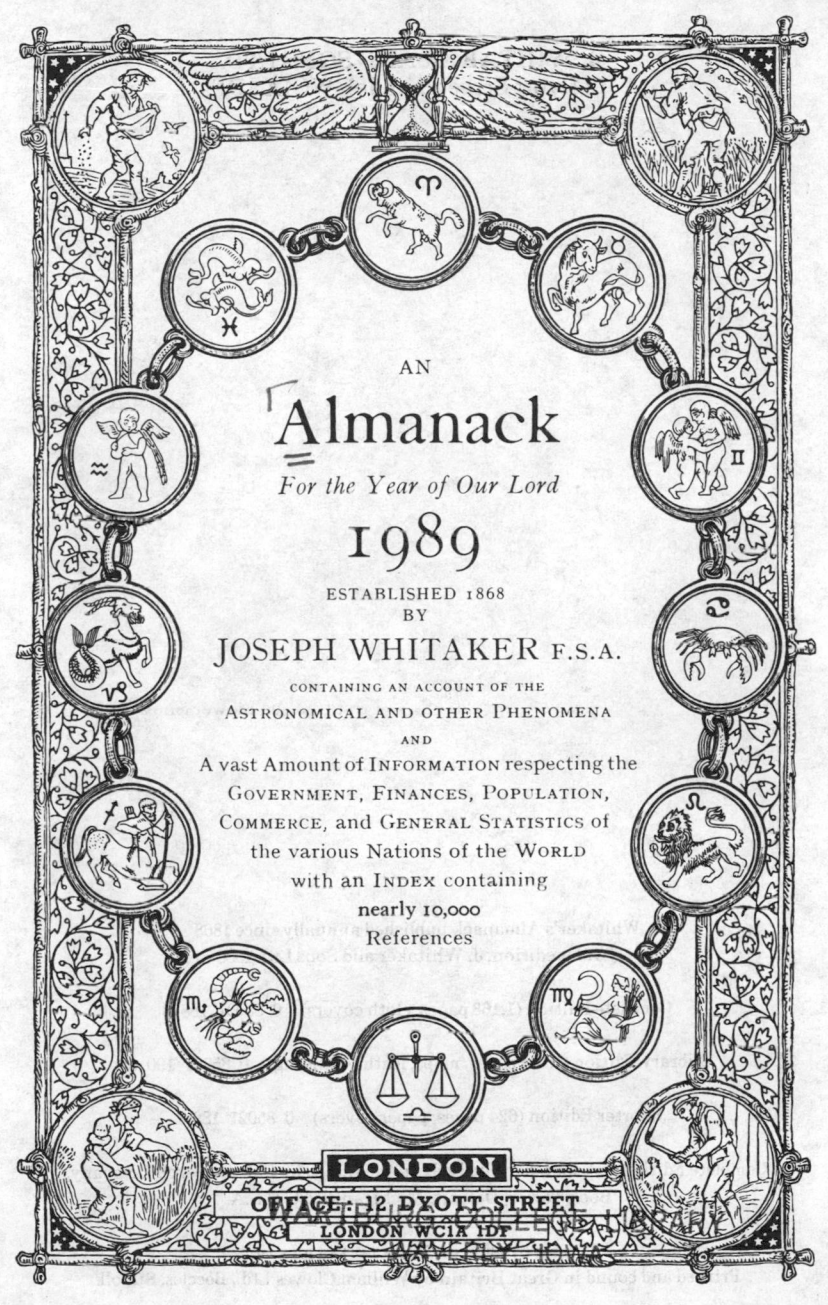

AN

'Almanack

For the Year of Our Lord

1989

ESTABLISHED 1868
BY

JOSEPH WHITAKER F.S.A.

CONTAINING AN ACCOUNT OF THE
ASTRONOMICAL AND OTHER PHENOMENA
AND
A vast Amount of INFORMATION respecting the
GOVERNMENT, FINANCES, POPULATION,
COMMERCE, and GENERAL STATISTICS of
the various Nations of the WORLD
with an INDEX containing
nearly 10,000
References

LONDON
OFFICE: 12 DYOTT STREET
LONDON WC1A 1DF

160937

J. WHITAKER AND SONS LTD.
12 Dyott Street, London WC1A 1DF

Complete Edition (1,168 pages, cloth covers)   0 85021 188 3

Library Edition (1,168 pages, maps, leather binding)   0 85021 190 5

Shorter Edition (624 pages, paper covers)   0 85021 189 1

Complete Edition distributed exclusively in the U.S.A. by Gale Research Company,
Book Tower, Detroit, Michigan 48226, U.S.A.

Typeset by Clowes Computer Composition
Printed and bound in Great Britain by William Clowes Ltd., Beccles, Suffolk

CONTENTS

CONTENTS
(of the Complete Edition and Library Edition)
continued

PREFACE
to the 121st Annual Volume (1989)

The 121st edition of WHITAKER'S ALMANACK maintains the traditional contents of the Almanack, on which its users have come to rely. There are also a number of innovations in this new edition.

The major innovation in this edition of Whitaker's Almanack is the new Index. This has been completely re-compiled, and the use of computer technology has allowed a separate index for the Shorter Edition of Whitaker's Almanack to be abstracted. At the same time the opportunity has been taken of moving the Index to the end of the volume.

As a result of this change, more space has been given over to the Notes for the Year. Among other items, these pages now include the dates of public holidays in 1990 as well as in the forthcoming year. The number of enquiries on this subject received by the Almanack Office suggests that this information will be of great use to readers.

Other changes in this edition include the expansion of the former Architectural Conservation section into Conservation and Heritage, giving a wider coverage of the subject. The information on the police has been augmented, with the addition of an article describing the Police Service in the United Kingdom and giving details of police pay.

The 24th Olympic Games in Seoul occurred too late in the Almanack's printing schedule for results to be included in the Sports section. However, a list of gold medallists can be found at the end of the Index, and the controversial events during the Games are mentioned in **Occurrences During Printing** overleaf.

The Editor wishes again to thank the many individuals and organizations worldwide whose assistance and suggestions have been invaluable in the compilation of the Almanack.

12 Dyott Street, London WC1A 1DF
Telephone 01-836 8911
October, 1988

OCCURRENCES DURING PRINTING

EVENTS

Sept. 2. The Peruvian Cabinet resigned. **3.** The governing People's Action Party won the general election in Singapore. **5.** The TUC conference opened in Bournemouth: on the opening day the Electrical, Electronic, Telecommunication and Plumbing Union was expelled from the TUC. **6.** The inquest opened in Gibraltar into the deaths of three IRA terrorists: on Sept. 30 a verdict of lawful killing was given. The Dutch Defence Minister Willem van Eekelen resigned. The Conservative government in Nova Scotia, Canada, was returned to office in a provincial election. **7.** A Cabinet reshuffle occurred in New Zealand. **9.** Opponents of the government in Burma formed an alternative government and called for a general election to be held on Oct. 9. The TCCB cancelled the England cricket team's winter tour of India. **12.** The Cuban ambassador and another Cuban diplomat were expelled after a shooting incident in west London. **12–16.** Hurricane Gilbert, the strongest-ever hurricane recorded in the western hemisphere, caused devastation in the Caribbean and Mexico, leading to 300 deaths. **15.** The national postal strike was called off. A Cabinet reshuffle occurred in Canada. **17.** The SDP conference opened in Torquay. The Haiti government was overthrown in a coup by Brig.-Gen. Prosper Avril who declared himself President. The Iceland's coalition government resigned. The 24th Olympic Games opened in Seoul. **18.** Sweden's Social Democrat government was returned to power in the general election. The Burmese government was overthrown by Gen. Saw Maung who abolished the people's assembly. **19.** Thirteen Malaysian politicians resigned from the ruling coalition. The Polish parliament voted to accept the resignation of the Prime Minister, Zbigniew Messner: he was replaced by Mieczyslaw Rakowski on Sept. 27. **20.** Argentina's foreign minister, Dante Caputo, was elected President of the UN General Assembly. **21.** A Cabinet reshuffle occurred in Bolivia. **22.** Crown Prince Akihito of Japan took over the official duties of Emperor Hirohito as the Emperor's medical condition worsened. Legislative elections were held in Hong Kong. One crewman was killed by an explosion on the Ocean Odyssey oil rig in the North Sea. Three Czechoslovak envoys were expelled from Britain for spying: on the 28th British officials were expelled from Prague in retaliation. **23.** The SLD conference opened in Blackpool. **24.** Rev. Barbara Harris was elected Bishop Suffragan of Boston, Massachusetts. **25.** The President of the Maldives was elected for a third term in office. **26.** The Canadian sprinter Ben Johnson was stripped of his Olympic 100-metre gold medal after a drug test proved positive. **28.** Steingrimur Hermansson became Iceland's new Prime Minister, at the head of a tripartite coalition government. **29.** Alderman Christopher Collett was elected Lord Mayor of London for 1988–89. **30.** At an extraordinary session of the Supreme Soviet, Mr. Gromyko left office and on Oct. 1 was replaced as President of the USSR by Mr. Gorbachev: on Oct. 3 there were further extensive changes to membership of the politburo and the central committee.

Oct. 1. The Canadian Prime Minister called a general election for Nov. 21. **2.** The Labour Party conference began in Blackpool. Mr. Neil Kinnock and Mr. Roy Hattersley won the party leadership election. The 24th Olympic Games ended in Seoul. **5.** British boxer Duke McKenzie won the IBF world flyweight title. In a plebiscite Chileans voted against President Pinochet continuing in office for another term: on the 6th the Chilean Cabinet resigned. **9.** Over 200 were killed in several days of rioting in Algeria.

APPOINTMENTS

Royal Households

Mr. G. Salter to be temporary assistant private secretary to the Prince of Wales, in place of the Hon. Rupert Fairfax.

Government and Public Offices

Mr. P. Troughton to be a trustee of the National Gallery.

Mr. J. S. Flemming to be a director of the Bank of England.

Sir Nicholas Fairbairn, M.P., to be chairman of the Historic Buildings Council for Scotland from Dec.

Mr. D. Chalmers to be Deputy Keeper of Public Records, Public Records Office.

Legal

Mr. Scott Baker to be a Justice of the High Court (Queen's Bench Division).

Mr. Alan Hylton Ward to be a Justice of the High Court (Family Division).

Mr. Igor Judge to be a Justice of the High Court (Queen's Bench Division).

Knighthoods were conferred on Mr. Justice Carswell, Mr. Justice Higgins, Mr. Justice McCollum, Mr. Justice Murray and Mr. Justice Nicholson, judges of the High Court of Northern Ireland.

Mr. W. A. Campbell to be a judge of the High Court of Northern Ireland.

OBITUARIES

September

1. Prof. Luis Alvarez, *aged* 77.

2. Lord Cooper of Stockton Heath, *aged* 80.

4. Sir Leonard Huxley, *aged* 86.

12. Roger Hargreaves, creator of *Mr. Men* books, *aged* 53.

—. Gen. Lauris Norstad, *aged* 81.

14. Sir Donald Albery, *aged* 74.

15. Sir Frank Francis, *aged* 86.

17. Sir John Biggs-Davison, Conservative M.P. for Epping Forest, *aged* 70.

—. Lord Roberthall, *aged* 87.

—. Nat Jackley, *aged* 79.

20. Roy Kinnear, *aged* 54.

—. Lt.-Gen. Sir Alexander Drummond, *aged* 87.

—. Sir Frank Young, *aged* 80.

—. Air Vice Marshal C. V. Winn, *aged* 70.

21. Lord Balfour of Inchyre, P.C., *aged* 90.

23. Brig. Dame Mary Colvin, *aged* 80.

—. Sir William Harris, *aged* 78.

24. Basil de Ferranti, Conservative M.E.P. for Hampshire Central, *aged* 58.

27. 4th Baron Ailwyn, *aged* 91.

—. Sir Peter Troubridge, Bt., *aged* 61.

28. The Countess of Wemyss and March, *aged* 77.

October

1. Sir Sacheverell Sitwell, Bt., C.H., *aged* 90.

2. Sir Alec Issigonis, *aged* 81.

—. Gen. Sir Peter Hunt, *aged* 72.

3. Franz Josef Strauss, Minister-President of Bavaria, *aged* 73.

4. Geoffrey Household, *aged* 87.

—. 6th Earl of Powis, *aged* 84.

8. Sir Edward Hulton, *aged* 81.

9. Jackie Milburn, *aged* 64.

ABBREVIATIONS

Ψ = Seaport.

A

A.—Associate of.
A.A.—Alcoholics Anonymous; Automobile Association; Anti-Aircraft.
A.A.A.—Amateur Athletic Association.
A.B.—Able-bodied seaman.
A.B.A.—Amateur Boxing Association.
abbrev.—abbreviation.
A.B.M.—Anti-ballistic missile defence system.
abr.—abridged.
a.c.—alternating current.
a/c.—accounts.
A.C.—Companion, Order of Australia; Aircraftman.
A.C.A.S.—Advisory, Conciliation and Arbitration Service.
A.C.T.—Australian Capital Territory.
A.C.T.T.—Association of Cinematograph, Television and Allied Technicians.
ad(vert)—advertisement.
A.D.—(*Anno Domini*) In the year of our Lord.
A.D.C.—Aide-de-Camp.
A.D.C. (P).—Personal A.D.C. to The Queen.
adj.—adjective.
Adjt.—Adjutant.
ad lib.—(*ad libitum*) at pleasure.
Adm.—Admiral; Admission.
adv.—adverb.
A.E.—Air Efficiency Award.
A.E.A.—Atomic Energy Authority.
A.E.M.—Air Efficiency Medal.
A.E.R.E.—Atomic Energy Research Establishment.
A.F.C.—Air Force Cross; Association Football Club.
A.F.M.—Air Force Medal.
A.F.V.—Armoured fighting vehicle.
A.G.—Adjutant-General.
a.g.m.—annual general meeting.
A.H.—(*Anno Hegirae*) In the year of the Hegira.
A.I.D.S.—Acquired Immune Deficiency Syndrome.
alt.—altitude.
a.m.—(*ante meridiem*) before noon.
A.M.—(*Anno mundi*) In the year of the world.
A.M.D.G.—(*Ad majorem Dei gloriam*) To the greater glory of God.
amp.—ampere.
A.N.C.—African National Congress.
anon.—anonymous.
A.N.Z.A.C.—Australian and New Zealand Army Corps.
A.O.—Officer, Order of Australia.
A.O.C.—Air Officer Commanding.
A.R.C.—Agricultural Research Council.
A.S.—Anglo-Saxon.
A.S.A.—Amateur Swimming Association.
A.S.B.—Alternative Service Book.
A.S.E.A.N.—Association of South East Asian Nations.
A.S.H.—Action on Smoking and Health.
A.S.L.E.F.—Associated Society of Locomotive Engineers and Firemen.
A.S.L.I.B.—Association for Information Management (*formerly* Association of Special Libraries and Information Bureaux).
A.S.T.M.S.—Association of Scientific, Technical and Managerial Staffs.
A.T.C.—Air Training Corps.
A.U.C.—(*ab urbe condita*) In the year from the foundation of Rome; (*anno urbis conditae*) In the year of the founding of the city.
A.U.E.W.—Amalgamated Union of Engineering Workers.
A.U.T.—Association of University Teachers.
A.V.—Authorized Version.
A.V.R.—Army Volunteer Reserve.
A.W.O.L.—Absent without leave.

B

b.—born; bowled.
B.A.—Bachelor of Arts.
B.A.A.—British Astronomical Association; British Airports Authority.
B. Acc.—Bachelor of Accountancy.
B.A.F.—British Athletic Federation.
B.A.F.T.A.—British Academy of Film and Television Arts.
B.A.O.R.—British Army of the Rhine.
B. Arch.—Bachelor of Architecture.
B.A.S.—British Antarctic Survey.
B.B.—Boys' Brigade.
B.B.C.—British Broadcasting Corporation.
B.C.—Before Christ; British Columbia.
B. Ch. (or Ch.B.)—Bachelor of Surgery.
B.C.L.—*do*, of Civil Law.
B. Com—*do*, of Commerce.
B.D.—*do*, of Divinity.
B.D.A.—British Dental Association.
B.D.S. (or B.Ch.D.)—Bachelor of Dental Surgery.
B. Ed.—*do*, of Education.
B.E.M.—British Empire Medal.
B. Eng.—Bachelor of Engineering.
B.F.I.—British Film Institute.
B.F.P.O.—British Forces Post Office.
B.I.M.—British Institute of Management.
B.L.A.I.S.E.—British Library Automated Information Service.
B. Litt.—Bachelor of Literature *or* of Letters.
B.M.—*do*, of Medicine; British Museum.
B.M.A.—British Medical Association.
B. Mus.—Bachelor of Music.
B.O.T.B.—British Overseas Trade Board.
Bp.—Bishop.
B. Pharm.—Bachelor of Pharmacy.
B. Phil.—*do*, of Philosophy.
Br. (*or* Brit.)—British.
B.R.—British Rail.
B.R.C.S.—British Red Cross Society.
Brig.—Brigadier.
B.Sc.—Bachelor of Science.
B.S.C.—British Steel Corporation.
B.S.I—British Standards Institution.
B.S.T.—British Summer Time.
Bt. (*or* Bart.)—Baronet.
B.T.G.—British Technology Group.
B. Th.—Bachelor of Theology.
B.t.u.—British thermal unit.
B.V.M.—Blessed Virgin Mary.
B.V.M.S.—Bachelor of Veterinary Medicine and Surgery.
B.W.B.—British Waterways Board.

C

c.—(*circa*) about.
C.—Celsius; Centigrade.
C. (*or* Con.)—Conservative.
C.A.—Chartered Accountant (*Scottish Institute*).
C.A.A.—Civil Aviation Authority.
C.A.B.—Citizens' Advice Bureau.
Cantab.—(of) Cambridge.
Cantuar.—of Canterbury (*Archbishop*).
C.A.P.—Common Agricultural Policy.
Capt.—Captain.
Caricom—Caribbean Community and Common Market.
Carliol.—of Carlisle (*Bishop*).
C.A.S.—Chief of Air Staff.
C.B.—Companion, Order of the Bath.
C.B.E.—Commander, Order of the British Empire.
C.B.I.—Confederation of British Industry.
cc.—cubic centimetres.

C.C.—County Council; County Councillor; Chamber of Commerce.
C.C.C.—County Cricket Club.
C. Chem.—Chartered Chemist.
C.D.—Civil Defence.
Cdr.—Commander.
Cdre.—Commodore.
C.D.S.—Chief of the Defence Staff.
C.E.—Civil Engineer.
C.E.G.B.—Central Electricity Generating Board.
C. Eng.—Chartered Engineer.
C.E.N.T.O.—Central Treaty Organization.
Cestr.—of Chester (*Bishop*).
C.E.T.—Common External Tariff; Central European Time.
cf.—confer; compare.
C.F.—Chaplain to the Forces.
C.G.M.—Conspicuous Gallantry Medal.
C.G.S.—Chief of General Staff; Centimetre-gramme-second (system).
C.H.—Companion of Honour.
Ch.B./M.—Bachelor/Master of Surgery.
C.I.—The Imperial Order of the Crown of India; Channel Islands.
C.I.A.—Central Intelligence Agency.
Cicestr.—of Chichester (*Bishop*).
C.I.D.—Criminal Investigation Department.
C.I.E.—Companion, Order of the Indian Empire.
c.i.f.—cost, insurance and freight.
C.-in-C.—Commander-in-Chief.
C.I.P.F.A.—Chartered Institute of Public Finance and Accountancy.
C.L. (*or* C. Litt.)—Companion of Literature.
C.L.J.—Commander, Order of St. Lazarus of Jerusalem.
C.M.—(*Chirurgiae Magister*) Master of Surgery.
C.M.G.—Companion, Order of St. Michael and St. George.
C.M.S.—Church Missionary Society.
C.N.A.A.—Council for National Academic Awards.
C.N.D.—Campaign for Nuclear Disarmament.
c/o—care of.
C.O.—Commanding Officer; conscientious objector.
C.O.D.—Cash on delivery.
C. of E.—Church of England.
C.O.H.S.E.—Confederation of Health Service Employees.
C.O.I.—Central Office of Information.
Col.—Colonel.
Comecon.—Council for Mutual Economic Assistance.
C.P.—Communist Party.
Cpl.—Corporal.
C.P.M.—Colonial Police Medal.
C.P.R.E.—Council for the Protection of Rural England.
C.P.V.E.—Certificate of Pre-Vocational Education.
C.R.E.—Council for Racial Equality.
C.S.E.—Certificate of Secondary Education.
C.S.I.—Companion, Order of the Star of India.
C.T.—Civic Trust.
C.T.C.—Cyclists' Touring Club.
C.V.O.—Commander, Royal Victorian Order.
cwt.—hundredweight.

D

d.—(*denarius*) penny.
D.B.E.—Dame Commander, Order of the British Empire.
d.c.—direct current.
D.C.—District of Columbia.
D.C.B.—Dame Commander, Order of the Bath.
D. Ch.—(*Doctor Chirurgiae*) Doctor of Surgery.
D.C.L.—Doctor of Civil Law.
D.C.M.—Distinguished Conduct Medal.
D.C.M.G.—Dame Commander, Order of St. Michael and St. George.

D.C.V.O.—Dame Commander, Royal Victorian Order.
D.D.—Doctor of Divinity.
D.D.S.—*do*, of Dental Surgery.
D.D.T.—dichlorodiphenyl-trichloroethane (insecticide).
del.—(*delineavit*) he/she drew it.
D.E.S.—Department of Education and Science.
D.F.C.—Distinguished Flying Cross.
D.F.M.—Distinguished Flying Medal.
D.G.—(*Dei gratia*) By the grace of God; Director-General.
D.H.Q.—District Headquarters.
D.H.S.S.—Department of Health and Social Security.
Dip. Ed.—Diploma in Education.
Dip. H. E.—Diploma in Higher Education.
Dip. Tech.—Diploma in Technology.
D.J.—Disc jockey.
D.L.—Deputy-Lieutenant.
D. Litt.—Doctor of Letters *or* of Literature.
D. Mus.—*do*, of Music.
D.N.A.—deoxyribonucleic acid.
D.N.B.—Dictionary of National Biography.
do.—(*ditto*) the same.
D.o.E.—Department of the Environment.
D.O.M.—(*Dominus Omnium Magister*) God the Master of All.
D. Phil.—Doctor of Philosophy.
D.P.P.—Director of Public Prosecutions.
Dr.—Doctor.
D.Sc.—Doctor of Science.
D.S.C.—Distinguished Service Cross.
D.S.M.—Distinguished Service Medal.
D.S.O.—Companion, Distinguished Service Order.
D.Th.—Doctor of Theology.
D.T.I.—Department of Trade and Industry.
Dunelm.—of Durham (*Bishop*).
D.V.—(*Deo volente*) God willing.

E

E. (*or* O.E.)—Errors and omissions excepted.
Ebor.—of York (*Archbishop*).
E.C.—European Community; Electricity Council.
E.C.G.—Electrocardiograph.
E.C.S.C.—European Coal and Steel Community.
E.C.T.U.—European Confederation of Trade Unions.
E.D.—Efficiency Decoration.
E.E.C.—European Economic Community.
E.E.G.—Electroencephalograph.
E.F.T.A.—European Free Trade Association.
e.g.—(*exempli gratia*) for the sake of example.
Elien.—of Ely (*Bishop*).
E.M.S.—European Monetary System.
E.N.E.A.—European Nuclear Energy Agency.
E.R.—Elizabeth Regina.
E.R.D.—Emergency Reserve Decoration.
E.R.N.I.E.—Electronic random number indicator equipment.
E.S.A.—European Space Agency.
E.S.P.—Extra-sensory perception.
E.S.R.C.—Economic and Social Research Council.
et al.—(*et alibi*) and elsewhere; (*et alii*) and others.
etc.—(*et cetera*) and the other things.
et seq.—(*et sequentia*) and the following.
Euratom—European Atomic Energy Commission.
ex lib.—(*ex libris*) from the books of.
Exon.—of Exeter (*Bishop*).

F

f (ff)—and the following page(s).
F.—Fahrenheit; Fellow of.
F.A.—Football Association.
F.A.N.Y.—First Aid Nursing Yeomanry.
F.A.O.—Food and Agriculture Organization.
F.B.A.—Fellow, British Academy.
F.B.A.A.—*do*, British Association of Accountants.
F.B.I.—Federal Bureau of Investigation.
F.B.I.M.—Fellow, British Institute of Management.

F.B.S.—*do*, Botanical Society.
F.C.A.—*do*, Institute of Chartered Accountants (of England and Wales).
F.C.C.A.—*do*, Association of Certified Accountants.
F.C.G.I.—*do*, City and Guilds Institute.
F.C.I.A.—*do*, Corporation of Insurance Agents.
F.C.I.B.—*do*, Chartered Institute of Bankers; Corporation of Insurance Brokers.
F.C.I.B.S.—*do*, Chartered Institution of Building-Services Engineers.
F.C.I.I.—*do*, Chartered Insurance Institute.
F.C.I.S.—*do*, Chartered Institute of Secretaries and Administrators.
F.C.I.T.—*do*, Chartered Institute of Transport.
F.C.M.A.—*do*, Institute of Cost and Management Accountants.
F.C.O.—Foreign and Commonwealth Office.
fcp.—foolscap.
F.C.P.—Fellow, College of Preceptors.
F.D.—(*Fidei Defensor*) Defender of the Faith.
fec.—(*fecit*) he did it/made it.
F.Eng.—Fellow, Fellowship of Engineering.
F.F.A.—*do*, Faculty of Actuaries.
F.F.A.S.—*do*, Faculty of Architects and Surveyors.
F.G.S.—*do*, Geological Society.
F.H.—Fire hydrant.
F.H.S.—Fellow, Heraldry Society.
F.H.S.M.—*do*, Institute of Health Service Management.
F.I.A.—*do*, Institute of Actuaries.
F.I.Arb.—*do*, Institute of Arbitrators.
F.I.Biol.—*do*, Institute of Biology.
F.I.C.E.—*do*, Institution of Civil Engineers.
F.I.C.S.—*do*, Institution of Chartered Shipbrokers.
F.I.E.E.—*do*, Institution of Electrical Engineers.
F.I.E.R.E.—*do*, Institution of Electronic and Radio Engineers.
F.I.F.A.—International Association Football Federation.
F.I.M.—Fellow, Institute of Metals.
F.I.M.M.—*do*, Institution of Mining and Metallurgy.
F.Inst.F.—*do*, Institute of Fuel.
F.Inst.P.—*do*, Institute of Physics.
F.I.Q.S.—*do*, Institute of Quantity Surveyors.
F.I.S.—*do*, Institute of Statisticians.
F.J.I.—*do*, Institute of Journalists.
fl.—(*floruit*) he/she flourished.
F.L.A.—Fellow, Library Association.
F.L.S.—*do*, Linnean Society.
F.M.—Field Marshal.
fo.—folio.
F.O.—Flying Officer.
f.o.b. free on board.
F.P.A.—Family Planning Association.
F.Ph.S.—Fellow, Philosophical Society.
F.P.S.—*do*, Pharmaceutical Society.
F.R.A.D.—*do*, Royal Academy of Dancing.
F.R.Ae.S.—*do*, Royal Aeronautical Society.
F.R.A.I.—*do*, Royal Anthropological Institute.
F.R.A.M.—*do*, Royal Academy of Music.
F.R.A.S.—*do*, Royal Astronomical Society.
F.R.B.S.—*do*, Royal Society of British Sculptors.
F.R.C.G.P.—*do*, Royal College of General Practitioners.
F.R.C.M.—*do*, Royal College of Music.
F.R.C.O.—*do*, Royal College of Organists.
F.R.C.O.G.—*do*, Royal College of Obstetricians and Gynaecologists.
F.R.C.P., (Ed.), (I.)—*do*, Royal College of Physicians, of London (of Edinburgh), (in Ireland).
F.R.C.Path.—*do*, Royal College of Pathologists.
F.R.C.P.S.G.—*do*, Royal College of Physicians and Surgeons of Glasgow.
F.R.C.Psych.—*do*, Royal College of Psychiatrists.
F.R.C.R.—*do*, Royal College of Radiologists.
F.R.C.S., (Eng.), (Ed.), (I.)—*do*, Royal College of Surgeons of England (of Edinburgh), (in Ireland).

F.R.C.V.S.—*do*, Royal College of Veterinary Surgeons.
F.R.Econ.S.—*do*, Royal Economic Society.
F.R.G.S.—*do*, Royal Geographical Society.
F.R.Hist.S.—*do*, Royal Historical Society.
F.R.H.S.—*do*, Royal Horticultural Society.
F.R.I.B.A.—*do*, Royal Institute of British Architects.
F.R.I.C.S.—*do*, Royal Institution of Chartered Surveyors.
F.R.Met.S.—*do*, Royal Meteorological Society.
F.R.M.S.—*do*, Royal Microscopical Society.
F.R.N.S.—*do*, Royal Numismatic Society.
F.R.P.S.—*do*, Royal Photographic Society.
F.R.S.—*do*, Royal Society.
F.R.S.A.—*do*, Royal Society of Arts.
F.R.S.C.—*do*, Royal Society of Chemistry.
F.R.S.E.—*do*, Royal Society of Edinburgh.
F.R.S.L.—*do*, Royal Society of Literature.
F.R.T.P.I.—*do*, Royal Town Planning Institute.
F.S.A.—*do*, Society of Antiquaries.
F.S.S.—*do*, Statistical Society.
F.S.V.A.—*do*, Society of Valuers and Auctioneers.
F.T.—*Financial Times*.
F.T.I.—Fellow, Textile Institute.
F.T.I.I.—*do*, Taxation Institute Inc.
F.Z.S.—*do*, Zoological Society.

G

G.A.T.T.—General Agreement on Tariffs and Trade.
G.B.E.—Knight/Dame Grand Cross, Order of the British Empire.
G.C.—George Cross.
G.C.B.—Knight/Dame Grand Cross, Order of the Bath.
G.C.E. General Certificate of Education.
G.C.H.Q.—Government Communications Headquarters.
G.C.I.E.—Knight Grand Commander, Order of the Indian Empire.
G.C.L.J.—Knight Grand Cross, Order of St. Lazarus of Jerusalem.
G.C.M.G.—Knight/Dame Grand Cross, Order of St. Michael and St. George.
G.C.S.E.—General Certificate of Secondary Education.
G.C.S.I.—Knight Grand Commander, Order of the Star of India.
G.C.V.O.—Knight/Dame Grand Cross, Royal Victorian Order.
G.D.I.—Gross domestic income.
G.D.P.—Gross domestic product.
G.D.R.—German Democratic Republic (E. Germany).
Gen.—General.
G.H.Q.—General Headquarters.
Gib.—Gibraltar.
G.M.—George Medal.
G.M.T.—Greenwich Mean Time.
G.N.P.—Gross national product.
G.O.C.—General Officer Commanding.
G.P. General Practitioner.
Gp. Capt.—Group Captain.
G.S.O.—General Staff Officer.

H

H.A.C.—Honourable Artillery Company.
H.B.M.—Her Britannic Majesty('s).
H.C.F.—Highest common factor.
H.E.—His/Her Excellency; His Eminence; high explosive.
H.H.—His/Her Highness.
H.I.M.—His/Her Imperial Majesty.
H.J.S.—(*hic jacet sepultus*) here lies buried.
H.M.—His/Her Majesty.
H.M.A.S.—Her Majesty's Australian Ship.
H.M.C.—Headmasters' Conference.
H.M.I.—Her Majesty's Inspector.
H.M.L.—Her Majesty's Lieutenant.

H.M.S.—Her Majesty's Ship.
H.M.S.O.—Her Majesty's Stationery Office.
H.N.C.—Higher National Certificate.
H.N.D.—Higher National Diploma.
H.O.L.M.E.S.—Home Office Large Major Enquiry System.
Hon.—Honourable; Honorary.
h.p.—horse power.
H.P.—Hire purchase.
H.Q.—Headquarters.
H.R.H.—His/Her Royal Highness.
H.S.E.—(*hic sepultus est*) here lies buried. *cf.* H.J.S.
H.T.R.—High temperature reactor.
H.W.M.—High water mark.

I

I.A.A.S.—Incorporated Association of Architects and Surveyors.
I.A.E.A.—International Atomic Energy Agency.
I.A.T.A.—International Air Transport Association.
I.B.A.—Independent Broadcasting Authority.
Ibid.—(*ibidem*) in the same place.
I.B.R.D.—International Bank for Reconstruction and Development.
I.C.A.O.—International Civil Aviation Organization.
I.C.B.M.—Inter-continental ballistic missile.
I.C.J.—International Court of Justice.
I.C.R.C.—International Committee of the Red Cross.
Id.—(*idem*) the same.
i.e.—(*id est*) that is.
I.E.A.—International Energy Agency.
I.F.C.—International Finance Corporation.
I.H.S.—(*Iesus Hominum Salvator*) Jesus the Saviour of Mankind; originally, these were the Greek capital letters, I H Σ.
I.L.E.A.—Inner London Education Authority.
I.L.O.—International Labour Organization.
I.M.F.—International Monetary Fund.
I.M.O.—International Maritime Organization.
Inc.—Incorporated.
Incog.—(*incognito*) unknown, unrecognized.
I.N.L.A.—Irish National Liberation Army.
In loc.—(*in loco*) its place.
I.N.R.I.—(*Iesus Nazarenus Rex Iudaeorum*) Jesus of Nazareth, King of the Jews.
Inst.—(*instant*) current month.
Intelsat—International Telecommunications Satellite Consortium.
Interpol—International Criminal Police Commission.
I.O.M.—Isle of Man.
I.O.U.—I owe you.
I.O.W.—Isle of Wight.
I.Q.—Intelligence quotient.
I.R.A.—Irish Republican Army.
I.R.C.—International Red Cross.
I.S.B.N.—International Standard Book Number.
I.S.O.—Imperial Service Order.
I.T.U.—International Telecommunication Union.
I.T.V.—Independent Television.

J

J.—Judge.
J.P.—Justice of the Peace.

K

K.—Köchel numeration (of Mozart's works).
K.A.N.U.—Kenyan African National Union.
K.B.E.—Knight Commander, Order of the British Empire.
K.C.B.—*do*, Order of the Bath.
K.C.I.E.—*do*, Order of the Indian Empire.
K.C.L.J.—*do*, Order of St. Lazarus of Jerusalem.
K.C.M.G.—*do*, Order of St. Michael and St. George.
K.C.S.I.—*do*, Order of the Star of India.
K.C.V.O.—*do*, Royal Victorian Order.

K.G.—Knight of the Garter.
K.G.B.—Soviet State Security Service.
K.K.K.—Ku Klux Klan.
K.L.J.—Knight, Order of St. Lazarus of Jerusalem.
k.o.—knock out (boxing).
K.P.—Knight, Order of St. Patrick.
K.St.J.—Knight, Order of St. John of Jerusalem.
Kt.—Knight.
K.T.—Knight, Order of the Thistle.
K.V.—Kilovolt.
K.W.—Kilowatt.
K.W.h.—Kilowatt hour.

L

L. (*or* Lib.)—Liberal.
Lab.—Labour.
L.A.M.D.A.—London Academy of Music and Dramatic Art.
Lat.—Latitude.
lb.—(*libra*) pound weight.
l.b.w.—leg before wicket.
l.c.—lower case (*printing*).
L.C.J.—Lord Chief Justice.
L.C.M.—Least common multiple.
L.D.S.—Licentiate in Dental Surgery.
L.E.A.—Local Education Authority.
L.H.D.—(*Litterarum Humaniorum Doctor*) Doctor of Humane Letters.
Lic. Med.—Licentiate in Medicine.
Lic. S.—*do*, in Surgery.
Lit.—Literary.
Lit. Hum.—(*Litterae Humaniores*) study of the classics.
Litt. D.—Doctor of Letters.
L.J.—Lord Justice.
LL.B.—Bachelor of Laws.
LL.D.—Doctor of Laws.
LL.M.—Master of Laws.
L.M.—Licentiate in Midwifery.
L.M.S.S.A.—*do*, in Medicine and Surgery, Society of Apothecaries.
loc. cit.—(*loco citato*) in the place cited.
log.—logarithm.
Londin.—of London (*Bishop*).
L.S.—(*loco sigilli*) place of the seal.
L.S.A.—Licentiate of Society of Apothecaries.
L.s.d.—(*Librae, solidi, denarii*) £, shillings and pence.
L.S.E.—London School of Economics.
L.S.O.—London Symphony Orchestra.
Lt.—Lieutenant.
L.T.A.—Lawn Tennis Association.
Ltd.—Limited liability.
L.Th.—Licentiate in Theology.
L.V.O.—Lieutenant, Royal Victorian Order.
L.W.M.—Low water mark.

M

M.—Member of; Monsieur.
M.A.—Master of Arts.
M.A.F.F.—Ministry of Agriculture, Fisheries and Food.
Maj.—Major.
max.—maximum.
M.B./D.—Bachelor/Doctor of Medicine.
M.B.E.—Member, Order of the British Empire.
M.C.—Master of Ceremonies; Military Cross.
M.C.C.—Marylebone Cricket Club.
M.Ch.(D.)—Master of (Dental) Surgery.
M.D.S.—*do*, of Dental Surgery.
M.E.—Middle English.
M.E.C.—Member of Executive Council.
M.Ed.—Master of Education.
mega—one million times.
M.E.P.—Member of the European Parliament.
M.F.H.—Master of Foxhounds.
Mgr.—Monsignor.
M.I.—Military Intelligence.

micro—one-millionth part.
milli—one-thousandth part.
min.—minimum.
M.L.A.—Member of Legislative Assembly.
M.L.C.—Member of Legislative Council.
Mlle.—Mademoiselle.
M.L.R.—Minimum lending rate.
M.M.—Military Medal.
Mme.—Madame.
M.N.—Merchant Navy.
M.O.—Medical Officer/Orderly.
M.o.D.—Ministry of Defence.
M.o.T.—Ministry of Transport.
M.P.—Member of Parliament; Military Police.
m.p.h.—miles per hour.
M.R.—Master of the Rolls.
M.R.C.—Medical Research Council.
M.S.—Master of Surgery; Manuscript (pl. MSS).
M.Sc.—*do*, of Science.
M.S.C.—Manpower Services Commission.
M.T.B.—Motor torpedo boat.
M.Th.—Master of Theology.
Mus. B./D.—Bachelor/Doctor of Music.
M.V.—million volts (*or* megavolts); Merchant Vessel; Motor Vessel.
M.V.O.—Member, Royal Victorian Order.
M.W.—million watts (*or* megawatts).

N

N.A.A.F.I.—Navy Army and Air Force Institutes.
N.A.L.G.O.—National and Local Government Officers Association.
N.A.S.A.—National Aeronautics and Space Administration.
N.A.T.O.—North Atlantic Treaty Organization.
N.B.—(*Nota bene*) note well; New Brunswick.
N.C.O.—Non-commissioned officer.
n.d.—no date (*of books*).
N.E.B.—New English Bible.
N.E.D.C./NEDDY.—National Economic Development Council.
Nem. con.—(*Nemine contradicente*) no one contradicting.
N.E.R.C.—Natural Environment Research Council.
N.F.T.—National Film Theatre.
N.G.A.—National Graphical Association.
N.H.S.—National Health Service.
N.I.—Northern Ireland.
No.—(*numero*) number.
Non seq.—(*Non sequitur*) it does not follow.
Norvic.—of Norwich (*Bishop*).
N.P.—Notary Public.
N.R.A.—National Rifle Association.
N.S.—New Style (calendar); Nova Scotia.
N.S.P.C.C.—National Society for the Prevention of Cruelty to Children.
N.S.W.—New South Wales.
N.T.—National Theatre; New Testament.
N.U.J.—National Union of Journalists.
N.U.M.—*do*, of Mineworkers.
N.U.P.E.—*do*, of Public Employees.
N.U.R.—*do*, of Railwaymen.
N.U.S.—*do*, of Seamen; *do*, of Students.
N.U.T.—*do*, of Teachers.
N.V.Q.—National Vocational Qualification.
N.W.T.—Northwest Territory.
N.Y.—New York.
N.Z.—New Zealand.

O

O. and M.—Organization and method.
O.A.P.E.C.—Organization of Arab Petroleum Exporting Countries.
O.A.S.—Organization of American States.
O.A.U.—Organization of African Unity.
Ob. (*or* obit.)—died.
O.B.E.—Officer, Order of the British Empire.
O.C.—Officer Commanding.
O.E.—Old English.
O.E.C.D.—Organization for Economic Co-operation and Development.
O.E.D.—Oxford English Dictionary.
O.F.M.—Order of Friars Minor (Franciscans).
O.H.M.S.—On Her Majesty's Service.
O.M.—Order of Merit.
O.P.—Order of Preachers (Dominicans); opposite prompt side (of theatre); out of print (of books).
op.—(*opus*) work.
op. cit.—(*opere citato*) in the work cited.
O.P.C.S.—Office of Population Censuses and Surveys.
O.P.E.C.—Organization of Petroleum Exporting Countries.
O.S.—Old Style (calendar).
O.S.A.—Order of St. Augustine.
O.S.B.—Order of St. Benedict.
O. St. J.—Officer, Order of St. John of Jerusalem.
O.T.—Old Testament.
O.T.C.—Officer Training Corps.
Oxon.—(of) Oxford; Oxfordshire.
Oz.—ounce.

P

P.A.—Press Association.
P.A.Y.E.—Pay as You Earn.
p.c.—per cent.
P.C.—Privy Counsellor; Police Constable.
P.C.A.S.—Polytechnics Central Admission System.
P.D.S.A.—People's Dispensary for Sick Animals.
P.E.—Physical Education.
Petriburg—of Peterborough (*Bishop*).
Ph.D.—Doctor of Philosophy.
pinx(it)—he/she painted it.
P.L.A.—Port of London Authority.
P.L.C.—Public Limited Company.
P.L.O.—Palestine Liberation Organization.
p.m.—(*post meridiem*) after noon.
P.M.—Prime Minister.
P.M.R.A.F.N.S.—Princess Mary's Royal Air Force Nursing Service.
P.O.—Post Office; postal order; Petty Officer; Pilot Officer.
P.O.U.N.C.—Post Office Users' National Council.
P.O.W.—Prisoner of War.
p.p. (*or* per pro)—(*per procurationem*) by proxy.
P.P.S.—Parliamentary Private Secretary.
P.R.—Proportional Representation; Public Relations.
P.R.A.—President of the Royal Academy.
Pro tem.—(*pro tempore*) for the time being.
Prox.—(*proximo*) next month.
P.R.S.—President of the Royal Society.
P.R.S.E.—*do*, of Edinburgh.
Ps.—Psalm.
P.S.—(*Post scriptum*) postscript.
P.S.B.R.—Public sector borrowing requirement.
p.s.c.—passed Staff College.
Pte.—Private.
P.T.O.—Please turn over.

Q

Q.A.R.A.N.C.—Queen Alexandra's Royal Army Nursing Corps.
Q.A.R.N.N.S.—Queen Alexandra's Royal Naval Nursing Service.
Q.B.—Queen's Bench.
Q.C.—Queen's Counsel.
Q.e.d.—(*quod erat demonstrandum*) which was to be proved.
Q.G.M.—Queen's Gallantry Medal.
Q.H.C.—Honorary Chaplain to the Queen.
Q.H.D.S.—Honorary Dental Surgeon to the Queen.
Q.H.N.S.—Honorary Nursing Sister to the Queen.
Q.H.P.—Honorary Physician to the Queen.
Q.H.S.—Honorary Surgeon to the Queen.

Q.M.G.—Quartermaster General.
Q.P.M.—Queen's Police Medal.
Q.S.—Quarter Sessions.
Q.S.O.—Quasi-stellar object (quasar).
Q.S.S.s—Quasi-stellar radio sources (quasar).
q.v.—*(quod vide)* which see.

R

R.—*(Rex)* King; *(Regina)* Queen.
R.A.—Royal Artillery; Royal Academy/Academician.
R.A.C.—Royal Armoured Corps; Royal Automobile Club.
R.A.D.A.—Royal Academy of Dramatic Art.
R.A.D.C.—Royal Army Dental Corps.
R.A.E.—Royal Aircraft Establishment.
R.A.E.C.—Royal Army Education Corps.
R.Ae.S.—Royal Aeronautical Society.
R.A.F.—Royal Air Force.
R.A.M.—Royal Academy of Music.
R.A.M.C.—Royal Army Medical Corps.
R.A.N.—Royal Australian Navy.
R. and D.—Research and development.
R.A.O.C.—Royal Army Ordnance Corps.
R.A.P.C.—Royal Army Pay Corps.
R.A.V.C.—Royal Army Veterinary Corps.
R.B.A.—Royal Society of British Artists.
R.B.S.—Royal Society of British Sculptors.
R.C.—Roman Catholic; Red Cross.
R.C.M.—Royal College of Music.
R.C.N.—Royal Canadian Navy.
R.C.N.C.—Royal Corps of Naval Constructors.
R.C.T.—Royal Corps of Transport.
R.D.—Naval Reserve Decoration; Rural Dean; refer to drawer *(banking)*.
R.D.I.—Designer for Industry of the Royal Society of Arts.
R.E.—Royal Engineers.
R.E.M.E.—Royal Electrical and Mechanical Engineers.
Rep.—Republican; representative.
Rev.—Reverend.
R.G.N.—Registered General Nurse.
R.G.S.—Royal Geographical Society.
R.H.S.—Royal Horticultural Society; Royal Humane Society.
R.I.—Royal Institution; Royal Institute of Painters in Watercolours; Rhode Island.
R.I.A.—Royal Irish Academy.
R.I.B.A.—Royal Institute of British Architects.
R.I.P.—*(Requiescat in pace)* May he/she rest in peace.
R.L.—Rugby League.
R.M.—Royal Marines.
R.M.A.—Royal Military Academy.
R.M.S.—Royal Mail Steamer.
R.N.—Royal Navy.
R.N.I.B.—Royal National Institute for the Blind.
R.N.L.I.—Royal National Lifeboat Institution.
R.N.R.—Royal Naval Reserve.
R.N.V.R.—Royal Naval Volunteer Reserve.
R.N.Z.N.—Royal New Zealand Navy.
Ro.—*(Recto)* on the right-hand page.
R.O.C.—Royal Observer Corps.
Roffen.—of Rochester *(Bishop)*.
R.O.I.—Royal Institute of Oil Painters.
Ro. S.P.A.—Royal Society for the Prevention of Accidents.
R.P.—Royal Society of Portrait Painters.
r.p.m.—revolutions per minute.
R.R.C.—Lady of Royal Red Cross.
R.R.E.—Royal Radar Establishment.
R.S.A.—Royal Society of Arts; Royal Scottish Academician; Republic of South Africa.
R.S.C.—Royal Shakespeare Company.
R.S.E.—Royal Society of Edinburgh.
R.S.M.—Regimental Sergeant Major.
R.S.P.B.—Royal Society for the Protection of Birds.

R.S.P.C.A.—Royal Society for the Prevention of Cruelty to Animals.
R.S.V.P.—*(Respondez s'il vous plait)* Answer, if you please.
R.S.W.—Royal Scottish Society of Painters in Water-colours.
R.T.P.I.—Royal Town Planning Institute.
R.U.—Rugby Union.
R.U.C.—Royal Ulster Constabulary.
R.V.—Revised Version (of Bible).
R.W.S.—Royal Water Colour Society.
R.Y.S.—Royal Yacht Squadron.

S

s.—*(solidus)* shilling.
S.A.—Salvation Army; sex appeal; South Africa; South America; South Australia.
Salop.—Shropshire.
S.A.L.T.—Strategic Arms Limitation Treaty.
Sarum.—of Salisbury *(Bishop)*.
S.A.S.—Special Air Service Regiment.
S.B.S.—Special Boat Squadron.
Sc.D.—Doctor of Science.
S.C.M.—State Certified Midwife.
S.D.I.—Strategic Defence Initiative ("Star Wars").
S.D.L.P.—Social Democratic and Labour Party (N. Ireland).
S.D.P.—Social Democratic Party.
S.E.A.Q.—Stock Exchange Automated Quotations system.
S.E.A.T.O.—South East Asia Treaty Organization.
S.E.N.—State Enrolled Nurse.
S.E.R.C.—Science and Engineering Research Council.
S.E.R.P.S.—State Earnings Related Pension Scheme.
S.H.A.P.E.—Supreme Headquarters, Allied Powers, Europe.
S.I.—*(Système International d'Unités)* International System of Units; Statutory Instruments.
Sic.—So written.
Sig.—Signalman.
S.J.—Society of Jesus (Jesuits).
S.L.D.—Social and Liberal Democrats.
S.N.P.—Scottish National Party.
S.O.G.A.T.—Society of Graphical and Allied Trades.
S.O.S.—Save Our Souls (distress signal).
s.p.—*(sine prole)* without issue.
S.P.C.K.—Society for the Promotion of Christian Knowledge.
sp.gr.—specific gravity.
S.P.Q.R.—*(Senatus Populusque Romanus)* The Senate and People of Rome.
Sqn. Ldr.—Squadron Leader.
S.R.N.—State Registered Nurse.
S.R.O—Self Regulating Organization.
SS.—Saints.
S.S.—Steamship.
S.S.A.F.A.—Soldiers', Sailors', and Airmen's Families Association.
S.S.C.—Solicitor before Supreme Court (Scotland).
S.S.F.—Society of St. Francis.
St.—Saint; Street.
S.T.A.R.—Satellites for Telecommunications, Applications and Research.
Stet.—Let it stand.
S.T.D.—*(Sacrae Theologiae Doctor)* Doctor of Sacred Theology; Subscriber trunk dialling.
s.t.p.—Standard temperature and pressure.
S.T.P.—*(Sacrae Theologiae Professor)* Professor of Sacred Theology.
Sub Lt.—Sub-Lieutenant.
S.W.A.P.O.—South West Africa People's Organization.

T

T.A.—Territorial Army.
T.B.—Tuberculosis.

T.C.C.B.—Test and County Cricket Board.
T.D.—Territorial Decoration.
temp.—temperature; temporary employee.
T.E.S.—*Times Educational Supplement.*
T.G.W.U.—Transport and General Workers Union.
T.L.S.—*Times Literary Supplement.*
T.N.T.—trinitrotoluene (explosive).
Toc. H.—Talbot House.
tr.—transpose (*printing*).
Truron—of Truro (*Bishop*).
T.T.—Teetotal; Tubercular tested.
T.U.C.—Trades Union Congress.
T.V.—Television.

U

U.—Unionist.
U.A.E.—United Arab Emirates.
u.c.—upper case (*printing*).
U.C.C.A.—University Central Council on Admissions.
U.C.L.—University College, London.
U.D.I.—Unilateral Declaration of Independence.
U.D.M.—Union of Democratic Mineworkers.
U.D.R.—Ulster Defence Regiment.
U.E.F.A.—Union of European Football Associations.
U.F.O.—Unidentified flying object.
U.G.C.—University Grants Committee.
u.h.f.—ultra-high frequency.
U.K.—United Kingdom.
U.K.A.E.A.—United Kingdom Atomic Energy Authority.
Ult.—(*ultimo*) in the preceding month.
U.N.E.S.C.O.—United Nations Educational, Scientific and Cultural Organization.
U.N.I.C.E.F.—United Nations International Children's Emergency Fund.
Unita.—National Union for the Total Independence of Angola.
U.N.O.—United Nations Organization.
U.P.U.—Universal Postal Union.
U.S. (*or* U.S.A.)—United States (of America).
U.S.M.—Unlisted Securities Market.
U.S.P.G.—United Society for the Propagation of the Gospel.
U.S.S.R.—Union of Soviet Socialist Republics.
U.U.—Ulster Unionist.

V

v.—(*versus*) against.
V.—Volt.
V.A.—Vicar Apostolic; Victoria and Albert Order.
V.A.D.—Voluntary Aid Detachment.
V. and A.—Victoria and Albert Museum.
V.A.T.—Value added tax.
V.C.—Victoria Cross.
V.D.—Volunteer Officers' Decoration; venereal disease.
V.D.U.—Visual display unit.
Ven.—Venerable.
Verb. sap.—(*Verbum sapienti satis est*) A word to the wise is enough.
v.h.f.—very high frequency.
V.I.P.—Very important person.
Viz.—(*videlicet*) namely.
Vo.—(*Verso*) on the left-hand page.
V.R.D.—Volunteer Reserve Decoration.
V.S.O.—Voluntary Service Overseas.
V.T.O.L.—Vertical take-off and landing (*aircraft*).

W

W.C.C.—World Council of Churches.
W.E.U.—Western European Union.
W.H.O.—World Health Organization.
W.I.—West Indies; Women's Institutes.
Winton.—of Winchester (*Bishop*).
W.M.O.—World Meteorological Organization.
W.O.—Warrant Officer.
W.R.A.C.—Women's Royal Army Corps.
W.R.A.F.—Women's Royal Air Force.
W.R.N.S.—Women's Royal Naval Service.
W.R.V.S.—Women's Royal Voluntary Service.
W.S.—Writer to the Signet.

Y

Y.H.A.—Youth Hostels Association.
Y.M.C.A.—Young Men's Christian Association.
Y.T.S.—Youth Training Scheme.
Y.W.C.A.—Young Women's Christian Association.

Z

Z.A.N.U.—Zimbabwe African National Union.
Z.A.P.U.—Zimbabwe African People's Union.

CALENDAR FOR THE YEAR 1989

	January	February	March	April
Su.	.. 1 8 15 22 29	.. — 5 12 19 26	.. — 5 12 19 26	.. — 2 9 16 23 30
M.	.. 2 9 16 23 30	.. — 6 13 20 27	.. — 6 13 20 27	— 3 10 17 24 —
Tu.	.. 3 10 17 24 31	.. — 7 14 21 28	.. — 7 14 21 28	— 4 11 18 25 —
W.	.. 4 11 18 25 —	.. 1 8 15 22 —	.. 1 8 15 22 29	— 5 12 19 26 —
Th.	.. 5 12 19 26 —	.. 2 9 16 23 —	.. 2 9 16 23 30	— 6 13 20 27 —
F.	.. 6 13 20 27 —	.. 3 10 17 24 —	.. 3 10 17 24 31	— 7 14 21 28 —
S.	.. 7 14 21 28 —	.. 4 11 18 25 —	.. 4 11 18 25 —	1 8 15 22 29 —

	May	June	July	August
Su.	.. — 7 14 21 28	.. — 4 11 18 25	.. 2 9 16 23 30	— 6 13 20 27
M.	.. 1 8 15 22 29	.. — 5 12 19 26	.. 3 10 17 24 31	— 7 14 21 28
Tu.	.. 2 9 16 23 30	.. — 6 13 20 27	.. 4 11 18 25 —	.. 1 8 15 22 29
W.	.. 3 10 17 24 31	.. — 7 14 21 28	.. 5 12 19 26 —	.. 2 9 16 23 30
Th.	.. 4 11 18 25 —	.. 1 8 15 22 29	.. 6 13 20 27 —	.. 3 10 17 24 31
F.	.. 5 12 19 26 —	.. 2 9 16 23 30	.. 7 14 21 28 —	.. 4 11 18 25 —
S.	.. 6 13 20 27 —	.. 3 10 17 24 —	1 8 15 22 29 —	.. 5 12 19 26 —

	September	October	November	December
Su.	.. — 3 10 17 24	.. 1 8 15 22 29	.. — 5 12 19 26	— 3 10 17 24 31
M.	.. — 4 11 18 25	.. 2 9 16 23 30	.. — 6 13 20 27	— 4 11 18 25 —
Tu.	.. — 5 12 19 26	.. 3 10 17 24 31	.. — 7 14 21 28	— 5 12 19 26 —
W.	.. — 6 13 20 27	.. 4 11 18 25 —	.. 1 8 15 22 29	— 6 13 20 27 —
Th.	.. — 7 14 21 28	.. 5 12 19 26 —	.. 2 9 16 23 30	— 7 14 21 28 —
F.	.. 1 8 15 22 29	.. 6 13 20 27 —	.. 3 10 17 24 —	1 8 15 22 29 —
S.	.. 2 9 16 23 30	.. 7 14 21 28 —	.. 4 11 18 25 —	2 9 16 23 30 —

CALENDAR FOR THE YEAR 1990

	January	February	March	April
Su.	.. — 7 14 21 28	.. — 4 11 18 25	.. — 4 11 18 25	.. 1 8 15 22 29
M.	.. 1 8 15 22 29	.. — 5 12 19 26	.. — 5 12 19 26	.. 2 9 16 23 30
Tu.	.. 2 9 16 23 30	.. — 6 13 20 27	.. — 6 13 20 27	.. 3 10 17 24 —
W.	.. 3 10 17 24 31	.. — 7 14 21 28	.. — 7 14 21 28	.. 4 11 18 25 —
Th.	.. 4 11 18 25 —	.. 1 8 15 22 —	.. 1 8 15 22 29	.. 5 12 19 26 —
F.	.. 5 12 19 26 —	.. 2 9 16 23 —	.. 2 9 16 23 30	.. 6 13 20 27 —
S.	.. 6 13 20 27 —	.. 3 10 17 24 —	.. 3 10 17 24 31	.. 7 14 21 28 —

	May	June	July	August
Su.	.. — 6 13 20 27	.. — 3 10 17 24	.. 1 8 15 22 29	— 5 12 19 26
M.	.. — 7 14 21 28	.. — 4 11 18 25	.. 2 9 16 23 30	— 6 13 20 27
Tu.	.. 1 8 15 22 29	.. — 5 12 19 26	.. 3 10 17 24 31	— 7 14 21 28
W.	.. 2 9 16 23 30	.. — 6 13 20 27	.. 4 11 18 25 —	.. 1 8 15 22 29
Th.	.. 3 10 17 24 31	.. — 7 14 21 28	.. 5 12 19 26 —	.. 2 9 16 23 30
F.	.. 4 11 18 25 —	.. 1 8 15 22 29	.. 6 13 20 27 —	.. 3 10 17 24 31
S.	.. 5 12 19 26 —	.. 2 9 16 23 30	.. 7 14 21 28 —	.. 4 11 18 25 —

	September	October	November	December
Su.	— 2 9 16 23 30	.. — 7 14 21 28	.. — 4 11 18 25	— 2 9 16 23 30
M.	— 3 10 17 24 —	.. 1 8 15 22 29	.. — 5 12 19 26	— 3 10 17 24 31
Tu.	— 4 11 18 25 —	.. 2 9 16 23 30	.. — 6 13 20 27	— 4 11 18 25 —
W.	— 5 12 19 26 —	.. 3 10 17 24 31	.. — 7 14 21 28	— 5 12 19 26 —
Th.	— 6 13 20 27 —	.. 4 11 18 25 —	.. 1 8 15 22 29	— 6 13 20 27 —
F.	— 7 14 21 28 —	.. 5 12 19 26 —	.. 2 9 16 23 30	— 7 14 21 28 —
S.	1 8 15 22 29 —	.. 6 13 20 27 —	.. 3 10 17 24 —	1 8 15 22 29 —

PUBLIC HOLIDAYS

	1989 ENGLAND & WALES	1989 SCOTLAND	1989 N. IRELAND	1990 ENGLAND & WALES	1990 SCOTLAND	1990 N. IRELAND
New Year	Jan. 2	Jan. 2, 3	Jan. 2	Jan. 1	Jan. 1, 2	Jan. 1
St. Patrick's Day	—	—	March 17	—	—	Mar. 17
Good Friday	March 24*	March 24	March 24*	April 13*	April 13	April 13*
Easter Monday..	March 27	—	March 27	April 16	—	April 16
May Day	May 1	May 29	May 1	May 7	May 7	May 7
Spring	May 29	May 1	May 29	May 28	May 7	May 28
Battle of Boyne	—	—	July 12	—	—	July 12
Summer........	Aug. 28	Aug. 7	Aug. 28	Aug. 27	Aug. 6	Aug. 27
Christmas	Dec. 25*, 26	Dec. 25, 26	Dec. 25*, 26	Dec. 25*, 26	Dec. 25, 26	Dec. 25*, 26

*In England, Wales, and Northern Ireland, Christmas Day and Good Friday are common law holidays.
In the CHANNEL ISLANDS Liberation Day (May 9) is a bank and public holiday.

NOTES FOR THE YEAR 1989

BEING THE FIRST YEAR AFTER
BISSEXTILE OR LEAP YEAR

Dominical Letter	A	St. George's Day	April 23
Epact	22	Coronation of H.M. The Queen (1953)	June 2
Golden Number	XIV	Duke of Edinburgh's Birthday (1921)	June 10
Julian Period	6702	Queen's Official Birthday	June 17
Roman Indiction	12	Prince William of Wales' Birthday	
Solar Cycle	10	(1982)	June 21
Julian Day, Jan. 1 (begins at noon)	2,447,528	Princess of Wales' Birthday (1961)	July 1
		Queen Elizabeth the Queen Mother's	
New Year's Day	Jan. 1	Birthday (1900)	Aug. 4
Accession of H.M. The Queen (1952)	Feb. 6	Princess Royal's Birthday (1950)	Aug. 15
Ancient Chinese New Year (Snake)	Feb. 6	Princess Margaret's Birthday (1930)	Aug. 21
Duke of York's Birthday (1960)	Feb. 19	Prince Henry of Wales' Birthday (1984)	Sept. 15
St. David's Day	March 1	Lord Mayor's Day	Nov. 11
Prince Edward's Birthday (1964)	March 10	Remembrance Sunday	Nov. 12
Commonwealth Day	March 13	Prince of Wales' Birthday (1948)	Nov. 14
St. Patrick's Day	March 17	Wedding Day of H.M. The Queen (1947)	Nov. 20
Birthday of H.M. The Queen (1926)	April 21	St. Andrew's Day	Nov. 30

RELIGIOUS CALENDARS 1989

Epiphany	Jan. 6	Trinity Sunday	May 21
Ash Wednesday	Feb. 8	Corpus Christi	May 25
Good Friday	March 24	Feast of Weeks, first day	June 9
Easter Day	March 26	Islamic New Year (1410)	Aug. 4
Ramadan, first day	April 7	Jewish New Year (5750)	Sept. 30
Passover, first day	April 20	Day of Atonement (Yom Kippur)	Oct. 9
Rogation Sunday	April 29	Feast of Tabernacles, first day	Oct. 14
Greek Orthodox Easter	April 30	First Sunday in Advent	Dec. 3
Ascension Day	May 4	Christmas Day	Dec. 25
Whit Sunday (Pentecost)	May 14		

SEASONS 1989

Northern Hemisphere

Spring Equinox	Sun enters Sign Aries	March 20d 15h	
Summer Solstice	„ „ „ Cancer	June 21d 10h	G.M.T.
Autumn Equinox	„ „ „ Libra	Sept. 23d 01h	
Winter Solstice	„ „ „ Capricornus	Dec. 21d 21h	

Southern Hemisphere

Autumn Equinox	Sun enters Sign Aries	March 20d 15h	
Winter Solstice	„ „ „ Cancer	June 21d 10h	G.M.T.
Spring Equinox	„ „ „ Libra	Sept. 23d 01h	
Summer Solstice	„ „ „ Capricornus	Dec. 21d 21h	

British Summer Time in 1989 begins March 26d 01h GMT and ends on October 29d 01h GMT.

LAW TERMS 1989

Hilary Term begins Jan. 11 and ends March 22
Easter Term begins April 4 and ends May 26
Trinity Term begins June 6 and ends July 31
Michaelmas Term begins Oct. 2 and ends Dec. 21

QUARTER DAYS		**TERM DAYS**	
(England, Wales, N. Ireland)		(Scotland)	
Lady Day	March 25	Candlemas	Feb. 2
Midsummer	June 24	Whitsunday	May 15
Michaelmas	Sept. 29	Lammas	Aug. 1
Christmas	Dec. 25	Martinmas	Nov. 11
		(*Removal Terms* are May 28 and Nov. 28).	

DAY OF		
Month	Week	

Janus, god of the portal, facing two ways, past and future.

Sun's Longitude 300° ≈ 20ᵈ 02ʰ

Month	Week	
1	S.	**1st S. after Christmas.** Paul Revere b. 1735.
2	M.	**Naming of Jesus.** Gen. Wolfe b. 1727.
3	Tu.	Princeton 1777. Marshal Joffre d. 1931.
4	W.	Jacob Grimm b. 1785. Augustus John b. 1878.
5	Th.	Catherine de Medici d. 1589.*
6	F.	**The Epiphany.** Fanny Burney d. 1840.
7	S.	Calais regained by the French 1558.
8	S.	**1st S. after Epiphany.** Galileo d. 1642.
9	M.	Katherine Mansfield Murry d. 1923.
10	Tu.	Penny Post introduced 1840.
11	W.	HILARY LAW SITTINGS BEGIN.
12	Th.	Field Marshal Herman Goering b. 1893.
13	F.	Stephen Foster d. 1864. James Joyce d. 1941.
14	S.	Lewis Carroll d. 1898. Harold Abrahams d. 1978.
15	S.	**2nd S. after Epiphany.** Fanny Kemble d. 1893.
16	M.	Edward Gibbon d. 1794. Coruña 1809.
17	Tu.	Gen. Fairfax b. 1612. Lloyd George b. 1863.
18	W.	Arthur Ransome b. 1884. Sir Cecil Beaton d. 1980.
19	Th.	Edgar Allen Poe b. 1809. Paul Cezanne b. 1839.
20	F.	David Garrick d. 1779. George V d. 1936.
21	S.	Christian Dior b. 1905. Jack Nicklaus b. 1940.
22	S.	**9th S. before Easter.** Rorke's Drift 1879.
23	M.	Tripoli 1943. Vietnam War Treaty 1973.
24	Tu.	Spion Kop 1900. Dogger Bank 1915.
25	W.	**Conversion of St. Paul.** Robert Burns b. 1759.
26	Th.	Gen. Charles Gordon killed 1885.
27	F.	First demonstration of television 1926.
28	S.	Gen. Charles Gordon b. 1833. W. B. Yeats d. 1939.
29	S.	**8th S. before Easter.** V.C. instituted 1856.
30	M.	Charles I exec. 1649. Gandhi assas. 1948.
31	Tu.	Guy Fawkes exec. 1606. A. A. Milne d. 1956.

PHENOMENA

d	h	
1	22	Earth at perihelion (147 million km.)
6	04	Venus in conjunction with Moon. Venus 5°N.
9	02	Mercury at greatest elongation E.19°
9	05	Mercury in conjunction with Moon. Mercury 2°N.
14	22	Mars in conjunction with Moon. Mars 4°S.
16	16	Saturn in conjunction with Venus. Saturn 0°.6N.
17	00	Jupiter in conjunction with Moon. Jupiter 6°S.
25	00	Mercury in inferior conjunction.

CONSTELLATIONS

The following constellations are near the meridian at

	d	h		d	h
Dec.	1	24	Dec.	16	23
Jan.	1	22	Jan.	16	21
Feb.	1	20	Feb.	15	19

Draco (below the Pole), Ursa Minor (below the Pole), Camelopardus, Perseus, Auriga, Taurus, Orion, Eridanus and Lepus.

MINIMA OF ALGOL

d	h	d	h
1	17	18	21
4	13	21	18
7	10	24	15
10	7	27	12
13	4	30	9
16	1		

*Centenary

PHASES OF THE MOON

	d	h	m
● New Moon	7	19	22
☽ First Quarter	14	13	58
○ Full Moon	21	21	33
☾ Last Quarter	30	02	02

	d	h
Perigee (366,380 kilometres)	10	23
Apogee (405,100 „)	27	00

Mean Longitude of Ascending Node on Jan. 1, 338°.

MONTHLY NOTES

Jan. 2. Bank Holiday in England, Scotland, Wales and Northern Ireland.

3. Bank Holiday, Scotland.

26. Australia Day. Republic Day, India.

Day	THE SUN									Sidereal Time	Transit of First Point of Aries
	Right Ascension	Dec. −	Equation of Time	Rise		Transit	Set				
				52°	56°		52°	56°			
	h m s	° ′	m s	h m	h m	h m	h m	h m		h m s	h m s
1	18 45 54	23 01	− 3 24	8 08	8 31	12 04	15 59	15 36		6 42 30	17 14 40
2	18 50 19	22 56	− 3 52	8 08	8 31	12 04	16 00	15 37		6 46 26	17 10 44
3	18 54 43	22 51	− 4 20	8 08	8 31	12 05	16 01	15 39		6 50 23	17 06 48
4	18 59 07	22 45	− 4 48	8 08	8 30	12 05	16 03	15 40		6 54 19	17 02 53
5	19 03 31	22 38	− 5 15	8 07	8 30	12 05	16 04	15 42		6 58 16	16 58 57
6	19 07 54	22 32	− 5 42	8 07	8 29	12 06	16 05	15 43		7 02 13	16 55 01
7	19 12 17	22 24	− 6 08	8 07	8 29	12 06	16 06	15 44		7 06 09	16 51 05
8	19 16 40	22 16	− 6 34	8 06	8 28	12 07	16 08	15 46		7 10 06	16 47 09
9	19 21 02	22 08	− 6 59	8 06	8 27	12 07	16 09	15 48		7 14 02	16 43 13
10	19 25 23	22 00	− 7 24	8 05	8 26	12 08	16 11	15 49		7 17 59	16 39 17
11	19 29 44	21 51	− 7 48	8 04	8 25	12 08	16 12	15 51		7 21 55	16 35 21
12	19 34 04	21 41	− 8 12	8 04	8 24	12 08	16 14	15 53		7 25 52	16 31 25
13	19 38 23	21 31	− 8 35	8 03	8 24	12 09	16 15	15 54		7 29 48	16 27 29
14	19 42 42	21 21	− 8 57	8 02	8 22	12 09	16 17	15 56		7 33 45	16 23 33
15	19 47 01	21 10	− 9 19	8 01	8 21	12 09	16 18	15 58		7 37 42	16 19 37
16	19 51 18	20 59	− 9 40	8 00	8 20	12 10	16 20	16 00		7 41 38	16 15 42
17	19 55 35	20 47	−10 00	7 59	8 19	12 10	16 21	16 02		7 45 35	16 11 46
18	19 59 51	20 35	−10 20	7 58	8 18	12 10	16 23	16 04		7 49 31	16 07 50
19	20 04 06	20 23	−10 39	7 57	8 16	12 11	16 25	16 06		7 53 28	16 03 54
20	20 08 21	20 10	−10 57	7 56	8 15	12 11	16 26	16 08		7 57 24	15 59 58
21	20 12 35	19 57	−11 14	7 55	8 14	12 11	16 28	16 10		8 01 21	15 56 02
22	20 16 48	19 44	−11 31	7 54	8 12	12 12	16 30	16 12		8 05 17	15 52 06
23	20 21 00	19 30	−11 46	7 53	8 11	12 12	16 32	16 14		8 09 14	15 48 10
24	20 25 12	19 16	−12 01	7 52	8 09	12 12	16 33	16 16		8 13 11	15 44 14
25	20 29 23	19 01	−12 16	7 50	8 07	12 12	16 35	16 18		8 17 07	15 40 18
26	20 33 33	18 46	−12 29	7 49	8 06	12 13	16 37	16 20		8 21 04	15 36 22
27	20 37 42	18 31	−12 42	7 48	8 04	12 13	16 39	16 22		8 25 00	15 32 27
28	20 41 51	18 16	−12 54	7 46	8 02	12 13	16 40	16 24		8 28 57	15 28 31
29	20 45 58	18 00	−13 05	7 45	8 01	12 13	16 42	16 26		8 32 53	15 24 35
30	20 50 05	17 43	−13 15	7 43	7 59	12 13	16 44	16 29		8 36 50	15 20 39
31	20 54 11	17 27	−13 25	7 42	7 57	12 13	16 46	16 31		8 40 47	15 16 43

Duration of Civil (C), Nautical (N), and Astronomical (A), Twilight (in minutes)

Lat.	Jan. 1			Jan. 11			Jan. 21			Jan. 31		
°	C	N	A	C	N	A	C	N	A	C	N	A
52	41	84	125	40	82	123	38	80	120	37	78	117
56	47	96	141	45	93	138	43	90	134	41	87	130

ASTRONOMICAL NOTES

MERCURY is at greatest eastern elongation on the 9th and, after the first few days of the month, is visible for about a fortnight. It is then an evening object (magnitude −0·7 to +1), visible for a short while around the time of end of evening civil twilight, low in the south-western sky. Shortly after the middle of January it becomes lost in the evening twilight, inferior conjunction occurring on the 25th.

VENUS is a brilliant object in the morning sky, magnitude −3·9, and at the beginning of the month is visible low in the E.S.E. sky for nearly an hour before dawn. The old crescent Moon, only 1½ days before New, passes about 5°S. of the planet on the morning of the 6th. For the last week of the month Venus is too close to the Sun for observation.

MARS, with its magnitude fading during the month from −0·1 to +0·5, is visible as an evening object in the western sky until midnight. During January Mars moves from Pisces into Aries. On the evening of the 14th the Moon, at First Quarter, passes 4°N. of the planet.

JUPITER is an evening object, magnitude −2·6, almost stationary in the western part of Taurus. The gibbous Moon passes 6°N. of the planet on the night of the 16th–17th.

SATURN remains too close to the Sun to be observed during January.

THE MOON

Day	R.A.	Dec.	Hor. Par.	Semi-diam.	Sun's Co-long.	P.A. of Bright Limb	Phase	Age	Rise 52°	Rise 56°	Transit	Set 52°	Set 56°
	h m	°	′	′	°	°		d	h m	h m	h m	h m	h m
1	13 05	−10·7	54·5	14·9	191	112	43	22·8	1 24	1 34	6 34	11 32	11 20
2	13 50	−15·8	54·9	15·0	204	109	33	23·8	2 37	2 53	7 17	11 45	11 28
3	14 38	−20·4	55·5	15·1	216	105	24	24·8	3 54	4 17	8 04	12 03	11 39
4	15 30	−24·2	56·2	15·3	228	99	16	25·8	5 13	5 43	8 55	12 29	11 58
5	16 26	−26·9	56·9	15·5	240	92	10	26·8	6 30	7 07	9 50	13 08	12 30
6	17 26	−28·1	57·7	15·7	252	82	4	27·8	7 37	8 16	10 50	14 04	13 25
7	18 28	−27·7	58·4	15·9	265	65	1	28·8	8 28	9 03	11 51	15 19	14 44
8	19 30	−25·5	59·0	16·1	277	317	0	0·2	9 04	9 31	12 50	16 46	16 20
9	20 30	−21·7	59·5	16·2	289	265	2	1·2	9 29	9 48	13 47	18 18	18 00
10	21 27	−16·6	59·8	16·3	301	254	6	2·2	9 47	9 59	14 40	19 49	19 38
11	22 21	−10·5	59·8	16·3	313	249	13	3·2	10 01	10 07	15 30	21 17	21 13
12	23 13	− 3·9	59·8	16·3	325	246	22	4·2	10 13	10 14	16 19	22 44	22 46
13	0 04	+ 2·9	59·5	16·2	338	246	32	5·2	10 25	10 20	17 07	—	—
14	0 54	+ 9·5	59·2	16·1	350	247	44	6·2	10 38	10 28	17 56	0 10	0 18
15	1 46	+15·5	58·8	16·0	2	250	55	7·2	10 54	10 37	18 48	1 36	1 51
16	2 40	+20·7	58·3	15·9	14	254	66	8·2	11 15	10 51	19 42	3 04	3 26
17	3 37	+24·7	57·9	15·8	26	260	76	9·2	11 44	11 13	20 38	4 29	4 59
18	4 36	+27·2	57·4	15·6	38	267	84	10·2	12 25	11 48	21 36	5 47	6 23
19	5 35	+28·2	56·9	15·5	51	275	91	11·2	13 22	12 44	22 34	6 50	7 28
20	6 34	+27·6	56·5	15·4	63	284	96	12·2	14 32	13 58	23 29	7 36	8 11
21	7 31	+25·5	56·0	15·3	75	298	99	13·2	15 49	15 23	—	8 09	8 36
22	8 24	+22·2	55·5	15·1	87	36	100	14·2	17 07	16 48	0 20	8 31	8 51
23	9 14	+17·9	55·1	15·0	99	100	99	15·2	18 23	18 10	1 07	8 47	9 01
24	10 01	+12·9	54·7	14·9	111	109	96	16·2	19 37	19 29	1 51	8 59	9 08
25	10 44	+ 7·5	54·4	14·8	123	113	91	17·2	20 47	20 45	2 31	9 09	9 14
26	11 27	+ 2·0	54·2	14·8	135	115	85	18·2	21 57	22 00	3 11	9 19	9 18
27	12 09	− 3·6	54·1	14·7	148	115	78	19·2	23 07	23 15	3 50	9 28	9 23
28	12 51	− 9·1	54·2	14·8	160	114	69	20·2	—	—	4 29	9 38	9 28
29	13 34	−14·3	54·4	14·8	172	112	60	21·2	0 19	0 33	5 10	9 50	9 35
30	14 21	−19·0	54·9	14·9	184	109	51	22·2	1 34	1 54	5 55	10 05	9 44
31	15 10	−23·0	55·4	15·1	196	105	41	23·2	2 51	3 18	6 43	10 27	9 59

MERCURY ☿

Day	R.A.	Dec. −	Diam.	Phase	Transit	5° high 52°	5° high 56°	Day	R.A.	Dec. −	Diam.	Phase	Transit	
	h m	°	″		h m	h m	h m		h m	°	″		h m	
1	19 59	22·6	6	81	13 18	16 27	15 54	16	20 56	16·3	—	—	13 12	
4	20 17	21·4	6	75	13 24	16 43	16 14	19	20 52	15·6	—	—	12 55	Mercury is too
7	20 33	20·0	7	65	13 27	16 57	16 31	22	20 41	15·5	—	—	12 31	close to the
10	20 46	18·6	7	54	13 27	17 07	16 43	25	20 26	15·8	—	—	12 04	Sun for
13	20 54	17·3	8	41	13 23	17 11	16 50	28	20 11	16·4	—	—	11 38	observation
16	20 56	16·3	8	27	13 12	17 07	16 47	31	19 59	17·1	—	—	11 15	

VENUS ♀

Day	R.A.	Dec. −	Diam.	Phase	Transit	5° high 52°	5° high 56°
	h m	°	″		h m	h m	h m
1	17 07	22·1	11	93	10 25	7 14	7 47
6	17 34	22·7	11	93	10 33	7 27	8 01
11	18 01	23·0	11	94	10 40	7 37	8 13
16	18 29	22·9	11	95	10 48	7 45	8 21
21	18 56	22·3	10	95	10 55	7 50	8 25
26	19 23	21·5	10	96	11 02	7 53	8 26
31	19 50	21·3	10	97	11 09	7 53	8 24

MARS ♂

Day	R.A.	Dec. +	Diam.	Phase	Transit	5° high 52°	5° high 56°
	h m	°	″		h m	h m	h m
1	1 14	8·4	10	88	18 30	0 42	0 45
6	1 23	9·5	9	88	18 20	0 37	0 42
11	1 33	10·5	9	88	18 10	0 33	0 38
16	1 43	11·6	8	88	18 00	0 29	0 35
21	1 54	12·6	8	88	17 51	0 25	0 32
26	2 05	13·7	8	88	17 42	0 22	0 30
31	2 16	14·7	7	88	17 34	0 18	0 27

SUNRISE AND SUNSET

Day	London a.m. h m	London p.m. h m	Bristol a.m. h m	Bristol p.m. h m	Birmingham a.m. h m	Birmingham p.m. h m	Manchester a.m. h m	Manchester p.m. h m	Newcastle a.m. h m	Newcastle p.m. h m	Glasgow a.m. h m	Glasgow p.m. h m	Belfast a.m. h m	Belfast p.m. h m
1	8 06	4 02	8 16	4 12	8 18	4 03	8 25	4 00	8 31	3 48	8 48	3 54	8 47	4 08
2	8 06	4 03	8 16	4 13	8 18	4 04	8 25	4 01	8 31	3 49	8 47	3 55	8 47	4 09
3	8 06	4 04	8 16	4 14	8 18	4 05	8 25	4 02	8 31	3 50	8 47	3 56	8 47	4 10
4	8 06	4 05	8 15	4 15	8 18	4 07	8 25	4 04	8 31	3 52	8 47	3 58	8 47	4 12
5	8 06	4 06	8 15	4 16	8 17	4 08	8 24	4 05	8 30	3 53	8 46	3 59	8 46	4 13
6	8 06	4 07	8 15	4 17	8 17	4 09	8 24	4 06	8 30	3 54	8 46	4 00	8 46	4 14
7	8 05	4 08	8 15	4 19	8 16	4 11	8 23	4 08	8 29	3 56	8 45	4 02	8 45	4 16
8	8 04	4 09	8 14	4 20	8 16	4 12	8 23	4 09	8 28	3 57	8 44	4 03	8 44	4 17
9	8 04	4 11	8 14	4 22	8 15	4 14	8 22	4 11	8 28	3 59	8 44	4 05	8 44	4 19
10	8 04	4 12	8 13	4 23	8 15	4 15	8 22	4 12	8 27	4 01	8 43	4 07	8 43	4 21
11	8 03	4 14	8 13	4 24	8 14	4 17	8 21	4 14	8 26	4 02	8 42	4 08	8 42	4 22
12	8 02	4 15	8 12	4 26	8 13	4 18	8 20	4 15	8 25	4 04	8 41	4 10	8 41	4 24
13	8 02	4 16	8 12	4 27	8 13	4 19	8 20	4 16	8 24	4 06	8 40	4 12	8 40	4 26
14	8 01	4 18	8 11	4 29	8 12	4 21	8 19	4 18	8 23	4 07	8 39	4 14	8 39	4 27
15	8 00	4 20	8 10	4 30	8 11	4 23	8 18	4 20	8 22	4 09	8 38	4 15	8 38	4 29
16	7 59	4 21	8 09	4 32	8 10	4 24	8 17	4 21	8 21	4 11	8 37	4 17	8 37	4 31
17	7 58	4 23	8 08	4 33	8 09	4 26	8 16	4 23	8 20	4 13	8 36	4 19	8 36	4 33
18	7 57	4 24	8 07	4 35	8 08	4 27	8 15	4 24	8 19	4 14	8 35	4 21	8 35	4 34
19	7 56	4 26	8 06	4 36	8 07	4 29	8 14	4 26	8 18	4 16	8 33	4 23	8 34	4 36
20	7 55	4 28	8 05	4 38	8 06	4 31	8 13	4 28	8 17	4 18	8 32	4 25	8 33	4 38
21	7 54	4 29	8 04	4 39	8 05	4 32	8 12	4 30	8 16	4 20	8 31	4 27	8 32	4 40
22	7 53	4 31	8 03	4 41	8 04	4 34	8 10	4 32	8 14	4 22	8 29	4 29	8 30	4 42
23	7 52	4 33	8 02	4 43	8 03	4 36	8 09	4 33	8 13	4 24	8 28	4 31	8 29	4 43
24	7 50	4 35	8 00	4 45	8 01	4 38	8 08	4 35	8 11	4 26	8 26	4 33	8 28	4 45
25	7 49	4 36	7 59	4 46	8 00	4 39	8 06	4 37	8 09	4 28	8 24	4 35	8 26	4 47
26	7 48	4 38	7 58	4 48	7 59	4 41	8 05	4 39	8 08	4 30	8 23	4 37	8 25	4 49
27	7 46	4 40	7 56	4 50	7 57	4 43	8 03	4 41	8 06	4 32	8 21	4 39	8 23	4 51
28	7 45	4 42	7 55	4 52	7 56	4 45	8 02	4 43	8 05	4 34	8 20	4 42	8 22	4 54
29	7 44	4 44	7 54	4 54	7 55	4 47	8 00	4 45	8 03	4 36	8 18	4 44	8 20	4 56
30	7 42	4 45	7 52	4 55	7 53	4 48	7 59	4 47	8 02	4 38	8 16	4 46	8 18	4 58
31	7 41	4 47	7 51	4 57	7 52	4 50	7 57	4 49	8 00	4 40	8 14	4 48	8 16	5 00

JUPITER ♃   SATURN ♄

Day	R.A. h m	Dec. + °	Transit h m	5° high 52° h m	5° high 56° h m	R.A. h m	Dec. − °	Transit h m	
1	3 39	18·6	20 52	4 00	4 13	18 24	22·6	11 40	Saturn is too
11	3 37	18·5	20 11	3 19	3 31	18 29	22·6	11 06	close to the
21	3 36	18·5	19 31	2 39	2 52	18 34	22·5	10 31	Sun for
31	3 37	18·6	18 53	2 01	2 14	18 39	22·4	9 57	Observation

Equatorial diameter of Jupiter 44″; of Saturn 15″.   Diameters of Saturn's rings 34″ and 15″.

URANUS ♅   NEPTUNE ♆

Day	R.A. h m	Dec. − ° ′	Transit h m		R.A. h m	Dec. − ° ′	Transit h m	
1	18 07·7	23 39	11 23	Uranus is too	18 42·9	22 10	11 59	Neptune is too
11	18 10·2	23 39	10 47	close to the Sun	18 44·5	22 09	11 21	close to the Sun
21	18 12·7	23 38	10 10	for observation	18 46·1	22 07	10 43	for observation
31	18 15·0	23 37	9 33		18 47·6	22 05	10 05	

Diameter 4″   Diameter 2″

Februa, Roman festival
of Purification
Sun's Longitude 330° ♓ 18ᵈ 16ʰ

Month	Week	
1	W.	John Ford b. 1895. Buster Keaton d. 1966.
2	Th.	**Presentation of Christ.** Nell Gwyn b. 1651.
3	F.	Elizabeth Blackwell b. 1821. Gertrude Stein b. 1874.
4	S.	End of sweet rationing 1953.
5	S.	**7th S. before Easter.** Robert Peel b. 1788.
6	M.	QUEEN'S ACCESSION 1952. Ronald Reagan b. 1911.
7	Tu.	SHROVE TUESDAY. Sir Thomas More b. 1478.
8	W.	**Ash Wednesday.** John Ruskin b. 1819.
9	Th.	Alban Berg b. 1885. Jim Laker b. 1922.
10	F.	Boris Pasternak b. 1890. Harold Macmillan b. 1894.
11	S.	Mary Quant b. 1934. John Buchan d. 1940.
12	S.	**1st S. in Lent.** Marie Lloyd b. 1870.
13	M.	Accession of William III and Mary II 1689.*
14	Tu.	VALENTINE'S DAY. Cape St. Vincent 1797.
15	W.	Surrender of Singapore 1942.
16	Th.	Sir Geraint Evans b. 1922.
17	F.	Geronimo d. 1909. Graham Sutherland d. 1980.
18	S.	Michaelangelo d. 1564. Dame Ngaio Marsh d. 1982.
19	S.	**2nd S. in Lent.** DUKE OF YORK b. 1960.
20	M.	Henry James Pye b. 1745.
21	Tu.	Nicolai Gogol d. 1852. Verdun 1915.
22	W.	Olave, Lady Baden-Powell b. 1889.*
23	Th.	Stan Laurel d. 1965. L. S. Lowry d. 1976.
24	F.	Wilhelm Grimm b. 1786. Henry Cavendish d. 1810.
25	S.	Renoir b. 1841. Anthony Burgess b. 1917.
26	S.	**3rd S. in Lent.** Everton Weekes b. 1925.
27	M.	German Reichstag burnt down 1933.
28	Tu.	Relief of Ladysmith 1900.

*Centenary

PHENOMENA

d h
1 03 Venus in conjunction with Mercury. Venus 4°S.

3 15 Saturn in conjunction with Moon. Saturn 5°N.

4 18 Mercury in conjunction with Moon. Mercury 6°N.

12 07 Mars in conjunction with Moon. Mars 4°S.

13 07 Jupiter in conjunction with Moon. Jupiter 6° S.

18 16 Mercury at greatest elongation W.26°.

CONSTELLATIONS

The following constellations are near the meridian at

	d	h		d	h
Jan.	1	24	Jan.	16	23
Feb.	1	22	Feb.	15	21
Mar.	1	20	Mar.	16	19

Draco (below the Pole), Camelopardus, Auriga, Taurus, Gemini, Orion, Canis Minor, Monoceros, Lepus, Canis Major and Puppis.

MINIMA OF ALGOL

d	h	d	h
2	5	16	14
5	2	19	10
7	23	22	7
10	20	25	4
13	17	28	1

PHASES OF THE MOON

	d	h	m
● New Moon.........	6	07	37
☽ First Quarter	12	23	15
○ Full Moon	20	15	32
☾ Last Quarter.......	28	20	08

	d	h
Perigee (360,940 kilometres)	7	22
Apogee (405,940 „)	23	14

Mean Longitude of Ascending Node on Feb. 1, 336°

MONTHLY NOTES

Feb. 1. Pheasant and partridge shooting ends.

6. National Day, New Zealand.

Ancient Chinese New Year (Year of the Snake).

8. First Day of Lent

Day	THE SUN s.d. 16′·2								Sidereal Time	Transit of First Point of Aries
	Right Ascension	Dec. −	Equation of Time	Rise 52°	Rise 56°	Transit	Set 52°	Set 56°		
	h m s	° ′	m s	h m	h m	h m	h m	h m	h m s	h m s
1	20 58 16	17 10	−13 33	7 40	7 55	12 14	16 48	16 33	8 44 43	15 12 47
2	21 02 21	16 53	−13 41	7 38	7 53	12 14	16 50	16 35	8 48 40	15 08 51
3	21 06 24	16 35	−13 48	7 37	7 51	12 14	16 52	16 37	8 52 36	15 04 55
4	21 10 27	16 18	−13 55	7 35	7 49	12 14	16 53	16 40	8 56 33	15 00 59
5	21 14 29	16 00	−14 00	7 34	7 47	12 14	16 55	16 42	9 00 29	14 57 03
6	21 18 31	15 41	−14 05	7 32	7 45	12 14	16 57	16 44	9 04 26	14 53 07
7	21 22 31	15 23	−14 09	7 30	7 43	12 14	16 59	16 46	9 08 22	14 49 12
8	21 26 31	15 04	−14 12	7 28	7 41	12 14	17 01	16 48	9 12 19	14 45 16
9	21 30 29	14 45	−14 14	7 27	7 39	12 14	17 03	16 51	9 16 16	14 41 20
10	21 34 27	14 26	−14 15	7 25	7 37	12 14	17 05	16 53	9 20 12	14 37 24
11	21 38 25	14 06	−14 16	7 23	7 34	12 14	17 06	16 55	9 24 09	14 33 28
12	21 42 21	13 46	−14 16	7 21	7 32	12 14	17 08	16 57	9 28 05	14 29 32
13	21 46 17	13 26	−14 15	7 19	7 30	12 14	17 10	16 59	9 32 02	14 25 36
14	21 50 12	13 06	−14 13	7 17	7 28	12 14	17 12	17 02	9 35 58	14 21 40
15	21 54 06	12 45	−14 11	7 15	7 25	12 14	17 14	17 04	9 39 55	14 17 44
16	21 57 59	12 25	−14 08	7 13	7 23	12 14	17 16	17 06	9 43 51	14 13 48
17	22 01 52	12 04	−14 04	7 11	7 21	12 14	17 18	17 08	9 47 48	14 09 52
18	22 05 44	11 43	−13 59	7 09	7 19	12 14	17 19	17 10	9 51 45	14 05 57
19	22 09 35	11 22	−13 54	7 07	7 16	12 14	17 21	17 12	9 55 41	14 02 01
20	22 13 26	11 00	−13 48	7 05	7 14	12 14	17 23	17 15	9 59 38	13 58 05
21	22 17 16	10 39	−13 41	7 03	7 11	12 14	17 25	17 17	10 03 34	13 54 09
22	22 21 05	10 17	−13 34	7 01	7 09	12 14	17 27	17 19	10 07 31	13 50 13
23	22 24 54	9 55	−13 26	6 59	7 07	12 13	17 29	17 21	10 11 27	13 46 17
24	22 28 42	9 33	−13 18	6 57	7 04	12 13	17 30	17 23	10 15 24	13 42 21
25	22 32 29	9 11	−13 09	6 55	7 02	12 13	17 32	17 25	10 19 20	13 38 25
26	22 36 16	8 48	−12 59	6 53	6 59	12 13	17 34	17 28	10 23 17	13 34 29
27	22 40 02	8 26	−12 49	6 50	6 57	12 13	17 36	17 30	10 27 14	13 30 33
28	22 43 48	8 03	−12 38	6 48	6 54	12 13	17 38	17 32	10 31 10	13 26 37

Duration of Civil (C), Nautical (N), and Astronomical (A), Twilight (in minutes)

Lat. °	Feb. 1 C	N	A	Feb. 11 C	N	A	Feb. 21 C	N	A	Feb. 28 C	N	A
52	37	77	117	35	75	114	34	74	113	34	73	112
56	41	86	130	39	83	126	38	81	125	38	81	124

ASTRONOMICAL NOTES

MERCURY, although it attains its greatest western elongation on the 18th, is unsuitably placed for observation in these latitudes.

VENUS is unsuitably placed for observation.

MARS continues to be visible as an evening object, magnitude +0·8, and may be observed in the western sky until midnight. The Moon is near Mars on the evenings of the 11th and 12th. Mars is in the constellation of Aries. The slight reddish tint of the planet is a useful aid to its identification.

JUPITER, magnitude −2·4, continues to be visible as a brilliant evening object, moving very slowly eastwards in the constellation of Taurus, some 5°S. of the Pleiades. The four Galilean satellites are readily observable with any small telescope, or even a good pair of binoculars provided that they are held rigidly. Times of eclipses and shadow transits of these satellites are given on page 73.

SATURN is gradually becoming visible as a morning object, magnitude +0·6, low above the south-eastern horizon before the brightening morning twilight inhibits observation.

ECLIPSE. A total eclipse of the Moon occurs on the 20th. See page 74 for details.

ZODIACAL LIGHT. The evening cone may be observed in the western sky after the end of twilight from the beginning of the month to the 7th and again after the 21st. This faint phenomenon is only visible under good conditions, in the absence of both moonlight and artificial lighting.

THE MOON

Day	R.A.	Dec.	Hor. Par.	Semi-diam.	Sun's Co-long.	P.A. of Bright Limb	Phase	Age	Rise 52°	Rise 56°	Tran-sit	Set 52°	Set 56°
	h m	°	′	′	°	°		d	h m	h m	h m	h m	h m
1	16 03	−26·1	56·2	15·3	208	99	32	24·2	4 08	4 42	7 35	10 58	10 23
2	17 01	−27·9	57·0	15·5	221	92	22	25·2	5 18	5 58	8 32	11 44	11 05
3	18 01	−28·2	57·9	15·8	233	85	14	26·2	6 17	6 55	9 32	12 50	12 12
4	19 03	−26·8	58·8	16·0	245	77	7	27·2	6 59	7 31	10 32	14 12	13 41
5	20 04	−23·6	59·6	16·2	257	68	2	28·2	7 29	7 53	11 31	15 44	15 22
6	21 04	−18·9	60·2	16·4	269	49	0	29·2	7 50	8 06	12 27	17 18	17 04
7	22 00	−12·9	60·6	16·5	282	254	1	0·7	8 06	8 16	13 20	18 50	18 43
8	22 54	− 6·2	60·7	16·6	294	246	4	1·7	8 20	8 23	14 11	20 21	20 21
9	23 47	+ 0·8	60·6	16·5	306	244	10	2·7	8 32	8 30	15 01	21 50	21 57
10	0 39	+ 7·7	60·2	16·4	318	244	19	3·7	8 45	8 37	15 51	23 20	23 33
11	1 32	+14·1	59·6	16·2	330	246	28	4·7	9 00	8 45	16 43	—	—
12	2 27	+19·6	59·0	16·1	342	250	39	5·7	9 19	8 58	17 37	0 49	1 10
13	3 24	+24·0	58·3	15·9	355	255	50	6·7	9 46	9 16	18 34	2 17	2 45
14	4 22	+26·9	57·6	15·7	7	262	61	7·7	10 23	9 47	19 31	3 38	4 13
15	5 21	+28·2	56·9	15·5	19	269	71	8·7	11 14	10 36	20 28	4 46	5 24
16	6 20	+28·0	56·3	15·3	31	275	80	9·7	12 20	11 44	21 23	5 37	6 13
17	7 19	+26·2	55·8	15·2	43	282	88	10·7	13 35	13 06	22 15	6 12	6 42
18	8 10	+23·2	55·3	15·1	55	288	93	11·7	14 52	14 30	23 03	6 37	7 00
19	9 00	+19·2	54·9	15·0	68	293	97	12·7	16 08	15 53	23 47	6 54	7 11
20	9 47	+14·4	54·6	14·9	80	297	100	13·7	17 22	17 13	—	7 07	7 18
21	10 32	+ 9·1	54·3	14·8	92	113	100	14·7	18 34	18 30	0 29	7 18	7 24
22	11 14	+ 3·6	54·1	14·8	104	118	98	15·7	19 44	19 45	1 09	7 27	7 29
23	11 56	− 2·0	54·0	14·7	116	118	95	16·7	20 54	21 00	1 48	7 37	7 33
24	12 38	− 7·6	54·0	14·7	128	117	90	17·7	22 05	22 16	2 27	7 46	7 38
25	13 21	−12·9	54·1	14·7	140	116	84	18·7	23 18	23 35	3 07	7 57	7 44
26	14 06	−17·7	54·4	14·8	153	113	76	19·7	—	—	3 50	8 11	7 52
27	14 54	−21·9	54·8	14·9	165	109	68	20·7	0 33	0 57	4 36	8 29	8 04
28	15 45	−25·2	55·3	15·1	177	104	58	21·7	1 49	2 20	5 25	8 55	8 23

MERCURY ☿

Day	R.A.	Dec. −	Diam.	Phase	Tran-sit		Day	R.A.	Dec. −	Diam.	Phase	Tran-sit	
	h m	°	″		h m			h m	°	″		h m	
1	19 56	17·3	—	—	11 08		16	20 12	19·3	—	—	10 29	
4	19 50	18·0	—	—	10 52	Mercury is too	19	20 25	19·1	—	—	10 29	Mercury is too
7	19 50	18·6	—	—	10 41	close to the	22	20 39	18·8	—	—	10 31	close to the
10	19 55	19·0	—	—	10 34	Sun for	25	20 54	18·3	—	—	10 35	Sun for
13	20 02	19·2	—	—	10 30	observation	28	21 09	17·6	—	—	10 39	observation
16	20 12	19·3	—	—	10 29		31	21 26	16·7	—	—	10 44	

VENUS ♀

Day	R.A.	Dec. −	Diam.	Phase	Tran-sit	5° high. 52°	5° high. 56°
	h m	°	″		h m	h m	h m
1	19 55	21·3	—	—	11 11		
6	20 21	20·2	—	—	11 17		
11	20 47	18·8	—	—	11 24	Venus is too close to the
16	21 13	17·2	—	—	11 29	Sun for observation
21	21 37	15·4	—	—	11 34	
26	22 02	13·4	—	—	11 39	
31	22 26	11·2	—	—	11 34	

MARS ♂

Day	R.A.	Dec. +	Diam.	Phase	Tran-sit	5° high. 52°	5° high. 56°
	h m	°	″		h m	h m	h m
1	2 18	14·9	7	89	17 32	0 18	0 27
6	2 29	15·9	7	89	17 24	0 15	0 25
11	2 41	16·8	7	89	17 15	0 12	0 23
16	2 53	17·7	7	89	17 08	0 09	0 21
21	3 04	18·6	6	89	17 00	0 06	0 19
26	3 17	19·4	6	90	16 52	0 04	0 17
31	3 29	20·2	6	90	16 45	0 01	0 16

SUNRISE AND SUNSET

Day	London a.m.	London p.m.	Bristol a.m.	Bristol p.m.	Birmingham a.m.	Birmingham p.m.	Manchester a.m.	Manchester p.m.	Newcastle a.m.	Newcastle p.m.	Glasgow a.m.	Glasgow p.m.	Belfast a.m.	Belfast p.m.
	h m	h m	h m	h m	h m	h m	h m	h m	h m	h m	h m	h m	h m	h m
1	7 40	4 49	7 49	4 59	7 50	4 52	7 55	4 51	7 58	4 42	8 12	4 50	8 14	5 02
2	7 38	4 51	7 48	5 01	7 48	4 54	7 53	4 53	7 56	4 44	8 10	4 52	8 12	5 04
3	7 37	4 53	7 46	5 03	7 47	4 56	7 52	4 55	7 54	4 46	8 08	4 54	8 11	5 06
4	7 35	4 55	7 44	5 05	7 45	4 58	7 50	4 57	7 52	4 49	8 06	4 57	8 09	5 08
5	7 34	4 56	7 43	5 06	7 43	5 00	7 48	4 59	7 50	4 51	8 04	4 59	8 07	5 10
6	7 32	4 58	7 41	5 08	7 41	5 02	7 46	5 01	7 48	4 53	8 02	5 01	8 05	5 12
7	7 30	5 00	7 40	5 10	7 39	5 04	7 44	5 03	7 46	4 55	8 00	5 03	8 03	5 14
8	7 29	5 01	7 38	5 11	7 38	5 06	7 43	5 05	7 45	4 57	7 59	5 05	8 02	5 16
9	7 27	5 03	7 36	5 13	7 36	5 08	7 41	5 07	7 43	4 59	7 57	5 07	8 00	5 18
10	7 25	5 05	7 35	5 15	7 34	5 10	7 39	5 09	7 41	5 01	7 55	5 09	7 58	5 20
11	7 23	5 07	7 33	5 17	7 32	5 12	7 37	5 11	7 39	5 03	7 53	5 11	7 56	5 22
12	7 21	5 09	7 31	5 19	7 30	5 14	7 35	5 13	7 37	5 05	7 51	5 13	7 54	5 24
13	7 19	5 10	7 29	5 21	7 28	5 15	7 33	5 14	7 34	5 07	7 48	5 15	7 52	5 26
14	7 17	5 12	7 27	5 22	7 26	5 17	7 31	5 16	7 32	5 09	7 46	5 17	7 50	5 28
15	7 15	5 14	7 25	5 24	7 24	5 19	7 29	5 18	7 30	5 12	7 44	5 20	7 47	5 30
16	7 13	5 16	7 23	5 26	7 22	5 21	7 27	5 20	7 28	5 14	7 42	5 22	7 45	5 32
17	7 11	5 18	7 21	5 28	7 20	5 23	7 25	5 22	7 25	5 16	7 39	5 24	7 43	5 34
18	7 09	5 20	7 19	5 30	7 18	5 25	7 23	5 24	7 23	5 18	7 37	5 26	7 41	5 36
19	7 07	5 21	7 17	5 31	7 16	5 26	7 21	5 26	7 21	5 20	7 35	5 28	7 39	5 38
20	7 05	5 23	7 15	5 33	7 14	5 28	7 19	5 28	7 19	5 22	7 32	5 31	7 36	5 41
21	7 03	5 25	7 13	5 35	7 12	5 30	7 16	5 30	7 17	5 24	7 30	5 33	7 34	5 43
22	7 01	5 27	7 11	5 37	7 10	5 32	7 14	5 32	7 14	5 26	7 27	5 35	7 31	5 45
23	6 59	5 29	7 09	5 39	7 08	5 34	7 12	5 34	7 12	5 28	7 25	5 37	7 29	5 47
24	6 57	5 31	7 07	5 41	7 06	5 36	7 10	5 36	7 10	5 30	7 23	5 39	7 27	5 49
25	6 55	5 33	7 05	5 43	7 04	5 38	7 07	5 38	7 07	5 32	7 20	5 41	7 24	5 51
26	6 53	5 34	7 03	5 44	7 02	5 39	7 05	5 40	7 05	5 35	7 18	5 44	7 22	5 53
27	6 51	5 36	7 01	5 46	7 00	5 41	7 03	5 42	7 02	5 37	7 15	5 46	7 20	5 55
28	6 49	5 38	6 59	5 48	6 57	5 43	7 00	5 44	7 00	5 39	7 13	5 48	7 17	5 57

JUPITER ♃ / SATURN ♄

Day	JUPITER R.A.	Dec. +	Transit	5° high. 52°	5° high. 56°	SATURN R.A.	Dec. −	Transit	5° high. 52°	5° high. 56°
	h m	°	h m	h m	h m	h m	°	h m	h m	h m
1	3 37	18·6	18 49	1 57	2 10	18 39	22·4	9 53	6 46	7 19
11	3 39	18·8	18 12	1 21	1 34	18 44	22·4	9 18	6 10	6 43
21	3 43	19·0	17 36	0 47	1 00	18 48	22·3	8 43	5 34	6 07
31	3 47	19·3	17 02	0 14	0 27	18 51	22·2	8 07	4 58	5 31

Equatorial diameter of Jupiter 40″; of Saturn 16″. Diameters of Saturn's rings 35″ and 15″.

URANUS ♅ / NEPTUNE ♆

Day	URANUS R.A.	Dec. −	Transit	10° high. 52°	10° high. 56°	NEPTUNE R.A.	Dec. −	Transit	10° high. 52°	10° high. 56°
	h m	° ′	h m	h m	h m	h m	° ′	h m	h m	h m
1	18 15·3	23 37	9 29	7 30	8 53	18 47·7	22 05	10 01	7 44	8 40
11	18 17·3	23 37	8 52	6 53	8 15	18 49·1	22 03	9 23	7 05	8 01
21	18 19·2	23 36	8 14	6 15	7 37	18 50·4	22 02	8 45	6 27	7 22
31	18 20·7	23 36	7 36	5 37	6 59	18 51·4	22 00	8 07	5 48	6 44

Diameter 4″ / Diameter 2″

		Mars, Roman god of battle

Sun's Longitude 0° ♈ 20ᵈ 15ʰ

Month	Week	
1	W.	ST. DAVID'S DAY. Dixie Dean d. 1980.
2	Th.	Cardinal Archbishop of Westminster b. 1923.
3	F.	Abolition of serfdom in Russia 1861.
4	S.	Opening of Forth Railway Bridge 1890.
5	S.	**4th S. in Lent.** MOTHERING SUNDAY.
6	M.	Alamo ended 1836. Pearl Buck d. 1973.
7	Tu.	First patent of Bell telephone 1876.
8	W.	Count von Zeppelin d. 1917. R. A. Butler d. 1982.
9	Th.	Amerigo Vespucci b. 1451. Imogen Holst d. 1984.
10	F.	PRINCE EDWARD b. 1964. Owen Brannigan b. 1908.
11	S.	Outbreak of Russian Revolution 1917.
12	S.	**5th S. in Lent.** Vaslav Nijinsky b. 1890.
13	M.	Earl Grey b. 1764. Uranus discovered 1781.
14	Tu.	Maxim Gorky b. 1868. Karl Marx d. 1883.
15	W.	Julius Caesar assas. 44 B.C.
16	Th.	Sir Austen Chamberlain d. 1937.
17	F.	ST. PATRICK'S DAY. Bobby Jones b. 1902.
18	S.	**St. Joseph of Nazareth.** Dr. Livingstone b. 1813.
19	S.	**Palm Sunday.** Edgar Rice Burroughs d. 1950.
20	M.	Henry IV d. 1413. Henrik Ibsen b. 1828.
21	Tu.	J. S. Bach b. 1685. Modest Mussorgsky b. 1839.
22	W.	HILARY LAW SITTINGS END. Stendhal d. 1842.
23	Th.	**Maundy Thursday.** Donald Campbell b. 1921.
24	F.	**Good Friday.** Elizabeth I d. 1603.
25	S.	**Easter Eve.** Treaty of Rome 1957.
26	S.	**Easter Day.** Sir Noel Coward d. 1973.
27	M.	John Bright d. 1889.* Yuri Garagin d. 1968.
28	Tu.	Neil Kinnock b. 1942. Marc Chagall d. 1985.
29	W.	Towton Field 1461. Vera Brittain d. 1970.
30	Th.	Alaska sold to U.S.A. by Russia 1867.
31	F.	Eiffel Tower completed 1889.*

*Centenary

PHENOMENA

d h
3 06 Saturn in conjunction with Moon. Saturn 5°N.
6 04 Mercury in conjunction with Moon. Mercury 0°·8S.
12 08 Jupiter in conjunction with Mars. Jupiter 2°S.
12 19 Jupiter in conjunction with Moon. Jupiter 6°S.
12 19 Mars in conjunction with Moon. Mars 4°S.
20 15 Equinox.
30 16 Saturn in conjunction with Moon. Saturn 5°N.

CONSTELLATIONS

The following are near the meridian at

	d h		d h
Feb. 1	24	Feb. 15	23
Mar. 1	22	Mar. 16	21
Apr. 1	20	Apr. 15	19

Cepheus (below the Pole), Camelopardus, Lynx, Gemini, Cancer, Leo, Canis Minor, Hydra, Monoceros, Canis Major and Puppis.

MINIMA OF ALGOL

d	h	d	h
2	22	20	3
5	18	22	23
8	15	25	20
11	12	28	17
14	9	31	14
17	6		

PHASES OF THE MOON

		d	h	m
● New Moon		7	18	19
☽ First Quarter		14	10	11
○ Full Moon		22	09	58
☾ Last Quarter		30	10	21

	d	h
Perigee (357,540 kilometres)	8	08
Apogee (406,350 ,,)	22	18

Mean Longitude of Ascending Node on March 1, 335°.

Summer Time in 1989 (*see* p. 72).—Begins: March 26ᵈ 01ʰ G.M.T.
Ends: October 29ᵈ 01ʰ G.M.T.

MONTHLY NOTES

March 13. Commonwealth Day.
17. Bank Holiday in Northern Ireland.
24. Bank Holiday, Scotland.
25. Lent ends at Midnight.
       Lady Day. Quarter Day.
27. Bank Holiday, England, Wales and Northern Ireland.
31. Financial Year 1988–89 ends.

Day	THE SUN s.d. 16'·1								Sidereal Time	Transit of First Point of Aries
	Right Ascension	Dec.	Equation of Time	Rise 52°	Rise 56°	Transit	Set 52°	Set 56°		
	h m s	° ′	m s	h m	h m	h m	h m	h m	h m s	h m s
1	22 47 33	−7 41	−12 27	6 46	6 52	12 12	17 40	17 34	10 35 07	13 22 42
2	22 51 18	−7 18	−12 15	6 44	6 49	12 12	17 41	17 36	10 39 03	13 18 46
3	22 55 02	−6 55	−12 03	6 42	6 47	12 12	17 43	17 38	10 43 00	13 14 50
4	22 58 46	−6 32	−11 50	6 39	6 44	12 12	17 45	17 40	10 46 56	13 10 54
5	23 02 30	−6 09	−11 37	6 37	6 42	12 12	17 47	17 42	10 50 53	13 06 58
6	23 06 13	−5 45	−11 23	6 35	6 39	12 11	17 49	17 45	10 54 49	13 03 02
7	23 09 55	−5 22	−11 09	6 33	6 36	12 11	17 50	17 47	10 58 46	12 59 06
8	23 13 37	−4 59	−10 55	6 30	6 34	12 11	17 52	17 49	11 02 42	12 55 10
9	23 17 19	−4 35	−10 40	6 28	6 31	12 11	17 54	17 51	11 06 39	12 51 14
10	23 21 01	−4 12	−10 25	6 26	6 29	12 10	17 56	17 53	11 10 36	12 47 18
11	23 24 42	−3 48	−10 10	6 24	6 26	12 10	17 57	17 55	11 14 32	12 43 22
12	23 28 23	−3 25	− 9 54	6 21	6 23	12 10	17 59	17 57	11 18 29	12 39 27
13	23 32 03	−3 01	− 9 38	6 19	6 21	12 09	18 01	17 59	11 22 25	12 35 31
14	23 35 43	−2 38	− 9 21	6 17	6 18	12 09	18 03	18 01	11 26 22	12 31 35
15	23 39 23	−2 14	− 9 05	6 14	6 16	12 09	18 04	18 03	11 30 18	12 27 39
16	23 43 03	−1 50	− 8 48	6 12	6 13	12 09	18 06	18 05	11 34 15	12 23 43
17	23 46 42	−1 26	− 8 30	6 10	6 10	12 08	18 08	18 07	11 38 11	12 19 47
18	23 50 21	−1 03	− 8 13	6 08	6 08	12 08	18 10	18 10	11 42 08	12 15 51
19	23 54 00	−0 39	− 7 55	6 05	6 05	12 08	18 11	18 12	11 46 05	12 11 55
20	23 57 39	−0 15	− 7 38	6 03	6 03	12 07	18 13	18 14	11 50 01	12 07 59
21	0 01 18	+0 08	− 7 20	6 01	6 00	12 07	18 15	18 16	11 53 58	12 04 03
22	0 04 56	0 32	− 7 02	5 58	5 57	12 07	18 16	18 18	11 57 54	12 00 07
23	0 08 35	+0 56	− 6 44	5 56	5 55	12 07	18 18	18 20	12 01 51	11 56 12
24	0 12 13	+1 19	− 6 26	5 54	5 52	12 06	18 20	18 22	12 05 47	11 52 16
25	0 15 51	+1 43	− 6 07	5 51	5 49	12 06	18 22	18 24	12 09 44	11 48 20
26	0 19 29	+2 07	− 5 49	5 49	5 47	12 06	18 23	18 26	12 13 40	11 44 24
27	0 23 08	+2 30	− 5 31	5 47	5 44	12 05	18 25	18 28	12 17 37	11 40 28
28	0 26 46	+2 54	− 5 13	5 44	5 41	12 05	18 27	18 30	12 21 34	11 36 32
29	0 30 24	+3 17	− 4 54	5 42	5 39	12 05	18 29	18 32	12 25 30	11 32 36
30	0 34 03	+3 40	− 4 36	5 40	5 36	12 04	18 30	18 34	12 29 27	11 28 40
31	0 37 41	+4 04	− 4 18	5 37	5 34	12 04	18 32	18 36	12 33 23	11 24 44

Duration of Civil (C), Nautical (N), and Astronomical (A), Twilight (in minutes)

Lat. °	Mar. 1 C	N	A	Mar. 11 C	N	A	Mar. 21 C	N	A	Mar. 31 C	N	A
52	34	73	112	34	73	113	34	74	116	34	76	120
56	38	81	124	37	80	125	37	82	129	38	84	136

ASTRONOMICAL NOTES

MERCURY is unsuitably placed for observation.

VENUS is too close to the Sun for observation.

MARS is still visible as an evening object, magnitude +1·2. It is visible in the western sky until shortly before midnight. Mars enters Taurus at the beginning of the month and passes between the Pleiades and the Hyades, passing 2°N. of Jupiter on the 12th. On the evening of the 12th the crescent Moon passes 4°N. of the planet.

JUPITER, magnitude −2·2, is still a brilliant object in the western sky in the evenings. Jupiter is in Taurus. On the evening of the 12th the crescent Moon passes 6°N. of the planet.

SATURN, magnitude +0·6, is a morning object in the south-eastern sky. Saturn is in Sagittarius. On the morning of the 3rd the old crescent Moon passes 5°S. of the planet.

ECLIPSE. A partial eclipse of the Sun occurs on the 7th. See page 74 for details.

ZODIACAL LIGHT. The evening cone may be observed in the western sky after the end of twilight from the beginning of the month to the 8th and again after the 23rd.

THE MOON

Day	R.A.	Dec.	Hor. Par.	Semi-diam.	Sun's Co-long.	P.A. of Bright Limb	Phase	Age	Rise 52°	Rise 56°	Transit	Set 52°	Set 56°
	h m	°	′	′	°	°		d	h m	h m	h m	h m	h m
1	16 40	−27·5	56·0	15·3	189	98	49	22·7	3 01	3 39	6 19	9 34	8 56
2	17 38	−28·3	56·8	15·5	201	91	38	23·7	4 04	4 43	7 16	10 28	9 49
3	18 38	−27·6	57·8	15·7	213	84	28	24·7	4 52	5 28	8 14	11 41	11 06
4	19 38	−25·2	58·7	16·0	226	78	19	25·7	5 27	5 55	9 12	13 07	12 40
5	20 37	−21·2	59·7	16·3	238	72	11	26·7	5 52	6 12	10 09	14 39	14 21
6	21 34	−15·8	60·5	16·5	250	69	5	27·7	6 10	6 23	11 03	16 12	16 02
7	22 30	− 9·4	61·0	16·6	262	69	1	28·7	6 25	6 31	11 56	17 45	17 41
8	23 24	− 2·3	61·3	16·7	274	224	0	0·2	6 38	6 38	12 48	19 18	19 21
9	0 17	+ 4·9	61·3	16·7	287	238	2	1·2	6 51	6 45	13 39	20 50	21 00
10	1 12	+11·7	60·9	16·6	299	242	8	2·2	7 05	6 53	14 33	22 24	22 41
11	2 08	+17·8	60·3	16·4	311	246	15	3·2	7 23	7 04	15 28	23 56	—
12	3 06	+22·8	59·5	16·2	323	251	24	4·2	7 47	7 21	16 26	—	0 21
13	4 06	+26·2	58·6	16·0	335	257	35	5·2	8 21	7 47	17 24	1 23	1 56
14	5 06	+28·0	57·7	15·7	348	264	46	6·2	9 09	8 31	18 23	2 38	3 16
15	6 06	+28·1	56·9	15·5	360	271	56	7·2	10 11	9 34	19 19	3 35	4 12
16	7 04	+26·7	56·1	15·3	12	278	66	8·2	11 24	10 53	20 12	4 15	4 47
17	7 58	+24·0	55·5	15·1	24	283	75	9·2	12 41	12 17	21 01	4 42	5 07
18	8 49	+20·2	55·0	15·0	36	288	83	10·2	13 57	13 40	21 46	5 02	5 20
19	9 36	+15·6	54·6	14·9	48	290	90	11·2	15 11	15 00	22 28	5 16	5 29
20	10 21	+10·5	54·3	14·8	61	291	95	12·2	16 23	16 17	23 08	5 27	5 35
21	11 03	+ 5·0	54·1	14·7	73	289	98	13·2	17 33	17 32	23 47	5 37	5 40
22	11 45	− 0·5	54·0	14·7	85	270	100	14·2	18 43	18 47	—	5 46	5 45
23	12 27	− 6·1	54·0	14·7	97	138	100	15·2	19 53	20 03	0 26	5 56	5 49
24	13 10	−11·5	54·0	14·7	109	124	98	16·2	21 06	21 21	1 06	6 06	5 55
25	13 54	−16·4	54·2	14·8	121	119	94	17·2	22 20	22 42	1 48	6 19	6 02
26	14 41	−20·8	54·4	14·8	134	114	89	18·2	23 35		2 33	6 36	6 13
27	15 31	−24·4	54·8	14·9	146	108	82	19·2	—	0 04	3 21	6 59	6 29
28	16 25	−26·9	55·3	15·1	158	102	74	20·2	0 48	1 23	4 12	7 32	6 56
29	17 21	−28·1	55·9	15·2	170	95	65	21·2	1 53	2 32	5 06	8 19	7 40
30	18 18	−27·9	56·7	15·4	182	89	55	22·2	2 46	3 23	6 03	9 23	8 46
31	19 17	−26·1	57·5	15·7	194	82	44	23·2	3 25	3 56	6 59	10 41	10 11

MERCURY ☿

Day	R.A.	Dec. −	Diam.	Phase	Transit		Day	R.A.	Dec.	Diam.	Phase	Transit	
	h m	°	″		h m			h m	°	″		h m	
1	21 15	17·3	—	—	10 40		16	22 44	−10·5	—	—	11 10	
4	21 32	16·3	—	—	10 46	Mercury is too	19	23 02	− 8·6	—	—	11 18	Mercury is too
7	21 49	15·1	—	—	10 51	close to the	22	23 22	− 6·5	—	—	11 25	close to the
10	22 07	13·8	—	—	10 57	Sun for	25	23 42	− 4·2	—	—	11 33	Sun for
13	22 25	12·2	—	—	11 04	observation	28	0 02	− 1·8	—	—	11 42	observation
16	22 44	10·5	—	—	11 10		31	0 23	+ 0·8	—	—	11 51	

VENUS ♀

Day	R.A.	Dec.	Diam.	Phase	Transit	
	h m	°	″		h m	
1	22 16	−12·1	—	—	11 42	
6	22 40	− 9·9	—	—	11 46	
11	23 04	− 7·6	—	—	11 49	Venus is too
16	23 27	− 5·2	—	—	11 53	close to the
21	23 50	− 2·7	—	—	11 56	Sun for
26	0 12	− 0·2	—	—	11 59	observation
31	0 35	+ 2·3	—	—	12 02	

MARS ♂

Day	R.A.	Dec. +	Diam.	Phase	Transit	5° high. 52°	5° high. 56°
	h m	°	″		h m	h m	h m
1	3 24	19·9	6	90	16 48	0 02	0 16
6	3 37	20·7	6	90	16 41	23 59	0 14
11	3 49	21·4	6	90	16 34	23 56	0 12
16	4 02	22·0	6	91	16 27	23 53	0 10
21	4 15	22·6	5	91	16 20	23 50	0 08
26	4 28	23·1	5	91	16 13	23 46	0 05
31	4 41	23·6	5	92	16 07	23 42	0 02

SUNRISE AND SUNSET

Day	London a.m. h m	London p.m. h m	Bristol a.m. h m	Bristol p.m. h m	Birmingham a.m. h m	Birmingham p.m. h m	Manchester a.m. h m	Manchester p.m. h m	Newcastle a.m. h m	Newcastle p.m. h m	Glasgow a.m. h m	Glasgow p.m. h m	Belfast a.m. h m	Belfast p.m. h m
1	6 47	5 40	6 56	5 50	6 55	5 45	6 58	5 46	6 57	5 41	7 10	5 50	7 15	5 59
2	6 45	5 42	6 54	5 52	6 53	5 47	6 56	5 48	6 55	5 43	7 08	5 52	7 13	6 01
3	6 43	5 43	6 52	5 53	6 50	5 49	6 53	5 50	6 52	5 45	7 05	5 54	7 10	6 03
4	6 41	5 45	6 50	5 55	6 48	5 51	6 51	5 52	6 50	5 47	7 03	5 56	7 08	6 05
5	6 38	5 47	6 48	5 57	6 46	5 53	6 49	5 54	6 48	5 49	7 00	5 59	7 06	6 07
6	6 36	5 48	6 45	5 58	6 43	5 55	6 46	5 56	6 45	5 51	6 57	6 01	7 03	6 09
7	6 34	5 50	6 43	6 00	6 41	5 57	6 44	5 58	6 43	5 53	6 55	6 03	7 01	6 11
8	6 32	5 52	6 41	6 02	6 39	5 58	6 42	5 59	6 40	5 55	6 52	6 05	6 58	6 13
9	6 29	5 53	6 39	6 03	6 36	6 00	6 39	6 01	6 38	5 57	6 50	6 07	6 56	6 15
10	6 27	5 55	6 37	6 05	6 34	6 02	6 37	6 03	6 35	5 59	6 47	6 09	6 53	6 17
11	6 25	5 57	6 35	6 07	6 32	6 03	6 35	6 04	6 33	6 01	6 45	6 11	6 51	6 19
12	6 23	5 58	6 33	6 08	6 30	6 05	6 33	6 06	6 30	6 03	6 42	6 13	6 48	6 21
13	6 20	6 00	6 30	6 10	6 27	6 07	6 30	6 08	6 27	6 05	6 39	6 15	6 45	6 23
14	6 18	6 02	6 28	6 12	6 25	6 09	6 28	6 10	6 25	6 07	6 37	6 17	6 43	6 25
15	6 16	6 04	6 26	6 14	6 23	6 11	6 25	6 12	6 22	6 09	6 34	6 19	6 40	6 27
16	6 13	6 05	6 23	6 15	6 20	6 12	6 23	6 14	6 20	6 11	6 31	6 21	6 38	6 29
17	6 11	6 07	6 21	6 17	6 18	6 14	6 21	6 16	6 18	6 13	6 29	6 23	6 36	6 31
18	6 09	6 09	6 19	6 19	6 16	6 16	6 18	6 18	6 15	6 15	6 26	6 25	6 33	6 33
19	6 06	6 10	6 16	6 20	6 13	6 17	6 15	6 19	6 12	6 16	6 24	6 27	6 30	6 34
20	6 04	6 12	6 14	6 22	6 11	6 19	6 13	6 21	6 10	6 18	6 21	6 29	6 28	6 36
21	6 02	6 14	6 12	6 24	6 09	6 21	6 11	6 23	6 08	6 20	6 18	6 31	6 25	6 38
22	6 00	6 16	6 10	6 26	6 07	6 23	6 08	6 25	6 05	6 22	6 16	6 34	6 23	6 40
23	5 58	6 17	6 08	6 27	6 05	6 24	6 06	6 27	6 03	6 24	6 13	6 36	6 20	6 42
24	5 55	6 19	6 05	6 29	6 02	6 26	6 03	6 29	6 00	6 26	6 10	6 38	6 17	6 44
25	5 53	6 21	6 03	6 31	6 00	6 28	6 01	6 31	5 58	6 28	6 08	6 40	6 15	6 46
26	5 50	6 22	6 00	6 32	5 57	6 29	5 58	6 32	5 55	6 30	6 05	6 42	6 12	6 48
27	5 48	6 24	5 58	6 34	5 55	6 31	5 56	6 34	5 52	6 32	6 02	6 44	6 09	6 50
28	5 46	6 26	5 56	6 36	5 53	6 33	5 54	6 36	5 50	6 34	6 00	6 46	6 06	6 52
29	5 44	6 28	5 54	6 37	5 50	6 35	5 51	6 38	5 47	6 36	5 57	6 48	6 03	6 54
30	5 42	6 29	5 52	6 39	5 48	6 36	5 49	6 39	5 45	6 38	5 55	6 50	6 01	6 56
31	5 39	6 31	5 49	6 40	5 46	6 38	5 47	6 41	5 42	6 40	5 42	6 52	5 58	6 58

JUPITER ♃   SATURN ♄

Day	R.A. h m	Dec. + °	Transit h m	5° high. 52° h m	5° high. 56° h m	R.A. h m	Dec. − °	Transit h m	5° high. 52° h m	5° high. 56° h m
1	3 46	19·2	17 09	0 20	0 33	18 51	22·2	8 14	5 05	5 38
11	3 52	19·5	16 35	23 45	0 02	18 54	22·2	7 38	4 28	5 01
21	3 58	19·9	16 02	23 14	23 28	18 56	22·1	7 01	3 51	4 24
31	4 05	20·3	15 30	22 44	22 59	18 58	22·1	6 24	3 13	3 46

Equatorial diameter of Jupiter 37″; of Saturn 16″. Diameters of Saturn's rings 36″ and 15″.

URANUS ♅   NEPTUNE ♆

Day	R.A. h m	Dec. ° ′	Transit h m	10° high. 52° h m	10° high. 56° h m	R.A. h m	Dec. − ° ′	Transit h m	10° high. 52° h m	10° high. 56° h m
1	18 20·4	23 36	7 44	5 45	7 06	18 51·2	22 01	8 15	5 56	6 51
11	18 21·7	23 35	7 06	5 07	6 28	18 52·1	21 59	7 36	5 17	6 13
21	18 22·6	23 35	6 28	4 28	5 49	18 52·8	21 58	6 58	4 39	5 34
31	18 23·1	23 35	5 49	3 49	5 10	18 53·2	21 57	6 19	4 00	4 54

Diameter 4″   Diameter 2″

DAY OF		
Month	Week	

Aperire, to open. Earth opens to receive seed.

Sun's Longitude 30° ♉ 20ᵈ03ʰ

Month	Week	
1	S.	End of Spanish Civil War 1939.
2	S.	**1st S after Easter.** Sir Neville Cardus b. 1889.*
3	M.	**The Annunciation.** Brahms d. 1897.
4	Tu.	EASTER LAW SITTINGS BEGIN.
5	W.	Bette Davis b. 1908. Gen. Douglas MacArthur d. 1964.
6	Th.	U.S.A. enters World War I 1917.
7	F.	Wordsworth b. 1770. Phineas T. Barnum d. 1891.
8	S.	Sir Adrian Boult b. 1889.* Entente Cordiale 1904.
9	S.	**2nd S. after Easter.** Francis Bacon d. 1626.
10	M.	Toulouse 1814. Antonia White d. 1980.
11	Tu.	Abdication of Napoleon 1814.
12	W.	Alan Ayckbourn b. 1939. Joe Louis d. 1981.
13	Th.	Sir Arthur "Bomber" Harris b. 1892.
14	F.	Abraham Lincoln shot 1865. Arnold Toynbee b.
15	S.	Joe Davis b. 1901. Jean-Paul Sartre d. 1980. [1889.*
16	S.	**3rd S. after Easter.** Charlie Chaplin b. 1889.*
17	M.	Benjamin Franklin d. 1790. Khrushchev b. 1894.
18	Tu.	Judge Jeffreys d. 1689.* Leopold Stokowski b. 1882.
19	W.	Primrose Day. Lexington 1775.
20	Th.	Napoleon III b. 1808. Adolf Hitler b. 1889.*
21	F.	QUEEN ELIZABETH II b. 1926. Mark Twain d. 1910.
22	S.	Henry Fielding b. 1707. Sidney Nolan b. 1917.
23	S.	**4th S. after Easter.** ST. GEORGE'S DAY.
24	M.	Sir Stafford Cripps b. 1889.* Bill Edrich d. 1986.
25	Tu.	**St. Mark.** Gallipoli landings 1915.
26	W.	Daniel Defore d. 1731. Delacroix b. 1798.
27	Th.	Gen. Ulysses Grant b. 1822.
28	F.	Edward IV b. 1442. Mutiny on the *Bounty* 1789.*
29	S.	Jules Poincaré b. 1854. Duke Ellington b. 1899.
30	S.	**5th S. after Easter.** A. E. Housman d. 1936.

PHENOMENA

d	h	
4	14	Mercury in superior conjunction.
5	00	Venus in superior conjunction.
9	12	Jupiter in conjunction with Moon. Jupiter 6°S.
10	09	Mars in conjunction with Moon. Mars 4°S.
26	23	Saturn in conjunction with Moon. Saturn 5°N.

CONSTELLATIONS

The following constellations are near the meridian at

d	h		d	h
Mar. 1	24		Mar. 16	23
Apr. 1	22		Apr. 15	21
May 1	20		May 16	19

Cepheus (below the Pole), Cassiopeia (below the Pole), Ursa Major, Leo Minor, Leo, Sextans, Hydra and Crater.

MINIMA OF ALGOL

d	h		d	h
3	11		17	19
6	7		20	16
9	4		23	12
12	1		26	9
14	22		29	6

*Centenary

PHASES OF THE MOON

		d	h	m
● New Moon		6	03	33
☽ First Quarter		12	23	13
○ Full Moon		21	03	13
☾ Last Quarter		28	20	46

		d	h
Perigee (357,190 kilometres)		5	20
Apogee (406,170 „)		18	21

Mean Longitude of Ascending Node on April 1, 333°.

See note on *Summer Time*, p. 24.

MONTHLY NOTES

April 5. Income Tax Year (1988–89) ends.

7. First day of Ramadân.

20. First day of Passover.

30. Greek Orthodox Easter.

Day	THE SUN s.d. 16'·0								Sidereal Time	Transit of First Point of Aries

Day	Right Ascension	Dec. +	Equation of Time	Rise 52°	Rise 56°	Transit	Set 52°	Set 56°	Sidereal Time	Transit of First Point of Aries
	h m s	° '	m s	h m	h m	h m	h m	h m	h m s	h m s
1	0 41 20	4 27	− 4 00	5 35	5 31	12 04	18 34	18 38	12 37 20	11 20 48
2	0 44 59	4 50	− 3 42	5 33	5 28	12 04	18 35	18 40	12 41 16	11 16 52
3	0 48 37	5 13	− 3 25	5 31	5 26	12 03	18 37	18 42	12 45 13	11 12 57
4	0 52 16	5 36	− 3 07	5 28	5 23	12 03	18 39	18 44	12 49 09	11 09 01
5	0 55 56	5 59	− 2 50	5 26	5 20	12 03	18 40	18 46	12 53 06	11 05 05
6	0 59 35	6 22	− 2 32	5 24	5 18	12 02	18 42	18 48	12 57 03	11 01 09
7	1 03 15	6 44	− 2 15	5 21	5 15	12 02	18 44	18 50	13 00 59	10 57 13
8	1 06 54	7 07	− 1 59	5 19	5 13	12 02	18 46	18 52	13 04 56	10 53 17
9	1 10 34	7 29	− 1 42	5 17	5 10	12 02	18 47	18 54	13 08 52	10 49 21
10	1 14 15	7 52	− 1 26	5 15	5 07	12 01	18 49	18 56	13 12 49	10 45 25
11	1 17 55	8 14	− 1 10	5 12	5 05	12 01	18 51	18 58	13 16 45	10 41 29
12	1 21 36	8 36	− 0 54	5 10	5 02	12 01	18 52	19 01	13 20 42	10 37 33
13	1 25 17	8 58	− 0 38	5 08	5 00	12 01	18 54	19 03	13 24 38	10 33 37
14	1 28 58	9 19	− 0 23	5 06	4 57	12 00	18 56	19 05	13 28 35	10 29 42
15	1 32 40	9 41	− 0 08	5 04	4 55	12 00	18 58	19 07	13 32 32	10 25 46
16	1 36 22	10 02	+ 0 06	5 01	4 52	12 00	18 59	19 09	13 36 28	10 21 50
17	1 40 04	10 23	+ 0 20	4 59	4 50	12 00	19 01	19 11	13 40 25	10 17 54
18	1 43 47	10 45	+ 0 34	4 57	4 47	11 59	19 03	19 13	13 44 21	10 13 58
19	1 47 30	11 05	+ 0 48	4 55	4 45	11 59	19 04	19 15	13 48 18	10 10 02
20	1 51 14	11 26	+ 1 01	4 53	4 42	11 59	19 06	19 17	13 52 14	10 06 06
21	1 54 57	11 47	+ 1 13	4 51	4 40	11 59	19 08	19 19	13 56 11	10 02 10
22	1 58 42	12 07	+ 1 26	4 49	4 37	11 58	19 09	19 21	14 00 07	9 58 14
23	2 02 27	12 27	+ 1 37	4 47	4 35	11 58	19 11	19 23	14 04 04	9 54 18
24	2 06 12	12 47	+ 1 49	4 44	4 33	11 58	19 13	19 25	14 08 01	9 50 22
25	2 09 58	13 07	+ 2 00	4 42	4 30	11 58	19 15	19 27	14 11 57	9 46 27
26	2 13 44	13 26	+ 2 10	4 40	4 28	11 58	19 16	19 29	14 15 54	9 42 31
27	2 17 31	13 45	+ 2 20	4 38	4 25	11 58	19 18	19 31	14 19 50	9 38 35
28	2 21 18	14 05	+ 2 29	4 36	4 23	11 57	19 20	19 33	14 23 47	9 34 39
29	2 25 06	14 23	+ 2 38	4 34	4 21	11 57	19 21	19 35	14 27 43	9 30 43
30	2 28 54	14 42	+ 2 46	4 32	4 19	11 57	19 23	19 37	14 31 40	9 26 47

Duration of Civil (C), Nautical (N), and Astronomical (A), Twilight (in minutes)

Lat. °	Apr. 1 C	N	A	Apr. 11 C	N	A	Apr. 21 C	N	A	Apr. 30 C	N	A
52	34	76	121	35	79	128	37	84	138	39	89	152
56	38	85	137	40	90	148	42	96	167	44	105	200

ASTRONOMICAL NOTES

MERCURY becomes visible as an evening object (magnitude − 1·3 to + 0·4) halfway through the month and is then observable well into May. It may be located above the W.N.W horizon around the time of end of evening civil twilight. Greatest eastern elongation occurs on May 1st and this is the most favourable evening apparition of the year for observers in the northern hemisphere.

VENUS is unsuitably placed for observation, superior conjunction occuring on the 4th.

MARS, magnitude + 1·5, continues to be visible as an evening object in the western sky. At the end of the month Mars passes from Taurus into Gemini.

The crescent Moon is near Mars on the evenings of the 9th and 10th.

JUPITER continues to be visible as a bright object in the western skies in the early part of the evening, though by the end of the month it is too low in the sky to be seen after 21h. Jupiter is in the constellation of Taurus and at the beginning of the month passes almost exactly half-way between Aldebaran and the Pleiades.

SATURN, magnitude + 0·5, is visible as a morning object in the south-eastern sky. At the end of the month it is due south at sunrise. When rising on the morning of the 27th the Moon and Saturn will be only about 6° apart.

THE MOON

Day	R.A.	Dec.	Hor. Par.	Semi-diam.	Sun's Co-long.	P.A. of Bright Limb	Phase	Age	Rise 52°	Rise 56°	Transit	Set 52°	Set 56°
	h m	°	′	′	°	°		d	h m	h m	h m	h m	h m
1	20 14	−22·8	58·4	15·9	207	76	33	24·2	3 52	4 16	7 54	12 07	11 45
2	21 11	−18·1	59·3	16·2	219	72	23	25·2	4 13	4 29	8 48	13 37	13 23
3	22 05	−12·3	60·2	16·4	231	69	14	26·2	4 29	4 38	9 40	15 08	15 01
4	22 59	− 5·6	60·9	16·6	243	69	7	27·2	4 42	4 46	10 31	16 39	16 39
5	23 52	+ 1·5	61·3	16·7	256	74	2	28·2	4 55	4 53	11 23	18 12	18 18
6	0 47	+ 8·6	61·4	16·7	268	124	0	29·2	5 09	5 01	12 16	19 46	19 59
7	1 43	+15·2	61·2	16·7	280	230	1	0·9	5 26	5 11	13 11	21 22	21 43
8	2 41	+20·8	60·6	16·5	292	243	5	1·9	5 47	5 25	14 10	22 55	23 24
9	3 43	+25·0	59·8	16·3	304	251	12	2·9	6 18	5 47	15 11	..	..
10	4 45	+27·4	58·9	16·1	317	259	20	3·9	7 01	6 24	16 12	0 19	0 55
11	5 47	+28·1	58·0	15·8	329	267	30	4·9	8 00	7 22	17 11	1 25	2 03
12	6 47	+27·1	57·0	15·5	341	274	40	5·9	9 11	8 38	18 06	2 13	2 47
13	7 44	+24·7	56·2	15·3	353	280	50	6·9	10 28	10 02	18 57	2 45	3 12
14	8 36	+21·1	55·5	15·1	5	285	60	7·9	11 45	11 26	19 44	3 07	3 28
15	9 24	+16·7	54·9	15·0	18	289	70	8·9	13 00	12 47	20 27	3 23	3 38
16	10 09	+11·7	54·5	14·8	30	291	78	9·9	14 12	14 05	21 08	3 36	3 45
17	10 53	+ 6·4	54·2	14·8	42	292	85	10·9	15 23	15 20	21 47	3 46	3 50
18	11 35	+ 0·8	54·0	14·7	54	291	91	11·9	16 32	16 35	22 26	3 55	3 55
19	12 16	− 4·7	54·0	14·7	66	287	96	12·9	17 42	17 50	23 05	4 05	4 00
20	12 59	−10·1	54·0	14·7	79	277	99	13·9	18 54	19 07	23 47	4 15	4 06
21	13 43	−15·2	54·2	14·8	91	220	100	14·9	20 8	20 27	..	4 27	4 13
22	14 30	−19·7	54·4	14·8	103	134	99	15·9	21 23	21 50	0 31	4 43	4 22
23	15 19	−23·5	54·7	14·9	115	118	97	16·9	22 37	23 10	1 18	5 04	4 37
24	16 12	−26·3	55·1	15·0	127	108	92	17·9	23 45	..	2 08	5 34	5 00
25	17 07	−27·8	55·6	15·1	139	100	86	18·9	..	0 23	3 02	6 17	5 39
26	18 04	−27·9	56·1	15·3	152	93	79	19·9	0 41	1 19	3 57	7 15	6 38
27	19 02	−26·5	56·7	15·5	164	86	70	20·9	1 24	1 57	4 53	8 28	7 56
28	19 58	−23·7	57·4	15·7	176	79	59	21·9	1 54	2 20	5 47	9 49	9 25
29	20 53	−19·5	58·2	15·9	188	74	49	22·9	2 16	2 35	6 40	11 15	10 58
30	21 47	−14·2	59·0	16·1	200	70	38	23·9	2 33	2 45	7 30	12 42	12 32

MERCURY ☿

Day	R.A.	Dec. +	Diam.	Phase	Transit		Day	R.A.	Dec. +	Diam.	Phase	Transit	5° high 52°	5° high 56°
	h m	°	″		h m			h m	°	″		h m	h m	h m
1	0 30	1·7	—	—	11 54		16	2 22	15·2	6	85	12 48	19 39	19 49
4	0 52	4·4	—	—	12 04	Mercury is too	19	2 44	17·5	6	77	12 58	20 01	20 13
7	1 14	7·2	—	—	12 15	close to the	22	3 05	19·5	6	67	13 06	20 20	20 34
10	1 37	10·0	—	—	12 26	Sun for	25	3 24	21·0	7	57	13 13	20 35	20 51
13	2 00	12·7	—	—	12 37	observation	28	3 40	22·2	7	47	13 17	20 46	21 03
16	2 22	15·2	—	—	12 48		31	3 54	23·0	8	38	13 18	20 51	21 09

VENUS ♀ / MARS ♂

Day	R.A.	Dec. +	Diam.	Phase	Transit		Day	R.A.	Dec. +	Diam.	Phase	Transit	5° high 52°	5° high 56°
	h m	°	″		h m			h m	°	″		h m	h m	h m
1	0 40	2·8	—	—	12 03		1	4 44	23·7	5	92	16 06	23 42	0 01
6	1 02	5·3	—	—	12 06		6	4 57	24·0	5	92	15 59	23 38	23 57
11	1 25	7·8	—	—	12 09	Venus is too	11	5 11	24·3	5	93	15 53	23 33	23 53
16	1 49	10·1	—	—	12 12	close to the	16	5 24	24·6	5	93	15 47	23 28	23 48
21	2 12	12·4	—	—	12 16	Sun for	21	5 38	24·7	5	93	15 41	23 23	23 43
26	2 36	14·6	—	—	12 20	observation	26	5 51	24·8	5	94	15 35	23 18	23 38
31	3 00	16·5	—	—	12 25		31	6 05	24·8	4	94	15 29	23 11	23 32

SUNRISE AND SUNSET

Day	London a.m.	London p.m.	Bristol a.m.	Bristol p.m.	Birmingham a.m.	Birmingham p.m.	Manchester a.m.	Manchester p.m.	Newcastle a.m.	Newcastle p.m.	Glasgow a.m.	Glasgow p.m.	Belfast a.m.	Belfast p.m.
	h m	h m	h m	h m	h m	h m	h m	h m	h m	h m	h m	h m	h m	h m
1	5 37	6 33	5 47	6 42	5 43	6 40	5 44	6 43	5 39	6 42	5 49	6 54	5 57	7 00
2	5 35	6 34	5 45	6 43	5 41	6 42	5 42	6 45	5 37	6 44	5 47	6 56	5 55	7 02
3	5 33	6 36	5 43	6 45	5 39	6 43	5 40	6 46	5 35	6 45	5 44	6 58	5 53	7 03
4	5 31	6 38	5 41	6 47	5 36	6 45	5 37	6 48	5 32	6 47	5 41	7 00	5 50	7 05
5	5 28	6 39	5 38	6 49	5 34	6 47	5 35	6 50	5 30	6 49	5 39	7 02	5 48	7 07
6	5 26	6 41	5 36	6 50	5 31	6 49	5 32	6 52	5 27	6 51	5 36	7 04	5 45	7 09
7	5 24	6 42	5 34	6 52	5 29	6 51	5 30	6 54	5 24	6 53	5 33	7 06	5 43	7 11
8	5 21	6 44	5 31	6 54	5 26	6 53	5 27	6 56	5 22	6 55	5 31	7 08	5 40	7 13
9	5 19	6 45	5 29	6 55	5 24	6 54	5 25	6 58	5 19	6 57	5 28	7 10	5 38	7 15
10	5 17	6 47	5 27	6 57	5 22	6 56	5 22	6 59	5 17	6 59	5 26	7 12	5 35	7 17
11	5 15	6 49	5 25	6 59	5 20	6 58	5 20	7 01	5 14	7 01	5 23	7 14	5 33	7 18
12	5 12	6 50	5 22	7 00	5 17	6 59	5 18	7 03	5 12	7 03	5 21	7 16	5 31	7 20
13	5 10	6 52	5 20	7 02	5 15	7 01	5 15	7 05	5 09	7 05	5 18	7 18	5 28	7 22
14	5 08	6 54	5 18	7 04	5 13	7 03	5 13	7 07	5 07	7 07	5 16	7 20	5 26	7 24
15	5 06	6 56	5 16	7 06	5 11	7 05	5 11	7 09	5 05	7 09	5 13	7 22	5 23	7 26
16	5 03	6 57	5 13	7 07	5 08	7 06	5 08	7 11	5 02	7 11	5 11	7 24	5 21	7 28
17	5 01	6 59	5 11	7 09	5 06	7 08	5 06	7 12	5 00	7 13	5 08	7 26	5 18	7 30
18	4 59	7 01	5 09	7 11	5 04	7 10	5 04	7 14	4 57	7 15	5 05	7 29	5 16	7 32
19	4 57	7 02	5 07	7 12	5 02	7 11	5 01	7 16	4 55	7 17	5 03	7 31	5 13	7 34
20	4 55	7 04	5 05	7 14	5 00	7 13	4 59	7 18	4 53	7 19	5 01	7 33	5 11	7 36
21	4 53	7 06	5 03	7 16	4 58	7 15	4 57	7 20	4 50	7 21	4 58	7 35	5 09	7 38
22	4 51	7 07	5 01	7 17	4 56	7 16	4 55	7 21	4 48	7 23	4 56	7 37	5 06	7 40
23	4 49	7 09	4 59	7 19	4 54	7 18	4 53	7 23	4 45	7 25	4 53	7 39	5 04	7 42
24	4 47	7 11	4 57	7 21	4 52	7 20	4 51	7 25	4 43	7 27	4 51	7 41	5 02	7 44
25	4 45	7 13	4 55	7 22	4 49	7 22	4 48	7 27	4 41	7 28	4 49	7 42	5 00	7 45
26	4 43	7 14	4 53	7 24	4 47	7 23	4 46	7 28	4 38	7 30	4 46	7 44	4 57	7 47
27	4 41	7 16	4 51	7 25	4 45	7 25	4 44	7 30	4 36	7 32	4 44	7 46	4 55	7 49
28	4 39	7 18	4 49	7 27	4 43	7 27	4 42	7 32	4 34	7 34	4 42	7 48	4 53	7 51
29	4 37	7 19	4 47	7 28	4 41	7 29	4 40	7 34	4 32	7 36	4 40	7 50	4 51	7 53
30	4 35	7 21	4 45	7 30	4 39	7 31	4 38	7 36	4 30	7 38	4 38	7 52	4 48	7 55

JUPITER ♃

Day	R.A.	Dec. +	Transit	5° high. 52°	5° high. 56°
	h m	°	h m	h m	h m
1	4 06	20·3	15 27	22 41	22 56
11	4 14	20·7	14 56	22 12	22 27
21	4 23	21·1	14 25	21 44	21 59
31	4 32	21·4	13 54	21 16	21 32

SATURN ♄

Day	R.A.	Dec. −	Transit	5° high. 52°	5° high. 56°
	h m	°	h m	h m	h m
1	18 59	22·1	6 20	3 10	3 42
11	19 00	22·1	5 42	2 31	3 03
21	19 00	22·0	5 03	1 52	2 25
31	19 00	22·1	4 24	1 13	1 45

Equatorial diameter of Jupiter 34″; of Saturn 17″. Diameters of Saturn's rings 38″ and 16″.

URANUS ♅

Day	R.A.	Dec. −	Transit	10° high. 52°	10° high. 56°
	h m	° ′	h m	h m	h m
1	18 23·2	23 35	5 45	3 45	5 07
11	18 23·3	23 35	5 06	3 06	4 27
21	18 23·0	23 35	4 26	2 27	3 48
31	18 22·4	23 36	3 46	1 47	3 09

Diameter 4″

NEPTUNE ♆

R.A.	Dec. −	Transit	10° high. 52°	10° high. 56°
h m	° ′	h m	h m	h m
18 53·3	21 57	6 15	3 56	4 50
18 53·5	21 57	5 36	3 16	4 11
18 53·4	21 57	4 56	2 37	3 32
18 53·1	21 57	4 17	1 57	2 52

Diameter 2″

DAY OF		
Month	Week	*Maia*, goddess of growth and increase. *Sun's Longitude* 60° II 21ᵈ 02ʰ

Maia, goddess of growth and increase.

Sun's Longitude 60° II 21ᵈ 02ʰ

1	M.	**SS. Philip and James.** Joseph Goebbels d. 1945.
2	Tu.	Nancy, Viscountess Astor d. 1964.
3	W.	Start of Festival of Britain 1951.
4	Th.	**Ascension Day.** Marshal Tito d. 1980.
5	F.	Field Marshal Earl Wavell b. 1883.
6	S.	First issue of postage stamps 1840.
7	S.	**S. after Ascension (6th after Easter).**
8	M.	V.E. Day 1945. Lord Shinwell d. 1986.
9	Tu.	Treaty of Windsor signed 1386.
10	W.	Indian Mutiny begins at Meerut 1857.
11	Th.	Spencer Perceval assas. 1812. Paul Nash b. 1889.*
12	F.	Collapse of the General Strike 1926.
13	S.	Daphne du Maurier b. 1907. Nansen d. 1930.
14	S.	**Pentecost. Whit Sunday.**
15	M.	**St. Matthias.** Joseph Whitaker d. 1895.
16	Tu.	Academy Awards first presented 1929.
17	W.	Paganini d. 1840. Relief of Mafeking 1900.
18	Th.	Pope John Paul II b. 1920. Fred Perry b. 1909.
19	F.	James Boswell d. 1795. Ogden Nash d. 1971.
20	S.	First Chelsea Flower Show 1913.
21	S.	**Trinity Sunday.** Henry VI killed 1471.
22	M.	Victor Hugo d. 1885. Blackwall Tunnel opened 1897.
23	Tu.	Coalition Ministry dissolved 1945.
24	W.	British Legion founded 1921.
25	Th.	CORPUS CHRISTI. Gustav Holst d. 1934.
26	F.	EASTER LAW SITTINGS END. Pepys d. 1703.
27	S.	Evacuation from Dunkirk began 1940.
28	S.	**1st S. after Trinity.** George I b. 1660.
29	M.	Constantinople captured by Turks 1453.
30	Tu.	Rubens d. 1640. Alfred Austin b. 1835.
31	W.	Jutland 1916. Jack Dempsey d. 1983.

PHENOMENA

d	h	
1	03	Mercury at greatest elongation E.21°.
4	07	Pluto at opposition.
6	22	Mercury in conjunction with Moon. Mercury 3°S.
7	07	Jupiter in conjunction with Moon. Jupiter 5°S.
9	01	Mars in conjunction with Moon. Mars 3°S.
16	07	Venus in conjunction with Mercury. Venus 0°·6 S.
23	04	Jupiter in conjunction with Venus. Jupiter 0°·8 S.
23	22	Mercury in inferior conjunction.
24	04	Saturn in conjunction with Moon. Saturn 4°N.

CONSTELLATIONS

The following constellations are near the meridian at

d	h		d	h
Apr. 1	24		Apr. 15	23
May 1	22		May 16	21
June 1	20		June 15	19

Cepheus (below the Pole), Cassiopeia (below the Pole), Ursa Minor, Ursa Major, Canes Venatici, Coma Berenices, Bootes, Leo, Virgo, Crater, Corvus, and Hydra.

ALGOL

ALGOL is inconveniently situated for observation during May.

* Centenary.

PHASES OF THE MOON

	d	h	m
● New Moon	5	11	46
☽ First Quarter	12	14	19
○ Full Moon	20	18	16
☾ Last Quarter	28	04	01

	d	h
Perigee (359,780 kilometres)	4	05
Apogee (405,370 „)	16	09

Mean Longitude of Ascending Node on May 1, 331°.

See note on *Summer Time*, p. 24.

MONTHLY NOTES

May   1. Bank Holiday, England, Wales, N. Ireland and Scotland.

        9. Liberation Day, Channel Islands.

     15. Whitsunday (Scotland). Scottish Term Day.

     28. Removal Day, Scotland.

     29. Bank Holiday, England, Wales, N. Ireland and Scotland.

Day	THE SUN						s.d. 15′·8			Sidereal Time	Transit of First Point of Aries
	Right Ascension	Dec. +	Equation of Time	Rise		Transit	Set				
				52°	56°		52°	56°			
	h m s	° ′	m s	h m	h m	h m	h m	h m	h m s	h m s
1	2 32 43	15 00	+ 2 54	4 30	4 16	11 57	19 25	19 39	14 35 36	9 22 51
2	2 36 32	15 18	+ 3 01	4 29	4 14	11 57	19 26	19 41	14 39 33	9 18 55
3	2 40 22	15 36	+ 3 07	4 27	4 12	11 57	19 28	19 43	14 43 30	9 14 59
4	2 44 13	15 54	+ 3 13	4 25	4 10	11 57	19 30	19 45	14 47 26	9 11 03
5	2 48 04	16 11	+ 3 19	4 23	4 07	11 57	19 31	19 47	14 51 23	9 07 07
6	2 51 55	16 28	+ 3 24	4 21	4 05	11 57	19 33	19 49	14 55 19	9 03 12
7	2 55 48	16 45	+ 3 28	4 19	4 03	11 56	19 35	19 51	14 59 16	8 59 16
8	2 59 41	17 01	+ 3 32	4 18	4 01	11 56	19 36	19 53	15 03 12	8 55 20
9	3 03 34	17 18	+ 3 35	4 16	3 59	11 56	19 38	19 55	15 07 09	8 51 24
10	3 07 28	17 34	+ 3 38	4 14	3 57	11 56	19 40	19 57	15 11 05	8 47 28
11	3 11 22	17 49	+ 3 40	4 13	3 55	11 56	19 41	19 59	15 15 02	8 43 32
12	3 15 17	18 05	+ 3 41	4 11	3 53	11 56	19 43	20 01	15 18 59	8 39 36
13	3 19 13	18 20	+ 3 42	4 09	3 51	11 56	19 44	20 03	15 22 55	8 35 40
14	3 23 09	18 34	+ 3 43	4 08	3 49	11 56	19 46	20 05	15 26 52	8 31 44
15	3 27 06	18 49	+ 3 43	4 06	3 47	11 56	19 47	20 07	15 30 48	8 27 48
16	3 31 03	19 03	+ 3 42	4 05	3 45	11 56	19 49	20 08	15 34 45	8 23 52
17	3 35 01	19 17	+ 3 41	4 03	3 44	11 56	19 50	20 10	15 38 41	8 19 57
18	3 38 59	19 30	+ 3 39	4 02	3 42	11 56	19 52	20 12	15 42 38	8 16 01
19	3 42 58	19 43	+ 3 37	4 00	3 40	11 56	19 53	20 14	15 46 34	8 12 05
20	3 46 57	19 56	+ 3 34	3 59	3 39	11 56	19 55	20 16	15 50 31	8 08 09
21	3 50 57	20 08	+ 3 30	3 58	3 37	11 57	19 56	20 17	15 54 28	8 04 13
22	3 54 58	20 20	+ 3 26	3 56	3 35	11 57	19 58	20 19	15 58 24	8 00 17
23	3 58 59	20 32	+ 3 22	3 55	3 34	11 57	19 59	20 21	16 02 21	7 56 21
24	4 03 00	20 43	+ 3 17	3 54	3 32	11 57	20 00	20 22	16 06 17	7 52 25
25	4 07 02	20 54	+ 3 11	3 53	3 31	11 57	20 02	20 24	16 10 14	7 48 29
26	4 11 05	21 05	+ 3 05	3 52	3 29	11 57	20 03	20 26	16 14 10	7 44 33
27	4 15 08	21 15	+ 2 59	3 51	3 28	11 57	20 04	20 27	16 18 07	7 40 37
28	4 19 12	21 25	+ 2 52	3 50	3 27	11 57	20 06	20 29	16 22 03	7 36 42
29	4 23 16	21 35	+ 2 44	3 49	3 25	11 57	20 07	20 30	16 26 00	7 32 46
30	4 27 20	21 44	+ 2 36	3 48	3 24	11 57	20 08	20 32	16 29 57	7 28 50
31	4 31 25	21 53	+ 2 28	3 47	3 23	11 58	20 09	20 33	16 33 53	7 24 54

Duration of Civil (C), Nautical (N), and Astronomical (A), Twilight (in minutes)

Lat.	May 1			May 11			May 21			May 31		
°	C	N	A	C	N	A	C	N	A	C	N	A
52	39	90	154	41	97	179	44	106	T.A.N.	46	116	T.A.N.
56	45	106	209	49	121	T.A.N.	53	143	T.A.N.	57	T.A.N.	T.A.N.

ASTRONOMICAL NOTES

MERCURY continues to be visible as an evening object (magnitude +0·4 to +3) for the first two weeks of May. It may be detected low above the W.N.W. horizon around the time of end of evening civil twilight. Thereafter it is unsuitably placed for observation, inferior conjunction occuring on the 23rd. The thin crescent Moon, only 1½ days old, will be seen approaching the planet on the evening of the 6th.

VENUS becomes a brilliant object in the evening sky, magnitude −3·9, after the first few days of the month. It may be seen low above the western horizon for a short while after sunset. Venus is moving eastwards relative to the stars and passes just south of Mercury on the 16th, and just north of Jupiter on the 23rd.

MARS, magnitude +1·7, is still an evening object in the western sky but the period of observation is shortening noticeably as it moves steadily towards the Sun. Mars is in Gemini. On the evening of the 8th the crescent Moon will be seen approaching the planet.

JUPITER, magnitude −2·0, is coming to the end of its period of visibility as an evening object and will be lost in the long evening twilight by the middle of the month.

SATURN, magnitude +0·3, continues to be visible as a morning object and shortly after the middle of the month may be detected low above the south-eastern horizon by midnight. On the morning of the 24th the gibbous Moon passes 4°S. of the planet.

THE MOON

Day	R.A.	Dec.	Hor. Par.	Semi-diam.	Sun's Co-long.	P.A. of Bright Limb	Phase	Age	Rise 52°	Rise 56°	Transit	Set 52°	Set 56°
	h m	°	′	′	°	°		d	h m	h m	h m	h m	h m
1	22 39	− 8·0	59·7	16·3	213	68	27	24·9	2 47	2 53	8 20	14 09	14 06
2	23 31	− 1·3	60·3	16·4	225	68	17	25·9	3 00	3 00	9 09	15 38	15 41
3	0 23	+ 5·7	60·7	16·6	237	71	9	26·9	3 13	3 08	10 00	17 09	17 18
4	1 17	+12·4	60·9	16·6	249	78	3	27·9	3 28	3 17	10 54	18 43	19 00
5	2 15	+18·4	60·8	16·6	262	104	1	28·9	3 47	3 29	11 51	20 18	20 43
6	3 15	+23·2	60·5	16·5	274	220	1	0·5	4 13	3 47	12 51	21 49	22 22
7	4 18	+26·5	59·8	16·3	286	247	3	1·5	4 51	4 17	13 54	23 06	23 43
8	5 22	+27·9	59·0	16·1	298	259	9	2·5	5 44	5 06	14 56	—	—
9	6 25	+27·5	58·1	15·8	310	269	16	3·5	6 52	6 17	15 55	0 04	0 39
10	7 24	+25·5	57·2	15·6	323	276	24	4·5	8 10	7 41	16 49	0 43	1 13
11	8 19	+22·2	56·3	15·3	335	282	34	5·5	9 29	9 08	17 39	1 10	1 32
12	9 12	+17·9	55·6	15·1	347	287	44	6·5	10 46	10 31	18 24	1 28	1 45
13	9 56	+13·0	55·0	15·0	359	290	54	7·5	12 00	11 51	19 06	1 42	1 53
14	10 40	+ 7·7	54·5	14·9	12	292	64	8·5	13 11	13 07	19 45	1 53	1 59
15	11 23	+ 2·2	54·2	14·8	24	292	72	9·5	14 21	14 22	20 24	2 03	2 05
16	12 05	− 3·3	54·1	14·7	36	291	80	10·5	15 31	15 37	21 03	2 13	2 10
17	12 47	− 8·8	54·1	14·7	48	289	87	11·5	16 42	16 53	21 44	2 23	2 15
18	13 31	−13·9	54·3	14·8	60	285	93	12·5	17 55	18 12	22 27	2 35	2 22
19	14 17	−18·6	54·5	14·8	73	277	97	13·5	19 10	19 34	23 14	2 49	2 31
20	15 06	−22·6	54·8	14·9	85	257	99	14·5	20 25	20 56	—	3 09	2 44
21	15 58	−25·6	55·2	15·0	97	163	100	15·5	21 36	22 12	0 04	3 36	3 05
22	16 53	−27·4	55·7	15·2	109	115	98	16·5	22 37	23 14	0 57	4 15	3 39
23	17 51	−27·8	56·1	15·3	121	100	95	17·5	23 23	23 57	1 52	5 09	4 32
24	18 48	−26·8	56·6	15·4	133	90	89	18·5	23 57	—	2 48	6 19	5 45
25	19 45	−24·2	57·2	15·6	146	82	82	19·5	—	0 24	3 43	7 38	7 12
26	20 41	−20·3	57·7	15·7	158	76	73	20·5	0 21	0 41	4 36	9 02	8 43
27	21 34	−15·3	58·2	15·9	170	72	63	21·5	0 39	0 53	5 26	10 27	10 15
28	22 25	− 9·5	58·8	16·0	182	69	52	22·5	0 53	1 01	6 15	11 52	11 46
29	23 15	− 3·1	59·3	16·2	195	67	41	23·5	1 06	1 09	7 03	13 17	13 17
30	0 06	+ 3·6	59·7	16·3	207	68	30	24·5	1 19	1 16	7 51	14 44	14 50
31	0 58	+10·2	60·0	16·4	219	70	20	25·5	1 32	1 24	8 42	16 13	16 27

MERCURY ☿

Day	R.A.	Dec. +	Diam.	Phase	Transit	5° high 52°	5° high 56°	Day	R.A.	Dec. +	Diam.	Phase	Transit	
	h m	°	″		h m	h m	h m		h m	°	″		h m	
1	3 54	23·0	8	38	13 18	20 51	21 09	16	4 17	22·1	—	—	12 40	
4	4 05	23·5	8	29	13 17	20 52	21 10	19	4 14	21·1	—	—	12 24	Mercury is too
7	4 13	23·6	9	22	13 12	20 47	21 06	22	4 08	20·0	—	—	12 06	close to the
10	4 17	23·4	10	16	13 05	20 37	20 55	25	4 01	18·8	—	—	11 48	Sun for
13	4 19	22·9	11	10	12 54	20 22	20 40	28	3 55	17·7	—	—	11 31	observation
16	4 17	22·1	—	—	12 40	20 03	20 20	31	3 51	16·8	—	—	11 14	

VENUS ♀   MARS ♂

Day	R.A.	Dec. +	Diam.	Phase	Transit	5° high 52°	5° high 56°	Day	R.A.	Dec. +	Diam.	Phase	Transit	5° high 52°	5° high 56°
	h m	°	″		h m	h m	h m		h m	°	″		h m	h m	h m
1	3 00	16·5	10	99	12 25	19 21	19 32	1	6 05	24·8	4	94	15 29	23 11	23 32
6	3 25	18·4	10	99	12 30	19 36	19 49	6	6 19	24·7	4	94	15 22	23 05	23 25
11	3 50	20·0	10	99	12 36	19 51	20 05	11	6 32	24·6	4	95	15 16	22 58	23 18
16	4 16	21·4	10	98	12 42	20 05	20 21	16	6 46	24·4	4	95	15 10	22 50	23 10
21	4 42	22·5	10	98	12 48	20 18	20 36	21	6 59	24·1	4	95	15 04	22 42	23 01
26	5 08	23·4	10	97	12 55	20 30	20 49	26	7 13	23·7	4	96	14 58	22 33	22 52
31	5 35	24·0	10	97	13 02	20 41	21 00	31	7 26	23·3	4	96	14 51	22 24	22 42

SUNRISE AND SUNSET

Day	London a.m.	London p.m.	Bristol a.m.	Bristol p.m.	Birmingham a.m.	Birmingham p.m.	Manchester a.m.	Manchester p.m.	Newcastle a.m.	Newcastle p.m.	Glasgow a.m.	Glasgow p.m.	Belfast a.m.	Belfast p.m.
	h m	h m	h m	h m	h m	h m	h m	h m	h m	h m	h m	h m	h m	h m
1	4 33	7 23	4 43	7 32	4 37	7 32	4 36	7 37	4 27	7 40	4 35	7 54	4 47	7 56
2	4 32	7 25	4 42	7 33	4 35	7 34	4 34	7 39	4 25	7 42	4 33	7 56	4 45	7 58
3	4 30	7 26	4 40	7 35	4 33	7 36	4 32	7 41	4 23	7 44	4 31	7 58	4 43	8 00
4	4 28	7 27	4 38	7 37	4 31	7 38	4 30	7 43	4 21	7 46	4 29	8 00	4 41	8 02
5	4 26	7 29	4 36	7 38	4 29	7 39	4 28	7 45	4 19	7 48	4 26	8 02	4 38	8 04
6	4 24	7 30	4 34	7 40	4 27	7 41	4 26	7 47	4 17	7 50	4 24	8 04	4 36	8 06
7	4 22	7 32	4 32	7 42	4 25	7 43	4 24	7 48	4 15	7 51	4 22	8 06	4 34	8 08
8	4 20	7 33	4 30	7 43	4 23	7 44	4 22	7 50	4 13	7 53	4 20	8 08	4 32	8 10
9	4 19	7 35	4 29	7 45	4 22	7 46	4 20	7 52	4 11	7 55	4 18	8 10	4 30	8 12
10	4 17	7 36	4 27	7 46	4 20	7 47	4 18	7 54	4 09	7 57	4 16	8 12	4 28	8 14
11	4 16	7 38	4 26	7 48	4 18	7 49	4 16	7 55	4 07	7 59	4 14	8 14	4 26	8 15
12	4 14	7 40	4 24	7 50	4 17	7 51	4 14	7 57	4 05	8 01	4 12	8 16	4 24	8 17
13	4 12	7 41	4 22	7 51	4 15	7 52	4 13	7 59	4 03	8 03	4 10	8 18	4 23	8 19
14	4 10	7 43	4 20	7 53	4 13	7 54	4 11	8 01	4 01	8 04	4 08	8 19	4 21	8 21
15	4 09	7 44	4 19	7 54	4 12	7 55	4 09	8 02	3 59	8 06	4 06	8 21	4 19	8 22
16	4 07	7 46	4 17	7 56	4 10	7 57	4 07	8 04	3 57	8 08	4 04	8 23	4 17	8 24
17	4 06	7 47	4 16	7 57	4 09	7 58	4 06	8 05	3 56	8 09	4 02	8 25	4 16	8 25
18	4 04	7 49	4 15	7 59	4 07	8 00	4 04	8 07	3 54	8 11	4 01	8 27	4 14	8 27
19	4 03	7 50	4 14	8 00	4 06	8 02	4 03	8 08	3 53	8 13	3 59	8 29	4 13	8 29
20	4 02	7 52	4 12	8 02	4 05	8 03	4 02	8 10	3 51	8 14	3 57	8 30	4 11	8 30
21	4 00	7 53	4 11	8 03	4 03	8 05	4 00	8 11	3 50	8 16	3 56	8 32	4 10	8 32
22	3 59	7 55	4 10	8 05	4 02	8 06	3 59	8 13	3 48	8 18	3 54	8 34	4 08	8 34
23	3 58	7 56	4 09	8 06	4 01	8 08	3 58	8 14	3 46	8 20	3 52	8 36	4 06	8 36
24	3 57	7 57	4 07	8 07	3 59	8 09	3 56	8 16	3 45	8 21	3 51	8 37	4 05	8 37
25	3 55	7 59	4 06	8 09	3 58	8 10	3 55	8 17	3 43	8 23	3 49	8 39	4 03	8 39
26	3 54	8 00	4 05	8 10	3 57	8 11	3 54	8 18	3 42	8 24	3 48	8 40	4 02	8 40
27	3 53	8 01	4 04	8 11	3 56	8 13	3 53	8 20	3 41	8 26	3 46	8 42	4 01	8 42
28	3 53	8 03	4 03	8 12	3 55	8 14	3 52	8 21	3 40	8 27	3 45	8 44	4 00	8 43
29	3 52	8 04	4 02	8 13	3 53	8 16	3 50	8 23	3 38	8 29	3 44	8 45	3 58	8 45
30	3 51	8 05	4 01	8 14	3 52	8 17	3 49	8 24	3 37	8 30	3 43	8 47	3 57	8 46
31	3 50	8 06	4 00	8 15	3 51	8 18	3 48	8 25	3 36	8 31	3 42	8 48	3 56	8 47

JUPITER ♃   SATURN ♄

Day	R.A.	Dec. +	Transit	5° high 52°	5° high 56°	R.A.	Dec. −	Transit	5° high 52°	5° high 56°
	h m	°	h m	h m	h m	h m	°	h m	h m	h m
1	4 32	21·4	13 54	21 16	21 32	19 00	22·1	4 24	1 13	1 45
11	4 41	21·7	13 25	20 48	21 04	18 59	22·1	3 43	0 33	1 05
21	4 51	22·1	12 55	20 20	20 37	18 58	22·1	3 03	23 48	0 25
31	5 01	22·3	12 25	19 52	20 09	18 55	22·2	2 21	23 07	23 40

Equatorial diameter of Jupiter 33"; of Saturn 18".   Diameters of Saturn's rings 40" and 17".

URANUS ♅   NEPTUNE ♆

Day	R.A.	Dec. −	Transit	10° high 52°	10° high 56°	R.A.	Dec. −	Transit	10° high 52°	10° high 56°
	h m	° ′	h m	h m	h m	h m	° ′	h m	h m	h m
1	18 22·4	23 36	3 46	1 47	3 09	18 53·1	21 57	4 17	1 57	2 52
11	18 21·5	23 37	3 06	1 07	2 29	18 52·6	21 57	3 37	1 18	2 13
21	18 20·3	23 37	2 25	0 27	1 49	18 52·0	21 58	2 57	0 38	1 33
31	18 18·8	23 38	1 45	23 42	1 09	18 51·1	21 59	2 17	23 54	0 53

Diameter 4"   Diameter 2"

Month	Week	Junius, Roman gens (family). Sun's Longitude 90° ♋ 21ᵈ 10ʰ
1	Th.	Frank Whittle b. 1907. Helen Keller d. 1968.
2	F.	CORONATION DAY 1953. Thomas Hardy b. 1840.
3	S.	George V b. 1865. Samuel Plimsoll d. 1898.
4	S.	**2nd S. after Trinity.** Magenta 1859.
5	M.	Earl Kitchener of Khartoum d. 1916.
6	Tu.	TRINITY LAW SITTINGS BEGIN. D-Day 1944.
7	W.	E. M. Forster d. 1970. Henry Miller d. 1980.
8	Th.	Thomas Paine d. 1809. George Sand d. 1876.
9	F.	Charles Dickens d. 1870. Lord Beaverbrook d. 1964.
10	S.	DUKE OF EDINBURGH b. 1921. Judy Garland b. 1922.
11	S.	**3rd S. after Trinity. St. Barnabas.**
12	M.	Anthony Eden b. 1897. Sir Billy Butlin d. 1980.
13	Tu.	Boxer Rebellion began 1900.
14	W.	Argentinian surrender in Falklands 1982.
15	Th.	First non-stop transatlantic flight 1919.
16	F.	Quatre-Bras 1815. Tom Graveney b. 1927.
17	S.	Edward I b. 1239. Bunker Hill 1775.
18	S.	**4th S. after Trinity.** Waterloo 1815.
19	M.	Field Marshal Earl Haig b. 1861.
20	Tu.	Machiavelli b. 1527. William IV d. 1837.
21	W.	PRINCE WILLIAM OF WALES b. 1982.
22	Th.	Germany invaded U.S.S.R. 1941.
23	F.	Plassey 1757. Jean Anouilh b. 1910.
24	S.	**St. John the Baptist.** Bannockburn 1314.
25	S.	**5th S. after Trinity.** Korean War began 1950.
26	M.	United Nations Charter signed 1945.
27	Tu.	Dettingen 1743. Harriet Martineau d. 1876.
28	W.	Henry VIII b. 1491. Berlin airlift began 1948.
29	Th.	**St. Peter.** Trades Unions legalised 1871.
30	F.	Tower Bridge opened 1894.

*Centenary.

PHENOMENA

d	h	
5	01	Venus in conjunction with Moon. Venus 3°S.
6	18	Mars in conjunction with Moon. Mars 2°S.
9	09	Jupiter in conjunction with Sun.
18	12	Mercury at greatest elongation W.23°.
20	07	Saturn in conjunction with Moon. Saturn 4°N.
21	10	Solstice.
24	22	Uranus at opposition.

CONSTELLATIONS

The following constellations are near the meridian at

d	h		d	h
May 1	24		May 16	23
June 1	22		June 15	21
July 1	20		July 16	19

Cassiopeia (below the Pole), Ursa Minor, Draco, Ursa Major, Canes Venatici, Bootes, Corona, Serpens, Virgo and Libra.

ALGOL

ALGOL is inconveniently situated for observation during June.

PHASES OF THE MOON

	d	h	m
● New Moon	3	19	53
☽ First Quarter	11	06	59
○ Full Moon	19	06	57
☾ Last Quarter	26	09	09

	d	h
Perigee (364,390 kilometres)	1	05
Apogee (404,460 „)	13	02
Perigee (368,960 „)	28	04

Mean Longitude of Ascending Node on June 1, 330°.

See note on *Summer Time*, p. 24.

MONTHLY NOTES

June   9. First day of Feast of Weeks.

       17. Queen's Official Birthday.

       21. Longest day.

       24. Midsummer Day. Quarter Day.

Day	Right Ascension	Dec. +	Equation of Time	Rise 52°	Rise 56°	Transit	Set 52°	Set 56°	Sidereal Time	Transit of First Point of Aries
	h m s	° ′	m s	h m	h m	h m	h m	h m	h m s	h m s
1	4 35 31	22 01	+ 2 19	3 46	3 22	11 58	20 10	20 34	16 37 50	7 20 58
2	4 39 37	22 09	+ 2 10	3 45	3 21	11 58	20 11	20 36	16 41 46	7 17 02
3	4 43 43	22 17	+ 2 00	3 44	3 20	11 58	20 12	20 37	16 45 43	7 13 06
4	4 47 49	22 24	+ 1 50	3 44	3 19	11 58	20 13	20 38	16 49 39	7 09 10
5	4 51 56	22 31	+ 1 40	3 43	3 18	11 58	20 14	20 39	16 53 36	7 05 14
6	4 56 04	22 38	+ 1 29	3 42	3 17	11 59	20 15	20 41	16 57 32	7 01 18
7	5 00 11	22 44	+ 1 18	3 42	3 17	11 59	20 16	20 42	17 01 29	6 57 22
8	5 04 19	22 50	+ 1 06	3 41	3 16	11 59	20 17	20 43	17 05 26	6 53 26
9	5 08 27	22 55	+ 0 55	3 41	3 15	11 59	20 18	20 44	17 09 22	6 49 31
10	5 12 36	23 00	+ 0 43	3 41	3 15	11 59	20 19	20 44	17 13 19	6 45 35
11	5 16 44	23 04	+ 0 31	3 40	3 14	12 00	20 19	20 45	17 17 15	6 41 39
12	5 20 53	23 08	+ 0 19	3 40	3 14	12 00	20 20	20 46	17 21 12	6 37 43
13	5 25 02	23 12	+ 0 06	3 40	3 14	12 00	20 21	20 47	17 25 08	6 33 47
14	5 29 11	23 15	− 0 06	3 39	3 13	12 00	20 21	20 48	17 29 05	6 29 51
15	5 33 20	23 18	− 0 19	3 39	3 13	12 00	20 22	20 48	17 33 02	6 25 55
16	5 37 30	23 21	− 0 32	3 39	3 13	12 01	20 22	20 49	17 36 58	6 21 59
17	5 41 39	23 23	− 0 44	3 39	3 13	12 01	20 23	20 49	17 40 55	6 18 03
18	5 45 48	23 24	− 0 57	3 39	3 13	12 01	20 23	20 50	17 44 51	6 14 07
19	5 49 58	23 25	− 1 10	3 39	3 13	12 01	20 23	20 50	17 48 48	6 10 11
20	5 54 08	23 26	− 1 23	3 39	3 13	12 01	20 24	20 50	17 52 44	6 06 16
21	5 58 17	23 27	− 1 36	3 40	3 13	12 02	20 24	20 50	17 56 41	6 02 20
22	6 02 27	23 26	− 1 49	3 40	3 13	12 02	20 24	20 51	18 00 37	5 58 24
23	6 06 36	23 26	− 2 02	3 40	3 14	12 02	20 24	20 51	18 04 34	5 54 28
24	6 10 46	23 25	− 2 15	3 40	3 14	12 02	20 24	20 51	18 08 31	5 50 32
25	6 14 55	23 24	− 2 28	3 41	3 14	12 03	20 24	20 51	18 12 27	5 46 36
26	6 19 04	23 22	− 2 41	3 41	3 15	12 03	20 24	20 51	18 16 24	5 42 40
27	6 23 13	23 20	− 2 53	3 42	3 15	12 03	20 24	20 50	18 20 20	5 38 44
28	6 27 22	23 18	− 3 06	3 42	3 16	12 03	20 24	20 50	18 24 17	5 34 48
29	6 31 31	23 15	− 3 18	3 43	3 17	12 03	20 24	20 50	18 28 13	5 30 52
30	6 35 40	23 11	− 3 30	3 43	3 17	12 04	20 23	20 49	18 32 10	5 26 56

Duration of Civil (C), Nautical (N), and Astronomical (A), Twilight (in minutes)

Lat. °	June 1 C	N	A	June 11 C	N	A	June 21 C	N	A	June 30 C	N	A
52	47	117	T.A.N.	48	125	T.A.N.	49	128	T.A.N.	49	125	T.A.N.
56	58	T.A.N.	T.A.N.	61	T.A.N.	T.A.N.	63	T.A.N.	T.A.N.	62	T.A.N.	T.A.N.

ASTRONOMICAL NOTES

MERCURY is at greatest western elongation on the 18th but the long duration of twilight renders observation impossible.

VENUS is a brilliant object, magnitude −3·9, in the evening skies but only visible low above the W.N.W. horizon for about half-an-hour after sunset.

MARS is an evening object in the western sky but no longer the brilliant object it was at the beginning of the year its magnitude having fallen to +1·8. Mars is in Gemini passing south of the Heavenly Twins, Castor and Pollux. Before the end of the month it has become lost in the long evening twilight.

JUPITER is in conjunction on the 9th and thus unsuitably placed for observation.

SATURN is a morning object, magnitude +0·1, and now visible for the greater part of the night as it approaches opposition early next month. Saturn is in Sagittarius and thus visible in the southern skies, though never at a great altitude—even from southern Britain the maximum altitude is only 17°.

URANUS is at opposition on the 24th in the western part of Sagittarius. Uranus is barely visible to the naked eye since its magnitude is +5·6, but it is readily located with only small optical aid.

THE MOON

Day	R.A.	Dec.	Hor. Par.	Semi-diam.	Sun's Co-long.	P.A. of Bright Limb	Phase	Age	Rise 52°	Rise 56°	Transit	Set 52°	Set 56°
	h m	°	'	'	°	°		d	h m	h m	h m	h m	h m
1	1 52	+16·3	60·2	16·4	231	75	11	26·5	1 49	1 34	9 36	17 46	18 07
2	2 50	+21·5	60·1	16·4	243	83	5	27·5	2 11	1 49	10 33	19 17	19 47
3	3 52	+25·3	59·8	16·3	256	102	1	28·5	2 43	2 12	11 35	20 41	21 17
4	4 55	+27·4	59·3	16·2	268	199	0	0·2	3 28	2 52	12 37	21 49	22 25
5	5 59	+27·7	58·7	16·0	280	255	2	1·2	4 30	3 54	13 39	22 37	23 09
6	7 01	+26·3	57·9	15·8	292	269	6	2·2	5 46	5 14	14 36	23 09	23 34
7	7 58	+23·3	57·1	15·6	305	278	12	3·2	7 07	6 42	15 29	23 31	23 50
8	8 51	+19·3	56·3	15·3	317	284	20	4·2	8 27	8 10	16 17	23 47	—
9	9 40	+14·5	55·6	15·2	329	289	29	5·2	9 43	9 32	17 01	—	0 00
10	10 26	+ 9·2	55·0	15·0	341	292	38	6·2	10 57	10 51	17 42	0 0	0 07
11	11 09	+ 3·7	54·6	14·9	354	293	47	7·2	12 07	12 07	18 21	0 10	0 13
12	11 51	− 1·9	54·3	14·8	6	293	57	8·2	13 17	13 21	19 00	0 20	0 18
13	12 34	− 7·3	54·2	14·8	18	292	66	9·2	14 27	14 37	19 40	0 30	0 24
14	13 17	−12·5	54·3	14·8	30	290	75	10·2	15 40	15 55	20 23	0 41	0 30
15	14 02	−17·3	54·5	14·8	42	286	82	11·2	16 54	17 15	21 08	0 55	0 38
16	14 50	−21·5	54·8	14·9	55	281	89	12·2	18 10	18 38	21 56	1 12	0 50
17	15 42	−24·8	55·3	15·1	67	273	94	13·2	19 23	19 57	22 49	1 36	1 07
18	16 36	−27·0	55·8	15·2	79	261	98	14·2	20 28	21 06	23 45	2 11	1 36
19	17 34	−27·8	56·3	15·3	91	220	100	15·2	21 20	21 56	—	3 01	2 23
20	18 33	−27·1	56·9	15·5	103	111	99	16·2	21 58	22 28	0 41	4 06	3 31
21	19 31	−24·9	57·4	15·6	116	89	97	17·2	22 25	22 48	1 38	5 25	4 56
22	20 27	−21·2	57·9	15·8	128	79	92	18·2	22 45	23 01	2 32	6 49	6 28
23	21 21	−16·4	58·3	15·9	140	73	85	19·2	23 01	23 10	3 24	8 15	8 01
24	22 13	−10·6	58·7	16·0	152	69	76	20·2	23 14	23 17	4 13	9 40	9 33
25	23 03	− 4·3	59·0	16·1	164	67	66	21·2	23 26	23 24	5 01	11 04	11 03
26	23 53	+ 2·2	59·2	16·1	177	66	55	22·2	23 39	23 32	5 48	12 29	12 34
27	0 44	+ 8·8	59·4	16·2	189	67	43	23·2	23 54	23 41	6 37	13 56	14 07
28	1 36	+14·8	59·4	16·2	201	70	32	24·2	—	23 53	7 28	15 24	15 43
29	2 32	+20·2	59·4	16·2	213	75	22	25·2	0 13	—	8 23	16 54	17 20
30	3 31	+24·3	59·2	16·1	226	82	13	26·2	0 40	0 12	9 21	18 20	18 53

MERCURY ☿

Day	R.A.	Dec. +	Diam.	Phase	Transit		Day	R.A.	Dec. +	Diam.	Phase	Transit	
	h m	°	"		h m			h m	°	"		h m	
1	3 49	16·6	—	—	11 09		16	4 04	16·9	—	—	10 27	
4	3 47	16·1	—	—	10 56	Mercury is too	19	4 15	17·8	—	—	10 26	Mercury is too
7	3 48	15·8	—	—	10 45	close to the	22	4 28	18·7	—	—	10 27	close to the
10	3 51	15·9	—	—	10 36	Sun for	25	4 43	19·8	—	—	10 31	Sun for
13	3 56	16·3	—	—	10 30	observation	28	5 01	20·8	—	—	10 37	observation
16	4 04	16·9	—	—	10 27		31	5 21	21·8	—	—	10 46	

VENUS ♀　　　　　　　　MARS ♂

Day	R.A.	Dec. +	Diam.	Phase	Transit	5° high 52°	5° high 56°	Day	R.A.	Dec. +	Diam.	Phase	Transit	5° high 52°	5° high 56°
	h m	°	"		h m	h m	h m		h m	°	"		h m	h m	h m
1	5 40	24·1	10	97	13 03	20 43	21 02	1	7 29	23·2	4	96	14 50	22 22	22 40
6	6 07	24·4	10	96	13 10	20 51	21 11	6	7 42	22·7	4	96	14 44	22 13	22 30
11	6 34	24·3	10	95	13 17	20 58	21 17	11	7 55	22·1	4	97	14 37	22 02	22 19
16	7 00	24·0	10	94	13 24	21 02	21 21	16	8 08	21·5	4	97	14 31	21 52	22 08
21	7 27	23·3	11	94	13 31	21 04	21 22	21	8 21	20·8	4	97	14 24	21 41	21 56
26	7 53	22·4	11	93	13 37	21 05	21 21	26	8 34	20·0	4	97	14 17	21 29	21 44
31	8 19	21·2	11	92	13 43	21 03	21 18	31	8 47	19·2	4	98	14 10	21 18	21 31

SUNRISE AND SUNSET

Day	London a.m. h m	London p.m. h m	Bristol a.m. h m	Bristol p.m. h m	Birmingham a.m. h m	Birmingham p.m. h m	Manchester a.m. h m	Manchester p.m. h m	Newcastle a.m. h m	Newcastle p.m. h m	Glasgow a.m. h m	Glasgow p.m. h m	Belfast a.m. h m	Belfast p.m. h m
1	3 49	8 07	3 59	8 16	3 50	8 19	3 47	8 26	3 35	8 33	3 40	8 50	3 55	8 48
2	3 48	8 08	3 58	8 17	3 49	8 20	3 46	8 28	3 34	8 34	3 39	8 51	3 54	8 50
3	3 48	8 09	3 58	8 19	3 49	8 22	3 45	8 29	3 33	8 35	3 38	8 52	3 53	8 51
4	3 47	8 10	3 57	8 20	3 48	8 23	3 44	8 30	3 32	8 36	3 37	8 53	3 52	8 52
5	3 46	8 11	3 56	8 21	3 47	8 24	3 44	8 31	3 31	8 38	3 36	8 55	3 52	8 53
6	3 45	8 12	3 55	8 22	3 46	8 25	3 43	8 32	3 31	8 39	3 36	8 56	3 51	8 54
7	3 45	8 13	3 55	8 23	3 46	8 26	3 42	8 33	3 30	8 40	3 35	8 57	3 50	8 55
8	3 44	8 14	3 54	8 23	3 45	8 26	3 42	8 34	3 29	8 41	3 34	8 58	3 50	8 56
9	3 44	8 15	3 54	8 24	3 45	8 27	3 41	8 35	3 28	8 42	3 33	8 59	3 49	8 57
10	3 43	8 15	3 53	8 25	3 44	8 28	3 41	8 36	3 28	8 43	3 33	9 00	3 49	8 58
11	3 43	8 16	3 53	8 26	3 44	8 29	3 40	8 37	3 27	8 44	3 32	9 01	3 48	8 59
12	3 43	8 17	3 53	8 26	3 44	8 29	3 40	8 38	3 27	8 45	3 32	9 02	3 48	9 00
13	3 43	8 17	3 53	8 27	3 44	8 30	3 39	8 38	3 26	8 45	3 31	9 02	3 47	9 00
14	3 42	8 18	3 52	8 28	3 43	8 31	3 39	8 39	3 26	8 46	3 31	9 03	3 47	9 01
15	3 42	8 18	3 52	8 28	3 43	8 31	3 39	8 40	3 26	8 47	3 31	9 04	3 47	9 02
16	3 42	8 19	3 52	8 29	3 43	8 32	3 39	8 40	3 26	8 47	3 31	9 04	3 47	9 02
17	3 42	8 19	3 52	8 29	3 43	8 32	3 39	8 40	3 26	8 47	3 30	9 05	3 47	9 02
18	3 42	8 20	3 52	8 30	3 43	8 33	3 39	8 41	3 26	8 48	3 30	9 05	3 47	9 03
19	3 42	8 20	3 52	8 30	3 43	8 33	3 39	8 41	3 26	8 48	3 30	9 06	3 47	9 03
20	3 42	8 20	3 52	8 30	3 43	8 33	3 39	8 42	3 26	8 49	3 30	9 06	3 47	9 04
21	3 42	8 21	3 52	8 31	3 43	8 34	3 39	8 42	3 26	8 49	3 31	9 06	3 47	9 04
22	3 43	8 21	3 53	8 31	3 44	8 34	3 39	8 42	3 26	8 49	3 31	9 06	3 47	9 04
23	3 43	8 21	3 53	8 31	3 44	8 34	3 39	8 42	3 26	8 49	3 31	9 07	3 47	9 04
24	3 43	8 21	3 53	8 31	3 44	8 34	3 40	8 42	3 27	8 49	3 32	9 07	3 48	9 04
25	3 43	8 21	3 53	8 31	3 44	8 34	3 40	8 42	3 27	8 49	3 32	9 07	3 48	9 04
26	3 44	8 21	3 54	8 31	3 45	8 34	3 41	8 42	3 28	8 49	3 32	9 07	3 49	9 04
27	3 44	8 21	3 54	8 31	3 45	8 34	3 41	8 42	3 28	8 49	3 33	9 06	3 49	9 04
28	3 45	8 21	3 55	8 31	3 46	8 34	3 42	8 42	3 29	8 49	3 33	9 06	3 50	9 04
29	3 45	8 21	3 55	8 31	3 46	8 34	3 42	8 42	3 29	8 49	3 34	9 06	3 50	9 04
30	3 46	8 21	3 56	8 31	3 47	8 34	3 43	8 42	3 30	8 49	3 35	9 06	3 51	9 04

JUPITER ♃   SATURN ♄

Day	R.A. h m	Dec. + °	Transit h m		R.A. h m	Dec. − °	Transit h m	5° high 52° h m	5° high 56° h m
1	5 02	22·3	12 22	Jupiter is too	18 55	22·2	2 17	23 03	23 36
11	5 12	22·6	11 53	close to the	18 53	22·2	1 35	22 22	22 55
21	5 22	22·8	11 24	Sun for	18 50	22·3	0 53	21 40	22 13
31	5 32	22·9	10 54	observation	18 46	22·4	0 10	20 58	21 31

Equatorial diameter of Jupiter 32″; of Saturn 18″.   Diameters of Saturn's rings 41″ and 18″.

URANUS ♅   NEPTUNE ♆

Day	R.A. h m	Dec. − ° ′	Transit h m	10° high 52° h m	10° high 56° h m	R.A. h m	Dec. − ° ′	Transit h m	10° high 52° h m	10° high 56° h m
1	18 18·7	23 38	1 41	23 38	1 05	18 51·0	21 59	2 13	23 50	0 49
11	18 17·0	23 39	1 00	22 57	0 25	18 50·0	22 00	1 33	23 10	0 09
21	18 15·3	23 40	0 19	22 16	23 40	18 48·9	22 02	0 52	22 30	23 25
31	18 13·5	23 41	23 33	21 35	23 00	18 47·8	22 03	0 12	21 49	22 45

Diameter 4″   Diameter 2″

Julius Caesar, formerly *Quintilis*, 5th month (from March).

Sun's *Longitude* 120° ♌ 22ᵈ 21ʰ

Month	Week		
1	S.	Princess of Wales b. 1961. The Boyne 1690.	
2	S.	**6th S. after Trinity.** Archbp. Cranmer b. 1489.*	
3	M.	**St. Thomas.** Gettysburg ends 1863.	
4	Tu.	Independence Day, U.S.A., 1776.	
5	W.	Jean Cocteau b. 1889.* N.H.S. started 1948.	
6	Th.	Henry II d. 1189.* Sedgemoor 1685.	
7	F.	Edward I b. 1307. Allen Lane d. 1970.	
8	S.	Edward, the Black Prince d. 1376.	
9	S.	**7th S. after Trinity.** Edward Heath b. 1916.	
10	M.	John Calvin b. 1509. Marcel Proust b. 1871.	
11	Tu.	Courtrai 1302. Oudenarde 1708.	
12	W.	Acre Captured by Crusaders 1191.	
13	Th.	John Clare b. 1793. Sidney Webb b. 1859.	
14	F.	Fête Nationale, France. Bastille stormed 1789.*	
15	S.	St. Swithin's Day. Iris Murdoch b. 1919.	
16	S.	**8th S. after Trinity.** Amundsen b. 1872.	
17	M.	Adam Smith d. 1790. James Whistler d. 1903.	
18	Tu.	Jean Watteau d. 1721. Jane Austen d. 1817.	
19	W.	*Mary Rose* sank 1545. Edgar Degas b. 1834.	
20	Th.	Sir Edmund Hillary b. 1919. Paul Valéry d. 1945.	
21	F.	First men on the Moon 1969.	
22	S.	**St. Mary Magdalen.** Atlanta 1864.	
23	S.	**9th S. after Trinity.** Olivia Manning d. 1980.	
24	M.	Treaty of Lausanne 1923. Peter Sellers d. 1980.	
25	Tu.	**St. James.** Start of Sino-Japanese War 1894.	
26	W.	George Borrow d. 1881. Robert Graves b. 1895.	
27	Th.	Korean War ended 1953. James Mason d. 1984.	
28	F.	Cyrano de Bergerac d. 1655. J.S. Bach d. 1750.	
29	S.	Frans Hals d. 1666. Sir John Barbirolli d. 1970.	
30	S.	**10th S. after Trinity.** Bismarck d. 1898.	
31	M.	Trinity Law Sittings End. Liszt d. 1886.	

* Centenary.

PHENOMENA

d	h	
1	21	Mercury in conjunction with Moon. Mercury 6° S.
1	23	Jupiter in conjunction with Moon. Jupiter 5° S.
2	13	Saturn at opposition.
2	17	Jupiter in conjunction with Mercury. Jupiter 0°·6 N.
2	23	Neptune at opposition.
4	12	Earth at aphelion (152 million km.).
5	04	Venus in conjunction with Moon. Venus 0°·1 S.
5	12	Mars in conjunction with Moon. Mars 0°·1 S.
12	12	Mars in conjunction with Venus. Mars 0°·5 S.
17	12	Saturn in conjunction with Moon. Saturn 4° N.
18	08	Mercury in superior conjunction.
29	16	Jupiter in conjunction with Moon. Jupiter 5° S.

CONSTELLATIONS

The following constellations are near the meridian at

d	h		d	h
June 1	24		June 15	23
July 1	22		July 16	21
Aug. 1	20		Aug. 16	19

Ursa Minor, Draco, Corona, Hercules, Lyra, Serpens, Ophiuchus, Libra, Scorpius and Sagittarius.

MINIMA OF ALGOL

d	h		d	h
1	8		18	13
4	5		21	10
7	2		24	6
9	22		27	3
12	19		30	0
15	16			

PHASES OF THE MOON

		d	h	m
●	New Moon........	3	04	59
☽	First Quarter	11	00	19
○	Full Moon	18	17	42
☾	Last Quarter......	25	13	31

	d	h
Apogee (404,150 kilometres)	10	21
Perigee (368,430 ,,)	23	07

Mean Longitude of Ascending Node on July 1, 328°

See note on *Summer Time*, p. 24.

MONTHLY NOTES

July   1. National Day, Canada.

3. Dog Days begin (end Aug. 15).

5. Tynwald Day, Isle of Man.

12. Bank Holiday, Northern Ireland.

Day	THE SUN s.d. 15'·8								Sidereal Time	Transit of First Point of Aries
	Right Ascension	Dec. +	Equation of Time	Rise		Transit	Set			
				52°	56°		52°	56°		
	h m s	° '	m s	h m	h m	h m	h m	h m	h m s	h m s
1	6 39 48	23 08	−3 42	3 44	3 18	12 04	20 23	20 49	18 36 06	5 23 00
2	6 43 57	23 04	−3 54	3 45	3 19	12 04	20 23	20 48	18 40 03	5 19 05
3	6 48 04	22 59	−4 05	3 46	3 20	12 04	20 22	20 48	18 44 00	5 15 09
4	6 52 12	22 54	−4 16	3 46	3 21	12 04	20 22	20 47	18 47 56	5 11 13
5	6 56 19	22 49	−4 27	3 47	3 22	12 05	20 21	20 47	18 51 53	5 07 17
6	7 00 26	22 43	−4 37	3 48	3 23	12 05	20 21	20 46	18 55 49	5 03 21
7	7 04 33	22 37	−4 47	3 49	3 24	12 05	20 20	20 45	18 59 46	4 59 25
8	7 08 39	22 30	−4 57	3 50	3 25	12 05	20 19	20 44	19 03 42	4 55 29
9	7 12 45	22 23	−5 06	3 51	3 26	12 05	20 19	20 43	19 07 39	4 51 33
10	7 16 51	22 16	−5 15	3 52	3 28	12 05	20 18	20 42	19 11 35	4 47 37
11	7 20 55	22 08	−5 23	3 53	3 29	12 05	20 17	20 41	19 15 32	4 43 41
12	7 25 00	22 00	−5 31	3 54	3 30	12 06	20 16	20 40	19 19 29	4 39 45
13	7 29 04	21 52	5 39	3 55	3 32	12 06	20 15	20 39	19 23 25	4 35 50
14	7 33 08	21 43	−5 46	3 57	3 33	12 06	20 14	20 38	19 27 22	4 31 54
15	7 37 11	21 34	−5 52	3 58	3 35	12 06	20 13	20 36	19 31 18	4 27 58
16	7 41 13	21 24	−5 58	3 59	3 36	12 06	20 12	20 35	19 35 15	4 24 02
17	7 45 15	21 14	−6 04	4 00	3 38	12 06	20 11	20 34	19 39 11	4 20 06
18	7 49 17	21 04	−6 09	4 01	3 39	12 06	20 10	20 32	19 43 08	4 16 10
19	7 53 18	20 54	−6 13	4 03	3 41	12 06	20 09	20 31	19 47 04	4 12 14
20	7 57 18	20 43	−6 17	4 04	3 42	12 06	20 08	20 29	19 51 01	4 08 18
21	8 01 18	20 31	−6 20	4 05	3 44	12 06	20 06	20 28	19 54 58	4 04 22
22	8 05 17	20 20	−6 23	4 07	3 46	12 06	20 05	20 26	19 58 54	4 00 26
23	8 09 16	20 08	−6 25	4 08	3 47	12 06	20 04	20 24	20 02 51	3 56 30
24	8 13 14	19 55	−6 27	4 10	3 49	12 06	20 02	20 23	20 06 47	3 52 35
25	8 17 11	19 43	−6 28	4 11	3 51	12 06	20 01	20 21	20 10 44	3 48 39
26	8 21 08	19 30	−6 28	4 12	3 53	12 06	19 59	20 19	20 14 40	3 44 43
27	8 25 05	19 16	−6 28	4 14	3 54	12 06	19 58	20 17	20 18 37	3 40 47
28	8 29 01	19 03	−6 27	4 15	3 56	12 06	19 56	20 15	20 22 34	3 36 51
29	8 32 56	18 49	−6 26	4 17	3 58	12 06	19 55	20 14	20 26 30	3 32 55
30	8 36 51	18 34	−6 24	4 18	4 00	12 06	19 53	20 12	20 30 27	3 28 59
31	8 40 45	18 20	−6 22	4 20	4 02	12 06	19 52	20 10	20 34 23	3 25 03

Duration of Civil (C), Nautical (N), and Astronomical (A), Twilight (in minutes)

Lat. °	July 1			July 11			July 21			July 31		
	C	N	A	C	N	A	C	N	A	C	N	A
52	48	124	T.A.N.	46	116	T.A.N.	44	107	T.A.N.	41	98	180
56	61	T.A.N.	T.A.N.	58	T.A.N.	T.A.N.	53	144	T.A.N.	49	122	T.A.N.

ASTRONOMICAL NOTES

MERCURY is at a superior conjunction on the 18th and is thus unsuitably placed for observation.

VENUS is a brilliant object in the evening sky, magnitude −3·9, but only visible low above the western horizon for about half-an-hour after sunset. The crescent moon will be seen near the planet on the 4th and 5th.

MARS is unsuitably placed for observation.

JUPITER is too close to the Sun to be observed for the first week of July but then becomes visible as a morning object, magnitude −2·0. It may be seen low in the eastern sky after about 03h at the beginning of the period of visibility and after about 02h by the end of the month.

SATURN, magnitude +0·1, is at opposition on the 2nd and thus visible throughout the hours of darkness.

NEPTUNE is at opposition on the 2nd, in Sagittarius. It is not visible to the naked eye since its magnitude is +7·9.

TWILIGHT. Reference to the section just above these notes shows that astronomical twilight lasts all night for some time around the summer solstice (i.e. in June and July), even in southern England. Under these conditions the sky never gets completely dark since the Sun is always less than 18° below the horizon.

THE MOON

Day	R.A.	Dec.	Hor. Par.	Semi-diam.	Sun's Co-long.	P.A. of Bright Limb	Phase	Age	Rise 52°	Rise 56°	Transit	Set 52°	Set 56°
	h m	°	′	′	°	°		d	h m	h m	h m	h m	h m
1	4 33	+27·0	58·9	16·1	238	90	6	27·2	1 18	0 44	10 22	19 33	20 11
2	5 36	+27·9	58·5	15·9	250	103	2	28·2	2 12	1 35	11 23	20 29	21 04
3	6 38	+27·0	58·0	15·8	262	149	0	29·2	3 22	2 48	12 23	21 07	21 36
4	7 37	+24·5	57·4	15·6	275	263	1	0·8	4 42	4 15	13 18	21 33	21 55
5	8 32	+20·8	56·7	15·5	287	280	4	1·8	6 04	5 44	14 08	21 52	22 07
6	9 23	+16·2	56·1	15·3	299	287	9	2·8	7 23	7 09	14 54	22 06	22 15
7	10 10	+11·0	55·4	15·1	311	291	15	3·8	8 39	8 31	15 36	22 17	22 22
8	10 54	+ 5·4	54·9	15·0	324	293	23	4·8	9 51	9 48	16 17	22 27	22 27
9	11 37	− 0·2	54·5	14·9	336	294	31	5·8	11 02	11 04	16 56	22 37	22 32
10	12 19	− 5·7	54·3	14·8	348	294	41	6·8	12 12	12 19	17 36	22 47	22 38
11	13 02	−11·1	54·3	14·8	0	293	50	7·8	13 23	13 36	18 17	23 00	22 45
12	13 46	−16·0	54·4	14·8	13	290	59	8·8	14 36	14 55	19 01	23 15	22 55
13	14 33	−20·4	54·6	14·9	25	286	69	9·8	15 51	16 17	19 48	23 36	23 10
14	15 23	−23·9	55·1	15·0	37	281	77	10·8	17 06	17 38	20 38	—	23 33
15	16 17	−26·5	55·6	15·2	49	275	85	11·8	18 15	18 52	21 33	0 06	—
16	17 14	−27·8	56·3	15·3	61	268	91	12·8	19 13	19 50	22 30	0 49	0 12
17	18 12	−27·6	56·9	15·5	74	258	96	13·8	19 56	20 29	23 27	1 49	1 12
18	19 11	−25·8	57·6	15·7	86	243	99	14·8	20 28	20 53	—	3 04	2 32
19	20 09	−22·5	58·2	15·9	98	112	100	15·8	20 50	21 08	0 23	4 28	4 05
20	21 05	−17·8	58·8	16·0	110	77	98	16·8	21 07	21 19	1 17	5 56	5 40
21	21 59	−12·2	59·2	16·1	122	70	94	17·8	21 21	21 27	2 08	7 24	7 15
22	22 51	− 5·8	59·4	16·2	135	66	87	18·8	21 34	21 34	2 57	8 50	8 47
23	23 41	+ 0·8	59·5	16·2	147	65	78	19·8	21 46	21 41	3 46	10 16	10 19
24	0 32	+ 7·5	59·5	16·2	159	65	68	20·8	22 01	21 49	4 34	11 43	11 52
25	1 24	+13·7	59·4	16·2	171	68	57	21·8	22 18	22 00	5 25	13 11	13 27
26	2 19	+19·2	59·1	16·1	183	71	45	22·8	22 42	22 17	6 18	14 40	15 04
27	3 16	+23·5	58·8	16·0	196	77	34	23·8	23 15	22 43	7 14	16 06	16 37
28	4 16	+26·5	58·5	15·9	208	83	24	24·8	—	23 25	8 13	17 22	17 59
29	5 18	+27·9	58·1	15·8	220	90	15	25·8	0 02	—	9 13	18 23	19 00
30	6 19	+27·5	57·7	15·7	232	98	8	26·8	1 06	0 30	10 12	19 06	19 38
31	7 18	+25·5	57·2	15·6	245	106	3	27·8	2 22	1 51	11 08	19 36	20 00

MERCURY ☿

Day	R.A.	Dec. +	Diam.	Phase	Transit		Day	R.A.	Dec. +	Diam.	Phase	Transit	
	h m	°	″		h m			h m	°	″		h m	
1	5 21	21·8	—	—	10 46		16	7 30	23·2	—	—	11 58	
4	5 43	22·7	—	—	10 57	Mercury is too	19	7 58	22·3	—	—	12 13	Mercury is too
7	6 08	23·3	—	—	11 11	close to the	22	8 25	21·1	—	—	12 28	close to the
10	6 35	23·7	—	—	11 26	Sun for	25	8 50	19·6	—	—	12 41	Sun for
13	7 02	23·6	—	—	11 41	observation	28	9 14	17·9	—	—	12 53	observation
16	7 30	23·2	—	—	11 58		31	9 36	16·0	—	—	13 03	

VENUS ♀

Day	R.A.	Dec. +	Diam.	Phase	Transit	5° high. 52°	5° high. 56°
	h m	°	″		h m	h m	h m
1	8 19	21·2	11	92	13 43	21 03	21 18
6	8 44	19·8	11	91	13 49	21 00	21 14
11	9 09	18·1	11	90	13 54	20 55	21 07
16	9 33	16·3	11	88	13 58	20 49	20 59
21	9 56	14·2	12	87	14 02	20 41	20 50
26	10 19	12·1	12	86	14 05	20 33	20 39
31	10 42	9·7	12	85	14 08	20 24	20 28

MARS ♂

Day	R.A.	Dec. +	Diam.	Phase	Transit	
	h m	°	″		h m	
1	8 47	19·2	—	—	14 10	
6	9 00	18·3	—	—	14 03	Mars is too
11	9 12	17·4	—	—	13 56	close to the
16	9 25	16·5	—	—	13 49	Sun for
21	9 37	15·4	—	—	13 41	observation
26	9 49	14·4	—	—	13 34	
31	10 01	13·3	—	—	13 26	

SUNRISE AND SUNSET

Day	London a.m. h m	London p.m. h m	Bristol a.m. h m	Bristol p.m. h m	Birmingham a.m. h m	Birmingham p.m. h m	Manchester a.m. h m	Manchester p.m. h m	Newcastle a.m. h m	Newcastle p.m. h m	Glasgow a.m. h m	Glasgow p.m. h m	Belfast a.m. h m	Belfast p.m. h m
1	3 47	8 21	3 57	8 30	3 48	8 33	3 44	8 41	3 31	8 48	3 36	9 05	3 52	9 03
2	3 47	8 20	3 57	8 30	3 48	8 33	3 44	8 41	3 31	8 48	3 36	9 05	3 52	9 03
3	3 48	8 20	3 58	8 29	3 49	8 32	3 45	8 40	3 32	8 47	3 37	9 04	3 53	9 02
4	3 49	8 20	3 59	8 29	3 50	8 32	3 46	8 40	3 33	8 47	3 38	9 04	3 54	9 02
5	3 50	8 19	4 00	8 29	3 51	8 32	3 47	8 39	3 34	8 46	3 39	9 03	3 55	9 01
6	3 50	8 19	4 00	8 28	3 51	8 31	3 48	8 39	3 35	8 45	3 40	9 02	3 56	9 01
7	3 51	8 18	4 01	8 27	3 52	8 30	3 49	8 38	3 36	8 45	3 41	9 02	3 57	9 00
8	3 52	8 18	4 02	8 27	3 53	8 30	3 50	8 37	3 37	8 44	3 42	9 01	3 58	8 59
9	3 53	8 17	4 03	8 26	3 54	8 29	3 51	8 36	3 39	8 43	3 44	9 00	3 59	8 58
10	3 54	8 16	4 04	8 25	3 55	8 28	3 52	8 36	3 40	8 42	3 45	8 59	4 00	8 58
11	3 55	8 16	4 05	8 25	3 56	8 28	3 53	8 35	3 41	8 41	3 46	8 58	4 01	8 57
12	3 56	8 15	4 06	8 24	3 57	8 27	3 54	8 34	3 42	8 40	3 48	8 57	4 02	8 56
13	3 57	8 14	4 08	8 23	3 59	8 26	3 56	8 33	3 44	8 39	3 49	8 55	4 04	8 55
14	3 58	8 13	4 09	8 22	4 00	8 25	3 57	8 32	3 45	8 38	3 50	8 54	4 05	8 54
15	3 59	8 12	4 10	8 21	4 01	8 24	3 58	8 31	3 46	8 37	3 52	8 53	4 06	8 53
16	4 01	8 11	4 11	8 20	4 02	8 23	3 59	8 30	3 47	8 36	3 53	8 52	4 07	8 52
17	4 02	8 10	4 12	8 19	4 04	8 21	4 01	8 28	3 49	8 34	3 55	8 50	4 09	8 50
18	4 03	8 09	4 13	8 18	4 05	8 20	4 02	8 27	3 50	8 33	3 56	8 49	4 10	8 49
19	4 04	8 08	4 15	8 17	4 07	8 19	4 04	8 26	3 52	8 32	3 58	8 48	4 12	8 48
20	4 05	8 06	4 16	8 16	4 08	8 17	4 05	8 24	3 53	8 30	3 59	8 46	4 13	8 46
21	4 07	8 05	4 17	8 15	4 09	8 16	4 06	8 23	3 55	8 28	4 01	8 44	4 15	8 44
22	4 08	8 04	4 19	8 14	4 11	8 15	4 08	8 22	3 57	8 27	4 03	8 43	4 17	8 43
23	4 09	8 03	4 20	8 13	4 12	8 14	4 09	8 21	3 58	8 25	4 04	8 41	4 18	8 41
24	4 11	8 01	4 21	8 11	4 14	8 12	4 11	8 19	4 00	8 24	4 06	8 40	4 20	8 40
25	4 12	8 00	4 23	8 10	4 15	8 11	4 12	8 18	4 02	8 22	4 08	8 38	4 22	8 38
26	4 14	7 58	4 24	8 08	4 17	8 09	4 14	8 16	4 03	8 21	4 10	8 36	4 23	8 37
27	4 15	7 57	4 25	8 07	4 18	8 08	4 15	8 15	4 05	8 19	4 11	8 34	4 25	8 35
28	4 16	7 55	4 26	8 05	4 19	8 06	4 16	8 13	4 06	8 17	4 13	8 33	4 26	8 33
29	4 18	7 54	4 28	8 04	4 21	8 05	4 18	8 12	4 08	8 16	4 15	8 31	4 28	8 32
30	4 19	7 52	4 29	8 02	4 22	8 03	4 20	8 10	4 10	8 14	4 16	8 29	4 30	8 30
31	4 21	7 51	4 31	8 01	4 24	8 02	4 21	8 08	4 11	8 12	4 18	8 27	4 31	8 28

JUPITER ♃ / SATURN ♄

Day	Jupiter R.A. h m	Jupiter Dec. + °	Jupiter Transit h m	Jupiter 5° high. 52° h m	Jupiter 5° high. 56° h m	Saturn R.A. h m	Saturn Dec. − °	Saturn Transit h m	Saturn 5° high. 52° h m	Saturn 5° high. 56° h m
1	5 32	22·9	10 54	3 24	3 06	18 46	22·4	0 10	3 18	2 45
11	5 41	23·0	10 25	2 54	2 36	18 43	22·5	23 24	2 35	2 02
21	5 51	23·1	9 55	2 23	2 06	18 40	22·5	22 41	1 52	1 19
31	6 00	23·1	9 24	1 53	1 35	18 38	22·6	21 59	1 10	0 36

Equatorial diameter of Jupiter 33″; of Saturn 19″. Diameters of Saturn's rings 41″ and 18″.

URANUS ♅ / NEPTUNE ♆

Day	Uranus R.A. h m	Uranus Dec. − ° ′	Uranus Transit h m	Uranus 10° high. 52° h m	Uranus 10° high. 56° h m	Neptune R.A. h m	Neptune Dec. − ° ′	Neptune Transit h m	Neptune 10° high. 52° h m	Neptune 10° high. 56° h m
1	18 13·5	23 41	23 33	1 36	0 11	18 47·8	22 03	0 12		
11	18 11·8	23 41	22 52	0 55	23 25	18 46·6	22 04	23 27		
21	18 10·2	23 42	22 11	0 13	22 44	18 45·5	22 06	22 47		
31	18 8·7	23 42	21 31	23 29	22 03	18 44·4	22 07	22 06		

Diameter 4″   Diameter 2″

DAY OF		Julius Caesar *Augustus*, formerly *Sextilis*, 6th month (from March). *Sun's Longitude* 150° ♍ 23ᵈ 04ʰ

Month	Week	
1	Tu.	Minden 1759. The Nile 1798.
2	W.	William II d. 1100. Gen. von Hindenburg d. 1934.
3	Th.	Discovery of Lake Victoria 1858.
4	F.	QUEEN ELIZABETH THE QUEEN MOTHER b. 1900.
5	S.	Lord North d. 1792. Marilyn Monroe d. 1962.
6	S.	**Transfiguration. 11th S. after Trinity.**
7	M.	Joseph Jacquard d. 1834.
8	Tu.	Great Train Robbery 1963.
9	W.	Second atomic bomb dropped, Nagasaki 1945.
10	Th.	Charles Keene b. 1823. James Whistler b. 1834.
11	F.	H. J. Pye d. 1813. Edith Wharton d. 1937.
12	S.	Glorious Twelfth. William Blake d. 1827.
13	S.	**12th S. after Trinity.** Blenheim 1704.
14	M.	Surrender of Japan 1945.
15	Tu.	PRINCESS ROYAL b. 1950. E. Nesbit b. 1858.
16	W.	Peterloo Massacre 1819. Marvell d. 1678.
17	Th.	Davy Crockett b. 1786. Rudolf Hess d. 1987.
18	F.	Lord Russell b. 1792. Goldfrey Evans b. 1920.
19	S.	Allied raid on Dieppe 1942.
20	S.	**13th S. after Trinity.** Gen. Booth d. 1912.
21	M.	PRINCESS MARGARET b. 1930.
22	Tu.	Bosworth Field 1485. Jomo Kenyatta d. 1978.
23	W.	William Wallace exec. 1305.
24	Th.	**St. Bartholomew.** Vesuvius erupted A.D. 79.
25	F.	Liberation of Paris 1944.
26	S.	Crécy 1346. Prince Albert b. 1819.
27	S.	**14th S. after Trinity.** Mountbatten assas. 1979.
28	M.	Prince William of Gloucester d. 1972.
29	Tu.	John Locke b. 1632. de Valera d. 1975
30	W.	Mary Shelley b. 1797. Lord Rutherford b. 1871.
31	Th.	Clive Lloyd b. 1944. Henry Moore d. 1986.

*Centenary.

PHENOMENA

d	h	
3	02	Mercury in conjunction with Moon. Mercury 2°N.
3	08	Mars in conjunction with Moon. Mars 2°N.
4	13	Venus in conjunction with Moon. Venus 3°N.
5	22	Mars in conjunction with Mercury. Mars 0°·01 S.
13	18	Saturn in conjunction with Moon. Saturn 4°N.
26	07	Jupiter in conjunction with Moon. Jupiter 4°S.
29	10	Mercury at greatest elongation E.27°.

CONSTELLATIONS

The following constellations are near the meridian at

d	h		d	h
July 1	24		July 16	23
Aug. 1	22		Aug. 16	21
Sept. 1	20		Sept. 15	19

Draco, Hercules, Lyra, Cygnus, Sagitta, Ophiuchus, Serpens, Aquila and Sagittarius.

MINIMA OF ALGOL

d	h	d	h
1	21	19	2
4	18	21	23
7	15	24	19
10	11	27	16
13	8	30	13
16	5		

PHASES OF THE MOON

		d	h	m
●	New Moon	1	16	06
☽	First Quarter	9	17	28
○	Full Moon	17	03	07
☾	Last Quarter	23	18	40
●	New Moon	31	05	44

	d	h
Apogee (404,700 kilometres)	7	15
Perigee (363,570 „)	19	12

Mean Longitude of Ascending Node on Aug. 1, 327°.

See note on *Summer Time*, p. 24.

MONTHLY NOTES

Aug. 1. Lammas. Scottish Term Day.

4. Islamic New Year (A.H. 1410).

7. Bank Holiday, Scotland.

12. Grouse shooting begins.

28. Bank and General Holiday, England, Wales and N. Ireland.

Day	Right Ascension	Dec. +	Equation of Time	Rise 52°	Rise 56°	Transit	Set 52°	Set 56°	Sidereal Time	Transit of First Point of Aries
	h m s	° ′	m s	h m	h m	h m	h m	h m	h m s	h m s
1	8 44 38	18 05	− 6 19	4 21	4 04	12 06	19 50	20 08	20 38 20	3 21 07
2	8 48 31	17 50	− 6 15	4 23	4 06	12 06	19 48	20 06	20 42 16	3 17 11
3	8 52 24	17 34	− 6 11	4 25	4 07	12 06	19 47	20 04	20 46 13	3 13 15
4	8 56 15	17 18	− 6 06	4 26	4 09	12 06	19 45	20 01	20 50 09	3 09 19
5	9 00 06	17 02	− 6 00	4 28	4 11	12 06	19 43	19 59	20 54 06	3 05 24
6	9 03 57	16 46	− 5 54	4 29	4 13	12 06	19 41	19 57	20 58 03	3 01 28
7	9 07 47	16 29	− 5 47	4 31	4 15	12 06	19 39	19 55	21 01 59	2 57 32
8	9 11 36	16 13	− 5 40	4 32	4 17	12 06	19 38	19 53	21 05 56	2 53 36
9	9 15 24	15 55	− 5 32	4 34	4 19	12 05	19 36	19 51	21 09 52	2 49 40
10	9 19 12	15 38	− 5 24	4 36	4 21	12 05	19 34	19 48	21 13 49	2 45 44
11	9 23 00	15 21	− 5 15	4 37	4 23	12 05	19 32	19 46	21 17 45	2 41 48
12	9 26 47	15 03	− 5 05	4 39	4 25	12 05	19 30	19 44	21 21 42	2 37 52
13	9 30 33	14 45	− 4 55	4 41	4 27	12 05	19 28	19 42	21 25 38	2 33 56
14	9 34 19	14 26	− 4 44	4 42	4 29	12 05	19 26	19 39	21 29 35	2 30 00
15	9 38 04	14 08	− 4 32	4 44	4 31	12 04	19 24	19 37	21 33 32	2 26 04
16	9 41 48	13 49	− 4 20	4 45	4 33	12 04	19 22	19 35	21 37 28	2 22 09
17	9 45 33	13 30	− 4 08	4 47	4 35	12 04	19 20	19 32	21 41 25	2 18 13
18	9 49 16	13 11	− 3 55	4 49	4 36	12 04	19 18	19 30	21 45 21	2 14 17
19	9 52 59	12 51	− 3 41	4 50	4 38	12 04	19 16	19 27	21 49 18	2 10 21
20	9 56 42	12 32	− 3 27	4 52	4 40	12 03	19 14	19 25	21 53 14	2 06 25
21	10 00 24	12 12	− 3 13	4 54	4 42	12 03	19 12	19 22	21 57 11	2 02 29
22	10 04 06	11 52	− 2 58	4 55	4 44	12 03	19 09	19 20	22 01 07	1 58 33
23	10 07 47	11 32	− 2 43	4 57	4 46	12 03	19 07	19 18	22 05 04	1 54 37
24	10 11 28	11 11	− 2 27	4 58	4 48	12 02	19 05	19 15	22 09 01	1 50 41
25	10 15 08	10 51	− 2 11	5 00	4 50	12 02	19 03	19 13	22 12 57	1 46 45
26	10 18 48	10 30	− 1 54	5 02	4 52	12 02	19 01	19 10	22 16 54	1 42 49
27	10 22 28	10 09	− 1 37	5 03	4 54	12 01	18 59	19 07	22 20 50	1 38 54
28	10 26 07	9 48	− 1 20	5 05	4 56	12 01	18 56	19 05	22 24 47	1 34 58
29	10 29 46	9 27	− 1 02	5 07	4 58	12 01	18 54	19 02	22 28 43	1 31 02
30	10 33 24	9 05	− 0 44	5 08	5 00	12 01	18 52	19 00	22 32 40	1 27 06
31	10 37 03	8 44	− 0 26	5 10	5 02	12 00	18 50	18 57	22 36 36	1 23 10

THE SUN   s.d. 15′·8

Duration of Civil (C), Nautical (N), and Astronomical (A), Twilight (in minutes)

Lat. °	Aug. 1 C	N	A	Aug. 11 C	N	A	Aug. 21 C	N	A	Aug. 31 C	N	A
52	41	97	177	39	89	153	37	83	138	35	79	127
56	48	120	T.A.N.	45	106	205	42	96	166	40	89	147

ASTRONOMICAL NOTES

MERCURY is at greatest elongation on the 29th but even so it is unsuitably placed for observation.

VENUS continues to be visible as a brilliant object in the evening skies, magnitude − 4·0, but only visible for about half-an-hour after sunset, low above the western horizon. The crescent Moon will be seen near the planet on the evenings of the 3rd and 4th.

MARS is too close to the Sun for observation.

JUPITER, magnitude − 2·0, is a morning object in the constellation of Gemini and by the end of the month may be seen low on the eastern horizon shortly after midnight. On the morning of the 26th the old crescent Moon will be seen approaching the planet, passing 4°N. of it after sunrise.

SATURN remains a prominent object, magnitude + 0·2, in the southern skies and visible for most of the night.

ECLIPSE. A total eclipse of the Moon occurs on the 17th, visible from the British Isles. See page 74 for details.

ECLIPSE. A partial eclipse of the Sun occurs on the 31st. See page 74 for details.

METEORS. The maximum of the famous Perseid meteor shower occurs on the 12th. A bright Moon will seriously interfere with observation before midnight.

THE MOON

Day	R.A.	Dec.	Hor. Par.	Semi-diam.	Sun's Co-long.	P.A. of Bright Limb	Phase	Age	Rise 52°	Rise 56°	Transit	Set 52°	Set 56°
	h m	°	′	′	°	°		d	h m	h m	h m	h m	h m
1	8 14	+22·2	56·6	15·4	257	118	1	27·8	3 42	3 19	12 00	19 57	20 14
2	9 06	+17·8	56·1	15·3	269	271	0	0·3	5 03	4 46	12 47	20 12	20 24
3	9 54	+12·8	55·6	15·1	281	290	2	1·3	6 20	6 10	13 31	20 24	20 31
4	10 39	+ 7·3	55·1	15·0	294	294	5	2·3	7 34	7 29	14 12	20 35	20 36
5	11 22	+ 1·6	54·7	14·9	306	296	11	3·3	8 45	8 46	14 52	20 44	20 42
6	12 05	− 4·0	54·4	14·8	318	296	17	4·3	9 56	10 01	15 32	20 55	20 47
7	12 48	− 9·4	54·2	14·8	330	295	25	5·3	11 07	11 18	16 12	21 06	20 54
8	13 31	−14·5	54·2	14·8	342	293	34	6·3	12 19	12 35	16 55	21 20	21 02
9	14 17	−19·1	54·3	14·8	355	290	43	7·3	13 33	13 56	17 40	21 38	21 14
10	15 06	−22·9	54·6	14·9	7	286	53	8·3	14 47	15 17	18 28	22 03	21 33
11	15 57	−25·8	55·1	15·0	19	280	62	9·3	15 58	16 34	19 20	22 39	22 03
12	16 52	−27·6	55·8	15·2	31	274	72	10·3	17 01	17 39	20 15	23 31	22 53
13	17 50	−27·9	56·5	15·4	44	268	80	11·3	17 50	18 25	21 12	—	—
14	18 48	−26·7	57·3	15·6	56	261	88	12·3	18 27	18 55	22 09	0 39	0 04
15	19 47	−24·0	58·2	15·8	68	254	94	13·3	18 53	19 14	23 04	2 00	1 32
16	20 44	−19·8	58·9	16·1	80	249	98	14·3	19 12	19 26	23 58	3 28	3 08
17	21 39	−14·4	59·6	16·2	92	241	100	15·3	19 28	19 36	—	4 58	4 45
18	22 33	− 8·1	60·0	16·4	104	63	99	16·3	19 41	19 43	0 49	6 27	6 21
19	23 25	− 1·3	60·3	16·4	117	62	95	17·3	19 54	19 50	1 39	7 55	7 56
20	0 17	+ 5·6	60·3	16·4	129	62	89	18·3	20 08	19 58	2 29	9 24	9 32
21	1 10	+12·1	60·1	16·4	141	64	80	19·3	20 24	20 09	3 20	10 54	11 08
22	2 05	+18·0	59·7	16·3	153	68	70	20·3	20 46	20 23	4 13	12 25	12 47
23	3 03	+22·7	59·2	16·1	165	73	59	21·3	21 16	20 46	5 09	13 54	14 23
24	4 02	+26·0	58·7	16·0	178	79	48	22·3	21 59	21 22	6 08	15 14	15 50
25	5 03	+27·7	58·1	15·8	190	86	37	23·3	22 57	22 20	7 08	16 19	16 57
26	6 04	+27·8	57·5	15·7	202	93	27	24·3	—	23 36	8 06	17 07	17 40
27	7 03	+26·2	57·0	15·5	214	99	18	25·3	0 08	—	9 03	17 40	18 06
28	7 59	+23·2	56·4	15·4	227	105	10	26·3	1 27	1 01	9 55	18 03	18 23
29	8 51	+19·1	55·9	15·2	239	109	5	27·3	2 47	2 28	10 43	18 19	18 33
30	9 40	+14·3	55·5	15·1	251	110	2	28·3	4 04	3 52	11 27	18 32	18 41
31	10 26	+ 9·0	55·0	15·0	263	94	0	29·3	5 19	5 12	12 09	18 43	18 47

MERCURY ☿

Day	R.A.	Dec. +	Diam.	Phase	Transit		Day	R.A.	Dec.	Diam.	Phase	Transit	
	h m	°	″		h m			h m	°	″		h m	
1	9 43	15·3	—	—	13 06		16	11 12	+4·9	—	—	13 35	
4	10 03	13·3	—	—	13 15	Mercury is too	19	11 27	+2·9	—	—	13 38	Mercury is too
7	10 22	11·2	—	—	13 22	close to the	22	11 40	+1·0	—	—	13 39	close to the
10	10 40	9·1	—	—	13 27	Sun for	25	11 52	−0·9	—	—	13 39	Sun for
13	10 57	7·0	—	—	13 32	observation	28	12 03	−2·6	—	—	13 38	observation
16	11 12	4·9	—	—	13 35		31	12 13	−4·2	—	—	13 36	

VENUS ♀ / MARS ♂

Day	R.A.	Dec.	Diam.	Phase	Transit	5° high 52°	5° high 56°	Day	R.A.	Dec. +	Diam.	Phase	Transit	
	h m	°			h m	h m	h m		h m	°	″		h m	
1	10 47	+9·3	12	85	14 09	20 22	20 26	1	10 04	13·1	—	—	13 25	
6	11 09	+6·8	12	83	14 11	20 12	20 13	6	10 16	11·9	—	—	13 17	
11	11 31	+4·3	13	82	14 13	20 01	20 01	11	10 28	10·8	—	—	13 09	Mars is too
16	11 52	+1·8	13	81	14 15	19 50	19 47	16	10 40	9·6	—	—	13 01	close to the
21	12 14	−0·8	13	79	14 17	19 38	19 34	21	10 52	8·4	—	—	12 54	Sun for
26	12 35	−3·4	14	78	14 18	19 26	19 20	26	11 03	7·1	—	—	12 46	observation
31	12 57	−5·9	14	77	14 20	19 14	19 05	31	11 15	5·9	—	—	12 38	

SUNRISE AND SUNSET

Day	London a.m.	London p.m.	Bristol a.m.	Bristol p.m.	Birmingham a.m.	Birmingham p.m.	Manchester a.m.	Manchester p.m.	Newcastle a.m.	Newcastle p.m.	Glasgow a.m.	Glasgow p.m.	Belfast a.m.	Belfast p.m.
	h m	h m	h m	h m	h m	h m	h m	h m	h m	h m	h m	h m	h m	h m
1	4 22	7 49	4 32	7 59	4 25	8 00	4 23	8 06	4 13	8 10	4 20	8 25	4 33	8 26
2	4 24	7 47	4 34	7 57	4 27	7 58	4 25	8 05	4 15	8 08	4 22	8 23	4 35	8 25
3	4 26	7 46	4 36	7 56	4 29	7 57	4 26	8 03	4 17	8 06	4 24	8 21	4 36	8 23
4	4 27	7 44	4 37	7 54	4 30	7 55	4 28	8 01	4 19	8 04	4 26	8 19	4 38	8 21
5	4 29	7 42	4 39	7 52	4 32	7 53	4 30	7 59	4 21	8 02	4 28	8 17	4 40	8 19
6	4 30	7 41	4 40	7 50	4 33	7 51	4 31	7 57	4 22	8 00	4 30	8 15	4 42	8 17
7	4 32	7 39	4 42	7 48	4 35	7 49	4 33	7 55	4 24	7 58	4 32	8 12	4 44	8 14
8	4 33	7 37	4 43	7 47	4 36	7 48	4 35	7 53	4 26	7 56	4 34	8 10	4 46	8 12
9	4 35	7 35	4 45	7 45	4 38	7 46	4 37	7 51	4 28	7 54	4 36	8 08	4 48	8 10
10	4 37	7 33	4 47	7 43	4 40	7 44	4 39	7 49	4 30	7 52	4 38	8 06	4 50	8 08
11	4 38	7 32	4 48	7 41	4 41	7 42	4 40	7 47	4 32	7 50	4 40	8 04	4 51	8 06
12	4 40	7 30	4 50	7 39	4 43	7 40	4 42	7 45	4 34	7 47	4 42	8 01	4 53	8 04
13	4 41	7 28	4 51	7 37	4 45	7 38	4 44	7 43	4 36	7 45	4 44	7 59	4 55	8 02
14	4 43	7 26	4 53	7 35	4 47	7 36	4 46	7 41	4 37	7 43	4 45	7 57	4 57	8 00
15	4 44	7 24	4 54	7 34	4 48	7 33	4 47	7 38	4 39	7 40	4 47	7 54	4 58	7 57
16	4 46	7 22	4 56	7 32	4 50	7 31	4 49	7 36	4 41	7 38	4 49	7 52	5 00	7 55
17	4 47	7 20	4 57	7 30	4 52	7 29	4 51	7 34	4 43	7 36	4 51	7 50	5 02	7 53
18	4 49	7 18	4 59	7 28	4 54	7 27	4 53	7 32	4 45	7 34	4 53	7 48	5 04	7 51
19	4 50	7 16	5 00	7 26	4 55	7 25	4 54	7 30	4 47	7 32	4 55	7 46	5 06	7 49
20	4 52	7 14	5 02	7 24	4 57	7 23	4 56	7 28	4 48	7 29	4 56	7 43	5 07	7 46
21	4 53	7 12	5 03	7 22	4 58	7 21	4 57	7 26	4 50	7 27	4 58	7 41	5 09	7 44
22	4 55	7 10	5 05	7 20	5 00	7 19	4 59	7 24	4 52	7 25	5 00	7 39	5 11	7 42
23	4 57	7 07	5 07	7 17	5 02	7 16	5 01	7 21	4 54	7 22	5 02	7 36	5 13	7 40
24	4 58	7 05	5 08	7 15	5 03	7 14	5 02	7 19	4 56	7 19	5 04	7 33	5 14	7 37
25	5 00	7 03	5 10	7 13	5 05	7 12	5 04	7 17	4 58	7 17	5 06	7 31	5 16	7 35
26	5 02	7 01	5 12	7 11	5 07	7 10	5 06	7 14	5 00	7 15	5 08	7 29	5 18	7 32
27	5 03	6 59	5 13	7 09	5 08	7 08	5 08	7 12	5 02	7 12	5 10	7 26	5 20	7 30
28	5 05	6 57	5 15	7 07	5 10	7 06	5 10	7 10	5 04	7 10	5 12	7 23	5 22	7 27
29	5 07	6 54	5 17	7 04	5 12	7 03	5 11	7 07	5 05	7 07	5 14	7 21	5 24	7 25
30	5 08	6 52	5 18	7 02	5 13	7 01	5 13	7 05	5 07	7 05	5 16	7 18	5 26	7 22
31	5 10	6 50	5 20	7 00	5 15	6 59	5 15	7 03	5 09	7 03	5 18	7 16	5 28	7 20

JUPITER ♃ / SATURN ♄

Day	R.A.	Dec. +	Transit	5° high 52°	5° high 56°	R.A.	Dec. −	Transit	5° high 52°	5° high 56°
	h m	°	h m	h m	h m	h m	°	h m	h m	h m
1	6 01	23·1	9 21	1 50	1 32	18 37	22·6	21 55	1 06	0 32
11	6 09	23·1	8 51	1 19	1 01	18 35	22·6	21 14	0 24	23 45
21	6 17	23·1	8 19	0 48	0 30	18 33	22·7	20 33	23 38	23 04
31	6 25	23·0	7 47	0 16	23 55	18 32	22·7	19 52	22 57	22 23

Equatorial diameter of Jupiter 35″; of Saturn 18″.   Diameters of Saturn's rings 40″ and 18″.

URANUS ♅ / NEPTUNE ♆

Day	R.A.	Dec. −	Transit	10° high 52°	10° high 56°	R.A.	Dec. −	Transit	10° high 52°	10° high 56°
	h m	° ′	h m	h m	h m	h m	° ′	h m	h m	h m
1	18 8·6	23 42	21 27	23 25	21 59	18 44·3	22 07	22 02	0 24	23 23
11	18 7·4	23 42	20 46	22 44	21 18	18 43·4	22 09	21 22	23 39	22 43
21	18 6·6	23 42	20 06	22 04	20 38	18 42·6	22 10	20 42	22 59	22 02
31	18 6·0	23 42	19 26	21 24	19 58	18 42·1	22 11	20 02	22 19	21 22

Diameter 4″   Diameter 2″

Septem (seven), 7th month
of Roman (pre-Julian)
Calendar.

Sun's Longitude 180° ♎ 23ᵈ 01ʰ

Day of Month	Week	
1	F.	Sir Roger Casement b. 1864. Sedan 1870.
2	S.	Fire of London 1666. Omdurman 1898.
3	S.	**15th S. after Trinity.** World War II began 1939.
4	M.	Third French Republic proclaimed 1870.
5	Tu.	Jesse James b. 1847. Douglas Bader d. 1982.
6	W.	*Mayflower* sailed from Plymouth 1620.
7	Th.	Elizabeth I b. 1533. Borodino 1812.
8	F.	**Blessed Virgin Mary.** Richard I b. 1157.
9	S.	Flodden 1513. Salerno landings 1943.
10	S.	**16th S. after Trinity.** Arnold Palmer b. 1929.
11	M.	Malplaquet 1709. Khrushchev d. 1971.
12	Tu.	Cleopatra's Needle erected 1878.
13	W.	Quebec captured 1759. Gen. Pershing b. 1860.
14	Th.	Duke of Wellington d. 1852.
15	F.	PRINCE HENRY OF WALES b. 1984. BATTLE OF BRITAIN
16	S.	FIRE OF MOSCOW 1812. [DAY.
17	S.	**17th S. after Trinity.** Laura Ashley d. 1985.
18	M.	William Hazlitt d. 1830. Sean O'Casey d. 1964.
19	Tu.	Poitiers 1356. George Cadbury b. 1839.
20	W.	Valmy 1792. Alma 1854.
21	Th.	**St. Matthew.** Prestonpans 1745.
22	F.	Zutphen 1586. Michael Faraday b. 1791.
23	S.	Wilkie Collins d. 1889.* Sigmund Freud d. 1939.
24	S.	**18th S. after Trinity.** Horace Walpole b. 1717.
25	M.	Stamford Bridge 1066. Shostakovich b. 1906.
26	Tu.	*Queen Mary* launched 1934.
27	W.	Jesuits given Papal recognition 1540.
28	Th.	President Nasser d. 1970. W. H. Auden d. 1973.
29	F.	**St. Michael and All Angels.** Emile Zola d. 1902.
30	S.	Rudolf Diesel d. 1913. Storm Jameson d. 1986.

* Centenary.

PHENOMENA

d	h	
2	16	Mercury in conjunction with Moon. Mercury 0°·6N.
3	21	Venus in conjunction with Moon. Venus 4°N.
10	02	Saturn in conjunction with Moon. Saturn 4°N.
22	19	Jupiter in conjunction with Moon. Jupiter 4°S.
23	01	Equinox.
24	22	Mercury in inferior conjunction.
29	19	Mars in conjunction with Sun.

CONSTELLATIONS

The following constellations are near the meridian at

	d	h		d	h
Aug.	1	24	Aug.	16	23
Sept.	1	22	Sept.	15	21
Oct.	1	20	Oct.	16	19

Draco, Cepheus, Lyra, Cygnus, Vulpecula, Sagitta, Delphinus, Equuleus, Aquila, Aquarius and Capricornus.

MINIMA OF ALGOL

d	h	d	h
2	10	16	18
5	7	19	15
8	3	22	12
11	0	25	8
13	21	28	5

PHASES OF THE MOON

	d	h	m
☽ First Quarter	8	09	49
○ Full Moon	15	11	51
☾ Last Quarter	22	02	10
● New Moon	29	21	47

	d	h
Apogee (405,730 kilometres)	4	08
Perigee (359,050 „)	16	15

Mean Longitude of Ascending
Node on Sept. 1, 325°

See note on *Summer Time*, p. 24.

MONTHLY NOTES

Sept. 1. Partridge shooting begins.

29. Michaelmas. Quarter day.

30. Jewish New Year (A.M. 5750).

Day	Right Ascension	Dec.	Equation of Time	Rise 52°	Rise 56°	Transit	Set 52°	Set 56°	Sidereal Time	Transit of First Point of Aries
						THE SUN s.d. 15'·9				
	h m s	° '	m s	h m	h m	h m	h m	h m	h m s	h m s
1	10 40 40	+8 22	− 0 08	5 11	5 04	12 00	18 47	18 55	22 40 33	1 19 14
2	10 44 18	+8 00	+ 0 11	5 13	5 06	12 00	18 45	18 52	22 44 30	1 15 18
3	10 47 55	+7 38	+ 0 31	5 15	5 08	11 59	18 43	18 49	22 48 26	1 11 22
4	10 51 32	+7 16	+ 0 50	5 16	5 10	11 59	18 41	18 47	22 52 23	1 07 26
5	10 55 09	+6 54	+ 1 10	5 18	5 12	11 59	18 38	18 44	22 56 19	1 03 30
6	10 58 46	+6 32	+ 1 30	5 20	5 14	11 58	18 36	18 42	23 00 16	0 59 34
7	11 02 22	+6 09	+ 1 50	5 21	5 16	11 58	18 34	18 39	23 04 12	0 55 39
8	11 05 58	+5 47	+ 2 11	5 23	5 18	11 58	18 31	18 36	23 08 09	0 51 43
9	11 09 34	+5 24	+ 2 31	5 25	5 20	11 57	18 29	18 34	23 12 05	0 47 47
10	11 13 10	+5 02	+ 2 52	5 26	5 22	11 57	18 27	18 31	23 16 02	0 43 51
11	11 16 45	+4 39	+ 3 13	5 28	5 23	11 57	18 24	18 28	23 19 58	0 39 55
12	11 20 21	+4 16	+ 3 34	5 29	5 25	11 56	18 22	18 26	23 23 55	0 35 59
13	11 23 56	+3 53	+ 3 56	5 31	5 27	11 56	18 20	18 23	23 27 52	0 32 03
14	11 27 31	+3 30	+ 4 17	5 33	5 29	11 56	18 17	18 21	23 31 48	0 28 07
15	11 31 06	+3 07	+ 4 38	5 34	5 31	11 55	18 15	18 18	23 35 45	0 24 11
16	11 34 41	+2 44	+ 5 00	5 36	5 33	11 55	18 13	18 15	23 39 41	0 20 15
17	11 38 17	+2 21	+ 5 21	5 38	5 35	11 54	18 10	18 13	23 43 38	0 16 20
18	11 41 52	+1 58	+ 5 43	5 39	5 37	11 54	18 08	18 10	23 47 34	0 12 24
19	11 45 27	+1 35	+ 6 04	5 41	5 39	11 54	18 06	18 07	23 51 31	0 08 28
20	11 49 02	+1 11	+ 6 26	5 42	5 41	11 53	18 03	18 05	23 55 27	0 04 32
21	11 52 37	+0 48	+ 6 47	5 44	5 43	11 53	18 01	18 02	23 59 24	{ 0 00 36 / 23 56 40
22	11 56 12	+0 25	+ 7 08	5 46	5 45	11 53	17 59	17 59	0 03 21	23 52 44
23	11 59 48	+0 01	+ 7 29	5 47	5 47	11 52	17 56	17 57	0 07 17	23 48 48
24	12 03 24	−0 22	+ 7 50	5 49	5 49	11 52	17 54	17 54	0 11 14	23 44 52
25	12 06 59	−0 45	+ 8 11	5 51	5 51	11 52	17 52	17 51	0 15 10	23 40 56
26	12 10 35	−1 09	+ 8 32	5 52	5 53	11 51	17 49	17 49	0 19 07	23 37 00
27	12 14 11	−1 32	+ 8 52	5 54	5 55	11 51	17 47	17 46	0 23 03	23 33 05
28	12 17 48	−1 56	+ 9 12	5 56	5 57	11 51	17 45	17 43	0 27 00	23 29 09
29	12 21 24	−2 19	+ 9 32	5 57	5 59	11 50	17 42	17 41	0 30 56	23 25 13
30	12 25 01	−2 42	+ 9 52	5 59	6 01	11 50	17 40	17 38	0 34 53	23 21 17

Duration of Civil (C), Nautical (N), and Astronomical (A), Twilight (in minutes)

Lat. °	Sept. 1 C	N	A	Sept. 11 C	N	A	Sept. 21 C	N	A	Sept. 30 C	N	A
52	35	79	127	34	76	120	34	74	115	34	73	113
56	39	89	146	38	84	135	37	82	129	37	80	126

ASTRONOMICAL NOTES

MERCURY is at inferior conjunction on the 24th and is thus unsuitably placed for observation throughout the month.

VENUS is a brilliant object in the early evening sky, magnitude −4·0, but only visible for about half-an-hour after sunset, low above the south-western horizon. The crescent Moon passses about 5°S. of the planet on the evening of the 3rd.

MARS is unsuitably placed for observation, conjunction occurring on the 29th.

JUPITER, magnitude −2·2, continues to be visible as a morning object in the eastern sky. Jupiter is in Gemini.

SATURN, magnitude +0·4, continues to be visible as an evening object in the constellation of Sagittarius, though by the end of the month it is too low in the south-west to be seen after 21h. The rings of Saturn present a beautiful spectacle to the observer with only a small telescope. The rings are open to almost their maximum extent.

ZODIACAL LIGHT. The morning cone may be seen stretching up from the eastern horizon before the beginning of morning twilight from the beginning of the month until the 12th. This faint phenomenon is only visible under good conditions, in the absence of both moonlight and artificial lighting.

THE MOON

Day	R.A.	Dec.	Hor. Par.	Semi-diam.	Sun's Co-long.	P.A. of Bright Limb	Phase	Age	Rise 52°	Rise 56°	Transit	Set 52°	Set 56°
	h m	°	′	′	°	°		d	h m	h m	h m	h m	h m
1	11 09	+ 3·4	54·7	14·9	275	305	1	0·8	6 31	6 29	12 50	18 53	18 52
2	11 52	− 2·3	54·4	14·8	288	302	3	1·8	7 42	7 45	13 29	19 03	18 57
3	12 35	− 7·8	54·2	14·8	300	300	7	2·8	8 52	9 01	14 09	19 14	19 03
4	13 18	−13·0	54·0	14·7	312	297	13	3·8	10 04	10 18	14 51	19 27	19 11
5	14 03	−17·7	54·1	14·7	324	294	20	4·8	11 17	11 37	15 34	19 43	19 21
6	14 50	−21·5	54·2	14·8	337	290	28	5·8	12 30	12 57	16 21	20 05	19 37
7	15 40	−25·0	54·6	14·9	349	285	37	6·8	13 42	14 15	17 11	20 35	20 02
8	16 33	−27·1	55·0	15·0	1	279	46	7·8	14 47	15 25	18 04	21 19	20 41
9	17 29	−27·9	55·7	15·2	13	273	56	8·8	15 41	16 18	18 59	22 18	21 42
10	18 26	−27·3	56·5	15·4	25	266	66	9·8	16 23	16 54	19 54	23 32	23 01
11	19 23	−25·3	57·4	15·6	38	260	75	10·8	16 53	17 17	20 49	—	—
12	20 20	−21·7	58·3	15·9	50	255	84	11·8	17 15	17 32	21 43	0 56	0 32
13	21 16	−16·8	59·2	16·1	62	251	91	12·8	17 32	17 43	22 35	2 24	2 08
14	22 10	−10·9	60·0	16·4	74	251	97	13·8	17 46	17 51	23 26	3 54	3 45
15	23 03	− 4·2	60·7	16·5	86	262	100	14·8	18 00	17 59	—	5 24	5 21
16	23 56	+ 2·8	61·0	16·6	99	44	100	15·8	18 14	18 07	0 17	6 54	6 58
17	0 50	+ 9·7	61·0	16·6	111	57	97	16·8	18 29	18 17	1 09	8 27	8 38
18	1 46	+16·0	60·8	16·6	123	62	91	17·8	18 50	18 30	2 03	10 01	10 19
19	2 45	+21·3	60·3	16·4	135	68	83	18·8	19 17	18 50	3 00	11 34	12 00
20	3 46	+25·2	59·6	16·2	147	75	73	19·8	19 56	19 22	4 00	13 00	13 34
21	4 48	+27·4	58·9	16·0	159	82	62	20·8	20 50	20 13	5 01	14 12	14 49
22	5 50	+27·8	58·1	15·8	172	89	51	21·8	21 59	21 25	6 01	15 06	15 41
23	6 50	+26·6	57·3	15·6	184	96	40	22·8	23 16	22 48	6 59	15 43	16 12
24	7 47	+23·9	56·6	15·4	196	101	30	23·8	—	—	7 52	16 09	16 30
25	8 39	+20·1	55·9	15·2	208	106	21	24·8	0 35	0 14	8 41	16 27	16 42
26	9 28	+15·5	55·4	15·1	220	109	14	25·8	1 52	1 38	9 26	16 41	16 51
27	10 14	+10·3	55·0	15·0	233	110	8	26·8	3 07	2 59	10 08	16 52	16 57
28	10 58	+ 4·8	54·6	14·9	245	108	3	27·8	4 19	4 16	10 49	17 02	17 03
29	11 41	− 0·8	54·3	14·8	257	99	1	28·8	5 30	5 31	11 28	17 12	17 08
30	12 23	− 6·3	54·1	14·7	269	7	0	0·1	6 40	6 47	12 08	17 23	17 14

MERCURY ☿

Day	R.A.	Dec. −	Diam.	Phase	Transit		Day	R.A.	Dec.	Diam.	Phase	Transit	
	h m	°	″		h m			h m	°	″		h m	
1	12 16	4·7	—	—	13 35		16	12 29	−7·6	—	—	12 46	
4	12 24	6·0	—	—	13 30	Mercury is too close to the Sun for observation	19	12 22	−6·7	—	—	12 27	Mercury is too close to the Sun for observation
7	12 29	7·0	—	—	13 23		22	12 13	−5·2	—	—	12 06	
10	12 32	7·6	—	—	13 14		25	12 02	−3·2	—	—	11 43	
13	12 32	7·9	—	—	13 02		28	11 52	−1·1	—	—	11 22	
16	12 29	7·6	—	—	12 46		31	11 46	+0·7	—	—	11 05	

VENUS ♀   MARS ♂

Day	R.A.	Dec. −	Diam.	Phase	Transit	5° high 52°	5° high 56°	Day	R.A.	Dec.	Diam.	Phase	Transit	
	h m	°	″		h m	h m	h m		h m	°	″		h m	
1	13 01	16·4	14	76	14 21	19 12	19 02	1	11 18	+5·6	—	—	12 36	
6	13 22	8·9	15	74	14 22	19 00	18 48	6	11 29	+4·3	—	—	12 28	
11	13 44	11·4	15	73	14 24	18 47	18 33	11	11 41	+3·0	—	—	12 20	Mars is too close to the Sun for observation
16	14 06	13·7	16	71	14 27	18 36	18 18	16	11 53	+1·7	—	—	12 12	
21	14 28	15·9	16	70	14 29	18 24	18 03	21	12 05	+0·4	—	—	12 04	
26	14 51	18·0	17	68	14 32	18 12	17 49	26	12 16	−0·9	—	—	11 57	
31	15 14	19·9	17	66	14 35	18 02	17 34	31	12 28	−2·2	—	—	11 49	

SUNRISE AND SUNSET

Day	London a.m. h m	London p.m. h m	Bristol a.m. h m	Bristol p.m. h m	Birmingham a.m. h m	Birmingham p.m. h m	Manchester a.m. h m	Manchester p.m. h m	Newcastle a.m. h m	Newcastle p.m. h m	Glasgow a.m. h m	Glasgow p.m. h m	Belfast a.m. h m	Belfast p.m. h m
1	5 11	6 48	5 21	6 58	5 16	6 57	5 17	7 00	5 11	7 00	5 20	7 13	5 30	7 17
2	5 13	6 45	5 23	6 55	5 18	6 54	5 18	6 58	5 13	6 58	5 22	7 11	5 31	7 15
3	5 15	6 43	5 25	6 53	5 20	6 52	5 20	6 55	5 15	6 55	5 24	7 08	5 33	7 12
4	5 16	6 41	5 26	6 51	5 21	6 50	5 22	6 53	5 17	6 52	5 26	7 05	5 35	7 10
5	5 18	6 39	5 28	6 49	5 23	6 48	5 24	6 51	5 18	6 50	5 27	7 03	5 37	7 08
6	5 20	6 37	5 30	6 46	5 25	6 45	5 26	6 48	5 20	6 47	5 29	7 00	5 39	7 05
7	5 21	6 34	5 31	6 44	5 27	6 43	5 28	6 46	5 22	6 45	5 31	6 58	5 41	7 03
8	5 23	6 32	5 33	6 42	5 28	6 41	5 29	6 43	5 24	6 42	5 33	6 55	5 42	7 00
9	5 25	6 30	5 35	6 39	5 30	6 38	5 31	6 41	5 26	6 40	5 35	6 52	5 44	6 58
10	5 26	6 28	5 36	6 37	5 32	6 36	5 33	6 38	5 28	6 37	5 37	6 50	5 46	6 55
11	5 28	6 26	5 38	6 35	5 34	6 34	5 35	6 36	5 30	6 35	5 39	6 47	5 48	6 53
12	5 29	6 23	5 39	6 33	5 35	6 33	5 36	6 33	5 31	6 32	5 41	6 44	5 49	6 50
13	5 31	6 21	5 41	6 31	5 37	6 29	5 38	6 31	5 33	6 30	5 43	6 42	5 51	6 48
14	5 33	6 19	5 43	6 28	5 39	6 26	5 40	6 29	5 35	6 27	5 45	6 39	5 53	6 45
15	5 34	6 16	5 44	6 26	5 40	6 24	5 41	6 26	5 37	6 24	5 47	6 36	5 55	6 42
16	5 35	6 14	5 45	6 23	5 42	6 21	5 43	6 24	5 39	6 22	5 49	6 34	5 57	6 40
17	5 37	6 12	5 47	6 21	5 44	6 19	5 45	6 22	5 41	6 19	5 51	6 31	5 59	6 37
18	5 38	6 09	5 48	6 18	5 45	6 16	5 46	6 19	5 43	6 16	5 53	6 28	6 01	6 35
19	5 40	6 07	5 50	6 16	5 47	6 14	5 48	6 17	5 45	6 14	5 55	6 26	6 03	6 32
20	5 42	6 05	5 52	6 14	5 49	6 12	5 50	6 14	5 47	6 11	5 57	6 23	6 05	6 29
21	5 43	6 02	5 53	6 12	5 50	6 09	5 51	6 12	5 48	6 09	5 59	6 20	6 06	6 27
22	5 45	6 00	5 55	6 10	5 52	6 07	5 53	6 09	5 50	6 06	6 01	6 18	6 08	6 24
23	5 46	5 58	5 56	6 07	5 53	6 05	5 55	6 07	5 52	6 04	6 03	6 15	6 10	6 22
24	5 48	5 55	5 58	6 05	5 55	6 02	5 57	6 04	5 54	6 01	6 05	6 12	6 12	6 19
25	5 50	5 53	6 00	6 03	5 57	6 00	5 59	6 02	5 56	5 59	6 07	6 10	6 14	6 17
26	5 51	5 51	6 01	6 01	5 58	5 58	6 01	5 59	5 58	5 56	6 09	6 07	6 16	6 14
27	5 53	5 48	6 03	5 58	6 00	5 55	6 02	5 57	5 59	5 54	6 11	6 04	6 17	6 12
28	5 54	5 46	6 04	5 56	6 01	5 53	6 04	5 54	6 01	5 51	6 13	6 02	6 19	6 09
29	5 56	5 44	6 06	5 54	6 03	5 51	6 06	5 52	6 03	5 49	6 15	5 59	6 21	6 07
30	5 58	5 41	6 08	5 51	6 05	5 48	6 08	5 49	6 05	5 46	6 17	5 57	6 23	6 04

JUPITER ♃   SATURN ♄

Day	R.A. h m	Dec. + °	Transit h m	5° high 52° h m	5° high 56° h m	R.A. h m	Dec. − °	Transit h m	5° high 52° h m	5° high 56° h m
1	6 26	23·0	7 44	0 13	23 52	18 32	22·7	19 48	22 53	22 19
11	6 32	22·9	7 11	23 37	23 20	18 32	22·8	19 09	22 13	21 39
21	6 37	22·9	6 37	23 04	22 46	18 32	22·8	18 30	21 34	21 00
31	6 42	22·8	6 02	22 29	22 11	18 33	22·8	17 51	20 56	20 22

Equatorial diameter of Jupiter 37″; of Saturn 17″. Diameters of Saturn's rings 39″ and 17″.

URANUS ♅   NEPTUNE ♆

Day	R.A. h m	Dec. − ° ′	Transit h m	10° high 52° h m	10° high 56° h m	R.A. h m	Dec. − ° ′	Transit h m	10° high 52° h m	10° high 56° h m
1	18 6·0	23 42	19 22	21 20	19 54	18 42·0	22 11	22 02	0 24	23 23
11	18 5·8	23 42	18 43	20 41	19 15	18 41·7	22 11	21 22	23 29	22 43
21	18 6·1	23 42	18 04	20 02	18 36	18 41·5	22 12	20 42	22 59	22 02
31	18 6·7	23 42	17 25	19 23	17 57	18 41·7	22 12	20 02	22 19	21 22

Diameter 4″   Diameter 2″

Day of Month	Week	

Octo (eight), 8th month
of Roman (pre-Julian)
Calendar.
Sun's Longitude 210° ♏ 23ᵈ 11ʰ

1	S.	**19th S. after Trinity.** Stanley Holloway b. 1890.
2	M.	MICHAELMAS LAW SITTINGS BEGIN.
3	Tu.	Eleanora Duse b. 1859. William Morris d. 1896.
4	W.	Printing of first English bible 1535.
5	Th.	*R101* disaster 1930. Tea rationing ended 1952.
6	F.	Le Corbusier b. 1887. Tennyson d. 1892.
7	S.	Archbp. Laud b. 1573. Mario Lanza d. 1959.
8	S.	**20th S. after Trinity.** Attlee d. 1967.
9	M.	John Lennon b. 1940. André Maurois d. 1967.
10	Tu.	Harold Pinter b. 1930. Orson Welles d. 1985.
11	W.	Camperdown 1797. James Joule d. 1889.*
12	Th.	Elizabeth Fry d. 1845. Edith Cavell d. 1915.
13	F.	Margaret Thatcher b. 1925. Henry Irving d. 1905.
14	S.	Hastings 1066. Eisenhower b. 1890.
15	S.	**21st S. after Trinity.** Cole Porter d. 1964.
16	M.	Houses of Parliament burnt down 1834.
17	Tu.	Saratoga 1777. Eric Gill d. 1940.
18	W.	**St. Luke.** Leipzig 1813.
19	Th.	John I d. 1216. Charles I b. 1600.
20	F.	Ulm 1805. Sir Richard Burton d. 1890.
21	S.	Trafalgar 1805. Aberfan Disaster 1966.
22	S.	**22nd S. after Trinity.** Cézanne d. 1906.
23	M.	Edgehill 1642. El Alamein began 1942.
24	Tu.	Peace of Westphalia 1648.
25	W.	Agincourt 1415. Balaclava 1854.
26	Th.	Founding of Royal Marines 1664.
27	F.	Dylan Thomas b. 1914.
28	S.	**SS. Simon and Jude.** Evelyn Waugh b. 1903.
29	S.	**23rd S. after Trinity.** Wall Street Crash 1929.
30	M.	George II b. 1683. Ezra Pound b. 1885.
31	Tu.	HALLOWMASS EVE. Chiang Kai Shek b. 1887.

PHENOMENA

d	h	
4	01	Venus in conjunction with Moon. Venus 3°N.
7	11	Saturn in conjunction with Moon. Saturn 4°N.
10	12	Mercury at greatest elongation W.18°.
20	05	Jupiter in conjunction with Moon. Jupiter 4°S.

CONSTELLATIONS

The following constellations are near the meridian at

	d	h		d	h
Sept. 1	24		Sept. 15	23	
Oct. 1	22		Oct. 16	21	
Nov. 1	20		Nov. 15	19	

Ursa Major (below the Pole), Cepheus, Cassiopeia, Cygnus, Lacerta, Andromeda, Pegasus, Capricornus, Aquarius and Piscis Austrinus.

MINIMA OF ALGOL

d	h	d	h
1	2	18	7
3	23	21	4
6	20	24	1
9	16	26	21
12	13	29	18
15	10		

*Centenary.

PHASES OF THE MOON

	d	h	m
☽ First Quarter	8	00	52
○ Full Moon	14	20	32
☾ Last Quarter	21	13	19
● New Moon	29	15	27

	d	h
Apogee (406,530 kilometres)	1	20
Perigee (356,710 „)	15	01
Apogee (406,640)	28	22

Mean Longitude of Ascending Node on Oct. 1, 323°

MONTHLY NOTES

Oct.   1. Pheasant shooting begins.

      9. Jewish Day of Atonement (Yom Kippur).

    14. First day of Feast of Tabernacles..

    29. *Summer Time* ends at 01ʰ G.M.T.

Day	Right Ascension	Dec. −	Equation of Time	Rise 52°	Rise 56°	Transit	Set 52°	Set 56°	Sidereal Time	Transit of First Point of Aries
	h m s	° ′	m s	h m	h m	h m	h m	h m	h m s	h m s
1	12 28 38	3 06	+10 12	6 01	6 03	11 50	17 38	17 35	0 38 50	23 17 21
2	12 32 15	3 29	+10 31	6 02	6 05	11 49	17 35	17 33	0 42 46	23 13 25
3	12 35 53	3 52	+10 50	6 04	6 07	11 49	17 33	17 30	0 46 43	23 09 29
4	12 39 31	4 15	+11 08	6 06	6 09	11 49	17 31	17 28	0 50 39	23 05 33
5	12 43 09	4 38	+11 27	6 07	6 11	11 48	17 28	17 25	0 54 36	23 01 37
6	12 46 48	5 02	+11 44	6 09	6 13	11 48	17 26	17 22	0 58 32	22 57 41
7	12 50 27	5 25	+12 02	6 11	6 15	11 48	17 24	17 20	1 02 29	22 53 45
8	12 54 06	5 47	+12 19	6 13	6 17	11 48	17 22	17 17	1 06 25	22 49 50
9	12 57 46	6 10	+12 36	6 14	6 19	11 47	17 19	17 15	1 10 22	22 45 54
10	13 01 26	6 33	+12 52	6 16	6 21	11 47	17 17	17 12	1 14 19	22 41 58
11	13 05 07	6 56	+13 08	6 18	6 23	11 47	17 15	17 10	1 18 15	22 38 02
12	13 08 48	7 18	+13 24	6 19	6 25	11 46	17 13	17 07	1 22 12	22 34 06
13	13 12 30	7 41	+13 38	6 21	6 27	11 46	17 11	17 05	1 26 08	22 30 10
14	13 16 12	8 03	+13 53	6 23	6 29	11 46	17 08	17 02	1 30 05	22 26 14
15	13 19 55	8 26	+14 07	6 24	6 31	11 46	17 06	16 59	1 34 01	22 22 18
16	13 23 38	8 48	+14 20	6 26	6 33	11 46	17 04	16 57	1 37 58	22 18 22
17	13 27 22	9 10	+14 33	6 28	6 35	11 45	17 02	16 55	1 41 54	22 14 26
18	13 31 06	9 32	+14 45	6 30	6 37	11 45	17 00	16 52	1 45 51	22 10 30
19	13 34 51	9 54	+14 57	6 32	6 39	11 45	16 58	16 50	1 49 48	22 06 35
20	13 38 37	10 15	+15 07	6 33	6 41	11 45	16 55	16 47	1 53 44	22 02 39
21	13 42 23	10 37	+15 18	6 35	6 44	11 45	16 53	16 45	1 57 41	21 58 43
22	13 46 10	10 58	+15 27	0 37	0 46	11 44	16 51	16 42	2 01 37	21 54 47
23	13 49 58	11 19	+15 36	6 39	6 48	11 44	16 49	16 40	2 05 34	21 50 51
24	13 53 46	11 40	+15 44	6 40	6 50	11 44	16 47	16 38	2 09 30	21 46 55
25	13 57 35	12 01	+15 52	6 42	6 52	11 44	16 45	16 35	2 13 27	21 42 59
26	14 01 25	12 22	+15 59	6 44	6 54	11 44	16 43	16 33	2 17 23	21 39 03
27	14 05 15	12 42	+16 05	6 46	6 56	11 44	16 41	16 31	2 21 20	21 35 07
28	14 09 07	13 02	+16 10	6 47	6 58	11 44	16 39	16 28	2 25 17	21 31 11
29	14 12 59	13 22	+16 14	6 49	7 00	11 44	16 37	16 26	2 29 13	21 27 15
30	14 16 52	13 42	+16 18	6 51	7 02	11 44	16 35	16 24	2 33 10	21 23 20
31	14 20 45	14 02	+16 21	6 53	7 05	11 44	16 34	16 22	2 37 06	21 19 24

THE SUN s.d. 16′·1

Duration of Civil (C), Nautical (N), and Astronomical (A), Twilight (in minutes)

Lat. °	Oct. 1 C	N	A	Oct. 11 C	N	A	Oct. 21 C	N	A	Oct. 31 C	N	A
52	34	73	113	34	73	112	34	74	113	36	75	114
56	37	80	125	37	80	124	38	81	124	40	83	126

ASTRONOMICAL NOTES

MERCURY is at greatest western elongation on the 10th, and is visible as a morning object after the first few days of the month and remaining so for about three weeks. During this period its magnitude ranges from +1 to −1. The best time to detect the planet will be around the time of beginning of morning civil twilight, low above the E.S.E. horizon. This is the most favourable morning apparition of the year for observers in the northern hemisphere.

VENUS is a brilliant object in the early evenings, magnitude −4·2, but only visible for a short while after sunset, low above the south-western horizon.

MARS is unsuitably placed for observation.

JUPITER is a morning object, magnitude −2·3, moving slowly eastwards in Gemini and reaching a stationary point towards the end of the month. On the morning of the 20th the Moon, one day before Last Quarter, passes 4°N. of the planet.

SATURN is still visible as an evening object, magnitude +0·5.

THE MOON

Day	R.A.	Dec.	Hor. Par.	Semi-diam.	Sun's Co-long.	P.A. of Bright Limb	Phase	Age	Rise 52°	Rise 56°	Transit	Set 52°	Set 56°
	h m	°	′	′	°	°		d	h m	h m	h m	h m	h m
1	13 06	−11·6	54·0	14·7	282	312	1	1·1	7 51	8 03	12 49	17 35	17 21
2	13 51	−16·4	53·9	14·7	294	302	4	2·1	9 03	9 21	13 32	17 50	17 31
3	14 37	−20·6	54·0	14·7	306	295	9	3·1	10 16	10 41	14 17	18 10	17 44
4	15 26	−24·1	54·2	14·8	318	290	15	4·1	11 28	11 59	15 05	18 37	18 05
5	16 18	−26·5	54·5	14·9	330	283	22	5·1	12 35	13 11	15 56	19 15	18 39
6	17 12	−27·7	55·0	15·0	343	277	30	6·1	13 33	14 10	16 50	20 07	19 30
7	18 08	−27·5	55·6	15·1	355	270	40	7·1	14 18	14 52	17 43	21 14	20 40
8	19 03	−26·0	56·3	15·3	7	264	50	8·1	14 51	15 19	18 37	22 31	22 04
9	19 59	−23·0	57·2	15·6	19	258	60	9·1	15 16	15 37	19 30	23 54	23 35
10	20 53	−18·8	58·1	15·8	31	254	70	10·1	15 35	15 49	20 21	—	—
11	21 47	−13·4	59·1	16·1	44	251	80	11·1	15 50	15 58	21 11	1 21	1 08
12	22 39	− 7·2	60·0	16·4	56	250	88	12·1	16 04	16 06	22 01	2 48	2 43
13	23 32	− 0·4	60·8	16·6	68	252	95	13·1	16 18	16 14	22 53	4 17	4 18
14	0 25	+ 6·6	61·3	16·7	80	263	99	14·1	16 33	16 23	23 47	5 49	5 56
15	1 21	+13·3	61·5	16·7	92	3	100	15·1	16 51	16 35	—	7 24	7 38
16	2 20	+19·1	61·3	16·7	104	55	98	16·1	17 16	16 52	0 44	9 00	9 22
17	3 22	+23·7	60·8	16·6	116	67	93	17·1	17 51	17 20	1 44	10 33	11 04
18	4 26	+26·6	60·1	16·4	129	76	86	18·1	18 41	18 05	2 47	11 55	12 31
19	5 30	+27·7	59·2	16·1	141	84	77	19·1	19 46	19 11	3 50	12 58	13 34
20	6 33	+26·9	58·3	15·9	153	92	67	20·1	21 03	20 34	4 51	13 42	14 13
21	7 32	+24·5	57·4	15·6	165	99	56	21·1	22 23	22 01	5 47	14 12	14 36
22	8 26	+21·0	56·5	15·4	177	104	46	22·1	23 42	23 26	6 38	14 33	14 50
23	9 17	+16·5	55·8	15·2	189	108	36	23·1	—	—	7 25	14 48	15 00
24	10 03	+11·4	55·2	15·0	202	110	26	24·1	0 57	0 47	8 08	15 00	15 07
25	10 47	+ 6·0	54·7	14·9	214	111	18	25·1	2 10	2 05	8 48	15 11	15 13
26	11 30	+ 0·5	54·3	14·8	226	110	12	26·1	3 20	3 20	9 28	15 21	15 19
27	12 12	− 5·0	54·1	14·7	238	107	6	27·1	4 30	4 35	10 07	15 32	15 24
28	12 55	−10·3	54·0	14·7	250	100	3	28·1	5 40	5 51	10 48	15 43	15 31
29	13 39	−15·2	53·9	14·7	263	78	1	29·1	6 52	7 08	11 30	15 58	15 40
30	14 25	−19·6	54·0	14·7	275	340	0	0·4	8 05	8 27	12 15	16 16	15 53
31	15 14	−23·2	54·1	14·7	287	304	2	1·4	9 17	9 46	13 02	16 41	16 12

MERCURY ☿

Day	R.A.	Dec.	Diam.	Phase	Transit	5° high 52°	5° high 56°	Day	R.A.	Dec.	Diam.	Phase	Transit	5° high 52°	5° high 56°
	h m	°	″		h m	h m	h m		h m	°	″		h m	h m	h m
1	11 46	+0·7	9	10	11 05	5 35	5 37	16	12 26	0·6	6	74	10 49	5 25	5 29
4	11 45	+1·8	8	23	10 53	5 16	5 18	19	12 43	2·4	6	82	10 54	5 39	5 45
7	11 49	+2·2	8	36	10 46	5 07	5 08	22	13 01	4·4	5	88	11 00	5 56	6 03
10	11 58	+1·9	7	50	10 43	5 07	5 08	25	13 19	6·5	5	93	11 06	6 14	6 23
13	12 10	+0·9	7	62	10 45	5 13	5 16	28	13 37	8·6	—	—	11 13	6 32	6 44
16	12 26	−0·6	6	74	10 49	5 25	5 29	31	13 56	10·6	—	—	11 20	6 51	7 05

VENUS ♀   MARS ♂

Day	R.A.	Dec.	Diam.	Phase	Transit	5° high 52°	5° high 56°	Day	R.A.	Dec.	Diam.	Phase	Transit	
	h m	°	″		h m	h m	h m		h m	°	″		h m	
1	15 14	19·9	17	66	14 35	18 02	17 34	1	12 28	2·2	—	—	11 49	
6	15 37	21·6	18	64	14 39	17 52	17 20	6	12 40	3·5	—	—	11 41	Mars is too
11	16 00	23·1	19	62	14 42	17 43	17 07	11	12 52	4·8	—	—	11 33	close to the
16	16 24	24·4	20	60	14 46	17 35	16 54	16	13 04	6·1	—	—	11 26	Sun for
21	16 48	25·4	21	58	14 50	17 30	16 43	21	13 17	7·4	—	—	11 18	observation
26	17 11	26·2	22	56	14 54	17 26	16 35	26	13 29	8·7	—	—	11 11	
31	17 35	26·7	23	54	14 58	17 25	16 30	31	13 42	9·9	—	—	11 04	

SUNRISE AND SUNSET

Day	London a.m. h m	London p.m. h m	Bristol a.m. h m	Bristol p.m. h m	Birmingham a.m. h m	Birmingham p.m. h m	Manchester a.m. h m	Manchester p.m. h m	Newcastle a.m. h m	Newcastle p.m. h m	Glasgow a.m. h m	Glasgow p.m. h m	Belfast a.m. h m	Belfast p.m. h m
1	6 00	5 39	6 10	5 49	6 07	5 46	6 10	5 47	6 07	5 44	6 19	5 54	6 25	6 02
2	6 01	5 37	6 11	5 47	6 08	5 44	6 11	5 45	6 09	5 41	6 21	5 51	6 27	5 59
3	6 03	5 34	6 13	5 44	6 10	5 41	6 13	5 42	6 11	5 39	6 23	5 49	6 29	5 57
4	6 05	5 32	6 15	5 42	6 12	5 39	6 15	5 40	6 13	5 36	6 25	5 46	6 31	5 54
5	6 06	5 30	6 16	5 40	6 13	5 37	6 16	5 38	6 15	5 33	6 27	5 43	6 33	5 51
6	6 08	5 28	6 18	5 38	6 15	5 35	6 18	5 36	6 17	5 31	6 29	5 41	6 35	5 49
7	6 10	5 26	6 19	5 36	6 17	5 32	6 20	5 33	6 19	5 28	6 31	5 38	6 37	5 46
8	6 12	5 24	6 21	5 34	6 19	5 30	6 22	5 31	6 21	5 26	6 33	5 36	6 39	5 44
9	6 13	5 22	6 22	5 32	6 20	5 27	6 23	5 28	6 22	5 23	6 35	5 33	6 40	5 41
10	6 15	5 19	6 24	5 29	6 22	5 25	6 25	5 26	6 24	5 21	6 37	5 31	6 42	5 39
11	6 16	5 17	6 26	5 27	6 24	5 23	6 27	5 24	6 26	5 19	6 39	5 28	6 44	5 37
12	6 18	5 15	6 27	5 25	6 26	5 20	6 29	5 21	6 28	5 16	6 41	5 25	6 46	5 34
13	6 20	5 13	6 29	5 23	6 28	5 18	6 31	5 19	6 30	5 14	6 43	5 23	6 48	5 32
14	6 21	5 11	6 31	5 21	6 30	5 16	6 33	5 17	6 32	5 11	6 45	5 20	6 50	5 30
15	6 23	5 08	6 33	5 18	6 32	5 13	6 35	5 14	6 34	5 09	6 47	5 18	6 52	5 27
16	6 25	5 06	6 35	5 16	6 33	5 11	6 36	5 12	6 36	5 06	6 49	5 15	6 53	5 25
17	6 26	5 04	6 36	5 14	6 35	5 09	6 38	5 10	6 38	5 04	6 51	5 13	6 55	5 23
18	6 28	5 02	6 38	5 12	6 37	5 07	6 40	5 07	6 40	5 01	6 53	5 10	6 57	5 20
19	6 30	5 00	6 40	5 10	6 39	5 05	6 42	5 05	6 42	4 59	6 55	5 08	6 59	5 18
20	6 31	4 58	6 41	5 08	6 40	5 03	6 44	5 03	6 44	4 57	6 57	5 05	7 01	5 15
21	6 33	4 55	6 43	5 05	6 42	5 00	6 46	5 00	6 46	4 54	6 59	5 03	7 03	5 13
22	6 35	4 53	6 45	5 03	6 44	4 58	6 48	4 58	6 48	4 52	7 01	5 01	7 05	5 11
23	6 37	4 51	6 47	5 01	6 46	4 56	6 50	4 56	6 50	4 50	7 04	4 58	7 08	5 08
24	6 38	4 49	6 48	4 59	6 47	4 54	6 52	4 54	6 52	4 48	7 06	4 56	7 10	5 06
25	6 40	4 47	6 50	4 57	6 49	4 52	6 54	4 52	6 54	4 46	7 08	4 54	7 12	5 04
26	6 42	4 45	6 52	4 55	6 51	4 50	6 56	4 50	6 56	4 43	7 10	4 51	7 14	5 02
27	6 44	4 43	6 54	4 53	6 53	4 48	6 58	4 47	6 58	4 41	7 12	4 49	7 16	4 59
28	6 46	4 41	6 56	4 51	6 55	4 46	7 00	4 45	7 00	4 39	7 14	4 47	7 18	4 57
29	6 47	4 39	6 57	4 49	6 56	4 44	7 01	4 43	7 02	4 36	7 16	4 44	7 20	4 55
30	6 49	4 38	6 59	4 47	6 58	4 43	7 03	4 42	7 04	4 34	7 18	4 42	7 22	4 53
31	6 51	4 36	7 01	4 46	7 00	4 41	7 05	4 40	7 06	4 32	7 20	4 40	7 24	4 51

	JUPITER ♃			5° high.		SATURN ♄			5° high.	
Day	R.A.	Dec. +	Transit	52°	56°	R.A.	Dec. −	Transit	52°	56°
	h m	°	h m	h m	h m	h m	°	h m	h m	h m
1	6 42	22·8	6 02	22 29	22 11	18 33	22·8	17 51	20 56	20 22
11	6 45	22·8	5 26	21 53	21 36	18 35	22·8	17 14	20 19	19 44
21	6 47	22·8	4 48	21 16	20 58	18 37	22·8	16 37	19 42	19 07
31	6 47	22·8	4 09	20 36	20 19	18 40	22·7	16 01	19 06	18 31

Equatorial diameter of Jupiter 41″; of Saturn 16″. Diameters of Saturn's rings 37″ and 16″.

	URANUS ♅			10° high.		NEPTUNE ♆			10° high.	
Day	R.A.	Dec. −	Transit	52°	56°	R.A.	Dec. −	Transit	52°	56°
	h m	° ′	h m	h m	h m	h m	° ′	h m	h m	h m
1	18 6·7	23 42	17 25	19 23	17 57	18 41·7	22 12	18 00	20 16	19 19
11	18 7·6	23 42	16 47	18 45	17 19	18 42·0	22 12	17 21	19 37	18 40
21	18 8·9	23 42	16 09	18 07	16 42	18 42·6	22 12	16 42	18 59	18 02
31	18 10·5	23 41	15 31	17 29	16 04	18 43·4	22 12	16 04	18 20	17 23

Diameter 4″   Diameter 2″

DAY OF		
Month	Week	

Novem (nine), 9th month of Roman (pre-Julian) Calendar.

Sun's Longitude 240° ♐ 22ᵈ 08ʰ

1	W.	**All Saints.** First hydrogen bomb exploded 1952.
2	Th.	ALL SOULS. Balfour Declaration 1917.
3	F.	First dog in space in *Sputnik II* 1957.
4	S.	Mendelssohn d. 1847. Wilfred Owen d. 1918.
5	S.	**24th S. after Trinity.** Inkerman 1854.
6	M.	Colley Cibber b. 1671. Kate Greenaway d. 1901.
7	Tu.	October Revolution 1917. Gene Tunney d. 1978.
8	W.	Fred Archer d. 1886. Munich Putsch 1923.
9	Th.	Edward VII b. 1841. Neville Chamberlain d. 1940.
10	F.	Martin Luther b. 1483. William Hogarth b. 1697.
11	S.	ARMISTICE DAY 1918. Jerome Kern d. 1945.
12	S.	**25th S. after Trinity.** *Tirpitz* sunk 1944.
13	M.	Edward III b. 1312. R. L. Stevenson b. 1850.
14	Tu.	PRINCE OF WALES b. 1948. Jawaharlal Nehru b.
15	W.	Brazil declared a Republic 1889.*　　　　[1889.*
16	Th.	Lützen 1632. Arthur Askey d. 1982.
17	F.	Field Marshal Viscount Montgomery b. 1887.
18	S.	Louis Daguerre b. 1789.* Niels Bohr d. 1962.
19	S.	**26th S. after Trinity.** Schubert d. 1828.
20	M.	QUEEN'S WEDDING DAY 1947. Jellicoe d. 1935.
21	Tu.	Voltaire b. 1694. Andre Gide b. 1869.
22	W.	Gen. Charles de Gaulle b. 1890. Mae West d. 1981.
23	Th.	Perkin Warbeck d. 1499. Boris Karloff b. 1887.
24	F.	John Knox d. 1572. Toulouse Lautrec b. 1864.
25	S.	Charles Kemble b. 1775. Leonard Woolf b. 1880.
26	S.	**27th S. after Trinity.** John McAdam d. 1836.
27	M.	Fanny Kemble b. 1809. Eugene O'Neill d. 1953.
28	Tu.	Founding of Royal Society 1660.
29	W.	C. S. Lewis b. 1898. Graham Hill d. 1975.
30	Th.	**St. Andrew.** Sir Winston Churchill b. 1874.

PHENOMENA

d	h	
2	22	Venus in conjunction with Moon. Venus 0°·7 N.
3	21	Saturn in conjunction with Moon. Saturn 4° N.
7	13	Pluto in conjunction with Sun.
8	17	Venus at greatest elongation E. 47°.
10	19	Mercury in superior conjunction.
15	19	Saturn in conjunction with Venus. Saturn 4° N.
16	14	Jupiter in conjunction with Moon. Jupiter 3° S.
26	19	Mars in conjunction with Moon. Mars 6° N.

CONSTELLATIONS

The following constellations are near the meridian at

	d	h		d	h
Oct.	1	24	Oct.	16	23
Nov.	1	22	Nov.	15	21
Dec.	1	20	Dec.	16	19

Ursa Major (below the Pole), Cepheus Cassiopeia, Andromeda, Pegasus, Pisces, Aquarius and Cetus.

MINIMA OF ALGOL

d	h	d	h
1	15	18	20
4	12	21	17
7	9	24	13
10	5	27	10
13	2	30	7
15	23		

* Centenary.

PHASES OF THE MOON

	d	h	m
☽ First Quarter	6	14	11
○ Full Moon	13	05	51
☾ Last Quarter	20	04	44
● New Moon	28	09	41

	d	h
Perigee (357,470 kilometres)	12	13
Apogee (406,140　　,,　　)	25	04

Mean Longitude of Ascending Node on Nov. 1, 322°.

MONTHLY NOTES

Nov.　1. Fox-hunting begins.

　　11. Martinmas. Scottish Term Day.

　　11. Lord Mayor's Show.

　　12. Remembrance Sunday.

　　28. Removal Day, Scotland.

Day	Right Ascension	Dec. −	Equation of Time	Rise 52°	Rise 56°	Transit	Set 52°	Set 56°	Sidereal Time	Transit of First Point of Aries
	h m s	° ′	m s	h m	h m	h m	h m	h m	h m s	h m s
1	14 24 40	14 21	+16 23	6 55	7 07	11 44	16 32	16 20	2 41 03	21 15 28
2	14 28 35	14 40	+16 25	6 57	7 09	11 44	16 30	16 17	2 44 59	21 11 32
3	14 32 31	14 59	+16 25	6 58	7 11	11 44	16 28	16 15	2 48 56	21 07 36
4	14 36 28	15 18	+16 25	7 00	7 13	11 44	16 26	16 13	2 52 52	21 03 40
5	14 40 25	15 36	+16 24	7 02	7 15	11 44	16 25	16 11	2 56 49	20 59 44
6	14 44 24	15 55	+16 22	7 04	7 17	11 44	16 23	16 09	3 00 46	20 55 48
7	14 48 23	16 13	+16 19	7 06	7 20	11 44	16 21	16 07	3 04 42	20 51 52
8	14 52 23	16 30	+16 16	7 07	7 22	11 44	16 20	16 05	3 08 39	20 47 56
9	14 56 24	16 47	+16 12	7 09	7 24	11 44	16 18	16 03	3 12 35	20 44 00
10	15 00 25	17 05	+16 06	7 11	7 26	11 44	16 16	16 01	3 16 32	20 40 05
11	15 04 28	17 21	+16 01	7 13	7 28	11 44	16 15	15 59	3 20 28	20 36 09
12	15 08 31	17 38	+15 54	7 14	7 30	11 44	16 13	15 58	3 24 25	20 32 13
13	15 12 35	17 54	+15 46	7 16	7 32	11 44	16 12	15 56	3 28 21	20 28 17
14	15 16 40	18 10	+15 38	7 18	7 34	11 44	16 10	15 54	3 32 18	20 24 21
15	15 20 46	18 25	+15 28	7 20	7 36	11 45	16 09	15 52	3 36 15	20 20 25
16	15 24 53	18 41	+15 18	7 21	7 38	11 45	16 08	15 50	3 40 11	20 16 29
17	15 29 01	18 56	+15 07	7 23	7 40	11 45	16 06	15 49	3 44 08	20 12 33
18	15 33 09	19 10	+14 55	7 25	7 43	11 45	16 05	15 47	3 48 04	20 08 37
19	15 37 18	19 24	+14 42	7 27	7 45	11 45	16 04	15 46	3 52 01	20 04 41
20	15 41 28	19 38	+14 29	7 28	7 47	11 46	16 02	15 44	3 55 57	20 00 45
21	15 45 39	19 52	+14 14	7 30	7 49	11 46	16 01	15 43	3 59 54	19 56 50
22	15 49 51	20 05	+13 59	7 32	7 50	11 46	16 00	15 41	4 03 50	19 52 54
23	15 54 04	20 18	+13 43	7 33	7 52	11 46	15 59	15 40	4 07 47	19 48 58
24	15 58 17	20 30	+13 26	7 35	7 54	11 47	15 58	15 39	4 11 44	19 45 02
25	16 02 31	20 42	+13 09	7 37	7 56	11 47	15 57	15 37	4 15 40	19 41 06
26	16 06 46	20 54	+12 50	7 38	7 58	11 47	15 56	15 36	4 19 37	19 37 10
27	16 11 02	21 05	+12 31	7 40	8 00	11 48	15 55	15 35	4 23 33	19 33 14
28	16 15 19	21 16	+12 11	7 41	8 02	11 48	15 54	15 34	4 27 30	19 29 18
29	16 19 36	21 26	+11 51	7 43	8 03	11 48	15 54	15 33	4 31 26	19 25 22
30	16 23 54	21 36	+11 29	7 44	8 05	11 49	15 53	15 32	4 35 23	19 21 26

Duration of Civil (C), Nautical (N), and Astronomical (A), Twilight (in minutes)

Lat. °	Nov. 1 C	N	A	Nov. 11 C	N	A	Nov. 21 C	N	A	Nov. 30 C	N	A
52	36	75	115	37	78	117	38	80	120	39	82	123
56	40	84	127	41	87	130	43	90	134	45	93	137

ASTRONOMICAL NOTES

MERCURY is unsuitably placed for observation, superior conjunction occuring on the 10th.

VENUS continues to be visible as a brilliant object in the early evenings. It is getting brighter (now magnitude −4·5) and also gradually becoming visible for a little longer every evening, low above the south-western horizon, until by the end of the month it may be seen for almost two hours after sunset. The crescent Moon will be seen approaching Venus on the evening of the 2nd. On the evening of the 15th Venus passes 4° S. of Saturn.

MARS is too close to the Sun for observation at first but very gradually becomes visible as a difficult morning object, magnitude +1·6, low above the south-eastern horizon until the sky gets too bright for observation, during the last week of the month. Mars is in the constellation of Libra.

JUPITER, magnitude −2·6, continues to be visible as a morning object, rising above the E.N.E. horizon in the evenings and even at the beginning of the month it should be clearly visible before 21ʰ. Jupiter is retrograding slowly in Gemini. The gibbous Moon passes north of the planet on the 16th.

SATURN, magnitude +0·6, is still visible as an evening object in the south-western sky but the period available for observation is shortening rapidly. On the evening of the 3rd the thin crescent Moon sets shortly before the planet.

THE MOON

Day	R.A.	Dec.	Hor. Par.	Semi-diam.	Sun's Co-long.	P.A. of Bright Limb	Phase	Age	Rise 52°	Rise 56°	Transit	Set 52°	Set 56°
	h m	°	′	′	°	°		d	h m	h m	h m	h m	h m
1	16 05	−25·8	54·3	14·8	299	291	5	2·4	10 26	11 00	13 53	17 16	16 41
2	16 59	−27·1	54·6	14·9	312	282	10	3·4	11 26	12 03	14 45	18 03	17 27
3	17 54	−27·5	55·1	15·0	324	274	17	4·4	12 15	12 50	15 38	19 05	18 30
4	18 49	−26·3	55·6	15·1	336	267	25	5·4	12 51	13 21	16 31	20 17	19 49
5	19 43	−23·7	56·2	15·3	348	261	34	6·4	13 18	13 41	17 22	21 36	21 15
6	20 36	−20·0	57·0	15·5	0	256	44	7·4	13 38	13 55	18 12	22 58	22 43
7	21 28	−15·1	57·8	15·8	12	252	55	8·4	13 54	14 05	19 01	—	—
8	22 19	− 9·4	58·7	16·0	25	249	65	9·4	14 08	14 13	19 49	0 22	0 13
9	23 10	− 3·0	59·6	16·2	37	248	76	10·4	14 22	14 21	20 38	1 46	1 44
10	0 01	+ 3·7	60·4	16·4	49	250	85	11·4	14 36	14 29	21 29	3 14	3 17
11	0 55	+10·3	61·0	16·6	61	254	92	12·4	14 52	14 40	22 24	4 44	4 55
12	1 52	+16·5	61·3	16·7	73	264	97	13·4	15 13	14 54	23 23	6 19	6 37
13	2 52	+21·7	61·3	16·7	85	308	100	14·4	15 43	15 16	—	7 55	8 21
14	3 57	+25·4	61·0	16·6	97	54	99	15·4	16 27	15 53	0 25	9 25	9 58
15	5 03	+27·3	60·4	16·5	110	75	95	16·4	17 27	16 51	1 31	10 40	11 16
16	6 08	+27·2	59·6	16·2	122	86	89	17·4	18 42	18 10	2 35	11 34	12 07
17	7 11	+25·3	58·6	16·0	134	95	81	18·4	20 04	19 39	3 35	12 11	12 37
18	8 09	+22·0	57·6	15·7	146	101	72	19·4	21 26	21 08	4 30	12 36	12 55
19	9 01	+17·7	56·7	15·5	158	106	62	20·4	22 44	22 32	5 20	12 53	13 07
20	9 50	+12·7	55·9	15·2	170	110	52	21·4	23 58	23 52	6 05	13 07	13 15
21	10 35	+ 7·3	55·2	15·0	183	112	42	22·4	—	—	6 47	13 18	13 22
22	11 19	+ 1·8	54·7	14·9	195	112	33	23·4	1 10	1 09	7 27	13 29	13 28
23	12 01	− 3·8	54·3	14·8	207	111	24	24·4	2 20	2 23	8 06	13 39	13 34
24	12 44	− 9·1	54·1	14·7	219	109	17	25·4	3 30	3 38	8 46	13 51	13 40
25	13 27	−14·1	54·0	14·7	231	106	10	26·4	4 41	4 55	9 28	14 04	13 49
26	14 13	−18·6	54·0	14·7	243	100	5	27·4	5 53	6 13	10 12	14 22	14 00
27	15 01	−22·3	54·2	14·8	256	89	2	28·4	7 06	7 32	10 59	14 45	14 17
28	15 52	−25·2	54·4	14·8	268	55	0	29·4	8 16	8 49	11 49	15 17	14 44
29	16 45	−26·9	54·7	14·9	280	312	0	0·6	9 20	9 56	12 41	16 01	15 25
30	17 40	−27·4	55·1	15·0	292	284	3	1·6	10 12	10 48	13 34	16 59	16 24

MERCURY ☿

Day	R.A.	Dec. −	Diam.	Phase	Transit		Day	R.A.	Dec. −	Diam.	Phase	Transit	
	h m	°	″		h m			h m	°	″		h m	
1	14 02	11·3	—	—	11 22		16	15 37	20·0	—	—	11 58	
4	14 21	13·2	—	—	11 29	Mercury is too	19	15 56	21·3	—	—	12 05	Mercury is too
7	14 40	15·1	—	—	11 36	close to the	22	16 16	22·5	—	—	12 13	close to the
10	14 59	16·9	—	—	11 43	Sun for	25	16 35	23·5	—	—	12 21	Sun for
13	15 18	18·5	—	—	11 51	observation	28	16 55	24·3	—	—	12 29	observation
16	15 37	20·0	—	—	11 58		31	17 16	25·0	—	—	12 38	

VENUS ♀

Day	R.A.	Dec. −	Diam.	Phase	Transit	5° high 52°	5° high 56°
	h m	°	″		h m	h m	h m
1	17 40	26·8	23	53	14 59	17 25	16 29
6	18 03	26·9	24	51	15 02	17 26	16 30
11	18 25	26·9	26	48	15 05	17 30	16 35
16	18 47	26·5	27	46	15 07	17 36	16 43
21	19 07	26·0	29	43	15 07	17 43	16 54
26	19 26	25·2	31	40	15 07	17 50	17 06
31	19 44	24·3	33	36	15 04	17 57	17 17

MARS ♂

Day	R.A.	Dec. −	Diam.	Phase	Transit	5° high 52°	5° high 56°
	h m	°	″		h m	h m	h m
1	13 44	10·2	4	100	11 03	6 31	6 44
6	13 57	11·4	4	100	10 56	6 31	6 45
11	14 10	12·6	4	99	10 49	6 31	6 47
16	14 23	13·8	4	99	10 42	6 32	6 49
21	14 36	14·9	4	99	10 36	6 33	6 51
26	14 49	15·9	4	99	10 29	6 33	6 53
31	15 03	17·0	4	99	10 23	6 34	6 56

SUNRISE AND SUNSET

Day	London a.m.	London p.m.	Bristol a.m.	Bristol p.m.	Birmingham a.m.	Birmingham p.m.	Manchester a.m.	Manchester p.m.	Newcastle a.m.	Newcastle p.m.	Glasgow a.m.	Glasgow p.m.	Belfast a.m.	Belfast p.m.
	h m	h m	h m	h m	h m	h m	h m	h m	h m	h m	h m	h m	h m	h m
1	6 53	4 34	7 03	4 44	7 02	4 39	7 07	4 38	7 08	4 30	7 22	4 38	7 25	4 49
2	6 55	4 32	7 04	4 42	7 04	4 37	7 09	4 36	7 10	4 28	7 24	4 36	7 27	4 47
3	6 56	4 30	7 06	4 40	7 05	4 35	7 10	4 34	7 12	4 26	7 26	4 34	7 29	4 45
4	6 58	4 29	7 08	4 39	7 07	4 33	7 12	4 32	7 14	4 24	7 28	4 32	7 31	4 43
5	7 00	4 27	7 09	4 37	7 09	4 31	7 14	4 30	7 16	4 22	7 30	4 30	7 33	4 41
6	7 02	4 26	7 11	4 36	7 11	4 29	7 16	4 28	7 18	4 20	7 32	4 28	7 35	4 39
7	7 03	4 24	7 13	4 34	7 13	4 28	7 18	4 27	7 20	4 18	7 34	4 26	7 37	4 38
8	7 05	4 22	7 14	4 32	7 15	4 26	7 20	4 25	7 22	4 16	7 36	4 24	7 39	4 36
9	7 07	4 21	7 16	4 31	7 17	4 24	7 22	4 23	7 25	4 14	7 39	4 22	7 41	4 34
10	7 09	4 19	7 18	4 29	7 19	4 22	7 24	4 21	7 27	4 12	7 41	4 20	7 43	4 32
11	7 10	4 18	7 20	4 28	7 21	4 21	7 26	4 19	7 29	4 10	7 43	4 18	7 45	4 30
12	7 12	4 16	7 22	4 26	7 23	4 19	7 28	4 18	7 31	4 09	7 45	4 16	7 47	4 28
13	7 14	4 15	7 23	4 25	7 24	4 18	7 30	4 16	7 33	4 07	7 47	4 15	7 49	4 27
14	7 15	4 13	7 25	4 23	7 26	4 16	7 32	4 15	7 35	4 06	7 49	4 13	7 51	4 25
15	7 17	4 12	7 27	4 22	7 28	4 15	7 33	4 13	7 36	4 04	7 51	4 11	7 53	4 23
16	7 19	4 10	7 30	4 20	7 30	4 13	7 35	4 11	7 38	4 02	7 53	4 10	7 55	4 22
17	7 20	4 09	7 30	4 19	7 31	4 12	7 37	4 10	7 40	4 01	7 55	4 08	7 57	4 20
18	7 22	4 08	7 32	4 18	7 33	4 11	7 39	4 08	7 43	3 59	7 58	4 06	7 59	4 18
19	7 24	4 06	7 34	4 16	7 35	4 09	7 41	4 07	7 45	3 58	8 00	4 05	8 01	4 17
20	7 26	4 05	7 36	4 15	7 37	4 08	7 43	4 06	7 47	3 56	8 02	4 03	8 03	4 16
21	7 27	4 04	7 37	4 14	7 38	4 07	7 45	4 04	7 49	3 55	8 04	4 02	8 05	4 14
22	7 29	4 03	7 39	4 13	7 40	4 06	7 47	4 03	7 50	3 53	8 05	4 00	8 07	4 13
23	7 31	4 02	7 41	4 12	7 42	4 05	7 48	4 02	7 52	3 52	8 07	3 59	8 08	4 12
24	7 32	4 01	7 42	4 11	7 43	4 04	7 50	4 01	7 54	3 51	8 09	3 57	8 10	4 11
25	7 34	4 00	7 45	4 10	7 45	4 03	7 52	4 00	7 56	3 49	8 11	3 56	8 12	4 09
26	7 35	3 59	7 45	4 09	7 46	4 02	7 53	3 59	7 58	3 48	8 13	3 55	8 14	4 08
27	7 37	3 58	7 47	4 08	7 48	4 01	7 55	3 58	7 59	3 47	8 15	3 54	8 15	4 07
28	7 38	3 57	7 48	4 08	7 49	4 00	7 56	3 57	8 01	3 46	8 17	3 53	8 17	4 06
29	7 40	3 56	7 50	4 07	7 51	3 59	7 58	3 56	8 03	3 45	8 18	3 52	8 19	4 05
30	7 41	3 55	7 51	4 06	7 52	3 58	7 59	3 55	8 04	3 45	8 20	3 51	8 20	4 05

JUPITER ♃   SATURN ♄

Day	R.A.	Dec. +	Transit	5° high 52°	5° high 56°	R.A.	Dec. −	Transit	5° high 52°	5° high 56°
	h m	°	h m	h m	h m	h m	°	h m	h m	h m
1	6 47	22·8	4 05	20 32	20 15	18 40	22·7	15 57	19 02	18 28
11	6 46	22·8	3 25	19 52	19 34	18 44	22·7	15 21	18 27	17 53
21	6 43	22·9	2 43	19 09	18 52	18 48	22·6	14 46	17 52	17 18
31	6 40	22·9	2 00	18 26	18 08	18 52	22·6	14 11	17 18	16 44

Equatorial diameter of Jupiter 45″; of Saturn 16″. Diameters of Saturn's rings 35″ and 15″.

URANUS ♅   NEPTUNE ♆

Day	R.A.	Dec. −	Transit		R.A.	Dec. −	Transit	
	h m	° ′	h m		h m	° ′	h m	
1	18 10·7	23 41	15 27		18 43·5	22 12	16 00	
11	18 12·6	23 41	14 50	Uranus is too	18 44·5	22 11	15 22	Neptune is too
21	18 14·8	23 40	14 13	close to the Sun	18 45·7	22 10	14 44	close to the Sun
31	18 17·2	23 39	13 36	for observation	18 47·1	22 09	14 06	for observation

Diameter 4″   Diameter 2″

DAY OF		
Month	Week	

Decem (ten), 10th month
of Roman (pre-Julian)
Calendar.

Sun's Longitude 270° ♑ 21ᵈ 21ʰ

1	F.	Henry I d. 1135. Queen Alexandra b. 1844.
2	S.	Napoleon Bonaparte crowned Emperor 1804.
3	S.	**Advent Sunday.** Sir Oswald Mosley d. 1980.
4	M.	First issue of *The Observer* 1791.
5	Tu.	Repeal of Prohibition, U.S.A. 1933.
6	W.	Finland gained independence 1917.
7	Th.	Capt. Bligh d. 1817. Pearl Harbour 1941.
8	F.	Mary, Queen of Scots b. 1542.
9	S.	John Milton b. 1608. Dame Edith Sitwell d. 1964.
10	S.	**2nd S. in Advent.** Paolo Uccello d. 1475.
11	M.	Hector Berlioz b. 1803. Solzhenitsyn b. 1918.
12	Tu.	Robert Browning d. 1889.* Douglas Fairbanks d.
13	W.	Dr. Johnson d. 1784. River Plate 1939. [1939.
14	Th.	Amundsen arrived at South Pole 1911.
15	F.	John Paul Getty b. 1892. Walt Disney d. 1966.
16	S.	Boston Tea Party 1773. Jane Austen b. 1775.
17	S.	**3rd S. in Advent.** Simon Bolivar d. 1830.
18	M.	Charles Wesley b. 1707. Ben Travers d. 1980.
19	Tu.	Brezhnev b. 1906. Jean Genet b. 1910.
20	W.	Gen. Ludendorff d. 1937. Bill Brandt d. 1983.
21	Th.	MICHAELMAS LAW SITTINGS END. Boccaccio d. 1375.
22	F.	George Eliot d. 1880. Beatrix Potter d. 1943.
23	S.	Richard Arkwright b. 1732. Malthus d. 1834.
24	S.	**4th S. in Advent.** CHRISTMAS EVE.
25	M.	**Christmas Day.** W. C. Fields d. 1946.
26	Tu.	**St. Stephen.** BOXING DAY.
27	W.	**St. John.** Marlene Dietrich b. 1904.
28	Th.	**The Holy Innocents.** Mary II d. 1694.
29	F.	Gladstone b. 1809. Jameson Raid 1895.
30	S.	Rudyard Kipling b. 1865. L. P. Hartley b. 1895.
31	S.	**1st S. after Christmas.** Peter May b. 1929.

PHENOMENA

d	h	
1	07	Saturn in conjunction with Moon. Saturn 3°N.
2	08	Venus in conjunction with Moon. Venus 0°·8 S.
13	20	Jupiter in conjunction with Moon. Jupiter 3°S.
14	09	Venus at greatest brilliancy.
16	22	Saturn in conjunction with Mercury. Saturn 2°N.
21	21	Solstice.
23	08	Mercury at greatest elongation E.20°.
25	17	Mars in conjunction with Moon. Mars 5°N.
27	06	Uranus in conjunction with Sun.
27	14	Jupiter at opposition.
29	15	Mercury in conjunction with Moon. Mercury 2°N.
30	10	Venus in conjunction with Moon. Venus 2°N.

CONSTELLATIONS

The following constellations are near the meridian at

	d	h			d	h
Nov.	1	24		Nov.	15	23
Dec.	1	22		Dec.	16	21
Jan.	1	20		Jan.	16	19

Ursa Major (below the Pole), Ursa Minor (below the Pole), Cassiopeia, Andromeda, Perseus, Triangulum, Aries, Taurus, Cetus and Eridanus.

MINIMA OF ALGOL

d	h	d	h
3	4	20	9
6	1	23	6
8	22	26	2
11	18	28	23
14	15	31	20
17	12		

* Centenary.

PHASES OF THE MOON

		d	h	m
☽	First Quarter	6	01	26
○	Full Moon	12	16	30
☾	Last Quarter......	19	23	54
●	New Moon........	28	03	20

	d	h
Perigee (361,310 kilometres)	10	23
Apogee (405,220 ,,)	22	19

Mean Longitude of Ascending
Node on Dec. 1, 320°.

MONTHLY NOTES

Dec. 10. Grouse shooting ends.

21. Shortest day.

25. Christmas Day. Quarter Day.

25, 26. Bank Holiday, England, Wales, N. Ireland and Scotland.

31. Various licences expire.

Day	THE SUN								Sidereal Time	Transit of First Point of Aries
	Right Ascension	Dec. −	Equation of Time	Rise 52°	Rise 56°	Transit	Set 52°	Set 56°		
	h m s	° ′	m s	h m	h m	h m	h m	h m	h m s	h m s
1	16 28 12	21 46	+11 07	7 46	8 07	11 49	15 52	15 31	4 39 19	19 17 30
2	16 32 31	21 55	+10 45	7 47	8 08	11 49	15 52	15 30	4 43 16	19 13 34
3	16 36 51	22 04	+10 21	7 48	8 10	11 50	15 51	15 29	4 47 13	19 09 39
4	16 41 11	22 12	+ 9 58	7 50	8 12	11 50	15 51	15 29	4 51 09	19 05 43
5	16 45 32	22 20	+ 9 33	7 51	8 13	11 51	15 50	15 28	4 55 06	19 01 47
6	16 49 54	22 28	+ 9 08	7 52	8 15	11 51	15 50	15 27	4 59 02	18 57 51
7	16 54 16	22 35	+ 8 43	7 53	8 16	11 51	15 49	15 27	5 02 59	18 53 55
8	16 58 38	22 42	+ 8 17	7 55	8 17	11 52	15 49	15 26	5 06 55	18 49 59
9	17 03 01	22 48	+ 7 51	7 56	8 19	11 52	15 49	15 26	5 10 52	18 46 03
10	17 07 25	22 54	+ 7 24	7 57	8 20	11 53	15 49	15 26	5 14 48	18 42 07
11	17 11 48	22 59	+ 6 57	7 58	8 21	11 53	15 48	15 25	5 18 45	18 38 11
12	17 16 13	23 04	+ 6 29	7 59	8 22	11 54	15 48	15 25	5 22 42	18 34 15
13	17 20 37	23 08	+ 6 01	8 00	8 23	11 54	15 48	15 25	5 26 38	18 30 19
14	17 25 02	23 12	+ 5 33	8 01	8 24	11 55	15 48	15 25	5 30 35	18 26 24
15	17 29 27	23 15	+ 5 04	8 02	8 25	11 55	15 49	15 25	5 34 31	18 22 28
16	17 33 52	23 18	+ 4 35	8 03	8 26	11 56	15 49	15 25	5 38 28	18 18 32
17	17 38 18	23 21	+ 4 06	8 03	8 27	11 56	15 49	15 25	5 42 24	18 14 36
18	17 42 44	23 23	+ 3 37	8 04	8 28	11 57	15 49	15 25	5 46 21	18 10 40
19	17 47 10	23 25	+ 3 07	8 05	8 28	11 57	15 50	15 26	5 50 18	18 06 44
20	17 51 36	23 26	+ 2 38	8 05	8 29	11 58	15 50	15 26	5 54 14	18 02 48
21	17 56 03	23 26	+ 2 08	8 06	8 30	11 58	15 50	15 27	5 58 11	17 58 52
22	18 00 29	23 27	+ 1 38	8 06	8 30	11 59	15 51	15 27	6 02 07	17 54 56
23	18 04 56	23 26	+ 1 08	8 07	8 31	11 59	15 51	15 28	6 06 04	17 51 00
24	18 09 22	23 26	+ 0 38	8 07	8 31	12 00	15 52	15 28	6 10 00	17 47 04
25	18 13 48	23 24	+ 0 08	8 07	8 31	12 00	15 53	15 29	6 13 57	17 43 08
26	18 18 15	23 23	− 0 21	8 08	8 31	12 01	15 54	15 30	6 17 53	17 39 13
27	18 22 41	23 20	− 0 51	8 08	8 32	12 01	15 54	15 31	6 21 50	17 35 17
28	18 27 07	23 18	− 1 21	8 08	8 32	12 02	15 55	15 32	6 25 47	17 31 21
29	18 31 33	23 15	− 1 50	8 08	8 32	12 02	15 56	15 33	6 29 43	17 27 25
30	18 35 59	23 11	− 2 20	8 08	8 32	12 03	15 57	15 34	6 33 40	17 23 29
31	18 40 25	23 07	− 2 49	8 08	8 32	12 03	15 58	15 35	6 37 36	17 19 33

s.d. 16″·3

Duration of Civil (C), Nautical (N), and Astronomical (A), Twilight (in minutes)

Lat. °	Dec. 1 C	N	A	Dec. 11 C	N	A	Dec. 21 C	N	A	Dec. 31 C	N	A
52	40	82	123	41	84	125	41	85	126	41	84	125
56	45	93	138	47	96	141	47	97	142	47	96	141

ASTRONOMICAL NOTES

MERCURY is at greatest eastern elongation on the 23rd but as it is then 23° S. of the equator observation will not be easy. It may be glimpsed, magnitude −0·2, low above the S.W horizon, around the time of ending of evening civil twilight, between the 25th and the 29th. If it can be detected on the 29th observers should note the proximity of the thin crescent Moon, only 1½ days old.

VENUS is still a magnificent object in the early evening sky, magnitude −4·7, and attaining its greatest brilliancy on the 14th. It is visible low above the south-western horizon for about two hours after sunset. Observers with telescopes can witness the decreasing crescent phase during the month (falling from 36 per cent to 11 per cent illuminated) while the diameter increases from 33″ to 54″. The crescent Moon is near Venus on the evenings of the 1st and 2nd and again on the 30th.

MARS, magnitude +1·6, is a difficult morning object low above the south-eastern horizon by about 06ʰ 30ᵐ from southern England and half-an-hour later in Scotland. During the month Mars moves from Libra, through Scorpius and into Ophiuchus, passing 5° N. of Antares on the 30th.

JUPITER is at opposition on the 27th, magnitude −2·7, and thus visible throughout the hours of darkness. Jupiter is in the western part of the constellation of Gemini. On the evening of the 13th the Moon, only 1 day past Full, passes 3° N. of the planet.

SATURN, magnitude +0·5, is becoming an increasingly difficult object to detect low above the south-western horizon in the early evening and is unlikely to be seen after the first week of the month.

METEORS. The maximum of the well-known Geminid meteor shower occurs on the 13th. The Full Moon will be a serious hindrance to observations.

THE MOON

Day	R.A.	Dec.	Hor. Par.	Semi-diam.	Sun's Co-long.	P.A. of Bright Limb	Phase	Age	Rise 52°	Rise 56°	Transit	Set 52°	Set 56°
	h m	°	′	′	°	°		d	h m	h m	h m	h m	h m
1	18 36	−26·5	55·5	15·1	304	272	6	2·6	10 52	11 23	14 27	18 08	17 39
2	19 31	−24·2	55·9	15·2	317	264	12	3·6	11 22	11 46	15 19	19 26	19 02
3	20 24	−20·7	56·5	15·4	329	258	20	4·6	11 43	12 01	16 09	20 46	20 29
4	21 15	−16·2	57·1	15·6	341	253	29	5·6	12 00	12 12	16 57	22 07	21 57
5	22 05	−10·7	57·7	15·7	353	249	39	6·6	12 14	12 21	17 44	23 28	23 24
6	22 54	− 4·7	58·4	15·9	5	248	49	7·6	12 27	12 28	18 30	—	—
7	23 44	+ 1·7	59·1	16·1	17	247	61	8·6	12 40	12 36	19 18	0 51	0 53
8	0 35	+ 8·1	59·7	16·3	30	249	71	9·6	12 55	12 45	20 09	2 17	2 24
9	1 28	+14·3	60·2	16·4	42	252	81	10·6	13 13	12 57	21 04	3 46	4 00
10	2 26	+19·7	60·6	16·5	54	258	90	11·6	13 38	13 14	22 04	5 18	5 40
11	3 27	+24·0	60·7	16·5	66	267	96	12·6	14 13	13 43	23 07	6 50	7 20
12	4 32	+26·7	60·5	16·5	78	287	99	13·6	15 05	14 29	—	8 13	8 49
13	5 39	+27·4	60·1	16·4	90	45	100	14·6	16 14	15 40	0 12	9 19	9 53
14	6 43	+26·2	59·5	16·2	102	85	98	15·6	17 35	17 07	1 16	10 04	10 33
15	7 44	+23·4	58·7	16·0	114	97	93	16·6	19 00	18 39	2 15	10 35	10 57
16	8 41	+19·3	57·8	15·7	127	104	86	17·6	20 23	20 08	3 09	10 56	11 12
17	9 32	+14·3	56·9	15·5	139	109	78	18·6	21 41	21 32	3 57	11 12	11 22
18	10 20	+ 8·9	56·0	15·3	151	112	69	19·6	22 55	22 52	4 41	11 24	11 30
19	11 05	+ 3·3	55·3	15·1	163	113	60	20·6	—	—	5 23	11 36	11 36
20	11 48	− 2·3	54·8	14·9	175	113	50	21·6	0 06	0 08	6 03	11 46	11 42
21	12 31	− 7·7	54·4	14·8	187	112	41	22·6	1 17	1 24	6 43	11 57	11 48
22	13 14	−12·8	54·2	14·8	200	110	32	23·6	2 27	2 40	7 24	12 10	11 56
23	13 59	−17·5	54·1	14·7	212	107	23	24·6	3 39	3 57	8 07	12 26	12 07
24	14 46	−21·4	54·2	14·8	224	103	16	25·6	4 52	5 16	8 53	12 47	12 21
25	15 37	−24·6	54·4	14·8	236	96	9	26·6	6 04	6 34	9 42	13 15	12 44
26	16 29	−26·6	54·8	14·9	248	88	5	27·6	7 10	7 46	10 34	13 55	13 20
27	17 25	−27·4	55·2	15·0	260	76	1	28·6	8 07	8 43	11 28	14 49	14 13
28	18 21	−26·8	55·7	15·2	273	23	0	29·6	8 52	9 24	12 22	15 57	15 25
29	19 16	−24·9	56·1	15·3	285	277	1	0·9	9 25	9 51	13 15	17 13	16 48
30	20 11	−21·6	56·6	15·4	297	261	4	1·9	9 49	10 08	14 06	18 34	18 16
31	21 03	−17·1	57·1	15·6	309	254	9	2·9	10 07	10 20	14 55	19 56	19 44

MERCURY ☿

Day	R.A.	Dec. −	Diam.	Phase	Transit		Day	R.A.	Dec. −	Diam.	Phase	Transit	5° high 52°	5° high 56°
	h m	°	″		h m			h m	°	″		h m	h m	h m
1	17 16	25·0	—	—	12 38		16	18 54	25·1	6	79	13 17	16 02	15 19
4	17 36	25·4	—	—	12 46	Mercury is too	19	19 12	24·5	6	73	13 23	16 14	15 34
7	17 56	25·7	—	—	12 54	close to the	22	19 28	23·7	7	65	13 26	16 25	15 48
10	18 16	25·7	—	—	13 03	Sun for	25	19 40	22·7	7	55	13 26	16 34	16 00
13	18 36	25·5	—	—	13 10	observation	28	19 49	21·7	8	43	13 22	16 37	16 06
16	18 54	25·1	—	—	13 17		31	19 51	20·8	8	30	13 11	16 34	16 05

VENUS ♀

Day	R.A.	Dec. −	Diam.	Phase	Transit	5° high 52°	5° high 56°
	h m	°	″		h m	h m	h m
1	19 44	24·3	33	36	15 04	17 57	17 17
6	19 59	23·2	36	33	15 00	18 02	17 27
11	20 13	22·0	39	29	14 53	18 06	17 34
16	20 23	20·8	42	25	14 43	18 06	17 37
21	20 30	19·5	46	20	14 30	18 03	17 37
26	20 34	18·3	50	16	14 14	17 55	17 31
31	20 33	17·2	54	11	13 53	17 42	17 20

MARS ♂

Day	R.A.	Dec.	Diam.	Phase	Transit	5° high 52°	5° high 56°
	h m	°	″		h m	h m	h m
1	15 03	17·0	4	99	10 23	6 34	6 56
6	15 17	17·9	4	99	10 17	6 35	6 58
11	15 31	18·8	4	98	10 12	6 36	7 01
16	15 45	19·7	4	98	10 06	6 36	7 03
21	15 59	20·5	4	98	10 01	6 37	7 06
26	16 14	21·2	4	98	9 56	6 38	7 08
31	16 29	21·8	4	97	9 51	6 38	7 10

SUNRISE AND SUNSET

Day	London a.m.	London p.m.	Bristol a.m.	Bristol p.m.	Birmingham a.m.	Birmingham p.m.	Manchester a.m.	Manchester p.m.	Newcastle a.m.	Newcastle p.m.	Glasgow a.m.	Glasgow p.m.	Belfast a.m.	Belfast p.m.
	h m	h m	h m	h m	h m	h m	h m	h m	h m	h m	h m	h m	h m	h m
1	7 43	3 55	7 53	4 06	7 54	3 58	8 01	3 55	8 06	3 44	8 22	3 50	8 22	4 04
2	7 44	3 54	7 54	4 05	7 55	3 57	8 02	3 54	8 08	3 43	8 24	3 49	8 24	4 03
3	7 46	3 53	7 56	4 04	7 57	3 56	8 04	3 53	8 09	3 42	8 25	3 48	8 25	4 02
4	7 47	3 53	7 57	4 04	7 58	3 56	8 05	3 53	8 11	3 41	8 27	3 47	8 27	4 01
5	7 48	3 53	7 58	4 04	8 00	3 55	8 07	3 52	8 12	3 40	8 28	3 46	8 28	4 00
6	7 50	3 52	7 59	4 03	8 01	3 55	8 08	3 52	8 14	3 40	8 30	3 46	8 30	4 00
7	7 51	3 52	8 01	4 03	8 02	3 54	8 09	3 51	8 15	3 39	8 31	3 45	8 31	3 59
8	7 52	3 51	8 02	4 02	8 04	3 54	8 11	3 51	8 17	3 39	8 33	3 44	8 33	3 59
9	7 53	3 51	8 03	4 02	8 05	3 53	8 12	3 50	8 18	3 38	8 34	3 43	8 34	3 58
10	7 54	3 51	8 04	4 02	8 06	3 53	8 13	3 50	8 19	3 38	8 35	3 43	8 35	3 58
11	7 56	3 51	8 05	4 01	8 07	3 53	8 14	3 50	8 20	3 38	8 36	3 43	8 36	3 58
12	7 57	3 51	8 06	4 01	8 08	3 53	8 15	3 50	8 21	3 38	8 38	3 43	8 37	3 58
13	7 58	3 51	8 07	4 01	8 09	3 53	8 16	3 50	8 22	3 38	8 39	3 43	8 38	3 58
14	7 58	3 51	8 08	4 01	8 10	3 53	8 17	3 50	8 23	3 38	8 40	3 43	8 39	3 58
15	7 59	3 51	8 09	4 01	8 11	3 53	8 18	3 50	8 24	3 38	8 41	3 43	8 40	3 58
16	8 00	3 51	8 09	4 02	8 12	3 53	8 19	3 50	8 25	3 38	8 42	3 43	8 41	3 58
17	8 01	3 52	8 10	4 02	8 13	3 53	8 20	3 50	8 26	3 38	8 43	3 43	8 42	3 58
18	8 02	3 52	8 11	4 02	8 14	3 53	8 21	3 50	8 27	3 38	8 44	3 43	8 43	3 58
19	8 02	3 52	8 12	4 02	8 15	3 53	8 22	3 50	8 28	3 38	8 44	3 44	8 44	3 58
20	8 03	3 53	8 12	4 03	8 15	3 54	8 22	3 50	8 28	3 38	8 45	3 44	8 44	3 58
21	8 04	3 53	8 13	4 03	8 16	3 54	8 23	3 51	8 29	3 39	8 46	3 44	8 45	3 59
22	8 04	3 54	8 13	4 04	8 16	3 55	8 24	3 52	8 30	3 40	8 46	3 45	8 46	4 00
23	8 05	3 54	8 14	4 04	8 17	3 55	8 24	3 52	8 30	3 40	8 47	3 45	8 46	4 00
24	8 05	3 55	8 14	4 05	8 17	3 56	8 24	3 53	8 30	3 41	8 47	3 46	8 46	4 01
25	8 06	3 55	8 15	4 05	8 18	3 57	8 25	3 54	8 31	3 42	8 47	3 47	8 47	4 02
26	8 06	3 56	8 15	4 06	8 18	3 57	8 25	3 54	8 31	3 42	8 48	3 48	8 47	4 02
27	8 06	3 57	8 15	4 07	8 18	3 58	8 25	3 55	8 31	3 43	8 48	3 48	8 47	4 03
28	8 06	3 58	8 15	4 08	8 18	3 59	8 25	3 56	8 31	3 44	8 48	3 49	8 47	4 04
29	8 06	3 59	8 16	4 09	8 18	4 00	8 25	3 57	8 31	3 45	8 48	3 50	8 47	4 05
30	8 06	3 59	8 16	4 10	8 18	4 01	8 25	3 58	8 31	3 46	8 48	3 51	8 47	4 06
31	8 06	4 00	8 16	4 11	8 18	4 02	8 25	3 59	8 31	3 47	8 48	3 52	8 47	4 07

JUPITER ♃ / SATURN ♄

Day	R.A.	Dec. +	Transit	5° high. 52°	5° high. 56°	R.A.	Dec. −	Transit	
	h m	°	h m	h m	h m	h m	°	h m	
1	6 40	22·9	2 00	18 26	18 08	18 52	22·6	14 11	Saturn is too
11	6 35	23·0	1 16	17 41	17 23	18 57	22·5	13 36	close to the
21	6 29	23·1	0 31	16 55	16 37	19 02	22·4	13 02	Sun for
31	6 23	23·2	23 41	16 10	15 52	19 07	22·3	12 28	observation

Equatorial diameter of Jupiter 47″; of Saturn 15″. Diameters of Saturn's rings 34″ and 15″.

URANUS ♅ / NEPTUNE ♆

Day	R.A.	Dec. −	Transit	R.A.	Dec. −	Transit	
	h m	° ′	h m	h m	° ′	h m	
1	18 17·2	23 39	13 36	18 47·1	22 09	14 06	
11	18 19·7	23 38	12 59	18 48·6	22 07	13 28	Uranus is too close to the Sun for observation / Neptune is too close to the Sun for observation
21	18 22·2	23 37	12 22	18 50·1	22 05	12 50	
31	18 24·9	23 35	11 45	18 51·8	22 03	12 12	

Diameter 4″   Diameter 2″

INTRODUCTION TO ASTRONOMICAL SECTION

GENERAL

The astronomical data are given in a form suitable for those who practise naked-eye astronomy or use small telescopes. No attempt has been made to replace the *Astronomical Almanac* for professional astronomers. Positions of the heavenly bodies are given only to the degree of accuracy required by amateur astronomers for setting telescopes, or for plotting on celestial globes or star atlases. Where intermediate positions are required, linear interpolation may be employed.

All data are, unless otherwise stated, for 0^h Greenwich Mean Time (G.M.T.), i.e. at the midnight at the beginning of the day named.

(*See also* notes on British Summer Time, *p. 72*).

Definitions of the terms used cannot be given in an ephemeris of this nature. They must be sought in astronomical literature and text-books. Probably the best source for the amateur is Norton's *Star Atlas and Reference Book* (Longman, 17th edition, 1987; £12·95), which contains an excellent introduction to observational astronomy, and the finest series of star maps yet produced for showing stars visible to the naked eye. Certain more extended ephemerides are available in the British Astronomical Association Handbook, an annual very popular among amateur astronomers. (Secretary: Burlington House, Piccadilly, London, W1V 9AG)

A special feature has been made of the times when the various heavenly bodies are visible in the British Isles. Since two columns, calculated for latitudes 52° and 56°, are devoted to risings and settings, the range 50° to 58° can be covered by interpolation and extrapolation. The times given in these columns are G.M.T.'s for the meridian of Greenwich. An observer west of this meridian must add his longitude (in time) and vice versa.

In accordance with the usual convention in astronomy, + and − indicate respectively north and south latitudes or declinations.

PAGE ONE OF EACH MONTH

The Zodiacal signs through which the Sun is passing during each month are illustrated. The date of transition from one sign to the next, to the nearest hour, is also given.

The **festivals and holy days** in black-letter type are those observed by the Church of England.

Under the heading PHENOMENA will be found particulars of the more important conjunctions of the Sun, Moon and planets with each other, and also the dates of eclipses and other astronomical phenomena of special interest.

The CONSTELLATIONS listed each month are those that are near the meridian at the beginning of the month at 22^h local mean time. Allowance must be made for Summer Time if necessary. The fact that any star crosses the meridian 4^m earlier each night or 2^h earlier each month may be used, in conjunction with the lists given each month, to find what constellations are favourably placed at any moment.

The table preceding the list of constellations may be extended indefinitely at the rate just quoted.

Times of MINIMA OF ALGOL are approximate times of the middle of the period of diminished light.

The Principal PHASES OF THE MOON are the G.M.T.'s when the difference between the longitude of the Moon and that of the Sun is 0°, 90°, 180° or 270°. The times of perigee and apogee are those when the Moon is nearest to, and farthest from, the Earth, respectively. The nodes or points of intersection of the Moon's orbit and the ecliptic make a complete retrograde circuit of the ecliptic in about 19 years. From a knowledge of the longitude of the ascending node and the inclination, whose value does not vary much from 5°, the path of the Moon among the stars may be plotted on a celestial globe or star atlas.

The MONTHLY NOTES are self-explanatory.

PAGE TWO OF EACH MONTH

The Sun's semi-diameter, in arc, is given once a month.

The right ascension given is that of the true Sun. The right ascension of the mean Sun is obtained by applying the equation of time, with the sign given, to the right ascension of the true Sun, or, more easily, by applying 12^h to the column Sidereal Time. The direction in which the equation of time has to be applied in different problems is a frequent source of confusion and error. Apparent Solar Time is equal to the Mean Solar Time plus the Equation of Time. For example at noon on Aug. 8 the Equation of Time is $-5^m\ 36^s$ and thus at 12^h Mean Time on that day the Apparent Time is $12^h - 5^m\ 36^s = 11^h\ 54^m\ 24^s$.

The Greenwich Sidereal Time at 0^h and the Transit of the First Point of Aries (which is really the mean time when the sidereal time is 0^h) are used for converting mean time to sidereal time and vice versa.

The G.M.T. of transit of the Sun at Greenwich may also be taken as the local mean time (L.M.T.) of transit in any longitude. It is independent of latitude. The G.M.T. of transit in any longitude is obtained by adding the longitude to the time given if west, and vice versa.

The legal importance of SUNRISE and SUNSET is that the Road Vehicles Lighting Regulations 1984 (S.I. 1984 No. 812) requires lights on vehicles to be used during the hours of darkness; that means the time between half an hour after sunset and half an hour before sunrise, throughout the year. In all laws and regulations "sunset" refers to the local sunset, i.e. the time at which the Sun sets at the place in question. This common-sense interpretation has been upheld by legal tribunals. Thus the necessity for providing for different latitudes and longitudes, as already described, is evident.

The times of SUNRISE and SUNSET are those when the Sun's upper limb, as affected by refraction, is on the true horizon of an observer at sea-level. Assuming the mean refraction to be 34′, and the Sun's semi-diameter to be 16′, the time given is that when the true zenith distance of the Sun's centre is 90° + 34′ + 16′ or 90° 50′, or, in other words, when the depression of the Sun's centre below the true horizon is 50′. The upper limb is then 34′ below the true horizon, but is brought there by refraction. It is true, of course, that an observer on a ship might see the Sun for a minute or so longer, because of the dip of the horizon, while another viewing the sunset over hills or mountains would record an earlier time. Nevertheless, the moment when the true zenith distance of the Sun's centre is 90° 50′ is a precise time dependent only on the latitude and longitude of the place, and independent of its altitude above sea-level, the contour of its horizon, the vagaries of refraction or the small seasonal change in the Sun's semi-diameter; this moment is suitable in every way as a definition of sunset (or sunrise) for all statutory purposes. On page 70 is given a method for calculating sunrise and sunset times for any other place.

It is well known that light reaches us before sunrise and also continues to reach us for some time after sunset. The interval between darkness and sunrise or sunset and darkness is called twilight. Astronomically speaking, twilight is considered to begin or end when the Sun's centre is 18° below the horizon, as no light from the Sun can then reach the observer. As thus defined twilight may last several hours; in high latitudes at the summer solstice the depression of 18° is not reached, and twilight lasts from sunset to sunrise.

The need for some sub-division of twilight was met some years ago by dividing the gathering darkness into four steps.

(1) *Sunrise or Sunset*, defined as above.

(2) *Civil twilight*, which begins or ends when the Sun's centre is 6° below the horizon. This marks the time when operations requiring daylight may commence or must cease. In England it varies from about 30 to 60 minutes after sunset and the same interval before sunrise.

"Lighting-up time" is a crude attempt to approximate to civil twilight over the British Isles.

(3) *Nautical twilight*, which begins or ends when the Sun's centre is 12° below the horizon. This marks the time when it is, to all intent and purposes, completely dark.

(4) *Astronomical twilight*, which begins or ends when the Sun's centre is 18° below the horizon. This marks theoretical perfect darkness. It is of little practical importance, especially if nautical twilight is tabulated.

To assist observers the durations of civil, nautical and astronomical twilights are given at intervals of ten days. The beginning of a particular twilight is found by subtracting the duration from the time of sunrise, while the end is found by adding the duration to the time of sunset. Thus the beginning of astronomical twilight in latitude 52°, on the Greenwich meridian, on March 11 is found as 06^h 24^m − 113^m = 04^h 31^m and similarly the end of civil twilight as 17^h 57^m + 34^m = 18^h 31^m.

The letters T.A.N. (twilight all night) are printed when twilight lasts all night.

Under the heading ASTRONOMICAL NOTES will be found notes describing the position and visibility of all the planets and also of other phenomena; these are intended to guide naked-eye observers, or those using small telescopes.

PAGE THREE OF EACH MONTH

The Moon moves so rapidly among the stars that its position is given only to the degree of accuracy that permits linear interpolation. The right ascension and declination are geocentric, i.e. for an imaginary observer at the centre of the Earth. To an observer on the surface of the Earth the position is always different, as the altitude is always less on account of parallax which may reach 1°.

The lunar terminator is the line separating the bright from the dark part of the Moon's disk. Apart from irregularities of the lunar surface, the terminator is elliptical, because it is a circle seen in projection. It becomes the full circle forming the limb, or edge, of the Moon at New and Full Moon. The selenographic longitude of the terminator is measured from the mean centre of the visible disk, which may differ from the visible centre by as much as 8°, because of libration.

Instead of the longitude of the terminator the Sun's selenographic colongitude is tabulated. It is numerically equal to the selenographic longitude of the morning terminator, measured eastward from the mean centre of the disk. Thus its value is approximately 270° at New Moon, 360° at First Quarter, 90° at Full Moon and 180° at Last Quarter.

The Position Angle of the Bright Limb is the position angle of the midpoint of the illuminated limb, measured eastward from the north point on the disk. The column PHASE shows the percentage of the area of the Moon's disk illuminated; this is also the illuminated percentage of the diameter at right angles to the line of cusps. The terminator is a semi-ellipse whose major axis is the line of cusps, and whose semi-minor axis is determined by the tabulated percentage; from New Moon to Full Moon the east limb is dark, and vice versa.

The times given as moonrise and moonset are those when the upper limb of the Moon is on the horizon of an observer at sea-level. The Sun's horizontal parallax is about 9″, and is negligible when considering sunrise and sunset, but that of the Moon averages about 57′. Hence the computed time represents the moment when the true zenith distance of the Moon is 90° 50′ (as for the Sun) minus the horizontal parallax. The time required for the Sun or Moon to rise or set is about four minutes (except in high latitudes). On page 71 is given a method for calculating moonrise and moonset times for any other place.

The tables have been constructed for the meridian of Greenwich, and for latitudes 52° and 56°. They give Greenwich Mean Time (G.M.T.) throughout the year. To obtain the G.M.T. of the phenomenon as seen from any other latitude and longitude, first interpolate or extrapolate for latitude by the usual rules of proportion. To the time thus found the longitude (expressed in time) is to be *added* if west (as it usually is in Great Britain) or *subtracted* if east. If the longitude is expressed in degrees and minutes of arc, it must be converted to time at the rate of 1° = 4^m and 15′ = 1^m.

The G.M.T. of transit of the Moon over the meridian of Greenwich is given: these times are independent of latitude, but must be corrected for longitude. For places in the British Isles it suffices to add the longitude if west, and vice versa. For more remote places a further correction is necessary because of the rapid movement of the Moon relative to the stars. The entire correction is conveniently determined by first finding the west longitude λ of the place. If the place is in west longitude, λ is the ordinary west longitude; if the place is in east longitude λ is the complement to 24^h (or $360°$) of the longitude and will be greater than 12^h (or $180°$). The correction then consists of two positive portions, namely λ and the fraction $\lambda/24$ (or $\lambda°/360$) multiplied by the difference between consecutive transits. Thus for Sydney, N.S.W., the longitude is $10^h 05^m$ east, so $\lambda = 13^h 55^m$ and the fraction $\lambda/24$ is 0·58. The transit on the local date 1989 November 6 is found as follows:

	d	h	m
G.M.T. of transit at Greenwich .....Jan.	5	17	22
λ		13	55
$0·58 \times (18^h 12^m - 17^h 22^m)$			29
G.M.T. of transit at Sydney		6 07	46
Corr. to N.S.W. Standard Time		10	00
Local standard time of transit		6 17	46

It is evident of course, that for any given place the quantities λ and the correction to local standard time may be combined permanently, being here $23^h 55^m$.

Positions of Mercury are given for every third day, and those of Venus and Mars for every fifth day; they may be interpolated linearly. The column PHASE shows the illuminated percentage of the disk. In the case of the inner planets this approaches 100 at superior conjunction and 0 at inferior conjunction. When the phase is less than 50 the planet is crescent-shaped or horned; for greater phases it is gibbous. In the case of the exterior planet Mars, the phase approaches 100 at conjunction and opposition, and is a minimum at the quadratures.

Since the planets cannot be seen when on the horizon, the actual times of rising and setting are not given; instead, the time when the planet has an apparent altitude of 5° has been tabulated. If the time of transit is between 00^h and 12^h the time refers to an altitude of 5° above the eastern horizon: if between 12^h and 24^h, to the western horizon. The phenomenon tabulated is the one that occurs between sunset and sunrise; unimportant exceptions to these rules may occur because changes are not made during a month, except in the case of Mercury. The times given may be interpolated for latitude and corrected for longitude as in the case of the Sun and Moon.

The G.M.T. at which the planet transits the Greenwich meridian is also given. The times of transit are to be corrected to local meridians in the usual way, as already described.

PAGE FOUR OF EACH MONTH

The G.M.T.'s of Sunrise and Sunset may be used not only for these phenomena, but also for lighting-up times, which, under the Road Vehicles Lighting Regulations, 1984, are from half an hour after sunset to half an hour before sunrise throughout the year.

The particulars for the four outer planets resemble those for the planets on Page Three of each month,

except that, under Uranus and Neptune, times when the planet is 10° high instead of 5° high are given; this is because of the inferior brightness of these planets. The polar diameter of Jupiter is about 3″ less than the equatorial diameter, while that of Saturn is about 2″ less. The diameters given for the rings of Saturn are those of the major axis (in the plane of the planet's equator) and the minor axis respectively. The former has a small seasonal change due to the slightly varying distance of the Earth from Saturn, but the latter varies from zero when the Earth passes through the ring plane every 15 years to its maximum opening half-way between these periods. The rings were open at their widest extent in 1988.

TIME

From the earliest ages, the natural division of time into recurring periods of day and night has provided the practical time scale for the everyday activities of mankind. Indeed, if any alternative means of time measurement is adopted, it must be capable of adjustment so as to remain in general agreement with the natural time scale defined by the diurnal rotation of the Earth on its axis. Ideally the rotation should be measured against a fixed frame of reference; in practice it must be measured against the background provided by the celestial bodies. If the Sun is chosen as the reference point, we obtain Apparent Solar Time, which is the time indicated by a sundial. It is not a uniform time, but is subject to variations which amount to as much as a quarter of an hour in each direction. Such wide variations cannot be tolerated in a practical time scale, and this has led to the concept of Mean Solar Time in which all the days are exactly the same length and equal to the average length of the Apparent Solar Day.

The positions of the stars in the sky are specified in relation to a fictitious reference point in the sky known as the First Point of Aries (or the Vernal Equinox). It is therefore convenient to adopt this same reference point when considering the rotation of the Earth against the background of the stars. The time scale so obtained is known as Apparent Sidereal Time.

Greenwich Mean Time

The daily rotation of the Earth on its axis causes the Sun and the other heavenly bodies to appear to cross the sky from East to West. It is convenient to represent this relative motion as if the Sun really performed a daily circuit around a fixed Earth. Noon in Apparent Solar Time may then be defined as the time at which the Sun transits across the observer's meridian. In Mean Solar Time, noon is similarly defined by the meridian transit of a fictitious Mean Sun moving uniformly in the sky with the same average speed as the true Sun. Mean Solar Time observed on the meridian of the transit circle telescope of the Old Royal Observatory at Greenwich is called Greenwich Mean Time (G.M.T.). The mean solar day is divided into 24 hours and, for astronomical and other scientific purposes, these are numbered 0 to 23, commencing at midnight. Civil time is usually reckoned in two periods of 12 hours, designated a.m. (*ante meridiem*, i.e. before noon) and p.m. (*post meridiem*, i.e. after noon).

Universal Time

Before 1925 January 1 G.M.T. was reckoned in 24 hours commencing at noon: since that date it has been reckoned from midnight. In view of the risk of confusion in the use of the designation G.M.T. before and after 1925, the International Astronomical Union recommended in 1928 that astronomers should employ the term Universal Time, U.T. (or Weltzeit, W.Z.) to denote G.M.T. measured from Greenwich Mean Midnight.

In precision work it is necessary to take account of small variations in Universal Time. These arise from small irregularities in the rotation of the Earth. Observed astronomical time is designated U.T.0. Observed time corrected for the effects of the motion of the poles (giving rise to a "wandering" in longitude) is designated U.T.1. There is also a seasonal fluctuation in the rate of rotation of the Earth arising from meteorological causes, often called the annual fluctuation. U.T.1 corrected for this effect is designated U.T.2 and provides a time scale free from short-period fluctuations. It is still subject to small secular and irregular changes.

Apparent Solar Time

As has been mentioned on page 66, the time shown by a sundial is called Apparent Solar Time. It differs from Mean Solar Time by an amount known as the Equation of Time, which is the total effect of two causes which make the length of the apparent solar day non-uniform. One cause of variation is that the orbit of the Earth is not a circle, but an ellipse, having the Sun at one focus. As a consequence, the angular speed of the Earth in its orbit is not constant; it is greatest at the beginning of January when the Earth is nearest the Sun. The other cause is due to the obliquity of the ecliptic; the plane of the equator (which is at right-angles to the axis of rotation of the Earth) does not coincide with the ecliptic (the plane defined by the apparent annual motion of the Sun around the celestial sphere) but is inclined to it at an angle of 23° 26′. As a result, the apparent solar day is shorter than average at the equinoxes and longer at the solstices. From the combined effects of the components due to obliquity and eccentricity, the equation of time reaches its maximum values in February (−14 mins.) and early November (+16 mins.). It has a zero value on four dates during the year, and it is only on these dates (approx. April 15, June 14, Sept. 1, and Dec. 25) that a sundial shows Mean Solar Time.

Sidereal Time

A sidereal day is the duration of a complete rotation of the Earth with reference to the First Point of Aries. The term sidereal (or "star") time is perhaps a little misleading since the time scale so defined is not exactly the same as that which would be defined by successive transits of a selected star, as there is a small progressive motion between the stars and the First Point of Aries due to the precession of the Earth's axis. This makes the length of the sidereal day shorter than the true period of rotation by 0·008 seconds. Superimposed on this steady precessional motion are small oscillations called nutation, giving rise to fluctuations in apparent sidereal time amount-

ing to as much as 1·2 seconds. It is therefore customary to employ Mean Sidereal Time, from which these fluctuations have been removed. The conversion of G.M.T. to Greenwich sidereal time (G.S.T.) may be performed by adding the value of the G.S.T. at 0^h on the day in question (Page Two of each month) to the G.M.T. converted to sidereal time using the table on p. 72.

Example. To find the G.S.T. at August 8^d 02^h 41^m 11^s G.M.T.

				h m s
G.S.T. at 0^h	..	..	..	21 05 56
G.M.T.	..	..	..	2 41 11
Acceleration for 2^h	..	..	..	20
„ „ 41^m 11^s	..	..	..	7
Sum = G.S.T. =	..	..	..	23 47 34

If the observer is not on the Greenwich meridian then his longitude, measured positively westwards from Greenwich, must be subtracted from the G.S.T. to obtain Local Sidereal Time (L.S.T.). Thus, in the above example, an observer 5^h east of Greenwich, or 19^h west, would find his L.S.T. as 4^h 47^m 34^s.

Ephemeris Time

In the study of the motions of the Sun, Moon and planets, observations taken over an extended period are used in the preparation of tables giving the apparent position of the body each day. A table of this sort is known as an ephemeris, and may be used in the comparison of current observations with tabulated positions. A detailed examination of the observations made over the past 300 years shows that the Sun, Moon and planets appear to depart from their predicted positions by amounts proportional to their mean motions. The only satisfactory explanation is that the time scale to which the observations were referred was not uniform as had been supposed. Since the time scale was based on the rotation of the Earth, it follows that this rotation is subject to irregularities. The fact that the discrepancies between the observed and ephemeris positions were proportional to the mean motions of the bodies made it possible to secure agreement by substituting a revised time scale and recomputing the ephemeris positions. The time scale which brings the ephemeris into agreement with the observations is known as Ephemeris Time (E.T.).

The new unit of time has been defined in terms of the apparent annual motion of the Sun. Thus the second is now defined in terms of the annual motion of the Earth in its orbit around the Sun (1/31556925·9747 of the Tropical Year for 1900 January 0^d 12^h E.T.) instead of in terms of the diurnal rotation of the Earth on its axis (1/86 400 of the Mean Solar Day). In many branches of scientific work other than astronomy there has been a demand for a unit of time that is invariable, and the second of Ephemeris time was adopted by the Comité International des Poids et Mésures in 1956. The length of the unit has been chosen to provide general agreement with U.T. throughout the 19th and 20th centuries. During 1989 the estimated difference E.T. − U.T. is 57 seconds. The precise determination of E.T. from astronomical observations is a lengthy process, as the accuracy with which a single observation of the Sun can be made is far less than that obtainable in, for instance, a comparison between clocks. It is therefore necessary to average the observations over an extended period. Largely on account of its faster motion, the position of the Moon may be observed with greater accuracy, and a close approximation to Ephemeris Time may be obtained by comparing observations of the moon with its ephemeris position. Even in this case, however, the requisite standard of accuracy can only be achieved by averaging over a number of years.

Atomic Time

The fundamental standards of time and frequency must be defined in terms of a periodic motion adequately uniform, enduring and susceptible of measurement. This has led in the past to the adoption of standards based on the observed motions in the Solar System. Recent progress has made it possible to consider the use of other natural standards, such as atomic or molecular oscillations. The oscillations so far employed are not in fact continuous periodic motions such as the revolution of the electrons in their orbits around the nuclei. The continuous oscillations are generated in an electrical circuit, the frequency of which is then compared or brought into coincidence with the frequency characteristic of the absorption or emission by the atoms or molecules when they change between two selected energy levels. At the National Physical Laboratory regular comparisons have been made since the middle of 1955 between quartz clocks of high stability and a frequency defined by atoms of caesium. The standard has proved of great value in the precise calibration of frequencies and time intervals: it has also been possible to build up a scale of "atomic time" by using continuously-running quartz clocks calibrated in ter_____ he caesium frequency standard.

Terrestrial Dynamical Time

A new time scale, known as Terrestrial Dynamical Time (T.D.T.) has recently been defined in terms of international atomic time in such a way that, for most purposes, it can be regarded as a continuation of atomic time.

Radio Time Signals

The establishment of a uniform time system by the assessment of the performance of standard clocks in terms of astronomical observations is the work of a national observatory, and standard time is then made

generally available by means of radio time signals. In the United Kingdom, the Royal Greenwich Observatory controls the "6-pips" radio signals emitted by the British Broadcasting Corporation. The British Telecom Speaking Clock is corrected by the National Physical Laboratory caesium beam atomic frequency standard at the British Telecom International Radio Station at Rugby.

For survey and scientific purposes, in which the highest accuracy is required, special signals are transmitted on behalf of the National Physical Laboratory from Rugby Radio Station. The signals consist of a standard frequency carrier of 60 kHz (MSF) which switches off for half a second to denote the passing of one minute and for a tenth of a second to denote the passing of one second. Also transmitted are two binary coded decimal (BCD) time codes giving time of day and calendar information. The service is continuous except for a maintenance period from 1000–1400 UTC on the first Sunday of each month.

In addition, a standard frequency and time service is transmitted for 5 minutes in every 10 minutes on 2·5, 5 and 10 MHz (MSF). This facility, however, was scheduled to be withdrawn on February 29, 1988.

The Coordinated Universal Time (UTC) system standard frequency emissions and radio time signals are broadcast on MSF, GBR, and by other national transmitters, eg. by WWV and WWVH in the U.S.A. in conformity with the International Atomic Time Scale. The time intervals between pips correspond exactly to the seconds defined as follows: "The second is the duration of 9 192 631 770 periods of the radiation corresponding to the transition between the 2 hyperfine levels of the ground state of the caesium 133 atom."

As the rate of rotation of the Earth is variable the time signals are adjusted by the introduction of a leap second when necessary in order that UTC shall not depart from UT by more than $0^s·9$. For convenience leap seconds are introduced when necessary, on the last second of a month, preferably on Dec. 31 and/or June 30. In the case of a positive leap second $23^h 59^m 60^s$ is followed one second later by $0^h 00^m 00^s$ of the first day of the month. In the case of a negative leap second (required if the Earth were to have a sudden change of rate and begin to gain relative to UTC) $23^h 59^m 58^s$ is followed one second later by $0^h 00^m 00^s$ of the first day of the month.

From 1972 Jan. 1 the six pips on the BBC have consisted of 5 short pips from second 55 to second 59 followed by one lengthened pip, the start of which indicates the exact minute.

STANDARD TIME

In the year 1880 it was enacted by statute that the word "time", when it occurred in any legal document relating to Great Britain, was to be interpreted, unless otherwise specifically stated, as the Mean Time of the Greenwich meridian.* Since the year 1883 the system of Standard Time by Zones has been

---

* Summer Time is the "legal" time during the period in which its use is ordained.

gradually accepted, and now almost throughout the world a Standard Time which differs from that of Greenwich by an integral number of hours, either fast or slow, is used.

The large territories of the United States and Canada are divided into zones approximately $7\frac{1}{2}°$ on either side of central meridians. The important ones are given below; there are in addition zones from 3 to 12 hours fast in the U.S.S.R.

Variations from the standard time of some countries occurs during part of the year: they are decided annually and are usually referred to as Summer Time or Daylight Saving Time. These variations occur in:

The Commonwealth.—Parts of Australia; Bahamas; Bermuda; Canada, Channel Islands; Cyprus; Gibraltar; Malta; New Zealand; U.K.

Foreign Countries.—Albania; Austria; Azores; Belgium; Brazil; Bulgaria; Canary Is.; Chile; parts of China; Corsica; Cuba; Czechoslovakia; Denmark; Faroe; Finland; France; Germany; Greece; Greenland; Guatemala; Haiti; Hungary; Iraq; Irish Republic; Israel; Italy; Jordan; Lebanon; Libya; Luxembourg; Madeira; Monaco; Mongolia; Netherlands; New Caledonia; Norway; Paraguay; Peru; Poland; Portugal; Romania; Sicily; Sweden; Switzerland; Syria; Taiwan; Turkey; Uruguay; parts of U.S.A.; U.S.S.R; Vanuatu; Yugoslavia.

Fast on Greenwich Time

12 hours fast
Fiji; Kiribati; Marshall Is.; Nauru; New Zealand.

11¾ hours fast
Norfolk I.

11 hours fast
New Caledonia; Pohnpei; Sakhalin; Solomon Is.; Vanuatu.

10 hours fast
Admiralty Is.; Australian Capital Territory; Mariana Is.; New South Wales (except Broken Hill Area); Queensland; Tasmania; Truk Is.; Victoria; Yap Is.

9½ hours fast
New South Wales (Broken Hill Area); Northern Territory (Aus); South Australia.

9 hours fast
Irian Jaya; Japan; Korea; Kuril Is.; Molucca Is; Palau Is.

8 hours fast
Bali; China; Hong Kong; Kalimantan*; Macao; Malaysia; Philippines; Sulawesi; Taiwan; Timor; Western Australia.

7 hours fast
Christmas I. (Indian Ocean); Java; Kampuchea; Laos; Sumatra; Thailand; Vietnam.

6½ hours fast
Burma; Cocos-Keeling Is.

6 hours fast
Bangladesh.

5¾ hours fast
Nepal.

5½ hours fast
India; Sri Lanka.

5 hours fast
Pakistan.

4½ hours fast
Afghanistan.

4 hours fast
Mauritius; Réunion; Seychelles; United Arab Emirates.

3½ hours fast
Iran.

3 hours fast
Bahrain; Comoro Is.; Ethiopia; Iraq; Kenya; Madagascar; Qatar; Somalia; Tanzania; Uganda; Yemen.

2 hours fast
Botswana; Bulgaria; Burundi; Crete; Cyprus; Egypt; Finland; Greece; Israel, Jordan, Lebanon; Lesotho; Malawi; Mozambique; Romania; Rwanda; South Africa; Sudan; Syria; Turkey; Zambia; Zimbabwe.

1 hour fast
Albania; Algeria; Angola; Austria; Belgium; Benin; Cameroon; Central African Republic; Czechoslovakia; Denmark; France; Germany; Gibraltar; Hungary; Ireland (Republic); Italy; Libya; Luxembourg; Malta; Monaco; Netherlands; Niger; Nigeria; Norway; Poland; Spain; Svalbard; Sweden; Switzerland; Tunisia; Yugoslavia; Zaire.

Greenwich Time

Ascension I.; Canary Is.; Channel Is.; Côte d'Ivoire; Faroe Is.; Gambia; Ghana; Guinea; Guinea Bissau; Iceland; Liberia; Madeira; Mali; Mauritania; Morocco; Portugal; St. Helena; São Tomé & Principe I.; Senegal; Sierra Leone; Togo; U.K.

Slow on Greenwich time

1 hour slow
Azores; Cape Verde Is.

2 hours slow
Fernando Noronha I.; South Georgia.

3 hours slow
Argentina; Brazil (eastern); French Guiana; Greenland (except Thule); Guyana; Uruguay.

3½ hours slow
Newfoundland; Suriname.

4 hours slow (Atlantic time)
Bermuda; Bolivia; Brazil (central); Canada (E. of 68° W); Chile; Dominican Republic; Falkland Is.; Greenland (west); Labrador; Paraguay; Puerto Rico; Venezuela; Windward Is.

5 hours slow
Bahama Is.; Brazil (western); Canada (68° W. to 85° W.); Cayman Is.; Colombia; Cuba; Ecuador; Haiti; Jamaica; Panama; Peru; U.S.A. (eastern time).

6 hours slow
Canada (85° W. to 102° W.); Costa Rica, Guatemala; Honduras; Mexico (eastern); Nicaragua; El Salvador; U.S.A. (central time).

7 hours slow
Canada (102° W. to 120° W.); Mexico (central); U.S.A. (mountain time).

8 hours slow
Alaska (S.E. coast); Canada (W. of 120° W.); Mexico (western); U.S.A. (Pacific time); Yukon.

8½ hours slow
Pitcairn I.

9 hours slow
Alaska (E. of 169°30′ W.).

10 hours slow
Aleutian Is. (W. of 169°30′ W.); Christmas I. (Pacific Ocean); Hawaii; Society Is.; Tuamotu archipelago; Tubuai Is.

11 hours slow
Midway Is.; Samoa.

11½ hours slow
Banaba (Kiribati).

12 hours slow
Tabuaeran Atoll (Kiribati).

In the Tonga Islands the time 13h fast and in Chatham Is. 12h 45m fast on Greenwich is used, as the Date line is to the East of them.

---

*The Indonesian territory on Borneo I.

RISING AND SETTING TIMES

Table 1. Hour Angle

Dec.	Latitude and Declination of Opposite Signs						0°	Latitude and Declination of Same Signs					
	50°	45°	40°	30°	20°	10°	0°	10°	20°	30°	40°	45°	50°
°	h m	h m	h m	h m	h m	h m	h m	h m	h m	h m	h m	h m	h m
0	6 00	6 00	6 00	6 00	6 00	6 00	6 00	6 00	6 00	6 00	6 00	6 00	6 00
1	5 55	5 56	5 57	5 58	5 59	5 59	6 00	6 01	6 01	6 02	6 03	6 04	6 05
2	5 50	5 52	5 53	5 55	5 57	5 58	6 00	6 02	6 03	6 05	6 07	6 08	6 10
3	5 45	5 48	5 50	5 53	5 56	5 58	6 00	6 02	6 04	6 07	6 10	6 12	6 15
4	5 40	5 44	5 46	5 51	5 54	5 57	6 00	6 03	6 06	6 09	6 14	6 16	6 20
5	5 36	5 40	5 43	5 48	5 52	5 56	6 00	6 04	6 08	6 12	6 17	6 20	6 24
6	5 31	5 36	5 39	5 46	5 51	5 56	6 00	6 04	6 09	6 14	6 21	6 24	6 29
7	5 26	5 32	5 36	5 44	5 50	5 55	6 00	6 05	6 10	6 16	6 24	6 28	6 34
8	5 21	5 27	5 33	5 41	5 48	5 54	6 00	6 06	6 12	6 19	6 27	6 33	6 39
9	5 16	5 23	5 29	5 39	5 47	5 53	6 00	6 07	6 13	6 21	6 31	6 37	6 44
10	5 11	5 19	5 26	5 37	5 45	5 53	6 00	6 07	6 15	6 23	6 34	6 41	6 49
11	5 06	5 15	5 22	5 34	5 44	5 52	6 00	6 08	6 16	6 26	6 38	6 45	6 54
12	5 01	5 11	5 19	5 32	5 42	5 51	6 00	6 09	6 18	6 28	6 41	6 49	6 59
13	4 56	5 06	5 15	5 29	5 40	5 51	6 00	6 09	6 20	6 31	6 45	6 54	7 04
14	4 51	5 02	5 12	5 27	5 39	5 50	6 00	6 10	6 21	6 33	6 48	6 58	7 09
15	4 46	4 58	5 08	5 24	5 38	5 49	6 00	6 11	6 22	6 36	6 52	7 02	7 14
16	4 40	4 53	5 04	5 22	5 36	5 48	6 00	6 12	6 24	6 38	6 56	7 07	7 20
17	4 35	4 49	5 00	5 19	5 35	5 48	6 00	6 12	6 25	6 41	7 00	7 11	7 25
18	4 29	4 44	4 57	5 17	5 33	5 47	6 00	6 13	6 27	6 43	7 03	7 16	7 31
19	4 23	4 39	4 53	5 14	5 31	5 46	6 00	6 14	6 29	6 46	7 07	7 21	7 37
20	4 17	4 35	4 49	5 11	5 30	5 45	6 00	6 15	6 30	6 49	7 11	7 25	7 43
21	4 11	4 30	4 44	5 09	5 28	5 44	6 00	6 16	6 32	6 51	7 16	7 30	7 49
22	4 04	4 25	4 40	5 06	5 26	5 44	6 00	6 16	6 34	6 54	7 20	7 35	7 56
23	3 58	4 19	4 36	5 03	5 24	5 43	6 00	6 17	6 36	6 57	7 24	7 41	8 02
24	3 52	4 14	4 32	5 00	5 23	5 42	6 00	6 18	6 37	7 00	7 28	7 46	8 08
25	3 45	4 09	4 28	4 58	5 21	5 41	6 00	6 19	6 39	7 02	7 32	7 51	8 15
26	3 38	4 03	4 24	4 55	5 19	5 40	6 00	6 20	6 41	7 05	7 36	7 57	8 22
27	3 30	3 57	4 19	4 52	5 17	5 39	6 00	6 21	6 43	7 08	7 41	8 03	8 30
28	3 23	3 51	4 14	4 48	5 15	5 38	6 00	6 22	6 45	7 12	7 46	8 09	8 37
29	3 15	3 45	4 09	4 45	5 14	5 38	6 00	6 22	6 46	7 15	7 51	8 15	8 45

SUNRISE AND SUNSET

The local mean time of sunrise or sunset (as defined on page 64) may be found by determining the appropriate hour angle from the table above and applying it to the time of transit given in the ephemeris for each month. The hour angle is negative for sunrise and positive for sunset. A small correction to the hour angle, which always has the effect of increasing it numerically, is necessary to allow for the Sun's semi-diameter (16′) and for refraction (34′). This correction may be obtained from Table 2. The resulting local mean time may be converted into the standard time of the country by taking the difference between the longitude of the standard meridian of the country and that of the place, and adding it to the local mean time if the place is west of the standard meridian, and subtracting it if the place is east of the standard meridian.

Example.—Required the N.Z. Mean Time (12ʰ fast on G.M.T.) of sunset on May 24 at Auckland. The latitude is 36° 50′ south (or minus) and the longitude 11ʰ 39ᵐ east. Taking the declination as +20°·7, we find

	h m
Tabular entry for 30° Lat. and Dec. 20°, opposite signs	+ 5 11
Proportional part for 6° 50′ of Lat.	− 15
Proportional part for 0°·7 of Dec.	− 3
Correction (Table 2)	+ 6
Hour angle	4 59
Sun transits	11 57
Longitudinal correction	+ 21
N.Z. Mean Time	17 17

Table 2. Correction for Refraction and Semi-Diameter

Latitude	Declination			
	0°	10°	20°	29°
°	m	m	m	m
0	3	3	4	4
20	4	4	4	4
30	4	4	4	5
40	4	4	5	6
50	5	5	6	8

MOONRISE AND MOONSET

It is possible to calculate the times of moonrise and moonset using Table 1 though the method is more complicated because the apparent motion of the Moon is much more rapid and also more variable than that of the Sun.

Table 3. Longitude Correction

A \ X	40^m	45^m	50^m	55^m	60^m	65^m	70^m
h	m	m	m	m	m	m	m
1	2	2	2	2	3	3	3
2	3	4	4	5	5	5	6
3	5	6	6	7	8	8	9
4	7	8	8	9	10	11	12
5	8	9	10	11	13	14	15
6	10	11	13	14	15	16	18
7	12	13	15	16	18	19	20
8	13	15	17	18	20	22	23
9	15	17	19	21	23	24	26
10	17	19	21	23	25	27	29
11	18	21	23	25	28	30	32
12	20	23	25	28	30	33	35
13	22	24	27	30	33	35	38
14	23	26	29	32	35	38	41
15	25	28	31	34	38	41	44
16	27	30	33	37	40	43	47
17	28	32	35	39	43	46	50
18	30	34	38	41	45	49	53
19	32	36	40	44	48	51	55
20	33	38	42	46	50	54	58
21	35	39	44	48	53	57	61
22	37	41	46	50	55	60	64
23	38	43	48	53	58	62	67
24	40	45	50	55	60	65	70

Notation

φ = latitude of observer
λ = longitude of observer (measured positively towards the west)
T_{-1} = time of transit of Moon on previous day
T_0 = time of transit of Moon on day in question
T_1 = time of transit of Moon on following day
δ_0 = approximate declination of Moon
δ_R = declination of Moon at moonrise
δ_S = declination of Moon at moonset
h_0 = approximate hour angle of Moon
h_R = hour angle of Moon at moonrise
h_S = hour angle of Moon at moonset
t_R = time of moonrise
t_S = time of moonset

The parallax of the Moon, about 57′, is near to the sum of the semi-diameter and refraction but has the opposite effect on these times. It is thus convenient to neglect all three quantities in the method outlined below.

Method

1. With arguments φ, δ_0 enter Table 1 on p. 70 to determine h_0 where h_0 is negative for moonrise and positive for moonset.

2. Form approximate times from
$$t_R = T_0 + \lambda + h_0$$
$$t_S = T_0 + \lambda + h_0$$

3. Determine δ_R, δ_S for times t_R, t_S respectively.

4. Re-enter Table 1 on p. 70 with—
   (a) arguments φ, δ_R to determine h_R
   (b) arguments φ, δ_S to determine h_S

5. Form $t_R = T_0 + \lambda + h_R + AX$
$$t_S = T_0 + \lambda + h_S + AX$$

where $A = (\lambda + h)$

and $X = (T_0 - T_{-1})$ if $(\lambda + h)$ is negative
$X = (T_1 - T_0)$ if $(\lambda + h)$ is positive

AX is the respondent in Table 3.

Example.—To find the times of moonrise and moonset at Vancouver ($\varphi = +49°$, $\lambda = +8^h 12^m$) on 1989 Jan. 4. The starting data (from p. 18) are

$$\begin{aligned} & \quad\quad\quad\quad\quad h \quad\; m \\ T_{-1} &= \quad 8 \quad 04 \\ T_0 &= \quad 8 \quad 55 \\ T_1 &= \quad 9 \quad 50 \\ \delta &= -24° \end{aligned}$$

1. $h_0 = 3^h 56^m$

2. Approximate values
$$\begin{aligned} t_R &= 4^d 08^h 55^m + 8^h 12^m + (-3^h 56^m) \\ &= 4^d 13^h 11^m \\ t_S &= 4^d 08^h 55^m + 8^h 12^m + (+3^h 56^m) \\ &= 4^d 21^h 03^m \end{aligned}$$

3. $\delta_R = -25°.7$
   $\delta_S = -26°.6$

4. $h_R = -3^h 45^m$
   $h_S = +3^h 38^m$

5. $t_R = 4^d 08^h 55^m + 8^h 12^m + (-3^h 45^m) + 9^m$
   $= 4^d 13^h 31^m$
   $t_S = 4^d 08^h 55^m + 8^h 12^m + (+3^h 38^m) + 28^m$
   $= 4^d 21^h 13^m$

To get the L.M.T. of the phenomenon the longitude is subtracted from the G.M.T. thus

Moonrise $= 4^d 13^h 31^m - 8^h 12^m = 4^d 05^h 19^m$
Moonset $= 4^d 21^h 13^m - 8^h 12^m = 4^d 13^h 01^m$

ASTRONOMICAL CONSTANTS

Solar Parallax	8″·794
Precession for the year 1989	50″·288
„ in R.A.	3^s·074
„ in Declination	20″·044
Constant of Nutation	9″·202
Constant of Aberration	20″·496
Mean Obliquity of Ecliptic (1989)	23° 26′ 26″
Moon's Equatorial Hor. Parallax	57′ 02″·70
Velocity of Light in vacuo *per sec*	299792·5 km.
Solar motion *per sec*	20·0 km.
Equatorial radius of the Earth	6378·140 km.
Polar radius of the Earth	6356·755 km.

North Galactic Pole } R.A. 12^h 49^m (1950·0).
(I.A.U. *Standard*). } Dec. 27°·4 N.
Solar Apex .... R.A. 18^h 06^m Dec. +30°

Length of Year ...	Tropical	365·24220
(*In Mean*	Sidereal	365·25636
Solar Days)	Anomalistic ...	365·25964
	(*Perihelion to Perihelion*)	
	Eclipse	346·6200

		d h m s
Length of Month	New Moon to New	29 12 44 02·9
(*Mean Values*)	Sidereal	27 07 43 11·5
	Anomalistic	27 13 18 33·2
	(*Perigee to Perigee*)	

MEAN AND SIDEREAL TIME

Acceleration						Retardation					

h	m s	h	m s	m s	s	h	m s	h	m s	m s	s
1	0 10	13	2 08	0 00	0	1	0 10	13	2 08	0 00	0
2	0 20	14	2 18	3 02	1	2	0 20	14	2 18	3 03	1
3	0 30	15	2 28	9 07	2	3	0 29	15	2 27	9 09	2
				15 13	3					15 15	3
4	0 39	16	2 38	21 18	4	4	0 39	16	2 37	21 21	4
5	0 49	17	2 48	27 23	5	5	0 49	17	2 47	27 28	5
6	0 59	18	2 57	33 28	6	6	0 59	18	2 57	33 34	6
7	1 09	19	3 07	39 34	7	7	1 09	19	3 07	39 40	7
8	1 19	20	3 17	45 39	8	8	1 19	20	3 17	45 46	8
9	1 29	21	3 27	51 44	9	9	1 28	21	3 26	51 53	9
				57 49	10					57 59	10
10	1 39	22	3 37	60 00		10	1 38	22	3 36	60 00	
11	1 48	23	3 47			11	1 48	23	3 46		
12	1 58	24	3 57			12	1 58	24	3 56		

MEAN REFRACTION

Alt.	Ref.	Alt.	Ref.
1 20	21	4 30	10
1 30	20	5 06	9
1 41	19	5 50	8
1 52	18	6 44	7
2 05	17	7 54	6
2 19	16	9 27	5
2 35	15	11 39	4
2 52	14	15 00	3
3 12	13	20 42	2
3 34	12	32 20	1
4 00	11	62 17	0
4 30		90 00	

The length of a sidereal day in mean time is 23h 56m 04s·09. Hence 1h M.T. = 1h + 9s·86 S.T. and 1h S.T. = 1h − 9s·83 M.T.

To convert an interval of mean time to the corresponding interval of sidereal time, enter the acceleration table with the given mean time (taking the hours and the minutes and seconds separately) and add the acceleration obtained to the given mean time. To convert an interval of sidereal time to the corresponding interval of mean time, take out the retardation for the given sidereal time and subtract.

The columns for the minutes and seconds of the argument are in the form known as Critical Tables. To use these tables, find in the appropriate left-hand column the two entries between which the given number of minutes and seconds lies; the quantity in the right-hand column between these two entries is the required acceleration or retardation. Thus the acceleration for 11m26s (which lies between the entries 9m07s and 15m13s) is 2s. If the given number of minutes and seconds is a tabular entry, the required acceleration or retardation is the entry in the right-hand column *above* the given tabular entry; e.g. the retardation for 45m46s is 7s.

Example.—Convert 14h27m35s from S.T. to M.T.

	h	m	s
Given S.T.	14	27	35
Retardation for 14h		2	18
Retardation for 27m35s			5
Corresponding M.T.	14	25	12

For further explanation, see p. 67.
The refraction table is also in the form of a critical table.

THE SUMMER TIME ACTS

In 1916 an Act ordained that during a defined period of that year the legal time for general purposes in Great Britain should be one hour in advance of Greenwich mean Time. The *Summer Time Acts*, 1922 to 1925, defined the period during which Summer Time was to be in force, stabilizing practice until the war.

During the Second World War the duration of Summer Time was extended and in the years 1941–45 and in 1947, Double Summer Time (2 hrs. in advance of Greenwich Mean Time) was in force. After the war, Summer Time was extended in each year from 1948–1952 and 1961–1964 by Order in Council. British Standard Time, during which clocks were kept one hour ahead of Greenwich Mean Time throughout the year, was in force between Oct. 27, 1968 and Oct. 31, 1971.

The most recent legislation is the Summer Time Act, 1972, which enacted that "the period of summer time for the purposes of this Act is the period beginning at two o'clock, Greenwich mean time, in the morning of the day after the third Saturday in March or, if that day is Easter Day, the day after the second Saturday in March, and ending at two o'clock, Greenwich mean time, in the morning of the day after the fourth Saturday in October."

The duration of Summer Time can be varied by Order in Council and in recent years alterations have been made to bring the operation of Summer Time in Britain closer to similar provisions in other countries of the European Community. The latest Order in Council is the Summer Time Order, 1988, stipulating the duration of Summer Time in 1989. In 1989 Summer Time will be in force from March 26 to October 29 and, as in recent years, the hour of changeover will be 01h Greenwich Mean Time.

The duration of Summer Time during the last few years is given in the following table.

1978 Mar. 19—Oct. 29	1984 Mar. 25—Oct. 28
1979 Mar. 18—Oct. 28	1985 Mar. 31—Oct. 27
1980 Mar. 16—Oct. 26	1986 Mar. 30—Oct. 26
1981 Mar. 29—Oct. 25	1987 Mar. 29—Oct. 25
1982 Mar. 28—Oct. 24	1988 Mar. 27—Oct. 23
1983 Mar. 27—Oct. 23	

ASTRONOMERS ROYAL

John Flamsteed, first Astronomer Royal	1675–1719
Edmund Halley	1720–1742
James Bradley	1742–1762
Nathaniel Bliss	1762–1764
Nevil Maskelyne	1765–1811
John Pond	1811–1835
Sir George Biddell Airy	1835–1881
Sir William Henry Mahoney Christie	1881–1910
Sir Frank Watson Dyson	1910–1933
Sir Harold Spencer Jones	1933–1955
Sir Richard van der Riet Woolley	1955–1971
Sir Martin Ryle	1972–1982
Prof. Sir Francis Graham Smith	1982–

PHENOMENA OF JUPITER'S SATELLITES, 1989

January

d h m	Sat	Phen
1 02 08	I	Ec.R.
1 18 45	III	Ec.R.
1 21 05	I	Sh.I.
1 23 15	I	Sh.E.
2 20 37	I	Ec.R.
3 17 44	I	Sh.E.
5 23 18	II	Sh.I.
6 01 37	II	Sh.E.
7 19 49	II	Ec.R.
8 20 32	III	Ec.D.
8 22 47	III	Ec.R.
8 23 01	I	Sh.I.
9 01 11	I	Sh.E.
9 22 32	I	Ec.R.
10 17 30	I	Sh.I.
10 19 40	I	Sh.E.
11 17 01	I	Ec.R.
13 01 54	II	Sh.I.
14 22 27	II	Ec.R.
16 00 33	III	Ec.D.
16 00 57	I	Sh.I.
16 02 49	III	Ec.R
16 17 31	II	Sh.E.
17 00 27	I	Ec.R.
17 19 25	I	Sh.I.
17 21 35	I	Sh.E.
18 18 56	I	Ec.R.
21 22 44	II	Ec.D.
22 01 05	II	Ec.R.
23 17 49	II	Sh.I.
23 20 08	II	Sh.E.
24 21 21	I	Sh.I.
24 23 31	I	Sh.E.
25 20 51	I	Ec.R.
26 18 00	I	Sh.E.
26 18 33	III	Sh.I.
26 20 48	III	Sh.E.
29 01 22	II	Ec.D.
30 20 25	II	Sh.I.
30 22 44	II	Sh.E.
31 23 17	I	Sh.I.

February

d h m	Sat	Phen
1 22 47	I	Ec.R.
2 17 46	I	Sh.I.
2 19 56	I	Sh.E.
2 22 35	III	Sh.I.
3 00 50	III	Sh.E.
6 23 01	II	Sh.I.
7 01 20	II	Sh.E.
8 19 41	II	Ec.R.

February

d h m	Sat	Phen
9 19 42	I	Sh.I.
9 21 51	I	Sh.E.
10 19 11	I	Ec.R.
13 18 56	III	Ec.R.
15 19 57	II	Ec.D.
15 22 19	II	Ec.R.
16 21 37	I	Sh.I.
16 23 47	I	Sh.E.
17 21 06	I	Ec.R.
18 18 16	I	Sh.E.
20 20 38	III	Ec.D.
20 22 58	III	Ec.R
22 22 35	II	Ec.D.
23 00 58	II	Ec.R.
23 23 33	I	Sh.I.
24 19 51	I	Sh.E.
24 23 02	I	Ec.R.
25 20 12	I	Sh.E.

March

d h m	Sat	Phen
3 20 07	II	Sh.I.
3 22 27	II	Sh.E.
4 19 58	I	Sh.I.
4 22 08	I	Sh.E.
5 19 26	I	Ec.R.
10 18 41	III	Sh.I.
10 21 01	III	Sh.E.
10 22 42	II	Sh.I.
11 21 54	I	Sh.I.
12 00 04	I	Sh.E.
12 19 36	I	Ec.R.
12 21 21	I	Ec.R.
17 22 42	III	Sh.I.
19 19 51	II	Ec.D.
19 22 15	II	Ec.R.
19 23 16	I	Ec.R.
20 20 29	I	Sh.E.
27 20 14	I	Sh.I
27 22 25	I	Sh.E.
28 19 07	III	Ec.R.
28 19 33	II	Sh.E.
28 19 40	I	Ec.R.

April

d h m	Sat	Phen
3 22 10	I	Sh.I.
4 19 46	II	Sh.I.
4 20 44	III	Ec.D.
4 21 35	I	Ec.R.
4 22 09	II	Sh.E.
4 23 09	III	Ec.R.
11 22 22	II	Sh.I.

April

d h m	Sat	Phen
12 20 46	I	Sh.E.
19 20 30	I	Sh.I.
22 21 13	III	Sh.E.
27 21 49	I	Ec.R.

November

d h m	Sat	Phen
3 04 31	I	Ec.D.
4 01 37	II	Sh.I.
4 01 47	II	Sh.I.
4 03 59	I	Sh.E.
4 04 13	II	Sh.E.
4 23 00	I	Ec.D.
5 20 15	II	Ec.D.
5 20 15	I	Sh.I.
5 20 32	III	Ec.D.
5 22 27	I	Sh.E.
5 23 25	III	Ec.E.
10 06 25	I	Ec.D.
11 03 40	I	Sh.I.
11 04 13	II	Sh.I.
11 05 53	I	Sh.E.
12 00 54	I	Ec.D.
12 22 09	I	Sh.I.
12 22 48	II	Ec.D.
13 00 21	I	Sh.E.
13 00 31	III	Ec.D.
13 03 25	III	Ec.R.
14 20 09	II	Sh.E.
18 05 33	I	Sh.I.
19 02 48	I	Ec.D.
20 00 02	I	Sh.I.
20 01 22	II	Ec.D.
20 02 15	I	Sh.E.
20 04 30	III	Ec.D.
20 21 16	I	Ec.D.
21 20 08	I	Sh.I.
21 20 43	I	Sh.E.
21 22 46	III	Sh.E.
23 21 21	III	Sh.E.
26 04 42	I	Ec.D.
26 20 38	IV	Ec.R.
26 21 13	IV	Ec.R.
27 01 55	I	Sh.I.
27 03 56	II	Ec.D.
27 04 08	I	Sh.E.
27 23 11	I	Ec.D.
28 20 24	I	Sh.I.
28 22 37	I	Sh.E.
28 22 45	II	Sh.I.
29 01 23	II	Sh.E.
30 22 26	III	Sh.I.

December

d h m	Sat	Phen
1 01 21	III	Sh.E.
4 03 49	I	Sh.I.
4 06 02	II	Ec.D.
4 06 30	II	Sh.I.
5 01 05	I	Ec.D.
5 22 17	I	Sh.I.
6 01 21	II	Sh.I.
6 04 00	II	Sh.E.
6 19 34	I	Ec.D.
7 18 59	I	Sh.E.
7 19 47	II	Sh.E.
8 02 25	III	Sh.I.
8 05 21	III	Sh.E.
11 05 42	I	Sh.I.
12 03 00	I	Ec.D.
13 02 24	I	Sh.E.
13 03 58	II	Sh.I.
13 06 37	II	Sh.E.
13 21 28	I	Ec.D.
14 18 39	I	Sh.I.
14 20 53	I	Sh.E.
14 22 21	II	Ec.D.
16 19 56	II	Sh.E.
18 20 27	III	Ec.D.
19 04 54	I	Ec.D.
20 02 05	I	Sh.I.
20 04 19	I	Sh.E.
20 23 23	I	Ec.D.
21 20 33	I	Sh.I.
21 22 47	I	Sh.E.
22 00 55	II	Ec.D.
22 01 09	IV	Sh.I.
22 02 37	IV	Sh.E.
22 17 51	I	Ec.D.
23 19 53	II	Sh.I.
23 22 33	II	Sh.E.
26 00 27	III	Ec.D.
27 03 59	I	Sh.I.
27 06 13	I	Sh.E.
28 03 32	I	Ec.R.
28 22 27	I	Sh.I.
29 00 41	I	Sh.E.
29 06 08	II	Ec.R.
29 17 21	III	Sh.E.
29 22 01	I	Ec.R.
30 16 56	I	Sh.I.
30 19 10	I	Sh.E.
30 22 30	II	Sh.I.
31 01 10	II	Sh.E.
31 16 30	I	Ec.R.

Jupiter's satellites transit across the disk from east to west, and pass behind the disk from west to east. The shadows that they cast also transit across the disk. With the exception at times of Satellite IV, the satellites also pass through the shadow of the planet, i.e. they are eclipsed. Just before opposition the satellite disappears in the shadow to the west of the planet, and reappears from occultation on the east limb. Immediately after opposition the satellite is occulted at the west limb, and reappears from eclipse to the east of the planet. At times approximately two to four months before and after opposition, both phases of eclipses of Satellite III may be seen. When Satellite IV is eclipsed, both phases may be seen.

The list of phenomena gives most of the eclipses and shadow transits visible in the British Isles under favourable conditions.

Ec. = Eclipse	R	= Reappearance
Sh. = Shadow transit	I	= Ingress
D = Disappearance	E	= Egress

CELESTIAL PHENOMENA FOR OBSERVATION IN 1989

ECLIPSES

There will be four eclipses during 1989, two of the Sun and two of the Moon. (Penumbral eclipses are not mentioned in this section as they are difficult to observe).

1. A total eclipse of the Moon on February 20 is visible from the north-western part of North America, the arctic regions, Australasia, Asia, the extreme eastern part of Africa and the north-eastern part of Europe. The eclipse begins at 13^h 45^m and ends at 17^h 27^m. Totality lasts from 14^h 57^m to 16^h 15^m.

2. A partial eclipse of the Sun on March 7 is visible from the Hawaiian Islands, the eastern part of the North Pacific Ocean, the north-western half of North America, most of Greenland, the extreme north-eastern part of Asia and the arctic regions. The eclipse begins at 16^h 17^m and ends at 19^h 58^m. The time of maximum eclipse is 18^h 07^m, when 0·83 of the Sun's diameter is obscured.

3. A total eclipse of the Moon on August 17 is visible from the extreme western part of Asia, Europe (including the British Isles) but excluding the northern part of Scandinavia, Africa, Iceland, Greenland except the northern part, the Americas except the north-western part of North America, and most of Antarctica. The eclipse begins at 01^h 21^m and ends at 04^h 55^m. Totality lasts from 02^h 20^m to 03^h 56^m.

4. An partial eclipse of the Sun on August 31 is visible from the extreme south-east of Africa, Madagascar, part of Antarctica and the southern part of the Indian Ocean. The eclipse begins at 03^h 34^m and ends at 07^h 28^m. The time of maximum eclipse is 05^h 30^m, when 0·63 of the Sun's diameter is obscured.

LUNAR OCCULTATIONS

No planets or bright stars are occulted by the Moon in 1989.

Observations of the times of these occultations are made by both amateur and professional astronomers. Such observations are later analysed to yield accurate positions of the Moon: this is one method of determining the difference between ephemeris time and universal time.

Many of the observations made by amateurs are obtained with the use of a stop-watch which is compared with a time signal immediately after the observation. Thus an accuracy of about one-fifth of a second is obtainable, though the observer's personal equation may amount to one-third or one-half of a second.

The list on the opposite page includes most of the occultations visible under favourable conditions in

the British Isles. No occultation is included unless the star is at least 10° above the horizon and the Sun sufficiently far below the horizon to permit the star to be seen with the naked eye or in a small telescope. The altitude limit is reduced from 10° to 2° for stars and planets brighter than magnitude 2·0 and such occultations are also predicted in daylight.

The column Phase shows whether a disappearance (D) or reappearance (R) is to be observed. The column headed "El. of Moon" gives the elongation of the Moon from the Sun, in degrees. The elongation increases from 0° at New Moon to 180° at Full Moon and on to 360° (or 0°) at New Moon again. Times and position angles (*P*), reckoned from the north point in the direction north, east, south, west, are given for Greenwich (Lat. 51° 30′, Long. 0°) and Edinburgh (Lat. 56° 00′, Long. 3° 12′ west).

The coefficients *a* and *b* are the variations in the G.M.T. for each degree of longitude (positive to the west) and latitude (positive to the north) respectively: they enable approximate times (to within about 1^m generally) to be found for any point in the British Isles. If the point of observation is $\Delta\lambda$ degrees west and $\Delta\phi$ degrees north, the approximate time is found by adding $a.\Delta\lambda + b.\Delta\phi$ to the given G.M.T.

As an illustration the reappearance of z.c. 537 on September 19 at Liverpool will be found from both Greenwich and Edinburgh.

	Greenwich	Edinburgh
	°	°
Longitude	0·0	+3·2
Long. of Liverpool	+3·0	+3·0
$\Delta\lambda$	+3·0	−0·2
Latitude	+51·5	+56·0
Lat. of Liverpool	+53·4	+53·4
$\Delta\phi$	+1·9	−2·6
	h　m	h　m
G.M.T.	22 32·6	22 44·1
$a.\Delta\lambda$	+1·8	−0·1
$b.\Delta\phi$	+4·6	−5·5
	22 39·0	22 38·5

If the occultation is given for one station but not the other, the reason for the suppression is given by the following code.

N = star not occulted.

A = star's altitude less than 10° (2° for bright stars and planets).

S = Sun not sufficiently below the horizon.

G = occultation is of very short duration.

It will be noticed that in some cases the coefficients *a* and *b* are not given: this is because the occultation is so short that prediction for other places by means of these coefficients would not be reliable.

LUNAR OCCULTATIONS, 1989

Date		Z.C. No.	Mag.	Phase	El. of Moon	GREENWICH				EDINBURGH			
					°	U.T.	a	b	P	U.T.	a	b	P
						h m	m	m	°	h m	m	m	°
Jan.	14	244	6·9	D.D.	94	20 47·7	−1·0	−0·3	64	20 44·5	−0·9	0·2	48
	17	536	5·4	D.D.	123	A				3 27·9	0·4	−1·5	104
	17	539	4·4	D.D.	123	A				3 38·3	0·2	−1·0	67
	17	541	4·0	D.D.	123	A				3 50·3	0·4	−1·3	93
	18	701	6·5	D.D.	134	1 32·0	−0·8	−0·5	53	1 27·9	−0·9	−0·1	42
	19	840	6·5	D.D.	145	0 12·9	−0·9	−2·1	119	0 1·6	−1·0	−1·6	107
Feb.	8	3474	6·0	D.D.	34	18 39·7	−0·2	0·6	24	18 44·2	0·0	1·8	1
	10	197	7·0	D.D.	62	19 41·4	−0·7	0·3	39	19 42·2	−0·6	1·0	21
	12	470	7·0	D.D.	88	19 58·0	−1·3	−0·4	73	19 53·7	−1·1	0·2	58
	14	773	6·9	D.D.	112	18 21·7	−1·7	−0·6	117	18 16·6	−1·3	0·4	99
	15	958	6·7	D.D.	127	..				23 35·3	..	..	177
	17	1208	6·4	D.D.	147	17 55·7	−0·4	2·5	66	18 8·8	−0·1	4·1	43
	23	1815	4·8	R.D.	216	23 20·3	0·2	−2·0	359	23 7·6	..	..	22
Mar.	11	438	6·7	D.D.	58	21 28·9	0·0	−1·6	97	21 21·7	−0·2	−1·5	86
	13	746	6·8	D.D.	84	21 38·9	−0·5	−1·9	106	21 29·3	−0·6	−1·6	97
	14	909	6·1	D.D.	96	22 3·5	−0·5	−2·2	121	21 52·5	−0·6	−1·9	113
	16	1195	6·7	D.D.	120	23 6·0	−1·3	−1·1	83	22 57·3	−1·3	−0·9	77
	17	1200	6·9	D D	121	1 4·1	−0·3	−1·7	99	0 55·1	−0·4	−1·7	97
	17	1304	6·6	D.D.	129	18 59·0	−1·4	0·6	101	S			
	28	2383	2·9	D.B.	244	4 9·9	−1·6	−0·1	111	4 5·1	−1·3	0·1	110
	28	2383	2·9	R.D.	244	5 30·3	−1·5	−0·7	267	A			
Apr.	10	840	6·5	D.D.	64	19 37·8	−0·9	−1·3	89	S			
	12	1155	6·3	D.D.	89	21 46·5	−0·7	−1·7	105	21 36·7	−0·7	−1·6	101
	12	1157	6·0	D.D.	90	22 18·7	−0·4	−1·9	115	22 8·8	−0·5	−1·9	112
	13	1269	7·0	D.D.	100	19 53·7	−1·2	−1·6	124	S			
	13	1277	5·5	D.D.	101	23 1·6	0·1	−2·5	155	22 50·6	0·0	−2·4	153
	15	1476	7·0	D.D.	123	20 30·8	−0·9	−1·8	146	20 20·9	−1·0	−1·3	140
	16	1573	7·0	D.D.	133	20 4·3	−0·9	−1·4	149	S			
May	12	1449	6·7	D.D.	93	21 18·5	..	..	50	21 11·2	..	..	44
	14	1635	5·4	D.D.	115	20 34·7	−0·7	−1·9	155	S			
	14	1637	6·0	D.D.	116	22 3·0	−0·4	−2·3	166	21 52·1	−0·4	−2·0	165
Jun.	7	1312	6·8	D.D.	52	21 40·9	0·3	−1·8	132	S			
July	16	2617	4·7	D.D.	157	21 20·2	−1·6	0·9	55	A			
Aug.	11	2406	6·0	D.D.	114	20 46·9	−1·7	−1·3	145	A			
	22	440	4·6	R D	259	21 39·4	0·5	1·5	221	21 47·7	0·5	1·5	226
Sep.	10	2805	7·0	D.D.	118	19 21·3	..	..	139	A			
	13	3105	6·2	D.D.	146	0 11·8	0·4	1·6	0	..			
	14	3253	5·4	D.D.	159	0 8·2	−1·1	−0·2	68	0 4·5	−0·9	0·0	55
	19	537	3·8	R.D.	242	22 32·6	0·6	2·4	199	22 44·1	0·3	2·1	211
	19	539	4·4	R.D.	242	23 1·0	−0·4	1·4	271	23 6·1	−0·4	1·4	280
	19	541	4·0	R.D.	243	23 12·8	−0·1	1·8	241	23 20·3	−0·2	1·7	250
Oct.	10	3177	6·0	D.D.	126	22 28·7	−0·6	0·3	34	22 29·4	−0·3	0·6	19
	10	3181	5·9	D.D.	126	..				22 43·7	..	..	128
	11	3322	6·4	D.D.	140	23 44·3	−0·8	−0·2	57	23 41·7	−0·6	0·1	42
	12	3467	6·5	D.D.	154	24 0·6	−1·3	−0·7	81	23 55·1	−1·0	−0·2	66
	17	552	3·0	D.B.	217	A				10 1·8	..	..	146
Nov.	7	3253	5·4	D.D.	105	..				19 17·8	..	..	121
	8	3380	6·2	D.D.	118	19 43·1	−0·5	1·6	15	19 50·0	0·0	1·9	359
	8	3385	6·7	D.D.	119	20 56·1	..	..	125	20 41·7	−1·7	−0·7	100
	13	552	3·0	D.B.	189	18 56·6	−0·3	1·3	99	19 2·2	−0·1	1·5	90
	13	552	3·0	R.D.	190	19 45·6	0·0	2·0	223	19 54·3	−0·1	1·9	234
Dec.	5	3334	6·3	D.D.	86	17 49·6	−1·3	0·5	65	17 48·4	−1·0	0·7	54
	6	3467	6·5	D.D.	98	..				17 15·8	..	..	133
	31	3173	5·3	D.D.	43	18 9·4	−1·4	−2·2	106	17 58·2	−1·0	−1·3	87

MEAN PLACES OF STARS, 1989·5

Name	Mag.	R.A.	Dec.	Spectrum
		h m	° ′	
α Andromedæ *Alpheratz*	2·1	0 07·8	+29 02	A0p
β Cassiopeiæ *Caph*	2·3	0 08·6	+59 06	F5
γ Pegasi *Algenib*	2·8	0 12·7	+15 08	B2
α Phœnicis	2·4	0 25·8	−42 22	K0
α Cassiopeiæ *Schedar*	2·2	0 39·9	+56 29	K0
β Ceti *Diphda*	2·0	0 43·1	−18 03	K0
γ Cassiopeiæ*	Var.	0 56·1	+60 40	B0p
β Andromedæ *Mirach*	2·1	1 09·1	+35 34	M0
δ Cassiopeiæ	2·7	1 25·1	+60 11	A5
α Eridani *Achernar*	0·5	1 37·3	−57 17	B5
β Arietis *Sheratan*	2·6	1 54·1	+20 45	A5
γ Andromedæ *Almak*	2·3	2 03·3	+42 17	K0
α Arietis *Hamal*	2·0	2 06·6	+23 25	K2
α Ursæ Minoris *Polaris*	2·0	2 20·7	+89 13	F8
β Persei *Algol**	Var.	3 07·5	+40 55	B8
α Persei *Mirfak*	1·8	3 23·6	+49 49	F5
η Tauri *Alcyone*	2·9	3 46·9	+24 04	B5p
α Tauri *Aldebaran*	0·9	4 35·3	+16 29	K5
β Orionis *Rigel*	0·1	5 14·0	− 8 13	B8p
α Aurigæ *Capella*	0·1	5 15·9	+45 59	G0
γ Orionis *Bellatrix*	1·6	5 24·6	+ 6 20	B2
β Tauri *Elnath*	1·7	5 25·6	+28 36	B8
δ Orionis	2·2	5 31·5	− 0 18	B0
α Leporis	2·6	5 32·3	−17 50	F0
ε Orionis	1·7	5 35·7	− 1 12	B0
ζ Orionis	1·8	5 40·2	− 1 57	B0
κ Orionis	2·1	5 47·3	− 9 40	B0
α Orionis *Betelgeuse**	Var.	5 54·6	+ 7 24	M0
β Aurigæ *Menkalinan*	1·9	5 58·8	+44 57	A0p
β Canis Majoris *Mirzam*	2·0	6 22·2	−17 57	B1
α Carinæ *Canopus*	−0·7	6 23·7	−52 41	F0
γ Geminorum *Alhena*	1·9	6 37·1	+16 25	A0
α Canis Majoris *Sirius*	−1·5	6 44·7	−16 42	A0
ε Canis Majoris	1·5	6 58·2	−28 57	B1
δ Canis Majoris	1·9	7 08·0	−26 23	F8p
α Geminorum *Castor*	1·6	7 33·9	+31 55	A0
α Canis Minoris *Procyon*	0·4	7 38·8	+ 5 15	F5
β Geminorum *Pollux*	1·1	7 44·7	+28 03	K0
ζ Puppis	2·3	8 03·2	−39 58	Od
γ Velorum	1·8	8 09·2	−47 18	Oap
ε Carinæ	1·9	8 22·3	−59 29	K0
δ Velorum	2·0	8 44·4	−54 40	A0
λ Velorum *Suhail*	2·2	9 07·6	−43 23	K5
β Carinæ	1·7	9 13·1	−69 40	A0
ι Carinæ	2·2	9 16·8	−59 14	F0
α Hydræ *Alphard*	2·0	9 27·1	− 8 37	K2
α Leonis *Regulus*	1·3	10 07·8	+12 01	B8
γ Leonis *Algeiba*	1·9	10 19·4	+19 54	K0
β Ursæ Majoris *Merak*	2·4	11 01·2	+56 26	A0
α Ursæ Majoris *Dubhe*	1·8	11 03·1	+61 48	K0

* γ Cassiopeiæ, 1988 mag. 2·5. β Persei, mag. 2·2 to 3·2.
α Orionis, mag. 0·1 to 1·2.

The positions of heavenly bodies on the celestial sphere are defined by two co-ordinates, right ascension and declination, which are analogous to longitude and latitude on the surface of the Earth. If we imagine the plane of the terrestrial equator extended indefinitely, it will cut the celestial sphere in a great circle known as the celestial equator. Similarly the plane of the Earth's orbit, when extended, cuts in the great circle called the ecliptic. The two intersections of these circles are known as the First Point of Aries and the First Point of Libra. If from any star a perpendicular be drawn to the celestial equator, the length of this perpendicular is the star's declination. The arc, measured eastwards along the equator from the First Point of Aries to the foot of this perpendicular, is the right ascension. An alternative definition of right ascension is that it is the angle at the celestial pole (where the Earth's axis, if prolonged, would meet the sphere) between the great circles to the First Point of Aries and to the star.

The plane of the Earth's equator has a slow movement, so that our reference system for right ascension and declination is not fixed. The consequent alteration in these quantities from year to year is called precession. In right ascension it is an increase of about 3s a year for equatorial stars, and larger or smaller changes in either direction for stars near the poles, depending on the right ascension of the star. In declination it varies between +20″ and −20″ according to the right ascension of the star.

A star or other body crosses the meridian when the sidereal time is equal to its right ascension. The altitude is then a maximum, and may be deduced by remembering that the altitude of the elevated pole is numerically equal to the latitude, while that of the equator at its intersection with the meridian is equal to the co-latitude, or complement of the latitude.

MEAN PLACES OF STARS, 1989·5

Name	Mag.	R.A.	Dec.	Spectrum
		h m	° ′	
δ Leonis	2·6	11 13·6	+20 35	A3
β Leonis *Denebola*	2·1	11 48·5	+14 38	A2
γ Ursæ Majoris *Phecda*	2·4	11 53·3	+53 45	A0
γ Corvi	2·6	12 15·3	−17 29	B8
α Crucis	1·0	12 26·0	−63 02	B1
γ Crucis	1·6	12 30·6	−57 03	M3
γ Centauri	2·2	12 40·9	−48 54	A0
γ Virginis *Spica*	2·7	12 41·1	− 1 24	F0
β Crucis	1·3	12 47·1	−59 38	B1
ε Ursæ Majoris *Alioth*	1·8	12 53·6	+56 01	A0p
α Canum Venaticorum	2·9	12 55·5	+38 22	A0p
ζ Ursæ Majoris *Mizar*	2·1	13 23·5	+54 59	A2p
α Virginis *Spica*	1·0	13 24·6	−11 06	B2
η Ursæ Majoris *Alkaid*	1·9	13 47·1	+49 22	B3
β Centauri *Hadar*	0·6	14 03·1	−60 19	B1
θ Centauri	2·1	14 06·1	−36 19	K0
α Boötis *Arcturus*	0·0	14 15·2	+19 14	K0
α Centauri *Rigil Kent*	0·1	14 38·9	−60 48	G0
ε Boötis	2·4	14 44·5	+27 07	K0
β Ursæ Minoris *Kochab*	2·1	14 50·7	+74 12	K5
α Coronæ Borealis *Alphecca*	2·2	15 34·2	+26 45	A0
δ Scorpii	2·3	15 59·7	−22 36	B0
β Scorpii	2·6	16 04·8	−19 47	B1
α Scorpii *Antares*	1·0	16 28·8	−26 25	M0
α Trianguli Australis	1·9	16 47·5	−69 01	K2
ε Scorpii	2·3	16 49·5	−34 16	K0
α Herculis*	Var.	17 14·2	+14 24	M3
λ Scorpii	1·6	17 32·9	−37 06	B2
α Ophiuchi *Rasalhague*	2·1	17 34·4	+12 34	A5
θ Scorpii	1·9	17 36·6	−43 00	F0
κ Scorpii	2·4	17 41·8	−39 02	B2
γ Draconis	2·2	17 56·4	+51 29	K5
ε Sagittarii *Kaus Australis*	1·9	18 23·5	−34 23	A0
α Lyræ *Vega*	0·0	18 36·6	+38 46	A0
σ Sagittarii	2·0	18 54·6	−26 19	B3
β Cygni *Albireo*	3·1	19 30·3	+27 56	K0
α Aquilæ *Altair*	0·8	19 50·3	+ 8 50	A5
α Capricorni	3·8	20 17·5	−12 35	G5
γ Cygni	2·2	20 21·9	+40 13	F8p
α Pavonis	1·9	20 24·8	−56 46	B3
α Cygni *Deneb*	1·3	20 41·1	+45 15	A2p
α Cephei *Alderamin*	2·4	21 18·3	+62 32	A5
ε Pegasi	2·4	21 43·7	+ 9 50	K0
δ Capricorni	2·9	21 46·5	−16 11	A5
α Gruis	1·7	22 07·6	−47 01	B5
δ Cephei*	3·7	22 28·8	+58 22	*
β Gruis	2·1	22 42·0	−46 56	M3
α Piscis Austrini *Fomalhaut*	1·2	22 57·1	−29 41	A3
β Pegasi *Scheat*	2·4	23 03·3	+28 02	M0
α Pegasi *Markab*	2·5	23 04·2	+15 09	A0

* α Herculis, mag. 3·1 to 3·9.

δ Cephei, mag. 3·7 to 4·4, Spectrum F5 to G0.

Thus in London (Lat. 51° 30′) the meridian altitude of *Sirius* is found as follows:

	°	′
Altitude of equator	38	30
Declination south	16	42
Difference	21	48

The altitude of *Capella* (Dec. +45° 59′) at lower transit is:

Altitude of pole	51	30
Polar distance of star	44	01
Difference	7	29

The brightness of a heavenly body is denoted by its magnitude. Omitting the exceptionally bright stars *Sirius* and *Canopus*, the twenty brightest stars are of the first magnitude, while the faintest stars visible to the naked eye are of the sixth magnitude. The magnitude scale is a precise one, as a difference of five magnitudes represents a ratio of 100 to 1 in brightness. Typical second magnitude stars are *Polaris* and the stars in the Belt of Orion. The scale is most easily fixed in memory by comparing the stars with Norton's *Star Atlas* (see page 64). The stars *Sirius* and *Canopus* and the planets Venus and Jupiter are so bright that their magnitudes are expressed by negative numbers. A small telescope will show stars down to the ninth or tenth magnitude, while stars fainter than the twentieth magnitude may be photographed by long exposures with the largest telescopes.

Some of the astronomical information in this ALMANACK has been taken from *Astronomical Phenomena*, and is published here by arrangement with, and with the permission of, the Controller of H.M. Stationery Office.

ELEMENTS OF THE SOLAR SYSTEM

Orb	Mean Distance from Sun (Earth=1)	Mean Distance from Sun km. 10⁶	Sidereal Period	Synodic Period	Incl. of Orbit to Ecliptic	Diameter	Mass (Earth=1)	Period of Rotation on Axis
			y d	Days	° '	km.		d h m
Sun	...	...	...	...	...	1,392,000	332,948	25 09
Mercury	0·39	58	88	116	7 00	4,880	0·055	59
Venus	0·72	108	225	584	3 24	12,100	0·815	243
Earth	1·00	150	1 0	...	...	12,756eq.	1·00	23 56
Mars	1·52	228	1 322	780	1 51	6,790	0·107	24 37
Jupiter	5·20	778	11 315	399	1 18	{142,800eq. / 134,200p.	318	{9 50 / 9 56
Saturn	9·54	1427	29 167	378	2 29	{120,000eq. / 108,000p.	95	{10 14 / 10 38
Uranus	19·19	2870	84 6	370	0 46	52,000	14·6	16–28
Neptune	30·07	4497	164 288	367	1 46	48,400	17·2	18–20
Pluto	39·46	5950	247 255	367	17 09	3,000?	0·01	6 09

THE SATELLITES

Name	Star Mag.	Mean distance from Primary	Sidereal Period of Revolution	Name	Star mag.	Mean distance from Primary	Sidereal Period of Revolution
Earth		km.	d	*Saturn*		km.	d
Moon	—	384,400	27·322	Janus	14	151,000	0·695
				Epimetheus	15	151,000	0·694
Mars				Mimas	13	186,000	0·942
Phobos	12	9,400	0·319	Enceladus	12	238,000	1·370
Deimos	13	23,500	1·262	Tethys	10	295,000	1·888
				Telesto	19	295,000	1·888
Jupiter				Calypso	18	295,000	1·888
XVI. Metis	17	128,000	0·295	Dione	10	377,000	2·737
XV. Adrastea	19	129,000	0·298	—	18	377,000	2·737
V. Amalthea	14	181,000	0·498	Rhea	10	527,000	4·518
XIV. Thebe	15	222,000	0·675	Titan	8	1,222,000	15·945
I. Io	5	422,000	1·769	Hyperion	14	1,481,000	21·277
II. Europa	5	671,000	3·551	Iapetus	11	3,561,000	79·331
III. Ganymede	5	1,070,000	7·155	Phoebe	16	12,954,000	550·4
IV. Callisto	6	1,880,000	16·689				
XIII. Leda	20	11,090,000	239	*Uranus*			
VI. Himalia	15	11,480,000	251	Miranda	17	129,000	1·414
X. Lysithea	18	11,720,000	259	Ariel	14	191,000	2·520
VII. Elara	17	11,740,000	260	Umbriel	15	266,000	4·144
XII. Ananke	19	21,200,000	631	Titania	14	436,000	8·706
XI. Carme	18	22,600,000	692	Oberon	14	583,000	13·463
VIII. Pasiphae	18	23,500,000	735				
IX. Sinope	18	23,700,000	758	*Neptune*			
				Triton	14	355,000	5·877
Saturn				Nereid	19	5,510,000	360·21
Atlas	18	138,000	0·602				
—	16	139,000	0·613	*Pluto*			
—	16	142,000	0·629	Charon	17	19,700	6·387

THE EARTH

The shape of the Earth is that of an oblate spheroid or solid of revolution whose meridian sections are ellipses not differing much from circles, whilst the sections at right angles are circles. The length of the equatorial axis is about 12,756 kilometres, and that of the polar axis is 12,714 kilometres. The mean density of the Earth is 5·5 times that of water, although that of the surface layer is less. The Earth and Moon revolve about their common centre of gravity in a lunar month; this centre in turn revolves round the Sun in a plane known as the ecliptic, that passes through the Sun's centre. The Earth's equator is inclined to this plane at an angle of $23\frac{1}{2}°$. This tilt is the cause of the seasons. In mid-latitudes, and when the Sun is high above the Equator, not only does the high noon altitude make the days longer, but the Sun's rays fall more directly on the Earth's surface; these effects combine to produce summer. In equatorial regions the noon altitude is large throughout the year, and there is little variation in the length of the day. In higher latitudes the noon altitude is lower, and the days in summer are appreciably longer than those in winter.

The average velocity of the Earth in its orbit is 30 kilometres a second. It makes a complete rotation on its axis in about $23^h 56^m$ of mean time, which is the sidereal day. Because of its annual revolution round the Sun, the rotation with respect to the Sun, or the solar day, is more than this by about four minutes (*see* p. 66). The extremity of the axis of rotation, or the North Pole of the Earth, is not rigidly fixed, but wanders over an area roughly 20 metres in diameter.

TERRESTRIAL MAGNETISM

A magnetic compass points along the horizontal component of a magnetic line of force. These directions converge on the "magnetic dip-poles". At these poles a freely suspended magnetized needle would become vertical. Not only do the positions of these poles change with time, but their exact location is ill-defined, particularly so in the case of the north dip-pole where the lines of force, on the north side of it, instead of converging radially, tend to bunch into a channel. Although it is therefore unrealistic to attempt to specify the locations of the dip-poles exactly, the present adopted positions are $77°\cdot0$ N., $102°\cdot4$ W. and $65°\cdot3$ S., $139°\cdot2$ E. The two magnetic dip-poles are thus not antipodal, the line joining them passing the centre of the Earth at a distance of about 1,200 kilometres. The distances of the magnetic dip-poles from the north and south geographical poles are about 1,400 and 2,700 kilometres respectively.

There is also a "magnetic equator", at all points of which the vertical force is zero and a magnetized needle remains horizontal. This line runs between $2°$ and $10°$ north of the geographical equator in the eastern hemisphere, turns sharply south off the West African coast, and crosses South America through Brazil, Bolivia and Peru; it recrosses the geographical equator in mid-Pacific.

Reference has already been made to secular changes in the Earth's field. The following table indicates the changes in magnetic declination (or variation of the compass). Similar, though much smaller, changes have occurred in "dip" or magnetic inclination. Secular changes differ throughout the world. Although the London observations strongly suggest a cycle of several hundred years, an exact repetition is unlikely.

London				Greenwich			
1580	11°	15′	E.	1850	22°	24′	W.
1622	5	56	E.	1900	16	29	W.
1665	1	22	W.	1925	13	10	W.
1730	13	00	W.	1950	9	07	W.
1773	21	09	W.	1975	6	39	W.

In order that up-to-date information on the variation of the compass may be available, many governments publish magnetic charts on which there are lines (called isogonic) passing through all places at which specified values of declination will be found at the date of the chart.

In the British Isles, isogonic lines now run approximately north-east to south-west. Though there are considerable local deviations due to geological causes, a rough value of magnetic declination may be obtained by assuming that at 50° N. on the meridian of Greenwich, the value in 1989 is 4° 24′ west and allowing an increase of 10′ for each degree of latitude northwards and one of 25′ for each degree of longitude westwards. For example, at 53° N., 5° W., declination will be about 4° 24′ + 30′ + 125′, i.e. 6° 59′ west. The average annual change at the present time is about 9′ decrease.

The number of magnetic observatories now approaches 200—widely scattered over the globe. There are three in Great Britain maintained by the Government: at Hartland, North Devon, at Eskdalemuir in Dumfriesshire, Scotland, and at Lerwick, Shetland Islands. Some recent annual mean values of the magnetic elements for Hartland are given below.

The normal worldwide terrestrial magnetic field corresponds approximately to that of a very strong small bar magnet near the centre of the Earth but with appreciable smooth spatial departures. The origin and slow secular change of the normal field is not yet fully understood but is generally ascribed to electric currents associated with fluid motions within the Earth's core. Superposed on the normal field are local and regional anomalies whose magnitudes may in places exceed that of the normal field; these are due to the influence of mineral deposits in the Earth's crust. A small proportion of the field is of external origin, mostly associated with electric currents in the ionosphere. The configuration of the external field and the ionization of the atmosphere depend on the incident particle and radiation flux. There are, therefore, short-term and non-periodic as well as diurnal, 27-day, seasonal and 11-year periodic changes in the magnetic field, dependent upon the position of the Sun and the degree of solar activity.

Year	Declina-tion West	Dip or Inclina-tion	Hori-zontal Force	Vertical Force
	° ′	° ′	oersted	oersted
1950	11 06	66 54	0·1848	0·4334
1955	10 30	66 49	0·1859	0·4340
1960	9 59	66 44	0·1871	0·4350
1965	9 30	66 34	0·1887	0·4354
1970	9 06	66 26	0·1903	0·4364
1975	8 32	66 17	0·1921	0·4373
1980	7 44	66 10	0·1933	0·4377
1985	6 56	66 08	0·1938	0·4380
1987	6 39	66 08	0·1939	0·4382

Magnetic Storms. Occasionally—sometimes with great suddenness—the Earth's magnetic field is subject for several hours to marked disturbance. In extreme cases, departures in field intensity as much as one tenth the normal value are experienced. In many instances, such disturbances are accompanied by widespread displays of aurorae, marked changes in the incidence of cosmic rays, an increase in the reception of "noise" from the Sun at radio frequencies together with rapid changes in the ionosphere and induced electric currents within the earth which adversely affect radio and telegraphic communications. The disturbances are generally ascribed to flux changes in the stream of neutral and ionized particles which emanates from the Sun and through which the Earth is continuously passing. Some of these changes are associated with visible eruptions on the

Sun, usually in the region of sun-spots. There is a marked tendency for disturbances to recur after intervals of about 27 days, the apparent period of rotation of the Sun on its axis, which is consistent with the sources being located on particular areas of the Sun.

Artificial Satellites Launched in 1987

Designation	Satellite	Launch date	i	P	e	Perigee height (km)
1987–		1987				
01	Meteor 2-15, rocket	January 5	82·5	104·1	0·001	942
02	Cosmos 1811, rocket	January 9	64·8	89·7	0·013	172
03	Cosmos 1812, rocket	January 14	82·5	97·8	0·002	635
04	Cosmos 1813, rocket, engine	January 15	72·8	92·3	0·004	356
05	Progress 27, rocket	January 16	51·6	90·0	0·006	240
06	Cosmos 1814, rocket	January 21	74·1	100·7	0·003	771
07	Cosmos 1815, rocket	January 22	50·7	93·5	0·015	345
08	Molniya 3–31, launcher rocket, launcher, rocket	January 22	62·8	735·9	0·748	438
09	Cosmos 1816, rocket	January 29	82·9	104·9	0·003	965
10	Cosmos 1817, launcher	January 30	51·6	89·1	0·003	212
11	Cosmos 1818, rocket	February 1	65·0	100·7	0·001	786
12	Ginga, rocket	February 5	31·1	96·7	0·014	515
13	Soyuz TM2, rocket	February 5	51·6	90·1	0·003	263
14	Cosmos 1819, rocket, engine	February 7	72·8	89·2	0·003	209
15	SDS 11(?), rocket	February 12	?	?	?	?
16	Cosmos 1820, rocket	February 14	64·8	88·8	0·005	179
17	Cosmos 1821, rocket	February 18	82·9	105·0	0·004	963
18	Momo 1, rocket	February 19	99·1	103·3	0·000	910
19	Cosmos 1822, rocket, engine	February 19	72·8	89·7	0·004	228
20	Cosmos 1823, rocket	February 20	73·6	116·1	0·003	1479
21	Cosmos 1824, rocket	February 26	67·1	89·6	0·013	167
22	GOES 7	February 26	0·5	1436·1	0·005	35583
23	Progress 28, rocket	March 3	51·6	90·4	0·006	257
24	Cosmos 1825, rocket	March 3	82·5	97·7	0·002	632
25	Cosmos 1826, rocket, engine	March 11	72·9	90·3	0·014	194
26	Cosmos 1827–1832, rocket	March 13	82·6	113·9	0·001	1396
27	Cosmos 1833, rocket	March 18	71·0	102·0	0·000	849
28	Reduga 20, launcher	March 19	1·2	1436·0	0·000	35768
29	Palapa 5	March 20	0·1	1436·0	0·001	35763
30	Kvant	March 31	51·6	89·1	0·010	170
31	Cosmos 1834, rocket	April 8	65·0	92·8	0·001	404
32	Cosmos 1835, rocket	April 9	64·8	89·6	0·013	171
33	Cosmos 1836, rocket	April 16	64·8	89·8	0·004	241
34	Progress 29, rocket	April 21	51·6	90·3	0·010	221
35	Cosmos 1837, rocket, engine	April 22	82·3	89·3	0·002	226
36	Cosmos 1838–1840	April 24	64·8	312·2	0·569	191
37	Cosmos 1841, rocket, engine	April 24	62·8	90·5	0·012	217
38	Cosmos 1842, rocket	April 27	82·5	97·8	0·002	634
39	Cosmos 1843, rocket, engine	May 5	70·3	89·4	0·006	205
40	Gorizont 14, launcher	May 11	0·9	1436·0	0·000	35781
41	Cosmos 1844, rocket	May 13	71·0	102·0	0·000	849
42	Cosmos 1845, rocket, engine	May 13	70·4	90·4	0·013	207
43	NOSS 8, rocket, USA 23–25	May 15	?	?	?	?
44	Progress 30, rocket	May 19	51·6	90·8	0·004	288
45	Cosmos 1846, rocket, engine	May 21	82·3	89·2	0·008	181
46	Cosmos 1847, rocket	May 26	67·1	89·6	0·014	162
47	Cosmos 1848, rocket, engine	May 28	72·8	90·2	0·012	203
48	Cosmos 1849, launcher, launcher rocket, rocket	June 4	62·9	717·8	0·736	627
49	Cosmos 1850, rocket	June 9	74·0	100·8	0·002	783
50	Cosmos 1851, launcher rocket, launcher, rocket	June 12	62·9	717·7	0·737	611

Artificial Satellites Launched in 1987—(*cont.*)

Desig-nation	Satellite	Launch date	i	P	e	Perigee height (km)
1987–		1987				
51	Cosmos 1852–1859, rocket	June 16	74·0	115·7	0·002	1473
52	Cosmos 1860, rocket, platform	June 18	65·0	104·0	0·000	945
53	DMSP 2–03	June 20	98·8	102·0	0·001	840
54	Cosmos 1861, rocket	June 23	82·9	105·0	0·001	985
55	Cosmos 1862, rocket	July 1	82·5	97·8	0·002	633
56	Cosmos 1863, rocket, engine	July 4	72·9	92·3	0·004	357
57	Cosmos 1864, rocket	July 6	82·9	104·8	0·003	961
58	Cosmos 1865, rocket	July 8	64·7	89·3	0·005	208
59	Cosmos 1866, rocket	July 9	67·2	89·8	0·014	166
60	Cosmos 1867, rocket	July 10	65·0	100·7	0·001	786
61	Cosmos 1868, rocket	July 14	74·0	94·6	0·031	284
62	Cosmos 1869, rocket	July 16	82·5	97·8	0·002	634
63	Soyuz TM3, rocket	July 22	51·6	89·9	0·005	236
64	Cosmos 1870	July 25	71·9	89·4	0·001	237
65	Cosmos 1871, rocket	August 1	97·0	88·3	0·002	177
66	Progress 31, rocket	August 3	51·6	90·2	0·003	268
67	China 20, rocket	August 5	62·9	90·2	0·017	171
68	Meteor 2–16, rocket	August 18	82·6	104·2	0·001	944
69	Cosmos 1872, rocket, engine	August 19	72·9	89·3	0·002	225
70	Kiku 5	August 27	0·1	1435·9	0·000	35779
71	Cosmos 1873, rocket	August 28	64·8	88·8	0·005	178
72	Cosmos 1874, rocket, engine	September 3	72·9	89·7	0·005	226
73	Ekram 16, launcher	September 3	0·4	1435·7	0·000	35769
74	Cosmos 1875–1880, rocket	September 7	82·6	113·8	0·002	1387
75	China 21, rocket	September 9	63·0	89·7	0·008	206
76	Cosmos 1881, rocket	September 11	64·8	89·6	0·003	231
77	Cosmos 1882, rocket, engine	September 15	82·3	89·9	0·002	256
78	Aussat 3, ECS 4	September 16	0·0	1436·0	0·000	35779
79	Cosmos 1883–1885, launcher	September 16	64·9	675·7	0·001	19110
80	Transit 21–22	September 16	90·3	107·3	0·011	1017
81	Cosmos 1886, rocket	September 17	67·1	89·8	0·014	167
82	Progress 32, rocket	September 23	51·6	90·1	0·008	229
83	Cosmos 1887, rocket	September 29	62·8	90·5	0·013	216
84	Cosmos 1888, launcher	October 1	1·4	1435·9	0·000	35765
85	Cosmos 1889, rocket, engine	October 9	70·0	92·2	0·005	348
86	Cosmos 1890, rocket	October 10	65·0	92·8	0·001	403
87	Cosmos 1891, rocket	October 14	82·9	105·0	0·005	954
88	Cosmos 1892, rocket	October 20	82·5	97·8	0·002	635
89	Cosmos 1893, rocket	October 22	67·2	89·6	0·013	167
90	USA 27, rocket	October 26	?	?	?	?

SATELLITE ORBITS

To consider the orbit of an artificial satellite it is best to imagine that one is looking at the Earth from a distant point in space. The Earth would then be seen to be rotating about its axis inside the orbit described by the rapidly revolving satellite. The inclination of a satellite orbit to the Earth's equator (which generally remains almost constant throughout the satellite's lifetime) gives at once the maximum range of latitudes over which the satellite passes. Thus a satellite whose orbit has an inclination of 53° will pass overhead all latitudes between S. 53° and N. 53°, but would never be seen in the zenith of any place nearer the poles than these latitudes. If we consider a particular place on the earth, whose latitude is less than the inclination of the satellite's orbit then the Earth's rotation carries this place first under the northbound part of the orbit and then under the southbound position of the orbit, these two occurrences being always less than 12 hours apart for satellites moving in direct orbits (i.e. to the east). (For satellites in retrograde orbits the words "northbound" and "southbound" should be interchanged in the preceding statement.) As the value of the latitude of the observer increases and approaches the value of the inclination of the orbit, so this interval gets shorter until (when the latitude is equal to the inclination) only one overhead passage occurs each day.

SATELLITE LAUNCHINGS

Apart from their names, e.g. Cosmos 6 Rocket, the satellites are also classified according to their date of launch. Thus 1961 α refers to the first satellite launching of 1961. A number following the Greek letter indicated the relative brightness of the satellites put in orbit. From the beginning of 1963 the Greek letters were replaced by numbers and the numbers by roman letters e.g. 1963–01A. In this table are given the designation and names of the main objects in orbit (in the order A, B, C ... etc.), the launch date and some initial orbital data. These are the inclination to the equator (i), the nodal period of revolution (P), the eccentricity, e, and the perigee height.

OBSERVATION OF SATELLITES

The regression of the orbit around the Earth causes alternate periods of visibility and invisibility, though this is of little concern to the radio or radar observer. To the visual observer the following cycle of events normally occurs (though the cycle may start in any position): invisibility, morning observations before dawn, invisibility, evening observations after dusk, invisibility, morning observations before dawn, and so on. With reasonably high satellites and for observers in high latitudes around the summer solstice the evening observations follow the morning observations without interruption as sunlight passing over the polar regions can still illuminate satellites which are passing over temperate latitudes at local midnight. At the moment all satellites rely on sunlight to make them visible though a satellite with a flashing light has been suggested for a future launching. The observer must be in darkness or twilight in order to make any useful observations and the durations of twilight and the sunrise, sunset times given on page 2 of each month will be a useful guide.

Some of the satellites are visible to the naked eye and much interest has been aroused by the spectacle of a bright satellite disappearing into the Earth's shadow. The event is even more fascinating telescopically as the disappearance occurs gradually as the satellite traverses the Earth's penumbral shadow, and during the last few seconds before the eclipse is complete the satellite may change colour (under suitable atmospheric conditions) from yellow to red. This is because the last rays of sunlight are refracted through the denser layers of our atmosphere before striking the satellite.

Some satellites rotate about one or more axes so that a periodic variation in brightness is observed. This was particularly noticeable in several of the U.S.S.R. satellites.

Satellite research has provided some interesting results. Among them may be mentioned a revised value of the Earth's oblateness, 1/298·2, and the discovery of the Van Allen radiation belts.

ROYAL OBSERVATORIES

Royal Greenwich Observatory
Herstmonceux, East Sussex, BN27 1RP
[0323 833171]

The Royal Observatory was founded at Greenwich by Charles II in 1675. Because of smog and light pollution, the Observatory was moved to Herstmonceux in East Sussex after the Second World War. The traditional work in positional astronomy remains an important activity of the Observatory. The well-known "Greenwich 6 pips" are sent from Herstmonceux to the B.B.C. by land line. The rate of rotation of the Earth and other geophysical parameters are monitored by the satellite laser ranging telescope. Various almanacs and other astronomical data are prepared by H.M. Nautical Almanac Office, which is part of the Royal Greenwich Observatory. However, as an establishment of the Science and Engineering Research Council, the main task of the Observatory now is the provision of facilities for research in optical astronomy for astronomers in the universities. In particular, this involves the running of the Isaac Newton group of telescopes with its associated instrumentation at the Roque de los Muchachos Observatory on the island of La Palma in the Canary Islands. This group comprises the 4·2 m. William Herschel telescope, the 2·5 m. Isaac Newton telescope and the 1·0 m Jacobus Kapteyn telescope. The running of these is shared with the Netherlands, and, in the case of the Jacobus Kapteyn telescope, with the Republic of Ireland also. At Herstmonceux, there are facilities for the processing of astronomical data obtained from the telescopes on La Palma and elsewhere; these include a node of the STARLINK computing network. The Royal Greenwich Observatory is to move from Herstmonceux to Cambridge. Relocation will take until at least 1990.
Dir., Prof. A. Boksenberg, F.R.S.

Royal Observatory
Blackford Hill, Edinburgh EH9 3HJ

The Observatory was founded by the Astronomical Institution in 1818 and its Royal Charter dates from 1822. It is now responsible for some major national astronomical facilities funded by the Science and Engineering Research Council, including a 1·2 m. Schmidt telescope in Australia, a 15·0 m. millimetre-wave telescope and a 3·8 m. infra-red telescope in Hawaii and COSMOS, a fast automatic plate measuring machine, in Edinburgh. The Observatory is also part of the U.K. Starlink network for astronomical image and data processing. The Observatory specializes in the development of advanced technologies and the application of these to studies of the properties of matter in extreme environments in space.
Dir., and Astronomer Royal for Scotland, Prof. M. S. Longair.

Stations whose latest reports are
broadcast in the 5 min. forecasts

BL   Butt of Lewis
C   Channel Light-Vessel
D   Dowsing
J   Jersey
LE   Land's End
M   Malin Head
R   Ronaldsway
RS   Royal Sovereign
SA   St. Abb's Head
Su   Sumburgh
T   Tiree
V   Dover
Va   Valentia

TIDAL CONSTANTS

The time of high water at the undermentioned Ports and Places may be *approximately* found by taking the appropriate Time of High Water at the Standard Port (as shown on pp. 86, 87, etc.) and adding thereto the quantities annexed. The columns headed "Springs" and "Neaps" show the height of the tide above datum for Mean High Water Springs and Mean High Water Neaps respectively.

EXAMPLE.—Required times of high water at Stranraer on *January* 1, 1989:—

(a) *Morning Tide.*		(b) *Afternoon Tide.*	
Appropriate time of high		Appropriate time of high	
water at *Greenock*	0629 hrs. (*Jan.* 1)	water at *Greenock*	1826 hrs. (*Jan* 1).
Tidal difference	−0020 hrs.	Tidal difference	−0020 hrs.
H.W at *Stranraer* ...	0609 hrs.	H.W. at *Stranraer* ..	1806 hrs.

Port	Diff.	Springs	Neaps	Port	Diff.	Springs	Neaps
	h.m.	metres	metres		h.m.	metres	metres
Aberdeen......... *Leith*	−1 19	4·3	3·4	Coulport ...... *Greenock*	−0 05	3·4	2·9
Aberdovey..... *Liverpool*	−3 00	5·0	3·5	Coverack .... *Avonmouth*	−2 02	5·3	4·2
Aberystwyth .. *Liverpool*	−3 30	5·0	3·5	Cowes.......... *London*	−2 23	4·2	3·5
Aldeburgh...... *London*	−3 05	2·8	2·7	Cromarty.......... *Leith*	−2 56	4·3	3·4
Alloa.............. *Leith*	+0 47	5·6	4·2	Cromer.......... *Hull*	+0 19	5·2	4·1
Amlwch....... *Liverpool*	−0 33	7·3	5·8	Dartmouth ..... *London*	+4 37	4·7	3·8
Anstruther Easter . *Leith*	−0 22	5·5	4·4	Deal .... *London*	−2 37	6·1	5·0
Antwerp .... *London*	+0 50	5·8	4·2	Dieppe .... *London*	−3 03	9·3	7·2
Appledore ... *Avonmouth*	−1 15	7·5	5·2	Dingle Hbr.... *Liverpool*	+5 38	3·9	2·9
Arbroath......... *Leith*	−0 33	5·0	4·1	Donegal Hbr.... *Liverpool*	−5 24	3·9	3·0
Ardrossan .... *Greenock*	−0 15	3·2	2·7	Douglas .... *Liverpool*	−0 04	6·9	5·4
†Arundel...... *London*	−2 03	3·1	2·2	Dover .... *London*	−2 52	6·7	5·3
Avonmouth ....*A'mouth*	0 00	13·2	10·0	Duclair......... *London*	−1 13	7·7	6·5
Ayr .... *Greenock*	−0 25	3·0	2·6	Duddon Bar ... *Liverpool*	+0 03	8·5	6·6
Baie de Lampaul . *London*	+2 30	7·5	5·8	Dunbar .... *Leith*	−0 07	5·2	4·2
Ballycotton.. *Avonmouth*	−1 43	4·2	3·3	Dundalk (Sldr's Pt) *L'pool*	+0 22	5·1	4·2
Banff.............. *Leith*	−2 44	3·5	2·8	Dundee .... *Leith*	+0 11	5·3	4·3
Bantry ...... *Liverpool*	+5 59	3·5	2·6	Dungeness....... *London*	−3 04	7·7	5·9
Bardsey Island . *Liverpool*	−3 18	4·5	3·3	Dunkirk ...... *London*	−1 54	5·8	4·8
Barmouth ..... *Liverpool*	−2 57	5·0	3·5	Eastbourne ..... *London*	−2 50	7·3	5·6
Barnstaple .. *Avonmouth*	−1 00	4·1	1·4	East Loch Tarbert *G'nock*	+0 05	3·4	2·9
Barrow .... *Liverpool*	+0 15	9·1	7·1	Exmouth Dock .. *London*	+4 55	4·0	2·8
Barry .... *Avonmouth*	−0 22	11·4	8·7	Eyemouth .... *Leith*	−0 20	4·7	3·7
Belfast .... *London*	−2 45	3·5	3·0	Falmouth ...... *London*	+3 35	5·3	4·2
Berwick .... *Leith*	−0 02	4·7	3·8	Ferryside.... *Avonmouth*	−0 58	6·7	4·5
Bideford..... *Avonmouth*	−1 15	5·9	3·6	Filey Bay .... *Leith*	+1 50	5·8	4·9
Blackpool ..... *Liverpool*	−0 10	8·9	7·0	Fishguard ..... *Liverpool*	−4 00	4·8	3·4
Blacktoft .... *Hull*	+0 32	5·7	3·9	Flushing ...... *London*	−0 40	4·9	4·0
Blakeney .... *Hull*	+0 44	3·4	2·0	Folkestone ..... *London*	−3 04	7·1	5·7
Blyth .... *Leith*	+0 50	5·0	3·9	Formby ...... *Liverpool*	−0 12	9·0	7·3
Boscastle .... *Avonmouth*	−1 20	7·3	5·6	Fowey .... *London*	+3 53	5·4	4·3
Boulogne....... *London*	−2 44	8·9	7·2	Fraserburgh ...... *Leith*	−2 19	3·9	3·1
Bovisand Pier... *London*	+3 55	5·3	4·3	*Freshwater Bay *London*	−4 33	2·6	2·3
Bowling .... *Greenock*	+0 15	4·0	3·4	Galway ...... *Liverpool*	−6 08	5·1	3·9
Braye .... *London*	+5 33	6·3	4·7	Glasgow ...... *Greenock*	+0 28	4·7	4·1
Brest.......... *London*	+2 28	7·5	5·9	Goole .... *Hull*	+0 59	5·7	3·7
Bridgwater . *Avonmouth*	−0 22	4·6	1·9	Gorleston ...... *London*	−5 00	2·4	2·0
Bridlington........ *Leith*	+2 03	6·1	4·7	Granton.......... *Leith*	0 00	5·6	4·5
Bridport .... *London*	+4 37	4·1	3·0	Granville...... *London*	+4 32	12·8	9·6
Brighton .. *London*	−2 50	6·5	5·1	Grimsby.......... *Hull*	−0 28	7·0	5·6
Buckie .... *Leith*	−2 56	4·1	3·2	Hartlepool......... *Leith*	+0 58	5·1	4·0
Bude Haven . *Avonmouth*	−1 33	7·7	5·8	Harwich .... *London*	−2 02	4·0	3·4
Bull Sand Fort ..... *Hull*	−0 46	6·9	5·5	Hastings .... *London*	−2 57	7·5	5·8
Burntisland ...... *Leith*	0 00	5·6	4·5	Haverfordwest . *Liverpool*	−4 50	2·2	0·3
Calais.......... *London*	−2 04	7·2	6·0	Hestan Islet .. *Liverpool*	+0 25	8·3	6·3
Campbeltown .. *Greenock*	+0 07	2·9	2·6	Hilbre Island... *Liverpool*	−0 13	9·0	7·2
Cape Cornwall ..*A'mouth*	−2 30	6·0	4·3	Holyhead ..... *Liverpool*	−0 48	5·7	4·5
Cardiff ...... *Avonmouth*	−0 15	12·2	9·4	Hook of Holland . *London*	−0 01	2·3	1·8
Cardigan, Port . *Liverpool*	−3 37	4·7	3·4	*Hurst Point .. *London*	−3 38	2·7	2·3
Carmarthen . *Avonmouth*	−0 48	2·6	0·4	Ijmuiden .... *London*	+1 04	2·0	1·7
Cayeux....... *London*	−2 55	10·2	7·9	Ilfracombe .. *Avonmouth*	−1 10	9·2	6·9
Chatham(N.Lock)*London*	−1 10	6·0	4·9	Inveraray ..... *Greenock*	+0 11	3·3	3·0
Chepstow.... *Avonmouth*	+0 20	No Data		Invergordon....... *Leith*	−2 49	4·4	3·5
Cherbourg...... *London*	−6 00	6·3	5·0	Ipswich .... *London*	−1 42	4·2	3·4
Chester ..... *Liverpool*	+1 05	4·0	2·0	Itchenor .... *London*	−2 23	4·8	3·8
Chichester Hbr. . *London*	−2 25	4·9	4·0	Kinsale ...... *Liverpool*	−6 03	4·1	3·2
Christchurch Hbr. *L'don*	−4 53	1·8	1·4	Kirkcudbright . *Liverpool*	+0 15	7·5	5·9
Cobh .... *Liverpool*	−5 56	4·1	3·3	Kirkwall .... *Leith*	−4 15	2·9	2·2

† Very Approximate.   * 1st H.W. (Springs).

Port	Diff.	Springs	Neaps	Port	Diff.	Springs	Neaps
	h.m.	metres	metres		h.m.	metres	metres
Knights Town . *Liverpool*	+5 36	3.9	3.0	Ramsey (I.O.M.) *Liverpool*	+0 04	7.2	5.7
Lamlash....... *Greenock*	−0 26	3.2	2.7	Ramsgate....... *London*	−2 32	4.9	3.8
Le Havre .... *London*	−3 55	7.8	6.5	†Rosslare...... *Liverpool*	−5 23	1.9	1.4
Lerwick ....*Leith*	−3 49	2.2	1.6	Rosyth ....*Leith*	+0 07	5.8	4.7
Limerick Dock . *Liverpool*	−4 24	5.9	4.5	Ryde .... *London*	−2 23	4.5	3.7
Littlehampton .. *London*	−2 33	5.5	4.3	St. Helier .... *London*	+4 48	11.1	8.1
Lizard Point . *Avonmouth*	−2 17	5.3	4.2	St. Ives ... *Avonmouth*	−1 55	6.6	4.9
Llanddwyn Island *L'pool*	−1 53	5.0	4.0	St. Malo ...... *London*	+4 27	12.1	9.1
Llanelli ..... *Avonmouth*	−0 56	7.8	5.8	St. Peter Port ... *London*	+4 54	9.0	6.7
Loch Moidart .. *Greenock*	+6 00	4.8	3.5	Salcombe .... *London*	+4 10	5.3	4.1
Londonderry ... *London*	−5 37	2.7	2.0	Saltash......... *London*	+4 10	5.6	4.5
Looe .... *London*	+3 55	5.4	4.2	Scarborough.......*Leith*	+1 33	5.7	4.6
Lossiemouth ....*Leith*	−3 01	4.1	3.2	Scheveningen... *London*	+0 24	2.1	1.8
Lowestoft ...... *London*	−4 25	2.4	2.1	Scrabster........*Leith*	+6 04	5.0	3.7
Lulworth Cove.. *London*	+5 00	2.3	1.5	Seaham ....*Leith*	+0 53	5.2	4.1
Lundy Island *Avonmouth*	−1 23	8.0	5.9	Selsey Bill ...... *London*	−2 28	5.3	4.4
Lyme Regis ..... *London*	+4 55	4.3	3.1	Sennen Cove . *Avonmouth*	−2 30	6.1	4.8
*Lymington .... *London*	−3 33	3.0	2.6	Sharpness Dock .*A'mouth*	+0 42	9.3	5.8
Margate .... *London*	−1 52	4.8	3.9	Sheerness ...... *London*	−1 16	5.7	4.8
Maryport...... *Liverpool*	+0 24	8.6	6.6	Shoreham ...... *London*	−2 43	6.2	5.0
Menai Bridge .. *Liverpool*	−0 28	7.4	5.9	Silloth .... *Liverpool*	+0 35	9.2	7.1
Mevagissey ..... *London*	+3 53	5.4	4.3	Southampton ... *London*	−2 52	4.5	3.7
Middlesbrough.....*Leith*	+1 09	5.6	4.5	Southend....... *London*	−1 22	5.7	4.8
Milford Haven . *Liverpool*	−5 07	7.0	5.2	Southwold...... *London*	−3 50	2.5	2.2
Minehead ... *Avonmouth*	−0 40	10.6	8.1	Stirling ....*Leith*	+1 13	2.9	1.6
Montrose..........*Leith*	−0 19	4.8	3.9	Stonehaven........*Leith*	−1 09	4.5	3.6
Morecambe..., *Liverpool*	+0 01	9.5	7.6	Stornoway ....*Liverpool*	−4 15	4.8	3.7
Mostyn Quay .. *Liverpool*	+0 17	8.5	6.7	Stranraer ..... *Greenock*	0 20	3.0	2.5
Newburgh ....*Leith*	+0 48	4.1	3.0	Stromness ....*Leith*	−5 34	3.6	2.7
Newcastle on Tyne . *Leith*	+0 54	5.3	4.1	Sunderland ....*Leith*	+0 51	5.2	4.2
Newhaven...... *London*	−2 48	6.6	5.2	*Swanage ......*Leith*	−5 13	2.0	1.6
Newlyn .... *Avonmouth*	−2 24	5.6	4.4	Swansea..... *Avonmouth*	−0 49	9.6	7.3
Newport(Gwent)*A'mouth*	−0 15	12.1	9.0	Tarn Point .... *Liverpool*	+0 05	8.3	6.4
Newquay ..... *Avonmouth*	−1 58	7.0	5.3	Tay River (Bar) ....*Leith*	−0 21	5.2	4.2
New Quay (Card.) . *L'pool*	−3 30	4.9	3.4	Tees R. (Ent.) ......*Leith*	+1 08	5.5	4.3
North Shields ......*Leith*	+0 51	5.0	3.9	Teignmouth ... *London*	+4 37	4.8	3.6
North Sunderland.. *Leith*	+0 05	4.8	3.7	Tenby....... *Avonmouth*	−1 05	8.4	6.3
N. Woolwich .... *London*	−0 20	7.0	5.7	Tilbury......... *London*	−0 49	6.4	5.3
Oban.......... *Greenock*	+5 45	4.0	2.9	Tobermory ... *Liverpool*	−5 12	4.4	3.3
Old Lynn Road..... *Hull*	+0 45	7.3	5.8	Torquay........ *London*	+4 40	4.9	3.7
Orfordness ...... *London*	−2 50	2.8	2.7	*Totland Bay ... *London*	−3 53	2.7	2.3
Ostend .... *London*	−1 32	5.1	4.2	Troon .... *Greenock*	−0 25	3.2	2.7
Padstow ..... *Avonmouth*	−1 45	7.3	5.6	Truro .... *London*	+3 43	5.3	4.2
Peel........... *Liverpool*	−0 02	5.3	4.2	Tyne River (Ent.)...*Leith*	+0 56	5.1	3.9
Peterhead ....*Leith*	−1 59	3.8	3.1	Walton-on-Naze. *London*	−2 10	4.2	3.4
Plymouth ..... *London*	+4 05	5.5	4.4	Waterford Hbr . *Liverpool*	−4 54	4.6	3.6
Poole (Entrance) *London*	−5 03	2.0	1.6	Weston S. Mare .*A'mouth*	−0 25	12.0	9.0
Porlock Bay . *Avonmouth*	−0 50	10.2	7.8	†Wexford Hbr.. *Liverpool*	−5 03	1.7	1.4
Porthcawl ... *Avonmouth*	−0 53	9.9	7.5	Whitby ....*Leith*	+1 22	5.4	4.3
Portmadoc..... *Liverpool*	−2 45	5.1	3.4	Whitehaven ... *Liverpool*	+0 10	8.0	6.3
Portland ...... *London*	+5 10	2.1	1.4	Wick...............*Leith*	−3 26	3.4	2.7
Portpatrick.... *Liverpool*	+0 22	3.8	3.0	Wisbech Cut .... *Hull*	+0 01	7.0	5.1
Portsmouth...... *London*	−2 23	4.7	3.8	Workington ... *Liverpool*	+0 20	8.2	6.4
Port Talbot .. *Avonmouth*	−0 53	9.6	7.3	Worthing ...... *London*	−2 38	6.1	4.8
Preston ...... *Liverpool*	+0 10	5.3	3.3	*Yarmth.(I.O.W.) *London*	−2 53	3.1	2.5
Pwllheli .... *Liverpool*	−3 07	5.0	3.4	Youghal....... *Liverpool*	−5 50	4.2	3.3

† Very Approximate.   * 1st H.W. (Springs).

Tidal data is no longer available for a number of places which formerly appeared in the list above. These places (with the name of the substitute now recorded) are: *Air Point* (Mostyn Quay); *Alderney* (Braye); *Ardrishaig* (East Loch Tarbert); *Arisaig* (Loch Moidart); *Ayr Pt., I.o.M.* (Peel); *Beachy Head* (Eastbourne); *Beaumaris* (Menai Bridge); *Brieile* (Scheveningen); *Broughty Ferry* (Newburgh); *Burryport* (Whiteford Lighthouse); *Caen* (Cayeux); *Caernarvon* (Llanddwyn Is.); *Devonport* (Plymouth); *Dumbarton* (Bowling); *Fareham* (Itchenor); *Fifeness* (Anstruther Easter); *Glasson Dock* (Tarn Pt.); *Gravesend* (Tilbury); *Greenwich* (R. Albert Dock); *Honfleur Harbour* (Duclair); *Hythe* (Totland Bay); *Lancaster* (Duddon Bar); *Loch Long* (Coulport); *Lynmouth* (Porlock Bay); *Nash Pt.* (Chepstow); *Neath* (Porthcawl); *Needles Pt.* (Freshwater Bay); *Nore Lt.* (Chatham); *Pembroke Dock* (Milford Haven); *Penzance* (Newlyn); *Plymouth Breakwater* (Bovisand Pier); *Port Harrington* (Hestan Islet); *Portishead* (Avonmouth); *St. Agnes* (Coverack); *St. Annes* (Blackpool); *St. Mary's* (Sennen Cove); *Spurn Head* (Bull Sand Fort); *Start Pt.* (Lulworth Cove); *Stockton* (Seaham); *Sutton Bridge* (Blacktoft); *Torbay* (Torquay); *Ushant* (Baie de Lampaul); *Valentia Harbour* (Knights Town); *Woolwich* (N. Woolwich); *Worms Head* (Ferryside); *Yarmouth Roads* (Gorleston).

Tidal predictions (pp. 86–97) for London Bridge, Liverpool, Avonmouth, Hull, Dún Laoghaire and Leith are computed by the Proudman Oceanographic Laboratory, copyright reserved. Those for Greenock have been supplied by the Hydrographer of the Navy and are crown copyright.

JANUARY, 1989

High Water at the undermentioned Places (G.M.T.*)—

Day of Month	Day of Week	London Bridge †Datum 3·20 m. below Mn. h.m.	Ht. m.	Aft. h.m.	Ht. m.	Liverpool †Datum 4·93 m. below Mn. h.m.	Ht. m.	Aft. h.m.	Ht. m.	Avonmouth †Datum 6·50 m. below Mn. h.m.	Ht. m.	Aft. h.m.	Ht. m.	Hull (Albert Dock) †Datum 3·90 m. below Mn. h.m.	Ht. m.	Aft. h.m.	Ht. m.	Greenock †Datum 1·62 m. below Mn. h.m.	Ht. m.	Aft. h.m.	Ht. m.	Leith †Datum 2·90 m. below Mn. h.m.	Ht. m.	Aft. h.m.	Ht. m.	Dun Laoghaire ‡Datum 0·20 m. above Mn. h.m.	Ht. m.	Aft. h.m.	Ht. m.
1	Su	0730	5.6	2015	5.7	0504	7.2	1725	7.3	0032	10.0	1257	10.2			1222	5.7	0629	2.8	1826	3.1	0845	4.4	2104	4.5	0557	3.2	1814	3.3
2	M	0834	5.5	2114	5.7	0608	7.1	1832	7.3	0137	9.7	1408	10.2	0045	5.9	1331	5.8	0731	2.9	1929	3.0	0942	4.5	2205	4.4	0701	3.1	1919	3.3
3	Tu	0938	5.5	2213	5.8	0716	7.3	1941	7.4	0250	9.8	1515	10.2	0158	5.9	1439	6.1	0840	2.9	2034	3.1	1044	4.5	2310	4.5	0757	3.2	2018	3.4
4	W	1038	5.7	2309	6.0	0816	7.6	2042	7.7	0355	10.3	1617	10.7	0307	6.0	1539	6.4	0937	3.0	2134	3.2	1145	4.6			0847	3.5	2109	3.5
5	Th	1137	5.9			0910	8.1	2134	8.1	0454	10.9	1718	11.2	0407	6.4	1633	6.7	1023	3.1	2229	3.2	0012	4.7	1241	4.8	0930	3.7	2156	3.6
6	F	0007	6.2	1235	6.2	0956	8.5	2220	8.5	0549	11.6	1812	11.8	0501	6.5	1719	7.0	1106	3.2	2320	3.5	0109	4.9	1331	5.0	1011	3.8	2240	3.6
7	Sa	0102	6.5	1328	6.6	1041	8.9	2305	8.8	0639	12.2	1903	12.2	0549	6.7	1803	7.2	1147	3.4			0159	5.1	1457	5.4	1053	4.0	2323	3.7
8	Su	0151	6.8	1416	6.9	1125	9.2	2350	9.1	0727	12.6	1949	12.6	0634	7.0	1843	7.5	0011	3.2	1231	3.7	0245	5.3	1539	5.6	1133	4.1		
9	M	0236	7.0	1503	7.2			1210	9.5	0811	13.0	2034	13.0	0716	7.2	1924	7.7	0101	3.3	1315	3.7	0328	5.5	1622	5.6	0006	3.9	1216	4.2
10	Tu	0318	7.1	1546	7.4	0034	9.2	1253	9.6	0854	13.3	2117	13.2	0759	7.4	2004	7.7	0151	3.3	1401	3.8	0410	5.5	1708	5.6	0051	3.9	1300	4.3
11	W	0400	7.2	1630	7.3	0119	9.2	1338	9.5	0936	13.3	2159	13.2	0840	7.4	2044	7.6	0239	3.3	1447	3.8	0453	5.5	1756	5.6	0137	3.9	1347	4.3
12	Th	0441	7.1	1715	7.1	0204	9.1	1423	9.3	1020	13.3	2242	12.9	0924	7.4	2127	7.4	0325	3.4	1533	3.8	0540	5.3	1847	5.4	0225	3.8	1436	4.3
13	F	0522	6.9	1801	6.8	0250	8.8	1510	8.8	1105	12.9	2327	12.3	1009	7.6	2212	7.1	0410	3.4	1619	3.6	0630	5.2	1941	5.2	0317	3.7	1529	4.2
14	Sa	0607	6.7	1852	6.5	0338	8.5	1600	8.4	1153	12.2			1058		2304	6.2	0452	3.2	1708	3.4	0723	5.1	2038	5.0	0414	3.6	1628	4.0
15	Su	0656	6.5	1949	6.3	0433	8.1	1659	8.1	0015	11.0	1246	11.5	1157				0537	3.2	1805	3.2	0820	4.9	2146	4.9	0520	3.5	1738	3.8
16	M	0758	6.4	2057	6.3	0539	7.7	1810	7.8	0113	11.0	1352	11.0	0007		1309	6.1	0630	3.0	1916	3.1	0924	4.7	2302	4.7	0633	3.6	1854	3.7
17	Tu	0912	6.4	2209	6.3	0656	7.6	1928	7.8	0226	10.5	1511	10.6	0123	6.6	1425	6.3	0741	3.0	2041	3.0	1036	4.7			0743	3.6	2007	3.6
18	W	1034	6.1	2320	6.2	0811	7.8	2042	8.1	0346	10.6	1627	10.8	0243	6.3	1539	6.5	0902	3.1	2157	3.1	1146	4.8	1249	5.0	0845	3.6	2114	3.7
19	Th	1151	6.1			0917	8.1	2145	8.5	0458	11.0	1733	11.2	0404	6.5	1642	6.7	1006	3.4	2300	3.1	0013	5.1	1342	5.1	0939	3.7	2209	3.7
20	F	0025	6.3	1252	6.3	1010	8.5	2235	8.9	0557	12.1	1828	12.1	0511	6.5	1732	7.0	1059	3.2	2355	3.2	0115	5.3	1429	5.3	1028	4.0	2256	4.0
21	Sa	0117	6.5	1342	6.5	1057	8.9	2319	9.1	0648	12.4	1914	12.3	0601	6.4	1814	7.1	1146	3.2			0207	5.3	1509	5.3	1110	4.1	2338	4.0
22	Su	0201	6.7	1425	6.7	1136	9.1	2358	9.1	0730	12.7	1955	12.4	0645	6.7	1850	7.2	0046	3.1	1230	3.6	0253	5.2	1545	5.2	1150	3.7		
23	M	0248	6.8	1504	6.9			1212	9.0	0808	12.6	2032	12.4	0721	6.7	1924	7.4	0131	3.1	1311	3.7	0332	5.1	1618	5.1	0015	3.6	1226	4.1
24	Tu	0315	6.8	1539	7.0	0032	9.0	1246	8.8	0843	12.5	2105	12.3	0754	6.8	1955	7.4	0211	3.1	1349	3.5	0405	5.1	1651	4.9	0050	3.6	1303	4.0
25	W	0349	6.8	1613	6.9	0104	8.8	1319	8.7	0914	12.3	2135	12.1	0825	6.8	2025	7.1	0247	3.1	1424	3.5	0438	4.8	1725	4.8	0123	3.5	1339	3.9
26	Th	0420	6.8	1645	6.8	0135	8.7	1349	8.6	0943	12.1	2203	11.7	0854	6.8	2057	6.8	0318	3.1	1457	3.4	0509	4.7	1800	4.7	0157	3.5	1413	3.8
27	F	0451	6.6	1718	6.6	0208	8.6	1420	8.2	1012	11.8	2231	11.1	0925	6.7	2131	6.4	0348	3.0	1532	3.3	0544	4.5	1836	4.5	0232	3.4	1447	3.6
28	Sa	0522	6.4	1751	6.2	0240	8.2	1453	7.9	1041	11.1	2259	10.5	0959	6.5	2207	6.0	0416	3.1	1608	3.3	0619	4.4	1916	4.6	0308	3.4	1525	3.6
29	Su	0557	6.2	1828	6.1	0314	7.9	1528	7.5	1113	11.2	2329	9.9	1035	6.3	2247	5.7	0446	3.0	1649	3.2	0658	4.5	2004	4.5	0352	3.3	1610	3.4
30	M	0635	5.9	1910	5.6	0356	7.5	1614	7.1	1149	10.5			1118	5.9	2337		0522	2.9	1735	3.2	0742	4.4	2004	4.3	0443	3.2	1706	3.3
31	Tu	0721	5.5	2004	5.6	0452	7.1	1719		0007	9.8	1241	9.9			1215		0608	2.9	1831	3.1	0838	4.3	2107	4.3	0550	3.1	1821	3.2

*All times shown are Greenwich Mean Time.   †Difference of height in metres from Ordnance Datum (Newlyn).   ‡Difference of height in metres from Ordnance Datum (Dublin).

FEBRUARY, 1989

High Water at the undermentioned Places (G.M.T.*)—

Day of Month	Day of Week	London Bridge (†Datum of Predictions 3·20 m. below) Mn. h.m.	Ht. m.	Aft. h.m.	Ht. m.	Liverpool (†Datum of Predictions 4·93 m. below) Mn. h.m.	Ht. m.	Aft. h.m.	Ht. m.	Avonmouth (†Datum of Predictions 6·50 m. below) Mn. h.m.	Ht. m.	Aft. h.m.	Ht. m.	Hull (Albert Dock) (†Datum of Predictions 3·90 m. below) Mn. h.m.	Ht. m.	Aft. h.m.	Ht. m.	Greenock (†Datum of Predictions 1·62 m. below) Mn. h.m.	Ht. m.	Aft. h.m.	Ht. m.	Leith (†Datum of Predictions 2·90 m. below) Mn. h.m.	Ht. m.	Aft. h.m.	Ht. m.	Dun Laoghaire (‡Datum of Predictions 0·20 m. above) Mn. h.m.	Ht. m.	Aft. h.m.	Ht. m.
1	W	0829	5·3	2111	5·5	0611	7·0	1848	7·0	0117	9·3	1404	9·5	0050	5·7	1341	5·6	0708	2·9	1936	3·0	0948	4·3	2228	4·3	0703	3·2	1940	3·2
2	Th	0946	5·4	2223	5·6	0734	7·2	2011	7·2	0258	9·4	1532	9·8	0225	5·7	1501	5·8	0833	2·9	2053	3·0	1106	4·4	2349	4·4	0810	3·3	2047	3·4
3	F	1102	5·6	2337	5·9	0843	7·7	2115	7·8	0419	10·2	1649	10·6	0342	5·9	1607	6·1	0949	3·1	2207	3·1			1217	4·6	0905	3·6	2141	3·5
4	Sa			1217	6·1	0939	8·4	2207	8·4	0526	11·6	1756	11·6	0445	6·3	1701	6·6	1045	3·4	2308	3·2	0054	4·7	1313	4·6	0952	3·8	2228	3·7
5	Su	0043	6·4	1314	6·5	1027	8·9	2254	9·0	0622	12·2	1849	12·4	0536	6·7	1746	6·7	1133	3·4			0147	5·1	1401	5·2	1036	4·0	2310	3·9
6	M	0135	6·8	1404	6·7	1112	9·5	2337	9·4	0712	13·0	1935	13·1	0621	7·1	1827	7·1	0003	3·2	1220	3·6	0232	5·4	1442	5·6	1117	4·2	2351	4·0
7	Tu	0220	7·2	1449	7·2	1156	9·8			0755	13·7	2019	14·0	0702	7·7	1904	7·9	0054	3·3	1307	3·7	0311	5·6	1521	5·8	1159	4·3		
8	W	0303	7·4	1531	7·5	0019	9·6	1238	10·1	0837	14·1	2100	14·0	0741	7·7	1944	8·2	0142	3·4	1353	3·9	0350	5·7	1602	5·9	0033	4·0	1242	4·4
9	Th	0342	7·5	1613	7·6	0102	9·7	1320	10·1	0919	14·3	2141	13·9	0820	7·7	2025	8·2	0227	3·4	1437	3·9	0431	5·7	1646	5·9	0115	4·0	1328	4·4
10	F	0421	7·4	1655	7·6	0144	9·5	1402	9·9	1000	14·0	2220	13·5	0901	7·6	2105	8·1	0308	3·5	1520	3·9	0516	5·6	1733	5·8	0200	4·0	1414	4·4
11	Sa	0502	7·2	1737	7·3	0225	9·0	1444	9·5	1041	13·4	2259	12·9	0942	7·2	2150	7·7	0346	3·5	1601	3·8	0604	5·5	1822	5·5	0249	3·9	1506	4·2
12	Su	0543	7·0	1822	6·9	0308	8·7	1531	8·9	1123	12·4	2340	11·6	1027	6·8	2240	7·2	0423	3·5	1646	3·6	0654	5·3	1914	5·2	0342	3·7	1601	4·0
13	M	0629	6·6	1913	6·5	0357	8·1	1627	8·1			1210	11·2	1120	6·4	2342	6·6	0502	3·4	1737	3·3	0748	4·8	2011	4·9	0445	3·5	1710	3·7
14	Tu	0727	6·3	2015	6·0	0501	7·6	1742	7·5	0028	10·7	1312	10·2			1228	6·0	0548	3·2	1841	3·0	0853	4·6	2126	4·7	0559	3·4	1834	3·5
15	W	0842	6·0	2129	5·8	0628	7·2	1916	7·3	0141	9·9	1439	9·7	0100	6·1	1354	5·8	0547	2·9	2020	2·8	1015	4·5	2254	4·6	0719	3·4	2000	3·4
16	Th	1012	5·9	2257	5·9	0759	7·4	2040	7·4	0317	9·8	1610	10·0	0239	6·0	1524	6·0	0626	2·9	2201	2·8	1138	4·6			0831	3·5	2112	3·5
17	F	1139	6·1			0910	7·9	2141	8·0	0442	10·4	1722	10·8	0406	6·0	1630	6·3	0726	3·0	2308	3·0	0013	4·8	1244	4·8	0931	3·6	2208	3·6
18	Sa	0008	6·2	1241	6·4	1002	8·4	2227	8·4	0546	11·3	1815	11·5	0505	6·3	1718	6·7	1055	3·0	2358	3·1	0112	5·0	1336	5·0	1019	3·9	2252	3·6
19	Su	0102	6·4	1328	6·7	1044	8·8	2305	8·7	0634	12·0	1857	12·5	0550	6·7	1757	7·2	1140	3·4			0200	5·2	1455	5·3	1100	3·9	2326	3·7
20	M	0145	6·6	1409	6·9	1119	9·1	2339	8·9	0713	12·7	1935	12·7	0627	6·7	1829	7·4	0039	3·1	1219	3·5	0240	5·2	1525	5·4	1136	4·0	2357	4·0
21	Tu	0222	6·8	1444	7·0	1151	9·2			0748	12·9	2009	12·8	0659	7·0	1900	7·6	0117	3·1	1257	3·6	0313	5·2	1551	5·4			1206	4·0
22	W	0254	6·9	1517	7·0	0008	9·0	1222	9·2	0819	12·9	2039	12·8	0727	7·0	1930	7·6	0151	3·1	1332	3·6	0340	5·2	1620	5·3	0023	4·0	1237	4·0
23	Th	0324	6·9	1545	7·0	0050	9·0	1250	9·0	0847	13·0	2107	12·8	0755	7·1	1959	7·5	0221	3·1	1403	3·5	0407	5·1	1650	5·3	0050	3·7	1307	4·0
24	F	0352	6·9	1613	6·9	0106	8·9	1319	9·0	0915	13·0	2132	12·6	0822	7·1	2029	7·5	0247	3·1	1432	3·5	0435	5·1	1722	5·2	0118	3·6	1337	3·9
25	Sa	0420	6·8	1642	6·8	0134	8·7	1345	8·7	0942	12·9	2157	12·1	0851	7·1	2101	7·2	0310	3·1	1501	3·5	0505	5·0	1756	5·1	0150	3·6	1410	3·8
26	Su	0449	6·6	1713	6·6	0202	8·5	1413	8·5	1009	12·1	2221	11·5	0922	6·8	2134	6·8	0334	3·2	1533	3·4	0538	4·8	1833	4·7	0224	3·5	1506	3·6
27	M	0522	6·4	1746	6·3	0232	8·2	1446	8·2	1034	11·4	2242	10·7	0953	6·5	2207	6·4	0401	3·2	1611	3·3	0612	4·6	1921	4·4	0304	3·4	1528	3·4
28	Tu	0558	6·1	1824	6·1	0308	7·8	1527	7·8	1102	10·6	2312	10·0	1028	6·1	2251	6·1	0436	3·1	1657	3·2	0653	4·4			0353	3·3	1621	3·2

* All times shown are Greenwich Mean Time.   †Difference of height in metres from Ordnance Datum (Newlyn).   ‡Difference of height in metres from Ordnance Datum (Dublin).

MARCH, 1989

High Water at the undermentioned Places (G.M.T.*)—

Day of Month	Day of Week	London Bridge †3·20 m. below Mn.	Ht.	Aft.	Ht.	Liverpool †4·93 m. below Mn.	Ht.	Aft.	Ht.	Avonmouth †6·50 m. below Mn.	Ht.	Aft.	Ht.	Hull (Albert Dock) †3·90 m. below Mn.	Ht.	Aft.	Ht.	Greenock †1·62 m. below Mn.	Ht.	Aft.	Ht.	Leith †2·90 m. below Mn.	Ht.	Aft.	Ht.	Dun Laoghaire ‡0·20 m. above Mn.	Ht.	Aft.	Ht.
1	W	0641	5·7	1909	5·7	0357	7·3	1627	7·1	1144	9·9	1300	9·3	1116	5·8	2356	5·6	0518	3·1	1750	3·1	0747	4·3	2030	4·2	0457	3·2	1739	3·1
2	Th	0740	5·4	2013	5·4	0516	7·0	1804	6·8	0007	9·4	1447	9·4	0149		1235	5·6	0611	3·0	1853	3·0	0902	4·3	2201	4·2	0616	3·1	1909	3·1
3	F	0903	5·3	2141	5·4	0656	7·0	1945	7·1	0157	9·4	1623	10·3	0322	5·5	1426	5·8	0729	2·9	2020	2·9	1033	4·2	2329	4·4	0734	3·3	2025	3·3
4	Sa	1037	5·6	2312	5·8	0818	7·6	2056	7·8	0343	9·8	1734	11·6	0428	5·8	1541	6·0	0920	3·0	2156	3·0	1152	4·5	—	—	0838	3·5	2124	3·5
5	Su	1157	6·2	—	—	0918	8·4	2149	8·5	0502	11·1	1828	12·7	0518	6·1	1637	6·6	1027	3·0	2257	3·1	0034	4·7	1252	4·9	0930	3·8	2209	3·7
6	M	0021	6·4	1255	6·6	1007	9·1	2234	9·6	0600	12·4	1914	13·1	0600	6·8	1722	7·1	1117	3·4	2348	3·2	0127	4·9	1337	5·3	1015	4·0	2252	3·9
7	Tu	0113	6·9	1342	7·4	1051	9·7	2318	9·6	0649	13·4	1958	14·1	0639	7·2	1801	8·1	1204	3·6	—	—	0210	5·1	1419	5·7	1056	4·2	2328	4·1
8	W	0158	7·3	1427	7·6	1134	10·1	2358	9·8	0734	14·1	2039	14·3	0717	7·7	1841	8·4	0035	3·3	1252	3·8	0248	5·4	1458	5·9	1138	4·4	—	—
9	Th	0239	7·6	1508	7·7	—	—	1217	10·3	0816	14·5	2117	14·2	0755	7·7	1920	8·4	0121	3·5	1338	3·9	0326	5·7	1538	6·1	0008	4·1	1221	4·5
10	F	0318	7·7	1550	7·6	0039	9·9	1257	10·2	0857	14·5	2156	13·6	0834	7·9	2002	8·1	0204	3·5	1420	3·9	0407	5·8	1622	6·0	0049	4·1	1304	4·5
11	Sa	0359	7·6	1631	7·3	0119	9·7	1338	9·9	0938	14·1	2234	13·6	0915	7·9	2044	7·6	0242	3·6	1501	3·9	0451	5·8	1710	5·8	0133	4·0	1353	4·4
12	Su	0440	7·4	1712	6·9	0159	9·7	1420	9·4	1017	13·2	2311	13·2	1000	7·7	2131	6·9	0318	3·6	1541	3·8	0538	5·6	1759	5·5	0220	3·8	1443	4·1
13	M	0522	7·0	1754	6·5	0240	8·8	1507	8·7	1058	12·3	2354	11·4	1051	7·4	2223	6·3	0352	3·6	1625	3·5	0628	5·4	1852	5·1	0311	3·5	1540	3·8
14	Tu	0610	6·6	1841	6·1	0328	8·1	1603	7·8	1142	10·7	—	—	1156	6·3	2326	5·6	0430	3·6	1713	3·3	0723	5·0	1953	4·8	0413	3·4	1650	3·5
15	W	0706	6·2	1938	5·8	0433	7·5	1723	7·2	0107	9·4	1241	9·7	0050	5·9	1323	5·8	0515	3·2	1816	2·9	0829	4·4	2112	4·5	0530	3·4	1820	3·3
16	Th	0818	5·9	2051	5·6	0605	7·3	1904	7·4	0250	9·3	1411	9·5	0237	5·6	1503	6·2	0610	3·1	2011	2·7	0955	4·3	2246	4·5	0656	3·4	1953	3·3
17	F	0948	5·8	2227	5·7	0742	7·3	2027	7·8	0421	10·1	1548	10·5	0336	5·8	1609	6·9	0743	3·0	2300	2·6	1123	4·5	—	—	0814	3·6	2102	3·4
18	Sa	1118	6·1	—	—	0851	7·8	2122	8·3	0523	11·9	1659	11·1	0448	6·1	1654	6·4	0944	2·8	2317	2·7	0001	4·6	1228	4·7	0914	3·9	2153	3·5
19	Su	0038	6·5	1306	6·9	0941	8·3	2204	8·7	0608	12·4	1750	12·1	0527	6·4	1730	7·2	1040	2·9	2340	3·0	0056	4·8	1317	4·9	1002	3·9	2232	3·6
20	M	0120	6·7	1345	7·0	1019	8·7	2240	9·0	0648	12·7	1832	12·4	0600	7·0	1803	7·4	1121	3·2	—	—	0138	4·8	1357	5·2	1049	3·9	2302	3·6
21	Tu	0157	6·9	1419	7·0	1052	8·9	2311	9·1	0721	12·9	1907	12·8	0629	7·0	1834	7·5	0015	3·1	1158	3·3	0214	5·1	1428	5·3	1110		2327	3·7
22	W	0227	6·9	1447	7·0	1123	9·1	2339	9·0	0751	12·9	1940	12·9	0656	7·3	1903	7·3	0048	3·1	1233	3·4	0243	5·1	1456	5·3	1140		2352	3·7
23	Th	0256	6·9	1514	6·9	1153	9·1	—	—	0819	13·0	2009	12·9	0724	7·3	1933	7·2	0118	3·1	1306	3·4	0310	5·2	1521	5·3	0018	3·7	1208	3·9
24	F	0321	6·9	1539	6·9	0007	9·0	1221	9·1	0846	13·0	2036	12·7	0751	7·2	2004	7·0	0146	3·1	1335	3·4	0334	5·2	1548	5·3	0044	3·7	1236	3·8
25	Sa	0349	6·8	1607	6·9	0035	9·0	1249	9·0	0914	12·6	2103	12·2	0820	7·0	2034	6·7	0210	3·1	1402	3·4	0401	5·2	1618	5·3	0115	3·6	1306	3·7
26	Su	0421	6·7	1640	6·7	0102	8·9	1316	8·8	0941	12·2	2128	11·5	0849	6·5	2105	6·5	0231	3·2	1430	3·3	0430	5·1	1651	5·1	0152	3·5	1339	3·6
27	M	0455	6·5	1712	6·6	0130	8·7	1344	8·5	1006	11·5	2150	10·8	0918	6·3	2141	6·3	0255	3·2	1503	3·3	0502	4·9	1726	4·9	0232	3·4	1417	3·4
28	Tu	0533	6·3	1750	6·2	0202	8·4	1418	8·1	1035	11·2	2214	10·2	0952	6·2	2226	6·0	0325	3·2	1543	3·2	0537	4·7	1806	4·7	0321	3·2	1501	3·4
29	W	0618	6·0	1836	5·9	0239	8·0	1501	7·7	1120	10·5	2245	9·6	1041	5·8	2332	5·6	0401	3·2	1630	3·2	0620	4·5	1900	4·4	0424		1559	3·2
30	Th	0716	5·6	1938	5·6	0331	7·5	1603	7·2		9·9	2344	9·4	1157	5·5			0445	3·2	1722	3·1	0717	4·3	2012	4·3	0539		1714	3·1
31	F					0447	7·2	1739	6·9	1157		1238						0537	3·0	1825	2·9	0734	4·2	2140	4·2			1844	

*All times shown are Greenwich Mean Time.   †Difference of height in metres from Ordnance Datum (Newlyn).   ‡Difference of height in metres from Ordnance Datum (Dublin).

A P R I L, 1989

High Water at the undermentioned Places (G.M.T.*)—

Day of Month	Day of Week	LONDON BRIDGE †Datum 3·20 m. below				LIVERPOOL †Datum 4·93 m. below				AVONMOUTH †Datum 6·50 m. below				HULL (Albert Dock) †Datum 3·90 m. below				GREENOCK †Datum 1·62 m. below				LEITH †Datum 2·90 m. below				DUN LAOGHAIRE ‡Datum 0·20 m. above			
		Mn. h.m.	Ht.	Aft. h.m.	Ht.	Mn. h.m.	Ht.	Aft. h.m.	Ht.	Mn. h.m.	Ht.	Aft. h.m.	Ht.	Mn. h.m.	Ht.	Aft. h.m.	Ht.	Mn. h.m.	Ht.	Aft. h.m.	Ht.	Mn. h.m.	Ht.	Aft. h.m.	Ht.	Mn. h.m.	Ht.	Aft. h.m.	Ht.
1	Sa	0839	5·5	2107	5·8	0624	7·2	1917	7·2	0127	9·3	1418	9·6	0123	5·6	1349	5·6	0648	2·9	1957	2·8	1001	4·3	2301	4·4	0659	3·3	2202	3·3
2	Su	1014	5·8	2242	6·4	0747	7·8	2029	7·9	0311	10·1	1553	10·5	0257	5·9	1507	6·1	0849	3·0	2140	2·9	1120	4·6			0809	3·5	2258	3·6
3	M	1132	6·4	2353		0849	8·5	2122	8·6	0431	11·3	1705	11·8	0402	6·5	1604	6·6	1001	3·1	2236	3·1	0005	4·8	1220	5·0	0902	3·8	2145	3·8
4	Tu	0046	7·0	1231	7·3	0949	9·2	2209	9·2	0533	12·6	1801	12·9	0452	7·0	1651	7·2	1053	3·4	2322	3·2	0056	5·1	1307	5·4	0949	4·1	2225	4·0
5	W	0131	7·3	1319	7·5	1024	9·7	2251	9·6	0624	13·5	1850	13·6	0534	7·4	1733	7·7	1141	3·6			0140	5·5	1349	5·7	1032	4·3	2303	4·1
6	Th	0213	7·5	1402	7·6	1109	10·1	2333	10·0	0710	14·1	1934	14·1	0612	7·7	1815	8·1	0007	3·5	1229	3·7	0220	5·7	1431	5·9	1114	4·4	2343	4·2
7	F	0254	7·6	1444	7·6	1151	10·2			0754	14·3	2015	14·3	0650	7·8	1857	8·3	0051	3·5	1316	3·8	0259	5·8	1513	6·0	1158	4·4		
8	Sa	0336	7·6	1525	7·4	0014	9·8	1235	10·1	0834	14·3	2054	13·9	0730	7·8	1942	8·2	0132	3·5	1359	3·8	0341	5·7	1553	5·7	0023	4·2	1243	4·4
9	Su	0420	7·4	1606	7·2	0055	9·6	1317	9·7	0917	13·7	2134	13·2	0811	7·6	2029	7·8	0211	3·6	1440	3·7	0426	5·6	1648	5·7	0107	4·1	1333	4·2
10	M	0506	7·2	1648	7·0	0135	9·2	1401	9·1	0957	12·9	2212	12·2	0853	7·2	2119	7·2	0246	3·7	1521	3·6	0514	5·3	1740	5·0	0154	4·0	1425	4·0
11	Tu	0556	7·0	1730	6·6	0219	8·7	1449	8·4	1038	11·5	2251	11·1	0938	6·8	2213	6·6	0323	3·7	1606	3·3	0605	5·0	1836	4·7	0249	3·8	1524	3·7
12	W	0650	6·6	1815	6·2	0308	8·1	1548	7·7	1123	10·3	2337	10·0	1028	6·3	2316	5·9	0403	3·5	1655	3·0	0701	4·7	1938	4·4	0350	3·6	1635	3·4
13	Th	0757	6·2	1910	5·9	0412	7·5	1704	7·1			1222	9·4	1129	5·9			0448	3·5	1757	2·7	0806	4·4	2053	4·3	0503	3·4	1803	3·2
14	F	0915	5·9	2018	5·7	0537	7·2	1836	7·0	0046	9·3	1341	9·0	0036	5·5	1246	5·6	0543	3·4	1957	2·6	0925	4·3	2216	4·4	0628	3·4	1930	3·2
15	Sa	1044	5·7	2143	6·0	0706	7·2	1952	7·3	0215	9·3	1505	9·4	0215	5·4	1423	5·7	0703	3·4	2048	2·7	1048	4·4	2327	4·4	0744	3·5	2035	3·3
16	Su	1147	6·0	2309	6·4	0815	7·7	2047	7·8	0339	10·0	1620	10·3	0327	5·6	1534	6·0	0904	3·5	2200	2·8	1154	4·6			0844	3·5	2122	3·4
17	M	0005	6·4	1235	6·8	0904	8·1	2129	8·1	0444	11·2	1713	11·5	0417	6·1	1620	6·6	1005	3·5	2306	3·0	0019	4·7	1242	4·8	0930	3·7	2159	3·6
18	Tu	0049	6·8	1313	6·9	0943	8·5	2204	8·5	0532	11·6	1756	11·8	0465	6·3	1658	6·8	1047	3·7	2339	3·1	0102	4·9	1321	5·0	1007	3·7	2228	3·6
19	W	0126	6·9	1347	6·9	1019	8·7	2237	8·7	0612	12·1	1834	12·3	0527	6·7	1732	7·1	1124	3·2			0137	5·1	1353	5·1	1039	3·8	2253	3·7
20	Th	0157	6·9	1415	6·8	1051	8·8	2306	8·8	0648	12·4	1907	12·5	0557	7·1	1804	7·2	0040	3·1	1204	3·1	0206	5·2	1422	5·3	1107	3·8	2319	3·8
21	F	0223	6·8	1440	6·8	1122	8·9	2336	8·9	0719	12·6	1938	12·7	0625	7·1	1835	7·3	0106	3·1	1240	3·1	0233	5·2	1450	5·3	1137	3·8	2345	3·8
22	Sa	0253	6·8	1508	6·8	1151	9·0			0749	12·6	2006	12·6	0653	7·2	1907	7·2	0131	3·1	1302	3·2	0300	5·3	1520	5·3	0015	3·8	1206	3·7
23	Su	0324	6·8	1539	6·7	0005	9·0	1221	9·0	0819	12·6	2036	12·4	0723	7·1	1940	7·0	0155	3·1	1332	3·2	0330	5·2	1553	5·2	0049	3·7	1240	3·7
24	M	0359	6·7	1613	6·7	0036	8·9	1252	8·9	0849	12·2	2104	12·0	0752	6·9	2013	6·8	0223	3·2	1403	3·2	0403	5·2	1628	5·2	0128	3·7	1317	3·6
25	Tu	0435	6·6	1649	6·5	0109	8·7	1326	8·5	0919	11·6	2132	11·4	0823	6·6	2049	6·5	0256	3·2	1441	3·2	0439	5·0	1709	4·9	0211	3·6	1400	3·5
26	W	0518	6·5	1729	6·2	0144	8·5	1405	8·1	0952	10·9	2204	10·9	0856	6·5	2129	6·3	0336	3·3	1524	3·3	0517	4·8	1757	4·5	0301	3·5	1449	3·4
27	Th	0607	6·2	1817	6·0	0226	8·2	1453	7·4	1030	10·6	2248	10·4	0935	6·2	2219	6·0	0422	3·3	1612	3·1	0604	4·6	1853	4·5	0354	3·5	1546	3·3
28	F	0706	6·0	1920	5·9	0321	7·8	1557	7·4	1123	10·2			1027	6·0	2325	5·8	0515	3·3	1706	3·0	0703	4·5	1959	4·4	0400	3·4	1656	3·2
29	Sa	0823	5·9	2043		0433	7·5	1720	7·3	0116	10·1	1357	10·1	1139	5·8			0515	3·1	1807	2·9	0813	4·4	2113	4·5	0510	3·4	1817	3·2
30	Su					0556	7·6	1845	7·5			1234	10·2	0057	5·8	1310	5·9	0625	3·0	1935	2·8	0929	4·5	2227	4·6	0626	3·5	1932	3·4

*All times shown are Greenwich Mean Time. †Difference of height in metres from Ordnance Datum (Newlyn). ‡Difference of height in metres from Ordnance Datum (Dublin).

MAY, 1989

High Water at the undermentioned Places (G.M.T.*)—

Day of Month	Day of Week	LONDON BRIDGE †Datum of Predictions 3·20 m. below				LIVERPOOL †Datum of Predictions 4·93 m. below				AVONMOUTH †Datum of Predictions 6·50 m. below				HULL (Albert Dock) †Datum of Predictions 3·90 m. below				GREENOCK †Datum of Predictions 1·62 m. below				LEITH †Datum of Predictions 2·90 m. below				DUN LAOGHAIRE ‡Datum of Predictions 0·20 m. above			
		Mn. h.m.	Ht.	Aft. h.m.	Ht.	Mn. h.m.	Ht.	Aft. h.m.	Ht.	Mn. h.m.	Ht.	Aft. h.m.	Ht.	Mn. h.m.	Ht.	Aft. h.m.	Ht.	Mn. h.m.	Ht.	Aft. h.m.	Ht.	Mn. h.m.	Ht.	Aft. h.m.	Ht.	Mn. h.m.	Ht.	Aft. h.m.	Ht.
1	M	0948	6·1	2209	6·0	0710	8·1	1954	8·0	0242	10·7	1522	11·0	0222	6·1	1426	6·3	0812	3·0	2108	2·9	1040	4·7	2328	4·9	0734	3·6	2028	3·6
2	Tu	1102	6·6	2319	6·5	0813	8·6	2050	8·6	0359	11·6	1634	11·9	0327	6·5	1527	6·8	0928	3·2	2203	3·0	1141	5·1			0832	3·8	2116	3·8
3	W			1203	7·0	0907	9·1	2139	9·1	0502	12·6	1733	12·7	0420	6·9	1619	7·2	1022	3·4	2249	3·2	0020	5·1	1234	5·4	0924	4·0	2159	4·0
4	Th	0015	6·9	1253	7·2	0956	9·5	2224	9·5	0557	13·2	1824	13·3	0505	7·2	1706	7·6	1113	3·5	2334	3·3	0107	5·4	1321	5·6	1008	4·2	2237	4·1
5	F	0104	7·1	1338	7·2	1044	9·6	2309	9·6	0646	13·6	1909	13·6	0547	7·4	1754	7·8	1202	3·6			0150	5·6	1406	5·8	1053	4·2	2317	4·1
6	Sa	0149	7·2	1422	7·2	1130	9·6	2351	9·6	0731	13·6	1952	13·6	0628	7·5	1842	7·9	0018	3·4	1251	3·6	0234	5·6	1453	5·8	1138	4·2	2359	4·2
7	Su	0233	7·3	1503	7·1			1215	9·6	0816	13·5	2034	13·4	0710	7·5	1931	7·7	0100	3·5	1337	3·6	0317	5·6	1542	5·8			1226	4·1
8	M	0319	7·3	1546	7·0	0035	9·4	1300	9·4	0900	13·0	2117	12·8	0752	7·3	2020	7·3	0140	3·6	1421	3·6	0405	5·5	1633	5·6	0046	4·1	1317	4·0
9	Tu	0406	7·3	1630	6·8	0119	9·1	1347	9·1	0942	12·2	2157	11·9	0837	7·1	2111	6·8	0219	3·7	1505	3·5	0454	5·3	1725	5·3	0136	4·0	1411	3·8
10	W	0454	7·0	1712	6·5	0204	8·7	1436	8·8	1026	11·3	2238	10·9	0921	6·7	2203	6·3	0258	3·7	1551	3·3	0546	5·0	1820	5·0	0229	3·9	1510	3·6
11	Th	0543	6·6	1756	6·1	0253	8·2	1531	8·2	1111	10·3	2325	10·2	1009	6·4	2259	5·9	0340	3·6	1642	3·1	0640	4·7	1918	4·5	0329	3·7	1616	3·3
12	F	0634	6·3	1845	5·9	0350	7·7	1634	7·7			1201	9·6	1101	6·1			0426	3·3	1742	2·7	0739	4·5	2020	4·5	0435	3·5	1731	3·3
13	Sa	0730	6·3	1944	5·6	0458	7·4	1747	7·3	0022	9·8	1303	9·4	0003	5·9	1203	5·9	0520	3·1	1909	2·6	0843	4·4	2128	4·4	0549	3·4	1849	3·2
14	Su	0834	5·8	2054	5·6	0611	7·2	1859	7·2	0131	9·7	1412	9·6	0119	5·4	1317	5·4	0628	2·9	2045	2·6	0952	4·4	2232	4·4	0701	3·5	1951	3·2
15	M	0950	5·8	2214	5·7	0719	7·5	1957	7·5	0242	10·0	1524	10·1	0236	5·4	1436	5·6	0800	2·9	2141	2·8	1057	4·6	2327	4·6	0800	3·5	2040	3·3
16	Tu	1101	5·9	2320	5·9			2044	7·9	0346	10·6	1620	10·7	0331	5·8	1535	5·8	0911	2·8	2222	2·9	1150	4·6			0848	3·5	2116	3·5
17	W	1153	6·4			0900	8·2	2124	8·5	0442	11·3	1711	11·3	0413	6·1	1620	6·5	1000	3·0	2256	2·9	0012	4·7	1233	4·8	0928	3·6	2148	3·6
18	Th	0008	6·5	1234	6·6	0939	8·3	2200	8·5	0529	11·6	1754	11·8	0449	6·5	1659	6·7	1041	3·0	2329	3·0	0051	4·8	1311	4·9	1003	3·6	2218	3·7
19	F	0048	6·5	1307	6·7	1016	8·6	2234	8·7	0610	12·1	1832	12·0	0522	6·7	1736	6·9	1119	3·1	2359	3·0	0127	5·0	1347	5·1	1036	3·7	2247	3·7
20	Sa	0121	6·6	1340	6·7	1051	8·6	2308	8·8	0646	12·1	1907	12·1	0554	6·9	1811	6·9	1156	3·1			0157	5·0	1422	5·2	1109	3·7	2317	3·7
21	Su	0154	6·6	1411	6·7	1126	8·7	2342	8·9	0723	12·1	1941	12·1	0627	6·9	1848	6·9	0028	3·1	1231	3·1	0233	5·1	1459	5·2	1144	3·7	2352	3·7
22	M	0229	6·6	1446	6·6			1201	8·7	0758	12·1	2016	12·1	0700	6·9	1924	6·9	0057	3·1	1307	3·1	0306	5·1	1538	5·2			1222	3·6
23	Tu	0307	6·7	1521	6·7	0017	8·9	1238	8·8	0833	11·9	2051	11·9	0734	6·8	2002	6·8	0126	3·2	1345	3·1	0344	5·1	1618	5·1	0029	3·8	1303	3·6
24	W	0346	6·8	1559	6·7	0055	8·8	1317	8·7	0910	11·7	2128	11·4	0809	6·7	2043	6·7	0200	3·3	1427	3·1	0424	5·1	1702	5·0	0111	3·8	1349	3·5
25	Th	0427	6·8	1638	6·7	0135	8·7	1401	8·4	0950	11·4	2210	11·0	0849	6·6	2127	6·6	0238	3·3	1513	3·1	0507	5·0	1750	4·9	0157	3·8	1439	3·5
26	F	0512	6·7	1720	6·7	0222	8·4	1451	8·0	1035	11·1	2259	11·0	0932	6·5	2217	6·3	0321	3·4	1603	3·1	0556	4·9	1843	4·7	0247	3·7	1533	3·4
27	Sa	0600	6·5	1808	6·5	0315	8·2	1550	7·8	1127	11·0	2356	10·8	1021	6·4	2315	6·2	0409	3·4	1655	3·0	0652	4·8	1941	4·6	0342	3·7	1636	3·3
28	Su	0657	6·3	1904	6·3	0417	8·1	1658	7·7			1227	10·9	1122	6·2			0502	3·3	1752	2·9	0752	4·7	2043	4·7	0443	3·7	1746	3·3
29	M	0804	6·1	2016	6·1	0525	8·1	1810	7·8	0100	11·0	1334	11·2	0028	6·1	1234	6·3	0606	3·1	1902	2·9	0855	4·8	2147	4·7	0552	3·7	1855	3·4
30	Tu	0919	6·3	2132	6·3	0634	8·3	1917	8·1	0215	11·2	1450	11·2	0142	6·3	1347	6·5	0732	3·2	2024	2·9	1001	4·9	2250	4·9	0701	3·7	1957	3·6
31	W	1030	6·6	2244	6·6	0738	8·6	2018	8·4	0328	11·7	1602	11·7	0249	6·5	1451	6·8	0850	3·1	2142	3·0	1104	5·1	2345	5·1	0803	3·8	2048	3·7

*All times shown are Greenwich Mean Time.   †Difference of height in metres from Ordnance Datum (Newlyn).
‡Difference of height in metres from Ordnance Datum (Dublin).

JUNE, 1989

High Water at the undermentioned Places (G.M.T.*)—

Day of Month	Day of Week	London Bridge (†3·20 m. below) Mn	Ht	Aft	Ht	Liverpool (†4·93 m. below) Mn	Ht	Aft	Ht	Avonmouth (†6·50 m. below) Mn	Ht	Aft	Ht	Hull Albert Dock (†3·90 m. below) Mn	Ht	Aft	Ht	Greenock (†1·62 m. below) Mn	Ht	Aft	Ht	Leith (†2·90 m. below) Mn	Ht	Aft	Ht	Dun Laoghaire (‡0·20 m. above) Mn	Ht	Aft	Ht
1	Th	1133	6·7	2347	6·6	0837	8·9	2111	8·8	—	—	1704	12·2	0346	6·8	1550	7·1	0950	3·2	2215	3·1	—	—	1202	5·3	0858	3·9	2134	3·9
2	F	0042	6·7	1229	6·8	0932	9·1	2202	9·0	0434	12·1	1758	12·6	0440	7·0	1648	7·3	1046	3·3	2303	3·2	0038	5·2	1257	5·4	0949	4·0	2216	4·0
3	Sa	0133	6·7	1319	6·7	1024	9·3	2249	9·2	0532	12·5	1849	12·8	0527	7·1	1743	7·4	1139	3·3	2349	3·4	0127	5·4	1349	5·5	1037	4·0	2259	4·0
4	Su	0222	6·9	1404	6·7	1115	9·3	2337	9·3	0625	12·7	1935	12·9	0614	7·2	1836	7·3	1231	3·3	—	—	0214	5·4	1441	5·6	1126	4·0	2344	4·1
5	M	0310	7·0	1447	6·8	—	—	1203	9·3	0716	12·7	2019	12·9	0657	7·2	1927	7·1	0034	3·5	1320	3·3	0302	5·5	1532	5·5	—	—	1215	3·9
6	Tu	0356	7·1	1531	6·8	0022	9·2	1249	9·0	0802	12·6	2103	12·4	0741	7·1	2015	6·9	0117	3·6	1409	3·2	0351	5·4	1623	5·4	0032	4·1	1306	3·8
7	W	0441	7·0	1614	6·8	0106	9·0	1334	8·7	0847	12·4	2145	11·9	0823	6·9	2101	6·6	0159	3·7	1455	3·1	0439	5·3	1711	5·3	0122	4·0	1357	3·7
8	Th	0526	6·8	1655	6·8	0149	8·8	1419	8·3	0931	11·9	2226	11·3	0904	6·9	2146	6·3	0240	3·7	1541	3·0	0527	5·1	1800	5·0	0213	3·9	1450	3·5
9	F	0610	6·4	1736	6·3	0234	8·5	1505	8·0	1013	11·3	2304	10·8	0945	6·7	2230	6·1	0322	3·6	1628	2·9	0616	4·9	1848	4·7	0306	3·7	1546	3·3
10	Sa	0657	6·2	1818	6·1	0321	8·1	1553	7·6	1052	10·7	2347	10·3	1028	6·5	2316	5·8	0406	3·4	1717	2·8	0705	4·7	1938	4·5	0400	3·7	1646	3·2
11	Su	0749	5·9	1906	5·9	0412	7·8	1648	7·4	1133	10·3	—	—	1118	6·3	—	—	0455	3·2	1813	2·7	0756	4·5	2030	4·4	0459	3·5	1750	3·1
12	M	0850	5·8	2005	5·7	0508	7·5	1749	7·2	0041	10·1	1316	10·0	0008	5·7	1217	6·0	0549	3·0	1921	2·6	0850	4·4	2126	4·4	0602	3·4	1851	3·2
13	Tu	0952	5·8	2111	5·7	0610	7·4	1852	7·3	0141	10·0	1418	10·0	0110	5·6	1324	5·9	0653	2·8	2030	2·7	0946	4·4	2222	4·4	0703	3·3	1944	3·2
14	W	1051	6·0	2216	5·8	0713	7·4	1949	7·5	0244	10·1	1519	10·3	0218	5·7	1434	6·0	0803	2·8	2125	2·7	1045	4·5	2315	4·5	0758	3·4	2028	3·3
15	Th	1140	6·1	2313	5·9	0811	7·6	2040	7·6	0343	10·5	1617	10·7	0317	5·7	1535	6·0	0903	2·8	2208	2·8	1139	4·6	—	—	0845	3·4	2108	3·5
16	F	0003	6·1	1224	6·3	0901	7·9	2125	8·2	0440	11·0	1711	11·2	0404	6·2	1626	6·3	0955	2·9	2246	2·9	0004	4·7	1230	4·7	0927	3·5	2144	3·6
17	Sa	0046	6·2	1307	6·5	0945	8·1	2206	8·5	0530	11·3	1758	11·6	0447	6·4	1711	6·5	1040	3·0	2322	3·0	0049	4·8	1317	4·8	1007	3·5	2219	3·7
18	Su	0130	6·4	1349	6·6	1028	8·3	2245	8·7	0618	11·6	1842	11·8	0526	6·6	1753	6·6	1124	3·0	2356	3·1	0131	4·8	1403	4·9	1046	3·6	2255	3·8
19	M	0213	6·6	1432	6·8	1106	8·5	2325	8·9	0702	11·8	1924	12·0	0605	6·7	1834	6·7	1206	3·0	—	—	0212	5·1	1446	5·1	1126	3·6	2334	3·9
20	Tu	0257	6·9	1512	6·8	1143	8·7	—	—	0744	11·9	2004	12·1	0643	6·9	1914	6·8	0031	3·2	1250	3·0	0251	5·2	1528	5·1	—	—	1208	3·6
21	W	0339	7·0	1553	6·8	0005	9·1	1228	8·7	0825	12·0	2044	12·2	0723	6·9	1955	6·9	0108	3·2	1335	3·0	0331	5·3	1610	5·3	0015	3·9	1250	3·6
22	Th	0421	7·0	1633	6·8	0046	9·1	1310	8·7	0907	12·2	2125	12·3	0801	7·0	2037	6·8	0147	3·3	1421	3·1	0412	5·3	1652	5·2	0057	4·0	1336	3·6
23	F	0505	6·9	1712	6·7	0130	9·0	1355	8·6	0948	12·2	2209	12·3	0842	7·0	2121	7·0	0229	3·4	1509	3·1	0456	5·2	1736	5·2	0143	4·0	1422	3·6
24	Sa	0550	6·7	1756	6·6	0215	8·8	1443	8·5	1031	12·2	2255	12·2	0924	6·9	2206	6·8	0313	3·5	1555	3·1	0544	5·2	1824	5·1	0229	4·0	1514	3·6
25	Su	0641	6·5	1845	6·5	0303	8·8	1534	8·3	1118	11·9	2343	11·9	1009	6·8	2255	6·5	0359	3·5	1643	3·1	0635	5·1	1917	5·0	0321	4·0	1610	3·6
26	M	0738	6·3	1945	6·4	0355	8·6	1628	8·1	—	—	1208	11·6	1101	6·8	2354	6·8	0449	3·4	1731	3·1	0728	5·1	2012	4·8	0417	3·9	1713	3·5
27	Tu	0846	6·3	2057	6·3	0452	8·5	1732	7·9	0039	11·6	1306	11·3	0103	6·3	1201	6·3	0545	3·3	1824	3·0	0826	5·0	2112	4·8	0521	3·8	1820	3·5
28	W	0956	6·4	2212	6·3	0558	8·3	1841	7·9	0144	11·2	1418	11·1	0212	6·4	1312	6·4	0654	3·1	1932	2·9	0927	5·0	2215	4·8	0631	3·7	1925	3·5
29	Th	1105	6·4	2325	6·4	0707	8·3	1949	8·3	0257	11·2	1531	11·2	0319	6·5	1423	6·5	0814	3·0	2045	2·9	1035	5·0	2320	4·9	0740	3·7	2023	3·6
30	F	—	—	—	—	0816	8·4	2053	8·3	0407	11·3	1640	11·4	—	—	1534	6·5	0926	3·0	2147	3·0	1143	5·1	—	—	0844	3·7	2116	3·8

* All times shown are Greenwich Mean Time.   † Difference of height in metres from Ordnance Datum (Newlyn).
‡ Difference of height in metres from Ordnance Datum (Dublin).

JULY, 1989

High Water at the undermentioned Places (G.M.T.*)—

Day of Month	Day of Week	London Bridge †Datum 3·20 m. below Mn. h.m.	Ht. m.	Aft. h.m.	Ht.	Liverpool †Datum 4·98 m. below Mn. h.m.	Ht.	Aft. h.m.	Ht.	Avonmouth †Datum 6·50 m. below Mn. h.m.	Ht.	Aft. h.m.	Ht.	Hull (Albert Dock) †Datum 3·90 m. below Mn. h.m.	Ht.	Aft. h.m.	Ht.	Greenock †Datum 1·62 m. below Mn. h.m.	Ht.	Aft. h.m.	Ht.	Leith †Datum 2·90 m. below Mn. h.m.	Ht.	Aft. h.m.	Ht.	Dun Laoghaire ‡Datum 0·20 m. above Mn. h.m.	Ht.	Aft. h.m.	Ht.
1	Sa	0031		1208	6·4	0919	8·5	2149	8·7	0513	11·6	1740	11·8	0421	6·7	1642	6·9	1028	3·0	2240	3·1	0020	5·0	1247	5·2	0939	3·8	2205	3·9
2	Su	0127	6·4	1304	6·4	1016	8·7	2241	8·9	0614	11·8	1835	12·1	0516	6·8	1743	6·9	1126	3·1	2331	3·3	0115	5·2	1345	5·3	1033	3·8	2252	4·0
3	M	0216	6·4	1354	6·4	1108	8·9	2329	9·1	0706	12·1	1924	12·5	0604	7·0	1835	6·9	1222	3·1			0207	5·3	1439	5·4	1121	3·8	2336	4·0
4	Tu	0301	6·6	1437	6·6	1154	8·9			0752	12·2	2009	12·4	0648	7·0	1921	6·8	0018	3·4	1315	3·0	0255	5·3	1528	5·4	0022	4·1	1209	3·7
5	W	0343	6·7	1518	6·7	0012	9·2	1238	8·9	0836	12·4	2050	12·4	0728	7·1	2004	6·6	0104	3·5	1403	3·0	0340	5·4	1612	5·4	0107	4·1	1254	3·6
6	Th	0424	6·8	1557	6·8	0053	9·1	1317	8·8	0915	12·1	2128	12·0	0805	7·1	2042	6·6	0146	3·6	1447	3·0	0422	5·3	1654	5·3	0152	4·0	1339	3·6
7	F	0502	7·0	1634	6·7	0131	9·0	1355	8·5	0952	11·8	2203	11·7	0842	7·1	2118	6·5	0227	3·6	1527	3·0	0504	5·2	1734	5·0	0236	3·9	1422	3·5
8	Sa	0540	6·8	1711	6·6	0210	8·7	1432	8·3	1026	11·5	2235	11·4	0917	6·9	2153	6·4	0306	3·6	1605	2·9	0545	5·1	1814	4·6	0320	3·8	1506	3·4
9	Su	0618	6·6	1746	6·4	0246	8·5	1510	8·0	1059	11·2	2311	11·2	0955	6·9	2230	6·3	0344	3·4	1643	2·9	0626	4·8	1854	4·5	0406	3·6	1552	3·3
10	M	0702	6·6	1825	6·1	0325	8·1	1552	7·7	1134	10·8	2349	10·4	1035	6·3	2312	6·0	0425	3·4	1721	2·8	0708	4·7	1936	4·5	0456	3·4	1640	3·2
11	Tu	0752	6·3	1913	5·9	0410	7·8	1641	7·4	0038	10·5	1217	9·9	0001	5·8	1224	5·9	0510	3·1	1804	2·7	0753	4·5	2022	4·5	0555	3·3	1738	3·2
12	W	0849	5·8	2012	5·6	0502	7·4	1742	7·2	0138	10·1	1310	9·7	0106	5·7	1338	5·9	0559	2·9	1856	2·7	0841	4·3	2115	4·5	0701	3·2	1838	3·3
13	Th	0946	5·7	2114	5·5	0607	7·2	1850	7·2	0247	9·9	1419	9·9	0215	5·7	1451	5·9	0657	2·8	2003	2·7	0940	4·1	2214	4·5	0802	3·2	1936	3·3
14	F	1044	5·7	2214	5·5	0720	7·4	1958	7·4	0353	10·2	1528	10·2	0319	6·2	1556	6·0	0801	2·8	2111	2·8	1047	4·4	2318	4·4	0855	3·3	2028	3·4
15	Sa	1143	6·0	2316	5·7	0826	7·8	2054	7·8	0458	10·6	1633	11·1	0417	6·7	1652	6·2	0907	2·9	2205	3·0	1156	4·5			0944	3·5	2114	3·6
16	Su	0018	5·9	1242	5·8	0921	8·2	2143	8·3	0556	11·7	1732	12·2	0505	6·7	1739	6·7	1006	2·9	2251	3·1	0018	4·6	1256	4·6	1028	3·6	2156	3·7
17	M	0112	6·3	1333	6·0	1009	8·2	2228	8·7	0646	11·7	1822	13·2	0549	7·3	1821	7·0	1059	2·9	2332		0112	4·8	1349	4·9	1110	3·7	2236	3·9
18	Tu	0201	6·7	1419	6·4	1052	8·5	2311	8·5	0731	12·6	1907	13·3	0628	7·5	1902	7·1	1150	2·9			0157	5·0	1435	5·1	1151	3·8	2316	4·0
19	W	0244	7·0	1501	6·8	1134	8·9	2353	8·9	0813	13·1	1951	13·3	0707	7·5	1942	7·3	0014	3·2	1239	2·9	0238	5·3	1515	5·3			2357	4·1
20	Th	0328	7·0	1541	7·0	0035	9·6	1217	9·2	0854	13·0	2032	13·1	0745	7·4	2022	7·3	0066	3·2	1328	3·0	0318	5·5	1555	5·5	0039	4·1	1233	3·9
21	F	0409	7·2	1619	7·2	0116	9·5	1259	9·6	0935	12·6	2114	12·5	0825	7·1	2103	7·1	0139	3·5	1414	3·1	0357	5·5	1635	5·5	0123	4·3	1315	3·8
22	Sa	0449	7·3	1657	7·3	0159	9·3	1341	9·5	1017	11·9	2155	11·2	0905	6·8	2145	6·5	0222	3·6	1459	3·2	0439	5·5	1717	5·5	0208	4·3	1401	3·8
23	Su	0532	7·1	1736	7·1	0242	9·0	1423	9·3	1058	11·7	2238	10·9	0948	6·2	2228	6·3	0305	3·6	1541	3·2	0526	5·3	1804	5·3	0259	4·2	1449	3·8
24	M	0617	6·9	1821	6·8	0328	8·5	1508	9·0	1143	11·7	2322	10·7	1035	6·1	2320	6·5	0348	3·5	1622	3·2	0613	5·1	1852	5·1	0352	4·0	1540	3·7
25	Tu	0709	6·6	1914	6·4	0421	8·1	1557	8·7	0011	11·7	1234	11·3	1133	6·2	2320	6·5	0434	3·3	1704	3·0	0704	5·3	1944	4·9	0455	4·0	1639	3·6
26	W	0811	6·3	2025	6·1	0527	7·8	1657	8·3	0110	10·9	1341	11·5	0025	6·2	1245	6·1	0524	3·3	1750	2·9	0759	5·1	2042	4·8	0607	3·9	1746	3·5
27	Th	0922	6·1	2146	6·1	0646	7·7	1811	7·9	0229	10·4	1504	11·2	0141	6·1	1408	6·3	0624	3·1	1846	2·9	0902	4·9	2150	4·7	0726	3·7	1858	3·6
28	F	1040	6·1	2312	6·1	0808	7·8	1931	7·7	0349	10·9	1623	10·7	0301	6·3	1535	6·5	0744	2·9	2005	2·9	1019	4·8	2305	4·7	0838	3·6	2006	3·6
29	Sa	1153	6·2			0918	8·1	2046	8·0	0505	10·9	1732	11·3	0413	6·4	1648	6·5	0914	2·8	2129	3·0	1139	4·9			0941	3·6	2107	3·7
30	Su			1253	6·3	1014	8·5	2146	8·1	0607	11·4	1828	11·9	0509	6·7	1743	6·7	1029	2·8	2232	3·2	0014	5·0	1249	5·0	1035	3·7	2159	3·8
31	M	0024	6·3	1253	6·3		8·5	2235	8·5									1130	2·9	2324		0114	5·2	1346	5·2			2246	4·0

* All times shown are Greenwich Mean Time. † Difference of height in metres from Ordnance Datum (Newlyn).
‡ Difference of height in metres from Ordnance Datum (Dublin).

AUGUST, 1989

High Water at the undermentioned Places (G.M.T.*)—

Day of Month	Day of Week	London Bridge †Datum 3·20 m. below				Liverpool †Datum 4·93 m. below				Avonmouth †Datum 6·50 m. below				Hull (Albert Dock) †Datum 3·90 m. below				Greenock †Datum 1·62 m. below				Leith †Datum 2·90 m. below				Dun Laoghaire ‡Datum 0·20 m. above			
		Mn. h.m.	Ht. m.	Aft. h.m.	Ht. m.	Mn. h.m.	Ht. m.	Aft. h.m.	Ht. m.	Mn. h.m.	Ht. m.	Aft. h.m.	Ht. m.	Mn. h.m.	Ht. m.	Aft. h.m.	Ht. m.	Mn. h.m.	Ht. m.	Aft. h.m.	Ht. m.	Mn. h.m.	Ht. m.	Aft. h.m.	Ht. m.	Mn. h.m.	Ht. m.	Aft. h.m.	Ht. m.
1	Tu	0121	6·5	1342	6·5	1101	8·8	2319	9·1	0657	11·9	1913	12·3	0554	6·9	1829	6·8	1223	2·9			0205	5·2	1437	5·3	1119	3·7	2328	4·1
2	W	0208	6·7	1425	6·6	1142	8·9	2357	9·3	0740	12·3	1954	12·6	0634	7·1	1907	6·9	0011	3·3	1311	3·0	0248	5·3	1518	5·4	1159	3·7		
3	Th	0249	6·9	1501	6·8			1218	9·0	0819	12·7	2030	12·7	0709	7·3	1942	6·9	0055	3·5	1354	3·0	0326	5·4	1555	5·3	0009	4·1	1236	3·7
4	F	0325	7·0	1536	6·9	0034	9·3	1253	8·9	0853	12·5	2104	12·7	0742	7·4	2015	6·9	0135	3·5	1430	3·0	0401	5·3	1630	5·2	0047	4·1	1311	3·7
5	Sa	0400	7·0	1609	6·8	0106	9·2	1324	8·8	0925	12·3	2135	12·6	0815	7·4	2046	6·9	0212	3·5	1504	2·9	0437	5·3	1703	4·9	0125	4·1	1346	3·6
6	Su	0433	6·9	1640	6·7	0138	9·0	1355	8·6	0955	12·3	2203	12·4	0847	7·3	2117	6·8	0245	3·5	1534	2·9	0511	5·1	1736	4·7	0201	4·0	1421	3·6
7	M	0505	6·7	1711	6·6	0209	8·7	1427	8·3	1023	11·9	2233	11·9	0921	7·1	2148	6·6	0319	3·4	1603	2·9	0547	5·0	1811	4·5	0239	3·8	1459	3·5
8	Tu	0537	6·5	1746	6·3	0242	8·4	1503	8·0	1051	11·3	2304	11·3	0956	6·9	2223	6·3	0353	3·3	1633	2·9	0623	4·8	1851	4·4	0315	3·5	1540	3·4
9	W	0612	6·2	1825	6·0	0317	7·9	1542	7·6	1120	10·6	2337	10·5	1035	6·3	2304	6·0	0431	3·1	1708	2·8	0703	4·6	1928	4·4	0359	3·5	1629	3·3
10	Th	0655	5·9	1912	5·7	0359	7·5	1635	7·2	1156	9·8			1123	5·8	2357	5·7	0515	2·9	1750	2·8	0748	4·4	2018	4·2	0453	3·3	1730	3·2
11	F	0744	5·6	2012	5·4	0501	7·0	1750	7·0	0022	9·8	1252	9·2	0121	5·5	1413	5·5	0606	2·8	1843	2·7	0848	4·3	2123	4·2	0603	3·2	1842	3·2
12	Sa	0846	5·4	2124	5·3	0629	6·8	1917	7·1	0133	9·1	1427	9·1	0243	5·7	1534	5·7	0707	2·8	1957	3·0	1007	4·3	2241	4·5	0723	3·3	1950	3·4
13	Su	0955	5·4	2238	5·4	0758	7·6	2029	7·6	0305	9·3	1556	9·7	0350	6·1	1635	6·1	0821	2·8	2125	3·1	1132	4·3	2354	4·9	0830	3·3	2045	3·6
14	M	1111	5·7	2356	5·7	0903	8·2	2124	8·2	0428	10·1	1706	10·7	0444	6·4	1723	6·4	0941	2·9	2226	3·3			1239	4·8	0925	3·5	2132	3·8
15	Tu			1221	6·1	0952	8·7	2210	8·8	0534	11·0	1801	11·8	0527	6·8	1805	6·9	1045	2·9	2314	3·3	0052	4·8	1332	5·2	1009	3·7	2215	4·0
16	W	0053	6·4	1314	6·6	1035	9·2	2252	9·3	0627	11·9	1848	12·6	0607	7·1	1843	7·3	1137	2·9	2358	3·0	0139	5·1	1417	5·5	1052	3·9	2255	4·2
17	Th	0142	7·1	1359	7·3	1116	9·5	2333	9·7	0713	13·0	1931	13·3	0645	7·6	1921	7·6	1226	2·9			0220	5·4	1456	5·7	1131	4·0	2336	4·3
18	F	0226	7·3	1440	7·3	1157	9·5			0755	13·3	2013	13·8	0723	7·9	1958	7·7	0043	3·5	1313	3·1	0258	5·7	1534	5·7			1209	4·1
19	Sa	0307	7·5	1518	7·5	0014	9·6	1238	9·6	0836	13·7	2054	14·0	0801	8·1	2037	8·0	0128	3·6	1359	3·1	0336	5·8	1611	5·6	0016	4·4	1250	4·1
20	Su	0348	7·5	1556	7·5	0055	10·0	1317	9·9	0915	13·5	2135	13·4	0842	8·0	2117	7·3	0211	3·7	1441	3·3	0418	5·9	1653	5·4	0058	4·5	1333	4·1
21	M	0428	7·3	1634	7·3	0135	9·9	1358	9·9	0955	13·5	2216	13·4	0925	7·2	2200	7·2	0252	3·7	1519	3·3	0503	5·8	1739	5·2	0146	4·3	1418	4·0
22	Tu	0509	6·9	1715	7·0	0218	9·6	1440	9·4	1034	12·5	2258	12·5	1014	7·2	2251	6·5	0334	3·7	1557	3·4	0552	5·6	1828	4·9	0235	4·3	1508	3·9
23	W	0551	6·5	1758	6·7	0303	9·1	1527	8·8	1115	11·8	2343	11·3	1112	6·6	2354	6·1	0416	3·5	1636	3·3	0643	5·3	1921	4·7	0329	4·1	1607	3·7
24	Th	0639	6·2	1853	6·3	0355	8·4	1627	7·8			1201	10·8	0119	5·9	1411	5·9	0504	3·0	1719	3·3	0740	5·3	2020	4·5	0433	3·6	1717	3·6
25	F	0738	5·9	2005	6·1	0505	7·7	1750	7·0	0041	10·3	1310	9·8	0251	6·0	1542	6·1	0602	3·0	1812	3·3	0840	4·7	2135	4·6	0552	3·6	1837	3·5
26	Sa	0851	5·8	2129	6·1	0638	7·3	1924	7·5	0205	9·8	1443	9·7	0404	6·3	1645	6·4	0726	2·7	1929	3·1	1017	4·6	2301	4·6	0720	3·5	1954	3·6
27	Su	1016	5·8	2301	6·1	0809	7·8	2042	8·0	0338	9·8	1613	10·3	0457	6·7	1733	6·6	0925	2·8	2121	3·0	1142	4·8			0840	3·5	2058	3·9
28	M	1136	6·1			0915	8·5	2138	8·5	0457	10·6	1723	11·2	0537	7·0	1811	6·8	1041	2·9	2230	2·7	0013	4·8	1248	5·0	0941	3·7	2152	4·1
29	Tu	0012	6·5	1238	6·5	1004	8·8	2223	8·8	0554	11·5	1814	12·0	0612	7·3	1845	7·0	1132	2·9	2318	3·2	0109	5·0	1341	5·1	1029	3·8	2237	4·1
30	W	0107	6·8	1326	6·7	1045	9·2	2301	9·0	0641	12·1	1856	12·5					1215	2·9			0155	5·2	1424	5·3	1107	3·8	2314	4·1
31	Th	0151	7·0	1405	7·0	1120	9·0	2334	9·0	0719	12·5	1933	12·8					0001	3·3	1245	3·0	0233	5·4	1500	5·3	1140	3·8	2350	4·2

*All times shown are Greenwich Mean Time.   †Difference of height in metres from Ordnance Datum (Newlyn).   ‡Difference of height in metres from Ordnance Datum (Dublin).

SEPTEMBER, 1989

High Water at the undermentioned Places (G.M.T.*)—

Datum of Predictions (below Ordnance Datum unless stated):
London Bridge † 3·20 m. below · Liverpool † 4·93 m. below · Avonmouth † 6·50 m. below · Hull (Albert Dock) † 3·90 m. below · Greenock † 1·62 m. below · Leith † 2·90 m. below · Dun Laoghaire ‡ 0·20 m. above

Day	DoW	LB Mn	Ht	LB Aft	Ht	Liv Mn	Ht	Liv Aft	Ht	Avon Mn	Ht	Avon Aft	Ht	Hull Mn	Ht	Hull Aft	Ht	Greenock Mn	Ht	Greenock Aft	Ht	Leith Mn	Ht	Leith Aft	Ht	Dun L. Mn	Ht	Dun L. Aft	Ht
1	F	0229	7·0	1440	6·9	1153	9·1	—	—	0754	12·8	2005	13·0	0643	7·5	1914	7·1	0041	3·4	1330	3·0	0305	5·4	1531	5·3	0021	4·2	1209	3·8
2	Sa	0301	7·0	1511	7·0	0007	9·3	1222	9·1	0826	12·9	2036	13·1	0716	7·6	1942	7·2	0117	3·5	1403	3·0	0336	5·4	1559	5·3	0053	4·1	1237	3·8
3	Su	0332	6·9	1539	6·9	0036	9·3	1252	9·0	0856	12·9	2104	13·0	0747	7·6	2011	7·1	0151	3·5	1432	3·0	0405	5·3	1627	5·0	0125	4·0	1307	3·8
4	M	0359	6·8	1606	6·8	0104	9·1	1320	9·1	0922	12·7	2131	12·7	0818	7·1	2040	7·0	0220	3·4	1457	3·0	0436	5·2	1657	4·9	0159	3·8	1339	3·7
5	Tu	0427	6·7	1635	6·7	0133	8·8	1348	8·6	0948	12·1	2157	12·1	0849	7·1	2108	6·8	0249	3·4	1522	2·9	0508	5·1	1730	4·7	0235	3·7	1413	3·6
6	W	0457	6·6	1709	6·5	0201	8·5	1419	8·2	1012	11·4	2223	11·1	0919	6·8	2139	6·1	0320	3·2	1550	2·9	0543	4·9	1804	4·5	0315	3·5	1452	3·5
7	Th	0530	6·4	1746	6·1	0232	8·0	1454	7·8	1033	10·6	2249	10·4	0953	6·2	2212	5·7	0356	3·0	1623	2·9	0621	4·7	1843	4·2	0409	3·3	1539	3·4
8	F	0607	6·1	1829	5·7	0311	7·5	1542	7·3	1057	9·2	2325	9·6	1035	5·4	2257	5·3	0438	2·9	1705	2·9	0710	4·4	1934	4·2	0521	3·2	1639	3·3
9	Sa	0650	5·7	1923	5·4	0407	7·0	1655	7·0	1143	9·0	1317	8·8	1137	5·5	1338	5·6	0529	2·9	1755	2·8	0815	4·2	2042	4·5	0649	3·2	1753	3·3
10	Su	0748	5·4	2037	5·2	0543	6·7	1836	6·7	0031	8·8	1517	8·5	0011	5·6	1507	6·2	0628	2·8	1901	2·7	0940	4·2	2207	4·6	0806	3·6	1911	3·4
11	M	0908	5·3	2209	5·4	0728	6·7	1959	6·8	0211	9·1	1635	9·0	0206	5·9	1612	6·7	0745	2·7	2044	2·8	1107	4·3	2325	5·3	0902	3·8	2014	3·6
12	Tu	1042	5·6	2332	6·0	0839	7·7	2057	7·7	0356	10·0	1733	10·7	0319	6·5	1659	7·1	0925	2·9	2202	2·9	—	—	1215	5·6	0948	4·0	2107	3·9
13	W	1156	6·2	—	—	0928	8·4	2143	8·3	0506	11·1	1822	12·0	0414	7·0	1740	7·5	1029	3·0	2253	3·0	0025	4·8	1307	5·6	1028	4·3	2151	4·1
14	Th	0029	6·8	1248	6·8	1012	9·5	2227	9·0	0601	12·3	1907	13·1	0501	7·5	1818	7·8	1117	3·0	2338	3·2	0113	5·6	1351	5·8	1105	4·6	2230	4·4
15	F	0117	7·2	1333	7·2	1052	9·8	2308	9·6	0648	13·1	1949	14·0	0540	7·9	1855	8·0	1204	3·0	1249	3·3	0153	5·8	1429	5·7	1143	4·5	2310	4·5
16	Sa	0201	7·5	1413	7·5	1132	10·0	2349	10·0	0731	13·8	2032	14·2	0618	8·2	1931	8·2	0025	3·6	1333	3·4	0231	6·0	1507	5·5	—	—	2351	4·6
17	Su	0243	7·5	1451	7·7	—	—	1212	10·2	0812	14·1	2112	14·4	0656	8·3	2011	8·3	0110	3·7	1413	3·5	0310	6·0	1546	5·5	0035	4·5	1221	4·3
18	M	0322	7·5	1531	7·5	0029	10·3	1252	9·7	0851	13·6	2153	14·1	0737	8·1	2051	8·1	0154	3·8	1451	3·5	0353	5·6	1629	4·9	0122	4·3	1303	4·2
19	Tu	0403	7·1	1613	7·1	0112	10·0	1333	9·4	0931	12·7	2235	13·3	0820	7·7	2135	7·4	0236	3·8	1530	3·3	0439	4·9	1715	4·6	0213	4·0	1350	4·0
20	W	0444	6·9	1657	7·0	0154	10·0	1415	9·5	1012	11·5	2322	12·0	0907	7·0	2226	6·5	0317	3·5	1609	3·3	0531	4·6	1806	4·8	0310	3·8	1442	3·8
21	Th	0527	6·5	1744	6·5	0240	9·5	1503	8·4	1051	9·7	1250	10·8	0957	6·3	2329	5·8	0400	3·3	1653	3·0	0625	4·6	1901	5·0	0416	3·7	1542	3·6
22	F	0615	6·3	1841	6·3	0336	8·4	1606	8·1	1139	9·2	1423	9·5	1101	5·8	1225	5·7	0448	3·3	1747	2·8	0727	4·8	2004	5·2	0542	3·6	1653	3·6
23	Sa	0713	5·8	1951	5·9	0452	8·1	1733	7·4	0022	10·5	1556	9·4	0056	6·7	1413	6·3	0547	2·9	1902	2·8	0842	5·0	2123	5·3	0716	3·7	1818	3·7
24	Su	0823	5·6	2111	5·8	0631	7·4	1910	7·2	0147	11·5	1701	10·2	0236	7·3	1534	6·6	0722	2·6	2109	3·0	1012	5·2	2249	5·4	0832	3·8	1939	4·0
25	M	0949	5·7	2242	6·1	0758	7·2	2025	8·1	0319	12·3	1750	11·2	0345	7·5	1630	6·8	0934	2·8	2216	3·2	1132	5·3	2359	5·4	0928	3·9	2045	4·1
26	Tu	1113	6·1	2353	6·6	0858	8·1	2117	8·5	0437	12·9	1829	12·1	0434	—	1711	7·3	1034	2·9	2301	3·3	—	—	1232	5·4	1009	3·9	2135	4·0
27	W	—	—	1214	6·6	0943	8·5	2157	8·9	0530	13·1	1904	12·6	0512	6·7	1746	7·2	1115	3·0	2340	3·1	0051	5·0	1319	5·0	1044	4·0	2216	4·1
28	Th	0043	7·0	1300	6·9	1020	8·8	2234	9·2	0614	—	1937	13·1	0546	7·3	1815	—	1150	3·0	1257	—	0134	5·2	1358	5·2	1112	4·1	2253	4·2
29	F	0126	7·1	1340	7·0	1052	9·2	2306	9·3	0650	—	—	—	0617	7·5	1843	—	1224	3·4	—	—	0209	5·3	1431	5·3	1137	4·1	2323	4·2
30	Sa	0202	7·1	1412	7·0	1123	9·1	2336	9·3	0726	—	—	—	—	—	—	—	0017	3·4	—	—	0239	5·4	1500	5·4	—	—	2352	4·1

* All times shown are Greenwich Mean Time.   †Difference of height in metres from Ordnance Datum (Newlyn).   ‡Difference of height in metres from Ordnance Datum (Dublin).

OCTOBER, 1989

High Water at the undermentioned Places (G.M.T.*)—

Datum of Predictions below Ordnance Datum (metres): London Bridge 3·20 m. below · Liverpool 4·93 m. below · Avonmouth 6·50 m. below · Hull (Albert Dock) 3·90 m. below · Greenock 1·62 m. below · Leith 2·90 m. below · Dun Laoghaire 0·20 m. above.

Day	Wk	LB Mn h.m	Ht	LB Aft h.m	Ht	Liv Mn h.m	Ht	Liv Aft h.m	Ht	Avon Mn h.m	Ht	Avon Aft h.m	Ht	Hull Mn h.m	Ht	Hull Aft h.m	Ht	Gree Mn h.m	Ht	Gree Aft h.m	Ht	Leith Mn h.m	Ht	Leith Aft h.m	Ht	Dun L Mn h.m	Ht	Dun L Aft h.m	Ht
1	Su	0233	7·0	1442	7·0	0004	9·1	1219	9·1	0755	13·0	2006	13·1	0648	7·5	1910	7·3	0052	3·4	1328	3·1	0305	5·4	1525	5·3	0021	—	1202	3·9
2	M	0300	6·9	1507	6·9	0032	9·2	1248	9·1	0825	13·0	2033	13·0	0719	7·5	1938	7·2	0122	3·4	1354	3·1	0334	5·4	1552	5·2	0051	4·0	1230	3·9
3	Tu	0324	6·9	1535	6·8	0100	9·0	1316	9·0	0850	12·7	2100	12·6	0749	7·2	2005	6·8	0151	3·3	1419	3·1	0404	5·3	1621	5·1	0125	3·9	1301	3·9
4	W	0350	6·8	1606	6·7	0130	8·8	1347	8·7	0915	12·1	2127	11·9	0820	7·0	2033	6·5	0219	3·2	1443	3·1	0435	5·1	1653	5·0	0201	3·8	1336	3·8
5	Th	0421	6·7	1640	6·6	0202	8·5	1422	8·4	0939	11·4	2152	11·1	0851	6·5	2101	6·2	0250	3·1	1512	3·2	0512	4·9	1728	4·8	0246	3·7	1417	3·7
6	F	0455	6·5	1718	6·3	0242	8·1	1510	8·0	1000	10·6	2219	10·4	0924	6·2	2132	5·8	0327	3·1	1548	3·2	0553	4·7	1810	4·6	0342	3·5	1504	3·6
7	Sa	0532	6·2	1801	6·0	0339	7·6	1620	7·6	1027	10·0	2257	9·7	1006	5·8	2216	5·4	0411	3·1	1631	3·1	0646	4·4	1904	4·4	0452	3·4	1603	3·5
8	Su	0615	5·9	1855	5·7	0509	7·1	1756	7·1	1116	9·4	—	—	1106	5·8	2325	—	0502	2·9	1722	2·9	0753	4·2	2014	4·3	0617	3·4	1714	3·4
9	M	0712	5·5	2006	5·5	0650	6·7	1920	6·7	0003	9·2	1248	9·1	0120	5·5	1257	5·5	0601	2·9	1826	2·9	0915	4·2	2133	4·2	0736	3·3	1831	3·5
10	Tu	0832	5·4	2139	5·6	0802	7·1	2020	7·1	0137	9·4	1434	10·9	0240	6·0	1430	6·0	0718	2·8	2004	2·9	1035	4·4	2249	4·4	0834	3·3	1940	3·7
11	W	1009	5·7	2301	6·2	0856	7·7	2111	7·7	0318	10·1	1559	10·9	0338	6·5	1536	6·3	0902	2·9	2132	3·1	1141	4·7	2349	4·9	0919	3·7	2035	4·0
12	Th	1122	6·3	—	—	0941	8·5	2156	8·5	0433	11·4	1701	12·3	0426	7·1	1627	6·8	1003	3·0	2226	3·4	—	—	1233	5·1	0959	3·9	2122	4·2
13	F	0001	6·8	1217	6·9	1023	9·1	2240	9·1	0530	12·6	1754	13·3	0509	7·6	1709	7·1	1049	3·1	2314	3·5	0040	5·3	1318	5·4	1037	4·1	2205	4·4
14	Sa	0050	7·2	1303	7·3	1105	9·6	2323	9·6	0621	13·4	1842	13·9	0551	7·8	1749	7·6	1133	3·2	1219	3·5	0122	5·6	1359	5·7	1114	4·3	2246	4·5
15	Su	0134	7·4	1345	7·5	1147	9·9	—	—	0706	13·9	1927	14·2	0634	8·2	1827	7·8	0001	3·7	1302	3·6	0203	5·9	1438	5·8	1154	4·3	2327	4·6
16	M	0216	7·5	1426	7·7	0007	9·9	1228	9·8	0748	14·1	2009	14·2	0717	7·9	1906	8·1	0048	3·6	1345	3·6	0244	6·0	1520	5·8	0012	4·4	1237	4·4
17	Tu	0257	7·4	1508	7·7	0050	9·8	1310	9·5	0830	14·0	2053	13·8	0805	7·6	1947	7·9	0034	3·7	1424	3·7	0331	6·0	1605	5·7	0101	4·5	1326	4·3
18	W	0339	7·1	1555	7·5	0135	9·5	1355	9·1	0911	13·4	2136	13·4	0854	7·3	2029	7·4	0217	3·7	1503	3·7	0421	5·6	1653	5·5	0154	4·5	1418	4·1
19	Th	0424	6·9	1642	7·2	0226	9·1	1447	8·7	0953	12·5	2221	11·8	0949	6·5	2115	6·5	0300	3·6	1545	3·7	0514	5·2	1746	5·1	0254	4·2	1520	3·8
20	F	0509	6·5	1734	6·7	0324	8·7	1549	7·9	1037	11·3	2309	11·3	1052	6·1	2206	6·1	0346	3·6	1632	3·6	0612	4·9	1842	4·9	0403	4·3	1632	3·8
21	Sa	0557	6·1	1831	6·3	0438	7·9	1711	7·4	1127	10·3	—	—	0019	5·9	2305	5·9	0436	3·3	1727	3·4	0715	4·6	1946	4·7	0527	3·5	1755	3·7
22	Su	0652	5·8	1934	6·0	0605	7·4	1836	7·2	0008	9·2	1232	9·6	0158	5·9	1212	5·6	0537	2·9	1839	2·9	0827	4·6	2101	4·6	0656	3·5	1913	3·7
23	M	0757	5·6	2046	5·8	0726	7·2	1948	7·2	0120	9·2	1351	9·5	0311	6·2	1349	6·1	0717	2·7	2032	2·7	0948	4·7	2218	4·8	0807	3·5	2017	3·8
24	Tu	0914	5·6	2210	6·0	0825	7·5	2042	7·5	0240	9·4	1514	10·0	0402	6·5	1504	6·5	0911	2·7	2143	2·7	1100	4·9	2327	—	0900	3·5	2108	3·8
25	W	1040	5·9	2322	6·4	0910	7·9	2124	7·9	0356	10·4	1623	11·0	0442	6·7	1557	6·7	1004	2·9	2228	2·9	1158	5·0	1243	5·1	0941	3·7	2149	4·0
26	Th	1143	6·4	—	—	0948	8·3	2200	8·3	0454	11·3	1713	11·9	0516	7·1	1640	6·9	1042	3·0	2308	3·0	0020	5·0	1322	5·1	1012	3·8	2223	4·0
27	F	0014	6·8	1229	6·8	1020	8·8	2234	8·8	0539	12·4	1756	12·5	0550	7·1	1713	7·1	1117	3·1	2345	3·1	0101	5·1	1355	5·2	1040	3·9	2253	4·0
28	Sa	0056	7·0	1309	7·0	1051	8·9	2305	8·9	0618	12·5	1834	12·7	0622	7·3	1743	7·2	1149	3·1	1250	3·3	0136	5·2	1424	5·3	1106	3·9	2323	4·0
29	Su	0131	7·0	1342	7·0	1120	9·0	2336	9·0	0653	12·8	1906	12·8	0653	7·3	1811	7·3	1221	3·3	1317	3·3	0206	5·3	1452	5·3	1133	4·0	2352	3·9
30	M	0201	6·9	1411	6·9	1150	9·1	—	—	0726	12·8	1937	12·8	0724	7·3	1839	7·2	0020	3·3	2345	3·2	0235	5·3	1452	5·3	1106	3·9	2323	3·9
31	Tu	0226	6·9	1439	6·9	—	—	—	—	0755	12·7	2006	12·6	0755	7·1	1909	7·1	0052	3·3	1317	3·2	0306	5·3	1522	5·3	1133	4·0	1202	4·0

* All times shown are Greenwich Mean Time.   † Difference of height in metres from Ordnance Datum (Newlyn).
‡ Difference of height in metres from Ordnance Datum (Dublin).

NOVEMBER, 1989

High Water at the undermentioned Places (G.M.T.*)—

Datum of Predictions:
- London Bridge — †3·20 m. below
- Liverpool — †4·93 m. below
- Avonmouth — †6·50 m. below
- Hull (Albert Dock) — †3·90 m. below
- Greenock — †1·62 m. below
- Leith — †2·90 m. below
- Dun Laoghaire — ‡0·20 m. above

(h.m. = time in hours and minutes; Ht. = height in metres)

Day	Day of Week	LB Mn	Ht	LB Aft	Ht	Liv Mn	Ht	Liv Aft	Ht	Avon Mn	Ht	Avon Aft	Ht	Hull Mn	Ht	Hull Aft	Ht	Green Mn	Ht	Green Aft	Ht	Leith Mn	Ht	Leith Aft	Ht	Dun L Mn	Ht	Dun L Aft	Ht
1	W	0253	6·9	1510	6·8	0005	8·9	1221	9·0	0823	12·5	2036	12·3	0726	7·0	1937	7·0	0122	3·3	1344	3·2	0337	5·2	1554	5·2	0025	3·8	1235	4·0
2	Th	0322	6·8	1543	6·7	0036	8·7	1252	8·8	0851	12·0	2104	11·7	0758	6·8	2006	6·8	0153	3·2	1411	3·3	0414	5·1	1628	5·1	0100	3·8	1311	3·9
3	F	0355	6·7	1620	6·6	0109	8·4	1326	8·5	0918	11·2	2135	11·2	0833	6·6	2037	6·6	0227	3·2	1443	3·3	0454	4·8	1706	4·9	0142	3·6	1354	3·8
4	Sa	0431	6·6	1659	6·5	0145	8·1	1405	8·2	0948	10·4	2209	10·6	0910	6·2	2114	6·3	0308	3·1	1522	3·3	0538	4·6	1750	4·6	0227	3·5	1442	3·8
5	Su	0509	6·4	1744	6·3	0229	7·8	1454	7·9	1024	10·0	2255	10·2	0955	5·8	2159	6·1	0353	3·1	1607	3·3	0632	4·4	1844	4·4	0321	3·4	1538	3·7
6	M	0553	6·1	1838	6·0	0327	7·4	1559	7·6	1120	10·0	2357	9·9	1054	5·8	—	—	0445	3·1	1658	3·2	0734	4·4	1948	4·5	0428	3·3	1640	3·6
7	Tu	0648	5·8	1945	5·8	0442	7·2	1718	7·6	—	—	1401	9·9	—	—	1215	5·8	0541	3·0	1759	3·1	0843	4·4	2057	4·6	0543	3·4	1752	3·7
8	W	0801	5·7	2108	5·9	0607	7·4	1835	8·0	0113	10·0	1522	10·3	0028	5·8	1345	6·1	0651	3·1	1925	3·1	0954	4·6	2208	5·0	0658	3·5	1901	3·8
9	Th	0929	5·9	2226	6·3	0719	7·9	1940	8·5	0242	10·5	1628	11·3	0151	6·1	1453	6·3	0823	3·0	2054	3·2	1059	4·8	2308	5·0	0800	3·7	2002	4·0
10	F	1044	6·3	2329	6·8	0818	8·5	2036	9·0	0357	11·5	1726	12·3	0254	6·6	1549	6·7	0927	3·1	2153	3·4	1153	5·1	—	—	0848	3·9	2053	4·2
11	Sa	1143	6·8	—	—	0908	9·0	2127	9·5	0459	12·5	1818	13·0	0350	7·1	1637	7·1	1016	3·2	2245	3·6	0002	5·3	1242	5·4	0931	4·1	2139	4·3
12	Su	0022	7·1	1235	7·1	0956	9·4	2214	9·9	0553	13·1	1906	13·5	0441	7·5	1722	7·6	1101	3·5	2335	3·6	0052	5·6	1328	5·6	1011	4·2	2223	4·4
13	M	0100	7·1	1321	7·2	1041	9·7	2302	9·9	0642	13·5	1952	13·7	0529	7·7	1804	7·6	1147	3·7	—	—	0138	5·8	1412	5·7	1052	4·3	2309	4·4
14	Tu	0154	7·1	1406	7·2	1126	9·7	2349	9·8	0728	13·6	2039	13·6	0618	7·9	1848	7·8	0025	3·7	1233	3·6	0225	5·9	1458	5·8	1133	4·4	2357	4·3
15	W	0237	7·0	1454	7·4	—	—	1211	9·4	0812	13·5	2125	13·2	0707	7·8	1930	7·5	0115	3·6	1318	3·8	0315	5·9	1545	5·9	—	—	1218	4·4
16	Th	0322	6·9	1543	7·2	0036	9·6	1256	9·6	0857	13·1	2210	12·6	0758	7·5	2015	7·0	0202	3·6	1359	3·8	0407	5·7	1637	5·7	0047	4·0	1308	4·3
17	F	0407	6·6	1634	6·9	0124	9·6	1342	9·0	0941	11·5	2257	11·7	0849	7·0	2100	6·6	0249	3·5	1442	3·7	0501	5·5	1729	5·5	0142	4·0	1403	4·2
18	Sa	0454	6·3	1725	6·5	0215	8·9	1433	8·6	1026	10·7	2347	10·8	0941	6·6	2146	6·6	0337	3·3	1526	3·7	0557	5·2	1824	5·2	0240	3·8	1501	4·0
19	Su	0542	6·1	1810	6·1	0308	8·0	1529	8·2	1113	10·0	—	—	1035	6·6	2237	5·9	0427	3·1	1614	3·5	0656	4·9	1922	4·9	0345	3·6	1607	3·9
20	M	0629	5·8	1910	5·9	0410	7·6	1633	7·8	—	—	1307	10·1	1136	5·8	2336	6·0	0525	2·9	1707	3·3	0757	4·7	2025	4·7	0459	3·4	1718	3·7
21	Tu	0724	5·8	2011	5·9	0519	7·3	1743	7·7	0043	9·7	1415	10·2	—	—	1253	6·0	0640	2·8	1810	3·1	0903	4·7	2130	4·6	0618	3·4	1833	3·7
22	W	0829	5·7	2121	5·7	0631	7·3	1853	7·3	0147	9·8	1524	10·0	0048	6·0	1411	6·3	0813	2·8	1933	3·0	1009	4·7	2235	4·6	0727	3·4	1939	3·7
23	Th	0948	5·8	2235	5·9	0735	7·9	1954	7·9	0254	10·8	1626	11·3	0212	6·3	1511	6·5	0916	2·9	2050	3·0	1109	4·7	2331	4·7	0821	3·5	2031	3·8
24	F	1059	6·1	2333	6·4	0826	8·2	2043	8·4	0400	11·4	1716	11·8	0315	6·5	1557	6·8	1001	3·1	2145	3·2	1158	4·9	—	—	0904	3·6	2115	3·8
25	Sa	1153	6·4	—	—	0910	8·5	2125	8·5	0455	12·0	1758	12·1	0404	6·8	1637	6·9	1038	3·2	2229	3·2	0018	4·9	1241	4·9	0938	3·7	2153	3·8
26	Su	0018	6·6	1235	6·6	0946	8·5	2203	8·7	0542	12·3	1838	12·3	0447	6·9	1711	7·0	1112	3·2	2309	3·3	0058	5·1	1319	5·0	1009	3·9	2226	3·8
27	M	0055	6·7	1310	6·7	1021	8·7	2238	8·7	0621	12·3	1913	12·3	0525	6·9	1743	7·0	1145	3·3	2347	3·3	0134	5·1	1353	5·1	1039	3·9	2259	3·8
28	Tu	0127	6·7	1344	6·7	1055	8·9	2312	8·9	0657	12·4	1947	12·4	0600	7·0	1814	7·0	1218	3·3	—	—	0210	5·1	1427	5·2	1109	4·0	2331	3·8
29	W	0158	6·8	1416	6·7	1129	9·0	2347	9·0	0731	12·4	2019	12·2	0635	6·9	1845	6·9	0023	3·3	1246	3·3	0246	5·2	1500	5·2	1141	4·0	—	—
30	Th	0230	6·8	1453	6·7	—	—	1203	9·0	0804	12·2	—	—	0709	6·8	1917	6·8	0058	3·2	1316	3·3	0324	5·2	1535	5·3	0008	3·8	1216	4·0

* All times shown are Greenwich Mean Time.   †Difference of height in metres from Ordnance Datum (Newlyn).   ‡Difference of height in metres from Ordnance Datum (Dublin).

DECEMBER, 1989

High Water at the undermentioned Places (G.M.T.*)—

Day of Month	Day of Week	LONDON BRIDGE †Datum of Predictions 3·20 m. below				LIVERPOOL †Datum of Predictions 4·93 m. below				AVONMOUTH †Datum of Predictions 6·50 m. below				HULL (Albert Dock) †Datum of Predictions 3·90 m. below				GREENOCK †Datum of Predictions 1·62 m. below				LEITH †Datum of Predictions 2·90 m. below				DUN LAOGHAIRE ‡Datum of Predictions 0·20 m. above			
		Mn.	Ht.	Aft.	Ht.	Mn.	Ht.	Aft.	Ht.	Mn.	Ht.	Aft.	Ht.	Mn.	Ht.	Aft.	Ht.	Mn.	Ht.	Aft.	Ht.	Mn.	Ht.	Aft.	Ht.	Mn.	Ht.	Aft.	Ht.
		h.m.	m.	h.m.	m.	h.m.	m.	h.m.	m.	h.m.	m.	h.m.	m.	h.m.	m.	h.m.	m.	h.m.	m.	h.m.	m.	h.m.	m.	h.m.	m.	h.m.	m.	h.m.	m.
1	F	0305	6·8	1531	6·8	0021	8·7	1238	8·9	0837	12·0	2054	11·8	0745	6·8	1952	6·9	0135	3·2	1348	3·4	0402	5·2	1613	5·2	0046	3·7	1254	4·0
2	Sa	0342	6·8	1610	6·8	0057	8·5	1316	8·8	0911	11·8	2129	11·6	0823	6·7	2029	6·8	0214	3·1	1424	3·4	0443	5·1	1653	5·1	0128	3·7	1337	4·0
3	Su	0419	6·7	1651	6·7	0137	8·3	1358	8·6	0948	11·6	2210	11·4	0904	6·5	2107	6·7	0256	3·1	1505	3·5	0527	5·0	1737	5·0	0213	3·6	1422	3·9
4	M	0458	6·5	1734	6·5	0222	8·1	1444	8·4	1031	11·3	2255	11·1	0949	6·2	2152	6·5	0342	3·2	1546	3·5	0616	4·8	1827	4·9	0303	3·5	1513	3·9
5	Tu	0540	6·4	1824	6·3	0314	7·9	1539	8·2	1120	11·1	2347	10·9	1040	6·1	2245	6·2	0430	3·2	1640	3·4	0708	4·7	1922	4·9	0400	3·5	1609	3·9
6	W	0628	6·2	1923	6·1	0414	7·7	1642	8·1	—	10·8	1219	10·9	—	—	1150	6·1	0521	3·2	1737	3·4	0808	4·7	2021	4·9	0504	3·5	1713	3·8
7	Th	0730	6·1	2034	6·1	0523	7·7	1750	8·2	0049	10·8	1328	11·0	0102	6·4	1253	6·4	0619	3·1	1848	3·3	0910	4·7	2123	4·9	0616	3·5	1821	3·8
8	F	0847	6·1	2149	6·3	0634	7·9	1857	8·4	0205	11·0	1446	11·3	0212	6·7	1405	6·6	0732	3·1	2012	3·3	1014	4·7	2227	5·2	0722	3·6	1929	3·9
9	Sa	1004	6·3	2258	6·6	0740	8·2	2002	8·7	0322	11·3	1557	11·9	0317	7·0	1510	7·0	0845	3·1	2122	3·4	1116	5·0	2330	5·2	0817	3·8	2028	4·0
10	Su	1112	6·6	2357	6·7	0834	8·4	2057	9·0	0430	11·7	1701	11·9	0420	7·2	1609	7·4	0942	3·3	2220	3·5	—	—	1213	5·2	0907	3·9	2122	4·1
11	M	—	—	1212	6·7	0934	8·6	2157	9·3	0529	11·9	1758	12·5	0519	7·5	1702	7·5	1054	3·4	2315	3·5	0028	5·4	1305	5·4	0952	4·1	2211	4·1
12	Tu	0050	6·8	1307	6·7	1024	8·9	2249	9·4	0624	12·5	1852	12·9	0614	7·4	1750	7·5	1122	3·5	1211	3·6	0123	5·5	1355	5·5	1036	4·2	2259	4·1
13	W	0140	6·8	1358	6·7	1113	9·3	2340	9·5	0714	13·1	1942	13·0	0704	7·4	1836	7·4	0010	3·5	1258	3·8	0216	5·6	1445	5·5	1120	4·3	2348	4·3
14	Th	0226	6·8	1447	7·1	—	—	1201	9·5	0801	13·1	2029	13·1	0754	7·2	1920	7·4	0103	3·5	1343	3·8	0307	5·7	1533	5·6	—	—	1208	4·3
15	F	0311	6·9	1536	7·2	0028	9·3	1248	9·4	0846	13·1	2114	12·9	0840	7·3	2002	7·2	0153	3·4	1427	3·9	0358	5·6	1622	5·5	0039	4·0	1257	4·3
16	Sa	0356	6·9	1623	7·2	0114	9·0	1333	9·2	0929	12·6	2157	12·6	0924	7·1	2044	7·1	0234	3·4	1511	3·9	0448	5·5	1711	5·3	0130	3·9	1349	4·2
17	Su	0438	6·8	1708	7·0	0159	8·7	1416	8·9	1010	11·9	2238	11·4	1007	7·0	2125	6·9	0328	3·2	1556	3·7	0537	5·2	1759	5·2	0222	3·7	1442	4·1
18	M	0520	6·6	1753	6·7	0244	8·3	1501	8·5	1051	11·3	2318	11·1	1051	6·7	2206	6·7	0414	3·1	1643	3·6	0626	5·0	1850	5·0	0317	3·6	1536	3·9
19	Tu	0603	6·3	1838	6·3	0331	7·9	1549	8·1	1132	11·1	—	—	—	—	2252	5·8	0500	3·1	1735	3·5	0717	4·7	1940	4·8	0416	3·4	1635	3·8
20	W	0648	6·0	1928	6·0	0421	7·6	1642	7·8	0000	10·8	1218	10·8	0052	6·1	1139	6·1	0551	2·9	1836	3·3	0809	4·6	2032	4·5	0520	3·3	1739	3·6
21	Th	0741	5·8	2025	5·8	0519	7·3	1743	7·5	0050	10·3	1314	10·5	0151	6·1	1418	6·1	0650	2·9	1945	3·1	0905	4·5	2129	4·5	0628	3·3	1845	3·5
22	F	0846	5·7	2128	5·8	0625	7·2	1850	7·4	0151	10·1	1418	10·2	0256	6·1	1524	6·4	0752	2·8	2050	3·0	1004	4·5	2228	4·5	0729	3·3	1946	3·5
23	Sa	0955	5·9	2233	5·9	0730	7·3	1955	7·5	0256	10·0	1524	10·6	0402	6·1	1628	6·5	0854	2·9	2147	3·0	1103	4·5	2327	4·6	0818	3·5	2038	3·5
24	Su	1101	5·9	2329	6·1	0827	7·7	2050	7·7	0402	10·1	1628	10·9	0502	6·5	1725	6·7	0946	3·0	2319	3·1	1156	4·7	—	—	0901	3·6	2122	3·6
25	M	1154	6·0	—	—	0915	8·0	2136	8·3	0502	11·1	1725	11·3	0543	6·7	1812	6·9	1034	3·1	—	—	0021	4·7	1244	4·8	0939	3·8	2202	3·6
26	Tu	0015	6·3	1239	6·2	0957	8·4	2219	8·5	0553	11·6	1812	11·7	0621	6·9	1853	7·1	1114	3·2	1223	3·3	0108	4·8	1328	4·9	1014	3·9	2240	3·6
27	W	0056	6·5	1321	6·6	1035	8·7	2257	8·7	0635	12·1	1853	11·9	0657	7·0	1933	7·1	1149	3·3	1257	3·3	0153	4·9	1408	5·1	1050	4·0	2316	3·7
28	Th	0137	6·6	1402	6·6	1113	8·9	2334	8·7	0714	12·1	1933	12·0	0735	7·0	2009	6·9	0001	3·2	1327	3·4	0234	5·1	1446	5·2	1124	4·0	2354	3·7
29	F	0218	6·6	1443	7·0	1150	9·1	—	—	0751	12·3	2009	12·1	0815	6·9	2047	7·0	0042	3·1	1357	3·5	0314	5·2	1523	5·3	—	—	1201	4·0
30	Sa	0257	6·9	1524	7·0	0011	9·1	1228	9·1	0827	12·4	2047	12·3	—	—	1334	7·3	0124	3·1	1334	3·5	0351	5·3	1559	5·3	0032	3·7	1240	4·1
31	Su	0335	6·9	1603	7·0	0049	8·8	1307	9·2	0904	12·6	2124	12·4	0296	7·0	2019	7·3	0206	3·2	1413	3·6	0429	5·3	1638	5·4	0113	3·7	1320	4·1

* All times shown are Greenwich Mean Time.   † Difference of height in metres from Ordnance Datum (Newlyn).   ‡ Difference of height in metres from Ordnance Datum (Dublin).

WEATHER IN THE UNITED KINGDOM, 1987–88

(1987) July.—Rainfall totals were above normal in most parts of the United Kingdom except for south-west England, central and southern Wales and parts of the Midlands where it was rather dry. Most of England and Wales was dry throughout the first half of the month, with no measurable rain in many areas south of a line from south Wales to the Wash until the 13th. Then outbreaks of rain with isolated thunderstorms spread from the southwest into Wales and southern England, becoming persistent and heavier in eastern areas of England on the 16th. On the 6th dust devils were seen at Minehead (Somerset). Rain or showers occurred in northern areas on most days during the second week when 70 mm. (2·8 in.) fell at Girvan (Strathclyde) on the 10th. Hail was reported at Weymouth (Dorset) on the 16th, and on the 17th 88 mm. (3·5 in.) of rain fell at Slapton (Devon) in five hours. Hail fell at Long Sutton (Hants.) on the 18th and winds reached gale force over the Isles of Scilly on the 19th. From the 27th to 31st belts of rain crossed all areas from the west but in parts of Cornwall the 22nd to 29th was mostly dry and the Isles of Scilly had 12 consecutive days without rain. Thunderstorms were accompanied by heavy rain in East Anglia and south-east England on the 29th. These storms were heaviest in the Epping (Essex) area where more than 1 m. (3·3 ft.) of flood water left some people marooned in their homes. Hail fell at Levington (Suffolk) and Finningley (S. Yorks.) on the 29th. Monthly mean temperatures were generally near normal but on the 5th and 6th it was hot, particularly over England and Wales where several stations recorded over 29°C. (84·2°F.) on the 6th. On the 18th Sheffield with 12·7°C. (54·9°F.) recorded its lowest July maximum temperature since 1962. On the 21st the temperature in Glasgow reached 25°C. (77·0°F.) while in Essex and Kent it was only 16°C. (60·8°F.). The lowest temperature of the month was 1·0°C. (33·8°F.) at Lowtown (Co. Antrim) on the 9th. Sunshine amounts were about normal nearly everywhere in the United Kingdom apart from northern Scotland where it was rather dull. The highest daily amount was 16 hours at Worthing (W. Sussex) on the 4th and the highest monthly total was 255 hours at Penzance (Cornwall).

August.—Rainfall totals were above normal in southern Scotland, Northern Ireland, north and east England, parts of the Midlands and northern Wales but below normal elsewhere. East Anglia had its wettest August for over 30 years while south-west England had its driest since 1981. On the 6th gales were reported in north and north-east areas and there were waterspouts off Yarmouth (Isle of Wight). One was 600 m. (1,969 ft.), nearly twice the height of the previous British record. On the 9th thunderstorms brought heavy rain to parts of south and west Yorkshire causing flooding and disrupting traffic. Tornadoes were reported in the Rochdale (Lancs.) area. On the 16th northern areas had heavy rain and storms and some minor roads in the Highlands were almost impassable because of floods. 87 mm. (3·43 in.) fell at Creebridge (Dumfries & Galloway) on the 16th. Desert sand was deposited in rain during the 16th/17th from the Isle of Wight to north-west England. On the 21st and 22nd widespread and sometimes violent thunderstorms gave very heavy rain causing floods in eastern and northern England and the Midlands. Many roads in Lancashire and Greater Manchester were closed by floods, the M61 motorway near Preston being under more than 1 m. (3·3 ft.) of floodwater. On the 22nd a landslide blocked the railway line at Manningtree (Essex) and the area from Chelmsford to Ipswich had one of its worst storms in living memory. Flooding was caused by

torrential rain with hailstones, some the size of golfballs, lying up to 30 cm. (11·8 in.) deep in places. At Isleworth (Greater London) one man was killed and nine injured by lightning at a cricket match. Also on the 22nd 73 mm. (2·9 in.) of rain fell at Birmingham Airport. Gales were again reported in northern and north-eastern areas on the 26th. Monthly mean temperatures were near normal in most parts of the United Kingdom. On the 18th southern counties of England had their warmest August night since 1980 with temperatures averaging more than 21°C. (69·8°F.) in parts of Sussex, Kent and Hampshire. The highest temperature recorded during the month was 30·2°C. (86·4°F.) at Liphook (Hants.) on the 21st and the lowest was −4·4°C. (24·1°F.) at Inverinan (Strathclyde) on the 5th. Sunshine totals were generally above normal in south Wales, south-west England and eastern Scotland but below normal elsewhere. The highest daily sunshine total was 14·9 hours at Cumnock (Strathclyde) on the 5th and the highest monthly total was 260 hours at St. Helier (Jersey).

September.—Rainfall totals were generally below normal in England and Wales but above normal in parts of western Scotland. Oxford had its driest September since 1979 with a total of 25·4 mm. (1·0 in.) for the month. On the 1st there was heavy rain in the London area. Thunderstorms occurred over eastern England and south-east Scotland on the 5th. A gust of 78 knots (89·8 mph) was recorded in a squall at Camborne (Cornwall) on the 5th, the highest September gust there since records began in 1979. On the 11th and 12th rain was widespread over central England, with gales in the west and south west on the 11th. On the 14th there were gales in north-eastern areas when a mean hourly speed of 36 knots (41·5 mph) was recorded at Butt of Lewis (Western Isles) and Fraserburgh (Grampian), while 34 knots (39·2 mph) was recorded at Blyth (Northumbs.). It was wet in England and Wales on the 16th and early on the 17th, followed by widespread fog. There were thunderstorms in south-east England on the 19th and it was showery in most areas on the 23rd and 24th with some hail and thunder, particularly in central and south-east England. Hail was widespread over the United Kingdom on the 24th and 25th. Hailstones of 10–20 mm. (0·4–0·8 in.) in diameter fell at Rugby (Warwicks.) on the 24th, and even larger ones fell at Prabost (Highland) on the 23rd. Monthly mean temperatures were below normal in northern areas and above normal in the south. The temperature rose to 26·5°C. (79·7°F.) at Christchurch (Dorset) on the 5th and at Margate and Elmstone (Kent) on the 17th. Overnight frosts occurred from the 25th to 30th and the temperature fell to −3·3°C. (26·1°F.) at Braemer (Grampian) on the 28th. Sunshine totals were generally above normal except in central southern and south-west England where they were near or below normal. It was the sunniest September at Tiree since 1927 and the second sunniest at Lerwick (Shetland) since 1922. The highest daily total was 12·4 hours at Cumnock (Strathclyde) on the 2nd and the highest monthly total was 187 hours at Dunbar (Lothian).

October.—Rainfall totals were well above normal generally but near normal in north-west Scotland. It was the fourth wettest October in England and Wales since 1727. On the 8th hailstones of 10–20 mm. (0·4–0·8 in.) fell at Slaidburn (Lancs.) On the 9th torrential rain caused flooding and road accidents in south-eastern areas as gales swept the south coast. Floods brought commuter traffic in London to a halt. Snow fell at Alwen (Clwyd) on the 9th. Further heavy rain brought more severe flooding to many parts of the south east on the 10th. In Essex some villages were almost cut off when the river Stour burst its banks, and flooding to a depth of 4 m. (13·1 ft.) occurred near Colchester. On the 16th a violent storm with heavy rain brought chaos to southern England. The winds were probably the strongest for 250 years. Millions of trees were uprooted or broken, many crashed into power lines and houses, or fell across roads and railway lines. The damage and disruption was enormous and the cost almost incalculable: the insured loss from the storm, about £1·5 billion, was the greatest on record for a natural disaster anywhere in the world (including earthquakes and tropical hurricanes). Some large areas were without electricity for up to a fortnight. The violent winds produced several gusts of over 90 knots (104 mph) and at Shoreham-by-Sea (W. Sussex) a mean hourly wind of 72 knots (83 mph) was recorded just before a power failure stopped the recorder. This is the highest mean wind ever recorded below 200 m. (656 ft.) in the United Kingdom. A gust of 100 knots (115 mph) was estimated from the recorder just after the power failure. On the 17th and 18th there were strong winds and heavy rain in western and northern Wales. Trecastle (Powys) had 22·2 cm. (8·7 in.) of rain from the 14th to the 18th, 77 mm. (3·0 in.) more than the normal amount for the month. There was widespread flooding, worst around Carmarthen and in the areas of the rivers Teifi and Tywi. At Glanrhyd near Llandeilo a Swansea to Shrewsbury train plunged into the river when the bridge gave way, killing four people. On the 20th torrential rain brought flooding to large areas of Northern Ireland, with floodwater up to 3 m. (9·8 ft.) deep in Strabane (Co. Londonderry). Patchy overnight fog occurred frequently in many parts of England from the 23rd to the end of the month. Sand was deposited in rain over southern England on the 27th. Monthly mean temperatures were below normal everywhere apart from one or two places in southern England. The highest temperature of the month was 22·1°C (71·8°F.) at Aldenham School (Herts.) on the 4th and the lowest temperature was −7·0°C. (19·4°F.) at St. Harmon (Powys) on the 24th. Sheffield had its lowest October day maximum temperatures since 1975 and its lowest mean temperature since 1981. Sunshine totals were above normal in most areas except for parts of the south coast of England and northern and eastern Scotland. The highest daily total was 10 hours at Ryde (Isle of Wight) and Jersey on the 1st and the highest monthly total was 135·7 hours at Faversham (Kent).

November.—Rainfall totals were below normal in most areas although one or two places had more than average. Overnight fog became widespread during the first week with southern and central England most affected. There was widespread rain on the 8th, heavy in places, and from the 10th onwards some places had rain almost every day of the month. There were gales in many areas on the 11th especially in the south and south west where mean hourly speeds were recorded of 42 knots (48·4 mph) at Shoreham-by-Sea (W. Sussex) and 48 knots (55·3 mph) at Gwennap Head (Cornwall). A gust of 71 knots (81·8 mph) was recorded at Gwennap Head. Snow was reported on high ground in Scotland and northern England on the 11th. There were further gales, mainly in the north west, on the 12th and fresh snow was reported in northern Wales on the 13th. On the 20th severe gales affected north and north-east Scotland with mean winds of 44 knots (50·7 mph) at Fraserburgh (Grampian) and 41 knots (47·2 mph) at Sumburgh (Shetland) and Butt of Lewis (Western Isles) being recorded. A gust of 70 knots (80·6 mph) was recorded at Fair Isle (Shetland). Snow fell widely down to near sea level on the 23rd and 25th with falls

as far south as Cornwall. Further rain reached all areas except south-east England on the 29th, with substantial falls in Devon, Cornwall and Dyfed. In central and south-east England some patches of freezing fog persisted all day on the 29th. Monthly mean temperatures were near normal everywhere in the United Kingdom. Oxford recorded its lowest maximum temperature for November since 1957 and its fourth lowest since 1881 with 12·6°C. (54·7°F.) on the 15th and 19th. The highest temperature of the month was 15·7°C. (60·3°F.) at Jersey on the 1st and the lowest was −10·0°C. (14·0°C.) at St. Harmon (Powys) on the 28th. Sunshine totals were below normal in most areas, except for parts of southern and eastern Scotland, south-west England and west Wales where it was quite sunny. The highest daily total was 8·5 hours at Boulmer (Northumbs.) on the 2nd, at Aberporth (Dyfed) on the 3rd, at Swansea (W. Glamorgan) on the 4th and at Long Sutton and Southsea (Hants.) on the 14th. The highest monthly total was 89·5 hours at Swansea.

December.—Rainfall totals were below normal in all areas except southern Scotland. Most of the area south of a line from Torbay (Devon) to the Wash was rather dry with about half the average rainfall. It was the driest December at Brooms Barn (Suffolk) and Hampstead (Gtr. London) since 1963. There was extensive and persistent fog in north-east Scotland on the first few days of the month. On the 2nd and 3rd snow fell in parts of the south west and in south Wales. Snow showers occurred in Shetland on the 5th, 6th and 7th and in other parts of Scotland between the 6th and 10th. In northern England snow fell in Durham on the 4th and in Tyne and Wear on the 6th. Between the 7th and 11th there was snow in East Anglia and on the 9th in parts of Middlesex, Essex and Buckinghamshire. There was snow in Gwynedd on the 11th and areas of dense fog in the Midlands. On the 19th 89 mm. (3·5 in.) of rain fell at Onich (Highland). Strong gales occurred in northern and western parts of Scotland on the 21st and 22nd when a gust of 71 knots (82 mph) was recorded at Sumburgh (Shetland). At Butt of Lewis (Western Isles) a mean wind of 47 knots (54 mph) was recorded on the 21st and mean winds of more than 40 knots (46 mph) were recorded in Orkney and Shetland on the 22nd. Hailstones of between 10 and 20 mm. (0·4 and 0·8 in.) in diameter fell at Colonsay (Strathclyde) on the 29th and there was further snow in Shetland on the 30th. Monthly mean temperatures were above normal nearly everywhere in the United Kingdom but the early part of the month was cold. On the 3rd the Moray Firth area of Scotland had temperatures below freezing all day. Frost was extensive at night between the 6th and 14th and on the 9th it was freezing all day in parts of Scotland and Northern Ireland. The frost was severe in Scotland on the 14th. The highest temperature recorded during the month was 15·9°C. (60·6°F.) at Minehead (Somerset) on the 17th and the lowest was −11·9°C. (10·6°F.) at Newry (Co. Down) on the 11th. Sunshine totals were generally below normal except in north-west Scotland and Northern Ireland. It was the dullest December at Sheffield since 1958 and at Coventry since 1964. The highest daily total was 7·9 hours at Jersey, Gorey Castle and St. Helier (Channel Is.) on the 9th. The highest monthly total was 58·3 hours at Valley (Gwynedd).

Year (1987).—The year 1987 will be remembered for the very cold spell in January, when the 12th was probably the coldest day this century in many parts of England and Wales, and for the very violent storm of October 16th when the winds were probably the strongest for 250 years. January was the driest in Hampstead (Gtr. London) since 1914. On the 4th, after torrential rain, the river Dovey burst its banks and flood-water blocked roads between Aberystwyth (Dyfed) and Machynlleth (Powys). On the 8th freezing fog closed Heathrow and Gatwick airports and disrupted traffic in the south east. On the 12th 15·35 in. of snow were measured at Penzance (Cornwall) and there were drifts over 20 feet deep in Kent. On the 13th conditions in Kent were the worst for 20 years and 20·5 inches of snow were measured at East Malling. On the 14th very heavy snow brought traffic to a halt in the Midlands and Wales. February was a changeable month. On the 3rd and 4th fog was thick and caused three collisions at sea. At Grizedale (Cumbria) 6·5 inches of rain fell in the last three days of the month to give a total for the month of 10·5 in. Gusts of 83 mph were recorded at Leeds and Blyth (Northumbs.) on the 6th. March was an unsettled month. Western Scotland had nearly two and a half times the normal rainfall. There were gales in the north and west on the 6th and 7th with heavy snow, and roads across the Pennines were blocked; many minor roads in the west were closed and traffic was disrupted on the M4 in Wiltshire. On the 19th traffic was again disrupted by snow in Avon, Wiltshire, Dorset and Hampshire. On the 27th many roads in north Wales were flooded and a 98 mph gust was recorded at Rhoose (S. Glamorgan), the highest ever recorded there. A gust of 107 mph was recorded at Gwennap Head (Cornwall) and at Oxford a mature beech tree was uprooted outside Keble College, while the spire of Waresley Church (Cambs.) was demolished. The Severn Bridge was closed to all traffic for only the second time in 20 years. On the 28th lightning struck a B.B.C. outside broadcast tower as rain, hail and wind accompanied the Boat Race. April was a month of contrast with almost daily rain in the first half and a record-breaking dry spell in the second half. By the 6th some places in the south west had received almost twice the normal April rainfall. There was considerable flooding around Exeter and in other areas of Devon and Cornwall. On the 10th there was flooding at Whitchester (Borders). However, after the 12th some places in central and southern England had no rain for 16 days. On the 17th, London with 72·7°F. and Bristol with 70·7°F. had one of the warmest Good Friday's since the 1940's. Bidston (Merseyside) had its warmest April since 1867. May was a generally unsettled month. On the 1st, two cross-channel ferries collided in thick fog outside Dover. Gales were reported on western coasts on the 2nd but otherwise it was a quiet month. June was a particularly wet month with many places in eastern areas having more than twice the average amount of rainfall. Ringway (Gtr. Manchester) had nearly three times the normal amount. Sheffield had its greatest consecutive number of days with rain since 1935. There was much flooding, particularly in southern areas, on the 6th, 7th, 14th and 15th. On the 14th 7 people were injured when lightning struck a tree in Stroud (Glos.) and on the 26th a whirlwind uprooted apple trees and destroyed greenhouses at Aston (S. Yorks.). On the 28th fog closed Jersey airport, stranding holiday makers. July was a very settled month with no measurable rain in many southern areas before the 13th. Despite this rainfall totals were above normal in most areas except south-west England and parts of Wales and the Midlands. After severe thunderstorms on the 29th flood-water was over three feet deep in the Epping (Essex) area. August was generally a wet month, except for south-west England where it was particularly dry. East Anglia had its wettest August for 30 years while North Wyke (Devon) had its driest since 1959. There were floods in south and west Yorkshire on the 9th and in the Highlands of Scotland on the 16th. On the 21st/22nd violent thunderstorms caused floods in eastern and northern England and the Midlands

with many roads affected. On the 22nd a landslide blocked the railway at Manningtree (Essex), and from Chelmsford to Ipswich torrential rain and hail more than a foot deep caused floods and chaos. At a cricket match at Isleworth (Gtr. London) one man was killed and nine injured by lightning. September was quite a dry month even though there was occasional heavy rain in places. Hailstones of over ½ inch in diameter fell at Rugby (Warwicks.) on the 24th. It was the sunniest September at Tiree since 1927 and the second sunniest at Lerwick (Shetland) since 1922. October was a very wet month with some places in the south east having up to three times the normal amount of rainfall. England and Wales had the 4th wettest October since 1727. On the 9th torrential rain caused flooding and accidents in south-eastern areas and London was almost brought to a standstill. There was further severe flooding in the area on the 10th. In Essex the river Stour burst its banks causing flooding near Colchester up to 13 feet deep. On the 16th a violent storm brought winds which were probably the strongest for 250 years over southern England. The damage was enormous and the insured loss was the greatest on record for a natural disaster anywhere in the world. Shoreham-by-Sea (W. Sussex) recorded a mean hourly wind of 83 mph., the highest mean wind ever recorded at a low-level station in the United Kingdom. There were numerous gusts of over 100 mph across southern England. Between the 14th and 18th Trecastle (Powys) had 8·7 inches of rain and there was widespread flooding around Carmarthen and near the Teifi and Tywi rivers. Floods were nearly 10 feet deep in Strabane (Co. Londonderry) on the 20th. November was a windy month with gales in many areas on the 11th, in the north west on the 12th, and in north and east Scotland on the 20th. There were widespread snowfalls from the 23rd to 25th as far south as Cornwall. December was a dry month except in southern Scotland but there were frequent falls of snow in many parts of the country.

(1988) January.—Rainfall was above normal everywhere except in Shetland and the far north of Scotland. Parts of East Anglia had more than two and a half times the average amount. It was the wettest January in England and Wales since 1948 and the wettest at Hampstead (Gtr. London) since 1909. Heavy rain on the 2nd caused a landslip on the road between Bideford and Torrington (Devon), and gale force winds in the south west brought down several large trees and caused a power failure in north Devon. On the 4th there were further gales in the south west and a tanker was blown from its moorings at Milford Haven (Dyfed). Three women were injured in Cardiff when glass panels were blown from the roof of the central market. Also on the 4th there was fairly heavy snow over the Pennines and hailstones 10–20 mm. (0·4–0·8 in.) in diameter were reported at Oxford. On the 5th thunderstorms in south-west Wales caused power cuts, and lightning demolished the steeple of a Swansea chapel. On the 6th further gales caused the closure of the Severn Bridge for only the third time in its history when a high-sided lorry overturned. 12 cm. (4·7 in.) of snow was reported on Great Dun Fell (Cumbria) on the 6th and on the 11th 87 mm. (3·4 in.) of rain fell at Inverailort (Highland). Heavy rain fell in north-western parts of the United Kingdom on the 17th, and 85 mm. (3·3 in.) at Trassey Slievenaman (Co. Down) on the 18th. On the 21st/22nd snow fell in the north and there was considerable snowfall in central England with depths of up to 18 cm. (7·1 in.) being reported. On the 23rd snow was heavy for a time over Lincolnshire and north-east England. There was dense fog on the 25th in parts of the Midlands and northern England. On the 29th torrential rain fell in the south causing flooding in areas as far apart as Gloucestershire and Wiltshire in the west and Essex and Kent in the east. Monthly mean temperatures were above normal nearly everywhere except north-west Scotland where they were near normal. The highest temperature recorded during the month was 14·9°C. (58·8°F.) at Aber (Gwynedd) on the 8th and the lowest was −8·9°C. (16·0°F.) at Kinbrace (Highland) on the 6th. Sunshine totals were near or above normal everywhere except parts of southern Scotland and parts of eastern England where they were below normal. The highest daily total was 8·2 hours at the Lizard (Cornwall) on the 28th and the highest monthly total was 82 hours at Penzance (Cornwall).

February.—Rainfall totals were above normal in Scotland and Northern Ireland but below normal in England and Wales. On the 1st and 2nd gales were widespread across England and Wales with gusts over 70 knots (81 mph) on exposed west and south-west coasts. On the 9th severe gales affected many parts of the country. A gust of 96 knots (111 mph) was recorded at Gwennap Head (Cornwall) and at Plymouth a gust of 72 knots (83 mph) was the highest ever recorded there in February. North-west England was the worst hit with damage to many buildings, including the roof of the town hall at Bury (Gtr. Manchester). Road and rail traffic was disrupted and a bus was blown over at Chesterfield (Derbys.) Rail services between Glasgow and London were disrupted when electrical equipment was damaged. On the 9th and 10th heavy drifting snow blocked major roads across the Pennines and there was heavy snow in north Devon. There was prolonged snowfall in the Grampians on the 10th/11th. Hail was widespread and frequent during the first half of the month. There was rain in most areas, heavy in parts of the south and west, on the 12th and 13th but after that many southern areas of England had no rain at all. Parts of eastern England had a covering of snow on the 25th. On the 28th the Grampian region had about 30 cm. (11·8 in.) of level snow blocking some major roads. Monthly mean temperatures were above normal everywhere but there was widespread frost on the 12th with temperatures below −5°C. (23·0°F.) in central areas of Scotland. There was widespread frost over England and Wales on the 26th. The highest temperature recorded during the month was 16·6°C. (61·9°F.) at Betws-y-Coed (Gwynedd) and Prestatyn (Clwyd) on the 15th. The lowest was −9·4°C. (15·1°F.) at Glenlivet (Grampian) on the 12th. Sunshine was above normal everywhere except in north-west Scotland. It was a very sunny month with many places in central and southern areas in particular having the highest February amounts since records began. Bablake (Warwicks.) had its highest total since 1895 and Sheffield its highest since 1949. Brighton (E. Sussex), Bognor Regis (W. Sussex), Swanage (Dorset), Torbay and Teignmouth (Devon) had around 144 hours. The highest daily total was 10·2 hours at Starcross (Devon) and the highest monthly total was 144·4 hours at Teignmouth.

March.—Rainfall was above normal in most places and was two and a half times the normal amount in parts of the Midlands and the north west. Silsoe (Beds.) had its wettest March since 1982 despite having 13 days without rain. It was the wettest March in Northern Ireland since 1903. There were 39 cm. (15·3 in.) of level snow at Fealar Lodge (Grampian) on the 1st. The 3rd was a windy day in the north of Scotland with gales in many places. At the Forth Road Bridge (Lothian) a mean speed of 38 knots (44 mph) was recorded with a gust of 60 knots (69 mph). On the 4th snow showers in the north of Scotland gave 17 cm. (6·7 in.) of snow at Kinbrace

(Highland). On the 15th winds were very strong over a wide area of the country and 66 knots (76 mph) was the highest gust ever recorded for March at Culdrose (Cornwall). A gust of 85 knots (98 mph) was recorded at Gwennap Head. Fog formed over a wide area on the 19th and 21st, mainly in southern England, but with a few patches in Lincolnshire, Yorkshire and Northern Ireland. On the 22nd fog was widespread over eastern Scotland and on the 24th 81·5 mm.(3·2 in.) of rain fell at Killin (Central). Gales occurred over a wide area on the 24th and a gust of 66 knots (76 mph) was recorded at Leith Harbour (Lothian). There was widespread thunder from southern Scotland to East Anglia, and lightning caused damage to property at Donington (Lincs.). Hail was reported frequently during the month. Monthly mean temperatures were above normal in all areas except northern Scotland. There was severe overnight frost on the 1st and it became very cold in north Scotland on the 12th, with severe night frosts from the 13th–15th. The highest temperature recorded was 15·6°C. (60·1°F.) at Leeming (N. Yorks.) on the 19th and the lowest was −10·2°C. (13·6°F.) at Tummel Bridge (Tayside) on the 14th. Sunshine totals were above normal only in the coastal areas of north-east England and eastern Scotland, Orkney and Shetland: otherwise it was a dull month everywhere. Oxford had nearly 30 hours less than the average amount. The highest daily total was 11·6 hours at Hazelrigg and Morecambe (Lancs.) and at Starcross (Devon) on the 30th. The highest monthly total was 147·3 hours at Leuchars (Fife).

April.—Rainfall totals were generally above normal north of a line from the Isle of Man to Tynemouth, except for western Scotland. South of the line it was generally dry except for some places in central and south-east England and the extreme south of Cornwall. Arbroath (Grampian) had nearly three times the normal amount of rainfall. It was the driest April since 1984 in parts of Northern Ireland. On the 2nd snow fell on high ground in Scotland to give 24 cm. (9·5 in.) at Cairngorm (Highland). On the 3rd thunderstorms occurred in the Midlands, notably over Nottinghamshire and Derbyshire. There was snow over much of eastern Wales and central and southeastern England on the 9th. On the 10th and 14th gales in the north gave a mean wind speed of 38 knots (44 mph) at Butt of Lewis (Western Isles). Rain fell in the extreme west on the 13th and spread to all but the extreme east of England during the next two days. On the 18th thunder was reported over a wide area of eastern and southern England and 75 mm. (2·9 in.) of rain fell at Arbroath (Tayside). Rain in the extreme east and south-east of England on the 19th gave over 26 mm. (1·0 in.) at Anvil Green (Kent). On the 20th there were thunderstorms in Northern Ireland and on the 23rd there were gales in western Cornwall when a mean speed of 44 knots (51 mph) with gusts of 59 knots (68 mph) was recorded at Gwennap Head. On the 27th there was thunder over much of central southern and south-west England, and hail was widespread in the north Midlands and in places from Dorset to Kent. Monthly mean temperatures were above normal everywhere except the far north of Scotland and on some east-facing coasts in the south and west. On the 5th temperatures in the north were well above normal and places in central Scotland had maxima 7°C. (12·6°F.) above normal. On the 6th a temperature of 20°C. (68°F.) was recorded at Aviemore (Highland) but on the 8th the maximum at Aviemore was only 5°C. (41°F.) followed by a minimum of −7°C. (19·4°F.). The highest temperature of the month was 21·9°C. (71·4°F.) at March (Cambs.) on the 18th and the lowest was −8·2°C. (17·2°F.) at Braemar (Grampian). Sunshine totals were generally below normal except in the far north of Scotland, south-east England and south Wales. The sunniest day was the 13th when most of England and Wales and eastern Scotland enjoyed between 10 and 13 hours of sunshine. The highest daily total was 14 hours at Hastings (E. Sussex) on the 24th and the highest monthly total was 204·7 hours at Hayling Island (Hants.).

May.—Rainfall totals were below normal in all areas except parts of East Anglia, south-west England, south Wales and a few places in the north of Scotland and the Borders. The first 26 days of the month yielded only half the normal amount of rainfall at many places in the south east, and in the United Kingdom as a whole it was the driest May for six years. On the 1st a climber was killed by lightning near Grasmere (Cumbria), and a severe thunderstorm occurred at Moel-y-Crio (Clwyd) with hailstones 15 mm. (0·6 in.) in diameter causing much damage to trees and hedges. Also on the 1st a gust of 56 knots (65 mph) was recorded at Camborne (Cornwall), the highest wind speed recorded in the United Kingdom during the month. There was very little rain between the 4th and 18th in many parts of south and south-west England, with parts of Dorset, Hampshire and the Isle of Wight completely dry. By contrast there was widespread flooding in the Thames valley and north-west London during thunderstorms on the 8th. At Northwood (Gtr. London) 48·5 mm.(1·9 in.) of rain fell in three hours, followed by 23 mm. (0·9 in.) later in the day. On the 7th coloured dust was deposited in places as far apart as North Yorkshire, Dyfed, Essex and the south coast. Overnight fog occurred mainly in England and Wales, between the 9th and 13th, and again on the 27th and 28th. Snow fell in parts of central and northern Scotland between the 17th and 19th. A funnel cloud was seen at Rhoose (S. Glamorgan) on the 19th. Monthly mean temperatures were above normal nearly everywhere for the sixth successive month. Coventry had its warmest May since 1970 and it was also the first May in Coventry without any frost since 1970. Hampstead (Gtr. London) had its warmest May since 1976. The highest temperature of the month was 26·5°C. (79·7°F.) at Inverailort (Highland) on the 15th and the lowest was −3·5°C. (25·7°F.) at Leadhills (Strathclyde) on the 18th. Sunshine totals were near or above normal

in all areas ranging from 93 per cent. of normal in East Anglia to 135 per cent. in eastern Scotland. The United Kingdom had 10 to 14 hours sunshine each day from the 15th to 17th. The highest daily total was 15·9 hours at Kirkwall (Orkney) on the 22nd and the highest monthly total was 271·4 hours at Valley (Gwynedd).

June.—Rainfall totals were generally below normal except in parts of south Wales, the Midlands and East Anglia where rainfall was above normal. Over England and Wales as a whole, rainfall averaged 56 per cent. of normal, making it the driest June since 1976. At Abbotsinch (Strathclyde) the 10 mm. (0·4 in.) total equalled amounts for 1921 and 1926, the driest June since 1868 when records began in the Glasgow area. Morecambe (Lancs.) had its driest June since 1949. Showers or spells of rain affected western areas on the 1st and extended eastwards to most areas by the 3rd with some heavy local falls. There was thunder somewhere in the United Kingdom from the 2nd to the 4th. On the 20th there were heavy showers and thunderstorms with hail in parts of East Anglia, London, south-east and central southern England. The area around Chelmsford (Essex) had a prolonged period of heavy rain with thunder. Showers over the Pennines on the 25th turned to more general and heavy rain for a time, spreading to western England to end two weeks of dry weather there. There were widespread thunderstorms on the 30th. Monthly mean temperatures were slightly above normal in most areas but below normal in parts of the west Midlands, East Anglia and south-east England. It became very warm in Scotland on the 13th and 14th with temperatures of over 25°C. (77·0°F.) in central Scotland. The 23rd was generally the warmest day of the year so far. The highest temperature recorded during the month was 27·7°C. (81·2°F.) at Ardtalnaig (Tayside) on the 13th and the lowest was −0·8°C. (30·6°F.) at St. Harmon (Powys) on the 6th. Sunshine totals were generally above normal in northern Wales, northern England and most of Scotland but below normal in northern Scotland, southern Wales and the remaining areas of England. The highest daily total was 16·7 hours at Prestwick (Strathclyde) on the 12th and the highest monthly total was 237·3 hours at Valley (Gwynedd).

BUCHAN'S WEATHER PERIODS OR RECURRENCES OF WEATHER

Dr. Alexander Buchan, F.R.S., Secretary of the Scottish Meteorological Society, published in 1867 a paper in the Journal of that Society entitled "Interruptions in the regular rise and fall of temperature in the course of the year". Buchan gave six cold periods and three warm periods, based on his examination of the mean daily temperature as recorded at stations in Scotland covering long periods. The cold periods were February 7–14, April 11–14, May 9–14, June 29–July 4, August 6–11, November 6–13, and the warm periods July 12–15, August 12–15, and December 3–14. This early work aroused considerable interest later. It should be noted, however, that Buchan claimed no more than the existence of tendencies for short spells of relatively cold and warm weather to occur at certain times of the year.

In recent years these smaller fluctuations of weather super-imposed on the normal seasonal changes have been examined from the aspect of tendencies to stormy or anticyclonic spells over the British Isles and have been referred to as "singularities". Stormy periods are relatively warm in winter and cool in summer. The following tendencies have been given:—Jan. 5–17 stormy; Jan. 18–24 anticyclonic; Jan. 24–Feb. 1 stormy; Feb. 8–16 anticyclonic; Feb. 21–25 cold; Feb. 26–Mar. 9 stormy; Mar. 12–19 anticyclonic; Mar. 24–31 stormy; April 10–15 stormy; April 23–26 unsettled; June 1–21 summer monsoon; July 10–24 warm; Aug. 20–30 stormy; Sept. 1–17 anticyclonic; Sept. 17–24 stormy; Sept. 24–Oct. 4 anticyclonic; Oct. 5–12 stormy; Oct. 16–20 anticyclonic; Oct. 24–Nov. 13 stormy; Nov. 15–21 anticyclonic; Nov. 24–Dec. 14 stormy; Dec. 18–24 anticyclonic; Dec. 25–Jan. 1 stormy.

AVERAGE AND GENERAL VALUES, 1986–1988 (June)

Month	Rainfall (mm.)				Temperature (°C.)				Bright Sunshine (hrs. per day)			
	Aver. 1941–1970	1986	1987	1988	Aver. 1951–1980	1986	1987	1988	Aver. 1951–1980	1986	1987	1988
England and Wales												
January	86	120	30	154	4·0	4·1	1·4	5·8	1·6	1·9	1·7	1·7
February	65	17	58	63	4·1	−0·4	4·1	5·2	2·3	2·7	2·3	3·7
March	59	80	83	94	5·9	5·4	4·6	6·6	3·6	4·0	3·3	3·1
April	58	84	66	42	8·2	6·2	10·3	8·5	5·1	4·5	5·3	4·6
May	67	85	48	62	11·3	11·3	10·3	12·0	6·3	6·4	6·3	6·6
June	61	43	102	38	14·3	14·8	13·1	14·6	6·7	6·8	4·1	5·8
July	73	54	77	—	16·0	16·1	16·2	—	5·9	5·4	5·6	—
August	90	117	72	—	15·9	14·1	16·0	—	5·5	4·6	5·1	—
September	83	26	67	—	14·0	11·9	14·2	—	4·6	5·7	5·1	—
October	83	95	171	—	11·0	11·4	10·3	—	3·3	3·7	3·4	—
November	97	124	81	—	7·1	8·3	7·2	—	2·1	2·5	1·8	—
December	90	143	59	—	5·1	6·3	6·1	—	1·5	1·7	1·1	—
YEAR	912	988	914	—	9·8	9·1	9·5	—	4·1	4·2	3·8	—
Scotland												
January	137	192	70	193	3·5	2·9	2·0	4·2	1·3	1·1	1·2	1·4
February	104	21	95	149	3·4	0·5	3·5	4·5	2·4	2·9	2·2	2·2
March	92	169	142	159	5·1	5·0	3·8	5·0	3·3	3·7	3·5	3·1
April	90	80	76	85	7·1	5·2	8·5	7·2	5·0	4·3	4·1	4·1
May	91	176	77	57	9·9	10·0	9·3	10·5	5·7	5·1	5·7	6·5
June	92	63	101	33	12·7	13·0	11·0	13·6	5·9	6·5	4·6	6·1
July	112	87	120	—	13·9	13·8	14·3	—	4·9	4·2	3·9	—
August	129	120	126	—	13·9	12·1	13·8	—	4·6	4·5	4·2	—
September	137	63	160	—	12·2	10·7	11·9	—	3·7	4·3	4·9	—
October	149	161	165	—	9·8	9·8	8·2	—	2·6	3·2	2·7	—
November	142	232	107	—	6·0	7·1	6·4	—	1·7	1·6	1·5	—
December	156	277	114	—	4·5	4·7	5·2	—	1·1	0·9	1·1	—
YEAR	1431	1641	1353	—	8·5	7·9	8·2	—	3·5	3·5	3·3	—

TEMPERATURE, RAINFALL AND WIND SPEED RECORDS

WORLD: The maximum air temperature recorded is 57·8°C. (136°F.) at San Louis, Mexico on August 11, 1933; the minimum air temperature recorded is −89·2°C. (−128·56°F.) at Vostok, Antarctica on July 21, 1983. The greatest rainfall recorded in one day is 1,870 mm. (73·62 in.) at Cilaos, Isle de Réunion on March 16, 1952; the greatest rainfall in one calendar month is 9,300 mm. (366·14 in.) at Cherrapunji, Assam in July 1861, the greatest annual total being 22,990 mm. (905·12 in.) also at Cherrapunji in 1861. The highest gust recorded was 201 knots (231 mph) at Mount Washington Observatory, New Hampshire, U.S.A. on April 12, 1934.

UNITED KINGDOM: The maximum air temperature recorded is 38·1°C. (100·5°F.) at Tonbridge, Kent on July 22 1868; the minimum air temperature recorded is −27·2°C. (−17°F.) at Braemar (Grampian) on February 11, 1895 and 10th January 1982. The greatest rainfall recorded in one day is 280 mm. (11 in.) at Martinstown, Dorset on July 18, 1955. The greatest annual total is 6,528 mm. (257 in.) at Sprinkling Tarn, Cumbria in 1954. The highest gust recorded was 150 knots (173 mph) at Cairngorm (Highland) on March 20, 1986. The highest low-level (below 200 m. (656 ft.)) gust was 118 knots (136 mph) at Kirkwall (Shetland) on February 7, 1969. The highest mean hourly speed was 92 knots (106 mph) at Great Dun Fell (Cumbria) in December 1974. The highest low-level mean hourly speed was 72 knots (83 mph) at Shoreham-by-Sea (Sussex) on October 16, 1987.

WIND FORCE MEASURES

The **Beaufort Scale** of wind force has been accepted internationally and is used in communicating weather conditions. Devised originally by Admiral Sir Francis Beaufort in 1805, it now consists of the numbers 0–17, each representing a certain strength or velocity of wind at 10 m. (33 ft.) above ground in the open.

Scale No.	Wind Force	M.p.h.	Knots	Scale No.	Wind Force	M.p.h.	Knots
0	Calm	1	1	9	Strong gale	47–54	41–47
1	Light air	1–3	1–3	10	Whole gale	55–63	48–55
2	Slight breeze	4–7	4–6	11	Storm	64–72	56–63
3	Gentle breeze	8–12	7–10	12	Hurricane	73–82	64–71
4	Moderate breeze	13–18	11–16	13	—	83–92	72–80
5	Fresh breeze	19–24	17–21	14	—	93–103	81–89
6	Strong breeze	25–31	22–27	15	—	104–114	90–99
7	High wind	32–38	28–33	16	—	115–125	100–108
8	Gale	39–46	34–40	17	—	126–136	109–118

TEMPERATURE, RAINFALL AND SUNSHINE
IN THE UNITED KINGDOM

The following table gives mean air temperature (°C.), total monthly rainfall (mm.) and mean daily bright sunshine (hrs.) at a representative selection of climatological reporting stations in the United Kingdom during the year July 1987 to June 1988 and the calendar year 1987. The heights (in metres) of the reporting stations above mean sea level are also given.

		1987											
		July			August			September			October		
Station	Ht. in mtrs.	Temp. °C.	Rain mm.	Sun hrs.	Temp. °C.	Rain mm.	Sun hrs.	Temp. °C.	Rain mm.	Sun hrs.	Temp. °C.	Rain mm.	Sun hrs.
Aberdeen (Dyce) .	65	13.9	107	3.7	13.7	60	4.7	11.5	39	5.7	7.7	125	2.7
Aberporth	134	14.7	46	5.7	14.9	57	6.0	13.5	78	5.1	9.8	219	3.7
Aldergrove	68	15.3	65	4.1	14.1	131	3.9	12.1	78	5.1	8.1	119	3.7
Aspatria	61	15.1	132	6.1	14.5	90	5.0	12.5	88	5.5	8.7	147	2.9
Bala	163	14.3	45	4.7	14.1	69	4.2	12.2	110	4.3	8.5	296	2.9
Birmingham (Elmdon)	98	15.7	31	5.1	15.5	120	4.5	13.3	49	4.8	9.1	113	3.6
Boulmer	23	14.2	64	5.6	13.9	120	5.2	12.3	35	6.0	8.5	91	3.1
Bournemouth (Hurn)	10	16.5	75	6.7	16.1	26	6.2	14.5	37	4.9	10.4	153	3.6
Bradford	134	15.3	69	4.6	14.9	56	—	12.9	58	—	8.9	114	2.6
Braemar	339	13.3	76	—	12.5	51	4.6	9.3	56	4.7	5.6	104	1.8
Buxton..........	307	14.1	87	4.6	14.1	97	4.0	11.5	90	4.9	7.7	196	3.3
Cambridge.......	24	16.3	70	4.8	16.1	72	4.2	14.5	31	5.1	10.1	116	3.9
Cheltenham	65	16.7	41	5.4	16.3	48	4.8	14.3	57	4.5	10.4	151	3.3
Clacton-on-Sea ...	16	16.7	97	5.9	16.6	73	5.7	15.5	26	5.5	11.9	104	3.8
Douglas	85	14.7	122	—	14.1	109	—	12.5	113	—	9.5	171	—
Dumfries	49	14.9	100	5.7	14.1	182	4.8	11.9	90	5.2	8.0	145	2.8
Dundee	45	15.2	62	—	14.7	69	—	12.3	41	5.8	8.1	106	2.6
Durham	102	15.1	85	4.6	14.7	54	3.8	12.6	46	5.6	8.5	100	2.8
East Malling	33	16.7	91	6.3	16.6	55	5.6	14.9	29	5.0	10.9	146	3.8
Edinburgh.......	134	14.7	67	4.7	14.5	87	5.5	12.2	49	5.6	8.1	86	2.8
Glasgow	107	15.1	66	4.5	13.9	127	4.2	11.9	95	4.8	7.4	129	2.4
Gogerddan	31	15.1	93	5.8	15.1	68	5.4	13.7	70	4.9	10.3	206	3.4
Hastings	45	16.7	107	7.0	16.7	99	6.6	15.5	38	5.1	12.5	201	3.7
Hull	2	16.4	31	—	16.1	79	—	14.3	70	—	10.0	104	—
Inverness	4	14.7	82	2.8	14.5	41	3.5	12.3	40	5.1	7.5	72	2.7
Leeming.........	32	15.8	57	4.8	15.4	57	3.8	13.3	43	4.7	8.7	107	2.8
Lerwick	82	11.9	43	3.7	11.7	78	4.5	10.3	97	5.0	8.5	245	1.9
London (Heathrow)	25	17.5	77	5.7	17.1	57	5.6	15.3	37	4.9	11.3	175	3.9
Long Ashton	51	16.3	59	6.3	16.3	23	6.5	14.4	72	4.7	10.4	190	3.4
Lowestoft	25	16.2	77	5.3	16.5	118	4.3	14.9	37	5.1	11.5	95	3.7
Manchester (Ringway).....	75	15.9	86	5.1	15.5	86	4.4	13.3	77	5.3	9.7	135	3.5
Manston	44	16.8	109	6.2	16.8	91	6.1	15.5	15	5.3	11.6	133	3.7
Melbury	143	14.7	60	6.5	14.9	35	6.3	13.3	85	4.3	9.6	267	3.5
Morecambe	7	16.0	118	6.3	15.3	81	4.6	13.4	109	5.9	9.8	193	2.9
Nottingham (Watnall)......	117	15.9	42	4.9	15.5	51	4.1	13.3	53	4.4	9.2	119	3.3
Oxford	63	16.9	29	5.8	16.7	34	5.1	14.7	25	4.4	10.3	139	3.5
Penzance	19	16.3	40	8.4	16.5	81	7.6	15.0	64	4.2	11.1	225	4.2
Plymouth	27	16.6	53	7.6	16.3	10	7.1	14.7	46	4.7	11.3	185	3.4
Prestwick	16	14.8	88	5.7	13.5	121	5.2	12.1	79	6.0	8.3	136	3.3
Rhoose	65	16.1	77	6.7	16.0	33	6.9	14.1	70	4.7	10.3	180	3.5
St. Mawgan......	103	15.9	48	7.2	16.1	31	7.2	14.5	59	4.6	10.9	217	3.9
Shawbury........	72	15.3	56	5.1	15.1	72	4.9	13.0	40	4.7	8.9	113	3.6
Sheffield.........	131	16.0	51	5.4	15.9	45	4.8	13.3	67	5.1	9.3	119	2.5
Skegness	5	15.7	50	5.6	—	81	4.3	—	34	5.5	9.7	107	4.1
Southampton	3	17.6	47	6.5	17.3	17	6.2	15.9	38	4.8	11.6	193	3.6
Stornoway	15	12.9	60	2.7	12.5	70	3.1	11.3	145	5.1	8.1	130	3.8
Tenby...........	5	15.4	48	7.1	15.2	55	6.8	13.7	70	5.5	10.3	233	3.7
Tiree	9	13.5	108	4.1	12.9	115	3.9	12.1	119	5.9	9.1	165	3.8
Torbay	8	17.3	52	7.2	17.1	6	6.9	15.1	68	4.3	11.5	158	3.5
Trawscoed.......	63	14.7	100	4.7	14.7	61	4.3	13.2	95	4.4	9.7	226	3.1
Ventnor.........	135	16.5	43	7.3	16.5	37	6.5	15.5	43	4.8	12.3	187	3.7
Waddington	68	15.7	62	5.3	15.5	77	4.1	13.6	44	5.3	9.5	96	3.7
Weymouth	21	16.5	42	7.4	16.7	24	7.5	15.4	35	5.1	11.9	135	3.5
Whitby..........	41	15.0	59	5.4	14.7	79	4.2	12.7	43	6.1	8.7	104	3.9
Worthing	2	16.6	49	7.1	16.1	45	6.7	14.9	42	5.1	11.9	215	3.6
Writtle..........	35	16.1	76	—	16.1	129	—	—	31	—	10.4	139	—

TEMPERATURE, RAINFALL AND SUNSHINE IN THE UNITED KINGDOM—*contd.*

Mean Temperature of the air (°C.), Rainfall (mm.) and Bright Sunshine (as mean hours per day) at a representative selection of reporting stations during the year July 1987 to June 1988. Fuller details of the weather are given in the *Monthly Weather Report* published by the Meteorological Office.

| | 1987 | | | | | | | | | 1988 | | | | | |
| | November | | | December | | | Year | | | January | | | February | | |
Station	Temp. °C.	Rain mm.	Sun hrs.	Temp. °C.	Rain mm.	Sun hrs.	Temp. °C.	Rain mm.	Sun hrs.	Temp. °C.	Rain mm.	Sun hrs.	Temp. °C.	Rain mm.	Sun hrs.
Aberdeen (Dyce)	5·2	51	2·1	4·7	61	1·3	7·6	868	3·5	3·2	149	1·9	3·9	66	2·9
Aberporth	7·3	103	3·0	6·2	65	1·8	9·1	852	4·2	5·8	164	1·7	5·0	47	2·9
Aldergrove	6·7	67	1·9	5·9	50	1·3	8·7	827	3·5	4·4	127	2·0	4·3	69	2·4
Aspatria	5·9	52	2·1	5·0	117	1·4	8·3	1043	4·0	4·9	137	1·7	4·5	77	2·8
Bala	6·1	106	1·2	4·7	141	0·5	7·9	1200	3·0	5·1	246	1·0	4·4	119	1·9
Birmingham (Elmdon)	6·1	58	1·3	5·1	31	0·9	8·7	715	3·5	5·0	103	1·7	4·6	47	3·5
Boulmer	6·6	51	2·3	6·3	51	1·0	8·3	799	4·0	4·5	97	1·2	4·5	36	3·4
Bournemouth (Hurn)	6·9	81	2·2	6·1	50	1·4	9·5	728	4·5	6·1	161	2·0	4·8	53	4·8
Bradford	6·3	70	1·2	5·5	48	0·6	8·5	792	—	4·5	135	1·3	4·5	89	2·9
Braemar	3·5	64	1·0	2·4	47	0·3	5·8	741	—	1·3	124	0·7	1·9	83	1·4
Buxton	5·1	99	1·1	4·3	84	0·7	7·4	1316	3·3	3·6	239	1·3	2·9	100	2·5
Cambridge	6·5	40	1·4	5·7	23	0·9	—	617	3·4	5·3	100	1·9	4·9	21	4·2
Cheltenham	7·2	77	1·1	6·1	32	1·4	9·7	728	3·3	6·1	137	1·7	5·1	46	3·6
Clacton-on-Sea	7·3	66	2·2	6·1	17	1·0	9·7	622	3·9	5·6	160	2·2	4·9	26	4·7
Douglas	7·5	116	—	6·7	109	—	8·9	1197	—	5·7	182	—	5·3	70	—
Dumfries	5·7	81	2·0	4·7	124	0·8	—	1182	3·5	4·1	164	1·6	4·6	83	2·9
Dundee	6·3	26	2·4	5·4	51	0·9	8·6	746	—	4·1	102	1·0	4·7	31	—
Durham	6·1	61	1·8	5·6	35	0·8	8·3	730	3·4	4·1	80	1·8	4·5	34	3·9
East Malling	7·1	55	1·7	6·1	16	1·1	9·7	671	3·9	6·0	151	1·9	5·3	38	4·2
Edinburgh	6·3	28	2·0	5·5	54	0·8	8·3	731	3·4	4·0	78	1·7	4·3	39	2·5
Glasgow	5·9	73	1·8	4·5	108	0·7	8·1	1032	3·7	3·5	121	1·2	4·3	82	2·5
Gogerddan	7·3	136	2·5	6·3	122	1·4	9·3	1125	4·0	6·7	151	1·6	5·7	52	2·6
Hastings	8·1	79	2·5	6·4	31	1·3	10·1	854	4·4	6·0	186	2·1	5·7	58	4·3
Hull	7·2	54	—	6·3	44	—	9·5	718	—	5·4	81	—	5·1	47	—
Inverness	6·3	31	1·3	4·2	39	0·8	8·3	606	3·0	3·9	114	2·0	4·9	62	1·8
Leeming	6·3	51	1·5	5·5	29	1·0	8·7	623	3·2	4·3	73	1·6	4·7	53	3·8
Lerwick	6·0	113	1·1	5·6	94	0·3	7·1	1166	2·9	3·9	104	1·1	3·6	143	2·0
London (Heathrow)	6·9	43	1·3	6·5	14	1·1	10·3	653	3·8	5·9	107	1·7	5·3	26	4·0
Long Ashton	7·3	79	1·7	6·1	51	1·1	9·7	822	4·1	6·3	131	1·8	5·2	71	4·0
Lowestoft	7·3	51	1·5	6·3	27	0·8	9·5	647	3·5	5·5	108	1·5	4·8	57	3·8
Manchester (Ringway)	6·6	59	1·3	6·0	45	1·4	9·2	897	3·6	5·3	115	1·7	4·6	32	2·5
Manston	7·8	62	2·0	6·1	31	1·3	9·8	671	4·1	5·9	114	2·3	4·9	35	4·5
Melbury	7·3	162	1·1	6·2	123	1·1	8·9	1227	4·1	6·3	255	1·8	5·3	111	3·6
Morecambe	6·9	59	1·7	5·8	106	1·2	9·1	1101	3·9	5·5	142	1·9	5·3	61	3·6
Nottingham (Watnall)	6·1	49	1·7	5·5	49	1·0	8·8	711	3·4	4·7	98	1·6	4·4	42	3·9
Oxford	6·7	58	1·5	5·9	26	1·4	9·7	595	3·7	5·7	100	1·5	5·2	34	3·6
Penzance	9·5	145	2·7	8·7	85	1·3	10·9	1107	4·7	8·3	240	2·7	7·1	89	4·0
Plymouth	8·5	115	2·7	7·7	81	1·1	10·3	891	4·6	7·7	212	2·4	6·1	104	4·7
Prestwick	6·4	61	1·6	5·0	87	1·4	8·3	968	4·0	4·6	133	1·5	4·8	92	2·4
Rhoose	7·3	110	2·1	5·9	59	1·3	9·5	926	4·4	6·2	160	2·1	5·2	66	4·4
St. Mawgan	8·6	130	2·9	7·5	66	1·5	10·1	903	4·6	7·6	202	2·1	6·0	83	3·9
Shawbury	6·2	65	1·4	5·1	34	1·1	8·6	679	3·5	5·0	110	2·0	4·5	44	3·8
Sheffield	6·3	53	1·5	5·9	38	0·5	9·1	788	3·5	4·9	174	1·2	4·7	81	3·3
Skegness	6·7	37	1·7	6·3	29	0·9	—	644	—	5·1	108	1·6	4·9	43	4·6
Southampton	7·9	79	2·3	6·8	43	1·4	10·5	748	4·3	6·5	140	2·0	5·7	49	4·5
Stornoway	6·9	88	1·1	5·6	126	1·4	7·9	1053	3·3	4·3	141	1·3	4·6	120	2·1
Tenby	8·4	165	2·7	7·1	119	1·5	9·6	1132	4·5	7·1	229	2·1	5·7	84	3·5
Tiree	7·9	102	1·6	6·5	121	1·6	8·7	1205	4·0	4·9	150	1·7	5·3	121	2·5
Torbay	8·7	77	2·1	8·3	87	0·9	10·7	729	4·3	7·6	182	2·4	6·1	103	4·7
Trawscoed	6·7	142	2·1	6·1	87	0·9	8·9	1187	3·2	6·1	189	1·1	5·0	61	2·3
Ventnor	8·5	83	2·5	6·9	33	1·7	10·1	743	4·7	6·9	159	2·4	5·9	51	4·8
Waddington	6·1	37	1·5	5·5	31	0·9	8·8	695	3·7	4·7	99	1·8	4·5	31	4·2
Weymouth	8·5	81	2·7	6·8	41	1·6	10·1	649	4·8	7·3	147	2·3	5·9	61	4·8
Whitby	6·5	32	1·7	6·1	29	1·1	8·5	679	3·7	4·7	71	1·7	4·5	62	4·1
Worthing	7·8	85	2·2	6·4	27	1·4	9·9	801	4·5	6·4	154	2·3	5·4	61	4·8
Writtle	6·6	49	—	5·9	16	—	—	691	—	5·4	138	—	4·6	24	—

TEMPERATURE, RAINFALL AND SUNSHINE IN THE UNITED KINGDOM—*contd.*

Mean Temperature of the air (°C.), Rainfall (mm.) and Bright Sunshine (as mean hours per day) at a representative selection of reporting stations during the year July 1987 to June 1988. Fuller details of the weather are given in the *Monthly Weather Report* published by the Meteorological Office.

| | 1988 | | | | | | | | | | | |
| | March | | | April | | | May | | | June | | |
Station	Temp. °C.	Rain mm.	Sun hrs.	Temp. °C.	Rain mm.	Sun hrs.	Temp. °C.	Rain mm.	Sun hrs.	Temp. °C.	Rain mm.	Sun hrs.
Aberdeen (Dyce)	4·5	89	4·0	6·7	77	4·2	9·7	43	7·5	13·0	17	6·1
Aberporth	6·5	103	3·5	8·1	40	6·4	10·8	62	7·3	13·5	77	6·8
Aldergrove	6·0	114	2·6	8·7	35	5·3	10·9	43	6·7	14·1	40	6·7
Aspatria	5·3	87	2·5	7·7	56	4·6	11·1	47	7·7	14·3	23	7·9
Bala	5·7	141	2·2	7·5	49	4·4	10·3	82	6·3	13·2	42	5·8
Birmingham (Elmdon)	6·3	74	3·2	7·7	31	3·5	11·5	34	6·1	14·3	59	5·2
Boulmer...........	5·3	52	4·4	6·9	35	4·2	9·4	35	5·7	12·6	24	6·6
Bournemouth (Hurn)	7·1	87	3·3	8·1	35	6·2	12·5	29	7·7	14·8	20	5·9
Bradford	5·5	86	2·7	7·8	35	3·1	11·0	55	—	14·1	59	—
Braemar	2·5	96	3·1	5·1	56	3·6	8·6	36	6·3	13·5	20	7·4
Buxton...........	4·0	225	2·5	6·5	51	3·2	10·3	65	6·1	13·3	57	5·3
Cambridge.........	6·4	59	2·8	8·1	37	4·0	12·3	39	5·2	14·1	48	4·7
Cheltenham	7·3	47	2·7	9·1	37	4·3	12·7	57	5·5	15·7	35	—
Clacton-on-Sea.....	6·5	64	3·4	8·2	41	5·3	12·3	36	6·9	13·9	21	4·6
Douglas	5·9	142	—	7·5	75	—	10·9	32	—	14·5	15	—
Dumfries	5·1	98	2·7	7·1	55	3·7	10·4	59	6·6	14·3	10	7·6
Dundee	5·4	60	4·6	7·6	101	3·9	10·7	46	6·2	13·9	17	6·6
Durham...........	5·3	55	3·7	7·7	26	4·2	10·3	58	5·6	13·9	16	6·3
East Malling	7·3	59	3·1	8·5	34	5·1	12·7	56	6·5	14·3	9	4·7
Edinburgh.........	5·3	49	3·2	7·3	71	4·3	10·3	46	6·1	13·7	16	6·6
Glasgow	4·7	122	2·1	7·3	67	3·2	10·7	55	6·3	13·1	17	5·6
Gogerddan	6·9	147	2·5	8·7	39	6·2	11·5	74	7·3	14·5	27	7·0
Hastings	7·1	92	3·2	8·7	31	6·2	13·1	75	7·1	14·3	29	5·7
Hull	6·1	73	—	8·5	18	—	11·5	37	—	14·5	39	—
Inverness	5·3	82	3·2	7·5	48	3·7	10·8	39	6·3	14·1	13	5·9
Leeming...........	5·9	49	3·2	8·1	26	4·0	10·9	44	6·0	14·7	22	6·5
Lerwick	3·1	132	3·2	4·6	63	5·1	8·1	53	5·1	10·4	13	4·8
London (Heathrow)	7·2	59	2·8	9·3	26	4·9	13·5	42	6·5	15·5	44	5·3
Long Ashton........	7·2	96	3·4	8·6	36	5·3	12·3	55	7·0	15·0	41	6·1
Lowestoft	6·2	83	2·6	8·1	50	4·8	11·9	46	6·3	13·7	20	4·7
Manchester (Ringway)........	5·9	125	2·7	8·5	39	4·0	12·1	47	6·8	14·8	61	5·8
Manston	6·5	81	3·5	8·7	45	5·8	12·3	32	7·1	13·9	12	5·3
Melbury	6·9	144	2·8	7·8	45	6·1	10·5	88	6·6	—	—	—
Morecambe	5·9	95	2·9	8·7	53	4·9	12·6	61	7·3	15·5	21	7·8
Nottingham (Watnall).........	5·7	82	3·2	7·7	36	3·2	11·5	44	6·1	14·1	55	5·3
Oxford	7·0	59	2·7	8·6	30	4·4	12·5	32	5·7	14·5	60	4·7
Penzance..........	8·7	149	4·0	9·5	64	4·8	12·0	70	7·8	14·9	43	6·6
Plymouth	7·8	105	3·3	9·0	51	5·6	12·4	45	7·6	15·3	25	7·1
Prestwick	5·5	132	2·5	7·7	54	4·6	10·9	42	7·7	13·8	28	7·8
Rhoose	6·8	107	3·4	8·5	39	5·9	11·9	66	7·1	15·1	43	6·3
St. Mawgan........	7·5	148	3·2	9·1	42	6·1	11·5	67	7·3	14·8	45	7·2
Shawbury	6·1	80	3·4	7·8	32	3·7	11·4	59	6·6	14·1	46	6·3
Sheffield..........	6·1	97	3·4	8·3	44	3·0	11·7	50	6·3	14·9	56	4·9
Skegness	5·9	75	3·2	8·0	20	4·3	11·3	38	7·1	13·4	48	5·3
Southampton.......	7·5	70	3·2	9·2	46	6·1	13·6	24	7·5	15·8	26	5·7
Stornoway	5·0	147	3·2	6·8	76	4·1	9·9	43	5·9	11·9	26	4·4
Tenby	7·1	142	3·4	8·4	49	6·3	11·5	60	7·0	14·7	66	6·8
Tiree..............	5·8	145	3·4	7·9	30	5·5	10·9	42	7·2	12·4	56	6·3
Torbay............	8·3	95	3·5	9·0	41	5·3	12·7	69	7·3	15·7	35	6·4
Trawscoed.........	6·4	176	2·1	8·5	39	5·3	11·2	93	5·6	13·9	33	6·1
Ventnor...........	6·9	100	3·7	8·8	56	6·5	12·9	18	8·0	14·7	22	6·3
Waddington	5·9	71	3·1	8·0	25	4·0	11·5	50	6·3	13·9	38	5·6
Weymouth	7·7	95	3·5	8·5	37	6·3	12·7	42	7·9	15·2	22	5·9
Whitby............	5·5	71	3·6	7·5	42	3·7	9·7	32	5·7	13·1	19	6·3
Worthing	7·3	82	2·9	8·3	29	6·1	12·9	37	7·9	14·7	9	5·5
Writtle............	6·6	69	—	8·3	19	—	12·3	29	—	14·1	41	—

Weather Record, July, 1987 / Weather Record, August, 1987

Day	Max. °C	Min. °C	Wind Speed knots	Rain-fall mm	Sun-shine hrs.	Max. °C	Min. °C	Wind Speed knots	Rain-fall mm	Sun-shine hrs.	Day
1	21.0	11.2	5.3	0.0	10.6	21.6	13.3	7.3	4.5	7.4	1
2	22.0	11.2	4.5	0.0	9.5	20.9	13.9	5.5	0.4	2.1	2
3	23.4	12.6	5.3	0.0	13.3	21.2	12.5	4.3	0.6	6.4	3
4	26.0	12.1	4.4	0.0	14.6	18.5	10.2	4.2	0.0	9.4	4
5	27.8	13.1	6.3	0.0	15.1	19.1	9.2	3.2	0.0	7.7	5
6	28.3	15.3	3.0	0.0	6.2	19.9	9.0	3.3	0.0	10.6	6
7	25.3	16.2	5.9	0.0	8.4	19.5	9.4	6.1	0.0	7.7	7
8	23.1	12.7	4.6	0.0	13.3	17.2	11.5	4.8	0.0	0.2	8
9	22.4	12.9	4.5	0.0	10.1	19.6	13.2	3.2	0.9	1.5	9
10	26.6	15.9	6.7	0.0	3.9	20.8	9.8	3.3	0.0	8.2	10
11	25.9	15.3	8.1	0.0	7.0	19.1	10.1	3.8	1.6	4.4	11
12	23.2	11.1	4.4	0.0	9.6	21.4	12.2	5.0	0.0	1.6	12
13	25.8	13.2	4.7	0.0	7.8	22.6	16.5	6.0	0.0	0.6	13
14	24.9	15.9	8.0	6.3	0.6	23.5	12.5	5.4	0.0	8.3	14
15	22.7	16.6	8.1	6.5	2.7	26.2	12.7	5.0	0.0	13.1	15
16	19.4	13.4	3.4	5.1	1.9	28.1	13.7	4.0	0.1	12.7	16
17	16.0	13.1	3.1	4.7	0.0	24.2	16.2	2.1	1.0	0.4	17
18	17.4	12.8	4.2	15.9	0.0	23.7	15.9	5.0	0.0	3.1	18
19	17.8	12.9	7.6	12.7	0.6	25.3	12.6	4.7	0.0	6.6	19
20	20.3	14.4	9.1	0.7	2.6	29.1	14.9	6.8	0.0	12.7	20
21	15.5	13.3	6.6	3.2	0.0	29.2	17.8	4.0	5.3	7.7	21
22	17.7	14.0	7.6	0.1	0.0	24.4	17.6	5.6	24.7	3.4	22
23	15.3	13.1	5.4	0.3	0.0	22.1	12.5	4.8	0.0	9.4	23
24	19.9	10.9	3.9	0.3	0.1	19.3	13.1	6.3	7.1	2.2	24
25	18.1	10.3	4.8	0.0	5.5	15.4	10.9	7.0	8.8	0.0	25
26	20.8	8.2	6.6	1.4	10.2	18.1	9.9	5.4	2.1	2.4	26
27	21.3	13.4	8.9	0.4	8.9	16.1	11.2	5.8	0.1	1.2	27
28	22.7	12.0	4.4	9.2	4.5	25.1	8.5	4.6	0.0	8.2	28
29	21.9	16.0	5.5	8.8	2.2	21.1	14.0	2.6	0.0	1.4	29
30	19.3	13.8	4.9	1.7	0.6	22.8	11.1	3.1	0.0	4.9	30
31	25.1	14.4	6.5	0.0	6.7	19.3	13.5	6.9	0.0	6.8	31
Total	—	—	—	77.3	176.1	—	—	—	57.2	172.3	Total
Mean	21.8	13.3	5.7	—	—	21.8	12.6	4.8	—	—	Mean
Temp. °F.	71.2	55.9	—	—	—	71.2	54.7	—	—	—	Temp. °F.
Average	22.0	12.9	8.2	51.0	189.7	21.6	12.7	8.0	58.0	176.4	Average

Weather Record, September, 1987 / Weather Record, October, 1987

Day	Max. °C	Min. °C	Wind Speed knots	Rain-fall mm	Sun-shine hrs.	Max. °C	Min. °C	Wind Speed knots	Rain-fall mm	Sun-shine hrs.	Day
1	24.4	11.8	2.4	5.7	3.7	17.5	7.2	5.3	0.0	9.7	1
2	20.5	16.9	3.2	0.0	0.0	19.0	9.3	7.1	0.2	4.0	2
3	22.2	15.5	5.7	1.2	1.9	18.2	13.4	8.2	10.3	5.3	3
4	21.0	10.5	5.3	1.8	8.4	20.5	12.2	4.6	0.0	4.2	4
5	19.8	12.7	7.0	2.0	4.8	20.0	12.6	5.1	0.2	2.5	5
6	19.5	10.0	9.2	1.0	0.5	15.7	11.6	6.5	5.3	3.0	6
7	18.9	11.9	4.1	0.2	5.5	16.0	7.3	8.6	13.8	0.0	7
8	20.2	8.5	3.2	0.0	9.0	13.4	8.9	11.0	0.3	6.3	8
9	20.4	11.5	6.6	1.5	6.3	14.5	6.3	9.3	53.1	0.2	9
10	20.1	14.0	8.0	0.0	8.3	9.4	9.4	5.2	12.5	0.0	10
11	19.5	12.5	7.6	0.5	4.2	14.1	4.5	4.7	0.0	7.2	11
12	21.6	17.6	11.0	6.5	1.0	15.0	6.0	3.9	1.8	9.1	12
13	17.3	12.4	3.1	0.0	0.5	14.7	7.5	5.3	1.0	6.4	13
14	20.9	10.3	7.3	0.0	9.3	12.1	5.9	6.4	10.4	3.5	14
15	19.7	9.0	4.1	0.0	4.0	11.1	8.6	7.7	17.3	0.0	15
16	18.0	13.1	3.7	0.1	0.0	14.8	8.2	16.4	6.3	5.1	16
17	24.7	14.0	5.2	1.9	5.3	15.5	8.4	6.1	0.1	5.6	17
18	20.6	15.6	3.9	0.6	8.7	17.1	9.9	13.0	1.4	5.4	18
19	16.2	13.3	3.2	5.2	0.0	17.3	12.1	6.9	1.2	1.2	19
20	23.1	14.5	5.0	0.0	6.8	14.4	11.1	4.0	35.5	0.0	20
21	21.6	16.7	6.1	0.1	3.4	14.3	11.2	6.8	0.4	2.8	21
22	19.0	13.0	6.4	0.0	8.1	14.4	6.7	3.2	0.0	8.8	22
23	19.9	10.4	5.8	6.6	4.9	11.1	2.5	3.6	0.0	1.4	23
24	16.0	10.1	6.0	2.0	7.5	12.5	4.5	2.3	0.0	8.6	24
25	16.0	5.9	2.7	0.0	8.1	14.0	0.5	3.2	0.0	6.8	25
26	15.4	3.6	5.0	0.0	8.4	12.3	4.3	3.7	2.4	0.0	26
27	14.5	5.7	2.4	0.0	5.6	16.0	11.0	6.2	0.2	0.0	27
28	13.8	9.4	2.5	0.0	0.8	12.8	5.5	2.9	0.0	9.0	28
29	15.1	5.7	4.3	0.0	5.8	12.4	1.4	2.9	0.0	4.5	29
30	16.6	8.1	5.1	0.0	6.4	13.0	5.7	4.3	0.2	0.0	30
31						13.9	11.7	2.5	0.9	0.0	31
Total	—	—	—	36.9	147.2	—	—	—	174.8	120.6	Total
Mean	19.2	11.5	5.1	—	—	14.7	7.9	6.0	—	—	Mean
Temp. °F.	66.6	52.7	—	—	—	58.5	46.2	—	—	—	Temp. °F.
Average	19.2	10.6	7.9	56.0	144.7	15.2	7.6	7.8	56.0	104.4	Average

Entries of Maximum Temperature cover the day period 9–21 h.; Minimum Temperature the night period 21–9 h. entered to the day of reading; Rainfall is for the 24 hours commencing at 9 h. on the day of entry; Sunshine is for the 24 hours 0–24 h.; Mean Wind Speed is 10 metres above the ground. 100 knots = 115.1 m.p.h.; 100 mm. = 3.94 ins.; °F. = 9/5°C. + 32.
Averages are for the period 1951–1980 except for mean wind speed which is for 1961–1980.

Weather Record, November, 1987

Day	Temperature Max. °C.	Temperature Min. °C.	Wind Speed knots	Rainfall mm.	Sunshine hrs.
1	12·3	9·7	2·3	0·0	0·0
2	9·3	2·2	2·1	0·0	0·0
3	11·6	6·5	4·8	0·0	0·1
4	12·2	9·3	7·3	0·0	0·1
5	12·4	7·8	5·6	0·0	4·4
6	9·4	2·7	2·3	0·0	0·0
7	7·4	5·6	2·1	0·0	0·0
8	7·6	5·3	2·5	8·8	0·0
9	8·7	6·7	5·6	0·2	0·0
10	10·3	7·0	3·5	1·9	0·0
11	13·1	4·0	7·1	15·2	0·0
12	9·3	5·6	10·6	0·0	4·2
13	9·0	5·0	5·3	0·5	0·2
14	10·4	1·7	5·0	2·2	7·5
15	13·1	3·8	6·7	0·4	0·0
16	13·8	10·3	10·4	0·0	4·9
17	12·9	5·7	4·7	0·0	2·9
18	13·0	5·7	4·9	1·5	0·6
19	13·2	10·7	7·2	9·0	0·0
20	11·4	4·0	7·7	0·0	2·7
21	9·5	2·2	4·0	0·5	2·0
22	9·4	7·2	5·1	2·9	0·1
23	6·3	3·1	5·3	0·2	0·0
24	8·9	3·3	9·0	0·0	0·6
25	7·7	5·7	11·0	0·0	1·0
26	7·1	4·9	8·3	0·0	0·0
27	7·5	0·5	3·6	0·0	6·9
28	5·0	−2·6	2·1	0·0	1·6
29	2·5	−2·8	2·0	0·0	0·0
30	6·5	2·1	2·2	0·0	0·0
31					
Total	—	—	—	43·3	39·8
Mean	9·7	4·8	5·3	—	—
Temp. °F.	49·5	40·6	—	—	—
Average	10·2	3·9	8·9	62·0	64·0

Weather Record, December, 1987

Temperature Max. °C.	Temperature Min. °C.	Wind Speed knots	Rainfall mm.	Sunshine hrs.	Day
7·6	3·7	6·0	0·4	0·1	1
5·9	4·4	12·3	0·0	0·0	2
3·5	2·9	11·6	0·0	0·0	3
7·0	2·4	8·0	0·0	0·1	4
7·8	5·3	7·3	0·0	0·0	5
6·6	5·8	8·5	0·0	0·0	6
5·8	4·2	6·6	0·0	0·0	7
5·4	−1·6	4·3	0·2	6·1	8
4·5	−0·8	2·9	0·0	3·0	9
5·0	−1·4	2·0	0·0	6·3	10
5·0	−3·7	1·9	0·0	0·0	11
5·8	−0·3	3·3	0·0	0·1	12
6·4	0·6	8·1	0·0	6·6	13
2·8	0·2	6·6	0·0	0·0	14
7·5	1·0	5·0	7·4	0·0	15
12·8	7·4	8·2	0·9	0·2	16
13·8	10·0	8·1	0·4	0·0	17
13·0	11·9	9·6	0·0	0·5	18
10·8	5·3	5·5	0·0	0·3	19
11·4	9·5	7·5	0·0	0·0	20
11·5	8·9	5·6	0·0	0·0	21
9·8	4·3	2·7	0·0	5·0	22
5·6	1·6	2·8	0·0	1·1	23
8·9	3·9	4·6	0·1	0·0	24
9·8	6·0	3·7	0·0	1·9	25
11·6	4·6	9·3	0·0	0·0	26
12·7	10·5	9·6	0·0	0·0	27
13·5	11·7	10·9	0·0	0·0	28
13·7	11·2	13·0	1·2	0·0	29
12·5	7·6	6·0	3·8	0·2	30
11·5	9·4	10·1	0·0	2·9	31
—	—	—	14·4	34·4	Total
8·7	4·7	6·8	—	—	Mean
47·7	40·5	—	—	—	Temp. °F.
7·9	2·2	7·0	55·0	43·9	Average

Weather Record, January, 1988

Day	Temperature Max. °C.	Temperature Min. °C.	Wind Speed knots	Rainfall mm.	Sunshine hrs.
1	13·2	5·9	11·1	1·2	0·0
2	12·6	11·5	16·4	3·3	1·8
3	9·3	7·0	12·7	3·0	2·5
4	10·9	6·2	13·5	8·6	4·5
5	10·2	6·2	5·0	2·0	0·0
6	9·7	6·9	15·4	0·2	1·3
7	7·0	1·6	6·4	0·0	6·0
8	9·7	−2·3	5·5	0·6	0·0
9	12·7	9·4	9·1	0·6	0·0
10	8·9	7·1	3·7	0·0	0·2
11	7·8	1·0	5·4	0·0	7·1
12	8·2	4·2	9·6	2·4	0·6
13	9·0	4·4	5·5	3·0	0·0
14	9·7	3·5	4·2	2·8	5·3
15	4·7	1·9	2·2	0·0	0·0
16	2·7	0·3	2·0	0·0	0·0
17	4·9	− 1·5	2·4	0·0	3·1
18	7·7	1·9	6·1	0·0	0·1
19	10·0	5·9	7·2	0·5	0·1
20	8·5	4·0	5·2	1·6	1·9
21	6·8	−2·2	4·0	12·4	5·5
22	4·6	1·0	10·0	0·2	2·3
23	11·1	−2·0	5·7	5·6	0·0
24	10·5	8·3	8·9	11·1	4·2
25	8·8	4·6	4·3	1·3	0·6
26	8·0	5·8	3·3	0·0	0·0
27	6·9	4·0	7·3	10·0	0·3
28	9·6	3·0	4·9	10·4	0·0
29	7·5	6·4	6·1	14·9	0·0
30	7·5	3·1	8·2	0·0	0·7
31	8·2	1·4	9·1	11·2	6·6
Total	—	—	—	106·9	54·7
Mean	8·6	3·8	7·1	—	—
Temp. °F.	47·5	38·8	—	—	—
Average	6·7	1·1	8·6	51·0	48·8

Weather Record, February, 1988

Temperature Max. °C.	Temperature Min. °C.	Wind Speed knots	Rainfall mm.	Sunshine hrs.	Day
9·8	3·6	16·3	1·7	1·2	1
7·8	5·2	13·6	3·5	4·4	2
10·2	2·2	8·6	4·1	1·1	3
7·8	2·4	10·7	0·4	2·8	4
10·1	2·6	5·4	0·0	4·6	5
7·9	0·7	3·2	0·0	6·1	6
6·8	−1·8	8·3	3·6	5·6	7
7·2	1·0	10·7	3·1	8·1	8
7·3	2·9	15·2	2·3	4·9	9
7·7	2·0	15·3	1·7	2·8	10
7·4	1·5	6·6	0·0	6·2	11
7·6	−1·6	4·6	0·0	7·8	12
8·4	−1·3	11·3	1·6	0·0	13
12·1	7·9	7·7	0·0	2·3	14
14·5	3·0	3·6	0·0	7·9	15
8·4	2·9	4·5	0·0	8·4	16
9·6	−0·1	4·3	0·0	7·7	17
10·9	1·2	5·1	0·0	3·0	18
12·3	5·8	4·3	0·0	5·8	19
9·7	6·0	2·3	0·0	0·0	20
9·8	6·4	2·1	0·0	0·1	21
9·2	2·1	2·8	0·0	0·3	22
7·2	2·1	8·3	0·0	5·4	23
5·8	1·6	8·5	1·5	2·4	24
5·0	0·7	5·6	0·7	5·0	25
5·5	−1·9	5·0	0·0	6·0	26
7·4	−1·3	2·7	0·4	0·0	27
9·2	5·2	8·7	1·4	1·0	28
4·7	0·5	12·4	0·0	5·3	29
					30
					31
—	—	—	26·0	115·9	Total
8·5	2·1	7·5	—	—	Mean
47·3	35·8	—	—	—	Temp. °F.
7·3	1·3	9·3	38·0	62·6	Average

Weather Record. March, 1988

Day	Temperature Max. °C.	Min. °C.	Wind Speed knots	Rainfall mm.	Sunshine hrs.
1	5·9	−0·7	8·5	0·0	6·3
2	7·2	−4·0	5·1	0·5	7·8
3	8·9	1·6	6·1	3·9	1·4
4	5·6	−0·8	5·3	0·0	7·2
5	5·9	−4·0	5·0	0·0	3·9
6	9·9	4·4	7·9	2·1	0·3
7	8·6	5·0	6·0	0·0	0·9
8	9·0	3·6	2·1	0·0	0·0
9	12·5	3·4	3·6	2·1	7·8
10	10·2	4·9	5·7	0·0	3·5
11	11·6	1·5	6·8	0·0	0·8
12	11·7	8·2	7·3	0·0	0·6
13	11·0	5·2	6·8	3·4	0·1
14	9·9	6·4	4·8	4·7	0·0
15	11·5	8·6	13·5	6·2	1·6
16	11·7	5·8	8·9	0·1	1·6
17	9·8	3·7	2·7	0·9	4·2
18	10·1	3·7	7·4	5·9	3·5
19	12·2	5·3	9·4	1·7	0·0
20	12·1	7·7	6·6	9·5	0·4
21	14·2	7·8	5·8	0·6	3·3
22	13·2	3·3	6·2	1·4	3·1
23	13·0	4·9	9·8	0·0	3·5
24	13·5	7·3	11·9	7·3	3·4
25	13·1	6·1	11·7	0·2	6·4
26	11·2	5·4	11·2	0·0	6·3
27	12·4	5·0	7·0	0·0	4·3
28	10·3	2·7	5·8	0·6	0·1
29	8·8	5·6	3·6	8·4	0·0
30	9·7	5·3	3·8	0·0	1·2
31	12·2	2·7	3·6	0·0	4·6
Total	—	—	—	59·5	88·1
Mean	10·5	4·1	6·8	—	—
Temp. °F.	50·9	39·4	—	—	—
Average	10·2	2·6	9·5	43·0	110·8

Weather Record, April, 1988

Temperature Max. °C.	Min. °C.	Wind Speed knots	Rainfall mm.	Sunshine hrs.	Day
12·2	0·0	4·5	0·0	6·3	1
13·6	6·9	5·1	0·0	2·8	2
14·7	3·6	4·2	0·0	6·6	3
12·1	4·6	9·4	0·0	5·0	4
9·1	5·0	9·5	0·0	0·5	5
13·1	5·2	9·7	0·0	7·7	6
13·6	3·7	7·1	0·0	1·9	7
13·0	5·0	5·3	4·9	2·0	8
6·2	1·1	5·8	0·3	0·0	9
13·1	−2·2	4·3	0·0	10·7	10
16·0	1·5	2·2	0·0	11·4	11
15·4	5·1	8·1	0·0	10·1	12
11·1	2·5	7·1	0·0	12·8	13
11·5	1·4	5·1	0·0	1·7	14
13·5	6·5	4·7	2·9	0·0	15
15·0	11·3	6·7	2·7	0·1	16
17·2	10·6	4·9	0·0	3·2	17
18·9	9·6	5·0	4·8	1·0	18
16·1	11·8	2·8	4·6	0·1	19
17·2	9·4	6·4	0·0	9·7	20
15·9	7·9	3·9	0·0	0·5	21
12·0	8·5	8·3	0·0	0·1	22
10·3	4·5	10·4	0·0	9·9	23
11·6	1·6	6·8	0·0	13·1	24
12·4	1·0	5·4	0·0	11·2	25
15·2	2·3	2·8	1·0	8·1	26
12·0	7·6	3·9	0·0	2·3	27
12·4	5·5	3·0	0·4	2·3	28
11·0	6·6	7·3	1·9	0·0	29
16·6	8·2	7·6	4·2	4·7	30
					31
—	—	—	27·7	145·8	Total
13·4	5·2	5·9	—	—	Mean
56·1	41·4	—	—	—	Temp. °F.
13·2	4·6	8·3	41·0	146·9	Average

Weather Record, May, 1988

Day	Temperature Max. °C.	Min. °C.	Wind Speed knots	Rainfall mm.	Sunshine hrs.
1	16·1	9·6	8·0	1·5	5·6
2	15·8	9·0	9·4	0·7	5·0
3	14·7	8·2	7·8	1·5	2·7
4	16·1	10·0	8·6	1·1	5·1
5	17·1	6·6	3·2	0·0	10·9
6	20·3	6·6	5·7	0·0	13·2
7	19·1	9·5	8·7	18·8	6·4
8	22·7	13·6	4·1	0·8	1·5
9	13·1	12·6	6·0	0·0	0·0
10	16·8	10·7	5·7	0·0	9·8
11	13·5	8·2	3·4	5·3	2·7
12	18·7	10·4	3·6	0·0	0·2
13	21·2	9·8	3·4	0·0	2·9
14	23·9	9·7	5·7	0·0	11·9
15	23·4	10·9	7·3	0·0	8·5
16	22·4	9·9	7·8	0·0	12·9
17	21·0	6·9	5·8	1·1	14·2
18	11·5	7·3	6·2	0·0	0·0
19	13·7	6·8	4·7	0·0	8·5
20	16·1	3·2	3·1	0·0	8·8
21	17·8	6·9	3·1	0·0	6·2
22	18·6	7·5	9·5	0·0	14·1
23	17·1	9·5	7·1	0·5	0·6
24	18·9	9·3	9·1	0·0	10·8
25	21·0	11·9	4·6	0·0	4·1
26	18·1	11·5	4·1	0·1	3·8
27	19·8	7·3	3·0	0·0	8·9
28	19·5	8·5	7·5	1·5	12·2
29	16·4	10·4	10·2	0·7	5·8
30	15·5	10·0	6·0	8·0	2·3
31	17·8	10·2	7·7	0·0	2·4
Total	—	—	—	41·6	202·0
Mean	18·0	9·1	6·1	—	—
Temp. °F.	64·4	48·4	—	—	—
Average	17·1	7·8	8·5	48·0	196·1

Weather Record, June, 1988

Temperature Max. °C.	Min. °C.	Wind Speed knots	Rainfall mm.	Sunshine hrs.	Day
19·4	6·8	6·3	0·3	6·2	1
17·6	11·5	7·4	0·0	0·0	2
17·4	8·2	7·5	8·8	5·2	3
15·8	8·9	4·3	8·3	4·7	4
16·1	7·1	3·5	0·0	3·0	5
17·5	9·7	2·9	0·0	5·0	6
18·6	7·6	4·3	1·8	8·9	7
16·9	10·3	3·2	9·4	0·0	8
13·6	11·9	5·8	0·2	0·0	9
14·1	11·5	5·4	0·0	0·0	10
14·9	10·3	7·5	0·0	0·0	11
19·5	10·6	11·1	0·0	8·5	12
23·3	11·4	7·3	0·0	11·1	13
23·2	10·0	6·3	0·0	14·7	14
20·8	11·1	5·2	0·0	8·4	15
20·2	12·5	5·6	0·0	4·5	16
16·4	11·4	6·5	0·1	0·0	17
19·8	11·1	6·3	0·0	10·1	18
25·1	11·8	4·3	0·0	11·5	19
23·7	12·9	3·7	2·0	1·5	20
23·5	13·5	3·7	0·0	2·3	21
21·2	13·5	5·6	0·0	14·1	22
24·7	10·4	5·5	0·0	14·5	23
21·3	12·5	4·5	0·0	0·9	24
23·5	14·6	7·0	0·1	9·6	25
20·3	15·4	5·1	0·0	1·7	26
16·7	12·0	5·0	4·9	0·0	27
16·0	12·2	3·2	2·4	0·0	28
21·9	14·0	4·9	0·0	5·2	29
25·2	13·8	6·3	6·0	8·3	30
					31
—	—	—	44·3	159·9	Total
19·6	11·3	5·5	—	—	Mean
67·3	52·3	—	—	—	Temp. °F.
20·5	10·9	8·4	51·0	206·0	Average

CHRONOLOGICAL NOTES

GEOLOGICAL TIME

The earth is thought to have come into existence approximately 4,600 million years ago, but for nearly half this time, the ARCHEAN era, it was uninhabited; life is generally believed to have emerged in the succeeding PROTEROZOIC era. The Archean and the Proterozoic eras are often together referred to as the PRECAMBRIAN. Although primitive forms of life e.g. algae and bacteria, existed during the Proterozoic era, it is not until the strata of Palaeozoic rocks is reached that abundant fossilized remains appear, initially of small shellfish, followed by plants, primitive fishes and, in the Devonian period (c.400 million B.C.), land-living plants and amphibia.

Since the Precambrian, there have been three great geological eras:

PALAEOZOIC ("ancient life") c.570–c.250 million B.C.

(i) *Cambrian.* Mainly sandstones, slate and shales; limestones in Scotland. Shelled fossils and invertebrates e.g. trilobites and brachiopods appear.

(ii) *Ordovician.* Mainly shales and mudstones e.g. in N. Wales; limestones in Scotland.

(iii) *Silurian.* Shales, mudstones and some limestones, found mostly in Wales and southern Scotland.

(iv) *Devonian.* Old red sandstone, shale, limestone and slate, e.g. in S. Wales and the West Country. "The age of fishes"—proliferation of fish fossils. First traces of land-living life.

(v) *Carboniferous.* Coal-bearing rocks, millstone grit, limestone and shale.

(vi) *Permian.* Marls, sandstones and clays, named after the area of Russia where these strata are widespread. First large-scale appearance of reptile fossils.

There were two great phases of mountain building in the Palaeozoic area: the *Caledonian*, characterized in Britain by N.E.–S.W. lines of hills and valleys; and the later *Hercyian*, widespread in W. Germany and adjacent areas, and in Britain exemplified in E.–W. lines of hills and valleys.

The end of the Palaeozoic was marked by the extensive glaciations of the Permian period in the southern continents and the decline of amphibians; it was succeeded by an era of warm conditions.

MESOZOIC ("middle forms of life") c.250-c.65 million B.C.

(i) *Triassic.* Mostly sandstone, e.g. in the W. Midlands.

(ii) *Jurassic.* Mainly limestones and clays, typically displayed in the Jura Mts. and in England in a N.E.–S.W. belt from Lincolnshire and the Wash to the Severn and the Dorset coast.

(iii) *Cretaceous.* Mainly chalk, clay and sands, e.g. in Kent and Sussex.

Giant reptiles were dominant during the Mesozoic, but it was at this time that marsupial mammals first appeared, as well as *Archaeopteryx lithographica*, the earliest known species of bird. Coniferous trees and flowering plants also developed during the era and, with the birds and the mammals, were the main species to survive into the Caenozoic (or Cenozoic) era. The giant reptiles became extinct.

CAENOZOIC ("recent life") from c.65 million B.C.

(i) *Eocene.* The emergence of new forms of life, i.e. existing species.

(ii) *Oligocene.* Fossils of a few still existing species.

(iii) *Miocene.* Fossil remains show a balance of existing and extinct species.

(iv) *Pliocene.* Fossil remains show a majority of still existing species.

(v) *Pleistocene.* The majority of remains are those of still existing species.

(vi) *Holocene.* The present, post-glacial period. Existing species only, except for a few exterminated by man.

In the last 25 million years, from the Miocene through the Pliocene, the Alpine-Himalayan and the circum-Pacific phases of mountain building reached their climax. During the Pleistocene period ice sheets repeatedly locked up masses of water as land ice; its weight depressed the land, but the locking-up of the water lowered the sea-level by 100–200 metres. The glaciations and interglacials of the Ice Age are extremely difficult to date and classify, but recent scientific opinion considers the Pleistocene to have begun approximately 1·7 million years ago. The last glacial retreat, merging into the Holocene period, was 10,000 years ago.

EARLY MAN

Any consideration of the history of man must start with the fact that all members of the human race belong to one species of animal, i.e. *Homo sapiens*, the definition of a species being in biological terms that all its members can interbreed. As a species of mammal it is possible to group man with other similar types, known as the primates. Amongst these is found a sub-group, the apes, which includes, in addition to man, the chimpanzees, gorillas, orang-utans and gibbons. All lack a tail, have shoulder blades at the back, and a Y-shaped chewing pattern on the surface of their molars, as well as showing the more general primate characteristics of four incisors, a thumb which is able to touch the fingers of the same hand, and finger and toe nails instead of claws. All the factors available to scientific study suggest that human beings have chimpanzees and gorillas as their nearest relatives in the animal world. However, there remains the possibility that there once lived creatures, now extinct, which were closer to modern man than the chimpanzees and gorillas. To decide whether or not this is the case it is necessary to consider the fossil evidence to see if any extinct ape-like forms shared with modern man the characteristics of having flat faces (i.e. the absence of a pronounced muzzle), being bipedal, and possessing large brains.

There are two broad groups of extinct apes recognised by specialists. First the ramapithecines, the remains of which, mainly jaw fragments, have been found in East Africa, Asia, and Turkey. They lived about 14 to 8 million years ago, and from the evidence of their teeth it seems they chewed more in the manner of modern man than the other presently living apes. The second group, the australopithecines, have left much more numerous remains amongst which sub-groups may be detected, although the geographic spread is limited to South and East Africa. Living between 5 and 1·5 million years ago, they were closer relatives of modern man to the extent that they walked upright, did not have an extensive muzzle, and had similar types of pre-molars. The first australopithecine remains were recognised at Taung in South Africa in 1924, and subsequent discoveries include those at the famous site of Olduvai Gorge in Tanzania. Perhaps the most impressive discovery was made at Hadar in Ethiopia in 1974 when about half a skeleton, known as "Lucy", was found.

Also in East Africa, between 2 million and 1·5 million years ago, lived a hominid group which not only walked upright, had a flat face, and a large brain case, but also made simple pebble and flake stone tools. On present evidence these habilines seem to have been the first people to make tools, however crude. This facility is related to the larger brain size and human beings are the only animals to make implements to be used in other processes. These early pebble tool users, because of their distinctive characteristics, have been grouped as a separate sub-species, now extinct, of the genus *Homo*, and are known as *Homo habilis*.

The use of fire, again a human characteristic, is associated with another group of extinct hominids whose remains, about a million years old, are found in South and East Africa, China, Indonesia, North Africa and Europe. No doubt the mastery of the techniques of making fire helped the colonisation of the colder northern areas and in this respect the site of Vertesszollos in Hungary is of particular importance. *Homo erectus* is the name given to this group of fossils and it now includes a number of famous individual discoveries from earlier decades, for example, Solo Man, Heidelberg Man, and especially Peking Man who lived at the cave site at Choukoutien, which has yielded evidence of fire and burnt bone.

The well known group, Neanderthal Man, or *Homo sapiens neanderthalensis*, is an extinct form of modern man who lived between about 100,000 and 40,000 years ago, thus spanning the last Ice Age. Indeed, its ability to adapt to the cold climate on the edge of the ice sheets is one of its characteristic features, the remains being only found in Europe, Asia and the Middle East. Complete neandertthal skeletons were found during excavations at Tabun in Israel together with evidence of tool-making and the use of fire. Distinguished by very large brains, it seems that neanderthal man was the first to develop recognisable social customs, especially deliberate burial rites. Why the neanderthalers became extinct is not clear, but it may be connected with the climatic changes at the end of the Ice Ages which would have seriously affected their food supplies; possibly they became too specialised for their own good.

The Swanscombe skull is the only known human fossil remains found in England. Some specialists see Swanscombe Man (or, more probably, woman) as a neanderthaler. Others group these remains together with the Steinheim skull from Germany, seeing both as a separate sub-species, *Homo sapiens steinheimenses*. Unfortunately there is just too little evidence as yet on which to form a final judgment.

Modern Man, *Homo sapiens sapiens*, the surviving sub-species of *Homo sapiens*, had evolved to our present physical condition and had colonised much of the world by about 30,000 years ago. There are many previously distinguished individual specimens, for example Cromagnon Man, which may now be grouped together as *Homo sapiens sapiens*. It was modern man who spread to the New World by crossing the landbridge between Siberia and Alaska and thence moved south through North and into South America. Equally it is modern man who over the last 30,000 years has been responsible for the major developments in technology, art and civilisation generally.

One of the problems for those studying fossil man is the lack in many cases of sufficient quantities of fossil bone for analysis. It is important that theories should be tested against evidence, and not the evidence made to fit the theory. The celebrated Piltdown hoax is perhaps the best known example of

"fossils" being forged to fit what was seen in some quarters as the correct theory of man's evolution.

HUMAN CULTURAL DEVELOPMENT

The Eurocentric bias of early archaeologists meant that the search for a starting point for the development and transmission of cultural ideas, especially by migration, trade and warfare, concentrated unduly on Europe and the Near East. The Three Age System, whereby pre-history was divided into a Stone Age, Bronze Age, and Iron Age, was devised by Christian Thomsen, curator of the National Museum of Denmark in the early nineteenth century, to facilitate the classification of the Museum's collections. The descriptive adjectives referred to the materials from which the implements and weapons were made, and came to be regarded as the dominant features of the societies to which they related. The refinement of the Three Age System once dominated archaeological thought and still remains a generally accepted concept in the popular mind. However, it is now seen by archaeologists as an inadequate model for human development.

Common sense alone suggests that there were no complete breaks between one so-called "Age" and another, any more than contemporaries would have regarded 1485 as a complete break between medieval and modern English history. Nor can the Three Age System be applied universally. In some areas it is necessary to insert a Copper Age, while in Africa south of the Sahara there would seem to be no Bronze Age at all; in Australia, Old Stone Age societies survived, while in South America, New Stone Age communities existed into modern times. The civilisations in other parts of the world clearly invalidate a Eurocentric theory of human development.

The concept of the "Neolithic Revolution", associated with the domestication of plants and animals, was a development of particular importance in the human cultural pattern. It reflected change from the primitive hunter/gatherer economies to a more settled agricultural way of life and therefore, so the argument goes, made possible the development of urban civilisation. However, it can no longer be argued that this "Revolution" took place only in one area from which all development stemmed. Though it appears that the cultivation of wheat and barley was first undertaken, together with the domestication of cattle and goats/sheep in the Fertile Crescent, there is evidence that rice was first deliberately planted and pigs domesticated in South East Asia; maize first cultivated in Central America and llamas first domesticated in South America. It has been recognized increasingly in recent years that cultural changes can take place independently of each other in different parts of the world at different rates and different times. There is no need for a general diffusionist theory.

Although scholars will continue to study the particular societies which interest them, it may be possible to obtain a reliable chronological framework, in absolute terms of years, against which the cultural development of any particular area may be set. The development and refinement of radiocarbon dating and other scientific methods of producing absolute chronologies is enabling the cross-referencing of societies to be undertaken. As the techniques of dating become more rigorous in application and the number of scientifically obtained dates increases, the attainment of an absolute chronology for prehistoric societies throughout the world comes closer to being achieved.

TIME MEASUREMENT AND CALENDARS
MEASUREMENTS OF TIME

Measurements of Time are based on the time taken by the earth to rotate on its axis (*Day*); by the moon to revolve round the earth (*Month*); and by the earth to revolve round the sun (*Year*). From these, which are not commensurable, certain average or mean intervals have been adopted for ordinary use.

The Day begins at midnight and is divided into 24 hours of 60 minutes, each of 60 seconds. The hours are counted from midnight up to 12 noon (when the sun crosses the meridian), and these hours are designated A.M. (*ante meridiem*); and again from noon up to 12 midnight, which hours are designated P.M. (*post meridiem*), except when the *twenty-four hour* reckoning is employed. The 24-hour reckoning ignores A.M. and P.M., and the hours are numbered 0 to 23 from midnight to midnight.

Colloquially the 24 hours are divided into *day* and *night*, day being the time while the sun is above the horizon (including the four stages of twilight defined on p. 65). Day is subdivided further into *morning*, the early part of daytime, ending at noon; *afternoon* from noon to 6 p.m. and *evening*, which may be said to extend from 6 p.m. until midnight. *Night*, the dark period between day and day, begins at the close of Astronomical Twilight (*see* p. 65) and extends beyond midnight to sunrise the next day.

The names of the Days—Sunday, Monday, Tuesday (Tyr or Tiw = god of war), Wednesday (Woden or Odin), Thursday (Thor), Friday (Frigga = wife of Odin, or Freyja = goddess of love), and Saturday—are derived from Old English translations or adaptions of the Roman titles (Sol, Luna, Mars, Mercurius, Jupiter, Venus and Saturnius).

The Week is a period of 7 days.

The Month in the ordinary calendar is approximately the twelfth part of a year, but the lengths of the different months vary from 28 (or 29) days to 31.

The Year.—The *Equinoctial* or *Tropical Year* is the time that the earth takes to revolve round the sun from equinox to equinox, or 365·2422 mean solar days. The *Calendar Year* consists of 365 days, but a year the date of which is divisible by 4, without remainder, is called *bissextile* (see Roman Calendar) or *Leap Year* and consists of 366 days, one day being added to the month February, so that a date "leaps over" a day of the week. The last year of a century is not a leap year unless its number is divisable by 400 (e.g. the years 1800 and 1900 had only 365 days).

The Solstice.—A Solstice is the point in the Tropical Year at which the Sun attains its greatest distance, north or south, from the Equator. In the northern hemisphere the greatest distance north of the Equator is the Summer Solstice and the greatest distance south is the Winter Solstice.

The Summer Solstice is also the *Longest Day*, measured from sunrise to sunset. At the Solstice the Sun, reaching its greatest northern declination, appears to stand still, the times of sunrise and sunset and the consequent length of the day showing no variation for several days together, before and after the longest day (June 21 or 22). For the remainder of this century the longest day will fall each year on June 21.

The date of the Solstice varies according to locality. If the Solstice falls on June 21 late in the day by Greenwich time, that day will be the longest day of the year at Greenwich even though it may be by only a second of time or a fraction thereof, but it will be on June 22, local date, in Japan, and so June 22 will be the longest day there and at places in eastern longitudes.

Leaving aside the question of locality, the date of the Solstice is also affected by the length of the Tropical Year, which is 365¼ days less about 11 minutes. If a Solstice happens late on June 21 in one year, it will be nearly six hours later in the next, i.e. early on June 22, and that will be the longest day. This delay of the Solstice is not permitted to continue because the extra day in Leap Year brings it back a day in the Calendar.

However, because of the 11 minutes above mentioned, the additional day in Leap Year brings the Solstice back too far by 44 minutes, and the time of the Solstice in the Calendar is earlier as the century progresses. (In the year 2000 the Summer Solstice reaches its earliest date for 100 years, i.e., June 21^d 02^h.) To remedy this the last year of a century is in most cases not a Leap Year, and the omission of the extra day puts the date of the Solstice later by about six hours too much, compensation for which is made by making the fourth centennial year a Leap Year.

Similar considerations apply to the day of the Winter Solstice, or the *Shortest Day* of the year. For the remainder of this century the shortest day will fall on Dec. 21 in two years of four and on Dec. 22 in the remaining two years. In the year 2000 the Winter Solstice reaches its earliest date, i.e., Dec. 21^d 13^h. The difference due to locality also prevails in the same sense as for the longest day.

At Greenwich the Sun sets at its earliest by the clock about ten days before the shortest day, which is a circumstance that may require explanation. The daily change in the time of sunset is due in the first place to the Sun's movement southwards at this time of the year, which diminishes the interval between the Sun's transit, and its setting, and, secondly, because of the daily decrease of the Equation of Time which causes the time of Apparent noon to be continuously later, day by day, and so in a measure counteracts the first effect. The rates of the change of these two quantities are not equal, nor are they uniform, but are such that their combination causes the date of earliest sunset to be Dec. 12 or 13 at Greenwich. In more southerly latitudes the effect of the movement of the Sun is less, and the change in the time of sunset depends on that of the Equation of Time to a greater degree, and the date of earliest sunset is earlier than it is at Greenwich.

The Equinox is the point at which the Sun crosses the Equator and day and night are of equal length all over the world. This occurs in March (Vernal Equinox—about March 21) and September (Autumnal Equinox—about September 21).

The Historical Year.—Before the year 1752, two Calendar systems were in use in England. The Civil or Legal Year began on March 25, while the Historical Year began on January 1. Thus the Civil or Legal date March 24 1658, was the same day as the Historical date March 24, 1659; and a date in that portion of the year is written as: March 24 165⅜, the lower figure showing the Historical year.

The New Year.—In England in the seventh century, and as late as the thirteenth, the year was reckoned from Christmas Day, but in the twelfth century the Anglican Church began the year with the Feast of The Annunciation of the Blessed Virgin (Lady Day) on March 25 and this practice was adopted generally in the fourteenth century. The Civil or Legal year in the British Dominions (exclusive of Scotland) began with "Lady Day" until 1751. But in and since 1752 the civil year has begun with Jan. 1. Certain dividends are still paid by the Bank of England on dates based on Old Style. New Year's Day in *Scotland* was changed from March 25 to Jan. 1 in 1600.

On the Continent of Europe Jan. 1 was adopted as the first day of the year by Venice in 1522, Germany in 1544, Spain, Portugal, and the Roman Catholic Netherlands in 1556, Prussia, Denmark and Sweden in 1559, France 1564, Lorraine 1579, Protestant Netherlands 1583, Russia 1725, and Tuscany 1751.

The Masonic Year.—Two dates are quoted in warrants, dispensations etc., issued by the United Grand Lodge of England, those for the current year being expressed as *Anno Domini* 1989—*Anno Lucis* 5989. This *Year of Light* is based on the Book of Genesis I: 3, the 4000 year difference being derived, in modified form, from *Ussher's Notation*, published in 1654, which places the Creation of the World in 4,004 B.C.

Regnal Years.—These are the years of a sovereign's reign, and each begins on the anniversary of his or her accession: e.g. Regnal year 38 of the present Queen begins on Feb. 6, 1989. The *Summer Time Act* of 1925, for example, is quoted as 15 and 16 Geo. V. c. 64, because it became law in the session which extended over part of both of these regnal years. The regnal years of Edward VII began on January 22, which was the day of Queen Victoria's death in 1901, so that Acts passed in that reign are, in general, quoted with only one year number, but year 10 of the series ended on May 6, 1910, being the day on which King Edward died, and Acts of the Parliamentary Session 1910 are headed 10 Edw. VII. and 1 Geo. V.; Acts passed in 1936 were dated 1 Edw. VIII. and 1 Geo. VI.; Acts passed in 1952 were dated 16 Geo. VI. and 1 Elizabeth II.

The system was used for dating Acts of Parliament until 1962. Since 1962 Acts of Parliament have been dated by the calendar year.

Lord Mayor's Day.—The Lord Mayor of London was previously elected on the Feast of St. Simon and St. Jude (Oct. 28), and from the time of Edward I, at least, was presented to the King or to the Barons of the Exchequer on the following day, except that day be a Sunday. The day of election was altered to Oct. 16 in 1346, and after some further changes was fixed for Michaelmas Day in 1546, but the ceremonies of admittance and swearing-in of the Lord Mayor continued to take place on Oct. 28 and 29 respectively until 1751. In 1752, at the reform of the Calendar (*see* page 114), the Lord Mayor was continued in office until Nov. 8, the "New Style" equivalent of Oct. 28. The Lord Mayor is now presented to the Lord Chief Justice at the Royal Courts of Justice on the second Saturday in November to make the final declaration of office, having been sworn in at Guildhall on the preceding day.

Dog Days.—The days about the heliacal rising of the Dog Star, noted from ancient times as the hottest and most unwholesome period of the year in the northern hemisphere. Their incidence has been variously calculated as depending on the Greater or Lesser Dog Star (Sirius or Procyon) and their duration has been reckoned as from 30 to 54 days. A generally accepted period is from July 3 to Aug. 15.

Metonic (Lunar, or Minor) **Cycle.**—In the year 432 B.C. Meton, an Athenian astronomer, found that 235 Lunations are very nearly, though not exactly equal in duration to 19 Solar Years, and, hence, after 19 years the Phases of the Moon recur on the same days of the month (nearly). The dates of Full Moon in a cycle of nineteen years were inscribed in figures of gold on public monuments in Athens, and the number showing the position of a year in the Cycle is called the **Golden Number** of that year.

Roman Indication.—A period of fifteen years, instituted for fiscal purposes about A.D. 300.

Solar (or Major) **Cycle.**—A period of twenty-eight years, in any corresponding year of which the days of the week recur on the same day of the month.

Julian Period.—Proposed by Joseph Scaliger in 1582. The period is 7980 Julian years, and its first year coincides with the year 4713 B.C. 7980 is the product of the number of years in the Solar Cycle, the Metonic Cycle and the cycle of the Roman Indication (28 × 19 × 15).

Epact.—The age of the calendar Moon, diminished by one day, on January 1, in the ecclesiastical lunar calendar.

THE FOUR SEASONS

Spring, the first season of the year, is defined astronomically to begin in the northern hemisphere at the Vernal Equinox when the Sun enters the sign Aries and to terminate at the Summer Solstice. In Great Britain, Spring in popular parlance comprises the months of February, March and April. In the southern hemisphere Spring corresponds with Autumn in the northern hemisphere.

Summer, the second and warmest season, begins astronomically in the northern hemisphere at the Summer Solstice when the Sun enters the sign of Cancer, and terminates at the Autumnal Equinox. In popular parlance Summer in Great Britain includes the months of May, June, July and August. In the southern hemisphere Summer corresponds with Winter in the northern hemisphere.

Autumn, the third season, begins astronomically in the northern hemisphere at the Autumnal Equinox when the Sun enters the sign Libra and ends at the Winter Solstice. In Great Britain it is popularly held to include the months of September and October. A warm period sometimes occurs round about St. Luke's Day (Oct. 18) and is known as "St. Luke's Summer." In the southern hemisphere it corresponds with Spring of the northern.

Winter, the fourth and coldest season, begins astronomically in the northern hemisphere at the Winter Solstice when the Sun enters the sign of Capricornus, and ends at the Vernal Equinox. In Great Britain the season is popularly held to comprise the months of November, December and January. A warm period sometimes occurs round about Martinmas (Nov. 11) and is known as "St. Martin's Summer." In the southern hemisphere it corresponds with Summer of the northern.

THE CHRISTIAN CALENDAR

In the Christian chronological system the years are distinguished by cardinal numbers before or after the Incarnation, the period being denoted by the letters B.C. (Before Christ) or, more rarely, A.C. (*Ante Christum*), and A.D. (*Anno Domini*—In the Year of Our Lord). The correlative dates of the epoch are the 4th year of the 194th Olympiad, the 753rd year from the Foundation of Rome, A.M. 3761 (Jewish Chronology), and the 4714th year of the Julian Period.

The system was introduced into Italy in the sixth century, and though first used in France in the seventh it was not universally established there until about the eighth century. It has been said that the system was introduced into England by St. Augustine (A.D. 596), but was probably not generally used until some centuries later. It was ordered to be used by the Bishops at the Council of Chelsea, A.D. 816. The actual date of the birth of Christ is somewhat uncertain.

The Julian Calendar.—In the Julian Calendar all the centennial years were Leap Years, and for this reason towards the close of the sixteenth century there was a difference of 10 days between the tropical and calendar years; the equinox fell on March 11 of the Calendar, whereas at the time of the Council of Nicaea, A.D. 325, it had fallen on March 21. In 1582 Pope Gregory ordained that Oct. 5th should be called Oct. 15th and that of the end-century years only the fourth should be a Leap Year (*see* p. 112).

The Gregorian Calendar was adopted by Italy, France, Spain, and Portugal in 1582; by Prussia, the German Roman Catholic States, Switzerland, Holland, and Flanders on Jan. 1, 1583, Poland 1586, Hungary 1587, the German and Netherland Protestant States and Denmark 1700, Sweden (gradually) by the omission of eleven leap days, 1700–1740; Great Britain and her Dominions (including the North American Colonies) in 1752, by the omission of eleven days (Sept. 3 being reckoned as Sept. 14). Japan adopted the calendar in 1872, China in 1912, Bulgaria in 1915, Turkey and Soviet Russia in 1918, Yugoslavia and Romania in 1919, and Greece in February, 1923.

In the same year that the change was made in England from the Julian to the Gregorian Calendar, the beginning of the new year was also changed from March 25 to January 1 (*see* p. 112).

The Orthodox Churches.—Some Orthodox Churches still use the Julian reckoning, but the majority of Greek Churches and the Romanian Orthodox Church have adopted a modified "New Calendar", observing the Gregorian Calendar for fixed feasts and the Julian for movable feasts.

The Orthodox Church year begins on September 1. There are four fast periods, and in addition to Pascha (Easter), twelve great feasts, as well as numerous commemorations of the Saints of the Old and New Testaments throughout the year.

The Dominical Letter is one of the letters A–G which are used to denote the Sundays in successive years. If the first day of the year is a Sunday the letter is A; if the second, B; the third, C; and so on. Leap year requires two letters, the first for Jan. 1—Feb. 29, the second for March 1—Dec. 31.

Epiphany.—The Feast of the Epiphany, commemorating the manifestation of Christ, later became associated with the offering of gifts by the Magi. The day was of exceptional importance from the time of the Council of Nicaea (A.D. 325) as the primate of Alexandria was charged at every Epiphany Feast with the announcement in a letter to the Churches of the date of the forthcoming Easter. The day was of considerable importance in Britain as it influenced

dates, ecclesiastical and lay, e.g. **Plow Monday**, when work was resumed in the fields, falls upon the Monday in the first full week after the Epiphany.

Lent.—The Teutonic word *Lent*, which denotes the Fast preceding Easter, originally meant no more than the Spring season; but from Anglo-Saxon times, at least, it has been used as the equivalent of the more significant Latin term **Quadragesima**, meaning the "Forty Days" or, more literally, the fortieth day. As early as the fifth century some of the Fathers of the Church put forward the view that the forty days Fast is of Apostolic origin, but this is not supported or believed by modern scholars; and it appears to some that it dates from the early years of the fourth century. There is some suggestion that the Fast was kept originally for only forty hours. **Ash Wednesday** is the first day of Lent, which ends at midnight before Easter Day.

Sexagesima and Septuagesima.—It has been suggested that the unmeaning application of the names *Sexagesima* and *Septuagesima* to the second and third Sundays before Lent was made by analogy with the names *Quadragesima* and *Quinquagesima*. Another less likely conjecture is that *Septuagesima* means the seventh day before the Octave of Easter. It is not certain whether the name *Quinquagesima* is due to the fact that the Sunday in question is the fiftieth day before Easter (reckoned inclusive) or was simply formed on the analogy of *Quadragesima* (*New English Dictionary*).

Mothering Sunday is the fourth Sunday in Lent.

Palm Sunday, the Sunday before Easter and the beginning of Holy Week, commemorates the triumphal entry of Christ into Jerusalem and is celebrated in Britain (when palm is not available) by branches of willow gathered for use in the decoration of churches on that day.

Maundy Thursday is the day before Good Friday, the name itself being a corruption of *dies mandati* (day of the mandate) when Christ washed the feet of the disciples and gave them the mandate to love one another.

Easter Day is the first Sunday after the full moon which happens upon, or next after, the 21st day of March; and if the full moon happens upon a Sunday, Easter Day is the Sunday after. This definition is contained in an Act of Parliament (24 Geo. II., cap. 23), and explanation is given in the preamble to the Act that the day of Full Moon depends on certain tables that have been prepared. These are the tables whose essential points are given in the early pages of the Book of Common Prayer. The Moon referred to is not the real Moon of the heavens, but a hypothetical Moon on whose "Full" the date of Easter depends, and the lunations of this "Calendar" Moon consist of twenty-nine and thirty days alternately with certain necessary modifications to make the date of its Full agree as nearly as possible with that of the real Moon, which is known as the **Paschal Full Moon**. As at present ordained, Easter falls on one of 35 days— (March 22–April 25).

A Fixed Easter.—On June 15, 1928, the House of Commons agreed to a motion for the third reading of the Bill that Easter Day shall, in the Calendar year next but one after the commencement of the Act and in all subsequent years, be *the first Sunday after the second Saturday in April.* Easter would thus fall between April 9 and 15, both inclusive—that is, on the second or third Sunday in April. A clause in the Bill provided that before it shall come into operation regard shall be had to any opinion expressed officially by the various Christian Churches. Efforts by the World Council of Churches to secure a unanimous choice of date for Easter by its member Churches have so far been unsuccessful.

Holy Days and Saints Days were the normal factors in early times for settling the dates of future and recurrent appointments, e.g. the **Quarter Days** in England and Wales are the Feast of the Nativity, the Feast of the Annunciation, the Feast of St. John the Baptist and the Feast of St. Michael and All Angels, while **Term Days** in Scotland are Candlemas (Feast of the Purification), Whitsunday (a fixed date), Lammas (Loaf Mass) and Martinmas (St. Martin's Day). **Law Sittings** in England and Wales commence on the Feast of St. Hilary and the term which begins on Old Michaelmas Day ends on the former feast of St. Thomas the Apostle.

Red Letter Days (*see also* p. 155) were Holy Days and Saints Days indicated in early ecclesiastical calendars by letters printed in red ink. The days to be distinguished in this way were finally approved at the Council of Nicaea, A.D. 325.

Rogation Days.—These are the Monday, Tuesday and Wednesday preceding Ascension Day (Holy Thursday) and in the fifth century were ordered by the Church to be observed as public fasts with solemn processions and supplications. The processions were discontinued as religious observances at the Reformation, but survive in the ceremony known as

"Beating the Parish Bounds". **Rogation Sunday** is the Sunday before Ascension Day.

Ascension Day is forty days after Easter Day.

Ember Days.—The Ember Days at the Four Seasons are the Wednesday, Friday and Saturday (*a*) before the third Sunday in Advent, (*b*) before the second Sunday in Lent, and (*c*) before the Sundays nearest to the Festivals of St. Peter, and St. Michael and All Angels.

Whit Sunday or **Pentecost** is seven weeks after Easter Day. It is generally said that this name is a variant of White Sunday, and was so called from the albs or white robes of the newly baptized, but other derivations have been suggested.

Trinity Sunday is eight weeks after Easter Day, on the Sunday following Whit Sunday, and subsequent Sundays are sometimes reckoned in the Church of England as "after Trinity".

Thomas Becket (1118–1170) was consecrated Archbishop of Canterbury on the Sunday after Whit Sunday and his first act was to ordain that the day of his consecration should be held as a new festival in honour of the Holy Trinity. The observance thus originated spread from Canterbury throughout the whole of Christendom.

Advent Sunday is the Sunday nearest to St. Andrew's Day, Nov. 30, which allows three Sundays between Advent and Christmas Day in all cases.

A TABLE OF THE MOVABLE FEASTS TO THE YEAR 2010

Year	Ash Wednesday	Easter	Ascension	Whit Sunday	Sundays after Trinity	Advent Sunday
1985........	Feb. 20	April 7	May 16	May 26	25	Dec. 1
1986........	Feb. 12	March 30	May 8	May 18	26	Nov. 30
1987........	March 4	April 19	May 28	June 7	23	Nov. 29
1988........	Feb. 17	April 3	May 12	May 22	25	Nov. 27
1989........	Feb. 8	March 26	May 4	May 14	27	Dec. 3
1990........	Feb. 28	April 15	May 24	June 3	24	Dec. 2
1991........	Feb. 13	March 31	May 9	May 19	26	Dec. 1
1992........	March 4	April 19	May 28	June 7	23	Nov. 29
1993........	Feb. 24	April 11	May 20	May 30	24	Nov. 28
1994........	Feb. 16	April 3	May 12	May 22	25	Nov. 27
1995........	March 1	April 16	May 25	June 4	24	Dec. 3
1996........	Feb. 21	April 7	May 16	May 26	25	Dec. 1
1997........	Feb. 12	March 30	May 8	May 18	26	Nov. 30
1998........	Feb. 25	April 12	May 21	May 31	24	Nov. 29
1999........	Feb. 17	April 4	May 13	May 23	25	Nov. 28
2000........	March 8	April 23	June 1	June 11	23	Dec. 3
2001........	Feb. 28	April 15	May 24	June 3	24	Dec. 2
2002........	Feb. 13	March 31	May 9	May 19	26	Dec. 1
2003........	March 5	April 20	May 29	June 8	23	Nov. 30
2004........	Feb. 25	April 11	May 20	May 30	24	Nov. 28
2005........	Feb. 9	March 27	May 5	May 15	26	Nov. 27
2006........	March 1	April 16	May 25	June 4	24	Dec. 3
2007........	Feb. 21	April 8	May 17	May 27	25	Dec. 2
2008........	Feb. 6	March 23	May 1	May 11	27	Nov. 30
2009........	Feb. 25	April 12	May 21	May 31	24	Nov. 29
2010........	Feb. 17	April 4	May 13	May 23	25	Nov. 28

NOTES CONCERNING TABLE OF MOVABLE FEASTS

Ash Wednesday (first day in Lent) can fall at earliest on February 4 and at latest on March 10.
Easter Day can fall at earliest on March 22 and at latest on April 25.
Ascension Day can fall at earliest on April 30 and at latest on June 3.
Whit Sunday can fall at earliest on May 10 and at latest on June 13.
Trinity Sunday is the Sunday after *Whit Sunday.*
Corpus Christi falls on the Thursday after *Trinity Sunday.*
There are not less than 22 and not more than 27 *Sundays after Trinity.*
Advent Sunday is the Sunday nearest to November 30.

A TABLE OF EASTER DAYS AND SUNDAY LETTERS, 1500 TO 2025

		1500—1599	1600—1699	1700—1799	1800—1899	1900—1999	2000—2025
d	Mar. 22	1573	1668	1761	1818		
e	„ 23	1505-16	1600	1788	1845-56	1913	2008
f	„ 24		1611-95	1706-99		1940	
g	„ 25	1543-54	1627-38-49	1722-33-44	1883-94	1951	
A	„ 26	1559-70-81-92	1654-65-76	1749-58-69-80	1815-26-37	1967-78-89	
b	Mar. 27	1502-13-24-97	1608-87-92	1785-96	1842-53-64	1910-21-32	2005-16
c	„ 28	1529-35-40	1619-24-30	1703-14-25	1869-75-80	1937-48	
d	„ 29	1551-62	1635-46-57	1719-30-41-52	1807-12-91	1959-64-70	
e	„ 30	1567-78-89	1651-62-73-84	1746-55-66-77	1823-34	1902-75-86-97	
f	„ 31	1510-21-32-83-94	1605-16-78-89	1700-71-82-93	1839-50-61-72	1907-18-29-91	2002-13-24
g	April 1	1526-37-48	1621-32	1711-16	1804-66-77-88	1923-34-45-56	2018
A	„ 2	1553-64	1643-48	1727-38-52(NS)	1809-20-93-99	1961-72	
b	„ 3	1575-80-86	1659-70-81	1743-63-68-74	1825-31-36	1904-83-88-94	
c	„ 4	1507-18-91	1602-13-75-86-97	1708-79-90	1847-58	1915-20-26-99	2010-21
d	„ 5	1523-34-45-56	1607-18-29-40	1702-13-24-95	1801-63-74-85-96	1931-42-53	2015
e	April 6	1539-50-61-72	1634-45-56	1729-35-40-60	1806-17-28-90	1947-58-69-80	
f	„ 7	1504-77-88	1667-72	1751-65-76	1822-33-44	1901-12-85-96	
g	„ 8	1509-15-20-99	1604-10-83-94	1705-87-92-98	1849-55-60	1917-28	2007-12
A	„ 9	1531-42	1615-26-37-99	1710-21-32	1871-82	1939-44-50	2023
b	„ 10	1547-58-69	1631-42-53-64	1726-37-48-57	1803-14-87-98	1955-66-77	
c	April 11	1501-12-63-74-85-96	1658-69-80	1762-73-84	1819-30-41-52	1909-71-82-93	2004
d	„ 12	1506-17-28	1601-12-91-96	1789	1846-57-68	1903-14-25-36-98	2009-20
e	„ 13	1533-44	1623-28	1707-18	1800-73-79-84	1941-52	
f	„ 14	1555-60-66	1639-50-61	1723-34-45-54	1805-11-16-95	1963-68-74	
g	„ 15	1571-82-93	1655-66-77-88	1750-59-70-81	1827-38	1900-06-79-90	2001
A	April 16	1503-14-25-36-87-98	1609-20-82-93	1704-75-86-97	1843-54-65-76	1911-22-33-95	2006-17
b	„ 17	1530-41-52	1625-36	1715-20	1808-70-81-92	1927-38-49-60	2022
c	„ 18	1557-68	1647-52	1731-42-56	1802-13-24-97	1954-65-76	
d	„ 19	1500-79-84-90	1663-74-85	1747-67-72-78	1829-35-40	1908-81-87-92	
e	„ 20	1511-22-95	1606-17-79-90	1701-12-83-94	1851-62	1919-24-30	2003-14-25
f	April 21	1527-38-49	1622-33-44	1717-28	1867-78-89	1935-46-57	2019
g	„ 22	1565-76	1660	1739-53-64	1810-21-32	1962-73-84	
A	„ 23	1508	1671		1848	1905-16	2000
b	„ 24	1519	1603-14-98	1709-91	1859		2011
c	„ 25	1546	1641	1736	1886	1943	

THE JEWISH CALENDAR

Origin.—The story in the Book of Genesis that the Flood began on the seventeenth day of the second month; that after the end of 150 days the waters were abated; and that on the seventeenth day of the seventh month the Ark rested on Mount Ararat, indicates a calendar of some kind and that the writers recognized 30 days as the length of a lunation. There is other mention of months by their original numbers in the Book of Genesis and in establishing the rite of the Passover Moses spoke of *Abib* as the month when the Israelites came out from Egypt and Abib was to be the first month of the year. In the first Book of Kings three months are mentioned by name, Živ the second month, Ethanim the seventh and Bul the eighth, but these are not names now in use. After the Dispersion, Jewish communities were left in considerable doubt as to the times of Fasts and Festivals, and this led to the formation of the Jewish Calendar as used today, which, it is said, was done in A.D. 358 by Rabbi Hillel II, a descendant of Gamaliel—though some assert that it did not happen until much later. This calendar is luni-solar, and is based on the lengths of the lunation and of the tropical year as found by Hipparchus (*c.* 120 B.C.) which differ little from those adopted at the present day. The year 5749 A.D. (1988–89) is the 11th year of the 303rd *Metonic* (Minor or Lunar) *Cycle* of 19 years and the 9th year of the 206th *Solar* (or Major) *Cycle* of 28 years since the Era of the Creation, which the Jews hold to have occurred at the time of the Autumnal Equinox in the year known in the Christian Calendar as 3760 B.C. (954 of the Julian Period). The epoch or starting point of Jewish Chronology corresponds to Oct. 7, 3761 B.C. At the beginning of each Solar Cycle the *Tekufah* of Nisan (the vernal equinox) returns to the same day and to the same hour.

The hour is divided into 1080 *minims* and the month between one new moon and the next is reckoned as 29 days, 12 hours, 793 minims. The normal calendar year, called a Common Regular year, consists of 12 months of 30 days and 29 days alternately. Since 12 months such as these comprise only 354 days, in order that each of them shall not diverge greatly from an average place in the solar year, a thirteenth month is occasionally added after the fifth month of the Civil year (which commences on the first day of the month Tishri), or as the penultimate month of the Ecclesiastical (which commences on the first day of month Nisan), the years when this happens being called Embolismic or Leap years. Of the 19 years that form a Metonic cycle, 7 are leap years; they occur at places in the cycle indicated by the numbers 3, 6, 8, 11, 14, 17, 19, these places being chosen so that the accumulated excesses of the solar years should be as small as possible. The first of each month is called the day of New Moon, though it is not necessarily the day of astronomical New Moon, that being the day on which conjunction of Sun and Moon occurs, but there is generally a difference of a day or two. In practice, in a month which follows one of 30 days, the day preceding its first day is also observed as a day of New Moon. The dates on which the first days of the months fall depend on that of the first of Tishri, which therefore controls the dates of fasts and festivals in the Jewish year. For certain ceremonial reasons connected with these, the first of Tishri must not fall on a Sunday, Wednesday or Friday, and if this should happen as the result of the computation it is postponed to the following day. Also, if the New Moon of Tishri falls on any day of the week at noon or later than noon, then the following day is to be taken for the celebration of that New Moon and is Tishri 1, provided that it is not one of the forbidden days, in which case there is a further postponement of a day. These rules and others have been considered

in detail, and finally a calendar scheme has been drawn up in which a Jewish year is of one of the following six types: Minimal Common (353 days), Regular Common (354 days), Full Common (355 days), Minimal Leap (383 days), Regular Leap (384 days), or Full Leap (385 days).

The Regular year has an alternation of 30 and 29 days. In a full year, whether Common or Leap, Marcheshvan, the second month of the Civil year, has 30 days instead of 29; in Minimal years Kislev, the third month, has 29 days instead of 30. The additional month in Leap years which is called Adar I, and precedes the month called Adar in Common years and Adar II, or Ve-Adar, in Leap, always has 30 days, but neither this, nor the other variations mentioned, is allowed to change the number of days in the other months which still follow the alternation of the normal twelve. In Leap years the month intercalated precedes Adar and usurps its name, but the usual Adar festivals are kept in Ve-Adar.

These are the main features of the Jewish Calendar which must be considered permanent, because as a Jewish law it cannot be altered except by a great Sanhedrin.

The Jewish day begins between sunset and nightfall. The time used is that of the meridian of Jerusalem, which is $2h.21m.$ in advance of Greenwich Mean Time. Rules for the beginning of Sabbaths and Festivals were laid down for the latitude of London in the eighteenth century and hours for nightfall are now fixed annually by the Chief Rabbi.

Jewish Calendar 5749–50

Jewish Month					A.M. 5749				A.M. 5750	
Tishri	1	..	..	..	1988 September	12	..	..	1989 September	30
Marcheshvan	1	..	..	..	October	12	..	..	October	30
Kislev	1	..	..	..	November	10	..	..	November	29
Tebet	1	..	..	..	December	9	..	..	December	29
Shebat	1	..	..	..	1989 January	7	..	..	1990 January	27
*Adar	1	..	..	..	February	6	..	..	February	26
Ve-Adar	1	..	..	..	March	8	..	..		
Nisan	1	..	..	..	April	6	..	..	March	27
Iyar	1	..	..	..	May	6	..	..	April	26
Sivan	1	..	..	..	June	4	..	..	May	25
Tammuz	1	..	..	..	July	4	..	..	June	24
Ab	1	..	..	..	August	2	..	..	July	23
Elul	1	..	..	..	September	1	..	..	August	22

A.M. 5749 (749) is a Minimal Leap Year of 13 months, 54 Sabbaths and 383 days. A.M. 5750 (750) is a Full Common Year of 12 months, 51 Sabbaths and 355 days.
*Known as Adar Rishon in Leap Years.

Jewish Fasts and Festivals

Tishri	1–2	Rosh Hashanah (New Year).	*Tebet*	10	Fast of Tebet.
,,	3	*Fast of Gedaliah.	†*Adar*	13	§Fast of Esther.
,,	10	Yom Kippur (Day of Atonement).	,, ,,	14	Purim.
,,	15–21	Succoth (Feast of Tabernacles).	,, ,,	15	Shushan Purim.
,,	21	Hoshana Rabba.	*Nisan*	15–22	Pesach (Passover).
,,	22	Shemini Atseret (Solemn Assembly).	*Sivan*	6–7	Shavuot (Feast of Weeks).
,,	23	Simchat Torah (Rejoicing of the Law).	*Tammuz*	17	*Fast of Tammuz.
Kislev	25	Chanukah (Dedication of the Temple) begins.	*Ab*	9	*Fast of Ab.

NOTES.—* If these dates fall on the Sabbath the Fast is kept on the following day.
† Ve-Adar in Leap Years.
§ This fast is observed on Adar 11 (or Ve-Adar 11 in Leap Years) if Adar 13 falls on a Sabbath.

THE ROMAN CALENDAR

Roman historians adopted as an epoch the Foundation of Rome, which is believed to have happened in the year 753 B.C., and the ordinal number of the years in Roman reckoning is followed by the letters A.U.C. (*Ab Urbe Condita*), so that the year 1989 is 2742 A.U.C. (MMDCCXLII). The Calendar that we know has developed from one established by Romulus, who is said to have used a year of 304 days divided into ten months, beginning with March, to which Numa added January and February, making the year consist of 12 months of 30 and 29 days alternately, with an additional day so that the total was 355. It is also said that Numa ordered an intercalary month of 22 or 23 days in alternate years, making 90 days in eight years, to be inserted after Feb. 23, but there is some doubt as to the origination and the details of the intercalation in the Roman Calendar, though it is certain that some scheme of this kind was inaugurated and not fully carried out, for in the year 46 B.C. Julius Cæsar, who was then Pontifex Maximus,

found that the Calendar had been allowed to fall into some confusion. He therefore sought the help of the Egyptian astronomer Sosigenes, which led to the construction and adoption (45 B.C.) of the Julian Calendar, and, by a slight alteration, to the Gregorian now in use. The year 46 B.C. was made to consist of 445 days, and is called the *Year of Confusion*. In the Roman (Julian) Calendar the days of the month were counted backwards from three fixed points, or days, and an intervening day was said to be so many days *before* the next coming point, the first *and* last being counted. These three points were (*a*) the Kalends; (*b*) the Nones; and (*c*) the Ides. Their positions in the months and the method of counting from them will be seen in the table below. The year containing 366 days was called *bissextillis annus*, as it had a doubled sixth day (*bissextus dies*) before the March Kalends on Feb. 24—*ante diem sextum Kalendas Martias*, or a.d. VI Kal. Mart.

Present Days of the Month	March, May, July, October have thirty-one days	January, August, December have thirty-one days	April, June, September, November have thirty days	February has twenty-eight days, and in Leap Year twenty-nine
1	Kalendis.	Kalendis.	Kalendis.	Kalendis.
2	VI. ⎱ ante	IV. ante	IV. ⎱ Nonas.	IV. ⎱ ante
3	V. ⎰	III. Nonas.	III. ⎰ Nonas.	III. ⎰ Nonas.
4	IV. ⎱ Nonas.	pridie Nonas.	pridie Nonas.	pridie Nonas.
5	III. ⎰	Nonis.	Nonis.	Nonis.
6	pridie Nonas.	VIII.	VIII.	VIII.
7	Nonis.	VII.	VII.	VII.
8	VIII.	VI. ⎱ ante	VI. ⎱ ante.	VI. ⎱ ante
9	VII.	V. ⎰ Idus.	V. ⎰ Idus.	V. ⎰ Idus.
10	VI. ⎱ ante	IV.	IV.	IV.
11	V. ⎰ Idus.	III.	III.	III.
12	IV.	pridie Idus.	pridie Idus.	pridie Idus.
13	III.	Idibus.	Idibus.	Idibus.
14	pridie Idus.	XIX.	XVIII.	XVI.
15	Idibus.	XVIII.	XVII.	XV.
16	XVII.	XVII.	XVI.	XIV.
17	XVI.	XVI.	XV.	XIII.
18	XV.	XV.	XIV.	XII.
19	XIV.	XIV.	XIII.	XI.
20	XIII.	XIII.	XII.	X.
21	XII.	XII.	XI.	IX.
22	XI.	XI.	X.	VIII.
23	X.	X.	IX.	VII.
24	IX.	IX.	VIII.	*VI.
25	VIII.	VIII.	VII.	V.
26	VII.	VII.	VI.	IV.
27	VI.	VI.	V.	III.
28	V.	V.	IV.	pridie Kalendas Martias.
29	IV.	IV.	III.	
30	III.	III.	pridie Kalendas (Maias, Quinctilis, Octobris, Decembris).	
31	pridie Kalendas (Aprilis, Iunias, Sextilis, Novembris).	pridie Kalendas (Februarias, Septembris, Ianuarias).		* (repeated in Leap Year).

Note: Columns 2-4 carry the bracketed label "ante Kalendas (of the month following)." for days 14-30 (or 14-29/28). Column 5 carries the label "ante Kalendas Martias." for days 14-27.

ROMAN NUMERALS

1 I	9 IX	17 XVII	70 LXX	600 ....DC
2 II	10 X	18 XVIII	80 LXXX	700 ......DCC
3 III	11 XI	19 XIX	90 XC	800 .....DCCC
4 IV	12 XII	20 XX	100 C	900 ....CM
5 V	13 XIII	30 XXX	200 CC	1000 ....M
6 VI	14 XIV	40 XL	300 CCC	1500 ......MD
7 VII	15 XV	50 L	400 ....CD	1900 ....MCM
8 VIII	16 XVI	60 LX	500 ....D	2000 ....MM

Other Examples: 43 = XLIII; 66 = LXVI; 98 = XCVIII.
339 = CCCXXXIX; 619 = DCXIX; 988 = CMLXXXVIII; 996 = CMXCVI.
1674 = MDCLXXIV; 1962 = MCMLXII; 1989 = MCMLXXXIX.
A bar placed over a numeral has the effect of multiplying the number by 1,000, e.g.:

6,000 = $\overline{\text{VI}}$; 16,000 = $\overline{\text{XVI}}$; 160,000 = CLX; 666,000 = $\overline{\text{DCLXVI}}$.

THE MOSLEM CALENDAR

The basic date of the Moslem Calendar is the *Hejira*, or Flight of Muhammad from Mecca to Medina, the corresponding date of which is A.D. 622, July 16, in the Julian Calendar. Hejira years are used principally in Iran, Turkey, Egypt, in various Arabian states, in certain parts of India and in Malaysia. The system was adopted about A.D. 632, commencing from the first day of the month preceding the Hejira. The years are purely lunar and consist of 12 months containing in alternate sequence 30 or 29 days, with the intercalation of one day at the end of the 12th month at stated intervals in each cycle of 30 years, the object of the intercalation being to reconcile the date of the first of the month with the date of the actual New Moon. Some adherents still take the date of the evening of the first visibility of the crescent as that of the first of the month. In each cycle of 30 years 19 are common and contain 354 days and 11 are intercalary (355 days), the latter being called *kabishah*.

The mean length of the Hejira year is 354 days, 8 hours, 48 minutes and the period of mean lunation is 29 days, 12 hours, 44 minutes.

To ascertain if a Hejira year is common or *kabishah* divide it by 30; the quotient gives the number of completed cycles and the remainder shows the place of the year in the current cycle. If the remainder is 2, 5, 7, 10, 13, 16, 18, 21, 24, 26 or 29 the year is *kabishah* and consists of 355 days.

Hejira year A.H. 1409 (remainder 29) is a *kabishah* year and A.H. 1410 (no remainder) is a common year.

Hejira Years 1409 and 1410

Name and Length of Month	A.H. 1409		A.H. 1410	
Muharram (30)......1988	Aug.	14	1989 Aug.	4
Safar (29)...........	Sept.	13	Sept.	3
Rabia I (30)	Oct.	12	Oct.	2
Rabia II (29)	Nov.	11	Nov.	1
Jumâda I (30)	Dec.	10	Nov.	30
Jumâda II (29) 1989	Jan.	9	1990 Dec.	30
Rajab (30)	Feb.	7	Jan.	28
Shaabân (29)........	Mar.	9	Feb.	27
Ramadân (30)	April	7	Mar.	28
Shawwâl (29)	May	7	April	27
Dhû'l-Qa'da (30).....	June	5	May	26
Dhû'l-Hijja (29 or 30)	July	5	June	25

OTHER EPOCHS AND CALENDARS

China.—Until the year A.D. 1911 a lunar calendar was in force in China, but with the establishment of the Republic the Government adopted the Gregorian Calendar, and the new and old systems were used simultaneously by the people for several years. Since 1930 the publication and use of the old Calendar have been banned by the Government, and an official Chinese Calendar, corresponding with the European or Western system, is compiled, but the old lunar calendar is still in use to some extent in China. The old Chinese Calendar, with a cycle of 60 years, is still in use in Tibet, Hong Kong, Singapore, Malaysia and elsewhere in South-East Asia.

Ethiopia.—In the Coptic Calendar, which is used by part of the population of Egypt and Ethiopia, the year is made up of 12 months of 30 days each, followed, in general, by 5 complementary days. Every fourth year is an Intercalary or Leap year and in these years there are 6 complementary days. The Intercalary year of the Coptic Calendar immediately precedes the Leap year of the Julian Calendar. The Era is that of Diocletian or the Martyrs, the origin of which is fixed at A.D. 284, Aug. 29 (Julian date).

Greece.—Ancient Greek chronology was reckoned in *Olympiads*, cycles of 4 years corresponding with the periodic Olympic Games held on the plain of Olympia in Elis once in 4 years, the intervening years being the first, second, etc., of the Olympiad which received the name of the victor at the Games. The first recorded Olympiad is that of Choroebus, 776 B.C.

India.—In addition to the Moslem reckoning there are six eras used in India. The principal astronomical system was the *Kaliyuga Era*, which appears to have been adopted in the fourth century A.D. It began on Feb. 18, 3102 B.C. The chronological system of Northern India, known as the *Vikrama Samvat Era*, prevalent in Western India, began on Feb. 23, 57 B.C. The year A.D. 1989 is, therefore, the year 2046 of the Vikrama Era.

The *Saka Era* of Southern India dating from A.D. 78, March 3, was declared the uniform national calendar of the Republic of India with effect from March 22, 1957, to be used concurrently with the Gregorian Calendar. As revised, the year of the new

Saka Era begins at the spring equinox, with five successive months of 31 days and seven of 30 days in ordinary years; six months of each length in leap years. The year A.D. 1989 is 1911 of the revised *Saka Era*.

In the Hills, the *Saptarshi Era* dates from the moment when the Saptarshi, or saints, were translated and became the stars of the Great Bear in 3076 B.C.

The *Buddhists* reckoned from the death of Buddha in 543 B.C. (the actual date being 487 B.C.); and the epoch of the *Jains* was the death of Vardhamana, the founder of their faith, in 527 B.C.

Iran.—The chronology of Iran is the Era of Hejira, which began on A.D. 622, July 16. The *Zoroastrian Calendar* was used in pre-Moslem days and is still employed by Zoroastrians in Iran and India (Parsees) with an era beginning A.D. 632, June 16.

Japan.—The Japanese Calendar is the Gregorian, and is essentially the same as that in use by Western nations, the years, months and weeks being of the same length and beginning on the same days as those of the Western Calendar. The numeration of the years is different, for Japanese chronology is based on a system of epochs or periods, each of which begins at the accession of an Emperor or other important occurrence, the method being not unlike the former British system of Regnal years, but differing from it in the particular that each year of a period closes on Dec. 31. The Japanese scheme begins about A.D. 650 and the three latest epochs are defined by the reigns of Emperors, whose actual names are not necessarily used:

Epoch Meiji	from 1868 Oct. 13 to 1912 July 31
„ Taishō „	1912 Aug. 1 to 1926 Dec. 25
„ Shōwa „	1926 Dec. 26

Hence the year Shōwa 64 begins Jan. 1, 1989. The months are not named. They are known as First Month, Second Month, etc., first month being the equivalent to January. The days of the week are Nichiyōbi (Sun-day), Getsuyōbi (Moon-day), Kayōbi (Fire-day), Suiyōbi (Water-day), Mokuyōbi (Wood-day), Kinyōbi (Metal-day), Doyōbi (Earth-day).

for any year between 1770 and 2025 together with the dates of Easter in each of those years.
To select the correct calendar for any year consult the Index below

INDEX TO CALENDARS

Year		Year		Year		Year		Year		Year	
1770	C	1813	K	1856	F*	1899	A	1942	I	1985	E
1771	E	1814	M	1857	I	1900	C	1943	K	1986	G
1772	H*	1815	A	1858	K	1901	E	1944	N*	1987	I
1773	E	1816	D*	1859	M	1902	G	1945	C	1988	L*
1774	M	1817	G	1860	B*	1903	I	1946	E	1989	A
1775	A	1818	I	1861	E	1904	L*	1947	G	1990	C
1776	D*	1819	K	1862	G	1905	A	1948	J*	1991	E
1777	I	1820	N*	1863	I	1906	C	1949	M	1992	H*
1778	I	1821	C	1864	L*	1907	E	1950	A	1993	K
1779	K	1822	E	1865	A	1908	H*	1951	C	1994	M
1780	N*	1823	G	1866	C	1909	K	1952	F*	1995	A
1781	C	1824	J*	1867	E	1910	M	1953	I	1996	D*
1782	E	1825	M	1868	H*	1911	A	1954	K	1997	G
1783	G	1826	A	1869	K	1912	D*	1955	M	1998	I
1784	J*	1827	C	1870	M	1913	G	1956	B*	1999	K
1785	M	1828	F*	1871	A	1914	I	1957	E	2000	N*
1786	A	1829	I	1872	D*	1915	K	1958	G	2001	C
1787	C	1830	K	1873	G	1916	N*	1959	I	2002	E
1788	F*	1831	M	1874	I	1917	C	1960	L*	2003	G
1789	I	1832	B*	1875	K	1918	E	1961	A	2004	J*
1790	K	1833	E	1876	N*	1919	G	1962	C	2005	M
1791	M	1834	G	1877	C	1920	J*	1963	E	2006	A
1792	B*	1835	I	1878	E	1921	M	1964	H*	2007	C
1793	E	1836	L*	1879	G	1922	A	1965	K	2008	F*
1794	G	1837	A	1880	J*	1923	C	1966	M	2009	I
1795	I	1838	C	1881	M	1924	F*	1967	A	2010	K
1796	L*	1839	E	1882	A	1925	I	1968	D*	2011	M
1797	A	1840	H*	1883	C	1926	K	1969	G	2012	B*
1798	C	1841	K	1884	F*	1927	M	1970	I	2013	E
1799	E	1842	M	1885	I	1928	B*	1971	K	2014	G
1800	I	1843	G	1886	K	1929	E	1972	N*	2015	I
1801	I	1844	D*	1887	M	1930	G	1973	C	2016	L*
1802	K	1845	G	1888	B*	1931	I	1974	E	2017	A
1803	M	1846	I	1889	E	1932	L*	1975	G	2018	C
1804	B*	1847	K	1890	G	1933	A	1976	J*	2019	E
1805	E	1848	N*	1891	I	1934	C	1977	M	2020	H*
1806	G	1849	C	1892	L*	1935	E	1978	A	2021	K
1807	I	1850	E	1893	A	1936	H*	1979	C	2022	M
1808	L*	1851	G	1894	C	1937	K	1980	F*	2023	A
1809	A	1852	J*	1895	E	1938	M	1981	I	2024	D*
1810	C	1853	M	1896	H*	1939	A	1982	K	2025	G
1811	E	1854	A	1897	K	1940	D*	1983	M		
1812	H*	1855	C	1898	M	1941	G	1984	B*		

* Leap Year

A

January
```
Su. ..  1  8 15 22 29
M.  ..  2  9 16 23 30
Tu. ..  3 10 17 24 31
W.  ..  4 11 18 25
Th. ..  5 12 19 26
F.  ..  6 13 20 27
S.  ..  7 14 21 28
```

February
```
Su.        5 12 19 26
M.         6 13 20 27
Tu.        7 14 21 28
W.      1  8 15 22
Th.     2  9 16 23
F.      3 10 17 24
S.      4 11 18 25
```

March
```
Su.        5 12 19 26
M.         6 13 20 27
Tu.        7 14 21 28
W.      1  8 15 22 29
Th.     2  9 16 23 30
F.      3 10 17 24 31
S.      4 11 18 25
```

April
```
Su.     2  9 16 23 30
M.      3 10 17 24
Tu.     4 11 18 25
W.      5 12 19 26
Th.     6 13 20 27
F.      7 14 21 28
S.   1  8 15 22 29
```

May
```
Su.        7 14 21 28
M.      1  8 15 22 29
Tu.     2  9 16 23 30
W.      3 10 17 24 31
Th.     4 11 18 25
F.      5 12 19 26
S.      6 13 20 27
```

June
```
Su.     4 11 18 25
M.      5 12 19 26
Tu.     6 13 20 27
W.      7 14 21 28
Th.  1  8 15 22 29
F.   2  9 16 23 30
S.   3 10 17 24
```

July
```
Su.     2  9 16 23 30
M.      3 10 17 24 31
Tu.     4 11 18 25
W.      5 12 19 26
Th.     6 13 20 27
F.      7 14 21 28
S.   1  8 15 22 29
```

August
```
Su.        6 13 20 27
M.         7 14 21 28
Tu.     1  8 15 22 29
W.      2  9 16 23 30
Th.     3 10 17 24 31
F.      4 11 18 25
S.      5 12 19 26
```

September
```
Su.     3 10 17 24
M.      4 11 18 25
Tu.     5 12 19 26
W.      6 13 20 27
Th.     7 14 21 28
F.   1  8 15 22 29
S.   2  9 16 23 30
```

October
```
Su.     1  8 15 22 29
M.      2  9 16 23 30
Tu.     3 10 17 24 31
W.      4 11 18 25
Th.     5 12 19 26
F.      6 13 20 27
S.      7 14 21 28
```

November
```
Su.        5 12 19 26
M.         6 13 20 27
Tu.        7 14 21 28
W.      1  8 15 22 29
Th.     2  9 16 23 30
F.      3 10 17 24
S.      4 11 18 25
```

December
```
Su.     3 10 17 24 31
M.      4 11 18 25
Tu.     5 12 19 26
W.      6 13 20 27
Th.     7 14 21 28
F.   1  8 15 22 29
S.   2  9 16 23 30
```

B (Leap year)

January
```
Su. ..  1  8 15 22 29
M.  ..  2  9 16 23 30
Tu. ..  3 10 17 24 31
W.  ..  4 11 18 25
Th. ..  5 12 19 26
F.  ..  6 13 20 27
S.  ..  7 14 21 28
```

February
```
Su.        5 12 19 26
M.         6 13 20 27
Tu.        7 14 21 28 29
W.      1  8 15 22 29
Th.     2  9 16 23
F.      3 10 17 24
S.      4 11 18 25
```

March
```
Su.     4 11 18 25
M.      5 12 19 26
Tu.     6 13 20 27
W.      7 14 21 28
Th.  1  8 15 22 29
F.   2  9 16 23 30
S.   3 10 17 24 31
```

April
```
Su.  1  8 15 22 29
M.   2  9 16 23 30
Tu.     3 10 17 24
W.      4 11 18 25
Th.     5 12 19 26
F.      6 13 20 27
S.      7 14 21 28
```

May
```
Su.        6 13 20 27
M.         7 14 21 28
Tu.     1  8 15 22 29
W.      2  9 16 23 30
Th.     3 10 17 24 31
F.      4 11 18 25
S.      5 12 19 26
```

June
```
Su.     3 10 17 24
M.      4 11 18 25
Tu.     5 12 19 26
W.      6 13 20 27
Th.     7 14 21 28
F.   1  8 15 22 29
S.   2  9 16 23 30
```

July
```
Su.  1  8 15 22 29
M.   2  9 16 23 30
Tu.     3 10 17 24 31
W.      4 11 18 25
Th.     5 12 19 26
F.      6 13 20 27
S.      7 14 21 28
```

August
```
Su.        5 12 19 26
M.         6 13 20 27
Tu.        7 14 21 28
W.      1  8 15 22 29
Th.     2  9 16 23 30
F.      3 10 17 24 31
S.      4 11 18 25
```

September
```
Su.     2  9 16 23 30
M.      3 10 17 24 31
Tu.     4 11 18 25
W.      5 12 19 26
Th.     6 13 20 27
F.      7 14 21 28
S.   1  8 15 22 29
```

October
```
Su.        7 14 21 28
M.      1  8 15 22 29
Tu.     2  9 16 23 30
W.      3 10 17 24 31
Th.     4 11 18 25
F.      5 12 19 26
S.      6 13 20 27
```

November
```
Su.     4 11 18 25
M.      5 12 19 26
Tu.     6 13 20 27
W.      7 14 21 28
Th.  1  8 15 22 29
F.   2  9 16 23 30
S.   3 10 17 24
```

December
```
Su.     2  9 16 23 30
M.      3 10 17 24 31
Tu.     4 11 18 25
W.      5 12 19 26
Th.     6 13 20 27
F.      7 14 21 28
S.   1  8 15 22 29
```

Easter Days

March 26.	1815	1826	1837	1967	1978 1989.
April 2.	1809	1893	1899	1961.	
April 9.	1871	1882	1939	1950	2023.
April 16.	1775	1786	1797	1843	1854 1865 1911
April 23.	1905.	[1922	1933	1995	2006 2017.

Easter Days

April 1.	1804	1888	1956.	
April 8.	1792	1860	1928	2012.
April 22.	1832	1984.		

C

	January	February	March
Su.	.. 7 14 21 28	4 11 18 25	4 11 18 25
M.	.. 1 8 15 22 29	5 12 19 26	5 12 19 26
Tu.	.. 2 9 16 23 30	6 13 20 27	6 13 20 27
W.	.. 3 10 17 24 31	7 14 21 28	7 14 21 28
Th.	.. 4 11 18 25	1 8 15 22	1 8 15 22 29
F.	.. 5 12 19 26	2 9 16 23	2 9 16 23 30
S.	.. 6 13 20 27	3 10 17 24	3 10 17 24 31

	April	May	June
Su.	.. 1 8 15 22 29	6 13 20 27	3 10 17 24
M.	.. 2 9 16 23 30	7 14 21 28	4 11 18 25
Tu.	.. 3 10 17 24	1 8 15 22 29	5 12 19 26
W.	.. 4 11 18 25	2 9 16 23 30	6 13 20 27
Th.	.. 5 12 19 26	3 10 17 24 31	7 14 21 28
F.	.. 6 13 20 27	4 11 18 25	1 8 15 22 29
S.	.. 7 14 21 28	5 12 19 26	2 9 16 23 30

	July	August	September
Su.	.. 1 8 15 22 29	5 12 19 26	2 9 16 23 30
M.	.. 2 9 16 23 30	6 13 20 27	3 10 17 24
Tu.	.. 3 10 17 24 31	7 14 21 28	4 11 18 25
W.	.. 4 11 18 25	1 8 15 22 29	5 12 19 26
Th.	.. 5 12 19 26	2 9 16 23 30	6 13 20 27
F.	.. 6 13 20 27	3 10 17 24 31	7 14 21 28
S.	.. 7 14 21 28	4 11 18 25	1 8 15 22 29

	October	November	December
Su.	.. 7 14 21 28	4 11 18 25	2 9 16 23 30
M.	.. 1 8 15 22 29	5 12 19 26	3 10 17 24 31
Tu.	.. 2 9 16 23 30	6 13 20 27	4 11 18 25
W.	.. 3 10 17 24 31	7 14 21 28	5 12 19 26
Th.	.. 4 11 18 25	1 8 15 22 29	6 13 20 27
F.	.. 5 12 19 26	2 9 16 23 30	7 14 21 28
S.	.. 6 13 20 27	3 10 17 24	1 8 15 22 29

Easter Days

March 25.	1883	1894	1951.			
April 1.	1866	1877	1923	1934	1945	2018.
April 8.	1787	1798	1849	1855	1917	2007.
April 15.	1770	1781	1827	1838	1900	1906 1979
April 22.	1810	1821	1962	1973.		[1990 2001.

D (Leap year)

	January	February	March
Su.	.. 7 14 21 28	4 11 18 25	3 10 17 24 31
M.	.. 1 8 15 22 29	5 12 19 26	4 11 18 25
Tu.	.. 2 9 16 23 30	6 13 20 27	5 12 19 26
W.	.. 3 10 17 24 31	7 14 21 28	6 13 20 27
Th.	.. 4 11 18 25	1 8 15 22 29	7 14 21 28
F.	.. 5 12 19 26	2 9 16 23	1 8 15 22 29
S.	.. 6 13 20 27	3 10 17 24	2 9 16 23 30

	April	May	June
Su.	.. 7 14 21 28	5 12 19 26	2 9 16 23 30
M.	.. 1 8 15 22 29	6 13 20 27	3 10 17 24
Tu.	.. 2 9 16 23 30	7 14 21 28	4 11 18 25
W.	.. 3 10 17 24	1 8 15 22 29	5 12 19 26
Th.	.. 4 11 18 25	2 9 16 23 30	6 13 20 27
F.	.. 5 12 19 26	3 10 17 24 31	7 14 21 28
S.	.. 6 13 20 27	4 11 18 25	1 8 15 22 29

	July	August	September
Su.	.. 7 14 21 28	4 11 18 25	1 8 15 22 29
M.	.. 1 8 15 22 29	5 12 19 26	2 9 16 23 30
Tu.	.. 2 9 16 23 30	6 13 20 27	3 10 17 24
W.	.. 3 10 17 24 31	7 14 21 28	4 11 18 25
Th.	.. 4 11 18 25	1 8 15 22 29	5 12 19 26
F.	.. 5 12 19 26	2 9 16 23 30	6 13 20 27
S.	.. 6 13 20 27	3 10 17 24 31	7 14 21 28

	October	November	December
Su.	.. 6 13 20 27	3 10 17 24	1 8 15 22 29
M.	.. 7 14 21 28	4 11 18 25	2 9 16 23 30
Tu.	.. 1 8 15 22 29	5 12 19 26	3 10 17 24 31
W.	.. 2 9 16 23 30	6 13 20 27	4 11 18 25
Th.	.. 3 10 17 24 31	7 14 21 28	5 12 19 26
F.	.. 4 11 18 25	1 8 15 22 29	6 13 20 27
S.	.. 5 12 19 26	2 9 16 23 30	7 14 21 28

Easter Days

March 24.	1940.			
March 31.	1872	2024.		
April 7.	1776	1844	1912	1996.
April 14.	1816	1968.		

E

	January	February	March
Su.	.. 6 13 20 27	3 10 17 24	3 10 17 24 31
M.	.. 7 14 21 28	4 11 18 25	4 11 18 25
Tu.	.. 1 8 15 22 29	5 12 19 26	5 12 19 26
W.	.. 2 9 16 23 30	6 13 20 27	6 13 20 27
Th.	.. 3 10 17 24 31	7 14 21 28	7 14 21 28
F.	.. 4 11 18 25	1 8 15 22	1 8 15 22 29
S.	.. 5 12 19 26	2 9 16 23	2 9 16 23 30

	April	May	June
Su.	.. 7 14 21 28	5 12 19 26	2 9 16 23 30
M.	.. 1 8 15 22 29	6 13 20 27	3 10 17 24
Tu.	.. 2 9 16 23 30	7 14 21 28	4 11 18 25
W.	.. 3 10 17 24	1 8 15 22 29	5 12 19 26
Th.	.. 4 11 18 25	2 9 16 23 30	6 13 20 27
F.	.. 5 12 19 26	3 10 17 24 31	7 14 21 28
S.	.. 6 13 20 27	4 11 18 25	1 8 15 22 29

	July	August	September
Su.	.. 7 14 21 28	4 11 18 25	1 8 15 22 29
M.	.. 1 8 15 22 29	5 12 19 26	2 9 16 23 30
Tu.	.. 2 9 16 23 30	6 13 20 27	3 10 17 24
W.	.. 3 10 17 24 31	7 14 21 28	4 11 18 25
Th.	.. 4 11 18 25	1 8 15 22 29	5 12 19 26
F.	.. 5 12 19 26	2 9 16 23 30	6 13 20 27
S.	.. 6 13 20 27	3 10 17 24 31	7 14 21 28

	October	November	December
Su.	.. 6 13 20 27	3 10 17 24	1 8 15 22 29
M.	.. 7 14 21 28	4 11 18 25	2 9 16 23 30
Tu.	.. 1 8 15 22 29	5 12 19 26	3 10 17 24 31
W.	.. 2 9 16 23 30	6 13 20 27	4 11 18 25
Th.	.. 3 10 17 24 31	7 14 21 28	5 12 19 26
F.	.. 4 11 18 25	1 8 15 22 29	6 13 20 27
S.	.. 5 12 19 26	2 9 16 23 30	7 14 21 28

Easter Days

March 24.	1799.					
March 31.	1771 1782	1793 1839 1850 1861 1907			[1918 1929 1991 2002 2013.	
April 7.	1822	1833	1901	1985.		
April 14.	1805	1811	1895	1963	1974.	
April 21.	1867	1878	1889	1935	1946 1957	2019.

F (Leap year)

	January	February	March
Su.	.. 6 13 20 27	3 10 17 24	2 9 16 23 30
M.	.. 7 14 21 28	4 11 18 25	3 10 17 24 31
Tu.	.. 1 8 15 22 29	5 12 19 26	4 11 18 25
W.	.. 2 9 16 23 30	6 13 20 27	5 12 19 26
Th.	.. 3 10 17 24 31	7 14 21 28	6 13 20 27
F.	.. 4 11 18 25	1 8 15 22	7 14 21 28
S.	.. 5 12 19 26	2 9 16 23	1 8 15 22 29

	April	May	June
Su.	.. 6 13 20 27	4 11 18 25	1 8 15 22 29
M.	.. 7 14 21 28	5 12 19 26	2 9 16 23 30
Tu.	.. 1 8 15 22 29	6 13 20 27	3 10 17 24
W.	.. 2 9 16 23 30	7 14 21 28	4 11 18 25
Th.	.. 3 10 17 24	1 8 15 22 29	5 12 19 26
F.	.. 4 11 18 25	2 9 16 23 30	6 13 20 27
S.	.. 5 12 19 26	3 10 17 24 31	7 14 21 28

	July	August	September
Su.	.. 6 13 20 27	3 10 17 24 31	7 14 21 28
M.	.. 7 14 21 28	4 11 18 25	1 8 15 22 29
Tu.	.. 1 8 15 22 29	5 12 19 26	2 9 16 23 30
W.	.. 2 9 16 23 30	6 13 20 27	3 10 17 24
Th.	.. 3 10 17 24 31	7 14 21 28	4 11 18 25
F.	.. 4 11 18 25	1 8 15 22 29	5 12 19 26
S.	.. 5 12 19 26	2 9 16 23 30	6 13 20 27

	October	November	December
Su.	.. 5 12 19 26	2 9 16 23 30	7 14 21 28
M.	.. 6 13 20 27	3 10 17 24	1 8 15 22 29
Tu.	.. 7 14 21 28	4 11 18 25	2 9 16 23 30
W.	.. 1 8 15 22 29	5 12 19 26	3 10 17 24 31
Th.	.. 2 9 16 23 30	6 13 20 27	4 11 18 25
F.	.. 3 10 17 24 31	7 14 21 28	5 12 19 26
S.	.. 4 11 18 25	1 8 15 22 29	6 13 20 27

Easter Days

March 23.	1788	1856	2008.
April 6.	1828	1980.	
April 13.	1884	1952.	
April 20.	1924.		

G

	January	February	March
Su.	5 12 19 26	2 9 16 23	2 9 16 23 30
M.	6 13 20 27	3 10 17 24	3 10 17 24 31
Tu.	7 14 21 28	4 11 18 25	4 11 18 25
W.	1 8 15 22 29	5 12 19 26	5 12 19 26
Th.	2 9 16 23 30	6 13 20 27	6 13 20 27
F.	3 10 17 24 31	7 14 21 28	7 14 21 28
S.	4 11 18 25	1 8 15 22	1 8 15 22 29

	April	May	June
Su.	6 13 20 27	4 11 18 25	1 8 15 22 29
M.	7 14 21 28	5 12 19 26	2 9 16 23 30
Tu.	1 8 15 22 29	6 13 20 27	3 10 17 24
W.	2 9 16 23 30	7 14 21 28	4 11 18 25
Th.	3 10 17 24	1 8 15 22 29	5 12 19 26
F.	4 11 18 25	2 9 16 23 30	6 13 20 27
S.	5 12 19 26	3 10 17 24 31	7 14 21 28

	July	August	September
Su.	6 13 20 27	3 10 17 24 31	7 14 21 28
M.	7 14 21 28	4 11 18 25	1 8 15 22 29
Tu.	1 8 15 22 29	5 12 19 26	2 9 16 23 30
W.	2 9 16 23 30	6 13 20 27	3 10 17 24
Th.	3 10 17 24 31	7 14 21 28	4 11 18 25
F.	4 11 18 25	1 8 15 22 29	5 12 19 26
S.	5 12 19 26	2 9 16 23 30	6 13 20 27

	October	November	December
Su.	5 12 19 26	2 9 16 23 30	7 14 21 28
M.	6 13 20 27	3 10 17 24	1 8 15 22 29
Tu.	7 14 21 28	4 11 18 25	2 9 16 23 30
W.	1 8 15 22 29	5 12 19 26	3 10 17 24 31
Th.	2 9 16 23 30	6 13 20 27	4 11 18 25
F.	3 10 17 24 31	7 14 21 28	5 12 19 26
S.	4 11 18 25	1 8 15 22 29	6 13 20 27

Easter Days

March 23.	1845 1913.
March 30.	1777 1823 1834 1902 1975 1986 1997.
April 6.	1806 1817 1890 1947 1958 1969.
April 13.	1800 1873 1879 1941. [2014 2025.
April 20.	1783 1794 1851 1862 1919 1930 2003

H (Leap year)

	January	February	March
Su.	5 12 19 26	2 9 16 23	1 8 15 22 29
M.	6 13 20 27	3 10 17 24	2 9 16 23 30
Tu.	7 14 21 28	4 11 18 25	3 10 17 24 31
W.	1 8 15 22 29	5 12 19 26	4 11 18 25
Th.	2 9 16 23 30	6 13 20 27	5 12 19 26
F.	3 10 17 24 31	7 14 21 28	6 13 20 27
S.	4 11 18 25	1 8 15 22 29	7 14 21 28

	April	May	June
Su.	5 12 19 26	3 10 17 24 31	7 14 21 28
M.	6 13 20 27	4 11 18 25	1 8 15 22 29
Tu.	7 14 21 28	5 12 19 26	2 9 16 23 30
W.	1 8 15 22 29	6 13 20 27	3 10 17 24
Th.	2 9 16 23 30	7 14 21 28	4 11 18 25
F.	3 10 17 24	1 8 15 22 29	5 12 19 26
S.	4 11 18 25	2 9 16 23 30	6 13 20 27

	July	August	September
Su.	5 12 19 26	2 9 16 23 30	6 13 20 27
M.	6 13 20 27	3 10 17 24 31	7 14 21 28
Tu.	7 14 21 28	4 11 18 25	1 8 15 22 29
W.	1 8 15 22 29	5 12 19 26	2 9 16 23 30
Th.	2 9 16 23 30	6 13 20 27	3 10 17 24
F.	3 10 17 24 31	7 14 21 28	4 11 18 25
S.	4 11 18 25	1 8 15 22 29	5 12 19 26

	October	November	December
Su.	4 11 18 25	1 8 15 22 29	6 13 20 27
M.	5 12 19 26	2 9 16 23 30	7 14 21 28
Tu.	6 13 20 27	3 10 17 24	1 8 15 22 29
W.	7 14 21 28	4 11 18 25	2 9 16 23 30
Th.	1 8 15 22 29	5 12 19 26	3 10 17 24 31
F.	2 9 16 23 30	6 13 20 27	4 11 18 25
S.	3 10 17 24 31	7 14 21 28	5 12 19 26

Easter Days

March 29.	1812 1964.
April 5.	1896.
April 12.	1868 1936 2020.
April 19.	1772 1840 1908 1992.

I

	January	February	March
Su.	4 11 18 25	1 8 15 22	1 8 15 22 29
M.	5 12 19 26	2 9 16 23	2 9 16 23 30
Tu.	6 13 20 27	3 10 17 24	3 10 17 24 31
W.	7 14 21 28	4 11 18 25	4 11 18 25
Th.	1 8 15 22 29	5 12 19 26	5 12 19 26
F.	2 9 16 23 30	6 13 20 27	6 13 20 27
S.	3 10 17 24 31	7 14 21 28	7 14 21 28

	April	May	June
Su.	5 12 19 26	3 10 17 24 31	7 14 21 28
M.	6 13 20 27	4 11 18 25	1 8 15 22 29
Tu.	7 14 21 28	5 12 19 26	2 9 16 23 30
W.	1 8 15 22 29	6 13 20 27	3 10 17 24
Th.	2 9 16 23 30	7 14 21 28	4 11 18 25
F.	3 10 17 24	1 8 15 22 29	5 12 19 26
S.	4 11 18 25	2 9 16 23 30	6 13 20 27

	July	August	September
Su.	5 12 19 26	2 9 16 23 30	6 13 20 27
M.	6 13 20 27	3 10 17 24 31	7 14 21 28
Tu.	7 14 21 28	4 11 18 25	1 8 15 22 29
W.	1 8 15 22 29	5 12 19 26	2 9 16 23 30
Th.	2 9 16 23 30	6 13 20 27	3 10 17 24
F.	3 10 17 24 31	7 14 21 28	4 11 18 25
S.	4 11 18 25	1 8 15 22 29	5 12 19 26

	October	November	December
Su.	4 11 18 25	1 8 15 22 29	6 13 20 27
M.	5 12 19 26	2 9 16 23 30	7 14 21 28
Tu.	6 13 20 27	3 10 17 24	1 8 15 22 29
W.	7 14 21 28	4 11 18 25	2 9 16 23 30
Th.	1 8 15 22 29	5 12 19 26	3 10 17 24 31
F.	2 9 16 23 30	6 13 20 27	4 11 18 25
S.	3 10 17 24 31	7 14 21 28	5 12 19 26

Easter Days

March 22.	1818.
March 29.	1807 1891 1959 1970. [1953 2015.
April 5.	1795 1801 1863 1874 1885 1931 1942
April 12.	1789 1846 1857 1903 1914 1925 1998
April 19.	1778 1829 1835 1981 1987. [2009.

J (Leap year)

	January	February	March
Su.	4 11 18 25	1 8 15 22 29	7 14 21 28
M.	5 12 19 26	2 9 16 23	1 8 15 22 29
Tu.	6 13 20 27	3 10 17 24	2 9 16 23 30
W.	7 14 21 28	4 11 18 25	3 10 17 24 31
Th.	1 8 15 22 29	5 12 19 26	4 11 18 25
F.	2 9 16 23 30	6 13 20 27	5 12 19 26
S.	3 10 17 24 31	7 14 21 28	6 13 20 27

	April	May	June
Su.	4 11 18 25	2 9 16 23 30	6 13 20 27
M.	5 12 19 26	3 10 17 24 31	7 14 21 28
Tu.	6 13 20 27	4 11 18 25	1 8 15 22 29
W.	7 14 21 28	5 12 19 26	2 9 16 23 30
Th.	1 8 15 22 29	6 13 20 27	3 10 17 24
F.	2 9 16 23 30	7 14 21 28	4 11 18 25
S.	3 10 17 24	1 8 15 22 29	5 12 19 26

	July	August	September
Su.	4 11 18 25	1 8 15 22 29	5 12 19 26
M.	5 12 19 26	2 9 16 23 30	6 13 20 27
Tu.	6 13 20 27	3 10 17 24 31	7 14 21 28
W.	7 14 21 28	4 11 18 25	1 8 15 22 29
Th.	1 8 15 22 29	5 12 19 26	2 9 16 23 30
F.	2 9 16 23 30	6 13 20 27	3 10 17 24
S.	3 10 17 24 31	7 14 21 28	4 11 18 25

	October	November	December
Su.	3 10 17 24 31	7 14 21 28	5 12 19 26
M.	4 11 18 25	1 8 15 22 29	6 13 20 27
Tu.	5 12 19 26	2 9 16 23 30	7 14 21 28
W.	6 13 20 27	3 10 17 24	1 8 15 22 29
Th.	7 14 21 28	4 11 18 25	2 9 16 23 30
F.	1 8 15 22 29	5 12 19 26	3 10 17 24 31
S.	2 9 16 23 30	6 13 20 27	4 11 18 25

Easter Days

March 28.	1880 1948.
April 4.	1920.
April 11.	1784 1852 2004.
April 18.	1824 1976.

K

	January	February	March
Su.	3 10 17 24 31	7 14 21 28	7 14 21 28
M.	4 11 18 25	1 8 15 22	1 8 15 22 29
Tu.	5 12 19 26	2 9 16 23	2 9 16 23 30
W.	6 13 20 27	3 10 17 24	3 10 17 24 31
Th.	7 14 21 28	4 11 18 25	4 11 18 25
F.	1 8 15 22 29	5 12 19 26	5 12 19 26
S.	2 9 16 23 30	6 13 20 27	6 13 20 27

	April	May	June
Su.	4 11 18 25	2 9 16 23 30	6 13 20 27
M.	5 12 19 26	3 10 17 24 31	7 14 21 28
Tu.	6 13 20 27	4 11 18 25	1 8 15 22 29
W.	7 14 21 28	5 12 19 26	2 9 16 23 30
Th.	1 8 15 22 29	6 13 20 27	3 10 17 24
F.	2 9 16 23 30	7 14 21 28	4 11 18 25
S.	3 10 17 24	1 8 15 22 29	5 12 19 26

	July	August	September
Su.	4 11 18 25	1 8 15 22 29	5 12 19 26
M.	5 12 19 26	2 9 16 23 30	6 13 20 27
Tu.	6 13 20 27	3 10 17 24 31	7 14 21 28
W.	7 14 21 28	4 11 18 25	1 8 15 22 29
Th.	1 8 15 22 29	5 12 19 26	2 9 16 23 30
F.	2 9 16 23 30	6 13 20 27	3 10 17 24
S.	3 10 17 24 31	7 14 21 28	4 11 18 25

	October	November	December
Su.	3 10 17 24 31	7 14 21 28	5 12 19 26
M.	4 11 18 25	1 8 15 22 29	6 13 20 27
Tu.	5 12 19 26	2 9 16 23 30	7 14 21 28
W.	6 13 20 27	3 10 17 24	1 8 15 22 29
Th.	7 14 21 28	4 11 18 25	2 9 16 23 30
F.	1 8 15 22 29	5 12 19 26	3 10 17 24 31
S.	2 9 16 23 30	6 13 20 27	4 11 18 25

Easter Days

March 28.	1869 1875 1937.		[2010 2021.
April 4.	1779 1790 1847 1858 1915	1926 1999	
April 11.	1773 1819 1830 1841 1909	1971 1982	
April 18.	1802 1813 1897 1954 1965.		[1993.
April 25.	1886 1943.		

L (Leap year)

	January	February	March
Su.	3 10 17 24 31	7 14 21 28	6 13 20 27
M.	4 11 18 25	1 8 15 22 29	7 14 21 28
Tu.	5 12 19 26	2 9 16 23	1 8 15 22 29
W.	6 13 20 27	3 10 17 24	2 9 16 23 30
Th.	7 14 21 28	4 11 18 25	3 10 17 24 31
F.	1 8 15 22 29	5 12 19 26	4 11 18 25
S.	2 9 16 23 30	6 13 20 27	5 12 19 26

	April	May	June
Su.	3 10 17 24	1 8 15 22 29	5 12 19 26
M.	4 11 18 25	2 9 16 23 30	6 13 20 27
Tu.	5 12 19 26	3 10 17 24 31	7 14 21 28
W.	6 13 20 27	4 11 18 25	1 8 15 22 29
Th.	7 14 21 28	5 12 19 26	2 9 16 23 30
F.	1 8 15 22 29	6 13 20 27	3 10 17 24
S.	2 9 16 23 30	7 14 21 28	4 11 18 25

	July	August	September
Su.	3 10 17 24 31	7 14 21 28	4 11 18 25
M.	4 11 18 25	1 8 15 22 29	5 12 19 26
Tu.	5 12 19 26	2 9 16 23 30	6 13 20 27
W.	6 13 20 27	3 10 17 24 31	7 14 21 28
Th.	7 14 21 28	4 11 18 25	1 8 15 22 29
F.	1 8 15 22 29	5 12 19 26	2 9 16 23 30
S.	2 9 16 23 30	6 13 20 27	3 10 17 24

	October	November	December
Su.	2 9 16 23 30	6 13 20 27	4 11 18 25
M.	3 10 17 24 31	7 14 21 28	5 12 19 26
Tu.	4 11 18 25	1 8 15 22 29	6 13 20 27
W.	5 12 19 26	2 9 16 23 30	7 14 21 28
Th.	6 13 20 27	3 10 17 24	1 8 15 22 29
F.	7 14 21 28	4 11 18 25	2 9 16 23 30
S.	1 8 15 22 29	5 12 19 26	3 10 17 24 31

Easter Days

March 27.	1796 1864 1932 2016.
April 3.	1836 1904 1988.
April 17.	1808 1892 1960.

M

	January	February	March
Su.	2 9 16 23 30	6 13 20 27	6 13 20 27
M.	3 10 17 24 31	7 14 21 28	7 14 21 28
Tu.	4 11 18 25	1 8 15 22	1 8 15 22 29
W.	5 12 19 26	2 9 16 23	2 9 16 23 30
Th.	6 13 20 27	3 10 17 24	3 10 17 24 31
F.	7 14 21 28	4 11 18 25	4 11 18 25
S.	1 8 15 22 29	5 12 19 26	5 12 19 26

	April	May	June
Su.	3 10 17 24	1 8 15 22 29	5 12 19 26
M.	4 11 18 25	2 9 16 23 30	6 13 20 27
Tu.	5 12 19 26	3 10 17 24 31	7 14 21 28
W.	6 13 20 27	4 11 18 25	1 8 15 22 29
Th.	7 14 21 28	5 12 19 26	2 9 16 23 30
F.	1 8 15 22 29	6 13 20 27	3 10 17 24
S.	2 9 16 23 30	7 14 21 28	4 11 18 25

	July	August	September
Su.	3 10 17 24 31	7 14 21 28	4 11 18 25
M.	4 11 18 25	1 8 15 22 29	5 12 19 26
Tu.	5 12 19 26	2 9 16 23 30	6 13 20 27
W.	6 13 20 27	3 10 17 24 31	7 14 21 28
Th.	7 14 21 28	4 11 18 25	1 8 15 22 29
F.	1 8 15 22 29	5 12 19 26	2 9 16 23 30
S.	2 9 16 23 30	6 13 20 27	3 10 17 24

	October	November	December
Su.	2 9 16 23 30	6 13 20 27	4 11 18 25
M.	3 10 17 24 31	7 14 21 28	5 12 19 26
Tu.	4 11 18 25	1 8 15 22 29	6 13 20 27
W.	5 12 19 26	2 9 16 23 30	7 14 21 28
Th.	6 13 20 27	3 10 17 24	1 8 15 22 29
F.	7 14 21 28	4 11 18 25	2 9 16 23 30
S.	1 8 15 22 29	5 12 19 26	3 10 17 24 31

Easter Days

March 27.	1785 1842 1853 1910 1921 2005.
April 3.	1774 1825 1831 1983 1994.
April 10.	1803 1814 1887 1898 1955 1966 1977.
April 17.	1870 1881 1927 1938 1949 2022.
April 24.	1791 1859 2011.

N (Leap year)

	January	February	March
Su.	2 9 16 23 30	6 13 20 27	5 12 19 26
M.	3 10 17 24 31	7 14 21 28	6 13 20 27
Tu.	4 11 18 25	1 8 15 22 29	7 14 21 28
W.	5 12 19 26	2 9 16 23	1 8 15 22 29
Th.	6 13 20 27	3 10 17 24	2 9 16 23 30
F.	7 14 21 28	4 11 18 25	3 10 17 24 31
S.	1 8 15 22 29	5 12 19 26	4 11 18 25

	April	May	June
Su.	2 9 16 23 30	7 14 21 28	4 11 18 25
M.	3 10 17 24	1 8 15 22 29	5 12 19 26
Tu.	4 11 18 25	2 9 16 23 30	6 13 20 27
W.	5 12 19 26	3 10 17 24 31	7 14 21 28
Th.	6 13 20 27	4 11 18 25	1 8 15 22 29
F.	7 14 21 28	5 12 19 26	2 9 16 23 30
S.	1 8 15 22 29	6 13 20 27	3 10 17 24

	July	August	September
Su.	2 9 16 23 30	6 13 20 27	3 10 17 24
M.	3 10 17 24 31	7 14 21 28	4 11 18 25
Tu.	4 11 18 25	1 8 15 22 29	5 12 19 26
W.	5 12 19 26	2 9 16 23 30	6 13 20 27
Th.	6 13 20 27	3 10 17 24 31	7 14 21 28
F.	7 14 21 28	4 11 18 25	1 8 15 22 29
S.	1 8 15 22 29	5 12 19 26	2 9 16 23 30

	October	November	December
Su.	1 8 15 22 29	5 12 19 26	3 10 17 24 31
M.	2 9 16 23 30	6 13 20 27	4 11 18 25
Tu.	3 10 17 24 31	7 14 21 28	5 12 19 26
W.	4 11 18 25	1 8 15 22 29	6 13 20 27
Th.	5 12 19 26	2 9 16 23 30	7 14 21 28
F.	6 13 20 27	3 10 17 24	1 8 15 22 29
S.	7 14 21 28	4 11 18 25	2 9 16 23 30

Easter Days

March 26.	1780.
April 2.	1820 1972.
April 9.	1944.
April 16.	1876.
April 23.	1848 1916 2000.

The World

The **superficial area** of the Earth is estimated to be 196,836,000 square miles, of which 55,786,000 square miles are land and 141,050,000 square miles water. The **diameter** of the Earth at the Equator is 7,926·5 English miles, and at the Poles 7,900 English miles. The **equatorial circumference** is 24,901·8 English miles, divided into 360 *degrees of longitude*, each of 69·17 English (or 60 geographical) miles; these degrees are measured from the Meridian of Greenwich, and numbered East and West of that point to meet in the Antipodes at the 180th degree. Distance North and South of the Equator is marked by *parallels of latitude*, which proceed from zero (at the Equator) to 90° at the Poles.

The velocity of a given point of the Earth's surface at the Equator exceeds 1,000 miles an hour (24,901·8 miles in 24 hours); the Earth's velocity in its orbit round the Sun is about 66,600 miles an hour (584,000,000 miles in 365¼ days). The Earth is distant from the Sun 93,000,000 miles, on the average.

AREA AND POPULATION

The total population of the world in mid-1985, was estimated at 4,837,500,000, compared with 3,003,000,000 in 1960 and 2,070,000,000 in 1930.

Continent, etc.	Area		Estimated Population, mid-1985
	Sq. miles '000	Sq. km. '000	
Africa	11,704	30,313	555,000,000
North America[1]	8,311	21,525	264,000,000
Latin America[2]	7,933	20,547	405,000,000
Asia[3]	10,637	27,549	2,813,000,000
Europe[4]	1,915	4,961	497,000,000
U.S.S.R.	8,649	22,402	279,000,000
Oceania[5]	3,286	8,510	24,500,000
TOTAL	52,435	135,807	4,837,500,000

[1] Includes Greenland and Hawaii.
[2] Mexico and the remainder of the Americas south of the U.S.A.
[3] Includes Asiatic Turkey, excludes U.S.S.R.
[4] Includes European Turkey, excludes U.S.S.R.
[5] Includes Australia, New Zealand and the islands inhabited by Micronesian, Melanesian and Polynesian peoples.
Source: *U.N. Demographic Yearbook 1985 (pub. 1987).*

A United Nations report (*The Future Growth of World Population*) in 1958, pointed out that the population of the world had increased since the beginning of the 20th Century at an unprecedented rate: in 1850 it was estimated at 1,094,000,000 and in 1900 at 1,550,000,000, an increase of 42 per cent in 50 years. By 1925 it had risen to 1,907,000,000—23 per cent in 25 years—and by 1950 it had reached 2,500,000,000, an increase of 31 per cent in 25 years. Levels of population and the trend in distribution of the population by continents as forecast for the year 2000 were:—

Continent, etc.	[millions] 2000	
	Estimated Population	Per cent
Africa	517	8·2
N. America	312	5·0
Latin America†	592	9·4
Asia (excluding U.S.S.R.)...	3,870	61·8
Europe (including U.S.S.R.)	947	15·1
Oceania	29	0·5
World	6,267	100

† Mexico and the remainder of America south of U.S.A.

THE CONTINENTS

Africa is the second largest continent. It is surrounded by sea except for the narrow isthmus of Suez in the north-east, through which is cut the Suez Canal. The Equator passes through the middle of the continent. Its extreme longitudes are 17° 20′ W. at Cape Verde, Senegal, and 51° 24′ E. at Ras Hafun, Somalia. The extreme latitudes are 37° 20′ N. at Cape Blanco, Tunisia, and 34° 50′ S. at Cape Agulhas, South Africa, about 5,000 miles apart.

North America, including Mexico, is surrounded by ocean except in the south, where the isthmian states of Central America link North America with South America. Its extreme longitudes are 168° 5′ W. at Cape Prince of Wales, Alaska, and 55° 40′ W. at Cape Charles, Newfoundland. The extreme latitudes are about 82° N. in the Arctic Ocean and 15° N. in the south of Mexico. The West Indies, about 65,000 square miles in area, extend from about 27° N. to 10° N. latitude.

South America lies mostly in the southern hemisphere: the Equator passes through the north of the continent. It is surrounded by ocean except where it is joined to Central America in the north by the narrow isthmus through which is cut the Panama Canal. Its extreme longitudes are 34° 47′ W. at Cape Branco in Brazil and 81° 20′ W. at Punta Pariña, Peru. The extreme latitudes are 12° 25′ N. at Punta Gallinas, Colombia, and 55° 59′ S. at Cape Horn.

Antarctica lies almost entirely within the Antarctic Circle (66° 33′ S.) and is too hostile an environment for unsupported human habitation. (*See also* p. 134.)

Asia is the largest continent and occupies about a third of the world's land surface. The extreme longitudes are about 26° E. on the west coast of Asia Minor and 169° 45′ W. at Mys Dežneva (East Cape), U.S.S.R., a distance of about 6,000 miles. Its extreme northern latitude is 77° 45′ N. at Cape Čeljuskin, U.S.S.R., and it extends over 5,000 miles south to about 1° 15′ N. of the Equator. The islands of Japan, the Philippines and Indonesia ring the continent to the east and south-east.

Australia is the smallest of the continents and lies in the southern hemisphere. It is entirely surrounded by ocean. Its extreme longitudes are 113° 9′ E. at Steep Point and 153° 38′ E. at Cape Byron. The extreme latitudes are 10° 40′ S. at Cape York and 39° S. at South East Point.

Europe, including European Russia, is the smallest continent in the northern hemisphere. Its extreme latitudes are 71° 11′ N. at North Cape in Norway, and 36° 23′ N. at Cape Matapan in southern Greece, a distance of about 2,400 miles. Its breadth from Cape da Roca in Portugal (9° 30′ W.) in the west to the Urals is about 3,300 miles. The division between Europe and Asia is generally regarded as being the Ural Mountains and, in the south, the valley of the Manych, which stretches from the Caspian Sea to the mouth of the Don.

Countries and Their Capitals

No complete survey of many countries has yet been achieved and consequently accurate area figures are not always available. Similarly, many countries have not recently, or have never, taken a census. The areas and populations of countries given below are derived from estimated figures published by the United Nations. The conversion factors used are: (i) to convert square miles to square km.—multiply by 2·589988; (ii) to convert square km. to square miles—multiply by 0·3861022.

Accurate and up-to-date data for the populations of capital cities are scarce, and definitions of cities' extent differ. The figures given below are the latest estimates available, and where it is known that the figure applies to an urban agglomeration this is indicated.

Where later information becomes available during printing, the new figures are given in the overseas sections of the ALMANACK.

*latest census result　　*u.a.* urban-agglomeration　Ψ seaport*

AFRICA

COUNTRY	AREA Sq. Miles	AREA Sq. Km.	POPULATION	CAPITAL	POPULATION OF CAPITAL
Algeria	919,595	2,381,741	22,971,558*	Ψ Algiers	3,250,000
Angola	481,354	1,246,700	8,754,000	Ψ Luanda	1,000,000
Benin	43,484	112,622	3,932,000	Ψ Porto Novo	208,258
Botswana	224,607	581,730	1,127,880	Gaborone	103,000
Burkina	105,869	274,200	8,846,929	Ouagadougou	375,001
Burundi	10,747	27,834	4,718,000	Bujumbura	150,000
Cameroon	183,569	475,442	10,106,000	Yaoundé	522,000
Cape Verde Islands	1,557	4,033	326,000	Ψ Praia	57,748
Central African Rep.	240,535	622,984	2,608,000	Bangui	473,817
Chad	495,755	1,284,000	5,018,000	Ndjaména	402,000
Comoros	838	2,171	440,000	Moroni	17,267
Congo	132,047	342,000	1,740,000	Brazzaville	600,000
Côte d'Ivoire	124,503	322,463	10,056,000	Ψ Abidjan	2,000,000
Djibouti	8,494	22,000	430,000	Ψ Djibouti	200,000
Egypt	386,662	1,001,449	52,000,000	Cairo	14,000,000
Equatorial Guinea	10,830	28,051	392,000	Ψ Malabo	34,980
Ethiopia	471,778	1,221,900	43,350,000	Addis Ababa	1,464,901
Gabon	103,347	267,667	1,151,000	Ψ Libreville	251,000
Gambia	4,361	11,295	695,886*	Ψ Banjul (*u.a.*)	44,536*
Ghana	92,100	238,537	13,588,000	Ψ Accra (*u.a.*)	1,420,066*
Guinea	94,926	245,857	6,075,000	Ψ Conakry	763,000
Guinea-Bissau	13,948	36,125	890,000	Ψ Bissau	109,486*
Kenya	224,961	582,646	20,333,000	Nairobi	1,103,554
Lesotho	11,720	30,355	1,443,853*	Maseru	288,951*
Liberia	43,000	111,369	2,189,000	Ψ Monrovia	425,000
Libya	679,362	1,759,540	3,800,000	Ψ Tripoli	1,000,000
Madagascar	226,669	587,041	11,000,000	Antananarivo	1,000,000
Malawi	45,747	118,484	7,059,000	Lilongwe	175,000
Mali	478,791	1,240,000	8,206,000	Bamako	600,000
Mauritania	397,955	1,030,700	1,888,000	Nouakchott	500,000
Mauritius	790	2,045	1,054,200	Ψ Port Louis	138,272
Mayotte	144	372	67,000	Mamoundzou	12,000
Morocco	172,414	446,550	23,602,000	Ψ Rabat	893,402*
Western Sahara	102,703	266,000	155,000	Laayoune	24,000
Mozambique	309,495	801,590	14,000,000	Ψ Maputo	1,000,000
Namibia	318,261	824,292	1,184,000	Windhoek	61,260
Niger	489,191	1,267,080	6,317,550	Niamey	399,100
Nigeria	356,669	923,768	100,000,000	Ψ Lagos	3,000,000
Réunion	969	2,510	531,000	St. Denis	109,072
Rwanda	10,169	26,338	6,070,000	Kigali	156,000
St. Helena	47	122	5,564	Ψ Jamestown	1,330
Ascension I.	34	88	1,155	Ψ Georgetown	..
Tristan da Cunha	40	104	311	Ψ Edinburgh	..
Sao Tomé & Príncipe	372	964	108,000	Ψ São Tomé	25,000
Senegal	75,750	196,192	6,540,000	Ψ Dakar	1,000,000
Seychelles	108	280	65,032	Ψ Victoria	24,733
Sierra Leone	27,699	71,740	3,700,000*	Ψ Freetown	470,000*
Somalia	246,201	637,657	5,800,000	Ψ Mogadishu	1,000,000
South Africa	471,445	1,221,031	32,392,000	Pretoria (*u.a.*)	822,925
				{ Ψ Cape Town (*u.a.*)	1,911,521
Sudan	967,500	2,505,813	21,550,000	Khartoum (*u.a.*)	2,000,000
Swaziland	6,704	17,363	647,000	Mbabane	30,000
Tanzania	364,900	945,087	21,733,000	Ψ Dar-es-Salaam	1,096,000
Togo	21,925	56,785	3,030,000	Ψ Lomé	366,476
Tunisia	63,170	163,610	7,205,106	Ψ Tunis	1,394,749
Uganda	91,259	236,036	15,477,000	Kampala (*u.a.*)	460,000
Zaire	905,567	2,345,409	34,671,607	Kinshasa	2,778,281
Zambia	290,586	752,614	6,666,000	Lusaka (*u.a.*)	641,000
Zimbabwe	150,804	390,580	8,660,000	Harare	658,364

AMERICA

(For symbols, etc., *see* introductory note on page 125.)

COUNTRY	AREA		POPULATION	CAPITAL	POPULATION OF CAPITAL
	Sq. Miles	Sq. Km.			
North America					
Canada................	3,849,646	9,970,537	25,309,330	Ottawa (*u.a.*)	819,263
Greenland	840,004	2,175,600	52,940	Ψ Godthab	8,425
Mexico	761,605	1,972,547	78,524,000	Mexico City (*u.a.*) .	18,748,000
St. Pierre and Miquelon	93	242	6,500	Ψ St. Pierre	..
United States	3,618,787	9,372,614	239,283,000	Washington, D.C. (*u.a.*)	3,563,000
Central America and the West Indies					
Anguilla	35	91	7,000	The Valley	500
Antigua and Barbuda..	170	440	80,000	Ψ St. John's	30,000
Aruba................	75	193	62,000	Ψ Oranjestad	17,000
Bahamas	5,380	13,935	237,090*	Ψ Nassau............	135,437*
Barbados	166	431	253,000	Ψ Bridgetown	7,466
Belize	8,867	22,965	166,000	Belmopan	2,935
Bermuda	20	53	56,000	Ψ Hamilton	1,669
Cayman Islands	100	259	23,400	Ψ George Town	10,000
Costa Rica	19,575	50,700	2,816,558	San José (*u.a.*)	1,031,102
Cuba	42,804	110,861	10,356,400	Ψ Havana	2,100,000
Dominica	290	751	76,000	Ψ Roseau..........	8,346*
Dominican Republic ...	18,816	48,734	6,416,000*	Ψ Santo Domingo (*u.a.*)	1,313,172*
Grenada..............	133	344	112,000	Ψ St. George's	7,500
Guadeloupe...........	687	1,779	334,000	Ψ Basse-Terre	15,778
Guatemala	42,042	108,889	7,963,000	Guatemala City	1,300,000
Haiti.................	10,714	27,750	6,585,000	Ψ Port au Prince	1,000,000
Honduras	43,277	112,088	4,372,000	Tegucigalpa	539,600
Jamaica	4,244	10,991	2,355,100	Ψ Kingston (*u.a.*) ...	696,300
Martinique	425	1,102	328,566	Ψ Fort de France....	100,576
Montserrat	38	98	11,900	Ψ Plymouth	3,000
Netherlands Antilles ..	371	961	183,000	Ψ Willemstad	50,000
Nicaragua	50,193	130,000	3,272,000	Managua	615,000
Panama	29,762	77,082	2,227,254	Ψ Panama City	608,890
Puerto Rico..........	3,435	8,897	3,279,231	Ψ San Juan (*u.a.*) ...	1,816,300
St. Christopher and Nevis	101	261	45,100	Ψ Basseterre	15,000
St. Lucia	238	616	138,000	Ψ Castries..........	50,798
St. Vincent and the Grenadines	150	388	104,000	Ψ Kingstown	33,694
El Salvador	8,124	21,041	5,480,000	San Salvador	425,119
Trinidad and Tobago ..	1,981	5,130	1,185,000	Ψ Port of Spain	59,649
Turks and Caicos Is. ...	166	430	14,000	Ψ Grand Turk	3,146
Virgin Islands:—					
British	59	153	13,000	Ψ Road Town	2,479
U.S...............	132	342	107,500	Ψ Charlotte Amalie .	11,842
South America					
Argentina	1,068,302	2,766,889	30,564,000	Ψ Buenos Aires (*u.a.*)	9,967,826
Bolivia	424,165	1,098,581	6,429,000	La Paz	1,000,000
Brazil	3,286,488	8,511,965	135,564,000	Brasilia	1,576,657
Chile................	292,258	756,945	12,074,000	Santiago	4,132,293
Colombia	439,737	1,138,914	26,525,670*	Bogotá............	3,967,988*
Ecuador	109,484	283,561	9,379,000	Quito	1,003,875
Falkland Islands	4,700	12,173	1,916	Ψ Stanley	1,231
French Guiana........	35,135	91,000	82,000	Ψ Cayenne	38,135
Guyana	83,000	214,969	750,000	Ψ Georgetown	185,000
Paraguay.............	157,048	406,752	3,930,000	Asunción (*u.a.*) ...	729,307*
Peru	496,225	1,285,216	19,700,000	Lima (*u.a.*)	5,258,600
South Georgia	1,580	4,092	500		..
Suriname.............	63,037	163,265	375,000	Ψ Paramaribo	110,000
Uruguay	68,037	176,215	3,012,000	Ψ Montevideo	1,355,312
Venezuela	352,144	912,050	17,323,000	Caracas	1,816,901

ASIA

(For symbols, etc., *see* introductory note on page 125.)

COUNTRY	AREA		POPULATION	CAPITAL	POPULATION OF CAPITAL
	Sq. Miles	Sq. Km.			
Afghanistan	250,000	647,497	18,136,000	Kabul.............	2,000,000
Bahrain	240	622	417,210	Ψ Manama	121,986
Bangladesh	55,598	143,998	100,000,000	Dhaka	4,047,000
Bhutan	18,147	47,000	1,417,000	Thimphu	8,922
Brunei	2,226	5,765	226,000	Bandar Seri Begawan	58,000
Burma	261,218	676,552	37,153,000	Ψ Rangoon	2,458,712*
China[1]	3,705,408	9,596,961	1,080,000,000	Beijing (Peking) ..	5,970,000
Taiwan	13,800	35,742	19,135,254	Taipei	2,507,620
Hong Kong	413	1,071	5,600,000	Ψ Victoria	767,000
India................	1,269,346	3,287,590	750,900,000	Delhi	6,222,000*
Indonesia	735,358	1,904,569	165,030,000	Ψ Jakarta	6,503,449
Iran	636,296	1,648,000	49,765,000	Tehran	6,000,000
Iraq................	167,925	434,924	16,278,316	Baghdad	3,205,645
Israel	8,019	20,770	4,404,000	Jerusalem	506,200
Japan	145,834	377,708	121,740,000	Tokyo (*u.a.*)	11,806,729
Jordan	37,738	97,740	2,670,000	Amman	1,100,000
Kampuchea	69,898	181,035	7,284,000	Ψ Phnom Penh	500,000
Korea D.P.R. (North) ..	46,540	120,538	20,385,000	Pyongyang	1,500,000
Korea Rep. of (South) ..	38,025	98,484	41,209,000	Seoul	10,000,000
Kuwait	6,880	17,818	1,695,128*	Ψ Kuwait (city)	400,000
Laos	91,429	231,800	4,117,000	Vientiane	120,000
Lebanon.............	4,015	10,400	2,668,000	Ψ Beirut	702,000
Macao	6	16	343,000	Ψ Macao	..
Malaysia	127,317	329,749	16,544,000	Kuala Lumpur	1,103,200*
Maldives	115	298	189,400	Ψ Malé	46,334
Mongolia	604,250	1,565,000	1,900,000	Ulan Bator	480,000
Nepal	54,342	140,747	17,500,000	Kathmandu	235,000
Oman	82,030	212,457	1,500,000	Ψ Muscat	400,000
Pakistan	307,374	746,045	96,180,000	Islamabad (*u.a.*) ..	350,000
Philippines	115,831	300,000	57,000,000	Ψ Manila	1,630,485
Qatar	4,247	11,000	315,000	Ψ Doha	220,000
Saudi Arabia	830,000	2,149,640	12,400,000	Riyadh	1,000,000
Singapore	224	581	2,612,800	..	..
Sri Lanka	25,332	65,610	15,837,000	Ψ Colombo	643,000
Syria................	71,498	185,180	10,267,000	Damascus	2,250,000
Thailand	198,457	514,000	52,970,000	Ψ Bangkok	5,400,000
Turkey (in Asia)	292,261	756,953	44,485,734*	Ankara	3,196,460
U.S.S.R. (in Asia)......	6,498,486	16,831,000	63,070,000	..	..
United Arab Emirates .	32,278	83,600	1,600,000	..	..
Vietnam	127,242	329,556	62,300,000	Hanoi.............	925,000
Yemen A.R. (North) ...	75,290	195,000	9,250,000	Sana'a	427,185
Yemen P.D.R. (South) .	128,560	332,968	2,500,000	Ψ Aden	270,000

[1] Including Tibet.

THE SEVEN WONDERS OF THE WORLD

I.   THE PYRAMIDS OF EGYPT.—From Gizeh (near Cairo) to a southern limit 60 miles distant. The oldest is that of Zoser, at Saqqara, built about 2,700 B.C. The Great Pyramid of Cheops covers more than 12 acres and was originally 481 ft. in height and 756 × 756 ft. at the base.

II.   THE HANGING GARDENS OF BABYLON.—Adjoining Nebuchadnezzar's palace, 60 miles south of Baghdad. Terraced gardens, ranging from 75 to 300 ft. above ground level, watered from storage tanks on the highest terrace.

III.   THE TOMB OF MAUSOLUS.—At Halicarnassus, in Asia Minor. Built by the widowed Queen Artemisia about 350 B.C. The memorial originated the term mausoleum.

IV.   THE TEMPLE OF ARTEMIS AT EPHESUS.—Ionic temple erected about 350 B.C. in honour of the goddess and burned by the Goths in A.D. 262.

V.   THE COLOSSUS OF RHODES.—A bronze statue of Apollo, set up about 280 B.C. According to legend it stood at the harbour entrance of the seaport of Rhodes.

VI.   THE STATUE OF ZEUS.—At Olympia in the plain of Elis, constructed of marble inlaid with ivory and gold by the sculptor Phidias, about 430 B.C.

VII.   THE PHAROS OF ALEXANDRIA.—A marble watch tower and lighthouse on the island of Pharos in the harbour of Alexandria.

EUROPE AND THE MEDITERRANEAN

(For symbols, etc., *see* introductory notes on page 125.)

COUNTRY	AREA Sq. Miles	AREA Sq. Km.	POPULATION	CAPITAL	POPULATION OF CAPITAL
Albania	11,099	28,748	3,000,000	Tirana	210,757
Andorra..............	175	453	40,000	Andorra La Vella .	16,000
Austria	32,374	83,849	7,566,000	Vienna	1,531,346
Belgium..............	11,781	30,513	9,858,895	Brussels (*u.a.*)	976,536
Bulgaria	42,823	110,912	8,948,388*	Sofia..............	1,114,759
Cyprus	3,572	9,251	673,100	Nicosia	164,400
Czechoslovakia	49,370	127,869	15,500,000	Prague...........	1,190,576
Denmark	16,629	43,069	5,124,794	Ψ Copenhagen (*u.a.*) .	469,706
Faroe Is.	540	1,399	46,000	Ψ Thorshavn	..
Finland	137,851	337,032	4,908,000	Ψ Helsinki	485,626
France	211,208	547,026	55,279,000	Paris (*u.a.*)	8,707,000
German D.R. (East)	41,768	108,178	16,644,000	East Berlin	1,202,895
Germany, F.R. (West)[1] .	95,976	248,577	61,149,000	Bonn	290,800
Gibraltar.............	2	6	29,692	Ψ Gibraltar	..
Greece	50,944	131,944	9,935,000	Athens (*u.a.*)	3,027,331*
Hungary	35,919	93,030	10,658,000	Budapest.........	2,072,000
Iceland	39,768	103,000	247,024	Ψ Reykjavik (*u.a.*) ..	93,270
Ireland, Republic of....	27,136	70,283	3,540,643*	Ψ Dublin	502,749*
Italy	116,304	301,225	57,193,708	Rome (*u.a.*)	2,821,420
Liechtenstein	61	157	27,714	Vaduz	4,890
Luxembourg	998	2,586	365,900	Luxembourg	77,500
Malta and Gozo	122	316	383,000	Ψ Valletta.........	14,013
Monaco	0·4	1	28,000	Monaco-ville	1,443
Netherlands	15,770	40,844	14,615,000	Ψ Amsterdam (*u.a.*) .	1,031,000
Norway[2]	125,181	324,219	4,198,637	Ψ Oslo	450,808
Poland	120,725	312,677	37,203,000	Warsaw	1,644,626
Portugal[3]	35,553	92,082	10,229,000	Ψ Lisbon	807,937
Romania	91,699	237,500	22,823,500	Bucharest........	1,961,189
San Marino...........	23	61	22,361	San Marino	..
Spain[4]	194,897	504,782	38,818,355	Madrid (*u.a.*)	3,188,297
Sweden	173,732	449,964	8,358,139	Ψ Stockholm (*u.a.*) ..	1,435,474
Switzerland	15,943	41,293	6,532,400	Berne (*u.a.*)	301,000
Turkey (in Europe)	9,121	23,623	6,942,780*	..	..
UNITED KINGDOM[5]	94,227	244,046	56,972,700	Ψ London (*u.a.*)	6,775,200
England.............	50,363	130,439	47,254,000		
Wales	8,018	20,768	2,821,000	Ψ Cardiff	279,500
Scotland	30,414	78,772	5,121,000	Ψ Edinburgh	438,232
Northern Ireland	5,452	14,121	1,575,200	Ψ Belfast	303,800
U.S.S.R. (in Europe) ...	2,150,975	5,571,000	218,607,000	Moscow	8,815,000
Vatican City State	0·2	0·44	1,000	Vatican City	..
Yugoslavia	98,766	255,804	23,123,000	Belgrade	1,455,000

[1] Data include West Berlin.
[2] Excludes Svalbard and Jan Mayen Is. (approx. 24,101 sq. miles (62,422 sq. km.) and 3,000 population).
[3] Includes Madeira (314 sq. miles) and the Azores (922 sq. miles).
[4] Includes Balearic Is., Canary Is., Ceuta and Melilla.
[5] Includes Isle of Man (227 sq. miles (588 sq. km.), 64,282 population), and Channel Is. (75 sq. miles (195 sq. km.), 137,196 population).

OCEANIA

(For symbols, etc., *see* introductory notes on page 125.)

COUNTRY	AREA		POPULATION	CAPITAL	POPULATION OF CAPITAL
	Sq. Miles	Sq. Km.			
Australia.............	2,967,909	7,686,848	16,263,319*	Canberra.........	281,000*
Norfolk Island	14	36	2,000	Ψ Kingston.........	..
Fiji	7,055	18,274	715,373*	Ψ Suva.............	75,000
French Polynesia	1,544	4,000	176,400	Ψ Papeete	22,967
Guam	212	549	120,977	Agaña	896
Kiribati	281	728	63,800*	Tarawa	24,400
Marshall Is...........	70	181	35,000	Majuro	14,500
Micronesia, Fed. States of.	271	701	88,000	Kolonia	6,000
Nauru	8	21	8,042*	Ψ Nauru	..
New Caledonia........	7,358	19,058	153,000	Ψ Noumea	60,112*
New Zealand..........	103,736	268,676	3,307,084	Ψ Wellington	351,000
Cook Islands	91	236	17,400	Avarua	..
Niue	100	259	3,002	Alofi.............	956
*Ross Dependency** ...	286,696	750,310	..	..	..
Northern Mariana Is ..	184	476	22,000	Saipan	17,000
Palau	192	497	14,000	Koror............	6,500
Papua New Guinea	178,260	461,691	3,329,000	Ψ Port Moresby	139,300
Pitcairn Islands	1·9	5	57	..	..
Samoa:—					
Eastern (U.S.)	76	197	34,500	Ψ Pago Pago	3,055
Western	1,097	2,842	163,000	Ψ Apia	33,100
Solomon Islands.......	10,983	28,446	285,176*	Ψ Honiara	30,499*
Tonga	270	699	97,000	Ψ Nuku'alofa	27,815
Tuvalu	10	25	8,229	Ψ Funafuti	2,856
Vanuatu	5,700	14,763	140,154	Ψ Vila	14,184
Wallis and Futuna Is...	106	274	13,100	Ψ Mata-Utu	..

* Includes permanent shelf ice.

THE LARGEST CITIES OF THE WORLD

Ψ = Seaport	Population
MEXICO CITY, Mexico	18,748,000
CAIRO, Egypt	14,000,000
TOKYO, Japan	11,806,729
SEOUL, S. Korea	10,000,000
Ψ BUENOS AIRES, Argentina	9,967,826
Ψ Calcutta, India	9,166,000
MOSCOW, U.S.S.R.	8,815,000
PARIS, France	8,707,000

Ψ = Seaport	Population
São Paulo, Brazil	8,490,763
Ψ Bombay, India	8,202,000
Ψ New York, U.S.A.	7,262,000
Ψ Shanghai, China	7,100,000
Ψ LONDON, U.K.	6,775,000
Ψ JAKARTA, Indonesia	6,503,449
DELHI, India	6,222,000
TEHRAN, Iran	6,000,000

WORLD GEOGRAPHICAL STATISTICS

North America
River.......	Mississippi–Missouri– Red Rock	3,741 miles
Lake	Superior	31,000 sq miles
Mountain ..	McKinley	20,320 ft
Waterfall ..	Yosemite, California	2,425 ft

South America
River.......	Amazon	4,007 miles
Lake	Titicaca	3,205 sq miles
Mountain ..	Aconcagua	22,834 ft
Waterfall ...	Angel, Venezuela	3,212 ft

Africa
River.......	Nile	4,145 miles
Lake	Victoria	26,800 sq miles
Mountain ..	Kilimanjaro	19,340 ft
Waterfall ...	Tugela, Natal	3,110 ft

Europe
River.......	Volga, USSR	2,293 miles
Lake	Ladoga, USSR	6,826 sq miles
Mountain ..	Elbruz, Caucasus	18,481 ft
Waterfall ...	Utigard, Norway	2,625 ft

Asia
River.......	Yenisei, Mongolia– USSR	3,442 miles
Lake	Aral Sea, USSR	25,500 sq miles
Mountain ..	Everest	29,028 ft
Waterfall ...	Gersoppa, India	830 ft

Oceania
River.......	Murray-Darling, Australia	2,350 miles
Lake	Eyre, Australia	3,700 sq miles
Mountain ..	Cook, New Zealand	12,349 ft
Waterfall ...	Sutherland, New Zealand	1,904 ft

OCEAN AREAS AND DEPTHS

Oceans

Name	Area of Basin (sq. miles)	Greatest Depth (feet)
Pacific	63,800,000	Mariana Trench, 36,198
Atlantic	31,830,000	Milwaukee Deep 30,238
Indian	28,360,000	Java Trench 25,344
Arctic.........	5,500,000	 18,050

Seas

Name	Area of Basin (sq. miles)	Greatest Depth (feet)
South China ...	1,148,500	 16,452
Caribbean[1] ...	1,020,000	Cayman Trench, 25,216

Seas

Name	Area of Basin (sq. miles)	Greatest Depth (feet)
Mediterranean.[2]	966,750	Ionian Basin, 16,801
Bering	875,750	 13,442
Gulf of Mexico .	590,000	Sigsbee Deep, 17,070
Okhotsk.......	589,800	Kuril Trough, 11,069
East China	482,300	Okinawa Trench, 8,914
Hudson Bay ...	475,800	.... c. 1,500
Japan	389,000	 12,276
Andaman	308,000	 14,500
North Sea	222,125	Skaggerak, 2,400
Banda Sea	180,000	Weber Basin, 24,400
Black Sea (and Sea of Azov) .	178,500	 7,257
Red Sea	169,000	 8,984

[1] Excluding the Gulf of Mexico.
[2] Excluding the Black Sea.

PRINCIPAL LAND AREAS OF THE WORLD BELOW SEA LEVEL
(With approx. greatest depth in feet below Mean Sea Level.)

Europe: Netherlands coastal areas (15).
Asia: Jordan Valley, Dead Sea (1290)*.
  China: Sinkiang, Turfan Basin (980).
  U.S.S.R.–Iran: Caspian Sea (85)*.
  Arabia: Trucial Oman-U.A.E. (70).
Africa: Libyan Desert Depressions:—
  Qattara (440), Faiyum (150).
  Wadi Ryan (140), Sittra (110).

Africa: Libyan Desert Depressions (*continued*)—
  Areg (80), Wadi Natrun (75).
  Melfa (60), Siwa (55), Bahrain (50).
  Eritrea: Salt Plains depression (385).
  Algeria-Tunisia: Shott Melghir and El Gharsa (90)*.
America: Death Valley (275), Salton Sea (245)*.
Australia: Lake Eyre (40).

* Water surface

PRINCIPAL HEIGHTS ABOVE SEA LEVEL

	Feet
Europe: Elbruz............................	18,481
Alps—Mont Blanc	15,771
England: Scafell Pike....................	3,210
Wales: Snowdon	3,560
Scotland: Ben Nevis	4,406
Ireland: Carrantuohill..................	3,414
Asia: Everest	29,028
Africa: Kilimanjaro	19,340
North America: McKinley	20,320

	Feet
South America: Aconcagua	22,834
Australia: Kosciusko	7,316
New Zealand: Cook	12,349
Oceania: Jayakusumu[1]	16,500
Antarctica: Vinson Massif	16,864

[1] Variously known as Ngga Pulu, Carstensz Pyramid, Puntjak Sukarno.

THE LARGEST ISLANDS

Name of Island	Ocean	Area in Sq. Miles
Greenland	Arctic	840,004
New Guinea	Pacific	300,000
Borneo	Pacific	280,100
Madagascar	Indian	226,658
Baffin Island	Arctic	183,810
Sumatra	Indian	182,860
Honshu	Pacific	88,031
Great Britain[1]	Atlantic	84,186
Victoria Island.............	Arctic	81,930
Ellesmere Island	Arctic	75,767

Name of Island	Ocean	Area in Sq. Miles
Celebes (Sulawesi)	Indian	72,987
South Island, N.Z.	Pacific	58,093
Java (Indian)	Indian	48,763
North Island, N.Z.	Pacific	44,281
Newfoundland	Atlantic	43,359
Cuba	Atlantic	42,804
Luzon	Pacific	40,420
Iceland	Atlantic	39,769
Mindanao	Pacific	36,381
Ireland	Atlantic	32,595

[1] Mainland only.

THE WORLD'S LARGEST LAKES

The areas of some of these lakes are subject to seasonal variation.

Name	Locality	Length (Miles)	Area (Sq. Miles)	Name	Locality	Length (Miles)	Area (Sq. Miles)
Caspian Sea	Asia	760	143,000	Balkhash	U.S.S.R.	376	6,700
Superior	North America	383	31,800	Nettilling	Baffin Island	120	5,000
Victoria	Africa	210	26,800	Amadjuak	Baffin Island	75	4,000
Aral	U.S.S.R.	280	25,500	Bangweulu[1]	Africa	150	3,800
Huron	North America	206	23,100				(max)
Michigan	North America	321	22,300	Onega	U.S.S.R.	145	3,753
Tanganyika	Africa	430	12,700	Eyre[1]	Australia	130	3,700
Great Bear	Canada	200	12,275	Titicaca	South America	110	3,205
Baikal	U.S.S.R.	395	12,200	Nicaragua	Nicaragua	110	3,190
Malawi	Africa	363	11,430	Athabasca	Canada	208	3,120
Great Slave	Canada	300	11,030	Gairdner	Australia	100	3,000
Erie	North America	241	9,910	Turkana			
Winnipeg	Canada	264	9,465	(Rudolf)	Africa	154	2,473
Chad[1]	Africa	175	9,000	Reindeer	Canada	152	2,467
			(max)	Issyk-Kul	U.S.S.R.	115	2,445
Ontario	North America	193	7,550	Koko-Nor[1]	China	68	2,300
Ladoga	U.S.S.R.	136	6,826				(max)

[1] Area varies considerably according to season.

THE WORLD'S HIGHEST VOLCANOES

ACTIVE

Volcano	Locality	Height in Feet	Volcano	Locality	Height in Feet
Antofalla	Argentina	21,162	Nyamuragira	Zaire	10,150
Guallatiri	Chile	19,882	Mt. St. Helens	Cascade Range, U.S.A.	9,677
Cotopaxi	Ecuador	19,347	Tambora	Indonesia	9,351
Kluchevskaya	U.S.S.R.	15,913	Villarrica	Chile	9,325
Mt Wrangell	Alaska	14,000	Ruapehu	New Zealand	9,175
Mauna Loa	Hawaii	13,680	Paricutin	Mexico	9,100
Cameroon	Cameroon	13,350	Asama	Japan	8,340
Erebus	Antarctica	12,450	Ngauruhoe	New Zealand	7,515
Nyiragongo	Zaire	11,385	Hecla	Iceland	4,747
Iliamna	Aleutian Range, U.S.A.	11,000	Vesuvius	Italy	4,198
Etna	Sicily	10,853	Kilauea	Hawaii	4,077
Chillan	Chile	10,500	Stromboli	Lipari Is. Italy	3,038

DORMANT

Llullaillaco	Chile	22,057	Haleakala	Hawaii	10,022
Cayembe	Ecuador	18,982	The Peak	Tristan da Cunha	6,760
Demavend	Iran	18,384	Tongariro	New Zealand	6,458
Popocatepetl	Mexico	17,887	Pelée	Martinique	4,800
Pico de Teide	Tenerife	12,198	Soufrière	St Vincent Is., W.I.	4,200
Semerou	Java	12,060			

BELIEVED EXTINCT

Aconcagua	Andes	22,834	Antisana	Ecuador	18,713
Chimborazo	Ecuador	20,561	Citlaltepetl	Mexico	18,700
Kilimanjaro	Tanzania	19,340	Elbruz	Caucasus	18,481

THE WORLD'S HIGHEST MOUNTAINS

The following list contains some of the principal peaks of such ranges as the Himalayas and the Andes, and the highest mountains in other ranges.

Name	Range or Country	Height in Feet	Name	Range or Country	Height in Feet
Everest	Himalayas	29,028	Llullaillaco	Andes	22,057
K2	Karakoram	28,250	Sajama	Andes	21,463
Kanchenjunga	Himalayas	28,208	Illimani	Andes	21,200
Makalu I	Himalayas	27,824	Chimborazo	Andes	20,561
Dhaulagiri	Himalayas	26,810	McKinley	Alaska	20,320
Nanga Parbat	Himalayas	26,660	Logan	Yukon	19,850
Annapurna	Himalayas	26,504	Cotopaxi	Andes	19,347
Nanda Devi	Himalayas	25,646	Kilimanjaro	Tanzania	19,340
Kamet	Himalayas	25,446	Citlaltepetl	Sierra Madre	18,700
Namcha Barwa	China	25,445	Elbruz	Caucasus	18,481
Minya Konka	China	24,890	St. Elias	Alaska	18,008
Communism Peak	Pamirs	24,590	Popocatepetl	Mexico	17,887
Pobedy Peak	Tian Shan	24,406	Foraker	Alaska	17,395
Lenin Peak	Pamirs	23,406	Lucania	Yukon	17,150
Aconcagua	Andes	22,834	Kenya	Kenya	17,058
Ojos del Salado	Andes	22,588	Ararat	Armenia	16,945
Bonete	Andes	22,545	Vinson Massif	Antarctica	16,864
Huascaran	Andes	22,204	Mont Blanc	Alps	15,771

THE WORLD'S LARGEST WATERFALLS

Greatest in height		Total height ft.	Greatest single drop ft.
Angel	Venezuela	3,212	2,648
Tugela	S. Africa	3,110	1,350
Utigard	Norway	2,625	1,970
Mongefossen	Norway	2,540	
Yosemite	California, U.S.A.	2,425	1,430
Mardalsfoss	Norway	2,154	974
Tyssestrengane	Norway	2,120	948
Kukenaam	Venezuela	2,000	
Sutherland	New Zealand	1,904	815
Takkakaw	Canada	1,650	1,200
Ribbon	California, U.S.A.	1,612	1,612
King George VI	Guyana	1,600	
Wollomombi	Australia	1,580	1,100
Roraima	Guyana	1,500	
Gavarnie	France	1,385	

Greatest in height		Total height ft.	Greatest single drop ft.
BRITISH ISLES			
Eas Coul Aulin	Scotland	658	
Caldron Snout*	England	450	
Powerscourt	Ireland	350	
Pistyll Rhaeadr	Wales	300	

* Cataracts—no sheer drop.

Greatest in volume		Width yd.
Khone Cataracts	Laos	11,667
Guayra	Brazil	5,300
Victoria	Zimbabwe-Zambia	1,534
Niagara	Canada–U.S.A.	1,200

THE LONGEST RIVERS

River	Outflow	Length in Miles
Nile	Mediterranean	4,145
Amazon	Atlantic	4,007
Mississippi-Missouri–Red Rock	Gulf of Mexico	3,741
Yenisei	Arctic	3,442
Yangtze	North Pacific	3,436
Ob-Irtysh	Arctic	3,362
Hwang-ho (Yellow River)	North Pacific	3,000
Zaire (Congo)	Atlantic	2,920
Lena	Arctic	2,734
Amur	North Pacific	2,700
Mackenzie-Peace	Beaufort Sea	2,635
Mekong	China Sea	2,600
Niger	Gulf of Guinea	2,600
Rio de la Plata-Parana	Atlantic	2,485
Murray-Darling	Southern Ocean	2,350
Volga	Caspian Sea	2,293
Zambezi	Indian Ocean	2,200
Madeira	(1)	2,100
Purus (Coxiuara)	(1)	2,000
Yukon	Bering Sea	1,979
St. Lawrence	Gulf of St. Lawrence	1,945
Rio Grande del Norte	Gulf of Mexico	1,885
Ganges-Brahmaputra	Bay of Bengal	1,800
São Francisco	Atlantic	1,800
Indus	Arabian Sea	1,790
Danube	Black Sea	1,770
Salween (No Chiang)	Gulf of Martaban	1,750
Tigris-Euphrates	Persian Gulf	1,700
Tocantins	Pará River	1,700
Orinoco	Atlantic	1,700

Great Britain

Severn	Bristol Channel	220
Thames	North Sea	215

(1) Tributaries of the Amazon.

SOME FAMOUS BRIDGES

Among the outstanding *suspension bridges* of the World are the Verrazano Narrows Bridge, New York (main span, 4,260 ft.); the Golden Gate Bridge, San Francisco (4,200 ft.); Mackinac Bridge, Michigan (3,800 ft.); Bosporus, Turkey (3,523 ft.); George Washington Bridge, New York (3,500 ft.); the Ponte 25 April (Tagus Bridge), Portugal (3,323 ft.); Forth Road Bridge, Scotland (3,300 ft.); Severn Bridge, England (3,240 ft.); Tacoma Bridge, Washington, U.S.A. (2,800 ft.); Orinoco Bridge, Venezuela (2,336 ft.) and the Kanmon Bridge, Japan (2,336 ft.). Lengths shown above are all those of the main or longest span. The Humber Bridge was opened in 1981 and has the longest single central span, 4,626 ft., of any suspension bridge in the world.

The Transbay Bridge (*suspension and cantilever*), crossing San Francisco Bay from Oakland to San Francisco is 7½ miles long, with spans of 2,310 ft. each.

Among important *steel arch* bridges are the New River Gorge Bridge, Virginia, U.S.A. (1,700 ft); the Bayonne Bridge, from New Jersey to Staten Island, U.S.A. (1,652 ft.); Sydney Harbour Bridge, Australia (1,650 ft.); the Runcorn-Widnes Bridge, England (1,082 ft.); and the Glen Canyon Bridge over the Colorado River, U.S.A. (1,028 ft.). Major *concrete trestle* bridges include the Lake Pontchartrain Causeway, U.S.A. of 2,170 spans extending 23·87 miles and the Oosterscheldebrug, Netherlands, 3·12 miles long. The Chesapeake Bay Bridge-Tunnel (17·6 miles long) has 12·5 miles of *concrete trestle*. Gladesville Bridge, Sydney, Australia, is a *concrete arch* bridge of 1,000 ft. span. The Tay Bridge in Scotland is a *steel box girder* bridge supported on twin piers (42 spans), 7,365 ft long.

GREAT SHIP CANALS OF THE WORLD

Canal	Opened	Length, miles	Depth (ft.)†	Width (ft.)†
North Sea (Netherlands)	1876	14·5	43	148
Corinth (Greece)	1893	4	26	72
Kiel (Germany)	1895	61	31	132
Manchester (England)	1894	35·5	30	120
Panama	1914	50·5	39·5	500
Suez (Egypt)	1869	100	42	197
Terneuzen-Ghent (Netherlands–Belgium)	1895	18·5	38	102
St. Lawrence Seaway (Canada)	1959	378*	27	200

† Of largest vessels permitted.   * Includes Lake Ontario and Welland Canal.

INLAND WATERWAYS.—The British Waterways Board are the navigational authority for nearly 2,000 miles of canals and river navigations in England, Scotland and Wales. Some 340 miles are maintained and are being developed as Commercial Waterways for use by freight-carrying vessels, and another 1,200 miles, the Cruising Waterways, are being developed for boating, fishing and other leisure activities. The remaining 500 miles, the Remainder Waterways, are maintained with due regard to safety, public health and the preservation of amenities. Over a third of this remaining mileage is being, or has been, restored to navigation. The Manchester Ship Canal, Bridgewater Canal, Rochdale Canal, River Thames and Fenland Waterways are among those which are the responsibility of other authorities.

LONGEST RAILWAY TUNNELS

E.R. = Eastern Region; L.M.R. = London Midland Region;
S.R. = Southern Region; W.R. = Western Region

United Kingdom

		Miles	Yards			Miles	Yards
Severn	W.R.	4	484	Bradway	E.R.	1	267
Totley	E.R.	3	950	Sough	L.M.R.	1	255
Standedge	E.R.	3	66	Watford, New	L.M.R.	1	230
Sodbury	W.R.	2	924	Llangyfelach	W.R.	1	193
Disley	L.M.R.	2	346	Caerphilly	W.R.	1	173
Ffestiniog	L.M.R.	2	338	Abbot's Cliff	S.R.	1	182
Bramhope	E.R.	2	241	Halton	L.M.R.	1	176
Cowburn	L.M.R.	2	182	Corby	L.M.R.	1	160
Sevenoaks	S.R.	1	1693	Wenvoe	W.R.	1	107
Morley	E.R.	1	1609	Sapperton	W.R.	1	100
Box	W.R.	1	1452	Wymington	L.M.R.	1	100
Dove Holes	L.M.R.	1	1224				

The London Underground *Northern Line* between Morden and East Finchley by the City Branch serves 25 stations and uses tunnels totalling 17¼ miles in length).

		Miles	Yards
Littleborough (Summit)	L.M.R.	1	1125
Anderston	S.R.	1	1010
Ponsbourne	E.R.	1	924
Bleamoor	L.M.R.	1	869
Polhill	S.R.	1	851
Queensbury	E.R.	1	741
Kilsby	L.M.R.	1	666
Lydden	S.R.	1	609
Strood	S.R.	1	569
Oxted	S.R.	1	501
Clayton	S.R.	1	499
Penge	S.R.	1	381
Merstham New (Quarry)	S.R.	1	353
Greenock	Scottish Region	1	351

The World
(Submarine tunnels are not included)

		Miles	Yards
Simplon	Switzerland–Italy	12	560
Apennine	Italy	11	880
St. Gotthard	Switzerland	9	550
Lötschberg	Switzerland	9	130
Mont Cenis	Italy	8	870
Cascade	United States	7	1410
Arlberg	Austria	6	650
Moffat	United States	6	200
Shimizu	Japan	6	70

THE ARCTIC OCEAN

The Arctic Ocean consists of a deep sea over 2,000 fathoms, on the southern margin of which there is a broad continental shelf with numerous islands. Into this deeper sea there is only one broad channel, about 700 miles, between Greenland and Scandinavia. Bering Strait is only 49 miles wide and 27 fathoms deep. The southern boundary of the Arctic Ocean is the Wyville-Thomson and Faeroe-Icelandic submarine ridge, which separates the North Atlantic from the Norwegian and Greenland Seas. The Norwegian Deep lies between Norway and Jan Mayen and Iceland; it exceeds 1,500 fathoms. The Greenland Deep, of similar depth, lies between Spitsbergen and Greenland. These two depressions are separated by a somewhat deeply submerged ridge from the east of Jan Mayen to Bear Island, south of Spitsbergen. A shallow ridge from the north-west of Spitsbergen to Greenland separates the Greenland Sea from the deep North Polar Basin. This extends from the north of Spitsbergen and Franz Josef Land to the north of the New Siberia Islands and of the North American Arctic Archipelago. Another more shallow depression is Baffin Bay, less than 1,000 fathoms. This is separated from the North Atlantic by a submarine ridge. Barent's Sea, between Spitsbergen, Norway and Novaya Zemlya, and the Kara Sea, between Novaya Zemlya and the Siberian coast, are respectively below 200 and 100 fathoms. The total area of the Arctic Sea is about 5·5 million square miles, of which 2·3 million square miles are probably covered with floating ice.

DISTANCE OF THE HORIZON

The limit of distance to which one can see varies with the height of the spectator. The greatest distance at which an object on the surface of the sea, or of a level plain, can be seen by a person whose eyes are at a height of five feet from the same level is nearly three miles. At a height of 20 feet the range is increased to nearly six miles, and an approximate rule for finding the range of vision for small heights is to increase the square root of the number of feet that the eye is above the level surface by a third of itself, the result being the distance of the horizon in miles, but is slightly in excess of that in the table below, which is computed by a more precise formula. The table may be used conversely to show the distance of an object of given height that is just visible from a point in the surface of the earth or sea. Refraction is taken into account both in the approximate rule and in the Table.

At a height of	the range is	At a height of	the range is	At a height of	the range is
5 ft.	2·9 miles	500 ft	29·5 miles	4,000 ft	83·3 miles
20 „	5·9 „	1,000 „	41·6 „	5,000 „	93·1 „
50 „	9·3 „	2,000 „	58·9 „	20,000 „	186·2 „
100 „	13·2 „	3,000 „	72·1 „		

THE ANTARCTIC

THE ANTARCTIC is generally defined as the area lying within the Antarctic Convergence—the zone where cold northward-flowing Antarctic sea water sinks below warmer southward-flowing water. This zone is at about lat. 50° S. in the Atlantic Ocean and lat. 55°–62° S. in the Pacific Ocean. The continent itself lies almost entirely within the Antarctic Circle, an area of about 5·5 million square miles, 99 per cent of which is permanently ice-covered. The average thickness of the ice is 7,100 ft. but in places exceeds 14,500 ft., submerging entire mountain ranges; some mountains protrude—the highest being Vinson Massif, 16,066 ft. The ice amounts to some 7·2 million cubic miles and represents more than 90 per cent of the world's fresh water.

Along one-third of the Antarctic coastline, land-ice flowing outwards forms extensive ice shelves, fragments of which break off to form tabular icebergs, leaving ice cliffs up to 150 ft. high. Much of the sea freezes in winter, forming fast ice which breaks up in summer and drifts north as pack ice. The presence of ice and continuous darkness in winter restrict access to the coastline by sea to the summer months.

The most conspicuous physical features of the continent are its high inland plateau (much of it over 10,000 ft.), the Transantarctic Mountains (which together with the large embayments of the Weddell Sea and Ross Sea mark the approximate boundary between Greater and Lesser Antarctica), and the mountainous Antarctic Peninsula and off-lying islands (which extend northwards towards South America). The continental shelf averages about 20 miles in width (half the global mean, and in places it is non-existent) and reaches exceptional depths (1,300–2,600 ft., which is 3–6 times the global mean).

Climate.—On land, summer temperatures range from just below freezing around the coast to −34° C. (about −30° F.) on the plateau, and in winter −20° C. (about −4° F.) on the coast to −65° C. (about −85° F.) inland. Over a large area the maxima do not exceed −15° C. (+5° F.).

Precipitation is scanty over the plateau but amounts to 25–76 cms. (10–30 ins.) (water equivalent) along the coast and some scientific stations are permanently buried by snow. Some rain falls over the more northerly areas in summer. Gravity winds on the plateau slopes and cyclonic storms further north can both exceed 100 m.p.h. and gusts have been known to reach 150 m.p.h. Visibility can be reduced to zero in blizzards.

Flora and Fauna.—Although a small number of flowering plants, ferns and clubmosses occur on the sub-Antarctic islands, only two (a grass and a pearlwort) extend south of 60° S. Antarctic vegetation is dominated by lichens and mosses, with a few liverworts, algae, and fungi. Most of these occur around the coast or on islands, but lichens and some mosses also occur inland.

The only land animals are tiny insects and mites with nematodes, rotifers, and tardigrades in the mosses, but large numbers of seals, penguins, and other sea-birds go ashore to breed in the summer. The emperor penguin is the only species which breeds ashore throughout the winter. In contrast, the Antarctic seas abound with life—a wide variety of invertebrates (including krill) and fish providing food for the seals, penguins, and other sea birds and a residual population of whales.

Exploration and Antarctic Treaty.—In the 180 years from Captain James Cook's circumnavigation of the Antarctic in 1772–75 to the mid-1950's, about half of all expeditions to the Antarctic were British and a number of these made major contributions to geographical and scientific knowledge of the area. Notable were the expeditions of Sir James Clark Ross, Captain Robert Scott, and Sir Ernest Shackleton.

Apart from four years during World War II, British Antarctic research has been continuous since 1925, and most of it is now organized and carried out by the British Antarctic Survey (a component of the Natural Environment Research Council).

The world-wide International Geophysical Year, 1957–58, gave great impetus to Antarctic research. Prior to the mid-1950's, only 17 stations were operated in the Antarctic by four nations and vast areas of the continent were still unknown. By 1957, 44 stations had been established by 12 nations. The co-operative scientific effort proved so fruitful that the 12 nations involved pledged themselves to continue to promote scientific and technical co-operation unhampered by politics (territorial claims being left in abeyance) and agreed that the continent should be used for peaceful purposes only. These aims were embodied in the Antarctic Treaty (covering the area south of lat. 60° S., excluding the high seas but including the ice shelves), which came into force in 1961. It has since been signed by a further 25 acceding nations, 7 of which are active in the Antarctic and have therefore been accorded consultative status.

Potential resources.—Increasing pressure on the world's food and mineral supplies has stimulated the search for new sources even in the extremely hostile polar environment. Minerals have been found in great variety but not in commercially exploitable concentrations in accessible localities. (For example, coal seams occur in the Theron Mountains and Horlick Mountains.)

There are indications that off-shore hydrocarbons could be present but mostly below great depths of stormy, ice-infested seas. However, the Antarctic Treaty nations and their scientific advisors are already considering the environmental implications of possible mineral exploration and exploitation.

Currently, the chief interest is in marine protein, including the shrimp-like krill already fished commercially by Japan, Poland and U.S.S.R. Basic research to ensure rational management of stocks of this key organism is being continued by international groups, but it is estimated that they could sustain a yield equal to the present total annual world fish catch.

Scientific research.—At present, five British stations are maintained in the British Antarctic Territory and at South Georgia. Two are biological stations, two geophysical observatories, and one is the centre for airborne earth sciences.

There are a number of permanently occupied stations operated by other nations including one maintained at the South Pole by the U.S.A

The staff of these stations and summer field-workers are the only people present on the continent and off-lying islands. There are no indigenous inhabitants. (British Antarctic Survey, *see* entry on p. 351).

THE UNITED KINGDOM

The United Kingdom comprises Great Britain (England, Wales and Scotland) and Northern Ireland.

AREA

The land area of the United Kingdom* is 93,005 sq. miles. The area of inland water in the United Kingdom is 1,242 sq. miles. Total 94,247 sq. miles.

Sq. miles	England	Wales	Scotland	N. Ireland
Land..........................	50,070	7,968	29,761	5,206
Inland Water	293	50	653	246
Total..........................	50,363	8,018	30,414	5,452

* Excludes the Isle of Man (221 sq. miles) and the Channel Islands (75 sq. miles)

POPULATION

CENSUS RESULTS, 1801–1981

Before 1801 there existed no official return of the population of either England or Scotland. Estimates of the population of England at various periods, calculated from the number of baptisms, burials and marriages, are: in 1570, 4,160,221; 1600, 4,811,718; 1630, 5,600,517; 1670, 5,773,646; 1700, 6,045,008; 1750, 6,517,035.

Thousands

	United Kingdom			England and Wales			Scotland			Northern Ireland†		
	Total	Male	Female	Total	Male	Female	Total	Male	Female	Total	Male	Female
1801	11,944	5,692	6,252	8,893	4,255	4,638	1,608	739	869	1,443	698	745
1811	13,368	6,368	7,000	10,165	4,874	5,291	1,806	826	980	1,397	668	729
1821	15,472	7,498	7,974	12,000	5,850	6,150	2,092	983	1,109	1,380	665	715
1831	17,835	8,647	9,188	13,897	6,771	7,126	2,364	1,114	1,250	1,574	762	812
1841	20,183	9,819	10,364	15,914	7,778	8,137	2,620	1,242	1,378	1,649	800	849
1851	22,259	10,855	11,404	17,928	8,781	9,146	2,889	1,376	1,513	1,443	698	745
1861	24,525	11,894	12,631	20,066	9,776	10,290	3,062	1,450	1,612	1,396	668	728
1871	27,431	13,309	14,122	22,712	11,059	11,653	3,360	1,603	1,757	1,359	647	712
1881	31,015	15,060	15,955	25,974	12,640	13,335	3,736	1,799	1,936	1,305	621	684
1891	34,264	16,593	17,671	29,003	14,060	14,942	4,026	1,943	2,083	1,236	590	646
1901	38,237	18,492	19,745	32,528	15,729	16,799	4,472	2,174	2,298	1,237	590	647
1911	42,082	20,357	21,725	36,070	17,446	18,625	4,761	2,309	2,452	1,251	603	648
1921	44,027	21,033	22,994	37,887	18,075	19,811	4,882	2,348	2,535	1,258	610	648
1931	46,038	22,060	23,978	39,952	19,133	20,819	4,843	2,326	2,517	1,243	601	642
1951	50,225	24,118	26,107	43,758	21,016	22,742	5,096	2,434	2,662	1,371	668	703
1961	52,709	25,481	27,228	46,105	22,304	23,801	5,179	2,483	2,697	1,425	694	731
1971	55,515	26,952	28,562	48,750	23,683	25,067	5,229	2,515	2,714	1,536	755	781
1981	55,776	27,064	28,701	49,154	23,873	25,281	5,130	2,466	2,664	1,491	725	756

NOTES.— 1. Because of the War there was no Census in 1941.

2. The last official Census of Population in respect of England and Wales, Scotland, Northern Ireland, the Isle of Man and Guernsey, was taken on the night of April 5, 1981.

3. † All figures refer to the area which is now Northern Ireland. Figures for N. Ireland in 1921 and 1931 are estimates based on the Censuses held in 1926 and 1937.

ISLANDS

The figures given above do not include islands of the British Seas. Populations of these islands at census years since 1900 were:—

	ISLE OF MAN			JERSEY			GUERNSEY		
	Total	Male	Female	Total	Male	Female	Total	Male	Female
1901............	54,752	25,496	29,256	52,576	23,940	28,636	43,042	21,140	21,902
1911............	52,016	23,937	28,079	51,898	24,014	27,884	45,001	22,215	22,786
1921............	60,284	27,329	32,955	49,701	22,438	27,263	40,529	19,303	21,226
1931............	49,308	22,443	26,865	50,462	23,424	27,038	42,743	20,675	22,068
1951............	55,123	25,749	29,464	57,296	27,282	30,014	45,747	22,094	23,380
1961............	48,151	22,060	26,091	57,200	27,200	30,000	47,178	22,890	24,288
1971............	56,289	26,461	29,828	72,532	35,423	37,109	52,708	25,382	27,326
1981............	64,679	30,901	33,778	77,000	37,000	40,000	56,000	27,000	29,000

Births and Marriages (Thousands)

	Live births				Marriages				
	United Kingdom	England and Wales		Scotland	Northern Ireland	United King-dom	England and Wales		Scotland	Northern Ireland
		Total	Wales				Total	Wales		
1980	753·7	656·2	37·4	68·9	28·6	418·4	370·0	21·1	38·5	9·9
1981	730·8	634·5	35·8	69·1	27·3	397·8	352·0	19·8	36·2	9·6
1982	719·2	625·9	35·7	66·2	27·0	387·0	342·2	19·0	34·9	9·9
1983	721·5	629·1	35·5	65·1	27·3	389·3	344·3	19·9	35·0	10·0
1984	729·6	636·8	35·9	65·1	27·7	395·8	349·0	19·2	36·3	10·4
1985	750·7	656·4	36·8	66·7	27·6	393·1	346·4	19·1	36·4	10·3
1986	755·0	661·0	37·0	65·8	28·2	393·9	347·9	19·5	35·8	10·2
1987	755·6	681·5	37·8	66·2†	27·9†	—	—	—	35·8†	10·4†
1987 1st quarter	185·8†	162·7	9·2	16·1†	7·0†	55·2†	48·8†	2·7†	5·1†	1·3†
2nd quarter	199·1†	174·9	9·6	16·7†	7·4†	114·5†	101·7†	5·5†	9·9†	3·0†
3rd quarter	200·8†	176·6	9·7	17·0†	7·1†	—	135·3†	7·6†	13·3†	4·4†
4th quarter	190·0	167·3†	9·3	16·4†	6·3†	—	—	—	7·5†	1·7†

† Provisional.

Divorce

	1980	1981	1982	1983	1984	1985	1986
England and Wales							
Decrees absolute granted:							
Number	148,301	145,713	146,698	147,479	144,501	160,300	153,903
Rate per 1,000 married population ...	*12·0*	*11·9*	*12·0*	*12·2*	*12·0*	*13·4*	*12·8†*
Scotland							
Decrees absolute, granted:							
Number	10,528	9,894	11,288	13,238	11,906	13,371	13,063
Rate per 1,000 married population ...	*8·6*	*8·0*	*9·2*	*11·0*	*9·9*	*11·2*	*11·1†*
Northern Ireland							
Petitions filed							
Nullity of marriage	9	9	5	—	6	6	6
Divorce	1,620	1,645	1,734	1,577	1,749	1,986	1,630
Judicial separation	4	2	2	9	5	15	17

† Provisional.

Deaths Registered* (Thousands)

	Total					Infants under one year				
	United Kingdom	England and Wales		Scotland	Northern Ireland	United King-dom	England and Wales		Scotland	North-ern Ireland
		Total	Wales				Total	Wales		
1980	661·5	581·4	35·1	63·3	16·8	9·11	7·90	0·43	0·83	0·38
1981	658·0	577·9	35·0	63·8	16·3	8·16	7·02	0·45	0·78	0·36
1982	662·8	581·9	35·2	65·0	15·9	7·90	6·78	0·38	0·75	0·37
1983	659·1	579·6	35·2	63·5	16·0	7·36	6·38	0·38	0·65	0·33
1984	644·9	566·9	33·7	62·3	15·7	7·00	6·04	0·31	0·67	0·29
1985	670·6	590·7	35·5	64·0	16·0	7·03	6·14	0·36	0·62	0·27
1986	660·7†	581·2	34·7	63·5†	16·1	7·18†	6·31	0·35	0·58	0·29
1987	644·3†	567·0	33·9	62·0†	15·3†	7·08	6·27	0·36	0·56†	0·24†
1987 1st quarter	175·0†	153·9	9·3	16·9†	4·1†	1·96†	1·73	0·10	0·15†	0·08†
2nd quarter	154·0†	135·4	8·1	14·9†	3·7†	1·64†	1·46	0·08	0·13†	0·05†
3rd quarter	146·3†	128·8	7·7	14·1†	3·5†	1·54†	1·35	0·08	0·13†	0·06†
4th quarter	169·1†	148·9	8·8	16·1†	4·1†	1·93†	1·72	0·10	0·15†	0·05†

* Excluding stillbirths.   † Provisional.

DEATHS ANALYSED BY CAUSE

	England and Wales		Scotland	
	1985	1986	1985	1986
Total deaths	580,734	581,203	63,967	63,467
Deaths from natural causes	571,725	562,449	61,148	60,562
Infections and parasitic diseases	2,381	2,470	278	268
Cholera	—	—	—	—
Typhoid fever	—	—	—	—
Shigellosis and amoebiasis	2	4	—	—
Enteritis and other diarrhoeal diseases	124	128	14	9
Tuberculosis of respiratory system	408	376	47	41
Other tuberculosis, including late effects	366	357	57	47
Plague	—	—	—	—
Diphtheria	—	—	—	—
Whooping cough	4	3	—	—
Streptococcal sore throat and scarlatina	1	1	1	—
Meningococcal infection	97	141	9	11
Acute poliomyelitis	—	1	—	—
Smallpox	—	—	—	—
Measles	11	10	1	—
Louse-borne typhus and other rickettsioses	2	—	—	—
Malaria	5	3	—	1
Syphilis	40	38	2	3
Neoplasms	141,618	140,801	14,618	14,686
Malignant neoplasm of stomach	9,971	9,714	1,010	961
Malignant neoplasm of trachea, bronchus and lung	35,792	35,257	4,307	4,149
Malignant neoplasm of breast	13,592	13,746	1,264	1,326
Malignant neoplasm of uterus	3,494	3,466	353	334
Leukaemia	3,696	3,572	352	315
Benign and unspecified neoplasms	1,346	1,311	113	116
Endocrine, nutritional and metabolic diseases & immunity disorders	9,798	10,158	723	707
Diabetes mellitus	7,452	7,912	534	518
Nutritional deficiencies	130	123	21	15
Diseases of blood and blood-forming organs	2,422	2,366	181	167
Anaemias	1,522	1,409	83	89
Mental disorders	12,011	12,410	965	949
Diseases of nervous system and sense organs	11,414	11,182	810	827
Meningitis	306	271	18	20
Diseases of the circulatory system	287,054	278,749	32,319	31,424
Acute rheumatic fever	6	3	—	—
Chronic rheumatic heart disease	2,889	2,616	252	258
Hypertensive disease	4,581	4,173	391	372
Ischaemic heart disease	163,104	158,667	18,758	18,138
Diseases of pulmonary circulation & other forms of heart disease	22,835	21,930	2,620	2,337
Cerebrovascular disease	73,219	71,454	8,505	8,590
Diseases of the respiratory system	64,607	63,052	7,156	7,469
Influenza	662	587	54	121
Pneumonia	27,931	27,624	3,880	4,113
Bronchitis, emphysema	14,255	12,119	969	791
Asthma	1,972	1,990	146	152
Diseases of the digestive system	18,148	17,974	2,038	2,011
Ulcer of stomach and duodenum	4,861	4,528	470	448
Appendicitis	147	137	18	6
Hernia of abdominal cavity	2,001	2,013	201	165
Chronic liver disease and cirrhosis	2,582	2,527	423	380
Diseases of the genito-urinary system	8,012	7,926	897	887
Nephritis, nephrotic syndrome and nephrosis	4,640	4,556	555	538
Hyperplasia of prostate	668	585	37	41
Complications of pregnancy, child birth etc.	46	45	9	7
Abortion	9	3	1	2
Diseases of the skin and subcutaneous tissue	670	743	89	86
Diseases of the musculo-skeletal system	5,452	5,448	269	289
Congenital anomalies	2,909	1,871	265	224
Certain conditions originating in the perinatal period	2,293	225	246	250
Birth trauma, hypoxia, birth asphyxia & other respiratory conditions	1,293	85	122	142
Signs, symptoms and other ill-defined conditions	2,890	3,540	285	311
Deaths by violence	19,009	18,754	2,819	2,905
All accidents	12,475	12,369	1,981	2,055
Motor vehicle accidents	4,914	4,900	609	608
Suicide and self-inflicted injury	4,419	4,126	569	568
All other external causes	2,115	2,259	269	282

Resident Population by Sex and Age 1986

Thousands

	All ages	0–4	5–14	15–44	45–59/64*	60/65†–74	75 or over
Males							
United Kingdom	27,647·0	1,867·0	3,676·5	12,642·6	6,033·6	2,200·7	1,226·6
England	23,034·4	1,540·5	3,020·5	10,532·7	5,049·8	1,851·3	1,039·6
Wales	1,369·1	91·6	184·7	606·5	306·6	117·3	62·2
Scotland	2,475·0	165·3	337·1	1,154·0	535·9	183·6	99·1
Northern Ireland .	768·4	69·5	134·3	349·4	141·2	48·4	25·7
Females							
United Kingdom	29,116·3	1,774·6	3,480·8	12,363·7	4,644·1	4,401·7	2,451·4
England	24,220·0	1,463·7	2,859·2	10,306·9	3,856·8	3,668·6	2,064·8
Wales	1,451·9	87·2	173·8	596·2	231·9	236·0	126·9
Scotland	2,646·0	157·7	320·0	1,124·2	439·0	395·4	209·8
Northern Ireland .	798·4	66·0	127·9	336·5	116·3	101·7	50·0

*59 for women, 64 for men.
†60 for women, 65 for men.

Birth Rates 1986

Live births per 1,000 women in age groups:

	15–19*	20–24	25–29	30–34	35–39	40–44†
United Kingdom	30	93	125	78	25	5
England	30	92	124	78	25	5
Wales	36	103	127	73	22	4
Scotland	31	91	120	70	20	4
Northern Ireland	30	122	164	112	52	12

*Includes also births to mothers under 15.
†Includes also births to mothers 45 or over.

Death Rates 1986

Deaths per 1,000 population in age groups:

	0–4	5–14	15–24	25–34	35–44	45–54	55–64	65–74	75 or over
Males									
United Kingdom	2·6	0·2	0·8	0·9	1·7	5·5	17·0	43·6	117·6
England	2·6	0·2	0·8	0·9	1·6	5·2	16·4	42·6	116·2
Wales	2·8	0·2	0·8	0·8	1·9	5·9	18·1	45·2	119·1
Scotland	2·4	0·3	0·9	1·2	2·3	7·1	20·7	49·9	126·3
Northern Ireland .	2·5	0·2	1·0	1·2	2·0	6·4	20·6	49·2	126·9
Females									
United Kingdom	2·0	0·2	0·3	0·5	1·1	3·3	9·5	24·0	87·4
England	2·0	0·2	0·3	0·5	1·1	3·2	9·1	23·3	86·7
Wales	2·0	0·1	0·3	0·5	1·1	3·2	10·1	24·7	86·1
Scotland	1·9	0·1	0·3	0·5	1·3	4·0	11·5	29·0	92·8
Northern Ireland .	2·2	0·2	0·3	0·4	1·2	3·4	10·6	26·4	95·5

MIGRATION
Acceptances for settlement by nationality

Geographical region and nationality	Number of persons			Geographical region and nationality	Number of persons		
	1984	1985	1986		1984	1985	1986
Belgium	120	100	110	Nigeria	320	500	560
Denmark	140	150	140	Sierra Leone	80	70	90
France	590	580	490	Somalia	20	20	70
Germany (Federal				South Africa	690	790	730
Republic)	640	750	550	Sudan	50	110	50
Greece	220	250	220	Tanzania	300	330	240
Italy	520	540	400	Tunisia	60	40	50
Luxembourg	—	—	—	Uganda	40	50	80
Netherlands	540	460	410	Zambia	110	100	120
Portugal	230	230	200	Zimbabwe	280	320	270
Spain	530	440	360				
				Africa: total	4,380	4,710	4,000
European Community	3,530	3,490	2,880				
				Bangladesh	4,180	5,330	4,760
Austria	140	120	80	India	5,140	5,500	4,140
Cyprus	470	420	370	Pakistan	5,510	6,680	5,530
Finland	100	110	110				
Malta	210	180	160	**Indian sub-continent**	14,840	17,510	14,430
Norway	210	230	170				
Sweden	400	390	350	Iran	1,670	2,210	1,640
Switzerland	180	170	160	Iraq	400	550	430
Turkey	530	480	400	Israel	290	340	320
Yugoslavia	130	130	130	Jordan	120	90	140
				Kuwait	10	10	10
Other Western Europe	2,370	2,240	1,950	Lebanon	260	250	190
				Saudi Arabia	50	30	30
Bulgaria	10	20	20	Syria	70	90	80
Czechoslovakia	30	20	20				
German Democratic				**Middle East**	2,870	3,580	2,840
Republic	10	10	—				
Hungary	40	50	40	China	140	140	100
Poland	310	370	250	Indonesia	60	60	60
Romania	20	20	20	Japan	1,100	1,010	890
U.S.S.R.	50	50	40	Malaysia	680	630	560
				Philippines	630	780	990
Eastern Europe	470	540	380	Singapore	160	160	110
				Sri Lanka	760	930	800
Europe: total	6,370	6,270	5,220	Thailand	300	340	410
				BDTC Hong Kong*	1,040	950	860
Argentina	40	50	50				
Barbados	50	60	40	**Remainder of Asia**	4,860	5,000	4,780
Brazil	190	170	160				
Canada	1,400	1,500	1,200	**Asia: total**	22,570	26,090	22,040
Chile	60	70	40				
Colombia	140	170	140				
Cuba	—	—	—	Australia	3,590	3,780	2,850
Guyana	190	200	140	New Zealand	2,460	2,880	2,510
Jamaica	290	350	490				
Mexico	70	70	70	**Australasia: total**	6,040	6,660	5,360
Peru	60	80	50				
Trinidad and Tobago	150	160	160				
U.S.A.	3,750	4,170	3,740	British Overseas Citizens	2,690	2,180	1,670
Uruguay	—	10	—	Other countries not else-			
Venezuela	50	50	40	where specified	860	900	700
West Indies Associated				Stateless†	1,600	1,420	1,520
States	—	—	—				
				All nationalities	50,950	55,360	46,820
Americas: total	6,440	7,130	6,310				
				Foreign	24,230	26,840	23,270
Algeria	60	70	60	Commonwealth	26,720	28,520	23,550
Egypt	350	350	240				
Ethiopia	40	30	50	Old Commonwealth	7,440	8,160	6,560
Ghana	690	660	520	New Commonwealth and			
Kenya	610	520	340	Pakistan	24,800	27,050	22,520
Libya	70	170	130	Foreign excluding			
Mauritius	470	410	260	Pakistan	18,720	20,150	17,740
Morocco	130	160	140				

*British Dependant Territories Citizens.   †Includes refugees from South-East Asia.

ENGLISH KINGS AND QUEENS A.D. 827 TO 1603

Name	DYNASTY	MARRIED	Access.	Died	Age	Rgnd. Yrs.
	Saxons and Danes					
EGBERT	King of Wessex and all England		827	839	—	12
ETHELWULF	Son of Egbert		839	858	—	19
ETHELBALD	Son of Ethelwulf		858	860	—	2
ETHELBERT	Son of Ethelwulf		858	866	—	8
ETHELRED	Son of Ethelwulf		866	871	—	5
ALFRED THE GREAT	Son of Ethelwulf	Ealhswith of Gaini	871	899	52	28
EDWARD THE ELDER	Son of Alfred the Great	1st, Egwyn; 2nd, Elfed; 3rd, Eadgifu	899	925	55	26
ATHELSTAN	Eldest son of Edward the Elder (by 1)		925	940	45	15
EDMUND	Third son of Edward the Elder (by 3)	1st, Elgiu; 2nd, Ethelfled	940	946	25	6
EDRED	Fourth son of Edward the Elder (by 3)		946	955	32	9
EDWY	Son of Edmund (by 1)	1st, Ethelfled; 2nd, Elfthryth	955	959	18	3
EDGAR	Second son of Edmund (by 1)		959	975	32	17
EDWARD THE MARTYR	Son of Edgar (by 1)		975	978	17	4
ETHELRED II	Younger son of Edgar (by 2)	1st, Elfgifu; 2nd, Emma, dau. of Richard, Duke of Normandy	978	1016	48	37
EDMUND IRONSIDE	Eldest son of Ethelred II (by 1)	1st, Elfgifu of Deira; 2nd, Emma, widow of Ethelred II	1016	1016	27	0
CANUTE THE DANE	By conquest and election		1017	1035	40	18
HAROLD I	Son of Canute (by 1)		1035	1040	—	5
HARDICANUTE	Son of Canute (by 2)		1040	1042	24	2
EDWARD THE CONFESSOR	Son of Ethelred II (by 2)	Edith, dau. of Earl Godwin	1042	1066	62	24
HAROLD II	Son of Earl Godwin		1066	1066	44	0
	The House of Normandy					
WILLIAM I	Obtained the Crown by conquest	Matilda, dau. of Baldwin, Count of Flanders	1066	1087	60	21
WILLIAM II	Third son of William I	(Died unmarried)	1087	1100	43	13
HENRY I	Youngest son of William I	1st Matilda, dau. of Malcolm Canmore, K. of Scotland; 2nd Adelicia, dau. of Godfrey, D. of Louvaine	1100	1135	67	35
STEPHEN	Third son of Stephen, Count of Blois, by Adela, fourth dau. of William I	Matilda, dau. of Eustace, Count of Boulogne	1135	1154	50	19
	The House of Plantagenet					
HENRY II	Son of Geoffrey Plantagenet by Matilda, only dau. of Henry I; his grandmother, Matilda of Scotland, was a lineal descendant of Alfred and Egbert.	Eleanor, dau. of Guienne and divorced Queen of Louis VII of France	1154	1189	56	35
RICHARD I	Eldest surviving son of Henry II	Berengaria, dau. of Sancho VI, K. of Navarre	1189	1199	42	10
JOHN	Sixth and youngest son of Henry II	1st Avisa, dau. of E. of Gloucester, divorced upon grounds of consanguinity; 2nd Isabella dau. of Aymer, Count of Angoulême	1199	1216	50	17
HENRY III	Elder son of John	Eleanor, dau. of Raymond, Count of Provence	1216	1272	65	56
EDWARD I	Eldest surviving son of Henry III	1st Eleanor, dau. of Ferdinand III, K. of Castile; 2nd Margaret, dau. of Philip III, the Hardy, K. of France	1272	1307	68	35
EDWARD II	Eldest surviving son of Edward I	Isabella, dau. of Philip IV, the Fair, K. of France	1307	1327	43	20

Name	DYNASTY	MARRIED	Access.	Died	Age	Rgnd.
						Yrs.
EDWARD III	Eldest son of Edward II	Philippa, dau. of William, Count of Holland and Hainault.	1327	1377	65	50
RICHARD II	Son of the Black Prince, eldest son of Edward III	1st Anne, dau. of Emp. Charles IV; 2nd Isabel, dau. of Charles VI of France.	1377	dep. 1399 (d. 1400)	34	22
	The House of Lancaster					
HENRY IV	Son of John of Gaunt, 4th son of Edward III	1st Mary de Bohun, dau... of the E. of Hereford; 2nd Joanna of Navarre, widow of John de Montfor-, D. of Brittany.	1399	1413	47	13
HENRY V	Eldest surviving son of Henry IV	Katherine, dau. of Charles VI, K. of France	1413	1422	34	9
HENRY VI	Only son of Henry V (died 1471)	Margaret of Anjou, dau. of René, D. of Anjou. ..	1422	dep. 1461	49	39
	The House of York					
EDWARD IV	Son of Richard, grandson of Edmund, fifth son of Edward III; and of Anne, great-grand-daughter of Lionel, third son of Edward III	Elizabeth Widvile (or Woodville), dau. of Sir Richard Widvile and widow of Sir John Grey of Groby.	1461	1483	41	22
EDWARD V	Eldest son of Edward IV	(Died unmarried)	1483	1483	13	75 days
RICHARD III	Younger brother of Edward IV	Anne, dau. of the E. of Warwick, and widow of Edward, Prince of Wales, son of Henry VI	1483	1485	32	2
	The House of Tudor					
HENRY VII	Son of Edmund, eldest son of Owen Tudor, by Katherine, widow of Henry V; his mother, Margaret Beaufort, was great-grand-daughter of John of Gaunt	Elizabeth, dau. of Edward IV	1485	1509	53	24
HENRY VIII	Only surviving son of Henry VII	1st Katherine of Aragon, widow of his elder brother Arthur, (divorced); 2nd Anne, dau. of Sir Thomas Boleyn, (beheaded); 3rd Jane, dau. of Sir John Seymour, (died in childbirth of a son, aft. Edward VI); 4th Anne, sister of William, D. of Cleves, (divorced); 5th Catherine Howard niece of the Duke of Norfolk, (beheaded) 6th Catherine, dau. of Sir Thomas Parr and widow of Edward Nevill, Lord Latimer.	1509	1547	56	38
EDWARD VI	Son of Henry VIII by Jane Seymour	(Died unmarried)	1547	1553	16	6
JANE	Grand-daughter of Mary, younger sister of Henry VIII, (beheaded Feb. 12, 1554).	Lord Guildford Dudley	1553	1554	17	14 days
MARY I	Daughter of Henry VIII by Katherine of Aragon	Philip II of Spain	1553	1558	43	5
ELIZABETH I	Daughter of Henry VIII by Anne Boleyn	(Died unmarried)	1558	1603	69	44

BRITISH KINGS AND QUEENS FROM 1603

Name	DYNASTY	MARRIED	Access.	Died	Age	Rgnd.
						Yrs.
JAMES I (VI OF SCOT.)	*The House of Stuart* Son of Mary, Queen of Scots, grand-daughter of James IV and Margaret, daughter of Henry VII.	Anne, dau. of Frederick II of Denmark	1603	1625	59	22
CHARLES I	Only surviving son of James I	Henrietta-Maria, dau. of Henry IV of France	1625	Beh. 1649	48	24
	Commonwealth declared May 19, 1649 *Oliver Cromwell, Lord Protector, 1653–8: Richard Cromwell, Lord Protector, 1658–9*					
CHARLES II	Eldest son of Charles I (restored 1660)	The Infanta Catharine of Portugal, dau. of John IV and sister of Alphonso VI.	1649	1685	55	36
JAMES II (VII OF SCOT.)	Second son of Charles I (Interregnum, Dec. 11, 1688—Feb. 13, 1689)	1st Lady Anne Hyde, dau. of Edward, E. of Clarendon, who died before James ascended the throne; 2nd Mary Beatrice Eleanor d'Este, dau. of Alphonso, D. of Modena.	1685	dep. 1688 (d. 1701)	68	3
WILLIAM III and MARY II	Son of William, Prince of Orange and grandson of Charles I. Eldest daughter of James II	}	1689	{1702 1694}	51 33	13 6
ANNE	Second daughter of James II	Prince George of Denmark	1702	1714	49	12
GEORGE I	*The House of Hanover* Son of Elector of Hanover, by Sophia, daughter of Elizabeth, daughter of James I	Sophia, dau. of George William, D. of Celle.	1714	1727	67	13
GEORGE II	Only son of George I	Wilhelmina Caroline, dau. of John Frederick, Margrave of Brandenburg-Anspach.	1727	1760	77	33
GEORGE III	Grandson of George II	Charlotte Sophia, dau. of Charles Lewis Frederick, D. of Mecklenburg-Strelitz	1760	1820	81	59
GEORGE IV	Eldest son of George III (Regent from February 5, 1811)	Caroline, dau. of Charles William Ferdinand, D. of Brunswick-Wolfenbuttel.	1820	1830	67	10
WILLIAM IV	Third son of George III	Adelaide, dau. of George Frederick Charles, D. of Saxe-Meiningen.	1830	1837	71	7
VICTORIA	Daughter of Edward, 4th son of George III	Francis Albert Augustus Charles Emmanuel, D. of Saxe, Pr. of Saxe-Cobourg and Gotha.	1837	1901	81	63
EDWARD VII	*The House of Saxe-Coburg* Eldest son of Victoria	Alexandra, dau. of Christian IX, K. of Denmark	1901	1910	68	9
GEORGE V	*The House of Windsor* Surviving son of Edward VII	Victoria Mary, dau. of Francis, D. of Teck.	1910	1936	70	25
EDWARD VIII	Eldest son of George V (abdicated 1936)	Mrs. Wallis Warfield (after abdication)	1936	1972	77	325 days
GEORGE VI	Second son of George V	Lady Elizabeth Angela Marguerite Bowes-Lyon, dau. of the 14th Earl of Strathmore and Kinghorne (HER MAJESTY QUEEN ELIZABETH THE QUEEN MOTHER).	1936	1952	56	15
ELIZABETH II	Elder daughter of George VI	Philip, son of Prince Andrew of Greece (H.R.H. THE DUKE OF EDINBURGH).	1952	WHOM GOD PRESERVE.		

SCOTTISH KINGS AND QUEENS A.D. 1057 to 1603

Name	SOVEREIGN	MARRIED	Access.	Died
MALCOLM III (CANMORE)	Son of Duncan I	1st Ingibiorg, widow of Thorfinn, Earl of Orkney; 2nd Margaret, sister of Edgar the Atheling.	1057	1093
DONALD BÁN	Brother of Malcolm Canmore		1093	—
DUNCAN II	Son of Malcolm Canmore, by first marriage		1094	1094
DONALD BÁN	(Restored)		1094	1097
EDGAR	Son of Malcolm Canmore, by second marriage	(Died unmarried)	1097	1107
ALEXANDER I	Son of Malcolm Canmore	Sybilla, natural daughter of Henry I of England	1107	1124
DAVID I	Son of Malcolm Canmore	Matilda, daughter of Waltheof, Earl of Northumbria widow of Simon, Earl of Northampton	1124	1153
MALCOLM IV (THE MAIDEN)	Son of Henry, eldest son of David I	(Died unmarried)	1153	1165
WILLIAM I (THE LION)	Brother of Malcolm the Maiden	Ermengarde, daughter of Richard, Viscount of Beaumont	1165	1214
ALEXANDER II	Son of William the Lion	1st Joanna, daughter of King John; 2nd Mary, daughter of Ingelram de Coucy (*Picardy*)	1214	1249
ALEXANDER III	Son of Alexander II, by second marriage	1st Margaret, daughter of Henry III of England; 2nd Joleta, daughter of the Count de Dreux	1249	1286
MARGARET (THE MAID OF NORWAY)	Daughter of Eric II of Norway, grand-daughter of Alexander III.	(Died unmarried)	1286	1290
JOHN BALIOL	Grandson of eldest daughter of David, Earl of Huntingdon, brother of William the Lion		1292	1296
ROBERT I (BRUCE)	Great-grandson of 2nd daughter of David, Earl of Huntingdon, brother of William the Lion	1st Isabella, daughter of Donald, Earl of Mar; 2nd Elizabeth de Burgh, sister of Earl of Ulster.	1306	1329
DAVID II	Son of Robert I, by second marriage	1st Joanna, daughter of Edward II of England; 2nd Margaret, widow of Sir John Logie (divorced, 1369).	1329	1371
ROBERT II (STEWART)	Son of Marjorie, daughter of Robert I by first marriage, and Walter the Steward.	1st Elizabeth, dau. of Sir Robert Mure (or More) of Rowallan; 2nd Euphemia, dau., of Hugh, Earl of Ross, widow of John, Earl of Moray.	1371	1390
ROBERT III	(John, Earl of Carrick) son of Robert II	Annabella, daughter of Sir John Drummond of Stobhall, niece of Margaret Logie.	1390	1406
JAMES I	Son of Robert III	Jane Beaufort, daughter of John, Earl of Somerset, 4th son of John of Gaunt and grandson of Edward III of England.	1406	1437
JAMES II	Son of James I	Mary, daughter of Arnold, Duke of Gueldres	1437	1460
JAMES III	Eldest son of James II	Margaret, daughter of Christian I of Denmark, Norway and Sweden.	1460	1488
JAMES IV	Eldest son of James III	Margaret Tudor, daughter of Henry VII	1488	1513
JAMES V	Son of James IV	1st Madeleine, daughter of Francis I of France; 2nd Mary of Lorraine, daughter of Duc de Guise, widow of Duc de Longueville.	1513	1542
MARY	Daughter of James V, by second marriage	1st Francis, Dauphin of France; 2nd Henry, Lord Darnley; 3rd James, Earl of Bothwell	1542	1587
JAMES VI (Ascended the Throne of England 1603)	Son of Mary, by second marriage	Anne, daughter of Frederick II of Denmark	1567	1625

WELSH SOVEREIGNS AND PRINCES

WALES was ruled by Sovereign Princes from the "earliest times" until the death of Llywelyn in 1282. The first English Prince of Wales was the son of Edward I, and was born in Caernarvon town on April 25, 1284. According to a discredited legend, he was presented to the Welsh chieftains as their Prince, in fulfilment of a promise that they should have a Prince who "could not speak a word of English" and should be native born. This son, who afterwards became Edward II, was created "Prince of Wales and Earl of Chester" at the famous Lincoln Parliament on February 7, 1301. The title Prince of Wales is borne after individual conferment and is not inherited at birth, though some Princes have been declared and styled Prince of Wales but never formally so created (s.). The title was conferred on Prince Charles by Her Majesty the Queen on July 26, 1958. He was invested at Caernarvon on July 1, 1969.

Independent Princes, A.D. 844 to 1282

Rhodri the Great	844–878
Anarawd, son of Rhodri	878–916
Hywel Dda, the Good	916–950
Iago ab Idwal (or Ieuaf)	950–979
Hywel ab Ieuaf, the Bad	979–985
Cadwallon, his brother	985–986
Maredudd ab Owain ap Hywel Dda	986–999
Cynan ap Hywel ab Ieuaf	999–1008
Llywelyn ap Seisyll	1018–1023
Iago ab Idwal ap Meurig	1023–1039
Gruffydd ap Llywelyn ap Seisyll	1039–1063
Bleddyn ap Cynfyn	1063–1075
Trahaern ap Caradog	1075–1081
Gruffydd ap Cynan ab Iago	1081–1137
Owain Gwynedd	1137–1170
Dafydd ab Owain Gwynedd	1170–1194
Llywelyn Fawr, the Great	1194–1240
Dafydd ap Llywelyn	1240–1246
Llywelyn ap Gruffydd ap Llywelyn	1246–1282

English Princes, since A.D. 1301

Edward, b. 1284 (Edwd. II), cr. Pr. of Wales	1301
Edward the Black Prince, s. of Edward III	1343
Richard (Richard II), s. of the Black Prince	1376
Henry of Monmouth (Henry V)	1399
Edward of Westminster, son of Henry VI	1454
Edward of Westminster (Edward V)	1471
Edward, son of Richard III (d. 1484)	1483
Arthur Tudor, son of Henry VII	1489
Henry Tudor (Hen. VIII), s. of Henry VII	1504
Henry Stuart, son of James I (d. 1612)	1610
Charles Stuart (Charles I), s. of James I	1616
Charles (Charles II), son of Charles I (s.) c.	1638
James Francis Edward, "The Old Pretender" (d. 1766) (s.)	1688
George Augustus (Geo. II), s. of George I	1714
Frederick Lewis, s. of George II (d. 1751)	1729
George William Frederick (George III)	1751
George Augustus Frederick (George IV)	1762
Albert Edward (Edward VII)	1841
George (George V)	1901
Edward (Edward VIII)	1910
Charles Philip Arthur George	1958

THE FAMILY OF QUEEN VICTORIA

QUEEN VICTORIA *was born* May 24, 1819; *succeeded* to the Throne June 20, 1837; *married* Feb. 10, 1840 Albert, PRINCE CONSORT (*born* Aug. 26, 1819, *died* Dec. 14, 1861); *died* Jan. 22, 1901. Her Majesty had *issue*:—

1. H.R.H. Princess Victoria (*Princess Royal*) (1840–1901), *m.*, 1858, Frederick, *German Emperor* 1888. *Issue*:—

(1) H.I.M. William II (1859–1941), *German Emperor* 1888–1918, *m.*, 1st, 1881, Princess Augusta Victoria of Schleswig-Holstein-Sonderburg-Augustenburg (1858–1921), and 2nd, 1922, Princess Hermine of Reuss (1887–1947). *Issue*:—

(a) Prince William (1882–1951), (*Crown Prince* 1888–1918), *m.* Duchess Cecilia of Mecklenburg-Schwerin (d. 1954); *issue*:—Prince Wilhelm (1906–40); Prince Louis Ferdinand (b. 1907), *m.*, 1938, Grand Duchess Kira (*see* p. 145); Prince Hubertus (1909–50); Prince Frederick George (1911–66); Princess Alexandrine Irene (b. 1915); Princess Cecilia (1917–75).

(b) Prince Eitel Frederick (1883–1942), *m.* Duchess Sophie of Oldenburg (marriage dissolved 1926).

(c) Prince Adalbert (1884–1948), *m.* Duchess Adelaide of Saxe-Meiningen; *issue*:—Princess Victoria Marina (b. 1917); Prince William Victor (b. 1919).

(d) Prince Augustus William (1887–1949), *m.* Princess Alexandra of Schleswig-Glucksburg (marriage dissolved 1920); *issue*:—Prince Alexander (b. 1912).

(e) Prince Oscar (1888–1958), *m.* Countess von Ruppin; *issue*:—Prince Oscar (1915–39); Prince Burchard (b. 1917); Princess Herzeleide (b. 1918); Prince William (b. 1922).

(f) Prince Joachim (1890–1920), *m.* Princess Marie of Anhalt; *issue*:—Prince Karl Franz Joseph (1916–75).

(g) Princess Victoria (1892–1980), *m.*, 1913, Ernst, Duke of Brunswick; *issue*:—Prince Ernest (1914–87); Prince George (b. 1915); Princess Frederica (1917–81), *m.* Paul I, King of the Hellenes (*see* below); Prince Christian Oskar (1919–81); Prince Welf Heinrich (b. 1923).

(2) Princess Charlotte (1860–1919), *m.*, 1878, Bernhard, Duke of Saxe-Meiningen (1851–1914). *Issue*:—Princess Feodora (1879–1945), *m.*, 1898, the Prince Henry XXX of Reuss.

(3) Prince Henry (1862–1929), *m.*, 1888, Princess Irene of Hesse. *Issue*:—

(a) Prince Waldemar (1889–1945), *m.* Princess Calixsta of Lippe.

(b) Prince Sigismund (1896–1978), *m.* Princess Charlotte of Saxe-Altenberg; *issue*:—Princess Barbe (b. 1920); Prince Alfred (b. 1924).

(4) Princess Victoria (1866–1929), *m.*, 1st, 1890, Prince Adolphus of Schaumburg-Lippe, and 2nd, 1927, Alexander Zubkov.

(5) Prince Waldemar (1868–79).

(6) Princess Sophia (1870–1932), *m.*, 1889, Constantine I, *King of the Hellenes*, 1913–17, 1920–22. *Issue*:—

(a) George II (1890–1947), *King of the Hellenes* 1922–24 and 1935–47, *m.*, 1921, Princess Elisabeth of Roumania (marriage dissolved 1935).

(b) Alexander (1893–1920), *King of the Hellenes* 1917–20, *m.*, 1919, Aspasia Manos; *issue*:—Princess Alexandra (b. 1921), *m.*, 1944, King Petar II of Yugoslavia.

(c) Princess Helena (1896–1982), *m.*, 1921, King Carol of Roumania, (marriage dissolved 1928); *issue*:—Michael (b. 1921), *King of Roumania* 1927–30, 1940–47, *m.*, 1948, Princess Anne of Bourbon Parma, and has issue (five daughters).

(d) Paul I (1901–64), *King of the Hellenes* 1947–64, *m.*, 1938, Princess Frederica of Brunswick (*see* above); *issue*:—King Constantine (*Constantine XIII*), b. 1940, *m.*, 1964, Princess Anne-Marie of

Denmark, and has issue; Princess Sophia, b. 1938, m., 1962, Juan Carlos I, KING OF SPAIN, and has issue; Princess Irene, b. 1942.

(e) Princess Eirene (1904–74), m., 1939, 4th Duke of Aosta; issue:—Prince Amedeo (b. 1943).

(f) Princess Katherine (Lady Katherine Brandram) (b. 1913), m., 1947, Major R. C. A. Brandram; issue:—R. Paul G. A. Brandram (b. 1948).

(7) Princess Margarete (1872–1954), m., 1893, Prince Frederick Charles of Hesse (1863–1940). Issue:—

(a) Prince Frederick William (1893–1916).

(b) Prince Maximilian (1894–1914).

(c) Prince Philipp (1896–1980), m., 1925, Princess Mafalda of Italy; issue:—three sons and one daughter.

(d) Prince Wolfgang (b. 1896), m., 1st, 1924, Princess Marie of Baden, and 2nd, 1948, Ottilie Möller.

(e) Prince Richard (1901–).

(f) Prince Christoph (1901–43), m., 1930, Princess Sophie of Greece (see p. 146).

2. H.M. KING EDWARD VII (see p. 146).

3. H.R.H. Princess Alice (1843–78), m., 1862, Prince Louis, Grand Duke of Hesse, 1877–92. Issue:—

(1) Victoria Alberta (1863–1950), m., 1884, Admiral of the Fleet the Marquess of Milford Haven. Issue:—

(a) Alice (1885–1969), m., 1903, Prince Andrew of Greece, having issue (see p. 146).

(b) Louise (1889–1965), m., 1923, Gustav VI Adolf, King of Sweden 1950–73.

(c) George, 2nd Marquess of Milford Haven, G.C.V.O., (1892–1938), Capt. R.N., m., 1916, Countess Nadejda, daughter of Grand Duke Michael of Russia; issue:—Lady Tatiana (1917–88); David Michael, 3rd Marquess (1919–70).

(d) Louis, 1st Earl Mountbatten of Burma (1900–79), m., 1922, Edwina Ashley, daughter of Lord Mount Temple; issue:—Patricia (b. 1924), Pamela (b. 1929).

(2) Elizabeth (1864–1918), m., 1884, Grand Duke Sergius of Russia.

(3) Irene (1866–1953), m. Prince Henry of Prussia (see p. 144).

(4) Ernest Ludwig (1868–1937), Grand Duke of Hesse 1892–1918, m., 1st, 1894, Princess Victoria of Saxe-Coburg, and 2nd, 1905, Princess Eleonore of Solms-Hohensolmslich. Issue:—

(a) George, Grand Duke of Hesse (1906–37), m. Princess Cecilie of Greece and Denmark (see p. 146).

(b) Ludwig, Grand Duke of Hesse (1908–68), m., 1937, Margaret, daughter of 1st Lord Geddes.

(5) Frederick William (1870–73).

(6) Alix (Tsaritsa of Russia) (1872–1918), m., 1894, Nicholas II (Tsar of All the Russias), assassinated July 16, 1918. Issue:—

(a) Grand Duchess Olga (b. 1895).

(b) Grand Duchess Tatiana (b. 1897).

(c) Grand Duchess Marie (b. 1899).

(d) Grand Duchess Anastasia (b. 1901).

(e) Alexis, Tsarevitch of Russia (b. 1904).

(7) Mary (1874–1878).

4. Admiral of the Fleet H.R.H. Prince Alfred, Duke of Edinburgh (1844–1900), m., 1874, Grand Duchess Marie Alexandrovna of Russia; succeeded as Duke of Saxe-Coburg and Gotha Aug. 22, 1893. Issue:—

(1) Alfred (Prince of Saxe-Coburg) (1874–1899).

(2) Marie (1875–1938), m., 1893, King Ferdinand of Roumania. Issue:—

(a) Carol II (1893–1953), King of Roumania 1930–40, m., 1st, 1918, Joana Lambrino, 2nd, 1921, Princess Helena of Greece (see p. 144), and 3rd, 1947, Mrs. Elena Tampeanu.

(b) Elizabeth (1894–1956), m., 1921, King George II of the Hellenes (see p. 144).

(c) Marie (1900–61), m., 1922, King Alexander of Yugoslavia; issue:—Petar, King of Yugoslavia (1923–70); Prince Tomislav (b. 1928), m., 1957, Princess Margarita of Baden (see p. 146); Prince Andrej (b. 1929).

(d) Prince Nicolas (b. 1903).

(e) Princess Ileana (b. 1909), m., 1st, 1931, Archduke Anton of Austria, and 2nd, 1954, Dr. Stefan Issarescu; issue:—two sons and three daughters.

(f) Prince Mircea (1913–16).

(3) Victoria (1876–1936), m., 1st, 1894, Grand Duke of Hesse, and 2nd, 1905, the Grand Duke Cyril of Russia. Issue:—

(a) Marie (1907–51), m., 1925, Prince Friedrich Carl of Leiningen; issue:—three sons and three daughters.

(b) Kira Cyrillovna (1909–67), m., 1938, Prince Ludwig of Germany; issue:—four sons and two daughters.

(c) Vladimir Cyrillovitch (b. 1917), m., 1948, Princess Leonida Bagration-Moukhransky; issue:—a daughter.

(4) Alexandra (1878–1942), m., 1896, Prince of Hohenlohe Langenburg. Issue:—

(a) Gottfried (1897–1960), m., Princess Margarita of Greece (see p. 146); issue:—three sons and one daughter.

(b) Maria (1899–1967), m. Prince Frederick of Holstein-Glucksburg; issue:—one son and one daughter.

(c) Princess Alexandra (1901–63).

(d) Princess Irma (b. 1902).

(5) Princess Beatrice (1884–1966), m., 1909, Prince Alfonso, Infante of Spain. Issue:—

(a) Prince Alvaro (b. 1910), m. Carla Parodi-Delfino; issue:—two sons and two daughters.

(b) Prince Alonso (b. 1912).

(c) Prince Ataulfo (b. 1913).

5. H.R.H. Princess Helena Augusta Victoria (1846–1923), m., 1866, Prince Christian of Schleswig-Holstein. Issue:—

(1) Prince Christian Victor (1867–1900).

(2) Prince Albert (1869–1931).

(3) Princess Helena Victoria (1870–1948).

(4) Princess Marie Louise (1872–1956).

(5) Prince Harold (May 12–20, 1876).

6. H.R.H. Princess Louise (1848–1939), m., 1871, the Marquess of Lorne, afterwards 9th Duke of Argyll (1845–1914); without issue.

7. Field Marshal H.R.H. Prince Arthur, Duke of Connaught (1850–1942), m., 1879, Princess Louisa of Prussia (1860–1917). Issue:—

(1) Princess Margaret (1882–1920), m., 1905, Gustav VI Adolf, King of Sweden 1950–73. Issue:—

(a) Duke of Westerbotten (1906–47), m., 1932, Princess Sybil of Saxe-Coburg-Gotha; issue:—Carl XVI Gustaf, KING OF SWEDEN, and four daughters.

(b) Duke of Upland (Count Sigvard Bernadotte) (b. 1907).

(c) Princess Ingrid (Queen Mother of Denmark) (b. 1910), m., 1935, Frederick IX, King of Denmark (1899–72); issue:—Margrethe II, QUEEN OF DENMARK (b. 1940); Princess Benedikte (b. 1944); Princess Anne-Marie (Queen of the Hellenes) (b. 1946).

(d) Duke of Halland (b. 1912).

(e) Duke of Dalecarlia (Count Carl Bernadotte) (b. 1916).

(2) Prince Arthur (1883–1938), m., 1913, H.H. the Duchess of Fife (see p. 146).

(3) Princess Patricia (1886–1974), m., 1919, Adm. Hon. Sir Alexander Ramsay. Issue:—Hon. Alexander Ramsay of Mar (b. 1919), m., 1956, Hon. Flora Fraser (Lady Saltoun).

8. H.R.H. Prince Leopold, Duke of Albany (1853–84), m., 1882, Princess Helena of Waldeck (d. 1922). Issue:—

(1) Princess Alice (1883–1981), *m.*, 1904, Prince Alexander of Teck, afterwards *1st Earl of Athlone.* Issue:—
    (*a*) Lady May (*b.* 1906), *m.*, 1931, Sir Henry Abel-Smith, K.C.M.G., K.C.V.O., D.S.O.; *issue:*—one son and two daughters.
    (*b*) *Viscount Trematon* (1907–28).
(2) Charles Edward (1884–1954), *Duke of Saxe-Coburg-Gotha* 1900–18, *m.*, 1905, Princess Victoria of Schleswig-Holstein. *Issue:*—Prince Johann (1906–72); Princess Sibylle (1908–); Prince Dietmar (1909–); Princess Caroline (1912–83); Prince Frederick (*b.* 1918).

9. H.R.H. Princess Beatrice (1857–1944), *m.*, 1885, Prince Henry of Battenberg (1858–96). *Issue:*—
    (1) Alexander, *1st Marquess of Carisbrooke* (1886–1960), *m.*, 1917, Lady Irene Denison. *Issue:*—Lady Iris Mountbatten (1920–82).
    (2) Victoria Eugénie (1887–1969), *m.*, 1906, Alfonso XIII (1886–1941) *King of Spain* 1886–1931. *Issue:*—Prince Alfonso (1907–); Prince Jaime (1908–75); Princess Beatrice (*b.* 1909); Princess Maria (*b.* 1911); Prince Juan (*b.* 1913); Prince Gonzale (1914–).
    (3) Major Lord Leopold Mountbatten (1889–1922).
    (4) Maurice (1891–1914), died of wounds received in action.

THE FAMILY OF KING EDWARD VII

KING EDWARD VII, eldest son of Queen Victoria, *born* Nov. 9, 1841; *married* March 10, 1863, Her Royal Highness Princess Alexandra of Denmark (*Queen Alexandra, born* Dec. 1, 1844; *died* Nov. 20, 1925); *succeeded* to the Throne Jan. 22, 1901; *died* May 6, 1910. *Issue:*—

1. H.R.H. Prince Albert Victor, *Duke of Clarence and Avondale and Earl of Athlone* (1864–92).

2. H.M. KING GEORGE V (*see* below). Assumed by Royal Proclamation (June 17, 1917) for his House and Family as well as for all descendants in the male line of Queen Victoria who are subjects of these Realms, the name of WINDSOR; (*see* p. 147).

3. H.R.H. Louise, *Princess Royal* (1867–1931), *m.*, 1889, *1st Duke of Fife* (1849–1912). *Issue:*—
    (1) H.H. Princess Alexandra, Duchess of Fife (1891–1959), *m.*, 1913, H.R.H. Prince Arthur of Connaught (*see,* p. 145). *Issue:*—
        (*a*) Alastair Arthur, Duke of Connaught (1914–43).
    (2) H.H. Princess Maud (1893–1945), *m.*, 1923, 11th

Earl of Southesk. *Issue:*—
    (*a*) THE DUKE OF FIFE (*b.* 1929).

4. H.R.H. Princess Victoria (1868–1935).

5. H.R.H. Princess Maud (1869–1938), *m.*, 1896, Haakon VII, *King of Norway* 1905–57. *Issue:*—
    (1) H.M. Olav V., K.G., K.T., G.C.B., G.C.V.O., KING OF NORWAY (*b.* 1903), *m.*, 1929, H.R.H. Princess Marthe of Sweden (died 1954). Issue:—
        (*a*) H.R.H. Princess Ragnhild (*b.* 1930).
        (*b*) H.R.H. Princess Astrid (*b.* 1932).
        (*c*) H.R.H. Harald, Crown Prince of Norway, G.C.V.O. (*b.* 1937).

6. H.R.H. Prince Alexander John Charles Albert (April 6–7, 1871).

THE FAMILY OF PRINCE ANDREW OF GREECE

Prince Andrew of Greece (1882–1944), *m.*, 1903, Princess Alice of Battenberg (*H.R.H. Princess Andrew of Greece*), (1885–1969) (*see* p. 145); *issue:*—

(1) Princess Margarita (1905–1981), *m.*, 1931, Prince Gottfried of Hohenlohe-Langenburg (*see* p. 145); *issue:*—Prince Kraft, *b.* 1935, Princess Beatrix, *b.* 1936, Prince George, *b.* 1938, Prince Ruprecht and Prince Albrecht, *b.* 1944.
(2) Princess Theodora (1906–1969), *m.*, 1931, Prince Berthold of Baden (*d.* 1963); *issue:*—Princess Margarita, *b.* 1932 (*m.*, 1957, Prince Tomislav of Yugoslavia (*see* p. 145)), Prince Max, *b.* 1933, Prince Louis, *b.* 1937.
(3) Princess Cecilie (1911–1937), *m.*, George, Grand

Duke of Hesse (*see* p. 145), accidentally killed with husband and two sons, 1937.
(4) Princess Sophie, *b.* 1914, *m.*, 1st, 1930, Prince Christopher of Hesse (*see* p. 145); *issue:*—Princess Christina, *b.* 1933, Princess Dorothea, *b.* 1934, Prince Charles, *b.* 1937, Prince Rainer, *b.* 1939, Princess Clarissa, *b.* 1944; *m.*, 2nd, 1946, Prince George of Hanover; *issue:*—Prince George (*b.* 1949); Princess Friederike (*b.* 1954).
(5) Prince Philip (H.R.H. THE PRINCE PHILIP, DUKE OF EDINBURGH), *b.* 1921 (*see* p. 148).

THE FAMILY OF KING GEORGE V

KING GEORGE V., second son of King Edward VII., *born* June 3, 1865; *married* July 6, 1893, Her Serene Highness Princess Victoria Mary Augusta Louise Olga Pauline Claudine Agnes (*Queen Mary, born* May 26, 1867; *died* March 24, 1953); *succeeded* to the Throne May 6, 1910; *died* Jan. 20, 1936. *Issue:*—

H.R.H. The Duke of Windsor (Edward Albert Christian George Andrew Patrick David), *born* June 23, 1894, *succeeded* to the Throne as KING EDWARD VIII., Jan. 20, 1936; *abdicated* Dec. 11, 1936; *married* June 3, 1937, Mrs. Wallis Warfield (Her Grace The Duchess of Windsor, *born* June 19, 1896; *died* April 24, 1986), *died* May 28, 1972.

H.M. KING GEORGE VI. (Albert Frederick Arthur George) *born* at York Cottage, Sandringham, Dec. 14, 1895; *married* April 26, 1923, Lady Elizabeth Bowes-Lyon (HER MAJESTY QUEEN ELIZABETH THE QUEEN MOTHER), daughter of the 14th Earl of Strathmore and Kinghorne, *succeeded* to the throne Dec. 11, 1936; *died* Feb. 6, 1952, having had issue (*see* pp. 147 and 149).

H.R.H. The Princess Royal (Victoria Alexandra Alice MARY), *born* April 25, 1897, *married* Feb. 28, 1922, the 6th Earl of Harewood (*born* Sept. 9, 1882; *died* May 24, 1947), *died* Mar. 28, 1965, leaving issue:—
    (1) George Henry Hubert Lascelles, 7TH EARL OF HAREWOOD, K.B.E., *born* Feb. 7, 1923; *married* 1st, Sept. 29, 1949, Maria (Marion) Stein (marriage dissolved 1967); *issue,* (i) David Henry George, Viscount Lascelles, *born* Oct. 21, 1950; (ii) James Edward, *born* Oct. 5, 1953; (iii) Robert Jeremy Hugh, *born* Feb. 14, 1955; 2nd, July 31, 1967, Mrs. Patricia Tuckwell; *issue,* Mark Hubert, *born* July 5, 1964.

(2) Gerald David Lascelles, *born* Aug. 21, 1924, *married* 1st, July 15, 1952, Miss Angela Dowding (marriage dissolved, 1978); *issue*, Henry Ulick, *born* May 19, 1953; 2nd, Nov. 17, 1978, Mrs. Elizabeth Colvin; *issue*, Martin David, born Feb. 9, 1962.

H.R.H. The Duke of Gloucester (Henry William Frederick Albert), Duke of Gloucester, Earl of Ulster and Baron Culloden, *born* March 31, 1900, *married* Nov. 6, 1935, Lady Alice Christabel Montagu-Douglas-Scott, daughter of the 7th Duke of Buccleuch (H.R.H. Princess Alice, Duchess of Gloucester, G.C.B., C.I., G.C.V.O., G.B.E., Grand Cordon of Al Kamal, Air Marshal, Colonel-in-Chief of The Royal Hussars (Prince of Wales's Own), The King's Own Scottish Borderers, Royal Corps of Transport, Royal Australian Corps of Transport, Royal New Zealand Corps of Transport, Deputy Colonel-in-Chief, The Royal Anglian Regt., Air Chief Commandant W.R.A.F., *born* Dec. 25, 1901); *died* June 10, 1974. Issue:
- (1) H.R.H. Prince William Henry Andrew Frederick, *born* Dec. 18, 1941; *accidentally killed* Aug. 28, 1972.
- (2) H.R.H. Prince Richard Alexander Walter George (H.R.H. The Duke of Gloucester), G.C.V.O., Colonel-in-Chief, The Gloucestershire Regiment, Royal Pioneer Corps, Honorary Colonel Royal Monmouthshire Royal Engineers (Militia), Grand Prior of the Order of St. John of Jerusalem. *Born* Aug. 26, 1944, *married* July 8, 1972, Birgitte Eva van Deurs (H.R.H. The Duchess of Gloucester), Colonel-in-Chief, Royal Army Educational Corps, Royal Australian Army Educational Corps, Royal New Zealand Educational Corps, and has issue, (i) Alexander Patrick Gregers Richard, Earl of Ulster, *born* Oct. 24, 1974, (ii) Davina Elizabeth Alice Benedikte (Lady Davina Windsor), *born* Nov. 19, 1977 and (iii) Rose Victoria Birgitte Louise (Lady Rose Windsor), *born* March 1, 1980. *Residences*—Kensington Palace, W.8.; Barnwell Manor, Peterborough.

H.R.H. The Duke of Kent (George Edward Alexander Edmund), Duke of Kent, Earl of St. Andrews and Baron Downpatrick, *born* Dec. 20, 1902, *married* Nov. 29, 1934, H.R.H. Princess Marina of Greece and Denmark (*born* Nov. 30, O.S., 1906; *died* Aug. 27, 1968); *killed on Active Service*, Aug. 25, 1942. Issue:—
- (1) H.R.H. Prince Edward George Nicholas Paul Patrick (H.R.H. The Duke of Kent), K.G., G.C.M.G., G.C.V.O., Personal A.D.C. to the Queen, Major General, Hon. Air Vice-Marshal, Colonel-in-Chief The Royal Regiment of Fusiliers, The Devonshire and Dorset Regiment, The Lorne Scots Regiment (Peel, Dufferin and Hamilton Regiment), Colonel Scots Guards. *Born* Oct. 9, 1935, *married* June 8, 1961, Katharine Lucy Mary Worsley (H.R.H. The Duchess of Kent, G.C.V.O., *born* Feb. 22, 1933), Hon. Major General, Colonel-in-Chief 4th/7th Royal Dragoon Guards, The Prince of Wales's Own Regiment of Yorkshire, Army Catering Corps, Controller Commandant Women's Royal Army Corps, Hon. Colonel The Yorkshire Volunteers, daughter of Sir William Worsley, Bt., and has issue, (i) George Philip Nicholas, Earl of St. Andrews, *born* June 26, 1962, *married* Jan. 9, 1988, Sylvana Tomaselli; (ii) Helen Marina Lucy (Lady Helen Windsor), *born* April 28, 1964; (iii) Nicholas Charles Edward Jonathan (Lord Nicholas Windsor), *born* July 25, 1970. *Residences*—York House, St. James's Palace, S.W.1.; Anmer Hall, Norfolk.
- (2) H.R.H. Princess Alexandra Helen Elizabeth Olga Christabel (H.R.H. Princess Alexandra, the Hon. Mrs. Angus Ogilvy), G.C.V.O., Colonel-in-Chief, 17th/21st Lancers, The King's Own Royal Border Regiment, The Queen's Own Rifles of Canada, The Canadian Scottish Regiment (Princess Mary's), Deputy Colonel-in-Chief The Light Infantry, Deputy Hon. Colonel The Royal Yeomanry, Patron and Air Chief Commandant Princess Mary's Royal Air Force Nursing Service, Patron Queen Alexandra's Royal Naval Nursing Service. *Born* Dec. 25, 1936, *married* April 24, 1963, Hon. Angus Ogilvy, 2nd son of the 12th Earl of Airlie (*born* Sept. 14, 1928) and has issue, (i) James Robert Bruce, *born* Feb. 29, 1964, *married* July 30, 1988, Miss Julia Rawlinson; and (ii) Marina Victoria Alexandra, *born* July 31, 1966. *Residence*—Thatched House Lodge, Richmond Park, Surrey. *Office*—22 Friary Court, St. James's Palace, SW1A 1BJ.
- (3) H.R.H. Prince Michael George Charles Franklin (H.R.H. Prince Michael of Kent), *born* July 4, 1942, *married* June 30, 1978, Baroness Marie-Christine Agnes Hedwig Ida von Reibnitz (H.R.H. Princess Michael of Kent), and has issue, (i) Frederick Michael George David Louis (Lord Frederick Windsor), *born* April 6, 1979; and (ii) Gabriella Marina Alexandra Ophelia (Lady Gabriella Windsor), *born* April 23, 1981. *Residences*—Kensington Palace, W.8.; Nether Lypiatt Manor, Stroud, Glos.

H.R.H. Prince John Charles Francis, *born* July 12, 1905; *died* Jan. 18, 1919.

THE HOUSE OF WINDSOR

Her Most Excellent Majesty **ELIZABETH THE SECOND** (Elizabeth Alexandra Mary of Windsor) by the Grace of God, of the United Kingdom of Great Britain and Northern Ireland and of Her other Realms and Territories Queen, Head of the Commonwealth, Defender of the Faith, Sovereign of the British Orders of Knighthood and Sovereign Head of the Order of St. John, Lord High Admiral of the United Kingdom, Colonel-in-Chief of The Life Guards, The Blues and Royals (Royal Horse Guards and 1st Dragoons), The Royal Scots Dragoon Guards (Carabiniers and Greys), 16th/5th The Queen's Royal Lancers, Royal Tank Regiment, Corps of Royal Engineers, Grenadier Guards, Coldstream Guards, Scots Guards, Irish Guards, Welsh Guards, The Royal Welch Fusiliers, The Queen's Lancashire Regiment, The Argyll and Sutherland Highlanders (Princess Louise's), The Royal Green Jackets, Royal Army Ordnance Corps, Corps of Royal Military Police, The Queen's Own Mercian Yeomanry, The Duke of Lancaster's Own Yeomanry, Canadian Forces Military Engineers Branch, The King's Own Calgary Regiment, Royal 22e Regiment, Governor-General's Foot Guards, The Canadian Grenadier Guards, Le Régiment de la Chaudière, 2nd Bn. Royal New Brunswick Regt. (North Shore), The 48th Highlanders of Canada, The Argyll and Sutherland Highlanders of Canada (Princess Louise's), The Calgary Highlanders, Royal Australian Engineers, Royal Australian Infantry Corps, Royal Australian Army Ordnance Corps, Royal Australian Army Nursing Corps, The Corps of Royal New Zealand Engineers, Royal New Zealand Infantry Regiment, Royal New Zealand Army Ordnance Corps, Royal Malta Artillery, The Malawi Rifles, Captain-General of Royal Regiment of Artillery, The Honourable Artillery Company, Combined Cadet Force, Royal Regiment of Canadian Artillery, Royal Regiment of Australian Artillery, Royal Regiment of New Zealand Artillery, Royal New Zealand Armoured Corps, Air-Commodore-in-Chief, R. Aux.A.F., R.A.F. Regiment, Royal Observer Corps, Air Reserve (of Canada), Australian Citizen Air Force, Commandant-in-Chief, Royal Air Force College, Cranwell, Hon. Air Commodore, R.A.F. Marham,

Hon. Commissioner, Royal Canadian Mounted Police, Master of the Merchant Navy and Fishing Fleets, Head of the Civil Defence Corps.

Elder daughter of His late Majesty King George VI and of Her Majesty Queen Elizabeth the Queen Mother; *born* at 17 Bruton Street, London, W.1, April 21, 1926, *succeeded* to the throne February 6, 1952, *crowned* June 2, 1953; having *married*, November 20, 1947, in Westminster Abbey, Philip, Duke of Edinburgh, Earl of Merioneth and Baron Greenwich (H.R.H. THE PRINCE PHILIP, DUKE OF EDINBURGH, *born* June 10, 1921), K.G., K.T., O.M., G.B.E., P.C., Admiral of the Fleet, Field Marshal, Marshal of the Royal Air Force, Admiral of the Fleet, Royal Australian Navy, Field Marshal, Australian Military Forces, Marshal of the Royal Australian Air Force, Admiral of the Fleet, Royal New Zealand Navy, Field Marshal New Zealand Army, Marshal of the Royal New Zealand Air Force, Captain General, Royal Marines, Colonel-in-Chief, The Queen's Royal Irish Hussars, The Duke of Edinburgh's Royal Regiment (Berkshire and Wiltshire), The Queen's Own Highlanders (Seaforth and Camerons), Corps of Royal Electrical and Mechanical Engineers, Intelligence Corps, Army Cadet Force, The Royal Canadian Regiment, The Royal Hamilton Light Infantry (Wentworth Regt.), The Cameron Highlanders of Ottawa, The Queen's Own Cameron Highlanders of Canada, The Seaforth Highlanders of Canada, The Royal Canadian Army Cadets, The Royal Australian Electrical and Mechanical Engineers, The Australian Cadet Corps, Corps of Royal New Zealand Electrical and Mechanical Engineers, Colonel of Grenadier Guards, Hon. Colonel, Edinburgh and Heriot-Watt Universities Officers' Training Corps, The Trinidad and Tobago Regiment, Admiral, Royal Canadian Sea Cadets, Air Commodore-in-Chief, Royal New Zealand Air Force, Air Training Corps, Royal Canadian Air Cadets, Hon. Air Commodore, R.A.F. Kinloss, Master of the Corporation of Trinity House, Ranger of Windsor Park, Admiral Sea Cadet Corps, Hon. Colonel Leicester and Derbyshire Yeomanry PAQ Sqn. *See* p. 146.

Residences—Buckingham Palace, S.W.1.; Windsor Castle, Berks.; Balmoral Castle, Aberdeenshire; Sandringham, Norfolk.

CHILDREN OF HER MAJESTY

H.R.H. THE PRINCE OF WALES (CHARLES Philip Arthur George), K.G., K.T., G.C.B, P.C., A.D.C., Prince of Wales and Earl of Chester, Duke of Cornwall and Duke of Rothesay, Earl of Carrick and Baron Renfrew, Lord of the Isles and Great Steward of Scotland, Personal A.D.C. to the Queen, Great Master of the Order of the Bath, Commander Royal Navy, Wing Commander Royal Air Force, Colonel-in-Chief 5th Royal Inniskilling Dragoon Guards, The Cheshire Regiment, The Royal Regiment of Wales (24th/41st Foot), The Gordon Highlanders, The Parachute Regiment, 2nd King Edward VII's Own Gurkha Rifles (The Sirmoor Rifles), The Royal Canadian Dragoons, Lord Strathcona's Horse (Royal Canadians), Royal Regiment of Canada, Royal Winnipeg Rifles, Royal Australian Armoured Corps, The Royal Pacific Islands Regiment, Colonel, Welsh Guards, Air Commodore-in-Chief Royal New Zealand Air Force, Hon. Air Commodore, R.A.F. Brawdy.

Born November 14, 1948, *married* July 29, 1981, Lady Diana Frances Spencer (H.R.H. THE PRINCESS OF WALES, *born* July 1, 1961), Colonel-in-Chief The Royal Hampshire Regiment, The Princess of Wales's Own Regiment (of Canada), Hon. Air Commodore, R.A.F. Wittering, youngest daughter of the 8th Earl Spencer and the Hon. Mrs. Shand Kydd; and has issue, (i) William Arthur Philip Louis (H.R.H. PRINCE WILLIAM OF WALES), *born* June 21, 1982, and (ii) Henry Charles Albert David (H.R.H. PRINCE HENRY OF WALES), *born* Sept. 15, 1984.

Residences—Highgrove, Doughton, Tetbury, Glos.; Kensington Palace, W.8. *Office*—St. James's Palace, S.W.1.

H.R.H. THE PRINCESS ROYAL (ANNE Elizabeth Alice Louise), G.C.V.O. Chief Commandant Women's Royal Naval Service, Colonel-in-Chief 14th/20th King's Hussars, Royal Corps of Signals, The Royal Scots (The Royal Regiment), The Worcestershire and Sherwood Foresters Regiment (29th/45th Foot), 8th Canadian Hussars (Princess Louise's), Canadian Forces Communications and Electronics Branch, Grey and Simcoe Foresters Militia, The Royal Regina Rifle Regiment, Royal Australian Corps of Signals, Royal New Zealand Corps of Signals, Royal New Zealand Nursing Corps, Hon. Air Commodore, R.A.F. Lyneham, Commandant-in-Chief, (Ambulance and Nursing Cadets) St. John Ambulance, Commandant-in-Chief, Women's Transport Service (FANY), Dame of Justice, Order of St. John.

Born August 15, 1950, *married* Nov. 14, 1973, Capt. Mark Anthony Peter Phillips, C.V.O. (*born* Sept. 22, 1948), Personal A.D.C. to the Queen; and has issue, (i) Peter Mark Andrew, *born* Nov. 15, 1977, and (ii) Zara Anne Elizabeth, *born* May 15, 1981.

Residence—Gatcombe Park, Minchinhampton, Stroud, Glos. *Office*—Buckingham Palace, S.W.1.

H.R.H. THE DUKE OF YORK (ANDREW Albert Christian Edward), Duke of York, Earl of Inverness and Baron Killyleagh, C.V.O., Personal A.D.C. to the Queen, Lieutenant, Royal Navy. *Born* Feb. 19, 1960, *married* July 23, 1986, Miss Sarah Margaret Ferguson (H.R.H. THE DUCHESS OF YORK, *born* October 15, 1959), younger daughter of Major Ronald Ferguson and Mrs. Hector Barrantes; and has issue, Beatrice Elizabeth Mary (H.R.H. PRINCESS BEATRICE OF YORK), *born* Aug. 8, 1988.

H.R.H. PRINCE EDWARD ANTONY RICHARD LOUIS, *born* March 10, 1964.

MOTHER OF HER MAJESTY

H.M. QUEEN ELIZABETH THE QUEEN MOTHER (Elizabeth Angela Marguerite) (daughter of the 14th Earl of Strathmore and Kinghorne), Lady of the Garter, Lady of the Thistle, Order of the Crown of India, Grand Master of the Royal Victorian Order, Dame Grand Cross of the Order of the British Empire, Dame, Grand Cross of the Order of St. John, Royal Victorian Chain, Doctor of Civil Law, Doctor of Literature, Colonel-in-Chief 1st The Queen's Dragoon Guards, The Queen's Own Hussars, 9th/12th Royal Lancers (Prince of Wales's) The King's Regiment, The Royal Anglian Regiment, The Light Infantry, The Black Watch (Royal Highland Regiment), Royal Army Medical Corps, The Black Watch (Royal Highland Regiment) of Canada, The Toronto Scottish Regiment, Canadian Forces Medical Services, Royal Australian Army Medical Corps, Royal New Zealand Army Medical Corps, Hon. Colonel The Royal Yeomanry, The London Scottish, University of London Officers' Training Corps, Commandant-in-Chief R.A.F. Central Flying School, W.R.N.S., W.R.A.C.,

W.R.A.F., Patron St. Andrew's Ambulance Association, Commandant-in-Chief Nursing Corps and Divisions, Commandant-in-Chief (Nursing) St. John's Ambulance, Lord Warden and Admiral of the Cinque Ports and Constable of Dover Castle. *Born* August 4, 1900, *married* April 26, 1923, Prince Albert Frederick Arthur George of Windsor, Duke of York (*see* King GEORGE VI).

Residences.—Clarence House, St. James's Palace, S.W.1.; Royal Lodge, Windsor Great Park, Berks.; Castle of Mey, Caithness, Scotland.

SISTER OF HER MAJESTY

H.R.H. THE PRINCESS MARGARET, COUNTESS OF SNOWDON (Margaret Rose), C.I., G.C.V.O., Colonel-in-Chief, 15th/19th The King's Royal Hussars, The Royal Highland Fusiliers (Princess Margaret's Own Glasgow and Ayrshire Regiment), Queen Alexandra's Royal Army Nursing Corps, The Highland Fusiliers of Canada, The Princess Louise Fusiliers, The Bermuda Regiment, Deputy Colonel-in-Chief, The Royal Anglian Regiment, Hon. Air Commodore, R.A.F. Coningsby, Grand President, St. John Ambulance Association and Brigade, Dame Grand Cross of the Order of St. John of Jerusalem, President of the Girl Guides Association.

Born Aug. 21, 1930; *married* May 6, 1960 Anthony Charles Robert Armstrong-Jones, G.C.V.O. (*born* March 7, 1930, son of the late Ronald Armstrong-Jones, Q.C. and the Countess of Rosse, *created* Earl of Snowdon, 1961, Constable of Caernarvon Castle, *marriage dissolved*, 1978); and has issue, (i) David Albert Charles, Viscount Linley, *born* Nov. 3, 1961, and (ii) Sarah Frances Elizabeth (Lady Sarah Armstrong-Jones), *born* May 1, 1964.

Residence.—Kensington Palace, W.8.

Order of Succession to the Throne

1. H.R.H. The Prince of Wales; 2. H.R.H. Prince William of Wales; 3. H.R.H. Prince Henry of Wales; 4. H.R.H. The Duke of York; 5. H.R.H. Princess Beatrice of York; 6. H.R.H. Prince Edward; 7. H.R.H. The Princess Royal; 8. Master Peter Phillips; 9. Miss Zara Phillips; 10. H.R.H. Princess Margaret, Countess of Snowdon; 11. Viscount Linley; 12. Lady Sarah Armstrong-Jones; 13. H.R.H. the Duke of Gloucester; 14. Earl of Ulster; 15. Lady Davina Windsor; 16. Lady Rose Windsor; 17. H.R.H. The Duke of Kent; 18. Lord Nicholas Windsor; 19. Lady Helen Windsor; 20. Lord Frederick Windsor; 21. Lady Gabriella Windsor; 22. H.R.H. Princess Alexandra, Hon. Mrs. Angus Ogilvy; 23. Mr. James Ogilvy; 24. Miss Marina Ogilvy.

Precedence in England

THE SOVEREIGN.
The Prince Philip, Duke of Edinburgh.
The Prince of Wales.
The Sovereign's younger Sons.
The Sovereign's Grandsons.
The Sovereign's Cousins.
Archbishop of Canterbury.
Lord High Chancellor.
Archbishop of York.
The Prime Minister.
Lord President of the Council.
Speaker of the House of Commons.
Lord Privy Seal.
High Commissioners of Commonwealth Countries and Ambassadors of Foreign States.
Dukes, according to their Patents of Creation:
(1) Of England; (2) of Scotland; (3) of Great Britain; (4) of Ireland; (5) those created since the Union.
Ministers and Envoys.
Eldest sons of Dukes of Blood Royal.
Marquesses, in same order as Dukes.
Dukes' eldest Sons.
Earls, in same order as Dukes.
Younger sons of Dukes of Blood Royal.
Marquesses' eldest Sons.
Dukes' younger Sons.
Viscounts, in same order as Dukes.
Earls' eldest Sons.
Marquesses' younger Sons.
Bishops of London, Durham and Winchester.
All other English Bishops, according to their seniority of

Consecration.
Secretaries of State, if of the degree of a Baron.
Barons, in same order as Dukes.
Treasurer of H.M.'s Household.
Comptroller of H.M.'s Household.
Vice-Chamberlain of H.M.'s Household.
Secretaries of State under the degree of Baron.
Viscounts' eldest Sons.
Earls' younger Sons.
Barons' eldest Sons.
Knights of the Garter if Commoners.
Privy Counsellors if of no higher rank.
Chancellor of the Exchequer.
Chancellor of the Duchy of Lancaster.
Lord Chief Justice of England.
Master of the Rolls.
President of the Family Division.
Vice-Chancellor.
The Lords Justices of Appeal.
Judges of the High Court.
Vice-Chancellor of County Palatine of Lancaster.
Viscounts' younger Sons.
Barons' younger Sons.
Sons of Life Peers.
Baronets of either Kingdom, according to date of Patents.
Knights of the Thistle if Commoners.
Knights Grand Cross of the Bath.
Members of the Order of Merit.
Knights Grand Commanders of the Star of India.
Knights Grand Cross of St.

Michael and St. George.
Knights Grand Commanders of the Indian Empire.
Knights Grand Cross of the Royal Victorian Order.
Knights Grand Cross of Order of the British Empire.
Companions of Honour.
Knights Commanders of the above Orders.
Knights Bachelor.
Official Referees of The Supreme Court.
Circuit judges and judges of the Mayor's and City of London Court.
Companions and Commanders e.g. C.B.; C.S.I.; C.M.G.; C.I.E.; C.V.O.; C.B.E.; D.S.O.; L.V.O.; O.B.E.; I.S.O.
Eldest Sons of younger Sons of Peers.
Baronets' eldest Sons.
Eldest Sons of Knights in the same order as their Fathers.
M.V.O.; M.B.E.
Younger Sons of the younger Sons of Peers.
Baronets' younger Sons.
Younger Sons of Knights in the same order as their Fathers.
Naval, Military, Air, and other Esquires by Office.

WOMEN

Women take the same rank as their husbands or as their brothers; but the daughter of a Peer marrying a Commoner retains her title as Lady or Honourable.

THE QUEEN'S HOUSEHOLD

Lord Chamberlain, The Earl of Airlie, K.T., P.C., G.C.V.O.
Lord Steward, The Duke of Northumberland, K.G., P.C., G.C.V.O., T.D., F.R.S.
Master of the Horse, The Earl of Westmorland, K.C.V.O.
Treasurer of the Household, D. Hunt, M.B.E.
Comptroller of the Household, T. Garel-Jones, M.P.
Vice Chamberlain, M. Neubert, M.P.

Gold Stick, Maj.-Gen. Lord Michael Fitzalan Howard, G.C.V.O., C.B., C.B.E., M.C.; Gen. Sir Desmond Fitzpatrick, G.C.B., D.S.O., M.B.E., M.C.
Vice-Adm. of the United Kingdom, Adm. Sir Derek Empson, G.B.E., K.C.B.
Rear-Adm. of the United Kingdom, Adm. Sir Anthony Griffin, G.C.B.
First and Principal Naval Aide-de-Camp, Adm. Sir William Staveley, G.C.B.
Flag Aide de Camp, Adm. Sir John Woodward, K.C.B.
Aides-de-Camp General, Field Marshal Sir Nigel Bagnall, G.C.B., C.V.O., M.C.; Gen. Sir John Chapple, G.C.B., C.B.E.; Gen. Sir David Mostyn, K.C.B., C.B.E.
Air Aides-de-Camp, Marshal of the R.A.F. Sir David Craig, G.C.B., O.B.E.; Air Chief Marshal Sir Michael Knight, K.C.B., A.F.C.

Mistress of the Robes, The Duchess of Grafton, G.C.V.O.
Ladies of the Bedchamber, The Countess of Airlie, C.V.O.; The Lady Farnham, (temp.).
Extra Ladies of the Bedchamber, The Marchioness of Abergavenny, D.C.V.O.; The Countess of Cromer, C.V.O.
Women of the Bedchamber, Hon. Mary Morrison, D.C.V.O.; Lady Susan Hussey, D.C.V.O.; The Lady Elton, (temp.); Mrs. John Dugdale, D.C.V.O.
Extra Women of the Bedchamber, Mrs. John Woodroffe, C.V.O.; Lady Rose Baring, D.C.V.O., Mrs. Michael Wall, D.C.V.O.; Lady Abel Smith, D.C.V.O.; Mrs Robert de Pass, (temp.).
Extra Equerries, Vice-Adm. Sir Peter Ashmore, K.C.B., K.C.V.O., D.S.C.; Rear-Adm. the Earl Cairns, G.C.V.O., C.B.; Lt.-Col. The Lord Charteris of Amisfield, P.C., G.C.B., G.C.V.O., O.B.E., Q.S.O.; Vice-Adm. Sir Peter Dawnay, K.C.V.O., C.B., D.S.C.; Sir Edward Ford, K.C.B., K.C.V.O., E.R.D.; Rear-Adm. John Garnier, C.B.E., L.V.O.; Rear-Adm. Sir Paul Greening, K.C.V.O.; Brig. Sir Geoffrey Hardy-Roberts, K.C.V.O., C.B., C.B.E.; The Rt. Hon. Sir William Heseltine, G.C.V.O., K.C.B.; Rear-Adm. Sir Hugh Janion, K.C.V.O.; Lt.-Col. Sir John Johnston, G.C.V.O., M.C.; Air Cdre. Sir Dennis Mitchell, K.B.E., C.V.O., D.F.C., A.F.C.; The Lord Moore of Wolvercote G.C.B., G.C.V.O., C.M.G., Q.S.O.; Rear-Adm. Sir Patrick Morgan, K.C.V.O., C.B., D.S.C.; Lt.-Col. Sir Eric Penn, G.C.V.O., O.B.E., M.C.; Cdr. Sir Philip Row, K.C.V.O., O.B.E., R.N.; Air Vice-Marshal John Severne, L.V.O., O.B.E., A.F.C.; Group Capt. Peter Townsend, C.V.O., D.S.O., D.F.C.; Rear Adm. Sir Richard John Trowbridge, K.C.V.O.; Lt.-Col. G. West; Air Cdre. Sir Archie Little Winskill, K.C.V.O., C.B.E., D.F.C., A.E.

THE PRIVATE SECRETARY'S OFFICE
Buckingham Palace, S.W.1.

Private Secretary to The Queen, The Rt. Hon. Sir William Heseltine, G.C.V.O., K.C.B.
Deputy Private Secretary, R. Fellowes, C.B., L.V.O.
Assistant Private Secretary, K. Scott, C.M.G.
Press Secretary, R. Janvrin, L.V.O.
Deputy Press Secretary, J. Haslam, L.V.O.
Assistant Press Secretaries, G. Crawford; R. W. Arbiter.
Chief Clerk, Mrs P. G. Coulson, M.V.O.
Secretary to the Private Secretary, Miss E. Pearce, M.V.O.
Head of Information and Correspondence Section, Mrs. J. Bean, M.V.O.
Clerks, Mrs. J. Atwell, M.V.O.; Mrs. C. H. Good; Miss A. Kennedy; Miss K. E. Mays-Smith; J. Mordant, M.V.O.; Mrs. P. Bachelier.
Press Office, Miss K. McGrigor; Mrs. R. Murdo-Smith, L.V.O.; Mrs. A. Neal, L.V.O.
Lady in Waiting's Office, Mrs. D. Phillips; Mrs. A. Vince.

The Queen's Archives
Round Tower, Windsor Castle.

Keeper of The Queen's Archives, The Rt. Hon. Sir William Heseltine, G.C.V.O., K.C.B.
Assistant Keeper, O. Everett, L.V.O.
Registrar, Miss E. Cuthbert, M.V.O.
Assistant Registrars, Lady de Bellaigue; Miss P. Clark, L.V.O.
Curator of the Photographic Collection, Miss F. Dimond, M.V.O.

THE PRIVY PURSE AND TREASURER'S OFFICE
Buckingham Palace, S.W.1.

Keeper of the Privy Purse and Treasurer to The Queen, Major S. Blewitt, C.V.O.
Deputy Keeper of the Privy Purse and Deputy Treasurer, J. Parsons.
Chief Accountant and Paymaster, F. Mintram, L.V.O.
Personnel Officer, G. Franklin, L.V.O.
Administrative Officer, D. Waters, C.V.O.
Asst. Chief Accountant and Paymaster, D. Walker, L.V.O.
Assistant Personnel Officer, Mrs. D. Larkins.
Assistant Administrative Officer, Miss R. Ashton.
Superintendent of Public Enterprises, E. Hewlett.
Accountants, J. Atwell; Mrs. J. Maitland, L.V.O.; Mrs. D. Mowbray, M.V.O.
Clerks, Mrs. C. Auton, M.V.O.; Miss F. Juniper; Miss C. McCarthy; Miss N. Mooney; Miss H. Pearce; Miss G. Wickham, M.V.O.
Reprographic Unit, D. Groves; E. Williams.
Clerk of Stationery, W. Cotton.
Land Agent, Sandringham, J. Loyd, C.V.O.
Resident Factor, Balmoral, M. Leslie, L.V.O.

Royal Almonry

Lord High Almoner, The Rt. Rev. the Lord Bishop of St. Albans, L.V.O.
Hereditary Grand Almoner, The Marquess of Exeter.
Sub-Almoner, Rev. Canon A. D. Caesar, L.V.O., F.R.C.O.
Secretary, P. Wright, C.V.O.
Assistant Secretary, D. Waters, C.V.O.

THE LORD CHAMBERLAIN'S OFFICE
Buckingham Palace, S.W.1.

Comptroller, Lt.-Col. G. West, c.v.o.
Assistant Comptroller, Lt.-Col. M. Ross, o.b.e.
Secretary, J. E. P. Titman, c.v.o.
Assistant Secretary, P. D. Hartley, m.v.o.
State Invitations Assistant, Maj. J. C. Leech.
Registrar, Capt. D. Rankin-Hunt.
Clerks, Miss S. Hay, m.v.o.; Miss S. Bowring; Miss E. Paine; Miss E. Fellowes; Miss C. Britton; Mrs. J. Marsham.
Permanent Lords in Waiting, Lt. Col. The Lord Charteris of Amisfield, p.c., g.c.b., g.c.v.o., o.b.e., q.s.o.; The Lord Maclean, p.c., k.t., g.c.v.o., k.b.e.
Lords in Waiting, The Lord Somerleyton; The Viscount Boyne; The Viscount Long; The Lord Hesketh; The Earl of Dundee; The Earl of Arran; The Lord Strathclyde.
Gentlemen Ushers, C. Greig, c.v.o., c.b.e.; Lt.-Col. Sir Julian Paget, Bt., c.v.o.; Air Chief Marshal Sir Neville Stack, k.c.b., c.v.o., c.b.e., a.f.c.; Group Capt. J. Slessor; Maj. N. Chamberlayne-Macdonald, l.v.o., o.b.e.; Air Chief Marshal Sir Roy Austen-Smith, k.b.e., c.b., d.f.c.; Vice-Adm. Sir David Loram, k.c.b., l.v.o.; Capt. M. Barrow, d.s.o., r.n.; Capt. M. Fulford-Dobson, r.n.; Lt. Gen. Sir Richard Vickers, k.c.b., l.v.o., o.b.e.
Extra Gentlemen Ushers, Capt. A. Yates, l.v.o., r.n.; Maj. T. Harvey, c v o , n s o ; Air Vice-Marshal Sir Ranald Reid, k.c.b., d.s.o., m.c.; E. Butler, c.v.o.; Maj.-Gen. Sir Cyril Colquhoun, k.c.v.o., c.b., o.b.e.; Lt.-Col. Sir John Hugo, k.c.v.o., o.b.e.; Vice-Adm. Sir Ronald Brockman, k.c.b., c.s.i., c.i.e., c.v.o., c.b.e.; Air Marshal Sir Maurice Heath, k.b.e., c.b., c.v.o.; Maj.-Gen. Sir Peter Gillett, k.c.v.o., c.b., o.b.e.; Sir James Scholtens, k.c.v.o.; Sir Patrick O'Dea, k.c.v.o.; Brig.-Gen. S. Cooper, c.v.o., o.b.e., c.d.; Adm. Sir David Williams, g.c.b.; Capt. M. Tufnell, c.v.o., d.s.c., r.n.; H. Davis, c.v.o., c.m.; Maj.-Gen. R. Reid, c.v.o., m.c., c.d.; Lt.-Cdr. J. Holdsworth, c.v.o., o.b.e., r.n.; Capt. P. Blackman, r.a.n.; Col. G. Leigh, c.v.o., c.b.e.; Lt.-Cdr. Sir Russell Wood, k.c.v.o., v.r.d.; Col. D. Lawrence.
Gentleman Usher to the Sword of State, Gen. Sir Edward Burgess, k.c.b., o.b.e.
Gentleman Usher of the Black Rod, Air Chief Marshal Sir John Gingell, g.b.e., k.c.b.
Serjeants at Arms, F. Mintram, l.v.o.; J. E. P. Titman, c.v.o.; M. Tims, c.v.o.

Marshal of the Diplomatic Corps, Lt.-Gen. Sir John Richards, k.c.b.
Vice-Marshal, R. Hervey, c.m.g.

Constable & Governor of Windsor Castle, Adm. Sir David Hallifax, k.c.b., k.b.e.
Keeper of the Jewel House, Tower of London, Maj. Gen. Patrick MacLellan, c.b., m.b.e.
Master of The Queen's Music, Malcolm Williamson, c.b.e.
Poet Laureate, Ted Hughes, o.b.e.
Bargemaster, E. Hunt.
Keeper of the Swans, F. J. Turk, m.v.o.
Superintendent of the State Apartments, St. James's Palace, T. Taylor, m.v.o., m.b.e.

ROYAL COLLECTION DEPARTMENT
St. James's Palace, S.W.1.

Director of Royal Collection and Surveyor of The Queen's Works of Art, Sir Geoffrey de Bellaigue, k.c.v.o., f.s.a.
Surveyor of The Queen's Pictures, C. Lloyd.
Librarian, The Royal Library, Windsor Castle, O. Everett, l.v.o.
Deputy Surveyor of The Queen's Works of Art, H. Roberts.

Adviser for The Queen's Works of Art, Sir Francis Watson, k.c.v.o., f.s.a.
Librarian Emeritus, Sir Robin Mackworth-Young, g.c.v.o., f.s.a.
Curator of the Print Room, The Hon. Mrs. Roberts, m.v.o.
Registrar, M. Bishop, m.v.o.
Assistant to Registrar, Miss C. Hunter-Craig.
Assistant to Director, Mrs. J. Harland, m.v.o.
Personal Sec. to Director, Miss V. Colfox.
Assistants to Surveyor of The Queen's Pictures, C. Noble, Miss C. Crichton-Stuart.
Personal Sec. to Surveyor of Pictures, Miss C. Neville.
Sec. to Deputy Surveyor of Works of Art, Miss J. Impey.
Inventory Clerk, Miss S. de Falbe.

ASCOT OFFICE
St. James's Palace, S.W.1.

Her Majesty's Representative at Ascot, Col. Sir Piers Bengough, k.c.v.o., o.b.e.
Secretary, Miss L. Thompson-Royd.

ECCLESIASTICAL HOUSEHOLD
The College of Chaplains.

Clerk of the Closet, Rt. Rev. John Bickersteth.
Deputy Clerk of the Closet, Rev. Canon A. D. Caesar, l.v.o., f.r.c.o.
Chaplains to The Queen, Ven. E. J. G. Ward, l.v.o.; Rev. J. R. W. Stott; Rev. A. H. H. Harbottle, l.v.o.; Prof. Canon G. R. Dunstan, d.d., f.s.a.; Ven. D. N. Griffiths, r.d.; Canon A. Glendining, l.v.o.; Canon J. G. Grimwade; Canon D. Landreth, t.d.; Canon J. V. Bean; Canon P. A. Welsby, ph.d.; Canon P. W. Miller; Canon G. Carnell; Rev. K. Huxley; Ven. R. Simpson, l.v.o.; Ven. P. Ashford; Canon G. A. Elcoat; Canon D. C. Gray, t.d.; Canon S. Wilkinson; Canon J. Treadgold; Ven. D. Scott; Canon A. Russell, d.phil.; Canon E. James; Canon J. Hester; Rev. S. Pedley; Rev. D. Tonge; Rev. Canon C. Craston; Rev. Canon N. M. Ramm; Rev. Canon D. N. Hole; Rev. M. A. Moxon; Canon R. J. W. Bevan; Canon R. T. W. McDermid; Canon R. H. C. Lewis; Rev. D. J. Burgess; Rev. E. R. Ayerst; Rev. C. G. R. Hall; Rev. R. S. Clarke; Rev. Canon C. J. Hill; Rev. J. H. Williams.
Extra Chaplains, Canon J. S. D. Mansel, k.c.v.o., f.s.a.; Preb. S. A. Williams, c.v.o.

Chapels Royal

Dean of the Chapels Royal, The Bishop of London.
Sub-Dean of Chapels Royal, Rev. Canon A. D. Caesar, l.v.o., f.r.c.o.
Priests in Ordinary, Rev. W. Booth; Rev. A. Ford; Rev. G. Watkins.
Organist, Choirmaster and Composer, R. J. Popplewell, f.r.c.o., f.r.c.m.
Domestic Chaplain—Buckingham Palace, Rev. Canon A. D. Caesar, l.v.o., f.r.c.o.
Domestic Chaplain—Windsor Castle, The Dean of Windsor.
Domestic Chaplain—Sandringham, Canon G. R. Hall.
Chaplain—Royal Chapel, Windsor Great Park, Rev. Canon J. Treadgold.
Chaplain—Hampton Court Palace, Rev. Canon M. Moore.
Chaplain—Tower of London, Rev. J. F. M. Llewellyn, l.v.o.
Organist and Choirmaster—Hampton Court Palace, Gordon Reynolds, l.v.o., a.r.c.m.

MEDICAL HOUSEHOLD

Head of the Medical Household and Physician, Sir John Batten, k.c.v.o., m.d., f.r.c.p.

Physicians, A. M. Dawson, M.D., F.R.C.P.; R. W. Davey, M.B., B.S.
Serjeant Surgeon, W. Slack, M.Ch., F.R.C.S.
Surgeon Oculist, P. Holmes Sellors, B.M., B.Ch., F.R.C.S.
Surgeon Gynaecologist, G. D. Pinker, C.V.O., F.R.C.S.(Edin.), F.R.C.O.G.
Surgeon Dentist, N. A. Sturridge, C.V.O., L.D.S., B.D.S., D.D.S.
Orthopaedic Surgeon, D. R. Sweetnam, F.R.C.S.
Physician to the Household, R. Thompson, D.M., F.R.C.P.
Surgeon to the Household, B. Jackson, M.S., F.R.C.S.
Surgeon Oculist to the Household, T. J. ffytche, F.R.C.S., L.R.C.P.
Apothecary to The Queen and to the Household, N. R. Southward, L.V.O., M.B., B.chir., M.R.C.P.
Apothecary to the Household at Windsor, J. H. D. Briscoe, M.A., M.B., B.chir., M.R.C.G.P., D.obst., R.C.O.G.
Apothecary to the Household at Sandringham, H. K. Ford, L.V.O., M.B., F.R.C.G.P.
Coroner of The Queen's Household, J. Burton, M.B., B.S., M.R.C.S., L.R.C.P..

CENTRAL CHANCERY OF THE ORDERS OF KNIGHTHOOD
St. James's Palace, S.W.1.

Secretary, Maj. Gen. D. H. G. Rice, C.V.O., C.B.E.
Assistant Secretary, Sqn. Ldr. B. Sowerby, M.V.O.
Insignia Clerk, M. G. P. Kelly, L.V.O.
Clerks, J. McGurk, M.V.O.; Miss S. Koller; Miss R. A. Wells; Miss T. Perfect; Miss H. Weir; Mrs. L. Marshall.

The Honorable Corps of Gentlemen at Arms
St. James's Palace, S.W.1.

Captain, The Lord Denham, P.C.; *Lieutenant*, Maj. D. Jamieson, V.C.; *Standard Bearer*, Col. A. Way, M.C.; *Clerk of the Cheque & Adjutant*, Maj. T. St. Aubyn; *Harbinger*, Lt.-Col. R. Steele, M.B.E.

Gentlemen of the Corps

Brigadier, A. N. Breitmeyer.
Colonels, T. Hall, O.B.E.; Sir Piers Bengough, K.C.V.O., O.B.E.; Hon. N. Crossley, T.D.; T. Wilson; D. Fanshawe, O.B.E.; J. Baker.
Lieutenant-Colonels, P. Hodgson; W. S. P. Lithgow; Sir James Scott, Bt.; R. Mayfield, D.S.O.; B. Lockhart; Hon. P. H. Lewis.
Majors, Sir Richard Carne Rasch, Bt.; J. D. Dillon, D.S.C., R.M.; The Lord Suffield, M.C.; Sir Torquhil Matheson of Matheson, Bt.; F. J. H. Matheson; J. A. J. Nunn; Sir Philip Duncombe, Bt.; I. B. Ramsden, M.B.E.; M. J. Drummond-Brady; A. Arkwright; G. M. B. Colenso-Jones; T. Gooch, M.B.E.; J. B. B. Cockcroft.
Captain, The Lord Monteagle of Brandon.

The Queen's Bodyguard of the Yeoman of the Guard
St. James's Palace, S.W.1.

Captain, The Viscount Davidson; *Lieutenant*, Col. A. B. Pemberton, C.V.O., M.B.E.; *Clerk of the Cheque and Adjutant*, Col. G. W. Tufnell; *Ensign*, Lt.-Col. R. S. Longsdon; *Exons.*, Maj. C. Marriott; Maj. C. Enderby.

MASTER OF THE HOUSEHOLD'S DEPARTMENT
Board of Green Cloth
Buckingham Palace, S.W.1.

Master of the Household, Rear-Adm. Sir Paul Greening, K.C.V.O.
Deputy Master of the Household, Lt.-Col. B. A. Stewart-Wilson, L.V.O.
Assistants to the Master of the Household, M. D. Tims, C.V.O.; M. Parker.

Chief Clerk, A. Hancock, M.V.O.
Deputy to Assistant, M. Jephson, M.V.O.
Senior Clerks, M. Dibben; S. Stacey.
Clerks, Miss S. Derry, M.V.O.; Miss S. Fergus, M.V.O.; Miss J. Colville; Miss S. Crossley.
Superintendent, Windsor Castle, Maj. B. Eastwood, M.B.E.
Assistant to Superintendent, Capt. R. McClosky, M.V.O.
Palace Steward, C. S. Dickman, R.V.M.
Chief Housekeeper, Miss H. Colebrook.

ROYAL MEWS DEPARTMENT
Buckingham Palace, S.W.1.

Crown Equerry, Lt.-Col. S. Gilbart-Denham.
Equerries, Lt.-Col. B. A. Stewart-Wilson, L.V.O.; Lt.-Cdr. T. Laurence; Capt. A. Johnston (*temp.*).
Veterinary Surgeon, P. S. Dunn, L.V.O., M.R.C.V.S.
Supt. Royal Mews, Buckingham Palace, Maj. A. Smith, M.B.E.
Comptroller of Stores, Maj. L. Marsham, M.V.O..
Chief Clerk, P. Almond.
Deputy Chief Clerk, J. Spencer.
Office Keeper, P. M. Goodman, M.V.O.

HER MAJESTY'S HOUSEHOLD IN SCOTLAND

Hereditary Lord High Constable, The Earl of Erroll.
Hereditary Master of the Household, The Duke of Argyll.
Lord Lyon King of Arms, Malcolm R. Innes of Edinight, C.V.O., W.S.
Hereditary Bearer of the Royal Banner of Scotland, The Earl of Dundee.
Hereditary Bearer of the Scottish National Flag, The Earl of Lauderdale.
Hereditary Keepers:—
Holyrood, The Duke of Hamilton and Brandon.
Falkland, N. J. Crichton-Stuart.
Stirling, The Earl of Mar and Kellie.
Dunstaffnage, The Duke of Argyll.
Hereditary Carver, Sir Ralph Anstruther, K.C.V.O., M.C.
Keeper of Dumbarton Castle, Brig. A. S. Pearson, C.B., D.S.O., O.B.E., M.C., T.D.
Governor of Edinburgh Castle, Lt.-Gen. Sir John MacMillan, K.C.B.
Dean of the Order of the Thistle, The Very Rev. Prof. J. McIntyre, C.V.O., D.D., D.Litt, F.R.S.E.
Dean of the Chapel Royal, Very Rev. Prof. R. A. S. Barbour, M.C., D.D.
Chaplains in Ordinary, Very Rev. R. A. S. Barbour, M.C., D.D.; Rev. W. J. Morris, D.D., LL.D., Ph.D.; Rev. H. W. M. Cant; Rev. K. MacVicar, M.B.E., D.F.C., T.D.; Rev. A. J. C. Macfarlane; Rev. J. McLeod; Rev. G. I. Macmillan; Very Rev. W. B. Johnston, D.D.; Rev. M. D. Craig; Rev. W. B. R. Macmillan.
Extra Chaplains, Very Rev. the Lord MacLeod of Fuinary, M.C., D.D.; Very Rev. Prof. J. S. Stewart, D.D.; Rev. Prof. E. P. Dickie, M.C., D.D.; Very Rev. R. L. Small, C.B.E., D.D.; Very Rev. W. R. Sanderson, D.D.; Very Rev. R. W. V. Selby Wright, C.V.O., T.D., D.D., F.R.S.E., F.S.A.(scot.); Rev. T. J. T. Nicol, M.V.O., M.B.E., M.C., T.D.; Very Rev. G. T. H. Reid, M.C., D.D.; Very Rev. Prof. J. McIntyre, C.V.O., D.D., F.R.S.E.; Rev. C. Forrester-Paton.
Domestic Chaplain, Balmoral, Rev. J. A. K. Angus, T.D.
Historiographer, Prof. G. Donaldson, C.B.E., F.B.A., F.R.S.E.
Botanist, Prof. D. Henderson, C.B.E., F.R.S.E.
Painter and Limner, D. A. Donaldson, R.S.A., R.P.
Sculptor in Ordinary, Prof. E. Paolozzi.
Astronomer, Prof. M. S. Longair, Ph.D.

Physicians in Scotland, P. Brunt, M.D., F.R.C.P.; A. L. Muir, M.D., F.R.C.P.

Surgeons in Scotland, I. B. Macleod, M.B., ch.B., F.R.C.S.; J. Engeset, ch.M., F.R.C.S.

Extra Surgeons in Scotland, Prof. Sir Charles Illingworth, C.B.E., M.D., F.R.C.S.Ed.; Prof. Sir Donald Douglas, M.B.E., ch.M., M.S., D.SC., F.R.C.S.

Apothecary to the Household at Balmoral, D. J. A. Glass, M.B., ch.B.

Apothecary to the Household at the Palace of Holyroodhouse, Dr. H. Gebbie, M.B., M.R.C.G.P.

THE QUEEN'S BODY GUARD FOR SCOTLAND

Royal Company of Archers.
Archers' Hall, Edinburgh.

Captain-General and Gold Stick for Scotland, Col. The Lord Clydesmuir, K.T., C.B., M.B.E., T.D.

Captains, Maj. The Lord Home of the Hirsel, K.T.; The Duke of Buccleuch and Queensberry, K.T., V.R.D.; Lt.-Col. Sir John Gilmour, Bt., D.S.O., T.D.

Lieutenants, Maj. Sir Hew Hamilton-Dalrymple, Bt., K.C.V.O.; Maj. The Earl of Wemyss and March, K.T.; The Earl of Airlie, K.T., G.C.V.O.; The Earl of Dalhousie, K.T., G.C.V.O., G.B.E., M.C.

Ensigns, Capt. Sir Iain Tennant, K.T.; Maj.-Gen. The Earl Cathcart, C.B., D.S.O., M.C.; Capt. N. E. F. Dalrymple-Hamilton, C.V.O., M.B.E., D.S.C., R.N.; The Marquess of Lothian, K.C.V.O.

Brigadiers, Cdre. Sir John Clerk of Penicuik, Bt., C.B.E., V.R.D.; The Earl of Elgin and Kincardine, K.T.; Col. G. R. Simpson, D.S.O., L.V.O., T.D.; Maj. D. H. Butter, M.C.; The Earl of Minto, O.B.E.; Maj.-Gen. Sir John Swinton, K.C.V.O., O.B.E.; Gen. Sir Michael Gow, G.C.B.; The Hon. Lord Elliott, M.C.; Maj. The Hon. L. H. C. Maclean; The Rt. Hon. George Younger, T.D., M.P.; Capt. G. Burnet, L.V.O.; The Marquess of Graham; Lt.-Gen. Sir Norman Arthur, K.C.B..

Adjutant, Maj. The Hon. L. H. C. Maclean.

Surgeon, Dr. M. D. L. Finlay, M.D.

Chaplain, Very Rev. R. Selby Wright, C.V.O., T.D., D.D., F.R.S.E.

President of the Council and Silver Stick for Scotland, Maj. Sir Hew Hamilton-Dalrymple, Bt., K.C.V.O.

Vice-President, The Earl of Dalhousie, K.T., G.C.V.O., G.B.E., M.C.

Secretary, Col. H. F. O. Bewsher, O.B.E..

Treasurer, R. A. G. Douglas-Miller.

HOUSEHOLD OF THE PRINCE PHILIP, DUKE OF EDINBURGH

Private Secretary and Treasurer, B. H. McGrath, C.V.O.

Assistant Private Secretary, Brig. C. Robertson.

Equerry, Maj. Sir Guy Acland, Bt.

Extra Equerries, J. B. V. Orr, C.V.O.; Sir Richard Davies, K.C.V.O., C.B.E.; Lord Buxton of Alsa.

Temporary Equerries, Capt. A. J. Fraser; Capt. M. O. M. Chitty.

Chief Clerk and Accountant, V. G. Jewell, M.V.O.

HOUSEHOLD OF QUEEN ELIZABETH THE QUEEN MOTHER

Lord Chamberlain, Maj. the Earl of Dalhousie, K.T., G.C.V.O., G.B.E., M.C.

Comptroller and Extra Equerry, Capt. Sir Alastair Aird, C.V.O.

Private Secretary and Equerry, Lt.-Col. Sir Martin Gilliat, G.C.V.O., M.B.E.

Treasurer and Equerry, Maj. Sir Ralph Anstruther, Bt., K.C.V.O., M.C.

Equerry, Maj. R. Seymour, L.V.O.

Press Secretary and Extra Equerry, Maj. A. J. S. Griffin, C.V.O.

Extra Equerry, The Lord Sinclair, L.V.O.

Equerry (Temp.), Capt. G. A. C. Bassett.

Apothecary to the Household, Dr. N. Southward, L.V.O., M.D., B.chir., M.R.C.P.

Surgeon-Apothecary to the Household (Royal Lodge, Windsor), Dr. J. Briscoe, M.R.C.G.P., D.obst., R.C.O.G.

Mistress of the Robes, The Dowager Duchess of Abercorn, G.C.V.O.

Ladies of the Bedchamber, The Dowager Viscountess Hambleden, D.C.V.O.; The Lady Grimthorpe, C.V.O.

Women of the Bedchamber, Ruth, Lady Fermoy, D.C.V.O., O.B.E.; Mrs Patrick Campbell-Preston, C.V.O.; Lady Elizabeth Basset, C.V.O.; Lady Angela Oswald.

Extra Women of the Bedchamber, Lady Victoria Wemyss, C.V.O.; Lady Jean Rankin, D.C.V.O.; Miss Jane Walker-Okeover

Clerk Comptroller, M. Blanch, L.V.O.

Clerk Accountant, J. P. Kyle, L.V.O.

Clerks, Mrs. R. Murphy, L.V.O.; Miss F. Fletcher, M.V.O.

HOUSEHOLD OF THE PRINCE AND PRINCESS OF WALES

Private Secretary and Treasurer to The Prince and Princess of Wales Sir John Riddell, Bt.

Deputy Private Secretary, D. Wright.

Assistant Private Secretary to The Prince of Wales, The Hon. Rupert Fairfax, M.V.O.

Assistant Private Secretary to The Prince and Princess of Wales, Cdr. R. J. Aylard, R.N.

Secretary to the Duchy of Cornwall and Keeper of the Records, D. Landale.

Equerry to The Prince of Wales, Maj. C. Lavender.

Extra Equerries to The Prince of Wales, The Hon. Edward Adeane, C.V.O.; Sqn. Ldr. Sir David Checketts, K.C.V.O.; G. J. Ward.

Lady in Waiting and Assistant Private Secretary to The Princess of Wales, Miss Anne Beckwith-Smith.

Equerry to The Princess of Wales, Lt. Cdr. P. D. C. J. Jephson, R.N.

Extra Ladies in Waiting, Mrs. George West; Viscountess Campden; Mrs. Max Pike; Miss Alexandra Loyd; The Hon. Mrs. Vivian Baring.

HOUSEHOLD OF THE DUKE AND DUCHESS OF YORK

Private Secretary and Equerry to The Duke and Duchess of York, Lt.-Col. S. O'Dwyer.

Equerry, Capt. G. W. McLean.

Ladies in Waiting, Mrs. John Spooner; Mrs. John Floyd.

HOUSEHOLD OF THE PRINCE EDWARD

Private Secretary and Equerry to the Prince Edward, Lt.-Col. S. O'Dwyer.

HOUSEHOLD OF THE PRINCESS ROYAL

Private Secretary, Lt.-Col. P. Gibbs.

Assistant Private Secretary, The Hon. Madeleine Dillon.

Ladies in Waiting, Mrs. Richard Carew Pole, L.V.O.; The Hon. Mrs. Legge-Bourke, L.V.O.; Mrs. Malcolm Wallace; Mrs. Timothy Holderness-Roddam; Mrs. Charles Ritchie.

Extra Ladies in Waiting, Mrs. Andrew Feilden, L.V.O.; Miss Victoria Legge-Bourke, L.V.O.; Mrs. Malcolm Innes; The Countess of Lichfield.

HOUSEHOLD OF THE PRINCESS MARGARET, COUNTESS OF SNOWDON

Private Secretary and Comptroller, The Lord Napier and Ettrick, C.V.O.

Personal Secretary, Miss M. Murray Brown, c.v.o.
Extra Ladies in Waiting, Lady Elizabeth Cavendish, L.V.O.; Mrs. Alastair Aird, L.V.O.; Mrs. Robin Benson, L.V.O.; Lady Juliet Townsend, L.V.O.; Mrs. Jane Stevens; The Hon. Mrs. Wills, L.V.O.; The Lady Glenconner; The Hon. Mrs. Whitehead, L.V.O.; The Countess Alexander of Tunis; Mrs. Elizabeth Blair.

HOUSEHOLD OF THE DUKE AND DUCHESS OF GLOUCESTER

Comptroller, Private Secretary and Equerry, Lt.-Col. Sir Simon Bland, K.C.V.O.
Secretary to The Duchess of Gloucester, Miss Suzanne Marland.
Ladies in Waiting, Mrs. Michael Wigley, L.V.O.; Mrs. Euan McCorquodale; Mrs. Howard Page.
Extra Lady in Waiting, Miss Jennifer Thomson.

HOUSEHOLD OF PRINCESS ALICE, DUCHESS OF GLOUCESTER

Comptroller, Private Secretary and Equerry, Lt.-Col. Sir Simon Bland, K.C.V.O.
Ladies in Waiting, Dame Jean Maxwell-Scott, D.C.V.O.; Mrs. Michael Harvey.
Extra Ladies in Waiting, Miss Dorothy Meynell, C.V.O.; Miss Diana Harrison; The Hon. Jane Walsh, L.V.O.; Miss Jane Egerton Warburton, L.V.O.

HOUSEHOLD OF THE DUKE AND DUCHESS OF KENT

Private Secretary, A. Palmer, C.M.G., C.V.O.
Ladies in Waiting, Mrs. Alan Henderson, C.V.O.; Mrs. David Napier, L.V.O.; Miss Sarah Partridge.
Extra Lady in Waiting, Mrs. Peter Wilmot-Sitwell.

HOUSEHOLD OF PRINCESS ALEXANDRA

Private Secretary and Extra Lady in Waiting, Miss Mona Mitchell, C.V.O.
Lady in Waiting, Lady Mary Mumford, C.V.O.
Extra Equerry, Maj. P. C. Clarke, C.V.O.
Extra Lady in Waiting, Mrs. Peter Afia.

HOUSEHOLD OF PRINCE AND PRINCESS MICHAEL OF KENT

Private Secretary, Cdr. M. Clarke.
Ladies in Waiting, The Hon. Mrs. Leatham; Miss Anne Frost.

THE QUEEN'S BIRTHDAY, 1989

The date for the observance of the Queen's Birthday in 1989 both at home and abroad will be Saturday, June 17.

ROYAL SALUTES

On the Anniversaries of the Birth, Accession and Coronation of the Sovereign and on the Anniversaries of the birth of H.M. the Queen Mother and H.R.H. the Duke of Edinburgh a salute of 62 guns is fired on the wharf at the Tower of London.

On extraordinary and triumphal occasions, such as on the occasion of the Sovereign opening, proroguing or dissolving Parliament in Person, or when passing through London in procession, except when otherwise ordered, 41 guns only are fired.

On the occasion of the birth of a Royal infant a salute of 41 guns is fired from the two Saluting Stations in London, i.e. Hyde Park and the Tower of London.

Constable of the Royal Palace and Fortress of London, Field Marshal Sir Roland Gibb, G.C.B., C.B.E., D.S.O., M.C.
Lieutenant of the Tower of London, Gen. Sir Peter Hudson, K.C.B., C.B.E.
Resident Governor and Keeper of the Jewel House, Maj.-Gen. A. P. W. MacLellan, C.B., M.B.E.
Master Gunner of St. James's Park, Lt.-Gen. Sir Thomas Morony, K.C.B., O.B.E.
Master Gunner within the Tower, Col. G. E. Codbold, T.D.

THE ROYAL ARMS

QUARTERLY.—1st and 4th *gules*, three lions passant guardant in pale *or* (*England*); 2nd *or*, a lion rampant within a double tressure flory counter-flory *gules* (*Scotland*); 3rd *azure*, a harp *or*, stringed *argent* (*Ireland*); the whole encircled with the Garter.

SUPPORTERS.—*Dexter*: a lion rampant guardant *or*, imperially crowned. *Sinister*: a unicorn *argent*, armed crined and unguled *or*, gorged with a coronet composed of crosses patées and fleurs de lis, a chain affixed passing between the forelegs and reflexed over the back.

BADGES.—The red and white rose united (*England*), a thistle (*Scotland*); a harp *or*, the strings *argent*, with a shamrock leaf *vert* (*Ireland*); upon a mount *vert*, a dragon passant wings elevated *gules* (*Wales*).

THE UNION FLAG

The national flag of the United Kingdom is the Union Flag, generally known as the Union Jack, the name deriving from the use of the Union Flag on the jack-staff of naval vessels. It is a combination of the cross of the patron saint of England, St. George (*cross gules in a field argent*), the cross of the patron saint of Scotland, St. Andrew (*saltire argent in a field azure*) and a cross similar to that of St. Patrick, patron saint of Ireland (*saltire gules in a field argent*). The Union Flag was first introduced in 1606 after the union of England and Scotland, the cross of St. Patrick being added in 1801.

ANNUITIES TO THE ROYAL FAMILY

The annuity payable to Her Majesty is known as the Civil List, and is payable out of the Consolidated Fund under the authority of a Civil List Act following the recommendation of a Parliamentary Select Committee.

The allocation for the calendar year 1988 was as follows:—

The Queen	£4,500,000
Queen Elizabeth The Queen Mother	390,300
The Duke of Edinburgh	217,700
Duke of York	86,500
Prince Edward	20,000
The Princess Royal	135,600
The Princess Margaret	132,100
Princess Alice, Duchess of Gloucester	53,500
*Duke of Gloucester	106,300
*Duke of Kent	143,500
*Princess Alexandra	136,800
	5,922,300
*Refunded by The Queen	386,600
Total	5,535,700

These figures combine the sums payable directly from the Consolidated Fund with the supplements provided by the Royal Trustees from the grant made to them in the vote for economic and financial administration in the Estimates.

THE FLYING OF FLAGS

Days for hoisting the Union Flag on Government Buildings (from 8 a.m. to sunset).

February 6 (1952).—Her Majesty's Accession.

February 19 (1960).—Birthday of The Duke of York.

March 1.—St. David's Day (in Wales only).

March 10 (1964).—Birthday of The Prince Edward.

March 13.—Commonwealth Day 1989.

April 21 (1926).—Birthday of Her Majesty the Queen.

April 23.—St. George's Day (in England only). Where a building has two or more flagstaffs the Cross of St. George may be flown in addition to the Union Jack but not in a superior position.

June 2 (1953).—Coronation Day.

June 10 (1921).—Birthday of The Duke of Edinburgh.

June 17.—Queen's Official Birthday, 1989.

July 1 (1961).—Birthday of The Princess of Wales.

Aug. 4 (1900).—Birthday of Her Majesty Queen Elizabeth the Queen Mother.

Aug. 15 (1950). Birthday of The Princess Royal.

Aug. 21 (1930).—Birthday of The Princess Margaret.

Nov. 12.—Remembrance Sunday, 1989.

Nov. 14 (1948).—Birthday of The Prince of Wales.

Nov. 20 (1947).—Her Majesty's Wedding Day.

Nov. 30.—St. Andrew's Day (in Scotland only).

And on the occasion of the opening and closing of Parliament by the Queen, flags should be flown on Government buildings in the Greater London area, whether or not Her Majesty performs the ceremony in person.

The only additions to the above list will be those notified to the Department of the Environment by Her Majesty's command and communicated by the Ministry to the other Departments. The list applies to all Government Buildings in London and elsewhere in the United Kingdom. In cases where it has been the practice to fly the Union Flag daily, e.g. on some Custom Houses, that practice may continue.

Flags will be flown at half-mast on the following occasions:...

(*a*) From the announcement of the death up to the funeral of the Sovereign, except on Proclamation Day, when they are hoisted right up from 11 A.M. to sunset.

(*b*) The funerals of members of the Royal Family, subject to special commands from Her Majesty in each case.

(*c*) The funerals of Foreign Rulers, subject to special commands from Her Majesty in each case.

(*d*) The funerals of Prime Ministers and ex-Prime Ministers of the United Kingdom.

(*e*) Other occasions by special command of Her Majesty.

On occasions when days for flying flags coincide with days for flying flags at half mast the following rules will be observed. Flags will be flown: (*a*) although a member of the Royal Family, or a near relative of the Royal Family, may be lying dead, unless special commands be received from Her Majesty to the contrary, and (*b*) although it may be the day of the funeral of a Foreign Ruler. If the body of a very distinguished subject is lying at a Government Office the flag may fly at half mast on that office until the body has left (provided it is a day on which the flag would fly) and then the flag is to be hoisted right up. On all other Government Buildings the flag will fly as usual.

The *Royal Standard* is only to be hoisted when the Queen is actually present in the building, and never when Her Majesty is passing in procession.

RED-LETTER DAYS

Scarlet Robes are worn by the Judges of the Queen's Bench Division on *Red-Letter Days*.

RED-LETTER DAYS AND STATE OCCASIONS, 1989.

Jan. 25. Conversion of St. Paul.	„ 14. St. Matthias.	*July* 25. St. James.
Feb. 2. Purification.	*June* 2. Coronation Day.	*Aug.* 4. Birthday of Queen Elizabeth the Queen Mother.
„ 6. Queen's Accession.	„ 10. Birthday of The Duke of Edinburgh.	
„ 8. Ash Wednesday.		*Oct.* 18. St. Luke.
Mar. 1. St. David.	„ 11. St. Barnabas.	„ 28. St. Simon and St. Jude.
„ 25. Annunciation.	„ 17. Queen's Official Birthday (1989).	*Nov.* 1. All Saints.
Apr. 21. Queen's Birthday.	„ 24. St. John the Baptist.	„ 11. Lord Mayor's Day.
„ 25. St. Mark.	„ 29. St. Peter.	„ 14. Birthday of The Prince of Wales.
May 2. St. Philip and St. James.	*July* 3. St. Thomas.	„ 30. St. Andrew.
„ 4. Ascension Day.		

THE MILITARY KNIGHTS OF WINDSOR

Founded in 1348 after the Wars in France to assist English Knights, who, having been prisoners in the hands of the French, had become impoverished by the payments of heavy ransoms. They received a pension and quarters in Windsor Castle. Edward III founded the Order of the Garter later in the same year, incorporating the Knights of Windsor and the College of St. George into its foundation and raising the number of Knights to 26 to correspond with the number of the Knights of the Garter. Known later as the Alms Knights or Poor Knights of Windsor, their establishment was reduced under the will of King Henry VIII to 13 and Statutes were drawn up by Queen Elizabeth I.

In 1833 King William IV changed their designation to The Military Knights and granted them their present uniform which consists of a scarlet tail-coat with white cross sword-belt, crimson sash and cocked hat with plume. The badges are the Shield of St. George and the Star of the Order of the Garter. The Knights receive a small stipend in addition to their Army pensions and quarters in Windsor Castle. They take part in all ceremonies of the Noble Order of the Garter and attend Sunday morning service in St. George's Chapel as representatives of the Knights of the Garter.

Applications for appointment should be made to The Military Secretary, Ministry of Defence, Army Dept.

Governor, Maj.-Gen. Sir Peter Gillett, K.C.V.O., C.B., O.B.E. (retires early 1989. Replaced Feb. 1989 by Maj.-Gen. Peter Downward, C.B., D.S.O., D.F.C.)

Military Knights, Lt.-Col. R. W. Dobbin, O.B.E.; Maj. H. Smith, M.B.E., R.V.M.; Maj. A. E. Wollaston, M.V.O.; Brig. A. L. Atkinson, O.B.E.; Brig. J. F. Linders, O.B.E., M.C; Brig. A. C. Tyler, C.B.E., M.C., D.L.; Maj. W. L. Thompson, M.V.O., M.B.E., D.C.M.; Maj. L. W. Dickerson; Maj. J. C. Cowley, D.C.M.; Lt.-Col. N. L. West; Lt.-Col. R. L. C. Tamplin.

Supernumerary, Lt.-Col. A. R. Clark, M.C.

THE PEERAGE

The rules which govern the creation and succession of Peerages are extremely complicated. There are, technically, five separate Peerages, the Peerage of England, of Scotland, of Ireland, of Great Britain, and of the United Kingdom. The Peerage of Great Britain dates from 1707 when an Act of Union combined the two Kingdoms of England and Scotland and separate Peerages were discontinued; and the Peerage of the United Kingdom from 1801 when Great Britain and Ireland were combined under an Act of Union. Some Scottish Peers have received additional Peerages of Great Britain or of the United Kingdom since 1707, and some Irish Peers additional Peerages of the United Kingdom since 1801. The Peerage of Ireland was not entirely discontinued from 1801 but holders of Irish Peerages, whether pre-dating or created subsequent to the Union of 1801, are not entitled to sit in the House of Lords if they have no additional English, Scottish, Great Britain or United Kingdom Peerage. (However, they are eligible for election to the House of Commons and to vote in Parliamentary elections, which other Peers are not.) An Irish Peer holding a Peerage of a lower grade which enables him to sit in the House of Lords is introduced there by the title which enables him to sit, though for all other purposes he is known by his higher title. In the Peerage of Scotland there is no rank of Baron; the equivalent rank is Lord of Parliament, abbreviated to "Lord" (the female equivalent is "Lady"). All Peers of England, Scotland, Great Britain or the United Kingdom who are of full age (21 years) and of British nationality are entitled to sit in the House of Lords. Most hereditary peerages pass on death to the nearest male heir; but certain ancient Peerages pass on death to the nearest heir, male or female, and several are held by women (see also pp. 176–7). Since the Peerage Act, 1963, Peeresses in their own Right have been entitled to sit in the House of Lords, subject to the qualifications applying to Peers.

Non-hereditary or Life Peerages, in the degree of Baron or Baroness, have been conferred by the Crown since 1876 on eminent judges, the Lords of Appeal or Law Lords, to enable them to carry out the judicial functions of the House of Lords, and since 1958 on men and women of distinction in public life, giving them seats in the House of Lords. Life Peers and Peeresses are addressed identically as an hereditary Peer or Peeress, and their children have the same courtesy style as the children of an hereditary Peer or Peeress.

No fees for Dignities have been payable since 1937. The House of Lords surrendered the ancient right of peers to be tried for treason or felony by their peers in 1948.

Peerages Extinct Since the Last Issue

MARQUESSATES.—Dufferin and Ava (cr. 1888).
EARLDOMS.—Ypres (cr. 1922).
VISCOUNTCIES.—Ward of Witley (cr. 1960).
BARONIES.—Armstrong (cr. 1903); Drumalbyn (cr. 1963); Greville (cr. 1869); Blackford (cr. 1935).
LIFE PEERAGES.—See p. 182.

Disclaimer of Peerages

The Peerage Act, 1963, enables Peers or Peeresses to disclaim their Peerages for life. Peers alive in 1963 could disclaim within 12 months after the passing of the Act (July 31, 1963); a person subsequently succeeding to a Peerage may disclaim within 12 months (one month if an M.P.) after the date of succession, or of attaining his or her majority, if later. The disclaimer is irrevocable but does not affect the descent of the Peerage after the disclaimant's death, and children of a disclaimed Peer may, if they wish, retain their precedence and any courtesy titles and styles borne as children of a Peer.

EARLS: Durham (1970); Home (1963); Sandwich (1964).
VISCOUNTS: Hailsham (1963); Stansgate (1963).
BARONS: Altrincham (1963); Archibald (1975); Merthyr (1977); Reith (1972); Sanderson of Ayot (1971); Silkin (1972); Southampton (1964).

Peers Who Are Minors

EARLS (1): Hardwicke (b. 1971).
VISCOUNTS (1): Dillon (b. 1973).

COMPOSITION OF THE HOUSE OF LORDS (At Aug. 31, 1988)

Archbishops and Bishops	26	
Peers by Succession	759	(20 women)
Hereditary Peers of first creation (including the Prince of Wales)	26	
Life Peers under the Appellate Jurisdiction Act 1876	22	
Life Peers under the Life Peerages Act 1958	354	(46 women)
TOTAL	1187	

Of whom:

Peers without Writs of Summons	81
Peers on Leave of Absence from the House	177

Contractions and Symbols.—S. or I. appended to the date of creation denotes a *Scottish* or *Irish* title, the further addition of a * implies that the Peer in question holds also an *Imperial* title, which is specified (after the name) by its more definite description as *Engl.*, *Brit.*, or *U.K.* When both titles are alike, as in the case of Argyll, this star is appended to the conjoined date below, and it then denotes that such date is that of the imperial creation. The mark ° signifies that there is no "of" in the Marquessate or Earldom so designated; *b.* signifies born; *s.*, succeeded; *m.*, married; *w.*, widower or widow; *M.*, minor; † Information on *Eldest Son or Heir* not ascertained at time of going to press.

ROYAL DUKES

Style, His Royal Highness The Duke of ——.
Addressed as, Sir, or more formally, May it please your Royal Highness.

1947 *Edinburgh,* The Prince Philip, Duke of Edinburgh, K.G., K.T., O.M., G.B.E., P.C., *b.* 1921, *m.* (see p. 148).
1337 *Cornwall,* Charles, Prince of Wales, Duke of Cornwall (*Scottish Duke, Rothesay,* 1398). K.G., K.T., G.C.B., P.C., *b.* 1948, *m.* (see p. 148).
1986 *York,* The Prince Andrew, Duke of York, C.V.O., *b.* 1960, *m.* (see p. 148).
1928 *Gloucester* (2nd), Richard, Duke of Gloucester, G.C.V.O., *b.* 1944, *s.* 1974, *m.* (see p. 147).
1934 *Kent* (2nd), Edward, Duke of Kent, K.G., G.C.M.G., G.C.V.O., *b.* 1935, *s.* 1942, *m.* (see p. 147).

ARCHBISHOPS

Style, The Most Rev. His Grace The Lord Archbishop of——.
Addressed as, My Lord Archbishop; or, Your Grace.

Introd. to House of Lords

1973   *Canterbury* (102nd), Robert Alexander Kennedy Runcie, M.C., P.C., *b.* 1921, *m. Consecrated Bishop of St. Albans,* 1970, *trans.* 1980.

1973   *York* (95th), John Stapylton Habgood, P.C., PH.D., *b.* 1927, *m. Consecrated Bishop of Durham,* 1973, *trans.* 1983.

DUKES

Style, His Grace The Duke of——. *Addressed as,* My Lord Duke; or, Your Grace. The eldest sons of Dukes and Marquesses take, by courtesy, their father's second title. The other sons and the daughters are styled Lord Edward, Lady Caroline. etc.

Created.	*Title, Order of Succession, Name, etc.*	*Eldest Son or Heir.*
1868 I.*	*Abercorn* (5th), James Hamilton (6th *Brit. Marq.,* 1790, and 14th *Scott. Earl,* 1606 both *Abercorn*), *b.* 1934, *s.* 1979, *m.*	Marquess of Hamilton, *b.* 1969.
1701 s. 1892*	*Argyll,* Ian Campbell (12th *Scottish* and 5th *U.K. Duke, Argyll*), *b.* 1937, *s.* 1973, *m.*	Marquess of Lorne, *b.* 1968.
1703 s.	*Atholl* (10th), George Iain Murray, *b.* 1931, *s.* 1957.	Godfrey P. *M.,* D.S.O., *b.* 1901.
1682	*Beaufort* (11th), David Robert Somerset, *b.* 1928, *s.* 1984, *m.*	Marquess of Worcester, *b.* 1952.
1694	*Bedford* (13th), John Robert Russell, *b.* 1917, *s.* 1953, *m.*	Marquess of Tavistock, *b.* 1940.
1663 s.*	*Buccleuch* (9th) & (11th) *Queensberry* (1684), Walter Francis John Montagu Douglas Scott, K.T., V.R.D. (8th *Engl. Earl, Doncaster,* 1662), *b.* 1923, *s.* 1973, *m.*	Earl of Dalkeith, *b.* 1954.
1694	*Devonshire* (11th), Andrew Robert Buxton Cavendish, M.C., P.C., *b.* 1920, *s.* 1950, *m.*	Marquess of Hartington, *b.* 1944.
1900	*Fife* (3rd), James George Alexander Bannerman Carnegie, *b.* 1929, *s.* 1959. *(see* p. 146).	Earl of Macduff, *b.* 1961.
1675	*Grafton* (11th), Hugh Denis Charles FitzRoy, K.G., *b.* 1919, *s.* 1970, *m.*	Earl of Euston, *b.* 1947.
1643 s.*	*Hamilton* (15th) & *Brandon* (12th) (*Brit.* 1711), Angus Alan Douglas Douglas-Hamilton (*Premier Peer of Scotland*), *b.* 1938, *s.* 1973, *m.*	Marquess of Douglas and Clydesdale, *b.* 1978.
1766 I.*	*Leinster* (8th), Gerald FitzGerald (*Premier Duke, Marquess and Earl of Ireland;* 8th *Brit. Visct., Leinster,* 1747) *b.* 1914, *s.* 1976, *m.*	Marquess of Kildare, *b.* 1948.
1719	*Manchester* (12th), Angus Charles Drogo Montagu, *b.* 1938, *s.* 1985, *m.*	Viscount Mandeville, *b.* 1962.
1702	*Marlborough* (11th), John George Vanderbilt Henry Spencer-Churchill, *b.* 1926, *s.* 1972, *m.*	Marquess of Blandford, *b.* 1955.
1707 s.*	*Montrose* (7th), James Angus Graham (5th *Brit. Earl, Graham,* 1722), *b.* 1907, *s.* 1954, *m.*	Marquess of Graham, *b.* 1935.
1756	*Newcastle* (*under Lyme*) (9th), Henry Edward Hugh Pelham-Clinton-Hope, O.B.E., *b.* 1907, *s.* 1941, *m.*	Edward C. *Pelham-Clinton, b.* 1920
1483	*Norfolk* (17th), Miles Francis Stapleton Fitzalan-Howard, K.G., G.C.V.O., C.B., C.B.E., M.C. (*Premier Duke and Earl;* 12th *Eng. Baron Beaumont,* 1309, *s.* 1971; 4th *U.K. Baron Howard of Glossop,* 1860, *s.* 1972), *b.* 1915, *s.* 1975, *m.* (*Earl Marshal*).	Earl of Arundel and Surrey, *b.* 1956.
1766	*Northumberland* (10th), Hugh Algernon Percy, K.G., G.C.V.O., T.D., P.C., F.R.S., *b.* 1914, *s.* 1940, *m.* (*Lord Steward*).	Earl Percy, *b.* 1953.
1716	*Portland* (9th), Victor Frederick William Cavendish-Bentinck, C.M.G. *b.* 1897, *s.* 1980, *m.*	(None to Dukedom), to Earldom of Portland, Henry N. B., *b.* 1919.
1675	*Richmond* (9th) & *Gordon* (4th, 1876), Frederick Charles Gordon Lennox (9th *Scott. Duke, Lennox.* 1675), *b.* 1904, *s.* 1935, *m.*	Earl of March and Kinrara, *b.* 1929.
1707 s.*	*Roxburghe* (10th), Guy David Innes-Ker (5th *U.K. Earl, Innes,* 1837), *b.* 1954, *s.* 1974, *m.* (*Premier Baronet of Scotland*).	Marquess of Bowmont, *b.* 1981.
1703	*Rutland* (10th), Charles John Robert Manners, C.B.E., *b.* 1919, *s.* 1940, *m.*	Marquess of Granby, *b.* 1959.
1684	*St. Albans* (13th), Charles Frederick Aubrey de Vere Beauclerk, O.B.E., *b.* 1915, *s.* 1964, *m.*	Earl of Burford, *b.* 1939.
1547	*Somerset* (19th), John Michael Edward Seymour, *b.* 1952, *s.* 1984, *m.*	Lord Seymour, *b.* 1982.
1833	*Sutherland* (6th), John Sutherland Egerton, T.D. (5th *U.K. Earl Ellesmere,* 1846), *b.* 1915, *s.* 1963, *m.*	Cyril R. *E., b.* 1905.
1814	*Wellington* (8th), Arthur Valerian Wellesley, M.V.O., O.B.E., M.C. (9th *Irish Earl, Mornington,* 1760), *b.* 1915, *s.* 1972, *m.*	Marquess of Douro, *b.* 1945.
1874	*Westminster* (6th), Gerald Cavendish Grosvenor, *b.* 1951, *s.* 1979, *m.*	(None to Dukedom), to Marquessate of Westminster, Earl of Wilton, *b.* 1921 (*see,* p. 163).

MARQUESSES

Style, The Most Hon. The Marquess of——. *Addressed as,* My Lord Marquess.
In titles marked ° the "of" is *not* used. For the style of Marquesses' sons and daughters, *see* under "DUKES," above.

Created.	Title, Order of Succession, Name, etc.	Eldest Son or Heir.
1916	*Aberdeen and Temair* (6th), Alastair Ninian John Gordon (12th *Scott. Earl, Aberdeen,* 1682), *b.* 1920, *s.* 1984, *m.*	Earl of Haddo, *b.* 1955.
1876	*Abergavenny* (5th), John Henry Guy Nevill, K.G., O.B.E., *b.* 1914, *s.* 1954, *m.*	Guy R. G. *N., b.* 1945.
1821	*Ailesbury* (8th), Michael Sidney Cedric Brudenell-Bruce, *b.* 1926, *s.* 1974, *m.*	Earl of Cardigan, *b.* 1952.
1831	*Ailsa* (7th), Archibald David Kennedy, O.B.E., (19th *Scott. Earl, Cassillis,* 1509), *b.* 1925, *s.* 1957, *m.*	Earl of Cassillis, *b.* 1956.
1815	*Anglesey* (7th), George Charles Henry Victor Paget, *b.* 1922, *s.* 1947, *m.*	Earl of Uxbridge, *b.* 1950.
1789	*Bath* (6th), Henry Frederick Thynne, *b.* 1905, *s.* 1946, *m.*	Viscount Weymouth, *b.* 1932.
1826	*Bristol* (7th), Frederick William John Augustus Hervey, *b.* 1954, *s.* 1985.	Lord Frederick W. C. N. W. *H., b.* 1961.
1796	*Bute* (6th), John Crichton-Stuart (11th *Scott. Earl, Dumfries,* 1633), *b.* 1933, *s.* 1956, *m.*	Earl of Dumfries, *b.* 1958.
1812	°*Camden* (6th), David George Edward Henry Pratt, *b.* 1930, *s.* 1983.	Earl of Brecknock, *b.* 1965.
1815	*Cholmondeley* (6th), George Hugh Cholmondeley, G.C.V.O., M.C. (10th *Irish Viscount, Cholmondeley,* 1661), *b.* 1919, *s.* 1968, *m.* (*Lord Great Chamberlain*).	Earl of Rocksavage, *b.* 1960.
1816 I.*	°*Conyngham* (7th), Frederick William Henry Francis Conyngham (7th *U.K. Baron, Minster, U.K.* 1821), *b.* 1924, *s.* 1974, *w.*	Earl of Mount Charles, *b.* 1951.
1791 I.*	*Donegall* (7th), Dermot Richard Claud Chichester, L.V.O. (7th *Brit. Baron, Fisherwick,* 1790, 6th *Brit. Baron, Templemore,* 1831), *b.* 1916, *s.* to Marquessate, 1975: to Templemore Barony, 1953, *m.*	Earl of Belfast, *b.* 1952.
1789 I.*	*Downshire* (7th), Arthur Wills Percy Wellington Blundell Trumbull Sandys Hill (7th *Brit. Earl, Hillsborough,* 1772), *b.* 1894, *s.* 1918, *w.*	A. Robin I. *H., b.* 1929.
1801 I.*	*Ely* (8th) Charles John Tottenham (8th *U.K. Baron, Loftus,* 1801), *b.* 1913, *s.* 1969, *m.*	Viscount Loftus, *b.* 1943.
1801	*Exeter* (8th), (William) Michael Anthony Cecil, *b.* 1935, *s.* 1988, *m.*	Lord Burghley, *b.* 1970.
1800 I.*	*Headfort* (6th), Thomas Geoffrey Charles Michael Taylour (4th *U.K. Baron, Kenlis,* 1831), *b.* 1932, *s.* 1960, *m.*	Earl of Bective, *b.* 1959.
1793	*Hertford* (8th), Hugh Edward Conway Seymour (9th *Irish Baron, Conway,* 1712), *b.* 1930, *s.* 1940, *m.*	Earl of Yarmouth, *b.* 1958.
1599 S.*	*Huntly* (13th), Granville Charles Gomer Gordon (*Premier Marquess of Scotland*) (5th *U.K. Baron, Meldrum,* 1815), *b.* 1944, *s.* 1987, *m.*	Earl of Aboyne, *b.* 1973.
1784	*Lansdowne* (8th), George John Charles Mercer Nairne Petty-Fitzmaurice, P.C. (8th *Irish Earl. Kerry,* 1723), *b.* 1912, *s.* 1944, *w.*	Earl of Shelburne, *b.* 1941.
1902	*Linlithgow* (4th), Adrian John Charles Hope (10th *Scott. Earl, Hopetoun* 1703), *b.* 1946, *s.* 1987, *m.*	Earl of Hopetoun, *b.* 1969.
1816 I.*	*Londonderry* (9th), Alexander Charles Robert Vane-Tempest-Stewart (6th *U.K. Earl, Vane,* 1823), *b.* 1937, *s.* 1955, *m.*	Viscount Castlereagh, *b.* 1972.
1701 S.*	*Lothian* (12th), Peter Francis Walter Kerr, K.C.V.O. (6th *U.K. Baron, Kerr,* 1821), *b.* 1922, *s.* 1940, *m.*	Earl of Ancram, *b.* 1945.
1917	*Milford Haven* (4th), George Ivar Louis Mountbatten, *b.* 1961, *s.* 1970.	Lord Ivar A. M. *M., b.* 1963.
1838	*Normanby* (4th), Oswald Constantine John Phipps, K.G., C.B.E. (8th *Irish Baron, Mulgrave,* 1767), *b.* 1912, *s.* 1932, *m.*	Earl of Mulgrave, *b.* 1954.
1812	*Northampton* (7th), Spencer Douglas David Compton, *b.* 1946, *s.* 1978, *m.*	Earl Compton, *b.* 1973.
1825 I.*	*Ormonde* (7th), James Hubert Theobald Charles Butler, M.B.E. (7th *U.K. Baron, Ormonde,* 1821), *b.* 1899, *s.* 1971, *w.*	(None to Marquessate), to Earldoms of Ormonde and Ossory, Viscount Mountgarret, *b.* 1936 (see, p. 165).
1682 S.	*Queensberry* (12th), David Harrington Angus Douglas, *b.* 1929, *s.* 1954.	Viscount Drumlanrig, *b.* 1967.
1926	*Reading* (4th), Simon Charles Henry Rufus Isaacs, *b.* 1942, *s.* 1980, *m.*	Viscount Erleigh, *b.* 1986.
1789	*Salisbury* (6th), Robert Edward Peter Gascoyne-Cecil, *b.* 1916, *s.* 1972, *m.*	Viscount Cranborne, *b.* 1946.
1800 I.*	*Sligo* (10th), Denis Edward Browne (10th *U.K. Baron, Monteagle,* 1806), *b.* 1908, *s.* 1952, *m.*	Earl of Altamont, *b.* 1939.
1787	°*Townshend* (7th), George John Patrick Dominic Townshend, *b.* 1916, *s.* 1921, *w.*	Viscount Raynham, *b.* 1945.
1694 S.*	*Tweeddale* (13th), Edward Douglas John Hay (4th *U.K. Baron, Tweeddale,* 1881), *b.* 1947, *s.* 1979.	Lord Charles D. M. *H., b.* 1947.
1789 I.*	*Waterford* (8th), John Hubert de la Poer Beresford (8th *Brit. Baron, Tyrone,* 1786), *b.* 1933, *s.* 1934, *m.*	Earl of Tyrone, *b.* 1958.
1551	*Winchester* (18th), Nigel George Paulet (*Premier Marquess of England*), *b.* 1941, *s.* 1968, *m.*	Earl of Wiltshire, *b.* 1969.
1892	*Zetland* (3rd), Lawrence Aldred Mervyn Dundas (5th *U.K. Earl of Zetland,* 1838, 6th *Brit. Baron Dundas,* 1794), *b.* 1908, *s.* 1961, *m.*	Earl of Ronaldshay, *b.* 1937.

EARLS

Style (see also note, p. 187). The Right Hon. The Earl of ——. *Addressed as,* My Lord. The eldest sons of Earls take, by courtesy, their father's second title, the younger sons being styled the Hon., *e.g.* the Hon. John ——, but the daughters Lady Elizabeth ——, etc. Where marked ° the "of" is not used.

Created.	*Title, Order of Succession, Name, etc.*	*Eldest Son or Heir.*
1639 s.	*Airlie* (13th), David George Coke Patrick Ogilvy, K.T., G.C.V.O., P.C., *b.* 1926, *s.* 1968, *m.* (*Lord Chamberlain*).	Lord Ogilvy, *b.* 1958.
1696	*Albemarle* (10th), Rufus Arnold Alexis Keppel, *b.* 1965, *s.* 1979.	Crispian W. J. K., *b.* 1948.
1952	°*Alexander of Tunis* (2nd), Shane William Desmond Alexander, *b.* 1935, *s.* 1969, *m.*	Hon. Brian J. A., *b.* 1939.
1826	°*Amherst* (5th), Jeffery John Archer Amherst, M.C., *b.* 1896, *s.* 1927.	(None.)
1662 s.	*Annandale and Hartfell* (11th), Patrick Andrew Wentworth Hope Johnstone, *b.* 1941, *claim established* 1985, *m.*	Lord Johnstone, *b.* 1971.
1789 I.	°*Annesley* (10th), Patrick Annesley, *b.* 1924, *s.* 1979, *m.*	Hon. Philip H.A., *b.* 1927.
1785 I.	*Antrim* (9th), Alexander Randal Mark McDonnell, *b.* 1935, *s.* 1977, *m.* (*Viscount Dunluce.*)	Hon. Randal A. St. J. M., *b.* 1967.
1762 I.*	*Arran* (9th), Arthur Desmond Colquhoun Gore (5th *U.K. Baron Sudley,* 1884), *b.* 1938, *s.* 1983, *m.*	Paul A. G., C.M.G., C.V.O., *b.* 1921.
1955	°*Attlee* (2nd), Martin Richard Attlee, *b.* 1927, *s.* 1967.	Viscount Prestwood, *b.* 1956.
1714	*Aylesford* (11th), Charles Ian Finch-Knightley, *b.* 1918, *s.* 1958, *m.*	Lord Guernsey, *b.* 1947.
1937	°*Baldwin of Bewdley* (4th), Edward Alfred Alexander Baldwin, *b.* 1938, *s.* 1976, *m.*	Viscount Corvedale, *b.* 1973.
1922	*Balfour* (4th), Gerald Arthur James Balfour, *b.* 1925, *s.* 1968, *m.*	Eustace A. G. B., *b.* 1921.
1772	°*Bathurst* (8th), Henry Allen John Bathurst, *b.* 1927, *s.* 1943, *m.*	Lord Apsley, *b.* 1961.
1919	°*Beatty* (3rd), David Beatty, *b.* 1946, *s.* 1972.	Viscount Borodale, *b.* 1973.
1797 I.	*Belmore* (8th), John Armar Lowry-Corry, *b.* 1951, *s.* 1960, *m.*	Viscount Corry, *b.* 1985.
1739 I.* } 1937 }	*Bessborough,* Frederick Edward Neuflize Ponsonby (10th *Irish* and 2nd *U.K. Earl Bessborough*), *b.* 1913, *s.* 1956, *m.*	Arthur M. L. P., *b.* 1912 (to Irish Earldom only).
1815	*Bradford* (7th), Richard Thomas Orlando Bridgeman, *b.* 1947, *s.* 1981, *m.*	Viscount Newport, *b.* 1980.
1677 s.	*Breadalbane and Holland* (10th), John Romer Boreland Campbell, *b.* 1919, *s.* 1959.	(None.)
1469 s.*	*Buchan* (17th), Malcolm Harry Erskine, (8th *U.K. Baron Erskine* 1806), *b.* 1930, *s.* 1984, *m.*	Lord Cardross, *b.* 1960.
1740	*Buckinghamshire* (10th), (George) Miles Hobart-Hampden, *b.* 1944, *s.* 1983, *m.*	Sir Robert Hobart, Bt., *b.* 1915.
1800	°*Cadogan* (7th), William Gerald Charles Cadogan, M.C., *b.* 1914, *s.* 1933, *m.*	Viscount Chelsea, *b.* 1937.
1878	°*Cairns* (5th), David Charles Cairns, G.C.V.O., C.B., *b.* 1909, *s.* 1946, *m.*	Viscount Garmoyle, *b.* 1939.
1455 s.	*Caithness* (20th), Malcolm Ian Sinclair, *b.* 1948, *s.* 1965, *m.*	Lord Berriedale, *b.* 1981.
1800 I.	*Caledon* (7th), Nicholas James Alexander, *b.* 1955, *s.* 1980.	Earl Alexander of Tunis (*see* above.)
1661	*Carlisle* (12th), Charles James Ruthven Howard, M.C. (12th *Scott. Baron, Ruthven of Freeland,* 1651), *b.* 1923, *s.* 1963, *m.*	Viscount Morpeth, *b.* 1949.
1793	*Carnarvon* (7th), Henry George Reginald Molyneux Herbert, K.C.V.O., K.B.E., *b.* 1924, *s.* 1987, *m.*	Lord Porchester, *b.* 1956.
1748 I.*	*Carrick* (9th), Brian Stuart Theobald Somerset Caher Butler (3rd *U.K. Baron, Butler,* 1912), *b.* 1931, *s.* 1957.	Viscount Ikerrin, *b.* 1953.
1800 I.	°*Castle Stewart* (8th), Arthur Patrick Avondale Stuart, *b.* 1928, *s.* 1961, *m.*	Viscount Stuart, *b.* 1953.
1814	°*Cathcart* (6th), Alan Cathcart, C.B., D.S.O., M.C. (15th *Scott. Baron, Cathcart,* 1447), *b.* 1919, *s.* 1927, *m.*	Lord Greenock, *b.* 1952.
1647 I.	*Cavan* (12th), Michael Edward Oliver Lambart, T.D., *b.* 1911, *s.* 1950, *m.*	Roger C. L., *b.* 1944.
1827	°*Cawdor* (6th), Hugh John Vaughan Campbell, *b.* 1932, *s.* 1970, *m.*	Viscount Emlyn, *b.* 1962.
1801	*Chichester* (9th), John Nicholas Pelham, *b.* 1944, *s.* 1944, *m.*	Richard A. H. P., *b.* 1952.
1803 I.*	*Clancarty* (8th), William Francis Brinsley Le Poer Trench (7th *U.K. Visct. Clancarty,* 1823), *b.* 1911, *s.* 1975, *m.*	Nicholas P. R. *Le P. T.,* *b.* 1952.
1776 I.*	*Clanwilliam* (6th), John Charles Edmund Carson Meade (4th *U.K. Baron Clanwilliam,* 1828), *b.* 1914, *s.* 1953, *m.*	John H. *M.,* *b.* 1919.
1776	*Clarendon* (7th), George Frederick Laurence Hyde Villiers, *b.* 1933, *s.* 1955, *m.*	Lord Hyde, *b.* 1976.
1620 I.*	*Cork* (13th) *& Orrery* (13th)(I. 1660), Patrick Reginald Boyle (9th *Brit. Baron, Boyle of Marston,* 1711), *b.* 1910, *s.* 1967, *m.*	Hon. John W. *B.,* D.S.C., *b.* 1916.
1850	*Cottenham* (8th), Kenelm Charles Everard Digby Pepys, *b.* 1948, *s.* 1968, *m.*	Viscount Crowhurst, *b.* 1983.
1762 I.*	*Courtown* (9th), James Patrick Montagu Burgoyne Winthrop Stopford (8th *Brit. Baron, Saltersford,* 1796), *b.* 1954, *s.* 1975, *m.*	Viscount Stopford, *b.* 1988.
1697	*Coventry* (11th), George William Coventry, *b.* 1934, *s.* 1940, *m.*	Viscount Deerhurst, *b.* 1957.
1857	°*Cowley* (7th), Garret Graham Wellesley, *b.* 1934, *s.* 1975, *m.*	Viscount Dangan, *b.* 1965.
1892	*Cranbrook* (5th), Gathorne Gathorne-Hardy, *b.* 1933, *s.* 1978, *m.*	Lord Medway, *b.* 1968.
1801	*Craven* (8th), Simon George Craven, *b.* 1961, *s.* 1983.	Rupert J. E. C., *b.* 1926.
1398 s.*	*Crawford* (29th) *& Balcarres* (12th) (s. 1651), Robert Alexander Lindsay, P.C., (*Premier Earl on Union Roll,* 5th *U.K. Baron, Wigan,* 1826, *and Baron Balniel* (*Life Peer*)), *b.* 1927, *s.* 1975, *m.*	Lord Balniel, *b.* 1958.

Created.	Title, Order of Succession, Name, etc.	Eldest Son or Heir.
1861	*Cromartie* (4th), Roderick Grant Francis Mackenzie, M.C., T.D., *b.* 1904, *s.* 1962, *m.*	Viscount Tarbat, *b.* 1948.
1901	*Cromer* (3rd), George Rowland Stanley Baring, K.G., G.C.M.G., M.B.E., P.C., *b.* 1918, *s.* 1953, *m.*	Viscount Errington, *b.* 1946.
1633 S.*	*Dalhousie* (16th), Simon Ramsay, K.T., G.C.V.O., G.B.E., M.C. (4th *U.K. Baron, Ramsay*, 1875), *b.* 1914, *s.* 1950, *m.*	Lord Ramsay, *b.* 1948.
1725 I.*	*Darnley* (11th), Adam Ivo Stuart Bligh (20th *English Baron, Clifton of Leighton Bromswold*, 1608), *b.* 1941, *s.* 1980, *m.*	Lord Clifton, *b.* 1968.
1711	*Dartmouth* (9th), Gerald Humphry Legge, *b.* 1924, *s.* 1962, *m.*	Viscount Lewisham, *b.* 1949.
1761	°*De La Warr* (11th), William Herbrand Sackville, *b.* 1948, *s.* 1988, *m.*	Lord Buckhurst, *b.* 1979.
1622	*Denbigh* (11th) *& Desmond* (10th) (I. 1622), William Rudolph Michael Feilding, *b.* 1943, *s.* 1966, *m.*	Viscount Feilding, *b.* 1970.
1485	*Derby* (18th), Edward John Stanley, M.C., *b.* 1918, *s.* 1948, *m.*	Edward R. W. S., *b.* 1962.
1553	*Devon* (17th), Charles Christopher Courtenay, *b.* 1916, *s.* 1935, *m.*	Lord Courtenay, *b.* 1942.
1800 I.*	*Donoughmore* (8th), Richard Michael John Hely-Hutchinson (8th *U.K. Visct., Hutchinson*, 1821), *b.* 1927, *s.* 1981, *m.*	Viscount Suirdale, *b.* 1952.
1661 I.*	*Drogheda* (11th), Charles Garrett Ponsonby Moore, K.G., K.B.E. (2nd *U.K. Baron. Moore*, 1954), *b.* 1910, *s.* 1957, *m.*	Viscount Moore, *b.* 1937.
1837	*Ducie* (6th), Basil Howard Moreton, *b.* 1917, *s.* 1952, *m.*	Lord Moreton, *b.* 1951.
1860	*Dudley* (4th), William Humble David Ward, *b.* 1920, *s.* 1969, *m.*	Viscount Ednam, *b.* 1947.
1660 S.*	*Dundee* (12th), Alexander Henry Scrymgeour, (2nd *U.K. Baron, Glassary*, 1954), *b.* 1949, *s.* 1983, *m.*	Lord Scrymgeour, *b.* 1982.
1669 S.	*Dundonald* (15th), Iain Alexander Douglas Blair Cochrane, *b.* 1961, *s.* 1986, *m.*	Baron Cochrane of Cults, *b.* 1922 (*see*, p. 169).
1686 S.	*Dunmore* (11th), Kenneth Randolph Murray, *b.* 1913, *s.* 1981, *w.*	Viscount Fincastle, *b.* 1946.
1822 I.	*Dunraven and Mount-Earl* (7th), Thady Windham Thomas Wyndham-Quin, *b.* 1939, *s.* 1965, *m.*	(None).
1837	*Effingham* (6th), Mowbray Henry Gordon Howard (16th *E. Baron, Howard of Effingham*, 1554), *b.* 1905, *s.* 1946, *m.*	Lt.-Cdr. David P. M. A. H., *b.* 1939.
1507 S. ⎫ 1859* ⎭	*Eglinton* (18th) *& (9th) Winton* (1600), Archibald George Montgomerie (6th *U.K. Earl Winton*, 1859), *b.* 1939, *s.* 1966, *m.*	Lord Montgomerie, *b.* 1966.
1733 I.*	*Egmont* (11th), Frederick George Moore Perceval (9th *Brit. Baron, Lovel & Holland*, 1762), *b.* 1914, *s.* 1932, *m.*	Viscount Perceval, *b.* 1934.
1821	*Eldon* (5th), John Joseph Nicholas Scott, *b.* 1937, *s.* 1976, *m.*	Viscount Encombe, *b.* 1962.
1633 S.*	*Elgin* (11th), *& Kincardine* (15th) (S. 1647), Andrew Douglas Alexander Thomas Bruce, (4th *U.K. Baron, Elgin*, 1849), K.T., *b.* 1924, *s.* 1968, *m.*	Lord Bruce, *b.* 1961.
1789 I.*	*Enniskillen* (6th), David Lowry Cole, M.B.E., (4th *U.K. Baron, Grinstead*, 1815) *b.* 1918, *s.* 1963, *m.*	Viscount Cole, *b.* 1942.
1789 I.*	*Erne* (6th), Henry George Victor John Crichton (3rd *U.K. Baron, Fermanagh*, 1876), *b.* 1937, *s.* 1940, *m.*	Viscount Crichton, *b.* 1971.
1452 S.	*Erroll* (24th), Merlin Sereld Victor Gilbert Hay (*Hereditary Lord High Constable and Knight Marischal of Scotland*), *b.* 1948, *s.* 1978, *m.*	Lord Hay, *b.* 1984.
1661	*Essex* (10th), Robert Edward de Vere Capell, *b.* 1920, *s.* 1981, *m.*	Viscount Malden, *b.* 1944.
1711	°*Ferrers* (13th), Robert Washington Shirley, P.C., *b.* 1929, *s.* 1954, *m.*	Viscount Tamworth, *b.* 1952.
1789	°*Fortescue* (7th), Richard Archibald Fortescue, *b.* 1922, *s.* 1977.	Viscount Ebrington, *b.* 1951.
1841	*Gainsborough* (5th), Anthony Gerard Edward Noel, *b.* 1923, *s.* 1927, *m.*	Viscount Campden, *b.* 1950.
1623 S.*	*Galloway* (13th), Randolph Keith Reginald Stewart (6th *Brit. Baron, Stewart of Garlies*, 1796), *b.* 1928, *s.* 1978, *m.*	Andrew C. S., *b.* 1949.
1703 S.*	*Glasgow* (10th), Patrick Robin Archibald Boyle (4th *U.K. Baron, Fairlie*, 1897), *b.* 1939, *s.* 1984, *m.*	Viscount of Kelburn, *b.* 1978.
1806 I.*	*Gosford* (7th), Charles David Nicholas Alexander John Sparrow Acheson (5th *U.K. Baron, Worlingham*, 1835), *b.* 1942, *s.* 1966, *m.*	Hon. Patrick B. V. M. A., *b.* 1915.
1945	*Gowrie* (2nd), Alexander Patric Greysteil Hore-Ruthven, P.C. (3rd *U.K. Baron, Ruthven of Gowrie*, 1919), *b.* 1939, *s.* 1955, *m.*	Viscount Ruthven of Canberra, *b.* 1964.
1684 I.*	*Granard* (9th), Arthur Patrick Hastings Forbes, A.F.C. (4th *U.K. Baron, Granard*, 1806), *b.* 1915, *s.* 1948, *m.*	Peter A. E. H. F., *b.* 1957.
1833	°*Granville* (5th), Granville James Leveson-Gower, M.C., *b.* 1918, *s.* 1953, *m.*	Lord Leveson, *b.* 1959.
1806	°*Grey* (6th), Richard Fleming George Charles Grey, *b.* 1939, *s.* 1963, *m.*	Philip K. G., *b.* 1940.
1752	*Guilford* (9th), Edward Francis North, *b.* 1933, *s.* 1949, *m.*	Lord North, *b.* 1971.
1619 S.	*Haddington* (13th), John George Baillie-Hamilton, *b.* 1941, *s.* 1986, *m.*	Lord Binning, *b.* 1985.
1919	°*Haig* (2nd), George Alexander Eugene Douglas Haig, O.B.E., *b.* 1918, *s.* 1928, *m.*	Viscount Dawick, *b.* 1961.
1944	*Halifax* (3rd), Charles Edward Peter Neil Wood (5th *U.K. Viscount, Halifax*, 1866), *b.* 1944, *s.* 1980, *m.*	Lord Irwin, *b.* 1977.
1898	*Halsbury* (3rd), John Anthony Hardinge Giffard, F.R.S., *b.* 1908, *s.* 1943, *w.*	Adam E. G., *b.* 1934.
1754	*Hardwicke* (10th), Joseph Philip Sebastian Yorke, *b.* 1971, *s.* 1974, *M.*	Richard C. J. Y., *b.* 1916.
1812	*Harewood* (7th), George Henry Hubert Lascelles, K.B.E., *b.* 1923, *s.* 1947, *m.* (*See also* p. 146).	Viscount Lascelles, *b.* 1950.

Created.	*Title, Order of Succession, Name, etc.*	*Eldest Son or Heir.*
1742	*Harrington* (11th), William Henry Leicester Stanhope (8th *Brit. Viscount, Stanhope of Mahon*, 1717), *b.* 1922, *s.* 1929, *m.*	Viscount Petersham, *b.* 1945.
1809	*Harrowby* (7th), Dudley Danvers Granville Coutts Ryder, T.D., *b.* 1922, *s.* 1987, *m.*	Viscount Sandon, *b.* 1951.
1821	°*Howe* (7th), Frederick Richard Penn Curzon, *b.* 1951, *s.* 1984, *m.*	Charles M. P. C., *b.* 1967.
1529	*Huntingdon* (15th), Francis John Clarence Westenra Plantagenet Hastings, *b.* 1901, *s.* 1939, *m.*	Lt.-Col. Robin H. W. S. H., D.S.O., O.B.E., M.C., *b.* 1917.
1885	*Iddesleigh* (4th), Stafford Henry Northcote, *b.* 1932, *s.* 1970, *m.*	Viscount St. Cyres, *b.* 1957.
1756	*Ilchester* (9th), Maurice Vivian de Touffreville Fox-Strangways, *b.* 1920, *s.* 1970, *m.*	Hon. Raymond G. F.-S., *b.* 1921.
1929	*Inchcape* (3rd), Kenneth James William Mackay, *b.* 1917, *s.* 1939, *m.*	Viscount Glenapp, *b.* 1943.
1919	*Iveagh* (3rd), Arthur Francis Benjamin Guinness, *b.* 1937, *s.* 1967.	Viscount Elveden, *b.* 1969.
1925	°*Jellicoe* (2nd), George Patrick John Rushworth Jellicoe, K.B.E., D.S.O., M.C., P.C., *b.* 1918, *s.* 1935, *m.*	Viscount Brocas, *b.* 1950.
1697	*Jersey* (9th), George Francis Child-Villiers (12th *Irish Visct., Grandison*, 1620), *b.* 1910, *s.* 1923, *m.*	Viscount Villiers, *b.* 1948.
1822 I.	*Kilmorey* (6th), Richard Francis Needham, M.P., *b.* 1942, *s.* 1977, *m.*	Viscount Newry and Morne, *b.* 1966.
1866	*Kimberley* (4th), John Wodehouse, *b.* 1924, *s.* 1941, *m.*	Lord Wodehouse, *b.* 1951.
1768 I.	*Kingston* (11th), Barclay Robert Edwin King-Tenison, *b.* 1943, *s.* 1948.	Viscount Kingsborough, *b.* 1969.
1633 S.*	*Kinnoull* (15th), Arthur William George Patrick Hay (9th *Brit. Baron, Hay of Pedwardine*, 1711), *b.* 1935, *s.* 1938, *m.*	Viscount Dupplin, *b.* 1962.
1677 S.*	*Kintore* (12th), (James) Ian Keith (2nd *U.K. Visct., Stonehaven*, 1938), *b.* 1908, *s.* to Viscountcy, 1941, to Earldom, 1974, *m.*	Lord Inverurie, *b.* 1939.
1914	°*Kitchener of Khartoum* (3rd), Henry Herbert Kitchener, T.D., *b.* 1919, *s.* 1937.	(None.)
1756 I.	*Lanesborough* (9th), Denis Anthony Brian Butler, T.D., *b.* 1918, *s.* 1950.	Cdr. Terence B. J. D. B., *b.* 1913.
1624 S.	*Lauderdale* (17th), Patrick Francis Maitland, *b.* 1911, *s.* 1968, *m.*	Viscount Maitland, *b.* 1937.
1837	*Leicester* (6th), Anthony Louis Lovel Coke, *b.* 1909, *s.* 1976, *m.*	Viscount Coke, *b.* 1936.
1641 S.	*Leven* (14th) & *Melville* (13th) (s. 1690), Alexander Robert Leslie Melville, *b.* 1924, *s.* 1947, *m.*	Lord Balgonie, *b.* 1954.
1831	*Lichfield* (5th), Thomas Patrick John Anson, *b.* 1939, *s.* 1960.	Viscount Anson, *b.* 1978.
1803 I.*	*Limerick* (6th), Patrick Edmund Pery, K.B.E. (6th *U.K. Baron, Foxford*, 1815), *b.* 1930, *s.* 1967, *m.*	Viscount Glentworth, *b.* 1963.
1633 S.	*Lindsay* (15th), David Lindesay-Bethune, *b.* 1926, *s.* 1985, *m.*	Viscount Garnock, *b.* 1955.
1626	*Lindsey* (14th) *and Abingdon* (9th) (1682), Richard Henry Rupert Bertie, *b.* 1931, *s.* 1963, *m.*	Lord Norreys, *b.* 1958.
1776 I.	*Lisburne* (8th), John David Malet Vaughan, *b.* 1918, *s.* 1965, *m.*	Viscount Vaughan, *b.* 1945.
1822 I.*	*Listowel* (5th), William Francis Hare, G.C.M.G., P.C., (3rd *U.K. Baron, Hare*, 1869), *b.* 1906, *s.* 1931, *m.*	Viscount Ennismore, *b.* 1964.
1905	*Liverpool* (5th), Edward Peter Bertram Savile Foljambe, *b.* 1944, *s.* 1969, *m.*	Viscount Hawkesbury, *b.* 1972.
1945	°*Lloyd George of Dwyfor* (3rd), Owen Lloyd George, *b.* 1924, *s.* 1968, *m.*	Viscount Gwynedd, *b.* 1951.
1785 I.*	*Longford* (7th), Francis Aungier Pakenham, K.G., P.C. (6th *U.K. Baron, Silchester*, 1821; 1st *U.K. Baron, Pakenham*, 1945), *b.* 1905, *s.* 1961, *m.*	Thomas F. D. P., *b.* 1933.
1807	*Lonsdale* (7th), James Hugh William Lowther, *b.* 1922, *s.* 1953, *m.*	Viscount Lowther, *b.* 1949.
1838	*Lovelace* (5th), Peter Axel William Locke King (12th *British Baron, King*, 1725), *b.* 1951, *s.* 1964, *m.*	(None.)
1795 I.*	*Lucan* (7th), Richard John Bingham (3rd *U.K. Baron, Bingham*, 1934), *b.* 1934, *s.* 1964, *m.*	Lord Bingham, *b.* 1967.
1880	*Lytton* (5th), John Peter Michael Scawen Lytton (18th *English Baron, Wentworth*, 1529), *b.* 1950, *s.* 1985, *m.*	Hon. T. Roland C. L. L. *b.* 1954.
1721	*Macclesfield* (8th), George Roger Alexander Thomas Parker, *b.* 1914, *s.* 1975, *m.*	Viscount Parker, *b.* 1943.
1800	*Malmesbury* (6th), William James Harris, T.D., *b.* 1907, *s.* 1950, *m.*	Viscount FitzHarris, *b.* 1946.
1776 & 1792	*Mansfield and Mansfield* (8th), William David Mungo James Murray (14th *Scott. Visct., Stormont*, 1621), *b.* 1930, *s.* 1971, *m.*	Viscount Stormont, *b.* 1956.
1565 S.	*Mar* (13th) & *Kellie* (15th) (s. 1616), John Francis Hervey Erskine, *b.* 1921, *s.* 1955, *m.*	Lord Erskine, *b.* 1949.
1785 I.	*Mayo* (10th), Terence Patrick Bourke, *b.* 1929, *s.* 1962, *m.*	Lord Naas, *b.* 1953.
1627 I.*	*Meath* (14th), Anthony Windham Normand Brabazon (5th *U.K. Baron, Chaworth*, 1831), *b.* 1910, *s.* 1949, *m.*	Lord Ardee, *b.* 1941.
1766 I.	*Mexborough* (8th), John Christopher George Savile, *b.* 1931, *s.* 1980, *m.*	Viscount Pollington, *b.* 1959.
1813	*Minto* (6th), Gilbert Edward George Lariston Garnet Elliot-Murray-Kynynmound, O.B.E., *b.* 1928, *s.* 1975, *w.*	Viscount Melgund, *b.* 1953.
1562 S.*	*Moray* (20th) Douglas John Moray Stuart (12th *Brit. Baron, Stuart of Castle Stuart*, 1796), *b.* 1928, *s.* 1974, *m.*	Lord Doune, *b.* 1966.
1815	*Morley* (6th), John St. Aubyn Parker, *b.* 1923, *s.* 1962, *m.*	Visct. Boringdon, *b.* 1956.
1458 S.	*Morton* (22nd), John Charles Sholto Douglas, *b.* 1927, *s.* 1976, *m.*	Lord Aberdour, *b.* 1952.
1789	*Mount Edgcumbe* (8th), Robert Charles Edgcumbe, *b.* 1939, *s.* 1982, *m.*	Piers V. E., *b.* 1946.

Created.	Title, Order of Succession, Name, etc.	Eldest Son or Heir.
1831	*Munster* (7th), Anthony Charles FitzClarence, *b.* 1926, *s.* 1983, *m.*	(None).
1805	°*Nelson* (9th), Peter John Horatio Nelson, *b.* 1941, *s.* 1981, *m.*	Viscount Merton, *b.* 1971.
1660 s.	*Newburgh* (12th), Prince Filippo Giambattista Camillo Francesco Aldo Maria Rospigliosi, *b.* 1942, *s.* 1986, *m.*	Princess Benedetta F. M. *R.*, *b.* 1974.
1827 I.	*Norbury* (6th), Noel Terence Graham-Toler, *b.* 1939, *s.* 1955, *m.*	Viscount Glandine, *b.* 1967.
1806 I.*	*Normanton* (6th), Shaun James Christian Welbore Ellis Agar (9th *Brit. Baron, Mendip,* 1791) (4th *U.K. Baron, Somerton,* 1873), *b.* 1945, *s.* 1967, *m.*	Viscount Somerton, *b.* 1982.
1647 s.	*Northesk* (13th), Robert Andrew Carnegie, *b.* 1926, *s.* 1975, *m.*	Lord Rosehill, *b.* 1954.
1801	*Onslow* (7th), Michael William Coplestone Dillon Onslow, *b.* 1938, *s.* 1971, *m.*	Viscount Cranley, *b.* 1967.
1696 s.	*Orkney* (8th), Cecil O'Bryen Fitz-Maurice, *b.* 1919, *s.* 1951, *m.*	Oliver P. St. John, *b.* 1938
1925	*Oxford and Asquith* (2nd), Julian Edward George Asquith, K.C.M.G., *b.* 1916, *s.* 1928, *m.*	Viscount Asquith, *b.* 1952.
1929	°*Peel* (3rd), William James Robert Peel (4th *U.K. Viscount Peel,* 1895), *b.* 1947, *s.* 1969, *m.*	Viscount Clanfield, *b.* 1976.
1551	*Pembroke* (17th) & *Montgomery* (14th) (1605), Henry George Charles Alexander Herbert, *b.* 1939, *s.* 1969, *m.*	Lord Herbert, *b.* 1978.
1605 s.	*Perth* (17th), John David Drummond, P.C., *b.* 1907, *s.* 1951, *m.*	Viscount Strathallan, *b.* 1935.
1905	*Plymouth* (3rd), Other Robert Ivor Windsor-Clive (15th *English Baron, Windsor,* 1529), *b.* 1923, *s.* 1943, *m.*	Viscount Windsor, *b.* 1951.
1785 I.	*Portarlington* (7th), George Lionel Yuill Seymour Dawson-Damer, *b.* 1938, *s.* 1959, *m.*	Viscount Carlow, *b.* 1965.
1743	*Portsmouth* (10th), Quentin Gerard Carew Wallop, *b.* 1954, *s.* 1984, *m.*	Viscount Lymington, *b.* 1981.
1804	*Powis* (6th), Christian Victor Charles Herbert (7th *Irish Baron, Clive,* 1762), *b.* 1904, *s.* 1974.	George W. *H.*, *b.* 1925.
1765	*Radnor* (8th), Jacob Pleydell-Bouverie, *b.* 1927, *s.* 1968, *m.*	Viscount Folkestone, *b.* 1955.
1831 I.*	*Ranfurly* (6th), Thomas Daniel Knox, K.C.M.G. (7th *U.K. Baron, Ranfurly,* 1826), *b.* 1913, *s.* 1933, *m.*	Gerald F. N. *K.*, *b.* 1929.
1771 I.	*Roden* (9th), Robert William Jocelyn, *b.* 1909, *s.* 1956, *m.*	Viscount Jocelyn, *b.* 1938.
1801	*Romney* (7th), Michael Henry Marsham, *b.* 1910, *s.* 1975, *m.*	Julian C. *M.*, *b.* 1948.
1703 s.*	*Rosebery* (7th), Neil Archibald Primrose (3rd *U.K. Earl, Midlothian,* 1911), *b.* 1929, *s.* 1974, *m.*	Lord Dalmeny, *b.* 1967.
1806 I.	*Rosse* (7th), William Brendan Parsons, *b.* 1936, *s.* 1979, *m.*	Lord Oxmantown, *b.* 1969.
1801	*Rosslyn* (7th), Peter St. Clair-Erskine, *b.* 1958, *s.* 1977, *m.*	Lord Loughborough, *b.* 1986.
1457 s.	*Rothes* (21st), Ian Lionel Malcolm Leslie, *b.* 1932, *s.* 1975, *m.*	Lord Leslie, *b.* 1958.
1861	°*Russell* (5th), Conrad Sebastian Robert Russell, *b.* 1937, *s.* 1987, *m.*	Viscount Amberley, *b.* 1968.
1915	°*St. Aldwyn* (2nd), Michael John Hicks Beach, G.B.E., T.D., P.C., *b.* 1912, *s.* 1916, *m.*	Viscount Quenington, *b.* 1950.
1815	*St. Germans* (10th), Peregrine Nicholas Eliot, *b.* 1941, *s.* 1988, *m.*	Lord Eliot, *b.* 1966.
1690	*Scarbrough* (12th), Richard Aldred Lumley (13th *Irish Visct., Lumley,* 1628), *b.* 1932, *s.* 1969, *m.*	Viscount Lumley, *b.* 1973.
1701 s.	*Seafield* (13th), Ian Derek Francis Ogilvie-Grant, *b.* 1939, *s.* 1969, *m.*	Visct. Reidhaven, *b.* 1963.
1882	*Selborne* (4th), John Roundell Palmer, K.B.E., *b.* 1940, *s.* 1971, *m.*	Viscount Wolmer, *b.* 1971.
1646 s.	*Selkirk* (10th), (George) Nigel Douglas-Hamilton, K.T., G.C.M.G., G.B.E., A.F.C., P.C., Q.C., *b.* 1906, *s.* 1940, *m.*	The Master of Selkirk, *b.* 1939.
1672	*Shaftesbury* (10th), Anthony Ashley-Cooper, *b.* 1938, *s.* 1961, *m.*	Lord Ashley, *b.* 1977.
1756 I.*	*Shannon* (9th), Richard Bentinck Boyle (8th *Brit. Bn., Carleton* 1786), *b.* 1924, *s.* 1963.	Viscount Boyle, *b.* 1960.
1442	*Shrewsbury & Waterford* (22nd) (I. 1446), Charles Henry John Benedict Crofton Chetwynd Chetwynd-Talbot (*Premier Earl of England and Ireland; Earl Talbot,* 1784), *b.* 1952, *s.* 1980, *m.*	Viscount Ingestre, *b.* 1978.
1961	*Snowdon* (1st), Antony Charles Robert Armstrong-Jones, G.C.V.O., *b.* 1930, *m.* (*See also* p. 149).	Viscount Linley, *b.* 1961 (*see also* p. 149).
1880	°*Sondes* (5th), Henry George Herbert Milles-Lade, *b.* 1940, *s.* 1970.	(None.)
1633 s.*	*Southesk* (11th), Charles Alexander Carnegie, K.C.V.O. (3rd *U.K. Baron, Balinhard,* 1869), *b.* 1893, *s.* 1941, *m.*	The Duke of Fife, *b.* 1929 (*see* pp. 146 and 157).
1765	°*Spencer* (8th), Edward John Spencer, L.V.O., *b.* 1924, *s.* 1975, *m.*	Viscount Althorp, *b.* 1964.
1703 s.*	*Stair* (13th), John Aymer Dalrymple, K.C.V.O., M.B.E (6th *U.K. Baron, Oxenfoord,* 1841), *b.* 1906, *s.* 1961, *m.*	Viscount Dalrymple, *b.* 1961.
1984	*Stockton* (2nd), Alexander Daniel Alan Macmillan, *b.* 1943, *s.* 1986, *m.*	Viscount Macmillan of Ovenden, *b.* 1974.
1821	*Stradbroke* (6th), Robert Keith Rous, *b.* 1937, *s.* 1983, *m.*	Viscount Dunwich, *b.* 1961.
1847	*Strafford* (8th), Thomas Edmund Byng, *b.* 1936, *s.* 1984, *m.*	Viscount Enfield, *b.* 1964.
1606 s.*	*Strathmore and Kinghorne* (18th), Michael Fergus Bowes Lyon (16th *Scottish Earl, Strathmore,* 1677, & 18th *Kinghorne,* 1606; 5th *U.K. Earl, Strathmore & Kinghorne,* 1937), *b.* 1957, *s.* 1987, *m.*	Lord Glamis, *b.* 1986.
1603	*Suffolk* (21st) & *Berkshire* (14th) (1626), Michael John James George Robert Howard, *b.* 1935, *s.* 1941, *m.*	Viscount Andover, *b.* 1974.
1955	*Swinton* (2nd), David Yarburgh Cunliffe-Lister, *b.* 1937, *s.* 1972, *m.*	Hon. Nicholas J. *C.-L.*, *b.* 1939.
1714	*Tankerville* (10th), Peter Grey Bennet, *b.* 1956, *s.* 1980.	Rev. the Hon. George A. G. *B.*, *b.* 1925.

Created.	Title, Order of Succession, Name, etc.	Eldest Son or Heir.
1822	°*Temple of Stowe* (8th), (Walter) Grenville Algernon Temple-Gore-Langton, *b.* 1924, *s.* 1988, *m.*	Hon. James G. *T.-G.-L.*, *b.* 1955.
1815	*Verulam* (7th), John Duncan Grimston (11th *Irish Visct.*, *Grimston*, 1719; 16th *Scott. Baron*, *Forrester of Corstorphine*, 1633), *b.* 1951, *s.* 1973, *m.*	Viscount Grimston, *b.* 1978.
1729	°*Waldegrave* (12th), Geoffrey Noel Waldegrave, K.G., G.C.V.O., T.D., *b.* 1905, *s.* 1936, *m.*	Viscount Chewton, *b.* 1940.
1759	*Warwick* & °*Brooke* (8th) (*Brit.* 1746), David Robin Francis Guy Greville (8th *Earl Brooke* and 8th *Earl of Warwick*), *b.* 1934, *s.* 1984.	Lord Brooke, *b.* 1957.
1633 s.*	*Wemyss* (12th) & *March* (8th) (s. 1697), Francis David Charteris, K.T. (5th *U.K. Baron*, *Wemyss*, 1821), *b.* 1912, *s.* 1937, *m.*	Lord Neidpath, *b.* 1948.
1621 I.	*Westmeath* (13th), William Anthony Nugent, *b.* 1928, *s.* 1971, *m.*	Lord Delvin, *b.* 1965.
1624	*Westmorland* (15th), David Anthony Thomas Fane, K.C.V.O., *b.* 1924, *s.* 1948, *m.* (*Master of the Horse*).	Lord Burghersh, *b.* 1951.
1876	*Wharncliffe* (5th), Richard Alan Montagu Scott Wortley, *b.* 1953, *s.* 1987, *m.*	Viscount Carlton, *b.* 1980.
1801	*Wilton* (7th), Seymour William Arthur John Egerton, *b.* 1921, *s.* 1927, *m.*	Baron Ebury, *b.* 1934 (*see* p. 170).
1628	*Winchilsea* (16th) & *Nottingham* (11th) (1675), Christopher Denys Stormont Finch Hatton, *b.* 1936, *s.* 1950, *m.*	Viscount Maidstone, *b.* 1967.
1766 I.	°*Winterton* (7th), Robert Chad Turnour, *b.* 1915, *s.* 1962, *m.*	N. Cecil *T.*, D.F.M., C.D., *b.* 1919.
1956	*Woolton* (3rd), Simon Frederick Marquis, *b.* 1958, *s.* 1969, *m.*	(None.)
1837	*Yarborough* (7th), John Edward Pelham, *b.* 1920, *s.* 1966, *m.*	Lord Worsley, *b.* 1963.

VISCOUNTS

Style (see also note, p. 187), The Right Hon. The Viscount ——. *Addressed as*, My Lord. The eldest sons of Viscounts and Barons have no distinctive title; they, as well as their brothers and sisters, are styled the Hon. Robert, Hon. Mary, &c.

Created.	Title, Order of Succession, Name, etc.	Eldest Son or Heir.
1945	*Addison* (3rd), Michael Addison, *b.* 1914, *s.* 1976, *m.*	Hon. William M. W. *A.*, *b.* 1945.
1946	*Alanbrooke* (3rd), Alan Victor Harold Brooke, *b.* 1932, *s.* 1972.	(None).
1919	*Allenby* (3rd), Lt.-Col. Michael Jaffray Hynman Allenby, *b.* 1931, *s.* 1984, *m.*	Hon. Henry J. H. *A.*, *b.* 1968.
1911	*Allendale* (3rd), Wentworth Hubert Charles Beaumont, *b.* 1922, *s.* 1956, *m.*	Hon. Wentworth P. I. *B.*, *b.* 1948.
1642 s.	*of Arbuthnott* (16th), John Campbell Arbuthnott, C.B.E., D.S.C., *b.* 1924, *s.* 1966, *m.*	Master of Arbuthnott, *b.* 1950.
1751 I.	*Ashbrook* (10th), Desmond Llowarch Edward Flower, K.C.V.O., M.B.E., *b.* 1905. *s.* 1936, *m.*	Hon. Michael L. W. *F.*, *b.* 1935.
1917	*Astor* (4th), William Waldorf Astor, *b.* 1951, *s.* 1966, *m.*	Hon. William W. *A.*, *b.* 1979.
1781 I.	*Bangor* (7th), Edward Henry Harold Ward, *b.* 1905, *s.* 1950, *m.*	Hon. William M. D. *W.*, *b.* 1948.
1720 I.*	*Barrington* (11th), Patrick William Daines Barrington (5th *U.K. Baron Shute*, 1880), *b.* 1908, *s.* 1960.	(None.)
1925	*Bearsted* (4th), Peter Montefiore Samuel, M.C., T.D., *b.* 1911, *s.* 1986, *m.*	Hon. Nicholas A. *S.*, *b.* 1950.
1963	*Blakenham* (2nd), Michael John Hare, *b.* 1938, *s.* 1982, *m.*	Hon. Caspar J. *H.*, *b.* 1972.
1935	*Bledisloe* (3rd), Christopher Hiley Ludlow Bathurst, Q.C., *b.* 1934, *s.* 1979.	Hon. Rupert E. L. *B.*, *b.* 1964.
1712	*Bolingbroke* & *St. John* (7th) (1716), Kenneth Oliver Musgrave St. John, *b.* 1927, *s.* 1974, *m.*	Hon. Henry F. *St. J.*, *b.* 1957.
1960	*Boyd of Merton* (2nd), Simon Donald Rupert Neville Lennox-Boyd, *b.* 1939, *s.* 1983, *m.*	Hon. Benjamin A. *L.-B.*, *b.* 1964.
1717 I.*	*Boyne* (10th), Gustavus Michael George Hamilton-Russell (4th *U.K. Baron, Brancepeth*, 1866), *b.* 1931, *s.* 1942, *m.*	Hon. Gustavus M. S. *H.-R.*, *b.* 1965.
1929	*Brentford* (4th), Crispin William Joynson-Hicks, *b.* 1933, *s.* 1983, *m.*	Hon. Paul W. *J.-H.*, *b.* 1971.
1929	*Bridgeman* (3rd), Robin John Orlando Bridgeman, *b.* 1930, *s.* 1982, *m.*	Hon. William O. C. *B.*, *b.* 1968.
1868	*Bridport* (4th), Alexander Nelson Hood (7th *Duke of Bronté in Sicily*, 1799, *and* 6th *Irish Baron, Bridport* 1794), *b.* 1948, *s.* 1969, *m.*	Hon. Peregrine A. N. *H.*, *b.* 1974.
1952	*Brookeborough* (3rd), Alan Henry Brooke, *b.* 1952, *s.* 1987, *m.*	Hon. Christopher A. *B.*, *b.* 1954.
1933	*Buckmaster* (3rd), Martin Stanley Buckmaster, O.B.E., *b.* 1921, *s.* 1974.	Hon. Colin J. *B.*, *b.* 1923.
1939	*Caldecote* (2nd), Robert Andrew Inskip, K.B.E., D.S.C., *b.* 1917, *s.* 1947, *m.*	Hon. Piers J. H. *I.*, *b.* 1947.
1941	*Camrose* (2nd), (John) Seymour Berry, T.D., *b.* 1909, *s.* 1954, *m.*	Baron Hartwell, M.B.E., T.D., *b.* 1911 (*see* p. 179).
1952	*Chandos* (3rd), Thomas Orlando Lyttelton, *b.* 1953, *s.* 1980, *m.*	Hon. Matthew P. A. *L.*, *b.* 1956.

Created.	Title, Order of Succession, Name, etc.	Eldest Son or Heir.
1665 I.	*Charlemont* (14th), John Day Caulfeild (18th *Irish Baron, Caulfeild of Charlemont*, 1620), *b.* 1934, *s.* 1985, *m.*	Hon. John D. C., *b.* 1966.
1921	*Chelmsford* (3rd), Frederic Jan Thesiger, *b.* 1931, *s.* 1970, *m.*	Hon. Frederic C. P. T., *b.* 1962.
1717 I.	*Chetwynd* (10th), Adam Richard John Casson Chetwynd, *b.* 1935, *s.* 1965, *m.*	Hon. Adam D. C., *b.* 1969.
1911	*Chilston* (4th), Alastair George Akers-Douglas, *b.* 1946, *s.* 1982, *m.*	Hon. Oliver I. A.-D., *b.* 1973.
1902	*Churchill* (3rd), Victor George Spencer (5th *U.K. Baron Churchill,* 1815), *b.* 1934, *s.* 1973.	(None to Viscountcy), to Barony, R. Harry R. S., *b.* 1926.
1718	*Cobham* (11th), John William Leonard Lyttelton (8th *Irish Baron, Westcote*, 1776), *b.* 1943, *s.* 1977, *m.*	Hon. Christopher C. L., *b.* 1947.
1902	*Colville of Culross* (4th), John Mark Alexander Colville, Q.C. (13th *Scott. Baron, Colville of Culross*, 1604), *b.* 1933, *s.* 1945, *m.*	Master of Colville, *b.* 1959.
1826	*Combermere* (5th), Michael Wellington Stapleton-Cotton, *b.* 1929, *s.* 1969, *m.*	Hon. Thomas R. W. S.-C., *b.* 1969.
1917	*Cowdray* (3rd), Weetman John Churchill Pearson, T.D. (3rd *U.K. Baron, Cowdray*, 1910), *b.* 1910, *s.* 1933, *m.*	Hon. Michael O. W. P., *b.* 1944.
1927	*Craigavon* (3rd), Janric Fraser Craig, *b.* 1944, *s.* 1974.	(None).
1886	*Cross* (3rd), Assheton Henry Cross, *b.* 1920, *s.* 1932, *m.*	(None).
1943	*Daventry* (3rd), Francis Humphrey Maurice FitzRoy Newdegate, *b.* 1921, *s.* 1986, *m.*	Hon. James E. F-N., *b.* 1960.
1937	*Davidson* (2nd), John Andrew Davidson, *b.* 1928, *s.* 1970, *m.*	Hon. Malcolm W. M. D., *b.* 1934.
1956	*De L'Isle* (1st), William Philip Sidney, V.C., K.G., G.C.M.G., G.C.V.O., P.C., (6th *Baron De L'Isle and Dudley*, 1835), *b.* 1909, *m.*	Maj. Hon. Philip J. A. S., M.B.E., *b.* 1945.
1776 I.	*De Vesci* (7th), Thomas Eustace Vesey (8th *Irish Baron, Knapton,* 1750), *b.* 1955, *s.* 1983.	Nicholas I. V., *b.* 1954.
1917	*Devonport* (3rd), Terence Kearley, *b.* 1944, *s.* 1973.	Chester D. H. K., *b.* 1932.
1964	*Dilhorne* (2nd), John Mervyn Manningham-Buller, *b.* 1932, *s.* 1980, *m.*	Hon. James E. M.-B., *b.* 1956.
1622 I.	*Dillon* (22nd), Henry Benedict Charles Dillon, *b.* 1973, *s.* 1982, *M.*	Hon. Richard A. L. D., *b.* 1948.
1785 I.	*Doneraile* (10th), Richard Allen St. Leger, *b.* 1946, *s.* 1983, *m.*	Hon. Nathaniel W. R. St. J. St. L., *b.* 1971.
1680 I.*	*Downe* (11th), John Christian George Dawnay (4th *U.K. Baron, Dawnay*, 1897), *b.* 1935, *s.* 1965, *m.*	Hon. Richard H. D., *b.* 1967.
1959	*Dunrossil* (2nd), John William Morrison, C.M.G., *b.* 1926, *s.* 1961, *m.*	Hon. Andrew W. R. M., *b.* 1953.
1964	*Eccles* (1st), David McAdam Eccles, C.H., K.C.V.O., P.C., *b.* 1904, *m.*	Hon. John D. E., C.B.E., *b.* 1931.
1897	*Esher* (4th), Lionel Gordon Baliol Brett, C.B.E., *b.* 1913. *s.* 1963, *m.*	Hon. Christopher L. B. B., *b.* 1936.
1816	*Exmouth* (10th), Paul Edward Pellew, *b.* 1940, *s.* 1970, *m.*	Hon. Edward F. P., *b.* 1978.
1620 s.	*Falkland* (15th), Lucius Edward William Plantagenet Cary (*Premier Scottish Viscount on the Roll*), *b.* 1935, *s.* 1984, *m.*	Master of Falkland, *b.* 1963.
1720	*Falmouth* (9th), George Hugh Boscawen (26th *Eng. Baron, Le Despencer*, 1264), *b.* 1919, *s.* 1962, *m.*	Hon. Evelyn A. H. B., *b.* 1955.
1918	*Furness* (2nd), William Anthony Furness, *b.* 1929, *s.* 1940.	(None.)
1720 I.*	*Gage* (7th), George John St. Clere Gage, (6th *Brit. Baron, Gage*, 1790), *b.* 1932, *s.* 1982, *m.*	Hon. Henry N G., *b.* 1934.
1727 I.	*Galway* (12th), George Rupert Monckton-Arundell, *b.* 1922, *s.* 1980, *m.*	Hon. John P. M.-A., *b.* 1952.
1478 I.*	*Gormanston* (17th), Jenico Nicholas Dudley Preston (*Premier Viscount of Ireland*; 5th *U.K. Baron, Gormanston*, 1868), *b.* 1939, *s.* 1940, *w.*	Hon. Jenico F. T. P., *b.* 1974.
1816 I.	*Gort* (8th), Colin Leopold Prendergast Vereker, *b.* 1916, *s.* 1975, *m.*	Hon. Foley R.S.P. V., *b.* 1951.
1900	*Goschen* (4th), Giles John Harry Goschen, *b.* 1965, *s.* 1977.	(None.)
1849	*Gough* (5th), Shane Hugh Maryon Gough, *b.* 1941, *s.* 1951.	(None.)
1937	*Greenwood* (2nd), David Henry Hamar Greenwood, *b.* 1914, *s.* 1948.	Hon. Michael G. H. G., *b.* 1923.
1891	*Hambleden* (4th), William Herbert Smith, *b.* 1930, *s.* 1948.	Hon. William H. B. S., *b.* 1955.
1884	*Hampden* (6th), Anthony David Brand, *b.* 1937, *s.* 1975.	Hon. Francis A. B., *b.* 1970.
1936	*Hanworth* (2nd), David Bertram Pollock, *b.* 1916, *s.* 1936, *m.*	Hon. David S. G. P., *b.* 1946.
1791 I.	*Harberton* (10th), Thomas de Vautort Pomeroy, *b.* 1910, *s.* 1980, *m.*	Hon. Robert W. P., *b.* 1916.
1846	*Hardinge* (6th), Charles Henry Nicholas Hardinge, *b.* 1956, *s.* 1984.	Hon. Andrew H. H., *b.* 1960.
1791 I.	*Hawarden* (8th), Robert Leslie Eustace Maude, *b.* 1926, *s.* 1958, *m.*	Hon. Robert C. W. L. M., *b.* 1961.
1960	*Head* (2nd), Richard Antony Head, *b.* 1937, *s.* 1983, *m.*	Hon. Henry J. H., *b.* 1980.
1550	*Hereford* (18th), Robert Milo Leicester Devereux (*Premier Viscount of England*), *b.* 1932, *s.* 1952.	Hon. Charles R. de B. D., *b.* 1975.
1842	*Hill* (8th), Antony Rowland Clegg-Hill, *b.* 1931, *s.* 1974, *m.*	Peter D. R. C. C.-H., *b.* 1945.
1796	*Hood* (7th), Alexander Lambert Hood (7th *Irish Baron, Hood,* 1782), *b.* 1914, *s.* 1981, *m.*	Hon. Henry L. A. H., *b.* 1958.
1956	*Ingleby* (2nd), Martin Raymond Peake, *b.* 1926, *s.* 1966, *m.*	(None.)
1945	*Kemsley* (2nd), (Geoffrey) Lionel Berry, *b.* 1909, *s.* 1968, *m.*	Richard G. B., *b.* 1951.

Created.	Title, Order of Succession, Name, etc.	Eldest Son or Heir.
1911	*Knollys* (3rd), David Francis Dudley Knollys, b. 1931, s. 1966, m.	Hon. Patrick N. M. K., b. 1962.
1895	*Knutsford* (6th), Michael Holland-Hibbert, b. 1926, s. 1986, m.	Hon. Henry T. H.-H., b. 1959.
1945	*Lambert* (2nd), George Lambert, T.D., b. 1909, s. 1958, m.	Hon. Michael J. L., b. 1912.
1954	*Leathers* (2nd), Frederick Alan Leathers, b. 1908, s. 1965, m.	Hon. Christopher G. L., b. 1941.
1922	*Leverhulme* (3rd), Philip William Bryce Lever, K.G., T.D., b. 1915, s. 1949, w.	(None.)
1781 I.	*Lifford* (9th), (Edward) James Wingfield Hewitt, b. 1949, s. 1987, m.	Hon. James T. W. H., b. 1979.
1921	*Long* (4th), Richard Gerard Long, b. 1929, s. 1967, m.	Hon. James R. L., b. 1960.
1957	*Mackintosh of Halifax* (3rd), (John) Clive Mackintosh, b. 1958, s. 1980, m.	Hon. Thomas H. G. M., b. 1985.
1955	*Malvern* (3rd), Ashley Kevin Godfrey Huggins, b. 1949, s. 1978.	Hon. M. James H., b. 1928.
1945	*Marchwood* (3rd), David George Staveley Penny, b. 1936, s. 1979, m.	Hon. Peter G. W. P., b. 1965.
1942	*Margesson* (2nd), Francis Vere Hampden Margesson, b. 1922, s. 1965, m.	Capt. Hon. Richard F. D. M., b. 1960.
1660 I.*	*Massereene* (13th) & (6th) *Ferrard* (1797), John Clotworthy Talbot Foster Whyte-Melville Skeffington (6th *U.K. Baron, Oriel,* 1821), b. 1914, s. 1956, m.	Hon. John D. C. W.-M. F. S., b. 1940.
1802	*Melville* (9th), Robert David Ross Dundas, b. 1937, s. 1971, m.	Hon. Robert H. K. D., b. 1984.
1916	*Mersey* (4th), Richard Maurice Clive Bigham, b. 1934, s. 1979, m.	Hon. Edward J. H. B., b. 1966.
1717 I.*	*Midleton* (11th), Trevor Lowther Brodrick (8th *Brit. Baron, Brodrick of Peper Harow,* 1796), b. 1903, s. 1979, m.	Alan H. B., b. 1949.
1962	*Mills* (2nd), Roger Clinton Mills, b. 1919, s. 1968, m.	Hon. Christopher P. R. M., b. 1956.
1716 I.	*Molesworth* (11th), Richard Gosset Molesworth, b. 1907, s. 1961, w.	Hon. Robert B. K. M., b. 1959.
1801 I.*	*Monck* (7th), Charles Stanley Monck (4th *U.K. Baron, Monck,* 1866), b. 1953, s. 1982.	Hon. George S. M., b. 1957.
1957	*Monckton of Brenchley* (2nd), Gilbert Walter Riversdale Monckton, C.B., O.B.E., M.C., b. 1915, s. 1965, m.	Hon Christopher W. M., b. 1952.
1935	*Monsell* (2nd), Henry Bolton Graham Eyres Monsell, b. 1905, s. 1969.	(None.)
1946	*Montgomery of Alamein* (2nd), David Bernard Montgomery, C.B.E, b. 1928, s. 1976, m.	Hon. Henry D. M., b. 1954.
1550 I.*	*Mountgarret* (17th), Richard Henry Piers Butler (4th *U.K. Baron, Mountgarret,* 1911), b. 1936, s. 1966, m.	Hon. Piers J. R. B., b. 1961.
1964	*Muirshiel* (1st), John Scott Maclay, K.T., C.H., C.M.G., P.C., b. 1905, w.	(None.)
1952	*Norwich* (2nd), John Julius Cooper, b. 1929, s. 1954.	Hon. Jason C. D. B. C., b. 1959.
1651 S.	*of Oxfuird* (13th), George Hubbard Makgill, b. 1934, s. 1986, m.	Master of Oxfuird, b. 1969.
1873	*Portman,* (9th), Edward Henry Berkeley Portman, b. 1934, s. 1967, m.	Hon. Christopher E. B. P., b. 1958.
1743 I.*	*Powerscourt* (10th), Mervyn Niall Wingfield (4th *U.K. Baron, Powerscourt,* 1885), b. 1935, s. 1973, m.	Hon. Mervyn A. W., b. 1963.
1900	*Ridley* (4th), Matthew White Ridley, T.D., b. 1925, s. 1964, m.	Hon. Matthew W. R., b. 1958.
1960	*Rochdale* (1st), John Durival Kemp, O.B.E., T.D. (2nd U.K. Baron, Rochdale, 1913), b. 1906, m.	Hon. St. John D. K., b. 1938.
1919	*Rothermere* (3rd), Vere Harold Esmond Harmsworth, b. 1925, s. 1978, m.	Hon. Harold J. E. V. H., b. 1967.
1937	*Runciman of Doxford* (2nd), Walter Leslie Runciman, O.B.E., A.F.C. (3rd *U.K. Baron, Runciman,* 1933), b. 1900, s. 1949, m.	Hon. Walter G. R., C.B.E., F.B.A., b. 1934.
1918	*St. Davids* (2nd), Jestyn Reginald Austen Plantagenet Philipps (19th *English Baron, Strange of Knokin* 1299, 7th *English Baron, Hungerford,* 1426 *and De Moleyns,* 1445), b. 1917, s. 1938, m.	Hon. Colwyn J. J. P., b. 1939.
1801	*St. Vincent* (7th), Ronald George James Jervis, b. 1905, s. 1940, m.	Hon. Edward R. J. J., b. 1951.
1937	*Samuel* (3rd), David Herbert Samuel, Ph.D., b. 1922, s. 1978, m.	Hon. Dan J. S., b. 1925.
1911	*Scarsdale* (3rd), Francis John Nathaniel Curzon (7th *Brit. Baron, Scarsdale,* 1761), b. 1924, s. 1977, m.	Hon. Peter G. N. C., b. 1949.
1905	*Selby* (4th), Michael Guy John Gully, b. 1942, s. 1959, m.	Hon. Edward T. W. G., b. 1967.
1805	*Sidmouth* (7th), John Tonge Anthony Pellew Addington, b. 1914, s. 1976, m.	Hon. Jeremy F. A., b. 1947.
1940	*Simon* (2nd), John Gilbert Simon, C.M.G., b. 1902, s. 1954, m.	Hon. Jan D. S., b. 1940.
1960	*Slim* (2nd), John Douglas Slim, O.B.E., b. 1927, s. 1970, m.	Hon. Mark W. R. S., b. 1960.
1954	*Soulbury* (2nd), James Herwald Ramsbotham, b. 1915, s. 1971, w.	Hon. Sir Peter E. R., G.C.M.G., G.C.V.O., b. 1919.
1776 I.	*Southwell* (7th), Pyers Anthony Joseph Southwell, b. 1930, s. 1960, m.	Hon. Richard A. P. S., b. 1956.
1959	*Stuart of Findhorn* (2nd), David Randolph Moray Stuart, b. 1924, s. 1971, m.	Hon. James D. S., b. 1948.

Created.	Title, Order of Succession, Name, etc.	Eldest Son or Heir.
1957	*Tenby* (3rd), William Lloyd George, *b.* 1927, *s.* 1983, *m.*	Hon. Timothy H. G. *L. G., b.* 1962.
1952	*Thurso* (2nd), Robin Macdonald Sinclair, *b.* 1922, *s.* 1970, *m.*	Hon. John A. *S., b.* 1953.
1983	*Tonypandy* (1st), (Thomas) George Thomas, P.C., *b.* 1909.	(None).
1721	*Torrington* (11th), Timothy Howard St. George Byng, *b.* 1943, *s.* 1961, *m.*	John L. *B.*, M.C., *b.* 1919.
1936	*Trenchard* (3rd), Hugh Trenchard, *b.* 1951, *s.* 1987, *m.*	Hon. Alexander T. *T., b.* 1978.
1921	*Ullswater* (2nd), Nicholas James Christopher Lowther, *b.* 1942, *s.* 1949, *m.*	Hon. Benjamin J. *L., b.* 1975.
1621 I.	*Valentia* (15th), Richard John Dighton Annesley, *b.* 1929, *s.* 1983, *m.*	Hon. Francis W. D. *A., b.* 1959.
1964	*Watkinson* (1st), Harold Arthur Watkinson, C.H., P.C., *b.* 1910, *m.*	(None.)
1952	*Waverley* (2nd), David Alastair Pearson Anderson, *b.* 1911, *s.* 1958, *m.*	Hon. John D. F. *A., b.* 1949.
1938	*Weir* (3rd), William Kenneth James Weir, *b.* 1933, *s.* 1975, *m.*	Hon. James W. H. *W., b.* 1965.
1983	*Whitelaw* (1st), William Stephen Ian Whitelaw, C.H., M.C., P.C., *b.* 1918, *m.*	(None).
1918	*Wimborne* (3rd), Ivor Fox-Strangways Guest (4th *U.K. Baron, Wimborne,* 1880), *b.* 1939, *s.* 1967, *m.*	Hon. Ivor M.V.*G., b.* 1968.
1923	*Younger of Leckie* (3rd), Edward George Younger, O.B.E., T.D., *b.* 1906, *s.* 1946, *w.*	Rt. Hon. George K. H. *Y.,* T.D., M.P., *b.* 1931.

BISHOPS

Style, The Right Rev. The Lord Bishop of ——. *Addressed as,* My Lord.

The Bishops of London, Durham and Winchester always have seats in the House of Lords: the other 21 seats are filled by the remaining diocesan Bishops in order of seniority. The Bishop of Sodor and Man and the Bishop of Gibraltar are not eligible to sit in the House of Lords.

Introd. to House of Lords		Election as Diocesan Bp. confirmed	Trans. to present See
1977	*London* (130th), Graham Douglas Leonard, P.C., *b.* 1921, *cons.* 1964, *m.*	1973	1981
1984	*Durham* (92nd), David Edward Jenkins, *b.* 1925, *cons.* 1984, *m.*	1984	—
1982	*Winchester* (95th), Colin Clement Walter James, *b.* 1926, *cons.* 1973, *m.*	1977	1985
1976	*Carlisle* (64th), Henry David Halsey, *b.* 1919, *cons.* 1968, *m.*	1972	
1976	*Southwark* (7th), Ronald Oliver Bowlby, *b.* 1926, *cons.* 1973, *m.*	1973	1980
1979	*Hereford* (102nd), John Richard Gordon Eastaugh, *b.* 1920, *cons.* 1974, *m.*	1974	
1979	*Chichester* (102nd), Eric Waldram Kemp, D.D., *b.* 1915, *cons.* 1974, *m.*	1974	
1980	*Liverpool* (6th), David Stuart Sheppard, *b.* 1929, *cons.* 1969, *m.*	1975	
1981	*Gloucester* (37th), John Yates, *b.* 1925, *cons.* 1972, *m.*	1975	
1984	*Ripon* (11th), David Nigel de Lorentz Young, *b.* 1931, *cons.* 1977, *m.*	1977	
1984	*Ely* (66th), Peter Knight Walker, *b.* 1919, *cons.* 1972, *m.*	1977	
1985	*Chelmsford* (7th), John Waine, *b.* 1930, *cons.* 1975, *m.*	1978	1986
1985	*Manchester* (9th), Stanley Eric Francis Booth-Clibborn, *b.* 1924, *cons.* 1979, *m.*	1979	
1985	*Leicester* (4th), Cecil Richard Rutt, C.B.E., *b.* 1925, *cons.* 1966, *m.*	1979	
1985	*Sheffield* (5th), David Ramsay Lunn, *b.* 1930, *cons.* 1980.	1980	
1985	*St. Albans* (8th), John Bernard Taylor, *b.* 1929, *cons.* 1980, *m.*	1980	
1985	*Newcastle* (10th), Andrew Alexander Kenny Graham, *b.* 1929, *cons.* 1977.	1981	
1985	*Truro* (12th), Peter Mumford, *b.* 1922, *cons.* 1974, *m.*	1981	
1986	*Salisbury* (76th), John Austin Baker, *b.* 1928, *cons.* 1982, *m.*	1982	
1986	**Blackburn* (6th), David Stewart Cross, *b.* 1928, *cons.* 1976, *m.*	1982	
1987	*Worcester* (111th), Philip Harold Ernest Goodrich, *b.* 1929, *cons.* 1973, *m.*	1982	
1987	*Chester* (39th), Michael Alfred Baughen, *b.* 1930, *cons.* 1982, *m.*	1982	
1988	*Guildford* (7th), Michael Edgar Adie, *b.* 1929, *cons.* 1983, *m.*	1983	
1988	*Bradford* (7th), Robert Kerr Williamson, *b.* 1932, *cons.* 1984, *m.*	1984	

Bishops awaiting seats, in order of seniority

	Lichfield (97th), Keith Norman Sutton, *b.* 1934, *cons.* 1978, *m.*	1984	
	Peterborough (36th), William John Westwood, *b.* 1925, *cons.* 1975, *m.*	1984	
	Portsmouth (7th), Timothy John Bavin, *b.* 1935, *cons.* 1974.	1985	
	Exeter (69th), (Geoffrey) Hewlett Thompson, *b.* 1929, *cons.* 1974, *m.*	1985	
	Bristol (54th), Barry Rogerson, *b.* 1936, *cons.* 1979, *m.*	1985	
	Wakefield (10th), David Michael Hope, D.PHIL., *b.* 1940, *cons.* 1985.	1985	
	Coventry (7th), Simon Barrington-Ward, *b.* 1930, *cons.* 1985, *m.*	1985	
	Norwich (70th), Peter John Nott, *b.* 1933, *cons.* 1977, *m.*	1985	
	St. Edmundsbury and Ipswich (8th), John Dennis, *b.* 1931, *cons.* 1979, *m.*	1986	

	Election as Diocesan Bp. confirmed	Trans. to present See
Lincoln (70th), Robert Maynard Hardy, *b.* 1936, *cons.* 1980, *m.*	1986	
Oxford (41st), Richard Douglas Harries, *b.* 1936, *cons.* 1987, *m.*	1987	
Birmingham (7th), Mark Santer, *b.* 1936, *cons.* 1981, *m.*	1987	
Bath and Wells (75th), George Leonard Carey, PH.D., *b.* 1935, *cons.* 1988, *m.*	1987	
Derby (5th), Peter Spencer Dawes, *b.* 1928, *cons.* 1988, *m.*	1988	
Southwell (9th), Patrick Burnet Harris, *b.* 1934, *cons.* 1973, *m.*	1988	
Rochester (105th), (Anthony) Michael (Arnold) Turnbull, *b.* 1935, *cons.* 1988, *m.*	1988	

* The Bishop of Blackburn retires in Oct. 1988.

BARONS

Style (see *also* note, p. 187), The Right Hon. The Lord ——.
Addressed as, My Lord.

Created.	Title, Order of Succession, Name, etc.	Eldest Son or Heir.
1911	*Aberconway* (3rd), Charles Melville McLaren, *b.* 1913, *s.* 1953, *m.*	Hon. Henry C. *McL.*, *b.* 1948.
1873	*Aberdare* (4th), Morys George Lyndhurst Bruce, K.B.E., P.C., *b.* 1919, *s.* 1957, *m.*	Hon. Alastair J. L. *B.*, *b.* 1947.
1835	*Abinger* (8th), James Richard Scarlett, *b.* 1914, *s.* 1943, *m.*	Hon. James H. *S.*, *b.* 1959.
1869	*Acton* (3rd), John Emerich Henry Lyon-Dalberg-Acton, C.M.G., M.B.E., T.D., *b.* 1907, *s.* 1924, *m.*	Hon. Richard G. *L.-D.-A.*, *b.* 1941.
1887	*Addington* (6th), Dominic Bryce Hubbard, *b.* 1963, *s.* 1982.	Hon. Michael W. L. *H.*, *b.* 1965.
1955	*Adrian* (2nd), Richard Hume Adrian, F.R.S., *b.* 1927, *s.* 1977, *m.*	(None.)
1921	*Ailwyn* (4th), Carol Arthur Fellowes, T.D., *b.* 1896, *s.* 1976, *w.*	(None.)
1907	*Airedale* (4th), Oliver James Vandeleur Kitson, *b.* 1915, *s.* 1958.	(None.)
1896	*Aldenham* (6th), and (4th) *Hunsdon of Hunsdon* (1923), Vicary Tyser Gibbs, *b.* 1948, *s.* 1986, *m.*	Hon. George H. P. *G.*, *b.* 1950.
1962	*Aldington* (1st), Toby Austin Richard William Low, K.C.M.G., C.B.E., D.S.O., T.D., P.C., *b.* 1914, *m.*	Hon Charles H. S. *L.*, *b.* 1948.
1902	*Allerton* (3rd), George William Lawies Jackson, *b.* 1903, *s.* 1925, *m.*	(None).
1929	*Alvingham* (2nd), Maj.-Gen. Robert Guy Eardley Yerburgh, C.B.E., *b.* 1926, *s.* 1955, *m.*	Capt. Hon. Robert R. G. *Y.*, *b.* 1956.
1892	*Amherst of Hackney* (4th), William Hugh Amherst Cecil, *b.* 1940, *s.* 1980, *m.*	Hon. Hugh W. A. *C.*, *b.* 1968.
1881	*Ampthill* (4th), Geoffrey Denis Erskine Russell, C.B.E., *b.* 1921, *s.* 1973, *m.*	Hon. David W. E. *R.*, *b.* 1947.
1947	*Amwell* (2nd), Frederick Norman Montague, *b.* 1912, *s.* 1966, *m.*	Hon. Keith N. *M.*, *b.* 1943.
1863	*Annaly* (5th), Luke Robert White, *b.* 1927, *s.* 1970, *m.*	Hon. Luke R. *W.*, *b.* 1954.
1885	*Ashbourne* (4th), Edward Barry Greynville Gibson, *b.* 1933, *s.* 1983, *m.*	Hon. Edward C. D'O. *G.*, *b.* 1967.
1835	*Ashburton* (6th), Alexander Francis St. Vincent Baring, K.G., K.C.V.O., *b.* 1898, *s.* 1938, *w.*	Hon. Sir John F. H. *B.*, C.V.O., *b.* 1928.
1892	*Ashcombe* (4th), Henry Edward Cubitt, *b.* 1924, *s.* 1962, *m.*	M. Robin *C.*, *b.* 1936.
1911	*Ashton of Hyde* (3rd), Thomas John Ashton, T.D., *b.* 1926, *s.* 1983, *m.*	Hon. Thomas H. *A.*, *b.* 1958.
1800 I.	*Ashtown* (6th), Christopher Oliver Trench, *b.* 1931, *s.* 1979.	Sir Nigel C. C. *T.*, K.C.M.G., *b.* 1916.
1956	*Astor of Hever* (3rd), John Jacob Astor, *b.* 1946, *s.* 1984, *m.*	Hon. Philip D. P. *A.*, *b.* 1959.
1789 I. 1793* }	*Auckland* (9th), Ian George Eden (9th *Brit. Baron, Auckland*), *b.* 1926, *s.* 1957, *m.*	Hon. Robert I. B. *E.*, *b.* 1962.
1313	*Audley* (25th), Richard Michael Thomas Souter, *b.* 1914, *s.* 1973, *m.*	Three co-heiresses.
1900	*Avebury* (4th), Eric Reginald Lubbock, *b.* 1928, *s.* 1971.	Hon. Lyulph A. J. *L.*, *b.* 1954.
1718 I.	*Aylmer* (13th), Michael Anthony Aylmer, *b.* 1923, *s.* 1982, *m.*	Hon. A. Julian *A.*, *b.* 1951.
1929	*Baden-Powell* (3rd), Robert Crause Baden-Powell, *b.* 1936, *s.* 1962, *m.*	Hon. David M. *B.-P.*, *b.* 1940.
1780	*Bagot* (9th), Heneage Charles Bagot, *b.* 1914, *s.* 1979, *m.*	Hon. Charles H. S. *B.*, *b.* 1944.
1953	*Baillieu* (3rd), James William Latham Baillieu, *b.* 1950, *s.* 1973, *m.*	Hon. Robert L. *B.*, *b.* 1979.
1607 S.	*Balfour of Burleigh* (8th), Robert Bruce, *b.* 1927, *s.* 1967, *m.*	Hon. Victoria *B.*, *b.* 1973.
1945	*Balfour of Inchrye* (1st), Harold Harington Balfour, M.C., P.C., *b.* 1897, *m.*	Hon. Ian *B.*, *b.* 1924.
1924	*Banbury of Southam* (3rd), Charles William Banbury, *b.* 1953, *s.* 1981, *m.*	(None.)
1698	*Barnard* (11th), Harry John Neville Vane, T.D., *b.* 1923, *s.* 1964, *m.*	Hon. Henry F. C. *V.*, *b.* 1959.
1887	*Basing* (5th), Neil Lutley Sclater-Booth, *b.* 1939, *s.* 1983, *m.*	Hon. Stuart W. *S.-B.*, *b.* 1969.
1917	*Beaverbrook* (3rd), Maxwell William Humphrey Aitken, *b.* 1951, *s.* 1985, *m.*	Hon. Maxwell F. A, *b.* 1977.
1647 S.	*Belhaven and Stenton* (13th), Robert Anthony Carmichael Hamilton, *b.* 1927, *s.* 1961, *m.*	Master of Belhaven, *b.* 1953.
1848 I.	*Bellew* (7th), James Bryan Bellew, *b.* 1920, *s.* 1981, *m.*	Hon. Bryan E. *B.*, *b.* 1943.
1856	*Belper* (4th), (Alexander) Ronald George Strutt, *b.* 1912, *s.* 1956.	Hon. Richard H. *S.*, *b.* 1941.
1938	*Belstead* (2nd), John Julian Ganzoni, P.C., *b.* 1932, *s.* 1958.	(None.)

Created.	Title, Order of Succession, Name, etc.	Eldest Son or Heir.
1922	*Bethell* (4th), Nicholas William Bethell, *b.* 1938, *s.* 1967.	Hon. James N. *B.*, *b.* 1967.
1938	*Bicester* (3rd), Angus Edward Vivian Smith, *b.* 1932, *s.* 1968.	Hugh C. V. *S.*, *b.* 1934.
1903	*Biddulph* (4th), Robert Michael Christian Biddulph, *b.* 1931, *s.* 1972, *m.*	Hon. Anthony N. C. M.*B.*, *b.* 1959.
1938	*Birdwood* (3rd), Mark William Ogilvie Birdwood, *b.* 1938, *s.* 1962, *m.*	(None.)
1958	*Birkett* (2nd), Michael Birkett, *b.* 1929, *s.* 1962, *m.*	Hon. Thomas *B.*, *b.* 1982.
1907	*Blyth* (4th), Anthony Audley Rupert Blyth, *b.* 1931, *s.* 1977, *m.*	Hon. Riley A. J. *B.*, *b.* 1955.
1797	*Bolton* (7th), Richard William Algar Orde-Powlett, *b.* 1929, *s.* 1963, *m.*	Hon. Harry A. N. *O.-P.*, *b.* 1954.
1452 s.	*Borthwick* (23rd), John Henry Stuart Borthwick, T.D., *b.* 1905, *claim* succeeded 1986, *w.*	Master of Borthwick, *b.* 1940.
1922	*Borwick* (4th), James Hugh Myles Borwick, M.C., *b.* 1917, *s.* 1961, *m.*	Hon. George S. *B.*, *b.* 1922.
1761	*Boston* (10th), Timothy George Frank Boteler Irby, *b.* 1939, *s.* 1978, *m.*	Hon. George W. E. B. *I.*, *b.* 1971.
1942	*Brabazon of Tara* (3rd), Ivon Anthony Moore-Brabazon, *b.* 1946, *s.* 1974, *m.*	Hon. Benjamin R. *M.-B.*, *b.* 1983.
1880	*Brabourne* (7th), John Ulick Knatchbull, *b.* 1924, *s.* 1943, *m.*	Lord Romsey, *b.* 1947, *see* p. 176.
1925	*Bradbury* (2nd), John Bradbury, *b.* 1914, *s.* 1950, *m.*	Hon. John *B.*, *b.* 1940.
1962	*Brain* (2nd), Christopher Langdon Brain, *b.* 1926, *s.* 1966, *m.*	Hon. Michael C. *B.*, D.M., *b.* 1928.
1938	*Brassey of Apethorpe* (3rd), David Henry Brassey, *b.* 1932, *s.* 1967, *m.*	Hon. Edward *B.*, *b.* 1964.
1788	*Braybrooke* (9th), Henry Seymour Neville, *b.* 1897, *s.* 1943, *w.*	Hon. Robin H. C. *N.*, *b.* 1932.
1957	*Bridges* (2nd), Thomas Edward Bridges, G.C.M.G., *b.* 1927, *s.* 1969, *m.*	Hon. Mark T. *B.*, *b.* 1954.
1945	*Broadbridge* (3rd), Peter Hewett Broadbridge, *b.* 1938, *s.* 1972, *m.*	Martin H. *B.*, *b.* 1929.
1933	*Brocket* (3rd), Charles Ronald George Nall-Cain, *b.* 1952, *s.* 1967, *m.*	Hon. Alexander C. C. *N.-C.*, *b.* 1984.
1860	*Brougham and Vaux* (5th), Michael John Brougham, *b.* 1938, *s.* 1967.	Hon. Charles W. *B.*, *b.* 1971.
1945	*Broughshane* (2nd), Patrick Owen Alexander Davison, *b.* 1903, *s.* 1953, *m.*	Hon. Alexander *D.*, *b.* 1936.
1776	*Brownlow* (7th), Edward John Peregrine Cust, *b.* 1936, *s.* 1978, *m.*	Hon. Peregrine E. Q. *C.*, *b.* 1974.
1942	*Bruntisfield* (1st), Victor Alexander George Anthony Warrender, M.C., *b.* 1899, *m.*	Col. Hon. John R. *W.*, O.B.E., M.C., T.D., *b.* 1921.
1950	*Burden* (2nd), Philip William Burden, *b.* 1916, *s.* 1970, *m.*	Hon. Andrew P. *B.*, *b.* 1959.
1529	*Burgh* (7th), Alexander Peter Willoughby Leith, *b.* 1935, *s.* 1959, *m.*	Hon. Alexander G. D. *L.*, *b.* 1958.
1903	*Burnham* (5th), William Edward Harry Lawson, *b.* 1920, *s.* 1963, *m.*	Hon. Hugh J. F. *L.*, *b.* 1931.
1897	*Burton* (3rd), Michael Evan Victor Baillie, *b.* 1924, *s.* 1962, *m.*	Hon. Evan M. R. *B.*, *b.* 1949.
1643	*Byron* (12th), Richard Geoffrey Gordon Byron, D.S.O., *b.* 1899, *s.* 1983, *w.*	Hon. Robert J. *B.*, *b.* 1950.
1937	*Cadman* (3rd), John Anthony Cadman, *b.* 1938, *s.* 1966, *m.*	Hon. Nicholas A. J. *C.*, *b.* 1977.
1796	*Calthorpe* (10th), Peter Waldo Somerset Gough-Calthorpe, *b.* 1927, *s.* 1945, *m.*	(None.)
1945	*Calverley* (3rd), Charles Rodney Muff, *b.* 1946, *s.* 1971, *m.*	Hon. Jonathan E. *M.*, *b.* 1975.
1383	*Camoys* (7th), (Ralph) Thomas (Campion George Sherman) Stonor, *b.* 1940, *s.* 1976, *m.*	Hon. William *S.*, *b.* 1974.
1715 I.	*Carbery* (11th), Peter Ralfe Harrington Evans-Freke, *b.* 1920, *s.* 1970, *m.*	Hon. Michael P. *E.-F.*, *b.* 1942.
1834 I. 1838*	} *Carew* (6th), William Francis Conolly-Carew, C.B.E. (6th *U.K. Baron*, *Carew*, 1838), *b.* 1905, *s.* 1927, *m.*	Hon. Patrick T. *C.-C.*, *b.* 1938.
1916	*Carnock* (4th), David Henry Arthur Nicolson, *b.* 1920, *s.* 1982.	Nigel *N.*, M.B.E., *b.* 1917.
1796 I. 1797*	} *Carrington* (6th), Peter Alexander Rupert Carington, K.G., G.C.M.G., C.H., M.C., P.C., (6th *Brit. Baron, Carrington*, 1797), *b.* 1919, *s.* 1938, *m.*	Hon. Rupert F. J. *C.*, *b.* 1948.
1812 I.	*Castlemaine* (8th), Roland Thomas John Handcock, *b.* 1943, *s.* 1973, *m.*	Terence R. *H.*, *b.* 1902.
1936	*Catto* (2nd), Stephen Gordon Catto, *b.* 1923, *s.* 1959, *m.*	Hon. Innes G. *C.*, *b.* 1950.
1918	*Cawley* (3rd), Frederick Lee Cawley, *b.* 1913, *s.* 1954, *m.*	Hon. John F. *C.*, *b.* 1946.
1937	*Chatfield* (2nd), Ernle David Lewis Chatfield, *b.* 1917, *s.* 1967, *m.*	(None.)
1858	*Chesham* (5th), John Charles Compton Cavendish, P.C., *b.* 1916, *s.* 1952, *m.*	Hon. Nicholas C. *C.*, *b.* 1941.
1945	*Chetwode* (2nd), Philip Chetwode, *b.* 1937, *s.* 1950.	Hon. Roger *C.*, *b.* 1968.
1945	*Chorley* (2nd), Roger Richard Edward Chorley, *b.* 1930, *s.* 1978, *m.*	Hon. Nicholas R. D. *C.*, *b.* 1966.
1858	*Churston* (4th), Richard Francis Roger Yarde-Buller, V.R.D., *b.* 1910, *s.* 1930, *m.*	Hon. John F. *Y.-B.*, *b.* 1934.
1946	*Citrine* (2nd), Norman Arthur Citrine, *b.* 1914, *s.* 1983, *m.*	Hon. Ronald E. *C.*, *b.* 1919.
1800 I.	*Clanmorris* (8th), Simon John Ward Bingham, *b.* 1937, *s.* 1988, *m.*	†
1672	*Clifford of Chudleigh* (14th), Thomas Hugh Clifford, *b.* 1948, *s.* 1988, *m.*	Hon. Rollo H. *C.*, *b.* 1954.
1299	*Clinton* (22nd), Gerard Nevile Mark Fane Trefusis, *b.* 1934, *title called out of abeyance* 1965, *m.*	Hon. Charles P. R. F. *T.*, *b.* 1962.
1955	*Clitheroe* (2nd), Ralph John Assheton, *b.* 1929, *s.* 1984, *m.*	Hon. Ralph C. *A.*, *b.* 1962.
1919	*Clwyd* (3rd), (John) Anthony Roberts, *b.* 1935, *s.* 1987, *m.*	Hon. John M. *R.*, *b.* 1971.
1948	*Clydesmuir* (2nd), Ronald John Bilsland Colville, K.T., C.B., M.B.E., T.D., *b.* 1917, *s.* 1954, *m.*	Hon. David R. *C.*, *b.* 1949.

Created.	Title, Order of Succession, Name, etc.	Eldest Son or Heir.
1960	*Cobbold* (2nd), David Antony Fromanteel Lytton-Cobbold, *b.* 1937, *s.* 1987, *m.*	Hon. Henry F. *L.-C.*, *b.* 1962.
1919	*Cochrane of Cults* (3rd), Thomas Charles Anthony Cochrane, *b.* 1922, *s.* 1968.	Hon. R. H. Vere *C.*, *b.* 1926.
1954	*Coleraine* (2nd), (James) Martin (Bonar) Law, *b.* 1931, *s.* 1980, *m.*	Hon. James P. B. *L.*, *b.* 1975.
1873	*Coleridge* (5th), William Duke Coleridge, *b.* 1937, *s.* 1984, *m.*	Hon. James D. *C.*, *b.* 1967.
1946	*Colgrain* (3rd), David Colin Campbell, *b.* 1920, *s.* 1973, *m.*	Hon. Alastair C. L. *C.*, *b.* 1951.
1917	*Colwyn* (3rd), (Ian) Anthony Hamilton-Smith, *b.* 1942, *s.* 1966, *m.*	Hon. Craig P. *H.-S.*, *b.* 1968.
1956	*Colyton* (1st), Henry Lennox D'Aubigné Hopkinson, C.M.G., P.C., *b.* 1902, *m.*	Hon. Nicholas H. E. *H.*, *b.* 1932.
1841	*Congleton* (8th), Christopher Patrick Parnell, *b.* 1930, *s.* 1967, *m.*	Hon. John P. C. *P.*, *b.* 1959.
1927	*Cornwallis* (3rd), Fiennes Neil Wykeham Cornwallis, O.B.E., *b.* 1921, *s.* 1982, *m.*	Hon. F. W. Jeremy *C.*, *b.* 1946.
1874	*Cottesloe* (4th), John Walgrave Halford Fremantle, G.B.E., T.D., *b.* 1900, *s.* 1956, *m.*	Hon. John T. *F.*, *b.* 1927.
1929	*Craigmyle* (3rd), Thomas Donald Mackay Shaw, *b.* 1923, *s.* 1944, *m.*	Hon. Thomas C. *S.*, *b.* 1960.
1899	*Cranworth* (3rd), Philip Bertram Gurdon, *b.* 1940, *s.* 1964, *m.*	Hon. Sacha W. R. *G.*, *b.* 1970.
1959	*Crathorne* (2nd), Charles James Dugdale, *b.* 1939, *s.* 1977, *m.*	Hon. Thomas A. J. *D.*, *b.* 1977.
1892	*Crawshaw* (4th), William Michael Clifton Brooks, *b.* 1933, *s.* 1946.	Hon. David G. *B.*, *b.* 1934.
1940	*Croft* (2nd), Michael Henry Glendower Page Croft, *b.* 1916, *s.* 1947, *w.*	Hon. Bernard W. H. P. *C.*, *b.* 1949.
1797 I.	*Crofton* (6th), Charles Edward Piers Crofton, *b.* 1949, *s.* 1974, *m.*	Hon. Guy P. G. *C.*, *b.* 1951.
1375	*Cromwell* (7th), Godfrey John Bewicke-Copley, *b.* 1960, *s.* 1982.	Hon. Thomas D. *B.-C.*, *b.* 1964.
1947	*Crook* (1st), Reginald Douglas Crook, *b.* 1901, *w.*	Hon. Douglas E. *C.*, *b.* 1926.
1920	*Cullen of Ashbourne* (2nd), Charles Borlase Marsham Cokayne, M.B.E., *b.* 1912, *s.* 1932, *m.*	Hon. Edmund W. M. *C.*, *b.* 1916.
1914	*Cunliffe* (3rd), Roger Cunliffe, *b.* 1932, *s.* 1963, *m.*	Hon. Henry *C.*, *b.* 1962.
1927	*Daresbury* (2nd), Edward Greenall, *b.* 1902, *s.* 1938, *w.*	Hon. Edward G. *G.*, *b.* 1928.
1924	*Darling* (2nd), Robert Charles Henry Darling, *b.* 1919, *s.* 1936, *m.*	Hon. Robert J. H. *D.*, *b.* 1944.
1946	*Darwen* (2nd), Cedric Percival Davies, *b.* 1915, *s.* 1950, *m.*	Hon. Roger M. *D.*, *b.* 1938.
1923	*Daryngton* (2nd), Jocelyn Arthur Pike Pease, *b.* 1908, *s.* 1949.	(None.)
1932	*Davies* (3rd), David Davies, *b.* 1940, *s.* 1944, *m.*	Hon. David D. *D.*, *b.* 1975.
1812 I.	*Decies* (6th), Arthur George Marcus Douglas de la Poer Beresford, *b.* 1915, *s.* 1944, *m.*	Hon. Marcus H. T. *de la P.B.*, *b.* 1948.
1299	*de Clifford* (27th), John Edward Southwell Russell, *b.* 1928, *s.* 1982, *m.*	Hon. William S. *R.*, *b.* 1930.
1851	*De Freyne* (7th), Francis Arthur John French, *b.* 1927, *s.* 1935, *m.*	Hon. Fulke C. A. J. *F.*, *b.* 1957.
1821	*Delamere* (5th), Hugh George Cholmondeley, *b.* 1934, *s.* 1979, *m.*	Hon. Thomas P. G. *C.*, *b.* 1968.
1838	*de Mauley* (6th), Gerald John Ponsonby, *b.* 1921, *s.* 1962, *m.*	Col. Hon. Thomas M. *P.*, T.D., *b.* 1930.
1937	*Denham* (2nd), Bertram Stanley Mitford Bowyer, P.C., *b.* 1927, *s.* 1948, *m.*	Hon. Richard G. *B.*, *b.* 1959.
1834	*Denman* (5th), Charles Spencer Denman, C.B.E., M.C., T.D., *b.* 1916, *s.* 1971, *m.*	Hon. Richard T. S. *D.*, *b.* 1946.
1885	*Deramore* (6th), Richard Arthur de Yarburgh-Bateson, *b.* 1911, *s.* 1964, *m.*	(None.)
1887	*De Ramsey* (3rd), Ailwyn Edward Fellowes, K.B.E., T.D., *b.* 1910, *s.* 1925, *w.*	Hon. John A. *F.*, *b.* 1942.
1264	*de Ros* (28th), Peter Trevor Maxwell, *b.* 1958, *s.* 1983, *m.* (*Premier Baron of England*).	Hon. Diana E. *M.*, *b.* 1957.
1881	*Derwent* (5th), Robin Evelyn Leo Vanden-Bempde-Johnstone, L.V.O., *b.* 1930, *s.* 1986, *m.*	Hon. Francis P. H. *V.-B.-J.*, *b.* 1965.
1831	*De Saumarez* (6th), James Victor Broke Saumarez, *b.* 1924, *s.* 1969, *m.*	Hon. Eric D. *S.*, *b.* 1956.
1910	*de Villiers* (3rd), Arthur Percy de Villiers, *b.* 1911, *s.* 1934.	Hon. Alexander C. *de V.*, *b.* 1940.
1930	*Dickinson* (2nd), Richard Clavering Hyett Dickinson, *b.* 1926, *s.* 1943, *m.*	Hon. Martin H. *D.*, *b.* 1961.
1620 I. 1765* }	*Digby* (12th), Edward Henry Kenelm Digby, (6th *Brit. Baron*, *Digby*), *b.* 1924, *s.* 1964, *m.*	Hon. Henry N. K. *D.*, *b.* 1954.
1615	*Dormer* (16th), Joseph Spencer Philip Dormer, *b.* 1914, *s.* 1975.	Geoffrey H. *D.*, *b.* 1920.
1943	*Dowding* (2nd), Derek Hugh Tremenheere Dowding, *b.* 1919, *s.* 1970, *m.*	Hon. Piers H. T. *D.*, *b.* 1948.
1800 I.	*Dufferin and Clandeboye* (10th), Francis George Blackwood, *b.* 1916, *s.* 1988, *m.*	Hon. John F. *B.*, *b.* 1944.
1929	*Dulverton* (2nd), (Frederick) Anthony Hamilton Wills, C.B.E., T.D., *b.* 1915, *s.* 1956, *m.*	Hon. G. Michael H. *W.*, *b.* 1944.
1800 I.	*Dunalley* (6th), Henry Desmond Graham Prittie, *b.* 1912, *s.* 1948, *m.*	Hon. Henry F. C. *P.*, *b.* 1948.
1324 I.	*Dunboyne* (28th), Patrick Theobald Tower Butler, *b.* 1917, *s.* 1945, *m.*	Hon. John F. *B.*, *b.* 1951.
1802	*Dunleath* (4th), Charles Edward Henry John Mulholland, T.D., *b.* 1933, *s.* 1956, *m.*	Sir Michael H. *M.*, Bt., *b.* 1915.

Created.	*Title, Order of Succession, Name, etc.*	*Eldest Son or Heir.*
1439 I.	*Dunsany* (19th), Randal Arthur Henry Plunkett (20th *Irish*, *Baron*, *Killeen*, 1449), b. 1906, s. 1957, m.	Hon. Edward J. C. P., b. 1939.
1780	*Dynevor* (9th), Richard Charles Uryan Rhys, b. 1935, s. 1962.	Hon. Hugo G. U. R., b. 1966.
1928	*Ebbisham* (2nd), Rowland Roberts Blades, T.D., b. 1912, s. 1953, m.	(None.)
1857	*Ebury* (6th), Francis Egerton Grosvenor, b. 1934, s. 1957, m.	Hon. Julian F. M. G., b. 1959.
1643	*Elibank* (14th), Alan d'Ardis Erskine-Murray, b. 1923, s. 1973, m.	Master of Elibank, b. 1964.
1802	*Ellenborough* (8th), Richard Edward Cecil Law, b. 1926, s. 1945, m.	Capt. Hon. Rupert E. H. L., b. 1955.
1509 s.*	*Elphinstone* (18th), James Alexander Elphinstone (4th *U.K. Baron Elphinstone*, 1885), b. 1953, s. 1975, m.	Master of Elphinstone, b. 1980.
1934	*Elton* (2nd), Rodney Elton, T.D., b. 1930, s. 1973, m.	Hon. Edward P. E., b. 1966.
1964	*Erroll of Hale* (1st), Frederick James Erroll, T.D., P.C., b. 1914, m.	(None.)
1964	*Erskine of Rerrick* (2nd), Iain Maxwell Erskine, b. 1926, s. 1980, m.	(None).
1627 s.	*Fairfax of Cameron* (14th), Nicholas John Albert Fairfax, b. 1956, s. 1964, m.	Hon. Edward N. T. F., b. 1984.
1961	*Fairhaven* (3rd), Ailwyn Henry George Broughton, b. 1936, s. 1973, m.	Hon. James H. A. B., b. 1963.
1916	*Faringdon* (3rd), Charles Michael Henderson, b. 1937, s. 1977, m.	Hon. James H. H., b. 1961.
1756 I.	*Farnham* (12th), Barry Owen Somerset Maxwell, b. 1931, s. 1957, m.	Hon. Simon K. M., b. 1933.
1856 I.	*Fermoy* (6th), Patrick Maurice Burke Roche, b. 1967, s. 1984.	Hon. E. Hugh B. R., b. 1972.
1826	*Feversham* (6th), Charles Antony Peter Duncombe, b. 1945, s. 1963, m.	Hon. Jasper O. S. D., b. 1968.
1798 I.	*ffrench* (8th), Robuck John Peter Charles Mario ffrench, b. 1956, s. 1986.	Hon. John C. M. J. F. ff., b. 1928.
1909	*Fisher* (3rd), John Vavasseur Fisher, D.S.C., b. 1921, s. 1955, m.	Hon. Patrick V. F., b. 1953.
1295	*Fitzwalter* (21st), Fitzwalter Brook Plumptre, b. 1914, *called out of abeyance*, 1953, m.	Hon. Julian B. P., b. 1952.
1776	*Foley* (8th), Adrian Gerald Foley, b. 1923, s. 1927, m.	Hon. Thomas H. F., b. 1961.
1445 s.	*Forbes* (22nd), Nigel Ivan Forbes, K.B.E. (*Premier Baron of Scotland*), b. 1918, s. 1953, m.	Master of Forbes, b. 1946.
1821	*Forester* (8th), (George Cecil) Brooke Weld-Forester, b. 1938, s. 1977, m.	Hon. Charles R. G. W.-F., b. 1975.
1922	*Forres* (4th), Alastair Stephen Grant Williamson, b. 1946, s. 1978, m.	Hon. George A. M. W., b. 1972.
1917	*Forteviot* (3rd), Henry Evelyn Alexander Dewar, M.B.E., b. 1906, s. 1947, w.	Hon. John J. E. D., b. 1938.
1951	*Freyberg* (2nd), Paul Richard Freyberg, O.B.E., M.C., b. 1923, s. 1963, m.	Hon. Valerian B. F., b. 1970.
1917	*Gainford* (3rd), Joseph Edward Pease, b. 1921, s. 1971, m.	Hon. George P., b. 1926.
1818 I.	*Garvagh* (5th), (Alexander Leopold Ivor) George Canning, b. 1920, s. 1956, m.	Hon. Spencer G. S. de R. C., b. 1953.
1942	*Geddes* (3rd), Euan Michael Ross Geddes, b. 1937, s. 1975, m.	Hon. James G. N. G., b. 1969.
1876	*Gerard* (4th), Robert William Frederick Alwyn Gerard, b. 1918, s. 1953.	Anthony R. H. G., b. 1949.
1824	*Gifford* (6th), Anthony Maurice Gifford, Q.C., b. 1940, s. 1961, m.	Hon. Thomas A. G., b. 1967.
1917	*Gisborough* (3rd), Thomas Richard John Long Chaloner, b. 1927, s. 1951, m.	Hon. Thomas P. L. C., b. 1961.
1960	*Gladwyn* (1st), (Hubert Miles) Gladwyn Jebb, G.C.M.G., G.C.V.O., C.B., b. 1900, m.	Hon. Miles A. G. J., b. 1930.
1899	*Glanusk* (4th), David Russell Bailey, b. 1917, s. 1948, m.	Hon. Christopher R. B., b. 1942.
1918	*Glenarthur* (4th), Simon Mark Arthur, b. 1944, s. 1976, m.	Hon. Edward A. A., b. 1973.
1911	*Glenconner* (3rd), Colin Christopher Paget Tennant, b. 1926, s. 1983, m.	Hon. Charles E. P. T., b. 1957.
1964	*Glendevon* (1st), John Adrian Hope, P.C., b. 1912, m.	Hon. Julian J. S. H., b. 1950.
1922	*Glendyne* (3rd), Robert Nivison, b. 1926, s. 1967, m.	Hon. John N., b. 1960.
1939	*Glentoran* (2nd), Daniel Stewart Thomas Bingham Dixon, K.B.E., P.C. (N.I.), b. 1912, s. 1950, w.	Hon. Thomas R. V. D., M.B.E., b. 1935.
1909	*Gorell* (4th), Timothy John Radcliffe Barnes, b. 1927, s. 1963, m.	Hon. Ronald A. H. B., b. 1931.
1953	*Grantchester* (2nd), Kenneth Bent Suenson-Taylor, C.B.E., Q.C., b. 1921, s. 1976, m.	Hon. Christopher J. S-.T., b. 1951.
1782	*Grantley* (7th), John Richard Brinsley Norton, M.C., b. 1923, s. 1954, m.	Hon. Richard W. B. N., b. 1956.
1794 I.	*Graves* (8th), Peter George Wellesley Graves, b. 1911, s. 1963, m.	Evelyn P. G., b. 1926.
1445 s.	*Gray* (22nd), Angus Diarmid Ian Campbell-Gray, b. 1931, s. 1946, w.	Master of Gray, b. 1964.
1950	*Greenhill* (2nd), Stanley Ernest Greenhill, M.D., b. 1917, s. 1967, m.	Hon. Malcolm G., b. 1924.
1927	*Greenway* (4th), Ambrose Charles Drexel Greenway, b. 1941, s. 1975, m.	Hon. Mervyn S. K. G., b. 1942.
1902	*Grenfell* (3rd), Julian Pascoe Francis St. Leger Grenfell, b. 1935, s. 1976, m.	Francis P. J. G., b. 1938.
1944	*Gretton* (3rd), John Henrik Gretton, b. 1941, s. 1982, m.	Hon. John L. G., b. 1975.
1955	*Gridley* (2nd), Arnold Hudson Gridley, b. 1906, s. 1965, m.	Hon. Richard D. A. G., b. 1956.
1964	*Grimston of Westbury* (2nd), Robert Walter Sigismund Grimston, b. 1925, s. 1979, m.	Hon. Robert J. S. G., b. 1951.
1886	*Grimthorpe* (4th), Christopher John Beckett, O.B.E., b. 1915, s. 1963, m.	Hon. Edward J. B., b. 1954.
1945	*Hacking* (3rd), Douglas David Hacking, b. 1938, s. 1971, m.	Hon. Douglas F. H., b. 1968.

Created.	Title, Order of Succession, Name, etc.	Eldest Son or Heir.
1950	*Haden-Guest* (4th), Peter Haden Haden-Guest, *b.* 1913, *s.* 1987, *m.*	Hon. Christopher *H.-G.*, *b.* 1948.
1886	*Hamilton of Dalzell* (3rd), John d'Henin Hamilton, G.C.V.O., M.C., *b.* 1911, *s.* 1952, *m.*	Hon. James L. *H.*, *b.* 1938.
1874	*Hampton* (6th), Richard Humphrey Russell Pakington, *b.* 1925, *s.* 1974, *m.*	Hon. John H. A. *P.*, *b.* 1964.
1939	*Hankey* (2nd), Robert Maurice Alers Hankey, K.C.M.G., K.C.V.O., *b.* 1905, *s.* 1963, *m.*	Hon. Donald R. A. *H.*, *b.* 1938.
1958	*Harding of Petherton* (1st), John Harding, G.C.B., C.B.E., D.S.O., M.C., Field-Marshal, *b.* 1896, *w.*	Hon. John C. *H.*, *b.* 1928.
1910	*Hardinge of Penshurst* (3rd), George Edward Charles Hardinge, *b.* 1921, *s.* 1960, *m.*	Hon. Julian A. *H.*, *b.* 1945.
1876	*Harlech* (6th), Francis David Ormsby-Gore, *b.* 1954, *s.* 1985.	Hon. John J. S. *O.-G.*, *b.* 1925.
1939	*Harmsworth* (2nd), Cecil Desmond Bernard Harmsworth, *b.* 1903, *s.* 1948, *m.*	Hon. Eric B. N. *H.*, *b.* 1905.
1815	*Harris* (6th), George Robert John Harris, *b.* 1920, *s.* 1984.	Derek M. *H.*, *b.* 1916.
1954	*Harvey of Tasburgh* (2nd), Peter Charles Oliver Harvey, *b.* 1921, *s.* 1968, *m.*	Hon. John W. *H.*, *b.* 1923.
1295	*Hastings* (22nd), Edward Delaval Henry Astley, *b.* 1912, *s.* 1956, *m.*	Hon. Delaval T. H. *A.*, *b.* 1960.
1835	*Hatherton* (8th), Edward Charles Littleton, *b.* 1950, *s.* 1985, *m.*	Hon. Thomas E. *L.*, *b.* 1977.
1776	*Hawke* (10th), (Julian Stanhope) Theodore Hawke, *b.* 1904, *s.* 1985, *m.*	Hon. Edward G. *H.*, *b.* 1950.
1927	*Hayter* (3rd), George Charles Hayter Chubb, K.C.V.O., C.B.E., *b.* 1911, *s.* 1967, *m.*	Hon. George W. M. *C.*, *b.* 1943.
1945	*Hazlerigg* (2nd), Arthur Grey Hazlerigg, M.C., *b.* 1910, *s.* 1949, *w.*	Hon. Arthur G. *H.*, *b.* 1951.
1797 I.	*Headley* (7th), Charles Rowland Allanson-Winn, *b.* 1902, *s.* 1969, *m.*	Hon. John R. *A.-W.*, *b.* 1934.
1943	*Hemingford* (3rd), Dennis Nicholas Herbert, *b.* 1934, *s.* 1982, *m.*	Hon. Christopher D. C. *H.*, *b.* 1973.
1906	*Hemphill* (5th), Peter Patrick Fitzroy Martyn Martyn-Hemphill, *b.* 1928, *s.* 1957, *m.*	Hon. Charles A. M. *M.-H.*, *b.* 1954.
1799 I.*	*Henley* (8th), Oliver Michael Robert Eden (6th *U.K. Baron, Northington*, 1885), *b.* 1953, *s.* 1977, *m.*	Hon. Andrew F. *E.*, *b.* 1955.
1800 I.*	*Henniker* (8th), John Patrick Edward Chandos Henniker-Major, K.C.M.G., C.V.O., M.C. (4th *U.K. Baron, Hartismere*, 1866), *b.* 1916, *s.* 1980, *m.*	Hon. Mark I. P. C. *H.-M.*, *b.* 1947.
1886	*Herschell* (3rd), Rognvald Richard Farrer Herschell, *b.* 1923, *s.* 1929, *m.*	(None.)
1935	*Hesketh* (3rd), Thomas Alexander Fermor-Hesketh, *b.* 1950, *s.* 1955, *m.*	Hon. Robert *F.-H.*, *b.* 1951.
1828	*Heytesbury* (6th), Francis William Holmes à Court, *b.* 1931, *s.* 1971, *m.*	Hon. James W. *H. à C.*, *b.* 1967.
1886	*Hindlip* (5th), Henry Richard Allsopp, *b.* 1912, *s.* 1966, *m.*	Hon. Charles H. *A.*, *b.* 1940.
1950	*Hives* (2nd), John Warwick Hives, *b.* 1913, *s.* 1965, *m.*	Matthew P. *H.*, *b.* 1971.
1912	*Hollenden* (3rd), Gordon Hope Hope-Morley, *b.* 1914, *s.* 1977, *m.*	Hon. Ian H. *H.-M.*, *b.* 1946.
1897	*Holm Patrick* (3rd), James Hans Hamilton, *b.* 1928, *s.* 1942, *m.*	Hon. Hans J. D. *H.*, *b.* 1955.
1933	*Horder* (2nd), Thomas Mervyn Horder, *b.* 1910, *s.* 1955.	(None.)
1797 I.	*Hotham* (8th), Henry Durand Hotham, *b.* 1940, *s.* 1967, *m.*	Hon. William B. *H.*, *b.* 1972.
1881	*Hothfield* (5th), George William Anthony Tufton, T.D., *b.* 1904, *s.* 1986, *m.*	Hon. Anthony C. S. *T.*, *b.* 1939.
1597	*Howard de Walden* (9th), John Osmael Scott-Ellis (5th *U.K. Baron, Seaford*, 1826), *b.* 1912, *s.* 1946, *m.*	Co-heiresses. To U.K. Barony, Colin H. F. *Ellis*, *b.* 1946.
1930	*Howard of Penrith* (2nd), Francis Philip Howard, *b.* 1905, *s.* 1939, *m.*	Hon. Philip E. *H.*, *b.* 1945.
1960	*Howick of Glendale* (2nd), Charles Evelyn Baring, *b.* 1937, *s.* 1973, *m.*	Hon. David E. C. *B.*, *b.* 1975.
1796 I.	*Huntingfield* (6th), Gerard Charles Arcedeckne Vanneck, *b.* 1915, *s.* 1969, *m.*	Hon. Joshua C. *V.*, *b.* 1954.
1866	*Hylton* (5th), Raymond Hervey Jolliffe, *b.* 1932, *s.* 1967, *m.*	Hon. William H. M. *J.*, *b.* 1967.
1933	*Iliffe* (2nd), Edward Langton Iliffe, *b.* 1908, *s.* 1960, *m.*	Robert P. R. *I.*, *b.* 1944.
1543 I.	*Inchiquin* (18th), Conor Myles John O'Brien, *b.* 1943, *s.* 1982, *m.*	Murrough R. *O'B.*, *b.* 1910.
1962	*Inchyra* (1st), Frederick Robert Hoyer Millar, G.C.M.G., C.V.O., *b.* 1900, *m.*	Hon. Robert C. R. H. *M.*, *b.* 1935.
1964	*Inglewood* (1st), William Morgan Fletcher-Vane, T.D., *b.* 1909, *w.*	Hon. W. Richard *F.-V.*, *b.* 1951.
1919	*Inverforth* (4th), Andrew Peter Weir, *b.* 1966, *s.* 1982.	Hon. John V. *W.*, *b.* 1935.
1941	*Ironside* (2nd), Edmund Oslac Ironside, *b.* 1924, *s.* 1959, *m.*	Hon. Charles E. G. *I.*, *b.* 1956.
1952	*Jeffreys* (3rd), Christopher Henry Mark Jeffreys, *b.* 1957, *s.* 1986.	Hon. Alexander C. D. *J.*, *b.* 1959.
1924	*Jessel* (2nd), Edward Herbert Jessel, C.B.E., *b.* 1904, *s.* 1950, *m.*	(None.)
1906	*Joicey* (4th), Michael Edward Joicey, *b.* 1925, *s.* 1966, *m.*	Hon. James M. *J.*, *b.* 1953.
1937	*Kenilworth* (4th), John Randle Siddeley, *b.* 1954, *s.* 1981, *m.*	(None.)
1935	*Kennet* (2nd), Wayland Hilton Young, *b.* 1923, *s.* 1960, *m.*	Hon. William A. T. *Y.*, *b.* 1957.
1776 I. } 1886*	*Kensington* (8th), Hugh Ivor Edwardes (5th *U.K. Baron, Kensington*), *b.* 1933, *s.* 1981, *m.*	Hon. William O. A. *E.*, *b.* 1964.
1951	*Kenswood* (2nd), John Michael Howard Whitfield, *b.* 1930, *s.* 1963, *m.*	Hon. Michael C. *W.*, *b.* 1955.

Created.	Title, Order of Succession, Name, etc.	Eldest Son or Heir.
1788	*Kenyon* (5th), Lloyd Tyrell-Kenyon, C.B.E., *b.* 1917, *s.* 1927, *m.*	Hon. Lloyd *T.-K.*, *b.* 1947.
1947	*Kershaw* (4th), Edward John Kershaw, *b.* 1936, *s.* 1962, *m.*	Hon. John C. E. *K.*, *b.* 1971.
1943	*Keyes* (2nd), Roger George Bowlby Keyes, *b.* 1919, *s.* 1945, *m.*	Hon. Charles W. P. *K.*, *b.* 1951.
1909	*Kilbracken* (3rd), John Raymond Godley, D.S.C., *b.* 1920, *s.* 1950, *m.*	Hon. Christopher J. *G.*, *b.* 1945.
1900	*Killanin* (3rd), Michael Morris, M.B.E., T.D., *b.* 1914, *s.* 1927, *m.*	Hon. G. Redmond F. *M.*, *b.* 1947.
1943	*Killearn* (2nd), Graham Curtis Lampson, *b.* 1919, *s.* 1964, *m.*	Hon. Victor M. G. A. *L.*, *b.* 1941.
1789 I.	*Kilmaine* (7th), John David Henry Browne, *b.* 1948, *s.* 1978, *m.*	Hon. John F. S. *B.*, *b.* 1983.
1831	*Kilmarnock* (7th), Alastair Ivor Gilbert Boyd, *b.* 1927, *s.* 1975, *m.*	Hon. Robin J. *B.*, *b.* 1941.
1941	*Kindersley* (3rd), Robert Hugh Molesworth Kindersley, *b.* 1929, *s.* 1976, *m.*	Hon. Rupert J. M. *K.*, *b.* 1955.
1223 I.	*Kingsale* (35th), John de Courcy (*Premier Baron of Ireland*), *b.* 1941, *s.* 1969.	Nevinson R. *de C.*, *b.* 1920.
1682 s. } 1860* }	*Kinnaird* (13th), Graham Charles Kinnaird (5th *U.K. Baron, Kinnaird*), *b.* 1912, *s.* 1972, *m.*	(None.)
1902	*Kinross* (5th), Christopher Patrick Balfour, *b.* 1949, *s.* 1985, *m.*	Hon. Alan I. *B.*, *b.* 1978.
1951	*Kirkwood* (3rd), David Harvie Kirkwood, PH.D., *b.* 1931, *s.* 1970, *m.*	Hon. James S. *K.*, *b.* 1937.
1800 I	*Langford* (9th), Geoffrey Alexander Rowley-Conwy, O.B.E., *b.* 1912, *s.* 1953, *m.*	Hon. Owen G. *R.-C.*, *b.* 1958.
1942	*Latham* (2nd), Dominic Charles Latham, *b.* 1954, *s.* 1970.	Anthony M. *L.*, *b.* 1954.
1431	*Latymer* (8th), Hugo Nevill Money-Coutts, *b.* 1926, *s.* 1987, *m.*	Hon. Crispin J. A. N. *M.-C.*, *b.* 1955.
1869	*Lawrence* (5th), David John Downer Lawrence, *b.* 1937, *s.* 1968.	(None.)
1947	*Layton* (2nd), Michael John Layton, *b.* 1912, *s.* 1966, *m.*	Hon. Geoffrey M. *L.*, *b.* 1947.
1859	*Leconfield* (7th), John Max Henry Scawen Wyndham (2nd *U.K. Baron, Egremont*, 1963), *b.* 1948, *s.* 1972, *m.*	Hon. George R. V. *W.*, *b.* 1983.
1839	*Leigh* (5th), John Piers Leigh, *b.* 1935, *s.* 1979, *m.*	Hon. Christopher D. P. *L.*, *b.* 1960.
1962	*Leighton of St. Mellons* (2nd), (John) Leighton Seager, *b.* 1922, *s.* 1963, *m.*	Hon. Robert W. H. L. *S.*, *b.* 1955.
1797	*Lilford* (7th), George Vernon Powys, *b.* 1931, *s.* 1949, *m.*	Hon. Mark V. *P.*, *b.*, 1975.
1945	*Lindsay of Birker* (2nd), Michael Francis Morris Lindsay, *b.* 1909, *s.* 1952, *m.*	Hon. James F. *L.*, *b.* 1945.
1758 I.	*Lisle* (7th), John Nicholas Horace Lysaght, *b.* 1903, *s.* 1919, *m.*	Patrick J. *L.*, *b.* 1931.
1895	*Loch* (4th), Spencer Douglas Loch, M.C., *b.* 1920, *s.* 1982, *m.*	(None.)
1850	*Londesborough* (9th), Richard John Denison, *b.* 1959, *s.* 1968, *m.*	(None.)
1541 I.	*Louth* (16th), Otway Michael James Oliver Plunkett, *b.* 1929, *s.* 1950, *m.*	Hon. Jonathan O. *P.*, *b.* 1952.
1458 s. } 1837* }	*Lovat* (15th), Simon Christopher Joseph Fraser, D.S.O., M.C., T.D. (4th *U.K. Baron, Lovat*), *b.* 1911, *s.* 1933, *m.*	Master of Lovat, *b.* 1939.
1946	*Lucas of Chilworth* (2nd), Michael William George Lucas, *b.* 1926, *s.* 1967, *m.*	Hon. Simon W. *L.*, *b.* 1957.
1929	*Luke* (2nd), Ian St. John Lawson-Johnston, K.C.V.O., T.D., *b.* 1905, *s.* 1943, *m.*	Hon. Arthur C. St. J. *L.-J.*, *b.* 1933.
1839	*Lurgan* (5th), John Desmond Cavendish Brownlow, O.B.E., *b.* 1911, *s.* 1984.	(None.)
1914	*Lyell* (3rd), Charles Lyell, *b.* 1939, *s.* 1943.	(None.)
1859	*Lyveden* (6th), Ronald Cecil Vernon, *b.* 1915, *s.* 1973, *m.*	Hon. Jack L. *V.*, *b.* 1938.
1959	*MacAndrew* (2nd), Colin Nevil Glen MacAndrew, *b.* 1919, *s.* 1979, *m.*	Hon. Christopher A. C. *MacA.*, *b.* 1945.
1776 I.	*Macdonald* (8th), Godfrey James Macdonald, *b.* 1947, *s.* 1970, *m.*	Hon. Godfrey E. H. T. *M.*, *b.* 1982.
1949	*Macdonald of Gwaenysgor* (2nd), Gordon Ramsay Macdonald, *b.* 1915, *s.* 1966, *m.*	Hon. Kenneth L. *M.*, *b.* 1921.
1937	*McGowan* (3rd), Harry Duncan Cory McGowan, *b.* 1938, *s.* 1966, *m.*	Hon. Harry J. C. *McG.*, *b.* 1971.
1922	*Maclay* (3rd), Joseph Paton Maclay, *b.* 1942, *s.* 1969, *m.*	Hon. Joseph P. *M.*, *b.* 1977.
1955	*McNair* (2nd), (Clement) John McNair, *b.* 1915, *s.* 1975, *m.*	Hon. Duncan J. *McN.*, *b.* 1947.
1951	*Macpherson of Drumochter* (2nd), (James) Gordon Macpherson, *b.* 1924, *s.* 1965, *m.*	Hon. James A. *M.*, *b.* 1979.
1937	*Mancroft* (3rd), Benjamin Lloyd Stormont Mancroft, *b.* 1957, *s.* 1987.	(None.)
1807	*Manners* (5th), John Robert Cecil Manners, *b.* 1923, *s.* 1972, *m.*	Hon. John H. R. *M.*, *b.* 1956.
1922	*Manton* (3rd), Joseph Rupert Eric Robert Watson, *b.* 1924, *s.* 1968, *m.*	Capt. Hon. Miles R. M. *W.*, *b.* 1958.
1908	*Marchamley* (3rd), John William Tattersall Whiteley, *b.* 1922, *s.* 1949, *m.*	Hon. William F. *W.*, *b.* 1968.
1964	*Margadale* (1st), John Granville Morrison, T.D., *b.* 1906, *w.*	Hon. James I. *M.*, T.D., *b.* 1930.
1961	*Marks of Broughton* (2nd), Michael Marks, *b.* 1920, *s.* 1964, *m.*	Hon. Simon R. *M.*, *b.* 1950.
1930	*Marley* (2nd), Godfrey Pelham Leigh Aman, *b.* 1913, *s.* 1952, *m.*	(None.)

Created.	*Title, Order of Succession, Name, etc.*	*Eldest Son or Heir.*
1964	*Martonmere* (1st), (John) Roland Robinson, G.B.E., K.C.M.G., P.C.,b. 1907, m.	John S. R., b. 1963.
1776 I.	*Massy* (9th), Hugh Hamon John Somerset Massy, b. 1921, s. 1958, m.	Hon. David H. S. M., b. 1947.
1935	*May* (3rd), Michael St. John May, b. 1931, s. 1950, m.	Hon. Jasper B. St. J. M., b. 1965.
1928	*Melchett* (4th), Peter Robert Henry Mond, b. 1948, s. 1973.	(None.)
1925	*Merrivale* (3rd), Jack Henry Edmond Duke, b. 1917, s. 1951, m.	Hon. Derek J. P. D., b. 1948.
1919	*Meston* (3rd), James Meston, b. 1950, s. 1984, m.	Hon. Thomas J. D. M., b. 1977.
1838	*Methuen* (6th), Anthony John Methuen, b. 1925, s. 1975.	Hon. Robert A. H. M., b. 1931.
1711	*Middleton* (12th), (Digby) Michael Godfrey John Willoughby, M.C., b. 1921, s. 1970, m.	Hon. Michael C. J. W., b. 1948.
1939	*Milford* (2nd), Wogan Philipps, b. 1902, s. 1962, m.	Hon. Hugo J. L. P., b. 1929.
1933	*Milne* (2nd), George Douglass Milne, T.D., b. 1909, s. 1948, m.	Hon. George A. M., b. 1941.
1951	*Milner of Leeds* (2nd), Arthur James Michael Milner, b. 1923, s. 1967, m.	Hon. Richard J. M., b. 1959.
1947	*Milverton* (2nd), Rev. Fraser Arthur Richard Richards, b. 1930, s. 1978, m.	Hon. Michael H. R., b. 1936.
1873	*Moncreiff* (5th), Harry Robert Wellwood Moncreiff, b. 1915, s. 1942, w.	Hon. Rhoderick H. W. M., b. 1954.
1884	*Monk Bretton* (3rd), John Charles Dodson, b. 1924, s. 1933, m.	Hon. Christopher M. D., b. 1958.
1885	*Monkswell* (5th), Gerard Collier, b. 1947, s. 1984, m.	Hon. James A. C., b. 1977.
1728	*Monson* (11th), John Monson, b. 1932, s. 1958, m.	Hon. Nicholas J. M., b. 1955.
1885	*Montagu of Beaulieu* (3rd), Edward John Barrington Douglas-Scott-Montagu, b. 1926, s. 1929, m.	Hon. Ralph D.-S.-M., b. 1961.
1839	*Monteagle of Brandon* (6th), Gerald Spring Rice, b. 1926, s. 1946, m.	Hon. Charles J. S. R., b. 1953.
1943	*Moran* (2nd), (Richard) John (McMoran) Wilson, K.C.M.G., b. 1924, s. 1977, m.	Hon. James McM. W., b. 1952.
1918	*Morris* (3rd), Michael David Morris, b. 1937, s. 1975, m.	Hon. Thomas A. S. M., b. 1982.
1950	*Morris of Kenwood* (2nd), Philip Geoffrey Morris, b. 1928, s. 1954, m.	Hon. Jonathan D. M., b. 1968.
1945	*Morrison* (2nd), Dennis Morrison, b. 1914, s. 1953.	(None.)
1831	*Mostyn* (5th), Roger Edward Lloyd Lloyd-Mostyn, M.C., b. 1920, s. 1965, m.	Hon. Llewellyn R. L. L.-M., b. 1948.
1933	*Mottistone* (4th), David Peter Seely, C.B.E., b. 1920, s. 1966, m.	Hon. Peter J. P. S., b. 1949.
1945	*Mountevans* (3rd), Edward Patrick Broke Evans, b. 1943, s. 1974, m.	Hon. Jeffrey de C. R. E., b. 1948.
1283	*Mowbray* (26th), *Segrave* (27th) (1283), & *Stourton* (23rd) (1448), Charles Edward Stourton, C.B.E., b. 1923, s. 1965, m.	Hon. Edward W. S. S., b. 1953.
1932	*Moyne* (2nd), Bryan Walter Guinness, b. 1905, s. 1944, m.	Hon. Jonathan B. G., b. 1930.
1929	*Moynihan* (3rd), Antony Patrick Andrew Cairnes Berkeley Moynihan, b. 1936, s. 1965.	Hon. Colin B. M., M.P., b. 1955.
1781 I.	*Muskerry* (8th), Hastings Fitzmaurice Tilson Deane, b. 1907, s. 1966, m.	Hon. Robert F. D., b. 1948.
1627 S.	*Napier* (14th) & *Ettrick* (5th) (*U.K.* 1872), Francis Nigel Napier, C.V.O. (5th *U.K. Baron, Ettrick*, 1872), b. 1930, s. 1954, m.	Master of Napier, b. 1962.
1868	*Napier of Magdala* (6th), Robert Alan Napier, b. 1940, s. 1987, m.	Hon. James R. N., b. 1966.
1940	*Nathan* (2nd), Roger Carol Michael Nathan, b. 1922, s. 1963, m.	Hon. Rupert H. B. N., b. 1957.
1960	*Nelson of Stafford* (2nd), Henry George Nelson, b. 1917, s. 1962, m.	Hon. Henry R. G. N., b. 1943.
1959	*Netherthorpe* (3rd), James Frederick Turner, b. 1964, s. 1982.	Hon. Patrick A. T., b. 1971.
1946	*Newall* (2nd), Francis Storer Eaton Newall, b. 1930, s. 1963, m.	Hon. Richard H. E. N., b. 1961.
1776 I.	*Newborough* (7th), Robert Charles Michael Vaughan Wynn, D.S.C., b. 1917, s. 1965, m.	Hon. Robert V. W., b. 1949.
1892	*Newton* (4th), Peter Richard Legh, b. 1915, s. 1960, m.	Hon. Richard T. L., b. 1950.
1930	*Noel-Buxton* (3rd), Martin Connal Noel-Buxton, b. 1940, s. 1980.	Hon. Charles C. N.-B., b. 1975.
1957	*Norrie* (2nd), (George) Willoughby Moke Norrie, b. 1936, s. 1977, m.	Hon. Mark W. J. N., b. 1972.
1884	*Northbourne* (5th), Christopher George Walter James, b. 1926, s. 1982, m.	Hon. Charles W. H. J., b. 1960.
1866	*Northbrook* (5th), Francis John Baring, b. 1915, s. 1947, m.	Hon. Francis T. B., b. 1954.
1878	*Norton* (7th), John Arden Adderley, O.B.E., b. 1915, s. 1961, m.	Hon. James N. A. A., b. 1947.
1906	*Nunburnholme* (4th), Ben Charles Wilson, b. 1928, s. 1974, m.	Hon. Charles T. W., b. 1935.
1950	*Ogmore* (2nd), Gwilym Rees Rees-Williams, b. 1931, s. 1976, m.	Hon. Morgan R.-W., b. 1937.
1870	*O'Hagan* (4th), Charles Towneley Strachey, b. 1945, s. 1961.	Hon. Richard T. S., b. 1950.
1868	*O'Neill* (4th), Raymond Arthur Clanaboy O'Neill, T.D., b. 1933, s. 1944, m.	Hon. Shane S. C. O'N., b. 1965.
1836 I.*	*Oranmore and Browne* (4th), Dominick Geoffrey Edward Browne (2nd *U.K. Baron Mereworth*, 1926), b. 1901, s. 1927, m.	Hon. Dominick G. T. B., b. 1929.
1933	*Palmer* (3rd), Raymond Cecil Palmer, O.B.E., b. 1916, s. 1950, m.	Hon. Gordon W. N. P., O.B.E., T.D., b. 1918.
1914	*Parmoor* (4th), (Frederick Alfred) Milo Cripps, b. 1929, s. 1977.	M. Anthony L. C., C.B.E., D.S.O., T.D., Q.C., b. 1913.

Created.	Title, Order of Succession, Name, etc.	Eldest Son or Heir.
1937	*Pender* (3rd), John Willoughby Denison-Pender, *b.* 1933, *s.* 1965, *m.*	Hon. Henry J. R. *D.-P.*, *b.* 1968.
1866	*Penrhyn* (6th), Malcolm Frank Douglas-Pennant, D.S.O., M.B.E., *b.* 1908, *s.* 1967, *m.*	Hon. Nigel *D.-P.*, *b.* 1909.
1603	*Petre* (17th), Joseph William Lionel Petre, *b.* 1914, *s.* 1915, *m.*	Hon. John P. L. *P.*, *b.* 1942.
1918	*Phillimore* (3rd), Robert Godfrey Phillimore, *b.* 1939, *s.* 1947.	Hon. Claud S. *P.*, *b.* 1911.
1945	*Piercy* (3rd), James William Piercy, *b.* 1946, *s.* 1981.	Hon. Mark E. P. *P.*, *b.* 1953.
1827	*Plunket* (8th), Robin Rathmore Plunket, *b.* 1925, *s.* 1975, *m.*	Hon. Shaun A. F. S. *P.*, *b.* 1931.
1831	*Poltimore* (7th), Mark Coplestone Bampfylde, *b.* 1957, *s.* 1978, *m.*	Hon. Henry A. W. *B.*, *b.* 1985.
1690 s.	*Polwarth* (10th), Henry Alexander Hepburne-Scott, T.D., *b.* 1916, *s.* 1944, *m.*	Master of Polwarth, *b.* 1947.
1930	*Ponsonby of Shulbrede* (3rd), Thomas Arthur Ponsonby, *b.* 1930, *s.* 1976, *m.*	Hon. Frederick M. T. *P.*, *b.* 1958.
1958	*Poole* (1st), Oliver Brian Sanderson Poole, C.B.E., T.D., P.C., *b.* 1911, *m.*	Hon. David C. *P.*, *b.* 1945.
1852	*Raglan* (5th), FitzRoy John Somerset, *b.* 1927, *s.* 1964.	Hon. Geoffrey *S.*, *b.* 1932.
1932	*Rankeillour* (4th), Peter St. Thomas More Henry Hope, *b.* 1935, *s.* 1967.	Michael R. *H.*, *b.* 1940.
1953	*Rathcavan* (2nd), Phelim Robert Hugh O'Neill, P.C. (N.I.), *b.* 1909, *s.* 1982, *m.*	Hon. Hugh D. T. *O'N.*, *b.* 1939.
1916	*Rathcreedan* (2nd), Charles Patrick Norton, T.D., *b.* 1905, *s.* 1930, *m.*	Hon. Christopher J. *N.*, *b.* 1949.
1868 I.	*Rathdonnell* (5th), Thomas Benjamin McClintock–Bunbury, *b.* 1938, *s.* 1959, *m.*	Hon. William L. McC.-*B.*, *b.* 1966.
1911	*Ravensdale* (3rd), Nicholas Mosley, M.C., *b.* 1923, *s.* 1966, *m.*	Hon. Shaun N. *M.*, *b.* 1949.
1821	*Ravensworth* (8th), Arthur Waller Liddell, *b.* 1924, *s.* 1950, *m.*	Hon. Thomas A. H. *L.*, *b.* 1954.
1821	*Rayleigh* (6th), John Gerald Strutt, *b.* 1960, *s.* 1988.	Hon. Hedley V. *S.*, *b.* 1915.
1937	*Rea* (3rd), John Nicolas Rea, M.D., *b.* 1928, *s.* 1981, *m.*	Hon. Matthew J. *R.*, *b.* 1956.
1628 s.	*Reay* (14th), Hugh William Mackay, *b.* 1937, *s.* 1963, *m.*	Master of Reay, *b.* 1965.
1902	*Redesdale* (5th), Clement Napier Bertram Mitford, *b.* 1932, *s.* 1963, *m.*	Hon. Rupert B. *M.*, *b.* 1967.
1928	*Remnant* (3rd), James Wogan Remnant, C.V.O., *b.* 1930, *s.* 1967, *m.*	Hon. Philip J. *R.*, *b.* 1954.
1806 I.	*Rendlesham* (8th), Charles Anthony Hugh Thellusson, *b.* 1915, *s.* 1943, *w.*	Hon. Charles W. B. *T.*, *b.* 1954.
1933	*Rennell* (3rd), (John Adrian) Tremayne Rodd, *b.* 1935, *s.* 1978, *m.*	Hon. James R. D. T. *R.*, *b.* 1978.
1964	*Renwick* (2nd), Harry Andrew Renwick, *b.* 1935, *s.* 1973, *m.*	Hon. Robert J. *R.*, *b.* 1966.
1885	*Revelstoke* (4th), Rupert Baring, *b.* 1911, *s.* 1934.	Hon. John *B.*, *b.* 1934.
1905	*Ritchie of Dundee* (5th), (Harold) Malcolm Ritchie, *b.* 1919, *s.* 1978, *m.*	Hon. Charles R. R. *R.*, *b.* 1958.
1935	*Riverdale* (2nd), Robert Arthur Balfour, *b.* 1901, *s.* 1957, *m.*	Hon. Mark R. *B.*, *b.* 1927.
1961	*Robertson of Oakridge* (2nd), William Ronald Robertson, *b.* 1930, *s.* 1974, *m.*	Hon. William B. E. *R.*, *b.* 1975.
1938	*Roborough* (2nd), Massey Henry Edgcumbe Lopes, *b.* 1903, *s.* 1938, *m.*	Hon. Henry M. *L.*, *b.* 1940.
1931	*Rochester* (2nd), Foster Charles Lowry Lamb, *b.* 1916, *s.* 1955, *m.*	Hon. David C. *L.*, *b.* 1944.
1934	*Rockley* (3rd), James Hugh Cecil, *b.* 1934, *s.* 1976, *m.*	Hon. Anthony R. *C.*, *b.* 1961.
1782	*Rodney* (9th), John Francis Rodney, *b.* 1920, *s.* 1973, *m.*	Hon. George B. *R.*, *b.* 1953.
1651 s.*	*Rollo* (13th), Eric John Stapylton Rollo (4th *U.K. Baron, Dunning,* 1869), *b.* 1915, *s.* 1947, *m.*	Master of Rollo, *b.* 1943.
1959	*Rootes* (2nd), William Geoffrey Rootes, *b.* 1917, *s.* 1964, *m.*	Hon. Nicholas G. *R.*, *b.* 1951.
1796 I. ⎫ 1838* ⎭	*Rossmore* (7th), William Warner Westenra (6th *U.K. Baron, Rossmore*), *b.* 1931, *s.* 1958, *m.*	Hon. Benedict W. *W.*, *b.* 1983.
1939	*Rotherwick* (2nd), (Herbert) Robin Cayzer, *b.* 1912, *s.* 1958, *w.*	Hon. H. Robin *C.*, *b.* 1954.
1885	*Rothschild* (3rd), Nathaniel Mayer Victor Rothschild, G.B.E., G.M., F.R.S., *b.* 1910, *s.* 1937, *m.*	Hon. N. C. Jacob *R.*, *b.* 1936.
1911	*Rowallan* (3rd), Arthur Cameron Corbett, *b.* 1919, *s.* 1977.	Hon. John P. C. *C.*, *b.* 1947.
1947	*Rugby* (2nd), Alan Loader Maffey, *b.* 1913, *s.* 1969, *m.*	Hon. Robert C. *M.*, *b.* 1951.
1919	*Russell of Liverpool* (3rd), Simon Gordon Jared Russell, *b.* 1952, *s.* 1981, *m.*	Hon. Edward C. S. *R.*, *b.* 1985.
1876	*Sackville* (6th), Lionel Bertrand Sackville-West, *b.* 1913, *s.* 1965, *m.*	Hugh R. I. *S.-W.*, M.C., *b.* 1919.
1964	*St. Helens* (2nd), Richard Francis Hughes-Young, *b.* 1945, *s.* 1980, *m.*	Hon. Henry T. *H.-Y.*, *b.* 1986.
1559	*St. John of Bletso* (21st), Anthony Tudor St. John, *b.* 1957, *s.* 1978.	Edmund O. *St. J.*, *b.* 1927.
1887	*St. Levan* (4th), John Francis Arthur St. Aubyn, D.S.C., *b.* 1919, *s.* 1978, *m.*	Hon. O. Piers *St. A.*, M.C., *b.* 1920.
1885	*St. Oswald* (5th), Derek Edward Anthony Winn, *b.* 1919, *s.* 1984, *m.*	Hon. Charles R. A. *W.*, *b.* 1959.
1945	*Sandford* (2nd), Rev. John Cyril Edmondson, D.S.C., *b.* 1920, *s.* 1959, *m.*	Hon. James J. M. *E.*, *b.* 1949.
1871	*Sandhurst* (5th), (John Edward) Terence Mansfield, D.F.C., *b.* 1920, *s.* 1964, *m.*	Hon. Guy R. J. *M.*, *b.* 1949.
1802	*Sandys* (7th), Richard Michael Oliver Hill, *b.* 1931, *s.* 1961, *m.*	Marcus T. *H.*, *b.* 1931.
1888	*Savile* (3rd), George Halifax Lumley-Savile, *b.* 1919, *s.* 1931.	Hon. Henry L. T. *L.-S.*, *b.* 1923.
1447	*Saye and Sele* (21st), Nathaniel Thomas Allen Fiennes, *b.* 1920, *s.* 1968, *m.*	Hon. Richard I. *F.*, *b.* 1959.
1932	*Selsdon* (3rd), Malcolm McEacharn Mitchell-Thomson, *b.* 1937, *s.* 1963, *m.*	Hon. Callum M. M. *M.-T.*, *b.* 1969.
1916	*Shaughnessy* (3rd), William Graham Shaughnessy, *b.* 1922, *s.* 1938, *m.*	Hon. Michael J. *S.*, *b.* 1946.

Created.	Title, Order of Succession, Name, etc.	Eldest Son or Heir.

1783 I. ⎫ *Sheffield* (8th), Thomas Henry Oliver Stanley (8th *U.K. Baron, Stanley* — Hon. Richard O. S., b. 1956.
1839* ⎬ *of Alderley and* 7th *U.K. Baron Eddisbury*, 1848), b. 1927, s. 1971, m.

1946 *Shepherd* (2nd), Malcolm Newton Shepherd, P.C., b. 1918, s. 1954, m. — Hon. Graeme G. S., b. 1949.

1964 *Sherfield* (1st), Roger Mellor Makins, G.C.B., G.C.M.G., b. 1904, m. — Hon. Christopher J. M., b. 1942.

1902 *Shuttleworth* (5th), Charles Geoffrey Nicholas Kay-Shuttleworth, b. 1948, s. 1975, m. — Hon. Thomas E. K.-S., b. 1976.

1963 *Silsoe* (2nd), David Malcolm Trustram Eve, Q.C., b. 1930, s. 1976, m. — Hon. Simon R. T. E., b. 1966.

1947 *Simon of Wythenshawe* (2nd), Roger Simon, b. 1913, s. 1960, m. — Hon. Matthew S., b. 1955.

1449 S. *Sinclair* (17th), Charles Murray Kennedy St. Clair, L.V.O., b. 1914, s. 1957, m. — Master of Sinclair, b. 1968.

1957 *Sinclair of Cleeve* (3rd), John Lawrence Robert Sinclair, b. 1953, s. 1985. — (None.)

1919 *Sinha* (3rd), Sudhindro Prosanno Sinha, b. 1920, s. 1967, m. — Hon. Sushanto S., b. 1953.

1828 *Skelmersdale* (7th), Roger Bootle-Wilbraham, b. 1945, s. 1973, m. — Hon. Andrew B.-W., b. 1977.

1916 *Somerleyton* (3rd), Savile William Francis Crossley, b. 1928, s. 1959, m. — Hon. Hugh F. S. C., b. 1971.

1784 *Somers* (8th), John Patrick Somers Cocks, b. 1907, s. 1953, m. — Philip S. S. C., b. 1948.

1917 *Southborough* (4th), Francis Michael Hopwood, b. 1922, s. 1982, w. — (None.)

1959 *Spens* (3rd), Patrick Michael Rex Spens, b. 1942, s. 1984, m. — Hon. Patrick N. G. S., b. 1968.

1640 *Stafford* (15th), Francis Melfort William Fitzherbert, b. 1954, s. 1986, m. — Hon. Benjamin F., b. 1983.

1938 *Stamp* (4th), Trevor Charles Bosworth Stamp, M.D., F.R.C.P., b. 1935, s. 1987, m. — Hon. Nicholas C. T. S., b. 1978.

1318 *Strabolgi* (11th), David Montague de Burgh Kenworthy, b. 1914, s. 1953, m. — Rev. the Hon. Jonathan M. A. K., b. 1916.

1954 *Strang* (2nd), Colin Strang, b. 1922, s. 1978, m. — (None.)

1955 *Strathalmond* (3rd), William Roberton Fraser, b. 1947, s. 1976, m. — Hon. William G. F., b. 1976.

1936 *Strathcarron* (2nd), David William Anthony Blyth Macpherson, b. 1924, s. 1937, m. — Hon. Ian D. P. M., b. 1949.

1955 *Strathclyde* (2nd), Thomas Galloway Dunlop du Roy de Blicquy Galbraith, b. 1960, s. 1985. — Hon. Charles W. du R. de B. G., b. 1962.

1900 *Strathcona and Mount Royal* (4th), Donald Euan Palmer Howard, b. 1923, s. 1959, m. — Hon. Donald A. S. H., b. 1961.

1836 *Stratheden & Campbell* (1841) (5th), Gavin Campbell, b. 1901, s. 1981, m. — Hon. Donald C., b. 1934.

1884 *Strathspey* (5th), Donald Patrick Trevor Grant, b. 1912, s. 1948, m. — Hon. James P. G., b. 1943.

1838 *Sudeley* (7th), Merlin Charles Sainthill Hanbury-Tracy, b. 1939, s. 1941, m. — Desmond A. J. H-T., b. 1928.

1786 *Suffield* (11th), Anthony Philip Harbord-Hamond, M.C., b. 1922, s. 1951, m. — Hon. Charles A. A. H.-H., b. 1953.

1893 *Swansea* (4th), John Hussey Hamilton Vivian, b. 1925, s. 1934, m. — Hon. Richard A. H. V., b. 1957.

1907 *Swaythling* (3rd), Stuart Albert Samuel Montagu, O.B.E., b. 1898, s. 1927, m. — Hon. David C. S. M., b. 1928.

1919 *Swinfen* (3rd), Roger Mynors Swinfen Eady, b. 1938, s. 1977, m. — Hon. Charles R. P. S. E., b. 1971.

1935 *Sysonby* (3rd), John Frederick Ponsonby, b. 1945, s. 1956. — (None.)

1831 I. *Talbot of Malahide* (10th), Reginald John Richard Arundell, b. 1931, s. 1987, m. — Hon. Richard J. T. A., b. 1957.

1946 *Tedder* (2nd), John Michael Tedder, SC.D., PH.D., D.SC., b. 1926, s. 1967, m. — Hon. Robin J. T., b. 1955.

1884 *Tennyson* (4th), Harold Christopher Tennyson, b. 1919, s. 1951. — Hon. Mark A. T., D.S.C., b. 1920.

1918 *Terrington* (4th), (James Allen) David Woodhouse, b. 1915, s. 1961, m. — Hon. C. Montague W., D.S.O., O.B.E., b. 1917.

1940 *Teviot* (2nd), Charles John Kerr, b. 1934, s. 1968, m. — Hon. Charles R. K., b. 1971.

1616 *Teynham* (20th), John Christopher Ingham Roper-Curzon, b. 1928, s. 1972, m. — Hon. David J. H. I. R.-C., b. 1965.

1964 *Thomson of Fleet* (2nd), Kenneth Roy Thomson, b. 1923, s. 1976, m. — Hon. David K. R. T., b. 1957.

1792 *Thurlow* (8th), Francis Edward Hovell-Thurlow-Cumming-Bruce, K.C.M.G., b. 1912, s. 1971, m. — Hon. Roualeyn R. H.-T.-C.-B., b. 1952.

1876 *Tollemache* (5th), Timothy John Edward Tollemache, b. 1939, s. 1975, m. — Hon. Edward J. H. T., b. 1976.

1564 S. *Torphichen* (15th), James Andrew Douglas Sandilands, b. 1946, s. 1975, m. — Douglas R. A. S., b. 1926.

1947 *Trefgarne* (2nd), David Garro Trefgarne, b. 1941, s. 1960, m. — Hon. George G. T., b. 1970.

1921 *Trevethin* (4th), *and Oaksey* (2nd), John Geoffrey Tristram Lawrence (2nd *U.K. Baron, Oaksey*, 1947), b. 1929, s. 1971, m. — Hon. Patrick J. T. L., b. 1960.

1880 *Trevor* (4th), Charles Edwin Hill-Trevor, b. 1928, s. 1950, m. — Hon. Marke C. H.-T., b. 1970.

1461 I. *Trimlestown* (19th), Charles Aloysius Barnewall, b. 1899, s. 1937, m. — Hon. Anthony E. B., b. 1928.

1940 *Tryon* (3rd), Anthony George Merrik Tryon, b. 1940, s. 1976, m. — Hon. Charles G. B. T., b. 1976.

1935 *Tweedsmuir* (2nd), John Norman Stuart Buchan, C.B.E., C.D., b. 1911, s. 1940, m. — Hon. William B., b. 1916.

1523 *Vaux of Harrowden* (10th), John Hugh Philip Gilbey, b. 1915, s. 1977, m. — Hon. Anthony W. G., b. 1940.

Created.	Title, Order of Succession, Name, etc.	Eldest Son or Heir.
1800 I.	*Ventry* (8th), Andrew Wesley Daubeny de Moleyns, *b.* 1943, *s.* 1987, *m.*	Hon. Francis W. *D. de M.*, *b.* 1965.
1762	*Vernon* (10th), John Lawrance Vernon, *b.* 1923, *s.* 1963, *m.*	Robert *Vernon-Harcourt*, *b.* 1918.
1922	*Vestey* (3rd), Samuel George Armstrong Vestey, *b.* 1941, *s.* 1954, *m.*	Hon. William G. *V.*, *b.* 1983.
1841	*Vivian* (5th), Anthony Crespigny Claude Vivian, *b.* 1906, *s.* 1940, *w.*	Hon. Nicholas *V.*, *b.* 1935.
1934	*Wakehurst* (3rd), (John) Christopher Loder, *b.* 1925, *s.* 1970, *m.*	Hon. Timothy W. *L.*, *b.* 1958.
1723	*Walpole* (9th), Robert Henry Montgomerie Walpole, T.D., *b.* 1913, *s.* 1931, *m.*	Hon. Robert H. *W.*, *b.* 1938.
1780	*Walsingham* (9th), John de Grey, M.C., *b.* 1925, *s.* 1965, *m.*	Hon. Robert *de G.*, *b.* 1969.
1936	*Wardington* (2nd), Christopher Henry Beaumont Pease, *b.* 1924, *s.* 1950, *m.*	Hon. William S. *P.*, *b.* 1925.
1792 I.	*Waterpark* (7th), Frederick Caryll Philip Cavendish, *b.* 1926, *s.* 1948, *m.*	Hon. Roderick A. *C.*, *b.* 1959.
1942	*Wedgwood* (4th), Piers Anthony Weymouth Wedgwood, *b.* 1954, *s.* 1970.	John *W.*, C.B.E., M.D., *b.* 1919.
1861	*Westbury* (5th), David Alan Bethell, M.C., *b.* 1922, *s.* 1961, *m.*	Hon. Richard N. *B.*, M.B.E., *b.* 1950.
1944	*Westwood* (2nd), William Westwood, *b.* 1907, *s.* 1953, *m.*	Hon. William G. *W.*, *b.* 1944.
1935	*Wigram* (2nd), (George) Neville (Clive) Wigram, M.C., *b.* 1915, *s.* 1960, *w.*	Maj. Hon. Andrew F. C. *W.*, *b.* 1949.
1491	*Willoughby de Broke* (21st), Leopold David Verney, *b.* 1938, *s.* 1986, *m.*	Hon. Rupert G. *V.*, *b.* 1966.
1946	*Wilson* (2nd), Patrick Maitland Wilson, *b.* 1915, *s.* 1964, *m.*	(None.)
1937	*Windlesham* (3rd), David James George Hennessy, C.V.O., P.C., *b.* 1932, *s.* 1962, *w.*	Hon. James *H.*, *b.* 1968.
1951	*Wise* (2nd), John Clayton Wise, *b.* 1923, *s.* 1968, *m.*	Hon. Christopher J. C. *W.*, PH.D., *b.* 1949.
1869	*Wolverton* (7th), Christopher Richard Glynn, *b.* 1938, *s.* 1988, *m.*	Hon. Andrew J. *G.*, *b.* 1943.
1928	*Wraxall* (2nd), George Richard Lawley Gibbs, *b.* 1928, *s.* 1931.	Hon. Eustace H. B. *G.*, C.M.G., *b.* 1929.
1915	*Wrenbury* (3rd), John Burton Buckley, *b.* 1927, *s.* 1940, *m.*	Hon. William E. *B.*, *b.* 1966.
1838	*Wrottesley* (6th), Clifton Hugh Lancelot de Verdon Wrottesley, *b.* 1968, *s.* 1977.	Hon. Mark *W.*, *b.* 1951.
1919	*Wyfold* (3rd), Hermon Robert Fleming Hermon-Hodge, *b.* 1915, *s.* 1942.	(None.)
1829	*Wynford* (8th), Robert Samuel Best, M.B.E., *b.* 1917, *s.* 1943, *m.*	Hon. John P. *B.*, *b.* 1950.
1308	*Zouche* (18th), James Assheton Frankland, *b.* 1943, *s.* 1965, *m.*	Hon. William T. A. *F.*, *b.* 1984.

PEERESSES IN THEIR OWN RIGHT

Peerages falling under this heading are the result of regular inheritance in lines which are open to females in default of males. A Peeress in her Own Right retains her title after marriage, and if her husband's rank is the superior she is designated by the two titles jointly, the inferior one last: her hereditary claim still holds good in spite of any marriage whether higher or lower. No rank held by a woman can confer any title or even precedence upon her husband but the rank of a Peeress in her Own Right is inherited by her eldest son (or perhaps daughter), to whomsoever she may have been married.

COUNTESSES IN THEIR OWN RIGHT

Style, The Countess of —— *Addressed as,* My Lady.

Created.	Title, Name, etc.	Eldest Son or Heir.
1643 s.	*Dysart* (11th in line), Rosamund Agnes Greaves, *b.* 1914, *s.* 1975.	Lady Katherine *Grant of Rothiemurchus*, *b.* 1918.
1633 s.	*Loudoun* (13th in line), Barbara Huddleston Abney-Hastings, *b.* 1919, *s.* 1960, *m.*	Lord Mauchline, *b.* 1942.
c. 1115 s.	*Mar* (31st in line), Margaret of Mar (*Premier Earldom of Scotland*), *b.* 1940, *s.* 1975, *m.*	The Mistress of Mar, *b.* 1963.
1947	*Mountbatten of Burma* (2nd in line), Patricia Edwina Victoria Knatchbull, *b.* 1924, *s.* 1979, *m.*	Lord Romsey, *b.* 1947.
c. 1235 s.	*Sutherland* (24th in line), Elizabeth Millicent Sutherland, *b.* 1921, *s.* 1963, *m.*	Lord Strathnaver, *b.* 1947.

BARONESSES IN THEIR OWN RIGHT

Style, The Baroness —— *Addressed as,* My Lady.

Created.	Title, Name, etc.	Eldest Son or Heir.
1421	*Berkeley* (17th in line), Mary Lalle Foley-Berkeley, *b.* 1905, *title called out of abeyance,* 1967.	Hon. Cynthia E. *Gueterbock*, *b.* 1909.
1455	*Berners* (15th in line), Vera Ruby Williams, *b.* 1901, *s.* 1950, *m.*	Two co-heiresses.

Created.	Title, Name, etc.	Eldest Son or Heir.
1529	*Braye* (8th in line), Mary Penelope Aubrey-Fletcher, *b*. 1941, *s*. 1985, *m*.	Hon. Ambrose J. Verney-Cave, *b*. 1906.
1321	*Dacre* (27th in line), Rachel Leila Douglas-Home, *b*. 1929, *title called out of abeyance*, 1970, *m*.	Hon. James T. A. *D.-H.*, *b*. 1952.
1332	*Darcy de Knayth* (18th in line), Davina Marcia Ingrams, *b*. 1938, *s*. 1943, *w*.	Hon. Caspar D. *I.*, *b*. 1962.
1439	*Dudley* (14th in line), Barbara Amy Felicity Hamilton, *b*. 1907, *s*. 1972, *m*.	Hon. Jim. A. H. *Wallace*, *b*. 1930.
1490 s.	*Herries of Terregles* (14th in line), Anne Elizabeth Fitzalan-Howard, *b*. 1938, *s*. 1975, *m*.	Lady Mary K. *Mumford*, c.v.o., *b*. 1940.
1602 s.	*Kinloss* (12th in line), Beatrice Mary Grenville Freeman-Grenville, *b*. 1922, *s*. 1944, *m*.	Master of Kinloss, *b*. 1953.
1663	*Lucas of Crudwell* (10th in line) & *Dingwall* (13th in line) (Scottish Lordship 1609), Anne Rosemary Palmer, *b*. 1919, *s*. 1958, *m*.	Hon. Ralph M. *P.*, *b*. 1951.
1681 s.	*Nairne* (12th in line), Katherine Evelyn Constance Bigham (*Katherine, Viscountess Mersey*), *b*. 1912, *s*. 1944, *m*.	Viscount Mersey, *b*. 1934 (*see* p. 165).
1945	*Portal of Hungerford* (2nd in line), Rosemary Ann Portal, *b*. 1923, *s*. 1971.	(None).
1445 s.	*Saltoun* (20th in line), Flora Marjory Fraser, *b*. 1930, *s*. 1979, *m*.	Hon. Katharine I. M. I. *F.*, *b*. 1957.
1489 s.	*Sempill* (20th in line), Ann Moira Sempill, *b*. 1920, *s*. 1965, *m*.	Master of Sempill, *b*. 1949.
1628	*Strange* (16th in line), Jean Cherry Drummond, *b*. 1928, *title called out of abeyance*, 1986, *m*.	Hon. Adam H. *D.*, *b*. 1953.
1313	*Willoughby de Eresby* (27th in line), Nancy Jane Marie Heathcote-Drummond-Willoughby, *b*. 1934, *s*. 1983.	Two co-heiresses.

LIFE PEERS

Created under the Appellate Jurisdiction Act, 1876 (as amended)

BARONS

Created

1986	*Ackner*, Desmond James Conrad Ackner, p.c., *b*. 1920, *m*.	Lord of Appeal in Ordinary.
1981	*Brandon of Oakbrook*, Henry Vivian Brandon, m.c., p.c., *b*. 1920, *m*.	Lord of Appeal in Ordinary.
1980	*Bridge of Harwich*, Nigel Cyprian Bridge, p.c., *b*. 1917, *m*.	Lord of Appeal in Ordinary.
1982	*Brightman*, John Anson Brightman, p.c., *b*. 1911, *m*.	Lord of Appeal (retired).
1971	*Cross of Chelsea*, (Arthur) Geoffrey (Neale) Cross, p.c., *b*. 1904, *m*.	Lord of Appeal (retired).
1957	*Denning*, Alfred Thompson Denning, p.c., *b*. 1899, *m*.	Lord of Appeal (retired).
1961	*Devlin*, Patrick Arthur Devlin, p.c., f.b.a., *b*. 1905, *m*.	Lord of Appeal (retired).
1974	*Edmund-Davies*, (Herbert) Edmund Edmund-Davies, p.c., *b*. 1906, *m*.	Lord of Appeal (retired).
1975	*Fraser of Tullybelton*, Walter Ian Reid Fraser, p.c., *b*. 1911, *m*.	Lord of Appeal (retired).
1986	*Goff of Chieveley*, Robert Lionel Archibald Goff, p.c., *b*. 1926, *m*.	Lord of Appeal in Ordinary.
1985	*Griffiths*, (William) Hugh Griffiths, m.c., p.c., *b*. 1923, *m*.	Lord of Appeal in Ordinary.
1987	*Jauncey of Tullichettle*, Charles Eliot Jauncey, p.c., *b*. 1925, *m*.	Lord of Appeal in Ordinary.
1977	*Keith of Kinkel*, Henry Shanks Keith, p.c., *b*. 1922, *m*.	Lord of Appeal in Ordinary.
1971	*Kilbrandon*, Charles James Dalrymple Shaw, p.c., *b*. 1906, *m*.	Lord of Appeal (retired).
1979	*Lane*, Geoffrey Dawson Lane, a.f.c., p.c., *b*. 1918, *m*.	Lord of Appeal (Lord Chief Justice).
1986	*Oliver of Aylmerton*, Peter Raymond Oliver, p.c., *b*. 1921, *m*.	Lord of Appeal in Ordinary.
1962	*Pearce*, Edward Holroyd Pearce, p.c., *b*. 1901, *w*.	Lord of Appeal (retired).
1980	*Roskill*, Eustace Wentworth Roskill, p.c., *b*. 1911, *m*.	Lord of Appeal in Ordinary.
1972	*Salmon*, Cyril Barnet Salmon, p.c., *b*. 1903, *m*	Lord of Appeal (retired).
1977	*Scarman*, Leslie George Scarman, o.b.e., p.c., *b*. 1911, *m*.	Lord of Appeal (retired).
1982	*Templeman*, Sydney William Templeman, m.b.e., p.c., *b*. 1920, *m*.	Lord of Appeal in Ordinary.
1964	*Wilberforce*, Richard Orme Wilberforce, c.m.g., o.b.e., p.c., *b*. 1907, *m*.	Lord of Appeal (retired).

Created under Life Peerages Act, 1958

BARONS

Life Peerages were conferred on the following: in the New Years Honours List 1988, Sir Robert Armstrong, Sir John Donaldson, Sir Immanuel Jakobovits; in the Queen's Birthday Honours List 1988, R. S. Alexander, Sir John Butterfield, Hon. Lord Mackenzie Stuart, Sir William Rees-Mogg.

1974	*Alexander of Potterhill*, William Picken Alexander, ph.d., *b*. 1905, *m*.
1988	*Alexander of Weedon*, Robert Scott Alexander, q.c., *b*. 1936, *m*.
1976	*Allen of Abbeydale*, Philip Allen, g.c.b., *b*. 1912, *m*.
1961	*Alport*, Cuthbert James McCall Alport, t.d., p.c., *b*. 1912, *w*.

1965 *Annan*, Noel Gilroy Annan, O.B.E., *b.* 1916, *m.*
1970 *Ardwick*, John Cowburn Beavan, *b.* 1910, *m.*
1988 *Armstrong of Ilminster*, Robert Temple Armstrong, G.C.B., C.V.O., *b.* 1927, *m.*
1973 *Ashby*, Eric Ashby, D.SC., F.R.S., *b.* 1904, *m.*
1967 *Aylestone*, Herbert William Bowden, C.H., C.B.E., P.C., *b.* 1905, *m.*
1982 *Bancroft*, Ian Powell Bancroft, G.C.B., *b.* 1922, *m.*
1974 *Banks*, Desmond Anderson Harvie Banks, C.B.E., *b.* 1918, *m.*
1974 *Barber*, Anthony Perrinott Lysberg Barber, T.D., P.C., *b.* 1920, *w.*
1983 *Barnett*, Joel Barnett, P.C., *b.* 1923, *m.*
1987 *Basnett*, David Basnett, *b.* 1924, *m.*
1982 *Bauer*, Prof. Peter Thomas Bauer, *b.* 1915.
1967 *Beaumont of Whitley*, Timothy Wentworth Beaumont, *b.* 1928, *m.*
1979 *Bellwin*, Irwin Norman Bellow, *b.* 1923, *m.*
1981 *Beloff*, Max Beloff, *b.* 1913, *m.*
1981 *Benson*, Henry Alexander Benson, G.B.E., *b.* 1909, *m.*
1969 *Bernstein*, Sidney Lewis Bernstein, *b.* 1899, *m.*
1971 *Blake*, Robert Norman William Blake, F.B.A., *b.* 1916, *m.*
1983 *Blanch*, Rt. Rev. Stuart Yarworth Blanch, P.C., *b.* 1918, *m.*
1978 *Blease*, William John Blease, *b.* 1914, *m.*
1980 *Boardman*, Thomas Gray Boardman, M.C., T.D., *b.* 1919, *m.*
1986 *Bonham-Carter*, Hon. Mark Raymond Bonham Carter, *b.* 1922, *m.*
1976 *Boston of Faversham*, Terence George Boston, Q.C.,*b.* 1930, *m.*
1983 *Bottomley*, Arthur George Bottomley, O.B.E., P.C., *b.* 1907, *m.*
1963 *Bowden*, Bertram Vivian Bowden, PH.D., *b.* 1910.
1972 *Boyd-Carpenter*, John Archibald Boyd-Carpenter, P.C., *b.* 1908, *m.*
1987 *Bramall*, Edwin Noel Westby Bramall, G.C.B., O.B.E., M.C., *Field Marshal*, *b.* 1923, *m.*
1976 *Briggs*, Asa Briggs, *b.* 1921, *m.*
1974 *Briginshaw*, Richard William Briginshaw, *m.*
1976 *Brimelow*, Thomas Brimelow, G.C.M.G., O.B.E., *b.* 1915, *m.*
1975 *Brookes*, Raymond Percival Brookes, *b.* 1909, *m.*
1979 *Brooks of Tremorfa*, John Edward Brooks, *b.* 1927, *m.*
1983 *Broxbourne*, Derek Colclough Walker-Smith, T.D., P.C., Q.C., *b.* 1910, *m.*
1974 *Bruce of Donington*, Donald William Trevor Bruce, *b.* 1912, *m.*
1983 *Bruce-Gardyne*, John, (Jock), Bruce-Gardyne, *b.* 1930, *m.*
1976 *Bullock*, Alan Louis Charles Bullock, F.B.A., *b.* 1914, *m.*
1988 *Butterfield*, (William) John (Hughes) Butterfield, O.B.E., D.M., *b.* 1920, *m.*
1985 *Butterworth*, John Blackstock Butterworth, C.B.E., *b.* 1918, *m.*
1978 *Buxton of Alsa*, Aubrey Leland Oakes Buxton, M.C., *b.* 1918, *m.*
1965 *Caccia*, Harold Anthony Caccia, G.C.M.G., G.C.V.O., *b.* 1905, *m.*
1987 *Callaghan of Cardiff*, (Leonard) James Callaghan, K.G., P.C., *b.* 1912, *m.*
1984 *Cameron of Lochbroom*, Kenneth John Cameron, P.C., Q.C., *b.* 1931, *m.*
1981 *Campbell of Alloway*, Alan Robertson Campbell, Q.C., *b.* 1917, *m.*
1974 *Campbell of Croy*, Gordon Thomas Calthrop Campbell, M.C., P.C., *b.* 1921, *m.*
1966 *Campbell of Eskan*, John Middleton Campbell, *b.* 1912, *w.*
1964 *Caradon*, Hugh Mackintosh Foot, G.C.M.G., K.C.V.O., O.B.E., P.C., *b.* 1907, *w.*
1987 *Carlisle of Bucklow*, Mark Carlisle, P.C., Q.C., *b.* 1929, *m.*
1983 *Carmichael of Kelvingrove*, Neil George Carmichael, *b.* 1921, *m.*
1975 *Carr of Hadley*, (Leonard) Robert Carr, P.C., *b.* 1916, *m.*
1987 *Carter*, Denis Victor Carter, *b.* 1932, *m.*
1977 *Carver*, (Richard) Michael (Power) Carver, G.C.B., C.B.E., D.S.O., M.C., *Field Marshal*, *b.* 1915, *m.*
1982 *Cayzer*, (William) Nicholas Cayzer, *b.* 1910, *m.*
1964 *Chalfont*, (Alun) Arthur Gwynne Jones, O.B.E., M.C., P.C., *b.* 1919, *m.*
1985 *Chapple*, Frank Joseph Chapple, *b.* 1921, *m.*
1978 *Charteris of Amisfield*, Martin Michael Charles Charteris, G.C.B., G.C.V.O., O.B.E., P.C., *b.* 1913, *m.*
1963 *Chelmer*, Eric Cyril Boyd Edwards, M.C., T.D., *b.* 1914, *m.*
1974 *Chelwood*, Tufton Victor Hamilton Beamish, M.C., *b.* 1917, *m.*
1987 *Chilver*, (Amos) Henry Chilver, F.R.S., *b.* 1926, *m.*
1977 *Chitnis*, Pratap Chidamber Chitnis, *b.* 1936, *m.*
1979 *Cledwyn of Penrhos*, Cledwyn Hughes, C.H., P.C., *b.* 1916, *m.*
1978 *Cockfield*, (Francis) Arthur Cockfield, P.C., *b.* 1916, *m.*
1987 *Cocks of Hartcliffe*, Michael Francis Lovell Cocks, P.C., *b.* 1929, *m.*
1980 *Coggan*, Rt. Rev. (Frederick) Donald Coggan, P.C., D.D., Royal Victorian Chain, *b.* 1909, *m.*
1964 *Collison*, Harold Francis Collison, C.B.E., *b.* 1909, *m.*
1987 *Colnbrook*, Humphrey Edward Gregory Atkins, K.C.M.G., P.C., *b.* 1922, *m.*
1981 *Constantine of Stanmore*, Theodore Constantine, C.B.E., *b.* 1910, *m.*
1966 *Cooper of Stockton Heath*, John Cooper, *b.* 1908, *m.*
1959 *Craigton*, Jack Nixon Browne, C.B.E., P.C., *b.* 1904, *m.*
1987 *Crickhowell*, (Roger) Nicholas Edwards, P.C., *b.* 1934, *m.*
1978 *Croham*, Douglas Albert Vivian Allen, G.C.B., *b.* 1917, *m.*
1974 *Cudlipp*, Hugh Cudlipp, O.B.E., *b.* 1913, *m.*
1979 *Dacre of Glanton*, Hugh Redwald Trevor-Roper, *b.* 1914, *m.*
1986 *Dainton*, Frederick Sydney Dainton, PH.D., SC.D., F.R.S., *b.* 1914, *m.*
1974 *Davies of Penrhys*, Gwilym Elfed Davies, *b.* 1913, *m.*
1983 *Dean of Beswick*, Joseph Jabez Dean, *b.* 1923.
1986 *Deedes*, William Francis Deedes, M.C., P.C., *b.* 1913, *m.*
1976 *Delfont*, Bernard Delfont, *b.* 1909, *m.*
1970 *Diamond*, John Diamond, P.C., *b.* 1907, *m.*

1967 *Donaldson of Kingsbridge*, John George Stuart Donaldson, O.B.E., *b.* 1907, *m.*
1988 *Donaldson of Lymington*, John Francis Donaldson, P.C., *b.* 1920, *m.* (*Master of the Rolls*).
1985 *Donoughue*, Bernard Donoughue, D.Phil., *b.* 1934, *m.*
1987 *Dormand of Easington*, John Donkin Dormand, *b.* 1919, *m.*
1983 *Eden of Winton*, John Benedict Eden, P.C., *b.* 1925, *m.*
1985 *Elliott of Morpeth*, Robert William Elliott, *b.* 1920, *m.*
1972 *Elworthy*, (Samuel) Charles Elworthy, K.G., G.C.B., C.B.E., D.S.O., L.V.O., D.F.C., A.F.C., *Marshal of the Royal Air Force, b.* 1911, *w.*
1974 *Elwyn-Jones*, Frederick Elwyn-Jones, C.H., P.C., *b.* 1909, *m.*
1981 *Elystan-Morgan*, Dafydd Elystan Elystan-Morgan, *b.* 1932, *m.*
1980 *Emslie*, George Carlyle Emslie, M.B.E., P.C., *b.* 1919, *m.* (*Lord Justice-General of Scotland*).
1983 *Ennals*, David Hedley Ennals, P.C., *b.* 1922, *m.*
1978 *Evans of Claughton*, (David Thomas) Gruffydd Evans, *b.* 1928, *m.*
1983 *Ezra*, Derek Ezra, M.B.E., *b.* 1919, *m.*
1983 *Fanshawe of Richmond*, Anthony Henry Fanshawe Royle, K.C.M.G., *b.*, 1927, *m.*
1958 *Ferrier*, Victor Ferrier Noel-Paton, E.D., *b.* 1900, *m.*
1983 *Fitt*, Gerard Fitt, *b.* 1926, *m.*
1970 *Fletcher*, Eric George Molyneux Fletcher, P.C., LL.D., *b.* 1903, *m.*
1979 *Flowers*, Brian Hilton Flowers, F.R.S., *b.* 1924, *m.*
1967 *Foot*, John Mackintosh Foot, *b.* 1909, *m.*
1982 *Forte*, Charles Forte, *b.* 1908, *m.*
1962 *Franks*, Oliver Shewell Franks, O.M., G.C.M.G., K.C.B., K.C.V.O., C.B.E., P.C., F.B.A., *b.* 1905, *m.*
1974 *Fraser of Kilmorack*, (Richard) Michael Fraser, C.B.E., *b.* 1915, *m.*
1982 *Gallacher*, John Gallacher, *b.* 1920, *m.*
1979 *Galpern*, Myer Galpern, *b.* 1903.
1963 *Gardiner*, Gerald Austin Gardiner, C.H., P.C., *b.* 1900, *m.*
1975 *Gibson*, (Richard) Patrick (Tallentyre) Gibson, *b.* 1916, *m.*
1979 *Gibson-Watt*, (James) David Gibson-Watt, M.C., P.C., *b.* 1918, *m.*
1977 *Glenamara*, Edward Watson Short, C.H., P.C., *b.* 1912, *m.*
1965 *Goodman*, Arnold Abraham Goodman, C.H., *b.* 1913.
1987 *Goold*, James Duncan Goold, *b.* 1934, *m.*
1982 *Gormley*, Joseph Gormley, O.B.E., *b.* 1917, *m.*
1976 *Grade*, Lew Grade, *b.* 1906, *m.*
1983 *Graham of Edmonton*, (Thomas) Edward Graham, *b.*1925, *m.*
1967 *Granville of Eye*, Edgar Louis Granville, *b.* 1899, *m.*
1983 *Gray of Contin*, James (Hamish) Hector Northey Gray, P.C., *b.* 1927, *m.*
1974 *Greene of Harrow Weald*, Sidney Francis Greene, C.B.E., *b.* 1910, *m.*
1974 *Greenhill of Harrow*, Denis Arthur Greenhill, G.C.M.G., O.B.E., *b.* 1913, *m.*
1975 *Gregson*, John Gregson, *b.* 1924.
1968 *Grey of Naunton*, Ralph Francis Alnwick Grey, G.C.M.G., G.C.V.O., O.B.E., *b.* 1910, *m.*
1983 *Grimond*, Joseph Grimond, T.D., P.C., *b.* 1913, *m.*
1970 *Hailsham of St. Marylebone*, Quintin McGarel Hogg, K.G., C.H., P.C., *b.* 1907, *m.*
1983 *Hanson*, James Edward Hanson, *b.* 1922, *m.*
1974 *Harmar-Nicholls*, Harmar Harmar-Nicholls, *b.* 1912, *m.*
1974 *Harris of Greenwich*, John Henry Harris, *b.* 1930, *m.*
1979 *Harris of High Cross*, Ralph Harris, *b.* 1924, *m.*
1968 *Hartwell*, (William) Michael Berry, M.B.E., T.D., *b.* 1911, *w.*
1971 *Harvey of Prestbury*, Arthur Vere Harvey, C.B.E., *b.* 1906, *m.*
1974 *Harvington*, Robert Grant Grant-Ferris, P.C., *b.* 1907, *m.*
1978 *Hatch of Lusby*, John Charles Hatch, *b.* 1917.
1987 *Havers*, (Robert) Michael (Oldfield) Havers, P.C., *b.* 1923, *m.*
1983 *Henderson of Brompton*, Peter Gordon Henderson, K.C.B., *b.* 1922, *m.*
1967 *Heycock*, Llewellyn Heycock, C.B.E., *b.* 1905, *m.*
1963 *Hill of Luton*, Charles Hill, P.C., M.D., *b.* 1904, *m.*
1979 *Hill-Norton*, Peter John Hill-Norton, G.C.B., *Admiral of the Fleet, b.* 1915, *m.*
1967 *Hirshfield*, Desmond Barel Hirshfield, *b.* 1913, *m.*
1979 *Holderness*, Richard Frederick Wood, P.C., *b.* 1920, *m.*
1974 *Home of the Hirsel*, Alexander Frederick Douglas-Home, K.T., P.C., *b.* 1903, *m.*
1979 *Hooson*, (Hugh) Emlyn Hooson, Q.C., *b.* 1925, *m.*
1974 *Houghton of Sowerby*, (Arthur Leslie Noel) Douglas Houghton, C.H., P.C., *b.* 1898, *m.*
1978 *Howie of Troon*, William Howie, *b.* 1924, *m.*
1961 *Hughes*, William Hughes, C.B.E., P.C., *b.* 1911, *m.*
1966 *Hunt*, (Henry Cecil) John Hunt, K.G., G.C.B., D.S.O., *b.* 1910, *m.*
1980 *Hunt of Tanworth*, John Joseph Benedict Hunt, G.C.B., *b.* 1919, *m.*
1978 *Hunter of Newington*, Robert Brockie Hunter, M.B.E., F.R.C.P., *b.* 1915, *m.*
1978 *Hutchinson of Lullington*, Jeremy Nicolas Hutchinson, Q.C., *b.* 1915, *m.*
1982 *Ingrow*, John Aked Taylor, O.B.E., T.D., *b.* 1917, *m.*
1987 *Irvine of Lairg*, Alexander Andrew Mackay Irvine, Q.C., *b.* 1940, *m.*
1979 *Irving of Dartford*, Sydney Irving, P.C., *b.* 1918, *m.*
1968 *Jacques*, John Henry Jacques, *b.* 1905, *m.*
1988 *Jakobovits*, Immanuel Jakobovits, *b.* 1921, *m.*
1959 *James of Rusholme*, Eric John Francis James, *b.* 1909, *m.*
1987 *Jay*, Douglas Patrick Thomas Jay, P.C., *b.* 1907, *m.*
1987 *Jenkin of Roding*, (Charles) Patrick (Fleeming) Jenkin, P.C., *b.* 1926, *m.*
1987 *Jenkins of Hillhead*, Roy Harris Jenkins, P.C., *b.* 1920, *m.*
1981 *Jenkins of Putney*, Hugh Gater Jenkins, *b.* 1908, *m.*
1981 *John-Mackie*, John John-Mackie, *b.* 1909, *m.*

1987 *Johnston of Rockport,* Charles Collier Johnston, T.D., b. 1915, m.
1987 *Joseph,* Keith Sinjohn Joseph, C.H., P.C., b. 1918.
1983 *Kaberry of Adel,* Donald Kaberry, T.D., b. 1907, m.
1981 *Kadoorie,* Lawrence Kadoorie, C.B.E., b. 1899, m.
1976 *Kagan,* Joseph Kagan, b. 1915, m.
1965 *Kahn,* Richard Ferdinand Kahn, C.B.E., F.B.A., b. 1905.
1970 *Kearton,* (Christopher) Frank Kearton, O.B.E., F.R.S., b. 1911, m.
1980 *Keith of Castleacre,* Kenneth Alexander Keith, b. 1916, m.
1985 *Kimball,* Marcus Richard Kimball, b. 1928, m.
1983 *King of Wartnaby,* John Leonard King, m.
1965 *Kings Norton,* Harold Roxbee Cox, PH.D., b. 1902, m.
1975 *Kirkhill,* John Farquharson Smith, b. 1930, m.
1974 *Kissin,* Harry Kissin, b. 1912, m.
1987 *Knights,* Philip Douglas Knights, C.B.E., Q.P.M., b. 1920, m.
1964 *Leatherland,* Charles Edward Leatherland, O.B.E., b. 1898, m.
1979 *Lever of Manchester,* Harold Lever, P.C., b. 1914, m.
1982 *Lewin,* Terence Thornton Lewin, K.G., G.C.B., L.V.O., D.S.C., *Admiral of the Fleet,* b. 1920, m.
1965 *Lloyd of Hampstead,* Dennis Lloyd, Q.C., LL.D., b. 1915, m.
1973 *Lloyd of Kilgerran,* Rhys Gerran Lloyd, C.B.E., Q.C., b. 1907, m.
1974 *Lovell-Davis,* Peter Lovell Lovell-Davis, b. 1924, m.
1979 *Lowry,* Robert Lynd Erskine Lowry, P.C., b. 1919, w. (*Lord of Appeal in Ordinary*).
1980 *McAlpine of Moffat,* (Robert) Edwin McAlpine, b. 1907, m.
1983 *McAlpine of West Green,* (Robert) Alistair McAlpine, b. 1942, m.
1975 *McCarthy,* William Edward John McCarthy, b. 1925, m.
1976 *McCluskey,* John Herbert McCluskey, Q.C., b. 1929, m.
1966 *McFadzean,* William Hunter McFadzean, K.T., b. 1903, m.
1980 *McFadzean of Kelvinside,* Francis Scott McFadzean, b. 1915, m.
1978 *McGregor of Durris,* Oliver Ross McGregor, b. 1921, m.
1982 *McIntosh of Haringey,* Andrew Robert McIntosh, b. 1933, m.
1979 *Mackay of Clashfern,* James Peter Hymers Mackay, P.C., Q.C., b. 1927, m. (*Lord High Chancellor*).
1974 *Mackie of Benshie,* George Yull Mackie, C.B.E., D.S.O., D.F.C., b. 1919, w.
1971 *Maclean,* Charles Hector Fitzroy Maclean, K.T., G.C.V.O., K.B.E., Royal Victorian Chain, P.C., b. 1916, m.
1982 *MacLehose of Beoch,* (Crawford) Murray MacLehose, K.T., G.B.E., K.C.M.G., K.C.V.O., b. 1917, m.
1967 *MacLeod of Fuinary,* Very Rev. George Fielden MacLeod, M.C., D.D., b. 1895, m.
1967 *Mais,* Alan Raymond Mais, G.B.E., T.D., E.R.D., b. 1911, m.
1981 *Marsh,* Richard William Marsh, P.C., b. 1928, m.
1985 *Marshall of Goring,* Walter Charles Marshall, C.B.E., F.R.S., b. 1932, m.
1980 *Marshall of Leeds,* Frank Shaw Marshall, b. 1915, m.
1987 *Mason of Barnsley,* Roy Mason, P.C., b. 1924, m.
1980 *Matthews,* Victor Collin Matthews, b. 1919, m.
1983 *Maude of Stratford-upon-Avon,* Angus Edmund Upton Maude, T.D., P.C., b. 1912, m.
1981 *Mayhew,* Christopher Paget Mayhew, P.C., b. 1915, m.
1985 *Mellish,* Robert Joseph Mellish, P.C., b. 1913, m.
1979 *Miles,* Bernard James Miles, C.B.E., b. 1907, m.
1978 *Mishcon,* Victor Mishcon, b. 1915, m.
1981 *Molloy,* William John Molloy, b. 1918, m.
1961 *Molson,* (Arthur) Hugh (Elsdale) Molson, P.C., b. 1903, m.
1986 *Moore of Wolvercote,* Philip Brian Cecil Moore, G.C.B., G.C.V.O., C.M.G., P.C., b. 1921, m.
1967 *Morris of Grasmere,* Charles Richard Morris, K.C.M.G., b. 1898, w.
1985 *Morton of Shuna,* Hugh Drennan Baird Morton, Q.C., b. 1930, m.
1971 *Moyola,* James Dawson Chichester-Clark, P.C. (N.I.), b. 1923, m.
1983 *Mulley,* Frederick William Mulley, P.C., b. 1918, m.
1985 *Murray of Epping Forest,* Lionel Murray, O.B.E., P.C., b. 1922, m.
1964 *Murray of Newhaven,* Keith Anderson Hope Murray, K.C.B., PH.D., b. 1903.
1979 *Murton of Lindisfarne,* (Henry) Oscar Murton, O.B.E., T.D., P.C., b. 1914, m.
1975 *Northfield,* (William) Donald Chapman, b. 1923.
1966 *Nugent of Guildford,* (George) Richard (Hodges) Nugent, P.C., b. 1907, m.
1973 *O'Brien of Lothbury,* Leslie Kenneth O'Brien, G.B.E., P.C., b. 1908, m.
1970 *Olivier,* Laurence Kerr Olivier, O.M., b. 1907, m.
1970 *O'Neill of the Maine,* Terence Marne O'Neill, P.C. (N.I.), b. 1914, m.
1976 *Oram,* Albert Edward Oram, b. 1913, m.
1971 *Orr-Ewing,* (Charles) Ian Orr-Ewing, O.B.E., b. 1912, m.
1974 *Paget of Northampton,* Reginald Thomas Paget, Q.C., b. 1908, m.
1975 *Parry,* Gordon Samuel David Parry, b. 1925, m.
1967 *Penney,* William George Penney, O.M., K.B.E., PH.D., D.S.C., F.R.S., b. 1909, m.
1982 *Pennock,* Raymond (William) Pennock, b. 1920, m.
1979 *Perry of Walton,* Walter Laing Macdonald Perry, O.B.E., M.D., D.SC., F.R.S.E., F.R.C.P., b. 1921, m.
1987 *Peston,* Maurice Harry Peston, b. 1931, m.
1983 *Peyton of Yeovil,* John Wynne William Peyton, P.C., b. 1919, m.
1975 *Pitt of Hampstead,* David Thomas Pitt, b. 1913, m.
1959 *Plowden,* Edwin Noel Plowden, G.B.E., K.C.B., b. 1907, m.
1987 *Plumb,* Charles Henry Plumb, b. 1925, m.
1981 *Plummer of St. Marylebone,* (Arthur) Desmond (Herne) Plummer, T.D., b. 1914, m.
1973 *Porritt,* Arthur Espie Porritt, G.C.M.G., G.C.V.O., C.B.E., b. 1900, m.
1987 *Prior,* James Michael Leathes Prior, P.C., b. 1927, m.
1975 *Pritchard,* Derek Wilbraham Pritchard, b. 1910, m.
1982 *Prys-Davies,* Gwilym Prys Prys-Davies, b. 1923, m.

1987 *Pym*, Francis Leslie Pym, M.C., P.C., *b.* 1922, *m.*
1982 *Quinton*, Anthony Meredith Quinton, *b.* 1925, *m.*
1978 *Rawlinson of Ewell*, Peter Anthony Grayson Rawlinson, P.C., Q.C., *b.* 1919, *m.*
1976 *Rayne*, Max Rayne, *b.* 1918, *m.*
1983 *Rayner*, Derek George Rayner, *b.* 1926.
1987 *Rees*, Peter Wynford Innes Rees, P.C., Q.C., *b.* 1926, *m.*
1988 *Rees-Mogg*, William Rees-Mogg, *b.* 1928, *m.*
1970 *Reigate*, John Kenyon Vaughan-Morgan, P.C., *b.* 1905, *m.*
1978 *Reilly*, Paul Reilly, *b.* 1912, *m.*
1979 *Renton*, David Lockhart-Mure Renton, K.B.E., T.D., P.C., Q.C., *b.* 1908, *w.*
1979 *Richardson*, John Samuel Richardson, L.V.O., M.D., F.R.C.P., *b.* 1910, *m.*
1983 *Richardson of Duntisbourne*, Gordon William Humphreys Richardson, K.G., M.B.E., T.D, P.C., *b.* 1915, *m.*
1987 *Rippon of Hexham*, (Aubrey) Geoffrey (Frederick) Rippon, P.C., Q.C., *b.* 1924, *m.*
1961 *Robens of Woldingham*, Alfred Robens, P.C., *b.* 1910, *m.*
1969 *Roberthall*, Robert Lowe Roberthall, K.C.M.G., C.B., *b.* 1901, *m.*
1977 *Roll of Ipsden*, Eric Roll, K.C.M.G., C.B., *b.* 1907, *m.*
1987 *Ross of Newport*, Stephen Sherlock Ross, *b.* 1926, *m.*
1975 *Ryder of Eaton Hastings*, Sydney Thomas Franklin (Don) Ryder, *b.* 1916, *m.*
1962 *Sainsbury*, Alan John Sainsbury, *b.* 1902, *m.*
1977 *Saint Brides*, John Morrice Cairns James, G.C.M.G., C.V.O., M.B.E., P.C., *b.* 1916, *m.*
1987 *St. John of Fawsley*, Norman Antony Francis St. John-Stevas, P.C., *b.* 1929.
1985 *Sanderson of Bowden*, Charles Russell Sanderson, *b.* 1933, *m.*
1979 *Scanlon*, Hugh Parr Scanlon, *b.* 1913, *m.*
1976 *Schon*, Frank Schon, *b.* 1912, *m.*
1972 *Seebohm*, Frederic Seebohm, T.D., *b.* 1909, *m.*
1978 *Sefton of Garston*, William Henry Sefton, *b.* 1915, *m.*
1958 *Shackleton*, Edward Arthur Alexander Shackleton, K.G., O.B.E., P.C., *b.* 1911, *m.*
1959 *Shawcross*, Hartley William Shawcross, G.B.E., P.C., Q.C., *b.* 1902, *w.*
1980 *Sieff of Brimpton*, Marcus Joseph Sieff, O.B.E., *b.* 1918, *m.*
1971 *Simon of Glaisdale*, Jocelyn Edward Salis Simon, P.C., *b.* 1911. *m. (Lord of Appeal, retired).*
1978 *Smith*, Rodney Smith, K.B.E., F.R.C.S., *b.* 1914, *m.*
1965 *Soper*, Rev. Donald Oliver Soper, Ph.D., *b.* 1903, *m.*
1983 *Stallard*, Albert William Stallard, *b.* 1921, *m.*
1987 *Stevens of Ludgate*, David Robert Stevens, *b.* 1936, *m.*
1979 *Stewart of Fulham*, Robert Michael Maitland Stewart, C.H., P.C., *b.* 1906, *w.*
1981 *Stodart of Leaston*, James Anthony Stodart, P.C., *b.* 1916, *m.*
1983 *Stoddart of Swindon*, David Leonard Stoddart, *b.* 1926, *m.*
1969 *Stokes*, Donald Gresham Stokes, T.D., *b.* 1914, *m.*
1979 *Strauss*, George Russell Strauss, P.C., *b.* 1901, *m.*
1981 *Swann*, Michael Meredith Swann, Ph.D., F.R.S., *b.* 1920, *m.*
1971 *Tanlaw*, Simon Brooke Mackay, *b.* 1934, *m.*
1978 *Taylor of Blackburn*, Thomas Taylor, C.B.E., *b.* 1929, *m.*
1968 *Taylor of Gryfe*, Thomas Johnston Taylor, *b.* 1912, *m.*
1982 *Taylor of Hadfield*, Francis Taylor, *b.* 1905, *m.*
1966 *Taylor of Mansfield*, Harry Bernard Taylor, C.B.E., *b.* 1895, *w.*
1987 *Thomas of Gwydir*, Peter John Mitchell Thomas, P.C., Q.C., *b.* 1920, *w.*
1981 *Thomas of Swynnerton*, Hugh Swynnerton Thomas, *b.* 1931, *m.*
1977 *Thomson of Monifieth*, George Morgan Thomson, K.T., P.C., *b.* 1921, *m.*
1967 *Thorneycroft*, (George Edward) Peter Thorneycroft, C.H., P.C., *b.* 1909, *m.*
1962 *Todd*, Alexander Robertus Todd, O.M., D.SC., D.Phil., F.R.S., *b.* 1907, *w.*
1981 *Tordoff*, Geoffrey Johnson Tordoff, *b.* 1928, *m.*
1987 *Trafford*, Joseph Anthony Porteous Trafford, *b.* 1932, *m.*
1974 *Tranmire*, Robert Hugh Turton, K.B.E.,M.C., P.C., *b.* 1903, *m.*
1979 *Underhill*, (Henry) Reginall Underhill, C.B.E., *b.* 1914, *m.*
1985 *Vinson*, Nigel Vinson, L.V.O., *b.* 1931, *m.*
1964 *Wade*, Donald William Wade, *b.* 1904, *m.*
1974 *Wallace of Campsie*, George Wallace, *b.* 1915, *m.*
1974 *Wallace of Coslany*, George Douglas Wallace, *b.* 1906, *m.*
1961 *Walston*, Henry David Leonard George Walston, C.V.O., *b.* 1912, *m.*
1972 *Watkins*, Tudor Elwyn Watkins, *b.* 1903, *m.*
1977 *Wedderburn of Charlton*, Kenneth William Wedderburn, *b.* 1927, *m.*
1976 *Weidenfeld*, (Arthur) George Weidenfeld, *b.* 1919.
1980 *Weinstock*, Arnold Weinstock, C.B.E., *b.* 1924, *m.*
1965 *Wells-Pestell*, Reginald Alfred Wells-Pestell, *b.* 1910, *m.*
1978 *Whaddon*, John Derek Page, *b.* 1927, *m.*
1974 *Wigoder*, Basil Thomas Wigoder, Q.C., *b.* 1921, *m.*
1985 *Williams of Elvel*, Charles Cuthbert Powell Williams, C.B.E., *b.* 1933, *m.*
1963 *Willis*, Edward Henry Willis, *b.* 1918, *m.*
1969 *Wilson of Langside*, Henry Stephen Wilson, P.C., Q.C., *b.* 1916, *m.*
1983 *Wilson of Rievaulx*, (James) Harold Wilson, K.G., O.B.E., P.C., F.R.S., *b.* 1916, *m.*
1975 *Winstanley*, Michael Platt Winstanley, *b.* 1918, *m.*
1965 *Winterbottom*, Ian Winterbottom, *b.* 1913, *m.*
1985 *Wolfson*, Leonard Gordon Wolfson, *b.* 1927, *m.*
1987 *Wyatt of Weeford*, Woodrow Lyle Wyatt, *b.* 1918, *m.*
1978 *Young of Dartington*, Michael Young, Ph.D., *b.* 1915, *m.*
1984 *Young of Graffham*, David Ivor Young, P.C., *b.* 1932, *m.*
1971 *Zuckerman*, Solly Zuckerman, O.M., K.C.B., F.R.S., M.D., D.SC., *b.* 1904, *m.*

BARONESSES

1979 *Airey of Abingdon,* Diana Josceline Barbara Neave Airey, *b.* 1919, *w.*
1970 *Bacon,* Alice Martha Bacon, C.B.E., P.C., *b.* 1911.
1967 *Birk,* Alma Birk, *b.* 1921, *m.*
1987 *Blackstone,* Tessa Ann Vosper Blackstone, PH.D., *b.* 1942.
1987 *Blatch,* Emily May Blatch, C.B.E., *b.* 1937, *m.*
1964 *Brooke of Ystradfellte,* Barbara Muriel Brooke, D.B.E., *b.* 1908, *w.*
1962 *Burton of Coventry,* Elaine Frances Burton, *b.* 1904.
1982 *Carnegy of Lour,* Elizabeth Patricia Carnegy of Lour, *b.* 1925.
1982 *Cox,* Caroline Anne Cox, *b.* 1937, *m.*
1978 *David,* Nora Ratcliff David, *b.* 1913, *m.*
1974 *Delacourt-Smith of Alteryn,* Margaret Rosalind Delacourt-Smith, *b.* 1916, *m.*
1978 *Denington,* Evelyn Joyce Denington, D.B.E., *b.* 1907, *m.*
1972 *Elles,* Diana Louie Elles, *b.* 1921, *m.*
1958 *Elliot of Harwood,* Katharine Elliot, D.B.E., *b.* 1903, *w.*
1981 *Ewart-Biggs,* (Felicity) Jane Ewart-Biggs, *b.* 1929, *w.*
1975 *Faithfull,* Lucy Faithfull, O.B.E., *b.* 1910.
1974 *Falkender,* Marcia Matilda Falkender, *b.* 1932.
1974 *Fisher of Rednal,* Doris Mary Gertrude Fisher, *b.* 1919, *w.*
1963 *Gaitskell,* Anna Dora Gaitskell, *w.*
1981 *Gardner of Parkes,* (Rachel) Trixie (Anne) Gardner, *b.* 1927, *m.*
1988 *Hart of South Lanark,* Judith Constance Mary Hart, D.B.E., P.C., *b.* 1924, *m.*
1985 *Hooper,* Gloria Hooper, *b.* 1939.
1965 *Hylton-Foster,* Audrey Pellew Hylton-Foster, *b.* 1908, *w.*
1979 *Jeger,* Lena May Jeger, *b.* 1915, *m.*
1970 *Lee of Asheridge,* Janet Bevan, P.C., *b.* 1904, *w.*
1967 *Llewelyn-Davies of Hastoe,* Annie Patricia Llewelyn-Davies, P.C., *b.* 1915, *w.*
1978 *Lockwood,* Betty Lockwood, *b.* 1924, *m.*
1979 *McFarlane of Llandaff,* Jean Kennedy McFarlane, *b.* 1926.
1971 *Macleod of Borve,* Evelyn Hester Macleod, *b.* 1915, *w.*
1970 *Masham of Ilton,* Susan Lilian Primrose Cunliffe-Lister, *b.* 1935, *m.* (*Countess of Swinton*).
1982 *Nicol,* Olive Mary Wendy Nicol, *b.* 1923, *m.*
1964 *Phillips,* Norah Phillips, *b.* 1910, *w.*
1974 *Pike,* (Irene) Mervyn (Parnicott) Pike, D.B.E., *b.* 1918.
1981 *Platt of Writtle,* Beryl Catherine Platt, C.B.E., *b.* 1923, *m.*
1974 *Robson of Kiddington,* Inga-Stina Robson, *b.* 1919, *w.*
1979 *Ryder of Warsaw,* (Margaret) Susan Cheshire, C.M.G., O.B.E., *b.* 1924, *m.*
1971 *Seear,* (Beatrice) Nancy Seear, P.C., *b.* 1913.
1967 *Serota,* Beatrice Serota, *b.* 1919, *m.*
1973 *Sharples,* Pamela Sharples, *b.* 1923, *m.*
1974 *Stedman,* Phyllis Stedman, O.B.E., *b.* 1916, *m.*
1980 *Trumpington,* Jean Alys Barker, *b.* 1922, *w.*
1985 *Turner of Camden,* Muriel Winifred Turner, *b.* 1927, *m.*
1974 *Vickers,* Joan Helen Vickers, D.B.E., *b.* 1907.
1985 *Warnock,* Helen Mary Warnock, D.B.E., *b.* 1924, *m.*
1970 *White,* Eirene Lloyd White, *b.* 1909, *w.*
1971 *Young,* Janet Mary Young, P.C., *b.* 1926, *m.*

LIFE PEERAGES EXTINCT SINCE LAST ISSUE.—Rhodes (*cr.* 1964); Soames (*cr.* 1978); Blyton (*cr.* 1964); Duncan-Sandys (*cr.* 1974); Hunt of Fawley (*cr.* 1973); Taylor (*cr.* 1958); Lane-Fox (*cr.* 1981); Ramsey of Canterbury (*cr.* 1974); Brockway (*cr.* 1964); Ross of Marnock (*cr.* 1979); Wootton of Abinger (*cr.* 1958); Wheatley (*cr.* 1970); Jacobson (*cr.* 1975); Silkin of Dulwich (*cr.* 1985); Peart (*cr.* 1976).

COURTESY TITLES

Holders of Courtesy Titles are addressed in the same manner as holders of substantive titles.

From this list it will be seen that, for example, the "Marquess of Blandford" is heir to the Dukedom of Marlborough, and "Viscount Althorp" to the Earldom of Spencer. Titles of second heirs are also given, and the Courtesy Title of the father of a second heir is indicated by *; e.g., Earl of Burlington, eldest son of *Marquess of Hartington.

Marquesses
Blandford—*Marlborough*
Bowmont—*Roxburghe*
Douglas and Clydesdale—
    Hamilton
*Douro—*Wellington*
*Graham—*Montrose*
Granby—*Rutland*
Hamilton—*Abercorn*
*Hartington—*Devonshire*
*Kildare—*Leinster*
Lorne—*Argyll*
*Tavistock—*Bedford*
Worcester—*Beaufort*

Earls
*Aboyne—*Huntly*
Altamont—*Sligo*
Ancram—*Lothian*
Arundel and Surrey—
    Norfolk
Bective—*Headfort*
Belfast—*Donegall*
*Brecknock—*Camden*
*Burford *St. Albans*
Burlington—*Hartington*
Cardigan—*Ailesbury*
Cassillis—*Ailsa*
Compton—*Northampton*
Dalkeith—*Buccleuch*
Dumfries—*Bute*
*Euston—*Grafton*
Haddo—*Aberdeen and*
    Temair
*Hopetoun—*Linlithgow*
Macduff—*Fife*
*March and Kinrara—
    Richmond
*Mount Charles
    Conyngham
Mornington—*Douro*
Mulgrave—*Normanby*
Offaly—*Kildare*
Percy—*Northumberland*
Rocksavage —
    Cholmondeley
*Ronaldshay—*Zetland*
St. Andrews—*Kent*
*Shelburne—*Lansdowne*
Tyrone—*Waterford*
Ulster—*Gloucester*
Uxbridge—*Anglesey*
Wiltshire—*Winchester*
Yarmouth—*Hertford*

Viscounts
Althorp—*Spencer*
Amberley—*Russell*
Andover—*Suffolk and*
    Berkshire

Anson—*Lichfield*
Asquith—*Oxford &*
    Asquith
Boringdon—*Morley*
Borodale—*Beatty*
Boyle—*Shannon*
Brocas—*Jellicoe*
Calne and Calstone—
    Shelburne
Campden—*Gainsborough*
Carlow—*Portarlington*
Carlton—*Wharncliffe*
Castlereagh—
    Londonderry
Chelsea—*Cadogan*
Chewton—*Waldegrave*
Clanfield—*Peel*
Coke—*Leicester*
Cole—*Enniskillen*
Corry—*Belmore*
Corvedale—*Baldwin of*
    Bewdley
Cranborne—*Salisbury*
Cranley—*Onslow*
Crichton—*Erne*
Crowhurst—*Cottenham*
Dalrymple—*Stair*
Dangan—*Cowley*
Dawick—*Haig*
Deerhurst—*Coventry*
Drumlanrig—
    Queensberry
Dunwich—*Stradbroke*
Dupplin—*Kinnoull*
Ebrington—*Fortescue*
Ednam—*Dudley*
Elveden—*Iveagh*
Emlyn—*Cawdor*
Encombe—*Eldon*
Ennismore—*Listowel*
Enfield—*Strafford*
Erleigh—*Reading*
Errington—*Cromer*
Feilding—*Denbigh*
Fincastle—*Dunmore*
FitzHarris—*Malmesbury*
Folkestone—*Radnor*
Garmoyle—*Cairns*
Garnock—*Lindsay*
Glandine—*Norbury*
Glenapp—*Inchcape*
Glentworth—*Limerick*
Grimstone—*Verulam*
Gwynedd—*Lloyd George*
    of Dwyfor
Hawkesbury—*Liverpool*
Ikerrin—*Carrick*
Ingestre—*Shrewsbury*
Ipswich—*Euston*
Jocelyn—*Roden*

Kelburn—*Glasgow*
Kingsborough—*Kingston*
Lascelles—*Harewood*
Lewisham—*Dartmouth*
Linley—*Snowdon*
Loftus—*Ely*
Lowther—*Lonsdale*
Lumley—*Scarbrough*
Lymington—*Portsmouth*
Macmillan of Ovenden—
    Stockton
Maidstone — *Winchilsea*
    and Nottingham
Maitland—*Lauderdale*
Malden—*Essex*
Mandeville—*Manchester*
Melgund—*Minto*
Merton—*Nelson*
Moore—*Drogheda*
Morpeth—*Carlisle*
Newport—*Bradford*
Newry and Mourne—
    Kilmorey
Parker—*Macclesfield*
Perceval—*Egmont*
Petersham—*Harrington*
Pollington—*Mexborough*
Prestwood—*Attlee*
Quenington—*St. Aldwyn*
Raynham—*Townshend*
Reidhaven—*Seafield*
Ruthven of Canberra—
    Gowrie
St. Cyres—*Iddesleigh*
Sandon—*Harrowby*
Slane—*Mount Charles*
Somerton—*Normanton*
Stopford—*Courtown*
Stormont—*Mansfield*
Strathallan—*Perth*
Stuart—*Castle Stewart*
Suirdale—*Donoughmore*
Tamworth—*Ferrers*
Tarbat—*Cromartie*
Tiverton—*Halsbury*
Vaughan—*Lisburne*
Villiers—*Jersey*
Weymouth—*Bath*
Windsor—*Plymouth*
Wolmer—*Selborne*

Barons (Lord—)
Aberdour—*Morton*
Apsley—*Bathurst*
Ardee—*Meath*
Ashley—*Shaftesbury*
Balgonie—*Leven &*
    Melville
Balniel—*Crawford and*
    Balcarres

Berriedale—*Caithness*
Bingham—*Lucan*
Binning—*Haddington*
Brooke—*Warwick*
Bruce—*Elgin*
Buckhurst—*De La Warr*
Burghersh—
    Westmorland
Burghley—*Exeter*
Cardross—*Buchan*
Clifton—*Darnley*
Courtenay—*Devon*
Dalmeny—*Rosebery*
Delvin—*Westmeath*
Doune—*Moray*
Dundas—*Ronaldshay*
Eliot—*St. Germans*
Erskine—*Mar & Kellie*
Fintrie—*Graham*
Glamis—*Strathmore*
Greenock—*Cathcart*
Guernsey—*Aylesford*
Hay—*Erroll*
Herbert—*Pembroke*
Howland—*Tavistock*
Hyde—*Clarendon*
Inverurie—*Kintore*
Irwin—*Halifax*
Johnstone—*Annandale*
    and Hartfell
Leslie—*Rothes*
Leveson—*Granville*
Loughborough—*Rosslyn*
Mauchline—*Loudoun*
Medway—*Cranbrook*
Montgomerie—*Eglinton*
    and Winton
Moreton—*Ducie*
Naas—*Mayo*
Neidpath—*Wemyss &*
    March
Norreys—*Lindsey &*
    Abingdon
North—*Guilford*
Ogilvy—*Airlie*
Oxmantown—*Rosse*
Porchester—*Carnarvon*
Ramsay—*Dalhousie*
Romsey—*Mountbatten of*
    Burma
Rosehill—*Northesk*
Scrymgeour—*Dundee*
Settrington—*March*
    and Kinrara
Seymour—*Somerset*
Strathnaver—*Sutherland*
Vere of Hanworth—
    Burford
Wodehouse—*Kimberley*
Worsley—*Yarborough*

Surnames of Peers and Peeresses differing from their Titles

The following symbols indicate the rank of the peer/peeress holding each title: *C.* Countess; *D.* Duke; *E.* Earl; *M.* Marquess; *V.* Viscount; *Life Peer/Peeress. Where no designation is given, the title is that of an hereditary Baron or Baroness.

Abney-Hastings—*Loudoun, C.*
Acheson—*Gosford, E.*
Adderley—*Norton*
Addington—*Sidmouth, V.*
Agar—*Normanton, E.*
Airey—*A. of Abingdon**
Aitken—*Beaverbrook*
Akers-Douglas—*Chilston, V.*
Alexander—*A. of Potterhill**
Alexander—*A. of Tunis, E.*
Alexander—*A. of Weedon**
Alexander—*Caledon, E.*
Allen—*A. of Abbeydale**
Allen—*Croham**
Allanson-Winn—*Headley*
Allsopp—*Hindlip*
Aman—*Marley*
Anderson—*Waverley, V.*
Annesley—*Valentia, V.*
Anson—*Lichfield, E.*
Armstrong—*A. of Ilminster**
Armstrong-Jones—*Snowdon, E.*
Arthur—*Glenarthur*
Arundell—*Talbot of Malahide*
Ashley-Cooper—*Shaftesbury, E.*
Ashton—*A. of Hyde*
Asquith—*Oxford & Asquith, E.*
Assheton—*Clitheroe*
Astley—*Hastings*
Astor—*A. of Hever*
Atkins—*Colnbrook**
Aubrey-Fletcher—*Braye*
Bailey—*Glanusk*
Baillie—*Burton*
Baillie Hamilton—*Haddington, E.*
Baldwin—*B. of Bewdley, E.*
Balfour—*B. of Inchrye*
Balfour—*Kinross*
Balfour—*Riverdale*
Bampfylde—*Poltimore*
Banbury—*B. of Southam*
Baring—*Ashburton*
Baring—*Cromer, E.*
Baring—*Howick of Glendale*
Baring—*Northbrook*
Baring—*Revelstoke*
Barker—*Trumpington**
Barnes—*Gorell*
Barnewall—*Trimlestown*
Bathurst—*Bledisloe, V.*
Beamish—*Chelwood**
Beauclerk—*St. Albans, D.*
Beaumont—*Allendale, V.*
Beaumont—*B. of Whitley**
Beavan—*Ardwick**
Beckett—*Grimthorpe*

Bellow—*Bellwin**
Bennet—*Tankerville, E.*
Beresford—*Decies*
Beresford—*Waterford, M.*
Berry—*Camrose, V.*
Berry—*Hartwell**
Berry—*Kemsley, V.*
Bertie—*Lindsey, E.*
Best—*Wynford*
Bethell—*Westbury*
Bevan—*Lee of Asheridge**
Bewicke-Copley—*Cromwell*
Bigham—*Mersey, V.*
Bigham—*Nairne*
Bingham—*Clanmorris*
Bingham—*Lucan, E.*
Blackwood—*Dufferin & Clandeboye*
Blades—*Ebbisham*
Bligh—*Darnley, E.*
Bootle-Wilbraham—*Skelmersdale*
Boscawen—*Falmouth, V.*
Boston—*Boston of Faversham**
Bourke—*Mayo, E.*
Bowden—*Aylestone**
Bowes Lyon—*Strathmore, E.*
Bowyer—*Denham*
Boyd—*Kilmarnock*
Boyle—*Cork & Orrery, E.*
Boyle—*Glasgow, E.*
Boyle—*Shannon, E.*
Brabazon—*Meath, E.*
Brand—*Hampden, V.*
Brandon—*B. of Oakbrook**
Brassey—*B. of Apethorpe*
Brett—*Esher, V.*
Bridge—*B. of Harwich**
Bridgeman—*Bradford, E.*
Brodrick—*Midleton, V.*
Brooke—*Alanbrooke, V.*
Brooke—*Brookeborough, V.*
Brooke—*B. of Ystradfellte**
Brooks—*B. of Tremorfa**
Brooks—*Crawshaw*
Brougham—*Brougham and Vaux*
Broughton—*Fairhaven*
Browne—*Craigton**
Browne—*Kilmaine*
Browne—*Oranmore and Browne*
Browne—*Sligo, M.*
Brownlow—*Lurgan*
Bruce—*Aberdare*
Bruce—*Balfour of Burleigh*
Bruce—*B. of Donington**
Bruce—*Elgin and Kincardine, E.*
Brudenell-Bruce—*Ailesbury, M.*
Buchan—*Tweedsmuir*
Buckley—*Wrenbury*

Burton—*B. of Coventry**
Butler—*Carrick, E.*
Butler—*Dunboyne*
Butler—*Lanesborough, E.*
Butler—*Mountgarret, V.*
Butler—*Ormonde, M.*
Buxton—*B. of Alsa**
Byng—*Strafford, E.*
Byng—*Torrington, V.*
Callaghan—*C. of Cardiff**
Cameron—*C. of Lochbroom**
Campbell—*Argyll, D.*
Campbell—*Breadalbane and Holland, E.*
Campbell—*C. of Alloway**
Campbell—*C. of Croy**
Campbell—*C. of Eskan**
Campbell—*Cawdor, E.*
Campbell—*Colgrain*
Campbell—*Stratheden and Campbell*
Campbell-Gray—*Gray*
Canning—*Garvagh*
Capell—*Essex, E.*
Carington—*Carrington*
Carlisle—*C. of Bucklow**
Carmichael—*C. of Kelvingrove**
Carnegie—*Fife, D.*
Carnegie—*Northesk, E.*
Carnegie—*Southesk, E.*
Carr—*C. of Hadley**
Cary—*Falkland, V.*
Caulfeild—*Charlemont, V.*
Cavendish—*Chesham*
Cavendish—*Devonshire, D.*
Cavendish—*Waterpark*
Cavendish-Bentinck—*Portland, D.*
Cayzer—*Rotherwick*
Cecil—*Amherst of Hackney*
Cecil—*Exeter, M.*
Cecil—*Rockley*
Cecil—*Salisbury, M.*
Chaloner—*Gisborough*
Chapman—*Northfield**
Charteris—*C. of Amisfield**
Charteris—*Wemyss and March, E.*
Cheshire—*Ryder of Warsaw**
Chetwynd-Talbot—*Shrewsbury, E.*
Chichester—*Donegall, M.*
Chichester-Clark—*Moyola**
Child-Villiers—*Jersey, E.*
Cholmondeley—*Delamere*
Chubb—*Hayter*
Clegg-Hill—*Hill, V.*
Clifford—*Clifford of Chudleigh*
Cochrane—*C. of Cults*
Cochrane—*Dundonald, E.*

Cocks—*C. of Hartcliffe**
Cocks—*Somers*
Cokayne—*Cullen of Ashbourne*
Coke—*Leicester, E.*
Cole—*Enniskillen, E.*
Collier—*Monkswell*
Colville—*Clydesmuir*
Colville—*C. of Culross, V.*
Compton—*Northampton, M.*
Conolly-Carew—*Carew*
Constantine—*C. of Stanmore**
Cooper—*C. of Stockton Heath**
Cooper—*Norwich, V.*
Corbett—*Rowallan*
Courtenay—*Devon, E.*
Cox—*Kings Norton**
Craig—*Craigavon, V.*
Crichton—*Erne, E.*
Crichton-Stuart—*Bute, M.*
Cripps—*Parmoor*
Cross—*C. of Chelsea**
Crossley—*Somerleyton*
Cubitt—*Ashcombe*
Cunliffe-Lister—*Masham of Ilton**
Cunliffe-Lister—*Swinton, E.*
Curzon—*Howe, E.*
Curzon—*Scarsdale, V.*
Cust—*Brownlow*
Dalrymple—*Stair, E.*
Daubeny de Moleyns—*Ventry*
Davies—*Darwen*
Davies—*D. of Penrhys**
Davison—*Broughshane*
Dawnay—*Downe, V.*
Dawson-Damer—*Portarlington, E.*
Dean—*D. of Beswick**
Deane—*Muskerry*
de Courcy—*Kingsale*
de Grey—*Walsingham*
Delacourt-Smith—*Delacourt Smith of Alteryn**
Denison—*Londesborough*
Denison-Pender—*Pender*
Devereux—*Hereford, V.*
Dewar—*Forteviot*
De Yarburgh-Bateson—*Deramore*
Dixon—*Glentoran*
Dodson—*Monk Bretton*
Donaldson—*D. of Kingsbridge**
Donaldson—*D. of Lymington**
Dormand—*D. of Easington**
Douglas—*Morton, E.*
Douglas—*Queensberry, M.*
Douglas-Hamilton—*Hamilton, D.*

Douglas-Hamilton—Selkirk, E.
Douglas-Home—Dacre
Douglas-Home—Home of the Hirsel*
Douglas-Pennant—Penrhyn
Douglas-Scott-Montagu—Montagu of Beaulieu
Drummond—Perth, E.
Drummond—Strange
Dugdale—Crathorne
Duke—Merrivale
Duncombe—Feversham
Dundas—Melville, V.
Dundas—Zetland, M.
Eady—Swinfen
Eden—Auckland
Eden—E. of Winton*
Eden—Henley
Edgcumbe—Mount Edgcumbe, E.
Edmondson—Sandford
Edwardes—Kensington
Edwards—Chelmer*
Edwards—Crickhowell*
Egerton—Sutherland, D.
Egerton—Wilton, E.
Eliot—St. Germans, E.
Elliot—E. of Harwood*
Elliot-Murray-Kynynmound—Minto, E.
Elliott—E. of Morpeth*
Erroll—E. of Hale
Erskine—Buchan, E.
Erskine—E. of Rerrick
Erskine—Mar & Kellie, E.
Erskine-Murray—Elibank
Evans—E. of Claughton*
Evans—Mountevans
Evans-Freke—Carbery
Eve—Silsoe
Eyres Monsell—Monsell, V.
Fairfax—F. of Cameron
Fane—Westmorland, E.
Feilding—Denbigh, E.
Fellowes—Ailwyn
Fellowes—De Ramsey
Fermor-Hesketh—Hesketh
Fiennes—Saye & Sele
Finch Hatton—Winchilsea, E.
Finch-Knightley—Aylesford, E.
Fisher—F. of Rednal*
Fitzalan Howard Herries of Terregles
Fitzalan-Howard—Norfolk, D.
FitzClarence—Munster, E.
FitzGerald—Leinster, D.
Fitzherbert—Stafford
Fitz-Maurice—Orkney, E.
FitzRoy—Grafton, D.
FitzRoy Newdegate—Daventry, V.
Fletcher-Vane—Inglewood

Flower—Ashbrook, V.
Foley-Berkeley—Berkeley
Foljambe—Liverpool, E.
Foot—Caradon*
Forbes Granard, E.
Fox-Strangways—Ilchester, E.
Frankland—Zouche
Fraser—F. of Kilmorack*
Fraser—F. of Tullybelton*
Fraser—Lovat
Fraser—Saltoun
Fraser—Strathalmond
Freeman-Grenville—Kinloss
Fremantle—Cottesloe
French—De Freyne
Galbraith—Strathclyde
Ganzoni—Belstead
Gardner—G. of Parkes*
Gascoyne-Cecil—Salisbury, M.
Gathorne-Hardy—Cranbrook, E.
Gibbs—Aldenham
Gibbs—Wraxall
Gibson—Ashbourne
Giffard—Halsbury, E.
Gilboy Vaux of Harrowden
Glyn—Wolverton
Godley—Kilbracken
Goff—G. of Chieveley*
Gordon—Aberdeen, M.
Gordon—Huntly, M.
Gordon Lennox—Richmond, D.
Gore—Arran, E.
Gough-Calthorpe—Calthorpe
Graham—G. of Edmonton*
Graham—Montrose, D.
Graham-Toler—Norbury, E.
Grant—Strathspey
Grant-Ferris—Harvington*
Granville—G. of Eye*
Gray—G. of Contin*
Greaves—Dysart, C.
Greenall—Daresbury
Greene—G. of Harrow Weald*
Greenhill—G. of Harrow*
Greville—Warwick, E.
Grey—G. of Naunton*
Grimston—G. of Westbury
Grimston—Verulam, E.
Grosvenor—Ebury
Grosvenor—Westminster, D.
Guest—Wimborne, V.
Guinness—Iveagh, E.
Guinness—Moyne
Gully—Selby, V.
Gurdon—Cranworth
Gwynne Jones—Chalfont*
Hamilton—Abercorn, D.
Hamilton—Belhaven and Stenton
Hamilton—Dudley
Hamilton—H. of Dalzell

Hamilton—Holm Patrick
Hamilton-Russell—Boyne, V.
Hamilton-Smith—Colwyn
Hanbury-Tracy—Sudeley
Handcock—Castlemaine
Harbord-Hamond—Suffield
Harding—H. of Petherton
Hardinge—H. of Penshurst
Hare—Blakenham, V.
Hare—Listowel, E.
Harmsworth—Rothermere, V.
Harris—H. of Greenwich*
Harris—H. of High Cross*
Harris—Malmesbury, E.
Hart—H. of South Lanark*
Harvey—H. of Prestbury*
Harvey—H. of Tasburgh
Hastings—Huntingdon, E.
Hatch—H. of Lusby*
Hay—Erroll, E.
Hay—Kinnoull, E.
Hay—Tweeddale, M.
Heathcote-Drummond-Willoughby—Willoughby de Eresby
Hely-Hutchinson—Donoughmore, E.
Henderson—Faringdon
Henderson H. of Brompton*
Hennessy—Windlesham
Henniker-Major—Henniker
Hepburne-Scott—Polwarth
Herbert—Carnarvon, E.
Herbert—Hemingford
Herbert—Pembroke, E.
Herbert—Powis, E.
Hermon-Hodge—Wyfold
Hervey—Bristol, M.
Hewitt—Lifford, V.
Hicks Beach—St. Aldwyn, E.
Hill—Downshire, M.
Hill—H. of Luton*
Hill—Sandys
Hill-Trevor—Trevor
Hobart-Hampden—Buckinghamshire, E.
Hogg—Hailsham of St. Marylebone*
Holland-Hibbert—Knutsford, V.
Holmes à Court—Heytesbury
Hood—Bridport, V.
Hope—Glendevon
Hope—Linlithgow, M.
Hope—Rankeillour
Hope Johnstone—Annandale and Hartfell, E.
Hope-Morley—Hollenden
Hopkinson—Colyton
Hopwood—Southborough
Hore Ruthven—Gowrie, E.

Houghton—H. of Sowerby*
Hovell-Thurlow-Cumming-Bruce—Thurlow
Howard—Carlisle, E.
Howard—Effingham, E.
Howard—H. of Penrith
Howard—Strathcona
Howard—Suffolk and Berkshire, E.
Howie—H. of Troon*
Hubbard—Addington
Huggins—Malvern, V.
Hughes—Cledwyn of Penrhos*
Hughes-Young—St. Helens
Hunt—H. of Tanworth*
Hunter—H. of Newington*
Hutchinson—H. of Lullington*
Ingrams—Darcy de Knayth
Innes-Ker—Roxburghe, D.
Inskip—Caldecote, V.
Irby—Boston
Irvine—I. of Lairg*
Irving—I. of Dartford*
Isaacs—Reading, M.
Jackson—Allerton
James—J. of Rusholme*
James—Northbourne
James Saint Brides*
Jauncey—J. of Tullichettle*
Jebb—Gladwyn
Jenkin—J. of Roding*
Jenkins—J. of Hillhead*
Jenkins—J. of Putney*
Jervis—St. Vincent, V.
Jocelyn—Roden, E.
Johnston—J. of Rockport*
Jolliffe—Hylton
Joynson-Hicks—Brentford, V.
Kaberry—K. of Adel*
Kay-Shuttleworth—Shuttleworth
Kearley—Devonport, V.
Keith—K. of Castleacre*
Keith—K. of Kinkel*
Keith—Kintore, E.
Kemp—Rochdale, V.
Kennedy—Ailsa, M.
Kenworthy—Strabolgi
Keppel—Albemarle, E.
Kerr—Lothian, M.
Kerr—Teviot
King—Lovelace, E.
King—K. of Wartnaby*
King-Tenison—Kingston, E.
Kitchener—K. of Khartoum, E.
Kitson—Airedale
Knatchbull—Brabourne
Knatchbull-Mountbatten of Burma, C.
Knox—Ranfurly, E.

C. Countess; D. Duke; E. Earl; M. Marquess; V. Viscount; * Life Peer & Peeress.

Lamb—*Rochester*
Lambart—*Cavan, E.*
Lampson—*Killearn*
Lascelles—*Harewood, E.*
Law—*Coleraine*
Law—*Ellenborough*
Lawrence—*Trevethin and Oaksey*
Lawson—*Burnham*
Lawson-Johnston—*Luke*
Lee—*L. of Asheridge**
Legge—*Dartmouth, E.*
Legh—*Newton*
Leith—*Burgh*
Lennox-Boyd—*Boyd of Merton; V.*
Le Poer Trench—*Clancarty, E.*
Leslie—*Rothes, E.*
Leslie Melville—*Leven and Melville, E.*
Lever—*Leverhulme, V.*
Lever—*L. of Manchester**
Leveson-Gower—*Granville, E.*
Liddell—*Ravensworth*
Lindesay-Bethune—*Lindsay, E.*
Lindsay—*Crawford, E.*
Lindsay—*L. of Birker*
Littleton—*Hatherton*
Llewelyn-Davies—*Llewelyn-Davies of Hastoe**
Lloyd—*L. of Hampstead**
Lloyd—*L. of Kilgerran**
Lloyd George—*Lloyd George of Dwyfor, E.*
Lloyd George—*Tenby, V.*
Lloyd-Mostyn—*Mostyn*
Loder—*Wakehurst*
Lopes—*Roborough*
Low—*Aldington*
Lowry-Corry—*Belmore, E.*
Lowther—*Lonsdale, E.*
Lowther—*Ullswater, V.*
Lubbock—*Avebury*
Lucas—*L. of Chilworth*
Lumley—*Scarbrough, E.*
Lumley-Savile—*Savile*
Lyon-Dalberg-Acton—*Acton*
Lysaght—*Lisle*
Lyttelton—*Chandos, V.*
Lyttelton—*Cobham, V.*
Lytton-Cobbold—*Cobbold*
McAlpine—*M. of Moffat**
McAlpine—*M. of West Green**
McClintock-Bunbury—*Rathdonnell*
Macdonald—*M. of Gwaenysgor*
McDonnell—*Antrim, E.*
McFadzean—*M. of Kelvinside**
McFarlane—*M. of Llandaff**
McGregor—*M. of Durris**
McIntosh—*M. of Haringey**
Mackay—*Inchcape, E.*

Mackay—*M. of Clashfern**
Mackay—*Reay*
Mackay—*Tanlaw**
Mackenzie—*Cromartie, E.*
Mackie—*John-Mackie**
Mackie—*M. of Benshie**
Mackintosh—*M. of Halifax, V.*
McLaren—*Aberconway*
Maclay—*Muirshiel, V.*
MacLehose—*M. of Beoch**
Macleod—*M. of Borve**
MacLeod—*M. of Fuinary**
Macmillan—*Stockton, E.*
Macpherson—*M. of Drumochter*
Macpherson—*Strathcarron*
Maffey—*Rugby*
Maitland—*Lauderdale, E.*
Makgill—*Oxfuird, V.*
Makins—*Sherfield*
Manners—*Rutland, D.*
Manningham-Buller—*Dilhorne, V.*
Mansfield—*Sandhurst*
Marks—*M. of Broughton*
Marquis—*Woolton, E.*
Marshall—*M. of Goring**
Marshall—*M. of Leeds**
Marsham—*Romney, E.*
Martyn-Hemphill—*Hemphill*
Mason—*M. of Barnsley**
Maude—*Hawarden, V.*
Maude—*M. of Stratford-upon-Avon**
Maxwell—*de Ros*
Maxwell—*Farnham*
Meade—*Clanwilliam, E.*
Mercer Nairne Petty-Fitzmaurice—*Lansdowne, M.*
Millar—*Inchyra*
Milles-Lade—*Sondes, E.*
Milner—*M. of Leeds*
Mitchell-Thomson—*Selsdon*
Mitford—*Redesdale*
Monckton—*M. of Brenchley, V.*
Monckton-Arundell—*Galway, V.*
Mond—*Melchett*
Money-Coutts—*Latymer*
Montagu—*Manchester, D.*
Montagu—*Swaythling*
Montagu Douglas Scott—*Buccleuch, D.*
Montagu Stuart Wortley—*Wharncliffe, E.*
Montague—*Amwell*
Montgomerie—*Eglinton, E.*
Montgomery—*M. of Alamein, V.*
Moore—*Drogheda, E.*
Moore—*M. of Wolvercote**

Moore-Brabazon—*Brabazon of Tara*
Moreton—*Ducie, E.*
Morris—*Killanin*
Morris—*M. of Grasmere**
Morris—*M. of Kenwood*
Morrison—*Dunrossil, V.*
Morrison—*Margadale*
Morton—*M. of Shuna**
Mosley—*Ravensdale*
Mountbatten—*Milford Haven, M.*
Muff—*Calverley*
Mulholland—*Dunleath*
Murray—*Atholl, D.*
Murray—*Dunmore, E.*
Murray—*Mansfield and Mansfield, E.*
Murray—*M. of Epping Forest**
Murray—*M. of Newhaven**
Murton—*M. of Lindisfarne**
Nall-Cain—*Brocket*
Napier—*Napier and Ettrick*
Napier—*N. of Magdala*
Needham—*Kilmorey, E.*
Nelson—*N. of Stafford*
Nevill—*Abergavenny, M.*
Neville—*Braybrooke*
Nicolson—*Carnock*
Nivison—*Glendyne*
Noel—*Gainsborough, E.*
Noel-Paton—*Ferrier**
North—*Guilford, E.*
Northcote—*Iddesleigh, E.*
Norton—*Grantley*
Norton—*Rathcreedan*
Nugent—*N. of Guildford**
Nugent—*Westmeath, E.*
O'Brien—*Inchiquin*
O'Brien—*O'Brien of Lothbury**
Ogilvie-Grant—*Seafield, E.*
Ogilvy—*Airlie, E.*
Oliver—*O. of Aylmerton**
O'Neill—*O'Neill of the Maine**
O'Neill—*Rathcavan*
Orde-Powlett—*Bolton*
Ormsby-Gore—*Harlech*
Page—*Whaddon**
Paget—*Anglesey, M.*
Paget—*P. of Northampton**
Pakenham—*Longford, E.*
Pakington—*Hampton*
Palmer—*Lucas of Crudwell*
Palmer—*Selborne, E.*
Parker—*Macclesfield, E.*
Parker—*Morley, E.*
Parnell—*Congleton*
Parsons—*Rosse, E.*
Paulet—*Winchester, M.*
Peake—*Ingleby, V.*
Pearson—*Cowdray, V.*
Pease—*Daryngton*
Pease—*Gainford*
Pease—*Wardington*
Pelham—*Chichester, E.*
Pelham—*Yarborough, E.*

Pelham-Clinton-Hope—*Newcastle, D.*
Pellew—*Exmouth, V.*
Penny—*Marchwood, V.*
Pepys—*Cottenham, E.*
Perceval—*Egmont, E.*
Percy—*Northumberland, D.*
Perry—*P. of Walton**
Pery—*Limerick, E.*
Peyton—*P. of Yeovil**
Philipps—*Milford*
Philipps—*St. Davids, V.*
Phipps—*Normanby, M.*
Pitt—*P. of Hampstead**
Platt—*P. of Writtle**
Pleydell-Bouverie—*Radnor, E.*
Plummer—*P. of St. Marylebone**
Plumptre—*Fitzwalter*
Plunkett—*Dunsany*
Plunkett—*Louth*
Pollock—*Hanworth, V.*
Pomeroy—*Harberton, V.*
Ponsonby—*Bessborough, E.*
Ponsonby—*de Mauley*
Ponsonby—*P. of Shulbrede*
Ponsonby—*Sysonby*
Portal—*P. of Hungerford*
Powys—*Lilford*
Pratt—*Camden, M.*
Preston—*Gormanston, V.*
Primrose—*Rosebery, E.*
Prittie—*Dunalley*
Ramsay—*Dalhousie, E.*
Ramsbotham—*Soulbury, V.*
Rawlinson—*R. of Ewell**
Rees-Williams—*Ogmore*
Rhys—*Dynevor*
Richards—*Milverton*
Richardson—*R. of Duntisbourne**
Rippon—*R. of Hexham**
Ritchie—*R. of Dundee*
Robens—*R. of Woldingham**
Roberts—*Clwyd*
Robertson—*R. of Oakridge*
Robinson—*Martonmere*
Robson—*R. of Kiddington**
Roche—*Fermoy*
Rodd—*Rennell*
Roll—*R. of Ipsden**
Roper-Curzon—*Teynham*
Rospigliosi—*Newburgh, E.*
Ross—*R. of Newport**
Rous—*Stradbroke, E.*
Rowley-Conwy—*Langford*
Royle—*Fanshawe of Richmond**
Runciman—*R. of Doxford, V.*
Russell—*Ampthill*
Russell—*Bedford, D.*
Russell—*de Clifford*
Russell—*R. of Liverpool*
Ryder—*Harrowby, E.*

Ryder—*R. of Eaton Hastings**
Sackville—*De La Warr, E.*
Sackville-West—*Sackville*
St. Aubyn—*St. Levan*
St. Clair—*Sinclair*
St. Clair-Erskine—*Rosslyn, E.*
St. John—*Bolingbroke and St. John, V.*
St. John—*St. John of Blesto*
St. John-Stevas—*St. John of Fawsley**
St. Leger—*Doneraile, V.*
Samuel—*Bearsted, V.*
Sanderson—*S. of Bowden**
Sandilands—*Torphichen*
Saumarez—*De Saumarez*
Savile—*Mexborough, E.*
Scarlett—*Abinger*
Sclater-Booth—*Basing*
Scott—*Eldon, E.*
Scott-Ellis—*Howard de Walden*
Scrymgeour—*Dundee, E.*
Seager—*Leighton of St. Mellons*
Seely—*Mottistone*
Sefton—*S. of Garston**
Seymour—*Hertford, M.*
Seymour—*Somerset, D.*
Shaw—*Craigmyle*
Shaw—*Kilbrandon**
Shirley—*Ferrers, E.*
Short—*Glenamara**
Siddeley—*Kenilworth*
Sidney—*De L'Isle, V.*
Sieff—*S. of Brimpton**
Simon—*S. of Glaisdale**
Simon—*S. of Wythenshawe*

Sinclair—*Caithness, E.*
Sinclair—*S. of Cleeve*
Sinclair—*Thurso, V.*
Skeffington—*Massereene, V.*
Smith—*Bicester*
Smith—*Hambleden, V.*
Smith—*Kirkhill**
Somerset—*Beaufort, D.*
Somerset—*Raglan*
Souter—*Audley*
Spencer—*Churchill, V.*
Spencer-Churchill—*Marlborough, D.*
Spring Rice—*Monteagle of Brandon*
Stanhope—*Harrington, E.*
Stanley—*Derby, E.*
Stanley—*Sheffield*
Stapleton-Cotton—*Combermere, V.*
Stevens—*S. of Ludgate**
Stewart—*Galloway, E.*
Stewart—*S. of Fulham**
Stodart—*S. of Leaston**
Stoddart—*S. of Swindon**
Stonor—*Camoys*
Stopford—*Courtown, E.*
Stourton—*Mowbray*
Strachey—*O'Hagan*
Strutt—*Belper*
Strutt—*Rayleigh*
Stuart—*Castle Stewart, E.*
Stuart *Moray, E.*
Stuart—*S. of Findhorn, V.*
Suenson-Taylor—*Grantchester*
Taylor—*Ingrow**
Taylor—*T. of Blackburn**
Taylor—*T. of Gryfe**
Taylor—*T. of Hadfield**
Taylor—*T. of Mansfield**
Taylour—*Headfort, M.*

Temple-Gore-Langton—*Temple of Stowe, E.*
Tennant—*Glenconner*
Thellusson—*Rendlesham*
Thesiger—*Chelmsford, V.*
Thomas—*T. of Gwydir**
Thomas—*T. of Swynnerton**
Thomas—*Tonypandy, V.*
Thomson—*T. of Fleet*
Thomson—*T. of Monifieth**
Thynne—*Bath, M.*
Tottenham—*Ely, M.*
Trefusis—*Clinton*
Trench—*Ashtown*
Trevor-Roper—*Dacre of Glanton**
Tufton—*Hothfield*
Turner—*Netherthorpe*
Turner—*T. of Camden**
Turnour—*Winterton, E.*
Turton—*Tranmire**
Tyrell-Kenyon—*Kenyon*
Vanden-Bempde-Johnstone—*Derwent*
Vane—*Barnard*
Vane-Tempest-Stewart—*Londonderry, M.*
Vanneck—*Huntingfield*
Vaughan—*Lisburne, E.*
Vaughan-Morgan—*Reigate**
Vereker—*Gort, V.*
Verney—*Willoughby de Broke*
Vernon—*Lyveden*
Vesey—*De Vesci, V.*
Villiers—*Clarendon, E.*
Vivian—*Swansea*
Walker-Smith—*Broxbourne**
Wallace—*W. of Campsie**
Wallace—*W. of Coslany**
Wallop—*Portsmouth, E.*
Ward—*Bangor, V.*

Ward—*Dudley, E.*
Warrender—*Bruntisfield*
Watson—*Manton*
Wedderburn—*W. of Charlton**
Weir—*Inverforth*
Weld-Forester—*Forester*
Wellesley—*Cowley, E.*
Wellesley—*Wellington, D.*
Westenra—*Rossmore*
White—*Annaly*
Whiteley—*Marchamley*
Whitfield—*Kenswood*
Williams—*Berners*
Williams—*W. of Elvel**
Williamson—*Forres*
Willoughby—*Middleton*
Wills—*Dulverton*
Wilson—*Moran*
Wilson—*Nunburnholme*
Wilson—*W. of Langside**
Wilson—*W. of Rievaulx**
Windsor—*Gloucester, D.*
Windsor—*Kent, D.*
Windsor-Clive—*Plymouth, E.*
Wingfield—*Powerscourt, V.*
Winn—*St. Oswald*
Wodehouse—*Kimberley, E.*
Wood—*Halifax, E.*
Wood—*Holderness**
Woodhouse—*Terrington*
Wyatt—*W. of Weeford**
Wyndham—*Leconfield*
Wyndham-Quin—*Dunraven, E.*
Wynn—*Newborough*
Yarde-Buller—*Churston*
Yerburgh—*Alvingham*
Yorke—*Hardwicke, E.*
Young—*Kennet*
Young—*Y. of Dartington**
Young—*Y. of Graffham**
Younger—*Y. of Leckie, V.*

C. Countess; *D.* Duke; *E.* Earl; *M.* Marquess; *V.* Viscount; * Life Peer & Peeress.

THE PREFIX RIGHT HONOURABLE

By established custom, members of the Privy Council are entitled to the style "The Right Honourable", usually abbreviated to The Right (or Rt.) Hon. All Cabinet Ministers must be members of the Privy Council. The Archbishops of Canterbury and York, the Bishop of London, the Lord Chancellor and the Lords Justices of Appeal are admitted to the Privy Council upon their appointment to office.

In the case of Privy Counsellors who are peers the prefix The Right Honourable may be absorbed in the prefix of a higher dignity (e.g. His Royal Highness, His Grace, or Most Honourable). The style of peers below the rank of Marquess is "Right Honourable" whether or not they are Privy Counsellors. Because it is not apparent from the use of a prefix whether a peer is a Privy Counsellor, it is common practice to add the initials P.C. after their name. In any other circumstances it is incorrect to use the initials P.C. after a person's name. (If used, the letters P.C. follow all honours and decorations awarded by the Crown.)

ORDERS OF CHIVALRY

The Most Noble Order of the Garter (1348)—K.G.

Ribbon, Garter Blue. *Motto*, Honi soit qui mal y pense (*Shame on him who thinks evil of it*).
The number of Knights Companions is limited to 24.

SOVEREIGN OF THE ORDER—THE QUEEN

Lady of the Garter—H.M. QUEEN ELIZABETH THE QUEEN MOTHER, 1936.
Extra Ladies of the Garter—PRINCESS JULIANA OF THE NETHERLANDS, 1958
H.M. THE QUEEN OF DENMARK, 1979

Royal Knights

H.R.H. The Duke of Edinburgh, 1947.
H.R.H. The Prince of Wales, 1958.
H.R.H. The Duke of Kent, 1985.

Extra Knights

H.M. The King of Norway, 1959.
H.M. The King of The Belgians, 1963.
H.I.M. The Emperor of Japan, 1971.
H.R.H. The Grand Duke of Luxemburg, 1972.
H.M. The King of Sweden, 1983

Knights Companions

The Duke of Northumberland, 1959.
The Viscount De L'Isle, 1968.
The Lord Ashburton, 1969.
Sir Cennydd Traherne, 1970.
The Earl Waldegrave, 1971.
The Earl of Longford, 1971.
The Earl of Drogheda, 1972.
The Lord Shackleton, 1974.
The Marquess of Abergavenny, 1974.
The Lord Wilson of Rievaulx, 1976.
The Duke of Grafton, 1976.
The Earl of Cromer, 1977.
The Lord Elworthy, 1977.
The Lord Hunt, 1979.
Sir Paul Hasluck, 1979.
Sir Richard Hull, 1980
The Duke of Norfolk, 1983
The Lord Lewin, 1983
The Lord Richardson of Duntisbourne, 1983
The Marquess of Normanby, 1985
The Lord Carrington, 1985
The Lord Callaghan of Cardiff, 1987.
The Viscount Leverhulme, 1988.
The Lord Hailsham of St. Marylebone, 1988.
Prelate, The Bishop of Winchester.
Chancellor, The Marquess of Abergavenny, K.G., O.B.E.
Register, The Dean of Windsor.
Garter King of Arms, Lt.-Col. Sir Colin Cole, K.C.V.O., T.D.
Gentleman Usher of the Black Rod, Air Chief Marshal Sir John Gingell, G.B.E., K.C.B.
Secretary, D. H. B. Chesshyre, L.V.O.

The Most Ancient and Most Noble Order of the Thistle—K.T.

Ribbon, Green. *Motto*, Nemo me impune lacessit (*No one provokes me with impunity*).
The number of Knights is limited to 16.

SOVEREIGN OF THE ORDER—THE QUEEN

Lady of the Thistle—H.M. QUEEN ELIZABETH THE QUEEN MOTHER, 1937

Royal Knights

H.R.H. The Duke of Edinburgh, 1952.
H.R.H. The Prince of Wales (*Duke of Rothesay*), 1977.

Extra Knight

H.M. The King of Norway, 1962.

Knights

The Lord Home of the Hirsel, 1962.
The Earl of Wemyss and March, 1966.
The Lord Maclean, 1969.
The Earl of Dalhousie, 1971.
The Lord Clydesmuir, 1972.
The Viscount Muirshiel, 1973.
Sir Donald Cameron of Lochiel, 1973.
The Earl of Selkirk, 1976.
The Lord McFadzean, 1976.
The Hon. Lord Cameron, 1978.
The Duke of Buccleuch and Queensberry, 1978.
The Earl of Elgin and Kincardine, 1981.
The Lord Thomson of Monifieth, 1981.
The Lord MacLehose of Beoch, 1983.
The Earl of Airlie, 1985.
Capt. Sir Iain Tennant, 1986.
Chancellor, The Lord Home of the Hirsel.
Dean, The Very Rev. Prof. J. McIntyre, C.V.O., D.Litt.
Secretary and Lord Lyon King of Arms, Malcolm R. Innes of Edingight, C.V.O., W.S.
Usher of the Green Rod, Rear-Admiral D.A. Dunbar-Nasmith, C.B., D.S.C.

The Most Honourable Order of the Bath (1725)

Ribbon, Crimson. *Motto*, Tria juncta in uno (*Three joined in one*). (Remodelled 1815, and enlarged many times since. The Order is divided into civil and military divisions.)

G.C.B. Mil.   G.C.B. Civ.   K.C.B. Mil.   K.C.B. Civ.   C.B. Mil.

THE SOVEREIGN; *Great Master and First or Principal Knight Grand Cross*, H.R.H. The Prince of Wales, K.G., K.T., G.C.B.; *Dean of the Order*, The Dean of Westminster; *Bath King of Arms*, Air Chief Marshal Sir David Evans, G.C.B., C.B.E.; *Registrar and Secretary*, Air Marshal Sir Denis Crowley-Milling, K.C.B., C.B.E., D.S.O., D.F.C.; *Genealogist*, Dr. C. Swan, C.V.O., PH.D.; *Gentleman Usher of the Scarlet Rod*, Rear-Admiral D. E. Macey, C.B.; *Deputy Secretary*, Maj.-Gen. D. H. G. Rice, C.V.O., C.B.E.; *Chancery*, Central Chancery of the Orders of Knighthood, St. James's Palace, SW1A 1BH.—G.C.B., Knight (or Dame) Grand Cross; K.C.B., Knight Commander; D.C.B., Dame Commander; C.B., Companion. Women became eligible for the Order from Jan. 1, 1971.

The Order of Merit (1902)—O.M.
Ribbon, Blue and Crimson.

O.M.Mil.   This Order is designed as a special distinction for eminent men and women—without   O.M.Civ.
conferring a knighthood upon them. The Order is limited in numbers to 24, with the
addition of foreign honorary members. Membership is of two kinds, Military and Civil,
the badge of the former having crossed swords, and the latter oak leaves. Membership is
denoted by the suffix O.M., which follows the first class of the Order of the Bath and
precedes the letters designating membership of the inferior classes of the Bath and all
classes of the lesser Orders of Knighthood.

THE SOVEREIGN
H.R.H. THE DUKE OF EDINBURGH (1968)

Dorothy Hodgkin, 1965.
The Lord Zuckerman, 1968.
The Lord Penney, 1969.
Dame Veronica Wedgwood, 1969.
Sir Isaiah Berlin, 1971.
Sir George Edwards, 1971.
Sir Alan Hodgkin, 1973.
Sir Ronald Syme, 1976.
The Lord Todd, 1977.

The Lord Franks, 1977.
The Lord Olivier, 1981.
Gp. Capt. L. Cheshire, V.C., 1981.
Sir Andrew Huxley, 1983.
Sir Sidney Nolan, 1983.
Sir Michael Tippett, 1983.
Rev. Prof. Owen Chadwick, K.B.E.,
1983.

Graham Greene, 1986.
Frederick Sanger, 1986.
Air Commodore Sir Frank Whittle,
1986.
Sir Yehudi Menuhin, 1987.
Prof. Sir Ernst Gombrich, 1988.
Dr. Max Perutz, 1988.

Secretary and Registrar, Sir Edward Ford, K.C.B., K.C.V.O.
Chancery, Central Chancery of the Orders of Knighthood, St. James's Palace, SW1A 1BH.

The Most Exalted Order of the Star of India (1861)

Ribbon, Light Blue, with White Edges. *Motto*, Heaven's Light our Guide.
G.C.S.I.   THE SOVEREIGN; *Registrar*, Maj.-Gen. D. H. G. Rice, C.V.O., C.B.E.; G.C.S.I. Knight Grand
Commander; K.C.S.I., Knight Commander; C.S.I., Companion. No conferments since 1947.

The Most Distinguished Order of St. Michael and St. George (1818)

Ribbon, Saxon Blue, with Scarlet centre. *Motto*, Auspicium melioris ævi (Token of a better age)
THE SOVEREIGN; *Grand Master*, H.R.H. The Duke of Kent, K.G., G.C.M.G., G.C.V.O., A.D.C.; *Prelate*,
The Rt. Rev. R. Woods, K.C.V.O.; *Chancellor*, The Lord Carrington, K.G., G.C.M.G., C.H., M.C., P.C.;
Secretary, Sir Patrick Wright, K.C.M.G.; *Registrar*, Sir John Graham, Bt., G.C.M.G.; *King of Arms*, Sir
Oliver Wright, G.C.M.G., G.C.V.O., D.S.C.; *Gentleman Usher of the Blue Rod*, Sir John Moreton, K.C.M.G.,
K.C.V.O., M.C.; *Dean*, The Dean of St. Paul's; *Deputy Secretary*, Maj.-Gen. D. H. G. Rice, C.V.O., C.B.E.
Chancery, Central Chancery of the Orders of Knighthood, St. James's Palace, SW1A 1BH.—G.C.M.G.,
Knight (or Dame) Grand Cross; K.C.M.G., Knight Commander; D.C.M.G., Dame Commander;
C.M.G., Companion.

The Most Eminent Order of the Indian Empire (1868)

Ribbon, Imperial Purple. *Motto*, Imperatricis auspiciis (*Under the auspices of the Empress*).
G.C.I.E.   THE SOVEREIGN; *Registrar*, Maj.-Gen. D. H. G. Rice, C.V.O., C.B.E.; G.C.I.E., Knight Grand
Commander; K.C.I.E., Knight Commander; C.I.E., Companion. No conferments since 1947.

The Imperial Order of the Crown of India (for Ladies)—C.I.

Instituted Dec. 31, 1877. Badge, the royal cipher in jewels within an oval, surmounted by an Heraldic Crown
and attached to a bow of light blue watered ribbon, edged white. The honour does not confer any rank or title
upon the recipient. No conferments have been made since 1947.

H.M. THE QUEEN, 1947.
H.M. Queen Elizabeth the Queen
Mother, 1931.

H.R.H. The Princess Margaret,
Countess of Snowdon, 1947.

H.R.H. The Princess Alice, Duchess
of Gloucester, 1937.
H.H. Maharani of Travancore, 1929.

The Royal Victorian Order (1896)

Ribbon, Blue, with Red and White Edges. *Motto*, Victoria.
THE SOVEREIGN; *Grand Master*, H.M. Queen Elizabeth The Queen Mother; *Chancellor*,
The Lord Chamberlain; *Secretary*, The Keeper of the Privy Purse; *Registrar*, The Secretary
of the Central Chancery of the Orders of Knighthood; *Chaplain*, The Rev. J. H. Williams.
Hon. Genealogist, D. H. B. Chesshyre, L.V.O.; G.C.V.O., Knight or Dame Grand Cross;
K.C.V.O., Knight Commander; D.C.V.O., Dame Commander; C.V.O., Commander; L.V.O.,
Lieutenant; M.V.O., Member.

The Most Excellent Order of the British Empire (1917)

Ribbon, Rose pink edged with pearl grey with vertical pearl stripe in centre (Military Division); without vertical pearl stripe (Civil Division). *Motto*, For God and the Empire.

G.B.E.

K.B.E.

THE SOVEREIGN: *Grand Master*, H.R.H. The Prince Philip, Duke of Edinburgh, K.G., P.C., K.T., O.M., G.B.E., F.R.S.; *Prelate*, The Bishop of London; *King of Arms*, Admiral Sir Anthony Morton, G.B.E., K.C.B.; *Registrar*, Maj.-Gen. D. H. G. Rice, C.V.O., C.B.E.; *Secretary*, Sir Robin Butler, K.C.B., C.V.O.; *Dean*, The Dean of St. Paul's; *Gentleman Usher of the Purple Rod*, Sir Robin Gillett, Bt., G.B.E.; *Chancery*, Central Chancery of the Orders of Knighthood, St. James's Palace, SW1A 1BH. G.B.E., Knight or Dame Grand Cross; K.B.E. Knight Commander; D.B.E., Dame Commander; C.B.E., Commander; O.B.E., Officer; M.B.E., Member. The Order was divided into *Military* and *Civil* divisions in Dec. 1918.

Order of the Companions of Honour (June 4, 1917)—C.H.

Ribbon, Carmine, with Gold Edges.

This Order consists of one Class only and carries with it no title. It ranks after the 1st Class of the Order of the British Empire, *i.e.*, Knights and Dames Grand Cross (Mil. and Civ. Div.). The number of awards is limited to 65 (excluding honorary members) and the Order is open to both sexes. *Secretary and Registrar*, The Secretary of the Central Chancery of the Orders of Knighthood.

Anthony, Rt. Hon. John, 1982.
Ashley, Rt. Hon. Jack, 1975.
Aylestone, The Lord, 1975.
Brenner, Sydney, 1987.
Carrington, The Lord, 1983.
Casson, Sir Hugh, 1985.
Cledwyn of Penrhos, The Lord, 1977.
de Valois, Dame Ninette, 1982.
Eccles, The Viscount, 1984.
Elwyn-Jones, The Lord, 1976.
Fraser, Rt. Hon. Malcolm, 1977.
Freud, Lucian, 1983.
Gardiner, The Lord, 1975.
Gielgud, Sir John, 1977.
Glenamara, The Lord, 1976.
Goodman, The Lord, 1972.
Gorton, Rt. Hon. Sir John, 1971.
Greene, Graham, 1966.

Hailsham of St. Marylebone, The Lord, 1974.
von Hayek, *Prof.* Friedrich, 1984.
Healey, Rt. Hon. Denis, 1979.
Houghton of Sowerby, The Lord, 1967.
Jones, James, 1978.
Joseph, The Lord, 1986.
Marshall, Rt. Hon. Sir John, 1973.
Muirshiel, TheViscount, 1962.
Muldoon, Rt. Hon. Sir Robert, 1977.
Pasmore, Victor, 1981.
Perutz, *Prof.* Max Ferdinand, 1975.
Piper, John, 1972.
Popper, *Prof.* Sir Karl, 1982.
Powell, Anthony, 1987.
Powell, Sir Philip, 1984.
Rahman, Tunku Abdul, 1960.

Runciman, *Hon.* Sir Steven, 1984.
Rylands, George, 1987.
Sanger, Frederick, 1981.
Scott, Sir Peter, 1987.
Sitwell, Sir Sacheverell, 1984.
Smith, Arnold Cantwell, 1975.
Somare, Rt. Hon. Michael, 1978.
Stewart of Fulham, The Lord, 1969.
Summerson, Sir John, 1987.
Talboys, Rt. Hon. Brian, 1981.
Tebbit, Rt. Hon. Norman, 1987.
Thorneycroft, The Lord, 1980
Tippett, Sir Michael, 1979.
Trudeau, Rt. Hon. Pierre, 1984.
Watkinson, The Viscount, 1962.
Whitelaw, The Viscount, 1974.
Honorary Members, Lee Kuan Yew, 1970; Dr. Joseph Luns, 1971.

THE DISTINGUISHED SERVICE ORDER (1886)—D.S.O.

Ribbon, Red, with Blue Edges.

Bestowed in recognition of especial services in action of commissioned officers in the Navy, Army and Royal Air Force and (1942) Mercantile Marine. The members are Companions only and rank immediately before the 4th Class of the Royal Victorian Order. A Bar may be awarded for any additional act of service.

The Imperial Service Order (1902)—I.S.O.

Ribbon, Crimson, with Blue Centre.

Appointment of Companion of this Order shall be open to those members of the Civil Services whose eligibility shall be determined by the grade held by such persons. The Order consists of THE SOVEREIGN and Companions (not exclusively male) to a number not exceeding 1,700 of whom 1,100 may belong to the Home Civil Services and 600 to Overseas Civil Services. *Secretary*, Sir Robin Butler, K.C.B., C.V.O. *Registrar*, Maj.-Gen. D. H. G. Rice, C.V.O., C.B.E., St. James's Palace, SW1A 1BH.

The Royal Victorian Chain (1902)

Founded by King Edward VII, in 1902. It confers no precedence on its holders.

H.M. THE QUEEN

H.M. QUEEN ELIZABETH THE QUEEN MOTHER (1937).

Princess Juliana of the Netherlands (1950).
H.M. The King of Norway (1955).
H.M. The King of Thailand (1960).
H.I.H. The Crown Prince of Ethiopia (1965).
H.M. The King of Jordan (1966).
H.M. King Zahir Shah of Afghanistan (1971).

Rt. Hon. Roland Michener (1973).
H.M. The Queen of Denmark (1974).
H.M. The King of Nepal (1975).
H.M. The King of Sweden (1975).
The Right Rev. The Lord Coggan (1980).
Ratu Sir George Cakobau (1982).

H.M. The Queen of the Netherlands (1982).
The Lord Maclean (1984).
General Antonio Eanes (1985).
H.M. The King of Spain (1986).
H.M. The King of Saudi Arabia (1987).

BARONETS, KNIGHTS GRAND CROSS, KNIGHTS GRAND COMMANDERS, KNIGHTS COMMANDERS AND KNIGHTS BACHELOR

Badge of Baronets
of England, Great Britain, U.K.,
(and Ireland marked I.).

Badge of Baronets
of Scotland or Nova Scotia
(marked s. or N.S.).

NOTES CONCERNING BARONETS

Clause II. of the Royal Warrant of February 8, 1910, ordains as follows:—"That no person whose name is not entered upon the Official Roll shall be received as a Baronet, or shall be addressed or mentioned by that title in any Civil or Military Commission, Letters Patent or other official document."

Baronets are addressed as "Sir" (with Christian name) and in writing as "Sir Robert A—, Bt." Baronet's wives are addressed (formally) as "Your Ladyship" or "Lady A—," without any Christian name unless a daughter of a Duke, Marquess or Earl, in which case "The Lady Mary A—"; if daughter of a Viscount or Baron "The Hon. Lady A—."

NOTES CONCERNING KNIGHTS GRAND CROSS, ETC.

Knights Grand Cross, Knights Grand Commanders and Knights Commanders are addressed in the same manner as Baronets (*q.v.*), but in writing the appropriate initials (G.C.B., K.C.B., &c.) are appended to surname after "Bt." if they are also baronets or in place of "Bt." if they are not. Knights Bachelor are addressed as "Sir —— (first or Christian name)" and in writing as "Sir —— B ——." The wife of a Knight Grand Cross, Knight Grand Commander, Knight Commander or Knight Bachelor.is addressed as stated for the wife of a Baronet.

NOTES CONCERNING KNIGHTS BACHELOR

The Knights Bachelor do not constitute a Royal Order, but comprise the surviving representation of the ancient State Orders of Knighthood. The Register of Knights Bachelor, instituted by James I in the 17th century, lapsed, and in 1908 a voluntary Association under the title of "The Society of Knights" (now "The Imperial Society of Knights Bachelor" by Royal command) was formed with the primary objects of continuing the various registers dating from 1257 and obtaining the uniform registration of every created Knight Bachelor. In 1926 a design for a badge to be worn by Knights Bachelor was approved and adopted, a miniature reproduction being shown above; in 1974 a neck badge and miniature were added. The Officers of the Society are:—*Knight Principal*, Sir Colin Cole, K.C.V.O., T.D.; *Chairman of Council*, Sir David Napley; *Prelate*, Rt. Rev. and Rt. Hon. Graham D. Leonard, D.D.; *Hon. Registrar*, Sir Roger Falk, O.B.E.; *Hon. Treasurer*, Sir Peter Lane; *Clerk to the Council*, R. M. Esden; *Deputy Clerk*, Lt. Col. G. H. H. Coles; *Office*, 21 Old Buildings, Lincoln's Inn, WC2A 3UJ.

BARONETAGE AND KNIGHTAGE
(Revised to Aug. 31, 1988)
Peers are not included in this list

When an obelisk (†) precedes a name it indicates that, *at the time of going to press*, the Baronet concerned has not been registered on the Official Roll of the Baronetage. The date of creation of the Baronetcy is given in parenthesis ( ).

A full entry in italic type indicates that the recipient of a Knighthood died during the year in which the honour was conferred. The name is included for purposes of record.

Aarvold, *Hon.* Sir Carl Douglas, Kt., O.B.E., T.D.

Abal, Sir Tei, Kt., C.B.E.

Abbott, Sir Albert Francis, Kt., C.B.E.

Abdy, Sir Valentine Robert Duff, Bt. (1850).

Abel, Sir Seselo (Cecil) Charles Geoffrey, Kt., O.B.E.

Abeles, Sir (Emil Herbert) Peter, Kt.

Abell, Sir Anthony Foster, K.C.M.G.

Abell, Sir George Edmond Brackenbury, K.C.I.E., O.B.E.

Abercromby, Sir Ian George, Bt. (s. 1636).

Abraham, Sir Edward Penley, Kt., C.B.E., F.R.S.

Acheson, *Prof.* Sir (Ernest) Donald, K.B.E.

Ackers, Sir James George, Kt.

Ackroyd, Sir John Robert Whyte, Bt. (1956).

Acland, Sir Antony Arthur, G.C.M.G., K.C.V.O.

Acland, *Maj.* Sir (Christopher) Guy (Dyke), Bt. (1890).

Acland, *Maj.-Gen.* Sir John Hugh Bevil, K.C.B., C.B.E.

Acland, Sir Richard Thomas Dyke, Bt. (1644).

Acton, Sir Harold Mario Mitchell, Kt., C.B.E.

Adam, Sir Christopher Eric Forbes, Bt. (1917).

Adams, Sir Philip George Doyne, K.C.M.G.

Adams-Schneider, *Rt. Hon.* Sir Lancelot Raymond, K.C.M.G.

Adamson, Sir (William Owen) Campbell, Kt.

Adcock, Sir Robert Henry, Kt., C.B.E.

Addison, Sir William Wilkinson, Kt.

Ademola, *Rt. Hon.* Sir Adetokunbo Adegboyega, K.B.E.

Adrien, *Hon.* Sir Maurice Latour-, Kt.

Agnew, Sir Crispin Hamlyn, Bt. (s. 1629).

Agnew, Sir (John) Anthony Stuart, Bt. (1895).

Agnew, *Cdr.* Sir Peter Garnett, Bt. (1957).

Agnew, Sir (William) Godfrey, K.C.V.O., C.B.

Ah-Chuen, Sir Moi Lin Jean Etienne, Kt.

Aiken, *Air Chief Marshal* Sir John Alexander Carlisle, K.C.B.

Ainley, Sir (Alfred) John, Kt., M.C.

Ainsworth, Sir (Thomas) David, Bt. (1916).

Aird, *Capt.* Sir Alastair Sturgis, K.C.V.O.

Aird, Sir (George) John, Bt. (1901).

Airey, Sir Lawrence, K.C.B.

Aisher, Sir Owen Arthur, Kt.

Aitchison, Sir Charles Walter de Lancey, Bt. (1938).

Aitken, Sir Robert Stevenson, Kt., M.D., D.Phil.

Akehurst, *Gen.* Sir John Bryan, K.C.B., C.B.E.

Akers-Jones, Sir David, K.B.E., C.M.G.

Albert, Sir Alexis François, Kt., C.M.G., V.R.D.

Albery, Sir Donald Arthur Rolleston, Kt.

Albu, Sir George, Bt. (1912).

Aldington, Sir Geoffrey William, K.B.E., C.M.G.

Aldous, *Hon.* Sir William, Kt.

Alexander, Sir Alexander Sandor, Kt.

Alexander, Sir Charles Gundry, Bt. (1945).

Alexander, Sir Claud Hagart-, Bt. (1886).

Alexander, *Hon.* Sir Darnley Arthur Raymond, Kt., C.B.E.

Alexander, Sir Douglas, Bt. (1921).

Alexander, Sir (John) Lindsay, Kt.

Alexander, *Prof.* Sir Kenneth John Wilson, Kt.

Alexander, Sir Michael O'Donal Bjarne, K.C.M.G.

Alexander, Sir Norman Stanley, Kt., C.B.E.

†Alexander, Sir Patrick Desmond William Cable-, Bt. (1809).

Allan, Sir Anthony James Allan Havelock-, Bt. (1858).

Allan, Sir Colin Hamilton, K.C.M.G., O.B.E.

Allard, Sir Gordon Laidlaw, Kt.

Allcroft, Sir Philip Magnus-, Bt., C.B.E. (1917).

Allen, *Prof.* Sir Geoffrey, Kt., Ph.D., F.R.S.

Allen, Sir George Oswald Browning, Kt., C.B.E., T.D.

Allen, *Hon.* Sir Peter Austin Philip Jermyn, Kt.

Allen, Sir Peter Christopher, Kt.

Allen, Sir Richard Hugh Sedley, K.C.M.G.

Allen, Sir William Guilford, Kt.

Allen, Sir (William) Kenneth (Gwynne), Kt.

Alleyne, *Rev.* Sir John Olpherts Campbell, Bt., (1769).

Allinson, Sir (Walter) Leonard, K.C.V.O., C.M.G.

Alliott, *Hon.* Sir John Downes, Kt.

Alment, Sir (Edward) Anthony John, Kt.

Alun-Jones, Sir (John) Derek, Kt.

Ambo, *Rt. Rev.* George, K.B.E.

Anderson, *Prof.* Sir (James) Norman (Dalrymple), Kt., O.B.E., Q.C., F.B.A.

Anderson, *Maj.-Gen.* Sir John Evelyn, K.B.E.

Anderson, Sir John Muir, Kt., C.M.G.

Anderson, Sir Kenneth, K.B.E., C.B.

Anderson, *Hon.* Sir Kevin Victor, Kt.

Anderson, *Vice-Adm.* Sir Neil Dudley, K.B.E., O.B.E.

Anderson, *Prof.* Sir (William) Ferguson, Kt., O.B.E.

Andrew, Sir Robert John, K.C.B.

Andrewes, Sir Christopher Howard, Kt., M.D., F.R.S.

Andrews, *Hon.* Sir Dormer George, Kt.

Ansell, *Col.* Sir Michael Picton, Kt., C.B.E., D.S.O.

Anson, *Vice-Adm.* Sir Edward Rosebery, K.C.B.

Anson, *Rear-Adm.* Sir Peter, Bt., C.B (1831).

Anstey, *Brig.* Sir John, Kt., C.B.E., T.D.

Anstruther, Sir Ralph Hugo, Bt. K.C.V.O., M.C. (s. 1694).

Anthony, Sir (Michael) Mobolaji Bank-, K.B.E.

Antico, Sir Tristan Venus, Kt.

Antrobus, Sir Philip Coutts, Bt. (1815).

Appleyard, Sir Raymond Kenelm, K.B.E.

Arbuthnot, Sir John Sinclair-Wemyss, Bt., M.B.E., T.D. (1964).

Arbuthnot, Sir Keith Robert Charles, Bt. (1823).

Archdale, *Cdr.* Sir Edward Folmer, Bt., D.S.C., R.N. (1928).

Archer, *Gen.* Sir (Arthur) John, K.C.B., O.B.E.

Archer, Sir Clyde Vernon Harcourt, Kt.

Arculus, Sir Ronald, K.C.M.G., K.C.V.O.

Armitage, *Air Chief Marshal* Sir Michael John, K.C.B., C.B.E.

Armitage, Sir Robert Perceval, K.C.M.G., M.B.E.

Armstrong, Sir Andrew Clarence Francis, Bt., C.M.G. (1841).

Armstrong, Sir Thomas Henry Wait, Kt., D.MUS.

Armytage, Sir John Martin, Bt. (1738).

Arnold, *Rt. Hon.* Sir John Lewis, Kt.

Arnott, Sir Alexander John Maxwell, Bt. (1896).

Arnott, *Prof.* Sir (William) Melville, Kt., T.D., M.D.

Arrindell, Sir Clement Athelston, G.C.M.G., G.C.V.O.

Arrowsmith, Sir Edwin Porter, K.C.M.G.

Arthur, Sir Stephen John, Bt. (1841).

Arthur, *Lt.-Gen.* Sir (John) Norman Stewart, K.C.B.

Arundell, *Brig.* Sir Robert Duncan Harris, K.C.M.G., O.B.E.

Ashburnham, Sir Denny Reginald, Bt. (1661).

Ashe, Sir Derick Rosslyn, K.C.M.G.

Ashley, Sir Bernard Albert, Kt.

Ashmore, *Admiral of the Fleet* Sir Edward Beckwith, G.C.B., D.S.C.

Ashmore, *Vice-Adm.* Sir Peter William Beckwith, K.C.B., K.C.V.O., D.S.C.

Ashworth, Sir Herbert, Kt.

Aske, *Rev.* Sir Conan, Bt. (1922).

Astley, Sir Francis Jacob Dugdale, Bt. (1821).

Aston, Sir Harold George, Kt., C.B.E.

Aston, *Hon.* Sir William John, K.C.M.G.

Astor, *Hon.* Sir John Jacob, Kt., M.B.E.

Astwood, *Hon.* Sir James Rufus, Kt.

Astwood, *Lt.-Col.* Sir Jeffrey Carlton, Kt., C.B.E., E.D.

Atcherley, Sir Harold Winter, Kt.

Atiyah, Sir Michael Francis, Kt., Ph.D., F.R.S.

Atkins, Sir William Sydney Albert, Kt., C.B.E.

Atkinson, *Air Marshal* Sir David William, K.B.E.

Atkinson, Sir Frederick John, K.C.B.

Atkinson, Sir John Alexander, K.C.B., D.F.C.

Atkinson, Sir (John) Kenneth, Kt.

Atkinson, *Maj.-Gen.* Sir Leonard Henry, K.B.E.

Atkinson, Sir Robert, Kt., D.S.C.

Attenborough, Sir David Frederick, Kt., C.B.E., F.R.S.

Attenborough, Sir Richard Samuel, Kt., C.B.E.

Atwell, Sir John William, Kt., C.B.E., F.R.S.E.

Atwill, Sir (Milton) John (Napier), Kt.

Audland, Sir Christopher John, K.C.M.G.

Audley, Sir George Bernard, Kt.

Auld, *Hon.* Sir Robin Ernest, Kt.

Austin, Sir William Ronald, Bt. (1894).

Austin, *Vice-Adm.* Sir Peter Murray, K.C.B.

Ayer, *Prof.* Sir Alfred Jules, Kt., F.B.A.

Aykroyd, Sir Cecil William, Bt. (1929).

Aykroyd, Sir William Miles, Bt., M.C. (1920).

†Aylmer, Sir Richard John, Bt. (1 1622).

Backhouse, Sir Jonathan Roger, Bt. (1901).

Bacon, Sir Nicholas Hickman Ponsonby, Bt. *Premier Baronet of England* (1611 and 1627).

Bacon, Sir Sidney Charles, Kt., C.B.

Baddeley, Sir John Wolsey Beresford, Bt. (1922).

Baddiley, *Prof.* Sir James, Kt., Ph.D., D.SC., F.R.S., F.R.S.E.

Badenoch, Sir John, Kt., D.M., F.R.C.P.

Badger, Sir Geoffrey Malcolm, Kt.

Bagge, Sir John Alfred Picton, Bt. (1867).

Bagnall, *Field Marshal* Sir Nigel Thomas, G.C.B., C.V.O., M.C.

Bailey, Sir Alan Marshall, K.C.B.

Bailey, Sir Brian Harry, Kt., O.B.E.

Bailey, Sir Derrick Thomas Louis, Bt., D.F.C. (1919).

Bailey, *Prof.* Sir Harold Walter, Kt., D.Phil., F.B.A.

Bailey, Sir John Bilsland, K.C.B.

Bailey, Sir Richard John, Kt., C.B.E.

Bailey, Sir Stanley Ernest, Kt., C.B.E., Q.P.M.

Baillie, Sir Gawaine George Hope, Bt. (1823).

Baines, *Prof.* Sir George Grenfell-, Kt., O.B.E.

Baird, Sir David Charles, Bt. (1809).

Baird, *Lt.-Gen.* Sir James Parlane, K.B.E., M.D.

Baird, Sir James Richard Gardiner, Bt., M.C. (s. 1695).

Baird, *Vice-Adm.* Sir Thomas Henry Eustace, K.C.B.

Bairsto, *Air Marshal* Sir Peter Edward, K.B.E., C.B.

Baker, Sir (Allan) Ivor, Kt., C.B.E.

Baker, Sir Humphrey Dodington Benedict Sherston-, Bt. (1796).

Baker, Sir (Stanislaus) Joseph, Kt., C.B.

Balcombe, *Rt. Hon.* Sir (Alfred) John, Kt.

Balderstone, Sir James Schofield, Kt.

Baldwin, Sir Peter Robert, K.C.B.

Balfour, *Gen.* Sir (Robert George) Victor FitzGeorge-, K.C.B., C.B.E., D.S.O., M.C.

Ball, *Air Marshal* Sir Alfred Henry Wynne, K.C.B., D.S.O., D.F.C.

Ball, Sir Charles Irwin, Bt. (1911).

Ball, Sir Christopher John Elinger, Kt.

Ball, *Prof.* Sir Robert James, Kt., Ph.D.

Balmer, Sir Joseph Reginald, Kt.

Banks, Sir Maurice Alfred Lister, Kt.

Banner, Sir George Knowles Harmood-, Bt. (1924).

Bannerman, *Lt.-Col.* Sir Donald Arthur Gordon, Bt. (s. 1682).

Bannister, Sir Roger Gilbert, Kt., C.B.E., D.M., F.R.C.P.

Barber, Sir Derek Coates, Kt.

Barber, *Hon.* Sir (Edward Hamilton) Esler, Kt.

Barber, Sir William Francis, Bt., T.D. (1960).

Barclay, Sir Colville Herbert Sanford, Bt. (s. 1668).

Barclay, Sir Roderick Edward, G.C.V.O., K.C.M.G.

Barford, Sir Leonard, Kt.

Baring, Sir Charles Christian, Bt. (1911).

Baring, *Hon.* Sir John Francis Harcourt, Kt., C.V.O.

Barker, Sir Alwyn Bowman, Kt., C.M.G.

Barker, Sir Harry Heaton, Kt., K.B.E.

Barker, Sir William, K.C.M.G., O.B.E.

Barlow, Sir Christopher Hilaro, Bt. (1803).

Barlow, Sir (George) William, Kt.

Barlow, Sir John Kemp, Bt. (1907).

Barlow, Sir Thomas Erasmus, Bt., D.S.C. (1902).

Barnard, Sir (Arthur) Thomas, Kt., C.B., O.B.E.

Barnard, *Capt.* Sir George Edward, Kt.

Barnard, Sir Joseph Brian, Kt.

Barnes, Sir Denis Charles, K.C.B.

Barnes, Sir (Ernest) John (Ward), K.C.M.G., M.B.E.

Barnes, Sir James George, Kt., M.B.E.

Barnes, Sir Kenneth, K.C.B.

Barnett, *Air Chief Marshal* Sir Denis Hensley Fulton, G.C.B., C.B.E., D.F.C.

Barnett, Sir Oliver Charles, Kt., C.B.E., Q.C.

Barnewall, Sir Reginald Robert, Bt. (I. 1623).

Barraclough, *Air Chief Marshal* Sir John, K.C.B., C.B.E., D.F.C., A.F.C.

Barraclough, Sir Kenneth James Priestley, Kt., C.B.E., T.D.

Barran, Sir David Haven, Kt.

Barran, Sir John Napoleon Ruthven, Bt. (1895).

Barratt, Sir Lawrence Arthur, Kt.

Barratt, Sir Richard Stanley, Kt., C.B.E., Q.P.M.

Barrett, *Lt.-Gen.* Sir David William Scott-, K.B.E., M.C.

Barrett, *Lt.-Col.* Sir Dennis Charles Titchener, Kt., T.D.

Barrie, Sir Walter, Kt.

Barrington, Sir Alexander (Fitzwilliam Croker), Bt. (1831).

Barritt, Sir David Thurlow, Kt.

Barron, Sir Donald James, Kt.

Barrow, *Capt.* Sir Richard John Uniacke, Bt. (1835).

Barrowclough, Sir Anthony Richard, Kt., Q.C.

Barry, Sir (Lawrence) Edward (Anthony Tress), Bt. (1899).

Barry, Sir (Philip) Stuart Milner-, K.C.V.O., C.B., O.B.E.

Bartlett, Sir Henry David Hardington, Bt., M.B.E. (1913).

Barton, Sir Charles Newton, Kt., O.B.E., E.D.

Barton, *Prof.* Sir Derek Harold Richard, Kt., F.R.S., F.R.S.E.

Barttelot, *Lt.-Col.* Sir Brian Walter de Stopham, Bt., O.B.E. (1875).

Barwick, *Rt. Hon.* Sir Garfield Edward John, G.C.M.G.

Basten, Sir Henry Bolton, Kt., C.M.G.

Batchelor, Sir Ivor Ralph Campbell Kt., C.B.E.

Bate, Sir David Lindsay, K.B.E.

Bate, Sir (Walter) Edwin, Kt., O.B.E.

Bateman, Sir Cecil Joseph, K.B.E.

Bateman, Sir Geoffrey Hirst, Kt., F.R.C.S.

Bateman, Sir Ralph Melton, K.B.E.

Bates, *Prof.* Sir David Robert, Kt., D.SC., F.R.S.

Bates, *Maj.-Gen.* Sir (Edward) John (Hunter), K.B.E., C.B., M.C.

Bates, Sir Geoffrey Voltelin, Bt., M.C. (1880).

Bates, Sir John David, Kt., C.B.E., V.R.D.

Bates, Sir (John) Dawson, Bt., M.C. (1937).

Bates, Sir (Julian) Darrell, Kt., C.M.G., C.V.O.

Batho, Sir Maurice Benjamin, Bt. (1928).

Bathurst, *Vice-Adm.* Sir (David) Benjamin, K.C.B.

Bathurst, Sir Frederick Peter Methuen Hervey-, Bt. (1818).

Bathurst, Sir Maurice Edward, Kt., C.M.G., C.B.E., Q.C.

Batsford, Sir Brian Caldwell Cook, Kt.

Batten, Sir John Charles, K.C.V.O.

Batty, Sir William Bradshaw, Kt., T.D.

Baxendell, Sir Peter Brian, Kt., C.B.E.

Baxter, *Prof.* Sir (John) Philip, K.B.E., C.M.G.

Bayliss, *Prof.* Sir Noel Stanley, Kt., C.B.E.

Bayliss, Sir Richard Ian Samuel, K.C.V.O., M.D., F.R.C.P.

Bayly, *Vice-Adm.* Sir Patrick Uniacke, K.B.E., C.B., D.S.C.

Baynes, Sir John Christopher Malcolm, Bt. (1801).

Bazley, Sir Thomas Stafford, Bt. (1869).

Beach, *Gen.* Sir (William Gerald) Hugh, G.B.E., K.C.B., M.C.

Beale, Sir William Francis, Kt., O.B.E.

Beament, Sir James William Longman, Kt., SC.D., F.R.S.

Beattie, *Hon.* Sir Alexander Craig, Kt.

Beattie, *Hon.* Sir David Stuart, G.C.M.G., G.C.V.O.

Beauchamp, Sir Christopher Radstock Proctor-, Bt. (1745).

Beaumont, Sir George (Howland Francis), Bt. (1661).

Beaumont, Sir Richard Ashton, K.C.M.G., O.B.E.

Beavis, *Air Chief Marshal* Sir Michael Gordon, K.C.B., C.B.E., A.F.C.

Becher, Sir William Fane Wrixon, Bt., M.C. (1831).

Beck, Sir Edgar Charles, Kt., C.B.E.

Beck, Sir Edgar Philip, Kt.

Beckett, *Capt.* Sir (Martyn) Gervase, Bt., M.C. (1921).

Beckett, Sir Terence Norman, Kt., K.B.E.

Bedbrook, Sir George Montario, Kt., O.B.E.

Bedingfeld, *Capt.* Sir Edmund George Felix Paston-, Bt. (1661).

Beecham, John Stratford Roland, Bt. (1914).

Beeley, Sir Harold, K.C.M.G., C.B.E.

Beetham, *Marshal of the Royal Air Force* Sir Michael James, G.C.B., C.B.E., D.F.C., A.F.C.

Beevor, Sir Thomas Agnew, Bt. (1784).

Begg, Sir Neil Colquhoun, K.B.E.

Begg, *Admiral of the Fleet* Sir Varyl Cargill, G.C.B., D.S.O., D.S.C.

Beit, Sir Alfred Lane, Bt. (1924).

Beith, Sir John Greville Stanley, K.C.M.G.

Beldam, *Hon.* Sir (Alexander) Roy (Asplan), Kt.

Bell, Sir Gawain Westray, K.C.M.G., C.B.E.

Bell, Sir (George) Raymond, K.C.M.G., C.B.

Bell, Sir John Lowthian, Bt. (1885).

Bell, Sir (William) Ewart, K.C.B.

Bell, Sir William Hollin Dayrell Morrison-, Bt. (1905).

Bellew, *Hon.* Sir George Rothe, K.C.B., K.C.V.O., F.S.A.

Bellew, Sir Henry Charles Gratton-, Bt. (1838).

Bellinger, Sir Robert Ian, G.B.E.

Bellingham, Sir Noel Peter Roger, Bt. (1796).

Bengough, *Col*. Sir Piers, K.C.V.O., O.B.E.

Benn, *Capt*. Sir (Patrick Ion) Hamilton, Bt. (1920).

Benn, Sir James Jonathan, Bt. (1914).

Bennett, *Rt. Hon*. Sir Charles Moihi Te Arawaka, Kt., D.S.O.

Bennett, *Rt. Hon*. Sir Frederic Mackarness, Kt.

Bennett, Sir Hubert, Kt.

Bennett, Sir John Mokonuiarangi, Kt.

Bennett, *Lt.-Gen*. Sir Phillip Harvey, K.B.E.

Bennett, Sir Reginald Frederick Brittain, Kt., V.R.D.

Bennett, Sir Ronald Wilfrid Murdoch, Bt. (1929).

Benson, Sir Christopher John, Kt.

Benson, Sir (William) Jeffrey, Kt.

Benthall, Sir (Arthur) Paul, K.B.E.

Bentley, Sir William, K.C.M.G.

Berger, *Vice-Adm*. Sir Peter Egerton Capel, K.C.B., M.V.O., D.S.C.

Berkeley, Sir Lennox Randal Francis, Kt., C.B.E.

Berlin, Sir Isaiah, Kt., O.M., C.B.E.

Bernard, Sir Dallas Edmund, Bt. (1954).

Berney, Sir Julian Reedham Stuart, Bt. (1620).

Berrill, Sir Kenneth Ernest, G.B.E., K.C.B.

Berthon, *Vice-Adm*. Sir Stephen Ferrier, K.C.B.

Berthoud, Sir Eric Alfred, K.C.M.G.

Berthoud, Sir Martin Seymour, K.C.V.O., C.M.G.

Bethune, Sir Alexander Maitland Sharp, Bt. (s. 1683).

Bethune, *Hon*. Sir (Walter) Angus, Kt.

Bevan, Sir Martyn Evan Evans, Bt. (1958).

Bevan, Sir Timothy Hugh, Kt.

Beynon, *Prof*. Sir (William John) Granville, Kt., C.B.E., Ph.D., D.SC., F.R.S.

Bibby, Sir Derek James, Bt., M.C. (1959).

Biddulph, Sir Ian D'Olier, Bt. (1664).

Bide, Sir Austin Ernest, Kt.

Biggs, Sir Norman Paris, Kt.

Biggs-Davison, Sir John Alec, Kt., M.P.

Billiere, *Lt. Gen*. Sir Peter Edgar de la Cour de la, K.C.B., C.B.E., D.S.O., M.C.

Bing, Sir Rudolf Franz Josef, K.B.E.

Bingham, *Hon*. Sir Eardley Max, Kt., Q.C.

Bingham, *Rt. Hon*. Sir Thomas Henry, Kt.

Bird, Sir Richard Geoffrey Chapman, Bt. (1922).

Bird, *Col*. Sir Richard Dawnay Martin-, Kt., C.B.E., T.D.

Birkin, Sir John Christian William, Bt. (1905).

Birkmyre, Sir Henry, Bt. (1921).

Birtwistle, Sir Harrison, Kt.

Bishop, Sir Frederick Arthur, Kt., C.B., C.V.O.

Bishop, Sir George Sidney, Kt., C.B., O.B.E.

Bishop, *Instructor Rear-Adm*. Sir William, K.B.E., C.B.

Bjelke-Petersen, *Hon*. Sir Johannes, K.C.M.G.

Black, Sir Cyril Wilson, Kt.

Black, *Prof*. Sir Douglas Andrew Kilgour, Kt., M.D., F.R.C.P.

Black, Sir Hermann David, Kt.

Black, Sir James Whyte, Kt., F.R.C.P., F.R.S..

Black, *Vice-Adm*. Sir John Jeremy, K.C.B., D.S.O., M.B.E.

Black, Sir Robert Brown, G.C.M.G., O.B.E.

Black, Sir Robert David, Bt. (1922).

Blacker, *Gen*. Sir Cecil Hugh, G.C.B., O.B.E., M.C.

Blackett, Sir George William, Bt. (1673).

Blackman, Sir Frank Milton, K.C.V.O., O.B.E.

Blackwell, Sir Basil Davenport, Kt.

Blair, Sir Alastair Campbell, K.C.V.O., T.D., W.S.

Blair, *Lt.-Gen*. Sir Chandos, K.C.V.O., O.B.E., M.C.

Blair, Sir Edward Thomas Hunter, Bt. (1786).

Blake, Sir Alfred Lapthorn, K.C.V.O., M.C.

Blake, Sir Francis Michael, Bt. (1907).

Blake, Sir (Thomas) Richard (Valentine), Bt. (I. 1622).

Blaker, Sir John, Bt. (1919).

Blaker, *Rt. Hon*. Sir Peter Allan Renshaw, K.C.M.G., M.P.

Blakiston, Sir Ferguson Arthur James, Bt. (1763).

Bland, Sir Henry Armand, Kt., C.B.E.

Bland, *Lt.-Col*. Sir Simon Claud Michael, K.C.V.O.

Blaxter, Sir Kenneth Lyon, Kt., F.R.S., F.R.S.E.

Blelloch, Sir John Nial Henderson, K.C.B.

Blennerhassett, Sir (Marmaduke) Adrian Francis William, Bt. (1809).

Blois, Sir Charles Nicholas Gervase, Bt. (1686).

Blomefield, Sir Thomas Charles Peregrine, Bt. (1807).

Bloomfield, *Hon*. Sir John Stoughton, Kt., Q.C.

Bloomfield, Sir Kenneth Percy, K.C.B.

Blosse, *Capt*. Sir Richard Hely Lynch-, Bt. (1622).

Blount, Sir Walter Edward Alpin, Bt., D.S.C. (1642).

Blundell, Sir Michael, K.B.E.

Blunden, Sir George, Kt.

Blunden, Sir Philip Overington, Bt. (I. 1766).

Blunt, Sir David Richard Reginald Harvey, Bt. (1720).

Blyth, Sir James, Kt.

Boardman, Sir Kenneth Ormrod, Kt.

Bodilly, *Hon*. Sir Jocelyn, Kt., V.R.D.

Bodmer, Sir Walter Fred, Kt., Ph.D., F.R.S.

Body, Sir Richard Bernard Frank Stewart, Kt., M.P.

Boevey, Sir Thomas Michael Blake Crawley-, Bt. (1784).

Boileau, Sir Guy (Francis), Bt. (1838).

Boles, Sir Jeremy John Fortescue, Bt. (1922).

Boles, Sir John Dennis, Kt., M.B.E.

Bolland, Sir Edwin, K.C.M.G.

Bollers, *Hon*. Sir Harold Brodie Smith, Kt.

Bolte, *Hon*. Sir Henry Edward, G.C.M.G.

Bolton, Sir Frederic Bernard, Kt., M.C.

Bonallack, Sir Richard Frank, Kt., C.B.E.

Bonar, Sir Herbert Vernon, Kt., C.B.E.

Bond, Sir Kenneth Raymond Boyden, Kt.

Bondi, *Prof*. Sir Hermann, K.C.B., F.R.S.

Bonham, *Maj*. Sir Antony Lionel Thomas, Bt. (1852).

Bonsall, Sir Arthur Wilfred, K.C.M.G., C.B.E.

Bonsor, Sir Nicholas Cosmo, Bt., M.P. (1925).

Boolell, Sir Satcam, Kt.

Boon, Sir Peter Coleman, Kt.

Boord, Sir Nicolas John Charles, Bt. (1896).

Boorman, *Lt.-Gen*. Sir Derek, K.C.B.

Booth, Sir Angus Josslyn Gore-, Bt. (I. 1760).

Booth, Sir Christopher Charles, Kt., M.D., F.R.C.P.

Booth, Sir Douglas Allen, Bt. (1916).

Booth, Sir Gordon, K.C.M.G., C.V.O.

Booth, Sir Robert Camm, Kt., C.B.E., T.D.

Boothby, Sir Brooke Charles, Bt. (1660).

Boreel, Sir Francis David, Bt. (1645).

Boreham, Sir (Arthur) John, K.C.B.

Boreham, *Hon*. Sir Leslie Kenneth Edward, Kt.

Bornu, The Waziri of, K.C.M.G., C.B.E.

Borrie, Sir Gordon Johnson, Kt., Q.C.

Borthwick, Sir John Thomas, Bt. M.B.E. (1908).

Bossom, *Hon*. Sir Clive, Bt. (1953).

Boswall, Sir (Thomas) Alford Houstoun-, Bt. (1836).

Boswell, *Lt.-Gen*. Sir Alexander Crawford Simpson, K.C.B., C.B.E.

Bosworth, Sir Neville Bruce Alfred, Kt., C.B.E.

Bottomley, Sir James Reginald Alfred, K.C.M.G.

Boughey, Sir John George Fletcher, Bt. (1798).

Boulton, Sir (Harold Hugh) Christian, Bt. (1905).

Boulton, Sir William Whytehead, Bt., C.B.E., T.D. (1944).

Bourne, Sir (John) Wilfrid, K.C.B.

Bovell, *Hon*. Sir (William) Stewart, Kt.

Bowater, Sir (John) Vansittart, Bt. (1914).

Bowater, Sir Euan David Vansittart, Bt. (1939).

Bowden, Sir Frank, Bt. (1915).

Bowen, Sir Geoffrey Fraser, Kt.

Bowen, *Hon.* Sir Nigel Hubert, K.B.E.

Bowen, Sir Thomas Frederic Charles, Bt. (1921).

Bower, *Air Marshal* Sir Leslie William Clement, K.C.B., D.S.O., D.F.C.

Bower, *Lt.-Gen.* Sir Roger Herbert, K.C.B., K.B.E.

Bowlby, Sir Anthony Hugh Mostyn, Bt. (1923).

Bowman, Sir George, Bt. (1961).

Bowman, Sir John Paget, Bt. (1884).

Bowman-Shaw, Sir (George) Neville, Kt.

Bowmar, Sir Charles Erskine, Kt.

Bowness, Sir Alan, Kt., C.B.E.

Bowness, Sir Peter Spencer, Kt., C.B.E.

Boxer, *Air Vice-Marshal* Sir Alan Hunter Cachemaille, K.C.V.O., C.B., D.S.O., D.F.C.

Boyce, Sir Robert Charles Leslie, Bt. (1952).

Boyd, Sir Alexander Walter, Bt. (1916).

Boyd, Sir John McFarlane, Kt., C.B.E.

Boyd, *Prof.* Sir Robert Lewis Fullarton, Kt., C.B.E., D.SC., F.R.S.

Boyes, Sir Brian Gerald Barratt-, K.B.E.

Boyle, *Marshal of the Royal Air Force* Sir Dermot Alexander, G.C.B., K.C.V.O., K.B.E., A.F.C.

Boyle, Sir Lawrence, Kt., PH.D.

Boyle, Sir Stephen Gurney, Bt. (1904).

Boyne, Sir Henry Brian, Kt., C.B.E.

Boynton, Sir John Keyworth, Kt., M.C.

Boyson, *Rt. Hon.* Sir Rhodes, Kt., M.P.

Brabham, Sir John Arthur, Kt., O.B.E.

Bradbeer, Sir John Derek Richardson, Kt., O.B.E., T.D.

Bradbury, *Surgeon Vice-Adm.* Sir Eric Blackburn, K.B.E., C.B.

Bradford, Sir Edward Alexander Slade, Bt. (1902).

Bradlaw, *Prof.* Sir Robert Vivian, Kt., C.B.E.

Bradman, Sir Donald George, Kt.

Bradshaw, Sir Kenneth Anthony, K.C.B.

Bradshaw, *Lt.-Gen.* Sir Richard Phillip, K.B.E.

Brain, Sir (Henry) Norman, K.B.E., C.M.G.

Braine, *Rt. Hon.* Sir Bernard Richard, Kt., M.P.

Braithwaite, Sir (Joseph) Franklin Madders, Kt.

Braithwaite, Sir Rodric Quentin, K.C.M.G.

Bramall, Sir (Ernest) Ashley, Kt.

Bramley, *Prof.* Sir Paul Anthony, Kt.

Branch, Sir William Allan Patrick, Kt.

Brancker, Sir (John Eustace) Theodore, Kt., Q.C.

Branigan, Sir Patrick Francis, Kt., Q.C.

Brassey, *Col.* Sir Hugh Trefusis, K.C.V.O., O.B.E., M.C.

Bray, Sir Theodor Charles, Kt., C.B.E.

Braynen, Sir Alvin Rudolph, Kt.

Brearley, Sir Norman, Kt., C.B.E., D.S.O., M.C., A.F.C.

Bremridge, Sir John Henry, K.B.E.

Brennan, *Hon.* Sir (Francis) Gerard, K.B.E.

Brett, Sir Lionel, Kt.

Brickwood, Sir Basil Greame, Bt. (1927).

Bridges, *Hon.* Sir Phillip Rodney, Kt., C.M.G.

Brierley, Sir Ronald Alfred, Kt.

Brierley, Sir Zachry, Kt., C.B.E.

Briggs, *Hon.* Sir Geoffrey Gould, Kt.

Bright, Sir Keith, Kt.

Brinckman, Sir Theodore George Roderick, Bt. (1831).

Brisco, Sir Donald Gilfrid, Bt. (1782).

Briscoe, Sir John Leigh Charlton, Bt., D.F.C. (1910).

Brise, Sir John Archibald Ruggles-, Bt., C.B., O.B.E., T.D. (1935).

Bristow, *Hon.* Sir Peter Henry Rowley, Kt.

Britton, Sir Edward Louis, Kt., C.B.E.

Broackes, Sir Nigel, Kt.

Broadbent, Sir Ewen, K.C.B., C.M.G.

Broadbent, Sir George Walter, Bt. (1893).

Broadhurst, *Air Chief Marshal* Sir Harry, G.C.B., K.B.E., D.S.O., D.F.C., A.F.C.

Brockhoff, Sir Jack Stuart, Kt.

Brocklebank, Sir Aubrey Thomas, Bt. (1885).

Brockman, *Vice-Adm.* Sir Ronald Vernon, K.C.B., C.V.O., C.S.I., C.I.E., C.B.E.

Brockman, *Hon.* Sir Thomas Charles Drake-, Kt., D.F.C.

Brodie, Sir Benjamin David Ross, Bt. (1834).

Brogan, *Lt.-Gen.* Sir Mervyn Francis, K.B.E., C.B.

Bromhead, Sir John Desmond Gonville, Bt. (1806).

Bromley, Sir Rupert Charles, Bt. (1757).

Bromley, Sir Thomas Eardley, K.C.M.G.

Brook, Sir Robin, Kt., C.M.G., O.B.E.

†Brooke, Sir Alistair Weston, Bt. (1919).

Brooke, Sir Francis George Windham, Bt. (1903).

Brooke, *Hon.* Sir Henry, Kt.

Brooke, Sir (Norman) Richard (Rowley), Kt., C.B.E.

Brooke, Sir Richard Neville, Bt. (1662).

Brookes, Sir Wilfred Deakin, Kt., C.B.E., D.S.O.

Brooksbank, Sir (Edward) Nicholas, Bt. (1919).

Broom, *Air Marshal* Sir Ivor Gordon, K.C.B., C.B.E., D.S.O., D.F.C., A.F.C.

Broughton, *Air Marshal* Sir Charles, K.B.E., C.B.

Broughton, Sir Evelyn Delves, Bt. (1661).

Broun, Sir Lionel John Law, Bt. (b. 1686).

Brown, Sir Allen Stanley, Kt., C.B.E.

Brown, Sir (Arthur James) Stephen, K.B.E.

Brown, *Lt.-Col.* Sir Charles Frederick Richmond, Bt. (1863).

Brown, Sir (Cyril) Maxwell Palmer, K.C.B., C.M.G.

Brown, Sir David, Kt.

Brown, *Vice-Adm.* Sir David Worthington, K.C.B.

Brown, Sir Derrick Holden-, Kt.

Brown, Sir Douglas Denison, Kt.

Brown, Sir Edward Joseph, Kt., M.B.E.

Brown, *Prof.* Sir (Ernest) Henry Phelps, Kt., M.B.E., F.B.A.

Brown, Sir (Frederick Herbert) Stanley, Kt., C.B.E.

Brown, *Prof.* Sir (George) Malcolm, Kt., F.R.S

Brown, Sir John Douglas Keith, Kt.

Brown, Sir John Gilbert Newton, Kt., C.B.E.

Brown, Sir Mervyn, K.C.M.G., O.B.E.

Brown, *Hon.* Sir Ralph Kilner, Kt., O.B.E., T.D.

Brown, Sir Raymond Frederick, Kt., O.B.E.

Brown, Sir Robert Crichton-, K.C.M.G., C.B.E., T.D.

Brown, *Hon.* Sir Simon Denis, Kt.

Brown, *Rt. Hon.* Sir Stephen, Kt.

Brown, Sir Thomas, Kt.

Brown, Sir William Brian Piggott-, Bt. (1903).

Browne, *Rt. Hon.* Sir Patrick Reginald Evelyn, Kt., O.B.E., T.D.

Browne, Sir Thomas Anthony Gore, Kt.

Brownrigg, Sir Nicholas (Gawen), Bt. (1816).

Bruce, Sir Arthur Atkinson, K.B.E., M.C.

Bruce, Sir (Francis) Michael Ian, Bt. (s. 1628).

Bruce, Sir Hervey James Hugh, Bt. (1804).

Bruce, *Rt. Hon.* Sir (James) Roualeyn Hovell-Thurlow-Cumming-, Kt.

Brunner, Sir John Henry Kilian, Bt. (1895).

Brunton, Sir (Edward Francis) Lauder, Bt. (1908).

Brunton, Sir Gordon Charles, Kt.

Bryan, Sir Arthur, Kt.

Bryan, Sir Paul Elmore Oliver, Kt., D.S.O., M.C.

Bryce, *Hon.* Sir (William) Gordon, Kt., C.B.E.

Bryson, *Vice-Adm.* Sir Lindsay Sutherland, K.C.B.

Buchan, Sir John, Kt., C.M.G.

Buchanan, Sir Charles Alexander James Leith-, Bt. (1775).

Buchanan, Sir Andrew George, Bt. (1878).

Buchanan, *Prof.* Sir Colin Douglas, Kt., C.B.E.

Buchanan, *Vice-Adm.* Sir Peter William, K.B.E.

Buck, Sir (Philip) Antony (Fyson), Kt., Q.C., M.P.

Buckley, *Rt. Hon.* Sir Denys Burton, Kt., M.B.E.

Buckley, Sir John William, Kt.

Buckley, *Rear-Adm.* Sir Kenneth Robertson, K.B.E.

Buckley, *Lt.-Cdr.* Sir (Peter) Richard, K.C.V.O.

Bulkeley, Sir Richard Harry David Williams-, Bt., T.D. (1661).

Bull, Sir Simeon George, Bt. (1922).

Bull, Sir Walter Edward Avenon, K.C.V.O.

Bullard, Sir Giles Lionel, K.C.V.O., G.M.G.

Bullard, Sir Julian Leonard, G.C.M.G.

Bullus, Sir Eric Edward, Kt.

Bulmer, Sir William Peter, Kt.

Bultin, Sir Bato, Kt., M.B.E.

Bunbury, Sir Michael William, Bt. (1681).

Bunbury, Sir (Richard David) Michael Richardson-, Bt. (I. 1787).

Bunch, Sir Austin Wyeth, Kt., C.B.E.

Bunting, Sir (Edward) John, K.B.E.

Burbidge, Sir Herbert Dudley, Bt. (1916).

Burbury, *Hon.* Sir Stanley Charles, K.C.M.G., K.C.V.O., K.B.E.

Burdett, Sir Savile Aylmer, Bt. (1665).

Burgen, Sir Arnold Stanley Vincent, Kt., F.R.S.

Burgess, *Gen.* Sir Edward Arthur, K.C.B., O.B.E.

Burgh, Sir John Charles, K.C.M.G., C.B.

Burke, Sir Aubrey Francis, Kt., O.B.E.

Burke, *Prof.* Sir Joseph Terence, K.B.E.

Burke, Sir Thomas Stanley, Bt. (I. 1797).

Burley, Sir Victor George, Kt., C.B.E.

Burman, Sir (John) Charles, Kt.

Burman, Sir Stephen France, Kt., C.B.E.

Burnet, Sir James William Alexander (Sir Alastair Burnet), Kt.

Burnett, *Air Chief Marshal* Sir Brian Kenyon, G.C.B., D.F.C., A.F.C.

Burnett, Sir David Humphery, Bt., M.B.E., T.D. (1913).

Burnett, Sir John Harrison, Kt.

Burnett, Sir Walter John, Kt.

Burney, Sir Anthony George Bernard, Kt., O.B.E.

Burney, Sir Cecil Denniston, Bt. (1921).

Burns, Sir Charles Ritchie, K.B.E., M.D.

Burns, Sir John Crawford, Kt.

Burns, Sir Terence, Kt.

Burns, *Maj.-Gen.* Sir (Walter Arthur) George, K.C.V.O., C.B., D.S.O., O.B.E., M.C.

Burrell, Sir John Raymond, Bt. (1774).

Burrenchobay, Sir Dayendranath, K.B.E., C.M.G., C.V.O.

Burrows, Sir Bernard Alexander Brocas, G.C.M.G.

Burston, Sir Samuel Gerald Wood, Kt., O.B.E.

Burt, *Hon.* Sir Francis Theodore Page, K.C.M.G.

Burton, Sir Carlisle Archibald, Kt., O.B.E.

Burton, Sir George Vernon Kennedy, Kt., C.B.E.

Burton, *Air Marshal* Sir Harry, K.C.B., C.B.E., D.S.O.

Burton-Chadwick, Sir Joshua Kenneth, Bt. (1935).

Busby, Sir Matthew, Kt., C.B.E.

Bush, *Hon.* Sir Brian Drex, Kt.

Bush, *Adm.* Sir John Fitzroy Duyland, G.C.B., D.S.C.

Busk, Sir Douglas Laird, K.C.M.G.

Butler, *Rt. Hon.* Sir Adam Courtauld, Kt.

Butler, Sir Clifford Charles, Kt., Ph.D., F.R.S.

Butler, Sir (Frederick) (Edward) Robin, K.C.B., C.V.O.

Butler, Sir Michael Dacres, G.C.M.G.

Butler, Sir (Reginald) Michael (Thomas), Bt. (1922).

Butler, *Hon.* Sir Richard Clive, Kt.

Butler, *Col.* Sir Thomas Pierce, Bt., C.V.O., D.S.O., O.B.E. (1628).

Butt, Sir (Alfred) Kenneth Dudley, Bt. (1929).

Butterworth, Sir (George) Neville, Kt.

Buxton, Sir Thomas Fowell Victor, Bt. (1840).

Buzzard, Sir Anthony Farquhar, Bt. (1929).

Byatt, Sir Hugh Campbell, K.C.V.O., C.M.G.

Byers, Sir Maurice Hearne, Kt., C.B.E., Q.C.

Byford, Sir Lawrence, Kt., C.B.E., Q.P.M.

Byrne, Sir Clarence Askew, Kt., O.B.E., D.S.C.

Cable, Sir James Eric, K.C.V.O., C.M.G.

Cadbury, Sir (George) Adrian (Hayhurst), Kt.

Cadell, *Vice-Adm.* Sir John Frederick, K.B.E.

Cadwallader, Sir John, Kt.

Caffyn, *Brig.* Sir Edward Roy, K.B.E., C.B., T.D.

Cahn, Sir Albert Jonas, Bt. (1934).

Cain, Sir Edward Thomas, Kt., C.B.E.

Cain, Sir Henry Edney Conrad, Kt.

Caine, Sir Michael Harris, Kt.

Caine, Sir Sydney, K.C.M.G.

Cairncross, Sir Alexander Kirkland, K.C.M.G.

Cakobau, *Ratu* Sir George, G.C.M.G., G.C.V.O., O.B.E., Royal Victorian Chain.

Caldicott, *Hon.* Sir John Moore, Kt., C.M.G.

Caldwell, *Surgeon Vice-Adm.* Sir (Eric) Dick, K.B.E., C.B.

Callaghan, Sir Allan Robert, Kt., C.M.G.

Callaghan, Sir Bede Bertrand, Kt., C.B.E.

Callard, Sir Eric John, Kt.

Callaway, *Prof.* Sir Frank Adams, Kt., C.M.G., O.B.E.

Calley, Sir Henry Algernon, Kt., D.S.O., D.F.C.

Callinan, Sir Bernard James, Kt., C.B.E., D.S.O., M.C.

Calne, *Prof.* Sir Roy Yorke, Kt., F.R.S.

Calthorpe, Sir Euan Hamilton Anstruther-Gough-, Bt. (1929).

Cameron of Lochiel, Sir Donald Hamish, K.T., C.V.O., T.D.

Cameron, Sir (Eustace) John, Kt., C.B.E.

Cameron, Sir James Clark, Kt., C.B.E., T.D.

Cameron, *Hon.* Sir John, Kt., D.S.C., Q.C. (Lord Cameron).

Cameron, Sir John Watson, Kt., O.B.E.

Camilleri, *His Hon.* Sir Luigi Antonio, Kt, Ll.D.

Campbell, Sir Alan Hugh, G.C.M.G.

Campbell, Sir Clifford Clarence, G.C.M.G., G.C.V.O.

Campbell, Sir Colin Moffat, Bt., M.C. (s. 1668)

Campbell, *Col.* Sir Guy Theophilus Halswell, Bt., O.B.E., M.C. (1815).

Campbell, *Maj.-Gen.* Sir Hamish Manus, K.B.E., C.B.

Campbell, *Cdr.* Sir Ian Tofts, C.B.E., V.R.D.

Campbell, Sir Ilay Mark, Bt. (1808).

Campbell, Sir Matthew, K.B.E., C.B., F.R.S.E.

Campbell, Sir Niall Alexander Hamilton, Bt. (1831).

Campbell, Sir Ralph Abercromby, Kt.

Campbell, Sir Robin Auchinbreck, Bt. (s. 1628).

Campbell, Sir Thomas Cockburn-, Bt. (1821).

Campbell, *Hon.* Sir Walter Benjamin, Kt.

Campion, Sir Harry, Kt., C.B., C.B.E.

Cantley, *Hon.* Sir Joseph Donaldson, Kt., O.B.E.

Carden, *Lt.-Col.* Sir Henry Christopher, Bt., O.B.E. (1887).

Carden, Sir John Craven, Bt. (I. 1787).

Carew, Sir Rivers Verain, Bt. (1661).

Carey, Sir Peter Willoughby, G.C.B.

Carlill, *Vice-Adm.* Sir Stephen Hope, K.B.E., C.B., D.S.O.

Carlisle, Sir John Michael, Kt.

Carmichael, Sir David Peter William Gibson-Craig-, Bt. (s. 1702 and 1831).

Carmichael, Sir John, K.B.E.

Carnac, *Rev. Canon* Sir (Thomas) Nicholas Rivett-, Bt. (1836).

Carnegie, *Lt.-Gen.* Sir Robin Macdonald, K.C.B., O.B.E.

Carnegie, Sir Roderick Howard, Kt.

Carnwath, Sir Andrew Hunter, K.C.V.O.

Caro, Sir Anthony Alfred, Kt., C.B.E.

Carpenter, *Very Rev.* Edward Frederick, K.C.V.O.

Carr, Sir (Albert) Raymond (Maillard), Kt.

Carr, *Air Marshal* Sir John Darcy Baker-, K.B.E., C.B., A.F.C.

Carreras, *Lt.-Col.* Sir James, K.C.V.O., M.B.E.

Carrick, *Hon.* Sir John Leslie, K.C.M.G.

Carter, Sir Charles Frederick, Kt., F.B.A.

Carter, Sir Derrick Hunton, Kt., T.D.

Carter, *Hon.* Sir Douglas Julian, K.C.M.G.

Carter, Sir John, Kt., Q.C.

Carter, Sir William Oscar, Kt.

Cartland, Sir George Barrington, Kt., C.M.G.

Cartledge, Sir Bryan George, K.C.M.G.

Cary, Sir Roger Hugh, Bt. (1955).

Cash, Sir Gerald Christopher, G.C.M.G., G.C.V.O., O.B.E.

Cass, Sir John Patrick, Kt., O.B.E.

Cassel, Sir Harold Felix, Bt., T.D., Q.C. (1920)

Cassels, *Field Marshal* Sir (Archibald) James Halkett, G.C.B., K.B.E., D.S.O.

Cassels, Sir John Seton, Kt., C.B.

Cassels, *Adm.* Sir Simon Alastair Cassillis, K.C.B., C.B.E.

Cassidi, *Adm.* Sir (Arthur) Desmond, G.C.B.

Casson, Sir Hugh Maxwell, C.H., K.C.V.O., P.P.R.A., F.R.I.B.A.

Cater, Sir Jack, K.B.E.

Cater, Sir John Robert, Kt.

Catherwood, Sir (Henry) Frederick (Ross), Kt.

Catling, Sir Richard Charles, Kt., C.M.G., O.B.E.

Cato, *Hon.* Sir Arnott Samuel, K.C.M.G.

Caughey, Sir Thomas Harcourt Clarke, K.B.E.

Caulfield, *Hon.* Sir Bernard, Kt.

Cave, Sir Charles Edward Coleridge, Bt. (1896).

Cave, Sir (Charles) Philip Haddon-, K.B.E., C.M.G.

Cave, Sir Robert Cave-Browne-, Bt. (1641).

Cawley, Sir Charles Mills, Kt., C.B.E., Ph.D.

Cayley, Sir Digby William David, Bt. (1661).

Cayzer, Sir James Arthur, Bt. (1904).

Cazalet, *Hon.* Sir Edward Stephen, Kt.

Cecil, *Rear-Adm.* Sir (Oswald) Nigel Amherst, K.B.E., C.B.

Chacksfield, *Air Vice-Marshal* Sir Bernard Albert, K.B.E., C.B.

Chadwick, *Rev. Prof.* (William) Owen, O.M., K.B.E., F.B.A.

Chalk, *Hon.* Sir Gordon William Wesley, K.B.E.

Chamberlain, *Hon.* Sir Reginald Roderic St. Clair, Kt.

Chan, *Rt. Hon.* Sir Julius, K.B.E.

Chance, Sir (George) Jeremy ffolliott, Bt. (1900).

Chancellor, Sir Christopher John, Kt., C.M.G.

Chandler, Sir Colin Michael, Kt.

Chandler, Sir Geoffrey, Kt., C.B.E.

Chaney, *Hon.* Sir Frederick Charles, K.B.E., A.F.C.

Chapman, Sir David Robert Macgowan, Bt. (1958).

Chapman, Sir George Alan, Kt.

Chapman, *Hon.* Sir Stephen, Kt.

Chapple, *Gen.* Sir John Lyon, G.C.B., C.B.E.

Charles, Sir Joseph Quentin, Kt.

Charnley, Sir (William) John, Kt., C.B.

Chau, *Hon.* Sir Sik-Nin, Kt., C.B.E.

Chaytor, Sir George Reginald, Bt. (1831).

Cheadle, Sir Eric Wallers, Kt., C.B.E.

Cheeketts, *Sqn. Ldr.* Sir David John, K.C.V.O.

Cheetham, Sir Nicolas John Alexander, K.C.M.G.

Chesterman, Sir (Dudley) Ross, Kt., Ph.D.

Chesterton, Sir Oliver Sidney, Kt., M.C.

Chetwood, Sir Clifford Jack, Kt.

Chetwynd, Sir Arthur Ralph Talbot, Bt. (1795).

Cheung, Sir Oswald Victor, Kt., C.B.E.

Cheyne, Sir Joseph Lister Watson, Bt., O.B.E. (1908).

Chichester, Sir (Edward) John, Bt. (1641).

Child, Sir (Coles John) Jeremy, Bt. (1919).

Chilton, *Air Marshal* Sir (Charles) Edward, K.B.E., C.B.

Chilton, *Brig.* Sir Frederick Oliver, Kt., C.B.E., D.S.O.

Chitty, Sir Thomas Willes, Bt. (1924).

Cholmeley, Sir Montague John, Bt. (1806).

Christie, Sir George William Langham, Kt.

Christie, *Hon.* Sir Vernon Howard Colville, Kt.

Christie, Sir William, Kt., M.B.E.

Christison, *Gen.* Sir (Alexander Frank) Philip, Bt., G.B.E., C.B., D.S.O., M.C. (1871).

Christofas, Sir Kenneth Cavendish, K.C.M.G., M.B.E.

Christopherson, Sir Derman Guy, Kt., O.B.E., D.Phil., F.R.S.

Chung, Sir Sze-yuen, Kt., C.B.E.

Clapham, Sir Michael John Sinclair, K.B.E.

Claringbull, Sir (Gordon) Frank, Kt., Ph.D.

Clark, Sir George Anthony, Bt. (1917).

Clark, Sir John Allen, Kt.

Clark, Sir John Douglas, Bt. (1886).

Clark, Sir John Stewart-, Bt. (1918).

Clark, Sir Robert Anthony, Kt., D.S.C.

Clark, Sir Robin Chichester-, Kt.

Clark, Sir Thomas Edwin, Kt.

Clark, Sir William Gibson, Kt., M.P.

Clarke, Sir (Charles Mansfield) Tobias, Bt. (1831).

Clarke, *Prof.* Sir Cyril Astley, K.B.E., M.D., SC.D., F.R.S., F.R.C.P.

Clarke, Sir Ellis Emmanuel Innocent, G.C.M.G.

Clarke, Sir (Henry) Ashley, G.C.M.G., G.C.V.O.

Clarke, Sir Jonathan Dennis, Kt.

Clarke, Sir Rupert William John, Bt., M.B.E. (1882).

Clay, Sir Richard Henry, Bt. (1841).

Clayson, Sir Eric Maurice, Kt.

Clayton, Sir David Robert, Bt., (1732).

Clayton, *Air Marshal* Sir Gareth Thomas Butler, K.C.B., D.F.C.

Clayton, Sir Robert James, Kt., C.B.E.

Cleary, Sir Joseph Jackson, Kt.

Clegg, Sir Walter, Kt.

Cleminson, Sir James Arnold Stacey, Kt., M.C.

Clerk, Sir John Dutton, Bt., C.B.E., V.R.D. (s. 1679).

Clerke, Sir John Edward Longueville, Bt. (1660).

Clifford, Sir Roger Joseph, Bt. (1887).

Clothier, Sir Cecil Montacute, K.C.B., Q.C.

Clowes, *Col.* Sir Henry Nelson, K.C.V.O., D.S.O., O.B.E.

Clucas, Sir Kenneth Henry, K.C.B.

Clutterbuck, *Vice-Adm.* Sir David Granville, K.B.E., C.B.

Coates, Sir Ernest William, Kt., C.M.G.

Coates, Sir Frederick Gregory Lindsay, Bt. (1921).

Coats, Sir Alastair Francis Stuart, Bt. (1905).

Coats, Sir William David, Kt.

Cobban, Sir James Macdonald, Kt., C.B.E., T.D.

Cochrane, Sir (Henry) Marc (Sursock), Bt. (1903).

Cockburn, Sir John Elliot, Bt. (s. 1671).

Cockburn, Sir Robert, K.B.E., C.B., Ph.D.

Cockcroft, Sir Wilfred Halliday, Kt., D.Phil.

Cockerell, Sir Christopher Sydney, Kt., C.B.E., F.R.S.

Cockram, Sir John, Kt.

Cocks, Sir (Thomas George) Barnett, K.C.B., O.B.E.

Codrington, Sir Simon Francis Bethell, Bt. (1876).

Codrington, Sir William Alexander, Bt. (1721).

Coghill, Sir Egerton James Nevill Tobias, Bt. (1778).

Cohen, Sir Bernard Nathaniel Waley-, Bt. (1961).

Cohen, Sir Edward, Kt.

Coldstream, Sir George Phillips, K.C.B., K.C.V.O., Q.C.

Cole, Sir (Alexander) Colin, K.C.V.O., T.D.

Cole, Sir David Lee, K.C.M.G., M.C.

Cole, Sir (Robert) William, Kt.

Coles, Sir Norman Cameron, Kt.

Colfox, Sir (William) John, Bt. (1939).

Collett, Sir Ian Seymour, Bt. (1934).

Collins, Sir Arthur James Robert, K.C.V.O.

Collins, *Vice-Adm.* Sir John Augustine, K.B.E., C.B.

Collyear, Sir John Gowen, Kt.

Colman, Sir Michael Jeremiah, Bt. (1907).

Colquhoun, *Maj.-Gen.* Sir Cyril Harry, K.C.V.O., C.B., O.B.E.

Colquhoun of Luss, Sir Ivar Iain, Bt. (1786).

Colt, Sir Edward William Dutton Bt. (1694).

Colthurst, Sir Richard La Touche, Bt. (1744).

Combs, Sir Willis Ide, K.C.V.O., C.M.G.

Compston, *Vice-Adm.* Sir Peter Maxwell, K.C.B.

Compton, Sir Edmund Gerald, G.C.B., K.B.E.

Compton Miller, Sir John (Francis), Kt., M.B.E., T.D.

Comyn, *Hon.* Sir James, Kt.

Conant, Sir John Ernest Michael, Bt. (1954).

Conran, Sir Terence Orby, Kt.

Constable, Sir Robert Frederick Strickland-, Bt. (1641).

Constantine, *Air Chief Marshal* Sir Hugh Alex, K.B.E., C.B., D.S.O.

Cook, *Prof.* Sir Alan Hugh, Kt.

Cook, Sir Christopher Wymondham Rayner Herbert, Bt. (1886).

Cook, Sir (Philip) Halford, Kt., O.B.E.

Cooke, Sir Charles Fletcher-, Kt., Q.C.

Cooke, *Lt.-Col.* Sir David William Perceval, Bt. (1661).

Cooke, Sir John Fletcher-, Kt., C.M.G.

Cooke, *Rt. Hon.* Sir Robin Brunskill, K.B.E.

Cooley, Sir Alan Sydenham, Kt., C.B.E.

Coop, Sir Maurice Fletcher, Kt.

Cooper, *Rt. Hon.* Sir Frank, G.C.B., C.M.G.

Cooper, *Gen.* Sir George Leslie Conroy, G.C.B., M.C.

Cooper, Sir Gilbert Alexander, Kt., C.B.E., E.D.

Cooper, Sir Patrick Graham Astley, Bt. (1821).

Cooper, Sir Richard Powell, Bt. (1905).

Cooper, Sir William Daniel Charles, Bt. (1863).

Cooper, Sir William Henry, Kt., C.B.E.

Cooper, *Prof.* Sir (William) Mansfield, Kt.

Coote, Sir Christopher John, Bt., *Premier Baronet of Ireland* (I. 1621).

Copas, *Most Rev.* Virgil, K.B.E., D.D.

Copisarow, Sir Alcon Charles, Kt.

Corbet, Sir John Vincent, Bt., M.B.E. (1808).

Corfield, *Rt. Hon.* Sir Frederick Vernon, Kt., Q.C.

Corfield, Sir Kenneth George, Kt.

Cork, Sir Kenneth Russell, G.B.E.

Corley, Sir Kenneth Sholl Ferrand, Kt.

Cormack, Sir Magnus Cameron, K.B.E.

Corness, Sir Colin Ross, Kt.

Cornford, Sir (Edward) Clifford, K.C.B.

Cornforth, Sir John Warcup, Kt., C.B.E., D.Phil., F.R.S.

†Corry, Sir William James, Bt. (1885).

Cortazzi, Sir (Henry Arthur) Hugh, G.C.M.G.

Cory, Sir Clinton James Donald, Bt. (1919).

Coslett, *Air Marshal* Sir (Thomas) Norman, K.C.B., O.B.E.

Costar, Sir Norman Edgar, K.C.M.G.

Cotter, *Lt.-Col.* Sir Delaval James Alfred, Bt., D.S.O. (I. 1763).

Cotterell, Sir John Henry Geers, Bt. (1805).

Cotton, Sir John Richard, K.C.M.G., O.B.E.

Cotton, *Hon.* Sir Robert Carrington, K.C.M.G.

Cotton, Sir (Thomas) Henry, Kt., M.B.E.

Cottrell, Sir Alan Howard, Kt., Ph.D., F.R.S.

Cotts, Sir (Robert) Crichton Mitchell, Bt. (1921).

Coulson, Sir John Eltringham, K.C.M.G.

Couper, Sir (Robert) Nicholas (Oliver), Bt. (1841).

Court, *Hon.* Sir Charles Walter Michael, K.C.M.G., O.B.E.

Coutts, Sir Walter Fleming, G.C.M.G., M.B.E.

Couzens, Sir Kenneth Edward, K.C.B.

Covacevich, Sir (Anthony) Thomas, Kt., D.F.C.

Cowen, *Rt. Hon. Prof.* Sir Zelman, G.C.M.G., G.C.V.O., Q.C.

Cowley, *Lt.-Gen.* Sir John Guise, K.B.E., C.B.

Cowper, Sir Norman Lethbridge, Kt., C.B.E.

Cowperthwaite, Sir John James, K.B.E., C.M.G.

Cox, Sir Anthony Wakefield, Kt., C.B.E., F.R.I.B.A.

Cox, *Prof.* Sir David Roxbee, Kt., F.R.S.

Cox, Sir (Ernest) Gordon, K.B.E., T.D., D.S.C., F.R.S.

Cox, Sir Geoffrey Sandford, Kt., C.B.E.

Cox, Sir (George) Trenchard, Kt., C.B.E., F.S.A.

Cox, *Vice-Adm.* Sir John Michael Holland, K.C.B.

Cox, Sir John William, Kt., C.B.E.

Cox, Sir Mencea Ethereal, Kt.,

Cradock, Sir Percy, G.C.M.G.

Craig, Sir (Albert) James (Macqueen), G.C.M.G.

Craig, *Marshal of the R.A.F.* Sir David Brownrigg, G.C.B., O.B.E.

Cramer, *Hon.* Sir John Oscar, Kt.

Crane, Sir James William Donald, Kt., C.B.E.

Craufurd, Sir Robert James, Bt. (1781).

Craven, *Air Marshal* Sir Robert Edward, K.B.E., C.B., D.F.C.

Crawford, *Prof.* Sir Frederick William, Kt.

Crawford, *Hon.* Sir George Hunter, Kt.

Crawford, Sir (Robert) Stewart, G.C.M.G., C.V.O

Crawford, *Prof.* Sir Theodore, Kt.

Crawford, *Vice-Adm.* Sir William Godfrey, K.B.E., C.B., D.S.C.

Crawshaw, *Hon.* Sir (Edward) Daniel (Weston), Kt.

Crawshay, *Col.* Sir William Robert, Kt., D.S.O., E.R.D., T.D.

Creagh, *Maj.-Gen.* Sir (Kilner) Rupert Brazier-, K.B.E., C.B., D.S.O.

Crichton, Sir Andrew James Maitland-Makgill-, Kt.

Crill, Sir Peter Leslie, Kt., C.B.E.

Cripps, Sir John Stafford, Kt., C.B.E.

Crisp, Sir (John) Peter, Bt. (1913).

Critchett, Sir Ian (George Lorraine), Bt. (1908).

Croft, Sir John Archibald Radcliffe, Bt. (1818).

Croft, Sir Owen Glendower, Bt. (1671).

†Crofton, Sir Hugh Denis, Bt. (1801).

Crofton, *Prof.* Sir John Wenman, Kt.

Crofton, Sir Malby Sturges, Bt. (1838).

Croker, Sir Walter Russell, K.B.E.

Crookenden, *Lt.-Gen.* Sir Napier, K.C.B., D.S.O., O.B.E.

Croom-Johnson, *Rt. Hon.* Sir David Powell, Kt., D.S.C., V.R.D.

Cross, Sir Cecil Lancelot Stewart, Kt., C.B.E.

Cross, *Air Chief Marshal* Sir Kenneth Brian Boyd, K.C.B., C.B.E., D.S.O., D.F.C.

Crossland, Sir Leonard, Kt.

Crossley, Sir Christopher John, Bt. (1909).

Crossman, Sir Douglas Peter, Kt., T.D.

Crosthwaite, Sir (Ponsonby) Moore, K.C.M.G.

Crouch, Sir David Lance, Kt.

Crowe, Sir Colin Tradescant, G.C.M.G.

Cruthers, Sir James Winter, Kt.

Cubbon, Sir Brian Crossland, G.C.B.

Cubitt, Sir Hugh Guy, Kt., C.B.E.

Cuckney, Sir John Graham, Kt.

Cumber, Sir John Alfred, Kt., C.M.G., M.B.E., T.D.

Cumming, Sir William Gordon Gordon-, Bt. (1804).

Cunard, Sir Guy Alick, Bt. (1859).

Cuninghame, Sir John Christopher Foggo Montgomery-, Bt. (N.S. 1672).

†Cuningham, Sir William Henry Fairlie-, Bt., (s. 1630).

Cunliffe, Sir David Ellis, Bt. (1759)

Cunningham, Sir Charles Craik, G.C.B., K.B.E., C.V.O.

Cunningham, *Lt.-Gen.* Sir Hugh Patrick, K.B.E.

Cunynghame, Sir Andrew David Francis, Bt. (s. 1702).

Cunynghame, Sir James Ogilvy Blair-, Kt., O.B.E.

Curle, Sir John Noel Ormiston, K.C.V.O., C.M.G.

Curran, Sir Samuel Crowe, Kt., D.SC., Ph.D., F.R.S., F.R.S.E.

Currie, *Prof.* Sir Alastair Robert, Kt., F.R.C.P., F.R.C.P.E., F.R.S.E.

Currie, Sir Neil Smith, Kt., C.B.E.

Currie, Sir William George Cubitt, Bt. (1847).

Curtis, Sir (Edward) Leo, Kt.

Curtis, Sir William Peter, Bt. (1802).

Curtiss, *Air Marshal* Sir John Bagot, K.C.B., K.B.E.

Curwen, Sir Christopher Keith, K.C.M.G.

Cuthbertson, Sir David Paton, Kt., C.B.E., M.D., D.SC.

Cuthbertson, Sir Harold Alexander, Kt.

Cutler, Sir (Arthur) Roden, V.C., K.C.M.G., K.C.V.O., C.B.E.

Cutler, Sir Charles Benjamin, K.B.E., E.D.

Cutler, Sir Horace Walter, Kt., O.B.E.

Dacie, *Prof.* Sir John Vivian, Kt., M.D., F.R.S.

Daldry, Sir Leonard Charles, K.B.E.

Dale, Sir William Leonard, K.C.M.G.

Dalrymple, *Maj.* Sir Hew Fleetwood Hamilton-, Bt., K.C.V.O. (s. 1697).

Dalton, Sir Alan Nugent Goring, Kt., C.B.E.

Dalton, *Maj.-Gen.* Sir Charles James George, Kt., C.B., C.B.E.

Dalton, *Vice-Adm.* Sir Geoffrey Thomas James Oliver, K.C.B.

Dalton, *Vice-Adm.* Sir Norman Eric, K.C.B., O.B.E.

Daly, *Lt.-Gen.* Sir Thomas Joseph, K.B.E., C.B., D.S.O.

Dalyell, Sir Tam, Bt., M.P. (N.S. 1685).

Daniel, Sir Goronwy Hopkin, K.C.V.O., C.B., D.Phil.

Daniell, Sir Peter Averell, Kt., T.D.

Danks, Sir Alan John, K.B.E.

Darby, *Prof.* Sir Henry Clifford, Kt., C.B.E.

Darby, Sir Peter Howard, Kt., C.B.E., Q.F.S.M.

Darell, Sir Jeffrey Lionel, Bt., M.C. (1795).

Dargie, Sir William Alexander, Kt., C.B.E.

Darling, Sir Clifford, Kt.

Darling, Sir James Ralph, Kt., C.M.G., O.B.E.

Darling, *Gen.* Sir Kenneth Thomas, G.B.E., K.C.B., D.S.O.

Darlington, *Rear-Adm.* Sir Charles Roy, K.B.E.

Darvall, Sir (Charles) Roger, Kt., C.B.E.

Dashwood, Sir Francis John Vernon Hereward, Bt., *Premier Baronet of Great Britain* (1707).

Dashwood, Sir Richard James, Bt. (1684).

Davenport, *Lt.-Col.* Sir Walter Henry Bromley-, Kt., T.D.

David, Sir Jean Marc, Kt., C.B.E., Q.C.

Davie, Sir Antony Francis Ferguson-, Bt. (1847).

Davie, Sir Paul Christopher, Kt.

Davies, *Air Marshal* Sir Alan Cyril, K.C.B., C.B.E.

Davies, *Hon.* Sir (Alfred William) Michael, Kt.

Davies, Sir Alun Talfan, Kt., Q.C.

Davies, Sir (David) Arthur, K.B.E.

Davies, Sir David Henry, Kt.

Davies, *Hon.* Sir (David Herbert) Mervyn, Kt., M.C., T.D.

Davies, Sir David Joseph, Kt.

Davies, *Vice-Adm.* Sir Lancelot Richard Bell, K.B.E.

Davies, Sir Oswald, Kt., C.B.E.

Davies, Sir Peter Maxwell, Kt., C.B.E.

Davies, Sir Richard Harries, K.C.V.O., C.B.E.

Davies, Sir Victor Caddy, Kt., O.B.E.

Davis, Sir Charles Sigmund, Kt., C.B.

Davis, Sir Colin Rex, Kt., C.B.E.

Davis, *Hon.* Sir (Dermot) Renn, Kt., O.B.E.

Davis, Sir (Ernest) Howard, Kt., C.M.G., O.B.E.

Davis, Sir John Gilbert, Bt. (1946).

Davis, *Air Chief Marshal* Sir John Gilbert, G.C.B., O.B.E.

Davis, Sir John Henry Harris, Kt.

Davis, Sir Maurice Herbert, Kt., O.B.E.

Davis, Sir Rupert Charles Hart-, Kt.

Davis, *Hon.* Sir Thomas Robert Alexander Harries, K.B.E.

Davis, Sir (William) Allan, G.B.E.

Davison, *Rt. Hon.* Sir Ronald Keith, G.B.E., C.M.G.

Dawbarn, Sir Simon Yelverton, K.C.V.O., C.M.G.

Dawnay, *Vice-Adm.* Sir Peter, K.C.V.O., C.B., D.S.C.

Dawson, *Hon.* Sir Daryl Michael, K.B.E., C.B.

Dawson, Sir Hugh Michael Trevor, Bt. (1920).

Dawson, *Air Chief Marshal* Sir Walter Lloyd, K.C.B., C.B.E., D.S.O.

Dawtry, Sir Alan (Graham), Kt., C.B.E., T.D.

Day, Sir Derek Malcolm, K.C.M.G.

Day, Sir Robin, Kt.

Deakin, Sir (Frederick) William (Dampier), Kt., D.S.O.

Dean, Sir (Arthur) Paul, Kt., M.P.

Dean, Sir Patrick Henry, G.C.M.G.

Deane, *Hon.* Sir William Patrick, K.B.E.

Dearing, Sir Ronald Ernest, Kt., C.B.

de Bellaigue, Sir Geoffrey, K.C.V.O.

Debenham, Sir Gilbert Ridley, Bt. (1931).

De Bunsen, Sir Bernard, Kt., C.M.G.

Deer, Sir (Arthur) Frederick, Kt., C.M.G.

de Hoghton, Sir (Richard) Bernard (Cuthbert), Bt. (1611).

De la Bère, Sir Cameron, Bt. (1953).

Delacombe, *Maj.-Gen.* Sir Rohan, K.C.M.G., K.C.V.O., K.B.E., C.B., D.S.O.

de la Mare, Sir Arthur James, K.C.M.G., K.C.V.O.

de la Rue, Sir Eric Vincent, Bt. (1898).

de Lotbinière, *Lt.-Col.* Sir Edmond Joly, Kt.

Delve, Sir Frederick William, Kt., C.B.E.

de Montmorency, Sir Arnold Geoffroy, Bt. (1 1631).

Denman, Sir (George) Roy, K.C.B., C.M.G.

Denning, *Lt.-Gen.* Sir Reginald Francis Stewart, K.C.V.O., K.B.E., C.B.

Denny, Sir Alistair Maurice Archibald, Bt. (1913).

Denny, Sir Anthony Coningham de Waltham, Bt. (1 1782).

Dent, Sir John, Kt., C.B.E.

Denton, *Prof.* Sir Eric James, Kt., C.B.E., F.R.S.

Derbyshire, Sir Andrew George, Kt.

Derham, Sir Peter John, Kt.

de Trafford, Sir Dermot Humphrey, Bt. (1841).

Deverell, Sir Colville Montgomery, G.B.E., K.C.M.G., C.V.O.

Devesi, Sir Baddeley, G.C.M.G., G.C.V.O.

Devitt, Sir Thomas Gordon, Bt. (1916).

Dewey, Sir Anthony Hugh, Bt. (1917).

Dewhurst, *Prof.* Sir (Christopher) John, Kt.

†d'Eyncourt, Sir Giles Gervais Tennyson-, Bt. (1930).

de Zulueta, Sir Philip Francis, Kt.

Dhenin, *Air Marshal* Sir Geoffrey Howard, K.B.E., A.F.C., G.M., M.D.

Dhrangadhra, H.H. the Maharaja Raj Saheb of, K.C.I.E.

Dibela, *Hon.* Sir Kingsford, G.C.M.G.

Dick, Sir John Alexander, M.C.

Dickinson, Sir Harold Herbert, Kt.

Dickinson, Sir Samuel Benson, Kt.

Dilbertson, Sir Geoffrey, C.B.E.

Dilke, Sir John Fisher Wentworth, Bt. (1862).

Dill, Sir Nicholas Bayard, Kt., C.B.E.

Dillon, *Rt. Hon.* Sir (George) Brian (Hugh), Kt.

Dillon, Sir John Vincent, Kt., C.M.G.

Dillon, Sir Max, Kt.

Diver, *Hon.* Sir Leslie Charles, Kt.

Dixon, *Air Vice-Marshal* Sir (Francis Wilfred) Peter, K.B.E.

Dixon, Sir John George, Bt. (1919).

Dobson, Sir Denis William, K.C.B., O.B.E., Q.C.

Dobson, *Gen.* Sir Patrick John Howard-, G.C.B.

Dobson, Sir Richard Portway, Kt.

Dodds, Sir Ralph Jordan, Bt. (1964).

Dodson, Sir Derek Sherborne Lindsell, K.C.M.G., M.C.

Dodsworth, Sir John Christopher Smith-, Bt. (1784).

Doll, *Prof.* Sir (William) Richard (Shaboe), Kt., O.B.E., F.R.S., D.M., M.D., D.SC.

Dollery, Sir Colin Terence, Kt.

Donald, Sir Alan Ewen, K.C.M.G.

Donald, *Air Marshal* Sir John George, K.B.E.

Donaldson, Sir Dawson, K.C.M.G.

Donne, *Hon.* Sir Gaven John, K.B.E.

Donne, Sir John Christopher, Kt.

Dookun, Sir Dewoonarain, Kt.

Dorman, *Lt.-Col.* Sir Charles Geoffrey, Bt., M.C. (1923).

Dorman, Sir Maurice Henry, G.C.M.G., G.C.V.O.

Dos Santos, Sir Errol Lionel, Kt., C.B.E.

Dougherty, *Maj.-Gen.* Sir Ivan Noel, Kt., C.B.E., D.S.O., E.D.

Douglas, *Prof.* Sir Donald Macleod, Kt., M.B.E.

Douglas, Sir (Edward) Sholto, Kt.

Douglas, Sir Robert McCallum, Kt., O.B.E.

Douglas, *Rt. Hon.* Sir William Randolph, K.C.M.G.

Dover, *Prof.* Sir Kenneth James, Kt., D.Litt., F.B.A., F.R.S.E.

Down, Sir Alastair Frederick, Kt., O.B.E., M.C., T.D.

Downey, Sir Gordon Stanley, K.C.B.

Downs, Sir Diarmuid, Kt., C.B.E.

Downward, Sir William Atkinson, Kt.

Dowson, Sir Philip Manning, Kt., C.B.E., A.R.A.

†D'Oyly, Sir Nigel Hadley Miller, Bt. (1663).

Drake, Sir (Arthur) Eric (Courtney), Kt., C.B.E.

Drake, *Hon.* Sir (Frederick) Maurice, Kt., D.F.C.

Drake, Sir James, Kt., C.B.E.

Drew, Sir Arthur Charles Walter, K.C.B.

Drew, *Lt.-Gen.* Sir (William) Robert (Macfarlane), K.C.B., C.B.E., F.R.C.P.

Dreyer, *Adm.* Sir Desmond Parry, G.C.B., C.B.E., D.S.C.

Dring, *Lt.-Col.* Sir Arthur John, K.B.E., C.I.E.

Drinkwater, Sir John Muir, Kt., Q.C.

Driver, Sir Antony Victor, Kt.

Driver, Sir Arthur John, Kt.

Driver, Sir Eric William, Kt.

Drummond, *Lt.-Gen.* Sir (William) Alexander (Duncan), K.B.E., C.B.

Dryden, Sir John Stephen Gyles, Bt. (1733 and 1795).

du Cann, *Rt. Hon.* Sir Edward Dillon Lott, K.B.E.

Duckmanton, Sir Talbot Sydney, Kt., C.B.E.

Duckworth, *Maj.* Sir Richard Dyce, Bt. (1909).

du Cros, Sir Claude Philip Arthur Mallet, Bt. (1916).

Duff, *Rt. Hon.* Sir (Arthur) Antony, G.C.M.G., C.V.O., D.S.O., D.S.C.

Duffus, *Hon.* Sir William Algernon Holwell, Kt.

Dugdale, Sir William Stratford, Bt., M.C. (1936).

Duke, *Maj.-Gen.* Sir Gerald William, K.B.E., C.B., D.S.O.

Dunbar, Sir Archibald Ranulph, Bt. (s. 1700).

Dunbar, Sir David Hope-, Bt. (s. 1664).

Dunbar, Sir Drummond Cospatrick Ninian, Bt., M.C. (s. 1698).

Dunbar, Sir Jean Ivor, Bt. (s. 1694).

Dunbar of Hempriggs, Dame Maureen Daisy Helen, Bt. (s. 1706).

Duncan, Sir James Blair, Kt.

Duncombe, Sir Philip Digby Pauncefort-, Bt. (1859).

Dundas, Sir Hugh Spencer Lisle, Kt., C.B.E., D.S.O., D.F.C.

Dunham, Sir Kingsley Charles, Kt., Ph.D., F.R.S., F.R.S.E.

Dunlop, Sir (Ernest) Edward, Kt., C.M.G., O.B.E.

Dunlop, Sir Thomas, Bt. (1916).

Dunlop, Sir William Norman Gough, Kt.

Dunn, *Air Marshal* Sir Eric Clive, K.B.E., C.B., B.E.M.

Dunn, *Lt.-Col.* Sir (Francis) Vivian, K.C.V.O., O.B.E.

Dunn, *Air Marshal* Sir Patrick Hunter, K.B.E., C.B., D.F.C.

Dunn, *Rt. Hon.* Sir Robin Horace Walford, Kt., M.C.

Dunnett, Sir (Ludovic) James, G.C.B., C.M.G.

Dunning, Sir Simon William Patrick, Bt. (1930).

Dunphie, *Maj.-Gen.* Sir Charles Anderson Lane, Kt., C.B., C.B.E., D.S.O.

Dunstan, *Lt.-Gen.* Sir Donald Beaumont, K.B.E., C.B.

Duntze, Sir John Alexander, Bt. (1774).

Dupree, Sir Peter, Bt. (1921).

Dupuch, Sir (Alfred) Etienne (Jerome), Kt., O.B.E.

Durand, *Rev.* Sir (Henry Mortimer) Dickon, Bt. (1892).

Durham, Sir Kenneth, Kt.

Durie, Sir Alexander Charles, Kt., C.B.E.

Durkin, *Air Marshal* Sir Herbert, K.B.E., C.B.

Durrant, Sir William Henry Estridge, Bt. (1784).

Duthie, *Prof.* Sir Herbert Livingston, Kt.

Duthie, Sir Robert Grieve (Robin), Kt., C.B.E.

Duval, Sir (Charles) Gaetan, Kt.

Duxbury, *Air Marshal* Sir (John) Barry, K.C.B., C.B.E.

Dyer, *Prof.* Sir (Henry) Peter (Francis) Swinnerton-, Bt., K.B.E., F.R.S. (1678).

Dyke, Sir David William Hart, Bt. (1677).

Earle, *Air Chief Marshal* Sir Alfred, G.B.E., C.B.

Earle, Sir (Hardman) George (Algernon), Bt. (1869).

East, Sir (Lewis) Ronald, Kt., C.B.E.

Eastham, *Hon.* Sir (Thomas) Michael, Kt.

Eastick, *Brig.* Sir Thomas Charles, Kt., C.M.G., D.S.O., E.D.

Easton, *Adm.* Sir Ian, K.C.B., D.S.C.

Easton, *Air Cdre.* Sir James Alfred, K.C.M.G., C.B., C.B.E.

Eastwood, Sir John Bealby, Kt.

Eberle, *Adm.* Sir James Henry Fuller, G.C.B.

Ebrahim, Sir (Mahomed) Currimbhoy, Bt. (1910).

Eburne, Sir Sidney Alfred William, Kt., M.C.

Eccles, Sir John Carew, Kt., D.Phil., F.R.S.

Echlin, Sir Norman David Fenton, Bt. (I. 1721).

Eckersley, Sir Donald Payze, Kt., O.B.E.

Edden, *Vice-Adm.* Sir (William) Kaye, K.B.E., C.B.

†Edge, Sir William, Bt. (1937).

Edmenson, Sir Walter Alexander, Kt., C.B.E.

Edmonstone, Sir Archibald Bruce Charles, Bt. (1774).

Edwardes, Sir Michael Owen, Kt.

Edwards, Sir Christopher John Churchill, Bt. (1866).

Edwards, Sir George Robert, Kt., O.M., C.B.E., F.R.S.

Edwards, Sir (John) Clive (Leighton), Bt. (1921).

Edwards, Sir Llewellyn Roy, Kt.

Edwards, *Prof.* Sir Samuel Frederick, Kt., F.R.S.

Egan, Sir John Leopold, Kt.

Egerton, Sir John Alfred Roy, Kt.

Egerton, Sir (Philip) John (Caledon) Grey-, Bt. (1617).

Egerton, Sir Seymour John Louis, G.C.V.O.

Egerton, Sir Stephen Loftus, K.C.M.G.

Eggleston, *Hon.* Sir Richard Moulton, Kt.

Eley, Sir Geoffrey Cecil Ryves, Kt., C.B.E.

Eliott of Stobs, Sir Arthur Francis Augustus Boswell, Bt. (s 1666).

Elliot, Sir Gerald Henry, Kt.

Elliot, Sir John Blumenfeld, Kt.

Elliott, Sir Hugh Francis Ivo, Bt., O.B.E. (1917).

Elliott, Sir Norman Randall, Kt., C.B.E.

Elliott, Sir Randal Forbes, K.B.E.

Elliott, *Prof.* Sir Roger James, Kt., F.R.S.

Elliott, Sir Ronald Stuart, Kt.

Ellis, Sir John Rogers, Kt., M.B.E., M.D., F.R.C.P.

Ellis, Sir Ronald, Kt.

Ellison, *Rt. Rev.* and *Rt. Hon.* Gerald Alexander, K.C.V.O.

Ellison, *Col.* Sir Ralph Harry Carr-, Kt., T.D.

Ellwood, *Air Marshal* Sir Aubrey Beauclerk, K.C.B., D.S.C.

Elphinstone, Sir John, Bt. (s 1701).

Elphinstone, Sir (Maurice) Douglas (Warburton), Bt., T.D. (1816).

Elstub, Sir St. John de Holt, Kt., C.B.E.

Elton, Sir Arnold, Kt., C.B.E.

Elton, Sir Charles Abraham Grierson, Bt. (1717).

Elton, *Prof.* Sir Geoffrey Rudolph, Kt., F.B.A.

Elworthy, Sir Peter Herbert, Kt.

Elyan, Sir (Isadore) Victor, Kt.

Emery, Sir Peter Frank Hannibal, Kt., M.P.

Empson, *Adm.* Sir (Leslie) Derek, G.B.E., K.C.B.

Emson, *Air Marshal* Sir Reginald Herbert, K.B.E., C.B., A.F.C.

Engholm, Sir Basil Charles, K.C.B.

Engineer, Sir Noshirwan Phirozshah, Kt.

Engle, Sir George Lawrence Jose, K.C.B., Q.C.

English, Sir Cyril Rupert, Kt.

English, Sir David, Kt.

Entwistle, Sir (John Nuttall) Maxwell, Kt.

Ereaut, Sir (Herbert) Frank Cobbold, Kt.

Errington, *Col.* Sir Geoffrey Frederick, Bt. (1963).

Errington, Sir Lancelot, K.C.B.

Erskine, Sir (Thomas) David, Bt. (1821).

†Esmonde, Sir Thomas Francis Grattan, Bt. (I. 1629).

Espie, Sir Frank Fletcher, Kt., O.B.E.

Esplen, Sir William Graham, Bt. (1921).

Eustace, Sir Joseph Lambert, G.C.M.G., G.C.V.O.

Evans, Sir Anthony Adney, Bt. (1920).

Evans, Sir Athol Donald, K.B.E.

Evans, *Hon.* Sir Anthony Howell Meurig, Kt., R.D.

Evans, *Air Chief Marshal* Sir David George, G.C.B., C.B.E.

Evans, Sir Geraint Llewellyn, Kt., C.B.E.

Evans, Sir Richard Mark, K.C.M.G., K.C.V.O.

Evans, Sir (Robert) Charles, Kt.

Evans, Sir (William) Vincent (John), G.C.M.G., M.B.E., Q.C.

Eveleigh, *Rt. Hon.* Sir Edward Walter, Kt., E.R.D.

Everard, *Maj.-Gen.* Sir Christopher Earle Welby-, K.B.E., C.B.

Everard, Sir Robin Charles, Bt. (1911).

Everson, Sir Frederick Charles, K.C.M.G.

Every, Sir John Simon, Bt. (1641).

Evetts, *Lt.-Gen.* Sir John Fullerton, Kt., C.B., C.B.E., M.C.

Ewans, Sir Martin Kenneth, K.C.M.G.

Ewart, Sir (William) Ivan (Cecil), Bt., D.S.C. (1887).

Ewbank, *Hon.* Sir Anthony Bruce, Kt.

Ewin, Sir (David) Ernest Thomas Floyd, Kt., O.B.E., M.V.O.

Ewing, *Vice-Adm.* Sir (Robert) Alastair, K.B.E., C.B., D.S.C.

Ewing, Sir Ronald Archibald Orr-, Bt. (1886).

Eyre, *Maj.-Gen.* Sir James Ainsworth Campden Gabriel, K.C.V.O., C.B.E.

Eyre, Sir Reginald Edwin, Kt.

Faber, Sir Richard Stanley, K.C.V.O., C.M.G.

Fadahunsi, Sir Joseph Odeleye, K.C.M.G.

Fagge, Sir John William Frederick, Bt. (1660).

Fairbairn, *Hon.* Sir David Eric, K.B.E., D.F.C.

Fairbairn, Sir (James) Brooke, Bt. (1869).

Fairbairn, Sir Nicholas Hardwick, Kt., Q.C., M.P.

Fairfax, Sir Vincent Charles, Kt., C.M.G.

Fairgrieve, Sir (Thomas) Russell, Kt., C.B.E., T.D.

Fairhall, *Hon.* Sir Allen, K.B.E.

Falconer, *Hon.* Sir Douglas William, Kt., M.B.E.

Falk, Sir Roger Salis, Kt., O.B.E.

Falkiner, Sir Edmond Charles, Bt. (I. 1778).

Falkner, Sir (Donald) Keith, Kt.

Falle, Sir Samuel, K.C.M.G., K.C.V.O., D.S.C.

Falvey, *Hon.* Sir John Neil, K.B.E., Q.C.

Faridkot, *Col.* H.H. the Raja of, K.C.S.I.

Farmer, Sir (Lovedin) George Thomas, Kt.

Farndale, *Gen.* Sir Martin Baker, K.C.B.

Farquhar, Sir Michael Fitzroy Henry, Bt. (1796).

Farquharson, *Hon.* Sir Donald Henry, Kt.

Farquharson, Sir James Robbie, K.B.E.

Farr, Sir John Arnold, Kt., M.P.

Farrar-Hockley, *Gen.* Sir Anthony Heritage, G.B.E., K.C.B., D.S.O., M.C.

Farrer, Sir Charles Matthew, K.C.V.O.

Farrington, Sir Henry Francis Colden, Bt. (1818).

Faulkner, Sir Eric Odin, Kt., M.B.E.

Faulkner, Sir Percy, K.B.E., C.B.

Fawcus, Sir (Robert) Peter, K.B.E., C.M.G.

Fawkes, Sir Randol Francis, Kt.

Fawcett, Sir James Edmund Sandford, Kt., D.S.C., Q.C.

Fayrer, Sir John Lang Macpherson, Bt., (1896).

Feilden, Sir Bernard Melchior, Kt., C.B.E.

Feilden, Sir Henry Wemyss, Bt., (1846).

Feldman, Sir Basil Samuel, Kt.

Fell, Sir Anthony, Kt.

Fennessy, Sir Edward, Kt., C.B.E.

Ferens, Sir Thomas Robinson, Kt., C.B.E.

Ferguson, *Lt.-Col.* Sir Neil Edward Johnson-, Bt., T.D. (1906).

Fergusson of Kilkerran, Sir Charles, Bt. (s. 1703).

Fergusson, Sir Ewan Alastair John, K.C.M.G.

Fergusson, Sir James Herbert Hamilton Colyer-, Bt. (1866).

Feroze, Sir Rustam Moolan, Kt., F.R.C.S.

ffolkes, Sir Robert Francis Alexander, Bt. (1774).

Fieldhouse, Sir Harold, K.B.E., C.B.

Fieldhouse, *Admiral of the Fleet* Sir John David Elliott, G.C.B., G.B.E.

Fielding, Sir Colin Cunningham, Kt., C.B.

Fielding, Sir Leslie, K.C.M.G.

Fiennes, Sir John Saye Wingfield Twisleton-Wykeham-, K.C.B., Q.C.

Fiennes, Sir Maurice Alberic Twisleton-Wykeham-, Kt.

Fiennes, Sir Ranulph Twisleton-Wykeham-, Bt. (1916).

Figg, Sir Leonard Clifford William, K.C.M.G.

Figgess, Sir John George, K.B.E., C.M.G.

Figgures, Sir Frank Edward, K.C.B., C.M.G.

Figures, Sir Colin Frederick, K.C.M.G., O.B.E.

Fingland, Sir Stanley James Gunn, K.C.M.G.

Finlay, Sir David Ronald James Bell, Bt. (1964).

Finley, Sir Peter Hamilton, Kt., O.B.E., D.F.C.

Finniston, Sir (Harold) Montague, Kt., Ph.D., F.R.S.

Finsberg, Sir Geoffrey, Kt., M.B.E., M.P.

Firth, *Prof.* Sir Raymond William, Kt., Ph.D., F.B.A.

Fisher, *Sir Antony George Anson, Kt., A.F.C.

Fisher, Sir George Read, Kt., C.M.G.

Fisher, *Hon.* Sir Henry Arthur Pears, Kt.

Fisher, Sir Nigel Thomas Loveridge, Kt., M.C.

Fison, Sir (Richard) Guy, Bt., D.S.C. (1905).

Fitch, *Adm.* Sir Richard George Alison, K.C.B.

Fitzgerald, *Rev.* (Sir) Edward Thomas, Bt. (1903).

FitzGerald, Sir George Peter Maurice, Bt., M.C., *The Knight of Kerry* (1880).

FitzGerald, Sir William James, Kt., M.C., Q.C.

FitzHerbert, Sir John Richard Frederick, Bt. (1784).

Fitzmaurice, *Lt.-Col.* Sir Desmond FitzJohn, Kt., C.I.E.

Fitzpatrick, *Gen.* Sir (Geoffrey Richard) Desmond, G.C.B., D.S.O., M.B.E., M.C.

Fitzpatrick, *Air Marshal* Sir John Bernard, K.B.E., C.B.

Flanagan, Sir James Bernard, Kt., C.B.E.

Flavelle, Sir (Joseph) David Ellsworth, Bt. (1917).

Fleming, Sir Charles Alexander, K.B.E., F.R.S.

Fleming, *Instructor Rear-Adm.* Sir John, K.B.E., D.S.C.

Fleming, *Rt. Rev.* (William) Launcelot Scott, K.C.V.O., D.D.

Fletcher, *Hon.* Sir Alan Roy, Kt.

Fletcher, Sir Alexander MacPherson, Kt.

Fletcher, Sir James Muir Cameron, Kt.

Fletcher, Sir John Henry Lancelot Aubrey-, Bt. (1782).

Fletcher, Sir Leslie, Kt., D.S.C.

Fletcher, Sir Norman Seymour, Kt.

Fletcher, *Air Chief Marshal* Sir Peter Carteret, K.C.B., O.B.E., D.F.C., A.F.C.

Floyd, Sir Giles Henry Charles, Bt. (1816).

Foley, Sir (Thomas John) Noel, Kt., C.B.E.

Foot, Sir Geoffrey James, Kt.

Foots, Sir James William, Kt.

Forbes, *Hon.* Sir Alastair Granville, Kt.

Forbes, Sir Archibald Finlayson, G.B.E.

Forbes of Pitsligo, Sir Charles Edward Stuart-, Bt. (s. 1626).

Forbes of Brux, *Hon.* Sir Ewan, Bt. (s. 1630).

Forbes, *Vice-Adm.* Sir John Morrison, K.C.B.

Forbes, *Maj.* Sir Hamish Stewart, Bt., M.B.E., M.C. (1823).

Ford, *Capt.* Sir Aubrey St. Clair-, Bt., D.S.O., R.N. (1793).

Ford, Sir David Robert, K.B.E., L.V.O., O.B.E.

Ford, *Maj.* Sir Edward William Spencer, K.C.B., K.C.V.O.

Ford, *Air Marshal* Sir Geoffrey Harold, K.B.E., C.B.

Ford, Sir Henry Russell, Bt. (1929).

Ford, *Prof.* Sir Hugh, Kt., F.R.S.

Ford, Sir John Archibald, K.C.M.G., M.C.

Ford, *Maj.-Gen.* Sir Peter St. Clair-, K.B.E., C.B., D.S.O.

Ford, Sir Richard Brinsley, Kt., C.B.E.

Ford, *Gen.* Sir Robert Cyril, G.C.B., C.B.E.

Foreman, Sir Philip Frank, Kt., C.B.E.

Forman, Sir John Denis, Kt., O.B.E.

Forrest, *Prof.* Sir (Andrew) Patrick (McEwen), Kt.

Forrest, Sir James Alexander, Kt.

Forrest, *Rear-Adm.* Sir Ronald Stephen, K.C.V.O.

Forster, Sir Archibald William, Kt.

Forster, Sir Oliver Grantham, K.C.M.G., M.V.O.

Forwood, Sir Dudley Richard, Bt. (1895).

Foster, *Prof.* Sir Christopher David, Kt.

Foster, Sir John Gregory, Bt. (1930).

Foster, Sir Robert Sidney, G.C.M.G., K.C.V.O.

Foulis, Sir Ian Primrose Liston-, Bt. (s. 1634).

Foulkes, Sir Nigel Gordon, Kt.

Fowden, Sir Leslie, Kt., F.R.S.

†Fowke, Sir David Frederick Gustavus, Bt. (1814).

Fowler, Sir (Edward) Michael Coulson, Kt.

Fox, Sir (Henry) Murray, G.B.E.

Fox, Sir (John) Marcus, Kt., M.B.E., M.P.

Fox, *Rt. Hon.* Sir Michael John, Kt.

Fox, Sir Theodore Fortescue, Kt., M.D., Ll.D.

Frame, Sir Alistair Gilchrist, Kt.

France, Sir Arnold William, G.C.B.

Francis, Sir Frank Chalton, K.C.B., F.S.A.

Frank, Sir Douglas George Horace, Kt., Q.C.

Frank, Sir (Frederick) Charles, Kt., O.B.E., F.R.S.

†Frank, Sir Robert Andrew, Bt. (1920).

Frankel, Sir Otto Herzberg, Kt., D.S.C., F.R.S.

Franklin, Sir Eric Alexander, Kt., C.B.E.

Franklin, Sir Michael David Milroy, K.C.B., C.M.G.

Franks, Sir Arthur Temple, K.C.M.G., T.D.

Fraser, Sir Angus McKay, K.C.B., T.D.

Fraser, Sir Basil Malcolm, Bt. (1921).

Fraser, Sir Bruce Donald, K.C.B.

Fraser, *Gen.* Sir David William, G.C.B., O.B.E.

Fraser, Sir Douglas Were, Kt., I.S.O.

Fraser, *Air Marshal Rev.* Sir (Henry) Paterson, K.B.E., C.B., A.F.C.

Fraser, Sir Ian, Kt., D.S.O., O.B.E.

Fraser, Sir Ian James, Kt., C.B.E., M.C.

Fraser, Sir (James) Campbell, Kt.

Fraser, *Prof.* Sir James David, Bt. (1943).

Fraser, Sir William Kerr, G.C.B.

Frederick, Sir Charles Boscawen, Bt. (1723).

Freeland, Sir John Redvers, K.C.M.G.

Freeman, *His Eminence Cardinal* James Darcy, K.B.E.

Freeman, Sir James Robin, Bt. (1945).

Freeman, Sir Ralph, Kt., C.V.O., C.B.E.

Freer, *Air Chief Marshal* Sir Robert William George, G.B.E., K.C.B.

Freeth, *Hon.* Sir Gordon, K.B.E.

French, *Hon.* Sir Christopher James Saunders, Kt.

Fretwell, Sir George Herbert, K.B.E., C.B.

Fretwell, Sir (Major) John (Emsley), G.C.M.G.

Freud, Sir Clement Raphael, Kt.

Froggatt, Sir Leslie Trevor, Kt.

Froggatt, Sir Peter, Kt.

Frossard, Sir Charles Keith, Kt.

Frost, *Hon.* Sir (Thomas) Sydney, Kt.

Fry, *Hon.* Sir William Gordon, Kt.

Fryberg, Sir Abraham, Kt., M.B.E.

Fuchs, Sir Vivian Ernest, Kt., Ph.D.

Fuller, *Hon.* Sir John Bryan Munro, Kt.

Fuller, Sir John William Fleetwood, Bt. (1910).

Fung, *Hon.* Sir Kenneth Ping-Fan, Kt., C.B.E.

Furness, Sir Stephen Roberts, Bt. (1913).

Gadsden, Sir Peter Drury Haggerston, G.B.E.

Gage, Sir Berkeley Everard Foley, K.C.M.G.

Gairy, *Rt. Hon.* Sir Eric Matthew, Kt.

Gaius, *Rt. Rev.* Saimon, K.B.E.

Gallwey, Sir Philip Frankland Payne-, Bt. (1812).

Galsworthy, Sir John Edgar, K.C.V.O., C.M.G.

Gamble, Sir David Hugh Norman, Bt. (1897).

Gandell, Sir Alan Thomas, Kt., C.B.E.

Ganilau, *Ratu* Sir Penaia Kanatabatu, G.C.M.G., K.C.V.O., K.B.E., D.S.O.

Gardner, Sir Douglas Bruce Bruce-, Bt. (1945).

Gardner, Sir Edward Lucas, Kt., Q.C.

Gardner-Thorpe, *Col.* Sir Ronald, G.B.E., T.D.

Garland, *Hon.* Sir Patrick Neville, Kt.

Garland, *Hon.* Sir Ransley Victor, K.B.E.

Garlick, Sir John, K.C.B.

Garner, Sir Anthony Stuart, Kt.

Garran, Sir (Isham) Peter, K.C.M.G.

Garrett, *Hon.* Sir Raymond William, Kt., A.F.C.

Garrioch, Sir (William) Henry, Kt.

Garrod, *Lt. Gen.* Sir John Martin Carruthers, K.C.B., O.B.E.

Garthwaite, Sir William Francis Cuthbert, Bt., D.S.C. (1919).

Garvey, Sir Ronald Herbert, K.C.M.G., K.C.V.O., M.B.E.

Gascoigne, *Maj.-Gen.* Sir Julian Alvery, K.C.M.G., K.C.V.O., C.B., D.S.O.

Gatehouse, *Hon.* Sir Robert Alexander, Kt.

Geddes, Sir (Anthony) Reay (Mackay), K.B.E.

Gentry, *Maj.-Gen.* Sir William George, K.B.E., C.B., D.S.O.

George, Sir Arthur Thomas, Kt.

Gerken, *Vice-Adm.* Sir Robert William Frank, K.C.B., C.B.E.

Gethin, *Lt.-Col.* Sir Richard Patrick St. Lawrence, Bt. (1 1665).

Ghurburrun, Sir Rabindrah, Kt.

Gibb, Sir Francis Ross (Frank), Kt., C.B.E.

Gibbon, *Gen.* Sir John Houghton, G.C.B., O.B.E.

Gibbons, Sir (John) David, K.B.E.

Gibbons, Sir William Edward Doran, Bt. (1752).

Gibbs, *Hon.* Sir Eustace Hubert Beilby, K.C.V.O., C.M.G.

Gibbs, *Air Marshal* Sir Gerald Ernest, K.B.E., C.I.E., M.C.

Gibbs, *Rt. Hon.* Sir Harry Talbot, G.C.M.G., K.B.E.

Gibbs, *Rt. Hon.* Sir Humphrey Vicary, G.C.V.O., K.C.M.G., O.B.E.

Gibbs, *Field Marshal* Sir Roland Christopher, G.C.B., C.B.E., D.S.O., M.C.

Gibson, Sir Alexander Drummond, Kt., C.B.E.

Gibson, Sir Christopher Herbert, Bt. (1931).

Gibson, *Rev.* Sir David, Bt. (1926).

Gibson, *Vice-Adm.* Sir Donald Cameron Ernest Forbes, K.C.B., D.S.C.

Gibson, Sir Donald Evelyn Edward, Kt., C.B.E.

Gibson, *Hon.* Sir Peter Leslie, Kt.

Gibson, *Rt. Hon.* Sir Ralph Brian, Kt.

Gibson, Sir Ronald George, Kt., C.B.E., F.R.C.S.

Giddings, *Air Marshal* Sir (Kenneth Charles) Michael, K.C.B., O.B.E., D.F.C., A.F.C.

Gielgud, Sir (Arthur) John, Kt., C.H.

Giffard, Sir (Charles) Sydney (Rycroft), K.C.M.G.

Gilbert, *Brig.* Sir Herbert Ellery, K.B.E., D.S.O.

Gilbert, *Air Chief Marshal* Sir Joseph Alfred, K.C.B., C.B.E.

Gilbertson, Sir Geoffrey, Kt., C.B.E.

Gilbey, Sir (Walter) Derek, Bt. (1893).

Gilchrist, Sir Andrew Graham, K.C.M.G.

Giles, Sir Alexander Falconer, K.B.E., C.M.G.

Gilkison, Sir Alan Fleming, Kt., C.B.E.

Gillett, *Maj.-Gen.* Sir Peter Bernard, K.C.V.O., C.B., O.B.E.

Gillett, Sir Robin Danvers Penrose, Bt., G.B.E., R.D. (1959).

Gilliat, *Lt.-Col.* Sir Martin John, G.C.V.O., M.B.E.

Gilmour, *Rt. Hon.* Sir Ian Hedworth John Little, Bt., M.P. (1926).

Gilmour, Sir John Edward, Bt., D.S.O., T.D. (1897).

Gingell, *Air Chief Marshal* Sir John, G.B.E., K.C.B.

Girolami, Sir Paul, Kt.

Gladstone, Sir (Erskine) William, Bt. (1846).

Glass, Sir Leslie Charles, K.C.M.G.

Glasspole, Sir Florizel Augustus, G.C.M.G., G.C.V.O.

Glen, Sir Alexander Richard, K.B.E., D.S.C.

Glenn, Sir (Joseph Robert) Archibald, Kt., O.B.E.

Glidewell, *Rt. Hon.* Sir Iain Derek Laing, Kt.

Glock, Sir William Frederick, Kt., C.B.E.

Glover, *Gen.* Sir James Malcolm, K.C.B., M.B.E

Glyn, Sir Anthony Geoffrey Leo Simon, Bt. (1927).

Glyn, Sir Richard Lindsay, Bt., (1759 and 1800).

Goad, Sir (Edward) Colin (Viner), K.C.M.G.

Godber, Sir George Edward, G.C.B., D.M.

Goff, Sir Robert (William) Davis-, Bt. (1905).

Gold, Sir Arthur Abraham, Kt., C.B.E.

Gold, Sir Joseph, Kt.

Goldberg, *Prof.* Sir Abraham, Kt., M.D., D.SC., F.R.C.P.

Golding, Sir John Simon Rawson, Kt., O.B.E

Golding, Sir William Gerald, Kt., C.B.E.

Goldman, Sir Samuel, K.C.B.

Goldsmith, Sir James Michael, Kt.

Gombrich, *Prof.* Sir Ernst Hans Josef, Kt., C.B.E., PH.D., F.B.A., F.S.A.

Gooch, Sir (Richard) John Sherlock, Bt. (1746).

Gooch, Sir Robert Douglas, Bt. (1866).

Goodall, Sir (Arthur) David Saunders, K.C.M.G.

Goodall, Sir Reginald, Kt., C.B.E.

Goodenough, Sir Richard Edmund, Bt. (1943).

Goodhart, Sir Philip Carter, Kt., M.P.

Goodhart, Sir Robert Anthony Gordon, Bt. (1911).

Goodhew, Sir Victor Henry, Kt.

Goodison, Sir Alan Clowes, K.C.M.G.

Goodison, Sir Nicholas Proctor, Kt.

Goodson, Sir Mark Weston Lassam, Bt. (1922).

Goody, *Most Rev.* Launcelot John, K.B.E.

Goold, Sir George Leonard, Bt. (1801).

Goold, Sir James Duncan, Kt.

Gordon, Sir Alexander John, Kt., C.B.E.

Gordon, Sir Andrew Cosmo Lewis Duff-, Bt. (1813).

Gordon, Sir Charles Addison Somerville Snowden, K.C.B.

Gordon, Sir Keith Lyndell, Kt., C.M.G.

Gordon, Sir (Lionel) Eldred (Peter) Smith-, Bt. (1838).

Gordon, Sir Robert James, Bt. (s. 1706).

Gordon, Sir Sidney Samuel, Kt., C.B.E.

Gore, Sir Richard Ralph St. George, Bt. (I. 1622).

Goring, Sir William Burton Nigel, Bt. (1627).

Gorton, *Rt. Hon.* Sir John Grey, G.C.M.G., C.H.

Goschen, Sir Edward Christian, Bt., D.S.O. (1916).

Gosling, Sir (Frederick) Donald, Kt.

Goulding, Sir (Ernest) Irvine, Kt.

Goulding, Sir (William) Lingard Walter, Bt. (1904).

Gourlay, *Gen.* Sir (Basil) Ian (Spencer), K.C.B., O.B.E., M.C., R.M.

Govan, Sir Lawrence Herbert, Kt.

Gow, *Gen.* Sir (James) Michael, G.C.B.

Gowans, *Hon.* Sir (Urban) Gregory, Kt.

Gowans, Sir James Learmonth, Kt., C.B.E., F.R.C.P., F.R.S.

Gower, Sir (Herbert) Raymond, Kt., M.P.

Gowing, *Prof.* Sir Lawrence Burnett, Kt., C.B.E.

Graaff, Sir de Villiers, Bt., M.B.E. (1911).

Grabham, Sir Anthony Henry, Kt.

Graesser, *Col.* Sir Alastair Stewart Durward, Kt., D.S.O., O.B.E., M.C., T.D.

Graham, Sir Charles Spencer Richard, Bt. (1783).

Graham, Sir James Bellingham, Bt. (1662).

Graham, Sir John Alexander Noble, Bt., K.G.M.G. (1906).

Graham, Sir John Moodie, Bt. (1964).

Graham, Sir (John) Patrick, Bt., C.B.

Graham, Sir Norman William, Kt., C.B.

Graham, Sir Peter Alfred, Kt., O.B.E.

Graham, Sir Ralph Wolfe, Bt. (1629).

Graham, *Hon.* Sir Samuel Horatio, Kt., C.M.G., O.B.E.

Grandy, *Marshal of the Royal Air Force* Sir John, G.C.B., G.C.V.O., K.B.E., D.S.O.

Grant, Sir Archibald, Bt. (s. 1705).

Grant, Sir Clifford, Kt.

Grant, Sir (John) Anthony, Kt., M.P.

Grant, Sir Kenneth Lindsay, Kt., O.B.E.

Grant, Sir Patrick Alexander Benedict, Bt. (s. 1688).

Grantham, *Adm.* Sir Guy, G.C.B., C.B.E., D.S.O.

Granville, Sir Keith, Kt., C.B.E.

Gray, Sir John Archibald Browne, Kt., SC.D., F.R.S.

Gray, *Vice-Adm.* Sir John Michael Dudgeon, K.B.E., C.B.

Gray, *Lt.-Gen.* Sir Michael Stuart, K.C.B., O.B.E.

Gray, Sir William Hume, Bt. (1917).

Gray, Sir William Stevenson, Kt.

†Grayson, Sir Rupert Stanley Harrington, Bt. (1922).

Greatbatch, Sir Bruce, Kt., K.C.V.O., C.M.G., M.B.E.

Green, Sir (Edward) Stephen (Lycett), Bt., C.B.E. (1886).

Green, Sir George Ernest, Kt.

Green, *Hon.* Sir Guy Stephen Montague, K.B.E.

Green, Sir Kenneth, Kt.

Green, Sir Owen Whitley, Kt.

Green, Sir Peter James Frederick, Kt.

Greenaway, Sir Derek Burdick, Bt., C.B.E. (1933).

Greenborough, Sir John, K.B.E.

Greene, Sir (John) Brian Massy-, Kt.

Greengross, Sir Alan David, Kt.

Greening, *Rear-Adm.* Sir Paul Woollven, K.C.V.O.

Greenwell, Sir Edward Bernard, Bt. (1906).

Greeves, *Maj.-Gen.* Sir Stuart, K.B.E., C.B., D.S.O., M.C.

Gregson, Sir Peter Lewis, K.C.B.

Grenside, Sir John Peter, Kt., C.B.E.

Gretton, *Vice-Adm.* Sir Peter William, K.C.B., D.S.O., O.B.E., D.S.C.

Grey, Sir Anthony Dysart, Bt. (1814).

Grey, Sir Paul Francis, K.C.M.G.

†Grierson, Sir Michael John Bewes, Bt. (s. 1685).

Grieve, *Prof.* Sir Robert, Kt.

Griffin, *Adm.* Sir Anthony Templer Frederick Griffith, G.C.B.

Griffin, Sir (Charles) David, Kt., C.B.E.

Griffin, Sir John Bowes, Kt., Q.C.

Griffiths, Sir Eldon Wylie, Kt., M.P.

Griffiths, Sir (Ernest) Roy, Kt.

Griffiths, Sir Percival Joseph, K.B.E., C.I.E.

Griffiths, Sir John Norton-, Bt. (1922).

Griffiths, Sir Reginald Ernest, Kt., C.B.E.

Grimwade, Sir Andrew Sheppard, Kt., C.B.E.

Grindrod, *Most Rev.* John Basil Rowland, K.B.E.

Grinstead, Sir Stanley Gordon, Kt.

Groom, Sir (Thomas) Reginald, Kt.

Groom, *Air Marshal* Sir Victor Emmanuel, K.C.V.O., K.B.E., C.B., D.F.C.

Grotrian, Sir Philip Christian Brent, Bt. (1934).

Grove, Sir Charles Gerald, Bt. (1874).

Grove, Sir Edmund Frank, K.C.V.O.

Groves, Sir Charles Barnard, Kt., C.B.E.

Grugeon, Sir John Drury, Kt.

Guinness, Sir Alec, Kt., C.B.E.

Guinness, Sir Howard Christian Sheldon, Kt., V.R.D.

Guinness, Sir Kenelm Ernest Lee, Bt. (1867).

Guise, Sir John, G.C.M.G., K.B.E.

Guise, Sir John Grant, Bt. (1783).

Gujadhur, Sir Radhamohun, Kt., C.M.G.

Gull, Sir Michael Swinnerton Cameron, Bt. (1872).

Gunn, *Prof.* Sir John Currie, Kt., C.B.E.

Gunn, Sir William Archer, K.B.E., C.M.G.

Gunning, Sir Robert Charles, Bt. (1778).

Gunston, Sir Richard Wellesley, Bt. (1938).

Gurden, Sir Harold Edward, Kt.

Guthrie, Sir Malcolm Connop, Bt., (1936)

Guthrie, *Hon.* Sir Rutherford Campbell, Kt., C.M.G.

Guy, *Gen.* Sir Roland Kelvin, G.C.B., C.B.E., D.S.O.

Gwynne-Evans, Sir Francis Loring, Bt. (1913).

Habakkuk, Sir John Hrothgar, Kt., F.B.A.

Hackett, *Gen.* Sir John Winthrop, G.C.B., C.B.E., D.S.O., M.C.

Hadley, Sir Leonard Albert, Kt.

Hadow, Sir Gordon, Kt., C.M.G., O.B.E.

Hadow, Sir (Reginald) Michael, K.C.M.G.

Hague, *Prof.* Sir Douglas Chalmers, Kt., C.B.E.

Halberg, Sir Murray Gordon, Kt., M.B.E.

Hale, *Prof.* Sir John Rigby, Kt

Hall, Sir Arnold Alexander, Kt., F.R.S.

Hall, Sir Basil Brodribb, K.C.B., M.C., T.D.

Hall, *Air Marshal* Sir Donald Percy, K.C.B., C.B.E., A.F.C.

Hall, Sir Douglas Basil, Bt., K.C.M.G. (s. 1687)

Hall, Sir (Frederick) John (Frank), Bt. (1923).

Hall, Sir John Bernard, Bt. (1919).

Hall, Sir Peter Reginald Frederick, Kt., C.B.E.

Hall, Sir Robert de Zouche, K.C.M.G.

Hall, *Brig.* Sir William Henry, K.B.E., D.S.O., E.D.

Halliday, Sir George Clifton, Kt.

Halliday, *Vice-Adm.* Sir Roy William, K.B.E., D.S.C.

Hallifax, *Adm.* Sir David John, K.C.B., K.B.E.

Hallinan, Sir (Adrian) Lincoln, Kt.

Halpern, Sir Ralph Mark, Kt.

Halsey, *Rev.* Sir John Walter Brooke, Bt. (1920).

Halstead, Sir Ronald, Kt., C.B.E.

Hambling, Sir (Herbert) Hugh, Bt. (1924).

Hamburger, Sir Sidney Cyril, Kt., C.B.E.

Hamer, *Hon.* Sir Rupert James, K.C.M.G., E.D.

Hamill, Sir Patrick, Kt., Q.P.M.

Hamilton, Sir Edward Sydney, Bt. (1776 and 1819).

Hamilton, Sir James Arnot, K.C.B., M.B.E.

Hamilton, *Adm.* Sir John Graham, G.B.E., C.B.

Hamilton, Sir Michael Aubrey, Kt.

Hamilton, Sir Patrick George, Bt. (1937).

Hamilton, Sir (Robert Charles) Richard Caradoc, Bt. (s. 1646).

Hamilton, Sir Bruce Stirling-, Bt. (s. 1673).

Hammett, *Hon.* Sir Clifford James, Kt.

Hammick, Sir Stephen George, Bt. (1834).

Hampshire, Sir Stuart Newton, Kt., F.B.A.

Hanbury, Sir John Capel, Kt., C.B.E.

Hancock, *Lt.-Col.* Sir Cyril Percy, K.C.I.E., O.B.E., M.C.

Hancock, Sir David John Stowell, K.C.B.

Hancock, *Air Marshal* Sir Valston Eldridge, K.B.E., C.B., D.F.C.

Hand, *Most Rev.* Geoffrey David, K.B.E.

Handley, Sir David John Davenport-, Kt., O.B.E.

Hanham, Sir Michael William, Bt., D.F.C. (1667).

Hanley, Sir Michael Bowen, K.C.B.

Hanmer, Sir John Wyndham Edward, Bt. (1774).

Hannay, Sir David Hugh Alexander, K.C.M.G.

Hanson, Sir Anthony Leslie Oswald, Bt. (1887).

Hanson, Sir (Charles) John, Bt. (1918).

Harcourt-Smith, *Air Chief Marshal* Sir David, K.C.B., D.F.C.

Harders, Sir Clarence Waldemar, Kt., O.B.E.

Hardie, Sir Charles Edgar Mathewes, Kt., C.B.E.

Harding, Sir George William, K.C.M.G., C.V.O.

Harding, *Air Chief Marshal* Sir Peter Robin, G.C.B.

Harding, Sir Roy Pollard, Kt., C.B.E.

Hardinge, Sir Robert Arnold, Bt. (1801).

Hardingham, Sir Robert Ernest, Kt., C.M.G., O.B.E.

Hardman, Sir Fred, Kt., M.B.E.

Hardman, Sir Henry, K.C.B.

Hardy, Sir James Gilbert, Kt., O.B.E.

Hardy, Sir Rupert John, Bt., (1876).

Hare, Sir Thomas, Bt. (1818).

Harford, Sir James Dundas, K.B.E., C.M.G.

Harford, Sir (John) Timothy, Bt. (1934).

Hargroves, *Brig.* Sir Robert Louis, Kt., C.B.E.

Harington, *Gen.* Sir Charles Henry Pepys, G.C.B., C.B.E., D.S.O., M.C.

Harington, Sir Nicholas John, Bt. (1611).

Harland, *Air Marshal* Sir Reginald Edward Wynyard, K.B.E., C.B.

Harley, Sir Thomas Winlack, Kt., M.B.E., M.C.

Harman, *Gen.* Sir Jack Wentworth, G.C.B., O.B.E., M.C.

Harman, *Hon.* Sir Jeremiah LeRoy, Kt.

Harmer, Sir Frederic Evelyn, Kt., C.M.G.

Harmer, Sir (John) Dudley, Kt., O.B.E.

Harmsworth, Sir Hildebrand Harold, Bt. (1922).

Harper Gow, Sir Leonard Maxwell, Kt., M.B.E.

Harpham, Sir William, K.B.E., C.M.G.

Harris, *Prof.* Sir Alan James, Kt., C.B.E.

Harris, Sir Anthony Kyrle Travers, Bt. (1953).

Harris, *Prof.* Sir Charles Herbert Stuart-, Kt., C.B.E., M.D.

Harris, *Lt.-Gen.* Sir Ian Cecil, K.B.E., C.B., D.S.O.

Harris, Sir Jack Wolfred Ashford, Bt. (1932).

Harris, Sir Philip Charles, Kt.

Harris, Sir Ronald Montague Joseph, K.C.V.O., C.B.

Harris, Sir William Gordon, K.B.E., C.B.

Harris, Sir William Woolf, Kt., O.B.E.

Harrison, Sir Ernest Thomas, Kt., O.B.E..

Harrison, Sir Francis Alexander Lyle, Kt., M.B.E., Q.C.

Harrison, Sir Geoffrey Wedgwood, G.C.M.G., K.C.V.O.

Harrison, *Surgeon Vice-Adm.* Sir John Albert Bews, K.B.E.

Harrison, *Hon.* Sir (John) Richard, Kt., E.D.

Harrison, Sir Michael James Harwood, Bt. (1961).

Harrison, *Prof.* Sir Richard John, Kt., F.R.S.

Harrison, Sir (Robert) Colin, Bt. (1922).

Harrop, Sir Peter John, K.C.B.

Hart, Sir Byrne, Kt., C.B.E., M.C.

Hart, Sir Francis Edmund Turton-, K.B.E.

Hartley, *Air Marshal* Sir Christopher Harold, K.C.B., C.B.E., D.F.C., A.F.C.

Hartley, Sir Frank, Kt., C.B.E., Ph.D.

Hartopp, Sir John Edmund Cradock-, Bt. (1796).

Hartwell, Sir Brodrick William Charles Elwin, Bt. (1805).

Harvey, Sir Charles Richard Musgrave, Bt. (1933).

Harvey-Jones, Sir John Henry, Kt., M.B.E.

Haskard, Sir Cosmo Dugal Patrick Thomas, K.C.M.G., M.B.E.

Haslam, *Hon.* Sir Alec Leslie, Kt.

Haslam, *Rear-Adm.* Sir David William, K.B.E., C.B.

Haslam, Sir Robert, Kt.

Hasluck, *Rt. Hon.* Sir Paul Meernaa Caedwalla, K.G., G.C.M.G., G.C.V.O.

Hassan, Sir Joshua Abraham, G.B.E., K.C.M.G., L.V.O., Q.C.

Hassett, *Gen.* Sir Francis George, K.B.E., C.B., D.S.O., M.V.O.

Hastings, Sir Stephen Lewis Edmonstone, Kt., M.C.

Hatty, *Hon.* Sir Cyril James, Kt.

Haughton, Sir James, Kt., C.B.E., Q.P.M.

Havelock, Sir Wilfrid Bowen, Kt.

Hawker, Sir (Frank) Cyril, Kt.

Hawkings, Sir (Francis) Geoffrey, Kt.

Hawkins, Sir Arthur Ernest, Kt.

Hawkins, Sir Humphry Villiers Caesar, Bt. (1778).

Hawkins, Sir Paul Lancelot, Kt., T.D.

Hawley, Sir Donald Frederick, K.C.M.G., M.B.E.

†Hawley, Sir Henry Nicholas, Bt. (1795).

Haworth, Sir Philip, Bt. (1911).

Hawthorne, *Prof.* Sir William Rede, Kt., C.B.E., SC.D., F.R.S.

Hay, Sir Arthur Thomas Erroll, Bt., I.S.O. (s. 1663).

Hay, Sir David Osborne, Kt., C.B.E., D.S.O.

Hay, Sir Hamish Grenfell, Kt.

Hay, Sir James Brian Dalrymple-, Bt. (1798).

†Hay, Sir Ronald Nelson, Bt. (s. 1703).

Hayday, Sir Frederick, Kt., C.B.E.

Haydon, Sir Walter Robert, K.C.M.G.

Hayes, Sir Brian David, G.C.B.

Hayes, Sir Claude James, K.C.M.G.

Hayes, *Vice-Adm.* Sir John Osier Chattock, K.C.B., O.B.E.

Hayhoe, *Rt. Hon.* Sir Bernard John (Barney), Kt., M.P.

Hayman, Sir Peter Telford, K.C.M.G., C.V.O., M.B.E.

Hayr, *Air Marshal* Sir Kenneth William, K.C.B., C.B.E., A.F.C.

Hayter, Sir William Goodenough, K.C.M.G.

Hayward, Sir Alfred, K.B.E.

Hayward, Sir Anthony William Byrd, Kt.

Hayward, Sir Jack Arnold, Kt., O.B.E.

Hayward, Sir Richard Arthur, Kt., C.B.E.

Haywood, Sir Harold, K.C.V.O., O.B.E.

Hazan, *Hon.* Sir John Boris Roderick, Kt.

Head, Sir Francis David Somerville, Bt. (1838).

Healey, Sir Charles Edward Chadwyck-, Bt. (1919).

Heap, Sir Desmond, Kt.

Heath, Sir Mark Evelyn, K.C.V.O., C.M.G.

Heath, *Air Marshal* Sir Maurice Lionel, K.B.E., C.B., C.V.O.

Heathcoat Amory, Sir Ian, Bt. (1874).

Heathcote, *Brig.* Sir Gilbert Simon, Bt., C.B.E. (1733).

Heathcote, Sir Michael Perryman, Bt. (1733).

Heaton, Sir Yvo Robert Henniker-, Bt. (1912).

Heiser, Sir Terence Michael, K.C.B.

Hele, Sir Ivor Thomas Henry, Kt., C.B.E.

Hellaby, Sir (Frederick Reed) Alan, Kt.

Hellings, *Gen.* Sir Peter William Cradock, K.C.B., D.S.C., M.C., R.M.

Henare, Sir James Clendon Tau, K.B.E., D.S.O.

Henderson, Sir Guy Wilmot McLintock, Kt., Q.C.

Henderson, Sir James Thyne, K.B.E., C.M.G.

Henderson, Sir (John) Nicholas, G.C.M.G.

Henderson, *Adm.* Sir Nigel Stuart, G.B.E., K.C.B.

Henderson, Sir William MacGregor, Kt., D.SC., F.R.S.

Henley, Sir Douglas Owen, K.C.B.

Henley, *Rear-Adm.* Sir Joseph Charles Cameron, K.C.V.O., C.B.

Hennessy, Sir James Patrick Ivan, K.B.E., C.M.G.

Hennessy, Sir John Wyndham Pope-, Kt., C.B.E., F.B.A., F.S.A.

Henniker, *Brig.* Sir Mark Chandos Auberon, Bt., C.B.E., D.S.O., M.C. (1813).

Henry, Sir Denis Aynsley, Kt., O.B.E., Q.C.

Henry, *Hon.* Denis Robert Maurice, Kt.

Henry, Sir James Holmes, Bt., C.M.G., M.C., T.D., Q.C. (1923).

Henry, *Hon.* Sir Trevor Ernest, Kt.

Hepburn, Sir Ninian Buchan Archibald John Buchan-, Bt. (1815).

Herbecq, Sir John Edward, K.C.B.

Herbert, *Adm.* Sir Peter Geoffrey Marshall, K.C.B., O.B.E.

Hermon, Sir John Charles, Kt., O.B.E., Q.P.M.

Heron, Sir Conrad Frederick, K.C.B., O.B.E.

Herries, Sir Michael Alexander Robert Young-, Kt., O.B.E., M.C.

Heseltine, *Rt. Hon.* Sir William Frederick Payne, G.C.V.O., K.C.B.

Hetherington, Sir Arthur Ford, Kt., D.S.C.

Hetherington, Sir Thomas Chalmers, K.C.B., C.B.E., T.D., Q.C.

Heward, *Air Chief Marshal* Sir Anthony Wilkinson, K.C.B., O.B.E., D.F.C., A.F.C.

Hewetson, Sir Christopher Raynor, Kt., T.D.

Hewetson, *Gen.* Sir Reginald Hackett, G.C.B., C.B.E., D.S.O.

Hewett, Sir John George, Bt., M.C. (1813).

Hewitt, Sir (Cyrus) Lenox (Simson), Kt., O.B.E.

Hewitt, Sir Nicholas Charles Joseph, Bt. (1921).

Heygate, Sir George Lloyd, Bt. (1831).

Heyman, Sir Horace William, Kt.

Heywood, Sir Oliver Kerr, Bt. (1838).

Hezlet, *Vice-Adm.* Sir Arthur Richard, K.B.E., C.B., D.S.O., D.S.C.

Hibbert, Sir Reginald Alfred, G.C.M.G.

Hickey, Sir Justin, Kt.

Hickman, Sir (Richard) Glenn, Bt. (1903).

Hicks, Sir John Richard, Kt., F.B.A.

Hielscher, Sir Leo Arthur, Kt.

Higgins, Sir Christopher Thomas, Kt.

Higgs, Sir (John) Michael (Clifford), Kt.

Hildreth, *Maj.-Gen.* Sir (Harold) John (Crossley), K.B.E.

Hildyard, Sir David Henry Thoroton, K.C.M.G., D.F.C.

Hiley, *Hon.* Sir Thomas Alfred, K.B.E.

Hilgendorf, Sir Charles, Kt., C.M.G.

Hill, *Prof.* Sir Austin Bradford, Kt., C.B.E., Ph.D., D.SC., F.R.S.

Hill, Sir James Frederick, Bt. (1917).

Hill, Sir John McGregor, Kt., Ph.D.

Hill, Sir John Maxwell, Kt., C.B.E., D.F.C.

Hill, Sir Richard George Rowley, Bt., M.B.E. (I. 1779).

Hill, Sir Robert Erskine-, Bt. (1945).

Hillary, Sir Edmund, K.B.E.

Hills, Sir Graham John, Kt.

Himsworth, Sir Harold Percival, K.C.B., M.D., F.R.S.

Hine, *Air Chief Marshal* Sir Patrick Bardon, K.C.B.

Hines, Sir Colin Joseph, Kt., O.B.E.

Hinsley, *Prof.* Sir Francis Harry, Kt., O.B.E., F.B.A.

Hirsch, *Prof.* Sir Peter Bernhard, Kt., Ph.D., F.R.S.

Hirst, *Hon.* Sir David Cozens-Hardy, Kt.

Hoare, Sir Peter Richard David, Bt. (1786).

Hoare, Sir Timothy Edward Charles, Bt. (I. 1784).

Hobart, *Lt.-Cdr.* Sir Robert Hampden, Bt., R.N. (1914).

Hobday, Sir Gordon Ivan, Kt.

Hobhouse, Sir Charles Chisholm, Bt., T.D. (1812).

Hobhouse, *Hon.* Sir John Stewart, Kt.

Hobson, Sir Harold, Kt., C.B.E.

Hockaday, Sir Arthur Patrick, K.C.B., C.M.G.

Hodge, Sir John Rowland, Bt., M.B.E. (1921).

Hodge, Sir Julian Stephen Alfred, Kt.

Hodges, *Air Chief Marshal* Sir Lewis MacDonald, K.C.B., C.B.E., D.S.O., D.F.C.

Hodgkin, *Prof.* Sir Alan Lloyd, O.M., K.B.E., F.R.S., SC.D.

Hodgkinson, *Air Chief Marshal* Sir (William) Derek, K.C.B., C.B.E., D.F.C., A.F.C.

Hodgson, Sir Maurice Arthur Eric, Kt.

Hodgson, *Hon.* Sir (Walter) Derek (Thornley), Kt.

Hodson, Sir Michael Robin Adderloy, Bt. (I. 1789).

Hoffenberg, *Prof.* Sir Raymond, K.B.E.

Hoffman, *Hon.* Sir Leonard Hubert, Kt.

Hogg, *Maj.* Sir Arthur Ramsay, Bt., M.B.E. (1846).

Hogg, Sir Christopher Anthony, Kt.

†Hogg, Sir Edward William Lindsay-, Bt. (1905).

Hogg, *Vice-Adm.* Sir Ian Leslie Trower, K.C.B., D.S.C.

Hogg, Sir John Nicholson, Kt., T.D.

Holcroft, Sir Peter George Culcheth, Bt. (1921).

Holden, Sir David Charles Beresford, K.B.E., C.B., E.R.D.

Holden, Sir Edward, Bt. (1893).

Holden, Sir John David, Bt. (1919).

Holder, Sir John Henry, Bt. (1898).

Holder, *Air Marshal* Sir Paul Davie, K.B.E., C.B., D.S.O., D.F.C., Ph.D.

Holderness, Sir Richard William, Bt. (1920).

Holdsworth, Sir (George) Trevor, Kt.

Holland, Sir Clifton Vaughan, Kt.

Holland, Sir Guy (Hope), Bt. (1917).

Holland, Sir Kenneth Lawrence, Kt., C.B.E., Q.F.S.M.

Holland, Sir Philip Welsby, Kt.

Hollings, *Hon.* Sir (Alfred) Kenneth, Kt., M.C.

Hollis, *Hon.* Sir Anthony Barnard, Kt.

Hollom, Sir Jasper Quintus, K.B.E.

Holloway, *Hon.* Sir Barry Blyth, K.B.E.

Holm, Sir Carl Henry, Kt., O.B.E.

Holmes, *Prof.* Sir Frank Wakefield, Kt.

Holmes, Sir Maurice Andrew, Kt.

Holmes, Sir Peter Fenwick, Kt., M.C.

Holt, Sir James Richard, K.B.E.

Holt, Sir John Anthony Langford-, Kt.

Home, Sir David George, Bt. (s. 1671).

Hone, *Maj.-Gen.* Sir (Herbert) Ralph, K.C.M.G., K.B.E., M.C., T.D., Q.C.

Honywood, Sir Filmer Courtenay William, Bt. (1660).

Hood, Sir Alexander William Fuller-Acland-, Bt. (1806).

Hood, Sir Harold Joseph, Bt., T.D. (1922).

Hookway, Sir Harry Thurston, Kt.

Hoole, Sir Arthur Hugh, Kt.

Hooper, Sir Leonard James, K.C.M.G., C.B.E.

Hooper, Sir Robin William John, D.S.O., D.F.C.

Hope, Sir (Charles) Peter, K.C.M.G., T.D.

Hope, Sir John Carl Alexander, Bt. (s 1628).

Hope, Sir Robert Holms-Kerr, Bt. (1932)

Hopkin, Sir David Armand, Kt.

Hopkin, Sir (William Aylsham) Bryan, Kt., C.B.E.

Hopkins, *Adm.* Sir Frank Henry Edward, K.C.B., D.S.O., D.S.C.

Hopkins, Sir James Sidney Rawdon Scott-, Kt.

Hopkinson, Sir (Henry) Thomas, Kt., C.B.E.

Hordern, Sir Michael Murray, Kt., C.B.E.

Hordern, Sir Peter Maudslay, Kt., M.P.

Horlick, *Vice-Adm.* Sir Edwin John, K.B.E.

Horlick, Sir John James Macdonald, Bt. (1914).

Hornby, Sir Simon Michael, Kt.

Horne, Sir Alan Gray Antony, Bt. (1929).

Horsfall, Sir John Musgrave, Bt., M.C., T.D. (1909).

Horsley, *Air Marshal* Sir (Beresford) Peter (Torrington), K.C.B., C.B.E., M.V.O., A.F.C.

Hort, Sir James Fenton, Bt. (1767).

Hoskyns, Sir Benedict Leigh, Bt. (1676).

Hoskyns, Sir John Austin Hungerford Leigh, Kt.

Houldsworth, Sir (Harold) Basil, Bt. (1956).

Houldsworth, Sir Reginald Douglas Henry, Bt., O.B.E., T.D. (1887).

Hounsfield, Sir Godfrey Newbold, Kt., C.B.E.

House, *Lt.-Gen.* Sir David George, G.C.B., K.C.V.O., C.B.E., M.C.

Houssemayne du Boulay, Sir Roger William, K.C.V.O., C.M.G.

How, Sir Friston Charles, Kt., C.B.

Howard, Sir (Hamilton) Edward de Coucey, Bt., G.B.E. (1955).

Howard, *Prof.* Sir Michael Eliot, Kt., C.B.E., M.C.

Howard, *Maj.-Gen.* Lord Michael Fitzalan-, G.C.V.O., C.B., C.B.E., M.C.

Howard, Sir Walter Stewart, Kt., M.B.E.

Howe, *Rt. Hon.* Sir (Richard Edward) Geoffrey, Kt., Q.C., M.P.

Howie, Sir James William, Kt., M.D.

Howlett, *Gen.* Sir Geoffrey Hugh Whitby, K.B.E., M.C.

Hoyle, *Prof.* Sir Fred, Kt., F.R.S.

Hoyos, *Hon.* Sir Fabriciano Alexander, Kt.

Huckle, Sir (Henry) George, Kt., O.B.E.

Huddie, Sir David Patrick, Kt.

Hudleston, *Air Chief Marshal* Sir Edmund Cuthbert, G.C.B., C.B.E.

Hudson, Sir Havelock Henry Trevor, Kt.

Hudson, *Lt.-Gen.* Sir Peter, K.C.B., C.B.E.

Huggins, *Hon.* Sir Alan Armstrong, Kt.

Hugh-Jones, Sir Wynn Normington, Kt., M.V.O.

Hughes, Sir David Collingwood, Bt. (1773).

Hughes, *Prof.* Sir Edward Stuart Reginald, Kt., C.B.E.

Hughes, Sir Jack William, Kt.

Hughes, *Air Marshal* Sir (Sidney Weetman) Rochford, K.C.B., C.B.E., A.F.C.

Hughes, Sir Trevor Poulton, K.C.B.

Hughes, Sir Trevor Denby Lloyd-, Kt.

Hugo, *Lt.-Col.* Sir John Mandeville, K.C.V.O., O.B.E.

Hull, *Field Marshal* Sir Richard Amyatt, K.G., G.C.B., D.S.O.

Hulme, *Hon.* Sir Alan Shallcross, K.B.E.

Hulse, Sir (Hamilton) Westrow, Bt. (1739).

Hulton, Sir Edward George Warris, Kt.

Hulton, Sir Geoffrey Alan, Bt. (1905).

Hume, Sir Alan Blyth, Kt., C.B.

Humphreys, Sir Olliver William, Kt., C.B.E.

Humphreys, Sir (Raymond Evelyn) Myles, Kt.

Hunn, Sir Jack Kent, Kt., C.M.G.

Hunt, Sir David Wathen Stather, K.C.M.G., O.B.E.

Hunt, *Adm.* Sir Nicholas John Streynsham, G.C.B., L.V.O.

Hunt, *Gen.* Sir Peter Mervyn, G.C.B., D.S.O., O.B.E.

Hunt, Sir Rex Masterman, Kt., C.M.G.

Hunt, Sir Robert Frederick, Kt., C.B.E.

Hunter, *Hon.* Sir Alexander Albert, K.B.E.

Hunter, Sir Ian Bruce Hope, Kt., M.B.E.

Hurley, Sir John Garling, Kt., C.B.E.

Hurrell, Sir Anthony Gerald, K.C.V.O., C.M.G.

Hutchinson, *Hon.* Sir Ross, Kt., D.F.C.

Hutchison, *Lt.-Cdr.* Sir (George) Ian Clark, Kt., R.N.

Hutchison, *Hon.* Sir Michael, Kt.

Hutchison, Sir Peter, Bt. (1939).

Hutchison, Sir Peter Craft, Bt. (1956).

Hutchison, Sir (William) Kenneth, Kt., C.B.E., F.R.S.

Hutson, Sir Francis Challenor, Kt., C.B.E.

Hutton, *Hon.* Sir (James) Brian Edward, Kt.

Hutton, Sir Leonard, Kt.

Huxley, *Prof.* Sir Andrew Fielding, Kt., O.M., F.R.S.

Huxley, Sir Leonard George Holden, K.B.E., D.Phil., Ph.D.

Huxtable, *Gen.* Sir Charles Richard, K.C.B., C.B.E.

Hyatali, *Hon.* Sir Isaac Emanuel, Kt.

Ibbs, Sir (John) Robin, Kt., K.B.E.

Illingworth, *Prof.* Sir Charles Frederick William, Kt., C.B.E.

Imbert, Sir Peter Michael, Kt., Q.P.M.

Inch, Sir John Ritchie, Kt., C.V.O., C.B.E.

Inge, *Lt. Gen.* Sir Peter Anthony, K.C.B.

Ingilby, Sir Thomas Colvin William, Bt. (1866).

Inglefield, Sir Gilbert Samuel, G.B.E., T.D.

Inglefield, *Col.* Sir John Frederick Crompton-, Kt., T.D.

Inglis, Sir Brian Scott, Kt.

Inglis of Glencorse, Sir Roderick John, Bt. (s. 1703).

Ingram, Sir James Herbert Charles, Bt. (1893).

Innes, Sir Charles Kenneth Gordon, Bt. (N.S. 1686).

†Innes, Sir Peter Alexander Berowald, Bt. (s. 1628).

Inniss, *Hon.* Sir Clifford de Lisle, Kt.

Irish, Sir Ronald Arthur, Kt., O.B.E.

Irvine, *Rt. Hon.* Sir Bryant Godman, Kt.

Irving, *Rear-Adm.* Sir Edmund George, K.B.E., C.B.

Irwin, Sir James Campbell, Kt., O.B.E., E.D.

Isaac, Sir Neil, Kt.

Isham, Sir Ian Vere Gyles, Bt. (1627).

Issigonis, Sir Alec Arnold Constantine, Kt., C.B.E., F.R.S.

Jack, *Hon.* Sir Alieu Sulayman, Kt.

Jackman, *Air Marshal* Sir (Harold) Douglas, K.B.E., C.B.

Jackson, *Air Marshal* Sir Brendan James, K.C.B.

Jackson, Sir (John) Edward, K.C.M.G.

Jackson, *Hon.* Sir Lawrence Walter, K.C.M.G.

Jackson, Sir Michael Roland, Bt. (1902).

Jackson, Sir Nicholas Fane St. George, Bt. (1913).

Jackson, *Air Vice-Marshal* Sir Ralph Coburn, K.B.E., C.B.

Jackson, Sir Robert, Bt. (1815).

Jackson, *Cdr.* Sir Robert Gillman Allen, K.C.V.O., C.M.G., O.B.E.

Jackson, *Gen.* Sir William Godfrey Fothergill, G.B.E., K.C.B., M.C.

Jackson, Sir William Thomas, Bt. (1869).

Jacob, *Lt.-Gen.* Sir (Edward) Ian (Claud), G.B.E., C.B.

Jacob, Sir Isaac Hai, Kt., Q.C.

Jacobs, Sir David Anthony, Kt.

Jacobs, *Hon.* Sir Kenneth Sydney, K.B.E.

Jacobs, Sir Wilfred Ebenezer, G.C.M.G., G.C.V.O., O.B.E., Q.C.

Jacomb, Sir Martin Wakefield, Kt.

Jaffray, Sir William Otho, Bt. (1892).

Jagatsingh, *Hon.* Sir Kher, Kt.

Jakeway, Sir (Francis) Derek, K.C.M.G., O.B.E.

James, Sir Cynlais Morgan, K.C.M.G.

James, Sir Gerard Bowes Kingston, Bt. (1823).

Jamieson, *Air Marshal* Sir David Ewan, K.B.E., C.B.

Janion, *Rear-Adm.* Sir Hugh Penderel, K.C.V.O.

Janvrin, *Vice-Adm.* Sir (Hugh) Richard Benest, K.C.B., D.S.C.

Jardine, *Maj.* Sir (Andrew) Rupert (John) Buchanan-, Bt., M.C. (1885).

Jardine, Sir Andrew Colin Douglas, Bt. (1916).

Jardine of Applegirth, Sir Alexander Maule, Bt. (s. 1672).

Jarratt, Sir Alexander Anthony, Kt., C.B.

Jarrett, Sir Clifford George, K.B.E., C.B.

Jawara, *Hon.* Sir Dawda Kairaba, Kt.

Jay, Sir Antony Rupert, Kt.

Jeewoolall, Sir Ramesh, Kt.

Jeffcoate, Sir (Thomas) Norman (Arthur), Kt., M.D., F.R.C.S.

Jefferson, Sir George Rowland, Kt., C.B.E.

Jefferson, Sir Mervyn Stewart Dunnington-, Bt. (1958).

Jeffreys, Sir Harold, Kt., D.S.C., F.R.S.

Jehangir, Sir Hirji, Bt. (1908).

Jejeebhoy, Sir Rustom, Bt. (1857).

Jellicoe, Sir Geoffrey Alan, Kt., C.B.E., F.R.I.B.A.

Jenkins, Sir Owain Trevor, Kt.

Jenkinson, Sir Anthony Banks, Bt. (1661).

Jenks, Sir Richard Atherley, Bt. (1932).

Jennings, Sir Albert Victor, Kt.

Jennings, Sir Raymond Winter, Kt., Q.C.

Jennings, *Prof.* Sir Robert Yewdall, Kt., Q.C.

Jenour, Sir (Arthur) Maynard (Chesterfield), Kt., T.D.

Jephcott, *Hon.* Sir Bruce Reginald, Kt., C.B.E.

Jephcott, Sir (John) Anthony, Bt. (1962).

Jessel, Sir Charles John, Bt. (1883).

Joel, *Hon.* Sir Asher Alexander, K.B.E.

John, Sir Rupert Godfrey, Kt.

Johnson, Sir John Rodney, K.C.M.G.

Johnson, Sir Peter Colpoys Paley, Bt. (1755).

†Johnson, Sir Robin Eliot, Bt. (1818).

Johnson, Sir Ronald Ernest Charles, Kt., C.B.

Johnson Smith, Sir Geoffrey, Kt., M.P.

Johnston, Sir Alexander, G.C.., K.B.E.

Johnston, Sir Charles Collier, Kt., T.D.

Johnston, Sir (David) Russell, Kt., M.P.

Johnston, Sir John Baines, G.C.M.G., K.C.V.O.

Johnston, *Lt.-Col.* Sir John Frederick Dame, G.C.V.O., M.C.

Johnston, *Lt.-Gen.* Sir Maurice Robert, K.C.B., O.B.E.

Johnston, Sir Thomas Alexander, Bt. (s. 1626).

Johnstone, Sir Frederic Allan George, Bt. (s. 1700).

Jolliffe, Sir Anthony Stuart, G.B.E.

Jones, Sir Brynmor, Kt., Ph.D., SC.D.

Jones, Sir Christopher Lawrence-, Bt. (1831).

Jones, *Air Marshal* Sir Edward Gordon, K.C.B., C.B.E., D.S.O., D.F.C.

Jones, Sir (Edward) Martin Furnival, Kt., C.B.E.

Jones, *Rt. Hon.* Sir Edward Warburton, Kt.

Jones, Sir Ewart Ray Herbert, Kt., D.SC., Ph.D., F.R.S.

Jones, Sir Francis Avery, Kt., C.B.E., F.R.C.P.

Jones, *Air Marshal* Sir George, K.B.E., C.B., D.F.C.

Jones, Sir Glyn Smallwood, G.C.M.G., M.B.E.

Jones, Sir Harry Ernest, Kt., C.B.E.

Jones, Sir James Duncan, K.C.B.

Jones, Sir (John) Kenneth (Trevor), Kt., C.B.E., Q.C.

Jones, Sir John Lewis, K.C.B., C.M.G.

Jones, Sir John Prichard-, Bt. (1910).

Jones, Sir Keith Stephen, Kt.

Jones, *Hon.* Sir Kenneth George Illtyd, Kt.

Jones, *Air Marshal* Sir Laurence Alfred, K.C.B., C.B., A.F.C.

Jones, Sir (Owen) Trevor, Kt.

Jones, Sir Simon Warley Frederick Benton, Bt. (1919).

Jones, Sir (Thomas) Philip, Kt., C.D.

Jones, Sir (William) Elwyn (Edwards), Kt.

Jones, Sir (William) Emrys, Kt.

Jordan, *Air Marshal* Sir Richard Bowen, K.C.B., D.F.C.

Joseph, *Maj.* Sir (Herbert) Leslie, Kt.

Jugnauth, *Rt. Hon.* Sir Anerood, K.C.M.G., Q.C.

Jungius, *Vice-Adm.*, Sir James George, K.B.E.

Junor, Sir John Donald Brown, Kt.

Jupp, *Hon.* Sir Kenneth Graham, Kt., M.C.

Kalo, Sir Kwamala, Kt., M.B.E.

Kan Yuet-Keung, Sir, G.B.E.

Kapi, *Hon.* Sir Mari, Kt., C.B.E.

Karimjee, Sir Tayabali Hassanali Alibhoy, Kt.

Katsina, The Emir of, K.B.E., C.M.G.

Katz, Sir Bernard, Kt., F.R.S.

Kavali, Sir Thomas, Kt., O.B.E.

Kay, *Prof.* Sir Andrew Watt, Kt.

Kaye, Sir Emmanuel, Kt., C.B.E.

Kaye, Sir John Phillip Lister Lister-, Bt. (1812).

Kaye, Sir David Alexander Gordon, Bt. (1923).

Keane, Sir Richard Michael, Bt. (1801).

Keating, Sir Edgar Mayne, Kt., C.B.E.

Keeble, Sir (Herbert Ben) Curtis, G.C.M.G.

Keith, *Prof.* Sir James, K.B.E.

Kellett, Sir Brian Smith, Kt.

Kellett, Sir Stanley Charles, Bt. (1801).

Kelliher, Sir Henry Joseph, Kt.

Kelly, *Rt. Hon.* Sir (John William) Basil, Kt.

Kelly, Sir William Theodore, Kt., O.B.E.

Kemsley, *Col.* Sir Alfred Newcombe, K.B.E., C.M.G., E.D.

Kendrew, *Maj.-Gen.* Sir Douglas Anthony, K.C.M.G., C.B., C.B.E., D.S.O.

Kendrew, Sir John Cowdery, Kt., C.B.E., SC.D., F.R.S.

Kenilorea, *Rt. Hon.* Sir Peter, K.B.E.

Kennard, *Lt.-Col.* Sir George Arnold Ford, Bt. (1891)

Kennaway, Sir John Lawrence, Bt. (1791).

Kennedy, Sir Albert Henry, Kt.

Kennedy, Sir Clyde David Allen, Kt.

Kennedy, Sir Francis, K.C.M.G., C.B.E.

Kennedy, *Hon.* Sir Ian Alexander, Kt.

Kennedy, Sir Michael Edward, Bt., (1836).

Kennedy, *Hon.* Sir Paul Joseph Morrow, Kt.

Kennedy, *Air Chief Marshal* Sir Thomas Lawrie, G.C.B., A.F.C.

Kennedy-Good, Sir John, K.B.E.

Kennon, *Vice-Adm.* Sir James Edward Campbell, K.C.B., C.B.E.

Kenny, *Gen.* Sir Brian Leslie Graham, K.C.B., C.B.E.

Kenny, Sir Patrick John, Kt.

Kent, Sir Harold Simcox, G.C.B., Q.C.

Kenyon, Sir George Henry, Kt.

Kermode, Sir Ronald Graham Quale, K.B.E.

Kerr, *Rt. Hon.* Sir (John) Robert, G.C.M.G., G.C.V.O.

Kerr, *Rt. Hon.* Sir Michael Robert Emanuel, Kt.

Kerr, *Hon.* Sir Alastair Blair-, Kt.

Kerruish, Sir (Henry) Charles, Kt., O.B.E.

Kerry, Sir Michael James, K.C.B., Q.C.

Kershaw, Sir (John) Anthony, Kt., M.C.

Keswick, Sir William Johnston, Kt.

Keville, Sir (William) Errington, Kt., C.B.E.

Kidd, Sir Robert Hill, K.B.E., C.B.

Kidu, *Hon.* Sir Buri (William), Kt.

Kikau, *Ratu* Sir Jone Latianara, K.B.E.

Kiki, *Hon.* Sir (Albert) Maori, K.B.E.

Killen, *Hon.* Denis James, K.C.M.G.

Killick, Sir John Edward, G.C.M.G.

Kilpatrick, *Prof.* Sir Robert, Kt., C.B.E.

Kilpatrick, Sir William John, K.B.E.

Kimber, Sir Charles Dixon, Bt. (1904).

Kinahan, Sir Robert George Caldwell, Kt., E.R.D.

King, Sir Albert, Kt., O.B.E.

King, *Gen.* Sir Frank Douglas, G.C.B., M.B.E.

King, Sir James Granville Le Neve, Bt., T.D. (1888).

King, Sir Richard Brian Meredith, K.C.B., M.C.

King, Sir Sydney Percy, Kt., O.B.E.

King, Sir Wayne Alexander, Bt. (1815).

Kingman, *Prof.* Sir John Frank Charles, Kt., F.R.S.

Kingsland, Sir Richard, Kt., C.B.E., D.F.C.

Kingsley, Sir Patrick Graham Toler, K.C.V.O.

Kinloch, Sir David, Bt. (s. 1686).

Kinloch, Sir John, Bt. (1873).

Kirby, *Hon.* Sir Richard Clarence, Kt.

Kirkley, Sir (Howard) Leslie, Kt., C.B.E.

Kirkpatrick, Sir Ivone Elliott, Bt. (s. 1685).

Kirwan, Sir (Archibald) Laurence Patrick, K.C.M.G., T.D.

Kitson, *Gen.* Sir Frank Edward, G.B.E., K.C.B., M.C.

Kitson, Sir Timothy Peter Geoffrey, Kt.

Kitto, *Rt. Hon.* Sir Frank Walters, K.B.E.

Kleinwort, Sir Kenneth Drake, Bt. (1909).

Klug, Sir Aaron, Kt.

Knight, Sir Allan Walton, Kt., C.M.G.

Knight, Sir Arthur William, Kt.

Knight, Sir Harold Murray, K.B.E., D.S.C.

Knight, *Air Marshal* Sir Michael William Patrick, K.C.B., A.F.C.

Knill, Sir John Kenelm Stuart, Bt. (1893).

Knipe, Sir Leslie Francis, Kt., M.B.E.

Knott, Sir John Laurence, Kt., C.B.E.

Knowles, Sir Charles Francis, Bt. (1765).

Knowles, Sir Leonard Joseph, Kt., C.B.E.

Knox, *Hon.* Sir John Leonard, Kt.

Knox, *Hon.* Sir William Edward, Kt.

Kornberg, *Prof.* Sir Hans Leo, Kt., D.SC., SC.D., Ph.D., F.R.S.

Krusin, Sir Stanley Marks, Kt., C.B.

Kurongku, *Most. Rev.* Peter, K.B.E.

Labouchere, Sir George Peter, G.B.E., K.C.M.G.

Lacon, Sir Edmund Vere, Bt. (1818).

Lacy, Sir Hugh Maurice Pierce, Bt. (1921).

Lagesen, *Air Marshal* Sir Philip Jacobus, K.C.B., D.F.C., A.F.C.

Laidlaw, Sir Christophor Charles Fraser, Kt.

Laing, Sir Hector, Kt.

Laing, Sir (John) Maurice, Kt.

Laing, Sir (William) Kirby, Kt.

Lake, Sir (Atwell) Graham, Bt. (1711).

Laker, Sir Frederick Alfred, Kt.

Lakin, Sir Michael, Bt. (1909).

Laking, Sir George Robert, K.C.M.G.

Lamb, Sir Albert (Larry), Kt.

Lamb, Sir Albert Thomas, K.B.E., C.M.G., D.F.C.

Lamb, Sir Lionel Henry, K.C.M.G., O.B.E.

Lambert, Sir Anthony Edward, K.C.M.G.

Lambert, Sir Edward Thomas, K.B.E., C.V.O.

Lambert, Sir Greville Foley, Bt. (1711).

Lambert, Sir John Henry, K.C.V.O., C.M.G.

Lancaster, *Vice-Adm.* Sir John Strike, K.B.E., C.B.

Landau, Sir Dennis Marcus, Kt.

Lane, Sir David William Stennis Stuart, Kt.

Lane, Sir Peter Stewart, Kt.

Lang, *Lt.-Gen.* Sir Derek Boileau, K.C.B., D.S.O., M.C.

Langham, Sir James Michael, Bt. (1660).

Langley, *Maj.-Gen.* Sir Henry Desmond Allen, K.C.V.O., M.B.E.

Langrishe, Sir Hercules Ralph Hume, Bt. (I. 1777).

Lapsley, *Air Marshal* Sir John Hugh, K.B.E., C.B., D.F.C., A.F.C.

Lapun, *Hon.* Sir Paul, Kt.

Larcom, Sir (Charles) Christopher Royde, Bt. (1868).

Larmour, Sir Edward Noel, K.C.M.G.

Lartigue, Sir Louis Cools-, Kt., O.B.E.

Lasdun, Sir Denys Louis, Kt., C.B.E., F.R.I.B.A.

Latey, *Rt. Hon.* Sir John Brinsmead, Kt., M.B.E.

Latham, Sir Richard Thomas Paul, Bt. (1919).

Latimer, Sir (Courtenay) Robert, Kt., C.B.E.

Latimer, Sir Graham Stanley, K.B.E.

Laucke, *Hon.* Sir Condor Louis, K.C.M.G.

Lauder, Sir Piers Robert Dick-, Bt. (s. 1690).

Laughton, Sir Anthony Seymour, Kt.

Laurantus, Sir Nicholas, Kt., M.B.E.

Laurence, Sir Peter Harold, K.C.M.G., M.C.

Laurie, Sir Robert Bayley Emilius, Bt. (1834).

Lavan, *Hon.* Sir John Martin, Kt.

Law, *Adm.* Sir Horace Rochfort, G.C.B., O.B.E., D.S.C.

Lawes, Sir (John) Michael Bennet, Bt. (1882).

Lawler, Sir Peter James, Kt., O.B.E.

Lawrence, Sir David Roland Walter, Bt. (1906).

Lawrence, Sir Guy Kempton, Kt., D.S.O., O.B.E., D.F.C.

Lawrence, Sir John Patrick Grosvenor, Kt., C.B.E.

Lawrence, Sir John Waldemar, Bt., O.B.E. (1858).

Lawrence, Sir William Fettiplace, Bt. (1867).

Lawson, Sir Christopher Donald, Kt.

Lawson, *Col.* Sir John Charles Arthur Digby, Bt., D.S.O., M.C. (1900).

Lawson, *Hon.* Sir Neil, Kt.

Lawson, *Gen.* Sir Richard George, K.C.B., D.S.O., O.B.E.

Lawson, Sir William Howard, Bt. (1841).

Lawton, *Prof.* Sir Frank Ewart, Kt.

Lawton, *Rt. Hon.* Sir Frederick Horace, Kt.

Layden, Sir John (Jack), Kt.

Layfield, Sir Frank Henry Burland Willoughby, Kt., Q.C.

Lazarus, Sir Peter Esmond, K.C.B.

Lea, *Lt.-Gen.* Sir George Harris, K.C.B., D.S.O., M.B.E.

Lea, *Vice-Adm.*, Sir John Stuart Crosbie, K.B.E.

†Lea, Sir (Thomas) Julian, Bt. (1892).

Leach, *Prof.* Sir Edmund Ronald, Kt., Ph.D., F.B.A.

Leach, *Admiral of the Fleet* Sir Henry Conyers, G.C.B.

Leach, Sir Ronald George, G.B.E.

Leahy, Sir John Henry Gladstone, K.C.M.G.

Lean, Sir David, Kt., C.B.E.

Leask, *Lt.-Gen.* Sir Henry Lowther Ewart Clark, K.C.B., D.S.O., O.B.E.

Leather, Sir Edwin Hartley Cameron, K.C.M.G., K.C.V.O.

Leaver, Sir Christopher, G.B.E.

Le Bailly, *Vice-Adm.* Sir Louis Edward Stewart Holland, K.B.E., C.B.

Le Cheminant, *Air Chief Marshal* Sir Peter de Lacey, G.B.E., K.C.B., D.F.C.

Lechmere, Sir Berwick Hungerford, Bt. (1818).

Ledger, Sir Frank, (Joseph Francis), Kt.

Ledwidge, Sir (William) Bernard (John), K.C.M.G.

Lee, Sir Arthur James, K.B.E., M.C.

Lee, *Air Chief Marshal* Sir David John Pryer, G.B.E., C.B.

Lee, Sir (Henry) Desmond (Pritchard), Kt.

Lee, *Brig.* Sir Leonard Henry, Kt., C.B.E.

Lee, Sir Quo-wei, Kt., C.B.E.

Lee, *Col.* Sir William Allison, Kt., O.B.E., T.D.

Leeds, Sir Christopher Anthony, Bt. (1812).

Lees, *Air Marshal* Sir Ronald Beresford, K.C.B., C.B.E., D.F.C.

Lees, Sir Thomas Edward, Bt. (1897).

Lees, Sir Thomas Harcourt Ivor, Bt. (1804).

Lees, Sir (William) Antony Clare, Bt. (1937).

Leese, Sir John Henry Vernon, Bt. (1908).

Le Fanu, *Maj.* Sir (George) Victor (Sheridan), K.C.V.O.

le Fleming, Sir William Kelland, Bt. (1705).

Legard, Sir Charles Thomas, Bt. (1660).

Leggatt, *Hon.* Sir Andrew Peter, Kt.

Leggatt, Sir Hugh Frank John, Kt.

Leggett, Sir Clarence Arthur Campbell, K.t., M.B.E.

Leigh, Sir John, Bt. (1918).

Leigh, Sir Neville Egerton, K.C.V.O.

Leighton, Sir Michael John Bryan, Bt. (1693).

Leitch, Sir George, K.C.B., O.B.E.

Leith, Sir Andrew George Forbes-, Bt. (1923).

Le Marchant, Sir Francis Arthur, Bt. (1841).

Le Masurier, Sir Robert Hugh, Kt., D.S.C.

Lemon, Sir (Richard) Dawnay, Kt., C.B.E.

Leng, *Gen.* Sir Peter John Hall, K.C.B., M.B.E., M.C.

Lennard, *Rev.* Sir Hugh Dacre Barrett-, Bt. (1801).

Leon, Sir John Ronald, Bt. (1911).

Leonard, *Hon.* Sir (Hamilton) John, Kt.

Lepping, Sir George Geria Dennis, G.C.M.G., M.B.E.

Le Quesne, Sir (Charles) Martin, K.C.M.G.

Le Quesne, Sir (John) Godfray, Kt., Q.C.

Leslie, Sir Colin Alan Bettridge, Kt.

Leslie, Sir John Norman Ide, Bt. (1876).

†Leslie, Sir (Percy) Theodore, Kt. (s. 1625).

Lethbridge, Sir Thomas Periam Hector Noel, Bt. (1804).

Leuchars, Sir William Douglas, K.B.E.

Leupena, Sir Tupua, G.C.M.G., M.B.E.

Lever, Sir (Tresham) Christopher Arthur Lindsay, Bt. (1911).

Levey, Sir Michael Vincent, Kt., M.V.O.

Levine, Sir Montague Bernard, Kt.

Levinge, Sir Richard George Robin, Bt. (I. 1704).

Levy, Sir Ewart Maurice, Bt. (1913).

Lewando, Sir Jan Alfred, Kt., C.B.E.

Lewis, Sir Allen Montgomery, G.C.M.G., G.C.V.O., Q.C.

Lewis, *Adm.* Sir Andrew Mackenzie, K.C.B.

Lewis, Sir Ian Malcolm, Kt.

Lewis, *Prof.* Sir Jack, Kt., F.R.S.

Lewis, Sir Kenneth, Kt.

Lewis, Sir Terence Murray, Kt., O.B.E., Q.P.M.

Lewis, Sir William Arthur, Kt.

Lewthwaite, Sir William Anthony, Bt. (1927).

Ley, Sir Francis Douglas, Bt., M.B.E., T.D. (1905).

Leyland, Sir Philip Vyvyan Naylor-, Bt. (1895).

Lickley, Sir Robert Lang, Kt., C.B.E.

Lidbury, Sir John Towersey, Kt.

Lidderdale, Sir David William Shuckburgh, K.C.B.

Liddle, Sir Donald Ross, Kt.

Liggins, Sir Edmund Naylor, Kt., T.D.

Lighthill, Sir (Michael) James, Kt., F.R.S.

Lighton, Sir Christopher Robert, Bt., M.B.E. (I. 1791).

Lim, Sir Han-Hoe, Kt., C.B.E.

Linacre, Sir (John) Gordon (Seymour), Kt., C.B.E., A.F.C., D.F.M.

Lincoln, Sir Anthony Handley, K.C.M.G., C.V.O.

Lincoln, *Hon.* Sir Anthony Leslie Julian, Kt.

Lindley, Sir Arnold Lewis George, Kt.

Lindop, Sir Norman, Kt.

Lindsay, Sir James Harvey Kincaid Stewart, Kt.

Lindsay, Sir Ronald Alexander, Bt. (1962).

Lintott, Sir Henry John Bevis, K.C.M.G.

Lithgow, Sir William James, Bt. (1925).

Little, *Hon.* Sir Douglas Macfarlan, Kt

Little, *Most Rev.* Thomas Francis, K.B.E.

Littler, Sir (James) Geoffrey, K.C.B.

Livermore, Sir Harry, Kt.

Llewellyn, Sir David Treharne, Kt.

Llewellyn, Sir (Frederick) John, K.C.M.G.

Llewellyn, Sir Henry Morton, Bt., C.B.E. (1922).

Llewelyn, Sir John Michael Dillwyn-Venables-, Bt. (1890).

Llewellyn, *Lt.-Col.* Sir Michael Rowland Godfrey, Bt. (1959).

Lloyd, *Rt. Hon.* Sir Anthony John Leslie, Kt.

Lloyd, Sir Ian Stewart, Kt., M.P.

Lloyd, Sir (John) Peter (Daniel), Kt.

Lloyd, Sir Richard Ernest Butler, Bt., (1960).

Lloyd Jones, Sir Richard Anthony, K.C.B.

Loader, Sir Leslie Thomas, Kt., C.B.E.

Loane, *Most Rev.* Marcus Lawrence, K.B.E.

Lobo, Sir Rogerio Hyndman, Kt., C.B.E.

Lock, *Cdr.* Sir (John) Duncan, Kt.

†Lockhart, Sir Simon John Edward Francis Sinclair-, Bt. (s. 1636).

Lockspeiser, Sir Ben, K.C.B., F.R.S.

Lockwood, Sir Joseph Flawith, Kt.

Loder, Sir Giles Rolls, Bt. (1887).

Lodge, Sir Thomas, Kt.

Loehnis, Sir Clive, K.C.M.G.

Logan, Sir Donald Arthur, K.C.M.G.

Logan, Sir Raymond Douglas, Kt.

Lokoloko, Sir Tore, G.C.M.G., G.C.V.O., O.B.E.

Longden, Sir Gilbert James Morley, Kt., M.B.E.

Longland, Sir David Walter, Kt., C.M.G.

Longland, Sir John Laurence, Kt.

Longley, Sir Norman, Kt., C.B.E.

Looker, Sir Cecil Thomas, Kt.

Loram, *Vice-Adm.* Sir David Anning, K.C.B., M.V.O.

Lorimer, Sir (Thomas) Desmond, Kt.

Lousada, Sir Anthony Baruh, Kt.

Love, Sir Makere Rangiatea Ralph, Kt.

Lovell, Sir (Alfred Charles) Bernard, Kt., O.B.E., F.R.S.

Lovelock, Sir Douglas Arthur, K.C.B.

Loveridge, Sir John Henry, Kt., C.B.E.

Loveridge, Sir John Warren, Kt.

Lovill, Sir John Roger, Kt., C.B.E.

Low, Sir Alan Roberts, Kt.

Low, Sir James Richard Morrison-, Bt. (1908).

Lowe, *Air Chief Marshal* Sir Douglas Charles, G.C.B., D.F.C., A.F.C.

Lowe, *Air Vice-Marshal* Sir Edgar Noel, K.B.E., C.B.

Lowe, Sir Thomas William Gordon, Bt. (1918).

Lowry, Sir John Patrick, Kt., C.B.E.

Lowson, Sir Ian Patrick, Bt. (1951).

Lowther, *Maj.* Sir Charles Douglas, Bt. (1824).

Loyd, Sir Francis Alfred, K.C.M.G., O.B.E.

Lu, Sir Tseng Chi, Kt.

Lubbock, Sir Alan, Kt., F.S.A.

Lucas, Sir Cyril Edward, Kt., C.M.G., F.R.S.

Lucas, Sir Thomas Edward, Bt. (1887).

Luckhoo, *Hon.* Sir Joseph Alexander, Kt.

Luckhoo, Sir Lionel Alfred, K.C.M.G., C.B.E., Q.C.

Lucy, Sir Edmund John William Hugh Cameron-Ramsay-Fairfax-, Bt. (1836).

Luddington, Sir Donald Collin Cumyn, K.B.E., C.M.G., C.V.O.

Luke, *Hon.* Sir Emile Fashole, K.B.E.

Lumby, Sir Henry, Kt., C.B.E.

Lumsden, Sir David James, Kt.

Lus, *Hon.* Sir Pita, Kt., O.B.E.

Lush, *Hon.* Sir George Hermann, Kt.

Lushington, Sir Henry Edmund Castleman, Bt. (1791).

Lusty, Sir Robert Frith, Kt.

Luyt, Sir Richard Edmonds, G.C.M.G., K.C.V.O., D.C.M.

Lyell, Sir Nicholas Walter, Kt., Q.C., M.P.

Lygo, *Adm.* Sir Raymond Derek, K.C.B.

Lyle, Sir Gavin Archibald, Bt. (1929).

Lyons, Sir Edward Houghton, Kt.

Lyons, Sir (Isidore) Jack, Kt., C.B.E.

Lyons, Sir James Reginald, Kt.

Lyons, Sir John, Kt.

Lyons, *His Hon.* Sir Rudolph, Kt., Q.C.

McAdam, Sir Ian William James, Kt., O.B.E.

Macadam, Sir Peter, Kt.

McAlpine, Sir Robin, Kt., C.B.E.

Macara, Sir (Charles) Douglas, Bt. (1911).

Macartney, Sir John Barrington, Bt. (I. 1799).

McAvoy, Sir (Francis) Joseph, Kt., C.B.E.

McCaffrey, Sir Thomas Daniel, Kt.

McCall, Sir (Charles) Patrick Home, Kt., M.B.E., T.D.

McCallum, Sir Donald Murdo, Kt., C.B.E.

McCamley, Sir Graham Edward, Kt., M.B.E.

McCarthy, *Rt. Hon.* Sir Thaddeus Pearcey, K.B.E.

McCauley, *Air Marshal* Sir John Patrick Joseph, K.B.E., C.B.

McCaw, *Hon.* Sir Kenneth Malcolm, Kt., Q.C.

McClellan, *Col.* Sir Herbert Gerard Thomas, Kt., C.B.E., T.D.

McClintock, Sir Eric Paul, Kt.

McConnell, *Cdr.* Sir Robert Melville Terence, Bt., V.R.D. (1900).

McCowan, *Hon.* Sir Anthony James Denys, Kt.

McCowan, Sir Hew Cargill, Bt. (1934).

McCrea, *Prof.* Sir William Hunter, Kt., F.R.S.

McCullough, *Hon.* Sir (Iain) Charles (Robert), Kt.

McCusker, Sir James Alexander, Kt.

MacDermot, Sir Dermot Francis, K.C.M.G., C.B.E.

MacDermott, *Rt. Hon.* Sir John Clarke, Kt.

McDermott, Sir (Lawrence) Emmet, K.B.E.

MacDonald, *Gen.* Sir Arthur Leslie, K.B.E., C.B.

McDonald, *Air Chief Marshal* Sir Arthur William Baynes, K.C.B., A.F.C.

McDonald, Sir Duncan, Kt., C.B.E.

Macdonald, Sir Herbert George deLorme, K.B.E.

Macdonald of Sleat, Sir Ian Godfrey Bosville, Bt. (s. 1625).

McDonald, Sir James, K.B.E.

Macdonald, *Vice-Adm.* Sir Roderick Douglas, K.B.E.

McDonald, *Hon.* Sir William John Farquhar, Kt.

MacDougall, Sir (George) Donald (Alastair), Kt., C.B.E., F.B.A.

McDowell, Sir Henry McLorinan, K.B.E.

McEvoy, *Air Chief Marshal* Sir Theodore Newman, K.C.B., C.B.E.

McEwen, Sir John Roderick Hugh, Bt. (1953).

McEwin, *Hon.* Sir (Alexander) Lyell, K.B.E.

McFarland, Sir John Talbot, Bt. (1914).

Macfarlane, Sir (David) Neil, Kt., M.P.

McFarlane, Sir Ian, Kt.

Macfarlane, Sir George Gray, Kt., C.B.

Macfarlane, Sir James Wright, Kt.

Macfarlane, Sir Norman Somerville, Kt.

McGeoch, *Vice-Adm.* Sir Ian Lachlan Mackay, K.C.B., D.S.O., D.S.C.

Macgregor, Sir Edwin Robert, Bt. (1828).

MacGregor of MacGregor, Sir Gregor, Bt. (1795).

McGregor, Sir Ian Alexander, Kt., C.B.E., F.R.S.

MacGregor, Sir Ian Kinloch, Kt.

McGrigor, *Capt.* Sir Charles Edward, Bt. (1831).

McInerney, *Hon.* Sir Murray Vincent, Kt.

McIntosh, *Vice-Adm.* Sir Ian Stewart, K.B.E., C.B., D.S.O., D.S.C.

Macintosh, Sir Robert Reynolds, Kt., M.D.

McIntosh, Sir Ronald Robert Duncan, K.C.B.

McKaig, *Adm.* Sir (John) Rae, K.C.B., C.B.E.

McKay, *Hon.* Sir Donald Norman, K.C.M.G.

Mackay, Sir (George Patrick) Gordon, Kt., C.B.E.

McKay, Sir James Wilson, Kt.

McKay, Sir John Andrew, Kt., C.B.E.

Mackay, Sir William Calder, Kt., O.B.E., M.C.

McKee, *Air Marshal* Sir Andrew, K.C.B., C.B.E., D.S.O., D.F.C., A.F.C.

McKee, *Maj.* Sir (William) Cecil, Kt., E.R.D.

MacKenna, Sir Bernard Joseph Maxwell, Kt.

McKenzie, Sir Alexander, K.B.E.

Mackenzie, Sir Alexander Alwyne Henry Charles Brinton Muir-, Bt. (1805).

Mackenzie, Sir (Alexander George Anthony) Allan, Bt. (1890).

Mackenzie, *Vice-Adm.* Sir Hugh Stirling, K.C.B., D.S.O., D.S.C.

Mackenzie, Sir Robert Evelyn, Bt. (s. 1673).

†Mackenzie, Sir Roderick McQuhae, Bt. (s. 1703).

Mackeson, Sir Rupert Henry, Bt. (1954).

Mackie, Sir Maitland, Kt., C.B.E.

MacKinlay, Sir Bruce, Kt., C.B.E.

McKinnon, *Hon.* Sir Stuart Neil, Kt.

McKissock, Sir Wylie, Kt., O.B.E., F.R.C.S.

Macklin, Sir Bruce Roy, Kt., O.B.E.

Mackworth, *Cdr.* Sir David Arthur Geoffrey, Bt. (1776).

Maclaren, Sir Hamish Duncan, K.B.E., C.B., D.F.C.

Maclean, Sir Donald Og Grant, Kt.

Maclean, Sir Fitzroy Hew, Bt., C.B.E. (1957).

McLean, Sir Francis Charles, Kt., C.B.E.

MacLean, *Vice-Adm.* Sir Hector Charles Donald, K.B.E., C.B., D.S.C.

Maclean, Sir Robert Alexander, K.B.E.

MacLellan, Sir (George) Robin (Perronet), Kt., C.B.E.

McLennan, Sir Ian Munro, K.C.M.G., K.B.E.

McLeod, Sir Charles Henry, Bt. (1925).

McLeod, Sir Ian George, Kt.

McLintock, Sir Michael William, Bt. (1934).

Maclure, Sir John Robert Spencer, Bt. (1898).

McMahon, Sir Brian Patrick, Bt. (1817).

McMahon, Sir Christopher William, Kt.

McMichael, Sir John, Kt., M.D., F.R.S., F.R.C.P.

MacMillan, *Lt. Gen.* Sir John Richard Alexander, K.C.B., C.B.E.

MacMillan, Sir Kenneth, Kt.

Macmillan, Sir Alexander McGregor Graham, Kt.

Macmillan, Sir (James) Wilson, K.B.E.

McMullin, *Rt. Hon.* Sir Duncan Wallace, Kt.

Macnab, *Brig.* Sir Geoffrey Alex Colin, K.C.M.G., C.B.

Macnaghten, Sir Patrick Alexander, Bt. (1836).

McNair-Wilson, Sir (Robert) Michael Conal, Kt., M.P.

McNamara, *Air Chief Marshal* Sir Neville Patrick, K.B.E.

Macnaughton, *Prof.* Sir Malcolm Campbell, Kt.

McNee, Sir David Blackstock, Kt., Q.P.M.

McNeice, Sir (Thomas) Percy (Fergus), Kt., C.M.G., O.B.E.

McNeill, *Hon.* Sir David Bruce, Kt.

McPetrie, Sir James Carnegie, K.C.M.G., O.B.E.

MacPherson, Sir Keith Duncan, Kt.

Macpherson of Cluny, *Hon.* Sir William Alan, Kt., T.D.

McQuarrie, Sir Albert, Kt.

Macready, Sir Nevil John Wilfrid, Bt. (1923).

Macrory, Sir Patrick Arthur, Kt.

McShine, *Hon.* Sir Arthur Hugh, Kt.

Mactaggart, Sir John Auld, Bt. (1938).

McTiernan, *Rt. Hon.* Sir Edward Aloysius, K.B.E.

Madden, *Adm.* Sir Charles Edward, Bt., G.C.B. (1919).

Maddock, Sir Ieuan, Kt., C.B., O.B.E., F.R.S.

Maddocks, Sir Kenneth Phipson, K.C.M.G., K.C.V.O.

Maddox, Sir (John) Kempson, Kt., V.R.D., M.D.

Madigan, Sir Russel Tullie, Kt., O.B.E.

Magarey, Sir James Rupert, Kt.

Maguire, *Air Marshal* Sir Harold John, K.C.B., D.S.O., O.B.E.

Mahon, Sir (John) Denis, Kt., C.B.E.

†Mahon, Sir William Walter, Bt. (1819).

Main, Sir Peter Tester, Kt., E.R.D.

Maini, Sir Amar Nath, Kt., C.B.E.

Mais, *Hon.* Sir (Robert) Hugh, Kt.

Maitland, Sir Donald James Dundas, G.C.M.G., O.B.E.

Maitland, Sir Richard John, Bt. (1818).

Makins, Sir Paul Vivian, Bt. (1903).

Malcolm, Sir David Peter Michael, Bt. (s. 1665).

Malet, *Col.* Sir Edward William St. Lo, Bt., O.B.E. (1791).

Mallaby, Sir Christopher Leslie George, K.C.M.G.

Mallet, Sir (William) Ivo, G.B.E., K.C.M.G.

Mallinson, Sir (William) Paul, Bt. (1935).

Malone, *Hon.* Sir Denis Eustace Gilbert, Kt.

Mamo, Sir Anthony Joseph, Kt., O.B.E.

Manchester, Sir William Maxwell, K.B.E.

Mander, Sir Charles Marcus, Bt. (1911).

Mann, *Rt. Hon.* Sir Michael, Kt.

Mann, Sir Rupert Edward, Bt. (1905).

Mansel, *Rev. Canon* James Seymour Denis, K.C.V.O.

Mansel, Sir Philip, Bt. (1622).

Mansergh, *Vice-Adm.* Sir (Cecil) Aubrey (Lawson), K.B.E., C.B., D.S.C.

Mansfield, *Vice-Adm.* Sir (Edward) Gerard (Napier), K.B.E., C.V.O.

Mansfield, Sir Philip (Robert Aked), K.C.M.G.

Mant, Sir Cecil George, Kt., C.B.E.

Manzie, Sir (Andrew) Gordon, K.C.B.

Mara, *Rt. Hon. Ratu* Sir Kamisese Kapaiwai Tuimacilai, G.C.M.G., K.B.E.

March, Sir Derek Maxwell, K.B.E.

Marchant, Sir Herbert Stanley, K.C.M.G., O.B.E.

Margetson, Sir John William Denys, K.C.M.G.

Marjoribanks, Sir James Alexander Milne, K.C.M.G.

Mark, Sir Robert, G.B.E.

Markham, Sir Charles John, Bt. (1911).

Marking, Sir Henry Ernest, K.C.V.O., C.B.E., M.C.

Marling, Sir Charles William Somerset, Bt., (1882).

Marr, Sir Leslie Lynn, Bt. (1919).

Marre, Sir Alan Samuel, K.C.B.

Marriner, Sir Neville, Kt., C.B.E.

†Marriott, Sir Hugh Cavendish Smith-, Bt. (1774).

Marsack, Sir Charles Croft, K.B.E.

Marsden, Sir Nigel John Denton, Bt., (1924).

Marshall, Sir Arthur Gregory George, Kt., O.B.E.

Marshall, Sir Colin Marsh, Kt.

Marshall, Sir Denis Alfred, Kt.

Marshall, *Prof.* Sir (Oshley) Roy, Kt., C.B.E.

Marshall, Sir Peter Harold Reginald, K.C.M.G.

Marshall, Sir Robert Braithwaite, K.C.B., M.B.E.

Mars-Jones, *Hon.* Sir William Lloyd, Kt., M.B.E.

Martell, *Vice-Adm.* Sir Hugh Colenso, K.B.E., C.B.

Martin, *Air Marshal* Sir Harold Brownlow, K.C.B., D.S.O., D.F.C., A.F.C.

Martin, *Vice-Adm.* Sir John Edward Ludgate, K.C.B., D.S.C.

Martin, *Prof.* Sir (John) Leslie, Kt., Ph.D.

Martin, Sir John Miller, K.C.M.G., C.B., C.V.O.

Martin, *Col.* Sir Robert Andrew St. George, K.C.V.O., O.B.E.

Martin, Sir Sidney Launcelot, Kt.

Marwick, Sir Brian Allan, K.B.E., C.M.G.

Marychurch, Sir Peter Harvey, K.C.M.G.

Masefield, Sir Peter Gordon, Kt.

Mason, *Hon.* Sir Anthony Frank, K.B.E.

Mason, Sir (Basil) John, Kt., C.B., D.SC., F.R.S.

Mason, Sir Frederick Cecil, K.C.V.O., C.M.G.

Mason, Sir John Charles Moir, K.C.M.G.

Mason, *Prof.* Sir Ronald, K.C.B., F.R.S.

Matane, Sir Paulias Nguna, Kt., C.M.G., O.B.E.

Mather, Sir (David) Carol (Macdonell), Kt., M.C.

Mather, *Prof.* Sir Kenneth, C.B.E., D.SC., F.R.S.

Mather, Sir William Loris, Kt., C.V.O., O.B.E., M.C., T.D.

Mathers, Sir Robert William, Kt.

Matheson, Sir (James Adam) Louis, K.B.E., C.M.G.

Matheson of Matheson, Sir Torquhil Alexander, Bt. (1882).

Mathias, Sir Richard Hughes, Bt. (1917).

Matthews, Sir Peter Alec, Kt.

Matthews, Sir Peter Jack, Kt., C.V.O., O.B.E., Q.P.M.

Matthews, Sir Russell, Kt., O.D.E.

Matthews, Sir Stanley, Kt., C.B.E.

Mavor, *Air Marshal* Sir Leslie Deane, K.C.B., A.F.C.

†Maxwell, Sir Michael Eustace George, Bt. (s. 1681).

Maxwell, Sir Nigel Mellor Heron-, Bt. (s. 1683).

Maxwell, Sir Robert Hugh, K.B.E.

May, *Rt. Hon.* Sir John Douglas, Kt.

May, Sir Kenneth Spencer, Kt., C.B.E.

Mayall, Sir (Alexander) Lees, K.C.V.O., C.M.G.

Mayhew, *Rt. Hon.* Sir Patrick Barnabas Burke, Kt., Q.C., M.P.

Mayhew-Sanders, Sir John Reynolds, Kt.

Maynard, *Air Chief Marshal* Sir Nigel Martin, K.C.B., C.B.E., D.F.C., A.F.C.

Meade, Sir (Richard) Geoffrey (Austin), K.B.E., C.M.G., C.V.O.

Meaney, Sir Patrick Michael, Kt.

Medlycott, Sir Mervyn Tregonwell, Bt. (1808).

Megarry, *Rt. Hon.* Sir Robert Edgar, Kt., F.B.A.

Megaw, *Rt. Hon.* Sir John, Kt., C.B.E., T.D.

Meinertzhagen, Sir Peter, Kt., C.M.G.

Mellon, Sir James, K.C.M.G.

Mellor, Sir John Francis, Bt. (1924).

Melville, Sir Harry Work, K.C.B., Ph.D., D.SC., F.R.S.

Melville, Sir Leslie Galfreid, K.B.E.

Melville, Sir Ronald Henry, K.C.B.

Mensforth, Sir Eric, Kt., C.B.E., F.Eng.

Menter, Sir James Woodham, Kt., Ph.D., SC.D., F.R.S.

Menteth, Sir James Wallace Stuart-, Bt. (1838).

Menuhin, Sir Yehudi, O.M., K.B.E.

Menzies, Sir Peter Thomson, Kt.

Merrison, Sir Alexander Walter, Kt., F.R.S.

Messervy, Sir (Roney) Godfrey (Collumbell), Kt.

Meyer, Sir Anthony John Charles, Bt., M.P. (1910).

Meyjes, Sir Richard Anthony, Kt.

Meyrick, *Lt.-Col.* Sir George David Elliott Tapps-Gervis-, Bt., M.C. (1791).

Meyrick, Sir David John Charlton, Bt. (1880).

Micklethwait, Sir Robert Gore, Kt., Q.C.

Middleton, Sir George Humphrey, K.C.M.G.

Middleton, Sir Peter Edward, K.C.B.

Middleton, Sir Stephen Hugh, Bt. (1662).

Miers, Sir (Henry) David Alastair Capel, K.B.E., C.M.G.

Milbank, Sir Anthony Frederick, Bt. (1882).

Milburn, Sir Anthony Rupert, Bt. (1905).

Miles, Sir Peter Tremayne, K.C.V.O.

Miles, Sir William Napier Maurice, Bt. (1859).

Millais, Sir Ralph Regnault, Bt. (1885).

Millar, Sir Oliver Nicholas, G.C.V.O., F.B.A.

Millar, Sir Ronald Graeme, Kt.

Millard, Sir Guy Elwin, K.C.M.G., C.V.O.

Miller, Sir Douglas Sinclair, K.C.V.O., C.B.E.

Miller, Sir Hilary Duppa (Hal), Kt., M.P.

Miller, Sir (Ian) Douglas, Kt.

Miller, Sir John Holmes, Bt. (1705).

Miller, *Lt.-Col.* Sir John Mansel, G.C.V.O., D.S.O., M.C.

Miller, Sir (Joseph) Holmes, Kt., O.B.E.

Miller, Sir (Oswald) Bernard, Kt.

Miller, Sir Peter North, Kt.

Miller, Sir Richard Hope, Kt.

Miller, Sir Stephen James Hamilton, K.C.V.O., M.D., F.R.C.S.

Miller of Glenlee, Sir (Frederick William) Macdonald, Bt. (1788).

Millett, *Hon.* Sir Peter Julian, Kt.

Milling, *Air Marshal* Sir Denis Crowley-, K.C.B., C.B.E., D.S.O., D.F.C.

Mills, *Vice-Adm.* Sir Charles Piercy, K.C.B., C.B.E., D.S.C.

Mills, Sir Frank, K.C.V.O., C.M.G.

Mills, Sir John Lewis Ernest Watts, Kt., C.B.E.

Mills, Sir Peter Frederick Leighton, Bt. (1921).

Mills, Sir Peter McLay, Kt.

Milman, Sir Dermot Lionel Kennedy, Bt. (1800).

Milne, Sir John Drummond, Kt.

Milner, Sir (George Edward) Mordaunt, Bt. (1717).

Milnes Coates, Sir Anthony Robert, Bt. (1911).

Milton-Thompson, *Surgeon Vice-Adm.* Sir Godfrey James, K.B.E.

Minhinnick, Sir Gordon Edward George, K.B.E.

Minogue, *Hon.* Sir John Patrick, Kt., Q.C.

Miskin, *Hon.* Sir James William, Kt., Q.C.

Mitchell, *Air Cdre.* Sir (Arthur) Dennis, K.B.E., C.V.O., D.F.C., A.F.C.

Mitchell, Sir David Bower, Kt., M.P.

Mitchell, Sir Derek Jack, K.C.B., C.V.O.

Mitchell, Sir Hamilton, K.B.E.

Mitchell, Sir (Seton) Steuart Crichton, K.B.E., C.B.

Mobbs, Sir (Gerald) Nigel, Kt.

Moberly, Sir John Campbell, K.B.E., C.M.G.

Moberly, Sir Patrick Hamilton, K.C.M.G.

Mocatta, Sir Alan Abraham, Kt., O.B.E.

Moffat, *Lt.-Gen.* Sir (William) Cameron, K.B.E.

Mogg, *Gen.* Sir (Herbert) John, G.C.B., C.B.E., D.S.O.

Moir, Sir Ernest Ian Royds, Bt. (1916).

Moller, *Hon.* Sir Lester Francis, Kt.

†Molony, Sir Thomas Desmond, Bt. (1925).

Monro, Sir Hector Seymour Peter, Kt., M.P.

Monson, Sir (William Bonnar) Leslie, K.C.M.G., C.B.

Montgomery, Sir (Basil Henry) David, Bt. (1801).

Montgomery, Sir (William) Fergus, Kt., M.P.

Mookerjee, Sir Birendra Nath, Kt.

Moollan, Sir Abdool Hamid Adam, Kt.

Moollan, *Hon.* Sir Cassam (Ismael), Kt.

Moon, Sir Edward, Bt., M.C. (1887).

Moon, Sir Peter James Scott, K.C.V.O., C.M.G.

Moon, Sir Peter Wilfred Giles Graham-, Bt. (1855).

Moore, Sir Edward Stanton, Bt., O.B.E. (1923).

Moore, Sir Francis Thomas, Kt.

Moore, Sir Henry Roderick, Kt., C.B.E.

Moore, *Hon.* Sir John Cochrane, Kt.

Moore, *Maj.-Gen.* Sir (John) Jeremy, K.C.B., O.B.E., M.C.

Moore, Sir John Michael, K.C.V.O., C.B., D.S.C.

Moore, *Prof.* Sir Norman Winfrid, Bt. (1919).

Moore, Sir William Roger Clotworthy, Bt., T.D. (1932).

Moores, Sir John, Kt., C.B.E.

Mootham, Sir Orby Howell, Kt.

Mordaunt, Sir Richard Nigel Charles, Bt. (1611).

Moreton, Sir John Oscar, K.C.M.G., K.C.V.O., M.C.

Morgan, *Maj.-Gen.* Sir David John Hughes-, Bt., C.B., C.B.E. (1925).

Morgan, Sir Ernest Dunstan, K.B.E.

Morgan, *Rear-Adm.* Sir Patrick John, K.C.V.O., C.B., D.S.C.

Morgan-Giles, *Rear-Adm.* Sir Morgan Charles, Kt., D.S.O., O.B.E., G.M.

Morony, *Gen.* Sir Thomas Lovett, K.C.B., O.B.E.

Morpeth, Sir Douglas Spottiswoode, Kt., T.D.

Morris, *Air Marshal* Sir Arnold Alec, K.B.E., C.B.

Morris, *Air Marshal* Sir Douglas Griffith, K.C.B., C.B.E., D.S.O., D.F.C.

Morris, Sir Robert Byng, Bt. (1806).

Morrison, *Hon.* Sir Charles Andrew, Kt., M.P.

Morritt, *Hon.* Sir (Robert) Andrew, Kt.

Morrow, Sir Ian Thomas, Kt.

Morse, Sir Christopher Jeremy, K.C.M.G.

Morton, *Adm.* Sir Anthony Storrs, G.B.E., K.C.B.

Morton, Sir Brian, Kt.

Morton, Sir Ralph John, K.C.M.G., O.B.E., M.C.

Moseley, Sir George Walker, K.C.B.

Moser, *Prof.* Sir Claus Adolf, K.C.B., C.B.E., F.B.A.

Moss, Sir John Herbert Theodore Edwards-, Bt. (1868).

Mostyn, Sir Jeremy John Anthony, Bt. (1670).

Mostyn, *Gen.* Sir (Joseph) David Frederick, K.C.B., C.B.E.

Mott, Sir John Harmer, Bt. (1930).

Mott, Sir Nevill Francis, Kt., F.R.S.

Mount, Sir James William Spencer, Kt., C.B.E., B.E.M.

Mount, Sir William Malcolm, Bt. (1921).

Mountain, Sir Denis Mortimer, Bt. (1922).

Mowbray, Sir John, Kt.

Mowbray, Sir John Robert, Bt. (1880).

Moynihan, Sir Noel Henry, Kt.

Muir, Sir John Harling, Bt. (1892).

Muir, Sir Laurence Macdonald, Kt.

Muir Wood, Sir Alan Marshall, Kt., F.R.S.

Muirhead, Sir David Francis, K.C.M.G., C.V.O.

Muldoon, *Rt. Hon.* Sir Robert David, G.C.M.G., C.H.

Mulholland, Sir Michael Henry, Bt. (1945).

Mumford, Sir Albert Henry, K.B.E.

Munn, Sir James, Kt., O.B.E.

Munro, Sir Alasdair Thomas Ian, Bt. (1825).

Munro, Sir Ian Talbot, Bt. (s. 1634).

Munro, *Hon.* Sir Robert Lindsay, Kt., C.B.E.

Munro, Sir Sydney Douglas Gun-, G.C.M.G., M.B.E.

Murley, Sir Reginald Sydney, K.B.E., T.D., F.R.C.S.

Murphy, Sir Leslie Frederick, Kt.

Murray, *Rear-Adm.* Sir Brian Stewart, K.C.M.G.

Murray, Sir Donald Frederick, K.C.V.O., C.M.G.

Murray, *Gen.* Sir Horatius, G.C.B., K.B.E., D.S.O.

Murray, Sir James, K.C.M.G.

Murray, Sir John Antony Jerningham, Kt., C.B.E.

Murray, Sir Nigel Andrew Digby, Bt. (s. 1628).

Murray, Sir Patrick Ian Keith, Bt. (s. 1673).

Murray, Sir Rowland William Patrick, Bt. (s. 1630).

Murrie, Sir William Stuart, G.C.B., K.B.E.

Mursell, Sir Peter, Kt., M.B.E.

Musgrave, Sir Christopher Patrick Charles, Bt. (1611).

Musgrave, Sir Richard James, Bt. (I. 1782).

Musker, Sir John, Kt.

Musson, *Gen.* Sir Geoffrey Randolph Dixon, G.C.B., C.B.E., D.S.O.

Mustill, *Rt. Hon.* Sir Michael John, Kt.

Myers, Sir Kenneth Ben, Kt., M.B.E.

Myers, Sir Philip Alan, Kt., O.B.E., Q.P.M.

Myers, *Prof.* Sir Rupert Horace, K.B.E.

Mynors, Sir Humphrey Charles Baskerville, Bt. (1964).

Mynors, *Prof.* Sir Roger Aubrey Baskerville, Kt., F.B.A.

Nabarro, Sir John David Nunes, Kt., M.D., F.R.C.P.

Nairn, Sir Michael, Bt. (1904).

Nairn, Sir Robert Arnold Spencer-, Bt. (1933).

Nairne, *Rt. Hon.* Sir Patrick Dalmahoy, G.C.B., M.C.

Nalder, *Hon.* Sir Crawford David, Kt.

Nall, Sir Michael Joseph, Bt., R.N. (1954).

Napier, Sir Oliver John, Kt.

Napier, Sir Robin Surtees, Bt. (1867).

Napier, Sir William Archibald, Bt. (s 1627).

Napley, Sir David, Kt.

Narain, Sir Sathi, K.B.E.

Neal, Sir Eric James, Kt.

Neal, Sir Leonard Francis, Kt., C.B.E.

Neale, Sir Alan Derrett, K.C.B., M.B.E.

Neave, Sir Arundell Thomas Clifton, Bt. (1795).

Nedd, *Hon.* Sir Robert Archibald, Kt.

Neill, *Rt. Hon.* Sir Brian Thomas, Kt.

Neill, Sir Francis Patrick, Kt., Q.C.

Neill, *Rt. Hon.* Sir Ivan, Kt.

Nelson, *Maj.-Gen.* Sir (Eustace) John (Blois), K.C.V.O., C.B., D.S.O., O.B.E., M.C.

Nelson, *Air Marshal* Sir (Sidney) Richard (Carlyle), K.C.B., O.B.E., M.D.

Nelson, *Maj.* Sir William Vernon Hope, Bt., O.B.E. (1912).

Nepean, *Lt.-Col.* Sir Evan Yorke, Bt. (1802).

Ness, *Air Marshal* Sir Charles Ernest, K.C.B., C.B.E.

Neville, Sir Richard Lionel John Baines, Bt. (1927).

Newbold, Sir Charles Demorée, K.B.E., C.M.G., Q.C.

Newman, Sir Francis Hugh Cecil, Bt. (1912).

Newman, Sir Geoffrey Robert, Bt. (1836).

Newman, Sir Jack, Kt., C.B.E.

Newman, Sir Kenneth Leslie, Kt., G.B.E.

Newns, Sir (Alfred) Foley (Francis Polden), K.C.M.G., C.V.O.

Newsam, Sir Peter Anthony, Kt.

Newton, Sir (Harry) Michael (Rex), Bt. (1900).

Newton, Sir Hubert, Kt.

Newton, Sir Kenneth Garnar, Bt., O.B.E., T.D. (1924).

Newton, Sir (Leslie) Gordon, Kt.

Ngata, Sir Henare Kohere, K.B.E.

Niall, Sir Horace Lionel Richard, Kt., C.B.E.

Nicholas, Sir Herbert Richard, Kt., O.B.E.

Nicholas, Sir John William, K.C.V.O., C.M.G.

Nicholls, *Rt. Hon.* Sir Donald James, Kt.

Nicholls, *Air Marshal* Sir John Moreton, K.C.B., C.B.E., D.F.C., A.F.C.

Nichols, Sir Edward Henry, Kt., T.D.

Nicholson, Sir Bryan Hubert, Kt.

Nicholson, *Hon.* Sir David Eric, Kt.

Nicholson, Sir Godfrey, Bt. (1958).

Nicholson, Sir John Norris, Bt., K.B.E., C.I.E. (1912).

Nicholson, Sir Robin Buchanan, Kt., Ph.D., F.R.S.

Nickerson, Sir Joseph, Kt.

Nickson, Sir David Wigley, K.B.E.

Nicolson, Sir David Lancaster, Kt.

Nield, Sir Basil Edward, Kt., C.B.E., Q.C.

Nield, Sir William Alan, G.C.M.G., K.C.B.

Nightingale, Sir Charles Manners Gamaliel, Bt. (1628).

Nightingale, Sir John Cyprian, Kt., C.B.E., B.E.M., Q.P.M.

Nimmo, *Hon.* Sir John Angus, Kt., C.B.E.

Niven, Sir (Cecil) Rex, Kt., C.M.G., M.C.

Nixon, Sir Edwin Ronald, Kt., C.B.E.

Nixon, *Rev.* Sir Kenneth Michael John Basil, Bt. (1906).

Noad, Sir Kenneth Beeson, Kt., M.D.

Noble, Sir Iain Andrew, Bt., O.B.E. (1923).

Noble, Sir Marc Brunel, Bt. (1902).

Noble, Sir (Thomas Alexander) Fraser, Kt., M.B.E.

Nock, Sir Norman Lindfield, Kt.

Noel, Sir Claude, Kt., C.M.G.

Nolan, *Hon.* Sir Michael Patrick, Kt.

Nolan, Sir Sidney Robert, Kt., O.M., C.B.E.

Nordmeyer, *Hon.* Sir Arnold Henry, K.C.M.G.

Norman, Sir Arthur Gordon, K.B.E., D.F.C.

Norman, *Vice-Adm.* Sir (Horace) Geoffrey, K.C.V.O., C.B., C.B.E.

Norman, Sir Mark Annesley, Bt. (1915).

Norman, *Prof.* Sir Richard Oswald Chandler, K.B.E., F.R.S.

Norman, Sir Robert Wentworth, Kt.

Normanton, Sir Tom, Kt., T.D.

Norris, Sir Alfred Henry, K.B.E.

Norris, *Vice-Adm.* Sir Charles Fred Wivell, K.B.E., C.B., D.S.O.

Norris, *Air Chief Marshal* Sir Christopher Neil Foxley-, G.C.B., D.S.O., O.B.E.

Norris, Sir Eric George, K.C.M.G.

Norris, *Hon.* Sir John Gerald, Kt., E.D.

North, Sir Thomas Lindsay, Kt.

North, Sir (William) Jonathan (Frederick), Bt. (1920).

Northam, Sir William Herbert, Kt., C.B.E.

Norton, Sir Clifford John, K.C.M.G., C.V.O.

Norwood, Sir Walter Neville, Kt.

Nossal, Sir Gustav Joseph Victor, Kt., C.B.E.

Nosworthy, Sir John Reeve, Kt., C.B.E.

Nott, *Rt. Hon.* Sir John William Frederic, K.C.B.

Nourse, *Rt. Hon.* Sir Martin Charles, Kt.

Nugent, Sir John Edwin Lavallin, Bt. (I. 1795).

Nugent, *Maj.* Sir Peter Walter James, Bt. (1831).

Nugent, Sir Robin George Colborne, Bt. (1806).

Nuttall, Sir Nicholas Keith Lillington, Bt. (1922).

Nutting, *Rt. Hon.* Sir (Harold) Anthony, Bt. (1903).

Oakeley, Sir John Digby Atholl, Bt. (1790).

Oakes, Sir Christopher, Bt. (1939).

Oakshott, Hon. Sir Anthony Hendrie, Bt. (1959).

Oates, Sir Thomas, Kt., C.M.G., O.B.E.

Oatley, Sir Charles William, Kt., O.B.E., F.R.S.

Obolensky, *Prof.* Sir Dimitri, Kt.

O'Brien, Sir Frederick William Fitzgerald, Kt.

O'Brien, Sir Timothy John, Bt. (1849).

O'Brien, Sir Richard, Kt., D.S.O., M.C.

O'Brien, *Adm.* Sir William Donough, K.C.B., D.S.C.

O'Connell, Sir Morgan Donal Conail, Bt. (1869).

O'Connor, *Rt. Hon.* Sir Patrick McCarthy, Kt.

O'Dea, Sir Patrick Jerad, K.C.V.O.

Odell, Sir Stanley John, Kt.

Ogilvie, Sir Alec Drummond, Kt.

Ogilvy, Sir David John Wilfrid, Bt. (s. 1626).

Ognall, *Hon.* Sir Harry Henry, Kt.

O'Halloran, Sir Charles Ernest, Kt.

Ohlson, Sir Brian Eric Christopher, Bt. (1920).

Okeover, *Capt.* Sir Peter Ralph Leopold Walker-, Bt. (1886).

Oldman, *Col.* Sir Hugh Richard Deare, K.B.E., M.C.

Olewale, *Hon.* Sir Niwia Ebia, Kt.

Oliphant, Sir Mark (Marcus Laurence Elwin), K.B.E., F.R.S.

Oliver, Sir (Frederick) Ernest, Kt., C.B.E., T.D.

O'Loghlen, Sir Colman Michael, Bt. (1838).

Olver, Sir Stephen John Linley, K.B.E., C.M.G.

O'Neil, *Hon.* Sir Desmond Henry, Kt.

Ongley, *Hon.* Sir Joseph Augustine, Kt.

Onslow, Sir John Roger Wilmot, Bt. (1797).

Oppenheim, Sir Alexander, Kt., O.B.E., D.S.C., F.R.S.E.

Oppenheim, Sir Duncan Morris, Kt.

Oppenheimer, Sir Michael Bernard Grenville, Bt. (1921).

Oppenheimer, Sir Philip Jack, Kt.

Opperman, *Hon.* Sir Hubert Ferdinand, Kt., O.B.E.

Orde, Sir John Alexander Campbell-, Bt. (1790).

O'Regan, *Hon.* Sir John Barry, Kt.

Organe, *Prof.* Sir Geoffrey Stephen William, Kt., M.D.

Ormond, Sir John Davies Wilder, Kt., B.E.M.

Ormrod, *Rt. Hon.* Sir Roger Fray Greenwood, Kt.

Orr, *Rt. Hon.* Sir Alan Stewart, Kt., O.B.E.

Orr, Sir David Alexander, Kt., M.C.

Orr, Sir John Henry, Kt., O.B.E., Q.P.M.

Osborn, Sir Richard Henry Danvers, Bt. (1662).

Osborn, Sir John Holbrook, Kt.

Osborne, Sir Basil, Kt., C.B.E.

Osborne, Sir Peter George, Bt. (I. 1629).

Osifelo, Sir Frederick Aubarua, Kt., M.B.E.

Osman, Sir (Abdool) Raman Mahomed, G.C.M.G., C.B.E.

Osmond, Sir Douglas, Kt., C.B.E.

Osmond, Sir (Stanley) Paul, Kt., C.B.

Oswald, *Adm.* Sir John Julian Robertson, K.C.B.

Otton, Sir Geoffrey John, K.C.B.

Otton, *Hon.* Sir Philip Howard, Kt.

Oulton, Sir Antony Derek Maxwell, K.C.B., Q.C.

Outram, Sir Alan James, Bt. (1858).

Pilditch, Sir Richard Edward, Bt. (1929).

Pile, Sir Frederick Devereux, Bt. M.C. (1900).

Pile, Sir William Dennis, G.C.B., M.B.E.

Pilkington, Sir Lionel Alexander Bethune, (Sir Alastair), Kt., F.R.S.

Pilkington, Sir Thomas Henry Milborne-Swinnerton-, Bt. (s. 1635).

Pill, *Hon.* Sir Malcolm Thomas, Kt.

Pillar, *Adm.* Sir William Thomas, G.B.E, K.C.B.

Pindling, *Rt. Hon.* Sir Lynden Oscar, K.C.M.G.

Pinsent, Sir Christopher Roy, Bt. (1938).

Piper, Sir David Towry, Kt., C.B.E.

Pippard, *Prof.* Sir (Alfred) Brian, Kt., F.R.S.

Pirbhai, Sir Eboo, Kt., O.B.E.

Pirie, *Gp. Capt.* Sir Gordon Hamish, Kt., C.V.O., C.B.E.

Pitblado, Sir David Bruce, K.C.B., C.V.O.

Pitoi, Sir Sere, Kt., C.B.E.

Pitt, Sir Harry Raymond, Kt., Ph.D., F.R.S.

Pitts, Sir Cyril Alfred, Kt.

Pixley, Sir Neville Drake, Kt., M.B.E., V.R.D.

Pizey, *Adm.* Sir (Charles Thomas) Mark, G.B.E., C.B., D.S.O.

Plaister, Sir Sydney, Kt., C.B.E.

Plastow, Sir David Arnold Stuart, Kt.

†Platt, Sir (Frank) Lindsey, Bt. (1958).

Platt, *Prof.* Hon. Sir Peter, Bt. (1959).

Playfair, Sir Edward Wilder, K.C.B.

Pleass, Sir Clement John, K.C.M.G., K.C.V.O., K.B.E.

Pliatzky, Sir Leo, K.C.B.

Plimmer, Sir Clifford Ulric, K.B.E.

Plowman, Sir (John) Anthony, Kt.

Plowman, *Hon.* Sir John Robin, Kt., C.B.E.

Plumb, Sir (Charles) Henry, Kt.

Plumb, *Prof.* Sir John Harold, Kt.

Pochin, Sir Edward Eric, Kt., C.B.E., M.D., F.R.C.P.

Poett, *Gen.* Sir (Joseph Howard) Nigel, K.C.B., D.S.O.

Pole, *Col.* Sir John Gawen Carew, Bt., D.S.O., T.D. (1628).

Pole, Sir Peter Van Notten, Bt. (1791).

Pollard, Sir (Charles) Herbert, Kt., C.B.E.

Pollen, Sir John Michael Hungerford, Bt. (1795).

Pollock, Sir George, Kt., Q.C.

Pollock, Sir George Frederick, Bt. (1866).

Pollock, Sir Giles Hampden Montagu-, Bt. (1872).

Pollock, *Admiral of the Fleet* Sir Michael Patrick, G.C.B., M.V.O., D.S.C.

Pollock, Sir William Horace Montagu-, K.C.M.G.

Ponsonby, Sir Ashley Charles Gibbs, Bt., M.C. (1956).

Pontin, Sir Frederick William, Kt.

Poore, Sir Herbert Edward, Bt. (1795).

Pope, *Vice-Adm.* Sir (John) Ernle, K.C.B.

Pope, Sir Joseph Albert, Kt., D.SC., Ph.D.

Popper, *Prof.* Sir Karl Raimund, Kt., C.H., Ph.D., F.R.S.

Popplewell, *Hon.* Sir Oliver Bury, Kt.

Portal, Sir Jonathan Francis, Bt. (1901).

Porter, Sir John Simon Horsbrugh-, Bt. (1902).

Porter, *Prof.* Sir George, Kt., F.R.S., Ph.D., Sc.D.

Porter, Sir Leslie, Kt.

Porter, *Air Marshal* Sir (Melvin) Kenneth (Drowley), K.C.B., C.B.E.

Porter, *Hon.* Sir Murray Victor, Kt.

Porter, *Rt. Hon.* Sir Robert Wilson, Kt., Q.C.

Posnett, Sir Richard Neil, K.B.E., C.M.G.

Potter, Sir (Joseph) Raymond (Lynden), Kt.

Potter, *Hon.* Sir Mark Howard, Kt.

Potter, *Maj.-Gen.* Sir (Wilfrid) John, K.B.E., C.B.

Potter, Sir (William) Ian, Kt.

Potts, *Hon.* Sir Francis Humphrey, Kt.

Pound, Sir John David, Bt. (1905).

Pountain, Sir Eric John, Kt.

Powell, Sir (Arnold Joseph) Philip, Kt., C.H., O.B.E., R.A., F.R.I.B.A.

Powell, Sir Nicholas Folliott Douglas, Bt. (1897).

Powell, Sir Richard Royle, G.C.B., K.B.E., C.M.G.

Power, Sir Alastair John Cecil, Bt. (1924).

Powles, Sir Guy Richardson, K.B.E., C.M.G., E.D.

Poynton, Sir (Arthur) Hilton, G.C.M.G.

Prain, Sir Ronald Lindsay, Kt., O.B.E.

Prendergast, Sir John Vincent, K.B.E., C.M.G., G.M.

Prentice, *Rt. Hon.* Sir Reginald Ernest, Kt.

Prentice, *Hon.* Sir William Thomas, Kt., M.B.E.

Prescott, Sir Mark, Bt. (1938).

Preston, Sir Kenneth Huson, Kt.

Preston, Sir Peter Sansome, K.C.B.

Preston, Sir Ronald Douglas Hildebrand, Bt. (1815).

Pretyman, Sir Walter Frederick, K.B.E.

Prevost, Sir Christopher Gerald, Bt. (1805).

Price, Sir Charles Keith Napier Rugge-, Bt. (1804).

Price, Sir David Ernest Campbell, Kt., M.P.

Price, Sir Francis Caradoc Rose, Bt. (1815).

Price, Sir Frank Leslie, Kt.

Price, Sir (James) Robert, K.B.E.

Price, Sir Leslie Victor, Kt., O.B.E.

Price, Sir Norman Charles, K.C.B.

Price, Sir Robert John Green-, Bt. (1874).

Prichard, Sir Montague Illtyd, Kt., C.B.E., M.C.

Prickett, *Air Chief Marshal* Sir Thomas Other, K.C.B., D.S.O., D.F.C.

Prideaux, Sir Humphrey Povah Treverbian, Kt., O.B.E.

Prideaux, Sir John Francis, Kt., O.B.E.

Primrose, Sir Alasdair Neil, Bt. (1903).

Pringle, *Air Marshal* Sir Charles Norman Seton, K.B.E.

Pringle, *Lt.-Gen.* Sir Steuart (Robert), Bt., K.C.B., R.M. (s. 1683).

Pritchard, Sir Asa Hubert, Kt.

Pritchard, Sir John Michael, Kt., C.B.E.

Pritchard, Sir Neil, K.C.M.G.

Pritchett, Sir Victor Sawdon, Kt., C.B.E.

Proby, Sir Peter, Bt. (1952).

Proctor, Sir Roderick Consett, Kt., M.B.E.

Proud, Sir John Seymour, Kt.

Pryke, Sir David Dudley, Bt. (1926).

Pugh, Sir Idwal Vaughan, K.C.B.

Pugsley, *Prof.* Sir Alfred Grenvile, Kt., O.B.E., D.SC., F.R.S.

Pullen, Sir William Reginald James, K.C.V.O.

Pullinger, Sir (Francis) Alan, Kt., C.B.E.

Pumphrey, Sir (John) Laurence, K.C.M.G.

Purchas, *Rt. Hon.* Sir Francis Brooks, Kt.

Quayle, Sir (John) Anthony, Kt., C.B.E.

Quicke, Sir John Godolphin, Kt., C.B.E.

Quilliam, *Hon.* Sir (James) Peter, Kt.

Quilter, Sir Anthony Raymond Leopold Cuthbert, Bt. (1897).

Quinlan, Sir Michael Edward, K.C.B.

Quirk, *Prof.* Sir (Charles) Randolph, C.B.E., F.B.A.

Rabukawaqa, Sir Josua Rasilau, K.B.E., M.V.O.

Raby, Sir Victor Harry, K.B.E., C.B., M.C.

Radcliffe, Sir Sebastian Everard, Bt. (1813).

Radclyffe, Sir Charles Edward Mott-, Kt.

Radford, Sir Ronald Walter, K.C.B., M.B.E.

Radzinowicz, *Prof.* Sir Leon, Kt., LL.D.

Rae, *Hon.* Sir Wallace Alexander Ramsay, Kt.

Raeburn, Sir Michael Edward Norman, Bt. (1923).

Raeburn, *Maj.-Gen.* Sir (William) Digby (Manifold), K.C.V.O., C.B., D.S.O., M.B.E.

Raffray, Sir Piat Joseph Raymond Andre, Kt.

Raikes, *Vice-Adm.* Sir Iwan Geoffrey, K.C.B., C.B.E., D.S.C.

Ralli, Sir Godfrey Victor, Bt., T.D. (1912).

Ramphal, Sir Shridath Surendranath, Kt., C.M.G.

Ramphul, Sir Baalkhristna, Kt.

Rampton, Sir Jack Leslie, K.C.B.

Ramsay, Sir Alexander William Burnett, Bt. (1806).

Ramsay, Sir Thomas Meek, Kt., C.M.G.

Ramsbotham, *Lt.-Gen.* Sir David John, K.C.B., C.B.E.

Ramsbotham, *Hon.* Sir Peter Edward, G.C.M.G., G.C.V.O.

Ramsden, Sir Geoffrey Charles Frescheville, Kt., C.I.E.

Ramsden, Sir John Charles Josslyn, Bt. (1689).

Ramsey, Sir Alfred Ernest, Kt.

Randle, *Prof.* Sir Philip John, Kt.

Ranger, Sir Douglas, Kt., F.R.C.S.

Rank, Sir Benjamin Keith, Kt., C.M.G.

†Rankin, Sir Ian Niall, Bt. (1898).

Raper, *Vice-Adm.* Sir (Robert) George, K.C.B.

Rasch, *Maj.* Sir Richard Guy Carne, Bt. (1903).

Rashleigh, Sir Richard Harry, Bt. (1831).

Rault, Sir Louis Joseph Maurice, Kt.

Rawlins, *Surgeon Vice-Adm.* Sir John Stuart Pepys, K.B.E.

Rawlinson, Sir Anthony Henry John, Bt. (1891).

Rayne, Sir Edward, Kt., C.V.O.

Read, *Air Marshal* Sir Charles Frederick, K.B.E., C.B., D.F.C., A.F.C.

Read, *Gen.* Sir (John) Antony (Jervis), G.C.B., C.B.E., D.S.O., M.C.

Read, Sir John Emms, Kt.

Reade, Sir Clyde Nixon, Bt. (1661).

Readhead, Sir James Templeman, Bt. (1922).

Reay, *Lt.-Gen.* Sir (Hubert) Alan John, K.B.E.

Redgrave, *Maj.-Gen.* Sir Roy Michael Frederick, K.B.E., M.C.

Redmayne, Sir Nicholas, Bt. (1964).

Redmond, Sir James, Kt.

Redshaw, Sir Leonard, Kt.

Redwood, Sir Peter Boverton, Bt. (1911).

Reece, Sir Charles Hugh, Kt.

Reece, Sir James Gordon, Kt.

Reed, *Hon.* Sir Nigel Vernon, Kt., C.B.E.

Rees, Sir (Charles William) Stanley, Kt., T.D.

Reeve, *Hon.* Sir (Charles) Trevor, Kt.

Reeves, *Most Rev.* Paul Alfred, G.C.M.G., G.C.V.O.

Reffell, *Adm.* Sir Derek Roy, K.C.B.

Refshauge, *Maj-Gen.* Sir William Dudley, Kt., C.B.E.

Reid, Sir Alexander James, Bt. (1897).

Reid, *Hon.* Sir George Oswald, Kt., Q.C.

Reid, *Air Vice-Marshal* Sir (George) Ranald Macfarlane, K.C.B., D.S.O., M.C.

Reid, Sir (Harold) Martin (Smith), K.B.E., C.M.G.

Reid, Sir Hugh, Bt. (1922).

Reid, Sir John James Andrew, K.C.M.G., C.B., T.D.

Reid, Sir Norman Robert, Kt.

Reid, Sir Robert Basil, Kt., C.B.E.

Reilly, Sir (D'Arcy) Patrick, G.C.M.G., O.B.E.

Reilly, *Lt.-Gen.* Sir Jeremy Calcott, K.C.B., D.S.O.

Reiss, Sir John Anthony Ewart, Kt., B.E.M.

Renals, Sir Stanley, Bt. (1895).

Rendell, Sir William, Kt.

Rennie, Sir Alfred Baillie, Kt.

Rennie, Sir John Shaw, G.C.M.G., O.B.E.

Renouf, Sir Clement William Bailey, Kt.

Renouf, Sir Francis Henry, Kt.

Renshaw, Sir (Charles) Maurice Bine, Bt. (1903).

Renwick, Sir Richard Eustace, Bt. (1921).

Reporter, Sir Shapoor Ardeshirji, K.B.E.

Revans, Sir John, Kt., C.B.E.

Rex, *Hon.* Sir Robert Richmond, K.B.E., C.M.G.

Reynolds, Sir David James, Bt. (1923).

Reynolds, Sir Peter William John, Kt., C.B.E.

Rhodes, Sir Basil Edward, Kt., C.B.E., T.D.

Rhodes, Sir John Christopher Douglas, Bt. (1919).

Rhodes, Sir Peregrine Alexander, K.C.M.G.

Richards, *Hon.* Sir Edward Trenton, Kt., C.B.E.

Richards, Sir (Francis) Brooks, K.C.M.G., D.S.C.

Richards, Sir James Maude, Kt., C.B.E.

Richards, *Lt.-Gen.* Sir John Charles Chisholm, K.C.B., R.M.

Richards, Sir Rex Edward, Kt., D.SC., F.R.S.

Richardson, Sir Anthony Lewis, Bt. (1924).

Richardson, *Gen.* Sir Charles Leslie, G.C.B., C.B.E., D.S.O.

Richardson, *Air Marshal* Sir (David) William, K.B.E.

Richardson, Sir Egerton Rudolf, Kt., C.M.G.

Richardson, Sir (Horace) Frank, Kt.

Richardson, *Rt. Hon.* Sir Ivor Lloyd Morgan, Kt.

Richardson, Sir (John) Eric, Kt., C.B.E.

Richardson, Sir (Lionel) Earl George, Kt.

Richardson, *Lt.-Gen.* Sir Robert Francis, K.C.B., D.S.O., C.B.E.

Richardson, Sir Simon Alaisdair Stewart-, Bt. (s. 1630).

Riches, Sir Derek Martin Hurry, K.C.M.G.

Riches, *Gen.* Sir Ian Hurry, K.C.B., D.S.O.

Richmond, Sir Alan James, Kt.

Richmond, *Rt. Hon.* Sir Clifford Parris, K.B.E.

Richmond, Sir John Christopher Blake, K.C.M.G.

Richmond, Sir John Frederick, Bt. (1929).

Richmond, *Prof.* Sir Mark Henry, Kt., F.R.S.

Rickett, Sir Denis Hubert Fletcher, K.C.M.G., C.B.

Ricketts, Sir Robert Cornwallis Gerald St. Leger, Bt. (1828).

Ricks, Sir John Plowman, Kt.

Riddell, Sir John Charles Buchanan, Bt. (s. 1628).

Ridley, Sir Adam (Nicholas), Kt.

Ridley, Sir Sidney, Kt.

Ridsdale, Sir Julian Errington, Kt., M.P.

Rigby, *Lt.-Col.* Sir (Hugh) John (Macbeth), Bt. (1929).

Riley, Sir Ralph, Kt., F.R.S.

Ring, Sir Lindsay Roberts, G.B.E.

Ringadoo, *Hon.* Sir Veerasamy, G.C.M.G.

Ripley, Sir Hugh, Bt. (1880).

Risk, Sir Thomas Neilson, Kt.

Risson, *Maj.-Gen.* Sir Robert Joseph Henry, Kt., C.B., C.B.E., D.S.O., E.D.

Ritchie, Sir James Edward Thomson, Bt., T.D. (1918).

Rix, Sir Brian Norman Roger, Kt., C.B.E.

Rix, Sir John, Kt., M.B.E.

Roberts, Sir Bryan Clieve, K.C.M.G., Q.C.

Roberts, *Hon.* Sir Denys Tudor Emil, K.B.E., Q.C.

Roberts, Sir (Edward Fergus) Sidney, Kt., C.B.E.

Roberts, Sir Frank Kenyon, G.C.M.G., G.C.V.O.

Roberts, Sir Geoffrey Newland, Kt., C.B.E., A.F.C.

Roberts, *Brig.* Sir Geoffrey Paul Hardy-, K.C.V.O., C.B., C.B.E.

Roberts, Sir Gilbert Howland Rookehurst, Bt. (1809).

Roberts, Sir Gordon James, Kt., C.B.E.

Roberts, Sir Samuel, Bt. (1919).

Roberts, Sir Stephen James Leake, Kt.

Roberts, Sir William James Denby, Bt. (1909).

Robertson, *Prof.* Sir Alexander, Kt., C.B.E.

Robertson, Sir James Anderson, Kt., C.B.E.

Robertson, *Prof.* Sir Rutherford Ness, Kt., C.M.G.

Robins, Sir Ralph Harry, Kt.

Robinson, Sir Albert Edward Phineas, Kt.

Robinson, Sir Dove-Myer, Kt.

Robinson, *Prof.* Sir (Edward) Austin (Gossage), Kt., C.M.G., O.B.E., F.B.A.

Robinson, Sir John Beverley, Bt. (1854).

Robinson, Sir John James Michael Laud, Bt. (1660).

Robinson, *Rt. Hon.* Sir Kenneth, Kt.

Robinson, Sir Niall Bryan Lynch-, Bt., D.S.C. (1920).

Robinson, Sir Wilfred Henry Frederick, Bt. (1908).

Robotham, *Hon.* Sir Lascelles Lister, Kt.

Robson, *Prof.* Sir James Gordon, Kt., C.B.E.

Robson, Sir Thomas Buston, Kt., M.B.E.

Robson, *Vice-Adm.* Sir (William) Geoffrey (Arthur), K.B.E., C.B., D.S.O., D.S.C.

Roch, *Hon.* Sir John Ormond, Kt.

Roche, Sir David O'Grady, Bt. (1838).

Rodger, Sir William Glendinning, Kt., O.B.E.

Rodgers, Sir John Charles, Bt. (1964).

Rodrigues, Sir Alberto Maria, Kt., C.B.E., E.D.

Roe, *Air Chief Marshal* Sir Rex David, G.C.B., A.F.C.

Rogers, Sir Frank Jarvis, Kt.

Rogers, *Air Chief Marshal* Sir John Robson, K.C.B., C.B.E.

Rogers, Sir Philip, G.C.B., C.M.G.

Rogers, Sir Philip James, Kt., C.B.E.

Roll, *Rev.* Sir James William Cecil, Bt. (1921).

Rooke, Sir Denis Eric, Kt., C.B.E.

Roper, *Hon.* Sir Clinton Marcus, Kt.

Ropner, Sir John Bruce Woollacott, Bt. (1952).

Ropner, Sir Robert Douglas, Bt. (1904).

Roscoe, Sir Robert Bell, K.B.E.

Rose, Sir Alec Richard, Kt.

Rose, *Hon.* Sir Christopher Dudley Roger, Kt.

Rose, Sir Clive Martin, G.C.M.G.

Rose, Sir David Lancaster, Bt. (1874)

Rose, Sir Julian Day, Bt. (1872 and 1909).

Rosier, *Air Chief Marshal* Sir Frederick Ernest, G.C.B., C.B.E., D.S.O.

Roskill, Sir Ashton Wentworth, Kt., Q.C.

Ross, Sir Alexander, Kt.

Ross, Sir Archibald David Manisty, K.C.M.G.

Ross, Sir (James) Keith, Bt., R.D., F.R.C.S. (1960).

Ross, Sir Lewis Nathan, Kt., C.M.G.

Rosser, Sir Melvyn Wynne, Kt.

Rossi, Sir Hugh Alexis Louis, Kt., M.P.

Rostron, Sir Frank, Kt., M.B.E.

Roth, *Prof.* Sir Martin, Kt., M.D., F.R.C.P.

Rothenstein, Sir John Knewstub Maurice, Kt., C.B.E., Ph.D.

Rothnie, Sir Alan Keir, K.C.V.O., C.M.G.

Rougier, *Hon.* Sir Richard George, Kt.

Rous, Sir Anthony Gerald Roderick, K.C.M.G., O.B.E.

Row, *Hon.* Sir John Alfred, Kt.

Row, *Cdr.*, Sir Philip John, K.C.V.O., O.B.E., R.N.

Rowe, Sir Henry Peter, K.C.B., Q.C.

Rowe-Ham, Sir David Kenneth, G.B.E.

Rowell, Sir John Joseph, Kt., C.B.E.

Rowland, *Air Marshal* Sir James Anthony, K.B.E., D.F.C., A.F.C.

Rowlands, *Air Marshal* Sir John Samuel, K.B.E., G.C.

Rowley, Sir Charles Robert, Bt. (1836).

Rowley, Sir Joshua Francis, Bt. (1786).

Rowling, *Rt. Hon.* Sir Wallace Edward, K.C.M.G.

Rowntree, Sir Norman Andrew Forster, Kt.

Roxburgh, *Vice-Adm.* Sir John Charles Young, K.C.B., C.B.E., D.S.O., D.S.C.

Royden, Sir Christopher John, Bt. (1905).

Rucker, Sir Arthur Nevil, K.C.M.G., C.B., C.B.E.

Rumbold, Sir (Horace) Algernon (Fraser), K.C.M.G., C.I.E.

Rumbold, Sir Henry John Sebastian, Bt. (1779).

Rumbold, Sir Jack Seddon, Kt.

Runciman, *Hon.* Sir Steven (James Cochran Stevenson), Kt., C.H.

Rusby, *Vice-Adm.* Sir Cameron, K.C.B., M.V.O.

Russell, Sir Archibald Edward, Kt., C.B.E., F.R.S.

Russell, Sir Charles Ian, Bt. (1916).

Russell, Sir Evelyn Charles Sackville, Kt.

Russell, Sir George Michael, Bt. (1812).

Russell, Sir (Robert) Mark, K.C.M.G.

Russell, Sir Spencer Thomas, Kt.

Russell, *Rt. Hon.* Sir (Thomas) Patrick, Kt.

Russo, Sir Peter George, Kt., C.B.E.

Rutter, Sir Frank William Eden, K.B.E.

Ryan, Sir Derek Gerald, Bt. (1919).

Rycroft, Sir Richard Newton, Bt. (1784).

Rymill, Sir Arthur Campbell, Kt.

Ryrie, Sir William Sinclair, K.C.B.

Sainsbury, *Hon.* Sir John Davan, Kt.

Sainsbury, Sir Robert James, Kt.

St. Aubyn, Sir (John) Arscott Molesworth-, Bt. (1689).

St. George, Sir Denis Howard, Bt. (l. 1766).

St. Johnston, Sir Kerry, Kt.

Sainty, Sir John Christopher, K.C.B.

Sakzewski, Sir Albert, Kt.

Salt, Sir Anthony Houlton, Bt. (1869).

Salt, Sir (Thomas) Michael John, Bt. (1899).

Samuel, Sir Jon Michael Glen, Bt. (1898).

Samuelson, Sir (Bernard) Michael (Francis), Bt. (1884).

Sandberg, Sir Michael Graham Ruddock, Kt., C.B.E.

Sanders, Sir Robert Tait, K.B.E., C.M.G.

Sanderson, Sir (Frank Philip) Bryan, Bt. (1920).

Sandilands, Sir Francis Edwin Prescott, Kt., C.B.E.

Sarei, Sir Alexis Holyweek, Kt., C.B.E.

Sarell, Sir Roderick Francis Gisbert, K.C.M.G., K.C.V.O.

Sargant, Sir (Henry) Edmund, Kt.

Saunders, *Hon.* Sir John Anthony Holt, Kt., C.B.E., D.S.O., M.C.

Saunders, Sir Owen Alfred, Kt., D.S.C., F.R.S.

Saunders, Sir Peter, Kt.

Sauzier, Sir (André) Guy, Kt., C.B.E., E.D.

Savage, Sir Ernest Walter, Kt.

Saville, *Hon.* Sir Mark Oliver, Kt.

Savory, Sir Reginald Charles Frank, Kt., C.B.E.

Say, *Rt. Rev.* Richard David, K.C.V.O.

Schiemann, *Hon.* Sir Konrad Hermann Theodor, Kt.

Scholey, Sir David Gerald, Kt., C.B.E.

Scholey, Sir Robert, Kt., C.B.E.

Scholtens, Sir James Henry, K.C.V.O.

Schubert, Sir Sydney, Kt.

Schultz, Sir (Joseph) Leopold, Kt., O.B.E.

Schuster, Sir (Felix) James Moncrieff, Bt., O.B.E. (1906).

Scipio, Sir Hudson Rupert, Kt.

Scoon, Sir Paul, G.C.M.G., G.C.V.O., O.B.E.

Scoones, *Maj.-Gen.* Sir Reginald Laurence, K.B.E., C.B., D.S.O.

Scopes, Sir Leonard Arthur, K.C.V.O., C.M.G., O.B.E.

Scott, Sir Anthony Percy, Bt. (1913).

Scott, Sir (Charles) Hilary, Kt.

Scott, Sir (Charles) Peter, K.B.K., C.M.G.

Scott, Sir David Aubrey, G.C.M.G.

Scott, Sir George Edward, Kt., C.B.E.

Scott, Sir Ian Dixon, K.C.M.G., K.C.V.O., C.I.E.

Scott, Sir James Walter, Bt. (1962).

Scott, Sir Michael, K.C.V.O., C.M.G.

Scott, Sir Michael Fergus Maxwell, Bt. (1642).

Scott, Sir Oliver Christopher Anderson, Bt. (1909).

Scott, Sir Peter Markham, Kt., C.H., C.B.E., D.S.C.

Scott, *Prof.* Sir Philip John, K.B.E.

Scott, *Hon.* Sir Richard Rashleigh Folliott, Kt.

Scott, Sir Terence Charles Stuart Morrison-, Kt., D.S.C., D.SC.

Scott, Sir Walter, Bt. (1907).

Scott, *Rear-Adm.* Sir (William) David (Stewart), K.B.E., C.B.

Scowen, Sir Eric Frank, Kt., M.D., D.S.C., LL.D., F.R.C.P., F.R.C.S.

Scragg, *Air Vice-Marshal* Sir Colin, K.B.E., C.B., A.F.C.

Scrivenor, Sir Thomas Vaisey, Kt., C.M.G.

Seale, Sir John Henry, Bt. (1838).

Seaman, Sir Keith Douglas, K.C.V.O., O.B.E.

Sebright, Sir Peter Giles Vivian, Bt. (1626).

Seccombe, Sir (William) Vernon Stephen, Kt.

Secombe, Sir Harry Donald, Kt., C.B.E.

Seconde, Sir Reginald Louis, K.C.M.G., C.V.O.

Seely, Sir Nigel Edward, Bt. (1896).

Seeto, Sir Ling James, Kt., M.B.E.

Seeyave, Sir Rene Sow Choung, Kt., C.B.E

Selby, Sir Kenneth, Kt.

Seligman, Sir Peter Wendel, Kt., C.B.E.

Sells, Sir David Perronet, Kt.

Senior, Sir Edward Walters, Kt., C.M.G.

Sergeant, Sir Patrick, Kt.

Series, Sir (Joseph Michel) Emile, Kt., C.B.E.

Serpell, Sir David Radford, K.C.B., C.M.G., O.B.E.

†Seton, Sir Iain Bruce, Bt. (s. 1663).

Seton, Sir Robert James, Bt. (s. 1683).

Sewell, Sir (John) Allan, Kt., I.S.O.

Seymour, *Cdr.* Sir Michael Culme-Bt., R.N. (1809).

Shakerley, Sir Geoffrey Adam, Bt. (1838).

Shakespeare, Sir William Geoffrey, Bt. (1942).

Shapland, Sir William Arthur, Kt.

Sharp, Sir Adrian, Bt. (1922).

Sharp, Sir Eric, Kt., C.B.E.

Sharp, Sir George, Kt., O.B.E.

Sharp, Sir Kenneth Johnston, Kt., T.D.

Sharp, Sir Milton Reginald, Bt. (1920).

Sharp, Sir Richard Lyall, K.C.V.O., C.B.

Sharp, Sir (William Harold) Angus, K.B.E., Q.P.M.

Sharpe, Sir Frank Victor, Kt., C.M.G., O.B.E., E.D.

Sharpe, *Hon.* Sir John Henry, Kt., C.B.E.

Sharpe, Sir Reginald Taaffe, Kt., Q.C.

Shattock, Sir Gordon, Kt.

Shaw, Sir Brian Piers, Kt.

Shaw, Sir (Charles) Barry, Kt., C.B., Q.C.

Shaw, Sir (John) Giles (Dunkerley), Kt., M.P.

Shaw, Sir John Michael Robert Best-, Bt. (1665).

Shaw, Sir Michael Norman, Kt., M.P.

Shaw, Sir Robert, Bt. (1821).

Shaw, Sir Roy, Kt.

Shaw, Sir Run Run, Kt., C.B.E.

Sheen, *Hon.* Sir Barry Cross, Kt.

Sheffield, Sir Reginald Adrian Berkeley, Bt. (1755).

Shehadie, Sir Nicholas Michael, Kt., O.B.E.

Shelbourne, Sir Philip, Kt.

Sheldon, *Hon.* Sir (John) Gervase (Kensington), Kt.

Shelley, Sir John Richard, Bt. (1611).

Shepheard, Sir Peter Faulkner, Kt., C.B.E.

Shepheard, Sir Victor George, K.C.B.

Shepherd, Sir Peter Malcolm, Kt., C.B.E.

Sherlock, Sir Philip Manderson, K.B.E.

Sherman, Sir Alfred, Kt.

Sherman, Sir Louis, Kt., O.B.E.

Shields, Sir Neil Stanley, Kt., M.C.

Shiffner, Sir Henry David, Bt. (1818).

Shillington, Sir (Robert Edward) Graham, Kt., C.B.E.

Shock, Sir Maurice, Kt.

Sholl, *Hon.* Sir Reginald Richard, Kt.

Shone, Sir Robert Minshull, Kt., C.B.E.

Short, *Brig.* Sir Noel Edward Vivian, Kt., M.B.E., M.C.

Shuckburgh, Sir (Charles Arthur) Evelyn, G.C.M.G., C.B.

†Shuckburgh, Sir Rupert Charles Gerald, Bt. (1660).

Sich, Sir Rupert Leigh, Kt., C.B.

Siddall, Sir Norman, Kt., C.B.E.

Sidey, *Air Marshal* Sir Ernest Shaw, K.B.E., C.B., M.D.

Sie, Sir Banja Tejan-, G.C.M.G.

Simeon, Sir John Edmund Barrington, Bt. (1815).

Simonet, Sir Louis Marcel Pierre, Kt., C.B.E.

Simpson, *Hon.* Sir Alfred Henry, Kt.

Simpson, Sir William James, Kt.

Sinclair, Sir Clive Marles, Kt.

Sinclair, Sir George Evelyn, Kt., C.M.G., O.B.E.

Sinclair, Sir Ian McTaggart, K.C.M.G., Q.C.

Sinclair, Sir John Rollo Norman Blair, Bt. (s. 1704).

Sinclair, *Prof.* Sir Keith, Kt., C.B.E.

Sinclair, *Air Vice-Marshal* Sir Laurence Frank, G.C., K.C.B., C.B.E., D.S.O.

Sinclair, Sir Ronald Ormiston, K.B.E.

Singh, *Hon.* Sir Vijay Raghubir, Kt.

Singhania, Sir Padampat, Kt.

Singleton, Sir Edward Henry Sibbald, Kt.

Sinnamon, Sir Hercules, Kt., O.B.E.

Sisson, Sir Roy, Kt.

Sitwell, Sir Sacheverell, Bt., C.H. (1808).

Skeet, Sir Trevor Herbert Harry, Kt., M.P.

Skeggs, Sir Clifford George, Kt.

Skellerup, Sir Valdemar Reid, Kt., C.B.E.

Skingsley, *Air Marshal* Sir Anthony Gerald, K.C.B.

Skinner, Sir Thomas Edward, K.B.E.

Skinner, Sir (Thomas) Keith (Hewitt), Bt. (1912).

Skipwith, Sir Patrick Alexander d'Estoteville, Bt. (1622).

Skyrme, Sir (William) Thomas (Charles), K.C.V.O., C.B., C.B.E.,T.D.

Slade, Sir Benjamin Julian Alfred, Bt. (1831).

Slade, *Rt. Hon.* Sir Christopher John, Kt.

Slaney, *Prof.* Sir Geoffrey, K.B.E.

Slater, *Vice-Adm.* Sir John Cunningham Kirkwood, K.C.B., L.V.O.

Slattery, *Rear-Adm.* Sir Matthew Sausse, K.B.E., C.B.

Sleight, Sir John Frederick, Bt. (1920).

Slimmings, Sir William Kenneth MacLeod, Kt., C.B.E.

Sloman, Sir Albert Edward, Kt., C.B.E.

Slynn, *Hon.* Sir Gordon, Kt.

Smallpeice, Sir Basil, K.C.V.O.

Smallwood, *Air Chief Marshal* Sir Denis Graham, G.B.E., K.C.B., D.S.O., D.F.C.

Smart, *Prof.* Sir George Algernon, Kt., M.D., F.R.C.P.

Smart, Sir Jack, Kt., C.B.E.

Smedley, Sir Harold, K.C.M.G., M.B.E.

Smeeton, *Vice-Adm.* Sir Richard Michael, K.C.B., M.B.E.

Smiley, Sir Hugh Houston, Bt. (1903).

Smirk, Sir (Frederick) Horace, K.B.E., M.D.

Smith, Sir Alan, Kt., C.B.E., D.F.C.

Smith, Sir Alexander Mair, Kt., Ph.D.

Smith, Sir Arthur Henry, Kt.

Smith, Sir Charles Bracewell-, Bt. (1947).

Smith, Sir Christopher Sydney Winwood, Bt. (1809).

Smith, Sir Cyril, Kt., M.B.E., M.P.

Smith, *Prof.* Sir David Cecil, Kt., F.R.S.

Smith, Sir Dudley (Gordon), Kt., M.P.

Smith, *Maj.-Gen.* Sir (Francis) Brian Wyldbore-, Kt., C.B., D.S.O., O.B.E.

Smith, *Prof.* Sir (Francis) Graham, Kt., F.R.S.

Smith, Sir (Frank) Ewart, Kt.

Smith, *Col.* Sir Henry Abel, K.C.M.G., K.C.V.O., D.S.O.

Smith, Sir Howard Frank Trayton, G.C.M.G.

Smith, *Hon.* Sir James Alfred, Kt., C.B.E., T.D.

Smith, Sir (James) Eric., Kt., C.B.E., SC.D., F.R.S.

Smith, Sir John Hamilton-Spencer-, Bt. (1804).

Smith, Sir John Kenneth Newson-, Bt. (1944).

Smith, Sir John Lindsay Eric., Kt., C.B.E.

Smith, Sir Laurence Barton Grafftey-, K.C.M.G., K.B.E.

Smith, Sir Leonard Herbert, Kt., C.B.E.

Smith, Sir Leslie Edward George, Kt.

Smith, Sir Raymond Horace, K.B.E.

Smith, Sir Reginald Beaumont, Kt.

Smith, Sir Richard Rathbone Vassar-, Bt., T.D. (1917).

Smith, Sir (Richard) Robert Law-, Kt., C.B.E., A.F.C.

Smith, Sir Robert Courtney, Kt., C.B.E.

Smith, Sir Robert Hill, Bt., (1945).

Smith, *Air Marshal* Sir Roy David Austen-, K.B.E., C.B., D.F.C.

Smith, *Prof.* Sir Thomas Broun, Kt., Q.C.

Smith, Sir (Thomas) Gilbert, Bt. (1897).

Smith, *Adm.* Sir Victor Alfred Trumper, K.B.E., C.B., D.S.C.

Smith, Sir William Reardon Rear-don-, Bt. (1920).

Smith, Sir (William) Reginald Verdon, Kt.

Smith, Sir (William) Richard Prince-, Bt. (1911).

Smithers, *Prof.* Sir David Waldron, Kt., M.D.

Smithers, Sir Peter Henry Berry Otway, Kt., V.R.D., D.Phil.

Smithers, *Hon.* Sir Reginald All-free, Kt.

Smyth, Sir Thomas Weyland Bowyer-, Bt., (1661).

Smyth, Sir Timothy John, Bt. (1955).

Snelling, Sir Arthur Wendell, K.C.M.G., K.C.V.O.

Snelson, Sir Edward Alec Abbott, K.B.E.

Soame, Sir Charles John Buckworth-Herne-, Bt. (1697).

Sobell, Sir Michael, Kt.

Sobers, Sir Garfield St. Auburn, Kt.

Solomon, Sir David Arnold, Kt., M.B.E.

Solomons, *Hon.* Sir (Louis) Adrian, Kt.

Solti, Sir Georg, K.B.E.

Somerset, Sir Henry Beaufort, Kt., C.B.E.

Somerville, *Brig.* Sir John Nicholas, Kt., C.B.E.

Somerville, Sir Robert, K.C.V.O.

Sopwith, Sir Charles Ronald, Kt.

Sopwith, Sir Thomas Octave Murdoch, Kt., C.B.E.

Sorsbie, Sir Malin, Kt., C.B.E.

Soutar, *Air Marshal* Sir Charles John Williamson, K.B.E.

South, Sir Arthur, Kt.

†Southby, Sir John Richard Bilbe, Bt. (1937).

Southern, Sir Richard William, Kt., F.B.A.

Southern, Sir Robert, Kt., C.B.E.

Southey, Sir Robert John, Kt., C.M.G.

Southward, Sir Leonard Bingley, Kt., O.B.E.

Southward, Sir Ralph, K.C.V.O., F.R.C.P.

Southwood, *Prof.* Sir (Thomas) Richard (Edmund), Kt., F.R.S.

Southworth, Sir Frederick, Kt., Q.C.

Souyave, *Hon.* Sir (Louis) Georges, Kt.

Sowrey, *Air Marshal* Sir Frederick Beresford, K.C.B., C.B.E., A.F.C.

Soysa, Sir Warusahennedige Abraham Bastian, Kt., C.B.E.

Sparkes, Sir Robert Lyndley, Kt.

Sparrow, Sir John, Kt.

Spearman, Sir Alexander Young Richard Mainwaring, Bt. (1840).

Speed, Sir Robert William Arney, Kt., C.B., Q.C.

Speelman, Sir Cornelis Jacob, Bt. (1686).

Speight, *Hon.* Sir Graham Davies, Kt.

Speir, Sir Rupert Malise, Kt.

Spencer, Sir Kelvin Tallent, Kt., C.B.E., M.C.

Spender, *Prof.* Sir Stephen Harold, Kt., C.B.E.

Spicer, Sir James Wilton, Kt., M.P.

Spicer, Sir Peter James, Bt. (1906).

Spooner, Sir James Douglas, Kt.

Spotswood, *Marshal of the Royal Air Force* Sir Denis Frank, G.C.B., C.B.E., D.S.O., D.F.C.

Spratt, *Col.* Sir Greville Douglas, G.B.E., T.D.

Springer, Sir Hugh Worrell, G.C.M.G., G.C.V.O., C.B.E.

Spry, *Brig.* Sir Charles Chambers Fowell, Kt., C.B.E., D.S.O.

Spry, *Hon.* Sir John Farley, Kt.

Stabb, *Hon.* Sir William Walter, Kt., Q.C.

Stack, *Air Chief Marshal* Sir (Thomas) Neville, K.C.B., C.V.O., C.B.E., A.F.C.

Staine, *Hon.* Sir Albert Llewellyn, Kt., C.B.E.

Stainton, Sir Anthony Nathaniel, K.C.B., Q.C.

Stainton, Sir (John) Ross, Kt., C.B.E.

Stakis, Sir Reo Argiros, Kt.

Stallard, Sir Peter Hyla Gawne, K.C.M.G., C.V.O., M.B.E.

Stallworthy, Sir John Arthur, Kt., F.R.C.S.

Stamer, Sir (Lovelace) Anthony, Bt. (1809).

Stanbridge, *Air Vice-Marshal* Sir Brian Gerald Tivy, K.C.V.O., C.B.E., A.F.C.

Stanford, *Adm.* Sir Peter Maxwell, G.C.B., L.V.O.

Stanier, *Brig.* Sir Alexander Beville Gibbons, Bt., D.S.O., M.C. (1917).

Stanier, *Field Marshal* Sir John Wilfred, G.C.B., M.B.E.

Stanley, *Rt. Hon.* Sir John Paul, Kt., M.P.

Staples, Sir John Richard, Bt. (I. 1628).

Stapleton, Sir (Henry) Alfred, Bt. (1679).

Stark, Sir Andrew Alexander Steel, K.C.M.G., C.V.O.

Starke, *Hon.* Sir John Erskine, Kt.

Starkey, Sir John Philip, Bt. (1935).

Starritt, Sir James, K.C.V.O.

Statham, Sir Norman, K.C.M.G., C.V.O.

Staughton, *Rt. Hon.* Sir Christopher Stephen Thomas Jonathan Thayer, Kt.

Staveley, Sir John Malfroy, K.B.E., M.C.

Staveley, *Adm.* Sir William Doveton Minet, G.C.B.

Stebbings, Sir John Chalmer, Kt.

Steedman, *Air Chief Marshal* Sir Alasdair (Alexander McKay Sinclair), G.C.B., C.B.E., D.F.C.

Steel, Sir David Edward Charles, Kt., D.S.O., M.C., T.D.

Steel, *Maj.* Sir (Fiennes) William Strang, Bt. (1938).

Steel, Sir James, Kt., C.B.E.

Steele, Sir (Philip John) Rupert, Kt.

Steere, Sir Ernest Henry Lee-, K.B.E.

Stenhouse, Sir Nicol, Kt.

Stening, *Col.* Sir George Grafton Lees, Kt., E.D.

Stephen, *Rt. Hon.* Sir Ninian Martin, G.C.M.G., G.C.V.O., K.B.E.

Stephens, Sir David, K.C.B., C.V.O.

Stephenson, Sir Henry Upton, Bt. (1936).

Stephenson, *Rt. Hon.* Sir John Frederick Eustace, Kt.

Stephenson, Sir William Samuel, Kt., M.C., D.F.C.

Sterling, Sir Jeffrey Maurice, Kt., C.B.E.

Sternberg, Sir Sigmund, Kt.

Stevens, *Vice-Adm.* Sir John Felgate, K.B.E., C.B.

Stevens, Sir Laurence Houghton, Kt., C.B.E.

Stevenson, *Vice-Adm.* Sir (Hugh) David, K.B.E.

Stevenson, Sir Simpson, Kt.

Stewart, Sir Alan, K.B.E.

Stewart, Sir Alan d'Arcy, Bt. (I. 1623).

Stewart, Sir David Brodribb, Bt., T.D. (1960).

Stewart, Sir David James Henderson-, Bt. (1957).

Stewart, Sir Edward Jackson, Kt.

Stewart, *Prof.* Sir Frederick Henry, Kt., Ph.D., F.R.S., F.R.S.E.

Stewart, Sir Herbert Ray, Kt., C.I.E.

Stewart, Sir Houston Mark Shaw-, Bt., M.C., T.D. (S. 1667).

Stewart, Sir Hugh Charlie Godfray, Bt. (1803).

Stewart, Sir James Douglas, Kt.

Stewart, Sir John Keith Watson, Bt. (1920).

Stewart, Sir Michael Norman Francis, K.C.M.G., O.B.E.

Stewart, Sir Robertson Huntly, Kt., C.B.E.

Stewart, Sir Ronald Compton, Bt. (1937).

Steyn, *Hon.* Sir Johan Van Zyl, Kt.

Stibbon, *Gen.* Sir John James, K.C.B., O.B.E.

Stinson, Sir Charles Alexander, K.B.E.

Stirling, Sir Alexander John Dickson, K.B.E., C.M.G.

Stockdale, Sir Arthur Noel, Kt.

Stockdale, Sir Edmund Villiers Minshull, Bt. (1960).

Stocker, *Rt. Hon.* Sir John Dexter, Kt., M.C., T.D.

Stoker, *Prof.* Sir Michael George Parke, Kt., C.B.E., F.R.C.P., F.R.S., F.R.S.E.

Stokes, Sir John Heydon Romaine, Kt., M.P.

Stone, *Prof.* Sir (John) Richard (Nicholas), KT., C.B.E.

Stonhouse, Sir Philip Allan, Bt. (1628).

Storey, *Hon.* Sir Richard, Bt. (1960).

Stormonth Darling, Sir James Carlisle, Kt., C.B.E., M.C., T.D.

Stott, Sir Adrian George Ellingham, Bt. (1920).

Stow, Sir Christopher Philipson-, Bt., D.F.C. (1907).

Stow, Sir John Montague, G.C.M.G., K.C.V.O.

Stowe, Sir Kenneth Ronald, G.C.B., C.V.O.

Stracey, Sir John Simon, Bt. (1818).

Strachey, Sir Charles, Bt. (1801).

Stradling Thomas, Sir John, Kt., M.P.

Straker, Sir Michael Ian Bowstead, Kt., C.B.E.

Strasser, Sir Paul, Kt.

Stratton, *Lt.-Gen.* Sir William Henry, K.C.B., C.V.O., C.B.E., D.S.O.

Strawson, *Prof.* Sir Peter Frederick, Kt., F.B.A.

Street, *Hon.* Sir Laurence Whistler, K.C.M.G.

Strong, Sir Roy Colin, Kt., PH.D., F.S.A.

Stronge, Sir James Anselan Maxwell, Bt. (1803).

Strutt, Sir Nigel Edward, Kt., T.D.

Stuart, Sir James Keith, Kt.

Stuart, Sir Kenneth Lamonte, Kt.

†Stuart, Sir Phillip Luttrell, Bt. (1660).

Stuart-Smith, *Rt. Hon.* Sir Murray, Kt.

Stubblefield, Sir (Cyril) James, Kt., D.SC., F.R.S.

Stubbs, Sir James Wilfrid, K.C.V.O., T.D.

Stucley, *Lt.* Sir Hugh George Coplestone Bampfylde, Bt. (1859).

Studd, Sir Edward Fairfax, Bt. (1929).

Studd, Sir Peter Malden, G.B.E., K.C.V.O.

†Studholme, Sir Paul Henry William, Bt. (1956).

Style, *Lt. Cdr.* Sir Godfrey William, Kt., C.B.E., D.S.C., R.N.

†Style, Sir William Frederick, Bt. (1627).

Suffield, Sir (Henry John) Lester, Kt.

Sugden, Sir Arthur, Kt.

Sullivan, Sir Desmond John, Kt.

Sullivan, Sir Richard Arthur, Bt. (1804).

Summerfield, *Hon.* Sir John Crampton, Kt., C.B.E.

Summers, Sir Felix Roland Brattan, Bt. (1952).

Summerson, Sir John Newenham, Kt., C.H., C.B.E., F.B.A., F.S.A.

Sunderland, *Prof.* Sir Sydney, Kt., C.M.G.

Surridge, Sir (Ernest) Rex (Edward), Kt., C.M.G.

Sutherland, Sir John Brewer, Bt. (1921).

Sutherland, Sir Maurice, Kt.

Sutherland, Sir William George MacKenzie, Kt., M.P.

Suttie, Sir (George) Philip Grant-, Bt. (s. 1702).

Sutton, Sir Frederick Walter, Kt., O.B.E.

Sutton, *Air Marshal* Sir John Matthias Dobson, K.C.B.

Sutton, Sir Richard Lexington, Bt. (1772).

Sutton, Sir Stafford William Powell Foster-, K.B.E., C.M.G., Q.C.

Swaffield, Sir James Chesebrough, Kt., C.B.E., R.D.

Swallow, Sir William, Kt.

Swan, *Lt. Col.* Sir William Bertram, K.C.V.O., C.B.E., T.D.

Swann, Sir Anthony Charles Christopher, Bt., C.M.G., O.B.E., (1906).

Swanwick, Sir Graham Russell, Kt., M.B.E.

Swartz, *Hon.* Sir Reginald William Colin, K.B.E., E.D.

Swayne, Sir Ronald Oliver Carless, Kt., M.C.

Swinson, Sir John Henry Alan, Kt., O.B.E.

Swinton, *Maj.-Gen.* Sir John, K.C.V.O., O.B.E.

Swire, Sir Adrian Christopher, Kt.

Swiss, Sir Rodney Geoffrey, Kt., O.B.E.

Swynnerton, Sir Roger John Massy, Kt., C.M.G., O.B.E., M.C.

Sykes, Sir Francis Godfrey, Bt. (1781).

Sykes, Sir John Charles Anthony le Gallais, Bt. (1921).

Sykes, Sir Tatton Christopher Mark, Bt. (1783).

Syme, Sir Ronald, Kt., O.M., F.B.A.

Symington, *Prof.* Sir Thomas, Kt., M.D., F.R.S.E.

Symons, *Vice-Adm.* Sir Patrick Jeremy, K.B.E.

Synge, Sir Robert Carson, Bt. (1801).

Tait, *Adm.* Sir (Allan) Gordon, K.C.B., D.S.C.

Tait, Sir James Sharp, Kt., D.SC., LlD., PH.D.

Tait, Sir Peter, K.B.E.

Tait, *Air Vice-Marshal* Sir Victor Hubert, K.B.E., C.B.

Talbot, *Vice-Adm.* Sir (Arthur Allison) FitzRoy, K.B.E., C.B., D.S.O.

Talbot, *Hon.* Sir Hilary Gwynne, Kt.

Tallack, Sir Hugh Mackay, Kt.

Tancred, Sir Henry Lawson-, Bt. (1662).

Tang, Sir Shiu-kin, Kt., C.B.E.

Tangaroa, *Hon.* Sir Tangaroa, M.B.E.

Tange, Sir Arthur Harold, Kt., C.B.E.

Tansley, Sir Eric Crawford, Kt., C.M.G.

Tapp, *Maj.-Gen.* Sir Nigel Prior Hanson, K.B.E., C.B., D.S.O.

Tapsell, Sir Peter Hannay Bailey, Kt., M.P.

Tate, *Lt.-Col.* Sir Henry, Bt. (1898).

Taukala, Sir David Dawea, Kt., M.B.E.

Tavaiqia, *Ratu* Sir Josaia, K.B.E.

Taylor, *Lt.-Gen.* Sir Allan Macnab, K.B.E., M.C.

Taylor, Sir Alvin Burton, Kt.

Taylor, Sir (Arthur) Godfrey, Kt.

Taylor, Sir Charles Stuart, Kt., T.D.

Taylor, Sir George, Kt., D.SC., F.R.S., F.R.S.E.

Taylor, Sir Henry Milton, Kt.

Taylor, Sir James, Kt., M.B.E., D.SC.

Taylor, Sir John Lang, K.C.M.G.

Taylor, Sir Nicholas Richard Stuart, Bt. (1917).

Taylor, *Rt. Hon.* Sir Peter Murray, Kt.

Tebbit, Sir Donald Claude, G.C.M.G.

Te Heuheu, Sir Hepi Hoani, K.B.E.

Telford, Sir Robert, Kt., C.B.E.

Temple, Sir Ernest Sanderson, Kt., M.B.E., Q.C.

Temple, Sir John Meredith, Kt.

Temple, Sir Rawden John Afamado, Kt. C.B.E., Q.C.

Temple, *Maj.* Sir Richard Anthony Purbeck, Bt., M.C. (1876).

Templeton, Sir John Marks, Kt.

Tennant, *Capt.* Sir Iain Mark, Kt.

Tennant, Sir Mark Dalcour, K.C.M.G., C.B.

Tennant, Sir Peter Frank Dalrymple, Kt., C.M.G., O.B.E.

Teo, Sir Fiatau Penitala, G.C.M.G., G.C.V.O., I.S.O., M.B.E.

Terry, Sir George Walter Roberts, Kt., C.B.E., Q.P.M.

Terry, Sir John Elliott, Kt.

Terry, Sir Michael Edward Stanley Imbert-, Bt. (1917).

Terry, *Air Chief Marshal* Sir Peter David George, G.C.B., A.F.C.

Tetley, Sir Herbert, K.B.E., C.B.

Tett, Sir Hugh Charles, Kt.

Thiess, Sir Leslie Charles, Kt., C.B.E.

Thomas, Sir Derek Morison David, K.C.M.G.

Thomas, Sir Frederick William, Kt.

Thomas, Sir (Godfrey) Michael (David) Bt. (1694).

Thomas, Sir Jeremy Cashel, K.C.M.G.

Thomas, Sir John Maldwyn, Kt.

Thomas, Sir Keith Vivian, Kt.

Thomas, Sir Patrick Muirhead, Kt., D.S.O., T.D.

Thomas, Sir Robert Evan, Kt.

Thomas, *Hon.* Sir Swinton Barclay, Kt.

Thomas, Sir William James Cooper, Bt., T.D. (1919).

Thomas, Sir (William) Michael (Marsh), Bt. (1918).

Thomas, *Vice-Adm.* Sir William Richard Scott, K.C.B., O.B.E.

Thompson, Sir Christopher Peile, Bt. (1890).

Thompson, Sir Edward Hugh Dudley, Kt., M.B.E., T.D.

Thompson, Sir Edward Walter, Kt.

Thompson, *Vice-Adm.* Sir Hugh Leslie Owen, K.B.E.

Thompson, Sir (Humphrey) Simon Meysey-, Bt. (1874).

Thompson, *Hon.* Sir John, Kt.

Thompson, Sir Paul Anthony, Bt. (1963).

Thompson, Sir Peter Anthony, Kt.

Thompson, Sir Ralph Patrick, Kt.

Thompson, Sir Richard Hilton Marler, Bt. (1963).

Thompson, Sir Robert Grainger Ker, K.B.E., C.M.G., D.S.O., M.C.

Thompson, Sir (Thomas) Lionel Tennyson, Bt. (1806).

Thomson, Sir Adam, Kt., C.B.E.

Thomson, Sir Evan Rees Whitaker, Kt.

Thomson, Sir (Frederick Douglas) David, Bt. (1929).

Thomson, Sir Ivo Wilfrid Home, Bt. (1925).

Thomson, Sir John, K.B.E., T.D.

Thomson, Sir John Adam, G.C.M.G.

Thomson, Sir John (Ian) Sutherland, K.B.E., C.M.G.

Thorley, Sir Gerald Bowers, Kt., T.D.

Thorn, Sir John Samuel, Kt., O.B.E.

Thorne, *Maj.-Gen.* Sir David Calthrop, K.B.E.

Thorne, Sir Peter Francis, K.C.V.O., C.B.E.

Thornton, *Lt.-Gen.* Sir Leonard Whitmore, K.C.B., C.B.E.

Thornton, Sir Peter Eustace, K.C.B.

Thorold, Sir Anthony Henry, Bt., O.B.E., D.S.C. (1642).

Thorpe, *Hon.* Sir Mathew Alexander, Kt.

Thouron, Sir John Rupert Hunt, K.B.E.

Throckmorton, Sir Robert George Maxwell, Bt. (1642).

Thwaites, Sir Bryan, Kt., PH.D.

Thwin, Sir U, Kt.

Tibbits, *Capt.* Sir David Stanley, Kt., D.S.C.

Tickell, Sir Crispin Charles Cervantes, K.C.V.O.

Tikaram, Sir Moti, K.B.E.

Tilney, Sir John Dudley Robert Tarleton, Kt., T.D.

Tippet, *Vice-Adm.* Sir Anthony Sanders, K.C.B.

Tippett, Sir Michael Kemp, Kt., O.M., C.H., C.B.E.

Tirvengadum, Sir Harry Krishnan, Kt.

Titterton, *Prof.* Sir Ernest William, Kt., C.M.G.

Tizard, Sir John Peter Mills, Kt.

Tod, *Air Marshal* Sir John Hunter Hunter-, K.B.E., C.B.

Todd, *Hon.* Sir (Reginald Stephen) Garfield, Kt.

Tollomache, *Maj.-Gen.* Sir Humphry Thomas, Bt., C.B., C.D.E., R.M. (1793).

Tololo, Sir Alkan, K.B.E.

Tombs, Sir Francis Leonard, Kt.

Tomkins, Sir Alfred George, Kt., C.B.E.

Tomkins, Sir Edward Emile, G.C.M.G., C.V.O.

Tomlinson, *Prof.* Sir Bernard Evans, Kt., C.B.E.

Tomlinson, Sir (Frank) Stanley, K.C.M.G.

Tooley, Sir John, Kt.

†Tooth, Sir Hugh John Lucas-, Bt. (1920).

Tooth, *Hon.* Sir (Seymour) Douglas, Kt.

ToRobert, Sir Henry Thomas, K.B.E.

Tory, Sir Geofroy William, K.C.M.G.

Touche, Sir Anthony George, Bt. (1920).

Touche, Sir Rodney Gordon, Bt. (1962).

Tovey, Sir Brian John Maynard, K.C.M.G.

ToVue, Sir Ronald, Kt., O.B.E.

Townley, Sir John Barton, Kt.

Townsend, *Rear-Adm.* Sir Leslie William, K.C.V.O., C.B.E.

Townsing, Sir Kenneth Joseph, Kt., C.M.G.

Trafford, Sir (Joseph) Anthony Porteous, Kt.

Traherne, Sir Cennydd George, K.G., T.D.

Traill, Sir Alan Towers, G.B.E.

Trant, *Gen.* Sir Richard Brooking, K.C.B.

Travancore, *Maj.-Gen.* H.H. the Maharajah of, G.C.S.I., G.C.I.E.

Travers, Sir Thomas à'Beckett, Kt.

Treacher, *Adm.* Sir John Devereux, K.C.B.

Trehane, Sir (Walter) Richard, Kt.

Trelawny, Sir John Barry Salusbury-, Bt. (1628).

Trench, Sir David Clive Crosbie, G.C.M.G., M.C.

Trench, Sir Nigel Clive Cosby, K.C.M.G.

Trench, Sir Peter Edward, Kt., C.B.E., T.D.

Trescowthick, Sir Donald Henry, K.B.E.

Trethowan, Sir (James) Ian (Raley), Kt.

Trethowan, *Prof.* Sir William Henry, Kt. C.B.E., F.R.C.P.

Trevaskis, Sir (Gerald) Kennedy (Nicholas), K.C.M.G., O.B.E.

Trevelyan, Sir George Lowthian, Bt. (1874).

Trevelyan, Sir Norman Irving, Bt. (1662).

Trewby, *Vice-Adm.* Sir (George Francis) Allan, K.C.B.

Trinder, Sir (Arnold) Charles, G.B.E.

Tritton, Sir Anthony John Ernest, Bt. (1905).

†Trollope, Sir Anthony Simon, Bt. (1642).

Trotter, Sir Ronald Ramsay, Kt.

Troubridge, Sir Peter, Bt. (1799).

Troughton, Sir Charles Hugh Willis, Kt., C.B.E., M.C., T.D.

Troup, *Vice-Adm.* Sir (John) Anthony (Rose), K.C.B., D.S.C.

Trowbridge, *Rear-Adm.* Sir Richard John, K.C.V.O.

Truscott, Sir Denis Henry, G.B.E., T.D.

Truscott, Sir George James Irving, Bt. (1909).

Tuck, Sir Bruce Adolph Reginald, Bt. (1910).

Tucker, *Hon.* Sir Richard Howard, Kt.

Tuckwell, Sir Edward George, K.C.V.O., F.R.C.S.

Tudor, *Hon.* Sir James Cameron, K.C.M.G.

Tudor Evans, *Hon.* Sir Haydn, Kt.

Tuite, Sir Christopher Hugh, Bt., PH.D. (1622).

Tuivaga, Sir Timoci Uluiburotu, Kt.

Tuke, Sir Anthony Favill, Kt.

Tupper, Sir Charles Hibbert, Bt. (1888).

Turbott, Sir Ian Graham, Kt., C.M.G., C.V.O.

Turing, Sir John Dermot, Kt. (s 1638).

Turnbull, *Prof.* Sir Alexander Cuthbert, Kt., C.B.E.

Turnbull, Sir Francis Fearon, K.B.E., C.B., C.I.E.

Turnbull, Sir Richard Gordon, G.C.M.G.

Turner, *Rt. Hon.* Sir Alexander Kingcome, K.B.E.

Turner, *Adm.* Sir (Arthur) Francis, K.C.B., D.S.C.

Turner, *Hon.* Sir Michael John, Kt.

Turner, *Lt.-Gen.* Sir William Francis Robert, K.B.E., C.B., D.S.O.

Tuti, *Rev.* Dudley, K.B.E.

Tuttle, *Air Marshal* Sir Geoffrey William, K.B.E., C.B., D.F.C.

Tuzo, *Gen.* Sir Harry Craufurd, G.C.B., O.B.E., M.C.

Twiss, *Adm.* Sir Frank Roddam, K.C.B., K.C.V.O., D.S.C.

Tyler, *Maj.-Gen.* Sir Leslie Norman, K.B.E., C.B.

Tyree, Sir (Alfred) William, Kt., O.B.E.

Tyrrell, Sir Murray Louis, K.C.V.O., C.B.E.

Tyrwhitt, Sir Reginald Thomas Newman, Bt. (1919).

Udoma, *Hon.* Sir (Egbert) Udo, Kt.

Unsworth, Hon. Sir Edgar Ignatius Godfrey, Kt., C.M.G.

Unwin, Sir Keith, K.B.E., C.M.G.

Ure, Sir John Burns, K.C.M.G., L.V.O.

Urquhart, Sir Andrew, K.C.M.G., M.B.E.

Urquhart, Sir Brian Edward, K.C.M.G., M.B.E.

Urwick, Sir Alan Bedford, K.C.V.O., C.M.G.

Usher, Sir Leonard Gray, K.B.E.

Usher, Sir Peter Lionel, Bt. (1899).

Vallat, Sir Francis Aimé, G.B.E., K.C.M.G., Q.C.

Vallings, *Vice-Adm.* Sir George Montague Francis, K.C.B.

Vanderfelt, Sir Robin Victor, K.B.E.

van der Post, Sir Laurens Jan, Kt., C.B.E.

Vane, Sir John Robert, Kt., D.Phil., D.SC., F.R.S.

Vangeke, *Most Rev.* Louis, K.B.E.

Vanneck, *Air Cdre.* Hon. Sir Peter Beckford Rutgers, G.B.E., C.B., A.F.C.

van Straubenzee, Sir William Radcliffe, Kt., M.B.E.

Vasquez, Sir Alfred Joseph, Kt., C.B.E., Q.C.

Vaughan, Sir (George) Edgar, K.B.E.

Vaughan, Sir Gerard Folliott, Kt., M.P., F.R.C.P.

Vavasour, *Cdr.* Sir Geoffrey William, Bt., D.S.C., R.N. (1828).

Veale, Sir Alan John Ralph, Kt.

Veira, Sir Philip Henry, K.B.E.

Verco, Sir Walter John George, K.C.V.O.

Verney, Sir John, Bt., M.C., T.D. (1946).

Verney, Sir Ralph Bruce, Bt., K.B.E. (1818).

Vernon, Sir James, Kt., C.B.E.

Vernon, Sir Nigel John Douglas, Bt. (1914).

Vesey, Sir (Nathaniel) Henry (Peniston), Kt., C.B.E.

Vestey, Sir (John) Derek, Bt. (1921).

Vial, Sir Kenneth Harold, Kt., C.B.E.

Vick, Sir (Francis) Arthur, Kt., O.B.E., PH.D.

Vickers, *Lt.-Gen.* Sir Richard Maurice Hilton, K.C.B., M.V.O., O.B.E.

Victoria, Sir (Joseph Aloysius) Donatus, Kt., C.B.E.

Villiers, Sir Charles Hyde, Kt., M.C.

Villiers, *Vice-Adm.* Sir (John) Michael, K.C.B., O.B.E.

Vincent, *Gen.* Sir Richard Frederick, K.C.B., D.S.O.

Vincent, Sir William Percy Maxwell, Bt. (1936).

Vinelott, *Hon.* Sir John Evelyn, Kt.

Vines, Sir William Joshua, Kt., C.M.G.

Wheeler, *Hon.* Sir Kenneth Henry, Kt.

Wheler, Sir Edward Woodford, Bt. (1660).

Whishaw, Sir Charles Percival Law, Kt.

Whitaker, *Maj.* Sir James Herbert Ingham, Bt. (1936).

White, Sir Christopher Robert Meadows, Bt. (1937).

White, Sir Dick Goldsmith, K.C.M.G., K.B.E.

White, Sir Frederick William George, K.B.E., Ph.D., F.R.S.

White, Sir George Stanley James, Bt. (1904).

White, Sir Harold Leslie, Kt., C.B.E.

White, *Wg-Cdr.* Sir Henry Arthur Dalrymple-, Bt., D.F.C. (1926).

White, *Hon.* Sir John Charles, Kt., M.B.E.

White, Sir John Woolmer, Bt. (1922).

White, Sir Lynton Stuart, Kt., M.B.E.. T.D.

White, *Adm.* Sir Peter, G.B.E.

White, Sir Thomas Astley Woollaston, Bt. (1802).

White, Sir (Vincent) Gordon (Lindsay), K.B.E.

Whitehead, Sir John Stainton, K.C.M.G., C.V.O.

Whitehead, Sir Rowland John Rathbone, Bt. (1889).

Whiteley, Sir Hugo Baldwin Huntington-, Bt. (1918).

Whiteley, *Gen.* Sir Peter John Frederick, G.C.B., O.B.E., R.M.

Whitford, *Hon.* Sir John Norman Keates, Kt.

Whitley, *Air Marshal* Sir John René, K.B.E., C.B., D.S.O., A.F.C.

Whitmore, Sir Clive Anthony, G.C.B., C.V.O.

Whitmore, Sir John Henry Douglas, Bt. (1954).

Whitteridge, Sir Gordon Coligny, K.C.M.G., O.B.E.

Whittle, *Air Cdre.* Sir Frank, O.M., K.B.E., C.B., F.R.S.

Whyte, Sir William Erskine Hamilton, K.C.M.G.

Wickerson, Sir John Michael, Kt.

Wicks, *Hon.* Sir James, Kt.

Wicks, Sir James Albert, Kt.

Wigan, Sir Alan Lewis, Bt. (1898).

Wiggin, Sir John Henry, Bt., M.C. (1892).

Wigglesworth, Sir Vincent Brian, Kt., C.B.E., M.D., F.R.S.

Wigram, *Rev. Canon* Sir Clifford Woolmore, Bt. (1805).

Wilbraham, Sir Richard Baker, Bt. (1776).

Wilford, Sir (Kenneth) Michael, G.C.M.G.

Wilkins, Sir Graham John, Kt.

Wilkins, *Lt.-Gen.* Sir Michael Compton Lockwood, K.C.B., O.B.E.

Wilkinson, Sir (David) Graham (Brook) Bt. (1941).

Wilkinson, *Prof.* Sir Denys Haigh, Kt., F.R.S.

Wilkinson, *Prof.* Sir Geoffrey, Kt., F.R.S.

Wilkinson, *Rt. Hon.* Sir Nicolas Christopher Henry Browne-, Kt.

Wilkinson, Sir Peter Allix, K.C.M.G., D.S.O., O.B.E.

Wilkinson, Sir Philip William, Kt.

Wilkinson, Sir (Robert Francis) Martin, Kt.

Willatt, Sir (Robert) Hugh, Kt.

Willcocks, Sir David Valentine, Kt., C.B.E., M.C.

Williams, Sir Alastair Edgcumbe James Dudley-, Bt. (1964).

Williams, Sir Alwyn, Kt., Ph.D., F.R.S.

Williams, Sir Anthony James, K.C.M.G.

†Williams, Sir (Arthur) Gareth Ludovic Emrys Rhys, Bt. (1918).

Williams, *Prof.* Sir Bruce Rodda, K.B.E.

Williams, *Adm.* Sir David, G.C.B.

Williams, Sir David Innes, Kt.

Williams, *Hon.* Sir Denys Ambrose, Kt.

Williams, Sir Donald Mark, Bt. (1866).

Williams, Sir Edgar Trevor, Kt., C.B., C.B.E., D.S.O.

Williams, *Hon.* Sir Edward Stratten, K.C.M.G., K.B.E.

Williams, Sir Francis John Watkin, Bt., Q.C. (1798).

Williams, Sir Gwilym Tecwyn, Kt., C.B.E.

Williams, Sir Henry Morton Leech, Kt., M.B.E.

Williams, Sir Henry Sydney, Kt., O.B.E.

Williams, Sir (John) Leslie, Kt., C.B.E.

Williams, *Capt.* Sir John Protheroe, Kt., C.M.G., O.B.E.

Williams, Sir John Robert, K.C.M.G.

Williams, Sir Leonard, K.B.E., C.B.

Williams, Sir Osmond, Bt., M.C. (1909).

Williams, Sir Peter Watkin, Kt.

Williams, *Prof.* Sir Robert Evan Owen, Kt., M.D., F.R.C.P.

Williams, Sir (Robert) Philip Nathaniel, Bt. (1915).

Williams, Sir Robin Philip, Bt. (1953).

Williams, Sir (William) Maxwell (Harries), Kt.

Williamson, *Marshal of the Royal Air Force* Sir Keith Alec, G.C.B., A.F.C.

Williamson, Sir (Nicholas Frederick) Hedworth, Bt. (1642).

Willink, Sir Charles William, Bt. (1957).

Willis, *Hon.* Sir Eric Archibald, K.B.E., C.M.G.

Willis, *Vice-Adm.* Sir (Guido) James, K.B.E.

Willis, Sir John Ramsay, Kt.

Willison, *Lt.-Gen.* Sir David John, K.C.B., O.B.E., M.C.

Willison, Sir John Alexander, Kt., O.B.E.

Willoughby, *Maj.-Gen.* Sir John Edward Francis, K.B.E., C.B.

Wills, Sir David Seton, Bt. (1904).

Wills, Sir (Hugh) David Hamilton, Kt., C.B.E., T.D.

Wills, Sir John Spencer, Kt.

Wills, Sir John Vernon, Bt., T.D. (1923).

Wilmot, Sir Henry Robert, Bt. (1759).

Wilmot, *Cdr.* Sir John Assheton Eardley-, Bt., M.V.O., D.S.C., R.N. (1821).

Wilson, Sir Alan Herries, Kt., F.R.S.

Wilson, *Lt.-Gen.* Sir (Alexander) James, K.B.E., M.C.

Wilson, Sir Angus Frank Johnstone, Kt., C.B.E.

Wilson, Sir Anthony, Kt.

Wilson, Sir Austin George, Kt., O.B.E.

Wilson, Sir Charles Haynes, Kt.

Wilson, Sir David, Bt. (1920).

Wilson, Sir David Clive, K.C.M.G.

Wilson, Sir David Mackenzie, Kt.

Wilson, Sir Geoffrey Masterman, K.C.B., C.M.G.

Wilson, Sir James William Douglas, Bt. (1906).

Wilson, Sir John Foster, Kt., C.B.E.

Wilson, Sir John Gardiner, Kt., C.B.E.

Wilson, Sir John Martindale, K.C.B.

Wilson, Sir Keith Cameron, Kt.

Wilson, Sir (Mathew) Martin, Bt. (1874).

Wilson, Sir Reginald Holmes, Kt.

Wilson, Sir Robert Donald, Kt.

Wilson, *Rt. Rev.* Roger Plumpton, K.C.V.O., D.D.

Wilson, Sir Roland, K.B.E.

Wilson, *Hon.* Sir Ronald Darling, K.B.E., C.M.G.

Wilton, Sir (Arthur) John, K.C.M.G., K.C.V.O., M.C.

Wiltshire, Sir Frederick Munro, Kt., C.B.E.

Windeyer, Sir Brian Wellingham, Kt.

Wingate, *Capt.* Sir Miles Buckley, K.C.V.O.

Winnifrith, Sir (Alfred) John (Digby), K.C.B.

Winnington, Sir Francis Salwey William, Bt. (1755).

Winskill, *Air Cdre.* Sir Archibald Little, K.C.V.O., C.B.E., D.F.C.

Winterbottom, Sir Walter, Kt., C.B.E.

Wiseman, Sir John William, Bt. (1628).

Wolfson, Sir David, Kt.

Wolfson, Sir Isaac, Bt., F.R.S. (1962).

Wolseley, Sir Charles Garnet Richard Mark, Bt. (1628).

Wolseley, Sir Garnet, Bt. (1 1745).

Wolstenholme, Sir Gordon Ethelbert Ward, Kt., O.B.E.

Wombwell, Sir George Philip Frederick, Bt. (1778).

Womersley, Sir Peter John Walter, Bt. (1945).

Wontner, Sir Hugh Walter Kingwell, G.B.E., C.V.O.

Wood, Sir Anthony John Page, Bt. (1837).

Wood, Sir David Basil Hill-, Bt. (1921).

Wood, Sir Frederick Ambrose Stuart, Kt.

Wood, Sir Henry Peart, Kt., C.B.E.

Wood, *Prof.* Sir John Crossley, Kt., C.B.E.

Wood, *Hon.* Sir John Kember, Kt., M.C.

Wood, Sir Martin Francis, Kt., O.B.E.

Wood, Sir Russell Dillon, K.C.V.O., V.R.D.

Wood, Sir William Alan, K.C.V.O., C.B.

Woodfield, Sir Philip John, K.C.B., C.B.E.

Woodhouse, *Rt. Hon.* Sir (Arthur) Owen, K.B.E., D.S.C.

Woodroffe, *Most Rev.* George Cuthbert Manning, K.B.E.

Woodroofe, Sir Ernest George, Kt., Ph.D.

Woodruff, *Prof.* Sir Michael Francis Addison, Kt., D.SC., F.R.S., F.R.C.S.

Woods, Sir Colin Philip Joseph, K.C.V.O., C.B.E.

Woods, *Most Rev.* Frank, K.B.E., D.D.

Woods, *Rt. Rev.* Robert Wilmer, K.C.V.O.

Woodward, *Hon.* Sir (Albert) Edward, Kt., O.B.E.

Woodward, *Adm.* Sir John Forster, K.C.B.

Woolf, *Rt. Hon.* Sir Harry Kenneth, Kt.

Woolf, Sir John, Kt.

Woollaston, Sir (Mountford) Tosswill, Kt.

Wordie, Sir John Stewart, Kt., C.B.E., V.R.D.

Worsley, *Gen.* Sir Richard Edward, G.C.B., O.B.E.

Worsley, Sir (William) Marcus (John), Bt. (1838).

Worthington, *Air Vice Marshal* Sir Geoffrey Luis, K.B.E., C.B

Wraight, Sir John Richard, K.B.E., C.M.G.

Wraxall, Sir Charles Frederick Lascelles, Bt. (1813).

Wrey, Sir (Castel Richard) Bourchier, Bt. (1628).

Wright, Sir Allan Frederick, K.B.E.

Wright, Sir Denis Arthur Hepworth, G.C.M.G.

Wright, Sir Edward Maitland, Kt., D.Phil.,Ll.D., D.SC., F.R.S.E.

Wright, Sir (John) Oliver, G.C.M.G., G.C.V.O., D.S.C.

Wright, Sir Patrick Richard Henry, K.C.M.G.

Wright, Sir Paul Hervé Giraud, K.C.M.G., O.B.E.

Wright, *Hon.* Sir Reginald Charles, Kt.

Wright, Sir Richard Michael Cory-, Bt. (1903).

Wright, Sir Rowland Sydney, Kt., C.B.E.

Wrightson, Sir Charles Mark Garmondsway, Bt. (1900).

Wykeham, *Air Marshal* Sir Peter Guy, K.C.B., D.S.O., O.B.E., D.F.C., A.F.C.

Wylie, Sir Campbell, Kt., E.D., Q.C.

Wyndham, Sir Harold Stanley, Kt., C.B.E.

†Wynn, Sir David Watkin Williams-, Bt. (1688).

Wynter, Sir Luther Reginald, Kt., C.B.E.

Yang, *Hon.* Ti Liang, Kt.

Yapp, Sir Stanley Graham, Kt.

Yarrow, Sir Eric Grant, Bt., M.B.E. (1916).

Yeend, Sir Geoffrey John, Kt., C.B.E.

Yellowlees, Sir Henry, K.C.B.

Yocklunn, Sir John (Soong Chung), K.C.V.O.

Youens, Sir Peter William, Kt., C.M.G., O.B.E.

Young, Sir Brian Walter Mark, Kt.

Young, *Lt.-Gen.* Sir David Tod, K.B.E., C.B., D.F.C.

Young, *Prof.* Sir Frank George, Kt., D.SC., Ph.D., F.R.S.

Young, Sir George Samuel Knatchbull, Bt., M.P. (1813).

Young, *Hon.* Sir Harold William, K.C.M.G.

Young, Sir John Kenyon Roe, Bt. (1821).

Young, *Hon.* Sir John McIntosh, K.C.M.G.

Young, Sir Leslie Clarence, Kt., C.B.E.

Young, Sir Norman Smith, Kt.

Young, Sir Richard Dilworth, Kt.

Young, Sir Robert Christopher Mackworth-, G.C.V.O.

Young, Sir Roger William, Kt.

Young, Sir Stephen Stewart Templeton, Bt. (1945).

Young, Sir William Neil, Bt. (1769).

Younger, *Maj.-Gen.* Sir John William, Bt., C.B.E. (1911).

Younger, Sir William McEwan, Bt., D.S.O. (1964).

Zeidler, Sir David Ronald, Kt. C.B.E.

Zoleveke, Sir Gideon Pitabose, K.B.E.

Zurenuo, *Rt. Rev.* Zurewe Kamong, Kt., O.B.E.

Baronetcies Extinct (Since last issue).—d'Avigdor-Goldsmid (U.K., 1934); Mason (U.K., 1918), by the death of 4th Baron Blackford; Adair (U.K., 1838).

Dames Grand Cross and Dames Commanders of the Order of the Bath, the Order of St. Michael and St. George, the Royal Victorian Order and the Order of the British Empire

NOTE.—Dames Grand Cross (G.C.B., G.C.M.G., G.C.V.O. or G.B.E.) and Dames Commanders (D.C.B., D.C.M.G., D.C.V.O. or D.B.E.) are addressed in a manner similar to that of Knights Grand Cross or Knights Commanders, *e.g.* "Miss Florence Smith" after receiving the honour would be addressed as "Dame Florence", and in writing as "Dame Florence Smith, G. (or D.) C.B., G. (or D.) C.M.G., G. (or D.) C.V.O., OR G. (or D.) B.E." Where such award is made to a lady already in enjoyment of a higher title the appropriate letters are appended to her name, *e.g.* "The Countess of —— G.C.V.O." Peeresses in their own right, and Life Peeresses, are not included in this list. Dames Grand Cross rank after wives of Baronets and before wives of Knights Grand Cross. Dames Commanders rank after the wives of Knights Grand Cross and before the wives of Knights Commanders.

DAMES GRAND CROSS AND DAMES COMMANDERS

H.M. Queen Elizabeth The Queen Mother, K.G., K.T., C.I., G.M.V.O.

H.R.H. The Princess Margaret, Countess of Snowdon, C.I., G.C.V.O.

H.R.H. The Princess Alice, Duchess of Gloucester, G.C.B., C.I., G.C.V.O., G.B.E.

H.R.H. The Princess Alexandra of Kent, G.C.V.O.

H.R.H. The Princess Royal, G.C.V.O.

H.R.H. The Duchess of Kent, G.C.V.O.

Abel Smith, Lady, D.C.V.O.

Abercorn, Mary, Duchess of, G.C.V.O.

Abergavenny, The Marchioness of, D.C.V.O.

Albemarle, The Countess of, D.B.E.

Anderson, Dame Judith, D.B.E.

Anderson, *Brig.* Hon. Dame Mary Mackenzie (Mrs. Pihl), D.B.E.

Anglesey, The Marchioness of, D.B.E.

Ashcroft, Dame Peggy, D.B.E.

Baker, Dame Janet Abbott (Mrs. Shelley), D.B.E.

Baring, Lady Rose Gwendolen Louisa, D.C.V.O.

Barnes, Dame (Alice) Josephine (Mary Taylor), (Dame Josephine Warren), D.B.E., F.R.C.P., F.R.C.S.

Bate, Dame Zara Kate, D.B.E.

Beaurepaire, Dame Beryl Edith, D.B.E.

Berry, Dame Alice Miriam, D.B.E.

Raven, Dame Kathleen Annie (Mrs. Ingram), D.B.E.

Reader, Dame Audrey Tattie Hinchcliff, D.B.E.

Reader-Harris, Dame (Muriel) Diana, D.B.E.

Rees, Dame Dorothy Mary, D.B.E.

Riddelsdell, Dame Mildred, D.C.B., C.B.E.

Ridley, Dame (Mildred) Betty, D.B.E.

Rivett-Drake, *Brig.* Dame Jean Elizabeth Rivett, D.B.E.

Roberts, Dame Jean, D.B.E.

Roberts, Dame Joan Howard, D.B.E.

Roberts, Dame Shelagh Marjorie, D.B.E.

Robertson, *Cmdt.* Dame Nancy Margaret, D.B.E.

Roe, Dame Raigh Edith, D.B.E.

Russell-Smith, Dame Enid Mary Russell, D.B.E.

Salas, Dame Margaret Laurence, D.B.E.

Saunders, Dame Cicely Mary Strode, D.B.E., F.R.C.P.

Scott, Dame Catherine Campbell, D.B.E.

Scott, Dame Margaret, (Dame Catherine Margaret Mary Denton), D.B.E.

Seccombe, Dame Joan Anna Dalziel, D.B.E.

Shenfield, Dame Barbara Estelle, D.B.E.

Shepherd, Dame Margaret Alice, D.B.E.

Sherlock, *Prof.* Dame Sheila Patricia Violet, D.B.E., M.D., F.R.C.P.

Smieton, Dame Mary Guillan, D.B.E.

Smith, Dame Margot, D.B.E.

Snagge, Dame Nancy Marion, D.B.E.

Soames, The Lady, D.B.E.

Stark, Dame Freya (Mrs. Perowne), D.B.E.

Stephens, *Air Cmdt.* Dame Anne, D.B.E.

Stewart, Dame Muriel Acadia, D.B.E.

Sutherland, Dame Joan (Mrs. Bonynge), D.B.E.

Taylor, Dame Jean Elizabeth, D.C.V.O.

Te Atairangikaahu, Arikinui, D.B.E.

Te Kanawa, Dame Kiri Janette (Mrs. Park), D.B.E.

Tilney, Dame Guinevere (Lady Tilney), D.B.E.

Tizard, Dame Catherine Anne, D.B.E.

Tokiel, Dame Rosa, D.B.E.

Turner, Dame Eva, D.B.E.

Turner, *Brig.* Dame Margot, D.B.E., R.R.C.

Tyrwhitt, *Brig.* Dame Mary Joan Caroline, D.B.E., T.D.

Uatioa, Dame Mere, D.B.E.

Uvarov, Dame Olga, D.B.E.

Van Praagh, Dame Peggy, D.B.E.

Varley, Dame Joan Fleetwood, D.B.E.

Vaughan, Dame Janet Maria (Mrs. Gourlay), D.B.E., F.R.S.

Wakehurst, Margaret, Lady, D.B.E.

Walker, Dame Susan Armour, D.B.E.

Wall, (Alice) Anne, (Mrs. Michael Wall), D.C.V.O.

Warburton, Dame Anne Marion, D.C.V.O., C.M.G.

Wedega, Dame Alice, D.B.E.

Wedgwood, Dame (Cicely) Veronica, O.M., D.B.E.

Weston, Dame Margaret Kate, D.B.E.

Williamson, Dame (Elsie) Marjorie, D.B.E., Ph.D.

Wormald, Dame Ethel May, D.B.E.

Yarwood, Dame Elizabeth Ann, D.B.E.

Yonge, Dame (Ida) Felicity (Ann), D.B.E.

THE VICTORIA CROSS, V.C.

For Conspicuous Bravery

The ribbon *is Crimson* for all Services (until 1918 it was *Blue* for Royal Navy).

Instituted on January 29, 1856, the Victoria Cross was awarded retrospectively to 1854, the first being held by Lieut. C. D. Lucas, R.N. for bravery in the Baltic Sea on June 21, 1854 (gazetted Feb. 24, 1857). The first 62 Crosses were presented by Queen Victoria in Hyde Park, London, on June 26, 1857.

The V.C. is worn before all other decorations, on the left breast, and consists of a cross-pattée of bronze, 1¼ inches in diameter, with the Royal Crown surmounted by a lion in the centre, and beneath there is the inscription "For Valour." Holders of the V.C. receive a tax-free annuity of £100, irrespective of need or other conditions. In 1911, the right to receive the Cross was extended to Indian soldiers, and in 1920 a Royal Warrant extended the right to Matrons, Sisters and Nurses, and the Staff of the Nursing Services and other services pertaining to Hospitals and Nursing, and to Civilians of either sex regularly or temporarily under the orders, direction or supervision of the Naval, Military, or Air Forces of the Crown.

Surviving Recipients of the Victoria Cross

Agansing Rai, *Havildar* (Gurkha Rifles), *World War* 1944

Ali Haidar, *Jemadar* (Frontier Force Rifles), *World War* 1945

Anderson, *Lt.-Col.* C. G. W., M.C. (Australian M.F.), *World War* 1942

Annand, *Capt.* R. W. (Durham L.I.), *World War* 1940

Bhanbhagta Gurung, *Capt.* (2nd Gurkha Rifles), *World War* 1945

Bhandari Ram, *Capt.* (Baluch R.), *World War* . . 1944

Burton, *Corpl.* R. H. (Duke of Wellington's R.), *World War* 1944

Campbell, *Brigadier* L. M., D.S.O., O.B.E., T.D. (A. & S. Highrs.), *World War* 1943

Chapman, *Sergt.* E. T., B.E.M. (Monmouthshire R.), *World War* 1945

Cheshire, *Group Capt.* G. L., O.M., D.S.O., D.F.C. (R.A.F.), *World War* 1944

Cruickshank, *Fl. Lt.* J. A. (R.A.F.V.R.), *World War* 1944

Cutler, Sir A. R., K.C.M.G., K.C.V.O., C.B.E. (Australia), *World War* 1941

De L'Isle, *Maj.* The Viscount, K.G., P.C., G.C.M.G., G.C.V.O. (*Hon.* W. P. Sidney) (Gren. Gds.), *World War* 1944

Eardley, *Sergt.* G. H., M.M. (K.S.L.I.), *World War* 1944

Elliott, *Lt.* the Rev. K. (N.Z.M.F.), *World War* . . 1942

Ervine-Andrews, *Lt.-Col.* H. M. (E. Lancs. R.), *World War* 1940

Foote, *Maj.-Gen.* H. R. B., C.B., D.S.O. (R. Tank R.), *World War* 1942

Fraser, *Cdr.* I. E., D.S.C. (R.N.R.), *World War* . . 1945

Ganju Lama, *Jemadar*, M.M. (Gurkha Rifles), *World War* 1944

Gardner, *Capt.* P. J., M.C. (R.T.R.), *World War* . . 1941

Ghale, *Subedar* Gaje (Gurkha Rifles), *World War* 1943

Gian Singh, *Jemadar* (Punjab R.), *World War* . . 1945

Gould, *Lt.* T. W. (R.N.), *World War* 1942

Hinton, *Sergt.* J. D. (N.Z.M.F.), *World War* 1941

Jackson, *W.O.* N. C. (R.A.F.V.R.), *World War* . . . 1944

Jamieson, *Maj.* D. A. (R. Norfolk R.), *World War* 1944

Kenna, *Pte.* E. (Australian M.F.), *World War* . . . 1945

Kenneally, *C.-Q.-M.-S.* J. P. (Irish Gds.), *World War* 1943

Lachiman Gurung, *Rifleman* (Gurkha Rifles), *World War* 1945

Learoyd, *Wing-Cmdr.* R. A. B. (R.A.F.), *World War* 1940

Mahony, *Lt.-Col.* J. K., C.D. (Westminster R., Canada), *World War* 1944

Merritt, *Lt.-Col.* C. C. I., C.D. (S. Saskatchewan R.), *World War* 1942

Norton, *Capt.* G. R., M.M. (S.A.M.F.), *World War* 1944

Parkash Singh, *Maj.* (Punjab R.), *World War* ... 1943

Payne, *W.O.* K. (Australian Army), *Vietnam* ... 1969

Place, *Rear-Adm.* B. C. G., C.B., D.S.C. (R.N.), *World War* 1943

Porteous, *Col.* P. A. (R.A.), *World War* 1942

Rambahadur Limbu, *Lt.* M.V.O. (Gurkha Rifles), *Sarawak* 1965

Reid, *Fl.-Lt.* W. (R.A.F.V.R.), *World War* 1943

Rutherford, *Capt.* C. S., M.C., M.M. (Quebec R.), *Gt. War* 1918

Smith, *Sergt.* E. A., C.D. (Seaforth Highrs. of Canada), *World War* 1944

Smythe, *Capt.* Q. G. M. (S.A.M.F.), *World War* .. 1942

Speakman, *Sergt.* W. (Black Watch), *Korea* 1951

Starcevich, *Pte.* L. T. (Australia), *World War* 1945

Tilston, *Maj.* F. A. (Essex Scottish, Canada), *World War* 1945

Tulbahadur Pun, *W.O. I.* (Gurkha Rifles), *World War* 1944

Umrao Singh, *Sub-Major* (I.A.), *World War* 1944

Upham, *Capt.* C. H. (and Bar, 1942), (N.Z.M.F.), *World War* 1941

Watkins, *Maj. Rt. Hon.* Sir Tasker (Welch R.), *World War* 1944

Wilson, *Lt.-Col.* E. C. T. (E. Surrey R.), *World War* 1940

Wright, *C.S.M.* P. H. (Coldstream Gds.), *World War* 1943

THE GEORGE CROSS, G.C. (1940)

FOR GALLANTRY

The ribbon is *dark blue* threaded through a bar adorned with laurel leaves.

INSTITUTED *September, 24th,* 1940 (with amendments, *November 3rd,* 1942).

The George Cross is worn before all other decorations (except the V.C.) on the left breast § and consists of a plain silver cross with four equal limbs, the cross having in the centre a circular medallion bearing a design showing St. George and the Dragon. The inscription "For Gallantry" appears round the medallion and in the angle of each limb of the cross is the Royal cypher "G VI" forming a circle concentric with the medallion. The reverse is plain and bears the name of the recipient and the date of the award. The cross is suspended by a ring from a bar adorned with laurel leaves on dark blue ribbon 1½ inches wide.

The cross is intended primarily for civilians and awards to the fighting services are confined to actions for which purely military honours are not normally granted. It is awarded only for acts of the greatest heroism or of the most conspicuous courage in circumstances of extreme danger. From April 1, 1965, holders of the Cross have received a tax-free annuity of £100.

§ When worn by a woman it may be worn on the left shoulder from a ribbon of the same width and colour fashioned into a bow.

Empire Gallantry Medal.—The Royal Warrant which ordained that the grant of the Empire Gallantry Medal should cease authorized holders of that medal to return it to the Central Chancery of the Orders of Knighthood and to receive in exchange the George Cross. A similar provision applied to posthumous awards of the Empire Gallantry Medal made after the outbreak of war in 1939.

In October 1971 all surviving holders of the Albert Medal and the Edward Medal exchanged those decorations for the George Cross.

THE ORDER OF ST. JOHN

The Most Venerable Order of the Hospital of St. John of Jerusalem

St. John's Gate, Clerkenwell, EC1M 4DA

Grand Prior, H.R.H. The Duke of Gloucester, G.C.V.O.

Lord Prior, The Lord Grey of Naunton, G.C.M.G., G.C.V.O., O.B.E.
Chancellor, The Lord Vestey.

PRINCIPAL DECORATIONS AND MEDALS (in order of Precedence)

Victoria Cross. (V.C.)—1856.
George Cross. (G.C.)—1940.
British Orders of Knighthood, Etc. (for order in which worn, *see* pp. 188–90).
Baronet's Badge
Knight Bachelor's Badge
Decorations
   Royal Red Cross. (Class I—R.R.C.)—1883.—For ladies.
   Distinguished Service Cross. (D.S.C.)—1914.—For officers of R.N. below the rank of Captain, and Warrant Officers.
   Military Cross. (M.C.)—Dec. 1914.—Awarded to Captains, Lieutenants, and Warrant Officers (Cl I. and II.) in the Army and Indian and Colonial Forces.
   Distinguished Flying Cross. (D.F.C.)—1918.—For officers and Warrant Officers in the R.A.F. (and Fleet Air Arm from April 9, 1941) for acts of gallantry when flying in active operations against the enemy.
   Air Force Cross. (A.F.C.)—1918.—Instituted as preceding but for acts of courage or devotion to duty when flying, although not in active operations against the enemy (extended to Fleet Air Arm since April 9, 1941).
   Royal Red Cross (Class II—A.R.R.C.).
   Order of British India.
   Kaisar-i-Hind Medal.
   Order of St. John.
Medals for Gallantry and Distinguished Conduct
   Union of South Africa Queen's Medal for Bravery, in Gold.
   Distinguished Conduct Medal. (D.C.M.)—1854.—Awarded to warrant officers, non-commissioned officers and men of the Army and R.A.F.
   Conspicuous Gallantry Medal. (C.G.M.)—1874.—Is bestowed upon warrant officers and men of the R.N. and since 1942 of Mercantile Marine and R.A.F.
   The George Medal. (G.M.)—1940.
   Queen's Police Medal for Gallantry.
   Queen's Fire Service Medal for Gallantry.
   Royal West African Frontier Force Distinguished Conduct Medal.
   King's African Rifles Distinguished Conduct Medal.
   Indian Distinguished Service Medal.
   Union of South Africa Queen's Medal for Bravery, in Silver.
   Distinguished Service Medal. (D.S.M.)—1914.—For chief petty officers, petty officers and men, of all branches of the Royal Navy, and since 1942 of Mercantile Marine; non-commissioned officers and men of the Royal Marines; all other persons holding corresponding positions in Her Majesty's Service afloat.
   Military Medal. (M.M.)—1916.—For warrant and noncommissioned officers and men and serving women.
   Distinguished Flying Medal. (D.F.M.)—1918.—and the **Air Force Medal.** (A.F.M.)—For warrant and noncommissioned officers and men for equivalent services as for D.F.C. and A.F.C. (extended to Fleet Air Arm, 1941).
   Constabulary Medal (Ireland).
   Medal for Saving Life at Sea.
   Indian Order of Merit (Civil).
   Indian Police Medal for Gallantry.
   Ceylon Police Medal for Gallantry.
   Sierra Leone Police Medal for Gallantry.
   Sierra Leone Fire Brigades Medal for Gallantry.
   Colonial Police Medal for Gallantry. (C.P.M.)
   Queen's Gallantry Medal.—1974.
   Royal Victorian Medal.—(Gold, Silver and Bronze).
British Empire Medal. (B.E.M.)—(formerly the Medal of the Order of the British Empire, for Meritorious Service; also includes the Medal of the Order awarded before Dec. 29, 1922).
Queen's Police (Q.P.M.) and Fire Services Medals for Distinguished Service, (Q.F.S.M.).

Queen's Medal for Chiefs.
War Medals and Stars (in order of date).
Polar Medals (in order of date).
Imperial Service Medal.
Police Medals for Valuable Service.
Badge of Honour.
Jubilee, Coronation and Durbar Medals.
   King George V, King George VI and Queen Elizabeth II Long and Faithful Service Medals.
Efficiency and Long Service Decorations and Medals.
   Medal for Meritorious Service.
   Long Service and Good Conduct Medal—(Military).
   Naval Long Service and Good Conduct Medal.
   Royal Marine Meritorious Service Medal.
   Royal Air Force Meritorious Service Medal.
   Royal Air Force Long Service and Good Conduct Medal.
   Medal for Long Service and Good Conduct (Ulster Defence Regiment).
   Police and Fire Brigade Long Service and Good Conduct Medal.
   Colonial Police and Fire Brigades Long Service Medal.
   Colonial Prison Service Medal.
   Army Emergency Reserve Decoration.—(E.R.D.)
   Volunteer Officer's Decoration.—(V.D.)
   Volunteer Long Service Medal.
   Volunteer Officer's Decoration (for India and the Colonies).
   Volunteer Long Service Medal (for India and the Colonies).
   Colonial Auxiliary Forces Officer's Decoration.
   Colonial Auxiliary Forces Long Service Medal.
   Medal for Good Shooting (Naval).
   Militia Long Service Medal.
   Imperial Yeomanry Long Service Medal.
   Territorial Decoration.—(T.D.)—1908.
   Efficiency Decoration.—(E.D.)
   Territorial Efficiency Medal.
   Efficiency Medal.
   Special Reserve Long Service and Good Conduct Medal.
   Decoration for Officers, Royal Navy Reserve. (R.D.)—1910.
   Decoration for Officers, R.N.V.R.—(V.R.D.)
   Royal Naval Reserve Long Service and Good Conduct Medal.
   R.N.V.R. Long Service and Good Conduct Medal.
   Royal Naval Auxiliary Sick Berth Reserve Long Service and Good Conduct Medal.
   Royal Fleet Reserve Long Service and Good Conduct Medal.
   Royal Naval Wireless Auxiliary Reserve Long Service and Good Conduct Medal.
   Air Efficiency Award. (A.E.)—1942.
   Ulster Defence Regiment Medal.
   The Queen's Medal.—(For champion shots in the R.N., R.M., R.N.Z.N., Army, R.A.F.).
   Cadet Forces Medal.—1950.
   Coast Life Saving Corps Long Service Medal.—1911.
   Special Constabulary Long Service Medal.
   Royal Observer Corps Medal.
   Civil Defence Long Service Medal.
   Royal Ulster Constabulary Service Medal.
   Service Medal of the Order of St. John.
   Badge of the Order of the League of Mercy.
   Voluntary Medical Service Medal.—1932.
   Women's Royal Voluntary Service Medal.
   Colonial Special Constabulary Medal.
Foreign Orders, Decorations and Medals (in order of date).

THE PRIVY COUNCIL

Apart from Cabinet Ministers, who must be Privy Counsellors and are sworn in on first assuming office, membership of the Council (retained for life) is accorded by the Sovereign on the recommendation of the Prime Minister to eminent people in independent monarchical countries of the Commonwealth.

H.R.H. The Duke of Edinburgh	1951	Caradon, Lord	1968	Ferrers, Earl	1982
H.R.H. The Prince of Wales	1977	Carlisle of Bucklow, Lord	1979	Fletcher, Lord	1967
		Carr of Hadley, Lord	1963	Foot, Michael	1974
		Carrington, Lord	1959	Fowler, Norman	1979
Aberdare, Lord	1974	Casey, M. Eugene	1986	Fox, Sir Michael	1981
Ackner, Lord	1980	Castle, Barbara	1964	Franks, Lord	1949
Adams-Schneider, Sir Lancelot	1980	Cato, Robert	1981	Fraser of Tullybelton, Lord	1975
Ademola, Sir Adetokunbo	1963	Chalfont, Lord	1964	Fraser, Malcolm	1976
Airlie, Earl of	1984	Chalker, Lynda	1987	Fraser, Thomas	1964
Aldington, Lord	1954	Chan, Sir Julius	1981	Freeman, John	1966
Alebua, Ezekial	1988	Channon, Paul	1980	Freeson, Reginald	1976
Alison, Michael	1981	Charteris of Amisfield, Lord	1972	Gairy, Sir Eric	1977
Alport, Lord	1960	Chataway, Christopher	1970	Gardiner, Lord	1964
Amery, Julian	1960	Chesham, Lord	1964	Georges, Telford	1986
Anthony, John Douglas	1971	Clarke, Kenneth	1983	Gibbs, Sir Harry	1972
Archer, Peter	1977	Cledwyn of Penrhos, Lord	1966	Gibbs, Sir Humphrey	1969
Armstrong, Ernest	1979	Cockfield, Lord	1982	Gibson, Sir Ralph	1985
Arnold, Sir John	1979	Cocks of Hartcliffe, Lord	1976	Gibson-Watt, Lord	1974
Ashley, Jack	1979	Coggan, Rt. Rev. Lord	1961	Gilbert, John William	1978
Avonside, Lord	1962	Colman, Fraser	1986	Gilmour, Sir Ian, Bt	1973
Aylestone, Lord	1962	Colnbrook, Lord	1973	Glenamara, Lord	1964
Azikiwe, Nnamdi	1960	Colyton, Lord	1952	Glendevon, Lord	1959
Dacon, Daroness	1966	Compton, John	1983	Glidewell, Sir Iain	1985
Baker, Kenneth	1984	Concannon, John	1978	Goff of Chieveley, Lord	1982
Balcombe, Sir John	1985	Cooke, Sir Robin	1977	Gordon, John Bowie	1978
Balfour of Inchrye, Lord	1941	Cooper, Sir Frank	1983	Gorton, Sir John Grey	1968
Barber, Lord	1963	Cope, John	1988	Gowrie, Earl of	1984
Barnett, Lord	1975	Corfield, Sir Frederick	1970	Gray of Contin, Lord	1982
Barwick, Sir Garfield	1964	Cowen, Sir Zelman	1981	Griffiths, Lord	1980
Belstead, Lord	1983	Craigton, Lord	1961	Grimond, Lord	1961
Benn, Anthony	1964	Crawford and Balcarres, Earl of	1972	Gummer, John	1986
Bennett, Sir Frederic	1985	Crickhowell, Lord	1979	Hailsham of St. Marylebone, Lord	1956
Bevins, John Reginald	1959	Cromer, Earl of	1966	Harrison, Walter	1977
Biffen, John	1979	Croom-Johnson, Sir David	1984	Hart of South Lanark, Baroness	1967
Bingham, Sir Thomas	1986	Cross of Chelsea, Lord	1969	Harvington, Lord	1971
Bird, Vere	1982	Cumming-Bruce, Sir Roualeyn	1977	Hasluck, Sir Paul	1966
Blaize, Herbert	1986	Davies, Denzil	1978	Hattersley, Roy	1975
Blaker, Sir Peter	1983	Davison, Sir Ronald	1978	Havers, Lord	1977
Blanch, Rt. Rev. Lord	1975	Deedes, Lord	1962	Hayhoe, Sir Barney	1985
Booth, Albert	1976	De L'Isle, Viscount	1951	Healey, Denis	1964
Bottomley, Lord	1952	Dell, Edmund	1970	Heath, Edward	1955
Boyd-Carpenter, Lord	1954	Denham, Lord	1981	Herbison, Margaret	1964
Boyson, Sir Rhodes	1987	Denning, Lord	1948	Heseltine, Michael	1979
Braine, Sir Bernard	1985	Devlin, Lord	1960	Heseltine, Sir William	1986
Brandon of Oakbrook, Lord	1978	Devonshire, Duke of	1964	Higgins, Terence	1979
Bridge of Harwich, Lord	1975	Diamond, Lord	1965	Hill of Luton, Lord	1955
Brightman, Lord	1979	Dillon, Sir Brian	1982	Holderness, Lord	1959
Brittan, Leon	1981	Donaldson of Lymington, Lord	1979	Home of the Hirsel, Lord	1951
Brooke, Peter	1988	Douglas, Sir William	1977	Houghton of Sowerby, Lord	1964
Brown, Sir Stephen	1983	du Cann, Sir Edward	1964	Howe, Sir Geoffrey	1972
Browne, Sir Patrick	1974	Duff, Sir Antony	1980	Howell, David	1979
Browne-Wilkinson, Sir Nicolas	1983	Dunn, Sir Robin	1980	Howell, Denis	1976
Broxbourne, Lord	1957	Eccles, Viscount	1951	Hughes, Lord	1970
Buchanan-Smith, Alick	1981	Eden of Winton, Lord	1972	Hurd, Douglas	1982
Buckley, Sir Denys	1970	Edmund-Davies, Lord	1966	Irvine, Sir Bryant Godman	1982
Butler, Sir Adam	1984	Ellison, Rt. Rev. Gerald	1973	Irving of Dartford, Lord	1969
Butler-Sloss, Dame Elizabeth	1988	Elwyn-Jones, Lord	1964	Jauncey of Tullichettle, Lord	1988
Callaghan of Cardiff, Lord	1964	Emslie, Lord	1972	Jay, Lord	1952
Cameron of Lochbroom, Lord	1984	Ennals, Lord	1970	Jellicoe, Earl	1963
Campbell of Croy, Lord	1970	Erroll of Hale, Lord	1960	Jenkin of Roding, Lord	1973
Canterbury, The Archbishop of	1980	Esquivel, Manuel	1986	Jenkins of Hillhead, Lord	1964
		Eveleigh, Sir Edward	1977	Jones, Aubrey	1955
		Fernyhough, Ernest	1970	Jones, Sir Edward	1979

THE UNITED KINGDOM CONSTITUTION

The United Kingdom constitution is not contained in any single document but has evolved in the course of time, formed partly by statute, partly by common law and partly by convention. A constitutional monarchy, the United Kingdom is governed by Ministers of the Crown in the name of the Sovereign, who is head both of the state and the government.

The organs of government are the *legislature* (Parliament), the *executive* and the *judiciary*. The executive consists of Her Majesty's Government (Cabinet and other Ministers), government departments (*see* pp. 297–377), local authorities (*see* Index), and public corporations operating nationalised industries or social or cultural services (*see* pp. 297–377). The judiciary, i.e. judges, pronounce on the law, both written and unwritten, interpret statutes and are responsible for the enforcement of the law; the judiciary is independent of both the legislature and the executive (*see* Law Courts and Offices).

THE MONARCHY

The Sovereign personifies the state and is, in law, an integral part of the legislature, head of the executive, head of the judiciary, the Commander-in-Chief of all armed forces of the Crown and the 'Supreme Governor' of the Church of England. The seat of the monarchy is in the United Kingdom. In the Channel Islands and the Isle of Man, which are Crown dependencies, the Sovereign is represented by a Lieutenant-Governor; in the member states of the Commonwealth of which the Sovereign is head of state, her representative is a Governor-General (*see also* p. 625); in United Kingdom dependencies the Sovereign is usually represented by a Governor, who is responsible to the British Government.

Although the powers of the monarchy are now very limited, restricted mainly to the advisory and ceremonial, there are important acts of government which require the participation of the Sovereign. These include summoning, proroguing and dissolving Parliament, giving Royal Assent to Bills passed by Parliament, appointing important office-holders, e.g. government ministers, judges, bishops, and governors, conferring peerages, knighthoods and other honours, and granting pardon to a person wrongly convicted of a crime. An important function is appointing a Prime Minister, by convention the leader of the political party which enjoys, or can secure, a majority of votes in the House of Commons. In international affairs the Sovereign as head of State has the power to declare war and make peace, to recognise foreign states and governments, to conclude treaties and to annex or cede territory. However, as the Sovereign entrusts executive power to Ministers of the Crown and acts on the advice of her Ministers, which she cannot ignore, in practice royal prerogative powers are exercised by Ministers, who are responsible to Parliament.

Ministerial responsibility does not diminish the Sovereign's importance to the smooth working of government. She holds meetings of the Privy Council, gives audiences to her Ministers and other officials at home and overseas, receives accounts of Cabinet decisions, reads dispatches and signs state papers; she must be informed and consulted on every aspect of national life; and she must show complete impartiality.

In the event of the Sovereign's absence abroad, it is necessary to appoint *Counsellors of State* under Letters Patent to carry out the chief functions of the Monarch, including the holding of Privy Councils and giving Royal Assent to Acts passed by Parliament. The normal procedure is to appoint as Counsellors three or four members of the Royal Family among those remaining in the United Kingdom. In the event of the Sovereign on accession being under the age of eighteen years, or at any time unavailable or incapacitated by infirmity of mind or body for the performance of the royal functions, provision is made for a Regency.

THE PRIVY COUNCIL

The Sovereign in Council, or Privy Council, was the chief source of executive power until the system of Cabinet government developed. Now its main function is to advise the Sovereign to approve Orders in Council and to advise on the issue of royal proclamations. The Council's own statutory responsibilities (independent of the powers of the Sovereign in Council) include powers of supervision over the registering bodies for the medical and allied professions. A full Council is summoned only on the death of the Sovereign or when the Sovereign announces his or her intention to marry (for full list of Counsellors, *see* pp. 229–230).

There are a number of advisory Privy Council committees, whose meetings the Sovereign does not attend. Some are prerogative committees, such as those dealing with legislative matters submitted by the legislatures of the Channel Islands and the Isle of Man or with applications for charters of incorporation; and some are provided for by statute, e.g. those for the universities of Oxford and Cambridge and the Scottish universities.

The Judicial Committee of the Privy Council is the final court of appeal from courts of the United Kingdom dependencies, courts of independent Commonwealth countries which have retained the right of appeal, courts of the Channel Islands and the Isle of Man, some professional and disciplinary committees, and church sources. The Committee is composed of all Privy Counsellors who hold, or have held, high judicial office, although usually only three or five hear each case.

Administrative work is carried out by the Privy Council Office under the direction of the Lord President of the Council, a Cabinet Minister.

PARLIAMENT

Parliament is the supreme law-making authority and can legislate for the United Kingdom as a whole or for any parts of it separately (the Channel Islands and the Isle of Man are Crown dependencies and not part of the United Kingdom). The main functions of Parliament are to pass laws, to provide (by voting taxation) the means of carrying on the work of government and to scrutinise government policy and administration, particularly proposals for expenditure. International treaties and agreements are by custom presented to Parliament before ratification.

Parliament emerged during the late thirteenth and early fourteenth centuries. The nucleus of early Parliaments were the officers of the King's household and the King's judges, joined by such ecclesiastical and lay magnates as the King might summon to form a prototype "House of Lords", and occasionally by the knights of the shires, burgesses and proctors of the lower clergy. By the end of Edward III's reign a "House of Commons" was beginning to appear: the first known Speaker was elected in 1377.

Parliamentary procedure is based on custom and precedent, partly formulated in the Standing Orders of both Houses (*see* p. 237), and each House has the right to control its own internal proceedings and to commit for contempt. The system of debate in the two Houses is similar; when a motion has been moved, the Speaker proposes the question as the subject of a debate. Members speak from wherever they have been sitting. Questions are decided by a vote on a simple majority. Draft legislation is introduced, in either House, as a Bill. Bills can be introduced by a Government Minister or a private Member, but in practice the majority of Bills which become law are introduced by the Government. To become law, a Bill must be passed by each House (for parliamentary stages, *see* Bill, p. 235) and then sent to the Sovereign for the Royal Assent, after which it becomes an Act of Parliament.

Proceedings of both Houses are public, except on extremely rare occasions. The minutes (called Votes and Proceedings in the Commons, and Minutes of Proceedings in the Lords) and the speeches (The Official Report of Parliamentary Debates, *Hansard*) are published daily. Proceedings are also recorded for sound transmission on radio and television and preserved by the Parliamentary Sound Archive. Since January 1985, the House of Lords has allowed television cameras into its debates and Select Committees: television broadcasting of House of Commons proceedings is about to start for an experimental period.

By the Parliament Act of 1911, the maximum duration of a Parliament is five years, if not previously dissolved, the term being reckoned from the date given on the writs for the new Parliament. The maximum life has been prolonged by legislation in such rare circumstances as the two world wars (Jan. 31, 1911–Nov. 25, 1918; Nov. 26, 1935–June 15, 1945). Dissolution and writs for a general election are ordered by the Queen on the advice of the Prime Minister. The life of a Parliament is divided into *sessions*, usually of one year in length, beginning and ending most often in October or November.

THE HOUSE OF LORDS

The House of Lords consists of the Lords Spiritual and Temporal. The Lords Spiritual are the Archbishops of Canterbury and York, the Bishops of London, Durham and Winchester, and the 21 senior diocesan Bishops of the Church of England. The Lords Temporal consist of all hereditary Peers and Peeresses of England, Scotland, Great Britain and the United Kingdom who have not disclaimed their Peerages, Life Peers and Peeresses created under the Life Peerages Act 1958, and those Lords of Appeal in Ordinary created Life Peers under the Appellate Jurisdiction Act 1876, as amended (Law Lords). Disclaimants of an hereditary Peerage lose their right to sit in the House of Lords but gain the right to vote at Parliamentary elections and to offer themselves for election to the House of Commons. (*See also* p. 156). Peers who do not wish to attend sittings of the House of Lords may apply for leave of absence for the duration of a Parliament.

Until the beginning of this century the House of Lords had considerable power, being able to veto any Bill submitted to it by the House of Commons, but those powers were greatly reduced by the Parliament Act of 1911 and subsequently by the Parliament Act of 1949 (*see* **Parliament Acts 1911 and 1949**, p. 236).

Combined with its legislative role, the House of Lords has judicial powers as the ultimate Court of Appeal for Courts in Great Britain and Northern Ireland, except for criminal cases in Scotland. These powers are exercised by the Lord Chancellor and the Law Lords.

Members of the House of Lords are unpaid. However, they are entitled to reimbursement of travelling expenses on parliamentary business within the U.K. and certain other expenses incurred for the purpose of attendance at sittings of the House, within a maximum for each day of £57·00 for overnight subsistence, £21·00 for day subsistence and incidental travel, and £23·00 for secretarial costs, postage and certain additional expenses.

The House is presided over by the Lord Chancellor, who is *ex officio* Speaker of the House. A panel of deputy Speakers is appointed by Royal Commission. The first deputy Speaker is the Lord Chairman of Committees, appointed at the beginning of each session, a salaried officer of the House who takes the chair in Committee of the whole House and in some Select Committees. He is assisted by a panel of Deputy Chairmen, headed by the salaried Principal Deputy Chairman of Committees, who is also Chairman of the European Communities Committee of the House. The permanent officers include the Clerk of the Parliaments and other Clerks who, with other officers of the House, are collectively known as the Parliament Office; the Gentleman-Usher of the Black Rod, who is also Serjeant-at-Arms in attendance upon the Lord Chancellor and is responsible for security and for accommodation and services in the House of Lords; and the Yeoman Usher who is Deputy Serjeant-at-Arms and assists Black Rod in his duties.

OFFICERS OF THE HOUSE OF LORDS

Speaker, The Rt. Hon. the Lord Mackay of Clashfern £12,215
  Private Secretary, J. P. Stockton.
Chairman of Committees, The Rt. Hon. the Lord Aberdare, K.B.E. £34,688
Principal Deputy Chairman of Committees, The Baroness Serota £31,578

Clerk of the Parliaments, Sir John Sainty,
  K.C.B. £68,500
Clerk Assistant and Clerk of the Journals,
  M. A. J. Wheeler-Booth . . . . £45,800–£57,000
Reading Clerk and Principal Clerk, Public
  Bills, J. M. Davies . . . . £35,800–£45,300
Counsel to Chairman of Committees,
  D. Rippengal, C.B., Q.C. . . . . £45,800–£57,000
Second Counsel, Mrs. E. Denza, C.M.G.
  . . . . £35,800–£45,300
Assistant Counsel, G. A. Preston . . . £27,506–£32,394
Principal Clerks, J. A. Vallance White
  (*Judicial Office and Fourth Clerk at the*
  Table); M. G. Pownall (*Private Bill and*
  Overseas Offices); P. D. G. Hayter (*Com-*
  mittees) . . . . £35,800–£45,300

Chief Clerks, C. A. J. Mitchell; B. P. Keith;
  R. H. Walters, D.PHIL. (*Seconded as Sec-*
  retary to the Leader of the House and
  Chief Whip); D. R. Beamish; Mrs. F. M.
  Martin . . . . £27,506–£32,394
Senior Clerks, D. F. Slater; Miss F. P.
  Tudor; E. C. Ollard; Miss M. E. De Groose
  . . . . £17,381–£23,686
Clerk of the Records, H. S. Cobb, F.S.A.
  . . . . £27,506–£32,394
Deputy Clerk of the Records, D. J. Johnson,
  F.S.A. . . . . £21,287–£29,138
Assistant Clerks of the Records, J. C.
  Morgan (*Sound Archives*); S. K. Ellison
  . . . . £17,381–£23,686
Accountant, C. Preece . . . . £17,381–£29,138

Assistant Accountant, Miss J. M.
 Lansdown .... £14,556–£18,239
Judicial Taxing Clerk, C. G. Osborne
 £14,556–£18,239
Librarian, R. H. V. C. Morgan ..... £27,506–£32,394
Deputy Librarian, D. L. Jones. ..... £21,287–£29,138
Library Clerks, P. G. Davis, PH.D.; Miss I. L.
 Victory, PH.D. .... £17,381–£23,686
Examiners of Petitions for Private Bills,
 M. G. Pownall; R. J. Willoughby.
Gentleman-Usher of the Black Rod and
 Serjeant-at-Arms, Air Chief Marshal Sir
 John Gingell, G.B.E., K.C.B. .... £35,800–£45,300
Yeoman Usher of the Black Rod and Deputy
 Serjeant-at-Arms, Brig. D. M. Stileman,
 O.B.E. .... £17,381–£23,686
Staff Superintendent, Maj. F. P. Horsfall, M.B.E.
Shorthand Writer, Mrs. E. M. C. Holland ...... *fees*
Editor, Official Report (Hansard), Mrs.
 M. E. Villiers .... £25,961–£30,555
Deputy do. G. R. Goodbarne .... £19,333–£26,399

THE HOUSE OF COMMONS

The Members of the House of Commons are elected by universal adult suffrage. For electoral purposes, the United Kingdom is divided into constituencies, each of which returns one Member to the House of Commons, the Member being the candidate who obtains the largest number of votes cast in the constituency. To ensure equitable representation the four Boundary Commissions keep constituency boundaries under review and recommend any redistribution of seats which may seem necessary due to population movements, etc. The number of seats was raised to 640 in 1945, then reduced to 625 in 1948, and subsequently rose to 630 in 1955, 635 in 1970 and 650 in 1983. Of the present 650 seats there are 523 for England, 38 for Wales, 72 for Scotland and 17 for Northern Ireland. Elections are by secret ballot, each elector casting one vote: voting is not compulsory. When a seat becomes vacant between General Elections, a by-election is held.

British subjects and citizens of the Irish Republic can stand for election as Members of Parliament (M.P.s) provided they are 21 or over and not subject to disqualification. Those disqualified from sitting in the House include undischarged bankrupts, people sentenced to more than one year's imprisonment, clergy of the Church of England, Church of Scotland, Church of Ireland and Roman Catholic Church, peers, and holders of certain offices listed in the House of Commons Disqualification Act 1975 (e.g. members of the judiciary, Civil Service, regular armed forces, police forces, some local government officers and some members of public corporations and government commissions). A candidate does not require any party backing but his or her nomination for election must be supported by the signatures of ten people registered in the constituency. A candidate must also deposit with the returning officer £500, which is forfeit if the candidate does not receive more than 5 per cent of the votes cast. All election expenses, except the candidate's personal expenses, are subject to a statutory limit of £3,370, plus 2·9 pence for each elector in a borough constituency or 3·8 pence for each elector in a county constituency. (*See* pp. 241–248 for an alphabetical list of M.P.s, pp. 249–275 for the results of the last General Election and subsequent by-elections).

The week's business of the House is outlined each Thursday by the Leader of the House, after consultation between the Chief Government Whip and the Chief Opposition Whip. A quarter to a third of the time will be taken up by the Government's legislative programme, and the rest by other business, e.g. question time. As a rule Bills likely to raise political controversy are introduced in the Commons before going on to the Lords, and the Commons claims exclusive control in respect of national taxation and expenditure. Bills such as the Finance Bill, which imposes taxation, and the Consolidated Fund Bills, which authorise expenditure, must begin in the Commons. A Bill of which the financial provisions are subsidiary may begin in the Lords; and the Commons may waive their rights in regard to Lords' amendments affecting finance.

The Commons has a public register of M.P.s' financial, and certain other, interests. Members must also disclose any relevant financial interest or benefit in a matter before the House when taking part in a debate, in certain other proceedings of the House or in consultations with other Members, with Ministers or civil servants.

Since 1911 Members of the House of Commons have received payments and travelling facilities; they are entitled to claim income tax relief on expenses incurred in the course of their Parliamentary duties. Salary rates since 1911 as follows:

	p.a.		p.a.
1911	£400	1979 June	£9,450
1937	600	1980 June	11,750
1946	1,000	1981 June	13,950
1957	1,750	1982 June	14,510
1964	3,250	1983 June	15,308
1972 Jan	4,500	1984 Jan	16,106
1975 June	5,750	1985 Jan	16,904
1976 June	6,062	1986 Jan	17,702
1977 July	6,270	1987 Jan	18,500
1978 June	6,897	1988 Jan	22,548

In October 1969 Members were granted an allowance for secretarial and research expenses. In 1987 this became known as the Office Costs Allowance.

	p.a.		p.a.
1969 Oct	£500	1980 Aug	£8,000
1972 Jan	1,000	1981 June	8,480
1974 Aug	1,750	1982 June	8,820
1975 June	3,200	1983 June	12,000
1976 June	3,512	1984 June	12,546
1977 June	3,687	1985 April	13,211
1978 June	4,200	1986 April	20,140
1979 June	4,600	1987 April	21,302
1980 Feb	6,750		

Also, since January 1972, Members can claim reimbursement for the additional cost of staying overnight away from their main residence while on Parliamentary business. Since 1984 this has been non-taxable.

	p.a.		p.a.
1972	£750	1981 Aug	£5,206
1974 Aug	1,050	1982 Aug	5,674
1975 July	1,814	1983 Aug	6,163
1976 July	2,038	1984 Aug	6,696
1977 July	2,534	1985 Aug	7,351
1978 July	3,046	1986 Aug	7,855
1979 July	3,866	1987 Aug	8,674
1980 Aug	4,903		

From March 1980 provision was made enabling each Member in receipt of Secretarial and Research Allowance to contribute sums to an approved pension scheme for the provision of a pension, or other benefits, for or in respect of persons whose salary is met by him, from the office secretarial research allowance, now the Office Costs Allowance.

To March 31 1981	£786 p.a.	1985	£1,200 p.a.
1982	838	1986	1,321
1983	875	1987	2,014
1984	1,136	1988	2,130

The cost of travel allowances for 1987–88 was stated in July 1988 to be £4,956,290 (car mileage claims £3,259,966, rail travel £585,683 and air travel £484,198, spouse/children travel £361,722, extended travel within U.K. £70,779, and secretarial travel £193,892).

The Ministerial Salaries and Members' Pensions Act 1965 established a contributory pension fund providing pensions for former Members of Parliament and for dependents of deceased former Members. The Fund was reconstituted and the scheme restructured to bring it into line with pension schemes in the public sector by the Parliamentary and Other Pensions Acts 1972: further Acts modifying the arrangements for Members, Ministers and certain office-holders were passed in 1976, 1978, 1981, 1984 and 1987. The Parliamentary and Other Pensions Act 1987 is an enabling measure which provides that the detailed provisions may be contained in subordinate legislation. The arrangements now provide a pension of one-fiftieth of salary for each year of pensionable service with a maximum of two-thirds of salary at age 65. Pension is normally payable at age 65, for men and women, or on later retirement. Pensions may be paid earlier e.g. on ill-health retirement. The widow/widower of a former Member receives a pension of one-half of the late Member's pension. Pensions are index-linked. Members contribute 9 per cent of salary to the pension fund : there is an Exchequer contribution, currently twice the amount contributed by Members.

The House of Commons Members' Fund provides for annual or lump sum grants to ex-Members, their widows or widowers, and children whose incomes are below certain limits. Alternatively, payments of £1,488 per annum to ex-Members with at least ten years service and who left the House of Commons before October 1964 and £744 per annum to their widows or widowers are made as of right. Members contribute £24 per annum and the Exchequer £115,000 per annum to the Fund. The income of the Fund in 1986–87 was £214,561 and estimated expenditure on grants and payments was £131,741. The net assets of the Fund as at September 30, 1987 amounted to £1,693,989.

The House of Commons is presided over by the Speaker, who has considerable powers to maintain order in the House. His deputy, the Chairman of Ways and Means, and two Deputy Chairmen may preside over sittings of the House of Commons; they are elected by the House, and, like the Speaker, neither speak nor vote other than in their official capacity. The staff of the House are employed by a Commission chaired by the Speaker. The Heads of House of Commons Departments (*see* below) are permanent officers of the House, not M.P.s. The Clerk of the House is the principal adviser to the Speaker on the privileges and procedures of the House, the conduct of the business of the House, and Committees. The Serjeant-at-Arms is responsible for security, ceremonial, and for accommodation in the Commons part of the Palace of Westminster.

OFFICERS AND OFFICIALS OF THE HOUSE OF COMMONS

Speaker, The Rt. Hon. Bernard Weatherill, M.P. for Croydon North East £48,750
Chairman of Ways and Means, The Rt. Hon. Harold Walker, M.P. for Doncaster Central £37,773
First Deputy Chairman of Ways and Means, Sir Paul Dean, M.P. for Woodspring £34,763
Second Deputy Chairman of Ways and Means, Miss Betty Boothroyd, M.P. for West Bromwich West .. £34,763

Offices of the Speaker and Chairman of Ways and Means

Speaker's Secretary, P. J. Kitcatt, C.B.
                   £27,506–£31,394
Speaker's Counsel, H. Knorpel, C.B., Q.C.;
  G. E. Gammie, C.B. .... £35,800–£39,000
Chaplain to the Speaker, The Rev. Canon D. Gray, T.D.
Secretary to the Chairman of Ways and Means, R. I. S Phillips

Department of the Clerk of the House

Clerk of the House of Commons, C. J. Boulton,
  C.B. £68,500
Clerk Asst., J. F. Sweetman, T.D. ... £45,800–£48,000
Clerk of Committees, M. T. Ryle .... £45,800–£48,000
Principal Clerks—
  Public Bills, H. M. Barclay
  Table Office, D. W. Limon
  Journal Office, W. R. McKay
  Select Committees, C. B. Winnifrith
  Overseas Office, R. B. Sands
  Financial Committees, G. Cubie
  Second Clerk of Select Committees,
    A. J. Hastings
  Standing Committees, J. R. Rose
  Private Bills, R. J. Willoughby ... £32,094–£39,000
Deputy Principal Clerks, S. A. L. Panton;
  M. R. Jack, PH.D.; D. G. Millar; Mrs. J.
  Sharpe; Ms. A. Milner-Barry; R. W. G.
  Wilson; W. A. Proctor; F. A. Cranmer; R.
  J. Rogers; C. R. M. Ward, PH.D.; Ms. H. E.
  Irwin; D. W. N. Doig; A. Sandall; D. L.
  Natzler; E. P. Silk .... £27,506–£31,394
Senior Clerks, Mrs. S. A. de Ste. Croix; A. R.
  Kennon; D. W. Robson; L. C. Laurence-

Smyth; A. R. Gren; S. J. Patrick; D. J.
Gerhold; C. J. Poyser; D. F. Harrison; S. J.
Priestley; A. H. Doherty; P. A. Evans; R.
I. S. Phillips; R. G. James; Miss E. J. Baker;
Miss P. A. Helme; J. B. Ingram (*acting*); I.
C. Gilbert (*acting*); J. Darling (*acting*); J.
M. Hope (*acting*). .... £17,381–£22,854
Clerk of Services Sub-Committees, K. J.
  Brown .... £16,599–£21,799
Examiners of Petitions for Private Bills, R. J.
  Willoughby; M. G. Pownall.
Registrar of Members' Interests, A. J. Hastings
Taxing Officer, R. J. Willoughby.

Department of the Serjeant-at-Arms

Serjeant-at-Arms, Sir Victor Le Fanu, K.C.V.O.
                 £35,800–£39,000
Deputy Serjeant-at-Arms, P. N. W.
  Jennings .... £27,506–£31,094
Assistant Serjeant-at-Arms, M. J. A.
  Cummins .... £20,310–£26,781
Deputy Assistant Serjeants-at-Arms, P. A. J.
  Wright; J. F. Collins .... £17,381–£22,854

Department of the Library

Librarian, D. Menhennet, D.Phil ... £35,800–£39,000
Deputy Librarian, D. J. T. Englefield
                 £32,094–£33,594

Library and Information Service

Assistant Librarians, G. F. Lock; Miss
  J. B. Tanfield .... £27,506–£31,094
Deputy Assistant Librarians, S. Z. Young;
  Mrs. H. R. Coates; Miss P. J. Baines; K. G.
  Cuninghame; Mrs. J. M. Wainwright;

C. C. Pond, PH.D.; Mrs. C. B. Andrews; R.
C. Clements; Mrs. J. M. Lourie .. £21,827–£28,098
Senior Library Clerks, Ms. F. Poole; Mrs. J.
M. Fiddick; C. R. Barclay; Mrs. C. M.
Gillie; R. J. Ware, D.Phil; Ms. D. Gore,
PH.D; R. J. Twigger; B. K. Winctrobe; T.
N. Edmonds; R. J. Cracknell; Miss O. M.
Gay; Miss E. M. McInnes; Mrs. G. L. Allen
£17,381–£22,854

Vote Office

Deliverer of the Vote, G. R. Russell . £21,287–£28,098
Deputy Deliverer of the Vote, H. C. Foster
£17,381–£22,854

Administration Department

Head of Administration Department, G. A.
Roberts .... £35,800–£39,000
Accountant, J. L. G. Dobson .... £32,094–£33,594
Deputy Accountant, A. J. Lewis..... £27,506–£31,094
Senior Assistant Accountant, G. P. Brown
£21,287–£28,098
Assistant Accountants, A. R. Marskell; M. J.
Barram; Miss M. M. McColl; M. Fletcher
£17,381–£22,854

Head of Establishments Office, (*vacant*)
£27,506–£31,094
Deputy Head of Establishments Office, J. A.
Robb .... £21,287–£28,098
Computer Officer, R. S. Morgan .... £27,506–£31,094
Internal Auditor, A. A. Cameron... £17,381–£22,854
Staff Inspector, R. C. Collins .... £17,381–£22,854

Department of the Official Report

Editor, K. S. Morgan .... £32,094–£33,594
Deputy Editor, I. D. Church .... £21,287–£28,098
Principal Assistant Editors, R. V. Hadlow;
J. Gourley; F. G. Brotherston, O.B.E.;
J. Withers .... £19,919–£26,254
Assistant Editors, P. Walker; E. Holland; W.
G. Garland; Miss. V. Grainger... £17,966–£23,619

Refreshment Department

General Manager, W. J. J. Smillie .. £21,287–£28,098
Deputy General Manager, E. J. Nash
£17,381–£22,854
Catering Accountant, D. R. W. Wood
£17,381–£22,854

PARLIAMENTARY INFORMATION
The following is a short glossary of aspects of work of Parliament:
(*Unless otherwise stated, references are to* House of Commons *procedures.*)

Adjournment Debate.—Usually a half-hour debate introduced by a backbencher at the end of business for the day. The subjects raised are often local or personal issues.

Bill.—Proposed legislation is termed a *Bill.* The stages of a Public Bill (for Private Bills, *see* below) in the House of Commons are as follows:
First Reading: There is no debate at this stage, which nowadays merely constitutes an order to have the Bill printed.
Second Reading: The debate on the principles of the Bill.
Committee Stage: The detailed examination of a Bill, clause by clause. In most cases this takes place in a *Standing Committee*, or the whole House may act as a Committee. A *Special Standing Committee* may take evidence before embarking on detailed scrutiny of the Bill. Very rarely, a Bill may be examined by a *Select Committee* (*see* below).
Report Stage: Detailed review of a Bill as amended in Committee.
Third Reading: Final debate on a Bill.
Public Bills go through the same stages in the House of Lords, except that in almost all cases the Committee Stage is taken in the Committee of the Whole House.
A Bill may start in either House, and has to pass through both Houses to become law.
Both Houses have to agree the same text of a Bill, so that the *Amendments* made by the second House are then considered in the originating House and if not agreed, sent back or themselves amended, until agreement is reached.

Chiltern Hundreds.—A legal fiction, a nominal office of profit under the Crown, the acceptance of which requires a Member to vacate his seat. The Manor of Northstead is similar. These are the only means by which an M.P. may resign.

Closure & Guillotine.—To prevent deliberate waste of time of either House, a motion may be made that the question be now put. In the House of Commons, if the Speaker decides that the rights of a minority are not being prejudiced and 100 members support the closure motion in a division, if carried, the original motion is put to the House, without further debate. The *Guillotine* represents a more rigorous and systematic application of the Closure. Under this system, a Bill proceeds in accordance with a rigid timetable and discussion is limited to the time allotted to each group of clauses. The Closure is hardly ever used in the Lords, and there is no procedure for a guillotine. The completion of business in the Lords is traditionally ensured by mutual agreement from all sides of the House.

Consolidated Fund Bill. A Bill to authorize issue of money to maintain Government services. The Bill is dealt with without debate, but afterwards members may raise topics of public or local importance.

Delegated Legislation.—Many Statutes empower Ministers to make delegated legislation, with little or no reference back to Parliament, usually by means of Statutory Instruments. These fall into four broad categories:—(i) Affirmative Instruments, which are subject to approval by resolutions of both Houses before they can come into or remain in force; (ii) Negative Instruments, which are subject to annulment by resolution of either House; (iii) General Instruments, which include those not required to be laid before Parliament and those which are required to be so laid but are not subject to approval or annulment; (iv) Special Procedure Orders, against which parties outside Parliament may lodge petitions.

Dissolution.—Parliament comes to an end either by Dissolution by the Sovereign, on the advice of the Prime Minister, or the expiration of the term of five years for which the House of Commons was elected. Dissolution is normally effected by a Royal Proclamation.

Early Day Motion.—A motion put on the Notice Paper by an M.P. without in general the real prospect of its being debated. Such motions are expressions of backbench opinion.

Emergency Debate.—In the Commons a method of obtaining prompt discussion of a matter of urgency is by moving the adjournment under Standing Order No. 20 for the purpose of discussing a specific and important matter that should have urgent consideration. A member may ask leave to make this motion by giving written notice to the Speaker, usually before 12 noon, and if the Speaker considers the matter of sufficient importance and it obtains the support of 40 members, it is discussed usually at 7 p.m. on the following day.

Father of the House.—The Member whose continuous service in the House of Commons, is the longest. The present Father of the House is the Rt. Hon. Sir Bernard Braine, elected first in 1950.

General Synod Measure.—A measure passed by the national assembly of the Church of England under the Church of England Assembly (Powers) Act 1919. These measures are considered by the Joint Ecclesiastical Committee, who make a report. They are then considered by both Houses, and if approved, sent for the Royal Assent.

Hansard.—The official report of debates in both Houses (and in Standing Committees) published by H.M.S.O., normally on the day after the sitting concerned.

Hours of Meeting.—The House of Commons meets on Monday, Tuesday, Wednesday and Thursday at 2.30 p.m., and on Friday at 9.30 a.m. The House of Lords normally meets at 2.30 p.m. on Monday, Tuesday and Wednesday and at 3 p.m. on Thursday. In the latter part of the Session, the House sometimes sits on Fridays at 11 a.m.

Hybridity.—A Public Bill which is considered to affect specific private or local interests, as distinct from *all* such interests of a single category, is called a Hybrid Bill and is subject to a special form of scrutiny.

Leader of the Opposition.—In 1937 the office of Leader of the Opposition was recognized and a salary of £2,000 per annum was assigned to the post, thus following a practice which had prevailed in the Dominion of Canada since 1906. In June 1988 the salary was £48,148. The present Leader of the Opposition is the Rt. Hon. Neil Kinnock.

The Lord Chancellor.—The Lord High Chancellor of Great Britain is (*ex officio*) the Speaker of the House of Lords. Unlike the Speaker of the House of Commons, he is a member of the Government, takes part in debates and votes in divisions. He has none of the powers to maintain order that the Speaker in the Commons has, these powers being exercised in the Lords by the House as a whole. The Lord Chancellor sits in the Lords on one of the *Woolsacks*, couches covered with red cloth and stuffed with wool. If he wishes to address the House in any way except formally as Speaker, he leaves the Woolsack and steps towards his place as a peer.

Naming.—When a member has been named by the Speaker for a breach of order, i.e. contrary to the practice of the House called by surname and not addressed as the "Hon. Member for ... (his/her constituency)", the Leader of the House moves that the offender "be suspended from the service of the House" for (in the case of a first offence) a period of a week. Should the member offend again, the period of suspension is increased.

Opposition Day.—A day on which the topic for debate is chosen by the Opposition. There are 20 such days in a normal session. On 17 days, subjects are chosen by the Leader of the Opposition; on the remaining three days by the leader of the next largest opposition party.

Parliament Acts 1911 and 1949.—Under these Acts Bills may become law without the consent of the Lords.

Since at least the 18th century the Commons have had the privilege of having bills concerned with supply (i.e. taxation and money matters) passed without amendment by the Lords; though until 1911 the Lords retained the right to reject such bills outright.

By the Parliament Act 1911 a Bill which has been endorsed by the Speaker of the House of Commons as a Money Bill and has been passed by the Commons and sent up to the Lords at least one month before the end of a session can become law without the consent of the Lords if it is not passed by them without amendment within a month.

Under the Parliament Acts 1911 and 1949, if the Lords reject any other Public Bill (except one to prolong the life of a Parliament) which has been passed by the Commons in two successive sessions then that Bill shall (unless the Commons direct to the contrary) become law without the consent of the Lords. The Lords have power, therefore, to delay a Public Bill for thirteen months from its first Second Reading in the House of Commons.

Prime Minister's Questions.—The Prime Minister answers questions from 3.15 to 3.30 pm on Tuesdays and Thursdays. Nowadays the "open question" predominates. Members tend to ask the Prime Minister what are his or her official engagements for the day: a supplementary question on virtually any topic can then be put.

Private Bill.—A Bill promoted by a body or an individual to give powers additional to, or in conflict with, the general law, and to which a separate procedure applies.

Private Members' Bill.—A Public Bill promoted by a Member who is not a member of H.M. Government.

Private Notice Question.—A question adjudged of urgent importance on submission to Mr. Speaker, answered at the end of oral questions—usually at 3.30 p.m.

Privilege.—The following are covered by the privilege of Parliament: (i) freedom from interference in going to, attending at, and going from, Parliament; (ii) freedom of speech in Parliamentary proceedings; (iii) the printing and publishing of anything relating to the proceedings of the two Houses is subject to privilege; (iv) each House is the guardian of its dignity and may punish any insult to the House as a whole.

Prorogation.—The bringing to an end, by the Sovereign on the advice of the Government, of a Session of Parliament. Public Bills which have not completed all their stages lapse on Prorogation.

Queen's Speech.—The Speech delivered by H.M. The Queen at the State Opening of Parliament, in which the Government's programme for the session is set forth. The Speech is, of course, drafted for and approved by the Cabinet.

Question Time.—Oral questions are answered by Ministers in the Commons from 2.30 to 3.30 pm every day except Friday. They are also taken at the start of the Lords sittings, with a daily limit of four oral questions.

Royal Assent.—The Royal Assent is signified by Letters Patent to such Bills and Measures as have passed both Houses of Parliament (or Bills which have been passed under the Parliament Acts 1911 and 1949). The Sovereign has not given Royal Assent in person since 1854. On occasion, for instance in the Prorogation of Parliament, Royal Assent may be pronounced to the two Houses by Lords Commissioners; but more usually Royal Assent is notified to each House sitting separately in accordance with the Royal Assent Act 1967. The Norman formulae for Royal Assent are then endorsed on the Acts by the Clerk of the Parliaments.

The power to withhold assent (colloquially known as the Royal Veto) resides with the Sovereign, but has not been exercised in the United Kingdom since 1707, in the reign of Queen Anne.

Select Committees consisting usually of 10–15 members of all parties are a means used by both Houses in order to investigate certain matters.

Most Select Committees in the House of Commons are now tied to Departments—each Committee investigates subjects within a Government Department's remit. These are: Agriculture, Defence, Education Science and Arts, Employment, Energy, Environment, Foreign Affairs, Home Affairs, Social Services, Trade and Industry, Transport, Treasury and Civil Service, Welsh Affairs. The Scottish Affairs Committee is in temporary abeyance.

There are other House of Commons Select Committees dealing with Public Accounts (i.e. the spending by H.M. Government of money voted by Parliament) and European Legislation, and also domestic committees dealing, for example, with Privilege and Services. Major Select Committees usually take evidence in public: their evidence and reports are published by H.M.S.O.

The principal Select Committee in the House of Lords is that on the European Communities, which has, at present, six sub-committees dealing with all areas of community policy. The House of Lords also has a Select Committee on Science and Technology, which appoints sub-committees to deal with specific subjects. In addition, *ad hoc* Select Committees have been set up from time to time to investigate specific subjects, e.g. unemployment, overseas trade. There are also some Joint Committees of the two Houses, e.g. the Joint Committee on Statutory Instruments.

The Speaker.—The Speaker of the House of Commons is the spokesman and president of the Chamber. He is elected by the House at the beginning of each Parliament or when the previous Speaker retires or dies. He neither speaks in debates nor votes in divisions except when the voting is equal.

Standing Orders.—Rules which have from time to time been agreed by each House of Parliament to regulate the conduct of its business. These orders are not irrevocable, may be revised, amended or repealed, and are from time to time suspended or dispensed with.

State Opening.—This marks the start of each new session of Parliament. Parliament is normally opened, in the presence of both Houses, by the Queen in person, who makes the Speech from the Throne which outlines the Government's policies for the coming session (*see* **Queen's Speech**). In the absence of the Queen, Parliament is opened by Royal Commission, and the Queen's Speech is read by one of the Lords Commissioners specially appointed by Letters Patent for the occasion.

Strangers.—Anyone who is not a Member or Officer of the House is a *stranger*. Visitors are generally admitted to debates of both Houses but may be excluded if the House so decides. In practice this happens only in time of war.

Ten Minute Rule.—A colloquial term for Standing Order No. 19, under which backbenchers have an opportunity on Tuesdays and Wednesdays to state for about ten minutes why a Bill on a certain subject should be introduced. Time is also available for a short opposing speech.

Vacant Seats.—When a vacancy occurs in the House of Commons during a session of Parliament the Writ for the by-election is moved, by a Whip of the party to which the member whose seat has been vacated belonged. If the House is in recess, the Speaker can issue a warrant for a writ, should two members certify to him that a seat is vacant.

Whips.—In order to secure the attendance of Members of a particular party in Parliament on all occasions, and particularly on the occasion of an important vote, Whips (originally known as "Whippers-in") are appointed. The written appeal or circular letter issued by them is also known as a "whip", its urgency being denoted by the number of times it is underlined. Failure to respond to a three-line whip, headed "Most important", is tantamount in the Commons to secession (at any rate temporarily) from the party. Whips are officially recognized by Parliament and are provided with office accommodation in both Houses. In both Houses, Government and some Opposition Whips receive salaries from public funds.

PUBLIC INFORMATION SERVICE.—Enquiries from the general public and organizations of all kinds about the work, practices, composition and history of the House of Commons are answered by the Public Information Office, House of Commons, SW1A 0AA (01-219 4272). This office also edits the House of Commons Weekly Information Bulletin (published by H.M.S.O.). A series of factsheets on the work and processes of the House is available. The Journal and Information Office, House of Lords, SW1A 0PW (01-219 3107) answers queries relating to the procedure and practice of the Lords.

HER MAJESTY'S GOVERNMENT

Her Majesty's Government is the body of Ministers responsible for the administration of national affairs, determining policy and introducing into Parliament any legislation necessary to give effect to government policy. The majority of Ministers are members of the House of Commons but members of the House of Lords may also hold Ministerial responsibility. The Lord Chancellor is always a member of the House of Lords. The Prime Minister is, by recent convention, always a member of the House of Commons.

THE PRIME MINISTER

The office of Prime Minister, which had been in existence for nearly 200 years, was officially recognised in 1905 and its holder was granted a place in the Table of Precedence. The Prime Minister, by tradition also First Lord of the Treasury and Minister for the Civil Service, is appointed by the Sovereign and is usually the leader of the party which enjoys, or can secure, a majority in the House of Commons. Other Ministers are appointed by the Sovereign on the recommendation of the Prime Minister, who also allocates functions amongst Ministers and has the power to obtain their resignation or dismissal individually.

The Prime Minister informs the Sovereign of state and political matters, advises on the dissolution of Parliament, and makes recommendations for important Crown appointments, the award of honours, etc.

As the chairman of Cabinet meetings and leader of a political party, the Prime Minister is responsible for translating party policy into government activity: and as leader of the Government the Prime Minister is responsible to Parliament and to the electorate for the policies and their implementation.

The Prime Minister also represents the nation in international affairs, e.g. summit conferences.

THE CABINET

The Cabinet developed during the 18th century as an inner committee of the Privy Council, which was the chief source of executive power until that time. It is composed of about 20 Ministers chosen by the Prime Minister, usually the heads of government departments (generally known as Secretaries of State unless they have a special title, e.g. Chancellor of the Exchequer) and the holders of various traditional offices.

The Cabinet's functions are the final determination of policy, control of government and co-ordination of government departments. The exercise of its functions is dependent upon enjoying majority support in the House of Commons. Cabinet meetings are held in private, taking place once or twice a week during parliamentary sittings and less often during a recess. Proceedings are confidential, the members being bound by their oath as Privy Counsellors not to disclose information about the proceedings.

The convention of collective responsibility means that the Cabinet acts unanimously even when Cabinet Ministers do not all agree on a subject. The policies of departmental Ministers must be consistent with the policies of the Government as a whole, and once the Government's policy has been decided, each Minister is expected to support it or resign.

The convention of Ministerial responsibility holds a Minister, as the political head of his or her department, accountable to Parliament for the department's work. Departmental Ministers usually decide all matters within their responsibility, although on matters of political importance they normally consult their colleagues collectively. A decision by a departmental Minister is binding on the Government as a whole.

HER MAJESTY'S GOVERNMENT

THE CABINET

Prime Minister, First Lord of the Treasury and Minister for the Civil Service, THE RT. HON. MARGARET HILDA THATCHER, M.P., *born* Oct. 13, 1925.
Secretary of State for Foreign and Commonwealth Affairs, The Rt. Hon. Sir (Richard Edward) Geoffrey Howe, Q.C., M.P., *born* Dec. 20, 1926.
Chancellor of the Exchequer, The Rt. Hon. Nigel Lawson, M.P., *born* March 11, 1932.
Lord High Chancellor, The Rt. Hon. the Lord Mackay of Clashfern, *born* July 2, 1927.
Secretary of State for the Home Department, The Rt. Hon. Douglas Richard Hurd, C.B.E., M.P., *born* March 8, 1930.
Secretary of State for Wales, The Rt. Hon. Peter Edward Walker, M.B.E., M.P., *born* March 25, 1932.
Secretary of State for Defence, The Rt. Hon. George Kenneth Hotson Younger, T.D., M.P., *born* Sept. 22, 1931.
Secretary of State for Employment, The Rt. Hon. (Peter) Norman Fowler, M.P., *born* Feb. 2, 1938.
Secretary of State for Northern Ireland, The Rt. Hon. Thomas Jeremy King, M.P., *born* June 13, 1933.
Secretary of State for the Environment, The Rt. Hon. Nicholas Ridley, M.P., *born* Feb. 17, 1929.
Secretary of State for Trade and Industry, The Rt. Hon. the Lord Young of Graffham, *born* Feb. 27, 1932.
Secretary of State for Education and Science, The Rt. Hon. Kenneth Wilfred Baker, M.P., *born* Nov. 3, 1934.
Secretary of State for Health, The Rt. Hon. Kenneth Henry Clarke, Q.C., M.P., *born* July 2, 1940.
Minister of Agriculture, Fisheries and Food, The Rt. Hon. John Roddick Russell MacGregor, O.B.E., M.P., *born* Feb. 14, 1937.
Secretary of State for Scotland, The Rt. Hon. Malcolm Leslie Rifkind, Q.C., M.P., *born* June 21, 1946.
Secretary of State for Transport, The Rt. Hon. (Henry) Paul Guinness Channon, M.P., *born* Oct. 9, 1935.
Secretary of State for Social Security, The Rt. Hon. John Edward Michael Moore, M.P., *born* Nov. 26, 1937.
Lord President of the Council and Leader of the House of Commons, The Rt. Hon. John Wakeham, M.P., *born* June 22, 1932.
Lord Privy Seal and Leader of the House of Lords, The Rt. Hon. The Lord Belstead, *born* Sept. 30, 1932.
Secretary of State for Energy, The Rt. Hon. Cecil Edward Parkinson, M.P., *born* Sept. 1, 1931.
Chief Secretary to the Treasury, The Rt. Hon. John Major, M.P., *born* March 29, 1943.
Chancellor of the Duchy of Lancaster and Minister of Trade and Industry, The Rt. Hon. Antony Harold Newton, O.B.E.., M.P., *born* Aug. 29, 1937.

LAW OFFICERS

Attorney-General, The Rt. Hon. Sir Patrick Barnabas Burke Mayhew, Q.C., M.P.
Lord Advocate, The Rt. Hon. The Lord Cameron of Lochbroom, Q.C.
Solicitor-General, Sir Nicholas Walter Lyell, Q.C., M.P.
Solicitor-General for Scotland, Peter Lovat Fraser, Q.C.*
    (* not a member of the House of Commons)

OTHER MINISTERS

Parliamentary Secretary to the Treasury, The Rt. Hon. David Waddington, Q.C., M.P.
Paymaster General, The Rt. Hon. Peter Brooke, M.P.
Financial Secretary to the Treasury, The Rt. Hon. Norman Lamont, M.P.

MINISTERS OF STATE

Agriculture, Fisheries and Food, (no appointment made).
Defence, The Lord Trefgarne (*Defence Procurement*);

The Hon. Archibald Hamilton, M.P. (*Armed Forces*).
Education and Science, Mrs. Angela Rumbold, C.B.E., M.P.
Employment, The Rt. Hon. John Cope, M.P.
Energy, The Rt. Hon. Peter Morrison, M.P.
Environment, Michael Howard, Q.C., M.P. (*Water, Planning*); The Earl of Caithness (*Housing, Environment Protection, Countryside and Heritage*); The Rt. Hon. John Gummer, M.P. (*Local Government*).

Foreign and Commonwealth Affairs, The Rt Hon. Lynda Chalker, M.P.; Christopher Patten, M.P. (*Minister for Overseas Development*); Hon. William Waldegrave, M.P.; The Lord Glenarthur.

Health, David Mellor, Q.C., M.P.

Home Office, The Rt. Hon. the Earl Ferrers; John Patten, M.P.; Timothy Renton, M.P.

Northern Ireland, Ian Stewart, R.D., M.P.

Privy Council Office, The Rt. Hon. Richard Luce, M.P. (*Minister for the Arts*).

Scottish Office, Ian Lang, M.P.; The Lord Sanderson of Bowden.

Social Security, Nicholas Scott, M.B.E., M.P.

Trade and Industry, The Hon. Alan Clark, M.P. (*Trade*).

Transport, Michael Portillo, M.P. (*Public Transport*).

Treasury, Peter Lilley, M.P. (*Economic Secretary*).

Welsh Office, Wyn Roberts, M.P.

UNDER-SECRETARIES OF STATE

Agriculture, Fisheries and Food, Donald Thompson, M.P.; The Baroness Trumpington; Richard Ryder, O.B.E., M.P.

Defence, Roger Freeman, M.P. (*Armed Forces*); The Hon. Timothy Sainsbury, M.P. (*Defence Procurement*).

Education and Science, John Butcher, M.P.; Robert Jackson, M.P.

Employment, John Lee, M.P.; Patrick Nicholls, M.P.

Energy, Michael Spicer, M.P.; The Baroness Hooper.

Environment, Christopher Chope, O.B.E., M.P.; The Hon. Colin Moynihan, M.P. (*Minister for Sport*); Mrs. Virginia Bottomley, M.P.; David Trippier, R.D., M.P.

Foreign and Commonwealth Affairs, Timothy Eggar, M.P.

Health, Mrs. Edwina Currie, M.P.

Home Office, The Hon. Douglas Hogg, M.P.

Northern Ireland Office, The Lord Lyell; Dr. Brian Mawhinney, M.P.; Richard Needham, M.P.; Peter Viggers, M.P.

Scottish Office, Michael Forsyth, M.P.; Lord James Douglas-Hamilton, M.P.

Social Security, Peter Lloyd, M.P., The Lord Skelmersdale.

Trade and Industry, Robert Atkins, M.P.; The Hon. Francis Maude, M.P.; Eric Forth, M.P.

Transport, Peter Bottomley, M.P. The Lord Brabazon of Tara.

Treasury, The Lords Commissioners (*see* Government Whips).

Welsh Office, Ian Grist, M.P.

GOVERNMENT WHIPS

HOUSE OF LORDS

Captain of the Honourable Corps of Gentlemen-at-Arms (Chief Whip), The Rt. Hon. The Lord Denham.

Captain of the Queen's Bodyguard of the Yeoman of the Guard (Deputy Chief Whip), The Viscount Davidson.

Lords in Waiting, The Viscount Long; The Lord Hesketh; The Earl of Dundee; The Earl of Arran; The Lord Strathclyde.

HOUSE OF COMMONS

Parliamentary Secretary to the Treasury (Chief Whip), The Rt. Hon. David Waddington, Q.C., M.P.

Treasurer of the H.M. Household (Deputy Chief Whip), David Hunt, M.B.E., M.P.

Comptroller of H.M. Household, Tristan Garel-Jones, M.P.

Vice-Chamberlain of H.M. Household, Michael Neubert, M.P.

Lords Commissioners, Kenneth Carlisle, M.P.; Anthony Durant, M.P.; Alan Howarth, C.B.E., M.P.; David Lightbown, M.P.; David Maclean, M.P.

Assistant Whips, Stephen Dorrell, M.P.; Michael Fallon, M.P.; David Heathcoat-Amory, M.P.; The Hon. Thomas Sackville, M.P.; John Taylor, M.P.

GOVERNMENT BY PARTY

Before the reign of William and Mary the principal Officers of State were chosen by and were responsible to the Sovereign alone and not to Parliament or the nation at large. Such officers acted sometimes in concert with one another, but more often independently, and the fall of one did not, of necessity, involve that of others, although all were liable to be dismissed at any moment.

In 1693 the Earl of Sunderland recommended to William III the advisability of selecting a Ministry from the political party which enjoyed a majority in the House of Commons and the first united Ministry was drawn in 1696 from the Whigs, to which party the King owed his throne, the principal members being Russell (the Admiral), Somers (the Advocate), Lord Wharton and Charles Montague (afterwards Chancellor of the Exchequer). This group became known as the *Junto* and was regarded with suspicion as a novelty in the political life of the nation, being a small section meeting in secret apart from the main body of Ministers. It may be regarded as the forerunner of the *Cabinet* and in course of time it led to the establishment of the principle of joint responsibility of Ministers, so that internal disagreement caused a change of personnel or resignation of the whole body of Ministers.

The accession of George I, who was unfamiliar with the English language, led to a disinclination on the part of the Sovereign to preside at meetings of his Ministers and caused the appearance of a *Prime*

Minister, a position first acquired by Robert Walpole in 1721 and retained without interruption for 20 years and 326 days.

In 1828 the old party of the Whigs became known as *Liberals*, a name originally given to it by its opponents to imply laxity of principles, but gradually accepted by the party to indicate its claim to be pioneers and champions of political reform and progressive legislation. In 1861 a Liberal Registration Association was founded and Liberal Associations became widespread. In 1877 a National Liberal Federation was formed, with headquarters in London. The Liberal Party was in power for long periods during the second half of the nineteenth century and for several years during the first quarter of the twentieth century, but after a split in the party the numbers elected were small from 1931. In March 1988, the Liberals and the Social Democratic Party merged under the title *Social and Liberal Democrats* (*see* below).

Soon after the change from Whig to Liberal the Tory Party became known as *Conservative*, a name traditionally believed to have been invented by John Wilson Croker in 1830 and to have been generally adopted about the time of the passing of the Reform Act of 1832 to indicate that the preservation of national institutions was the leading principle of the party. After the Home Rule crisis of 1886 the dissentient Liberals entered into a compact with the Conservatives, under which the latter undertook not to contest their seats, but a separate *Liberal Unionist* organization was maintained until 1912, when it was united with the Conservatives.

The Labour Party.—Labour candidates for Parliament made their first appearance at the General Election of 1892, when there were 27 standing as "Labour" or "Liberal-Labour."

In 1900 the *Labour Representation Committee* was set up in order to establish a distinct Labour Group in Parliament, with its own whips, its own policy, and a readiness to co-operate with any party which might be engaged in promoting legislation in the direct interest of labour. In 1906 the L.R.C. became known as *The Labour Party.*

Social Democratic Party.—The Council for Social Democracy was announced by four former Labour Cabinet Ministers on Jan. 25, 1981. Subsequently a number of sitting Labour Members of Parliament, together with one Conservative, joined the new group, and on March 26, 1981 the Social Democratic Party was launched. Later in the year the S.D.P. and

the Liberal Party formed an electoral *Alliance.* In 1988 a majority of the S.D.P. agreed on a merger with the Liberal Party but a minority continue as a separate party under the S.D.P. title.

The government of the day is formed by the party which wins the largest number of seats in the House of Commons at a General Election, or which has the support of a majority of members in the House of Commons. By tradition, the leader of the majority party is asked by the Sovereign to form a government, while the largest minority party becomes the official Opposition with its own leader and own "Shadow Cabinet". Leaders of the Government and Opposition sit on the front benches of the Commons with their supporters (the back-benchers) sitting behind them.

When a party is in Opposition and its leadership becomes vacant, it makes its free choice among the various personalities available; but if the party is in office, the Sovereign's choice may anticipate, and in a certain sense forestall, the decision of the party.

POLITICAL PARTIES

CONSERVATIVE AND UNIONIST PARTY, Central Office, 32 Smith Square, SW1P 3HH. (Tel : 01-222 9000).—*Party Chairman,* The Rt. Hon. P. Brooke, M.P.; *Deputy Chairman,* The Rt. Hon. P. Morrison, M.P.; *Vice Chairmen,* T. Arnold, M.P.; Dame Joan Seccombe, O.B.E.; J. Spicer, M.P.; *Hon. Treasurers,* Lord McAlpine of West Green; Sir Oulton Wade; Sir Hector Laing.

SCOTTISH CONSERVATIVE PARTY, Central Office, 3 Chester Street, Edinburgh EH3 7RF. (Tel: 031-226 4426).—*Chairman,* The Lord Goold; *Deputy Chairman,* Sir Donald Maclean; *Hon. Treasurer,* M. D. Goodwin, C.B.E.; *Chief Exec.,* J. J. MacKay.

LABOUR PARTY, 150 Walworth Road, SE17 1JT. (Tel: 01-703 0833).—*Chair,* The Rt. Hon. N. Kinnock, M.P.; *Vice Chair,* D. Skinner, M.P.; *Treasurer,* S. McCluskie; *Gen. Sec.,* L. Whitty; *Parliamentary Party Leader,* The Rt. Hon. N. Kinnock, M.P.; *Deputy Leader,* The Rt. Hon. R. Hattersley, M.P.; *Leader of the Labour Peers,* Lord Cledwyn of Penrhos, C.H.

SHADOW CABINET, 1987–88.—The Rt. Hon. N. Kinnock, M.P. (*Leader of the Opposition*); The Rt. Hon. J. Smith, M.P. (*Treasury and Economic Affairs*); The Rt. Hon. G. Kaufman, M.P. (*Foreign and Commonwealth Affairs*); The Rt. Hon. R. Hattersley, M.P. (*Home Affairs*); F. Dobson, M.P. (*Leader of the House and Campaigns Co-ordinator*); B. Gould, M.P. (*Trade and Industry*); Dr. J. Cunningham, M.P. (*Environment*); M. Meacher, M.P. (*Employment*); R. Hughes, M.P. (*Transport*); M. O'Neill, M.P. (*Defence, Disarmament and Arms Control*); K. McNamara, M.P. (*Northern Ireland*); The Rt. Hon. A. Williams, M.P. (*Wales*); D. Dewar, M.P. (*Scotland*); R. Cook, M.P. (*Health and Social Security*); J. Straw, M.P. (*Education*); J. Prescott, M.P. (*Energy*); Dr. D. Clark, M.P. (*Agriculture and Rural Affairs*); Ms. J. Richardson, M.P. (*Women*); G. Brown, M.P. (*Chief Secretary to the Treasury*).

Labour Whips in the House of Lords are: *Chief Whip,* Lord Ponsonby of Shulbrede; *Deputy Chief Whip,* Baroness Nichol. Labour Whips in the House of Commons are: *Chief Whip,* D. Foster, M.P.; *Deputy Chief Whip,* D. Dixon, M.P.

PLAID CYMRU, 51 Cathedral Road, Cardiff CF1 9HD. (Tel: 0222-31944).—*Chairman,* D. Huws; *Deputy Chairman,* I. W. Jones, M.P.; *Hon. Treasurer,* D. Watkins; *Sec.,* D. Williams; *Party President,* D. E. Thomas, M.P.; *Vice-President,* D. Iwan.

SCOTTISH NATIONAL PARTY, 6 North Charlotte Street, Edinburgh EH2 4JH. (Tel: 031-226 3661).—*Chairman,* G. Wilson; *Deputy Chairman,* A. Salmond, M.P.; *Hon. Treasurer,* A. Morgan; *National Sec.,* J.

Swinney; *Parliamentary Party Leader,* Mrs. M. Ewing, M.P.; *Chief Whip,* A. Welsh, M.P.

SOCIAL AND LIBERAL DEMOCRATS, 4 Cowley Street, SW1P 3NB. (Tel: 01-222 7999).—*President,* I. W. Wrigglesworth; *Deputy Chair,* T. McNally; *Hon. Treasurer,* T. Razzell; *Chief Executive,* A. Ellis, O.B.E.; *Leader of the Party,* J. J. D. (Paddy) Ashdown, M.P.; *Leader of the S.L.D. Peers,* The Rt. Hon. the Lord Jenkins of Hillhead.

SCOTTISH SOCIAL AND LIBERAL DEMOCRATS, 4 Clifton Terrace, Edinburgh EH12 5DR. (Tel: 031-337 2314).—*Chairman,* J. Bannerman; *Hon. Treasurer,* K. Smith; *Party President,* Sir Russell Johnston, M.P.; *Party Leader,* M. G. Bruce, M.P.

WELSH SOCIAL AND LIBERAL DEMOCRATS, 91 St. Mary Street, Cardiff CF1 1DW. (Tel: 0222-382210).—*Chairman (interim),* G. Jones; *Hon. Treasurers (interim),* Dr. G. Morrison; P. Davies; *Party President,* T. Ellis; *Party Leader,* R. Livsey, M.P.

S.L.D. Whips in the House of Lords are: *Chief Whip,* Lord Tordoff; *Deputy Whips,* Viscount Falkland, Lord McNair. S.L.D. Whips in the House of Commons are: *Chief Whip,* J. R. Wallace, M.P.; *Deputy Whip,* R. C. Fearn, M.P.

SOCIAL DEMOCRATIC PARTY, 25–28 Buckingham Gate, SW1E 6LD. (Tel: 01-821 9661).—*President,* J. Cartwright, M.P.; *National Sec.,* Ms. F. Wilson; *Parliamentary Leader,* The Rt. Hon. Dr. D. Owen, M.P.; *Leader of the S.D.P. Peers,* Baroness Stedman.

The S.D.P. Whip in the House of Lords is Lord Walston. The S.D.P. Whip in the House of Commons is J. Cartwright, M.P.

NORTHERN IRELAND

SOCIAL DEMOCRATIC AND LABOUR PARTY, 38 University Street, Belfast BT7 1FZ. (Tel: 0232-323428).—*Chairman,* A. Maginness; *Deputy Chairmen,* M. Durkan, S. Doyle; *Hon. Treasurer,* P. Brannigan; *Gen. Sec.,* P. McGlone; *Parliamentary Party Leader,* J. Hume, M.P.; *Deputy Leader,* S. Mallon, M.P.; *Chief Whip,* E. McGrady, M.P.

ULSTER DEMOCRATIC UNIONIST PARTY, 296 Albertbridge Road, Belfast BT5 4GW. (Tel: 0232-458597).—*Chairman,* J. McClure; *Deputy Chairman,* S. Gibson; *Hon. Treasurer,* D. Herron; *Sec.,* A. Kane; *Parliamentary Party Leader,* Dr. I. Paisley, M.P.; *Deputy Leader,* P. Robinson, M.P.

ULSTER UNIONIST COUNCIL, 3 Glengall Street, Belfast BT12 5AE. (Tel: 0232-324601).—*Chairman,* J. Allen; *Vice Chairman,* Dr. W. Brownlees; *Hon. Treasurer,* J. Cunningham; *Party Sec.,* J. Wilson; *Party Leader,* The Rt. Hon. J. H. Molyneaux, M.P.

ALPHABETICAL LIST OF MEMBERS OF THE HOUSE OF COMMONS
(as at end July 1988)
S.L.D. = Social and Liberal Democrat. For other abbreviations, *see* page 249

	Maj.
*Walker, Rt. Hon. Harold (*b.* 1927), *Lab.,* Doncaster, Central	8,196
*Walker, Rt. Hon. Peter E., M.B.E. (*b.* 1932), *C., Worcester*	10,453
*Walker, William C. (*b.* 1929), *Tayside, N.*	5,016
Wall, C. Patrick (*b.* 1933), *Lab., Bradford, N.*	1,633
*Wallace, James R. (*b.* 1954), *S.L.D., Orkney and Shetland*	3,922
*Waller, Gary P. A. (*b.* 1945), *C., Keighley*	5,606
Walley, Ms. Joan L. (*b.* 1949), *Lab., Stoke-on-Trent, N.*	8,513
*Walters, Sir Dennis, M.B.E. (*b.* 1928), *C., Westbury*	10,097
*Ward, John D., C.B.E. (*b.* 1925), *C., Poole*	14,808
*Wardell, Gareth L. (*b.* 1944), *Lab., Gower*	5,764
*Wardle, Charles F. (*b.* 1939), *C., Bexhill and Battle*	20,519
*Wareing, Robert N. (*b.* 1930), *Lab., Liverpool, West Derby*	20,496
*Warren, Kenneth R. (*b.* 1926), *C., Hastings and Rye*	7,347
*Watts, John A. (*b.* 1947), *C., Slough*	4,090
*Weatherill, Rt. Hon. B. Bernard (*b.* 1920), *The Speaker, Croydon, N.E.*	12,519
*Wells, Bowen (*b.* 1935), *C., Hertford and Stortford*	17,140
Welsh, Andrew (*b.* 1944), *S.N.P., Angus, E.*	1,544
*Welsh, Michael C. (*b.* 1926), *Lab., Doncaster, N.*	19,935
*Wheeler, John D. (*b.* 1940), *C., Westminster, N.*	3,310
*Whitney, Raymond W., O.B.E. (*b.* 1930), *C., Wycombe*	13,819
Widdecombe, Miss Ann N. (*b.* 1947), *C., Maidstone*	10,364

	Maj.
*Wiggin, A. W. (Jerry), T.D. (*b.* 1937), *C., Weston-super-Mare*	7,998
*Wigley, Dafydd W. (*b.* 1943), *P.C., Caernarfon*	12,802
*Wilkinson, John A. D. (*b.* 1940), *C., Ruislip-Northwood*	16,971
*Williams, Rt. Hon. Alan J. (*b.* 1930), *Lab., Swansea, W.*	7,062
Williams, Alan W. (*b.* 1945), *Lab., Carmarthen*	4,317
Wilshire, David (*b.* 1943), *C., Spelthorne*	20,050
Wilson, Brian D. H. (*b.* 1948), *Lab., Cunninghame, N.*	4,467
*Winnick, David J. (*b.* 1933), *Lab., Walsall, N.*	1,790
*Winterton, Mrs. J. Ann (*b.* 1941), *C., Congleton*	7,969
*Winterton, Nicholas R. (*b.* 1938), *C., Macclesfield*	19,092
Wise, Mrs. Audrey (*b.* 1935), *Lab., Preston*	10,645
*Wolfson, G. Mark (*b.* 1934), *C., Sevenoaks*	17,345
*Wood, Timothy J. R. (*b.* 1940), *C., Stevenage*	5,340
*Woodcock, Michael (*b.* 1943), *C., Ellesmere Port and Neston*	1,853
Worthington, Anthony (*b.* 1941), *Lab., Clydebank and Milngavie*	16,304
Wray, James (*b.* 1938), *Lab., Glasgow, Provan*	18,372
*Yeo, Timothy S. K. (*b.* 1945), *C., Suffolk, S.*	16,243
*Young, David W. (*b.* 1930), *Lab., Bolton, S.E.*	11,381
*Young, Sir George, Bt. (*b.* 1941), *C., Ealing, Acton*	12,243
*Younger, Rt. Hon. George K. H., T.D. (*b.* 1931), *C., Ayr*	182

SMALL MAJORITIES

The following Members were returned in June 1987 with majorities of fewer than 1,000 votes.

*Richard Livsey (*L/All., Brecon and Radnor*)	56
Alan Meale (*Lab., Mansfield*)	56
*Conal Gregory (*C., York*)	147
*Gerald Bowden (*C., Dulwich*)	180
*Rt. Hon. George Younger (*C., Ayr*)	182
Mrs. Maureen Hicks (*C., Wolverhampton N.E.*)	204
David Martin (*C., Portsmouth, S.*)	205
*Mrs. Lynda Chalker (*C., Wallasey*)	279
Robert Cryer (*Lab., Bradford S.*)	309
John Garrett (*Lab., Norwich, S.*)	336
Mrs. Ann Taylor (*Lab., Dewsbury*)	445
*Michael Knowles (*C., Nottingham, E.*)	456

Elliott Morley (*Lab., Glanford and Scunthorpe*)	512
Timothy Janman (*C., Thurrock*)	690
Edward McGrady (*S.D.L.P., Down, S.*)	731
Timothy Devlin (*C., Stockton, S.*)	774
*Christopher Smith (*Lab., Islington, S. and Finsbury*)	805
*Peter Thurnham (*C., Bolton, N.E.*)	813
Ronald Campbell (*Lab., Blyth Valley*)	853
John Bowis (*C., Battersea*)	857
Michael Irvine (*C., Ipswich*)	874
Eric Martlew (*Lab., Carlisle*)	916
*Michael Forsyth (*C., Stirling*)	948
*Peter Snape (*Lab., West Bromwich, E*)	983

WOMEN MEMBERS

The number of women M.P.s returned in June 1987 (41) was the highest ever.

Ms. Diane Abbott (*Lab., Hackney N. and Stoke Newington*); Ms. Hilary Armstrong (*Lab., Durham N.W.*); *Mrs. Rosemary Barnes (*SDP/All., Greenwich*); *Mrs. Margaret Beckett (*Lab., Derby S.*); *Miss Betty Boothroyd (*Lab., West Bromwich W.*); *Mrs. Virginia Bottomley (*C., Surrey S.W.*); *Mrs. Lynda Chalker (*C., Wallasey*); *Mrs. Ann Clwyd (*Lab., Cynon Valley*); *Mrs. Edwina Currie (*C., Derbyshire S.*); *Hon. Mrs. Gwyneth Dunwoody (*Lab., Crewe and Nantwich*); Mrs. Margaret Ewing (*S.N.P., Moray*); *Dame Peggy Fenner (*C., Medway*); *Miss Janet Fookes (*C., Plymouth Drake*); Mrs. Maria Fyfe (*Lab., Glasgow Maryhill*); *Mrs. Llinos Golding (*Lab., Newcastle-under-Lyme*); Mrs. Mildred Gordon (*Lab., Bow and Poplar*); Mrs. Theresa Gorman (*C., Billericay*); *Ms. Harriet Harman (*Lab., Peckham*); Mrs. Maureen Hicks (*C., Wolverhampton N.E.*); *Mrs. Elaine Kellett-Bowman (*C., Lancaster*); *Dame Jill Knight (*C., Birmingham Edgbaston*).

Miss Joan Lestor (*Lab., Eccles*); Mrs. Alice Mahon (*Lab., Halifax*); Mrs. Ray Michie (*L./All., Argyll and Bute*); Dr. Marjorie Mowlam (*Lab., Redcar*); Miss Emma Nicholson (*C., Devon W. and Torridge*); *Mrs. Elizabeth Peacock (*C., Batley and Spen*); Ms. Dawn Primarolo (*Lab., Bristol S.*); Miss Joyce Quin (*Lab., Gateshead E.*); *Ms. Jo Richardson (*Lab., Barking*); *Mrs. Marion Roe (*C., Broxbourne*); Ms. Joan Ruddock (*Lab., Lewisham Deptford*); *Mrs. Angela Rumbold (*C., Mitcham and Morden*); Mrs. Gillian Shephard (*C., Norfolk S.W.*); *Ms. Clare Short (*Lab., Birmingham Ladywood*); Mrs. Ann Taylor (*Lab., Dewsbury*); *Rt. Hon. Mrs. Margaret Thatcher (*C., Finchley*); Ms. Joan Walley (*Lab., Stoke-on-Trent*); Miss Ann Widdecombe (*C., Maidstone*); *Mrs. Ann Winterton (*C., Congleton*); Mrs. Audrey Wise (*Lab., Preston*).

THE HOUSE OF COMMONS BY CONSTITUENCIES, JUNE 1987

The figures following the name of each Constituency denote the total number of *Electors* in the Parliamentary Division at the General Election of June 11, 1987.

An asterisk * denotes membership of the last House. The majority in the 1983 General Election (and in any subsequent by-election) is shown below the 1987 result. For **by-elections** since the 1987 General Election, *see* p. 275.

Abbreviations — *C.* = Conservative; *D.U.P.* = Democratic Unionist Party; *Ind.* = Independent; *L./All.*, *S.D.P./All.* = Liberal and Social Democratic Alliance; *Lab.* = Labour; *O.U.P.* = Official Unionist Party; *P.C.* = Plaid Cymru; *S.D.L.P.* = Social Democratic and Labour Party; *S.F.* = Sinn Fein; *S.N.P.* = Scottish National Party; *U.P.U.P* = Ulster Popular Unionist Party.

All. = Alliance Party (N.I.); *B.N.* = British Nationalist; *Bread* = Creek Road Fresh Bread Party; *B.T.* = Blancmange Thrower; *C.D.* = Christian Democrat; *C.M.N.H.Y.* = Common Market No, Hanging Yes; *Comm.* = Communist Party; *C.P.R.P.* = Capital Punishment Referendum Party; *C.P.W.S.M.L.* = Capital Punishment Will Save More Lives; *C.S.* = Christian Socialist Opposing Secret Masonic Government; *D.C.* = Democratic Commonwealth Party; *Dem.* = Independent Democrat; *Ecol.* = Ecology (N.I.); *Ex. Lab. Mod.* = Ex Labour Moderate; *Falk.* = Right of Falkland Islands to elect Westminster M.P.; *F.D.P.* = Fancy Dress Party; *Fell.* = Fellowship Party; *F.P.* = Feudal Party; *Gait. Lab.* = Gaitskell Labour; *Gold* = Gold Party; *Grem.* = Gremloid; *Grn.* = Green Party; *H.P.* = Human Party; *I.C.C.* = Independent Community Campaigner, East Oxford People; *I.C.N.* = Independent Christian Nationalist; *L.A.O.* = Law and Order; *L.A.P.P.* = Let's Have Another Party Party; *L.M.* = Loony Official Monster Raving Party; *M.L.* = Moderate Labour Party; *N.F.F.G.* = National Front Flag Group; *N.P.R.* = National People's Rally; *O.F.P.* = Official Fidgeyitous Party; *O.O.B.P.C.* = Only Official Best Party Candidate; *O.S.M.* = Orkney and Shetland Movement; *P.I.P.* = Public Independent Plaintiff; *Prot. U.* = Protestant Unionist; *P.R.P.* = Protestant Reformation Party; *R.A.B.I.E.S.* = Rainbow Alliance Brixton Insane Extremist Section; *R.C.P.* = Return Capital Punishment; *Real U.* = Real Unionist; *R.F.* = Red Front; *Ret.* = Retired; *R.R.P.R.C.* = Revolutionary Reform Party Representative of Christ; *S.E.* = Spare the Earth; *S.L.D.* = Social and Liberal Democrat; *S.P.G.B.* = Socialist Party of Great Britain; *W.P.* = Workers' Party (N.I.); *W.R.P.* = Workers' Revolutionary Party.

ENGLAND

Aldershot (Hants)
E. 80,797

*J. M. G. Critchley, C.	35,272
R. A. Hargreaves, *L./All.*	17,488
I. H. Pearson, *Lab.*	7,061
C. maj.	17,784
(June '83, C. maj. 12,218)	

Aldridge-Brownhills
(W. Midlands)
E. 62,129

*R. C. S. Shepherd, C.	26,434
C. Duncan, *Lab.*	14,038
G. Betteridge, *S.D.P./All.*	9,084
C. maj.	12,396
(June '83, C. maj. 12,284)	

Altrincham and Sale
(Gtr. Manchester)
E. 67,611

*Sir F. Montgomery, C.	27,746
J. Mulholland, *L./All.*	13,518
D. Hinder, *Lab.*	10,617
C. Maj.	14,228
(June '83, C. maj. 10,911)	

Amber Valley (Derbys)
E. 68,478

*P. A. C. L. Oppenheim, C.	28,603
D. M. Bookbinder, *Lab.*	19,103
S. Reynolds, *L./All.*	7,904
C. maj.	9,500
(June '83, C. maj. 3,318)	

Arundel (W. Sussex)
E. 78,683

*R. M. Marshall, C.	34,356
Dr. J. M. M. Walsh, *L./All.*	15,476
P. Slowe, *Lab.*	6,177
C. maj.	18,880
(June '83, C. maj. 15,705)	

Ashfield (Notts)
E. 70,937

*D. F. Haynes, Lab.	22,812
B. G. Coleman, *C.*	18,412
Mrs. F. B. Stein, *L./All.*	13,542
Lab. maj.	4,400
(June '83, Lab. maj. 6,087)	

Ashford (Kent)
E. 70,052

*H. K. Speed, C.	29,978
N. N. Macmillan, *S.D.P./All.*	14,490
M. J. Wiggins, *Lab.*	7,775
Dr. C. A. Porter, *Grn.*	778
C. maj.	15,488
(June '83, C. maj. 13,911)	

Ashton-under-Lyne
(Gtr. Manchester)
E. 58,440

*Rt. Hon. R. E. Sheldon, Lab.	22,389
H. L. Cadman, *C.*	13,103
M. J. Hunter, *L./All.*	7,760
Lab. maj.	9,286
(June '83, Lab. maj. 7,697)	

Aylesbury (Bucks)
E. 76,919

*Rt. Hon. T. H. F. Raison, C.	32,970
M. A. Soole, *S.D.P./All.*	16,412
Ms. J. Larner, *Lab.*	7,936
C. maj.	16,558
(June '83, C. maj. 14,920)	

Banbury (Oxon)
E. 69,455

*A. B. Baldry, C.	29,716
D. C. Rowland, *S.D.P./All.*	12,386
J. A. Honeybone, *Lab.*	10,789
C. maj.	17,330
(June '83, C. maj. 13,025)	

Barking (Gtr. London)
E. 51,639

*Ms. J. Richardson, Lab.	15,307
W. K. Sharp, *C.*	11,898
J. K. Gibb, *L./All.*	7,336
Lab. maj.	3,409
(June '83, Lab. maj. 4,026)	

Barnsley (S. Yorks)

CENTRAL   *E.* 55,902

E. E. *Illsley, Lab.*	26,139
Mrs. V. Prais, *C.*	7,088
Mrs. S. A. M. Holland, *L./All.*	5,928
Lab. maj.	19,051
(June '83, Lab. maj. 14,173)	

EAST   *E.* 53,505

*T. Patchett, Lab.	28,948
W. J. Clappison, *C.*	5,437
G. J. Griffiths, *L./All.*	4,482
Lab. maj.	23,511
(June '83, Lab. maj. 17,492)	

WEST AND PENISTONE   *E.* 61,091

*A. McKay, Lab.	26,498
A. J. C. Duncan, *C.*	12,307
R. Hall, *S.D.P./All.*	7,409
Lab. maj.	14,191
(June '83, Lab. maj. 10,342)	

Barrow and Furness (Cumbria)
E. 69,288

*C. S. Franks, C.	25,431
P. Phizacklea, *Lab.*	21,504
R. W. Phelps, *S.D.P./All.*	7,799
C. maj.	3,927
(June '83, C. maj. 4,577)	

Basildon (Essex)
E. 68,500

*D. A. A. Amess, C.	21,858
J. G. H. Fulbrook, *Lab.*	19,209
R. M. Auvray, *L./All.*	9,139
C. maj.	2,649
(June '83, C. maj. 1,379)	

Basingstoke (Hants)
E. 78,003

*A. R. F. Hunter, C.		33,657
D. Bennett, S.D.P./All.		15,764
P. Daden, Lab.		10,632
C. maj.		17,893
(June '83, C. maj. 12,450)		

Bassetlaw (Notts)
E. 68,043

*J. W. Ashton, Lab.		25,385
D. R. J. Selves, C.		19,772
W. G. Smith, S.D.P./All.		7,616
Lab. maj.		5,613
(June '83, Lab. maj. 3,831)		

Bath (Avon)
E. 65,246

*C. F. Patten, C.		23,515
J. M. Dean, S.D.P./All.		22,103
Mrs. J. Smith, Lab.		5,507
D. N. Wall, Grn.		687
C. maj.		1,412
(June '83, C. maj. 5,304)		

Batley and Spen (W. Yorks)
E. 74,347

*Mrs. E. J. Peacock, C.		25,512
K. J. Woolmer, Lab.		24,150
K. Burke, S.D.P./All.		8,372
A. Harrison, M.L.		689
C. maj.		1,362
(June '83, C. maj. 870)		

Battersea (Gtr. London)
E. 66,979

J. C. Bowis, C.		20,945
*A. Dubs, Lab.		20,088
D. I. Harries, S.D.P./All.		5,634
Ms. S. G. Willington, Grn.		559
A. B. Bell, W.R.P.		116
C. maj.		857
(June '83, Lab. maj. 3,276)		

Beaconsfield (Bucks)
E. 67,713

*T. J. Smith, C.		33,324
D. H. Ive, L./All.		11,985
K. J. Harper, Lab.		5,203
C. maj.		21,339
(June '83, C. maj. 18,300)		

Beckenham (Gtr. London)
E. 60,110

*Sir P. C. Goodhart, C.		24,903
C. G. Darracott, L./All.		11,439
K. G. Ritchie, Lab.		7,888
C. maj.		13,464
(June '83, C. maj. 12,670)		

Bedfordshire

MID E. 80,673

*N. W. Lyell, Q.C., C.		37,411
N. C. Hills, S.D.P./All.		14,560
J. Heywood, Lab.		11,463
C. maj.		22,851
(June '83, C. maj. 17,381)		

NORTH E. 73,536

*Sir T. H. H. Skeet, C.		29,845
Mrs. J. V. Lennon, L./All.		13,340
C. B. Henderson, Lab.		13,140
C. D. Slee, O.O.B.P.C.		435
C. maj.		16,505
(June '83, C. maj. 13,849)		

SOUTH WEST E. 78,956

*W. D. Madel, C.		36,140
J. R. Burrow, S.D.P./All.		13,835
P. H. Dimoldenberg, Lab.		11,352
P. J. Rollings, Grn.		822
C. maj.		22,305
(June '83, C. maj. 15,731)		

Berkshire East
E. 87,820

*A. J. MacKay, C.		39,094
Mrs. L. A. Murray, S.D.P./All.		16,468
R. J. E. Evans, Lab.		9,287
C. maj.		22,626
(June '83, C. maj. 16,099)		

Berwick-upon-Tweed (Nthmb)
E. 54,378

*A. J. Beith, L./All.		21,903
T. Middleton, C.		12,400
S. Lambert, Lab.		7,360
N. Pamphilion, Grn.		379
L./All. maj.		9,503
(June '83, L./All. maj. 8,215)		

Bethnal Green and Stepney
(Gtr. London)
E. 55,769

*Rt. Hon. P. D. Shore, Lab.		15,490
J. A. Shaw, L./All.		10,206
Lady O. H. Maitland, C.		6,176
Ms. S. Gasquoine, Comm.		232
Lab. maj.		5,284
(June '83, Lab. maj. 6,358)		

Beverley (Humberside)
E. 78,923

J. D. Cran, C.		31,459
J. Bryant, L./All.		18,864
M. Shaw, Lab.		9,901
C. maj.		12,595
(June '83, C. maj. 13,869)		

Bexhill and Battle
(E. Sussex)
E. 65,288

*C. F. Wardle, C.		33,570
R. Kiernan, S.D.P./All.		13,051
D. K. Watts, Lab.		3,903
C. maj.		20,519
(June '83, C. maj. 19,746)		

Bexleyheath
(Gtr. London)
E. 59,448

*C. D. Townsend, C.		24,866
B. C. Standen, L./All.		13,179
J. F. Little, Lab.		8,218
C. maj.		11,687
(June '83, C. maj. 10,258)		

Billericay (Essex)
E. 79,535

Mrs. T. E. Gorman, C.		33,741
M. Birch, S.D.P./All.		15,755
R. Howitt, Lab.		11,942
C. maj.		17,986
(June '83, C. maj. 14,615)		

Birkenhead (Merseyside)
E. 65,662

*F. Field, Lab.		27,883
K. J. Costa, C.		12,511
R. Kemp, L./All.		7,095
Lab. maj.		15,372
(June '83, Lab. maj. 9,714)		

Birmingham (W. Midlands)

EDGBASTON E. 54,416

*Dame J. C. J. Knight, D.B.E., C.		18,595
J. Wilton, Lab.		10,014
J. C. Binns, S.D.P./All.		7,843
P. Simpson, Grn.		559
S. T. Hardwick, Ind. C.		307
C. maj.		8,581
(June '83, C. maj. 11,418)		

ERDINGTON E. 54,179

*R. Corbett, Lab.		17,037
P. J. Johnston, C.		14,570
N. Biddlestone, S.D.P./All.		5,530
Lab. maj.		2,467
(June '83, Lab. maj. 231)		

HALL GREEN E. 61,148

A. R. Hargreaves, C.		20,478
Mrs. E. Brook, Lab.		12,857
M. Wilkes, S.D.P./All.		12,323
C. maj.		7,621
(June '83, C. maj. 9,373)		

HODGE HILL E. 59,296

*T. A. G. Davis, Lab.		19,872
S. Eyre, C.		15,083
K. G. Hardeman, L./All.		5,868
Lab. maj.		4,789
(June '83, Lab. maj. 5,092)		

LADYWOOD E. 58,761

*Ms. C. Short, Lab.		21,971
S. T. Lee, C.		11,943
G. S. Sangha, S.D.P./All.		3,532
Ms. J. Millington, Grn.		650
Lab. maj.		10,028
(June '83, Lab. maj. 9,030)		

NORTHFIELD E. 73,319

*R. D. King, C.		24,024
J. F. Spellar, Lab.		20,889
J. Gordon, S.D.P./All.		8,319
C. maj.		3,135
(June '83, C. maj. 2,760)		

PERRY BARR E. 73,767

*J. W. Rooker, Lab.		25,894
J. D. B. Taylor, C.		18,961
D. D. Webb, L./All.		6,514
Lab. maj.		6,933
(June '83, Lab. maj. 7,402)		

SELLY OAK *E.* 72,213
A. M. Beaumont-Dark, C.	23,305
A. Bore, *Lab.*	20,721
Mrs. C. Cane, *L./All.*	8,128
Ms. M. Hackett, *Grn*	611
C. maj.	2,584
(June '83, C. maj. 5,396)	

SMALL HEATH *E.* 56,722
Rt. Hon. D. H. Howell, *Lab.*	22,787
P. Nischal, *C.*	7,266
J. A. M. Hemming, *L./All.*	3,600
A. Clawley, *Grn.*	559
P. R. Sheppard, *Comm.*	154
Lab. maj.	15,521
(June '83, Lab. maj. 15,252)	

SPARKBROOK *E.* 53,093
Rt. Hon. R. S. G. Hattersley, *Lab.*	20,513
N. A. Khan, *C.*	8,654
R. Dimmick, *S.D.P./All.*	3,803
R. Ambler, *Grn.*	526
P. Khan, *R.F.*	229
Lab. maj.	11,859
(June '83, Lab. maj. 10,548)	

YARDLEY *E.* 56,957
A. D. G. Bevan, C.	17,931
G. Edge, *Lab.*	15,409
L. Smith, *L./All.*	8,734
C. maj.	2,522
(June '83, C. maj. 2,865)	

Bishop Auckland (Durham)
E. 72,147
D. Foster, Lab.	25,648
R. Wight, *C.*	18,613
G. Irwin, *L./All.*	9,195
Lab. maj.	7,035
(June '83, Lab. maj. 4,306)	

Blaby (Leics)
E. 77,094
Rt. Hon. N. Lawson, C.	37,732
R. E. Lustig, *L./All.*	15,556
J. M. Roberts, *Lab.*	9,046
C. maj.	22,176
(June '83, C. maj. 17,116)	

Blackburn (Lancs)
E. 74,801
J. W. Straw, Lab.	27,965
Mrs. A. C. Cheetham, *C.*	22,468
M. A. Ali, *S.D.P./All.*	5,602
Lab. maj.	5,497
(June '83, Lab. maj. 3,055)	

Blackpool (Lancs)

NORTH *E.* 58,893
N. A. Miscampbell, Q.C., C.	20,680
E. Kirton, *Lab.*	13,359
C. J. Heyworth, *L./All.*	9,032
C. maj.	7,321
(June '83, C. maj. 10,152)	

SOUTH *E.* 57,567
Rt. Hon. Sir P. A. R. Blaker, *K.C.M.G., C.*	20,312
Mrs. S. Baugh, *Lab.*	13,568
J. Allitt, *S.D.P./All.*	8,405
C. maj.	6,744
(June '83, C. maj. 10,138)	

Blaydon (Tyne & Wear)
E. 66,301
J. D. McWilliam, Lab.	25,277
V. P. Nunn, *S.D.P./All.*	12,789
P. R. Pescod, *C.*	12,147
Lab. maj.	12,488
(June '83, Lab. maj. 7,222)	

Blyth Valley (Nthmb)
E. 59,104
R. Campbell, *Lab.*	19,604
Miss R. M. Brownlow, *S.D.P./All.*	18,751
Dr. R. Kinghorn, *C.*	7,823
Lab. maj.	853
(June '83, Lab. maj. 3,243)	

Bolsover (Derbys)
E. 65,452
D. E. Skinner, Lab.	28,453
M. R. Lingens, *C.*	14,333
M. H. Fowler, *S.D.P./All.*	7,836
Lab. maj.	14,120
(June '83, Lab. maj. 13,848)	

Bolton (Gtr. Manchester)

NORTH EAST *E.* 59,382
P. G. Thurnham, C.	20,742
F. R. White, *Lab.*	19,929
J. H. Alcock, *S.D.P./All.*	6,060
C. maj.	813
(June '83, C. maj. 2,443)	

SOUTH EAST *E.* 65,932
D. W. Young, Lab.	26,791
S. Windle, *C.*	15,410
F. Harasiwka, *L./All.*	7,161
Lab. maj.	11,381
(June '83, Lab. maj. 8,753)	

WEST *E.* 69,843
T. G. Sackville, C.	24,779
G. J. Harkin, *Lab.*	20,186
D. T. Eccles, *S.D.P./All.*	10,936
C. maj.	4,593
(June '83, C. maj. 7,152)	

Boothferry (Humberside)
E. 75,176
D. M. Davis, *C.*	31,716
Mrs. J. D. Davies, *L./All.*	12,746
R. Donson, *Lab.*	12,498
C. maj.	18,970
(June '83, C. maj. 17,420)	

Bootle (Merseyside)
E. 71,765
A. Roberts, Lab.	34,975
P. R. Papworth, *C.*	10,498
P. Denham, *S.D.P./All.*	6,820
Lab. maj.	24,477
(June '83, Lab. maj. 15,139)	

Bosworth (Leics)
E. 77,186
D. A. S. Tredinnick, *C.*	34,145
D. C. Bill, *L./All.*	17,129
R. S. Hall, *Lab.*	10,787
Mrs. D. Freer, *Grn*	660
C. maj.	17,016
(June '83, C. maj. 17,294)	

Bournemouth (Dorset)

EAST *E.* 75,232
D. A. Atkinson, C.	30,925
Dr. J. Millward, *L./All.*	16,242
I. A. Taylor, *Lab.*	5,885
C. maj.	14,683
(June '83, C. maj. 11,416)	

WEST *E.* 74,444
J. V. Butterfill, C.	30,117
P. G. M. Craven, *S.D.P./All.*	17,466
R. W. Jones, *Lab.*	7,018
C. maj.	12,651
(June '83, C. maj. 13,331)	

Bow and Poplar (Gtr. London)
E. 59,178
Ms. M. Gordon, *Lab.*	15,746
E. Flounders, *L./All.*	11,115
D. C. Hughes, *C.*	6,810
P. S. Chappell, *W.R.P.*	274
Lab. maj.	4,631
(June '83, Lab. maj. 5,861)	

Bradford (W. Yorks)

NORTH *E.* 67,430
C. P. Wall, Lab.	21,009
G. J. Lawler, C.	19,376
A. M. Berkeley, *S.D.P./All.*	8,656
Lab. maj.	1,633
(June '83, C. maj. 1,602)	

SOUTH *E.* 69,588
G. R. Cryer, Lab.	21,230
G. T. Hall, *C.*	20,921
T. Lindley, *S.D.P./All.*	9,109
Lab. maj.	309
(June '83, Lab. maj. 110)	

WEST *E.* 70,763
M. F. Madden, Lab.	25,775
I. Duncan-Smith, *C.*	18,224
M. Moghal, *S.D.P./All.*	5,657
Lab. maj.	7,551
(June '83, Lab. maj. 3,337)	

Braintree (Essex)
E. 76,994
A. H. Newton, O.B.E., C.	32,978
I. G. Bing, *S.D.P./All.*	16,121
B. Stapleton, *Lab.*	11,764
C. maj.	16,857
(June '83, C. maj. 13,441)	

Brent (Gtr. London)

EAST *E.* 61,020
K. R. Livingstone, *Lab.*	16,772
Miss H. S. Crawley, *C.*	15,119
D. W. Finkelstein, *S.D.P./All.*	5,710
R. Q. Dooley, *Ind. Lab.*	1,035
M. Litvinoff, *Grn.*	716
Lab. maj.	1,653
(June '83, Lab. maj. 4,834)	

NORTH *E.* 63,081
Dr. R. Boyson, C.	26,823
P. Patel, *Lab.*	11,103
C. Mularczyk, *S.D.P./All.*	6,868
C. maj.	15,720
(June '83, C. maj. 14,651)	

SOUTH *E.* 62,772
P. Y. Boateng, *Lab.*		21,140
A. J. Paterson, *C.*		13,209
M. T. Harskin, *L./All.*		6,375
Lab. maj.		7,931

(June '83, Lab. maj. 10,519)

Brentford and Isleworth
(Gtr. London)
E. 71,715

Rt. Hon. Sir B. J. Hayhoe, C.		26,230
Ms. A. Keen, *Lab.*		18,277
Dr. D. M. W. Wilks, *S.D.P./All.*		9,626
T. Cooper, *Grn.*		849
C. maj.		7,953

(June '83, C. maj. 9,387)

Brentwood and Ongar (Essex)
E. 67,521

R. A. McCrindle, C.		32,258
N. R. Amor, *L./All.*		13,337
J. W. Orpe, *Lab.*		7,042
Mrs. M. E. Willis, *Grn.*		686
C. maj.		18,921

(June '83, C. maj. 14,202)

Bridgwater (Somerset)
E. 67,480

Rt. Hon. T. J. King, C.		27,177
C. Clarke, *S.D.P./All.*		15,982
J. Turner, *Lab.*		9,594
C. maj.		11,195

(June '83, C. maj. 10,697)

Bridlington (Humberside)
E. 80,126

J. E. Townend, C.		32,351
E. I. Marshall, *S.D.P./All.*		15,030
L. M. Bird, *Lab.*		10,653
R. D. Myerscough, *Grn.*		983
C. maj.		17,321

(June '83, C. maj. 16,609)

Brigg and Cleethorpes
(Humberside)
E. 80,096

M. R. Brown, C.		29,723
I. Powney, *L./All.*		17,475
T. Geraghty, *Lab.*		13,876
C. maj.		12,248

(June '83, C. maj. 12,189)

Brighton (E. Sussex)
KEMPTOWN *E.* 60,271

A. Bowden, M.B.E., C.		24,031
J. S. Bassam, *Lab.*		14,771
C. Berry, *L./All.*		6,080
C. maj.		9,260

(June '83, C. maj. 9,378)

PAVILION *E.* 58,910

Rt. Hon. H. J. Amery, C.		22,056
D. S. Hill, *Lab.*		12,914
K. F. Carey, *S.D.P./All.*		8,459
C. maj.		9,142

(June '83, C. maj. 11,132)

Bristol (Avon)
EAST *E.* 63,840

J. Sayeed, C.		21,906
R. R. Thomas, *Lab.*		17,783
D. M. E. Foster, *L./All.*		10,247
P. M. Kingston, *N.F.F.G.*		286
C. maj.		4,123

(June '83, C. maj. 1,789)

NORTH WEST *E.* 72,836

M. C. Stern, C.		26,953
T. W. Walker, *Lab.*		20,001
J. M. G. Kirkaldy, *S.D.P./All.*		10,885
C. maj.		6,952

(June '83, C. maj. 6,327)

SOUTH *E.* 68,733

Ms. D. Primarolo, *Lab.*		20,798
P. S. Cutcher, *C.*		19,394
Mrs. H. S. Long, *S.D.P./All.*		9,952
G. R. Vowles, *Grn.*		600
Ms. C. M. Meghji, *R.F.*		149
Lab. maj.		1,404

(June '83, Lab. maj. 4,419)

WEST *E.* 72,357

Hon. W. A. Waldegrave, C.		24,695
G. R. P. Ferguson, *L./All.*		16,992
Mrs. M. C. Georghiou, *Lab.*		11,337
Mrs. G. A. Dorey, *Grn.*		1,096
Ms. V. Ralph, *Comm.*		134
C. maj.		7,703

(June '83, C. maj. 10,178)

Bromsgrove (H & W)
E. 69,494

H. D. Miller, C.		29,051
J. D. Ward, *Lab..*		12,366
D. L. Cropp, *S.D.P./All.*		11,663
C. maj.		16,685

(June '83, C. maj. 17,175)

Broxbourne (Herts)
E. 70,631

Mrs. M. A. Roe, C.		33,567
Mrs. E. Yates, *L./All.*		10,572
P. Parry, *Lab.*		8,984
C. maj.		22,995

(June '83, C. maj. 17,466)

Broxtowe (Notts)
E. 71,780

J. T. Lester, C.		30,462
K. Fleet, *Lab.*		13,811
K. M. Melton, *L./All.*		12,562
C. maj.		16,651

(June '83, C. maj. 15,078)

Buckingham
E. 70,036

G. G. H. Walden, C.M.G., C.		32,162
C. M. Burke, *L./All.*		13,636
M. Groucutt, *Lab.*		9,053
C. maj.		18,526

(June '83, C. maj. 13,968)

Burnley (Lancs)
E. 65,956

P. L. Pike, Lab.		25,140
H. Elletson, *C.*		17,583
R. H. Baker, *S.D.P./All.*		9,241
Lab. maj.		7,557

(June '83, Lab. maj. 770)

Burton (Staffs)
E. 73,252

I. J. Lawrence, Q.C., C.		29,160
D. Heptonstall, *Lab.*		19,330
K. A. Hemsley, *L./All.*		9,046
C. maj.		9,830

(June '83, C. maj. 11,647)

Bury (Gtr. Manchester)
NORTH *E.* 67,961

A. J. H. Burt, C.		28,097
D. Crausby, *Lab.*		21,186
D. Vasmer, *L./All.*		6,804
C. maj.		6,911

(June '83, C. maj. 2,792)

SOUTH *E.* 65,039

D. A. G. Sumberg, C.		23,878
D. Boden, *Lab.*		21,199
D. A. Eyre, *S.D.P./All.*		6,772
C. maj.		2,679

(June '83, C. maj. 3,720)

Bury St. Edmunds (Suffolk)
E. 76,619

Sir E. W. Griffiths, C.		33,672
Sir R. Harland, *S.D.P./All.*		12,214
C. L. Greene, *Lab.*		9,841
Ms. I. M. J. Wakelam, *Grn.*		1,057
C. maj.		21,458

(June '83, C. maj. 16,122)

Calder Valley (W. Yorks)
E. 73,398

D. Thompson, C.		25,892
D. M. Chaytor, *Lab.*		19,847
D. T. Shutt, *L./All.*		13,761
C. maj.		6,045

(June '83, C. maj. 7,999)

Cambridge
E. 69,336

R. V. Rhodes James, C.		21,624
Mrs. S. V. T. B. Williams, *S.D.P./All.*		16,564
C. J. Howard, *Lab.*		15,319
Ms. M. E. Wright, *Grn.*		597
C. maj.		5,060

(June '83, C. maj. 5,968)

Cambridgeshire
NORTH EAST *E.* 74,231

M. D. Moss, *C.*		26,983
C. R. Freud, L./All.		25,555
R. J. Harris, *Lab.*		4,891
C. maj.		1,428

(June '83, L./All. maj. 5,195)

SOUTH EAST *E.* 73,216

J. E. T. Paice, *C.*		32,901
P. C. Lee, *S.D.P./All.*		15,399
T. G. Ling, *Lab.*		7,694
C. maj.		17,502

(June '83, C. maj. 13,764)

SOUTH WEST *E.* 81,658
Sir J. A. Grant, C. 36,622
D. C. Nicholls, *L./All.* 18,371
Ms. J. Billing, *Lab.* 8,434
  C. maj. 18,251
  (June '83, C. maj. 13,867)

Cannock and Burntwood (Staffs)
E. 68,137
J. G. D. Howarth, C. 24,186
G. E. Roberts, *Lab.* 21,497
N. Stanley, *L./All.* 8,698
  C. maj. 2,689
  (June '83, C. maj. 2,045)

Canterbury (Kent)
E. 76,062
J. W. H. Brazier, *C.* 30,273
J. Purchese, *L./All.* 15,382
Ms. L. A. Keen, *Lab.* 9,494
S. Dawe, *Grn.* 947
Miss J. M. White, *I.C.N.* .. 157
  C. maj. 14,891
  (June '83, C. maj. 15,742)

Carlisle (Cumbria)
E. 55,053
E. A. Martlew, *Lab.* 18,311
W. G. Hodgson, *C.* 17,395
R. S. Hunt, *S.D.P./All* 7,655
  Lab. maj. 916
  (June '83, Lab. maj. 71)

Carshalton and Wallington
(Gtr. London) *E.* 69,120
F. N. Forman, C. 27,984
J. D. Grant, *S.D.P./All.* .. 13,575
Mrs. J. G. Baker, *Lab.* 9,440
R. W. Steel, *Grn.* 843
  C. maj. 14,409
  (June '83, C. maj. 10,755)

Castle Point (Essex) *E.* 65,992
*Rt. Hon. Sir B. R. Braine,
C.* 29,681
Miss A. P. Bastow, *S.D.P./
All.* 10,433
W. A. Deal, *Lab.* 9,422
  C. maj. 19,248
  (June '83, C. maj. 15,417)

Cheadle
(Gtr. Manchester)
E. 68,332
S. R. Day, *C.* 30,484
A. B. Leah, *L./All.* 19,853
Ms. A. Coffey, *Lab.* 5,037
  C. maj. 10,631
  (June '83, C. maj. 9,380)

Chelmsford (Essex)
E. 82,564
S. H. M. Burns, *C.* 35,231
S. G. Mole, *L./All.* 27,470
C. E. Playford, *Lab.* 4,642
A. C. Slade, *Grn.* 486
  C. maj. 7,761
  (June '83, C. maj. 378)

Chelsea (Gtr. London)
E. 49,534
N. P. Scott, M.B.E., C. 18,443
Mrs. J. M. Ware, *L./All.* .. 5,124
D. J. Ward, *Lab.* 4,406
Ms. N. Kortvelyessy, *Grn.* .. 587
  C. maj. 13,319
  (June '83, C. maj. 12,021)

Cheltenham (Glos)
E. 79,234
C. G. Irving, C. 31,371
R. G. Holme, *L./All.* 26,475
M. Luker, *Lab.* 4,701
  C. maj. 4,896
  (June '83, C. maj. 5,518)

Chertsey and Walton (Surrey)
E. 71,448
G. E. Pattie, C. 32,119
Mrs. S. K. Stapely, *S.D.P./
All.* 14,650
H. G. Trace, *Lab.* 7,185
  C. maj. 17,469
  (June '83, C. maj. 15,699)

Chesham and Amersham
(Bucks) *E.* 71,751
*Rt. Hon. Sir I. H. J. L.
Gilmour, BT., C.* 34,504
A. T. Ketteringham, *L./All.* 15,064
P. A. Goulding, *Lab.* 5,170
Mrs. A. G. Darnbrough,
Grn. 760
  C. maj. 19,440
  (June '83, C. maj. 15,879)

Chester, City of
E. 65,845
Hon. P. H. Morrison, C. .. 23,582
D. Robinson, *Lab.* 18,727
R. A. Stunell, *L./All.* 10,262
  C. maj. 4,855
  (June '83, C. maj. 9,099)

Chesterfield (Derbys)
E. 70,357
*Rt. Hon. A. N. W. Benn,
Lab.* 24,532
A. H. Rogers, *L./All.* 15,955
R. P Grant, *C.* 13,472
  Lab. maj. 8,577
  (June '83, Lab. maj. 7,763)
  (March '84, Lab. maj. 6,264)

Chichester (W. Sussex)
E. 81,019
R. A. Nelson, C. 37,274
P. F. Weston, *L./All.* 17,097
D. Morrison, *Lab.* 4,751
I. F. N. Bagnall, *Grn.* 1,196
  C. maj. 20,177
  (June '83, C. maj. 20,117)

Chingford (Gtr. London)
E. 56,797
Rt. Hon. N. B. Tebbit, C. .. 27,110
J. G. Williams, *L./All.* 9,155
Ms. M. I. Cosin, *Lab.* 6,650
Ms. E. Newton, *Grn.* 634
  C. maj. 17,955
  (June '83, C. maj. 12,414)

Chipping Barnet (Gtr. London)
E. 60,876
S. B. Chapman, C. 24,686
J. Skinner, *L./All.* 9,815
D. Perkin, *Lab.* 8,115
  C. maj. 14,871
  (June '83, C. maj. 12,393)

Chislehurst (Gtr. London)
E. 55,535
R. E. Sims, C. 24,165
R. A. Younger-Ross, *L./All.* 9,658
S. H. Ward, *Lab.* 8,115
  C. maj. 14,507
  (June '83, C. maj. 12,061)

Chorley (Lancs)
E. 78,541
D. R. Dover, C. 29,015
A. J. Watmough, *Lab.* 20,958
I. A. Simpson, *L./All.* 9,706
A. S. Holgate, *Grn.* 714
  C. maj. 8,057
  (June '83, C. maj. 10,275)

Christchurch (Dorset)
E. 70,964
R. J. Adley, C. 35,656
Miss H. J. McKenzie,
S.D.P./All. 13,282
Ms C E. Longhurst, *Lab.* 5,174
  C. maj. 22,374
  (June '83, C. maj. 19,738)

Cirencester and Tewkesbury
(Glos)
E. 84,071
Rt. Hon. N. Ridley, C. 36,272
P. T. Beckerlegge, *L./All.* . 23,610
J. D. Naysmith, *Lab.* 5,342
M. A. Curtis, *Male O.A.P.* 283
  C. maj. 12,662
  (June '83, C. maj. 13,827)

**The City of London and
Westminster South**
E. 57,428
Hon. P. L. Brooke, C. 19,333
Ms. J. C. G. Smithard,
S.D.P./All. 7,291
Ms. R. E. Bush, *Lab.* 6,821
  C. maj. 12,042
  (June '83, C. maj. 13,387)

Colchester (Essex)
NORTH *E.* 82,420
Sir P. A. F. Buck, Q.C., C. .. 32,747
A. Hayman, *S.D.P./All.* .. 19,124
R. A. Green, *Lab.* 10,768
  C. maj. 13,623
  (June '83, C. maj. 15,048)

SOUTH, AND MALDON *E.* 84,392
Rt. Hon. J. Wakeham, C. .. 34,894
J. W. Stevens, *S.D.P./All.* 19,411
Ms. S. Bigwood, *Lab.* 9,229
  C. maj. 15,483
  (June '83, C. maj. 12,165)

Colne Valley (W. Yorks)
E. 70,199

G. E. G. Riddick, C.	......	20,457
N. J. Priestley, L./All.	....	18,780
J. A. Harman, Lab.	......	16,353
M. R. Mullany, Grn.	.....	614
C. maj.	....	1,677

(June '83, L./All. maj. 3,146)

Congleton (Cheshire)
E. 68,172

*Mrs. J. A. Winterton, C.	..	26,513
I. M. Brodie-Browne, L./All.	....	18,544
M. Knowles, Lab.	....	9,810
C. maj.	....	7,969

(June '83, C. maj. 8,459)

Copeland (Cumbria)
E. 54,695

*Dr. J. A. Cunningham, Lab.	....	20,999
A. R. M. Toft, C.	......	19,105
E. T. Colgan, S.D.P./All.	.	4,052
R. A. Gibson, Grn.	....	319
Lab. maj.		1,894

(June '83, Lab. maj. 1,837)

Corby (Northants)
E. 66,119

*W. R. Powell, C.	....	23,323
H. A. Feather, Lab.	......	21,518
T. G. Whittington, L./All.	....	7,805
C. maj.		1,805

(June '83, C. maj. 3,168)

Cornwall
NORTH   E. 72,375

*G. A. Neale, C.	....	29,862
M. N. Mitchell, L./All.	...	24,180
Ms. C. Herries, Lab.	.....	3,719
C. maj.		5,682

(June '83, C. maj. 5,059)

SOUTH EAST   E. 70,248

*R. A. Hicks, C.	....	28,818
I. P. Tunbridge, L./All.	...	22,211
P. A. Clark, Lab.	....	4,847
C. maj.		6,607

(June '83, C. maj. 8,354)

Coventry (W. Midlands)
NORTH EAST   E. 67,479

J. Hughes, Lab.	....	25,832
C. Prior, C.	....	13,965
S. Wood, L./All.	......	7,502
A. McNally, Comm.	......	310
Lab. maj.	....	11,867

(June '83, Lab. maj. 8,775)

NORTH WEST   E. 53,090

*G. Robinson, Lab.	....	19,450
J. Powell, C.	....	13,787
T. Jones, S.D.P./All.	.....	6,455
Lab. maj.	....	5,663

(June '83, Lab. maj. 3,038)

SOUTH EAST   E. 51,880

*D. J. Nellist, Lab.	....	17,969
A. Grant, C.	....	11,316
F. Devine, S.D.P./All.	....	8,095
N. Hutchinson, Grn.	.....	479
Lab. maj.		6,653

(June '83, Lab. maj. 2,682)

SOUTH WEST   E. 65,567

*J. P. Butcher, C.	....	22,318
R. E. G. Slater, Lab.	......	19,108
R. Wheway, L./All.	......	10,166
C. maj.		3,210

(June '83, C. maj. 6,447)

Crawley (W. Sussex)
E. 72,076

*Hon. A. N. W. Soames, C.	..	29,259
P. J. Leo, Lab.	....	17,121
D. N. Simmons, S.D.P./All.		12,674
C. maj.		12,138

(June '83, C. maj. 11,814)

Crewe and Nantwich (Cheshire)
E. 72,961

*Hon. Mrs. G. P. Dunwoody, Lab.	....	25,457
Mrs. A. F. Browning, C.	..	24,365
Dr. K. N. Roberts, S.D.P./All.		8,022
Lab. maj.	....	1,092

(June '83, Lab. maj. 290)

Crosby (Merseyside)
E. 83,914

*G. M. Thornton, C.	......	30,836
A. F. S. Donovan, S.D.P./All.		23,989
C. W. Cheetham, Lab.	....	11,992
C. maj.		6,847

(June '83, C. maj. 3,401)

Croydon (Gtr. London)
CENTRAL   E. 55,410

*Rt. Hon. J. E. M. Moore, C.		22,133
Ms. B. T. Prentice, Lab.	..	9,516
T. Burgess, S.D.P./All.	...	7,435
C. maj.		12,617

(June '83, C. maj. 11,821)

NORTH EAST   E. 63,129

*Rt. Hon. B. B. Weatherill, (The Speaker)		24,188
Miss C. Patrick, Lab.	....	11,669
J. D. Goldie, S.D.P./All.	..	8,128
The Speaker maj.		12,519

(June '83, C. maj. 11,627)

NORTH WEST   E. 57,369

*H. J. Malins, C.	....	18,665
M. H. Wicks, Lab.	......	14,677
L. A. Rowe, L./All.	......	6,363
C. maj.		3,988

(June '83, C. maj. 4,092)

SOUTH   E. 65,085

*Sir W. G. Clark, C.	......	30,732
I. Morrison, L./All.	......	11,669
G. R. Davies, Lab.	......	4,679
P. C. Baldwin, Grn.	......	900
C. maj.		19,063

(June '83, C. maj. 17,440)

Dagenham (Gtr. London)
E. 61,714

*B. C. Gould, Lab.	....	18,454
R. J. M. Neill, C.	....	15,985
J. Carter, S.D.P./All	.....	7,088
Lab. maj.	....	2,469

(June '83, Lab. maj. 2,997)

Darlington (Durham)
E. 65,940

*M. Fallon, C.	....	24,831
O. O'Brien, Lab.	....	22,170
A. Collinge, L./All.	......	6,289
C. maj.		2,661

(June '83, C. maj. 3,438)

Dartford (Kent)
E. 72,632

*R. J. Dunn, C.	....	30,685
B. J. Clarke, Lab.	....	15,756
M. G. Bruce, S.D.P./All.	..	10,439
K. J. Davenport, F.D.P.	..	491
C. maj.		14,929

(June '83, C. maj. 13,563)

Daventry (Northants)
E. 69,241

T. E. Boswell, C.	....	31,353
I. R. Miller, L./All.	....	11,663
Mrs. L. M. A. W. Koumi, Lab.		11,097
C. maj.		19,690

(June '83, C. maj. 13,136)

Davyhulme (Gtr. Manchester)
E. 65,558

*W. S. Churchill, C.	....	23,633
J. Nicholson, Lab.	....	15,434
D. I. Wrigley, L./All.	.....	11,637
C. maj.		8,199

(June '83, C. maj. 9,014)

Denton and Reddish
(Gtr. Manchester)
E. 69,533

*A. F. Bennett, Lab.	......	26,023
P. Slater, C.	....	17,773
T. I. Huffer, S.D.P./All.	..	8,697
Lab. maj.		8,250

(June '83, Lab. maj. 5,125)

Derby
NORTH   E. 71,738

*G. Knight, C.	....	26,561
P. Whitehead, Lab.	......	20,236
S. F. Connolly, L./All.	....	7,268
E. Wall, Grn.	....	291
C. maj.		6,325

(June '83, C. maj. 3,506)

SOUTH   E. 68,825

*Mrs. M. M. Beckett, Lab.	.	21,003
P. F. Leighton, C.	....	19,487
Ms. P. N. Mellor, S.D.P./All.		7,608
Lab. maj.	....	1,516

(June '83, Lab. maj. 421)

Derbyshire
NORTH EAST   E. 70,314

H. Barnes, Lab.	....	24,747
J. H. Hayes, C.	....	21,027
S. P. Hardy, S.D.P./All.	..	9,985
Lab. maj.	....	3,720

(June '83, Lab. maj. 2,006)

SOUTH   E. 80,045

*Mrs. E. Currie, C.	....	31,927
J. D. Whitby, Lab.	....	21,616
J. Edgar, S.D.P./All.	.....	11,509
C. maj.		10,311

(June '83, C. maj. 8,613)

WEST *E.* 70,782
*P. A. McLoughlin, C. 31,224
C. R. Walmsley, *L./All.* ... 20,697
W. Moore, *Lab.* 6,875
C. maj. 10,527
(June '83, C. maj. 15,325)
(May '86, C. maj. 100)

Devizes (Wilts)
E. 86,047

*Hon. C. A. Morrison, C. .. 36,372
Mrs. L. E. Siegle, *L./All.* .. 18,542
R. W. Buxton, *Lab.* 11,487
C. maj. 17,830
(June '83, C. maj. 15,624)

Devon

NORTH *E.* 67,474
*A. Speller, C 28,071
M. A. Pinney, *L./All.* 23,602
Ms. A. Marjoram, *Lab.* ... 3,467
C. maj. 4,469
(June '83, C. maj. 8,727)

WEST AND TORRIDGE *E.* 74,550
Miss E. H. Nicholson, *C.* .. 29,484
J. P. A. Burnett, *L./All.* .. 23,016
D. G. Brenton, *Lab.* 4,990
F. Williamson, *Grn.* 1,168
C. maj. 6,468
(June '83, C. maj. 12,351)

Dewsbury (W. Yorks)
E. 70,836

Mrs. W. A. Taylor, Lab. .. 23,668
*J. Whitfield, C. 23,223
A. Mills, *S.D.P./All.* 8,907
Lab. maj. 445
(June '83, C. maj. 2,086)

Doncaster (S. Yorks)

CENTRAL *E.* 69,699
*Rt. Hon. H. Walker, Lab. . 26,266
Miss P. E. Rawlings, *C.* ... 18,070
J. A. Gore-Browne, *S.D.P./
All.* 7,004
Lab. maj. 8,196
(June '83, Lab. maj. 2,508)

NORTH *E.* 72,986
*M. C. Welsh, Lab. 32,950
R. J. Shepherd, *C.* 13,015
P. Norwood, *S.D.P./All.* ... 7,394
Lab. maj. 19,935
(June '83, Lab. maj. 12,711)

Don Valley (S. Yorks)
E. 74,500

*M. Redmond, Lab. 29,200
C. H. Gallagher, *C.* 17,733
W. K. Whitaker, *L./All.* ... 8,027
Lab. maj. 11,467
(June '83, Lab. maj. 6,466)

Dorset

NORTH *E.* 72,844
*N. B. Baker, C. 32,854
Dr. G. W. Tapper, *L./All.* . 20,947
J. Hanley, *Lab.* 3,819
C. maj. 11,907
(June '83, C. maj. 11,380)

SOUTH *E.* 72,855
I. C. Bruce, *C.* 30,184
B. Ellis, *L./All.* 15,117
Ms. B. Dench, *Lab.* 9,494
A. Hayler, *Ind.* 244
C. maj. 15,067
(June '83, C. maj. 15,098)

WEST *E.* 64,360
*J. W. Spicer, C. 28,305
T. Jones, *L./All.* 15,941
D. Watson, *Lab.* 6,123
C. maj. 12,364
(June '83, C. maj. 13,952)

Dover (Kent)
E. 68,997

D. L. Shaw, *C.* 25,343
S. S. E. W. Love, *Lab.* 18,802
G. Nice, *S.D.P./All.* 10,942
C. maj. 6,541
(June '83, C. maj. 9,220)

Dudley (W. Midlands)

EAST *E.* 75,206
**Rt. Hon. Dr. J. W. Gilbert,
Lab.* 24,942
Mrs. E. Jones, *C.* 21,469
K. Monks, *S.D.P./All.* 7,965
Lab. maj. 3,473
(June '83, Lab. maj. 5,816)

WEST *E.* 81,789
*J. G. Blackburn, C. 32,224
G. Titley, *Lab.* 21,980
G. P. T. Lewis, *L./All.* 10,477
C. maj. 10,244
(June '83, C. maj. 8,723)

Dulwich (Gtr. London)
E. 56,355

*G. F. Bowden, C. 16,563
Miss C. L. Hoey, *Lab.* 16,383
Dr. A. N. G. Harris, *S.D.P./
All.* 5,664
A. Goldie, *Grn.* 432
C. maj. 180
(June '83, C. maj. 1,859)

Durham

CITY OF *E.* 66,567
G. N. Steinberg, *Lab.* 23,382
D. Stoker, *S.D.P./All.* 17,257
C. M. Colquhoun, *C.* 11,408
Lab. maj. 6,125
(June '83, Lab. maj. 1,973)

NORTH *E.* 72,115
*G. H. Radice, Lab. 30,798
Dr. D. Jeary, *S.D.P./All.* .. 12,365
N. C. Gibbon, *C.* 11,602
Lab. maj. 18,433
(June '83, Lab. maj. 13,437)

NORTH WEST *E.* 61,302
Ms. H. J. Armstrong, *Lab.* . 22,947
D. Iceton, *C.* 12,785
C. Foote Wood, *L./All.* ... 9,349
Lab. maj. 10,162
(June '83, Lab. maj. 6,356)

Ealing (Gtr. London)

ACTON *E.* 67,176
*Sir G. S. K. Young, BT., C. . 25,499
P. J. Portwood, *Lab.* 13,256
S. R. D. Brooks, *S.D.P./All.* 8,973
C. maj. 12,243
(June '83, C. maj. 10,092)

NORTH *E.* 71,634
*H. Greenway, C. 30,100
H. J. Benn, *Lab.* 14,947
A. H. J. Miller, *L./All.* 8,149
Mrs. K. Fitzherbert, *Grn.* . 577
C. maj. 15,153
(June '83, C. maj. 6,291)

SOUTHALL *E.* 74,843
*S. J. Bidwell, Lab. 26,480
M. A. Truman, *C.* 18,503
Mrs. M. Howes, *L./All.* ... 6,947
R. F. Lugg, *W.R.P.* 256
Lab. maj. 7,977
(June '83, Lab. maj. 11,116)

Easington (Durham)
E. 64,863

J. S. Cummings, *Lab.* 32,396
W. J. Perry, *C.* 7,757
G. Morpeth, *L./All.* 7,117
Lab. maj. 24,639
(June '83, Lab. maj. 14,792)

Eastbourne (E. Sussex)
E. 74,144

*I. Gow, T.D., C. 33,587
P. G. Driver, *L./All.* 16,664
A. Patel, *Lab.* 4,928
Ms. R. Addison, *Grn.* 867
C. maj. 16,923
(June '83, C. maj. 13,486)

Eastleigh (Hants)
E. 87,552

*Sir D. E. C. Price, C. 35,584
M. J. Kyrle, *L./All.* 22,229
D. J. C. Bull, *Lab.* 11,599
C. maj. 13,355
(June '83, C. maj. 13,008)

Eccles (Gtr. Manchester)
E. 66,961

Miss J. Lestor, *Lab.* 25,346
Mrs. M. E. J. Packalow, *C.* 15,647
P. C. W. Beatty, *S.D.P./All.* 8,924
Lab. maj. 9,699
(June '83, Lab. maj. 6,005)

Eddisbury (Cheshire)
E. 73,894

*A. R. Goodlad, C. 29,474
R. I. Fletcher, *L./All.* 13,639
Mrs. C. Grigg, *Lab.* 13,574
A. Basden, *Grn.* 976
C. maj. 15,835
(June '83, C. maj. 14,846)

Edmonton (Gtr. London)
E. 66,080

*Dr. I. D. Twinn, C. 24,556
B. G. Grayston, *Lab.* 17,270
M. Lawson, *S.D.P./All.* ... 6,115
C. maj. 7,286
(June '83, C. maj. 1,193)

Ellesmere Port and Neston
(Cheshire)
E. 71,344

*M. Woodcock, C.	25,664
Miss H. M. Jones, Lab.	23,811
S. A. Holbrook, S.D.P./All.	8,143
D. J. E. Carson, P.R.P.	185
C. maj.	1,853
(June '83, C. maj. 7,087)	

Elmet (W. Yorks)
E. 69,024

*S. L. Batiste, C.	25,658
C. Burgon, Lab.	20,302
J. D. Macarthur, S.D.P./All.	8,755
C. maj.	5,356
(June '83, C. maj. 7,856)	

Eltham (Gtr. London)
E. 54,063

*P. J. Bottomley, C.	19,752
D. Vaughan, Lab.	13,292
E. J. Randall, L./All.	8,542
C. maj.	6,460
(June '83, C. maj. 7,592)	

Enfield (Gtr. London)
NORTH E. 69,488

*T. J. C. Eggar, C.	28,758
M. Upham, Lab.	14,743
Ms. H. Leighter, S.D.P./All.	7,633
M. Chantler, Grn.	644
C. maj.	14,015
(June '83, C. maj. 11,716)	

SOUTHGATE E. 66,600

*M. D. X. Portillo, C.	28,445
N. Harvey, L./All.	10,100
R. Course, Lab.	9,114
S. Rooney, Grn.	696
C. maj.	18,345
(June '83, C. maj. 15,819)	
(Dec. '84, C. maj. 4,711)	

Epping Forest (Essex)
E. 67,804

*Sir J. A. Biggs-Davison, C.	31,536
A. Humphris, S.D.P./All.	10,023
S. Murray, Lab.	9,499
R. Denhard, Grn.	695
C. maj.	21,513
(June '83, C. maj. 15,378)	

Epsom and Ewell (Surrey)
E. 70,683

*Hon. A. G. Hamilton, C.	33,145
Mrs. M. J. Joachim, L./All.	12,384
Mrs. D. B. Follett, Lab.	7,751
C. maj.	20,761
(June '83, C. maj. 17,195)	

Erewash (Derbys)
E. 76,545

*P. L. Rost, C.	28,775
R. W. Jones, Lab.	19,021
Ms. C. P. Moss, S.D.P./All.	11,442
C. maj.	9,754
(June '83, C. maj. 11,319)	

Erith and Crayford
(Gtr. London)
E. 59,292

*D. A. Evennett, C.	20,203
C. F. Hargrave, Lab.	13,209
*A. J. Wellbeloved, S.D.P./All.	11,300
C. maj.	6,994
(June '83, C. maj. 920)	

Esher (Surrey)
E. 62,117

I. C. Taylor, M.B.E., C.	31,334
A. J. Barnett, L./All.	12,266
N. J. V. Lucas, Lab.	4,197
C. maj.	19,068
(June '83, C. maj. 15,912)	

Exeter (Devon)
E. 75,208

*J. G. Hannam, C.	26,922
M. S. Thomas, S.D.P./All.	19,266
J. A. Vincent, Lab.	13,643
R. J. Vail, Grn.	597
N. D. Byles, L.A.P.P.	209
C. maj.	7,656
(June '83, C. maj. 9,880)	

Falmouth and Camborne
(Cornwall)
E. 68,612

*W. D. Mudd, C.	23,725
J. C. Marks, S.D.P./All.	18,686
J. Cosgrove, Lab.	11,271
F. Zapp, L.M.	373
C. maj.	5,039
(June '83, C. maj. 11,025)	

Fareham (Hants)
E. 76,974

*P. R. C. Lloyd, C.	36,781
T. Slack, L./All.	17,986
M. Merritt, Lab.	5,451
C. maj.	18,795
(June '83, C. maj. 16,316)	

Faversham (Kent)
E. 79,039

*R. D. Moate, C.	31,074
E. M. Goyder, S.D.P./All.	17,096
P. Dangerfield, Lab.	12,616
C. maj.	13,978
(June '83, C. maj. 14,597)	

Feltham and Heston
(Gtr. London)
E. 81,062

*R. P. Ground, Q.C., C.	27,755
C. Hinds, Lab.	22,325
J. Daly, S.D.P./All.	9,623
C. maj.	5,430
(June '83, C. maj. 2,148)	

Finchley (Gtr. London)
E. 57,727

*Rt. Hon. Mrs. M. H. Thatcher, C.	21,603
J. Davies, Lab.	12,690
D. Howarth, L./All.	5,580
Lord Buckethead, Grem.	131
Miss M. St. Vincent, Gold	59
C. maj.	8,913
(June '83, C. maj. 9,314)	

Folkestone and Hythe (Kent)
E. 64,406

*M. Howard, Q.C., C.	27,915
J. R. MacDonald, L./All.	18,789
V. S. Anand, Lab.	3,720
C. maj.	9,126
(June '83, C. maj. 11,670)	

Fulham (Gtr. London)
E. 54,498

M. H. M. Carrington, C.	21,752
*W. R. N. Raynsford, Lab.	15,430
P. A. C. Marshall, S.D.P./All.	4,365
Ms. J. Grimes, Grn.	465
C. maj.	6,322
(June '83, C. maj. 4,789)	
(April '86, Lab. maj. 3,503)	

Fylde (Lancs)
E. 63,246

J. M. Jack, C.	29,559
Mrs. E. A. Smith, L./All.	11,787
G. Smith, Lab.	6,955
H. Fowler, R.C.P.	405
C. maj.	17,772
(June '83, C. maj. 17,102)	

Gainsborough and Horncastle
(Lincs)
E. 69,760

*E. J. E. Leigh, C.	28,621
D. A. Grace, L./All.	18,898
R. Naylor, Lab.	6,156
C. maj.	9,723
(June '83, C. maj. 5,067)	

Gateshead East (Tyne & Wear)
E. 67,953

Miss J. G. Quin, Lab.	28,895
F. W. Rogers, C.	11,667
N. G. Rippeth, S.D.P./All.	8,231
Lab. maj.	17,228
(June '83, Lab. maj. 10,322)	

Gedling (Notts)
E. 68,398

A. J. B. Mitchell, C.	29,492
V. R. Coaker, Lab.	12,953
D. Morton, S.D.P./All.	11,684
C. maj.	16,539
(June '83, C. maj. 14,664)	

Gillingham (Kent)
E. 71,847

*J. R. Couchman, C.	28,711
L. R. Andrews, L./All.	16,162
D. J. Bishop, Lab.	9,230
C. maj.	12,549
(June '83, C. maj. 10,843)	

Glanford and Scunthorpe
(Humberside)
E. 72,816

E. A. Morley, Lab.	24,733
*R. S. Hickmet, C.	24,221
C. Nottingham, S.D.P./All.	7,762
K. S. Trivedi, Ind.	104
Lab. maj.	512
(June '83, C. maj. 637)	

Gloucester
E. 76,910

D. C. French, *C.*	....	29,826
D. Hulme, *Lab.*	....	17,791
J. Hilton, *L./All.*	....	12,417
C. maj.	....	12,035

(June '83, C. maj. 12,537)

Gloucestershire West
E. 77,994

*P. Marland, *C.*	....	29,257
P. E. S. Nielson, *Lab.*	......	17,578
J. T. Watkinson, *S.D.P./All.*		16,440
C. maj.	....	11,679

(June '83, C. maj. 9,652)

Gosport (Hants)
E. 68,113

*P. J. Viggers, *C.*	....	29,804
P. J. Chegwyn, *L./All.*	...	16,081
A. Lloyd, *Lab.*	....	5,053
C. maj.	....	13,723

(June '83, C. maj. 14,451)

Grantham (Lincs)
E. 79,434

*Hon. D. M. Hogg, *C.*	.....	33,988
J. P. Heppell, *L./All.*	.....	12,685
M. B. Gent, *Lab.*	....	12,197
Mrs. P. A. Hewis, *Grn.*	...	700
C. maj.	....	21,303

(June '83, C. maj. 18,911)

Gravesham (Kent)
E. 72,759

J. A. Arnold, *C.*	....	28,891
M. A. Coleman, *Lab.*	.....	20,099
R. I. Crawford, *L./All.*	...	8,724
C. maj.	....	8,792

(June '83, C. maj. 8,463)

Great Grimsby (Humberside)
E. 68,501

*A. V. Mitchell, *Lab.*	......	23,463
C. F. Robinson, *C.*	....	14,679
P. W. Genney, *S.D.P./All.*		13,457
Lab. maj.	....	8,784

(June '83, Lab. maj. 731)

Great Yarmouth
(Norfolk)
E. 65,770

*M. R. H. Carttiss, *C.*	.....	25,336
J. Cannell, *Lab.*	....	15,253
S. D. Maxwell, *S.D.P./All.*		8,387
C. maj.	....	10,083

(June '83, C. maj. 11,200)

Greenwich (Gtr. London)
E. 50,830

*Mrs. R. S. Barnes, *S.D.P./All.*		15,149
Mrs. D. F. M. Wood, *Lab.*	.	13,008
J. G. C. Antcliffe, *C.*	.....	8,695
Ms. J. Thomas, *Grn.*	.....	346
R. Mallone, *Fell.*	....	59
Ms. P. Clinton, *Comm.*	...	58
S.D.P./All. maj.	....	2,141

(June '83, Lab. maj. 1,211)
(Feb. '87, S.D.P./All. maj. 6,611)

Guildford (Surrey)
E. 77,872

*Rt. Hon. D. A. R. Howell, *C.*		32,504
Mrs. M. L. Sharp, *S.D.P./All.*		19,897
R. J. Wolverson, *Lab.*	.....	6,216
C. maj.	....	12,607

(June '83, C. maj. 11,824)

Hackney (Gtr. London)

NORTH AND STOKE NEWINGTON
E. 66,771

Ms. D. J. Abbott, *Lab.*	....	18,912
O. Letwin, *C.*	....	11,234
S. H. Taylor, *S.D.P./All.*	..	7,446
D. J. Fitzpatrick, *Grn.*	...	997
Ms. Y. T. Anwar, *R.F.*	....	228
Lab. maj.	....	7,678

(June '83, Lab. maj. 8,545)

SOUTH AND SHOREDITCH *E.* 70,873

*B. C. J. Sedgemore, *Lab.*	..	18,799
M. C. Northcroft-Brown, *C.*		11,277
J. D. Roberts, *L./All.*	......	8,812
D. Green, *Comm.*	....	403
Lab. maj.	....	7,522

(June '83, Lab. maj. 7,691)

Halesowen and Stourbridge
(W. Midlands)
E. 78,017

*J. H. R. Stokes, *C.*	....	31,037
T. J. Sunter, *Lab.*	....	17,229
D. C. A. Simon, *S.D.P./All.*		13,658
C. maj.	....	13,808

(June '83, C. maj. 13,316)

Halifax (W. Yorks)
E. 73,392

Mrs. A. Mahon, *Lab.*	.....	24,741
*R. Galley, *C.*	....	23,529
F. L. Cockcroft, *S.D.P./All.*		8,758
Lab. maj.	....	1,212

(June '83, C. maj. 1,869)

Halton (Cheshire)
E. 73,848

*Rt. Hon. G. J. Oakes, *Lab.*	.	32,065
J. Hardman, *C.*	....	17,487
Ms. H. Clucas, *S.D.P./All.*		8,272
Lab. maj.	....	14,578

(June '83, Lab. maj. 6,829)

Hammersmith (Gtr. London)
E. 48,285

*C. S. Soley, *Lab.*	....	15,811
N. J. A. Deva, *C.*	....	13,396
S. H. J. A. Knott, *L./All.*	..	5,241
D. P. Kirk, *Grn.*	....	453
P. J. F. Fitzpatrick, *R.F.*	..	125
Miss M. M. A. Carrick, *Humanist*	....	98
Lab. maj.	....	2,415

(June '83, Lab. maj. 1,954)

Hampshire

EAST *E.* 86,363

*M. J. Mates, *C.*	....	43,093
R. Booker, *L./All.*	....	19,307
C. Lloyd, *Lab.*	....	4,443
C. maj.	....	23,786

(June '83, C. maj. 18,327)

NORTH WEST *E.* 69,965

*D. B. Mitchell, *C.*	....	31,470
I. H. Wills, *L./All.*	....	18,033
Ms. A. Burnage, *Lab.*	....	4,980
C. maj.	....	13,437

(June '83, C. maj. 12,122)

Hampstead and Highgate
(Gtr. London)
E. 63,301

*Sir G. Finsberg, *M.B.E., C.*	.	19,236
P. J. Turner, *Lab.*	....	17,015
Mrs. A. Sofer, *S.D.P./All.*		8,744
G. Weiss, *Rainbow*	....	137
Ms. S. Ellis, *Humanist*	....	134
C. maj.	....	2,221

(June '83, C. maj. 3,370)

Harborough (Leics)
E. 74,700

*Sir J. A. Farr, *C.*	....	35,216
T. J. Swift, *L./All.*	....	16,406
P. Harley, *Lab.*	....	7,646
C. maj.	....	18,810

(June '83, C. maj. 18,485)

Harlow (Essex)
E. 70,286

*J. J. J. Hayes, *C.*	....	26,017
A. S. Newens, *Lab.*	......	20,140
Mrs. M. C. Eden-Green, *S.D.P./All.*	....	8,915
C. maj.	....	5,877

(June '83, C. maj. 3,674)

Harrogate (N. Yorks)
E. 75,761

*R. G. Banks, *C.*	....	31,167
J. R. Leach, *S.D.P./All.*	..	19,265
A. J. Wright, *Lab.*	....	5,671
C. maj.	....	11,902

(June '83, C. maj. 15,888)

Harrow (Gtr. London)

EAST *E.* 81,124

*H. J. M. Dykes, *C.*	....	32,302
D. J. Brough, *Lab.*	....	14,029
Mrs. Z. Gifford, *L./All.*	...	13,251
C. maj.	....	18,273

(June '83, C. maj. 12,668)

WEST *E.* 74,041

R. G. Hughes, *C.*	....	30,456
S. P. Bayliss, *S.D.P./All.*	..	15,012
C. Bastin, *Lab.*	....	9,665
C. maj.	....	15,444

(June '83, C. maj. 11,021)

Hartlepool (Cleveland)
E. 68,686

*E. Leadbitter, *Lab.*	......	24,296
P. C. Catchpole, *C.*	....	17,007
A. Preece, *L./All.*	....	7,047
I. J. Cameron, *Ind.*	....	1,786
Lab. maj.	....	7,289

(June '83, Lab. maj. 3,090)

Harwich (Essex)
E. 77,149

*Sir J. E. Ridsdale, *C.B.E., C.*		29,344
Miss E. Lynne, *L./All.*	....	17,262
R. Knight, *Lab.*	....	9,920
C. A. Humphrey, *O.F.P.*	..	161
C. maj.	....	12,082

(June '83, C. maj. 12,502)

Hastings and Rye (E. Sussex)
E. 72,758

*K. R. Warren, C.	26,163
D. J. Amies, L./All.	18,816
Ms. J. Hurcombe, Lab.	6,825
D. Howell, L.M.	242
S. P. Davies, N.P.R.	194
C. maj.	7,347

(June '83, C. maj. 10,980)

Havant (Hants)
E. 76,344

*Sir I. S. Lloyd, C.	32,527
Mrs. E. E. Cleaver, S.D.P./All.	16,017
J. A. Phillips, Lab.	8,030
G. W. Fuller, Bread	373
C. maj.	16,510

(June '83, C. maj. 11,956)

Hayes and Harlington
(Gtr. London)
E. 58,240

*T. P. Dicks, C.	21,355
P. F. Fagan, Lab.	15,390
Ms. S. Slipman, S.D.P./All.	6,641
C. maj.	5,965

(June '83, C. maj. 4,234)

Hazel Grove (Gtr. Manchester)
E. 65,717

*T. R. Arnold, C.	24,396
A. M. Vos, L./All.	22,556
J. G. Ford, Lab.	6,354
Ms. F. K. Chapman, Grn.	346
C. maj.	1,840

(June '83, C. maj. 2,022)

Hemsworth (W. Yorks)
E. 54,951

G. J. Buckley, Lab.	27,859
E. H. Garnier, C.	7,159
J. D. Wooffindin, L./All.	6,568
Lab. maj.	20,700

(June '83, Lab. maj. 14,190)

Hendon (Gtr. London)
NORTH   E. 55,095

*J. M. Gorst, C.	20,155
Ms. J. Manson, Lab.	9,223
Ms. E. Davies, S.D.P./All.	6,859
C. maj.	10,932

(June '83, C. maj. 9,025)

SOUTH   E. 54,560

J. L. Marshall, C.	19,341
M. O. Palmer, L./All.	8,217
Miss L. Christian, Lab.	7,261
C. maj.	11,124

(June '83, C. maj. 6,433)

Henley (Oxon)
E. 65,443

*Rt. Hon. M. R. D. Heseltine, C.	29,978
J. Madeley, L./All.	12,896
M. B. Barber, Lab.	6,173
C. maj.	17,082

(June '83, C. maj. 13,781)

Hereford
E. 67,075

*C. R. Shepherd, C.	24,865
C. F. Green, L./All.	23,452
V. S. Woodell, Lab.	4,031
C. maj.	1,413

(June '83, C. maj. 2,277)

Hertford and Stortford
E. 75,508

*B. Wells, C.	33,763
R. E. Wotherspoon, S.D.P./All.	16,623
Mrs. P. R. E. Sumner, Lab.	7,494
G. C. Cole, Grn.	814
C. maj.	17,140

(June '83, C. maj. 12,929)

Hertfordshire
NORTH   E. 78,694

*B. H. I. H. Stewart, R.D., C.	31,750
G. W. Binney, L./All.	20,308
A. Gorst, Lab.	11,782
C. maj.	11,442

(June '83, C. maj. 9,943)

SOUTH WEST   E. 75,643

*R. L. Page, C.	32,791
I. M. Blair, L./All.	17,007
I. Willmore, Lab.	8,966
C. maj.	15,784

(June '83, C. maj. 12,194)

WEST   E. 78,966

*R. B. Jones, C.	31,760
N. A. Hollinghurst, S.D.P./All.	16,836
A. McBrearty, Lab.	15,317
C. maj.	14,924

(June '83, C. maj. 9,576)

Hertsmere (Herts)
E. 73,367

*Rt. Hon. C. E. Parkinson, C.	31,278
L. S. Brass, L./All.	13,172
F. Ward, Lab.	10,835
C. maj.	18,106

(June '83, C. maj. 14,870)

Hexham (Nthmb)
E. 56,360

A. T. Amos, C.	22,370
E. M. Robson, L./All.	14,304
M. R. Wood, Lab.	8,103
Mrs. S. M. Wood, Grn.	336
C. maj.	8,066

(June '83, C. maj. 8,308)

Heywood and Middleton
(Gtr. Manchester)
E. 59,487

*J. Callaghan, Lab.	21,900
R. E. Walker, C.	15,052
I. Greenhalgh, S.D.P./All.	6,953
Lab. maj.	6,848

(June '83, Lab. maj. 3,974)

High Peak (Derbys)
E. 69,926

*C. J. Hawkins, C.	25,715
Mrs. J. McCrindle, Lab.	16,199
Dr. J. Oldham, S.D.P./All.	14,389
C. maj.	9,516

(June '83, C. maj. 9,940)

Holborn and St. Pancras
(Gtr. London)
E. 70,589

*F. G. Dobson, Lab.	22,966
P. J. Luff, C.	14,113
S. McGrath, L./All.	7,994
M. J. Gavan, R.F.	300
Lab. maj.	8,853

(June '83, Lab. maj. 7,259)

Holland with Boston (Lincs)
E. 65,539

*Sir R. B. F. S. Body, C.	27,412
Mrs. C. Le Brun, L./All.	9,817
J. D. Hough, Lab.	9,734
D. James, Local Voice	405
C. maj.	17,595

(June '83, C. maj. 11,736)

Honiton (Devon)
E. 77,259

*Sir P. F. H. Emery, C.	34,931
G. Tatton-Brown, S.D.P./All.	18,369
S. Pollentine, Lab.	4,988
S. Hughes, L.M.	747
C. maj.	16,562

(June '83, C. maj. 14,769)

Hornchurch (Gtr. London)
E. 62,397

*R. C. Squire, C.	24,039
A. R. Williams, Lab.	13,345
M. L. C. Long, L./All.	9,609
C. maj.	10,694

(June '83, C. maj. 9,184)

Hornsey and Wood Green
(Gtr. London)
E. 80,594

*Sir H. A. L. Rossi, C.	25,397
Mrs. B. M. R. Roche, Lab.	23,618
D. Eden, S.D.P./All.	8,928
Ms. E. Crosbie, Grn.	1,154
C. maj.	1,779

(June '83, C. maj. 3,899)

Horsham (W. Sussex)
E. 86,135

*Sir P. M. Hordern, C.	39,775
Mrs. J. Pearce, S.D.P./All.	15,868
M. Shrimpton, Lab.	5,435
T. Metheringham, Grn.	1,383
C. maj.	23,907

(June '83, C. maj. 21,785)

Houghton and Washington
(Tyne & Wear)
E. 77,906

*R. Boyes, Lab.	32,805
J. M. Callanan, C.	12,612
R. F. Kenyon, S.D.P./All.	10,090
Lab. maj.	20,193

(June '83, Lab. maj. 13,821)

Hove (E. Sussex)
E. 72,626

Hon. T. A. D. Sainsbury, C.		28,952
Mrs. M. E. Collins, *S.D.P./*		
All.		10,734
D. K. Turner, *Lab.*		9,010
T. A. Layton, *S.E.*		522
C. maj.		18,218
(June '83, C. maj. 17,219)		

Huddersfield (W. Yorks)
E. 66,413

B. J. Sheerman, Lab.		23,019
N. J. Hawkins, *C.*		15,741
J. Smithson, *L./All.*		10,773
N. A. L. Harvey, *Grn.*		638
Lab. maj.		7,278
(June '83, Lab. maj. 3,955)		

Huntingdon (Cambs)
E. 86,186

Rt. Hon. J. Major, C.		40,530
A. J. Nicholson, *S.D.P./All.*		13,486
D. M. Brown, *Lab.*		8,883
B. Lavin, *Grn.*		874
C. maj.		27,044
(June '83, C. maj. 20,348)		

Hyndburn (Lancs)
E. 60,529

J. K. Hargreaves, C.		21,606
K. Coombes, *Lab.*		19,386
J. Strak, *S.D.P./All.*		7,423
F. Smith, *Grn.*		297
C. maj.		2,220
(June '83, C. maj. 21)		

Ilford (Gtr. London)

NORTH E. 60,433

V. W. H. Bendall, C.		24,110
P. Jeater, *Lab.*		12,020
G. Tobbell, *S.D.P./All.*		7,757
C. maj.		12,090
(June '83, C. maj. 11,201)		

SOUTH E. 58,572

N. G. Thorne, O.B.E., T.D., C.		20,351
K. Jones, *Lab.*		15,779
R. J. Scott, *L./All.*		5,928
C. maj.		4,572
(June '83, C. maj. 4,566)		

Ipswich (Suffolk)
E. 68,165

M. F. Irvine, *C.*		23,328
K. T. Weetch, Lab.		22,454
H. P. Nicholson, *S.D.P./All.*		6,596
D. T. Lettice, *W.R.P.*		174
C. maj.		874
(June '83, Lab. maj. 1,077)		

Isle of Wight
E. 98,694

B. J. A. Field, *C.*		40,175
M. Young, *L./All.*		33,733
K. Pearson, *Lab.*		4,626
C. maj.		6,442
(June '83, L./All. maj. 3,503)		

Islington (Gtr. London)

NORTH E. 58,917

J. B. Corbyn, Lab.		19,577
E. G. Noad, *C.*		9,920
A. Whelan, *S.D.P./All.*		8,560
C. Ashby, *Grn.*		1,131
Lab. maj.		9,657
(June '83, Lab. maj. 5,607)		

SOUTH AND FINSBURY E. 57,910

C. R. Smith, Lab.		16,511
G. Cunningham, *S.D.P./*		
All.		15,706
A. Mitchell, *C.*		8,482
P. Powell, *Grn.*		382
S. Dowsett, *S.P.G.B.*		81
Ms. J. Early, *H.P.*		56
Lab. maj.		805
(June '83, Lab. maj. 363)		

Jarrow (Tyne & Wear)
E. 62,845

D. Dixon, Lab.		29,651
P. Yeoman, *C.*		10,856
P. Freitag, *L./All.*		6,230
Lab. maj.		18,795
(June '83, Lab. maj. 13,877)		

Keighley (W. Yorks)
E. 65,831

G. P. A. Waller, C.		23,903
A. Rye, *Lab.*		18,297
J. H. Wells, *L./All.*		10,041
C. maj.		5,606
(June '83, C. maj. 2,774)		

Kensington (Gtr. London)
E. 48,212

Sir B. M. Rhys Williams,		
BT., *C.*		14,818
B. T. Bousquet, *Lab.*		10,371
W. H. Goodhart, *S.D.P./*		
All.		5,379
R. E. Shorter, *Grn.*		528
Miss L. Carrick, *Humanist*		65
Mrs. M. Hughes, *P.I.P.*		30
C. maj.		4,447
(June '83, C. maj. 5,101)		
(*see also* p. 275)		

Kent Mid
E. 72,456

A. J. B. Rowe, C.		28,719
G. D. Colley, *L./All.*		13,951
J. A. Hazelgrove, *Lab.*		9,420
C. maj.		14,768
(June '83, C. maj. 12,543)		

Kettering (Northants)
E. 65,965

R. N. Freeman, C.		26,532
Mrs. C. M. Goodhart,		
S.D.P./All.		15,205
A. M. Minto, *Lab.*		10,229
C. maj.		11,327
(June '83, C. maj. 8,586)		

Kingston-upon-Hull

EAST E. 68,657

J. L. Prescott, Lab.		27,287
P. Jackson, *C.*		12,598
T. Wright, *L./All.*		8,572
Lab. maj.		14,689
(June '83, Lab. maj. 10,074)		

NORTH E. 73,288

J. K. McNamara, Lab.		26,123
Miss A. O'Brien, *C.*		13,954
S. W. Unwin, *S.D.P./All.*		10,962
Lab. maj.		12,169
(June '83, Lab. maj. 6,028)		

WEST E. 55,636

S. J. Randall, Lab.		19,527
M. R. C. Humphrys, *C.*		11,397
M. Bond, *S.D.P./All.*		6,669
Lab. maj.		8,130
(June '83, Lab. maj. 3,654)		

Kingston upon Thames
(Gtr. London)
E. 54,839

Rt. Hon. N. S. H. Lamont,		
C.		24,198
R. M. Hayes, *L./All.*		13,012
R. Markless, *Lab.*		5,676
J. Baker, *C.P.W.S.M.L.*		175
C. maj.		11,186
(June '83, C. maj. 8,872)		

Kingswood (Avon)
E. 73,089

R. A. Hayward, C.		26,300
R. L. Berry, *Lab.*		21,907
Mrs. P. Whittle, *S.D.P./All.*		10,382
C. maj.		4,393
(June '83, C. maj. 1,797)		

Knowsley (Merseyside)

NORTH E. 52,960

G. E. Howarth, Lab.		27,454
Ms. R. Cooper, *L./All.*		6,356
R. C. A. Brown, *C.*		4,922
D. Hallsworth, *R.F.*		538
Lab. maj.		21,098
(June '83, Lab. maj. 17,191)		
(Nov. '86, Lab. maj. 6,724)		

SOUTH E. 65,643

S. F. Hughes, Lab.		31,378
A. J. Hall, *C.*		10,532
Mrs. R. Watmough, *S.D.P./*		
All.		6,760
Lab. maj.		20,846
(June '83, Lab. maj. 11,769)		

Lancashire West
E. 76,094

K. H. Hind, C.		26,500
C. Pickthall, *Lab.*		25,147
R. Jermyn, *S.D.P./All.*		8,972
C. maj.		1,353
(June '83, C. maj. 6,858)		

Lancaster (Lancs)
E. 57,229

Mrs. M. E. Kellett-Bow-		
man, C.		21,142
J. Gallacher, *Lab.*		14,689
Mrs. K. C. Brooks, *L./All.*		9,003
P. F. F. Jones, *Grn.*		473
C. maj.		6,453
(June '83, C. maj. 10,636)		

Langbaurgh (Cleveland)
E. 79,193

*J. R. Holt, C.	26,047
P. Harford, Lab.	23,959
R. A. J. Ashby, L./All.	12,405
C. maj.	2,088

(June '83, C. maj. 6,024)

Leeds (W. Yorks)
CENTRAL E. 59,019

*D. J. Fatchett, Lab.	21,270
D. Schofield, C.	9,765
Dr. Karen Lee, S.D.P./All.	6,853
W. Innis, Comm.	355
Lab. maj.	11,505

(June '83, Lab. maj. 8,222)

EAST E. 61,178

*Rt. Hon. D. W. Healey, C.H., M.B.E., Lab.	20,932
J. S. W. Sheard, C.	11,406
Miss M. G. Clay, L./All.	10,630
Lab. maj.	9,526

(June '83, Lab. maj. 6,095)

NORTH EAST E. 64,631

T. J. R. Kirkhope, C.	22,196
P. M. Crystal, S.D.P./All.	13,777
O. B. Glover, Lab.	12,292
Ms. C. D. Nash, Grn.	416
C. maj.	8,419

(June '83, C. maj. 8,995)

NORTH WEST E. 68,227

*Dr. K. Hampson, C.	22,480
B. Peters, L./All.	17,279
Ms. J. Thomas, Lab.	11,210
A. Stevens, Grn.	663
C. maj.	5,201

(June '83, C. maj. 8,537)

SOUTH AND MORLEY E. 60,726

*Rt. Hon. M. Rees, Lab.	21,551
Mrs. T. C. Holdroyd, C.	14,840
E. J. V. Dawson, S.D.P./All.	7,099
Lab. maj.	6,711

(June '83, Lab. maj. 5,854)

WEST E. 66,344

J. D. Battle, Lab.	21,032
*M. J. Meadowcroft, L./All.	16,340
P. D. Allott, C.	11,276
Lab. maj.	4,692

(June '83, L./All. maj. 2,048)

Leicester
EAST E. 66,372

N. K. A. S. Vaz, Lab.	24,074
*P. N. E. Bruinvels, C.	22,150
Mrs. A. M. Ayres, S.D.P./All.	5,935
Lab. maj.	1,924

(June '83, C. maj. 933)

SOUTH E. 73,236

J. Marshall, Lab.	24,901
*D. H. Spencer, Q.C., C.	23,024
R. Pritchard, L./All.	7,773
B. Fewster, Grn.	390
M. M. Mayat, Ind. Lab.	192
Ms. R. F. Manners, W.R.P.	96
Lab. maj.	1,877

(June '83, C. maj. 7)

WEST E. 67,829

*G. E. Janner, Q.C., Lab.	22,156
J. S. W. Cooper, C.	20,955
W. Edgar, S.D.P./All.	6,708
Lab. maj.	1,201

(June '83, Lab. maj. 1,712)

Leicestershire North West
E. 70,633

*D. G. Ashby, C.	27,872
Mrs. S. A. Waddington, Lab.	20,044
D. S. Emmerson, L./All.	10,034
Miss H. T. Michetschlager, Grn.	570
C. maj.	7,828

(June '83, C. maj. 6,662)

Leigh (Gtr. Manchester)
E. 69,155

*L. F. Cunliffe, Lab.	30,064
L. B. A. Browne, C.	13,458
S. D. Jones, S.D.P./All.	7,743
Lab. maj.	16,606

(June '83, Lab. maj. 12,314)

Leominster (H & W)
E. 69,977

*P. Temple-Morris, C.	31,396
S. C. Morris, L./All.	17,321
A. C. R. Chappell, Lab.	4,444
Mrs. F. M. Norman, Grn.	1,102
C. maj.	14,075

(June '83, C. maj. 9,786)

Lewes (E. Sussex)
E. 73,181

*J. R. Rathbone, C.	32,016
D. F. Bellotti, L./All.	18,396
R. P. Taylor, Lab.	4,973
A. G. P. Sherwood, Grn.	970
C. maj.	13,620

(June '83, C. maj. 13,904)

Lewisham (Gtr. London)
DEPTFORD E. 58,151

Ms. J. M. Ruddock, Lab.	18,724
M. C. Punyer, C.	11,953
Ms. A. M. E. Braun, S.D.P./All.	6,513
P. K. Makepeace, Grn.	568
Lab. maj.	6,771

(June '83, Lab. maj. 6,032)

EAST E. 59,627

*Hon. C. B. Moynihan, C.	19,873
M. R. Profitt, Lab.	15,059
Mrs. V. W. Stone, S.D.P./All.	9,118
C. maj.	4,814

(June '83, C. maj. 1,909)

WEST E. 62,923

*J. C. Maples, C.	20,995
J. P. Dowd, Lab.	17,223
Ms. S. C. Titley, L./All.	7,247
C. maj.	3,772

(June '83, C. maj. 2,506)

Leyton (Gtr. London)
E. 57,662

*H. M. Cohen, Lab.	16,536
S. Banks, L./All.	11,895
D. N. Gilmartin, C.	11,692
Lab. maj.	4,641

(June '83, Lab. maj. 4,516)

Lincoln
E. 77,049

*K. M. Carlisle, C.	27,097
N. J. Butler, Lab.	19,614
P. Zentner, S.D.P./All.	11,319
T. B. Kyle, R.R.P.R.C.	232
C. maj.	7,483

(June '83, C. maj. 10,286)

Lindsey East (Lincs)
E. 74,027

*Sir P. H. B. Tapsell, C.	29,048
J. C. L. Sellick, L./All.	20,432
K. Stevenson, Lab.	6,206
C. maj.	8,616

(June '83, C. maj. 7,517)

Littleborough and Saddleworth
(Gtr. Manchester)
E. 66,074

*G. K. Dickens, C.	22,027
C. Davies, L./All.	15,825
P. Stonier, Lab.	13,299
C. maj.	6,202

(June '83, C. maj. 5,650)

Liverpool
BROADGREEN E. 63,091

*T. Fields, Lab.	23,262
R. Pine, L./All.	17,215
M. R. G. Seddon, C.	7,413
Lab. maj.	6,047

(June '83, Lab. maj. 3,800)

GARSTON E. 61,280

*E. Loyden, Lab.	24,848
P. B. Feather, C.	11,071
R. Isaacson, S.D.P./All.	10,370
K. Timlin, W.R.P.	98
Lab. maj.	13,777

(June '83, Lab. maj. 4,002)

MOSSLEY HILL E. 60,954

*D. P. P. Alton, L./All.	20,012
J. A. Devaney, Lab.	17,786
W. M. Lightfoot, C.	8,005
L./All. maj.	2,226

(June '83, L./All. maj. 4,195)

RIVERSIDE E. 53,328

*R. Parry, Lab.	25,505
S. Fitzsimmons, C.	4,816
B. S. Chahal, S.D.P./All.	3,912
Ms. C. A. Gardner, Comm.	601
Lab. maj.	20,689

(June '83, Lab. maj. 17,378)

WALTON E. 73,118

*E. S. Heffer, Lab.	34,661
P. R. Clark, L./All.	11,408
I. A. Mays, C.	7,738
Lab. maj.	23,253

(June '83, Lab. maj. 14,115)

West Derby   E. 60,522
*R. N. Wareing, Lab.	......	29,021
J. E. Backhouse, C.	......	8,525
M. Ferguson, S.D.P./All.		6,897
Lab. maj.	....	20,496
(June '83, Lab. maj. 11,843)		

Loughborough (Leics)
E. 73,660

*S. J. Dorrell, C.	....	31,931
C. J. Wrigley, Lab.	....	14,283
R. G. Fox, S.D.P./All.	...	11,499
R. Gupta, Grn.	....	656
C. maj.	....	17,648
(June '83, C. maj. 16,180)		

Ludlow (Salop)
E. 66,187

C. J. F. Gill, R.D., C.	......	27,499
D. Phillips, L./All.	......	15,800
K. Harrison, Lab.	....	7,724
C. maj.	....	11,699
(June '83, C. maj. 11,303)		

Luton (Beds)
North   E. 74,235

*J. R. Carlisle, C.	....	30,997
M. Wright, Lab.	....	15,424
J. D. Stephen, S.D.P./All.	...	11,166
C. maj.	....	15,573
(June '83, C. maj. 11,981)		

South   E. 71,231

*G. F. J. Bright, C.	......	24,762
W. D. McKenzie, Lab.	...	19,647
P. Chapman, L./All.	......	9,146
C. maj.	....	5,115
(June '83, C. maj. 4,621)		

Macclesfield (Cheshire)
E. 76,093

*N. R. Winterton, C.	......	33,208
A. B. Haldane, L./All.	......	14,116
Ms. C. Pinder, Lab.	......	11,563
C. maj.	....	19,092
(June '83, C. maj. 20,679)		

Maidstone (Kent)
E. 72,987

Miss A. N. Widdecombe, C.		29,100
C. J. Sutton-Mattocks, L./		
All.	....	18,736
K. P. Brooks, Lab.	......	6,935
Mrs. P. A. Kemp, Grn.	....	717
C. maj.	....	10,364
(June '83, C. maj. 7,226)		

Makerfield (Gtr. Manchester)
E. 70,819

I. McCartney, Lab.	....	30,190
L. A. Robertson, C.	......	14,632
B. Hewer, L./All.	....	8,838
Lab. maj.	....	15,558
(June '83, Lab. maj. 10,876)		

Manchester
Blackley   E. 58,814

*K. Eastham, Lab.	....	22,476
K. Nath, C.	....	12,354
H. Showman, S.D.P./All.	...	8,041
Lab. maj.	....	10,122
(June '83, Lab. maj. 6,456)		

Central   E. 62,928

*R. K. Litherland, Lab.	...	27,428
M. R. W. Banks, C.	....	7,561
B. W. McColgan, S.D.P./		
All.	....	5,250
Lab. maj.	....	19,867
(June '83, Lab. maj. 18,485)		

Gorton   E. 64,243

*Rt. Hon. G. B. Kaufman,		
Lab.	....	24,615
J. Kershaw, C.	....	10,550
K. A. Whitmore, L./All.	...	9,830
Ms. P. Lawrence, R.F.	....	253
Lab. maj.	....	14,065
(June '83, Lab. maj. 9,965)		

Withington   E. 65,343

K. J. C. Bradley, Lab.	....	21,650
*F. J. Silvester, C.	....	18,259
Mrs. A. Jones, L./All.	....	9,978
M. T. Abberton, Grn.	.....	524
Lab. maj.	....	3,391
(June '83, C. maj. 2,373)		

Wythenshawe   E. 58,287

*Rt. Hon. A. Morris, Lab.	..	23,881
D. G. Sparrow, C.	....	12,026
Ms. J. Butterworth,		
S.D.P./All.	....	5,021
Ms. S. Connelly, R.F.	.....	216
Lab. maj.	....	11,855
(June '83, Lab. maj. 10,684)		

Mansfield (Notts)
E. 66,764

J. A. Meale, Lab.	....	19,610
C. Hendry, C.	....	19,554
B. Answer, S.D.P./All.	...	11,604
B. Marshall, M.L.	....	1,580
Lab. maj.	....	56
(June '83, Lab. maj. 2,216)		

Medway (Kent)
E. 64,103

*Dame P. Fenner, D.B.E., C.		23,889
V. Hull, Lab.	....	13,960
Mrs. J. Horne-Roberts,		
S.D.P./All.	....	8,450
Ms. J. V. Rosser, Grn.	....	504
C. maj.	....	9,929
(June '83, C. maj. 8,656)		

Meriden (W. Midlands)
E. 78,444

*I. C. Mills, C.	....	31,935
R. H. Burden, Lab.	....	15,115
Ms. C. E. Parkinson,		
S.D.P./All.	....	10,896
C. maj.	....	16,820
(June '83, C. maj. 15,018)		

Middlesbrough (Cleveland)
E. 60,789

*S. Bell, Lab.	....	25,747
R. J. Orr-Ewing, C.	....	10,789
P. A. Hawley, L./All.	.....	6,594
Lab. maj.	....	14,958
(June '83, Lab. maj. 9,669)		

Milton Keynes (Bucks)
E. 97,041

*W. R. Benyon, C.	....	35,396
W. T. Rodgers, S.D.P./All.		21,695
Ms. Y. V. A. Brownfield-		
Pope, Lab.	....	16,111
A. H. Francis, Grn.	......	810
C. maj.	....	13,701
(June '83, C. maj. 11,522)		

Mitcham and Morden
(Gtr. London)
E. 63,089

*Mrs. A. C. R. Rumbold,		
c.b.e., C.	....	23,002
Ms. S. McDonagh, Lab.	...	16,819
B. L. H. Douglas-Mann,		
S.D.P./All.	....	7,930
C. maj.	....	6,183
(June '83, C. maj. 6,451)		

Mole Valley (Surrey)
E. 67,715

*Rt. Hon. K. W. Baker, C.	..	31,689
Mrs. S. P. Thomas, L./All.		15,613
C. M. B. King, Lab.	......	4,846
C. maj.	....	16,076
(June '83, C. maj. 14,718)		

Morecambe and Lunesdale
(Lancs)
E. 55,718

*Hon. M. A. Lennox-Boyd,		
C.	....	22,327
Mrs. J. Greenwell, S.D.P./		
All.	....	10,542
D. Smith, Lab.	....	9,535
C. maj.	....	11,785
(June '83, C. maj. 12,194)		

Newark (Notts)
E. 67,555

*R. T. Alexander, C.	......	28,070
D. Barton, Lab.	....	14,527
G. A. Emerson, S.D.P./All.		9,833
C. maj.	....	13,543
(June '83, C. maj. 14,283)		

Newbury (Berks)
E. 75,187

*R. M. C. McNair-Wilson, C.		35,266
D. D. Rendel, L./All.	......	18,608
R. C. Stapley, Lab.	......	4,765
C. maj.	....	16,658
(June '83, C. maj. 13,038)		

Newcastle-under-Lyme (Staffs)
E. 66,053

*Mrs. L. Golding, Lab.	....	21,618
A. L. Thomas, L./All.	.....	16,486
P. C. J. Ridgway, C.	......	14,863
M. J. Nicklin, Ex Lab.		
Mod.	....	397
Lab. maj.	....	5,132
(June '83, Lab. maj. 2,804)		
(July '86, Lab. maj. 799)		

Newcastle upon Tyne
Central   E. 63,682

J. M. Cousins, Lab.	......	20,416
*P. R. G. Merchant, C.	...	17,933
Dr. N. Martin, S.D.P./All.		7,304
R. J. Bird, Grn.	....	418
K. Williams, R.F.	....	111
Lab. maj.	....	2,483
(June '83, C. maj. 2,228)		

EAST E. 59,369

*N. H. Brown, Lab.	....	23,677
Miss J. G. A. Riley, C.	....	11,177
P. J. Arnold, L./All.	......	6,728
J. Keith, Comm.	....	362
Lab. maj.	....	12,500
(June '83, Lab. maj. 7,492)		

NORTH E. 69,178

D. J. Henderson, Lab.	....	22,424
J. W. Shipley, L./All.	.....	17,181
J. W. Tweddle, C.	......	12,915
Lab. maj.	....	5,243
(June '83, Lab. maj. 2,556)		

New Forest (Hants)
E. 75,083

*P. M. E. D. McNair-Wilson,		
C.	....	37,188
R. Karn, L./All.	....	15,456
J. I. Hampton, Lab.	......	4,856
C. maj.	....	21,732
(June '83, C. maj. 20,925)		

Newham (Gtr. London)

NORTH EAST E. 60,787

*R. Leighton, Lab.	....	20,220
P. Davis, C.	....	11,984
Ms. H. Steele, L./All.	.....	6,772
Lab. maj.	....	8,236
(June '83, Lab. maj. 8,509)		

NORTH WEST E. 47,568

*T. L. Banks, Lab.	....	15,677
J. C. Wylie, C.	....	7,181
R. H. Redden, S.D.P./All.	.	4,920
Ms. A. V. Degrandis-		
Harrison, Grn.	....	497
Lab. maj.	....	8,496
(June '83, Lab. maj. 6,918)		

SOUTH E. 50,244

*N. J. Spearing, Lab.	......	12,935
J. Fairrie, C.	....	10,169
A. J. Kellaway, S.D.P./All.		6,607
Lab. maj.	....	2,766
(June '83, Lab. maj. 7,311)		

Norfolk

MID E. 73,893

*R. A. Ryder, O.B.E., C.	....	32,758
G. J. E. Graham, S.D.P./		
All.	....	14,750
K. Luckey, Lab.	....	10,272
C. maj.	....	18,008
(June '83, C. maj. 15,515)		

NORTH E. 69,790

*R. F. Howell, C.	....	28,822
N. R. Anthony, S.D.P./All.		13,512
A. Earle, Lab.	....	10,765
M. G. Filgate, Grn.	....	960
C. maj.	....	15,310
(June '83, C. maj. 13,223)		

NORTH WEST E. 73,739

*H. C. Bellingham, C.	.....	29,393
C. Brocklebank-Fowler,		
S.D.P./All.	....	18,568
F. Dignan, Lab.	....	10,184
C. maj.	....	10,825
(June '83, C. maj. 3,147)		

SOUTH E. 78,372

*Rt. Hon. J. R. R. Mac-		
Gregor, O.B.E., C.	....	33,912
R. A. P. Carden, L./All.	...	21,494
L. Addison, Lab.	....	8,047
C. maj.	....	12,418
(June '83, C. maj. 12,135)		

SOUTH WEST E. 74,240

Mrs. G. P. Shephard, C.	..	32,519
M. Scott, L./All.	....	12,083
Ms. M. Page, Lab.	....	11,844
C. maj.	....	20,436
(June '83, C. maj. 14,910)		

Normanton (W. Yorks)
E. 62,899

*W. O'Brien, Lab.	....	23,303
M. D. M. Smith, C.	....	16,016
R. J. Macey, S.D.P./All.	..	7,717
Lab. maj.	....	7,287
(June '83, Lab. maj. 4,183)		

Northampton

NORTH E. 69,294

*A. R. Marlow, C.	....	24,816
O. J. Granfield, Lab.	.....	15,560
A. S. Rounthwaite, L./All.		10,690
M. Green, Grn.	....	471
S. Colling, W.R.P.	....	156
C. maj.	....	9,256
(June '83, C. maj. 9,860)		

SOUTH E. 76,071

*M. W. L. Morris, C.	.....	31,864
J. Dickie, Lab.	....	14,061
G. Hopkins, S.D.P./All.	..	10,639
Mrs. M. Hamilton, Grn.	..	647
C. maj.	....	17,803
(June '83, C. maj. 15,126)		

Northavon (Avon)
E. 78,483

*J. A. Cope, C.	....	34,224
Mrs. C. Willmore, L./All.	.	19,954
D. Norris, Lab.	....	8,762
C. maj.	....	14,270
(June '83, C. maj. 12,983)		

Norwich (Norfolk)

NORTH E. 62,725

*H. P. Thompson, C.	.....	22,772
Miss M. H. R. Honeyball,		
Lab.	....	14,996
T. P. Nicholls, L./All.	....	11,922
C. maj.	....	7,776
(June '83, C. maj. 5,879)		

SOUTH E. 64,421

J. L. Garrett, Lab.	....	19,666
*J. A. Powley, C.	....	19,330
C. J. M. Hardie, S.D.P./All.	12,896
Lab. maj.	....	336
(June '83, C. maj. 1,712)		

Norwood (Gtr. London)
E. 56,602

*J. D. Fraser, Lab.	....	18,359
D. C. R. Grieve, C.	....	13,636
M. M. Noble, S.D.P./All.	..	12,579
F. M. Jackson, R.A.B.I.E.S.		171
R. J. Hammond, C.D.	......	151
Lab. maj.	....	4,723
(June '83, Lab. maj. 2,883)		

Nottingham

EAST E. 68,266

*M. Knowles, C.	....	20,162
M. Aslam, Lab.	....	19,706
S. Parkhouse, L./All.	.....	6,887
K. Malik, R.F.	....	212
C. maj.	....	456
(June '83, C. maj. 1,464)		

NORTH E. 69,620

G. W. Allen, Lab.	....	22,713
*R. G. J. Ottaway, C.	.....	21,048
S. C. Fernando, S.D.P./All.	5,912
J. H. Peck, Comm.	....	879
Lab. maj.	....	1,665
(June '83, C. maj. 362)		

SOUTH E. 72,807

*M. M. Brandon-Bravo, C.	.	23,921
A. Simpson, Lab.	....	21,687
L. V. Williams, S.D.P./All.		7,517
C. maj.	....	2,234
(June '83, C. maj. 5,715)		

Nuneaton (Warwicks)
E. 68,287

*L. D. Stevens, M.B.E., C.	...	24,630
Mrs. V. A. Veness, Lab.	..	18,975
A. Trembath, S.D.P./All.	.	10,550
Dr. J. Morrissey, Grn.	....	719
C. maj.	....	5,655
(June '83, C. maj. 5,061)		

Old Bexley and Sidcup
(Gtr. London)
E. 50,831

*Rt. Hon. E. R. G. Heath,		
M.B.E., C.	....	24,350
T. H. Pearce, L./All.	......	8,076
H. J. A. Stoate, Lab.	.....	6,762
C. maj.	....	16,274
(June '83, C. maj. 12,718)		

Oldham (Gtr. Manchester)

CENTRAL AND ROYTON
E. 65,277

*J. A. Lamond, Lab.	......	21,759
J. A. Farquhar, C.	....	15,480
Mrs. A. Dunn, S.D.P./All.		7,956
Lab. maj.	....	6,279
(June '83, Lab. maj. 3,312)		

WEST E. 57,178

*M. H. Meacher, Lab.	.....	20,291
Mrs. J. M. Jacobs, C.	.....	14,324
Miss M. R. Mason, L./All.	.	6,478
Lab. maj.	....	5,967
(June '83, Lab. maj. 3,180)		

Orpington (Gtr. London)
E. 59,608

*I. R. Stanbrook, C.	......	27,261
J. H. Fryer, L./All.	....	14,529
S. J. Cowan, Lab.	....	5,020
C. maj.	....	12,732
(June '83, C. maj. 10,151)		

Oxford

EAST E. 62,145

A. D. Smith, Lab.	....	21,103
*S. J. Norris, C.	....	19,815
Mrs. M. Godden, L./All.	..	7,648
D. Dalton, Grn.	....	441
P. S. Mylvaganam, I.C.C.	.	60
Lab. maj.	....	1,288
(June '83, C. maj. 1,267)		

WEST AND ABINGDON *E.* 69,193
*J. H. C. Patten, C. 25,171
C. M. P. Huhne, *S.D.P./All.* 20,293
J. G. Power, *Lab.* 8,108
D. Smith, *Grn.* 695
C. maj. 4,878
(June '83, C. maj. 7,151)

Peckham (Gtr. London)
E. 59,261

*Ms. H. Harman, Lab. 17,965
Mrs. L. K. F. Ingram, *C.* .. 8,476
R. H. Shearman, *L./All.* ... 5,878
Miss D. Robinson, *Grn.* ... 628
Lab. maj. 9,489
(June '83, Lab. maj. 8,824)

Pendle (Lancs)
E. 63,588

*J. R. L. Lee, C. 21,009
Mrs. S. Renilson, *Lab.* 18,370
A. G. Lishman, *L./All.* ... 12,662
C. maj. 2,639
(June '83, C. maj. 6,135)

Penrith and the Border
(Cumbria)
E. 70,994

*D. J. Maclean, C. 33,148
D. J. Ivison, *L./All.* 15,782
J. M. P. Hutton, *Lab.* 6,075
C. maj. 17,366
(June '83, C. maj. 15,421)
(July '83, C. maj. 552)

Peterborough (Cambs)
E. 84,284

*Dr. B. S. Mawhinney, C. .. 30,624
A. MacKinlay, *Lab.* 20,840
D. W. Green, *L./All.* 9,984
N. A. Callaghan, *Grn.* 506
C. maj. 9,784
(June '83, C. maj. 10,439)

Plymouth (Devon)
DEVONPORT *E.* 64,741
*Rt. Hon. Dr. D. A. L. Owen,
S.D.P./All. 21,039
T. Jones, *C.* 14,569
I Flintoff, *Lab.* 14,166
S.D.P./All. maj. 6,470
(June '83, S.D.P./All. maj. 4,936)

DRAKE *E.* 51,186
*Miss J. E. Fookes, C. 16,195
D. Astor, *S.D.P./All.* 13,070
D. Jamieson, *Lab.* 9,451
Ms. P. Barber, *Grn.* 493
C. maj. 3,125
(June '83, C. maj. 8,585)

SUTTON *E.* 64,120
*Hon. A. K. M. Clark, C. .. 23,187
B. Tidy, *L./All.* 19,174
R. D. Maddern, *Lab.* 8,310
C. maj. 4,013
(June '83, C. maj. 11,687)

Pontefract and Castleford
(W. Yorks)
E. 64,414

*G. Lofthouse, Lab. 31,656
J H Mallins, *C.* 10,030
M. F. Taylor, *L./All.* 5,334
D. M. Lees, *R.F.* 295
Lab. maj. 21,626
(June '83, Lab. maj. 13,691)

Poole (Dorset)
E. 76,673

*J. D. Ward, C.B.E., C. 34,159
R. J. Whitley, *S.D.P./All.* . 19,351
M. Shutler, *Lab.* 5,901
C. maj. 14,808
(June '83, C. maj. 14,429)

Portsmouth (Hants)
NORTH *E.* 80,501
*P. H. S. Griffiths, C. 33,297
Mrs. E. Mitchell, *S.D.P./*
All. 14,896
D. Miles, *Lab.* 12,016
C. maj. 18,401
(June '83, C. maj. 17,999)

SOUTH *E.* 76,292
D. Martin, *C.* 23,534
*M. T. Hancock, S.D.P./All. 23,329
K. Gardiner, *Lab.* 7,047
R. Hughes, *657 Party* 455
C. maj. 205
(June '83, S.D.P./All. maj. 12,335)
(June '84, S.D.P./All. maj. 1,341)

Preston (Lancs)
E. 64,459

Mrs. A. Wise, *Lab.* 23,341
Dr. R. T. Chandran, *C.* ... 12,696
J. P. Wright, *L./All.* 8,452
Lab. maj. 10,645
(June '83, Lab. maj. 6,978)

Pudsey (W. Yorks)
E. 71,681

*J. G. D. Shaw, C. 25,457
J. P. F. Cummins, *L./All.* . 19,021
N. Taggart, *Lab.* 11,461
C. maj. 6,436
(June '83, C. maj. 5,314)

Putney (Gtr. London)
E. 63,108

*D. J. Mellor, C. 24,197
P. G. Hain, *Lab.* 17,290
Ms. S. Harlow, *L./All.* 5,934
S. Desorgher, *Grn.* 508
C. maj. 6,907
(June '83, C. maj. 5,019)

Ravensbourne (Gtr. London)
E. 59,365

*J. L. Hunt, C. 28,295
G. Campbell, *S.D.P./All.* .. 11,376
M. D'Arcy, *Lab.* 5,087
A. Waide, *B.N.* 184
C. maj. 16,919
(June '83, C. maj. 15,512)

Reading (Berks)
EAST *E.* 72,311
*Sir G. Vaughan, C. 28,515
Mrs. S. M. Baring, *S.D.P./*
All. 12,298
M. J. Salter, *Lab.* 11,371
P. J. Unsworth, *Grn.* 667
A. B. Shone, *C.S.* 125
C. maj. 16,217
(June '83, C. maj. 11,508)

WEST *E.* 70,391
*R. A. B. Durant, C. 28,122
K. H. Lock, *L./All.* 11,369
M. E. Orton, *Lab.* 10,819
E. P. Wilson, *Grn.* 542
C. maj. 16,753
(June '83, C. maj. 11,399)

Redcar (Cleveland)
E. 63,393

Dr. Marjorie Mowlam, *Lab.* 22,824
P. J. Bassett, *C.* 15,089
G. Nightingale, *S.D.P./All.* 10,298
Lab. maj. 7,735
(June '83, Lab. maj. 3,104)

Reigate (Surrey)
E. 71,940

*G. A. Gardiner, C. 30,925
Mrs. E. A. Pamplin, *S.D.P./*
All. 12,752
R. P. Spencer, *Lab.* 7,460
G. Brand, *Grn.* 1,026
C. maj. 18,173
(June '83, C. maj. 16,307)

Ribble Valley (Lancs)
E. 62,644

*Rt. Hon. D. C. Waddington,
Q.C., *C.* 30,136
M. Carr, *S.D.P./All.* 10,608
G. Pope, *Lab.* 8,781
C. maj. 19,528
(June '83, C. maj. 18,591)

Richmond and Barnes
(Gtr. London)
E. 54,700

*J. J. Hanley, C. 21,729
A. J. Watson, *L./All.* 19,963
M. D. Gold, *Lab.* 3,227
Miss C. M. Matthews, *Grn.* 610
C. maj. 1,766
(June '83, C. maj. 74)

Richmond (N. Yorks)
E. 79,277

*Rt. Hon. L. Brittan, Q.C.,
C. 34,995
D. Lloyd-Williams, *L./All.* 15,419
F. Robson, *Lab.* 6,737
C. maj. 19,576
(June '83, C. maj. 18,066)

Rochdale (Gtr. Manchester)
E. 68,703

*C. Smith, M.B.E., L./All. ... 22,245
D. Williams, *Lab.* 19,466
C. Condie, *C.* 9,561
L./All. maj. 2,779
(June '83, L./All. maj. 7,587)

Rochford (Essex)
E. 76,048

*Dr. M. Clark, C.	....	35,872
P. Young, L./All.	....	16,178
D. Weir, Lab.	....	7,308
C. maj.	....	19,694
(June '83, C. maj. 13,102)		

Romford (Gtr. London)
E. 55,668

*M. J. Neubert, C.	....	22,745
N. J. M. Smith, Lab.	.....	9,274
J. H. Bates, L./All.	....	8,195
F. J. Gibson, Grn.	....	385
C. maj.	....	13,471
(June '83, C. maj. 10,574)		

Romsey and Waterside (Hants)
E. 79,136

*M. K. B. Colvin, C.	....	35,303
A. T. Bloss, S.D.P./All.	...	20,031
S. J. Roberts, Lab.	....	7,213
C. maj.	....	15,272
(June '83, C. maj. 13,690)		

Rossendale and Darwen (Lancs)
E. 75,038

*D. A. Trippier, C.	....	28,056
Mrs. J. Anderson, Lab.	....	23,074
P. J. Hulse, L./All.	....	9,097
C. maj.	....	4,982
(June '83, C. maj. 8,821)		

Rotherham (S. Yorks)
E. 61,521

*J. S. Crowther, Lab.	......	25,422
J. C. C. Stevens, C.	....	9,410
P. J. Bowler, L./All.	......	7,766
Lab. maj.	....	16,012
(June '83, Lab. maj. 11,709)		

Rother Valley (S. Yorks)
E. 66,416

*K. J. Barron, Lab.	....	28,292
P. R. Rayner, C.	....	12,502
J. R. Boddy, S.D.P./All.	..	9,240
M. R. Driver, W.R.P.	.....	145
Lab. maj.	....	15,790
(June '83, Lab. maj. 8,625)		

Rugby and Kenilworth
(Warwicks)
E. 76,654

*J. F. Pawsey, C.	....	31,485
J. Airey, Lab.	....	15,221
D. R. Owen-Jones, L./All.	.	14,343
C. maj.	....	16,264
(June '83, C. maj. 14,241)		

Ruislip-Northwood
(Gtr. London)
E. 56,365

*J. A. D. Wilkinson, C.	....	27,418
Mrs. D. Darby, L./All.	....	10,447
Ms. H. A. Smith, Lab.	....	5,913
C. maj.	....	16,971
(June '83, C. maj. 12,982)		

Rushcliffe (Notts)
E. 72,797

*Rt. Hon. K. H. Clarke, Q.C.,		
C.	....	34,214
L. George, S.D.P./All.	....	13,375
P. Tipping, Lab.	....	9,631
Ms. H. Wright, Grn.	.....	991
C. maj.	....	20,839
(June '83, C. maj. 20,220)		

Rutland and Melton (Leics)
E. 77,846

*M. A. Latham, C.	....	37,073
R. C. Renold, L./All.	.....	14,051
L. C. Burke, Lab.	....	8,680
C. maj.	....	23,022
(June '83, C. maj. 18,353)		

Ryedale (N. Yorks)
E. 83,205

J. R. Greenway, C.	....	35,149
*Mrs. E. L. Shields, L./All.	.	25,409
J. Beighton, Lab.	....	5,340
C. maj.	....	9,740
(June '83, C. maj. 16,142)		
(May '86, L./All. maj. 4,940)		

Saffron Walden (Essex)
E. 73,185

*A. G. B. Haselhurst, C.	...	33,354
M. P. Hayes, L./All.	......	16,752
R. Gifford, Lab.	....	6,674
G. B. Hannah, Grn.	......	816
W. O. Smedley, C.M.N.H.Y.		217
C. maj.	....	16,602
(June '83, C. maj. 15,363)		

St. Albans (Herts)
E. 75,281

*P. B. Lilley, C.	....	31,726
A. S. B. Walkington, L./All.		20,845
A. McWalter, Lab.	....	6,922
Ms. E. V. Field, Grn.	.....	788
W. H. Pass, C.P.R.P.	.....	110
C. maj.	....	10,881
(June '83, C. maj. 8,561)		

St. Helens (Merseyside)

NORTH E. 70,836

*J. Evans, Lab.	....	28,989
Miss M. J. Libby, C.	.....	14,729
N. P. Derbyshire, L./All.	..	10,300
Lab. maj.	....	14,260
(June '83, Lab. maj. 9,259)		

SOUTH E. 69,449

*G. E. Bermingham, Lab.	..	27,027
A. J. Brown, C.	....	13,226
P. J. Briers, S.D.P./All.	..	9,252
Lab. maj.	....	13,801
(June '83, Lab. maj. 9,662)		

St. Ives (Cornwall)
E. 67,448

*D. A. Harris, C.	....	25,174
H. H. J. Carter, S.D.P./All.		17,619
I. Hope, Lab.	....	9,275
C. maj.	....	7,555
(June '83, C. maj. 7,859)		

Salford East
(Gtr. Manchester)
E. 58,087

*Rt. Hon. S. Orme, Lab.	...	22,555
C. W. H. McFall, C.	......	10,499
P. Keaveney, S.D.P./All.	.	5,105
S. G. Murray, W.R.P.	....	201
Lab. maj.	....	12,056
(June '83, Lab. maj. 9,541)		

Salisbury (Wilts)
E. 76,221

*S. R. Key, C.	....	31,612
P. A. Mitchell, S.D.P./All.		20,169
Ms. T. E. Seabourne, Lab.		5,455
S. W. Fletcher, Ind.	......	372
C. maj.	....	11,443
(June '83, C. maj. 7,174)		

Scarborough (N. Yorks)
E. 74,612

*Sir M. N. Shaw, C.	....	27,672
Mrs. H. Callan, S.D.P./All.		14,046
M. Wolstenholme, Lab.	..	12,913
C. maj.	....	13,626
(June '83, C. maj. 13,929)		

Sedgefield (Durham)
E. 60,866

*A. C. L. Blair, Lab.	.....	25,965
N. B. S. Hawkins, C.	.....	12,907
R. I. Andrew, S.D.P./All.	.	7,477
Lab. maj.	....	13,058
(June '83, Lab. maj. 8,281)		

Selby (N. Yorks)
E. 71,378

*Rt. Hon. M. J. H. Alison,		
C.	....	28,611
J. T. Grogan, Lab.	....	14,832
J. E. F. Longman, L./All.	.	12,010
C. maj.	....	13,779
(June '83, C. maj. 15,965)		

Sevenoaks (Kent)
E. 73,179

*G. M. Wolfson, C.	....	32,945
S. R. Jakobi, L./All.	......	15,600
G. A. Green, Lab.	....	7,379
C. maj.	....	17,345
(June '83, C. maj. 15,706)		

Sheffield (S. Yorks)

ATTERCLIFFE E. 67,051

*A. E. P. Duffy, Lab.	......	28,266
G. J. Perry, C.	....	11,075
Ms. H. E. Woolley, S.D.P./		
All.		9,549
Lab. maj.	....	17,191
(June '83, Lab. maj. 11,612)		

BRIGHTSIDE E. 64,982

D. Blunkett, Lab.	....	31,208
Miss M. C. Glyn, C.	......	7,017
J. A. Leeman, L./All.	.....	6,434
Lab. maj.	....	24,191
(June '83, Lab. maj. 15,209)		

CENTRAL *E.* 61,156
*R. G. Caborn, *Lab.* 25,872
B. Oxley, *C.* 6,530
Ms. F. C. Hornby, *S.D.P.*/
  All. 5,314
C. T. Dingle, *R.F.* 278
K. E. Petts, *Comm.* 203
  Lab. maj. 19,342
  (June '83, Lab. maj. 16,790)

HALLAM *E.* 74,158
C. I. Patnick, *C.* 25,649
P. J. Gold, *L.*/*All.* 18,012
M. C. Savani, *Lab.* 11,290
Ms. L. M. Spencer, *Grn.* .. 459
  C. maj. 7,637
  (June '83, C. maj. 11,774)

HEELEY *E.* 73,931
*W. Michie, *Lab.* 28,425
N. P. Mearing-Smith, *C.* .. 13,985
P. Moore, *S.D.P.*/*All.* 10,811
  Lab. maj. 14,440
  (June '83, Lab. maj. 8,368)

HILLSBOROUGH *E.* 76,312
*M. H. Flannery, *Lab.* 26,208
D. Chadwick, *L.*/*All.* 22,922
J. D. Sykes, *C.* 10,396
  Lab. maj. 3,286
  (June '83, Lab. maj. 1,546)

Sherwood (Notts)
E. 71,378

*A. S. Stewart, *C.* 26,816
W. S. G. Bach, *Lab.* 22,321
S. R. Thompstone, *S.D.P.*/
  All. 9,343
  C. maj. 4,495
  (June '83, C. maj. 658)

Shipley (W. Yorks)
E. 68,705

*Sir J. M. Fox, M.B.E., *C.* ... 26,941
W. J. L. Wallace, *L.*/*All.* ... 14,311
C. R. B. Butler, *Lab.* 12,669
C. M. Harris, *Grn.* 507
  C. maj. 12,630
  (June '83, C. maj. 11,445)

Shoreham (W. Sussex)
E. 71,318

*Rt. Hon. R. N. Luce, *C.* ... 33,660
J. A. Ingram, *L.*/*All.* 16,590
P. Godwin, *Lab.* 5,053
  C. maj. 17,070
  (June '83, C. maj. 15,766)

Shrewsbury and Atcham (Salop)
E. 70,689

*D. L. Conway, *C.* 26,027
R. Hutchison, *L.*/*All.* 16,963
Mrs. E. Owen, *Lab.* 10,797
G. Hardy, *Grn.* 660
  C. maj. 9,064
  (June '83, C. maj. 8,624)

Shropshire North
E. 77,122

*Rt. Hon. W. J. Biffen, *C.* .. 30,385
G. Smith, *L.*/*All.* 15,970
R. Hawkins, *Lab.* 11,866
  C. maj. 14,415
  (June '83, C. maj. 11,667)

Skipton and Ripon
(N. Yorks)
E. 72,199

D. M. Curry, *C.* 33,128
S. J. Cooksey, *L.*/*All.* 15,954
T. L. Whitfield, *Lab.* 6,264
Ms. L. S. Williams, *Grn.* .. 825
  C. maj. 17,174
  (June '83, C. maj. 15,046)

Slough (Berks)
E. 73,424

*J. A. Watts, *C.* 26,166
E. Lopez, *Lab.* 22,076
M. Goldstone, *S.D.P.*/*All* . 7,490
  C. maj. 4,090
  (June '83, C. maj. 3,106)

Solihull (W. Midlands)
E. 78,123

*J. M. Taylor, *C.* 35,844
G. E. Gadie, *L.*/*All.* 14,058
Mrs. S. E. Knowles, *Lab.* . 8,791
  C. maj. 21,786
  (June '83, C. maj. 17,394)

Somerton and Frome
(Somerset)
E. 68,773

*Hon. R. T. Boscawen, M.C.,
  C. 29,351
R. G. Morgan, *L.*/*All.* 19,813
I. S. Kelly, *Lab.* 5,461
  C. maj. 9,538
  (June '83, C. maj. 9,227)

Southampton (Hants)
ITCHEN *E.* 72,687
*C. R. Chope, O.B.E., *C.* ... 24,419
J. Y. Denham, *Lab.* 17,703
R. C. Mitchell, *S.D.P.*/*All.* 13,006
  C. maj. 6,716
  (June '83, C. maj. 5,290)

TEST *E.* 73,918
*S. J. A. Hill, *C.* 25,722
A. P. V. Whitehead, *Lab.* .. 18,768
Mrs. V. Rayner, *L.*/*All.* ... 11,950
  C. maj. 6,954
  (June '83, C. maj. 9,346)

Southend (Essex)
EAST *E.* 59,073
*E. M. Taylor, *C.* 23,753
H. J. Berkeley, *S.D.P.*/*All.* 9,906
D. R. Scully, *Lab.* 7,296
  C. maj. 13,847
  (June '83, C. maj. 10,691)

WEST *E.* 68,415
*Rt. Hon. H. P. G. Channon,
  C. 28,003
G. Grant, *L.*/*All.* 19,603
Mrs. A. Smith, *Lab.* 3,899
  C. maj. 8,400
  (June '83, C. maj. 8,033)

South Hams (Devon)
E. 78,583

*A. D. Steen, *C.* 34,218
R. F. Chave, *L.*/*All.* 21,072
*W. W. Hamilton, *Lab.* 5,060
C. G. Titmuss, *Grn.* 1,178
T. C. Langsford, *L.M.* 277
  C. maj. 13,146
  (June '83, C. maj. 12,401)

Southport (Merseyside)
E. 71,443

R. C. Fearn, *L.*/*All.* 26,110
N. M. Thomas, *C.* 24,261
Mrs. A. Moore, *Lab.* 3,483
J. R. G. Walker, *Grn.* 653
  L./*All. maj.* 1,849
  (June '83, C. maj. 5,039)

South Ribble (Lancs)
E. 72,177

*R. J. Atkins, *C.* 28,133
D. F. Roebuck, *Lab.* 19,703
J. A. Holleran, *L.*/*All.* 11,746
  C. maj. 8,430
  (June '83, C. maj. 12,659)

South Shields (Tyne & Wear)
E. 60,754

*Dr. D. G. Clark, *Lab.* 24,882
M. L. D. Fabricant, *C.* 11,031
Ms. M. Meling, *S.D.P.*/*All.* 6,654
E. G. Dunn, *Dem.* 408
  Lab. maj. 13,851
  (June '83, Lab. maj. 6,402)

Southwark and Bermondsey
(Gtr. London)
E. 55,438

*S. H. W. Hughes, *L.*/*All.* .. 17,072
J. Bryan, *Lab.* 14,293
O. Heald, *C.* 4,522
P. N. Power, *Comm.* 108
  L./*All. maj.* 2,779
  (June '83, L./All. maj. 5,164)

Spelthorne (Surrey)
E. 72,967

D. Wilshire, *C.* 32,440
Mrs. M. Cunningham,
  S.D.P./*All.* 12,390
D. F. J. Welfare, *Lab.* 9,227
  C. maj. 20,050
  (June '83, C. maj. 13,506)

Stafford
E. 72,431

*W. N. P. Cash, *C.* 29,541
C. B. Phipps, *S.D.P.*/*All.* .. 15,834
Ms. N. Hafccz, *Lab.* 12,177
  C. maj. 13,707
  (June '83, C. maj. 14,277)
  (May '84, C. maj. 3,980)

Staffordshire
MID *E.* 71,252
*B. J. Heddle, *C.* 28,644
C. R. St. Hill, *Lab.* 13,990
T. A. Jones, *L.*/*All.* 13,114
J. G. Bazeley, *Ind.* *C.* 836
  C. maj. 14,654
  (June '83, C. maj. 13,880)

MOORLANDS *E.* 74,302
*D. L. Knox, *C.* 31,613
Mrs. V. Ivers, *Lab.* 17,186
J. P. Corbett, *S.D.P.*/*All.* . 10,950
  C. maj. 14,427
  (June '83, C. maj. 16,566)

SOUTH *E.* 79,261
*P. T. Cormack, *C.* 37,708
Mrs. F. Oborski, *L.*/*All.* .. 12,440
P. Bateman, *Lab.* 11,805
  C. maj. 25,268
  (June '83, C. maj. 19,760)

SOUTH EAST *E.* 66,176
*D. L. Lightbown, C. 25,115
Miss E. Gluck, *S.D.P./All.* 14,230
D. Spilsbury, *Lab.* 13,874
C. maj. 10,885
(June '83, C. maj. 10,898)

Stalybridge and Hyde
(Gtr. Manchester)
E. 67,983

*T. Pendry, Lab. 24,401
R. N. Greenwood, *C.* 18,738
P. J. Ashenden, *S.D.P./All.* 7,311
Lab. maj. 5,663
(June '83, Lab. maj. 4,362)

Stamford and Spalding (Lincs)
E. 70,560

J. Q. Davies, *C.* 31,000
Miss R. Bryan, *L./All.* 17,009
P. E. Lowe, *Lab.* 6,882
C. maj. 13,991
(June '83, C. maj. 11,756)

Stevenage (Herts)
E. 69,525

*T. J. R. Wood, C. 23,541
B. R. M. Stoneham, *S.D.P./All.* 18,201
M. R. C. Withers, *Lab.* ... 14,229
C. maj. 5,340
(June '83, C. maj. 1,755)

Stockport (Gtr. Manchester)
E. 60,059

*A. R. Favell, C. 19,410
Mrs. S. Haines, *Lab.* 16,557
J. L. Begg, *S.D.P./All.* 10,365
M. Shipley, *Grn.* 573
C. maj. 2,853
(June '83, C. maj. 5,786)

Stockton (Cleveland)
NORTH *E.* 70,329
*F. Cook, Lab. 26,043
D. J. C. Faber, *C.* 17,242
N. F. G. Bosanquet, *S.D.P./All.* 9,712
Lab. maj. 8,801
(June '83, Lab. maj. 1,870)

SOUTH *E.* 75,279
T. R. Devlin, *C.* 20,833
*I. W. Wrigglesworth, S.D.P./All. 20,059
J. M. Scott, *Lab.* 18,600
C. maj. 774
(June '83, S.D.P./All. maj. 102)

Stoke-on-Trent (Staffs)
CENTRAL *E.* 65,987
*M. Fisher, Lab. 23,842
D. Stone, *C.* 14,072
I. Cundy, *S.D.P./All.* 7,462
Lab. maj. 9,770
(June '83, Lab. maj. 8,250)

NORTH *E.* 74,184
Ms. J. L. Walley, *Lab.* 25,459
R. Davies, *C.* 16,946
S. J. Simmonds, *S.D.P./All.* 11,665
Lab. maj. 8,513
(June '83, Lab. maj. 8,203)

SOUTH *E.* 70,806
*Rt. Hon. J. Ashley, C.H., Lab. 24,794
D. Hartshorne, *C.* 19,741
P. Wild, *L./All.* 7,669
Lab. maj. 5,053
(June '83, Lab. maj. 7,105)

Stratford-upon-Avon (Warwicks)
E. 81,263

*A. T. Howarth, C.B.E., C. ... 38,483
D. G. Cowcher, *L./All.* ... 17,318
R. H. Rhodes, *Lab.* 6,335
C. maj. 21,165
(June '83, C. maj. 17,917)

Streatham (Gtr. London)
E. 60,519

*W. J. M. Shelton, C. 18,916
Ms. A. Tapsall, *Lab.* 16,509
M. Tuffrey, *L./All.* 6,663
C. maj. 2,407
(June '83, C. maj. 5,902)

Stretford (Gtr. Manchester)
E. 57,568

*A. J. Lloyd, Lab. 22,831
D. Dougherty, *C.* 13,429
D. Lee, *S.D.P./All.* 5,125
Lab. maj. 9,402
(June '83, Lab. maj. 4,342)

Stroud (Glos)
E. 81,275

R. M. Knapman, *C.* 32,883
A. A. Walker-Smith, *L./All.* 20,508
T. Levitt, *Lab.* 12,145
C. maj. 12,375
(June '83, C. maj. 11,714)

Suffolk
CENTRAL *E.* 79,199
*M. N. Lord, C. 32,422
T. Dale, *L./All.* 16,132
M. Walker, *Lab.* 11,817
C. maj. 16,290
(June '83, C. maj. 14,731)

COASTAL *E.* 75,684
*Rt. Hon. J. S. Gummer, C. 32,834
Mrs. J. M. Miller, *S.D.P./All.* 17,554
Mrs. S. A. Reeves, *Lab.* ... 7,534
J. W. Holloway, *Grn.* 1,049
C. maj. 15,280
(June '83, C. maj. 15,622)

SOUTH *E.* 81,954
*T. S. K. Yeo, C. 33,972
C. M. N. Bradford, *L./All.* 17,729
A. C. Bavington, *Lab.* 11,876
C. maj. 16,243
(June '83, C. maj. 11,269)

Sunderland
(Tyne & Wear)
NORTH *E.* 75,674
*R. A. Clay, Lab. 29,767
I. S. Picton, *C.* 15,095
T. Jenkinson, *L./All.* 8,518
Lab. maj. 14,672
(June '83, Lab. maj. 7,196)

SOUTH *E.* 74,947
C. J. Mullin, *Lab.* 28,823
G. E. Howe, *C.* 16,210
K. Hudson, *S.D.P./All.* ... 7,768
D. N. Jacques, *Grn.* 516
Lab. maj. 12,613
(June '83, Lab. maj. 5,548)

Surbiton (Gtr. London)
E. 45,428

*R. P. Tracey, C. 19,861
D. T. Burke, *S.D.P./All.* .. 10,120
A. McGowan, *Lab.* 5,111
Ms. J. Vidler, *Grn.* 465
C. maj. 9,741
(June '83, C. maj. 8,749)

Surrey
EAST *E.* 59,528
*Rt. Hon. Sir R. E. G. Howe, Q.C., C. 29,126
M. A. J. Anderson, *L./All.* 11,000
M. Davis, *Lab.* 4,779
D. Newell, *Grn.* 1,044
C. maj. 18,126
(June '83, C. maj. 15,436)

NORTH WEST *E.* 83,083
*W. M. J. Grylls, C. 38,535
C. Brodie, *L./All.* 14,960
J. Cooper, *Lab.* 6,751
C. maj. 23,575
(June '83, C. maj. 21,018)

SOUTH WEST *E.* 73,018
*Mrs. V. H. B. M. Bottomley, C. 34,024
G. D. Scott, *L./All.* 19,681
J. K. P. Evers, *Lab.* 3,224
M. J. Green, *Ind. C.* 299
C. maj. 14,343
(June '83, C. maj. 14,351)
(May '84, C. maj. 2,599)

Sussex Mid
E. 80,147

*R. T. Renton, C. 37,781
N. S. E. Westbrook, *L./All.* 19,489
R. Hughes, *Lab.* 4,573
C. maj. 18,292
(June '83, C. maj. 16,744)

Sutton and Cheam
(Gtr. London)
E. 63,850

*D. N. Macfarlane, C. 29,710
R. D. Grieg, *L./All.* 13,992
Ms. L. Monk, *Lab.* 5,202
C. maj. 15,718
(June '83, C. maj. 10,264)

Sutton Coldfield (W. Midlands)
E. 72,329

*Rt. Hon. P. N. Fowler, C. . 34,475
T. Bick, *L./All.* 13,292
P. McLoughlin, *Lab.* 6,104
C. maj. 21,183
(June '83, C. maj. 18,984)

Swindon (Wilts)
E. 86,150

*S. C. Coombs, C.	....	29,385
Ms. G. Johnston, *Lab.*	....	24,528
D. J. Scott, *S.D.P./All.*	..	13,114
C. maj.	....	4,857
(June '83, C. maj. 1,395)		

Tatton (Cheshire)
E. 71,904

*M. N. Hamilton, C.	......	30,128
Ms. B. Gaskin, *S.D.P./All.*		13,034
Ms. H. A. Blears, *Lab.*	....	11,760
M. G. Gibson, *F.P.*	....	263
C. maj.	....	17,094
(June '83, C. maj. 13,960)		

Taunton (Somerset)
E. 74,145

D. J. Nicholson, C.	....	30,248
M. A. K. Cocks, *S.D.P./All.*		19,868
Dr. G. Reynolds, *Lab.*	....	8,754
C. maj.	....	10,380
(June '83, C. maj. 12,567)		

Teignbridge (Devon)
E. 71,872

*P. C. M. Nicholls, C.	.....	30,693
R. D. Ryder, *L./All.*	....	20,268
J. Greenwood, *Lab.*	......	6,413
A. Hope, *L.M.*	....	312
C. maj.	....	10,425
(June '83, C. maj. 8,218)		

Thanet (Kent)
NORTH   E. 69,723

*R. J. Gale, C.	....	29,225
N. R. M. Cranston, *S.D.P./ All.*		11,745
A. M. Bretman, *Lab.*	.....	8,395
D. R. Condor, *Grn.*	....	996
C. maj.	....	17,480
(June '83, C. maj. 14,545)		

SOUTH   E. 62,761

*J. W. P. Aitken, C.	....	25,135
W. H. Pitt, *L./All.*	....	11,452
C. Wright, *Lab.*	....	9,673
C. maj.	....	13,683
(June '83, C. maj. 14,051)		

Thurrock (Essex)
E. 67,594

T. S. Janman, C.	....	20,527
Dr. O. A. McDonald, *Lab.*		19,837
D. S. Benson, *S.D.P./All.*	.	7,970
C. maj.	....	690
(June '83, Lab. maj. 1,722)		

Tiverton (Devon)
E. 68,210

*R. J. Maxwell-Hyslop, C.	.	29,875
D. J. Morrish, *L./All.*	....	20,663
Mrs. J. A. Northam, *Lab.*	..	3,400
W. J. Jones, *L.A.O.*	......	434
C. maj.	....	9,212
(June '83, C. maj. 7,886)		

Tonbridge and Malling (Kent)
E. 76,797

*Rt. Hon. J. P. Stanley, C.	.	33,990
M. J. Ward, *S.D.P./All.*	..	17,561
D. G. Still, *Lab.*	....	7,803
M. D. S. Easter, *B.N.*	.....	369
C. maj.	....	16,429
(June '83, C. maj. 13,520)		

Tooting (Gtr. London)
E. 68,116

*T. M. Cox, *Lab.*	....	21,457
M. A. Winter, *C.*	....	20,016
J. N. Ambache, *S.D.P./All.*		6,423
Ms. M. Vickery, *Grn.*	.....	621
Lab. maj.	....	1,441
(June '83, Lab. maj. 2,659)		

Torbay (Devon)
E. 70,435

R. W. S. Allason, C.	......	29,029
N. D. Bye, *L./All.*	....	20,209
G. R. Taylor, *Lab.*	....	4,538
C. maj.	....	8,820
(June '83, C. maj. 6,555)		

Tottenham (Gtr. London)
E. 76,092

B. A. L. Grant, *Lab.*	......	21,921
P. L. Murphy, *C.*	....	17,780
S. Etherington, *L./All.*	...	8,983
D. Nicholls, *Grn.*	....	744
P. Nealon, *Gait. Lab.*	.....	638
Ms. C. L. Dixon, *W.R.P.*	..	205
Lab. maj.	....	4,141
(June '83, Lab. maj. 9,396)		

Truro (Cornwall)
E. 72,432

*M. O. J. Taylor, *L./All.*	...	28,368
N. F. St. Aubyn, *C.*	......	23,615
J. R. King, *Lab.*	....	5,882
L./All. maj	....	4,753
(June '83, L./All. maj. 10,480)		
(March '87, L./All. maj. 14,617)		

Tunbridge Wells (Kent)
E. 76,291

*Sir P. B. B. Mayhew, Q.C., C.		33,111
Mrs. D. A. Buckrell, *L./All.*		16,989
P. L. Sloman, *Lab.*	....	6,555
C. maj.	....	16,122
(June '83, C. maj. 15,126)		

Twickenham (Gtr. London)
E. 64,661

*T. F. H. Jessel, C.	....	27,331
J. Waller, *L./All.*	....	20,204
Ms. V. C. M. Vaz, *Lab.*	..	4,415
D. S. Batchelor, *Grn.*	.....	746
C. maj.	....	7,127
(June '83, C. maj. 4,792)		

Tyne Bridge
(Tyne & Wear)
E. 58,152

*D. G. Clelland, *Lab.*	......	23,131
M. W. Bates, *C.*	....	7,558
J. C. Mansfield, *S.D.P./All.*		6,005
Lab. maj.	....	15,573
(June '83, Lab. maj. 11,693)		
(Dec '85, Lab. maj. 6,575)		

Tynemouth
(Tyne & Wear)
E. 74,407

*N. G. Trotter, C.	....	25,113
P. Cosgrove, *Lab.*	....	22,530
D. F. Mayhew, *L./All.*	....	10,446
C. maj.	....	2,583
(June '83, C. maj. 9,609)		

Upminster (Gtr. London)
E. 66,613

*Sir N. C. Bonsor, bt., C.	..	27,946
J. Martin, *S.D.P./All.*	....	11,089
D. R. O'Flynn, *Lab.*	......	11,069
C. maj.	....	16,857
(June '83, C. maj. 12,814)		

Uxbridge (Gtr. London)
E. 63,157

*J. M. Shersby, C.	....	27,292
D. Keys, *Lab.*	....	11,322
A. Goodman, *S.D.P./All.*	.	9,164
I. Flindall, *Grn.*	....	549
C. maj.	....	15,970
(June '83, C. maj. 12,837)		

Vauxhall (Gtr. London)
E. 66,538

*S. K. Holland, *Lab.*	......	21,364
D. R. Lidington, *C.*	......	12,345
S. H. V. Acland, *S.D.P./All.*		7,764
Ms. J. Owens, *Grn.*	......	770
D. J. S. Cook, *Comm.*	.....	223
K. Oluremi, *R.F.*	....	117
Lab. maj.	....	9,019
(June '83, Lab. maj 7,780)		

Wakefield (W. Yorks)
E. 69,580

D. M. Hinchliffe, *Lab.*	....	24,509
N. J. Hazell, *C.*	....	21,720
Dr. L. Kamal, *S.D.P./All*	.	6,350
Lab. maj.	....	2,789
(June '83, Lab. maj. 360)		

Wallasey (Merseyside)
E. 67,216

*Mrs. L. Chalker, C.	......	22,791
L. Duffy, *Lab.*	....	22,512
J. K. Richardson, *S.D.P./ All.*		8,363
C. maj.	....	279
(June '83, C. maj. 6,708)		

Wallsend (Tyne & Wear)
E. 76,688

*W. E. Garrett, *Lab.*	....	32,709
D. Milburn, *C.*	....	13,325
Mrs. J. Phylactou, *S.D.P./ All.*		11,508
Lab. maj.	....	19,384
(June '83, Lab. maj. 12,514)		

Walsall (W. Midlands)
NORTH   E. 68,331

*D. J. Winnick, *Lab.*	......	21,458
Mrs. L. Hertz, *C.*	....	19,668
I. Shires, *L./All.*	....	9,285
Lab. maj.	....	1,790
(June '83, Lab. maj. 2,824)		

SOUTH   E. 66,746

*B. T. George, *Lab.*	....	22,629
G. E. Postles, *C.*	....	21,513
L. A. King, *L./All.*	....	6,241
Lab. maj.	....	1,116
(June '83, Lab. maj. 702)		

Walthamstow (Gtr. London)
E. 48,691

H. H. F. Summerson, *C.*	..	13,748
*E. P. Deakins, *Lab.*	......	12,236
P. L. Leighton, *S.D.P./All.*		8,852
Dr. Z. I. Malik, *D.C.*	......	396
C. maj.	....	1,512
(June '83, Lab. maj. 1,305)		

Wansbeck (Nthmb)
E. 62,639

*J. Thompson, *Lab.*	......	28,080
Mrs. S. Mitchell, *L./All.*	..	11,291
D. Walton, *C.*	....	9,490
Lab. maj.	....	16,789
(June '83, Lab. maj. 7,831)		

Wansdyke (Avon)
E. 75,239

*J. H. Aspinwall, *C.*	....	31,537
R. B. Blackmore, *L./All.*	..	15,393
I. White, *Lab.*	....	14,231
C. maj.	....	16,144
(June '83, C. maj. 13,066)		

Wanstead and Woodford
(Gtr. London)
E. 57,921

J. N. Arbuthnot, *C.*	......	25,701
J. R. Bastick *L./All.*	......	9,289
Mrs. L. Hilton, *Lab.*	.....	6,958
C. maj.	....	16,412
(June '83, C. maj. 14,354)		

Wantage (Oxon)
E. 66,499

*R. V. Jackson, *C.*	....	27,951
Mrs. W. Tumin, *S.D.P./All.*		15,795
S. Ladyman, *Lab.*	....	8,055
C. maj.	....	12,156
(June '83, C. maj. 10,125)		

Warley (W. Midlands)

EAST E. 55,706

*A. M. W. Faulds, *Lab.*	...	19,428
A. Antoniou, *C.*	....	13,843
J. J. Jordan, *S.D.P./All.*	..	5,396
Lab. maj.	....	5,585
(June '83, Lab. maj. 3,391)		

WEST E. 57,526

*Rt. Hon. P. K. Archer, Q.C., *Lab.*		19,825
W. Williams, *C.*	....	14,432
Miss E. Todd, *L./All.*	.....	6,027
Lab. maj.	....	5,393
(June '83, Lab. maj. 5,268)		

Warrington (Cheshire)

NORTH E. 75,627

*E. D. H. Hoyle, *Lab.*	......	27,422
L. Jones, *C.*	....	19,409
C. Bithel, *S.D.P./All.*	....	10,046
Lab. maj.	....	8,013
(June '83, Lab. maj. 5,277)		

SOUTH E. 76,219

C. J. Butler, *C,*	....	24,809
A. Booth, *Lab.*	....	21,200
I. Marks, *L./All.*	....	13,112
C. maj.	....	3,609
(June '83, C. maj. 6,465)		

Warwick and Leamington
E. 72,763

*Sir D. G. Smith, *C.*	....	27,530
K. P. O'Sullivan, *S.D.P./All.*		13,548
Ms. A. Christina, *Lab.*	...	13,019
Ms. J. A. Alty, *Grn.*	......	1,214
C. maj.	....	13,982
(June '83, C. maj. 13,032)		

Warwickshire

NORTH E. 70,687

*Hon. F. A. A. Maude, *C.*	..	25,453
M. O'Brien, *Lab.*	....	22,624
Mrs. S. J. Neale, *S.D.P./All.*		8,382
C. maj.	....	2,829
(June '83, C. maj. 2,585)		

Watford (Herts)
E. 73,540

*W. A. T. T. Garel-Jones, *C.*	....	27,912
M. J. Jackson, *Lab.*	......	16,176
Mrs. F. M. Beckett, *S.D.P./All.*	....	13,202
C. maj.	....	11,736
(June '83, C. maj. 12,006)		

Waveney (Suffolk)
E. 81,889

D. J. Porter, *C.*	....	31,067
J. A. Lark, *Lab.*	....	19,284
D. Beaven, *S.D.P./All.*	...	13,845
C. maj.	....	11,783
(June '83, C. maj. 14,298)		

Wealden (E. Sussex)
E. 73,057

*Sir G. J. Johnson Smith, *C.*	....	35,154
D. Sinclair, *S.D.P./All.*	..	15,044
C. Ward, *Lab.*	....	4,563
C. maj.	....	20,110
(June '83, C. maj. 17,185)		

Wellingborough (Northants)
E. 70,450

*P. D. Fry, *C.*	....	29,038
J. Currie, *Lab.*	....	14,968
L. E. Stringer, *L./All.*	....	11,047
C. maj.	....	14,070
(June '83, C. maj. 12,056)		

Wells (Somerset)
E. 67,195

*D. P. Heathcoat-Amory, *C.*		28,624
A. A. S. Butt Philip, *L./All.*		20,083
P. James, *Lab.*	....	4,637
J. S. Fish, *Falk.*	....	134
C. maj.	....	8,541
(June '83, C. maj. 6,575)		

Welwyn Hatfield (Herts)
E. 73,607

D. J. Evans, *C.*	....	27,164
Miss L. P. Granshaw, *S.D.P./All.*		16,261
C. R. Pond, *Lab.*	....	15,699
B. I. Dyson, *Ind. C.*	......	401
C. maj.	....	10,903
(June '83, C. maj. 12,246)		

Wentworth (S. Yorks)
E. 63,886

*P. Hardy, *Lab.*	....	30,205
W. J. Hague, *C.*	....	10,113
D. M. Eglin, *S.D.P./All.*	..	6,031
Lab. maj.	....	20,092
(June '83, Lab. maj. 15,935)		

West Bromwich (W. Midlands)

EAST E. 58,239

*P. C. Snape, *Lab.*	....	18,162
R. F. Woodhouse, *C.*	.....	17,179
M. G. Smith, *L./All.*	......	7,268
Lab. maj.	....	983
(June '83, Lab. maj. 298)		

WEST E. 58,944

*Miss B. Boothroyd, *Lab.*	...	19,925
F. A. Betteridge, *C.*	......	14,672
A. Collingbourne, *S.D.P./All.*	....	4,877
Lab. maj.	....	5,253
(June '83, Lab. maj. 6,639)		

Westbury (Wilts)
E. 84,860

*D. M. Walters, M.B.E., *C.*	..	34,256
D. J. Hughes, *L./All.*	.....	24,159
H. W. Thomas, *Lab.*	......	7,982
C. maj.	....	10,097
(June '83, C. maj. 8,506)		

Westminster North
(Gtr. London)
E. 59,263

*J. D. Wheeler, *C.*	....	19,941
Ms. J. F. Edwards, *Lab.*	..	16,631
R. J. De Ste Croix, *S.D.P./All.*	......	5,116
D. Stutchfield, *Grn.*	......	450
C. maj.	....	3,310
(June '83, C. maj. 1,710)		

Westmorland and Lonsdale
(Cumbria)
E. 70,237

*Rt. Hon. T. M. Jopling, *C.* ..		30,259
S. Collins, *L./All.*	....	15,339
C. Halfpenny, *Lab.*	......	6,968
C. maj.	....	14,920
(June '83, C. maj. 16,587)		

Weston-super-Mare (Avon)
E. 76,341

*A. W. Wiggin, T.D., *C.*	...	28,547
J. R. Crockford-Hawley, *S.D.P./All.*	....	20,549
P. J. Loach, *Lab.*	....	6,584
Dr. R. H. Lawson, *Grn.*	...	2,067
C. maj.	....	7,998
(June '83, C. maj. 9,491)		

Wigan (Gtr. Manchester)
E. 72,064

*R. Stott, C.B.E., *Lab.*	......	33,955
K. R. Wade, *C.*	....	13,493
K. J. White, *L./All.*	......	7,732
Lab. maj.	....	20,462
(June '83, Lab. maj. 17,305)		

Wiltshire North
E. 80,712

*R. F. Needham, C.	35,309
C. S. M. Graham, L./All.	24,370
Mrs. C. Reid, Lab.	4,343
C. maj.	10,939
(June '83, C. maj. 7,232)	

Wimbledon (Gtr. London)
E. 63,353

Dr. C. Goodson-Wickes, C.	24,538
A. C. Slade, L./All.	13,237
Ms. C. M. Bickerstaff, Lab.	10,428
C. maj.	11,301
(June '83, C. maj. 11,546)	

Winchester (Hants)
E. 76,507

*J. E. D. D. Browne, C.	32,195
J. L. MacDonald, S.D.P./All.	24,716
F. C. Inglis, Lab.	4,028
Ms. J. P. Walker, Grn.	565
C. maj.	7,479
(June '83, C. maj. 13,047)	

Windsor and Maidenhead
(Berks)
E. 79,319

*Dr. A. Glyn, E.R.D., C.	33,980
S. J. Jackson, L./All.	16,144
Ms. H. B. De Lyon, Lab.	6,678
W. O. Board, Ind. C.	1,938
P. Gordon, Grn.	711
Ms. P. H. Stephenson, B.T.	328
C. maj.	17,836
(June '83, C. maj. 18,203)	

Wirral (Merseyside)

SOUTH E. 62,251

*G. B. Porter, C.	24,821
J. S. Swarbrooke, Lab.	13,858
P. N. Gilchrist, L./All.	10,779
C. maj.	10,963
(June '83, C. maj. 13,838)	

WEST E. 63,597

*D. J. F. Hunt, M.B.E., C.	25,736
A. H. Dunn, Lab.	13,013
A. J. Brame, L./All.	10,015
D. Burton, Grn.	806
C. maj.	12,723
(June '83, C. maj. 15,151)	

Witney (Oxon)
E. 75,284

*Rt. Hon. D. R. Hurd, C.B.E., C.	33,458
Miss M. E. Burton, L./All.	14,994
Ms. C. Collette, Lab.	9,733
C. maj.	18,464
(June '83, C. maj. 12,712)	

Woking (Surrey)
E. 82,476

*C. G. D. Onslow, C.	35,990
P. Goldenberg, L./All.	19,446
Miss A. J. Pollack, Lab.	6,537
C. maj.	16,544
(June '83, C. maj. 16,237)	

Wokingham (Berks)
E. 85,474

J. A. Redwood, C.	39,808
J. C. Leston, L./All.	19,421
P. J. Morgan, Lab.	5,622
C. maj.	20,387
(June '83, C. maj. 15,698)	

Wolverhampton (W. Midlands)
NORTH EAST E. 63,464

Mrs. M. P. Hicks, C.	19,857
K. Purchase, Lab.	19,653
M. Pearson, L./All.	7,623
C. maj.	204
(June '83, Lab. maj. 214)	

SOUTH EAST E. 55,710

D. Turner, Lab.	19,760
J. P. Mellor, C.	13,362
R. F. Whitehouse, L./All.	7,258
Lab. maj.	6,398
(June '83, Lab. maj. 5,012)	

SOUTH WEST E. 68,586

*N. W. Budgen, C.	26,235
R. Lawrence, Lab.	15,917
B. Lamb, S.D.P./All.	9,616
C. maj.	10,318
(June '83, C. maj. 11,520)	

Woodspring (Avon)
E. 76,289

*Sir P. Dean, C.	34,134
Mrs. C. R. Coleman, L./All.	16,282
D. L. T. Chapple, Lab.	8,717
Dr. B. R. Keeble, Grn.	1,208
C. maj.	17,852
(June '83, C. maj. 15,132)	

Woolwich (Gtr. London)
E. 58,071

*J. C. Cartwright, S.D.P./All.	17,137
J. Austin Walker, Lab.	15,200
A. Salter, C.	8,723
S.D.P./All. maj.	1,937
(June '83, S.D.P./All. maj. 2,725)	

Worcester
E. 68,980

*Rt. Hon. P. E. Walker, M.B.E., C.	25,504
M. J. Webb, Lab.	15,051
J. J. Caiger, S.D.P./All.	12,386
C. maj.	10,453
(June '83, C. maj. 10,871)	

Worcestershire

MID E. 80,591

*M. E. Forth, C.	31,854
P. Pinfield, Lab.	16,943
E. Harwood, S.D.P./All.	12,954
C. maj.	14,911
(June '83, C. maj. 14,205)	

SOUTH E. 77,237

*W. M. H. Spicer, C.	32,277
P. J. Chandler, L./All.	18,632
R. J. Garnett, Lab.	6,374
G. M. H. Woodford, Grn.	1,089
C. maj.	13,645
(June '83, C. maj. 11,389)	

Workington (Cumbria)
E. 56,911

*D. N. Campbell-Savours, Lab.	24,019
Miss A. C. B. McIntosh, C.	17,000
G. W. Badger, L./All.	4,853
Lab. maj.	7,019
(June '83, Lab. maj. 7,128)	

Worsley (Gtr. Manchester)
E. 73,208

*T. Lewis, Lab.	27,157
Mrs. V. Horman, C.	19,820
D. Cowpe, L./All.	9,507
Lab. maj.	7,337
(June '83, Lab. maj. 4,139)	

Worthing (W. Sussex)
E. 77,000

*Rt. Hon. T. L. Higgins, C.	34,573
B. A. Clare, L./All.	16,072
J. Deen, Lab.	5,387
C. maj.	18,501
(June '83, C. maj. 15,253)	

The Wrekin (Salop)
E. 82,520

B. J. Grocott, Lab.	27,681
*P. W. Hawksley, C.	26,225
G. Cook, S.D.P./All.	10,737
Lab. maj.	1,456
(June '83, C. maj. 1,331)	

Wycombe (Bucks)
E. 71,918

*R. W. Whitney, O.B.E., C.	28,209
T. E. G. Hayhoe, S.D.P./All.	14,390
J. R. W. Huddart, Lab.	9,773
C. maj.	13,819
(June '83, C. maj. 13,197)	

Wyre (Lancs)
E. 67,066

K. D. R. Mans, C.	26,800
I. C. Murdoch, S.D.P./All.	12,139
P. Ainscough, Lab.	10,725
R. Brown, Grn.	874
C. maj.	14,661
(June '83, C. maj. 14,811)	

Wyre Forest (H & W)
E. 70,784

A. M. V. Coombs, C.	25,877
A. J. Batchelor, L./All.	18,653
N. Knowles, Lab.	10,365
C. maj.	7,224
(June '83, C. maj. 8,177)	

Yeovil (Somerset)
E. 70,390

*J. J. D. Ashdown, L./All.	28,841
G. D. S. Sandeman, C.	23,141
J. Fitzmaurice, Lab.	4,099
L./All. maj.	5,700
(June '83, L./All. maj. 3,406)	

York (N. Yorks)
E. 79,297

*C. R. Gregory, C.	25,880
H. Bayley, Lab.	25,733
J. V. Cable, S.D.P./All.	9,898
A. D. Dunnett, Grn.	637
C. maj.	147
(June '83, C. maj. 3,647)	

WALES

Aberavon (W. Glam)
E. 52,280

*Rt. Hon. J. Morris, Q.C., Lab. 27,126
Mrs. M. Harris, L./All. ... 6,517
P. Warrick, C. 5,861
Miss A. Howells, P.C. 1,124
　Lab. maj. 20,609
　(June '83, Lab. maj. 15,539)

Alyn and Deeside (Clwyd)
E. 58,674

*S. B. Jones, Lab. 22,916
N. J. Twilley, C. 16,500
E. C. H. Owen, S.D.P./All. 7,273
J. D. Rogers, P.C. 478
　Lab. maj. 6,416
　(June '83, Lab. maj. 1,368)

Blaenau Gwent
E. 56,011

*Rt. Hon. M. M. Foot, Lab. .. 32,820
A. R. Taylor, C. 4,959
D. I. McBride, L./All. 3,847
S. Morgan, P.C. 1,621
　Lab. maj. 27,861
　(June '83, Lab. maj. 23,705)

Brecon and Radnor (Powys)
E. 49,394

*R. A. L. Livsey, L./All. ... 14,509
J. P. Evans, C. 14,453
F. R. Willey, Lab. 12,180
J. H. Davies, P.C. 535
　L./All. maj. 56
　(June '83, C. maj. 8,784)
　(July '84, L./All. maj. 559)

Bridgend (Mid Glam)
E. 57,389

W. J. Griffiths, Lab. 21,893
*P. C. Hubbard-Miles, C. .. 17,513
R. Smart, S.D.P./All. 5,590
Miss L. McAllister, P.C. .. 1,065
　Lab. maj. 4,380
　(June '83, C. maj. 1,327)

Caernarfon (Gwynedd)
E. 45,661

*D. W. Wigley, P.C. 20,338
F. F. E. Aubel, C. 7,536
D. Rhys Williams, Lab. ... 5,632
J. H. Parsons, L./All. 2,103
　P.C. maj. 12,802
　(June '83, P.C. maj. 10,989)

Caerphilly (Mid Glam)
E. 64,154

*R. Davies, Lab. 28,698
M. E. Powell, C. 9,531
M. G. Butlin, L./All. 6,923
L. G. Whittle, P.C. 3,955
　Lab. maj. 19,167
　(June '83, Lab. maj. 11,553)

Cardiff (S. Glam)
CENTRAL　E. 52,980

*I. Grist, C. 15,241
J. O. Jones, Lab. 13,255
M. J. German, L./All. 12,062
Ms. S. M. Caiach, P.C. 535
　C. maj. 1,986
　(June '83, C. maj. 3,452)

NORTH　E. 54,704

*G. H. Jones, C. 20,061
S. H. Tarbet, Lab. 11,827
A. W. Jeremy, S.D.P./All. 11,725
Ms. E. M. Bush, P.C. 692
　C. maj. 8,234
　(June '83, C. maj. 6,848)

SOUTH AND PENARTH　E. 58,714
A. E. Michael, Lab. 20,956
G. J. J. Neale, C. 16,382
Mrs. J. E. Randerson, L./All. 6,900
Ms. S. A. Edwards, P.C. .. 599
　Lab. maj. 4,574
　(June '83, Lab. maj. 2,276)

WEST　E. 57,363
H. R. Morgan, Lab. 20,329
*S. Terlezki, C. 16,284
R. G. Drake, S.D.P./All. .. 7,300
P. J. Keelan, P.C. 736
　Lab. maj. 4,045
　(June '83, C. maj. 1,774)

Carmarthen (Dyfed)
E. 65,252

A. W. Williams, Lab. 19,128
R. Richards, C. 14,811
H. T. Edwards, P.C. 12,457
G. G. Jones, S.D.P./All. .. 7,203
G. E. Oubridge, Grn. 481
　Lab. maj. 4,317
　(June '83, Lab. maj. 1,154)

Ceredigion and Pembroke North (Dyfed)
E. 63,141

*G. W. Howells, L./All. 17,683
O. J. Williams, C. 12,983
J. R. Davies, Lab. 8,965
C. G. Davis, P.C. 7,848
Mrs. M. A. Wakefield, Grn. 821
　L./All. maj. 4,700
　(June '83, L./All. maj. 5,639)

Clwyd
NORTH WEST　E. 66,118

*Sir A. J. C. Meyer, BT., C. . 24,116
K. L. Thomas, Lab. 12,335
O. G. Griffiths, L./All. 11,279
R. K. Davies, P.C. 1,966
　C. maj. 11,781
　(June '83, C. maj. 9,989)

SOUTH WEST　E. 58,158
M. D. Jones, Lab. 16,701
*R. L. Harvey, C. 15,673
R. T. Ellis, S.D.P./All. ... 10,778
E. L. Jones, P.C. 3,987
　Lab. maj. 1,028
　(June '83, C. maj. 1,551)

Conwy (Gwynedd)
E. 52,862

*I. W. P. Roberts, C. 15,730
J. R. Roberts, L./All. 12,706
Ms. E. Williams, Lab. 9,049
R. Davies, P.C. 3,177
　C. maj. 3,024
　(June '83, C. maj. 4,268)

Cynon Valley (Mid Glam)
E. 49,621

*Mrs. A. Clwyd, Lab. 26,222
K. D. Butler, S.D.P./All. . 4,651
M. A. Bishop, C. 4,638
Mrs. D. L. Richards, P.C. . 2,549
　Lab. maj. 21,571
　(June '83, Lab. maj. 13,074)
　(May '84, Lab. maj. 12,835)

Delyn (Clwyd)
E. 63,541

*K. W. T. Raffan, C. 21,728
D. G. Hanson, Lab. 20,504
D. J. Evans, L./All. 8,913
D. J. Owen, P.C. 1,329
　C. maj. 1,224
　(June '83, C. maj. 5,944)

Gower (W. Glam)
E. 58,871

*G. L. Wardell, Lab. 22,138
G. A. L. Price, C. 16,374
D. H. O. Elliott, S.D.P./All. 7,645
J. G. M. Edwards, P.C. ... 1,341
　Lab. maj. 5,764
　(June '83, Lab. maj. 1,205)

Islwyn (Gwent)
E. 50,414

*Rt. Hon. N. G. Kinnock, Lab. 28,901
J. Twitchen, C. 5,954
Ms. J. Gasson, S.D.P./All. 1,932
A. Richards, P.C. 1,932
　Lab. maj. 22,947
　(June '83, Lab. maj. 14,380)

Llanelli (Dyfed)
E. 63,845

*Rt. Hon. D. J. D. Davies, Lab. 29,506
P. J. Circus, C. 8,571
M. J. Shrewsbury, L./All. . 6,714
A. Price, P.C. 5,088
　Lab. maj. 20,935
　(June '83, Lab. maj. 13,606)

Meirionnydd Nant Conwy (Gwynedd)
E. 31,632

*D. E. Thomas, P.C. 10,392
D. T. Jones, C. 7,366
H. G. Roberts, Lab. 4,397
D. L. Roberts, S.D.P./All. . 3,847
　P.C. maj. 3,026
　(June '83, P.C. maj. 2,643)

Merthyr Tydfil and Rhymney (Mid Glam)
E. 58,285

*E. Rowlands, Lab. 33,400
N. M. Walters, C. 5,270
P. Verma, L./All. 3,573
Mrs. J. Davies, P.C. 2,085
　Lab. maj. 28,130
　(June '83, Lab. maj. 22,730)

Monmouth (Gwent)
E. 58,468

*Sir J. Stradling Thomas, C. 22,387
Ms. K. Gass, Lab. 13,037
C. Lindley, S.D.P./All. .. 11,313
Mrs. S. Meredudd, P.C. .. 363
 C. maj. 9,350
(June '83, C. maj. 9,343)

Montgomery (Powys)
E. 39,808

*A. C. Carlile, Q.C. L./All. .. 14,729
D.M. Evans, C. 12,171
E. D. W. Llewellyn Jones,
 Lab. 3,304
C. Clowes, P.C. 1,412
 L./All. maj. 2,558
(June '83, L./All. maj. 668)

Neath (W. Glam)
E. 55,261

*D. R. Coleman, Lab. 27,612
M. R. T. Howe, C. 7,034
J. Warman, S.D.P./All. .. 6,132
H. John, P.C. 2,792
 Lab. maj. 20,578
(June '83, Lab. maj. 13,604)

Newport (Gwent)
EAST E. 52,199
*R. J. Hughes, Lab. 20,518
G. R. Webster-Gardiner, C. 13,454
Mrs F A David, S.D.P./
 All. 7,383
G. Butler, P.C. 458
 Lab. maj. 7,064
(June '83, Lab. maj. 2,630)

WEST E. 55,455
P. P. Flynn, Lab. 20,887
*M. N. F. Robinson, C. 18,179
G. W. Roddick, L./All. 5,903
D. J. Bevan, P.C. 377
 Lab. maj. 2,708
(June '83, C. maj. 581)

Ogmore (Mid Glam)
E. 51,255

*R. Powell, Lab. 28,462
M. F. Barratt, C. 6,170
Ms. M. James, S.D.P./All. 3,954
J. G. Jones, P.C. 1,791
T. H. Spence, Ind. Lab. ... 652
 Lab. maj. 22,292
(June '83, Lab. maj. 17,364)

Pembroke (Dyfed)
E. 70,360

N. J. Bennett, C. 23,314
B. J. Rayner, Lab. 17,614
P. E. C. Jones, L./All. 14,832
O. Osmond, P.C. 1,119
 C. maj. 5,700
(June '83, C. maj. 9,356)

Pontypridd (Mid Glam)
E. 61,255

*B. T. John, Lab. 26,422
D. Swayne, C. 9,145
P. G. Sain-Ley-Berry,
 S.D.P./All. 8,865
D. L. Bowen, P.C. 2,498
 Lab. maj. 17,277
(June '83, Lab. maj. 8,744)

Rhondda (Mid Glam)
E. 60,931

*A. R. Rogers, Lab. 35,015
G. R. Davies, P.C. 4,261
J. R. YorkWilliams, S D P./
 All. 3,930
S. H. Reid, C. 3,611
A. True, Comm. 869
 Lab. maj. 30,754
(June '83, Lab. maj. 21,370)

Swansea (W. Glam)
EAST E. 57,200
*D. Anderson, Lab. 27,478
R. D. Lewis, C. 8,140
Rev. D. W. Thomas, L./All. 6,380
C. Reid, P.C. 1,145
 Lab. maj. 19,338
(June '83, Lab. maj. 13,535)

WEST E. 59,836
*Rt. Hon. A. J. Williams,
 Lab. 22,089
N. M. Evans, C. 15,027
M. Ford, L./All. 7,019
N. Williams, P.C. 902
Mrs. J. V. Harman, Grn. .. 469
 Lab. maj. 7,062
(June '83, Lab. maj. 2,350)

Torfaen (Gwent)
E 59,896

P. P. Murphy, Lab. 26,577
G. R. Blackburn, L./All. .. 9,027
R. Gordon, C. 8,632
J. Evans, P.C. 577
M. Witherden, Grn. 450
 Lab. maj. 17,550
(June '83, Lab. maj. 8,285)

Vale of Glamorgan (S. Glam)
E. 65,310

*Sir H. R. Gower, C. 24,229
J. W. P. Smith, Lab. 17,978
D. K. Davies, S.D.P./All. . 8,633
P. G. Williams, P.C. 946
 C. maj. 6,251
(June '83, C. maj. 10,393)

Wrexham (Clwyd)
E. 62,401

*Dr. J. C. Marek, Lab. 22,144
R. H. W. Graham-Palmer,
 C. 17,992
M. Thomas, L./All. 9,808
D. Watkins, P.C. 539
 Lab. maj. 4,152
(June '83, Lab. maj. 424)

Ynys Môn/Anglesey
(Gwynedd)
E. 52,633

I. W. Jones, P.C. 18,580
R. Evans, C. 14,282
C. Parry, Lab. 7,252
I. L. Evans, S.D.P./All. ... 2,863
 P.C. maj. 4,298
(June '83, P.C. maj. 1,684)

SCOTLAND
Aberdeen (Grampian)
NORTH E. 63,214
*R. Hughes, Lab. 24,145
R. Smith, S.D.P./All. 7,867
Mrs. G. E. C. Scanlan, C. . 6,330
P. Greenhorn, S.N.P. 5,827
 Lab. maj. 16,278
(June '83, Lab. maj. 9,144)

SOUTH E. 62,943
F. Doran, Lab. 15,917
*G. P. Malone, C. 14,719
I. G. Philip, S.D.P./All. ... 8,844
M. F. Weir, S.N.P. 2,776
 Lab. maj. 1,198
(June '83, C. maj. 3,581)

Angus East (Tayside)
E. 61,060

A. Welsh, S.N.P. 19,536
*P. L. Fraser, Q.C., C. 17,992
R. Mennie, Lab. 4,971
I. Mortimer, S.D.P./All. ... 3,592
 S.N.P. maj. 1,544
(June '83, C. maj. 3,527)

Argyll and Bute (S'clyde)
E. 48,700

Mrs. J. R. Michie, L./All. . 13,726
*J. J. MacKay, C 12,332
R. Shaw, S.N.P. 6,297
D. Tierney, Lab. 4,437
 L./All. maj. 1,394
(June '83, C. maj. 3,844)

Ayr (S'clyde)
E. 66,450

*Rt. Hon. G. K. H. Younger,
 T.D., C. 20,942
K. MacDonald, Lab. 20,760
K. M. Moody, L./All. 7,859
C. Weir, S.N.P. 3,548
 C. maj. 182
(June '83, C. maj. 7,987)

Banff and Buchan (Grampian)
E. 62,149

A. E. A. Salmond, S.N.P. . 19,462
*A. McQuarrie, C. 17,021
G. M. Burness, S.D.P./All. 4,211
J. Livie, Lab. 3,281
 S.N.P. maj. 2,441
(June '83, C. maj. 937)

Caithness and Sutherland
(H'land)
E. 31,279

*R. A. R. Maclennan,
 S.D.P./All. 12,338
R. L. Hamilton, C. 3,844
A. Byron, Lab. 3,437
K. MacGregor, S.N.P. 2,371
W. A. Mowat, Ind. L. 686
B. Planterose, Grn. 333
 S.D.P./All. maj. 8,494
(June '83, S.D.P./All. maj. 6,843)

Carrick, Cumnock and Doon Valley (S'clyde)
E. 56,360

*G. Foulkes, Lab.	25,669
S. Stevenson, C.	8,867
Mrs. M. Ali, S.D.P./All.	4,106
C. D. Calman, S.N.P.	4,094
Lab. maj.	16,802
(June '83, Lab. maj. 11,370)	

Clackmannan (Central)
E. 49,083

*M. J. O'Neill, Lab.	20,317
Dr. A. Macartney, S.N.P.	7,916
J. Parker, C.	5,620
Mrs. A. Watters, S.D.P./All.	3,961
Lab. maj.	12,401
(June '83, Lab. maj. 9,639)	

Clydebank and Milngavie (S'clyde)
E. 50,152

A. Worthington, Lab.	22,528
K. Hirstwood, C.	6,224
R. Ackland, S.D.P./All.	5,891
S. Fisher, S.N.P.	4,935
Lab. maj.	16,304
(June '83, Lab. maj. 7,715)	

Clydesdale (S'clyde)
E. 61,620

J. Hood, Lab.	21,826
R. Robertson, C.	11,324
J. Boyle, S.D.P./All.	7,909
M. Russell, S.N.P.	7,125
Lab. maj.	10,502
(June '83, Lab. maj. 4,866)	

Cumbernauld and Kilsyth (S'clyde)
E. 45,427

*N. Hogg, Lab.	21,385
T. Johnston, S.N.P.	6,982
C. S. Deans, S.D.P./All.	4,059
Mrs. A. E. Thomson, C.	3,227
Lab. maj.	14,403
(June '83, Lab. maj. 9,928)	

Cunninghame (S'clyde)

NORTH E. 54,817

B. D. H. Wilson, Lab.	19,061
*J. A. Corrie, C.	14,594
D. J. Herbison, S.D.P./All.	5,185
M. Brown, S.N.P.	4,076
Lab. maj.	4,467
(June '83, C. maj. 1,637)	

SOUTH E. 49,842

*D. Lambie, Lab.	22,728
E. R. Gibson, C.	6,095
J. A. Boss, L./All.	4,426
Mrs. K. Ullrich, S.N.P.	4,115
Lab. maj.	16,633
(June '83, Lab. maj. 11,768)	

Dumbarton (S'clyde)
E. 58,968

J. McFall, Lab.	19,778
R. F. Graham, C.	14,556
R. Mowbray, S.D.P./All.	6,060
Ms. J. Herriot, S.N.P.	5,564
Lab. maj.	5,222
(June '83, Lab. maj. 2,115)	

Dumfries (D & G)
E. 59,347

*Sir H. S. P. Monro, C.	18,785
Ms. C. W. Phillips, Lab.	11,292
J. R. McCall, S.D.P./All.	8,064
T. McAlpine, S.N.P.	6,391
P. M. Thomas, Grn.	349
C. maj.	7,493
(June '83, C. maj. 8,694)	

Dundee (Tayside)

EAST E. 60,805

J. McAllion, Lab.	19,539
*R. G. Wilson, S.N.P.	18,524
P. Cook, C.	5,938
Mrs. M. von Romberg, L./All.	2,143
Lab. maj.	1,015
(June '83, S.N.P. maj. 5,016)	

WEST E. 61,926

*E. Ross, Lab.	24,916
J. A. Donnelly, C.	8,390
A. N. Morgan, S.N.P.	7,164
Ms. R. Lonie, S.D.P./All.	5,922
S. R. Mathewson, Comm.	308
Lab. maj.	16,526
(June '83, Lab. maj. 10,150)	

Dunfermline (Fife)

EAST E. 51,175

*Dr. J. G. Brown, Lab.	25,381
C. Shenton, C.	5,792
Ms. E. Harris, L./All.	4,122
Mrs. A. McGarny, S.N.P.	3,901
Lab. maj.	19,589
(June '83, Lab. maj. 11,301)	

WEST E. 51,063

*R. G. Douglas, Lab.	18,493
P. R. Gallie, C.	9,091
F. A. Moyes, S.D.P./All.	8,288
G. Hughes, S.N.P.	3,435
Lab. maj.	9,402
(June '83, Lab. maj. 2,474)	

East Kilbride (S'clyde)
E. 63,097

A. P. Ingram, Lab.	24,491
D. R. E. Sullivan, S.D.P./All.	11,867
P. M. Walker, C.	7,344
J. H. Taggart, S.N.P.	6,275
Lab. maj.	12,624
(June '83, Lab. maj. 4,336)	

East Lothian
E. 65,046

*J. D. Home Robertson, Lab.	24,583
S. M. Langdon, C.	14,478
A. Robinson, L./All.	7,929
A. Burgon-Lyon, S.N.P.	3,727
A. Marland, Grn.	451
Lab. maj.	10,105
(June '83, Lab. maj. 6,241)	

Eastwood (S'clyde)
E. 61,872

*J. A. Stewart, C.	19,388
R. Leishman, S.D.P./All.	13,374
P. A. Grant-Hutchison, Lab.	12,305
J. Findlay, S.N.P.	4,033
C. maj.	6,014
(June '83, C. maj. 8,595)	

Edinburgh (Lothian)

CENTRAL E. 59,529

A. M. Darling, Lab.	16,502
*Sir A. Fletcher, C.	14,240
A. Myles, L./All.	7,333
B. Shaw, S.N.P.	2,559
Mrs. L. M. Hendry, Grn.	438
Lab. maj.	2,262
(June '83, C. maj. 2,566)	

EAST E. 48,895

*G. S. Strang, Lab.	18,257
J. F. Renz, C.	8,962
Mrs. J. Aitken, L./All.	5,592
M. Bovey, S.N.P.	3,434
Lab. maj.	9,295
(June '83, Lab. maj. 5,866)	

LEITH E. 60,359

*R. D. M. Brown, Lab.	21,104
D. A. Y. Menzies, C.	9,777
Mrs. S. Wells, S.D.P./All.	7,843
W. Morrison, S.N.P.	4,045
Lab. maj.	11,327
(June '83, Lab. maj. 4,973)	

PENTLANDS E. 58,125

*Rt. Hon. M. L. Rifkind, Q.C., C.	17,278
M. Lazarowicz, Lab.	13,533
K. A. Smith, S.D.P./All.	11,072
D. N. MacCormick, S.N.P.	3,264
C. maj.	3,745
(June '83, C. maj. 4,309)	

SOUTH E. 63,842

N. Griffiths, Lab.	18,211
*M. A. F. J. K. Ancram (Earl of Ancram), C.	16,352
D. A. Graham, S.D.P./All.	10,900
Mrs. R. Moore, S.N.P.	2,455
Mrs. R. Clark, Grn.	440
Lab. maj.	1,859
(June '83, C. maj. 3,655)	

WEST E. 62,214

*Lord James Douglas-Hamilton, C.	18,450
D. G. King, L./All.	17,216
M. McGregor, Lab.	10,957
N. Irons, S.N.P.	2,774
C. maj.	1,234
(June '83, C. maj. 498)	

Falkirk (Central)

EAST E. 52,564

*H. Ewing, Lab.	21,379
K. H. Brookes, C.	7,356
R. N. F. Halliday, S.N.P.	6,056
Mrs. E. G. Dick, S.D.P./All.	4,624
Lab. maj.	14,023
(June '83, Lab. maj. 10,061)	

WEST E. 50,222

*D. A. Canavan, Lab.	20,256
D. R. D. Thomas, C.	6,704
I. R. Goldie, S.N.P.	6,696
M. J. Harris, L./All.	4,841
Lab. maj.	13,552
(June '83, Lab. maj. 8,978)	

Fife

CENTRAL *E.* 56,090
H. B. McLeish, *Lab.* 22,827
R. E. Aird, *C.* 7,118
Mrs. T. M. Little, *L./All.* .. 6,487
D. Hood, *S.N.P.* 6,296
Lab. maj. 15,709
(June '83, Lab. maj. 7,794)

NORTH EAST *E.* 52,266
W. M. Campbell, C.B.E., Q.C.,
L./All. 17,868
*J. S. B. Henderson, *C.* 16,421
A. M. E. Gannon, *Lab.* 2,947
F. D. Roche, *S.N.P.* 2,616
L./All. maj. 1,447
(June '83, C. maj. 2,185)

Galloway and Upper Nithsdale
(D & G)
E. 53,429

*I. B. Lang, *C.* 16,592
S. F. Norris, *S.N.P.* 12,919
J. McKercher, *L./All.* 6,001
J. Gray, *Lab.* 5,298
D. Kenny, *Ret.* 230
C. maj. 3,673
(June '83, C. maj. 5,461)

Glasgow (S'clyde)

CATHCART *E.* 49,307
*J. A. Maxton, *Lab.* 19,623
W. A. Harvey, *C.* 8,420
Miss M. Craig, *S.D.P./All.* 5,722
W. A. Steven, *S.N.P.* 3,883
Lab. maj. 11,203
(June '83, Lab. maj. 4,230)

CENTRAL *E.* 51,137
*R. McTaggart, *Lab.* 21,619
B. Jenkin, *C.* 4,366
Dr. J. Bryden, *L./All.* 3,528
A. Wilson, *S.N.P.* 3,339
A. Brooks, *Grn.* 290
J. P. McGoldrick, *Comm.* . 265
D. Owen, *R.F.* 126
Lab. maj. 17,253
(June '83, Lab. maj. 10,962)

GARSCADDEN *E.* 47,958
*D. C. Dewar, *Lab.* 23,178
A. Brophy, *S.N.P.* 4,201
T. N. A. Begg, *C.* 3,660
S. Callison, *S.D.P./All.* ... 3,211
Lab. maj. 18,977
(June '83, Lab. maj. 13,474)

GOVAN *E.* 50,616
*Rt. Hon. B. Millan, *Lab.* ... 24,071
A. Ferguson, *S.D.P./All.* .. 4,562
Mrs. J. R. Girsman, *C.* 4,411
F. McCabe, *S.N.P.* 3,851
D. Chalmers, *Comm.* 237
Lab. maj. 19,509
(June '83, Lab. maj. 13,057)

HILLHEAD *E.* 57,836
G. Galloway, *Lab.* 17,958
*Rt Hon. R. H. Jenkins,
S.D.P./All. 14,707
B. D. Cooklin, *C.* 6,048
W. Kidd, *S.N.P.* 2,713
A. Whitelaw, *Grn.* 443
Lab. maj. 3,251
(June '83, S.D.P./All. maj. 1,164)

MARYHILL *E.* 52,371
Mrs. M. Fyfe, *Lab.* 23,482
Miss E. M. A. Attwooll, *L./
All.* 4,118
G. Roberts, *S.N.P.* 3,895
S. R. R. Kirk, *C.* 3,307
D. Spaven, *Grn.* 539
Lab. maj. 19,364
(June '83, Lab. maj. 11,203)

POLLOK *E.* 51,396
J. Dunnachie, *Lab.* 23,239
Mrs. G. French, *C.* 5,256
J. Shearer, *L./All.* 4,445
A. Doig, *S.N.P.* 3,528
D. Fogg, *Grn.* 362
Lab. maj. 17,983
(June '83, Lab. maj. 11,532)

PROVAN *E.* 43,744
J. Wray, *Lab.* 22,032
W. Ramsay, *S.N.P.* 3,660
Miss A. Strutt, *C.* 2,336
J. Morrison, *S.D.P./All.* .. 2,189
Lab. maj. 18,372
(June '83, Lab. maj. 15,385)

RUTHERGLEN *E.* 57,313
T. McAvoy, *Lab.* 24,790
R. E. Brown, *L./All.* 10,795
G. Hamilton, *C.* 5,088
J. Higgins, *S.N.P.* 3,584
Lab. maj. 13,995
(June '83, Lab. maj. 9,126)

SHETTLESTON *E.* 53,604
*D. Marshall, *Lab.* 23,991
J. M. S. Fisher, *C.* 5,010
J. MacVicar, *S.N.P.* 4,807
Miss P. Clarke, *L./All.* ... 3,942
Lab. maj. 18,981
(June '83, Lab. maj. 12,416)

SPRINGBURN *E.* 51,563
*M. J. Martin, *Lab.* 25,617
B. O'Hara, *S.N.P.* 3,554
M. Call, *C.* 2,870
D. Rennie, *L./All.* 2,746
Lab. maj. 22,063
(June '83, Lab. maj. 17,599)

Gordon (Grampian)
E. 73,479

*M. G. Bruce, *L./All.* 26,770
P. R. Leckie, *C.* 17,251
Mrs. M. C. Morrell, *Lab.* .. 6,228
G. E. Wright, *S.N.P.* 3,876
L./All. maj. 9,519
(June '83, L./All. maj. 850)

Greenock and Port Glasgow
(S'clyde)
E. 57,756

*Dr. N. A. Godman, *Lab.* ... 27,848
J. H. Moody, *L./All.* 7,793
T. J. D. Pearson, *C.* 4,199
T. Lenehan, *S.N.P.* 3,721
Lab. maj. 20,055
(June '83, Lab. maj. 4,625)

Hamilton (S'clyde)
E. 62,205

*G. I. M. Robertson, *Lab.* .. 28,563
G. S. Mond, *C.* 6,901
T. Mackay, *L./All.* 6,302
C. Crossley, *S.N.P.* 6,093
Lab. maj. 21,662
(June '83, Lab. maj. 15,019)

Inverness, Nairn and Lochaber
(H'land)
E. 66,743

*Sir D. R. Johnston, *L./All.* 17,422
D. Stewart, *Lab.* 11,991
Mrs. A. T. Keswick, *C.* ... 10,901
N. P. Johnson, *S.N.P.* 7,001
L./All. maj. 5,431
(June '83, L./All. maj. 7,298)

Kilmarnock and Loudoun
(Grampian)
E. 62,648

*W. McKelvey, *Lab.* 23,713
Mrs. A. K. Bates, *C.* 9,586
G. Leslie, *S.N.P.* 8,881
P. Kerr, *S.D.P./All.* 6,698
Lab. maj. 14,127
(June '83, Lab. maj. 8,800)

Kincardine and Deeside
(Grampian)
E. 63,587

*Rt. Hon. A. L. Buchanan-
Smith, *C.* 19,438
N. R. Stephen, *L./All.* 17,375
J. K. Thomaneck, *Lab.* 7,624
Mrs. F. E. Duncan, *S.N.P.* 3,082
Mrs. L. M. Perica, *Grn.* ... 299
C. maj. 2,063
(June '83, C. maj. 7,796)

Kirkcaldy (Fife)
E. 53,439

Dr. L. G. Moonie, *Lab.* ... 20,281
I. G. Mitchell, *C.* 8,711
D. Stewart, *S.D.P./All.* ... 7,118
W. A. R. Mullin, *S.N.P.* .. 4,794
Lab. maj. 11,570
(June '83, Lab. maj. 5,331)

Linlithgow (Lothian)
E. 59,542

*T. Dalyell, *Lab.* 21,869
J. Sillars, *S.N.P.* 11,496
T. R. Armstrong Wilson, *C.* 6,828
Mrs. H. McDade, *S.D.P./
All.* 5,840
J. Glassford, *Comm.* 154
Lab. maj. 10,373
(June '83, Lab. maj. 11,361)

Livingston (Lothian)
E. 56,583

*R. F. Cook, *Lab.* 19,110
R. McCreadle, *L./All.* 8,005
Dr. M. N. A. Mayall, *C.* .. 7,860
K. MacAskill, *S.N.P.* 6,969
Lab. maj. 11,105
(June '83, Lab. maj. 4,951)

Midlothian
E. 60,549

*A. Eadie, B.E.M., *Lab.* 22,553
A. R. Dewar, *S.D.P./All.* . 10,300
Dr. F. Riddell, *C.* 8,527
I. Chisholm, *S.N.P.* 4,947
I. Smith, *Grn.* 412
Lab. maj. 12,253
(June '83, Lab. maj. 6,156)

Monklands (S'clyde)

EAST *E.* 49,644

*Rt. Hon. J. Smith, Q.C., *Lab.*		22,649
J. Love, *C.*		6,260
K. Gibson, *S.N.P.*		4,790
Mrs. S. Grieve, *L./All.*		3,442
	Lab. maj.	16,389
(June '83, Lab. maj. 9,799)		

WEST *E.* 50,874

*T. Clarke, C.B.E., *Lab.*		24,499
G. Lind, *C.*		6,166
Ms. A. McQueen, *S.D.P./All.*		4,408
K. Bovey, *S.N.P.*		4,260
	Lab. maj.	18,333
(June '83, Lab. maj. 12,264)		

Moray (Grampian)

E. 62,201

Mrs. M. Ewing, S.N.P.		19,510
*A. Pollock, C.		15,825
C. R. C. Smith, *Lab.*		5,118
D. G. M. Skene, *L./All.*		4,724
	S.N.P. maj.	3,685
(June '83, C. maj. 1,713)		

Motherwell (S'clyde)

NORTH *E.* 57,632

Dr. J. Reid, Lab.		29,825
A. Currie, *S.N.P.*		6,230
R. Hargrave, *C.*		4,939
G. Swift, *L./All.*		3,558
	Lab. maj.	23,595
(June '83, Lab. maj. 17,894)		

SOUTH *E.* 52,127

*Dr. J. W. Bray, Lab.		22,957
J. Wright, *S.N.P.*		6,027
J. S. Bercow, *C.*		5,702
W. R. MacGregor, *S.D.P./ All.*		4,463
R. Somerville, *Comm.*		223
	Lab. maj.	16,930
(June '83, Lab. maj. 12,349)		

Orkney and Shetland (Islands)

E. 31,047

*J. R. Wallace, L./All.		8,881
R. W. A. Jenkins, *C.*		4,959
J. H. Aberdein, *Lab.*		3,995
J. Goodlad, *O.S.M.*		3,095
G. K. Collister, *Grn.*		389
	L./All. maj.	3,922
(June '83, L./All. maj. 4,150)		

Paisley (S'clyde)

NORTH *E.* 49,487

*A. S. Adams, Lab.		20,193
Mrs. E. F. Laing, *C.*		5,751
Miss E. P. McCartin, *S.D.P./All.*		5,741
I. Taylor, *S.N.P.*		4,696
	Lab. maj.	14,442
(June '83, Lab. maj. 7,587)		

SOUTH *E.* 51,127

*N. F. Buchan, Lab.		21,611
A. M. Carmichael, *L./All*		5,826
Miss D. A. Williamson, *C.*		5,644
J. R. Mitchell, *S.N.P.*		5,398
	Lab. maj.	15,785
(June '83, Lab. maj. 6,529)		

Perth and Kinross (Tayside)

E. 63,443

*N. H. Fairbairn, Q.C., *C.*		18,716
J. M. Fairlie, *S.N.P.*		13,040
S. Donaldson, *L./All.*		7,969
J. W. McConnell, *Lab.*		7,490
	C. maj.	5,676
(June '83, C. maj. 6,733)		

Renfrew West and Inverclyde
(S'clyde)

E. 56,189

T. Graham, *Lab.*		17,525
*Mrs. A. A. McCurley, C.		13,472
Dr. J. D. Mabon, *S.D.P./ All.*		9,669
C. Campbell, *S.N.P.*		4,578
	Lab. maj.	4,053
(June '83, C. maj. 1,322)		

Ross, Cromarty and Skye
(H'land)

E. 52,369

*C. P. Kennedy, S.D.P./All.		18,809
F. Spencer Nairn, *C.*		7,490
M. M. MacMillan, *Lab.*		7,287
R. M. Gibson, *S.N.P*		4,492
	S.D.P./All. maj.	11,319
(June '83, S.D.P./All. maj. 1,704)		

Roxburgh and Berwickshire
(Borders)

E. 43,140

*A. J. Kirkwood, L./All.		16,388
Dr. L. Fox, *C.*		12,380
T. Luckhurst, *Lab.*		2,944
M. Douglas, *S.N.P.*		1,586
	L./All. maj.	4,008
(June '83, L./All. maj. 3,396)		

Stirling (Central)

E. 57,836

*M. B. Forsyth, C.		17,591
M. Connarty, *Lab.*		16,643
I. McFarlane, *L./All.*		6,804
I. M. Lawson, *S.N.P.*		4,897
	C. maj.	948
(June '83, C. maj. 5,133)		

Strathkelvin and Bearsden
(S'clyde)

E. 62,676

S. L. Galbraith, *Lab.*		19,639
*M. W. Hirst, C.		17,187
J. Bannerman, *L./All.*		11,034
G. Paterson, *S.N.P.*		3,654
	Lab. maj.	2,452
(June '83, C. maj. 3,700)		

Tayside North

E. 53,985

*W. C. Walker, C.		18,307
K. J. N. Guild, *S.N.P.*		13,291
P. F. Regent, *L./All.*		5,201
J. Whytock, *Lab.*		3,550
	C. maj.	5,016
(June '83, C. maj. 10,099)		

Tweeddale, Ettrick and Lauder-
dale (Borders)

E. 37,875

*Rt. Hon. D. M. S. Steel, L./ All.		14,599
Mrs. S. Finlay-Maxwell, *C.*		8,657
N. Glen, *Lab.*		3,320
A. Lumsden, *S.N.P.*		2,660
	L./All. maj.	5,942
(June '83, L./All. maj. 8,539)		

Western Isles (Islands)

E. 23,507

C. A. MacDonald, *Lab.*		7,041
I. Smith, *S.N.P.*		4,701
K. MacIver, *S.D.P./All.*		3,419
M. Morrison, *C.*		1,336
	Lab. maj.	2,340
(June '83, S.N.P. maj. 3,712)		

NORTHERN IRELAND

Antrim

EAST *E.* 60,587

*J. R. Beggs, O.U.P.		23,942
S. Neeson, *All.*		8,582
A. Kelly, *W.P.*		936
	O.U.P. maj.	15,360
(June '83, OUP. maj. 367)		
(Jan. '86, O.U.P. maj. 24,981)		

NORTH *E.* 65,733

*Rev. I. R. K. Paisley, D.U.P.		28,383
S. Farren, *S.D.L.P.*		5,149
G. Williams, *All.*		5,140
S. Reagan, *S.F.*		2,633
	D.U.P. maj.	23,234
(June '83, D.U.P. maj. 13,173)		
(Jan. '86, D.U.P. maj. 33,024)		

SOUTH *E.* 61,649

*C. Forsythe, O.U.P.		25,395
G. Mawhinney, *All.*		5,808
D. McClelland, *S.D.L.P.*		3,611
H. Cushinan, *S.F.*		1,592
	O.U.P. maj.	19,587
(June '83, O.U.P. maj. 6,792)		
(Jan. '86, O.U.P. maj. 28,217)		

Belfast

EAST *E.* 54,628

*P. D. Robinson, D.U.P.		20,372
Dr. J. Alderdice, *All.*		10,574
F. Cullen, *W.P.*		1,314
J. O'Donnell, *S.F.*		649
	D.U.P. maj.	9,798
(June '83, D.U.P. maj. 7,989)		
(Jan. '86, D.U.P. maj. 21,690)		

NORTH *E.* 59,124

*A. C. Walker, O.U.P.		14,355
A. Maginness, *S.D.L.P.*		5,795
G. Seawright, *Prot. U.*		5,671
P. McManus, *S.F.*		5,062
S. Lynch, *W.P.*		3,062
T. Campbell, *All.*		2,871
	O.U.P. maj.	8,560
(June '83, O.U.P. maj. 7,079)		
(Jan. '86, O.U.P. maj. 16,577)		

SOUTH *E.* 54,208
Rev. W. M. Smyth, O.U.P. 18,917
D. Cook, *All.* 6,963
Dr. A. McDonnell, *S.D.L.P.* 4,268
G. Carr, *W.P.* 1,528
S. McKnight, *S.F.* 1,030
O.U.P. maj. 11,954
(June '83, O.U.P. maj. 9,724)
(Jan. '86, O.U.P. maj. 14,136)

WEST *E.* 59,324
G. Adams, S.F. 16,862
Dr. J. G. Hendron, *S.D.L.P.* 14,641
F. Miller, *O.U.P.* 7,646
Mrs. M. McMahon, *W.P.* . 1,819
S.F. maj. 2,221
(June '83, S.F. maj. 5,445)

Down

NORTH *E.* 65,018
J. A. Kilfedder, U.P.U.P. . 18,420
R. McCartney, *Real U.* ... 14,467
J. Cushnahan, *All.* 7,932
U.P.U.P. maj. 3,953
(June '83, U.P.U.P. maj. 13,846)
(Jan. '86, U.P.U.P. maj. 22,727)

SOUTH *E.* 71,235
E. K. McGrady, *S.D.L.P.* . 26,579
Rt. Hon. J. E. Powell, M.B.E.,
O.U.P. 25,848
Ms. G. Ritchie, *S.F.* 2,363
Miss S. E. Laird, *All.* ... 1,069
D. O'Hagan, *W.P.* 675
S.D.L.P. maj. 731
(June '83, O.U.P. maj. 548)
(Jan. '86, O.U.P. maj. 1,842)

Fermanagh and South Tyrone
E. 68,979
K. Maginnis, O.U.P. 27,446
P. Corrigan, *S.F.* 14,623
Mrs. R. Flanagan, *S.D.L.P.* 10,581
D. Kettyles, *W.P.* 1,784
J. Haslett, *All.* 941
O.U.P. maj. 12,823
(June '83, O.U.P. maj. 7,676)
(Jan. '86, O.U.P. maj. 12,579)

Foyle
E. 70,519
J. Hume, S.D.L.P. 23,743
G. Campbell, *D.U.P.* 13,883
M. McGuiness, *S.F.* 8,707
Mrs. E. Zammitt, *All.* 1,276
E. Melaugh, *W.P.* 1,022
S.D.L.P. maj. 9,860
(June '83, S.D.L.P. maj. 8,148)

Lagan Valley
E. 64,873
Rt. Hon. J. H. Molyneaux,
O.U.P. 29,101
S. A. Close, *All.* 5,728
B. McDonnell, *S.D.L.P.* .. 2,888
P. J. Rice, *S.F.* 2,656
J. T. Lowry, *W.P.* 1,215
O.U.P. maj. 23,373
(June '83, O.U.P. maj. 17,216)
(Jan. '86, O.U.P. maj. 29,186)

Londonderry East
E. 71,031
W. Ross, O.U.P. 29,532
A. Doherty, *S.D.L.P.* 9,375
J. Davey, *S.F.* 5,464
P. McGowan, *All.* 3,237
F. Donnelly, *W.P.* 935
M. H. Samuel, *Ecol.* 281
O.U.P. maj. 20,157
(June '83, O.U.P. maj. 7,262)
(Jan. '86, O.U.P. maj. 28,921)

Newry and Armagh
E. 66,027
S. Mallon, S.D.L.P. 25,137
J. F. Nicholson, O.U.P. ... 19,812
J. McAllister, *S.F.* 6,173
W. H. Jeffrey, *All.* 664
J. O'Hanion, *W.P.* 482
S.D.L.P. maj. 5,325
(June '83, O.U.P. maj. 1,554)
(Jan. '86, S.D.L.P. maj. 2,583)

Strangford
E. 64,429
Rt. Hon. J. D. Taylor,
O.U.P. 28,199
A. J. Morrow, *All.* 7,553
Miss I. E. Hynds, *W.P.* ... 1,385
O.U.P. maj. 20,646
(June '83, O.U.P. maj. 7,370)
(Jan. '86, O.U.P. maj. 30,634)

Ulster, Mid-
E. 67,256
Rev. R. T. W. McCrea,
D.U.P. 23,004
P. D. Haughey, *S.D.L.P.* .. 13,644
S. Begley, *S.F.* 12,449
P. Bogan, *All.* 1,846
P. J. McClean, *W.P.* 1,133
D.U.P. maj. 9,360
(June '83, D.U.P. maj. 78)
(Jan. '86, D.U.P. maj. 9,697)

Upper Bann
E. 64,540
J. H. McCusker, O.U.P. .. 26,037
Mrs. B. Rodgers, *S.D.L.P.* 8,676
B. P. Curran, *S.F.* 3,126
Mrs. M. F. A. Cook, *All.* .. 2,487
T. French, *W.P.* 2,004
O.U.P. maj. 17,361
(June '83, O.U.P. maj. 17,081)
(Jan. '86, O.U.P. maj. 22,333)

BY-ELECTIONS (Since 1987 General Election)

Kensington (Gtr. London)
(July 14, 1988)

J. D. Fishburn, *C.* 9,829
Mrs. A. Holmes, *Lab.* 9,014
W. Goodhart, *S.L.D.* 2,546
J. Martin, *S.D.P.* 1,190
P. Hobson, *Green Party* 572
Mrs. C. Payne, *Rainbow Al-*
liance Payne and Pleasure
Party 193

Lord David Sutch, *Monster*
Raving Loony Rock Music
Party 61
J. Duignan, *London Class*
War 60
B. Goodier, *Anti Left Wing*
Fascist 31
B. McDermott, *Free Trade*
Liberal Party—Europe
Out 31

R. Edey, *Fair Wealth Distri-*
bution Fair Housing Pro-
vision 30
W. Scola, *The Leveller Party* 27
J. Crowley, *Anti-Yuppie*
Revolutionary Crowleyist
Vegetarian Visionary ... 24
J. Connell, *Peace—Stop ITN*
Manipulation 20
Dr. K. Trivedi, *Independent*
Janata Party 5
C. maj. 815

PRIME MINISTERS AND SPEAKERS

PRIME MINISTERS SINCE 1782

Marquess of Rockingham, *Whig,* March 27, 1782.
Earl of Shelburne, *Whig,* July 13, 1782.
Duke of Portland, *Coalition,* April 4, 1783.
William Pitt, *Tory,* Dec. 7, 1783.
Henry Addington, *Tory,* March 21, 1801.
William Pitt, *Tory,* May 16, 1804.
Lord Grenville, *Whig,* Feb. 10, 1806.
Duke of Portland, *Tory,* March 31, 1807.
Spencer Perceval, *Tory,* Dec. 6, 1809.
Earl of Liverpool, *Tory,* June 16, 1812.
George Canning, *Tory,* April 30, 1827.
Viscount Goderich, *Tory,* Sept. 8, 1827.
Duke of Wellington, *Tory,* Jan. 26, 1828.
Earl Grey, *Whig,* Nov. 24, 1830.
Viscount Melbourne, *Whig,* July 13, 1834.
Sir Robert Peel, *Tory,* Dec. 26, 1834.
Viscount Melbourne, *Whig,* March 18, 1835.
Sir Robert Peel, *Tory,* Sept. 6, 1841.
Lord John Russell, *Whig,* July 6, 1846.
Earl of Derby, *Tory,* Feb. 28, 1852.
Earl of Aberdeen, *Peelite,* Dec. 28, 1852.
Viscount Palmerston, *Liberal,* Feb. 10, 1855.
Earl of Derby, *Conservative,* Feb. 25, 1858.
Viscount Palmerston, *Liberal,* June 18, 1859.
Earl Russell, *Liberal,* Nov. 6, 1865.
Earl of Derby, *Conservative,* July 6, 1866.
Benjamin Disraeli, *Conservative,* Feb. 27, 1868.
W. E. Gladstone, *Liberal,* Dec. 9, 1868.
Benjamin Disraeli, *Conservative,* Feb. 21, 1874.
W. E. Gladstone, *Liberal,* April 28, 1880.
Marquess of Salisbury, *Conservative,* June 24, 1885.
W. E. Gladstone, *Liberal,* Feb. 6, 1886.
Marquess of Salisbury, *Conservative,* Aug. 3, 1886.
W. E. Gladstone, *Liberal,* Aug. 18, 1892.
Earl of Rosebery, *Liberal,* March 3, 1894.
Marquess of Salisbury, *Conservative,* July 2, 1895.
A. J. Balfour, *Conservative,* July 12, 1902.
Sir H. Campbell-Bannerman, *Liberal,* Dec. 5, 1905.
H. H. Asquith, *Liberal,* April 8, 1908.
H. H. Asquith, *Coalition,* May 26, 1915.
D. Lloyd-George, *Coalition,* Dec. 7, 1916.
A. Bonar Law, *Conservative,* Oct. 23, 1922.
S. Baldwin, *Conservative,* May 22, 1923.
J. R. MacDonald, *Labour,* Jan. 22, 1924.
S. Baldwin, *Conservative,* Nov. 4, 1924.
J. R. MacDonald, *Labour,* June 8, 1929.
J. R. MacDonald, *Coalition,* Aug. 25, 1931.
S. Baldwin, *Coalition,* June 7, 1935.
N. Chamberlain, *Coalition,* May 28, 1937.
W. S. Churchill, *Coalition,* May 11, 1940.
W. S. Churchill, *Conservative,* May 23, 1945.
C. R. Attlee, *Labour,* July 26, 1945.
Sir W. S. Churchill, *Conservative,* Oct. 26, 1951.
Sir A. Eden, *Conservative,* April 6, 1955.
H. Macmillan, *Conservative,* Jan. 13, 1957.
Sir A. Douglas-Home, *Conservative,* Oct. 19, 1963.
J. H. Wilson, *Labour,* Oct. 16, 1964.
E. R. G. Heath, *Conservative,* June 19, 1970.

J. H. Wilson, *Labour,* March 4, 1974.
L. J. Callaghan, *Labour,* April 5, 1976.
Mrs. M. H. Thatcher, *Conservative,* May 4, 1979.

SPEAKERS OF THE COMMONS SINCE 1660

PARLIAMENT OF ENGLAND

1660 Sir Harbottle Grimston.
1661 Sir Edward Turner.
1673 Sir Job Charlton.
1673 Sir Edward Seymour.
1678 Sir Robert Sawyer.
1679 Sir William Gregory.
1680 Sir William Williams.
1685 Sir John Trevor.
1688 Henry Powle.
1694 Paul Foley.
1698 Sir Thomas Lyttelton.
1700 Robert Harley (*Earl of Oxford and Mortimer*).
1702 John Smith.

PARLIAMENT OF GREAT BRITAIN

1708 Sir Richard Onslow (*Lord Onslow*).
1710 William Bromley.
1713 Sir Thomas Hanmer.
1715 Spencer Compton (*Earl of Wilmington*).
1727 Arthur Onslow.
1761 Sir John Cust.
1770 Sir Fletcher Norton.
1780 Charles Cornwall.
1788 Hon. William Grenvill (*Lord Grenville*).
1789 Henry Addington (*Viscount Sidmouth*).

PARLIAMENT OF UNITED KINGDOM

1801 Sir John Mitford (*Lord Redesdale*).
1802 Charles Abbot (*Lord Colchester*).
1817 Charles M. Sutton (*Viscount Canterbury*).
1835 James Abercromby (*Lord Dunfermline*).
1839 Charles Shaw-Lefevre (*Viscount Eversley*).
1857 J. Evelyn Denison (*Viscount Ossington*).
1872 Sir Henry Brand (*Viscount Hampden*).
1884 Arthur Wellesley Peel (*Viscount Peel*).
1895 William Court Gully (*Viscount Selby*).
1905 James W. Lowther (*Viscount Ullswater*).
1921 John Henry Whitley.
1928 Hon. Edward Algernon FitzRoy.
1943 Col. D. Clifton Brown (*Viscount Ruffside*).
1951 William Shepherd Morrison (*Viscount Dunrossil*).
1959 Sir Harry Hylton-Foster.
1965 Horace Maybray King, PH.D. (*Lord Maybray-King*).
1971 (John) Selwyn (Brooke) Lloyd (*Lord Selwyn-Lloyd*).
1976 (Thomas) George Thomas (*Viscount Tonypandy*).
1983 (Bruce) Bernard Weatherill.

EUROPEAN PARLIAMENT—U.K. MEMBERS

An asterisk* denotes membership of the previous Parliament

*Adam, Gordon J. (b. 1934), Lab., Northumbria
*Balfe, Richard A. (b. 1944), Lab., London, S. Inner
*Battersby, Robert C., M.B.E. (b. 1924), C., Humberside
Beazley, Christopher J. P. (b. 1952), C., Cornwall and Plymouth
*Beazley, Peter G. (b. 1922), C., Bedfordshire S.
*Bethell, The Lord (b. 1938), C., London N.W.
Bird, John (b. 1926), Lab., Midlands W.
*Brookes, Miss Beata A. (b. 1932), C., Wales N.
*Buchan, Miss Janey (b. 1926), Lab., Glasgow
Cassidy, Bryan M. D. (b. 1934), C., Dorset E. and Hampshire W.
*Castle, Rt. Hon. Mrs. Barbara A. (b. 1910), Lab., Greater Manchester W.
*Catherwood, Sir H. Frederick R. (b. 1925), C., Cambridge and Bedfordshire N.
*Collins, Kenneth D. (b. 1939), Lab., Strathclyde E.
*Cottrell, Richard J. (b. 1943), C., Bristol
Crawley, Mrs. Christine M. (b. 1950), Lab., Birmingham E.
Cryer, G. Robert, M.P. (b. 1934), Lab., Sheffield
*Curry, David M., M.P. (b. 1944), C., Essex N.E.
Daly, Mrs. Margaret E. (b. 1938), C., Somerset and Dorset W.
*De Courcy Ling, John (b. 1933), C., Midlands Central
*De Ferranti, Basil R. V. Z. (b. 1930), C., Hampshire Central
*Douro, The Marquess of (b. 1945), C., Surrey W.
*Elles, The Baroness (b. 1921), C., Thames Valley
Elles, James E. M. (b. 1949), C., Oxford and Buckinghamshire
Elliott, Michael N. (b. 1932), Lab., London W.
*Ewing, Mrs. Winifred M. (b. 1929), S.N.P., Highlands and Islands
Faith, Mrs. I. Sheila (b. 1928), C., Cumbria and Lancashire N.
Falconer, Alec (b. 1940), Lab., Scotland Mid and Fife
Ford, J. Glyn (b. 1950), Lab., Greater Manchester E.
*Griffiths, Winston J., M.P. (b. 1943), Lab., Wales S.
Hindley, Michael J. (b. 1947), Lab., Lancashire E.
Hoon, Geoffrey W. (b. 1953), Lab., Derbyshire
*Howell, Paul F. (b. 1951), C., Norfolk
Huckfield, Leslie J. (b. 1942), Lab., Merseyside E.
Hughes, Stephen S. (b. 1952), Lab., Durham
*Hume, John, M.P. (b. 1937), S.D.L.P., Northern Ireland
*Hutton, Alasdair H., M.B.E., T.D. (b. 1940), C., Scotland S.
Jackson, Mrs. Caroline F. (b. 1946), C., Wiltshire
*Jackson, Christopher M. (b. 1935), C., Kent E.
Kilby, Michael L. (b. 1924), C., Nottingham
*Lomas, Alfred (b. 1928), Lab., London N.E.
McGowan, Michael (b. 1940), Lab., Leeds

McMahon, Hugh R. (b. 1938), Lab., Strathclyde W.
McMillan-Scott, Edward H. C. (b. 1949), C., York
*Marshall, John L., M.P. (b. 1940), C., London N.
Martin, David W. (b. 1954), Lab., Lothians
*Megahy, Thomas (b. 1929), Lab., Yorkshire S.W.
Moorhouse, C. James O. (b. 1924), C., London S. and Surrey E.
Morris, D. Richard (b. 1930), Lab., Wales Mid and W.
Newens, A. Stanley (b. 1930), Lab., London Central
Newman, Edward (b. 1953), Lab., Greater Manchester Central
*Newton Dunn, William F. (b. 1941), C., Lincolnshire
*Normanton, Sir Tom, T.D. (b. 1917), C., Cheshire E.
*O'Hagan, The Lord (b. 1945), C., Devon
*Paisley, Rev. Ian R. K., M.P. (b. 1926), D.U.P., Northern Ireland
*Patterson, George B. (b. 1939), C., Kent W.
*Pearce, Andrew (b. 1937), C., Cheshire W.
*Plumb, Lord (b. 1925), C., The Cotswolds
*Prag, Derek (b. 1923), C., Hertfordshire
*Price, Peter N. (b. 1942), C., London S.E.
*Prout, Christopher J. (b. 1942), C., Shropshire and Stafford
*Provan, James L. C. (b. 1936), C., Scotland N.E.
*Quin, Miss Joyce G., M.P. (b. 1944), Lab., Tyne and Wear
*Roberts, Dame Shelagh M., D.B.E. (b. 1924), C., London S.W.
*Scott-Hopkins, Sir James (b. 1921), C., Hereford and Worcester
*Seal, Barry H. (b. 1937), Lab., Yorkshire W.
*Seligman, R. Madron (b. 1918), C., Sussex W.
*Sherlock, Dr. Alexander (b. 1922), C., Essex S.W.
*Simmonds, Richard J. (b. 1944), C., Wight and Hampshire E.
*Simpson, Anthony M. H., T.D. (b. 1935), C., Northamptonshire
Smith, Llewellyn (b. 1944), Lab., Wales S.E.
Stevenson, George W. (b. 1938), Lab., Staffordshire E.
Stewart, Kenneth (b. 1925), Lab., Merseyside W.
*Stewart-Clark, Sir John, Bt. (b. 1929), C., Sussex E.
*Taylor, Rt. Hon. John D., M.P. (b. 1937), O.U.P., Northern Ireland
Tomlinson, John E. (b. 1939), Lab., Birmingham W.
Tongue, Miss Carole (b. 1955), Lab., London E.
*Tuckman, Frederick A. (b. 1922), C., Leicester
*Turner, Amédée E, Q.C. (b. 1929), C., Suffolk
*Vanneck, Hon. Sir Peter B. R. (b. 1922), C., Cleveland and Yorkshire N.
*Welsh, Michael J. (b. 1942), C., Lancashire Central
West, Norman (b. 1935), Lab., Yorkshire S.

UNITED KINGDOM ELECTIONS TO EUROPEAN PARLIAMENT (June 14, 1984)

(Eco. = Ecology Party; W. Reg. = Wessex Regionalists; for other abbreviations, see p. 249)

Bedfordshire, South
E. 524,974

*P. G. Beazley, C.	72,088
W. Cochrane, Lab.	57,106
P. A. Dixon, L./All.	36,444
C. maj.	14,982

Birmingham, East
E. 548,899

Mrs. C. M. Crawley, Lab.	76,377
*Miss N. E. Forster, C.	54,994
D. A. Bennett S.D.P./All.	21,927
Miss D. Howell, Ind.	1,440
Lab. maj.	21,383

Birmingham, West
E. 518,707

J. E. Tomlinson, Lab.	61,946
C. Hart, C.	55,702
J. C. Binns, S.D.P./All.	19,422
Lab. maj.	6,244

Bristol
E. 569,765

*R. J. Cottrell, C.	94,652
R. L. Berry, Lab.	77,008
P. J. Farley, S.D.P./All.	33,698
C. maj.	17,644

Cambridge and Bedfordshire North
E. 523,899

*Sir Frederick Catherwood, C.	86,117
H. G. Bottomley, Lab.	38,901
A. N. Duff, L./All.	36,341
C. maj.	47,216

Cheshire, East
E. 498,568

*T. Normanton, C.	71,182
A. Stephenson, Lab.	52,806
J. P. Corbett, S.D.P./All.	31,374
C. maj.	18,376

Cheshire, West
E. 539,761

*A. Pearce, C.		74,579
D. G. Hanson, *Lab.*		64,887
E. C. H. Owen, *S.D.P./All.*		30,470
C. maj.		*9,692*

Cleveland and Yorkshire North
E. 566,083

*Hon. Sir P. Vanneck,, C.		73,217
P. F. Tinnion, *Lab.*		70,592
C. Beever, *S.D.P./All.*		35,916
C. maj.		*2,625*

Cornwall and Plymouth
E. 506,004

C. J. P. Beazley, C.		81,627
J. C. Marks, *S.D.P./All.*		63,876
J. D. Cosgrove, *Lab.*		35,952
A. I. Parkin, *Ind.*		5,645
R. J. Trevallion, *Ind.*		2,981
J. Whetter, *Ind.*		1,892
C. maj.		*17,751*

The Cotswolds
E. 527,081

*Sir H. Plumb, C.		94,740
Miss M. E. Burton, *L./All.*		45,798
Miss J. A. Royall, *Lab.*		36,738
C. maj.		*48,942*

Cumbria and Lancashire North
E. 547,433

Mrs. I. S. Faith, C.		86,127
J. R. Atkinson, *Lab.*		62,332
Mrs. K. C. Brooks, *L./All.*		39,622
C. maj.		*23,795*

Derbyshire
E. 553,020

G. W. Hoon, *Lab.*		79,466
*T. N. B. Spencer, C.		72,613
Miss J. M. Elles, *S.D.P./All.*		30,824
Lab. maj.		*6,853*

Devon
E. 560,807

*Lord O'Hagan, C.		110,129
P. G. Driver, *L./All.*		53,519
D. A. Gorbutt, *Lab.*		30,017
P. S. Christie, *Eco.*		6,919
Lady Rous, *W. Reg.*		659
C. maj.		*56,610*

Dorset East and Hampshire West
E. 565,709

B. M. D. Cassidy, C.		109,072
J. M. Goss, *L./All.*		49,181
D. T. James, *Lab.*		31,223
C. maj.		*59,891*

Durham
E. 530,104

S. S. Hughes, *Lab.*		106,073
Hon. W. R. Fletcher-Vane, C.		44,846
C. Foote Wood, *L./All.*		32,307
Lab. maj.		*61,227*

Essex, N.E.
E. 574,022

*D. M. Curry, C.		97,138
B. L. Stapleton, *Lab.*		42,836

A. E. Ross, *S.D.P./All.*		34,769
C. maj.		*54,302*

Essex, S.W.
E. 557,704

*Dr. A. Sherlock, C.		72,190
C. O'Brien, *Lab.*		56,169
A. F. C. Morris, *L./All.*		29,385
C. maj.		*16,021*

Glasgow
E. 518,178

*Mrs. J. Buchan, *Lab.*		91,015
Miss S. Chadd, C.		25,282
C. Mason, *L./All.*		20,867
N. MacLeod, *S.N.P.*		16,456
Lab. maj.		*65,733*

Greater Manchester, Central
E. 507,941

E. Newman, *Lab.*		76,830
T. R. M. Sewell, C.		48,753
G. E. A. O. Weddell, *L./All.*		24,192
K. J. Martin, *Ind.*		1,430
Lab. maj.		*28,077*

Greater Manchester, East
E. 510,586

J. G. Ford, *Lab.*		65,101
T. K. Thornber, C.		56,450
Mrs. B. Gaskin, *S.D.P./All.*		27,801
M. J. Shipley, *Eco.*		3,158
Lab. maj.		*8,651*

Greater Manchester, West
E. 528,896

*Rt. Hon. Mrs. B. A. Castle, *Lab.*		93,740
*W. J. Hopper, C.		56,042
J. R. Boddy, *S.D.P./All.*		17,894
Lab. maj.		*37,698*

Hampshire, Central
E. 524,649

*B. R. V. Z. de Ferranti, C.		84,086
F. B. Jacobs, *S.D.P./All.*		39,265
M. V. Castle, *Lab.*		39,228
C. maj.		*44,821*

Hereford and Worcester
E. 560,654

*Sir J. Scott-Hopkins, C.		84,077
P. E. S. Nielson, *Lab.*		44,143
I. D. Phillips, *L./All.*		37,854
Mrs. F. M. Norman, *Eco.*		8,179
C. maj.		*39,934*

Hertfordshire
E. 505,206

*D. Prag, C.		87,603
A. McWalter, *Lab.*		41,671
Mrs. F. M. Beckett, *S.D.P./All.*		40,877
C. maj.		*45,932*

Highlands and Islands
E. 307,265

*Mrs. W. M. Ewing, *S.N.P.*		49,410
D. R. Johnston, *L./All.*		33,133
D. Webster, C.		18,847
Rev. J. McArthur, *Lab.*		16,644
S.N.P. maj.		*16,277*

Humberside
E. 503,080

*R. C. Battersby, C.		61,952
P. D. Crampton, *Lab.*		53,937
S. W. Unwin, *S.D.P./All.*		27,318
C. maj.		*8,015*

Kent, East
E. 554,808

*C. M. Jackson, C.		92,340
D. A. Enright, *Lab.*		43,473
A. Kinch, *S.D.P./All.*		34,601
S. Dawe, *Eco.*		5,405
C. maj.		*48,867*

Kent, West
E. 565,693

*G. B. Patterson, C.		85,414
A. Woodhams, *Lab.*		50,784
P. H. Billenness, *L. All.*		33,306
Mrs. C. A. Bunyan, *Eco.*		4,991
C. maj.		*34,630*

Lancashire, Central
E. 524,132

*M. J. Welsh, C.		82,370
Miss H. M. Jones, *Lab.*		56,175
*M. Gallagher, *S.D.P./All.*		24,936
C. maj.		*26,195*

Lancashire, East
E. 534,542

M. J. Hindley, *Lab.*		75,711
*E. T. Kellett-Bowman, C.		67,806
A. G. Lishman, *L./All.*		26,320
Lab. maj.		*7,905*

Leeds
E. 527,653

M. McGowan, *Lab.*		70,535
J. G. Holt, C.		60,178
S. J. Cooksey, *L./All.*		36,097
Lab. maj.		*10,357*

Leicester
E. 564,350

*F. A. Tuckman, C.		72,508
P. A. Soulsby, *Lab.*		69,616
D. N. Simmonds, *S.D.P./All.*		29,656
A. G. Barrett, *Ind.*		3,249
C. maj.		*2,892*

Lincolnshire
E. 551,904

*W. F. Newton Dunn, C.		92,606
C. W. Sewell, *Lab.*		47,161
G. Purves, *L./All.*		37,244
C. maj.		*45,445*

London, Central
E. 543,825

A. S. Newens, *Lab.*		77,842
*A. D. Fergusson, C.		64,545
E. Wistrich, *S.D.P./All.*		30,269
J. E. Porritt, *Eco.*		5,945
R. J. Maynard, *Ind.*		1,569
Lab. maj.		*13,297*

London, East
E. 537,831

Miss C. Tongue, *Lab.*		73,870
*A. R. Tyrrell, C.		61,711
Mrs. J. Horne, *S.D.P./All.*		26,379
Lab. maj.		*12,159*

London, North
E.564,359

*J. L. Marshall, C.	74,846
E. Large, Lab.	69,993
J. Skinner, L./All.	31,344
P. S. J. Lang, Eco.	4,682
C. maj.	*4,853*

London, N.E.
E.513,781

*A. Lomas, Lab.	79,907
M. Batchelor, C.	27,242
J. P. Heppell, L./All.	17,344
Mrs. J. Lambert, Eco.	4,797
Lab. maj.	*52,665*

London, N.W.
E.518,365

*The Lord Bethell, C.	69,803
Ms. P. Healy, Lab.	62,381
A. Ketteringham, L./All.	29,609
C. maj.	*7,422*

London, S.E.
E.561,984

*P. N. Price, C.	81,508
S. J. Cowan, Lab.	61,493
J. H. Fryer, L./All.	38,614
W. E. Turner, Ind.	989
C. maj.	*20,015*

London, S.W.
E.499,273

*Dame Shelagh M. Roberts, C.	70,490
Miss A. J. Pollack, Lab.	63,623
D. J. Twigg, L./All.	32,268
Mrs. S. G. Willington, Eco.	3,066
C. maj.	*6,867*

London South and Surrey East
E.505,393

*C. J. O. Moorhouse, C.	82,122
A. S. MacKinlay, Lab.	37,465
J. G. Parry, L./All.	34,522
C. maj.	*44,657*

London, South Inner
E.530,672

*R. A. Balfe, Lab.	77,661
Mrs. D. Miller, C.	46,180
J. Daly, S.D.P./All.	25,391
Mrs. J. Owens, Eco.	3,281
Lab. maj.	*31,481*

London, West
E.516,661

M. N. Elliot, Lab.	79,554
*B. H. Hord, C.	74,325
C. Layton, S.D.P./All.	36,687
Mrs. D. M. Sutherland, Eco.	4,361
Lab. maj.	*5,229*

Lothians
E.516,068

D. W. Martin, Lab.	74,989
I. J. Henderson, C.	49,065
Dr. J. D. Mabon, S.D.P./All.	36,636
Dr. D. Stevenson, S.N.P.	22,331
Miss L. Hendry, Eco.	2,560
Lab. maj.	*25,924*

Merseyside, East
E.537,285

L. J. Huckfield, Lab.	87,086
T. G. D. R. B. Galbraith, C.	38,047
T. Bishop, S.D.P./All.	17,259
Lab. maj.	*49,039*

Merseyside, West
E.551,532

K. Stewart, Lab.	65,915
*Miss G. D. Hooper, C.	52,718
P. R. Clark, L./All.	37,303
Lab. maj.	*13,197*

Midlands, Central
E.533,798

*J. de Courcy Ling, C.	67,884
D. J. Blackman, Lab.	55,155
P. Langmead, S.D.P./All.	27,912
A. Enstone, Ind.	1,494
C. maj.	*12,729*

Midlands, West
E.533,796

T. J. Pitt, Lab.	74,091
A. T. Burnside, C.	54,406
C. Carter, L./All.	17,709
Lab. maj.	*19,685*
(see p. 280 for by-election result)	

Norfolk
E.543,214

*P. F. Howell, C.	95,459
A. E. B. Heading, Lab.	58,602
L. Williams, S.D.P./All.	37,703
C. maj.	*36,857*

Northamptonshire
E.547,188

*A. M. H. Simpson, C.	88,668
J. Dickie, Lab.	48,809
Mrs. C. M. Goodhart, S.D.P./All.	37,421
Mrs. A. Bryant, Ind.	3,330
C. maj.	*39,859*

Northumbria
E.512,979

*G. J. Adam, Lab.	78,417
C. M. M. Crichton, C.	62,717
G. Scott, L./All.	42,946
Lab. maj.	*15,700*

Nottingham
E.554,473

M. L. Kilby, Lab.	82,500
K. Coates, Lab.	66,374
K. M. Melton, L./All.	33,169
C. maj.	*16,126*

Oxford and Buckinghamshire
E.542,343

J. E. M. Elles, C.	94,136
R. J. Liddle, S.D.P./All.	45,055
J. G. Power, Lab.	39,164
C. maj.	*49,081*

Scotland, Mid and Fife
E.528,529

A. Falconer, Lab.	80,038
*J. R. Purvis, C.	52,872
Mrs. J. T. Jones, S.N.P.	30,511
A. A. I. Wedderburn, S.D.P./All.	24,220
Lab. maj.	*27,166*

Scotland, North-East
E.548,711

*J. L. C. Provan, C.	53,809
F. Doran, Lab.	44,638
D. Hood, S.N.P.	33,448
I. G. Philip, S.D.P./All.	25,490
C. maj.	*9,171*

Scotland, South
E.484,760

*A. H. Hutton, C.	60,843
R. Stewart, Lab.	57,706
Mrs. E. M. Buchanan, L./All.	23,598
I. R. Goldie, S.N.P.	22,242
C. maj.	*3,137*

Sheffield
E.558,984

G. R. Cryer, Lab.	93,530
D. R. Grayson, C.	47,247
Miss M. Holmstedt, L./All.	23,935
Lab. maj.	*46,283*

Shropshire and Stafford
E.562,823

*C. J. Prout, C.	82,291
D. J. A. Hallam, Lab.	57,359
R. M. Burman, L./All.	37,209
C. maj.	*24,932*

Somerset and Dorset West
E.540,393

Mrs. M. Daly, C.	98,928
R. G. Moore, L./All.	58,677
Mrs. J. Linden, Lab.	36,836
C. maj.	*40,251*

Staffordshire, East
E.563,376

G. W. Stevenson, Lab.	76,753
*R. J. Moreland, C.	68,886
R. Fox, S.D.P./All.	26,093
Lab. maj.	*7,867*

Strathclyde, East
E.498,458

*K. D. Collins, Lab.	90,792
G. Leslie, S.N.P.	27,330
P. R. Leckie, C.	24,857
Ms. P. de Seume, L./All.	11,883
Lab. maj.	*63,462*

Strathclyde, West
E.499,162

H. McMahon, Lab.	70,234
Miss J. Lait, C.	47,196
Mrs. J. Herriot, S.N.P.	28,866
D. J. Herbison, S.D.P./All.	25,955
Lab. maj.	*23,038*

Suffolk
E.516,050

*A. E. Turner, C.	88,243
W. Moszczynski, Lab.	41,145
C. Leakey, L./All.	34,084
C. maj.	*47,098*

Surrey, West
E.504,923

*The Marquess of Douro, C.	96,675
E. Mortimer, S.D.P./All.	44,087
N. K. A. S. Vaz, Lab.	22,531
C. maj.	*52,588*

Sussex, East
E.537,397

Sir J. Stewart-Clark, Bt.,	
C.	102,287
J. Busby, *S.D.P./All.*	36,666
H. Spillman, *Lab*	32,213
Mrs. E. Evelyn, *Eco.*	5,401
C.maj.	*65,621*

Sussex, West
E.531,934

R. M. Seligman, C.	104,257
Dr. J. M. M. Walsh, *L./All.*	46,755
G. C. Rees, *Lab.*	22,857
D. Aherne, *Eco.*	3,842
C.maj.	*57,502*

Thames Valley
E.519,564

The Baroness Elles, C.	74,928
R. B. Bastin, *Lab.*	36,123
R. W. Bradnock, *L./All.* ...	32,704
C.maj.	*38,805*

Tyne and Wear
E.543,955

Miss J. G. Quin, Lab.	89,024
R. R. Cook, *C.*	39,610
B. P. Carroll, *S.D.P./All.* ...	19,081
Lab.maj.	*49,414*

Wales, Mid and West
E.533,644

D. R. Morris, *Lab.*	89,362
D. Lewis, *C.*	52,910
D. Lloyd, *L./All.*	35,168
Dr. P. Williams, *P.C.*	32,880
Miss M. A. Smith, *Eco.*	4,266
Lab.maj.	*36,452*

Wales, North
E.516,153

Miss B. A. Brooks, C.	69,139
R. T. Ellis, *S.D.P./All.* ...	56,861
C. I. Campbell, *Lab.*	54,768
D. Iwan, *P.C.*	38,117
C.maj.	*12,278*

Wales, South
E.509,434

W. J. Griffiths, Lab.	99,936
Miss J. R. Pattman, *C.*	55,678
Mrs. J. Davis, *L./All.*	26,588
Dr D. Huws, *P.C.*	13,201
Lab.maj.	*44,258*

Wales, S.E.
E.565,739

L. Smith, *Lab.*	131,916
R. Whyatt, *C.*	36,359
C. D. Lindley, *S.D.P./All.* .	28,330
S. Morgan, *P.C.*	18,833
Lab.maj.	*95,557*

Wight and Hampshire, East
E.544,189

R. J. Simmonds, C.	96,666
Mrs. S. Ludford, *L./All.* ...	53,738
J. A. Phillips, *Lab.*	36,445
C.maj.	*42,928*

Wiltshire
E.531,501

Mrs. C. F. Jackson, *C.*	86,873
J. B. Ainslie, *L./All.*	60,404
P. Whiteside, *Lab.*	35,457
C.maj.	*26,469*

York
E.517,592

E. H. C. McMillan-Scott, *C.*	80,636
Mrs. S. Haines, *Lab.*	44,234
M. G. Howard, *S.D.P./All.*	33,356
C.maj.	*36,402*

Yorkshire, South
E.516,431

N. West, *Lab.*	98,020
Mrs. R. P. N. Pockley, *C.* .	30,271
D. Eden, *S.D.P./All.*	19,306
Lab.maj.	*67,749*

Yorkshire, S.W.
E.518,423

T. Megahy, Lab.	88,464
A. J. A. Lodge, *C.*	44,291
J. F. Crossley, *L./All.*	26,964
Lab.maj.	*44,173*

Yorkshire, West
E.560,190

B. H. Seal, Lab.	86,259
I. C. Bruce, *C.*	65,405
E. Lyons, *S.D.P./All.*	28,709
Lab.maj.	*20,854*

Northern Ireland
E.1,077,605

	First Preference
Rev. I. R. K. Paisley,	
D.U.P.	230,251
J. Hume, S.D.L.P.	151,399
Rt. Hon. J. D. Taylor,	
O.U.P.	147,169
D. Morrison, *S.F.*	91,476
D. Cook, *All.*	34,046
J. Kilfedder, *U.P.U.P.*	20,092
S. Lynch, *W.P.*	8,712
C. McGuigan, *Eco.*	2,172

Rev. I. R. K. Paisley, J. Hume, and Rt. Hon. J. D. Taylor were elected by the single transferable voting system.

BY-ELECTIONS

Midlands, West
(March 5, 1987)

John Bird, *Lab.*	59,761
Michael Whitby, *C.*	55,736
Christopher Carter, *L.*	37,106
Lab.maj.	*4,025*

PARLIAMENTARY ASSOCIATIONS

COMMONWEALTH PARLIAMENTARY ASSOCIATION (1911)

The Commonwealth Parliamentary Association consists of 115 branches in the national, state, provincial or territorial parliaments in the countries of the Commonwealth. Commonwealth Parliamentary conferences and general assemblies are held every year in different countries of the Commonwealth.

President (1988–89), Hon. Lawson A. Weekes, M.P., Speaker of the House of Assembly (*Barbados*).

Vice President (1988–89), Hon. D. N. E. Mutasa, M.P., Speaker of the House of Assembly (*Zimbabwe*).

Secretary-General, Dr. the Hon. David Tonkin, 7 Old Palace Yard, S.W.1.

Secretary, United Kingdom Branch, P. Cobb, O.B.E., Westminster Hall, Houses of Parliament, S.W.1.

THE INTER-PARLIAMENTARY UNION (1889)

To facilitate personal contact between Members of all Parliaments in the promotion of representative institutions, peace and international co-operation.
Secretary General, P. Cornillon, Place du Petit-Saconnex, B.P. 99, 1211 Geneva 19, Switzerland.

BRITISH GROUP

Palace of Westminster, SW1A 0AA

Hon. Presidents, The Lord Chancellor; Mr. Speaker.
President, The Rt. Hon. Margaret Thatcher, M.P.
Chairman, M. Marshall, M.P.
Secretary, Capt. P. J. Shaw, R.N.

THE PRINCIPAL PARTIES IN PARLIAMENT (1931–1987)

General Election	Conservative	Liberal	Labour
1931	471	72 (a)	65 (b)
1935	387	54 (c)	166 (d)
1945	189	25 (e)	396 (f)
1950	298 (g)	9	315 (h)
1951	320 (i)	6	296 (h)
1955	344 (i)	6	277 (j)
1959	365 (i)	6	258 (k)
1964	303 (i)	9	317
1966	253 (i)	12	363 (l)
1970	330 (m)	6	287 (n)
1974 (February)	296	14	301 (o)
1974 (October)	276	13	319 (p)
1979	339	11	268 (q)
1983	397	23 (r)	209 (s)
1987	376	22 (t)	229 (u)

Notes.—(a) Liberal National 35 (Simon); Liberal 33 (Samuel); 4 (Lloyd George). (b) National Labour 13 (MacDonald); Labour 52 (Henderson). (c) Liberal National 33; Liberal 21. (d) National Labour 8; Labour 154; I.L.P. 4. (e) Liberal National 13; Liberal 12. (f) Labour 393; I.L.P. 3. (g) Incl. Nat. Liberal. (h) Irish Nationalists (2) and Speaker make total of 625.

(i) Including associates. (j) Sinn Fein (2) and Speaker make total of 630. (k) Independent (1) makes total of 630. (l) Republican Labour (1) makes total of 630. (m) Including Ulster Unionists. (n) Scottish Nationalists (1); Independent (5) and Speaker make total of 630. (o) United Ulster Unionist Council (11), Scottish Nationalists (7), Plaid Cymru (2); Social Democratic and Labour Party (1); Social Democrat (1); Independent Labour (1); and Speaker make total of 635. (p) Scottish Nationalists (11); United Ulster Unionist (10); Plaid Cymru (3); Social Democratic and Labour Party (1); Independent (1) and Speaker make a total of 635. (q) Ulster Unionist (5); Democratic Unionist (3); Plaid Cymru (2); Scottish Nationalists (2); Social Democratic and Labour (1); United Ulster Unionist (1); Independent (2) and Speaker make a total of 635. (r) Liberal 17; S.D.P. 6. (s) Official Unionist (11); Democratic Unionist (3); Scottish Nationalists (2); Plaid Cymru (2); Ulster Popular Unionist (1); Social Democratic and Labour Party (1) and Provisional Sinn Fein (1) make a total of 650. (t) Liberal 17; S.D.P. 5. (u) Ulster Unionist (9); Scottish Nationalists (3); Plaid Cymru (3); Democratic Unionist (3); Social Democratic and Labour Party (3); Ulster Popular Unionist (1); Sinn Fein (1) make a total of 650.

PARLIAMENTS SINCE 1945

Assembled	Dissolved	Duration yrs. m. d.	Assembled	Dissolved	Duration yrs. m. d.
1945 Aug. 1	1950 Feb. 3	4 6 2	1970 June 29	1974 Feb. 8	3 7 10
1950 March 1	1951 Oct. 5	1 7 4	1974 March 6	1974 Sept. 20	0 6 14
1951 Oct. 31	1955 May 6	3 6 6	1974 Oct. 22	1979 April 7	4 5 16
1955 June 7	1959 Sept. 18	4 3 11	1979 May 9	1983 May 13	4 0 4
1959 Oct. 20	1964 Sept. 25	4 11 5	1983 June 15	1987 May 18	3 11 3
1964 Oct. 27	1966 March 10	1 4 11	1987 June 17		
1966 April 18	1970 May 29	4 1 11			

MAJORITIES IN THE HOUSE OF COMMONS SINCE 1945

Year	Party	Majority	Year	Party	Majority
1945	*Labour*	146	1970	*Conservative*	31
1950	*Labour*	8	1974 (Feb.)	No Majority	
1951	*Conservative*	16	1974 (Oct.)	*Labour*	5
1955	*Conservative*	59	1979	*Conservative*	43
1959	*Conservative*	100	1983	*Conservative*	144
1964	*Labour*	5	1987	*Conservative*	102
1966	*Labour*	99			

VOTES CAST AT U.K. GENERAL ELECTIONS, 1974–87

General Election, October, 1974*

Labour	11,156,597
Conservative	10,464,675
Liberal	5,346,800
Scottish Nationalist	839,628
Plaid Cymru	166,321
Others	195,065

General Election, 1983*

Conservative	13,012,602
Labour	8,457,124
Liberal/S.D.P. Alliance	7,780,587
Scottish Nationalist	331,975
Plaid Cymru	125,309
Others	198,383

General Election, 1979*

Conservative	13,697,753
Labour	11,506,741
Liberal	4,305,324
Scottish Nationalist	504,259
National Front	191,706
Plaid Cymru	132,544
Others	188,063

General Election, 1987*

Conservative	13,760,525
Labour	10,029,944
Liberal/S.D.P. Alliance	7,341,152
Scottish Nationalist	416,873
Plaid Cymru	123,589
Green†	89,753
Others	37,576

*Excluding Northern Ireland   †Excluding Ecology candidate in Northern Ireland

PARLIAMENTARY SUMMARY 1987-88

The House of Lords re-assembled after the summer recess on Oct. 20 and the House of Commons on Oct. 21.

On Oct. 21 the Environment Secretary (Mr. Nicholas Ridley) outlined the assistance that the government would be offering to local authorities to help repair the damage caused by the storms on Oct. 15-16. On Oct. 22 the Prime Minister (Mrs. Margaret Thatcher) delivered a strong rejection of economic sanctions against South Africa. The Leader of the Opposition (Mr. Neil Kinnock) labelled Mrs. Thatcher "an ally of apartheid". On Oct. 26 Labour M.P.s offered to change the day's business to allow the Chancellor of the Exchequer (Mr. Nigel Lawson) to speak to the House on the crisis in the world stock markets. They expressed anger at the fact that Mr. Lawson was not in the House, but was instead speaking at the Stock Exchange. In the House of Lords that day, the Government won approval for a clause in the Criminal Justices Bill which gives the Attorney General the power to refer unduly lenient sentences to the Court of Appeal. The vote was won by a majority of 43.

On Oct. 27, at the start of a two-day debate on defence, the Defence Secretary (Mr. George Younger) told the Commons that NATO would plug any gaps in the West's nuclear defence following the removal of cruise and Pershing missiles as a result of the Intermediate Nuclear Force reduction agreement between the Soviet Union and the U.S.A. Labour's shadow defence secretary, Mr. Denzil Davies, said that this would make a mockery of the I.N.F. agreement. On the second day of the debate Labour M.P. Mr. Denis Healey said that Britain was now entirely dependent on the U.S.A. for its nuclear weapons, and incapable of standing up to Washington on any important defence or foreign policy issue. On Oct. 29 the Chancellor announced that the proposed British Petroleum share offer would go ahead despite the recent fall in the stock market. On Nov. 2 the Commons approved the second reading of the Social Security Bill, which is intended to end benefit for 16 and 17 year olds and expected to save the D.H.S.S. some £275 million. Labour's shadow social services secretary, Mr. Robin Cook, criticized the Bill, saying that it would extinguish the benefit rights of 400,000 people and reduce the benefits of a further 300,000.

FINANCIAL STATEMENT

On Nov. 3 the Chancellor of the Exchequer (Mr. Lawson) presented his autumn financial statement in the Commons, and said that his forecast of economic prospects for 1988 took account of the likely effect of the worldwide falls in the equity markets. He said that the public expenditure planning total looked likely to amount to £147·5 billion, around £1 billion less than was allowed for in the 1986 public expenditure White Paper. The Chancellor gave the main reason for this shortfall as higher capital receipts by local authorities and new towns. He expected total spending on programmes apart from this to be broadly in line with plans.

"Taking account of miscellaneous items not included in the planning total, the net shortfall on the expenditure side is likely to be slightly in excess of £0·5 billion. On the receipts side, total tax revenues are likely to exceed the Budget forecast by almost 2·5 billion. This buoyancy reflects higher-than-forecast economic growth, greater than expected profitability, and an oil price above the $15 a barrel assumed."

Mr. Lawson said that at the time of the Budget he had set a public sector borrowing requirement for

1987-88 of some £4 billion, or 1 per cent of G.D.P. However, as a result of higher tax revenues and lower spending, he now expected the P.S.B.R. for the current financial year to be only £1 billion, or one quarter per cent of G.D.P.

Mr. Lawson said that privatization proceeds had made an important contribution to this year's low P.S.B.R., and that even if there had been no privatization proceeds at all, it would still be the lowest P.S.B.R. for 17 years.

PUBLIC EXPENDITURE

Turning to the public expenditure plans for the next three years, the Chancellor said: "Since 1982-83 public spending, including and excluding privatization proceeds, has been declining as a proportion of national income. There is likely to be a further substantial reduction this year, which will make this the longest sustained fall in public expenditure as a proportion of national income since the early 1950s.

"In July, Cabinet reaffirmed the objective of ensuring that public spending as a share of national income continued to fall, and, in particular, did not exceed the ratios published in the last White Paper. The plans that I am about to announce secure that objective."

He went on to announce new planning totals of 156·75 billion for 1988-89 , and £167 billion for 1989-90, increases of £2·5 billion and £5·5 billion respectively over the totals previously published. For 1990-91, the planning total has been set at £176 billion. Mr. Lawson said that for the later years, he judged it prudent to set aside larger reserves within the planning totals than he had done previously. The reserves will rise from £3·5 billion in 1988-89 to £7 billion in 1989-90, and £10·5 billion in 1990-91.

Mr. Lawson said that the planning totals also incorporated an estimate for privatization proceeds of £5 billion a year, unchanged from the last White Paper. These plans meant that public spending, excluding privatization proceeds, would continue to fall as a share of national income, from nearly 47 per cent in 1982-83, to around 42·5 per cent this year, and to 41·25 per cent by 1990-91.

He said: "This progress has been founded on our success in reining back the rate of growth of public spending. In our first Parliament the real annual rate of growth averaged 2·25 per cent; in our second Parliament it was just under 1·75 per cent. In the succeeding four years, the real growth of public spending is planned to be around 1·25 per cent a year, well within the prospective growth of the economy as a whole."

SPENDING PROGRAMMES

Mr. Lawson added that with public spending growing more slowly, the substantial reduction in public borrowing the Government had brought about had made more room for programme spending. He went on to give figures for expenditure on various programmes which represented increases over the plans published in the last public expenditure White Paper.

An extra £700 million is to be provided for the National Health Service in England in 1988-89, and an extra £800 million in 1989-90. On top of this the health service is expected to benefit from additional resources as a result of cost improvement programmes and land sales.

On law and order the Chancellor said that provision had been made for the substantial increase and acceleration in the prison building programme which the Home Secretary announced in July 1987.

This is intended to provide 4,200 extra places by 1993. Provision for local authority spending on the police has also been increased.

An extra £60 million a year has been provided for the improvement of school buildings. Spending on the universities will also increase, by £115 million in 1988–89 and by £130 million in 1989–90. There will also be an additional £45 million in 1988–89 and £65 million in 1989–90 for science.

Mr. Lawson announced that gross provision for housing investment is to be increased by nearly £400 million in 1988–89. This is intended to sustain the rising trend of spending on local authority renovation, and provide additional resources for housing associations. He added that provision for Urban Development Corporations is being increased by £65 million in the next year to help tackle the problems of the inner cities.

Social security spending has been increased by £1 billion for 1988–89 and £1·9 billion for 1989–90. This is partly because the take-up of benefits is expected to be higher than was previously envisaged. It also takes account of the uprating of benefits announced the week before the Chancellor's statement, and of the cost of compensating income support claimants for their contributions to rates.

Defence spending is to be increased by £230 million in 1988–89 and £490 million in 1989–90, while additions to planned capital expenditure for the public sector amount to some £1 billion in each of the next two years. About half of this is for the nationalized industries, principally for the large-scale investment programmes of the electricity and water industries.

Turning to national insurance, Mr. Lawson said that the lower earnings limit would be increased in April 1988 to £41 a week, in line with the single person's pension. The upper earnings limit would be raised to £305 a week, and limits for the reduced rate bands would also be increased. The upper limit for the 5 per cent and 7 per cent bands would be raised to £70 and £105 a week respectively. The upper limit for the 9 per cent rate for employers will rise to £155 a week.

The taxpayer's contribution to the National Insurance Fund—the so-called Treasury supplement—would be reduced from 7 per cent to 5 per cent but this would not require any change in contribution rates.

The Economy

Mr. Lawson told M.P.s that economic growth in 1987 looked to be turning out at 4 per cent, compared with the 3 per cent forecast at the time of the Budget.

"Strong growth in domestic demand has been more than matched by the rapid rise in exports. Manufacturing industry is doing particularly well, with output rising by 5 per cent. This strong performance has led to a substantial fall in unemployment, which is now more than 400,000 lower than a year ago.

"As I forecast at the time of the Budget, inflation in the fourth quarter of this year is likely to be 4 per cent."

Mr. Lawson added that he saw no need to amend his Budget forecast of a modest current account deficit of some £2·5 billion or about 1⁄2 per cent of G.D.P.

Looking ahead to 1988, the Chancellor forecast a continuation of the steady growth in the economy with low inflation.

Referring to the recent stock market crisis, the Chancellor concluded by saying, "This is clearly a time when economic forecasting is a more than usually hazardous business. But the economy is forecast to grow next year by around 2·5 per cent. With North Sea oil output now declining, this implies 3 per cent growth for the non-North Sea economy."

Reaction to the Financial Statement

The financial statement received widespread praise from the Conservative back-benches: Mr. Neil Hamilton said that Mr. Lawson would be the envy of finance ministers throughout the developed world. The Opposition were fiercely critical, however. Mr. John Smith, Labour's chief spokeman on Treasury and economic affairs, described the statement as a "confidence trick". He claimed that the Chancellor had only adjusted spending by the inflation rate, and not committed any money to the various programmes above the amount the Government had originally planned to spend.

On Nov. 5, in a debate on the collapse of the financial market, Mr. John Smith urged international action to deal with the crisis. The Chancellor said that any international intervention before the United States had "put its house in order" would be disastrous. The Opposition motion that the Government institute international action was defeated by 333 votes to 213 votes. On Nov. 10 the Government endorsed the decision of the Speaker (Mr. Bernard Weatherill) to suspend from the precincts of the Commons a researcher working for Labour M.P. Jeremy Corbyn. The researcher, Mr. Ronan Bennett, had been convicted and then cleared of terrorist crimes in Northern Ireland. On Nov. 19 the Secretary of State for Transport (Mr. Paul Channon) announced a public inquiry into the King's Cross fire.

The Government was criticized for its Health Service record by Labour M.P.s on Nov. 26, and several Conservative M.P.s, including former Health Minister Sir Barney Hayhoe and Dame Jill Knight, called for increased funding for the N.H.S. The Government's attitude to the N.H.S. attracted further criticism on Dec. 7 when Labour M.P.s and several Conservative back-benchers condemned plans to impose charges for dental examinations and eye tests and some Conservative M.P.s voted against the Government. In a full day's debate on the N.H.S on Jan. 20 the Social Services Secretary (Mr. John Moore) resisted calls for additional funding for health, refusing to anticipate the findings of a major review of the N.H.S.

On Nov. 30 the Commons debated the Housing Bill. Mr. Clive Soley, for Labour, argued that the Bill could lead to the return of Rachmanism. The Environment Secretary (Mr. Nicholas Ridley) said that the Bill would "make a major contribution to ending the shortage of premises to rent in London and other places."

Education

During the Commons debate on the Education Reform Bill on Dec. 1, the Labour education spokesman, Mr. Jack Straw, accused the Education Secretary (Mr. Kenneth Baker) of transferring power from local authorities back to central government. He said that the move was towards education vouchers whereby parents would have to pay for everything except basic education. Former Prime Minister Mr. Edward Heath called the Bill "a confidence trick" on parents. Mr. Baker said that the Bill's qualities could be summed up in three words, "standards, choice and freedom".

On Dec. 3 Mr. Kenneth Clarke, Minister of Trade and Industry, announced in the Commons that British Steel was to be privatized. The announcement led to criticism from the Opposition and Mr. Brian Gould, Labour spokesman on trade and industry, called it "another case of privatization which is dogma-driven".

On Dec. 16 the Commons began a two day debate on the Local Government (Finance) Bill containing provisions for replacing the rating system with the community charge. The Environment Secretary, (Mr. Ridley) said that the Bill was intended "to abolish the inequities of the present domestic rating system". The shadow environment secretary, Mr. Jack Cunningham, described the Bill as mediaeval and a giant stride towards centralized government. Rebel Conservative M.P.s, led by Mr. Michael Heseltine, criticized the Bill. On Dec. 17 Mr. Edward Heath was barracked by members of the Conservative right wing when he said that the community charge would be "unfair and unworkable". Mr. Peter Walker, Welsh Secretary, said that a separate system would operate in Wales. Mr. David Owen, for the S.D.P., referred to the Bill as "the most massive act of maldistribution in centuries". The second reading of the Bill was passed but 17 Conservative M.P.s voted against it, reducing the Government majority to 72.

Another attempt to amend the Official Secrets Act was made this session with the introduction of a private member's Bill by Conservative M.P. Mr. Richard Shepherd. The Government opposed the Bill on the grounds that a White Paper on the reform of the Act was in preparation.. On Jan. 14 at Commons question time Mr. Neil Kinnock attacked the Prime Minister's wish that Conservative M.P.s vote down the Bill as "shallow, spiteful and spurious". On Jan. 15 the Bill was voted down but the Government had a majority of only 37.

The Stalker/Sampson Inquiry

On Jan. 25 the Attorney General (Sir Patrick Mayhew) told the Commons that there would be no prosecutions of R.U.C. officers as a result of the Stalker/Sampson inquiry into the fatal shooting of six people by the Royal Ulster Constabulary in 1982 which had led to allegations that the R.U.C. were operating a "shoot-to-kill" policy. The decision not to prosecute was taken despite evidence that officers had conspired to pervert the course of justice and drew immediate protests from Opposition M.P.s. Labour M.P. Mr. Ken Livingstone was suspended for five days for calling the Attorney General "an accomplice to murder". On Jan. 28 the Northern Ireland Secretary (Mr. Tom King) said that the decision not to prosecute was not the end of the matter and that the possibility of disciplinary proceedings against some individuals was being urgently considered. On Feb. 17 Mr. King told the House that the Chief Constable of Staffordshire had been asked to consider whether disciplinary charges should be brought against any R.U.C. officer.

On Feb. 1 Opposition peers launched a concerted attack on Clause 28 of the Local Government Bill which proposed to outlaw the promotion of homosexuality by local authorities, especially in schools. On Feb. 2 the Archbishop of York said that Clause 28 was a "dangerous" threat to civil liberties. However, the Lords passed the Bill by 202 votes to 122. On Feb. 4 the Education Secretary (Mr. Kenneth Baker) announced to the Commons that the Inner London Education Authority would be abolished in 1990. On Feb. 9 the Commons debated an all party motion which called for the approval in principle of the televising of proceedings in the Commons. The Prime Minister opposed the motion, saying that television would erode the reputation of the House, but the following day the House voted in favour of the motion.

On March 4 the Prime Minister (Mrs. Thatcher) told critics of the outcome of the recent NATO summit that the Soviet Union must initiate the next phase of disarmament in Europe by giving up its superiority in conventional weapons. This would be necessary before further nuclear reductions could be considered. On March 7 the Commons began a debate on the privatization of the electricity industry.

THE BUDGET

On March 15 the Chancellor of the Exchequer (Mr. Lawson) presented his fifth Budget to the House of Commons. During the course of the speech unprecedented interruptions occurred and the Deputy Speaker was at one stage forced to suspend proceedings for ten minutes.

In his Budget statement Mr. Lawson said: "The strength and durability of the economic upswing has now exceeded all postwar records. We are about to enter our eighth successive year of sustained growth, and the sixth in which this has been combined with low inflation. And even without looking to 1988, the six years to 1987 have been the longest period of steady growth, at a rate averaging 3 per cent a year, for half a century.

"In 1987 as a whole, output grew by getting on for 4·5 per cent, rather more than the rate of inflation, which averaged 4·2 per cent. At the same time unemployment fell faster than in any other year since the war, in every region of the country, and more than in any other major nation.

"Looking ahead, I expect 1988 to be yet another year of healthy growth with low inflation; and there is every prospect that unemployment will continue to fall, although probably not as rapidly as last year.

"As last year, inflation is forecast to end the year at 4 per cent. While this is still too high, it is a testimony to the soundness of our policies that the present strong and sustained upswing, unlike almost all its predecessors, has not led to a resurgence of inflation.

"With growth in the U.K. economy likely to continue to outpace that of most other major countries, particularly in continental Europe, and with our oil surplus falling as North Sea oil production declines, the current account of the balance of payments is forecast to remain in deficit this year, by some £4 billion, equivalent to less than 1 per cent of G.D.P.

"Given the strength of the economy in general, and of our public finances in particular, not to mention our massive net overseas assets, I foresee no difficulty in financing a temporary current account deficit of this scale."

MONETARY POLICY

Mr. Lawson continued: "The Medium-Term Financial Strategy, now entering its ninth year, will continue to provide the framework for reducing the growth of money G.D.P. and hence inflation, over the medium term. These will be achieved by maintaining firm monetary discipline, buttressed by a prudent fiscal stance.

"Achieving the gradual eradication of inflation requires a steady reduction in monetary growth in the medium term. While I shall continue to take account of broad money, or liquidity, as last year there will be no explicit target. For narrow money, M0, the target range for 1988–89 will be 1–5 per cent, as foreshadowed in last year's M.T.F.S."

Mr. Lawson said that short-term interest rates remain the essential instrument of monetary policy and that he would continue to set interest rates at the level necessary to ensure downward pressure on inflation.

PUBLIC SECTOR BORROWING

On public sector borrowing, Mr. Lawson told the House that in 1987–88 the Government was set to secure something previously achieved only on one occasion since the beginning of the 1950s: a balanced budget. He said that he expected the final outturn for 1987–88 to be a Budget surplus of £3 billion, and added that having achieved a balanced Budget, he intended to stick to it.

The Chancellor had announced, in the Autumn Statement in November 1987, a £2·5 billion increase in public expenditure plans for 1988–89, with resources allocated to programmes up by over £4·5 billion. These large increases in public expenditure programmes for the coming year will be financed partly from the saving in debt interest resulting from the reduction in Government borrowing. Debt interest payments now account for about three quarters of a percentage point less of G.D.P. than they did only three years ago, a saving of some £3 billion a year. The achievement of a balanced Budget this year will reduce debt interest payments still further.

TAX REFORM

Mr. Lawson said that in preparing the Budget he had been guided by four basic principles:

"First, the need to reduce tax rates where they are clearly too high. Second, the need to reduce or abolish unwarranted tax breaks. Third, the need to make life a little simpler for the taxpayer. And, fourth, the need to remove some manifest injustices from the system.

"My first reform concerns the taxation of marriage. I have decided to introduce, at the earliest practicable date, April 1990, a completely new system of independent taxation.

"Under this new system, a husband and wife will be taxed independently, on income of all kinds. All taxpayers, male or female, married or single will be entitled to the same personal allowance, which will be available against all income, whether from earnings, pensions or savings.

"In addition, there will be a married couple's allowance, equal to the difference under the present system between the married man's allowance and the single allowance. This new allowance will go in the first instance to the husband, so that his tax threshold does not fall. But if he does not have enough income to use it in full, he will be able to transfer any unused portion to his wife, to set against her income. At the same time, from 1990 married women will pay their own tax, on the basis of their own income, and have their own tax return, when one is necessary.

MORTGAGES

"Independent taxation by itself will remove the most common penalty—the taxation of a married woman's income at her husband's marginal rate. But there are other tax penalties on marriage, and I propose to abolish all of them. These changes need not await the introduction of independent taxation.

"Under the present system an unmarried couple can get twice as much mortgage interest relief as a married couple. This has attracted increasing—and justified—criticism. I propose to put a stop to it as from August this year. Thereafter, the £30,000 limit on mortgage interest relief will be related to the house or flat, irrespective of the number of borrowers. Existing mortgages will be unaffected.

"Another anomaly is that an unmarried couple with children can each claim the additional personal allowance intended for single parents, and thus get more tax relief than a married couple in the same position. I propose to confine them to a single additional personal allowance, with effect from April 1989."

TAXATION ON BUSINESS

Turning to business taxation Mr. Lawson said: "I do not propose any further changes to the structure of corporation tax. And the main corporation tax rate for 1988–89 will be unchanged at 35 per cent. But I do have some changes to propose to specific aspects of business taxation.

"I propose to simplify the system by making all business entertainment non-deductible for tax purposes, including for V.A.T.

"In conjunction with the Secretary of State for Energy (Mr. Parkinson), I propose to restructure the tax regime for the new generation of southern basin and onshore fields, so as to relate tax liability more closely to profitability. Accordingly, Mr. Parkinson will shortly be bringing forward legislation to abolish royalties, from July 1, for all such fields. At the same time, I propose to reduce the petroleum revenue tax oil allowance for these fields. This will mean the end of royalties for all future fields."

The Chancellor said that he intended to remove the tax charge which hitherto fell on building societies wishing to convert themselves into companies, and also to simplify the administrative arrangements for taxing Lloyd's members. Mr. Lawson added that he proposed to simplify the Section 482 rules for companies who wish to migrate overseas, so that in future companies will be considered resident in the U.K. if they are incorporated here.

The Chancellor then turned to a number of proposals to give further help to small businesses and new businesses.

"The rate of new business formation, net of failures, has averaged 500 a week since 1979. Many new businesses have been greatly assisted by the Business Expansion Scheme, which has now been running for nearly five years.

"However, the rapid growth of the venture capital market since 1983 has meant that companies seeking relatively large amounts of equity investment can now raise these readily, while smaller companies looking for more modest amounts can still find it difficult to do so.

"To improve the targeting of the B.E.S., I therefore propose to introduce a limit of £500,000 on the amount any company can raise under the scheme in any one year. Investment should thus be better directed at the smaller and newer businesses, particularly those outside the south-east of England. In the special circumstances of the ship-chartering industry, however, the limit will be £5 million.

"I have one further proposal affecting the Business Expansion Scheme. If successful firms are to expand further, and create still more jobs, we also have to make it easier for people to move to where the new jobs are. The Government's proposals to deregulate new rents are already going through the House. Deregulation will, over time, substantially increase the supply of housing for rent. But this will not happen overnight, and there is a case for a special incentive to speed up the process in the early years.

"I therefore propose to extend the Business Expansion Scheme to include companies specializing in the letting of residential property on the new assured tenancy basis.

RELIEF

"In last year's Budget I raised the ceiling for capital gains tax retirement relief from £100,000 of gain to £125,000. But I believe it is necessary to do more to help the small businessman whose wealth is tied up in his business and who is faced with the disincentive of a heavy capital gains tax bill when he sells up on retirement. I therefore propose to extend capital gains tax retirement relief so that, on top of the exemption, half of any gain between £125,000 and £500,000 will also be completely free of tax.

"Lastly, on the small business front, I propose to increase the V.A.T. threshold to £22,100, the maximum permitted under existing European Community law."

Mr. Lawson went on to announce the abolition of Capital Duty with effect from midnight, and, at the same time, the Unit Trust Instrument Duty. The cost of abolishing these two taxes will be of the order of £100 million in 1988–89.

PERSONAL TAXATION

"I now turn to an important area of personal taxation which is ripe for reform and simplification: the taxation of payments made under deeds of covenant and maintenance arrangements.

[Covenants to charity will be unaffected by the changes.]

"First, covenants. Charitable covenants apart, I propose to take all new covenants made by individuals on or after today out of the tax system altogether. In other words, people receiving payments under covenants will not be liable to tax on them, and those making the payments will not be able to claim tax relief on them. The tax treatment of existing covenants will continue unchanged.

"Next, maintenance. Here, too, we tax the recipient, only to give tax relief to the payer. The present rules can be complex and confusing for people going through separation and divorce.

"Accordingly, I propose that, for new maintenance arrangements, recipients will not be liable to any tax whatever on maintenance payments. Relief to the payer will be restricted to payments to a separated or divorced spouse, up to a limit equal to the difference between the married and single allowances.

"For existing maintenance arrangements, the present rules will continue to apply in 1988–89, except that a separated or divorced spouse will be exempt from tax on receipts up to the difference between the married and single allowances. Full relief will continue for all those who are making payments under existing court orders or agreements. The same protection will also apply to those who have already applied for court orders, provided these are made by June 30. From April 1989 there will be special transitional rules to continue protection for existing arrangements.

"The payroll giving scheme has now been running for nearly a year. In order to give further encouragement to charitable giving, and to assist the growth of the payroll giving scheme, I propose to double the annual limit on tax-allowable donations under the scheme to £240, or £20 a month.

TAXATION ON SPENDING

"I now turn to the taxation on spending. I have one change to propose today affecting the coverage of value-added tax, which will remain at 15 per cent. Recent legal decisions mean that some cereal bars are subject to V.A.T., while other are not. I propose to clarify the law so that all cereal bars are taxed.

"I propose to raise the excise duties as a whole broadly in line with inflation, but to make some modest adjustments within the total. The duty on cigarettes and hand-rolling tobacco will be increased, by the equivalent, including V.A.T., of between 3p and 4p for a package of 20 cigarettes. The duty on a packet of five small cigars will rise by 2p but that on pipe tobacco will remain unchanged.

"As to the alcohol duties, I propose increases which, including V.A.T., will put about 1p on the price of a pint of average-strength beer and cider, 4p on a bottle of table wine, and 6p on a bottle of sparkling or fortified wine. There will once again be no increase in the duty on spirits.

"I propose once again to leave the main rates of vehicle excise duty unchanged. To recover the revenue forgone, I propose increases in petrol and derv duty over and above the rate of inflation, which, including V.A.T., will raise the price of petrol by between 5p and 6p a gallon, and that of derv by a little under 5p a gallon.

"In my Budget last year, I sought to promote the use of lead-free petrol by introducing a duty differential in its favour. As a result, the number of garages selling lead-free petrol has more than trebled. But consumption remains disappointingly low. Accordingly, I propose to double the duty differential in its favour by exempting it altogether from the duty increase I have just announced for leaded petrol.

TAXES ON CAPITAL

"I have two proposals to encourage share ownership still further to announce today. First, personal equity plans are off to a successful start. To give further encouragement to this form of investment, I propose to increase the annual limit from £2,400 to £3,000."

The Chancellor also announced that the provisions of Section 79 of the 1972 Finance Act will be relaxed, making it easier for companies to provide shares to their employees outside the approved schemes without giving rise to an undue charge to tax.

Mr. Lawson continued:

"Last year, I reduced the number of inheritance tax rates from seven to four. This year, I propose to simplify the tax still further by levying it at a flat rate of 40 per cent. At the same time I propose to raise the threshold from £90,000 to £110,000. The increase in the threshold will reduce the number of estates liable to tax by a quarter, allowing many more people to inherit the family home free of tax. The cost of these changes will be £100 million in 1988–89.

"Lastly, capital gains tax. I have decided to bring the base date for the tax forward from 1965 to 1982. That is to say, for all disposals on or after April 6, that part of any capital gain which arose before April 1982 will be exempt from tax altogether, for individuals and companies alike." Mr. Lawson said that the capital gains tax threshold would also be reduced, to £5,000. He added that, subject to the new base date, capital gains will continue to be worked out as now, with the present exemptions and reliefs. In particular, the principal private residence will remain tax-free. But the indexed gain will be taxed at the income tax rate that would apply if it were the taxpayer's marginal slice of income. In other words, in future the same rate of tax will apply to income and capital gains alike.

TAXES ON INCOME

Finally the Chancellor turned to income tax. He dealt first with forestry and the much-criticized tax relief which could be obtained, particularly by top-rate taxpayers. Mr. Lawson announced that, subject to transitional provisions, expenditure on commercial woodlands would no longer be allowed as a deduction for income tax and corporation tax. He went on to announce an increase in the tax-exemption limit for payments from £25,000 to £30,000, and the abolition of the additional relief for larger amounts.

Also increased was the taxation on company cars, the car scales for 1988–89 being doubled, and tax relief was ended on all new home improvement schemes.

On income tax itself, the Chancellor said:

"The single allowance will go up not by £90, as required by indexation, but by £180, to £2,605; and the married allowance will go up not by £150 but by £300, to £4,095. The additional personal allowance and widow's bereavement allowance will thus rise by £120 to £1,490. Similarly the single age allowance will rise by £220 to £3,180 and the married age allowance by £360 to £5,035.

"The higher allowances for taxpayers aged 80 and over, which I introduced in the last Budget, will correspondingly be increased by £240 and £360 to £3,310 and £5,205 respectively, and the new age allowance income limit will be £10,600. The upper limit of taxable income for the basic rate band will be increased to £19,300.

"Given these substantial increases in the main allowances, I am taking the opportunity to simplify the system by abolishing three minor personal allowances which have been unchanged, in cash terms, for over 20 years: the housekeeper allowance, the dependent relative allowance, and the son's or daughter's services allowance.

"The basic rate of income tax for 1988–89 will be 25p in the pound. The small companies' rate of corporation tax will similarly be reduced to 25 per cent. This means that the basic rate of income tax, and the corporation tax rate for small companies, will both be at their lowest level since the war.

"After nine years at 60 per cent I believe the time has come to make a further reduction in the top rate of income tax. At present there are not fewer than five higher rates of income tax: 40 per cent, 45 per cent, 50 per cent, 55 per cent, and 60 per cent. I propose to abolish all the higher rates of tax above 40 per cent.

"The changes will take effect under P.A.Y.E. on the first pay day after June 14. They will cost £4·25 billion in 1988–89 over and above statutory indexation. The total cost of all the measures in this year's Budget, again on an indexed basis, is a shade under £4 billion."

The Chancellor concluded:

"After an autumn statement which substantially increased public spending in priority areas, I have once again cut the basic rate of income tax, fulfilling our manifesto pledge of a basic rate of 25p in the pound and setting a new target of 20p in the pound. And I have balanced the Budget."

Debate on the Budget

The Leader of the Opposition (Mr. Neil Kinnock) opened the debate on the Budget by saying that the Budget had generated anger and resentment because of the Chancellor's decision to award large tax concessions to the well-off while offering nothing at all to the National Health Service. Mr. Kinnock said "But I and my comrades shall take the view: don't get mad, get even." He continued to criticize the Chancellor for failing to help those attempting to export from Britain, for offering subsidies to landlords, thus reintroducing Rachmanism, and for failing to build a foundation for sustainable economic growth. Mr. Kinnock said that the Budget should have invested in production, in exports and sales, in research and development, in health and social justice. Conservative M.P. Mr. David Knox said that he would have preferred the Chancellor to have put more into public expenditure projects like the N.H.S.

When the debate continued the following day the shadow Chancellor Mr. John Smith predicted that the Budget would prove "the beginning of the end of Thatcherism." He called the Budget "an outrage. It is immoral. It is wrong. It is foolish. It is divisive. It is corrupting." Mr. John Major, Chief Secretary to the Treasury, condemned Labour for the "class conscious way" in which they referred to the rich. He claimed that the Budget was aimed primarily at the "meritocracy" of professionals who might otherwise leave the country.

Former Conservative Minister Sir Ian Gilmour made an extended critique of economic policy. He criticized the Government for failing to avert the spending boom: "it is your classic, authentic British consumption-led economic boom with imports rising far faster than exports". He concluded "the British economy has not been transformed. I therefore hope the Chancellor will now devote his very formidable powers and energies to effect the genuine transformation which is still so badly needed".

On March 17 former Conservative Minister Mr. John Biffen said that he would vote against the income-tax cuts as a "personal gesture", because of the risk of higher inflation. On March 21 former Prime Minister Mr. Edward Heath questioned the cut in income tax, both at base rate and at the higher rate, and asked how the two and a half million unemployed could look to the Budget for any benefit. The Budget proposal increasing duty on oil and petrol was carried with a Government majority of 306. The resolution reducing income tax rates was carried by a majority of 112.

Northern Ireland

On March 17 the Northern Ireland Secretary (Mr. Tom King), made a statement on the attack on mourners at an I.R.A. funeral at Milltown cemetery, Belfast, which left three people dead. He said "at this time of great emotion it is now incumbent on everybody in the province to play their part in ending the cycle of violence and retaliation and further violence". Members of the House agreed with Mr. King and said that the security forces had acted correctly in maintaining a low profile at the funeral. Labour M.P. Mr. Ken Livingstone called for a national referendum to decide whether Britain should remain in Northern Ireland.

On March 21 Mr. King told the Commons that, following the murder of two soldiers at an I.R.A. funeral in Belfast, the Chief Constable of the R.U.C., Sir John Hermon, was to undertake an urgent review of the policing of future I.R.A. funerals. He also announced that there would be a meeting of British and Irish Ministers and security chiefs in London later that week. Mr. Kevin McNamara, Labour spokesman on Northern Ireland, welcomed this move but said that Mrs. Thatcher should play a more active part in Irish affairs. Mr. King criticized Mr. James Molyneaux, leader of the Official Unionist Party, for comments made outside of the House about political interference, particularly as he considered that Mr. Molyneaux had a part to play in leadership. On March 22 Mrs. Thatcher condemned the reluctance of television stations and newspapers to allow the police to examine film of the murders and called on the media to assist in the search for the killers of the two soldiers.

In the House of Lords on March 21 the Government came under attack from bishops and Opposition peers for threatening family life by its proposal to take away the automatic right of immigrant men to bring their families to Britain. A cross-party amendment to the proposed Bill, seeking to extend the right to both men and women, was defeated by a Government majority of 25. An amendment to give those who arrived in Britain without proper papers the right to appeal against deportation was also defeated.

Education

On March 22 the Education Reform Bill began its report stage in the House of Commons. The Education Secretary (Mr. Kenneth Baker) introduced a series of amendments to the Bill to exclude children with special educational needs from the provisions of the national curriculum. Mr. Derek Fatchett, an Opposition spokesman on education, first moved a clause whereby local authorities could be required to provide allowances for pupils aged 16 to 19. This clause was withdrawn and another Opposition clause requiring the Education Secretary to give Parliament a report on education and training for 16 to 19 year olds within six months of the Bill receiving Royal Assent was defeated by 66 votes. A clause moved by Labour M.P. Mrs. Ann Clwyd, requiring local education authorities to provide nursery education for children under school age was rejected by 57 votes. During the debate Mr. Baker told the Commons that religious education would have the status of a core curriculum subject. However, parents would still have the right, as with the 1944 Act, to withdraw their children from R.E. lessons and collective worship. A series of amendments to establish R.E. as a core subject in such a way as to allow for differences of treatment from other core subjects were withdrawn once Mr. Baker made it clear he accepted the principle of the amendments.

In the House of Lords on March 23 former Labour Social Services Secretary Lord Ennals accused the Government of deliberately precipitating a crisis in the National Health Service to enable it to carry out radical restructuring of health provision. During the debate the Social Services Under-Secretary Lord Skelmersdale announced increased funding in London and the north-west. He also said that although no more funds were allocated in the Budget, this did not mean that more money would not be made available.

On March 28 the Education Minister (Mrs. Angela Rumbold) told the Commons that Inner London councils would get £13 million in grants over the next two years to ease their transition to education authority status following the abolition of the Inner London Education Authority.

Money Matters

In the House of Lords, the Trade and Industry Secretary, Lord Young of Graffham, announced that the Government would make a cash injection of £800 million into the Rover Group before selling its shares to British Aerospace for £150 million. He also said that the Government had agreed to eliminate £1·1 billion of Rover's trading tax losses. Lord Young's statement was later repeated in the House of Commons by Mr. Kenneth Clarke, Minister of Trade and Industry. The Opposition spokesman on trade and industry, Mr. Brian Gould, called the proposed sale "an act of political irresponsibility and industrial sabotage".

On April 12 the Speaker granted a three-hour emergency debate on the recently-introduced changes to social security payments. The debate was granted following arguments during Prime Minister's questions. The debate took place on April 13. The shadow social services secretary, Mr. Robin Cook, called on Conservative M.P.s to force the Government to ease the plight of those facing benefit cuts under the new system. The Social Services Secretary (Mr. John Moore) called the changes a "charter for self-respect", aimed at helping those most in need. Mr. Nicholas Scott, Minister of Social Services, wound up the debate by confirming that the Government would monitor "with great care and sympathy" the implementation of the reforms.

On April 18 the Local Government (Finance) Bill began a five-day report stage. A Conservative backbencher, Mr. Michael Mates, introduced an amendment to replace the flat rate community charge with a banded system related to ability to pay. The

Environment Secretary (Mr. Nicholas Ridley) dismissed the amendment as unworkable and said that "it would be a great mistake for the House to divert at this stage from the sensible balance which the Government proposed". Nevertheless, 38 Conservative M.P.s defied the party whip to vote for the amendment and at least ten Tories abstained, leaving the Government with a majority of only 25 when the amendment was put to the vote. The rebellion was the most serious in this Parliament and a humiliation for the Government.

The following day the Government rejected amendments from its own back-benchers intended to relieve people over 80 and the severely physically disabled from paying the charge. On April 20 the Government moved an amendment setting out in detail the arrangements for recovering unpaid charges. The amendment was passed by a majority of 111 votes.

At the end of the debate on April 18 Labour M.P. Mr. Ron Brown seized the Mace and threw it to the floor, causing damage. The following day he failed ten times to read a statement of apology agreed in advance with the Speaker and was led from the House by the Labour deputy chief whip, Mr. Don Dixon. On April 21 the House of Commons voted by 463 to 26 to suspend Mr. Brown for 20 days without pay.

On May 3 the former Education Secretary Lord Joseph led a revolt in the House of Lords. The occasion was an amendment to the Education Reform Bill intended to remove the Bill's mandatory rulings on the national curriculum: it was defeated by a Government majority of 74 votes.

Abortion Bill

On May 6 the private member's Bill sponsored by Mr. David Alton failed to complete its report state in the House of Commons. The Abortion (Amendment) Bill, intended to reduce the time limit for abortions from 28 to 18 weeks, had been the centre of controversy since its introduction in January. Delaying tactics by opponents on May 6 meant that proceedings on the Bill ended without a vote on amendments setting the legal limit at 20, 22 or 24 weeks. As a consequence Mr. Alton's Bill dropped to third place on the list of private members Bills to be considered on May 13, when progress was prevented by the length of debate on the third reading of a Bill proposing that the wearing of rear seat belts in cars by children should be compulsory. Mr. Alton accused opponents of filibustering to prevent consideration of the abortion Bill.

On May 11, during a Labour-inspired debate on the seamen's dispute, Mr. Michael Meacher, Labour's spokesman on employment, claimed that the Government's reluctance to launch an inquiry into ferry safety was connected with P. & O. contributing to Conservative Party funds. Mr. Meacher moved a motion calling on the Government to encourage P. & O. to come to the negotiating table and to accept binding arbitration. The Employment Secretary (Mr. Norman Fowler), said that the Government believed disputes should be settled by the parties concerned. The Opposition motion was rejected by 317 votes to 205. A Government amendment stating that the resolution of industrial disputes was a matter for the parties concerned was carried by a majority of 88 votes.

In the House of Lords on May 23 Conservative peers led by Lord Chelwood proposed an amendment to the Local Government (Finance) Bill requiring the Government to relate the community charge to ability to pay. The amendment was defeated by 314 votes to 183, a Government majority of 134, after the Government ensured the highest recorded attendance in the Lords for 17 years.

On May 25 in the House of Lords the Trade and Industry Secretary Lord Young defended his decision not to refer to the Monopolies Commission the bid for Rowntree by the Swiss group Nestlé. He said that he suspected that the Commission would have found no grounds for blocking the bid even if he had referred it. It was now a decision for the Rowntree shareholders.

Hanging

On June 7 a group of Conservative back-benchers proposed to add a clause to the Criminal Justice Bill which would reintroduce hanging as the maximum sentence for murder. Mr. Roger Gale, who proposed the amendment, said that the consistent refusal by M.P.s to sanction the return of hanging had "flown in the face of public opinion". The Home Secretary (Mr. Douglas Hurd) argued against the clause, warning that the return of the death penalty would lead to public executions in a circus of media publicity. Mr. Roy Hattersley, the Labour home affairs spokesman, said that capital punishment would institutionalize the most extreme violence. He continued "I expect the House of Commons to have a different standard of values from murderers". Mr. Merlyn Rees opposed the clause, saying that capital punishment was not the answer to the problems of murder in general or terrorism in particular. The amendment was defeated by 341 votes to 218.

On June 8 Labour introduced debates on two takeover bids, one concerning Rowntree and the other the Rover group. Mr. Brian Gould, the Labour spokesman on trade and industry, moved a motion criticizing the Government for failing to refer to the Monopolies Commission the bids by the Suchard and Nestlé companies for Rowntree. The motion called on the Government to adopt merger and competition policies that would allow industry to prepare for the completion of the single European market in 1992 without fear of hostile takeover bids. The motion was defeated by a majority of 98 votes. Mr. Gould also introduced a motion calling for the retention of the Rover group in public ownership. This was defeated by a Government majority of 109 votes.

Following a request from the Opposition spokesman on sport, Mr. Denis Howell, the Sports Minister Mr. Colin Moynihan made a statement to the House on June 16 about the behaviour of "certain so-called England football supporters" attending the European championships in West Germany. Mr. Moynihan said that the football authorities had been asked to meet Government ministers to discuss the problem. Mr. Howell offered full Labour support in dealing with what he defined as a law-and-order problem rather than a problem confined to football.

On June 23 the Associated Ports (No. 2) Bill, intended to empower Associated British Ports to extend facilities at Immingham, King's Lynn and Port Talbot, passed its second reading. Labour M.P.s criticized the Bill, stating that the extension of facilities at the ports would facilitate the importation of coal from South Africa.

End of Term

On July 5 the Social Services Secretary (Mr. Moore) outlined the main aims of the review of the National Health Service. The Labour health and social security spokesman, Mr. Robin Cook, claimed that some of the more radical proposals for reform of N.H.S. funding had been dropped in response to public opinion. Mr. Cook called for an immediate cash injection into the N.H.S. The Prime Minister rebuffed the Leader of the Opposition, Mr. Kinnock, when he made repeated calls for additional funding and told him that the Government was totally committed to the National Health Service.

Following publication of the report of the inquiry into the Cleveland child abuse cases, the Minister of Health, Mr. Tony Newton, announced on July 6 a package of measures aimed at ensuring a similar situation did not arise. Following Mr. Newton's statement the Labour spokesman, Mr. Robin Cook, called for urgent legislation to implement proposals put forward in the White Paper on child care which was presented in 1987.

On July 18 the Labour party put forward an amendment to the Education Reform Bill in an attempt to remove proposals, added in the Lords, that religious education and worship in schools should reflect Britain's predominantly Christian society. The amendment was defeated by 224 votes. On July 19 a series of Government amendments to the Bill were carried by a majority of 89 votes.

During Prime Minister's Questions on July 19 the Leader of the Opposition, Mr. Kinnock, asked Mrs. Thatcher if she would consider imposing sanctions on South Africa and increasing support for neighbouring states. Mrs. Thatcher condemned the call for sanctions and said that the people most likely to suffer would be the black people that Mr. Kinnock was supporting. At one stage during an unruly question time Labour M.P. Mr. David Winnick was heard to call Mrs. Thatcher a hypocrite.

On July 21 the Energy Secretary (Mr. Cecil Parkinson) told the Commons that a Government review of the commercial deployment of fast breeder reactors suggested that they would not be required for 30 to 40 years, so the Government had decided to put a five-year limit on its funding of the fast breeder reactor at Dounreay in Scotland. He said that funding for research and development and the operation of fast breeder reactors would continue at a reduced level.

In a debate on the Government's proposed reform of the Official Secrets Act on July 22, several Conservative back-benchers joined with Opposition M.P.s in attacking the reforms as a move towards more secrecy and authoritarianism. Mr. John Patten, the Home Office Minister, said that there was still scope for changes to the Government plans.

During Questions to the Minister for the Civil Service on July 25 Labour M.P. Tam Dalyell accused the Prime Minister of an "indispensable lie" to the House about the Westland affair. After refusing to withdraw the allegation he was suspended from the House for 15 days.

In a debate on immigration on July 27 the Labour deputy leader, Mr. Roy Hattersley, moved a motion disapproving of the Government's changes in immigration rules. He said that in a radio talk the Conservative M.P. Timothy Renton had raised the spectre of thousands of immigrants flooding Britain, an opinion akin to that of the National Front. The motion was defeated by 54 votes.

Both houses of Parliament rose for the summer recess on July 29.

BUDGET 1988 STATISTICS

The Finances of the Public Sector

	£ billion				£ billion		
	1987–88				1987–88		
	1987 Budget	Latest estimate	1988–89 Forecast		1987 Budget	Latest estimate	1988–89 Forecast
RECEIPTS				**EXPENDITURE**			
Income tax	40·0	41·5	42·1	DHSS—social security	46·0	46·3	48·5
Corporation tax excluding				DHSS—health and personal			
North Sea[1]	13·5	13·7	17·3	social services	19·1	19·7	20·7
Capital taxes	3·3	3·7	4·7	Defence	18·8	18·6	19·2
Expenditure taxes:				Education and science	16·6	17·1	18·0
VAT	23·3	24·1	26·2	Scotland, Wales and			
local authority rates	16·9	16·9	19·0	Northern Ireland	16·0	16·3	17·1
petrol, derv, etc	7·8	7·8	8·4	Other departments	33·6	33·0	34·9
cigarettes and other tobacco .	4·9	4·8	5·0	Privatisation proceeds	−5·0	−5·0	−5·0
spirits, beer, wine, etc	4·3	4·4	4·5	Reserve	3·5	—	3·5
stamp duties	2·1	2·4	2·0				
other	8·5	8·9	9·4				
Total expenditure taxes	67·8	69·3	74·4	**Public expenditure planning total . . . .**	148·6	146·0	156·8
North Sea revenues:	1·4	1·4	1·5				
North Sea corporation tax[2] . .	1·7	2·3	1·2				
petroleum revenue tax	0·8	1·0	0·6				
oil royalties	3·9	4·7	3·3				
Total North Sea	−0·8	−0·6	−0·7	General government gross			
Other[3]	127·8	132·3	141·2	debt interest	17·9	17·5	17·5
Total taxes and royalties . .				Other adjustments	7·0	8·3	8·6
National insurance and other	28·5	28·7	31·6				
contributions	5·7	6·3	5·6				
Interest and dividend receipts . .							
Gross trading surpluses and	3·3	3·0	3·5				
rent	3·5	3·4	2·9				
Other							
General government receipts	168·8	173·7	184·9	**General government expenditure . . . .**	173·5	171·8	182·9

Expenditure, Receipts and Borrowing[4]

	£ billion		
	1987–88		1988–89 Forecast
	1987 Budget	Latest estimate	
General government expenditure	173·5	171·8	182·9
General government receipts	168·8	173·7	184·9
General government borrowing requirements	4·7	−1·9	−2·0
Public corporations' market and overseas borrowing	−0·8	−1·2	−1·2
Public sector borrowing requirement	3·9	−3·1	−3·2

[1] Including advance corporation tax but excluding corporation tax on capital gains.
[2] Before advance corporation tax set off. See footnote[2] on following page.
[3] Adjustments for advance corporation tax set off against North Sea corporation tax plus accruals adjustment.
[4] Net borrowing: positive; net debt repayment: negative.

Consolidated Fund Expenditure

	£ million 1987–88 latest estimate
Supply Issues*	105,100
Standing services	
Payment to the National Loans Fund in respect of service of the national debt	9,800
Northern Ireland—share of taxes etc.	2,200
Payments to the European Communities	3,770
Other services	100
Total standing services	15,900
Total Consolidated Fund expenditure	121,000

* Supply Issues are monies paid from the Consolidated Fund to departments' cash accounts with the Paymaster General for spending on Supply.

Consolidated Fund Revenue

	£ million		
	1987–88		1988–89 Forecast
	1987 Budget	Latest estimate	
Inland Revenue			
Income tax	39,900	41,400	42,100
Corporation tax[1,2]	15,000	15,600	19,800
Petroleum revenue tax[3]	1,680	2,330	1,180
Capital gains tax	1,300	1,350	1,950
Development land tax	20	25	10
Inheritance tax[4]	1,100	1,070	1,000
Stamp duties	2,100	2,440	1,950
Total Inland Revenue	61,100	64,200	68,000
Customs and Excise			
Value added tax	23,300	24,100	26,200
Petrol, derv, etc.	7,800	7,800	8,400
Cigarettes and other tobacco	4,800	4,800	5,000
Spirits, beer, wine, cider and perry	4,300	4,400	4,500
Betting and gaming	800	810	890
Car tax	1,100	1,150	1,260
Other excise duties	20	20	20
E.C. own resources			
Customs duties, etc.	1,350	1,470	1,550
Agricultural levies	230	190	120
Total Customs and Excise	43,800	44,700	47,900
Vehicle excise duties	2,600	2,700	2,770
Gas levy	490	500	420
Broadcasting receiving licences	1,030	1,030	1,140
Interest and dividends	1,020	1,080	680
Other	7,600	9,100	7,300
Total Consolidated Fund revenue	117,500	123,200	128,200

[1] Includes advance corporation tax (net of repayments)	4,700	4,950	5,250
[2] North Sea corporation tax	1,400	1,360	1,500
of which satisfied by setting off ACT	800	730	780

Liability to corporation tax arising in respect of North Sea production may be satisfied by setting off ACT arising on dividends paid in previous periods in respect of both onshore and offshore activities. Dividends and ACT associated with North Sea activities alone cannot be identified.

[3] Includes advance petroleum revenue tax.
[4] Includes estate duty and capital transfer tax.

PUBLIC ACTS OF PARLIAMENT 1987–88

This list of Public Acts commences with one Public Act which received the Royal Assent before September 1987 and which was mentioned briefly in the last summary. Those Public Acts which follow received the Royal Assent after August 1987. The date stated after each Act is the date on which it came into operation.

Channel Tunnel Act 1987, c. 53 (July 23, 1987) provides for the construction and operation of a railway tunnel system under the English Channel together with associated works; for connected improvements in road (e.g. the A 20) and rail networks in S.E. England; incorporates the tunnel into the U.K. railway tunnel system; and for connected purposes.

Consolidated Fund (No. 2) Act 1987, c. 54 (Nov. 17, 1987) applies a sum out of the Consolidated Fund to the service of the year ending March 31, 1988.

Consolidated Fund (No. 3) Act 1987, c. 55 (Dec. 10, 1987) applies certain sums out of the Consolidated Fund to the service of the years ending March 31, 1988 and 1989.

Scottish Development Agency Act 1987, c. 56 (Dec. 17, 1987) makes provision with respect to the limit on sums borrowed by, or paid by the Secretary of State to, the Scottish Development Agency and its subsidiaries; on sums paid by the Treasury in pursuance of guarantees of loans to the Agency and on loans guaranteed by the Agency or its subsidiaries.

Urban Development Corporations (Financial Limits) Act 1987, c. 57 (Feb. 17, 1988) removes the limit on the amount of grants that may be made to urban development corporations and provides a new limit applicable only to the amounts for the time being outstanding in respect of sums borrowed by them and sums issued by the Treasury in fulfilment of guarantees of their debts.

Income and Corporation Taxes Act 1988, c. 1 (except as otherwise provided, for the year 1988–89 and subsequent years of assessment and for companies' accounting periods ending after April 5, 1988) consolidates certain of the enactments relating to income tax and corporation tax, including certain enactments relating also to capital gains tax and repeals as obsolete certain taxation provisions.

Arms Control and Disarmament (Privileges and Immunities) Act 1988, c. 2 (Feb. 9, 1988) provides for the conferring of privileges and immunities on observers, inspectors and auxiliary personnel exercising functions under international agreements or arrangements for furthering arms control or disarmament.

Land Registration Act 1988, c. 3 (day to be appointed) amends section 112 of the 1925 Act.

Norfolk and Suffolk Broads Act 1988, c. 4 (various dates, some to be appointed) establishes an authority to be known as the Broads Authority and makes provision with respect to its powers and for making grants to it. The area covered is that commonly known as the Broads and also Great Yarmouth Port and Haven and its Commissioners.

Welsh Development Agency Act 1988, c. 5 (March 15, 1988) increases the financial limit which applies by virtue of section 18 of the 1975 Act to the general external borrowing of the Agency and certain other amounts.

Consolidated Fund Act 1988, c. 6 (March 15, 1988) applies certain sums out of the Consolidated Fund to the service of the years ending on March 31, 1987 and 1988.

Social Security Act 1988, c. 7 (various dates, some to be appointed) amends the law relating to social security and makes fresh provision in relation to welfare foods; provides for the remission of charges for services provided under the N.H.S. Act 1977 and the N.H.S. (Scotland) Act 1978 and for the payment of travelling and overnight expenses for the purpose of persons availing themselves of services provided under those Acts.

Multilateral Investment Guarantee Act 1988, c. 8 (April 12, 1988) enables the U.K. to give effect to the Convention establishing the Multilateral Investment Guarantee Agency.

Local Government Act 1988, c. 9 (various dates) regulates certain functions of local and other public authorities in connection with public supply or works contracts; authorizes and regulates the provision of financial assistance by local authorities for certain housing purposes; prohibits the promotion of homosexuality by local authorities; and makes further provision as to publicity, administration, auditing and other matters connected with local authorities.

Duchy of Lancaster Act 1988, c. 10 (May 3, 1988) extends the leasing powers of the Chancellor and Council of the Duchy of Lancaster.

Regional Development Grants (Termination) Act 1988, c. 11 (May 3, 1988) precludes the making of grants under Part II of the Industrial Development Act 1982 after March 31, 1988 unless previously applied for, and restricts the payment of such grants in certain cases.

Merchant Shipping Act 1988, c. 12 (July 4, 1988) amends the law relating to the registration of ships; makes provision for giving financial assistance in connection with the training of seamen and crew relief costs; and for the establishment of a Merchant Navy Reserve; makes further provision in connection with shipping safety, liability and compensation for oil pollution and the financing and administration of the lighthouse service; and for connected purposes.

Coroners Act 1988, c. 13 (July 10, 1988) consolidates the Acts 1887–1980 and certain enactments with amendments to give effect to recommendations of the Law Commission.

Immigration Act 1988, c. 14 (July 10, 1988) makes further provision for the regulation of immigration in the U.K.

Public Utility Transfers and Water Charges Act 1988, c. 15 (various dates) confers powers on water authorities, electricity boards and the Electricity Council to act in relation to proposals for the transfer of any of the property or functions of water authorities or electricity boards or other corporate bodies; and also provides for the fixing of charges by water undertakers.

Farm Land and Rural Development Act 1988, c. 16 (May 10, 1988) provides for the payment of grants for certain purposes connected with farm business or with the conversion of agricultural land to woodlands; provides for the increase in the limit on the number of members of the Development Commission.

Licensing Act 1988, c. 17 (days to be appointed) amends the 1964 Act.

Matrimonial Proceedings (Transfers) Act 1988, c. 18 (May 19, 1988) empowers the High Court to transfer certain matrimonial proceedings to county courts and to validate certain High Court orders purporting to transfer such proceedings to county courts.

Employment Act 1988, c. 19 (various dates) makes provision with respect to trade unions, their members and their property; provides with respect to things done for the purpose of enforcing membership of a trade union, to trade union ballots and elections, and to proceedings involving trade unions. Provision is made with respect to the Manpower Services Commission, including changing its name to the Training Commission. The Act also provides for additional members to be appointed to industrial training boards and the Agricultural Training Board and for the terms on which certain persons hold office or employment under the Crown to be treated as if, for certain purposes, as contained in contracts of employment.

Dartford–Thurrock Crossing Act 1988, c. 20 (day to be appointed) provides for the construction of a bridge over the Thames between Dartford and Thurrock and for associated works; for the Secretary of State to be the highway authority for the tunnels between the two towns; the levying of tolls; and for several other related and connected matters.

Consumer Arbitration Agreements Act 1988, c. 21 (days to be appointed) extends certain rights to consumers in connection with agreements to refer future differences to arbitration.

Scotch Whisky Act 1988, c. 22 (various dates) makes provision as to the definition of Scotch Whisky and as to the production and sale of whisky.

Motor Vehicles (Wearing of Rear Seat Belts by Children) Act 1988, c. 23 (days to be appointed) makes provision for the wearing of rear seat belts by children.

Community Health Council (Access to Information) Act 1988, c. 24 (April 1, 1989) provides for access by the public to meetings and to certain documents and information relating to Community Health Councils and their committees, and for related purposes.

Licensing (Retail Sales) Act 1988, c. 25 (day to be appointed) amends the definition of "sale by retail" in the Licensing Act 1964, s. 201; and for connected purposes.

Landlord and Tenant Act 1988, c. 26 (Sept. 29, 1988) makes new provision for imposing statutory duties in connection with covenants in tenancies against assigning, underletting, charging or parting with possession of premises without consent.

Malicious Communications Act 1988, c. 27 (Sept. 29, 1988) provides for the punishment of persons who send or deliver letters or other articles for the purpose of causing distress or anxiety.

Access to Medical Reports Act 1988, c. 28 (Jan. 1, 1989) establishes a right of access by individuals to reports relating to themselves by medical practitioners for employment or insurance purposes and makes provision for related matters.

Protection of Animals (Amendment) Act 1988, c. 29 (Sept. 29, 1988) enables a court to disqualify a person for having custody of an animal on a first conviction of cruelty; increases the penalties for offences relating to animal fights; makes further provision with respect to attendance at such fights in England and Wales and penalizes attendance at such fights in Scotland.

Environment and Safety Information Act 1988, c. 30 (April 1, 1989) establishes public registers of certain notices served concerning health, safety and environmental protection and for related purposes.

Protection Against Cruel Tethering Act 1988, c. 31 (Sept. 29, 1988) protects horses, asses and mules against cruel tethering and for connected purposes.

Civil Evidence (Scotland) Act 1988, c. 32 (day to be appointed) makes fresh provision in relation to civil proceedings in Scotland concerning corroboration of evidence and the admissibility of hearsay and other evidence; and for connected purposes.

Criminal Justice Act 1988, c. 33 (various dates) makes fresh provision for extradition; amends the rules of evidence for criminal proceedings; provides for the reference by the Attorney General of certain questions relating to sentencing to the Court of Appeal; amends the law relating to the jurisdiction and power of criminal courts, the collection, enforcement and remission of fines imposed by coroners, juries, supervision orders, the detention of children and young persons, probation and the probation service, criminal appeals, anonymity in cases of rape and similar cases; and amends or makes fresh provision in many other areas of the criminal law, including witnesses, compensation under the Criminal Injuries Compensation Board, compensation for wrongful conviction, creating a summary offence of possession of an indecent photograph of a child, computer data on fingerprints; and for connected purposes.

Legal Aid Act 1988, c. 34 (day or days to be appointed) makes new provision for the administration of and revises the law relating to legal aid advice and assistance.

British Steel Act 1988, c. 35 (various dates) provides for the vesting of the property, rights and liabilities of the British Steel Corporation in a company nominated by the Secretary of State, for the subsequent dissolution of the Corporation and for connected purposes.

Court of Session Act 1988, c. 36 (Sept. 29, 1988) consolidates with amendments to give effect to the recommendations of the Scottish Law Commission certain enactments relating to the construction, administration and procedure of the Court of Session and procedure on appeal therefrom to the House of Lords; and repeals, in accordance with recommendations of the Scottish Law Commission, certain enactments relating to those matters which are no longer of practical utility.

Electricity (Financial Provisions) (Scotland) Act 1988, c. 37 (July 29, 1988) raises the financial limit imposed by virtue of section 29(1) of the Electricity (Scotland) Act 1979.

Appropriation Act 1988, c. 38 (July 29, 1988) applies a sum out of the Consolidated Fund to the service of the year ending March 31, 1989 and appropriates the supplies granted in this Session of Parliament. It also repeals certain Consolidated Fund and Appropriation Acts.

Finance Act 1988, c. 39 (July 29, 1988) grants certain duties, alters others and amends the law relating to the National Debt and the Public Revenue. Amongst other provisions, the Act provides for capital gains to be taxed only on the increase since 1982, for the reduction of the basic rate of income tax

to 25 per cent., and for mortgage interest relief to be limited to £30,000 per house unit instead of per borrower.

Education Reform Act 1988, c. 40 (various dates) amends the law relating to education.

Local Government (Finance) Act 1988, c. 41.

Solicitors (Scotland) Act 1988, c. 42 (Jan. 29, 1989) amends the 1980 Act; and for connected purposes.

CIVIL SERVICE STAFF

Analysis by ministerial responsibility at April 1 in each year

† Full-time equivalents (thousands)

	1981	1982	1983	1984	1985	1986	1987
Total civil and defence departments	689·6	666·4	648·9	624·0	599·0	594·4	597·8
of which Non-industrials	539·9	528·0	518·5	504·3	498·0	498·2	507·5
	149·7	138·4	130·4	119·7	101·0	96·2	90·3
Total civil departments	460·0	449·4	440·0	424·8	425·0	424·9	433·8
Agriculture, Fisheries and Food	13·6	13·1	12·7	12·1	12·1	11·7	11·3
Chancellor of the Exchequer's Departments:	114·9	121·0	117·4	112·4	111·9	110·0	110·1
Customs and Excise	26·8	26·2	25·4	25·1	25·4	25·1	25·8
Inland Revenue	75·6	74·0	73·1	69·8	69·8	69·3	67·8
Department for National Savings	10·0	9·1	8·3	8·0	7·8	7·8	7·7
Treasury and others	2·5	11·7	10·6	9·5	8·9	8·8	8·8
Education and Science	3·6	3·5	3·5	2·4	2·4	2·4	2·4
Employment	53·8	58·7	57·9	56·4	54·7	55·7	60·5
Energy	1·2	1·1	1·1	1·1	1·1	1·0	1·0
Environment	47·0	42·1	39·4	36·6	35·8	34·9	34·2
Foreign and Commonwealth	11·4	11·1	11·1	10·0	9·8	9·6	9·5
Home	35·4	34·6	35·1	36·4	36·6	37·5	37·6
Industry	8·8	8·3	7·7	–	–	–	–
Scotland	13·6	13·4	13·1	12·8	13·0	12·9	13·0
Social Services	100·1	98·0	96·4	92·6	94·9	94·9	97·7
Trade	9·3	8·9	8·9	–	–	–	–
Trade and Industry	–	–	–	14·7	14·8	14·8	14·8
Transport	13·7	13·0	13·0	14·2	14·4	14·7	12·3
Wales	2·3	2·3	2·2	2·2	2·3	2·3	2·3
Other civil departments	31·3	20·2	20·5	20·9	21·2	21·5	25·1
Total Ministry of Defence	229·6	216·9	208·9	199·2	174·0	169·5	164·0

† Part-time employees are counted as half units.

DEFENCE MANPOWER STRENGTHS

At April 1   Thousands

	1981	1982	1983	1984	1985	1986	1987
U.K. SERVICE PERSONNEL							
All services: total	333·8	327·6	320·6	325·9	326·2	322·5	319·8
Female	16·9	15·7	15·4	16·2	16·4	16·0	16·2
Royal Navy: total	66·4	65·1	64·0	63·7	62·8	60·3	58·7
Female	4·1	4·0	3·9	3·9	3·7	3·4	3·4
Royal Marines: total	7·9	7·9	7·8	7·6	7·6	7·6	7·8
Army: total..........................	166·0	163·2	159·1	161·5	162·4	161·4	159·7
Female	6·6	6·0	6·1	6·6	6·8	6·6	6·5
Royal Air Force: total	93·5	91·5	89·8	93·1	93·4	93·2	93·6
Female	6·3	5·8	5·4	5·7	6·0	6·0	6·3
Personnel locally entered overseas:							
total	9·7	10·1	10·1	10·1	10·2	10·1	9·8
Regular Reserves*: total	196·5	196·4	193·4	198·0	205·5	211·4	–
Royal Navy........................	26·8	24·8	23·9	23·5	23·3	24·2	–
Royal Marines	2·2	2·2	2·2	2·2	2·2	2·3	–
Army	137·5	140·2	138·3	143·2	150·1	153·8	–
Royal Air Force	30·1	29·3	28·9	29·0	29·8	31·2	–
Volunteer Reserves and Auxiliary Forces*: total	84·0	86·3	87·5	85·9	88·6	95·4	–
Royal Navy	5·4	5·4	5·4	5·2	5·2	5·5	–
Royal Marines	0·9	1·0	1·1	1·1	1·1	1·2	–
Territorial Army..................	69·5	72·1	72·8	71·4	73·7	77·7	–
Ulster Defence Regiment............	7·5	7·1	7·1	6·8	6·4	6·6	–
Home Service Force	–	–	0·3	0·3	0·9	3·0	–
Royal Air Force	0·6	0·6	0·8	1·1	1·2	1·4	–
Cadet Forces*: total	150·6	148·7	149·0	146·5	144·7	143·4	–
Royal Navy........................	31·1	28·7	29·4	28·4	28·4	28·0	–
Army	75·1	74·1	74·5	73·8	72·1	70·9	–
Royal Air Force	44·4	45·9	45·1	44·3	44·1	44·5	–
Ministry of Defence civilians:							
total..............................	264·9	251·7	242·7	232·5	206·5	201·7	196·1
U.K. based	229·6	216·9	208·9	199·1	174·1	169·4	164·0
Non-industrial	113·5	108·1	105·6	103·2	94·9	93·8	93·3
Industrial	116·1	108·8	103·3	95·9	79·1	75·6	70·7
Locally engaged overseas	35·3	34·8	33·8	33·4	32·4	32·2	32·1
Non-industrial...................	10·9	10·7	10·5	10·4	10·2	10·3	10·3
Industrial	24·4	24·1	23·3	23·0	22·2	22·0	21·8

* figures unavailable for 1987.

Recruitment of U.K. Service personnel to each Service

                                                                                                    Number

1980–81	1980–81	1981–82	1982–83	1983–84	1984–85	1985–86	1986–87
All Services: total	50,488	22,607	21,647	36,991	34,721	32,651	34,049
Female	3,795	1,419	2,305	3,231	2,645	2,244	2,902
Royal Navy: total	9,088	3,805	3,584	4,785	4,582	4,276	5,336
Female	958	452	506	562	351	289	545
Royal Marines: total	1,674	699	447	447	954	1,093	1,233
Army: total	28,871	14,204	13,071	22,348	22,278	20,268	19,918
Female	1,630	601	1,392	1,537	1,364	1,095	1,200
Royal Air Force: total............	10,855	3,899	4,545	9,411	6,907	7,014	7,562
Female	1,207	366	407	1,132	930	860	1,157

IMPROVING MANAGEMENT IN GOVERNMENT

Various Government initiatives since 1979 have sought to increase efficiency within the Civil Service. The report *Improving Management in Government: The Next Steps* was commissioned in 1986 to investigate what further improvements were possible in the delivery of services and management of government. The scrutiny was carried out by members of the Efficiency Unit at the Cabinet Office under the supervision of Sir Robin Ibbs (Adviser on Efficiency).

The terms of reference for the scrutiny were:

(i) to assess the progress achieved in improving management in the Civil Service;

(ii) to identify what measures have been successful in changing attitudes and practices;

(iii) to identify the institutional, administrative, political and attitudinal obstacles;

(iv) to report to the Prime Minister on what further measures should be taken.

The scrutiny lasted for three months and involved interviews with Ministers and other government officials, visits to regional and local offices, an examination of past scrutinies of individual departments, and studies of large private sector organizations.

Findings

From discussions with Civil Servants it emerged that progress has been made in shifting the focus of attention away from processes towards results. Attitudes and practices have changed due to the introduction since 1979 of budgeting systems and manpower cuts. The development of management systems has given managers a greater freedom to make decisions and has forced them to define the results they wish to achieve. But these developments have been marred by a lack of flexibility within the Civil Service to changes in general.

The following were identified as obstacles to further progress:

(i) there is insufficient focus on the delivery of government services (as opposed to policy and ministerial support) even though 95 per cent. of civil servants work in service delivery or executive functions;

(ii) the careers of many senior civil servants develop their skills and experience in policy formulation rather than in service delivery and this affects their ability to manage the latter. The Unit concludes that a balance between the two skills is hard to achieve within the present framework;

(iii) short-term political priorities imposed by Ministers and the demands of Parliamentary business tend to squeeze out long-term planning;

(iv) there is too much emphasis on spending money and keeping to budgets and not enough on getting results. There is relatively little external pressure for improvement in performance;

(v) the Civil Service, with 600,000 employees, is too large and too diverse to be managed as a single organization. The main decisions on rules and regulations are formulated centrally, and fit everything in general and nothing in particular.

Recommendations

The Unit suggests that a different way of conducting the business of government should be established. It proposes that the central Civil Service should consist of a relatively small core engaged in the function of providing services for Ministers and managing government policies and services, but that the execution and delivery of these services should be the function of a range of agencies employing their own staff.

The departments would provide a detailed framework for the agencies, specifying policies, objectives, results and the resources available. Once this framework had been established, the total independence of the agencies should be guaranteed. Managers of agencies would be accountable for their agency's performance within the framework but each would have complete freedom on matters such as the structure of the agency and the recruitment and pay of staff. In some cases a whole department could be managed as an agency: in other instances, where the scale of activity is too small for an entirely separate organization, it may be better to have smaller agencies within a department.

The responsibility for ensuring that there is change and improvement rests with the Prime Minister and the Head of the Home Civil Service. They in turn need the commitment of Ministers and of Permanent Secretaries to ensure that the changes are not sacrificed to other priorities. The Unit recommends that a Project Manager, preferably of the rank of Permanent Secretary, should be designated. He or she would work with the authority of the Prime Minister and the Head of the Home Civil Service, to whom he or she would report, and would be responsible for planning and supervising the process of change.

The Unit suggests that within two years departments should have identified areas of their work where agencies would be the most effective form of management. Departments should also have altered their internal structures in line with these changes. Departments will need to be more flexible in training, moving and promoting their staff to improve their management skills in the delivery of services as well as ensuring experience of the political and policy aspects of the department's work. In time, management functions at the centre would diminish, though responsibility would be retained for allocating resources, applying external pressure on departments continually to improve results, ensuring that the overall shape of the Civil Service responds to changes in the needs of the government and country, and setting and policing rules on propriety for the public service in carrying out its essential functions.

Following 12 months' study, the report was published and was being considered by the Government during early 1988. Departments under consideration for agency status seem likely to include the Driver and Vehicle Licensing Centre, the Royal Parks, H.M. Stationery Office and the Meteorological Office.

GOVERNMENT AND PUBLIC OFFICES

SALARIES 1988–89

Ministerial Salaries
(as at April 1, 1988)

Prime Minister £34,157
Secretary of State £34,157
Minister of State (Lords) £34,688
Minister of State (Commons) £23,887
Parliamentary Under Secretary £17,877

(Ministers who are Members of the House of Commons receive a (reduced) parliamentary salary in addition to this ministerial salary.)

Civil Service Salaries
(from Oct. 1, 1988)

+ Secretary to the Cabinet and Head of the
 Home Civil Service................... £85,250
+ Permanent Secretary to the Treasury £79,750
+ Head of the Diplomatic Service £79,750
+ Grade 1 .... £68,500
+ Grade 1A £62,750
+ Grade 2 .... £45,800–£48,000
+ Grade 3 .... £35,800–£39,000
 Grade 4 .... £32,219–£35,457
        (as at April 1, 1988)
 Grade 5 .... £25,756–£29,344
 Grade 6 .... £19,537–£26,348
 Grade 7 .... £15,631–£21,104

+ These grades do not attract London Weighting.
London Weighting, since July 1, 1988, is:
 Inner zone .... £1,750 a year
 Intermediate zone .... £1,000 a year
 Outer zone .... £725 a year

The Home Civil Service's unified pay and grading structure for senior personnel represents the following:

Grade	Title
1	Permanent Secretary.
1A	Second Permanent Secretary.
2	Deputy Secretary.
3	Under Secretary.
4	Chief Scientific Officer B, Professional and Technology Directing A.
5	Assistant Secretary, Deputy Chief Scientific Officer, Professional and Technology Directing B.
6	Senior Principal, Senior Principal Scientific Officer, Professional and Technology Superintending Grade.
7	Principal.

ADVISORY, CONCILIATION AND ARBITRATION SERVICE
27 Wilton Street, SW1X 7AX
[01–210 3000]

The Advisory, Conciliation and Arbitration Service (ACAS) is an independent organization set up under the Employment Protection Act, 1975, under the management of a Council appointed by the Secretary of State for Employment. The functions of the Service are to provide facilities for conciliation, mediation and arbitration as a means of avoiding and resolving industrial disputes; and to provide advisory services to industry on industrial relations and quality of working life matters.
Chairman, D. B. Smith, c.b.
Chief Conciliation Officer, D. G. Boyd, c.b.e.
Director of Resources and General Policy Branch, E. Norcross.

MINISTRY OF AGRICULTURE, FISHERIES AND FOOD
Whitehall Place, SW1A 2HH†
[01–270 3000]

The Ministry of Agriculture, Fisheries and Food is responsible for administering government policy for agriculture, horticulture and fishing in England and for many food matters in the United Kingdom. Some of the Ministry's responsibilities for animal health and welfare extend to Great Britain. In association with the other Agricultural Departments in the U.K. and the Intervention Board for Agricultural Produce it is responsible for the administration of the E.C. common agricultural and fisheries policies and for various national support schemes. It deals with countryside matters within the responsibilities of the Ministry including agricultural land use and farm woodlands; diversification; pollution; environmental and conservation policy. It administers schemes for the control and eradication of animal and plant diseases and for assistance to capital investment in farm and horticultural businesses and flood defence; it exercises responsibilities relating to applied research and development. The Ministry sponsors the food and drink manufacturing industries and distribution trades. It is concerned with the supply and quality of food, food compositional standards, hygiene, labelling and advertising of food and has certain responsibilities for ensuring public health standards in the manufacture, preparation and distribution of basic foods. The Agricultural Development and Advisory Service (ADAS) is part of the Ministry.

Minister, THE RT. HON. JOHN MACGREGOR, O.B.E., M.P.
 Principal Private Secretary (G7), Mrs. S. Stagg.
 Asst. Private Secretary, Mrs. D. B. Haine.
 Parliamentary Private Secretary, A. Stewart, M.P.
 Special Adviser, R. Gueterbok.
Parliamentary Secretary (Lords), The Baroness Trumpington.
 Private Secretary, Miss K. J. Williams.
Parliamentary Secretary (Commons), D. Thompson, M.P.
 Private Secretary, Miss C. J. Bowles.
Parliamentary Secretary, R. Ryder, O.B.E., M.P.
Parliamentary Clerk Miss B. J. Richards.
Permanent Secretary (G1), D. H. Andrews, C.B., C.B.E.
 Private Secretary, W. F. G. Strang.

ESTABLISHMENT DEPARTMENT

Director of Establishments (G3), J. W. Hepburn.

Manpower Division
Victory House, 30–34 Kingsway, WC2B 6TU
[01–405 4310]
Head of Division (G5), M. T. Haddon.

Establishments (General) Division
Victory House, 30–34 Kingsway, WC2B 6TU
[01–405 4310]
Head of Division (G5), Mrs. A. M. Pickering.

Staff Training Branch*
Principal (G7), G. F. Buxton.

Welfare Branch
Victory House, 30–34 Kingsway, WC2B 6TU
[01–405 4310]
Chief Welfare Officer (S.E.O.), D. J. Jones.

†Unless otherwise stated, this is the main address of Divisions of the Ministry.
*At Nobel/Ergon House, 17 Smith Square, SW1P 3HX [01–238 3000].

Personnel Division
Victory House, 30–34 Kingsway, WC2B 6TU
[01-405 4310]
Head of Division (G5), Mrs. K. J. A. Brown.

FINANCE DEPARTMENT
Principal Finance Officer (G3), B. H. B. Dickinson.

Finance Planning Division*
Head of Division (G5), G. A. Hollis.

Finance Guidance Division*
Head of Division (G5), R. C. McIvor.

Financial Management Division*
Head of Division (G5), C. J. Lawson.

Audit Division*
Director of Audit (G5), D. V. Fisher.
Deputy Directors of Audit (G6), F. W. Martin;
(vacant).

Purchasing and Supply Unit
Director (G5), J. J. Frost.

LEGAL DEPARTMENT
55 Whitehall, SW1A 2EY
[01-270 3000]

Legal Adviser and Solicitor (G2), G. J. Jenkins.
Principal Assistant Solicitors (G3), A. E. Munir; J. McElheran.

Legal Division A1
Assistant Solicitor (G5), B. T. Atwood.

Legal Division A2
Assistant Solicitor (G5), A. Yavash.

Legal Division A3
Assistant Solicitor (G5), J. H. Jordan.

Legal Division A4
Assistant Solicitor (G5), Miss E. A. Stephens.

Legal Division A5
Assistant Solicitor (G5), J. E. G. Vaux.

Legal Division B1
Assistant Solicitor (G5), J. F. McCleary.

Legal Division B2
Assistant Solicitor (G5), D. J. Pearson.

Legal Division B3
Assistant Solicitor (G5), R. W. Dyer.

Legal Division B4
Assistant Solicitor (G5), Mrs. H. Cornwell-Kelly.

Investigation Unit
Chief Investigation Officer (SEO), A. F. N. Maloney.

MANAGEMENT SERVICES
Under Secretary (G3), M. Madden.

Computer Services Division
Government Buildings, Epsom Road,
Guildford, Surrey GU1 2LD
[0483-68121]
Head of Division (G5), D. V. Orchard.

Building Projects Unit*
Head of Division (G5), J. S. Buchanan.

Office Services Division
Head of Division (G6), J. E. Nunn, D.F.C.

Management Services Division*
Head of Division (G5), G. B. Hopley.

Information Division
Chief Information Officer (G5), J. Coe.
Chief Press Officer, Mrs. S. Cunningham.
Principal Librarian (G7), T. C. J. Norton.

Information Technology and Procedures Division
Victory House, 30–34 Kingsway, WC2B 6TU
[01-405 4310]
Head of Division (G5), R. J. Wheeler.

CHIEF SCIENTIST'S GROUP

Chief Scientist (Fisheries and Food) (G3), R. N. Crossett, D.Phil.*
Chief Scientist (Agriculture and Horticulture) (G3), D. W. F. Shannon, Ph.D.*

RESEARCH AND DEVELOPMENT REQUIREMENTS DIVISION*
Head of Division (G5), C. J. A. Barnes.

FOOD SCIENCE DIVISION*
Deputy Chief Scientific Officer (G5), M. E. Knowles, Ph.D.

AGRICULTURAL COMMODITIES
Deputy Secretary (G2), D. A. Hadley.

EUROPEAN COMMUNITY AND EXTERNAL TRADE POLICY
Under Secretary (G3), R. J. D. Carden.

European Community Division I
Head of Division (G5), R. S. Thomas.

European Community Division II
Head of Division (G6), D. Maskell.

External Trade Policy Division
Head of Division (G5), D. P. Hunter.

ARABLE CROPS, PIGS AND POULTRY
Under Secretary (G3), G. E. Myers, C.M.G.

Cereals Division
Head of Division (G5), C. J. Llewelyn.

Sugar, Oils and Fats Division
Head of Division (G5), Miss V. K. Timms.

Pigs, Eggs and Poultry Division
Head of Division (G5), M. Ring.

Set-aside and Extensification Unit
Head of Division (G5), R. E. Melville.

MEAT
Under Secretary (G3), S. Wentworth.

Beef Division
Head of Division (G5), J. R. Cowan.

Sheep Division
Head of Division (G5), A. T. Cahn.

Livestock Subsidies Division
Head of Division (G6), G. Belchamber.

MILK
Under Secretary (G3), P. W. Murphy.

*At Nobel/Ergon House, 17 Smith Square, SW1P 3HX [01-238 3000].

Milk and Milk Products Division I
Head of Division (G5), R. C. Lowson.

Milk and Milk Products Division II
Head of Division (G5), I. C. Redfern.

FISHERIES AND FOOD

Deputy Secretary (G2), W. E. Mason, c.b.

FISHERIES DEPARTMENT*

Fisheries Secretary (G3), C. R. Cann.

Marine Environmental Protection Division
Head of Division (G5), P. M. Boyling.

Fisheries Division I
Head of Division (G5), G. W. Noble.

Fisheries Division II
Head of Division (G5), A. R. Burne.

Fisheries Division III
Head of Division (G5), Mrs. A. M. Blackburn.

Sea Fisheries Inspectorate
Chief Inspector (G6), M. G. Jennings.

Fisheries Research
Director of Fisheries Research and Development for Great Britain (G4), H. W. Hill.
Deputy Directors of Fisheries Research (G5), D. J. Garrod, ph.d.; Dr. R. J. Pentreath.

Fisheries Laboratory
Pakefield Road, Lowestoft, Suffolk NR33 0HT
[0502–62244]

Fisheries Laboratory
Remembrance Avenue, Burnham-on-Crouch,
Essex CM0 8HA
[0621–782658]

Fisheries Experiment Station
Benarth Road, Conwy, Gwynedd LL32 8UB
[049–263 3883]

Fish Diseases Laboratory
The Nothe, Weymouth, Dorset DT4 8UB
[03057–72137]
Officer-in-charge (Principal Scientific Officer) (G7),
B. J. Hill, ph.d.

Torry Research Station
P.O. Box 31, 135 Abbey Road,
Aberdeen AB9 8DG
[0224–877071]
Director (G5), G. Hobbs, ph.d.

FOOD, DRINK AND MARKETING POLICY

Under Secretary (G3), D. H. Griffiths.

Food Policy Division
Head of Division (G5), J. D. Garnett.

Alcoholic Drinks Division
Head of Division (G5), C. R. Bodrell.

External Relations and Trade Promotion Division
Head of Division (G5), P. A. Cocking.

Tropical Foods*
Head of Division (G5), F. J. H. Scolles.

Marketing Policy and Potatoes Division*
Head of Division (G5), G. P. McLachlan.

EMERGENCIES, FOOD QUALITY AND PEST CONTROLS*

Under Secretary (G3), Mrs. E. A. J. Attridge.

Food Safety, Fertilizers and Feedstuffs Standards Division*
Head of Division (G5), R. C. McKinley.

Food Standards Division*
Head of Division (G5), C. A. Cockbill.

Emergencies Division
Head of Division (G5), A. Jeffrey Smith.

Pesticides Safety*
Head of Division (G5), G. M. Trevelyan.

LAND AND RESOURCES

Deputy Secretary (G2), E. J. G. Smith, c.b.

LANDS AND ENVIRONMENTAL AFFAIRS

Under Secretary (G3), J. A. Anderson.*

Rural Structures and Grants Division*
Head of Division (G5), Miss S. E. Brown.

Land Use and Tenure Division*
Head of Division (G5), Miss L. J. Neville-Rolfe.

Environmental Protection Division*
Head of Division (G5), P. P. Nash.

Conservation Policy Division*
Head of Division (G5), R. E. Mordue.

ANIMAL HEALTH

Under Secretary (G3), A. R. Cruickshank.

Animal Health Division
Government Buildings, Hook Rise South,
Tolworth, Surbiton, Surrey KT6 7NF
[01–337 6611]
Head of Division (G5), J. C. Suich.

Animal Welfare Division
Government Buildings, Hook Rise South,
Tolworth, Surbiton, Surrey KT6 7NF
[01–337 6611]
Head of Division (G5), H. B. Brown.

Animal Medicines Division
Tolworth Tower, Surbiton, Surrey KT6 7DX
[01–399 5191]
Head of Division (G5), K. W. Wilkes.

Meat Hygiene Division
Tolworth Tower, Surbiton, Surrey KT6 7DX
[01–399 5191]
Head of Division (G5), M. J. Griffiths.

HORTICULTURE, SEEDS, PLANT HEALTH AND FLOOD PROTECTION

Under Secretary (G3), G. P. Jupe.

Horticulture Division*
Head of Division (G5), Miss V. A. Smith.

Plant Variety, Rights Office and Seeds
White House Lane, Huntingdon Road,
Cambridge CB3 0LF
[0223–277151]
Head of Division (G5), J. Harvey.

Plant Health Division*
Head of Division (G5), J. C. Edwards.

Flood Defence and Land Sales Division*
Head of Division (G5), J. R. Park, p.h.d.

*At Nobel/Ergon House, 17 Smith Square, SW1P 3HX [01–238 3000].

ECONOMICS AND STATISTICS

Under Secretary (G3), C. W. Capstick, C.M.G.

Economics (Farm Business) Division
Senior Economic Adviser (G5), Mrs. S. M. Dickinson.

Economics (International) Division
Senior Economic Adviser (G5), R. W. Irving.

Economics (Resource Use) Division
Senior Economic Adviser (G5), A. P. Power, Ph.D.

Statistics (Agricultural Commodities) Division*
Chief Statistician (G5), P. J. Lund, Ph.D.

Statistics (Census and Prices) Division
Government Buildings, Epsom Road,
Guildford GU1 2LD
[0483–68121]
Chief Statistician (G5), D. E. Bradbury.

Economics and Statistics (Food)
Senior Economic Adviser (G5), J. M. Slater, Ph.D.

Agricultural Resources Policy Division
Head of Division (G5), H. R. Neilson.

AGRICULTURAL DEVELOPMENT AND ADVISORY SERVICE (A.D.A.S.) AND REGIONAL ORGANIZATION

Director General of A.D.A.S. and Regional Organization (G2), Prof. R. L. Bell, C.B., Ph.D.

ADAS AND REGIONAL ADMINISTRATION

Director of Regional Administration (G3), R. J. Packer.

Eastern, Block C, Government Buildings, Brooklands Avenue, Cambridge CB2 2DR (0223–358911).—*Regional Director (G4),* G. K. Bruce.

Northern, Block 2, Government Buildings, Lawnswood, Leeds LS16 5PY (0532–611223).—*Regional Director (G4),* A. F. Baines.

South Eastern, Block A, Government Offices, Coley Park, Reading RG1 6DT (0734–581222).—*Regional Director (G4),* J. A. Bamford.

South Western, Block 3, Government Bldgs., Burghill Road, Westbury-on-Trym, Bristol BS10 6NJ (0272–500000).—*Regional Director (G4),* B. F. Shorney.

Midlands and Western, Woodthorne, Wolverhampton WV6 8TQ (0902–754190).—*Regional Director (G4),* A. D. Bailey.

Wales, Plas Crug, Aberystwyth SY23 1PQ.—*Chief A.D.A.S. Officer (G5),* T. M. K. Evans.

A.D.A.S. and Regional Management Division
Head of Division (G5), A. H. Abbott.*

A.D.A.S. Marketing Unit
Head of Unit (G5), D. E. Bawcutt.*

A.D.A.S. Information Services Unit
Rivershill House, St. Georges Road
Cheltenham
Head of Unit (G5), R. W. Swain.

FARM AND COUNTRYSIDE SERVICE*

Director of F.C.S. (G3), P. Needham.
Head of Cropping Services (G4), D. J. Fuller.
Head of Livestock Services (G4), J. B. Finney.

* At Nobel/Ergon House, 17 Smith Square, SW1P 3HX [01–238 3000]

Head of Environmental Rural Development and Engineering Services Group (G4), B. D. Trafford.
Staff Officer (G5), I. M. Tring.

RESEARCH AND DEVELOPMENT SERVICE

Director of R.D.S. (G3), P. J. Bunyan, D.SC., Ph.D.*
Deputy Directors of R.D.S. (G4), (vacant)* *(Commercial Funding);* P. Needham* *(Public Funding).*
Staff Officer (G6), W. J. Stubbs.*

Slough Laboratory
London Road, Slough, Berks. SL3 7HJ
[0753–34626]
Director of Slough, Tolworth and Worplesdon Laboratories (G5), P. I. Stanley, Ph.D.

Harpenden Laboratory
Hatching Green, Harpenden, Herts. AL5 2BD
[0582–75241]
Director of Harpenden Laboratory (G5), H. J. Gould.

STATE VETERINARY SERVICE
Government Buildings, Hook Rise South,
Tolworth, Surbiton, Surrey KT15 3NB
[01–337 6611]

Chief Veterinary Officer (G3), K. C. Meldrum.
Director of Veterinary Field Services (G3), I. Crawford.
Staff Officer (G5), J. E. Morris.

Central Veterinary Laboratory, New Haw,
Weybridge, Surrey KT15 3NB
[09323–41111]
Director of Veterinary Laboratories (G3), W. A. Watson, Ph.D.

Lasswade Veterinary Laboratory,
East of Scotland College of Agriculture,
The Bush Estate, Penicuick,
Midlothian EH26 09N
[031–445 4811]

Cattle Breeding Centre, Shinfield, Reading,
Berks. RG2 9BZ
[0734–883157]

AGRICULTURAL AND FOOD RESEARCH COUNCIL
160 Great Portland Street, W1N 6DT
[01-580 6655]

The Agricultural and Food Research Council (A.F.R.C.) is an independent body established by Royal Charter. It is funded from the Science Budget of the Department of Education and Science, receives commissions from the Ministry of Agriculture, Fisheries and Food, and does research for industry and other bodies.

The Council is responsible for research done in its institutes and in U.K. university departments funded through its research grants scheme. It advises the Department of Agriculture and Fisheries for Scotland (D.A.F.S.) on research in the Scottish Agricultural Research Institutes.

The institutes funded through A.F.R.C. and D.A.F.S., and the university groups supported, form the Agricultural and Food Research Service.

Chairman, The Earl of Selborne, K.B.E.
Deputy Chairman and Secretary, Prof. W. D. P. Stewart, F.R.S.E., F.R.S.
Members, Prof. R. L. Bell, C.B.; Prof. T. L. Blundell, F.R.S.; Prof. D. Boulter; J. E. Cross; R. N. Crossett; Prof. J. M. M. Cunningham, C.B.E., F.R.S.E.; Prof. A. W. Cuthbert, F.R.S.; Prof. B. K. Follett, F.R.S.; A. C.

Green; L. P. Hamilton, C.B.; Prof. J. L. Harper, F.R.S.; M. Mackie; Prof. A. Nienow; J. A. Parry, C.B.E.; G. T. Pryce; B. C. Read, C.B.E.; Dr. D. W. F. Shannon; Prof. Sir David Smith, F.R.S.; E. J. G. Smith, C.B.; Prof. E. J. L. Soulsby; Prof. R. Whittenbury.
Assessors, Prof. E. C. Cocking, F.R.S.; Dr. R. F. Coleman, F.R.S.E.; J. I. Davies, M.B.E.; K. Meldrum; Dr. C. McMurray.
Deputy Secretary (G2), Prof. J. Hearn.
Director of Central Office (G3), B. G. Jamieson, PH.D.
Heads of Divisions (G5), R. Prideaux (*Finance*); J. Dickens (*Personnel*); R. J. Harris (*Research*); Dr. J. V. Lake (*Policy*).
Commercial Policy Section (G7), S. M. Lawrie.
Principal Information Officer (G7), M. F. Goodwin.
For institutes and units of the Agricultural and Food Research Service, *see* Index.

COLLEGE OF ARMS OR HERALDS COLLEGE
Queen Victoria Street, EC4V 4BT
[01-248 2762]

The College is the official repository of the Arms and pedigrees of English, Northern Irish, and Commonwealth families and their descendants, and its records include official copies of the records of Ulster King of Arms, the originals of which remain in Dublin. The 13 officers of the College specialize in genealogical and heraldic work for their respective clients.

Arms have been and still are granted by Letters Patent from the Kings of Arms under Authority delegated to them by the Sovereign, such authority having been expressly conferred on them since at least the fifteenth century. A right to Arms can only be established by the registration in the official records of the College of Arms of a pedigree showing direct male line descent from an ancestor already appearing therein as being entitled to Arms, or by making application through the College of Arms for a Grant of Arms.

The College of Arms is open Mon.–Fri. 10–4, when an Officer of Arms is in attendance to deal with enquiries by the public, though such enquiries may also be directed to any of the Officers of Arms, either personally or by letter.

Earl Marshal, His Grace the Duke of Norfolk, K.G., G.C.V.O., C.B., C.B.E., M.C.

Kings of Arms
Garter, Sir Colin Cole, K.C.V.O., T.D., F.S.A.
Clarenceux, Sir Anthony Wagner, K.C.B., K.C.V.O., F.S.A.
Norroy and Ulster, J. P. B. Brooke-Little, C.V.O., F.S.A.

Heralds
York (and Registrar), C. M. J. F. Swan, C.V.O., PH.D., F.S.A.
Chester, D. H. B. Chesshyre, F.S.A.
Windsor, T. D. Mathew.
Richmond, M. Maclagan, F.S.A.
Lancaster, P. L. Gwynn-Jones.
Somerset, T. Woodcock.

Earl Marshal's Secretary, Sir Walter Verco, K.C.V.O., Surrey Herald Extraordinary.

Pursuivants
Rouge Dragon, P. L. Dickinson.
Portcullis, P. B. Spurrier.
Bluemantle, T. D. McCarthy.
Rouge Croix, H. E. Paston-Bedingfeld.

COURT OF THE LORD LYON
H.M. New Register House, Edinburgh EH1 3YT
[031-556 7255]

The Court of the Lord Lyon is the Scottish Court of Chivalry, (including the genealogical jurisdiction of the *Ri-Sennachie* of Scotland's Celtic Kings) and adjudicates rights to arms and administration of The Scottish Public Register of All Arms and Bearings and Public Register of All Genealogies. The Lord Lyon presides and judicially establishes rights to existing arms or succession to Chiefship, or for cadets with scientific "differences" showing position in clan or family. Pedigrees are also established by decrees of Lyon Court, and by Letters Patent. As Royal Commissioner in Armory, he grants Patents of Arms (which constitute the grantee and heirs noble in the Noblesse of Scotland) to "virtuous and well-deserving" Scotsmen, and petitioners (personal or corporate) in Her Majesty's overseas realms of Scottish connection, and issues birthbrieves.
Lord Lyon King of Arms, Malcolm Rognvald Innes of Edingight, C.V.O., W.S., F.S.A. scot.

Heralds
Marchmont, Maj. D. M. Maitland-Titterton, T.D., F.S.A. scot.
Albany, J. A. Spens, R.D., W.S.
Rothesay, Sir Crispin Agnew of Lochnaw, Bt.

Pursuivants
Dingwall, C. J. Burnett, F.S.A. scot.
Kintyre, J. C. G. George, F.S.A. scot.
Unicorn, Alastair Campbell of Airds, younger, F.S.A. scot.

Lyon Clerk and Keeper of Records, Mrs. C. G. W. Roads, F.S.A. scot.
Procurator-Fiscal, I. R. Guild, C.B.E., W.S.
Herald Painter, Mrs. J. Phillips.
Macer, T. C. Gray.

ART GALLERIES, ETC.

OFFICE OF ARTS AND LIBRARIES
Horse Guards Road, SW1P 3AL
[01-270 3000]

The Office of Arts and Libraries, formerly part of the Department of Education and Science, became a separate department in 1983. It has general responsibilities for arts policy and its broad objectives are to assist the provision and development of the performing and visual arts, to maintain and enhance the collections of national museums and art galleries, to help preserve the national heritage and to sustain and develop national collections of literary and archive material. It directly funds some 20 bodies including the Arts Council, the eleven national museums and galleries, the British Library and its St. Pancras project. The Office of Arts and Libraries also has policy responsibilities towards the public library and local museum services. The Government Art Collection, which is responsible for the acquisition, maintenance and display of works of art in major government buildings in this country and abroad, forms part of the Office of Arts and Libraries.

Minister for the Arts, The Rt. Hon. Richard Luce, M.P.
Private Secretary, Miss E. M. Goodison.
Parliamentary Private Secretary, J. Hanley, M.P.
Head of the Office of Arts and Libraries (Deputy Secretary), R. W. L. Wilding, C.B.

Arts and Heritage

Assistant Secretary, R. H. Stone.
Principals, P. J. Fallon; Miss M. J. Lamont; D. H. A. Lodge; Miss C. R. Morrison.

Finance, Establishments and Museums

Assistant Secretary, Mrs. S. D. Brown.
Principals, N. A. Luck; D. M. Mainwood; E. A. Yeo.

Libraries and Information Services

Assistant Secretary, C. C. Leamy.
Principal, A. Poulter.
Library Advisers, P. J. Beauchamp; Miss C. R. Lutyens.

British Library Project St. Pancras

Project Director, J. R. W. Pardey.
Principal, E. T. James.

Government Art Collection

Curator, Dr. W. Baron.

ARTS COUNCIL OF GREAT BRITAIN
105 Piccadilly, W1V 0AU
[01-629 9495]

The Arts Council, an independent body established by Royal Charter in 1946, is Great Britain's principal channel for public financial support of the arts. It funds the major arts organizations in England, the Regional Arts Associations and the Scottish and Welsh Arts Councils. It also provides a service of advice, information and help to artists, arts organizations and the general public.

Its aims are to develop and improve the understanding and practice of the arts and to increase their accessibility to the public.

The Council receives a grant-in-aid from the Government, and for the year 1988–89 the amount is £150 million.

Chairman, The Lord Rees-Mogg.
Secretary-General, L. Rittner.

ROYAL FINE ART COMMISSION
7 St. James's Square, SW1Y 4JU
[01-839 6537]

Appointed in May, 1924, the Commission is required to advise Departments of State on, and call their attention to, any project or development which might affect national or public amenities.

Chairman, The Lord St. John of Fawsley, P.C.
Commissioners, The Countess of Airlie, C.V.O.; R. D. Carter, C.B.E.; Dame Elizabeth Chesterton, D.B.E.; Sir Philip Dowson, C.B.E.; M. Girouard, PH.D.; Sir Alexander Gordon, C.B.E.; The Duke of Grafton, K.G., F.S.A.; M. J. Hopkins; R. MacCormac; P. Nuttgens, C.B.E., PH.D.; Mrs. J. Nutting; D. Hamilton Fraser, R.A.; Sir Philip Powell, C.H., O.B.E., R.A.; J. Sutherland; Miss W. Taylor, C.B.E.; W. Whitfield, C.B.E.; J. Winter, M.B.E.; H. T. Moggridge, O.B.E.; S. A. Lipton.
Secretary (G6), S. Cantacuzino, C.B.E.

ROYAL FINE ART COMMISSION FOR SCOTLAND
9 Atholl Crescent,
Edinburgh EH3 8HA
[031-229 1109]

Chairman, Prof. A. J. Youngson, C.B.E.
Commissioners, Miss K. Borland; J. Boys, F.R.I.B.A.; B. Gasson, O.B.E.; Dr. Deborah Howard, PH.D., F.S.A.; W. K. Mackay; Prof. I. Metzstein; A. Morrocco, R.S.A.; G. Ogilvie-Laing; J. D. Richards, C.B.E.; R. R. Steedman, R.S.A.; Mrs. F. M. E. Walker.
Secretary, C. Prosser.

NATIONAL GALLERY
Trafalgar Square, WC2N 5DN
[01-839 3321]

Hours of opening.—Weekdays 10–6, Sun. 2–6. Closed on Good Friday, Christmas Eve, Christmas Day, Boxing Day, New Year's Day and May Day Bank Holiday.

The National Gallery was founded in 1824, following a Parliamentary grant of £60,000 for the purchase and exhibition of the Angerstein collection of pictures. The present site was first occupied in 1838 and enlarged and improved at various times throughout the years. A substantial extension to the north of the building with a public entrance in Orange Street was opened in 1975, and a new wing, the Sainsbury wing, is under construction. Expenses for 1988–89 are estimated at £11,238,000.

Board of Trustees

Chairman, Hon. J. Rothschild.
Trustees, H.R.H. The Prince of Wales, K.G., K.T., G.C.B., P.C.; Sir Rex Richards, F.R.S., D.Phil.; Mrs. C. Hubbard; M. Cowdy; Sir Nicholas Henderson, G.C.M.G.; Lord Alexander of Weedon, Q.C.; F. St. J. Gore, C.B.E.; B. Gascoigne; M. Andrews.

Officers

Salaries

Grade 3	£43,200
Grade 5	£32,137
Grade 6	£28,837

Director (G3), R. N. MacGregor.
Keeper and Deputy Director (G5), Dr. A. J. W. Braham.
Keeper, Education and Exhibitions (G5), A. J. W. Smith.
Deputy Keepers (G6), Dr. C. P. H. Brown; M. J. Wilson.
Chief Restorer (G5), M. H. Wyld.
Scientific Adviser (G6), Dr. J. S. Mills.
Bursar (G5), Ms. C. E. Macready.

NATIONAL PORTRAIT GALLERY
St. Martin's Place, WC2H 0HE
[01-930 1552]

Open Mon.–Fri. 10–5. Sat. 10–6. Sun. 2–6.

A grant was made in 1856 to form a gallery of the portraits of the most eminent persons in British history. The present building was opened in 1896, £80,000 being contributed to its cost by Mr. W. H. Alexander; an extension erected at the expense of Lord Duveen was opened in 1933.

Chairman, The Rev. Prof. W. O Chadwick, O.M., K.B.E., F.B.A.
Trustees, The Lord President of the Council (*ex officio*); The President of the Royal Academy of Arts (*ex officio*); Prof. Sir Lawrence Gowing, C.B.E.; The Duke of Grafton, K.G., F.S.A.; Sir Oliver Millar, K.C.V.O., F.B.A., F.S.A.; J. Roberts, D.Phil.; Prof. B. R. Morris, D.Phil.; Mrs. S. Crosland; Prof. M. Gowing, C.B.E., F.B.A.; The Marquess of Anglesey, F.S.A; H. Keswick; Prof. N. Lynton; The Lord Sieff of Brimpton, O.B.E.; The Lord Weidenfeld.

Director, J. T. Hayes, C.B.E., PH.D., F.S.A £32,094
Keeper and Deputy Director, M. Rogers, D.Phil.
                                                    £30.467

TATE GALLERY
Millbank, SW1P 4RG
[01-821 1313]

Hours of opening.—Weekdays 10–5.50. Sun. 2–5.50. Closed on New Year's Day, Good Friday, May Day

Holiday, Christmas Eve, Christmas Day and Boxing Day.

The Tate Gallery comprises the National Collections of British painting and 20th century painting and sculpture. Works are displayed at the Gallery as two collections: The British Collection and the Modern Collection. The Gallery was opened in 1897, the cost of erection (£80,000) being defrayed by Sir Henry Tate, who also contributed the nucleus of the present collection. The Turner Wing, built at the expense of Sir Joseph Duveen was opened in 1920. Lord Duveen defrayed the cost of galleries to contain the collection of modern foreign painting, completed in 1926, and a new sculpture hall, completed in 1937. The latest extension to the Tate Gallery, the Clore Gallery for the Turner Collection, was opened by H.M. The Queen on April 1, 1987. The Tate Gallery Liverpool, sited in the Albert Dock opened in May 1988. Expenses for 1988–89 are estimated at £10,895,000.

Board of Trustees

Chairman, R. Rogers.
Trustees, The Countess of Airlie, c.v.o.; Sir Anthony Caro, c.b.e.; G. de Botton; J. Golding; D. Puttnam, c.b.e.; Sir Rex Richards, d.sc., f.r.s.; Sir Mark Weinberg; Mrs. C. Hubbard; W. Govett; Mrs. P. Ridley.

Officers

Salaries

Director £43,200
Grade 5 .... £24,765–£29,465
Grade 6 .... £18,786–£25,335

Director (G3), N. Serota.
Keeper of the British Collection (G5), M. R. F. Butlin
Keeper of the Modern Collection (G5), R. Morphet
Keeper of Conservation (G5), The Viscount Dunluce
Curator of the Turner Collection (G6), A. Wilton
Curator, Tate Gallery Liverpool (G6), R. Francis.
Deputy Keepers (G6), L. A. Parris; Miss R. Rattenbury; R. Perry.
Secretary and Head of Administration (G6), R. Aylward.

WALLACE COLLECTION
Hertford House, Manchester Square, W1M 6BN
[01–935 0687]

Admission free. Open on weekdays 10–5: Sun. 2–5. Closed on Good Friday, December 24–26, January 1 and May Day.

The Wallace Collection was bequeathed to the nation by the widow of Sir Richard Wallace, Bt., on her death in 1897, and Hertford House was subsequently acquired by the Government. The collection includes pictures, drawings and miniatures, French furniture, sculpture, bronzes, porcelain, armour and miscellaneous *objets d'art*. The total net expenses were estimated at £1,570,000 in 1988–89.
Director, J. A. S. Ingamells.
Assistants to Director, P. Hughes; Miss R. J. Savill.
Head of Administration, A. W. Houldershaw.

NATIONAL GALLERIES OF SCOTLAND
The Mound, Edinburgh EH2 2EL
[031–556 8921]

Chairman of the Trustees, A. M. Grossart.
Trustees, The Countess of Rosebery; J. Packer, o.b.e.; A. R. Cole-Hamilton; Mrs. L. W. Gibbs; Sir Norman Macfarlane; J. D. Richards, c.b.e.; R. W. Begg.

Salaries

Director .... £30,344–£31,844
Keeper .... £18,786–£25,335
Assistant Keeper/Curator .... £12,024–£20,292
Director, T. Clifford.
Keeper of Conservation, J. P. Dick.
Keeper of Information (Asst. Keeper), R. Dalrymple.
Secretary (Asst. Keeper), W. J. Sinclair.

Comprising:

National Gallery of Scotland
The Mound, Edinburgh
[031–556 8921]

Open: Mon.–Sat. 10–5; Sun. 2–5; Closed December 25, 26, 31; January 1, 2, 3.
Keeper, M. Clarke.
Assistant Keepers, Miss L. M. Errington, ph.d.; Ms. J. Lloyd Williams.
Keeper of Prints and Drawings, H. Macandrew.

Scottish National Portrait Gallery
1 Queen Street, Edinburgh
[031–556 8921]

Hours—as for National Gallery of Scotland.
Keeper, D. Thomson, ph.d.
Assistant Keepers, Miss R. K. Marshall, ph.d.; J. E. Holloway.
Curator of Photography, Miss S. F. Stevenson.

Scottish National Gallery of Modern Art
Belford Road, Edinburgh EH4 3DR
[031–556 8921]

Hours—as for National Gallery of Scotland.
Keeper, R. Calvocoressi.
Assistant Keeper, K. S. Hartley.

(For other British Art Galleries, *see* Index.)

UNITED KINGDOM ATOMIC ENERGY AUTHORITY
11 Charles II Street, SW1Y 4QP
[01–930 5454]

Established by the Atomic Energy Authority Act, 1954, the Authority is responsible for providing research and development support for the U.K. nuclear power programme. It also undertakes work on other civil applications of nuclear energy and on various projects outside the nuclear field on repayment. Since April 1986 UKAEA has been required by the Government on a quasi-commercial footing. The UKAEA has eight laboratories and a London headquarters employing some 14,000 people.
Chairman, J. G. Collier £65,000
Members (Full-time), Dr. G. G. E. Low; C. C. S. Chapman; Dr. B. L. Eyre.
(Part-time) Prof. Sir Peter Hirsch, f.r.s.; J. Bullock; R. E. J. Roberts, c.b.e.; R. Sanderson, o.b.e.; J. N. Maltby, c.b.e.; Prof. Sir Roger Elliott, f.r.s. (*each* £5,650).
Secretary, M. A. W. Baker.

THE AUDIT COMMISSION FOR ENGLAND AND WALES
49 Whitehall, SW1A 2BX
[01–828 1212]

The Audit Commission was set up in 1983. Its main responsibility is for appointing external auditors for local authorities and certain other public bodies in England and Wales. The auditors may be from the District Audit Service or from a private firm of accountants. The Commission also tries to ensure that local authorities are getting, and giving, value for money through special studies of their services.

The Commission has 15–17 members appointed by the Secretary of State for the Environment in consultation with the Secretary of State for Wales. Though appointed by the Secretary of State the Commissioners are responsible to Parliament.

Chairman, D. J. S. Cooksey.
Deputy Chairman, H. S. Axton.
Controller of Audit, H. J. Davies.
Deputy Controller, J. C. Nicholson, C.B.E.

The Commission for Local Authority Accounts in Scotland
18 George Street, Edinburgh EH2 2QU
[031–226 7348]

The Commission was set up in 1975. It is responsible for securing the audit of the accounts of Scottish local authorities and certain joint boards and joint committees. Amongst its duties the Commission is required to deal with reports made by the Controller of Audit on items of account contrary to law; incorrect accounting; and losses due to misconduct, negligence and failure to carry out statutory duties.

Members are appointed by the Secretary of State for Scotland.

Chairman, Prof. J. R. Small.
Chief Executive and Controller of Audit, R. K. Simpson.
Secretary, K. Ferguson.

THE BANK OF ENGLAND
Threadneedle Street, EC2R 8AH

The Bank of England was incorporated in 1694 under Royal Charter. It is the banker of the Government on whose behalf it manages the Note Issue and the National Debt. As central reserve bank of the country, the Bank keeps the accounts of British banks, who maintain with it a proportion of their cash resources, and of most overseas central banks.

Governor, Rt. Hon. Robin Leigh-Pemberton.
Deputy Governor, Sir George Blunden.
Directors, Dr. D. V. Atterton, C.B.E.; Hon. Sir John Baring, C.V.O.; Sir Adrian Cadbury; F. B. Corby; Sir Colin Corness; R. D. Galpin; E. A. J. George; Sir Robert Haslam; Sir Martin Jacomb; Sir Hector Laing; G. H. Laird; A. D. Loehnis, C.M.G.; B. Quinn; Sir David Scholey, C.B.E.; D. A. Walker; D. V. Weyer, C.B.E.; Sir Leslie Young, C.B.E.
Associate Directors, P. H. Kent; J. S. Fleming; H. C. E. Harris; W. P. Cooke.
Advisers to the Governor, J. P. Charkham; A. L. Coleby.
Assistant Directors, I. Plenderleith; R. A. Barnes.
Chief of Banking Department (Chief Cashier), G. M. Gill.
Chief Registrar, J. G. Drake.
General Manager, Printing Works, A. W. Jarvis.
Secretary, G. A. Croughton.
Head of Information Division, P. J. Warland.
The Auditor, L. G. Lloyd.

BOUNDARY COMMISSIONS

The Commissions are constituted under the Parliamentary Constituencies Act, 1986. The Speaker of the House of Commons is ex-officio chairman of all four Commissions in the United Kingdom. Each of the four Commissions is required by law to keep the parliamentary constituencies in their part of the United Kingdom under review. Each of the three Commissions in Great Britain is required by law to keep the European Parliamentary constituencies in their part of Great Britain under review.

England
St. Catherines House, 10 Kingsway, WC2B 6JP
[01–242 0262]

Deputy Chairman, The Hon. Mr. Justice Knox.
Joint Secretaries, R. McLeod; Mrs. M. E. Moxon.

Wales
St. Catherines House, 10 Kingsway, WC2B 6JP
[01–242 0262]

Deputy Chairman, The Hon. Mr. Justice Kenneth Jones.
Joint Secretaries, R. McLeod; Mrs. M. E. Moxon.

Scotland
St. Andrew's House, Edinburgh EH1 3DE
[031–556 8400]

Deputy Chairman, The Hon. Lord Davidson.
Secretary, A. Simmen, O.B.E.

Northern Ireland
c/o Northern Ireland Office,
Whitehall, SW1A 2AZ
[01–210 6569]

Deputy Chairman, (vacant).
Secretary, J. R. Fisher.

BRITISH BROADCASTING CORPORATION
Broadcasting House, W1A 1AA
[01–580 4468]

The B.B.C. was incorporated under Royal Charter as successor to the British Broadcasting Company, Ltd., whose licence expired Dec. 31, 1926. Its present Charter came into force Aug. 1, 1981, for 15 years. The Chairman, Vice-Chairman and other Governors are appointed by the Queen in Council. The B.B.C. is financed by revenue from receiving licences for the Home services and by grant-in-aid from Parliament for the External services. The total number of receiving licences in the U.K. at March 31, 1988 was 19,354,000, of which 2,220,000 were for monochrome receivers and 17,134,000 for colour receivers. Annual television fees are: monochrome £21; colour £62.50. Television licence fees became index-linked from April 1, 1988.

Board of Governors
(as at Aug. 1, 1988)

Chairman, M. Hussey. £36,840
Vice-Chairman, The Lord Barnett, P.C. £9,475
Governors, W. Peat, C.B.E. (*Scotland*); J. Kincade, PH.D. (*N. Ireland*); J. Parry (*Wales*).. (*each*)£9,475
Miss J. Barrow, O.B.E.; The Lady Parkes; Sir Curtis Keeble; Dr. J. Roberts; W. B. Jordan; J. K. Oates; Miss P. D. James, O.B.E.............. (*each*) £4,725

Board of Management
(as at Aug. 1, 1988)

Director-General, M. Checkland.
Deputy Director-General, J. Birt.
Managing Directors, P. Fox (*Network Television*); D. Hatch (*Network Radio*); J. Tusa (*External Broadcasting*); G. Stanley Jones (*Regional Broadcasting*).
Directors, C. Martin (*Personnel*); W. Dennay (*Engineering*); H. James (*Corporate Affairs*); I. Phillips (*Finance*).

Other Senior Staff

Director, News and Current Affairs, R. Neil.
Director, Resources, Radio, D. Thomas.
Director, Resources, Television, C. Taylor.

Director of Programmes, Television, P. Ibbotson.
Deputy Managing Director, External Broadcasting, C. Bell.
Deputy Director of Engineering, C. Sandbank.
Deputy Director of Personnel, R. Chase.
Head of Policy and Planning Unit, Ms. P. Hodgson.
Controller, BBC-1, J. Powell.
Controller BBC-2, A. Yentob.
Controller Radio 1, J. Beerling.
Controller Radio 2, B. Marriott.
Controller Radio 3, J. Drummond.
Controller Radio 4, M. Green.
Controller, Scotland, P. Chalmers.
Controller, Wales, G. Price.
Controller, N. Ireland, Rev. Dr. C. Morris.
Chief Political Adviser, Ms. M. Douglas.
Controller, Editorial Policy, J. Wilson.
Controller Information Services, M. Bunce.
The Secretary, J. McCormick.
Legal Adviser, A. Jennings.
Chief Executive, B.B.C. Enterprises, J.Arnold-Baker.

BRITISH COAL CORPORATION
Hobart House, Grosvenor Place, SW1X 7AE
[01–235 2020]

The British Coal Corporation (formerly the National Coal Board) was constituted in 1946 and took over the mines on January 1, 1947.
Chairman, Sir Robert Haslam.
Deputy Chairmen, Sir Kenneth Couzens, K.C.B.; J. H. Northard, C.B.E.
Members, M. H. Butler; M. J. Edwards, C.B.E.; K. Moses, C.B.E.
Members (part-time), Sir Melvyn Rosser; C. Barker; Dr. D. V. Atterton, C.B.E.; Dr. T. J. Parker; Sir Ronald Dearing; D. B. Walker.
Secretary, D. G. Brandrick, C.B.E.

THE BRITISH COUNCIL
10 Spring Gardens, SW1A 2BN
[01–930 8466]

The British Council was established in 1934 and incorporated by Royal Charter in 1940.
It is an independent, non-political organization which promotes Britain abroad. It provides access to British ideas, talents and experience in education and training, books and periodicals, the English language, the arts, the sciences and technology.
The Council is represented in more than eighty countries and runs 138 offices, 116 libraries and 50 English language schools around the world.
The Council's annual turnover is £276 million, including grants from the Foreign and Commonwealth Office and the Overseas Development Administration. The Council's own earnings now exceed £64 million.
Chairman, Sir David Orr, M.C.
Director-General, R. Francis £59,500

BRITISH RAILWAYS BOARD
Euston Square, P.O. Box 100, NW1 2DZ
[01–928 5151]

The British Railways Board came into being on Jan. 1, 1963 under the terms of the Transport Act, 1962. The Board became responsible for the provision of railway services in Great Britain and for catering and other services formerly carried on by the British Transport Commission.
Chairman, Sir Robert Reid, C.B.E. £89,757
Vice-Chairmen, D. Fowler, C.B.E.; D. D. Kirby, C.B.E.
Members, H. G. DeVille, C.B.E.*; S. D. Jenkins*; D. P. Hornby*; A. J. G. Sheppard*; R. W. Tookey, C.B.E.*; Ms. A. Biss*; Miss K. T. Kantor*; D. L. Davies;

J. B. Cameron; J. K. Welsby, D. E. Rayner, J. J. O'Brien (*Joint Managing Directors, Railways*).
* Part-time members, paid *pro rata.*

BRITISH SHIPBUILDERS
197 Knightsbridge, SW7 1RB
[01–581 1393]

Established under the Aircraft and Shipbuilding Industries Act of 1977, British Shipbuilders is a national corporation responsible for all publicly-owned shipyards, etc. in England and Scotland. At the time of going to press the Government's plans to privatize the publicly-owned shipyards were well-advanced.
Chairman and Chief Executive, J. Lister, C.B.E.
Corporation Secretary, M. Day.

B.S.I. (BRITISH STANDARDS INSTITUTION)
2 Park Street, W1A 2BS
[Enquiry Section: B.S.I., Linford Wood, Milton Keynes, MK14 6LE. Tel. 0908–221166]

B.S.I. (the British Standards Institution) is the recognized authority in the U.K. for the preparation and publication of national standards for industrial and consumer products. In consultation with the interests concerned, B.S.I. prepares standards relating to nearly every sector of the nation's industry and trade.
British Standards are issued for voluntary adoption though in a number of cases compliance with a British Standard is required by legislation. B.S.I. operates certification schemes under which industrial and consumer products are certified as complying with the relevant British Standard and manufacturers satisfying the requirements of such schemes may use the Institution's certification trade marks known as the "Kitemark" and the "Safety Mark".
B.S.I. is financed by voluntary subscriptions, an annual Government grant, the sale of its publications and fees for testing and certification. There are more than 20,000 subscribing members of B.S.I.
Director General, Dr. I. Dunstan.

BRITISH STEEL CORPORATION
9 Albert Embankment, SE1 7SN
[01–735 7654]

The British Steel Corporation was established under the Iron and Steel Act 1967 which vested in the Corporation the shares of the fourteen major steel companies. Legislation was placed before Parliament in the 1987–88 session which will provide for the Corporation to be returned to the private sector, and the Government intends to follow this with a flotation of shares.
Chairman, Sir Robert Scholey, C.B.E. £105,000
Deputy Chairman (part-time), Sir Ronald Halstead, C.B.E.
Chief Executive, M. E. Llowarch.
Members (full-time), Dr. F. Fitzgerald; Dr. D. Grieves, C.B.E.; B. S. Moffat, O.B.E.; G. H. Sambrook, C.B.E.; J. G. Stewart.
Members (part-time), J. D. Birkin; J. F.Eccles, C.B.E.; The Lord Gregson; S. J. Gross, C.M.G.; H. L. I. Runciman; A. E. Wheatley.
Secretary, T. J. MacDonald.

BRITISH TECHNOLOGY GROUP
101 Newington Causeway, SE1 6BU
[01–403 6666]

British Technology Group (B.T.G.) is a self-financing public organization appointed by the Government to license new scientific and engineering products and processes discovered through research at U.K.

universities, polytechnics, research councils and Government research establishments. B.T.G. provides finance where further development is needed before inventions can be licensed to industry. B.T.G. can also offer finance to companies that want to develop new products and processes based on their own technology.
Chairman, C. Barker.
Chief Executive, I. A. Harvey.

BRITISH TOURIST AUTHORITY
Thames Tower, Black's Road, W6 9EL
[01–846 9000]

Under the Development of Tourism Act, 1969, four co-equal statutory Tourist Boards were established: the British Tourist Authority, the English Tourist Board, the Scottish Tourist Board and the Wales Tourist Board. Each is financed mainly by direct grant-in-aid from Government and is an independent statutory body. The British Tourist Authority has specific responsibility for promoting tourism to Great Britain from overseas. It also has a general responsibility for tourism within Great Britain as a whole.
Chairman, D. R. Y. Bluck, O.B.E. (*part-time*).
Chief Executive, M. G. Medlicott.

English Tourist Board
Thames Tower, Black's Road, W6 9EL

Scottish Tourist Board
23, Ravelston Terrace, Edinburgh EH4 3EU

Wales Tourist Board
Brunel House, 2 Fitzalan Street, Cardiff CF2 1UY

BRITISH WATERWAYS BOARD
Melbury House, Melbury Terrace, NW1 6JX
[01–262 6711]

Chairman, D. C. Ingman.
Vice-Chairman, Dr. A. Robertson, C.B.E. (*part-time*).
Members (all part-time), Sir Trevor Hughes, K.C.B.; J. Gordon; Sir Peter Hutchison, Bt.
Chief Executive, B. C. Dice.
Secretary and Parliamentary Adviser, T. T. Luckcuck.

BROADCASTING STANDARDS COUNCIL
c/o Broadcasting Department, The Home Office

The Council was set up in 1988 to develop a code on the use of sex and violence in all forms of broadcasting in consultation with producers; and to commission research into the effects of sex and violence in broadcasting upon viewers. Members of the Council are appointed by the Home Secretary. (The appointments are part-time.)
Chairman, The Lord Rees-Mogg £30,000
Deputy Chairman, Miss J. Barrow, O.B.E.
                                                                £15,000–£22,000
Members, R. Barker, O.B.E., R.D.; The Bishop of Peterborough; A. Dubs; Dr. R. Brinley Jones; Dr. Jean Curtis-Raleigh; Rev. C. Robertson ... £9,000

CABINET OFFICE
The Cabinet Office comprises the Secretariat, who support Ministers collectively in the conduct of Cabinet business; the Central Statistical Office; and the Office of the Minister for the Civil Service (O.M.C.S.) which is responsible for the management and organization of the Civil Service and recruitment into it, efficiency, and senior appointments. Other functions are from time to time laid on the Office, some ephemerally and some permanently. Non-departmental Ministers may be attached to the Office.

The functions of the Cabinet Office (O.M.C.S.) are in support of the Prime Minister in her capacity as Minister for the Civil Service, with responsibility for day-to-day supervision delegated to the Minister of State, Privy Council Office.

(For **Salaries,** *see* page 297)

PRIME MINISTER'S OFFICE
Prime Minister and Minister for the Civil Service, THE RT. HON. MARGARET THATCHER, M.P.
Principal Private Secretary to the Prime Minister, N. L. Wicks, C.B.E.
Private Secretaries to the Prime Minister, C. D. Powell (*Overseas Affairs*); P. R. C. Gray (*Economic Affairs*); P. A. Bearpark (*Parliamentary Affairs*); D. Morris (*Home Affairs*).
Personal Assistant to the Prime Minister, Mrs. T. Gaisman.
Secretary for Appointments, J. R. Catford.
Foreign Affairs Adviser, Sir Percy Cradock, G.C.M.G.
Political Secretary, J. Whittingdale.
Policy Unit, G. Guise; Miss C. Sinclair; P. J. Steader; G. D. Bourne; Prof. B. Griffiths; A. Dunlop; I. K. Whitehead.
Chief Press Secretary, B. Ingham.
Deputy Chief Press Secretary, T. J. Perks.
Assistant Private Secretaries to Prime Minister, Miss J. Drever; Mrs J. Cole.
Parliamentary Private Secretary, Hon. M. Lennox-Boyd, M.P.
Adviser on Efficiency, Sir Angus Fraser, K.C.B., T.D.

Efficiency Unit
70 Whitehall, SW1A 2AS

Head of Unit (G3), Miss K. Jenkins.
Assistant Secretaries (G5), Mrs. C. Dixon; J. M. Cunningham.

Secretary to the Cabinet and Head of Home Civil Service, Sir Robin Butler, K.C.B., C.V.O.

Ceremonial Branch
Ceremonial Officer (G5), J. Thompson.

SECRETARIAT
70 Whitehall, SW1A 2AS
[01–270 3000]

Deputy Secretaries (G2), Sir Colin Figures, K.C.M.G., O.B.E.; P. J. Weston, C.M.G.; R. G. Lavelle; R. T. J. Wilson.
Chief Scientific Adviser, J. W. Fairclough.
Under Secretaries (G3), J. H. Holroyd; A. J. Langdon; P.E. Hall, C.M.G.; G. Monger; N. H. Nicholls; H. V. B. Brown.
Assistant Secretaries (G5), G. Barrassi; C. R. Budd; Brig. J. A. J. Budd; H. Burke, C.B.E.; B. Dinwiddy; R. E. Escritt; F. M. Merrifield; J. Morrison; M. Nicholson; P. B. Preece; A. Quigley; R. P. Short; M. W. Townley.
Senior Principals (G6), A. R. Bell; Mrs. M. Bloom; C. K. Davies; Dr. G. W. D. Findlay; P. C. F. Gilbert; P. F. Tero.

ESTABLISHMENT OFFICER'S GROUP
Principal Establishment and Finance Officer, (G3), J. W. Stevens, C.B.

Information Services
Chief Press Officer (G6), J. B. Wright.

Establishment Division
Deputy Establishment Officer (G5), A. Phillips.

Finance Division
Senior Finance Officer (G6), Miss J. M. E. Buchan.

Internal Audit

Principal (G7), I. C. R. Boulton.

Historical Section
Hepburn House, Marsham Street, SW1P 4HW
[01–211 6605]

Departmental Records Adviser (G6), Miss. P. Andrews.

CENTRAL STATISTICAL OFFICE
Government Offices, Great George Street,
SW1P 3AQ
[01–270 3000]

Director and Head of the Government Statistical Service (G1A), J. Hibbert.
Private Secretary, Miss A. J. Large.
Under Secretaries (G3), D. W. Flaxen; M. J. M. Erritt; J. E. Kidgell.
Assistant Secretaries (G5), P. Altobell; B. J. Buckingham; Miss S. P. Carter; A. A. Croxford; T. J. Griffin; P. B. Kenny; K. Mansell; Dr. J. H. Ludley; D. Ramprakash; D. C. K. Stirling.

OFFICE OF THE MINISTER FOR THE CIVIL SERVICE
Horse Guards Road, SW1P 3AL
3AL
[01–270 3000]

Second Permanent Secretary (G1A), E. P. Kemp.
Director of Management Development and Training (G2), B. T. Gilmore.
Security Adviser, Air Vice Marshal B. G. Lock, C.B., C.B.E., A.F.C.

Personnel Management Group

Under Secretary and Director, Public Appointments Unit(G3), G. T. Morgan.
Assistant Secretaries (G5), E. Ferguson; G. J. Court; Mrs. S. Collins; G. H. Wollen.

Machinery of Government

Assistant Secretary (G5), Dr. J. P. Spencer.

Security Division

Assistant Secretary (G5), S. R. Davie.

Occupational Health Service
Tilbury House, Petty France, SW1H 9EU

Medical Adviser and Acting Director of Occupational Health Service, Dr. G. S. Sorrie.
Principal Medical Officers, Dr. P. J. Constable (*Deputy Medical Adviser*); Dr. A. N. Hepburn.

Civil Service Commission
Alencon Link, Basingstoke, Hants. RG21 1JB
[0256–29222]

First Commissioner (G2), D. J. Trevelyan, C.B.
Commissioners (G3), B. Walmsley; (*G4*), J. K. Moore (*Director, Civil Service Selection Board*).
Commissioners (part-time), D. P. Hornby; G. L. Dennis; Miss D. Whittingham.
Assistant Secretary (G5), C. J. Parry.
Senior Principals (G6), A. S. Halford; R. B. M. Payne; G. S. Royston; P. J. Wiggett.

Civil Service Selection Board
24 Whitehall, SW1A 2ED

Director (G4), J. K. Moore.
Deputy Director (G5), Mrs. D. C. Miller.
Chief Psychologist (G6), J. McLeod.

Top Management Programme

Director (G2), B. T. Gilmore.
Deputy Directors (G5), Miss V. M. Dews; J. S. Pitt-Brooke.

Training and Civil Service College
Sunningdale Park, Ascot, Berks. SL5 0QE
[0990–23444]
London: 11 Belgrave Road, SW1V 1RB
[01-834 6644]

Principal (G3), R. Jackling.
Head of Training Division (G5), P. R. Coster.
College Policy Planning Manager (G5), Mrs. E. A. Shaw.
Directors (G5), J. Allen; A. A. Carter; G. Gammon; Dr. P. Lund; Dr. R. J. Smith.
College Secretary (G6), P. Cook.

CABLE AUTHORITY

Gillingham House, 38–44 Gillingham Street,
SW1V 1HU
[01-821 6161]

The Cable Authority is the statutory body established by the Cable and Broadcasting Act, 1984 to grant franchises for the operation of new cable systems and to licence and regulate the provision of cable programme services.
Chairman, R. Burton.
Deputy Chairman, Prof. J. Ring, C.B.E.
Members, Mrs. A. Ballard; P. Johnson; Mrs. E. MacDonald-Brown; P. Paine, C.B.E., D.F.C; P. Darwin.
Director-General, J. Davey.
Secretary, E. Mercer.

CERTIFICATION OFFICE FOR TRADE UNIONS AND EMPLOYERS' ASSOCIATIONS
27 Wilton Street, SW1X 7AZ
[01–210 3733/4]

The Certification Officer is an independent statutory authority appointed by the Secretary of State for Employment. He is responsible for receiving and scrutinising annual returns from trade union and employers' associations; for reimbursing certain costs of trade unions' postal ballots; for dealing with complaints concerning trade union elections; for ensuring observance of statutory requirements governing political funds and trade union mergers; and for certifying the independence of trade unions.
Certification Officer, M. Wake.
Assistant Certification Officer, Mrs. S. Van Noorden.

Scotland
58 Frederick Street, Edinburgh EH2 1LN
[031–226 3224]

Assistant Certification Officer for Scotland, J. L. J. Craig.

CHARITY COMMISSION
St. Alban's House, 57–60 Haymarket, SW1Y 4QX
[01–210 3000]

Northern Office:
Graeme House, Derby Square, Liverpool L2 7SB
[051–227 3191]

The Charity Commissioners are appointed under the Charities Act, 1960, principally to further the work of charities in England and Wales by giving advice and information, and by investigating and checking abuses. The Commissioners maintain a register of charities; give consent to land transactions; help to modernize the purposes and administrative machinery of charities; and, in the name of one of their staff, the Official Custodian for Charities, hold investments for charities.

Salaries

Grade 5	£24,765–£28,215
Grade 6	£15,030–£25,335
Grade 7	£15,030–£20,292

Chief Commissioner, R. I. L Guthrie £40,058–£41,000
Commissioners, C. A. H. Parsons; J. Farquharson £30,334–£37,000
Deputy Commissioners (G5), R. W. Groves; J. A. Dutton; M. A. Rao; J. F. Claricoat; Mrs. J. F. Quint; G. S. Goodchild.
Assist. Commissioners (G6), Mrs. H. M. Phillips; Miss D. F. Taylor; S. K. Sen; K. M. Dibble; P. P. White; N. M. Mackenzie; D. C. Raikes; R. W. Tomlinson; Miss V. A. Nuttall; S. Slack; M. J. Harbottle; I. M. Davies; P. W. Somerfield.
Secretary and Asst. Commissioner (G5), D. Forrest.
Office Manager and Asst. Commissioner (G5), J. H. Vining.
Asst. Commissioners (G7), R. E. Hatton; A. O. Polak; Miss S. M. St. C. Smith; M. C. T. Seymour; Miss C. F. Byrne.
Official Custodian for Charities (G6), R. J. Crick.
Deputy Official Custodian (G7), R. E. Edwards.
Establishment Officer (G6), J. M. Samuels.

CHURCH COMMISSIONERS

1 Millbank, SW1P 3JZ
[01–222 7010]

The Church Commissioners were established on April 1, 1948, by the amalgamation of *Queen Anne's Bounty* (established 1704) and the *Ecclesiastical Commissioners* (established 1836).

The Commissioners' main task is to improve the stipends and housing of the Church of England clergy and to provide them and their widows with adequate pensions and assistance with housing in retirement. They also carry out administrative duties in connection with pastoral reorganization and redundant churches, and have been designated by the General Synod as the Central Stipends Authority of the Church of England.

The Commissioners' income for the year ended Dec. 31, 1987, was derived from the following sources:—

	£ million
Stock exchange investments	52·8
Land and property	54·5
Mortgages, loans, etc.	9·6
Trust income, and diocesan/parish contributions for stipends	55·9
	£172·8

This income was applied as follows:—

Clergy stipends	93·1
Clergy and widows' pensions	39·0
Clergy houses	20·4
Episcopal administration and payments to Chapters	6·0
Church buildings	3·1
Administrative expenses of the Commissioners and related bodies	8·5
Carried forward	2·7
	£172·8

Constitution

The 2 Archbishops, the 41 diocesan Bishops, 5 deans or provosts, 10 other clergy and 10 laymen appointed by the General Synod; 4 laymen nominated by the Queen; 4 persons nominated by the Archbishop of Canterbury; The Lord Chancellor; The Lord President of the Council; the First Lord of the Treasury; The Chancellor of the Exchequer; The Secretary of State for the Home Dept; The Speaker of the House of Commons; The Lord Chief Justice; The Master of the Rolls; The Attorney-General; The Solicitor-General; The Lord Mayor and two Aldermen of the City of London; The Lord Mayor of York and one representative from each of the Universities of Oxford and Cambridge.

Church Estates Commissioners

First, Sir Douglas Lovelock, K.C.B.
Second, Rt. Hon. Michael Alison, M.P.
Third, Mrs. B. E. Haworth.

Officers

Secretary, J. E. Shelley.
Deputy Secretary, P. Locke.
Assistant Secretaries, D. I. Archer *(Chief Accountant)*; P. H. P. Shaw, L.V.O. *(Estates)*; R. M. Hutchings *(Commercial Property)*; W. R. Herbert *(Establishment Officer)*; J. M. Davies *(Redundant Churches)*; D. J. Day *(Pastoral)*; M. D. Elengorn *(Stipends and Allocations)*; J. W. Ferguson *(Computer)*; D. N. Goodwin *(Houses)*; C. P. Canton *(Bishoprics)*; P. G. Brealey *(Investments)*.
Deputy Accountant and Trust Officer, G. C. Baines.
Deputy Establishment Officer, Mrs. B. A. Bartlett.
Press & Information Officer, R. S. Hopgood.
Principals, A. W. Atkins; P. D. Chadwick; M. G. S. Farrell; Miss A. M. Mackie; E. G. Peacock; G. Wills; J. A. W. Elloy; C. R. Bullen; N. M. Waring; J. M. Shirley.

Legal Department

Official Solicitor, E. W. Wills.
Deputy Solicitor, J. P. Guy.
Solicitors (G6), Miss J. M. Bland; Miss S. M. S. Jones; R. D. C. Murray.
Senior Legal Assistants, J. D. Carter; Mrs. S. E. Prosser.

Main Agents

Messrs. Cluttons, 5 Great College Street, SW1; Messrs. Smiths Gore, The King's Lodgings, Minster Precincts, Peterborough; Messrs. Chesterton, Lalonde, 54 Brooke Street, W1.

CIVIL AVIATION AUTHORITY

C.A.A. House, 45–59 Kingsway, WC2B 6TE
[01–379 7311]

The C.A.A. is responsible for the economic regulation of U.K. airlines by licensing air routes, air travel organizers and approving fares; for the safety regulation of U.K. civil aviation by the certification of airlines and aircraft, and by licensing aerodromes, flight crew and aircraft engineers; and, through the National Air Traffic Services, for the provision of air traffic control and telecommunications services.
Chairman, C. Tugendhat *(part-time)* £50,880
Managing Director, T. Murphy.
Secretary, Miss G. M. E. White.

COMMONWEALTH DEVELOPMENT CORPORATION

1 Bessborough Gardens, SW1V 2JQ
[01–828 4488]

The Corporation's area of operations covers British dependent territories and, with Ministerial approval, any Commonwealth or other developing country. At present, the Corporation is authorized to operate in

36 Commonwealth and 16 non-Commonwealth countries in addition to the remaining British dependent territories. The Corporation is authorized to borrow up to £750,000,000.

Chairman (part-time), The Lord Kindersley.
Deputy Chairman (part-time), Sir Colin Campbell, Bt., M.C.
Members (part-time), Mrs. A. Wright; V. Robertson, O.B.E.; Sir Michael Caine; M. D. Nightingale, O.B.E.; Prof. M. Faber.
General Manager, J. D. Eccles, C.B.E.

COMMONWEALTH SECRETARIAT
(see p. 626)

COMMONWEALTH WAR GRAVES COMMISSION
2 Marlow Road, Maidenhead, Berkshire SL6 7DX
[0628 34221]

The Commonwealth War Graves Commission (formerly Imperial War Graves Commission) was founded by Royal Charter in 1917. It is responsible for the commemoration of 1,695,000 members of the forces of the Commonwealth who fell in the two world wars. More than one million graves are maintained in 23,175 burial grounds throughout the world. Over three-quarters of a million men and women who have no known grave or who were cremated are commemorated by name on memorials built by the Commission.

The funds of the Commission are derived from the six Governments participating in its work—the U.K., Australia, Canada, India, New Zealand and South Africa.

President, H.R.H. The Duke of Kent, K.G., G.C.M.G., G.C.V.O.
Chairman, The Secretary of State for Defence in the U.K.
Vice-Chairman, Adm. Sir David Williams, G.C.B.
Members, The Secretary of State for the Environment in the U.K.; The High Commissioners for Australia, Canada, India, and New Zealand; the Ambassador for the Republic of South Africa; Gen. Sir Robert Ford, G.C.B., C.B.E.; Air Chief Marshal Sir John Gingell, G.B.E., K.C.B.; Capt. Sir Miles Wingate, K.C.V.O.; Maj.-Gen. D. Smith, C.B.E., D.S.O.; The Rt. Hon. J. D. Concannon; Miss J. Fookes, M.P.; Sir Derek Day, K.C.M.G.; Sir Nigel Mobbs.
Director-General, Sir Arthur Hockaday, K.C.B., C.M.G.
Deputy Director-Generals, D. Kennedy *(Administration);* J. Saynor *(Operations).*
Directors, R. Wilson *(Finance);* P. J. Noakes *(Horticulture);* H. Mackay *(Management Services);* T. F. Penfold *(Personnel);* R. J. Dalley *(Secretariat);* N. B. Osborn *(Works).*
Legal Adviser and Solicitor, G. C. Reddie.
Hon. Botanical Adviser, Prof. E. A. Bell, Ph.D.
Hon. Artistic Adviser, Prof. Sir Peter Shepheard, C.B.E.

Imperial War Graves Endowment Fund
Trustees, Admiral Sir David Williams, G.C.B.; H. U. A. Lambert; The Lord Remnant, C.V.O.
Hon. Secretary to the Trustees, R. Wilson.

COUNTRYSIDE COMMISSION
John Dower House, Crescent Place,
Cheltenham, Glos. GL50 3RA
[0242–521381]

The Countryside Commission is an independent agency set up in 1968 to promote the conservation and enhancement of landscape beauty in England and Wales, to encourage the provision and improvement of facilities in the countryside for enjoyment, including the need to secure access for open air recreation. Since April 1982 the Commission has been funded by annual grant from the Department of the Environment. Members of the Commission are appointed by the Secretary of State for the Environment and the Secretary of State for Wales acting jointly.

Chairman, Sir Derek Barber £18,902
Director (G3), A. A. C. Phillips.
Assistant Directors (G5), R. Clarke *(Policy);* M. J. Kirby *(Regions).*
National Heritage Adviser, Mrs. M. D. Laverack.
Secretary (G7), M. J. Burchell.
Head of Conservation Branch (G7), M. E. Taylor.
Head of Recreation & Access Branch (G7), J. W. B. Worth.
Head of Communications Branch (G7), C. Pugsley.
Regional Officers (G7), G. Taylor *(Newcastle);* B. Walbank *(Cambridge);* Dr. S. A. Bucknall *(Leeds);* E. Holdaway *(Bristol);* R. T. Thomas *(Manchester);* D. E. Coleman *(London);* F. S. Walmsley *(Birmingham).*

Office for Wales
Ladywell House, Newtown, Powys, SY16 1RD
[0686–26799]

Chairman, R. E. M. Rees £10,580
Principal Officer (G7), A. M. H. Fitton.

COUNTRYSIDE COMMISSION FOR SCOTLAND
Battleby, Redgorton, Perth, PH1 3EW
[0738–27921]

Established under the Countryside (Scotland) Act, 1967, with functions for the provision, development and improvement of facilities for the enjoyment of the Scottish countryside, and for the conservation and enhancement of its natural beauty and amenity.

Chairman, J. R. Carr *(part-time).*
Commissioners, J. M. S. Arnott *(Vice-Chairman);* Dr. D. J. Bennet; Prof. C. H. Gimingham; Prof. J. I. Cunningham; Q. Brown; D. Grainger; R. D. Cramond, C.B.E.; Mrs. S. Harvey; A. W. Henry; I. Miller; Dr. W. E. S. Mutch; W. M. Turnbull.
Director, D. Campbell.
Asst. Directors, J. M. Fladmark *(Research and Development);* J. R. Turner *(Planning);* M. A. Payne *(Communications and Training).*

COVENT GARDEN MARKET AUTHORITY
Covent House, New Covent Garden Market,
SW8 5NX
[01–720 2211]

The Covent Garden Market Authority is constituted under the Covent Garden Market Acts, 1961 to 1966, the members being appointed by the Minister of Agriculture, Fisheries and Food. The Authority owns and operates the 60-acre New Covent Garden Markets (fruit, vegetable, flowers) which have been trading since 1974.

Chairman, W. P. Bowman, O.B.E. *(part-time)* £22,100
Members (part-time), Sir Adrian Cadbury; P. J. Hunt; E. I. Kingston; R. Pierson; J. A. Harvey
£1,000–£5,000
General Manager, C. M. G. Allen, C.B.E.
Secretary, Dr. P. M. Liggins.

CRIMINAL INJURIES COMPENSATION BOARD

Whittington House, 19 Alfred Place, WC1E 7LG
[01–636 9501 and 01–636 2812]

The Board was constituted in 1964 to administer the Government scheme for *ex gratia* payments of compensation to victims of crimes of violence.

Chairman, M. Ogden, Q.C.
Members, J. F. A. Archer, Q.C.; Sir Derek Bradbeer; M. S. R. Bruce, Q.C.; D. Calcutt, Q.C.; H. Carlisle, Q.C.; B. W. Chedlow, Q.C.; Miss B. Cooper, Q.C.; J. D. Crowley, Q.C.; T. Dawson, Q.C.; C. Fawcett, Q.C.; W. Gage, Q.C.; B. Green, Q.C.; G. M. Hamilton, Q.C.; Sir Arthur Hoole; J. Law, Q.C.; M. E. Lewer, Q.C.; J. Leighton Williams, Q.C.; C. Lindsay, Q.C.; Sir Denis Marshall; M. Morland, Q.C.; The Lord Morton of Shuna, Q.C.; Sir John Palmer; I. M. S. Park, C.B.E.; Miss S. Ritchie, Q.C.; D. B. Robertson, Q.C.; C. Seagroatt, Q.C.; Mrs. J. Smith, Q.C.; L. Stuart Shields, Q.C.; D. M. Thomas, O.B.E., Q.C.; D. O. Thomas, Q.C.; P. Weitzman, Q.C.; C. H. Whitby, Q.C.
Secretary and Solicitor, D. M. North.
Deputy Secretary, D. J. White.

Scotland

Blythswood House, 200 West Regent Street, Glasgow G2 4SW
[041–221 0945]

Office Manager, M. Walker. (Initial enquiries should be directed to the London office.)

CROWN AGENTS FOR OVERSEAS GOVERNMENTS AND ADMINISTRATIONS

St. Nicholas House, St. Nicholas Road, Sutton, Surrey, SM1 1EL
[01–643 3311]

The Crown Agents act on behalf of governments and public authorities in the developing world Incorporated by Act of Parliament, they provide commercial, financial and professional services to public sector authorities and the major international development agencies. They do not act for individuals or for commercial concerns in the private sector.
Chairman, Sir Peter Graham, O.B.E.
Managing Director, P. F. Berry.

CROWN ESTATE COMMISSIONERS

13/16 Carlton House Terrace, SW1Y 5AH
[01–210 3000]

The Land Revenues of the Crown in England and Wales have been collected on the public account since 1760, when George III surrendered them and received a fixed annual payment or *Civil List.* At the time of the surrender the gross revenues amounted to about £89,000 and the net return to about £11,000.

In the year ended March 31, 1988, the gross income from the Crown Estate totalled £69,500,000. The total expenditure was £36,624,000. The sum of £35,000,000 was paid to the Exchequer in 1987–88 as Surplus Revenue.

The Land Revenues in Ireland have been carried to the Consolidated Fund since 1820; from April 1, 1923, as regards Southern Ireland, they have been collected and administered by the Irish Government.

The Land Revenues in Scotland were transferred to the Commissioners in 1833.

First Commissioner and Chairman (part-time), The Earl of Mansfield and Mansfield.
Second Commissioner (and Secretary), Dr. K. Dexter, C.B. £49,920
Commissioners (part-time), R. B. Caws, C.B.E.; P. Sober; O. H. Colburn; G. D. Lillingston, C.B.E.; Capt. Sir Iain Tennant, K.T.; J. N. C. James.

Deputy Chief Executive, H. B. Clarke £49,400
Deputy Commissioner, R. G. L. Osborne
.... £25,756–£30,644
Crown Estate Surveyor, C. F. Hynes £19,537–£27,388
Principals (G7), J. Stumbke; F. G. Parrish; J. S. Ellingford; J. E. Ford .... £15,631–£21,936
Organization and Establishments Officer (G7), R. Blake .... £15,631–£21,936
Accountant and Receiver-General, R. G. Bell
.... £25,756–£30,644
Legal Adviser and Assistant Solicitor, M. L. Davies
.... £30,344–£33,469
Senior Principal (G6), I. R. Colquhoun; H. Turnsek; J. B. Postgate.
Principal (G7), R. T. Hayward.
Senior Legal Assistants, M. A. J. Cordingley; A. M. G. Spratt.
Crown Estate Receiver for Scotland (G7), M. J. Gravestock (10 Charlotte Square, Edinburgh)
.... £15,631–£21,936
Solicitor, Scotland, D. F. Stewart.

Windsor Estate

Surveyor and Deputy Ranger, A. R. Wiseman, M.V.O.
.... £33,469
Crown Estate Forestry Officer and Chief Forester, Windsor (G7), J. J. Taylor .... £15,631–£21,936

BOARD OF CUSTOMS AND EXCISE

New King's Beam House, 22 Upper Ground, SE1 9PJ
[01–600 1313]

Commissioners of Customs were first appointed in 1671 and housed by the King in London. The present "Long Room" in the Custom House, Lower Thames Street, E.C.3, replaced that built by Charles II and was rebuilt after destruction by fire in 1718 and 1814. The Excise Department was formerly under the Inland Revenue Department and was amalgamated with the Customs Department on April 1, 1909.

H.M. Customs and Excise is responsible for collecting and administering customs and excise duties and value added tax and advises the Chancellor of the Exchequer on any matters connected with them. The Department is also responsible for preventing and detecting the evasion of revenue laws and for enforcing a range of prohibitions and restrictions on the importation of certain classes of goods. In addition, the Department undertakes certain agency work on behalf of other departments, including the compilation of U.K. overseas trade statistics from customs import and export documents.
(For **Salaries**, *see* page 297.)

The Board

Chairman (G1), J. B. Unwin, C.B.
    Private Secretaries, P. R. Stevenson; Mrs. M. A. Ward.
Deputy Chairmen (G2), Mrs. V. P. M. Strachan; P. Jefferson Smith.
Commissioners (G3), D. J. Howard; P. Nash; A. W. Russell; R. Weston, C.B.; C. C. Finlinson; P. G. Wilmott.

Headquarters Office

Assistant Secretaries (G5), I. D. Savins; P. R. H. Allen; J. Vaughan; P. Kent; D. A. Walton; R. A. Mechem; P. J. Webb; D. F. O. Battle; R. H. C. Stiff; V. Matthews; B. J. Cockerell; J. W. Tracey; G. F. Taylor; D. F. W. Fryett; R. D. Goddard; P. Hogg; D. E. Barratt; L. G. Bentley; J. C. Stevenson; F. D. Tweddle; P. Trevett; A. G. H. Paynter; Mrs. F. R. Boardman; D. Gaw; M. R. Brown; N. Hodson; R. Shepherd; I. Walton; A. Killikelly; R. Craggs; M. J. Eland; A. C. Sawyer.

Head of Press and Information Division (G7), G. G. Hammond.

V.A.T. Central Unit

Controller(G5), M. J. Wardle.
Deputy Controller (G6), B. Smith.

Solicitor's Office

Solicitor (G2), P. V. H. Smith.
Principal Assistant Solicitors (G3), G. F. Butt; D. E. J. Nissen.
Assistant Solicitors (G5), P. Breuer; P. J. C. Ellis; M. Michael; R. D. S. Wylie; M. A. Cooper; G. W. M. McFarlane; D. E. T. S. Keefe; M. C. K. Gasper; R. L. Barlow; Miss A. E. Bolt; G. Fotherby; D. Pratt.

Accountant and Comptroller-General's Office

Accountant and Comptroller-General (G5), P. A. Blomfield.
Deputy Accountants-General (G6), J. E. Ebery; L. J. Haugh.

Statistical Office

Controller (G5), M. E. Pratt.

Investigation Division

Chief Investigation Officer (G5), R. L. H. Lawrence.

Collectors of Customs and Excise (G5)
England and Wales

Birmingham: M. W. Summers.
Dover: R. Crossley.
East Anglia: R. N. Lewis.
East Midlands: C. J. Packman.
Leeds: W. J. G. Prollins.
Liverpool: C. Roberts.
London Airports: J. Bugge.
London City and South: A. Collie.
London Port: A. C. Morrow.
London North and West: C. A. Bray.
Manchester: D. Smith.
Northampton: P. E. St. Quentin.
Northern England: D. R. Inglis.
Reading: J. H. Tee.
Southampton: R. I. Bolt.
South Wales and the Borders: A. Ferguson.
South West England: M. W. G. Lloyd.

Scotland

Edinburgh: W. F. Coghill.
Glasgow & Clyde: I. McLeod.

Northern Ireland

Belfast: B. E. Barclay.

OFFICE OF THE DATA PROTECTION REGISTRAR
Springfield House, Water Lane, Wilmslow, Cheshire
SK9 5AX
[Admin.: 0625–535711; Enquiries: 0625–535777]

The Office of the Data Protection Registrar was created by the Data Protection Act, 1984. It is the Registrar's duty to compile and maintain the Register of Data Users and Computer Bureaux and provide facilities for members of the public to examine the Register; promote observance of the data protection principles; consider complaints made by data subjects; disseminate information about the Act; encourage the production of codes of practice by trade associations and other bodies, to guide data users in complying with the data protection principles; cooperate with other parties to the Council of Europe Convention and act as U.K. authority for the purposes of Article 13 of the Convention; report annually to Parliament on the performance of his functions under the Act.
Registrar, E. J. Howe.

MINISTRY OF DEFENCE
See **Armed Forces Section**

DESIGN COUNCIL
28 Haymarket, SW1Y 4SU
[01-839-8000]

The Design Council's aim is to improve the design of British products by: advising companies on up-to-date practice in engineering and industrial design; the annual British Design Awards; publishing information to help manufacturers, designers, and others professionally involved in design; and promoting improvements in design education at all levels. There are Design Centres in London, Glasgow and Cardiff, and offices in Belfast, Wolverhampton and Manchester. The Design Council is funded partly by a Government grant-in-aid and partly by earned revenues.
Chairman, S. Hornby.
Director, I. Owen.

THE DUCHY OF CORNWALL
10 Buckingham Gate, SW1E 6LA
[01-834 7346]

The Duchy of Cornwall was instituted by Edward III in 1337 for the support of his eldest son, Edward, the Black Prince, and since 1503 the eldest surviving son of the Sovereign has, as heir apparent, succeeded to the Dukedom by inheritance. As the oldest of the English Duchies, it has enjoyed a long association with the Crown. Before elevation to a dukedom, it was an earldom from 1227, when Richard, King of the Romans and younger brother of Henry III, was created Earl of Cornwall.

The Prince's Council

H.R.H. The Prince of Wales, K.G., K.T., G.C.B; Sir Nicholas Henderson, G.C.M.G. (*Lord Warden of the Stannaries*); Hon. Sir John Baring, C.V.O. (*Receiver General*); R. J. A. Carnwath, Q.C. (*Attorney-General to the Prince of Wales*); D. W. N. Landale (*Secretary and Keeper of the Records*); Sir John Riddell, Bt.; J. E. Pugsley; J. N. C. James; A. M. J. Galsworthy.

Other Officers of the Duchy of Cornwall

Auditors, J. H. Bowman; P. L. Ainger; H. Hughes.
Solicitor, M. H. Boyd-Carpenter.
Assistant Secretary, K. J. S. Knott.
Sheriff (1988–89), Mrs. D. E. Colville.

THE DUCHY OF LANCASTER
Lancaster Place, Strand, WC2E 7ED
[01-836 8277]

The estates and jurisdiction known as the Duchy and County Palatine of Lancaster have been attached to the Crown since 1399, when John of Gaunt's son came to the throne as Henry IV. As the Lancaster inheritance it goes back to 1265. Edward III erected Lancashire into a County Palatine in 1351.
Chancellor of the Duchy of Lancaster, THE RT. HON. ANTONY NEWTON, O.B.E., M.P.
Private Secretary, P. J. Smith.
Attorney-General and Attorney and Serjeant within the County Palatine of Lancaster, D. K. Rattee, Q.C.
Receiver-General, Maj. S. Blewitt, C.V.O.
Vice-Chancellor, The Hon. Mr. Justice Scott.
Clerk of the Council and Keeper of Records, M. K. Ridley.

Solicitor, W. O. Farrer.
Asst. Solicitor, I. J. Dicker.
Chief Clerk, P. C. Clarke, c.v.o.

ECONOMIC AND SOCIAL RESEARCH COUNCIL
Cherry Orchard East, Kembrey Park,
Swindon SN2 6UQ
[0793–513838]

The E.S.R.C. was set up by Royal Charter in 1965 for the promotion of social science research. The Council carries out its role by awarding research grants, by initiating research and research contracts, by funding designated research centres, and by awarding postgraduate studentships and bursaries. In addition, the Council provides advice and disseminates knowledge on the social sciences.
Chairman, (vacant).
Secretary, D. Stafford.

DEPARTMENT OF EDUCATION AND SCIENCE
Elizabeth House, York Road, SE1 7PH
[01–934 9000]

The Government Department of Education was, until the establishment of a separate office, a Committee of the Privy Council appointed in 1839 to supervise the distribution of certain grants which had been made by Parliament since 1834. The Act of 1899 established the Board of Education, with a President and Parliamentary Secretary, and created a Consultative Committee. The Education Act of 1944 established the Ministry of Education. In April 1964 the office of the Minister of Science was combined with the Ministry to form the Department of Education and Science. The cost of administration for the financial year 1988–89 was estimated at £67,735,000. (For *Salaries, see* page 297).

Secretary of State for Education and Science, THE RT. HON. KENNETH BAKER, M.P.
Private Sec., T. B. Jeffery.
Parliamentary Private Secretary, A. Burt, M.P.
Minister of State, MRS. ANGELA RUMBOLD, C.B.E., M.P.
Private Secretary, Ms. S. Scott.
Parliamentary Private Secretary, P. McLoughlin, M.P.
Parliamentary Under Secretaries of State, R. Jackson, M.P.; J. Butcher, M.P.
Permanent Secretary (*G1*), Sir David Hancock, K.C.B.
Private Secretary, M. Wardle.
Deputy Secretaries (*G2*), R. H. Bird, C.B.; N. W. Stuart; J. M. M. Vereker.
Under Secretaries (*G3*), M. M. Capey (*Director of Establishments*); Miss J. H. Bacon; A. E. D. Chamier; C. A. Clark (*Accountant General*); J. I. Langtry; D. G. Libby; B. M. Norbury; N. Summers; D. W. Tanner; W. B. Wakefield (*Director of Statistics*); A. J. Wiggins; D. M. Forrester; J. C. Hedger; C. H. Saville.

Schools Branch 1
Assistant Secretaries (*G5*), Mrs. H. K. Douglas; Miss J. A. Gilbey; R. J. Green; Miss C. E. Hodkinson.
Principals (*G7*), D. H. Griffiths; M. H. Sharpe; D. K. Timms; Mrs. S. J. Trundle; A. Wilshaw; P. Chorley; S. Adamson; Miss S. Phippard; Miss A. Brown; Miss C. Bienkowska.

Schools Branch 2
Assistant Secretaries (*G5*), Mrs. J. Reisz; Miss D. C. Fordham; Ms. J. F. Cramphorn.
Senior Principal (*G6*), P. S. Lewis.
Principals (*G7*), D. Barwick; W. M. Caldow; Mrs. G. W. Dishart; Mrs. K. H. Jameson; I. A. Loveless;

Mrs. P. A. Masters; J. N. Walmsley; J. F. Bird; N. Cornwell; C. Dee; S. Lee; D. Noble; M. McBride; A. Sevier.

Schools Branch 3
Assistant Secretaries (*G5*), Mrs. H. M. Williams; M. D. Phipps; Ms. S. Scales.
Staff Inspector (*G5*), A. Clegg.
H.M. Inspectors (*G6*), Mrs. J. McLean; P. J. Silvester.
Principals (*G7*), Miss M. d'Armenia; S. N. Jardine; Miss A. M. J. Benham; C. De Grouchy; L. B. Webb; Mrs. S. G. Evans; Miss K. J. Fleay; Mrs. S. Jetha; T. A. H. Tyler.

Schools Branch 4
Assistant Secretaries (*G5*), Miss A. Stewart; Miss J. Partington; A. Woollard; Miss P. Laidlaw.
Principals (*G7*), J. Lawrence; N. Flint; G. H. N. Evans; S. Kershaw; S. T. Crowne; Miss N. Bartman; Miss G. G. Beauchamp; Ms. S. Gane.

Architects and Building Branch
Chief Architect (*G4*), P. Benwell.
Deputy Chief Architect, R. L. Thompson.
Superintending Architects, R. Clynes; D. H. Griffin; M. S. Hacker; J. J. Wilson.
Superintending Engineer (*Mechanical and Electrical*), (vacant).
Chief Quantity Surveyor, B. G. Whitehouse.
Principals (*G7*), K. L. R. English; A. G. Myatt.
Principal Architects, R. W. U. Alcock; A. J. Branton; Miss C. G. Edwards; Miss E. J. Lloyd-Jones; P. Lenssen; D. S. Nightingale; G. J. Parker; T. W. Prosser; Miss B. M. T. Sanders; A. C. Thompson; D. F. Wicks.
Principal Quantity Surveyors, T. W. A. Carden; A. A. Jones; J. L. S. Sinclair.
Principal Engineer, M. J. Patel.
S.P.T.O. Architects, S. Aswat; A. J. Benson-Wilson; E. C. Bissell; J. R. C. Brooke; Mrs. D. Holt; G. E. Hughes; Miss L. Watson; T. J. Williamson.
S.P.T.O. Quantity Surveyors, E. W. Lawless; M. Sturt.
S.P.T.O. Engineers, R. Heard; R. L. Daniels.
S.P.T.O. Furniture Designer, N. J. Carter.

Further and Higher Education Branch 1
Assistant Secretaries (*G5*), A. N. Brown; R. D. Horne; E. R. Morgan.
Senior Principal (*G6*), E. J. Herbert.
Principals (*G7*), K. Baxter; A. Clarke; Miss L. M. Clarke; M. F. Hipkins; P. J. Hodgman; W. A. Irvine; M. Kerin; M. F. Neale.

Further and Higher Education Branch 2
Assistant Secretaries (*G5*), R. D. Hull; K. Clarke.
Principals (*G7*), J. K. Bushnell; A. J. Coles; S. A. Marston; D. R. Pollard; A. J. Shaw; R. E. Troedson; J. P. Vann; D. T. Wood.

Further and Higher Education Branch 3
Assistant Secretaries (*G5*), M. B. Baker; M. J. G. Smith; P. W. Syme.
Senior Principal (*G6*), D. I. B. Hardy.
Principals (*G7*), Miss L. Butler; C. J. Dowse; P. W. Fulford-Jones; Mrs. M. E. Jackson; A. J. Sargent; J. S. Street.

Science Branch
Assistant Secretaries (*G5*), G. J. Mungeam; R. P. Ritzema; P. J. Thorpe.
Principals (*G7*), A. Callaghan; K. C. Humphrey; L. J. R. Dando; K. D. J. Root; A. Smyth.

Information Branch
Assistant Secretary (*G5*), P. A. Shaw.
Chief Information Officers (*G7*), A. P. Duncan; C. R. Stephens.

Teachers Pay and General Branch

Assistant Secretary (G5), R. W. Chattaway.
Principals (G7), A. D. Adamson; R. S. Daruwalla;
Mrs. A. C. Jeffery; M. J. F. Rabarts; A. J. Wye.

Pensions Branch

Mowden Hall, Staindrop Road,
Darlington, Co. Durham DL3 9BG
[0325–460155]

Assistant Secretary (G5), J. Wilde.
Principals (G7), D. G. Halladay; K. M. Miles.

Teachers Supply and Training Branch

Assistant Secretaries (G5), M. J. Richardson; J. W.
Whitaker; Mrs. C. M. Chattaway.
Senior Economic Adviser (G5), B. D. Cullen.
Senior Principal Scientific Officer (G6), R. B. Ladley.
Principals (G7), B. D. Glickman; M. Williams.
Economic Advisers (G7), K. J. Sear; J. Tarsh.

Information Technology Branch

Assistant Secretary (G5), F. M. Scott.
Senior Principals (G6), B. Bekhradnia; A. Cowan.
Principals (G7), A. Allison; K. Coombs; A. M. Cooper;
B. Lillburn; Mrs. N. A. T. Malt; Mrs. J. D. Nisbet.

Statistics Branch

Chief Statisticians (G5), J. W. Gardner; H. M. Dale.
Statisticians (G7), W. H. Barron; R. E. Dew; R. K.
Jain; Mrs. S. Keith; T. C. Knight, Mrs. I. R. Magill;
Mrs. A. E. Mellor; Miss A. C. Brown; A. J. Barnett;
N. D. Rudoe.
Senior Principal (G6), P. D. Gott.
Principal Research Officer (G7), D. J. Hodges.

Legal Branch

Assistant Legal Adviser (G5), A. G. Jones.
Assistant Solicitors (G6), F. L. Croft; R. S. Cumming.
Senior Legal Assistant (G6), Miss M. E. Trefgarne; A.
D. Preston; M. A. Widdrington.

Library

Librarian, D. N. Allum.

Finance Branch

Assistant Secretaries (G5), R. L. Smith; N. J. Sanders
(*Deputy Accountant General*).
Senior Principals (G6), W. Gamble; P. Smith.
Principals (G7), E. A. Alcock; P. J. Edwards; B. M.
Ellington; J. P. Partington; G. R. E. Stewart; C. E.
Treen; B. G. Townsend; C. Walker; G. D. S.
Sandeman.

H.M. Inspectorate (England)

Senior Chief Inspector (G2), E. J. Bolton, c.b.
Chief Inspectors (G4), B. C. Arthur, c.b.e.; J. A.
Everson; A. R. Marshall; T. P. Melia; Miss A. C.
Millett; A. J. Rose; B. D. Short.
Divisional Inspectors (G5), B. A. Chaplin; Miss V. J.
Evans; B. W. Howes; L. Jackson; E. Scott; K. W.
Thomas; D. E. Walker.
Staff Inspectors (G5), T. H. Bennetts; R. G. Booth; P.
L. Bradbury; R. J. Brake; P. Brown; R. A.
Callender; P. R. Clarke; D. A. Cormican; A. T. Cox;
L. S. Crickmore; D. A. Denegri; B. Denton; Mrs. G.
M. Dolden; Mrs. V. E. Emmett; Mrs. G. Everson; J.
H. Fairhurst; D. Flanagan; G. R. Frater; A. Gibson;
G. Goldstein; J. G. Goulding; V. Green; R. A. S.
Hennessey; G. A. Hicks; P. Highfield; M. W.
Himsworth; D. Hollingsworth; D. A. Jones; D. G.
Labon; Miss B. J. Lewis; D. J. Marjoram; P. F.
Marlow; C. P. Marshall; J. H. Mayhew; R. W.
Mycock; P. J. Pearson; G. T. Peaker; C. M.
Richards; C. H. Selby; P. Singh; Mrs. M. M. Smart;
D. E. Soulsby; Mrs. B. Staniland; D. W. Taylor; M.
J. Tomlinson; D. R. Trainor; A. F. Turberfield; A.
D. J. Turner; Mrs. S. P. Twite; J. R. Ungoed-

Thomas; D. L. West; J. B. Willcock; T. Wylie; R. E.
Young.
H.M. Inspectors (G6), Mrs. C. A. Agambar; W. Agnew;
D. W. Airey; Mrs. G. M. V. Alexander; K. J.
Anglesey; P. L. Armitage; A. Ashworth; D. Baillie;
W. G. Bakehouse; Mrs. C. A. Baker; Mrs. E. M.
Baker; C. Banks; Miss D. M. L. Barlow; J. H.
Barnes; Mrs. J. M. Barnes; G. Barratt; R. E.
Barrett; Ms. E. P. Baxell; Mrs. J. M. Bell; P. E. B.
Belshaw; D. A. Bennett; J. F. Bennett; S. G. L.
Bignell; D. B. F. Billimore; Miss. V. Blackburn; A.
J. Boddington; Mrs. C. M. Bond; Miss J. M.
Bonner; Mrs. E. J. Boucher; Miss E. Bourne; Mrs.
M. T. Boyd-Clarke; D. J. Bradbury; M. H. Bradley;
Mrs. P. A. Brain; T. E. Brand; Mrs. H. S. Bridge;
E. F. H. Brittain; J. Broadbent; F. Brook; Mrs. J.
M. Brookes; Miss C. M. Brooks; A. W. Brown; Mrs.
M. A. Buckingham; D. G. Buckland; M. J. Buckley;
Miss K. Bull; J. M. Burgess; Mrs. G. M. Burke; J.
W. Butler; Ms. M. E. Caistor; M. J. Campbell; P.
Candlish; N. Carr; Mrs. J. Carswell; M. J. Caton;
B. Chandler; Miss J. A. Cheong; B. J. Chopping;
Miss D. H. Chorley; Mrs. M. S. Christie; D. Clare;
P. Clarke; G. Clay; R. S. W. Clements; D. G. Close;
D. A. Coe; J. E. M. Cohn; B. Colbeck; M. J. Collier;
Mrs. P. M. Collins; M. J. Convey; Mrs. M. A. Cooke;
P. Cradock; G. Cranmer; Mrs. G. K. Crawford; J.
Creedy; Mrs. M. E. Crisp; Miss K. Cross; Ms. B. J.
Cusdin; D. K. Dana; Mrs. J. Darroch; C. M. Davies;
T. Dickinson; T. Dillon; A. Dobson; Ms. C. R.
Donoughue; J. A. S. Dossett; P. W. Dougill; R. G.
Dyke; K. H. Dyson; Mrs. M. E. Eade; P. D. Edwards;
Mrs. C. Elliott; D. L. Elliott; J. A. Elliott; M. A.
Emery; Mrs. J. E. Ensing; K. J. Evans; Mrs. C.
Farrell; Mrs. B. E. Fawcett; Ms. F. D. Finlay; B. P.
Fitzgerald; J. Fitzpatrick; I. G. Forrest; D. H. M.
Foster; Ms. C. M. Fraser; D. Fraser; P. S. Friend;
Mrs. C. Frisby; B. Frost; C. C. Frost; D. J. Frost;
R. C. Frost; B. S. Furness; P. Gannon; D. A.
Gardiner; P. H. W. Garwood; I. Gera; Mrs. P. M.
Gibbon; Mrs. J. E. A. Gifford; G. A. Gill; C. R.
Gillings; C. Goodhead; Mrs E. M. Goodwin; Mrs.
K. N. Gosling; C. D. Gould; C. Goulding; Miss S.
Gracey; D. I. Grant; J. D. Green; B. Gregson-
Allcott; N. Grenyer; P. Griffiths; R. H. Griffiths;
Mrs. F. Hadley; Miss C. E. Hague; E. E. J. Haidon;
D. S. Hale; D. J. Halligan; N. J. Hallmark; J. A.
Hamer; P. G. Hancock; J. N. Hardwick; J. S.
Hardwick; R. A. Hargreaves; B. R. Harris; C. R.
Hart; D. J. Hart; R. Hartley; A. Harvey; R. C.
Harvey; Mrs. G. M. Hayes; G. M. Hearnshaw; Miss
L. M. Hencher; M. L. Hening; J. F. Herbert; Mrs.
J. S. Herbert; J. A. Hertrich; P. M. Hesketh; D.
Hibbert; J. M. Hibbs; J. F. H. Hilbourne; W. J. Hill;
Mrs. G. A. Hindhaugh; D. G. Holford; Mrs. M. H.
Hollingsworth; J. R. Holmes; C. Hooper; Mrs. P. E.
Hooper; F. X. Horan; J. E. Hosegood; D. J. House;
M. J. Howarth; B. A. F. Hubbard; B. R. Hudson; V.
C. Hughes; J. E. Hunt; P. J. Hunt; J. B. Huskins;
J. N. Hutchinson; Mrs. M. A. V. Huxley; J. S.
Ingleson; P. F. J. Irvine; A. R. Ivatts; M. J. Ive; H.
A. James; R. K. James; T. M. Jardine; B. D. Jelly;
D. W. John; Miss S. H. Johns; P. W. R. Johnson;
H. B. Joicey; B. Jones; Mrs. M. E. Jones; M. G.
Jones; R. Kapadia; W. D. Kaye; Mrs. A. C. Keelan-
Towner; M. Kerrigan; M. A. Khan; B. L. King; D.
P. King; K. King; A. V. Kirwan; D. Knighton; J.
B. Knox; A. J. Lacey; G. N. E. Lageard; B. M. Lane;
Miss E. J. M. Layson; J. W. F. Learmonth; J. P.
Leigh; D. Lewis; D. F. Lewis; D. J. Lewis; Mrs. J.
M. Lingard; E. R. B. Little; G. R. Little; A. W.
Littlewood; W. G. K. Lloyd; Miss B. M. Lockwood;
A. B. Lomax; R. Long; J. A. Low; Mrs. E. M. Lowe;
T. L. Lusty; J. A. Mabey; B. McCafferty; Mrs. H.
M. Macdonald; Mrs. P. R. Maclay; C. McCall; Mrs.
J. C. McGinty; D. C. McIntosh; M. McLaughlin;
Mrs. J. McLean; I. A. McNally; M. E. Madden; R.

H. Manser; J. R. Marriott; G. D. Marrow; J. G. Marshall; E. S. Martin; Mrs. M. M. Martin; W. P. Massam; Miss E. M. Matthews; J. E. Mattick; M. R. E. Mealing; B. R. Meech; Miss B. E. Megson; G. Merlane; B. E. Merton; K. Miller; H. Millington; D. Mills; Miss H. A. Moffat; Mrs. J. L. Mokades; A. R. H. Monk; D. Moon; D. L. Moore; P. R. Moore; S. H. Morris; S. A. M. Muir; Miss F. A. Munday; P. Muschamp; H. Myers; C. Needham; Miss D. A. Nelson; R. Nicholls; Ms. S. M. Nicholls; A. J. Nisbett; P. M. Nixon; M. Norman; Mrs. G. I. Oldham; P. I. Orr; B. C. O'Sullivan; Mrs. P. S. O'Sullivan; W. E. Owen; H. M. Page; R. L. Page-Jones; Miss P. Park; K. Parker; D. J. Parks; J. M. Parsons; Mrs. E. L. Passmore; I. M. Paterson; Mrs. D. M. Penn; Miss J. M. Phillips; P. Piddock; K. Pinder; M. W. A. Pitts; E. A. Pollard; M. R. Potter; C. Potts; C. P. Power; A. E. Prick; Mrs. M. P. Pryce; M. E. Pullee; W. J. Rea; C. J. Redman; J. C. Richardson; P. H. Roberts; A. S. Robertson; C. Robinson; G. Robson; I. A. Rodger; S. J. A. Rogers; A. C. Rowe; C. Rowe; D. H. Rutt; M. J. Ryder; W. H. Salaman; Mrs. J. Sartain; Mrs. K. J. Saunders; B. Sayer; Ms. M. Sayer; J. C. Schenk; D. J. Scott; P. L. Seaborne; G. W. Searle; Mrs. P. J. Selwood; D. T. V. Sharman; R. V. L. Sharman; D. I. Shelton; A. R. Shirley; J. R. Shirtcliff; Mrs. V. M. Sida; P. J. Silvester; Mrs. D. E. Simmonds; Mrs. P. A. Simpson; D. Singleton; G. Sleightholme; B. J. Smeaton; B. J. Smith; P. J. C. Smith; P. R. Smith; J. D. Stannard; Ms. O. M. Stannard; J. Stanyer; J. W. Steel; J. M. Steels; J. B. Stevenson; Miss M. T. Stiles; R. W. Stockdale; M. M. Stone; C. F. Stoneman; Mrs. J. E. Storrie; R. Storrs; Ms. M. E. Stride; R. Summersby; D. P. Swain; A. Sykes; D. W. Sylvester; F. Taylor; J. A. Taylor; R. S. Taylor; A. F. Thomas; D. L. Thorburn; R. M. Thorpe; J. Tierney; M. J. Todd; P. N. Toft; B. D. Tomkins; J. V. Townshend; J. E. Trickey; Ms. L. J. Tumman; Mrs. J. W. Turner; E. A. Vallis; B. C. L. Walker; C. V. Wall; A. Walmsley; Miss P. Walters; M. Wardlow; Mrs. A. P. Warren; R. K. Warren; N. G. Warwick; J. M. Watson; M. R. Webb; Mrs. J. M. Webberley; R. R. Weir; D. J. Wells; P. E. Weston; K. J. Wheeldon; R. Whitburn; Miss F. White; J. White; F. Whiteman; D. G. Whittaker; Mrs. O. Whittingham; C. C. B. Wightwick; Ms. S. M. Wiles; J. B. Willcock; D. G. Williams; J. R. Williams; K. G. Williams; Mrs. S. A. Williams; G. R. Wilson; J. D. Woodhouse; Mrs. S. A. Woodroffe; J. A. Woodrow; J. I. Wragg; Miss B. M. Wright; D. Wynne; Miss A. P. Yeomans; F. P. Young; A. J. Youngs.

H.M. Inspectorate Support Services

Principals (G7), C. Boxall; G. A. Holley.

H.M. Inspectorate (Wales)
(*See* Welsh Office)

Establishments and Organization Branch

Assistant Secretaries (G5), E. B. Granshaw; D. A. Wilkinson.
Senior Principal (G6), H. H. Barrick.
Principals (G7), Miss S. A. Clarke; K. R. Fitzgerald; P. L. Jones; R. M. King; P. Ramsden; B. C. Willett; D. A. Robins.

ELECTRICITY AUTHORITIES

THE ELECTRICITY COUNCIL
30 Millbank, SW1P 4RD
[01–834 2333]

The Electricity Council, a non-trading body, is the central council of the supply industry for the formulation of general policy. It is a federal body with representation from both the generation and distribution boards which provides a forum for common problems to be resolved with independent guidance from Central Members and their supporting staff. The Council's main functions are to advise the Secretary of State for Energy on matters affecting the supply industry and "to promote and assist the maintenance and development by electricity boards in England and Wales of an efficient, co-ordinated and economical system of electricity supply".

Chairman, Sir Philip Jones, C.B. £80,000
Deputy Chairman, D. G. Jefferies .. £55,000–£61,000
Members, R. W. Orson, C.B.E.; R. A. Farrance, C.B.E.;
 D. G. C. Gronow. .... £49,000–£54,000
Members from the Central Electricity Generating Board, The Lord Marshall of Goring, C.B.E., F.R.S.; G. A. W. Blackman, C.B.E.
Secretary, R. Savinson.

CENTRAL ELECTRICITY GENERATING BOARD
Sudbury House, 15 Newgate Street, EC1A 7AU
[01–634 5111]

The Central Electricity Generating Board owns and operates the power stations and grid system of main transmission lines. It is responsible for bulk supply of electricity to the twelve area boards; and also, for traction purposes, to the railways. Its duties also include (i) planning the provision of new generating and transmission capacity, including research, (ii) siting and constructing new power stations (conventional and nuclear) and (iii) siting and constructing extensions to the transmission network. The C.E.G.B. is a highly capitalized process industry—engaged in converting primary fuels into electricity, of which they are the "wholesalers". Among its main problems are the choice of primary fuels for the power stations; the development of new technology (for example, nuclear generation); and problems concerned with amenity, as in siting of power stations and grid-lines, the disposal of effluents, and smoke elimination.

Chairman, The Lord Marshall of Goring, C.B.E., F.R.S.
Deputy Chairman, G. A. W. Blackman, C.B.E.
Corporate Managing Director, J. W. Baker.
Members, D. A. Davis; F. Ledger, O.B.E.
Part-time Members, R. V. Giordano; Sir Terence Beckett, K.B.E.; W. H. N. Wilkinson; D. A. Walker.
Secretary, G. H. Hadley.

ELECTRICITY BOARDS
The 12 Area Electricity Boards

(The Chairmen of Area Boards receive a salary of £30,000–£45,000).
London, Templar House, 81–87 High Holborn, WC1V 6NU. *Chairman*, J. J. Wilson. *Sec.*, M. W. Saunders.
South Eastern, Grand Avenue, Hove, East Sussex BN3 2LS. *Chairman*, G. A. Squair. *Sec.*, S. M. Wide.
Southern, Southern Electricity House, Littlewick Green, Maidenhead, Berks. *Chairman*, D. A. Ross. *Sec.*, C. J. May.
South Western, Electricity House, Colston Avenue, Bristol BS1 4TS. *Chairman*, A. W. Nicol. *Sec. and Solicitor*, S. G. Marshall.
Eastern, P.O. Box 40, Wherstead, Ipswich, Suffolk IP9 2AQ. *Chairman*, J. C. Smith. *Sec.*, W. N. Moss.
East Midlands, P.O. Box 4, North P.D.O., 398 Coppice Road, Arnold, Nottingham NG5 7HX. *Chairman*, J. F. Harris. *Sec.*, T. F. C. Walker.
Midlands, P. O. Box 8 Mucklow Hill, Halesowen, West Midlands B62 8BP. *Chairman*, B. S. Townsend. *Sec.*, G. Degg.
South Wales, St. Mellons, Cardiff CF3 9XW. *Chairman*, J. Wynford Evans. *Sec.*, A. Worth.
Merseyside and North Wales, Sealand Road, Chester. *Chairman*, B. H. Weston, *Sec.*, C. W. Leonard.

Yorkshire, Wetherby Road, Scarcroft, Leeds LS14 3HS. *Chairman,* J. Porteous. *Dir. of Administration,* J. M. Chatwin.

North Eastern, Carliol House, Newcastle upon Tyne NE99 1SE. *Chairman,* T. Rutherford, C.B.E., *Sec.,* R. Dixon.

North Western, Talbot Road, Manchester M16 0HQ. *Chairman,* B. R. Hastings. *Sec.,* B. Benson.

NORTH OF SCOTLAND HYDRO-ELECTRIC BOARD
16 Rothesay Terrace, Edinburgh EH3 7SE
[031–225 1361]

Chairman, M. Joughin, C.B.E. *(part-time)*
Chief Executive, K. R. Vernon, C.B.E.
Members (part-time), A. T. H. Tulloch; Ms. C. A. M. Davis *(Chairman of Consultative Council).*; M. G. N. Walker, C.B.E.; D. J. Miller; C. S. Macphie; D. F. Myles, C.B.E.; G. Barrie (£3,750 to £5,750).
Secretary, J. E. M. Watts.

SOUTH OF SCOTLAND ELECTRICITY BOARD
Spean Street, Glasgow G44 4BE
[041–637 7177]

Chairman, D. J. Miller £55,700
Deputy Chairman, I. M. H. Preston £46,750
Non-Executive Members, A. Barr, O.B.E.; N. C. Kuenssberg; I. H. Macdonald, O.B.E.; J. Neumann, C.B.E.; Mrs. J. A. Thomson (£4,150); M. Joughin, C.B.E.; G. B. Whyte *(unpaid).*
Secretary, D. A. S. MacLaren.

DEPARTMENT OF EMPLOYMENT
Caxton House, Tothill Street, SW1H 9NF
[01–213 3000]

The Department of Employment is responsible for Government policies on the working of the labour market and the needs and conditions of people at work. Its main tasks are to prepare people for work, to help unemployed people find work, to encourage the creation of small firms and assist in their expansion, and to encourage industries to provide jobs and to train their workforce.

Many of the executive functions carried out in the Department's area of policy interest are exercised by separate public agencies reporting to the Secretary of State for Employment. These include the Training Commission, the Health and Safety Commission and A.C.A.S.

(For **Salaries,** *see* page 297).

Secretary of State for Employment, THE RT. HON. NORMAN FOWLER, M.P.
Principal Private Secretary (G5), N. Wilson.
Parliamentary Private Secretary, P. Thurnam, M.P.
Minister of State, THE RT. HON. JOHN COPE, M.P.
Private Secretaries, R. Ledsome; Mrs. J. Campbell.
Under Secretaries of State, J. Lee, M.P.; P. Nicholls, M.P.
Private Secretaries, Miss A. Lys *(to Mr. Lee);* Mrs.E. Norman *(to Mr. Nicholls).*
Parliamentary Clerk, R. Ledsome.
Permanent Secretary (G1), G. Holland, C.B.
Private Secretary, Ms. J. Rutherford.
Deputy Secretaries (G2), I. Manley, C.B.; G. Reid.
Legal Adviser (G3), H. R. L. Purse.
Special Adviser, W. Lightfoot.

Industrial Relations
Grade 3, R. S. Allison; E. G. Whybrew.
Grade 5, D. W. Brown; N. H. Reed; A. G. Johnson.

Chief Wages Inspector (G6), J. A. Dyble.
Secretary of Wages Councils, S. Cottingham.

Training Policy
Grade 3 (Division 1), C. R. Walker.
Grade 3 (Division 2), M. E. G. Fogden.
Chief Executive of Unemployment Benefit Service (G4), J. W. Cooper.
Grade 5, M. J. Miller; R. A. David; L. Lewis; H. Miller.

Overseas Division
Grade 3, W. R. B. Robinson.
Grade 5, J. B. Sahw; G. Kahan.

Economic and Social Division
Chief Economic Adviser (G4), D. Stanton.
Grade 5, P. Brannen; Ms. P. Meadows; J. Stern.

Employment Policy Division
Grade 3, C. F. Tucker.

Personnel and Business Services Division
Director of Personnel (G3), A. W. Brown.
Head of Business Services (G4), M. Davies.
Head of Group Personnel Unit (G5), S. Tolson.
Director of Computing (G5), S. Elliott.
Head of Personnel Services Branch (G5), D. Lifton.

Information Division
Head of Information (G5), B. Sutlieff.
Deputy Head of Information (G6), S. Reardon.

Finance Division
Director of Finance and Resource Management (G3), D. G. Talintyre.
Grade 5, R. H. Chambers; K. J. Jordan.

Solicitor's Office
Legal Adviser (G3), H. R. L. Purse.

Statistics Division
Director of Statistics (G3), P. D. Dworkin.
Chief Statisticians (G5), M. J. Hughes; Mrs. A. V. Wheatcroft; D. J. Sellwood; D. E. Allnutt.

Small Firms and Tourism Division
Grade 3, J. Turner.
Grade 5, I. M. Jones; Dr. P. J. Graham; Mrs. J. Peretz.

DEPARTMENT OF ENERGY
Thames House South,
Millbank, SW1P 4QJ (unless otherwise stated)
[01–211 3000]

The Department of Energy is responsible within the Government for the development of policies in relation to all forms of energy. It also discharges governmental functions connected with the publicly-owned coal and electricity industries. It is responsible for the Atomic Energy Authority; is the sponsoring Department for the nuclear power industry and is responsible for the development of oil and gas resources on the British sector of the Continental Shelf. It is the sponsoring Department for the oil industry and is responsible for international aspects of energy problems, including relations and co-operation with oil producing countries. The Department is the co-ordinating body for energy efficiency policy and for encouraging the development of new sources of energy.

(For **Salaries**, *see* page 297).

Head of P.E.D. £48,147
Reservoir Evaluation Specialist I £42,205
Reservoir Evaluation Specialist II .. £31,665–£39,742
Petroleum Specialist II ....£28,479–£35,718

Secretary of State for Energy, THE RT. HON. CECIL
    PARKINSON, M.P.
    Principal Private Secretary, S. H. Haddrill.
    Parliamentary Private Secretary, J. Butterfill, M.P.
Minister of State for Energy, THE RT. HON. PETER
    MORRISON, M.P.
    Private Secretary, S. J. Whiting.
    Parliamentary Private Secretary, Dr. I. Twinn, M.P.
Parliamentary Under-Secretaries of State, M. Spicer,
    M.P.; The Baroness Hooper.
Permanent Under Secretary of State (G1), Sir Peter
    Gregson, K.C.B.
    Private Secretary, C. P. Nichols.
Deputy Secretaries (G2), J. R. S. Guinness; G. H.
    Chipperfield.
Chief Scientific Adviser, Sir Sam Edwards, F.R.S.
Parliamentary Clerk, A. D. Proud.

Establishment and Finance Division

Principal Establishment and Finance Officer (G3), C.
    E. Henderson.
Director of Resource Management (G4), C. C. Wilcock.
Assistant Secretaries (G5), R. Beasley; J. Morris; P.
    D. Atkinson; Ms. P. Boys; Dr. D. P. Hauser.

Electricity Division

Under Secretary (G3), W. I. Macintyre.
Assistant Secretaries (G5), G. W. Thynne; Dr. A.
    Eggington; W. J. Rickett; G. S. Dart.
Chief Electrical Engineering Inspector (G7), D. C.
    Gore.

Coal Division

Under Secretary (G3), M. S. Buckley.
Assistant Secretaries (G5), M. H. Atkinson; E. Pash.

Atomic Energy Division

Under Secretary (G3), D. I. Morphet.
Assistant Secretaries (G5), P. H. Agrell; B. Hampton;
    Dr. J. G. Wright; A. J. T. Steele.

Energy Technology Division

Chief Scientist (G3), Dr. J. Rae.
Deputy Chief Scientific Officers (G5), Dr. R. G. S.
    Skipper; G. Bevan.
Assistant Secretary (G5), Dr. W. D. Evans.
Senior Principal Scientific Officers (G6), H. F. Fergu-
    son; R. A. Meir; Dr. S. E. R. Hiscocks; G. S.
    Dearnley; W. Macpherson; Dr. D. Fairmaner.

International Unit

Assistant Secretary (G5), S. W. Freemantle.

Energy Efficiency Office

Director General (G3), Dr. E. G. Finer.
Directors (G5), P. G. P. D. Fullerton; M. Keay; J. E.
    P. Miles.
Director (G6), Dr. D. Hauser.

Economics and Statistics Division

Under Secretary (G3), E. H. M. Price.
Chief Statistician (G5), T. S. Simmons.
Senior Economic Advisers (G5), S. A. Price; S. F. D.
    Powell; G. R. Horton.

Oil and Gas Division

Under Secretary (G3), D. R. Davis.
Assistant Secretaries (G5), P. T. Harding; W. C. F.
    Butler; Ms. A. Beaton; N. A. C. Hirst; J. R. Wakely.

Gas and Oil Measurement Branch
Government Buildings, Saffron Road, Wigston,
Leicester
[0533–785354]

Director (G5), J. Plant.
Senior Chief Examiner (G6), G. A. Paul-Clark.

Petroleum Engineering Division

Director of P.E.D., P. J. Walmsley, M.B.E..
Reservoir Evaluation Specialist I, I. W. G. Hughes.
Reservoir Evaluation Specialists II, J. R. V. Brooks;
    D. W. Mann.
Reservoir Evaluation Specialist I, J. R. Petrie.
Petroleum Specialists II, R. Giles; D. R. Clementson;
    B. B. Moore; N. G. Marguerie.
Senior Principal Scientific Officer (G6), J. N. Mans-
    field.
Assistant Director Engineer (G6), G. N. Marriott.

Offshore Supplies Office
Alhambra House, 45 Waterloo Street,
Glasgow G2 6AS
[041–221 8777]

Director General (G3), J. E. d'Ancona.
Director Industry (G5), W. E. Allison.
Director Policy and Administration (G5), A. E. Maule.
Director Research and Development (G5), C. P. Carter.
Director China Unit (G6), Dr. K. P. Forrest.
Senior Principal Business Development (G6), H.
    Holden.
Senior Principal Scientific Officer (G6), Dr. K. Tregon-
    ning.
Assistant Director Engineers (G6), H. M. Whiteside;
    P. R. Taylor.

Information Division

Head of Information (G5), M. S. D. Granatt.
Deputy Head of Information (G6), Mrs. A. Wadsworth.
Chief Press Officer (G7), N. Hayes.

DEPARTMENT OF THE ENVIRONMENT
2 Marsham Street, SW1P 3EB
[01–276 3000]

The Department of the Environment is responsible
for planning and land use; local government; housing, construction; inner city areas; new towns;
environmental protection; conservation areas and
countryside affairs; royal parks and palaces; historic
buildings and ancient monuments; sport and recreation. The Property Services Agency is responsible
for all construction activities, supplies and transport
at home and abroad for all Government departments
including the Ministry of Defence and some repayment clients including British Telecom.
(For **Salaries**, *see* page 297)

Secretary of State for the Environment, THE RT. HON.
    NICHOLAS RIDLEY, M.P.
    Private Secretary, R. F. M. Bright.
    Special Adviser, Mrs. K. Ramsay.
    Parliamentary Private Secretary, The Hon. N.
        Soames, M.P.

Minister for Local Government, THE RT. HON. JOHN
    GUMMER, M.P.
    Private Secretary, (vacant).
Minister for Water Privatization and Planning,
    MICHAEL HOWARD, M.P.
    Private Secretary, A. G. Riddell.
    Parliamentary Private Secretary, R. King, M.P.

Minister for Environment, Countryside and Housing,
    THE EARL OF CAITHNESS.
    Private Secretary, S. Watts.
Parliamentary Under Secretaries of State:—
    The Hon. Colin Moynihan, M.P. (*also Minister for*

Sport); D. Trippier, R.D., M.P.; C. Chope, O.B.E., M.P.;
Mrs. V. Bottomley, M.P.
Private Secretaries, P. J. Heron (*to Hon. C. Moynihan*); Mrs. S. J. Bishop (*to D. Trippier*); Miss I.
Ogilvie (*to C. Chope*); E. Brice (*to Mrs. Bottomley*).
Lord in Waiting, The Lord Hesketh.
  Private Secretary, J. Bishop.
  Parliamentary Clerk, A. Mitcheson.
Permanent Secretary (*G1*), Sir Terence Heiser, K.C.B.
  Private Secretary, M. J. Bailey.
Second Permanent Secretary, (*G1*A), Sir Gordon
Manzie, K.C.B.
  Private Secretary, J. A. Hammond.

Information

Director (*G4*), Miss J. Caines.
Head of News and Administration (*G5*), J. Gee (*temp.*).
Head of Promotions and Publicity (*G6*), Ms. P.
Alexander (*temp.*).

Merseyside Task Force

Under Secretary (*G3*), (vacant).
Controllers (*G5*), D. J. Morrison; R. K. Madders.

PLANNING, INNER CITIES, REGIONAL
DEVELOPMENT, LAND AND PROPERTY

Deputy Secretary (*G2*), J. Delafons, C.B.

Inner Cities

Under Secretary (*G3*), A. J. Butler.
Head of Divisions (*G5*), W. B. Solesbury; C. P. Evans;
A. C. B. Ramsay.

Land and Property

Director (*G4*), C. K. Howes.
Grade 6, J. C. White.

Planning Land Use Policy

Under Secretary (*G3*), N. W. Summerton.
Grade 5, D. N. Donaldson; A. H. Corner; R. S.
Horsman.

Planning Services

Director (*G4*), J. B. Wilson.
Grade 5, R. A. Bird; R. C. Mabey; J. A. Zetter.
Grade 6, P. Morgan; D. C. Stroud.

HOUSING, CONSTRUCTION AND
THE BUILT HERITAGE

Deputy Secretary (*G2*), P. F. Owen.

Housing Associations and Private Rented
Sector

Director (*G3*), R. U. Young.
Heads of Divisions (*G5*), P. J. J. Britton; R. J. Gibson;
G. L. Laufer; P. F. Everall; M. J. C. Faulkner; D.
R. Ritchie.
Grade 6, J. S. Gill.

Housing Monitoring and Analysis

Under Secretary (*G3*), D. C. L. Wroe.
Grade 5, J. E. Turner; A. E. Holmans; W. H. Stott; R.
F. Sellwood; D. T. I. G. Davies; N. Dorling.
Grade 6, Mrs. J. Littlewood.

Public Housing Management and Resources

Under Secretary (*G3*), A. G. Watson.
Heads of Divisions (*G5*), J. F. Stoker; J. K. Stoker; D.
V. Teasdale; I. H. Nicol; J. Jacobs.
Grade 6, J. D. Harvey.

Construction Industry

Director (*G3*), D. A. McDonald.
Heads of Divisions (*G5*), A. D. Fagin; G. I. Fuller; I.
C. Macpherson; F. D. Sando.

Sports and Recreation Directorate

Director (*G3*), D. A. McDonald.
Head of Division (*G5*), N. A. J. Kingham.

Building Research Establishment

Director (*G3*), R. G. Courtney.
Deputy Director (*G4*), J. M. Baker.
Heads of Departments and Stations (*G5*), Dr. J. B.
Menzies; N. O. Milbank; K. N. Palmer; B. O. Hall.
Heads of Services/Research (*G6*), A. J. M. Harrison;
I. L. Freeman; Mrs. J. Lemessany; Dr. H. W. Pratt;
Dr. R. F. Stevens; J. B. Bowden; Dr. J. K. Eaton;
Dr. J. F. A. Moore; Dr. A. B. Birtles; R. E. Baldwin;
Dr. V. A. C. Crisp; C. J. D. Webster; Dr. W. H. Gutt;
Dr. L. H. Everett; B. B. Pigott; P. F. Thorne; Dr.
W. D. Woolley; J. F. S. Carruthers; Dr. J. M. W.
Morgan; Dr. A. J. Majumdar, M.B.E.
Heads of Laboratories and Services (*G7*), P. W. Staff;
A. J. Butler; R. L. Hawes; Dr. J. P. Cornish; J.
Hartup.

Heritage and Royal Estate

Director (*G3*), Ms. E. C. Turton.
Head of Royal Parks and Palaces Division (*G5*), J. J.
Rendell.
Grade 6, A. Cornwell.
Grade 7, G. A. Wheeldon.
Bailiff of the Royal Parks Office (*G6*), R. A. Stephenson,
M.V.O.
Grade 7, Miss M. E. Green.

Heritage Sponsorship Division

Head of Division (*G5*), T. E. Radice.
Grade 7, L. Packer; M. A. L. Ross; P. H. Denton.

CHIEF ARCHITECTURAL ADVISER
ON THE BUILT ENVIRONMENT

Grade 2, J. B. Jefferson, C.B.E.
Grade 5, J. E. Turner.

FINANCE AND LOCAL GOVERNMENT

Deputy Secretary, Principal Finance Officer (*G2*), F.
A. Osborn.

Local Government Finance Policy

Under Secretary (*G3*), C. J. S. Brearley.
Grade 4, Mrs. D. S. Phillips.
Heads of Divisions (*G5*), D. L. H. Roberts; P. D. Ward;
J. E. Roberts; J. Adams; R. Jones; J. S. Parker;
Mrs. C. Wells.

Housing, Water and Central Finance

Under Secretary (*G3*), P. J. Fletcher.
Heads of Divisions (*G5*), B. Redfern; D. A. C. Heigham;
R. S. Dudding; (*G6*), G. Knowles.

Local Government

Under Secretary (*G3*), R. J. A. Sharp.
Heads of Divisions (*G5*), R. Compton; A. H. Davis; A.
J. C. Simcock; (*G6*), P. G. Iredale.

CHIEF ENVIRONMENTAL SCIENTISTS

Chief Scientist (*G3*), Dr. D. J. Fisk.
Head of Division (*G5*), C. L. Robson.

ENVIRONMENT PROTECTION

Deputy Secretary (G2), D. J. Burr.
Deputy Secretary, Water (G2), A. P. Brown.

H.M. Inspectorate of Pollution

Director (G3), B. D. Ponsford.
Chief Inspector (Air, Wastes, Water), R. J. Perriman.
Chief Inspectors (Radioactive Substances) (G5), F. S. Feates; D. A. Mills.
Deputy Chief Inspectors, J. M. Thayer; M. F. Tunnicliffe; L. N. Stuffins.
Grade 6, Dr. P. D. Johnston; A. Windsor; Dr. A. G. Duncan; Dr. M. Jones; I. Handyside.

District Inspectors, G. G. Jones; M. R. Walters; J. Downs; Dr. L. A. Hales; J. E. Hooper; B. T. Head; Dr. K. Speakman; E. F. Tomlinson; A. H. Brown; Dr. E. Hutton; J. Barrett; D. D. B. H. Munns; Dr. J. K. Allen.

Central Directorate of Environmental Protection

Under Secretary (G3), J. Hobson.
Grade 5, Miss F. McConnell; Dr. N. J. King; P. S. MacCormack; G. N. Bendon.
Grade 6, Dr. D. L. Simms.

Air, Noise and Wastes Directorate

Under Secretary (G3), Dr. D. J. Fisk.
Grade 5, N. Sanders; F. C. Argent.

Directorate of Rural Affairs

Under Secretary (G3), R. J. Green.
Grade 5, A. Flexman; R. Bunce.
Grade 6, J. C. Peters.

Water Privatization Directorate

Director (G3), J. A. L. Gunn.
Head of Division (G5), A. D. Whetnall; J. P. Henry; L. B. Hicks; C. Bolt.

Water Directorates

Director (G3), Miss D. A. Nichols.
Heads of Divisions (G5), R. J. Dorrington; M. G. Healey; J. W. Smith; Mrs. J. M. Williams.

National Rivers Authority Advisory Committee

Chief Executive (G3), D. C. Renshaw.
Grade 5, D. P. Whalley.

LEGAL

Solicitor and Legal Adviser (G2), M. J. Ware.
Deputy Solicitors (G3), J. G. Medcalf; J. G. Roscoe.
Assistant Solicitors (G5), Ms. S. D. Underman; J. L. Comber; Mrs. J. L. Weinberg; J. A. Catlin; Mrs. I. M. Watson; P. J. Szell; D. J. Serjeant; I. D. Day; Miss A. Brett-Holt; C. M. Vine; Mrs. S. Headley.

PROPERTY SERVICES AGENCY

Chief Executive (G1 A), Sir Gordon Manzie, K.C.B..
Private Secretary, J. Hammond.

DEPUTY CHIEF EXECUTIVE 1

Deputy Chief Executive (G2), A. R. Atherton.

Home Regional Services

Director (G3), P. J. M. Butter.
Assistant Directors (G5), J. W. Deane; R. Kent; E. R. Turtle.
Head of Works Division (G6), M. J. Riley.

Scottish Services

Director (G3), A. G. Gosling.
Assistant Directors (G5), D. R. Smith; J. S. Wilson; B. A. Taylor.

Central Office for Wales

Director (G4), J. H. Clemits.
Deputy Director (G5), A. N. Towers.
Admin. Officer (G6), A. L. S. Richard.

Regions (Home)

London Region:
Director (G4), G. Hopkinson.
Assistant Directors (G5), Mrs. M. Clare, C. A. K. Pain; P. M. Livesey; W. J. Purdie; R. E. Kendrick.
Eastern Region:
Director (G4), A. J. B. Staveley.
Deputy Director (G5), J. E. Jolly.
Admin. Officer (G6), A. J. Hazeldine.
Midland Region:
Director (G4), R. M. Jordan.
Deputy Director (G5), W. Shelton.
Admin. Officer (G6), J. Knott.
North East Region:
Director (G4), G. Flanagan.
Deputy Director (G5), G. H. Sowden.
Admin. Officer (G6), W. M. McAndrew.
North West Region:
Director (G4), M. M. Harrison.
Deputy Director (G5), D. A. R. Reeson.
Admin. Officer (G6), F. Smith.
South East Region:
Director (G4), S. P. Todd.
Deputy Director (G5), P. M. Pryke.
Admin. Officer (G6), R. G. S. Leeson.
South West Region:
Director (G4), M. Baggott.
Deputy Director (G5), J. Mitchell.
Admin. Officer (G6), E. A. Reid.
Southern Region:
Director (G4), M. R. Newey.
Deputy Director (G5), F. Rymill.
Admin. Officer (G6), G. R. Byers.

DEPUTY CHIEF EXECUTIVE 2

Deputy Chief Executive (G2), J. P. G. Rowcliffe.

Civil Accommodation

Director (G3), R. G. S. Johnston.
Chief Estate Surveyor (G4), R. P. Hore.
Grade 5, F. Boonham; D. J. Phillips; W. H. M. Clarke; R. Holland; M. R. Sutton.
Grade 6, R. M. Hosangady; M. Nelson.

Defence Services I

Director (G3), R. A. Gomme.
Grade 5, H. L. Froome-Lewis; M. Clayton; D. C. P. Izzatt; R. G. Jones.
Grade 6, R. K. Houghton.
Germany:
Director (G4), R. B. Perry.
Regional Works Officer (G5), P. W. Berrington.
Regional Admin. Officer (G6), D. C. Falvey.

Defence Services II

Director (G3), A. S. Kennedy.
Grade 5, M. B. Chammings; G. D. Miles; J. G. Dillaway; J. G. Chisnell; S. G. D. Duguid; A. K. W. Morgan; M. S. Barratt.
Grade 6, K. A. Holme.

Defence Estates Services Division

Grade 5, M. D. Clarke.

DIRECTOR GENERAL OF DESIGN SERVICES
Director General (G2), J. B. Jefferson, C.B.E.

Directorate of Architectural Services
Director (G4), J. E. Jeavons.
Director (G5), C. A. P. Crooke.

Building and Quantity Surveying Services
Director (G4), K. A. Miles.
Grade 5, M. Barnes; M. G. Stuart.

Civil Engineering Services
Director (G4), H. P. Webber.
Grade 5, D. A. Woodward.

Mechanical and Electrical Engineering Services
Director (G4), R. C. Cracknell.
Grade 5, J. Fisher.

PSA ESTABLISHMENTS AND INFORMATION
TECHNOLOGY MANAGEMENT OFFICE
SERVICES
Principal Establishment Officer (G3), P. S. Draper.
Grade 5, R. A. Stead; G. J. Skinner; D. S. Ashworth.

Information Technology and Office Systems
Grade 4, Mrs. E. M. Causley Cooper.
Computing Division:
Grade 5, D. Evans.
Grade 6, F. J. H. Brown; A. L. Cole.

PSA FINANCE

Principal Finance Officer (G3), R. A. Munday.
Grade 5, M. L. Taylor; I. G. Urquhart.
Controller of Accounts (G5), J. A. Pearson.
Director of Contracts (G4), M. J. Wanstall.
Deputy Director (G5), (vacant).
Head of Internal Audit (G5), M. Reece.
Public Expenditure (G5), I. G. Urquhart.
Grade 6, P. Ashton.

THE CROWN SUPPLIERS

Controller (G3), D. T. Routh.
Financial Controller (G5), J. Cousins.
Assistant Controllers (G5), E. L. Pinfold; A. H. Pollington; B. G. Rosser.
Grade 6, R. Thrower.

DEPARTMENTS OF THE ENVIRONMENT
AND TRANSPORT REGIONAL OFFICES

West Midlands, Birmingham.—*Regional Director (G3),* H. F. Ellis-Rees. *Regional Controllers (G5),* J. E. Northover; D. L. Saunders; Mrs. P. M. Holland.
Yorkshire and Humberside, Leeds.—*Regional Director (G3),* J. F. Ballard. *Regional Controllers (G5),* I. H. Crowther; K. Beaumont.
North West, Manchester.—*Regional Director (G3),* F. Kendall. *Regional Controllers (G5),* B. C. Isherwood; J. W. Glester; *(G6),* P. Walton.
Northern, Newcastle upon Tyne.—*Regional Director (G3),* J. A. Owen. *Regional Controllers (G5),* J. A. M. Hastings; R. G. Bell.
South West, Bristol.—*Regional Director (G3),* G. M. Wedd. *Regional Controllers (G5),* S. McQuillin; *(G6),* J. M. Rollinson; R. Pritchard.
East Midlands, Nottingham.—*Regional Director (G4),* P. M. Hewitt, O.B.E. *Regional Controller (G5),* G. Meynell, M.B.E.
South East, W.14.—*Regional Director (G3),* D. Gruffydd Jones. *Regional Controllers (G5),* N. Thompson; R. Williams; J. A. Colley; *(G6),* P. J. Beque.

Eastern, W.14.—*Regional Director (G3),* G. D. Crane. *Regional Controllers (G5),* A. Z. Levy; A. F. Richardson.

GREATER LONDON REGIONAL OFFICES

Under Secretary (G3), A. A. Pelling.
Grade 5, J. G. Grevatt; A. Buchanan; D. R. Bradley; B. Strong.

DEPARTMENTS OF THE ENVIRONMENT
AND TRANSPORT—COMMON SERVICES
2 Marsham Street, SW1P 3EB
[01-276 3000]

ORGANIZATION AND ESTABLISHMENTS

Director General of Organization and Establishments (G2), P. C. McQuail.

Establishments Organization Division
Grade 5, P. D. Burgess.

Senior Staff Management
Director (G5), E. B. C. Osmotherly.
Grade 5, H. D. Hallett; B. E. Fensome.
Chief Librarian (G6), P. Kirwan.

Personnel Management and Training
Director (G3), K. E. C. Sorensen.
Grade 5, P. Stringfellow; G. D. Edmonds; A. S. D. Whybrow; Mrs. A. Heath.
Grade 6, B. L. W. Dexter; Dr. J. C. Miles; G. Bray; Miss J. A. Clark; R. E. Vidler; K. Wright.
Chief Welfare Officer (G7), R. J. Lintern.

Directorate of Administrative Resources
Director (G3), Mrs M. McDonald.
Grade 4, P. Leonard.
Grade 5, Miss L. F. Bell; D. M. Smith; Miss S. Booth; D. A. R. Peel.
Grade 6, R. H. Cheeseman; D. Tridwell; C. M. Shreeves.

PLANNING INSPECTORATE

Chief Planning Inspector (G3), H. S. Crow.
Deputy Chief Planning Inspector (G4), J. R. Mossop.
Director of Operations (G4), A. J. M. Morgan.
Assistant Chief Planning Inspectors (G5), Miss G. M. Pain; G. Lidbury; J. G. Greenfield; J. T. Graham.
Head of Administration (G5), D. A. C. Marshall.

ROYAL COMMISSION ON
ENVIRONMENTAL POLLUTION
Church House, Great Smith Street, SW1P 3BL
[01-276 2080]

Set up on Feb. 20, 1970, "to advise on matters, both national and international, concerning the pollution of the environment; on the adequacy of research in this field; and the future possibilities of danger to the environment."
Chairman, Prof. Sir Jack Lewis, F.R.S.
Members, Prof. B. E. Clayton; Prof. G. R. Conway; The Earl of Cranbrook; J. W. Edmonds; The Lord Nathan; Prof. D. E. Newland; J. J. R. Pope, O.B.E.; Dr. C. W. Suckling, F.R.S.; Prof. M. P. Vessey; Prof. H. Charnock, F.R.S.; L. C. G. Gilling, O.B.E.; Prof. E. M. Rothschild; Prof. Z. A. Silberston, O.B.E.; Prof. W. D. P. Stewart, F.R.S.
Secretary, B. Glicksman.

EQUAL OPPORTUNITIES COMMISSION
Overseas House, Quay Street, Manchester M3 3HN
[061–833 9244]

PRESS OFFICE: 1 Bedford Street. WC2 [01–379 6323]

REGIONAL OFFICES: St. Andrew House, 141 West Nile Street, Glasgow G1 2RN [041–332 8018]
Caerwys House, Windsor Place, Cardiff [0222–43552]

The Commission was set up by Parliament in 1975 as a result of the passing of the Sex Discrimination Act. It works towards the elimination of discrimination by virtue of sex or marital status and to promote equality of opportunity between men and women generally.

Chair, Mrs. J. Foster £39,270
Deputy Chair, Mrs. J. O'Dell £16,485
Members, K. Boardman; Mrs. R. Brown; D. Guereca; Prof. G. Powell; A. Simpkin; Mrs. P. Turner; Mrs. E. Walker; Dame Anne Warburton, D.C.V.O., C.M.G.; Miss M. Monk; Mrs. M. Prosser; Baroness Turner of Camden; Mrs. D. Brittan; Mrs. A. Hasan.
Chief Executive, A. E. Hart.

EXCHEQUER AND AUDIT DEPARTMENT
See National Audit Office

EXPORT CREDITS GUARANTEE DEPARTMENT
P.O. Box 272, Export House,
50 Ludgate Hill, EC4M 7AJ
[01–382 7000]
Crown Buildings, Cathays Park,
Cardiff CF1 3NH
[0222–824000]

The Export Credits Guarantee Department is a separate government department responsible to the Secretary of State for Trade and functions under the Export Guarantees and Overseas Investment Act 1978. This enables E.C.G.D. to encourage U.K. exports by making available export credit insurance to British firms engaged in selling overseas and to guarantee repayment to banks in Britain providing finance for export credit for goods sold on credit terms of two years or more. Guarantees under Section 1 of the Act are given after consultation with an Advisory Council of bankers and businessmen.

The Act also empowers E.C.G.D. to insure British private investment overseas against political risks, such as war, expropriation and restrictions on remittances.

Chief Executive, M. G. Stephens.
Directors (G3), G. E. J. Breach; R. G. Codd; C. Foxall; M. T. Hawtin; D. H. Twyford .... £34,000–£37,000
Heads of Divisions (G5), C. M. Bossom; G. Bromley; J. G. M. Cochrane; R. Wild; R. A. Ranson; J. K. Sedman; A. J. Bray; J. R. Weiss; A. P. Fowell; A. J. Holloway; Dr. R. Van Slooten; R. I. Fear; M. J. Long; R. W. MacGregor; D. R. Coombe; D. C. Cooper; T. M. Jaffray; R. F. Lethbridge; V. P. Lunn-Rockliffe; K. G. Lockwood; M. D. Pentecost.
Senior Principals (G6), G. C. Bird; D. Q. Bryars; P. J. Callaghan; J. D. Cameron; D. Collins; D. A. Green; K. Dixey; A. P. G. Hare; L. S. W. Montgomery.
Principals (G7), Miss J. Albutt; J. S. Astruc; J. E. Atkinson; D. D. Baird; G. Blackburn; D. I. Calvert; A. L. Childs; Mrs. H. V. Cieslik; Mrs. A. C. Cowie; D. M. Cox; A. B. Coyne; M. J. Crane; R. P. D. Crick; J. C. W. Croall; R. A. Dew; L. Easterbrook; J. B. Eilbeck; D. Elliott; R. X. Fear; J. M. Foster; Mrs. J. A. Fulwood; P. C. Gaudoin; N. F. George; R. Gotts; R. T. Griffiths; P. Hambleton; R. Hardy; G. H. Hill; R. Holloway; P. Jackson; P. F. Jennings; Miss S. J. Johnson; C. D. Jones; G. G. Jones; K. Jones; R. Jones; N. A. Lambert; Mrs. F. M. Lewis;

I. Mackay; J. S. McKibbin; Mrs. M. Maddox; S. Merchack; D. W. Miller; D. J. Morris; A. J. E. Muckersie; P. L. Neal; G. A. Newhouse; R. C. Parry; R. J. Pomeroy; S. C. Pond; A. B. Redmayne; S. Rosenthal; M. Russell; M. Scales; R. Scott; B. M. Sidwell, T.D.; K. R. Smith; R. G. Smith; J. S. Snowdon; B. C. Southwell; I. J. Summers; R. S. Summers; J. Sweeney; Ms. P. K. Terry; C. M. Thorogood; D. A. H. Tickner; J. A. Tyler; E. J. Walsby; A. R. Watt; R. A. Watt; Miss J.West; T. J. M. West; F. Whitehead; J. M. Willis; D. L. Wyatt; J. A. Youd; G. A. Young.
Principal Information Officer, G. Hicks.

Regional Offices
Belfast: Windsor House, 9–15 Bedford Street, BT2 7EG (0232–231743); Birmingham: Colmore Centre, 115 Colmore Row, B3 3SB (021–233 1771); Bristol: Robinson Building, 1 Redcliffe Street, BS1 6NP (0272–299971); Cambridge: Three Crowns House, 72–80 Hills Road, CB2 1NJ (0223–68801); City of London: Export House, 50 Ludgate Hill, EC4M 7AY (01–726 4050); Croydon: Sunley House, Bedford Park, Croydon, CR9 4HL (01–680 5030); Glasgow: Berkeley House, 285 Bath Street, G2 4JL (041–332 8707); Leeds: West Riding House, 67 Albion Street, LS1 5AA (0532–450631); Manchester: Townbury House, Blackfriars Street, Salford M3 5AL (061–834 8181).

Export Guarantees Advisory Council
Chairman, P. E. Leslie.
Deputy Chairman, T. W. B. Sallitt.
Other Members, E. L. Brooks; P. W. Bulfield; The Hon. D. Douglas-Home; R. H. George, C.B.E; A. G. Gormley; S. M. F. Harris; W. Hogbin; Dr. K. Scholes.

OFFICE OF FAIR TRADING
Field House, Bream's Buildings, EC4A 1PR
[01–242 2858]

The Office of Fair Trading is a government department responsible for the administration of the Fair Trading Act, 1973, the Consumer Credit Act, 1974, the Restrictive Trade Practices Act, 1976, the Estate Agents Act, 1979, the Competition Act, 1980, and the Control of Misleading Advertisements Regulations, 1988. Under the supervision of the Director General of Fair Trading the office keeps under review commercial activities in the U.K. and aims to protect the consumer against unfair practices and is divided between five main areas: consumer affairs, consumer credit, monopolies and mergers, restrictive trade practices and anti-competitive practices.
Director General (G1), Sir Gordon Borrie, Q.C.
Deputy Director General (G2), A. J. Lane.

Consumer Affairs Division
Director (G3), R. J. Thomas.
Assistant Directors (G5), H. J. Charman; S. G. Linstead, M. Z. Wasilewski.

Competition Policy Division
Director (G3), Dr. M. Howe.
Assistant Directors (G5), Dr. A. Marshall; D. W. Lightfoot; J. C. Octon.

Legal Division
Director (G3), R. Woolman.
Assistant Directors (G5), A. J. Perrett; G. Vaughan Davies.

Chief Information Officer (G6), J. E. Perry.
Senior Economic Adviser (G6), (vacant).
Establishment and Finance Officer (G7), B. A. Hennah.

FOREIGN AND COMMONWEALTH OFFICE
Downing Street, SW1A 2AL
[01-270 3000]

The Foreign and Commonwealth Office provides, mainly through diplomatic missions, the means of communication between the British Government and other governments and international governmental organizations for the discussion and negotiation of all matters falling within the field of international relations. It is responsible for alerting the British Government to the implications of developments overseas; for protecting British interests overseas; for protecting British citizens abroad; for explaining British policies to, and cultivating friendly relations with, Governments overseas and for the discharge of British responsibilities to the dependent territories.

Salaries

For Ministerial salaries, *see* page 297

Diplomatic Service

Permanent Under Secretary and Head of the Diplomatic Service	£79,750
Senior Grade Salary Point 1 (SP1)	£68,500
Deputy to the Permanent Under Secretary	£62,750
Senior Grade Salary Point 2 (SP2)	£57,000
Senior Grade Salary Point 3 (SP3)	£45,800–£48,000
Senior Grade Salary Point 4 (SP4)	£43,200
Senior Grade Salary Point 5 (SP5)	£35,800–£39,000
Diplomatic Service Grade 4 (DS4)	£27,087–£30,387
Diplomatic Service Grade 5 (DS5)	£16,692–£21,737

Secretary of State, THE RT. HON. SIR GEOFFREY HOWE, Q.C., M.P.
 Private Secretary, J. S. Wall, L.V.O.
 Assistant Private Secretaries, L. Parker; R. N. Peirce.
 Social Secretary, Mrs. L. McBride.
Ministers of State for Foreign and Commonwealth Affairs, THE RT. HON. LYNDA CHALKER, M.P.; THE LORD GLENARTHUR; THE HON. WILLIAM WALDEGRAVE, M.P.
 Private Secretaries, M. J. Lyall Grant (*to Mrs. Chalker*); R. V. Court (*to Lord Glenarthur*); N. K. Darroch (*to Mr. Waldegrave*).
 Parliamentary Private Secretaries:
 To Mrs. Chalker, D. French, M.P.
 To Mr. Waldegrave, A. Mitchell, M.P.
Minister of State for Foreign and Commonwealth Affairs (Minister for Overseas Development), CHRISTOPHER PATTEN, M.P.
 Private Secretary, M. A. Wickstead.
 Parliamentary Private Secretary, S. R. Key, M.P.
Parliamentary Under Secretary of State, T. Eggar, M.P.
 Private Secretary, R. E. Makepeace.
Parliamentary Relations Unit, J. D. F. Holt (*Head*); C. A. Hamilton (*Deputy Head and Parliamentary Clerk*).

Permanent Under Secretary of State and Head of the Diplomatic Service, Sir Patrick Wright, K.C.M.G.
 Private Secretary, G. D. Adams.
Deputy to the Permanent Under Secretary and Political Director, Sir John Fretwell, G.C.M.G.
Deputy Under Secretaries (SP2), Sir Mark Russell, K.C.M.G. (*Chief Clerk*); D. H. Gillmore, C.M.G.; A. G. Munro, C.M.G.; N. P. Bayne, C.M.G.; J. D. I. Boyd, C.M.G.
H.M. Vice-Marshal of the Diplomatic Corps, R. Hervey, C.M.G.
Assistant Under Secretaries (SP5), Miss C. E. Pestell, C.M.G.; P. R. Fearn, C.M.G.; P. J. Goulden; D. J. Moss (*Deputy Chief Clerk*); W. R. Tomkys, C.M.G. (*Principal Finance Officer and Chief Inspector*); R. J. Carrick, C.M.G., L.V.O.; Sir David Miers, K.B.E., C.M.G.; D. J. E. Ratford, C.M.G., C.V.O.; P. S. Fairweather, C.M.G.; J. O. Kerr, C.M.G.; D. Slater, C.M.G.; R. J. T. McLaren, C.M.G.; I. S. Winchester, C.M.G. (*Director of Communications & Technical Services*).
Legal Adviser, A. D. Watts, C.M.G.
Second Legal Adviser, H. G. Darwin, C.M.G.
Deputy Legal Advisers, D. H. Anderson, C.M.G.; F. D. Berman, C.M.G.
Legal Counsellors, F. D. Berman, C.M.G.; M. C. Wood; A. I. Aust; I. D. Hendry; K. J. Chamberlain; J. Siddle.
International Labour Adviser, A. E. Smith.
Overseas Police Adviser (DS4), J. W. Kelland, L.V.O., Q.P.M.

Signals Department (Government Communications Headquarters)
Priors Road, Cheltenham, Glos. GL52 5AJ
[0242–221491]

Director (G2), Sir Peter Marychurch, K.C.M.G.
Principal Establishment Officer (G3), J. Adye.

Heads of Departments (DS4) and Assistant Heads of Department (DS5)

Aid Policy Dept., C. Raleigh; *Asst.*, T. J. David.
Arms Control and Disarmament Dept., P. D. R. Davies; *Asst.*, P. Dun.
Central African Dept., C. A. K. Cullimore; *Asst.*, N. R. Jarrold.
Claims Dept., J. Thomas.
Commercial Management and Exports Dept., G. A. Duggan; *Asst.*, Miss P. M. Kelly, M.B.E.
Commonwealth Co-ordination Dept., T. C. S. Stitt.
Communications Administration Dept., P. M. Piddington; *Assts.*, R. J. Saltwell: D. Hughes.
Communications Engineering Dept., R. Castle-Smith, M.B.E.
Communications Operations Dept., B. P. Austin; *Asst.*, E. G. B. Jarman.
Communications Planning Staff, D. J. Briggs.
Conference on Security and Co-operation in Europe Unit, P. W. Summerscale.
Consular Dept., J. Harrison, L.V.O.; *Assts.*, J. R. Jamieson; J. W. MacDonald.
Cultural Relations Dept., J. N. Elam; *Assts.*, J. M. Candlish; S. F. Howarth.
Defence Dept., P. Yarnold; *Asst.*, R. D. Lavers.
East African Dept., W. Marsden; *Asst.*, M. R. Crompton.
Eastern European Dept., C. Hulse, O.B.E.; *Asst.*, Miss A. W. Lewis.
Economic Advisers, S. H. Broadbent; *Deputy Head*, J. M. C. Rollo.
Economic Relations Dept., T. L. Richardson; *Asst.*, J. White.
Energy Science and Space Dept., P. H. D. Wetton; *Asst.*, M. J. Robinson.
European Community Dept. (External), Miss R. J. Spencer; *Asst.*, P. S. Collecott.
European Community Dept. (Internal), J. S. Wall, L.V.O.; *Asst.*, M. I P. Webb.
Falkland Islands Dept., D. E. Tatham; *Deputy Head*, D. Broad.
Far Eastern Dept., R. F. Cooper, M.V.O.; *Asst.*, (vacant).
Finance Dept., C. D. Crabbie; *Deputy Head of Dept.*, G. F. Griffiths; *Assts.*, I. Knight Smith; F. Calleghan.
Hong Kong Dept., C. O. Hum; *Asst.*, A. R. Paul.
Information Dept., R. J. S. Muir; *Assts.* S. D. R. Brown; C. K. Woodfield, O.B.E.

Information Technology Dept., K. R. Willis; *Asst.*, N. O. Rampton.

*Internal Audit Unit, L. E. Fitzpatrick.

Library and Records Dept., Miss P. M. Barnes; *Assts.*, R. L. E. Foreman; Miss M. Clay, O.B.E.

*Management Review Staff, A. F. Smith; *Deputy Head*, J. Anning.

Maritime, Aviation and Environment Dept., R. C. Beetham, L.V.O.; *Asst.*, H. G. Hogger.

Mexico and Central America Dept., A. L. S. Coltman; *Asst.*, D. F. C. Ridgway.

Middle East Dept., J. R. Young; *Asst.*, I. L. Blackley.

Migration and Visa Dept., D. M. Harrison, O.B.E.; *Asst.*, J. Smith-Laittan.

Narcotics Control and Aids Dept., J. Poston.

Nationality and Treaty Dept., P. V. Rollitt; *Asst.*, A. Harrington.

Near East and North Africa Dept., A. F. Goulty; *Asst.*, J. S. Laing.

News Dept., C. J. R. Meyer, C.M.G.; *Deputy Head*, M. A. Price.

North America Dept., D. A. Burns.

Nuclear Energy Dept., J. K. Gordon; *Asst.*, D. C. B. Beaumont.

Office Services and Transport Dept., I. McCluney; *Asst.*, A. E. Gay.

Overseas Estate Dept., M. H. R. Bertram; *Deputy Head*, M. E. Cook.

Overseas Inspectorate, W. R. Tomkys, C.M.G. (*Chief Inspector and Principal Finance Officer*); *Inspectors*, R. Thomas; Miss M. I. Rothwell; G. M. Gowlland, L.V.O.; B. Smith, O.B.E.

Permanent Under Secretary's Dept., C. C. R. Battiscombe; *Deputy Head*, P. J. Torry.

Personnel Operations Dept., D. B. C. Logan; *Deputy Head*, R. P. Ralph; *Assts.*, H. J. S. Pearce; P. A. Heald, M.B.E.; J. R. Cowling.

Personnel Policy Dept., A. M. Goodenough; *Asst.*, D. W. Fall.

Personnel Services Dept., A. P. F. Bache; *Assts.*, B. E. Bowley; G. C. Fedrick.

Policy Planning Staff, Hon. D. Gore-Booth; *Asst.*, Dr. V. Caton.

Protocol Dept., D. MacLeod; *Assts.*, J. S. Jasper, O.B.E.; S. W. F. Martin, L.V.O. (*First Assistant Marshal of the Diplomatic Corps*).

Republic of Ireland Dept., T. J. B. George.

Research Dept., Director, J. Ling; *Regional Directors*, C. J. S. Rundle, O.B.E. (*Africa & Middle East*); K. C. Walker (*Asia*); R. M. Bone (*Atlantic*); J. R. Banks (*Soviet Union & E. Europe*).

Security Dept., A. Ford; *Asst.*, D. A. Wright, O.B.E.

Security Co-ordination Dept., I. A. Roberts; *Asst.*, D. R. Upton.

Security Policy Dept., P. Lever; *Asst.*, W. G. Ehrman.

South America Dept., C. R. L. de Chassiron; *Asst.*, J. M. Cresswell.

South Asian Dept., R. A. Burns; *Asst.*, W. B. Sinton.

South-East Asian Dept., D. H. Colvin; *Asst.*, P. K. C. Thomas.

Southern African Dept., W. K. Prendergast; *Asst.*, R. J. Dalton.

Southern European Dept., M. C. S. Weston, C.V.O.

South Pacific Dept., A. E. Furness; *Asst.*, M. J. Peart, L.V.O.

Soviet Dept., S. N. P. Hemans, C.V.O.; *Asst.*, J. E Holmes.

Technical Security Dept., P. Mason, C.B.E.; *Assts.*, R. Read; J. Gould.

Training Dept., T. T. Macan; *Director of Language Centre*, J. Moore.

United Nations Dept., P. K. Williams; *Asst.*, N. A. Thorne.

---

*Joint Foreign and Commonwealth Office/Overseas Development Administration Dept.

West African Dept., Miss M. G. Fort; *Asst.*, F. X. Gallagher, O.B.E.

West Indian and Atlantic Dept., R. S. Gorham; *Asst.*, P. A. Penfold, O.B.E.

Western European Dept., D. J. M. Dain; *Assts.*, G. H. Fry; J. W. Guy, O.B.E.

CORPS OF QUEEN'S MESSENGERS
Foreign and Commonwealth Office, SW1A 2AH

Superintendent of the Corps of Queen's Messengers, Maj. I. G. M. Bamber.

Queen's Messengers, Maj. J. E. A. Andre; Col. B. C. F. Arkle, M.B.E., T.D.; Cdr. R. D. D. Bamford; Cdr. D. H. Barraclough; Maj. G. M. Benson; Lt.-Cdr. B. R. Bezance; Capt. D. F. A. Bloom, G.M.; Lt.-Col. M. B. de S. Clayton; Lt.-Col. J. B. B. Clee; Capt. G. Courtauld; Maj. F. C. W. Courtenay-Thompson; Col. J. M. Deans; Maj. P. T. Dunn; Maj. A. M. Farmer; Lt.-Col. J. W. A. Fleming, O.B.E.; Capt. N. C. E. Gardner; J. W. Hannah, M.B.E.; J. O. Hollis; Wg. Cdr. J. O. Jewiss; Lt.-Col. P. S. Kerr-Smiley; Lt.-Col. J. M. C. Kimmins; Lt.-Col. R. C. Letchworth; G. F. Miller; Lt.-Col. A. R. Murray; Maj. D. R. Nevile; Maj. L. M. Phillips; Maj. M. R. Senior; Lt.-Col. H. M. L. Smith; Maj. P. M. O. Springfield; Col. D. W. F. Taylor; Sqn. Ldr. J. A. Watson.

FOREIGN COMPENSATION COMMISSION
Alexandra House, Kingsway, WC2B 6TT
[01–438 7045]

The Commission was set up by the Foreign Compensation Act 1950 primarily to distribute under Orders in Council funds received from other governments in accordance with agreements to pay compensation for expropriated British property and other losses sustained by British nationals.

The Commission has the further duty of registering claims for British-owned property in contemplation of agreements with other countries, and it has done so in seven instances since 1950.

Chairman, A. W. E. Wheeler, C.B.E.

Commissioners, J. A. S. Hall, D.F.C., Q.C.; Sir Alan Leslie; I. M. P. Evans.

Secretary and Chief Examiner, D. H. Wright.

FORESTRY COMMISSION
231 Corstorphine Road, Edinburgh EH12 7AT
[031–334 0303]

The Forestry Commissioners are charged with the general duty of promoting in Great Britain the interests of forestry, the development of afforestation, the production and supply of timber and, in discharging their functions, endeavouring to achieve a reasonable balance between the needs of forestry and conservation. The Commission manages some 890,000 hectares of productive forest and has a continuing policy of developing its forests for recreation by the general public. It is also the Forestry Authority for Great Britain with responsibility for a range of regulatory functions, including the administration of grant-aid schemes for planting by private owners, the licensing of tree felling and the control of tree pests and diseases.

Chairman, Sir David Montgomery (*part-time*)
.... £25,824

Director-General and Deputy Chairman, G. J. Francis £48,000

Commissioner for Private Forestry and Development, R. T. Bradley £39,000

Commissioner for Administration and Finance, D. T. J. Rutherford £39,000

Commissioner for Operations, D. L. Foot £37,400

Secretary to the Commissioners, P. J. Clarke . £30,387

REGISTRY OF FRIENDLY SOCIETIES
15 Great Marlborough Street, W1V 2AX
[01–437 9992]

The Registry of Friendly Societies is a Government department serving two statutory bodies, the Building Societies Commission, and the Central Office of the Registry of Friendly Societies, together with the Assistant Registrar of Friendly Societies for Scotland.

The Building Societies Commission was established by the Building Societies Act, 1986. The Commission is responsible for the supervision of building societies, and administers the system of regulations. It also advises the Treasury and other Government departments on matters relating to building societies.

The Central Office of the Registry of Friendly Societies provides a public registry for mutual organizations registered under the Building Societies Act, 1986, Friendly Societies Act, 1974, and the Industrial and Provident Societies Act, 1965. It is responsible for the supervision of friendly societies and credit unions, and advises the Government on issues affecting those societies. The Chief Registrar has certain powers to arbitrate in disputes between members and registered societies. He also acts as the Industrial Assurance Commissioner.

(For **Salaries**, *see* page 297)

Building Societies Commission

Chairman, J. M. Bridgeman, C.B..
Deputy Chairman, G. W. Watson.
Commissioners, R. L. Devlin; D. Hobson; S. Proctor, C.B.E.; G. Sammons; H. R. C. Walden, C.B.E.

Central Office

Chief Registrar, J. M. Bridgeman.
Assistant Registrars, A. Wilson; P. D. Davis; R. N. Williams.

The Registry

First Commissioner and Chief Registrar (G2), J. M. Bridgeman.
Staff serving the Building Societies Commission:
Grade 3, G. W. Watson.
Grade 5, R. L. Devlin; T. Mathews; Mrs. P. Diggle.
Grade 7, A. G. Tebbutt.
Staff serving the Central Office:
Assistant Registrar (G4), A. Wilson.
Grade 7, R. E. Merrick; F. da Rocha.

Central Services
Assistant Registrar (G5), P. D. Davis.
Legal Staff (G6), Miss V. Mayson.
Establishment and Finance Officer (G6), M. L. Battenti.
Computer Project Manager (G7), F. Gold.

Registry of Friendly Societies, Scotland
58 Frederick Street, Edinburgh, EH2 1NB
[031–226 3224]

Assistant Registrar (G5), J. L. J. Craig, W.S.

GAMING BOARD FOR GREAT BRITAIN
Berkshire House, 168–173 High Holborn,
WC1V 7AA
[01–240 0821]

Established on October 25, 1968, to maintain a broad oversight of developments in gaming in Great Britain, to check prospective gaming licensees management and staff, and to advise the Home Secretary

on making regulations which may be needed for the further control of gaming.
Chairman, N. A. Ward Jones, V.R.D. *(part-time)*
£21,630
Members, P. B. Kavanagh, C.B.E., Q.P.M.; Lady Ibbs; W. N. Hunter Smart; M. H. Hogan *(part-time)*
£8,670
Secretary, P. Burleigh.

OFFICE OF GAS SUPPLY
Southside, 105 Victoria Street, SW1E 6QT
[01–828 0898]

The Office of Gas Supply (OFGAS) is a regulatory body set up under the Gas Act 1986. It is headed by the Director General of Gas Supply who is independent of Ministerial control.

The principal function of OFGAS is to monitor British Gas' activities as a public gas supplier and, where necessary, enforce the conditions of that company's authorization to act as a public gas supplier. Other functions are to grant authorizations to other suppliers of gas through pipes; to investigate complaints on matters where enforcement powers may be exercisable; to fix and publish maximum charges for reselling gas; to publish information and advice for the benefit of tariff customers; to keep under review developments concerning the gas supply industry; to settle the terms on which other suppliers have access to British Gas' pipelines in the event of disagreement.
Director General, J. McKinnon.
Deputy Director General, Dr. D. H. Metz.
Legal Adviser, D. R. M. Long.
Business Adviser, P. T. Gittins.
Public Affairs Adviser, I. Cooke.
Consumer Affairs Adviser, W. Macleod.
Administration Manager, P. Schrapel.

THE GOVERNMENT ACTUARY
22 Kingsway, WC2B 6LE
[01–242 6828]

The Government Actuary provides a consulting service to Government departments, nationalized industries and Commonwealth Governments. His actuaries advise on social security schemes and superannuation arrangements within the public sector at home and abroad, on population and other statistical studies, and on Government supervision of insurance companies and friendly societies.
Government Actuary, E. A. Johnston, C.B. . . . £56,160
Directing Actuaries, C. D. Daykin; D. H. Loades; G. G. Newton £44,720
Chief Actuaries, D. G. Ballantine; J. L. Field; R. T. Foster; P. H. Hinton; M. A. Pickford; A. G. Young
£33,594–£35,219
Senior Actuaries, E. I. Battersby; P. L. Burt; B. J. Coode; C. A. Harris*; T. W. Hewitson*; F. A. Honeysett; A. I. Johnston*; Mrs. I. W. Lane; J. M. MacLeod; A. P. Pavelin; D. F. Renn*; Miss P. M. Webster
£23,938–£29,138

*£29,794–£32,394

GOVERNMENT HOSPITALITY FUND
8 Cleveland Row, SW1A 1DH
[01–210 3000]

Instituted in 1908 for the purpose of organizing official hospitality on a regular basis, with a view to the promotion of international goodwill.
Minister in Charge, The Lord Glenarthur.
Secretary, Brig. A. Cowan, M.B.E.

HEALTH AND SAFETY COMMISSION
Baynards House, 1 Chepstow Place,
Westbourne Grove, W2 4TF
[01–229 3456]

The Health and Safety Commission is made up of eight representatives of trade unions, employers and local authorities and a full-time chairman appointed by the Secretary of State for Employment. Its primary functions are: to secure the health, safety and welfare of people at work; to protect the public from risks arising from work activities; to control the storage and use of explosives, highly flammable or other dangerous substances.
Chairman, Dr. E. J. Cullen.
Members, D. Mason; Dr. M. C. Shannon; Dr. C. M. Thomas; R. Eberlie; P. Jacques; Dr. A. H. Raper; Miss A. Maddocks; A. Tuffin.
Secretary, A. J. Lord

Health and Safety Executive
Broad Lane, Sheffield S3 7HQ
[0742–768141]

The Health and Safety Executive is a statutory body consisting of a director general and two other people appointed by the Commission. It advises the Commission, and its staff are the primary instrument for carrying out the Commission's policies.

Through a network of 20 area offices, H.S.E. inspectors visit and review work activities, giving expert advice and guidance and, where necessary, issuing enforcement notices and initiating prosecutions. The Employment Medical Advisory Services, the operational arm of the Medical Division, is also based on the area offices. Other inspectorates within H.S.E. monitor or enforce standards and give advice and guidance in specific sectors of industry or employment.
Director General, J. D. Rimington.
Deputy Director General, J. D. G. Hammer.
Director, Resources and Planning Division, D. C. T. Eves.

Responsible to the Director General:

H.M. Factory Inspectorate
H.M. Chief Inspector of Factories, A. J. Linehan.

H.M. Agricultural Inspectorate
H.M. Chief Agricultural Inspector, C. Boswell.

H.M. Mines and Quarries Inspectorate
H.M. Chief Inspector of Mines and Quarries, Dr. M. B. Jones.

H.M. Nuclear Installations Inspectorate
H.M. Chief Inspector of Nuclear Installations (G3), E. A. Ryder.

Safety Policy and Information Services Division
Director, D. J. Hodgkins.

Hazardous Substances Division
Director, C. D. Burgess.

Responsible to the Deputy Director General:

Technology Division
(includes H.M. Explosives Inspectorate and Major Hazards Unit).
Director, A. C. Barrell.

Research and Laboratory Services Division
Director (G3), Dr. J. McQuaid.

Medical Division
(includes the Employment Medical Advisory Service).
Director of Medical Services, Dr. J. T. Carter.

Responsible to Director, Resources and Planning Division:

Resources and Planning Division
(including the Accident Prevention Advisory Unit).
Director, A. B. Martin.

Public enquiry points: London (01–221 0870); Sheffield (0742–753259); Bootle (051–951 4381).

DEPARTMENT OF HEALTH
Richmond House, 79 Whitehall, SW1A 2NS
[01–210 3000]

The Department of Health was formed in July 1988 by the division of the Department of Health and Social Security into two separate departments.

The Department is responsible for the administration of the National Health Service in England and for the personal social services run by local authorities in England for children, the elderly, infirm, handicapped and other persons in need. It has functions relating to food hygiene and welfare foods. The Department is also concerned with the medical treatment of war pensioners, and is responsible for the ambulance and first aid services in emergency, under the Civil Defence Act, 1948. The Department represents the U.K. on the World Health Organization. Responsibility for the administration of the Health Services in Wales was transferred to the Welsh Office on April 1, 1969.
(For **Salaries,** *see* page 297)
Secretary of State for Health, THE RT. HON. KENNETH CLARKE, Q.C., M.P.
Private Secretary, G. J. F. Podger.
Special Adviser to the Secretary of State, J. Hill.
Minister of State, DAVID MELLOR, Q.C., M.P.
Private Secretary, Miss J. Harper.
Parliamentary Under Secretary of State, Mrs. E. Currie, M.P.
Private Secretary, Mrs. M. Kirk.
The reorganization of the divisions of the Department of Health and Social Security into the two separate departments created in late July 1988 is expected to take at least until late autumn 1988. The following details show the postings and personnel of the D.H.S.S. at June 1988. Details of Ministerial appointments at the Department of Social Security are shown on page 365.
Permanent Secretary (G1), C. W. France, C.B.
Private Secretary (G7), B. Slater.
Chief Medical Officer (G1A), Prof. Sir Donald Acheson, K.B.E.
Chief Scientist, Prof. F. W. O'Grady, C.B.E., T.D.

NATIONAL HEALTH SERVICE MANAGEMENT BOARD

Chairman, The Secretary of State.
Deputy Chairman, Sir Roy Griffiths.
Chief Executive and Director of Personnel, L. H. Peach.
Chief Medical Officer, Sir Donald Acheson, K.B.E.
Director of Operations, G. A. Hart, C.B.
Director of Planning & Information Technology, M. J. Fairey.
Director of Operations (Personnel), P. J. Wormald.
Director of Financial Management, G. I. Mills.
Director of Health Authority Finance, J. James.
Director of Health Authority Liaison, A. J. Merifield.
Director of N.H.S. Procurement, T. Critchley.
Chief Nursing Officer, Mrs A. A. B. Poole.
Property Adviser, D. N. I. Pearce.
Non Executive Director, D. Nichol.
Secretary, Mrs. L. Westbrook.
Assistant Secretary, Miss S. Harris.

SOCIAL SECURITY OPERATIONS GROUP

Deputy Secretary (G2), N. E. Clarke.

Regional Directorate

Under Secretary (G3), B. W. Taylor.
Assistant Secretaries (G5), O. C. L. Thorpe; J. F. Jones; J. R. Moyes.

Operational Strategy Directorate

Director (G3*), E. Caines.
Assistant Directors (G4), W. A. Healey; (G5), Miss S. Frankel; A. Scott.
Assistant Secretary, NUBS (G5), B. Gibb.
Assistant Secretary, LOP (G5), P. F. Dunn.

North Fylde Central Office

Controller (G5), J. M. Bankier.

Newcastle upon Tyne Central Office

Controller (G3), S. Thorpe-Tracey.
Assistant Secretaries (G5), J. Wailes; B. Heaney; A. Laurance.

NHS Information Technology and Planning Division

Director of Planning and Information Technology (G2), M. J. Fairey.
Family Practitioner Services Information Technology (G3), J. F. Shaw.
Assistant Secretaries (G5), C. M. O'Rourke; R. T. Rogers; Ms. L. Loekyear.
Senior Principals (G6), M. A. O'Flynn; Mrs. L. Masterman.

International Relations (Health)

Assistant Secretary (G5), G. C. M. Lupton.

Health Service Division

Under Secretary (G3), J. P. Cashman.
Assistant Secretaries (G5), M. A. Harris; Miss P. M. C. Winterton; J. A. Thompson.
Senior Principal (G6), L. G. T. Weir.

Community/Childrens Services Division

Under Secretary (G3), J. Halliday.
Assistant Secretaries (G5), C. E. Stone; J. H. Garlick; R. P. S. Hughes; Mrs. L. Fosh.

Priority Care Division

Under Secretary (G3), C. Graham.
Assistant Secretaries (G5), Miss M. R. Edwards; A. D. Bacon; Miss I. Nisbet.

Child Health, Maternity and Prevention Division and Aids Unit

Under Secretary (G3), N. M. Hale.
Assistant Secretaries (G5), N. Teller; W. Burroughs; R. Cunningham; A. Barton.

Procurement Directorate

Director of Procurement and Distribution (G3), T. Critchley.
Technical Director of Supplies Technology Division, (G4), (vacant).
Assistant Directors (G5), Miss M. N. Duncan; Dr. D. C. Potter; E. H. W. Luxton; B. Love; E. Sutherland.

Regional Liaison Division

Under Secretary (G3), A. Merifield.
Assistant Secretaries (G5), A. J. Davies; N. Glass; Mrs. K. Caines.

FAMILY PRACTITIONERS SERVICES AND MEDICINES

Deputy Secretary (G2), B. R. Rayner.

Division FPS1

Under Secretary (G3), J. F. Shaw.
Assistant Secretaries (G5), J. A. Parker; J. Sharpe; Mrs. P. Petrie; B. A. R. Smith.

Division IIAP

Under Secretary (G3), N. B. U. Gurney.
Assistant Secretaries (G4), R. M. Drury; (G5), J. H. Rogers; R. M. Orton; I. Jewesbury.

Division FPS2

Under Secretary (G3), J. I. Langtry.
Assistant Secretaries (G5), P. Allen; K. J. Guinness; B. A. Harrison.

Medicines Division

Under Secretary (G3), C. H. Wilson.
Assistant Secretaries (G5), D. O. Hagger; W. Robertson.

ADMINISTRATION AND FINANCE GROUP

Principal Establishments and Finance Officer (G2), J. F. Mayne, C.B.

Finance Division A

Under Secretary (Health) (G3), J. H. James.
Assistant Secretaries (G5), Ms. P. Stewart; R. K. Alder.

Finance Division B

Under Secretary (Health) (G4), M. G. Lillywhite.
Assistant Secretaries (G5), Mrs. R. Grimshaw; H. Jones; P. F. Slade; S. Lord.

Financial Management Directorate

Director of Financial Management (G2), I. Mills.
Deputy Directors (G3), A. Black; R. Spurgeon.

Finance Division C

Under Secretary (Social Security) (G3), D. V. Chislett.
Assistant Secretaries (G5), J. T. Hughes; J. R. Simpson; D. E. Carter; J. M. Wray.

Statistics and Research Division

Director of Statistics and Information Management (G3), Dr. R. Gibbs.
Chief Statisticians (G5), Miss P. W. Annesley; R. J. Scott; C. P. Hogan; J. N. Lithgow; R. Willmer; T. Orchard; G. J. O. Phillpotts.
Senior Statistician (G6), Miss A. J. Cleveland.

Economic Adviser's Office

Chief Economic Adviser (G3), C. H. Smee.
Senior Economic Advisers (G5), G. C. Fiegehen; J. W. Hurst; D. Todd.

Operational Research Service

Under Secretary (G3), C. H. Smee.
Director (G4), Dr. A. A. Holt.
Branch Heads (G6), F. M. Gayton; Dr. G. H. D. Royston; Dr. D. J. Hughes; Dr. L. D. Mayhew.

Departmental Personnel Management

Principal Establishment Officer (G3), N. L. J. Montagu.
Assistant Secretaries (G5), R. J. Tilney; P. E. Turner; I. Magee; B. K. Gilbert.

Central Management Support

Assistant Secretary (G5), R. W. D. Venning.
Senior Principals (G6), D. E. Matthews; J. Parker.

N.H.S. Superannuation Branch

Executive Director (Personnel) (G4), R. M. Drury.
Assistant Secretary (G5), J. M. Bankier.
Senior Principal (G6), D. Napier.

SOCIAL SECURITY POLICY GROUP

Deputy Secretary (G2), Mrs. A. E. Bowtell.

Social Security Division A

Under Secretary (G3), D. G. Storer.
Assistant Secretaries (G5), J. E. Knight; P. L. Adeane; Mrs. A. De Peyer.

Social Security Division B

Under Secretary (G3), R. Birch.
Assistant Secretaries (G5), J. W. White; S. H. F. Hickey; Mrs. S. P. Maunsell; Miss K. E. W. Blunt.

Social Security Division C

Under Secretary (G3), Mrs. J. M. Firth.
Assistant Secretaries (G5), Mrs. M. Evans; D. S. Fanning.
Senior Principal (G6), P. I. Blakey.

Social Security Division D

Under Secretary (G3), M. L. Whippman.
Assistant Secretaries (G5), D. Brereton; Mrs. E. A. Woods; R. Brown.
Senior Principal (G6), Mrs. C. E. Limm.

Research Management Division

Chief Scientist (G2), Prof. F. W. O'Grady, C.B.E., T.D.
Deputy Chief Scientist, Director of Research Management (G3), Dr. J. S. Metters.
Assistant Secretary (G5), D. M. Woolley.
Senior Medical Officers (G5), Dr. M. B. Dastgir; Dr. D. Rothman, O.B.E.; Dr. M. E. Smith.
Senior Principal Research Officers (G6), P. J. Hennessy; Ms. H. Canter.

Solicitor's Office

Solicitor (G2), J. St. L. Brockman, C.B.
Principal Assistant Solicitors (G3), P. K. J. Thompson; Mrs. M. A. Morgan.
Proceedings Operational Director (G4), G. E. Beaven.

MEDICAL DIVISIONS (HEALTH AND PERSONAL SOCIAL SERVICES)

Chief Medical Officer (G1A), Sir Donald Acheson, K.B.E.
Deputy Chief Medical Officers (G2), Dr. M. E. Abrams; Dr. R. M. Oliver; Dr. E. L. Harris, C.B.

Division CDPNM

Senior Principal Medical Officer (G3), Dr. P. R. Greenfield.
Principal Medical Officer (G4), Dr. J. M. Graham.
Senior Medical Officers (G5), Dr. E. Cloake; Dr. B. S. Ely; Dr. D. Ernaelsteen; Dr. P. Clarke; Dr. L. B. Hunt; Dr. W. J. Modle; Dr. S. Munday; Dr. A. Rawson; Dr. I. A. F. Lister Cheese.
Medical Officers (G6), Dr. J. G. Ablett; Dr. R. Young.
Principal Research Officer (G7), R. Wenlock.

Division MHI

Senior Principal Medical Officer (G3), Dr. J. L. Reed.
Principal Medical Officers (G4), Dr. J. Shanks; Dr. R. Jenkins.
Senior Medical Officers (G5), Dr. D. F. M. Black; Dr. P. G. Mason; Dr. L. J. F. Warnants; D. J. Brooksbank.

Division PCR

Senior Principal Medical Officer (G3), Dr. G. C. Rivett.
Principal Medical Officer (G4), Dr. R. H. Smith.
Senior Medical Officers (G5), Dr. W. G. Griffiths; Dr. W. Miller; Dr. M. F. Cuthbert; Dr. J. D. F. Bellamy.

Toxicology and Environmental Health

Senior Principal Medical Officer (G3), Dr. J. Steadman.
Principal Medical Officer (G4), Dr. G. Matthew.

Division E

Principal Medical Officer (G4), Dr. J. L. Hunt, O.B.E.
Medical Officer (G6), Dr. R. Young.

Division HPS

Senior Principal Medical Officer (G3), Dr. N. P. Halliday.
Principal Medical Officer (G4), Dr. G. Pincherle.
Senior Medical Officers (G5), Dr. M. Prophet; Dr. N. Melia; Dr. P. Bourdillon; Dr. P. Simpson.
Medical Officer (G6), Dr. J. Mettle.
Principal Scientific Officer (G7), M. R. Godfrey.

Division MPO

Senior Principal Medical Officer (G4), Dr. G. Winyard.
Senior Medical Officers (G5), Dr. J. P. Doyle; Dr. L.J. Martin; Dr. W. Thorne; Dr. G. N. Brown; Dr. D. Holt; Dr. J. Lloyd.
Medical Officer (G6), Dr. D. Macpherson.

Division MME

Senior Principal Medical Officers (G3), Dr. A. J. Isaacs.
Senior Medical Officers (G5), Dr. C. Swinson; Dr. D. McInnes; Dr. D. P. Mason; Dr. J. R. Lissamore; Dr. M. Smith.
Assistant Secretary (G5), J. C. Dobson.
Principals (G7), Mrs. V. Keating; P. W. D. Lawrence.

Division MD

Senior Principal Medical Officer (G3), Dr. G. Jones.
Principal Medical Officer (G4), Dr. D. Jefferys; Dr. W. J. Jenkins; Dr. R. D. Mann.
Senior Medical Officers (G5), Dr. P. N. Adams; Dr. G. H. Burton; Dr. T. H. Corn; Dr. K. Fowler; Dr. J. Hilton; Dr. D. Looi; Dr. A. Nath; Dr. J. A. Nicholson; Dr. J. M. Raine; Dr. L. Robinson; Dr. F. Rotblat; Dr. R. Shah; Dr. D. I. Slovick; Dr. K. A. Winship; Dr. S. Wood.
Medical Officer (G6), Dr. M. Glen-Bott.

Division IMCD

Senior Principal Medical Officer (G3), Dr. D. Walford.
Principal Medical Officer (G4), (vacant).
Senior Medical Officers (G5), Dr. J. Barnes; Dr. A. Fenton Lewis; Dr. P. A. Hyzler; Dr. H. Murrell; Dr. R. G. Penn; Dr. P. Exon; Dr. J. Berrie; Dr. G. Greenberg; Dr. D. M. Salisbury; Dr. H. Williams.
Medical Officers (G6), Dr. A. Dawson; Dr. H. Nicholas.
Environmental Health Officers, M. Jacob; E. W. Kingcott.

Division SEB

Senior Principal Medical Officer (G3), (vacant).
Chief Scientific Officer, Dr. F. P. Woodford.
Principal Medical Officer (G4), Dr. H. Pickles.
Senior Medical Officers (G5), Dr. P. R. Dendy; Dr. P. M. Furnell; Dr. S. P. Vahl; Dr. H. Sutton; Dr. S. Lader.
Medical Officer (G6), Dr. J. Chodera.

Medical Division (Social Security)

Chief Medical Adviser (G3), Dr. W. R. O. Eggington.
Principal Medical Officers, Dr. K. A. Cameron; Dr. P. Castaldi; T. J. G. Phillips; Dr. D. R. Findlay.

Dental Division

Chief Dental Officer, Dr. M. C. Downer.
Deputy Chief Dental Officer, D. R. Whittington.
Senior Dental Officers, W. G. Everett; Dr. A. S. Atkinson; R. B. Mouatt; C. Howard; G. A. Wells.

Nursing Division

Chief Nursing Officer, Mrs. A. A. B. Poole ... £38,480
Deputy Chief Nursing Officer, Miss S. P. C. Wright-Warren.
Principal Nursing Officers, M. A. Clark; Mrs. D. A. Patey; J. Tait; Mrs. A. Dawar; Miss C. Clifford.

Social Services Inspectorate

Chief Inspector (G2), W. B. Utting.
Deputy Chief Inspectors (G4), J. H. Barnes; Ms. M. Stuart.
Assistant Chief Inspectors (HQ), Miss J. Baraclough; J. Cypher; Mrs. P. K. Hall; J. G. Smith; Mrs. W. Rose.
Assistant Chief Inspectors (Regions), S. Allard; J. K. Corcoran; D. Gilroy; B. D. Harrison; Miss C. M. Hey; D. G. Lambert; Miss S. Markham; B. E. Stimpson; Miss A. Taylor .... £21,070–£26,409

Pharmaceutical Division

Chief Pharmaceutical Officer, Dr. B. A. Wills £33,080
Deputy Chief Pharmaceutical Officers (G5), B. H. Hartley; Dr. P. R. Noyce; Dr. A. R. Rogers; A. G. Stewart.
Superintending Pharmaceutical Officers (G6), K. J. Ayling; A. C. Cartwright; Miss D. Hepburn; Dr. R. C. Hutton; Dr. B. R. Matthews; J. R. V. Merrills; Dr. J. Purves; Miss M. L. Rabouhans; S. L. Turner.

Hotel and Dietetic Services Branch

Chief Officer, D. G. Thomson.
Deputy Chief Officer, Hotel and Dietetic Services (G7), R. Brown.
Deputy Chief Officer, Domestic Services (G7), Miss I. D. Oliver.

Information Division

Director of Information (G4), Miss R. Christopherson.
Deputy Directors (G6), C. P. Wilson (*news*); G. Meredith (*publicity*).

HEALTH BUILDING DIRECTORATE

Director of Health Building (G3), M. A. Meager.

HBD1—NHS Building Procurement

Assistant Director (G5) and Chief Surveyor, D. A. Butler.
Superintending Architect (G6), B. Hitchcox.
Superintending Engineer (G6), R. S. Body.
Superintending Surveyor (G6), R. W. Davis.

HBD2—NHS Building Procurement

Assistant Director (G5), G. G. Mayers.
Superintending Architects (G6), A. J. Noakes; W. R. Hyslop.
Superintending Engineer (G6), G. D. Fisher.

HBD3—Nucleus Development

Assistant Director (G5) and Chief Architect, P. L. Ward.
Superintending Architect (G6), (vacant).
Superintending Engineer (G6), J. M. Singh.
Superintending Surveyors (G6), D. A. Eastwood; K. J. I. McSweeney.

HBD4—Technology and Safety

Assistant Director (G5) and Chief Engineer, I. E. G. Mahon.
Superintending Engineers (G6), B. C. Oliver; L. W. Arrowsmith.
Superintending Surveyor (G6), D. W. Luscombe.

HBD5—Administrative Support

Assistant Secretary (G5), P. R. Gant.
Superintending Engineer (G6), R. J. Tuthill.

ESTATE AND PROPERTY MANAGEMENT DIRECTORATE

Property Adviser to the NHS Management Board (G2), D. N. I. Pearce.

Policy Branch

Assistant Secretary (G5), T. Whiteley.
Superintending Estate Surveyor (G6), J. C. Ellis.
Superintending Engineer (G6), T. Wagstaff.

Performance Branch

Assistant Director (G5), C. Davies.
Superintending Estate Surveyor (G6), M. Bridgeford (*temp.*).

REGIONAL ORGANIZATION
Scotland

Argyle House, 3 Lady Lawson Street, Edinburgh
Controller (G4), R. Walton.

England and Wales

North Eastern, Government Buildings, Lawnswood, Leeds. *Regional Controller (G5)*, P. Nelmes.
London North, Olympic House, Olympic Way, Wembley, Middx. *Regional Controller*, Mrs. M. A. Robinson (*Middx.*).
London South, Sutherland House, 29–37 Brighton Road, Sutton, Surrey and Grosvenor House, Basing View, Basingstoke, Hants. *Regional Controller*, M. F. Archer.
Wales and South Western, Gabalfa, Cardiff. *Regional Controller*, G. Griffiths.
Midlands, Five Ways Tower, Frederick Road, Edgbaston, Birmingham. *Regional Controller*, J. T. Green.
North Western, St. Martin's House, Stanley Precinct, Bootle, Merseyside. *Regional Controller*, J. B. Griffin.

INDUSTRIAL INJURIES ADVISORY COUNCIL
Friars House, 157–168 Blackfriars Road,
SE1 8EU
[01–703 6380]

The Industrial Injuries Advisory Council is a statutory body under the Social Security Act, 1975, which considers and advises the Secretary of State for Social Services on Regulations and other questions relating to industrial injuries benefits or their administration.
Chairman, Prof. J. M. Harrington.
Members, G. Applebey; Miss J. C. Brown; Prof. M. J. Cinnamond; Dr. D. Coggon; Dr. R. J. Donaldson, O.B.E.; Dr. G. A. Hard; P. R. A. Jacques; Dr. C. P. Juniper; G. Lloyd, C.B.E.; T. W. Mawer; Dr. A. J. Newman Taylor; Mrs. M. Prosser; Dr. E. Roman; Dr. A. Sinclair; Miss B. Swiadkowska; G. M. Thompson.
Secretary, A. L. Perl.

NATIONAL INSURANCE
JOINT AUTHORITY
151 Great Titchfield Street, W1P 8AD
[01–636 1696]

The Authority's function is to co-ordinate the operation of social security legislation in Great Britain and Northern Ireland, including the necessary financial adjustments between the two National Insurance Funds.
Members, The Secretary of State for Social Services; the Head of the Department of Health and Social Services for Northern Ireland.
Secretary, Miss K. E. W. Blunt.

SOCIAL SECURITY—OFFICE OF THE
CHIEF ADJUDICATION OFFICER
Cumberland House,
15/17 Cumberland Place, Southampton SO9 2DD
[0703–330066]

The Chief Adjudication Officer is an independent authority under the Social Security Act, 1975 (as amended) appointed by the Secretary of State for Social Services to give advice to adjudication officers (who make decisions of first instance on all claims for Social Security cash benefits), to keep under review the operation of the system of adjudication and to report annually to the Secretary of State on adjudication standards. The Office also enters written observations on all appeals made to the Social Security Commissioners.
Chief Adjudication Officer, M. E. H. Platt.

SOCIAL SECURITY ADVISORY COMMITTEE
New Court, Carey Street, WC2A 2LS
[01–831 6111]

The Social Security Advisory Committee (SSAC) was established by the Social Security Act 1980 to advise the Secretary of State for Social Services and the Department of Health and Social Services for Northern Ireland on all Social Security matters except those relating to benefits for industrial injuries and diseases and occupational pensions. The Social Security Housing Benefit Act 1982 added housing benefit to the Committee's responsibilities.
Chairman, P. M. Barclay, C.B.E.
Members, Prof. J. Cheetham; Mrs. E. A. Denholm; Dr. R. J. Donaldson, O.B.E.; Mrs. S. Flather; Rev. G. H. Good, O.B.E.; H. Hodge; J. Hughes; P. Jacques; P. F. Naish; Hon. Mrs. R. H. P. Price; Dr. A. V. Stokes, O.B.E.; Prof. Olive Stevenson; R. G. Wendt.
Secretary, N. Cockett.

NATIONAL HEALTH SERVICE
Regional Health Authorities

The Chairmen, and members of Regional Health Authorities are appointed by the Secretary of State for Social Services.

Northern, Benfield Road, Walker Gate, Newcastle upon Tyne. *Chairman*, Prof. Sir Bernard Tomlinson, C.B.E., M.D. *Regional General Manager*, D. Hague.
Yorkshire, Park Parade, Harrogate. *Chairman*, B. Askew. *Regional General Manager*, A. Foster.
Trent, Fulwood House, Old Fulwood Road, Sheffield. *Chairman*, Sir Michael Carlisle. *Regional General Manager*, B. Edwards, C.B.E.
East Anglia, Union Lane, Chesterton, Cambridge. *Chairman*, C. Walker. *Regional General Manager*, A. Liddell.
North East Thames, 40 Eastbourne Terrace, W2. *Chairman*, D. Berriman. *Regional General Manager*, T. Hunt.

North West Thames, 40 Eastbourne Terrace, W2. *Chairman*, W. Doughty. *Regional General Manager*, D. J. Kenny.
South East Thames, Thrift House, Collington Avenue, Bexhill-on-Sea, E. Sussex. *Chairman*, Sir Peter Baldwin, K.C.B. *Regional General Manager*, P. A. Griffiths.
South West Thames, 40 Eastbourne Terrace, W2. *Chairman*, Sir Antony Driver. *Regional General Manager*, A. J. Kember.
Wessex, Highcroft, Romsey Road, Winchester, Hants. *Chairman*, Prof. Sir Bryan Thwaites, PH.D. *Regional General Manager*, J. Hoare.
Oxford, Old Road, Headington, Oxford. *Chairman*, Sir Gordon Roberts, C.B.E. *Regional General Manager*, R. M. Nicolls.
South Western, King Square House, 26–27 King Square, Bristol. *Chairman*, Sir Vernon Seccombe. *Regional General Manager*, Miss C. E. Hawkins.
West Midlands, Arthur Thompson House, 146–150 Hagley Road, Birmingham. *Chairman*, Sir James Ackers. *Regional General Manager*, K. F. Bales.
Mersey, Hamilton House, 24 Pall Mall, Liverpool. *Chairman*, Sir Donald Wilson. *Regional General Manager*, D. Nichol.
North Western, Gateway House, Piccadilly South, Manchester. *Chairman*, Sir John Page, O.B.E. *Regional General Manager*, D. Allison.

Special Health Authorities

Health Education Authority, 78 New Oxford Street, WC1A 1AH. *Chairman*, Sir Brian Bailey, O.B.E.; *Chief Executive*, Dr. Spencer Hagard.
Disablement Services Authority, 14 Russell Square, WC1. *Chairman*, Lord Holdermess, P.C.; *Chief Executive*, M. G. Jeremiah.

The Special Hospitals Service is provided by four hospitals: Rampton; Broadmoor; Moss Side; and Park Lane. The Boards of these hospitals are Special Health Authorities. (There is a single Board for Moss Side and Park Lane). Chairmen and members are appointed by the Secretary of State for Social Services.

Rampton Hospital, Retford, Notts. *Chairman*, Dr. D. E. Edmond. *Administrator*, D. Atha.
Broadmoor Hospital, Crowthorne, Berks. *Chairman*, Sir David Brown, K.C.B. *Administrator*, J. R. Roberts.
Moss Side and Park Lane Hospitals, Maghull, Liverpool. *Chairman*, R. F. McConnell. *Administrator*, C. P. Tattersall.

SCOTTISH HOME AND HEALTH
DEPARTMENT
and
NATIONAL HEALTH SERVICE, SCOTLAND
See Scottish Office

NATIONAL HERITAGE MEMORIAL FUND
10 St James's Street, SW1A 1EF
[01–930 0963]

The National Heritage Memorial Fund was established in 1980 as an independent body, and is intended as a memorial to those who have died for the U.K. The Fund is empowered, by the National Heritage Act 1980, to give financial assistance towards the cost of acquiring, maintaining or preserving land, buildings, works of art and other objects of outstanding interest which are also of importance to the national heritage. The Fund is administered by up to eleven Trustees, appointed by the Prime Minister.
The Fund's major sources of money are the Department of the Environment and the Office of Arts and Libraries, each of which gives annual

grants. In its first eight years, the Fund spent £90 million in carrying out its responsibilities.

Trustees

The Lord Charteris of Amisfield (*Chairman*); The Marquess of Anglesey; Sir Nicholas Goodison; Prof. F. G. T. Holliday; Sir Martin Jacomb; C. Kinahan; Sir Oliver Millar, G.C.V.O., F.B.A.; Prof. B. R. Morris; Sir Norman Macfarlane; M. McCrum; Cdr. L. M. M. Saunders Watson.
Director, O. B. Harris.

HIGHLANDS AND ISLANDS DEVELOPMENT BOARD
Bridge House, 27 Bank Street,
Inverness IV1 1QR
[0463–234171]

The Board, a grant-aided body, responsible to the Secretary of State for Scotland, has two broad objectives. These are (1) to assist the people of the Highlands and Islands to improve their economic and social conditions; (2) to enable the Highlands and Islands to play a more effective part in the economic and social development of the nation. To this end the Board will concert, promote, assist or undertake measures for economic and social development.
Chairman, R. Cowan.
Secretary, J. A. MacAskill.

HISTORIC BUILDINGS AND MONUMENTS COMMISSION FOR ENGLAND
Fortress House,
23 Savile Row, W1X 2HE
[01–734 6010]

Under the National Heritage Act, 1983, the duties of the Commission are: (i) to secure the preservation of ancient monuments and historic buildings; (ii) to promote the preservation and enhancement of conservation areas; (iii) to promote the public's enjoyment of, and advance their knowledge of, ancient monuments and historic buildings and their preservation. The Commission has advisory committees on historic buildings, ancient monuments, historic areas, and London.
Chairman, The Lord Montagu of Beaulieu.
Deputy Chairman, H.R.H. The Duke of Gloucester, G.C.V.O.
Commissioners, Prof. R. Cramp; Prof. B. Cunliffe; A. H. Emery; D. W. Insall; S. D. Jenkins; Sir George Moseley; J. Newman; The Earl of Shelburne; R. L. Vigars.
Chief Executive, P. W. Rumble, C.B.

HISTORIC BUILDINGS COUNCIL FOR WALES
Brunel House, 2 Fitzalan Road,
Cardiff CF2 1UY
[0222–465511]

Chairman, The Marquess of Anglesey, F.S.A.
Members, W. Lindsay Evans; Prof. J. Eynon, F.R.I.B.A., F.S.A.; The Earl Lloyd George of Dwyfor; T. Lloyd; Prof. G. Williams, C.B.E., D.Litt., F.S.A.; R. Haslam.
Secretary, S. R. Williams.

HISTORIC BUILDINGS COUNCIL FOR SCOTLAND
20 Brandon Street, Edinburgh EH3 5RA
[031–556 8400]

Chairman, The Marquess of Bute.
Members, R. Clow; Prof. J. Dunbar-Nasmith, C.B.E.; M. Ellington; I. Hutchison, O.B.E.; The Hon. Lord Jauncey; K. Martin; K. Newis, C.B., C.V.O.; Rev. K. Nugent, S.J.; Mrs. M. Richards; H. F. Smith, M.B.E.
Secretary, I. G. Dewar.

ROYAL COMMISSION ON THE HISTORICAL MONUMENTS OF ENGLAND
Fortress House, 23 Savile Row, W1X 2JQ
[01–734 9847]

The Royal Commission on the Historical Monuments of England was established in 1908. The Royal Commission is the national body charged with the recording and analysing of ancient and historical monuments and buildings. It compiles, preserves and makes publicly available the national archive of such material, which is housed in the National Monuments Record.
Chairman, (vacant).
Commissioners, Prof. M. W. Beresford, F.B.A.; Prof. R. Bradley, F.S.A.; R. A. Buchanan, Ph.D.; Prof. J. D. Evans, Ph.D., Litt.D, F.B.A., F.S.A.; D. J. Keene, Ph.D.; Prof. G. H. Martin, C.B.E., D.Phil., F.S.A.; Prof. G. I. Meirion-Jones, Ph.D., F.S.A.; Prof. J. K. Downes, Ph.D., F.S.A.; Prof. A. C. Thomas, D.Litt., F.S.A.; Prof. M. Biddle, F.B.A., F.S.A.; Prof. P. E. Lasko, C.B.E., F.B.A., F.S.A.; Prof. M. Todd, F.S.A.; Mrs. B. K. Cherry, F.S.A.; R. D. H. Gem, Ph.D., F.S.A.
Secretary, T. G. Hassall, F.S.A.

ROYAL COMMISSION ON ANCIENT AND HISTORICAL MONUMENTS IN WALES
Edleston House, Queens Road,
Aberystwyth SY23 2HP
[Aberystwyth: 4381]

The Commission was appointed in 1908 to make an inventory of the ancient and historical monuments in Wales and Monmouthshire. The Commission also includes the National Monuments Record for Wales.
Chairman, Prof. G. Williams C.B.E., F.B.A., F.S.A.
Commissioners, Prof. L. Alcock, F.S.A.; M. R. Apted, Ph.D., F.S.A.; G. C. Boon, F.S.A.; R. W. Brunskill, Ph.D.; Prof. D. Ellis Evans, D.Phil., F.B.A.; R. M. Haslam, F.S.A.; J. G. Jenkins, D.SC., F.S.A.; J. B. Smith; G. J. Wainwright, Ph.D., F.S.A.; Prof. J. G. Williams.
Secretary, P. Smith, F.S.A.

ROYAL COMMISSION ON ANCIENT AND HISTORICAL MONUMENTS OF SCOTLAND
54 Melville Street, Edinburgh EH3 7HF
[031–225 5994]

The Commission was appointed in 1908 to make an inventory of the ancient and historical monuments of Scotland and to specify those that seem most worthy of preservation. The Commission also includes the National Monuments Record of Scotland.
Chairman, The Earl of Crawford and Balcarres, P.C.
Commissioners, Prof. A. A. M. Duncan, F.B.A., F.R.S.E.; Prof. J. D. Dunbar-Nasmith, C.B.E., F.R.I.B.A.; Prof. Rosemary Cramp, C.B.E., F.S.A.; H. M. Colvin, C.V.O., C.B.E., F.B.A.; Prof. L. Alcock, F.S.A., F.R.S.E.; Prof. G. Jobey, D.S.O., F.S.A; Mrs. P. E. Durham; Prof. T. C. Smout, Ph.D.; The Hon. Lord Cullen.
Secretary, J. G. Dunbar, F.S.A.

ANCIENT MONUMENTS BOARD FOR WALES
Brunel House, 2 Fitzalan Road, Cardiff CF2 1UY
[0222–465511]

Chairman, Prof. G. Williams, C.B.E., F.B.A., F.S.A.
Members, G. C. Boon, F.S.A.; R. B. Heaton, F.R.I.B.A.; Prof. R. R. Davies, D.Phil.; R. G. Keen; Mrs. F. Lynch-Llewellyn, F.S.A.; D. Moore, R.D., F.S.A.; P. Smith, F.S.A.
Secretary, I. Gibson.

ANCIENT MONUMENTS BOARD FOR SCOTLAND
20 Brandon Street, Edinburgh EH3 5RA
[031 244 3076]

Chairman, M. Magnusson, F.R.S.E., F.S.A.scot.
Members, J. G. Dunbar, F.S.A., F.S.A.scot.; A. Fenton, C.B.E., D.Litt., F.S.A., F.S.A.scot.; H. F. Smith, M.B.E.; The Lady Grimond; Prof. L. Alcock, F.S.A., F.R.S.E., F.S.A.scot.; J. Simpson, F.S.A.scot.; Sir Jamie Stormonth Darling, C.B.E., M.C., T.D., W.S.; Prof. J. J. Wilkes, Ph.D., F.S.A., F.S.A.scot.; Prof. E. C. Fernie, F.S.A., F.S.A.scot.; Mrs. E. W. Proudfoot, F.S.A., F.S.A.scot.; Miss R. Fothergill, F.S.A.scot.
Secretary, J. C. Judson.

HOME-GROWN CEREALS AUTHORITY
Hamlyn House, Highgate Hill, N19 5PR

Constituted under the Cereals Marketing Act, 1965, the Authority consists of 9 members representing U.K. cereal growers, 9 representing dealers in, or processors of, grain and 3 independent members. The purpose of the Authority is to improve the production and marketing of U.K. grain. The Authority also acts as the agent of the Intervention Board for Agricultural Produce in respect of intervention buying, storage and disposal of cereals and oilseed rape within the U.K. under the Common Agricultural Policy and for certain other aspects of the E.C. arrangements for cereals in the U.K.
Chairman, A. Laing, C.B.E.
General Manager, C. J. Ames.

British Cereal Exports
Chairman, R. J. Cherrington.
Adviser, J. B. Rose.

HOME OFFICE
50 Queen Anne's Gate, SW1H 9AT
[01–273 3000]

The Home Office deals with those internal affairs in England and Wales which have not been assigned to other Government Departments. The Home Secretary is particularly concerned with the administration of justice; criminal law; the treatment of offenders including probation and the prison service; the police; immigration and nationality; passport policy matters; community relations; certain public safety matters; fire and civil defence services and also with broad questions of national broadcasting policy. He personally is the link between The Queen and the public and exercises certain powers on her behalf including that of the Royal Pardon.

Other subjects dealt with include electoral arrangements; addresses and petitions to The Queen; ceremonial and formal business connected with honours; requests for extradition of criminals; scrutiny of local authority byelaws; grant of licences for scientific experiments on animals; cremations, burials and exhumations; firearms; dangerous drugs and poisons, general policy on laws relating to shops, liquor licensing, gaming and lotteries, charitable collections and marriage; theatre and cinema licensing; co-ordination of government action in relation to the voluntary social services; and sex discrimination and race relations policy.

The Home Secretary is also the link between the U.K. Government and the governments of the Channel Islands and the Isle of Man.

(For **Salaries,** *see* page 297)

H.M. Chief Inspector of Constabulary £48,154
H.M. Inspectors of Constabulary £43,539

Secretary of State for the Home Department, THE RT. HON. DOUGLAS HURD, C.B.E., M.P.
Principal Private Secretary (G5), P. C. J. Mawer.
Private Secretaries, Miss C. Bannister; N. C. Sanderson.
Parliamentary Private Secretary, T. Yeo, M.P.
Parliamentary Clerk, J. Gilbert.
Ministers of State, THE RT. HON. THE EARL FERRERS; TIMOTHY RENTON, M.P.; JOHN PATTEN, M.P.
Parliamentary Under Secretary of State, The Hon. Douglas Hogg, M.P.
Parliamentary Private Secretaries:
To Lord Ferrers and Mr. Patten, H. Malins, M.P.
To Mr. Renton and Mr. Hogg, M. Brandon-Bravo, M.P.
Permanent Under Secretary of State (G1), Sir Clive Whitmore, G.C.B., C.V.O.
Private Secretary, R. G. Yates.
Chief Medical Officer (at Department of Health), Prof. Sir Donald Acheson, K.B.E.

Legal Adviser's Branch
Legal Adviser (G2), (vacant).
Principal Assistant Legal Advisers (G3), D. J. Bentley; A. H. Hammond.
Assistant Legal Advisers, R. J. Clayton; Miss P. Edwards; Mrs. S. A. Evans; D. Seymour; A. W. D. Wilson.
Senior Principal Legal Assistants, J. O'Meara; C. M. L. Osborne.

CRIMINAL AND STATISTICS DEPARTMENTS
Deputy Under Secretary (G2), D. E. R. Faulkner, C.B.

Criminal Policy Department
Assistant Under Secretary of State (G3), W. J. Bohan, C.B.
Heads of Divisions (G5), D. M. Ackland; R. J. Baxter; P. C. Edwards; W. R. Fittall; Miss J. M. Goose; N. R. Varney.
Principals (G7), N. Benger; T. K. Cobley; A. Cogbill; Miss K. Collins; R. G. W. Cook; F. H. Eggleston; R. E. Hawkes; Mrs. R. M. Mitev; T. C. Morris; A. Pickersgill; J. M. Potts; Miss J. B. Rumble; P. A. Stanton; G. Sutton; G. L. Thomas; R. J. Weatherill; Mrs. V. M. Wilsdon; R. B. Woodland.
Chief Inspector, Drugs Branch (G6), P. G. Spurgeon.

Research and Planning Unit
Head of Unit (G5), Mrs. M. Tuck.
Grade 6, J. A. Ditchfield; R. Tarling; G. R. Walmsley.
Principals (G7), Dr. P. J. Ekblom; T. J. Hope; Mrs. P. Mayhew; Ms. P. M. Morgan; Miss J. W. Mott; Dr. G. I. U. Mair; J. F. Mcleod; A. D. Moxon; W. E. Saulsbury; Dr. L. J. F. Smith; F. P. E. Southgate; Ms. J. Vennard.

Statistical Department
Assistant Under Secretary of State (G3), Miss R. J. Maurice.
Chief Statisticians (G5), C. G. Lewis; P. W. Ward.
Statisticians (G7), Ms. A. Barber; G. G. Barclay; T. Benn; Dr. A. V. Bishop; L. Davidoff; H. P. Redway; Mrs. P. Dowdeswell; P. F. Collier; B. J. Derry; Mrs. R. Passmore; P. H. Atkinson; Z. J. Frosztega; K. M. Jackson; Ms. C. D. Morgan; Mrs. P. A. Penneck; P. E. Ramell; R. M. Taylor; C. F. Woolf.

Criminal Justice and Constitutional Department

Assistant Under Secretary of State (G3), M. E. Head.
Heads of Divisions (G5), S. S. Bampton; G. K. Sandiford; Miss P. C. Drew.
Principals (G7), Miss M. V. A. Allibone; R. M. Bradley; M. P. Cook; M. Copley; J. L. Gilhespy; M. J. Gillespie; Miss G. M. Griffith; J. M. Hough; A. J. Lewis; A. D. MacFarlane; Miss S. R. Muir; Mrs. E. A. Sandars; C. P. Stevens; J. Wake.
Chief Inspector of Probation (G4), C. H. Thomas, O.B.E.
Assistant Chief Inspectors of Probation (G6), R. A. Betteridge; D. F. Duchemin, T.D.

Animals (Scientific Procedure) Inspectorate

Chief Inspector, Dr. R. W. Watt.
Superintending Inspectors, C. B. Hart; Dr. W. D. Tavernor.

POLICE DEPARTMENT

Deputy Under Secretary (G2), J. A. Chilcot.

Police Department

Assistant Under Secretaries of State (G3), G. L. Angel; S. G. Norris; G. J. Wasserman.
Heads of Divisions (G5), M. J. Addison; Mrs. P. G. W. Catto; Mrs. E. I. France; J. A. Ingram; E. Soden; F. J. Warne.
Senior Principals (G6), Dr. H. Goldman; K. H. Heal, J. W. Cane.
Principals (G7), C. E. Birt; Mrs. F. Clarkson; T. P. R. Crompton; P. R. Curwen; S. W. Davidson; D. R. Dewick; J. C. Dilling; C. M. Dolphin; G. E. Dunkley; N. F. M. Home; C. C. R. Hudson; L. T. Hughes; Dr. G. K. Laycock; K. Mackenzie; Miss E. B. Moody; J. F. Nicholson; A. Norbury; Miss P. Ransford; A. C. Sinfield; R. E. Smith; P. R. C. Storr; K. D. Sutton; A. Townsend; P. F. Vallance; S. C. Wells; A. Wolfenden; Miss M. S. Wooldridge; R. C. Yeates.

Scientific Research and Development Branch
Horseferry House,
Dean Ryle Street, S.W.1
[01–211 3000]

Director (G5), A. N. Rapsey.
Deputy Directors (G6), T. R. Mann; Dr. D. M. S. Peace; Dr. J. R. Stealey; Dr. G. Turnbull; Dr. P. A. Young.
Principal Scientific Officers (G7), C. J. Aldridge; Dr. B. J. Blain; E. C. Brown; Dr. G. A. Carr-Hill; R. H. Doney; Dr. J. A. Harwood; T. Kent; Dr. S. R. Lewis; D. J. Meakin; Mrs. M. B. Manolias; D. D. O'Brien; R. Oliver; C. D. Payne; Dr. F. Preston; Dr. G. E. Scott; R. C. Stephen; Dr. I. P. Williamson.

Headquarters Forensic Science Service
Horseferry House
Dean Ryle Street, S.W.1.
[01–211 3000]

Director General (G4), (vacant).
Chief Forensic Scientist (G5), Dr. A. Scaplehorn.
Assistant to Director General (G6), Dr. D. G. Sanger.
Principals (G7), J. Glaze; D. S. Loxley.

Police National Computer Organization
Horseferry House,
Dean Ryle Street, S.W.1
[01–211 3000]

Technical Development Director (G5), A. Holt.
Deputy Assistant Commissioner, J. F. Newing, Q.P.M.
Senior Principals (G6), G. M. Cole; D. W. Punshon.
Principals (G7), E. L. Brannan; Mrs. P. Cocks; G. T. Coulthard; D. H. Faulks; P. D. Hill-Jones; A. F. G. Hitchman; D. C. Moulton; D. A. Quamby; B. G. Stocking; R. H. Watt; M. H. Williams; T. W. Wrighton.

Directorate of Telecommunications
Horseferry House,
Dean Ryle Street, S.W.1
[01–211 3000]

Director of Telecommunications (G5), G. E. Guy.
Deputy Directors (G6), I. Aitken; N. K. Finlayson; D. A. Hendon; R. M. Hughes.
Head of Purchasing Supply and Contract Unit, M. P. Gore.
Principals (G7), C. J. Barron; R. C. Eaton; R. Harry; W. Hogg; A. Hulme; A. N. Kent; J. Leary; D. Mullarky; J. L. Mumford; M. A. Parker; T. R. Peters; M. J. Phillips; D. A. Pooley; A. A. Sipson; K. Staves; D. C. J. Theobald; P. M. Tomlinson.

H.M. Inspectorate of Constabulary

H.M. Chief Inspector of Constabulary, Sir Richard Barratt, C.B.E., Q.P.M.
H.M. Inspectors, J. H. Brownlow, C.B.E., Q.P.M.; D. Elliott, Q.P.M.; C. McLachlan, C.B.E., Q.P.M.; Sir Philip Myers, O.B.E., Q.P.M.; J. Woodcock, C.B.E., Q.P.M.

Police Staff College
Bramshill House, Basingstoke, Hampshire
RG27 0JW
[Hartley Wintney 2931]

Commandant, R. S. Bunyard, C.B.E., Q.P.M.
Deputy Commandant and Director of Courses, D. P. Griffiths.
Secretary (G7), K. J. Sheehan.

BROADCASTING, EQUAL OPPORTUNITIES, IMMIGRATION AND NATIONALITY DEPARTMENTS

Deputy Under Secretary (G2), W. N. Hyde.

Broadcasting and Miscellaneous Department

Assistant Under Secretary of State (G3), Q. J. Thomas.
Heads of Divisions (G5), E. A. Grant; N. M. Johnson; L. P. Wright.
Principals (G7), D. A. L. Cooke; J. P. Emery; N. M. McLean; C. R. Miller; Mrs. P. W. Nice; J. Sibson; R. B. Snow.

Equal Opportunities and General Department

Assistant Under Secretary of State (G3), R. J. Fries.
Heads of Divisions (G5), Mrs. P. A. Lee, C.B.E.; G. P. Pratt.
Principals (G7), J. P. Casey; A. Harnett; M. J. I. Hill; P. J. Honour; Mrs. G. Moody; Mrs. M. E. Moxon; D. J. Rigby.

Voluntary Services Unit

Assistant Secretary (G5), Mrs. B. H. Fair.
Senior Principal (G6), B. Gange.
Principals (G7), A. C. Cook; G. H. Marriage.

Immigration and Nationality Department
Lunar House, 40 Wellesley Road, Croydon, Surrey,
CR9 2BY
[01–686 0688/686 3441]

Assistant Under Secretaries of State (G3), R. M. Morris; T. C. Platt.
Heads of Divisions (G5), J. I. Chisholm; T. J. Flesher; R. A. Harrington; T. G. Kavanagh; N. R. Varney.
Senior Principal (G6), D. M. McQueen.
Principals (G7), Mrs. H. Bayne; B. D. Bishop; M. Boyle; W. F. Bryant; J. G. Burgess; J. G. Daley; P. Durbin; Mrs. C. Kellas; Mrs. J. M. Kidd; Mrs. E. C. L. Pallett; D. A. Peters; S. Spence; R. S. Weekes; P. N. Wrench.

Immigration Service

Chief Inspector (*G4*), P. Tompkins.
Deputy Chief Inspectors (*G6*), G. Boiling; A. A. Holton; D. J. McDonough.
Assistant Chief Inspectors (*G7*), J. M. Durose; T. Farrage; V. Hogg; J. D. Smith.

Passport Department
Clive House, Petty France, SW1H 9HD
[01–271 3000]

Heads of Divisions (*G5*), A. Holmes, c.b.e.; E. B. Nicholls.
Deputy Head of Division (*G6*), W. R. Mann.
Principals (*G7*), Miss M. A. N. Ashton; R. M. Bowley; R. I. Henderson; T. Lonsdale.

PRISON SERVICE
Cleland House, Page Street, SW1P 4LN
[01–211 3000]

Non-Civil Service grade salaries

H. M. Chief Inspector of Prisons £41,000
Prison Service Grade 1 (PSI) £31,542
Prison Service Grade 2 (PSII) £28,979
Prison Service Grade 3 (PSIII) £25,541
Prison Service Grade 4 (PSIV) ..... £20,329–£21,893

Director-General of the Prison Service (*G2*), C. J. Train, c.b.
Deputy Director-General of the Prison Service (*G3*), B. A. Emes.

Prisons Department

Assistant Under Secretaries of State (Directors) (*G3*), J. G. Pilling (*Personnel and Finance*); W. J. A. Innes (*Operational Policy*); Miss M. A. Clayton (*Directorate of Services*); Dr. J. L. Kilgour, c.b. (*Medical Services*).
Non-Executive Members, Miss P. Downs; C. J. Ganderton.
Heads of Divisions (*G5*), S. W. Boys-Smith; B. O. Bubbear; B. M. Caffarey; Mrs. V. V. R. Harris; R. J. D. Hazell; W. A. Jeffrey; J. Lynch; Miss J. McNaughton; A. J. Pearson; Miss C. J. Stewart; Miss J. Thompson.
Deputy Director of Prison Medical Services (*G4*), Dr. P. J. Hynes.
Principal Medical Officers (*G4*), Dr. P. Arrowsmith; N. Glendinning; Dr. J. M. Sinclair; Dr. R. J. Wool.
Senior Principals (*G6*), D. R. Birleson; D. A. Brown; P. Cook; M. Ireson; L. A. Scudder, o.b.e. Miss A. Smith.
Governors (*PSI*), G. D. Dadds; J. E. Simmons; W. R. Booth.
Principals (*G7*), W. M. Black; Miss M. E. Bowden; M. J. Brown; G. Boiling, m.b.e.; A. D. Burgess; B. Charlson; N. M. Clowes; Mrs. M. A. Cooper; A. D. Cory; Mrs. C. Crawford; H. M. C. Crudge; M. J. Davies; P. Done; J. Duke-Evans; R. W. G. Dyce; R. Eagle; D. H. Gannon; Miss L. F. Gill; N. F. M. Home; J. C. Imber; M. W. Jarvis; Mrs. S. Jarvis; F. N. Jasper; B. Johnson; Miss B. Latimer; Miss D. Loudon; M. J. Murphy; Mrs. S. Murray; K. R. North; J. S. Nottingham; K. O'Sullivan; Ms. C. Pelham; P. G. V. Pike; J. Plumridge; J. R. K. de Quidt; M. J. A. Prowse; Miss G. Romney; P. M. Scott; J. Simpson; A. G. Thomson; R. J. Weatherill; H. S. Webber; Miss S. Weinel; W. F. Whiting; Miss P. Whitson; T. J. Wilson; D. I. M. Wright; E. Wright; R. A. Wright.
Governors (*PSII*), B. G. Chaplin; M. R. J. Gander; D. G. Longley; B. McLuckie; J. Marriott; M. Mogg; S. C. A. Prior; A. K. Rawson; J. Shulman.
Prison Service Chaplaincy (*G6*), Ven. K. S. Pound.
Director of Psychological Services, P. H. Shapland.

Chief Education Officer, I. G. Benson.
Chief Physical Education Officer (*G6*), M. W. Denton.
Governors (*PSII*), B. Clark; R. Daly; Miss M. Gorman; D. V. Hickson; F. Masserick; W. R. Quirie; R. J. Talbot; M. F. V. Watson-Jackson; C. P. Welsh; D. Wilson.

Directorate of Works
Abell House, John Islip Street, SW1P 4LH
[01–211 3000]

Chief Architect and Director of Works (*G4*), W. L. Sparks.
Superintending Architects (*G6*), J. H. Cooper; A. W. Gillman; R. W. T. Haines; D. W. Harris; S. Mahraj.
Principal Professional and Technology Officers (*G7*), O. P. Astaniotis; P. J. Attwater; D. G. Baines; G. F. Burgess; J. K. Chamberlain; B. D. Charlson; G. W. Chrisp; C. R. Cope; H. J. Davies; J. A. Doohan; C. F. Drewitt; M. C. Hayes; G. E. Hickey; J. V. R. Hillyer; F. Home; M. J. Ireson; J. F. Keeler; R. T. Lewis; A. A. Newman; A. W. Orchard; R. J. Perham; C. A. G. Poole; R. S. Putland; K. T. Stannard; B. A. Stickley; M. Sweeny.
Principals (*G7*), D. Mannings; P. Luscombe.

Prison Service Industries and Farms
Lunar House, Wellesley Road, Croydon,
Surrey CR9 2BY
[01–686 0688/686 3441]

Director (*G5*), Miss A. M. Edwards.
Group Managers (*G6*), J. D. Cleary; M. Codd; G. C. Robertson; J. H. Smith.
Principals (*G7*), J. A. Byrd; R. Cunningham; A. Gillcrist; W. Heppolette; N. F. Montgomery-Pott; D. E. Neville; J. A. Ward; A. S. Wilson.
Principal Professional & Technology Officers (*G7*), R. Fisher; T. Senior; A. Sweeney.

Supply and Transport Branch
Crown House, 52 Elizabeth Street,
Corby, Northants.
[Corby 202101]

Director (*G6*), D. J. Hardwick.
Principals (*G7*), R. C. Brett; M. Fitzgerald; J. Harvey; A. S. Thompson.

Prison Service Regional Offices

Midland, Birmingham:
Regional Director (*G5*), J. R. Sandy.
Deputy Regional Director, R. R. Tilt.
Assistant Regional Directors (*PSII*), W. L. Mowbray (*Administration*); J. Blakey (*Young Offenders*); J. R. Wilkinson (*Operations*).

South West, Bristol:
Regional Director (*G5*), I. Dunbar.
Deputy Regional Director, A. H. Rayfield.
Assistant Regional Directors (*PSII*), T. C. Newell (*Adult Offenders*); M. Carr (*Administration*); J. W. Plumb (*Young Offenders*).

North, Manchester:
Regional Director (*G5*), A. W. Driscoll, q.g.m..
Deputy Regional Director, C. J. Jones.
Assistant Regional Directors (*PSII*), L. Edgar (*Administration*); F. V. Weigh (*Locals/Reception Centres*); G. A. Shore (*Trainers/Dispersal/Open*); P. J. Rudgard (*Female/Young Offenders*).

South East, Woking:
Regional Director (*G5*), C. P. Honey.
Deputy Regional Director, J. F. Perriss.
Assistant Regional Directors (*PSII*), J. L. Harrison; J. Dugdale (*Operations*); K. M. Brewer (*Young Offenders*); (vacant) (*Women*).
Assistant Regional Director (*G7*), J. Walsh (*Administration*).

PRISONS
Governors

Acklington, Northumberland, C. Harder.
Albany, I o W, P J. Kitteridge.
Aldington, Kent, H. G. Bagshaw.
Ashwell, Leics., R. Curtis.
Askham Grange, Yorks., R. Smith.
Bedford, J. L. Uzzell.
Birmingham, P. Buxton.
Blantyre House, J. Semple.
Blundeston, Suffolk, Miss J. M. Fowler.
Bristol, T. M. O'Sullivan.
Brixton, SW2., Miss J. Kinsley.
Camp Hill, I.o.W., D. M. Morrison.
Canterbury, J. M. Reid.
Cardiff, J. M. Williams.
Channings Wood, Devon, C. G. Clark.
Chelmsford, D. B. Sinclair.
Coldingley, Surrey, Mrs. M. M. Donnelly.
Cookham Wood, P. J. Meakings.
Dartmoor, R. J. May.
Dorchester, B. Coatsworth.
Drake Hall, Stafford, R. J. Crouch.
Durham, H. D. Jones.
East Sutton Park, G. Gibson.
Erlestoke Park, R. S. Brandon.
Exeter, D. Alderson.
Featherstone, Wolverhampton, L. M. Wiltshire.
Ford, Sussex, G. W. E. Ellington.
Frankland, Durham, A. H. Papps.
Full Sutton, B. V. Smith.
Garth, T. A. Bone.
Gartree, Leics., R. S. Duncan.
Gloucester, N. W. A. Wall.
Grendon and Spring Hill, Bucks., M. F. G. Selby.
Haverigg, Cumbria, D. I. Lockwood.
Highpoint, Newmarket, J. Hunter.
Hindley, Lancs., J. H. M. Anderson.
Holloway, N7, C. Allen.
Hull, P. M. Wheatley.
Kingston, Portsmouth, Miss M. R. Allen.
Kirkham, Lancs., Maj. R. B. Coombs.
Lancaster, W. J. Ginn.
Leeds, W. A. Martin, O.B.E.
Leicester, J. R. Wilkinson.
Lewes, R. Jacques.
Leyhill, Glos., W. E. McEvoy.
Lincoln, P. L. Harrap.
Lindholme, Doncaster, C. F. Lambert.
Littlehay, S. J. Twinn.
Liverpool, A. N. Joseph.
Long Lartin, Worcs., J. Whitty.
Maidstone, G. Gregory-Smith.
Manchester, F. B. O'Friel.
Medomsley, D. G. McNaughton.
Morton Hall, Lincoln, T. Davies.
New Hall, H. G. Owen.
Northeye, Sussex, D. C. Ozanne.
North Sea Camp, (vacant).
Norwich, A. J. Barclay.
Nottingham, H. Reid.
Oxford, J. M. A. Thomas-Ferrand.
Parkhurst, I.o.W., R. E. Withers.
Pentonville N7, R. J. Kendrick.
Preston, B. A. Wilson.
Ranby, F. Abbott.
Reading, D. Myers.
Rochester, M. Manning.
Rudgate, W. Yorks., J. D. Yates.
Send, Surrey, A. C. Smith.
Shepton Mallet, R. D. Dixon.
Shrewsbury, G. Ross.
Stafford, (vacant).
Standford Hill, W. J. Cooper.
Stocken, E. P. Polkinghorne.
Styal, Cheshire, G. Walker.

Sudbury, Derbys., L. Stones.
Swansea, S. R. Robinson.
Thorp Arch, W. Yorks, D. Whitehead.
The Verne, Dorset, D. L. Long.
Wakefield, T. J. Gadd.
Wakefield Service College, J. W. Staplon.
Wandsworth, SW18., D. A. Marsden.
Wayland, T. C. H. Newth.
Winchester, M. V. Roberts.
Wormwood Scrubs, W12., D. Brooke.
Wymott, Preston, C. B. Scott.

YOUNG OFFENDERS INSTITUTIONS
Governors

Aylesbury, J. W. Dring.
Buckley Hall, Lancs., C. R. Griffiths.
Bullwood Hall, Essex, Miss U. M. B. McCollam.
Campsfield House, Oxford, K. B. Owen.
Castington, R. Mitchell.
Deerbolt, P. A. Whitehouse.
Dover, D. Aram.
Drake Hall, R. J. Crouch.
East Sutton Park, Kent, G. Gibson.
Eastwood Park, Glos., T. B. Thomas.
Everthorpe, Humberside, T. M. Turner.
Exeter, D. Alderson.
Feltham, A. M. E. de Frisching.
Glen Parva, Leics., H. Jones.
Grendon/Spring Hill, M. F. G. Selby.
Gringley, B. Tyreman.
Guys Marsh, Dorset, G. Brunskill.
Haslar, Hants., J. J. O'Neill.
Hatfield, Yorks., W. J. Clark.
Hewell Grange, Worcs., Miss M. A. Carden.
Hollesley Bay Colony, Suffolk, Miss S. F. McCormick.
Huntercombe and Finnamore Wood, Oxon, E. Crowe.
Kirklevington, Cleveland, R. J. E Wright.
Lowdham Grange, Notts., R. S. Radcliffe.
The Mount, I. Ward.
New Hall, H. G. Owen.
Northallerton, M. A. Mogg.
Onley, Warwicks., R. Doughty.
Portland, Dorset, M. Langdon.
Rochester, M. Manning.
Stoke Heath, Salop, A. Cruikshank.
Styal, Cheshire, G. Walker.
Swinfen Hall, Staffs., J. B. Pudney.
Thorn Cross, D. Hall.
Usk, Gwent, J. Capel.
Wellingborough, P. Atherton.
Werrington, Staffs., M. K. Pascoe.
Wetherby, Yorks., A. Holman.
Whatton, Notts., M. A. Lewis.

REMAND CENTRES
Governors

Ashford, Middx., S. C. A. Pryor.
Brockhill, Worcs., P. T. Hanglin.
Cardiff, J. M. Williams.
Feltham, A. M. E. de Frisching.
Glen Parva, J. Rumball.
Latchmere House, Surrey, G. Barnard.
Low Newton, Co. Durham, W. J. Mansfield.
Pucklechurch, Bristol, D. C. Leach.
Risley, Cheshire, I. Boon.

Inspectorate of Prisons

H.M. Chief Inspector of Prisons, His Hon. Judge Tumim.
H.M. Deputy Chief Inspector of Prisons (G5), M. D. Jenkins.
H.M. Inspectors (G5), D. F. Campbell; S. C. Handley; D. J. Jarvis; D. Shaw; B. G. Thulborn; B. J. Wells.
Principal (G7), Mrs. C. L. Lehman.

ESTABLISHMENT, FINANCE AND MANPOWER, FIRE AND EMERGENCY PLANNING DEPARTMENTS

Deputy Under Secretary (G2), M. J. Moriarty, C.B..

Establishment Department

Assistant Under Secretary of State (G3), A. R. Rawsthorne (*Personnel, Organization and Management Services*).
Heads of Divisions (G5), B. W. Buck; P. Canovan; J. L. Goddard; Mrs. E. J. Grimsey; F. H. Keens, O.B.E.; J. S. Smedley.
Senior Principals (G6), D. J. Grant; F. R. Hayhurst; M. H. Rumble.
Principals (G7), K. Aylen; W. Black; D. J. Blackwood; P. Bolt; J. W. Bradley; M. Carr; R. C. Case; Mrs. C. A. Cowley; G. J. Edwards; B. Elliott; R. G. Ferguson; A. Fishwick; D. H. Gannon; J. A. Greenland; H. D. Hillier; B. J. Jordan; J. F. Love; Miss S. Marshall; Mrs. J. Morgan; R. Ritchie; K. E. R. Rogers; D. G. Ross; J. S. Sarjantson; M. P. Scandrett; A. Silver; J. C. Smith; R. E. Stockdale; S. E. Wharton.

Home Office Unit at Civil Service Selection Board
Kirkland House, 24 Whitehall, SW1A 2ED
[01–210 plus extension]

Assistant Secretary (G5), R. J. Miles.
Principal Psychologist, F. D. Bedford.

Public Relations Branch

Director of Information Services (G4), B. L. Mower.
Deputy Director, P. G. Rose.
Principal Information Officers (G7), C. R. Seabrook; R. Windsor.

Finance and Manpower Department

Assistant Under Secretary of State (Principal Finance Officer) (G3), M. C. Malone Lee.
Heads of Divisions (G5), C. Farrington; A. Harding; J. E. Hayzelden; N. A. Nagler.
Senior Principals (G6), D. W. Diamond; R. M. Hoare; A. K. Holman.
Principals (G7), I. J. Acton; Mrs. P. R. Atkins; G. Brindle; I. N. Bruce; A. D. Chadwick; C. I. Dickinson; G. B. Fox; F. Gorton; S. B. Hickson; J. Le Vay; J. W. Maloney; M. R. Matthews; D. J. Moon; G. Stadlen; A. V. H. Stainer.

Fire and Emergency Planning Department

Assistant Under Secretary of State (G3), A. H. Turney.
Assistant Secretaries (G5), P. E. Bolton; R. R. G. Watts; R. M. Whalley.
Grade 6, B. S. Luetchford.
Principals (G7), F. J. Archer; A. Browne; D. H. Evans; Mrs. D. M. Grice; R. Kornick; B. Lockett; D. J. Moss; D. J. Mould; T. E. Russell; G. Underwood; A. Walmsley; Mrs. S. M. K. Willington.

H.M. Fire Service Inspectorate

H.M. Chief Inspector, R. D. Doyle, C.B.E.
H.M. Inspectors, C. G. Burgon; S. D. Christian; J. Dukelow; C. Green; T. Greenwood; A. F. Kilford; P. A. Kilshaw; W. C. Perry, M.B.E.; H. V. Reed; N. F. Roundell, Q.F.S.M.; C. H. Sanders; G. J. Tinley.
Senior Engineering Inspector, R. M. Simpson

Fire Service College
Moreton-in-Marsh, Gloucestershire GL56 0RH
[Moreton-in-Marsh: 50831]

Commandant, G. Clarke, C.B.E.
Deputy Commandant, F. N. David.
Secretary (G7), J. A. Gunderson.

Civil Defence College
The Hawkhills, Easingwold, Yorks. YO6 3EG
[Easingwold: 21406]

Head of College (G5), J. B. Bettridge, C.B.E.
Vice-Principal, J. D. Shallow, M.C.

Home Office H.Q. U.K. Warning and Monitoring Organization
James Wolfe Road, Cowley, Oxford OX4 2PT
[Oxford 776005]

Director (G6), R. F. Cooke.
Deputy Director I (G7), W. P. Lawrie.
Deputy Director II (G7), D. L. Warden.

Women's Royal Voluntary Service
234–244 Stockwell Road, SW9 9SP
[01–733 3388]

National Chairman, Dame Barbara Shenfield, D.B.E.

HORSERACE TOTALISATOR BOARD
74 Upper Richmond Road, SW15 2SU
[01–874 6411]

Established by the Betting, Gaming and Lotteries Act, 1963, as successor in title to the Racecourse Betting Control Board established by the Racecourse Betting Act, 1928.

Its function is to operate totalisators on approved racecourses in Great Britain, and it also provides off-course cash and credit offices. Under the Horserace Totalisator and Betting Levy Board Act, 1972, it is further empowered to offer bets at starting price (or other bets at fixed odds) on any sporting event.

Chairman, Lord Wyatt of Weeford £57,000
Members, The Lord Chapple; Mrs. P. Hastings; Hon. D. Montagu; P. S. Winfield; J. F. Sanderson; H.R.H. Prince Michael of Kent.

HOUSING CORPORATION
149 Tottenham Court Road, W1P 0BN
[01–387 9466]

Established by Parliament in 1964, the Housing Corporation has since had its functions broadened by the Housing Acts of 1974 and 1980. It registers, supervises and funds non-profit making housing associations.

The Corporation supports housing associations in the rehabilitation of older houses and in new building to help people with special needs, including the elderly, the disabled, and single homeless people, and backs initiatives by housing associations to provide homes for sale to people on lower incomes, through schemes for shared equity, leasehold for the elderly and improvement for sale.

Chairman, Sir Hugh Cubitt, C.B.E.

INDEPENDENT BROADCASTING AUTHORITY
70 Brompton Road, S.W.3
[01–584 7011]

The Independent Television Authority was created by Act of Parliament in 1954 to provide an additional television broadcasting service to that provided by the British Broadcasting Corporation. In 1972 it was renamed the Independent Broadcasting Authority and its functions were extended to cover the provision of independent local radio.

The main functions of the Authority are to appoint the ILR and ITV programme companies; to own and operate transmitters; to supervise the programmes provided by contractors and the Channel Four Television Company and their scheduling; and to control advertising. The programme companies pay the Authority a rental to enable it to carry out its duties.

Fifteen ITV programme companies provide programmes in 14 regions (two companies operate in London, one at the weekends, the other during the week). By June, 1988, 49 Independent Local Radio contractors were broadcasting in the U.K. (in London, there are two companies, one providing a news and information service, and the second general entertainment and information). Both ITV and ILR are financed mainly by the sale of advertizing time.

The Authority consists of a Chairman and eleven members appointed by the Home Secretary and a permanent staff under the Director General.

Chairman, The Lord Thomson of Monifieth, K.T., P.C.
Deputy Chairman, Sir Donald Maitland, G.C.M.G., O.B.E.
Members, Mrs. P. Ridley; Sir Michael Caine; R. A. Grantham; Prof. J. F. Fulton (*Northern Ireland*); J. R. Purvis (*Scotland*); G. R. Peregrine (*Wales*); Prof. A. Cullen, O.B.E., F.R.S., Sir Anthony Jolliffe; Lady Popplewell; R. Sondhi.
Director General, J. Whitney.
Deputy Director General, Lady Littler.
Director of Television, D. Glencross.
Director of Radio, P. A. C. Baldwin.
Director of Engineering, Dr. J. Forrest.
Director of Finance, P. Rogers.
Controller of Advertising, F. Willis.
Controller of Public Affairs, Miss C. Bowe.
Secretary, K. Blyth.
Regional Officers, M. J. Fay (*Yorkshire*), E. Lewis (*Wales and West of England*); A. D. Fleck (*Northern Ireland*); S. Perkins (*East of England*); D. Lee (*North-West England*); B. Marjoribanks (*Scotland*); J. Dougray (*North-East England and the Borders*); N. J. Reedy (*East and West Midlands*); J. B. Scott (*South of England and Channel Islands*).

CENTRAL OFFICE OF INFORMATION
Hercules Road, SE1 7DU
[01–928 2345]

The Central Office of Information is a common service department which produces information and publicity material, and supplies publicity services, for other Government departments on a repayment basis. In the U.K. it conducts Government display press, television and poster advertizing, produces and distributes booklets, leaflets, films, television material, exhibitions, photographs and other visual material; and distributes departmental press notices. For the overseas departments it supplies British Information posts overseas with press, radio and television material, booklets, magazines, reference services, films, exhibitions, photographs, display and reading room material; arranges tours in the U.K. for official visitors from overseas. Administrative responsibility for the Central Office of Information rests with H.M. Treasury Ministers, while the ministers whose departments it serves are responsible for the policy expressed in its work.
(For **Salaries**, *see* page 297)

Director-General (*G3*), N. Taylor.
 Private Secretary, Mrs. M. M. Habershon.
Head of Information Officer Management Unit (*G5*), Ms. A. Nash.
Deputy Director-General (*G4*), G. M. Devereau.

CENTRAL SERVICES GROUP

Client Services
Director (*G6*), Miss J. Luke.

Communications Services
Director (*G6*), J. A. Leys.

OVERSEAS PUBLICITY GROUP
Group Director (*G5*), P. T. Brazier.

Overseas Press Services
Director (*G6*), G. L. Stickland.

Overseas Publications & Foreign Languages
Director (*G6*), R. Smith.

Overseas Visitors & Information Studies
Director (*G6*), D. A. Smith.

VISUAL MEDIA AND RADIO GROUP
Group Director (*G5*), R. N. Hooper.

Films & Television
Director (*G6*), R. J. Hall.

Exhibitions and Photographs
Director (*G6*), D. A. Loxley.

HOME PUBLICITY GROUP
Group Director (*G5*), J. Bolitho.

Advertising
Director (*G6*), K. C. Belben.

Home Publications
Director (*G6*), D. A. Low.

Research
Director (*G6*), M. C. Warren.

ADMINISTRATION SERVICES GROUP
Principal Establishment and Finance Officer (*G5*), D. A. Truman.
Personnel and Office Services Director (*G6*), W. J. Colwill.
Finance and Management Services Director (*G6*), K. E. Williamson.

REGIONAL OFFICES

North Eastern, Wellbar House, Gallowgate, Newcastle upon Tyne.—*Regional Director* (*G7*), R. P. Haslam.
Yorkshire and Humberside, City House, New Station Street, Leeds.—*Regional Director* (*G6*), A. S. Poole, L.V.O.
Eastern, Three Crowns House, 72–80 Hills Road, Cambridge.—*Regional Director* (*G7*), D. Dowle.
London and South Eastern, Hercules Road, SE1 7DU.—*Regional Director* (*G6*), G. E. Moggridge.
South Western, The Pithay, Bristol.—*Regional Director* (*G7*), P. D. Yorke.
Midlands, Five Ways Tower, Frederick Road, Edgbaston, Birmingham.—*Regional Director* (*G6*), P. J. Woodford.
North Western, Sunley Building, Piccadilly Plaza, Manchester.—*Regional Director* (*G6*), O. J. B. Prince-White.

BOARD OF INLAND REVENUE
Somerset House, WC2R 1LB
[01–438 6622]

The Board of Inland Revenue was constituted under the Inland Revenue Board Act, 1849, by the consolidation of the Board of Excise and the Board of Stamps and Taxes. In 1909 the administration of excise duties was transferred to the Board of Customs. The Board of Inland Revenue administers and collects direct taxes—mainly income tax, corporation tax, capital gains tax, inheritance tax, stamp duty, development land tax and petroleum revenue tax—

and advises the Chancellor of the Exchequer on policy questions involving them. The Head Office is in London and there are Inspectors of Taxes offices and Collection offices throughout the United Kingdom. The Department's Valuation Office is responsible for valuing property for tax purposes, for compensation and for compulsory purchase and (in England and Wales) for local rating purposes. In 1986–87 Inland Revenue collected over £57,000 million tax.

(For **Salaries,** *see* page 297)

The Board

Chairman (G1), A. M. W. Battishill.
 Private Secretary, R. F. S. Evers.
Deputy Chairmen (G2), A. J. G. Isaac, C.B.; T. J. Painter.
 Private Secretary, M. F. Bolland.
Directors General (G2), D. B. Rogers, C.B.; J. H. Beighton.
Commissioner: Chief Valuer (G2), A. B. Fallows, C.B.

Policy/Technical Divisions

Directors (G3), P. Lewis; C. W. Corlett; B. T. Houghton; E. McGivern; D. Y. Pitts; M. A. Johns; K. V. Deacon; J. H. Roberts.
Senior Principal Inspector of Taxes (G4), J. C. Campbell; K. A. Skinner, C.B.E.; R. E. German; J. Moule; M. D. E. Newstead; E. K. Pearson; G. F. Hamilton; W. Northend; J. M. L. Davenport; J. K. Duxbury; D. W. Hugo; I. N. Hunter; B. Sadler; J. F. Hall; J. M. Phalp.
Grade 5, B. A. Mace; Miss A. M. Rhodes; M. Prescott; J. D. Farmer; D. L. Shaw; H. B. Thompson; M. F. Cayley; J. H. Read; M. J. G. Elliott; I. R. Spence; J. P. B. Bryce; P. W. Fawcett; J. B. Shepherd; Miss M. A. Hill; B. O'Connor; L. E. Jaundoo; M. A. Keith.
Principal Inspectors of Taxes (G5), O. J. O'Brien; R. C. Mountain; M. L. Gordon; M. Templeman; J. W. Calder; J. Potter; T. R. Evans; R. E. Creed; J. White; P. C. Fielder; R. Thomas; A. Beauchamp; R. E. Haigh; Mrs. M. E. Williams; D. F. Parratt; D. A. Smith; J. T. Caldron; A. C. Williams.
Controller of Oil Taxation Office (G4), R. M. Elliss.
Controller of Development Land Tax Office (G7), P. Lakhanpaul.

Central Division

Grade 3, G. H. Bush.
Grade 5, S. J. McManus.
Senior Economic Adviser (G5), R. Weeden.

Management Divisions

Director of Personnel (G3), P. B. G. Jones.
Assistant Directors (G4), G. Findley; G. J. Lyall; (G5) R. A. Hutton, J. T. Tudor; R. Neilson; N. C. Munro; Mrs. C. Hubbard; M. K. Robins.
Controller of Office Services (G6), B. R. Spooner.
Director of Manpower and Support Services (G3), J. M. Crawley.
Assistant Directors (G5); D. Ward; R. R. Martin; A. W. Bryant.
Head of Operational Research (G5), R. P. R. Tilley.
Director of Information Technology (G3), S. C. T. Matheson.
Assistant Directors (G5), R. A. Hamilton; J. C. Cockcroft; D. Selwood; J. A. Pinder; C. J. Thompson; B. T. Glassberg; A. M. Paterson.
Director of Operations (G3), C. Cherry.
Deputy Director of Operations (G4), D. W. Muir.
Assistant Directors (G4), R. N. Page; (G5) J. E. Yard; J. C. Jones; Miss M. James; J. M. Thomas; M. Hodgson; R. S. Hurcombe; D. J. Timmons.
Controller, Enforcement Office (G5), R. F. Bruford.
Head of Communications Group (G5), P. C. Tharby.
Press Secretary (G7), Miss F. A. McFarlane.

Finance Division

Principal Finance Officer (G3), J. M. Crawley.
Assistant Secretary (G5), A. G. Nield.
Controller, Central Accounting Office (G6), J. Gray.
Chief Internal Auditor (G6), N. Buckley.

Statistics Division

Director (G3), J. R. Calder.
Chief Statisticians (G5), J. B. Dearman; R. J. Eason; F. A. Fitzpatrick; W. Gonzalez, C.B.E.
Computing (G6), R. James.

Office of the Controller of Stamps
South-West Wing, Bush House, Strand, WC2B 4QN and Barrington Road, Worthing, W. Sussex BN12 4XH

Controller (G6), D. E. Pipe, O.B.E.

Capital Taxes Office
Minford House, Rockley Road, W14 0DF

Controller (G4), G. A. Spencer.
Deputy Controllers (G5), B. D. Kent; R. J. Draper.
Asst. Controllers (G6), A. S. Johnson; M. Swann; A. L. Barton; I. P. Gunn; D. J. Ferley; C. A. Oldridge; H. V. Capon; R. T. Kablean; J. Blagden; T. J. Plumb; R. Shanks.
Boards Actuarial Adviser (G6), D. R. Erasmus.

Solicitor of Inland Revenue
Somerset House, WC2R 1LB

Solicitor (G2), R. K. Miller.
Principal Assistant Solicitors (G3), B. E. Cleave; J. D. H. Johnston; P. L. Ridd.
Assistant Solicitors (G5), R. J. Alderman; C. J. C. Baron; J. C. H. Bates; S. Bousher; K. Brown; K. O. Butterfield; B. R. D. Clarke; A. J. Gunz; J. F. W. Hinson; N. R. Phillips; A. K. S. Shaw; R. W. Thornhill; Miss A. E. Wyman.

Superannuation Funds Office
Lynwood Road, Thames Ditton, Surrey KT7 0DP

Controller (G5), R. G. Lusk.
Assistant Controllers (G6), I. A. Young; R. C. Fullbrook.

Inspector of Foreign Dividends Office
Lynwood Road, Thames Ditton, Surrey KT7 0DP

Inspector of Foreign Dividends (G6), J. Steele.

Office of the Chief Valuer
New Court, Carey Street, WC2A 2JE

Chief Valuer (G2), A. B. Fallows, C.B..
Deputy Chief Valuers (G3), P. G. Heard, C.B.; R. R. B. Shutler.
Assistant Chief Valuers (G4), S. H. Keith; A. J. Langford; R. J. Pawley.
Superintending Valuers (G5), R. Burrows; P. R. Garrett; W. A. M. Jones; M. J. Loveridge; O. T. Morgan; W. J. Reed; A. B. Prior.
Assistant Directors (G5), J. H. Ebdon; D. K. Park; T. R. Peckham.

INLAND REVENUE (SCOTLAND)
80 Lauriston Place, Edinburgh EH3 9SL

Controller (G4), W. S. Linkie.
Group Controllers (G5), J. Brown; H. S. MacRae; G. M. McGregor; R. I. Ford.

Controller (Stamps)
16 Picardy Place, Edinburgh EH1 3NF

Controller, D. G. Hunter.

Capital Taxes Office
16 Picardy Place, Edinburgh EH1 3NF

Registrar (G5), J. B. M. McKean, C.B.E.
Deputy Registrar (G6), P. G. Bruce, M.B.E.

Chief Examiners (G7), G. Mackie; Mrs. J. A. Templeton; W. Young; J. Telford; T. E. Naysmith; C. G. Hogg; Miss A. Forbes.

Solicitor's Office
80 Lauriston Place, Edinburgh EH3 9SL
Solicitor, T. H. Scott.
Senior Principals (Legal) (G6), I. K. Laing; D. S. Wishart.
Principal (Legal), H. M. Milne.

Office of the Chief Valuer, Scotland
15 Drumsheugh Gardens, Edinburgh EH3 7UN
Chief Valuer (G4), J. A. Sutherland.
Assistant Chief Valuer (G5), M. A. Newbury.

INTERVENTION BOARD FOR AGRICULTURAL PRODUCE
Fountain House, 2 Queen's Walk,
Reading RG1 7QW
[0734–583626]

The Intervention Board for Agricultural Produce was formed as a Government Department on November 22, 1972, and became operational on Feb. 1, 1973. The Board is responsible for the implementation of European Community regulations covering the market support arrangements of the Common Agricultural Policy. Members of the Board are appointed by and responsible to the Agricultural Ministers of the U.K.
(For **Salaries**, *see* page 297)

Chairman, A. J. Ellis, C.B.E.
Chief Executive (G3), G. Stapleton.
Finance Officer and Director General of Corporate Services (G4), D. J. Coates.

Heads of Divisions
Finance Division (G5), J. Diserens.
External Trade Division (G5), G. N. Dixon.
Crops Division (G5), D. M. L. Macgregor.
Livestock Products Division (G5), R. A. Saunderson.
Establishments Services (G6), J. Bird.
Computer Services (G6), E. M. Abbott.
Secretariat and Procurement Services (G6), G. R. Holloway.

U.K. Seeds Executive
Chairman, Prof. J. C. Murdoch, O.B.E., Ph.D.
Members, T. M. Clucas; J. Harvey; Prof. J. D. Hayes, Ph.D.; P. R. Hayward, O.B.E.; I. C. Henderson; G. G. Lyall; D. J. Palmer; W. P. Watt.

H.M. LAND REGISTRY
Lincoln's Inn Fields, WC2A 3PH
[01–405 3488]

The registration of title to land was first introduced in England and Wales by the Land Registry Act, 1862: H.M. Land Registry operates today under the Land Registration Acts, 1925 to 1986. The object of registering title to land is to create and maintain a register of land owners whose title is guaranteed by the State and so to simplify the transfer, mortgage and other dealings with real property. In certain areas of the country registration of title is compulsory on sale: voluntary registration in the non-compulsory areas has been common and it is still possible to register building estates, upon certain conditions, in any part of England or Wales. However, under the Land Registration Act, 1966, the voluntary first registration of land in non-compulsory areas was curtailed to accelerate the extension of the compulsory system to all built-up areas of the country. The intention is that registration of title shall ultimately be universal throughout England and Wales.

H.M. Land Registry is administered under the Lord Chancellor by the Chief Land Registrar and the work is decentralized to a number of regional offices. The Chief Land Registrar is also responsible for the Land Charges Department and the Agricultural Credits Department.
(For **Salaries**, *see* page 297)

Headquarters Office
Chief Land Registrar (G2), E. J. Pryer.
Chief Executive (G3), J. J. Manthorpe.
Senior Land Registrar (G5), Mrs. J. G. Totty.
Principal Establishment Officer (G5), E. G. Beardsall.
Controller (Registration) (G5), G. N. French.
Controller (Management Services) (G5), R. J. Fenn.
Land Registrar (G5), M. G. Garwood.

Birkenhead District Land Registry
Old Market House, Hamilton Street,
Birkenhead L41 5JW
[051–647 2377]
District Land Registrar (G5), J. L. Inskipp.
Area Manager (G6), J. Eccles.

Croydon District Land Registry
Sunley House, Bedford Park, Croydon CR9 3LE
[01–686 8833]
District Land Registrar (G5), D. M. J. Moss.
Area Manager (G6), G. Hix.

Durham District Land Registry
Southfield House, Southfield Way,
Durham DH1 5TR
[091–3866151]
District Land Registrar (G5), P. H. Curnow.
Area Manager (G6), D. F. Price.

Gloucester District Land Registry
Twyver House, Bruton Way,
Gloucester GL1 1DQ
[0452–28666]
District Land Registrar (G5), W. W. Budden.
Area Manager (G6), M. H. Spooner.

Harrow District Land Registry
Lyon House, Lyon Road, Harrow,
Middx. HA1 2EU
[01–427 8811]
District Land Registrar (G5), M. L. Wood.
Area Manager (G6), D. I. Whyte.

Kingston upon Hull District Land Registry
Earle House, Portland Street, Hull HU2 8JN
[0482–223244]
District Land Registrar (G5), S. R. G. Coveney.
Area Manager (G7), E. Howard.

Land Charges and Agricultural Credits Department
Burrington Way, Plymouth PL6 3LP
[0752–779831]
Superintendent of Land Charges (G7), J. C. O'Brien.

Lytham District Land Registry
Birkenhead House, Lytham St. Annes,
Lancs. FY8 5AB
[0253–736999]
District Land Registrar (G5), J. G. Cooper.
Area Manager (G6), E. J. Stringer.

Nottingham District Land Registry
Chalfont Drive, Nottingham NG8 3RN
[0602–291166]
District Land Registrar (G5), P. J. Timothy.
Area Manager, (G6), W. Whitaker.

Peterborough District Land Registry
Touthill Close, City Road,
Peterborough PE1 1XN
[0733 555666]

District Land Registrar (G5), M. Avens.
Area Manager (G6), B. J. Andrews.

Plymouth District Land Registry
Plumer House, Tailyour Road,
Crownhill, Plymouth PL6 5HY
[0752–701234]

District Land Registrar (G5), P. A. Meehan.
Area Manager(G6), K. Robinson.

Stevenage District Land Registry
Brickdale House, Danestrete, Stevenage,
Herts. SG1 1XG
[0438–313003]

District Land Registrar (G5), D. M. T. Mullett.
Area Manager (G6), A. Gould.

Swansea District Land Registry
Tybryn Glas High Street,
Swansea, Glam. SA1 1PW
[0792–458877]

District Land Registrar (G5), G. A. Hughes.
Area Manager (G6), B. E. G. Martin.

Telford District Land Registry
Stafford Park 15, Telford,
Shropshire TF3 3BB
[0952–290355]

District Land Registrar (G5), M. A. Roche.
Area Manager (G7), R. D. Moseley.

Tunbridge Wells District Land Registry
Curtis House, Hawkenbury, Tunbridge Wells,
Kent TN2 5AQ
[0892–510015]

District Land Registrar (G5), C. J. West.
Area Manager (G6), B. E. Kitching.

Weymouth District Land Registry
1 Cumberland Drive, Weymouth,
Dorset DT4 9TT
[03057–76161]

District Land Registrar (G5), K. L. Charles.
Area Manager (G6), R. R. C. Green.

Computer Services Division
Burrington Way,
Plymouth PL5 3LP
[0752–779831]

Head of Division (G6), A. A. Restorick.

LAW COMMISSION

England and Wales
Conquest House, 37–38 John Street,
Theobalds Road, WC1N 2BQ
[01–242 0861]

Set up on June 16, 1965, under the Law Commissions Act, 1965, to make proposals to the Government for the examination of the law and for its revision where it is unsuited for modern requirements, obscure, or otherwise unsatisfactory. It recommends to the Lord Chancellor programmes for the examination of different branches of the law and suggests whether the examination should be carried out by the Commission itself or by some other body. The Commission is also responsible for the preparation of Consolidation and Statute Law (Repeals) Bills.
Chairman, The Hon. Mr. Justice Beldam.
Members, T. M. Aldridge; B. J. Davenport, Q.C.; Prof. J. T. Farrand; Prof. B. M. Hoggett.
Secretary, M. H. Collon.

Scottish Law Commission
140 Causewayside, Edinburgh EH9 1PR
[031-668 2131]

Chairman, The Hon. Lord Davidson.
Commissioners, Dr. E. M. Clive; C. G. B. Nicholson, Q.C. (*full-time*); Prof. P. N. Love, C.B.E.; W. Nimmo Smith, Q.C.
Secretary, K. S. Barclay.

LAW OFFICERS' DEPARTMENT
Attorney-General's Chambers,
Royal Courts of Justice, WC2A 2LL
[01–936 6602]

The Law Officers of the Crown for England and Wales (the Attorney General and the Solicitor General) are the legal advisers of the Government and represent the Crown in court. The Attorney General also superintends the Director of Public Prosecutions for England and Wales (who is head of the Crown Prosecution Service), the Director of Public Prosecutions for Northern Ireland and the Director of the Serious Fraud Office, and is the Attorney General for Northern Ireland.
Attorney General, THE RT. HON. SIR PATRICK MAYHEW, Q.C., M.P. . . . . £36,277†
Parliamentary Private Secretary, D. A. Sumberg, M.P.
Solicitor General, SIR NICHOLAS LYELL, Q.C., M.P.
£29,557†
Parliamentary Private Secretary, P. Ground, Q.C., M.P.
Legal Secretary (G2), M. L. Saunders.
Asst. Legal Secretary (G5), C. W. P. Newell.
† Excluding Parliamentary salary.

THE LAY OBSERVER'S OFFICE
Royal Courts of Justice, Strand, WC2A 2LL
[01–936 6695]

The Lay Observer's Office was established in 1975 and is funded by the Lord Chancellor's Department. The function of the Lay Observer is to monitor the Solicitor's Complaints Bureau's handling of complaints made to it about the conduct of solicitors or solicitors' employees. The Lay Observer is independent and is appointed by the Lord Chancellor.
Lay Observer, L. Lightman £22,000
Clerk, J. S. Twist.

Solicitors Complaints Bureau
Portland House, Stag Place, SW1E 5BL
[01–834 2288]

Director, J. P. S. Thompson.

LIBRARIES

OFFICE OF ARTS AND LIBRARIES
(*see* entry on pages 301–2)

THE BRITISH LIBRARY
2 Sheraton Street, W1V 4BH
[01–636 1544]

The British Library is the U.K.'s national library and occupies the central position in the library and information network. The Library aims to serve scholarship, research, industry, commerce and all other major users of information. Its services are based on collections which include over 16 million volumes (books, manuscripts, maps, newspapers and other serials, stamps and music), 1 million discs, 45,000 hours of tape recordings, in more than 20 buildings in London and one complex in West

Yorkshire, amounting to over 367 miles of shelving growing at the rate of 8 miles every year.

The British Library was established on July 1, 1973 under the British Library Act, 1972. It brought together the library departments of the British Museum, the National Central Library, the National Lending Library for Science and Technology, the British National Bibliography Ltd and, in 1974, the functions of the Office for Scientific and Technical Information. Subsequently the Library took responsibility for other organisations: the India Office Library and Records and the H.M.S.O. Binderies in 1982; and the National Sound Archive in 1983. Since 1985 they have all been regrouped into three service areas, a Research and Development Department plus a corporate administrative centre.

Access to the Humanities and Social Sciences reading rooms in Great Russell Street is limited to holders of a British Library Reader's Pass, and information about eligibility (basically, academic researchers and investigative professionals) is available from the Reader Admissions Office. The Aldwych and Holborn reading rooms of the Science Reference and Information Service are open to the general public without charge or formality.

The Library's exhibition galleries are housed in the British Museum building in Great Russell Street. On permanent display are famous items from the national written archive including the Magna Carta, the Lindisfarne Gospels and Shakespeare's First Folio.

Board Members

Chairman, The Lord Quinton.
Chief Executive and Deputy Chairman, K. R. Cooper.
Directors General, J. M. Smethurst; P. R. Lewis; D. Russon.
Part-time Members, The Lord Adrian, M.D., F.R.S.; The Lord Windlesham, C.V.O., P.C.; Prof. A. S. Forty, PH.D., D.SC.; Prof. B. Morris; D. Owen; Miss D. Park; Sir Robin Mackworth-Young, K.C.V.O., F.S.A.; N. Higham; R. E. Utiger, C.B.E.; T. J. Rix.

HUMANITIES AND SOCIAL SCIENCES

Director General, J. M. Smethurst.

Planning and Administration

Great Russell Street WC1B 3DG
[01-636 1544]

Director, A. Phillips.

Preservation Service

Great Russell Street WC1B 3DG
[01-636 1544]

Director, Dr. D. W. Clements.

Collection Development

Director, B. C. Bloomfield.

Oriental Collections
Store Street WC1E 7DG
[01-636 1544]

India Office Library and Records
197 Blackfriars Road SE1 8NG
[01-928 9531]

English Language, Western, Eastern European Printed Books
Great Russell Street WC1B 3DG
[01-636 1544]

Special Collections

Director, Mrs. S. J. Tyacke.

Western Manuscripts, Maps, Manuscript and Printed Music, Stamps
Great Russell Street WC1B 3DG
[01-636 1544]

The National Sound Archive
29 Exhibition Road SW7 2AS
[01-589 6603]

Public Services

Director, A. Phillips.

Reading rooms for Great Russell Street collections, Official Publications
Great Russell Street WC1B 3DG
[01-636 1544]

Information Sciences Service
7 Ridgmount Street WC1E 7AE
[01-323 7688]

SCIENCE, TECHNOLOGY AND INDUSTRY

Director General, D. Russon.

Document Supply Centre

Boston Spa, Wetherby, W. Yorks. LS23 7BQ
[0937 843434]

Director, (vacant).

Science Reference and Information Service

25 Southampton Buildings, Chancery Lane WC2A 1AW
[01-636 1544]
and 9 Kean Street WC2B 4AT
[01-636 1544]

Director, A. Gomersall.

BIBLIOGRAPHIC SERVICES

2 Sheraton Street W1V 4BH
[01-636 1544]

Director General, P. R. Lewis.
Director of Automated Services, J. Mahoney.

Research and Development Department

2 Sheraton Street W1V 4BH
[01-636 1544]

Director, B. J. Perry.

NATIONAL LIBRARY OF SCOTLAND

George IV Bridge, Edinburgh EH1 1EW
[031-226 4531]

Open free. Reading Room, weekdays, 9.30–8.30; Sat. 9.30–1. Map Room, weekdays, 9.30–5; Sat. 9.30–1. Exhibition, weekdays, 9.30–5; Sat. 9.30–1; Sun. 2–5 (closed on Sun. Oct.–April).

The Library, which had been founded as the Advocates' Library in 1682, became the National Library of Scotland by Act of Parliament in 1925. It continues to share the rights conferred by successive Copyright Acts since 1710. Its collections of printed books and MSS., augmented by purchase and gift, are very large and it has an unrivalled Scottish collection. The present building was opened by H.M. the Queen in 1956.

The Reading Room is for reference and research which cannot conveniently be pursued elsewhere. Admission is by ticket issued to an approved applicant.

Salaries

Librarian	£32,219–£33,819
Keeper	£19,905–£28,154
Curator Grade C	£16,692–£21,737

Chairman of the Trustees, M. F. Strachan, C.B.E. F.R.S.E.
Librarian and Secretary to the Trustees, Prof. E. F. D. Roberts, Ph.D., F.R.S.E.
Secretary of the Library, I. D. McGowan.
Curators Grade C, M. C. Graham; J. E. McIntyre.
Keepers of Printed Books, R. Donaldson, Ph.D.; A. M. Marchbank, Ph.D.; Ms. A. Matheson, Ph.D.
Curators Grade C, A. M. Cain, Ph.D.; T. A. Cherry; R. Duce; Ms. A. E. Harvey Wood; B. P. Hillyard, D.Phil.; S. Holland; Ms. R. I. Hope; Ms. A. F. Howe; W. A. Kelly; J. M. Morris; Ms. J. M. Wilkes.
Keepers of Manuscripts, P. M. Cadell; T. I. Rae, Ph.D.
Curators Grade C, I. G. Brown, Ph.D., F.S.A.; I. C. Cunningham; I. F. Maciver; S. M. Simpson; Ms. E. D. Yeo.
Director of Scottish Library Network (SCOLCAP) (Keeper), B. Gallivan.
Curator Grade C, R. F. Guy.
Director of Scottish Science Library (Keeper), Ms. A. J. Bunch.

THE NATIONAL LIBRARY OF WALES

Llyfrgell Genedlaethol Cymru
Aberystwyth, Dyfed SY23 3BU
[0970–623816]

Readers' room open on weekdays, 9.30 a.m. to 6 p.m. (Saturdays, 5 p.m.); closed on Sundays and Bank Holidays. Admission by Reader's Ticket.

Founded by Royal Charter, 1907, and maintained by annual grant from the Treasury. One of the six libraries entitled to privileges under Copyright Act. Contains about 3,000,000 printed books, 40,000 manuscripts, 4,000,000 deeds and documents, and numerous maps, prints and drawings, and audio-visual collection. Specializes in manuscripts and books relating to Wales and the Celtic peoples. Repository for pre-1858 Welsh probate records. Approved by the Master of the Rolls as a repository for manorial records and tithe documents, and by the Lord Chancellor for certain legal records. Bureau of the Regional Libraries Scheme for Wales.
Librarian, B. F. Roberts, Ph.D., F.S.A.
Secretary, D. B. Lloyd.
Heads of Departments, D. Huws (*Manuscripts and Records*); J. L. Madden (*Printed Books*); D. H. Owen (*Pictures and Maps*).

LIGHTHOUSE AUTHORITIES

CORPORATION OF TRINITY HOUSE
Trinity House, Tower Hill, EC3N 4DH
[01–480 6601]

Trinity House, the first General Lighthouse and Pilotage Authority in the Kingdom, was a body of importance when Henry VIII granted the institution its first charter in 1514. The Corporation is the General Lighthouse Authority for England, Wales and the Channel Islands, with certain statutory jurisdiction over aids to navigation maintained by local harbour authorities. It is also responsible for dealing with wrecks dangerous to navigation, except those occurring within port limits or wrecks of H.M. ships. The Trinity House Lighthouse Service is maintained out of the General Lighthouse Fund which is provided from light dues levied on ships at ports of the U.K. and Republic of Ireland. The Corporation was, until Sept. 30, 1988, the principal pilotage authority in the U.K. is responsible for

London and 39 other districts. Under the terms of the Pilotage Act 1987, responsibility for pilotage was transferred to harbour authorities with effect from Oct. 1, 1988.

The affairs of the Corporation are controlled by a board of Elder Brethren, who are master mariners with long experience of command in the Royal and Merchant Navy together with figures from the world of commerce, and the Secretary. A separate Board, which comprises Elder Brethren, senior staff and outside representatives currently controls the Lighthouse Service. The Board is assisted by administrative and technical staff. The Elder Brethren also act as nautical assessors in marine cases in the Admiralty Division of the High Court of Justice.

Elder Brethren

Master, H.R.H. the Duke of Edinburgh, K.G.
Deputy Master, Capt. P. M. Edge.
Elder Brethren, Capt. I. R. C. Saunders; Capt. P. F. Mason, C.B.E.; H.R.H. the Prince of Wales, K.G.; Capt. G. P. McGraith; Capt. Sir George Barnard; Capt. R. N. Mayo, C.B.E.; Capt. Sir David Tibbits, D.S.C., R.N.; Capt. D. A. G. Dickens; Capt. J. E. Bury; Capt. J. A. N. Bezant, D.S.C., R.D., R.N.R. (*ret.*); Capt. Sir Miles Wingate, K.C.V.O.; Capt. D. J. Cloke; The Lord Wilson of Rievaulx, K.G., O.B.E., F.R.S.; Rt. Hon. Edward Heath, M.B.E., M.P.; The Viscount Runciman of Doxford, O.B.E., A.F.C.; Capt. T. Woodfield, O.B.E.; Sir Arthur Drake, C.B.E.; The Lord Simon of Glaisdale, P.C.; Admiral of the Fleet the Lord Lewin, K.G., G.C.B., M.V.O., D.S.C.; Capt. D. T. Smith, R.N.; Commander Sir Robin Gillett, G.B.E., R.D., R.N.R.; The Lord Shackleton, K.G., O.B.E., P.C.; Sir John Cuckney; Capt. D. J. Orr; The Lord Carrington, K.G., C.H., K.C.M.G., M.C., P.C.

Officers

Secretary, J. R. Backhouse.
Deputy Secretary, J. B. Fuller.
Director of Engineering, D. A. S. Vennings.
Director of Finance, K. W. Clark.
Operations Manager, Mrs. B. C. Heesom.
Personnel Manager, M. J. Faulkner.
Finance Manager, J. B. Burke.
Engineering Manager, F. E. J. Holden.
Surveyor of Shipping, J. K. Rankin.
Principal, Corporate Department, J. A. Liddle.
Information Officer, Mrs. L. A. Dennison.

CLYDE PORT AUTHORITY
16 Robertson Street, Glasgow G2 8DS
[041-221 8733]

The Authority is a self-governing statutory body established by individual Act of Parliament and provides sea port facilities within a 450 sq. mile area of jurisdiction which encompasses the River Clyde, its estuary and sea lochs.
Chairman, R. W. S. Easton, C.B.E.
Managing Director, J. Mather.
Director and Secretary, G. P. Johnston.
Director and Marine Operations, Capt. D. B. McMurray.

COMMISSIONERS OF NORTHERN LIGHTHOUSES
84 George Street, Edinburgh EH2 3DA.
[031-226 7051]

The Commissioners of Northern Lighthouses are the General Lighthouse Authority for Scotland and the Isle of Man. The present Board owes its origin to an Act of Parliament passed in 1786. At present the Commissioners operate under the Merchant Shipping Act, 1894 and are 19 in number.

The Commissioners control 36 major manned lighthouses, 54 major unmanned lighthouses, 106 minor lights and many lighted and unlighted buoys. They have a fleet of 2 motor vessels.

Commissioners

The Lord Advocate, the Solicitor General for Scotland, the Lords Provost of Edinburgh, Glasgow and Aberdeen; the Provost of Inverness; the Chairman of Argyll & Bute District Council; the Sheriffs-Principal of North Strathclyde; Tayside, Central & Fife; Grampian, Highlands & Islands: South Strathclyde, Dumfries & Galloway; Lothians & Borders; and Glasgow & Strathkelvin; W. D. H. Gregson, C.B.E.; T. Macgill; Capt. J. A. MacLeod; Capt. A. F. Dickson, O.B.E.; Capt. W. B. Kinley; A. J. Struthers.

Officers

General Manager, Cdr. J. M. Mackay, M.B.E.
Secretary, I. A. Dickson.
Engineer-in-Chief, W. Paterson.

LOCAL COMMISSIONERS

COMMISSION FOR LOCAL ADMINISTRATION IN ENGLAND
21 Queen Anne's Gate, SW1H 9BU
[01–222 5622]

Local Commissioners (Local Ombudsmen) are responsible for investigating complaints from members of the public against local authorities (but not town and parish councils); water authorities; police authorities; the Commission for New Towns and new town development corporations (housing functions); and urban development corporations (town and country planning functions). The Commissioners are appointed by the Crown on the recommendation of the Secretary of State for the Environment.

Certain types of action are excluded from investigation, particularly personnel matters and commercial transactions unless they relate to the purchase or sale of land. Complaints can be sent direct to the Local Ombudsman or through a councillor, although the Local Ombudsman will not consider a complaint unless the Council has had an opportunity to investigate and reply to a complainant.

A free booklet "Your Local Ombudsman" is available from the Commission's office.
Chairman of the Commission and Local Commissioner, D. C. M. Yardley, D.Phil. £65,000
Vice Chairman and Local Commissioner, F. G. Laws
£46,500
Local Commissioner, Mrs. P. A. Thomas £45,500
Member, The Parliamentary Commissioner for Administration
Secretary, G. D. Adams £30,666

COMMISSION FOR LOCAL ADMINISTRATION IN WALES
Derwen House, Court Road, Bridgend CF31 1BN
[0656–61325]

The Local Commissioner for Wales has similar powers to the Local Commissioners in England. The Commissioner is appointed by the Crown on the recommendation of the Secretary of State for Wales. A free booklet "Your Local Ombudsman in Wales" is available from the Commission's office.
Local Commissioner, H. F. Jones.
Secretary, D. Bowen.

COMMISSIONER FOR LOCAL ADMINISTRATION IN SCOTLAND
5 Shandwick Place, Edinburgh EH2 4RG
[031–229 4472]

The Local Commissioner for Scotland has similar powers to the Local Commissioners in England, and is appointed by the Crown on the recommendation of the Secretary of State for Scotland.
Local Commissioner, R. G. E. Peggie, C.B.E.
Secretary, K. Bratton

LONDON REGIONAL TRANSPORT
55 Broadway, SW1H 0BD
[01–222 5600]

Subject to the financial objectives and principles approved by the Secretary of State for Transport, London Regional Transport has a general duty to provide or secure the provision of public transport services for Greater London.
Chairman, Sir Keith Bright £64,000
Members, Dr. T. M. Ridley (£60,000); J. Telford Beasley; M. Marsh £55,000

LORD ADVOCATE'S DEPARTMENT
Fielden House, 10 Great College Street,
SW1P 3SL
[01–276 3000]

The Law Officers for Scotland are the Lord Advocate and the Solicitor-General for Scotland. The Lord Advocate's Department is responsible for drafting Scottish legislation, for providing legal advice to other departments on Scottish questions and for assistance to the Law Officers for Scotland in certain of their legal duties.
Lord Advocate, THE RT. HON. THE LORD CAMERON OF LOCHBROOM, P.C., Q.C. £40,508
Solicitor-General for Scotland, PETER FRASER, Q.C.
£34,956
Legal Secretary and First Parliamentary Draftsman, N. J. Adamson, C.B., Q.C. £47,320
Senior Asst. Legal Secs. and Parliamentary Draftsmen, G. M. Clark; D. J. S. Duncan; G. Kowalski; P. J. Layden, T.D.; J. C. McCluskie .. £32,596–£39,000
Asst. Legal Secs. and Deputy Parliamentary Draftsmen, J. D. Harkness; D. C. Macrae; C. A. M. Wilson
£24,139–£28,215

LORD CHANCELLOR'S DEPARTMENT
House of Lords, SW1A 0PW
[01–219 3000]

The Lord Chancellor is responsible for promoting general reforms in the civil law, for the procedure of the civil courts and for the administration of the Supreme Court (Court of Appeal, High Court and Crown Court) and county courts in England and Wales, and for legal aid schemes. He is responsible for advising the Crown on the appointment of judges and certain other officers and is himself responsible for the appointment of Masters and Registrars of the High Court and District and County Court Registrars and magistrates. He is responsible for ensuring that letters patent and other formal documents are passed in the proper form under the Great Seal of the Realm, of which he is the custodian. The work in connection with this is carried out under his direction in the Office of the Clerk of the Crown in Chancery.
(For **Salaries,** *see* page 297)
Lord Chancellor, THE RT. HON. THE LORD MACKAY OF CLASHFERN £87,250
Private Secretary, J. P. Stockton.
Permanent Secretary (GI), Sir Derek Oulton, K.C.B., Q.C.
Private Secretary, E. S. Adams.

Crown Office

Clerk of the Crown in Chancery (G1), Sir Derek Oulton, K.C.B., Q.C.
Deputy Clerk of the Crown in Chancery (G2), T. S. Legg, C.B.
Clerk of the Chamber, Miss J. L. Waine.

COURT SERVICE POLICY AND LEGAL SERVICES
Trevelyan House, 30 Great Peter Street, SW1P 2BY
[01–210 8872]

Deputy Secretary (G2), R. Potter.

Court Service Management Group

Head of Group (G4), J. F. Brindley.
Heads of Divisions (G5), D. E. Staff; R. A. Vincent; R. J. Clark.

Policy and Legal Services Group

Head of Group (G3), J. G. H. Gasson.
Heads of Divisions (G5), W. Arnold; M. W. Sayers; M. Kron; R. H. H. White; C. W. V. Everett.

JUDICIAL APPOINTMENTS AND LEGISLATION
House of Lords, SW1A 0PW
[01–219 4311]

Deputy Secretary (G2), T. S. Legg, C.B.

Judicial Appointments Group
House of Lords, SW1A 0PW
[01–219 3000]

Head of Group (G3), B. Cooke.
Heads of Divisions (G5), R. C. Stoate; J. R. A. Hanratty, R.D.

26–28 Old Queen Street, SW1H 2HP
[01–210 3537]

Grade 5, R. V. Gobler; G. Norman.

Legislation Group
26–28 Old Queen Street, SW1H 2HP
[01–210 3508]

Head of Group (G3), C. R. Seaton.
Heads of Divisions (G5), P. Graham Harris; M. H. Collon; M. C. L. Carpenter.

Establishment and Finance Group
Trevelyan House, 30 Great Peter Street, SW1P 2BY
[01–210 8512]

Principal Establishment and Finance Officer (G3), M. D. Huebner.
Heads of Divisions (G5), Miss J. E. Court; D. S. Mortimer; D. Nooney; Mrs. N. A. Oppenheimer.
Principal Information Officer (G7), Miss J. Morley.

Public Trust Office
Stewart House, 24 Kingsway, WC2B 6JX
[01–405 4300]

Public Trustee and Accountant General (G3), J. Boland.
Asst. Public Trustee and Deputy Accountant General (G5), P. J. Farmer.
Asst. Public Trustee (G5), R. C. Annis.

22 Kingsway, WC2B 6LE
[01–936 6000]

Head of Courts Funds Office (G7), I. J. MacBean.

Ecclesiastical Patronage
10 Downing Street, S.W.1
[01–233 3000]

Secretary for Ecclesiastical Patronage, J. R. Catford.
Assistant Secretary for Ecclesiastical Patronage (G7), N. Wheeler.

See also Law Courts and Offices

LORD GREAT CHAMBERLAIN'S OFFICE
House of Lords, SW1A 0PW
[01–219 3100]

The Lord Great Chamberlain is a Great Officer of State, the office being hereditary since the grant of Henry I to the family of De Vere, Earls of Oxford.
Lord Great Chamberlain, The Marquess of Cholmondeley, G.C.V.O., M.C.
Secretary to the Lord Great Chamberlain, Air Chief Marshal Sir John Gingell, G.B.E., K.C.B.
Clerk to the Lord Great Chamberlain, Miss J. M. Drewett.

LORD PRIVY SEAL'S OFFICE
Privy Council Office,
Whitehall, SW1A 2AT

As leader of the House of Lords, the Lord Privy Seal is responsible to the Prime Minister for the arrangement of government business in the House. He also has a responsibility to the House itself to advise it on procedural matters and other difficulties which arise.
Lord Privy Seal, and Leader of the House of Lords, THE RT. HON. THE LORD BELSTEAD.
Private Secretary, N. F. J. Gibbons.
Assistant Private Secretaries, R. Appleton; E. R. Wilson.

OFFICE OF MANPOWER ECONOMICS
22 Kingsway, WC2B 6JY
[01–405 5944]

The Office of Manpower Economics was set up in 1971. It is an independent non-statutory organization which is responsible for servicing independent review bodies which advise on the pay of various public service groups (*see* entries under "Review Bodies"), the Pharmacists Review Panel, the Police Negotiating Board and the Civil Service Arbitration Tribunal. The Office is also responsible for servicing *ad hoc* bodies of inquiry and for undertaking research into pay and associated matters as requested by Government.
Director, N. Covington.
Assistant Secretaries (G5), D. W. R. Lewis; K. R. Perry; P. J. H. Edwards.

MEDICAL RESEARCH COUNCIL
20 Park Crescent, W1N 4AL
[01–636 5422]

The Medical Research Council is the main Government agency for the promotion of medical and related biological research. The Council employs its own research staff and also provides grants for other institutions and for individuals who are not members of its own staff, thus complementing the research resources of the universities and hospitals.
Chairman, The Earl Jellicoe, K.B.E., D.S.O., M.C., P.C.
Deputy Chairman and Secretary, D. A. Rees, Ph.D., D.SC., F.R.S.
Members, Sir Donald Acheson, K.B.E., D.M., F.R.C.P.; Belinda Banham, C.B.E.; Sir Austin Bide; S. Brenner, D.Phil., F.R.C.P., F.R.S.; J. T. Carter; D. L. Crouch, M.P.; M. J. Crumpton, Ph.D., F.R.S.; Prof. C. J. Dickinson, D.M., F.R.C.P.; I. S. Macdonald, M.D.; Prof. P. J. Morris, Ph.D., F.R.C.S.; Prof. J. M.

Newsom-Davis, M.D., F.R.C.P.; Prof. F. W. O'Grady, C.B.E.; Prof. J. K. Wing, M.D., Ph.D.
Administrative Secretary, D. Noble.

Neurobiology and Mental Health Board
Chairman, A. D. Baddeley, Ph.D.

Cell Biology and Disorders Board
Chairman, Prof. G. Radda.

Physiological Systems and Disorders Board
Chairman, Prof. D. K. Peters, F.R.C.P.

Tropical Medicine Research Board
Chairman, Prof. M. A. Epstein, C.B.E., F.R.S.

HEADQUARTERS OFFICE

Medical Division
Principal Medical Officers, Katherine Levy; D. James, Ph.D.; J. Alwen, Ph.D.

Administrative Division
Administrative Secretary, D. Noble.
Assistant Secretaries, Norma Morris; N. H. Winterton; J. E. A. Hay.

Secretariat, Grants and Training Awards
Assistant Secretary, B. C. Dodd.

Headquarters Establishments
Head of Section, M. Wood, Ph.D.

National Institute for Medical Research
Mill Hill, N.W.7
[01–959 3666]
Director, J. Stohel, Ph.D., F.R.S.

Clinical Research Centre
Watford Road, Harrow, Middlesex
[01–864 5311]
Director, (vacant).

Research Units
Anatomical Neuropharmacology Unit, Dept. of Pharmacology, University of Oxford, South Park Road, Oxford OX1 3QT. *Director,* Prof. A. D. Smith, D.Phil.
Applied Psychology Unit, 15 Chaucer Road, Cambridge CB2 2EF. *Director,* A. D. Baddeley, Ph.D.
Biostatistics Unit, 5 Shaftesbury Road, Cambridge CB2 2BW. *Director,* N. E. Day, Ph.D.
Blood Group Unit, University College, London, Wolfson House, 4 Stephenson Way, NW1 2EH. *Director,* Patricia Tippett, Ph.D.
Blood Pressure Unit, Western Infirmary, Glasgow G11 6NT. *Director,* A. F. Lever, F.R.C.P., F.R.S.E.
Brain Metabolism Unit, University Dept. of Pharmacology, 1 George Square, Edinburgh EH8 9JZ. *Director,* G. Fink, M.D., D.Phil.
Cell Biophysics Unit, Dept. of Biophysics, King's College, 26–29 Drury Lane, WC2. *Director,* Prof. B. B. Boycott, F.R.S.
Cell Mutation Unit, University of Sussex, Falmer, Brighton BN1 9RR. *Director,* Prof. B. A. Bridges, Ph.D.
Cellular Immunology Unit, Sir William Dunn School of Pathology, Oxford OX1 3RE. *Director,* Dr. A. F. Williams, Ph.D.
Child Psychiatry Unit, Institute of Psychiatry, De Crespigny Park, Denmark Hill, SE5 8AF. *Director,* Prof. M. Rutter, C.B.E., M.D., F.R.C.P.
Clinical and Population Cytogenetics Unit, Western General Hospital, Crewe Road, Edinburgh EH4 2XU. *Director,* Prof. H. J. Evans, Ph.D., F.R.S.E.
Clinical Oncology and Radiotherapeutics Unit, M.R.C. Centre, Hills Road, Cambridge CB2 2QH. *Hon. Director,* Prof. N. M. Bleehen, F.R.C.P., F.R.C.R.

Clinical Pharmacology Unit, University Department of Clinical Pharmacology, Radcliffe Infirmary, Woodstock Road, Oxford OX2 6HE. *Hon. Director,* Prof. D. G. Grahame-Smith, Ph.D., F.R.C.P.
Cognitive Development Unit, 17 Gordon Street, WC1. *Director,* Prof. J. Morton. Ph.D.
Cyclotron Unit, Hammersmith Hospital, Ducane Road, W12. *Director,* D. D. Vonberg, C.B.E.
Dental Research Unit, London Hospital Medical College, 30/32 Newark Street, E1 2AA. *Director,* Prof. N. W. Johnson, Ph.D.
Unit on the Development and Integration of Behaviour, Subdept. of Animal Behaviour, Madingley, Cambridge CB3 8AA. *Hon. Director,* Prof. R. A. Hinde, D.Phil., Sc.D., F.R.S
Dunn Nutrition Unit, Downhams Lane, Milton Road, Cambridge. *Director,* R. G. Whitehead, Ph.D.
Environmental Epidemiology Unit, Southampton General Hospital, Southampton SO9 4XY. *Director,* Prof. D. J. P. Barker, M.D., M.D., F.R.C.P.
Epidemiology and Medical Care Unit, Northwick Park Hospital, Watford Road, Harrow, Middx. *Director,* T. W. Meade, D.M., F.R.C.P.
Epidemiology Unit (South Wales), 4 Richmond Road, Cardiff. *Director,* P. C. Elwood, M.D., F.R.C.P.
Unit for Epidemiological Studies in Psychiatry, University Dept. of Psychiatry, Royal Edinburgh Hospital, Morningside Park, Edinburgh EH10 5HF. *Director,* N. B. Kreitman, M.D.
Experimental Embryology and Teratology Unit, M.R.C. Laboratories, Woodmansterne Road, Carshalton, Surrey. *Director,* D. G. Whittingham, D.Sc.
Human Biochemical Genetics Unit, Galton Laboratory, University College London, Wolfson House, 4 Stephenson Way, NW1. *Hon. Director,* D. A. Hopkinson, M.D.
M.R.C. Human Movement and Balance Unit, Institute of Neurology, National Hospital, Queens Square, WC1. *Director,* J. D. Hood, Ph.D., D.Sc.
Immunochemistry Unit, University Department of Biochemistry, South Parks Road, Oxford OX1 3QU. *Director,* K. B. M. Reid, Ph.D.
Institute of Hearing Research, University of Nottingham, Nottingham NG7 2RD. *Director,* M. P. Haggard, Ph.D.
M.R.C. Laboratories, Carshalton, Woodmansterne Road, Carshalton, Surrey, SM5 4EF. *Laboratory Manager,* T. B. Pendry.
M.R.C. Laboratories, The Gambia, Fajara, near Banjul, The Gambia, W. Africa. *Director,* B. M. Greenwood, M.D., F.R.C.P.
M.R.C. Laboratories, Jamaica, University of the West Indies, Mona, Kingston, Jamaica. *Director,* Prof. G. R. Serjeant, C.M.G., M.D., F.R.C.P.
Leukaemia Unit, Royal Postgraduate Medical School, Ducane Road, W12 0HS. *Hon. Director,* Prof. L. Luzzatto, M.D., F.R.C.P.
Mammalian Development Unit, University College London, Wolfson House, 4 Stephenson Way, NW1. *Director,* Anne McLaren, D.Phil., F.R.S.
Medical Sociology Unit, 6, Lilybank Gardens, Glasgow, G12 8QQ. *Director,* Sally Macintyre, Ph.D.
Laboratory of Molecular Biology, Hills Road, Cambridge CB2 2QH. *Director,* Sir Aaron Klug, Ph.D., F.R.S.
Molecular Genetics Unit, M.R.C. Centre, Hills Road, Cambridge CB2 2QH. *Director,* S. Brenner, D.Phil., D.Sc., F.R.C.P., F.R.S.
Molecular Haematology Unit, John Radcliffe Hospital, Headington, Oxford OX3 9DU. *Director,* Prof. D. J. Weatherall, M.D., F.R.C.P., F.R.S.
M.R.C. Molecular Immunopathology Unit, University Medical School, Hills Road, Cambridge CB2 2QH. *Director,* Prof. P. J. Lachmann, Sc.D., F.R.C.P., F.R.S.

Molecular Neurobiology Unit, University Medical School, Hills Road, Cambridge CB2 2QH. *Director*, Prof. E. A. Barnard.

Neurochemical Pathology Unit, Newcastle General Hospital, Westgate Road, Newcastle upon Tyne NE4 6BE. *Director*, Prof. J. A. Edwardson, Ph.D.

Neurological Prostheses Unit, Institute of Psychiatry, De Crespigny Park, Denmark Hill, SE5. *Hon. Director*, Prof. G. S. Brindley, M.D., F.R.C.P., F.R.S.

A.F.R.C./M.R.C. Neuropathogenesis Unit, Ogston Building, West Mains Road, Edinburgh. *Director*, (vacant).

Perceptual and Cognitive Performance Unit, Experimental Psychology Laboratory, University of Sussex, Falmer, Brighton. *Director*, Prof. W. P. Colquhoun, Ph.D.

Radiobiology Unit, Chilton, Didcot, Oxon. OX11 0RD *Director*, Prof. G. E. Adams, Ph.D., D.Sc.

Reproductive Biology Unit, Centre for Reproductive Biology, 37 Chalmers St., Edinburgh EH3 9EW. *Director*, D. W. Lincoln, D.Sc.

Social and Applied Psychology Unit, Dept. of Psychology, University of Sheffield S10 2TN. *Director*, P. B. Warr, Ph.D.

Social Psychiatry Unit, Institute of Psychiatry, De Crespigny Park, Denmark Hill, SE5. *Director*, Prof. J. K. Wing, M.D., Ph.D.

Toxicology Unit, M.R.C. Laboratories, Woodmansterne Road, Carshalton, Surrey SM5 4EF. *Director*, T. A. Connors, D.SC., Ph.D.

Tuberculosis and Related Infections Unit, Hammersmith Hospital, Du Cane Road, W12 0HS. *Director*, Dr. J. Ivanyi, M.D., Ph.D.

Virology Unit, Institute of Virology, Church Street, Glasgow G11 5JR. *Hon. Director*, Prof. J. H. Subak-Sharpe, Ph.D., F.R.S.E.

THE ROYAL MINT
Llantrisant, nr. Pontyclun,
Mid-Glamorgan CF7 8YT
[0443–222111]

Master Worker and Warden, The Chancellor of the Exchequer (*ex officio*).
Deputy Master and Comptroller, A. D. Garrett.

MONOPOLIES AND MERGERS COMMISSION
New Court, 48 Carey Street, WC2A 2JT
[01–831 6111]

The Commission was established in 1948 as the Monopolies and Restrictive Practices Commission and was reconstituted on subsequent occasions. It became the Monopolies and Mergers Commission in 1973. The Commission has the duty of investigating and reporting on questions referred to it with respect to (*a*) the existence or possible existence of monopolies not registrable under the Restrictive Trade Practices Act, 1976, and relating to the supply of goods or services in the U.K. or part of the U.K. or to the supply of goods for export; (*b*) the transfer of a newspaper or newspaper's assets; (*c*) the creation or possible creation of a merger qualifying for investigation within the meaning of the Fair Trading Act, 1973.

References may be made to the Commission on the general effect on the public interest of specified monopoly or other uncompetitive practices and of restrictive labour practices.

The Competition Act, 1980, provides for the reference to the Commission of particular anti-competitive practices and of questions of efficiency, costs, service provided and possible abuse of monopolies in the public sector. In respect of recently-privatized industries, references to the Commission may be made in certain circumstances, with regard to their respec-

tive industries, by the Director General of Telecommunications, the Civil Aviation Authority and the Director General of Gas Supply.

Chairman, M. S. Lipworth £68,500
Deputy Chairmen, H. H. Hunt, C.B.E. (£24,010); D. G. Richards (£27,612); R. G. Smethurst (£24,010).
Members, Sir James Ackers; C. C. Baillieu; L. Britz; M. B. Bunting; K. S. Carmichael, C.B.E.; Sir Robert Clayton, C.B.E.; P. H. Dean; A. Ferry, M.B.E.; P. S. G. Flint; D. G. Goyder; Miss A. M. Head; J. D. Keir, Q.C.; L. Kelly; Prof. S. C. Littlechild; Miss P. K. R. Mann; S. McDowall, C.B.E.; L. A. Mills; B. C. Owens; N. L. Salmon; D. P. Thomson; C. A. Unwin, M.B.E.; S. Wainwright, C.B.E.; Prof. G. Whittington; R. Young . . . . *each* £9,666
Secretary, S. N. Burbridge.

MUSEUMS

MUSEUMS AND GALLERIES COMMISSION
7 St. James's Square, SW1Y 4JU
[01–839 9341]

The Commission was established in 1931 as an advisory body. Since 1981 it has, at the Government's instance, taken on several new executive functions. The Chairman and 14 Commissioners are appointed by the Prime Minister and represent all parts of the U.K. The Commission is funded by the Office of Arts and Libraries and has an annual budget of £6 million, of which nearly 90 per cent is distributed as grants.

The Commission advises the Government and others on a wide range of matters relating to museums and galleries. In addition to its advisory role the Commission's executive functions include the services of the National Museums Security Adviser; funding of the seven Area Museum Councils in England and the Museum Documentation Association; administration of capital and conservation grant schemes for non-national museums, and transitional grants occasioned by the abolition of the G.L.C. and metropolitan county councils. The Commission also administers the arrangements for government indemnities and the acceptance of works of art in lieu of Inheritance Tax, and has responsibility for the two Purchase Funds for local museums administered on its behalf by the V. & A. and Science Museums. The Commission has recently established a conservation unit and an information service on travelling exhibitions.

Chairman, Prof. B. Morris, D.Phil.
Members, The Marchioness of Anglesey, D.B.E.; F. Atkinson, O.B.E.; R. Begg, C.B.E.; L. Brandes, C.B.E.; The Lord Dainton, F.R.S.; Prof. Sir John Hale, F.B.A.; T. W. I. Hodgkinson, C.B.E.; J. Last; Sir Hugh Leggatt; The Lord O'Neill, T.D.; The Lord Rees, P.C., Q.C.; R. H. Smith; Dame Margaret Weston, D.B.E.; Adm. Sir David Williams, G.C.B.
Secretary, P. Longman.

THE BRITISH MUSEUM
Great Russell Street, WC1B 3DG
[01–636 1555]

Antiquities collections, coins and medals, prints and drawings. Open weekdays (including Bank Holidays) 10–5 and Sun. 2.30–6. Closed on Good Friday, Christmas Eve, Christmas Day, Boxing Day, New Year's Day and the first Monday in May. The ethnographical collections are displayed in The Museum of Mankind at 6 Burlington Gardens, W1. Opening times as above.

The British Museum may be said to date from 1753, when Parliament granted funds to purchase the collections of Sir Hans Sloane and the Harleian manuscripts, and for their proper housing and maintenance. The building (Montagu House) was opened in 1759. The present buildings were erected between 1823 and the present day, and the original collection has increased to its present dimensions by gifts and purchases. The administrative expenses, including work and building in progress, were estimated at £15,665,000 in 1988–89.

Board of Trustees

Appointed by the Sovereign: H.R.H. The Duke of Gloucester, G.C.V.O. *Appointed by the Prime Minister:* The Lord Windlesham, C.V.O., P.C. (*Chairman*); The Lord Charteris of Amisfield, G.C.B., G.C.V.O., O.B.E, P.C.; Graham C. Greene, C.B.E.; Prof. E. T. Hall, D.Phil., F.S.A., F.B.A.; C. E. A. Hambro; Sir Peter Harrop, K.C.B.; Prof. Sir Harry Hinsley, O.B.E., F.B.A.; Hon. Mrs. Marten, O.B.E.; Mrs. M. Moore; Prof. G. H. Treitel, D.C.L., F.B.A., Q.C.; Sir Ian Trethowan; The Lord Weinstock; Prof. W. Whitfield, C.B.E.; Sir Oliver Wright, G.C.M.G., G.C.V.O., D.S.C.

Nominated by the learned Societies: The Lord Adrian, M.D., F.R.S. (*Royal Society*); Dame Elisabeth Frink, D.B.E., R.A. (*Royal Academy*); The Lord Blake, F.B.A. (*British Academy*); Prof. W. Watson, C.B.E., F.S.A., F.B.A. (*Society of Antiquaries*)

Appointed by the Trustees of the British Museum: Sir David Attenborough, C.B.E., F.R.S.; Prof. Rosemary Cramp, F.S.A.; Prof. Sir John Hale, F.S.A., F.B.A.; Prof. P. Lasko, C.B.E., F.S.A., F.B.A.

Salaries

Grade 2	£45,000
Grade 5	£24,765–£28,215
Grade 6	£18,786–£25,335
Grade 7	£15,030–£20,292
Head of Press and P.R.	£13,005–£15,823
Press and P.R. Officer	£10,622–£13,005

Officers

Director (G2), Sir David Wilson.
Deputy Director (G4), Ms. J. M. Rankine.
Secretary (G5), G. B. Morris.
Assistant to the Director (G7), Ms. M. L. Caygill.
Head of Public Services (G6), G. A. L. House.
Head of Design (G6), Margaret Hall, O.B.E.
Head of Education (G7), J. F. Reeve.
Head of Press and Public Relations, A. E. Hamilton.
Press and Public Relations Officer, Ms. K. Hudson.
Head of Administration (G6), B. A. Wilson.
Head of Building and Security Services (G6), P. E. Youngs.
Head of Architectural and Building Services (G7), C. J. Walker.
Head of Finance and Personnel (G7), G. E. Cooper.
Head of Management Services (G7), D. E. Williams.
Keeper of Prints and Drawings (G5), J. K. Rowlands.
Deputy Keeper (G6), A. V. Griffiths.
Assistant Keepers (G7), Ms. F. A. Carey; N. J. L. Turner; Ms. L. Stainton; M. B. Royalton-Kisch.
Keeper of Coins and Medals (G5), J. P. C. Kent.
Deputy Keeper (G6), M. J. Price.
Assistant Keepers (G7), M. G. Powell-Jones; Ms. M. M. Archibald; A. M. Burnett; B. J. Cook.
Keeper of Egyptian Antiquities (G6), W. V. Davies (acting).
Assistant Keepers (G7), M. L. Bierbrier; A. J. Spencer.
Keeper of Western Asiatic Antiquities (G5), T. C. Mitchell.
Assistant Keepers (G7), J. E. Curtis; C. B. F. Walker; I. L. Finkel.
Keeper of Greek and Roman Antiquities (G5), B. F. Cook.
Deputy Keeper (G6), K. S. Painter.
Assistant Keepers (G7), Ms. S. E. C. Walker; Ms. V. Tatton-Brown; D. J. R. Williams.

Keeper of Medieval and Later Antiquities (G5), N. M. Stratford.
Deputy Keepers (G6), G. H. Tait; J. Cherry; Ms. L. E. Webster.
Assistant Keepers (G7), D. Kidd; D. Buckton; T. H. Wilson.
Keeper of Prehistoric and Romano-British Antiquities (G5), I. H. Longworth.
Deputy Keeper (G6), I. M. Stead.
Assistant Keepers (G7), I. A. Kinnes; T. W. Potter; Ms. J. M. Cook.
Keeper of Japanese Antiquities (G5), L. R. H. Smith.
Keeper of Oriental Antiquities (G5), Ms. J. M. Rawson.
Deputy Keeper (G6), J. M. Rogers.
Assistant Keepers (G7), W. Zwalf; Ms. A. S. L. Farrer; J. R. Knox.
Keeper of Ethnography (G5), M. D. McLeod.
Deputy Keeper (G6), B. Durrans.
Assistant Keepers (G7), Ms. E. M. Carmichael; Ms. S. G. Weir; Ms. D. Starzecka; J. C. H. King; J. B. Mack; N. F. Barley.
Keeper of Scientific Research (G5), M. Tite.
Principal Scientific Officers (G7), P. T. Craddock; M. J. Hughes; I. C. Freestone; Ms. S. G. E. Bowman; E. J. Neville.
Keeper of Conservation (G5), W. A. Oddy.
Principal Scientific Officer (G7), V. D. Daniels.
Principal Conservator (G7), Ms. H. P. Lane.

THE BRITISH MUSEUM (NATURAL HISTORY)
Cromwell Road, SW7 5BD
[01-938 9123]

Open Mon. Sat. (except New Year's Day, Good Friday, May Day, Christmas Eve, Christmas Day and Boxing Day) 10–6, Sun. 1–6. Admission, £2.

The Natural History Museum originates from the natural history departments of the British Museum. During the 19th century the natural history collections grew extensively and in 1881 they were moved to South Kensington. In 1963, the Natural History Museum became completely independent with its own body of Trustees. The Zoological Museum, Tring, bequeathed by the second Lord Rothschild, has formed part of the Museum since 1938. The Geological Museum merged with the Natural History Museum in 1985 (opening times are as given above). Research workers are admitted to the libraries and study collections by Student's Ticket, applications for which should be made in writing to the Director.

The administrative expenses were estimated at £17,958,000 in 1987–88.

(For **Salaries**, *see* page 297).

Board of Trustees

Chairman, Prof. Sir Richard Harrison, M.D., F.R.S.
Appointed by the Prime Minister: The Lord Adrian, M.D., F.R.S.; Sir Walter Bodmer, F.R.S.; Prof. D. Spencer Smith; Sir Owen Green; Prof. J. M. Thomas, F.R.S.; G. M. Ronson; E. N. K. Clarkson, F.R.S.E.
Nominated by the Royal Society: Prof. Sir Andrew Huxley, O.M., F.R.S.
Appointed by the Trustees of the British Museum (Natural History): Prof. H. B. Whittington, F.R.S.; Sir James Hamilton, K.C.B., M.B.E.; R. J. Carter.
Director (G3), N. R. Chalmers, PH.D.
Deputy Director (G5), A. C. Bishop, PH.D.
Secretary (G5), C. J. E. Legg.
Head of Marketing and Development (G6), A. P. Harvey.
Assistant to the Director (G7), A. A. Fincham, PH.D.

Department of Zoology

Keeper (G5), J. F. Peake.
Deputy Keepers (G6), C. R. Curds, D.SC.; R. J. Lincoln, PH.D.

Grade 5 , P. H. Greenwood, D.SC., F.R.S.
Grade 6 , J. D. Taylor, PH.D.
Grade 7, E. N. Arnold, PH.D.; I. R. Bishop, O.B.E.; G. A. Boxhall, PH.D.; R. A. Bray, PH.D.; P. F. S. Cornelius, PH.D.; J. D. George, PH.D.; D. I. Gibson, PH.D.; R. W. Ingle, PH.D.; Mrs. J. Jewell, PH.D.; P. B. Mordan, PH.D.; H. M. Platt, PH.D.; D. M. Roberts, PH.D.; D. Rollinson, PH.D.; V. R. Southgate, PH.D.; A. C. Wheeler.

Bird Section
Park Street, Tring, Herts.
[Tring: 4181]

Grade 7, I. R. Bishop, O.B.E.

Department of Entomology

Keeper (G5), L. A. Mound, D.SC.
Deputy Keepers (G6), D. R. Ragge, PH.D.; R. I. Vane-Wright.
Grade 6, R. L. Blackman PH.D.; R. W. Crosskey, D.SC.
Grade 7, P. C. Barnard, PH.D.; B. Bolton; Mrs. J. M. Cox, PH.D.; M. G. Fitton, PH.D.; I. D. Gauld, PH.D.; P. M. Hammond; D. Hollis; W. J. Knight, PH.D.; A. C. Pont; G. S. Robinson, PH.D.; K. S. O. Sattler, PH.D.; A. J. Shelley, PH.D.; K. G. V. Smith; N. E. Stork, PH.D.; R. T. Thompson; W. G. Tremewan; Miss C. M. F. von Hayek.

Department of Botany

Keeper (G5), J. F. M. Cannon.
Deputy Keeper (G6), P. W. James.
Grade 7, S. Blackmore, PH.D.; A. O. Chater; A. Eddy; D. J. Galloway, PH.D.; C. J. Humphries, PH.D.; A. C. Jermy; D. M. John, PH.D.; R. J. Pankhurst; J. H. Price; I. Tittley.

Department of Palaeontology

Keeper (G5), L. R. M. Cocks, D.SC.
Deputy Keeper (G6), M. K. Howarth, PH.D.; H. G. Owen, PH.D.
Grade 6, C. Patterson, PH.D.; R. A. Fortey, SC.D.
Grade 7, P. J. Andrews, PH.D.; C. H. C. Brunton, PH.D.; P. L. Forey, PH.D.; A. W. Gentry, D.PHIL.; R. P. S. Jefferies, PH.D.; Miss T. I. Molleson; N. J. Morris, D.PHIL.; C. P. Nuttall; J. B. Richardson, PH.D.; B. R. Rosen, PH.D.; A. B. Smith, PH.D.; C. B. Stringer, PH.D.; P. D. Taylor, PH.D.; J. E. P. Whittaker, PH.D.

Department of Mineralogy

Keeper (G5), A. C. Bishop, PH.D.
Deputy Keeper (G6), P. Henderson, D.PHIL.
Grade 6, R. Hutchison, PH.D.
Grade 7, A. M. Clark, PH.D.; G. Cressey, PH.D.; A. J. Criddle; A. L. Graham, PH.D.; R. R. Harding, D.PHIL.; R. F. Symes, PH.D.; A. R. Woolley, PH.D.

Department of Administrative Services

Head and Finance and Establishment Officer (G5), C. J. E. Legg.
Building Manager (G6), R. H. Essex.
Administration Officer (G7), K. Davey, PH.D.
Finance and Organization (G7), E. G. Hartman.
Estates Manager (G7), R. G. Nash.
Publications Officer (G7), C. A. P. Reynard.

Department of Library Services

Head (G6), R. E. R. Banks (*acting*).
Deputy Head (G7), Miss P. Gilbert (*acting*).

Department of Public Services

Head (G5), R. S. Miles, D.SC.
Deputy Head (G6), G. C. S. Clarke, PH.D.
Operations Manager (G7), M. J. Grant.
Technical Services (G7), B. S. Martin.

Geological Museum
Exhibition Road, South Kensington, SW7 2DE
[01-938 8932]

The Museum's three public galleries have major displays of gems and basic earth science.

MUSEUM OF LONDON
London Wall, EC2Y 5HN
[01-600 3699]

The Museum of London opened in 1976. It is based on the amalgamation of the former Guildhall Museum and London Museum. The Museum is controlled by a Board of Governors, appointed (9 each) by the Government and the Corporation of London. The exhibition illustrates the history of London from prehistoric times to the present day.
Chairman of Board of Governors, R. M. Robbins, C.B.E., F.S.A.
Director, M. G. Hebditch, F.S.A.

THE SCIENCE MUSEUM
South Kensington, SW7 2DD
[01-938 8000]

Open on Mon.-Sat. 10-6; Sun. 2.30-6. Closed on New Year's Day, Good Friday, May Day Bank Holiday, Christmas Eve, Christmas Day and Boxing Day. Admission Charge.

The Science Museum, part of the National Museum of Science & Industry, houses the national collections of science, technology, industry and medicine. The Museum began as the Science Collection of the South Kensington Museum and first opened in 1857. In 1883, it acquired the collections of the Patent Museum and in 1909 the Science Collections were transferred to the new Science Museum, leaving the Art Collections with the Victoria and Albert Museum.

Some of the Museum's commercial aircraft, agricultural machinery, and road and rail transport collections are at Wroughton, near Swindon, Wilts., and are open for public viewing on selected weekends during the summer.

The Museum is responsible for the Concorde Exhibition at the Fleet Air Arm Museum, Yeovilton.

The administrative expenses of the Museum, the Science Museum Library, the National Railway Museum and the National Museum of Photography, Film and Television are estimated at £16,257,000 for 1988–89.

Salaries

Director	£35,800–£45,300
Keeper/Grade 5	£27,087–£35,371
Curator B/Grade 6	£19,905–£31,563
Curator C/Grade 7	£16,692–£25,921

Director, Dr. N. Cossons, O.B.E.

RESOURCE MANAGEMENT DIVISION

Assistant Director (G5), (vacant).
Personnel and Training Manager (G7), (vacant).
Finance Officer (G7), Miss J. M. Quickfall.
Buildings Manager (G7), I. Brown.
Curator C, J. C. Robinson.

COLLECTIONS MANAGEMENT DIVISION

Director (G5), Dr. B. Bracegirdle.

Department of Physical Sciences

Keeper, Dr. D. A. Robinson.
Curator B, Dr. R. F. Bud.

Curators C, Dr. D. Vaughan; Dr. A. Q. Morton; Dr. A. K. Newmark; Dr. J. Darius; C. N. Brown.

Department of Medical Sciences

Keeper, Dr. B. Bracegirdle.
Curator C, Dr. G. M. Lawrence.

Department of Engineering

Keeper, Dr. E. J. S. Becklake.
Curators C, Dr. B. P. Bowers; A. E. Butcher; P. D. Stephens; D. D. Swade.

Department of Transport

Keeper, Dr. T. Wright.
Curators C, J. A. Bagley; A. Hall-Patch; P. R. Mann.

MARKETING DIVISION

Assistant Director (G5), C. M. Pemberton.
Marketing Executive (G7), Ms. K. Booth.

Public Services Division

Assistant Director (G5), T. Suthers.
Curators C, I. M. Ball; Dr. A. W. Wilson.

RESEARCH AND INFORMATION SERVICES DIVISION

A national library of science, specializing in the history of science and technology. Bibliographies supplied. Photocopying and microfilm service.—Open Mon.–Sat. 10–5.30. Closed on Sundays and Bank Holiday weekends.
Assistant Director (G5), Prof. R. F. Fox.
Curator B, Dr. L. D. Will.

NATIONAL RAILWAY MUSEUM
Leeman Road, York YO2 4XJ
[0904–621261]

The Museum, opened in 1975, houses the national rail transport collection. Locomotives, rolling stock and carriages are displayed to illustrate the technical, social and economic story of the development of railways in Britain. Open Mon.–Sat. 10–6, Sun. 11–6.
Keeper , Dr. J. A. Coiley.
Curator C, R. Shorland-Ball.

NATIONAL MUSEUM OF PHOTOGRAPHY, FILM AND TELEVISION
Prince's View, Bradford BD5 0TR
[0274–727488]

The Museum, opened in 1983, collects, conserves and displays photography, film and television materials and equipment. The Museum has the only IMAX cinema in the U.K. Open Tues.–Sun. 11–6, with special exhibition galleries open to 7.30.
Keeper (Curator B), C. J. Ford.
Curator C, Miss M. Benton.

THE VICTORIA AND ALBERT MUSEUM
South Kensington, SW7 2RL
[01–938 8500]

Open Mon.–Sat. 10–5.30, Sun. 2.30–5.50. Closed Christmas Eve, Christmas Day, Boxing Day, New Year's Day and May Day. The National Art Library is open Tues.–Sat. 10–5 (closed 1–2 Sat.) and the Print Room Tues.–Fri. 10–5, Sat. 10–1, 2–4.30. Donations are invited.

A museum of all branches of fine and applied art, it descends directly from the Museum of Manufactures, which opened in Marlborough House in 1852 after the Great Exhibition of 1851. The Museum was moved in 1857 to become part of the collective South

Kensington Museum. It was renamed the Victoria and Albert Museum in 1899. The branch museum at Bethnal Green was opened in 1872 and the building is the most important surviving example of the type of glass and iron construction used by Paxton for the Great Exhibition. The Victoria and Albert Museum also administers the Wellington Museum (Apsley House), Ham House, Osterley Park, and the Theatre Museum.
Director and Secretary, Mrs. E. A. L. Esteve-Coll.

Department of Ceramics

Keeper (G5), J. V. Mallet.
Deputy Keeper, D. M. Archer.
Assistant Keeper, Dr. O. Watson.

Department of Conservation

Keeper (G5), Dr. J. Ashley-Smith.
Deputy Keeper, Mrs. G. F. Miles.

Far Eastern Department

Keeper (G5), Miss R. Kerr (*acting*).
Assistant Keeper, A. C. Clunas.

Department of Furniture and Interior Design

Keeper (G5), J. H. Morley.
Deputy Keeper, S. S. Jervis.

Indian Department

Keeper (G5), R. W. Skelton.
Assistant Keepers, Dr. D. Swallow; J. S. Guy.

National Art Library

Keeper (G5), J. F. van den Wateren.
Deputy Keeper, Dr. D. Haldane.
Assistant Keeper, Dr. R. Watson.

Metalwork Department

Keeper (G5), R. Lightbown.
Assistant Keepers, Mrs. P. Glanville; Miss M. Campbell; E. R. Edgecumbe.

Prints, Drawings, Photographs and Paintings Department

Keeper (G5), J. D. W. Murdoch.
Assistant Keepers, Miss S. B. Lambert; L. S. Lambourne; M. Haworth-Booth; M. Snodin.

Department of Sculpture

Keeper (G5), A. F. Radcliffe.
Assistant Keepers, M. Baker; P. E. D. Williamson.

Department of Textiles and Dress

Keeper (G5), Miss S. Levey.
Deputy Keeper, Miss N. K. A. Rothstein.
Assistant Keepers, Mrs. M. Ginsburg; Mrs. V. D. Mendes; Miss W. Hefford.

Administration

Chief Administrative Officer (G5), J. Close.

Department of Public Services

Keeper (G5), J. Earle.

Bethnal Green Museum of Childhood
Cambridge Heath Road, Bethnal Green, E2 9PA
[01–980 3204]

Open Mon.–Thurs. and on Sat. 10–6, Sun. 2.30–6. Closed every Friday, May Day, Christmas Eve, Christmas Day, Boxing Day and New Year's Day.
Keeper (G6), A. P. Burton.

Theatre Museum
1E Tavistock Street, WC2E 7PA
[01–836 7891]

Open Tues.–Sun. 11–7. Closed Mon. except Bank Holidays. Admission £2.25, concessions £1.25.

Keeper (G6), A. Schouvaloff.
Assistant Keeper, Dr. J. Fowler.

THE COMMONWEALTH INSTITUTE
Kensington High Street, W8
[01–603 4535]

The Commonwealth Institute is a centre for information about the Commonwealth. It is funded by the British Government with contributions from other Commonwealth Governments. The Institute is controlled by a Board of Governors which includes the High Commissioners of all Commonwealth countries represented in London. The Institute has permanent exhibitions on all Commonwealth nations, an arts centre, library and education department.
Open Mon.–Sat. 10–5.30, Sun. 2–5. Admission free. Closed Good Friday, May Day, Christmas Eve, Christmas Day, Boxing Day and New Year's Day.
Director, J. F. Porter.
Deputy Director, R. R. Bourne.
* *Chief Education Officer*, P. L. B. Woodroffe.
* *Chief Exhibition Officer*, A. E. Cobbold.
* *Art Director*, R. Atkins.
* *Chief Administration Officer*, M. J. Dunleavy.
** *Librarian*, M. J. Foster.
** *Senior Education Officer*, Miss M. Butcher.
** *Senior Exhibition Officer*, R. Varney.
(Salaries: * £16,392–£21,757; ** £13,599–£16,665).

IMPERIAL WAR MUSEUM
Lambeth Road, SE1 6HZ
[01–735 8922]

Open daily (except Good Friday, Christmas Eve, Christmas Day, Boxing Day, New Year's Day and May Bank Holiday) 10–5.50 (Sun. 2–5.50). Reference Depts. open Mon.–Fri. (except on public holidays), 10–5. The display galleries will be closed Oct. 31, 1988–March 19, 1989 for redevelopment; the reference departments will be open as usual.
The Museum, founded in 1917, illustrates and records all aspects of the two world wars and other military operations involving Britain and the Commonwealth since 1914. It was opened in its present home, formerly Bethlem Hospital or Bedlam, in 1936. The Museum also administers H.M.S. *Belfast* in the Pool of London, Duxford Airfield near Cambridge and The Cabinet War Rooms in Westminster.
Expenses for 1988–89 are estimated at £12,800,000.

Salaries

Grade 5	£25,756–£30,644
Grade 6	£19,537–£27,388
Grade 7	£15,631–£21,936

Director (G5), A. C. N. Borg, ph.d., f.s.a.
Deputy Director and Head of the Research and Information Office (G5), R. W. K. Crawford.
Secretary (G6), J. J. Chadwick.
Special Assistant to the Director, Mrs. S. R. Burgess.
Establishment Officer, G. A. Kelly.
Finance Officer, Mrs. P. A. Whitfield.
Museum Superintendent (G7), D. A. Needham.
Senior Keeper and Keeper of Audio-Visual Records (G5), G. T. C. Coultass.
Keeper of Duxford Airfield (G5), E. O. Inman.
Keeper of H.M.S. Belfast (G5), Capt. A. W. Wheeler, r.n.
Keeper of the Department of Museum Services (G6), C. Dowling, d.Phil.
Keeper of the Department of Documents (G6), R. W. A. Suddaby.

Keeper of the Department of Exhibits and Firearms (G6), D. J. Penn.
Keeper of the Department of Printed Books (G6), G. M. Bayliss, ph.d.
Keeper of the Department of Art (G6), Miss A. H. Weight.
Keeper of the Department of Film (G6), Miss A. E. Fleming.
Keeper of the Department of Information Retrieval (G6), R. B. N. Smither.
Keeper of the Department of Photographs (G6), Miss K. J. Carmichael.
Keeper of the Department of Sound Records (G7), Mrs. M. A. Brooks.
Curator of the Cabinet War Rooms, E. J. Wenzel.

NATIONAL MARITIME MUSEUM
Greenwich, SE10 9NF
[01–858 4422]

Open Mon.–Sat., 10–6 (10–5 in winter); Sun. 2–6 (2–5 in winter). Closed Jan. 1, Good Friday, May Day Bank Holiday and Dec. 24–26. Admission charge.
Reading Room open Mon.–Fri., 10–5; readers' tickets available on written application to Reader Services Section.
Established by Act of Parliament in 1934, the National Maritime Museum illustrates the maritime history of Great Britain in the widest sense, underlining the importance of the sea and its influence on the nation's power, wealth, culture, technology and institutions. The Museum is in two groups of buildings in Greenwich Park—the main buildings centred around the Queen's House (built by Inigo Jones, 1616–35) and the Old Royal Observatory (including Wren's Flamsteed House) to the south. The collections include paintings, actual craft and ship models, ships' lines, prints and drawings, atlases and charts, navigational and astronomical instruments, uniforms and relics, books and MSS.
Director, R. L. Ormond.

NATIONAL ARMY MUSEUM
Royal Hospital Road, SW3 4HT
[01–730 0717]

Established by Royal Charter (1960). History of five centuries of the British Army: includes the story of the Indian Army up to Independence in 1947. Open, Mon.–Sat., 10–5.30; Sun. 2–5.30. The Indian Army room at R.M.A. Sandhurst, Camberley, Surrey may be viewed by appointment.
Director, I. G. Robertson.
Personal Assistant to the Director, Miss E. Christie.
Deputy Director and Keeper of Records, B. Mollo, t.d.

ROYAL AIR FORCE MUSEUM
Grahame Park Way,
Hendon, NW9 5LL
[01–205 2266]

Situated on the former airfield at Hendon, the Museum illustrates the development of aviation from before the Wright brothers to the present-day R.A.F. Over 60 historic aircraft are on display from the Museum's collection. The complex includes Battle of Britain and Bomber Command halls.
Open daily, 10–6. Closed Dec. 24, 25, 26, Jan. 1, Admission charge.
Director, M. A. Fopp.
Keepers, R. F. Barker; D. C. R. Elliott; P. Murton; R. Simpson; A. Harold.

THE NATIONAL MUSEUMS AND GALLERIES ON MERSEYSIDE
William Brown Street, Liverpool L3 8EN
[051–207 0001]

On April 1, 1986 a corporate body, The National Museums and Galleries on Merseyside, was established, funded directly by the Government, to take over responsibility for the museums and galleries previously administered by Merseyside County Council. Various stores ancillary to the collections are also the responsibility of the body.

All properties, except the Large Objects Collection, are open all year except Jan. 1, Dec. 24–26 and Good Friday. Opening times for all properties (except the Maritime Museum and the Large Objects Collection) are Mon.–Sat. 10–5, Sun. 2–5. Opening times for the Merseyside Maritime Museum are daily 10.30–5.30. Admission charge. Opening times for the Large Objects Collection are; Easter–Sept., daily 10–5.
Chairman of the Board of Trustees, Sir Leslie Young, C.B.E.
Director, R. Foster.
Deputy Director, (vacant).

Liverpool Museum
William Brown Street, Liverpool
[051–207 0001]

Merseyside Maritime Museum
Pier Head, Liverpool
[051–709 1551]

Large Objects Collection
Princes Dock, Liverpool
[051–207 0001]

Museum of Labour History
County Sessions House, Islington, Liverpool
[051–207 0001]

Walker Art Gallery
William Brown Street, Liverpool
[051–207 0001]

Lady Lever Art Gallery
Port Sunlight Village, Bebington, Wirral
[051–645 3623]

Sudley Art Gallery
Mossley Hill Road, Liverpool
[051–207 0001]

(For other Museums in England—*see* Index)

THE NATIONAL MUSEUM OF WALES
(Amgueddfa Genedlaethol Cymru)
Cardiff CF1 3NP
[0222 397951]

Open Tues.–Sat., 10–5, Sun. 2.30–5. Closed on Mondays, Christmas Eve, Christmas Day, Boxing Day, New Year's Day, May Day and Good Friday. Admission charge.
President, Hon. J. Davies.
Vice-President, C. R. T. Edwards.
Director, D. W. Dykes, Ph.D., F.S.A.
Secretary, G. Morgan.
Keepers, M. G. Bassett, Ph.D. (*Geology*); B. A. Thomas, Ph.D. (*Botany*); P. M. Morgan (*Zoology*); H. S. Green, Ph.D. (*Archaeology*); T. J. Stevens (*Art*).

Welsh Folk Museum
(Amgueddfa Werin Cymru)
St. Fagans, Nr. Cardiff

Open April–Oct., daily 10–5; Nov.–March, Mon.–Sat. 10–5. Admission charge. Closed on Christmas Eve, Christmas Day, Boxing Day, New Year's Day, Good Friday and May Day.
Curator, J. G. Jenkins, Ph.D.
Keepers, V. H. Phillips; E. Scourfield, Ph.D.; E. William, Ph.D.

Roman Legionary Museum, Caerleon
Caerleon, Gwent.

Contains material found on the site of the Roman fortress of Isca and its suburbs. Admission charge.

Turner House Art Gallery
Plymouth Road, Penarth, Nr. Cardiff

Open Tues.–Sat. 11–12.45 and 2–5, Sun. 2–5. Closed Mondays, except Bank Holidays, and on Christmas Eve, Christmas Day, Boxing Day, New Year's Day, Good Friday, and May Day.

Museum of the North
Llanberis, Gwynedd

An environmental centre interpreting the natural history of Snowdonia. Open mid-June to mid-Sept.; weekdays 10–5; Sun. 2.30–5. Admission charge.

Welsh Slate Museum
Llanberis, Gwynedd

Open Easter–Sept. daily 9.30–5.30. Admission charge.

Segontium Roman Fort Museum
Beddgelert Road, Caernarfon, Gwynedd

Open weekdays at 9.30, Sundays at 2. Closes at 6 from May to September, at 5.30 in March, April and October, at 4 from November to February. Closed Christmas Eve, Christmas Day, Boxing Day, New Year's Day, Good Friday and May Day. On the site of the fort, the museum is in the guardianship of the Welsh Office. Contains mostly material excavated there.

Museum of the Welsh Woollen Industry
Dre-fach Felindre, nr. Llandysul, Dyfed

It occupies part of a working mill. Open April–Sept., Mon.–Sat. 10–5. Closed May Day. Admission charge.

Welsh Industrial and Maritime Museum
Bute Street, Cardiff

Open Tues.–Sat. 10–5; Sun. 2.30–5. Closed Mondays, Christmas Eve, Christmas Day, Boxing Day, New Year's Day, Good Friday and May Day. Admission charge.
Curator, S. Owen-Jones, Ph.D., (*acting*).

Yr Hen Gapel
Tre'r-ddôl, nr. Aberystwyth, Dyfed

The museum portrays 19th century religious life in Wales. Open 10–5 Monday–Saturday from April–September. Closed May Day. Admission free.

NATIONAL MUSEUMS OF SCOTLAND
Chambers Street, Edinburgh EH1 1JF
[031–225 7534]
and
Queen Street, Edinburgh EH2 1JD
[031–225 7534]

Open, Mon.–Sat., 10–5 and Sun., 2–5.
The National Museums of Scotland have one Director and one Board of Trustees, and include, besides the Royal Museum of Scotland (an amalgamation of the Royal Scottish Museum and the National Museum of Antiquities), the Scottish United Services Museum, the Scottish Agricultural Museum at Ingliston, the Museum of Flight at East Fortune, Shambellie House Museum of Costume near Dumfries, Leith Custom House Gallery and Biggar Gasworks Museum.

Director, R. G. W. Anderson, D.Phil. £31,844
Research Director, A. Fenton, C.B.E., D.Litt. ...£28,931
Keeper, Department of History & Applied Art, Miss D. Idiens.
Keeper, Department of Geology, W. D. I. Rolfe Ph.D.
Keeper, Department of Natural History, M. Shaw, D.Phil.
Keeper, Department of Science, Technology and Working Life, D. Bryden.
Deputy Keepers, Sheila Brock, Ph.D.; S. C. Wood; D. V. Clarke, Ph.D.; Ms C. V. Glenn.
(Salaries: Keepers £24,765–£28,215; Deputy Keepers £18,786–£25,335).

NATIONAL AUDIT OFFICE
157–197 Buckingham Palace Road, SW1W 9SP
[01–798 7000]

The National Audit Office came into existence under the National Audit Act 1983, to replace and continue the work of the former Exchequer and Audit Department. The Act reinforced the Office's total financial and operational independence from the Government and brought its head, the Comptroller and Auditor General, into a closer relationship with Parliament as an Officer of the House of Commons.

The National Audit Office provides independent information, advice and assurance to Parliament and the public about all aspects of the financial operations of government departments and many other bodies receiving public funds. This it does by examining and certifying the accounts of these organizations; and by regularly publishing reports to Parliament on the results of its value for money investigations of the economy, efficiency and effectiveness with which public resources have been used. The National Audit Office is also the auditor by agreement of the accounts of certain international and other organizations. In addition, the office authorizes the issue of public funds to Government departments.

Comptroller and Auditor General, J. B. Bourn, C.B.
  Private Secretary, T. J. Bristow.
Deputy Comptroller and Auditor General, H. D. Myland, C.B.
Assistant Auditor Generals, D. A. Dewar; M. J. Goodson; R. N. Le Marechal.
Directors, P. J. C. Keemer; G. W. Garside; M. R. J. Paul; P. J. Beck; J. A. Davies; I. R. W. Hargest; R. W. Locke; T. Dobson; P. O'Keefe; A. G. Brown; T. J. Lovett; A. C. Pyatt; G. J. S. Frith; A. I. A. Oyarzabal; C. L. Press; W. D. Turner; B. D. Baker; C. K. Beauchamp; J. A. Higgins; A. K. Bell; L. H. Hughes; M. C. Pfleger; R. M. Bennett; J. M. Pearce; R. E. Spurgeon.
Deputy Directors, A. W. Bird; E. J. Weeks; C. J. Day; D. C. Page; J. E. Smith; B. Hogg; R. J. McCourt; A. R. Murray; W. L. Ewing; G. J. McKeown; M. V. Pettet; A. G. Roberts; R. A. Skeen; A. Cunningham; D. S. Dodge; G. G. Jones; K. Maclean; M. L. Daynes; D. R. Corsby; R. W. Tycer; J. Parsons; S. Clayton; J. J. Jones; D. J. Woodward; J. Darling; R. J. Eales; Mrs. H. Jackson; R. A. Pocock; J. O. A. Thompson; P. G. Woodward.

NATIONAL CONSUMER COUNCIL
20 Grosvenor Gardens, SW1W 0DH
[01–730 3469]

The National Consumer Council was set up by the Government in 1975 and is funded by a grant-in-aid from the Department of Trade and Industry. The Council watches over consumers' interests and speaks up for the consumer to Government, nationalised industry, independent industry and commerce, and the public and private services.

Chairman, The Rt. Hon. Sally Oppenheim-Barnes.
Director, M. Healy.

NATIONAL DOCK LABOUR BOARD
22–26 Albert Embankment, SE1 7TE
[01–735 7271]

The National Dock Labour Board administers the scheme for giving permanent employment to dock workers under the Dock Workers (Regulation of Employment) (Amendment) Scheme 1967. The Board was reconstituted as a body corporate on August 1, 1977 under the Dock Work Regulation Act 1976 which made further provision for regulating the allocation and performance of the work of cargo-handling in and about the ports of Great Britain.
Chairman, R. H. Thompson.
General Manager, K. T. Percy.

NATIONAL ECONOMIC DEVELOPMENT OFFICE
Millbank Tower, Millbank, SW1P 4QX
[01–211 6998]

The National Economic Development Council brings together Government, management and unions to tackle issues vital to jobs and economic growth, by identifying obstacles to economic development and promoting change.

Council

Government Members, The Chancellor of the Exchequer (*Chairman*); the Secretaries of State for Education and Science, Employment, Energy, Environment, and Trade and Industry.
Management Members, J. M. M. Banham; Dr. J. S. McFarlane; D. A. G. Monk; Sir Trevor Holdsworth; T. J. O'Connor; Sir Thomas Risk.
Trade Union Members, R. Bickerstaffe; J. Edmonds; C. Jenkins; W. Jordan, R. Todd; N. Willis.
Independent Members, Sir Bryan Nicholson; Sir Robert Haslam; The Rt. Hon. Robin Leigh-Pemberton; Mrs. R. E. Waterhouse, C.B.E.
Director-General, Sir John Cassels, C.B.
Secretary, M. Couchman.
Operations Director, D. Fraser.
Economic Director, W. Eltis.

NATIONAL GALLERIES
See Art Galleries

NATIONAL INVESTMENT AND LOANS OFFICE
Royex House, Aldermanbury Square, EC2V 7LR
[01–606 7321]

The National Investment and Loans Office was set up on April 1, 1980 by merging the staffs of the National Debt Office and the Public Works Loan Board. The Department provides staff and services for the National Debt Commissioners and the Public Works Loan Commissioners.
Director, I. H. Peattie.
Establishment Officer, A. G. Ladd.

National Debt Office
Comptroller General, I. H. Peattie.

Public Works Loan Board
Chairman, J. E. A. R. Guinness, C.B.E.
Deputy Chairman, R. J. Dent.

Other Commissioners, Miss F. M. Cook; R. W. E. Law; Miss V. J. Di Palma, O.B.E.; G. Ross Russell; P. Brackfield; D. H. Adams; R. A. Chapman; J. Broadfoot; R. Emmott; B. Fieldhouse.
Secretary, I. H. Peattie.
Assistant Secretary, D. L. Hammond.

NATIONAL RADIOLOGICAL PROTECTION BOARD
Chilton, Didcot, Oxon. OX11 0RQ
[0235–831600]

The National Radiological Protection Board is an independent statutory body created by the Radiological Protection Act 1970. The Government's purpose was to establish a national point of authoritative reference in radiological protection.
Chairman, Sir Richard Southwood, F.R.S.
Director, Dr. R. H. Clarke.

DEPARTMENT FOR NATIONAL SAVINGS
Charles House, 375 Kensington High Street,
W14 8SD
[01–605 9300]

The Department for National Savings was established as a Government Department in 1969. The Department is responsible for the administration of a wide range of schemes for personal savers.
(For details of schemes, *see* **National Savings** section).
(For **Salaries,** *see* page 297)

Director of Savings (G2), J. A. Patterson.
Deputy Director (G3), G. R. Wilson.
Establishment Officer (G5), D. S. Speedie.
Finance Officer (G5), D. E. L. Whittall.
Controllers (G5), P. N. S. Hickman Robertson (*Marketing & Information*); R. S. Watts; J. Stamp; E. B. Senior; C. Ward.
Senior Principals (G6), D. W. Kellaway; I. T. Standen; R. H. Lee; J. K. Hill; I. Forsyth; D. H. Monaghan; Mrs. S. M. Cullen.
Principals (G7), A. G. Muir; M. A. Nicholls; Mrs. H. Brown; W. J. Herd; D. K. Paterson; A. J. V. Cummings; T. J. Bedeman; W. J. Ferrier; H. Johnson; J. W. Davison; D. Newton; A. B. Wood; P. Finnie; C. E. Funk; I. Jordinson; A. Brown; K. R. Tyerman; T. Threlfall; B. Paley; A. T. Stevenson; H. Webster; J. Wheatley; A. S. McGill; T. J. F. McMahon; C. McVey; R. A. Nichol; N. Thistlethwaite; J. B. Dunphy; R. J. McLelland; J. C. Foreman; D. Wilson; J. Wheatley; P. B. Robinson; G. V. Wise; A. S. Lamond; D. Jeffrey; R. H. Mitchell; Miss A. Fort.

NATIONAL THEATRE BOARD
South Bank, SE1 9PX
[01–928 2033]

Chairman, The Lord Rayne.
Chairman–designate, The Lady Soames, D.B.E.
Members, R. Baird; T. Burrill; The Lord Chorley; R. Clutton; J. Hannam, M.P.; Sonia Melchett; R. M. Mills; The Lord Mishcon; Sir Derek Mitchell, K.C.B., C.V.O.; J. Mortimer, Q.C.; The Lady Plowden, D.B.E.; Lois Sieff; J. Whitney; Sir Peter Parker, M.V.O.
Secretary, D. Gosling.

NATURAL ENVIRONMENT RESEARCH COUNCIL
Polaris House, North Star Avenue,
Swindon, Wilts. SN2 1EU
[0793–40101]

The Natural Environment Research Council was established in 1965, to encourage, plan and conduct research in the physical and biological sciences which relate to man's natural environment and its resources.
The Council carries out research and training through its own institutes and grant-aided institutes, and by grants, fellowships and post-graduate awards to universities and other institutions of higher education.
Chairman, Prof. J. Knill, Ph.D., D.Sc.
Secretary, J. C. Bowman, C.B.E., Ph.D.
Director of Earth Sciences, Prof. J. C. Briden, Ph.D.
Director of Terrestrial and Fresh Water Sciences, P. B. Tinker, D.Sc., Ph.D.
Director of Marine Sciences, J. D. Woods, Ph.D.
Director of Policy, Planning and External Affairs, J. McGinnety, Ph.D.

RESEARCH INSTITUTES

British Antarctic Survey
Madingley Road, Cambridge CB3 0ET
[0223–61188]
Director, Dr. D. J. Drewry, Ph.D.

British Geological Survey
Nicker Hill, Keyworth, Nottingham NG12 5GG
[06077–6111]
Director, F. G. Larminie, C.B.E.

Institute of Oceanographic Sciences
Deacon Laboratory, Wormley, nr. Godalming
GU8 5UB
[042879–4141]
Director, Dr. A. Rees (*acting*).

Institute of Marine Biochemistry
St. Fittick's Road, Aberdeen AB1 3RA
[0224–875695]
Director, C. B. Cowey, Ph.D. (*acting*).

Plymouth Marine Laboratory
Prospect Place, The Hoe, Plymouth PL1 3DH
Citadel Hill, Plymouth PL1 2PB
[0752–222772]
Director, B. L. Bayne, Ph.D.
Deputy Director, M. Whitfield.

Proudman Oceanographic Laboratory
Bidston, Birkenhead L43 7RA
[051–653 8633]
Director, B. S. McCartney, Ph.D.

Sea Mammal Research Unit
c/o British Antarctic Survey,
[0223–311354]
Head of Unit, J. Harwood, Ph.D.

Institute of Hydrology
Maclean Building, Crowmarsh Gifford,
Wallingford, Oxon. OX10 8BB
[0491–38800]
Director, Prof. B. Wilkinson.

Institute of Terrestrial Ecology (North)
Bush Estate, Penicuik, Midlothian EH26 0QB,
[031–445 4343]
Director, O. W. Heal, Ph.D.

Institute of Terrestrial Ecology (South)
Monks Wood Experimental Station, Abbots Ripton,
Huntingdon PE17 2LS
[04873–381/8]
Director, J. P. Dempster, ph.d; d.sc.

Institute of Virology
Mansfield Road, Oxford OX1 3SR
[0865–512361]
Director, Prof. D. H. L. Bishop, ph.d.

GRANT-AIDED INSTITUTES

Freshwater Biological Association
The Ferry House, Far Sawrey,
Ambleside, Cumbria LA22 0LP
[09662–2468/9]
Director, J. G. Jones, ph.d.

Marine Biological Association of the U.K.
The Laboratory, Citadel Hill, Plymouth PL1 2PB
[0752–222772]
Director, M. Whitfield, m.d.

Scottish Marine Biological Association
Dunstaffnage Marine Research Laboratory
P.O. Box 3, Oban, Argyll PA34 4AD
[0631–62244]
Director, Prof. J. B. L. Matthews (*acting*).

Unit of Comparative Plant Ecology
Dept. of Plant Sciences, Sheffield University,
Sheffield S10 2TN
[0742–768555]
Head of Unit, Prof. I. H. Rorison, d.phil.

CENTRAL SERVICES

N.E.R.C. Scientific Services
Polaris House, North Star Avenue, Swindon,
Wilts. SN2 1EU
[0793–40104]
Director, B. J. Hinde.

Research Vessel Services
No. 1 Dock, Barry, S. Glamorgan
[0446–737451]
Head, L. M. Skinner, ph.d.

N.E.R.C. Computer Service
Holbrook House, Station Road,
Swindon, Wilts. SN1 1DE
[0793–40101]
Director, H. J. Down.

NATURE CONSERVANCY COUNCIL
Northminster House, Peterborough PE1 1UA
[0733–40345]

Establishes, maintains and manages National Nature Reserves, advises generally on nature conservation, gives advice to the Government on nature conservation policies and on how other policies may affect nature conservation, and supports, commissions and undertakes relevant research.
Chairman, W. H. N. Wilkinson.
Deputy Chairman, Sir John Burnett.
Director General, T. R. Hornsby.
Chief Scientist, Dr. D. A. Ratcliffe.
Country Headquarters:
England: Northminster House, Peterborough
PE1 1UA.—*Director*, Dr. F. B. O'Connor.
Scotland: 12 Hope Terrace, Edinburgh EH9 2AS.—
Director, Dr. J. Francis.
Wales: Plas Penrhos, Penrhos Road, Bangor, Gwynedd LL57 2LQ.—*Director*, Dr. T. Pritchard.

NORTHERN IRELAND OFFICE
Whitehall, SW1A 2AZ
[01–210 3000]
Stormont House, Belfast BT4 3ST
[0232–63255]
Stormont Castle, Belfast BT4 3ST
[0232–63011]
Dundonald House,
Upper Newtownards Road, Belfast BT4 3SU
[0232–63255]

The Northern Ireland Office is the U.K. government department in which the Secretary of State for Northern Ireland has overall responsibility for the government of Northern Ireland. The Secretary of State is directly responsible for constitutional developments, law and order, security and electoral matters. Under the Northern Ireland Act 1974, the Northern Ireland departments are also subject to the direction and control of the Secretary of State during direct rule.
Secretary of State for Northern Ireland, THE RT. HON.
THOMAS KING, M.P.
Parliamentary Private Secretary, A. Mackay, M.P.
Minister of State, IAN STEWART, R.D., M.P.
Parliamentary Private Secretary, M. G. Wolfson,
M.P.
Parliamentary Under Secretaries of State, The Lord
Lyell; R. Needham, M.P.; Dr. B. Mawhinney, M.P.;
P. Viggers, M.P.
Permanent Under Secretary of State, Sir John Blelloch, K.C.B.
*Second Permanent Under Secretary of State, Head of
the NICS*, Sir Kenneth Bloomfield, K.C.B.

OMBUDSMAN, *see* LOCAL
COMMISSIONERS, and PARLIAMENTARY
COMMISSIONER
(For non-statutory Ombudsmen, *see* Index)

ORDNANCE SURVEY
Romsey Road, Maybush, Southampton SO9 4DH
[0703–79200]

The Ordnance Survey is the national mapping agency for Britain and it produces over 220,000 large scale maps of the country at three basic scales. These are 1:1,250 (50 inches to 1 mile) for urban areas; 1:2,500 (25 inches to 1 mile) for rural areas; and 1:10,000 (6 inches to 1 mile) for mountain and moorland. Additionally, Ordnance Survey produces a range of small scale maps and other products for general use.
Director-General, P. McMaster.
Directors:
Surveys and Production, A. S. Macdonald.
Marketing, Planning and Development, J.
Leonard.
Overseas Surveys, B. E. Furmston.
Establishments and Finance, K. Nolan.
Heads of Functions:
Production, E. Gilbert.
Topographic Surveys, P. Wesley.
Marketing, D. Toft.
Research and Development, M. Sowton.
Head of Finance, J. Evenett.
Establishments, I. Lock.
Information and Computer Service, B. W. Nanson.

OVERSEAS DEVELOPMENT ADMINISTRATION
Eland House, Stag Place, SW1E 5DH
[01–273 3000]
Abercrombie House, Eaglesham Road, East Kilbride,
Glasgow G75 8EA
[03552–41199]

The Overseas Development Administration deals with British development assistance to overseas countries. This includes both capital aid on concessional terms and technical assistance (mainly in the form of specialist staff abroad and training facilities in the United Kingdom), whether provided directly to developing countries or through the various multilateral aid organizations, including the United Nations and its specialized agencies.
(For **Salaries**, *see* page 297)

Minister for Overseas Development, THE RT. HON. CHRISTOPHER PATTEN, M.P.
  Private Secretary (G7), M. A. Wickstead.
  Parliamentary Private Secretary, R. Key, M.P.
Permanent Secretary (G1A), J. Caines, C.B.
  Private Secretary, Ms. S. A. Howes.
Deputy Secretary (G2), R. M. Ainscow.
Under Secretaries (G3), N. B. Hudson; J. L. F. Buist; B. R. Ireton; J. V. Kerby; Dr. J. M. Healey; R. G. Manning; A. J. Bennett; Dr. D. G. Osborne.

Economic and Social Division
Head of the Economic Service (G3), Dr. J. M. Healey.
Senior Economic Advisers (G5), J. B. Wilmshurst; J. C. H. Morris; G. P. Sandersley; A. G. Coverdale; B. P. Thomson.
Economic Advisers (G7), P. J. Ackroyd; P. D. Balacs; B. Carstairs; C. R. Clift; J. Clarke; D. B. Crapper; P. J. Dearden; M. G. Foster; K. E. Gubbins; Dr. S. Haley; E. Hawthorn; P. G. Hill; W. Kingsmill; P. J. A. Landymore; A. Moon; P. L. Owen; J. N. Stevens; Mrs. J. M. White.
Chief Statistician (G5), R. M. Allen.
Statisticians (G7), A. B. Williams; Miss M. O'Connor; J. R. B. King; M. V. Wilson.
Principal Finance and Management Adviser (G5), K. L. Sparkhall.
Senior Finance and Management Advisers (G6), E. A. Gill; D. W. Heffer.
Senior Social Development Adviser (G6), Dr. S. R. Conlin.
Social Development Adviser (G7), Dr. R. J. Eyben.

Information Department
Head of Information Dept. (G5), J. C. Machin.
Principal Information Officer (G7), Ms L. J. Sinclair.

Heads of Development Divisions (G5)
Caribbean (Bridgetown), M. G. Bawden; *East Africa (Nairobi)*. M. C. McCulloch; *Pacific (Suva)*, J. Hodges; *South-East Asia (Bangkok)*, M. J. Dinham; *Southern Africa (Lilongwe)*, G. M. Stegmann.
Assistant Secretaries (G5), Miss A. M. Archbold; G. A. Beattie; P. D. M. Freeman; K. G. W. Frost; R. M. Graham-Harrison; W. Hobman; C. R. O. Jones; Mrs. B. M. Kelly; J. C. Machin; V. J. McLean; R. G. Pettitt; M. A. Power; C. P. Raleigh; D. Sands Smith; D. L. Stanton; D. F. Turner; Ms. S. Unsworth; Mrs. P. M. Wilkinson; R. J. Wilson; R. W. Wootton.
Senior Principals (G6), F. Crampsey; L. E. Fitzpatrick; B. W. Hammond; S. Ray; D. G. Bell; G. A. Williams.
Principals (G7), J. D. Aitken; S. I. Alexander; J. A. Anning; G. A. Armstrong; D. W. Baker; D. J. Batt; D. G. Bell; W. T. Birrell; H. Britton; W. A. Brownlie; P. J. Burton; R. O. Carter; J. H. S. Chard; P. H. Charters; Miss D. W. Cherry; D. J. Church; T. F. G. Connor; B. Cook; G. Crabtree; D.

R. Curran; A. D. Davis; P. Dean; J. R. Drummond; J. R. Gilbert; K. D. Grimshaw; Miss J. V. Hanna; P. Harris; Ms. V. M. Harris; Ms. P. J. Hilton; M. I. Holland; N. Hoult; W. Jardine; Mrs. J. Laurance; D. Lawless; G. G. Leader; G. H. Malley; C. A. Metcalf; J. C. Millett; J. D. Moye; G. A. Mustard; C. Myhill; P. T. Perris; B. G. Peskett; G. M. Porter; S. Ray; D. T. Richards; R. S. Ridgwell; S. R. J. Robbins; G. F. Roberts; M. K. Robson; C. R. Roth; J. M. Scoular; R. J. Smith; M. J. Sexton; I. F. Stickels; I. D. Stuart; A. J. Sutherland; C. M. Taylor; E. C. N. Taylor; N. Thomas; B. A. Thorpe; R. G. Toulmin; D. Trotter; Miss M. H. Vowles; C. W. Warren; S. A. Wheeler; C. J. White; R. S. White; D. M. Whitecross; M. A. Wickstead; P. M. Wilson; J. M. Winter; A. K. C. Wood.

Advisory and Specialist Staff
Principal Education Adviser (G5), Dr. R. O. Iredale.
Education Advisers (G6), M. D. Francis; M. E. Seath; Dr. D. G. Swift.
Principal Engineering Adviser (G5), T. D. Pike.
Engineering Advisers (G6), J. N. Bulman; A. G. Colley; D. Gillett; B. Dolton; P. H. Hilton; H. B. Jackson; B. G. Little.
Engineering Advisers (G7), C. I. Ellis; R. J. Cadwallader; C. S. Reid; M. F. Sergeant; P. W. D. H. Roberts; A. Coulthart; A. Barker; J. R. Plumb.
Energy Adviser (G6), Dr. J. L. D. Harrison.
Electrical and Mechanical Engineering Adviser (G6), R. P. Jones.
Senior Architectural Adviser (G6), M. W. Parkes.
Senior Architectural & Planning Adviser (G6), H. W. Housego-Woolgar.
Senior Medical Adviser (G6), Dr. P. Key.
Principal Nursing and Health Services Adviser, Miss M. Pollock.
Nursing and Health Services Adviser, Miss A. Rutter.
Chief Natural Resources Adviser (G3), A. J. Bennett.
Deputy Chief National Resources Adviser (G5), P. R. Weare.
Deputy Chief Natural Resources Adviser (G5), Dr. J. C. Davies (*Research*).
Senior Agricultural Advisers (G6), J. R. F. Hansell; R. W. Smith (*Research*); P. Tuley; J. M. Scott; A. R. Stobbs; A. J. Tainsh; R. L. Waddell; M. F. Watson; M. J. Wilson.
Agricultural Advisers (G7), Dr. B. E. Grimwood; D. J. Salmon; D. A. Trotman.
Animal Health Advisers (G6), G. G. Freeland; Dr. A. D. Irvin.
Fisheries Advisers (G6), J. Stoneman; Dr. J. Tarbit.
Forestry Advisers (G6), R. H. Kemp; W. J. Howard.
Financial Management Advisers (G6), E. A. Gill; D. W. Heffer.
Senior Procurement Adviser (G6), R. C. Morgan.

Overseas Development Natural Resources Institute
Central Avenue, Chatham Maritime,
Chatham, Kent ME4 4TB
[0634–880088]

Director (G5), G. A. Beattie.

OFFICE OF THE PARLIAMENTARY COMMISSIONER AND HEALTH SERVICE COMMISSIONER
Church House, Great Smith Street, SW1P 3BW
[01–212 7676]

The Parliamentary Commissioner for Administration is responsible for investigating complaints referred to him by Members of the House of Commons from members of the public who claim to have sustained injustice in consequence of maladministration in connection with administrative action taken by or on behalf of Government Departments and certain non-departmental public bodies. Certain types of action by Government Departments or bodies are excluded from investigation. Actions taken by other public bodies (such as local authorities, the police, the Post Office and nationalized industries) are outside the Commissioner's scope.

The Health Service Commissioners for England, for Scotland and for Wales are responsible for investigating complaints against National Health Service authorities that are not dealt with by those authorities to the satisfaction of the complainant. Complaints can be referred direct by the member of the public who claims to have sustained injustice or hardship in consequence of the failure in a service provided by a relevant body, failure of that body to provide a service or in consequence of any other action by that body. Certain types of action are excluded, in particular, action taken solely in consequence of the exercise of clinical judgment. The three offices are presently held by the Parliamentary Commissioner.

Parliamentary Commissioner and Health Service Commissioner, Sir Anthony Barrowclough, Q.C.
£68,500
Secretaries (G3), D. G. Allen, C.M.G.; G. V. Marsh
Directors (G5), K. H. Green; Mrs. J. M. Fowler; M. D. Randall; J. C. Bateman; M. A. Johnson; M. P. Cornwell-Kelly.
Principals (G7), P. J. Belsham; G. M. Keil; A. Watson; Mrs. C. Bentley; N. J. Jordan; R. L. Fenner; Miss D. M. Pace; R. Paxton; T. J. Corkett; D. S. Burn; A. C. Beer (*Establishment Officer*); R. V. Siese; J. D. Jarvis; D. Hall; B. P. Jones.

PARLIAMENTARY COUNSEL
36 Whitehall, SW1A 2AY
[01–210 6633]

Parliamentary Counsel draft all Government Bills (i.e. primary legislation) except common form ones and those relating exclusively to Scotland. They also advise on all aspects of parliamentary procedure in connection with such Bills and draft Government amendments to them as well as any motions (including financial resolutions) necessary to secure their introduction into, and passage through, Parliament.
First Counsel, C. H. de Waal, C.B., Q.C. £65,000
Second Counsel, P. Graham, C.B. £54,000
Counsel, J. D. M. Rennie, C.B.; J. C. Jenkins, C.B.; J. S. Mason, C.B.; Miss S. P. Burns; D. W. Saunders; E. G. Caldwell; E. G. Bowman; G. B. Sellers. *up to* £45,500

PAROLE BOARD
Abell House, John Islip Street, SW1P 4LH
[01–211 3000]

The Board was constituted under section 59 of the Criminal Justice Act, 1967.

The function of the Board is to advise the Secretary of State for the Home Department with respect to: (1) Release on licence under section 60 (i) or 61 and recall under section 62 of the Criminal Justice Act, 1967 of persons whose cases have been referred to the Board by the Secretary of State; (2) The conditions of such licences, and the variation and cancellation of such conditions; and (3) any other matter so referred which is connected with release on licence or recall of persons to whom section 60 or 61 of the Act applies.
Chairman, The Viscount Colville of Culross, Q.C.
Vice-Chairman, The Hon. Mr. Justice Wood.
Secretary, T. J. Wilkie.

PATENT OFFICE
(and Industrial Property and Copyright Department)
Department of Trade and Industry,
State House, 66–71 High Holborn,
WC1R 4TP
[01–831 2525]
Sale Branch: Orpington, Kent

The duties of the Department consist in the administration of the Patent Acts, the Registered Designs Act and the Trade Marks Act and in dealing with questions relating to the Copyright Acts. The Department also provides an information service about patent specifications. In 1986 the Office granted 16,206 patents and registered 7,167 designs and 17,089 trade marks.
Comptroller-General (G3), P. J. Cooper £38,530
Assistant Comptrollers, T. W. Sage; V. Tarnofsky
£32,414
Superintending Examiners, N. G. Tarnofsky; J. P. Britton; M. F. Vivian; A. Sugden; J. Sharrock; G. K. Lindsey; E. F. Blake; K. E. Panchen; W. J. Lyon £29,745
Principal Examiners, C. S. Richenberg; A. J. Needs; P. L. Eggington; Miss C. M. Edwards; D. R. Barratt; B. C. Faulkner; S. J. Rutland; C. D. Kopkin; D. H. Rowland; E. J. Lawrence; B. J. Phillips; D. B. Johnson; C. G. M. Hoptroff; S. Southworth; B. G. Harden; M. W. Hills; L. Lewis; P. S. Michaelis; N. M. Miles; K. C. Thomas; R. S. Vidler; Miss Y. J. Pegler; P. Ferdinando; M. F. Pilgrim; P. J. Herbert; J. K. Dugnolle; G. C. Brown; D. L. Wood; C. Corney; D. Davenport . . . . £26,469–£28,629
Assistant Registrar, Trade Marks, J. M. Myall
£25,260–£28,595
Senior Principals (G6), R. V. Egan; A. Holt
£20,316–£26,865

Manchester Office
Room 921A, Sunley Buildings,
Piccadilly Plaza, M1 4BA
[01–236 2171]

PAYMASTER GENERAL
H.M. Treasury, Parliament Street, SW1P 3AG
[01–270 4350]
Sutherland House, Russell Way, Crawley, West
Sussex RH10 1UH
[0293–560999]

The Paymaster General's Office was formed by the consolidation in 1835 of various separate pay departments then existing, some of which dated back at least to the Restoration of 1660. Its function is that of paying agent for Government Departments, other than the Revenue Departments. Most of its payments are made through banks, to whose accounts the necessary transfers are made at the Bank of England. The payment of over one million public service pensions is an important feature of its work.
Paymaster General, THE RT. HON. PETER BROOKE, M.P.
Assistant Paymaster General (G5), L. A. Andrews.
Senior Principals (G6), D. R. L. Breed; A. J. McClatchey.
Principals (G7), D. R. Alexander; T. R. George; J. A. Payne; K. Sullens; G. Thomas; C. A. Ulph; M. D. West.

POLICE COMPLAINTS AUTHORITY
10 Great George Street, SW1P 3AB
[01–273 6403]

The Police Complaints Authority was established under the Police and Criminal Evidence Act 1984 to introduce a further independent element into the procedure for dealing with complaints by members of the public against police officers in England and Wales. The Authority has powers to supervise the investigation of certain categories of serious complaints and certain statutory functions in relation to the disciplinary aspects of complaints.

Chairman, Sir Cecil Clothier, K.C.B., Q.C.

Deputy Chairman (Discipline), Brig. J. Pownall.

Deputy Chairman (Investigations), Rt. Hon. R. Moyle.

Members, Air Vice-Marshal D. Clark; V. Clements; J. Crawford; B. A. Gillman; B. V. Moore; P. W. Moorhouse; K. Singh; Capt. N. Taylor; Mrs. R. Vickers; Mrs. R. Wolff.

POLITICAL HONOURS SCRUTINY COMMITTEE
Cabinet Office, 53 Parliament Street, SW1A 2NG
[01–210 3000]

The function of the Political Honours Scrutiny Committee is set out in an Order in Council dated May 31, 1979. The Prime Minister submits certain particulars to the Committee about persons proposed to be recommended for honour for their political services. The Committee, after such enquiry as they think fit, report to the Prime Minister whether, so far as they believe, the persons whose names are submitted to them are fit and proper persons to be recommended.

Chairman, The Lord Shackleton, K.G., P.C., O.B.E.

Members, The Lord Grimond, T.D., P.C.; The Lord Pym, M.C., P.C.

Secretary, Mrs. M. E. Hedley-Miller, C.B.

OFFICE OF POPULATION CENSUSES AND SURVEYS
St. Catherine's House, 10 Kingsway,
WC2B 6JP
[01–242 0262]

The Office of Population Censuses and Surveys was created by a merger in May 1970 of the General Register Office and the Government Social Survey Department. The Registrar General controls the local registration service in England and Wales in the exercise of its registration and marriage duties. Copies of the original registrations of births, still-births, marriages and deaths are kept in London. A register of adopted children is held at Titchfield. Central indexes are compiled annually and certified copies of entries may be obtained on payment of certain fees. Since 1841 the Registrar General has been responsible for taking the census of population. She also prepares and publishes a wide range of statistics and appropriate commentary relating to population, fertility, births, still-births, marriages, deaths and cause of death, infectious diseases, sickness and injuries. The Registrar General also maintains, at Southport, a central register of persons on doctors' lists, for the purposes of the National Health Service.

Hours of public access, Mon.–Fri., 8.30 a.m.–4.30 p.m.

Director and Registrar General (G2), Mrs. G. T. Banks.

Deputy Directors (G3), F. E. Whitehead; B. J. Ellis *(Establishment Officer).*

Chief Medical Statistician (G3), A. J. Fox, PH.D.

Grade 5, R. Barnes; J. Craig; M. L. Pennington; J. V. Ribbins *(Deputy Registrar General);* I. K. G. Arnold; J. A. Rowntree; B. H. Mahon.

Senior Statisticians (Medical), J. S. A. Ashley; A. G. McCormick; A. J. Swerdlow £29,344

Grade 6, B. S. T. Alcock; M. S. Britton; R. J. Butcher; A. M. Clark; J. Denton; Mrs. K. H. Dunnell; Mrs. W. Jenkins; I. B. Knight; D. L. Pearce; R. K. Thomas; R. McLeod.

Grade 7, R. I. Armitage; F. L. Ashwood; Mrs. P. E. Astbury; Ms J. Atkinson; N. E. Auckland; R. A. P. Bailey; E. Barton; R. J. Beacham; D. E. Birch; Mrs. M. R. Bone; Mrs. B. J. Botting; A. Bradbury; M. J. Bradley; T. B. Bryson; L. Bulusu; D. Capron; R. J. Carpenter; J. Cloyne; C. J. Denham; T. L. F. Devis; J. M. Dixie; Mrs. J. C. Dobbs; Ms. E. M. Goddard; I. Golds; Mrs. H. A. Green; Mrs. J. R. Gregory; P. C. Gregory; J. Haskey; P. J. Heady; A. F. Jones; B. G. Little; Miss C. S. J. Lloyd; Mrs. S. M. McCartney; Miss E. M. McCrossan; Mrs. I. MacDonald-Davies; A. J. Manners; Mrs. J. Martin; B. W. Meakings; I. D. Mills; Mrs. J. S. Morris; R. M. Nicholls; A. Parr *(Chief Inspector of Registration);* J. A. Rampton; Mrs. I. Rauta; R. U. Redpath; Miss J. M. R. Rosenbaum; T. A. Russell; J. A. Salveti; C. Shaw; D. Stewart; Mrs. D. M. Stobbart; Mrs. L. M. Street; A. W. Tester; Miss J. Todd; Mrs. M. J. Waggett; Miss S. Wallace *(Press Officer);* P. H. White.

PORT OF LONDON AUTHORITY
Head Office: Europe House, World Trade Centre,
E1 9AA
[01–481 8484]

The Port of London Authority is a public trust constituted under the Port of London Act 1968 and a Harbour Revision Order of 1975. The Board comprises a Chairman and up to ten non-executive members appointed by the Secretary of State for Transport, and up to six executive members appointed by the Board.

Chairman, Sir Brian Kellett.

Vice-Chairman, R. Crawford.

Chief Executive, River, D. Jeffery.

Chief Executive, Property, J. C. Jenkinson, M.V.O.

Chief Executive Tilbury, J. S. McNab.

Secretary, G. E. Ennals.

THE POST OFFICE
33 Grosvenor Place, SW1X 1PX
[01–235 8000]

Crown services for the carriage of Government despatches were set up about 1516. The conveyance of public correspondence began in 1635 and the mail service was made a Parliamentary responsibility with the setting up of a Post Office in 1657. Telegraphs came under the Post Office control in 1870 and the Post Office Telephone Service began in 1880. The National Girobank service of the Post Office began in 1968. The Post Office ceased to be a Government Department on October 1, 1969 and responsibility for the running of the postal, telecommunications, and giro and remittance services was transferred to a public authority called the Post Office. The 1981 British Telecommunications Act separated the functions of the Post Office, making it solely responsible for postal services and National Girobank.

The Chairman and members of the Post Office Board are appointed by the Secretary of State but responsibility for the running of the Post Office as a whole rests with the Board in its corporate capacity.

Financial Results

	1986–87 £m.	1987–88 £m.
Post Office Group		
Turnover	3,473·3	3,790·8
Trading profit before tax	170·0	212·2
Letters and Parcels		
Turnover	2,781·9	3,037·0
Trading profit before tax	131·2	151·3
Counters		
Turnover	770·0	769·2
Trading profit before tax	19·1	33·6

Girobank

Income	153·5	190·9
Operating profit before tax ...	23·1	23·5

Post Office Board

Chairman, Sir Bryan Nicholson
Vice-Chairman and Member for Personnel and Corporate Resources, K. M. Young, C.B.E.
Members, W. Cockburn, T.D. (*Managing Director, Letters*); N. Nelson (*Managing Director, Parcels*); A. J. Roberts (*Managing Director, Counters*); P. E. Sellers (*Corporate Finance and Planning*); G. M. Williamson (*Managing Director, Girobank* P.L.C.).
Part-time Members, A. B. Butler; Miss E. M. L. Cole, C.B.E.; D. O. Gladwin, C.B.E.; D. Hodson.
Secretary, Miss M. MacDonald.

PRIVY COUNCIL OFFICE
Whitehall, SW1A 2AT
[01-270 3000]

The Office is responsible for the arrangements leading to the making of all Royal Proclamations and Orders in Council; for certain formalities connected with Ministerial changes; for considering applications for the grant (or amendment) of Royal Charters; the scrutiny and approval of bye-laws and statutes of Chartered Bodies; for the appointment of High Sheriffs and many Crown and Privy Council appointments to governing bodies.

Lord President of the Council (and Leader of the House of Commons), THE RT. HON. JOHN WAKEHAM, M.P.
Private Secretary, N. F. J. Gibbons.
Minister of State, THE RT. HON. RICHARD LUCE, M.P.
Clerk of the Council, G. I. de Deney, C.V.O. £38,480
Deputy Clerk of the Council, C. E. S. Horsford, C.V.O. £30,871
Senior Clerk, R. P. Bulling £19,904

PUBLIC HEALTH LABORATORY SERVICE
Headquarters Office:
61 Colindale Avenue, NW9 5DF
[01–200 1295]

The Public Health Laboratory Service comprises 52 regional or area laboratories distributed through England and Wales, and 23 reference and special laboratories or units. The P.H.L.S. gives a routine microbiological service to several hospitals, and provides reference facilities that are available nationally. It collates information on the incidence of infection, and when necessary it institutes special enquiries into outbreaks and the epidemiology of infectious disease, although executive responsibility for their control is the statutory responsibility of local authorities. It also undertakes bacteriological surveillance of the quality of food and water for local authorities and others. The P.H.L.S. is often called upon to advise central and local government and the hospital service on many aspects of infectious disease. It maintains close contact with veterinary organizations in areas of mutual interest, and collaborates with the World Health Organization and with national laboratory and epidemiological services overseas.

The Board

Chairman, Dr. C. E. Gordon Smith, C.B., M.D., D.SC. F.R.C.P., F.R.C.Path.
Members, A. E. Eames; P. W. Russell Eggitt, O.B.E., PH.D.; E. L. Harris, C.B., F.R.C.P.; P. Higham; Ms. D. J. Hine; Prof. Rosalinde Hurley, M.D.; M. J. Painter; Prof. H. Smith, PH.D., D.SC., F.R.S.; Prof. A. J. Zuckerman, D.SC., M.D., F.R.C.P.; J. Forsythe; N. E. Day, PH.D.; J. Godfrey; A. Graham-Dixon; P. R. Grob, M.D.; H. H. John.

Staff Assessors, J. F. R. Graves; R. Gross; D. M. Jones, M.D.
Secretary, K. M. Saunders.
Deputy Secretary, J. M. Harker.
Director, J. W. G. Smith, M.D.
Deputy Directors, Joan R. Davies, M.D.; C. Roberts, M.D.

Central Public Health Laboratory
Colindale Avenue, NW9 5HT

Director, Prof. A. A. Glynn, M.D., F.R.C.P.
Division of Enteric Pathogens, B. Rowe, T.D.
Division of Hospital Infection, E. M. Cooke, M.D.
Division of Microbiological Reagents and Quality Control, A. G. Taylor, PH.D.
Food Hygiene Laboratory, R. J. Gilbert, PH.D.
Hepatitis Epidemiology Unit (Division of Epidemiology), S. Polakoff, M.D.
Mycological Reference Laboratory, Prof. D. W. R. Mackenzie, PH.D.
National Collection of Type Cultures, L. R. Hill, D.SC.
Virus Reference Laboratory, P. P. Mortimer, M.D.

Centre for Applied Microbiology and Research
Porton Down, Salisbury,
Wilts, SP4 0JG

Director, P. M. Sutton.
Director of Pathology Division, A. Baskerville, D.V.SC., PH.D.
Director of Biologics Division, Prof. J. Melling, PH.D.
Director of Biotechnology Division, Prof. A. Atkinson, PH.D.

Other Special Laboratories and Units

Anaerobe Reference Unit, Public Health Laboratory, Luton: A. T. Willis, M.D.
Communicable Disease Surveillance Centre (Division of Epidemiology), 61 Colindale Avenue, N.W.9: Dr. C. L. R. Bartlett.
Gonococcus Reference Unit, Public Health Laboratory, Bristol: A. E. Jephcott, M.D.
Influenza Research Unit, Public Health Laboratory, Guildford: J. R. Davies, M.D.
Leptospira Reference Unit, Public Health Laboratory, Hereford: S. A. Waitkins, PH.D.
Malaria Reference Laboratory, London School of Hygiene and Tropical Medicine, W.C.1: Prof. D. J. Bradley, D.M.; Prof. W. Peters, M.D., D.SC.
Mycobacterium Reference Unit, Public Health Laboratory, Cardiff: P. A. Jenkins, PH.D.

Regional Laboratories

Birmingham, J. G. P. Hutchison, M.D.; *Bristol*, A. E. Jephcott, M.D.; *Cambridge*, C. E. D. Taylor, M.D.; *Cardiff*, C. D. Ribeiro (*acting*); *Leeds*, R. N. Peel; *Liverpool*, G. C. Turner, M.D.; *Manchester*, D. M. Jones, M.D.; *Newcastle*, A. E. Wright, T.D., M.D.; *Oxford*, J. B. Selkon, T.D.; *Portsmouth*, O. A. Okubadejo, M.D.; *Sheffield*, B. W. Barton.

Area Laboratories

Ashford, C. Dulake; *Bath*, D. G. White; *Brighton*, B. T. Thom; *Carlisle*, M. A. Knowles; *Carmarthen*, H. D. S. Morgan; *Chelmsford*, R. E. Tettmar, D.Path.; *Chester*, J. H. Pennington, M.D.; *Coventry*, P. R. Mortimer, M.D.; *Dorchester*, P. Gill; *Epsom*, E. I. Tanner; *Exeter*, J. G. Cruickshank; *Gloucester*, K. A. V. Cartwright; *Guildford*, Prof. R. Y. Cartwright; *Hereford*, I. R. Ferguson; *Hull*, S. L. Mawer; *Ipswich*, P. H. Jones; *Leicester*, C. J. Mitchell; *Lincoln*, J. G. Wallace; *London*: *Central Middlesex Hospital*, D. A. McSwiggan; *Dulwich*, A. H. C. Uttley, PH.D.; *Tooting*,

D. G. Fleck, M.D.; *Whipps Cross*, B. Chattopadhyay, M.D.; *Luton*, A. T. Willis, M.D.; *Middlesbrough*, E. McKay-Ferguson, M.D.; *Norwich*, W. Shepherd, M.D.; *Nottingham*, M. J. Lewis, M.D.; *Peterborough*, R. S. Jobanputra, M.D.; *Plymouth*, P. J. Wilkinson; *Poole*, W. L. Hooper; *Preston*, D. N. Hutchinson; *Reading*, J. V. Dadswell; *Rhyl*, D. N. Looker; *Salisbury*, S. Patrick; *Shrewsbury*, C. A. Morris, M.D.; *Southampton*, J. A. Lowes; *Stoke-on-Trent*, J. Gray; *Swansea*, D. H. M. Joynson; *Taunton*, N. F. Lightfoot; *Truro*, W. A. Telfer Brunton; *Watford*, M. T. Moulsdale; *Wolverhampton*, R. G. Thompson.

REGISTRAR OF PUBLIC LENDING RIGHT
Bayheath House,
Prince Regent Street,
Stockton-on-Tees,
TS18 1DF
[0642–604699]

Under the Public Lending Right system, in operation since Jan. 1983, payment is made from public funds to authors whose books are lent out from public libraries. Payment is made once a year (in February) and the amount each author receives is proportionate to the number of times (established from a sample) that each registered book was lent out during the previous year.

The Registrar of PLR, who is appointed by the Minister for the Arts, compiles the register of authors and books. Only living authors resident in the U.K. or West Germany are eligible to apply. (The term "author" covers writers, illustrators, translators, and some editors/compilers.)

A payment of 1·12 pence was made in 1987–88 for each estimated loan of a registered book, up to a top limit of £5,000 for the books of any one registered author: the money for loans above this level is used to augment the remaining PLR payments.

In February 1988, the sum of £2,408,000 was made available for distribution to 12,260 registered authors and assignees as the fifth annual payment of PLR.
Registrar, J. W. Sumsion.

PUBLIC RECORD OFFICE
See **Record Offices**

PUBLIC TRUST OFFICE
Stewart House, 24 Kingsway, WC2B 6JX
[01 405 1300]

The Public Trustee is a trust Corporation created to undertake the business of executorship and trusteeship; he can act as executor or administrator of the estate of a deceased person, or as trustee of a will or settlement. The Public Trustee is also responsible for the performance of all the administrative, but not the judicial, tasks required of the Court of Protection under Part VII of the Mental Health Act, 1983, relating to the management and administration of the property and affairs of persons suffering from mental disorder. The Public Trustee also acts as Receiver when so directed by the Court, usually where there is no other person willing or able so to act.

The Accountant General of the Supreme Court, through the Court Funds Office, is responsible for the investment and accounting of funds in court for persons under a disability, monies in Court subject to litigation and statutory deposits.

The Court Funds Office is at 22 Kingsway, WC2B 6LE (01-936 6000).
Public Trustee and Accountant General, J. A. Boland.
Assistant Public Trustee (Administration) and Deputy Accountant General, P. J. Farmer.

Assistant Public Trustee (Legal), H. N. Mather.
Heads of Divisions:
Administration, M. J. Munt.
Court Funds, I. J. MacBean.
Finance, F. J. Eddy.
Investment, H. Stevenson
Property, A. Nightingale.
Protection, I. S. Price.
Receivership and Trust, R. A. Cunningham, T.D.

COMMISSION FOR RACIAL EQUALITY
Elliot House, 10–12 Allington Street, SW1E 5EH
[01–828 7022]

Established on June 13, 1977, under the Race Relations Act 1976, to work towards elimination of discrimination and promote equality of opportunity and good relations between different racial groups generally.
Chairman, M. Day, O.B.E.
Deputy Chairman, Prof. B. Parekh.
Members, G. E. B. Tyler; L. Crawford; Mrs. L. Khan; G. S. Sarang; Ethel M. Houston, O.B.E.; E. Gilmour Jones; K. R. Whitesides; Q. S. Anisuddin; Prof. B. Hepple; Mrs. E. Nam *(full-time)*; D. A. C. Lambert; Dr. D. Ray; C. Lloyd *(part-time)*.

RECORD OFFICES, ETC.

THE PUBLIC RECORD OFFICE
Chancery Lane, WC2A 1LR
[01-876 3444]
Ruskin Avenue, Kew,
Richmond, Surrey TW9 4DU
[01–876 3444]

The Office, originally established in 1838 under the Master of the Rolls, was placed by the Public Records Act 1958 under the direction of the Lord Chancellor. He appoints a Keeper of Public Records, whose duties are to co-ordinate and supervise the selection of records of government departments and the English Law Courts for permanent preservation, to safeguard the records under his charge, and to make them available to the public.

The Office holds records of central government dating from *Domesday Book* (1086) to 1987. Under the 1967 Public Records Act they are normally open to inspection when 30 years old, and are then available, without charge, in the reading rooms, Monday to Friday, 9.30–5.
Keeper of Public Records (G3), M. Roper.
Deputy Keeper (G5), (vacant).
Records Administration Officer (G5), C. D. Chalmers.
Establishment Officer (G7), J. G. Wickham.
Principal Assistant Keepers (G6), Mrs. J. M. Cox; Dr. N. G. Cox; N. E. Evans; Dr. A. A. H. Knightbridge; Mrs. A. N. Nicol; J. B. Post; J. L. Walford.
Assistant Keepers (G7), Mrs. M. K. Banton; Miss G L. Beech; Dr. A. S. Bevan; Dr. T. M. Chalmers; Miss M. M. Condon; C. R. H. Cooper; Miss A. Crawford; Dr. D. Crook; Dr. H. Forde; Dr. M. R. Foster; Dr. E. M. Hallam Smith; Ms. S. M. F. Healy; Dr. E. J. Higgs; Mrs. H. E. Jones; Dr. M. J. Jubb; A. J. McDonald; Mrs. A. E. Morton; T. R. Padfield; Dr. N. A. M. Rodger; Dr. D. L. Thomas.
Head, Repository and Reprographic Services (G7), K. J. Smith.
Principal Inspecting Officer (G7), A. W. H. Medlicott.
Inspecting Officers, D. Barlow; R. A. Blake; Miss C. J. Dimmer; J. S. Harley; F. McCall; Mrs. E. J. Baldwin; Mrs. M. A. Bull; C. J. Edwards; Mrs. H. R. Saw........................ £12,806–£16,489
Head of Information Technology Unit (G7), Mrs. M. Wilkinson.

ADVISORY COUNCIL ON PUBLIC RECORDS
Public Record Office, Chancery Lane, WC2A 1LR
[01–878 3666]

Council members are appointed by the Lord Chancellor, under the Public Records Act 1958, to advise him "on matters concerning public records in general and, in particular, on those aspects of the work of the Public Record Office which affect members of the public who make use of the facilities provided by the Public Record Office". The Council meets quarterly and produces an annual report which is published alongside the Report of the Keeper of Public Records as a House of Commons sessional paper.
Chairman, The Master of the Rolls.
Members, The Lord Bancroft, G.C.B.; Miss S. Beesley; Miss V. Cromwell; A. Gomersall; J. S. W. Gibson; Prof. P. D. A. Harvey; Sir Paul Osmond, C.B.; Prof. T. Ranger; Prof. H. Roseveare; Prof. W. Saunders; W. R. Serjeant; Prof. R. Skidelsky; R. S. Wainwright.
Assessors, D. J. Wiblin; Dr. G. H. Martin.
Secretary, Dr. M. J. Jubb.

HOUSE OF LORDS RECORD OFFICE
House of Lords, SW1A 0PW
[01–219 3074]

Since 1497, the records of Parliament have been kept within the Palace of Westminster. They are in the custody of the Clerk of the Parliaments, who in 1946 established a record department to supervise their preservation and their production to students. The Search Room of this office is open to the public Mon.–Fri., 9.30–5.

The records preserved number some 3,000,000 documents, and include Acts of Parliament from 1497, Journals of the House of Lords from 1510, Minutes and Committee proceedings from 1610, and Papers laid before Parliament from 1531. Amongst the records are the Petition of Right, the Death Warrant of Charles I, the Declaration of Breda and the Bill of Rights. The House of Lords Record Office also has charge of the Journals of the House of Commons (from 1547), and other surviving records of the Commons (from 1572), which include plans and annexed documents relating to Private Bill legislation from 1818. Among other documents are the records of the Lord Great Chamberlain, the political papers of certain members of the two Houses (including the papers of Lloyd George, Bonar Law and other statesmen previously preserved in the Beaverbrook Library), and documents relating to Parliament acquired on behalf of the nation. All the manuscripts and other records are preserved in the Victoria Tower of the Houses of Parliament. A permanent exhibition was established in the Royal Gallery in 1979.
Clerk of the Records, H. S. Cobb, F.S.A.
£27,506–£32,394
Deputy Clerk of the Records, D. J. Johnson, F.S.A.
£21,287–£29,138
Assistant Clerks of the Records, J. C. Morgan (*Sound Archives*); S. K. Ellison . . . . £17,381–£23,636

ROYAL COMMISSION ON HISTORICAL MANUSCRIPTS
Quality House, Quality Court, Chancery Lane, WC2A 1HP
[01–242 1198]

The Commission was set up by Royal Warrant in 1869 to enquire and report on collections of papers of value for the study of history in private hands. In 1959 a new warrant enlarged these terms of reference to include all historical records, wherever situated, outside the Public Records and gave it added responsibilities, as a central co-ordinating body, to promote, assist and advise on their proper preservation and storage. The Commission has published over 200 volumes of reports. It holds a further 30,000 unpublished reports in the National Register of Archives, available for consultation in its search room. It also administers the Manorial and Tithe Documents Rules on behalf of the Master of the Rolls.
Chairman, The Lord Blake, F.B.A.
Commissioners, The Lord Kenyon, C.B.E., F.S.A.; The Lord Fletcher, P.C., F.S.A.; ; The Duke of Northumberland, K.G., P.C., G.C.V.O., F.R.S.; J. P. W. Ehrman, F.B.A., F.S.A.; Prof. S. F. C. Milsom, F.B.A.; Sir John Habakkuk, F.B.A.; G. E. Aylmer, F.B.A.; P. T. Cormack, F.S.A., M.P.; H. M. Colvin, C.B.E., F.B.A., F.S.A.; Prof. G. W. S. Barrow, F.B.A.; Valerie L. Pearl, F.S.A.; The Marquess of Anglesey; Prof. Owen Chadwick, O.M., K.B.E., F.B.A.; D. G. Vaisey, F.S.A.; The Viscount of Arbuthnott, C.B.E., D.S.C.; The Lord Camoys.
Secretary, B. S. Smith, F.S.A.

SCOTTISH RECORD OFFICE
H.M. General Register House, Edinburgh EH1 3YY
[031–556 6585]

The history of the national archives of Scotland can be traced back to the 13th century. The present headquarters of the Scottish Record Office, the General Register House, was founded in 1774. Here are preserved the administrative records of pre-Union Scotland, the registers of central and local courts of law, the public registers of property rights and legal documents, and many collections of local and church records and private archives. Certain groups of records, mainly the modern records of government departments in Scotland, the Scottish railway records, and the plans collection, are preserved in the branch repository at the West Register House in Charlotte Square. The Search Rooms in both buildings open Mon.–Fri., 9–4.45. A permanent exhibition at the West Register House and changing exhibitions at the General Register House are open to the public on weekdays, 10–4. The National Register of Archives (Scotland), which is a branch of the Scottish Record Office, is based in the West Register House.
Keeper of the Records of Scotland, Dr. A. L. Murray.

DEPARTMENT OF THE REGISTERS OF SCOTLAND
Meadowbank House, 153 London Road, Edinburgh EH8 7AU
[031–661 6111]

The Registers of Scotland consist of:—
(1) General Register of Sasines and Land Register of Scotland; (2) Register of Deeds in the Books of Council and Session; (3) Register of Protests; (4) Register of English and Irish Judgments; (5) Register of Service of Heirs; (6) Register of the Great Seal; (7) Register of the Quarter Seal; (8) Register of the Prince's Seal; (9) Register of Crown Grants; (10) Register of Sheriffs' Commissions; (11) Register of the Cachet Seal; (12) Register of Inhibitions and Adjudications; (13) Register of Entails; (14) Register of Hornings.
The General Register of Sasines and the Land Register of Scotland form the chief security in Scotland of the rights of land and other heritable (or real) property.
Keeper of the Registers of Scotland (G4), J. Robertson.
Deputy Keeper (G5), R. C. Brown.
Senior Assistant Keepers (G6), A. G. Rennie; A. A. Snowdon; G. C. Warrender.

Assistant Keepers (G7), J. Anderson; R. C. Clark; J. Cogle; B. J. Corr; A. M. Falconer; A. B. Farmer; R. C. Fulton; J. Knox; D. Lorimer; Mrs. A. McDonald; A. G. T. New; D. L. Nicoll; A. W. Ramage; J. Rynn; I. M. Tainsh.

CORPORATION OF LONDON RECORDS OFFICE
Guildhall, EC2P 2EJ
[01–260 1251]

Contains the municipal archives of the City of London which are regarded as the most complete collection of ancient municipal records in existence. Includes charters of William the Conqueror, Henry II, and later Kings and Queens to 1957; ancient custumals: Liber Horn, Dunthorne, Custumarum, Ordinacionum, Memorandorum and Albus, Liber de Antiquis Legibus, and collections of Statutes; continuous series of judicial rolls and books from 1252 and Council minutes from 1275; records of the Old Bailey and Guildhall Sessions from 1603, and financial records from the 16th century, together with the records of London Bridge from the 12th century and numerous subsidiary series and miscellanea of historical interest. A Guide was published in 1951. Readers' Room open Mon.–Fri., 9.30–4.45.
Keeper of the City Records, The Town Clerk.
City Archivist, J. R. Sewell.
Deputy City Archivist, Mrs. J. M. Bankes.

REVIEW BODIES

The secretariat for these bodies is provided by the Office of Manpower Economics (*see separate entry*).

ARMED FORCES PAY

The Review Body on Armed Forces Pay was appointed in September 1971 to advise the Prime Minister on the pay and allowances of members of Naval, Military and Air Forces of the Crown and of any women's service administered by the Defence Council.

The members of the Review Body are: Sir Peter Matthews (*Chairman*); P. Ball; D. P. M. Hudson; Mrs. J. Hughes; R. Sanderson, O.B.E.; W. C. Thomson; Prof. J. White, C.B.E.

DOCTORS' AND DENTISTS' REMUNERATION

The Review Body on Doctors' and Dentists' Remuneration was appointed in July 1971 to advise the Prime Minister on the remuneration of doctors and dentists taking any part in the National Health Service.

The members of the Review Body are: Sir Graham Wilkins (*Chairman*); Dr. Anne Hogg; J. L. Kirkpatrick, C.B.E.; Prof. P. G. Moore, T.D.; D. G. Richards; Prof. G. F. Thomason, C.B.E.; J. K. Warburton, C.B.E.

NURSING STAFF, MIDWIVES, HEALTH VISITORS AND PROFESSIONS ALLIED TO MEDICINE

The Review Body for nursing staff, midwives, health visitors and professions allied to medicine was set up in July 1983 to advise the Prime Minister on the remuneration of nursing staff, midwives and health visitors employed in the National Health Service; and physiotherapists, radiographers, remedial gymnasts, occupational therapists, orthoptists, chiropodists, dietitians and related grades employed in the National Health Service.

The members of the Review Body are: Sir James Cleminson, M.C. (*Chairman*); Sir John Herbecq, K.C.B. (*Deputy Chairman*); Miss B. Cooper, Q.C.; Mrs. J. Hughes; I. H. Phillipps; Prof. G. F. Thomason, C.B.E.

TOP SALARIES

The Review Body on Top Salaries was appointed in May, 1971 to advise the Prime Minister on the remuneration of the higher judiciary and other judicial appointments; senior civil servants; and senior officers of the armed forces. Until August 1980 the remit also included the Chairmen and members of the Boards of nationalized industries. The Review Body has also been asked on a number of occasions to advise on the remuneration of Members of Parliament and of Ministers and on the level of parliamentary allowances.

The members of the Review Body are: The Lord Plowden, G.B.E., K.C.B. (*Chairman* until early 1989); Sir Terence Beckett, K.B.E.; J. D. Birkin, T.D.; Ms. L. Botting; The Lord Chorley; Sir Robin Ibbs; Sir Peter Matthews A.O.; Sir David Nickson, K.B.E. (*Chairman* from early 1989); J. J. R. Pope, O.B.E.; Sir Thomas Skyrme, K.C.V.O., C.B., C.B.E., T.D.

ROYAL BOTANIC GARDENS, EDINBURGH
Inverleith Row, Edinburgh EH3 5LR
[031–552 7171]

The Royal Botanic Garden Edinburgh, which originated as the Physic Garden established in 1670 beside the Palace of Holyroodhouse, became the direct responsibility of the Commissioners of Her Majesty's Works and Public Buildings (later the Department of Public Works) in 1889, transferring to the Department of Agriculture and Fisheries for Scotland in 1969. Since 1986, RBG Edinburgh has been administered by a Board of Trustees established under the National Heritage (Scotland) Act 1985.

RBG Edinburgh is an international centre for scientific research on plant diversity, maintaining collections of living plants and reference resources, including a herbarium of some 1.8 million specimens of preserved plants. Other statutory functions of RBG Edinburgh include provision of education and information on botany and horticulture, and the provision of public access to the living plant collections.

The Garden moved to its present site at Inverleith, Edinburgh in 1820. There are also three outstations of RBG Edinburgh: Younger Botanic Garden, Benmore, near Dunoon, Argyllshire; Logan Botanic Garden, near Stranraer, Wigtownshire; Dawyck Botanic Garden, near Stobo, Peeblesshire. Public opening hours: RBG Edinburgh – daily (except Dec. 25, Jan 1) 9 to sunset (1 hour earlier in summer) (Sun. 11 to sunset); Younger Botanic Garden – April–Oct. 10–6; Logan Botanic Garden – April–Sept. 10–5; Dawyck Botanic Garden – April–Oct. 9–5.

Chairman of the Board of Trustees, Sir Peter Hutchison, Bt.
Regius Keeper, Prof. J. McNeill.
Assistant Keeper, J. Cullen, PH.D.

ROYAL BOTANIC GARDENS, KEW
Richmond, Surrey TW9 3AB
[01-940 1171]
Also at: Wakehurst Place, Ardingly, near Haywards
Heath,
West Sussex RH17 6TN
[0444 892701]

The Royal Botanic Gardens (RBG), Kew were
founded in 1759 by H.R.H. Princess Augusta. In 1841,
they became a public institution; in 1847, the
Museums of Economic Botany were opened, and in
1852, the Herbarium and Library were established.
The Jodrell Laboratory opened in 1876. In 1965, the
garden at Wakehurst Place was acquired; it is owned
by the National Trust and managed by RBG Kew.
From 1903 to 1984, RBG Kew was part of the Ministry
of Agriculture, Fisheries and Food. Under the
National Heritage Act 1983, a Board of Trustees was
set up to administer the Gardens which in 1984
became an independent body supported by a grant-
in-aid.

The functions of RBG Kew are to carry out
research into plant sciences, to disseminate knowledge about plants and to provide the public with the
opportunity to gain knowledge and enjoyment from
the Gardens' collections. There are extensive national reference collections of living and preserved
plants and a comprehensive library and archive. The
main emphasis is on tropical and subtropical plants.
Open daily, except Christmas Day and New Year's
Day, from 9.30 a.m. The closing hour varies from 4
p.m. in mid-winter to 6.30 p.m. on week-days, and 8
p.m. on Sundays and Bank Holidays, in mid-summer.
Admission, 50p. Museums open 9.30 a.m.; Glass-
houses, 9.30–4.30 (weekdays); to 5.30 p.m. (Sundays).
No dogs except guide-dogs for the blind.

BOARD OF TRUSTEES
Chairman, Hon. J. D. Eccles, C.B.E.
Members, Sir Leslie Fowden, F.R.S.; Sir David Atten-
borough, C.B.E., F.R.S.; Prof. W. G. Chaloner, F.R.S.;
Prof. E. C. D. Cocking, F.R.S.; J. P. Cousins; Sir
Philip M. Dowson, C.B.E.; Prof. G. E. Fogg, C.B.E.; R.
A. E. Herbert; P. J. D. Marshall; Prof. Elizabeth B.
Robson, PH.D.; Cdr. L. M. Saunders Watson, R.N.
(*ret*).
Director, Dr. G. T. Prance.

ROYAL COMMISSION FOR THE
EXHIBITION OF 1851
Sherfield Building,
Imperial College of Science and Technology,
SW7 2AZ
[01–589 6483]

Incorporated by Supplemental Charter as a per-
manent Commission after winding up the affairs of
the Great Exhibition of 1851. It has for its object the
promotion of scientific and artistic education by
means of funds derived from its Kensington Estate,
purchased with the surplus left over from the Great
Exhibition.
President, H.R.H. The Duke of Edinburgh, K.G., K.T.,
O.M., G.B.E., P.C.
Chairman, Board of Management, Sir Denis Rooke,
C.B.E., F.R.S.
Secretary to Commissioners, M. C. Neale, C.B.

RURAL DEVELOPMENT COMMISSION
11 Cowley Street, SW1P 3NA
[01-276 6969]

The Rural Development Commission was formed
in 1988 by the merger of the Development Commission

for Rural England and the Council for Small Indus-
tries in Rural Areas. It is a statutory body funded by
Government grant-in-aid which undertakes to alle-
viate economic and social problems in rural areas and
advises the Government on related rural matters in
England. It concentrates its resources in Rural
Development Areas but some assistance is available
both within and outside the RDAs.
Chairman, The Lord Vinson, L.V.O.
Other Commissioners, Mrs. P. Batty Shaw, C.B.E.;
Prof. M. D. I. Chisholm; D. J. C. Davenport; The
Lord Gisborough; M. Schreiber; R. Thompson; A.
Leavett; J. L. Thompson; G. P. Gray; M. B. Ferris;
J. M. Galsworthy.
Chief Executive, J. V. Williams.

SCIENCE AND ENGINEERING
RESEARCH COUNCIL
Polaris House, North Star Avenue,
Swindon, Wilts. SN2 1ET
[0793–26222]

The Science and Engineering Research Council
(S.E.R.C.) is one of five research councils funded
through the Department of Education and Science
"to develop the natural and social sciences, including
engineering, to maintain a fundamental capacity of
research and scholarship and to support relevant
postgraduate education". S.E.R.C.'s role is to encour-
age and support research and advanced training in
U.K. universities and polytechnics in all the basic
areas of science and engineering.
Chairman, Prof. E. W. J. Mitchell.
Members, Prof. Sir Michael Atiyah; Dr. R. F.
Coleman; Prof. D. E. N. Davies; Prof. B. E. F.
Fender; C. A. P. Foxell; Prof. C. Humphreys; Prof.
M. A. Jeeves; Dr. C. Jordan; Dr. H. D. Law; D.
Nash; Prof. Sir Richard Norman; Prof. D. H.
Perkins; Dr. C. H. Reece; D. T. Shore; Prof. J. M.
Thomas; Dr. A. Williamson; Prof. R. Wilson; Prof.
A. Wolfendale.

SCOTTISH OFFICE
The Secretary of State for Scotland is responsible
in Scotland for a wide range of statutory functions
which in England and Wales are the responsibility of
a number of departmental ministers. He also works
closely with ministers in charge of Great Britain
departments on topics of special significance to
Scotland within their fields of responsibility. His
statutory functions are administered by five main
departments: Department of Agriculture and Fisheries for Scotland, Scottish Development Department, Scottish Education Department, Scottish
Home and Health Department, and Industry Department for Scotland. These Departments (plus Central
Services embracing the Solicitor's Office, the Scottish
Information Office, Establishment, Liaison and
Finance Divisions) are collectively known as the
Scottish Office. In addition there are a number of
other Scottish Departments for which the Secretary
of State has some degree of responsibility: these
include the Scottish Courts Administration, the
Department of the Registrar General for Scotland
(the General Register Office), the Scottish Record
Office and the Department of the Registers of
Scotland. The Secretary of State also bears Ministerial responsibility for the activities in Scotland of
several statutory bodies whose functions extend
throughout Great Britain such as the Training

Commission and the Forestry Commission.
(For **Salaries,** *see* page 297)

Dover House, Whitehall, SW1A 2AU
[01–270 3000]

Secretary of State for Scotland, THE RT. HON. MALCOLM RIFKIND, Q.C., M.P.
Private Secretary (G5), D. J. Crawley
Assistant Private Secretaries, Miss U. M. Jamieson; Mrs. M. S. Jones.
Ministers of State, IAN LANG, M.P. *(Industry and Local Government);* THE LORD SANDERSON OF BOWDEN *(Agriculture and Fisheries, Forestry, the Highlands and Islands, and Tourism).*
Private Secretaries, D. C. Henderson *(I. Lang);* A. C. McLaren *(Lord Sanderson of Bowden).*
Parliamentary Under Secretaries of State, Lord James Douglas–Hamilton, M.P.; M. Forsyth, M.P.*
Private Secretaries, M. Foulis *(Lord James Douglas–Hamilton);* D. B. Binnie *(M. Forsyth)*.
Parliamentary Clerk, Mrs. M. E. Thomson.
Permanent Under Secretary of State (G1), R. R. Hillhouse.
Private Secretary, R. M. Hay.
Liaison Staff:
  Assistant Secretary (G5), I. C. Freeman.
  Principals (G7), I. A. Sneddon; A. C. King.

St. Andrew's House,
Edinburgh EH1 3DG
[031–556 8400]

MANAGEMENT GROUP SUPPORT STAFF

Principal (G7), G. S. Pearson.

CENTRAL SERVICES

Deputy Secretary (Central Services) (G2), I. D. Penman, C.B..

Establishment Division
16 Waterloo Place Edinburgh, EH1 3DN
[031–556 8400]

Principal Establishment Officer (G3), A. H. Bishop.
Assistant Secretaries (G5), Miss M. Maclean; G. N. Munro.
Senior Principals (G6), D. J. Chalmers; J. N. Davison, O.B.E.; A. B. Fairweather, T.D.; G. W. Tucker.
Principals (G7), W. E. Bennet; D. A. Christie; J. H. F. Finnie; J. R. M. Flucker; H. J. Graham; C. D. Henderson; I. C. Henderson; J. Meldrum; A. McNaughton; G. R. Pearson; Mrs. C. Peden; A. Stephenson.

Directorate of Information Technology
Broomhouse Drive, Edinburgh EH11 3XD
[031–556 8400]

Computer Services
Director (G5), J. Duffy.
Deputy Director (G6), I. W. Goodwin.
Principals (G7), W. Ferguson; A. R. McCowan; B. U. Pearson.

Telecommunications
St. Andrew's House, Edinburgh EH1 3DE
(031–556 8400)

Director (G6), A. F. Harrison.

Finance Division
New St. Andrew's House, Edinburgh EH1 3SX
[031–556 8400]

---

*Based at New St. Andrew's House.

Finance Group
Principal Finance Officer (G3), K. J. MacKenzie.
Assistant Secretaries (G5), T. A. Cameron; E. W. Frizzell; I. G. F. Gray; T. E. McGreevy; G. Robson; A. J. Rushworth; A. M. Russell; W. T. Tait.
Senior Principal (G6), A. Walker.
Principals (G7), E. G. J. Bee; D. I. Dalgetty; S. W. E. Davidson; J. P. Garvie; D. A. Howe; T. Hunter; N. G. Ingrams; D. K. C. Jeffrey; W. A. Lamberton; I. A. McLeod; W. E. M. Maxwell; D. R. Mayer; R. E. Merrall; D. F. Middleton; D. Muir; G. S. Pearson; J. Porter; I. M. Smith; R. K. West.

Local Government Finance Group
Assistant Secretaries (G5), G. Robson; A. M. Russell.
Principals (G6), M. T. Affolter; D. J. Christie; P. S. Collings; A. G. Dickson; I. Melville; G. A. Paul.

Solicitor's Office
(For the Scottish Departments and certain U.K. services including H.M. Treasury, in Scotland.)

Solicitor (G2), R. Brodie.
Deputy Solicitor (G3), N. W. Boe.
Divisional Solicitors (G5), J. B. Allan;* K. F. Barclay; G. C. Duke; R. M. Henderson; G. Jackson; J. L. Jamieson; *Mrs. L. A. Lilliker; H. F. Macdiarmid; T. G. Walters.
  *Seconded to Scottish Law Commission

Scottish Information Office
(For the Scottish Departments and certain U.K. services)

Director (G5), C. F. Corbett.
Deputy Director (G6), D. C. M. Beveridge.

Statistics
Chief Statistician (G5), A. M. Burnside.

Inquiry Reporters
16 Waterloo Place, Edinburgh EH1 3DN
[031–556 8400]

Chief Reporter (G3), A. G. Bell.
Deputy Chief Reporter (G5), W. D. Campbell.

DEPARTMENT OF AGRICULTURE AND FISHERIES FOR SCOTLAND
Chesser House, 500 Gorgie Road, Edinburgh
EH1 3AW
[031–443 4020]

Dover House, Whitehall, London, SW1A 2AU
[01–270 3000]

Secretary (G2), L. P. Hamilton, C.B.
Under Secretary (G3), D. J. Essery.
Fisheries Secretary (G3), W. A. P. Weatherston.
Assistant Secretaries (G5), A. D. F. Findlay; R. S. B. Gordan; G. G. Lyall; L. V. McEwan; W. Moyes; N. E. Sharp; G. M. D. Thomson; E. J. Weeple; I. M. Whitelaw.
Principals (G7), D. J. Baird; J. G. Donnelly; J. H. B. Fleming, T.D.; A. W. Gladwin; R. A. Grant; A. Johnston; N. J. H. Kernohan; A. Lister; B. E. McAdam; I. F. McEwan; W. Malcolm; C. K. McIntosh; W. R. J. McQueen; B. Naylor; D. Reid; J. Reid, M.B.E., W. B. Ritchie; D. M. Rowand; N. A. Stewart; R. S. Stewart; T. A. Titterton; R. J. Walker.
Chief Agricultural Officer (G4), J. F. Hutcheson.
Deputy Chief Agricultural Officer (G5), W. A. Macgregor.
Assistant Chief Agricultural Officers (G6), D. R. J. Craven; J. A. Hardie; J. G. Muir; A. Robb; J. I. Woodrow.
Chief Agricultural Economist (G6), J. M. Dunn, D.Phil.
Chief Meat and Livestock Inspector (G7), A. Bain.

Chief Food and Dairy Officer (G7), M. E. M. Anderson.
Chief Surveyor (G6) N. Taylor.
Scientific Adviser (G5) A. M. Raven, PH.D.
Senior Principal Scientific Officers (G6), R. J. Dowdell, PH.D.; T. W. Hegarty, PH.D.; D. Thornton.

Agricultural Scientific Services
East Craigs, Edinburgh EH12 8NJ
[031–339 2355]

Director (G5), D. C. Graham, PH.D., F.R.S.E.
Deputy Director (G6), J. R. Cutler.
Senior Principal Scientific Officers (G6), J. L. Keppie; M. J. Richardson.

Fisheries Research Services
Marine Laboratory, P.O. Box 101,
Victoria Road, Torry, Aberdeen AB9 8DB
[0224 876544]

Director and Co-ordinator of U.K. Fisheries Research and Development, Prof. A. D. Hawkins, PH.D
Deputy Director (G5), D. N. MacLennan.
Senior Principal Scientific Officers (G6), J. M. Davies, PH.D.; R. Jones; A. L. S. Munro, PH.D.; P. A. M. Stewart, PH.D.; C. S. Wardle, PH.D.

Freshwater Fisheries Laboratory,
Faskally, Pitlochry, Perthshire PH16 5LB
[0796 2060]

Senior Principal Scientific Officers (G6), R. G. J. Shelton, PH.D.; J. E. Thorpe, PH.D.

Sea Fisheries Inspectorate

Chief Inspector of Sea Fisheries (G6), J. F. Fenton.
Inspector of Salmon and Freshwater Fisheries for Scotland (G7), R. B. Williamson.
Marine Superintendent, Captain D. R. Corse
£23,650 to £24,031

Crofters Commission
4/6 Castle Wynd, Inverness IV2 3EQ
[0463 237231]

Chairman (part-time), A. Macleod, O.B.E. £22,667
Members (part-time), A. I. Macarthur; B. T. Hunter; D. A. Morrison; P. Morrison; I. G. Munro; W. Lawson; A. Bremner.
Secretary (G6), I. A. Macpherson.

Red Deer Commission
Knowsley, 82 Fairfield Road, Inverness IV3 5LH
[0463 231751]

Chairman, I. K. Mackenzie £11,900
Secretary, N. H. McCulloch ...... £11,639 to £14,629

SCOTTISH DEVELOPMENT DEPARTMENT
St. Andrew's House, Edinburgh EH1 3DG
[031–556 8400]
Dover House, Whitehall, London, SW1A 2AU
[01–270 3000]

Secretary and Chief Economic Adviser (G2), Dr. R. C. L. McCrone, C.B., F.R.S.E.
Under Secretaries (G3), H. H. Mills; D. G. MacKay*.
Director, Historic Buildings and Monuments, D. Connelly.
Assistant Secretaries (G5), N. G. Campbell; Mrs. E. C. G. Craghill, C.B.E.; M. J. P. Cunliffe; J. S. Graham; Mrs. M. B. Gunn; Miss E. A. MacKay; J. S. B. Martin; I. Maxwell; K. W. Moore; R. E. S. Robinson; A. B. Scott; Mrs. G. M. Stewart.
Principals (G7), J. S. Aldridge; I. R. Anderson; M. T. S. Batho; A. G. Beattie; D. S. Chalmers; I. G. Dewar; Mrs. W. Dickson; P. G. Drumm; M. A. Duffy; W. M. Giles; J. C. Halley; J. L. Helm; I. P. Hetherington; W. A. Howat; J. C. Judson; D. G. Kerr; G. A. McHugh; I. J. MacKenzie; Mrs. J.

---

*At New St. Andrew's House.

Niven; J. B. Rodden; J. Symington; Miss T. S. Teale; T. Tumilty; J. O. Wastle.

Professional Staff
Chief Engineer (G3), R. MacGillivray.
Deputy Chief Engineer (G5), A. C. Paton.
Assistant Chief Engineers (G6), T. Bolton; T. D. Macdonald; N. G. Semple.
Director of Building and Chief Architect (G3), J. E. Gibbons, PH.D.
Deputy Director of Building and Deputy Chief Architect (G5), M. R. Miller.
Deputy Director of Building and Chief Quantity Surveyor (G5), D. C. Russell.
Assistant Director and Deputy Chief Quantity Surveyor (G6), A. Duncan, O.B.E.
Assistant Directors (G6), G. Gray; H. R. McCallum; R. W. Naismith.
Chief Planner (G3), A. Mackenzie.
Deputy Chief Planner (G5), D. R. Dare.
Assistant Chief Planners (G6), T. Williamson; A. W. Denham; I. R. Duncan; S. G. Fulton.
Chief Research Officer (G5), C. C. MacDonald.
Senior Principal Research Officers (G6), C. P. A. Levein, PH.D.; C. L. Wood.
Chief Road Engineer (G3), J. A. L. Dawson.
Deputy Chief Engineer (Roads) (G5), G. S. Marshall.
Deputy Chief Engineer (Bridges) (G5), W. R. Varley.
Assistant Chief Engineers (G6), J. Patience; R. D. Udall; J. Innes.
H.M. Chief Industrial Pollution Inspector (G5), I. W. W. Wright.
Chief Estates Officer (G6), R. I. K. White.
Principal Inspector of Ancient Monuments for Scotland, I. MacIvor .... £18,517–£21,343
Principal Inspector of Historic Buildings, D. M. Walker .... £18,517–£21,343

INDUSTRY DEPARTMENT
FOR SCOTLAND
New St. Andrew's House, Edinburgh EH1 3TA
[031–556 8400]
and
Dover House, Whitehall, SW1A 2AU
[01–270 3000]

Secretary (G2), J. A. Scott, C.B., L.V.O.
Under Secretaries (G3), J. F. Laing; W. W. Scott.
Assistant Secretaries (G5), P. A. Brady; G. D. Calder; Ms. L. Clare; R. S. Crofts; M. J. P. Cunliffe; J. D. Gallagher; Miss I. M. Low.
Senior Economic Advisers (G5), J. A. Peat; W. M. McNie.
Principals (G7), J. A. Brown; C. H. Coulthard; J. A. Ewing; S. W. Fox; M. J. Lowndes; J. Lugton; R. N. Irvine; A. McKean; A. K. MacLeod; N. MacLeod; B. R. Morgan; D. N. G. Reid; Mrs. A. Robson; D. A. Stewart; M. R. Wilson.

Industrial Expansion
Alhambra House, 45 Waterloo Street, Glasgow
G2 6AT
[041–248 2855]

Under Secretary (G3), H. Morison.
Industrial Adviser, Dr. K. Benington.
Assistant Secretaries (G5), A. W. Fraser; S. F. Hampson.
Senior Principals (G6), W. C. Alison; J. McGhee.
Principals (G7), D. A. Brew; J. A. Brown; D. J. Fowles; D. M. McFadyen; Ms. J. E. Morgan.

Locate in Scotland
120 Bothwell Street, Glasgow G2 7JP
[041–248 2700]

Director, Prof. N. Hood £36,500
Senior Principal (G6), W. Malone.
Principal (G7), (vacant).
H. Moody (U.S.A.)

SCOTTISH EDUCATION DEPARTMENT
New St. Andrew's House,
Edinburgh EH1 3SY
[031–556 8400]
and
Dover House, Whitehall, London, SW1A 2AU
[01–270 3000]

Secretary (G2), G. R. Wilson.
Under Secretaries (G3), P. MacKay, H. Robertson,
M.B.E.
Assistant Secretaries (G5), D. A. Campbell; J. R.
Cuthbert, PH.D. *(Chief Statistician)*; E. C. Davison;
I. W. Gordon; J. W. L. Lonie; K. Macrae; E. C.
Reavley; D. Wishart.
Senior Principal (G6), G. E. Brewerton.
Principals (G7), T. Blacklock; Mrs. M. Brannan; D.
G. Campbell; W. Davidson; M. Ewart; C. E.
Forsyth; J. B. Lyall; B. J. O'Connor; R. I. Perrett;
B. W. Sharry; B. V. Surridge; I. M. Watt; G. P.
Walker; A. W. Wallace.

H.M. Inspectors of Schools
Senior Chief Inspector (G3), T. N. Gallacher.
Deputy Senior Chief Inspectors (G4), D. W. Mack; S.
E. McCelland, PH.D.
Chief Inspectors (G5), W. T. Beveridge; W. F. L.
Bigwood; L. Clark; J. P. Donaldson; A. H. Fergu-
son; G. P. D. Gordon; J. Howgego; A. S. McGlynn;
D. W. Mack, D. A. Osler; A. M. Rankin.
Inspectors (G6), J. N. Alison; M. T. J. Axford; P.
Banks; Mrs. W. Binnie; A. D. Blair; J. Boyes; Miss
C. L. Boyle; M. J. Brown; Mrs. M. M. Browning; J.
W. Burdin; D. C. Burgess; Miss G. C. Campbell; T.
N. Carr; M. Q. Cramb; F. Crawford; A. H. B.
Davidson; G. A. Dell; R. F. Dick; J. C. Dignan; G.
H. C. Donaldson; D. W. Duncan; Miss K. M.
Fairweather; B. Fryer; A. R. Gallon; K. G. Gavin;
W. Geddes; A. B. Giovanazzi; G. D. Gray, PH.D.; T.
O. Greig; R. A. Hawke; J. Hay, PH.D.; K. A. Hope;
L. A. Hunter; M. Jack; J. Jackson, PH.D.; E. S.
Kelly; D. E. Kelso; Ms. A. Kennedy; D. G.
Kirkpatrick; I. Lawson; R. E. Lygo; M. McAllan;
I. M. MacAskill; L. McCallum; H. K. Mc-
Corkindale; J. J. McDonald; Mrs. M. A. Macfar-
lane; Ms. I. S. McGregor; H. M. MacLaren; C. R.
MacLean; M. Macleod; D. R. McNicoll; A. J.
Macpherson; A. Maltby; H. L. Martin; G. Mathi-
son; W. M. Mein; Mrs. J. M. Millar; A. Milne; J.
Mitchell; Miss E. R. Mowat; R. H. Nelson; B.
Nickerson, PH.D.; A. M. Noble, PH.D.; I. P. Pascoe;
W. M. Patterson; J. Picken; Miss A. H. M. Prain;
R. B. Prescott; T. A. Rankin; J. C. Rankine; S. A.
Ritchie; W. M. Roach, PH.D.; I. D. S. Robertson; A.
L. Robson; M. Roebuck; J. Rorrison; D. M. Russell;
A. L. Small; E. P. Spencer; H. M. Stalker; A. M.
Steele; W. Stevenson; A. Stewart; Mrs. J. A.
Stewart; W. P. Stewart; J. W. Thomson; R. M. S.
Tuck; R. S. Weir; Miss G. A. White; R. G. Wilson;
J. G. L. Wright; D. B. Young; R. W. J. Young, PH.D.

Social Work Services Group
43 Jeffrey Street, Edinburgh EH1 1DN
[031–556 8400]

The Social Work Services Group, which is attached
to the Scottish Education Department, administers
the provisions of the Social Work (Scotland) Act,
1968.
Under Secretary (G3), D. A. Leitch.
Assistant Secretaries (G5), D. A. Bennet; J. W.
Sinclair; R. E. Smith.
Principals (G7), J. R. Brown; M. J. Hunter; A.
Lindsey; G. A. McHugh; D. C. Meikle; D. R.
Semple; D. Stewart; R. Walker.
Chief Social Work Adviser, D. Colvin
£30,884–£32,980

Senior Advisers, Ms. M. L. Hunt; F. A. O'Leary; I. C.
Robertson; A. R. Sabine; J. I. Smith
£21,072–£26,409

SCOTTISH HOME AND HEALTH DEPARTMENT
St. Andrew's House,
Edinburgh EH1 3DE
[031–556 8400]
Dover House, Whitehall, London, SW1A 2AU
[01–270 3000]

Secretary (G2), W. K. Reid, C.B.
Under Secretaries (G3), D. Belfall; Miss P. A. Cox; J.
E. Fraser; J. Hamill.
Assistant Secretaries (G5), G. P. H. Aitken, T.D.; G. A.
Anderson; J. W. Barron; C. M. Baxter; W. J.
Fearnley; J. W. H. Irvine; R. D. Jackson; K. W.
McKay; D. Macniven, T.D.; Mrs. N. S. Munro; F.
H. Orr; B. V. Philp; P. M. Russell; R. H. Scott; N.
E. Sharp; D. Stevenson.
Senior Principal (G6), T. Collinson.
Principals (G7), A. G. Aitken; S. S. Anderson; J.
Ballantyne; Mrs. E. E. R. Barnwell; J. Black; H.
W. Bradford; D. H. Brown; J. T. Brown; A. J.
Cameron; L. C. Cunning; W. Davidson; D. H. F.
Dee; Miss W. M. Doonan; L. P. S. Dunbar; Dr. N.
Fojut; J. Gilmour; Miss A. E. Hamilton; N. Harvey;
D. M. Henderson; F. H. Hunter; S. M. Liddle; C. M.
A. Lugton; R. S. T. MacEwen; H. M. MacKenzie;
P. McLaren; D. C. Macnab; Mrs. V. M. Macniven;
Miss M. M. Marshall; A. J. Matheson; C. Naldrett;
D. J. Palmer; R. Patton; C. M. Reeves; A. J. Rennie;
D. A. Robertson; W. F. Robertson; A. Simmen,
O.B.E.; M. P. Sivell; T. Spence; D. Stephen; P. D.
Stephenson; I. C. Stewart; I. R. N. Stewart; R.
Tait; B. F. Warren; A. G. Young.

Medical Services
Chief Medical Officer (G2), I. S. Macdonald, C.B.
Deputy Chief Medical Officer (G3), G. A. Scott.
Principal Medical Officers, J. V. Basson; G. Gilray,
Margaret Hennigan; A. D. McIntyre; A. Rourke;
A. B. Young .... £29,965–£31,338
Senior Medical Officers, R. E. G. Aitken, T.D.; P. W.
Brooks; R. G. Covell; D. C. Drummond; J. B. P.
Ferguson; C. F. Fleming; G. I. Forbes; J. M.
Forrester; W. M. Gilmour; Ms. M. R. Halley; R. M.
Melville, O.B.E.; D. W. Sinclair; Ms. E. M. K. Sowler;
O. A. Thores; A. H. Watt £28,215
Senior Regional Medical Officers, I. G. Conn; H.
McBain .... £28,194 to £29,512
Regional Medical Officers, I. Arthurson; P. I. Brown;
Elspeth C. Carrick; J. A. Fergusson; T. E. S.
Fergusson; G. W. G. Hunter; K. Inglis; G. McKay;
A. S. Mackenzie; Elizabeth M. Melville; P. I. T.
Walker .... £17,593 to £24,926
Chief Scientist, Prof. R. D. Weir, O.B.E.
Chief Dental Officer, N. K. Colquhoun
£28,194 to £29,512
Deputy Chief Dental Officer, J. R. Wild £27.065
Regional Dental Officers, F. D. Murray; G. A. Reid
£17,593 to £24,926
Chief Nursing Officer, Mrs. Y. Moores..... £34,395
Chief Pharmacist (G6), G. Calder.

Miscellaneous Appointments
H.M. Chief Inspector of Constabulary, A. Morrison,
C.V.O., Q.P.M. £42,647
H.M. Chief Inspector of Prisons , T. B. Buyers, O.B.E.
£16,239
Commandant, Scottish Police College, T. J. Whitson,
O.B.E..................................... £31,860
H.M. Chief Inspector of Fire Services, R. J. Knowlton,
C.B.E., Q.F.S.M. .... £27,574–£30,759
Commandant, Scottish Fire Service Training School,
C. F. McManus, Q.F.S.M. .... £16,296–£17,046

Secretary, Scottish Health Service Planning Council,
W. J. Farquhar.

Prisons Group
St. Margaret's House, 151 London Road,
Edinburgh EH8 7TQ
[031–556 8400]

Director of Scottish Prison Service, P. McKinley
.... £30,793
Assistant Secretary, Deputy Director (Administration), J. W. H. Irvine .... £22,222 to £27,065
Assistant Controller, Deputy Director (Operations),
W. McVey £28,315
Deputy Director (Personnel and Supplies) (G5), W. J.
Fearnley.
Deputy Director (Regime Services) (G6), T. Collinson.
Deputy Director (Co-ordinator), T. J. Kelly.

Prison Governors

Governor I £31,542
Governor II £28,979
Governor III £25,541

Aberdeen (III), L. C. McBain.
Barlinnie (I), A. R. Walker.
Barlinnie Special Unit (III), D. E. Gunn.
Castle Huntly Young Offenders Institution (III), E. J.
Brownsmith.
Cornton Vale (II), J. Meiklejohn.
Dumfries Prison (III), G. R. Bond.
Dungavel, Strathaven (III), W. G. McKinlay.
Edinburgh (I), J. Pearce.
Friarton Prison, R. Park .... £20,329–£21,893
Glenochil Prison and Detention Centre (I), G. W.
Jackson.
Greenock Young Offenders Institution (III), I. A.
Bannatyne.
Inverness (III), W. G. Hewitson.
Longriggend Remand Institution (III), R. L. Houchim.
Low Moss (III), E. J. Campbell.
Noranside (III), J. C. Stuart.
Penninghame, M. Duffy .... £20,329–£21,893
Perth (II), R. Kite.
Peterhead (I), A. G. Coyle.
Polmont Young Offenders Institution (II), J. Milne.
Shotts (II), P. L. Abernethy.
Scottish Prison Service College (II), M. J. Milne.

Mental Welfare Commission for Scotland
25 Drumsheugh Gardens, Edinburgh EH3 7NS
[031–225 7034]

Chairman, P. C. Millar, o.b.e.
Commissioners, P. H. Brodie; Prof. T. D. Campbell; R.
G. Davis; Dr. L. Dunbar; A. Findlay, m.b.e.; Mrs.
A. M. Glen; Ms. A. M. Green; Mrs. A. I. Huggins;
D. A. Macdonald, o.b.e.; Mrs. H. S. Mein; Dr. A. N.
Munro; M. O'Reilly; Prof. P. Prophit; J. G.
Sutherland.
Medical Commissioners, H. C. Fowlie; W. Boyd.
Social Work Commissioner, J. H. L. Richards.
Secretary, J. S. Graham.

---

*Counsel to the Secretary of State for Scotland under
the Private Legislation Procedure (Scotland) Act,
1936* (50 Frederick Street, Edinburgh.—(031–226
6499)).
Senior Counsel, G. S. Douglas, q.c.
Junior Counsel, N. M. P. Morrison.

NATIONAL HEALTH SERVICE, SCOTLAND
Health Boards

Argyll and Clyde, Gilmour House, Paisley. *Chairman,* J. D. Ryan. *General Manager,* I. C. Smith.

Ayrshire and Arran, P.O. Box 13, Hunters Avenue,
Ayr. *Chairman,* W. S. Fyfe. *General Manager,* J.
M. Eckford.

Borders, Huntlyburn, Melrose, Roxburghshire.
Chairman, J. Gibb, c.b.e. *General Manager,* D. A.
Peters.

Dumfries and Galloway, Nithbank, Dumfries.
Chairman, J. A. M. McIntyre. *General Manager,*
M. D. Cook.

Fife, Glenrothes House, North Street, Glenrothes.
Chairman, Mrs. P. A. H. Ferguson. *General Manager,* Col. F. F. Gibb.

Forth Valley, 33 Spittal Street, Stirling. *Chairman,*
L. S. M. Hynd. *General Manager,* A. R. Robertson.

Grampian, 1–7 Albyn Place, Aberdeen. *Chairman,*
C. W. Ellis. *General Manager,* H. Fullerton.

Greater Glasgow, 225 Bath Street, Glasgow. *Chairman,* Dr. T. J. Thomson. *General Manager,* L.
Peterken.

Highland, Reay House, 17 Old Edinburgh Road,
Inverness. *Chairman,* J. McWilliam, o.b.e. *General
Manager,* R. R. W. Stewart.

Lanarkshire, 14 Beckford Street, Hamilton, Lanarkshire. *Chairman,* Mrs. B. M. Gunn, o.b.e. *General
Manager,* F. Clark.

Lothian, 11 Drumsheugh Gardens, Edinburgh.
Chairman, R. B. Weatherstone. *General Manager,*
W. J. Taylor.

Orkney, Balfour Hospital, New Scapa Road, Kirkwall, Orkney. *Chairman,* J. D. M. Robertson.
General Manager, Dr. J. I. Cromarty.

Shetland, 28 Burgh Road, Lerwick. *Chairman,* Mrs.
F. Grains. *General Manager,* D. C. March.

Tayside, P.O. Box 75, Vernonholme, Riverside Drive,
Dundee. *Chairman,* D. B. Grant. *General Manager,*
Dr. R. C. Graham.

Western Isles, 37 South Beach Street, Stornoway,
Isle of Lewis. *Chairman,* Mrs. M. A. Macmillan.
General Manager, J. J. Glover.

Common Services Agency
Trinity Park House, South Trinity Road,
Edinburgh EH5 3SE

Chairman, D. F. Macquaker.
General Manager, J. T. Donald.

GENERAL REGISTER OFFICE (Scotland)
New Register House, Edinburgh EH1 3YT
[031–556 3952]

Registrar General (G4), Dr. C. M. Glennie.
Deputy Registrar General (G5), J. N. Randall.
Senior Principal (G6), D. A. Orr.
Principals (G7), G. F. Baird; I. G. Bowie; D. M.
Robertson.
Statisticians (G7), J. Arrundale; F. G. Thomas.

SEA FISH INDUSTRY AUTHORITY
Sea Fisheries House, 10 Young Street,
Edinburgh EH2 4JQ
[031–225 2515]

Chairman, B. Davis.
Chief Executive, J. C. H. Richman.

Deputy Chief Executive, P. D. Chaplin.
Finance Director, A. Downie.
Technical Director, A. G. Hopper.
Marketing Director, R. M. Kennedy.
Secretary/Administration Director, R. A. Davie.

SECURITIES AND INVESTMENTS BOARD
3 Royal Exchange Buildings, EC3V 3NL
[01–283 2474]

The Securities and Investments Board was formed in 1985 and is the designated agency, under the Financial Services Act, 1986, to regulate the activities of investment businesses in the U.K. Although not a statutory body, the Board has transferred powers under the 1986 Act to recognize self-regulating organizations, professional bodies, investment exchanges and clearing houses, and directly to authorize firms to do investment business in the U.K. The Board also has the power to act as a prosecution authority in respect of persons carrying out authorizable business whilst unauthorized.

Members of the Board are appointed by agreement between the Secretary of State for Trade and Industry and the Governor of the Bank of England. The Chairman and Executive Director are full-time Board members; the others are part-time and non-executive.

The Board
Chairman, D. A. Walker.
Deputy Chairmen, Sir Mark Weinberg; R. N. Quartano, C.B.E.
Members (part-time), A. V. Alexander, C.B.E.; D. M. Child, C.B.E.; J. Clement; D. E. Fellows; R. G. Hodgson; P. J. Manser; W. Proudfoot; E. E. Ray, C.B.E.; The Hon. W. G. Runciman, C.B.E.; Mrs R. Waterhouse, C.B.E.; R. B. Williamson.
Executive Director and Chief Operating Officer, R. H. F. Croft, C.B.

Management
The Chairman.
The Executive Director.
Directors of Divisions:
  Finance, R. P. A. Purcell.
  Futures and Options, M. B. Gittins.
  Information Services, B. W. Smith.
  Intermediaries, M. J. Vile.
  International Securities Regulation, R. J. Britton.
  Investment Management and Products, J. Orme.
  Legal Services, M. Blair.
  Regulation, A. J. Thrall.
Deputy Directors:
  Futures and Options, P.E. Thompson.
  Intermediaries, A. Selman.
  International Securities Regulation, A. King.
  Investment Management, J. Hickman; M. Borland.
  Legal, J. B. Evans; A. Whittaker; J. Welch.
  Personnel and Administration, J. L. Clark.
  Press and Information, B. A. Conway.
  Regulation, R. L. Devlin; C. Hawker.
  Secretary to the Board, T. E. Allen.
  Special Adviser, P. Jackson.

RECOGNIZED BODIES
(as at July 1, 1988)

Self-regulating Organizations
The Association of Futures Brokers and Dealers Ltd. (A.F.B.D.).
The Financial Intermediaries, Managers and Brokers Regulatory Association Ltd. (F.I.M.B.R.A.).
*The Investment Management Regulatory Organization Ltd. (I.M.R.O.).
*The Life Assurance and Unit Trust Regulatory Organization Ltd. (L.A.U.T.R.O.).

The Securities Association Ltd. (T.S.A.).
*these two bodies are also recognized self-regulating organizations for friendly societies.

International Securities Self-regulating Organization
(recognized by D.T.I.)

The Association of International Bond Dealers (A.I.B.D.)

Recognized Investment Exchanges

U.K. Exchanges
The Baltic Futures Exchange (B.F.E.).
The International Petroleum Exchange of London Ltd. (I.P.E.).
The International Stock Exchange of Great Britain and the Republic of Ireland Ltd. (I.S.E.).
The London Commodity Exchange (1986) Ltd. (London FOX).
The London International Financial Futures Exchange Ltd. (L.I.F.F.E.).
LIFFE Options P.L.C.
The London Metal Exchange Ltd. (L.M.E.).

Overseas Exchanges (recognized by the Secretary of State for Trade and Industry)
The National Association of Securities Dealers Automated Quotations System.
Sydney Futures Exchange Ltd.

Recognized Professional Bodies
(†afforded only interim recognition at time of going to press)

The Institute of Chartered Accountants in England and Wales.
The Institute of Chartered Accountants of Scotland.†
The Institute of Chartered Accountants in Ireland.†
The Chartered Association of Certified Accountants.†
The Institute of Actuaries.†
The Insurance Brokers Registration Council.
The Law Society of England and Wales.†
The Law Society of Scotland.†
The Law Society of Northern Ireland.†

Recognized Clearing Houses
International Commodities Clearing House Ltd. (I.C.C.H.).
GAFTA Clearing House Company Ltd.

DEPARTMENT OF SOCIAL SECURITY
Richmond House, 79 Whitehall, SW1A 2NS
[01-210 3000]

The Department was formed in July 1988 by the division of the Department of Health and Social Security into two separate departments. The Department of Social Security is responsible for the social security services in England, Wales and Scotland.

(For **Salaries**, *see* page 297)

Secretary of State for Social Security, THE RT. HON. JOHN MOORE, M.P.
  Private Secretary, J. S. Lord.
Minister of State, NICHOLAS SCOTT, M.B.E., M.P.
  Private Secretary, N. Bromley.
Parliamentary Under Secretary of State, The Lord Skelmersdale.
  Private Secretary, Miss M. M. Dempster.
Parliamentary Under Secretary of State, P. Lloyd, M.P.
  Private Secretary, Ms. J. Rintoul.

Permanent Secretary (G1), M. J. A. Partridge.
Private Secretary, J. Nightingale.

The reorganization of the divisions of the Department of Health and Social Security into the two separate departments created in late July 1988 is expected to take at least until late autumn 1988. Details of the postings and personnel of the D.H.S.S. at end June 1988 are given on pages 324–7.

SPORTS COUNCIL
16 Upper Woburn Place, WC1H 0QP
[01–388 1277]

The Sports Council exists to promote the development of sport and foster the provision of facilities for sport and recreation in Great Britain.
Chairman, J. W. Smith, C.B.E.

HER MAJESTY'S STATIONERY OFFICE
St. Crispins, Duke Street, Norwich NR3 1PD
[0603–622211]

Her Majesty's Stationery Office was established in 1786 and is the British Government's central organization for the supply of printing, binding, office supplies and office machinery of all kinds, for the Public Service at home and abroad; H.M.S.O. is also the Government's publisher and has bookshops for the sale of Government publications in London, Edinburgh, Manchester, Bristol, Birmingham and Belfast. H.M.S.O. obtains most of its supplies from commercial sources by competitive tender, except that about 20 per cent of its printing requirements is done in its own printing works.

In 1980, H.M.S.O. became a trading fund established under the Government Trading Funds Act, 1973. From autumn 1988 H.M.S.O. will have executive agency status.

(For **Salaries**, *see* page 297)

Controller and Chief Executive (G2), J. A. Dole.
Executive Assistant, D. J. Howes.
Director General of Printing and Publishing (G4), E. B. McKendrick.
Director General of Corporate Services and Supply (G4), M. D. Lynn.

Heads of Divisions

Publications (G5), C. J. Penn.
Supply (G5), P. J. Macdonald.
Production (G5), D. G. Forbes.
Print Procurement (G5), B. Ekers.
Finance (G5), V. G. Bell.
Personnel Services (G5), D. W. Ray.
Industrial Personnel (G5), D. J. Wintle.
Marketing Services (G6), G. A. H. Turner.
Information Technology (G5), C. N. Southgate.

Scotland
Bankhead Avenue, Edinburgh EH11 4AB

Bookshop: 71 Lothian Road, Edinburgh EH3 9AZ
Director Edinburgh (G7), G. W. Bedford.

Northern Ireland
IDB House, Chichester Street, Belfast BT1 4PS

Retail and Trade Bookshop: 80 Chichester Street, Belfast BT1 4JY
Director Belfast (G7), Miss V. J. Wilson.

London
Publications Centre: 51 Nine Elms Lane, SW8 5DR.
Bookshops: Retail—49 High Holborn, WC1V 6HB.

Manchester
Broadway, Chadderton, Oldham, Lancs. OL9 9QH

Bookshop: 9–21 Princess Street, Manchester M60 8AS.

Bristol
Ashton Vale Road, Bristol BS3 2HN

Bookshop: Southey House, Wine Street, Bristol BS1 2BH.

Birmingham
Bookshop: 258 Broad Street, Birmingham B1 2HE.

STATUTE LAW COMMITTEE
House of Lords, SW1A 0PW

The Committee exercises a general supervision over the form of the statute law and of Statutory Instruments. It is also responsible for the publication of amended editions of the Statutes, including the current official revised edition of the Statutes in Force.
Chairman, The Lord Chancellor.
Vice-Chairman, The Hon. Mr. Justice Beldam.
Members, The Hon. Lord Maxwell; The Attorney General; The Lord Advocate; The Lord Scarman, P.C., O.B.E.; The Lord Lowry, P.C.; The Rt. Hon. J. Morris, Q.C., M.P.; The Rt. Hon. P. Archer, Q.C., M.P.; Sir Anthony Buck, Q.C., M.P.; Sir Derek Oulton, K.C.B.; D. Rippengal, C.B., Q.C.; H. Knorpel, C.B.; C. H. de Waal, C.B.; N. J. Adamson, C.B., Q.C.; Sir John Sainty, K.C.B.; Sir John Bailey, K.C.B.; Sir Brian Cubbon, G.C.B.; Sir Terence Heiser, K.C.B.; H. W. Gamon, C.B.E., M.C.; Sir Nicholas Lyell, Q.C., M.P.; The Lord Oliver of Aylmerton, P.C.; Sir Robin Butler, K.C.B., C.V.O.; C. Boulton, C.B.; K. F. Barclay; M. H. Collon; J. H. Willcox; E. McKendrick.
Secretary, B. P. Keith.

Statutory Publications Office
Queen Anne's Chambers,
28 Broadway, SW1H 9JS
[01–273 3000]

Editor, J. M. Gibson.

OFFICE OF TELECOMMUNICATIONS
Atlantic House, Holborn Viaduct, EC1N 2HQ
[01–353 4020]

OFTEL is a non-Ministerial Government Department headed by a Director General, which is responsible for supervising telecommunications activities in the U.K.

Its principal functions are to ensure that holders of telecommunications licences comply with their licence conditions; to maintain and promote effective competition in telecommunications; to promote, in respect of prices, quality and variety the interests of consumers, purchasers and other users of telecommunication services and apparatus.

The Director General has powers to deal with anti-competitive practices and monopoly situations. He also has a duty to consider all reasonable complaints and representations about telecommunication apparatus and services.
Director General, Prof. B. V. Carsberg.
Deputy Director General, W. R. B. Wigglesworth.
Director of P.T.O. Licensing, G. P. Knight.
Director of Apparatus Approval, J. P. Compton.
Head of Information, D. C. Redding.

DEPARTMENT OF TRADE AND INDUSTRY
1 Victoria Street, SW1H 0ET
[01–215 7877]

The Department is responsible for:
(a) international trade policy, including the promotion of U.K. trade interests in the European Community, G.A.T.T., O.E.C.D., U.N.C.T.A.D. and other international organizations.

(b) under the direction of the British Overseas Trade Board, the promotion of U.K. exports and assistance to exporters.

(c) policy in relation to industry, including the general promotion of the interests of industry and assistance to industry; specific interest in all manufacturing and service industries apart from those covered by other Departments; regional policy, Inner Cities Initiative, enterprise and deregulation, and regional industrial assistance (some of this applying only to England); and policy in relation to the public bodies British Shipbuilders, the British Steel Corporation, the Post Office and the British Technology Group.

(d) competition policy and consumer protection, including relations with the Office of Fair Trading and the Monopolies and Mergers Commission, and the National Weights and Measures Laboratory.

(e) policy on science and technology and research and development matters, standards and designs, support for innovation, and the administration of the National Physical Laboratory, National Engineering Laboratory, Warren Spring Laboratory and the Laboratory of the Government Chemist.

(f) the administration of company legislation and the Companies Registration Office; the Insolvency Service; the regulation of the insurance industry; the regulation of radio frequencies; and the Patent Office.

(g) the Business Statistics Office.

(For **Salaries,** *see* page 297).

Secretary of State for Trade and Industry and President of the Board of Trade, THE RT. HON. THE LORD YOUNG OF GRAFFHAM.
  Principal Private Secretary, N. R. Thornton.
  Parliamentary Private Secretary, N. Baker, M.P.
Chancellor of the Duchy of Lancaster and Minister of Trade and Industry, THE RT. HON. ANTONY NEWTON, O.B.E., M.P.
  Private Secretary, P. Smith.
Minister for Trade, THE HON. ALAN CLARK, M.P.
  Private Secretary, Miss M. E. K. Davies.
Parliamentary Under Secretary of State for Industry, Robert Atkins, M.P.
  Private Secretary, S. Gill.
Parliamentary Under Secretary of State for Corporate Affairs, The Hon. Francis Maude, Q.C., M.P.
  Private Secretary, G. Heyn.
Parliamentary Under Secretary of State for Industry and Consumer Affairs, Eric Forth, M.P.
  Private Secretary, M. Carvell.
Lord-in-Waiting, The Lord Strathclyde.
  Private Secretary, N. Mitchell.
Permanent Secretary (G1), Sir Brian Hayes, G.C.B.
  Private Secretary, T. Davy.
Deputy Secretaries (G2), D. M. Dell, C.B.; A. J. Macdonald; Dr. R. F. Coleman (*Chief Engineer and Scientist*); R. Mountfield, C.B.; Miss E. M. Llewellyn-Smith, C.B.; C. W. Roberts, C.B.; R. Williams; H. H. Liesner, C.B. (*Chief Economic Adviser*); G. A. Hosker, C.B. (*The Solicitor*); W. M. Knighton, C.B. (*Principal Establishment and Finance Officer*).
Parliamentary Clerk, T. A. Hardbattle.

Central Unit
1 Victoria Street, SW1H 0ET
[01-215 7877]

Head of Unit (G3), B. J. G. Hilton.
Heads of Branch (G5), Dr. R. C. Dobbie; P. D. J. Makeham; S. Spivey; J. Healey.

External European Policy Division
1 Victoria Street, SW1H 0ET
[01-215 7877]

Under Secretary (G3), A. C. Hutton.
Heads of Branch (G5), M. D. C. Johnson; D. E. Love; Miss A. E. Stoddart.

Overseas Trade Divisions
1 Victoria Street, SW1H 0ET
[01-215 7877]

Division 1 (*Projects and Export Policy*)
Under Secretary (G3), C. C. W. Adams.
Heads of Branch (G5), C. A. Palmer; F. B. Wheeler; C. E. Blundell.

Division 2
(*N. America, N.E. and S.E. Asia, China, Hong Kong and Export Licensing Operation*)
Under Secretary (G3), J. A. Cooke.
Heads of Branch (G5), W. J. Hall; J. V. Hagestadt; E. W. Beston.

Division 3
Under Secretary (G3), A. J. Hunter.

Administration and Finance
Head of Branch (G5), M. G. Roberts.

Exports to Europe Branch
Head of Branch (G5), K. D. Levinson.

Export Data Branch
Director (G6), (vacant).

Fairs and Promotions Branch
Head of Branch (G5), G. J. Bradshaw.

Eastern Europe Branch
Head of Branch (G5), K. W. N. George.

Division 4
(*Middle East, India and Pakistan, Africa, Latin America, the Caribbean and Australasia*)
Under Secretary (G3), T. Muir.
Heads of Branch (G5), H. R. Owen, C.B.E.; M. Petter; M. A. S. Garrod.

Internal Policy Division
1 Victoria Street, SW1H 0ET
[01-215 7877]

Under Secretary (G3), Miss M. T. Neville-Rolfe.
Heads of Branch (G5), P. Loughead; R. T. King; W. L. Stow.

Patent Office and Industrial Property and Copyright Department
see entry on p. 354

Insurance Division
10-18 Victoria Street, SW1H 0NN
[01-215 7877]

Under Secretary (G3), A. C. Russell.
Heads of Branch (G5), D. W. Hellings; D. G. Hyde; M. D. Oldham.

Financial Services Division
10-18 Victoria Street, SW1H 0NN
[01-215 7877]

Under Secretary (G3), W. B. Willott.
Heads of Branch (G5), A. C. G. Lowry; K. M. Long; D. T. Smith.

Companies Division
10-18 Victoria Street, SW1H 0NN
[01-215 7877]

Under Secretary (G3), Mrs. S. E. Brown.
Heads of Branch (G5), M. J. C. Butcher; D. L. Gatland; N. Worman.

Companies Registration Office
Companies House, Crown Way, Maindy, Cardiff CF4 3UZ
[0222-388588]

Registrar of Companies for England and Wales (G4), S. R. Curtis.

London Search Room, 55–71 City Road, EC1Y 1BB
[01–253 9393]

102 George Street, Edinburgh EH2 3DJ
[031–225 5774]

Registrar for Scotland, E. T. K. Lougheed.

Manufacturing Technology and Materials Division
Ashdown House, 123 Victoria Street, SW1E 6RB
[01–215 7877]

Under Secretary (G3), J. E. Cammell.
Heads of Branch (G5), H. M. Lanyon; R. C. McVickers.

The Insolvency Service
2–14 Bunhill Row, EC1Y 8LL
[01–606 4071]

Inspector General of the Insolvency Service, M. Clark.
Deputy Inspectors General, P. D. Pink; P. R. Joyce; A. K. Sales.
Head of Branch (G5), Miss A. J. Brimelow.

Consumer Affairs Division
10–18 Victoria Street, SW1H 0NN
[01–215 7877]

Under Secretary (G3), C. T. Newton.
Heads of Branch (G5), R. P. Hope; M. A. R. Lunn; R. E. Palmer.
Trading Standards Adviser (G5), D. Jones.

Air Division
Ashdown House, 123 Victoria Street, SW1E 6RB
[01–215 7877]

Under Secretary (G3), M. J. Michell.
Heads of Branch (G5), D. I. Richardson; D. Marsh.
Grade 6, M. O. Ralph; Dr. G. T. Coleman.

Research and Technology Policy Division
Ashdown House, 123 Victoria Street, SW1E 6RB
[01–215 7877]

Under Secretary (G3), B. Murray.
Heads of Branch (G5), J. H. Chapman; J. D. Howarth; Dr. A. W. Keddie; G. M. White.

National Physical Laboratory
Teddington, Middx. TW11 0LW
[01–977 3222]

Director (G3), Dr. P. Dean, C.B.

Laboratory of the Government Chemist
Cornwall House, Waterloo Road, SE1 8XY
[01–211 7900]

Government Chemist (G3), A. Williams.

National Engineering Laboratory
East Kilbride, Glasgow G75 0QU
[03552–20222]

Director (G3), Dr. D. A. Bell.

Warren Spring Laboratory
Gunnels Wood Road, Stevenage, Herts SG1 2BX
[0438–741122]

Director (G3), Dr. J. S. S. Reay.

National Weights and Measures Laboratory
Teddington, Middx. TW11 0JZ
[01–977 3222]

Director (G5), Dr. P. B. Clapham.

Competition Policy Division
1 Victoria Street, SW1H 0ET
[01–215 7877]

Under Secretary (G3), S. W. Treadgold.
Heads of Branch (G5), R. J. Allpress; R. E. Allen; G. C. Riggs.

Enterprise and Deregulation Unit
1 Victoria Street, SW1H 0ET
[01–215 7877]

Director (G3), R. Hewes.
Heads of Branch (G5), Mrs. G. Ashmore; Miss J. Morgan.

Quality Design and Education Division
Kingsgate House, 66–74 Victoria Street, SW1E 6SW
[01–215 7877]

Under Secretary (G3), Mrs. P. A. Denham.
Heads of Branch (G5), A. Berry; R. J. Brown; C. L. Jackson; M. E. Stanley.

Engineering Markets Division
Ashdown House, 123 Victoria Street, SW1E 6RB
[01–215 7877]

Under Secretary (G3), C. B. Benjamin.
Heads of Branch (G5), D. R. Coates; A. C. Conway; P. Goodman; B. N. Steele; Dr. H. M. Sutton.

British National Space Centre
Millbank Tower, Millbank, SW1P 4QU
[01–211 3000]

Director General (G2), A. J. Pryor.
Heads of Branch (G5), Dr. J. E. Harries; A. C. Nicholas.

Enterprise Initiative Division
Kingsgate House, 66–74 Victoria Street, SW1E 6SW
[01–215 7877]

Under Secretary (G3), A. R. Titchener.
Heads of Branches (G5), G. Kerfoot; R. M. Upson.

Telecommunications and Posts Division
Kingsgate House, 66–74 Victoria Street, SW1E 6SW
[01–215 7877]

Under Secretary (G3), R. J. Priddle.
Heads of Branch (G5), J. E. Avery; Mrs. E. C. Jones; J. F. Mills; S. R. Temple.

Radiocommunications Division
Waterloo Bridge House, Waterloo Road, SE1 8UA
[01–215 7877]

Under Secretary (G3), A. J. Nieduszynski.
Director (G4), Dr. K. C. Shotton.
Heads of Branch (G5), M. Goddard; M. P. Davies; M. V. Coolican; R. A. Bedford; B. A. Heatley; (G6) Dr. A. C. D. Whitehouse.

Information Engineering Directorate
Kingsgate House, 66–74 Victoria Street, SW1E 6SW
[01–215 7877]

Under Secretary (G3), Dr. T. E. H. Walker.
Heads of Branches (G5), R. L. Hird; R. Morland; D. G. Morgan; D. N. Shorter.

Industrial Materials Market Division
Ashdown House, 123 Victoria Street, SW1E 6RB
[01–215 7877]

Under Secretary (G3), J. F. Mogg.
Heads of Branch (G5), R. I. Rogers; V. F. Lane; Miss S. E. Harding; Dr. W. Vickers; Mrs. A. Wilks.

Consumer Market Division
Ashdown House, 123 Victoria Street, SW1E 6RB
[01–212 7676]

Under Secretary (G3), (vacant).
Heads of Branch (G5), P. Robinson; Miss V. E. Evans; M. S. Bremner; Dr. H. N. M. Stewart.

Vehicles Market Division
Ashdown House, 123 Victoria Street, SW1E 6RB
[01–215 7877]

Under Secretary (G3), M. J. A. Cochlin.
Heads of Branch (G5), S. J. Bowen; Mrs. C. E. D. Bell;
(G6) P. Neale.

Inner Cities Unit
1 Victoria Street, SW1H 0ET
[01–215 7877]

Director (G4), M. Gahagan.
Head of Branch (G5), Ms. S. Seymour.

Investment, Development and Accountancy Division
Kingsgate House, 66–74 Victoria Street,
SW1E 6SW
[01–215 7877]

Directors, I.D.A. (G3), A. J. N. Bray; P. L. Mason; P.
M. S. Corley.
Heads of Branch (G5), J. Phillips; R. H. S. Wells; G.
M. Field; J. C. S. Priston; C. P. Hicks; K. Holt;
(G6), N. A. T. Hobbs.

Information Technology Division
Kingsgate House, 66–74 Victoria Street,
SW1E 6SW
[01–215 7877]

Under Secretary (G3), Dr. J. C. J. Thynne.
Heads of Branch (G5), P. Casey; M. E. Farry; R.
Foster; H. L. Evans; J. P. Hobday; H. J. Ivey.

DEPARTMENT OF TRADE AND INDUSTRY SERVICES ORGANIZATION
Deputy Secretaries (G2), H. H. Liesner, C.B. *(Chief
Economic Adviser);* G. A. Hosker, C.B. *(The Solicitor);* W. M. Knighton, C.B. *(Principal Establishment
and Finance Officer).*

Personnel Management Division
Allington Towers,
17 Allington Street, SW1
[01–215 7877]

Under Secretary (G3), N. F. Ledsome, C.B.
Heads of Branch (G5), P. S. Salvidge; D. W. F.
Johnson; J. F. Bailes; T. Bryan.

Management Services and Manpower Division
29 Bressenden Place, SW1E 5DT
[01–215 7877]

Under Secretary (G3), R. M. Rumbelow.
Director of Information Technology (G4), N. Bernard.
Heads of Branch (G5), K. J. Doyle, C.B.E.; R. J.
Meadway; E. W. Pearcey; Mrs. E. M. Ryle.

Finance and Resource Management Division
Ashdown House, 123 Victoria Street, SW1E 6RB
[01–215 7877]

Under Secretary (G3), D. R. C. Durie.
Heads of Branch (G5), P. R. S. Hartnack; D. M.
Hoddinott; M. O'Shea.

Accounts Branch
P.O. Box 100, Government Buildings, Cardiff Road,
Newport, Gwent NP9 1ZA
[0633–810636]

Director of Accounts, D. M. Hoddinott.

Internal Audit
29 Bressenden Place, SW1E 5DT
[01–215 7877]

Head of Internal Audit, A. C. Elkington.

Solicitor's Office
10–18 Victoria Street, SW1H 0NQ
[01–215 7877]

The Solicitor (G2), G. A Hosker, C.B.

Investigations Divisions

Heads of Divisions (G3), J. R. Mallinson; C. S. Kerse;
(G4), J. M. Stanley.
Assistant Solicitors (G5), D. M. Bailey; H. H. Brad-
shaw; Mrs. N. M. P. Chappell; C. J. Cook; Mrs. T.
Dunston; R. D. Fayers; Miss P. A. E. Granados, R.
Higgins; I. K. Mathers; Miss K. Morton; Miss E.
N. O'Flynn; S. Parker; Miss J. Richardson; Miss J.
V. Stokes; A. M. Susman; E. A. Thompson; B.
Welch; A. Woods.
Head of Companies Investigation Branch, G. Clark.
*Head of Financial Services Act Investigation Group
(G5),* B. D. Winkett.

Information Division
1 Victoria Street, SW1H 0ET
[01–215 7877]

Head of Information (G4), A. E. Moorey.
Deputy Heads of Information Division (G6), B. Avery;
S. Lyle-Smythe; Miss A. MacLean.

Economics Divisions
1 Victoria Street, SW1H 0ET
[01–215 7877]

Chief Economic Adviser (G2), H. H. Liesner, C.B.

Division 1
Ashdown House, 123 Victoria Street, SW1E 6RB
[01–215 7877]

Under Secretary (G3), J. R. Shepherd.
Heads of Branch (G5), B. M. Nonehebel; J. M. Barber;
J. A. S. Robertson.

Division 2
1 Victoria Street, SW1H 0ET
[01–215 7877]

Under Secretary (G3), A. Whiting.
Heads of Branch (G5), P. J. Goate; M. S. Bradbury;
D. A. Miner.

Statistics Divisions
1 Victoria Street, SW1H 0ET
[01–215 7877]

Division 1
Millbank Tower, Millbank, SW1P 4QU
[01–211 3000]

Under Secretary (G3), N. Harvey.
Heads of Branch (G5), R. L. Butchart; J. Walker; J.
Astin.

Division 2
1 Victoria Street, SW1H 0ET
[01–215 7877]

Under Secretary (G3), P. J. Stibbard.
Heads of Branch (G5), W. E. Boyd; P. H. Richardson;
G. Jenkinson.

Business Statistics Office
Cardiff Road, Newport, Gwent, NP9 1XG
[0633–56111]

Director (G3), R. G. Ward.
Heads of Branch (G5), C. C. Maskall; Dr. B. Mitchell;
R. M. Norton; D. R. Lewis; C. J. Spiller.
Grade 6, W. D. Knight.

BRITISH OVERSEAS TRADE BOARD
1 Victoria Street, SW1H 0ET
[01–215 7877]

President, The Secretary of State for Trade and
Industry.
Chairman, Sir James Cleminson, M.C.
Vice-Chairman, H.R.H. The Duke of Kent, K.G.,
G.C.M.G., G.C.V.O.
Members, Mrs. P. A. Beckett; N. P. Bayne, C.M.G.; A.
B. Cleaver; D. M. Dell, C.B.; A. K. Edwards, M.B.E.;

T. P. Frost; Dr. A. Hayes; M. R. Hoffman; D. A. Holland, C.B.E.; D. P. Hornby; Sir Philip Jones, C.B.; W. B. Jordan; The Earl of Limerick, K.B.E.; J. W. Parsons, C.B.E.; M. S. Perry, O.B.E.; M. G. Stephens; B. D. Taylor; G. S. Tucker, C.B.E.
Chief Executive, D. M. Dell, C.B.
Secretary (*G5*), M. G. Roberts.

REGIONAL OFFICES

North East, Stanegate House, 2 Groat Market, Newcastle upon Tyne NE1 1YN. [091–232 4722].— *Regional Director* (*G3*), R. W. Simpson.

North West, Sunley Tower, Piccadilly Plaza, Manchester M1 4BA. [061–236 2171].—*Regional Director* (*G3*), M. M. Baker.

Yorkshire and Humberside, Priestley House, Park Row, Leeds LS1 5LF. [0532 443171].—*Regional Director* (*G3*), E. Wright.

West Midlands, Ladywood House, Stephenson Street, Birmingham B2 4DT. [021–631 6181].— *Regional Director* (*G3*), N. H. Perry.

East Midlands, Severns House, 20 Middle Pavement, Nottingham NG1 7DW. [0602 506181].—*Regional Director* (*G5*), R. M. Anderson.

South West, The Pithay, Bristol BS1 2PB. [0272– 272666].—*Regional Director* (*G5*), D. B. Lodge.

South East, Bridge Place, 88–89 Eccleston Square, SW1V 1PT. [01–215 7877].—*Regional Director* (*G5*), A. J. Mantle. *Director* (*G6*), Dr. H. A. P. Fisher.

TRAINING COMMISSION
Head Office: Moorfoot, Sheffield S1 4PQ
[0742–753275]

The Training Commission (Manpower Services Commission) came into existence on May 26, 1988. The Commission is separate from Government but accountable to the Secretary of State for Employment (and to the Secretaries for Scotland and Wales in respect of its operations in Scotland and Wales). The Commission has ten members who each serve for three years.
Chairman, B Wolfson £65,000
Members, M. Bett; M. O. Bury, O.B.E.; J. Gilchrist; R. Jackson; J. D. Pearman; K. Graham, O.B.E.; R. A. Grantham; J. M. Peake, C.B.E.; R. Todd.
Director General, R. Dawe, C.B., O.B.E. £59,000

Salaries

Grade 3 .... £34,000–£43,000
Grade 4 .... £31,069–£34,705
Grade 5 .... £24,765–£29,465
Grade 6 .... £18,786–£26,335

Resources and Personnel Division

Director (*G3*), Mrs. V. Bayliss.
Heads of Branches (*G5*):
Resource Control, C. P. Thomas.
Internal Audit (*G6*), C. Williams.
Finance Control, N. L. Gregory.
Information Systems and Management Services, I. Turl.
Personnel and Staff Development, D. Grover.

Skills Training Agency

Chief Executive (*G4*), T. R. R. O'Connor.
Heads of Branches (*G6*):
Skillcentre Operations (*G5*), S. Bishell.
Financial and Accounting Services, T. Kent.
Product Development, P. Wells.
Marketing and Mobile Training, J. Davies.

Training Standards Advisory Service

Director (*G5*), J. D. Tinsley.

Information Services
Head (*G5*), A. J. Brookes.

POLICY AND PROGRAMMES DIVISION

Deputy Director General and Director, Policy and Programmes Division, I. Johnston.

Youth Training

Director (*G3*), K. N. Atkinson.
Heads of Branches (*G5*):
Youth Programmes, J. F. Smith.
Youth Development, R. Niven.
Commission Secretariat, M. Twomey.

Quality Standards and Methods

Director (*G4*), G. Kendall.
Heads of Branches (*G5*):
Industry Bodies, J. Wiltshire.
Programme Quality, J. K. Fuller.
Occupational Standards, A. T. Wisbey.
Psychological Services, T. Edmonds (temp.).
Learning Technology, D. Mann.

Education Programmes

Director (*G3*), Mrs. A. Jones.
Heads of Branches (*G5*):
T.V.E.I (*Policy*), I. Fair.
T.V.E.I (*Operations*), Mrs. R. Le Guen.
Higher Education, G. Macnair.
Further Education, I. Randall.

Adult Training Programmes

Director (*G3*), J. Surr.
Heads of Branches (*G5*):
New Job Training Scheme, J. Walker.
Adult Training Programmes, Miss S. Newton.
Community Programmes, R. Lasko.
Policy and Project Management, N. Schofield.

Systems and Strategy

Director (*G3*), R. Hillier.
Heads of Branches (*G5*):
Policy and Analysis, N. Davis.
Evaluation and Research, Mrs. J. Marquand.
Labour Market Information, A. Davies.
Human Resources Development Promotion, P. Gregory.
Learning Systems and Access, (vacant).

Field Operations

Director (*G4*), J. Lambert.
Heads of Branches:
Field Support (*G5*), J. Franklin.
Field Development (*G6*), M. Christie.

DEPARTMENT OF TRANSPORT
2 Marsham Street, SW1P 3EB
[01–276 3000]

The Department of Transport has overall responsibility for land, sea and air transport. This entails general sponsorship of the transport industries, with particular responsibility for British Rail and London Regional Transport; domestic and international civil aviation policy; shipping policy and the ports industry; navigation lights; pilotage; H.M. Coastguard; oversight of road transport, including vehicle registration and licensing, driver licensing and road safety; responsibility for construction and maintenance of motorways and trunk roads; and general oversight of the transport planning of local authorities, including payments of grant from central Government.

(For **Salaries,** *see* page 297).

Secretary of State for Transport, THE RT. HON. PAUL CHANNON, M.P.
  Private Secretary, R. J. Griffin.
  Parliamentary Private Secretary, (vacant).
Minister of State for Public Transport, MICHAEL PORTILLO, M.P.
  Private Secretary, S. Bramall.
Parliamentary Under Secretaries, P. Bottomley, M.P. (*Roads and Traffic*); Lord Brabazon of Tara (*Aviation and Shipping*).
  Private Secretaries, S. L. Gooding; Miss S. J. Smith.
Lord in Waiting, The Viscount Davidson.
  Private Secretary. Miss S. J. Smith.
Parliamentary Clerk, Mrs. L. C. Jones.
Permanent Under Secretary of State (*G1*), Sir Alan Bailey, K.C.B.
  Private Secretary, J. Ware.

Information

Head of Information (G5), Miss G. P. Samuel.

PUBLIC TRANSPORT AND RESEARCH

Deputy Secretary (G2), J. Palmer, C.B.

Railways

Under Secretary (G3), J. R. Coates.
Heads of Division (G5), A. J. Nichols; P. G. Hewett; A. Fortnam.
Chief Inspecting Officer (G4), R. J. Seymour.

Public Transport London and Metropolitan

Under Secretary (G3), A. J. Goldman.
Heads of Division (G5), F. Gale; E. C. Neve; Miss S. J. Lambert.

Transport and Road Research Laboratory

Director (G3), D. F. Cornelius *(temp.).*
Deputy Director (G4), D. I. Robertson *(temp.).*
Grade 5, Dr. A. J. M. Hitchcock; Dr. P. H. Bly; R. S. Hinsley; Dr. G. P. Tilly.
Grade 6, J. S. Yerrell.

Science and Research Policy and Programmes

Grade 5, P. G. O'Neill.

CHIEF SCIENTIFIC ADVISER (G2): Dr. D. J. Fisk.

ROAD SAFETY AND LICENSING

Deputy Secretary and Principal Finance Officer (G2), R. C. M. Cooper, C.B.

Road and Vehicle Safety

Under Secretary (G3), Mrs. J. M. Bridgeman.
Heads of Division (G5), D. R. Instone; R. J. Oliver; Dr. C. M. Woodman; D. H. Worskett.
Grade 6, D. J. Spragg; J. David; K. Walton; D. Harvey.
Chief Mechanical Engineer (G4), D. V. Jones.
Grade 6, R. J. White.
Chief Mechanical Engineer (G4), E. Dunn.
Grade 6, R. J. White.

Driver and Vehicle Licensing

Director (G3), G. R. Wattley.
Deputy Director (G4), M. A. Robinson.
Heads of Division (G5), R. J. Verge; H. C. S. Derwent; P. G. Collis; J. K. Griffiths.
Grade 6, T. J. Horton.

Freight and Bus Licensing

Under Secretary (G3), W. P. Jackson.
Grade 5, H. C. T. Fawcett; L. Moyle.
Grade 6, J. Winder; D. J. Blackman.

Traffic Area Offices
Traffic Commissioners and Licensing Authorities

Eastern (*Nottingham and Cambridge*), Brig. C. M. Boyd.
Metropolitan (*Acton*), Air Vice-Marshal R. G. Ashford, C.B.E.
North Eastern (*Newcastle upon Tyne and Leeds*), F. Whalley.
North Western (*Manchester*), M. S. Albu.
Scottish (*Edinburgh*), H. McNamara.
South Eastern (*Eastbourne*), Brig. M. H. Turner.
West Midlands (*Birmingham*), J. M. C. Pugh.
Western (*Bristol*), Maj.-Gen. V. H. J. Carpenter, C.B., M.B.E.
South Wales (*Cardiff*), J. M. C. Pugh.

HIGHWAYS AND TRAFFIC

Deputy Secretary (G2), D. Holmes.

Highways Policy and Programme

Under Secretary (G3), P. Wood.
Heads of Division (G5), B. R. A. Blaxall; B. J. Billington; P. E. Pickering; Ms. A. Munro.
Grade 7, D. E. Gladding.

Highways, Contracts, Administration and Maintenance

Under Secretary (G3), P. Critchley.
Heads of Division (G5), P. R. Smith; J. H. Denning; P. G. Davies; B. J. Bennett; J. B. W. Robins.

Highways Engineering

Chief Highway Engineer (G3), F. J. Parker.
Deputy Chief Highway Engineer (G4), D. A. Holland.
Grade 5, R. S. Wilson; S. Rose; P. H. Dawe; D. Kershaw.
Grade 6, K. Softly.

Traffic and Greater London Roads

Under Secretary (G3), I. Yass.
Heads of Division (G5), R. M. C. Edridge; N. T. Rees; P. E. Butler; Dr. S. Chatterjee.

AVIATION, SHIPPING AND INTERNATIONAL

Deputy Secretary (G2), G. R. Sunderland.

Civil Aviation Policy

Under Secretary (G3), R. E. Clarke.
Grade 5, D. S. Evans; C. J. Harris; W. E. Kelly; S. C. Whiteley.

Shipping Policy and Emergency Planning

Under Secretary (G3), D. J. Lyness.
Heads of Division (G5), R. G. Jones; J. D. Henes; P. Kitchen; R. Bird.
Grade 6, J. R. Perrett.

Marine

Under Secretary (G3), J. W. S. Dempster.
Heads of Division (G5), J. R. Fells; M. W. Jackson.

Marine Emergency Operations and Marine Pollution Control Unit

Director (G4), Capt. W. H. H. McLeod.
Chief Coastguard (G5), Capt. P. C. K. Harris.
Surveyor General, G. Thompson.
Deputy Surveyors General (G5), P. J. Hambling; W. A. Graham; N. W. Scully.

International Aviation

Under Secretary (G3), D. C. Moss.
Heads of Division (G5), C. R. Hook; M. L. Fielder; Ms. E. A. Hopkins.

Accidents Investigation Branch
Chief Inspector of Accidents (G4), D. A. Cooper.
Deputy Chief Inspector of Accidents (G5), K. P. R. Smart.

International Transport
Under Secretary (G3), J. D. Noulton.
Grade 5, P. F. Emms; J. D. Henes.
Grade 6, R. Pounder.

Finance
Under Secretary (G3), H. M. G. Stevens.
Grade 4, H. B. Wenban-Smith.
Heads of Division (G5), P. R. Smethurst; C. R. Grimsey; D. J. Rowlands; D. Wadsworth.
Accounting Adviser (G5), A. R. Allum.
Grade 6, R. Eastman.

Internal Audit
Head of Branch (G6), J. Kingdom.

ECONOMICS AND STATISTICS (TRANSPORT)
Chief Economic Adviser (G2), Dr. J. H. Rickard.
Grade 5, G. A. C. Searle; C. T. B. Smith.

Statistics (Transport)
Under Secretary (G3), E. J. Thompson.
Grade 5, Miss B. J. Wood; H. Collings; G. R. Emes; R. P. Donachie.

DEPARTMENTS OF THE ENVIRONMENT AND TRANSPORT REGIONAL OFFICES AND COMMON SERVICES
See under **Department of the Environment**

THE TREASURY
Parliament Street, SW1P 3AG
[01–233 3000]

The Office of the Lord High Treasurer has been continuously in commission for well over 200 years: the Lord High Commissioners of H.M. Treasury consist of the First Lord of the Treasury (who is also the Prime Minister), the Chancellor of the Exchequer and five Junior Lords. This Board of Commissioners is assisted at present by the Chief Secretary, a Parliamentary Secretary who is the Chief Whip, a Financial Secretary, an Economic Secretary, a Paymaster General and by the Permanent Secretary.

The Prime Minister and First Lord is not primarily concerned in the day to day aspects of Treasury business. The Parliamentary Secretary and the Junior Lords are Government whips in the House of Commons. The management of the Treasury devolves upon the Chancellor of the Exchequer and, under him, the Chief Secretary, the Financial Secretary, the Economic Secretary and the Paymaster General. The Chief Secretary is responsible for the control of public expenditure; public services and industry groups; overseas aid and export credit; efficiency in the public sector; and procurement policy. The Financial Secretary discharges the traditional responsibility of the Treasury for the largely formal procedure for the voting of funds by Parliament. He also has responsibility for other Parliamentary financial business, Inland Revenue duties and taxes and privatization policy. The Economic Secretary has responsibility for monetary policy; international financial business; North Sea fiscal regime; Department for National Savings, Registry of Friendly Societies and the National Loans Office; and the Treasury research budget. The Paymaster General deals with Customs & Excise matters; European Community business; civil service pay; the Royal

Mint, H.M. Stationery Office, Central Office of Information, Government Actuary's Department and the Paymaster General's Office. All Treasury Ministers are concerned in tax matters.

Prime Minister and First Lord of the Treasury, THE RT. HON. MARGARET THATCHER, M.P.
Chancellor of the Exchequer, THE RT. HON. NIGEL LAWSON, M.P. £34,157
  Principal Private Secretary, A. C. S. Allan.
  Private Secretary, J. M. G. Taylor.
  Parliamentary Private Secretary, N. Forman, M.P.
  Parliamentary Clerk, B. O. Dyer.
Chief Secretary to the Treasury, THE RT. HON. JOHN MAJOR, M.P. £34,157
  Private Secretary, Miss G. C. Evans.
  Assistant Private Secretary, Miss Z. Everest-Phillips.
  Parliamentary Private Secretary, T. Favell, M.P.
Paymaster General, THE RT. HON. PETER BROOKE, M.P. £23,887
  Private Secretary, S. P. Judge.
  Parliamentary Private Secretary, M. Stern, M.P.
Financial Secretary to the Treasury, THE RT. HON. NORMAN LAMONT, M.P. £23,887
  Private Secretary, J. J. Heywood.
  Parliamentary Private Secretary, J. Maples, M.P.
Economic Secretary, PETER LILLEY, M.P. £17,877
  Private Secretary, P. D. P. Barnes.
Parliamentary Secretary to the Treasury and Government Chief Whip, THE RT. HON. DAVID WADDINGTON, Q.C., M.P. £28,267
  Private Secretary, M. Maclean.
Treasurer of H.M. Household and Deputy Chief Whip, David Hunt, M.B.E., M.P. £23,887
Lord Commissioners of the Treasury, A. Durant, M.P.; D. Lightbown, M.P.; K. Carlisle, M.P.; A. Howarth, C.B.E., M.P.; D. Maclean, M.P. £17,877
Assistant Whips, S. Dorrell, M.P.; M. Fallon, M.P.; D. Heathcoat-Amory, M.P.; The Hon. T. Sackville, M.P.; J. Taylor, M.P. £23,887
(NOTE.—(i) All salaries shown above do not include Parliamentary salary: (ii) The Prime Minister is entitled to draw a salary of £45,787.)
(For Civil Service **Salaries**, *see* page 297).

Permanent Secretary of the Treasury, Sir Peter Middleton, K.C.B.
  Private Secretary, S. D. H. Sargent.
Second Permanent Secretaries (G1a), Sir Geoffrey Littler, K.C.B. *(Overseas Finance)*; J. Anson *(Public Services)*; Dame Anne Mueller, D.C.B. *(Civil Service Management and Pay)*.
Head of Government Economics Service and Chief Economic Adviser to the Treasury, Sir Terence Burns.
Head of Government Accountancy Service, Sir Anthony Wilson.
Deputy Secretaries (G2), M. C. Scholar *(Public Finance)*; T. P. Lankester *(Overseas Finance)*; H. Phillips *(Public Services, and General Expenditure)*; N. J. Monck, C.B. *(Industry)*.
Deputy Chief Economic Adviser to the Treasury (G2), I. C. R. Byatt.

INDUSTRY
Industry, Agriculture and Employment Group
Under Secretary (G3), T. U. Burgner.
Assistant Secretaries (G5), R. J. Bonney; M. A. Waller; T. J. Burr.

Public Enterprises Group
Under Secretary (G3), D. J. L. Moore.
Assistant Secretaries (G5), M. L. Williams; Mrs. M. E. Brown.

FINANCIAL MANAGEMENT: PUBLIC SERVICES

Financial Management Group

Under Secretary (G3), L. J. Harris.
Assistant Secretaries (G5), C. J. Welsh; W. L. St. Clair.

Central Unit on Purchasing

Director, M. J. O. Willacy.
Deputy Director, F. Martin.

Social Services and Territorial Group

Under Secretary (G3), Miss M. E. Peirson.
Assistant Secretaries (G5), J. P. McInture; R. B. Saunders; A. M. White.

Local Government Group

Under Secretary (G3), A. J. C. Edwards.
Assistant Secretaries (G5), B. H. Potter; S. N. Woods.

Home Transport and Education Group

Under Secretary (G3), Miss A. F. Case.
Assistant Secretaries (G5), D. C. W. Revolta; C. Farthing.

Accounts and Purchasing

Under Secretary (G3), J. S. Beastall.
Assistant Secretary (G5), F. K. Jones.

Central Computer and Telecommunications Agency

Under Secretary (G3), P. I. Freeman.
Assistant Secretaries (G5), W. A. Beard; W. Houldsworth; R. Paynter; I. S. Thomson; P. Rayner; R. E. Dibble; D. E. Thomas.

GENERAL EXPENDITURE

General Expenditure Policy Group

Under Secretary (G3), A. Turnbull.
Assistant Secretaries (G5), Mrs. R. Butler; A. J. T. MacAuslan; M. G. Richardson.
Senior Principal (G6), E. I. Cooper.

Defence Policy and Material Group

Under Secretary (G3), S. A. Robson.
Assistant Secretaries (G5), B. M. Fox.

Civil Service Catering Organization

Executive Director (G3), D. S. B. Simpson.

OVERSEAS FINANCE

International Finance Group

Under Secretary (G3), H. P. Evans.
Assistant Secretaries (G5), H. G. Walsh; S. W. Matthews.

Aid and Export Finance Group

Under Secretary (G3), P. Mountfield.
Assistant Secretaries (G5), P. G. F. Davis; A. R. M. Bottrill.

European Community Group

Under Secretary (G3), R. I. G. Allen.
Assistant Secretaries (G5), J. E. Mortimer; M. C. Mercer.

Accountancy Advice Group

Grade 4, D. P. E. Mason.
Assistant Secretary (G5), D. Jamieson.
Senior Principals (G6), K. E. Bradley; R. Elias.

CHIEF ECONOMIC ADVISER'S DIVISIONS

Economic Assessment Group

Under Secretary (G3), P. N. Sedgewick.
Senior Economic Adviser (G5), J. S. Hibberd.

Medium Term and Policy Analysis

Under Secretary (G3), J. C. Odling-Smee.
Senior Economic Advisers (G5), C. Mellis; S. J. Davies.

DEPUTY CHIEF ECONOMIC ADVISER'S DIVISIONS

Deputy Secretary (G2), I. C. R. Byatt.
Assistant Secretary (G5), G. A. C. D. Houston.
Senior Economic Advisers (G5), Mrs. M. F. Haworth; C. J. Riley.
Public Expenditure Economics and Operational Research:
Under Secretary (G3), M. J. Spackman.
Assistant Secretaries (G5), M. A. Parsonage; A. J. Meyrick.
Deputy Chief Scientific Officer (G5), J. B. Jones.

PUBLIC FINANCE

Fiscal Policy

Under Secretary (G3), R. P. Culpin.
Assistant Secretary (G5), J. F. Gilhooly.

Monetary Group

Under Secretary (G3), D. L. C. Peretz.
Assistant Secretaries (G5), J. W. Grice; Miss M. O'Mara.

Financial Institutions and Market Group

Under Secretary (G3), Mrs. R. Lomax.
Assistant Secretaries (G5), Miss G. Noble; N. J. Ilett.

Public Sector Finance

Assistant Secretary (G5), C. J. Mowl.
Economic Advisers (G7), M. A. Franklin; A. W. Ritchie.

PAY GROUP

Deputy Secretary (G3), C. W. Kelly.
Assistant Secretaries (G5), Mrs. D. J. Seammen; C. J. A. Chivers; G. Jordan; I. Strachan.
Grade 6, L. G. Painting.

Running Costs and Superannuation

Under Secretary (G3), T. R. H. Luce.
Assistant Secretaries (G5), N. M. Hansford; I. Strachan; J. Dixon.
Grade 6, E. I. Cooper; W. G. Bristow; D. G. Pain.

CENTRAL DIVISIONS

Establishment and Organization Division

Under Secretary (G3), C. D. Butler.
Assistant Secretaries (G5), C. C. Allan; I. P. Wilson.
Senior Economic Adviser (G5), R. B. Stannard.
Senior Principals (G6), D. E. G. Griffiths; R. N. Edwards.

Economic Briefing

Assistant Secretary (G5), S. J. Pickford.

Information Division

Assistant Secretary (G5), E. J. W. Gieve.
Deputy Head of Division (G6), H. J. Bush.

TREASURY REPRESENTATIVES IN U.S.A.
Economic Minister and U.K. Representative IMF/ IBRD, F. Cassell.

RATING OF GOVERNMENT PROPERTY DEPARTMENT
Jameson House, 69 Notting Hill Gate, W11 3JU

Treasury Valuer, J. F. Olney.
Deputy Treasury Valuer, T. J. Cundall.

THE TREASURY SOLICITOR
Department of H.M. Procurator-General and Treasury Solicitor
Queen Anne's Chambers, 28 Broadway, SW1H 9JS
[01–210 3000]

The Treasury Solicitor's Department provides legal services for many Government Departments. Those that do not have their own lawyers are given legal advice, and both they and many other departments are provided with litigation and conveyancing services. The Department also deals with Bona Vacantia. The Treasury Solicitor is also the Queen's Proctor.

(For **Salaries**, *see* page 297).

Procurator-General and Treasury Solicitor (G1), J. Nursaw, C.B., Q.C.
Deputy Treasury Solicitor (G2), (vacant).

Central Advisory Division

Principal Assistant Solicitor (G3), Miss J. L. Wheldon.
Assistant Solicitors (G5), J. E. Collins; A. S. W. Hyett.
Grade 6, P. C. Jenkins; C. P. J. Muttukumaru; Mrs. P. Dayer; C. J. Gregory.

Litigation Divisions

Principal Assistant Solicitors (G3), T. J. G. Pratt; R. N. Ricks; J. H. Wilkinson.
Assistant Solicitors (G5), M. A. Blythe; M. Harris; D. A. Hogg; I. Hood; A. Leithead; C. G. Leonard; R. Lines; D. F. W. Pickup; A. J. Sandal; G. F. Sills.
Grade 6, Mrs. D. Babar; Mrs. G. Dagtoglou; J. N. Desai; I. R. S. Falconer; Mrs. S. J. Hay; R. A. D. Jackson; A. D. Lawton; Mrs. A. M. Morris; D. Palmer; R. J. Phillips; M. B. Sturdy; A. Turek; P. F. O. Whitehurst.
Senior Legal Assistants, A. P. M. Aylett; N. Beach; Miss P. J. Carroll; Miss. S. Cochrane; P. D. F. Grant; J. D. Howes; Mrs. C. Pearson; Miss J. E. Pemberton; R. E. Seely; Mrs. V. Selzer.
Principals (G7), M. W. Benney; Miss J. L. C. Brooks; S. P. Brockway; Miss R. M. Caudwell; A. K. Fraser; Miss J. A. Gensmantel; H. A. Kaya; Miss A. Lancaster; F. G. O'Connell; H. O. J. R. Shepheard; D. A. Stalker; J. C. Youdell.

Queen's Proctor Division

Queen's Proctor, J. Nursaw, C.B., Q.C.
Assistant Queen's Proctor, I. Hood.

Property Division

Principal Assistant Solicitor (G3), I. T. Lewis.
Assistant Solicitors (G5), D. E. T. Bevan; R. W. M. Cooper; P. L. Noble; A. M. Scarfe; R. M. C. Venables; J. Wyer.
Grade 6, M. H. M. Anderson; R. L. Coward; Miss R. C. Farmer; D. J. C. Garnett; Miss G. Gilder; D. M. Gleed; J. B. Howe; C. L. Oastler; G. E. Papes; R. M. Pierce; M. F. Rawlins; S. W. Rock; R. J. B. Stenhouse; Miss C. E. M. Troddyn.
Senior Legal Assistants, M. V. Cooper; M. Drayton; T. Forrester; A. R. Lilleystone; M. R. Rosenfeld; Miss P. E. Slatter; T. J. Sylvester-Jones; B. D. Thurley; S. A. Tobin; W. F. Williams.
Grade 7, I. Adams; H. S. Davis; Mrs. A. M. Foxhuntley; R. D. Harris; C. R. Irving; J. H. McFarland; G.

J. Norris; P. Page; A. W. Prior; N. P. Rex; J. M. Williamson.

Statutory Publications Office

Assistant Solicitor (G5), J. M. Gibson.
Grade 6, C. E. J. Carey.

Establishment, Finance and General Services Division

Establishment and Legal Personnel Officer (G5), G. Roberts.
Deputy Establishment Officer (G7), Mrs. P. L. Woods.
Head of Costs Branch (G6), A. M. Niven.
Chief Accountant (G7), B. C. Shephard.

Bona Vacantia Division

Assistant Solicitor (G5), Miss S. L. Sargant.
Senior Legal Assistant, M. R. M. Davies.
Grade 7, Miss H. Donnelly.

Ministry of Defence Branch
Neville House, Page Street, SW1P 4LS
[01–218 4691]

Grade 4, R. P. Ellis.
Grade 6, D. J. Aries; J. R. Braggins; M. J. Hemming; A. L. Norris.

Department of Education and Science Branch
Elizabeth House, York Road, SE1 7PH
[01–934 9958]

Principal Assistant Solicitor (G3), J. E. Coleman.
Assistant Solicitors (G5), A. G. Jones; F. L. Croft.
Grade 6, A. D. Preston; Miss M. Trefgarne; M. A. Widdrington.

Department of Employment Branch
Caxton House, Tothill Street, SW1H 9NF
[01–273 5851]

Principal Assistant Solicitor (G3), H. R. L. Purse.
Assistant Solicitors (G5), R. J. Baker; Mrs. A. Leale; S. G. Milligan; Miss V. Rice-Pyle.
Group 6, R. H. Britten; Mrs. C. V. Fox; G. W. M. Galliford; C. House; Miss R. A. Jeffreys; N. A. D. Lambert; C. B. D. Lucas; J. K. Winayak.
Senior Legal Assistants, Miss E. A. Barry; J. Hall.
Grade 7, P. H. Kilgarriff.

Department of Energy Branch
Thames House South, Millbank, SW1P 4QJ
[01–211 6046]

Principal Assistant Solicitor (G3), G. B. Claydon.
Assistant Solicitors (G5), D. Brummell; D. H. M. Ingham; D. J. Ecclestone; D. F. Pascho.
Grade 6, M. R. Brocklehurst; Miss V. F. Dewhurst; R. C. Perkins.

Department of Transport Branch
2 Marsham Street, SW1P 3EB
[01–276 5107]

Principal Assistant Solicitor (G3), G. H. Beetham.
Assistant Solicitors (G5), R. G. Bellis; P. D. Coopman; C. W. M. Ingram; B. W. James; L. Oates.
Grade 6, F. D. W. Clarke; Miss P. F. Henderson; Miss A. Lind-Smith; B. McHenry.
Senior Legal Assistants, B. J. Hammersley; A. K. Johnston.
Grade G7, S. T. Harker; A. W. Stewart.

COUNCIL ON TRIBUNALS
7th Floor, 22 Kingsway, WC2B 6LE
[01-936 7045]

The Council on Tribunals are an independent statutory body. It keeps under review the constitution and working of the various tribunals which have been placed under its general supervision, and considers and reports on administrative procedures relating to statutory inquiries. It must be consulted by Government departments on proposals for legislation affecting tribunals and inquiries and on proposals where the need for an appeals procedure may arise. It also offers advice on draft primary legislation.

Some 60 tribunals are currently under the Council's supervision. The matters with which they deal range from agriculture to immigration, pensions, road traffic, taxation, and the allocation of school places.

The Scottish Committee of the Council generally considers Scottish tribunals and matters relating only to Scotland.

Members of the Council are appointed by the Lord Chancellor and the Lord Advocate. The Scottish Committee is composed partly of members of the Council designated by the Lord Advocate and partly others appointed by him. The Parliamentary Commissioner for Administration is *ex officio* a member of both the Council and the Scottish Committee.

Chairman, Sir Cyril Philips.

Members, The Parliamentary Commissioner for Administration; D. Bruce; Miss S. M. Cameron, Q.C.; Mrs. M. P. Case; Sir Kenneth Clucas, K.C.B.; Prof. D. L. Foulkes; A. C. Heywood; Miss J. Horsham, C.B.E.; G. V. Hyde; Mrs. J. U. Kellock; R. N. M. MacLean, Q.C.; M. E. J. Rush; Mrs. S. H. Spence; Prof. A. Webb.

Secretary, C. W. Dyment.

Scottish Committee
20 Walker Street, Edinburgh EH3 7HR
[031–220 1236]

Chairman, R. N. M. MacLean, Q.C.

Members, The Parliamentary Commissioner for Administration; Mrs. E. Anderson; D. Bruce; W. J. Campbell; J. Langan; Mrs. E. Walker.

Secretary, Mrs. E. M. Chalmers.

TRIBUNALS
(see pages 389–90)

UNIVERSITY GRANTS COMMITTEE
14 Park Crescent, W1N 4DH
[01–636 7799]

The Committee was appointed in July, 1919 to enquire into the financial needs of university education in the U.K. and to advise the Government as to the application of any grants made by Parliament towards meeting them.

The Education Reform Act 1988 provides for the abolition of the U.G.C. and its replacement by the University Funding Council. The Council is expected formally to come into existence on April 1, 1989. The Chairman will be Lord Chilver, F.R.S., and the Chief Executive Sir Peter Swinnerton-Dyer.

Chairman, Sir Peter Swinnerton-Dyer, K.B.E., F.R.S.
£61,000

Other Members, Prof. E. W. Abel; Sir Peter Baxendell, C.B.E.; Prof. G. Brown; Prof. C. M. Campbell; Prof. J. Cannon, C.B.E.; Sir Robert Clayton, C.B.E.; Dr. S. Cotson; Prof. C. T. Dollery; Prof. T. A. Douglas; Prof. K. Entwistle; Prof. P. Haggett; R. S. Johnson, C.B.E.; Prof. P. R. G. Layard; Sir Donald McCallum; Prof. R. M. Needham, F.R.S.; Prof. M. J. O'Hara, F.R.S., F.R.S.E.; W. D. C. Semple; Prof. J. Sizer; Prof. R. Whittenbury.

Secretary, N. T. Hardyman, C.B. £38,000
Assistant Secretaries (G5), E. C. Appleyard; A. J. Davies; I. C. H. Powell.

Principals (G7), A. P. C. Bruce; C. R. Doherty; D. Farmer; J. G. Gooderham; M. C. Hutchison; P. K. James; T. Knight; J. Smith.

WELSH OFFICE

The Welsh Office has responsibility in Wales for ministerial functions relating to health and personal social services; education, except for terms and conditions of service, student awards and the University; the Welsh language and culture; local government; housing; water and sewerage; environmental protection; sport; agriculture and fisheries; forestry; land use, including town and country planning, countryside and nature conservation; new towns; ancient monuments and historic buildings; roads; tourism; a range of matters affecting the careers service and the activities of the Training Commission in Wales; financial assistance to industry; the urban programme in Wales; the operation of the European Regional Development Fund in Wales and other European Community matters; civil emergencies, and all financial aspects of these matters, including Welsh rate support grant. It has oversight responsibilities for economic affairs and regional planning in Wales.

(For **Salaries**, *see* page 297).

Principal Social Work Service Officer	£20,213–£25,332
Medical Officer	£17,593–£24,926
Dental Officer	£17,593–£24,926
Chief Nursing Officer	£27,420
Deputy Chief Nursing Officer	£24,125
Nursing Officer	£18,429–£21,676

Gwydyr House, Whitehall, SW1A 2ER
[01–270 300]

Secretary of State for Wales, THE RT. HON. PETER WALKER, M.B.E., M.P.
  Private Secretary, J. D. Shortridge.
  Assistant Private Secretaries, M. E. Powell; E. K. Davies.
  Parliamentary Private Secretary, C. Shepherd, M.P.
Minister of State, WYN ROBERTS, M.P.
  Private Secretary, C. M. Thomas.
Parliamentary Under-Secretary, I. Grist, M.P.
  Private Secretary, Miss J. M. Dominguez.
Parliamentary Clerk, V. R. Watkin.
Permanent Secretary (G1), Sir Richard Lloyd Jones, K.C.B.
  Private Secretary, J. Howells.
Head of Permanent Secretary's Division (G5), L. L. Ginn, T.D.

Cathays Park, Cardiff CF1 3NQ
[0222–825111]

Deputy Secretaries (G2), J. W. Lloyd; J. W. Preston.

Establishment Group

Principal Establishment Officer (G3), G. C. G. Craig.
Heads of Divisions (G5), W. L. Chapman; M. J. Clancy.
Senior Economic Adviser (G5), O. T. Hooker.
Chief Statistician (G5), Dr. M. P. G. Pepper.
Head of Health Intelligence Unit (G6), G. J. Cockell.
Principals (G7), P. Davenport; Miss C. M. Owen; M. J. Shanahan.
Economic Adviser (G7), V. W. F. McPherson.
Principal Research Officers (G7), I. I. Thomas; E. Darwin; Mrs. M. A. J. Gronow.
Statisticians (G7), M. R. Brand; Miss W. K. Fader; J. T. Fletcher; K. Francombe; P. J. Fullerton; E. Swires Hennessey; J. D. James; R. Jones; J. D. Kinder.

Cadw: Welsh Historic Monuments
Brunel House, Fitzalan Road, Cardiff CF2 1UY
[0222–465511]

Director, E. A. J. Carr.
Conservation Architect (G6), J. D. Hogg.
Principal Inspector of Ancient Monuments and Historic Buildings, J. R. Avent.

Cathay Park, Cardiff CF1 3NQ
Inspectors of Ancient Monuments and Historic Buildings, J. K. Knight; Dr. L. MacInnes; A. D. McLees; Dr. S. E. Rees.

Finance Group

Principal Finance Officer (G3), J. F. Craig.
Chief Accountant (G5), L. A. Pavelin.
Heads of Divisions (G5), C. L. Jones; L. Pritchard; B. Wilcox.
Principals (G7), Dr. M. Dunn; M. G. Horlock; J. Kilner; P. G. C. Lunn; D. T. Richards; C. E. Taylor; B. O. Valentine.
Head of Internal Audit (G7), B. R. Davies.
Head of N.H.S. Audit (G7), P. Brown.

Health Professional Group

Chief Medical Officer (G3), G. Crompton.
Deputy Chief Medical Officer (G4), A. M. George.
Senior Medical Officers (G5), G. J. Moses; D. Ferguson Lewis; Ms. M. Cotter; H. G. Penrhyn Jones; Ms. R. Jacobs; Ms. A. K. Thomas.
Chief Dental Officer, D. M. Heap.
Medical Officers, J. D. Andrews; R. Buntwal; J. W. Crossley; D. E. Davies; T. I. Evans; N. E. Thomas
.... £18,341–£25,985
Dental Officers, A. Cobb; J. D. O. Parkholm; T. A. Williams .... £18,341–£25,985
Scientific Adviser (G6), Dr. J. A. V. Pritchard.
Pharmaceutical Adviser (G6), Dr. G. B. A. Veitch.

Housing, Health and Social Services Policy Group

Head of Group (G3), R. W. Jarman.
Heads of Divisions (G5), R. J. Davies; S. H. Martin; A. E. Peat; D. I. Westlake.
Chief Social Work Service Officer (G5), D. G. Evans.
Chief Architect (G6), C. Eyres *(acting).*
Deputy Chief Social Work Service Officer, J. K. Fletcher *(acting).*
Principals (G7), L. Conway; A. C. Elmer; P. Godden-Kent; P. S. Gray; D. B. Hilbourne; A. G. Huwes; Miss E. M. Jones; Mrs. C. Peat; A. G. Thornton.
Social Work Service Officers (G7), D, Barker; G. H. Davies; I. Forster; J. F. Mooney; Miss A. M. Perrott; C. D. Vyvyan; R. C. Woodward.
Principal Professional and Technology Officers (G7), R. Broad; T. A. Campden; G. N. Harding; W. Ross.

National Health Service Directorate

Director of the NHS in Wales, J. W. Owen ... £46,787
Heads of Divisions (G5), P. R. Gregory; G. S. Podmore; N. E. Thomas.
Head of Division (G6), G. T. Evans.
Principals (G7), Mrs. J. Annand; C. J. Burdett; W. M. Cooper; W. G. Davies; J. Duggan; M. Harper; N. S. Jones, I.S.O.; D. McGlinn; K. Orchard; D. Quinlan; M. F. Webb.
Ambulance Adviser (G7), P. J. Hunt.
Principal Professional and Technology Officer (G7), M. W. Grist.

Nursing Division

Chief Nursing Officer, Miss M. Bull £32,314
Deputy Chief Nursing Officer, Mrs. G. M. Stephens
£28,432
Nursing Officers, Miss G. Harris; Dr. D. Keyzer; Mrs. B. Melvin; M. F. Tonkin; Mrs. D. J. Vass; Mrs. A. Wakin .... £21,841–£25,545

Legal Division

Legal Adviser (G3), A. J. Beale.
Assistant Solicitors (G5), D. G. Lambert; P. J. Murrin.
Grade 6, J. D. H. Evans; A. K. Gillard; C. P. Jones; C. G. Longville; Mrs. T. C. Shellens; J. H. Turnbull; A. J. Watkins.

Senior Legal Assistants (G7), A. J. Park; Mrs. A. T. Parkes; D. H. J. Williams.

Information Division

Director of Information (G5), H. G. Roberts.
Chief Press Officer (G7), E. M. Bowen, M.V.O.

Economic and Regional Policy Group

Head of Group (G3), O. Rees.
Heads of Divisions (G5), M. E. Bevan; Miss E. N. M. Davies; B. J. Mitchell; F. G. Watson.
Principals (G7), D. Beames; R. O. Evans; Ms. J. M. Gordon; J. A. Grimes; A. Lansdown; R. D. Macey; Miss J. E. Paulett; Ms. J. H. Roberts; G. A. Thomas.

Industry Department

Director (G3), C. D. Stevens.
Industrial Director (G4), T. E. Morgan, M.B.E.
Heads of Divisions (G5), R. M. Abel; R. C. Williams.
Senior Principal Scientific Officer (G6), Dr. J. N. M. Firth.
Principals (G7), P. Bishop; R. Callen; R. J. Masefield; D. A. Pritchard; D. Pugh (at Colwyn Bay); K. Smith; C. J. Tudor; R. Waller; J. W. Wallington.
Principal Scientific Officers (G7), P. Bragg; G. A. Madden.

Education Department

Head of Department (G3), R. H. Jones, C.V.O.
Heads of Divisions (G5), H. Evans; M. L. Evans.
Head of Division (G6), R. C. Simpson.
Principals (G7), Mrs. J. Booker; D. A. Bullen; J. B. Davies; B. Hayward-Blake; Mrs. J. Hopkins; J. W. Jones; Mrs. H. Thomas; A. Whittaker; Dr. B. M. J. Wilson.

H. M. Inspectorate

Chief Inspector (G4), I. R. Lloyd.
Staff Inspectors (G5), S. J. Adams; R. L. James; W. R. Jenkins; T. E. Parry; P. Thomas; R. Thomas; M. J. F. Wynn.
H. M. Inspectors (G6), C. Abbott; G. Adams; R. A. Charles; Mrs. G. Briwnant Jones; H. W. Dabies; R. G. Davies; D. G. Evans; J. R. N. Evans; N. B. Evans; Mrs. L. Gainsbury; A. G. George; J. Griffiths; M. G. Haines; A. Hamilton Jones; I. G. Higginbotham; A. Higgins; I. L. James; Mrs. R. James; W. R. Jenkins; M. John; G. D. Jones; G. T. J. Jones; O. E. Jones; Mrs A. Keane; J. M. Laugharne; M. J. Law; J. R. Lewis; Miss S. Lewis; Mrs. M. E. R. Lloyd; A. Morgan; I. G. Morgan; J. Nicholas; Miss P. A. Nicholas; Miss E. Ogwen; T. G. Prosser; W. H. Raybould; D. G. H. Rees; G. O. Roberts; Miss D. Selleck; Mrs. V. Scott; M. W. Stone; R. Taylor; G. Thomas; Mrs. I. Thomas; Miss L. Thomas; P. B. Walker; G. Warren; B. Wigley; E. L. Williams; D. P. Williams.

Transport, Planning, Water and Environment Group

Head of Group (G3), R. A. Wallace.
Director of Highways (G4), K. J. Thomas°.
Heads of Divisions (G5), A. H. H. Jones; J. C. Lewis; J. A. Morgan°; Mrs. E. Taylor°.
Chief Planner (G5), C. J. Curry.
Principal Planning Inspectors (G5), R. Pierce; D. Sheers.
Senior Principals (G6), D. M. Timlin; P. R. Marsden.
Superintending Engineers (G6), J. G. Evans°; B. H. Hawker*; R. Lober°.
Superintending Estates Officer (G6), G. K. Hoad.
Senior Housing and Planning Inspectors (G6), T. W. B. Barnes; J. H. Chadwick; R. Davies; J. I. T. Dunlop; P. Rosser; D. L. J. Robins; G. Sloan.

H. M. Inspectorate of Pollution

Inspectors for Wales, Dr. L. A. W. Hales (*Air*); H. G. Taylor (*Waste*); A. A. Houlden (*Water*).

Principals (*G7*), G. Davies; R. W. Jenkins°; A. V. Price; D. Powell°; G. R. Jones; D. Hadfield°; W. P. Roderick.

Principal Planning Officers (*G7*), D. B. Courtier; G. Fairhurst; J. O. Pryce.

Principal Research Officers (*G7*), A. S. Dredge; Ms. L. J. Roberts.

Principal Estates Officer (*G7*), M. L. Williams.

Principal Scientific Officer (*G7*), R. A. Page.

Principal Professional and Technology Officers (*G7*), J. A. Atkins; H. R. Payne; J. E. Saunders.

Principal Professional and Technology Officers, Highways Directorate (*G7*), T. A. Dockerty°; P. Dunstan°; J. A. L. Harries*; A. L. Howcraft°; D. G. Minas°; B. J. W. Martin°; S. D. Padfield°; A. L.

Based at:
°Ty Glas Road, Llanishen, Cardiff CF5 5PL (022–753271)
*Government Buildings, Dinerty Road, Rhos on Sea, Colwyn Bay LL28 4UL (0492–44261)
†Plas Crug, Aberystwyth SY23 1NG (0970–3162)

Perry°; R. H. Powell°; J. R. Rees°; D. P. Soane°; C. W. W. Smart°; J. Fitch*; J. Collins°; K. J. Alexander°.

Agriculture Department

Head of Department (*G3*), J. I. Davies, M.B.E.

Heads of Divisions (*G5*), H. R. Bollington; D. R. Thomas; L. K. Walford.

Principals (*G7*), P. Finnigan†; W. K. Griffiths; T. W. Hunter; R. F. Patterson†; J. M. Thomas.

Divisional Executive Officers (*G7*), J. C. Alexander (*Carmarthen*); D. W. Evans (*Ruthin*); D. Davies (*Cardiff*); D. R. Thomas (*Caernarfon*); R. J. E. Wilcox (*Llandrindod Wells*).

LAND AUTHORITY FOR WALES
The Custom House, Custom House Street,
Cardiff CF1 5AP
[0222–223444]

The Authority is responsible for acquiring and disposing of land needed for private development in Wales.

Chairman, G. D. Inkin, O.B.E. (*part-time*) £22,778
Chief Executive, B. Ryan.

LAW COURTS AND OFFICES

THE JUDICIAL COMMITTEE OF THE PRIVY COUNCIL

The Judicial Committee of the Privy Council is the final court of appeal from courts of the United Kingdom dependencies, courts of independent Commonwealth countries which have retained the right of appeal, courts of the Channel Islands and the Isle of Man, some professional and disciplinary committees and church sources. The Committee is composed of all Privy Counsellors who hold, or have held, high judicial office, although usually only three or five hear each case.

The Judicial Committee includes the Lord Chancellor, the Lords of Appeal in Ordinary (*see* below) and such other members of the Privy Council as shall from time to time hold or have held "high judicial office," and certain judges from the Commonwealth.

Office, Downing Street, S.W.1.
Registrar of the Privy Council, D. H. O. Owen.
Chief Clerk, D. Rushton.

THE JUDICATURE OF ENGLAND AND WALES

The legal system of England and Wales is separate from those of Scotland and Northern Ireland and differs from them in law, judicial procedure and court structure, although there is a common distinction between civil law (disputes between individuals) and criminal law (acts harmful to the community).

The supreme judicial authority for England and Wales is the House of Lords, which is the ultimate Court of Appeal from all courts in Great Britain and Northern Ireland (except criminal courts in Scotland). As a Court of Appeal it consists of the Lord Chancellor and the Lords of Appeal in Ordinary (Law Lords). The Supreme Court of Judicature comprises the Court of Appeal, the Crown Court and the High Court of Justice. The High Court of Justice is the superior civil court and is divided into three Divisions. The Chancery Division is concerned mainly with equity, bankruptcy and contentious probate business; the Queen's Bench Division deals with commercial and maritime law, with civil cases not assigned to other courts, and hears appeals from lower courts; and the Family Division, which deals with matters relating to family law. Sittings are held at the Royal Courts of Justice in London or at 24 Crown Court centres outside the capital. High Court judges sit alone to hear cases at first instance. Appeals from lower courts are heard by two or three judges, or by single judges of the appropriate Division.

The decision to prosecute in cases tried on indictment and in summary cases of a serious nature rests with the Crown Prosecution Service, an independent prosecuting body established in 1986 to serve all of England and Wales (*see* p. 384–5). At the head of the Service is the Director of Public Prosecutions, who discharges his duties under the superintendence of the Attorney General. Certain categories of offence continue to require the consent for prosecution of the Attorney General.

Minor criminal offences (summary offences) are dealt with in magistrates' courts, which usually consist of three unpaid lay magistrates (justices of the peace) sitting without a jury, who are advised on points of law and procedure by a legally-qualified clerk to the justices: in busier courts a full-time, salaried and legally-qualified stipendiary magistrate presides alone. Cases involving people under 17 are heard in juvenile courts, specially constituted magistrates' courts which sit apart from other courts.

Preliminary proceedings in a serious case to decide whether there is evidence to justify committal for trial in the Crown Court are also held in the magistrates' courts. Appeals from magistrates' courts against sentence or conviction are made to the Crown Court. Appeals upon a point of law are made to the High Court, and may go on to the House of Lords.

The Crown Court sits in about 90 centres, divided into six circuits, and is presided over by High Court judges, full-time circuit judges, and part-time recorders, sitting with a jury in all trials which are contested. It deals with trials of the more serious criminal offences, the sentencing of offenders committed for sentence by magistrates' courts (when the magistrates' consider their own power of sentence inadequate), and appeals from lower courts. Magistrates usually sit with a circuit judge or recorder to deal with appeals and committals for sentence. Appeals from the Crown Court, either against sentence or conviction, are made to the Court of Appeal (Criminal Division), presided over by the Lord Chief Justice. A further appeal from the Court of Appeal to the House of Lords can be brought if a point of law of general public importance is considered to be involved.

Most minor civil cases are dealt with by the county courts, of which there are about 300. For cases involving small claims there are special arbitration facilities and simplified procedures: cases involving claims which exceed set limits may be tried in the county courts with the consent of the parties, or in certain circumstances on transfer from the High Court. Undefended divorce cases and, outside London, bankruptcy proceedings can be heard in designated county courts. Magistrates' courts can deal with certain classes of civil case, mostly those relating to the family, and committees of magistrates licence public houses, clubs and betting shops. Appeals in matrimonial, adoption and guardianship proceedings heard in the magistrates' courts go to the Family Division of the High Court: affiliation appeals and appeals from decisions of the licensing committees of magistrates to the Crown Court. Appeals from the High Court and county courts are heard in the Court of Appeal (Civil Division), presided over by the Master of the Rolls, and may go on to the House of Lords, the final court of appeal in civil cases.

Coroners' courts investigate violent and unnatural deaths or sudden deaths where the cause is unknown. Cases may be brought before a local coroner (a senior lawyer or doctor) by doctors, the police, various public authorities or members of the public. Where a death is sudden and the cause is unknown the coroner may order a post-mortem examination to determine the cause of death rather than holding an inquest in court.

THE HOUSE OF LORDS
(as final Court of Appeal)

The Lord High Chancellor—
The Rt. Hon. the Lord Mackay of Clashfern
(*born* 1927, *apptd.* 1987), £87,250.

Lords of Appeal in Ordinary (each £78,750)

	Apptd.
Rt. Hon. Lord Keith of Kinkel, *born* 1922	1977
Rt. Hon. Lord Bridge of Harwich, *born* 1917 ..	1980
Rt. Hon. Lord Brandon of Oakbrook, M.C., *born* 1920....................................	1981
Rt. Hon. Lord Templeman, M.B.E., *born* 1920 ..	1982
Rt. Hon. Lord Griffiths, M.C., *born* 1923.........	1985
Rt. Hon. Lord Ackner, *born* 1920	1986
Rt. Hon. Lord Oliver of Aylmerton, *born* 1921 ..	1986

Rt. Hon. Lord Goff of Chieveley, *born* 1926 1986
Rt. Hon. Lord Jauncey of Tullichettle, *born*
  1925...1987
Rt. Hon. Lord Lowry, *born* 1919 1989
Registrar: The Clerk of the Parliaments, Sir John
  Sainty, K.C.B.

SUPREME COURT OF JUDICATURE
COURT OF APPEAL

Ex officio Judges.—The Lord High Chancellor, the
Lord Chief Justice of England, the Master of the
Rolls, the President of the Family Division, and the
Vice-Chancellor.
The Master of the Rolls (£78,750)
The Rt. Hon. the Lord Donaldson of Lymington
  (*born* 1920, *apptd.* 1982).
Secretary, Miss V. Seymour; *Clerk*, K. H. L. Smeeton.

Lords Justices of Appeal (each £75,750)

	Apptd.
Rt. Hon. Sir Tasker Watkins, V.C., *born* 1918 .	1980
Rt. Hon. Sir Patrick O'Connor, *born* 1914	1980
Rt. Hon. Sir Michael Fox, *born* 1921	1981
Rt. Hon. Sir Michael Kerr, *born* 1921	1981
Rt. Hon. Sir John May, *born* 1923	1982
Rt. Hon. Sir Christopher Slade, *born* 1927	1982
Rt. Hon. Sir Francis Purchas, *born* 1919	1982
Rt. Hon. Sir Brian Dillon, *born* 1923	1982
Rt. Hon. Sir Roger Parker, *born* 1923	1983
Rt. Hon. Sir David Croom-Johnson, D.S.C., v.R.D., *born* 1914	1984
Rt. Hon. Sir Anthony Lloyd, *born* 1929	1984
Rt. Hon. Sir Brian Neill, *born* 1923	1985
Rt. Hon. Sir Michael Mustill, *born* 1931	1985
Rt. Hon. Sir Martin Nourse, *born* 1932	1985
Rt. Hon. Sir Iain Glidewell, *born* 1924	1985
Rt. Hon. Sir John Balcombe, *born* 1925.......	1985
Rt. Hon. Sir Ralph Gibson, *born* 1922	1985
Rt. Hon. Sir John Stocker, M.C., T.D., *born* 1918	1986
Rt. Hon. Sir Harry Woolf, *born* 1933	1986
Rt. Hon. Sir Donald Nicholls, *born* 1933	1986
Rt. Hon. Sir Thomas Bingham, *born* 1933	1986
Rt. Hon. Sir Patrick Russell, *born* 1926	1986
Rt. Hon. Dame Elizabeth Butler-Sloss, D.B.E., *born* 1933	1988
Rt. Hon. Sir Peter Taylor, *born* 1930	1988
Rt. Hon. Sir Murray Stuart-Smith, *born* 1927.	1988
Rt. Hon. Sir Christopher Staughton, *born* 1933	1988
Rt. Hon. Sir Michael Mann, *born* 1930	1988

Court of Appeal (Criminal Division)

Judges, The Lord Chief Justice of England, The
Master of the Rolls, Lord Justices of Appeal and
the Judges of the Queen's Bench Division.

Courts-Martial Appeal Court

Judges, The Lord Chief Justice of England, The
Master of the Rolls, Lords Justice of Appeal, and
Judges of the Queen's Bench Division.

HIGH COURT OF JUSTICE

CHANCERY DIVISION
President, The Lord High Chancellor

The Vice-Chancellor (£75,750)
The Rt. Hon. Sir Nicolas Browne-Wilkinson
  (*born* 1930, *apptd.* 1985)

Secretary (vacant); *Clerk*, W. Northfield, B.E.M.

Judges (each £68,500)

	Apptd.
Hon. Sir John Vinelott, *born* 1923	1978
Hon. Sir Douglas Falconer, M.B.E., *born* 1914..	1981
Hon. Sir Jean-Pierre Warner, *born* 1924	1981
Hon. Sir Peter Gibson, *born* 1934	1981
Hon. Sir Mervyn Davies, M.C., T.D., *born* 1918 .	1982

Hon. Sir Jeremiah Harman, *born* 1930	1982
Hon. Sir Richard Scott, *born* 1934	1983
Hon. Sir Leonard Hoffman, *born* 1934........	1985
Hon. Sir John Knox, *born* 1925..............	1985
Hon. Sir Peter Millett, *born* 1932	1986
Hon. Sir Andrew Morritt, *born* 1938..........	1988
Hon. Sir William Aldous, *born* 1936	1988

High Court of Justice in Bankruptcy

Judges, The Master of the Rolls, The Vice-Chancellor,
the Lord Justices, and other members of the Court
of Appeal.

Companies Court

Judges, The Vice Chancellor; The Hon. Mr. Justice
Vinelott; The Hon. Mr. Justice Warner; The Hon.
Mr. Justice Mervyn Davies; The Hon. Mr. Justice
Harman; The Hon. Mr. Justice Scott; The Hon.
Mr. Justice Hoffman; The Hon. Mr. Justice Knox;
The Hon. Mr. Justice Millett; The Hon. Mr. Justice
Morritt.

Patent Court (Appellate Section)

Judges, The Hon. Mr. Justice Whitford; The Hon.
Mr. Justice Falconer.

QUEEN'S BENCH DIVISION
The Lord Chief Justice of England (£85,250)
The Rt. Hon. the Lord Lane, A.F.C.
  (*born* 1918, *apptd.* 1980)

Secretary, Mrs. J. Simpson; *Clerk*, G. Curtis.

Judges (each £68,500)

	Apptd.
Hon. Sir Bernard Caulfield, *born* 1914	1968
Hon. Sir William Mars-Jones, M.B.E., *born* 1915.	1969
Hon. Sir Leslie Boreham, *born* 1918..........	1972
Hon. Sir Michael Davies, *born* 1921	1973
Hon. Sir Kenneth Jones, *born* 1921	1974
Hon. Sir Haydn Tudor Evans, *born* 1920	1974
Hon. Sir Peter Pain, *born* 1913	1975
Hon. Sir Kenneth Jupp, M.C., *born* 1917	1975
Hon. Sir Derek Hodgson, *born* 1917..........	1977
Hon. Sir Ronald Waterhouse, *born* 1926......	1978
Hon. Sir Maurice Drake, D.F.C., *born* 1923	1978
Hon. Sir Barry Sheen, *born* 1918	1978
Hon. Sir David McNeill, *born* 1922	1979
Hon. Sir Christopher French, *born* 1925	1979
Hon. Sir Peter Webster, *born* 1924	1980
Hon. Sir Donald Farquharson, *born* 1928	1981
Hon. Sir Anthony McCowan, *born* 1928	1981
Hon. Sir Charles McCullough, *born* 1931	1981
Hon. Sir John Leonard, *born* 1926	1981
Hon. Sir Roy Beldam, *born* 1925	1981
Hon. Sir David Hirst, *born* 1925	1982
Hon. Sir John Stewart Hobhouse, *born* 1932..	1982
Hon. Sir Andrew Leggatt, *born* 1930........	1982
Hon. Sir Michael Nolan, *born* 1928	1982
Hon. Sir Oliver Popplewell, *born* 1927........	1983
Hon. Sir William Macpherson, T.D., *born* 1926	1983
Hon. Sir Philip Otton, *born* 1933	1983
Hon. Sir Paul Kennedy, *born* 1935	1983
Hon. Sir Michael Hutchison, *born* 1933	1983
Hon. Sir Simon Brown, *born* 1937	1984
Hon. Sir Anthony Evans, *born* 1934	1984
Hon. Sir Mark Saville, *born* 1936	1985
Hon. Sir Johan Steyn, *born* 1932	1985
Hon. Sir Christopher Rose, *born* 1937	1985
Hon. Sir Richard Tucker, *born* 1931	1985
Hon. Sir Robert Gatehouse, *born* 1924	1985
Hon. Sir Patrick Garland, *born* 1929	1985
Hon. Sir John Roch, *born* 1934	1985
Hon. Sir Michael Turner, *born* 1931	1985
Hon. Sir John Alliott, *born* 1932	1986
Hon. Sir Harry Ognall, *born* 1934	1986

Hon. Sir Konrad Schiemann, *born* 1937	1986
Hon. Sir John Owen, *born* 1925	1986
Hon. Sir Denis Henry, *born* 1931	1986
Hon. Sir Humphrey Potts, *born* 1931	1986
Hon. Sir Richard Rougier, *born* 1932	1986
Hon. Sir Ian Kennedy, *born* 1930	1986
Hon. Sir Nicholas Phillips, *born* 1938	1987
Hon. Sir Robin Auld, *born* 1937	1988
Hon. Sir Malcolm Pill, *born* 1938	1988
Hon. Sir Stuart McKinnon, *born* 1938	1988
Hon. Sir Mark Potter, *born* 1937	1988
Hon. Sir Henry Brooke, *born* 1936	1988

FAMILY DIVISION

President (£75,750)

Rt. Hon. Sir Stephen Brown
(*born* 1929, *apptd.* 1988).

Secretary, Mrs. S. Leung; *Clerk*, Mrs. S. Bell.

Judges (each £68,500)	Apptd.
Rt. Hon. Sir John Latey, M.B.E., *born* 1914 ...	1965
Hon. Sir Kenneth Hollings, M.C., *born* 1918 ...	1971
Hon. Sir Trevor Reeve, *born* 1915	1973
Hon. Sir Dame Rose Heilbron, D.B.E., *born* 1914 ...	1974
Hon. Sir Brian Bush, *born* 1925	1976
Hon. Sir John Wood, M.C., *born* 1922	1977
Hon. Sir Gervase Sheldon, *born* 1913	1978
Hon. Sir Michael Eastham, *born* 1920	1978
Hon. Dame Margaret Booth, D.B.E., *born* 1933 .	1979
Hon. Sir Anthony Lincoln, *born* 1920	1979
Hon. Sir Anthony Ewbank, *born* 1925	1980
Hon. Sir John Waite, *born* 1932	1982
Hon. Sir Anthony Hollis, *born* 1927..........	1982
Hon. Sir Swinton Thomas, *born* 1931	1985
Hon. Sir Mathew Thorpe, *born* 1938	1988
Hon. Sir Edward Cazalet, *born* 1936	1988

RESTRICTIVE PRACTICES COURT

Judicial Members, The Hon. Mr. Justice Anthony Lincoln (*Principal*); The Hon. Mr. Justice McNeill; The Hon. Mr. Justice Warner; Lord Sutherland; The Hon. Mr. Justice Murray.
Lay Members, N. L. Salmon; I. G. Stewart; B. M. Currie; L. Robertson; R. Garrick; Z. A. Silberston.

LORD CHANCELLOR'S DEPARTMENT
See **Government and Public Offices.**

SUPREME COURT DEPARTMENTS AND OFFICES
Royal Courts of Justice, WC2A 2LL

Administrator, S. Orchard .... £25,756–£29,344

Central Office of the Supreme Court
Royal Courts of Justice, WC2A 2LL

Senior Master of the Supreme Court (Q.B.D.), and Queen's Remembrancer, I. S. Warren £45,800
Masters of the Supreme Court (Q.B.D.), C. W. S. Lubbock; S. J. Waldman; P. B. Creightmore; K. W. Topley; D. L. Prebble; A. A. Grant; G. H. Hodgson; R. L. Turner; J. Trench; M. Tennant £37,500
Chief Clerk (Central Office), J. Bones
.... £15,631–£21,104
Chief Clerk to the Q.B. Judges in Chambers, C. F. Jones .... £15,631–£21,104

Crown Office of the Supreme Court
Royal Courts of Justice, WC2A 2LL

Master of the Crown Office, and Queen's Coroner and Attorney, M. McKenzie.

Official Referees of the Supreme Court

His Hon. Judge Hawser, Q.C.; His Hon. Judge Newey, Q.C.; His Hon. Judge Lewis, Q.C.; His Hon. Judge Davies, Q.C.; His Hon. Judge Fox-Andrews, Q.C.; His Hon. Judge Bowsher, Q.C.

Court of Appeal (Civil Division) Office
Royal Courts of Justice, WC2A 2LL

Registrar, J. D. R. Adams.

Criminal Appeal Office
Royal Courts of Justice, WC2A 2LL

Registrar, M. McKenzie £45,800
Assistant Registrars, (vacant) ..... £25,756–£29,344
Chief Clerk, J. Read............. £15,631–£21,104

Courts-Martial Appeals Office
Royal Courts of Justice, WC2A 2LL

Registrar, M. McKenzie £45,800
Chief Clerk, J. Read.

Supreme Court Taxing Office

Chief Master, F. G. Berkeley £45,800
Masters of the Supreme Court, A. J. Wright; C. R. N. Martyn; M. N. Devonshire, T.D.; P. T. Hurst; C. A. Prince £37,500
Principal Taxing Officers, D. Hutchings (*Chief Clerk*); A. J. Burroughs .... £15,631–£21,104

Examiners of the Court

(Empowered to take Examination of Witnesses in all Divisions of the High Court)
M. F. Meredith-Hardy; B. Rathbone; N. W. Briggs; R. Jacobs.

Chancery Chambers,
Royal Courts of Justice, WC2A 2LL

Chief Master of the Supreme Court, R. D. Munrow
£45,800
Masters of the Supreme Court, M. B. Cholmondeley Clarke; J. M. Dyson; J. S. Gowers; G. A. Barratt
£37,500
Chief Clerk, D. F. Jupe .... £15,631–£21,104
Conveyancing Counsel of the Supreme Court, J. Monckton; S. G. Maurice; M. J. Roth.

Bankruptcy Department
Thomas More Building, Royal Courts of Justice, Strand, WC2A 2LL

Chief Registrar, T. L. Dewhurst £45,800
Chief Clerk, T. Palmer.

Official Receivers' Department

Senior Official Receiver, A. K. Sales.
Official Receivers, D. E. Dolman; P. J. Chillery; M. J. Pugh; J. L. P. Pope; L. T. Cramp.

Companies Court
Thomas More Building, Royal Courts of Justice, WC2A 2LL

Registrar, M. Buckley.
Chief Clerk, C. A. N. Edinboro ..... £15,631–£21,104
Senior Official Receiver, Companies Department, A. K. Sales.

Restrictive Practices Court
Thomas More Building, Royal Courts of Justice, WC2A 2LL

Clerk of the Court, M. Buckley.
Chief Clerk, C. A. N. Edinboro.

Principal Registry (Family Division)
Somerset House, WC2R 1LP

Senior Registrar, C. F. Turner £45,800
Registrars, T. G. Guest; D. E. Morris; J. E. Artro-Morris; R. B. Rowe; G. B. N. A. Angel; B. P. F. Kenworthy-Browne; G. A. Terian; Mrs.

K. T. Moorhouse; D. T. A. Davies; Mrs. N. Pearce;
M. J. Segal; R. Conn £37,500
Secretary, G. J. Maple .... £15,631–£21,104

District Probate Registrars

Birmingham and Stoke-on-Trent, C. Marsh.
Brighton and Maidstone, M. N. Emery.
Bristol, Exeter and Bodmin, P. L. Speyer.
Ipswich, Norwich and Peterborough, E. R. Alexander.
Leeds, Lincoln and Sheffield, A. P. Dawson.
Liverpool, Lancaster and Chester, B. J. Thomas.
Llandaff, Bangor, Carmarthen and Gloucester,
D. W. Jones.
Manchester and Nottingham, M. A. Moran.
Newcastle, Carlisle, York and Middlesbrough, A.
Bertram.
Oxford and Leicester, Miss M. L. Farmborough.
Winchester, A. K. Biggs.

Admiralty and Commercial Registry and Marshal's Office
Royal Courts of Justice, WC2A 2LL

Registrar, W. K. Topley £37,500
Marshal and Chief Clerk, V. E. Ricks
£15,631–£21,104

Court of Protection
Stewart House, 24 Kingsway, WC2B 6HD

Master, Mrs. A. B. Macfarlane £45,800

Official Solicitor's Department
Penderel House, 287 High Holborn, W.C.1.

Official Solicitor to the Supreme Court, H. D. S.
Venables £39,000
Dep. do., H. J. Baker .... £25,756–£29,344
Chief Clerk, T. C. P. Molin .... £15,631–£21,104

OFFICE OF THE LORD CHANCELLOR'S VISITORS
Trevelyan House, 30 Great Peter Street, S.W.1.

Legal Visitor, M. H. Fauvelle.
Medical Visitors, W. A. Heaton-Ward; E. Carr; F. E.
Kenyon; R. J. Kerry; P. A. Morris; D. Parr; M.
Whittet.

OFFICE OF THE JUDGE ADVOCATE OF THE FLEET
The Law Courts, Barker Road, Maidstone ME16 8EQ

Judge Advocate of the Fleet, His Hon. Judge Waley,
V.R.D., Q.C.

OFFICE OF THE JUDGE ADVOCATE GENERAL OF THE FORCES
(*Joint Service for the Army and the Royal Air Force*)
22 Kingsway, WC2B 6LE

Judge Advocate General, J. Stuart-Smith, C.B., Q.C.
£50,900
Vice Judge Advocate General, G. L. Chapman
£45,800
Assistant Judge Advocates General, C. G. Gould; E.
G. Moelwyn-Hughes; A. P. Pitts; S. B. Spence; D.
M. Berkson .... £25,756–£29,344
Deputy Judge Advocates, M. A. Hunter; T. R. King;
J. P. Camp; T. G. Pontius .... £18,638–£25,363

HIGH COURT AND CROWN COURT CENTRES

First-tier centres deal with both civil and criminal
cases and are served by High Court and Circuit
Judges. Second-tier centres deal with criminal cases
only but are served by both High Court and Circuit

Judges. Third-tier centres deal with criminal cases
only and are served only by Circuit Judges.

Midland and Oxford Circuit

First-tier—Birmingham, Lincoln, Nottingham, Ox-
ford, Stafford, Warwick. *Second-tier*—Leicester,
Northampton, Shrewsbury, Worcester. *Third-tier*—
Coventry, Derby, Dudley, Grimsby, Peterborough,
Stoke-on-Trent.
Circuit Administrator, R. E. K. Holmes, 2 Newton
Street, Birmingham B4 7LU.
Courts Administrators, Birmingham Group, D. A.
Warner; *Nottingham Group*, P. H. Martin; *Stafford
Group*, A. F. Parker.

North Eastern Circuit

First-tier—Leeds, Newcastle upon Tyne, Sheffield,
Teesside. *Second-tier*—York. *Third-tier*—Beverley,
Doncaster, Durham, Huddersfield, Kingston-upon-
Hull, Wakefield.
Circuit Administrator, S. W. L. James, West Riding
House, 17th Floor, Albion Street, Leeds LS1 5AA.
Courts Administrators, Leeds Group, P. Delany;
Newcastle upon Tyne Group, F. I. Lance; *Sheffield
Group*, G. Bingham.

Northern Circuit

First-tier—Carlisle, Liverpool, Manchester, Pres-
ton. *Third-tier*—Barrow-in-Furness, Bolton, Burn-
ley, Kendal, Lancaster.
Circuit Administrator, P. M. Harris, Aldine House,
West Riverside, New Bailey Street, Salford
M3 5EU.
Courts Administrators, Manchester Group, A. H.
Howard; *Liverpool Group*, B. H. Whittaker; *Pres-
ton Group*, G. Davies.

South Eastern Circuit

First-tier—Greater London, Lewes, Norwich (The
High Court in Greater London sits at the Royal
Courts of Justice. The Crown Court in Greater
London sits at the following locations: Acton, Central
Criminal Court, Croydon, Inner London Sessions
House, Isleworth, Kingston upon Thames, Knights-
bridge, Snaresbrook, Southwark and Wood Green).
Second-tier—Chelmsford, Ipswich, Maidstone, Read-
ing, St. Albans. *Third-tier*—Aylesbury, Bury St.
Edmunds, Cambridge, Canterbury, Chichester,
Guildford, King's Lynn, Southend.
Circuit Administrator, J. L. Heritage, New Cavendish
House, 18 Maltravers Street, W.C.2.
Deputy Circuit Administrator, J. Howe.
Courts Administrators, Chelmsford Group, G. E.
Calvett; *Maidstone Group*, Mrs. H. Hartwell;
Kingston Group, P. M. Thomas; *London (Civil)*, S.
M. Orchard; *London (Crime)*, G. F. Addicott.

Wales and Chester Circuit

First-tier—Caernarfon, Cardiff, Chester, Mold,
Swansea. *Second-tier*—Carmarthen, Newport,
Welshpool. *Third-tier*—Dolgellau, Haverfordwest,
Knutsford, Merthyr Tydfil, Warrington.
Circuit Administrator, D. Howe, Churchill House,
Churchill Way, Cardiff.
Courts Administrators, Cardiff Group, G. Jones;
Chester Group, E. R. Walter.

Western Circuit

First-tier—Bodmin, Bristol, Exeter, Winchester.
Second-tier—Dorchester, Gloucester, Plymouth.
Third-tier—Barnstaple, Bournemouth/Poole, Dev-
izes, Newport (I.O.W.), Portsmouth, Salisbury,
Southampton, Swindon, Taunton.
Circuit Administrator, G. Jones, Bridge House, Clif-
ton, Bristol BS8 4BN.

Courts Administrators, *Bristol Group*, A. C. Butler; *Exeter Group*, (vacant); *Winchester Group*, K. Henderson.

CIRCUIT JUDGES
(*Senior Circuit Judges, £50,900; Circuit Judges, £45,800)

Midland and Oxford Circuit

W. A. L. Allardice; F. A. Allen; B. J. Appleby, Q.C.; M. J. Astill; I. J. Black, Q.C.; F. A. Blennerhassett, Q.C.; J. F. Blythe, T.D.; D. W. Brunning; F. L. Clark, Q.C.; P. Clark; R. Cole; J. M. Coulson; P. F. Crane; A. de Piro, Q.C.; T. M. Dillon, Q.C.; J. F. Evans, Q.C.; B. A. Farrer, Q.C.; J. E. Fletcher; H. G. A. Gosling; M. K. Harrison-Hall; T. R. Heald; J. R. Hopkin; R. H. Hutchinson; J. E. M. Irvine; J. G. Jones; *E. F. Jowitt, Q.C.; T. O. Kellock, Q.C.; J. T. C. Lee; M. H. Mander; K. Matthewman, Q.C.; R. G. May; P. W. Medd, O.B.E., Q.C.; K. S. W. Mellor, Q.C.; N. Micklem; A. J. H. Morrison; M. D. Mott; A. J. D. Nicholl; P. C. Northcote; C. J. Pitchers; F. M. Potter; D. E. Roberts; J. A. O. Shand; J. R. S. Smyth; P. J. Stretton; C. S. Stuart-White; H. C. Tayler, Q.C.; K. J. Taylor; R. J. Toyn; M. B. Ward; R. L. Ward, Q.C.; G. G. A. Whitehead, D.F.C.; D. J. R. Wilcox; D. H. Wild; H. Wilson; J. W. Wilson; B. Woods; G. H. Wootton; C. G. Young.

Northern Circuit

H. H. Andrew, Q.C.; J. R. Arthur, D.F.C.; A. W. Bell; M. S. Blackburn; A. S. Booth, Q.C.; D. D. Brown, Q.C.; R. Brown; I. B. Campbell; F. B. Carter, Q.C.; P. C. Clegg; G. P. Crowe, Q.C.; J. M. Davies, Q.C.; Miss A. E. Downey; B. Duckworth; Miss A. M. Ebsworth; A. A. Edmondson; D. M. Evans, Q.C.; S. J. D. Fawcus; J. FitzHugh, Q.C.; D. M. Forster; D. G. F. Franks; J. Hall; R. G. Hamilton; J. A. Hammond; R. J. Hardy; T. D. T. Hodson; Miss M. Holt; G. W. Humphries; A. C. Jolly; H. A. Kershaw; H. L. Lachs; C. N. Lees; J. M. Lever, Q.C.; R. Lockett; J. H. Lord; I. H. Morris-Jones, Q.C.; F. J. Nance; G. K. Naylor, T.D.; M. O' Donoghue; F. D. Paterson; R. E. I. Pickering; D. A. Pirie; *A. M. Prestt, Q.C. (*Recorder of Manchester*); M. A. G. Sachs; N. W. M. Sellers, V.R.D.; H. S. Singer; J. A. Stannard; Miss A. H. Steel; I. R. Taylor, Q.C.; *Sir Sanderson Temple, M.B.E., Q.C. (*Recorder of Liverpool*); J. P. Townsend; I. S. Webster; W. R. Wickham.

North Eastern Circuit

T. G. F. Atkinson; G. Baker, Q.C.; P. M. Baker, Q.C.; J. M. A. Barker; G. N. Barr Young; H. G. Bennett, Q.C.; B. Bush; M. C. Carr; Myrella Cohen, Q.C.; G. J. K. Coles, Q.C.; J. A. Cotton; J. Crabtree; W. H. R. Crawford, Q.C.; *C. R. Dean, Q.C.; P. J. Fox, Q.C.; A. N. Fricker, Q.C.; H. G. Hall; W. Hannah; G. F. R. Harkins; J. A. Henham; D. Herrod, Q.C.; H. Hewitt; R. Hunt; V. R. Hurwitz; A. E. Hutchinson, Q.C.; J. R. Johnson; G. M. Lightfoot; A. C. Macdonald; Miss M. B. M. MacMurray, Q.C.; A. L. Myerson, Q.C.; D. A. Orde; Miss H. E. Paling; R. A. Percy; J. Pickles; D. M. Savill, Q.C.; A. Simpson; L. B. Stephen; J. Stephenson; R. A. R. Stroyan, Q.C.; R. C. Taylor; G. M. Vos; J. D. Walker; M. Walker; P. H. C. Walker.

South Eastern Circuit

M. F. Addison; F. J. Aglionby; A. K. Allen, O.B.E.; M. J. Anwyl-Davies, Q.C.; J. A. Baker; J. B. Baker, Q.C.; P. V. Baker, Q.C.; A. F. Balston; R. M. N. Band, M.C., Q.C.; C. J. A. Barnett, Q.C.; R. A. Barr; N. G. A. Bathurst; P. T. S. Batterbury, T.D.; N. E. Beddard; F. E. Beezley; G. J. Binns; M. Birks; J. C. C. Blofeld, Q.C.; J. Bolland; P. C. Bowsher, Q.C.; P. N. Brandt; L.

J. Bromley, Q.C.; A. E. Brooks; G. N. Butler, Q.C.; *N. M. Butter, Q.C.; H. J. Byrt, Q.C.; C. V. Callman; B. E. Capstick, Q.C.; Sir Harold Cassel, Bt., T.D., Q.C.; A. W. Clark; D. J. Clarkson, Q.C.; Patricia Coles, Q.C.; C. C. Colston, Q.C.; C. D. Compston; M. J. Cook; R. K. Cooke, O.B.E.; G. H. Coombe; M. R. Coombe; Margaret D. Cosgrave; P. H. Counsell; A. E. Cox; P. V. Crocker; D. L. Croft, Q.C.; I. T. R. Davidson, Q.C.; I. H. Davies, T.D.; L. J. Davies, Q.C.; W. L. M. Davies, Q.C.; W. N. Denison, Q.C.; K. M. Devlin; G. L. S. Dobry, C.B.E., Q.C.; C. M. Edwards; Q. T. Edwards, Q.C.; F. P. L. Evans; J. K. Q. Evans; P. R. Faulks, M.C.; A. L. Figgis; J. A. R. Finlay, Q.C.; J. J. Finney; J. J. Fordham; G. C. F. Forrester; J. Fox-Andrews; A. Garfitt; L. Gerber; S. A. Goldstein; P. W. Goldstone; M. B. Goodman; J. H. Gower, Q.C.; M. Graham, Q.C.; P. B. Greenwood; D. J. Griffiths; R. B. Groves, T.D., V.R.D.; Miss J. G. Hall; P. J. Halnan; J. Hamilton; R. E. Hammerton; J. P. Harris, D.S.C., Q.C.; T. F. Hatton; C. L. Hawser, Q.C.; J. D. W. Hayman; A. H. Head; M. R. Hickman; J. C. Hicks, Q.C.; A. N. Hitching; D. Holden; A. C. W. Hordern, Q.C.; Sir David Hughes-Morgan, Bt., C.B., C.B.E.; J. Hunter; H. J. Hyam; C. P. James; W. Kee; M. Kennedy, Q.C.; A. M. Kenny; J. F. Kingham; L. G. Krikler; L. H. C. Lait; R. Laurie; T. Lawrence; C. G. Lea, M.C.; E. Lewis, Q.C.; A. C. L. Lewisohn; A. Lipfriend; D. T. Lloyd; G. D. Lovegrove, Q.C.; D. B. D. Lowe; R. H. Lownie; Mrs. N. M. Lowry; R. J. Lowry, Q.C.; R. D. Lymbery, Q.C.; K. M. McHale; K. A. Machin, Q.C.; I. G. McLean; J. L. E. MacManus, T.D., Q.C.; M. B. McMullan; M. J. P. Macnair; J. R. Main, Q.C.; B. A. Marder, Q.C.; O. S. Martin, Q.C.; N. A. Medawar, Q.C.; J. H. E. Mendl; A. L. Mildon, Q.C.; D. Q. Miller; Sir James Miskin, Q.C. (*Recorder of London*); E. F. Monier-Williams; D. Morton Jack; J. D. F. Moylan; J. I. Murchie; J. H. R. Newey, Q.C.; C. W. F. Newman, Q.C.; Mrs. M. F. Norrie; Suzanne F. Norwood; C. R. Oddie; A. Owen; D. A. Paiba; R. H. S. Palmer; M. C. Parker, Q.C.; Miss V. A. Pearlman; F. H. L. Petre; A. J. Phelan; T. H. Pigot, Q.C. (*Common Serjeant*); D. C. Pitman; R. B. Pollock; H. C. Pownall, Q.C.; B. H. Pryor, Q.C.; J. E. Pullinger; R. D. Ranking; J. W. Rant, Q.C.; E. V. P. Reece; G. K. Rice; K. A. Richardson, Q.C.; D. A. H. Rodwell, Q.C.; G. H. Rooke, T.D., Q.C.; P. C. R. Rountree; K. W. Rubin; T. R. G. Ryland; R. B. Sanders; J. H. A. Scarlett; J. D. Sheerin; *G. J. Shindler, Q.C.; D. R. A. Sich; M. Singh, Q.C.; J. K. E. Slack, T.D.; P. M. J. Slot; F. B. Smedley, Q.C.; R. J. Southan; *R. O. C. Stable, Q.C.; E. Stockdale; C. J. Sumner; J. B. Taylor, M.B.E., T.D.; D. A. Thomas, M.B.E.; A. H. Tibber; A. M. Troup; S. Tumim; J. T. Turner; J. E. Van der Werff; L. J. Verney, Q.C.; A. O. R. Vick, Q.C.; R. W. Vick; B. J. Wakley, M.B.E.; A. F. Waley, V.R.D., Q.C.; J. R. Warde; D. B. Watling, Q.C.; V. B. Watts; Sir David West-Russell; F. J. White; J. E. Williams; S. M. Willis; G. N. Worthington; E. G. Wrintmore.

Wales and Chester Circuit

T. R. Crowther, Q.C.; G. H. M. Daniel; R. D. G. David, Q.C.; Lord Elystan-Morgan; T. M. Evans, Q.C.; W. N. Francis; M. Gibbon, Q.C.; D. M. Hughes; G. Jones; G. E. Kilfoil; T. E. I. Lewis-Bowen; D. G. Morgan; D. A. Phillips; D. W. Powell; E. J. Prosser, Q.C.; H. W. J. ap Robert; H. E. P. Roberts, Q.C.; J. C. Rutter; S. M. Stephens, Q.C.; D. B. Williams, T.D., Q.C.; H. Williams, Q.C.; R. G. Woolley.

Western Circuit

G. B. Best; N. R. Blaker, Q.C.; C. L. Boothman; Miss J. W. Bracewell, Q.C.; M. J. L. Brodrick; Sir Jonathan Clarke; P. H. F. Clarke; Hazel Counsell; J. A. Cox; J. W. Da Cunha; M. Dyer; P. Fallon, Q.C.; P. D. Fanner; B. J. F. Galpin; I. S. Hill, Q.C.; G. B. Hutton; J. H. Inskip, Q.C.; A. C. Lauriston, Q.C.; Sir Ian Lewis; I. P. Llewellyn Jones; D. McCarraher, V.R.D.; H. E. L.

McCreery, Q.C.; Miss S. M. D. McKinney; J. G. McNaught; C. B. Mantell, Q.C.; E. G. Neville; D. A. Smith, Q.C.; K. C. L. Smithies; H. J. M. Tucker, Q.C.; D. M. Webster, Q.C.; J. R. Whitley; K. M. Willcock, Q.C.; J. H. Wroath.

RECORDERS

J. R. S. Adams; I. D. G. Alexander; W. P. Andreae-Jones, Q.C.; J. F. Appleton; J. F. A. Archer, Q.C.; Rt. Hon. P. K. Archer, Q.C., M.P.; A. J. Arlidge, Q.C.; R. Ashton; P. Ashworth, Q.C.; N. J. Atkinson; M. G. Austin-Smith; W. S. Aylen, Q.C.; P. Back, Q.C.; J. F. Badenoch; P. G. N. Badge; M. J. D. Baker; N. R. J. Baker, Q.C.; T. S. G. Baker, Q.C.; G. S. Barham; A. Barker, Q.C.; B. J. Barker; D. Barker, Q.C.; R. O. Barlow; D. M. W. Barnes, Q.C.; T. P. Barnes, Q.C.; W. E. Barnett, Q.C.; A. R. Barrowclough, Q.C.; J. E. Barry; J. C. T. Barton; K. Bassingthwaite; S. T. Bates, Q.C.; R. J. A. Batt; S. D. Batten; J. J. Baughan; P. M. Beard; C. H. Beaumont; P. J. L. Beaumont, Q.C.; C. O. M. Bedingfield, T.D., Q.C.; R. E. Bell, Q.C.; The Hon. M. J. Beloff, Q.C.; D. P. Bennett; P. Bennett, Q.C.; K. C. Bentall; D. R. Bentley, Q.C.; D. M. Berkson; Miss I. Bernstein; R. H. Bernstein, D.F.C., Q.C.; M. Bethel, Q.C.; J. P. V. Bevan; J. C. Beveridge, Q.C.; J. W. Black, Q.C.; D. M. Blair; J. A. Blair-Gould; A. N. H. Blake; C. Bloom, Q.C.; J. G. Boal; G. T. K. Bowyer; L. A. F. Borrett; I. R. Boyd; J. J. Boyle; R. W. A. Bray; D. J. Brennan, Q.C.; G. J. B. G. Brice, Q.C.; J. N. W. Bridges-Adams; A. J. Brigden; A. N. J. Briggs; P. J. Briggs; S. E. Brodie, Q.C.; H. Brooke, Q.C.; D. M. A. Bryant; R. J. Buckley, Q.C.; J. M. Bull, Q.C.; J. W. M. Bullimore; D. L. Bulmer; J. P. Burgess; J. K. Burke, Q.C.; J. P. Burke, Q.C.; M. A. B. Burke-Gaffney, Q.C.; R. D. H. Bursell, Q.C.; A. J. Butcher, Q.C.; A. N. L. Butterfield, Q.C.; R. J. Buxton, Q.C.; D. C. Calcutt, Q.C.; Mrs. B. A. Calvert, Q.C.; D. Calvert-Smith; Miss S. M. C. Cameron, Q.C.; The Lord Campbell of Alloway, Q.C.; G. M. C. Carey; A. C. Carlile, Q.C., M.P.; The Lord Carlisle of Bucklow, P.C., Q.C.; H. B. H. Carlisle, Q.C.; R. C. L. Carr; B. I. Caulfield; J. A. Chadwin, Q.C.; J. R. Chalkley; N. M. Chambers, Q.C.; F. A. Chapman; B. L. Charles, Q.C.; P. J. Charlesworth; B. W. Chedlow, Q.C.; J. M. Cherry, Q.C.; C. H. Clark; D. Clark; A. P. Clarke, Q.C.; D. C. Clarke, Q.C.; R. N. B. Clegg, Q.C.; G. M. Clifton; C. D. Cochrane, Q.C.; D. J. Cocks, Q.C.; J. R. Cole; N. B. C. Coles, Q.C.; S. H. Colgan; P. N. Collier; A. D. Collins, Q.C.; J. M. Collins; A. D. Colman, Q.C.; S. S. Coltart; J. S. Colyer, Q.C.; P. R. C. Coni, Q.C.; T. A. C. Coningsby, Q.C.; M. B. Connell, Q.C.; J. G. Connor; R. D. Connor; C. S. Cook; R. A. Cooke; Miss B. P. Cooper, Q.C.; S. M. Corkhill; T. G. E. Corrie; Miss D. R. Cotton, Q.C.; J. S. Coward, Q.C.; B. R. E. Cox, Q.C.; P. J. Cox, D.S.C., Q.C.; R. C. Cox; M. T. Cracknell; P. J. Crawford, Q.C.; C. J. Crespi, Q.C.; P. J. Cresswell, Q.C.; D. I. Crigman; M. L. S. Cripps; F. P. Crowder, Q.C.; J. D. Crowley, Q.C.; E. J. R. Crowther, O.B.E., Q.C.; W. R. H. Crowther, Q.C.; Miss E. A. M. Curnow, Q.C.; R. H. Curtis, Q.C.; S. C. Darwall-Smith; Mrs. S. P. Darwall-Smith; G. W. Davey; G. L. Davies; R. E. Davies, Q.C.; D. H. Day; J. J. Deave; J. B. Deby, Q.C.; C. F. Dehn, Q.C.; P. N. De Mille; W. E. Denny, C.B.E., Q.C.; S. C. Desch, Q.C.; M. N. Devonshire; A. E. J. Diamond, Q.C.; J. B. S. Diehl, Q.C.; A. M. Donne, Q.C.; D. P. Draycott, Q.C.; Sir John Drinkwater, Q.C.; R. Du Cann, Q.C.; S. B. Duncan; W. H. Dunn, Q.C.; C. H. Durman; A. H. Durrant; J. A. Dyson, Q.C.

D. Eady, Q.C.; T. K. Earnshaw; J. S. Eastwood; H. W. P. Eccles; D. E. H. Edwards; G. O. Edwards, Q.C.; D. F. Elfer, Q.C.; G. Elias, Q.C.; B. J. Elliott; R. M. Englehart, Q.C.; G. A. Ensor; D. A. Evans, Q.C.; D. R. Evans; Miss M. A. P. Evans; E. C. Evans-Lombe, Q.C.; G. N. Eyre, Q.C.; W. D. Fairclough; R. J. S. Fairley; J.

D. Farnworth; D. J. Farrer, Q.C.; E. J. Faulks; M. H. Fauvelle; J. D. A. Fennell, O.B.E., Q.C.; R. Fernyhough, Q.C.; P. Fingret; Miss E. N. Fisher; W. R. Fitch; G. D. Flather, Q.C.; P. E. J. Focke, Q.C.; T. J. Forbes, Q.C.; J. R. Foster; R. M. Foster; N. H. Freeman; R. H. K. Frisby, Q.C.; W. M. Gage, Q.C.; M. Gale, Q.C.; M. S. Garner; J. R. B. Geake; R. Gee; L. N. H. George; R. J. H. Gibbs, Q.C.; L. Giovene; A. T. Glass, Q.C.; W. J. Glover, Q.C.; Miss A. F. Goddard, Q.C.; H. K. Goddard, Q.C.; J. B. Goldring, Q.C.; A. R. Goldsack; A. J. J. Gompertz, Q.C.; A. A. Gordon; C. G. M. Gordon; J. P. Gorman, Q.C.; J. B. Gosschalk; T. J. C. Gouldie, Q.C.; The Lord Grantchester, Q.C.; G. Gray, Q.C.; J. M. Gray; R. I. Gray, Q.C.; R. M. K. Gray, Q.C.; B. S. Green, Q.C.; H. Green, Q.C.; S. P. Grenfell; R. D. Grey, Q.C.; D. L. Griffiths; J. C. Griffiths, Q.C.; L. Griffiths; G. D. Grigson; M. G. Grills; Mrs. H. M. Grindrod, Q.C.; A. S. Hacking, Q.C.; M. F. Haigh; V. E. Hall; G. Hallon; J. H. Hames, Q.C.; A. W. Hamilton, Q.C.; G. M. Hamilton, T.D., Q.C.; J. Hampton; C. R. H. Hardy; Miss R. S. A. Hare, Q.C.; B. Hargrove, O.B.E., Q.C.; R. D. Harman, Q.C.; D. M. Harris; R. M. Harrison, Q.C.; F. D. Hart, Q.C.; C. A. Hart-Leverton, Q.C.; C. S. Harvey, M.B.E., Q.C.; M. L. T. Harvey, Q.C.; R. O. Havery, Q.C.; T. S. A. Hawkesworth, Q.C.; R. G. Hawkins, Q.C.; R. W. P. Hay; R. Hayward-Smith, Q.C.; M. Heald, Q.C.; M. Hedley; T. B. Hegarty; G. E. Heggs; R. A. Henderson, Q.C.; R. H. Q. Henriques, Q.C.; P. J. M. Heppel; R. B. Hickman; A. B. Hidden, Q.C.; B. J. Higgs, Q.C.; A. M. Hill, Q.C.; E. M. Hill, Q.C.; A. J. H. Hilton; J. D. Hitchen; S. A. Hockman; C. R. Hodson; P. M. L. Hoffman; A. J. C. Hoggett, Q.C.; D. A. Hollis, V.R.D., Q.C.; A. T. Hoolahan, Q.C.; A. Hooper, Q.C.; The Lord Hooson, Q.C.; R. Houlker, Q.C.; M. Howard, Q.C., M.P.; M. J. Hubbard, Q.C.; A. P. G. Hughes; J. Hugill, Q.C.; J. G. Hull, Q.C.; P. J. Hunt, Q.C.; I. G. A. Hunter, Q.C.; B. A. Hytner, Q.C.; N. E. J. Inglis-Jones, Q.C.; The Lord Irvine of Lairg, Q.C.; F. C. Irwin, Q.C.; M. R. Jackson; P. J. E. Jackson; I. E. Jacob; C. E. F. James; N. F. B. Jarman, Q.C.; D. A. Jeffreys, Q.C.; J. Jeffs, Q.C.; R. P. V. Jenkins; D. B. Johnson; M. H. Johnson; R. L. Johnson, Q.C.; E. S. Jones, Q.C.; G. R. Jones; N. H. Jones, Q.C.; T. G. Jones; W. H. Joss; P. S. L. Joyce; I. Judge, Q.C.; M. D. L. Kalisher, Q.C.; J. W. Kay, Q.C.; D. St. J. Keane, Q.C.; M. L. Keane; R. W. M. Keeling; D. A. M. Kemp, Q.C.; T. D. Kent-Jones; P. M. Kershaw, Q.C.; G. M. Khayat; R. I. Kidwell, Q.C.; A. W. P. King; I. Kinnell, Q.C.; A. T. H. Kirkwood; R. C. Klevan, Q.C.; C. F. Kolbert.

D. G. Lane; G. J. H. Langley, Q.C.; D. N. R. Latham, Q.C.; R. B. Latham; G. F. B. Laughland, Q.C.; I. J. Lawrence, Q.C., M.P.; J. G. M. Laws; M. H. Lawson; L. D. Lawton, Q.C.; D. Lederman; M. K. Lee, Q.C.; F. L. Lee; C. H. de V. Leigh; Sir Godfrey Le Quesne, Q.C.; A. P. Lester, Q.C.; B. H. Leveson, Q.C.; S. Levine; M. E. Lewer, Q.C.; A. K. Lewis, Q.C.; M. ap G. Lewis, Q.C.; R. S. Lewis; C. C. D. Lindsay, Q.C.; B. J. E. Livesey; R. J. D. Livesey, Q.C.; C. G. Llewellyn-Jones; J. Lloyd-Eley, Q.C.; F. R. Lockhart; A. J. C. Lodge; R. P. Lowden; F. D. L. Loy; J. A. T. Loyd, Q.C.; Sir Nicholas Lyell, Q.C., M.P.; D. Lynch; E. Lyons, Q.C.; A. G. MacDuff; D. D. McEvoy, Q.C.; I. S. McKintosh; N. R. B. Macleod, Q.C.; N. J. C. McLusky; J. B. MacMillan; K. C. Macrae; E. A. Machin, Q.C.; B. C. Maddocks; C. J. Mahon; Miss V. H. Mairants; Miss A. Mallalieu, Q.C.; F. J. M. Marr-Johnson; R. G. Marshall-Andrews, Q.C.; D. N. N. Martineau; D. Matheson; P. B. Mauleverer, Q.C.; R. B. Mawrey, Q.C.; A. T. K. May, Q.C.; H. R. Mayor, Q.C.; M. Meggerson; D. J. Mellor, Q.C., M.P.; J. M. Meredith; J. T. Milford; R. A. Miller; Mrs. B. J. L. Mills, Q.C.; J. B. M. Milmo, Q.C.; N. A. Miscampbell, Q.C., M.P.; S. G. Mitchell, Q.C.; J. E. Mitting, Q.C.; H. J. Montlake; M. H. Morgan; J. A. Morgan; L. J. J. Morgan; W. G. O. Morgan, Q.C.; G. E. Moriarty, Q.C.; T. R. A. Morison, Q.C.; M. Morland, Q.C.; A. P. Morris; D. G. Morris; The Rt. Hon. J. Morris, Q.C., M.P.; J. I. Morris; T. H. Moseley,

Q.C.; A. G. Moses; P. C. Mott; J. Mulcahy, Q.C.; F. J. Muller, Q.C.; N. J. Mylne, Q.C.; M. H. D. Neligan; R. F. Nelson, Q.C.; R. E. Newbold; G. M. Newman, Q.C.; J. D. Newton; G. Nice; C. V. Nicholls, Q.C.; C. A. A. Nicholls, Q.C.; M. C. Nicholson; A. S. T. E. Nicol; J. G. Nutting; D. P. O'Brien, Q.C.; P. W. O'Brien; E. M. Ogden, Q.C.; B. R. Oliver; S. K. O'Malley; R. T. N. Orme; R. C. C. O'Rorke; J. F. F. Orrell; S. K. Overend; F. D. Owen; G. V. Owen, Q.C.; R. M. Owen, Q.C.; S. R. Page; D. C. J. Paget; A. W. Palmer, Q.C.; S. A. B. Parish; T. C. Parkin; E. O. Parry; N. S. K. Pascoe, Q.C.; A. Patience; J. G. Paulusz; Mrs. N. Pearce; D. H. Penry-Davey, Q.C.; J. R. Peppitt, Q.C.; Sir Ian Percival, Q.C.; D. S. Perrett, Q.C.; M. Pert; C. J. Pitchford, Q.C.; A. P. Pitts; Miss E. F. Platt, Q.C.; J. R. Playford, Q.C.; A. G. S. Pollock, Q.C.; D. A. Poole, Q.C.; M. J. Pratt, Q.C.; R. J. C. V. Prendergast; T. W. Preston, Q.C.; J. E. Previté; J. A. Price, Q.C.; N. P. L. Price; P. J. Price; A. J. Proctor; G. V. Pugh, Q.C.; C. P. B. Purchas; A. G. Purnell, Q.C.; N. R. Purnell, Q.C.; P. O. Purnell, Q.C.; J. R. Pyke.

D. A. Radcliffe; A. Rankin, Q.C.; A. D. Rawley, Q.C.; L. F. Read, Q.C.; A. R. F. Redgrave; P. Rees; J. R. Reid, Q.C.; R. E. Rhodes; M. S. Rich, Q.C.; D. W. Richards; H. A. Richardson; Miss S. A. Ritchie, Q.C.; G. Rivlin, Q.C.; S. D. Robbins; J. A. Roberts, Q.C.; J. H. Roberts; J. M. G. Roberts, Q.C.; P. B. Roberts; V. Robinson, Q.C.; D. E. H. Robson, Q.C.; G. W. Roddick, Q.C.; J. M. T. Rogers, Q.C.; J. W. Rogers, Q.C.; J. J. Rowe, Q.C.; R. J. Royce, Q.C.; J. H. Rucker; J. N. P. Rudd; A. A. Rumbelow; R. R. Russell; G. C. Ryan, Q.C.; J. E. A. Samuels, Q.C.; M. P. Sayers, Q.C.; R. J. Scholes, Q.C.; A. F. B. Scrivener, Q.C.; R. J. Seabrook, Q.C.; C. Seagroatt, Q.C.; H. M. Self, Q.C.; Brig. D. M. D. Selwood; R. M. Shawcross; S. J. Sher, Q.C.; M. D. Sherrard, Q.C.; L. Shield; L. S. Shields, Q.C.; J. M. Shorrock, Q.C.; S. R. Silber, Q.C.; K. T. Simpson; P. R. Simpson; J. P. Singer, Q.C.; A. T. Smith, Q.C.; C. M. Smith, Q.C.; J. H. Smith, Q.C.; R. S. Smith, Q.C.; R. E. Snape; R. F. Solman; R. C. E. Southwell; Miss J. M. Southworth, Q.C.; M. H. Spence, Q.C.; S. B. Spence; D. H. Spencer, Q.C.; M. G. Spencer; S. M. Spencer, Q.C.; J. A. C. Spokes, Q.C.; R. W. Spon-Smith; S. A. Stamler, Q.C.; D. P. Stanley; D. H. Stembridge; J. S. H. Stewart, Q.C.; R. M. Stewart, Q.C.; D. M. A. Stokes; E. D. R. Stone, Q.C.; P. L. Storr; M. Stuart-Moore; J. Stuart-Smith, Q.C.; G. C. Styler; F. R. C. Such; A. B. Suckling, Q.C.; D. M. Sumner; L. Swift, Q.C.; M. R. Swift, Q.C.; J. A. Tackaberry, Q.C.; A. B. Taylor; E. Taylor; N. Taylor, Q.C.; W. E. M. Taylor; M. I. Tennant; K. J. Tetley; D. M. Thomas, O.B.E., Q.C.; D. O. Thomas, Q.C.; J. Thomas, Q.C.; Lord Thomas of Gwydir, P.C., Q.C.; R. J. L. Thomas, Q.C.; R. L. Thomas; R. U. Thomas, Q.C.; W. F. C. Thomas; A. A. R. Thompson, Q.C.; C. H. Tilling; R. N. Titheridge, Q.C.; J. K. Toulmin, Q.C.; R. G. Toulson, Q.C.; J. B. S. Townend, Q.C.; S. L. Tuckey, Q.C.; H. W. Turcan; P. A. Twigg, Q.C.; C. J. M. Tyrer; A. R. Tyrrell, Q.C.; Mrs. A. P. Uziell-Hamilton; N. P. Valios; A. R. Vandermeer, Q.C.; Miss M. S. Viner, Q.C.; Rt. Hon. D. C. Waddington, Q.C., M.P.; J. P. Wadsworth, Q.C.; D. St. J. Wagstaff; R. M. Wakerley, Q.C.; W. H. Waldron, Q.C.; R. J. Walker, Q.C.; T. E. Walker, Q.C.; J. J. Walker-Smith; G. M. Waller, Q.C.; B. Walsh, Q.C.; A. H. Ward, Q.C.; C. D. G. P. Waud; P. A. Webster; M. Weisman; P. Weitzman, Q.C.; C. P. C. Whelon; C. H. Whitby, Q.C.; D. R. B. Whitehouse; P. J. M. Whiteman, T.D.; A. Whitfield, Q.C.; D. G. Widdicombe, Q.C.; A. D. F. Wilcken; D. B. Williams; G. H. G. Williams, Q.C.; G. W. Williams, Q.C.; J. G. Williams, Q.C.; J. L. Williams, Q.C.; The Hon. J. M. Williams, Q.C.; S. W. Williamson, Q.C.; J. C. Willis; A. M. Wilson, Q.C.; N. A. R. Wilson, Q.C.; C. Wilson-Smith, Q.C.; G. W. Wingate-Saul, Q.C.; M. E. Wolff; H. Wolton, Q.C.; D. A. Wood, Q.C.; L. G. Woodley, Q.C.; S. Woodley; D. R. Woolley, Q.C.; N. G. Wootton; A. M. Worrall; N. J. Worsley; P. F. Worsley; J. M. Wright, Q.C.; D. E. M. Young, Q.C.; K. H. Zucker, Q.C.

STIPENDIARY MAGISTRATES

Provincial

Greater Manchester, W. D. Fairclough (1982); C. T. Latham, O.B.E. (1976).
Humberside, N. H. White (1985).
Merseyside, N. G. Wootton (1976).
Mid Glamorgan, D. P. Rowland (1961); B. R. Oliver (1983).
South Glamorgan, Sir Lincoln Hallinan (1976).
South Yorkshire, I. W. Crompton (1983); J. E. Barry (1985).
West Midlands, F. H. Hatchard (1981); W. M. Probert (1983); G. H. Kamil (1987).
West Yorkshire, F. D. L. Loy (1972); I. R. Boyd (1982).

Metropolitan

Chief Metropolitan Stipendiary Magistrate and Chairman of Committee of Magistrates for Inner London Area, Sir David Hopkin (*Bow Street*) £45,800

Committee of Magistrates for Inner London Area

3rd Floor, North West Wing,
Bush House, Aldwych, WC2B 4PJ

Principal Chief Clerk and Clerk to the Committee, I. Fowler £36,102
Chief Clerk (Training), J. W. Greenhill £30,747

Magistrates
(*each £37,500*)

Bow Street, The Chief Magistrate; W. E. C. Robins; R. D. Bartle; G. L. Wicks.
Camberwell Green, R. D. Connor; P. Fingret; Mrs. H. Mitcham; G. B. Breen; A. W. Ormerod.
Clerkenwell, M. L. R. Romer; C. J. Bourke; M. A. Johnstone.
Greenwich and Woolwich, Miss P. M. Long; Mrs. K. R. Keating; T. G. Cowling.
Highbury Corner, D. Barr; G. E. Parkinson; Miss D. Quick; B. Morgan.
Horseferry Road, E. J. R. Crowther, O.B.E.; Sir Bryan Roberts, K.C.M.G., Q.C.; C. P. M. Davidson; Mrs. N. F. Negus.
Marlborough Street, K. J. H. Nichols; J. G. Connor.
Marylebone, G. L. J. Noel; J. Q. Campbell; S. G. Clixby; B. Black.
Old Street, T. Maher; D. B. Meier.
South Western, Miss D. A. Freedman; A. Cooray; M. H. D. Neligan.
Thames, B. J. Canham; T. M. English.
Tower Bridge, C. D. Voelcker; Mrs. J. R. Comyns; D. Kennett-Brown.
Wells Street, Miss A. M. Jennings; P. G. N. Badge; D. M. Fingleton; K. L. Maitland-Davies; N. Crichton.
West London, D. Fairbairn; H. J. Cook.
Unattached Magistrates, R. T. Moss; A. R. Davies; T. H. Workman.

CROWN PROSECUTION SERVICE
Headquarters: 4/12 Queen Anne's Gate, SW1H 9AZ
[01-273 3000: *Casework sections*, 01-222 7944]

Fraud Divisions
10 Furnival Street, EC4A 1PE
[01-831 3038]

The Crown Prosecution Service (C.P.S.) handles the prosecution of criminal proceedings instituted by police forces (excluding certain minor road traffic offences). The head of the C.P.S. is the Director of Public Prosecutions: day-to-day administration of the C.P.S. is handled by the Deputy Director. There are four Regional Directors responsible for the 31 areas: each area is headed by a Chief Crown Prosecutor.

Salaries

Grade 1	£68,500
Grade 2	£45,800–£48,000
Grade 3	£35,800–£39,000
Grade 4	£30,344–£31,844
Grade 5	£25,756–£29,344

London Weighting = £1,750 p.a.

Director of Public Prosecutions (G1), A. D. Green, Q.C..

Deputy Director and Chief Executive (G2), D. S. Gandy, O.B.E.

Principal Establishment and Finance Officer (G3), D. Wiblin.

Director, Headquarters Casework (G3), Mrs. M. Phillips.

Head, General Casework (G5), T. Taylor.

Head, Special Casework (G5), K. Horn.

Head, Policy Division (G5), K. Ashken.

Heads, Fraud Divisions (G5), T. Waring; G. Adams.

Head, Police Complaints Division (G5), C. Cleugh.

Head, Financial Services (G5), B. Spratt.

Head, Personnel and Training (G5), W. R. Mann.

Head, Office Services and Legal Costs (G6), B. Spear.

In addition, the four Regional Directors are based at C.P.S. headquarters: the Director, Northern Region also has an office in Manchester; the Director, London and South East Region also has an office in Surrey.

C.P.S. AREAS

Northern Region

Suite 101, Sunlight House, Quay Street
Manchester M3 3JU
Regional Director(G3), B. Crebbin

CHESHIRE, Hamilton House, Hamilton Place, Chester CH1 2BH.—*Chief Crown Prosecutor (G5),* Mrs. N. E. Hollingsworth.

CLEVELAND/N. YORKSHIRE, Rydale Buildings, 60 Piccadilly, York YO1 1NS.—*Chief Crown Prosecutor (G5),* D. Sharp.

GREATER MANCHESTER, P.O.Box 491, Sunlight House, Quay Street, Manchester M60 3LU.—*Chief Crown Prosecutor (G4),* A. Taylor.

LANCASHIRE/CUMBRIA, Red Rose House, Lancaster Road, Preston, Lancs. PR1 1ER.—*Chief Crown Prosecutor (G5),* J. V. Bates.

MERSEYSIDE, 7th Floor (South), Royal Liver Building, Liverpool L3 1HN.—*Chief Crown Prosecutor (G4),* E. C. Woodcock.

NORTHUMBRIA/DURHAM, Cuthbert House, All Saints Centre, Newcastle upon Tyne NE1 2DW.—*Chief Crown Prosecutor (G5),* G. Duff.

N. WALES/DYFED/POWYS, 491 Abergele Road, Old Colwyn, Colwyn Bay, Clwyd LL29 9AE.—*Chief Crown Prosecutor (G5),* A. S. R. Clarke.

S. YORKSHIRE, Belgrave House, 47 Bank Street, Sheffield S1 2EH.—*Chief Crown Prosecutor (G4),* M. J. Rose.

W. YORKSHIRE, Grove Hall, College Grove Road, Wakefield WF1 3RA.—*Chief Crown Prosecutor (G4),* R. Otley.

Midland Region

Regional Director (G3), R. Williamson.

CAMBRIDGESHIRE/LINCOLNSHIRE, The River Mill, St Ives, Huntingdon, Cambs. PE17 4HJ.—*Chief Crown Prosecutor (G5),* D. G. Lewis.

DERBYSHIRE, Celtic House, Heritage Gate, Friary Street, Derby DE1 1QX.—*Chief Crown Prosecutor (G5),* D. R. K. Seddon.

HUMBERSIDE, Queens House, Paragon Street, Hull HU3 3DA.—*Chief Crown Prosecutor (G5),* L. M. Bell.

LEICESTERSHIRE/NORTHAMPTONSHIRE, Leicester House, Lee Circle, Leicester LE1 3RE.—*Chief Crown Prosecutor (G5),* G. Etherington.

NORFOLK/SUFFOLK, Saxon House, 1 Cromwell Square, Ipswich, Suffolk IP1 1TR.—*Chief Crown Prosecutor (G5),* M. F. C. Harvey.

NOTTINGHAMSHIRE, Victoria House, 76 Milton Street, Nottingham NG1 3QZ.—*Chief Crown Prosecutor (G5),* D. C. Beal.

STAFFORDSHIRE/WARWICKSHIRE, Government Building, Millbank, Stafford ST16 8QU.—*Chief Crown Prosecutor (G5),* D. V. Dickenson.

WEST MIDLANDS, The McClaren Building, Dale End, Birmingham B4 7LN.—*Chief Crown Prosecutor (G3),* I. S. Manson.

South and West Region

Regional Director (G3), C. Hoad.

AVON/SOMERSET, Froomsgate House, Rupert Street, Bristol BS1 2PS.—*Chief Crown Prosecutor (G5),* C. T. Jones.

DEVON/CORNWALL, 54 Mary Arches Street, Exeter EX4 3BA.—*Chief Crown Prosecutor (G5),* R. J. Green.

DORSET/HAMPSHIRE, Black Horse House, 8–10 Leigh Road, Eastleigh, Hants. SO5 4FH.—*Chief Crown Prosecutor (G5),* P. Boeuf.

GLOUCESTERSHIRE/WILTSHIRE, Avonbridge House, Bath Road, Chippenham, Wiltshire SN15 2BB —*Chief Crown Prosecutor (G5),* R. A. Prickett.

S. WALES/GWENT, Pearl Assurance House, Greyfriars Road, Cardiff CF1 3AG.—*Chief Crown Prosecutor (G4),* H. G. Wallace.

SUSSEX, Unit 3, Clifton Mews, Clifton Hill, Brighton, E. Sussex BN1 3HR.—*Chief Crown Prosecutor (G5),* D. Thompson.

THAMES VALLEY, The Courtyard, Lombard Street, Abingdon, Oxon. OX14 5SE.—*Chief Crown Prosecutor (G5),* P. D. F. Higginbottom.

WEST MERCIA, Orchard House, Victoria Square, Droitwich, Worcester WR9 8QT.—*Chief Crown Prosecutor (G5),* D. R. Stott.

London and South East

Tolworth Tower (16th floor),
Surbiton, Surrey KT6 7DS

Regional Director (G3), R. Gwilliam.

ESSEX, Gemini Centre, 88 New London Road, Chelmsford, Essex CM2 0BR.—*Chief Crown Prosecutor (G5),* J. J. Goodwin.

HERTFORDSHIRE/BEDFORDSHIRE, Queens House, 58 Victoria Street, St Albans AL1 3HZ.—*Chief Crown Prosecutor (G5),* R. J. Chronnell.

KENT, Kent House, Lower Stone Street, Maidstone, Kent ME15 6JT.—*Chief Crown Prosecutor (G5),* R. A. Crabb.

LONDON (INNER), New Portland House, Stag Place, SW1.—*Chief Crown Prosecutor (G4),* B. McArdle.

LONDON (NORTH), Solar House, 1 Romford Road, Stratford E15 4LJ.—*Chief Crown Prosecutor (G4),* S. J. Wooler.

LONDON (SOUTH)/SURREY, Tolworth Tower, Surbiton KT6 7DS.—*Chief Crown Prosecutor (G4),* D. E. Dracup.

THE SCOTTISH JUDICATURE

Scotland has a legal system separate and differing greatly from the English legal system in enacted law, judicial procedure and the structure of courts.

There is in Scotland a system of public prosecution headed by the Lord Advocate which is independent of the police, who have no say in the decision to prosecute. The Lord Advocate, discharging his functions through the Crown Office in Edinburgh, is responsible for prosecutions in the High Court, sheriff courts and district courts. Prosecutions in the High Court are prepared by the Crown Office and conducted in court by one of the Law Officers or an advocate-depute. In the inferior courts the decision to prosecute is made and prosecution is preferred by procurators fiscal, who are lawyers and full-time civil servants, subject to the directions of the Crown Office. A permanent legally-qualified civil servant known as the Crown Agent is responsible for the running of the Crown Office and the organization of the Procurator Fiscal Service, of which he is the head.

Scotland is divided into six Sheriffdoms, each with a full-time Sheriff Principal. The Sheriffdoms are further divided into sheriff court districts, each of which has a legally-qualified, resident sheriff or sheriffs, who are the judges of the court.

In criminal cases sheriffs principal and sheriffs have the same powers: sitting with a jury of 15 members, they may try more serious cases on indictment, or, sitting alone, may try lesser cases under summary procedure. Minor summary offences are dealt with in district courts which are administered by the district and the islands local government authorities and presided over by lay justices of the peace, and, in Glasgow only, by stipendiary magistrates. Juvenile offenders (children under 16) may be brought before an informal children's hearing comprising three local lay people. The superior criminal court is the High Court of Justiciary which is both a trial and an appeal court. Cases on indictment are tried by a High Court Judge, sitting with a jury of 15, in Edinburgh and on circuit in other towns. Appeals from the lower courts against conviction or sentence are heard also by the High Court, which sits as an appeal court only in Edinburgh. There is no further appeal to the House of Lords in criminal cases.

In civil cases the jurisdiction of the sheriff court extends to most kinds of action. Appeal against decisions of the sheriff may be made to the Sheriff Principal and thence to the Court of Session, or direct to the Court of Session, which sits only in Edinburgh. The Court of Session is divided into the Inner and the Outer House. The Outer House is a court of first instance in which cases are heard by judges sitting singly, sometimes with a jury of 12. The Inner House, itself subdivided into two Divisions of equal status, is mainly an appeal court. Appeals may be made to the Inner House from the Outer House as well as from the sheriff court: an appeal may be made from the Inner House to the House of Lords.

The Judges of the Court of Session are the same as those of the High Court of Justiciary, the Lord President of the Court of Session also holding the office of Lord Justice General in the High Court.

The office of coroner does not exist in Scotland: the local procurator fiscal inquires privately into sudden and suspicious deaths and may report findings to the Crown Agent. In some cases a fatal accident inquiry may be held before the sheriff.

COURT OF SESSION (Established 1532) and HIGH COURT OF JUSTICIARY

The Lord President and Lord Justice General, The Rt. Hon. The Lord Emslie, M.B.E.

INNER HOUSE.—*First Division.*

The Lord President, The Rt. Hon. The Lord Emslie, (George Carlyle Emslie, M.B.E.) £78,750
Hon. Lord Grieve, (William Robertson Grieve, V.R.D.).
Hon. Lord Brand, (David William Robert Brand).
Hon. Lord Allanbridge (William Ian Stewart).

Second Division

Lord Justice Clerk, The Rt. Hon. Lord Ross, (Donald MacArthur Ross) £75,750
Hon. Lord Dunpark, (Alastair McPherson Johnston, T.D.)
Hon. Lord McDonald, (Robert Howat McDonald, M.C.)
Hon. Lord Maxwell, (Peter Maxwell) (*seconded to Scottish Law Commission*)

OUTER HOUSE

Hon. Lord Cowie, (William Lorn Kerr Cowie)
Rt. Hon. Lord Murray, (Ronald King Murray)
Hon. Lord Mayfield, (Ian MacDonald, M.C.)
Hon. Lord Davidson, (Charles Kemp Davidson)
Rt. Hon. Lord McCluskey, (John Herbert McCluskey).
Hon. Lord Morison, (Alastair Malcolm Morison)
Hon. Lord Sutherland, (Ranald Iain Sutherland)
Hon. Lord Weir, (David Bruce Weir)
Hon. Lord Clyde, (James John Clyde)
Hon. Lord Cullen, (William Douglas Cullen).
Hon. Lord Prosser (William David Prosser).
Hon. Lord Kirkwood (Ian Candlish Kirkwood).
Hon. Lord Coulsfield (John Taylor Cameron).
Hon. Lord Milligan (James George Milligan).
Hon. Lord Dervaird (John Murray).
(SALARIES: All Inner House judges other than the Lord President and Lord Justice Clerk, £75,750; Outer House judges, £68,500).

Court of Session and High Court of Justiciary
Parliament House, Parliament Square, Edinburgh

Principal Clerk of Session and Justiciary, A. M. Campbell .... £27,087–£31,563
Deputy Principal Clerk of Session and Principal Extractor, M. Weir .... £16,692–£22,715
Deputy Principal Clerk of Justiciary, J. Robertson £16,692–£22,715
Deputy Principal Clerk (Administration) and Keeper of the Rolls, H. S. Foley .... £16,692–£22,715
Depute Clerks of Session and Justiciary, W. Gillon; A. Hogg; N. J. Dowie; M. G. Bonar; I. Smith; J. A. R. Cowie; T. Higgins; E. A. Cumming; B. Watson; P. J. McGonigle; T. B. Cruickshank; Q. Oliver; F. Shannly; P. Crow; J. L. Anderson; R. D. Sinclair; Mrs. A. Leighton; J. Clark; T. M. Thomson; D. D. Mackay; A. S. Moffat; E. G. Appelbe ..... £12,806–£16,409

Scottish Courts Administration
26–27 Royal Terrace, Edinburgh EH7 5AH

Director, G. Murray.

Crown Office
5/7 Regent Road, Edinburgh EH7 5BL

Crown Agent, I. Dean, C.B. £48,000
Deputy Crown Agent, J. D. Lowe £33,469

Companies Registration Office
100–102 George Street, Edinburgh EH2 3DJ

Registrar, E. T. K. Lougheed.

Sheriff Court of Chancery
16 North Bank Street, Edinburgh

Sheriff of Chancery, Sir Frederick O'Brien, Q.C.

H.M. Commissary Office
16 North Bank Street, Edinburgh

Commissary Clerk, D. B. White.

SCOTTISH LAND COURT
1 Grosvenor Crescent, Edinburgh

Chairman, The Hon. Lord Elliott, M.C.
Members, A. B. Campbell, O.B.E.; D. D. McDiarmid; R. MacDonald.

SHERIFFS PRINCIPAL, SHERIFFS, SHERIFF CLERKS AND PROCURATORS FISCAL IN SCOTLAND

Sheriffdom and Sheriff Principal	Sheriffs	Sheriff Clerks	Procurators Fiscal
Grampian, Highland and Islands.— S. E. Bell, Q.C.	*Aberdeen, Stonehaven,* A. M. G. Russell, Q.C.; A. L. Stewart; D. J. Risk; D. Bogie; D. Kelbie.	J. Rodden .... I. P. Smith	S. W. Lockhart, C.B.E. (*Regional Procurator Fiscal*). J. D. McNaughton.
	Banff and Peterhead, A. J. Murphy.	W. H. Connon ...... A. H. Hempseed	A. J. M. Colley. I. S. McNaughtan.
	Elgin, N. McPartlin.	I. Munro	A. Wither.
	Inverness, Lochmaddy, Portree, Stornoway, Dingwall, Tain, Wick, Dornoch, W. J. Fulton; D. Booker-Milburn; J. O. A. Fraser; E. Stewart.	J. S. Doig† .... W. Dunn	D. R. Hingston. C. B. McClory. C. S. Mackenzie. H. T. Westwater. B. Heywood.
	Kirkwall, Lerwick, A. A. MacDonald.	J. Rodden	A. W. Wright. Miss A. Thom.
	Fort William, D. Noble (*also Oban and Campbeltown*)	J. S. Doig†	J. I. M. MacGillivray.
Tayside, Central and Fife.— R. R. Taylor, Q.C., Ph.D.	*Arbroath, Forfar,* S. O. Kermack	B. T. McCabe ...... P. Dougan	C. D. G. Hillary. A. L. Ingram.
	Dundee, G. L. Cox; E. F. Bowen	B. J. Young†	D. R. Smith (*Regional Procurator Fiscal*).
	Perth, J. F. Wheatley; C. Smith*.	Miss J. Telfer	M. MacPhail.
	Falkirk, A. V. Sheehan; A. B. Wilkinson.	P. Feeney..........	G. E. Scott.
	Stirling, W. C. Henderson; R. E. G. Younger	K. MacKenzie......	K. Valentine. Miss M. W. Robertson.
	Alloa, R. E. G. Younger	R. G. Young	
	Cupar, J. C. McInnes (*also Perth*)	B. Sullivan	R. A. S. Brown.
	Dunfermline, J. S. Forbes; W. M. Reid.	J. Ross	R. T. Hamilton.
	Kirkcaldy, W. J. Christie; C. R. Macarthur, Q.C.	T. Fyffe	Mrs. I. Guild.
Lothian and Borders.— Sir Frederick O'Brien, Q.C.	*Edinburgh,* N. E. D. Thomson; J. L. M. Mitchell; P. G. B. McNeill, Ph.D.; Miss H. J. Aronson; R. G. Craik, Q.C.; G. I. W. Shiach; Miss I. A. Poole; R. J. D. Scott; I. D. MacPhail; G. W. S. Presslie; J. A. Farrell*; I. A. Cameron*.	D. B. White†	J. D. Lowe (*Regional Procurator Fiscal*).
	Peebles, N. E. D. Thomson (*also Edinburgh*).	D. B. White†	F. J. M. Brown.
	Linlithgow, M. Stone	R. Sinclair.........	H. R. Annan.
	Haddington, G. W. S. Presslie (*also Edinburgh*)	B. W. S. Manthorpe.	I. D. Douglas.
	Jedburgh, Duns, J. V. Paterson.	J. R. Jenkins.......	J. C. Whitelaw.
	Selkirk, J. V. Paterson	J. R. Jenkins.......	
North Strathclyde.— P. I. Caplan, Q.C.	*Oban and Campbeltown,* D. Noble (*also Fort William*).	R. Twaddle .... Miss F. Petrie ...... B. J. Carroll	I. Henderson.
	Dumbarton, J. P. Murphy; J. T. Fitzsimons; C. W. Palmer; F. H. Hamilton*.	N. R. Weir	J. Cardle.
	Paisley, A. K. F. Hunter; H. R. MacLean; R. G. Smith.	A. A. Brown†	J. B. R. Mackinnon (*Regional Procurator Fiscal*).
	Greenock, J. Irvine Smith (*also Rothesay*); Sir Stephen Young.	A. P. MacPherson ..	A. T. W. Wilson. W. D. Stewart.
	Kilmarnock, T. M. Croan; D. B. Smith; T. F. Russell.	J. Shaw	J. L. McLeod.

*Floating Sheriffs.   †Regional Sheriff Clerk.

Sheriffdom and Sheriff Principal	Sheriffs	Sheriff Clerks	Procurators Fiscal
Glasgow and Strathkelvin.— N. D. MacLeod, Q.C.	*Glasgow,* J. J. Maguire; A. A. Bell, Q.C.; B. Kearney; G. H. Gordon, Q.C.; A. C. McKay; A. Lothian; J. C. M. Jardine; Mrs. D. J. B. Robertson; B. A. Lockhart; I. G. Pirie; Miss A. L. A. Smith; W. G. Stevenson, Q.C.; G. J. Evans; E. H. Galt; F. J. Keane; A. C. Henry; A. M. Bell; J. K. Mitchell; A. G. Johnston.	C. McLay†	A. S. Jessop *(Regional Procurator Fiscal).*
South Strathclyde, Dumfries and Galloway.— J. S. Mowat	*Hamilton,* J. R. Fiddes, Q.C.; L. S. Lovat; A. C. MacPherson; W. F. Lunny; I. A. MacMillan, C.B.E.; V. J. Canavan *(also Airdrie)*; R. H. Dickson*.	J. Cumming	W. G. Carmichael *(Regional Procurator Fiscal).*
	Lanark, J. D. Allan.	A. S. Morwood	S. R. Houston.
	Ayr, N. Gow, Q.C.; R. G. McEwan, Q.C.	T. D. McIntosh	N. G. O'Brien.
	Stranraer, Kirkcudbright, J. R. Smith.	L. McFarlane	F. Walkingshaw.
	Dumfries, K. G. Barr; L. Cameron.	W. Jones	J. T. MacDougall.
	Airdrie, J. H. Stewart; J. S. Boyle; V. J. Canavan *(also Hamilton).*	H. Findlay†	A. C. Normand.

*Floating Sheriffs. †Regional Sheriff Clerk.

NORTHERN IRELAND JUDICATURE

In Northern Ireland the legal system and the structure of courts closely resemble those of England and Wales; there are, however, often differences in enacted law.

The Supreme Court of Judicature of Northern Ireland comprises the Court of Appeal, the High Court of Justice and the Crown Court. The practice and procedure of these Courts is similar to those in England. The superior civil court is the High Court of Justice, from which an appeal lies to the Court of Appeal; the House of Lords is the final civil appeal court.

The decision to prosecute in cases tried on indictment and in summary cases of a serious nature rests in Northern Ireland with the Director of Public Prosecutions, who is responsible to the Attorney General. Minor summary offences are prosecuted by the police.

Minor criminal offences are dealt with in magistrates' courts by a full-time, legally qualified resident magistrate and, where an offender is under 17, by juvenile courts consisting of the resident magistrate and two lay members specially qualified to deal with juveniles (at least one of whom must be a woman). Appeals from magistrates' courts are heard by the county court. The Crown Court, served by High Court and county court judges, deals with criminal trials on indictment. Cases are heard before a judge and, except those involving offences specified under emergency legislation, a jury. Appeals from the Crown Court against conviction or sentence are heard by the Northern Ireland Court of Appeal; the House of Lords is the final court of appeal.

Magistrates' courts in Northern Ireland can deal with certain classes of civil case but most minor civil cases are dealt with in county courts. Judgments of all civil courts are enforceable through a centralized procedure administered by the Enforcement of Judgments Office.

SUPREME COURT OF JUDICATURE

The Royal Courts of Justice
Belfast.

Lord Chief Justice of Northern Ireland, The Hon. Sir Brian Hutton.

Judges, The Rt. Hon. Lord Justice (Turlough) O'Donnell; The Rt. Hon. Lord Justice (Sir John William Basil) Kelly; The Rt. Hon. Lord Justice (Sir John Clarke) MacDermott; The Hon. Mr. Justice (Donald Bruce) Murray; The Hon. Mr. Justice (John Patrick Basil) Higgins; The Hon. Mr. Justice (Robert Douglas) Carswell; The Hon. Mr. Justice (James Michael Anthony) Nicholson; The Hon. Mr. Justice (William Paschal) McCollum.

Lord Chief Justice's Office

Principal Secretary to the Lord Chief Justice and Clerk of the Crown for Northern Ireland, J. A. L. McLean, Q.C.

Legal Secretary to the Lord Chief Justice, R. T. Millar.

Heads of Departments of Supreme Court:
Master, Central Office, V. A. Care, Q.C.
Master, Office of Care and Protection, F. B. Hall.
Master, Chancery Office, V. G. Bridges.
Master, Bankruptcy and Companies Office, J. B. C. Glass.
Master, Probate and Matrimonial Office, D. W. G. Heatly.
Master, Taxing Office, A. E. Anderson, C.B.E.
Accountant, Court Funds Office, J. Teer.

Master, High Court, J. W. Wilson.

Recorders

Belfast, Judge Pringle, Q.C.
Londonderry, Judge Hart, Q.C.

County Court Judges

Judge Babington, D.S.C., Q.C.; Judge Chambers, Q.C.; Judge Curran, Q.C.; Judge Gibson, Q.C.; Judge Hart, Q.C.; Judge McKee, Q.C.; Judge Petrie, Q.C.; Rt. Hon. Judge Sir Robert Porter, Q.C.; Judge Rowland, Q.C.; Judge Russell, Q.C.; Judge Watt, Q.C.; Judge Higgins, Q.C.

Crown Solicitor, H. A. Nelson.
Director of Public Prosecutions, Sir Barry Shaw, C.B., Q.C.

ECCLESIASTICAL COURTS

Original jurisdiction is exercised by the Consistory Court of each Diocese in England, presided over by the Chancellor of that Diocese. Appellate jurisdiction is exercised by the Provincial Courts detailed below, and by the Court for Ecclesiastical Causes Reserved, and by Commissions of Review (the membership of these being newly constituted for each case).

Court of Arches
(Province of Canterbury)
Registry: 16 Beaumont Street, Oxford OX1 2LZ

Dean of the Arches, The Rt. Worshipful Sir John Owen.

Court of the Vicar-General of the Province of Canterbury
Registry: 16 Beaumont Street, Oxford OX1 2LZ

Vicar-General, The Rt. Worshipful Miss S. Cameron, Q.C.

Chancery Court of York
Registry: 22 High Petergate, York YO1 2EH

Auditor, The Rt. Worshipful Sir John Owen.

The Vicar-General of the Province of York
Registry: 22 High Petergate, York YO1 2EH

Vicar-General, The Rt. Worshipful T. A. C. Coningsby, Q.C.

Court of Faculties
Registry: 1 The Sanctuary, SW1P 3JT

Office for the issue of special and ordinary marriage licences, appointment of notaries public, etc. Office hours, Mon.–Fri., 10–4.
Master of the Faculties, The Rt. Worshipful Sir John Owen.

TRIBUNALS, ETC

Employment Appeal Tribunal
Central Office, 4 St. James's Square, SW1Y 4JU
Divisional Office, 11 Melville Crescent, Edinburgh, EH3 7LU.
President, The Hon. Mr. Justice Wood.
Registrar, Miss V. J. Selio.

The Industrial Tribunals
Central Office (England and Wales)
93 Ebury Bridge Road, SW1W 8RE

President, His Honour Judge Sir David West-Russell
£50,900

Central Office (Scotland)
St. Andrew House, 141 West Nile Street,
Glasgow G1 2RU

President, R. C. Hay, C.B.E., W.S. £50,900

Immigration Appellate Authorities
Thanet House, 231 Strand, WC2R 1DA

Immigration Appeal Tribunal
President, D. L. Neve.
Vice-Presidents, G. W. Farmer; Prof. D. C. Jackson.

Immigration Appeal Adjudicators
Chief Adjudicator, M. Patel, M.B.E.

Lands Tribunal
48/49 Chancery Lane, WC2A 1JR

President, Sir Douglas Frank, Q.C.
Members, V. G. Wellings, Q.C.; W. H. Rees; C. R. Mallett; W. Hall, D.F.C., J. C. Hill, T.D.
Registrar, C. A. McMullan.

Lands Tribunal for Scotland
1 Grosvenor Crescent, Edinburgh EH12 5ER

President, The Hon. Lord Elliott, M.C.
Members, W. Hall, D.F.C.; Sheriff A. C. Horsfall, Q.C. (*full-time*); W. D. C. Andrews, C.B.E., W.S.; T. Finlayson; D. A. Shepherd (*part-time*).
Clerk, D. McCallum.

N.H.S. Tribunal
Inquires into representations that the continued inclusion of a family practitioner (doctor, dentist, pharmacist or optician) on a Family Practitioner Committee's list would be prejudicial to the efficiency of the services concerned. The Tribunal sits when required, about eight times a year, and usually in London.

Chairman, B. Hargrove, Q.C.
Clerk, I. D. Keith, Martlets House, 25–26 Queens Square, Crawley, W. Sussex RH10 1EU.

Pensions Appeal Tribunals
48/49 Chancery Lane, WC2A 1JR

Responsibility for hearing appeals in connection with War Pensions.

President, M. H. Fauvelle.

Performing Right Tribunal
Room 1509, State House, 66–71 High Holborn, WC1R 4TP

Chairman, W. Aldous, Q.C.
Secretary, J. E. Owens.

The Office of the President of Social Security Appeal Tribunals and Medical Appeal Tribunals
Almack House, 26–28 King Street, SW1Y 6QW

An independent statutory authority which exercises judicial and administrative control over social security appeal tribunals and medical appeal tribunals.

President, His Hon. Judge J. Byrt, Q.C.
Secretary, J. Connelly.

The Office of the Social Security Commissioners
London: Harp House, 83/86 Farringdon Street, EC4A 4BL
Edinburgh: 23 Melville Street, EH3 7PW

The final statutory authority to decide social security and medical claims.

Chief Commissioner, Hon. Judge Bromley, Q.C.
Secretary, Miss H. A. R. Baker (*London*); I. Erskine (*Edinburgh*).

The Solicitors' Disciplinary Tribunal
60 Carey Street, WC2A 2JB

Independent body with members appointed by the Master of the Rolls.

President, G. B. Marsh.
Clerk, Mrs. S. C. Elson.

Special Commissioners of Income Tax
Turnstile House, 98 High Holborn, WC1V 6LQ

Independent body appointed by the Lord Chancellor to hear appeals concerning income taxes, etc.

Presiding Special Commissioner, R. H. Widdows
£45,240
Special Commissioners, B. M. F. O'Brien; T. H. K. Everett; D. A. Shirley £36,367
Deputy Special Commissioners, D. C. Potter, Q.C.; His Hon. Judge Medd, O.B.E., Q.C.
Clerk, R. P. Lester £17,306

Transport Tribunal
4th Floor, Golden Cross House,
Duncannon Street, WC2N 4JF

President, Judge Inskip, Q.C.
Secretary, E. J. Thomas.

V.A.T. Tribunals
15/17 Great Marlborough Street, W1V 2AP

V.A.T. Tribunals are administered by the Lord Chancellor's Department (the Secretary of State in Scotland) and are intended to determine disputes concerning V.A.T.

President, His Hon. Judge Medd, O.B.E., Q.C.
Vice-President, Scotland, R. A. Bennett, Q.C.
Registrar, J. M. Busby.

Tribunal Centres
London (including Belfast), 15/17 Great Marlborough Street, W1V 2AP.
Edinburgh, 44 Palmerston Place, Edinburgh EH12 5BJ.
Manchester, Warwickgate House, Warwick Road, Old Trafford, Manchester M16 0GP.

Parliamentary and Local Government Election Petitions Office
Room 120, Royal Courts of Justice, Strand, WC2A 2LL

Prescribed Officer, I. S. Warren.

THE POLICE SERVICE

There are 52 police forces in the United Kingdom, each responsible for law enforcement in its area. Most forces' area is coterminous with an English or Welsh county or Scottish region, though there are several combined forces. Law enforcement in London is carried out by the Metropolitan Police and the City of London Police; in Northern Ireland by the Royal Ulster Police; and by the Isle of Man, States of Jersey, and Guernsey forces in their respective islands and bailiwicks.

Each police force is maintained by a police authority. The authorities of English and Welsh forces comprise committees of local councillors and magistrates; in Scotland, the regional and islands councils are the authorities. The authority for the Metropolitan Police is the Home Secretary. In Northern Ireland the Secretary of State appoints the police authority.

Police authorities are financed by central and local government. Subject to the approval of the Home Secretary and to regulations, they appoint the chief constable and, decide the maximum size of the force and provide buildings and equipment.

The Home Secretary and the Secretaries of State for Scotland and Northern Ireland are responsible for the organization, administration and operation of the police service. They make regulations covering matters such as police ranks, discipline, hours of duty, and pay and allowances.

All police forces (except the Metropolitan Police) are subject to inspection by H.M. Inspectors of Constabulary, who report to the respective Secretary of State.

The investigation of a serious complaint against a police officer is supervised by the Police Complaints Authority in England and Wales. In Scotland, complaints are investigated by independent public prosecutors.

Basic rates of police pay
(since Sept. 1, 1987; *since Sept. 1, 1988; †since Oct. 1, 1988)

Chief Constable .... £36,906–£46,914
Deputy Chief Constable .... £32,511–£37,530
Assistant Chief Constable £30,960
Chief Superintendent............ £28,494–£30,255*
Superintendent .... £25,629–£27,831*
Chief Inspector .... £18,840–£20,958*
Inspector .... £16,593–£18,840*
Sergeant .... £14,466–£16,593*
Constable .... £8,352–£15,123*

Metropolitan Police

Metropolitan Commissioner .... £68,500†
Deputy Commissioner £49,983
Assistant Commissioner £44,097
Deputy Assistant Commissioner £35,277
Commander £30,960

POLICE AUTHORITIES IN THE UNITED KINGDOM

Police Force	Headquarters	Actual Strength	Chief Constable	Chairman of Police Authority/Committee
England				
Avon and Somerset	Bristol	3,030	R. Broome, O.B.E., Q.P.M.	R. Mullet
Bedfordshire	Bedford	1,006	A. Dyer, Q.P.M.	*
Cambridgeshire	Huntingdon	1,155	I. H. Kane, Q.P.M.	D. H. Morris
Cheshire	Chester	1,829	D. J. Graham, Q.P.M.	J. H. Collins, O.B.E.
Cleveland	Middlesbrough	1,474	C. F. Payne, C.B.E.,Q.P.M.	Mrs. I. Cole
Cumbria	Penrith	1,147	L. Sharp, Q.P.M.	Maj. T. R. Riley
Derbyshire	Ripley	1,798	A. O. Smith, Q.P.M.	A. Barnes
Devon and Cornwall	Exeter	2,810	(vacant)	B. R. Homer
Dorset	Dorchester	1,235	B. H. Weight, Q.P.M.	Maj. Gen. H. M. G. Bond
Durham	Durham	1,343	F. W. Taylor	A. Agar
Essex	Chelmsford	2,797	J. H. Burrow, O.B.E.	G. C. Waterer, M.B.E.
Gloucestershire	Cheltenham	1,156	A. H. Pacey, Q.P.M.	C. P. Hay
Hampshire	Winchester	3,085	J. C. Hoddinott, Q.P.M.	Capt. M. P. R. Boyle
Hertfordshire	Welwyn Garden City	1,621	T. A. Morris, Q.P.M.	D. R. Williams
Humberside	Hull	1,972	D. Hall, C.B.E., Q.P.M.	C. Brady
Kent	Maidstone	2,980	F. L. Jordan, Q.P.M.	J. A. Lawton, C.B.E.
Lancashire	Preston	3,157	R. B. Johnson, Q.P.M.	J. Entwistle
Leicestershire	Leicester	1,754	M. J. Hirst, Q.P.M.	R. R. Angrave
Lincolnshire	Lincoln	1,183	S. W. Crump, Q.P.M.	M. D. Kennedy
Greater Manchester	Manchester 16	6,961	C. J. Anderton, C.B.E., Q.P.M.	S. Murphy
Merseyside	Liverpool 69	4,685	Sir Kenneth Oxford, C.B.E., Q.P.M.	G. Bundred
Norfolk	Norwich	1,347	G. Charlton, Q.P.M.	J. S. Peel, M.C.
Northamptonshire	Northampton	1,094	D. J. O'Dowd, Q.P.M.	A. A. Morby
Northumbria	Newcastle upon Tyne	3,512	Sir Stanley Bailey, C.B.E., Q.P.M.	G. Gill
Nottinghamshire	Nottingham	2,259	R. Hadfield	F. Higgins
Staffordshire	Stafford	2,152	C. H. Kelly, C.B.E., Q.P.M.	Miss I. H. Moseley
Suffolk	Ipswich	1,183	S. L. Whiteley, C.B.E., Q.P.M.	Capt. R. J. Sheepshanks
Surrey	Guildford	1,712	B. Hayes, Q.P.M.	J. F. Whitfield
Sussex	Lewes	2,888	R. Birch, C.B.E., Q.P.M.	Mrs. P. A. Drake
Thames Valley	Oxford	3,576	C. Smith, C.V.O., Q.P.M.	Lt. Col. J. C. Walton
Warwickshire	Warwick	983	P. D. Joslin, Q.P.M.	H. W. De'Ath
West Mercia	Worcester	1,957	A. A. Mullett, Q.P.M.	Mrs. M. J. T. Hadley, O.B.E.
West Midlands	Birmingham 4	6,624	G. J. Dear, Q.P.M.	D. M. Ablett
Wiltshire	Devizes	1,069	W. R. Girven, Q.P.M.	J. E. H. Church.
Yorkshire, North	Northallerton	1,369	P. J. Nobes, Q.P.M.	J. H. G. Parfect, M.B.E.
Yorkshire, South	Sheffield	2,895	P. Wright, C.B.E.	J. Layden
Yorkshire, West	Wakefield	5,218	C. Sampson, O.B.E.	K. Wilson
Wales				
Dyfed-Powys	Carmarthen	920	D. J. Shattock, Q.P.M.	J. H. Lloyd
Gwent	Cwmbran	985	J. E. Over, Q.P.M., C.P.M	B. Sutton
North Wales	Colwyn Bay	1,316	D. Owen, Q.P.M.	M. H. Phillips
South Wales	Bridgend	3,115	D. A. East, Q.P.M.	J. Allison, C.B.E.
Scotland				
Central Scotland	Stirling	578	I. T. Oliver, Q.P.M., Ph.D.	S. Conner
Dumfries and Galloway	Dumfries	344	J. M. Boyd, Q.P.M.	K. A. Kelly
Fife	Kirkcaldy	754	W. M. Moodie, Q.P.M.	R. Gough
Grampian	Aberdeen	1,018	A. G. Lynn, C.B.E., Q.P.M.	W. A. Grant
Lothian and Borders	Edinburgh 4	2,435	Sir William Sutherland, Q.P.M.	W. G. Rankine
Northern	Inverness	620	H. C. MacMillan, Q.P.M.	J. S. Munro
Strathclyde	Glasgow 2	6,768	A. K. Sloan, Q.P.M.	W. Harley
Tayside	Dundee	1,001	J. W. Bowman, Q.P.M.	Mrs. P. Doran
Northern Ireland				
Royal Ulster Constabulary	Belfast 5	8,268	Sir John Hermon, O.B.E., Q.P.M.	T. Rainey
Islands				
Isle of Man	Douglas	191	R. E. N. Oake	E. G. Lowey, M.L.C.
States of Jersey	St. Helier	213	†D. Parkinson	R. J. Shenton
Guernsey	St. Peter Port	179	†M. Le Moignan	M. W. Torode

† Chief Officer   * Elected at every meeting

METROPOLITAN POLICE FORCE
New Scotland Yard, Broadway, SW1H 0BG

[01–230 1212]

Establishment: 28,115

Commissioner, Sir Peter Imbert, Q.P.M.
Deputy Commissioner, J. Dellow, C.B.E.
Receiver, D. H. J. Hilary £47,320
Deputy Receiver, J. E. Owen £31,844

Territorial Operations Department

Assistant Commissioner, G. D. McLean, C.B.E., Q.P.M.
Deputy Assistant Commissioner, D. Cree.
Head of Administration, Miss B. Arnold
£19,537–£26,348
Commanders, N. B. Dickens; J. P. Robinson, Q.P.M.;
W. E. E. Boreham.

Area Headquarters

Deputy Assistant Commissioners, D. H. Cree, Q.P.M.;
T. J. Siggs, O.B.E.; D. N. Meynell; R. Innes, Q.P.M.;
P. L. Condon; R. B. Wells, Q.P.M.; G. W. Jones,
Q.P.M.; M. J. Evans, Q.P.M.
Commanders, G. M. Ness; J. A. Coo; G. E. Howlett,
Q.P.M.; Miss T. M. Wagstaff; L. T. Roach; Miss J.
Hilton; D. N. Stevens; G. R. Lloyd, Q.P.M.; M. J.
Gough; M. J. Sullivan; A. G. Fry; C. J. Rideout,
Q.P.M.; K. W. Masterson; J. E. Metcalf; D. Flanders;
D. M. T. Kendrick; A. J. Speed.

Specialist Operations Department

Assistant Commissioner, H. N. Annesley, Q.P.M.
Deputy Assistant Commissioners, J. H. Cracknell,
L.V.O., Q.P.M.; S. R. A. Crawshaw, Q.P.M.; J. M. M.
Huins, Q.P.M.; P. Phelan, Q.P.M.
Commanders, M. R. Campbell; K. G. Churchill-
Coleman; A. W. F. Hemingway, Q.P.M.; J. M. Allain,
Q.P.M.; D. C. Veness; D. C. Gunn; R. A. Penrose; R.
C. Adams, B.E.M.; J. A. Howley.

Metropolitan Police Laboratory

Director, Dr. B. Sheard .... £25,756–£29,344
Deputy Directors, G. J. O. Lee; M. R. Loveland; P. D.
Martin; Dr. W. D. C. Wilson ..... £19,537–£26,348
Senior Principal Scientific Officer, B. B. Wheals
£19,537–26,348

Personnel and Training Department

Assistant Commissioner, C. B. J. Sutton, Q.P.M.
Deputy Assistant Commissioner, A. W. Young.
Commanders, D. M. Cansdale; E. Mitchell, Q.P.M.; D.
Y. Cooke.
Welfare Officer, K. F. T. Rivers, M.B.E.
£15,631–£21,104

Metropolitan Police Cadet Corps
Commander, D. M. Cansdale.

Medical and Dental Branch
Chief Medical Officer, Dr. E. C. A. Bott

Management Support Department

Assistant Commissioner, J. A. Smith, Q.P.M.
Deputy Assistant Commissioner, P. J. Winship.
Commander, A. E. Marnock, Q.P.M.

Complaints Investigation Bureau
Commander, K. J. Merton, Q.P.M.

Directorate of Public Affairs
Director of Public Affairs, B. D. Goodfellow
£25,756–£29,344
Deputy Director of Public Affairs, J. P. Stubbs
£19,537–£26,348

Directorate of Management Services
Director, N. E. Hand .... £25,756–£29,344

Deputy Directors, P. I. May; Mrs. S. M. Merchant
£19,537–£26,348

Force Inspectorate

Deputy Assistant Commissioner, R. A. Hunt, O.B.E.
Commanders, E. D. Humphrey; E. Jones.

Solicitor's Department

Solicitor, C. S. Porteous £31,844
Assistant Solicitors, R. E. Marsh; P. A. Shawdon; D.
S. Hamilton .... £25,756–£29,344

The following departments are responsible to the
Receiver through the Deputy Receiver.

"E" Department
Establishments and Secretariat

Establishment Officer, R. B. Jones .. £25,756–£29,344
Deputy Establishment Officers, D. F. F. Hannaford;
D. Wilson; A. M. J. Williams ..... £19,537–£26,348

"F" Department
Finance

Director of Finance, J. A. Crutchlow £25,756–£29,344
Deputy Directors of Finance, J. L. Davies; J. E. Tubb;
M. W. Maidment .... £19,537–£26,348

Supplies and Services Department
Director, N. N. I. Batten .... £19,537–£26,348

Catering Department
Director of Catering, R. J. Downing . £19,537–£26,348

Property Services Department
Director of Property Services, T. G. Lawrence
£25,756–£29,344
Deputy Directors, R. M. Boa; K. R. Sewell; D. F.
Hobart .... £19,537–£26,348

Chief Engineer's Department

Chief Engineer, N. Boothman ...... £25,756–£29,344
Deputy Chief Engineers, D. A. Woolgar; G. Sudbury;
J. T. Clifton; R. J. Perham .... £19,537–£26,348

Department of Computing Services

Director of Computing Services, R. G. Gregory
£25,756–£29,344
Deputy Directors of Computing Services, D. K. Dun-
kin; T. Egan .... £19,537–£26,348

CITY OF LONDON POLICE
26 Old Jewry, EC2R 8DJ

[01-601 2222]

Strength of Force (July 1988), 801

Commissioner, O. Kelly, Q.P.M. £48,507
Assistant Commissioner, W. Taylor £37,812
Commander, H. J. Moore £30,960
Chief Superintendents, E. Aggar *(Administration);* P.
Nove *(Traffic & Communications);* T. Hillier *("B"
Divn.);* R. Knevett *("C" Divn.);* P. Gwynn *(C.I.D.);*
G. Squires *(C.I.D/Fraud)* .... £26,262–£28,359

BRITISH TRANSPORT POLICE
15 Tavistock Place, WC1H 9SJ

[01-388 7541]

The Force provides a policing service to the British
Railways Board and its wholly-owned subsidiary
company, London Underground Ltd. Police posts are
located throughout England, Wales and Scotland.
Chief Constable, K. H. Ogram, Q.P.M.
Deputy Chief Constable, G. E. Coles.
Assistant Chief Constables, T. H. S. Buckle *(Admin-
istration);* W. I. McGregor *(Operations);* J. Nixon

(*Personnel & Training*); W. F. Palmer (*London Underground Division*); A. M. Mackenzie (*Scottish Division*).

MINISTRY OF DEFENCE POLICE
Ministry of Defence, Empress State Building,
Lillie Road, SW6 1TR
[01–385 1244]

The Ministry of Defence Police are responsible chiefly for the policing of naval, military, R.A.F. establishments, etc. in Great Britain.
Chief Constable, J. Aspinall.
Deputy Chief Constable, N. L. Chapple, Q.P.M.
Head of M.D.P. Secretariat, B. Aves.
Assistant Chief Constable (Operations), A. A. J. Scale.

Area Headquarters
Central Area, Campbell Block, R.A.F. Stafford, Staffs.—*Assistant Chief Constable*, A. F. Grant.
Northern Area, Hilton Road, Rosyth, Fife.—*Assistant Chief Constable*, C. Bucke.
Southern Area, Aldershot, Hants.—*Assistant Chief Constable*, R. E. Murray.
Western Area, Spring Quarry, Copenacre, Hawthorn, Wilts.—*Assistant Chief Constable*, S. G. Edwards.

STAFF ASSOCIATIONS
ASSOCIATION OF CHIEF POLICE OFFICERS OF ENGLAND, WALES AND NORTHERN IRELAND, Room 1133, New Scotland Yard, Broadway, SW1H 0BG.—Represents the Chief Constables, Deputy Chief Constables and Assistant Chief Constables of England, Wales and N. Ireland, and officers of the rank of Commander and above in the Metropolitan and City of London Police. *Gen. Sec.*, G. Maxted.

THE POLICE SUPERINTENDENTS' ASSOCIATION OF ENGLAND AND WALES, 67A Reading Road, Pangbourne RG8 7JD.—Represents officers of the rank of Superintendent and Chief Superintendent. *Sec.*, Chief Supt. K. A. Smith.

THE POLICE FEDERATION OF ENGLAND AND WALES, 15–17 Langley Road, Surbiton, Surrey KT6 6LP.—Represents officers up to and including the rank of Chief Inspector. *Gen. Sec.*, Insp. V. Nield.

ASSOCIATION OF CHIEF POLICE OFFICERS (SCOTLAND), Police Headquarters, Fettes Avenue, Edinburgh EH4 1RB.—Represents the Chief Constables, Deputy Chief Constables and Assistant Chief Constables of the Scottish police forces. *Hon. Sec.*, Chief Constable Sir William Sutherland, Q.P.M.

THE ASSOCIATION OF SCOTTISH POLICE SUPERINTENDENTS, Hon. Secretary's Office, Strathclyde Police, Divisional Headquarters, Campbell Street, Hamilton ML3 6AT.—Represents officers of the rank of Superintendent and Chief Superintendent. *Hon. Sec.*, Chief Supt. J. McNicol.

THE SCOTTISH POLICE FEDERATION, 5 Woodside Place, Glasgow G3 7PD.—Represents officers up to and including the rank of Chief Inspector. *Gen. Sec.*, A. W. A. Wallace.

THE SUPERINTENDENTS ASSOCIATION OF NORTHERN IRELAND, Ormiston House, Hawthornden Road, Belfast BT4 3NH.—Represents Superintendents and Chief Superintendents in the R.U.C. *Hon. Sec.*, W/Chief Supt. A. Donald.

THE POLICE FEDERATION FOR NORTHERN IRELAND, Royal Ulster Constabulary, Garnerville, Garnerville Road, Belfast BT4 2NX.—Represents officers up to and including the rank of Chief Inspector. *Gen. Sec.*, J. Elder.

POLICE FORCE STRENGTHS

Number

	1980	1981	1982	1983	1984	1985	1986
England and Wales							
Regular police							
Authorised establishment	118,930	120,008	120,125	120,447	120,679	120,903	121,785
Strength:							
Men	105,563	107,379	108,517	108,519	108,102	107,960	108,225
Women...................	10,355	10,702	10,935	10,995	11,001	11,213	11,600
Seconded:							
Men	1,430	1,424	1,419	1,407	1,388	1,439	1,617
Women...................	75	70	80	82	82	90	108
Additional constables:							
Men	96	90	89	84	83	79	88
Women...................	1	1	1	2	–	1	1
Scotland							
Regular police							
Authorised establishment:	13,187	13,195	13,205	13,261	13,283	13,377	13,489
Strength:							
Men	12,419	12,379	12,433	12,435	12,415	12,455	12,504
Women...................	771	749	719	713	722	761	838
Central service:							
Men	60	54	55	65	61	69	70
Women...................	5	2	2	2	2	1	2
Seconded:							
Men	69	78	73	68	67	67	88
Women...................	2	5	4	3	3	3	4
Additional regular police:							
Authorised establishment ..	72	67	62	60	88	88	86
Strength	71	66	62	60	88	88	86
Northern Ireland							
Royal Ulster Constabulary							
Strength:							
Men	6,224	6,622	7,017	7,328	7,487	7,610	7,581
Women...................	711	712	701	675	640	649	653

THE ARMED FORCES

MINISTRY OF DEFENCE
Main Building, Whitehall, SW1A 2HB
[01–218 9000]

Salaries

Secretary of State	£34,157
Minister of State, Commons	£23,887
Minister of State, Lords	£34,688
Parliamentary Under Secretaries	£17,897
Grade 1	£68,500
Grade 1A	£62,750
Grade 2	£45,800–£48,000
Grade 3	£35,800–£39,000
Grade 4	£30,344–£31,844

(For Services salaries, *see* pp. 404–9.)

Secretary of State for Defence, THE RT. HON. GEORGE YOUNGER, T.D., M.P.
Private Secretary, B. R. Hawtin.
Parliamentary Private Secretary, G. A. Neale, M.P.
Minister of State for the Armed Forces, HON. ARCHIBALD HAMILTON, M.P.
Private Secretary, Miss P. M. Aldred.
Parliamentary Under Secretary of State for the Armed Forces, R. N. Freeman, M.P.
Private Secretary, Dr. A. Cowpe.
Minister of State for Defence Procurement, THE LORD TREFGARNE.
Private Secretary, C. E. V. Hain-Cole.
Parliamentary Private Secretary, K. Hind, M.P.
Parliamentary Under Secretary of State for Defence Procurement, The Hon. T. Sainsbury, M.P.
Private Secretary, H. D. Kernohan.
Permanent Under Secretary of State (G1), Sir Michael Quinlan, K.C.B.
Private Sec., C. J. Wright.
Chief of Defence Staff, Marshal of the R.A.F. Sir David Craig, G.C.B., O.B.E.

Defence Staff

Vice Chief of the Defence Staff, Gen. Sir Richard Vincent, K.C.B., D.S.O.
Deputy Under Sec. of State (Policy) (G2), D. A. Nicholls, C.M.G.
Deputy Chief of the Defence Staff (Commitments), Lt.-Gen. Sir Antony Walker, K.C.B.
Asst. Under Sec. of State (Commitments) (G3), N. Bevan.
Asst. C.D.S. (N.A.T.O./U.K.), Air Vice-Marshal M. J. D. Stear, C.B.E.
Asst. C.D.S. (Overseas), Rear-Adm. E. S. J. Larken.
Asst. C.D.S. (Logistics), Maj.-Gen. I. S. Baxter, C.B.E.
Deputy C.D.S. (Systems), Vice-Adm. Sir Jeremy Black, K.C.B., D.S.O., M.B.E.
Asst. C.D.S. (Concepts), Maj.-Gen. J. R. Templer, O.B.E.
Asst. C.D.S., Operational Requirements (Sea), Rear-Adm. C. L. Wood.
Asst. C.D.S., Operational Requirements (Land), Maj.-Gen. A. R. G. Mullens, O.B.E.
Asst. C.D.S., Operational Requirements (Air), Air Vice-Marshal G. C. Williams, A.F.C.
Asst. C.D.S. (C.C.C.I.S.), Air Vice-Marshal D. A. Saunders, C.B.E.
Asst. C.D.S. (Policy and Nuclear), Air Vice-Marshal E. H. Macey, O.B.E.
Asst. Under Sec. of State (Policy) (G3), J. M. Legge.
Deputy C.D.S. (Programmes and Personnel), Air Marshal Sir David Parry-Evans, K.C.B., C.B.E.
Asst. C.D.S. (Programmes), Rear-Adm. B. N. Wilson.
Surgeon Gen. and Dir. Gen. Naval Medical Services, Vice-Adm. Sir Godfrey Milton-Thompson, K.B.E., Q.H.P.

Deputy Surgeon Gen. (Ops.), Dir. Gen. Medical Services (Army), Maj.-Gen. A. J. Shaw.
Deputy Surgeon Gen. (Research and Training), Medical Dir. Gen. (R.A.F.), Air Vice-Marshal N. H. Mills.

Defence Intelligence Staff

Chief of Defence Intelligence, Vice-Adm. J. B. Kerr.
Dir. Gen. Intelligence (Rest of World), Air Vice-Marshal R. J. Kemball, C.B.E.
Dir., Management and Support Intelligence, Maj.-Gen. I. O. J. Sprackling, O.B.E.
Dir., Scientific and Technical Intelligence (G3), Dr. J. W. Berry.
Dir., Economic and Logistic Intelligence (G4), D. H. Hills.

Naval Department

Chief of Naval Staff and First Sea Lord, Adm. Sir William Staveley, G.C.B., A.D.C.
Asst. Chief of Naval Staff, Rear-Adm. H. M. White, C.B.E.
Hydrographer of the Navy, Rear-Adm. R. O. Morris.
Cmdt. Gen. Royal Marines, Lt.-Gen. Sir Martin Garrod, K.C.B., O.B.E.
Chief of Naval Personnel and Second Sea Lord, Vice-Adm. B. T. Brown, C.B.E.
Naval Secretary, Rear-Adm. D. S. Dobson.
Dir. Gen., Naval Manpower and Training, Rear-Adm. N. Purvis.
Dir. Gen., Naval Personal Services, Rear-Adm. A. M. Norman.
Chief of Fleet Support, Vice-Adm. Sir Benjamin Bathurst, K.C.B.
Dir. Gen., Ship Refitting, Rear-Adm. D. R. Sherval.
Dir. Gen., Supplies and Transport (G3), J. T. Baugh.
Dir., Supplies and Transport (Armaments and Managements Services) (G4), W. N. Cooke.
Dir., Supplies and Transport (Stores, Moves and Victualling) (G4), G. E. Miller.
Dir. Gen., Fleet Support Policy and Services, Rear-Adm. R. T. Frere.
Dir. Gen., Aircraft (Navy), Rear-Adm. D. M. Pulvertaft.
Chaplain of The Fleet, Ven. N. D. Jones, C.B., Q.H.C.

Army Department

Chief of the General Staff, General Sir John Chapple, G.C.B., C.B.E.
Asst. Chief of the General Staff, Maj.-Gen. C. R. L. Guthrie, L.V.O., O.B.E.
Dir., Military Survey, Maj.-Gen. P. F. Fagan, M.B.E.
Dir. Gen., T.A. and Organization, Maj.-Gen. C. A. Ramsay, O.B.E.
Dir. Gen., Training and Doctrine (Army), Maj.-Gen. A. J. G. Pollard, C.B.E.
Dir., Royal Armoured Corps, Maj.-Gen. N. G. P. Ansell, O.B.E.
Dir., Royal Artillery, Maj.-Gen. P. R. F. Bonnet, M.B.E.
Dir., Infantry, Maj.-Gen. J. D. G. Pank.
Dir., Army Air Corps, Maj.-Gen. L. F. H. Busk.
Engineer in Chief (Army), Maj.-Gen. R. L. Peck.
Signal Officer in Chief (Army), Maj.-Gen. P. D. Alexander, M.B.E.
Military Secretary, Lt.-Gen. Sir Patrick Palmer, K.B.E.
Adjutant-General, Gen. Sir Robert Pascoe, K.C.B., M.B.E.
Dir. Gen., Army Manning & Recruiting, Maj.-Gen. A. B. Crowfoot, C.B.E.
Paymaster in Chief, Maj.-Gen. B. M. Bowen, C.B.

Dir. Gen., Personal Services (Army), Maj.-Gen. P. P. D. Stone, C.B.E.
Dir. Security (Army), Maj.-Gen. H. E. M. L. Garrett, C.B.E. (retd.).
Dir., Army Legal Services, Maj.-Gen. M. T. Fugard.
Dir., Army Education, Maj.-Gen. J. S. Lee, M.B.E.
Quartermaster General, Lt.-Gen. C. E. W. Jones, C.B.E.
Dir. Gen., Logistic Policy (Army), Maj.-Gen. P. W. E. Istead, O.B.E., G.M.
Dir. Gen., Transport and Movements, Maj.-Gen. C. E. G. Carrington, C.B.E.
Dir. Gen., Ordnance Services, Maj.-Gen. J. A. Hulme.
Dir. Gen., Electrical and Mechanical Engineering, Maj.-Gen. D. Shaw, C.B.E.
Chaplain General, Ven. Archd. W. F. Johnston, C.B., Q.H.C.

Air Force Department

Chief of the Air Staff, Air Chief Marshal Sir Peter Harding, K.C.B.
Asst. Chief of Air Staff, Air Vice-Marshal M. G. Simmons, C.B., A.F.C.
Cmdt. Gen. (R.A.F. Regt.) and Dir. Gen. of Security, Air Vice-Marshal J. H. Harris, C.B.E.
Controller of National Air Traffic Services, K. R. Mack, (C.A.A.)
Air Member for Personnel, Air Marshal Sir Laurence Jones, K.C.B., A.F.C.
Air Secretary, Air Vice-Marshal R. A. Mason, C.B.E.
Dir. Gen., R.A.F. Personal Services, Air Vice-Marshal D. W. Hann.
Dir. Gen., Training, Air Vice-Marshal M. J. Pilkington, C.B.E.
Air Member for Supply and Organization, Air Chief Marshal Sir Brendan Jackson, K.C.B.
Dir. Gen., Communications, Information Systems and Organization, Air Vice-Marshal J. A. Porter.
Chief Engineer, Air Marshal F. M. Holroyd, C.B.
Dir. Gen., Supply, Air Vice-Marshal R. C. Allerton.
Chaplain-in-Chief, Rev. B. N. Halfpenny, Q.H.C.

Defence Scientific Staff

Chief Scientific Adviser (G1A), Prof. E. R. Oxburgh.
Deputy Chief Scientific Adviser (G3), J. F. Barnes.
Asst. Chief Scientific Advisers (G3), D. E. Humphries (Projects and Research); Mrs. M. J. Bourne, O.B.E. (Capabilities); (G4) Dr. R. G. Ridley (Nuclear).
Dir., Defence Operational Analysis Establishment (G3), R. J. Poole.
Dir. Gen., Strategic Defence Initiative Participation Office (G3), Dr. S. Orman.

Office of Management and Budget

Second Permanent Under Secretary of State (G1A), K. C. Macdonald, C.B.
Deputy Under Secs. of State (G2), M. J. V. Bell (Finance); R. M. Hastie-Smith, C.B. (Civilian Management); R. L. L. Facer (Personnel and Logistics); C. T. McDonnell (Resources and Programmes).
Asst. Under Secs. of State (G3), T. J. Brack (Naval Personnel); J. E. Carruthers (Supply and Organization (Air)); B. H. Cousins, C.B.E. (General Finance); M. J. Cuiham (Civilian Management (Administrators)); I. D. Dawson (Resources); B. M. Day, C.B. (Fleet Support); M. Gainsborough (Adj. Gen.); K. W. B. Gooderham (Security and Common Services); Dr. M. J. Harte (Personnel (Air)); D. C. R. Heyhoe (Dir. Gen. of Management Audit); J. F. Howe (Personnel and Logistics); C. E. Johnson (Dir. Gen. of Defence Accounts); R. C. Mottram (Programmes); D. B. Omand; J. E. Pestell (Civilian Management (Specialists)); W. D. Reeves (Systems); J. Roberts; B. F. Rule (Dir. Gen. Information Technology Systems); B. A. E. Taylor (Quartermaster).

Public Relations

Chief of Public Relations (G4), H. B. Colver.

PROCUREMENT EXECUTIVE

Chief of Defence Procurement (G1), P. K. Levene.
Private Sec., S. French.

Procurement Executive Policy and Administration

Deputy Under Sec. of State (Defence Procurement) (G2), J. M. Stewart, C.B.
Asst. Under Sec. of State (Equipment Collaboration), (G3), J. L. Roberts.
Dir. Gen. Defence Quality Assurance (G3), B. Miller.
Dir. Gen. Defence Contracts (G3), B. J. Slade.
Principal Dir. Accountancy Services (P.E.) (G4), J. V. A. Crawford.
Principal Dir. Technical Costs (G4), R. E. Rowe.
Principal Dir. of Patents (G4), E. J. Mansfield.

Research and Development Controllerate

Controller Establishments, Research and Nuclear Programmes, D. M. Spiers, C.B., T.D.
Asst. Under Sec. of State Research Establishments and Research Admin. (G3), W. F. Mumford.
Deputy Controller (Nuclear) (G3), J. C. Mabberley.
Deputy Controller (Research) (G3), Dr. T. Buckley.
Dir., Admiralty Research Establishment (G3), P. D. Ewins.
Dir., Royal Signals and Radar Establishment (G2), N. H. Hughes.
Dir., Atomic Weapons Establishment (G2), Dr. T. P. McLean.
Dir., Chemical Defence Establishment (G3), Dr. G. F. Pearson.
Dir., Royal Armament Research and Development Establishment (G2/3), Dr. A. C. Baynham.
Commandant, Aeroplane and Armament Experimental Establishment, Air Cdre. P. D. L. Gover.
Dir., Royal Aircraft Establishment (G2), Dr. G. G. Pope, C.B.
Chief Engineer, (G4), R. H. Lovell.

Sea Systems Controllerate

Controller of the Navy, Adm. Sir Derek Reffell, K.C.B.
Asst. Under Sec. of State (Material-Naval) (G3), A. K. Bull.
Principal Dir., Navy and Nuclear Contracts (G4), A. J. Figes.
Chief Strategic Systems Executive, Rear-Adm. I. H. Pirnie.
Deputy Chief Strategic Systems Executive, Cdre. J. S. Kelly, O.B.E.
Dir. Gen. Strategic Weapon Systems, Cdre. T. W. Craven.
Deputy Controller Warships, Vice-Adm. Sir Hugh Thompson, K.B.E.
Dir. Gen. Surface Ships (G3), A. J. Creighton.
Dir. Gen. Submarines (G3), W. G. Sanders.
Chief Naval Architect (G3), B. O. Wall.
Chief Naval Weapons System Engineer (G4), D. McArthur.
Deputy Controller Warship Equipment (G3), P. E. Chamberlain.
Dir. Gen. Surface Weapons (G4), H. Perkins.
Dir. Gen. Underwater Weapons, Cdre. K. J. Eaton.
Dir. Gen. Marine Engineering, Chief Marine Systems Engineer, Rear-Adm. R. A. Issac.

Land Systems Controllerate

Master General of the Ordnance, Lt.-Gen. Sir John Stibbon, K.C.B., O.B.E.

Vice Master General of the Ordnance, Maj.-Gen. G. M. Hutchinson.

Asst. Under Sec. of State (Ordnance) (G3), M. D. Tidy.

Principal Dir., Contracts (Ordnance) (G4), R. G. Woodman, C.B.E.

Dir. Gen., Guided Weapons and Electronics (G3), J. D. Maines.

Dir. Gen., Fighting Vehicles and Engineer Equipment, Maj.-Gen. S. R. A. Stopford, C.B., M.B.E.

Dir. Gen., Weapons (Army), Maj.-Gen. E. G. Willmott, O.B.E.

Air Systems Controllerate

Controller Aircraft, Air Chief Marshal Sir David Harcourt-Smith, K.C.B., D.F.C.

Dep. Controller Aircraft (G2), M. T. Peters.

Asst. Under Sec. of State/Air (Procurement Executive) (G3), J. M. Moss.

Principal Dir., Contracts/Air (G4), D. Grassby.

Dir. Gen. Aircraft 1, Air Vice-Marshal, R. M. Austin.

Dir. Gen. Aircraft 2, D. G. Jones.

Dir. Gen. Aircraft 3, (G3), J. W. Britton.

Dir. Gen., Air Weapons Electronic Systems (G3), K. G. Hambleton.

Dir. Gen., Strategic Electronic Systems, Air Vice-Marshal M. J. D. Brown.

Defence Export Services Organization

Head of Defence Export Services (G2), Sir Colin Chandler.

Military Deputy to Head of D.E.S., Maj.-Gen. C. N. Last, O.B.E.

Dir. Gen. Saudi Airforce Projects, Air Vice-Marshal R. I. Stuart-Paul, M.B.E.

Dir. Gen., Marketing (G3), T. F. W. B. Knapp.

Asst. Under Sec. of State (D.E.S. Admin.) (G3), C. Henn.

METEOROLOGICAL OFFICE

London Road, Bracknell, Berks.

[Bracknell: 420242]

The Meteorological Office is the State Meteorological Service. It forms part of the Ministry of Defence, the Director General being ultimately responsible to the Secretary of State for Defence.

Except for the common services provided by other government departments as part of their normal functions, the cost of the Meteorological Office is borne by Defence Votes.

Of the expenditure chargeable to Defence Votes about £35,000,000 represents expenditure associated with staff and £34,000,000 on stores, communications and miscellaneous services. About £25,500,000 is recovered from outside bodies for special services rendered, sales of meteorological equipment, etc.

Dir. Gen., Dr. J. T. Houghton, C.B.E., D.Phil., F.R.S.

£45,800

Dir. of Services, Dr. D. N. Axford £39,000

Dir. of Research, A. Gilchrist £31,844

RELATIVE RANK—SEA, LAND AND AIR

Royal Navy	Army	Royal Air Force
1. Admiral of the Fleet.	1. Field Marshal.	1. Marshal of the R.A.F.
2. Admiral (Adm.).	2. General (Gen.).	2. Air Chief Marshal.
3. Vice-Admiral (Vice-Adm.).	3. Lieutenant-General (Lt.-Gen.).	3. Air Marshal.
4. Rear-Admiral (Rear-Adm.).	4. Major-General (Maj.-Gen.).	4. Air Vice-Marshal.
5. Commodore (1st & 2nd Class) (Cdre.).	5. Brigadier (Brig.).	5. Air Commodore (Air Cdre.).
6. Captain (Capt.).	6. Colonel (Col.).	6. Group Captain (Gp. Capt.).
7. Commander (Cdr.).	7. Lieutenant-Colonel (Lt.-Col.).	7. Wing Commander (Wg. Cdr).
8. Lieutenant Commander (Lt. Cdr.).	8. Major (Maj.).	8. Squadron Leader (Sqn. Ldr).
9. Lieutenant (Lt.).	9. Captain (Capt.).	9. Flight Lieutenant (Flt.-Lt.).
10. Sub-Lieutenant (Sub-Lt.).	10. Lieutenant (Lt.).	10. Flying Officer (F.O.).
11. Acting Sub-Lieutenant (Acting Sub-Lt.).	11. Second Lieutenant (2nd. Lt.).	11. Pilot Officer (P.O.).

THE ROYAL NAVY

THE QUEEN

Admirals of the Fleet

H.R.H. The Prince Philip, Duke of Edinburgh, K.G., K.T., O.M., G.B.E., P.C., *born* June 10, 1921 ..... Jan. 15, 1953
Sir Varyl Begg, G.C.B., D.S.O., D.S.C., *born* Oct. 1, 1908 .... Aug. 12, 1968
The Lord Hill-Norton, G.C.B., *born* Feb. 8, 1915 .... March 12, 1971
Sir Michael Pollock, G.C.B., L.V.O., D.S.C., *born* Oct. 19, 1916 .... March 1, 1974
Sir Edward Ashmore, G.C.B., D.S.C., *born* Dec. 11, 1919 .... Feb. 9, 1977
The Lord Lewin, K.G., G.C.B., L.V.O., D.S.C., *born* Nov. 19, 1920 .... July 6, 1979
Sir Henry Leach, G.C.B., *born* Nov. 18, 1923 .... Dec. 1, 1982
Sir John Fieldhouse, G.C.B., G.B.E., *born* Feb. 12, 1928 .... Aug. 2, 1985

Admirals

Staveley, Sir William, G.C.B., A.D.C., (*First Sea Lord and Chief of Naval Staff*).
Fitch, Sir Richard, K.C.B.
Woodward, Sir John, K.C.B., (*C.-in-C. Naval Home Command*).
Oswald, Sir Julian, K.C.B., (*C.-in-C. Fleet, Allied C.-in-C. Channel and C-in-C. Eastern Atlantic Area*).
Reffell, Sir Derek, K.C.B., (*Controller of the Navy*).

Vice-Admirals

Symons, Sir Patrick, K.B.E., (*Representative to SACLANT in Europe*).
Webster, Sir John, K.C.B. (*Flag Officer, Plymouth, Naval Base Commander Devonport, Commander Central Sub. Area, Eastern Atlantic and Plymouth Sub. Area Channel*).
Thompson, Sir Hugh, K.B.E., (*Deputy Controller Warships, Senior Naval Representative Bath and Chief Naval Engineer Officer*).
Black, Sir Jeremy, K.C.B., D.S.O., M.B.E., (*Deputy Chief of the Defence Staff (Systems)*).
Thomas, Sir William, K.C.B., O.B.E., (*Deputy Supreme Allied Commander Atlantic*).
Bathurst, Sir Benjamin, K.C.B., (*Chief of Fleet Support*).
Slater, Sir John, K.C.B., L.V.O., (*Flag Officer Scotland and N. Ireland, Commander Northern Sub. Area Eastern Atlantic, and Commander NORE Sub. Area Channel, and Naval Base Commander Rosyth*).
Kerr, J. B., (*Chief of Defence Intelligence*).
King, N. R. D., (*Chief of Staff to Commander, Allied Naval Forces Southern Europe*).
Brown, B. T., C.B.E. (*Second Sea Lord, Chief of Naval Personnel, and Admiral President Royal Naval College Greenwich.*
Milton-Thompson, Sir Godfrey, K.B.E., Q.H.P., (*Dir. Gen. Naval Medical Services and Surgeon Gen.*).

Rear-Admirals

Marsh, G. G. W., C.B., O.B.E., (*Project Manager N.F.R.90*)
Livesay, M. H.
Morris, R. O., (*Hydrographer of the Navy*).
Dimmock, R. C., C.B., (*Flag Officer Naval Air Command*).
Dingemans, P. G. V., D.S.O., (*Chief of Staff to C.-in-C. Fleet*).
Garnier, J., C.B.E., L.V.O., (*Flag Officer Royal Yachts*).
Sherval, D. R., (*Dir. Gen. Ship Refitting*).
Balfour, H. M., L.V.O., (*Commander, Sultan of Oman's Navy*).
Grenier, P. F., (*Flag Officer Submarines and COMSUBEAST-LANT*).
Wilson, B. N., (*Asst. C.D.S. (Programmes*)).
O'Riordan, J. P. B., C.B.E., (*Military Deputy Commandant, N.A.T.O. Defence College, Rome*).
Wood, C. L., (*Asst. C.D.S. Operational Requirements (Sea Systems*)).
Isaac, R. A., (*Dir. Gen. Marine Engineering*).
Layman, C. H., D.S.O., L.V.O., (*Asst. Dir. (Communications and Information Systems) on the I.M.S.*).
Grose, A., (*Flag Officer Third Flotilla*).
Norman, A. M., (*Dir. Gen. Naval Personal Services*).
Cole, M. C., (*Commander British Naval Staff Washington, Naval Attaché Washington and U.K. National Liaison Representative to SACLANT*).
Liardet, G. F., C.B.E.
Weatherall, J. L. (*Deputy Asst. Chief of Staff (Operations) on the Staff of the Supreme Allied Commander Europe*).
Purvis, N., (*Dir. Gen. Naval Manpower and Training*).
Howard, C. J., (*Chief of Staff to C.-in-C. Naval Home Command, and Chief Naval Instructor Officer*).
White, H. M., C.B.E., (*Asst. Chief of Naval Staff*).
Coward, J. F., D.S.O., (*Flag Officer First Flotilla*).
Eaton, K. J., (*Flag Officer Portsmouth, Naval Base Commander Portsmouth and Head of Establishment of the Fleet Maintenance and Repair Organization*).
Hill-Norton, N. J. (*Flag Officer Gibraltar, Gibraltar Naval Base Commander and COM-GIBMED*).
Hill, R. C. F. (*Chief Staff Officer (Engineering) to C.-in-C. Fleet*).
Pulvertaft, D. M. (*Dir. Gen. Aircraft (Naval*)).
Larken, E. S. J., D.S.O. (*Asst. C.D.S. (Overseas*)).
Dobson, D. S., (*Naval Secretary*).
Woodhead, A. P., (*Flag Officer Second Flotilla*).
Allen, D., C.B.E. (*Defence Services Secretary*).
Pirnie, I. H., (*Chief Strategic Systems Executive*).
Hilton, J. M. T., (*President of the Ordnance Board*).
Salt, J. F. T. G., (*Senior Naval Member of Directing Staff, Royal College of Defence Studies*).
Newman, R. T., (*Flag Officer Sea Training*).
Frere, R. T., (*Dir. Gen. Fleet Support Policy and Services*).
Layard, M. H. G., C.B.E., (*Flag Officer Naval Air Command*).
Snow, R. E., L.V.O., O.B.E., Q.H.P.
Lammiman, D. A., L.V.O., Q.H.S.

HER MAJESTY'S FLEET

Type/Class	No.	Operational or engaged in preparing for service or trials or training	No.	Undergoing restorative or major refit or conversion, on standby etc.
Submarines				
Polaris	3	*Repulse, Resolution, Revenge*	1	*Renown*
Fleet	13	*Churchill, Conqueror, Courageous, Sovereign, Swiftsure, Superb, Splendid, Sceptre, Trafalgar, Turbulent, Tireless, Torbay, Trenchant**	3	*Valiant, Warspite, Spartan*

Type/Class	No.	Operational or engaged in preparing for service or trials or training	No.	Undergoing restorative or major refit or conversion, on standby etc.
Type 2400	1	Upholder*		
Oberon Class	9	Olympus, Opportune, Odin, Onslaught, Otter, Otus, Ocelot, Onyx, Osiris	2	Oracle, Opossum
ASW Carriers	2	Illustrious, Ark Royal	1	Invincible
Assault Ships	1	Intrepid†	1	Fearless
Guided-Missile Destroyers				
Type 82	1	Bristol		
Type 42	10	Exeter, Birmingham, Southampton, Nottingham, Liverpool, Manchester, York, Gloucester, Edinburgh, Newcastle	2	Cardiff, Glasgow
Frigates				
Type 22	11	Battleaxe, Brazen, Boxer, Beaver, Brave, London, Sheffield†, Cornwall†, Coventry*, Cumberland*, Campbeltown*	2	Broadsword, Brilliant
Type 21	5	Amazon, Ambuscade, Active, Avenger†, Alacrity	1	Arrow
Leander Class	16	Achilles, Charybdis, Diomede, Euryalus, Penelope, Arethusa, Phoebe, Sirius, Minerva, Danae, Andromeda, Scylla, Apollo, Ariadne, Cleopatra, Jupiter	2	Hermione, Argonaut
Rothesay Class	1	Plymouth		
Navigation Training Ship	1	Juno†		
Offshore Patrol				
Castle Class	1	Dumbarton Castle	1	Leeds Castle
Island Class	7	Alderney, Guernsey, Lindisfarne, Orkney, Shetland, Anglesey, Jersey		
MCMVs				
Minesweepers	2	Cuxton, Soberton	2	Upton, Walkerton
River Class	12	Waveney, Carron, Dovey, Helford, Humber, Blackwater, Itchen, Helmsdale, Orwell, Ribble, Spey, Arun		
Minehunters Ton Class	10	Brereton†, Brinton, Bronington, Iveston, Kedleston, Kellington, Maxton, Nurton, Sheraton, Wilton	3	Kirkliston, Gavinton, Hubberston
Hunt Class	12	Brecon, Brocklesby, Ledbury, Cottesmore, Dulverton, Middleton, Chiddingfold, Hurworth, Bicester, Atherstone, Berkeley†, Quorn*	1	Cattistock
Patrol Craft				
Bird Class	5	Cygnet, Kingfisher, Peterel†, Sandpiper†, Redpole		
Coastal Training Craft	15	Attacker†, Fencer†, Hunter†, Chaser†, Striker†, Archer†, Biter†, Smiter†, Pursuer†, Blazer†, Dasher*, Puncher*, Charger*, Ranger*, Trumpeter*		
Peacock Class	5	Peacock, Plover, Starling, Swallow, Swift		
Gibraltar Search and Rescue Craft	2	Cormorant, Hart		
Support Ships				
Submarine Tender	1	Sentinel		
MCM Support Ship	1	Abdiel		
Seabed Operations Vessel	1	Challenger		
Royal Yacht/Hospital Ship	1	Britannia		
Training Ships				
Fleet Tenders	4	Manly†, Messina†, Milbrook†, Mentor†		
Ice Patrol Ship	1	Endurance		
Survey Ships	8	Bulldog, Fox, Hecate, Herald, Gleaner, Hecla, Roebuck, Beagle	1	Fawn

Notes:

(i) This table includes ships due for completion or disposal during the course of 1988/89; the numbers of each type are not therefore an accurate indication of the ships available at any one time. Ships solely engaged in harbour training duties are not included.

(ii) Ships marked * were under construction on April 1, 1988 and are planned to enter service during 1988/89.

(iii) Ships marked † are engaged partially on trials or training.

(iv) Ships approved during 1987/88 for disposal: Fife, Rothesay, Naiad, Aurora, Orpheus, Sealion, Stubbington, Wakeful.

Royal Naval Auxiliary Service.—The Royal Naval Auxiliary Service (RNXS) is a uniformed civilian volunteer service, administered by the Ministry of Defence and trained by the Royal Navy to operate at ports and anchorages, for duty in emergencies and war. RNXS units are situated on the coasts of the United Kingdom and organized and run by the Area Flag Officers. The role of the RNXS is to assist with the defence of ports and anchorages by manning local headquarters and supporting the Naval Control of Shipping Organization. The strength is 3,000.
Patron, H.R.H. Prince Michael of Kent.

ROYAL MARINES

The Corps of Royal Marines, about 7,000 strong, first formed in 1664, is part of the Naval Service. The Royal Marines provide Britain's sea soldiers and in particular 3 Commando Brigade Royal Marines, two thirds of which is trained and equipped for arctic warfare. Royal Marines also serve in H.M. Ships, provide landing craft crews, special boat sections and other detachments for naval and amphibious operations. They also provide the Naval Band Service.

The Royal Marines Reserve of about 1,350 volunteers consists of five main centres in London, Bristol, Liverpool, Newcastle and Glasgow.
Commandant General, Royal Marines, Lt.-Gen. Sir Martin Garrod, K.C.B., O.B.E.
Major-Generals, H. Y. La R. Beverley, O.B.E. (*Chief of Staff*); R. J. Ross, O.B.E. (*Training Reserve and Special Forces*); N. F. Vaux, D.S.O. (*Commando Forces*).

QUEEN ALEXANDRA'S ROYAL NAVAL NURSING SERVICE (Q.A.R.N.N.S.)

The first nursing sisters were appointed to naval hospitals in 1884 and the service gained its current title under the patronage of Queen Alexandra in 1902. Nursing ratings were introduced in 1960 and from 1982 a number of men have taken the opportunity to join Q.A.R.N.N.S. as both officers and ratings. Still largely based at the Royal Naval Hospitals, Q.A.R.N.N.S. continue their responsibility for the health and fitness of naval personnel. The strength is about 430.
Patron, H.R.H. Princess Alexandra.
Matron-in-Chief, Miss E. M. Northway, R.R.C., Q.H.N.S., Q.A.R.N.N.S.

WOMEN'S ROYAL NAVAL SERVICE (W.R.N.S.)

Originally founded in 1917, the W.R.N.S. were temporarily disbanded between World Wars I and II. The contribution of the Service is now firmly established as a professional and integral part of the Royal Navy with personnel serving in the United Kingdom and abroad in a wide range of specialist roles. Although W.R.N.S. do not serve at sea, they provide an essential nucleus of about 3,000 trained personnel ashore in order to release men to H.M. Ships.
Chief Commandant, H.R.H. Princess Anne.
Director W.R.N.S., Commandant A. Larken, A.D.C., W.R.N.S.

THE ARMY

THE QUEEN

Field Marshals

H.R.H. The Prince Philip, Duke of Edinburgh, K.G., K.T., O.M., G.B.E., P.C., *born* June 10, 1921	Jan. 15, 1953
The Lord Harding of Petherton, G.C.B., C.B.E., D.S.O., M.C., *born* Feb. 10, 1896	July 21, 1953
Sir Richard A. Hull, K.G., G.C.B., D.S.O., *born* May 7, 1907	Feb. 8, 1965
Sir A. James H. Cassels, G.C.B., K.B.E., D.S.O., *born* Feb. 28, 1907	Feb. 29, 1968
The Lord Carver, G.C.B., C.B.E., D.S.O., M.C., *born* April 24, 1915	July 18, 1973
Sir Roland Gibbs, G.C.B., C.B.E., D.S.O., M.C., *born* June 22, 1921	July 13, 1979
The Lord Bramall, G.C.B., O.B.E., M.C., *born* Dec. 18, 1923	Aug. 1, 1982
Sir John W. Stanier, G.C.B., M.B.E., *born* Oct. 6, 1925	July 10, 1985
Sir Nigel Bagnall, G.C.B., C.V.O., M.C., A.D.C. (*Gen.*), *born* Feb. 10, 1927	Sept. 9, 1988

Generals

Mostyn, Sir David, K.C.B., C.B.E., A.D.C. (*Gen.*), Col. Cmdt. A.L.C.

Howlett, Sir Geoffrey, K.B.E., M.C., Col. Cmdt. P.A.R.A., Col. Cmdt. A.C.C., (*C.-in-C. AFNORTH*).

Vincent, Sir Richard, K.C.B., D.S.O., Col. Cmdt. R.A., (*Vice Chief of the Defence Staff*).

Chapple, Sir John, G.C.B., C.B.E., A.D.C. (*Gen.*), Col. 2 GR (*Chief of the General Staff*).

Akehurst, Sir John, K.C.B., C.B.E., Col. R. Anglian, (*D. SACEUR*).

Huxtable, Sir Charles, K.C.B., C.B.E., Col. D.W.R. (*C.-in-C. U.K.L.F.*).

Kenny, Sir Brian, K.C.B., C.B.E., Col. Cmdt. R.A.V.C., Col. Q.R.I.H., Col. Cmdt. R.A.C., (*C.-in-C. B.A.O.R. and Commander Northern Army Group*).

Pascoe, Sir Robert, K.C.B., M.B.E., Col. Cmdt. 1 R.G.J., (*Adjutant General*).

Stibbon, Sir John, K.C.B., O.B.E., Col. Cmdt. R.A.P.C., Col. Cmdt. R.P.C., Col. Cmdt. R.E., (*Master General of the Ordnance*).

Lieutenant-Generals

Boorman, Sir Derek, K.C.B., Col. Staffords.

Reilly, Sir Jeremy, K.C.B., D.S.O., Col. Cmdt. The Queen's Division, Col.

R.R.F., (*Comd. Training and Arms Directors*).

Palmer, Sir Patrick, K.B.E., Col. A. & S.H., (*Military Secretary*).

Walker, Sir Antony, K.C.B., Col. Cmdt. R.T.R., (*Deputy Chief of the Defence Staff (Commitments)*).

Ramsbotham, Sir David, K.C.B., C.B.E., Col. Cmdt. 2GR, (*Comd. U.K. Fd. Army and Inspec. Gen. T.A.*).

Inge, Sir Peter, K.C.B., Col. Green Howards, Col. Cmdt. R.M.P., (*Comd. I (B.R.) Corps.*).

Billiere, Sir Peter de la, K.C.B., C.B.E., D.S.O., M.C., Col. Cmdt. The Light Division, (*G.O.C., S.E. District*).

MacMillan, Sir John, K.C.B., C.B.E., Col. Cmdt. The Scottish Division, (*G.O.C. Scotland and Governor Edinburgh Castle*).

Jones, C. E. W., C.B.E., Col. Cmdt. R.A.E.C., (*Quartermaster General*).

Waters, Sir Charles, K.C.B., C.B.E., Col. Glosters, (*G.O.C. & D. Mil. Ops. Northern Ireland*).

Major-Generals

Shortis, C. T., C.B., C.B.E., Col. Cmdt. P.O.W. Divn., Col. D and D, (*G.O.C. N.W. District*).

Cornock, C. G., C.B., M.B.E., Col. Cmdt. R.A., (*Chief of Staff LIVE OAK*).

Pank, J. D. G., Col. L.I., (*Dir. Infantry*).

Airy, C. J., C.B.E., (*G.O.C. London District and Maj.-Gen. Comd. The Household Divn.*).

Cooper, S. C., (*Cmdt. Royal Military Academy Sandhurst.*).

Guthrie, C. R. L., L.V.O., O.B.E., Col. Cmdt. Int. Corps., (*Asst. Chief of the General Staff*).

Jeapes, A. S., C.B., O.B.E., M.C., (*G.O.C. S.W. District*).

Johnson, G. D., O.B.E., M.C., Col. 10 G.R., (*C.B.F. Hong Kong and Maj.-Gen. Brigade of Gurkhas*).

Learmont, J. H., C.B.E., Col. Cmdt. A.A.C., (*Cmdt. Staff College*).

Mullens, A. R. G., O.B.E., (*Asst. Chief of Defence Staff O.R. (Land)*).

Ramsay, C. A., O.B.E., (*Dir. Gen., T.A. and Organization*).

Alexander, P. D., M.B.E., (*Signal Officer in Chief (Army)*).

Beckett, E. H. A., C.B., M.B.E., (*Col. Cmdt. The King's Division, (Head of British Defence Staff, Washington)*).

Brooking, P. G., C.B., M.B.E., (*G.O.C. Berlin*).

Evans, J. A. M., (*Senior Army Member, Royal College of Defence Studies*).

Stopford, S. R. A., C.B., M.B.E., (*Dir. Gen. Fighting Vehicles and Engineer Equipment*).

Shaw, A. J., C.B., C.B.E., Q.H.P., (*D.G.A.M.S. and D.S.G. (Ops.)*).

Bowen, B. M., C.B., (*Paymaster-in-Chief*).

Willmott, E. G., O.B.E., (*Col. Cmdt. R.E., (Dir. Gen. Weapons (Army))*).

Fawcus, G. B., (*Chief of Staff LIVE OAK (designate)*).

Ward, R. W., M.B.E., (*G.O.C. W. District*).

Bonnet, P. R. F., M.B.E., (*Dir. Royal Artillery*).

Crowfoot, A. B., C.B.E., (*Dir. Gen., Army Manning and Recruiting*).

Quayle, T. D. G., (*Comd. Arty 1 (B.R.) Corps*).

Templer, J. R., O.B.E., (*Asst. Chief of Defence Staff (Concepts)*).

Busk, L. F. H., (*Dir. Army Air Corps*).

Fugard, M. T., (*Dir. Army Legal Services*).

Graham, P. W., C.B.E., Col. Gordons, (*G.O.C. E. District*).

Pollard, A. J. G., C.B.E., Col. Cmdt. S.A.S.C., Dep. Col. R. Anglian, (*Dir. Gen. Training and Doctrine*).

Tyler, C., (*Dep. Chief of Staff (Support) H.Q. AFNORTH*).

Coakley, P. K., Q.H.S., (*Dir. Army Surgery*).

Ansell, N. G. P., O.B.E., (*Dir. Royal Armoured Corps*).

Baxter, I. S., C.B.E., (*Asst. Chief of Defence Staff (Logistics)*).

Davies, P. R., Col. King's, (*Comd. Comms. B.A.O.R.*).

Hodges, R. J., O.B.E., Col. Kings Own Border, (*C.L.F. and D.D. Ops. N. Ireland*).

Istead, P. W. E., O.B.E., G.M., (*Dir. Gen. Logistic Policy (Army)*).

Last, C. N., O.B.E., (*Mil. Dep. to the Head of Defence Export Services*).

Lee, J. S., M.B.E., (*Dir. Army Education*).

Sprackling, I. O. J., O.B.E., (*Dir. Gen. Management and Support Intelligence*).

Scott, R., (*Cmdt. Royal Army Medical College and Post Graduate Dᵉan*).

Blacker, A. S. J., C.B.E., Col. Cmdt. R.E.M.E., Col. Cmdt. R.T.R., (*Cmdt. R.M.C.S.*).

Carlier, A. N., O.B.E., (*Chief Jt. Services Liaison Organization Bonn*).

Fagan, P. F., M.B.E., (*D. G. Mil. Svy.*).

Llewellyn, R. M., O.B.E., (*G.O.C. Wales*).

Naylor, D. M., M.B.E., (*G.O.C. N.E. District Comd. 2 Inf. Divn.*).

Rous, The Hon. W. E., O.B.E., (*Comd. 4 Armd. Divn.*).

Swinburn, R. H., (*Comd. 1 Armd. Divn.*).

Macphie, D. L., Q.H.S., (*Comd. Med. B.A.O.R.*).

Beale, P. J., Q.H.P., (*Comd. Med. U.K.L.F.*).

Boyd-Carpenter, The Hon. T. P. J., M.B.E., (*Chief of Staff H.Q. B.A.O.R.*).

Hulme, J. A., (*Dir. Gen. Ordnance Services*).

Peck, R. L., (*Engineer-in-Chief (Army)*).

Shaw, D., C.B.E., (*Dir. Gen. Electrical and Mechanical Engineering*).

Stone, P. P. D., C.B.E., Dep. Col. R. Anglian, (*Dir. Gen. Personal Services (Army)*).

Wilsey, I. F. W., C.B.E., (*Chief of Staff H.Q. U.K.L.F.*).

Hutchinson, G. M., (*Vice Master General of the Ordnance*).

Brown, M.

Friedberger, J. P. W., C.B.E., (*Cdr. British Forces Cyprus and Admin. Sovereign Base Areas*).

Wilkes, M. J., O.B.E., (*Comd. 3 Armd. Divn.*).

Carrington, C. E. G., C.B.E., (*Dir. Gen. Transport and Movements*).

CONSTITUTION OF THE BRITISH ARMY

The Regular Forces include the following Arms, Branches and Corps. Soldiers' Record Offices are shown at the end of each group; records of officers are maintained at the Ministry of Defence.

The Arms

Household Cavalry.—The Life Guards; The Blues and Royals (Royal Horse Guards and 1st Dragoons). *Records,* Horse Guards, London, SW1.

Royal Armoured Corps.—Cavalry Regiments: 1st The Queen's Dragoon Guards; The Royal Scots Dragoon Guards (Carabiniers and Greys); 4th/7th Royal Dragoon Guards; 5th Royal Inniskilling Dragoon Guards; The Queen's Own Hussars; The Queen's Royal Irish Hussars; 9th/12th Royal Lancers (Prince of Wales's); The Royal Hussars (Prince of Wales's Own), 13th/18th Royal Hussars (Queen Mary's Own); 14th/20th King's Hussars; 15th/19th The King's Royal Hussars; 16th/5th The Queen's

Royal Lancers; 17th/21st Lancers; Royal Tank Regiment comprising four regular regiments. *Records,* Queen's Park, Chester.

Artillery.—Royal Regiment of Artillery. *Records,* Imphal Barracks, Fulford Road, York.

Engineers.—Corps of Royal Engineers. *Records,* Kentigern House, Brown Street, Glasgow.

Signals.—Royal Corps of Signals. *Records,* Kentigern House, Brown Street, Glasgow.

Infantry.—The Foot Guards and Regiments of Infantry of the Line are grouped in Divisions as follows:—

Guards Division—Grenadier, Coldstream, Scots, Irish and Welsh Guards. Divisional HQ: HQ Household Division, Horse Guards, SW1. *Depot:* Pirbright Camp, Brookwood, Surrey. *Records:* Imphal Barracks, Fulford Road, York.

Scottish Division—The Royal Scots (The Royal Regiment); The Royal Highland Fusiliers (Princess Margaret's Own Glasgow and Ayrshire Regiment);

The King's Own Scottish Borderers; The Black Watch (Royal Highland Regiment); Queen's Own Highlanders (Seaforth and Camerons); The Gordon Highlanders; The Argyll and Sutherland Highlanders (Princess Louise's). *Divisional HQ*, The Castle, Edinburgh. *Depots*, Scottish Divisional Depots, Glencorse, Milton Bridge, Midlothian and Albemarle Barracks, Ouston, Newcastle. *Records*, Imphal Barracks, Fulford, York.

Queen's Division—The Queen's Regiment, The Royal Regiment of Fusiliers, The Royal Anglian Regiment. *Divisional HQ*, Bassingbourn Barracks, Royston, Herts. *Depot*, Bassingbourn Barracks, Royston, Herts. *Records*, Higher Barracks, Exeter, Devon.

King's Division—The King's Own Royal Border Regiment, The King's Regiment; The Prince of Wales's Own Regiment of Yorkshire; The Green Howards (Alexandra, Princess of Wales's Own Yorkshire Regiment); The Royal Irish Rangers (27th (Inniskilling) 83rd and 87th); The Queen's Lancashire Regiment; The Duke of Wellington's Regiment (West Riding). *Divisional HQ*, Imphal Barracks, York. *Depots*, The King's Division Depot (Yorkshire), Queen Elizabeth Barracks, Strensall, Yorks., and Albemarle Barracks, Ouston, Newcastle. The King's Division Depot (Royal Irish Rangers), St. Patrick's Barracks, Ballymena, Northern Ireland. *Records*, Imphal Barracks, Fulford, York.

Prince of Wales's Division—The Devonshire and Dorset Regiment; The 22nd (Cheshire) Regiment; The Royal Welch Fusiliers, The Royal Regiment of Wales (24th/41st Foot); The Gloucestershire Regiment; The Worcestershire and Sherwood Foresters Regiment (29th/45th Foot); The Royal Hampshire Regiment; The Staffordshire Regiment (The Prince of Wales's); The Duke of Edinburgh's Royal Regiment (Berkshire and Wiltshire). *Divisional HQ*, Whittington Barracks, Lichfield, Staffs. *Depots*, The Prince of Wales's Division Depot, Whittington Barracks, Lichfield, Staffs. *Records*, Imphal Barracks, Fulford, York.

Light Division—The Light Infantry; The Royal Green Jackets. *Divisional HQ*, Sir John Moore Barracks, Winchester, Hants., *Depot*, Sir John Moore Barracks, Winchester, Hants. *Records*, Higher Barracks, Exeter.

Brigade of Gurkhas—2nd King Edward VII's Own Gurkha Rifles (The Sirmoor Rifles); 6th Queen Elizabeth's Own Gurkha Rifles; 7th Duke of Edinburgh's Own Gurkha Rifles; 10th Princess Mary's Own Gurkha Rifles, The Queen's Gurkha Engineers, Queen's Gurkha Signals, Gurkha Transport Regt.

Brigade HQ, H.M.S. *Tamar*, Hong Kong, B.F.P.O. 1. *Depot*, Training Depot, Brigade of Gurkhas, Malaya Lines, Sek Kong, B.F.P.O. 1. *Records*, Record Office, Brigade of Gurkhas, Hong Kong, B.F.P.O. 1.

The Parachute Regiment (Three regular battalions)—*Depot*, Browning Barracks, Aldershot, Hants. *Records*, Higher Barracks, Exeter.

Special Air Service Regiment—*Regimental HQ*, Duke of York's Headquarters, Sloane Square, SW3. *Depot*, Stirling Lines, Hereford. *Records*, Higher Barracks, Exeter, Devon.

Army Air Corps—Regimental H.Q. and Depot, Middle Wallop, Hants. *Records*, Higher Barracks, Exeter.

The Services

Royal Army Chaplain's Department—Regimental H.Q. and Depot, Bagshot Park, Surrey.

Royal Corps of Transport, *Records*, Kentigern House, Brown Street, Glasgow.

Royal Army Medical Corps, Royal Army Dental Corps, Queen Alexandra's Royal Army Nursing Corps, and Women's Royal Army Corps. *Records*, Queen's Park, Chester.

Royal Army Ordnance Corps, Corps of Royal Electrical and Mechanical Engineers. *Records*, Glen Parva Barracks, Saffron Road, Wigston, Leicester.

Small Arms School Corps. *Records*, Higher Barracks, Exeter.

General Service Corps. *Records*, Imphal Barracks, Fulford Road, York.

Corps of Royal Military Police, Royal Army Pay Corps, Royal Army Veterinary Corps, Royal Pioneer Corps, Intelligence Corps, Army Catering Corps, Military Provost Staff Corps, Royal Army Educational Corps, Army Physical Training Corps, Army Legal Corps, Sandhurst, Officers Training Corps. *Records*, Higher Barracks, Exeter, Devon.

The Territorial Army (T.A.) is designed to provide a highly trained and well equipped force which will complete the Regular Army order of battle in a time of national emergency. Its establishment is approximately 84,000 and it is planned that this will rise to 86,000 by 1990. A new element of the T.A., the Home Service Force, designed to produce a low cost guard force, is being expanded to some 5,000 posts by 1990.

The Ulster Defence Regiment (U.D.R.) was raised under authority of the *U.D.R. Act* 1969 and assists the Regular Army in Northern Ireland. H.Q., Magheralave Road, Lisburn, Co. Antrim. *Records*, Imphal Barracks, Fulford Road, York.

QUEEN ALEXANDRA'S ROYAL ARMY NURSING CORPS (Q.A.R.A.N.C.)

Founded in 1902 as Q.A.I.M.N.S., became Q.A.R.A.N.C. in 1959. Q.A.R.A.N.C. has trained nurses for the register and roll since 1950 and has four other employment categories. There was an introduction of a non-nursing officer element in 1959 for personnel work. The Q.A.R.A.N.C. provides service in military hospitals world-wide—United Kingdom (including N. Ireland), B.A.O.R., Hong Kong, Dharan, Cyprus, Falkland Islands and Belize.

Colonel-in-Chief, H.R.H. Princess Margaret.
Director of Defence Nursing Services, Brig. M. B. T. Hennessy, C.B.E., R.R.C., Q.H.N.S.

WOMEN'S ROYAL ARMY CORPS (W.R.A.C.)

The W.R.A.C. was formed on February 1, 1949 as a Corps of the Regular Army. The Corps predecessors were Q.M.A.A.C. in World War I, and A.T.S. in World War II. The present role of the W.R.A.C. is to be organized and trained, as an integral part of the Army, to carry out those tasks for which its members are best suited and qualified, so that it will contribute to the maximum efficiency of the Army as a whole. The Corps is approximately 8,500 (Regular and T.A.) and is employed by 36 sponsors in 30 employments in 500 units world-wide in the British Army.

Commandant-in-Chief, H.M. Queen Elizabeth The Queen Mother.
Controller Commandant, H.R.H. The Duchess of Kent.
Deputy Controller Commandant, Brig. A. Field, C.B.
Director, Women's Royal Army Corps, Brig. S. P. Nield, A.D.C.

THE ROYAL AIR FORCE

THE QUEEN

Marshals of the Royal Air Force

H.R.H. the Prince Philip, Duke of Edinburgh, K.G., K.T., O.M., G.B.E., P.C., *born* June 10, 1921 ...... Jan. 15, 1953
Sir Dermot A. Boyle, G.C.B., K.C.V.O., K.B.E., A.F.C., *born* Oct. 2, 1904 .... Jan 1, 1958
The Lord Elworthy, K.G., G.C.B., C.B.E., D.S.O., M.V.O., D.F.C., A.F.C., *born* March 23, 1911 .... April 1, 1967
Sir John Grandy, G.C.B., G.C.V.O., K.B.E., D.S.O., *born* Feb. 8, 1913 (*Governor and Constable of Windsor Castle*) .... April 1, 1971
Sir Denis Spotswood, G.C.B., C.B.E., D.S.O., D.F.C., *born* Sept. 26, 1916 .... March 31, 1974
Sir Michael Beetham, G.C.B., C.B.E., D.F.C., A.F.C., A.D.C., *born* May 17, 1923 .... Oct. 15, 1982
Sir Keith Williamson, G.C.B., A.F.C., *born* Feb. 25, 1928 .... Oct. 15, 1985
Sir David Craig, G.C.B., O.B.E. (*Chief of Defence Staff*), *born* Sept., 17, 1929 .... Nov. 14, 1988

Air Chief Marshals

Harding, Sir Peter, G.C.B., (*Chief of the Air Staff*).

Hine, Sir Patrick, K.C.B., (*A.O.C.-in-C. Strike Command*).

Knight, Sir Michael, K.C.B., A.F.C., A.D.C., (*U.K. Military Representative, H.Q. N.A.T.O.*).

Armitage, Sir Michael, K.C.B., C.B.E., (*Cmdt. Royal College of Defence Studies*).

Gilbert, Sir Joseph, K.C.B., C.B.E., (*Deputy C.-in-C., Allied Forces Central Europe*).

Harcourt-Smith, Sir David, K.C.B., D.F.C., (*Controller Aircraft*).

Air Marshals

Parry-Evans, Sir David, K.C.B., C.B.E., (*Deputy Chief of Defence Staff (Programmes and Personnel)*).

Sutton, Sir John, K.C.B., (*A.O.C.-in-C., R.A.F. Support Command*).

Skingsley, Sir Anthony, K.C.B., (*C.-in-C. R.A.F. Germany and Cmdr. 2 A.T.A.F.*).

Duxbury, Sir Barry, K.C.B., C.B.E., (*A.O.C. No. 18 Group*).

Jackson, Sir Brendan, K.C.B., (*Air Member for Supply and Organization*).

Jones, Sir Laurence, K.C.B., A.F.C., (*Air Member for Personnel*).

Hayr, Sir Kenneth, K.C.B., C.B.E., A.F.C., (*Chief of Staff and Deputy C.-in-C. Strike Command*).

Bennett, E. P., C.B., (*Commander Sultan of Oman's Air Force*).

Holroyd, F. M., C.B., (*Chief Engineer (R.A.F.)*).

Air Vice-Marshals

Spottiswood, J. D., C.B., C.V.O., A.F.C., (*Air Officer Training R.A.F. Support Command*).

Stuart-Paul, R. I., M.B.E., (*Dir. Gen. Saudi Air Force Project*).

Porter, J. A., O.B.E., (*Dir. Gen. of Communications Inf. Systems and Organization (R.A.F.)*).

Newton, B. H., C.B., O.B.E., (*Special Projects, R.C.D.S.*).

Simmons, M. G., C.B., A.F.C., (*Asst. Chief of the Air Staff*).

Hann, D. W., (*Dir. Gen of Personal Services*).

Bryant, D. T., C.B., O.B.E., (*Cmdt. R.A.F. Staff College, Bracknell*).

Macey, E. H., O.B.E., (*Asst. Chief of Defence Staff (Policy and Nuclear)*).

Stear, M. J. D., C.B.E., (*Asst. Chief of Defence Staff (N.A.T.O./U.K.)*).

Alcock, R. J. M., (*Air Officer Engineering Strike Command*).

Campbell, K. A., (*Air Officer Maintenance, R.A.F. Support Command*).

Walker, J. R., C.B.E., A.F.C., (*Deputy Chief of Staff (Ops.) Allied Forces Central Europe*).

Kemball, R. J., C.B.E., (*Dir. Gen. of Intelligence (Rest of World)*).

Palin, R. H., O.B.E., (*Air Officer Commanding No. 11 Group*).

Mason, R. A., C.B., C.B.E., (*Air Secretary and Air Officer Commanding R.A.F. Personnel Management Centre*).

Brook, D. C. G., C.B.E., (*Air Officer Scotland and N. Ireland*).

Whittaker, D., C.B., M.B.E., (*Air Officer Admin., R.A.F. Support Command*).

Pilkington, M. J., C.B.E., (*Dir. Gen. of Training (R.A.F.)*).

Graydon, M. J., C.B.E., (*Asst. Chief of Staff (Policy) Supreme H.Q. Allied Powers Europe*).

Brown, M. J. D., (*Dir. Gen. of Strategic Electronic Systems*).

Stonor, T. H., (*Deputy Controller, National Air Traffic Services*).

Roberts, A. L., C.B.E., A.F.C., (*Chief of Staff, H.Q. No. 18 Group*).

Wilson, R. A. F., A.F.C., (*Senior Air Strike Officer, Strike Command*).

Thomson, C. J., C.B.E., A.F.C., (*Air Officer Commanding No. 1 Group*).

Honey, R. J., C.B.E., (*Deputy Commander R.A.F. Germany*).

Williams, G. C., A.F.C., (*Asst. Chief of Defence Staff Operational Requirements (Air Systems)*).

Saunders, D. A., C.B.E., (*Asst. Chief of Defence Staff (Command, Control, Communications and Information Systems)*).

Allerton, R. C., (*Dir. Gen. of Supply (R.A.F.)*).

Austin, R. M., A.F.C., (*Dir. Gen. Aircraft 1*).

Wood, R. H., O.B.E., (*Air Officer Commanding and Cmdt. R.A.F. College, Cranwell*).

Woodford, A. A. G., (*Air Officer Administration, Strike Command*).

Harris, J. H., C.B.E., (*Cmdt. Gen. R.A.F. Regt. and Dir. Gen. of Security (R.A.F.)*).

Crwys-Williams, D. O., (*Commander British Forces Falkland Islands*).

Evans, C. E., C.B.E., (*Senior Directing Staff, Royal College of Defence Studies*).

Livingston, G., Q.H.S., (*Principal Medical Officer, R.A.F. Support Command*).

Simpson, C. E., Q.H.S., (*Principal Medical Officer, Strike Command*).

Jones, R. T. B., Q.H.S., (*Dean of Air Force Medicine*).

Mills, N. H., Q.H.P., (*Dep. Surgeon General (Research and Training) and Dir. Gen. R.A.F. Medical Services*).

Forman, G. N. (*Dir. of Legal Services (R.A.F.)*).

PRINCESS MARY'S ROYAL AIR FORCE NURSING SERVICE (P.M.R.A.F.N.S.)

The Princess Mary's Royal Air Force Nursing Service is open to suitable male and female candidates. Commissions are offered to those who are Registered General Nurses (R.G.N.) and possess a second qualification suitable to the needs of the service. R.G.N.s with no additional experience or qualification are also recruited as non-commissioned officers in the trade of Staff Nurse.

Matron-in-Chief, Princess Mary's R.A.F. Nursing Service, Group Captain E. A. I. Sandison, R.R.C., Q.H.N.S.

WOMEN'S ROYAL AIR FORCE (W.R.A.F.)

Formed on April 1, 1918, the Women's Royal Air Force was disbanded on April 1, 1920 and reformed on February 1, 1949 from the Women's Auxiliary Air Force, the World War II Service, which had been formed on June 28, 1939, and from the R.A.F. Companies of the Auxiliary Territorial Service.

W.R.A.F. officers and airwomen, respectively, serve in most of the R.A.F. ground branches and trades and also as Air Loadmaster aircrew. W.R.A.F. personnel are employed at R.A.F. stations and higher formations at home and abroad, and they compete, on equal terms, with their R.A.F. counterparts for appointments, promotion and places on training courses.

Commandant-in-Chief, H.M. Queen Elizabeth the Queen Mother.
Air Chief Commandant, H.R.H. Princess Alice, Duchess of Gloucester.
Director, Air Commodore S. A. Jones, A.D.C.

CONSTITUTION OF THE ROYAL AIR FORCE

The Royal Air Force consists of three Commands: Strike Command and Support Command in the United Kingdom, and R.A.F. Germany. Strike Command is responsible for providing the air defence of the United Kingdom and reinforcement forces for N.A.T.O.; its roles include strike/attack, air defence, control and reporting, maritime surveillance, air reconnaissance, air-to-air refuelling, offensive support, air transport, aero-medical facilities, and search and rescue. Support Command is responsible for air and ground training, communications, engineering support, logistics, hospitals and for providing a range of administrative support. R.A.F. Germany provides tactical air support in N.A.T.O.'s Central Region; its roles include strike/attack, interdiction, counter air operations, air defence, close air support of land forces, tactical reconnaissance and helicopter support.

To carry out its tasks, the Royal Air Force is equipped with Victor, Tornado, Buccaneer, Phantom, Harrier, Jaguar, Canberra, Nimrod, Shackleton, VC10, Tristar, Hercules, Hawk, Jet Provost, Tucano, Chipmunk and Bulldog aircraft; Puma, Wessex, Sea King and Chinook helicopters; miscellaneous communications aircraft, etc.; Bloodhound and Rapier missiles, and the Skyguard system.

ROYAL OBSERVER CORPS
Bentley Priory, Stanmore, Middlesex

Established 1925, the Royal Observer Corps is a uniformed voluntary civilian organization originally set up to identify and track the movement of aircraft in war. In 1955 the Corps assumed the modern role of detecting nuclear bursts and monitoring radioactive fall-out in support of the United Kingdom Warning and Monitoring Organization. The Corps is affiliated to the Royal Air Force and is administered by the Ministry of Defence.

Air Commodore-in-Chief, H.M. THE QUEEN.
Commandant, Air Commodore I. Horrocks

SERVICE SALARIES AND PENSIONS

The following rates of pay have been introduced as part of the 1988 pay award for Service personnel. The Government accepted the recommendations of the Armed Forces Pay Review Body, which advises on pay levels for all ranks from April 1, 1988. The Government, however, decided to introduce in two stages the recommendations of the Top Salaries Review Body, which advises on ranks above Brigadier. The first stage took effect from April 1, 1988, with the full amount (shown below) being introduced from Oct. 1, 1988.

Salaries for the Women's Services reflect equal pay for equal work and conditions, but because the X-Factor addition for women is lower than for men (9 per cent compared to 10 per cent) women's rates approximate to 99·08 per cent of the rates for men. Since 1970 the determining factor of the Review Bodies' recommendations has been the relation of forces' salaries to civilian earnings by a carefully detailed process of job evaluation.

ROYAL NAVY AND ROYAL MARINES
Normal Rates

Rank	Daily	Annual
	£	£
Midshipman		
On appointment............	17·36	6,336
After 1 year.................	21·58	7,877
Sub-Lieutenant and Acting Lieutenant RM		
On appointment.................	24·74	9,030
After 2 years in rank	32·55	11,881
After 3 years in rank	35·13	12,822
Lieutenant		
On appointment.............	41·06	14,987
After 1 year in rank	42·17	15,392
After 2 years in rank	43·28	15,797
After 3 years in rank	44·39	16,202
After 4 years in rank	45·50	16,608
After 5 years in rank	46·61	17,013
After 6 years in rank	47·72	17,418
Lieutenant Commander/Captain RM		
On appointment............	52·20	19,053
After 1 year in rank	53·50	19,528
After 2 years in rank	54·80	20,002
After 3 years in rank	56·10	20,476
After 4 years in rank	57·40	20,951
After 5 years in rank	58·70	21,426
After 6 years in rank	60·00	21,900
After 7 years in rank	61·30	22,375
After 8 years in rank	62·60	22,849
Commander/Major RM		
On appointment with less than 19 years service	72·49	26,459
After 2 years in rank or with 19 years service	74·40	27,156
After 4 years in rank or with 21 years service	76·31	27,853
After 6 years in rank or with 23 years service	78·22	28,550
After 8 years in rank or with 25 years service	80·13	29,247
Captain/Lieutenant-Colonel RM		
On appointment.............	83·60	30,514
After 2 years in rank	85·80	31,317
After 4 years in rank	88·00	32,120
With 6 years seniority/Colonel RM	100·15	36,555
Rear-Admiral/Major-General RM	106·85	39,000
Vice-Admiral/Lieutenant-General RM	131·51	48,000
Admiral/General RM	187·67	68,500
Admiral of the Fleet	233·56	85,250

ARMY
Normal Rates

Rank	Daily	Annual
	£	£
Second Lieutenant	24·74	9,030
Lieutenant		
On appointment.............	32·55	11,881
After 1 year in rank	33·41	12,195
After 2 years in rank	34·27	12,509
After 3 years in rank	35·13	12,822
After 4 years in rank	35·99	13,136
Captain		
On appointment.............	41·06	14,987
After 1 year in rank	42·17	15,392
After 2 years in rank	43·28	15,797
After 3 years in rank	44·39	16,202
After 4 years in rank	45·50	16,608
After 5 years in rank	46·61	17,013
After 6 years in rank	47·72	17,418
Major		
On appointment.............	52·20	19,053
After 1 year in rank	53·50	19,528
After 2 years in rank	54·80	20,002
After 3 years in rank	56·10	20,476
After 4 years in rank	57·40	20,951
After 5 years in rank	58·70	21,426
After 6 years in rank	60·00	21,900
After 7 years in rank	61·30	22,375
After 8 years in rank	62·60	22,849
Special List Lieutenant-Colonel	71·65	26,152
Lieutenant-Colonel		
On appointment with less than 19 years service	72·49	26,459
After 2 years in rank or with 19 years service	74·40	27,156
After 4 years in rank or with 21 years service	76·31	27,853
After 6 years in rank or with 23 years service	78·22	28,550
After 8 years or with 25 years service	80·13	29,247
Colonel		
On appointment.............	83·60	30,514
After 2 years in rank	85·80	31,317
After 4 years in rank	88·00	32,120
After 6 years in rank	90·20	32,923
After 8 years in rank	92·40	33,726
Brigadier......................	100·15	36,555
Major-General	106·85	39,000
Lieutenant-General	131·51	48,000
General	187·67	68,500
Field Marshal.................	233·56	85,250

ROYAL AIR FORCE, Normal Rates

Rank	Daily	Annual	Rank	Daily	Annual
	£	£		£	£
Acting Pilot Officer—On			After 7 years in rank	61·30	22,375
appointment..............	21·09	7,698	After 8 years in rank	62·60	22,849
After 6 months in the rank			Wing Commander—On appoint-		
(aircrew officers only)......	21·58	7,877	ment with less than 19 years		
Pilot Officer	24·74	9,030	service	72·49	26,459
Flying Officer—On appointment	32·55	11,881	After 2 years in rank or with		
After 1 year in rank	33·41	12,195	19 years service	74·40	27,156
After 2 years in rank	34·27	12,509	After 4 years in rank or with		
After 3 years in rank	35·13	12,822	21 years service	76·31	27,853
After 4 years in rank	35·99	13,136	After 6 years in rank or with		
Flight Lieutenant—On			23 years service	78·22	28,550
appointment..............	41·06	14,987	After 8 years in rank or with		
After 1 year in rank	42·17	15,392	25 years service	80·13	29,247
After 2 years in rank	43·28	15,797	Group Captain—On		
After 3 years in rank	44·39	16,202	appointment..............	83·60	30,514
After 4 years in rank	45·50	16,608	After 2 years in rank	85·80	31,317
After 5 years in rank	46·61	17,013	After 4 years in rank	88·00	32,120
After 6 years in rank	47·72	17,418	After 6 years in rank	90·20	32,923
Squadron Leader—On			After 8 years in rank	92·40	33,726
appointment..............	52·20	19,053	Air Commodore	100·15	36,555
After 1 year in rank	53·50	19,528	Air Vice-Marshal	106·85	39,000
After 2 years in rank	54·80	20,002	Air Marshal	131·51	48,000
After 3 years in rank	56·10	20,476	Air Chief Marshal	187·67	68,500
After 4 years in rank	57·40	20,951	Marshal of the Royal Air Force .	233·56	85,250
After 5 years in rank	58·70	21,426			
After 6 years in rank	60·00	21,900			

ROYAL NAVY AND ROYAL MARINES SPECIAL DUTIES LIST OFFICERS, ARMY MALE OFFICERS COMMISSIONED FROM THE RANKS, ROYAL AIR FORCE BRANCH OFFICERS

Years of Commissioned Service	Years of Non-Commissioned Service from age 18					
	Less than 12 years		12 years but less than 15 years		15 years or more	
	Daily	Annual	Daily	Annual	Daily	Annual
	£	£	£	£	£	£
On appointment...................	44·66	16,301	46·96	17,140	49·26	17,980
After 1 year service..............	45·81	16,721	48·11	17,556	50·12	18,294
After 2 years service.............	46·96	17,140	49·26	17,980	50·98	18,608
After 3 years service.............	48·11	17,556	50·12	18,294	51·84	18,922
After 4 years service.............	49·26	17,980	50·98	18,608	52·70	19,236
After 5 years service.............	50·12	18,294	51·84	18,922	53·56	19,549
After 6 years service.............	50·98	18,608	52·70	19,236	54·42	19,863
After 8 years service.............	51·84	18,922	53·56	19,549	55·28	20,177
After 10 years service............	52·70	19,236	54·42	19,863	55·28	20,177
After 12 years service............	53·56	19,549	55·28	20,177	55·28	20,177
After 14 years service............	54·42	19,863	55·28	20,177	55·28	20,177
After 16 years service............	55·28	20,177	55·28	20,177	55·28	20,177

ROYAL NAVY—ARTIFICERS, MEDICAL AND COMMUNICATIONS TECHNICIANS
Daily rates of pay for those committed to serve for:

Rating	Less than 6 years Scale A	6 years but less than 9 years Scale B	9 years or more Scale C
	£	£	£
FCPO Artificer/Technician	46·62	46·92	47·37
CCPO Artificer/Technician	44·79	45·09	45·54
CPO Artificer/1st Class Technician—Scale I	43·06	43·36	43·81
CPO Artificer/1st Class Technician—Scale II	41·41	41·71	42·16
PO Artificer/2nd Class Technician	36·51	36·81	37·26
Probationary or Acting PO Artificer/3rd Class			
Technician	34·82	35·12	35·57
4th Class Technician (Leading)	30·37	30·67	31·12
Leading Artificer/Acting or 4th Class Technician ...	28·47	28·77	29·22
Acting Leading Artificer...........................	25·69	25·99	26·44
5th Class Technician (Able)	24·06	24·36	24·81

ROYAL NAVY AND ROYAL MARINES—OTHER BRANCHES

Daily rates of pay for those committed to serve for:

Rank	Scale	Less than 6 years Scale A	6 years but less than 9 years Scale B	9 years or more Scale C
		£	£	£
Fleet Chief Petty Officer/Warrant Officer Class I	I	43·05	43·35	43·80
Chief Petty Officer	I	38·01	38·31	38·76
Chief Petty Officer	II	37·33	37·63	38·08
Petty Officer/Sergeant	I	33·81	34·11	34·56
Petty Officer/Sergeant	II	33·20	33·50	33·95
Leading Rating/Corporal	I	30·37	30·67	31·12
Leading Rating/Corporal	II	28·47	28·77	29·22
Able Rating/Marine 1st Class	I	24·06	24·36	24·81
Able Rating/Marine 1st Class	II	22·60	22·90	23·35
Able Rating/Marine 1st Class	III	19·69	19·99	20·44
Ordinary Rating/Marine 2nd Class	I	16·69	16·99	17·44
Ordinary Rating/Marine 2nd Class	II	15·33	15·63	16·08

ARMY

Daily rates of pay for those committed to serve for:

Rank	Less than 6 years Scale A			6 years but less than 9 years Scale B			9 years or more Scale C		
	Band 1	Band 2	Band 3	Band 1	Band 2	Band 3	Band 1	Band 2	Band 3
	£	£	£	£	£	£	£	£	£
Private Class IV ...	15·33	—	—	15·63	—	—	16·08	—	—
Class III ...	16·91	19·69	22·71	17·21	19·99	23·01	17·66	20·44	23·46
Class II ...	18·93	21·71	24·73	19·23	22·01	25·03	19·68	22·46	25·48
Class I	20·55	23·33	26·35	20·85	23·63	26·65	21·30	24·08	27·10
Lance Corporal									
Class III ...	20·55	23·33	26·35	20·85	23·63	26·65	21·30	24·08	27·10
Class II ...	22·16	24·94	27·96	22·46	25·24	28·26	22·91	25·69	28·71
Class I	23·86	26·64	29·66	24·16	26·94	29·96	24·61	27·39	30·41
Corporal Class II ...	25·69	28·47	31·49	25·99	28·77	31·79	26·44	29·22	32·24
Class I	27·59	30·37	33·69	27·89	30·67	33·99	28·34	31·12	34·14

	Band 4	Band 5	Band 6	Band 7	Band 4	Band 5	Band 6	Band 7	Band 4	Band 5	Band 6	Band 7
	£	£	£	£	£	£	£	£	£	£	£	£
Sergeant	30·18	33·20	36·51	—	30·48	33·50	36·81	—	30·93	33·95	37·26	—
Staff Sergeant	32·11	35·13	38·44	42·01	32·41	35·43	38·74	42·31	32·86	35·88	39·19	42·56
Warrant Officer Class II	34·33	37·35	40·66	44·23	34·63	37·65	40·96	44·53	35·08	38·10	41·41	44·98
Warrant Officer Class I	36·72	39·74	43·05	46·62	37·02	40·04	43·35	46·92	37·47	40·49	43·80	47·37

ROYAL AIR FORCE—AIRMEN (AIRCREW)

Daily rates for those committed to serve for:

Rank	Less than 6 years Scale A			6 years but less than 9 years Scale B			9 years or more Scale C		
	Band 5	Band 6	Band 7	Band 5	Band 6	Band 7	Band 5	Band 6	Band 7
	£	£	£	£	£	£	£	£	£
Pilots, Navigators, Air Electronics Operators and Air Engineers (A)									
Sergeant	—	36·51	—	—	36·81	—	—	37·26	—
Flight Sergeant	—	—	43·09	—	—	43·39	—	—	43·84
Master Aircrew	—	—	46·62	—	—	46·92	—	—	47·37
Air Signallers and Air Loadmasters									
Sergeant	33·20	—	—	33·50	—	—	33·95	—	—
Flight Sergeant	—	39·52	—	—	39·82	—	—	40·27	—
Master Aircrew	—	43·05	—	—	43·35	—	—	43·80	—

ROYAL AIR FORCE AIRMEN (GROUND TRADES, APPRENTICES AND P.M.R.A.F.N.S.)

Daily rates of pay for those committed to serve for:

Rank/Category	Less than 6 years Scale A			6 years but less than 9 years Scale B			9 years or more Scale C		
	Band 1	Band 2	Band 3	Band 1	Band 2	Band 3	Band 1	Band 2	Band 3
	£	£	£	£	£	£	£	£	£
Aircraftmen over 17 on entry	15·33	15·33	15·33	15·63	15·63	15·63	16·08	16·08	16·08
Leading Aircraftmen	16·91	19·69	22·71	17·21	19·99	23·01	17·66	20·44	23·46
Senior Aircraftmen	20·55	23·33	26·35	20·85	23·63	26·65	21·30	24·08	27·10
Junior Technician	23·86	26·64	29·66	24·16	26·94	29·96	24·61	27·39	30·41
Corporal	27·25	30·03	33·39	27·55	30·33	33·69	28·00	30·78	34·14

Rank/Category	Band 4	Band 5	Band 6	Band 7	Band 4	Band 5	Band 6	Band 7	Band 4	Band 5	Band 6	Band 7
	£	£	£	£	£	£	£	£	£	£	£	£
Sergeant	30·18	33·20	36·51	—	30·48	33·50	36·81	—	30·93	33·95	37·26	—
Chief Technician	31·68	34·70	38·01	41·58	31·98	35·00	38·31	41·88	32·43	35·45	38·76	42·33
Flight Sergeant	33·19	36·21	39·52	43·09	33·49	36·51	39·82	43·39	33·94	36·96	40·27	43·84
Warrant Officer	36·72	39·74	43·05	46·62	37·02	40·04	43·35	46·92	37·47	40·49	43·80	47·37

WOMEN'S SERVICES

OFFICERS OF W.R.N.S.

Rank	Daily	Annual
	£	£
Probationary 3rd Officer	24·52	8,950
Third Officer	27·10	9,892
On confirmation		
After 2 years	32·25	11,771
Second Officer	40·69	14,852
On appointment		
After 1 year in rank	41·79	15,253
After 2 years in rank	42·89	15,655
After 3 years in rank	43·99	16,056
After 4 years in rank	45·09	16,458
After 5 years in rank	46·19	16,859
After 6 years in rank	47·29	17,261
First Officer	51·73	18,881
On appointment		
After 1 year in rank	53·01	19,349
After 2 years in rank	54·30	19,820
After 3 years in rank	55·59	20,290
After 4 years in rank	56·88	20,761
After 5 years in rank	58·17	21,232
After 6 years in rank	59·45	21,699
After 7 years in rank	60·74	22,170
After 8 years in rank	62·03	22,641
Chief Officer	71·83	26,218
On appointment with less than 19 years service		
After 2 years in rank or with 19 years service	73·72	26,908
After 4 years in rank or with 21 years service	75·62	27,601
After 6 years in rank or with 23 years service	77·53	28,294
After 8 years in rank or with 25 years service	79·44	28,996
Superintendent	83·14	30,346
On appointment		
After 2 years in rank	85·34	31,149
After 4 years in rank	87·54	31,952
After 6 years in rank	89·74	32,755
After 8 years in rank	91·94	33,558
Director, W.R.N.S.	99·92	36,471

FEMALE OFFICERS OF Q.A.R.N.N.S.

Rank	Daily	Annual
	£	£
Nursing Officer		
On appointment	32·25	11,771
After 1 year in rank	33·11	12,085
After 2 years in rank	33·96	12,395
After 3 years in rank	34·81	12,706
After 4 years in rank	35·66	13,016
Senior Nursing Officer		
On appointment	40·69	14,852
After 1 year in rank	41·79	15,253
After 2 years in rank	42·89	15,655
After 3 years in rank	43·99	16,056
After 4 years in rank	45·09	16,458
After 5 years in rank	46·19	16,859
After 6 years in rank	47·29	17,261
Superintending Nursing Officer		
On appointment	51·73	18,881
After 1 year in rank	53·01	19,349
After 2 years in rank	54·30	19,820
After 3 years in rank	55·59	20,290
After 4 years in rank	56·88	20,761
After 5 years in rank	58·17	21,232
After 6 years in rank	59·45	21,699
After 7 years in rank	60·74	22,170
After 8 years in rank	62·03	22,641
Chief Nursing Officer		
On appointment with less than 19 years service	71·83	26,218
After 2 years in rank or with 19 years service	73·72	26,908
After 4 years in rank or with 21 years service	75·62	27,601
After 6 years in rank or with 23 years service	77·53	28,294
After 8 years in rank or with 25 years service	79·44	28,996
Principal Nursing Officer		
On appointment	83·14	30,346
After 2 years in rank	85·34	31,149
After 4 years in rank	87·54	31,952
After 6 years in rank	89·74	32,755
After 8 years in rank	91·94	33,558
Matron-in-Chief	99·92	36,471

OFFICERS OF W.R.A.C., AND Q.A.R.A.N.C.

Rank	Daily	Annual
	£	£
Second-Lieutenant	24·52	8,950
Lieutenant—On appointment	32·25	11,771
After 1 year in rank	33·11	12,085
After 2 years in rank	33·96	12,395
After 3 years in rank	34·81	12,706
After 4 years in rank	35·66	13,016
Captain—On appointment	40·69	14,852
After 1 year in rank	41·79	15,253
After 2 years in rank	42·89	15,655
After 3 years in rank	43·99	16,056
After 4 years in rank	45·09	16,458
After 5 years in rank	46·19	16,859
After 6 years in rank	47·29	17,261
Major—On appointment	51·73	18,881
After 1 year in rank	53·01	19,349
After 2 years in rank	54·30	19,820
After 3 years in rank	55·59	20,290
After 4 years in rank	56·88	20,761
After 5 years in rank	58·17	21,232
After 6 years in rank	59·45	21,699
After 7 years in rank	60·74	22,170
After 8 years in rank	62·03	22,641
Lieutenant-Colonel—On appointment with less than 19 years service	71·83	26,218
After 2 years in rank or with 19 years service	73·72	26,908
After 4 years in rank or with 21 years service	75·62	27,601
After 6 years in rank or with 23 years service	77·53	28,294
After 8 years in rank or with 25 years service	79·44	28,996
Colonel—On appointment........	83·14	30,346
After 2 years in rank	85·34	31,149
After 4 years in rank	87·54	31,952
After 6 years in rank	89·74	32,755
After 8 years in rank	91·94	33,558
Brigadier.......................	99·92	36,471

OFFICERS OF W.R.A.F. AND FEMALE OFFICERS OF THE P.M.R.A.F.N.S.

Rank	Daily	Annual
	£	£
Acting Pilot Officer..............	20·90	7,628
Pilot Officer	24·52	8,950
Flying Officer—On appointment ..	32·25	11,771
After 1 year in rank	33·11	12,085
After 2 years in rank	33·96	12,395
After 3 years in rank	34·81	12,706
After 4 years in rank	35·66	13,016
Flight Lieutenant—On appointment......................	40·69	14,852
After 1 year in rank	41·79	15·253
After 2 years in rank	42·89	15,655
After 3 years in rank	43·99	16,056
After 4 years in rank	45·09	16,458
After 5 years in rank	46·19	16,859
After 6 years in rank	47·29	17,261
Squadron Leader—On appointment......................	51·73	18,881
After 1 year in rank	53·01	19,349
After 2 years in rank	54·30	19,820
After 3 years in rank	55·59	20,290
After 4 years in rank	56·88	20,761
After 5 years in rank	58·17	21,232
After 6 years in rank	59·45	21,699
After 7 years in rank	60·74	22,170
After 8 years in rank	62·03	22,641
Wing Commander—On appointment with less than 19 years service	71·83	26,218
After 2 years in rank or with 19 years service.................	73·72	26,908
After 4 years in rank or with 21 years service.................	75·62	27,601
After 6 years in rank or with 23 years service.................	77·53	28,294
After 8 years in rank or with 25 years service.................	79·44	28,996
Group Captain—On appointment .	83·14	30,346
After 2 years in rank	85·34	31,149
After 4 years in rank	87·54	31,952
After 6 years in rank	89·74	32,755
After 8 years in rank	91·94	33,558
Air Commodore	99·92	36,471

W.R.N.S. RATINGS AND NAVAL NURSES
Daily rates for those who have served for:

Rank	Less than 6 years Scale A			6 years but less than 9 years Scale B			9 years or more Scale C		
	Band 1	Band 2	Band 3	Band 1	Band 2	Band 3	Band 1	Band 2	Band 3
	£	£	£	£	£	£	£	£	£
Ordinary Rating under 17½	11·48	—	—	—	—	—	—	—	—
Ordinary Rating at 17½	15·19	15·19	—	15·49	15·49	—	15·94	15·94	—
Able Rating Class III	16·76	19·51	22·50	17·06	19·81	22·80	17·51	20·26	23·25
Able Rating Class II	19·64	22·39	25·38	19·94	22·69	25·68	20·39	23·14	26·13
Able Rating Class I .	21·09	23·84	26·83	21·39	24·14	27·13	21·84	24·59	27·58
Leading Rating Class II	25·46	28·21	31·20	25·76	28·51	31·50	26·21	28·96	31·95
Leading Rating Class I	27·34	30·09	33·08	27·64	30·39	33·38	28·09	30·84	33·83

	Band 4	Band 5	Band 6	Band 7	Band 4	Band 5	Band 6	Band 7	Band 4	Band 5	Band 6	Band 7
	£	£	£	£	£	£	£	£	£	£	£	£
Petty Officer Class II	29·58	32·57	35·85	39·39	29·88	32·87	36·15	39·69	30·33	33·32	36·60	40·14
Petty Officer Class I	30·23	33·22	36·50	40·04	30·53	33·52	36·80	40·34	30·98	33·97	37·25	40·79
CPO Class II	32·05	35·04	38·32	41·86	32·35	35·34	38·62	42·16	32·80	35·79	39·07	42·61
CPO Class I	32·82	35·81	39·09	42·63	33·12	36·11	39·39	42·93	33·57	36·56	39·84	43·38
Warrant Officer Class I	36·39	39·38	42·66	46·20	36·69	39·68	42·96	46·50	37·14	40·13	46·41	46·95

W.R.A.C. and Q.A.R.A.N.C.
Daily rates of pay for those who have served for:

Rank	Less than 6 years			6 years but less than 9 years			9 years or more		
	Band 1	Band 2	Band 3	Band 1	Band 2	Band 3	Band 1	Band 2	Band 3
	£	£	£	£	£	£	£	£	£
Private Class IV Age 17–17½ ..	11·48	—	—	—	—	—	—	—	—
Class IV	15·19	—	—	15·49	—	—	15·94	—	—
Class III	16·76	19·51	22·50	17·06	19·81	22·80	17·51	20·26	23·25
Class II	18·76	21·51	24·50	19·06	21·81	24·80	19·51	22·26	25·25
Class I	20·37	23·12	26·11	20·67	23·42	26·41	21·12	23·87	26·86
Lance Corporal Class III	20·37	23·12	26·11	20·67	23·42	26·41	21·12	23·87	26·86
Class II	21·96	24·71	27·70	22·26	25·01	28·00	22·71	25·46	28·45
Class I	23·65	26·40	29·39	23·95	26·70	29·69	24·40	27·15	30·14
Corporal Class II	25·46	28·21	31·20	25·76	28·51	31·50	26·21	28·96	31·95
Class I	27·34	30·09	33·08	27·64	30·39	33·38	28·09	30·84	33·83

	Band 4	Band 5	Band 6	Band 7	Band 4	Band 5	Band 6	Band 7	Band 4	Band 5	Band 6	Band 7
	£	£	£	£	£	£	£	£	£	£	£	£
Sergeant	29·91	32·90	36·18	—	30·21	33·20	36·48	—	30·66	33·65	36·93	—
Staff Sergeant	31·82	34·81	38·09	41·63	32·12	35·11	38·39	41·93	32·57	35·56	38·84	42·38
Warrant Officer Class II	34·02	37·01	40·29	43·83	34·32	37·31	40·59	44·13	34·77	37·76	41·04	44·58
Class I	36·39	39·38	42·66	46·20	36·69	39·68	42·96	46·50	37·14	40·13	43·41	46·95

W.R.A.F. AIRWOMEN (Ground Trades) and P.M.R.A.F.N.S.
Daily rates of pay for those who have served for:

Rank/Category	Less than 6 years			6 years but less than 9 years			9 years or more		
	Band 1	Band 2	Band 3	Band 1	Band 2	Band 3	Band 1	Band 2	Band 3
	£	£	£	£	£	£	£	£	£
Aircraftwoman under age 17½	11·48	—	—	—	—	—	—	—	—
Aircraftwoman at age 17½	15·19	15·19	15·19	—	—	—	—	—	—
Leading Aircraftwoman	16·76	19·51	22·50	17·06	19·81	22·80	17·51	20·26	23·25
Senior Aircraftwoman	20·37	23·12	26·11	20·67	23·42	26·41	21·12	23·87	26·86
Junior Technician	23·65	26·40	29·39	23·95	26·70	29·69	24·40	27·15	30·14
Corporal	27·00	29·75	33·08	27·30	30·05	33·38	27·75	30·50	33·83

	Band 4	Band 5	Band 6	Band 7	Band 4	Band 5	Band 6	Band 7	Band 4	Band 5	Band 6	Band 7
	£	£	£	£	£	£	£	£	£	£	£	£
Sergeant	29·91	32·90	36·18	—	30·21	33·20	36·48	—	30·66	33·65	36·93	—
Chief Technician	31·39	34·39	37·67	41·20	31·69	34·69	37·97	41·50	32·14	35·14	38·42	41·95
Flight Sergeant	32·88	35·88	39·16	42·69	33·18	36·18	39·46	42·99	33·63	36·63	39·91	43·44
Warrant Officer	36·39	39·38	42·66	46·20	36·69	39·68	42·96	46·50	37·14	40·13	43·41	46·95

CHARGES FOR MARRIED AND SINGLE QUARTERS

Married Quarters

Type of quarter	Annual charge*			
	Grade 1	Grade 2	Grade 3	Grade 4
	£	£	£	£
Officers				
I	3,223	2,916	2,230	1,471
II	2,894	2,613	2,000	1,318
III	2,566	2,321	1,778	1,172
IV	2,219	2,008	1,555	1,011
V	1,924	1,745	1,329	891
Other Ranks				
D/WO	1,518	1,372	1,066	690
C	1,354	1,226	945	620
B	1,212	1,095	840	551
A	810	730	558	369

*Annual charges are derived from daily rates in whole pence and rounded to the nearest £.

Single Quarters

Rank	Annual charge*			
	Grade 1	Grade 2	Grade 3	Grade 4
	£	£	£	£
Major and above	1,256	1,135	869	573
Captain and below	1,040	938	719	485
Warrant Officer and Senior N.C.O.	745	675	515	339
Corporal and below	398	361	274	182
Young service-man receiving less than the minimum adult (i.e. Private IV) rate	299	266	204	139

SERVICE RETIREMENT BENEFITS, ETC.

NOTE—Those who leave the Forces having served at least five years, but not long enough to qualify for the appropriate immediate pension, now qualify for a preserved pension and terminal grant both of which are payable at age 60. The tax-free resettlement grants shown below are payable on release to those who qualify for a preserved pension and who have completed 9 years service from age 21 (officers) or 12 years from age 18 (other ranks).

RETIREMENT BENEFITS (MEN) Officers*—All Services

No. of years reckonable service over age 21	Capt. (incl. Q.M.) and below	Major (incl. Q.M.)	Lt.-Col.	Col. and Deputy Chaplain General	Brigadier	Major-General, etc.	Lieutenant-General, etc.	General, etc.
	£p.a.	£p.a.	£p.a.	£p.a.	£p.a.	£p.a.	£p.a.	£p.a.
16	4,964	5,971	7,739					
17	5,195	6,255	8,097					
18	5,425	6,539	8,455	9,751				
19	5,656	6,823	8,813	10,164				
20	5,887	7,107	9,171	10,577				
21	6,118	7,391	9,530	10,989				
22	6,348	7,675	9,888	11,402	12,855			
23	6,579	7,959	10,246	11,815	13,261			
24	6,810	8,243	10,604	12,228	13,667	14,582		
25	7,040	8,526	10,962	12,641	14,074	15,015		
26	7,271	8,810	11,320	13,054	14,480	15,449		
27	7,502	9,904	11,678	13,467	14,886	15,882	19,547	
28	7,733	9,378	12,036	13,880	15,292	16,315	20,080	
29	7,963	9,662	12,394	14,293	15,698	16,749	20,614	
30	8,194	9,946	12,753	14,705	16,104	17,182	21,147	30,178
31	8,425	10,230	13,111	15,118	16,511	17,615	21,680	30,939
32	8,656	10,514	13,469	15,531	16,917	18,048	22,213	31,701
33	8,886	10,798	13,827	15,944	17,323	18,482	22,747	32,462
34	9,117	11,082	14,185	16,357	17,729	18,915	23,280	33,223

* Including those male officers holding equivalent ranks in the Q.A.R.N.N.S.

Ratings, Soldiers and Airmen*

Number of years reckonable service	Below Corporal	Corporal	Sergeant	Staff Sergeant	Warrant Officer Class II	Warrant Officer Class I
	£p.a.	£p.a.	£p.a.	£p.a.	£p.a.	£p.a.
22	2,885	3,720	4,102	4,667	4,800	5,269
23	2,986	3,850	4,245	4,830	4,970	5,458
24	3,086	3,980	4,388	4,993	5,140	5,648
25	3,187	4,110	4,531	5,156	5,310	5,837
26	3,288	4,239	4,675	5,319	5,479	6,026
27	3,389	4,369	4,818	5,482	5,649	6,215
28	3,489	4,499	4,961	5,645	5,819	6,405
29	3,590	4,629	5,104	5,808	5,989	6,594
30	3,691	4,759	5,247	5,970	6,159	6,783
31	3,972	4,889	5,390	6,133	6,329	6,972
32	3,892	5,019	5,533	6,296	6,499	7,162
33	3,993	5,148	5,676	6,459	6,669	7,351
34	4,094	5,278	5,820	6,622	6,838	7,540
35	4,195	5,408	5,936	6,785	7,008	7,729
36	4,295	5,538	6,106	6,948	7,178	7,919
37	4,396	5,668	6,249	7,111	7,348	8,108

* Including male nurses serving in the Q.A.R.N.N.S. holding equivalent rank.

RETIREMENT BENEFITS (WOMEN)

Q.A.R.N.N.S., W.R.N.S., Q.A.R.A.N.C., W.R.A.C., P.M.R.A.F.N.S., W.R.A.F. (The annual rates for W.R.A.C. are given: these apply to equivalent ranks in all Services, including the Nursing Services).

OFFICERS (16–34 years' service).—Captain, £4,927–£9,049; Major, £5,926–£10,999; Lt.-Col., £7,681–£14,079; Colonel, £9,702–£16,275; Brigadier, £12,823–£17,685.

SERVICEWOMEN (22–37 years' service).—Below Corporal, £2,863–£4,363; Corporal, £3,692–£5,625; Sergeant, £4,071–£6,202; Staff Sergeant, £4,632–£7,058; Warrant Officer II, £4,764–£7,293; Warrant Officer I, £5,229–£8,047.

NOTES

Terminal grants are in each case three times the rate of retired pay or pension. There are special rates of retired pay for Chaplains, Flight Lieutenants (Specialist Aircrew), and certain other ranks not shown above. Deductions may be made in cases of voluntary retirement.

The normal rates of gratuity for officers with short service commissions are £1,690 (men) and £1,677 (women) for each year completed. Resettlement grants are: officers £5,806 (men) and £5,762 (women); non-commissioned ranks £3,878 (men), £3,849 (women).

THE CHURCHES

THE CHURCH OF ENGLAND

THE GENERAL SYNOD OF THE CHURCH OF ENGLAND

The General Synod was constituted in 1970, under the Synodical Government Measure 1969, in succession to the former Church Assembly. There are in total some 574 members of the General Synod, divided into three distinct houses—the House of Bishops, the House of Clergy and the House of Laity. It is presided over jointly by the Archbishops of Canterbury and York and normally meets three times each year—in February, July and November.

The function of the General Synod is to consider and make provision for all matters concerning the Church of England, and to consider and express opinion on any other matters of religious or public interest. The Synod appoints a number of Committees, Boards and Councils which deal with, or advise the Synod on, a wide range of matters affecting the Church and its Ministry.

Under the Church of England Assembly (Powers) Act 1919 the General Synod has the power—delegated by Parliament—to frame Statute Law on any matter concerning the Church of England, which are known as Measures. A Measure, once approved by General Synod, must be laid before both Houses of Parliament who may accept or reject it but may not amend it. If the Measure is accepted it is then submitted for Royal Assent and when this has been given the Measure has the full force of Law just as an Act of Parliament.

The Synod also has the power to make Canons and other ecclesiastical regulations provided that they do not conflict with statutory law. Canons have to be submitted to the Crown before they can come into effect.

OFFICES.—Church House, Dean's Yard, SW1P 3NZ— *Presidents,* The Archbishop of Canterbury; The Archbishop of York; *Sec. Gen.,* W. D. Pattinson. THE HOUSE OF BISHOPS.—*Chairman,* The Archbishop of Canterbury; *Vice Chairman,* The Archbishop of York. THE HOUSE OF CLERGY.—*Chairman,* The Archdeacon of Leicester; *Vice Chairman,* Canon P. H. Boulton. THE HOUSE OF LAITY, *Chairman,* Prof. J. D. McClean; *Vice Chairman,* Mrs. J. Dann.

Stipends (from April 1988)

Archbishop of Canterbury	£31,870
Archbishop of York	£27,820
Bishop of London	£25,870
Bishop of Durham	£22,745
Bishop of Winchester	£18,830
Diocesan Bishop	£16,915
Dean or Provost	£13,770
Canons Residentiary	£11,120

Province of Canterbury

CANTERBURY

102nd Archbishop and Primate of All England, Most Rev. and Rt. Hon. Robert Alexander Kennedy Runcie, M.C., *cons.* 1970, *trs.* 1980 (Lambeth Palace, SE1 7JU) [Signs Robert Cantuar] 1980

Bishops Suffragan

Dover, Rt. Rev. Richard Henry McPhail Third, *cons.* 1976 (Upway, St. Martin's Hill, Canterbury, CT1 1PR) 1980
Maidstone, Rt. Rev. David James Smith, *cons.* 1987 (Bishop's House, Pett Lane, Charing, Ashford TN27 0DL) 1987

Assistant Bishops

Rt. Rev. Harold Isherwood, M.V.O., O.B.E. (*cons.* 1974), 1979; Rt. Rev. The Lord Coggan, P.C. (*cons.* 1956), 1980; Rt. Rev. Ross Sydney Hook, M.C. (*cons.* 1965), 1986; Rt. Rev. William Alfred Franklin, O.B.E. (*cons.* 1972), 1987; Rt. Rev. Richard David Say, K.C.V.O. (*cons.* 1961), 1988.

Dean

Very Rev. John Arthur Simpson 1986

Canons Residentiary

J. H. R. De Sausmarez (1981); P. Brett (1983); Ven. M. Till (1986); C. A. Lewis (1987).
Organist, D. Flood (1988).

Archdeacons

Canterbury, Ven. M. Till 1986
Maidstone, Ven. A. M. P. Smith 1979
Clergy, 241
Vicar-General of Province and Diocese, Miss S. Cameron, Q.C.

Commissary General, J. H. R. Newey, Q.C. (1971).
Joint Registrars of the Province, F. E. Robson, 16 Beaumont Street, Oxford; B. J. T. Hanson, Church House, Dean's Yard, SW1P 3NZ.
Registrar of the Diocese of Canterbury, A. O. E. Davies, 9 The Precincts, Canterbury CT1 2EQ.

LONDON

130th Bishop, Rt. Rev. and Rt. Hon. Graham Douglas Leonard, *cons.* 1964, *trs.* 1973 and 1981 (8 Barton Street, SW1P 3NE) [Signs Graham Londin] 1981

Area Bishops

Edmonton, Rt. Rev. Brian John Masters, *cons.* 1982 (13 North Audley Street, W1Y 1FW) 1984
Kensington, Rt. Rev. John Hughes, PH.D., *cons.* 1987 (19 Campden Hill Square, W8 7JY) 1987
Stepney, Rt. Rev. James Lawton Thompson, *cons.* 1978 (23 Tredegar Square, E3 5AG) 1978
Willesden, Rt. Rev. Thomas Frederick Butler, PH.D., *cons.* 1985 (173 Willesden Lane, Brondesbury, NW6 7YN) 1985

Bishop Suffragan

Fulham, Rt. Rev. (Charles) John Klyberg, *cons.* 1985 (4 Cambridge Place, W8 5PB) 1985

Assistant Bishops

Rt. Rev. Maurice Wood, D.S.C. (*cons.* 1971), 1985; Rt. Rev. Michael Marshall (*cons.* 1975) 1984.

Dean of St. Paul's

Very Rev. Thomas Eric Evans 1988

Canons Residentiary

Rt. Rev. K. J. Woollcombe (1981); K. G. Routledge (1982); P. W. Ball (1984); Ven. G. Cassidy (1987).
Organist, C. H. Dearnley, F.R.C.O. (1968).
Receiver of St. Paul's, Commander C. Shears, O.B.E., R.N. *(retd.)*

Archdeacons

Hackney, Ven. R. E. D. Sharpley 1981
Hampstead, Ven. R. A. W. Coogan 1985
London, Ven. G. Cassidy 1987
Middlesex, Ven. T. J. Raphael 1983
Northolt, Ven. E. Shirras 1985
　　Beneficed Clergy, 403; *Curates, etc.,* 185
Chancellor and Commissary of the Dean and Chapter, G. H. Newsom, Q.C. (1971).
Registrar, D. W. Faull, 35 Great Peter Street, SW1P 3LR.

WESTMINSTER

The Collegiate Church of St. Peter—(A Royal Peculiar)
Dean, Michael Clement Otway Mayne 1986
Sub Dean and Archdeacon, A. E. Harvey (1987).

Canons Residentiary

S. Charles (1978); A. E. Harvey (1982); D. Gray (1987); C. Semper (1987).
Chapter Clerk and Receiver General, Rear-Adm. K. A. Snow, C.B. (1987).
Organist, M. Neary, F.R.C.O. (1988).
Legal Secretary, C. L. Hodgetts (1973).
Registrar, S. J. Holmes (1984), 20 Dean's Yard, SW1P 3PA.

WINCHESTER

95th Bishop, Rt. Rev. Colin Clement Walter James, *cons.* 1973, *trs.* 1977 and 1985 (Wolvesey, Winchester SO23 9ND) [Signs Colin Winton] 1985

Bishops Suffragan

Basingstoke, Rt. Rev. Michael Richard John Manktelow, *cons.* 1977 (1 The Close, Winchester SO23 9LS) 1977
Southampton, (vacant).

Assistant Bishop

Rt. Rev. Hassan Dehqani-Tafti *(cons.* 1961) 1982

Dean

Very Rev. Trevor Randall Beeson 1987

Dean of Jersey (A Peculiar), Very Rev. Basil Arthur O'Ferrall, C.B., R.N. 1985
Dean of Guernsey (A Peculiar), (vacant).

Canons Residentiary

E. G. Job (1979); P. A. Britton (1980); A. K. Walker (1987).
Organist, D. Hill, F.R.C.O. (1988).

Archdeacons

Basingstoke, Ven. T. G. Nash 1982
Winchester, Ven. A. G. Clarkson 1984
　　Beneficed Clergy, 220; *Curates, etc.,* 55
Chancellor, John Spokes, Q.C. (1985).
Registrar and Legal Secretary, P. M. White, 19 St. Peter Street, Winchester SO23 8BU.

BATH AND WELLS

75th Bishop, Rt. Rev. George Leonard Carey, PH.D., *cons.* 1987 (The Palace, Wells BA5 2PD) [Signs George Bath & Wells] 1987

Bishop Suffragan

Taunton, Rt. Rev. Nigel Simeon McCulloch, *cons.* 1986 (Sherford Farm House, Sherford, Taunton TA1 3RF)..................................1986

Assistant Bishop

Rt. Rev. John Stevens Waller *(cons.* 1979) 1987

Dean

Very Rev. Patrick Reynolds Mitchell, F.S.A. 1973

Canons Residentiary

S. R. Cutt (1979); C. E. Thomas (1983); P. de N. Lucas (1988).
Organist, A. Crossland, F.R.C.O. (1970).

Archdeacons

Bath, Ven. J. E. Burgess 1975
Taunton, Ven. L. E. Olyott 1977
Wells, Ven. C. E. Thomas 1983
　　Beneficed Clergy, 225; *Curates, etc.,* 45.
Chancellor, G. H. Newsom, Q.C. (1970).
Registrar, Sec. & Chapt. Clerk, N. M. Cavender, Diocesan Registry, Market Place, Wells BA5 2RE.

BIRMINGHAM

7th Bishop, Rt. Rev. Mark Santer, *cons.* 1981 (Bishop's Croft, Harborne, Birmingham B17 0BG) [Signs Mark Birmingham] 1987

Bishop Suffragan

Aston, Rt. Rev. Colin Ogilvie Buchanan, *cons.* 1985 (60 Handsworth Wood Road, Birmingham B20 2DT) 1985

Provost

Very Rev. Peter Austin Berry 1986

Canons Residentiary

D. McLean (1972); L. M. Davies (1981); Ven. J. L. Cooper (1982).
Organist, M. R. Huxley, F.R.C.O. (1986).

Archdeacons

Aston, Ven. J. L. Cooper 1982
Birmingham, Ven. J. Duncan..................1985
　　Beneficed Clergy, 165; *Curates, etc.,* 73
Chancellor, His Hon. Judge Aglionby (1970).
Registrar and Legal Secretary, M. Shaw, 85 Cornwall Street, Birmingham B3 3BZ.

BRISTOL

54th Bishop, Rt. Rev. Barry Rogerson, *cons.* 1979 (Bishop's House, Clifton Hill, Bristol BS8 1BW) [Signs Barry Bristol] 1985

Bishop Suffragan

Malmesbury, Rt. Rev. Peter James Firth, *cons.* 1983 (7 Ivywell Rd., Bristol BS9 1NX) 1983

Dean

Very Rev. Wesley Arthur Carr 1987

Canons Residentiary

J. M. Free (1982); J. Rogan (1983); A. L. J. Redfern (1987).
Organist, M. Archer, F.R.C.O., A.R.C.M. (1983).

Archdeacons

Bristol, Ven. A. J. Balmforth 1979
Swindon, Ven. K. J. Clark 1982
Beneficed Clergy, 126; *Curates,* 26; *Women Deacons,* 19
Chancellor, D. C. Calcutt, Q.C. (1971).

Registrar and Sec., T. R. Urquhart, 30 Queen Charlotte Street, Bristol BS13 8HE.

CHELMSFORD

7th Bishop, Rt. Rev. John Waine, *cons.* 1975 (Bishopscourt, Margaretting Ingatestone CM4 0HD) [Signs John Chelmsford] 1986

Bishops Suffragan

Barking, Rt. Rev. James William Roxburgh, *cons.* 1983 (28a Connaught Avenue, Loughton, IG10 4DS) 1983
Bradwell, Rt. Rev. Charles Derek Bond, *cons.* 1976 (21 Elmhurst Avenue, Benfleet SS7 5RY) 1976
Colchester, Rt. Rev. Michael Edwin Vickers, *cons.* 1988, (1 Fitzwalter Road, Lexden, Colchester CO3 3SS) 1988

Provost

Very Rev. J. H. Moses, ph.d. 1982

Canons Residentiary

A. W. Carr (1978); M. L. Yorke (1978); P. G. Brett (1985); P. G. Southwell-Sander (1985).
Organist, G. Elliott, ph.d., f.r.c.o. (1981).

Archdeacons

Colchester, Ven. E. C. F. Stroud 1983
Southend, Ven. J. S. Bailey 1982
West Ham, Ven. R. F. Sainsbury 1988
    Beneficed Clergy, 384; *Curates, etc.,* 99
Chancellor, Miss S. M. Cameron, q.c. (1970).
Diocesan Registrar, D. W. Faull, 35 Great Peter Street, Westminster SW1P 3LR.

CHICHESTER

102nd Bishop, Rt. Rev. Eric Waldram Kemp, d.d., *cons.* 1974 (The Palace, Chichester PO19 1PY) [Signs Eric Cicestr] 1974

Bishops Suffragan

Horsham, Rt. Rev. Ivor Colin Docker, *cons.* 1975 (Bishop's Lodge, Worth, nr. Crawley RH10 4RT) 1975
Lewes, Rt. Rev. Peter John Ball, *cons.* 1977 (Litlington Rectory, nr. Polegate BN26 5RB) .1977

Assistant Bishops

Rt. Rev. William Warren Hunt (*cons.* 1955), 1980; Rt. Rev. Mark Green (*cons.* 1972), 1982; Rt. Rev. Simon Wilton Phipps (*cons.* 1968), 1987; Rt. Rev. Edward George Knapp-Fisher (*cons.* 1960), 1987; Rt. Rev. Morris Henry St. John Maddocks (*cons.* 1972), 1987.

Dean

Very Rev. Robert Tinsley Holtby 1977

Canons Residentiary

R. T. Greenacre (1975); J. F. Hester (1985).
Organist, A. J. Thurlow, f.r.c.o. (1980).

Archdeacons

Chichester, Ven. K. Hobbs 1981
Horsham, Ven. W. C. L. Filby, ...1983
Lewes and Hastings, Ven. M. L. Godden 1975
    Beneficed Clergy, 312; *Curates, etc.,* 82
Chancellor, Q. T. Edwards, q.c. (1978).
Legal Secretary to the Bishop, and Diocesan Registrar, C. L. Hodgetts, 5 East Pallant, Chichester PO19 1TS.

COVENTRY

7th Bishop, Rt. Rev. Simon Barrington-Ward, *cons.* 1985 (The Bishop's House, 23 Davenport Road, Coventry CV5 6PW) [Signs Simon Coventry] 1985

Bishop Suffragan

Warwick, Rt. Rev. Keith Appleby Arnold, *cons.* 1980 (139 Kenilworth Rd., Coventry CV4 7AF) 1980

Assistant Bishops

Rt. Rev. John Charles Sydney Daly (*cons.* 1935), 1968; Rt. Rev. Vernon Sampson Nicholls (*cons.* 1974), 1984.

Provost

Very Rev. John Fitzmaurice Petty 1987

Canons Residentiary

P. Oestreicher (1986); M. Sadgrove (1987); D. A. Carrette (1988).
Organist, A. P. Wright, f.r.c.o. (1984).

Archdeacons

Coventry, Ven. A. W. Morgan 1983
Warwick, Ven. P. S. G. Bridges...............1983
    Beneficed Clergy, 104; *Curates, etc.,* 49
Chancellor, W. M. Gage (1980).
Registrar, D. J. Dumbleton, 8 The Quadrant, Coventry CV1 2EL.

DERBY

5th Bishop, Rt. Rev. Peter Spencer Dawes, *cons.* 1988 (The Bishop's House, 6 King Street, Duffield, Derby DE6 4EU) [Signs Peter Derby] 1988

Bishop Suffragan

Repton, Rt. Rev. Francis Henry Arthur Richmond, *cons.* 1986 (Repton House, Lea, Matlock DE4 5JP) 1986

Assistant Bishop

Rt. Rev. Cecil Allan Warren (*cons* 1965)........1983

Provost

Very Rev. Benjamin Hugh Lewers 1981

Canons Residentiary

Ven. R. S. Dell (1981); I. Gatford (1984); G. R. Orchard (1986).
Organist, P. Gould, f.r.c.o. (1982).

Archdeacons

Chesterfield, Ven. G. R. Phizackerley 1978
Derby, Ven. R. S. Dell 1973
    Beneficed Clergy, 182; *Curates, etc.,* 54
Chancellor, J. W. M. Bullimore (1981).
Registrar, J. S. Battie, Derby Church House, Full Street, Derby DE1 3DR.

ELY

66th Bishop, Rt. Rev. Peter Knight Walker, *cons.* 1972, *trs.* 1977 (The Bishop's House, Ely CB7 4DW) [Signs Peter Ely] 1977

Bishop Suffragan

Huntingdon, Rt. Rev. William Gordon Roe, d.Phil., *cons.* 1980 (Powchers Hall, The College, Ely CB7 4DL) 1980

Dean

Very Rev. William James Patterson 1984

Canons Residentiary

D. J. Green (1980); Rt. Rev. W. G. Roe (1980).
Organist, A. W. Wills, MUS.D., F.R.C.O. (1959).

Archdeacons

Ely, Ven. D. Walser 1981
Huntingdon, Ven. R. K. Sledge...............1978
Wisbech, Ven. D. Fleming 1984
    Incumbents, 158; *Curates, etc.,* 10
Chancellor, Rev. Canon K. G. Routledge.
Registrar, W. H. Godfrey, 18 The Broadway, St.
   Ives, Huntingdon PE17 4BS.
Joint Registrar, P. F. B. Beesley, 1 The Sanctuary,
   SW1P 3JT.

EXETER

69*th Bishop,* Rt. Rev. Geoffrey Hewlett Thompson, *cons.* 1974 (The Palace, Exeter EX1 1HY)
   [Signs Hewlett Exon] 1985

Bishops Suffragan

Crediton, Rt. Rev. Peter Coleman, *cons.* 1984 (10
   The Close, Exeter EX1 1EZ) 1984
Plymouth, Rt. Rev. Richard Stephen Hawkins,
   cons. 1988 (15 Stoneleigh Close, Pitt Hill Road,
   Newton Abbot TQ12 1PX) 1988

Assistant Bishops

Rt. Rev. John Armstrong, C.B., O.B.E. (*cons.* 1963),
   1969; Rt. Rev. Charles Robert Claxton (*cons.*
   1946), 1971; Rt. Rev. Ronald Cedric Osbourne
   Goodchild (*cons.* 1964), 1983; Rt. Rev. Philip
   John Pasterfield (*cons.* 1974), 1984.

Dean

Very Rev. Richard Montague Stephens Eyre . . . 1981

Canons Residentiary

J. A. Thurmer (1973); A. C. Mawson (1979); Ven.
   J. Richards (1981).
Organist, L. Nethsingha, F.R.C.O. (1972).
Chapter Clerk, J. F. Eden (1966).

Archdeacons

Barnstaple, (vacant).
Exeter, Ven. J. Richards 1981
Plymouth, Ven. R. G. Ellis 1982
Totnes, Ven. A. F. Tremlett..................1988
    Beneficed Clergy, 257; *Curates, etc.,* 35
Chancellor, D. C. Calcutt, Q.C. (1971).
Registrar, J. F. G. Michelmore, T.D., 18 Cathedral
   Yard, Exeter EX1 1HE.
Diocesan Secretary, Rev. R. R. Huddleson, Dioc-
   esan House, Palace Gate, Exeter EX1 1HX.

GIBRALTAR IN EUROPE

1*st Bishop,* Rt. Rev. John Richard Satterthwaite,
   cons. 1970 (5a Gregory Place, W8 4NG) [Signs
   John Gibraltar] 1970

Bishop Suffragan

In Europe, Rt. Rev. Edward Holland 1986

Auxiliary Bishops

Rt. Rev. E. M. H. Capper, O.B.E., (*cons.* 1967), 1973; Rt.
   Rev. D. de Pina Cabral, (*cons.* 1967), 1976; Rt. Rev.
   H. Isherwood, M.V.O., O.B.E., (*cons.* 1974), 1980.
Vicar-General, Rev. Canon P. O. Deacon.
Bishop's Commissaries, Canon J. A. Taylor; Canon
   L. Tyzack; Preb. D. W. C. Mossman, O.B.E.; Canon
   J. D. Beckwith.
Dean, Cathedral Church of the Holy Trinity, Gibraltar,
   Very Rev. A. L. Nind.
Chancellor, Pro-Cathedral of St. Paul, Valletta, Malta,
   Canon K. W. A. Roberts.

Chancellor, Pro-Cathedral of the Holy Trinity, Brus-
   sels, Belgium, Ven. J. Lewis.

Archdeacons

Aegean, Ven. G. B. Evans.
N.W. Europe, Ven. J. Lewis.
N. France, Ven. M. B. Lea.
Gibraltar, Rt. Rev. D. de Pina Cabral.
Italy, Ven. G. L. C. Westwell.
Riviera, Ven. J. Livingstone.
Scandinavia, Ven. B. Horlock, O.B.E.
Switzerland, Ven. P. J. Hawker.

Chancellor, D. Calcutt, Q.C.
Diocesan Registrar and Legal Secretary, J. G. Underwood, 37a Walbrook, EC4 8BS.

GLOUCESTER

37*th Bishop,* Rt. Rev. John Yates, *cons.* 1972
   (Bishopscourt, Gloucester GL1 2BQ) [Signs
   John Gloucestr] 1975

Bishop Suffragan

Tewkesbury, Rt. Rev. Geoffrey David Jeremy
   Walsh, *cons.* 1986 (Green Acre, Hempsted,
   Gloucester GL2 6LS) 1986

Dean

Very Rev. Kenneth Neal Jennings 1982

Canons Residentiary

D. C. St. V. Welander (1975); A. L. Dunstan
   (1978); R. D. M. Grey (1982); P. R. Greenwood
   (1986).
Organist, J. D. Sanders, F.R.C.O., A.R.C.M. (1967).

Archdeacons

Cheltenham, Ven. J. A. Lewis.................1988
Gloucester, Ven. C. J. H. Wagstaff 1982
    Beneficed Clergy, 184; *Curates, etc.,* 23
Chancellor & Vicar-Gen., Rev. E. Garth Moore (1957).
Registrar, C. G. Peak.
Diocesan Secretary, R. Anderton, 34 Brunswick
   Road, Gloucester GL1 1JW.

GUILDFORD

7*th Bishop,* Rt. Rev. Michael Edgar Adie, *cons.*
   1983 (Willow Grange, Woking Road, Guildford
   GU4 7QS) [Signs Michael Guildford] 1983

Bishop Suffragan

Dorking, Rt. Rev. David Peter Wilcox, *cons.* 1986
   (13 Pilgrims Way, Guildford GU4 8AD) 1986

Assistant Bishop

Rt. Rev. Kenneth Evans, (*cons.* 1968) 1986

Dean

Very Rev. Alexander Gillan Wedderspoon 1987

Canons Residentiary

F. S. Telfer (1973); P. G. Croft (1983); A. S. Leak
   (1986).
Organist, A. T. S. Millington, F.R.C.O. (1983).

Archdeacons

Dorking, Ven. P. G. Hogben 1982
Surrey, Ven. P. E. Barber.....................1980
    Beneficed Clergy, 148; *Curates, etc.,* 59
Chancellor, M. B. Goodman.
Legal Secretary and Registrar, P. F. B. Beesley, 1
   The Sanctuary, SW1P 3JT.

HEREFORD

102*nd Bishop,* Rt. Rev. John Richard Gordon
   Eastaugh, *cons.* 1974 (The Palace, Hereford
   HR4 9BN) [Signs John Hereford]............1974

Bishop Suffragan

Ludlow, Rt. Rev. Ian MacDonald Griggs, *cons.* 1987 (Halford Vicarage, Craven Arms, Shropshire SY7 9BT)............................1987

Dean

Very Rev. Peter Haynes......................1982

Canons Residentiary

Ven. A. H. Woodhouse (1982); P. Iles (1983); J. Tiller (1984).
Organist, R. Massey, F.R.C.O. (1974).

Archdeacons

Hereford, Ven. A. H. Woodhouse 1982
Ludlow, Ven. J. H. R. Lewis 1987
    Beneficed Clergy, 98; *Curates, etc.*, 43
Chancellor, J. M. Henty.
Joint Registrars, V. T. Jordan, 44 Bridge Street, Hereford; P. Beesley, 1 The Sanctuary, Westminster, SW1P 3JT.

LEICESTER

4th Bishop, Rt. Rev. Cecil Richard Rutt, C.B.E., *cons.* 1966 (Bishop's Lodge, Leicester LE2 3BD) [Signs Richard Leicester] 1979

Assistant Bishops

Rt. Rev. John Ernest Llewelyn Mort, O.B.E. (*cons.* 1952) 1972; Rt. Rev. Godfrey Ashby, 1980.

Provost

Very Rev. Alan Christopher Warren 1978

Canons Residentiary

M. T. H. Banks (1988); M. Wilson (1988).
Organist, P. White, F.R.C.O. (1968).

Archdeacons

Leicester, Ven. R. D. Silk 1980
Loughborough, Ven. T. H. Jones 1986
    Beneficed Clergy, 145; *Curates, etc.*, 36
Chancellor, N. H. Freeman (1979).
Registrar, G. K. J. Moore, 10 Friar Lane, Leicester LE1 5QD.

LICHFIELD

97th Bishop, Rt. Rev. Keith Norman Sutton, *cons.* 1978 (Bishop's House, The Close, Lichfield WS13 7LG) [Signs Keith Lichfield] 1984

Bishops Suffragan

Shrewsbury, Rt. Rev. John Dudley Davies, *cons.* 1987 (Athlone House, 68 London Road, Shrewsbury SY2 6PG) 1987
Stafford, Rt. Rev. Michael Charles Scott-Joynt, *cons.* 1987 (Ash Garth, Broughton Crescent, Barlaston ST12 9DD) 1987
Wolverhampton, Rt. Rev. Christopher John Mayfield, *cons.* 1985 (61 Richmond Road, Wolverhampton WV3 9JH) 1985

Dean

Very Rev. John Harley Lang 1980

Canons Residentiary

Ven. R. B. Ninis (1974); A. N. Barnard (1977); W. J. Turner (1983).
Organist, J. Rees-Williams, F.R.C.O. (1978).

Archdeacons

Lichfield, Ven. R. B. Ninis....................1974
Salop, Ven. G. Frost 1987
Stoke on Trent, Ven. J. D. Delight 1982
    Beneficed Clergy, 352; *Curates, etc.*, 76

Chancellor, Rev. Canon K. G. Routledge.
Diocesan Registrar and Bishop's Sec., J. P. Thorneycroft, St. Mary's House, The Close, Lichfield WS13 7LD.

LINCOLN

70th Bishop, Rt. Rev. Robert Maynard Hardy, *cons.* 1980 (Bishop's House, Eastgate, Lincoln LN2 1QQ) [Signs Robert Lincoln] 1987

Bishops Suffragan

Grantham, Rt. Rev. William Ind, *cons.* 1987 (Fairacre, Barrowby High Road, Grantham NG31 8NP) 1987
Grimsby, Rt. Rev. David Tustin, *cons.* 1979 (43 Abbey Park Road, Grimsby DN32 0HS) 1979

Assistant Bishop

Rt. Rev. Gerald Fitzmaurice Colin (*cons.* 1966), 1979

Dean

Very Rev. the Hon. Oliver William Twisleton-Wykeham-Fiennes 1969

Canons Residentiary

D. C. Rutter (1965); B. R. Davis (1977); J. S. Nurser, PH.D. (1977); Ven. J. H. C. Laurence (1985).
Organist, C. Walsh, F.R.C.O. (1988).

Archdeacons

Lincoln, Ven. M. P. Brackenbury 1988
Lindsey, Ven. J. H. C. Laurence...............1985
Stow, Ven. D. Scott 1975
    Beneficed Clergy, 250; *Curates, etc.*, 91
Chancellor, His Honour Judge M. B. Goodman (1971).
Registrar and Legal Secretary, D. M. Wellman, 28 West Parade, Lincoln LN1 1JT.

NORWICH

70th Bishop , Rt. Rev. Peter John Nott, *cons.* 1977 (Bishop's House, Norwich, NR3 1SB) [Signs Peter Norvic] 1985

Bishops Suffragan

Lynn, Rt. Rev. David Edward Bentley, *cons.* 1986 (The Old Vic., Castle Acre, King's Lynn PE32 2AA) 1986
Thetford, Rt. Rev. Timothy Dudley-Smith, *cons.* 1981 (Rectory Meadow, Bramerton, Norwich NR14 7DW)..............................1981

Dean

Very Rev. John Paul Burbridge...............1983

Canons Residentiary

D. H. Bishop (1980); C. Beswick (1984); M. S. McLean (1986).
Organist, M. B. Nicholas, F.R.C.O. (1971).

Archdeacons

Lynn, Ven. A. C. Foottit 1987
Norfolk, Ven. P. Dawson......................1977
Norwich, Ven. A. M. Handley 1981
    Beneficed Clergy, 210; *Curates, etc.*, 25
Chancellor, His Hon. J. H. Ellison, V.R.D. (1955).
Registrar and Sec., B. O. L. Prior, M.B.E., T.D., 74 The Close, Norwich NR1 4DE.

OXFORD

41st Bishop, Rt. Rev. Richard Douglas Harries, *cons.* 1987 (Diocesan Church House, North Hinksey, Oxford OX2 0NB) [Signs Richard Oxon] 1987

Area Bishops

Buckingham, Rt. Rev. Simon Hedley Burrows, cons. 1974 (Sheridan, Grimms Hill, Great Missenden HP16 9BD) 1974
Dorchester, Rt. Rev. Anthony Russell, cons. 1988 (The Rectory, Whitchurch, Stratford-on-Avon) 1988
Reading, Rt. Rev. Ronald Gregory Graham Foley, cons. 1982 (Greenbanks, Old Bath Road, Sonning, Reading RG4 0SY 1982

Assistant Bishops

Rt. Rev. Sydney Cyril Bulley, D.D. (cons. 1959), 1979; Rt. Rev. Albert Kenneth Cragg, D.D., (cons. 1970), 1982; Rt. Rev. Eric Wild, (cons. 1972), 1982; Rt. Rev. Leonard James Ashton, C.B., (cons. 1974), 1984; Rt. Rev. Richard Watson (cons. 1970), 1988.

Dean of Christ Church

Very Rev. Eric William Heaton 1979

Canons Residentiary

M. F. Wiles, (1970); J. C. Fenton (1978); Ven. F. V. Weston (1982); O. M. T. O'Donovan, D.Phil. (1982); R. D. Williams, D.Phil. (1985); J. M. Pierce (1987).
Organist, S. Darlington, F.R.C.O.

Archdeacons

Berkshire, Ven. D. Griffiths....................1987
Buckingham, Ven. J. F. E. Bone...............1978
Oxford, Ven. F. V. Weston 1982
    Stipendiary Clergy, 454; *Beneficed Clergy*, 380

Chancellor, P. T. S. Boydell, Q.C. (1958).
Registrar and Legal Secretary, F. E. Robson, 16 Beaumont Street, Oxford OX1 2LZ.

WINDSOR

(The Queen's Free Chapel of St. George within Her Castle of Windsor—A Royal Peculiar)
Dean, Rt. Rev. Michael Ashley Mann..........1976

Canons Residentiary

J. D. Treadgold (1981); J. A. White (1982); D. M. Stanesby (1985); A. A. Coldwells (1987).
Organist, C. J. Robinson, L.V.O., F.R.C.O. (1975).
Chapter Clerk, Maj.-Gen. R. L. C. Dixon, C.B., M.C. (1981).

PETERBOROUGH

36th Bishop, Rt. Rev. William John Westwood, cons. 1975 (The Palace, Peterborough PE1 1YA) [Signs William Petriburg] 1984

Bishop Suffragan

The new see of *Brixworth* was approved by the Queen in Aug. 1988. At the time of going to press no appointment had been made.

Dean

Very Rev. Randolph George Wise 1981

Canons Residentiary

Ven. B. Fernyhough (1977); T. R. Christie (1980); J. Higham (1983).
Organist, C. S. Gower, F.R.C.O. (1977).

Archdeacons

Northampton, Ven. B. R. Marsh...............1964
Oakham, Ven. B. Fernyhough 1977
    Beneficed Clergy, 181; *Curates, etc.*, 60
Chancellor, Rev. Canon K. C. Routledge.
Registrar and Legal Secretary, R. Hemingray, 10 Queen Street, Peterborough PE1 1PH.

PORTSMOUTH

7th Bishop, Rt. Rev. Timothy John Bavin, cons. 1974 (Bishopswood, Fareham, Hants. PO14 1NT) [Signs Timothy Portsmouth] 1985

Provost

Very Rev. David Staffurth Stancliffe 1982

Canons Residentiary

S. G. Platten (1983); R. Eckersley (1984); P. J. Cotton (1984); M. J. Gudgeon (1987).
Organist, A. Froggatt, F.R.C.O.

Archdeacons

Portsmouth, Ven. N. H. Crowder 1985
I. of Wight, Ven. A. H. M. Turner..............1986
    Beneficed Clergy, 90; *Curates, etc.*, 88
Chancellor, His Honour Judge Aglionby (1978).
Registrar, Miss H. A. G. Tyler, 132 High Street, Portsmouth PO1 2HR.

ROCHESTER

105th Bishop, Rt. Rev. Anthony Michael Arnold Turnbull, cons. 1988 (Bishopscourt, Rochester ME1 1TS) [Signs Michael Roffen] 1988

Bishop Suffragan

Tonbridge, Rt. Rev. David Henry Bartleet, cons. 1982 (Bishop's Lodge, St. Botolph's Road, Sevenoaks TN13 3AG) 1982

Dean

Very Rev. John Robert Arnold 1978

Canon Residentiary

E. R. Turner (1981).
Organist, B. Ferguson, F.R.C.O. (1977).

Archdeacons

Bromley, Ven. E. R. Francis 1979
Rochester, (vacant).
Tonbridge, Ven. R. J. Mason...................1977
    Beneficed Clergy, 200; *Curates, etc.*, 50
Chancellor, His Honour Judge M. B. Goodman (1971).
Registrar, O. R. Woodfield, The Precinct, Rochester ME1 1SZ.
Secretary, D. W. Faull, 35 Great Peter Street, SW1P 3LR.

ST. ALBANS

8th Bishop, Rt. Rev. John Bernard Taylor, cons. 1980 (Abbey Gate House, St. Albans AL3 4HD) [Signs John St. Albans] 1980

Bishops Suffragan

Bedford, Rt. Rev. David John Farmbrough, cons. 1981 (168 Kimbolton Road, Bedford MK41 8DN)..1981
Hertford, Rt. Rev. Kenneth Harold Pillar, cons. 1982 (Hertford House, Abbey Mill Lane, St. Albans AL3 4HE) 1982

Dean

Very Rev. Peter Clement Moore, D.Phil.........1973

Canons Residentiary

B. C. E. Pettifer; C. B. Slee (1982); C. Garner (1984); G. R. S. Ritson (1987); M. Sansom (1988).
Organist, B. Rose, F.R.C.O. (1988).

Archdeacons

Bedford, Ven. M. G. Bourke 1986
St. Albans, Ven. P. B. Davies 1987
    Beneficed Clergy, 249; *Curates, etc.*, 83

Chancellor, G. H. Newsom, Q.C. (1958).
Registrar and Legal Sec., D. N. Cheetham, Holywell Lodge, 41 Holywell Hill, St. Albans AL1 1HE.

ST. EDMUNDSBURY AND IPSWICH

8th Bishop, Rt. Rev. John Dennis, *cons.* 1979 (Bishop's House, Ipswich IP1 3ST) [Signs John St. Edmund & Ipswich] 1986

Bishop Suffragan

Dunwich, Rt. Rev. Eric Nash Devenport, *cons.* 1980 (The Old Vicarage, Stowupland, Stowmarket IP14 4BQ) 1980

Provost

Very Rev. Raymond Furnell 1981

Canons Residentiary

D. A. Payne (1973); G. J. Tarris (1982); R. Garrard (1987).
Organist, P. Treptre, F.R.C.O. (1985).

Archdeacons

Ipswich, Ven. T. A. Gibson 1987
Sudbury, Ven. D. J. Smith 1984
Suffolk, Ven. N. Robinson 1987
Beneficed Clergy, 139, *Curates, etc.*, 55
Chancellor, His Honour Judge Blofeld, Q.C. (1974).
Registrar, J. D. Mitson, 22–28 Museum Street, Ipswich IP1 1JA.

SALISBURY

76th Bishop, Rt. Rev. John Austin Baker, *cons.* 1982 (South Canonry, The Close, Salisbury SP1 2ER) [Signs John Sarum] 1982

Bishops Suffragan

Ramsbury, Rt. Rev. John Robert Geoffrey Neale, *cons.* 1974 (Bishop's House, Urchfont, Devizes, Wilts., SN10 4QH) 1974
Sherborne, Rt. Rev. John Dudley Galtrey Kirkham, *cons.* 1976 (Little Bailie, Sturminster Marshall, Wimborne BH21 4AD) 1976

Assistant Bishop

Rt. Rev. John Kingsmill Cavell, (*cons.* 1972) 1988

Dean

Very Rev. the Hon. Hugh Geoffrey Dickinson ..1986

Canons Residentiary

I. G. D. Dunlop, F.S.A. (1972); R. G. Askew (1983); D. J. C. Davies (1985).
Organist, R. G. Seal, F.R.C.O. (1968).

Archdeacons

Dorset, Ven. G. E. Walton 1982
Sarum, Ven. B. J. Hopkinson 1986
Sherborne, Ven. J. K. Oliver 1985
Wilts, Ven. B. J. Smith 1980
Beneficed Clergy, 255; *Curates, etc.*, 38
Chancellor of the Diocese, His Hon. J. H. Ellison, V.R.D. (1955).
Registrar and Legal Secretary, F. M. Broadbent, 42 Castle Street, Salisbury SP1 3TX.

SOUTHWARK

7th Bishop, Rt. Rev. Ronald Oliver Bowlby, *cons.* 1973, *trs.* 1980 (Bishop's House, 38 Tooting Bec Gardens, SW16 1QZ) [Signs Ronald Southwark] 1980

Bishops Suffragan

Croydon, Rt. Rev. Wilfred Denniston Wood, D.D., *cons.* 1985 (St. Matthew's House, George Street, Croydon CR0 1PE) 1985
Kingston upon Thames, Rt. Rev. Peter Stephen Maurice Selby, PH.D., *cons.* 1984 (24 Albert Drive, SW19 6LS) 1984
Woolwich, Rt. Rev. Albert Peter Hall, *cons.* 1984 (8b Hillyfields Crescent, SE4 1QA) 1984

Assistant Bishops

Rt. Rev. Edmund Michael Hubert Capper, O.B.E. (*cons.* 1967), 1981; Rt. Rev. Archibald Ronald McDonald Gordon (*cons.* 1975), 1984; Rt. Rev. John Hughes (*cons.* 1956), 1986; Rt. Rev. Hugh William Montefiore (*cons.* 1970), 1987; Rt. Rev. Simon Wilton Phipps (*cons.* 1976), 1987.

Provost

Very Rev. David Lawrence Edwards 1983

Canons Residentiary

P. H. Penwarden (1971); I. G. Smith-Cameron (1972); J. S. Cox (1983); P. B. Price (1988).
Organist, H. Bramma (1976).

Archdeacons

Croydon, Ven. F. R. Hazell 1984
Lambeth, Ven. C. R. B. Bird 1988
Lewisham, Ven. C. J. Lacey 1985
Reigate, (vacant).
Southwark, Ven. D. L. Bartles-Smith 1985
Wandsworth, Ven. P. B. Coombs 1975
Chancellor, Rev. E. Garth Moore (1948).
Registrar, D. W. Faull, 35 Great Peter Street, SW1P 3LR.

TRURO

12th Bishop, Rt. Rev. Peter Mumford, *cons.* 1974, (Lis Escop, Truro TR3 6QQ) [Signs Peter Truron] 1981

Bishop Suffragan

St. Germans, Rt. Rev. Richard Llewellin, *cons.* 1986 (32 Falmouth Road, Truro TR1 2HX) ...1985

Assistant Bishop

Rt. Rev. R. F. Cartwright (*cons.* 1972).........1982

Dean

Very Rev. David John Shearlock 1982

Canons Residentiary

W. J. P. Boyd, PH.D. (1985); Ven. R. L. Ravenscroft (1988); R. O. Osborne (1988).
Organist, (vacant).

Archdeacons

Cornwall, Ven. R. L. Ravenscroft 1988
Bodmin, Ven. G. F. Temple 1981
Beneficed Clergy, 164; *Curates, etc.*, 20
Chancellor, P. T. S. Boydell, Q.C. (1957).
Registrar and Secretary, M. J. Follett, 2 Princes Street, Truro TR1 2EZ.

WORCESTER

111th Bishop, Rt. Rev. Philip Harold Ernest Goodrich, *cons.* 1973 (The Bishop's House, Hartlebury Castle, Kidderminster DY11 7XX) [Signs Philip Worcester] 1982

Bishop Suffragan

Dudley, Rt. Rev. Anthony Charles Dumper, *cons.* 1977 (The Bishop's House, Brooklands, Halesowen Road, Cradley Heath B64 7JF) 1977

Assistant Bishops

Rt. Rev. David Howard Nicholas Allenby (*cons.* 1962), 1968; Rt. Rev. Oliver Stratford Tomkins (*cons.* 1959), 1975; Rt. Rev. John Arthur Arrowsmith Maund, C.B.E., M.C. (*cons.* 1950), 1984.

Dean

Very Rev. Robert Martin Colquhoun Jeffery . . . 1987

Canons Residentiary

J. R. Fenwick (1978); Ven. F. Bentley (1984).
Organist, D. Hunt, MUS.D., F.R.C.O. (1975).

Archdeacons

Dudley, Ven. J. Gathercole 1987
Worcester, Ven. F. Bentley 1984
  Beneficed Clergy, 120; *Curates, etc.*, 50
Chancellor, P. T. S. Boydell, Q.C. (1959).
Registrar, Rev. Canon J. A. Dale, Diocesan Registry, The Old Palace, Deansway, Worcester WR1 2JE.

Province of York

YORK

95th Archbishop and Primate of England Most Rev. and Rt. Hon. John Stapylton Habgood, PH.D., *cons.* 1973, *trs.* 1983 (Bishopthorpe, York YO2 1QE) [Signs John Ebor] 1983

Bishops Suffragan

Hull, Rt. Rev. Donald George Snelgrove, T.D., *cons.* 1981 (Hullen House, Woodfield Lane, Hessle, Hull HU13 0ES) 1981
Selby, Rt. Rev. Clifford Conder Barker, T.D., *cons.* 1976 (8 Bankside Close, Upper Poppleton, York YO2 6LH) 1983
Whitby, Rt. Rev. Gordon Bates, *cons.* 1983 (60 West Green, Stokesley, Middlesbrough TS9 5BD) 1983

Assistant Bishops

Rt. Rev. George Eyles Irwin Cockin (*cons.* 1959), 1969; Rt. Rev. Richard Knyvet Wimbush (*cons.* 1963), 1977; Rt. Rev. Richard James Wood (*cons.* 1973), 1985.

Dean

Very Rev. John Eliot Southgate 1984

Canons Residentiary

R. A. Hockley (1976); R. Mayland (1982); J. Toy, PH.D. (1983); R. Metcalfe (1988).
Organist, P. J. Moore, A.R.C.M., F.R.C.O.

Archdeacons

Cleveland, Ven. R. J. Woodley 1984
East Riding, Ven. H. F. Buckingham 1988
York, Ven. G. B. Austin 1988
  Beneficed Clergy, 257; *Curates, etc.*, 38
Official Principal and Auditor of the Chancery Court, J. A. D. Owen, Q.C.
Chancellor of the Diocese, T. A. C. Coningsby (1977).
Vicar-General of the Province and Official Principal of the Consistory Court, T. A. C. Coningsby.
Registrar and Legal Secretary, L. P. M. Lennox, 22 High Petergate, York YO1 2EH.

DURHAM

92nd Bishop, Rt. Rev. David Edward Jenkins, *cons.* 1984 (Auckland Castle, Bishop Auckland DL14 7NR) [Signs David Dunelm] 1984

Bishop Suffragan

Jarrow, Rt. Rev. Michael Thomas Ball, *cons.* 1980 (Melkridge House, Gilesgate, Durham DH1 1JB) 1980

Dean

Very Rev. Peter Richard Baelz 1980

Canons Residentiary

Ven. M. C. Perry (1970); R. L. Coppin (1974); Ven. J. D. Hodgson (1983); T. Hart (1983); D. W. Hardy (1986).
Organist, J. B. Lancelot, F.R.C.O. (1985).

Archdeacons

Auckland, Ven. J. D. Hodgson 1983
Durham, Ven. M. C. Perry 1970
  Clergy, 306
Chancellor, Rev. E. Garth Moore (1954).
Registrar and Legal Secretary, W. K. Wills, Diocesan Registry, 21a Elvet Bridge, Durham DH1 3AA (1975).

BLACKBURN

Bishop, (vacant).

Bishops Suffragan

Burnley, Rt. Rev. Ronald James Milner, *cons.* 1988 (Palace House, 458 Padiham Road, Burnley BB12 6TD) 1988
Lancaster, Rt. Rev. Ian Harland, *cons.* 1985 (Wheatfield, Dallas Road, Lancaster LA1 1TN) 1985

Provost

Very Rev. Lawrence Jackson 1973

Canons Residentiary

G. A. Williams (1965); J. M. Taylor (1976); B. M. Beaumont (1977); G. I. Hirst (1987).
Organist, D. A. Cooper, F.R.C.O. (1983).

Archdeacons

Blackburn, Ven. W. D. Robinson 1986
Lancaster, Ven. K. H. Gibbons 1981
  Beneficed Clergy, 230; *Curates, etc.*, 50
Chancellor, Q. T. Edwards, Q.C. (1977).
Registrar, L. Ranson, Diocesan Registry, Cathedral Close, Blackburn BB1 5AB (1954).

BRADFORD

7th Bishop, Rt. Rev. Robert Kerr Williamson, *cons.* 1984 (Bishopscroft, Ashwell Road, Heaton, Bradford BD9 4AU) [Signs Robert Bradford] 1984

Assistant Bishop

Rt. Rev. David Richard John Evans (*cons.* 1978) 1988

Provost

Very Rev. Brandon Donald Jackson 1977

Canons Residentiary

K. H. Cook (1977); C. J. Hayward (1983).
Organist, A. Horsey (1986).

Archdeacons

Bradford, Ven. D. H. Shreeve 1984
Craven, Ven. B. A. Smith 1987
  Beneficed Clergy, 114; *Curates, etc.*, 38
Chancellor, D. M. Savill, Q.C. (1976).
Registrar and Secretary, J. G. H. Mackrell, 6–14
  Devonshire Street, Keighley BD21 2AY (1977).

CARLISLE

64th Bishop, Rt. Rev. Henry David Halsey, *cons.*
  1968 (Rose Castle, Dalston, Carlisle CA5 7BZ),
  [Signs David Carliol] 1972

Bishop Suffragan

Penrith, Rt. Rev. George Lanyon Hacker, *cons.*
  1979 (The Rectory, Great Salkeld, Penrith
  CA11 9NA) 1979

Dean

Very Rev. Henry Edward Champneys Staple-
  ton 1988

Canons Residentiary

R. A. Chapman (1978); R. J. W. Bevan (1982); A.
  Smithson (1984); Ven. C. P. Stannard (1984).
Organist, R. A. Seivewright, A.R.C.O. (1960).

Archdeacons

Carlisle, Ven. C. P. Stannard 1984
West Cumberland, Ven. T. R. B. Hodgson 1979
Westmorland and Furness, Ven. P. St. G.
  Vaughan 1983
  Beneficed Clergy, 190
Chancellor, His Hon. D. J. Stinson (1971).
Registrar and Secretary, I. S. Sutcliffe, Castle
  Street, Carlisle CA3 8TW (1964).

CHESTER

39th Bishop, Rt. Rev. Michael Alfred Baughen,
  cons. 1982 (Bishop's House, Chester CH1 2JD)
  [Signs Michael Cestr] 1982

Bishops Suffragan

Birkenhead, Rt. Rev. Ronald Brown, *cons.* 1974
  (Trafford House, Queen's Park, Chester
  CH4 7AX) 1974
Stockport, Rt. Rev. Frank Pilkington Sargeant,
  cons. 1984 (32 Park Gate Drive, Cheadle Hulme,
  Cheshire SK8 7DF) 1984

Dean

Very Rev. Stephen Stewart Smalley 1986

Canons Residentiary

W. H. Vanstone (1978); L. R. Barker (1984); C. D.
  Biddell (1986).
Organist, R. A. Fisher, F.R.C.O. (1967).

Archdeacons

Chester, Ven. M. F. Gear 1988
Macclesfield, Ven. J. S. Gaisford 1986
Chancellor, H. H. Lomas (1977).
Registrar and Legal Secretary, A. K. McAllester,
  Friars, 20 White Friars, Chester CH1 1XS.

LIVERPOOL

6th Bishop, Rt. Rev. David Stuart Sheppard,
  cons. 1969 (Bishop's Lodge, Woolton Park,
  Liverpool L25 6DT) [Signs David Liverpool] . . 1975

Bishop Suffragan

Warrington, Rt. Rev. Michael Henshall, *cons.*
  1976 (Martinsfield, Elm Avenue, Great Crosby,
  Liverpool L23 2SX) 1976

Assistant Bishop

Rt. Rev. William Scott Baker (*cons.* 1943) 1968

Dean

Very Rev. R. D. C. Walters 1983

Canons Residentiary

M. M. Wolfe (1982); D. J. Hutton (1983); K. J.
  Riley (1983); H. Thomas (1988).
Organist, I. Tracey (1980).

Archdeacons

Liverpool, Ven. G. H. G. Spiers 1979
Warrington, Ven. C. D. S. Woodhouse 1981
  Beneficed Clergy, 246; *Curates, etc.*, 89
Chancellor, R. G. Hamilton.
Registrar and Cathedral Chapter Clerk, R. H.
  Arden, 1 Hanover Street, Liverpool L1 3DW.

MANCHESTER

9th Bishop, Rt. Rev. Stanley Eric Francis Booth-
  Clibborn, *cons.* 1979 (Bishopscourt, Bury New
  Road, Manchester M7 0LE) [Signs Stanley
  Manchester] 1979

Bishops Suffragan

Bolton, Rt. Rev. David George Galliford, *cons.*
  1984 (4 Sandfield Drive, Lostock, Bolton
  BL6 4DU) 1984
Hulme, Rt. Rev. Colin John Fraser Scott, *cons.*
  1984 (1 Raynham Avenue, Didsbury, Man-
  chester M20 0BW) 1984
Middleton, Rt. Rev. Donald Alexander Tytler,
  cons. 1982 (The Hollies, Manchester Road,
  Rochdale OL11 3QY) 1982

Assistant Bishops

Rt. Rev. Edward Ralph Wickham (*cons.* 1959),
  1982; Rt. Rev. Kenneth Venner Ramsey (*cons.*
  1953), 1975.

Dean

Very Rev. Robert Murray Waddington 1984

Canons Residentiary

Ven. R. B. Harris (1980); J. Nicholls (1983); J. R.
  Atherton, PH.D. (1984); B. Duncan (1986).
Organist, G. Stewart.

Archdeacons

Bolton, Ven. W. S. Brison 1985
Manchester, Ven. R. B. Harris 1980
Rochdale, Ven. D. Bonser 1982
  Beneficed Clergy, 300; *Curates, etc.*, 110
Chancellor, G. C. H. Spafford (1976).
Registrar and Bishop's Secretary, M. Darlington,
  90 Deansgate, Manchester M3 2GH (1986).

NEWCASTLE

10th Bishop, Rt. Rev. Andrew Alexander Kenny
  Graham, *cons.* 1977 (Bishop's House, 29 Moor
  Road South, Gosforth, Newcastle upon Tyne
  NE3 1PA) [Signs A. Newcastle] 1981

Assistant Bishop

Rt. Rev. Kenneth Edward Gill (*cons.* 1972) 1980

Provost

Very Rev. Christopher Garnett Howsin Spafford
  1976

Canons Residentiary

W. J. Thomas (1983); R. Langley (1985); P. R.
  Strange (1986); I. F. Bennett (1988).
Organist, T. Hone (1987).

Archdeacons

Lindisfarne, Ven. M. E. Bowering 1987
Northumberland, Ven. W. J. Thomas 1983
Beneficed Clergy, 117; *other Clergy of incumbent status*, 27; *Curates, etc.*, 34
Chancellor, His Hon. A. J. Blackett-Ord, C.V.O. (1971).
Registrar and Secretary, R. R. V. Nicholson, 46 Grainger Street, Newcastle upon Tyne NE1 5LB.

RIPON

11*th Bishop*, Rt. Rev. David Nigel de Lorentz Young, *cons.* 1977 (Bishop Mount, Ripon HG4 5DP) [Signs David Ripon] 1977

Bishop Suffragan

Knaresborough, Rt. Rev. Malcolm James Mennin, *cons.* 1986 (16 Shaftesbury Avenue, Roundhay, Leeds LS8 1DT) 1986

Assistant Bishops

Rt. Rev. John Howe (*cons.* 1955) 1983; Rt. Rev. Ralph Emmerson (*cons.* 1972) 1987.

Dean

Very Rev. Christopher Russell Campling 1984

Canons Residentiary

R. B. McFadden (1979); D. G. Ford (1980); P. J. Marshall (1985).
Organist, R. Perrin, F.R.C.O. (1966).

Archdeacons

Leeds, Ven. A. J. Comber 1982
Richmond, Ven. N. G. L. R. McDermid 1983
Beneficed Clergy, 132; *Curates, etc.*, 58
Chancellor, D. M. Savill, Q.C. (1987).
Registrar and Legal Secretary, J. R. Balmforth, York House, York Place, Knaresborough HG5 0AD.

SHEFFIELD

5*th Bishop*, Rt. Rev. David Ramsay Lunn, *cons.* 1980 (Bishopscroft, Snaithing Lane, Sheffield S10 3LG) [Signs David Sheffield] 1980

Bishop Suffragan

Doncaster, Rt. Rev. William Michael Dermot Persson, *cons.* 1982 (Bishops Lodge, Rotherham S65 4PF) 1982

Assistant Bishop

Rt. Rev. Kenneth John Fraser Skelton, C.B.E. (*cons.* 1962) 1984

Provost

Very Rev. John Warren Gladwin 1988

Canons Residentiary

G. Lacey (1981); T. M. Page (1982); Ven. S. R. Lowe (1988); J. R. Giles (1988).
Organist, G. Matthews, F.R.C.O. (1967).

Archdeacons

Doncaster, Ven. D. Carnelley 1985
Sheffield, Ven. S. R. Lowe 1988
Beneficed Clergy, 163; *Curates, etc.*, 46

Chancellor, G. B. Graham, Q.C. (1971).
Registrar and Legal Secretary, P. T. Ward, 30 Bank Street, Sheffield S1 2DS.

SODOR AND MAN

Bishop, (vacant).

Canons Residentiary

B. H. Kelly (1980); D. Baggaley (1980); J. D. Gelling (1980); B. H. Partington (1985).

Archdeacon

Isle of Man, Ven. D. A. Willoughby 1982
Beneficed Clergy, 20; *Curates, etc.*, 21
Vicar-General and Registrar, P. W. S. Farrant, 24 Athol Street, Douglas.

SOUTHWELL

9*th Bishop*, Rt. Rev. Patrick Burnet Harris, *cons.* 1973 (Bishop's Manor, Southwell NG25 0JR) [Signs Patrick Southwell] 1988

Bishop Suffragan

Sherwood, Rt. Rev. Harold Richard Darby, *cons.* 1975 (Applegarth, Halam, Newark NG22 8AN) 1975

Provost

Very Rev. John Murray Irvine 1978

Canons Residentiary

D. P. Keene (1981); I. G. Collins (1985).
Organist, K. Beard, F.R.C.O. (1959).

Archdeacons

Newark, Ven. D. Leaning 1980
Nottingham, Ven. G. C. Handford 1984
Beneficed Clergy, 180; *Curates, etc.*, 52
Chancellor, J. Shand (1981).
Registrar, P. H. Mellors, Diocesan Office, Westgate, Southwell NG25 0JL (1970).

WAKEFIELD

10*th Bishop*, Rt. Rev. David Michael Hope, D.Phil., *cons.* 1985 (Bishop's Lodge, Woodthorpe Lane, Wakefield WF2 6JJ) [Signs David Wakefield] 1985

Bishop Suffragan

Pontefract, Rt. Rev. Thomas Richard Hare, *cons.* 1971 (306 Barnsley Road, Wakefield WF2 6AX) 1971

Provost

Very Rev. John Edward Allen. 1982
Organist, J. L. Bielby, F.R.C.O. (1971).

Archdeacons

Halifax, Ven. A. D. Chesters 1985
Pontefract, Ven. K. Unwin 1981
Beneficed Clergy, 176; *Curates, etc.*, 27
Chancellor, G. B. Graham, Q.C. (1959).
Registrar and Sec., E. Chapman, Burton Street, Wakefield WF1 2DA (1979).

THE CHURCH IN WALES

9th Archbishop of Wales, Most Rev. George Noakes (Bishop of St. David's), *elected 1987.*

BANGOR

79th Bishop, Rt. Rev. John Cledan Mears, *b.* 1922, *cons.* 1982 (Tŷ'r Esgob, Bangor LL57 2SS) [Signs Cledan Bangor] 1982

LLANDAFF

101st Bishop, Rt. Rev. Roy Thomas Davies, *b.* 1934, *cons.* 1985 (Llys Esgob, The Cathedral Green, Llandaff, Cardiff CF5 2YE) [Signs Roy Landav] 1985

MONMOUTH

7th Bishop, Rt. Rev. Royston Clifford Wright, *b.* 1922, *cons.* 1986 (Bishopstow, Stow Hill, Newport NP9 4EA) [Signs Clifford Monmouth] . . . 1986

ST. ASAPH

74th Bishop, Rt. Rev. Alwyn Rice Jones, *b.*, 1934, *cons.* 1982 (Esgobty, St. Asaph, Clwyd LL17 0TW) [Signs Alwyn St. Asaph] 1982

ST. DAVID'S

124th Bishop and 9th Archbishop of Wales, Most Rev. George Noakes, *b.* 1924, *cons.* 1982 (Llys Esgob, Abergwili, Dyfed SA31 2JG) [Signs George Cambrensis] 1982

SWANSEA AND BRECON

7th Bishop, Rt. Rev. Dewi Morris Bridges, *b.* 1932, *cons.* 1988 (Ely Tower, Brecon, Powys LD3 9DE) [Signs Dewi Swansea & Brecon] . . . 1988

(Stipend of diocesan bishop of the Church of Wales is £16,155 p.a. from Jan. 1, 1989)

THE EPISCOPAL CHURCH IN SCOTLAND

Primus of the Episcopal Church in Scotland, Most Rev. Lawrence Edward Luscombe (Bishop of Brechin), *elected* 1985.

The Rt. Rev. Bishops

Aberdeen and Orkney, Frederick Charles Darwent, *b.* 1927, *cons.* 1978, *apptd.* 1978, *stipend* £11,088: *Clergy* 12.

Argyll and the Isles, George Kennedy Buchanan Henderson, *b.* 1921, *cons.* 1977, *apptd.* 1977, *stipend* £13,200: *Clergy* 11.

Brechin, Lawrence Edward Luscombe, *b.* 1924, *cons.* 1975, *apptd.* 1975, *stipend* £8,379: *Clergy* 18.

Edinburgh, Richard Frederick Holloway, *b.* 1933, *cons.* 1986, *apptd.* 1986, *stipend* £10,320: *Clergy* 62.

Glasgow and Galloway, Derek Alec Rawcliffe, O.B.E., *b.* 1921, *cons.* 1974, *apptd.* 1981, *stipend* £11,220: *Clergy* 43.

Moray, Ross and Caithness, George Minshull Sessford, *b.* 1928, *cons.* 1970, *apptd.* 1970, *stipend* £8,730: *Clergy* 17.

St. Andrews, Dunkeld and Dunblane, Michael Geoffrey Hare-Duke, *b.* 1925, *cons.* 1969, *apptd.* 1969, *stipend* £9,300: *Clergy* 29.

Registrar of the Episcopal Synod, I.R. Guild, 16 Charlotte Square, Edinburgh EH2 4YS Churches, Mission Stations, &c., 341. Clergy 203; Communicants, 36,033.

THE CHURCH OF IRELAND

Central Office: Church of Ireland House, Church Avenue, Rathmines, Dublin 6.

Province of Armagh

Archbishop of Armagh and Primate of All Ireland, Most Rev. Robert Henry Alexander Eames, PH.D., *b.* 1937, *cons.* 1975, *trs.* 1986: *Clergy* 50.

The Rt. Rev. Bishops

Clogher, Brian Desmond Anthony Hannon, *b.* 1936, *apptd.* 1986: *Clergy* 34.

Connor, Samuel Greenfield Poyntz, *b.* 1926, *apptd.* 1978, *trs.* 1987: *Clergy* 103.

Derry and Raphoe, James Mehaffey, PH.D., *b.* 1931, *apptd.* 1980: *Clergy* 55.

Down and Dromore, Gordon McMullan, PH.D., *b.* 1934, *apptd.* 1980, *trs.* 1986: *Clergy* 99.

Kilmore, Elphin and Ardagh, William Gilbert Wilson, PH.D., *b.* 1918, *apptd.* 1981: *Clergy* 20.

Tuam, Killala and Achonry, John Robert Winder Neill, *b.* 1945, *apptd.* 1986: *Clergy* 12.

Province of Dublin

Archbishop of Dublin, Bishop of Glendalough, and Primate of Ireland, Most Rev. Donald Arthur Caird, *b.* 1925, *cons.* 1970, *apptd.* 1985: *Clergy* 71.

The Rt. Rev. Bishops

Cashel and Ossory, Noel Vincent Willoughby, *b.* 1926, *apptd.* 1980: *Clergy* 35.

Cork, Cloyne and Ross, Robert Alexander Warke, *b.* 1930, *apptd.* 1988: *Clergy* 25.

Limerick and Killaloe, Edward Flewett Darling, *b.* 1933, *apptd.* 1985: *Clergy* 15.

Meath and Kildare, Walton Newcombe Francis Empey, *b.* 1934, *cons.* 1981, *trs.* 1985: *Clergy* 18.

St. Patrick's National Cathedral, Dublin: *Dean and Ordinary*, Very Rev. V. G. B. Griffin, PH.D.

ANGLICAN COMMUNION OVERSEAS

Sees	Apptd.

ANGLICAN CHURCH OF AUSTRALIA

Primate of Australia
The Most Rev. John Basil Rowland Grindrod, K.B.E.
(Archbishop of Brisbane).

Province of New South Wales

The Most Rev. Archbishop and Metropolitan

Sydney, Donald William Bradley Robinson, *cons.*
1973..1982
Asst. Bps., J. R. Reid, (1972); K. H. Short, (1975);
E. D. Cameron, (1975); R. H. Goodhew, (1982).

The Rt. Rev. Bishops

Armidale, P. Chiswell, *cons.* 1976..............1976
Bathurst, H. A. J. Witt, *cons.* 1965............1981
Canberra and Goulburn, O. D. Dowling, *cons.*
1981..1983
Grafton B. A. Schultz, *cons.* 1985..............1985
Newcastle, A. C. Holland, *cons.* 1970..........1978
Riverina, B. R. Hunter, *cons.* 1971............1971

Province of Queensland

The Most Rev. Archbishop and Metropolitan

Brisbane, John Basil Rowland Grindrod, K.B.E. .1980
Bp. for Southern Region, R. Wicks, O.B.E.,
(1973); Bp. for Western Region, A. O. Charles,
(1983); Bp. for Northern Region, G. V. Browning, (1985).

The Rt. Rev. Bishops

Carpentaria, A. F. B. Hall-Matthews 1984
N. Queensland, H. J. Lewis 1971
N. Territory, C. M. Wood.
Rockhampton, G. A. Hearn 1981

Province of South Australia

The Most Rev. Archbishop and Metropolitan

Adelaide, Keith Rayner, PH.D., *cons.* 1969 1975
Asst. Bp., L. E. W. Renfrey 1969

The Rt. Rev. Bishops

The Murray, R. G. Porter, O.B.E., *cons.* 1967....1970
Willochra, W. D. H. McCall, *cons.* 1987........1987

Province of Victoria

The Most Rev. Archbishop and Metropolitan

Melbourne, David John Penman, *cons.* 1982 1984
Bps. Coadj., J. A. Grant (1970); D. H. W. Shand
(1973); J. C. Stewart (1984); R. L. Butterss
(1985); P. J. Hollingworth (1985); J. W. Wilson
(1985).

The Rt. Rev. Bishops

Ballarat, J. Hazlewood, *cons.* 1975 1975
Bendigo, O. S. Heyward, *cons.* 1975 1975
Gippsland, C. D. Sheumack, *cons.* 1987........1987
Wangaratta, R. G. Beal, *cons.* 1985............1985

Province of Western Australia

The Most Rev. Archbishop and Metropolitan

Perth, Peter Frederick Carnley, PH.D., *cons.*
1981..1981
Asst. Bps., M. B. Challen (1978); B. R. Kyme (1982);
B. Wright (1988).

The Rt. Rev. Bishops

Bunbury, H. J. U. Jamieson, *cons.* 1974 1984
N. W. Australia, G. B. Muston, *cons.* 1971 1982

Sees	Apptd.

Extra-Provincial Diocese

Tasmania, P. K. Newell, *cons.* 1982 1982

EPISCOPAL CHURCH OF BRAZIL

The Most Rev. Primate

South Western Brazil, Olavo Ventura Luiz, *cons.*
1976 1986

The Rt. Rev. Bishops

Brasilia, A. G. Sória, *cons.* 1977 1985
Central Brazil, S. A. Ruiz, *cons.* 1985 1985
Northern Brazil, C. E. Rodrigues, *cons.* 1985 ..1986
South Central Brazil, S. Takatsu, *cons.* 1977 ...1977
Southern Brazil, C. V. S. Gastal, *cons.* 1984 ...1984
South Western Brazil, (see above).

CHURCH OF THE PROVINCE OF BURMA

The Most Rev. Archbishop

Rangoon, Andrew Mya Han, *cons.* 1988 1988

The Rt. Rev. Bishops

Mandalay, T. Mya Wah, *cons.* 1984 1984
Myitkyina, A. Hla Aung, *cons.* 1988............1988
Pa'an, G. Kyaw Mya, *cons.* 1979...............1979
Sittwe, B. Theaung Hawi, *cons.* 1978 1980

CHURCH OF THE PROVINCE OF BURUNDI, RWANDA AND ZAIRE

The Most Rev. Archbishop

Butare, Justin Ndandali, *cons.* 1975 1982

The Rt. Rev. Bishops

Boga Zaire, P. Njojo 1980
Bujumbura, S. Sindamuka 1975
Bukavu, B. Dirokpa 1982
Asst. Bp., K. Mbona 1980
Butare, (see above).
Asst. Bp. D. Nduhura 1985
Buye, S. Ndayisenga 1979
Gitega, J. Nduwayo...........................1985
Kigali, A. Sebununguri, (*cons.* 1965).
Kisangani, S. T. Mugera 1980
Shaba, K. Mbona, *cons.* 1980 1980
Shyira, A. Nshamihigo, (*cons.* 1984) 1984

ANGLICAN CHURCH OF CANADA

The Most Rev. Primate

Michael Geoffrey Peers, *cons.* 1977 1986

Province of British Columbia

The Most. Rev. Archbishop and Metropolitan

New Westminster, Douglas Walter Hambidge,
cons. 1969 1981

The Rt. Rev. Bishops

British Columbia R. F. Shepherd, *cons.* 1984 1984
Caledonia, J. E. Hannen, *cons.* 1981 1981
Cariboo, J. S. P. Snowden, *cons.* 1975 1975
Kootenay, R. E. F. Berry, *cons.* 1971...........1971
Yukon, R. C. Ferris, *cons.* 1981 1981

Province of Canada

The Most Rev. Archbishop and Metropolitan

Fredericton, Harold Lee Nutter, *cons.*1971 1980

The Rt. Rev. Bishops

Central Newfoundland, M. Genge, *cons.* 1976 ...1976
Eastern Newfoundland and Labrador, M. Mate,
cons. 1980.......................................1980

Sees	Apptd.
Montreal, R. Hollis, *cons.* 1974	1975
Nova Scotia, A. G. Peters, *cons.* 1981	1982
Quebec, A. Goodings, *cons.* 1977	1977
Western Newfoundland, S. S. Payne, *cons.* 1978	1978

Province of Ontario

The Most Rev. Archbishop and Metropolitan

Niagara, John Charles Bothwell, *cons.* 1971 1985

The Rt. Rev. Bishops

Algoma, L. E. Peterson, *cons.* 1983	1983
Huron, D. D. Jones, *cons.* 1982	1984
Moosonee, C. J. Lawrence, *cons.* 1980	1980
Ontario, A. A. Read, *cons.* 1972	1981
Ottawa, E. K. Lackey, *cons.* 1981	1981
Toronto L. S. Garnsworthy, *cons.* 1968	1972

Province of Rupert's Land

The Most Rev. Archbishop and Metropolitan

Rupert's Land, Walter Heath Jones, *cons.* 1970 . 1988

The Rt. Rev. Bishops

Arctic, J. R. Sperry, *cons.* 1974	1974
Athabasca , G. F. Woolsey, *cons.* 1983	1983
Brandon, J. F. S. Conlin, *cons.* 1975	1975
Calgary, J. B. Curtis, *cons.* 1983	1983
Edmonton, K. L. Genge, *cons.* 1988	1988
Keewatin, H. J. P. Allan, *cons.* 1974	1974
Qu' Appelle, E. Bays, *cons.* 1986	1986
Rupert's Land (see above).	
Saskatchewan, T. O. Morgan, *cons.* 1985	1985
Saskatoon, R. A. Wood, *cons.* 1981	1981

CHURCH OF THE PROVINCE OF CENTRAL AFRICA

The Most Rev. Archbishop

Botswana, Walter P. K. Makhulu, *cons.* 1979 ... 1980

The Rt. Rev. Bishops

Botswana (see above).	
Central Zambia, C. W. H. Shaba, *cons.* 1984	1984
Harare, R. P. Hatendi, *cons.* 1979	1981
Lake Malawi, P. N. Nyanja, *cons.* 1978	1978
Lundi, J. Siyachitema, *cons.* 1981	1981
Lusaka, S. S. Mumba, *cons.* 1981	1981
Manicaland, E. Masuko, *cons.* 1981	1981
Matabeleland, T. T. Naledi, *cons.* 1987	1987
Northern Zambia, (vacant).	
Southern Malawi, B. N. Aipa, *cons.* 1987	1987

CHURCH OF THE PROVINCE OF THE INDIAN OCEAN

The Most Rev. Archbishop

Seychelles, French Chang-Him | 1984

The Rt. Rev. Bishops

Antananarivo, R. Rabenirina, *cons.* 1984	1984
Antsiranana, K. Benzies, *cons.* 1982	1982
Mauritius, R. Donat, *cons.* 1984	1984
Seychelles, (see above).	
Toamasina, F. Razakariasy, *cons.* 1984	1984

THE HOLY CATHOLIC CHURCH IN JAPAN

(Nippon Sei Ko Kai)

The Most Rev. Primate

Osaka, Christopher Ichiro Kikawada, *cons.* 1975 | 1986

The Rt. Rev. Bishops

Chubu, S. W. Hoyo, *cons.* 1987	1987
Hokkaido, A. H. Amagi, *cons.* 1987	1987

Sees	Apptd.
North Kanto, J. T. Yashiro, *cons.* 1985	1985
Kobe, P. K. Yashiro, *cons.* 1984	1984
Kyoto, St. George J. Yagi, *cons.* 1979	1979
Kyushu, J. N. Iida, *cons.* 1982	1982
Okinawa, P. S. Nakamura, *cons.* 1972	1972
Osaka, (see above).	
Tohoku, C. Y. Tazaki, *cons.* 1979	1979
Tokyo, J. M. Takeda, *cons.* 1988	1988
Yokohama, R. S. Kajiwara, *cons.* 1984	1984

THE EPISCOPAL CHURCH IN JERUSALEM AND THE MIDDLE EAST

President-Bishop, Rt. Rev. S. Kafity	1986
Jerusalem, S. Kafity	1984
Iran, H. B. Dehqani-Tafti	1961
Egypt, G. Abdel Malik	1984
Cyprus and the Gulf, J. Brown	1986

CHURCH OF THE PROVINCE OF KENYA

The Most Rev. Archbishop

Nairobi, Manasses Kuria, *cons.* 1970 | 1980

The Rt. Rev. Bishops

Eldoret, A. K. Muge, *cons.* 1983	1983
Machakos, B. N. P. Nzimbi, *cons.* 1985	1985
Maseno North, J. Mundia, *cons.* 1970	1970
Maseno South, J. H. Okullu, *cons.* 1974	1974
Maseno West, D. J. Umolo, *cons.* 1982	1985
Mombasa, C. Nzano, *cons.* 1975	1981
Mount Kenya Central, J. Mahiaini, *cons.* 1984	1984
Mount Kenya East, D. Gitari, *cons.* 1975	1975
Mount Kenya South, G. M. Njuguna, *cons.* 1984	1985
Nairobi, (see above).	
Nakuru, L. Kamau, *cons.* 1984	1984
Nambale, I. Namango, *cons.* 1984	1987

CHURCH OF THE PROVINCE OF MELANESIA

The Most Rev. Archbishop

Central Melanesia, Amos Stanley Waiaru, *cons.* 1981 | 1988

The Rt. Rev. Bishops

Central Melanesia, (see above).	
Malaita, W. A. Pwaisiho, *cons.* 1981	1981
Temotu, L. S. Munamua, *cons.* 1987	1987
Vanuatu, H. S. Tevi, *cons.* 1979	1980
Ysabel, E. L. Pogo, *cons.* 1981	1981

CHURCH OF THE PROVINCE OF NEW ZEALAND

The Most Rev. Primate and Archbishop

Wellington, Brian Newton Davis, *cons.* 1980 1986

The Rt. Rev. Bishops

Aotearoa, W. Vercoe, *cons.* 1981	1981
Auckland, B. C. Gilberd, *cons.* 1985	1985
Christchurch, M. J. Goodall, *cons.* 1984	1984
Dunedin, P. W. Mann, *cons.* 1976	1976
Nelson, P. E. Sutton, *cons.* 1965	1965
Polynesia, J. L. Bryce, *cons.* 1975	1975
Waiapu, P. G. Atkins, *cons.* 1983	1983
Waikato, R. A. Herft, *cons.* 1986	1986
Wellington, (see above).	

CHURCH OF THE PROVINCE OF NIGERIA

The Most Rev. Archbishop

Ibadan, Timothy Omotayo Olufosoye, *cons.* 1965 | 1979

The Rt. Rev. Bishops

Aba, (vacant).	
Akigure/Orlu, S. C. N. Ebo	1985

Sees	Apptd.
Akoko, J. O. K. Olowokure	1986
Akure, E. B. Gbonigi	1983
Asaba, R. N. C. Nwosu	1977
Awka, M. S. C. Anikwenwa	1987
Benin, J. K. George	1985
Egba-Egbado, T. I. Akintayo	1977
Ekiti, C. A. Akinbola	1986
Enugu, G. N. Otubelu	1969
Ibadan, (see above).	
Ijebu, I. O. B. Akintemi	1976
Ijebu Remo, E. O. I. Ogundana	1984
Ilesha, G. I. O. Olajide	1981
Jos, T. E. I. Adesola	1985
Kaduna, T. Ogbonyomi	1975
Kano, B. B. Ayam	1980
Kwara, H. Haruna	1974
Lagos, J. A. Adetiloye	1985
The Niger, J. Arinzechukwu.	
Niger Delta, S. O. Elenwa	1981
Ondo, S. O. Aderin	1981
Owerri, B. Chukuemeka.	
Owo, A. O. Awosan	1983
Warri, J. O. Dafiewhare	1980

ANGLICAN CHURCH OF
PAPUA NEW GUINEA

The Most Rev. Archbishop
Popondota, George S. Ambo K.B.E., *cons.* 1960 ..1984

The Rt. Rev. Bishops
Aipo Rongo, P. Richardson, *cons.* 1987	1987
Dogura, R. Sanana, *cons.* 1976	1976
New Guinea Is., B. S. Meredith, *cons.* 1967	1967
Popondota, (see above).	
Port Moresby, I. R. Gadebo, *cons.* 1983	1983

CHURCH OF THE PROVINCE
OF SOUTHERN AFRICA

The Most Rev. Archbishop and Metropolitan
Cape Town, Desmond Mpilo Boy Tutu, *cons.*
1976 1986
Bps. Suff., C. H. Albertyn (1983); A. G. Quinlan (1988); E. Mackenzie (1988).

The Rt. Rev. Bishops
Bloemfontein, T. S. Stanage	1982
George, D. G. Damant	1985
Grahamstown, D. P. H. Russell	1986
Johannesburg, D. Buchanan	1986
Bps. Suff., M. S. Ndwandwe (1978); J. S. Nkoane (1982).	
Kimberley & Kuruman, G. A. Swartz	1983
Lebombo, D. S. Sengulane	1976
Lesotho, P. S. Mokuku	1978
Bp. Suff., D. P. Nestor	1980
Namibia, J. H. Kauluma	1981
Natal, M. Nuttall	1982
Niassa, P. T. Manhique	1986
Port Elizabeth, B. R. Evans	1974
Pretoria, R. A. Kraft	1982
St. Helena, J. N. Johnson	1985
St. John's, J. Z. Dlamini	1985
Swaziland, B. L. N. Mkhabela	1975
Zululand, L. B. Zulu	1975
Order of Ethiopia, S. Dwane	1983

ANGLICAN CHURCH OF THE
SOUTHERN CONE OF AMERICA

Presiding Bishop, Rt. Rev. David Leake.

The Rt. Rev. Bishops
Argentina and Uruguay, R. S. Cutts	1975
Chile, C. F. Bazley, *cons.* 1969	1977
Asst. Bp., I. Morrison	1977

Sees	Apptd.
Northern Argentina, D. Leake, *cons.* 1969	1980
Asst. Bp., M. Mariño	1975
Paraguay, J. Ellison.	
Peru and Bolivia, (vacant).	

CHURCH OF THE PROVINCE
OF THE SUDAN

The Most Rev. Archbishop, (vacant).

The Rt. Rev. Bishops
Bor, N. Garang.	
Juba, E. J. Ngalamu, *cons.* 1963	1976
Kadugli, M. Khamis.	
Kaji-Kaji, M. B. Dawidi.	
Khartoum, (vacant).	
Maridi, J. Marona.	
Mundri, E. Munda.	
Rumbek, B. W. Yugusuk, *cons.* 1971	1976
Yei, S. Solomona.	
Yambio, D. Zindo, *cons.* 1984	1984
Wau, (vacant).	

CHURCH OF THE PROVINCE OF TANZANIA

The Most Rev. Archbishop
Zanzibar and Tanga, John Acland Ramadhani,
cons. 1980 1984

The Rt. Rev. Bishops
Central Tanganyika, Y. Madinda, *cons.* 1971	1971
Dar es Salaam, C. Mlangwa, *cons.* 1984	1984
Kagera, C. Ruhuza, *cons.* 1985	1985
Mara, G. Nyaronga, *cons.* 1985	1985
Masasi, C. R. Norgate, *cons.* 1984	1984
Morogoro, D. Mageni, *cons.* 1987	1987
Mount Kilimanjaro, A. Mohamed, *cons.* 1982	1982
Ruvuma, M. Ngahyoma, *cons.* 1971	1971
South West Tanganyika, C. Mwaigoga, *cons.* 1983	1983
Victoria Nyanza, J. Rusibamayila, *cons.* 1976	1976
Western Tanganyika, G. E. Mpango, *cons.* 1983	1983
Zanzibar and Tanga, (see above).	

CHURCH OF THE PROVINCE OF UGANDA

The Most Rev Archbishop
Kampala, Dr. Yona Okoth *cons.* 1972 1984
Asst. Bp., A. L. Gonahasa 1985

The Rt. Rev. Bishops
East Ankole, A. Betungura	1970
Bukedi, N. E. Okille	1984
Bunyoro-Kitara, Y. Rwakaikara	1981
Busoga, C. Bamwoze	1972
Kampala, (see above).	
Karamoja, P. Lomongin	1987
Kigezi, (vacant).	
Asst. Bp., W. Rukirande	1975
Lango, M. Otim	1976
Asst. Bp., W. Okodi	1979
Madi and West Nile, R. Ringtho, *cons.* 1976	1977
Mbale, A. M. Wesonga	1981
Mityana, Y. Mukasa	1977
Mukono, L. Mpalanyi-Nkoyoyo	1985
Namirembe, M. Kauma	1985
North Kigezi, Y. Ruhindi	1981
Northern Uganda, B. Ogwal-Abwang	1974
Asst. Bp., G. Oboma	1979
Ruwenzori, E. Kamanyire	1981
Soroti, G. Ilukor	1976
West Ankole, Y. Bamunoba	1977
West Buganda, C. Senyonjo	1974

EPISCOPAL CHURCH IN THE U.S.A.

Presiding Bishop and Primate, Most Rev. Edmond Lee Browning, *cons.* 1986 *installed* 1986

Sees	Apptd.

Rt. Rev. Bishops
(*Missionary Diocese)

Province I

Connecticut, Arthur E. Walmsley, cons. 1979 ...1981
Maine, Edward C. Chalfont, cons. 1984........1986
Massachusetts, David E. Johnson, cons. 1985 ...1986
New Hampshire, Douglas E. Theuner, cons.
1986...1986
Rhode Island, George N. Hunt, cons. 1980 1980
Vermont, Daniel L. Swensen, cons. 1986........1987
Western Massachusetts, Andrew F. Wissemann,
cons. 1984...1984

Province II

Albany, David S. Ball, cons. 1984 1984
Central New York, O'Kelley Whitaker, cons.
1981..1983
Europe, Convocation of American Churches in,
Matthew P. Bigliardi, cons. 1974 1988
Haiti, Luc A. J. Garnier, cons. 1971 1971
Long Island, Robert C. Witcher, cons. 1975 1977
New Jersey, G. P. Mellick Belshaw, cons. 1975 ..1983
New York, Paul Moore (Jnr.), cons. 1964 1972
Newark, John S. Spong, cons. 1976 1979
Rochester, William G. Burrill, cons. 1984 1984
Virgin Islands, E. Donn Taylor, cons. 1987 1987
Western New York, David C. Bowman, cons.
1986...1987

Province III

Bethlehem, J. Mark Dyer, cons. 1982..........1983
Central Pennsylvania, Charles F. McNutt, cons.
1980..1982
Delaware, C. Cabell Tennis, cons. 1986 1986
Easton, Elliott L. Sorge, cons. 1971 1983
Maryland, A. Theodore Eastman, cons. 1982....1986
Northwestern Pennsylvania, Donald. J. Davis,
cons. 1973...1974
Pennsylvania, Allen L. Bartlett, cons. 1986 1987
Pittsburgh, Alden M. Hathaway, cons. 1981 1983
Southern Virginia, C. Charles Vache, cons.
1976...1978
Southwestern Virginia, Arthur H. Light, cons.
1979..1979
Virginia, Peter J. Lee, cons. 1984 1985
Washington, John T. Walker, cons. 1971 1977
West Virginia, Robert P. Atkinson, cons. 1973 ..1976

Province IV

Alabama, Furman C. Stough, cons. 1971 1971
Atlanta, C. Judson Child, cons. 1978 1983
Central Florida, William H. Folwell, cons. 1970 .1970
Central Gulf Coast, Charles F. Duvall, cons.
1981..1981
East Carolina, B. Sidney Sanders, cons. 1979 ...1983
East Tennessee, William E. Sanders, cons. 1979 .1985
Florida, Frank S. Cerveny, cons. 1974 1975
Georgia, Harry W. Shipps, cons. 1984 1985
Kentucky, David B. Reed, cons. 1964 1974
Lexington, Don A. Wimberly, cons. 1984 1985
Louisiana, James B. Brown, cons. 1976.........1976
Mississippi, Duncan M. Gray (Jnr.), cons. 1974 .1974
North Carolina, Robert W. Estill, cons. 1980 ...1983
San Joaquin, Victor M. Rivera, cons. 1968 1968
South Carolina, C. FitzSimons Allison, cons.
1980..1982
Southeast Florida, Calvin O. Schofield (Jnr.),
cons. 1979...1980
Southwest Florida, (vacant).
Tennessee, George L. Reynolds, cons. 1985......1985
Upper South Carolina, William A. Beckham,
cons. 1979...1979

West Tennessee, Alex D. Dickson (Jnr.), cons.
1983..1983
Western North Carolina, William G. Weinhauer,
cons. 1973...1975

Province V

Chicago, Frank T. Griswold III, cons. 1985 1987
Eau Claire, William C. Wantland, cons. 1980 ...1980
Fond Du Lac, William L. Stevens, cons. 1980 ...1980
Indianapolis, Edward W. Jones, cons. 1977 1977
Michigan, H. Coleman McGehee (Jnr.), cons.
1971...1973
Milwaukee, Roger J. White, cons. 1984.........1985
Missouri, William A. Jones (Jnr.), cons. 1975 ...1975
Northern Indiana, Francis C. Gray, cons. 1986 ..1987
Northern Michigan, Thomas K. Ray, cons. 1982 .1982
Ohio, James R. Moodey, cons. 1983 1984
Quincy, Donald J. Parsons, cons. 1973.........1973
Southern Ohio, William G. Black, cons. 1979 ...1980
Springfield, Donald M. Hultstrand, cons. 1982 ..1982
Western Michigan, (vacant).

Province VI

Colorado, William C. Frey, cons. 1967 1973
Iowa, Walter C. C. Righter, cons. 1972 1972
Minnesota, Robert M. Anderson, cons. 1978 1978
Montana, Charles I. Jones, cons. 1986 1986
Nebraska, James D. Warner, cons. 1976 1976
North Dakota, Harold A. Hopkins, cons. 1980 ..1980
South Dakota, Craig B. Anderson, cons. 1984 ...1984
Wyoming, Bob G. Jones, cons. 1977 1977

Province VII

Arkansas, Herbert A. Donovan (Jnr.), cons.
1980..1981
Dallas, Donis D. Patterson, cons. 1983 1983
Fort Worth, Clarence C. Pope (Jnr.), cons. 1985 .1986
Kansas, Richard F. Grein, cons. 1981 1981
Northwest Texas, Sam B. Hulsey, cons. 1980 1980
Oklahoma, Gerald N. McAllister, cons. 1977 1977
Rio Grande, Richard M. Trelease (Jnr.), cons.
1971...1972
Texas, Maurice M. Benitez, cons. 1980 1980
West Missouri, Arthur A. Vogel, cons. 1971.....1973
West Texas, John H. MacNaughton, cons. 1986 .1987
Western Kansas, John F. Ashby, cons. 1981.....1981

Province VIII

Alaska, George C. Harris, cons. 1981 1981
Arizona, Joseph T. Heistand, cons. 1976.......1979
California, William E. Swing, cons. 1979 1980
Central Philippines, Manuel C. Lumpias, cons.
1977..1978
Eastern Oregon, Rustin R. Kimsey, cons. 1980 ..1980
El Camino Real, C. Shannon Mallory, cons.
1972..1980
Hawaii, Donald P. Hart, cons. 1986 1986
Idaho, David B. Birney, cons. 1982 1982
Los Angeles, Frederick L. Borsch, cons. 1988 ...1988
*Navajoland Area Mission, (vacant).
Nevada, Stewart C. Zabriskie, cons. 1986 1986
Northern California, John L. Thompson III, cons.
1978..1978
Northern Luzon, Richard A. Abellon, cons.
1975..1986
Northern Philippines, Robert L. O. Longid, cons.
1983..1983
Olympia, Robert H. Cochrane, cons. 1976......1976
Oregon, Robert Louis Ladehoff, cons. 1985 1985
San Diego, C. Brinkley Morton, cons. 1982 1982
Southern Philippines, Narciso V. Ticobay, cons.
1986...1986

Sees	Apptd.
Spokane, Leigh A. Wallace, *cons.* 1979	1979
Taiwan, Chih-Tsung Chien, *cons.* 1988	1988
Utah, George E. Bates, *cons.* 1986	1986

*Province IX

Central and South Mexico, Jose G. Saucedo, *cons.* 1958 ... 1958
Colombia, Bernado Merino-Botero, *cons.* 1979 .. 1979
Dominican Republic, Telesforo A. Isaac, *cons.* 1972 ... 1972
Ecuador, Adrian D. Caceres-Villavicencio, *cons.* 1971 ... 1971
El Salvador, (vacant).
Guatemala, Armando Guerra-Soria, *cons.* 1982 . 1982
Honduras, Leopold Frade, *cons.* 1984 ... 1984
Nicaragua, Sturdie W. Downs-Higgs, *cons.* 1985 ... 1985
Northern Mexico, German Martinez-Marquez, *cons.* 1987 ... 1987
Panama, James H. Ottley, *cons.* 1984 ... 1984
Western Mexico, Samuel Espinoza-Venegas, *cons.* 1981 ... 1983

Extra-Provincial

Costa Rica, Cornelius J. Wilson, *cons.* 1978 ... 1978
Puerto Rico, Francisco Reus-Froylan, *cons.* 1964 ... 1964
Venezuela, Onell A. Soto, *cons.* 1987 ... 1987

CHURCH OF THE PROVINCE OF WEST AFRICA

The Most Rev Archbishop

Liberia, George Daniel Browne, D.D., *cons.* 1970 ... 1982
Bp. *Suff.*, Rt. Rev. Edward W. Neufville (1984).

The Rt. Rev. Bishops

Accra, F. W. B. Thompson, *cons.* 1983 ... 1983
Bo, M. Keili, *cons.* 1981 ... 1981
Cape Coast, (vacant)
Freetown, P. E. S. Thompson, *cons.* 1981 ... 1981
Gambia, (vacant).
Guinea, (vacant).
Koforidua, R. G. Okine, *cons.* 1981 ... 1981

Sees	Apptd.
Kumasi, E. K. Yeboah, *cons.* 1985	1985
Liberia, (see above)	
Sekondi, T. Annobil, *cons.* 1981	1981
Sunyani/Tamale, J. K. Dadson, *cons.* 1981	1981

As the Province of Nigeria came into being on Feb. 24, 1979, the rest of the Province of West Africa continues to function as the (On-going) Province of West Africa:

CHURCH IN THE PROVINCE OF THE WEST INDIES

The Most Rev. Archbishop

N.E. Caribbean and Aruba, Orland Lindsay, *cons.* 1970 ... 1986

The Rt. Rev. Bishops

Barbados, D. W. Gomez, *cons.* 1972 ... 1972
Belize, (vacant).
Guyana, R. O. George, *cons.* 1976 ... 1980
Jamaica, N. W. de Souza *cons.* 1973 ... 1979
    Bps. *Suff.* (*Mandeville*), W. A. Murray (1976);
    (*Montego Bay*), A. C. Reid (1980)
Nassau and the Bahamas, M. H. Eldon, C.M.G. *cons.* 1971 ... 1972
N.E. Caribbean and Aruba (see above).
Trinidad and Tobago, C. O. Abdulah *cons.* 1970 ... 1970
Windward Islands, P. Elder, *cons.* 1966.

OTHER CHURCHES AND EXTRA-PROVINCIAL DIOCESES

Under the Archbishop of Canterbury

The Rt. Rev. Bishops

Bermuda, C. C. Luxmoore.
Kuching, John Leong Chee Yun
Lusitanian Church in Portugal, F. Soares ... 1971
Pusan, Bundo Kim ... 1988
Sabah, Chhoa Heng Sze ... 1971
Seoul, S. S. Kim.
Singapore, M. Tay ... 1982
Spanish Reformed Episcopal Church, A. Sanchez ... 1982
Taejon, Paul Hwan Yoon ... 1988
West Malaysia, J. G. Savarimuthu ... 1973

THE PRESBYTERIAN CHURCH OF WALES

THE PRESBYTERIAN OR CALVINISTIC METHODIST CHURCH OF WALES is the only Church of purely Welsh origin, and embraces a large section of the Welsh-speaking population. Its form of government is Presbyterian, and it is a constituent of the World Alliance of Reformed Churches.

In 1988 the body numbered—chapels and other buildings, 1,064; ministers in pastoral charge, 149; elders, 4,624; communicants, 66,726; Sunday scholars, 20,949.

The *Association in the East* which includes nine of the English Presbyteries was formed in 1947.
Moderator of General Assembly (1988–89), Rev. R. G. Alun Richards, Morriston.
Moderators of Associations (1988–89) *South Wales*, Rev. J. D. Williams, Penygroes; *North Wales*, Rev. T. Jones, Caernarfon; *East Wales*, Rev. W. H. Whomsley, Llanelli.
General Secretary, Rev. D. H. Owen, 53 Richmond Road, Cardiff CF2 3UP

THE CHURCH OF SCOTLAND

Church Office, 121 George Street, Edinburgh EH2 4YN

THE CHURCH OF SCOTLAND is Presbyterian in constitution, and is governed by Kirk Sessions, Presbyteries, Synods, and the General Assembly, which consists of both representative ministers and elders, in equal numbers from each of the Presbyteries. It is presided over by a Moderator chosen annually by the Assembly. The Sovereign, if not present in person, is represented by a Lord High Commissioner, who is appointed each year by the Crown. The country, for Church purposes, is divided into 12 Synods and 46 Presbyteries, and there are about 1,400 ministers and licentiates engaged in ministerial and

other work. The figures at Dec. 31, 1987, were:—
Congregations, 1,727; total membership 838,659. There are 130 ministers and other personnel working with partner Churches and in expatriate charges in 26 countries.
LORD HIGH COMMISSIONER (1988–89), Capt. Sir Iain Tennant, K.T.
MODERATOR OF THE GENERAL ASSEMBLY (1988), Right Rev. Prof. J. A. White.
Principal Clerk, Rev. J. L. Weatherhead.
Deputy Clerk, Rev. A. G. McGillivray.
Procurator, G. Penrose, Q.C.

Law Agent and Solicitor of the Church, R. A. Paterson.
Parliamentary Agent, I. McCulloch (London).
General Treasurer, W. G. P. Colledge.

THE PRESBYTERIAN CHURCH IN IRELAND

The largest of the Presbyterian churches in Ireland consists of 22 presbyteries, 413 ministers, 564 congre-gations, with 131,471 communicants, 123,283 families and 6,100 Sunday-school teachers. During the 12 months ended Dec. 31, 1987, there was contributed by congregational effort £4,214,060 plus IR£281,432 for religious, charitable, and missionary purposes. The total income for the period raised by congregations for all purposes was £19,567,540 plus IR£1,541,665.—
General Sec., Very Rev. Dr. T. J. Simpson, Church House, Belfast BT1 6DW.

UNITED REFORMED CHURCH

THE UNITED REFORMED CHURCH was formed by the union of the Congregational Church in England and Wales and the Presbyterian Church of England on October 5, 1972. The Re-formed Association of Churches of Christ were joined to the U.R.C. on September 26, 1981. It is divided into 12 Provinces, each with a Provincial Moderator, and 70 Districts. There are 130,000 members and 1,000 serving minis-ters of whom 176 are auxiliary and give voluntary service. It shares an international mission through the Council for World Mission and is a member of the British and World Council of Churches. Its ministers are trained at five recognized colleges.
General Sec., Rev. B. G. Thorogood, 86 Tavistock Place, WC1H 9RT

The Congregational Federation

The majority of those members of the Congrega-tional Church who did not join the United Reformed Church comprise the Congregational Federation.
Gen. Sec., J. B. Wilcox, The Congregational Centre, 4 Castle Gate, Nottingham.

THE METHODIST CHURCH

THE METHODIST CHURCH was founded in 1739 by the two brothers Wesley and rapidly spread through-out the British Isles and to America before 1770. The Methodist Church in Great Britain was united in 1932 by the fusion of the Wesleyan Methodist Church (the original section), the Primitive Methodist Church (1810) and the United Methodist Church (a 1907 fusion of the Methodist New Connexion (1797), the Bible Christian Methodist Church (1815) and the United Methodist Free Churches (1828 and 1849)).

The World Methodist Council, founded 1881, reor-ganized 1951, associates Methodism throughout the world in 90 countries.

The Methodist Church in Great Britain is governed primarily by the Conference, secondarily by the District Synods (held in the autumn and the spring), consisting of all the ministers and of selected laypeople in each district, over which a chairman, who is a minister, is appointed by the Conference; and thirdly by the circuit meeting of the ministers and lay officers of each circuit. The authority of both Synods and Circuit Meetings is subordinate to the Conference, which has the supreme legislative and judicial power in Methodism.
President of the Conference (July 1988–89), Rev. Dr. R. G. Jones.
Vice-President of the Conference (July 1988–89), Mrs. J. M. Carpenter.
Secretary of the Conference, Rev. B. E. Deck, 1 Central Buildings, Westminster, SW1H 9NH.
President Designate 1989–90), Rev. Dr. J. J. Vincent.
Vice-President Designate (1989–90), J. B. Hindmarsh.
Statistics.—In 1987 in association with the Confer-ence in Great Britain there were 3,210 Ministers, 13,378 Local Preachers, 450,406 Members in 7,389 churches. (Statistics are published triennially.)

Methodist Church in Ireland

The Methodist Church in Ireland has 191 Minis-ters, 265 Lay Preacher., 20,118 Adult and 12,555 Junior Members.
President, (1988–89), Rev. T. Stanley Whittington.
Secretary, Rev. C. G. Eyre, 3 Upper Malone Road, Belfast BT9 6TD.

Independent Methodists

Independent Methodists.—This body is Congrega-tional in its organization, with an unpaid Ministry. Its first Conference was held in 1805. In 1987 there were in Great Britain 133 Ministers, 3,930 Members, 109 Churches and 3,711 Sunday scholars. *Gen. Sec.*, Rev. J. M. Day, The Old Police House, Croxton, Stafford ST21 6PE.

Wesleyan Reform Union

This Union is Methodist in doctrine, Congrega-tional in government, with, if any church desires it, a paid ministry. It is the remnant of the original Reformers expelled from Wesleyan Methodism in 1849. The adherents are mainly in the Midland and Northern counties. In 1988 there were in Great Britain 24 Ministers, 156 Lay Preachers, 3,157 Members, 130 Churches and 1,912 Sunday School scholars.—*President*, M. Radmall, 22 Harwood Close, Arnold, Notts.
General Secretary, Rev. D. A. Morris, Wesleyan Reform Church House, 123 Queen Street, Sheffield 1.

The Baptist Union

The Baptists have over 35,000,000 members in all countries. In Britain they are for the most part grouped in Associations of churches, and the majority of these belong to the Baptist Union, which was formed in 1812. Current statistics show that there are 2,132 churches and 170,610 members. There also exist separate Baptist Unions of Scotland (166 churches and 14,600 members); Wales (589 churches and 31,472 members); Ireland (92 churches and 8,550 members). *President of the Baptist Union of Great Britain*, (1988–89), Rev. Dr. Colin Marchant. *Secre-tary*, Rev. B. Green. *Office*, 4 Southampton Row, WC1B 4AB

LUTHERAN CHURCH

The Lutheran Church is one of the largest Protes-tant churches, with over 70 million members worldwide, although there are only about 27,000 adherents in Great Britain. The government and organization of the Lutheran Church varies from country to country, some having an episcopal and some a more congregational form.

Very few British people are Lutherans and services in Great Britain are held in many languages to serve members of different nationalities. English–language congregations in Great Britain are members either of the Lutheran Church in Great Britain— United Synod or of the Evangelical Lutheran Church of England. The United Synod and most of the "national churches" are members of the Lutheran Council of Great Britain and through the Council are related to the Lutheran World Federation.

LUTHERAN COUNCIL OF GREAT BRITAIN, 8 Collingham Gardens, SW5 0HW.—*Chairman*, Very Rev. R. J. Patkai.

ORTHODOX CHURCH

Greek Orthodox Church (*Archdiocese of Thyateira and Great Britain*), Most Rev. Archbishop Gregorios, 5 Craven Hill, W2 3EN.

Serbian Orthodox Church (*Patriarchate of Serbia*) Right Rev. Bishop Lavrentije, 89 Lancaster Road, W11 1QQ.

Russian Orthodox Church (*Patriarchate of Moscow*), Most Rev. Metropolitan Anthony of Sourozh, Russian Cathedral, Ennismore Gardens, SW7 1NH.

Russian Orthodox Church Outside Russia. His Grace Bishop Constantine, Dormition Cathedral, Emperor's Gate, SW7. *Mission Administrator*, Hegumen Seraphim, 14 St. Dunstan's Road, NW6.

The Poles, Ukrainians, Latvians, Byelorussians and Romanians also have congregations in this country.

OTHER RELIGIOUS DENOMINATIONS

The General Assembly of Unitarian and Free Christian Churches has about 95 ministers, 250 chapels and other places of worship in Great Britain and Ireland. *Gen. Sec.*, Dr. R. W. Smith, Essex Hall, 1–6 Essex Street, Strand, WC2R 3HY.

The Salvation Army, first known as the Christian Mission, was founded by William Booth in the East End of London in 1865. In 1878 it took its present name and adopted a quasi-military method of government. Since then it has become established in 90 countries of the world. The world leader, known as the General, is elected by a High Council, consisting of all active Commissioners and Territorial Commanders who have held the rank of Colonel for at least two years. In 1987 there were in Great Britain, 924 Corps (Churches), 139 Social Services Centres and 1,800 Officers engaged in evangelistic and social work. The latest world statistics (1987) are 14,362 Corps, 4,872 Social Services Centres (including institutions and schools) and 25,349 Officers. *General*, Eva Burrows. *International Headquarters:—* 101 Queen Victoria Street, EC4P 4EP.

The Religious Society of Friends (Quakers), founded in the 17th century, has no separated ministry. There are in Great Britain 458 places of worship and 18,087 members (world membership 213,800). *Central Offices (Great Britain)*, Friends House, Euston Road, NW1 2BJ; (*Ireland*), Swanbrook House, Morehampton Road, Dublin 4.

The First Church of Christ, Scientist, in Boston Massachusetts, U.S.A. (District Manager, Committees on Publication for Great Britain and Ireland, 108 Palace Gardens Terrace, W.8), has about 230 branch churches and societies in Great Britain and Ireland.

The Free Church of England (otherwise called The Reformed Episcopal Church) has 33 churches in England. *Gen. Sec.*, Rt. Rev. A. Ward, 28 Sedgebrook, Swindon, Wilts.

The Seventh Day Adventists (*Hdqrs.*, Stanborough Park, Watford, Herts. WD2 6JP), have more than 230 organized churches and companies and more than 16,500 members in the British Isles. *Executive Sec.*, D. W. McFarlane.

ARCHBISHOPS OF CANTERBURY SINCE 1501

1501 Henry Deane	1691 John Tillotson	1868 Archibald Campbell Tait
1503 William Warham	1695 Thomas Tenison	1883 Edward White Benson
1533 Thomas Cranmer	1716 William Wake	1896 Frederick Temple
1556 Reginald Pole	1737 John Potter	1903 Randall Thomas Davidson
1559 Matthew Parker	1747 Thomas Herring	1928 Cosmo Gordon Lang
1576 Edmund Grindal	1757 Matthew Hutton	1942 William Temple
1583 John Whitgift	1758 Thomas Secker	1945 Geoffrey Francis Fisher
1604 Richard Bancroft	1768 Frederick Cornwallis	1961 Arthur Michael Ramsey
1611 George Abbot	1783 John Moore	1974 Frederick Donald Coggan
1633 William Laud	1805 Charles Manners Sutton	1980 Robert Alexander Kennedy
1660 William Juxon	1828 William Howley	Runcie
1663 Gilbert Sheldon	1848 John Bird Sumner	
1678 William Sancroft	1862 Charles Thomas Longley	

THE ROMAN CATHOLIC CHURCH

His Holiness Pope John Paul II (Karol Wojtyla), *born* in Wadowice, Poland, May 18, 1920; *ordained priest* November 1, 1946; appointed *Archbishop of Krakow* January 13, 1964, created *Cardinal* at a Consistory on June 26, 1967. Formally assumed Pontificate October 16, 1978.

The Sacred College of Cardinals, when complete, consisted of six Cardinal Bishops, fifty Cardinal Priests and fourteen Cardinal Deacons. This number was fixed by Pope Sixtus V in 1586. Pope John XXIII created 52 new Cardinals. Pope Paul VI created 27 new Cardinals on Feb. 22, 1965, 27 on June 26, 1967, 33 on Apr. 28 1969, 30 on March 5, 1973, 20 on May 24, 1976, 4 on June 27, 1977; Pope John Paul II created 15 new Cardinals on June 30, 1979, 18 on Feb. 2, 1983, 28 on May 25, 1985, 25 on June 28, 1988. In Aug. 1988 there were 158 Cardinals. The Cardinals are advisers and assistants of the Sovereign Pontiff and form the supreme council or Senate of the Church. On the death of the Pope they elect his successor. The assembly of the Cardinals at the Vatican for the election of a new Pope is known as the Conclave in which, in complete seclusion, the Cardinals elect by secret ballot; a two-thirds majority is necessary before the vote can be accepted as final. When a Cardinal receives the necessary votes the Dean of the Sacred College formally asks him if he will accept election and the name by which he wishes to be known. On his acceptance of the office the Conclave is dissolved and the First Cardinal Deacon announces the election to the assembled crowd in St. Peter's Square. On the first Sunday or Holyday following the election the new Pope assumes the pontificate at High Mass in St. Peter's Square. A new pontificate is dated from the assumption of the pontificate.

Forms of Address: *Cardinal*, "His Eminence Cardinal ..." (if an Archbishop, "His Eminence the Cardinal Archbishop of ..."); *Archbishop*, "The Most Rev. Archbishop of ..."; *Bishop*, "The Rt. Rev. Bishop of ..."

THE CURIA

The Curia or governing body of the Roman Catholic Church is made up of various administrative departments headed by the Secretariat of State and the Sacred Council for the Public Affairs of the Church. Below these are congregations, secretariats and tribunals assisted by commissions and offices. All are headed by Cardinals who have as their British equivalent the Ministers or Secretaries of State heading the various government departments.

The Vatican State has, as with any nation, its own diplomatic service although its representatives are officially acknowledged in different ways throughout the countries of the world. Where the representation is only to the local churches and not to the government of that country then the man appointed is an Apostolic Delegate. However, where the representative is recognized as having diplomatic status by a particular government then he is known as either a nuncio, pro nuncio or inter nuncio. Nuncios are Papal Ambassadors who are given precedence over all other ambassadors by their appointed country and are the doyens of the diplomatic corps. In countries where precedence is not recognized, as in Britain, the papal representative is known as a pro nuncio.

THE BISHOPS' CONFERENCES

The Roman Catholic church in **England and Wales** is governed by:

1. **The Bishops' Conference** which consists of the local ordinaries (the Diocesan Bishops) of any rite; coadjutor bishops and auxiliaries; and titular bishops with special tasks. They are headed by the President, Cardinal Basil Hume, and Vice President, Archbishop Worlock, Archbishop of Liverpool.

2. **The Bishops' Standing Committee** made up of the Metropolitans (Archbishops) and department heads. It has general responsibility for continuity and policy between the Plenary Sessions of the Conference and for the preparation of the agenda and implementation of Conference decisions. This committee is serviced by the General Secretariat.

There are six departments, each with an episcopal chairman, which look after the life of the church within England and Wales. The departments and their heads are as follows:

(a) Department for Christian Life and Worship: Archbishop Bowen (*Southwark*).
(b) Department for Mission and Unity: Bishop Clark (*East Anglia*).
(c) Department for Christian Doctrine and Formation: Bishop Konstant (*Leeds*).
(d) Department for Social Responsibility: Bishop Harris (*Middlesbrough*).
(e) Department for Christian Citizenship: Bishop McCartie (*Auxiliary in Birmingham*).
(f) Department for International Affairs: Bishop O'Brien (*Hertfordshire*).

As well as the above the Conference has agencies and consultative bodies affiliated to it and all are serviced by the General Secretariat headed by a General Secretary namely:

England & Wales—Mgr. Vincent Nichols, 39 Eccleston Square, SW1V 1PD.

Scotland—Right Rev. Maurice Taylor, Bishop of Galloway, Candida Casa, 8 Corsehill Road, Ayr, Scotland, KA7 26T.

Ireland—(Executive Secretary) Rev. Gerard Clifford, Iona, 67 Newry Road, Dundalk, Co. Louth.

ENGLAND AND WALES

Apostolic Pro-Nuncio to the United Kingdom of Great Britain and Northern Ireland, The Most Rev. Luigi Barbarito.

The Most Revd. Archbishops	Cons.	Clgy.
Westminster, H.E. Cardinal Basil Hume (1976)	1976	926
Auxil., John Crowley	1986	
Auxil., Victor Guazzelli	1970	
Auxil., Philip Harvey	1977	
Auxil., Gerald Mahon	1970	
Auxil., James J. O'Brien	1977	
Birmingham, Maurice Couve de Murville (1982)	1982	526
Auxil., Joseph Cleary	1965	
Auxil., Crispian Hollis	1987	
Auxil., Patrick L. McCartie	1977	
Cardiff, John A. Ward (1983)	1981	186
Liverpool, Derek Worlock (1976)	1965	563
Auxil., Kevin O'Connor	1979	
Auxil., John Rawsthorne	1982	
Southwark, Michael Bowen (1977)	1970	573
Auxil., Charles Henderson	1972	
Auxil., Howard Tripp	1980	
Auxil., John Jukes	1980	

The Rt. Revd. Bishops		
Arundel and Brighton, Cormac Murphy-O'Connor	1977	331
Brentwood, Thomas McMahon (1980)	1980	214
Clifton, Mervyn Alexander (1975)	1972	246
East Anglia, Alan Clark (1976)	1969	125

	Cons.	Clgy.
Hallam, Gerald Moverley (1980) 1968		106
Hexham and Newcastle, Hugh Lindsay		
(1975) 1970		340
Auxil., Owen Swindelhurst 1977		
Lancaster, John Brewer (1971)..........1985		265
Leeds, David Konstant (1985)...........1977		299
Menevia (Wales), Daniel Mullins (1987) ..1970		
Middlesbrough, Augustine Harris (1978) .1966		208
Auxil., Thomas O'Brien 1982		
Northampton, Francis Thomas.........1982		182
Nottingham, James McGuinness (1975) ..1972		250
Plymouth, Christopher Budd 1986		187
Portsmouth, vacant		
Salford, Patrick Kelly 1984		490
Auxil., Geoffrey Burke...............1967		
Shrewsbury, Joseph Gray (1980) 1969		255
Wrexham (Wales), James Hannigan 1983		

SCOTLAND

The Most Revd. Archbishops

St. Andrews & Edinburgh, Keith Patrick		
O'Brian 1985		250
Auxil., James Monaghan 1970		
Glasgow, Thomas Winning (1974) 1972		374
Auxil., John Mone 1984		
Auxil., Charles Renfrew 1977		

The Rt. Revd. Bishops

Aberdeen, Mario Conti 1977		57
Argyll & Isles, Colin MacPherson 1969		39
Dunkeld, Vincent Logan 1981		75
Galloway, Maurice Taylor..............1981		82
Motherwell, Joseph Devine 1977		203
Paisley, John A. Mone 1984		94

IRELAND

There is one hierarchy for the whole of Ireland. Several of the Dioceses have territory partly in the Republic of Ireland and partly in Northern Ireland.
Nuncio to Ireland, Most Rev. Gaetano Alibrandi (Archbishop of Bindi)

The Most Revd. Archbishops

Armagh, H.E. Cardinal Thomas O'Fiaich 1977		290
Auxil., James Lennon 1980		
Cashel, Dermot Clifford 1986		
Dublin, Desmond Connell (1988) 1988		
Auxil., Joseph Carroll 1968		
Auxil., James Kavanagh 1973		
Auxil., Donal Murray................1982		
Auxil., Dermot O'Mahony 1975		
Auxil., Desmond Williams 1985		
Tuam, Joseph Cassidy (1987) 1979		182

The Rt. Revd. Bishops

Achony, Thomas Flynn 1975		75
Ardagh and Clonmacnois, Colm O'Reilly 1983		115
Clogher, Joseph Duffy.................1979		130
Clonfert, Joseph Kirby 1988		88
Cloyne, John Magee 1987		170
Cork and Ross, Michael Murphy 1976		389
Auxil., John Buckley 1984		
Derry, Edward Daly 1974		158
Auxil., Francis Lagan 1988		
Down and Connor, Cahal Daly..........1967		329
Auxil., Anthony Farquhar 1983		
Auxil., Patrick Walsh................1983		
Dromore, Francis Brooks...............1976		75
Elphin, Dominic Conway 1970		117
Ferns, Brendon Comiskey 1980		178
Galway and Kilmacduagh, Eamonn		
Casey 1969		162
Kerry, Dermot O'Sullivan 1985		167

Kildare and Leighlin, Patrick Lennon ...1966		246
Killala, Thomas Finnegan..............1970		55
Killaloe, Michael Harty 1967		204
Kilmore, Francis McKiernan 1972		139
Limerick, Jeremiah Newman 1974		247
Meath, John McCormack 1968		284
Auxil., Michael Smith 1984		
Ossory, Laurence Forristal 1980		149
Raphoe, Seamus Hegarty 1984		114
Waterford and Lismore, Michael Russell .1965		213

RESIDENTIAL ARCHBISHOPRICS
THROUGHOUT THE WORLD

NOTE: This list is set out with the name of the relevant country first; then the name of the diocese; and finally the Archbishop's name. It does not include England and Wales, Scotland or Ireland which are above.

Albania

Durrës, vacant. (Apostolic Administrator: Mgr. Nicola Troshani).
Shkodër, vacant. (Apostolic Administrator: Mgr. Ernesto Coba).

Algeria

Algiers, Henri Teissier.

Angola

Huambo, Francisco Viti.
Luanda, H.E. Cardinal Alexandre do Nascimento.
Lubango, Manuel Franklin da Costa.

Argentina

Bahia Blanca, Jorge Mayer.
Buenos Aires, H.E. Cardinal Juan Carlos Aramburu.
Córdoba, H.E. Cardinal Raúl Francisco Primatesta.
Corrientes, Fortunato A. Rossi.
La Plata, Antonio Quarracino.
Mendoza, Candido Genaro Rubiolo.
Paraná, Estanislao Esteban Karlich.
Resistencia, Juan J. Iriarte.
Rosario, Jorge Manuel López.
Salta, Moises J. Blanchoud.
San Juan de Cuyo, Italo Severino Di Stefano.
Santa Fe, Edgardo Gabriel Storni.
Tucumán, Horatio A. Bozzoli.

Australia

Adelaide, Leonard Anthony Faulkner.
Brisbane, Francis Roberts Rush.
Canberra, Francis P. Carroll.
Hobart, vacant.
Melbourne, Thomas Francis Little.
Perth, William J. Foley.
Sydney, H.E. Cardinal Edward B. Clancy.

Austria

Salzburg, Karl Berg.
Vienna, H.E. Cardinal Hans Hermann Groer.

Bangladesh

Dhaka, Michael Rozario.

Belgium

Malines-Bruxelles, H.E. Cardinal Godfried Danneels.

Benin

Cotonou, Christophe Adimou.

Bolivia

Cochabamba, Rene Fernandez Apaza.
La Paz, Luis Sainz Hinojosa.
Santa Cruz de la Sierra, Luis Rodriguez Pardo.
Sucre, vacant.

Brazil

Aparacida, Geraldo Maria de Morais Penido.
Aracaju, Luciano José Cabral Duarte.
Bélem do Pará, Alberto Guadêncio Ramos.
Belo Horizonte, Serafim Fernandes de Araújo.
Botucatu, Vincent Marchetti Zioni.
Brasilia, H.E. Cardinal Jose Freire Falcao.
Campinas, Gilberto Pereira Lopes.
Campo Grande, Vitorio Pavanello.
Cascavel, Armando Cirio.
Cuiaba, Bonifacio Piccinini.
Curitiba, Pedro Antonio Fedalto.
Diamantina, Geraldo Majelo Reis.
Florianópolis, Alfonso Niehues.
Fortaleza, H.E. Cardinal Aloisio Lorscheider.
Goiania, Antonio Ribeiro de Oliveira.
Juiz de Fora, Juvenal Roriz.
Londrina, Geraldo Majela Agnelo.
Maceió, Edvaldo G. Amaral.
Manaus, Clovis Frainer.
Mariana, Luciano Mendes de Almeida.
Maringá, Jaime Luis Coelho.
Natal, Alair V. Fernandes de Melo.
Niteroi, José Gonçalves da Costa.
Olinda & Recife, José Cardoso Sobrinho.
Paraiba, José M. Pires.
Porto Alegre, Claudio Colling.
Porto Velho, José Martins da Silva.
Pouso Alegre, José D'Angolo Neto.
Ribeirão Preto, Romeu Alberti.
São Luis do Maranhão, Paulo Eduardo Andrade Ponte.
São Paulo, H.E. Cardinal Paulo Evaristo Arns.
São Salvador da Bahia, H.E. Cardinal Lucas Moreira Neves.
São Sebastião do Rio de Janeiro, H.E. Cardinal Eugenio de Araújo Sales.
Teresina, Miguel F. Camara Filho.
Uberaba, Benedito de Ulhôa Vieira.
Vitória, Silvestre L. Scandian.

Burkina Faso

Ouagadougou, H.E. Cardinal Paul Zoungrana.

Burma

Mandalay, Alphonse U. Than Aung.
Rangoon, Gabriel Thohey Mahn Gaby.

Burundi

Gitega, Joachim Ruhuna.

Cameroon

Bamenda, Paul Verdzekov.
Douala, Simon Tonyé.
Garoua, H.E. Cardinal Christian W. Tumi.
Yaoundé, Jean Zoa.

Canada

Edmonton, Joseph N. MacNeil.
Grouard-McLennon, Henri Lègaré.
Halifax, James Martin Hayes.
Keewatin-Le Pas, Peter Alfred Sutton.
Kingston, Francis John Spence.
Moncton, Donat Chiasson.
Montreal, H.E. Cardinal Paul Grégoire.
Ottawa, Joseph Aurèle Plourde.
Quebec, H.E. Cardinal Louis-Albert Vachon.
Regina, Charles Halpin.
Rimouski, Gilles Ouellet.
St Boniface, Antoine Hacault.
St Johns, Newfoundland, Alphonsus L. Penney.
Sherbrooke, Jean Marie Fortier.
Toronto, H.E. Cardinal Gerald Emmett Carter.
Vancouver, James Francis Carney.
Winnipeg, Latin Rite–Adam Exner; Ukrainian Rite–Maxim Hermaniuk.

Central Africa

Bangui, Joachim N'Dayen.

Chad

N'Djamena, Charles Vandame.

Chile

Antofagasta, Carlos Oviedo Cavada.
Concepción, José Manuel Santos Ascarza.
La Serena, Bernardino Pinera Carvallo.
Puerto Montt, Savino B. C. Bertollo.
Santiago de Chile, H.E. Cardinal Juan F. Fresno Larrain.

China

Ankang, Huai-Ning, vacant.
Canton, Dominic Tang Yee-Ming.
Changsha, vacant.
Chungking, vacant.
Foochow, Min-Hou, vacant.
Hangchow, vacant.
Hankow, vacant.
Kaifeng, vacant.
Kunming, vacant.
Kweiyang, vacant.
Lanchow, vacant.
Mukden, vacant.
Nanchang, vacant.
Nanking, vacant.
Nanning, vacant.
Peking, vacant.
Sian, vacant.
Suiyüan, Francis Wang Hsueh-Ming.
Taiyuan, vacant; Bishop Emeritus Dominic Luke Capozi (expelled April 11, 1946, now living in Nazareth, Israel).
Tsinan, vacant.

Colombia

Barranquilla, Felix Maria Torres Parra.
Bogotá, H.E. Cardinal Mario Revollo Bravo.
Bucaramanga, Hector Rueda Hernández.
Cali, Pedro Rubiano Sáenz.
Cartagena, Carlos Jose Ruiseco Vieira.
Ibague, José Joaquin Flórez Hernández.
Manizales, José de Jesús Pimiento Rodriguez.
Medellin, H.E. Cardinal Alfonso López Trujillo.
Nueva Pamplona, Rafael Sarmiento Peralta.
Popayán, Samuel Silverio Buitrago Trujillo.
Tunja, Augusto Trujillo Arango.

Congo

Brazzaville, Barthélémy Batantu.

Costa Rica

San José, Román Arrieta Villalobos.

Côte d'Ivoire

Abidjan, H.E. Cardinal Bernard Yago.

Cuba

San Cristóbal de la Habana, Jaime Lucas Ortega y Alamino.
Santiago de Cuba, Pedro Meurice Estiu.

Czechoslovakia

Olomouc, vacant.
Praha, H.E. Cardinal František Tomášek.
Trnava, vacant.

Dominican Republic

Santo Domingo, Nicolás de Jesús López Rodriguez.

Ecuador

Cuenca, Alberto Luna Tobar.
Guayaquil, Bernardino Echeveria Ruiz.
Quito, Antonio J. González Zumárraga.

El Salvador
San Salvador, Arturo Rivera Damas.

Equatorial Guinea
Malabo, Rafael Nze Abuy.

Ethiopia
Addis Ababa, H.E. Cardinal Paul Tzadua.

France
Aix, Bernard Panafieu.
Albi, Joseph Rabine.
Auch, Gabriel Vanel.
Avignon, Raymond Bouchex.
Besançon, Lucien Daloz.
Bordeaux, Marius Maziers.
Bourges, Pierre Plateau.
Cambrai, Jacques Delaporte.
Chambéry, Claude Feidt.
Lyon, H.E. Cardinal Albert Decourtray.
Marseilles, Robert Coffey.
Paris, H. E. Cardinal J. M. Lustiger.
Reims, Jacques Ménager.
Rennes, Jacques Jullien.
Rouen, Joseph Duval.
Sens, Eugene Ernoult.
Toulouse, André Collini.
Tours, Jean Honoré.

French Polynesia
Papeete, Michel Coppenrath.

Gabon
Libreville, André Fernand Anguilé.

Germany (Federal Republic)
Bamberg, Elmar Maria Kredel.
Essen, H.E. Cardinal Franz Hengsbach.
Freiburg im Breisgau, Oskar Saier.
Munich & Freising, H.E. Cardinal Friedrich Wetter.
Paderborn, Johannes Joachim Degenhardt.

Ghana
Cape Coast, John Kodwo Amissah.
Tamale, Peter Poreiku Dery.

Greece
Athens, Nicholaos Foscolos.
Corfu, Antonio Varthalitis.
Naxos, Jean Perris.
Rhodes, vacant (Apostolic administrator: Michel Pierre Franzidis).

Guatemala
Guatemala, Prospero Penandos del Barrio.

Guinea
Conakry, Robert Sarah.

Haiti
Cap-Haitien, Francois Gayot.
Port au Prince, François-Wolff Ligondé.

Honduras
Tegucigalpa, Hector Enrique Santos Hernández.

Hong Kong
Hong Kong, H.E. Cardinal J. B. Wu Cheng Chung.

Hungary
Eger, Istvan Seregely.
Esztergom, H.E. Cardinal Laslo Paskai.
Kalocsa, Laszlo Danko.

India
Agra, Cecil de Sa.
Bangalore, Alphonsus Mathias.
Bhopal, Eugene D'Souza.
Bombay, H.E. Cardinal Simon Ignatius Pimenta.
Calcutta, Henry Sebastian D'Souza.
Changanacherry, Joseph Powathil.
Cuttack-Bhubaneswar, Raphael Cheenath.
Delhi, Angelo Innocent Fernandes.
Ernakulam, H.E. Cardinal Anthony Padiyara.
Goa and Daman, Raul Nicolau Gonsalves.
Hyderabad, Saminini Arulappa.
Madras and Mylapore, Casimir Gnanadickam.
Madurai, Marianus Arokiasamy.
Nagpur, Leobard D'Souza.
Pondicherry and Cuddalore, Venmani S. Selvanather.
Ranchi, Telesphore P. Toppo.
Shillong-Gauhati, Hubert D'Rosario.
Trivandrum, [Syrian Melekite Rite], Benedict Varghese Mar Gregorios Thangalathil.
Verapoly, Cornelius Elanjikal.

Indonesia
Ende, Donatus Djagom.
Jakarta, Leo Soekoto.
Medan, Alfred Gonti Pius Datubara.
Merauke, Jacobus Duivenvoorde.
Pontianak, Hieronymus Herculanus Bumbun.
Semarang, Julius R. Darmaatmadja.
Ujung Pandang, R. P. Francis van Roessel.

Iran
Ahváz, Hanna Zora.
Tehran, Youhannan Semaan Issayi.
Urmyā, Thomas Meram.

Iraq
Arbil, Stephane Babeka.
Baghdad, Paul Dahdah.
Basra, Yousif Thomas.
Kirkuk, André Sana.
Mosul, Georges Garmo.

Israel
Akka [Greek Melekite Catholic Rite], Maximos Salloum.

Italy
Acerenza, Michele Scandiffio.
Amalfi, Ferdinand Palatucci.
Ancona, Carlo Maccari.
Bari, Mariano Magrassi.
Benevento, Carlo Minchiatti.
Bologna, H.E. Cardinal Giacomo Biffi.
Brindisi, Settimio Todisco.
Cagliari, Otterino Pietro Alberti.
Camerino, Bruno Frattegiani.
Campobasso-Boiano, Pietro Santoro.
Capua, Luigi Diligenza.
Catania, Luigi Bommarito.
Catanzaro, Antonio Cantisani.
Chieti, Antonio Valentini.
Conza, Antonio Nuzzi.
Cosenza, Dino Trabalzini.
Crotone-Santa Severina, Giuseppi Agostino.
Fermo, Cleto Bellucci.
Ferrara, Luigi Maverna.
Florence, H.E. Cardinal Silvano Piovanelli,
Foggia, Giuseppe Casale.
Gaeta, Vincenzo Farano.
Genoa, H.E. Cardinal Giovanni Canestri.
Gorizia and Gradisca, Antonio Vitale Bommarco.
Lanciano, Enzio d'Antonio.
L'Aquila, Mario Peressin.
Lecce, Michele Mincuzzi.
Lucca, Guiliano Agresti.
Manfredonia, Valentino Vailati.
Matera, Ennio Appignanesi.
Messina, Ignazio Cannavó.

Milan, H.E. Cardinal Carlo Maria Martini.
Modena, Santo B. Quadri.
Monreale, Salvatore Cassisa.
Naples, H.E. Cardinal Michele Giordano.
Oristano, Pier Luigi Tiddia.
Otranto, Vincenzo Franco.
Palermo, H.E. Cardinal Salvatore Pappalardo.
Perugia, Cesare Pagani.
Pescara-Penne, Antonio Jannucci.
Pisa, Alessandro Plotti.
Potenza, Guiseppe Vairo.
Ravenna, Ersilio Tonini.
Reggio Calabria, Aurelio Sorrentino.
Rossano, Serafino Sprovieri.
Salerno, Guerino Grimaldi.
Sassari, Salvatore Isgrò.
Siena, Ismaele Mario Castellano.
Siracusa, Calogero Lauricella.
Sorrento, Antonio Zama.
Spoleto, Antonio Ambrosiano.
Taranto, Salvatore De Giorgi.
Turin, H.E. Cardinal Anastasio Alberto Ballestrero.
Trani and Barletta, Giuseppe Carata.
Trento, Giovanni Sartori.
Udine, Alfredo Battisti.
Urbino, Donato U. Bianchi.
Vercelli, Albino Mensa.

Jamaica

Kingston, Samuel Emmanuel Carter.

Japan

Nagasaki, H.E. Cardinal Joseph Asajiro Satowaki.
Osaka, Paul Hisao Yasuda.
Tōkyō, Peter Seiichi Shirayanagi.

Jordan

Petra and Filadelfia [Greek Melekite Catholic Rite], Saba Youakim.

Kenya

Nairobi, H.E. Cardinal Maurice Otunga.

Korea

Kwangju, Victorinus Kong-Hi Youn.
Seoul, H.E. Cardinal Stephen Sou Hwan Kim.
Taegu, Paul Moun-Hi Ri.

Lebanon

Baalbek, Eliopoli [Greek Melekite Catholic Rite], Elias Zoghbi.
Beirut [Greek Melekite Catholic Rite], Habib Bacha; [Maronite Rite] Khalil Abinader.
Cipro, Joseph Mohsen Bechara.
Saïda [Greek Melekite Catholic Rite], Georges Kwaiter.
Tripoli [Maronite Rite], Antoine Joubeir; [Greek Melekite Catholic Rite], Elias Nijmé.
Tyre [Greek Melekite Catholic Rite], vacant; [Maronite Rite], Joseph Khoury.
Zahle and Furzol [Greek Melekite Catholic Rite], Andre Haddad.

Lesotho

Maseru, Alfonso Ligouri Morapeli.

Liberia

Monrovia, Michael Kpakala Francis.

Lithuania

Abora, H.E. Cardinal Vincentas Sladkevicius.
Kaunas, vacant (Apostolic administrator: Mgr. Jouzas Preiksas).
Vilna, vacant (Apostolic administrator: Mgr. Edward Kisiel).

Luxembourg

Luxembourg, Jean Hengen.

Madagascar

Diego Suarez, Albert Joseph Tsiahoana.
Franarantsóa, Gilbert Ramanantoanina.
Tananarive, H.E. Cardinal Victor Razafimahatratra.

Malaysia

Kuching, Peter Chung Hoan Ting.

Mali

Bamako, Luc Auguste Sangaré.

Malta

Malta, Joseph Mercieca.

Martinique

Fort de France, Maurice Marie-Sainte.

Mauritius

Port Louis, H.E. Cardinal Jean Margeot.

Mexico

Acapulco, Rafael Bello Ruiz.
Antequera, Bartolomé Carrasco Briseno.
Chihuahua, Adalberto Almeida Merino.
Guadalajara, Juan J.P. Ocampo.
Hermosillo, Carlos Quintero Arce.
Jalapa, Sergio Obeso Rivera.
Mexico, H.E. Cardinal Ernesto Corripio Ahumada.
Monterrey, Adolfo Suarez Rivera.
Morelia, Estanislao Alcarez Figueroa.
Puebla de los Angeles, Rosendo Huesca Pacheco.
Yucatán, Manuel Castro Ruiz.

Monaco

Monaco, Joseph-Marie Sardou.

Morocco

Rabat, Hubert Michon.
Tanger, Antonio J. Peteiro Freire.

Mozambique

Maputo, H.E. Cardinal Alexandre José Maria dos Santos.
Nampula, Manuel Vieira Pinto.

Netherlands

Utrecht, H.E. Cardinal Adrianus J. Simonis.

New Zealand

Wellington, H.E. Cardinal Thomas Stafford Williams.

Nicaragua

Managua, H.E. Cardinal Miguel Obando Bravo.

Nigeria

Kaduna, Peter Yariyok Jatau.
Lugos, Anthony Okogie.
Onitsha, Stephen Nweke Ezeanya.

Oceania

Agaña, Anthony Sablan Apuron.
Honiara, Adrian Thomas Smith.
Nouméa, Michel-Marie-Bernard Calvet.
Samoa, Apia and Tokelau, H.E. Cardinal Pio Taofino'u.
Suva, Petero Mataca.

Pakistan

Karachi, H.E. Cardinal Joseph Cordeiro.

Panama

Panama, Marcos Gregorio McGrath.

Papua New Guinea

Madang, Benedict To Varpin.
Mount Hagen, Michael Meier.
Port Moresby, Peter Kurongku.
Rabaul, Albert Bundervoet.

Paraguay

Asuncion, Ismael Blas Rolon Silvero.

Peru

Arequipa, Fernando Vargas Ruiz de Somocurcio.
Ayacucho o Huamanga, Federico Richter Fernandez-Prada.
Cuzco, Alcides Mendoza Castro.
Huancayo, Emilio Vallebuona Merea.
Lima, H.E. Cardinal Juan Landózuri Ricketts.
Piura, Oscar Rolando Cantuarias Pastor.
Trujillo, Manuel Prado Pérez-Rosas.

Philippines

Caceres, Leonardo Legazpi.
Cagayan de Oro, Jesus B. Tuquia.
Capiz, Onesimo C. Gordoncillo.
Cebu, Nome di Gesù, H.E. Cardinal Ricardo Vidal.
Cotabato, Philip Frances Smith.
Davao, Antonio Mabutas.
Jaro, Alberto J. Piamonte.
Lingayan-Dagupen, Federico G. Limon.
Lipa, Mariano Gaviola.
Manila, H.E. Cardinal Jaime L. Sin.
Nueva Segovia, Orlando Quevedo.
Ozamiz, Jesus Dosado.
Palo, Pedro R. Dean.
San Fernando, Oscar Cruz.
Tuguegarao, Diosdado A. Talamayan.
Zamboanga, Francisco Raval Cruces.

Poland

Gniezno, H.E. Cardinal Józef Glemp. (See also Warsaw).
Kraków, H.E. Cardinal Franciszek Macharski.
Luców, vacant.
Poznan, Jerzy Stroba.
Warsaw, H.E. Cardinal Józef Glemp.
Wroclaw, H.E. Cardinal Henryk Roman Gulbinowicz.

Portugal

Braga, Eurico Dias Nogueira.
Evora, Maurilio Jorge Quintal de Gouveia.

Puerto Rico

San Juan, H.E. Cardinal Luis Aporte Martinez.

Romania

Bucarest, vacant.

Rwanda

Kigali, Vincent Nsengiyumva.

Senegal

Dakar, H.E. Cardinal Hyacinthe Thiandoum.

Sierra Leone

Freetown & Bo, Joseph Ganda.

Singapore

Singapore, Gregory Yong Sooi Nghean.

South Africa

Bloemfontein, Peter John Butelezi.
Cape Town, Stephen Naidoo.
Durban, Denis Eugene Hurley.
Pretoria, George Francis Daniel.

Spain

Barcelona, H.E. Cardinal Narciso Jubany Arnau.
Burgos, Theodoro C. Fernandez.

Granada, José Méndez Asensio.
Madrid, H.E. Cardinal Angel Suquia Goicoechea.
Oviedo, Gabino Diaz Merchán.
Pamplona, José Mariá Cirardo Lachiondo.
Santiago de Compostela, Antonio Rouco Varela.
Sevilla, Carlos Amigo Vallejo.
Tarragona, Ramon Torrella Cascante.
Toledo, H.E. Cardinal Marcelo González Martin.
Valencia, Miguel Roca Cabanellas.
Valladolid, José Delicado Baeza.
Zaragoza, Elíaz Yanez Alvarez.

Sri Lanka

Colombo, Nicholas Marcus Fernando.

Sudan

Khartoum, Gabriel Zubeir Wako.

Syria

Alep, Beroea, Halab [Greek Melekite Catholic Rite], Néophytes Edelby.
Baniyas, vacant.
Bosra, Bostra, Boulos Nassif Borkhoche.
Damascus [Greek Melekite Catholic Rite], vacant.
Hassaké-Nisibi, Georges Habib Hafouri.
Homs, Emesa [Syrian Catholic Rite], Jean Dahi.
Laodicea [Greek Melekite Catholic Rite], Michel Yatim.

Taiwan

Taipei, Matthew Kia Yen-Wen.

Tanzania

Dar es Salaam, H.E. Cardinal Laurean Rugambwa.
Tabora, Mario E. A. Mgulunde.

Thailand

Bangkok, H.E. Cardinal Michael Michai Kitbunchu.
Tharé and Nonseng, Lawrence Khai Saen-Phon-On.

Togo

Lomé, Robert Casimir Dosseh-Anyron.

Trinidad

Port of Spain, Gordon Anthony Pantin.

Turkey

Diarbekir, Paul Karatas.
Istanbul (Constantinople), Jean Tcholakian.
Izmir, Giuseppe G. Bernardini.

Uganda

Kampala, H.E. Cardinal Emmanuel Nsubuga.

Uruguay

Montevideo, José Gottardi Cristelli.

U.S.A.

Anchorage, Francis Thomas Hurley.
Atlanta, Eugene A. Marino.
Baltimore, William D. Borders.
Boston, H.E. Cardinal Bernard F. Law.
Chicago, H.E. Cardinal Joseph L. Bernardin.
Cincinnati, Daniel E. Pilarczyk.
Denver, James Francis Stafford.
Detroit, H.E. Cardinal Edmund C. Szoka.
Dubuque, Daniel W. Kucera.
Hartford, John F. Whealon.
Indianapolis, Edward T. O'Meara.
Kansas City, Ignatius J. Strecker.
Los Angeles, Roger M. Mahony.
Louisville, Thomas C. Kelly.
Miami, Edward A. McCarthy.
Milwaukee, Rembert G. Weakland.
Mobile, Oscar H. Lipscomb.
Newark, Theodore E. McCarrick.
New Orleans, Philip M. Hannan.

New York, H.E. Cardinal John J. O'Connor.
Oklahoma City, Charles A. Salatka.
Omaha, Daniel E. Sheehan.
Philadelphia, Anthony J. Beuilacqua.
Pittsburgh, Stephen J. Kocisko.
Portland (Oregon), William J. Levada.
St Louis (Missouri), John L. May.
St Paul & Minneapolis, John Robert Roach.
San Antonio, Patrick F. Flores.
San Francisco, John R. Quinn.
Santa Fe, Robert F. Sanchez.
Seattle, Raymond G. Hunthausen.
Washington, H.E. Cardinal James A. Hickey.

U.S.S.R.

There is an **unnamed** Apostolic Administrator in the following Russian Dioceses: Mohilev, Moscow, Leningrad, Kharkov, Kazan, Samara and Simbirsk.

Venezuela

Barquisimeto, Julio Manuel Chirivella Varela.
Caracas, H.E. Cardinal José Ali Lebrún Moratinos.
Ciudad Bolivar, Medardo Luzardo Romero.
Maracaibo, Domingo Roa Pérez.
Mérida, Miguel Antonio Salas Salas.
Valencia, Luis Eduardo Henriquez Jiménez.

Vietnam

Hanoi, H.E. Cardinal Joseph-Marie Trinh văn Căn.
Hue, vacant.
Thanh-Phô Hôchiminh, Paul Nguyên Van Binh.

West Indies

Castries, Kelvin Edward Felix.

Yugoslavia

Bar, Petar Perkolić.
Belgrade, Franc Perko.
Ljubljana, Alojzij Suštar.
Rijeka-Senj, Josip Paulišić.
Split-Makarska, Frane Franić.
Vrhbosna, Marco Jozinović.
Zadar, Marijan Oblak.
Zagreb, H.E. Cardinal Franjo Kuharić.

Zaire

Bukavu, Mulindwa Mutabesha.
Kananga, Bakole wa Ilunga.
Kinshasa, H.E. Cardinal Joseph Malula.
Kisangani, Fataki Alueka.
Lubumbashi, Kabanga Songasonga.
Mbandaka-Bikoro, Etsou-Nzabi-Bamungwabi.

Zambia

Kasama, Elias Mutale.
Lusaka, Adrian Mungandu.

Zimbabwe

Harare, Patrick Chakaipa.

ARCHBISHOPS OF TITULAR SEES

Acrida, Mario Schierano.
Adana [Greek Melekite Catholic Rite]: Gregoire Haddad.
Amasya, James Patrick Carroll.
Amida, Flavien Zacharie Melkie.
Aquileia, Michele Cecchini.
Beroe, Victor Sartre.
Cesariana, H.E. Cardinal Angelo Felici.
Cesarea in Palaestina [Greek Melekite Catholic Rite]: Hilarion Capucci.
Claudiopolis in Honoriade, Alfredo Bruniera.
Corinthus, Gennaro Verolino.
Dara, Nicholas T. Elko.
Doclea, Pier Luigi Celata.
Edessa in Osrhoëne [Greek Melekite Catholic Rite]: Pierre Rai; [Syrian Catholic Rite]: Gregoire Ephrem Jarjour.
Egina, Raffaele Forni.
Ephesus, John Henry Boccella.
Gabala, Gérard de Milleville.
Gangra, Antonio Ferreira de Macedo.
Gradum, José López Ortiz.
Hadrianopolis in Haemimonto, Lino Zanini.
Kaškar, Emmanuel-Karim Delly.
Macra, John Dooley.
Marcianopolis, Teofilo Camomot Bastida.
Mesembria, Loris Francesco Capovilla.
Meta, H.E. Cardinal Antonio M. J. Ortas.
Nazareth, Giuseppe Carata.
Neapoli, H.E. Cardinal Jacques Martin.
Nicaea Parva, Paolino Limongi.
Nicosia, Aurelio Signora.
Novaliciana, H.E. Cardinal Achille Silvestrini.
Nubia, Paul Antaki.
Razia Ria, Marian Oles.
Salamis, Joseph Kuo.
Scytopolis, Joseph Raya.
Selymbria, Emile Socquet.
Soteropolis, Ettore Cunial.
Tagora, H.E. Cardinal Eduardo M. Somalo.
Tarsus [Maronite Rite]: Abdallah Bared; [Greek Melekite Catholic Rite]: Loutfi Laham.
Tiburnia, Donato Squicciarini.
Velebusdo, Jose M. Estepa Llaurens.
Viminacium, Franco Brambilla.

THE JEWS

CHIEF RABBI—The Lord Jakobovits, KT., Ph.D.
Office, Adler House, Tavistock Square, WC1H 0EP. *Executive Officer*, S. Cohen.

It is estimated that about 410,000 Jews are resident in the U.K., some 280,000 in Greater London.

The *Board of Deputies of British Jews*, established in 1760, is the representative body of British Jewry and is recognized by H.M. Government. The basis of representation is mainly synagogal, but secular organizations are also represented. It is a deliberative body and its objects are to watch over the interests of British Jewry, to protect Jews against any disability which they may suffer by reason of their creed and to take such action as may be conducive to their welfare.
President, Dr. Lionel Kopelowitz.
Secretary General, H. Pinner, Woburn House, Upper Woburn Place, WC1H 0EP.

The *Beth Din* (Court of Judgment) is a rabbinic body consisting of *Dayanim* (Assessors) and the Chief Rabbi, who is President of the Court. The Court arbitrates when requested in cases between Jew and Jew, and Jew and non-Jew, and gives decisions on religious questions. The decisions are based on Jewish Law and practice and do not conflict with the law of the land. The *Beth Din* also deals with matters concerning dietary law and marriages and divorces, according to Jewish Law.
Dayanim, Rabbi C. Ehrentreu; Rabbi Dr. I. Lerner; Rabbi C. D. Kaplin; Rabbi I. D. Berger.
Clerk to the Court, Rabbi B. Berkovits, Adler House, Tavistock Square, WC1H 0EP.

EDUCATION IN THE UNITED KINGDOM

ENGLAND AND WALES

Aims

The Government's stated aims in education are to raise standards all round, to obtain the best possible value for money, to increase parental choice, and to widen access to further and higher education while linking them more closely to the needs of the economy. To achieve these objectives major education legislation was introduced and received the Royal Assent at the end of the 1987–88 session of Parliament.

Fall and rise in numbers

In primary education and, increasingly, in secondary education pupil numbers in England have continued to decline. However, for primary schools where pupil numbers peaked at around 4·9 million in the early 1970s and reached their lowest figure of 3·7 million in 1985, numbers are expected to increase gradually year by year until by the year 1991 they reach about 3·9 million. For secondary schools, where pupil numbers have fallen from 3·9 million in 1979 to 3·3 million in 1987 and will decline further to an expected 2·8 million in 1991, it is not expected that they will exceed about 3·1 million for the rest of the century.

Expenditure

In real terms (i.e. cash figures adjusted to 1986–87 price levels), expenditure on education was as follows (£million): 1985–86, 14,414; 1986–87, 15,691; 1987–88 (estimated), 17,169; and planned spending in 1988–89 is 17,971; 1989–90, 18,640; 1990–91, 19,170. Of the estimated expenditure on education of £17,169 million (in cash terms) in 1987–88, £10,633 million was spent on schools, £4,904 million on further and higher education, £975 million on miscellaneous education services and £657 million on the research councils and related bodies.

The unit cost, in real terms (1979–80=100), for maintained primary and secondary schools in England went up from 107 in 1980–81 to 120 in 1985–86, and to an estimated 131 in 1986–87.

Department of Education and Science

The Department of Education and Science (D.E.S.) is responsible for all aspects of education in England and for government policy and support for universities in England, Scotland and Wales. Responsibility in Wales for nursery, primary and secondary education, and for all non-university institutions of higher and further education, the youth and community services, and adult education lies with the Secretary of State for Wales.

The Department's main concerns are the formulation of national policies for education and the maintenance of consistency in educational standards. It is responsible for the broad allocation of resources for education, for the rate and distribution of educational building and for the supply, training and superannuation of teachers. Although the Department heretofore has not run any schools or colleges directly, nor employed any teachers, it may now be about to play a new role in funding individual schools under the provisions of the new Education Reform Act. This allows schools, if certain conditions are satisfied, to opt out of local education authority control and apply for direct funding from the Secretary of State. In addition, the Department together with sponsors from industry will fund the new City Technology Colleges and City Colleges for the Technology of the Arts.

The D.E.S. is also responsible for government support for civil science.

It acts within a framework of estimates approved by Parliament. The money which the Department itself spends is a small part of the total public expenditure on education, the major part being expenditure by local authorities (*see below*). This expenditure by local authorities is financed from rates and from the rate support grant payable from the national Exchequer.

The Department commissions research, related to policy interests of the D.E.S. and the L.E.A.s, from universities and other bodies such as the National Foundation for Educational Research.

H.M. Inspectorate

Her Majesty's Inspectors inspect schools and other educational establishments apart from universities. H.M.I.s assess standards and trends and advise the Secretaries of State on the performance of the system nationally. They identify and make more widely known good practice and promising developments and draw attention to weaknesses needing consideration. They provide advice and help to those with responsibilities for, or in, the institutions in the system through the H.M.I.s' day-to-day contacts, their contributions to training, and their publications. Inspection visits are the main, though not the only, way by which the H.M.I.s perform these functions. There were, in 1987–88, 472 H.M.I.s in England and 54 in Wales. In 1986 in England H.M.I.s visited about 15 per cent of primary schools, nearly 50 per cent of secondary schools in the maintained sector; and 22 per cent of independent schools. Nearly 90 per cent of public sector institutions of further and higher education (including those providing initial teacher training) also had inspection visits.

Local Education Authorities

The education service at present is a national service locally administered by local education authorities (L.E.A.s), although the provisions of the Education Reform Act will allow schools to opt out of L.E.A. control, and will remove non-university higher education from L.E.A. jurisdiction altogether. Among its main features are:—

(*a*) its administration is still largely decentralized, the day-to-day responsibility for providing state primary, secondary and some further education (but no longer the polytechnic sector) to meet the needs of their areas being that of the local education authorities (L.E.A.s). Subject to guidelines issued by the central education departments in England and Wales and the requirements of examination syllabuses, at present each educational establishment still has freedom to determine its own curriculum and the content of its courses. However, increased centralization is being introduced under the Education Reform Act in the form of a national curriculum which all schools will be obliged to teach and which will be introduced in schools over the next decade.

These local authorities appoint education committees consisting of some of their own members (a majority of the committee) and other people with experience in education and knowledge of the local education situation. The L.E.A.s own and maintain schools and colleges and build new ones, employ teachers and provide equipment. Most of the public money spent on education is disbursed by the local authorities. L.E.A.s are financed largely by rate support grants from the Department of the Environment and from the rates; teachers' salaries account for about half of local authority expenditure on education and related services.

(*b*) Voluntary agencies play an important part in

educational provision often in co-operation with the State. Some indication of its nature and extent is given below.

SCHOOLS AND PUPILS

Schooling is compulsory for all children between 5 and 16 years. Some provision is made for children under 5 and many pupils remain at school after the minimum leaving age. No fees are charged in any publicly maintained school.

There are two main categories of school: (*a*) those *maintained* by local education authorities, the authorities meeting their expenditure partly from local rates and partly from grants made by the Department of Education; (*b*) *independent* schools (which are liable to inspection by H.M. Inspectorate. To these categories may be added a third as a result of the Education Reform Act, namely that of schools which, although still providing free education, have applied to opt out of local education authority control to operate as autonomous institutions funded directly by the Secretary of State.

Maintained Schools

Maintained schools are of two types: (*i*) *county schools* (16,032 in 1987 in England) which are built, maintained and staffed by local education authorities. They are non-denominational and provide primary and secondary education. Their managers (primary schools) and governors (secondary schools) are appointed by the L.E.A.s. (*ii*) *voluntary schools* (7,621 in 1987 in England) also provide primary and secondary education. Although built by voluntary bodies (mainly religious denominations) they are financially maintained by an L.E.A.

Voluntary schools are of three kinds: controlled (3,146), aided (4,390), and special agreement (85). In *controlled* schools the L.E.A. nominates a majority of the managers or governors (the rest are nominated by the voluntary body), bears all costs and appoints the teachers. In *aided* schools the managers or governors (the majority appointed by the voluntary interest and the rest by the L.E.A.) are responsible for repairs to the outside of the school building and for improvements and alterations to it, though the Department of Education and Science may reimburse part of approved capital expenditure. The L.E.A. pays for internal maintenance and other running costs. The managers or governors control the appointment of teachers. *Special agreement* schools are those where the L.E.A. may, by special agreement, pay between one-half and three-quarters of the cost of building a new, or extending an existing, voluntary school, almost always a secondary school. A majority of the governors are appointed by the voluntary body and the remainder by the L.E.A. Expenditure is normally apportioned between the authority and the voluntary body.

Better Schools

New government policies were set out in 1985 in an important White Paper, *Better Schools* (Cmnd 9469) and over the last two years three pieces of educational legislation have given effect to most of these policies.

The first was the Education Act which received the Royal Assent in November 1986. It aims to raise standards by improving the management of schools and promoting teaching quality. Among other things, it gives parents a greater say in the running of their children's schools, provides for more effective in-service training of teachers and a new framework for the appraisal of teachers' performance, abolishes corporal punishment in the maintained sector, provides safeguards in the teaching of sex education and

political issues, and protects freedom of speech in universities, polytechnics and colleges.

The Education (No. 2) Act 1986 legislates for appraisal and more effective in-service training to promote the professional effectiveness of teachers and to improve the management and accountability of schools through new arrangements for the composition of governing bodies, increasing the influence of parents.

The Education Reform Act received the Royal Assent in July 1988. It provides for: the introduction of a national curriculum consisting of three core subjects, English, mathematics and science, together with seven other foundation subjects, supported by the establishment of attainment targets, programmes of study and systems of assessment and testing at the ages of seven (or thereabouts), eleven, fourteen and sixteen; curriculum aims and objectives to be reflected in school examinations; adequate information to be made available to parents, employers and others on the performance of pupils and of the education service at all levels; schools to admit pupils up to the limits of their capacity; L.E.A.s to develop schemes of resource allocation to schools and to delegate control for their budgets to all secondary schools and larger primary schools; all secondary schools and the largest primary schools to have the choice to opt out of local authority control and to operate as autonomous institutions with direct funding from central government, and the establishment of City Technology Colleges and City Colleges for the Technology of the Arts as independent secondary schools in urban areas to provide free education with special emphasis on science and technology.

Public Schools

By the term *public schools* is usually meant the independent schools in the membership of the Headmasters' Conference, the Governing Bodies Association or the Governing Bodies of Girls' Schools Association. Most public schools are for one sex (about half of them for girls) but there are some mixed schools and many boys' schools admit girls to their sixth forms.

Independent schools charge fees and do not receive grants from public funds. *Preparatory schools* are mainly for boys from about 7 to 13 years who wish to enter public schools. All independent schools are open to inspection by H.M. Inspectors (*see above*) and must register with the Department of Education and Science which lays down certain minimum standards and can make schools remedy any unacceptable features of their building or instruction and exclude any unsuitable teacher or proprietor. In 1987 there were in England 2,276 independent schools with 514,855 full-time pupils and a pupil–teacher ratio of 11·3 (which compares with 18·4 for maintained schools). The number of schools increased by only four over the previous year but full-time pupil numbers went up by 10,000. The arrangements by which independent schools could be "recognized as efficient", i.e. could satisfy the D.E.S. that their standards were broadly comparable with those of grant-aided schools, were discontinued in 1978.

Assisted places.—The Assisted Places Scheme enables bright children to benefit from attendance at good independent secondary schools which their parents could not otherwise afford. The take-up rate for places available at the 226 participating schools, at age 11 to 13, has risen to nearly 98 per cent and the proportion of pupils receiving full fee remission to 40 per cent. Some 33,200 places were offered in the academic year 1987–88.

The State System

Nursery Education is for children under 5 years who may attend a nursery school or a primary school.

516,800 pupils under 5 years of age were receiving education in maintained nursery and primary schools in January 1987, an increase of 8,000 on the previous year. Expressed as a percentage of the population aged 3 and 4 years, the 516,800 represented 43·8 per cent, compared to 43·3 in the previous year and 34·4 in 1978. 240,600 were in infant classes, 226,700 in nursery classes and 49,500 in nursery schools.

Primary Stage.—This begins at 5 years and the transfer to secondary school is generally made at 11 years. Primary schools consist mainly of *infants' schools* for children aged 5 to 7, *junior schools* for those aged 7 to 11 and *junior and infant schools* for both age groups. In addition *first schools* in some areas cater for ages from 5 to 8, 9 or 10. (They are the first stage of a three-tier system: first, middle and secondary.) Many primary schools provide nursery classes for children under 5 (*see above*).

Middle Schools.—Middle schools (which take children from first schools) cover varying age ranges between 8 and 14 and usually lead on to comprehensive upper schools.

Secondary Stage.—Secondary schools are for children aged 11 to 16 and over. The largest have over 2,000 pupils but 82 per cent of the schools take between 400 and 1,500 pupils. In January, 1987, when there were in England 3,239,500 pupils in maintained secondary schools the main types were: (*a*) *comprehensive* schools (85·8 per cent of pupils), whose admission arrangements are without reference to ability or aptitude; (*b*) *middle deemed secondary* schools (6·5 per cent); (*c*) *secondary modern* schools (4·1 per cent) providing mainly a general education with a practical bias; (*d*) *secondary grammar* schools (3·1 per cent) providing an academic course from 11 to 16–18 years; and (*e*) *technical* schools (0·5 per cent) providing an integrated academic and technical course.

Tertiary Colleges provide normal sixth form school courses as well as a range of courses for further education students over the age of 16.

Special Education is provided for children who require it because of physical or mental disability. In January 1987 there were 107,100 full-time pupils in special schools (of whom 2,949 were in hospital schools). Numbers have been going down since 1978 (131,500).

City Technology Colleges and City Colleges for the Technology of the Arts.—The first City Technology College opened in September 1988. These schools are state-aided but independent of L.E.A.s. Their aim is to widen the choice of secondary school for families in disadvantaged urban areas and to provide models for the effective teaching of a broad curriculum with an emphasis on science, technology, business understanding and arts technologies in a disciplined learning environment. Capital costs will be shared by government and sponsors from industry and commerce, and running costs will be covered by a per capita grant from the D.E.S. in line with comparable costs in a L.E.A. maintained school.

Primary and Secondary Schools

In 1987 there were 27,959 maintained and non-maintained schools in England, 216 fewer than in 1986. The total number of full-time pupils in them fell by 113,000 over the year to 7,450,000 in 1987. The number of maintained secondary schools (4,221 in 1987) fell slightly for the tenth successive year since the peak in 1977. Over the same period the number of primary schools has also fallen; in 1987 the total of 19,422 was 127 below the total for 1986.

Of the 7,450,000 full-time pupils in 1987, 11,600 were in maintained nursery schools, 3,576,000 in maintained primary schools (including 566,285 under 5 years), 3,239,800 in maintained secondary schools

(including 291,300 who were 16 or over), 514,855 in independent schools, and 107,100 in special schools.

Between 1984–85 and 1989–90 primary school pupil numbers are projected to rise by 5·2 per cent and secondary school pupil numbers by 19·5 per cent.

Boys and girls are taught together in almost all maintained primary schools. Most pupils in maintained secondary schools in England and Wales attend mixed schools.

Parents.—Parental involvement in publicly maintained schools is growing through parent/teacher associations and in other ways. There is now statutory provision for elected parent and teacher governors on school governing bodies and for parents to express a preference as to the school they would like their child to attend. They now have the power to decide whether their child's school should opt out of local authority control.

Pupil–teacher ratios.—In both maintained primary and secondary schools the steady year-by-year improvement continued, from 23·6 in primary schools in 1978 to 21·9 in 1987 and from 16·9 in secondary schools in 1978 to 15·6 in 1987. In independent schools, there was also a gradual improvement: from 12·9 in 1978 to 11 in 1987.

Class sizes.—The average size of classes "as taught" in maintained primary schools fell slightly from 25·9 in 1986 to 25·8 in 1987. Between 1977 and 1984 there had been a steady year-by-year improvement from 26·9 to 25·0, after which the class size began to increase. In secondary schools a steady annual improvement resumed after a rise in 1985 (to 21·4): 22·4 in 1977 to 20·9 in 1984 and 21·0 in 1987.

School meals.—Under the Social Security Act 1986, the duty of L.E.A.s to provide free school meals will from April 1988 be restricted to provision for children of families in receipt of Income Support.

Advanced levels.—In 1987 the number of pupils in all schools taking A-level courses was 224,391, almost equally divided between boys and girls. 26·1 per cent of them were studying maths/science subjects only, compared to 27·3 per cent in 1986, continuing the gradual decline from 29·5 in 1984.

In 1985–86, 20·8 per cent (proportion of 17 year old age group) achieved 1 or more passes at A level compared to 18·6 per cent ten years before, and 10·7 per cent achieved 3 or more passes compared to 9·0 per cent in 1975–76.

School-leavers.—38·1 per cent of those who left school in 1985–86 without A-levels had achieved one or more graded G.C.E. O-level or C.S.E. result, compared to 35·9 per cent 10 years before.

Examinations.—Secondary school pupils (and others) until the end of 1987 took the General Certificate of Education (G.C.E.) or the Certificate of Secondary Education (C.S.E.). The G.C.E. was introduced in 1951 (it replaced the School Certificate and Higher School Certificate) and the C.S.E. in 1965.

From 1987 a new single system of examinations—the *General Certificate of Secondary Education* (*G.C.S.E.*) was introduced. The last O-level, C.S.E. and joint 16+ examinations were held in summer and winter 1987, and the first G.C.S.E. courses started in the autumn of 1986 with the first examinations in summer 1988. National Criteria for the G.C.S.E. were approved by the Secretaries of State in 1985.

The purpose of the change was to improve the examination courses and to raise the standard of performance of all candidates. To achieve this, there are: fewer examining groups; syllabuses based on national criteria covering course objectives, content and assessment methods; differentiated assessment (i.e. different papers or questions for different ranges of ability); and grade-related criteria (i.e. grades to be awarded on absolute rather than relative performance). The G.C.S.E. is a single system of examinations, not a single examination.

The G.C.S.E. certificates are awarded with a seven-point scale: A to G. Grades A to C are the equivalent of the corresponding O-level grades A to C or C.S.E. grade 1. Grades D, E, F and G record achievement at least as high as that represented by C.S.E. grades 2, 3, 4 and 5. There is no restriction on entry to any examination. The G.C.S.E. examination is administered by six groups of examining boards in England, Wales and Northern Ireland. All G.C.S.E. syllabuses, assessment and grading procedures are monitored by the Secondary Examinations Council (*see below*) to ensure that they conform to the National Criteria. The National Criteria have two parts: the *General Criteria* which sets out the rules and principles for all courses and examinations; and *Subject Criteria* which set out the aims for the content and teaching of individual subjects.

The Secretary of State has said that the new examinations will: do more than O-levels to stretch the ablest pupils; do more than C.S.E. to motivate other pupils; promote more effectively worthwhile knowledge, understanding and skills; grade candidates by what they know, understand and can do; be clearer to candidates, their parents and employers than the previous system; and be more cost effective.

A-level examinations, taken two years after G.C.S.E., will continue though there are changes to the grading system. The Government set up, in February 1987, a small independent committee to review A-levels which reported in June 1988. It recommended that A-level students should study a broader spread of subjects.

In addition to A-level examinations, new *Advanced Supplementary level (AS-level) examinations* are being introduced. Their purpose is to broaden the curriculum for A-level students but without diluting academic standards. AS-levels are seen by the D.E.S. as "making a useful, if limited, contribution to the problems associated with overspecialisation." Courses leading to AS-level started in September 1987 and the first examinations will be held in summer 1989.

AS-levels will be for full-time A-level students but others can take them too. An AS-level syllabus will cover not less than half the amount of ground covered by the corresponding A-level syllabus and, where possible, will be related to it. An AS-level course will last two years and require not less than half the teaching time of the corresponding A-level course. It is envisaged that students hoping to go on to higher education would continue (where they do so now) to take A-level courses in the subjects they want to specialize in. AS-level courses will supplement and broaden these studies and examinations will be held at the same time as A-levels.

Technical and Vocational Education Initiative.— T.V.E.I., within a framework of general education, aims to give teenagers a curriculum more relevant to adult life and work. Following pilot projects, it is now a national scheme, with newly established curricular criteria, open to all maintained schools and colleges providing for young people, of all abilities, aged 14–18. T.V.E.I. is not an examination or a qualification.

The *Certificate of Pre-Vocational Education* is a one-year full-time (or two years part-time) course intended for a wide ability range at 16+ including pupils who do not intend to go on to A-levels but would like to continue their education on completion of their secondary schooling. This new national qualification is offered by the Business and Technician Education Council and the City and Guilds of London Institute operating together as the Joint Board for Pre-Vocational Education. Within guidelines laid down by that Board, schools and colleges design their own courses, which stress activity-based learning, basic numeracy and work-experience. The

C.P.V.E. is mainly for those who want to find out more about what work they may be good at and to prepare themselves for adult work, but who are not yet committed to a particular occupation.

In 1983 two new bodies were set up to replace the Schools Council—the *Secondary Examinations Council* (S.E.C.) and the *School Curriculum Development Committee* (S.C.D.C.). These bodies are now to be succeeded respectively by the School Examinations and Assessment Council and the National Curriculum Council, for both of which legislation is embodied in the new Education Reform Act. The School Examinations and Assessment Council will take over the S.E.C.'s role in co-ordinating and working to improve the school examination system and other forms of school-based assessment in England and Wales. It will also advise the Government on these policy areas, as well as taking care of the quality control arrangements for the national curriculum. The National Curriculum Council inherits its predecessor's responsibilities for the promotion and support of curriculum development and the identification of any important gaps, in addition to consulting educational interests and advising the Secretary of State on the national curriculum. The School Examinations and Assessment Council, like the S.E.C., will be funded wholly by central government. The National Curriculum Council will also be funded wholly by the D.E.S., unlike the S.C.D.C. which was jointly funded with the local authorities.

TEACHERS
(*see also* p. 470)

Teachers are appointed by local education authorities, school governing bodies or managers. Those in publicly maintained schools must be approved as "qualified" by the Department of Education and Science. To become a qualified teacher it is necessary to have successfully completed an initial course of teacher training. Teacher training is largely integrated with the rest of higher education with training places concentrated in polytechnics, institutes or colleges of education, and universities. Non-graduates usually qualify by way of a three- or four-year course leading to a B.Ed. degree while graduates take a one-year postgraduate certificate of education.

Entry requirements are high with a reduced number of training places available. On entry to a course of initial teacher training leading to qualified teacher status (whether at undergraduate or postgraduate level) students are expected to provide evidence of, inter alia, a level of competence in English and mathematics at least equivalent to passes at a minimum of Grade C at G.C.E. "O" level or Grade 1 in C.S.E.

For entry at undergraduate level candidates must also normally have five passes at the G.C.E. (two of which should be at "A" level) or four passes (three of which should be at "A" level).

With certain exceptions, the profession now has an all-graduate entry. Teachers in further education, however, are not required to have qualified teacher status but roughly half have a teaching qualification and most have industrial, commercial or professional experience.

The government-established Council for the Accreditation of Teacher Education (CATE) has been reviewing all initial teacher training courses to ensure that they meet stringent conditions.

Newly-Trained Teachers.—Of teachers who in 1986 had successfully completed initial training courses in public sector institutions in England and Wales, 85 per cent had obtained teaching posts in the U.K. (the same as in 1985 but an increase on the 1984 figure of 80 per cent), 7 per cent had taken up non-teaching employment in the U.K. or were working abroad, and 4 per cent were unemployed but seeking a teaching post (compared with 6 per cent in 1985 and 10 per cent in 1984). 96 per cent of all successful leavers had a postgraduate certificate in education or a bachelor's degree in education; 4 per cent had trained on a special further education course or taken some other course such as a one-year specialist certificate in education for mature students.

New Intake.—In the year to January 1987, 11,467 teachers took up first full-time appointments either permanent or for at least one term's duration, in maintained nursery, primary and secondary schools in England and Wales.

Shortage Subjects.—In recent years there have been shortages of teachers in a number of secondary subjects, particularly mathematics, the physical sciences and craft, design and technology (C.D.T.). There is a bursary scheme for trainee teachers in these three shortage areas for one- or two-year courses.

Serving Teachers.—In 1987 there were 520,517 teachers (full-time and full-time equivalent) in service with L.E.A.s in England. Of these, 402,280 (down from 402,932 in 1986) were in maintained schools (excluding special schools) and 118,237 (up from 117,166 in 1986) in further education, maintained special schools, etc. 1,522 were in nursery schools, 157,471 in primary schools, and 197,780 in secondary schools. 99,085 were in maintained and assisted further education, adult education centres and youth clubs and centres (16,191 of these in polytechnics), 17,167 in maintained special schools, and 1,985 provided out of school education.

A new scheme was launched in 1987 for the in-service training of teachers and others employed in the education service. In 1987–88 L.E.A.s were planning to devote £265 million to the scheme.

HIGHER EDUCATION

Higher Education consists of the education provided in universities and in advanced courses in polytechnics and colleges of higher education.

The Government is committed to quality and cost effectiveness in a higher education system which both plays its part in meeting the nation's economic and social needs and provides the necessary opportunities for the advancement of knowledge and the pursuit of scholarship. In addition, the Government is concerned to ensure that places are available to all who have the necessary intellectual competence, motivation and maturity to benefit from higher education and who wish to do so; and that the balance of skills required by the nation is ensured by a further shift towards science, engineering and vocational courses. The Education Reform Act legislates for important changes in the structure, national planning and especially the funding of higher education. Polytechnics and other major colleges are to be removed from local authority control and established as autonomous institutions; a Polytechnics and Colleges Funding Council is to be set up to make public funds available to the sector; and the University Grants Committee is to be reconstituted as the Universities Funding Council. The new Funding Councils are expected to secure more effective use of public funds allocated to higher education through: the implementation of new contract-based funding arrangments; further progress on targeting resources on strengths; and, in partnership with the institutions, continuing efforts to improve quality and efficiency in all their aspects.

Students.—In 1986–87, the number of home full-time and sandwich-course students in universities in Great Britain was 259,300 and in non-university higher education (including polytechnics) in England was 234,000. The university figure was an increase on the previous year of 2,800 and the non-university figure was the highest since 1980. To these figures must be added the number of overseas students (42,000 in 1986–87 in universities and 14,000 elsewhere) and 323,000 part-time students, including those studying at the Open University.

Between 1979 and 1986–87, the number of home students in higher education increased by almost 179,000, including an increase of 89,000 in the number of full-time students. The proportion of 18- and 19-year olds entering full-time higher education rose from 13·4 per cent in 1982–83 to 14·1 per cent in 1986–87; and the number of mature entrants to full-time higher education is up by 27 per cent on 1982. The proportion of home students on science courses increased from 37 per cent in 1979 to 40 per cent in 1985 and the proportion who are women from 44·9 per cent in 1985 to 45·4 per cent in 1986. Further increases in numbers over the next few years are envisaged.

Academic Staff.—In 1986–87 there were 45,000 full-time academic staff at universities in Great Britain and 26,500 (full-time equivalent) in local authority higher education in England. Student–staff ratios in 1985–86 were 10·3 in universities in Great Britain and 11·1 in local authority higher education in England, but these ratios are not comparable because of different methods of calculation.

Regional Technology Centres (R.T.C.s).—A national network of regional new technology centres is being set up in Great Britain, involving universities, polytechnics and colleges working with local firms. They will build on existing successful schemes to transfer technological innovations from the laboratory into new products for business and industry. The total funding for the Centres in 1987–88 was £1,546,000, made up of £687,000 from central government and around £859,000 from the participating educational institutions and industry.

Universities

Universities are self-governing institutions, usually established by Royal Charter, which are responsible for academic appointments, curriculum and student admissions. They depend on the State for much of their income.

There are 46 universities in the United Kingdom (*see* pp. 444–9). Of these, 35 are in England, eight in Scotland, two in Northern Ireland and one (a federal institution) in Wales.

The non-residential "*Open University*" provides courses leading to degrees by a combination of television, radio, correspondence, tutorials, short residential courses and local audio-visual centres. The Open University offers undergraduate (no qualifications needed for entry), post-experience and postgraduate courses. It is grant-aided directly by the Department of Education and Science and does not come within the University Grants Committee system.

The independent University at Buckingham provides a two-year course leading to a bachelor's degree and its tuition fees are £5,700 for 1988. (Fees for 1989 not available at time of going to press.) It receives no capital or recurrent income from the government but its students are eligible for mandatory awards from L.E.A.s. Its academic year consists of four terms of 10 weeks each.

Admission.—Students applying for admission to a first degree course at a university do so through the Universities Central Council on Admissions (U.C.C.A.) which was set up by the universities in 1961 on the initiative of the Committee of Vice-Chancellors and Principals. All universities participate in the U.C.C.A. scheme except the Open University and the University of Buckingham, which conduct their own admissions direct. The U.C.C.A. office is in Cheltenham.

The requirements for entry to first degree courses vary somewhat from one university to another, but the universities publish co-operatively an annual handbook, *University Entrance: the Official Guide,* which describes these requirements.

Fees.—Students with mandatory awards (*see* p. 453) do not pay tuition fees. Students from E.C. member states pay fees at home student rates. Since 1980–81 those from outside the E.C. have paid fees that are meant to cover the cost of their education.

The *University Grants Committee* advises the Secretary of State for Education and Science on university matters. Most of its members are academics or businessmen. The U.G.C. acts as a buffer between the Government from which it receives a block grant of money and the universities to which it allocates this grant.

Although the universities have freedom in academic matters, the government, through the U.G.C., determines the total size of the university student population, its distribution between arts, science, medicine, etc., and the part which the university sector plays in the whole higher education system. In February 1987, the Croham Committee, which had been set up by Government to review the work of the U.G.C., recommended that the U.G.C. should be replaced by a smaller body chaired by an eminent industrialist and with roughly equal numbers of academic and non-academic members. The Government subsequently announced that the new body would be called the Universities Funding Council and that its primary responsibility will be to allocate funds to the individual universities under new contractual arrangements. Legislation to this effect is included in the Education Reform Act.

Finance.—In 1986–87, the total recurrent income of universities in Great Britain was £2,484 million. Exchequer grants as a percentage of total income have dropped from 75 in 1976–77 to 55 in 1986–87. Income in 1986–87 from contracts with industry, commerce and public corporations rose by 16 per cent compared with the previous year. The exchequer grant of £1,367 million was, in real terms, 4 per cent lower than in 1985–86. The total *non*-recurrent exchequer grant for 1986–87 was £143 million.

Polytechnics, Colleges, etc.

Polytechnics and colleges of higher education provide both advanced and non-advanced courses. An *advanced course*—full-time, sandwich or part-time—is one that is of a standard higher than G.C.E. "A" level. It thus includes research, degree-level courses, higher diploma and higher certificate courses, and courses leading to a wide variety of professional qualifications. All other courses are regarded as *non-advanced.* Advanced courses are offered in some 400 institutions outside the universities, most of them maintained by L.E.A.s which are responsible for providing full-time and part-time courses of post-secondary education (other than university education) in their areas.

The Government announced in April 1987 that the polytechnics and 28 other higher education colleges in England would be re-established as free-standing institutions independent of local authority control. There will be a new Polytechnic and Colleges Funding Council which will succeed the National Advisory Body for Public Sector Higher Education (*see below*) and will contract with individual institutions for the provision of higher education. These changes are embodied in the Education Reform Act, 1988.

An important body is the *Council for National Academic Awards* (C.N.A.A.) which awards degrees to students taking courses approved by it in non-university institutions. Following a recommendation of the Robbins Committee it was established by Royal Charter in 1964 as a self-governing body. More than 100 colleges in Britain conduct courses leading to its degrees: B.A., B.Ed., B.Sc., and the higher degrees of M.A. and M.Sc. (for post-graduate course work) and M.Phil. and Ph.D. (for research which may be undertaken jointly in industry and college).

The *Diploma of Higher Education* (Dip.H.E.) is a two-year diploma intended to serve as either a terminal qualification or as a stepping stone to a degree or other further study; it has a normal entry requirement of two "A" levels. The Dip. H.E. is usually awarded by the Council for National Academic Awards (*see above*).

A *National Advisory Body for Public Sector Higher Education* advises the Secretary of State on a co-ordinated approach to the academic provision and the allocation of funds in polytechnics and other local authority and voluntary colleges in respect of courses leading to qualifications higher than A-level. It is to be succeeded by a new body with additional funding responsibilities, the Polytechnic and Colleges Funding Council for which legislation exists in the Education Reform Act.

Regional Advisory Councils. Responsibility for coordinating further education provision in different areas of England and Wales rests with 10 Regional Advisory Councils (*see* p. 471) set up by the local education authorities in each region. The councils bring together representatives of the L.E.A.s, colleges, universities, industry and commerce.

The 3,198 institutions other than universities in England may be grouped in the following main categories. All three are grant-aided and were in 1986 attended by a total of 3,558,000 students of whom 447,174 were on advanced courses and 594,000 were taking full-time or sandwich courses:—

1. *Polytechnics* (*see also* p. 450).—Twenty-nine major centres in England in which a wide range of full-time, sandwich and part-time courses are provided for students at all levels of higher education, and entirely or almost entirely for those of 18 years or more. They have governing bodies with a large measure of autonomy and are mainly teaching institutions though provision is made for certain research where it is essential to the proper fulfilment of teaching functions and the maintenance of close links with industry. A Polytechnics Central Admissions System (P.C.A.S.) was set up in 1984 in Cheltenham. It deals with admissions to full-time and sandwich first degree and Dip.H.E. courses in all polytechnics and in eight colleges and institutes of higher education in England and Wales, excluding art and design, and teacher training courses. In England in November 1986 there was a total of 246,442 students enrolled at polytechnics; of these 232,834 were on advanced courses (40 per cent of them women) and 13,008 on non-advanced courses; of those on advanced courses 159,617 were full-time or sandwich (42 per cent of them women).

2. *Other Major Establishments* (451).—Including all major establishments (maintained, assisted by L.E.A.s, direct grant from D.E.S. or voluntary), other than polytechnics, providing courses in teacher training, art, agricultural, commercial, technical and other subjects. In England there were 214,324 students on advanced courses including 87,883 on full-time or sandwich; and 1,615,846 on non-advanced courses.

3. *Adult Education Centres* (2,718).—Establishments maintained by local education authorities and offering a wide range of courses, many of them recreational, mainly for evening students, and often housed in premises used by day for other educational

purposes. 1,454,966 students in England; 73 per cent were women. *See also* pp. 455–7.

In 1983, the *Business and Technician Education Council* (B.T.E.C.) was set up by the Secretary of State for Education and Science to replace the Business Education Council (1974) and the Technician Education Council (1973) and to continue their work of developing a national system of non-degree vocational courses in these fields.

Vocational qualifications.—Following the report in 1986 of a working group, set up by Government, vocational qualifications in England and Wales will be brought within a new national framework to be called the National Vocational Qualification (N.V.Q.). A new National Council for Vocational Qualifications will develop the framework and secure change. The N.V.Q. framework, which will initially consist of four levels, is intended to come into operation in 1991.

The Youth Service provides for the spare-time activities of young people. The Local Education Authorities co-operate with voluntary bodies in their areas and may maintain their own youth clubs. There are various national voluntary youth organizations. There are some 4,500 full-time youth workers in England and Wales who are employed by local education authorities and voluntary youth organizations. In addition there are many thousands of part-time paid and unpaid workers. In 1987–88 the D.E.S. grant towards the headquarters' costs of national voluntary youth organizations was £3·7 million. There is a National Advisory Council for the Youth Service.

TRAINING

The main responsibility for carrying out industrial and commercial training lies with individual employers, but the Training Commission, which is separate from government but responsible to the Secretary of State for Employment, provides, with government support, opportunities for individuals to acquire new skills and helps to improve the effectiveness of training generally.

The *Youth Training Scheme* (Y.T.S.) is a major development. When it began in 1983, it offered a one-year programme of training and planned work experience for employed and unemployed 16-year old school-leavers and some unemployed 17-year old school-leavers.

From 1986 the Y.T.S. was expanded and developed to give 16-year old school-leavers two years of training and 17-year olds one year, with special arrangements for disabled young people. The two-year programme involves at least 20 weeks off-the-job training in a college or training centre, in addition to on-the-job training and planned work experience. The second year builds on the first year's foundations by providing specific skill training, leading to vocational qualifications. Entrants receive a tax-free weekly allowance. Since 1983 more than one million young people have joined the scheme. Three quarters of leavers go into work or further education/training.

The Y.T.S. is meant not just as an alternative to unemployment but as a permanent training scheme to help equip young people for working life. It is part of an overall Government policy whose aim is to ensure that all young people under 18 have a better opportunity than in the past either to continue in full-time education or to enter upon a period of planned work-experience combined with work-related training and education.

Other training programmes offered, under the aegis of the Department of Employment and the Training Commission formerly the Manpower Services Commission, include: *Employment Training*, which in September 1988 replaced the New Job Training Scheme, continuing its function as a programme of training to help people aged 18 or over who have been unable to get a job after six months' unemployment (with certain exceptions), with priority given to the under-25s; and the *Open Learning Programme* which aims to improve the skills of employed or unemployed people and thus to widen adult career and jobs opportunities at technician and supervisory management levels of skill.

Building on the experience of the Open Learning Programme, the Government has set up an *Open College* using radio and TV to support and deliver open-learning courses in all areas of vocational competence. It began broadcasting in September 1987, and it is planned that within 5 years it will give up to a million students a chance to progress towards vocational and technical qualifications, and that it will be self-financing as soon as practicable. Wherever appropriate, Open College courses will lead to nationally recognized qualifications or credits towards them.

SCOTLAND

The educational system of Scotland has developed independently to that of England and has a number of distinctive features. The general supervision of the national system of education, except for the universities, is the responsibility of the Secretary of State for Scotland acting through the Scottish Education Department. The duty of providing education locally rests with the nine regional councils and three island councils. Educational facilities of various kinds are also provided by the governing bodies of grant-aided schools, central institutions, colleges of education, and national voluntary organizations in the field of informal further education.

Schools.—Schools in Scotland fall into three main categories: *education authority schools* which are financed and managed by the regional and islands councils; *grant-aided schools*, conducted by voluntary managers who receive grants direct from the department; and *independent schools* which receive no direct grant, but which are subject to inspection and registration.

In 1986–87, there were 3,784 education authority and grant-aided schools and departments, of which 569 were nursery, 2,418 primary, 441 secondary and 356 special. There were also 108 registered independent schools. The total number of pupils in education authority and grant-aided schools and departments (including special) was 827,255 of which 38,585 received nursery education. There were a further 32,218 pupils in independent schools.

Schooling normally starts at the age of 5, and the primary school course lasts for 7 years. Primary schools usually take both boys and girls. Pupils transfer from the primary course to secondary courses about the age of 12.

Over 99 per cent of pupils in education authority secondary schools attend schools with a comprehensive intake. Most of these schools provide a full range of courses appropriate to all levels of ability from first to sixth year.

The Scottish Certificate of Education Examination is conducted by the Scottish Examination Board. Pupils may attempt as many of a wide range of subjects as they are capable of, on either the Ordinary/Standard grades which correspond to the Ordinary level of the General Certificate of Education, or on the Higher grade which is normally taken one year after Ordinary/Standard grades. The shorter length of course inevitably means that Higher grades are normally studied to a lesser depth than Advanced levels; on the other hand it is common for pupils to be presented for four or more Higher grades at a single diet of the examination. The Board grants a

Certificate of Sixth Year Studies designed to give direction and purpose to sixth-year work by encouraging pupils who have completed their main subjects at Higher grade to study a maximum of three such subjects in depth. Pupils may also use the sixth year to gain improved or additional Higher grades or Ordinary/Standard grades.

Further Education.—Facilities for further education are provided by 13 Central Institutions (grant-aided colleges administered by independent Boards of Governors) and by 49 further education colleges managed by education authorities. The Central Institutions provide mainly advanced courses in science and technology, commerce, art, music, domestic science, and other subjects, leading to their own diplomas, to professional qualifications or to degrees validated by C.N.A.A. or universities.

The further education colleges normally provide less advanced courses which are mainly part-time covering vocational and non-vocational subjects, but a few offer courses of degree level. Courses are offered in a wide variety of subjects but to make the most economic use of resources, provision of certain courses is made on a regional or even a national basis.

Teachers.—All teachers in public or grant-aided schools in Scotland are required to be registered with the General Teaching Council for Scotland (which is independent of the Scottish Education Department) and normally to hold a teaching qualification awarded by a Scottish College of Education. There are five of these colleges, four of which provide both one and four year courses leading to a Teaching Qualification (Primary Education), and a one year course leading to a Teaching Qualification (Secondary Education). The remaining college provides only courses leading to a Teaching Qualification (Primary Education). Physical education courses are provided at the Scottish Centre for Physical Education, Movement and Leisure Studies, which is incorporated in Moray House College of Education.

Unpromoted teachers in primary and secondary schools are paid on a single basic scale, while those in promoted posts receive higher salaries in recognition of their additional responsibilities.

NORTHERN IRELAND

Education in Northern Ireland is administered centrally by the Department of Education and locally by five Education and Library Boards. There are two main categories of school: controlled schools which are controlled by the Education and Library Boards

with all costs paid from public funds; and voluntary schools which get grants towards capital costs and running costs in whole or in part.

Nursery education for under-fives is provided in nursery schools or nursery classes in primary schools. Primary education is for children up to 11–12 years and is free, though children educated in preparatory departments of grammar schools pay fees. Entry, at 11–12 years, to a secondary (intermediate) school or grammar school is selective in most areas but children can subsequently transfer from one to the other. Grammar schools provide an academic type of secondary education with A-levels at the end of the seventh year, while secondary (intermediate) schools follow a curriculum suited to aptitudes and abilities leading to G.C.S.E. examinations. There are also eight independent schools. Northern Ireland has 26 institutions of further education (with 231 out-centres), two colleges of education, and two universities. The objective of the schools programme is to provide a broad, balanced and relevant curriculum appropriate to the needs and abilities of pupils. The application of government policies as contained in the Education Reform Act 1988, including proposals for a national curriculum, is being examined in consultation with education interests.

In January 1987 the total number of pupils enrolled in the 1,361 grant-aided schools was 341,600, of whom 3,600 were in nursery schools, 182,300 in primary schools, 153,200 in secondary schools and 2,500 in special schools. Between 1982 and 1985, primary school enrolments went down by 13,000, but have now begun to rise slowly, and secondary school enrolments by 9,000, pupil–teacher ratios improved from 23·6 to 23·4 (primary) and from 15·2 to 14·7 (secondary) and the staying-on rates for 16-year olds increased from 36 per cent in 1986 to 36·6 per cent in 1987, and the projected increase for 1988 is 38·7 per cent.

There were 18,500 full-time equivalent teachers of whom 200 were in nursery schools, 7,800 in primary, 7,400 in secondary, and 300 in special.

In 1985–86, there were 14,920 full time students and 6,995 part time students in universities and in advanced courses elsewhere. In addition, there were 14,634 full-time students and 31,532 part time students on non-advanced vocational courses of further education. In colleges of education there were 1,600 students.

Public expenditure on education and related services in 1986–87 was: current—£647,054,000; capital £49,498,000.

G.C.S.E. EXAMINATION BOARDS

LONDON AND EAST ANGLIA GROUP, The Lindens, Lexden Road, Colchester CO3 3RL (0206-549595) *Secretary,* Miss M. I. Thompson.

MIDLAND EXAMINING GROUP, Norfolk House, Smallbrook Queensway, Birmingham B5 4NJ (021-6312151) *Secretary,* Mr. B. Swift.

NORTHERN EXAMINING ASSOCIATION c/o Joint Matriculation Board, Manchester M15 6EU (061-2732565) *Joint Secretary,* Mr. C. Vickerman.

c/o North Regional Examinations Board, Wheatfield Road, Westerhope, Newcastle upon Tyne NE5 5JZ (091-2862711) *Joint Secretary,* Mr. D. Kelly.

c/o North West Regional Examinations Board, Orbit House, Albert Street, Eccles, Manchester M30 0WL (061-7889521) *Joint Secretary,* Ms. K. Tattersall.

SOUTHERN EXAMINING GROUP, Stag Hill House, Guildford, Surrey GU2 5XL (0483-503123) *Chief Executive,* Mr. P. K. Burke.

EDUCATION DIRECTORY

UNIVERSITIES

The universities have power to award their own degrees. They grant 70 per cent. of all first degrees awarded in Britain and 95 per cent. of all higher degrees. They provide most of the basic and much of the applied research undertaken in Britain, and are responsible for the initial training of virtually all research workers. The universities make the chief contribution to wholly new knowledge through fundamental research.

THE UNIVERSITY OF OXFORD

FULL TERMS, 1989

Hilary, Jan. 15 to March 11; *Trinity*, April 23 to June 18; *Michaelmas*, Oct. 8 to Dec. 2

Number of Undergraduates in Residence 1987–88: Men, 5,904; Women, 4,012

UNIVERSITY OFFICERS, etc.   Elect.

Chancellor, The Lord Jenkins of Hillhead, P.C., *Balliol* 1987
High Steward, The Lord Wilberforce, P.C., C.M.G., O.B.E., M.A., *All Souls* 1967
Vice-Chancellor, Sir Patrick Neill, Q.C., Warden of *All Souls* 1985
Proctors, D. L. Miller, D.Phil., *Nuffield*; D. J. Maberley, D.Phil., *Wadham* 1988
Assessor, C. J. Wells, St. *Edmund Hall* 1988
Public Orator, G. W. Bond, *Pembroke* 1980
Bodley's Librarian, D. G. Vaisey, *Exeter* 1986
Keeper of Archives, J. Hackney, *Wadham* 1988
Director of the Ashmolean Museum, C. J. White, *Worcester* 1985
Registrar of the University, A. J. Dorey, D.Phil., *Linacre* 1979
Surveyor to the University, D. W. Bending 1985
Secretary of Faculties, A. P. Weale *Worcester* .. 1984
Secretary of the Chest and Chief Accountant, I. G. Thompson, *Merton* 1986
Deputy Registrar (Admin.), D. W. Roberts, *Pembroke*

Oxford Colleges and Halls
(With dates of foundation)

All Souls (1438), Sir Patrick Neill, Q.C., *Warden* (1977).
Balliol (1263), A. J. P. Kenny, D.Phil., D.Litt., F.B.A., *Master* (1978).
Brasenose (1509) Prof. J. K. B. M. Nicholas *Principal* (1978).
Christ Church (1546), Very Rev. E. W. Heaton, *Dean*, (1979).
Corpus Christi (1517), Prof. Sir Keith Thomas, F.B.A., *President* (1986).
Exeter (1314), Sir Richard Norman, K.B.E., D.SC., F.R.S., *Rector* (1987).
Green (1979), Sir John Walton, D.SC., *Warden* (1983).
Hertford (1874), Prof. E. C. Zeeman, F.R.S., *Principal* (1988).
Jesus (1571), Dr. P. M. North, D.C.L. *Principal* (1984).
Keble (1868), (vacant)
Lady Margaret Hall (1878), D. M. Stewart, *Principal* (1979).
Linacre (1962). Sir Bryan Cartledge, K.C.M.G., *Principal* (1988).
Lincoln (1427), Sir Maurice Shock, *Rector* (1987).
Magdalen (1458), A. D. Smith, C.B.E., *President* (1988).
Merton (1264), J. M. Roberts, D.Phil., *Warden* (1985).
New College (1379), H. McGregor, Q.C., D.C.L. *Warden* (1985).
Nuffield (1937), Sir David Cox, F.R.S., *Warden* (1988).

Oriel (1326), The Rt. Hon. Sir Zelman Cowen, A.K., G.C.M.G., G.C.V.O., Q.C., D.C.L., *Provost* (1982).
Pembroke (1624), Sir Roger Bannister, C.B.E., D.M., F.R.C.P., *Master* (1985).
Queen's (1340), J. Moffatt, D.Phil., *Provost* (1987).
St. Anne's (1952) (Originally Society of Oxford Home-Students (1879)), Dr. C. Palley, PH.D., *Principal* (1984).
St. Antony's (1950), R. Dahrendorf, K.B.E., PH.D., F.B.A., *Warden* (1987).
St. Catherine's (1962), E. B. Smith, D.SC., *Master* (1988).
St. Cross (1965), R. C. Repp, D.Phil., *Master* (1987).
St. Edmund Hall (c. 1278), J. C. B. Gosling, *Principal* (1983).
St. Hugh's (1886), Miss M. R. Trickett, *Principal* (1973).
St. John's (1555), W. Hayes, D.Phil., *President* (1987).
St. Peter's (1929), Prof. G. E. Aylmer, D.Phil., F.B.A., *Master* (1978).
Trinity (1554), Sir John Burgh, K.C.M.G., C.B., *President* (1987).
University (1249), Kingman Brewster, *Master* (1986).
Wadham (1612), Sir Claus Moser, K.C.B., C.B.E., F.B.A., *Warden* (1984).
Wolfson (1966), Sir Raymond Hoffenberg, K.B.E., M.D., PH.D., *President* (1985).
Worcester (1714), The Lord Briggs, F.B.A., *Provost* (1976).
Campion Hall (1896), Rev. P. Hackett, *Master* (1984).
St. Benet's Hall (1897), Rev. P. D. Holdsworth, O.S.B., *Master* (1980).
Mansfield (1886), M. P. Mahony, D.Phil., *Acting Principal* (1988).
Regent's Park (1810), Rev. B. R. White, D.Phil., *Principal* (1972).
Greyfriars (1910), Rev. T. M. Mann, *Warden* (1981).

COLLEGES FOR WOMEN ONLY

St. Hilda's (1893), Mrs. G. M. Moore, *Principal* (1980).
Somerville (1879), Miss D. M. S. D. Park, C.M.G., O.B.E. *Principal* (1980).

THE UNIVERSITY OF CAMBRIDGE

FULL TERMS, 1989

Lent, Jan. 17 to March 17; *Easter*, April 25 to June 16; *Michaelmas*, Oct. 10 to Dec. 8

Number of Undergraduates in Residence 1987–88: Men, 6,156; Women, 3,706

UNIVERSITY OFFICERS, etc.   Elect.

Chancellor, H.R.H. The Duke of Edinburgh, K.G., K.T., O.M., G.B.E., P.C. 1977
† *Vice-Chancellor*, M. W. McCrum, *Master of Corpus Christi* 1985
High Steward, The Lord Devlin, P.C., F.B.A., *Christ's* 1966
Deputy High Steward, The Lord Richardson of Duntisbourne, P.C., M.B.E., T.D. 1983
Commissary, The Lord Salmon, P.C., *Pembroke*. 1979
Proctors, R. J. Richards, PH.D., *Downing*; T. H. Coaker, PH.D., *Queen's*. 1988
Orator, J. Diggle, LITT.D., *Queen's*. 1982
Registrary, S. G. Fleet, PH.D., *Downing* 1983
Deputy Registrary, R. F. Holmes, *Darwin* 1972

† Correspondence for the *Vice-Chancellor* and other administrative officers should be sent to the *University Offices*, The Old Schools, Cambridge.

Librarian, F. W. Ratcliffe, PH.D., *Corpus Christi* 1980
Treasurer, M. P. Halstead, PH.D.,*Caius* 1985
Secretary General of the Faculties, J. R. G.
  Wright, *St. Catharine's* 1987
Director of the Fitzwilliam Museum, Prof.
  A. M. Jaffé, LITT.D., *King's* 1973

Cambridge Colleges and Halls
(With dates of foundation)

Christ's (1505), Prof. Sir Hans Kornberg, SC.D., F.R.S., *Master* (1983).
Churchill (1960), Prof. Sir Hermann Bondi, K.C.B., F.R.S., *Master* (1982).
Clare (1326), Prof. R. C. O. Matthews, C.B.E., F.B.A., *Master* (1975).
Clare Hall (1966), Prof. D. A. Low, PH.D., *President* (1987).
Corpus Christi (1352), M. W. McCrum, *Master* (1980).
Darwin (1964), Sir Arnold Burgen, M.D., F.R.S.,*Master* (1982).
Downing (1800), P. Mathias, C.B.E., LITT.D., F.B.A., *Master* (1987).
Emmanuel (1584), Prof. D. S. Brewer, LITT.D., *Master* (1977).
Fitzwilliam (1966), Prof. G. C. Cameron, *Master* (1988).
Girton (1869), The Baroness Warnock, D.B.E., *Mistress* (1984).
Gonville & Caius (1348), Prof. P. Gray, SC.D., F.R.S., *Master* (1988).
Jesus (1496), Prof. A. C. Renfrew, SC.D. *Master* (1986).
King's (1441), Prof. P. P. G. Bateson, SC.D., F.R.S., *Provost* (1987).
Magdalene (1542), D. Calcutt, Q.C., *Master* (1985).
Pembroke (1347), Prof. The Lord Adrian, M.D., F.R.S., *Master* (1981).
Peterhouse (1284), Prof. H. Chadwick, D.D., F.B.A., *Master* (1987).
Queens' (1448), Prof. E. R. Oxburgh, PH.D., F.R.S., *President* (1982).
Robinson (1977), Prof. Sir Jack Lewis, SC.D., F.R.S., *Warden* (1977).
St. Catharine's (1473), *Master*, Prof. B. E. Supple, PH.D. (1984).
St. Edmund's (1896), R. M. Laws, C.B.E., PH.D, *Master* (1986).
St. John's (1511), Prof. Sir Harry Hinsley, O.B.E., *Master* (1979).
Selwyn (1882), Prof. Sir Alan Cook, SC.D., F.R.S., *Master* (1983).
Sidney Sussex (1596), Prof. D. H. Northcote, PH.D., SC.D., F.R.S., *Master* (1976).
Trinity (1546), Sir Andrew Huxley, O.M., F.R.S., *Master* (1984).
Trinity Hall (1350), Sir John Lyons, PH.D., *Master* (1984).
Wolfson (1965), Prof. D. G. T. Williams, *President* (1980).

COLLEGES FOR WOMEN ONLY

New Hall (1954), Mrs. V. L. Pearl, PH.D., *President* (1981).
Newnham (1871), Miss S. J. Browne, C.B., *Principal* (1983).

APPROVED SOCIETIES

Homerton (1824) (for B.Ed. Students), A. G. Bamford, *Principal* (1985).
Hughes Hall (1885), (for post-graduate students), B. M. Herbertson, M.D., *President* (1984).
Lucy Cavendish College (1965) (for women research students and mature undergraduates), Dame Anne Warburton, D.C.V.O., C.M.G., *President* (1985).

THE UNIVERSITY OF ASTON (1966)
Aston Triangle, Birmingham B4 7ET

Full-time Students (1987–88), 3,573.
Chancellor, Sir Adrian Cadbury (1979).
Vice-Chancellor Prof. Sir Frederick Crawford, PH.D., D.Eng., D.SC.
Registrar and Secretary, R. A. D. Packham.

UNIVERSITY OF BATH (1966)
Claverton Down, Bath BA2 7AY

Full-time Students (1987–88), 3,715.
Chancellor, The Lord Kearton, O.B.E., F.R.S. (1980).
Vice-Chancellor, Prof. J. R. Quayle, PH.D., F.R.S.
Secretary and Registrar, R. M. Mawditt, F.R.S.A.

THE UNIVERSITY OF BIRMINGHAM (1900)
P.O. Box 363, Birmingham B15 2TT

Full-time Students (1987-88), 9,116.
Chancellor, Sir Alex Jarratt, C.B. (1983).
Vice-Chancellor, Prof. M. W. Thompson, D.SC.
Registrar and Secretary, D. R. Holmes.

UNIVERSITY OF BRADFORD (1966)
Bradford BD7 1DP

Full-time Students (1987–88), 4,310.
Chancellor, Sir John Harvey-Jones, M.B.E. (1986).
Vice-Chancellor and Principal, Prof. J. C. West, C.B.E., D.SC. (1986).
Registrar and Secretary, I. M. Sanderson, M.B.E.

THE UNIVERSITY OF BRISTOL (1909)
Bristol BS8 1TH

Full-time Students (1987–88), 7,372.
Chancellor, (vacant).
Vice-Chancellor, Sir John Kingman, F.R.S.
Registrar, Mrs. C. M. Cunningham.
Secretary, J. H. M. Parry.

BRUNEL UNIVERSITY (1966)
Uxbridge, Middx. UB8 3PH

Full-time Students (1987–88), 2,997.
Chancellor, The Earl of Halsbury, F.R.S. (1966).
Vice-Chancellor, Prof. R. E. D. Bishop, C.B.E., F.R.S.
Registrar and Secretary, D. Neave.

UNIVERSITY OF BUCKINGHAM (1983)
(Founded 1976 as University College at Buckingham). Independent of state finance.
Buckingham MK18 1EG

Full-time Students (1987–88), 702.
Chancellor, The Lord Hailsham of St. Marylebone, C.H., P.C., F.R.S. (1983).
Vice-Chancellor, Dr. A. M. Barrett, PH.D.
Registrar, S. P. J. Ellis, F.R.S.A.
Secretary, Dr. M. Lavis.

THE CITY UNIVERSITY (1966)
Northampton Square, EC1V 0HB

Full-time Students (1987–88), 3,226.
Chancellor, The Rt. Hon. Lord Mayor of London.
Vice-Chancellor and Principal, Prof. R. N. Franklin, D.Phil., D.SC.
Registrar, A. H. Seville, PH.D.
Secretary, M. M. O'Hara.

THE UNIVERSITY OF DURHAM
(Founded 1832; re-organized 1908, 1937 and 1963)
Old Shire Hall, Durham DH1,3HP

Full-time Students (1987–88), 5,098.
Chancellor, Dame Margot Fonteyn de Arias (1982).
Vice-Chancellor and Warden, Prof. F. G. T. Holliday, C.B.E., F.R.S.E.
Registrar and Secretary, J. C. F. Hayward.

Colleges
Collingwood, G. H. Blake, PH.D.
Graduate Society, M. Richardson, PH.D.
Grey, E. Halladay, *Master*.
Hatfield, J. P. Barber, PH.D., *Master*.
St. Aidan's, P. H. Clarke, PH.D., *Principal*.
St. Chad's, (vacant).
St. Cuthbert's Society, J. D. Norton, *Principal*.
St. Hild and St. Bede, J. V. Armitage, PH.D., *Principal*.
St. John's, Rev. A. Thiselton, PH.D., *Principal*.
St. Mary's, Miss J. M. Kenworthy, *Principal*.
Trevelyan, Miss D. Lavin, *Principal*.
University, E. C. Salthouse, PH.D., *Master*
Ushaw, Rt. Rev. Mgr. P. F. J. Walton, *President*.
Van Mildert, Ms. J. Turner, PH.D., *Principal*.

THE UNIVERSITY OF EAST ANGLIA (1963)
Norwich NR4 7TJ

Full-time Students (1987–88), 4,384.
Chancellor, Rev. Prof. W. O. Chadwick, O.M., K.B.E., F.B.A. (1985).
Vice-Chancellor, Prof. D. C. Burke, PH.D.
Registrar and Secretary, M. G. E. Paulson-Ellis.

THE UNIVERSITY OF ESSEX (1964)
Wivenhoe Park, Colchester CO4 3SQ

Full-time Students (1987–88), 3,172.
Chancellor, The Rt. Hon. Sir Patrick Nairne G.C.B., M.C. (1983).
Vice-Chancellor, Prof. M. Harris, PH.D.
Registrar, E. Newcomb.

THE UNIVERSITY OF EXETER (1955)
Exeter EX4 4QJ

Full-time Students (1987–88), 5,112.
Chancellor, Sir Rex Richards, D.SC., F.R.S. (1981).
Vice-Chancellor, D. Harrison, PH.D., SC.D.
Registrar and Secretary, M. J. Hislop.

THE UNIVERSITY OF HULL (1954)
Cottingham Road, Hull HU6 7RX

Full-time Students (1987–88), 4,910.
Chancellor, The Lord Wilberforce, C.M.G., O.B.E., P.C. (1978).
Vice-Chancellor, Prof. W. Taylor, C.B.E., PH.D.
Registrar and Secretary, F. T. Mattison.

THE UNIVERSITY OF KEELE (1962)
Keele, Staffs. ST5 5BG

Full-time Students (1987–88), 2,900.
Chancellor, Sir Claus Moser, K.C.B., C.B.E., F.B.A. (1986).
Vice-Chancellor, Prof. B. E. F. Fender, C.M.G., PH.D.
Registrar, D. Cohen, PH.D.

UNIVERSITY OF KENT AT CANTERBURY (1965)
Canterbury CT2 7NZ

Full-time Students (1987–88), 4,187.
Chancellor, The Lord Grimond, T.D., P.C. (1969).
Vice-Chancellor, D. J. E. Ingram, D.Phil., D.SC.
Registrar, A. D. Linfoot.

THE UNIVERSITY OF LANCASTER (1964)
Bailrigg, Lancaster LA1 4YW

Full-time Students (1987–88), 4,755.
Chancellor, H.R.H. The Princess Alexandra, G.C.V.O. (1964).
Vice-Chancellor, Prof. H. J. Hanham, PH.D.
Registrar, M. D. Forster.
Secretary, G. M. Cockburn.

THE UNIVERSITY OF LEEDS (1904)
Leeds LS2 9JT

Full-time Students (1987–88), 10,110.
Chancellor, H.R.H. The Duchess of Kent, G.C.V.O. (1966).
Vice-Chancellor, Sir Edward Parkes, PH.D., SC.D.
Registrar, J. J. Walsh.
Bursar, R. Head.

THE UNIVERSITY OF LEICESTER (1957)
Leicester LE1 7RH

Full-time Students (1987–88), 4,851.
Chancellor, Sir George Porter, P.R.S., PH.D., SC.D. (1985).
Vice-Chancellor, K. J. R. Edwards, PH.D.
Registrar, Prof. G. Bernbaum.

THE UNIVERSITY OF LIVERPOOL (1903)
P.O. Box 147, Liverpool L69 3BX

Full-time Students (1987–88), 7,601.
Chancellor, The Viscount Leverhulme, K.G., T.D. (1980).
Vice-Chancellor, Prof. G. J. Davies, PH.D., SC.D.
Registrar, P. H. Gayward.
Academic Secretary, M. D. Carr.

THE UNIVERSITY OF LONDON (1836)
Senate House, WC1E 7HU

Internal Students (1986–87), 51,296, External Students, 22,134.
Visitor, H.M. The Queen in Council.
Chancellor, H.R.H. The Princess Royal, G.C.V.O., F.R.S. (1981).
Vice-Chancellor, The Lord Flowers, F.R.S.
Chairman of the Court, The Lord Goff of Chieveley, P.C., D.C.L.
Chairman of Convocation, Prof. J. P. Quilliam, O.B.E., D.SC.
Principal, P. Holwell.

Principal Officers
Clerk of the Court, P. J. Griffiths.
Clerk of the Senate, P. Taylor.
Academic Registrar, Mrs. G. F. Roberts.
Secretary to University Entrance and School Examinations Council, A. R. Stephenson.
Director of Central Library Services, V. T. H. Parry.

Schools of the University
Birkbeck College, Malet Street, WC1E 7HX, The Baroness Blackstone, PH.D., *Master*.
Goldsmiths' College, Lewisham Way, New Cross, SE14 6NW, A. Rutherford, *Warden*.
Imperial College of Science, Technology and Medicine, South Kensington, SW7 2AZ, Prof. E. A. Ash, C.B.E., PH.D., F.R.S., *Rector*.
Institute of Education, 20 Bedford Way, WC1H 0AL, Prof. D. Lawton, PH.D., *Dir*.
King's College London (includes former Chelsea College and Queen Elizabeth College), Strand, WC2R 2LS, Prof. S. R. Sutherland, *Principal*.
London School of Economics and Political Science, Houghton Street, WC2A 2AE, Dr. I. Patel, *Director*.

Queen Mary College, Mile End Road, E1 4NS, Prof. I. Butterworth, C.B.E., Ph.D., F.R.S., *Principal.*

Royal Holloway and Bedford New College, Egham Hill, Egham, Surrey TW20 0EX, Prof. Dorothy E. C. Wedderburn, D. Litt, *Principal.*

Royal Veterinary College, Royal College Street, NW1 0TU, A. O. Betts, Ph.D., *Principal and Dean.*

School of Oriental and African Studies, Malet Street, WC1E 7HP, Prof. C. D. Cowan, C.B.E., Ph.D., *Dir.*

School of Pharmacy, 29–39 Brunswick Square, WC1N 1AX, Prof. F. Fish, Ph.D., *Dean.*

University College, Gower Street, WC1E 6BT, Sir James Lighthill, F.R.S., *Provost.*

Westfield College, Kidderpore Avenue, Hampstead, NW3 7ST, Prof. J. E. Varey, Ph.D., D.Litt., F.B.A., *Principal.*

Wye College, Wye, Ashford, Kent TN25 5AH, Prof. J. H. D. Prescott, *Principal.*

*Heythrop College, 11–13 Cavendish Square, W1M 0AN, Rev. B. A. Callaghan, S.J., *Principal.*

Medical Schools

Charing Cross and Westminster Medical School, The Reynolds Building, St. Dunstan's Road, W6 8RP. *Dean*, Prof. T. W. Glenister, C.B.E., T.D., D.SC.; *Secretary*, G. K. Buckley.

The London Hospital Medical College, Turner Street, E1 2AD.—*Dean*, Prof. R. Duckworth, M.D., F.R.C.S., F.R.C. Path. *Secretary*, J. W. Walmsley.

Royal Free Hospital School of Medicine, Rowland Hill Street, NW3 2PF.—*Dean*, B. B. MacGillivray, F.R.C.P.; *Secretary*, B. A. Blatch.

St. Bartholomew's Hospital Medical College, West Smithfield, EC1A 7BE.—*Dean*, Dr. I. Kelsey Fry, D.M., F.R.C.P.; *Secretary*, D. J. Brown, M.B.E.

St. George's Hospital Medical School, Cranmer Terrace, Tooting, SW17 0RE.—*Dean*, (vacant); *Secretary*, R. B. Hill.

United Medical and Dental Schools of Guy's and St. Thomas's Hospitals, Guy's: London Bridge, SE1 9RT; St. Thomas's: Lambeth Palace Road, SE1 7EH.—*Dean*, Prof. T. J. H. Clark, M.D., F.R.C.P.; *Secretary*, C. S. Argles

Postgraduate Medical Schools

London School of Hygiene and Tropical Medicine, Keppel Street WC1E 7HT. Dr. C. E. Gordon Smith, C.B., M.D., F.R.C.P., *Dean.*

Royal Postgraduate Medical School, Du Cane Road W12 0SH. Prof. D. N. S. Kerr, F.R.C.P., *Dean.*

British Postgraduate Medical Federation (University of London), 33 Millman Street, WC1N 3EJ. Prof. M. J. Peckham, M.D., F.R.C.P.(G), F.R.C.R., *Director.*

Comprises:—

Institute of Cancer Research, Royal Cancer Hospital, 17A Onslow Gardens SW7 3AL. Prof. R. A. Weiss, Ph.D. *Director.*

Institute of Child Health, 30 Guilford Street, WC1N 1EH. Prof. P. J. Graham, F.R.C.P., *Dean.*

Institute of Dental Surgery, Eastman Dental Hospital, Gray's Inn Road, WC1X 8LD. Prof. G. B. Winter, D.Ch., F.D.S., *Dean.*

National Heart and Lung Institute, Fulham Road, SW3 6HP. M. Green, D.M., F.R.C.P., *Dean.*

Hunterian Institute, Royal College of Surgeons of England, Lincoln's Inn Fields, WC2A 3PN. Prof. Sir Gordon Robson, C.B.E., *Master*; Prof. G. P. Lewis, *Academic Dean.*

Institute of Neurology, National Hospital, Queen Square, WC1N 3BG. D. N. Landon, *Dean.*

Institute of Ophthalmology, Judd Street, WC1H 9QS. R. K. Blach, M.D., F.R.C.S., *Dean.*

Institute of Psychiatry, De Crespigny Park, Denmark Hill, SE5 8AF. Dr. R. M. Murray, M.D., *Dean.*

Senate Institutes

British Institute in Paris, 9–11 Rue de Constantine, 75007, Paris, Prof. C. L. Campos, L-ès-L., Ph.D., *Dir.* London office: Senate House, WC1E 7HU.

Courtauld Institute of Art, 20 Portman Square, W1H 0BE, Prof. C. M. Kauffman, Ph.D., *Dir.*

Institute of Advanced Legal Studies, Charles Clore House, 17 Russell Square, WC1B 5DR, Prof. T. C. Daintith, *Dir.*

Institute of Classical Studies, 31–34 Gordon Square, WC1H 0PY, Prof. J. P. Barron, F.S.A., *Dir.*

Institute of Commonwealth Studies, 27–28 Russell Square, WC1B 5DS, Prof. Shula E. Marks, Ph.D., *Dir.*

Institute of Germanic Studies, 29 Russell Square, WC1B 5DP, Prof. R. A. Wisbey, *Hon. Dir.*

Institute of Historical Research (including the Institute of United States Studies), Senate House, Malet Street, WC1E 7HU, Prof. F. M. L. Thompson, D.Phil., F.B.A., *Dir.*

Institute of Latin American Studies, 31 Tavistock Square, WC1H 9HA, Prof. L. M. Bethell, Ph.D., *Dir.*

School of Slavonic and E. European Studies, Senate House, WC1E 7HU, Prof. M. A. Branch, Ph.D., *Dir.*

Warburg Institute, Woburn Square, WC1H 0AB, Prof. J. B. Trapp, F.B.A., *Dir.*

Institutions having Recognized Teachers

Jews' College, 44A Albert Road, NW4 2SJ, Rabbi Dr. J. Sacks, *Principal.*

London Business School, Sussex Place, NW1 4SA, Prof. P. G. Moore, Ph.D., *Principal.*

Royal Academy of Music, Marylebone Road, NW1 5HT, Sir David Lumsden, D.Phil., F.R.C.M., *Principal.*

Royal College of Music, Prince Consort Road, SW7 2BS, M. G. Matthews, F.R.S.A., *Director.*

Trinity College of Music, Mandeville Place, W1M 6AQ, M. Davies, C.B.E., *Principal.*

LOUGHBOROUGH UNIVERSITY OF TECHNOLOGY (1966)
Loughborough LE11 3TU

Full-time Students (1987–88), 5,150.
Chancellor, Sir Arnold Hall, F.R.S. (1980).
Vice-Chancellor, Prof. D. E. N. Davies, C.B.E., Ph.D., D.SC., F.R.S.
Acting Registrar, D. E. Fletcher, Ph.D.

THE UNIVERSITY OF MANCHESTER
Oxford Road, Manchester MI3 9PL

(Founded 1851; re-organized 1880 and 1903).

Full-time Students (1987–88), 15,988.
Chancellor, Prof. J. A. G. Griffith, F.B.A. (1986).
Vice-Chancellor, Prof. Sir Mark Richmond, Ph.D., SC.D., F.R.S.
Registrar, K. E. Kitchen.

UNIVERSITY OF MANCHESTER INSTITUTE OF SCIENCE AND TECHNOLOGY (1824)
P.O. Box 88, Manchester M60 1QD

Full-time Students (1987–88), 4,270.
President, Sir John Mason, C.B., D.SC., F.R.S. (1986).
Principal, Prof. H. C. A. Hankins, Ph.D.
Registrar and Secretary, P. C. C. Stephenson.

---

*Not in receipt of U.G.C. grants.

THE UNIVERSITY OF NEWCASTLE UPON TYNE
(Founded 1852; re-organized 1908, 1937 and 1963)
6 Kensington Terrace, Newcastle upon Tyne
NE1 7RU

Full-time Students (1987–88), 7,777.
Chancellor, The Duke of Northumberland, K.G., P.C., G.C.V.O., T.D., F.R.S. (1963).
Vice-Chancellor, Prof. L. W. Martin, PH.D.
Registrar, D. E. T. Nicholson.

THE UNIVERSITY OF NOTTINGHAM (1948)
University Park, Nottingham NG7 2RD

Full-time Students (1987–88), 7,190.
Chancellor, Sir Gordon Hobday, PH.D. (1979).
Vice-Chancellor, C. M. Campbell.
Registrar, G. E. Chandler.

THE UNIVERSITY OF READING (1926)
Whiteknights, P.O. Box 217, Reading RG6 2AH

Full-time Students (1987–88), 6,080.
Chancellor, The Lord Sherfield, G.C.B., G.C.M.G., F.R.S. (1970).
Vice-Chancellor, E. S. Page, PH.D.
Registrar, T. Bottomley.

UNIVERSITY OF SALFORD (1967)
Salford M5 4WT

Full-time Students (1987–88), 3,600.
Chancellor, H.R.H. The Prince Philip, Duke of Edinburgh, K.G., K.T., O.M., G.B.E., P.C., F.R.S. (1967).
Vice-Chancellor, Prof. J. M. Ashworth, PH.D., D.SC.
Registrar, S. R. Bosworth, O.B.E.

THE UNIVERSITY OF SHEFFIELD (1905)
Western Bank, Sheffield S10 2TN

Full-time Students (1987–88), 7,914.
Chancellor, The Lord Dainton, PH.D., SC.D., F.R.S. (1979).
Vice-Chancellor, Prof. G. D. Sims, O.B.E., Ph.D.
Registrar and Secretary, Dr. J. S. Padley.

THE UNIVERSITY OF SOUTHAMPTON (1952)
Highfield, Southampton SO9 5NH

Full-time Students (1987–88), 6,592.
Chancellor, The Earl Jellicoe, K.B.E., D.S.O., M.C., P.C. (1984).
Vice-Chancellor, Dr. G. R. Higginson, PH.D.
Secretary and Registrar, D. A. Schofield.
Academic Registrar, Miss A. E. Clarke.

UNIVERSITY OF SURREY (1966)
Guildford, Surrey GU2 5XH

Full-time Students (1987–88), 3,522.
Chancellor, H.R.H. The Duke of Kent, K.G., G.C.M.G., G.C.V.O. (1977).
Vice-Chancellor, A. Kelly, C.B.E., PH.D., SC.D., F.R.S.
Academic Registrar, G. Haigh, PH.D.
Secretary, L. J. Kail.

THE UNIVERSITY OF SUSSEX (1961)
Falmer, Brighton BN1 9RH

Full-time Students (1987–88), 4,393.
Chancellor, The Earl of March and Kinrara (1985).
Vice-Chancellor, Sir Leslie Fielding, K.C.M.G.
Registrar and Secretary, G. Lockwood, D.Phil.

THE UNIVERSITY OF WARWICK (1965)
Coventry CV4 7AL

Full-time Students (1987–88), 7,400.
Chancellor, The Lord Scarman, O.B.E., P.C. (1977).
Vice-Chancellor, C. L. Brundin, PH.D.
Registrar, M. L. Shattock, O.B.E.

THE UNIVERSITY OF YORK (1963)
Heslington, York YO1 5DD

Full-time Students (1987–88), 3,650.
Chancellor, The Lord Swann, PH.D., F.R.S., F.R.S.E. (1979).
Vice-Chancellor, Prof. S. B. Saul, PH.D.
Registrar, D. J. Foster.

ROYAL COLLEGE OF ART (1837)
Kensington Gore, SW7 2EU

Under Royal Charter (1967) the Royal College of Art grants the degrees of Doctor, Doctor of Philosophy, Master of Arts and Master of Design (RCA).
Students (1987–88), 637 (all postgraduate).
Provost, The Earl of Gowrie, P.C. (1986).
Registrar, D. Bennington.

CRANFIELD INSTITUTE OF TECHNOLOGY (1969)
Central Business Exchange,
Central Milton Keynes MK9 2EN

Under Royal Charter (1969) the Cranfield Institute of Technology grants degrees in applied science, engineering, technology and management.
Full-time Students (1987–88), 2,300.
Chancellor, The Lord Kings Norton, PH.D. (1969).
Vice-Chancellor, The Lord Chilver, D.SC., F.R.S.
Secretary and Registrar, J. K. Pettifer.

THE OPEN UNIVERSITY (1969)
Walton Hall, Milton Keynes MK7 6AA

Students and clients (1987), 161,426.
Tuition by correspondence linked with special radio and television programmes, video and audio cassettes, residential schools and a locally-based tutorial and counselling service. Under Royal Charter the University awards degrees of B.A., B.Phil., M.A., M.B.A., M.SC., M.Phil., PH.D., D.SC. and D.Litt. There are seven faculties—arts, education, mathematics, science, social sciences, technology and management and a wide range of continuing education courses and study packs.
Chancellor, The Lord Briggs, F.B.A. (1978).
Vice-Chancellor, J. H. Horlock, PH.D., SC.D., F.R.S.
Secretary, D. J. Clinch.

THE UNIVERSITY OF WALES (1893)
Cathays Park, Cardiff CF1 3NS

Chancellor, H.R.H. The Prince of Wales, K.G., K.T., G.C.B., P.C. (1976).
Pro-Chancellor, The Lord Cledwyn of Penrhos, C.H., P.C. (1985).
Vice-Chancellor, Prof. B. L. Clarkson, PH.D.
Registrar, M. A. R. Kemp, PH.D.

Colleges

University College of Wales, Aberystwyth.—*Princ.*, G. Owen, C.B.E., D.SC. (1979).
University College of North Wales, Bangor.—*Princ.*, Prof. E. Sunderland, PH.D. (1984).
University of Wales College of Cardiff, Cardiff.—*Princ.*, A. F. Trotman-Dickenson, PH.D., D.SC. (1968).

Lampeter (*St. David's College*).—*Princ.*, Prof. B. R.
Morris, D.Phil. (1980).
Swansea (*University College*).—*Princ.*, Prof. B. L.
Clarkson, Ph.D., (1982).
University of Wales College of Medicine, Cardiff.—
Provost, Prof. Sir Herbert Duthic, M.D., Ch.M.,
F.R.C.S. (1979).

SCOTLAND

UNIVERSITY OF ABERDEEN (1495)
Regent Walk, Aberdeen AB9 1FX

Full-time Students (1987–88), 5,690.
Chancellor, Sir Kenneth Alexander, F.R.S.E. (1987).
Principal, Prof. G. P. McNicol, M.D., PH.D., F.R.S.E.,
F.R.C.P. (1981).
Secretary, W. M. Bradley.
Rector, W. Pickard (1988–91).

UNIVERSITY OF DUNDEE (1967)
Dundee DD1 4HN

Full-time Students (1987–88), 3,938.
Chancellor, The Earl of Dalhousie, K.T., G.C.V.O., G.B.E.,
M.C. (1977).
Vice-Chancellor, Prof. M. J. Hamlin.
Secretary, R. Seaton.
Rector, M. G. Bruce, M.P. (1986–89).

UNIVERSITY OF EDINBURGH (1583)
Old College, South Bridge, Edinburgh EH8 9YL

Full-time Students (1987–88), 10,235.
Chancellor, H.R.H. The Prince Philip, Duke of
Edinburgh, K.G., K.T., O.M., G.B.E., P.C., F.R.S. (1952).
Vice-Chancellor and Principal, Sir David Smith,
D.Phil., F.R.S.
Secretary, A. M. Currie, O.B.E.
Rector, Ms. M. Gray (1988–91).

UNIVERSITY OF GLASGOW (1451)
Glasgow G12 8QQ

Full-time Students (1987–88), 10,753.
Chancellor, Sir Alexander Cairncross, K.C.M.G., F.B.A.
(1972).
Vice-Chancellor, Sir William Fraser, G.C.B., F.R.S.E.
Registrar, J. M. Black.
Secretary, R. Ewen, O.B.E., T.D.
Rector, Mrs. W. Mandela, (1987–90).

HERIOT-WATT UNIVERSITY (1966)
Riccarton, Edinburgh EH14 4AS

Full-time Students (1987–88), 4,025.
Chancellor, (vacant).
Principal and Vice-Chancellor, T. L. Johnston, PH.D.,
F.R.S.E. (1981).
Secretary, D. I. Cameron.
Registrar, D. Sturgeon.

UNIVERSITY OF ST. ANDREWS (1411)
College Gate, St. Andrews KY16 9AJ

Full-time Students (1987–88), 3,837.
Chancellor, Sir Kenneth Dover, D.Litt., F.R.S.E., F.B.A.
(1981).
Vice-Chancellor, Prof. S. Arnott, PH.D., F.R.S., F.R.S.E.
Registrar and Secretary, Dr. M. J. B. Lowe.
Rector, S. Adams (1985–88).

UNIVERSITY OF STIRLING (1967)
Stirling FK9 4LA

Full-time Students (1987–88), 3,061.
Chancellor, The Lord Balfour of Burleigh, F.R.S.E.
(1988).
Vice-Chancellor, Prof. A. J. Forty, PH.D., D.SC., F.R.S.E.
Registrar, Dr. D. J. Farrington, D.Phil.
Secretary, R. G. Bomont.

UNIVERSITY OF STRATHCLYDE (1964)
16 Richmond Street, Glasgow G1 1XQ

Full-time Students (1987–88), 7,630.
Chancellor, The Lord Todd, O.M., D.SC., D.Phil., F.R.S.
(1965).
Principal and Vice-Chancellor, Sir Graham Hills,
PH.D., D.SC., F.R.S.E.
Registrar and Secretary, D. W. J. Morrell.

NORTHERN IRELAND

THE QUEEN'S UNIVERSITY OF BELFAST (1908)

Full-time Students (1987–88), 8,600.
Chancellor, Sir Rowland Wright, K.B., C.B.E., D.SC.
(1984).
President and Vice-Chancellor, Sir Gordon Bever-
idge, PH.D., F.R.S.E.
Registrar, (vacant).
Secretary, Dr. G. A. Baird.

UNIVERSITY OF ULSTER (1984)
Cromore Road, Coleraine BT52 1SA
(Amalgamation of New University of Ulster and
Ulster Polytechnic)

Full-time Students (1987–88), 7,968.
Chancellor, The Lord Grey of Naunton, G.C.M.G.,
G.C.V.O., O.B.E. (1985).
Vice-Chancellor, D. S. Birley.
Academic Registrar, P. J. Conway.
Secretary, J. A. Hunter.

REPUBLIC OF IRELAND

UNIVERSITY OF DUBLIN TRINITY COLLEGE (1592)
Dublin 2

Full-time Students (1987–88), 6,785.
Chancellor, F. J. C. O'Reilly (1985).
Provost, W. A. Watts, SC.D.
Registrar, W. R. Duncan.
Secretary, G. H. H. Giltrap.

NATIONAL UNIVERSITY OF IRELAND, DUBLIN (1908)
49 Merrion Square, Dublin 2

Full-time Students (1987–88), 19,419.
Chancellor, Dr. T. K. Whitaker (1976).
Vice-Chancellor, Dr. P. Masterton.
Registrar, Dr. J. Nolan.

Constituent Colleges
Presidents
Univ. Coll., Dublin, P. Masterson, PH.D.
Univ. Coll., Cork, T. ó Ciardha, PH.D.
Univ. Coll. Galway, C.ó h Eocha, PH.D.

THE ASSOCIATION OF COMMONWEALTH UNIVERSITIES
John Foster House, 36 Gordon Square, WC1H 0PF
[01-387 8572]

The Association holds quinquennial Congresses of the Universities of the Commonwealth and other meetings in the intervening years; publishes the *Commonwealth Universities Yearbook*; handbooks listing scholarships and fellowships, etc.; acts as a general information centre on universities in U.K. and other Commonwealth countries; provides an advisory service for the filling of university teaching staff appointments overseas; administers travelling fellowships for university administrators as well as the Overseas Development Administration Shared Scholarship Scheme and electives bursaries for medical students; and runs the Third World Academic Exchange Programme. It also supplies the secretariat for the Commonwealth Scholarship Commission in the U.K. and for the Marshall Aid Commemoration Commission.

Secretary General, A. Christodoulou, C.B.E., D.Univ.

COUNCIL FOR NATIONAL ACADEMIC AWARDS
344–354 Gray's Inn Road, WC1X 8BP
[01-278 4411]

Established in 1964 with powers to award degrees and other academic distinctions equivalent in standard to those awarded by universities. Courses are designed and taught in institutions of higher education (including polytechnics) which are not themselves empowered to award degrees. The Council awards degrees and honours degrees of B.A., B.Ed., B.Sc., LL.B., B.Eng. and M.Eng., and higher and research degrees and doctorates. On Sept. 1, 1974, the Council assumed responsibility for the work formerly undertaken by the National Council for Diplomas in Art and Design, and in September, 1976, for the Diploma of Management Studies.

Chairman, Sir Bryan Nicholson.
Chief Executive, M. Frazer, Ph.D.

POLYTECHNICS

The 30 polytechnics constitute a substantial part of the higher education system in England and Wales. Overall they provide an educational environment for some 330,000 students each year, about half of them following full-time or sandwich courses. Within the polytechnics and colleges sector their total entry includes over 70 per cent. of all first-year enrolments to degree courses and others recognised as being of the same standard. In addition the polytechnics play a major part in the national provision of other advanced courses including Higher National awards and professional qualifications. The polytechnics also provide opportunities for postgraduate study and research in most disciplines.

Courses have a vocational emphasis. Together engineering, science and technology currently account for some 42 per cent. of enrolments. A further 30 per cent. is involved in administrative, business and social studies and some 7 per cent. in education. The remaining 21 per cent. are spread over other professional and vocational subjects (e.g. architecture, librarianship and catering; music, drama and visual arts; languages (3 per cent.) and other arts (4 per cent.).

Full-time and sandwich course students for the year 1987–88 are shown in parentheses.

CITY OF BIRMINGHAM POLYTECHNIC, Perry Barr, Birmingham B42 2SU (5,903).—*Dir.,* P. C. Knight, D.Phil.
BRIGHTON POLYTECHNIC, Moulsecoomb, Brighton, E. Sussex BN2 4AT (5,854).—*Dir.,* Prof. G. R. Hall, C.B.E.

BRISTOL POLYTECHNIC, Coldharbour Lane, Frenchay, Bristol BS16 1QY (6,377).—*Dir.,* A. C. Morris.
COVENTRY POLYTECHNIC, Priory Street, Coventry CV1 5FB (6,090).—*Dir.,* M. Goldstein, Ph.D., D.SC., F.R.S.C.
HATFIELD POLYTECHNIC, College Lane, Hatfield, Herts AL10 9AB (4,500).—*Dir.,* Prof. N. K. Buxton, Ph.D.
HUDDERSFIELD POLYTECHNIC, Queensgate, Huddersfield HD1 3DH (5,000).—*Rector,* Prof. K. J. Durrands.
KINGSTON POLYTECHNIC, Kingston Hill Centre, Kenry House, Kingston upon Thames KT2 7LB (5,770).—*Dir.,* R. C. Smith, Ph.D.
LANCASHIRE POLYTECHNIC, Preston PR1 2TQ (5,500).—*Dir.,* E. E. Robinson.
LEEDS POLYTECHNIC, Calverley Street, Leeds LS1 3HE (6,269).—*Dir.,* C. Price.
LEICESTER POLYTECHNIC, P.O. Box 143, Leicester LE1 9BH (6,325).—*Dir.,* K. Barker.
LIVERPOOL POLYTECHNIC, Rodney House, 70 Mount Pleasant, Liverpool L3 5UX (7,244).—*Rector,* Prof. P. Toyne.
LONDON:
  CITY OF LONDON POLYTECHNIC, 31 Jewry Street, EC3N 2EY (3,592).—*Provost,* Prof. R. Floyd, D.Phil.
  MIDDLESEX POLYTECHNIC, Trent Park, Cockfosters Road, Barnet, Herts. EN4 0PT (7,134).—*Dir.,* R. M. W. Rickett, C.B.E., Ph.D.
  NORTH EAST LONDON POLYTECHNIC, Romford Road, E15 4LZ (5,150).—*Dir.,* Prof. G. T. Fowler.
  POLYTECHNIC OF CENTRAL LONDON, 309 Regent Street, W1R 8AL (4,828).—*Rector.,* Prof. T. E. Burlin, D.SC., Ph.D.
  POLYTECHNIC OF NORTH LONDON, Holloway Road N7 8DB (5,187).—*Dir.,* L. Wagner.
  SOUTH BANK POLYTECHNIC, 103 Borough Road, SE1 0AA (5,514).—*Dir.,* Mrs. P. Perry.
  THAMES POLYTECHNIC, Wellington Street, Woolwich, SE18 6PF (5,284).—*Dir.,* N. Singer, Ph.D.
MANCHESTER POLYTECHNIC, All Saints, Manchester M15 6BH (10,455)—*Dir.,* Sir Kenneth Green.
NEWCASTLE UPON TYNE POLYTECHNIC, Newcastle upon Tyne NE1 8ST (7,411)—*Dir.,* Prof. L. Barden, Ph.D., D.SC.
NORTH STAFFORDSHIRE POLYTECHNIC, Beaconside, Stafford ST18 0AD; College Road, Stoke-on-Trent, ST4 2DE (4,770).—*Dir.,* K. B. Thompson.
OXFORD POLYTECHNIC, Headington, Oxford OX3 0BP (4,919).—*Dir.,* Dr. Clive Booth.
PLYMOUTH POLYTECHNIC, Drake Circus, Plymouth PL4 8AA (5,040).—*Dir.,* R. F. M. Robbins, C.B.E., Ph.D.
PORTSMOUTH POLYTECHNIC, Ravelin House, Museum Road, Portsmouth PO1 2QQ (6,588).—*Pres.,* H. D. Law, Ph.D.
SHEFFIELD CITY POLYTECHNIC, Pond Street, Sheffield S1 1WB (8,248).—*Principal,* J. M. Stoddart.
SUNDERLAND POLYTECHNIC, Langham Tower, Ryhope Road, Sunderland SR2 7EE (4,417).—*Rector,* E. P. Hart, Ph.D.
TEESSIDE POLYTECHNIC, Middlesbrough, Cleveland TS1 3BA (3,760)—*Dir.,* M. D. Longfield, Ph.D.
TRENT POLYTECHNIC, Burton Street, Nottingham NG1 4BU (8,020).—*Dir.,* D. R. Cowell, R.D.
WOLVERHAMPTON POLYTECHNIC, Molineux Street, Wolverhampton WV1 1SB (5,167).—*Dir.,* M. J. Harrison.
POLYTECHNIC OF WALES, Pontypridd, Mid Glamorgan CF37 1DL (4,500).—*Dir.,* J. D. Davies, O.B.E., Ph.D., D.SC.

SCOTTISH CENTRAL INSTITUTIONS

There are no Polytechnics (*see above*) in Scotland but there are 15 Central Institutions which provide most of the advanced full-time courses of higher education there outside the universities and the colleges of education. Most Central Institutions are financed direct by the Scottish Education Department but the three agricultural colleges are funded by the Department of Agriculture and Fisheries for Scotland. Central Institutions are managed by independent boards of governors representing industrial, commercial, professional and educational interests. They are vocationally oriented and do not offer liberal arts courses. Most of their courses lead to degrees awarded by the C.N.A.A. (*see above*) or by neighbouring universities, or to diplomas and certificates granted by the Scottish Vocational Education Council (SCOTVEC) and other bodies. They also provide courses leading to other qualifications.

DUNCAN OF JORDANSTONE COLLEGE OF ART (*B.A., B.Sc., B.Arch.*), Perth Road, Dundee DD1 4HT.—*Principal*, R. Miller-Smith.

DUNDEE COLLEGE OF TECHNOLOGY (*B.A., B.Sc., B.Eng.*), Bell Street, Dundee DD1 1HG.—*Principal*, H. G. Cuming, C.B.E., PH.D.

EDINBURGH COLLEGE OF ART (*B.A., B.Sc., B.Arch.*), Lauriston Place, Edinburgh EH3 9DF.—*Principal*, J. L. Paterson.

EDINBURGH SCHOOL OF AGRICULTURE (*B.Sc.*), West Mains Road, Edinburgh EH9 3JG.—*Principal*, Prof. P. N. Wilson.

GLASGOW COLLEGE OF TECHNOLOGY (*B.A., B.Sc.*), Cowcaddens Road, Glasgow G4 0BA.—*Principal*, Dr. N. G. Meadows.

GLASGOW SCHOOL OF ART (*B.A., B.Arch.*), 167 Renfrew Street, Glasgow G3 6RQ.—*Director*, T. H. Pannell.

NAPIER COLLEGE (*B.A., B.Sc., B.Eng.*), Colinton Road, Edinburgh EH10 5DT.—*Principal*, W. A. Turmeau, PH.D.

NORTH OF SCOTLAND COLLEGE OF AGRICULTURE (School of Agriculture, Aberdeen) (*B.Sc.*), 581 King Street, Aberdeen AB9 1UD.—*Principal*, Prof. A. S. Jones, PH.D.

PAISLEY COLLEGE OF TECHNOLOGY (*B.A., B.Sc., B.Eng.*), High Street, Paisley PA1 2BE.—*Principal*, Prof. R. W. Shaw.

QUEEN MARGARET COLLEGE (*B.A., B.Sc.*), Clerwood Terrace, Edinburgh EH12 8TS.—*Principal*, D. F. Leach.

THE QUEEN'S COLLEGE, GLASGOW (*B.A., B.Sc.*), 1 Park Drive, Glasgow G3 6LP.—*Principal*, G. A. Richardson, PH.D.

ROBERT GORDON'S INSTITUTE OF TECHNOLOGY (*B.A., B.Sc., B.L.E., B.Eng.*), Schoolhill, Aberdeen AB9 1FR.—*Principal*, D. A. Kennedy, PH.D.

ROYAL SCOTTISH ACADEMY OF MUSIC AND DRAMA (*B.A.*), 100 Renfrew Street, Glasgow G2 3BD.—*Principal*, P. Ledger, C.B.E.

SCOTTISH COLLEGE OF TEXTILES (*B.A., B.Sc.*), Netherdale, Galashiels, Selkirkshire, TD1 3HF.—*Principal*, J. C. Furniss.

THE WEST OF SCOTLAND COLLEGE (*B.Sc.*), Auchincruive, Ayr KA6 5HW.—*Principal*, Prof. P. C. Thomas.

COLLEGES

It is not possible to name here all the colleges offering courses of higher or further education. The list that follows is confined to colleges providing at least one full-time course leading to a *first degree* granted by a university or by the Council for National Academic Awards (C.N.A.A.). It does not include colleges forming part of a polytechnic or a university, nor does it include Scottish central institutions.

After the name of each college the abbreviated title of the appropriate degree or degrees is given, but the very many *other* qualifications for which the colleges also provide courses are not listed.

BATH COLLEGE OF HIGHER EDUCATION (*B.A., B.Sc., B.Ed.*), Newton Park, Newton St. Loe, Bath BA2 9BN.—*Director*, B. L. Gomes da Costa.

BEDFORD COLLEGE OF HIGHER EDUCATION (*B.A., B.Ed.*), Cauldwell Street, Bedford MK42 9AH.—*Director*, P. Mansell, PH.D.

BISHOP GROSSETESTE COLLEGE (*B.Ed.*), Lincoln, Lincolnshire LN1 3DY.—*Principal*, Prof. L. Marsh, D.Phil.

BOLTON INSTITUTE OF HIGHER EDUCATION (*B.A., B.Sc., B.Ed., B.Eng.*), Deane Road, Bolton BL3 5AB.—*Principal*, R. Oxtoby, PH.D.

BRADFORD AND ILKLEY COMMUNITY COLLEGE (*B.A., B.Ed.*), Great Horton Road, Bradford BD7 1AY.—*Principal*, Dr. P. J. Gallagher.

BRETTON HALL COLLEGE OF HIGHER EDUCATION (*B.A., B.Ed.*), West Bretton, Wakefield, W. Yorkshire WF4 4LG.—*Principal*, Dr. J. L. Taylor.

THE BUCKINGHAMSHIRE COLLEGE (*B.A., B.Sc.*), Queen Alexandra Road, High Wycombe, Bucks. HP11 2JZ.—*Director*, D. J. Everett, LL.D.

BULMERSHE COLLEGE OF HIGHER EDUCATION (*B.A., B.Ed.*), Woodlands Avenue, Earley, Reading, Berks. RG6 1HY.—*Principal*, B. G. Palmer.

CAMBERWELL SCHOOL OF ART AND CRAFTS (*B.A.*), Peckham Road, London SE5 8UF—*Principal*, A. Harris.

CAMBORNE SCHOOL OF MINES (*B.Eng.*), Pool, Redruth, Cornwall TR15 3SE.—*Principal*, P. Hackett, PH.D.

CAMBRIDGESHIRE COLLEGE OF ARTS AND TECHNOLOGY (*B.A., B.Sc.*), East Road, Cambridge CB1 1PT—*Principal*, K. Swinhoe, PH.D.

CENTRAL SCHOOL OF ART AND DESIGN (*B.A.*), Southampton Row, London WC1B 4AP.—*Head of School*, D. C. Sherlock.

CENTRAL SCHOOL OF SPEECH AND DRAMA (B.A., B.Sc., B. Ed), Embassy Theatre, Eton Avenue, London NW3 3HY.—*Principal*, R. S. Fowler.

CHARLOTTE MASON COLLEGE OF EDUCATION (*B.Ed.*), Ambleside, Cumbria LA22 9BB.—*Principal*, J. Thorley, PH.D.

CHELSEA SCHOOL OF ART (*B.A.*), Manresa Road, London SW3 6LS—*Head of School*, J. Barnicoat.

CHESTER COLLEGE (*B.A., B.Sc., B.Ed.*), Cheyney Road, Chester CH1 4BJ.—*Principal*, Rev. E. J. Binks.

CHRIST CHURCH COLLEGE (*B.Ed.*), Canterbury, Kent CT1 1QU—*Principal*, M. H. A. Berry, T.D.

COLCHESTER INSTITUTE (*B.A.*), Sheepen Road, Colchester, Essex CO3 3LL.—*Director*, J. M. Threlfall.

CRAIGIE COLLEGE OF EDUCATION (*B.Ed.*), Ayr KA8 0SR.—*Principal*, G. M. Wilson, PH.D.

CREWE AND ALSAGER COLLEGE OF HIGHER EDUCATION (*B.A., B.Sc., B.Ed.*), Crewe Road, Crewe CW1 1DU.—*Director*, Miss B. R. P. Ward, C.B.E.

DARTINGTON COLLEGE OF ARTS (*B.A.*), Totnes, Devon TQ9 6EJ.—*Principal*, P. Hulton.

DERBYSHIRE COLLEGE OF HIGHER EDUCATION (*B.Comb.Studs., B.A., B.Sc., B.Eng., B.Ed.*), Kedleston Road, Derby DE3 1GB.—*Director*, J. May, T.D., PH.D.

DORSET INSTITUTE (*B.A., B.Sc.*), Wallisdown Road, Poole, Dorset BH12 5BB—*Director*, B. R. MacManus, PH.D.

DUNFERMLINE COLLEGE OF PHYSICAL EDUCATION (*B.A., B.Ed.*), Cramond Road North, Edinburgh EH4 6JD.—*Principal*, Miss J. A. Carroll.

EALING COLLEGE OF HIGHER EDUCATION (*B.A., LL.B.*), St. Mary's Road, Ealing, London W5 5RF—*Director*, N. Merritt.

EDGE HILL COLLEGE OF HIGHER EDUCATION (*B.A., B.Sc., B.Ed.*), St. Helens Road, Ormskirk, Lancs. L39 4QP.—*Director*, H. Webster.

ESSEX INSTITUTE OF HIGHER EDUCATION (*B.Sc., B.Ed., LL.B.*), Victoria Road South, Chelmsford, Essex CM1 1LL.—*Director*, M. Salmon.

EXETER COLLEGE OF ART AND DESIGN (*B.A.*), Earl Richards Road North, Exeter EX2 6AS.—*Principal,* Dr. D. Jeremiah.

FALMOUTH SCHOOL OF ART AND DESIGN (*B.A.*), Woodlane, Falmouth, Cornwall TR11 4RA—*Principal,* Prof. A. G. Livingston.

GLASGOW COLLEGE OF BUILDING AND PRINTING (*B.Sc.*), 60 North Hanover Street, Glasgow G1 2BP.—*Principal,* D. McEwan.

GLOUCESTERSHIRE COLLEGE OF ARTS AND TECHNOLOGY (GLOSCAT) (*B.A., B.Sc., B.Ed.*), Oxstalls Lane, Gloucester GL2 9HW.—*Principal,* D. Williams.

GWENT COLLEGE OF HIGHER EDUCATION (*B.A., B.Ed., B.Eng.*), Clarence Place, Newport, Gwent NP9 0UW.—*Principal,* M. I. Harris, O.B.E.

HARROW COLLEGE OF HIGHER EDUCATION (*B.A.*), Watford Road, Northwick Park, Harrow, Middlesex HA1 3TP.—*Principal,* H. R. Harris, PH.D.

HERTFORDSHIRE COLLEGE OF ART AND DESIGN (*B.A.*), 7 Hatfield Road, St. Albans, Herts. AL1 3RS. — *Principal,* C. Hunt.

HUMBERSIDE COLLEGE OF HIGHER EDUCATION (*B.A., B.Sc., B.Eng., B.Ed.*), Cottingham Road, Hull HU6 7RT.—*Director,* J. C. Earls, PH.D.

JEWS' COLLEGE (*B.A.*), Albert Road, Hendon, NW4 2SJ.—*Principal,* Rabbi Dr. J. Sacks.

JORDANHILL COLLEGE OF EDUCATION (*B.Ed., B.Sc.*), Southbrae Drive, Jordanhill, Glasgow G13 1PP.—*Principal,* T. R. Bone, C.B.E., PH.D.

KENT INSTITUTE OF ART AND DESIGN (*B.A.*), New Dover Road, Canterbury CT1 3AN; Oakwood Park, Maidstone ME16 8AG; Fort Pitt, Rochester ME1 1DZ.—*Director,* P. I. Williams.

KIDDERMINSTER COLLEGE (*B.A.*), Hoo Road, Kidderminster, Worcs. DY10 1LX.—*Principal,* Dr. T. Seddon.

KING ALFRED'S COLLEGE (*B.A., B.Ed.*), Winchester SO22 4NR.—*Principal,* J. A. Cranmer.

LABAN CENTRE FOR MOVEMENT AND DANCE (*B.A.*), Laurie Grove, New Cross, London SE14 6NH.—*Director,* Marion North.

LA SAINTE UNION COLLEGE OF HIGHER EDUCATION (*B.A., B.Th., B.Ed.*), The Avenue, Southampton SO9 5HB.—*Principal,* Sister Maria Bernard.

COLLEGE OF LIBRARIANSHIP WALES (*B.Lib.*), Aberystwyth, Dyfed SY23 3AS.—*Principal,* F. N. Hogg.

LIVERPOOL INSTITUTE OF HIGHER EDUCATION (*B.A., B.Ed.*), P.O. Box 6, Stand Park Road, Liverpool L16 9JD.—*Rector,* J. Burke, PH.D.

LONDON BIBLE COLLEGE (*B.A.*), Green Lane, Northwood, Middlesex HA6 2UW.—*Principal,* Dr. M. C. Griffiths.

LONDON COLLEGE OF PRINTING (*B.A.*), Elephant and Castle, London SE1 6SB.—*Head of College and Pro. Rector,* R. Hedley Lewis.

LONDON CONTEMPORARY DANCE SCHOOL (*B.A.*), 16 Flaxman Terrace, WC1H 9AT.—*Principal,* R. Ralph, D.Phil.

LOUGHBOROUGH COLLEGE OF ART AND DESIGN (*B.A.*), Redmoor, Loughborough, Leics. LE11 3BT—*Principal,* K. H. Smith.

LUTON COLLEGE OF HIGHER EDUCATION (*B.Sc.*), Park Square, Luton LU1 3JU.—*Director,* A. J. Wood, PH.D.

MORAY HOUSE COLLEGE OF EDUCATION (*B.Ed., B.A.*), Holyrood Road, Edinburgh EH8 8AQ.—*Principal,* G. Kirk.

NENE COLLEGE (*B.A., B.Sc., B.Ed.*), Moulton Park, Northampton NN2 7AL.—*Director,* E. Ogilvie, PH.D.

NEW COLLEGE (*B.A., B. Ed.*), Framwellgate Moor Centre, Durham DH1 5ES.—*Principal,* D. L. Turner.

NEWMAN COLLEGE (*B.Ed.*), Genners Lane, Bartley Green, Birmingham B32 3NT.—*Principal,* Joan S. Cuming, PH.D.

NORMAL COLLEGE OF HIGHER EDUCATION (*B.A., B.Ed.*), Bangor, North Wales LL57 2PX.—*Principal,* R. Williams.

NORTH CHESHIRE COLLEGE (*B.A.*), Fearnhead, Warrington WA2 0DB.—*Director,* T. R. Keen, PH.D.

NORTH EAST SURREY COLLEGE OF TECHNOLOGY (*B.Sc.*), Reigate Road, Ewell, Surrey KT17 3DS. *Principal,* J. A. Strickson, PH.D.

THE NORTH EAST WALES INSTITUTE (*B.A., B.Sc., B.Ed.*), Cartrefle, Wrexham, Clwyd LL13 9NL.—*Principal,* Prof. G. O. Phillips, PH.D., D.SC.

NORTHERN COLLEGE OF EDUCATION (*B.Ed.*). Hilton Place, Aberdeen AB9 1FA; Gardyne Road, Dundee DD5 1NY.—*Principal,* D. A. Adams.

NORTH RIDING COLLEGE (*B.Ed.*), Filey Road, Scarborough, N. Yorkshire YO11 3AZ.—*Principal,* F. W. Wright.

NORWICH CITY COLLEGE OF FURTHER AND HIGHER EDUCATION (*B.A.*), Ipswich Road, Norwich, Norfolk NR2 2LJ.—*Principal,* J. S. Lewis, R.D., PH.D.

NORWICH SCHOOL OF ART (*B.A.*), St. George Street, Norwich, Norfolk NR3 1BB.—*Principal,* B. Black.

OAK HILL COLLEGE (*B.A.*), Chase Side, Southgate, N14 4PS.—*Principal,* Rev. G. Bridger.

RAVENSBOURNE COLLEGE OF DESIGN AND COMMUNICATION (*B.A.*), Walden Road, Chislehurst, Kent BR7 5SN.—*Director,* N. J. Frewing.

RIPON AND YORK ST. JOHN COLLEGE OF HIGHER EDUCATION (*B.A., B.Sc., B.Ed.*), Lord Mayor's Walk, York YO3 7EX.—*Principal,* Dr. G. P. McGregor.

ROEHAMPTON INSTITUTE OF HIGHER EDUCATION (*B.A., B.Sc., B.Ed.*), Senate House, Roehampton Lane, London SW15 5PU.—*Rector,* Prof. S. C. Holt, PH.D.

ROLLE COLLEGE (*B.A., B.Ed.*), Exmouth, Devon EX8 2AT.

ROSE BRUFORD COLLEGE OF SPEECH AND DRAMA (*B.A.*), Lamorbey Park, Burnt Oak Lane, Sidcup, Kent DA15 9DF.—*Principal,* P. Robins.

ROYAL ACADEMY OF MUSIC (*B.Mus.*), Marylebone Road, London NW1 5HT.—*Principal,* Sir David Lumsden, D.Phil.

ROYAL COLLEGE OF MUSIC (*B.Mus.*), Prince Consort Road, London SW7 2BS.—*Director,* M. G. Matthews.

ROYAL NAVAL ENGINEERING COLLEGE (*B.Eng.*), Manadon, Plymouth PL5 3AQ.—*Dean,* Capt. G. C. George.

S. MARTIN'S COLLEGE OF HIGHER EDUCATION (*B.A., B.Ed.*), Bowerham, Lancaster LA1 3JD.—*Principal,* R. Clayton.

ST. ANDREW'S COLLEGE OF EDUCATION (*B.Ed.*), Duntocher Road, Bearsden, Glasgow G61 4QA.—*Principal,* B. J. McGettrick.

ST. JOHN'S SEMINARY (*B.Th.*), Wonersh, Guildford GU5 0QX.—*Rector,* Father P. Smith.

COLLEGE OF ST. MARK AND ST. JOHN (*B.A., B.Ed.*), Derriford Road, Plymouth PL6 8BH.—*Principal,* J. E. Anderson.

ST. MARTIN'S SCHOOL OF ART (*B.A.*), 107 Charing Cross Road, London WC2H 0DU.—*Head,* (vacant).

ST. MARY'S COLLEGE (*B.Ed.*), 191 Falls Road, Belfast BT12 6FE.—*Principal,* J. I. O'Connell.

ST. MARY'S COLLEGE (*B.A., B.Sc., B.Ed.*), Strawberry Hill, Twickenham, Middlesex TW1 4SX.—*Principal,* Rev. D. A. Beirne.

COLLEGE OF ST. PAUL AND ST. MARY (*B.A., B.Sc., B.Ed.*), The Park, Cheltenham, Glos. GL50 2RH.—*Principal,* Miss J. O. Trotter.

SALISBURY AND WELLS THEOLOGICAL COLLEGE (*B.Th.*), Salisbury SP1 2EE.—*Principal,* Rev. Canon P. A. Crowe.

SOUTHAMPTON INSTITUTE OF HIGHER EDUCATION (*B.A., B.Sc.*), East Park Terrace, Southampton SO9 4WW.—*Principal,* J. W. Longden.

SOUTH GLAMORGAN INSTITUTE OF HIGHER EDUCATION (*B.A.*, *B.Ed.*), Western Avenue, Llandaff, Cardiff CF5 2YB.—*Principal*, E. J. Brent, PH.D.

SPURGEON'S COLLEGE (*B.A.*), South Norwood Hill, SE25 6DJ.—*Principal*, P. Beasley-Murray, PH.D.

STOCKPORT COLLEGE OF TECHNOLOGY (*B.Sc.*, *B.Eng.*), Wellington Road South, Stockport SK1 3UQ. *Principal*, D. A. Humphreys, O.B.E.

STOURBRIDGE COLLEGE OF TECHNOLOGY AND ART (*B.A.*), Hagley Road, Stourbridge, W. Midlands DY8 1QU.—*Principal*, T. H. Jenkins.

STRANMILLIS COLLEGE (*B.Ed.*), Stranmillis Road, Belfast BT9 5DY.—*Principal*, R. J. Rodgers, PH.D.

THEOLOGICAL COLLEGE (*B.Th.*), Chichester PO19 1SG.—*Principal*, Rev. Canon J. W. Hind.

TRINITY AND ALL SAINTS' COLLEGE (*B.A.*, *B.Sc.*, *B.Ed.*), Brownberrie Lane, Horsforth, Leeds LS18 5HD.—*Principal*, H. Mary Hallaway, D.Phil.

TRINITY COLLEGE (*B.A.*), Stoke Hill, Bristol BS9 1JP.—*Principal*, Rev. D. Gillett.

TRINITY COLLEGE (*B.A.*, *B.Ed.*), Carmarthen, Dyfed, SA31 3EP.—*Principal*, D. C. Jones-Davies.

TRINITY COLLEGE OF MUSIC (*B.Mus.*), 11–13 Mandeville Place, London W1M 6AQ.—*Principal*, P. Jones, C.B.E.

WATFORD COLLEGE (*B.Sc.*), Hempstead Road, Watford, WD1 3EZ.—*Principal*, T. J. Howard, PH.D.

WELSH COLLEGE OF MUSIC AND DRAMA (*B.A.*, *B.Ed.*), Castle Grounds, Cathays Park, Cardiff CF1 3ER.—*Principal*, P. Fletcher.

WEST GLAMORGAN INSTITUTE OF HIGHER EDUCATION (*B.A.*, *B.Ed.*), Townhill Road, Swansea SA2 0UT.—*Principal*, G. Stockdale, PH.D.

WESTHILL COLLEGE (*B.Ed.*), Hamilton Building, Weoley Park Road, Selly Oak, Birmingham B29 6LL.—*Principal*, Rev. G. Benfield.

WEST LONDON INSTITUTE OF HIGHER EDUCATION (*B.A.*, *B.Sc.*, *B.Ed.*), Lancaster House, Borough Road, Isleworth, Middlesex TW7 5DU.—*Principal*, J. E. Kane, PH.D.

WEST MIDLANDS COLLEGE OF HIGHER EDUCATION (*B.Ed.*), Gorway, Walsall WS1 3BD.—*Principal*, T. J. Cox.

WESTMINSTER COLLEGE (*B.A.*, *B.Ed.*), North Hinksey, Oxford OX2 9AT.—*Principal*, Rev. Dr. K. B. Wilson.

WEST SURREY COLLEGE OF ART AND DESIGN (*B.A.*), Falkner Road, The Hart, Farnham, Surrey GU9 7DS.—*Principal*, N. J. Taylor.

WEST SUSSEX INSTITUTE OF HIGHER EDUCATION (*B.A.*, *B.Ed.*), The Dome, Upper Bognor Road, Bognor Regis, West Sussex PO21 1HR.—*Director*, J. F. Wyatt.

WIMBLEDON SCHOOL OF ART (*B.A.*), Merton Hall Road, Wimbledon, London SW19 3QA.—*Principal*, Dr. C. Painter.

WINCHESTER SCHOOL OF ART (*B.A.*), Park Avenue, Winchester, Hampshire SO23 8DL.—*Principal*, M. Sadler-Forster.

WORCESTER COLLEGE OF HIGHER EDUCATION (*B.A.*, *B.Sc.*, *B.Ed.*), Henwick Grove, Worcester WR2 6AJ.—*Principal*, D. R. Shadbolt, D.Phil.

GRANTS FOR STUDENTS

Post-School

Students in England and Wales who plan to take a full-time or sandwich course of further study after leaving school may be eligible for a grant from their local education authority (L.E.A.). Enquiries should be made to the authority in the area in which the student normally lives. There is a list on pages 454–455. Application forms are available from schools and L.E.A.s. Completed forms should be sent to the appropriate L.E.A. as early as possible. For courses beginning in the autumn, applications should, however, not be made earlier than the preceding January.

Types of grant. Grants are of two kinds: mandatory and discretionary. *Mandatory grants* (390,300 in 1985–86) are those which L.E.A.s *must* pay to students who are attending what are called "designated courses" and who can satisfy certain other conditions; such a grant is normally to enable the student to attend only one designated course and there is no general entitlement to an award for any particular number of years. *Discretionary grants* (47,400 full value awards in 1985–86) are those for which each L.E.A. has discretion to decide its own policy.

Designated courses include those which are *full-time or sandwich* and lead to a university or C.N.A.A. (see p. 450) degree; the diploma of higher education; the higher national diploma of the Business & Technician Education Council; and initial teacher-training courses including courses for the postgraduate certificate in education and the art teachers' certificate or diploma.

Eligibility. To be eligible for a grant, students admitted to a designated course must, *inter alia*:—

(a) have been ordinarily resident in the United Kingdom for the three years immediately preceding the academic year in which the course begins. (If the student was absent because his or her family was temporarily employed abroad, or if the student was in the UK primarily for full-time education (and would normally be elsewhere), the L.E.A. should be consulted for advice).

(b) have not previously attended a course of advanced further education of more than two years' duration. Attendance for one term and up to seven weeks of a second term on such a course is usually disregarded.

(c) apply for the grant before the end of the first term of the course.

Condition (b) above does not apply to students wishing to take a course leading to a postgraduate certificate in education or the art teachers' certificate.

Students attending designated courses who do not satisfy condition (a) above may be eligible for a mandatory grant if:—

a) they come from other member states of the E.C. and can establish "migrant worker" status, or whose parents are migrant workers.

b) they, or their spouses and children are asylees or refugees.

Value. A means-tested maintenance grant, usually paid once a term through the university or college office, covers periods of attendance during term and the Christmas and Easter vacations but not the summer vacation. It is subject to deduction on account of the student's own income and his/her parents' or spouse's income. Tuition fees in full are usually paid direct to the university or college by the L.E.A.

Cost. Local authority expenditure on student maintenance in 1985–86 was £526 million.

In Scotland corresponding awards are made by the Scottish Education Department and in Northern Ireland by Education and Library Boards.

Postgraduate awards

A number of schemes of postgraduate bursaries or studentships for U.K. residents are administered by the Department of Education and Science and the five research councils (agricultural and food, economic and social science, medical, natural environment, science and engineering). 16,200 awards were made in 1985–86.

LOCAL EDUCATION AUTHORITIES

English and Welsh Counties

AVON, P.O. Box 57, Avon House North, St. James Barton, Bristol BS99 7EB.—*Director*, P. Coleman.

BEDFORDSHIRE, County Hall, Bedford MK42 9AP.— *Chief Education Officer*, D. P. J. Browning, C.B.E.

BERKSHIRE, Shire Hall, Shinfield Park, Reading RG2 9XE.—*Director (acting)*, G. Williams.

BUCKINGHAMSHIRE, County Hall, Aylesbury HP20 1UA.—*Director*, S. Sharp.

CAMBRIDGESHIRE, Castle Court, Shire Hall, Cambridge CB3 0AP.—*Director*, G. H. Morris.

CHESHIRE, County Hall, Chester CH1 1SF.—*Director*, N. J. Fitton.

CLEVELAND, Woodlands Road, Middlesbrough TS1 3BN.—*County Education Officer*, A. H. R. Calderwood.

CLWYD, Shire Hall, Mold CH7 6NB.—*Director*, H. K. Evans.

CORNWALL, County Hall, Truro TR1 3AY.—*Secretary of Education*, D. W. Fryer.

CUMBRIA, 5 Portland Square, Carlisle CA1 1PU.— *Director*, P. C. Boulter.

DERBYSHIRE, County Offices, Matlock DE4 3AG.— *Director*, J. G. Evans.

DEVON, County Hall, Exeter EX2 4QD.—*Chief Education Officer*, J. G. Owen, C.B.E.

DORSET, County Hall, Dorchester DT1 1XJ.—*Director*, P. L. Gedling.

DURHAM, County Hall, Durham DH1 5UJ.—*Director*, K. B. Grimshaw.

DYFED, Pibwrlwyd, Carmarthen SA31 2NH.—*Director*, W. J. Phillips.

ESSEX, Threadneedle House, Market Road, Chelmsford CM1 1LD.—*County Education Officer*, J. O. Morris, C.B.E.

GLOUCESTERSHIRE, Shire Hall, Gloucester GL1 2TG.—*Director*, K. D. Anderson.

GWENT, County Hall, Cwmbran NP44 2XG.—*Director*, G. V. Drought.

GWYNEDD, County Offices, Caernarfon LL55 1SH.— *Director*, G. E. Humphreys.

HAMPSHIRE, The Castle, Winchester SO23 8UG.— *County Education Officer*, R. D. Clark.

HEREFORD AND WORCESTER, Castle Street, Worcester WR1 3AG.—*County Education Officer*, J. W. Turnbull.

HERTFORDSHIRE, County Hall, Hertford SG13 8DE.— *County Education Officer*, D. Fisher, C.B.E.

HUMBERSIDE, County Hall, Beverley HU17 9BA.— *Director*, Dr. M. J. Garnett.

ISLE OF WIGHT, County Hall, Newport PO30 1UD.— *Director*, R. O. Burton.

KENT, Springfield, Maidstone ME14 2LJ.—*Director*, B. Oatley.

LANCASHIRE, County Hall, Preston PR1 8RJ.—*Director*, A. J. Collier.

LEICESTERSHIRE, County Hall, Glenfield, Leicester LE3 8RF.—*Director*, K. H. Wood-Allum.

LINCOLNSHIRE, County Offices, Newland, Lincoln LN1 1YQ.—*Director*, A. M. Ridings, F.R.S.A.

MID GLAMORGAN, County Hall, Cathays Park, Cardiff CF1 3NF.—*Director*, E. Roberts.

NORFOLK, County Hall, Norwich NR1 2DH.—*Director*, M. H. Edwards.

NORTHAMPTONSHIRE, Northampton House, Northampton.—*County Education Officer*, J. R. Atkinson.

NORTHUMBERLAND, County Hall, Morpeth NE61 2EF.—*Director*, C. C. Tipple.

NOTTINGHAMSHIRE, County Hall, West Bridgford, Nottingham NG2 7QP.—*Director*, A. J. Fox.

OXFORDSHIRE, Macclesfield House, New Road, Oxford OX1 1NA.—*Chief Education Officer*, T. R. P. Brighouse.

POWYS, The Lindens, Spa Road, Llandrindod Wells LD1 5HA.—*Director*, R. W. Bevan.

SHROPSHIRE, The Shirehall, Abbey Foregate, Shrewsbury SY2 6ND.—*County Education Officer*, P. B. Caters.

SOMERSET, County Hall, Taunton TA1 4DY.—*Chief Education Officer*, Mrs. J. Wisker.

SOUTH GLAMORGAN, County Hall, Atlantic Wharf, Cardiff CF1 5UW.—*Director*, D. Orrell.

STAFFORDSHIRE, Tipping Street, Stafford ST16 2DH.— *Chief Education Officer*, Dr. P. J. Hunter.

SUFFOLK, St. Andrew House, County Hall, Ipswich IP4 1LJ.—*County Education Officer*, T. R. Cornthwaite.

SURREY, County Hall, Kingston upon Thames KT1 2DJ.—*County Education Officer*, M. C. Pinchin.

SUSSEX, EAST, P.O. Box 4, County Hall, St. Anne's Crescent, Lewes BN7 1SG.—*County Education Officer*, J. A. Carter.

SUSSEX, WEST, County Hall, Chichester PO19 1RF.— *Director*, R. D. C. Bunker.

WARWICKSHIRE, P.O. Box 24, 22 Northgate Street, Warwick CV34 4SR.—*Director*, M. L. Ridger.

WEST GLAMORGAN, County Hall, Swansea SA1 3SN.—*Director*, J. Beale.

WILTSHIRE, County Hall, Trowbridge BA14 8JB.— *Director*, I. M. Slocombe.

YORKSHIRE, NORTH, County Hall, Northallerton DL7 8AD.—*Director*, F. F. Evans.

London

INNER LONDON EDUCATION AUTHORITY.—*Chief Executive*, H. Ouseley. *Education Officer*, D. Mallen.

BARKING, Town Hall, Barking, Essex IG11 7LU.— A. W. Bush.

BARNET, Town Hall, Friern Barnet N11 3DL.—N. M. Gill.

BEXLEY, Town Hall, Crayford, Kent DA1 4EN.— *Education Officer*, G. Hall, D.med.

BRENT, Chesterfield House, Park Lane, Wembley, Middx. HA9 7RW.—*Director*, (vacant).

BROMLEY, Town Hall, Tweedy Road, Bromley, Kent BR1 1SB.—G. Grainge.

CROYDON, Taberner House, Park Lane, CR9 1TP.— *Director*, D. Naismith.

EALING, Hadley House, 79–81 Uxbridge Road, W5 5SU.—*Director*, U. Barlow.

ENFIELD, P.O. Box 56, Civic Centre, Silver Street, EN1 3XA.—G. Hutchinson.

HARINGEY, 48 Station Road, N22 4TY.—*Education Officer*, R. L. Jones.

HARROW, P.O. Box 2, Civic Centre, Harrow HA1 2UH.—*Director*, J. F. Mann.

HAVERING, Mercury House, Mercury Gardens, Romford, Essex RM1 3DR.—*Director*, B. H. Laister.

HILLINGDON, Civic Centre, Uxbridge, Middx. UB8 1UW.—*Education Officer*, T. Hinds.

HOUNSLOW, Civic Centre, Lampton Road, Hounslow, Middx. TW3 4DN.—*Education Officer*, J. D. Trickett.

KINGSTON UPON THAMES, Guildhall, KT1 1EU.— *Head of Schools*, R. L. Gan.

MERTON, Crown House, London Road, Morden, Surrey SM4 5DX.—*Director*, R. Davies.

NEWHAM, 379–383 High Street, E15 4RD.—*Education Officer*, A. Lockhart.

REDBRIDGE, 255–259 High Road, Ilford, Essex IG1 1NN.—*Director*, K. G. M. Ratcliffe.

RICHMOND UPON THAMES, Regal House, London Road, Twickenham TW1 3QB.—*Education Officer*, I. Waters.

SUTTON, The Grove, Carshalton, Surrey SM5 3AL.— *Director*, C. Melville.

WALTHAM FOREST, Municipal Offices, High Road, Leyton E10 5QJ.—*Director*, M. Shepherd.

Metropolitan District Councils

BARNSLEY, Berneslai Close, Barnsley.—*Director*, T. Brooks.

BIRMINGHAM, Council House, Margaret Street, B3 3BU.—*Director*, (vacant).

BOLTON, Paderborn House, Civic Centre, BL1 1JW.—*Education Officer*, B. Hughes.

BRADFORD, Provincial House, BD1 1NP.—*Director*, W. R. Knight, C.B.E.

BURY, Athenaeum House, Market Street, BL9 0BN.—*Education Officer*, M. Gray.

CALDERDALE.—Northgate House, Northgate, Halifax HX1 1UN.—*Education Officer*, A. Pickvance.

COVENTRY, Civic Centre 2, Earl Street, CV1 5RR.—*Education Officer*, C. Farmer.

DONCASTER, Princegate, Doncaster.—*Education Officer*, M. J. Pass.

DUDLEY, Westox House, 1 Trinity Road, DY1 1JQ.—*Education Officer*, R. K. Westerby.

GATESHEAD, Civic Centre, Regent Street, NE8 1HH.—*Education Officer*, H. Cubitt.

KIRKLEES, Oldgate House, 2 Oldgate, Huddersfield HD1 6QW.—*Education Officer*, P. G. Davies.

KNOWSLEY, Land and House Building, Huyton Hey Road, Huyton, Merseyside L36 5YH.—*Education Officer*, A. Culley.

LEEDS, Merrion House, Merrion Centre, LS2 8JY.—*Director*, R. S. Johnson, C.B.E.

LIVERPOOL, 14 Sir Thomas Street, L1 6DJ.—*Director*, K. A. Antcliffe.

MANCHESTER, Crown Square, Deansgate, M60 3BB.—*Education Officer*, G. Hainsworth.

NEWCASTLE UPON TYNE, Civic Centre, NE1 8PU.—*Education Officer*, M. R. Davies.

NORTH TYNESIDE, The Chase, North Shields NE29 1RW.—*Education Officer*, J. F. Partington.

OLDHAM, Town Hall, Chadderton, Oldham.—*Education Officer*, Dr. W. R. Kneen.

ROCHDALE, Municipal Offices, Smith Street, OL16 1YD.—*Education Officer*, A. N. Naylor.

ROTHERHAM, Norfolk House, Walker Place, Rotherham.—*Education Officer*, K. Snowden.

ST. HELENS, Century House, St. Helens WA10 1RN.—*Director*, N. D. Nelson.

SALFORD, Chapel Street, M3 5LT.—*Education Officer*, B. Grady.

SANDWELL, P.O. Box 41, Shaftesbury House, 402 High Street, West Bromwich B70 9LT.—*Director*, G. A. Brinsdon.

SEFTON, Town Hall, Bootle, Merseyside L20 7AE.—*Education Officer*, J. A. Marsden.

SHEFFIELD, Leopold Street, S1 1RJ.—*Education Officer*, W. Walton.

SOLIHULL, P.O. Box 20, Council House, B91 3QU.—*Education Officer*, M. E. Sweet.

SOUTH TYNESIDE, Town Hall and Civic Offices, South Shields, NE33 2RL.—*Education Officer*, K. Stringer.

STOCKPORT, Stopford House, Piccadilly, Stockport.—*Education Officer*, J. E. Hendy.

SUNDERLAND, Town Hall and Civic Centre, Burdon Road, SR2 7DN.—*Education Officer*, D. A. Bowers.

TAMESIDE, Level 2, Council Offices, Wellington Road, Ashton-under-Lyne OL6 6DL.—*Education Officer*, (vacant).

TRAFFORD, Town Hall, Sale M33 1YR.—*Chief Education Officer*, D. J. Hatfield, C.B.E.

WAKEFIELD, County Hall, WF1 2QW.—*Education Officer*, W. H. Wright.

WALSALL, Civic Centre, Darwall Street, WS1 1DQ.—*Education Officer*, Mrs D. M. Tuck.

WIGAN, Gateway House, Standishgate, WN1 1XL.—*Education Officer*, J. K. Hampson.

WIRRAL, Municipal Offices, Cleveland Street, Birkenhead L41 6NH.—*Education Officer*, M. G. Nichol.

WOLVERHAMPTON, Civic Centre, St. Peter's Square, WV1 1RR.—*Education Officer*, Dr. C. Saville.

Scottish Regional and Islands Councils

BORDERS, Regional Headquarters, Newtown St. Boswells, Melrose TD6 0SA.—*Director*, J. McLean.

CENTRAL, Regional Council H.Q., Viewforth, Stirling FK8 2ET.—*Director*, I. Collie.

DUMFRIES AND GALLOWAY, 30 Edinburgh Road, Dumfries DG1 1JQ.—*Director*, W. C. Fordyce.

FIFE, Fife House, North Street, Glenrothes KY7 5LT.—*Director*, M. More.

GRAMPIAN, Woodhill House, Westburn Road, Aberdeen AB9 2LU.—*Director*, J. A. D. Michie.

HIGHLAND, Regional Buildings, Glenurquhart Road, Inverness IV3 5NX.—*Director*, Dr. C. E. Stewart.

LOTHIAN, 40 Torphichen Street, Edinburgh EH3 8JJ.—*Director*, W. D. C. Semple.

ORKNEY, Council Offices, Kirkwall KW15 1NY.—*Director*, R. L. Henderson.

SHETLAND, Brentham Place, Lerwick.—*Director*, R. A. B. Barnes.

STRATHCLYDE, 20 India Street, Glasgow G2 4PF.—*Director*, (vacant).

TAYSIDE, Tayside House, 28 Crighton Street, Dundee DD1 3RJ.—*Director*, D. G. Robertson.

WESTERN ISLES, Council Offices, Stornoway, Isle of Lewis PA87 2BW.—*Director*, N. R. Galbraith.

Northern Ireland
Education and Library Boards

BELFAST, Board Headquarters, 40 Academy Street, Belfast BT1 2NQ.—*Chief Officer*, T. G. J. Moag.

NORTH-EASTERN, County Hall, 182 Galgorm Road, Ballymena, Co. Antrim BT42 1HN.—*Chief Officer*, R. A. Hamilton.

SOUTH-EASTERN, 18 Windsor Avenue, Belfast BT9 6EF.—*Chief Officer*, T. Nolan.

SOUTHERN, 3 Charlemont Place, The Mall, Armagh BT61 9AX.—*Chief Officer*, J. G. Kelly.

WESTERN, 1 Hospital Road, Omagh, Co. Tyrone BT79 0AW.—*Chief Officer*, M. H. F. Murphy, O.B.E.

Channel Islands, etc.

GUERNSEY, P.O. Box 32, La Couperderie, St. Peter Port.—*Director*, M. D. Hutchings.

JERSEY, P.O. Box 142, St. Saviour.—*Director*, J. S. Rodhouse.

ISLE OF MAN, Government Offices, Buck's Road, Douglas.—*Director*, A. Davies.

ISLES OF SCILLY, Town Hall, St. Mary's TR21 0LW.—*Secretary for Education*, L. W. Michell.

ADULT EDUCATION

'Adult Education' covers a broad spectrum of educational activities ranging from non-vocational courses of general interest, through the acquiring of special vocational skills needed in industry or commerce, to study for a degree at the Open University. It has been defined as "the provision of non-formal and informal education for adult people: that is, courses excluding the normal range of provision in colleges and universities for young people immediately following the statutory school leaving age, but including the full range of recurrent educational opportunities designed for people of more mature years, and related to any or all aspects of adult life".

Providers. Courses specifically for adults are provided by many bodies. They include local education authorities (regional authorities in Scotland, education and library boards in Northern Ireland), residential colleges, the Open University, the extra-mural departments of other universities (and Birkbeck College of the University of London), the BBC, ITV and local radio stations, and various voluntary bodies. The local education authorities operate through 'area' adult education centres, institutes or colleges and the adult studies departments of colleges of further education. The Open University, in partnership with the BBC, provides distance teaching leading to ordinary or honours first degrees, and also offers post-experience and higher degree courses. More than 30 other universities have extra-mural or adult education or continuing education departments which serve their local areas or regions. The BBC has a Continuing Education Advisory Council and the Independent Broadcasting Authority an Educational Advisory Council which has an Adult Education Section. Of the voluntary bodies the biggest and best-known is the Workers' Educational Association (*see below*). There are also the training and retraining facilities provided under the aegis of the Training Commission and of PICKUP (Professional, Industrial and Commercial Updating Programme).

Courses. Although lengths vary, most courses are part-time. Long-term residential colleges (*see below*) provide full-time courses lasting one or two years. Adult education courses are of two main kinds – those involving face-to-face teaching with teacher and student in the same room and the distance teaching provided through TV and radio, and/or correspondence courses.

Numbers. There are no comprehensive statistics covering all aspects of adult education but it is known that enrolments in November 1986 at L.E.A. adult education centres in England were about 1,455 million. During 1987, the Open University had 68,037 students studying for first degrees, 1,302 working for higher degrees, 11,734 associate students and 8,378 other students. In 1986–87, 299,269 students attended courses of liberal adult education provided by university extra-mural departments and the W.E.A. in England and Wales.

NATIONAL INSTITUTE OF ADULT CONTINUING EDUCATION (England and Wales), 19B De Montfort Street, Leicester LE1 7GE. The institute provides a means of consultation and co-operation between all the interests in adult continuing education. It provides information and advice to organizations and individuals in all aspects of adult continuing education; it conducts enquiries into problems of adult continuing education; organizes conferences and other meetings and issues publications. The Institute manages a number of agencies and special units which benefit from funding from the D.E.S. and the Welsh Office, including the Adult Literacy and Basic Skills Unit. It also manages a major part of the D.E.S./W.O.E.D. programme for the adult unemployed (REPLAN).—*Dir.*, A. Tuckett.

SCOTTISH INSTITUTE OF ADULT AND CONTINUING EDUCATION, 30 Rutland Square, Edinburgh EH1 2BW. The institute is a national voluntary organization which aims to advance education amongst adults. It makes policy, conducts research, provides information, arranges conferences, and produces publications.—*Dir.*, Dr. Elisabeth Gerver.

UNIVERSITIES COUNCIL FOR ADULT AND CONTINUING EDUCATION, Dept. of Adult Education, University of Leicester, University Road, Leicester LE1 7RH. The council, consisting of one or two representatives from each university, was established in 1947 for the interchange of ideas and the formulation of common policies on extra-mural education.—*Hon. Secretary*, Prof. W. Forster.

WORKERS EDUCATIONAL ASSOCIATION, Temple House, 9 Upper Berkeley Street, London W1H 8BY. Founded in 1903, the W.E.A. consists of about 900 branches and nearly 1,500 affiliated educational and workers' organisations. Non-sectarian and non-party-political, it aims to stimulate and to satisfy the demands of workers for education, and to further the advancement of education generally. The W.E.A. is organised in 20 districts. The D.E.S. and L.E.A.s make grants towards expenses.—*Gen. Sec.*, R. Lochrie.

RESIDENTIAL COLLEGES FOR ADULT EDUCATION

Long term:
The eight long-term colleges listed below offer one- and two-year courses for adults and are grant-aided by the Department of Education and Science, the Welsh Office or the Scottish Office. Students are eligible for grants under an Adult Education State Bursaries Scheme or, for certain specialized courses, for Local Education Authority grants.

COLEG HARLECH, Harlech, Gwynedd LL46 2PU. (For men and women).—*Warden*, J. W. England.

CO-OPERATIVE COLLEGE, Stanford Hall, Loughborough, Leics. LE12 5QR (For men and women).—*Principal*, Dr. R. Houlton.

FIRCROFT COLLEGE, 1018 Bristol Road, Selly Oak, Birmingham B29 6LH. (For men and women).—*Principal*, K. Jackson.

HILLCROFT COLLEGE, South Bank, Surbiton, Surrey KT6 6DF. (For women).—*Principal*, Ms. P. J. Lambert.

NEWBATTLE ABBEY COLLEGE, Dalkeith, Midlothian EH22 3LL. (For men and women).—*Principal*, A. D. Reid.

NORTHERN COLLEGE, Wentworth Castle, Stainborough, Barnsley, South Yorks. S75 3ET. (For men and women).—*Principal*, R. H. Fryer.

PLATER COLLEGE, Pullens Lane, Oxford OX3 0DT. (For men and women).—*Principal*, D. G. Chiles.

RUSKIN COLLEGE, Walton Street, Oxford OX1 2HE. (For men and women).—*Principal*, J. D. Hughes.

Short term:
The short-term colleges and centres listed below offer residential courses, lasting from a day or two to two or three weeks, in a wide range of subjects. L.E.A.s directly sponsor many of the colleges while others are sponsored by universities or voluntary organizations. A booklet listing such *Residential Short Courses* is published by the National Institute of Adult Continuing Education (see above).

ALSTON HALL COLLEGE, Longridge, nr. Preston PR3 3BP; AVONCROFT COLLEGE, Stoke Heath, Bromsgrove, Worcs. B60 4JS; BEAMISH HALL RESIDENTIAL COLLEGE FOR ADULT EDUCATION, Stanley, Co. Durham DH9 0RG; BELSTEAD HOUSE, Belstead, Ipswich, Suffolk IP8 3NA; BENSLOW MUSIC TRUST, Little Benslow Hills, Ibberson Way, Hitchin SG4 9RB; BRAZIERS ADULT COLLEGE, Ipsden, Oxford OX9 6AN; BURTON MANOR, Burton, South Wirral, Cheshire L64 5SJ; BURWELL HOUSE RESIDENTIAL CENTRE, North St., Burwell, Cambridge CB5 0BA; DEBDEN HOUSE, Debden Green, Loughton, Essex IG10 2PA; DENMAN COLLEGE, Marcham, Nr. Abingdon, Oxon. OX13 6NW; DEVON CENTRE FOR CONTINUING EDUCATION, Dartington Hall, Totnes; DILLINGTON COLLEGE FOR ADULT EDUCATION, Ilminster, Somerset TA19 9DT; DYFFRYN HOUSE, St. Nicholas, nr. Cardiff CF5 6SU; EARNLEY CONCOURSE, nr. Chichester, Sussex PO20 7JL; GRAFHAM WATER RESIDENTIAL CENTRE, West Perry, Huntingdon PE18 0BX; GRANTLEY HALL, Ripon, N. Yorks.; HIGHAM HALL, Bassenthwaite Lake, Cockermouth, Cumbria CA13 9SH;

THE HILL, Pen-y-Pound, Abergavenny, Gwent NP7 7RP; HOLLY ROYDE COLLEGE, West Didsbury, Manchester M20 9JP; HORNCASTLE RESIDENTIAL COLLEGE, Horncastle, Lincs. LN9 6BW; KINGSGATE HOUSE, Convent Road, Broadstairs, Kent CT10 3PX; KNUSTON HALL, Irchester, Wellingborough, Northants. NN9 7EU; LANCASHIRE COLLEGE FOR ADULT EDUCATION, Southport Road, Chorley PR7 1NB; LOSEHILL HALL, Castleton, Derbys. S30 2WB; MADINGLEY HALL, Madingley, Cambridge CB3 8AQ; MARYLAND, Woburn, Milton Keynes MK17 9JD; MISSENDEN ABBEY, Great Missenden, Bucks HP16 0BD; THE OLD RECTORY, Fittleworth, Pulborough, Sussex RH20 1HU; PENDRELL HALL, Codsall Wood, Wolverhampton WV8 1QP; REWLEY HOUSE, 1 Wellington Square, Oxford OX1 2JA; THEOBALDS COLLEGE, Waltham Cross, Herts. EN7 5HW; URCHFONT MANOR, nr. Devizes, Wilts.; WANSFELL COLLEGE, Theydon Bois, Epping, Essex CM16 7LF; WEDGWOOD MEMORIAL COLLEGE, Barlaston, Stoke-on-Trent, Staffs. ST12 9DG; WENSUM LODGE, King Street, Norwich, Norfolk NR1 1QW; WEST DEAN COLLEGE, West Dean, Chichester, Sussex; WESTHAM HOUSE COLLEGE, Barford, Warwick. CV35 8DP.

PROFESSIONAL EDUCATION
(excluding *postgraduate* study)

NOTE.—References to courses at universities, polytechnics and colleges in the sections following are not claimed to be comprehensive and cover only *full-time* courses leading to *first degrees*. Full lists appear in the new *University Entrance: the Official Guide* and in the *C.N.A.A. Directory of First Degree and Diploma of Higher Education Courses*. Both are produced annually.

POSTGRADUATE STUDY AND RESEARCH are not treated here. All universities provide facilities for postgraduate study and research. They co-operatively issue each year the *British Universities' Guide to Graduate Study* which lists all "taught courses" but does not cover research. In general, universities can provide facilities for research in at least some aspects of all the subjects in which first degrees are offered.

Courses at postgraduate level leading to master's-level degrees of the Council for National Academic Awards (C.N.A.A.) are offered by polytechnics and other colleges. They are listed in the C.N.A.A.'s annual *Directory of Postgraduate and Post-Experience Courses*. Research is also undertaken at polytechnics leading to an M. Phil. or Ph.D. granted by the C.N.A.A.

ACCOUNTANCY

(*See also* Business, Management and Administration).

First Degrees in *Accounting* or *Accountancy* are granted by the Universities of Aberdeen, Belfast, Birmingham, Bristol, Buckingham, City, Dundee, Durham, East Anglia (also *Computerized Accountancy*), Edinburgh, Essex, Exeter, Glasgow, Heriot Watt, Hull, Kent, Lancaster, Leeds, Liverpool, London (LSE), Loughborough, Manchester, Newcastle, Nottingham, Reading, Salford, Sheffield, Southampton, Stirling, Strathclyde, Ulster and Wales (Aberystwyth, Bangor and Cardiff University Colleges and Institute of Science and Technology), Warwick. At several universities one of these subjects can be combined with, e.g., Financial Administration, Finance or Economics.

Courses leading to first degrees in *Accounting, Accountancy* or *Accounting and Finance* granted by the C.N.A.A. are provided by City of Birmingham Polytechnic, Brighton Polytechnic, Bristol Polytechnic, City of London Polytechnic, Dorset Institute of Higher Education (*Financial Services*), Dundee College of Technology, Ealing College of Higher Education, Glasgow College of Technology, Huddersfield Polytechnic, Humberside College of Higher Education, Kingston Polytechnic, Lancashire Polytechnic, Leeds Polytechnic, Liverpool Polytechnic, Manchester Polytechnic, Middlesex Polytechnic, Napier College, Newcastle upon Tyne Polytechnic, North East London Polytechnic (*Finance with Accounting*), Polytechnic of North London, Plymouth Polytechnic, Portsmouth Polytechnic, Sheffield City Polytechnic (*Accounting and Financial Control*), Trent Polytechnic and Polytechnic of Wales.

Professional Bodies.—The main bodies granting membership on examination after a period of practical work are:

INSTITUTE OF CHARTERED ACCOUNTANTS IN ENGLAND AND WALES, Chartered Accountants Hall, P.O. Box 433, Moorgate Place, EC2P 2BJ.—*Dir. of Education and Training*, A. Colquhoun.

INSTITUTE OF CHARTERED ACCOUNTANTS OF SCOTLAND, 27 Queen Street, Edinburgh EH2 1LA.—*Sec.*, E. Tait, M.B.E.

CHARTERED ASSOCIATION OF CERTIFIED ACCOUNTANTS, 29 Lincolns Inn Fields, WC2A 3EE.—*Sec.*, A. W. Sansom.

CHARTERED INSTITUTE OF MANAGEMENT ACCOUNTANTS, 63 Portland Place, W1N 4AB.—*Sec.*, T. B. Degenhardt, O.B.E.

CHARTERED INSTITUTE OF PUBLIC FINANCE AND ACCOUNTANCY, 3 Robert Street, WC2N 6BH.—*Sec.*, N. P. Hepworth, O.B.E.

ACTUARIAL SCIENCE

First Degrees in *Actuarial Science* are granted by the City University and the Universities of Kent and London (London School of Economics and Political Science) and in *Actuarial Mathematics and Statistics* by Heriot-Watt University.

Two professional organizations grant qualifications after examination:

INSTITUTE OF ACTUARIES, Staple Inn Hall, High Holborn, WC1V 7QJ.—*Sec. Gen.*, C. D. A. Mackie.

FACULTY OF ACTUARIES IN SCOTLAND, 23 St. Andrew Square, Edinburgh EH2 1AQ.—*Sec.*, W. W. Mair.

AERONAUTICS
and Aeronautical Engineering

First Degrees in *Aeronautical Engineering* are granted by the Universities of Bath, Belfast, Bristol, Cambridge, the City University, the Universities of Glasgow (also *Avionics*), London (Imperial College of Science and Technology, Queen Mary College, also *Avionics—Aeronautical/Electrical*), Loughborough (*Aeronautical Engineering and Design*), Manchester, Salford and Southampton (*Aeronautics and Astronautics* and *Aerospace Systems Engineering*) and in *Air Transport Engineering* by the City University.

Courses leading to first degrees in *Aeronautical Engineering* granted by the C.N.A.A. are provided by Hatfield Polytechnic and North East Wales Institute of Higher Education (*Aerospace Studies*).

AGRICULTURE

First Degrees in *Agriculture* or *Agricultural Science(s)* are granted by the Universities of Aberdeen, Belfast, Edinburgh, Glasgow, Leeds, London (Wye College), Newcastle upon Tyne, Nottingham, Reading and Wales (University Colleges of Aberystwyth and Bangor); in *Agricultural Technology and Management* and *Agricultural Engineering* by Cranfield Institute of Technology (Silsoe College); and in *Horticulture* by Bath, London (Wye College), Nottingham, Reading and Strathclyde.

Courses leading to first degrees in *Agriculture* granted by the C.N.A.A. are provided by Plymouth Polytechnic/Seale Hayne College and (*Agricultural Technology*) Wolverhampton Polytechnic/Harper Adams Agricultural College.

ARCHAEOLOGY

First Degrees in *Archaeology* or *Archaeological Sciences/Studies* are granted by the Universities of Belfast (also Archaeological Conservation), Birmingham, Bradford, Bristol, Cambridge, Durham, Edinburgh, Exeter, Glasgow, Lancaster, Leicester, Liverpool, London (University College), Institute of Archaeology, King's College, School of Oriental and African Studies), Manchester, Newcastle upon Tyne, Nottingham, Reading, Southampton, Wales (University College Cardiff, also *Archaeological Conservation*, Bangor U.C., St. David's U.C.) and York. At several other universities archaeology can be combined with another subject, e.g. ancient history, classics or anthropology.

A course leading to a first degree in Archaeology granted by the C.N.A.A. is provided by King Alfred's College, Winchester.

ARCHITECTURE

(*See also* Building, and Town and Country Planning).

First Degrees in *Architecture/Architectural Studies* are granted by the universities of Bath, Belfast, Cambridge, Dundee, Edinburgh, Glasgow, Heriot-Watt, Leeds, Liverpool, London (University College), Manchester, Newcastle, Nottingham, Sheffield, Strathclyde, Wales (UWIST, Cardiff).

Courses leading to first degrees in *Architecture/Architectural Studies* granted by the C.N.A.A. are provided by City of Birmingham Polytechnic, Brighton Polytechnic (*Architectural Design*), Canterbury College of Art, Polytechnic of Central London, Huddersfield Polytechnic, Humberside College of Higher Education, Kingston Polytechnic, Leeds Polytechnic, Leicester Polytechnic, Liverpool Polytechnic, Manchester Polytechnic, North East London Polytechnic, Polytechnic of North London, Oxford Polytechnic, Plymouth Polytechnic, Portsmouth Polytechnic, Robert Gordon's Institute of Technology, Polytechnic of the South Bank, Thames Polytechnic.

Other schools of architecture include:
ARCHITECTURAL ASSOCIATION SCHOOL OF ARCHITECTURE, 34–36 Bedford Square, W.C.1.

The Education and Professional Development Committee of the Royal Institute of British Architects sets standards and guides the whole system of architectural education throughout the United Kingdom. Courses at Schools recognized by the R.I.B.A. exempt students from the R.I.B.A.'s own examinations.

THE ROYAL INSTITUTE OF BRITISH ARCHITECTS, 66 Portland Place, W1N 4AD.—*Pres.*, R. P. Hackney, PH.D.; *Dir.-Gen.* The Rt. Hon. W. Rodgers.

ART AND DESIGN

First Degrees in *Art, Fine Art* or *History of Art* are granted by the Universities of Aberdeen, Cambridge, East Anglia, Edinburgh, Essex, Glasgow, Lancaster (*Visual Arts*),Leeds, Leicester, London (Courtauld Institute of Art, Birkbeck, University and Westfield Colleges, School of Oriental and African Studies, Goldsmiths' College), Loughborough (*Design and Technology*), Manchester, Manchester Institute of Science and Technology (*Textile Design and Design Management*), Newcastle upon Tyne, Nottingham, Oxford, Reading, St. Andrews, Sussex, Ulster, Wales (University College, Aberystwyth—*Visual Art*) and Warwick. At several other universities art or history of art can be combined with another subject. Courses

in *Art and Design* leading to first degrees granted by the University of Leeds are provided at Bretton Hall College of Higher Education. The degrees in *Art* granted by the Royal College of Art are higher degrees.

Courses leading to first degrees in *Art and Design* (*Fine Art, Graphic Design, Textiles/Fashion or Three-Dimensional Design*) granted by the C.N.A.A. are provided by more than 40 colleges/schools of art and polytechnics some of which also offer C.N.A.A. degree courses in other subjects in the field of Art and Design, including *Furniture Design, Industrial Design* and *Interior Design*.

ASTRONOMY

First Degrees in *Astronomy* are granted by the Universities of Birmingham, Glasgow, Leicester, London (University College, Queen Mary College), Newcastle, St. Andrew's, Sheffield, Sussex, and in *Astrophysics* by the Universities of Birmingham, Edinburgh, Kent, London (Queen Mary College, King's College, Royal Holloway & Bedford New College), Manchester, Newcastle, St. Andrews and Wales (University College, Cardiff). Various combinations of Astronomy, Mathematics, Physics and Astrophysics are also available.

Astronomy may be taken as part of a C.N.A.A. degree course at certain polytechnics.

BANKING

First Degrees with specialization in *Banking and Finance* are granted by the Universities of Birmingham (*Money, Banking and Finance*), Loughborough, Ulster (*Banking and Finance*) and Wales (Institute of Science and Technology), Bangor University College (*Banking, Insurance and Finance*), and the City University (*Banking and International Finance*).

Banking may be taken as part of a C.N.A.A. degree course at certain polytechnics/colleges.

Professional organizations granting qualifications after examination:—
CHARTERED INSTITUTE OF BANKERS, 10 Lombard Street, EC3V 9AS.—*Sec. General*, E. Glover.
INSTITUTE OF BANKERS IN SCOTLAND, 20 Rutland Square, Edinburgh EH1 2DE.—*Sec.*, C. W. Munn.

BIOLOGY, CHEMISTRY, PHYSICS

First Degrees in these subjects are granted by many universities. Courses leading to first degrees, granted by the C.N.A.A., are provided by many polytechnics. Professional qualifications are awarded by:—

INSTITUTE OF BIOLOGY, 20 Queensberry Place, SW7 2DZ.—*President*, Dr. R. W. J. Keay, C.B.E., *Gen. Sec.*, P. N. O'Donoghue.
ROYAL SOCIETY OF CHEMISTRY, Burlington House, Piccadilly, W1V 0BN.—*President*, Prof. J. M. Ward, F.R.S.C., *Sec.*, J. S. Gow, PH.D., F.R.S.C., F.R.S.E.
INSTITUTE OF PHYSICS, 47 Belgrave Square, SW1X 8QX.—*Sec.*, Dr. L. Cohen.

BREWING

First Degrees in Brewing are granted by Heriot-Watt University.

BUILDING

(*See also* Architecture, Estate and Land Management and Surveying)

First Degrees in *Building, Building Engineering* or *Building Technology* are granted by the following Universities: Bath, Heriot-Watt (also *Building Services Engineering* and *Building Economics and Quantity Surveying*), Liverpool (*Building Technology, Building Services Engineering*), London (University College), Manchester (Manchester Institute of Science and Technology, also *Building Services Engi-*

neering and *Construction Management*), Reading (*Building Construction & Management*, *Quantity Surveying* and *Building Surveying*), Salford (*Building Surveying*, also *Quantity Surveying and Construction Economics*) Strathclyde (*Building Engineering Design*), and Ulster (also *Building Services Engineering* and *Quantity Surveying*).

Courses leading to first degrees in *Building* granted by the C.N.A.A. are provided by Brighton Polytechnic, Bristol Polytechnic, Polytechnic of Central London, Coventry (Lanchester) Polytechnic, Glasgow College of Technology with Glasgow College of Building and Printing, Leeds Polytechnic, Liverpool Polytechnic, Sheffield City Polytechnic (*Construction*), the Polytechnic of the South Bank, Trent Polytechnic, and Polytechnic of Wales; in *Building Surveying* by Leicester Polytechnic, Liverpool Polytechnic, Polytechnic of the South Bank, Thames Polytechnic; and in *Building Services Engineering* by Newcastle upon Tyne Polytechnic and the Polytechnic of the South Bank (*Environmental Engineering*).

Examinations are also conducted by:—

CHARTERED INSTITUTE OF BUILDING, Englemere, King's Ride, Ascot, Berks. SL5 8BJ.—*Chief Exec.*, K. Banbury.

INSTITUTE OF BUILDING CONTROL, 21 High Street, Ewell, Epsom, Surrey KT17 1SB.—*Sec.*, R. Raywood.

INSTITUTE OF CLERKS OF WORKS OF GREAT BRITAIN, 41 The Mall, Ealing, W5 3TJ.—*Sec.*, A. P. Macnamara.

BUSINESS, MANAGEMENT AND ADMINISTRATION

First Degrees in *Business Studies* are granted by the Universities of Bath (*Business Administration*), Bradford, Buckingham, the City University, the Universities of Edinburgh, Glasgow (*Business Administration*) Heriot-Watt (*Business Organization*), Salford (*Business and Management Studies*, *Business Operation and Control*), Sheffield, Stirling, Strathclyde (*Business and Administration*), Ulster (also *European Business Studies* and *International Business Communication*), Wales (University College, Aberystwyth and University College, Cardiff) (*Business Administration*) (University College, Swansea, also *European Business Studies*), (Institute of Science and Technology) (*Business Administration*, also *Business Economics*); in *Administration* by the Universities of Aston (*Managerial and Administrative Studies*), Birmingham (*Public Policy Making and Administration*) and Essex (*Policy-making and Administration*); in *Management Sciences/Studies* by the Universities of Aston (*Managerial and Administrative Studies*), Belfast, Bradford, Brunel, Cambridge, the City University (*Management & Systems*), the Universities of Hull, Keele, Kent (also *Public Administration and Management*, and *European Management Science*), Lancaster, Leeds (also *Textile Management*), Liverpool, London (King's College, Royal Holloway & Bedford New College, London School of Economics), Loughborough, Manchester (Institute of Science and Technology), St. Andrews, Salford (*Business and Management Studies*), Stirling, Wales (Cardiff University College; Swansea University College, also *American Management Studies* and *European Management Science*), and Warwick; in *Marketing* by the Universities of Lancaster, Salford, Stirling and Strathclyde; and in *Commerce* by the Universities of Birmingham and Ulster. A variety of other combinations in these fields are available at some of these universities and these subjects also form part of degree courses in other universities.

Courses leading to first degrees in *Public Administration* granted by the Universities of Birmingham (*Public Policymaking and Administration*) and Wales at Bangor Normal College.

Courses leading to first degrees in *Business Studies* or *Business Administration* granted by the C.N.A.A. are provided by City of Birmingham Polytechnic, Brighton Polytechnic, Bristol Polytechnic, Polytechnic of Central London, City of London Polytechnic, Coventry (Lanchester) Polytechnic, Dorset Institute of Higher Education, Dundee College of Technology (also *Commerce*), Ealing College of Higher Education, Glasgow College of Technology (also *Commerce*), Hatfield Polytechnic, Huddersfield Polytechnic, Humberside College of Higher Education, Kingston Polytechnic, Lancashire Polytechnic, Leeds Polytechnic, Leicester Polytechnic, Liverpool Polytechnic, Manchester Polytechnic, Middlesex Polytechnic, Napier College of Commerce and Technology (also *Commerce*), Newcastle upon Tyne Polytechnic, North East London Polytechnic (also *Manufacturing Studies*), Polytechnic of N. London, N. Staffordshire Polytechnic, Oxford Polytechnic, Paisley College of Technology (*Business Economics*), Plymouth Polytechnic, Portsmouth Polytechnic, Robert Gordon's Institute of Technology (also *Commerce*), Sheffield City Polytechnic (also *Industrial Studies*), Polytechnic of the South Bank, Sunderland Polytechnic, Teesside Polytechnic, Thames Polytechnic, Trent Polytechnic (also *Industrial Studies*), Polytechnic of Wales, West Glamorgan Institute of Higher Education and Wolverhampton Polytechnic.

Courses leading to first degrees in *Business Information Systems/Technology* granted by the C.N.A.A. are provided by Humberside College of Higher Education, Kingston Polytechnic, Lancashire Polytechnic and Manchester Polytechnic (*Information Technology in Business*).

Courses leading to first degrees in *European Business Studies/Administration* granted by the C.N.A.A. are provided by Brighton Polytechnic (*European Business with Technology*), Buckinghamshire College of Higher Education, Humberside College of Higher Education, Middlesex Polytechnic and Trent Polytechnic.

The Thames Polytechnic provides courses for C.N.A.A. first degrees in *International Marketing*; and Manchester Polytechnic in *Retail Marketing*. Huddersfield Polytechnic provides courses for C.N.A.A. degrees in *Marketing (Engineering)* and *Textile Marketing*. Humberside College of Higher Education provides courses for C.N.A.A. degrees in *Secretarial Studies and Office Systems Management*, and Newcastle upon Tyne Polytechnic in *Secretarial Studies*.

Leicester, Manchester, Sheffield City, Teesside and Trent Polytechnics, the Polytechnic of Wales, Glasgow College of Technology, Robert Gordon's Institute of Technology provide courses for C.N.A.A. first degrees in *Public Administration*.

Glasgow College of Technology provides courses for C.N.A.A. first degrees in *Risk Management*.

Professional bodies conducting training and/or examinations in Administration and Management include:

ROYAL INSTITUTE OF PUBLIC ADMINISTRATION, 3 Birdcage Walk, SW1H 9JH.—*Dir.-Gen.*, D. Falcon.

INSTITUTE OF ADMINISTRATIVE MANAGEMENT, 40 Chatsworth Parade, Petts Wood, Orpington, Kent BR5 1RW.—*Sec-Gen.*, M. J. Ainsworth.

INSTITUTE OF HEALTH SERVICES MANAGEMENT, 75 Portland Place, W1N 4AN.—*Dir.*, Maureen Dixon, PH.D.

INSTITUTE OF HOUSING, 9 White Lion Street, N1 9XJ.—*Asst. Dir., Education and Training*, Ms. A. Paterson.

INSTITUTION OF INDUSTRIAL MANAGERS, Rochester House, 66 Little Ealing Lane, W5 4XX.—*Chief Exec.*, Brig. P. V. Crooks.

INSTITUTE OF MARKETING, Moor Hall, Cookham, Maidenhead, Berks. SL6 9QH.—*Dir. Gen.*, P. B. Blood.

INSTITUTE OF PERSONNEL MANAGEMENT, IPM House, Camp Road, Wimbledon SW19 4UW.

HENLEY—THE MANAGEMENT COLLEGE, Greenlands, Henley on Thames, Oxon., RG9 3AU.—*Princ.*, Prof. T. Kempner.

LONDON BUSINESS SCHOOL, Sussex Place, Regent's Park, NW1 4SA.—*Princ.*, Prof. P. G. Moore, T.D., PH.D.

MANCHESTER BUSINESS SCHOOL, Booth Street West, Manchester M15 6PB.

SCOTTISH BUSINESS SCHOOLS, CONFEDERATION OF, 23 NELSON MANDELA PLACE, Glasgow G2 1EU.—*Director*, M. Makower.

Institutions awarding Professional Qualifications in Commerce:—

A. GENERAL

R. S. A. EXAMINATIONS BOARD, 8 John Adam Street WC2N 6EZ.—*Chief Exec.*, M. F. Cross.

LONDON CHAMBER OF COMMERCE AND INDUSTRY, Examinations Board, Marlowe House, Station Road, Sidcup, Kent DA15 7BJ.—*Dir.*, W. Bell.

EAST MIDLAND FURTHER EDUCATION COUNCIL, Robins Wood House, Robins Wood Road, Aspley, Nottingham NG8 3NH.—*Sec.*, R. Ainscough.

NORTH WESTERN REGIONAL ADVISORY COUNCIL FOR FURTHER EDUCATION, Town Hall, Walkden Road, Worsley, Manchester M28 4QE.—*Sec.*, D. W. Brown.

NORTHERN COUNCIL FOR FURTHER EDUCATION, 5 Grosvenor Villas, Grosvenor Road, Newcastle upon Tyne NE2 2RU.—*Sec.*, J. F. Pearce.

WELSH JOINT EDUCATION COMMITTEE, 245 Western Avenue, Cardiff CF5 2YX.—M. Lloyd Jones.

WEST MIDLANDS ADVISORY COUNCIL FOR FURTHER EDUCATION (incorporating Union of Educational Institutions), Norfolk House, Smallbrook Queensway, Birmingham B5 4NB.

YORKSHIRE AND HUMBERSIDE ASSOCIATION FOR FURTHER AND HIGHER EDUCATION, Bowling Green Terrace, Leeds LS11 9SX.

B. SPECIALIZED

INSTITUTE OF PRACTITIONERS IN ADVERTISING, 44 Belgrave Square SW1X 8QS.—*Sec.*, J. Raad.

CAM FOUNDATION, Abford House, 15 Wilton Road SW1V 1NJ.—*Registrar*, Mrs. S. J. Hurford.

INSTITUTE OF EXPORT, Export House, 64 Clifton Street, EC2A 4HB.—*Sec.*, D. J. Langham.

INSTITUTE OF MARKETING, Moor Hall, Cookham, Maidenhead, Berks. SL6 9QH.—*Dir. Gen.*, T. McBurnie.

INSTITUTE OF PERSONNEL MANAGEMENT, IPM House, Camp Road, Wimbledon, SW19 4UW.—*Dir.*, J. Miller, C.B.

INSTITUTE OF PURCHASING AND SUPPLY, Easton House, Easton on the Hill, Stamford, Lincs. PE9 3NZ.—*Dir.-Gen.*, I. G. S. Groundwater.

FACULTY OF SECRETARIES AND ADMINISTRATORS LTD., 15 Church Street, Godalming, Surrey GU7 1EL.—*Sec.*, Mrs. B. D. Lloyd.

INSTITUTE OF CHARTERED SECRETARIES AND ADMINISTRATORS, 16 Park Crescent, W1N 4AH.—*Sec.*, B. Barker, M.B.E.

INSTITUTE OF CHARTERED SHIPBROKERS, 24 St. Mary Axe, EC3A 8DE.—*Sec.*, J. H. Parker.

CHARTERED INSTITUTE OF TRANSPORT, 80 Portland Place, W1N 4DP.—*Dir. Gen.*, J. C. F. Cameron.

BUSINESS AND TECHNICIAN EDUCATION COUNCIL Central House, Upper Woburn Place, WC1H 0HH

The Business & Technician Education Council (BTEC) validates courses leading to nationally recognized qualifications in agriculture; business and finance; caring services; computing and information systems; construction; design; distribution; engineering; home economics; hotel and catering; leisure services; public administration and science, at colleges and polytechnics throughout England, Wales and Northern Ireland.

Chairman, P. Rogers.
Chief Executive, J. E. Sellars.

COMPUTER SCIENCE

First Degrees in *Computer/Computing Science(s)/ Computing, Computational Science* are granted by the Universities of Aberdeen, Aston, Bath (*Computer Software Technology*), Belfast (also *Information Technology*), Birmingham (*Software Engineering*), Bradford (also *Computing & Information Systems Science*), Bristol, Brunel (also *Applied Computer Systems* and *Information Technology*), Buckingham, Cambridge, the City University (also *Business Computing Systems*), Cranfield (*Command and Control Communications and Information Systems and Information Technology*) the Universities of Dundee, Durham, East Anglia, Edinburgh, Essex (also *Computer & Microprocessor Systems*), Exeter, Glasgow, Heriot-Watt, Hull, Keele, Kent (also *Computer Systems Engineering* and (provisional) *Computer Communications*) Lancaster, Leeds (also *Data Processing*), Leicester, Liverpool, London (Imperial (also *Software Engineering*), King's (also *Computer Systems with Microelectronics* and *Computer Science & Digital Electronics*), Queen Mary (also *Computer Systems with Microelectronics*), Royal Holloway and Bedford New, and University Colleges, London School of Economics and Political Science), Loughborough (also *Data Processing and Information Technology and Human Factors*), Manchester (also *Computing & Information Systems*), Manchester Institute of Science and Technology, Newcastle upon Tyne, Nottingham, Oxford, Reading, St. Andrews (also *Information Processing*), Salford (also *Electronic Computer Systems*), Sheffield, Southampton, Stirling, Strathclyde, Surrey, Sussex, Ulster (also *Computing Science (Information Systems)* and *Applied Computing*), Wales (University College, Aberystwyth; University College, Cardiff, also *Computer Systems*; University College, Swansea), Warwick and York (also *Computer Systems & Software Engineering*).

The University of Salford also grants a first degree in *Computer Studies* for which courses are provided at the North East Wales Institute of Higher Education.

Courses leading to first degrees in *Computer Science/Studies* or *Computing* granted by the C.N.A.A. are provided by City of Birmingham Polytechnic (*Computing Information Systems*), Brighton Polytechnic (also *Microelectronics & Information Processing*), Bristol Polytechnic (*Systems Analysis* and *Systems Design*), City of London Polytechnic (*Computing and Information Systems*), Coventry (Lanchester) Polytechnic (also *Information Systems Engineering*), Glasgow College of Technology (*Computer Information Systems*), Hatfield Polytechnic, Huddersfield Polytechnic (*Computing in Business*), Humberside College of Higher Education (*Business Information Systems*), Kingston Polytechnic (also *Information Systems Design*), Lancashire Polytechnic (*Business Information Technology*), Leeds Polytechnic (*Computing and Operational Research*), Leicester Polytechnic (also *Information Technology*), Liverpool Polytechnic, Napier College of Commerce and Technology (*Computing and Data Processing*), Newcastle Polytechnic (*Computing for Industry*), North East London Polytechnic, North Staffordshire Polytechnic (also *Information Systems* and *Information Technology*), Paisley College of Technology, Plymouth Polytechnic (*Computing and Informatics*), Portsmouth Polytechnic, Sheffield City Polytechnic (also *Information Technology*), Polytechnic of the South Bank (also *Computer and Information Engineering*), Sunderland Polytechnic (*Data Processing*), Teesside Polytechnic (also *Information Technology*), Thames Polytechnic (also *Computer and Communication Systems*), Wolverhampton Polytechnic and Polytechnic of Wales (also *Information Technology*).

These subjects also form part of other degree courses, often as *Mathematics/Statistics and Computer Science*, at many universities, polytechnics and colleges.

DANCE

(*See also* Recreation, Sport, etc.)

First degrees in *Dance in Society* are granted by the University of Surrey.

The University of Kent grants a first degree in *Contemporary Dance* for which courses are provided at the London Contemporary Dance School.

Courses leading to first degrees in *Dance Theatre* granted by the C.N.A.A. are provided by the Laban Centre for Movement and Dance in association with Goldsmiths' College. Dance also forms part of C.N.A.A. degree courses, often called *Performing Arts* or *Creative Arts*, at several polytechnics and colleges. For first degree courses in *Human Movement Studies* see under 'Recreation, Sport and Human Movement Studies'.

ROYAL ACADEMY OF DANCING, 48 Vicarage Crescent, SW11 3LT.—*Directors*, Ms. J. Farron, D. Wall, C.B.E., Ms. P. Yates.

ROYAL BALLET SCHOOL, 155 Talgarth Road, W14 9DE, and White Lodge, Richmond Park, Surrey TW10 5HR.—*Dir.*, Dame Merle Park, D.B.E.

IMPERIAL SOCIETY OF TEACHERS OF DANCING, Euston Hall, Birkenhead Street, WC1H 8BE.—*Gen. Sec.*, D. Osborne.

DEFENCE

First Degrees in *Peace Studies* are granted by the Universities of Bradford and Ulster, and in *Strategic Studies* by the Universities of Lancaster and Wales (University College, Aberystwyth).

Royal Naval Colleges

ROYAL NAVAL COLLEGE, Greenwich, SE10 9NN.— *Admiral President, Vice-Adm.* B. T. Brown, C.B.E.; *Dean of the College*, Prof. J. R. Lakey.

BRITANNIA ROYAL NAVAL COLLEGE, Dartmouth, Devon TQ6 0HJ.—Initial officer training. *Captain*, Capt. J. R. Brigstocke. *Dir. of Studies*, Dr. A. W. Machin.

ROYAL NAVAL ENGINEERING COLLEGE, Manadon, Plymouth PL5 3AQ.—B.Eng., M.Sc. and specialist training in naval engineering. Students are selected uniformed officers of the Royal Navy, Commonwealth and foreign navies, and civilians. *Captain*, Capt. J. A. Marshall.
Dean, Capt. G. C. George.
Executive Officer, Cdr. C. D. de Burgh.

INSTITUTE OF NAVAL MEDICINE, Alverstoke, Hants. PO12 2DL.—Higher professional and postgraduate training for officers of all three services, and some civilians.

Military Colleges

STAFF COLLEGE, CAMBERLEY, Surrey GU15 4NP.— *Commandant*, Maj.-Gen. J. H. Learmont, C.B.E.

ROYAL MILITARY ACADEMY, SANDHURST, Camberley, Surrey GU15 4PQ.—*Commandant*, Maj.-Gen. S. C. Cooper.

ROYAL MILITARY COLLEGE OF SCIENCE, Shrivenham, nr. Swindon, Wilts SN6 8LA.—Students from U.K. and overseas study from degree to post-graduate levels in management, science and technology. There is an increasing range of research and consultancy activity as the College is now a Faculty of the Cranfield Institute of Technology.
Commandant, Maj.-Gen. A. S. J. Blacker, C.B.E.
Dean, Prof. F. R. Hartley, D.Phil.
Academic Registrar, Lt.-Col. M. P. Groves (*retd*).

INSTITUTE OF ARMY EDUCATION, Court Road, Eltham, SE9 5NR.—*Director*, Maj.-Gen. J. S. Lee, M.B.E.

Royal Air Force Colleges

ROYAL AIR FORCE STAFF COLLEGE, Bracknell, Berks, RG12 3DD.—Prepares selected senior officers for high-grade command and staff appointments. The majority of students are R.A.F. officers but officers from the other U.K. services and from foreign air forces also attend.
Air Officer Commanding and Commandant, Air Vice-Marshal R. E. Johns, C.B.E., L.V.O.

ROYAL AIR FORCE COLLEGE, Cranwell, Sleaford, Lincs NG34 8HB.—Initial officer training for officers of the R.A.F., W.R.A.F. and P.M.R.A.F.N.S., and initial specialist training for officers of the Engineer and Supply Branches. Advanced specialist training is provided for officers of the General Duties, Engineer and Supply Branches and basic flying training for pilots of the General Duties Branch.
Air Officer Commanding and Commandant, Air Vice-Marshal R. H. Wood, O.B.E.

ROYAL AIR FORCE SCHOOL OF EDUCATION AND TRAINING SUPPORT, R.A.F. Newton, Nottingham NG13 8HL.—*Commanding Officer*, Gp. Capt. D. E. Priestley.

DENTISTRY

First Degrees in Dentistry are granted by the Universities of Belfast, Birmingham, Bristol, Dundee, Edinburgh, Glasgow, Leeds, Liverpool, London (United Medical and Dental Schools of Guy's and St. Thomas's Hospitals, King's College School of Medicine and Dentistry, London Hospital Medical College, University College & Middlesex Hospital Medical School), Manchester, Newcastle upon Tyne, Sheffield, Wales (College of Medicine).

To be entitled to be registered in the Dentists Register a person must hold the degree or diploma in dental surgery of a University in the U.K. or Republic of Ireland or the diploma of any of the Licensing Authorities (The Royal College of Surgeons of England, of Edinburgh and in Ireland, and the Royal College of Physicians and Surgeons of Glasgow). Nationals of an E.C. member state holding an appropriate European diploma, and holders of certain overseas diplomas, may also be registered. The Dentists Register is maintained by THE GENERAL DENTAL COUNCIL, 37 Wimpole Street, W1M 8DQ.

DIETETICS

(*See also* Food and Nutrition Science)

Courses in *Nutrition and Dietetics* leading to first degrees granted by the University of Wales are provided by South Glamorgan Institute of Higher Education. The University of Bradford grants a first degree in *Nutrition and Food Policy.* Courses leading to first degrees in *Dietetics* granted by the C.N.A.A. are provided by Leeds Polytechnic, Queen Margaret College, Paisley College of Technology with Queen's College and Robert Gordon's Institute of Technology (*Nutrition and Dietetics*).

The professional association is THE BRITISH DIE-TETIC ASSOCIATION, Daimler House, Paradise Circus, Queensway, Birmingham B1 2BJ. Full membership is open to dietitians holding a recognized qualification, who may also become State Registered Dietitians through the Council for Professions Supplementary to Medicine (*q.v.*).

DRAMA

First Degrees in *Drama* are granted by the Universities of Birmingham (*Drama and Theatre Arts*), Bristol, East Anglia, Exeter, Glasgow (*Dramatic Studies*—in conjunction with Royal Scottish Academy of Music and Drama), Hull, Kent (*Drama and Theatre Studies*), Lancaster (*Theatre Studies*), London (Royal Holloway and Bedford New College, *Drama and Theatre Studies*), Loughborough, Manchester and Wales (University College of Aberystwyth) and Warwick (*Theatre Studies and Dramatic Arts*). Drama also forms part of degree courses in other universities. Courses in Drama leading to first degrees granted by the University of Leeds are provided at Bretton Hall College of Higher Education.

Courses leading to first degrees granted by the C.N.A.A. are provided by Crewe and Alsager College of Higher Education (*Drama Studies*), Dartington College of Arts (*Theatre*), King Alfred's College of Higher Education (*Drama, Theatre and TV Studies*) and Rose Bruford College of Speech and Drama (*Theatre Arts*).

The national validating body for courses providing training in drama is THE NATIONAL COUNCIL FOR DRAMA TRAINING, 5 Tavistock Place, WC1H 9SS. It currently has accredited courses at the following: Academy of Live and Recorded Arts; Arts Educational Schools; Birmingham School of Speech Training & Dramatic Art; Bristol Old Vic Theatre School; Central School of Speech and Drama; Drama Centre, London; Drama Studio; Guildford School of Acting; Guildhall School of Music and Drama; London Academy of Music and Dramatic Art; Manchester Polytechnic School of Theatre; Mountview Theatre School; Rose Bruford College of Speech and Drama; Royal Academy of Dramatic Art; Royal Scottish Academy of Music and Drama; Webber Douglas Academy of Dramatic Art; Welsh College of Music and Drama.

ECONOMICS

Almost all universities grant first degrees in Economics. Courses leading to first degrees in Economics granted by the Council for National Academic Awards are provided by some 20 Polytechnics and Colleges.

ENGINEERING
(*See separate subjects below*)

The Council of Engineering Institutions ceased operations in Sept. 1983 and its major functions are now carried on by THE ENGINEERING COUNCIL, 10 Maltravers Street, WC2R 3ER.—*Sec.,* J. Carlill, O.B.E. The fifteen principal qualifying bodies are :—

ROYAL AERONAUTICAL SOCIETY, 4 Hamilton Place, W1V 0BQ.—*Sec.,* G. C. May.

ROYAL INSTITUTION OF NAVAL ARCHITECTS, 10 Upper Belgrave Street, SW1X 8BQ.—*Sec.,* P. W. Ayling.

INSTITUTION OF CHEMICAL ENGINEERS, 165/171 Railway Terrace, Rugby, Warwickshire CV21 3HQ.—*Gen. Sec.,* Dr. T. J. Evans.

INSTITUTION OF CIVIL ENGINEERS, Great George Street SW1P 3AA.—*Sec.,* J. C. McKenzie.

INSTITUTION OF ELECTRICAL ENGINEERS, Savoy Place, WC2R 0BL.—*Sec.,* H. H. W. Losty.

INSTITUTION OF ELECTRONIC AND RADIO ENGINEERS, 99 Gower Street, WC1E 6AZ.—*Sec.,* D. D. Duffett.

INSTITUTE OF ENERGY, 18 Devonshire Street, W1N 2AU.—*Sec.* C. Rigg, T.D.

INSTITUTION OF GAS ENGINEERS, 17 Grosvenor Crescent, SW1X 7ES.—*Sec.,* D. J. Chapman.

INSTITUTE OF MARINE ENGINEERS, 76 Mark Lane, EC3R 7JN.—*Sec.,* J. E. Sloggett.

INSTITUTION OF MECHANICAL ENGINEERS, 1 Birdcage Walk, SW1H 9JJ.—*Sec.* R. Mellor, C.B.E.

INSTITUTE OF METALS, 1 Carlton House Terrace, SW1Y 5DB.—*Sec.,* Dr. J. A. Catterall.

INSTITUTION OF MINING ENGINEERS, Danum House, 6A South Parade, Doncaster DN1 2DY.—*Sec.,* W. J. W. Bourne.

INSTITUTION OF MINING AND METALLURGY, 44 Portland Place, W1N 4BR.—*Sec.,* M. J. Jones.

INSTITUTION OF PRODUCTION ENGINEERS, Rochester House, 66 Little Ealing Lane, W5 4XX.—*Sec.,* Brig. P. V. Crooks.

INSTITUTION OF STRUCTURAL ENGINEERS, 11 Upper Belgrave Street, SW1X 8BH.—*Sec.,* D. J. Clark.

ENGINEERING, GENERAL AND ENGINEERING SCIENCE

First Degrees in *General Engineering* or *Engineering Science* are granted by the Universities of Aberdeen, Aston, Cambridge, Durham, Edinburgh, Exeter, Hull, Lancaster, Leicester, Liverpool, London (Queen Mary College), Loughborough, Oxford, Reading, Surrey, Sussex, Ulster, Wales (University College, Cardiff), and Warwick. Courses leading to first degrees in *Engineering* granted by the C.N.A.A. are provided by some 10 polytechnics and colleges.

Aeronautical Engineering

See main heading:
AERONAUTICS AND AERONAUTICAL ENGINEERING

Agricultural Engineering

First Degrees in *Agricultural Engineering* and *Agricultural Mechanization Management* are granted by the University of Newcastle upon Tyne. Courses in *Agricultural Engineering* and *Agricultural Technology & Management* leading to degrees granted by Cranfield Institute of Technology are provided at Silsoe College.

Chemical Engineering

First Degrees are granted by the Universities of Aston (*Chemical Process Engineering*), Bath, Belfast, Birmingham, Bradford, Cambridge, Edinburgh, Exeter, Heriot-Watt, Leeds, London (Imperial College of Science and Technology, University College), Loughborough, Manchester (Manchester Institute of Science and Technology), Newcastle upon Tyne, Nottingham, Salford, Sheffield (*Chemical Process Engineering*), Strathclyde, Surrey and Wales (University College, Swansea).

Courses leading to first degrees granted by the C.N.A.A. are provided by North East London Polytechnic, Polytechnic of the South Bank, Teesside Polytechnic and Polytechnic of Wales.

Civil, Electrical & Mechanical Engineering

First Degrees in *Civil,* (or *Civil and Structural*) *Electrical* (or *Electrical and Electronic*) and *Mechan-*

ical Engineering are granted by the Universities of Aberdeen, Aston, Bath, Belfast, Birmingham, Bradford, Bristol, Brunel (*E. & M.*), Cambridge, the City University, Cranfield Institute, the Universities of Dundee, Durham, Edinburgh, Exeter, Glasgow, Heriot-Watt, Lancaster, Leeds, Leicester, Liverpool, London (Imperial College of Science and Technology, King's College, Queen Mary College, University College), Loughborough, Manchester, *also* Manchester Institute of Science and Technology, Newcastle upon Tyne, Nottingham, Oxford, Reading (*E. & M.*), Salford, Sheffield, Southampton, Strathclyde, Surrey, Sussex, Ulster, Wales (University Colleges at Cardiff and Swansea, Institute of Science and Technology, Cardiff) and Warwick.

Some 28 polytechnics or colleges provide courses (in one or more of civil, electrical/electronic and mechanical engineering) leading to first degrees granted by the C.N.A.A.

Electronic Engineering & Electronics

First Degrees in *Electronic Engineering* or *Electronics* or *Electrical and Electronic Engineering* or *Electrical Engineering (including Electronics)* are granted by the following universities: Aberdeen, Aston, Bath, Belfast, Birmingham, Bradford, Bristol, Brunel, Cambridge, the City University, Cranfield Institute (*Electronic Systems Engineering*), the Universities of Dundee, Durham, East Anglia (*Electronic Systems Engineering*), Edinburgh, Essex, Exeter, Glasgow, Heriot-Watt, Hull, Keele, Kent, Lancaster, Leeds, Leicester, Liverpool, London (Imperial College of Science and Technology, King's, Queen Mary and University Colleges), Loughborough, Manchester (*also* Manchester Institute of Science and Technology), Newcastle upon Tyne, Nottingham, Oxford, Reading, Salford, Sheffield, Southampton, Strathclyde, Surrey, Sussex, Ulster, Wales (University Colleges of Bangor, Cardiff and Swansea, Institute of Science and Technology), Warwick (also *Engineering Electronics*), York.

Courses leading to first degrees in *Electronic Engineering* or in *Electrical and Electronic Engineering*, granted by the C.N.A.A. are provided by some 30 polytechnics or colleges.

Marine Engineering and Naval Architecture

First Degrees in *Marine Engineering* and *Naval Architecture and Shipbuilding* are granted by the University of Newcastle upon Tyne; in *Naval Architecture and Ocean Engineering* by the Universities of Glasgow and London (University College); in *Naval Architecture* by the University of Strathclyde; in *Offshore Engineering* by Heriot-Watt University; in *Ship Science* by the University of Southampton, and in *Maritime Studies* by the University of Wales (Institute of Science and Technology).

Courses leading to first degrees in *Mechanical Engineering (Marine)* granted by the C.N.A.A. are provided by Liverpool Polytechnic.

Nuclear Engineering

First Degrees are granted by the University of Manchester.

Production Engineering

First Degrees in *Production Engineering, Manufacturing Engineering* or *Industrial Engineering* are granted by the Universities of Aston, Bath, Belfast, Birmingham (*Engineering Production*), Brunel, Cambridge, Dundee, Exeter (*Engineering (Operations & Manufacturing)*), Hull (*Engineering Design and Manufacture*), Loughborough, Nottingham, Strath-

clyde, Ulster, Wales (Institute of Science and Technology) and Warwick (*Engineering (Manufacturing Systems)*).

Courses leading to first degrees in *Production Engineering* granted by the C.N.A.A. are provided by Coventry (Lanchester) Polytechnic, Kingston Polytechnic, Leeds Polytechnic, Trent Polytechnic; in *Industrial Engineering* by Hatfield Polytechnic, Paisley College of Technology; in *Manufacturing Engineering* by Liverpool Polytechnic; in *Manufacturing Systems Engineering* by Sheffield City Polytechnic; and in *Plant Engineering* by Trent Polytechnic.

Structural Engineering

First Degrees in *Civil and Structural Engineering* are granted by the Universities of Aberdeen, Bradford, Heriot-Watt (*Structural Engineering*), Liverpool, London (University College, *Civil, Structural and Environmental Engineering*), Sheffield, and Sussex (*Structural Engineering*).

ESTATE AND LAND MANAGEMENT, AND SURVEYING
(*See also* Building)

First Degrees are granted by the Universities of Aberdeen (*Land Economy*), Cambridge (*Land Economy*), Heriot-Watt (*Estate Management*), Reading (*Land Management* and *Rural Land Management*) Stirling (*Countryside Management*—provisional) and Ulster (*Estate Management*).

First Degrees in *Surveying Science* are granted by the University of Newcastle upon Tyne; in *Building Economics and Quantity Surveying* and in *Building Surveying* by Heriot-Watt University; in *Quantity Surveying* by Ulster University; in *Property Valuation and Management* by the City University; in *Quantity Surveying* and *Building Surveying* by the University of Reading and in *Quantity Surveying and Construction Economics* and *Building Surveying* by the University of Salford.

Courses leading to first degrees granted by the C.N.A.A. are provided by the following: in *Estate Management* by the City of Birmingham Polytechnic, Kingston Polytechnic, Newcastle upon Tyne Polytechnic, Oxford Polytechnic, Polytechnic of the South Bank and Thames Polytechnic; in *Housing* by Bristol Polytechnic; in *Housing Studies* by Sheffield City Polytechnic; in *Land Administration* by North East London Polytechnic; in *Land Economics* by Paisley College of Technology; in *Land Management* by Leicester Polytechnic; in *Minerals Estate Management* by Sheffield City Polytechnic; in *Quantity Surveying* by City of Birmingham Polytechnic, Bristol Polytechnic, Polytechnic of Central London, Dundee College of Technology, Glasgow College of Technology with Glasgow College of Building and Printing, Kingston Polytechnic, Leeds Polytechnic, Liverpool Polytechnic, Newcastle upon Tyne Polytechnic, Portsmouth Polytechnic, Robert Gordon's Institute of Technology, Polytechnic of the South Bank, Thames Polytechnic, Trent Polytechnic and Polytechnic of Wales; in *Surveying and Mapping Sciences* by North East London Polytechnic; in *Urban Estate Management* by Polytechnic of Central London, Liverpool Polytechnic and the Polytechnic of Wales; in *Urban Estate Surveying* by Trent Polytechnic; in *Urban Land Administration* by Portsmouth Polytechnic; in *Urban Land Economics* by Sheffield City Polytechnic; and in *Valuation and Estate Management* by Bristol Polytechnic.

Qualifying professional bodies include:

ROYAL INSTITUTION OF CHARTERED SURVEYORS (incorporating The Institute of Quantity Surveyors), 12 Great George Street, SW1P 3AD.—*Sec. Gen.*, M. Pattison.

FACULTY OF ARCHITECTS AND SURVEYORS, (incorporating the Institute of Registered Architects), 15 St. Mary Street, Chippenham, Wilts SN15 3JN.—*Sec.*, Mrs. J. E. Allen.

INCORPORATED ASSOCIATION OF ARCHITECTS AND SURVEYORS, Jubilee House, Billing Brook Road, Weston Favell, Northampton NN3 4NW.—*Hon. Sec.*, W. A. Black.

RATING AND VALUATION ASSOCIATION, 41 Doughty Street, WC1N 2LF.—*Dir.*, C. Farrington.

INCORPORATED SOCIETY OF VALUERS AND AUCTIONEERS, 3 Cadogan Gate, SW1X 0AS.—*Sec.*, M. Astbury.

FISHERY SCIENCE

First Degrees in *Wildlife and Fisheries Management* are granted by the University of Edinburgh.

Courses leading to first degrees in *Fishery Science/Studies* granted by the C.N.A.A. are provided by Humberside College of Higher Education, and Plymouth Polytechnic.

FOOD AND NUTRITION SCIENCE
(*See also* Dietetics, Home Economics and Hotelkeeping)

First Degrees in *Food Science* are granted by the Universities of Belfast (also *Food Technology*), Leeds, London (King's College), Newcastle (*Agricultural & Food Marketing*), Nottingham, Reading (also *Food Science, Food Economics & Marketing* and *Food Technology*), Strathclyde, Surrey (*Nutrition & Food Science*), Ulster (*Food Processing Technology*) and Wales (University College, Aberystwyth, *Agricultural & Food Marketing*); in *Nutrition* by the Universities of London (King's College), Southampton and Surrey; and in *Human Nutrition* by the Universities of Nottingham and Ulster.

Courses leading to first degrees in *Food Science* granted by the C.N.A.A. are provided by Manchester Polytechnic and by the Polytechnic of the South Bank; in *Catering and Applied Nutrition* by Huddersfield Polytechnic; in *Food and Accommodation Studies* by Leeds Polytechnic; in *Food Marketing Sciences* by Sheffield City Polytechnic; in *Food, Textiles & Consumer Studies* by the Polytechnic of the South Bank; in *Industrial Food Technology* by Humberside College of Higher Education; in *Nutrition and Dietetics* by Robert Gordon's Institute of Technology.

Scientific and professional bodies include:

NUTRITION SOCIETY, Grosvenor Gardens House, 35–37 Grosvenor Gardens, SW1W 0BS.—*Hon. Sec.*, Dr. M. Ashwell.

INSTITUTE OF FOOD SCIENCE & TECHNOLOGY (U.K.), 5 Cambridge Court, 210 Shepherd's Bush Road, W6 7NL.—*Exec. Sec.*, Ms. H. G. Wild.

FORESTRY AND TIMBER STUDIES

First Degrees in Forestry are granted by the Universities of Aberdeen, Edinburgh (also *Agriculture, Forestry & Rural Economy*), and Wales (University College, Bangor), (also *Wood Science and Agroforestry*).

Courses leading to first degrees in *Timber Technology* granted by the C.N.A.A. are provided by Buckinghamshire College of Higher Education.

Professional Organizations

ROYAL FORESTRY SOCIETY OF ENGLAND, WALES AND NORTHERN IRELAND, 102 High Street, Tring, Herts., HP23 4AH.—*Dir.*, E. H. M. Harris.

ROYAL SCOTTISH FORESTRY SOCIETY, 11 Atholl Crescent, Edinburgh EH3 8HE.—*Sec.*, W. B. C. Walker.

COMMONWEALTH FORESTRY ASSOCIATION, c/o Oxford Forestry Institute, South Parks Road, Oxford OX1 3RB.—*Sec.*, M. T. Rogers.

INSTITUTE OF CHARTERED FORESTERS, 22 Walker Street, Edinburgh EH3 7HR.—*Sec.*, Mrs. M. W. Dick.

FUEL AND ENERGY STUDIES
(*See also* Nuclear Engineering)

First Degrees in *Fuel and Combustion Science* and in *Fuel and Energy Engineering* are granted by the University of Leeds; in *Petroleum Engineering* by London (Imperial College of Science and Technology); in *Mining and Petroleum Engineering* by the University of Strathclyde; in *Natural Gas Engineering* by the University of Salford; in *Chemical Process Engineering, Fuel Technology* by the University of Sheffield; and in *Fuel and Energy—Management Studies* by the University of Leeds. These subjects may also form part of other degree courses.

Courses leading to first degrees in *Energy Engineering* granted by the C.N.A.A. are provided by Napier College of Commerce and Technology, and in *Power Engineering* by Derbyshire College of Higher Education.

Courses leading to certificates and qualification by professional bodies are available at many Technical Colleges.

The principal professional bodies are:—

INSTITUTE OF ENERGY, 18 Devonshire Street, W1N 2AU.—*Sec.*, C. Rigg, T.D.

INSTITUTION OF GAS ENGINEERS, 17 Grosvenor Crescent, SW1X 7ES.—*Sec.*, D. J. Chapman.

INSTITUTE OF PETROLEUM, 61 New Cavendish Street W1M 8AR.—*Dir. Gen.*, A. E. H. Williams.

GEOLOGY

First Degrees in *Geology* or *Geological Sciences* or *Applied Geology* are granted by the Universities of Aberdeen (also *Petroleum Geology*), Aston, Belfast, Birmingham, Bristol, Cambridge, Dundee, Durham, Edinburgh, Exeter, Glasgow, Hull, Keele, Leeds, Leicester (also *Mining Geology*), Liverpool, London (Birkbeck College, Goldsmiths' College, Imperial College of Science and Technology (also *Mining Geology*), Queen Mary College, Royal Holloway & Bedford New College, University College), Manchester, Newcastle upon Tyne, Nottingham, Oxford, Reading, St. Andrews, Sheffield, Southampton, Strathclyde, Wales (University Colleges at Aberystwyth, Cardiff and Swansea).

Degree courses in *Geophysics* and *Geophysical Sciences* are provided by the Universities of East Anglia, Edinburgh, Lancaster, Leeds, Leicester, Liverpool, Newcastle, Southampton and Wales (University College, Cardiff).

Courses leading to first degrees in *Geology* granted by the C.N.A.A. are provided by College of St. Paul and St. Mary (*Geography and Geology*), Derbyshire College of Higher Education (*Earth and Life Studies*), Kingston Polytechnic, Plymouth Polytechnic (*Applied Geology*), and Portsmouth Polytechnic; in *Earth Sciences* by Oxford Polytechnic and in *Engineering Geology and Geotechnics* by Portsmouth Polytechnic.

HOME ECONOMICS AND CATERING
(*See also* Dietetics, Food, Hotelkeeping and Institutional Management).

First Degrees are granted by the Universities of Ulster (*Home Economics* and *Catering Administration*), Wales (Cardiff University College, *Home Economics*), Strathclyde (*Hotel and Catering Management*) and Surrey (*Hotel and Catering Management*). Courses leading to first degrees in *Home*

Economics granted by the University of Bath are provided at Bath College of Higher Education.

Courses leading to first degrees granted by the C.N.A.A. are provided by Bradford and Ilkley Community College (*Home and Community Studies*), Brighton Polytechnic (*Hotel and Catering Management*), Dorset Institute of Higher Education (*Catering Administration*), Huddersfield Polytechnic (*Catering and Applied Nutrition, Hotel and Catering Administration*); Leeds Polytechnic (*Home Economics*); Liverpool Polytechnic (*Home Economics*), Manchester Polytechnic (*Home Economics* and *Hotel and Catering Studies*); Middlesex Polytechnic (*Hotel and Catering Administration*); Napier College of Commerce and Technology (*Catering and Accommodation Studies*); Newcastle upon Tyne Polytechnic (*Applied Consumer Science*); Oxford Polytechnic (*Catering*); Portsmouth Polytechnic/Highbury College of Technology (*Hotel and Catering Management*); Queen Margaret College (*Home Economics*); Queen's College (*Home Economics* and *Catering and Accommodation Management*); Robert Gordon's Institute of Technology (*Hotel, Catering and Institutional Administration*); and Sheffield City Polytechnic (*Catering Systems*).

HOTELKEEPING
(See also Institutional Management)

First Degrees are granted by the Universities of Strathclyde (*Hotel and Catering Management*), Surrey (*Hotel Management* and *Hotel and Catering Management*), Ulster (*Hotel and Tourism Management*) and Wales (Cardiff University College, *Hotel and Institutional Management*).

Courses leading to first degrees in *Hotel and Catering Administration / Studies / Management* granted by the C.N.A.A. are provided by Brighton, Huddersfield, Manchester and Middlesex Polytechnics and by Portsmouth Polytechnic/Highbury College of Technology; in *Hospitality Management* by Norwich City College of Further and Higher Education; and in *Hotel, Catering and Institutional Management* by Robert Gordon's Institute of Technology.

INDUSTRIAL RELATIONS

First Degrees in Industrial Relations are granted by the Universities of Kent, London (London School of Economics and Political Science), and Wales (Cardiff University College). Industrial relations also forms part of degree courses at other universities.

INSTITUTIONAL MANAGEMENT
(See also Hotelkeeping)

First Degrees in Hotel and Institutional Management are granted by the University of Wales (Cardiff University College).

Courses leading to first degrees in *Institutional Management* granted by the C.N.A.A. are provided by the Polytechnic of North London; and in *Hotel, Catering and Institutional Management* by Robert Gordon's Institute of Technology.

Qualifying professional body in the three subjects above is:
HOTEL, CATERING AND INSTITUTIONAL MANAGEMENT ASSOCIATION, 191 Trinity Road, SW17 7HN.—*Dir.*, Ms. E. Gadsby.

INSURANCE

First Degrees in *Banking, Insurance and Finance* are granted by the University of Wales (University College, Bangor) and in *Industrial Economics with Insurance* by the University of Nottingham.

Courses leading to first degrees in *Risk Management* granted by the C.N.A.A. are provided by the Glasgow College of Technology.

Organizations conducting examinations and awarding diplomas:—
ASSOCIATION OF AVERAGE ADJUSTERS, H.Q.S. "Wellington", Temple Stairs, Victoria Embankment, WC2R 2PN.—*Sec.*, J. G. Jacklin.
CHARTERED INSURANCE INSTITUTE, 20 Aldermanbury, EC2V 7HY.—*Sec. Gen.*, P. V. Saxton.
CHARTERED INSTITUTE OF LOSS ADJUSTERS, Manfield House, 376 Strand, WC2R 0LR.—*Dir.*, A. F. Clack.

JOURNALISM

Courses for trainee newspaper journalists are available at 11 centres. One-year full-time courses are available for selected students. Particulars of all these courses are available from the Director of the NATIONAL COUNCIL FOR TRAINING OF JOURNALISTS, Carlton House, Hemnall Street, Epping, Essex CM16 4NL. Short courses for experienced journalists are also arranged by the National Council.—*Dir.*, D. K. Hall.

For periodical journalists, there are four centres running courses approved by THE PERIODICALS TRAINING COUNCIL, Imperial House, 15–19 Kingsway, WC2B 6UN.—*Dir.*, A. R. Sumption.

LANGUAGES

First Degrees in English and in a very wide range of Foreign Languages (including Oriental and African languages) are granted by universities. Degrees in *Linguistics* are awarded by the Universities of Cambridge, East Anglia, Essex (also *Language Studies and Psycholinguistics*), Lancaster, Leeds (*Linguistics and Phonetics*), London (School of Oriental and African Studies and University College), Newcastle upon Tyne, Reading (also *Linguistics and Language Pathology*), Sussex and Wales (University College, Bangor, *Applied Linguistics* and *Theoretical Linguistics*); in *Applied Languages* by the University of Ulster; in *Language and Linguistic Science* by the University of York; and in *Languages (Interpreting and Translating*) by Heriot-Watt University. These subjects also form part of degree courses at many other universities.

Courses leading to first degrees in various *Foreign Languages* granted by the C.N.A.A. are provided by some 15 Polytechnics and Colleges and in *Applied Languages* by Brighton Polytechnic.

LAW

First Degrees in Law are granted by the Universities of Aberdeen, Belfast, Birmingham, Bristol, Brunel, Buckingham, Cambridge, Dundee, Durham, East Anglia, Edinburgh, Essex, Exeter, Glasgow, Hull, Kent (also *Industrial Relations (Law)*), Lancaster, Leeds, Leicester, Liverpool, London (King's College, London School of Economics and Political Science, Queen Mary College, School of Oriental and African Studies; University College), Manchester, Newcastle upon Tyne, Nottingham, Oxford, Reading, Sheffield, Southampton, Stirling (*Business Law*), Strathclyde (also *Business Law*), Sussex, Wales (University Colleges at Aberystwyth and Cardiff, Institute of Science and Technology) and Warwick.

Courses leading to first degrees in Law granted by the C.N.A.A. are provided by City of Birmingham Polytechnic, Bristol Polytechnic, Polytechnic of Central London, City of London Polytechnic (also *Business Law*), Coventry (Lanchester) Polytechnic (*Business Law*), Ealing College of Higher Education, Essex Institute of Higher Education, Huddersfield Polytechnic (*Business Law*), Kingston Polytechnic,

Lancashire Polytechnic, Leeds Polytechnic, Leicester Polytechnic, Liverpool Polytechnic, Manchester Polytechnic, Middlesex Polytechnic, Newcastle upon Tyne Polytechnic, North East London Polytechnic, Polytechnic of North London, North Staffordshire Polytechnic, Polytechnic of the South Bank, Trent Polytechnic and Wolverhampton Polytechnic; and Polytechnic of Wales.

The Bar

Qualifications for Barrister are obtainable only at one of the Inns of Court or Faculty of Advocates.

THE INNS OF COURT

THE GENERAL COUNCIL OF THE BAR
11 South Square, Gray's Inn, WC1R 5EL

The governing body of the Barristers' branch of the legal profession, established in 1987 in succession to the Senate of the Inns of Court and the Bar.
Chairman, R. Johnson, Q.C.
Vice-Chairman, D. Fennell, O.B.E., Q.C.
Treasurer, W. Blackburne, Q.C.
Chief Executive, J. Mottram, C.B., L.V.O., O.B.E.

THE INNER TEMPLE, EC4Y 7HL

Treasurer, Sir Godfray Le Quesne, Q.C.
Sub-Treasurer, Capt. P. T. Sheehan, C.B.E., R.N.

THE MIDDLE TEMPLE, EC4Y 9AT

Treasurer, P. Boydell, Q.C.
Deputy Treasurer, A. L. Price, Q.C.

GRAY'S INN, WC1R 5EU

Treasurer, The Lord Wigoder, Q.C.
Under-Treasurer, Rear Adm. C. M. Bevan, C.B.

LINCOLN'S INN, WC2A 3TL

Treasurer, The Rt. Hon. Sir Edward Eveleigh, E.R.D.
Under-Treasurer, Capt. P. M. Carver, R.N.

COUNCIL OF LEGAL EDUCATION
Inns of Court School of Law, 4 Gray's Inn Place, WC1R 5DX

Established by the four Inns of Court to superintend the Education and Examination of Students for the Bar of England and Wales.
Chairman, The Hon. Mr. Justice Hobhouse.
Inns of Court School of Law, Dean, Mrs. M. A. Phillips.
Registrar, R. H. Vaughan.

FACULTY OF ADVOCATES
Advocates Library, Parliament House, Edinburgh EH1 1RF

Application for admission as an Advocate of the Scottish Bar is made by Petition to the Court of Session. The candidate is remitted for examination to the Faculty of Advocates. Enquiries should be addressed to The Clerk of Faculty.
Dean of Faculty, J. A. D. Hope, Q.C.
Clerk of Faculty, P. B. Cullen.

NORTHERN IRELAND

Admission to the Bar of Northern Ireland is controlled by the Honorable Society of the Inn of Court of Northern Ireland, Royal Courts of Justice, Belfast BT1 3JF.
Treasurer, The Hon. Mr. Justice Carswell.
Under-Treasurer, J. A. L. McLean, Q.C.

Solicitors

Qualifications for Solicitor are obtainable only from the Law Society or its equivalent in Scotland or Northern Ireland.

LAW SOCIETY OF ENGLAND AND WALES
113 Chancery Lane, WC2A 1PL

The Society controls the education and examination of articled clerks, and the admission of solicitors in England and Wales. It also regulates professional standards and conduct. Number of members, over 40,000.
President of the Society (1988–89), R. K. H. Gaskell.
Vice-President (1988–89), D. Ward.
Secretary-General, J. W. Hayes.

THE COLLEGE OF LAW, Braboeuf Manor, St. Catherine's, Guildford, Surrey GU3 1HA (and at 33–35 Lancaster Gate, W2 3LU; 2 Breams Buildings, Chancery Lane, EC4A 1DP; and Christleton Hall, Chester CH3 7AB), provides courses for The Law Society examinations.

LAW SOCIETY OF SCOTLAND
Law Society's Hall, 26 Drumsheugh Gardens, Edinburgh EH3 7YR

The Society comprises all practising and non-practising solicitors in Scotland. It controls the examination of legal trainees and the admission of solicitors in Scotland and acts as Registrar of solicitors under the Solicitors (Scotland) Act, 1980.
President of the Society (1988–89), Prof. J. R. Harper, C.B.E.
Secretary, K. W. Pritchard.
Secretary (Legal Education), P. S. B. Niven.

LAW SOCIETY OF NORTHERN IRELAND
Law Society House, 90–106 Victoria Street, Belfast BT1 3JZ

The Society controls the education, examination and admission of all solicitors in Northern Ireland.
Secretary, M. Davey.

LIBRARIANSHIP AND INFORMATION SCIENCE

First Degrees are granted by the University of Belfast (*Information Studies*), Loughborough (*Library Studies*), and the University of Wales (Aberystwyth) (*Librarianship* with another subject) (jointly with the College of Librarianship, Wales), and by the University of Strathclyde (*Information Science*).

Courses leading to first degrees in *Librarianship/Library Studies* or *Librarianship/Library Studies and Information Studies/Science* granted by the C.N.A.A. are provided by City of Birmingham Polytechnic, Brighton Polytechnic, Ealing College of Higher Education, Leeds Polytechnic, Liverpool Polytechnic, Manchester Polytechnic, Newcastle upon Tyne Polytechnic, Polytechnic of North London and Robert Gordon's Institute of Technology.

THE LIBRARY ASSOCIATION, 7 Ridgmount Street, WC1E 7AE, maintains the professional register of Chartered Members.—*Chief Exec.,* G. Cunningham.

MATERIALS STUDIES (including Metallurgy)

First Degrees in *Materials Science, Materials Technology, or Materials Science and Technology* are granted by the Universities of Bath, Birmingham, Brunel, Cambridge (*Metallurgy and Materials Science*), Leeds, Liverpool, London (Imperial College of Science and Technology, Queen Mary College), Manchester and Manchester Institute of Science and

Technology, Sheffield (*Science and Engineering of Metals*), Strathclyde (*Science of Engineering Materials*), Surrey and Wales (University College, Swansea. First Degrees in *Polymer Science and Engineering* are granted by London (Queen Mary College) Manchester Institute of Science and Technology (*Polymer Science and Technology*), and Sheffield. First Degrees in *Ceramics Science and Engineering* are granted by the Universities of Leeds and Sheffield; and in *Science and Engineering of Glasses* by the University of Sheffield. First Degrees in *Metallurgy* and/or *Metallurgical Engineering* are granted by the Universities of Birmingham (*Metallurgy/Materials Engineering*), Brunel, Cambridge (*Metallurgy and Materials Science*), Leeds, Liverpool (*Metallurgy and Materials Science*), Manchester and Manchester Institute of Science and Technology, Oxford (*Metallurgy and Science of Materials*), Salford (*Engineering Metallurgy*), Sheffield, Strathclyde and Surrey.

Courses leading to first degrees in *Materials Science/Technology* or *Metallurgy* or *Metallurgy and Materials* granted by the C.N.A.A. are provided by the City of London Polytechnic, Coventry (Lanchester) Polytechnic, Sheffield City Polytechnic (*Metallurgy and Microstructural Engineering*), Sunderland Polytechnic, Thames Polytechnic and Wolverhampton Polytechnic (*Materials and Manufacture*). Courses leading to first degrees in *Polymer Science and Technology* granted by the C.N.A.A. are provided by Manchester Polytechnic and the Polytechnic of North London; in *Mineral Process Engineering* by Camborne School of Mines; and in *Timber Technology* by Buckinghamshire College of Higher Education.

INSTITUTE OF METALS, 1 Carlton House Terrace SW1Y 5DB, is a qualifying body—*Sec.*, Dr. J. A. Catterall.

MATHEMATICS

First Degrees in *Mathematics* and/or *Applied Mathematics* are granted by all universities.

Courses leading to first degrees in *Mathematics* granted by the C.N.A.A. are provided by about 16 Polytechnics and Colleges.

MEDICINE

First Degrees in *Medicine and Surgery* are granted by the Universities of Aberdeen, Belfast, Birmingham, Bristol, Cambridge, Dundee, Edinburgh, Glasgow, Leeds, Leicester, Liverpool, London (medical schools/colleges:— Charing Cross and Westminster M.S., King's College S.M.D., London H.M.C., Royal Free H.M.S., St. Bart's. H.M.C., St. George's H.M.S., St. Mary's H.M.S., United M.D.S. (Guy's and St. Thomas's), University College and Middlesex S.M.), Manchester, Newcastle upon Tyne, Nottingham, Oxford, Sheffield, Southampton, and University of Wales College of Medicine.

Licensing Corporations granting Diplomas

ROYAL COLLEGE OF PHYSICIANS OF LONDON AND THE ROYAL COLLEGE OF SURGEONS OF ENGLAND, Examining Board in England, 35–43 Lincoln's Inn Fields, WC2A 3PN.—*President*, I. P. Todd; *Sec.*, R. S. Johnson-Gilbert, O.B.E.

SOCIETY OF APOTHECARIES OF LONDON, Black Friars Lane, EC4V 6EJ.—*Clerk*, Major J. C. O'Leary; *Registrar*, D. H. C. Barrie.

ROYAL COLLEGE OF OBSTETRICIANS AND GYNÆCOLOGISTS, 27 Sussex Place, Regent's Park, NW1 4RG.—*President*, G. Pinker, C.V.O.; *Sec.*, P. Barnett.

ROYAL COLLEGE OF PHYSICIANS OF EDINBURGH, 9 Queen Street, Edinburgh EH2 1JQ.—*President*, Prof. M. F. Oliver, C.B.E.; *Sec.*, Dr. J. L. Anderton.

ROYAL COLLEGE OF SURGEONS OF EDINBURGH, Nicolson Street, Edinburgh EH8 9DW.—*President*, Prof. G. D. Chisholm; *Sec.*, Dr A. G. D. Maran.

ROYAL COLLEGE OF PHYSICIANS AND SURGEONS OF GLASGOW, 234–243 St. Vincent Street, Glasgow G2 5RJ.—*President*, J. McArthur, *Hon. Sec.*, Dr. A. D. Beattie.

SCOTTISH TRIPLE QUALIFICATION BOARD, Nicolson Street, Edinburgh EH8 9DW and 242 St. Vincent Street, Glasgow.

Professions Supplementary to Medicine

The standard of professional education in chiropody, dietetics, medical laboratory sciences, occupational therapy, orthoptics, physiotherapy and radiography is the responsibility of seven professional boards, which also publish an annual register of qualified practitioners. The work of the Boards is co-ordinated by THE COUNCIL FOR PROFESSIONS SUPPLEMENTARY TO MEDICINE, Park House, 184 Kennington Park Road, SE11 4BU. *Registrar*, F. Whitehill.

BIOMEDICAL SCIENCES

First Degrees in *Biomedical Sciences* are granted by the Universities of Bradford, London (King's College), and Ulster.

Courses leading to first degrees in *Medical Laboratory Science* granted by the C.N.A.A. are provided by Portsmouth Polytechnic (*Biomedical Sciences*).

Qualifications from higher or further education establishments and training in medical laboratories are required for progress to the professional examinations and qualifications of the INSTITUTE OF MEDICAL LABORATORY SCIENCES, 12 Queen Anne Street, W1M 0AU.

CHIROPODY

Professional qualifications are granted by THE SOCIETY OF CHIROPODISTS, 53 Welbeck Street, W1M 7HE, to students who have passed the qualifying examination after attending a course of full-time training for three years at one of the ten recognized schools in England and Wales, two in Scotland and one in Northern Ireland. Qualifications granted by the Society are approved by the Chiropodists Board for the purpose of State Registration, which is a condition of employment within the National Health Service. *Gen. Sec.*, J. G. C. Trouncer.

DIETETICS
(*See* main heading, p. 461)

OCCUPATIONAL HYGIENE

Courses leading to first degrees in *Occupational Hygiene* granted by the C.N.A.A. are provided by the Polytechnic of the South Bank.

OCCUPATIONAL THERAPY

First Degrees in *Occupational Therapy* are granted by the University of Ulster.

Courses leading to first degrees in *Occupation Therapy* granted by the C.N.A.A. are provided by Queen Margaret College.

Professional qualifications are awarded by THE COLLEGE OF OCCUPATIONAL THERAPISTS, 20 Rede Place, W2 4TU, upon completion of one of the 19 training courses approved by the College.

ORTHOPTICS

First Degrees in *Orthoptics* are granted by the University of Wales (College of Medicine).

Orthoptists undertake the diagnosis and treatment of all types of squint and other anomalies of binocular vision, working in close collaboration with ophthalmologists. The training and maintenance of professional standards are the responsibility of the Orthoptists Board of the Council for the Professions Supplementary to Medicine. The examining and qualifying body is the BRITISH ORTHOPTIC SOCIETY, Tavistock House North, Tavistock Square, WC1H 9HX. Training consists of a three-year course at one of nine approved Orthoptic Schools in England and Wales and one in Scotland.

(*See also* main heading Ophthalmic Optics, p. 469)

PHYSIOTHERAPY

First Degrees are granted by the University of Ulster.

Courses leading to first degrees in *Physiotherapy* granted by the C.N.A.A. are provided by North East London Polytechnic, Queen Margaret College and the Queen's College.

Full-time three- or four-year degree or diploma courses are available at 32 recognised Schools in the U.K. Information about examinations leading to eligibility for Membership of The Chartered Society of Physiotherapy and to State Registration is available from THE CHARTERED SOCIETY OF PHYSIOTHERAPY, 14 Bedford Row, London WC1R 4ED.—*Sec.*, T. Simon.

RADIOGRAPHY AND RADIOTHERAPY

First Degrees in *Diagnostic Radiography* and *Therapeutic Radiography* are granted by the University of Wales (College of Medicine).

Examinations leading to qualification are conducted by THE COLLEGE OF RADIOGRAPHERS, 14 Upper Wimpole Street, W1M 8BN.

There are recognized training centres in radiography and radiotherapy at many cities and towns in England and Wales, Scotland and Northern Ireland.

METEOROLOGY

First Degrees in *Meteorology* are granted by the University of Reading. The subject is also included in degree courses at some other universities.

MINING AND MINING ENGINEERING

First Degrees in *Mining* or *Mining Engineering* are granted by the following universities: Leeds (also *Mineral Engineering*), London (Imperial College of Science and Technology), Newcastle upon Tyne, Nottingham, Strathclyde (*Mining and Petroleum Engineering*), Wales (University College, Cardiff, also *Mineral Processing*).

Courses leading to first degrees granted by the C.N.A.A. are provided by Camborne School of Mines (*Mining Engineering* and *Mineral Processing Engineering*) and North Staffordshire Polytechnic (*Mining Engineering*).

Miscellaneous Authorities

ENGINEERING COUNCIL, 10 Maltravers Street, WC2R 3ER.

INSTITUTION OF MINING ENGINEERS, Danum House, 6A South Parade, Doncaster DN1 2DY—*Sec.*, W. J. W. Bourne.

MUSIC

First Degrees in *Music* are granted by the Universities of Aberdeen (also *History of Music*), Belfast, Birmingham, Bristol, Cambridge, the City University, the Universities of Durham, East Anglia, Edinburgh, Exeter, Glasgow (also *Music Education* and *Music Performance* in conjunction with Royal Scottish Academy of Music and Drama), Hull, Lancaster, Leeds (also at Bretton Hall College), Leicester (*Musicianship*), Liverpool, London (King's College, Royal Holloway and Bedford New College; *also* Goldsmiths' College, Royal Academy of Music, Royal College of Music, and Trinity College of Music), Manchester, Newcastle upon Tyne, Nottingham, Oxford, Reading, Sheffield, Southampton, Surrey (*Academic & Practical Applications of Music*; *Music & Sound Recording (Tonmeister)*), Sussex, Ulster, Wales (University Colleges at Aberystwyth, Bangor and Cardiff; also at Welsh College of Music and Drama), and York.

Courses leading to first degrees in Music granted by the C.N.A.A. are provided by Bath College of Higher Education, Cambridgeshire College of Arts and Technology, City of Birmingham Polytechnic, Colchester Institute, Dartington College of Arts, Huddersfield Polytechnic and Kingston Polytechnic (*Music Education*).

ASSOCIATED BOARD OF THE ROYAL SCHOOLS OF MUSIC, 14 Bedford Square, WC1B 3JG.—Conducts the local examinations in centres throughout the world in music and speech for the Royal Academy of Music and the Royal College of Music in London, the Royal Northern College of Music, Manchester and the Royal Scottish Academy of Music and Drama, Glasgow.

Chief Exec. and Dir. of Examinations, R. Smith.

ROYAL ACADEMY OF MUSIC, Marylebone Road, NW1 5HT.—*Principal*, Sir David Lumsden, D.Phil.

ROYAL COLLEGE OF MUSIC, Prince Consort Road, South Kensington, SW7 2BS.—*Director*, M. G. Matthews.

ROYAL NORTHERN COLLEGE OF MUSIC, 124 Oxford Road, Manchester M13 9RD.—*Principal*, J. Manduell, C.B.E.

ROYAL SCOTTISH ACADEMY OF MUSIC AND DRAMA, 100 Renfrew Street, Glasgow G2 3BD.—*Principal*, P. Ledger, C.B.E.

ROYAL COLLEGE OF ORGANISTS, Kensington Gore, SW7 2QS.—*Clerk*, K. B. Lyndon.

GUILDHALL SCHOOL OF MUSIC AND DRAMA, Barbican, EC2Y 8DT.—*Principal*, I. Horsbrugh.

LONDON COLLEGE OF MUSIC, 47 Great Marlborough Street, W1V 2AS.—*Director*, J. McCabe, C.B.E.

TRINITY COLLEGE OF MUSIC, 11–13 Mandeville Place, W1M 6AQ.—*Principal*, P. Jones, C.B.E.

NAUTICAL STUDIES

(*See also* Marine Engineering, Fishery Science)

The University of Wales grants first degrees in *Maritime Studies, Maritime Commerce* and *Maritime Geography* (courses at Institute of Science and Technology).

Courses leading to first degrees in *Nautical Studies* granted by the C.N.A.A. are provided by Liverpool Polytechnic (*Maritime Studies*), Plymouth Polytechnic and Sunderland Polytechnic.

Merchant Navy Training Schools
For Officers

MERCHANT NAVY COLLEGE, Greenhithe, Kent DA9 9NY.—*Principal*, G. Emmons, Ph.D.

THE COLLEGE OF MARITIME STUDIES, Warsash, Southampton SO3 6ZL. *Dean*, Capt. M. Longman.

For Seamen

INDEFATIGABLE AND NATIONAL SEA TRAINING SCHOOL FOR BOYS, Plas Llanfair, Llanfairpwll, Anglesey.—*Captain Headmaster*, Capt. T. R. Beggs.

NATIONAL SEA TRAINING COLLEGE, Denton, Gravesend, Kent DA12 2HR.—*Princ.*, Capt. C. G. W. Hunter.

NURSING

Courses in which academic study leading to a degree at a University may be combined with nursing training/practical nursing in hospitals are provided by the University of Brunel (*Mental Nursing*), the City University, the Universities of Edinburgh, Glasgow, Hull, Liverpool, London (King's College), Manchester, Southampton, Surrey, Ulster and Wales (College of Medicine).

Courses leading to first degrees in *Nursing* granted by the C.N.A.A. are provided by Bristol Polytechnic, Dundee College of Technology, Glasgow College of Technology, Leeds Polytechnic, Queen Margaret College, Sheffield City Polytechnic and Polytechnic of the South Bank.

Three-year courses for State Registration in general, sick children's mental and mental deficiency nursing. Two-year course for State enrolment. Training schools in many parts of Great Britain.

THE ROYAL COLLEGE OF NURSING
OF THE UNITED KINGDOM
20 Cavendish Square, W1M 0AB

The Royal College of Nursing, within its Institute of Advanced Nursing Education, provides education at post-basic level in hospital, occupational health and community health fields. Advanced courses are held in preparation for senior posts in management and teaching; and other short and special courses.
Director of Education and Principal of the Institute of Advanced Nursing Education, Miss M. D. Green, O.B.E.

ENGLISH NATIONAL BOARD FOR NURSING, MIDWIFERY AND HEALTH VISITING, 170 Tottenham Court Road, W1P 0HA.—*Chief Exec. Officer*, D. Jones, O.B.E.

NATIONAL BOARD FOR NURSING, MIDWIFERY AND HEALTH VISITING FOR SCOTLAND, 22 Queen Street, Edinburgh EH2 1JX.—*Chief Exec. Officer.*, Mrs. E. C. Mitchell.

WELSH NATIONAL BOARD FOR NURSING, MIDWIFERY AND HEALTH VISITING, Floor 13, Pearl Assurance House, Greyfriars Road, Cardiff CF1 3AG.—*Chief Exec.*, D. A. Ravey.

NATIONAL BOARD FOR NURSING, MIDWIFERY AND HEALTH VISITING FOR NORTHERN IRELAND, R.A.C. House, 79 Chichester Street, Belfast BT1 4JE.—*Chief Exec. Officer*, J. J. Walsh.

OPHTHALMIC OPTICS

First Degrees in *Ophthalmic Optics* or *Optometry* are granted by the Universities of Aston, Bradford, the City University, Manchester (Manchester Institute of Science and Technology), and Wales (Institute of Science and Technology).

Courses leading to first degrees in *Ophthalmic Optics* granted by the C.N.A.A. are provided by the Glasgow College of Technology.

THE BRITISH COLLEGE OF OPTOMETRISTS, 10 Knaresborough Place, SW5 0TG, grants qualifications as an optometrist.—*Gen. Sec.*, T. H. Collingridge.

THE ASSOCIATION OF BRITISH DISPENSING OPTICIANS, 22 Nottingham Place, W1M 4AT, grants qualifications as a dispensing optician.—*Sec.*, J. W. Roskill.

PHARMACY

First Degrees in *Pharmacy* are granted by the Universities of Aston, Bath, Belfast, Bradford, London (King's College and the School of Pharmacy), Manchester, Nottingham, Strathclyde, Wales (Institute of Science and Technology).

Courses leading to first degrees in Pharmacy granted by the C.N.A.A. are provided by Brighton Polytechnic, Leicester Polytechnic, Liverpool Polytechnic, Portsmouth Polytechnic, Robert Gordon's Institute of Technology, and Sunderland Polytechnic.

Information may be obtained from The Secretary and Registrar, ROYAL PHARMACEUTICAL SOCIETY OF GREAT BRITAIN, 1 Lambeth High Street, SE1 7JN. *Sec. and Registrar*, J. Ferguson.

PHOTOGRAPHY, FILM AND TV STUDIES

First Degrees are awarded by the Universities of Glasgow (*Drama/Film & TV Studies*), Kent (*Drama/Film Studies*), Stirling (*Film and Media Studies*), and Wales (College of Medicine, *Medical Photography* (provisional)). At some other universities *Film* may be studied as part of a first degree course.

Courses leading to first degrees granted by the C.N.A.A. are provided by Derbyshire College of Higher Education (*Photographic Studies*), Harrow College of Higher Education/Middlesex Polytechnic (*Applied Photography, Film and TV*), London College of Printing (*Photography*), Napier College of Commerce and Technology (*Photographic Studies*), Polytechnic of Central London (*Film, Video and Photographic Arts* and *Photographic Sciences*), Trent Polytechnic (*Photography*), West Surrey College of Art and Design (*Photography, Film and Video, Animation*).

BRITISH INSTITUTE OF PROFESSIONAL PHOTOGRAPHY, Amwell End, Ware, Herts. SG12 9HN.—*Secretary*, R. C. Reece.

PRINTING

First Degrees in *Typography and Graphic Communication* are awarded by the University of Reading.

Courses leading to first degrees in *Printing and Packaging Technology* granted by the C.N.A.A. are provided by Watford College of Technology.

Courses in technical and general, design and administrative aspects of printing are available at technical colleges throughout the United Kingdom. Details can be obtained from the Institute of Printing and the British Printing Industries Federation (*see below*).

In addition to the examining and organizing bodies listed below, examinations are held by various independent regional examining boards in further education.

INSTITUTE OF PRINTING, 8 Lonsdale Gardens, Tunbridge Wells, Kent TN1 1NU.—*Sec.*, C. F. Partridge.
BRITISH PRINTING INDUSTRIES FEDERATION, 11 Bedford Row, WC1R 4DX.—*Sec.*, D. Burch.

RECREATION, SPORT, AND HUMAN MOVEMENT STUDIES

(*See also* Dance)

First Degrees are granted by the University of Birmingham (*Sport and Recreation Studies*), Glasgow (*Physical Education and Sports Science*), Liverpool

(*Physical Education and Movement Science*), Loughborough (*Physical Education and Sports Science*; also *Physical Education, Sports Science and Recreation Management*) and Ulster (*Sport and Leisure Studies*). *Physical Education* may be studied as part of other first degree courses at several universities.

Courses in *Sports Science/Studies* leading to first degrees granted by the C.N.A.A. are provided by Bedford College of Higher Education, Brighton Polytechnic, Crewe and Alsager College of Higher Education, Dunfermline College of Physical Education, Jordanhill College of Education (*Sport in the Community* and *Physical Education and Human Movement*), Liverpool Polytechnic, Newcastle upon Tyne Polytechnic with Sunderland Polytechnic, North Staffordshire Polytechnic (*Sport and Recreation Studies*), Sheffield City Polytechnic, Trent Polytechnic (*Sport—Administration and Science*) and West Sussex Institute of Higher Education.

First Degrees in *Recreation and Environment* are granted by the University of Manchester (courses at North Cheshire College), in *Recreation Management* by the University of Loughborough; and in *Recreation* by the C.N.A.A. with courses at Dunfermline College of Physical Education, Leeds Polytechnic (*Leisure Studies*), North Staffordshire Polytechnic (*Sport and Recreation Studies*), and College of St. Mark and St. John (*Recreation and Community*), and in *Tourism* with courses at Dorset Institute of Higher Education and (*Travel and Tourism*) Newcastle upon Tyne Polytechnic.

First degrees in *Human Movement Studies* are granted by the University of Wales (courses at South Glamorgan Institute of Higher Education) and by the C.N.A.A. (courses at Leeds Polytechnic).

Physical Education and *Sports Science/Studies* also form part of a degree course at many other colleges/polytechnics.

ROBOTICS

(*See also* Computer Science)

First Degrees in *Electronic Control and Robot Engineering* are granted by the University of Hull.

SOCIAL WORK

First Degrees in *Social Studies* or in *Social Sciences* are granted by most universities. Courses leading to first degrees in *Social Science* or *Social Sciences/Applied Social Science or Sociology* granted by the C.N.A.A. are provided by some 30 polytechnics and colleges.

CENTRAL COUNCIL FOR EDUCATION AND TRAINING IN SOCIAL WORK, Derbyshire House, St. Chad's Street, London WC1H 8AD.—*Dir.*, A. Hall. The Council validates and approves courses, schemes and programmes leading to the C.C.E.T.S.W.'s awards, including the Certificate of Qualification in Social Work and the Certificate in Social Service.

SPEECH SCIENCE

(*See also* Languages)

First Degrees in *Speech* are awarded by the University of Newcastle upon Tyne; in *Speech Science* by the University of Sheffield; in *Speech Sciences* by the University of London (University College); in *Speech Pathology* by the University of Manchester; in *Speech Pathology and Therapeutics* (with courses at Jordanhill College of Education) by the University of Glasgow; and in *Speech Therapy* by the Universities of Manchester and Ulster and

(with courses at South Glamorgan Institute of Higher Education) by the University of Wales. First Degrees in *Clinical Communication Studies* are granted by the City University.

Courses leading to first degrees in *Speech Therapy* granted by the C.N.A.A. are provided by Central School of Speech and Drama, City of Birmingham Polytechnic (*Speech and Language Pathology and Therapeutics*), Leeds Polytechnic (*Clinical Language Sciences*), Leicester Polytechnic (*Speech Pathology and Therapy*), Manchester Polytechnic (*Speech Pathology and Therapy*) and Queen Margaret College (*Speech Pathology and Therapy*).

The Directory of qualified Speech Therapists is published biennially by THE COLLEGE OF SPEECH THERAPISTS, Harold Poster House, 6 Lechmere Road, NW2 5BU. Details of courses leading to certification by The College of Speech Therapists are available from the College, which also sponsors advanced clinical courses.

SURVEYING

(*See* Estate Management and Surveying)

TEACHING

There are two main ways to gain the qualification needed to become a teacher:

(a) The first is to follow a three- or four-year course leading to a B.Ed. degree. B.Ed. courses are provided by colleges of education/institutes of higher education/polytechnics. The degrees are awarded either by universities or by the C.N.A.A.

(b) The second, for those who are already graduates with a degree other than a B.Ed., is to follow a one-year course leading to a postgraduate certificate in education at a college, polytechnic or university.

There is, in addition, a third route which is to take a course at one of the few institutions, mainly universities, that offer concurrent courses (normally four years) leading to a degree (other than B.Ed.) *and* a teaching qualification.

Special arrangements exist for those wishing to teach craft design and technology.

TECHNICAL EDUCATION

First Degrees in one or more technologies are awarded by almost all universities; and many polytechnics and colleges of technology provide courses leading to first degrees granted by the C.N.A.A. Details are given under individual subject headings.

CITY AND GUILDS OF LONDON INSTITUTE
76 Portland Place, W1N 4AA

The Institute offers examinations on its published regulations and syllabuses, and awards certificates of pre-vocational and vocational training in a wide range of technical subjects. The Institute provides the administrative services for the National Examinations Board for Supervisory Studies and the National Examinations Board for Agriculture, Horticulture and Allied Industries. With the Business and Technician Education Council (*see* page 460), it has established the Joint Board for Pre-Vocational Education.

President, H.R.H. the Duke of Edinburgh, K.G., K.T.
Chairman, H. M. Neal.
Director-General, J. A. Barnes.
Secretary, S. J. Westacott.

Regional Advisory Councils for Further Education

The Councils issue handbooks, etc., giving information about the facilities available within a region or district for various types of technical, commercial, agricultural, art and other further education. They also have certain responsibilities in connection with the procedure for the approval by the Department of Education and Science of advanced courses.

EAST ANGLIAN REGIONAL ADVISORY COUNCIL FOR FURTHER EDUCATION, 2 Looms Lane, Bury St. Edmunds, Suffolk IP33 1HE.—*Sec.*, D. J. Lock.

EAST MIDLAND FURTHER EDUCATION COUNCIL, Robins Wood House, Robins Wood Road, Aspley, Nottingham NG8 3NH.—*Sec.*, R. Ainscough.

LONDON AND SOUTH EASTERN REGIONAL ADVISORY COUNCIL FOR FURTHER EDUCATION, Tavistock House South, Tavistock Square, WC1H 9LR.—*Dir.*, J. D. S. MacDougall.

NORTH WESTERN REGIONAL ADVISORY COUNCIL FOR FURTHER EDUCATION, Town Hall, Walkden Road, Worsley, Manchester M28 4QE.—*Sec.*, D. W. Brown.

NORTHERN COUNCIL FOR FURTHER EDUCATION, 5 Grosvenor Villas, Grosvenor Road, Newcastle upon Tyne NE2 2RU.—*Sec.*, J. F. Pearce.

SOUTHERN REGIONAL COUNCIL FOR FURTHER EDUCATION, 26 Bath Road, Reading RG1 6NT.—*Sec.*, T. A. Connor.

SOUTH WEST REGIONAL COUNCIL FOR FURTHER EDUCATION, Wessex Lodge, 11–13 Billetfield, Taunton TA1 3NN.—*Sec.*, F. S. Fisher.

WELSH JOINT EDUCATION COMMITTEE, 245 Western Avenue, Cardiff CF5 2YX.—*Sec.*, M. Lloyd Jones.

WEST MIDLANDS ADVISORY COUNCIL FOR FURTHER EDUCATION, Norfolk House, Smallbrook Queensway, Birmingham B5 4NB.

YORKSHIRE AND HUMBERSIDE ASSOCIATION FOR FURTHER AND HIGHER EDUCATION, Bowling Green Terrace, Leeds LS11 9SX.

Industry Training Boards

AGRICULTURAL, Summit House, Glebe Way, West Wickham, Kent BR4 0RF.—*Dir.*, D. C. Newman.

CLOTHING AND ALLIED PRODUCTS, Richardshaw Lane, Pudsey, Leeds LS28 6BN.—*Chief Exec.*, J. W. Dearden.

CONSTRUCTION, Dewhurst House, 24 West Smithfield, EC1A 9JA.—*Sec.*, J. A. Reynolds, O.B.E.

ENGINEERING, 54 Clarendon Road, Watford, Herts. WD1 1LB.—*Sec.*, E. P. Jones.

HOTEL AND CATERING, International House, High Street, Ealing, W5 5DB.—*Sec.*, W. A. Heaney.

LOCAL GOVERNMENT TRAINING BOARD, Arndale House, Arndale Centre, Luton, Beds. LU1 2TS.—*Dir.*, M. G. Clarke.

MAN-MADE FIBRES INDUSTRY TRAINING ADVISORY BOARD, Gable House, 40 High Street, Rickmansworth, Herts. WD3 1ER.—*Sec.*, P. Grice.

OFFSHORE PETROLEUM, Offshore Training Centre, Forties Road, Montrose, Angus DD10 9ET.—*Sec.*, P. J. Bing, O.B.E.

PLASTICS PROCESSING, Coppice House, Halesfield 7, Telford, Shropshire, TF7 4NA.—*Chief Exec.*, J. C. Shearman.

ROAD TRANSPORT, Capitol House, Empire Way, Wembley, Middx. HA9 0NG.—*Dir. Gen.*, D. C. Barnett.

TEXTILES

First Degrees in *Textiles* are awarded by the Universities of Leeds and Manchester (Manchester Institute of Science and Technology, *Textile Technology* and *Clothing Engineering*).

Courses leading to first degrees in *Textile Marketing* granted by the C.N.A.A. are provided by Huddersfield Polytechnic; in *Textile and Knitwear Technology* by Leicester Polytechnic; in *Textiles with Clothing Studies* by Scottish College of Textiles; in *Clothing Studies* by Manchester Polytechnic; in *Food, Textiles and Consumer Studies* by Polytechnic of the South Bank and Robert Gordon's Institute of Technology, and in various aspects of *Textiles/Fashion* by some 20 Polytechnics and Colleges.

THE TEXTILE INSTITUTE, 10 Blackfriars Street, Manchester M3 5DR.—*Gen. Sec.*, R. G. Denyer.

THEOLOGY

First Degrees in *Theology* or *Divinity* are granted by the Universities of Aberdeen, Belfast, Birmingham, Bristol (*Theology and Religious Studies*), Cambridge (*Theological and Religious Studies*), Durham, Edinburgh, Exeter, Glasgow, Hull, Kent, Leeds (*Theology and Religious Studies*), London (Heythrop and King's Colleges), Manchester (*Theology and Religious Studies*), Nottingham, Oxford, St. Andrews, Southampton (at La Sainte Union College of Higher Education), and Wales (Aberystwyth, Bangor, Cardiff, and, also *Theology and Religious Studies*, St. David's University Colleges); in *Biblical Studies* by the Universities of Belfast, London (Heythrop and King's Colleges), Manchester, Sheffield and Wales (Bangor University College); and in *Religious Studies* by the Universities of Bristol (*Theology and Religious Studies*), Cambridge (*Theological and Religious Studies*), Edinburgh, Lancaster, Leeds (*Theology and Religious Studies*), London (King's College), Manchester (*Theology and Religious Studies* and *Comparative Religion*), Newcastle upon Tyne, Stirling, and Wales (University Colleges, Bangor, Cardiff and St. David's University College).

Courses leading to first degrees in *Theology* or *Theological Studies* granted by the C.N.A.A. are provided by London Bible College, Spurgeon's College, Thames Polytechnic, Trinity College, Bristol and Westminster College, Oxford; in *Theological and Pastoral Studies* by Oak Hill College; and in *Jewish Studies* by Jews' College.

Theological Colleges

Church of England and Church in Wales

CHICHESTER THEOLOGICAL COLLEGE, Chichester, W. Sussex PO19 1SG. (56).—*Princ.*, Rev. Canon J. Hind.

CRANMER HALL, St. John's College, Durham DH1 3RJ. (80).—*Warden*, Rev. I. P. M. Cundy.

LINCOLN THEOLOGICAL COLLEGE, Drury Lane, Lincoln LN1 3BP. (70).—*Princ.*, Rev. Canon W. M. Jacob, PH.D.

OAK HILL COLLEGE, Chase Side, Southgate, N14 4PS. (105).—*Princ.*, Rev. G. Bridger.

COLLEGE OF THE RESURRECTION, Mirfield, W. Yorks. WF14 0BW. (43).—*Princ.*, Rev. Fr. D. Lloyd.

RIDLEY HALL, Cambridge CB3 9HG. (62).—*Princ.*, Rev. Canon H. F. de Waal.

RIPON COLLEGE, Cuddesdon, Oxford OX9 9EX. (70).—*Princ.*, Rev. Canon J. H. Garton.

ST. DEINIOL'S LIBRARY, Hawarden, Deeside, Clwyd CH5 3DF.—*Princ.*, Rev. P. J. Jagger.

ST. JOHN'S COLLEGE, Bramcote, Nottingham NG9 3DS. (120).—*Princ.*, Rev. Dr. J. Goldingay.

ST. MICHAEL'S THEOLOGICAL COLLEGE, Llandaff, Cardiff CF5 2YJ. (40).—*Warden*, Rev. J. H. L. Rowlands.

ST. STEPHEN'S HOUSE, 16 Marston Street, Oxford OX4 1JX. (55).—*Princ.*, Rev. E. R. Barnes.

SALISBURY AND WELLS THEOLOGICAL COLLEGE, 19 The Close, Salisbury, Wilts. SP1 2EE. (73).—*Princ.*, Rev. P. A. Crowe.

TRINITY COLLEGE, Stoke Hill, Bristol BS9 1JP. (141).—*Princ.*, Rev. D. Gillett.
WESTCOTT HOUSE, Jesus Lane, Cambridge CB5 8BP. (50).—*Princ.*, Rev. Dr. R. W. N. Hoare.
WYCLIFFE HALL, 54 Banbury Road, Oxford OX2 6PW. (90).—*Princ.*, Dr. R. T. France.

Scottish Episcopal Church

THEOLOGICAL COLLEGE, Rosebery Avenue, Edinburgh EH12 5JT. (24).—*Princ.*, Rev. Canon J. M. Armson.

Church of Scotland

CHRIST'S COLLEGE, Aberdeen AB11YD. (80).—*Master*, Rev. H. R. Sefton, PH.D.
NEW COLLEGE, Mound Place, Edinburgh EH1 2LU. (270).—*Princ.*, Rev. Prof. D. B. Forrester.
TRINITY COLLEGE, 4 The Square, University of Glasgow, GL12 8QQ. (160).—*Princ.*, Rev. Prof. R. Davidson, D.D.

Presbyterian Church of Wales

UNITED THEOLOGICAL COLLEGE, Aberystwyth SY23 2LT. (42).—*Princ.*, Rev. Prof. E. ap Nefydd Roberts.

Presbyterian

UNION THEOLOGICAL COLLEGE, Belfast BT7 1JT. (96).—*Princ.*, R. F. G. Holmes.

Methodist

EDGHILL THEOLOGICAL COLLEGE CHRISTIAN EDUCATION CENTRE, 9 Lennoxvale, Belfast BT9 5BY. (102).—*Princ.*, W. D. D. Cooke, PH.D.
WESLEY COLLEGE, Westbury-on-Trym, Bristol BS10 7QD. (70).—*Princ.*, Dr. H. McKeating.
WESLEY HOUSE, Cambridge. (33).—*Princ.*, Rev. Dr. I. H. Jones.

Baptist

BRISTOL BAPTIST COLLEGE, Woodland Road, Bristol BS8 1UN. (40).—*Princ.*, Rev. Dr. J. E. Morgan-Wynne.
NORTHERN BAPTIST COLLEGE, Brighton Grove, Rusholme, Manchester M14 5JP. (44).—*Princ.*, Rev. Dr. B. Haymes.
NORTH WALES BAPTIST COLLEGE, Ffordd Ffriddoedd, Bangor, Gwynedd LL57 2EH. (8).—*Princ.*, Rev. J. R. Rowlands.
REGENT'S PARK COLLEGE, Oxford OX1 2LB. (76).—*Princ.*, Rev. B. R. White, D.Phil.
THE SCOTTISH BAPTIST COLLEGE, 12 Aytoun Road, Glasgow G41 5RT. (19).—*Princ.*, Rev. I. J. N. Oakley, PH.D.
SOUTH WALES BAPTIST COLLEGE, 54 Richmond Road, Cardiff CF2 3UR. (20).—*Princ.*, Rev. N. Clark.
SPURGEON'S COLLEGE, South Norwood Hill, SE25 6DJ. (70).—*Princ.*, P. Beasley-Murray, PH.D.

Congregational and United Reformed

BALA-BANGOR INDEPENDENT COLLEGE, Bangor LL57 2EH. (15).—*Princ.*, R. T. Jones, D.Phil., D.D.
MANSFIELD COLLEGE, Oxford. (160).—*Princ.*, Rev. J. L. Womer.
MEMORIAL COLLEGE, Aberystwyth. (20).—*Princ.*, Rev. Dr. D. E. Davies.
NORTHERN COLLEGE, Luther King House, Brighton Grove, Rusholme, Manchester M14 5JP. (44).—*Princ.*, Rev. Dr. R. J. McKelvey.
SCOTTISH CONGREGATIONAL COLLEGE, Rosebery Crescent, Edinburgh EH12 5YN. (19).—*Princ.*, Rev. H. Smith.
WESTMINSTER COLLEGE, Madingley Road, Cambridge CB3 0AA. (42).—*Princ.*, Rev. M. H. Cressey.

Unitarian

UNITARIAN COLLEGE, Luther King House, Brighton Grove, Rusholme, Manchester M14 5JP. (4).—*Tutor-in-Charge*, Rev. L. Smith.

Interdenominational

QUEEN'S COLLEGE, Somerset Road, Edgbaston, Birmingham B15 2QH. (75).—*Princ.*, Rev. Dr. J. B. Walker.

Non-Denominational

COLLEGE OF ST. MARY, The University, St. Andrews KY16 9JU. (150).—*Princ.*, Rev. Prof. D. W. D. Shaw.

Roman Catholic

ALLEN HALL COLLEGE, 28 Beaufort Street, SW3 5AA. (80).—*Rector*, Mgr. P. O'Donoghue.
CAMPION HOUSE COLLEGE, 112 Thornbury Road, Osterley, Middx. TW7 4NN. (50).—*Princ.*, Rev. M. Barrow, S.J.
CHESTERS COLLEGE, 2 Chesters Road, Bearsden, Glasgow. (50).—*Rector*, Very Rev. P. Tartaglia.
OSCOTT COLLEGE, Chester Road, Sutton Coldfield, W. Midlands B73 5AA. (76).—*Rector*, Rt. Rev. Mgr. M. J. Kirkham.
ST. JOHN'S SEMINARY, Wonersh, Guildford, Surrey GU5 0QX. (90).—*Rector*, Rt. Rev. Mgr. P. Smith.
ST. JOSEPH'S UPHOLLAND NORTHERN INSTITUTE FOR ADULT CHRISTIAN EDUCATION, Upholland, Skelmersdale, Lancs. WN8 0PZ.—*Princ.*, Mgr. J. Butchard.
USHAW COLLEGE, Durham DH7 9RH. (140).—*Princ.*, Mgr. Canon P. Walton.

Jewish

JEWS' COLLEGE, Albert Road, Hendon, NW4 2SJ. (75).—*Princ.*, Rabbi Dr. J. Sacks.
LEO BAECK COLLEGE, The Manor House, 80 East End Road, N3 2SY (20).—*Princ.* Rabbi Dr. J. Magonet.

TOWN AND COUNTRY PLANNING

First Degrees are granted by the Universities of Belfast (*Environmental Planning*), Dundee (*Town and Regional Planning*), East Anglia (*Development Studies—Regional Analysis & Planning*), Glasgow (*Planning*), Heriot-Watt (*Town Planning*), Kent (*Urban Studies*), London (University College, *Environmental Studies* and *Planning*), Manchester (*Town and Country Planning*), Newcastle upon Tyne (*Town and Country Planning*), Sheffield (*Urban Studies*), Stirling (*Urban Studies and Social Policy*), Strathclyde (*Planning*), Sussex (*Urban Studies*), and Wales (Institute of Science and Technology, *Town Planning Studies*).

Courses leading to first degrees in *Town Planning* granted by the C.N.A.A. are provided by City of Birmingham Polytechnic, Leeds Polytechnic and Polytechnic of the South Bank; in *Town and Country Planning* by Bristol Polytechnic; in *Planning Studies* by Oxford Polytechnic; in *Environmental Planning* by Essex Institute of Higher Education; in *Urban Planning Studies* by the Polytechnic of Central London; and in *Urban and Regional Planning* by Coventry (Lanchester) Polytechnic.

The ROYAL TOWN PLANNING INSTITUTE, 26 Portland Place, W1N 4BE, recognizes a number of degree and diploma courses in town planning.

TRANSPORT

First Degrees are granted by the Universities of Aston (*Transport Management*), Loughborough (*Transport Management and Planning*), Wales (*Institute of Science and Technology: International Transport*) and Ulster (*Transport Technology*). The City University awards a first degree in *Air Transport Engineering*.

Courses leading to first degrees granted by the C.N.A.A. are provided by Coventry (Lanchester) Polytechnic (*Industrial Design—Transportation*), Huddersfield Polytechnic (*Transport and Distribution*) and Napier College of Commerce and Technology (*Transportation Engineering*).

THE CHARTERED INSTITUTE OF TRANSPORT, 80 Portland Place, London W1N 4DP, conducts qualifying examinations in transport management leading to chartered professional status. *Dir. Gen.,* J. C. F. Cameron.

VETERINARY STUDIES

First Degrees in *Veterinary Science/Medicine and Surgery* are granted by the Universities of Bristol, Cambridge, Edinburgh, Glasgow, Liverpool and London (Royal Veterinary College).

INDEPENDENT SCHOOLS

The following pages list those independent schools whose Head is a member of the Headmasters' Conference, the Society of Headmasters of Independent Schools or the Girls Schools Association.

THE HEADMASTERS' CONFERENCE

Chairman (1988), D. A. G. Smith (Bradford G.S.); *Sec.*, T. P. Snape, Chancery House, 107 St. Paul's Road, N1 2NB; *Deputy-Sec.*, R. N. P. Griffiths. The annual meetings are, as a rule, held at the end of September.

In considering applications for election to membership the Committee will have regard to the scheme or other instrument under which the school is administered (taking particularly into consideration the degree of independence enjoyed by the Headmaster and the Governing Body); the number of pupils over thirteen years of age in the school and the number of pupils in proportion to the size of the school who are in the sixth form, i.e. engaged on studies at the Advanced Level of the General Certificate of Education.

The Headmasters of some schools which do not meet the criteria for membership are by invitation additional members of the H.M.C. These include the following: Cavendish School; Devizes School; Easingwold School; High Wycombe Royal Grammar School; London Oratory School; Oxford Upper School; Prescot School; Richmond School; Royal Grammar School, Lancaster; Royal High School, Edinburgh; Sexey's School, Bruton; St. Bartholomew's School; Tiffin School; Verulam School; Watford Grammar School; Westcliffe High School.

Name of School	F'ded.	No. of Pupils	Annual Fees		Headmaster *(With date of Appointment)*
			B'ding	Day	
England and Wales					
Abbotsholme School, Staffs.	1889	260‡	£6,300	£4,200	D. J. Farrant (1984)
Abingdon School, Oxon.	1256	732	£5,832	£2,916	M. St. J. Parker (1975)
Aldenham School, Herts............	1597	350†	£7,290	£4,590	M. Higginbottom (1983)
Alleyn's School, SE22	1619	920‡	....	£3,240	D. A. Fenner (1976)
Allhallows School, Dorset	1515	305‡	£7,188	£3,594	P. S. Larkman, L.V.O. (1983)
Ampleforth College (*R.C.*), Yorks. ...	1802	700	£6,240	....	Rev. D. L. Milroy, O.S.B. (1980)
Ardingly College, W. Sussex*	1858	470‡	£7,040	£5,490	J. W. Flecker (1980)
Arnold School, Blackpool	1896	770‡	£4,368	£2,187	J. A. B. Kelsall (1987)
Ashville College, Harrogate	1877	450‡	£5,355	£2,910	M. H. Crosby (1987)
Bancroft's School, Essex	1727	700‡	....	£3,150	Dr. P. C. D. Southern (1985)
Barnard Castle School, Co. Durham .	1883	500†	£4,326	£2,316	F. S. McNamara (1980)
Bedales School, Hants.	1893	386‡	£6,825	£4,800	E. A. M. MacAlpine (1981)
Bedford School......................	1552	750	£6,174	£3,600	M. E. Barlen (1988)
Bedford Modern School	1566	950	£4,593	£2,508	P. J. Squire (1977)
Berkhamsted School, Herts.	1541	678	£5,772	£3,300	C. J. Driver (1983)
Birkenhead School, Merseyside.....	1860	720	....	£2,025	S. J. Haggett (1988)
Bishop's Stortford College, Herts. ...	1868	356†	£6,078	£4,317	S. G. G. Benson (1984)
Bloxham School, Oxon.*	1860	360†	£6,660	£4,440	M. W. Vallance (1982)
Blundell's School, Devon	1604	485†	£7,050	£4,290	A. J. D. Rees (1980)
Bolton School......................	1524	1000	....	£2,388	A. W. Wright (1983)
Bootham School, York.	1823	316‡	£5,697	£3,897	I. M. Small (1988)
Bradfield College, Berks.	1850	510†	£7,350	£5,510	P. B. Smith (1985)
Bradford Grammar School	1662	1040†	....	£2,298	D. A. G. Smith (1974)
Brentwood School, Essex...........	1557	809°†	£4,821°	£2,775°	J. A. E. Evans (1981)
Brighton College, E. Sussex	1845	475‡	£5,610	£3,645	J. D. Leach (1987)
Bristol Cathedral School	1542	459†	....	£2,241	C. S. Martin (1979)
Bristol Grammar School	1532	982°‡	....	£2,134°	C. E. Martin (1986)
Bromsgrove School, Worcs...........	1553	540‡	£5,697	£3,624	T. M. Taylor (1986)
Bryanston School, Dorset	1928	660‡	£7,728	£5,151	T. D. Wheare (1983)
Bury Grammar School, Lancs.	1634	640	....	£1,863	J. Robson (1969)
Canford School, Dorset	1923	530‡	£7,510	£5,260	M. Marriott (1976)
Caterham School, Surrey	1811	420†	£5,850	£3,180	R. Smith (1976)
Charterhouse, Surrey	1611	713†	£7,755	£6,399	P. J. Attenborough (1982)
Cheadle Hulme School, Cheshire	1855	870‡	£5,200	£2,500	DC. Firth (1977)
Cheltenham College, Glos...........	1841	570†	£7,140	£5,355	R. M. Morgan (1978)
Chigwell School, Essex............	1629	350‡	£5,430	£3,533	B. J. Wilson (1971)
Christ College, Brecon	1541	328†	£4,590	£3,480	S. W. Hockey (1982)
Christ's Hospital, W. Sussex	1553	825‡	various		R. C. Poulton (1987)
Churcher's College, Hants.	1722	480‡	£5,544	£2,985	G. W. Buttle (1988)
City of London, EC4	1442	800	....	£3,495	J. M. Hammond (1984)
City of London Freemen's School, Surrey	1854	340‡	£5,400	£3,438	D. C. Haywood (1987)
Clifton College, Bristol.............	1862	670‡	£7,560	£5,220	S. M. Andrews (1975)
Colfe's School, SE12	1652	680†	....	£2,715	V. S. Anthony (1976)
Colston's School, Bristol	1710	331†	£5,475	£3,300	S. B. Howarth (1988)

* A Woodard Corporation School.   † Girls in VI form.   ‡ Co-educational.   ° 1988 figure.

Name of School	F'ded.	No. of Pupils	Annual Fees B'ding	Annual Fees Day	Headmaster (With date of Appointment)
Coventry School	—	1690‡	....	£2,070	R. Cooke (*Director*) (1977)
Cranleigh School, Surrey	1863	560†	£7,635	£5,310	A. Hart (1984)
Culford School, Suffolk	1881	450‡	£5,736	£3,728	D. Robson (1971)
Dame Allan's School, Newcastle upon Tyne	1705	450	....	£2,199	T. A. Willcocks (*Principal*) (1988)
Dauntsey's School, Wiltshire	1543	580‡	£6,252	£3,780	C. R. Evans (1985)
Dean Close School, Cheltenham	1884	425‡	£7,020	£4,485	C. J. Bacon (1979)
Denstone College, Staffs.*	1873	360‡	£6,354	£4,632	R. M. Ridley (1986)
Douai School (*R.C.*), Berks.	1903	307	£5,769	£3,630	Dom. G. Scott, o.s.b. (1987)
Dover College, Kent	1871	340‡	£6,426	£4,248	J. K. Ind (1981)
Downside School (*R.C.*), Somerset	1607	481	£6,144	£4,014	Dom. P. Jebb, o.s.b. (1980)
Dulwich College, SE21	1619	1425	£7,200	£3,600	A. C. F. Verity (*Master*) (1986)
Durham School	1414	375†	£6,138	£4,038	M. A. Lang (1982)
Eastbourne College, E. Sussex	1867	561†	£7,074	£5,208	C. J. Saunders (1981)
Ellesmere College, Shropshire*	1884	400†	£6,540	£4,620	D. R. du Croz (1988)
Eltham College, SE9	1842	532†	£5,853	£2,745	C. D. Waller, ph.d. (1983)
Emanuel School, W11	1594	750	....	£2,688	P. F. Thomson (1984)
Epsom College, Surrey	1855	635†	£6,930	£4,830	Dr. J. B. Cook (1982)
Eton College, Berks.	1440	1250	£6,450	....	Dr. W. E. K. Anderson (1980)
Exeter School	1633	650†	£4,590	£2,490	G. T. Goodall (1979)
Felsted School, Essex	1564	480†	£7,194	£5,670	E. J. H. Gould (1983)
Forest School, E17	1834	445†	£4,839	£3,327	J. C. Gough (*Warden*) (1983)
Framlingham College, Suffolk	1864	500‡	£5,793	£3,714	L. I. Rimmer (1971)
Frensham Heights, Surrey	1925	270‡	£7,110	£4,650	A. L. Pattinson (1973)
Giggleswick School, N. Yorks.	1512	300‡	£6,285	£4,179	P. Hobson (1986)
Gresham's School, Norfolk	1555	470‡	£6,540	£4,440	H. R. Wright (1985)
Haberdashers' Aske's School, Herts.	1690	1107	....	£3,336	K. Dawson (1987)
Haileybury, Herts.	1862	685†	£6,591	£4,284	D. J. Jewell (1987)
Hampton School, Middx.	1557	840	....	£2,640	G. G. Able (1988)
Harrow School, Middx.	1571	770	£8,175	£6,132	I. D. S. Beer (1981)
Hereford Cathedral School	1384	606‡	£4,461	£2,250	Dr. H. C. Tomlinson (1988)
Highgate School, N6	1565	610	£6,810	£3,915	R. C. Giles (1974)
Hulme Grammar School, Oldham	1611	750	....	£1,995	G. F. Dunkin (1987)
Hurstpierpoint College, W. Sussex*	1849	415	£6,840	£5,310	S. A. Watson (1986)
Hymers College, Hull	1889	850†	....	£1,815	B. G. Bass (1983)
Ipswich School, Suffolk	1390	625†	£5,199	£3,030	Dr. J. M. Blatchly (1972)
John Lyon School, Middx.	1876	490	....	£2,865	Rev. T. J. Wright (1986)
Kelly College, Devon	1877	330†	£7,245	£2,646	C. H. Hirst (1984)
Kent College, Canterbury	1885	540‡	£5,790	£3,243	R. J. Wicks (1980)
Kimbolton School, Cambs.	1600	520‡	£5,472	£2,997	R. V. Peel (1987)
King Edward VI School, Southampton	1553	950†	....	£2,700	C. Dobson (1971)
King Edward VII School, Lytham	1908	544	....	£1,950	D. Heap (1982)
King Edward's School, Bath	1552	670†	....	£2,298	J. P. Wroughton (1982)
King Edward's School, Birmingham	1552	730	....	£2,430	M. J. W. Rogers (*Chief Master*) (1982)
King Edward's School, Witley, Surrey	1553	510‡	£5,340	£3,930	R. J. Fox (1988)
King's College, Taunton*	1880	490†	£6,870	£5,100	R. S. Funnell (1988)
King's College School, SW19	1829	650	....	£3,030	R. M. Reeve (1980)
King's School, Bruton, Somerset	1519	332†	£6,870	£4,905	A. H. Beadles (1985)
King's School, Canterbury	600	700†	£7,350	£5,145	Rev. Canon A. C. J. Phillips (1986)
King's School, Chester	1541	440	....	£2,448	A. R. D. Wickson (1981)
King's School, Ely, Cambs.	970	430‡	£6,990	£4,455	H. Ward (1970)
King's School, Macclesfield	1502	845†	....	£2,685	A. G. Silcock (1987)
King's School, Rochester, Kent	604	440†	£5,865	£3,525	Dr. I. R. Walker (1986)
King's School, Worcester	1541	718†	£4,773	£2,829	Dr. J. M. Moore (1983)
Kingston Grammar School, Surrey	1561	542‡	....	£2,955	A. B. Creber (1987)
Kingswood School, Bath	1748	485‡	£6,480	£4,200	G. M. Best (1987)
Lancing College, W. Sussex*	1848	555‡	£7,191	£5,004	J. S. Woodhouse (1981)
Latymer Upper School, W6	1624	950	....	£3,075	M. C. Pavey (1988)
Leeds Grammar School	1552	1182	....	£2,151	B. W. Collins (1976)
Leighton Park School, Reading	1890	360†	£6,435	£4,500	J. A. Chapman (1986)
The Leys School, Cambridge	1875	400†	£6,930	£5,145	T. G. Beynon (1986)
Liverpool College	1840	408†	£4,266	£2,307	R. V. Haygarth (1979)
Llandovery College, Dyfed	1848	250‡	£5,169	£3,153	Dr. C. E. Evans (1988)
Lord Wandsworth College, Hants.	1912	400†	£5,772	£4,512	G. A. G. Dodd (1982)
Loughborough Grammar School	1495	860	£5,079	£2,541	D. N. Ireland (1984)

* A Woodard Corporation School. † Girls in VI form. ‡ Co-educational. ° 1988 figure.

Name of School	F'ded	No. of Pupils	Annual Fees B'ding	Annual Fees Day	Headmaster (With date of Appointment)
Magdalen College School, Oxford ...	1480	500	£5,130	£2,667	W. B. Cook (*Master*) (1972)
Malvern College, Worcs.	1865	600	£7,080	£5,145	R. de C. Chapman (1983)
Manchester Grammar School	1515	1444	....	£2,298	J. G. Parker (*High Master*) (1985)
Marlborough College, Wilts.	1843	900†	£7,500	....	D. R. Cope (1986)
Merchant Taylors' School, Liverpool	1620	650	....	£2,460	S. J. R. Dawkins (1986)
Merchant Taylors' School, Middx. ...	1561	720	£5,700	£4,200	D. J. Skipper (1981)
Mill Hill School, NW7..............	1807	540†	£6,960	£4,600	A. C. Graham (1979)
Monkton Combe School, Bath	1868	323‡	£6,885	£5,025	R. A. C. Meredith (1978)
Monmouth School, Gwent...........	1614	542	£5,121	£2,871	R. D. Lane (1982)
Mount St. Mary's College (*R.C.*), Derbys...........................	1842	324‡	£5,436	£3,672	Rev. J. F. Grumitt, s.J. (1976)
Newcastle-under-Lyme School	1874	1176‡	....	£2,100	J. W. Donaldson (*Principal*) (1974)
Norwich School	1250	600	....	£2,625	C. D. Brown (1984)
Nottingham High School	1513	830	....	£2,280	Dr. D. T. Witcombe (1970)
Oakham School, Leics.	1584	933‡	£6,417	£3,351	G. Smallbone (1985)
The Oratory School (*R.C.*), Berks. ...	1859	350	£6,594	£4,614	M. Lynn (1989)
Oundle School, Northants	1556	740	£6,990	....	D. B. McMurray (1984)
Pangbourne College, Berks.	1917	360	£6,630	£4,650	A. B. E. Hudson (1988)
Perse School, Cambridge	1615	470	£4,944	£2,418	Dr. G. M. Stephen (1987)
Plymouth College	1877	700†	£4,860	£2,580	A. M. Joyce (1983)
Pocklington School, York.	1514	735°‡	£4,571°	£2,340°	A. D. Pickering (1981)
Portsmouth Grammar School	1732	750†	....	£2,340	A. C. V. Evans (1983)
Prior Park College (*R.C.*), Bath	1830	372‡	£5,410	£3,069	P. F. J. Tobin (1981)
Queen Elizabeth's G.S., Blackburn ..	1567	1052†	....	£2,220	P. F. Johnston (1978)
Queen Elizabeth G.S., Wakefield ...	1591	730	£4,038	£2,478	R. P. Mardling (1985)
Queen Elizabeth's Hospital, Bristol..	1590	480	£4,200	£2,385	Dr. R. Gliddon (1985)
Queen's College, Taunton	1843	440‡	£5,535	£3,645	A. P. Hodgson (1979)
Radley College, Oxon..............	1847	600	£7,350	....	D. R. W. Silk (*Warden*) (1968)
Ratcliffe College (*R.C.*), Leicester ...	1844	420‡	£5,499	£3,666	Rev. L. G. Hurdidge (1984)
Reed's School, Surrey	1813	350	£5,940	£4,290	D. E. Prince (1982)
Reigate Grammar School, Surrey ...	1675	850	....	£2,736	J. G. Hamlin (1982)
Rendcomb College, Glos.	1920	250‡	£6,426	....	J. Tolputt (1987)
Repton School, Derby	1557	570†	£7,110	£5,250	G. E. Jones (1987)
R.N.I.B. New College, Worcester	1987	110‡	£13,056	£8,616	Rev. B. R. Manthorp (1987)
Rossall School, Lancs.	1844	480°‡	£6,375°	£4,395°	R. D. W. Rhodes (1987)
Royal Grammar School, Guildford ..	1552	782	....	£3,090	J. Daniel (1975)
Royal Grammar School, Newcastle upon Tyne	1545	950	....	£2,178	A. S. Cox (1972)
Royal Grammar School, Worcester ..	1291	763	£4,800	£2,640	T. E. Savage, T.D. (1978)
Rugby School, Warwicks.	1567	720†	£7,575	£4,525	O. R. S. Bull (1985)
Rydal School, Clwyd	1885	347‡	£5,685	£4,275	P. F. Watkinson (1968)
Ryde School, Isle of Wight..........	1921	416‡	£4,590	£2,295	P. D. V. Wilkes (1983)
St. Albans School, Herts.	1570	660	....	£2,955	S. C. Wilkinson (1984)
St. Anselm's College, Birkenhead....	1933	630	....	£1,944	Rev. Br. C. J. Sreenan (1987)
St. Bees School, Cumbria	1583	380‡	£6,465	£4,515	P. A. Chamberlain (1988)
St. Benedict's School (*R.C.*), W5.....	1902	580†	....	£2,595	Dr. A. J. Dachs (1987)
St. Dunstan's College, SE6	1888	664	....	£2,820	B. D. Dance (1973)
St. Edmund's College (*R.C.*), Herts. ..	1568	500‡	£5,613	£3,612	D. J. J. McEwen (1984)
St. Edmund's School, Canterbury ...	1749	300‡	£6,945	£4,440	J. V. Tyson (1978)
St. Edward' College, Liverpool	1853	648†	....	£2,076	Rev. Br. B. D. Sassi (1984)
St. Edward's School, Oxford	1863	585†	£7,350	£5,520	D. Christie (1988)
St. George's College, (*R.C.*), Surrey ..	1869	600†	£5,562	£3,855	Rev. J. W. Munton (1987)
St. John's School, Surrey	1851	450°	£4,860°	£3,432°	D. E. Brown (1985)
St. Lawrence College, Kent........	1879	350‡	£6,465	£4,320	J. H. Binfield (1983)
St. Mary's College, Merseyside.....	1919	583†	....	£2,022	Rev. Br. P. E. Ryan (1987)
St. Paul's School, SW13	1509	770	£6,408	£3,954	Rev. Canon P. Pilkington (*High Master*) (1986)
St. Peter's School, York	627	490‡	£6,138	£3,574	R. N. Pittman (1985)
Sedbergh School, Cumbria	1525	480	£6,960	£4,890	Dr. R. G. Baxter (1982)
Sevenoaks School, Kent...........	1418	907‡	£6,894	£4,185	R. P. Barker (1981)
Sherborne School, Dorset	1550	650°	£6,740°	£4,200°	P. H. Lapping (1988)
Shrewsbury School	1552	650	£7,230	£5,100	F. E. Maidment (1988)
Silcoates School, W. Yorks.........	1820	302†	£4,944	£2,826	J. C. Baggaley (1978)
Solihull School, Warwicks	1560	840†	....	£2,355	A. Lee (1983)
Stamford School, Lincs.	1532	565	£4,800	£2,400	G. J. Timm (1978)
Stockport Grammar School	1487	1002‡	....	£2,394	D. R. J. Bird (1985)
Stonyhurst College (*R.C.*), Lancs. ...	1794	430	£6,678	£3,483	Dr. R. G. G. Mercer (1985)
Stowe School, Bucks.	1923	600†	£7,800	£5,460	C. G. Turner (1979)

* A Woodard Corporation School. † Girls in VI form. ‡ Co-educational. ° 1988 figure.

Name of School	F'ded.	No. of Pupils	B'ding	Day	Headmaster (With date of Appointment)
Sutton Valence School, Kent	1576	425‡	£6,579	£4,209	M. R. Haywood (1980)
Taunton School	1847	620‡	£6,525	£4,224	B. B. Sutton (1987)
Tettenhall College, Staffs.	1863	300°	£4,929°	£3,039°	W. J. Dale (1968)
Tonbridge School, Kent	1553	670	£7,200	£4,100	C. H. D. Everett, C.B.E. (1975)
Trent College, Derbys.	1868	625†	£6,255	£3,726	J. S. Lee (1988)
Trinity School, Surrey	1596	780	....	£2,970	R. J. Wilson (1972)
Truro School	1879	842°†	£4,350°	£2,400°	B. K. Hobbs (1986)
University College School, NW3	1830	520	....	£3,690	G. D. Slaughter (1983)
Uppingham School, Leics.	1584	680†	£6,900	....	N. R. Bomford (1982)
Warwick School	914	800	£5,445	£2,520	P. J. Cheshire (1988)
Wellingborough School, Northants	1595	420‡	£5,571	£3,408	G. Garrett (1973)
Wellington College, Berks.	1856	810†	£6,480	£4,710	Dr. D. H. Newsome (1980)
Wellington School, Somerset	1841	780‡	£4,755	£2,550	J. Kendall-Carpenter (1973)
Wells Cathedral School, Somerset	1180	742‡	£5,250	£2,970	J. S. Baxter (1986)
West Buckland School, Devon	1858	440‡	£5,250	£2,850	M. Downward (1979)
Westminster, SW1	1560	610†	£7,050	£4,650	D. M. Summerscale (1986)
Whitgift School, Surrey	1596	875	....	£3,120	D. A. Raeburn (1970)
William Hulme's G.S., Manchester	1887	780‡	....	£2,601	P. D. Briggs (1987)
Winchester College, Hants.	1382	650	£7,800	£5,850	J. P. Sabben-Clare (1985)
Wolverhampton Grammar School	1512	630†	....	£2,754	P. H. Hutton (1978)
Woodbridge School, Suffolk	1662	530‡	£5,520	£3,180	Dr. D. Younger (1985)
Woodhouse Grove School, Bradford	1812	560‡	£4,905	£2,994	D. A. Miller (1972)
Worksop College, Notts.*	1895	400‡	£6,390	£4,320	A. H. Monro (1986)
Worth School (*R.C.*), W. Sussex	1959	325	£6,525	....	Rev. R. S. Ortiger (1983)
Wrekin College, Shropshire	1880	400†	£6,750	£4,560	J. H. Arkell (1983)
Wycliffe College, Glos.	1882	328‡	£6,720	£4,365	A. P. Millard (1987)
Scotland					
Daniel Stewart's and Melville College, Edinburgh	1832	768	£4,920	£2,526	R. M. Morgan (1977)
Dollar Academy, Clackmannanshire	1818	887‡	£5,046	£2,352	L. Harrison (*Rector*) (1984)
Dundee High School, Tayside	1239	1172°‡	....	£2,034°	R. Nimmo (*Rector*) (1977)
The Edinburgh Academy	1824	600†	£6,300	£3,120	L. E. Ellis (*Rector*) (1977)
Fettes College, Edinburgh	1870	420‡	£7,455	£5,010	M. T. Thyne (1988)
George Heriot's College, Edinburgh	1659	1330‡	....	£2,355	K. P. Pearson (1983)
George Watson's College, Edinburgh	1741	1261‡	£4,896	£2,526	F. E. Gerstenberg (*Principal*) (1985)
Glasgow Academy	1845	550	....	£2,385	C. W. Turner (*Rector*) (1983)
Glenalmond College, Perth.	1841	380	£7,350	....	S. R. D. Hall (*Warden*) (1987)
Gordonstoun School, Morayshire	1934	470‡	£7,128	£4,578	M. B. Mavor, C.V.O. (1979)
The High School of Glasgow	1124	365‡	....	£2,175	R. G. Easton (1983)
Hutcheson's Grammar School, Glasgow	1641	1075‡	....	£1,650	D. R. Ward (*Rector*) (1987)
Kelvinside Academy, Glasgow	1878	500	....	£2,457	J. H. Duff (*Rector*) (1980)
Loretto School, E. Lothian	1827	300†	£6,300	£3,945	Rev. N. W. Drummond (1984)
Merchiston Castle School, Edinburgh	1833	360	£6,900	£4,440	D. M. Spawforth (1981)
Morrison's Academy, Perthshire	1860	600‡	£5,340	£2,040	H. A. Ashmall (*Rector*) (1979)
Robert Gordon's College, Aberdeen	1729	850‡	£4,315	£1,915	G. A. Allan (1978)
Strathallan School, Perth	1913	400‡	£6,750	£4,500	C. D. Pighills (1975)
Northern Ireland					
Bangor Grammar School, Co. Down	1856	890	....	£1,500	T. W. Patton (1979)
Belfast Methodist College	1868	1571‡	£3,696	£1,704	T. W. Mulryne (1988)
Belfast Royal Academy	1785	1250‡	....	£1,700	W. M. Sillery (1980)
Campbell College, Belfast	1894	420	£5,382	£2,406	Dr. R. J. I. Pollock (1987)
Coleraine Academical Institution	1856	980	£3,500	£1,500	R. S. Forsythe (1984)
Portora Royal School, Enniskillen	1618	342‡	£3,945	£1,995	R. L. Bennett (1983)
Royal Belfast Academical Institution	1810	900	....	£1,600	T. J. Garrett (1978)
Channel Islands and Isle of Man					
Elizabeth College, Guernsey	1563	523	£3,252	£1,152	J. H. F. Doulton (1988)
Victoria College, Jersey	1852	575	£4,995	£1,665	M. H. Devenport (1967)
King William's College, Isle of Man	1668	375‡	£2,055	£1,365	Dr. P. K. Bregazzi (1979)

* A Woodard Corporation School.   † Girls in VI form.   ‡ Co-educational.   ° 1988 figure.

H.M.C. SCHOOLS OVERSEAS
Fees are given in local currency.

Name of School	F'ded.	No. of Pupils	Annual Fees B'ding	Annual Fees Day	Headmaster (With date of Appointment)
Africa					
Diocesan College, Rondesbosch, S.A.	1849	629†	R10,268	R5,860	J. S. B. Peake (1983)
Falcon College, Esigodini, Zimbabwe	1954	450	Z$5,466	....	P. N. Todd (1985)
Kamuzu Academy, Malawi	—	360‡	K.7,600	....	M. J. Maloney (1986)
Peterhouse, Marondera, Zimbabwe	1955	580°	Z.$5,000°	Z.$3,500	Dr. A. J. Megahey (Rector) (1984)
St George's College, Harare, Zimbabwe	1896	850	Z.$3,240	Z.$1,320	J. C. Berry (1984)
St. John's College, Johannesburg, S.A.	—	580†	R10,095	R5,670	W. W. MacFarlane (1983)
St. Stithian's College, Randburg, S.A.	1953	570	R8,190	R4,635	M. Henning (1969)
Australia					
Brighton G.S., Victoria	1882	750	....	$A5,200	R. L. Rofe (1967)
Camberwell G.S., Victoria	1886	930	....	$A3,958	C. F. Black (1987)
Canberra G.S., A.C.T.	1929	884	$A8,480	$A3,692	T. C. Murray (1986)
Carey Baptist School, Victoria	1923	1167‡	....	$A4,953	G. L. Cramer (1965)
Caulfield G.S., Victoria	1881	1600‡	$A9,549	$A4,824	Rev. A. S. Holmes (Principal) (1977)
Christ Church G.S., W. Australia	1910	850	$A8,480	$A3,900	J. J. S. Madin (1988)
Anglican Church G.S., Queensland	1912	1290	$A6,600	$A2,850	C. V. Ellis (1987)
C. of E. G.S., Sydney, N.S.W.	1889	961	$A9,336	$A4,431	R. A. I. Grant (1984)
Cranbrook School, N.S.W.	1918	800	$A9,870	$A4,950	Dr. B. N. Carter (1985)
Geelong C. of E. G.S., Victoria	1855	1200‡	$A11,312	$A5,304	J. E. Lewis (1980)
The Geelong College, Victoria	1861	806‡	$A10,564	$A5,176	A. P. Sheahan (1986)
Guildford G.S., W. Australia	1896	800	$A8,400	$A4,000	J. M. Moody (1979)
Haileybury College, Victoria	1892	1743	....	$A4,875	A. M. H. Aikman (Principal) (1974)
Hale School, W. Australia	1858	650	$A9,000	$A4,500	J. Inverarity, O.B.E. (1989)
King's School, Parramatta, N.S.W.	1831	920	$A9,940	$A5,580	J. A. Wickham (1984)
Kinross Wolardi School, N.S.W.	—	579‡	$A8,940	$A4,185	A. E. S. Anderson (1978)
Knox, G.S., N.S.W.	1924	1214	$A9,940	$A4,800	Dr. I. W. Paterson (1969)
Melbourne C. of E. G.S., Victoria	1856	1093	$A9,360	$A4,960	A. J. de V. Hill (1988)
Newington College, N.S.W.	1863	1107	$A10,770	$A5,670	A. J. Rae (1972)
The Peninsula School, Victoria	1961	1046	$A10,196	$A5,897	H. A. Macdonald (1971)
St. Peter's College, S. Australia	1847	781	$A9,980	$A4,600	Dr. A. J. Shinkfield (1978)
Scotch College, Adelaide, S. Australia	1919	660°	$A9,300°	$A4,220°	W. M. Miles (1975)
Scotch College, Melbourne, Victoria	1851	1360	$A9,538	$A4,810	Dr. F. G. Donaldson (1983)
Scotch College, Swanbourne, W. Australia	1897	742	$A8,460	$A4,000	W. R. Dickinson (1972)
Scots College, Sydney, N.S.W.	1893	1050	$A10,500	$A5,500	G. A. W. Renney (Principal) (1980)
Sydney G.S., N.S.W.	1857	1119	....	$A1,935	A. M. Mackerras (1969)
Wesley College, Melbourne, Victoria	1866	1735‡	....	$A5,280	D. Prest (1972)
Canada					
Brentwood College School, Vancouver	1961	375‡	$13,675	$6,800	W. T. Ross (1976)
Hillfield Strathallan College, Ontario	1901	950‡	....	$6,807	M. B. Wansbrough (1969)
Pickering College, Ontario.	1842	200	$13,800	$6,900	S. H. Clark (1978)
St. Andrew's College, Ontario	1899	392	$15,180	$8,890	R. P. Bedard (1981)
Toronto French School, Ontario	1962	1240	....	$6,950	A. S. Troubetzkoy (1987)
Trinity College School, Ontario	1865	1865°	$13,700°	$8,100°	R. C. N. Wright (1983)
Upper Canada College, Toronto	1829	597	$15,000	$8,150	E. A. Barton (Principal) (1988)
Europe					
Aiglon College, Switzerland	1949	260°	n/a	n/a	P. Parsons (1976)
British School of Brussels	1970	1020‡	....	Frs.397,000	Dr. J. Jackson (1983)
British School in the Netherlands.	—	434‡	....	Fl.14,310	B. D. Davidson (1979)

† Girls in VI form.   ‡ Co-educational.   ° 1988 figures.

Name of School	F'ded.	No. of Pupils	Annual Fees B'ding	Annual Fees Day	Headmaster (With date of Appointment)
British School of Paris, France ...	—	280‡	Frs.84,000	Frs.55,500	A. W. Livingstone-Smith (1986)
Campion School, Athens, Greece ..	1970	379‡	Dr.1,300,000	Dr.660,000	C. D. Juckes (*acting*) (1988)
The English School, Nicosia, Cyprus......................	1900	820‡	....	C£1,102	A. M. Hudspeth (1988)
St. Columba's College, Dublin.....	1843	275‡	IR£4,350	IR£2,265	T. E. Macey (*Warden*) (1988)
St. George's English School, Rome	1958	500‡	....	L11,160,000	Dr. C. H. R. Niven (1988)
India					
Birla Public School, Pilani	—	360	Rs.8,750	Rs.2,800	B. K. Sood (1973)
Lawrence School, Ootacamund† ..	1858	450	Rs.10,000	....	B. S. Bhatnagar (1986)
Lawrence School, Sanawar†	1847	540	Rs.13,000	....	S. B. Singh (1988)
The Scindia School, Gualior	1897	500	Rs.10,500	....	Dr. S. D. Singh (1978)
Yadavindra Public School, Patiala	1947	1143	Rs.9,740	Rs.4,020	Dr. H. S. Dhillon (1987)
New Zealand					
Christchurch Boys' High School, Canterbury	1881	1080°	N.Z.$3,360°	N.Z.$44°	I. D. Leggat (1976)
Christ's College, Christchurch....	1850	600	N.Z.$2,550	N.Z.$1,385	Dr. M. J. Rosser (1985)
Collegiate School, Wanganui	1854	502	N.Z.$3,150	N.Z.$1,705	I. D. McKinnon (1980)
King's College, Auckland	1896	748†	N.Z.$2,865	N.Z.$1,720	J. S. Taylor (1988)
St. Andrew's College, Christchurch	1916	642	N.Z.$8,888	N.Z.$4,901	Dr. A. J. Rentoul (1982)
South America					
Markham College, Peru	1946	535	....	I.181,500	R. C. Pinchbeck, O.B.E. (1966)
St. Andrew's Scots School, Argentina....................		n/a	n/a	n/a	
St. George's College, Argentina ...	1898	225‡	A.4,800	A.3,300	G. R. Sims (1986)
St. Paul's School, Brazil	1926	240°	....	£1,500°	P. Gysin (1987)
United Arab Emirates					
Dubai College	1855	430‡	....	Dh.18,000	H. J. Deelman (1987)
U.S.A.					
The Rivers School, Massachusetts	1915	260	....	$9,250	R. A. Bradley (1981)

† Girls in VI form.   ‡ Co-educational.   ° 1988 figures.

SOCIETY OF HEADMASTERS OF INDEPENDENT SCHOOLS

Secretary, A. E. R. Dodds, Green Garth, Horsell Rise, Woking, Surrey GU21 4AY.

The Society was founded in 1961 and, in general, represents smaller boarding schools. A Headmaster may be a member of both H.M.C. and S.H.M.I.S. This is the case for the Headmasters of the following schools, details of which appear in the H.M.C. list:

Abbotsholme School, Bedales School, Churcher's College, City of London Freemen's School, Colston's School, Frensham Heights, Lord Wandsworth College, Pangbourne College, Rendcomb College, Ryde School, St. George's College, Weybridge, Silcoates School, Tettenhall College, Wells Cathedral School, West Buckland School and Woodbridge School.

Name of School	F'ded.	No. of Pupils	Annual Fees B'ding	Annual Fees Day	Headmaster (With date of Appointment)
Ackworth School, W. Yorks	1779	468‡	£5,373	£3,114	G. R. McKee (1971)
Austin Friars School (*R.C.*), Carlisle	1951	296‡	£3,927	£2,145	Rev. T. Lyons, O.S.A. (1981)
Bearwood College, Berks.	1827	340	£6,150	£3,600	The Hon. M. C. Penney (1980)
Bedstone College, Shropshire	1948	220‡	£5,295	£3,135	G. S. Wilson (1971)
Belmont Abbey (*R.C.*), Hereford	1926	250†	£5,145	£3,135	Rev. D. C. Jenkins, O.S.B. (1988)
Bembridge School, Isle of Wight	1919	266‡	£4,680	£2,592	J. High (1986)
Bentham School, N. Yorks	1726	290‡	£4,950	£2,490	J. E. Rigg (1988)
Bethany School, Kent	1866	275	£5,595	£3,735	W. M. Harvey (1988)

‡ Co-educational.   † Girls in VI form.

Name of School	F'ded.	No. of Pupils	Annual Fees B'ding	Annual Fees Day	Headmaster (With date of Appointment)
Box Hill School, Surrey	1959	265°‡	£5,805°	£3,405°	Dr. R. A. S. Atwood (1987)
Carmel College (*Jewish*), Oxon.	1948	325‡	£8,250	£4,470	P. D. Skelker (1984)
Chetham's School of Music, Manchester......................	1653	271‡	£9,555	£7,398	J. Vallins, O.B.E. (1975)
Clayesmore School, Dorset	1896	324‡	£6,885	£4,845	D. J. Beeby (1986)
Cokethorpe School, Oxon...........	1957	170†	£6,900	£4,950	D. F. Goldsmith (1979)
Cranbrook School, Kent	1518	720‡	£2,925	Nil	P. A. Close (1988)
Ewell Castle School, Surrey	—	n/a	n/a	n/a	R. A. Fewtell
Friends' School, Essex	1702	340°‡	£5,046°	£3,015°	J. C. Woods (1968)
Fulneck Boys' School, W. Yorks.	1753	305	£4,935	£2,541	I. D. Cleland (1980)
Grenville College, Devon*	1954	350	£5,775	£2,862	Dr. D. C. Powell-Price, T.D. (1975)
Keil School, Dumbarton	1915	196‡	£4,758	£2,760	C. H. Tongue (1984)
Kingham Hill School, Oxon.	1886	240	£4,860	£3,060	D. Shepherd (1981)
King's School, Gloucester	1541	450‡	£4,965	£2,940	Rev. A. C. Charters (1983)
King's School, Tynemouth	—	660†	....	£2,175	W. T. Gillen (1987)
Kirkham Grammar School, Lancs. ..	1549	478‡	£3,765	£2,025	M. J. Summerlee (1972)
Lindisfarne College, Clwyd	1891	200‡	£5,805	£3,225	T. R. Wilson (1986)
Lord Mayor Treloar College, Hants. .	1908	280‡	£16,686	£12,515	A. M. Macpherson (1974)
Milton Abbey School, Dorset	1954	285	£6,870	....	R. H. Hardy (1987)
Oswestry School, Shropshire	1407	310‡	£5,160	£3,075	I. G. Templeton (1985)
Pierrepont School, Surrey	1947	265‡	£5,964	£3,579	J. D. Payne (1983)
The Purcell School (music), Middx...	1962	175°‡	£6,045°	£3,075°	K. J. Bain (1983)
Rannoch School, Perthshire	1959	275‡	£5,460	£3,225	M. Barratt (1982)
Reading Blue Coat School, Berks. ...	1646	507†	£5,145	£2,871	A. C. E. Sanders (1974)
Rishworth School, W. Yorks.	1724	560°‡	£4,470°	£2,385°	A. J. Morsley (1986)
Rougemont School, Gwent	—	284‡	....	£2,640	F. W. Edwards (1975)
Royal Hospital School, Ipswich	1712	700	£3,474	....	M. A. B. Kirk (1983)
Royal Russell School, Surrey	1853	457‡	£5,175	£2,700	R. D. Balaam (1982)
Royal School, Dungannon, N. Ireland......................	—	600‡	£8,544	£2,994	P. D. Hewitt (1984)
Royal Wolverhampton School	1850	335‡	£5,100	£2,985	P. Gorring (1985)
Ruthin School, Clwyd	1574	187†	£5,685	£3,855	F. R. Ullmann (1986)
St. David's College, Gwynedd	1965	253	£5,940	£3,870	B. T. Culain Morris (1989)
Scarborough College, N. Yorks.	1898	363‡	£5,925	£3,174	Dr. D. S. Hempsall (1985)
Seaford College, W. Sussex	1884	430	£5,685	....	Rev. Canon C. Johnson (1944)
Shebbear College, Devon	1841	316	£5,115	£2,730	R. J. Buley (1983)
Shiplake College, Oxon.............	1959	342	£6,900	£4,500	N. V. Bevan (1988)
Sidcot School, Avon	1808	270‡	£5,985	£3,285	C. J. Greenfield (1986)
Stanbridge Earls School, Hants.	1952	170‡	£6,900	£4,600	H. Moxon (1984)
Warminster School, Wilts.	1707	320‡	£5,325	£3,195	D. M. Green (1984)

* A Woodard Corporation School.   ‡ Co-educational.   † Girls in VI form.   ° 1988 figure.

GIRLS' SCHOOLS ASSOCIATION

THE GIRLS' SCHOOLS ASSOCIATION, Chancery House, 107 St. Paul's Road, N1 2NB.—*President* (1988), Miss E. W. Evans; *Sec.*, Mrs. C. M. G. Kewell.

Name of School	F'ded.	No. of Pupils	Annual Fees B'ding	Annual Fees Day	Headmistress (a) Headmaster (With date of Appointment)
Abbey School, Reading.............	1887	950°	....	£2,277°	S. M. Hardcastle, M.B.E. (1960)
Abbots Bromley, Staffs	1874	255	£5,970	£3,760	(a) A. Grigg (1989)
Abbot's Hill, Herts.	1912	153°	£4,950°	£3,375°	Mrs. J. Kingsley (1979)
Adcote School, Shropshire	1907	110	£5,310	£3,150	Mrs. S. B. Cecchet (1979)
Alice Ottley School, Worcester	1883	550	£5,100	£2,625	C. Sibbit (1986)
All Hallows School, Suffolk	1864	173	£4,860	£3,060	A. C. Harris (1984)
Amberfield School, Ipswich........	—	150	....	£2,250	Mrs. P. Webb (1979)
Ashford School, Kent..............	1910	552	£4,398	£2,517	Mrs. A. T. D. Macaire (1984)
Assumption School, N. Yorks.	1852	175	£4,615	£2,574	Mrs. J. Coulthard (1987)
Atherley School, Southampton (*CSC*)	1926	320	....	£2,367	M. E. Taylor (1988)
Badminton School, Bristol	1858	300	£6,150	£3,450	(a) C. J. T. Gould (1981)
‡ Bath High School	1875	537	....	£2,085	M. A. Winfield (1986)

‡ Girls Public Day School Trust.   ° 1988 figure.

Name of School	F'ded.	No. of Pupils	Annual Fees B'ding	Annual Fees Day	Headmistress (a) Headmaster (With date of Appointment)
Battle Abbey School, E. Sussex.....	1912	140	£5,010	£3,120	(a) D. J. A. Teall (1982)
Bedford High School..............	1882	820	£5,247	£2,712	Mrs. D. M. Wilkes (1987)
Bedgebury School, Kent	1860	380	£6,237	£3,696	Mrs. M. E. A. Kaye (1987)
‡Belvedere School, Liverpool.......	1880	553	....	£2,085	S. Downs (1972)
Benenden School, Kent	1923	400	£6,450	....	Mrs. G. D. duCharme (1985)
Beresford House School, E. Sussex .	1902	162	£6,195	£3,510	S. B. Jackson (1988)
Berkhamsted School, Herts.	1888	461	£4,788	£2,634	V. E. M. Shepherd (1980)
‡Birkenhead High School	1901	933	....	£2,085	Mrs. K. R. Irving (1986)
‡Blackheath High School, SE3......	1880	539	....	£2,367	(vacant)
Bolton School, Lancs	1877	852	....	£2,388	Mrs. M. A. Spurr (1979)
Bradford Girls Grammar School ...	1875	700	....	£2,148	Mrs. L. J. Warrington (1987)
‡Brighton and Hove High School ...	1876	742	£4,653	£2,085	R. A. Woodbridge (1989)
‡Bromley High School, Kent	1883	700	....	£2,367	Mrs. A. B. Schofield (1984)
Bruton School, Somerset	1900	520	£4,050	£2,250	Mrs. J. W. Wade (1987)
Burgess Hill School, W. Sussex	1906	306	£5,370	£3,060	Mrs. B. H. Webb (1979)
Bury Grammar School, Lancs.	1884	773	....	£1,863	J. M. Lawley (1987)
Casterton School, Cumbria	1823	390	£5,301	£3,201	(a) G. Vinestock (1984)
‡Central Newcastle High School	1895	791	....	£2,085	Mrs. A. M. Chapman (1984)
Channing School, N6	1885	290	....	£3,150	Mrs. I. R. Raphael (1984)
‡Charters Ancaster College, E. Sussex	1906	282	£5,268	£2,700	Mrs. S. V. Chapman (1985)
Cheltenham Ladies' College, Glos...	1853	820	£7,080	£4,515	E. Castle (1987)
City of London School, EC2	1894	539	....	£2,850	Mrs. V. E. France (1986)
Clarendon School, Bedford	1898	232	£6,150	£3,570	J. L. Howell (1978)
Clifton High School, Bristol	1877	553	£4,380	£2,205	Mrs J. D. Walters (1985)
Cobham Hall, Kent	1962	310	£6,840	£4,560	S. Cameron (1985)
Colston's Girls' School, Bristol.....	1891	642	....	£2,015	A. C. Parkin (1981)
Combe Bank School, Kent	1868	245	£5,043	£2,943	Mrs. A. J. K. Austin (1982)
Commonweal Lodge School, Surrey	1916	130	....	£2,370	J. M. Brown (1982)
Cranborne Chase School, Wilts.....	1946	160	£6,450	£2,685	Mrs. M. Simmons (1983)
Cranford House School, Oxon......	1931	140	....	£2,445	T. A. Spencer (1980)
Croft House School, Dorset	1941	200	£5,700	£3,960	Mrs. S. Rawlinson (1985)
Croham Hurst School, Surrey	1899	360	....	£2,331	J. M. Shelmerdine (1986)
‡Croydon High School, Surrey	1874	1053	....	£2,367	A. M. Mark (1980)
Dame Alice Harpur School, Bedford	1882	830	....	£2,220	S. M. Morse (1970)
Dame Allan's Girls' School, Newcastle upon Tyne	1705	440°	....	£2,088°	J. Graham (1970)
Derby High School	1892	270	....	£2,700	(a) Dr. G. H. Goddard (1983)
Downe House, Berks.	1907	463	£6,900	£4,485	S. E. Farr (1978)
Dunottar School, Surrey	1926	300	....	£2,385	J. Burnell (1985)
Durham High School	1884	387°	....	£1,860°	B. E. Stephenson (1978)
Edgbaston Church of England College	1886	310	....	£2,232	(a) I. J. Walkley (1979)
Edgbaston High School	1876	528	....	£2,406	Mrs. S. J. Horsman (1987)
Edgehill College, Devon	1884	369	£4,830	£2,535	Mrs. E. M. Burton (1987)
Ellerslie, Worcs...................	1922	260	£6,450	£4,200	Mrs. E. Baker (1988)
Elmslie Girls' School, Lancs.	1918	400	....	£2,070	E. M. Smithies (1978)
Eothen School, Surrey (CSC)	1892	200	....	£2,637	D. C. Raine (1973)
Farlington, W. Sussex	1896	220	£5,400	£3,300	Mrs. P. Metham (1987)
Farnborough Hill, Hants.	1889	525	....	£2,640	Sr. E. McCormack (1988)
Farringtons, Kent	1911	400°	£4,959°	£2,790°	Mrs. B. J. Stock (1987)
Felixstowe College, Suffolk	1929	340	£6,360	£3,900	Mrs. A. F. Woodings (1989)
Fernhill Manor School, Hants......	1890	154°	£4,920	£3,135	(a) Rev. A. J. Folks (1985)
Francis Holland School, NW1......	1878	360	....	£2,844	Mrs. P. H. Parsonson (1988)
Francis Holland School, SW1	1881	176°	....	£2,961	Mrs. J. A. Anderson (1982)
Gateways School, Leeds	1941	200	....	£2,085	L. M. Brown (1984)
Godolphin School, Wilts...........	1726	320	£6,135	£3,645	E. A. S. Hannay (1980)
Godolphin and Latymer School, W6	1905	700°	....	£2,520°	M. Rudland (1986)
Greenacre School, Surrey	1933	365°	£4,515°	£2,370°	M. E. Haggerty (1977)
The Grove School, Hindhead, Surrey	1877	200	£4,716	£2,862	(a) C. Brooks (1984)
Guildford High School	1888	450	....	£2,805	J. E. Dutton (1977)
Haberdashers' Aske's School, Herts.	1873	830	....	£2,079	Mrs. S. Wiltshire (1974)
Haberdashers' Monmouth School, Gwent	1891	510	£4,710	£2,640	H. L. Gichard (1986)
Harrogate Ladies' College	1893	400	£5,445	£3,630	Mrs. J. C. Lawrance (1974)
Headington School, Oxford........	1915	550	£5,079	£2,604	E. M. Tucker (1982)
Heathfield School, Ascot, Berks. ...	1900	200	£6,300°	....	Mrs. S. E. Watkins (1982)

‡Girls Public Day School Trust. ° 1988 figure.

Name of School	F'ded.	No. of Pupils	Annual Fees B'ding	Annual Fees Day	Headmistress (a) Headmaster (With date of Appointment)
‡Heathfield School, Pinner, Middx. .	1900	398	....	£2,367	Mrs. J. Merritt (1988)
Hethersett Old Hall School, Norwich	1928	245	£4,305	£2,475	Mrs. V. M. Redington (1983)
Highclare School, W. Midlands ...	—	349†	....	£2,085	Mrs. C. A. Henson (1974)
Holy Child School, Birmingham ...	1933	230	£4,497	£2,445	J. M. Johnson (1987)
Holy Trinity Convent School, Bromley........................	—	380	....	£1,914	Sr. B. Wetz (1986)
Holy Trinity School, Kidderminster	—	400	....	£1,800	K. Butwilowska (1986)
Howell's School, Denbigh, Clwyd...	1859	300	£6,426	£4,020	(a) J. H. Delany (1987)
‡Howell's School, Landaff, Cardiff...	1860	651	£4,764	£2,196	J. P. Turner (1978)
Hull High School (CSC)............	1890	360	£3,426	£2,451	C. M. B. Radcliffe (1976)
Hulme Grammar School, Oldham ..	1895	460	....	£1,995	Mrs. A. Groom (1985)
Hunmanby Hall School, N. Yorks...	1928	230	£3,945	£2,340	J. Rutherford (1986)
Huyton College, Liverpool	1894	229	£5,556	£2,448	W. E. Edwards (1984)
‡Ipswich High School..............	1878	595	....	£2,085	P. M. Hayworth (1971)
James Allen's Girls' School, SE22 ..	1741	704	£6,060	£2,970	Mrs. B. Davies (1984)
School of Jesus and Mary, Suffolk ..	1860	200	....	£2,370	Mrs. E. A. McKay (1982)
Kent College......................	1885	302	£5,295	£3,135	(a) Rev. J. C. A. Barrett (1983)
King Edward VI High School, Birmingham	1883	550	....	£2,160	E. W. Evans (1977)
King's High School, Warwick	1879	540	....	£2,175	Mrs. J. M. Anderson (1987)
Kingsley School, Warwicks.	1884	336	£4,410	£2,295	Mrs. M. A. Webster (1988)
La Retraite School, Wilts.	1953	250	....	£2,238	Mrs. M. Paisey (1985)
La Sagesse Convent High School, Newcastle upon Tyne	1906	350	....	£2,094	Sr. Pauline (1967)
La Sagesse Convent School, Hants..	1896	250	£4,116	£1,764	Sr. Thomas (1977)
Lady Eleanor Holles School, Middx.	1711	610	....	£2,670	E. M. Candy (1981)
Lavant House School, W. Sussex ...	1952	130	£5,205	£3,090	Mrs. B. M. Gay (1987)
Lawnside, Worcs.	1818	150	£5,505	....	D. M. M. Stewart (1971)
Leeds Girls' High School	1876	961	....	£2,316	P. A. Randall (1977)
Leicester High School	1906	328	....	£2,310	Mrs. D. Buchan (1982)
Loughborough High School	1850	520	£3,822	£2,268	J. E. L. Harvatt (1978)
Luckley-Oakfield School, Berks. ...	1895	290°	£4,905	£3,135	(a) R. C. Blake (1984)
Malvern Girls' College, Worcs.	1893	520°	£5,130°	£3,420°	Dr. V. B. Payne (1986)
Manchester High School	1874	735	....	£2,277	M. M. Moon (1983)
Maynard School, Exeter	1877	462	....	£2,352	F. Murdin (1980)
Merchant Taylors' School, Liverpool......................	1888	550	....	£2,460	E. J. Panton (1988)
Micklefield School, E. Sussex	1910	200	£6,750	£3,420	(a) E. Reynolds (1987)
Moira House School, E. Sussex	1875	300	£6,000	£3,460	(a) A. R. Underwood (1975)
More House School, SW1..........	1953	248	....	£3,075	Mrs. P. M. Mathias (1973)
Moreton Hall, Shropshire	1913	345	£6,450	£4,275	(a) E. J. Cussell (1976)
Mount School, York	1831	301	£5,571	£3,798	B. J. Windle (1986)
New Hall, Essex	1642	555	£6,075	£3,206	Sr. M. M. Horton (1986)
Newcastle upon Tyne Church H.S. .	1885	400	....	£2,184	P. E. Davies (1974)
North Foreland Lodge, Hants.	1909	180°	£5,400°	....	D. Matthews (1983)
North London Collegiate School ...	1850	662	....	£2,730	Mrs. J. L. Clanchy (1986)
Northampton High School	1878	522	....	£2,181	Mrs. L. A. Mayne (1988)
Northwood College, Middx.	1878	470°	£4,038°	£2,388°	Mrs. D. K. Dalton (1986)
‡Norwich High School	1875	722	....	£2,085	Mrs. V. C. Bidwell (1985)
‡Notting Hill and Ealing High School	1873	781	....	£2,367	Mrs. C. J. Fitz (1983)
*Nottingham High School..........	1875	1002	....	£2,085	Mrs. C. Bowering (1984)
Oakdene, Beaconsfield, Bucks.	1911	340	£5,166	£3,057	A. M. Tippett (1987)
Ockbrook School, Derby	—	306	£3,861	£2,028	Dr. M. Rennie (1987)
Old Palace School, Surrey	1887	600	....	£1,980	K. L. Hilton (1974)
‡Oxford High School	1875	625	....	£2,085	Mrs. J. Townsend (1981)
Palmers Green High School, N21 ...	1905	104°	....	£2,091°	Mrs. A. F. E. Woodings (1984)
Park School, Somerset	1851	113	£4,860	£2,550	Mrs. M. J. Hannon (1987)
Parsons Mead, Surrey	1897	470	£5,280	£2,880	M. M. Dees (1979)
Penrhos College, Clwyd	1880	290	£5,820	£3,870	(a) N. C. Peacock (1974)
Perse School, Cambridge	1881	550	....	£2,547	M. R. Bateman (1980)
Pipers Corner School, Bucks.	1930	274	£5,130	£2,805	Dr. M. M. Wilson (1986)
Polam Hall, Co. Durham	1848	310	£5,130	£2,535	Mrs. H. C. Hamilton (1987)
‡Portsmouth High School	1882	672	....	£2,085	Mrs. J. M. Dawtrey (1984)
Princess Helena College, Herts.	1820	176	£6,000	£1,450	(a) Dr. D. Clarke (1971)
Prior's Field, Surrey	1902	228	£5,091	£3,141	Mrs. J. M. McCallum (1987)
‡Putney High School, SW15	1893	776	....	£2,367	Mrs. P. A. Penney (1987)

‡ Girls Public Day School Trust.   † Boys in VI form.   ° 1988 figure.   * Woodard Corporation School.

Name of School	F'ded.	No. of Pupils	Annual Fees		Headmistress (a) Headmaster (With date of Appointment)
			B'ding	Day	
Queen Anne's School, Berks.	1698	400	£5,985	£3,690	A. M. Scott (1977)
*Queen Ethelburga's School, Harrogate	1912	205	£5,925	£3,555	Mrs. J. M. Town (1988)
*Queen Margaret's School, York	1901	275°	£5,460°	£3,405	(a) C. S. McGarrigle (1983)
Queen Mary School, Lytham, Lancs.	1930	600	....	£1,950	M. C. Ritchie (1981)
Queen's College, W1	1848	385	£4,725	£2,925	Mrs. P. J. Fleming (1983)
Queen's Gate School, SW7	1891	177°	n/a	n/a	Mrs. C. M. Newnham (1971)
Queen's School, Chester	1878	420	....	£2,040	M. Farra (1973)
Queenswood, Herts.	1894	400	£6,465	....	Mrs. A. M. B. Butler (1981)
Redland High School, Bristol	1882	450	....	£2,184	E. Hobbs (1986)
Red Maids' School, Bristol	1634	480	£3,966	£1,950	S. Hampton (1988)
Rickmansworth Masonic School, Herts.	1788	596	£5,100	£2,829	(a) D. L. Curtis (1980)
Roedean School, E. Sussex	1885	475	£6,870	....	Mrs. A. R. Longley (1984)
Rosemead, W. Sussex	1919	200	£5,685	£3,180	Mrs. J. Bevis (*Principal*) (1987)
Royal Naval School, Surrey	1840	280	£5,544	£3,696	Dr. J. L. Clough (1987)
Royal School, Bath	1864	275	£5,250°	£3,150°	Dr. J. McClure (1987)
Runton Hill School, Norfolk	1911	155	£5,325	£3,525	Dr. A. Cardew (1987)
Rye St. Anthony School, Oxford ...	1930	350	£4,605	£2,520	P. M. Sumpter (1976)
Sacred Heart School, Kent	1915	208	£6,090	£3,450	(a) Dr. J. A. Fallon (1979)
St. Albans High School, Herts.	1889	500	....	£2,670	E. M. Diggory (1983)
St. Andrew's School, Bedford	1897	200	....	£1,845	Mrs. S. E. Cooke (1987)
St. Anne's School, Cumbria........	1863	310	£6,114	£4,035	(a) M. P. Hawkins (1986)
St. Anthony's-Leweston School, Dorset	1891	401	£5,985	£3,900	Mrs. P. Cartwright (1983)
St. Audries School, Somerset	1906	140	£5,589	£3,228	Mrs. A. Smith (1988)
St. Brandon's School, Avon	1831	240	£5,955	£2,985	(a) J. S. Davey (1978)
St. Catherine's School, Surrey	1885	435	£5,205	£3,180	(a) J. R. Palmer (1983)
*School of St. Clare, Penzance	1889	132	£4,455	£2,535	(a) I. Halford (1986)
St. David's School, Middx..........	1716	232°	£4,518°	£2,622°	Mrs. J. G. Osborne (1985)
St. Dunstan's Abbey, Devon	1850	246	£3,915	£2,325	H. L. Abley (1970)
St. Elphin's School, Derbys.	1844	230	£5,490	£3,105	(a) A. P. C. Pollard (1979)
St. Felix School, Suffolk	1897	360	£5,841	£3,615	M. A. Claydon (1987)
St. Francis' College, Herts.	1933	235	£4,980	£2,505	Mrs. J. Frith (1987)
S. Gabriel's School, Berks..........	1929	145	....	£2,949	Mrs. P. Gott (1980)
St. George's School, Ascot, Berks. ..	1923	270	£6,000	£3,375	Mrs. A. M. Griggs (1989)
School of St. Helen and St. Katharine, Oxon.	1903	518	£4,125	£2,145	Y. Paterson (1973)
St. Helen's School, Middx..........	1899	554	£5,115	£2,715	Dr. Y. A. Burne (1987)
*St. Hilary's School, Cheshire	1880	230	....	£2,453	Mrs. J. Tracey (1985)
St. Hilary's School, Sevenoaks, Kent	1942	160	....	£2,850	Mrs. P. Miles (1977)
St. James's and the Abbey, Worcs...	1896	160	£6,150	£4,101	E. M. Mullenger (1986)
St. Joseph's Convent School, Berks.	1909	510	....	£2,340	M. Ball (1985)
St. Joseph's School, Lincoln	1905	200	£4,350	£2,100	Mrs. A. Scott (1983)
St. Leonards-Mayfield School, E. Sussex	—	540	£5,805	£3,870	Sr. J. Sinclair (1980)
St. Margaret's School, Bushey, Herts	1749	393	£5,055	£3,114	Mrs. S. K. Law (1985)
*St. Margaret's School, Exeter	1904	375	£3,330	£2,025	Mrs. J. M. Giddings (1984)
St. Martin's, Solihull, W. Midlands .	1941	350	....	£2,415	Mrs. S. J. Williams (*acting*)
St. Mary's Hall, Brighton	1836	370	£5,682	£3,558	Mrs. M. T. Broadbent (1988)
St. Mary's School, Ascot, Berks. ...	1885	320	£6,237	£3,741	Sr. M. M. Orchard (1982)
St. Mary's School, Calne, Wilts.....	1872	320	£5,860	£3,480	D. H. Burns (1985)
St. Mary's School, Cambridge......	1898	550	£3,840	£2,160	Sr. M. C. Kenworthy-Browne (1977)
St. Mary's School, Colchester	1908	310	....	£2,130	Mrs. G. M. G. Mouser (1981)
St. Mary's School, Gerrards Cross ..	1872	340	....	£2,700	Mrs. J. P. G. Smith (1984)
St. Mary's School, Shaftesbury	1945	280	£5,628	£3,378	Sr. M. Campion Livesey (1985)
St. Mary's School, Wantage, Oxon..	1873	300	£6,150	....	Mrs. P. H. Johns (1980)
*St. Michael's, Burton Park, W. Sussex	1844	205	£5,850	£4,050	Mrs. M. Steeves (1981)
St. Michael's, Limpsfield, Surrey ...	1850	150	£5,655	£3,102	(a) Dr. B. Long (1983)
St. Paul's Girls' School, W6	1904	640	....	£3,720	Mrs. H. Brigstocke (*High Mistress*) (1974)
St. Stephen's College, Kent	1867	87	£5,490	£3,390	M. de Villiers (1987)

*Woodard Corporation School. °1988 figure.

Name of School	F'ded.	No. of Pupils	Annual Fees B'ding	Annual Fees Day	Headmistress (a) Headmaster (With date of Appointment)
St. Swithun's School, Hants.	1884	410	£6,510	£4,095	J. E. Jefferson (1986)
Selwyn School, Glos.	—	n/a	n/a	n/a	H. S. Beswick
‡Sheffield High School	1878	689	....	£2,085	D. M. Skilbeck (1983)
Sherborne School, Dorset	1899	460	£6,690	£4,455	J. M. Taylor (1985)
‡Shrewsbury High School	1885	546	....	£2,085	E. M. Gill (1982)
Sir William Perkins's School, Surrey	1725	470	....	£2,175	Mrs. A. F. Darlow (1982)
‡South Hampstead High School, NW3	1876	664	....	£2,367	Mrs. D. A. Burgess (1975)
Springfield Park, W Sussex	—	n/a	n/a	n/a	Mrs. H. D. Schofield
Stamford High School, Lincs.	1876	746	£4,344	£2,172	G. K. Bland (1978)
Stonar School, Wilts.	1921	331	£5,700	£3,060	Mrs. S. Hopkinson (1985)
Stover School, Devon	1932	265	£4,878	£2,664	Mrs. W. E. Lunel (1984)
Stratford House School, Kent	1912	250	....	£2,685	Mrs. A. Williamson (1974)
‡Streatham Hill and Clapham High School, SW2	1887	480	....	£2,367	G. M. Ellis (1979)
Sunderland Church High School (CSC)	1884	250†	....	£2,364	Mrs. M. Thrush (1980)
Surbiton High School (CSC), Surrey	1884	402°	....	£2,340°	Mrs. R. A. Thynne (1979)
‡Sutton High School, Surrey	1884	817	....	£2,367	A. E. Cavendish (1980)
‡Sydenham High School, SE26	1887	647	....	£2,367	(a) S. G. Baker (1988)
Talbot Heath, Dorset	1886	536	£4,863	£2,511	C. E. Austin-Smith (1976)
Teesside High School, Cleveland	1970	561	....	£2,214	Mrs. J. Coles (1982)
Tormead School, Surrey	1905	400	....	£2,526	Mrs. J. Crouch-Smith (1977)
Truro High School	1880	423	£4,458	£2,466	Mrs. J. F. Marshall (1984)
*Tudor Hall School, Oxon.	1850	225°	£6,150	£3,927	N. Godfrey (1984)
Upper Chine, Isle of Wight	1799	250	£5,175	£2,685	(a) S. H. Monard (1989)
Ursuline Convent School, Kent	1904	340	£5,646	£2,859	Sr. M. Murphy (1977)
Ursuline High School, Ilford	1903	420	....	£2,430	P. Dixon (1984)
Wadhurst College, E. Sussex	1930	230	£5,970	£3,705	D. Swatman (1972)
Wakefield Girls' High School	1878	750	....	£2,367	Mrs. P. A. Langham (1987)
Walthamstow Hall, Kent	1838	415	£5,520	£2,985	Mrs. J. S. Lang (1984)
Wentworth Milton Mount, Dorset	1962	350	£4,920	£2,925	M. Vokins (1982)
Westfield School, Newcastle upon Tyne	1962	220	....	£2,133	(a) J. S. Taylor (1986)
West Heath, Kent	1867	150	£5,775	£4,050	Mrs. D. Cohn-Sherbok (1988)
Westholme School, Lancs.	1923	600	....	£1,950	Mrs. L. Croston (1988)
Westonbirt, Glos.	1928	225	£6,420	£4,125	Mrs. G. Hylson-Smith (1986)
Westwood House School, Peterborough	—	250	£4,620	£2,280	Mrs. A. J. V. Storey (1977)
‡Wimbledon High School, SW19	1880	675	....	£2,367	Mrs. R. A. Smith (1982)
Wispers School, Surrey	1946	193	£4,875	£3,000	(a) L. H. Beltran (1979)
Withington Girls' School, Manchester	1890	465	....	£2,220	Mrs. M. Kenyon (1986)
Woldingham School, Surrey	1842	450	£6,165	£3,735	Dr. P. Dineen (1985)
Wroxhall Abbey School, Warwick	1872	150	£5,955	£3,588	Mrs. I. D. M. Iles (1980)
Wychwood School, Oxford	—	n/a	n/a	n/a	Mrs. M. L. Duffill
Wycombe Abbey School, Bucks.	1896	490	£7,200	....	Mrs. J. M. Goodland (1989)
York College (CSC)	1908	281	....	£2,619	Mrs. J. L. Clare (1982)
Scotland					
Laurel Bank School, Glasgow	1903	281	....	£2,619	L. G. Egginton (1984)
Mary Erskine School, Edinburgh	1694	560	£4,896	£2,526	R. M. Morgan (Principal) (1978)
Oxenfoord Castle School, Midlothian	—	70	£6,120	£2,235	M. Carmichael (1979)
Park School, Glasgow	1880	300	....	£2,277	Mrs. M. E. Myatt (1986)
St. Denis and Cranley School, Edinburgh	1858	195	£5,040	£2,535	Mrs. J. M. Munro (1984)
St. George's School, Edinburgh	1888	600	£5,100	£2,580	Mrs. J. G. Scott (1986)
St. Leonards School, St. Andrews	1877	362	£7,050	£3,525	Mrs. L. E. James (1988)
St. Margaret's School, Aberdeen	1846	315	£4,872	£2,073	L. Ogilvie (1989)
St. Margaret's School, Edinburgh	1890	575	£4,920	£2,580	Mrs. M. J. Cameron (1984)
Wellington School, Ayr		520	£5,088	£2,505	(a) A. J. Grigg (1983)
Channel Islands					
The Ladies' College, Guernsey	1872	350	....	£1,080	J. Honey (1976)

‡ Girls' Public Day School Trust, 26 Queen Anne's Gate, SW1H 9AN.   * Woodard Corporation School.
C.S.C. Church Schools Company, 1a Doughty Street, WC1N 2PH.   † Boys in VI form.   ° 1988 figure.

EVENTS OF THE YEAR
SEPT. 1, 1987—AUG. 31, 1988

THE ROYAL HOUSE

(1987). **Sept. 2.** The Princess Royal opened the British Olympic Medical Centre, Harrow. **9.** The Prince and Princess of Wales visited Caen and Bayeux in Normandy, France. **12.** The Duke and Duchess of York attended the last night of the Proms. **14.** The Princess Royal left R.A.F. Lyneham to visit West Germany and Cyprus. **16.** The Duke and Duchess of York left Heathrow Airport for the U.S.A. **22.** The Duchess of York arrived at Heathrow Airport from New York. The Princess Royal left Heathrow Airport for Brazil. **23.** The Duchess of York viewed the photographic entries for the Search '88 Cancer Trust book *One Day for Life*. **24.** The Princess of Wales attended a luncheon in aid of the British 1988 Paraolympics team. The Duke and Duchess of York left R.A.F. Northolt for Mauritius. **30.** The Princess Royal arrived at Heathrow Airport from Brazil.

Oct. 4. The Duke of Edinburgh left Dyce Airport for Geneva. **6.** Prince Edward attended the 1987 British Video Awards. **7.** The Princess Royal delivered the New Sarum lecture at Salisbury Cathedral. **8.** The Duke and Duchess of York arrived at Heathrow from Mauritius. **9.** The Queen and the Duke of Edinburgh left Heathrow Airport for Canada. **21.** The Prince and Princess of Wales visited the scenes of recent flooding in Wales. **25.** The Queen arrived at Heathrow Airport from Canada. **26.** The Duke of Edinburgh arrived at R.A.F. Marham from the U.S.A.

Nov. 1. The Prince and Princess of Wales left R.A.F. Northolt for West Germany. Prince Edward presented the 1987 Schools Design Prize at the Science Museum. **4.** The Queen attended a reception to mark the 60th anniversary of the Royal Television Society. **5.** The Queen opened the London City Airport. The Duchess of York attended the launch of the book *One Day for Life* in London. **6.** The Queen visited the Commonwealth Institute. **7.** The Prince and Princess of Wales arrived at R.A.F. Northolt from West Germany. The Queen and other members of the Royal Family were present at the Royal British Legion Festival of Remembrance at the Royal Albert Hall. **8.** The Queen and other members of the Royal Family laid wreaths at the Cenotaph on Remembrance Day. **9.** The Queen opened the Thames Valley Hospice. The Princess Royal left Gatwick Airport for South Korea. **10.** The Princess of Wales attended the Champion Children luncheon in London. **11.** The Duke of Edinburgh visited West Germany. **13.** The Princess Royal commenced visits to Singapore, Thailand, Laos and Burma. **16.** The Queen attended the premiere of the film *Melba*. **17.** The Prince and Princess

of Wales visited victims of the Remembrance Day bombing at the Erne Hospital, Enniskillen. **18.** Prince Edward switched on the Christmas lights in Regent Street, London. **20.** The Queen and the Duke of Edinburgh celebrated their 40th wedding anniversary. **24.** The Princess Royal arrived at Heathrow Airport from Burma. The Prince of Wales opened the International Conference on the Protection of the North Sea, in London. **25.** The Queen and the Duke of Edinburgh visited the Royal College of Defence Studies. **30.** Prince Edward attended a banquet in aid of the Mobility Trust.

Dec. 3. The Princess of Wales distributed Christmas presents at the Great Ormond Street Children's Hospital. **4.** The Princess of Wales opened a drugs detoxification unit at Cosham, Hants. The Prince and Princess of Wales attended a Royal Gala Performance at the London Palladium in aid of the Prince's Trust. **5.** The Princess of Wales was present at the King's Cross Fire Memorial Service. **6.** The Princess Royal left R.A.F. Lyneham for Paris. **7.** The Queen planted a tree at Runnymede for National Tree week. The Prince of Wales left R.A.F. Kemble for a one-day visit to Milan. **10.** The Duke of Edinburgh left Staverton airport for a one-day visit to Paris. **15.** Prince Edward attended the funeral of Prince Ernst August of Hanover. **16.** The Duchess of York presented the Children of Courage awards in Westminster Abbey. The Prince of Wales, accompanied by the Princess of Wales, attended a gala premiere of *Cinderella* at the Royal Opera House, Covent Garden. **17.** The Prince of Wales visited Brussels. **25.** The Queen made her traditional Christmas broadcast to the Commonwealth. **31.** The New Year's Honours List was published.

(1988). **Jan. 20.** The Duchess of York left Heathrow Airport for the U.S.A. **21.** The Princess of Wales visited the headquarters of the Turning Point charity in London. **22.** The Duchess of York arrived at Heathrow Airport from the U.S.A. **23.** The Prince and Princess of Wales left Heathrow Airport to visit Australia and Thailand. **24.** Prince Edward attended the Laurence Olivier Awards ceremony. **28.** The Duke of Edinburgh left Heathrow Airport to visit Costa Rica, Belize, Mexico and the Galapagos Islands. **31.** The Duchess of York left Heathrow Airport for France.

Feb. 5. The Duke of York launched "Youth in the Air 1988" at the Royal Aeronautical Society. **7.** The Duchess of York arrived at Heathrow Airport from France. The Princess of Wales arrived at Heathrow Airport from Thailand. **12.** The Queen visited the Wildfowl Trust at Slimbridge, Glos. The Princess Royal left Heathrow Airport for Canada. **15.** Prince Edward began work as a theatrical production assistant at the Palace Theatre, London. The Duke and Duchess of York visited Northern Ireland. **17.** The Queen attended a reception marking the 60th anniversary of the National Council for Voluntary Organizations. The Prince and Princess of Wales opened the "Suleyman the Magnificent" exhibition at the British Museum. **18.** The Duchess of York visited Harefield Hospital. The Queen Mother visited Lloyd's in London. **19.** The Queen opened the Guards Museum at Wellington Barracks, London. The Princess Royal arrived at Heathrow Airport from Canada. **20.** Prince Edward left R.A.F. Northolt for a one-day visit to France. **22.** The Princess Royal left Heathrow Airport to visit Uganda, Mozambique and Somalia. The Prince of Wales attended a dinner at 10 Downing Street. **26.** The Duke of Edinburgh arrived at Heathrow Airport from Morocco. The Duke and Duchess of York left Heathrow Airport for the U.S.A. The Princess of Wales started the Penguin Swimathon '88 in London.

March 4. The Duke of Edinburgh visited Cambridge University. The Prince of Wales left Heathrow Airport for the U.S.A. **5.** The Princess Royal arrived at R.A.F. Lyneham from Somalia. **7.** The Queen and the Duke of Edinburgh attended a preview of the *Daily Mail* Ideal Home Exhibition at Earls Court. The Duke and Duchess of York arrived at Heathrow Airport from the U.S.A. The Prince of Wales arrived at Heathrow Airport from the U.S.A. **8.** The Queen and the Duke of Edinburgh attended a reception at the Royal Institution to mark the 175th anniversary of the Royal Philharmonic Society. **10.** The Queen and the Duke of Edinburgh visited the Queen's Club to view the Centenary Tennis Exhibition. The Prince of Wales was a member of a ski party that was hit by an avalanche in Klosters, Switzerland : one member of the party, Maj. Hugh Lindsay, was killed. **11.** The Prince and Princess of Wales and the Duchess of York arrived at R.A.F. Northolt from Switzerland. **14.** The Queen and the Duke of Edinburgh attended the Commonwealth Day Observance Service in Westminster Abbey. **17.** The Queen and the Duke of Edinburgh attended a reception at Burlington House to mark the centenary of the Linnean Society of London. The Prince and Princess of Wales attended the funeral of Major Hugh Lindsay at Sandhurst. **18.** The Queen opened the new Rail/Air Link at Victoria Station. **19.** Prince Edward attended the Wales v France rugby international in Cardiff. **21.** The Queen attended the Royal Film Performance of *Empire of the Sun* in London. **26.** The Princess Royal and Captain Mark Phillips left Heathrow Airport for Australia. **28.** The Duchess of York opened the London International Book Fair. **29.** The

Duke of Edinburgh attended the 21st meeting of the Standing Conference on Countryside Sports in London. **30.** Prince Edward opened the new premises of the National Youth Theatre in London. **31.** The Queen and the Duke of Edinburgh attended the Maundy Service at Lichfield Cathedral. The Duchess of York was admitted as an Honorary Freeman of the Worshipful Company of Stationers and Newspaper Makers in London.

April 2. The Princess Royal and Captain Mark Phillips arrived at Heathrow Airport from Australia. **8.** The Princess Royal delivered the 1988 St. George's House Annual Lecture at St. George's Chapel, Windsor. **9.** The Princess Royal unveiled a statue of the racehorse Red Rum at Aintree Racecourse. **12.** The King of Norway arrived at Heathrow airport for a State visit. **15.** The Princess Royal launched the submarine *H.M.S. Talent* at Barrow-in-Furness. **17.** The Princess of Wales started the London Marathon. **18.** The Queen and the Duke of Edinburgh left Heathrow Airport for Australia. **21.** Lord Hailsham and Lord Leverhulme were appointed to the Order of the Garter. **22.** The Princess Royal left R.A.F. Lyneham for a two-day visit to Switzerland. **26.** The Queen Mother opened the new London Scottish Regimental Headquarters in London. **27.** Prince Edward left Heathrow Airport for Australia. The Princess of Wales attended the Gala Premiere of *Wall Street* at the Odeon Cinema, Haymarket. **29.** The Princess Royal visited the Spring Centre Pre-School Project in Gloucester.

May 2. The Duke and Duchess of York attended a performance of *Back with a Vengeance*. Prince Edward arrived at Heathrow airport from Australia. **3.** The Princess of Wales addressed the British/American Conference on Private Initiatives held in London. The Princess of Wales named a British Rail 125 locomotive "The Red Cross". **5.** The Princess of Wales attended a performance by the Moscow State Circus in London. **8.** The Prince of Wales left Heathrow Airport to visit France. **9.** The Princess Royal opened the new Regimental Museum of the 14th/20th King's Hussars in Preston. **11.** The Queen and the Duke of Edinburgh arrived at Heathrow Airport from Australia. Prince Edward attended the premiere of the film *Jane and the Lost City*. **12.** The Duchess of York attended the opening of the "Images de France" festival at the Barbican Centre. The Princess of Wales attended a gala performance of *The Magic Flute* at the London Coliseum. **14.** The Princess of Wales attended the F.A. Cup Final at Wembley Stadium. **16.** The Princess Royal visited Paris. The Princess of Wales attended a reception to mark the 25th year of the National Children's Bureau in London. **17.** The Queen and the Duke of Edinburgh attended a Service of the Order of the British Empire at St. Paul's Cathedral. The Princess of Wales visited the Royal Ballet School. **19.** The Queen attended a reception at St. James's Palace to mark the 10th anniversary of Motability. **23.** The Queen, the Duke of Edinburgh and the Princess Royal visited the Chelsea Flower Show. **24.** The Queen and the Duke of Edinburgh attended a service at St. Paul's Cathedral to celebrate the 250th anniversary of the conversion of John Wesley. The Princess Royal left R.A.F. Lyneham for Berlin. **31.** The Princess of Wales visited the counselling centre of Relate: Marriage Guidance in London.

June 1. The Queen and other members of the Royal Family visited Epsom Races. The Princess Royal visited the University of London Institute of Education. **4.** Prince Edward left Heathrow Airport to visit Canada. **6.** The Queen attended the Royal Gala Night of Ballet in honour of Dame Ninette de Valois at the Royal Opera House. The Princess Royal attended a dinner at the Institute of Directors in London. The Prince and Princess of Wales attended a rock concert at the Royal Albert Hall in aid of the Prince's Trust. **7.** The Duchess of York attended a Gala Performance of the Ballet Rambert at Sadlers Wells Theatre. The Princess of Wales visited Papworth Hospital, Cambridge, and Newmarket General Hospital. **10.** The Queen's Birthday Honours list was published. **11.** The Queen, accompanied by other members of the Royal Family, was present at The Queen's Birthday Parade on Horse Guard's Parade. Prince Edward arrived at Heathrow Airport from Canada. The Princess Royal attended the Festival of Youth 1988 at Battersea Park. **14.** The Queen, accompanied by other members of the Royal Family, visited Ascot Races. **19.** The Duke of Edinburgh attended a Royal Variety Show at the Adelphi Theatre in London. Prince Edward visited Northern Ireland. **23.** The Duke of Edinburgh attended a reception in London to mark the 70th anniversary of the English Speaking Union. **24.** The Prince of Wales visited the islands of Skokholm and Stomer. **28.** The Queen Mother opened the restored birthplace of Thomas Bewick at Cherryburn, Northumberland.

July 4. The Queen and the Duke of Edinburgh left Heathrow Airport for the Netherlands, to attend events commemorating the tercentary of the Glorious Revolution. **6.** The Queen and the Duke of Edinburgh arrived at Heathrow Airport from the Netherlands. The Princess Royal left R.A.F. Northolt for Munster, West Germany, returning the following day. **8.** The Princess Royal attended the Olympic Fundraising Ball at the Savoy hotel. **9.** The Princess Royal rode in a race at Les Landes Race Course, Jersey.

11. The Duke of Edinburgh attended a dinner given by the Royal Navy Club 1765 and 1785 to commemorate the 400th anniversary of the Armada. **12.** The President of the Republic of Turkey arrived in London on a State visit. **16.** The Prince and Princess of Wales attended a concert at Wembley Stadium in aid of the Wishing Well Appeal for Great Ormond Street Children's Hospital. **18.** The Queen, accompanied by the Duke of Edinburgh, attended the Royal Tournament at Earl's Court. Prince Edward started "An Extremely Trivial Pursuit 1988" at Hyde Park Corner, in aid of the Chemical Dependency Centre. The Princess of Wales attended a Gala Performance of the London Festival Ballet at the London Coliseum. **20.** On the occasion of the tercentenary of the Revolution of 1688–89 the Queen, accompanied by the Duke of Edinburgh, received addresses from both Houses of Parliament at Westminster. Later the Queen and the Duke of Edinburgh visited Torquay and subsequently embarked in H.M. Yacht *Britannia*. **21.** The Queen and the Duke of Edinburgh visited Brixham. **22.** The Queen and Duke of Edinburgh visited Devonport and Plymouth. **24.** The Prince of Wales opened the 1988 National Wheelchair Games in Buckinghamshire. **26.** The Queen attended a Gala Performance of the Australian Ballet at the Royal Opera House. **30.** The Duke of Edinburgh attended a dinner to celebrate the 150th anniversary of the Royal London Yacht Club at Cowes.

Aug. 1. The Princess of Wales attended the YMCA/Today Programme Best of British Youth Awards luncheon in London. **2.** The Queen visited the Armada Exhibition at Greenwich. **5.** The Queen left Southampton on H.M. Yacht *Britannia*, for Scotland. The Prince of Wales opened the National Waterways Museum in Gloucester. **8.** The Duchess of York gave birth to a daughter weighing 6 lb 12 ozs at the Portland Hospital, London; on Aug. 22, it was announced that the Princess would be called Beatrice Elizabeth Mary. **15.** The Queen and the Duke of Edinburgh met members of the rescue teams involved in the Piper Alpha disaster, in Edinburgh. **23.** Prince Edward attended the gala opening performance of the Furness Mystery Plays at Furness Abbey.

BRITISH POLITICS

(1987). Sept. 14. The Liberal Party annual conference began at Harrogate: on Sept. 17 party members voted to dissolve the Liberal Party and form a new party with the Social Democrats. **20.** The Northern Ireland Secretary (Mr. Tom King) left for a ten day visit to the U.S.A. **24.** The Foreign Secretary (Sir Geoffrey Howe) closed the Iranian military procurement office in London in response to an Iranian attack on a British oil tanker. On

Sept. 25 Iran retaliated by severing trade links with Britain. 26. David Alton resigned as Liberal chief whip to concentrate on his campaign for greater restrictions on abortion. 28. The Labour Party annual conference began at Brighton; delegates voted in favour of a major overhaul of policy and for an extension of the franchise for the selection and re-selection of parliamentary candidates: on Oct. 1 the conference called for a minimum wage of £120 or two thirds of the average wage, and a 35-hour week without loss of pay: on Oct. 2 the decision not to allow black sections to be formed within the party was reaffirmed.

Oct. 3. The Speaker of the House of Commons (Mr. Bernard Weatherill) suspended the rights of access to the parliamentary precincts of Mr. Ronan Bennett, research assistant of M.P. Jeremy Corbyn, because of his conviction in 1975 (later quashed) of the murder of an R.U.C. officer. The Northern Ireland Alliance Party elected John Alderdice to succeed John Cushnahan as leader. 5. Mr. Jim Wallace, M.P. for Orkney and Shetland, was elected the new Liberal chief whip. 6. The Conservative Party conference began at Blackpool: delegates rejected the Cabinet's plan to phase in the community charge in favour of immediate implementation: on Oct. 7 the Home Secretary (Mr. Douglas Hurd) announced new measures to curb the use of offensive weapons: on Oct 8 a review of the National Health Service was announced by the Social Services Secretary (Mr. John Moore). 26. The Lord Chancellor, Lord Havers, resigned due to ill health and was replaced by Lord Mackay of Clashfern. 30. The Labour Party's official newspaper *Labour Weekly* published its last issue.

Nov. 2. Sir Philip Woodfield was appointed part-time ombudsman for the security services. 3. Mr. Peter Brooke, a junior Treasury minister, was appointed chairman of the Conservative Party in succession to Mr. Norman Tebbit. 5. Mr. Richard Luce, Minister for the Arts, announced an increase in funding for the arts of 17 per cent. over the next three years. 11. Mr. William Rodgers, a vice-president of the S.D.P., resigned from his party post to become director-general of the Royal Institution of British Architects. 12. Labour M.P. Tam Dalyell was suspended from the House of Commons for five days for calling the Prime Minister a liar. Labour Party headquarters were closed by a strike over redundancy terms offered to *Labour Weekly* journalists. 15. The Communist Party of Great Britain severed its links with the *Morning Star* newspaper. 16. Labour M.P. Mr. Ken Livingstone was disowned by Labour Party leaders following his prediction that British troops would be forced to leave Ulster. 17. The Home Office announced that Mr.

Michael Day was to be the new chairman of the Commission for Racial Equality. The Government announced that the new community charge will be introduced on April 1, 1990 in England and Wales, except inner London and Waltham Forest. 20. The Prime Minister announced that Mr. Nicholas Serota was to be the new director of the Tate Gallery. 24. Mr. John Moore, Social Services Secretary, was re-admitted to hospital after being taken ill during a meeting at 10 Downing Street: he had only returned to work a few days earlier following a bout of pneumonia.

Dec. 1. The Prime Minister, Mrs. Thatcher, rebuked the French and Irish Governments for their attitude towards terrorism. 2. Broad agreement was reached on the constitution for a unified S.D.P.–Liberal party. 3. The Government said that it planned to privatize British Steel. 7. Mrs. Thatcher held talks with the Soviet leader Mr. Gorbachev at R.A.F. Brize Norton during a break in his flight to the Washington summit talks. 10. The Government admitted that a computer error had led to the publication of incorrect inflation figures for the previous 21 months. 14. Lord Whitelaw was taken to hospital after suffering a slight stroke. 16. The Minister of Health (Mr. Antony Newton) announced that £100 million in emergency funding was to be given to the National Health Service. 18. Mr. Kenneth Clarke, the Trade and Industry Minister, was named as the minister responsible for co-ordinating and presenting government policy on the inner cities.

(1988). Jan. 3. Mrs. Thatcher became the longest serving Prime Minister this century. 10. Viscount Whitelaw resigned from his parliamentary posts for health reasons: Lord Belstead became the new Leader of the House of Lords. 11. Labour M.P. John Hughes was suspended from the House of Commons for five days for disrupting the daily prayer session. 12. The Department of Trade and Industry published a White Paper *DTI—the department for Enterprise*. 13. Liberal M.P.s rejected a joint policy statement by their leader David Steel and S.D.P. leader Robert Maclennan: on Jan. 14 the two leaders abandoned the policy statement and said a new statement, drafted by members of both parties, would be issued: on Jan. 18 Liberal M.P.s accepted the new policy statement. 15. The Government defeated a Conservative backbench attempt to reform the Official Secrets Act. 19. The Secretary of State for Social Services (Mr. John Moore) said that no additional resources for the Health Service would be funded by taxation. 22. The Abortion (Amendment) Bill sponsored by Mr. David Alton passed its second reading in the Commons with a majority of 45. 24. The Liberal Party voted by a large majority to merge with the Social Democratic Party.

25. Labour M.P. Mr. Ken Livingstone was suspended from the House of Commons after calling the Attorney-General an "accomplice to murder" following the announcement of the decision not to prosecute R.U.C. officers involved in an alleged shoot-to-kill policy. 27. The Campaign group of left-wing Labour M.P.s voted to challenge the re-election of the party leader, Mr. Kinnock, and the deputy leader, Mr. Hattersley. 31. The S.D.P. voted to merge with the Liberals.

Feb. 2. A group of gay rights protesters abseiled into the chamber of the House of Lords to protest at Clause 28 of the Local Finance Bill. Labour M.P. Mr. Dale Campbell-Savours named three Northern Ireland police officers, Supts. Anderson, Flanagan and Browne, as the men who had allegedly been exempted from prosecution in the wake of the "shoot-to-kill" investigation: on Feb. 4 the Labour Party leader, Mr. Neil Kinnock, demanded a judical enquiry into the affair: on Feb. 5 the former Assistant Chief Constable of Greater Manchester, Mr. John Stalker, claimed that he was removed from the inquiry days before he was due to interview senior police officers about specific allegations; on Feb. 17 the Northern Ireland Secretary (Mr. Tom King) said that senior R.U.C. officers had been referred for possible disciplinary action. 4. Mrs. Thatcher redistributed Cabinet committee chairmanships previously held by Lord Whitelaw. 9. The House of Commons voted by a majority of 54 to allow its proceedings to be televised. 10. A Commons motion of no confidence was tabled against the Master of the Rolls, Sir John Donaldson, after he said in a Court of Appeal judgment that the security services were justified in using burglary and bugging. 12. Twenty Young Conservatives were barred from attending their own conference for fear that they might publicly embarrass the party. 14. Foreign Secretary Sir Geoffrey Howe visited Moscow. 16. The Government proposed to make the Prevention of Terrorism Act permanent. 18. The Government announced plans for a major reform of the Civil Service. 25. The Energy Secretary, Mr. Cecil Parkinson, released proposals for the privatization of the electricity supply industry in England and Wales.

March 9. The Prime Minister launched an inquiry into the leaking of a private letter from her office criticizing Department of Education plans for testing schoolchildren. 11. Forty Labour M.P.s signed a Commons motion that said that the shooting of three unarmed I.R.A. terrorists in Gibraltar was "tantamount to capital punishment without trial" and should be regarded as "an act of terrorism". 15. The Chancellor of the Exchequer (Mr. Lawson) presented his Budget in the Commons: the Budget proposals were passed

after a week of debate. 17. Opponents of the Abortion Bill sponsored by David Alton accused the Liberal M.P. of using dirty tactics in his campaign. 19. Mrs Thatcher, in a speech to Conservative Party members in Buxton, described Mr. Lawson's Budget as an "epitaph for socialism". The Social and Liberal Democratic Party was launched in London. 22. The Prime Minister condemned the BBC, ITN and the Irish television station RTE for refusing to release untransmitted film of the mob murder of two soldiers in Belfast: on March 23 the Royal Ulster Constabulary seized untransmitted film from the BBC and ITN. The Campaign Group of Labour M.P.s decided that Mr. Tony Benn and Mr. Eric Heffer would challenge the party leaders, Mr. Neil Kinnock and Mr. Roy Hattersley in the party leadership elections in the autumn. 29. The Government agreed to sell the Rover Group to British Aerospace for £150 million and to provide £800 million in cash towards writing off Rover's debts: the deal required the agreement of the European Commission because of the level of State aid involved. 29. Four Labour M.P.s resigned from the Campaign Group in protest at the decision of Mr. Benn and Mr. Heffer to contest the party leadership. 30. Mr. John Prescott declared that he would stand against Roy Hattersley in the elections for the deputy leadership of the Labour Party.

April 2. The Dalai Lama, the exiled spiritual leader of Tibet, was asked by the Foreign Office not to hold a press conference in London about the troubles in his homeland. 11. Pensioners demonstrated at Downing Street and D.H.S.S. clerical staff picketed in Whitehall in protest at changes in social security. 12. Following exchanges between the Prime Minister and Mr. Kinnock, the Speaker of the House of Commons granted a three-hour emergency debate on the social security changes. 13. Labour M.P. David Nellist was suspended from the Commons for five days for refusing to resume his seat when told to do so. 18. The Government's majority was reduced to 25 as an amendment to the Bill introducing the community charge was only narrowly defeated: after the adjournment of the sitting Labour M.P. Ron Brown picked up the Mace and threw it to the floor. 19. Mr. Ron Brown was ejected from the House of Commons after failing to read an agreed personal statement apologising for damaging the Mace: on April 20 Mr. Brown was suspended from the Commons for 20 days, and subsequently had the Labour Party whip withdrawn from him for three months. 25. The Government gave the go-ahead for the development of the Eurofighter aircraft for the R.A.F. 27. The Social Services Secretary (Mr. Moore) announced a number of changes to the new social security regulations following recent criticism and the threat of a

Conservative backbench rebellion. **28.** The Independent Broadcasting Authority ignored a request from the Foreign Secretary to postpone broadcasting a film about the killing of three I.R.A. members in Gibraltar. Labour M.P. Ken Livingstone withdrew from the House of Commons in protest at being still without an office nearly one year after the General Election.

May 5. Local council elections were held: the Labour Party made a net gain of 104 seats. The BBC, rejecting a request for postponement from the Foreign Secretary (Sir Geoffrey Howe), broadcast a documentary about the shooting of three I.R.A. members in Gibraltar. **6.** Due to lack of time Mr. David Alton's Abortion Bill failed to pass through the Commons. **12.** Mr. David Steel announced that he would not be standing for the leadership of the new Social and Liberal Democratic party. **16.** Sir William Rees-Mogg was appointed chairman of the new Broadcasting Standards Council. **17.** The Government published a Defence White Paper. **22.** Labour M.P. Bernie Grant made allegations of racial abuse by parliamentary staff to the House of Commons authorities. **24.** The Leader of the House of Commons (Mr. Wakeham) announced that opposition political parties were to receive a 70 per cent. increase in official funding. **30.** The Government and the Labour Party urged the publication in full of a report into the operation of anti-racist policies at Burnage High School, Manchester, where a young Asian boy was murdered by a fellow-pupil.

June 6. A change in Labour Party rules was passed by a party committee, making it necessary for any potential candidate for the leadership to have the backing of at least 20 per cent. of the party's M.P.s instead of the 5 per cent. needed at present. **7.** The House of Commons rejected an attempt to restore capital punishment as the maximum sentence for murder. **17.** An attache at the Israeli Embassy, Arie Regev, was ordered to leave Britain "for activities incompatible with his status". An official at the P.L.O. office in London was also expelled. **18.** The Labour deputy leader Mr. Roy Hattersley launched an attack on Mr. Tony Benn, the rival to Neil Kinnock in the forthcoming leadership election. Mr. Hattersley accused Mr. Benn of a "betrayal" of the Labour Party. **26.** Mr. Arthur Scargill, president of the National Union of Mineworkers, endorsed the candidacy of Mr. Benn for the Labour Party leadership, while acknowledging that his union would probably support Mr. Kinnock. **27.** The Government announced concessions on proposals in the Local Government Finance Bill which will exempt a further 25,000 people from paying the community charge. **29.** The Government published a White Paper

on the reform of the Official Secrets Act. **30.** The Prime Minister appointed Mr. Cecil Parkinson as chairman of the senior ministers who will adjudicate on Whitehall and Treasury spending for the forthcoming year.

July 3. In a speech at the celebrations of the 40th anniversary of the National Health Service, Mr. Kinnock accused Mrs. Thatcher of embodying "the values of Marie Antoinette" in her contempt for the N.H.S. **6.** Following the publication of the report of the inquiry into the Cleveland child abuse crisis, the Government announced a package of measures intended to prevent a repetition of the case. **11.** Mrs. Thatcher answered questions on the BBC World Service from listeners in the Soviet Union. **14.** The Conservative candidate, Mr. Dudley Fishburn, won the by-election at Kensington, with a reduced majority of 815 votes. **16.** Foreign Office Minister, Mr. David Mellor said that there was no hope of progress towards peace in the Middle East as long as Mr. Yitzhak Shamir remained Prime Minister of Israel: Mr. Mellor was quoted in an Arab newspaper of accusing Israel of becoming like South Africa. **17.** Mr. Neil Kinnock, his wife and three members of his staff were detained at gunpoint for more than an hour at an airstrip at Mutare, Zimbabwe, during a tour of southern Africa: Mr. Kinnock's party had arrived at Mutare instead of Grand Reef, where the official welcoming party was waiting. **21.** The Energy Secretary, Mr. Cecil Parkinson, announced cut-backs in Britain's research into nuclear fast-breeder reactor technology. **22.** The Prime Minister announced that Lord Cockfield would not be reappointed as Britain's senior European Commissioner. She said that Mr. Leon Brittan would replace him: on July 29 the Labour M.P. Mr. Bruce Millan was appointed Britain's other European Commissioner. **25.** Mrs. Thatcher made a number of Cabinet changes. The major change was the division of the Department of Health and Social Security into two departments: Mr. John Moore retained some of his responsibilities, as Secretary of State for Social Security; Mr. Kenneth Clarke, previously Minister of State for Trade and Industry, became Secretary of State for Health; Mr. Tony Newton replaced Mr. Clarke at the Department of Trade and Industry and as Chancellor of the Duchy of Lancaster. **28.** Mr. Paddy Ashdown was elected the first leader of the Social and Liberal Democrats: Mr. Ian Wrigglesworth was elected President of the party.

Aug. 12. The Home Secretary, Mr. Douglas Hurd, issued guidelines to the police, prosecuting authorities and the courts to ensure that people accused of violence and disorder are brought to trial within days of their offence. **21.** The Prime Minister ordered a security review and an examination of measures to strengthen the fight against terrorism after the killing of eight soldiers by an I.R.A. bomb in Omagh. **23.** The Ministry of Defence announced that the distinctive car number plates on British forces' cars in Europe will be changed to make servicemen's private vehicles indistinguishable from other cars, following the fatal shooting by I.R.A. gunmen on Aug. 12 of a British soldier travelling by car in Östend.

IRELAND

(1987). Sept. 2. The I.R.A. offered a two week amnesty to informers in the Irish Republic. **3.** Guns stolen from an Ulster Defence Regiment armoury were recovered in a loyalist area of Belfast.

Oct. 2. The Dublin District Court refused to extradite an Irish Embassy official, Kevin McDonald, to England: he was to face charges connected with selling passports. **18.** A bomb containing more than 3,000 lbs of explosives was defused by the army at a farm near Omagh, Co. Tyrone. **21.** The Government informed the Irish Government that there is no early prospect of the introduction of three judges to the juryless "Diplock" courts in Northern Ireland.

Nov. 5. Police freed an Irish dentist, Mr. John O'Grady, who had been kidnapped by terrorists, after a shoot-out in Dublin. **8.** Eleven people were killed and 63 injured when a bomb exploded in Enniskillen, Co. Fermanagh, as a crowd gathered for a Remembrance Day service: on Nov. 9 the I.R.A. admitted planting the bomb. **11.** A second I.R.A. Remembrance Day bomb that failed to explode was discovered and disarmed in the border village of Tullyhommon. **14.** The I.R.A. stated that it would continue its bombing and shooting campaign despite the public outrage at the Enniskillen bombing. **23.** A joint security operation between British and Irish police and army led to the arrest of 50 people on both sides of the border: the security forces were searching for arms shipments believed to have reached the I.R.A. from Libya. **24.** The Irish Government approved the text of a Bill that would impose restrictions on the extradition of suspected terrorists to Britain and Northern Ireland. **26.** Paul Kane, an I.R.A. man who escaped from the Maze prison, was re-arrested after being given bail by a court in the Irish Republic. **27.** Dessie O'Hare, known as the Border Fox, was captured by police and troops in Co. Kilkenny.

Dec. 3. Restrictions on the extradition of Irish suspects were approved in the Dail. **22.** John McMichael, the second-in-command of the Ulster Defence Association, was killed by an I.R.A. car bomb. **29.** Terrorism in Northern Ireland caused 93 deaths in 1987.

(1988). Jan. 2. Two people were hit by plastic bullets when police fired at rioters in Belfast. **5.** A judge in Northern Ireland, Andrew Donaldson, Q.C., resigned as he felt that his security protection was inadequate. **15.** An off-duty soldier was shot in Belfast and later died. **19.** The Irish Supreme Court ruled that members of the I.R.A. could not be protected from extradition by pleading that their offences were politically motivated. **26.** The Irish Government ordered the head of its police force to cancel a meeting with the head of the R.U.C. in protest at the decision not to investigate allegations of an R.U.C. shoot-to-kill policy. **28.** Irish police found a large cache of I.R.A. equipment at a remote beach in County Donegal.

Feb. 20. Former M.P. Owen Carron was ordered by an Irish court to be extradited to Northern Ireland to face firearms charges. **21.** An unarmed Roman Catholic man, Aidan McAnespie, was shot dead at the army checkpoint on the border at Aughnacloy: on Feb. 22 the Irish Government ordered its police force to conduct its own enquiry into the killing. **23.** A soldier, Private Ian Thain, who was sentenced to life imprisonment for the murder of a Roman Catholic in Belfast in 1983 was released after less than three years and returned to his regiment. **26.** The Irish Government banned any further talks between its senior police officers and Sir John Hermon, the Chief Constable of the R.U.C., until the Ulster Police Authority had completed its investigation into Hermon's role in the "shoot-to-kill" affair. **28.** The Irish Government ordered that the body of Aidan McAnespie be exhumed and a second post mortem be carried out. **29.** Two I.R.A. men were killed when their own bomb exploded prematurely near Crossmaglen.

March 1. It was revealed that one of the I.R.A. men who blew themselves up in Co. Armagh, was Brendan Burns, wanted in Northern Ireland for at least 25 killings. **4.** The BBC in Northern Ireland stopped broadcasting the Royal Ulster Constabulary's new confidential telephone number following death threats to their staff. **6.** Three suspected I.R.A. terrorists were shot dead in Gibraltar: on March 7 the three were named as Daniel McCann, Sean Savage and Mairead Farrell, all from West Belfast. Rioting broke out in Republican areas of Belfast following the killings. **8.** Spanish police found explosives in a car in Marbella used by the I.R.A. terrorists shot in Gibraltar. **11.** The Ulster Defence Association, a loyalist paramilitary group, sacked its chairman Andy Tyrie. **16.** Three people were killed when a loyalist gunman fired on and threw grenades at mourners at Milltown cemetery, Belfast, during the funeral of the three I.R.A. members killed in Gibraltar: a man was later captured by security forces. 19. Two British soldiers, Cpl. David Howes and Cpl. Derek Wood, were dragged from their car, beaten and shot dead in Belfast after driving into the path of the funeral of Kevin Brady, a victim of the Milltown cemetery attack. 21. The Northern Ireland Secretary (Mr. King) ordered a review of the policing of I.R.A. funerals. 25. British and Irish Ministers and police chiefs met in London to pursue new initiatives under the Anglo-Irish agreement. 28. Sinn Fein and the Social, Democratic and Labour Party announced a second round of secret talks.

April 7. The Democratic Unionist Party cancelled a meeting with U.S. Congressman Joseph Kennedy, on a visit to Northern Ireland, accusing him of having a pro-nationalist viewpoint. 12. The Annual Report of the Chief Constable of the R.U.C. showed that 93 people were killed in Ulster in 1987, shootings increased by 72 per cent. to nearly 700, and bombings by 43 per cent. to 400. 13. Dessie O'Hare, known as the "Border Fox", was sentenced to 40 years imprisonment for the kidnap and torture of dentist John O'Grady. 14. The Irish Government appealed for the release of the "Birmingham Six" on humanitarian grounds after the Court of Appeal rejected their case and their application for a hearing in the House of Lords was dismissed. 21. Thirteen people were being questioned about the killing of two soldiers during an I.R.A. funeral in Belfast. 25. A Londonderry man, Kevin Ramsay, was acquitted of the murder of two R.U.C. reservists. 26. The Prime Minister, Mrs. Thatcher, said in the Commons that the British Government would be seeking reassurances from the Irish Government that it was still committed to the Anglo–Irish agreement after the Irish Prime Minister, Mr. Haughey, criticized British policy in Northern Ireland during a visit to the U.S.A.

May 1. One R.A.F. serviceman was killed and two others injured in an I.R.A. machine-gun attack on their car in the Netherlands. In a separate incident 30 minutes later two R.A.F. servicemen were killed and one injured by an I.R.A. car-bomb. All six servicemen were based in West Germany and spending an evening off-duty in the Netherlands. 12. The wife of Dessie O'Hare, jailed for kidnapping a Dublin dentist, was cleared of a kidnap charge by a Dublin court. 15. Former I.R.A. informer Kevin McGrady was released from prison in Ulster less than six years after being sentenced to life imprisonment for murder. Three men were killed in a loyalist attack on a bar in Belfast. 18. Patrick McVeigh, an I.R.A. man wanted in Britain, was released from Portlaoise prison in the Irish Republic and immediately re-arrested.

June 13. A judge in the Irish Republic refused to authorize the extradition of a suspected I.R.A. terrorist Patrick McVeigh because no British police officer was present for the hearing. He said that the case for identification was flawed. 15. Five soldiers were killed and one wounded when an I.R.A. booby-trap bomb exploded in their van as they left Lisburn, Co. Antrim, after participating in a "fun run" for charity. 23. An army helicopter had to make a forced landing in South Armagh after being hit by terrorist gunfire. 28. The I.R.A. admitted planting a bomb in a school bus in Lisnaskea which injured five school-girls and the driver.

July 5. According to evidence released five days after the incident, a taxi driver who died after an I.R.A. attack on a Belfast police station was shot by R.U.C. officers who mistook him for a terrorist. 7. Two civilians died and four were injured when a bomb exploded outside a swimming pool in the Falls Road, Belfast. 13. A bomb planted by the I.R.A. exploded at a British Army base in West Germany, slightly injuring nine soldiers. 20. An I.R.A. terrorist, Thomas Mc-Mahon, was awarded damages of £3,500 in the Dublin High Court against the Portlaoise prison authorities after his arm was broken during a strip-search. Earlier McMahon had fired a shot in the court in an attempt to escape. 24. A family of three, the Hannas, were killed by a bomb planted by the I.R.A. on the Dublin-Belfast road. It is believed that the intended victim was Mr. Justice Higgins, a high court judge in Northern Ireland.

Aug. 1. A bomb planted by the I.R.A. exploded at the Inglis army barracks in North London, killing one soldier and seriously injuring two others. 2. An off-duty policeman was killed in Lisburn by a car bomb, and a part-time soldier in the Ulster Defence Regiment was shot dead in West Belfast. 4. Two men involved in construction work at an R.U.C. police station in Belleek, Co. Fermanagh, were shot dead by I.R.A. gunmen. 5. A bomb planted by the I.R.A. exploded on the perimeter of a British Army barracks at Ratingen, West Germany. 20. An I.R.A. bomb blew up a coach, taking soldiers to their barracks in Omagh: eight soldiers were killed and 27 injured. 22. A Royal Navy recruiting officer was killed by a booby-trap bomb in Belfast. 27. Robert Russell, an escapee from the Maze prison, was extradited from the Irish Republic to Northern Ireland. 30. Three suspected I.R.A. men were shot dead by security forces in an ambush near Omagh. 31. An elderly couple were killed by mistake by an I.R.A. booby-trap bomb in Londonderry. West German police arrested two men believed to be members of an I.R.A. cell involved in attacks in Europe.

ACCIDENTS AND DISASTERS

(1987). Sept. 5. Eight people were killed in a collision on the M6 motorway near Lancaster. **9.** Four people died and 74 were injured in a seven vehicle crash on the M4 motorway near Heston. **22.** Two earthquakes shook Ecuador, Peru and Colombia. **24.** Manila bay, in the Philippines, was set ablaze when chemicals leaked during a fire aboard a tanker and two barges. **27.** A landslide buried the Villa Tina shanty town in Medellin, Colombia, killing at least 120 people. **28.** Forty people died and thousands were made homeless by storms and rain in South Africa.

Oct. 1. An earthquake struck Los Angeles, killing seven. **11.** A Burmese Airways airliner crashed near Nyaung airport, killing all 49 people on board. **16.** A storm of hurricane force devastated large areas of southern England and caused 13 deaths: some homes were without electricity for weeks. **19.** Four people were killed when a passenger train fell from a collapsed bridge into a flood-swollen river at Glanrhyd, Dyfed: the accident followed severe flooding throughout West Wales. **21.** An American Air Force jet crashed into a hotel near Indianapolis airport, killing nine people. **28.** Twelve people were killed in a multi-vehicle accident on the M61 motorway in Lancashire: a thirteenth victim died later.

Nov. 2. Two R.A.F. Harrier jets collided near Otterburn, Northumberland, killing both pilots. **18.** A fire broke out at King's Cross underground station in London: the final death toll reached 31. The Prime Minister announced that a public enquiry would be held. **21.** Two men died when their rescue vessel, operating in British Gas's Morecambe gasfield, was involved in an unspecified accident. **22.** Freak storms in Vietnam killed 31 people and destroyed 19,000 homes. **26.** Typhoon Nina swept across the Philippines, causing 83 deaths. **28.** A South African Airways jumbo jet crashed into the Indian Ocean, killing all 160 people aboard. **29.** A South Korean airliner with 115 people on board went missing over Burma.

Dec. 7. Mudslides caused by heavy rain killed 33 people in the Junin area of Peru. A commuter jet of Pacific Southwest Airlines crashed in Central California, killing all 43 on board: it was later confirmed that the crash had been caused by a criminal act. **9.** A Peruvian naval plane crashed into the Pacific Ocean near Lima, killing 42 people, including the entire Alianza Lima football team. **19.** Four people died and eleven were injured in a series of house fires in Northern Ireland. **21.** A ferry collided with a tanker and sank off Mindoro Island in the Philippines: about 1,500 people were killed. **31.** A fire in a Bangkok hotel killed twelve people and injured many more.

(1988). Jan. 2. Floods in Honolulu caused some $29 million worth of damage and forced thousands to leave their homes. **4.** Heavy rain, gales and snow caused one death and much damage in Britain: on Jan. 6 bad weather conditions caused two deaths and several injuries, and on Jan. 23 snow seriously disrupted road and rail transport and caused two deaths. **8.** At least 60 people were killed when a massive snowstorm covered most of the eastern United States. **16.** Twenty cars were involved in a collision on the M4 motorway. **29.** A West German cargo ship, *Rolandia*, sank in bad weather in the Atlantic, with the loss of all 12 crewmen.

Feb. 9. Hurricane-force winds battered the British Isles. The death toll from storms rose to eight as bad conditions prevailed. **20.** Storms hit Rio de Janeiro, Brazil, causing 48 deaths and making 10,000 homeless: the death toll subsequently rose to over 250. **27.** A cliff collapsed on shanty homes near Fez, Mexico, killing more than 20 people.

March 4. Twenty-two people died when a French domestic airliner crashed on its approach to Paris's Orly Airport. **13.** Avalanches killed seven people in St. Anton, Austria. **17.** A plane crashed into a mountain in Colombia, killing all 137 people on board. **22.** A fire which began in a domestic kitchen spread to more than 2,000 buildings in a northern Burmese town, leaving 113 dead and 20,000 homeless.

April 1. Five people were killed when two cars collided with a tractor on the Glenshane Pass in Co. Londonderry. **4.** Four British schoolboys died when they fell on the Untersberg mountain near Salzburg, Austria. **5.** A fire at a hotel in Blackpool, used by the D.H.S.S. for homeless families, left five people dead. **11.** A 38-ton oil tanker overturned onto a car in Walton-on-Thames, trapping the motorist and spilling 6,000 gallons of petrol and 1,000 gallons of diesel. **29.** Boots the Chemist withdrew a cot safety pad from sale after a 21-month old boy died due to the ties on the pad becoming wrapped round his neck.

May 20. A passenger train collided with a lorry loaded with bricks in central Thailand, killing 22 people. **22.** Fire destroyed 60 acres of forest near Betws-y-Coed in the Snowdonia National Park. **23.** The death toll in floods in south-east China reached 78. **24.** A cross-channel cargo ferry, *Seafreight Freeway*, caught fire in mid-channel. One man died. The ferry was towed to Dunkirk. **29.** Four people were injured in a seven-car crash on the M11 motorway in Essex. Half a million people were driven from their homes in north-east Bangladesh by floods which killed five people.

June 1. An underground blast at a coal mine in Borken, West Germany, trapped 56 miners: on June 4 six men were rescued unharmed, 37 bodies were found and 14 men were still missing. **5.** At least 68 people were killed when a Soviet freight train carrying explosives blew up as it entered a station in Arzamas. **7.** A light aircraft crash-landed on the M62 motorway near Manchester. The two people in the plane and one motorist were hurt. **23.** A landslide overwhelmed the village of Catak in north-east Turkey: more than 150 people were feared dead, including foreign tourists. **26.** Following a crash by an airbus A320 near the Swiss-French border, British Airways and Air France suspended all flights by the aircraft: three people died and 133 were injured in the crash. **27.** A train packed with commuters was rammed by another train at the Gare de Lyon, Paris: at least 15 people were killed and more than 40 were injured. A British woman and her two young sons died after their car broke down in the Sahara Desert in Tunisia.

July 7. The Piper Alpha oil production platform in the North Sea exploded, killing 167 men, including three rescuers. The Government ordered an inquiry into the disaster. **22.** The Royal Devon and Exeter Hospital revealed that over a five-month period this year more than 150 cancer patients had accidentally received excessive doses of radiation during treatment.

Aug. 17. A mother and her three children died when their car caught fire after an accident on the M25 motorway near Reigate. **21.** An earthquake in the foothills of the Himalayas on the India-Nepal border killed at least 500 people. **25.** The historic Chiado district of Lisbon was gutted by fire. **27.** Six people died in road accidents, and there were four crashes involving 17 vehicles on the M6 and M62 motorways. **28.** Three Italian air force jets collided during an aerobatics display at a U.S. air base at Ramstein, West Germany, and fell into the crowd of spectators: over 40 people were killed and more than 500 injured.

CRIMES, TRIALS, ETC.

(1987). Sept. 1. Mr. Ernest Saunders, former chairman and chief executive of Guinness, was further remanded on bail at Bow Street Magistrates Court, charged with destroying and falsifying documents and perverting the course of justice. **2.** A man was jailed for four years at the Central Criminal Court for trying to extort £5 million from Cadbury by threatening to poison chocolate bars in supermarkets. **4.** Actress Maria Aitken was fined £500 for helping to import cocaine into Britain. **5.** Three alleged Irish terrorists, arrested near the home of the Northern Ireland Secretary, Tom King, were charged at Chippenham with

conspiring to murder Mr. King. **10.** Mr. Eric Butler, who defended himself with a swordstick against a drunken attacker, was sentenced to 28 days in prison, suspended for nine months. **24.** Two suspected drug runners were arrested after Customs investigators found 21 kg. of cocaine in a Venezuelan cargo ship in Liverpool. **29.** The jury at the Hungerford massacre inquest returned verdicts of unlawful killing on the 15 victims and also concluded that the murderer, Michael Ryan, killed himself. **30.** Former M.P. Keith Best was jailed for four months for attempting to obtain British Telecom shares by deception: on Oct 5 Best was set free by the Court of Appeal.

Oct. 4. A prison officer was taken hostage at Perth prison by inmates protesting at conditions. **6.** A bailiff and a solicitor's clerk were shot dead whilst attempting to evict a man from his home: the man was later found dead inside the house. **7.** Following a police undercover operation 36 football hooligans, were arrested in the West Midlands; on Oct. 14 a further eight men were taken into custody. **8.** At the inquest on the Zeebrugge ferry victims the jury found that the victims had been unlawfully killed. Businessman Sir Jack Lyons was charged with nine offences relating to the Guinness affair. **13.** Businessman Gerald Ronson was charged with stealing more than £6 million from Guinness. Mr. Ernest Saunders was charged with theft offences totalling over £20 million. **14.** A man killed four people in Bristol, two by bludgeoning and two by shooting: he was later arrested by two unarmed police officers. **23.** Former champion jockey Lester Piggott was found guilty of tax fraud involving £3·25 million and was sentenced to three years imprisonment. **27.** Gilbert McNamee was convicted of making the I.R.A. bomb that killed four soldiers in Hyde Park in 1982, and was jailed for 25 years. **28.** George Stephenson was given six life sentences for killing his former employers, their son and daughter-in-law and a nurse. His two accomplices, George and John Daly, received 22 years and life. **31.** The coaster *Eksund*, registered in Panama but with an Irish crew, was intercepted by French customs officers and found to be carrying 150 tons of arms, ammunition and explosives.

Nov. 1. Three footballers, Chris Woods, Graham Roberts and Frank McAvennie, were charged with conducting themselves in a manner likely to provoke a breach of the peace during the match between Rangers and Celtic in October. **11.** It was revealed that British Customs officers had seized the biggest ever haul of cocaine in Europe from a ship in Southampton. The find was kept secret for seven weeks so that the officers could continue their investigation: eight people were subsequently arrested in the Netherlands. British

Life Guards officer Simon Hayward failed in an appeal against his conviction for drug smuggling in Sweden. **13.** Four men were convicted at Southwark Crown Court of a £5 million VAT fraud. A rapist was jailed for eight years, the first conviction to be secured using the D.N.A. "genetic fingerprinting" technique as evidence. **22.** Police marksmen shot dead an armed man, Glyn Davis, following a 12-hour manhunt in Devon and Somerset. **23.** Police shot dead one armed robber and wounded another in Woolwich, south London. **24.** Eighteen adults were arrested in Congleton, Cheshire, as police and social workers attempted to break up an alleged child pornography ring. **26.** Stuart Burton, wanted by police for the murder of his daughter-in-law and for the assault of her daughter, was found dead in a car near Chippenham, Wilts.

Dec. 1. Sixteen men were arrested after a sex ring involving young boys was uncovered in Brent, London. **9.** The Court of Appeal reserved judgement on the appeal against conviction of the six men jailed for the Birmingham pub bombings in 1974. **10.** Russell Bishop was cleared at Lewes Crown Court of the murder of two Brighton schoolgirls. Two prisoners escaped from Gartree prison in a hijacked helicopter which was forced to land on the prison sports field. **12.** Five women were arrested as 600 protesters surrounded Greenham Common base to mark the eighth anniversary of the deployment of cruise missiles in Britain. **22.** Barry Seal, Labour M.E.P. for Yorkshire West, was convicted of shoplifting at Leeds Crown Court. **24.** Two sisters aged 87 and 77 were found murdered in their corner shop in Sparkhill, Birmingham. **26.** A police undercover operation led to the arrests of 87 people caught stealing from delivery vehicles in London.

(1988). Jan. 8. A girl of 15 was found guilty of manslaughter and grievous bodily harm to two elderly sisters: she was ordered to be detained for five years. **11.** P.C. Gordon Marshall was jailed for four years at Aylesbury for causing death by reckless driving: he was subsequently dismissed from the Force. **13.** A judge at the Central Criminal Court, sentencing a rapist to six years imprisonment, criticized the lenient approach of the Parole Board and called for an enquiry. **17.** A British woman, Maureen Paleschi, was jailed for 25 years in Cairo for smuggling heroin. **18.** Guinness challenged the Takeover Panel's ruling that it had breached the takeover code: in the High Court it was revealed that Guinness had induced a Swiss company, Pipetec, to purchase 10 million shares in Distillers in the final stages of the Guinness takeover bid: on Jan. 20 counsel for Guinness criticized the Takeover Panel's investigation

of the Pipetec share purchase: on Jan. 25 counsel for the Takeover Panel said that the Distillers shareholders were "short-changed" and should receive additional funds. **20.** A Merseyside teacher, Philip Ashcroft, and his alleged lover, 18 year-old Angela Page, were found guilty at Liverpool Crown Court of the murder of Ashcroft's wife. **26.** Jeremy Warner, business correspondent of *The Independent*, was fined £20,000 for refusing to reveal his confidential sources to government inspectors. **28.** The Court of Appeal rejected the appeals of six men jailed for the 1974 Birmingham pub bombings. **29.** At the Old Bailey Kenneth Erskine was found guilty of the murder of seven elderly people and jailed for life with a recommendation that he serves a minimum of 40 years. **31.** John Kendall, one of two prisoners who escaped from Gartree prison in a helicopter, was recaptured in London.

Feb. 1. At Hereford Magistrates Court Victor Miller confessed to the murder of newspaper delivery boy Stuart Gough. **10.** Crime figures for London for 1987 showed a drop of 4 per cent, the first fall in a decade. **13.** About 1·4 tons of top-grade heroin, valued at more than $2 billion, was seized in Bangkok. **16.** Former I.R.A. member William Quinn was jailed for life for the murder of P.C. Stephen Tibble 13 years ago. **19.** Anthony Taylor was convicted of the murder of a 16 year-old choirgirl and was jailed for life, with the recommendation that he serve a minimum of 20 years. **26.** John Duffy was sentenced to seven life terms at the Old Bailey for the two "railway murders" and five rapes.

March 4. A Briton, Keith Goldsworthy, was jailed for 22 years by a Miami judge for running a cocaine-smuggling organization. **8.** William Crowe was found guilty of murdering his wife by pushing her off a cliff and was sentenced to life imprisonment by a court in Stonehaven. **10.** Lord Spens was arrested by detectives investigating the Guinness affair. **14.** The family of Robert McHayle, stabbed to death in London in June 1986, announced that they planned to bring a private prosecution for murder against a 16-year old youth charged with murder, but not prosecuted. **18.** An Old Bailey judge sentenced Michael Chandler to life imprisonment after he was found guilty of six rapes. **19.** Three men were charged after police seized cannabis worth £1·5 million in London. **24.** Tony Parnes, charged with offences relating to the Guinness affair, was granted bail at Bow Street Magistrates Court, London, and was allowed to return to California. **25.** The Home Office announced that the crime rate in 1987 had shown its smallest increase, one per cent., for 30 years. A public schoolboy, Andrew Richens, was convicted of murdering a fellow pupil who allegedly raped his girlfriend, and was sentenced to be detained during Her Majesty's pleasure. **28.** Kevin Weaver was sentenced to life imprisonment in Broadmoor by a Bristol court after pleading guilty to the manslaughter of his mother, sister and two men.

April 4. The body of Bristol newly-wed Shirley Banks, who disappeared in October 1987, was found in the Great Wood Forest in Somerset. **5.** Erwin van Haarlem, an art dealer, appeared in court in London charged with an offence under the Official Secrets Act. **6.** Actress Maria Aitken was cleared of drug-smuggling charges at Southwark Crown Court. **7.** Mr. David Mayhew, a partner in the stockbroking firm Cazenove and Co., was charged with offences relating to his role in the Guinness affair. **12.** Six of the financiers and businessmen charged in the Guinness affair appeared at Bow Street Magistrates Court, London, and were bailed until June 1. **14.** An off-duty policeman was shot dead while attempting to foil a bank raid in Hemel Hempstead. **15.** Two England footballers, Terry Butcher and Chris Woods, were found guilty at Glasgow Sheriff Court of conducting themselves in a disorderly manner and committing a breach of the peace during a match in October 1987: they were fined £250 and £500 respectively. **19.** A Briton, Derrick Gregory, had his appeal against the death sentence for drug trafficking rejected by the Malaysian Supreme Court. **29.** Jeweller Robert Chatwin was jailed for 30 months after admitting that he stole £1 million from his own company.

May 4. Two policemen who beat to death a man in police custody were sentenced to life imprisonment at Liverpool Crown Court. **10.** The judge at Snaresbrook Crown Court told the jury to return verdicts of not guilty against 11 West Ham football supporters after it emerged during the trial that police surveillance records could have been fabricated. **13.** Sharon Head was jailed for four and a half years at Cardiff Crown Court after she admitted committing more than 2,257 crimes in four years. **16.** Mrs. Phyllis Hanlon, who won £1 million in *The Sun* bingo game, was cleared at Preston Crown Court of involvement in a fraud that led to her success. **18.** Eight Chelsea football supporters were freed at Knightsbridge Crown Court after the prosecution revealed that there were irregularities in the police records. **23.** The Crown Prosecution Service offered no evidence against five Millwall football supporters because of discrepancies in police paperwork. **24.** International arms dealer Michael Aspin was jailed for six years at the Central Criminal Court for leading a conspiracy to defraud a firm acting for the Iranian regime. Two other

men were jailed for three years and two years for their involvement in the conspiracy.

June 5. More than 100 inmates at Havering prison, Cumbria, rioted after they were ordered to remove pin-ups and other photographs from the walls: twenty-five prisoners escaped but were subsequently recaptured. **14.** Violence between German and English soccer fans broke out in Dusseldorf during the European football championships: on June 18 more than 200 fans were arrested in Frankfurt after renewed violence. **16.** A Palestinian, Ismael Sowan, who spied in Britain for the Israelis was convicted at the Old Bailey of possessing explosives, grenades and assault rifles and sentenced to 11 years imprisonment. **20.** Two I.R.A. men, Liam McCotter and Patrick McLaughlin, who hid a cache of explosives in a forest in the Midlands, were sentenced to a total of 37 years imprisonment at the Central Criminal Court. The body of a pregnant woman, Mrs. Marie Wilks, was found by the side of the M50, three miles from her broken-down car. **24.** Grahame Hunter was sentenced to life imprisonment at Leeds Crown Court for the murder of his two-year old foster child Gavin Maby. Wayne Hurrah, who shot three police officers during a raid on a security van, was sentenced at the Central Criminal Court to a total of 159 years in prison.

July 7. A London solicitor, Michael Relton, was jailed for twelve years for his part in the Brinks-Mat gold bullion case. **18.** Scotland Yard announced that charges against 89 alleged football hooligans were to be dropped. Everald Irons, known as the "Putney Rapist" was jailed for 18 years at the Central Criminal Court. **19.** More than 80 prisoners at Longriggend remand centre in Scotland climbed on to a roof and hurled missiles at prison staff and police. **20.** Miss Diana Maw was murdered with a crossbow outside her home in Ealing, West London. **25.** A drugs ring, allegedly the largest in the world, was broken in a multinational operation involving British, American and Spanish authorities. A Briton, Dennis Howard Marks, who was said to be the leader, was arrested in Majorca. **28.** Two prisoners being taken by van to high security prisons on the Isle of Wight hijacked the vehicle and then escaped.

Aug. 10. A security guard, Gerald Hall, was stabbed to death during an attempted robbery outside a bank in Birmingham. Comedian Ken Dodd appeared at Liverpool Magistrates Court accused of tax fraud involving more than £8 million and was ordered to surrender his passport. **17.** David Holmes, who murdered his estranged wife and her boyfriend by pouring petrol over them and setting it alight, was sentenced to two life terms at the Central Criminal Court.

ECCLESIASTICAL

(1987). Sept. 10. The Pope arrived in Miami at the start of an eleven-day tour of the U.S.A.

Oct. 1. The Pope opened a global synod of bishops in Rome to discuss the role of women in the Roman Catholic Church.

Nov. 22. The Pope beatified 85 Roman Catholics who were martyred in England during the 16th and 17th centuries for rejecting protestantism.

Dec. 2. The unsigned preface to the 1987 edition of *Crockford's Clerical Directory* contained an attack on the competence of the Archbishop of Canterbury: on Dec. 3 the Archbishop of York, condemned the article; on Dec. 4 Cardinal Hume, leader of the Roman Catholic Church in England, praised Dr. Runcie's leadership. **8.** It was confirmed that Dr. Gareth Bennett, a priest who had committed suicide the day before, was the author of the preface: on Dec. 10 the two Church officers who commissioned and published the preface were cleared of any wrongdoing or mismanagement by Church authorities. **29.** The Bishop of Ripon announced his intention to bar practising homosexual clergy from the ministry in his diocese.

(1988). Feb. 8. At the General Synod the House of Laity passed a motion requesting the House of Bishops to issue a clear statement of policy on sexual morality. **9.** The General Synod voted against discontinuing the Crockford Preface. **19.** The Pope issued an encyclical letter, *Sollicitudo Rei Socialis*, attacking both superpower blocks for their part in retarding the development of the Third World.

March 20. The Archbishop of Canterbury announced that he was sending an envoy, the Bishop of Lichfield, to South Africa in a show of support for Archbishop Desmond Tutu. **22.** In an apostolic letter, *Euntes in Mundum*, the Pope called for a reconciliation between the Roman Catholic and Orthodox churches.

April 2. The Bishop of Durham said that Mrs. Thatcher's Government was "wicked" in a interview on Radio 4, and was later criticized himself by members of the Conservative Party. **15.** Roman Catholic bishops announced plans to oppose provisions in the Education Reform Bill which threaten to change the nature of the Catholic school system. **16.** The head of the Greek Orthodox Church in Britain, Archbishop Methodios, was removed from his post by the Oecumenical Patriarch Dimitrios and replaced by Archbishop Grigorios.

May 24. A service was held at St. Paul's Cathedral to celebrate the 250th anniversary of the conversion of John Wesley. **26.** The Church of England announced that there will be no preface to *Crockford's Clerical Directory* in future editions.

June 30. The rebel Roman Catholic archbishop Marcel Lefebvre ordained four of his followers bishops in defiance of the Pope. Mgr. Lefebvre and his four bishops were excommunicated.

July 5. The General Synod approved in principle legislation providing for the ordination of women as priests. **17.** The inaugural service of the Lambeth Conference was held at Canterbury Cathedral.

Aug. 1. The Lambeth Conference agreed that it could not prevent the consecration of women as bishops but said that it was almost irreconcilably divided over whether women should be ordained at all. **7.** The Lambeth Conference ended.

EDUCATION

(1987). Sept. 4. Parents in Dewsbury, Yorks., refused to send their children to their allocated school where 85 per cent of the pupils are of Asian origin: on Sept. 7 the Education Secretary, Mr. Kenneth Baker, told the parents that he was unable to intervene in the dispute as there were no grounds for concluding that Kirklees Council had acted unreasonably. **11.** The Government published its proposals for the abolition of the Inner London Education Authority. **21.** The Open College began broadcasting its first programmes.

Oct. 28. The Education Secretary, Mr. Kenneth Baker, effectively limited the teachers' pay rise next year to about 4–5 per cent.

Nov. 3. A Government survey indicated that at least £2 billion would be needed to bring the fabric of schools up to a required standard by 1991. **20.** The Government published the Education Reform Bill which proposed, among other things, the introduction of a national curriculum and an end to artificial limits on parents' first choice of school.

Dec. 15. The National Association of Head Teachers lodged a pay claim of up to 21 per cent.

(1988). Jan. 19. The council of the Senate of Cambridge University agreed to set up a committee to investigate the way the university is governed. **24.** The University Grants Committee recommended a minimum rise of 7 per cent in fees for overseas students. **29.** The Government told the Inner London Education Authority that it must reduce its budget by 12 per cent.

Feb. 4. The Education Secretary, Mr. Kenneth Baker, announced that I.L.E.A. would be abolished in 1990. **9.** London teachers staged a one-day strike in protest at government-imposed spending cuts. **27.** Students marched in London in protest against the Education Reform Bill. **29.** A report published by the National Union of Teachers stated that nearly 75 per cent of state schools needed contributions from parents to buy sufficient books and equipment.

March 2. The Education Secretary issued a rebuttal of criticism of the Education Reform Bill made by the Roman Catholic Bishops. **8.** Mr. Baker announced that an independent inquiry into standards of discipline in schools, would be set up chaired by Lord Elton.

April 10. Several professional associations claimed that local authority services were unable to cope with requests from schools for G.C.S.E. source materials. **13.** A postal ballot of parents whose children attend schools in the I.L.E.A. area showed that nearly 95 per cent. were opposed to its abolition. **25.** A survey in *Teachers' Weekly* found that 22 per cent. of teachers had no training for G.C.S.E. and 23 per cent. had had one day or less. **29.** The official inquiry into the teaching of English, chaired by Sir John Kingman, published its report.

May 12. The House of Lords passed an amendment changing the voting procedures where schools wish to opt out of local education authority control. **13.** The Court of Appeal found Birmingham City Council guilty of sex discrimination in providing more grammar school places for boys than for girls. **17.** An amendment intended to postpone the abolition of the I.L.E.A. was defeated in the House of Lords.

June 1. Delegates at the annual conference of the National Association of Headteachers criticized Government proposals to give them more control of school budgets. **20.** Mr. Baker approved plans for senior staff currently employed by the I.L.E.A. to hold joint appointments with the 13 inner London boroughs who will take over responsibility for education from the I.L.E.A.

July 12. Parents in Dewsbury who had their children educated privately because they objected to the school allocated by Kirklees Metropolitan Council won a concession from the council, who offered places in the schools of their choice after the parents took action in the High Court: on July 13 the parents were awarded costs of £7,000.

Aug. 24. G.C.S.E. examination boards claimed that the results of the new exam showed that it was a success. **31.** G.C.S.E. examination boards were cleared by the Joint Council for the G.C.S.E. of rigging results to show that standards had risen.

ENVIRONMENT AND LOCAL AFFAIRS

(1987). Sept. 10. Parts of the railway station at Tonbridge in Kent were sealed off after liquid was seen dripping from a wagon carrying waste from Dungeness nuclear power station: it was later confirmed that there was no contamination.

Oct. 7. The Central Electricity Generating Board announced plans to reduce the amount of sulphur emitted from power stations. **21.** The Environment Secretary, Mr. Nicholas Ridley, announced that the Government would be allocating £3 million to restore woods and parks damaged in the recent storms. **23.** The Minister for Health, Mr. Antony Newton, announced that the London health authorities would receive £6·5 million in emergency funding to help them cope with the Aids crisis. **29.** The success of a campaign to eliminate the coypu was announced, none having been seen for several months.

Nov. 24. Following the King's Cross underground station fire, smoking was banned in all parts of London's underground system. A conference on North Sea pollution began in London: on Nov. 25 the British Government agreed to reduce the level of pollution coming from Britain.

Dec. 7. A £60 million package for urban renewal in Bristol, Leeds, Manchester and Wolverhampton was announced by Mr. Nicholas Ridley, Environment Secretary. **16.** An extra £90 million was allocated to the National Health Service for the 1987–88 financial year and the Government announced a major review of the N.H.S. in 1988.

(1988). Jan. 4. Three people died and two were seriously ill following an outbreak of meningitis in Malvern, Worcs.: on Jan. 5 further outbreaks in Kent, Warwickshire and Hampshire were brought to light, increasing the death toll to eight; and on Jan. 6 six new cases were confirmed in Wales. **11.** The Government banned the use of polyurethane foam in furniture manufacture from February 1989 following 10 deaths caused by the fumes emitted when polyurethane catches fire.

Feb. 15. Four Thames health authorities were granted an extra £7·08 million to help reduce operation waiting lists. **17.** Leading manufacturers of toiletries undertook to phase out chemicals in aerosol products which have been blamed for damage to the Earth's ozone layer. **29.** The Government announced an increase in prescription charges of 20p to £2·60 per item.

March 4. The Environment Secretary, Mr. Nicholas Ridley, announced that an independent auditor would investigate a deal whereby Westminster City Council sold off three cemeteries for 15p each. **7.** The Government launched "Action for Cities", a ten-year programme for urban renewal. **20.** The National Society for the Prevention of Cruelty to Children said that more than 2,300 child sexual abuse cases had been reported to the Society in the year ending September 1987. **22.** The Prince of Wales criticized the Government's approach to pollution control and environmental issues at the European Year of the Environment awards ceremony. **30.** The Government designated two areas, the Wash in East Anglia and Pagham harbour in West Sussex, as Special Protection Areas for Birds.

April 16. Surgeons at the Midland Centre for Neurosurgery in Birmingham announced that they had performed the first brain cell transplants in Britain.

May 3. The BBC confirmed that the bacteria which causes Legionnaires' disease was found in a cooling tower at Broadcasting House. Five confirmed and fifteen suspected cases of the disease had already been detected. **10.** The Environment Secretary (Mr. Ridley) said that increased demand for housing in south-east England would have to be met in part by building in green belt areas.

June 13. Derbyshire County Council began legal proceedings against the North West Water Authority, claiming that the Authority discharged excess sewage into the River Goyt. **17.** Mr. Ridley announced that the Government will give local authorities an extra £24.1 million to tackle homelessness and other housing problems.

July 8. British Telecom announced that it would freeze most of its charges until August 1989. **28.** Mr. Alan Lack, who eight years ago gave bone marrow to help cure his son of leukaemia, received an identical transplant from his son Stuart after contracting the disease himself.

Aug. 10. Concern grew about a mystery virus that has killed thousands of common seals in the North Sea: on Aug. 29 scientists announced the infection killing the seals was canine distemper rather than environmental pollution, though the latter may have affected the seals' immune systems. **22.** The change in licensing laws in England and Wales came

into effect, allowing public houses to remain open between 11 a.m. and 11 p.m. **27.** A ship carrying 2,000 tons of toxic waste tried to dock at a port in Britain after being expelled from Nigeria: on Aug. 30 the vessel, the *Karin B*, was banned from entering British ports by the Government.

FINANCE

(1987). Sept. 11. The U.S.A. announced its worst trade deficit: in July the gap between imports and exports showed a deficit of $16·47 billion. The Government and the banks announced a five-year agreement to lower bank earnings on government-backed export loans.

Oct. 16. The U.S. Dow Jones index fell by 108·35 points. **20.** The Dow Jones index fell by 508·32 points: stock markets worldwide suffered large falls. By Oct. 20 the London market had seen more than £93 billion cut from share values. **22.** The New York stock exchange cut trading time by two hours. **23.** Bank base rates were cut by half a per cent to 9·5 per cent. **30.** The British Petroleum share flotation opened with a 120p partly-paid price, but the stock market fall caused the shares to close at 85p: the Chancellor of the Exchequer gave investors the safety net of a 70p resale price.

Nov. 4. The high street banks cut their base lending rate from 9·5 to 9 per cent. **5.** The dollar fell to a record low as West Germany and the U.S.A. announced reductions in their interest rates. **30.** Share prices in London fell by 4·3 per cent, part of a worldwide response to the dollar reaching a post-war low against major currencies.

Dec. 3. The Bank of England approved a cut in interest rates to 8·5 per cent. **15.** Official figures indicated that manufacturing output in the U.K. is growing at 6·5 per cent a year. **28.** Over the Christmas weekend shares fell on the Tokyo stock exchange by 422·43 points: on Dec. 29 and 30 shares fell in other world markets.

(1988). Jan. 12. The Department of Trade and Industry announced an inquiry into the Burton Group. **23.** More than 1,600 jobs were lost after the October crash and more losses were forecast. **28.** Britain's balance of payments deteriorated sharply in 1987, giving a current account deficit of £2,692 million.

Feb. 8. Share prices fell sharply in London, cutting share values by more than £9 billion. **12.** The Midland Bank announced a pre-tax loss of £505 million. **26.** Lloyds Bank announced a pre-tax loss of £248 million.

March 17. Bank base rates dropped from 9 per cent. to 8·5 per cent. **29.** Sterling reached its highest level against all currencies for over two years.

April 8. Bank base rates dropped to 8 per cent., the lowest level for ten years. **26.** The Swiss foods group Nestlé launched a £2·1 billion take-over bid for Rowntree, the confectioners: on April 27 the Swiss group Suchard increased its shareholding in Rowntree to 16 per cent.

May 16. The Bank of England intervened to keep the pound below DM3·20. **17.** Bank base rates dropped from 8 per cent. to 7·5 per cent. **26.** The Swiss confectionery group Suchard launched a £2·3 billion bid for Rowntree, countering the take-over bid of Nestlé.

June 2. Interest rates rose from 7·5 per cent. to 8 per cent: on June 6 interest rates increased by a further half a point to 8·5 per cent. **7.** The Government announced that Girobank would be privatized by the end of the year. Barlow Clowes International, an investment management group based in Gibraltar, was closed and liquidators appointed to trace the whereabouts of £150 million of investors' money. **10.** Officials from the Department of Trade and Industry were asked to explain their decision to grant a licence to Barlow Clowes in 1985. **12.** Barlow Clowes chairman Peter Clowes admitted that he had channelled more than £100 million of investors' money into other businesses with which he was connected: on June 15 Mr. Clowes was arrested by fraud squad officers and charged with perverting the course of justice. **13.** Rowntree turned down a take-over bid of more than £2 billion from the Swiss company Suchard: on June 23 Rowntree accepted a bid of £2·55 billion from Nestlé. **22.** Interest rates rose to 9 per cent. **28.** Interest rates increased by half a point to 9·5 per cent.

July 4. Bank base rates rose by half a per cent. to 10 per cent. **11.** D. P. R. Futures, a company engaged in the high-pressure selling of futures contracts, was suspended by the Securities and Investments Board, who also froze the firm's business assets and launched an investigation into its activities. **14.** British Aerospace agreed to the European Commission's terms for its take-over of the Rover Group. **18.** Interest rates rose to 10·5 per cent.

Aug. 8. Interest rates rose to 11 per cent. **11.** Two dealers at County NatWest WoodMac, the investment banking arm of the National Westminster Bank, were sacked for insider dealing. **25.** The balance of trade figures showed a deficit of £2·15 billion in July. Interest rates rose to 12 per cent.

LABOUR AND TRADE UNIONS

(1987). Sept. 2. Air traffic control engineers began industrial action for improved pay and conditions: on Sept. 16 they called off their action after being awarded pay increases of up to 36 per cent. **7.** The T.U.C. annual conference began at Blackpool: the conference ordered the General Council to establish a Special Review Body to consider ways of increasing union strength and influence, and to examine the use of single-union agreements and no strike deals. On Sept. 8 delegates expressed unanimous opposition to Government plans to give union members the right to ignore a majority ballot to strike. **14.** All performances at the Royal Opera House, Covent Garden, were cancelled until further notice after the chorus rejected a new offer in its pay dispute: on Oct. 21 the dispute was settled when the chorus accepted an improved pay offer. **21.** Members of the National Union of Mineworkers began a limited overtime ban in protest at British Coal's code of conduct.

Oct. 13. Prison officers at several prisons refused to accept any more remand prisoners until prison numbers returned to manageable proportions: on Oct 28 the officers called off their action pending talks. **30.** Ford Motor Company presented its unions with a three-year pay deal conditional on changes in working practices.

Nov. 11. British Coal announced more pit closures and warned that the overtime ban by the N.U.M. could increase the rate of closures. **12.** Arthur Scargill resigned as president of the N.U.M. and immediately put himself forward for re-election: on Nov. 17 Mr. John Walsh was nominated to stand for election against Mr. Scargill. **25.** A dispute at two independent television companies escalated when the Association of Cinematograph, Television and Allied Technicians refused to give unconditional assurances that no industrial action would be taken over manning levels. **29.** The Association of Professional, Executive, Clerical and Computer Staff and the General, Municipal, Boilermakers and Allied Trades Union agreed to amalgamate, subject to a ballot of members.

Dec. 2. A series of 24-hour strikes by postal staff throughout the country caused many post boxes to be sealed up. **4.** Leaders of the Union of Communication Workers and the Post Office reached an agreement that will cut the working week by one and a half hours. **7.** TV-am's breakfast time programme was produced by management staff after A.C.T.T. members went on strike over manning levels. **15.** Electricians at Tyne Tees Television who were sacked for going on strike accepted a management charter and were immediately reinstated.

(1988). Jan. 7. Nurses and auxiliary staff at North Manchester General Hospital went on strike over Government proposals to cut special duty allowances. **11.** British Coal announced the closure of Seafield Colliery in Fife with the loss of 640 jobs. **14.** Scottish health workers, including nurses, staged a 24-hour strike in protest at the privatization of hospital ancillary services. **24.** Mr. Arthur Scargill was re-elected president of the National Union of Mineworkers. **29.** NACODS, the pit deputies' union, announced an immediate ban on overtime and a 24-hour strike after rejecting a 4·2 per cent pay offer made by British Coal.

Feb. 2. Ferry services in northern Britain were disrupted by a National Union of Seamen strike in support of 161 members dismissed by the Isle of Man Steam Packet Company. **3.** Health service workers began a month-long campaign of protests and strikes. British Coal cancelled a closed shop agreement with NACODS. **4.** The N.U.S. called an end to the ferry strike but disruption continued at Dover. Ford workers voted against a three-year pay productivity deal agreed by unions and management, but on Feb. 19 they accepted a pay offer of 14 per cent over two years and voted to return to work. **6.** Many of the striking seamen returned to work but some 2,000 P. & O. employees in Dover remained in dispute. **16.** TV-am sent dismissal notices to 229 technicians who had been on strike for five months in a dispute over working practices. **21.** The workforce at the Rover Group's Land-Rover plant rejected a pay offer of 14 per cent over two years and began an indefinite strike.

March 6. The N.U.M. voted to end its five-month ban on overtime. **15.** More than 2,000 members of the National Union of Seamen were served with dismissal notices by P. & O. after refusing to accept new contracts. **17.** The Ford motor company announced that it was abandoning its plans to build an electronics plant at Dundee because of an inter-union dispute over union representation at the new factory. Ford had made a single-union agreement with the A.E.W. in Oct. 1987 but the unions recognized at other Ford U.K. plants refused to accept a deal which contravened agreements at the other plants and threatened disruption if the single-union deal went ahead. **21.** The N.U.S. announced a ballot of its members on a national strike in support of sacked members in Dover and Belfast: P. & O. responded by threatening legal action for contempt of court. **25.** The N.U.S. was warned by a High Court judge that its assets could be seized if it continued with a national strike ballot. **28.** The Government announced a Monopolies Commission inquiry into restrictive labour practices in the television and film industry. **31.** T.U.C. general secretary Nor-man Willis failed in his attempts to resolve the inter-union dispute over Ford when unions at Ford plants refused to accept a single-union deal at the new Dundee factory.

April 3. Members of the N.U.S voted to continue industrial action at Dover: on April 12 P. & O. indicated their intention to recruit non-union labour in order to resume services: on April 17 N.U.S. members rejected an offer to end the dispute. **21.** Nurses were awarded pay increases linked to a regrading scheme, to be funded by the Government. **28.** The High Court ordered the freezing of N.U.S. funds. **29.** Two P. & O. ferries left Rotterdam for Dover manned by non-union crew.

May 1. The N.U.S. called a national strike after P. & O. sailed a strike-breaking ferry to Zeebrugge. **3.** The High Court fined the N.U.S. £150,000 and ordered the sequestration of the union's assets for repeated breaches of a court injunction. **12.** The N.U.S. called off their dispute with Sealink. **17.** Leaders of the engineering union, the A.E.U., and the electricians' union, the E.E.T.P.U., announced plans to merge in 1989. **21.** The Employment Secretary, Mr. Fowler, said that the Training Commission would be abolished unless the T.U.C. agreed to participate in programmes to assist the long-term unemployed: on May 25 the T.U.C. voted to co-operate with the scheme.

June 13. Workers at the VSEL shipyard in Barrow-in-Furness voted in favour of a strike: they returned to work on Aug. 30. **16.** John Golding, the general secretary of the National Communications Union, agreed to take early retirement in the wake of allegations that he had sex with a prostitute. **20.** The Special Review Body of the T.U.C. voted to adopt a code of conduct on single-union agreements which stated that unions must not sign such agreements in exchange for union recognition. **21.** The electricians union, the E.E.T.P.U., announced that it had signed three more no-strike agreements and intended signing a further seven. **22.** The E.E.T.P.U. were ordered to withdraw from two of the no-strike deals or face suspension from the T.U.C.: the union's leadership made it clear that they would not conform.

July 6. Members of the A.C.T.T. working at London Weekend Television accepted reforms of working practices. **8.** The E.E.T.P.U. was suspended from the T.U.C. for refusing to abandon two single-union no-strike agreements. **14.** Unemployment figures showed a fall to 2,375,300. **15.** The National Union of Seamen withdrew support for its members' mass picket of P. & O ferries at Dover because of the threat of a fine by the High Court. **19.** The E.E.T.P.U. declared its unilateral independence of the T.U.C. following a vote by its members.

Aug. 1. More than 200 prison officers at Holloway prison went on strike in a dispute over staffing levels: on Aug. 20 the officers voted to accept a Home Office offer on staffing levels but on Aug. 27 rejected a return-to-work plan. **2.** The E.E.P.T.U. beat the National Union of Railwaymen and other rail unions in a ballot on the representation of employees on the London Docklands Light Railway. **31.** Post Office workers began a national strike.

LEGAL

(1987). Sept. 1. The Cleveland inquiry, which opened on Aug. 11, resumed public session. **2.** The Home Secretary, Mr. Douglas Hurd, signed extradition warrants for 26 Liverpool fans to face manslaughter charges following the Heysel stadium riot. **25.** The Home Secretary announced that the police are to carry out random checks on jurors to ensure that they are not disqualified from serving.

Oct. 2. The Master of the Rolls, Sir John Donaldson, called for more judges and more court rooms to help speed up the hearing of civil appeals. **5.** Mr. Robert Humphreys was awarded record road accident damages of £750,000 at the High Court in London. **16.** Derbyshire County Council lost its High Court case and cannot place copies of *Spycatcher* in its libraries. **20.** In a child abuse case at the Old Bailey screening of witnesses from the defendants was used for the first time. **23.** Data protection officers used their powers to seize computer tapes for the first time when they raided the home of a police officer believed to be storing information about colleagues on his personal computer.

Nov. 10. The Lord Chancellor (Lord Mackay of Clashfern) said that he intends to increase the number of solicitors on the Bench. **26.** A High Court judge lifted reporting restrictions on the evidence of Sir Robert Armstrong in the *Spycatcher* case. **27.** The Attorney General, Sir Patrick Mayhew, obtained a High Court injunction preventing journalist Duncan Campbell from disclosing classified information about G.C.H.Q.

Dec. 3. The Government obtained a High Court injunction preventing the broadcast of a BBC Radio 4 series "My Country Right or Wrong" which includes interviews with members of the security services. **9.** The Government obtained injunctions to stop the British media from publishing any information about signals intelligence at G.C.H.Q. **11.** The commission of enquiry into the death of Kimberley Carlile at the hands of her

stepfather published its report. **13.** An American court ordered the manufacturers of the Dalkon Shield contraceptive device to set aside £1·35 billion to compensate women made infertile by the device. **16.** Dame Elizabeth Butler-Sloss was appointed the first woman judge on the Court of Appeal. **17.** The report into the death of Tyra Henry at the hands of her father was published: it said that professional mistakes and administrative incompetence were key factors in her death. **18.** A High Court judge awarded £10,000 to a six-year old girl and her mother who suffered a sex abuse investigation because of a hospital error. **21.** A High Court judge refused to grant the Government a permanent ban on media coverage of allegations from *Spycatcher*.

(1988). Jan. 2. In the High Court a ruling preventing the *Observer* quoting from the memoirs of former MI6 officer Anthony Cavendish was modified to a ban on the publication of material relating to his experience in security and intelligence services: the *Sunday Times* was allowed to use material already published. **12.** A family driven from their home when Hells Angels moved in next door were awarded £23,632 damages in the High Court. **29.** The Cleveland inquiry closed.

Feb. 1. The inquiry into the fire at King's Cross underground station chaired by Mr. Desmond Fennell, Q.C., began at Westminster Central Hall. **15.** Chief Inspector Brian Woollard was refused funds by the Police Federation to launch a judicial inquiry into the influence of freemasons in the Metropolitan Police: on Feb. 16 it was revealed that a group of senior officers had been investigating the matter behind the scenes. **23.** The Court of Session in Edinburgh turned down the Government's application to prevent publication of extracts from *Inside Intelligence*, the memoirs of former MI6 officer Anthony Cavendish. **25.** Ministry of Defence regulations which have been used to secure more than 1,000 convictions against Greenham Common peace campaigners were ruled illegal at Reading Crown Court.

March 1. The Government withdrew its objections to the first programme in the BBC Radio 4 series "My Country Right or Wrong" but the injunction against other parts of the series remained in force. **9.** The publishers Aurum Press and Transworld offered unlimited indemnity to booksellers following the threat by Robert Maxwell to take legal action against any store selling copies of two unauthorized biographies of him: on March 10 the chairman of Blackwell's of Oxford said that both books, along with the official biography, would be on sale in his company's shops: on March 12 a writ was issued against Blackwell's alleging libel. **24.** Unsold copies of the

Transworld biography of Robert Maxwell were withdrawn to be pulped following payment of undisclosed libel damages and an apology in open court by the authors, publishers and printers.

April 8. The Court of Session in Edinburgh rejected a Government appeal against a judge's refusal to grant an order banning publication of extracts from *Inside Intelligence*, the memoirs of former MI6 officer Anthony Cavendish. **28.** A report published by the Law Society said that county courts in England and Wales were failing to cope with their excessive workload.

May 17. Television presenter Anne Diamond reached an out-of-court settlement with her former agents, P.V.A. Management Ltd., and agreed to pay them an undisclosed sum for breach of contract.

June 2. The Government announced that it would proceed with its appeal to the House of Lords against the publication of *Spycatcher*. **10.** Mr. Michael Meacher, the Labour Party employment spokesman, lost a libel action against *The Observer*. **30.** Women warehouse workers at a mail order firm were granted the right by the House of Lords to bring a claim for equal pay for work of equal value before an industrial tribunal.

July 13. The Marre Committee report on the future of the legal profession was published. **28.** Guinness lost its appeal in the Court of Appeal against a Takeover Panel ruling that the company infringed City rules during its bid to take over Distillers.

Aug. 1. A boy who suffered irreversible brain damage after a hospital error was awarded £491,000 following a twelve-year battle for compensation.

SPORT

(1987). Sept. 9. Thirty English soccer fans were arrested in Dusseldorf, where England were playing West Germany. **13.** The world light-welterweight boxing champion Terry Marsh announced his retirement from boxing after discovering that he suffered from epilepsy. **20.** French racing driver Alain Prost established a record of 28 world championship grand prix wins when he won the Portuguese Grand Prix.

Oct. 16. Mike Weston resigned as England rugby union team manager after only six weeks in office.

Nov. 2. The Scottish Football Association announced an inquiry into violence at the Celtic–Rangers match in October. **19.** An open letter from the Minister of Sport, Colin

Moynihan, to the chairman of the Sports Council, John Smith, questioned whether the Council should be receiving Government funding. **20.** Watford's chairman, Elton John, sold the football club to Robert Maxwell's British Printing and Communication Corporation for £2 million: the Football League told Mr. Maxwell that if he wished to buy Watford he must sever his links with Derby County football club. **27.** England cricketer Chris Broad was reprimanded for questioning an umpire's decision given against him in the first Test match against Pakistan in Lahore: on Nov. 28 the England captain, Mike Gatting, attacked the umpiring of the match. **28.** A cannister of CS gas was fired into the crowd during the Hibernian–Celtic match, causing hundreds of spectators to run on to the field.

Dec. 8. In the second Test match between England and Pakistan, England captain Mike Gatting was involved in an argument with umpire Shakoor Rana over a decision given by the umpire: on Dec. 9 no play took place as Rana demanded an apology from Gatting: on Dec. 12 Gatting made a short handwritten apology and play resumed. **15.** Robert Maxwell was told by the Football League that he would have to sell his shares in three other football clubs before he could take over Watford: on Dec. 20 Elton John, chairman of Watford, asked Mr. Maxwell to withdraw his offer in view of the League Management Committee's opposition. **16.** Boxer Bobby Frankham was banned from boxing indefinitely for punching a referee.

(1988). Jan. 22. Watford chairman Elton John decided not to sell the club following the decision by the Football League not to allow him to sell his shareholding to Robert Maxwell.

Feb. 11. Nottingham Forest football club refused to allow their manager, Brian Clough, to become also the part-time manager of the Welsh national team. The Princess Royal was elected to the International Olympic Committee. **13.** The 15th Winter Olympics opened in Calgary, Canada. **17.** England cricketer Graham Dilley was fined £250 by the tour manager Peter Lush in New Zealand after swearing during a dispute over an umpiring decision.

March 3. Scottish rugby international John Jeffrey was suspended for five months for damaging the Calcutta Cup: on March 21 England player Dean Richards was banned from playing in the next international match for his part in the incident. **14.** The International Amateur Athletic Federation called on the British Amateur Athletic Board to withdraw Zola Budd from the team competing in the World Cross-Country championships in New Zealand pending an enquiry into her alleged participation in a race in South Africa in June 1987: on March 15 Budd presented a sworn affidavit to the BAAB refuting allegations of her involvement in the race and on March 16 she withdrew voluntarily from the British team. **28.** The Australian Cricket Board fined Ian Botham £2,000 for behaviour which led to him appearing in a civil court. **29.** The Queensland Cricket Association cancelled the remaining two years of Botham's contract.

May 6. Worcestershire batsman Graeme Hick scored 405 not out against Somerset, only the second time a score of over 400 has been achieved in a county championship match. **10.** Zola Budd announced that she was temporarily retiring from athletics and returning to South Africa. **12.** Snooker player Cliff Thorburn was banned from two tournaments and fined £10,000 for bringing the game into disrepute after failing a drugs test during the British Open tournament in March. **26.** West Indies batsman Phil Simmons had a blood clot removed from his brain after being hit on the head by a delivery in a match against Glamorgan. **28.** Graeme Hick became only the eighth batsman ever to score 1,000 runs before the end of May.

June 9. Mike Gatting was sacked as the England cricket captain for "irresponsible behaviour" following allegations in a national newspaper of involvement in a late-night drinking and sex party during the Test series. **10.** John Emburey was appointed as England cricket captain. **29.** World heavyweight boxing champion Mike Tyson announced his retirement.

July 4. F.I.F.A. announced that the 1994 World Cup will be held in the U.S.A. **7.** Tottenham Hotspur paid a record British fee of £2 million to buy Paul Gascoigne from Newcastle Utd. **8.** Twelve top soccer clubs threatened to form a breakaway super-league and accept a £32 million television deal from I.T.V.: on July 12 the B.B.C. and British Satellite Broadcasting made an offer of £42 million to all 92 clubs. **14.** Chris Cowdrey was appointed the England cricket captain for the last two Test matches against the West Indies. **25.** British international pole vaulter Jeff Gutteridge was suspended from competitions pending the result of a drugs test: on July 27 Gutteridge was banned for life following a positive result.

Aug. 2. Chris Cowdrey was dropped from the England cricket team through injury and replaced as captain by Graham Gooch for the final Test match against the West Indies. **3.** Mike Gatting was fined £5,000 by the Test and County Cricket Board for publishing a book without Board consent and in breach of his contract. **18.** Liverpool paid £2·8 million to sign Ian Rush from Juventus of Italy.

19. The British Amateur Athletic Board rejected an appeal by the president of the International Olympic Committee to reconsider the decision not to include Sebastian Coe in the British Olympic team.

TRANSPORT

(1987). Sept. 7. A public inquiry opened into the proposed route of the Oxfordshire section of the M40.

Oct. 14. Commercial flights from the City Airport in London's Docklands began.

Nov. 11. Members of Parliament backed the proposed merger of British Airways and British Caledonian: on Nov. 14 British Caledonian said that it was seeking a partnership with a European airline to avoid the British Airways takeover. The Scandinavian airline SAS subsequently emerged as the favourite to form a partnership with British Caledonian. **24.** The Government announced that four British Rail engineering workshops were to be sold as a single private business.

Dec. 3. The Government indicated that it would strongly oppose the attempt by SAS to merge with British Caledonian: on Dec. 10 British Airways increased its offer for British Caledonian to £200 million: on Dec. 22 an increased offer of £250 million was accepted. **18.** The Civil Aviation Authority ordered all flights between the London City airport and Paris to be halted because of fears of a mid-air collision.

(1988). Jan. 10. British Rail fares increased by an average of 6·5 per cent.

Feb. 3. The Transport Under Secretary Mr. Peter Bottomley announced several measures intended to reduce the number of accidents involving motor cyclists. **6.** Two passenger planes were involved in a near-miss incident over the south coast of England: on Feb. 21 another near-miss incident involving two passenger planes was reported.

March 2. The Civil Aviation Authority called in a team of independent management consultants to review the running of Britain's air traffic control system following criticism about delays and near-misses.

April 20. London Underground announced that safety measures costing £30 million would be introduced to prevent a recurrence of the King's Cross fire. **26.** British Airways began a trial smoking ban on its Glasgow-Heathrow flights.

July 2. Thousands of holidaymakers were delayed at airports throughout Britain because of air traffic control problems: on July 18 the Government announced moves to ease the crisis, including allowing charter flights to use Heathrow Airport.

AFRICA

(1987) Sept. 3. The President of Burundi, Colonel Bagaza, was deposed as head of state in his absence on a visit to Canada. **6.** Troops from Chad attacked an air base 60 miles inside Libya; on Sept. **7** French forces in Chad shot down a Libyan bomber. **10.** The provisional military council in Ethiopia was abolished and a republic was declared with Col. Mengistu Haile Mariam as President.

Oct. 8. An international conference of medical experts said that hundreds of thousands of people in Africa are believed to be developing Aids. **18.** The U.N. Food and Agricultural Organization said that Africa would need much more food aid if massive starvation was to be avoided. **25.** Eritrean rebels destroyed an entire food convoy in Ethiopia's Tigré province.

Nov. 5. Govan Mbeki, former chairman of the African National Congress, was released after 23 years in jail in South Africa. **8.** The Tunisian President, Habib Bourguiba, was removed from power after 31 years because of senility and the Prime Minister, Ben Ali, assumed the presidency. **10.** President Kountché of Niger died in a Paris hospital. **11.** South Africa admitted that its troops were fighting alongside Unita rebels in Angola.

Dec. 5. South Africa said that it was withdrawing its troops from Angola where they had been aiding the Unita rebels. **29.** The Ethiopian Ambassador in Geneva accused some western countries of withholding aid for political reasons. **30.** The Government of Transkei, one of South Africa's nominally independent homelands, was overthrown in a bloodless coup.

(1988) Jan. 8. The International Committee of the Red Cross revealed that it had ceased to give aid to refugees in Mozambique because of threats to attack Red Cross transport by the rebel Mozambique National Resistance. **24.** The President of Zanzibar, Idris Abdul Wakil, dismissed his government and took control of the army. **30.** Five people were killed and 1,500 left homeless after interfactional fighting in a Cape Town squatter camp; in Natal Province eight people died during fighting between rival groups of Zulus.

Feb. 1. Nineteen Zulus died in Natal as rival factions continued to fight. **10.** South African troops put down an attempted military coup in the homeland of Bophuthat-

swana and released President Lucas Mangope. **19.** A bomb killed 15 people in a bank on Oshakanti, northern Namibia; on Feb. 21 South Africa retaliated by bombing guerrilla bases in Angola. **24.** The South African government banned the activities of 17 anti-apartheid organizations. **29.** Police in Johannesburg broke up a march on Parliament by several hundred priests and briefly detained Archbishop Desmond Tutu and other senior clergymen. President Abdou Diouf of Senegal declared a state of emergency in an attempt to quell rioting.

March 15. Mrs. Thatcher, President Reagan and Chancellor Kohl all appealed to President Botha of South Africa to show clemency to the Sharpeville Six, due to be hanged on March 18 for complicity in a township murder; on March 17 the Supreme Court in Pretoria ordered a stay of execution of one month after doubt was cast on the evidence of a key prosecution witness. **28.** A South African commando unit killed four people in a raid on a house in Gaborone, Botswana. **29.** An African National Congress representative, Mrs. Dulcie September, was shot dead in Paris.

April 4. Ethiopia and Somalia announced a ten-point plan aimed at restoring diplomatic relations. Ethiopian Government forces suffered a heavy defeat at the hands of Eritrean rebels and lost control of their regional headquarters at Afabet. **25.** The Attorney General of Transvaal Province gave notice to the Supreme Court in Pretoria that he intended to contest an application by the Sharpeville Six to have their trial reopened.

May 3. A four-nation meeting aimed at ending the civil war in Angola took place in London. **21.** Seven princesses, imprisoned without trial in Ethiopia following the revolution in 1972, were released. **31.** Reports indicated that Ethiopian forces had failed in their attempted counter-offensive against Eritrean rebels, while the rebels claimed to have captured large areas of Tigré province.

June 3. A bomb exploded in Roodeport, near Johannesburg, killing four people. **6.** An estimated one million South African blacks began a strike in protest at political restrictions. **10.** President Botha announced an extension of the state of emergency in South Africa for another twelve months and the tightening of curbs on the media and on extra-parliamentary organizations. **20.** President Botha offered Bantu-speaking blacks a majority of the seats on an advisory and consultative council aimed at giving them "a voice in the processes of government". **27.** Fighting broke out between South African troops and a combined Angolan and Cuban force on the Angola-Namibia border.

July 2. A car bomb exploded in Johannesburg, killing two men. **12.** The South African Minister of Justice, Mr. Coetsee, announced an indefinite stay of execution for the Sharpeville Six. **13.** Representatives of Angola, Cuba and South Africa meeting in New York reached agreement on the withdrawal of Cuban troops from Angola and the ending of South African control of Namibia: on July 20 the South African Foreign Minister, R. F. Botha, released the text of a document setting out 14 principles, agreed with Angola and Cuba. **28.** The home of Mrs. Winnie Mandela in Soweto was set on fire by students. **29.** Police in South Africa seized all copies of the film *Cry Freedom* about the life of Steve Biko.

Aug. 3. A group of 143 white South Africans announced that they would not report for compulsory military service because they saw the South African Defence Force as an instrument of apartheid. **8.** South Africa, Cuba and Angola announced a ceasefire on the Angola-Namibia border. **12.** Nelson Mandela was admitted to hospital in Cape Town suffering from tuberculosis. **13.** The South African Foreign Minister, R. F. Botha, admitted that his country had the ability to produce nuclear weapons. **19.** Officials in Burundi confirmed that thousands of people had died in recent ethnic clashes.

COMMONWEALTH

(1987) Sept. 25. Lt.-Col. Sitiveni Rabuka staged a second bloodless coup in Fiji to prevent the formation of a bipartisan government and subsequently threatened to oust the Governor-General, Ratu Sir Penaia Ganilau, if he resisted the new government; on Sept. 29 a statement was issued by the Queen criticizing Rabuka's actions and saying that removing the Governor-General from office would be tantamount to a repudiation of allegiance to the Sovereign: after a week of confusion and contradictory statements from Rabuka, on Oct. 7 Rabuka declared Fiji a republic: on Oct. 14 Ratu Ganilau asked to be relieved of his position and his request was granted on Oct. 15, whereupon the Queen ceased to be head of state.

Oct. 10. Soldiers with the Indian peacekeeping force were killed in clashes with Tamil militants in Sri Lanka; on Oct. 20 Indian troops entered the Tamil militants' stronghold in Jaffna after ten days of heavy fighting. **13.** The 28th Commonwealth Summit began in Vancouver: on Oct. 16 the Commonwealth heads of government announced that Fiji's membership had lapsed as a result of the Queen's decision to step down as head of state. **27.** The Canadian House of Commons endorsed an accord intended to end Quebec's constitutional isolation from the rest of Canada. **28.** A security crackdown in Malaysia led to 63 arrests, the closure of three newspapers and a ban on public meetings.

Nov. 1. In Bangladesh opposition forces staged demonstrations against the government of President Ershad. **9.** A bomb exploded in Colombo, Sri Lanka, killing 32 people; on Nov. 10 Sinhalese demonstrators rioted during protests at the government's proposals for Tamil autonomy; on Nov. 20 the Indian Government declared a 48-hour ceasefire with the Tamil militants but the cease-fire was broken on Nov. 22 when Tamil Tiger guerrillas fired on two Indian patrols. **12.** In Australia a royal commission opened its investigations into the death of 63 aborigines in police custody since 1981. **27.** President Ershad declared a state of emergency in Bangladesh.

Dec. 1. Sir Johannes Bjelke-Petersen resigned as Premier of Queensland. **5.** Tamil rebels and Indian troops clashed in eastern Sri Lanka. **6.** President Ershad of Bangladesh dissolved parliament in the face of mounting protests against his rule. **9.** Gibraltar's Chief Minister, Sir Joshua Hassan, resigned. **17.** The Union Carbide Corporation was ordered to make an interim payment of £148 million to the victims of the Bhopal poison gas leak in 1984. **22.** Zimbabwe's two main political parties signed a merger agreement. **23.** The Chairman of Sri Lanka's ruling United National Party was shot dead in Colombo. **28.** Following a meeting between President Museveni and President Moi, Uganda and Kenya ended their two-week old border dispute.

(1988) Feb. 5. The Kenyan President, Daniel arap Moi, dissolved parliament and announced a general election for March 21. **10.** In Bangladesh fighting between rival groups contesting rural elections led to 85 deaths. **22.** George Vasiliou was elected President of Cyprus.

March 3. Five people were killed and at least 500 injured in rioting during parliamentary elections in Bangladesh. **14.** President Ershad of Bangladesh announced that Islam was to be the state religion. **16.** Indian troops stormed Tamil Tiger hideouts in northern Sri Lanka. **25.** Joe Bossano became chief minister of Gibraltar after his Socialist Labour Party won more than 60 per cent of the vote in the General Election on March 24. **29.** Sikh militants shot dead 17 people in the Punjab, bringing the total number of deaths for the first three months of 1988 to nearly 700. **31.** In Alice Springs, Australia, the equivalent of a year's rainfall fell in 24 hours, causing floods and forcing residents to evacuate their homes.

April 6. South-east Queensland, Australia, was declared a natural disaster area after 17

inches of rain fell in a week and caused floods.
29. Sri Lanka's ruling United National Party won control of all four councils in provincial elections.

May 11. Indian troops surrounded the Golden Temple in Amritsar; on May 15 troops took into custody 125 Sikh terrorists who surrendered; on May 18 the siege of the Golden Temple ended when the 46 Sikh rebels still alive inside surrendered. **29.** Sinhalese radicals killed 10 people, including candidates in the forthcoming elections, in southern Sri Lanka.

June 21. A bomb exploded near the Golden Temple in Amritsar, killing at least 15 people and injuring 20: the Indian authorities ordered an indefinite curfew.

July 4. The Prime Minister of Papua New Guinea, Mr. Paias Wingti, resigned after losing a vote of confidence. **6.** Five Supreme Court judges were suspended by the Malaysian government when they halted the work of a tribunal investigating the suspension of the head of the judiciary in May. **25.** The Gurkha National Liberation Front announced the end of its two-year separatist campaign in India after talks with federal government and West Bengali Ministers led to an agreement on the formation of a hill council giving the Gurkhas control of culture, education and local government.

Aug. 5. The bodies of 41 people tortured to death by Sikh extremists were found in the rubble of the Golden Temple at Amritsar. **31.** More than 25 million were left homeless in Bangladesh after the worst floods in the country's history.

EUROPEAN COMMUNITY

(1987) Sept. 2. An investigation by the Court of Auditors into the E.C. food aid programme revealed cases of fraud, lost consignments and contaminated food. **16.** Mrs. Thatcher's principal adviser to the E.C., David Williamson, was appointed Secretary-General of the Commission. **28.** The Commission agreed to a £4 billion science research programme over five years.

Oct. 4. E.C. foreign ministers failed to reach agreement on the next year's budget.

Nov. 4. The E.C. took emergency measures to combat the threat of swarms of locusts reaching parts of Europe from North Africa. **29.** Britain accused France and Germany of "ducking their responsibilities" when the foreign ministers of the two countries suggested that no attempt be made to agree price cuts for agricultural commodities.

Dec. 3. E.C. Environment ministers reached agreement on curbing the level of car exhaust emissions. **16.** The E.C. fishing quotas for 26 specimens of fish were increased. **19.** Following a lengthy dispute over the manufacture of counterfeits, the E.C. imposed punitive trade sanctions on South Korea.

(1988) Jan. 6. The European Commission agreed to pay farmers to take land out of agricultural production. **21.** The European Commission announced plans to limit the tar content of cigarettes. **24.** Britain and the Netherlands refused to endorse E.C. plans to curb farm spending because they did not consider the curbs strict enough.

Feb. 2. Mrs. Thatcher and Chancellor Kohl of West Germany met in London in an attempt to reach agreement before the extraordinary summit of the European Council on farm spending. **11.** The summit meeting on farm policy reform began in Brussels, closing on Feb. 13 after agreement had been reached. **25.** European Commission officials confirmed that Britain retained the right, for the time being, to be exempted from planned E.C. fiscal harmonization measures.

March. 7. An E.C. ban on the use of growth-promoting hormones in cattle was restored by Community agriculture ministers despite British objections. **10.** The European Parliament condemned the Israeli Army's violence in the occupied territories and renewed calls for an international peace conference. **23.** The Agriculture Commissioner, Frans Andriessen, revealed E.C. proposals for an across-the-board freeze on farm prices for the next year. **30.** E.C. farm ministers agreed new controls on subsidies in an attempt to reduce the Community's wine surplus.

April 11. A report by an E.C. consumers' organization said that cross-border transfers between banks in Europe are inept and disorganized. **25.** Ministerial talks between the E.C. and Turkey collapsed after the Turkish delegation objected to a reference to the situation in Cyprus.

May 3. It was announced that professional qualifications would be recognized throughout the European Community, enabling members of professions qualified in their own country to practise in any member state without having to gain further qualifications. **19.** The West German Economics Minister, Martin Bangemann, announced that he would resign his post and offer himself as a candidate for the presidency of the European Community Commission.

June 13. The Community agreed to negotiate with Hungary the lifting of import quotas for Hungarian goods by the end of

1995. **14.** E.C. foreign ministers agreed outstanding details of the finance and farm reform package, including details of the British budget rebate, set at £1·7 billion. **27.** An E.C. summit began in Hanover in West Germany: on June 28 the Community leaders agreed to consider new steps towards monetary fusion.

July 14. Britain forced the Community to withdraw a statement deploring the shooting down of an Iranian airliner by the U.S.A. **25.** E.C. foreign ministers agreed to allow the European Commission to explore closer economic ties with the Soviet Union and its allies.

MIDDLE EAST

(1987) Sept. 5. Israeli air raids on Palestinian targets in Southern Lebanon resulted in at least 40 deaths. **7.** A West German engineer, Alfred Schmidt, was released by his Lebanese kidnappers. Following a national referendum in Turkey, more than 200 politicians were allowed to return to political activity following a five year ban.

Oct. 6. President Mubarak of Egypt was re-elected with 97 per cent of the vote. **11.** In Jerusalem several thousand Palestinians rioted in protest at an attempt by militant Jews to enter the Temple Mount. **29.** Israeli military authorities closed Bethlehem University for three months following a student riot.

Nov. 13. Iraq and Egypt resumed full diplomatic relations after a nine-year break. **27.** Two French hostages, Jean-Louis Normandin and Roger Auque, were freed in Beirut by their captors, the Organization of Revolutionary Justice.

(1988) Jan. 20. In West Beirut the Shia militia lifted a three-year siege of Palestinian refugee camps. **28.** A West German engineer, Ralph Schray, was kidnapped in West Beirut. **29.** An Englishman working in Saudi Arabia was shot dead at a party in Riyadh.

Feb. 18. The trial of John Demjanjuk, accused of war crimes, ended in Jerusalem. **25.** A British businessman, John Smith, imprisoned in Iraq on a charge of bribery, was pardoned and released.

March 2. A West German engineer, Ralph Schray, kidnapped in Beirut in January, was released. **3.** Two Oxfam officials were kidnapped in South Lebanon; on March 8 the two men were released. **24.** In Jerusalem a former Israeli nuclear technician, Mordechai Vanunu, was convicted of espionage and

treason for revealing details of Israel's nuclear programme to the *Sunday Times*; on March 27 Vanunu was sentenced to 18 years imprisonment.

April 5. Arab gunmen hijacked a Kuwait Airways jet, diverted it to an airport in northeastern Iran and demanded the release of 17 Arabs jailed in Kuwait for terrorism; on April 6 most of the women passengers on the plane were released; on April 8 the hijacked plane was flown to Cyprus; one of the hostages was killed on April 9, and a second on April 11 when Cypriot authorities did not meet demands to have the plane refuelled; on April 12 twelve hostages were released in exchange for fuel; on April 13 the plane flew to Algeria, where the remaining 32 hostages were released; on April 20 the hijackers escaped. **19.** In Jerusalem John Demjanjuk was found guilty of war crimes against the Jewish people and humanity; on April 25 Demjanjuk was sentenced to death by hanging. **23.** A car bomb exploded in the city of Tripoli, Lebanon, killing more than fifty people.

May 4. Three Frenchmen kidnapped by the Islamic Jihad group three years previously were released to Syrian military authorities in Beirut. **7.** Rival Muslim groups fought for control of south Beirut, leaving 51 dead; on May 14 Syria ordered its troops to move into Beirut to end the fighting; figures released on May 24 showed that in the 19-day battle, 232 people died and 1,398 were injured.

THE GULF WAR.—**(1987) Sept. 1.** Iranian Revolutionary Guards attacked a Spanish tanker with grenades and machine guns. Iraq attacked Iranian oil tankers and other targets inside Iran; on Sept. 11 the U.N. Secretary General, Javier Perez de Cuellar, arrived in Tehran following an invitation from the Iranian Government; on Sept. 13 he left for Baghdad in Iraq: on Sept. 17 Iraq's unilateral ceasefire was broken when Iraqi aircraft attacked Kharg Island and on-shore oil fields. On Sept. 22, in a speech to the U.N., Seyed Ali Khamene'i, President of Iran, said that his country would continue the Gulf war until Iraq "had been punished". Throughout September and October attacks on shipping in the Gulf continued, with the loss of several lives, American naval forces adopted an aggressive attitude to Iranian attacks on shipping, capturing a mine-laying craft on Sept. 22, and in early Oct. sinking three Iranian speedboats that had attacked them. The American attack on two Iranian oil platforms on Oct. 19 provoked a near-declaration of war from Tehran.

Nov. 11. Delegates at an Arab summit conference condemned Iran for prolonging the Gulf War.

Dec. 3. Iran's deputy foreign minister, Mohammad Larijani, told the U.N. Security Council that his country would declare a ceasefire if the Council named Iraq as the aggressor in the war.

(1988) March 1. Iraqi missiles bombarded Tehran. **9.** Iran and Iraq deployed their air forces against each other's cities.

April 1. Iran claimed that 75 people had been killed in Iraqi chemical attacks on Kurdish villages. **18.** American forces attacked Iranian oil platforms and a frigate, and sank an Iranian patrol boat in the Gulf. **21.** Iraqi troops completed the recapture of the Fao Peninsula.

May 15. Iraqi bombers attacked the oil terminal at Larak, hitting four ships and killing 22 seamen. **29.** Ayatollah Khomeini ruled out a peace settlement in the Gulf War.

July 1. Iraq admitted that it had used chemical weapons in the war with Iran but claimed that the Iranians had used them first. **3.** A United States naval vessel, the USS *Vincennes*, shot down an Iranian airliner, killing all 290 civilians on board, after apparently mistaking it for an attacking jet fighter: on July 5 President Reagan told Congress that the shooting down of the airliner was justified in self-defence. **18.** Iran unconditionally accepted the U.N. Security Council Resolution 598 calling for a ceasefire with Iraq. **22.** Iraq launched a major offensive along a 100-mile stretch of the border with Iran. **26.** Representatives from the two nations began peace talks with U.N. Secretary General in New York.

Aug. 8. The U.N. Secretary General announced that Iran and Iraq had agreed to a ceasefire followed by direct talks under the auspices of the U.N. **10.** Advance teams of U.N. military observers arrived in Baghdad and Tehran. **20.** The ceasefire between Iran and Iraq came into effect.

PALESTINIAN UNREST.—**(1987) Dec. 9.** Two Palestinians were killed by Israeli troops in the Gaza Strip during demonstrations; by Dec. 16 the death toll had reached 21 as riots continued. On Dec. 22 the U.S.A. called for an end to the violence; on Dec. 23 Israel issued a strong rejection of the American criticism.

(1988) Jan. 3. Israel served deportation orders on nine Palestinians for hostile activity. **4.** British Foreign Office minister David Mellor condemned conditions at a Palestinian refugee camp in the Gaza Strip. **6.** British shadow Foreign Secretary Gerald Kaufman intervened to stop the arrest of an I.T.N. film crew in the Balata refugee camp. **10.** Israel sent troop reinforcements into the Gaza Strip

after renewed unrest left many wounded and two dead. **15.** Israeli security forces fired tear-gas into the Al-Haram Ash-Sharif mosque, known as the Noble Sanctuary. **19.** Israel banned foreign aid to Palestinians in the West Bank and Gaza Strip. **30.** It was revealed that a group calling itself the Unified National Leadership for the Uprising was co-ordinating unrest in the West Bank and Gaza Strip.

Feb. 1. As schools reopened in the Israeli occupied territories, violence erupted and two Palestinian youths were shot dead. **4.** The Prime Minister of Israel, Yitzhak Shamir, visited refugee camps in the Gaza Strip and promised to help improve conditions. By Feb. 12 the Palestinian death toll after two months of unrest had reached 56. **15.** Four Palestinians were buried alive by Israeli soldiers; military police launched an investigation, and on Feb. 27 four Israeli soldiers were detained and charged with brutality.

March 1. U.S. Secretary of State George Schultz and King Hussein of Jordan held talks in London about a peace plan for the Middle East. **7.** Three Israeli citizens were killed by Palestinian gunmen in southern Israel; the gunmen were later killed by Israeli troops. **11.** The Israeli Prime Minister categorically rejected the proposed peace plan drawn up by Mr. Schultz. **13.** Four hundred of Israel's Arab policemen resigned in response to a call from underground Arab leaders. **14.** The Israeli military authorities announced an indefinite nightly curfew in the Gaza Strip. **29.** The Israeli authorities sealed off the West Bank and the Gaza Strip for three days. **30.** The Arab-owned Palestinian Press Service was ordered to close for six months by the Israeli authorities.

April 5. Israeli troops killed two Palestinians attempting to enter Israel from the Lebanon. **6.** A 15-year-old Israeli girl was shot dead near the village of Beita. **16.** The military commander of the P.L.O., Abu Jihad, was assassinated in Tunis; following this, there were clashes between Israeli troops and Palestinian rioters which left 13 dead. **17.** Israel closed off Arab lands in Gaza and the West Bank. **26.** A Palestinian raiding party crossed into Israel from Lebanon and clashed with Israeli troops.

May 2. Israeli troops moved into south-east Lebanon in pursuit of Palestinian guerrillas; on May 4, all troops were withdrawn after a fierce battle with Hezbollah gunmen. **6.** Israel issued an expulsion order against Mubarak Awad, an American citizen who is the founder-leader of a Palestinian civil disobedience movement. **25.** Israeli troops entered Lebanon to attack Hezbollah strongholds.

June 13. Mubarek Awad was deported from Israel to the U.S.A. **17.** A raid on a shack in southern Beirut by pro-Iranian militiamen led to the release of three children held for ransom.

July 3. An archaeological dig in the Old City of Jerusalem caused Arab suspicions of an Israeli attempt to blow up the Al Aqsa mosque and the Dome of the Rock, and led to rioting by Arabs in Jerusalem. **4.** Israel closed all the schools on the West Bank. **31.** King Hussein of Jordan announced that Jordan would cut legal and administrative ties with the occupied West Bank, thereby acknowledging the P.L.O.'s aim of establishing an independent state in Palestine.

Aug. 25. Israeli air and naval forces attacked targets near Sidon, Lebanon, wounding five.

U.S.A.

(1987) Sept. 4. Thousands fled their homes as forest fires ravaged large areas of California; a state of emergency was declared in 22 counties. **14.** Elizabeth Dole resigned her cabinet post as Transportation Secretary to campaign for her husband, presidential contender Robert Dole. **23.** Senator Joseph Biden withdrew from the contest for the 1988 Democratic presidential nomination.

Oct. 6. The Senate Judiciary Committee recommended that the Senate reject the nomination of Judge Robert Bork as a Supreme Court Justice. **28.** President Reagan said that although the agreement to eliminate medium-range missiles had the highest priority, he would not abandon the Strategic Defence Initiative.

Nov. 5. Caspar Weinberger resigned as U.S. Secretary of Defence. **6.** The U.S. failed to reach agreement with Spain over the renewal of the leases of American military bases in southern Spain. **7.** President Reagan's second nominee as a member of the Supreme Court, Douglas Ginsburg, withdrew following his admission that he had smoked marijuana as a student. **9.** President Reagan said that the U.S. was ready to hold talks with the Nicaraguan government following its decision to negotiate with the U.S.-backed Contra rebels; on Nov. 10 Secretary of State George Schultz announced that military aid to the Contras would be frozen until 1988. **24.** The U.S. reached agreement with the Soviet Union on a treaty to eliminate all intermediate-range nuclear missiles.

Dec. 8. President Reagan and the Soviet leader Mikhail Gorbachev signed a treaty agreeing to eliminate all medium- and short-

range nuclear missiles. **16.** Gary Hart reentered the contest for the Democratic presidential nomination. **22.** Congress passed the budget for 1988 and agreed that the Nicaraguan Contra rebels should receive $8·1 million of "humanitarian" aid.

(1988) Jan. 15. Shares rose in London and New York and the dollar improved against the pound following a large reduction in the U.S. trade deficit. **23.** The United States tabled a draft treaty at Geneva on space defence, or "space wars". **27.** President Reagan submitted a request to Congress for $36·2 million aid for the Nicaraguan Contra rebels.

Feb. 4. Congress rejected plans to increase military aid to the Nicaraguan Contra rebels. **18.** President Reagan presented his budget to Congress; one of the main features of the budget was a restraint on military spending.

March 11. President Reagan suspended monthly U.S. payments for the use of the Panama Canal until "such a time as democratic government is restored" in Panama. **16.** Adm. John Poindexter and Lt.-Col. Oliver North were indicted on criminal charges arising from the Iran-Contra affair. **17.** U.S. troops flew in to Honduras after Nicaraguan incursions into Honduras; on March 28 the troops began to return to the U.S.

April 5. The governor of Arizona, Evan Mecham, was removed from office following the State Senate's vote to convict him of various misdemeanours. **13.** U.S. Marines fought off armed intruders at Howard air force base in the Panama Canal Zone.

May 27. The U.S. Senate formally approved the Intermediate Range Nuclear Forces Treaty on the eve of President Reagan's summit meeting in Moscow. **29.** The summit between President Reagan and Mikhail Gorbachev began in Moscow; on May 30 Mr. Gorbachev proposed a reduction of 500,000 troops in Europe; on May 31 President Reagan praised Mr. Gorbachev's reform plans in a speech to students at Moscow State University.

June 6. The Senate approved a $1,100 billion budget for the 1989 fiscal year that will leave a federal deficit of $135·3 billion. **15.** President Reagan called for an investigation of allegations of widespread bribery and fraud in the allocation of U.S. defence contracts.

July 3. Soviet inspection teams arrived at military bases in the U.S.A. to begin verification procedures under the I.N.F. treaty. **5.** Mr. Edwin Meese, the Attorney General, announced his resignation. **12.** Following the expulsion of eight American diplomats from Nicaragua, President Reagan ordered the expulsion of the Nicaraguan ambassador and seven of his staff from the U.S.A.

THE PRESIDENTIAL CAMPAIGN.—**Feb. 9.** The Republican caucus in the Iowa vote was won by Senator Robert Dole, with Vice-President George Bush achieving only third place; the Democrat vote was won by Senator Richard Gephardt. **12.** Gen. Alexander Haig withdrew his candidacy for the Republican nomination and pledged his support to Robert Dole. **17.** George Bush won the New Hampshire primary; Governor Michael Dukakis won the Democrat vote. **18.** Republican Pierre Dupont and Democrat Bruce Babbit withdrew from the presidential contest. **24.** Robert Dole won both the South Dakota primary and the Minnesota caucuses for the Republicans; Richard Gephardt won the Democrat vote in South Dakota and Michael Dukakis was victorious in Minnesota. **29.** George Bush won the Maine caucuses for the Republicans while Michael Dukakis received the Democrat vote.

March 8. George Bush won 16 of the 17 Republican contests; the Democrat vote was split evenly between Jesse Jackson, Michael Dukakis and Albert Gore. **10.** Congressman Jack Kemp withdrew from the contest for the Republican nomination. **11.** Gary Hart withdrew from the contest for the Democratic nomination. **13.** Jesse Jackson won the Democratic caucuses in his native South Carolina. **22.** In the Illinois primaries, George Bush won the Republican vote, while Senator Paul Simon was the leading Democrat. **26.** Jesse Jackson won the Democratic vote in the Michigan caucuses. **28.** Richard Gephardt withdrew from the contest for the Democratic nomination. **29.** Robert Dole withdrew from the contest for the Republican nomination. In the Connecticut primary Michael Dukakis won the Democratic vote.

April 6. Michael Dukakis won the Democratic vote in the Wisconsin elections. **8.** Democrat Paul Simon and Republican Pat Robertson both conceded that they had been defeated in their campaign for nomination but did not withdraw. **11.** Governor Cuomo of New York stated that he would not accept nomination as the Democratic candidate even if he was asked. **20.** Michael Dukakis won the New York primary. **21.** Albert Gore withdrew from the Democratic contest but did not release the delegates already pledged to him.

May 11. Michael Dukakis won victories in Nebraska and West Virginia. Pat Robertson ended his campaign for the Republican nomination and pledged his support for George Bush.

June 7. Governor Dukakis won the California, New Mexico and New Jersey primaries.

Vice-President Bush had uncontested victories in the Republican primaries.

July 12. Governor Dukakis chose Senator Lloyd Bentsen of Texas as his running mate. **17.** The Democratic convention began in Atlanta. **20.** Governor Michael Dukakis was confirmed as the Democratic presidential candidate.

Aug. 15. The Republican Convention began in New Orleans. **16.** Vice-President George Bush announced that Senator Dan Quayle would be his running mate in the presidential elections. **18.** Vice-President George Bush was confirmed as the Republican presidential candidate.

OTHER COUNTRIES

(1987) Sept. 7. In **Argentina** President Alfonsin's Radical Party lost its absolute majority in the Chamber of Deputies following elections. **10.** Queen Margrethe asked Poul Schlüter, leader of the centre-right coalition government in **Denmark**, to begin negotiations for the formation of a new government after elections left all parties without a working majority. **13.** In **Yugoslavia** 42 members of the ruling Communist Party were expelled and 28 faced criminal proceedings over a major financial scandal. The French Pacific territory of **New Caledonia** voted, in an independent referendum, to remain part of France. **24.** The government in **Nicaragua** released 17 non-Nicaraguan Contra prisoners. **27. Vietnam**'s leaders began a 15-month purge of corrupt and inefficient officials from the Communist Party.

Oct. 2. Riots followed the arrest of Buddhist monks in Lhasa, **Tibet**; on Oct. 4 the Chinese authorities imposed a strict curfew and press restrictions. **4.** President de la Madrid of **Mexico** named as his successor Carlos Salinas de Gortari. **6.** A new body to monitor human rights in the **U.S.S.R.** was founded by four leading dissidents. **8.** The American delegation to the U.N. walked out during an address by President Daniel Ortega of Nicaragua. **12.** In **Brazil** 41 people were taken to hospital suffering from the effects of radiation which was released when a capsule containing an isotope used in cancer therapy was stolen and dismantled. **19.** The **Belgian** Government resigned following its failure to resolve antagonism between the French and Flemish speaking communities. **23.** Five **Soviet** generals were killed in a helicopter crash.

Nov. 2. The **Soviet** leader, Mikhail Gorbachev, pledged to continue to reform Soviet society in a speech marking the start of celebrations of the 70th anniversary of the

Bolshevik Revolution. 6. Noboru Takeshita took office as **Japan's** new Prime Minister. 7. It was revealed that **Soviet** troops had secretly set up a base in the Seychelles. Federico Mayor of Spain was elected the new director-general of **Unesco**. 9. Edouard Saouma was elected director of the **Food and Agriculture Organization** for a third time. 11. Boris Yeltsin was dismissed from his job as **Moscow** Communist Party chief. 13. **West Germany** and **France** agreed on the establishment of joint councils on defence and economic and financial matters. 14. President Cossiga of **Italy** cancelled his state visit to Britain as a result of a sudden government crisis in his own country. 16. Dancer Rudolf Nureyev returned to the **Soviet Union** after 26 years in exile to visit his sick mother. 21. The **Italian** five-party coalition, led by Giovanni Goria, won a vote of confidence in the Senate a week after its apparent collapse. 24. **China** named Li Peng as acting prime minister, in place of Zhao Ziyang who was appointed general secretary of the Communist Party. 25. A general strike in **Italy** in protest at government budget plans brought all services to a standstill. 26. Troops were used to bring order to **Haiti** when violence erupted in the run up to elections; on Nov. 29 the elections were cancelled because of violence in Port-au-Prince which left 34 dead. 29. The **Polish** government failed to secure a mandate for political and economic reform in a national referendum when there was a turn-out of less than 50 per cent. The ruling **Turkish** Motherland Party was voted back into office with an absolute parliamentary majority.

Dec. 1. The **Kampuchean** leader, Hun Sen, met former ruler Prince Sihanouk in France for talks aimed at reconciliation. 7. A general strike against the military government in **Haiti** closed most businesses and shops in the capital. 10. **France** asked more than 50 members of the Mujahidin to leave Paris and return to Iraq. In **Haiti** the postponed elections were re-scheduled for January 17. 14. Elections in **Belgium** left no party with a clear mandate to govern. 16. President Ortega of **Nicaragua** announced a truce in the war with the Contra rebels over the Christmas period. 17. The **Czechoslovak** leader, Gustav Husak, resigned and was replaced by Milos Jakes. Roh Tae Woo won the presidential election in **South Korea**. 26. In **Afghanistan** fighting between rebels and Soviet and Government troops near the besieged garrison of Khost led to hundreds of casualties. 29. **Soviet** cosmonaut Yuri Romanenko returned to earth after a record 326 days in space.

(1988) Jan. 3. Soviet and **Afghan** army convoys reached the garrison town of Khost, ending a two-month siege. An **Argentine** foreign ministry communique renewed the country's claim to the Falkland Islands. 4. A

French journalist, Alain Guilly, was jailed for ten years in Afghanistan for spying. 8. The U.S. sent a top official to **Panama** to urge the Panamanian armed forces leader Gen. Noriega to allow free elections. 12. The six political parties in **Spain's** Basque region signed an anti-terrorist pact designed to isolate the E.T.A. movement. 13. President Chiang Ching-kuo of **Taiwan** died. 15. Rebel **Argentine** army colonel Aldo Rico escaped from house arrest before his trial for mutiny; on Jan. 18 Col. Rico surrendered to loyalist forces. 15. A **North Korean** woman, Kim Hyon Hi, admitted that she helped to place a bomb on a South Korean airliner that disappeared in mid-flight with 115 people on board. 17. President Ortega of **Nicaragua** made concessions to the Contra rebels in an attempt to keep the Central American peace plan alive. 18. The Jewish dissident Iosif Begun left the **Soviet Union** for Israel. Local elections took place in the **Philippines**. Presidential elections took place in **Haiti**. 20. Talks on **Kampuchea** resumed in Paris between Prince Sihanouk and Hun Sen. 22. Eight people were killed by car bombs at the funeral in **Afghanistan** of Khan Abdul Ghaffar Khan, an anti-colonialist campaigner. 23. **Italian** prime minister Giovanni Goria called for a vote of confidence after part of his government's budget package was defeated in Parliament. 25. The **Colombian** Attorney-General Carlos Mauro Hoyos was kidnapped and then executed by drug traffickers.

Feb. 7. Leslie Manigat took office as Head of State in **Haiti**, ending the period of military rule. 8. An independent historical commission investigating the wartime record of President Waldheim of **Austria** presented its report to the Austrian Chancellor: the report concluded that President Waldheim had known that atrocities were being committed in Greece and Yugoslavia. 10. The **Italian** Government collapsed when the Prime Minister Giovanni Goria resigned; on Feb. 13 Mr. Goria agreed to continue as Prime Minister. 14. The **Austrian** Chancellor, Franz Vranitzky, threatened to resign if the controversy surrounding President Waldheim continued. 17. In Bangkok **Thailand** and **Laos** signed a ceasefire agreement intended to end border hostilities. 16. The **Vietnamese** Government announced amnesties for 1,014 political prisoners as part of the new year celebrations. 18. The **Soviet** Communist Party Central Committee dismissed Boris Yeltsin from his position as a non-voting member. 25. Gen. Noriega was dismissed as **Panama's** chief of military staff by President Delvalle; on Feb. 26 President Delvalle was ousted by Gen. Noriega's supporters and replaced by former education minister, Manuel Solis Palma. 26. Massive demonstrations took place in Erevan, the capital of Soviet **Armenia**, as Armenians and

THE QUEEN IN AUSTRALIA

The Queen and the Duke of Edinburgh visited Australia in April to participate in the country's bicentennial celebrations.

THE QUEEN IN THE NETHERLANDS

The Queen is greeted by Queen Beatrix on her arrival in The Netherlands in July on a visit to commemorate the tercentenary of the Glorious Revolution.

THE ROYAL BABY

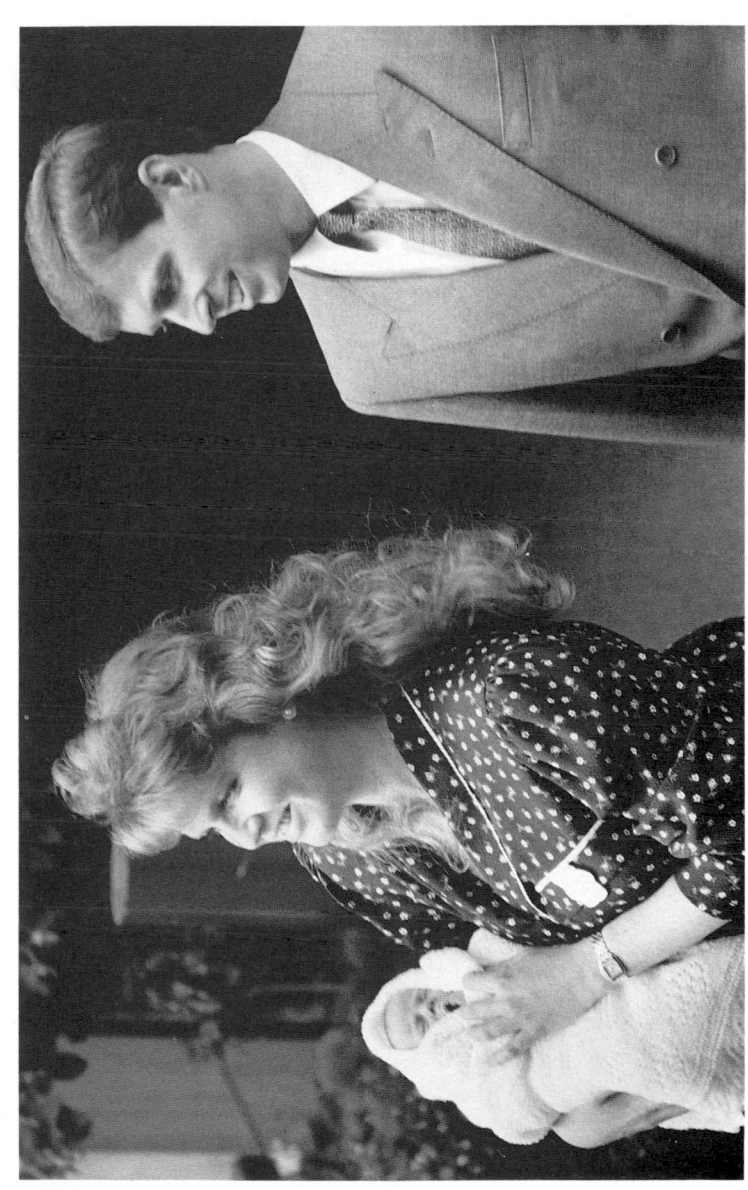

The Duke and Duchess of York leave hospital with Princess Beatrice after her birth in August.

THE LAMBETH CONFERENCE

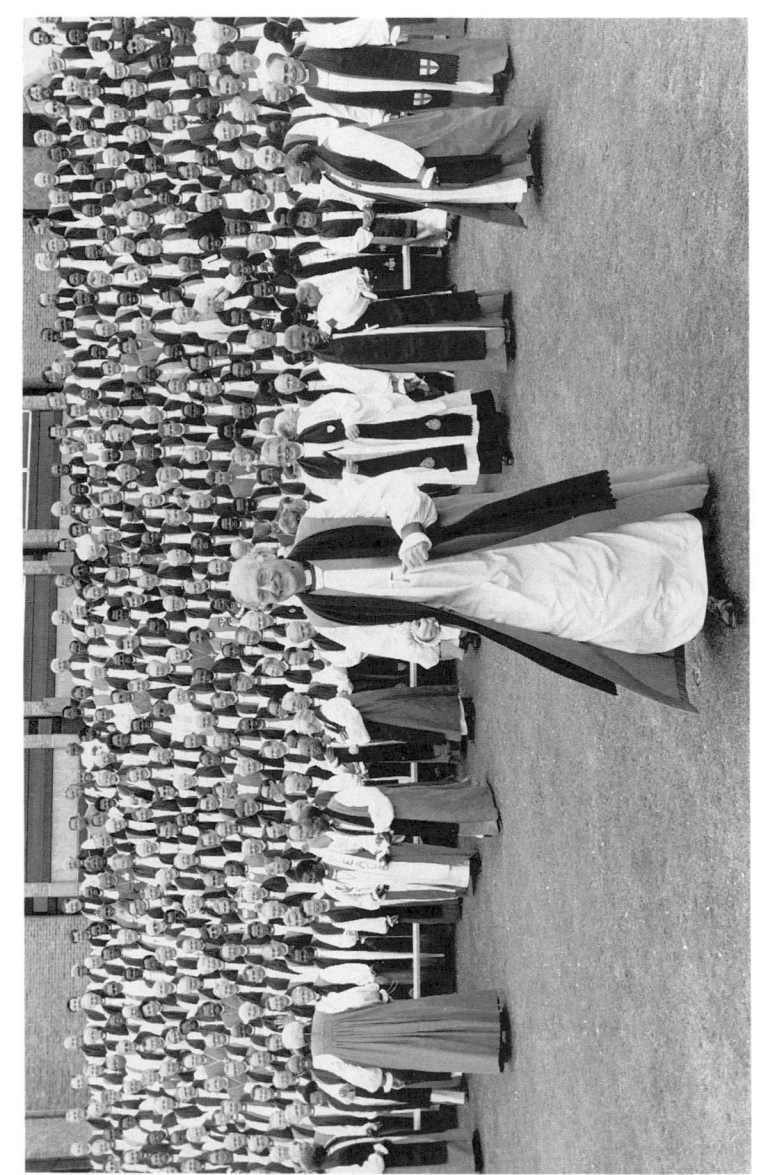

The decennial conference of archbishops and bishops of the Anglican Communion took place at Canterbury in July .

STORM DAMAGE

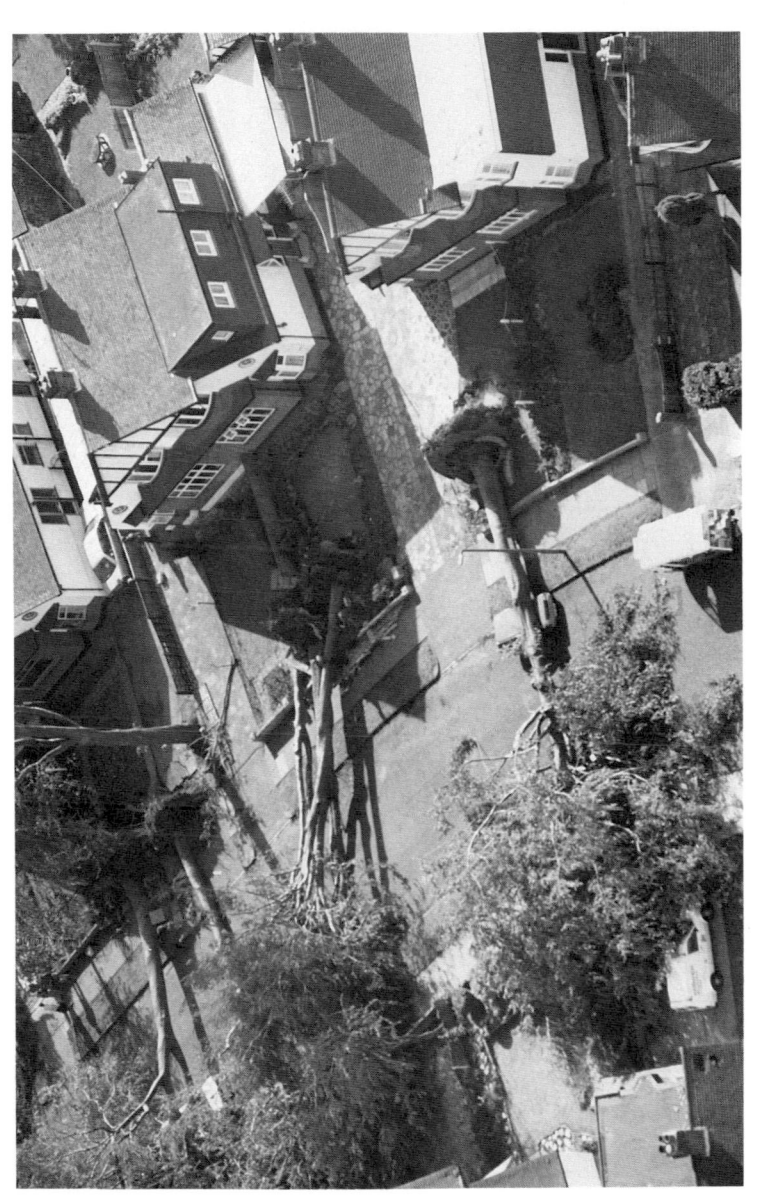

Hurricane-force winds on October 15–16 caused extensive damage throughout southern England.

THE KING'S CROSS FIRE

A fire at King's Cross underground station in November killed over thirty people.

THE PIPER ALPHA EXPLOSION

An explosion on the Piper Alpha oil rig in the North Sea in July killed 167 men.

THE ENNISKILLEN BOMBING

The funeral cortege of a victim passes the spot where a bomb exploded at a Remembrance Sunday ceremony, killing eleven people.

FUNERAL KILLINGS

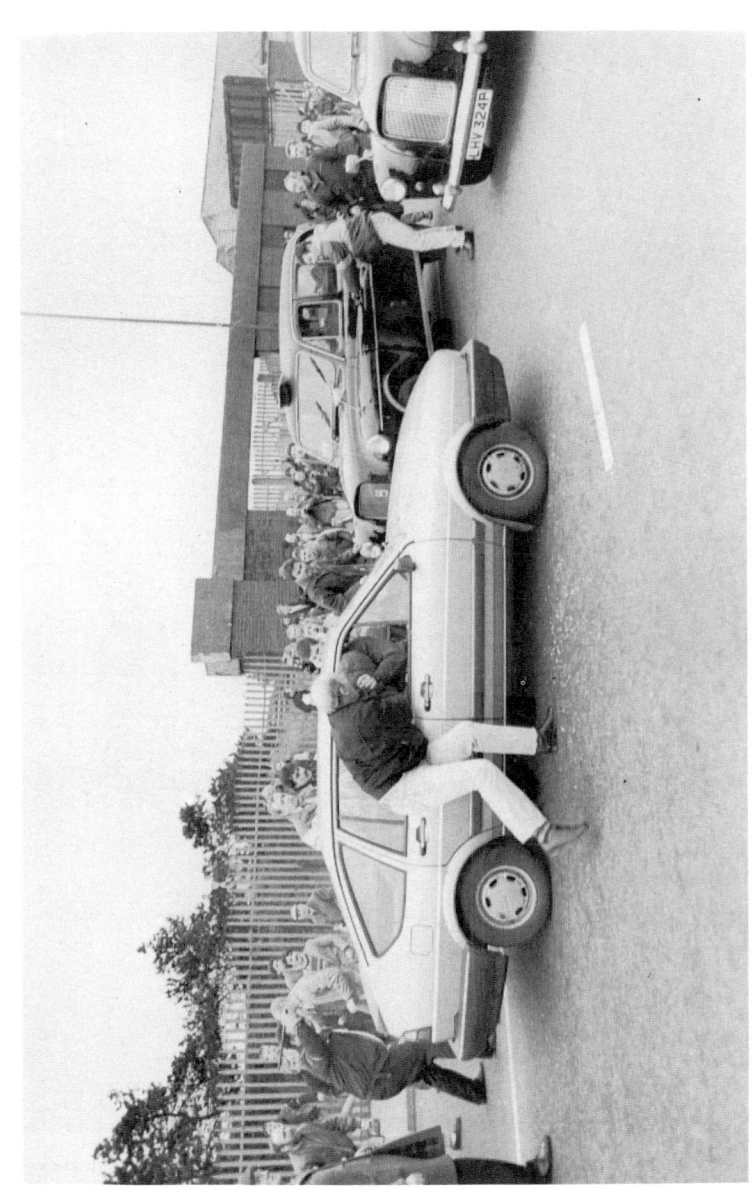

Two British soldiers were dragged from their car and killed after driving into the path of the funeral of a victim of the Milltown cemetery attack in March.

SOVIET WITHDRAWAL

Soviet troops began withdrawing from Afghanistan in May, eight years after the Soviet invasion of the country.

PALESTINIAN RIOTS

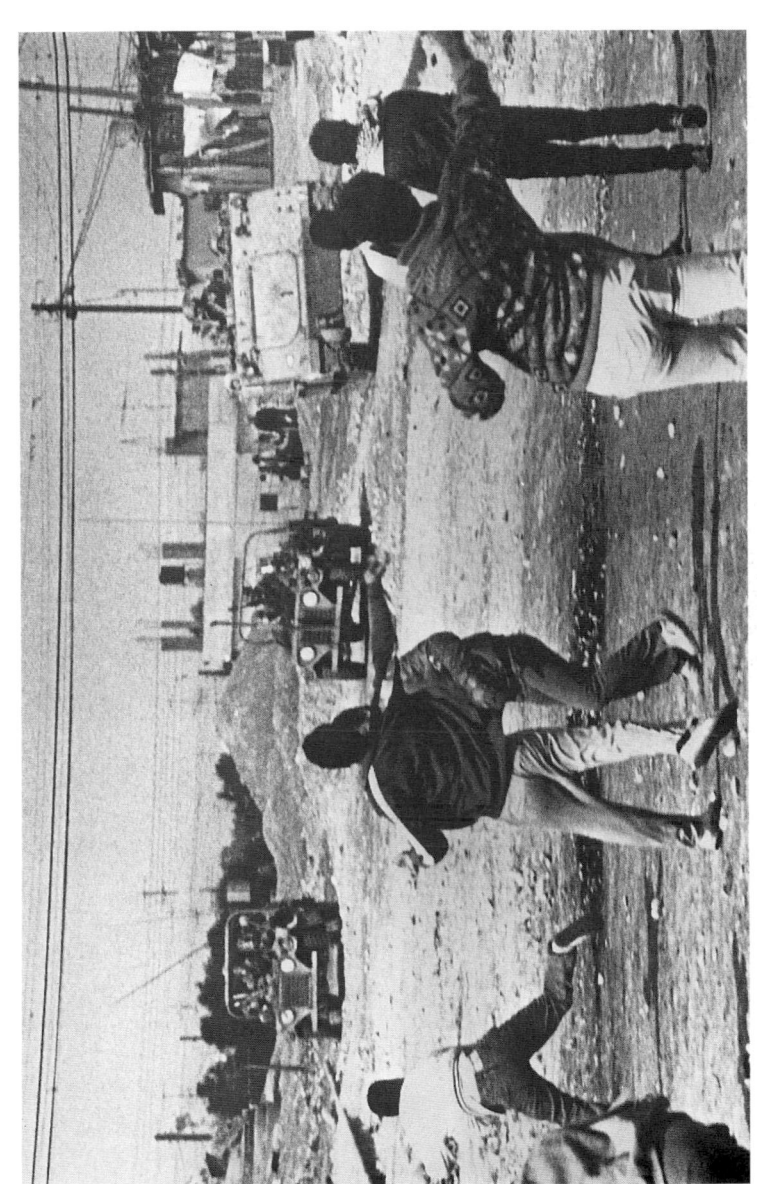

Demonstrations and rioting on the West Bank and in the Gaza Strip occurred sporadically throughout the year.

THE SUDAN FLOODS

The flooding of the Nile in Sudan in August left over a million people homeless.

OBITUARIES

Lord Silkin (*top left*), President Zia (*top right*), Sir Frederick Ashton (*bottom left*) and Lord Ramsey of Canterbury.

OBITUARIES

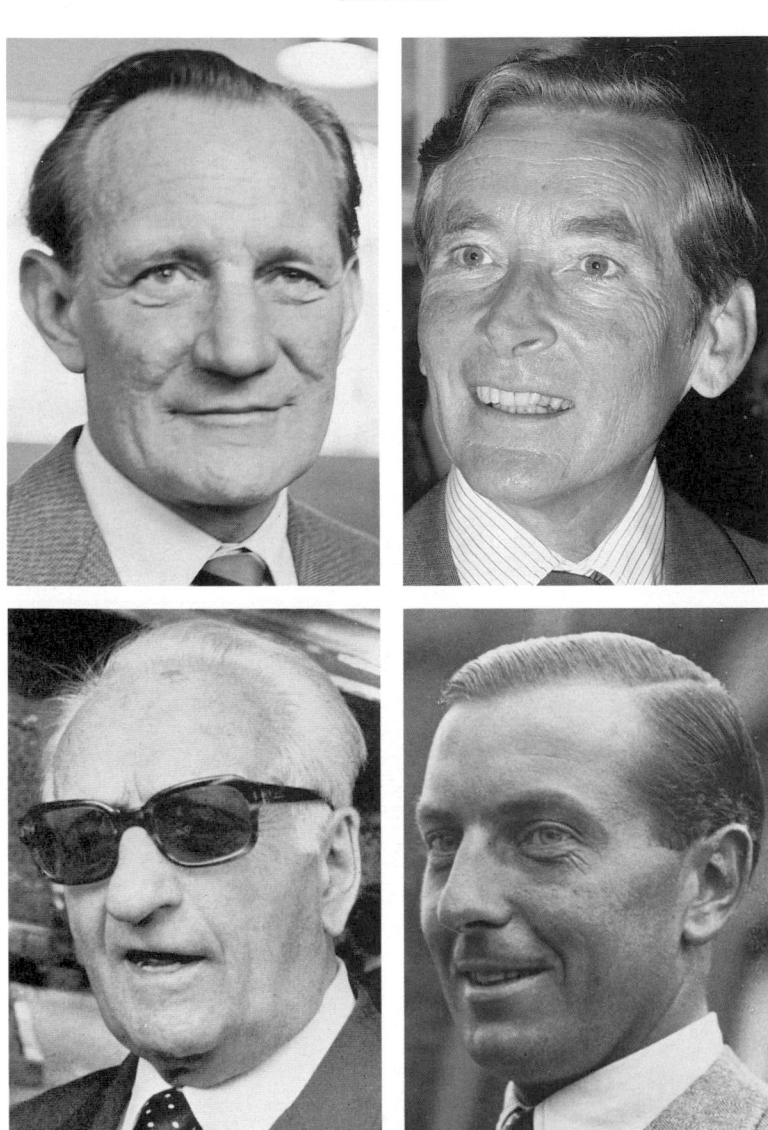

Trevor Howard (*top left*), Kenneth Williams (*top right*), Enzo Ferrari (*bottom left*) and Sir Henry Cotton.

Graeme Hick broke several batting records during the 1988 season and helped Worcestershire to their first county championship since 1974.

SPORTING TRIUMPHS

Sandy Lyle (*left*) became the first British golfer to win the U.S. Masters in April. American Harry Reynolds broke the 400-metre world record in August.

Azerbaidjanis disputed possession of the territory of Nagorno Karabakh; on Feb. 28 the **Soviet Union** announced that two Armenians had been killed in disorders in a border district.

March 1. In **Panama City** businesses shut in an attempt to paralyse the economy and bring about the fall of Gen. Noriega. **Soviet** troops were deployed in the Azerbaidjani city of Sumgait in an attempt to restore order after rioting. **4.** Following the U.S. Government's decision to freeze all Panamanian assets in the U.S.A., banks in **Panama** were forced to close for lack of cash. **5.** President Waldheim of **Austria** admitted that he knew that Allied commandos interrogated by his unit would be automatically executed. **7.** Chinese police sealed off **Tibet's** Jockhang Temple after the most serious outbreak of national unrest for 30 years. **11.** Italian Prime Minister Giovanni Goria resigned. **13.** Hundreds of Armenians gathered in Moscow to demand arbitration by the Government in the territorial dispute over Nagorno-Karabakh. **14.** Chinese and Vietnamese warships clashed in disputed waters in the South China Sea. **16.** Gen. Noriega retained control in **Panama** after suppressing an attempted rebellion by army officers. **21.** The **Nicaraguan** Government and the Contra rebels began discussions aimed at ending the seven year war. **24.** The **Soviet** authorities announced that there would be no redrawing of internal borders in the Nagorno-Karabakh region.

April 1. A 60-day ceasefire began between the **Nicaraguan** Government and the Contra rebels. **4.** The **Chinese** Government invited the Dalai Lama to return to Tibet on condition that he acknowledges Chinese sovereignty over Tibet. **8.** The **Chinese** Parliament named Yang Shangkun as the new President; on April 10 Li Peng was appointed Prime Minister. **10.** An ammunition dump in **Pakistan** exploded, raining bombs, rockets and shrapnel on the cities of Islamabad and Rawalpindi and killing over 70 people. **11.** A Briton, Andrew Bertie, was elected Grand Master of the Sovereign Military Order of **Malta**. **12.** The **Italian** Prime Minister designate, Ciriaco de Mita, formed the 48th post-war government. **14.** A bomb exploded in a U.S. naval club in Naples, killing 5 people. **19.** In **West Germany** an Arab terrorist, Abbas Ali Hamadei, was sentenced to 13 years imprisonment for kidnapping. The **Danish** Prime Minister, Poul Schlüter, called a general election for May 10 after his government was defeated in a vote on an opposition motion regarding nuclear weapons on foreign warships in Danish waters. **22.** Three gendarmes were killed and 27 taken hostage by Kanak separatists in the French Pacific territory of **New Caledonia**. **29.** **Thailand's** Prime Minister,

Gen. Prem Tinsulanonda, dissolved parliament and announced elections for July.

May 1. Violence broke out in six cities in **Poland** during unofficial May Day rallies. **2.** The leaders of five political parties in **Belgium** finalized an accord to form a new Government led by the outgoing Prime Minister Wilfred Martens. **5.** French troops in the French Pacific territory of **New Caledonia** released 23 hostages and killed 19 separatists in a battle on the island of Ouvea. **7.** It was revealed that in March Chinese police had stormed a temple in Lhasa, **Tibet**, and clubbed to death 30 monks. **8.** Francois Mitterrand was elected President of **France** for a second seven-year term. **9.** Rodrigo Borja won the presidential election in **Ecuador**. **10.** Workers at the Gdansk shipyard in **Poland** called off their week-long strike. **14.** President Mitterrand dissolved the **French** National Assembly and called a general election for early June. **22.** Janos Kadar was replaced as general secretary of the **Hungarian** Socialist Worker's Party by Karoly Grosz. **24.** **Nicaraguan** President Daniel Ortega announced a unilateral extension of the ceasefire with the Contra rebels. **25.** The **Vietnamese** announced that they would withdraw 50,000 troops from Kampuchea by the end of the year. **29.** President Zia of Pakistan dismissed the government and dissolved the national and provincial assemblies; on May 31 he announced that elections would not be held until 1989.

June 2. The **Brazilian** Constituent Assembly voted to grant a further five year term to President Sarney. **7.** The **Swedish** Justice Minister, Anna-Greta Leijon, resigned over her role in setting up an unofficial Social Democratic Party investigation into the assassination of the former Prime Minister Olaf Palme. **9.** President Zia of **Pakistan** announced a caretaker Cabinet. **10.** Peace talks between the Nicaraguan Government and the Contra rebels collapsed. **11.** Reports reached Moscow of new unrest in **Soviet** Azerbaijan which was said to have resulted in several deaths. **12.** Parliamentary elections in **France** left no party with a clear majority. **15.** President Zia of **Pakistan** proclaimed Islamic Sharia law the supreme law of the land and repealed all other laws. **20.** The President of **Haiti**, Mr. Leslie Manigat, was overthrown in a military coup and Gen. Henri Namphy formed a military Government. **21.** The **Burmese** authorities imposed a dusk-to-dawn curfew for two months in Rangoon after anti-government riots left six people dead. **26.** Workers in Nagorno-Karabakh in the **Soviet Union** voted to return to work after five weeks of strikes and unrest.

July 6. The **Armenian** capital of Yerevan was crippled by strikes as protests continued over the status of Nagorno-Karabakh. **8.** The ruling Institutional Revolutionary Party in **Mexico** claimed that their candidate, Carlos Salinas de Gortari, won the recent presidential election: on July 11 the Federal Election Commission announced that Sr. Salinas had won the election with 52·9 per cent. of the vote. **11.** Nine people died when masked gunmen attacked a **Greek** pleasure boat carrying tourists near the island of Aegina. Prince Sihanouk resigned as leader of the **Kampuchean** resistance alliance. **12.** The regional Communist party council of Nagorno-Karabakh voted for the region to secede from Azerbaijan and be transferred back to **Armenia**. **15. Afghan** rebels killed 20 people in a rocket attack on Kabul. **19.** President Ortega of **Nicaragua** extended the ceasefire with the Contra rebels for another month. **20.** President Zia of **Pakistan** announced that general elections would take place on November 16. **22.** Martial law was declared in the city of Prome, north **Burma**, following rioting. **26.** The **Burmese** party chairman Ne Win resigned and was replaced by Sein Lwin. Sein Lwin also replaced San Yu as President, and Tun Tin was appointed Prime Minister in place of Maung Maung. **27.** Gen. Prem Tinsulanonda declined an invitation to lead the new **Thai** government after recent elections.

Aug. 3. The Burmese leader Sein Lwin declared martial law in **Burma** as marches and demonstrations continued. **4.** Chatichai Choonhavan became Prime Minister of **Thailand**. **10.** More than 100 people were killed and several hundred were injured in Rangoon as civilians battled with government troops. **11.** Over 600 people were killed when a rocket attack on Kalagay by **Afghan** rebels ignited fuel and ammunition dumps. **12.** Sein Lwin resigned as leader of Burma: on Aug. 20 Maung Maung was appointed President, the first civilian to hold the position since 1962. **14. Afghan** rebel forces shelled three towns, killing 14 people and wounding 20. **16.** In **Poland** mineworkers went on strike demanding the legalization of the banned Solidarity trade union: on Aug. 17 strikes broke out in other industrial areas. **17.** President Zia ul-Haq was killed when his plane exploded and crashed in eastern **Pakistan**: also among the 39 dead were the American ambassador and several senior military officers. **21.** Thousands of protestors in Prague and hundreds in Moscow marked the 20th anniversary of the Soviet invasion of **Czechoslovakia** with demonstrations, which were broken up with great force by police. **24.** Martial law in **Burma** ended. **29.** Opposition groups in

Burma formed the Alliance for Democracy and Peace as unrest continued. **30.** President Pinochet, **Chile's** military ruler, was named as the sole candidate in the forthcoming presidential elections.

MISCELLANEOUS

(1987) Sept. 17. David Puttnam, the British film producer, resigned as chairman of Columbia Pictures after only one year in the post.

Oct. 2. The Tate Gallery acquired Picasso's *Weeping Woman* for £3·1 million. **30.** The London newspaper *The Evening News* closed after the circulation dropped to 39,000.

Nov. 11. A Van Gogh picture of a flower bed full of irises was sold for a record $53·9 million (£30·18 million) at Sotheby's in New York. **19.** A 1931 Bugatti Type 41 Sports Coupe was auctioned by Christie's for £5·5 million, the largest sum ever paid for a vintage car. **20.** The radical newspaper *News on Sunday* closed down.

Dec. 26. It was reported that a former M16 officer Anthony Cavendish had circumvented the ban on the publication of intelligence officers' memoirs by publishing his memoirs, "Inside Intelligence", privately and sending copies to friends as a Christmas card.

(1988) Feb. 6. The fund-raising event Comic Relief raised £7 million for famine relief in Africa and for deprived young people in Britain.

March 25. The explorer Sir Ranulph Fiennes was forced to abandon his attempt to walk to the North Pole because of frostbite.

April 21. Peter Levi, Oxford Professor of Poetry announced the discovery of verses which he ascribed to Shakespeare. **24.** Sotheby's in New York began the sale of the art collection of Andy Warhol.

June 2. Steven Venables became the first Briton to scale Mount Everest without oxygen. **5.** Australian yachtswoman Kay Cottee became the first woman to sail solo non-stop around the world.

July 11. Pop star Michael Jackson arrived in Britain to give a number of concerts.

Aug. 7. Harry Taylor of Britain and Russell Brice of New Zealand climbed Mount Everest's north-east ridge, the last remaining unclimbed route.

OBITUARIES
SEPT. 1, 1987–AUG. 31, 1988

Adair, *Maj.-Gen.* Sir Allan, Bt., G.C.V.O., C.B., D.S.O., M.C., *aged* 90—Aug. 4.

Anderson, *Gen.* Sir John, G.B.E., K.C.B., D.S.O., *aged* 79—April 16.

Andrews, Eamonn, Irish broadcaster, *aged* 64—Nov. 5, 1987.

Anouilh, Jean, French playwright, *aged* 77—Oct. 3, 1987.

Armstrong, 3rd Baron, *aged* 68—Oct. 1, 1987.

Arnott, *Most Rev.* Felix, C.M.G., Archbishop of Brisbane 1970–80, *aged* 77—July 27.

Arup, Sir Ove, C.B.E., civil engineer, *aged* 92—Jan. 5.

Ashton, Sir Frederick, O.M., C.H., C.B.E., choreographer, *aged* 83—Aug. 18.

Astor, John, Conservative M.P. for Newbury 1964–74, *aged* 64—Dec. 27, 1987.

Astor, Mary, American actress, *aged* 81—Sept. 25, 1987.

Baker, Chet, jazz trumpeter, *aged* 58—May 13.

Baldwin, James, American writer, *aged* 63—Nov. 30, 1987.

Barber, Noel, C.B.E., journalist and author, *aged* 78—July 10.

Bean, Robert, Labour M.P. for Rochester and Chatham 1974–79, *aged* 53—Dec. 1987.

Beecher, *Most Rev.* Leonard, C.M.G., Archbishop of East Africa 1960–70, *aged* 81—Dec. 16, 1987.

Bell, Sir Charles, C.B.E., industrialist, *aged* 80—March 12.

Bennett, Canon Gareth, Anglican priest and Oxford don, *aged* 58—Dec. 7, 1987.

Benson, Sir Arthur, G.C.M.G., Governor of Northern Rhodesia 1954–59, *aged* 79—Oct. 15, 1987.

Blackford, 4th Baron, *aged* 26—May 15.

Blyton, Lord, Labour M.P. for Houghton-le-Spring 1945–64, *aged* 88—Oct. 1987.

Boothroyd, Basil, writer and broadcaster, *aged* 77—Feb. 27.

Bowes, Bill, cricketer, *aged* 79—Sept. 5, 1987.

Boxer, Mark, editor and cartoonist, *aged* 57—July 20.

Bramwell-Booth, Catherine, Salvation Army Commissioner, *aged* 104—Oct. 4, 1987.

Brockway, Lord, Labour M.P. for East Leyton 1929–31 and Eton and Slough 1950–64, *aged* 99—April 28.

Cairns, *Rt. Hon.* Sir David, Lord Justice of Appeal 1970–74, *aged* 85—Sept. 8, 1987.

Carnarvon, 6th Earl of, *aged* 88—Sept. 22, 1987.

Carroll, Madeleine, film actress, *aged* 81—Oct. 1987.

Chiang, Ching-kuo, President of Taiwan since 1978, *aged* 77—Jan. 13.

Chipperfield, Dick, circus man, *aged* 83—March 3.

Chisholm, Judith, record-breaking aviator—July 8.

Clanmorris, 7th Baron, novelist (as John Bingham), *aged* 79—Aug. 6.

Clements, Sir John, C.B.E., actor-manager, *aged* 77—April 6.

Clifford of Chudleigh, 13th Baron, O.B.E., *aged* 71—March 17.

Cobbold, 1st Baron, K.G., G.C.V.O., P.C., Governor of the Bank of England 1949–61, *aged* 83—Nov. 1, 1987.

Cockayne, Dame Elizabeth, D.B.E., S.R.N., Chief Nursing Officer, Ministry of Health, 1948–58, *aged* 93—July 4.

Collins, *Gen.* J. Lawton, American army commander, *aged* 91—Sept. 12, 1987.

Colville, Sir John, C.B., C.V.O., private secretary to three Prime Ministers 1939–41, 1943–45, 1951–55, and to Princess Elizabeth 1947–49, and diplomat, *aged* 72—Nov. 19, 1987.

Cook, Sir William, K.C.B., F.R.S., civil servant, *aged* 82—Sept. 16, 1987.

Cotton, Sir Henry, M.B.E., golfer, *aged* 80—Dec. 22, 1987.

Cournand, Dr. André, French American physician and Nobel medicine prize winner, *aged* 92—Feb.

Courtney, *Cdr.* Anthony, Conservative M.P. for Harrow East 1959–66, *aged* 79—Jan. 24.

Crosby, John, C.M.G., L.V.O., British High Commissioner in Belize since 1984, *aged* 47—Jan. 22.

Cruickshank, Andrew, M.B.E., actor, *aged* 80—April 29.

d'Avigdor-Goldsmid, Sir James, Bt., C.B., O.B.E., M.C., Conservative M.P. for Lichfield and Tamworth 1970–74, *aged* 76—Sept. 6, 1987.

Darrell, Peter, C.B.E., founder-director of Scottish Ballet and choreographer, *aged* 58—Dec. 2, 1987.

Davis, *Adm.* Sir William, G.C.B., D.S.O., *aged* 86—Oct. 29, 1987.

De La Warr, 10th Earl, *aged* 66—Feb. 9.

de Rothschild, Baron Philippe, wine-producer, *aged* 85—Jan. 20.

Dickson, *Marshal of the Royal Air Force* Sir William, G.C.B., K.B.E., D.S.O., A.F.C., *aged* 88—Sept. 12, 1987.

Dien, *Most Rev.* Nguyen Kim, R.C. Archbishop of Hue, Vietnam, *aged* 67—June 8.

Donner, Sir Patrick, Conservative M.P. for West Islington 1931–35 and Basingstoke 1935–55, *aged* 83—Aug. 19.

Downie, *Prof.* Allan, F.R.C.Path., F.R.S., bacteriologist, *aged* 86—Jan. 26.

Drees, Dr. Willem, Hon. G.C.M.G., Prime Minister of the Netherlands 1948–58, *aged* 101—May.

Drumalbyn, 1st Baron, K.B.E., P.C., politician, *aged* 79—Oct. 11, 1987.

Dudley-Williams, Sir Rolf, Bt., Conservative M.P. for Exeter 1951–66, *aged* 79—Oct. 8, 1987.

Dufferin and Ava, 5th Marquess, *aged* 49—May 29.

Duncan-Sandys, Lord, C.H., P.C., Conservative M.P. 1935–45 and 1950–74, and Government Minister 1944–45 and 1951–64, *aged* 79—Nov. 26, 1987.

du Pré, Jacqueline, cellist, *aged* 42—Oct. 19, 1987.

Dwyer, *Most Rev.* George, R.C. Archbishop of Birmingham 1965–81, *aged* 78—Sept. 17, 1987.

Edwards, Jimmy, D.F.C., comedian, *aged* 68—July 7.

Emery, *Rt. Rev.* Anthony, R.C. Bishop of Portsmouth since 1976, *aged* 69—April 5.

Evans, Sir Hywel, K.C.B., Permanent Secretary, Welsh Office 1971–80, *aged* 68—June 2.

Exeter, 7th Marquess of, *aged* 78—Jan. 12.

Farwell, Dom Victor, Abbot of Worth Abbey since 1965, and Abbot President of English Benedictine Congregation 1967–85, *aged* 74—May 23.

Ferrari, Enzo, founder of Ferrari cars, *aged* 90—Aug. 14.

Feynman, *Prof.* Richard, American physicist and Nobel laureate, *aged* 69—Feb. 15.

Foote, *Lt. Col.* John, V.C., *aged* 83–May 2.

Ford, *Prof.* Edmund, F.R.S., geneticist, *aged* 86—Jan. 22.

Ford II, Henry, American motor manufacturer and philanthropist, *aged* 70—Sept. 29, 1987.

Fosse, Bob, American choreographer and film director, *aged* 60—Sept. 23, 1987.

Fraser, Bill, actor, *aged* 79—Sept. 5, 1987.

Fraser, Ian, M.C. Conservative M.P. for Plymouth Sutton 1959–66, *aged* 71—Nov. 8, 1987.

Fry, Maxwell, C.B.E., R.A., F.R.I.B.A., architect, *aged* 88—Sept. 3, 1987.

Fuchs, Klaus, German nuclear physicist and spy, *aged* 76—Jan. 28.

Gandar Dower, Eric, Conservative M.P. for Caithness and Sutherland 1945–50, *aged* 93—Oct. 1987.

Gibb, Bill, fashion designer, *aged* 44—Jan. 3.

Goossens, Leon, C.B.E., oboist, *aged* 90—Feb. 12.

Gorshkov, *Adm.* Sergei, commander-in-chief of the Soviet Navy 1956–85, *aged* 78—May 13.

Green, Roger Lancelyn, author, *aged* 68—Oct. 8, 1987.

Greene, Lorne, Canadian actor, *aged* 72—Sept. 11, 1987.

Greville, 4th Baron, *aged* 75—Dec. 9, 1987.

Haley, Sir William, K.C.M.G., director-general of the B.B.C. 1944–52, editor of *The Times* 1952–66, *aged* 86—Sept. 6, 1987.

Hamilton, Sir Dennis, D.S.O., T.D., editor-in-chief of Times Newspapers 1967–81, *aged* 69—April 7.

Hamilton, Hamish, publisher, *aged* 87—May 24.

Handl, Irene, actress, *aged* 85—Nov. 29, 1987.

Harty, Russell, broadcaster and writer, *aged* 53—June 8.

Hazan, *Hon.* Sir John, High Court judge since Jan. 1988, *aged* 61—Aug. 19.

Heath, Sir Barrie, D.F.C., industrialist, *aged* 71—Feb. 22.

Heinlein, Robert, American science fiction writer, *aged* 80—May 8.

Herman, Woody, band leader, *aged* 74—Oct. 28, 1987.

Hesketh, Roger, O.B.E., T.D., Conservative M.P. for Southport 1952–59, *aged* 85—Nov. 14, 1987.

Howard, *Lt. Cdr. Hon.* Greville, Conservative M.P. for St. Ives 1950–66, *aged* 78—Sept. 20, 1987.

Howard, Trevor, actor, *aged* 71—Jan. 7.

Hung, Pham, Chairman of Council of Ministers of Vietnam since 1987, *aged* 75—March 10.

Hunt of Fawley, Lord, C.B.E., D.M., *aged* 82—Dec. 28, 1987.

Hutchinson, Sir Joseph, C.M.G., F.R.S., plant geneticist, *aged* 85—Jan. 16.

Jacobson, Lord, M.C., journalist and editor, *aged* 79—Aug. 13.

John, Errol, Trinidadian actor and playwright, *aged* 64—July 10.

Jones, *Gen.* Sir Charles, G.C.B., C.B.E., M.C., *aged* 81—Jan. 4.

Kentner, Louis, C.B.E., pianist, *aged* 82—Sept. 22, 1987.

Kolmogorov, Andrei, Russian mathematician, *aged* 84—Oct. 20, 1987.

Kountché, *Gen.* Seyni, President of Niger since 1974, *aged* 56—Nov. 10, 1987.

Kyle, *Air Chief Marshal* Sir Wallace, G.C.B., K.C.V.O., C.B.E., D.S.O., D.F.C., Governor of Western Australia 1975–80, *aged* 78—Jan. 31.

L'Amour, Louis, American novelist, *aged* 80—June 10.

Lane, Dame Elizabeth, D.B.E., High Court judge 1965–79, *aged* 82—June.

Lane-Fox, Baroness, O.B.E., *aged* 69—April 17.

Laski, Marghanita, broadcaster and writer, *aged* 72—Feb. 6.

Laurent, Harry, V.C., *aged* 92—Dec. 9, 1987.

Levene, Harry, boxing promoter, *aged* 90—Jan. 28.

Levesque, Rene, Premier of Quebec 1976–85, *aged* 65—Nov. 1, 1987.

Lloyd, Sir Guy, Bt., D.S.O., Unionist M.P. for East Renfrewshire 1940–59, *aged* 97—Sept. 22, 1987.

Lockhart-Mummery, Sir Hugh, K.C.V.O., Serjeant-Surgeon to the Queen 1975–83, *aged* 70—June 24.

Loewe, Frederick, American composer of musicals, *aged* 86—Feb. 14.

Logan, Sir Douglas, Principal of the University of London 1948–75, *aged* 77—Oct. 19, 1987.

Luce, Clare Boothe, American writer and politician, *aged* 84—Oct. 9, 1987.

Luke, Sir Stephen, K.C.M.G., colonial administrator, *aged* 82—Feb. 27.

MacBride, Sean, Irish politician, human rights advocate and Nobel peace prize winner, *aged* 83—Jan. 15.

McMahon, *Rt. Hon.* Sir William, G.C.M.G., C.H., Prime Minister of Australia, 1971–72, *aged* 80—March 31.

McVittie, *Prof.* George, O.B.E., F.R.S.E., astronomer, *aged* 83—March 8.

Mancroft, 2nd Baron, K.B.E., T.D., *aged* 73—Sept. 14, 1987.

Marks, Kenneth, Labour M.P. for Manchester Gorton 1967–83, *aged* 67—Jan. 13.

Mason, *Vice-Adm.* Sir Frank, K.C.B., *aged* 88—Aug. 29.

Massigli, Rene, HON. G.C.V.O., HON. C.H., French Ambassador to Britain 1944–55, *aged* 99—Feb. 3.

Maudslay, *Maj.* Sir Rennie, G.C.V.O., K.C.B., M.B.E., Keeper of the Privy Purse and Treasurer to the Queen 1971–81, *aged* 72—June 8.

Medawar, Sir Peter, O.M., C.H., C.B.E., F.R.S., medical scientist and Nobel laureate, *aged* 72—Oct. 2, 1987.

Merchant, Vijay, Indian cricketer, *aged* 76—Oct. 27, 1987.

Miles, Sir Ashley, C.B.E., F.R.S., microbiologist, *aged* 83—Feb. 11.

Momigliano, *Prof.* Arnaldo, HON. K.B.E., F.B.A., Italian historian, *aged* 78—Sept. 1, 1987.

More, Sir Jasper, Conservative M.P. for Ludlow 1960–79, *aged* 80—Oct. 28, 1987.

Mulder, Dr. Connie, South African politician, *aged* 62—Jan. 12.

Napier of Magdala, 5th Baron, O.B.E., *aged* 83—Oct. 29, 1987.

Nicholls, Sir Douglas, K.C.V.O., O.B.E., Governor of South Australia 1976–77, *aged* 81—June 4.

O'Neill, *Hon.* Sir Con, G.C.M.G., diplomat, *aged* 75—Jan. 11.

Parker, John, C.B.E., Labour M.P. for Romford 1935–45 and for Dagenham 1945–83, *aged* 81—Nov. 24, 1987.

Patch, *Air Chief Marshal* Sir Hubert, K.C.B., C.B.E., *aged* 82—Nov. 18, 1987.

Paton, Alan, South African writer, *aged* 85—April 12.

Peart, Lord, P.C., Labour M.P. 1945–76, and Minister of Agriculture 1964–68 and 1974–76, *aged* 74—Aug. 26.

Philby, H.A.R. (Kim), British intelligence officer and Soviet spy, *aged* 76—May 11.

Pressburger, Emeric, Hungarian-born writer and film producer, *aged* 85—Jan. 5.

Rabi, Isidor, American physicist and Nobel laureate, *aged* 89—Jan. 11.

Ramsay, *Prof.* Arthur, M.B.E., F.R.S., biologist, *aged* 78—Jan. 5.

Ramsey of Canterbury, *Rt. Rev.* Lord, P.C., Archbishop of Canterbury 1961–74, *aged* 83—April 23.

Read, Al, radio comedian, *aged* 78—Sept. 1987.

Rhodes, Lord, K.G., P.C., D.F.C., industrialist, Labour M.P. for Ashton-under-Lyme 1945–64, *aged* 92—Sept. 11, 1987.

Rhys Williams, Sir Brandon, Bt., Conservative M.P. for Kensington South 1968–74 and Kensington since 1974, and M.E.P. for London South-East 1979–84, *aged* 60—May 18th.

Rose, Dr. Frank, C.B.E., F.R.S., chemist, *aged* 78—March 3.

Ross of Marnock, Lord, M.B.E., P.C., Labour M.P. for Kilmarnock 1946–79, and Secretary of State for Scotland 1964–70 and 1974–76, *aged* 77—June 10.

Ruska, *Prof* Ernst, German electrical engineer and Nobel physics prize winner, *aged* 81—May.

Russell, 4th Earl, *aged* 66—Dec. 16, 1987.

St. Germans, 9th Earl of, *aged* 74—March 11.

Sankara, *Capt.* Thomas, Head of State of Burkina since 1983, *aged* 37—Oct. 15, 1987.

Schwarz, Harvey, HON. C.B.E., American joint-originator of the Decca radio-navigation system, *aged* 82—April 23.

Scott, *Rt. Rev.* Moses, C.B.E., Archbishop of West Africa 1969–81, *aged* 76—May 9.

Silkin of Dulwich, Lord, P.C., Q.C., Labour M.P. 1964–83, and Attorney General 1974–79, *aged* 70—Aug. 17.

Skelhorn, Sir Norman, K.B.E., Q.C., Director of Public Prosecutions 1964–77, *aged* 78—May 28.

Soames, Lord, P.C., G.C.M.G., G.C.V.O., C.H., C.B.E., politician, diplomat, Governor of Southern Rhodesia 1979–80, *aged* 66—Sept. 16, 1987.

Solomon, C.B.E., pianist, *aged* 85—Feb. 2.

Stamp, 3rd Baron, bacteriologist, *aged* 80—Nov. 16, 1987.

Steptoe, Patrick, C.B.E., F.R.S., obstetrician and gynaecologist, *aged* 74—March 21.

Stevens, Dr. Siaka, HON. G.C.M.G., President of Sierra Leone 1971–85, *aged* 82—May 29.

Stevenson, *Rt. Hon* Sir Melford, High Court judge 1957–79, *aged* 85—Dec. 26, 1987.

Stonehouse, John, Labour M.P. for Wednesbury (later, Walsall North) 1957–76, Postmaster General 1968–69, *aged* 62—April 14.

Studholme, Sir Henry, Bt., C.V.O., Conservative M.P. for Tavistock 1942–66, *aged* 88—Oct. 9, 1987.

Taylor, Lord, M.D., psychiatrist, sociologist and politician, *aged* 77—Feb. 1.

Temple of Stowe, 7th Earl, *aged* 77—Aug. 28.

Templeman, Dr. Geoffrey, C.B.E., founding Vice-Chancellor of the University of Kent, *aged* 74—Feb. 22.

Thrower, Percy, M.B.E., gardener and broadcaster, *aged* 75—March 18.

Tomás, *Rear-Adm.* Americo, President of Portugal 1958–74, *aged* 92—Sept. 18, 1987.

Trevelyan, Julian, R.A., painter and etcher, *aged* 78—July 12.

Unstead, R. J., author and children's historian, *aged* 72—May 5.

Walton, Sir Raymond, High Court judge 1973–88, *aged* 72—Jan. 29.

Ward of Whitley, 1st Viscount, Conservative M.P. for Worcester 1945–60, and Secretary of State for Air 1957–60, *aged* 80—June 15.

Wavell, Countess (Eugenie), C.I., *aged* 100—Oct. 11, 1987.

West, *Air Cdre.* Ferdinand (Freddie), V.C., C.B.E., M.C., *aged* 92—July 7.

Wheatley, Lord, P.C., Lord Justice-Clerk 1972–85, *aged* 80—July 28.

Willey, *Rt. Hon.* Frederick, Labour M.P. for Sunderland 1945–50 and Sunderland North 1950–83, and Government Minister 1964–67, *aged* 77—Dec. 13, 1987.

Williams, Emlyn, actor and dramatist, *aged* 81—Sept. 25, 1987.

Williams, Kenneth, actor and comedian, *aged* 62—April 15.

Williams, *Prof.* Raymond, critic and novelist, *aged* 66—Jan. 26.

Windeyer, *Rt. Hon.* Sir. Victor, K.B.E., C.B., D.S.O., E.D., Australian soldier and High Court judge, *aged* 87—Nov. 1987.

Winner, Dame Albertine, D.B.E., physician and health service administrator, *aged* 81—May 13.

Winterton, *Maj. Gen.* Sir John, K.C.B., K.C.M.G., C.B.E., *aged* 89—Dec. 14, 1987.

Wolverton, 6th Baron, C.B.E., social scientist, *aged* 75—July 4.

Woodhouse, Barbara, animal trainer and television personality, *aged* 78—July 9.

Wootton of Abinger, Baroness, C.H., *aged* 91—July 11.

Wright, Basil, documentary film maker, *aged* 80—Oct. 14, 1987.

Young, *Most Rev.* Guildford, K.B.E., R.C. Archbishop of Hobart since 1955, *aged* 71—March 15.

Yourcenar, Marguerite, French author, *aged* 84—Dec. 19, 1987.

Ypres, 3rd Earl of, *aged* 66—March 4.

Zia ul-Haq, *Gen.* Muhammad, President of Pakistan since 1978, *aged* 64—Aug. 17.

CENTENARIES

One Hundred Years Ago (1889).—A selection follows of "Remarkable Occurrences" (as "Events of the Year" was then called) as printed in the 1890 and 1891 editions of *Whitaker's Almanack* covering the year 1889.

During this year more Whitechapel murders took place and, amid continuing home rule agitation, the Parnell Commission completed its investigation into the *Times'* allegations of Parnell's connivance at the Phoenix Park murders of 1882.

January

11. The German mission station at Dar-es-Salam attacked, and all the freed slaves and servants of the mission captured.

13. The German mission station at Tugu attacked and destroyed by Arabs.

21. Arrest of Mr. Sheehy, M.P., at Glasgow, on a warrant issued in Ireland.

25. Mr. O'Brien, M.P., in his absence, sentenced at Carrick-on-Suir to four months' imprisonment.

— Father McCarthy, parish priest of Kilmeen, sentenced to four months' imprisonment for inciting to boycotting.

30. The Crown Prince of Austria-Hungary found dead in his bed from suicide.

February

2. Mr. Cox, M.P., and Mr. Tulley sentenced to four months' imprisonment under the Crimes Act.

3. Arrest of Father M'Fadden at Gweedore, when the mob attacked the police with sticks and beat District-Inspector Martin to death.

5. Funeral of the Crown Prince Rudolph of Austria.

— Mr. Parnell's Scottish action against the *Times* dismissed, Lord Kinnear deciding that the Scotch Court had no jurisdiction.

8. Mr. Kilbride, M.P., sentenced to three months' imprisonment for conspiracy.

12. Proceedings opened against the Bishop of Lincoln in the Archbishop's Court for unlawful practices in the celebration of Divine Service.

— A new constitution for Japan proclaimed by the Mikado at Tokio, two Chambers being established on the German model.

18. A proposal in the Dominion Parliament, praying that Canada might be empowered to communicate directly with foreign States, defeated by 94 to 66.

— Resolutions passed by the South Wales Liberal Federation at Swansea and advocating the disestablishment of the Church and the application of the tithes to educational purposes.

19. Mr. O'Brien, M.P., sentenced to six months' imprisonment.

25. The marriage of the Emperor of China celebrated with great festivities at Pekin.

— Richard Pigott, a witness before the Parnell Special Commission, having failed to appear, a warrant was issued for his arrest.

March

1. Richard Pigott, on being arrested at Madrid, shot himself throught the head with a revolver.

— Dr. Tanner, M.P., arrested on a warrant when leaving the House of Commons.

6. King Milan of Servia announced his abdication in favour of his son, a boy of 13.

13. The British ironclad *Sultan*, after running on some rocks near Malta, sank while being towed off.

16. The Donegal Grand Jury awarded to the widow of Inspector Martin, who was murdered at Gweedore, the sum of £4,000, to be levied on the county.

— Violent hurricane at Samoa; three German vessels and three United States ships blown on shore, while the British warship *Calliope* put out to sea and escaped.

26. Prince Frederick of Hohenzollern, nephew of King Charles, officially proclaimed as heir to the throne of Roumania.

30. Funeral of Mr. John Bright at the Friends' Meeting-house, Rochdale.

— Rev. J. M'Fadden and 19 other persons committed for trial for the murder of Inspector Martin at Gweedore.

April

2. A communication received by the Dutch Chambers as to the King's inability to exercise the powers of Government. He, however, afterwards recovered.

8. The Court-martial on the officers of the ironclad *Sultan* reprimanded the captain for running his ship too close on a rocky shore.

12. Sir Charles Russell concluded a lengthy address before the Parnell Special Commission.

13. Mr. Justice Stephen with Baron Huddleston decided that women are not eligible for election to County Councils.

15. Patrick Molloy convicted of perjury before the Special Commission, and sentenced to six months' imprisonment.

16. Two Judges of the Queen's Bench Division decided that the practice of dishorning cattle is illegal.

24. M. Boulanger, with Count Dillon, M. Naquet, and others, arrived in London from Brussels.

30. Mr. Parnell called as a witness before the Special Commission.

May

3. Mr. Conybeare, M.P., sentenced to three months' imprisonment for inciting to disobedience to the law.

6. The Paris Exhibition formally opened by President Carnot.

7. The Inman steamer *City of Paris* arrived from New York after a passage of 5 days, 23 hours, 7 minutes, the shortest on record.

— The Town Council of Edinburgh confirmed a resolution, by 23 votes to 15, to confer the freedom of the city on Mr. Parnell.

11. The Archbishop of Canterbury decided in the case of the Bishop of Lincoln that he had jurisdiction to hear it.

— The Royal Stakes of £10,000 won at Kempton Park by the Duke of Portland's Ayrshire.

16. The Court of Appeal decided that women are not competent to be elected County Councillors.

18. The Queen laid the memorial-stone of new school buildings at Eton College.

21. Princess Henry of Battenberg delivered of a son at Windsor Castle.

— Meeting of peers and members of Parliament in favour of the abolition of the Irish Vice-royalty and the substitution of a Secretary of State.

31. Fearful floods in Pennysylvania: Johnstown, and other towns in the Conemaugh Valley, being swept away, and about 10,000 persons perished by water and fire.

June

5. The Derby Stakes at Epsom won by the Duke of Portland's Donovan.

11. Marriage of the Duke of Portland and Miss Dallas-Yorke at St. Peter's, Eaton Square.

12. Sad disaster to an excursion train conveying a party of children from Armagh to Warren Point; about 70 killed and many injured.

13. Thirteen men sentenced at Youghal to various periods of imprisonment for ploughing up growing crops on the Ponsonby estate.

16. Marriage of the Grand Duke Paul of Russia and the Princess Alexandra of Greece.

18. Captain Grimston, chief constable of Leicestershire, committed suicide by shooting himself through the head.

21. A verdict of culpable negligence returned by the Coroner's jury against six officials concerned in the catastrophe at Armagh.

— Letine, an acrobat, fatally stabbed at the door of the Canterbury Hall, Westminster Road.

July

1. The Shah of Persia arrived at Gravesend in the Royal yacht, where he was met by the Prince of Wales, and afterwards proceeded up the Thames to Westminster.

2. Colonel Wodehouse attacked and defeated the Dervish force at Arguin, killing and wounding 500 and taking 500 prisoners.

— The young King Alexander of Servia anointed at Zitcha.

12. The Shah of Persia visited the chief manufacturing establishments in Sheffield.

17. The dead body of another woman found in Whitechapel, she having been murdered by a wound in the stomach.

19. Verdict for the defendant returned in an action by Mr. O'Brien, M.P., against the Marquis of Salisbury for slander.

20. Mr. Parnell received the freedom of the city of Edinburgh.

27. Marriage of the Princess Louise of Wales and the Duke of Fife at Buckingham Palace.

29. The Shah of Persia left England for Paris.

— Dr. Tanner, M.P., convicted of spitting on a county inspector, sentenced to one month's imprisonment with hard labour.

August

1. The German Emperor arrived in the Downs, and next day visited the Queen at Osborne.

4. The Dervish force near Toski completely routed after seven hours' fighting by troops under the command of General Grenfell.

5. Great naval review at Spithead by the German Emperor and the Prince of Wales.

7. At Liverpool Mrs. Maybrick was found guilty of poisoning her husband. Sentenced to be hanged, but sentence afterwards commuted to imprisonment.

12. The High Court in Paris condemned General Boulanger and MM. Dillon and Rochefort in their absence to perpetual imprisonment in a fortified place.

26. After a prize fight held this day, one of the combatants died next morning.

30. Mr. Swaine, an English barrister, killed by falling from a mountain near Letterfrack, Connemara.

31. A letter-carrier charged at Bow Street with stealing 85 postal notes, and forging names to obtain payment.

September

2. A violent storm raged over Essex and West Kent, doing considerable damage and setting fire to several buildings.

6. Terrible explosion at a cartridge factory at Antwerp; 125 persons believed to have perished, and 200 suffered injuries.

11. The St. Leger won by the Duke of Portland's Donovan.

16. After a month's resistance the dock labourers' strike in London terminated with an agreement, to take effect from November 4th, to a rise of wages from 5d. to 6d. per hour.

17. The Rev. Father O'Dwyer sentenced to five months' imprisonment for intimidation and conspiracy.

— The mutilated trunk of another woman found in Pinchin Street, Whitechapel.

21. Mr. W. Redmond, M.P., sentenced to three months' imprisonment for conspiracy.

25. Annual conference of the Scottish Home Rule Association held at Dundee.

27. Escape of a lion from Wombwell's menagerie at Birmingham, and subsequent capture in a sewer.

October

4. Disasterous collision near Longsight station, three persons killed on the spot.

5. The Earl of Zetland formally sworn in as Lord-Lieutenant of Ireland.

7. Destructive storm throughout England; Holyhead breakwater damaged.

— Serious earthquake in Cornwall.

12. The tomb of Ralph Waldo Emerson, at Concord, violated by robbers.

24. A man having fired a revolver at the manager of a bank at Didsbury made off with £80 in notes, and subsequently shot himself.

27. Funeral of the King of Portugal at Lisbon.

29. General holiday in Russia to commemorate the Emperor's escape from accident last year.

30. Fifteen persons convicted for participation in the murder of Inspector Martin at Gweedore.

31. Mr. Davitt brought to a close a long speech before the Parnell Special Commission.

November

1. During a furious gale at Glasgow the wall of a carpet factory fell, crushing to death nearly 30 of the operatives.

5. Intelligence transmitted from Zanzibar of the massacre by natives of Dr. Peters and all the members of his party.

6. The Forth Bridge virtually completed, the last bolt having been driven.

— Paris Exhibition closed.

9. Death of a cotton-spinner at Todmorden, who is reported to have left a fortune of between three and four millions.

11. A lady in Leeds cut her throat, then bound up the wound, and afterwards went three miles and drowned herself.

— Jackson defeated Smith in a great glove fight at the Pelican Club in Soho.

12. A poacher when striking a keeper with the butt-end of his gun received its contents and died on the spot.

15. Queen Amelia, wife of the King of Portugal, gave birth to a son.

— Revolution in Brazil; Emperor deposed and Republic declared.

19. Attempted murder of His Honour Judge Bristow at Nottingham by a German dentist named Arnemann.

22. The Parnell Commission having sat for 129 days, the inquiry concluded with a speech by Sir Henry James lasting 11¼ days. About 493 witnesses were examined and 98,177 questions answered.

December

3. An elephant at Barnum's show attacked his keeper and trod him to death.

4. Mr. Stanley and Emin Pasha arrived at Bagamoyo from Central Africa.

10. An unfounded cry of "Fire" at a theatre in Johnstown, Pennsylvania, caused the death of 12 persons and severe injuries to 75 others.

11. Jefferson Davis's funeral at New Orleans attended by a vast concourse of people.

17. Mr. Parnell received by a large crowd at Nottingham.

18. Attempted revolution broke out in Rio de Janeiro.

20. Prince Albert Victor received with great demonstrations of loyalty at Rangoon.

28. Carlos proclaimed King of Portugal.

30. Ten thousand miners in North Wales resumed work, the masters having conceded an advance of 10 per cent. in wages.

THE CENTENARIES OF 1989

1889
Deaths

March 27	John Bright, statesman and orator.
Sept. 23	Wilkie Collins, novelist.
Oct. 11	James Joule, physicist.
Dec. 12	Robert Browning, poet.

Births

Feb. 22	Olave, Lady Baden-Powell.
April 2	Sir Neville Cardus, music critic and cricket writer.
April 8	Sir Adrian Boult, conductor.
April 14	Arnold Toynbee, writer and historian.
April 16	Sir Charles Chaplin, actor.
April 20	Adolf Hitler.
April 24	Sir Stafford Cripps, Labour statesman.
May 11	Paul Nash, artist.
July 5	Jean Cocteau, French writer.
Nov. 14	Jawaharlal Nehru.

Events

March 31	Eiffel Tower completed.
Nov. 15	Brazil declared a Republic.

1789
Births

Sept. 15	James Fenimore Cooper, American novelist.
Nov. 18	Louis Daguerre, French painter and pioneering photographer.

Events

April 28	Mutiny on the *Bounty*.
July 14	Storming of the Bastille.

1689
Deaths
April 18   Judge George Jeffreys.

Events
Feb. 13   Accession of William III and Mary II.
Dec.*   Bill of Rights.

1589
Deaths
Jan. 5   Catherine de Medici, Queen of France
           1547–1559.

1489
Births
July 2   Archbishop Thomas Cranmer.

1189
Deaths
July 6   Henry II.

*Exact date unknown.

THE CENTENARIES OF 1990

1890
Deaths
July 29   Vincent van Gogh, Dutch artist.
Oct. 20   Sir Richard Burton, explorer.
Nov. 8   César Franck, French composer.

Births
Feb. 10   Boris Pasternak, Russian writer.
March 12   Vaslav Nijinski, Russian dancer.
Sept. 15   Dame Agatha Christie, writer.
Oct. 1   Stanley Holloway, entertainer.
Oct. 14   Dwight D. Eisenhower, American general and President.
Nov. 22   Charles de Gaulle, French general and President.

Events
March 4   Opening of Forth Railway Bridge.

1790
Deaths
March 5   Flora Macdonald.
April 17   Benjamin Franklin, American statesman and scientist.
July 17   Adam Smith, Scottish economist.

1690
July 1   Battle of the Boyne.

WEDDING ANNIVERSARIES

First	Cotton	Twentieth	China
Second	Paper	Twenty-fifth	Silver
Third	Leather	Thirtieth	Pearl
Fourth	Fruit and Flower	Thirty-fifth	Coral
Fifth	Wood	Fortieth	Ruby
Sixth	Sugar	Forty-fifth	Sapphire
Seventh	Wool	Fiftieth	Gold
Tenth	Tin	Sixtieth	Diamond
Twelfth	Silk and Fine Linen	Seventieth	Platinum
Fifteenth	Crystal		

GROSS NATIONAL PRODUCT

By category of expenditure

£ million

	1981	1982	1983	1984	1985	1986
Expenditure at market prices						
Consumers' expenditure	153,027	167,599	183,068	195,912	213,720	234,167
General government final consumption	55,449	60,525	65,979	69,887	74,041	79,423
of which: central government	33,868	37,112	40,704	43,220	45,983	48,724
local authorities	21,581	23,413	25,275	26,667	28,058	30,699
Gross domestic fixed capital formation	41,309	44,763	48,594	55,108	60,477	64,227
Value of physical increase in stocks and work in progress	−2,735	−1,244	730	116	428	551
Total domestic expenditure	247,050	271,643	298,371	321,023	348,666	378,368
Exports of goods and services	67,819	73,003	80,322	91,967	102,110	97,835
Total final expenditure	314,869	344,646	378,693	412,990	450,776	476,203
less imports of goods and services[1]	−60,766	−68,237	−77,720	−92,870	−98,907	−101,308
Gross domestic product at market prices[2]	254,103	276,409	300,973	320,120	351,869	374,895
less taxes on expenditure	−42,672	−46,632	−49,389	−52,538	−56,735	−62,273
plus subsidies	6,296	5,801	6,275	7,555	7,300	6,467
Gross domestic product at factor cost[2]	217,727	235,578	257,859	275,137	302,434	319,089
Factor incomes						
Income from employment	149,525	158,568	169,558	180,053	194,434	209,445
Income from self-employment[3]	19,271	21,544	24,180	27,716	30,481	34,340
Gross trading profits of companies[3,4]	29,381	33,301	40,551	46,775	53,432	50,785
Gross trading surplus of public corporations[3]	7,821	9,389	9,949	8,231	7,077	8,126
Gross trading surplus of general government enterprises[3]	236	216	58	−71	260	161
Rent[5]	16,288	17,661	18,617	19,638	21,198	22,497
Imputed charge for consumption of non-trading capital	2,347	2,382	2,487	2,604	2,811	3,026
Total domestic income[3]	224,869	243,061	265,400	284,946	309,693	328,380
less stock appreciation	−5,915	−4,225	−4,998	−5,260	−3,332	−2,331
Gross domestic product (income-based)	218,954	238,836	260,402	279,686	306,361	326,049
Residual error	−1,227	−3,258	−2,543	−4,549	−3,927	−6,960
Net property income from abroad	945	1,078	2,479	4,216	2,992	4,686
Gross national product at factor cost	218,672	236,656	260,338	279,353	305,426	323,775
less capital consumption	−31,647	−33,676	−36,168	−38,892	−42,315	−46,004
National income (i.e. net national product)	187,025	202,980	224,170	240,461	263,111	277,771

[1] Excluding taxes on expenditure levied on imports.
[2] Including taxes on expenditure levied on imports.
[3] Before providing for depreciation and stock appreciation.
[4] Including financial institutions.
[5] Before providing for depreciation.

GROSS DOMESTIC PRODUCT BY INDUSTRY

(Before depreciation but after stock appreciation) £ million

	1980	1981	1982	1983	1984	1985	1986
Agriculture, forestry and fishing	4,303	4,837	5,530	5,365	6,222	5,627	5,902
Energy and water supply	20,200	24,201	26,914	30,697	30,605	33,131	24,445
Manufacturing (revised definition)	53,148	54,197	58,581	61,467	66,044	72,921	79,111
Construction	12,022	12,775	13,874	15,518	17,064	18,536	20,061
Distribution; hotels and catering; repairs	24,924	27,112	29,083	31,993	35,846	40,521	45,770
Transport	9,577	10,187	10,644	11,649	12,457	13,349	14,813
Communication	4,758	5,643	6,475	6,579	7,300	8,077	8,914
Banking, finance, insurance, business services and leasing	24,705	27,866	32,452	35,655	39,748	45,300	51,513
Ownership of dwellings	12,146	13,895	15,043	15,780	16,564	17,884	18,873
Public administration, national defence and compulsory social security	14,560	16,279	17,553	19,065	20,457	21,996	23,578
Education and health services	18,042	20,567	21,262	23,343	24,676	26,403	29,510
Other services	10,683	12,004	13,153	14,927	16,496	18,350	20,963
Total	209,068	229,563	250,564	272,038	293,479	322,095	343,453
Adjustment for financial services	−9,353	−10,609	−11,728	−11,636	−13,793	−15,734	−17,404
Gross domestic product at factor cost (income based)	199,715	218,954	238,836	260,402	279,686	306,361	326,049
Residual error	−57	−1,227	−3,258	−2,543	−4,549	−3,927	−6,960
Gross domestic product at factor cost (income-based)	199,658	217,727	235,578	257,859	275,137	302,434	319,089

GENERAL GOVERNMENT CURRENT ACCOUNT

£ million

	1980	1981	1982	1983	1984	1985	1986
Receipts							
Taxes on income	30,862	36,250	40,391	43,485	46,795	51,603	52,430
Taxes on expenditure	36,352	42,672	46,632	49,389	52,538	56,735	62,273
Social security contributions	13,939	15,916	18,095	20,787	22,301	24,200	26,067
Gross trading surplus*	180	236	216	58	−71	260	161
Rent, dividends and interest, etc.	8,074	9,087	10,101	9,917	10,482	11,629	9,878
Miscellaneous current transfers	164	164	184	214	226	209	241
Imputed charge for consumption of non-trading capital	1,746	1,944	1,973	2,070	2,172	2,353	2,541
Total	91,497	106,269	117,592	125,920	134,443	146,989	153,591
Expenditure							
Final consumption	49,027	55,449	60,525	65,979	69,887	74,041	79,423
Subsidies	5,588	6,296	5,801	6,275	7,555	7,300	6,467
National insurance benefits	21,394	26,564	31,063	32,123	34,515	37,587	40,616
Other current grants to personal sector	4,129	4,678	5,521	7,631	8,466	9,065	9,927
Current grants paid abroad (net)	1,779	1,606	1,789	1,929	2,100	3,336	2,235
Debt interest	10,873	12,701	13,972	14,187	15,758	17,473	17,022
Total current expenditure	92,791	107,295	118,672	128,123	138,281	148,801	155,690
Balance: current surplus*	−1,294	−1,026	−1,080	−2,203	−3,838	−1,812	−2,099
Total	91,497	106,269	117,592	125,920	134,443	146,989	153,591

* Before depreciation.

HOME FINANCE

Central government funds and accounts transactions £ million

	Consolidated Fund			National Loans Fund				Central government borrowing requirement
			Consolidated fund surplus/ deficit	Other transactions		Borrowing required	Other funds and accounts	
	Revenue	Expenditure		Receipts	Payments			
1984	95,194	103,385	−8,191	12,799	14,844	10,236	76	10,160
1985	104,193	110,497	−6,304	13,899	19,226	11,631	−173	11,804
1986	110,867	113,305	−2,438	14,984	20,397	7,851	−610	8,461
1987	119,517	120,712	−1,195	16,345	21,345	6,195	2,184	4,010
Financial years								
1984–85	98,247	105,608	−7,361	12,916	15,418	9,863	−301	10,164
1985–86	106,132	110,127	−3,995	14,213	20,592	10,374	−588	10,962
1986–87	111,211	116,451	−5,240	15,614	21,251	10,877	381	10,496
1988 1st quarter . .	36,329	31,874	4,455	4,732	6,054	−3,133	−1,066	−2,067
2nd quarter .	28,872	28,722	150	3,620	5,166	1,396		132
1987 June	9,231	8,750	481	674	1,091	−64	−26	−38
July	10,162	9,857	305	1,991	2,077	−219	80	−299
August	8,040	10,449	−2,409	1,144	1,004	2,269	1,424	845
September . .	10,353	9,679	674	1,497	1,493	−678	−489	−190
October	11,479	11,817	−338	1,220	1,285	403	1,063	−660
November . .	9,691	8,320	1,371	1,756	2,104	−1,023	−546	−477
December . .	10,423	9,498	925	689	774	−840	−378	−462
1988 January . .	16,873	9,123	7,750	388	2,005	−6,133	−263	−5,869
February . . .	9,795	8,356	1,439	412	1,617	−234	−388	155
March	9,661	14,395	−4,734	3,932	2,432	3,234	−415	3,647
April	9,633	10,455	−822	1,325	2,356	1,853	2,531	−675
May	10,340	9,927	413	1,607	1,785	−235		−216
June	8,899	8,340	559	688	1,025	−222		1,023

Public sector borrowing requirement £ million

	Total		Contributions by			Financed by				
						Non-bank private sector		Monetary sector	Overseas sector	
									External finance	
	Unadjusted	Seasonally adjusted†	Central government*	Local authorities	Public corporations	Notes and coin	Other	Borrowing in sterling from banks	Foreign currency borrowing from banks	Direct external finance
1984	−10,284		−10,160	470	−594	326	8,086	892	293	1,383
1985	−7,468		−11,804	957	957	523	7,643	−2,092	403	1,467
1986	−2,421		−8,461	5,192	848	738	4,430	−929	44	572
1987	1,410		−4,010	4,540	880	849	7,059	−200	−505	−6,386
Financial years										
1984–85	−10,100		−10,164	943	−879	522	15,051	−4,379	417	−710
1985–86	−5,654		−10,962	4,072	1,236	354	3,213	1,841	316	788
1986–87	−3,436		−10,496	5,645	1,415	−197	5,025	716	49	834
1987 1st quarter	867	401	−1,209	1,414	662	−662	2,943	−519	6	−1,886
2nd quarter	−1,451	442	−4,044	2,816	−223	356	4,535	−521	10	−1,346
3rd quarter	−473	8	−356	−408	291	111	−1,531	−472	−63	1,980
4th quarter	2,467	−2,334	1,599	718	150	1,004	1,112	1,312	−458	−5,134
1987 1st quarter	2,943	−1,602	2,067	−494	1,370	345	−1,666	−589	−636	−660
2nd quarter	1,640	−2,318	−132	1,379	393					

†Financial year constrained.   *An increase in debt is shown positive.

PERSONAL INCOME AND EXPENDITURE (£ million)

	1981	1982	1983	1984	1985	1986
Income before tax						
Income from employment:						
Wages and salaries	125,116	133,283	142,312	151,764	164,758	178,746
Pay in cash and kind of HM Forces	2,689	2,905	3,121	3,288	3,590	3,833
Total.........................	127,805	136,188	145,433	155,052	168,348	182,579
Employers' contributions:						
National insurance, etc.	8,814	9,344	10,540	11,263	12,208	13,257
Other......................	12,906	13,036	13,585	13,738	13,878	13,609
Total income from employment ...	149,525	158,568	169,558	180,053	194,434	209,445
Income from self-employment:						
After deducting stock						
appreciation	18,645	21,182	23,614	27,425	29,996	34,000
Stock appreciation	626	362	566	291	485	340
Total.........................	19,271	21,544	24,180	27,716	30,481	34,340
Rent, dividends and net interest:						
Receipts by life assurance and						
pension schemes	8,762	10,501	11,771	14,000	15,939	17,361
Imputed rent of owner-occupied						
dwellings.....................	9,114	10,160	11,013	11,759	12,838	13,610
Other receipts, net	2,881	2,797	2,365	615	−628	−913
Total.........................	20,757	23,458	25,149	26,374	28,149	30,058
Social security benefits and other current grants from general						
government	31,243	36,585	39,753	42,981	46,651	50,543
Current transfers from overseas	1,095	1,271	1,436	1,618	1,560	1,705
Current transfers to charities from companies....................	62	69	86	102	114	134
Imputed charge for capital consumption of private non-profit making bodies.........................	403	409	417	432	458	485
Total personal income	222,356	241,904	260,579	279,276	301,847	326,710
Deductions from income						
U.K. taxes on income	28,969	31,396	33,232	34,681	37,520	41,227
Social security contributions	15,916	18,095	20,787	22,301	24,200	26,067
Current transfers abroad	1,175	1,291	1,250	1,357	1,500	1,663
Miscellaneous current transfers	164	184	214	226	209	241
Personal disposable income	176,132	190,938	205,096	220,711	238,418	257,512
Expenditure						
Consumers' expenditure	153,027	167,599	183,068	195,912	213,720	234,167
Balance saving....................	23,105	23,339	22,028	24,799	24,698	23,345
Total.............................	176,132	190,938	205,096	220,711	238,418	257,512
Memorandum items						
Saving ratio (per cent)	*13.1*	*12.2*	*10.7*	*11.2*	*10.4*	*9.1*
Real personal disposable income:						
At 1980 prices	158,110	157,726	161,301	165,671	170,124	177,355
1980 = 100......................	98.6	98.4	100.6	103.4	106.1	110.6

CONSUMERS' EXPENDITURE

£ million

	Total consumers' expenditure	Durable goods				Other goods								Services	
		Total	Cars, motor cycles and other vehicles	Furniture and floor coverings	Other durable goods	Food (household expenditure)	Beer	Other alcoholic drink	Tobacco	Clothing other than footwear	Footwear	Energy products	Other goods	Rent, rates and water charges	Other services
At current prices															
1982	168,164	15,382	7,265	3,700	4,417	25,649	6,450	5,553	5,881	8,857	2,068	15,027	16,918	22,423	43,956
1983	183,864	17,987	8,767	3,985	5,235	27,385	7,138	6,232	6,209	9,876	2,315	16,312	18,458	23,541	48,411
1984	196,981	18,722	8,862	4,140	5,720	28,642	7,734	6,696	6,622	10,778	2,548	17,025	20,349	24,850	53,015
1985	215,052	20,733	10,006	4,312	6,415	30,064	8,416	7,367	7,006	12,080	2,799	18,629	22,656	26,993	58,309
1986	236,472	23,578	11,668	4,547	7,363	32,339	8,849	7,625	7,471	13,379	3,009	18,475	25,057	29,134	67,556
1987	257,498	26,443	13,621	4,883	7,939	33,643	9,206	8,216	7,653	14,580	3,226	18,724	27,788	31,149	76,870
Unadjusted															
1987 1st quarter	59,710	6,422	3,520	1,152	1,750	7,772	1,978	1,503	1,876	2,895	619	5,702	5,946	7,559	17,438
2nd quarter	61,951	6,035	3,274	1,127	1,634	8,328	2,355	1,758	1,900	3,301	802	4,108	6,471	7,753	19,140
3rd quarter	66,184	7,527	4,439	1,216	1,872	8,623	2,442	1,879	1,916	3,466	826	3,850	6,786	7,867	21,002
4th quarter	69,653	6,459	2,388	1,388	2,683	8,920	2,431	3,076	1,961	4,918	979	5,064	8,585	7,970	19,290
1988 1st quarter	65,834	7,521	4,278	1,302	1,941	8,459	2,220	1,579	1,948	3,172	677	5,574	6,755	8,062	19,867
Revalued at 1980 prices															
1982	138,812	14,401	6,712	3,426	4,263	22,642	4,825	4,545	4,128	8,333	1,813	11,007	14,713	16,402	35,823
1983	144,479	16,561	7,970	3,577	5,014	23,109	4,913	4,817	4,082	8,959	1,954	11,203	15,079	16,704	37,098
1984	147,687	16,698	7,633	3,534	5,531	22,801	4,943	5,040	3,943	9,497	2,065	11,329	15,851	16,953	38,477
1985	153,287	17,758	7,990	3,561	6,207	23,275	4,934	5,290	3,837	10,212	2,153	11,840	16,542	17,118	40,328
1986	162,450	19,606	8,595	3,620	7,391	24,162	4,935	5,362	3,731	11,046	2,233	12,317	17,571	17,290	44,197
1987	170,919	20,947	9,102	3,809	8,036	24,278	4,987	5,587	3,704	11,857	2,334	12,454	18,994	17,514	48,263
Unadjusted															
1987 1st quarter	39,818	5,116	2,433	913	1,770	5,651	1,083	1,028	909	2,375	452	3,634	4,116	4,358	11,096
2nd quarter	41,154	4,739	2,211	880	1,648	6,030	1,287	1,202	922	2,697	580	2,772	4,446	4,372	12,107
3rd quarter	43,715	5,768	2,910	952	1,906	6,257	1,328	1,270	930	2,853	600	2,658	4,631	4,386	13,034
4th quarter	46,232	5,324	1,548	1,064	2,712	6,340	1,289	2,087	943	3,932	702	3,390	5,801	4,398	12,026
1988 1st quarter	42,510	5,688	2,705	1,000	1,983	5,915	1,162	1,057	929	2,569	484	3,686	4,501	4,410	12,109
Seasonally adjusted															
1987 1st quarter	41,495	4,964	2,159	926	1,879	5,924	1,206	1,382	918	2,824	559	3,118	4,591	4,358	11,651
2nd quarter	42,275	5,092	2,172	947	1,973	5,992	1,255	1,379	935	2,923	579	3,020	4,691	4,372	12,037
3rd quarter	43,288	5,501	2,409	991	2,101	6,204	1,256	1,401	928	3,023	597	3,116	4,823	4,386	12,053
4th quarter	43,861	5,390	2,362	945	2,083	6,158	1,270	1,425	923	3,087	599	3,200	4,889	4,398	12,522
1988 1st quarter	44,444	5,525	2,409	1,014	2,102	6,199	1,294	1,418	937	3,039	597	3,193	5,025	4,410	12,807

EMPLOYMENT

Distribution of total working population

Thousands

At mid-June	1980	1981	1982	1983	1984	1985	1986
United Kingdom							
Total working population	26,839	26,740	26,677	26,594	27,090	27,624	27,772
Unemployed	1,513	2,395	2,770	2,984†	3,030	3,179	3,229
Employed labour force	25,327	24,344	23,908	23,610	24,060	24,445	24,542
HM Forces	323	334	324	322	326	326	322
Self-employed persons (with or without employees)...............................	2,013	2,119	2,170	2,221	2,496	2,610	2,627
Total employees in employment..............	22,991	21,891	21,414	21,067	21,238	21,509	21,594
of whom :							
Total, index of production and construction industries	8,906	8,061	7,610	7,217	7,062	6,976	6,770
Total, all manufacturing industries	6,937	6,222	5,863	5,525	5,409	5,365	5,239
Great Britain							
Total working population	26,176	26,076	26,012	25,924	26,413	26,944	27,096
Unemployed	1,444	2,299	2,664	2,871†	2,911	3,057	3,103
Employed labour force	24,731	23,777	23,348	23,054	23,502	23,887	23,993
HM Forces	323	334	324	322	326	326	322
Self-employed persons (with or without employees)...............................	1,950	2,058	2,109	2,160	2,435	2,550	2,567
Total employees in employment..............	22,458	21,386	20,916	20,572	20,741	21,011	21,105
of whom							
Total, index of production and construction industries	8,723	7,900	7,460	7,072	6,919	6,834	6,635
Total, all manufacturing industries	6,801	6,099	5,751	5,418	5,302	5,258	5,137

†From April 1983, the figures of unemployment reflect the effects of the provisions in the Budget for some men aged 60 and over who no longer have to sign on at an unemployment office.

Employees in employment: all industries

At June   Industries analysed according to the Standard Industrial Classification 1980   Thousands

	1979	1980	1981	1982	1983	1984	1985	1986	1987
Total employees in employment	23,173	22,991	21,891	21,414	21,067	21,238	21,506	21,581	21,810
Males........................	13,487	13,319	12,562	12,205	11,940	11,888	11,966	11,891	11,881
Females......................	9,686	9,672	9,330	9,209	9,127	9,350	9,540	9,691	9,930
of which: Total production and con-struction industries	9,213	8,906	8,061	7,610	7,217	7,062	6,977	6,766	6,650
Agriculture, forestry and fishing ..	380	373	363	358	350	340	341	329	322
Coal, oil and natural gas extraction and processing.................	354	355	344	328	311	289	271	230	196
Electricity, gas, other energy and water supply	368	371	366	352	338	328	317	308	301
Manufacturing industries	7,253	6,937	6,222	5,863	5,525	5,409	5,366	5,236	5,145
Construction....................	1,239	1,243	1,130	1,067	1,044	1,037	1,022	991	1,009
Wholesale distribution and repairs	1,138	1,173	1,137	1,140	1,150	1,181	1,194	1,207	1,235
Retail distribution	2,176	2,177	2,092	2,026	2,005	2,054	2,086	2,110	2,118
Hotels and catering	943	972	943	973	963	1,010	1,061	1,085	1,111
Transport......................	1,056	1,049	987	943	912	910	911	903	899
Postal services and communications	423	437	438	437	433	432	434	437	446
Banking, finance, insurance	1,647	1,695	1,738	1,798	1,875	1,969	2,083	2,202	2,328
Public administration	2,002	1,980	1,899	1,881	1,918	1,936	1,962	1,987	2,034
Education......................	1,660	1,642	1,615	1,598	1,592	1,602	1,619	1,656	1,704
Medical and other health services, veterinary services	1,233	1,258	1,293	1,304	1,294	1,298	1,308	1,305	1,312
Other services	1,303	1,327	1,324	1,348	1,358	1,446	1,530	1,592	1,652

Unemployment (Thousands)

		United Kingdom				Great Britain		
		Unemployed claimants		Seasonally adjusted excluding school-leavers		Unemployed		
		Total	% rate	Total	% rate	Total	% rate	Males	Females
1983		3,104·7	*11·7*	2,866·5	*10·8*	2,987·6	*11·5*	2,133·5	854·0
1984	Annual	3,159·8	*11·6*	2,998·7	*11·0*	3,038·4	*11·4*	2,109·6	928·8
1985	averages	3,271·2	*11·8*	3,113·5	*11·2*	3,149·4	*11·6*	2,163·7	985·7
1986		3,289·1	*11·7*	3,180·4	*11·4*	3,161·3	*11·6*	2,159·6	1,001·7
1987		2,953·4	*10·5*	2,880·0	*10·2*	2,826·9	*10·3*	1,953·8	873·1
1988 January 14 ...		2,722·2	*9·7*	2,563·1	*9·1*	2,600·4	*9·5*	1,803·3	797·1
February 11 ..		2,665·5	*9·5*	2,532·6	*9·0*	2,545·9	*9·3*	1,764·0	781·9
March 10		2,592·1	*9·2*	2,504·8	*8·9*	2,474·6	*9·0*	1,716·6	757·9
April 14		2,536·0	*9·0*	2,453·1	*8·7*	2,417·7	*8·8*	1,678·9	738·8
May 12		2,426·9	*8·6*	2,414·2	*8·6*	2,310·7	*8·4*	1,606·8	703·9
June 9		2,340·8	*8·3*	2,375·3	*8·4*	2,225·1	*8·1*	1,547·7	677·5

HOUSING

Stock of dwellings (Great Britain)

	1983	1984	1985	1986*
Estimated annual gains and losses (thousands)				
Gains: New construction	195·0	203·4	188·7	193·3
Other...	15·5	17·6	18·9	12·4
Losses: Slum clearance	17·4	12·4	12·1	10·5
Other...	9·1	14·2	16·0	9·5
Net gain...	183·8	194·4	179·5	185·6
Stock at end of year	21,521	21,716	21,896	22,076
Estimated tenure distribution at end of year (percentage)				
Owner occupied..	*59·9*	*60·9*	*61·9*	*62·9*
Rented: From local authorities and new towns	*28·6*	*27·9*	*27·3*	*26·7*
From housing associations	*2·3*	*2·4*	*2·5*	*2·5*
From private owners including other tenures	*9·1*	*8·7*	*8·3*	*7·9*

* Provisional.

Permanent dwellings completed

	United Kingdom				England and Wales			
	Total	For local housing authorities	For private owners	Other	Total	For local housing authorities	For private owners	Other
1964	383,192	154,754	221,264	7,174	336,505	119,468	210,432	6,605
1974	279,582	121,017	145,177	13,388	241,173	99,423	129,626	12,124
1979	251,814	88,485	144,055	19,274	220,722	77,192	125,306	18,224
1981	205,744	68,139	117,818	19,787	178,959	58,215	103,240	17,504
1982	180,065	39,879	126,553	13,633	157,552	33,349	112,352	11,851
1983	203,172	38,830	147,997	16,345	177,010	31,300	131,242	14,468
1984	212,356	37,271	157,883	17,202	184,580	31,050	139,157	14,373
1985	197,417	30,188	153,973	13,256	170,343	24,143	134,687	11,513

	Scotland				Northern Ireland			
	Total	For local housing authorities	For private owners	Other	Total	For local housing authorities	For private owners	Other
1964	37,171	29,156	7,662	353	9,516	6,130	3,170	216
1974	28,336	16,182	11,239	915	10,073	5,412	4,312	349
1979	23,782	7,857	15,175	750	7,310	3,436	3,574	300
1981	20,015	7,065	11,021	1,929	6,770	2,859	3,557	354
1982	16,429	3,716	11,529	1,184	6,084	2,814	2,672	598
1983	17,941	3,486	13,178	1,277	8,215	4,044	3,571	600
1984	18,839	2,633	14,116	2,090	8,937	3,588	4,610	739
1985	18,377	2,812	14,449	1,116	8,697	3,233	4,837	627

VALUE OF UNITED KINGDOM IMPORTS (cif)
Analysis by sections and divisions   (£ million)

	1983	1984	1985	1986*
Total U.K. imports	66,101·1	78,967·4	85,027·0	86,066·7
Food and live animals chiefly for food	6,907·2	7,820·4	8,106·5	8,719·9
Live animals chiefly for food	170·3	196·8	238·3	293·4
Meat and meat preparations	1,313.4	1,342·2	1,400·9	1,465·5
Dairy products and birds' eggs	629·2	604·6	606·3	653·3
Fish, crustaceans and molluscs, and preparations thereof	505·2	537·8	600·4	748·7
Cereals and cereal preparations	593·5	629·0	713·2	769·3
Vegetables and fruit	1,718·5	1,930·3	2,037·1	2,184·4
Sugar, sugar preparations and honey	443·2	524·3	508·1	530·3
Coffee, tea, cocoa, spices, and manufactures thereof	799·9	1,291·4	1,205·7	1,220·8
Feeding stuff for animals (not including un-milled cereals)	523·6	501·5	487·4	527·3
Miscellaneous edible products and preparations	210·4	262·6	309·0	326·9
Beverages and tobacco	962·0	1,112·5	1,230·8	1,347·0
Beverages	617·4	705·5	843·6	1,008·3
Tobacco and tobacco manufactures	344·6	407·1	387·2	338·8
Crude materials, inedible, except fuels	4,416·1	4,884·9	4,856·8	4,622·7
Hides, skins and furskins, raw	184·9	235·3	238·9	216·4
Oil seeds and oleaginous fruit	268·6	234·8	238·8	271·3
Crude rubber (including synthetic and re-claimed)	197·4	223·5	228·3	203·6
Cork and wood	937·8	1,009·3	895·3	1,000·4
Pulp and waste paper	428·0	611·7	505·9	523·3
Textile fibres (other than wool tops) and their wastes (not manufactured into yarn or fabric)	475·9	596·7	662·8	546·9
Crude fertilisers and crude minerals (excluding coal, petroleum and precious stones)	285·8	312·6	354·1	317·0
Metalliferous ores and metal scrap	1,357·8	1,343·8	1,371·8	1,139·8
Crude animal and vegetable materials	279·7	317·3	361·0	404·2
Mineral fuels, lubricants and related materials	7,076·1	10,333·8	10,663·6	6,294·1
Petroleum, petroleum products and related materials	5,743·3	8,219·8	8,316·2	4,393·5
Coal, coke, gas and electric current	1,333·1	2,114·0	2,347·4	1,900·5
Animal and vegetable oils, fats and waxes	358·8	533·2	531·5	365·1
Total manufactured goods	44,936·5	53,010·7	58,312·2	62,833·7
Chemicals and related products	5,118·9	6,322·1	6,900·8	7,345·7
Organic chemicals	1,456·3	1,874·4	1,893·8	1,830·9
Inorganic chemicals	560·8	709·8	897·0	952·5
Dyeing, tanning and colouring materials	235·1	269·7	310·9	396·5
Medicinal and pharmaceutical products	470·2	542·3	590·4	679·7
Essential oils and perfume materials; toilet, polishing and cleansing materials	305·3	377·1	443·3	480·3
Fertilisers, manufactured	171·1	219·4	217·3	212·7
Explosives and pyrotechnic products	14·1	19·0	20·0	21·2
Artificial resins and plastic materials, and cellu-lose esters and ethers	1,323·5	1,609·4	1,763·5	1,985·8
Chemical materials and products, not elsewhere specified	581·9	700·8	764·6	786·3

* provisional figures.

Value of United Kingdom Imports (cif) (£ million)—*Continued*

	1983	1984	1985	1986*
Total U.K. imports	66,101·1	78,967·4	85,027·0	86,066·7
Manufactured goods classified chiefly by material	11,846·6	13,447·4	14,342·3	15,327·9
Leather, leather manufactures, nes, and dressed furskins	183·9	245·1	250·3	247·9
Rubber manufactures, nes	419·6	457·1	527·4	589·8
Cork and wood manufactures (excluding furniture)	578·5	622·1	632·0	686·6
Paper, paperboard, and articles of paper pulp, of paper or of paperboard	1,905·8	2,280·4	2,532·0	2,703·0
Textile yarn, fabrics, made-up articles, nes, and related products	2,320·2	2,705·4	3,032·0	3,162·6
Non-metallic mineral manufactures, nes	2,085·4	2,269·3	2,242·6	2,661·7
Iron and steel	1,260·3	1,487·2	1,715·5	1,796·3
Non-ferrous metals	1,985·0	1,996·2	1,903·4	1,836·2
Manufactures of metal, nes	1,107·8	1,384·4	1,507·2	1,643·9
Machinery and transport equipment	20,260·7	23,781·7	26,937·5	28,769·2
Power generating machinery and equipment	1,568·7	1,782·4	1,997·5	2,238·0
Machinery specialised for particular industries	1,735·6	2,078·6	2,327·3	2,362·2
Metalworking machinery	342·3	432·7	525·1	645·7
General industrial machinery and equipment, nes, and machine parts, nes	1,845·2	2,249·9	2,603·9	2,755·4
Office machines and automatic data processing equipment	3,017·5	4,102·7	4,510·0	4,545·1
Telecommunications, sound recording and reproducing apparatus and equipment	1,915·9	1,848·3	2,130·6	2,402·3
Electrical machinery, apparatus and appliances, nes, and electrical parts thereof (including non-electrical counterparts, nes, of electrical household type equipment)	2,805·8	3,846·7	4,276·9	4,446·4
Road vehicles (including air cushion vehicles)	5,753·8	5,957·6	6,800·6	7,939·7
Other transport equipment	1,275·9	1,482·9	1,765·6	1,434·4
Miscellaneous manufactured articles	7,710·4	9,459·5	10,131·6	11,391·0
Sanitary, plumbing, heating and lighting fixtures and fittings, nes	126·7	151·2	177·2	216·7
Furniture and parts thereof	490·4	591·6	662·8	776·0
Travel goods, handbags and similar containers	131·1	161·9	174·9	199·9
Articles of apparel and clothing accessories	1,601·3	2,011·7	2,090·1	2,386·7
Footwear	542·0	642·0	671·1	735·0
Professional, scientific and controlling instruments and apparatus, nes	1,301·3	1,593·8	1,761·5	1,792·5
Photographic apparatus, equipment and supplies and optical goods, nes, watches and clocks	862·2	1,068·7	1,173·0	1,285·3
Miscellaneous manufactured articles, nes	2,655·5	3,238·7	3,420·9	3,998·9
Commodities and transactions not classified elsewhere	1,444·3	1,271·8	1,325·7	1,884·0

nes   not elsewhere specified   * provisional figures.

VALUE OF UNITED KINGDOM EXPORTS (fob)
Analysis by sections and divisions (£ million)

	1983	1984	1985	1986*
Total U.K. exports	60,684·3	70,488·3	78,391·8	73,009·0
Food and live animals chiefly for food	2,754·6	3,114·8	3,252·4	3,740·1
Live animals chiefly for food	187·4	191·0	262·0	299·9
Meat and meat preparations	495·7	491·1	497·4	521·9
Dairy products and birds' eggs	308·1	246·6	281·3	331·5
Fish, crustaceans and molluscs, and preparations thereof	203·2	224·4	260·3	323·6
Cereals and cereal preparations	740·9	992·7	833·0	1,177·1
Vegetables and fruit	163·2	190·8	205·3	251·7
Sugar, sugar preparations and honey	145·1	165·7	220·8	170·4
Coffee, tea, cocoa, spices and manufactures thereof	291·4	363·4	390·8	364·0
Feeding stuff for animals (not including un-milled cereals)	78·9	96·8	121·8	139·3
Miscellaneous edible products and preparations	140·8	152·3	179·7	160·6
Beverages and tobacco	1,486·2	1,577·9	1,719·1	1,737·9
Beverages	1,051·2	1,157·0	1,253·7	1,331·7
Tobacco and tobacco manufactures	435·0	420·9	465·4	406·3
Crude materials, inedible, except fuels	1,527·7	1,898·1	2,032·1	1,940·9
Hides, skins and furskins, raw	200·2	280·3	288·5	260·2
Oil seeds and oleaginous fruit	37·8	54·0	90·4	155·5
Crude rubber (including synthetic and re-claimed)	141·7	166·9	173·9	183·0
Cork and wood	24·1	25·5	25·7	22·9
Pulp and waste paper	15·8	27·2	24·7	25·0
Textile fibres (other than wool tops) and their wastes (not manufactured into yarn or fabric)	375·1	427·9	419·4	373·0
Crude fertilisers and crude minerals (excluding coal, petroleum and precious stones)	223·8	249·1	269·2	272·3
Metalliferous ores and metal scrap	444·2	591·4	645·8	538·6
Crude animal and vegetable materials	64·9	75·6	94·3	110·4
Mineral fuels, lubricants and related materials	13,102·7	15,308·4	16,795·5	8,683·4
Petroleum, petroleum products and related materials	12,501·2	14,851·8	16,133·9	8,221·2
Coal, coke, gas and electric current	601·4	456·8	661·6	462·1
Animal and vegetable oils, fats and waxes	59·1	91·0	95·9	105·3
Total manufactured goods	40,087·2	46,703·0	52,506·1	54,595·2
Chemicals and related products	6,933·0	8,216·8	9,411·7	9,691·8
Organic chemicals	1,930·2	2,381·7	2,742·8	2,585·3
Inorganic chemicals	699·6	811·1	976·6	1,123·5
Dyeing, tanning and colouring materials	568·8	633·3	692·0	763·3
Medicinal and pharmaceutical products	1,073·4	1,222·4	1,427·0	1,532·8
Essential oils and perfume materials; toilet, polishing and cleansing materials	574·5	690·5	767·9	807·8
Fertilisers, manufactured	69·7	64·4	74·8	67·4
Explosives and pyrotechnic products	40·1	47·6	45·7	42·8
Artificial resins and plastic materials, and cellu-lose esters and ethers	980·5	1,179·8	1,330·7	1,401·4
Chemical materials and products, not elsewhere specified	996·4	1,186·0	1,351·3	1,367·5

* provisional figures.

Value of United Kingdom Imports (fob) (£ million)—*Continued*

	1983	1984	1985	1986*
Total U.K. exports	60,533·7	70,488·3	78,391·8	73,009·0
Manufactured goods classified chiefly by material	9,016·4	10,010·6	10,430·2	10,979·0
Leather, leather manufactures, nes, and dressed furskins	233·3	312·5	295·2	321·6
Rubber manufactures, nes	451·6	481·8	554·4	611·9
Cork and wood manufactures (excluding furniture)	85·5	104·6	84·1	77·2
Paper, paperboard, and articles of paper pulp, of paper or of paperboard	543·1	678·6	767·6	824·3
Textile yarn, fabrics, made-up articles, nes, and related products	1,285·0	1,484·8	1,709·1	1,711·5
Non-metallic mineral manufactures, nes	1,995·5	2,298·7	2,164·5	2,549·2
Iron and steel	1,330·7	1,528·9	1,856·2	1,866·7
Non-ferrous metals	1,766·6	1,656·7	1,379·6	1,551·5
Manufactures of metal, nes	1,325·1	1,464·1	1,619·6	1,465·0
Machinery and transport equipment	18,324·8	21,520·5	24,667·5	25,348·9
Power generating machinery and equipment	2,472·7	2,709·0	3,061·3	3,248·6
Machinery specialised for particular industries	2,335·0	2,676·8	3,077·6	3,101·5
Metalworking machinery	416·2	503·8	521·1	581·2
General industrial machinery and equipment, nes, and machine parts, nes	2,334·2	2,577·1	2,937·5	3,035·2
Office machines and automatic data processing equipment	2,048·8	3,046·6	3,746·7	3,561·7
Telecommunications and sound recording and reproducing apparatus and equipment	991·6	1,117·0	1,295·1	1,402·3
Electrical machinery, apparatus and appliances, nes, and electrical parts thereof (including non-electrical counterparts, nes, of electrical household type equipment)	2,292·3	2,805·3	3,380·1	3,383·0
Road vehicles (including air cushion vehicles)	3,092·2	3,318·8	3,910·6	3,954·4
Other transport equipment	2,341·9	2,766·1	2,737·4	3,080·9
Miscellaneous manufactured articles	5,813·0	6,955·0	7,996·8	8,575·5
Sanitary, plumbing, heating and lighting fixtures and fittings, nes	108·4	118·9	135·0	126·3
Furniture and parts thereof	257·9	282·0	357·7	356·4
Travel goods, handbags and similar containers	19·3	22·4	29·4	30·6
Articles of apparel and clothing accessories	865·2	996·3	1,171·7	1,228·3
Footwear	123·4	142·7	159·2	167·2
Professional, scientific and controlling instruments and apparatus, nes	1,472·1	1,777·6	2,151·7	2,284·2
Photographic apparatus, equipment and supplies and optical goods, nes, watches and clocks	573·4	694·2	817·3	843·5
Miscellaneous manufactured articles, nes	2,393·4	2,290·8	3,174·9	3,539·1
Commodities and transactions not classified elsewhere	1,666·9	1,795·3	1,990·7	2,206·2

nes   not elsewhere specified   * provisional figures.

INSOLVENCY
Bankruptcies, etc.

	England and Wales				Northern Ireland			
	1983	1984	1985	1986	1983	1984	1985	1986
Number of bankruptcies, etc.								
Debtors adjudicated bankrupt	6,555	7,714	6,340	6,682	76	86	117	164
Compositions and schemes of arrangement	4	3	4	6	12	10	10	25
Administration orders of deceased debtors' estates	17	9	14	10	2	1	2	—
Liabilities (£ thousand)								
Debtors adjudicated bankrupt	226,277	556,484	337,090	449,143	4,650	4,010	7,389	10,286
Compositions and schemes of arrangement	81	149	27	777	533	662	882	909
Administration orders of deceased debtors' estates	709	2,299	364	1,641	342	54	90	—
Assets (£ thousand)								
Debtors adjudicated bankrupt	54,117	102,280	83,910	89,119	1,376	942	3,197	1,745
Compositions and schemes of arrangement	47	28	84	230	127	195	395	460
Administration orders of deceased debtors' estates	225	1,350	179	570	244	16	514	—

Sequestrations (bankruptcies) in Scotland

	1980	1981	1982	1983	1984	1985	1986
Number of sequestrations	111	117	144	174	197	160	392*
Liabilities (£ thousand)	4,843	12,266	9,757	18,434	11,055	13,093	50,328
Assets (£ thousand)	2,060	4,228	3,975	5,601	3,100	2,322	16,261

*Ninety-two sequestrations under The Bankruptcy (Scotland) Act 1913 and 347 under The Bankruptcy (Scotland) Act 1985.

Company Liquidations
Number

	1980	1981	1982	1983	1984	1985	1986
England and Wales							
Compulsory liquidations	2,935	2,771	3,745	4,807	5,260	5,761	5,204
Voluntary liquidations:							
Creditors'	3,955	5,825	8,322	8,599	8,461	9,137	9,201
Members'	3,970	3,638	3,908	3,808	3,772	3,946	4,525
Total liquidations notified (all types)	10,860	12,234	15,975	17,214	17,493	18,844	18,930
Scotland							
Compulsory liquidations	135	158	177	263	272	306	299
Voluntary liquidations:							
Creditors'	244	280	326	258	251	231	212
Members'	242	248	253	243	234	233	251
Total liquidations notified (all types)	621	686	756	764	757	770	762
Northern Ireland							
Compulsory liquidations	8	16	10	15	19	36	56
Voluntary liquidations:							
Creditors'	66	83	111	96	64	75	108
Members'	39	39	41	52	60	69	57
Total liquidations notified (all types)	113	138	162	163	143	180	221

AGRICULTURE

Estimated quantity of crops and grass harvested (thousand tonnes)

	1980	1981	1982	1983	1984	1985	1986
Cereals							
Wheat	8,470	8,710	10,320	10,800	14,970	12,050	13,910
Barley	10,320	10,230	10,960	9,980	11,070	9,740	10,010
Oats	600	620	575	465	515	615	505
Mixed corn for threshing	59	44	39	35	35	31	29
Rye for threshing	24	25	27	24	28	35	32
Potatoes							
Early crop‡	453	388	432	322	397	403	363*
Main crop‡	6,657	5,826	6,498	5,535	7,001	6,489	6,083*
Fodder crops							
Beans for stockfeeding	150	125	120	105	125	155	230
Turnips and swedes	5,065	4,795	4,575	3,655	3,960	3,300	3,855
Fodder beet and mangolds†	370	320	370	295	570	815	845
Maize for threshing or stockfeeding	785	635	635	550	580	770	915
Rape for stockfeeding, kale, cabbage, savoys and kohlrabi	2,115	2,195	1,985	1,660	1,805	1,555	1,380
Peas harvested dry for stockfeeding	—	—	—	85	170	215	330
Other crops							
Sugar beet	7,380	7,395	10,005	7,495	9,015	7,715	8,120
Rape grown for oilseed	300	325	580	565	925	895	965
Hops	10	9	10	9	8	6	5
Hay	6,975	6,775	6,550	6,000	5,700	4,650	4,675
Horticultural crops							
Vegetables grown in the open:							
Brussels sprouts	228	197	223	154	169	152	157
Cabbage (including savoys and spring greens)	576	546	610	518	670	683	698
Cauliflowers	367	325	353	298	344	356	360
Carrots	553	711	725	554	572	600	589
Parsnips	54	53	55	51	57	62	64
Turnips and swedes	163	109	145	135	142	142	160
Beetroot	109	97	105	94	115	114	104
Onions, dry bulb	224	232	231	175	238	268	279
Onions, salad	26	25	27	25	22	25	31
Leeks	40	40	43	44	53	60	61
Broad beans	18	17	19	17	21	19	16
Runner beans including French	62	69	92	65	77	66	65
Peas, green for market	18	25	28	23	27	26	25
Peas, green for processing	223	277	238	198	241	206	228
Celery	54	50	51	46	57	53	54
Lettuce	135	134	161	155	153	193	188
Rhubarb	43	41	39	29	26	26	26
Protected crops							
Tomatoes	129	125	118	118	129	116	125
Cucumbers	57	54	56	61	68	71	80
Lettuce	36	37	45	49	48	50	50
Fruit crops							
Total dessert apples	178	152	216	186	184	161	162
Cooking apples	179	80	147	126	163	141	149
Pears	44	49	40	54	48	51	47
Plums	47	16	34	36	34	24	34
Cherries	7	3	7	3	5	5	4
Soft Fruit	110	105	109	124	114	111	114

* provisional figures.
† from 1986 Scotland collected fodder beet separately.
‡ revised basis of calculation adopted in 1984 which prevents direct comparison with earlier years.

Cattle, Sheep, Pigs and Poultry on Agricultural Holdings

Thousands

At June each year	1980	1981	1982	1983	1984	1985	1986
Cattle and calves: total	13,426	13,138	13,244	13,290	13,213	12,911	12,533
Dairy herd	3,228	3,191	3,250	3,333	3,281	3,150	3,138
Beef herd	1,478	1,420	1,389	1,358	1,351	1,333	1,308
Heifers in calf (first calf)	838	863	851	847	811	874	879
Bulls for service	86	84	84	83	80	78	76
Other cattle:							
Two years old and over	1,005	963	937	904	905	852	769
One year old and under two	3,153	3,041	3,057	3,059	3,069	3,012	2,819
Six months old and under one year	1,866	1,876	1,890	1,924	1,949	1,905	1,876
Under six months old	1,770	1,699	1,786	1,783	1,768	1,707	1,668
Sheep and lambs: total	31,446	32,097	33,067	34,069	34,802	35,628	37,016
Breeding ewes	12,178	12,528	12,909	13,310	13,648	13,893	14,252
Rams for service	353	358	366	383	393	406	419
Other sheep	3,672	3,584	3,748	3,764	3,680	3,763	3,961
Lambs under one year old	15,243	15,628	16,044	16,612	17,080	17,566	18,384
Pigs: total	7,815	7,828	8,023	8,174	7,689	7,865	7,937
Breeding herd	831	836	864	856	800	828	824
Boars for service	42	43	45	45	42	44	44
Gilts not yet in pig	84	87	89	82	77	80	79
Barren sows for fattening	12	11	12	15	12	12	12
Other pigs:							
110 kg and over	102	90	117	100	91	89	80
80 kg and under 110 kg	657	638	630	605	599	589	603
50 kg and under 80 kg	1,772	1,776	1,824	1,868	1,787	1,813	1,863
20 kg and under 50 kg	2,240	2,227	2,281	2,362	2,198	2,260	2,270
Under 20 kg	2,074	2,119	2,163	2,241	2,082	2,151	2,163
Poultry: total	135,105	132,286	135,363	127,618	127,507	128,968	—
Fowls: total	127,063	122,639	126,091	117,854	118,846	119,456	120,740
Growing pullets	14,457	14,219	14,766	11,828	12,536	12,503	12,502
Laying flock	46,012	44,473	44,792	41,127	40,573	39,538	38,096
Breeding flock	6,678	6,117	6,457	6,012	6,396	6,104	6,334
Table birds	59,917	57,830	60,075	58,887	59,341	61,311	63,807
Ducks*	1,390	1,333	1,443	1,566	1,527	1,648	1,741
Geese*	133	148	157				
Turkeys	6,519	8,167	7,672	8,198	7,134	7,864	—

*Excludes Scotland except in 1983.

Agricultural land: area

Thousand hectares

	1980	1981	1982	1983	1984	1985	1986
Total tillage	5,031	5,071	5,127	5,124	5,196	5,265	5,287
All grasses under five years old	1,965	1,911	1,859	1,846	1,794	1,796	1,723
Total arable	6,996	6,982	6,986	6,970	6,990	7,061	7,010
All grasses five years old and over	5,140	5,103	5,097	5,107	5,105	5,019	5,077
Total crops and grass	12,136	12,085	12,083	12,078	12,095	12,080	12,088
Rough grazings							
Sole rights	5,119	5,021	4,984	4,927	4,895	4,872	4,829
Common (estimated)	1,214	1,214	1,214	1,212	1,212	1,216	1,216
Woodland on agricultural holdings	271	277	285	292	299	312	316
All other land on agricultural holdings	214	211	217	227	218	223	227
Total area of agricultural land	18,953	18,808	18,783	18,735	18,720	18,703	17,459
Total area of the United Kingdom	24,088	24,089	24,088	24,088	24,088	24,085	24,086

FISHERIES
Fishing fleet

Number

At December 31	1980	1981	1982	1983	1984	1985	1986p
England and Wales							
Trawlers	1,573	1,750	1,759	1,757	1,686	1,285	1,561
Seine nets	230	227	216	195	181	150	90
Lines	697	794	469	499	629	534	687
Purse seine	6	4	3	5	3	2	1
Other nets	88	133	89	111	114	99	257
Other and unknown	1,453	1,729	1,692	2,113	2,454	3,311	2,688
Scotland							
Total fishing vessels	2,514	2,370	2,233	2,214	2,180	2,198	2,183
Demersal trawl	359	339	315	291	244	253	235
Demersal pair trawl	38	72	70	76	104	116	122
Industrial trawl	6	9	19	17	12	10	6
Seine net	320	308	296	302	291	291	283
Lines	235	208	147	112	94	83	70
Purse seine	46	43	45	42	44	45	47
Pelagic trawl	42	35	34	26	23	20	12
Other nets*	15	22	27	43	48	46	43
Nephrops trawl	306	303	302	317	337	335	383
Other shellfishing†	1,147	1,031	978	988	983	999	982

p provisional figures
* Gill and cod nets, drift and ring nets.
† All shellfishing methods except nephrops trawl.

Landings of fish of British taking (Great Britain)

	Landed weight (Thousand tonnes)				Value (£ thousand)			
	1983	1984	1985	1986*	1983	1984	1985	1986*
Total all fish	748·4	733·7	762·1	716·9	280,263	297,863	323,825	361,680
Total wet fish	676·2	661·0	687·2	629·3	229,233	240,587	258,904	284,161
Demersal: total	427·5	395·0	402·3	383·2	202,084	211,713	227,175	256,705
Catfish	1·3	1·3	1·4	1·5	494	589	755	1,035
Cod	112·6	90·9	90·0	76·5	72,466	65,258	69,945	69,140
Dogfish	10·6	12·3	13·8	11·6	3,287	3,547	4,550	6,376
Haddock	122·6	107·5	132·2	131·0	57,361	64,204	67,757	79,019
Hake	2·3	2·5	2·7	3·0	2,519	2,794	3,851	4,549
Halibut	0·2	0·1	0·1	0·1	360	319	365	372
Lemon sole	5·9	5·7	5·7	5·0	5,493	5,972	7,137	8,265
Plaice	21·0	21·5	20·4	21·3	13,774	14,097	13,821	16,048
Redfish	0·3	0·4	0·2	0·1	73	98	75	56
Saithe (Coalfish)	12·8	12·1	14·4	17·7	3,520	2,759	3,874	6,361
Skate and ray	6·5	6·8	7·0	6·9	2,881	2,792	2,992	3,908
Sole	2·3	2·4	2·7	3·2	5,877	6,717	9,093	14,500
Turbot	0·5	0·5	0·5	0·6	1,426	1,660	1,976	2,607
Whiting	57·0	60·7	50·2	41·1	17,715	23,006	18,997	18,460
Livers	—	—	—	—	—	—	1	1
Roes	0·5	0·6	0·5	0·5	275	321	390	348
Other demersal	71·1	69·7	60·5	63·1	14,563	17,580	21,596	25,660
Pelagic: total	248·7	266·0	285·0	246·1	27,140	28,874	31,730	27,456
Herring	54·2	71·5	95·4	106·1	6,994	9,076	11,493	11,881
Mackerel	175·5	186·3	174·2	132·1	18,649	18,768	18,694	14,766
Other pelagic	19·0	8·2	15·4	7·9	1,506	1,030	1,543	809
Total shell fish	72·2	72·6	74·8	87·6	51,030	57,274	64,920	77,519
Cockles	5·8	5·4	7·8	19·4	327	311	476	1,165
Crab	11·3	14·0	13·5	12·6	6,373	8,422	8,557	9,599
Lobster	1·0	1·2	1·1	1·0	5,748	7,696	8,030	7,680
Mussels	5·9	4·3	5·8	6·3	468	314	467	541
Nephrop (Norway lobster)	22·1	22·2	24·8	25·4	24,061	24,545	31,548	39,119
Oysters	0·3	0·4	0·5	0·6	636	770	734	845
Shrimps	1·1	0·7	0·8	1·4	739	566	711	1,254
Whelks	1·3	2·2	1·6	2·0	226	456	355	418
Other shell fish	23·4	22·2	18·9	18·9	12,452	14,194	14,042	16,898

* Contains some provisional information.

MERCHANT SHIPPING

PRINCIPAL MERCHANT FLEETS OF THE WORLD. Source: *Lloyd's Register of Shipping*

Flag	1977 No.	1977 Gross Tonnage	1982 No.	1982 Gross Tonnage	1986 No.	1986 Gross Tonnage	1987 No.	1987 Gross Tonnage
Liberia	2,617	79,982,968	2,189	70,718,439	1,658	52,649,444	1,574	51,412,029
Panama	3,267	19,458,419	5,032	32,600,278	5,052	41,305,009	5,136	43,254,716
Japan	9,642	40,035,853	10,652	41,593,612	10,011	38,487,773	9,822	35,932,177
U.S.S.R.	8,167	21,438,291	7,513	23,785,698	6,726	24,960,888	6,705	25,232,091
Greece	3,344	29,517,059	3,501	40,035,204	2,255	28,390,800	1,948	23,559,852
*U.S.A.	4,740	15,299,681	6,133	19,111,092	6,263	18,300,337	6,427	20,178,236
Cyprus	900	2,787,908	557	2,149,869	940	10,616,809	1,341	15,650,207
China, People's Republic of	622	4,245,446	1,108	8,056,849	1,562	11,566,974	1,773	12,341,477
Bahamas	109	106,317	96	432,502	302	5,995,011	469	9,105,182
Philippines	504	1,146,529	882	2,773,855	1,131	6,922,499	1,394	8,681,227
United Kingdom	3,432	31,646,351	2,826	22,505,265	2,256	11,567,117	2,165	8,504,605
Hong Kong	113	609,679	255	3,495,512	416	8,179,670	409	8,034,668
Italy	1,690	11,111,182	1,663	10,374,966	1,569	7,896,569	1,571	7,817,353
Korea (South)	1,042	2,494,724	1,652	5,529,398	1,837	7,183,617	1,899	7,214,070
Singapore	872	6,791,398	849	7,183,326	736	6,267,627	700	7,098,116
India	566	5,482,176	644	6,213,489	2,107	6,540,121	803	6,725,776
Norway	2,738	27,801,471	2,409	21,861,635	697	9,394,630	1,979	6,359,349
Brazil	538	3,329,961	666	5,678,111	984	6,212,287	718	6,324,059
France	1,327	11,613,859	1,171	10,770,880	2,397	5,936,268	984	5,371,273
Spain	2,726	7,186,081	2,635	8,130,693	1,063	5,422,002	2,350	4,949,387
Denmark	1,407	5,331,165	1,152	5,214,063	587	4,661,224	1,256	4,873,466
China, Republic of (Taiwan)	443	1,558,713	511	2,225,377	1,352	4,272,295	1,494	4,512,749
Germany, Federal Republic of	1,975	9,592,314	1,782	7,706,661	1,334	5,965,214	1,414	3,976,873
Iran	193	1,002,061	235	1,312,104	749	4,324,359	370	3,908,031
Netherlands	1,254	5,290,360	1,328	3,653,104	825	4,324,135	1,307	3,469,670
Poland	473	3,447,817	816	3,690,615	426	3,457,242	719	3,336,093
Turkey	448	1,231,282	631	2,127,921	490	3,423,746	852	3,263,823
Romania	207	1,218,171	345	2,203,317	425	3,233,906	430	3,164,893
Yugoslavia	459	2,284,526	475	2,531,506	490	2,872,613	498	2,971,155
Canada	1,283	2,892,948	1,299	3,212,562	1,249	3,160,043	1,238	2,827,098
Gibraltar	6	10,549	18	15,708	100	1,612,948	113	2,692,044
Saudi Arabia	119	1,018,713	347	4,301,789	380	2,978,016	349	2,404,559
Australia	424	1,374,197	558	1,875,316	673	2,368,462	690	2,269,641
Sweden	728	7,449,394	697	3,787,567	660	2,516,614	642	2,268,383
Belgium	271	1,595,489	316	2,271,096	355	2,419,661	350	2,120,631
Indonesia	1,032	1,163,173	1,319	2,014,379	1,707	2,085,635	1,734	2,087,856
Kuwait	226	1,831,194	217	1,846,824	239	2,580,924	236	1,925,297
Bermuda	88	1,751,515	68	474,402	97	1,208,276	105	1,901,026
Argentina	401	1,677,169	523	2,255,758	454	2,117,017	434	1,725,984
Malta	44	100,420	93	425,563	246	2,014,947	271	1,668,823
Malaysia	179	563,666	329	1,195,411	498	1,743,629	498	1,650,176
Bulgaria	186	964,156	193	1,248,210	205	1,385,009	205	1,532,485
Mexico	311	673,964	545	1,351,630	642	1,386,246	651	1,494,039
German Democratic Republic	447	486,938	419	1,518,944	403	1,518,944	377	1,122,249
Finland	337	2,266,098	354	2,376,995	276	1,469,927	257	1,074,192
Egypt	176	407,818	341	635,801	422	1,063,020	428	1,048,197
Portugal	350	1,281,439	356	1,401,589	355	1,114,444	292	1,002,236
Iraq	110	1,135,245	155	1,521,491	149	1,016,343	142	—

* Including ships of the United States Reserve Fleet.

CLASSIFICATION WITH LLOYD'S REGISTER OF SHIPPING

Ships classed or to be classed with Lloyd's Register at 30th June, 1987, totalled 8,945 with an aggregate of over 92 million gross tonnage.

MERCHANT SHIPPING

MERCHANT SHIPS COMPLETED IN THE WORLD DURING 1987
Source: *Lloyd's Register of Shipping*

Country of Build	No.	Total Gross Tonnage	For Registration in	No.	Total Gross Tonnage
Japan	616	5,707,898	Japan	492	2,494,837
Korea (South)	99	2,090,966	Panama	78	2,128,519
Yugoslavia	18	350,406	Liberia	34	1,335,167
China, Republic of (Taiwan)	6	341,873	Korea (South)	55	796,414
Germany, Federal Republic of	56	341,319	U.S.A.	35	466,611
Spain	102	324,541	Norway	48	465,434
Italy	34	312,989	U.S.S.R.	73	389,611
German Democratic Republic	37	292,241	Greece	13	338,455
Poland	43	288,033	Singapore	16	325,646
*China, People's Republic of	19	285,721	Italy	31	312,289
Brazil	25	255,173	Denmark	37	239,115
Denmark	32	243,218	United Kingdom	36	218,617
*Romania	6	198,443	Romania	4	190,570
United Kingdom	31	194,231	India	41	182,642
Finland	14	167,919	China, Republic of (Taiwan)	8	178,355
France	21	167,027	Germany, Federal Republic of	38	173,481
U.S.A.	29	164,326	Yugoslavia	9	170,169
Bulgaria	7	84,822	Spain	58	165,244
Sweden	20	74,997	Philippines	5	149,810
Norway	55	62,264	China, People's Republic of	19	118,941
Netherlands	68	59,300	Netherlands	52	117,313
*U.S.S.R.	6	51,590	Bahamas	6	114,402
India	25	37,320	Sweden	16	112,592
Argentina	9	25,114	Poland	7	90,880
Mexico	4	23,914	Australia	23	89,340
Turkey	17	22,461	Hong Kong	12	88,704
Singapore	23	14,553	United Arab Emirates	6	70,144
Belgium	5	14,336	Mexico	9	67,579
Egypt	6	12,160	Bulgaria	6	60,592
Canada	20	11,691	Cyprus	4	59,689
Portugal	17	11,543	Brazil	25	57,860
Other Countries	58	27,030	Other Countries	232	490,497
WORLD TOTAL	1,528	12,259,419	WORLD TOTAL	1,528	12,259,419

Included in the tables above is 1 steamship of 81,000 gross tonnage to be built in Spain.

Of the steamships and motorships completed in the world during the year 2,26,420 gross tonnage (18·4%) is to be classed with Lloyd's Register.
 * Information incomplete.

TRANSPORT
Goods transport in Great Britain

	1981	1982	1983	1984	1985	1986
Total tonne kilometres (thousand millions)	168·8	174·1	179·0	179·3	183·5	182·4
Road	92·9	93·8	95·1	99·5	102·1	104·1
Rail (British Rail only)	17·5	15·9	17·1	12·7	15·3	16·5
Water: coastwise oil products*	36·0	38·1	38·4	39·5	37·9	32·5†
Water: other*	13·1	17·0	18·5	17·2	17·0	18·9†
Pipelines (except gases)	9·3	9·3	9·9	10·4	11·2	10·4
Total (million tonnes)	1,634	1,723	1,704	1,683	1,777	1,807
Road	1,286	1,376	1,344	1,385	1,435	1,455
Rail (British Rail only)	154	142	145	78	122	140
Water: coastwise oil products*	48	51	50	52	48	53†
Water: other*	71	76	83	80	83	80†
Pipelines (except gases)	75	78	82	88	89	79

*'other' comprises non-oil coastwise traffic and all coastwise traffic with Northern Ireland, Isle of Man and Channel Islands, and one-port traffic as well as traffic in inland waterways.
†provisional.

Seaport traffic of Great Britain

Million gross tonnes

	1981	1982	1983	1984	1985	1986*
Foreign traffic						
Imports						
Bulk fuel traffic	53·7	49·5	42·1	60·4	58·8	62·3
Other bulk traffic	32·8	31·8	34·3	34·6	36·7	37·9
Container and roll-on traffic	21·9	23·4	26·0	28·1	29·8	31·1
Semi-bulk traffic	12·3	14·1	14·6	14·7	14·6	15·9
Conventional traffic	3·0	2·3	2·3	2·3	1·7	1·5
All imports	123·7	121·2	119·3	140·2	141·6	148·7
Exports						
Bulk fuel traffic	86·9	92·0	95·8	97·3	103·0	102·0
Other bulk traffic	16·2	15·3	16·3	18·7	17·7	21·0
Container and roll-on traffic	16·5	17·1	18·6	20·2	21·3	22·1
Semi-bulk traffic	3·6	3·0	3·5	3·6	4·1	4·0
Conventional traffic	2·7	2·9	2·1	1·8	1·6	1·2
All exports	125·8	130·3	136·3	141·7	147·7	150·4
Domestic traffic						
Bulk fuel traffic	118·4	127·9	130·7	122·7	118·5	110·7
Other bulk traffic	29·5	30·3	31·7	30·9	31·7	32·6
Container and roll-on traffic	4·5	4·9	5·8	6·2	6·6	6·9
Semi-bulk traffic	0·3	0·2	0·2	0·4	0·3	0·2
Conventional traffic	2·8	0·4	0·3	0·2	0·3	0·3
Non-oil traffic with UK offshore installations	—	2·1	2·2	3·2	3·6	2·9
All domestic traffic	155·6	165·7	170·8	163·6	161·0	153·5
Total foreign and domestic traffic	405·1	417·2	426·4	445·6	460·4	452·6

Passenger transport in Great Britain

Thousand million passenger kilometres

	1981	1982	1983	1984	1985	1986
Total	457	463	471	487	494	516
Air (domestic scheduled services)	3	3	3	3	4	4
Rail*	34	31	34	35	36	37
Road:						
Public service vehicles	42	41	42	42	42	41
Cars and taxis	367	376	380	395	401	424
Motorcycles	7	7	7	7	6	6
Pedal cycles	4	5	5	5	5	4

*including London Regional Transport and Passenger Transport Executive railway systems.

BRITISH RAILWAYS

The British Railways Board was set up by the Transport Act, 1962, and assumed its responsibilities on January 1, 1963.

The railway business is broken down into five distinct business sectors each with its own Director. The sectors focus on three passenger businesses of InterCity; Network SouthEast; and Provincial; together with the Railfreight and Parcels businesses. In addition for the purposes of management and operation the railways are divided into Regions. They cover the following areas:

London Midland Region—bounded by a line joining Carlisle, Oldham, Nottingham, Bedford, London, Banbury, Kidderminster, Aberystwyth.

Western Region—west of a line joining Yeovil, Westbury, Reading, London and the southern border of the L.M. Region.

Southern Region—south of a line joining Dorchester, Salisbury, London and the Thames.

Eastern Region—east of a line joining London, Peterborough, Sheffield, Bradford and Carlisle, but excluding Anglia Region.

Anglia Region—east of a line joining London with Hertford East, Meldreth and Whittlesea.

Scottish Region—north of a line joining Carlisle and Berwick.

Financial Results, 1987–88.—The Profit and Loss Account for 1987–88 showed a surplus of £113·0 million, £47·3 million after interest, compared with a surplus of £2·4 million after interest in 1986–87. The railway working surplus was £108·7 million compared with a surplus of £71·8 million for the previous year.

	£ million
Railways	1987–88
Gross receipts:	
Passenger (including grants)	2,407·3
Freight (inc. parcels and mails)	628·1
TOTAL........................	3,089·4
Working expenses:	
Train services	1,282·2
Terminals	315·1
Miscellaneous traffic expenses	116·7
Track and signalling................	650·0
General expenses...................	540·8
Provision for replacement of assets ..	123·4
TOTAL........................	3,028·2
Railway net surplus	53·1
Surplus from subsidiaries, operational and non-operational property letting	55·4
GROUP OPERATING SURPLUS	108·5

Staff.—On March 31, 1988, British Rail employed 133,567 staff (140,069 at March 31, 1987). Including

B.R. Property Board, Travellers Fare Ltd, InterCity On Board Services, Freightliners Ltd., B.R. Engineering Ltd., Transmark, B.R. Maintenance Ltd., Hornwich Foundry Ltd. and B.R. Pension Trustee Co. Ltd., the group total at March 31, 1988, was 154,748 (166,989 at March 31, 1987).

OPERATING STATISTICS

At March 31, 1988, British Rail had 23,557 miles of standard gauge lines and sidings in use, representing 10,335 miles of route of which 2,614 miles were electrified. Standard rail on main line has a weight of 110 lb. per yard. British Rail had 2,270 locomotives (diesel and diesel electric, 2,040 and electric, 230); 2,382 diesel multiple-unit vehicles, 7,022 electric multiple-unit vehicles and 2,891 locomotive-hauled passenger carriages.

Loaded train miles run in passenger service totalled 216·6m. 727·2m passenger journeys were made during the year, including 324·9m made by holders of season tickets. The average distance of each passenger journey on ordinary fare was 35·6 miles; and on season ticket, 19·3 miles. Passenger stations in use in 1988 numbered 2,426 and freight stations 114.

Freight.—There were 28,908 freight-vehicles and 1,635 other vehicles in the non-passenger-carrying stock. Train miles run in freight service totalled 31·3m.

Accidents on Railways

	1985	1986
Train accidents: total	1,240	1,171
Persons killed : total	6	27
Passengers	—	8
Railway staff	—	5
Others	6	14
Persons injured : total	380	510
Passengers	261	342
Railway staff	88	137
Others	31	31
Other accidents through movement of railway vehicles		
Persons killed	55	41
Persons injured	2,489	2,443
Other accidents on railway premises		
Persons killed	13	4
Persons injured	6,295	6,528
Trespassers and suicides		
Persons killed	310	312
Persons injured	104	78

AIR

Air Traffic Between the United Kingdom and Abroad*

Thousands

	1981	1982	1983	1984	1985	1986
Flights: total	495·8	511·4	518·5	566·3	579·3	615·8
United Kingdom airlines						
Scheduled services	149·7	143·5	141·9	151·3	170·8	177·5
Non-scheduled services	162·2	176·3	184·9	214·0	196·2	198·8
Overseas airlines†						
Scheduled services	152·0	154·3	155·2	160·9	172·8	195·8
Non-scheduled services	31·9	37·3	36·5	40·2	39·5	43·6
Passengers carried: total	43,732·0	44,131·9	46,284·9	51,154·8	52,862·7	51,608·1
United Kingdom airlines						
Scheduled services	13,559·0	12,214·7	12,140·0	13,174·2	14,854·3	15,082·9
Non-scheduled services	12,128·9	13,216·6	14,661·9	16,643·7	15,529·0	12,929·7
Overseas airlines†						
Scheduled services	15,398·8	15,520·5	16,065·6	17,623·0	18,815·6	19,409·5
Non-scheduled services	2,645·4	3,180·1	3,417·4	3,713·9	3,663·8	4,186·0

*Excludes travel to and from the Channel Islands.
†Includes airlines of overseas U.K. Territories.

Activity at Civil Aerodromes

	1981	1982	1983	1984	1985	1986
Movement of civil aircraft (thousands)	2,103	2,113	2,238	2,363	2,354	2,439
Commercial: total	1,028	1,072	1,243	1,179	1,205	1,238
Transport	927	974	1,019	1,079	1,097	1,125
Other	101	98	224	100	108	113
Non-commercial	1,075	1,041	995	1,184	1,149	1,201
Passengers handled (thousands): total	58,979	60,033	62,301	68,830	71,812	76,593
Terminal	57,771	58,778	61,099	67,572	70,434	75,161
Transit	1,208	1,255	1,202	1,258	1,377	1,432
Commercial freight handled (tonnes): total	723,709	692,693	725,897	860,629	850,268	881,202
Set down	341,932	320,604	332,162	388,292	377,127	419,275
Picked up	381,777	372,088	393,737	472,335	473,140	461,927
Mail handled (tonnes): total	106,497	118,406	124,080	136,640	145,770	153,467
Set down	50,063	55,200	56,943	61,461	64,138	67,802
Picked up	56,434	63,206	67,138	75,179	81,632	85,665

Commercial Air Transport from Airports

	Passengers (thousands)						Freight (tonnes)	Mail (tonnes)
	Total*		International		Domestic			
	1981	1986	1981	1986	1981	1986	1986	1986
United Kingdom	58,978	76,592	43,732	57,431	14,039	17,742	861,076	153,469
North	1,246	1,662	631	912	551	615	1,051	957
Yorkshire & Humberside	410	690	163	311	214	302	346	1
East Midlands	747	1,134	518	852	221	271	20	7,596
East Anglia	160	194	77	73	79	98	808	725
South East	40,386	51,270	34,534	43,507	5,190	7,183	741,792	97,589
South West†	554	920	264	489	419	389	792	3,092
West Midlands	1,560	2,179	1,105	1,639	388	465	6,682	5
North West	5,466	8,400	3,811	6,151	1,479	2,098	52,501	17,648
England: total	50,529	66,449	41,104	53,934	8,542	11,421	803,992	127,613
Wales	331	508	232	437	65	51	241	376
Scotland	6,698	7,552	2,214	2,646	4,205	4,608	33,973	19,801
Northern Ireland	1,420	2,083	182	414	1,227	1,662	22,870	5,679

*includes passengers in transit.
†includes Bournemouth (Hurn) Airport, included in the South East prior to 1986.

AERODROMES AND AIRPORTS

Aerodromes in Great Britain, Northern Ireland, the Isle of Man and the Channel Islands which are either State owned, operated by the Highlands and Islands Airports Ltd. or licensed for use by civil aircraft. A number of unlicensed airfields not included in this list are also available for private use by permission of the owner or controlling authority.

Aerodromes designated as Customs airports are printed in bold type. Customs facilities are available at certain other aerodromes by special arrangement.

S = Owned and operated by the Government.
BAA = Owned by the British Airports Authority
  P.L.C.
M = Owned by the municipal authority.
HIAL = Operated by Highland and Islands Airports
  Ltd.

J = Military aerodromes available for civil use by
  prior permission.
H = Licensed helicopter station.

ENGLAND AND WALES
Aberporth, Dyfed. S
Abingdon, Oxon. J
Andrewsfield, Essex.
Barrow (Walney Island), Cumbria.
Bembridge, I.O.W.
Benson, Oxon. J
Biggin Hill, Kent.
Birmingham, W. Midlands. M
Blackbushe, Hants.
Blackpool, Lancs. M
Bodmin, Cornwall.
Bourn, Cambridge.
Bournemouth, (Hurn), Dorset. M
Bristol, Avon. M
Brize Norton, Oxford. J
Brough, N. Humberside. M
Caernarfon, Gwynedd.
Cambridge.
Cardiff, S. Glamorgan. M
Carlisle, Cumbria. M
Chichester (Goodwood), Sussex.
Chivenor, Devon. J
Church Fenton, N. Yorks. J
Clacton, Essex.
Compton Abbas, Dorset.
Cosford, Wolverhampton. J
Coventry, W. Midlands. M
Cranfield, Beds.
Cranwell, Lincs. J
Culdrose, Cornwall. J
Denham, Bucks.
Derby/Burnaston, Derby.
Dishforth, N. Yorks. J
Doncaster, S. Yorks.
Dunkeswell, Devon.
Dunsfold, Surrey. M
Duxford, Cambs. M
Earls Colne, Halstead.
East Midlands, Derbys. M
Elstree, Herts.
Exeter, Devon.
Fairoaks, Surrey.
Farnborough, Hants. S
Fenland, Lincs.
Filton, Bristol. M
Finningley, S. Yorks. J
Gloucester/Cheltenham
  (Staverton), Glos. M
Great Yarmouth (North Denes),
  Norfolk.
Halfpenny Green, Staffs.
Halton, Bucks. J
Hatfield, Herts.
Haverfordwest, Dyfed. M
Hawarden, Clwyd.
Hucknall, Notts.
Humberside. M
Ipswich, Suffolk.
Isle of Wight (Sandown).
Kemble, Glos. J

Land's End (St. Just), Cornwall.
Lashenden, Headcorn, Kent.
Leavesden, Herts.
Leeds and Bradford, Yorks. M
Lee-on-Solent, Hants. J
Leicester, Leics.
Linton-on-Ouse, Yorks. J
Liverpool, Merseyside. M
Llanbedr, Gwynedd. J.
London (City).
London (Gatwick). BAA
London (Heathrow). BAA
London (Stansted). BAA
London (Westland Heliport). H
Luton, Beds. M
Lydd, Kent.
Lyneham, Wilts. J
Manchester. M
Manchester (Barton).
Manston, Kent. J
Newcastle, Tyne and Wear. M
Newton, Notts. J
Northampton (Sywell), Northants.
Northolt, Mddx. J
Norwich, Norfolk. M
Nottingham, Notts.
Old Sarum, Wilts.
Oxford (Kidlington), Oxfordshire.
Panshanger, Herts.
Penzance, Cornwall. H
Peterborough (Conington).
Peterborough (Sibson), Cambs.
Plymouth (Roborough), Devon.
Portland Naval, Dorset. JH
Redhill, Surrey.
Retford/Gamston, Notts.
Rochester, Kent.
St. Mawgan, Cornwall. J
Sandtoft, Humberside.
Scilly Isles (St. Mary's).
Seething, Norfolk.
Shawbury, Shropshire. J
Sherburn-in-Elmet, N. Yorks.
Shipdham, Norfolk.
Shobdon, Herefordshire.
Shoreham, W. Sussex. M
Silverstone, Northants.
Skegness (Ingoldmells), Lincs.
Sleap, Shropshire.
Southampton, Eastleigh, Hants.
Southend, Essex. M
Stapleford, Essex.
Sturgate, Lincs.
Swansea, W. Glam. M
Tees-side, Cleveland. M
Thruxton, Hants.
Tresco, Isles of Scilly. H
Valley, Gwynedd. J
Warton, Lancs.
Wattisham, Suffolk. J

Wellesbourne Mountford,
  Warwick.
Weston, Avon. H
White Waltham, Berks.
Wickenby, Lincs.
Woodford, Gtr. Manchester.
Woodvale, Merseyside. J
Wycombe Air Park (Booker),
  Bucks.
Yeovil, Somerset.
Yeovilton, Somerset. J

SCOTLAND
Aberdeen (Dyce). BAA
Barra, Hebrides.
Benbecula, Hebrides. HIAL
Cumbernauld, Strathclyde.
Dounreay (Thurso). S
Dundee, Angus. M
Eday. M
Edinburgh. BAA
Fair Isle.
Fife/Glenrothes.
Flotta, Orkneys.
Glasgow. BAA
Inverness (Dalcross). HIAL
Islay (Port Ellen). HIAL
Isle of Skye. M
Kirkwall. HIAL
Lerwick (Tingwall). M
Machrihanish, Kintyre, J
North Ronaldsay, Orkneys. M
Papa Westray, Orkneys. M
Perth (Scone).
Prestwick. BAA
Sanday, Orkneys. M
Scatsta.
Stornoway, Hebrides. HIAL
Stronsay, Orkneys. M
Sumburgh, Shetlands. HIAL
Tiree. HIAL
Unst, Shetland. M
West Freugh, Wigtown. S
Westray, Orkneys. M
Whalsay, Shetlands.
Wick. HIAL

NORTHERN IRELAND
Belfast (Aldergrove). S
Belfast (Harbour).
Enniskillen (St. Angelo). M
Londonderry (Eglinton). M
Newtownards.

ISLE OF MAN
Ronaldsway. S

CHANNEL ISLANDS
Alderney. S
Guernsey. S
Jersey. S

ROADS

Highway Authorities

The powers and responsibilities of highway authorities in England and Wales are set out in the Highways Acts 1980: for Scotland there is separate legislation.

Responsibility for trunk road motorways and other trunk roads in Great Britain rests in England with the Secretary of State for Transport, in Scotland with the Secretary of State for Scotland and in Wales with the Secretary of State for Wales. The costs of construction, improvement and maintenance are paid for by central government. The highway authority for non-trunk roads in England and Wales is, in general, the county council in whose area the roads lie, and in Scotland the regional or islands council. In Northern Ireland the Northern Ireland Department of the Environment is responsible for public roads and their maintenance and construction.

Expenditure

Transport Supplementary Grant (T.S.G.) is a block grant and was introduced in England and Wales on April 1, 1975, to replace a variety of specific grants paid towards local transport expenditure.

In England grant was paid towards capital and current spending on transport by county councils and the G.L.C. from 1975–76 to 1984–85. From April 1, 1985, T.S.G. has only been paid towards capital spending on highways and the regulation of traffic, current expenditure having been subsumed by Rate Support Grant. With the abolition of the G.L.C. and the Metropolitan County Councils on April 1, 1986, grant has become payable to London Boroughs, the Common Council of the City of London and Metropolitan District Councils. In Wales, grant was also paid to the Welsh County Councils towards current and capital expenditure on transport. Since April 1982, T.S.G. became payable on capital expenditure only; current expenditure having been subsumed into the Rate Support Grant. From April 1, 1985 eligibility of new transport schemes for T.S.G. has been confined to those costing over £5 million.

Grant rates are determined by the respective Secretaries of State; at present grant is paid at 50 per cent. of expenditure accepted for grant in England and Wales. For the financial year 1988–89 local authorities in England will receive £191 million in T.S.G. In Wales local authorities will receive £19·5 million.

Total expenditure on roads (excluding New Town roads) during the financial year 1986–87 was £2,419 million in England, £403 million in Scotland and £267 million in Wales, a total of £3,089 million. Of this, some £1,091 million was spent on trunk roads and £1,998 million on principal and other roads. The amount spent on new construction and improvement of roads in the same financial year was £1,493 million.

Road Lengths (miles)
(at April 1987)

	Public Roads	Trunk Roads (incl. motorways)	*Trunk Motorways
England	166,811	6,505	1,578
Wales	20,326	1,057	75
Scotland ...	31,767	1,948	137
N. Ireland ..	14,777	1,364	70
U.K.	233,681	10,874	1,860

*There were in addition 48 miles of local authority motorway in England and 15 miles in Scotland.

Motorways

The network in England and Wales is based on five main routes—London–Yorkshire (M1), London–

South Wales (M4), Birmingham–Bristol–Exeter (M5), Birmingham–Carlisle (M6) and Lancashire–N. Humberside (M62).

Other important motorways in use include: Medway Towns (M2); London–Basingstoke (M3); London–Cambridge (M11); Rotherham–Goole (M18); London–Folkestone (M20); London orbital route (M25); London–Oxford (M40); North Cheshire (M56); and South Humberside (M180).

Motorways in use in Scotland include: Edinburgh–Glasgow–Greenock (M8); Edinburgh–Stirling (M9); Maryville–Mollisburn (M73); Millbank–Maryville (M74); Stirling–Haggs (M80); Friarton Bridge–Perth (M85); Inverkeithing–Perth (M90), and (M80)–Kincardine Bridge (M876).

Driving Tests

The number of driving tests conducted in Great Britain in 1987 was 1,951,016, of which 49·96 per cent resulted in a pass. In addition 73,632 H.G.V./P.S.V. tests were undertaken, of which 54·31 per cent. were successful. In 1987 3,471 Part I motorcycle tests were also conducted by Departmental examiners (49 per cent. successful) and 40,664 by Approved Training Bodies (96 per cent. successful).

Motor Vehicles

The number of vehicles in Great Britain with current licences in 1987 was:

Private and light goods	19,249,000
Motor cycles, scooters, mopeds	978,000
Public transport vehicles	129,000
Heavy goods vehicles	609,000
Agricultural tractors	374,000
Others	68,000
TOTAL	22,152,000

There were 744,000 Crown vehicles and vehicles exempt from licensing.

Buses and Coaches 1986–87
(Great Britain)

No. of vehicles (average)	69,500
Vehicle kilometres (millions)	3,407
Passenger journeys (millions)	5,913
Passenger receipts (£ million)	2,266

Road Accidents 1986

Road accidents	247,854
Vehicles involved:	
Pedal cycles	27,039
Motor vehicles	397,671
Total casualties	321,451
Pedestrians	60,875
Vehicle users	260,576
Killed*	5,382
Pedestrians	1,841
Pedal cycles	271
All two-wheeled motor vehicles	762
Cars & taxis	2,231
Others	277

*Died within 30 days of accident.

Year	Killed	Injured	Year	Killed	Injured
1965	7,952	389,985	1983	5,445	303,139
1970	7,499	355,869	1984	5,599	318,715
1975	6,366	318,584	1985	5,165	312,359
1980	6,010	323,000	1986	5,382	316,069

VEHICLE LICENCES, ETC.

Since October 1, 1974, registration and first licensing of vehicles has been done through local offices (known as Vehicle Registration Offices) of the Department of Transport's Driver and Vehicle Licensing Centre in Swansea. The records of existing vehicles are held at Swansea. Local facilities for relicensing are available as follows:—

(i) with a licence reminder (form V11) in person at any Post Office which deals with vehicle licensing or post it to the Post Office, shown on the form.

(ii) with a vehicle licence renewal (form V10). You may normally apply in person at any licensing Post Office. You will need to take your vehicle registration document with you: if this is not available you must complete form V62 which is held at Post Offices. Postal applications can be made to the Post Offices shown on form V100, available at any Post Office. This form also provides guidance on registering and licensing vehicles.

Details of the present duties chargeable on motor vehicles are available at Post Offices and Vehicle Registration Offices. The Vehicles (Excise) Act, 1971 provides *inter alia* that any vehicle kept on a public road but not used on roads is chargeable to excise duty as if it were in use.

Rates of duty for motor car and motor cycle licences are shown below. For Hackney Carriages the rates of duty are: Hackney Carriage with seating capacity not exceeding 20 persons, £52·50; additional for each person above 20 (excluding the driver) for which the vehicle has seating capacity, £1·05.

Type of Vehicle	Exceeding	Not Exceeding	12 Months	6 Months
MOTOR CARS			£	£
Those first constructed before January 1, 1947....	—	—	60·00	33·00
Other than above	—	—	100·00	55·00
MOTOR CYCLES				
With or without sidecar	—	150 c.c.	10·00	—
With or without sidecar	150 c.c.	250 c.c.	20·00	—
With or without sidecar	250 c.c.	—	40·00	22·00
If first constructed before 1 Jan. 1933 and weighs not more than 101·6 kgs.	250 c.c.	—	20·00	—
THREE WHEELERS				
Other than pedestrian-controlled	—	150 c.c.	10·00	—
Other than pedestrian-controlled	150 c.c.	—	40·00	22·00
PEDESTRIAN-CONTROLLED VEHICLES (Other than mowing machines)				
Three wheeled	—	150 c.c.	10·00	—
Three wheeled	150 c.c.	—	20·00	—
More than three wheels	—	—	20·00	—

Driving Licences—Fees

On or after 1.11.88

FULL LICENCE
First full licence .... £17·00*
Renewal of full licence if last full licence was:
(i) Issued before 1.1.76 .... £17·00*
(ii) Issued after 1.1.76 (not being an exchange licence and no additional entitlement claimed) .... free
New licence after a period of disqualification .... £5·00

PROVISIONAL LICENCE
First provisional licence .... £17·00*
First renewal of provisional licence issued before 1.10.82 .... £17·00

DUPLICATE LICENCE.................. £5·00
EXCHANGE LICENCE .... £5·00

* Once you have paid for *either* a provisional *or* a full licence all renewals are free except where additional entitlement is required.

Driving Test—Fees

For cars .... £16·50
For motor cycles, part I .... £17·94*
           part II .... £16·50

*When conducted by the Department of Transport. Appointed motor cycle training organizations, who conduct the majority of part I tests within the framework of their own training courses, are free to set their own fee.

Driving tests for invalid carriages are free.

M.o.T. Testing

Cars, motor cycles, motor caravans, light goods and dual-purpose vehicles more than 3 years old must be covered by an effective vehicle test certificate (often called the M.o.T. certificate). Copies of the legislation governing M.o.T. testing can be obtained from any bookshop which stocks H.M.S.O. publications. The legislation comprises The Road Traffic Act 1972 (Sections 44 and 45), The Motor Vehicles (Test) Regulations 1981, The Motor Vehicles (Extension) Order 1981, and The Motor Vehicles (Production of Test Certificate) Regulations 1969.

FUEL AND POWER

Coal: supply and demand

Million tonnes

	1981	1982	1983	1984	1985	1986
SUPPLY						
Production of deep-mined coal	110·5	106·2	101·7	35·2	75·2	90·4
Production of opencast coal	14·8	15·3	14·7	14·3	15·6	14·3
Recovered slurry, fines, etc.	2·2	3·3	2·8	1·6	3·3	3·5
Imports	4·3	4·1	4·5	8·9	12·6	10·6
Change in colliery stocks	+4·3	+0·2	+1·2	−7·9	−5·3	+0·3
Change in stocks at opencast sites	+0·5	−0·4	+0·8	+4·7	−6·3	−0·8
Total supply	127·0	128·9	121·7	63·2	118·2	119·2
HOME CONSUMPTION						
Electricity supply industry	87·2	80·2	81·6	53·4	73·9	82·6
Coke ovens	10·8	10·4	10·4	8·2	11·1	11·1
Low temperature carbonization plants	1·3	1·2	1·2	1·1	1·4	1·0
Manufactured fuel plants	1·1	1·1	0·9	0·2	0·8	1·0
Railways	0·1	0·1	—	—	—	—
Collieries	0·6	0·5	0·5	0·2	0·3	0·3
Industry (disposals to users)	7·0	7·1	7·2	6·1	7·4	8·1
Domestic (disposals to users)	8·4	8·6	8·0	6·5	8·6	8·4
Public services	1·4	1·4	1·4	1·3	1·3	1·3
Miscellaneous	0·4	0·5	0·4	0·5	0·4	0·2
Total home consumption	118·4	111·0	111·4	77·3	105·4	114·2
Overseas shipments and bunkers	9·1	7·4	6·6	2·3	2·4	2·7
Total consumption and shipments	127·5	118·4	+118·0	79·6	107·8	120·9
Change in distributed stocks*	−0·2	+10·3	+3·5	−17·1	+10·0	+4·0
Balance†	−0·3	+0·2	—	+0·7	+0·5	−1·8

*Stock change excludes industrial and domestic stocks.
†This is the balance between supply and consumption, shipments and changes in known distributed stocks.

Fuel input and gas output; gas sales

	1981	1982	1983	1984	1985	1986
FUEL INPUT TO GAS INDUSTRY:			million tonnes			
Petroleum	0·1	0·1	0·1	0·1	0·1	—
			million therms			
Petroleum gases	71	52	33	30	28	36
Natural gas	—	—	—	—	—	—
Coke oven gas	—	—	—	—	—	—
Total to gas works	100	85	61	56	57	55
Natural gas for direct supply	17,044	16,667	17,153	17,739	18,988	19,215
Total fuel input	17,144	16,752	17,214	17,794	19,046	19,270
GAS OUTPUT AND SALES			million therms			
Gas output:						
Town gas	31	26	23	21	20	18
Natural gas supplied direct	17,108	16,719	17,186	17,764	19,017	19,243
Gross total available	17,139	16,745	17,209	17,785	19,038	19,261
Own use	139	126	121	129	140	152
Statistical difference*	−378	+38	−244	−354	−508	−585
Total sales	16,622	16,657	16,844	17,302	18,390	18,524
Analysis of gas sales						
Power stations	78	76	77	178	197	75
Final users:						
Iron and steel industry	409	365	342	462	464	414
Other industries	5,261	5,319	5,295	5,258	5,319	4,677
Domestic	8,764	8,719	8,871	8,931	9,682	10,360
Public administration	966	1,003	1,050	1,071	1,183	1,279
Miscellaneous	1,144	1,175	1,210	1,337	1,474	1,652

*Supply greater than recorded demand (−). Includes losses in distribution.

Electricity: production and fuel used

	1981	1982	1983	1984	1985	1986
Electricity generated: total (GWh)	260,422	256,090	261,082	266,645	280,602	282,913
England and Wales	224,315	220,505	226,324	227,010	242,248	246,895
S. Scotland Electricity Board	25,331	23,276	20,332	22,938	25,771	23,748
N. Scotland Hydro-Electric Board	4,640	6,312	8,395	10,451	6,015	5,611
Northern Ireland	5,445	5,346	5,384	5,591	5,938	6,018
Railway and transport authorities	691	651	647	655	630	641
Method of generation (GWh)						
Steam plant, nuclear	34,043	40,001	45,776	49,498	56,354	54,005
Steam plant, other	220,849	210,545	209,116	209,711	216,830	221,981
Gas turbines and oil engines	610	580	401	2,012	1,138	609
Hydro-electric plant other than pumped storage plant	3,917	3,884	3,892	3,368	3,447	3,925
Pumped storage plant	1,003	1,080	1,897	2,055	2,831	2,394
Fuel used (Thousand tonnes)						
Coal	87,038	79,816	81,439	53,413	73,941	82,647
Coke and coke breeze	82	69	33	19	—	—
Oil	5,075	6,232	4,704	21,282	12,964	6,052
Natural gas*	313	304	311	712	762	285
Electricity sales total (GWh)	221,621	217,096	220,352	224,298	235,379	242,770
Domestic and farm premises	86,201	84,601	84,640	85,520	89,990	93,415
Domestic and commercial	2,129	2,014	1,979	1,984	1,416	1,416
Shops, offices, other commercial premises	45,359	46,134	49,019	51,039	55,420	59,200
Factories, other industrial premises	83,078	79,806	79,967	80,972	83,348	83,798
Public lighting	2,240	2,243	2,259	2,292	2,333	2,314
Traction	2,614	2,298	2,488	2,491	2,577	2,627

*Expressed in thousand tonnes of coal equivalent.

Electricity Council Finance 1986–88

	£ million	
	1986–87	1987–88
Turnover		
Electricity Supply	10,385·1	10,566·2
Contracting	183·8	199·3
Appliance Marketing	549·7	601·0
TOTAL	11,118·6	11,366·5
Operating Costs		
Electricity Supply	9,266·7	9,749·8
Contracting	174·8	189·9
Appliance Marketing	510·9	561·9
TOTAL	9,952·4	10,501·6
Operating profit/loss before monetary working capital adjustment		
Electricity Supply	1,118·4	816·4
Contracting	9·0	9·4
Appliance Marketing	38·8	39·1
TOTAL	1,166·2	864·9
Monetary working capital adjustment	16·5	50·2
Profit/loss on ordinary activities before interest	1,149·7	814·7
Interest payable	436·3	301·8
Profit/loss before taxation	713·4	512·9
Taxation	126·5	356·2
Minority interest	—	2·1
Profit/loss for the year transferred to reserves	586·9	154·6

British Coal Corporation Finance (£million)

	1986–87	1987–88
Operating Profit		
Turnover	4,515	4,388
Operating profit/(loss):		
Deep mines and related activities	67	(100)
Opencast	244	252
Total mining	311	152
Non-mining activities*	6	14
Profits from asset sales, etc.	52	50
TOTAL	369	216
Results after Interest		
Operating profit	369	216
Interest charges	(386)	(368)
LOSS	(17)	(152)
Overall result		
Loss after interest	(17)	(152)
Net restructuring costs	(259)	(387)
Taxation and extraordinary items	(12)	(1)
OVERALL DEFICIT	(288)	(540)
Government Grants		
Social cost grants	531	435
Contributions towards improved pension benefits	63	42
Total social grants	594	477
Deficit grant	288	200
TOTAL	882	677

*Includes British Coal Enterprise in 1986–87.

BRITISH GAS P.L.C.
152 Grosvenor Road, SW1V 3JL
[01–821 1444]

British Gas was privatised following the Gas Act, 1986. Its primary activities are the purchase, distribution and sale of gas. It also explores for and produces hydrocarbons.

Chairman, Sir Denis Rooke, C.B.E., F.R.S.
Chief Executive, R. Evans, C.B.E.
Secretary, G. C. Hogg.

Gas Regions

Scotland, Granton House, 4 Marine Drive, Edinburgh EH5 1YB. *Chairman*, R. W. Hill.
Northern, P.O. Box 1GB, Killingworth, Newcastle upon Tyne NE99 1GB. *Chairman*, J. H. S. Marris.
North Western, Welman House, Altrincham, Cheshire WA15 8AE. *Chairman*, R. H. Greenfield.
North Eastern, New York Road, Leeds LS2 7PE. *Chairman*, N. Blacker.
East Midlands, P.O. Box 145, De Montfort Street, Leicester LE1 9DB. *Chairman*, D. R. Atkinson.
West Midlands, Wharf Lane, Solihull, West Midlands B91 2JP. *Chairman*, C. H. Brown.
Wales, Helmont House, Churchill Way, Cardiff CF1 4NB. *Chairman*, G. H. Langshaw.
Eastern, Star House, Potters Bar, Herts. EN6 2PD. *Chairman*, G. Eccles, O.B.E.
North Thames, North Thames House, London Road, Staines, Middx. TW18 4AE. *Chairman*, A. A. Dove.
South Eastern, Katherine Street, Croydon CR9 1JU. *Chairman*, D. G. Wells.
Southern, 80 St. Mary's Road, Southampton SO9 5AT. *Chairman*, D. A. Young.
South Western, Riverside, Temple Street, Keynsham, Bristol BS18 1EQ. *Chairman*, A. I. D. Frith.

British Gas P.L.C. Finance (£ million)

	1987	1988
Turnover		
Gas supply	6,967	6,679
Installation and contracting	310	347
Appliance trading	300	307
Exploration subsidiaries	189	224
Other activities	28	27
	7,794	7,584
Less: intra-group sales	(184)	(220)
TOTAL....................	7,610	7,364
Operating costs		
Gas prime materials	3,024	2,717
Gas levy	503	469
Salaries, wages, associated costs	1,180	1,139
Cost of sales adjustment.......	2	4
Monetary working capital adjustment	(27)	(14)
Current cost depreciation	779	789
Lease rentals	34	27
Exploration expenditure	22	61
Research, testing & development	74	77
Employee profit-sharing scheme	—	38
Auditor's remuneration	0·581	0·635
Current cost pre-tax profit	1,058	1,008
Gearing adjustment	(8)	(23)
Total funds generated from operations	1,492	1,485
New Loans	—	225
Proceeds from disposal of tangible fixed assets	23	51
Total funds generated	1,515	1,761
Taxation paid	410	553
Dividends paid	—	270

BRITISH OIL STATISTICS

(million tonnes)

	1982	1983	1984	1985	1986
Oil production†					
Land	0·3	0·3	0·3	0·4	0·5
Offshore	103·1	114·6	125·6	127·1	126·5
Refinery output	70·7	70·9	73·2	72·9	74·1
Deliveries of petroleum products for inland consumption	67·2	64·5	81·4	70·1	69·2
Exports (including re-exports):					
Crude petroleum	60·4	68·3	75·9	79·6	82·1
Refined petroleum products and process oils	14·5	15·9	16·4	18·9	20·2
Imports:					
Crude petroleum	28·3	22·8	25·0	26·9	32·6
Refined petroleum products and process oils	17·2	17·3	28·5	25·0	22·9

† Crude oil plus condensates and petroleum gases derived at onshore treatment plants.

CRIMINAL STATISTICS

ENGLAND AND WALES
Notifiable offences recorded by the police (thousands)

	1982	1983	1984	1985	1986
Total	3,262·4	3,247·0	3,499·1	3,611·9	3,847·4
Violence against the person	108·7	111·3	114·2	121·7	125·5
Sexual offences	19·7	20·4	20·2	21·5	22·7
Burglary	810·6	813·4	897·5	871·3	931·6
Robbery	22·8	22·1	24·9	27·5	30·0
Theft and handling stolen goods	1,755·9	1,705·9	1,808·0	1,884·1	2,003·9
Fraud and forgery	123·1	121·8	126·1	134·8	133·4
Criminal damage	417·8	443·3	497·8	539·0	583·6
Other offences	3·8	8·7	10·4	12·2	16·7

SCOTLAND
Crimes and offences recorded by the police (thousands)

	1982	1983	1984	1985	1986
Total crimes and offences	762·5	799·6	809·4	800·4	822·4
Total crimes	435·1	448·3	474·9	462·0	463·8
Non-sexual crimes of violence against the person	12·1	13·0	13·7	15·1	15·7
Crimes involving indecency	5·0	5·5	5·7	5·7	5·4
Crimes involving dishonesty	340·1	342·5	359·2	342·3	342·5
Fire-raising, malicious and reckless conduct	66·0	73·1	79·1	79·5	78·9
Other crimes	11·9	14·3	17·3	19·2	21·4
Total offences	327·4	351·3	334·5	338·4	358·5
Miscellaneous offences	115·4	114·8	114·9	118·1	120·4
Motor vehicle offences	212·0	236·5	219·6	220·3	238·1

PRISONS

Receptions into prison: by number of previous convictions (England and Wales)

Number of previous convictions	1978	1979	1980	1981	1982	1983*†	1984*†	1985*†	1986*†
Males: total	34,832	36,412	38,016	43,388	46,779	42,716	39,930	43,626	40,004
None	1,936	1,634	1,731	1,518	1,773	1,848	1,765	1,686	2,004
1–2 sentences	2,500	2,484	2,685	3,002	3,164	2,969	2,924	3,394	3,165
3–5 sentences	5,399	5,652	6,092	7,161	7,312	6,104	5,694	6,273	5,727
6–10 sentences	9,470	9,412	9,665	11,152	11,845	10,048	9,009	9,861	8,695
11 or more sentences	11,011	11,340	11,905	13,343	14,057	13,632	13,169	13,835	11,855
Previous conviction information not recorded	4,516	5,890	5,938	7,212	8,628	8,115	7,369	8,577	8,558
Females: total	2,000	2,109	2,265	2,533	2,692	2,349	2,388	2,475	2,374
None	240	156	155	177	176	271	289	208	300
1–2 sentences	149	148	172	234	261	273	252	241	289
3–5 sentences	279	293	322	423	445	419	374	347	349
6–10 sentences	253	287	331	434	443	401	397	360	327
11 or more sentences	189	196	195	267	322	294	265	261	258
Previous conviction information not recorded	890	1,029	1,090	998	1,045	691	811	1,058	851

* From 1983 data are not comparable with previous years because of the Criminal Justice Act 1982.
† Youth custody for offenders aged 15–20 replaced imprisonment on May 24, 1983.

DUTY AND TAX-FREE ALLOWANCES

You are entitled to the allowances in either of the columns below (but not both) for any category of goods, as represented by the boxes (*see* Notes on Allowances). Passengers under 17 are not, however, entitled to tobacco and drinks allowances.

Column 1
Goods obtained duty and tax free in the E.C., or duty and tax free on a ship or aircraft, or goods obtained outside the E.C.

Column 2
Goods obtained duty and tax paid in the E.C.

Column 1	Column 2
Tobacco goods 200 cigarettes or 100 cigarillos or 50 cigars or 250 grammes of tobacco } double if you live outside Europe	**Tobacco goods** 300 cigarettes or 150 cigarillos or 75 cigars or 400 grammes of tobacco
Alcoholic drinks 2 litres of still table wine	**Alcoholic drinks** 5 litres of still table wine

plus

plus

Column 1	Column 2
1 litre over 22% vol. (e.g. spirits and strong liqueurs) or 2 litres not over 22% vol. (e.g. low strength liqueurs, fortified wine or sparkling wine) or A further 2 litres of still table wine	1½ litres over 22% vol. (e.g. spirits and strong liqueurs) or 3 litres not over 22% vol. (e.g. low strength liqueurs, fortified wine, or sparkling wine) or A further 3 litres of still table wine
Perfume 50 grammes (60 cc or 2 fl oz)	**Perfume** 75 grammes (90 cc or 3 fl oz)
Toilet water 250 cc (9 fl oz)	**Toilet water** 375 cc (13 fl oz)
Other goods £32 worth	**Other goods** £250 worth

N.B. A maximum of 50 litres of beer and 25 lighters may be imported duty-free, subject to the limitations of the 'Other goods' monetary allowance.

If you are visiting the United Kingdom for less than six months, you are also entitled to bring in, free of duty and tax, all personal effects (except tobacco goods, alcoholic drinks and perfume) which you intend to take with you when you leave.

NOTES ON ALLOWANCES

(1) The countries of the European Community are Belgium, Denmark, France, West Germany, Greece, the Irish Republic, Italy, Luxembourg, the Netherlands, Portugal, Spain (but not the Canary Islands), and the United Kingdom (but not the Channel Islands).
(2) The allowances apply only to goods carried and cleared by you at the time of your arrival.
(3) The allowances do not apply to goods brought in for sale or for other commercial purposes.
(4) Reduced allowances apply to certain persons crossing the Irish land boundary and to seamen and aircrew members.
(5) Whisky, gin, rum, brandy, vodka and most liqueurs normally exceed 22% vol. (38.8° proof) but advocaat, cassis, fraise, suze and aperitifs may be less. Fortified wines include port, sherry, vermouth and madeira. Sparkling wines include champagne, perelada, spumante and semi-sparkling wines. Still table wines include claret, Sauterne, Graves and Chianti. Burgundy, Chablis, hock and Moselle may be either sparkling or still, depending on manufacture.
(6) You may not mix goods obtained duty and tax free or outside the E.C. with goods of the same category (as represented by the boxes) obtained duty and tax paid in the E.C. to obtain the higher allowance, e.g. you will not get the higher allowance for Tobacco goods if *any* of the items in that category were obtained duty and tax free or outside the E.C.
(7) Where there are alternative quantities within a category of goods they may be apportioned. For example, 150 cigarettes (half allowance) plus 75 cigarillos (half allowance).
(8) One litre is approximately 1¾ pints or 35 fl oz.
(9) A cigarillo is a cigar with a maximum weight of 3 grammes.

PROHIBITED AND RESTRICTED GOODS

The customs officer will be able to provide full information. This is a list of more frequently met items:
    Controlled drugs, such as opium, heroin, morphine, cocaine, cannabis, amphetamines, lysergide (LSD) and barbiturates.
    Firearms (including gas pistols, electric shock batons and similar weapons), ammunition and explosives (including fireworks).
    Flick knives.

Counterfeit currency.

Horror comics. Indecent or obscene books, magazines, films, video cassettes and other articles.

Radio transmitters (walkie-talkies, Citizen's Band radios, cordless telephones, etc.) not approved for use in the U.K.

Meat and poultry, and most of their products, including ham, bacon, sausage, paté, eggs, milk and cream. (Exception: 1 kg. per passenger of fully cooked meat or poultrymeat products in cans or other hermetically-sealed containers of glass or foil).

Plants, parts thereof and plant produce, including trees and shrubs, potatoes and certain other vegetables, fruit, bulbs and seeds.

Animals and birds, whether alive or dead (e.g. stuffed), certain fish and fish eggs, whether live or dead, or bees; certain articles derived from rare species including furskins, ivory, reptile leather and goods made from them.

N.B.: Cats, dogs and other mammals must not be landed unless a British import licence (rabies) has previously been issued.

EXPORT CONTROL

The following are some of the goods subject to export control and should be declared to the customs officer. There are formalities to be completed in respect of these goods prior to your arrival at the port of exportation and further information is available through any local office of Customs and Excise (address in the telephone directory).

● Controlled drugs.

● Firearms and ammunition.

● Photographic material over 60 years old and valued at £400 or more.

● Portraits (including sculptures) of British historical personages which are over 50 years old and valued at £4,000 or more.

● Antiques, collectors' items, etc. (including paintings and other works of art) over 50 years old and valued at £16,000 or more.

● Certain archaeological material.

● Most live animals and birds, and items made from animals occurring wild in the U.K.

H.M. COASTGUARD

Founded in 1822 to guard our coasts against smuggling, H.M. Coastguard's role today is a very different one—that of complete dedication to the guarding and saving of all life at sea. Administered by the Department of Transport, it is responsible for co-ordinating all civil marine search and rescue operations around the 2,500 mile coastline of Great Britain and Northern Ireland, and 1,200 miles into the Atlantic as well as co-operating with search and rescue organizations of neighbouring countries both in Western Europe and around the Atlantic seaboard. In addition the Service maintains a 24-hour watch on the Dover Strait, providing a Channel Navigation Information Service for all shipping in one of the busiest sea lanes in the world.

Since 1978 H.M. Coastguard has been organized into six Regions, each with a Regional Controller operating from a Maritime Rescue Co-ordination Centre. Each Region is subdivided into Districts under District Controllers, operating from Maritime Rescue Sub-Centres. In all there are 24 of these major centres. They are on 24-hour watch and are fitted with a comprehensive range of communications and rescue equipment. They are supported by some 350 smaller stations manned by Auxiliary Coastguards under the direction of Regulars, each of which keeps its parent centre fully informed of day to day casualty risk, particularly on the more remote danger spots around the coast.

Between January 1 and December 31, 1987, the 560 Regular and 7,500 Auxiliary Coastguards co-ordinated 5,563 incidents requiring search and rescue facilities, resulting in assistance being given to 8,867 persons. All distress telephone and radio calls are centralized on the 24 centres, which are particularly on the alert for people or vessels in distress, shipping hazards and oil slicks. Using their modern telecommunications equipment and the facilities provided by British Telecom's Coast Radio Stations, they can alert and co-ordinate the most appropriate rescue facilities: RNLI lifeboats, Royal Navy, RAF or Coastguard helicopters, fixed-wing aircraft, Naval vessels, ships in the vicinity, and Coastguard shore and cliff rescue teams.

For those who regularly sail in local waters, or make longer passages, the Coastguard Yacht and Boat Safety Scheme provides a valuable free service. Its aim is to give the Coastguard a record of the details of craft, their normal operating areas and their passage plans. Yacht and Boat Safety Scheme Cards are available from all Coastguard stations, harbourmasters' offices and most yacht clubs and marinas.

Members of the public who see an accident or a potentially dangerous incident on or around the coast should without hesitation dial '999' and ask for the Coastguard.

LOCAL GOVERNMENT

ENGLAND AND WALES

The London Government Act, 1963, and the Local Government Acts of 1972 and 1985 have brought about the present system of local government in England and Wales. The system is based on two tiers of local authorities, county and district councils, in the non-metropolitan areas; and a single tier, of metropolitan district and London borough councils, in the six metropolitan areas of England and in London respectively.

Structures and Areas in England

England outside Greater London is divided into counties. Each county is divided into districts. Six *metropolitan counties* cover the main conurbations outside Greater London: Tyne and Wear, West Midlands, Merseyside, Greater Manchester, West Yorkshire and South Yorkshire. They are divided into 36 *metropolitan districts*, most of which have a population of over 200,000. There are 39 *non-metropolitan counties*; each of these is divided into *non-metropolitan districts*, of which there are 296. These districts have populations broadly in the range of 60,000 to 100,000: some however, have larger populations, because of the need to avoid dividing large towns, and some in mainly rural areas have smaller populations. Greater London is divided into 32 *London boroughs*, with populations between 134,000 and 390,000, and the *City*, with a daytime population of 340,000 but only 5,400 by night.

There are also about 10,000 parishes, in 219 of the non-metropolitan and 18 of the metropolitan districts.

A permanent Local Government Boundary Commission keeps the areas and electoral arrangements under review, and makes proposals to the Secretary of State for changes found necessary.

Constitution and Elections

For districts, non-metropolitan counties, London boroughs, the City, and for about 8,000 parishes, there are elected councils, consisting of directly elected councillors. Broadly, county councils range from 60–100 members; metropolitan district councils 50–80 members; non-metropolitan district councils 30–60 members. The councillors elect annually one of their number as chairman.

The general pattern in England is that councillors serve 4 years and there are no elections of district and parish councillors in county elections years. In metropolitan districts one-third of the councillors for each ward are elected each year except in the year of county elections. Non-metropolitan districts can choose whether to have elections by thirds or whole council elections. In the former case, one-third of the council, as nearly as may be, is elected in each year of metropolitan district elections. If whole council elections are chosen, these are held in the year midway between county elections. The London boroughs have whole council elections, in the year immediately following the county council election years. Local elections are normally held on the first Thursday in May.

Generally speaking, all British subjects or citizens of the Republic of Ireland of 18 years or over, resident on the qualifying date in the area for which the election is being held, are entitled to vote at local government elections. A register of electors is prepared and published annually by local electoral registration officers.

A returning officer has the overall responsibility for an election. Voting takes place at polling stations, arranged by the local authority and under the supervision of a presiding officer specially appointed for the purpose. Candidates, who are subject to various statutory qualifications and disqualifications designed to secure that they are suitable persons to hold office, must be nominated by electors for the electoral area concerned.

Internal Organization

Local authorities increasingly are organized along party political lines and over 80 per cent are now controlled by groups of councillors having allegiance to one of the main political parties. However, the council as a whole is the final decision-making body within any authority. Councils are free to a great extent to make their own internal organizational arrangements. Normally, questions of major policy are settled by the full council, while the administration of the various services is the responsibility of committees of members. Day to day decisions are delegated to the council's officers, who act within the policies laid down by the members.

Functions

Local authorities are empowered or required by various Acts of Parliament to carry out functions in their areas. The legislation concerned comprises public general Acts and "local" Acts which local authorities have promoted as private bills. In non-metropolitan areas, functions are divided between the districts and counties, those requiring the larger area or population for their efficient performance going to the county. The metropolitan district councils, with the larger population in their areas, already had wider functions than non-metropolitan councils, and following abolition of the metropolitan county councils have now been given most of their functions also. A few functions continue to be exercised over the larger area by joint bodies, made up of councillors from each district.

The allocation of functions is as follows:

county councils: education; strategic planning; traffic, transport and highways; police; fire service; consumer protection; refuse disposal; smallholdings; social services; libraries.

non-metropolitan district councils: local planning; housing; highways (maintenance of certain urban roads and off-street car parks); building regulations; environmental health; refuse collection; cemeteries and crematoria.

metropolitan district and London borough councils: their functions are all those listed above, except that fire, civil defence (and in some cases, refuse disposal) in all areas and police and passenger transport in the metropolitan counties only are exercised by joint bodies. Education in inner London is the responsibility of a special authority.

Functions exercised *concurrently* by county and district councils and London boroughs: recreation (parks, playing fields, swimming pools); museums; encouragement of the arts, tourism and industry.

The sewerage and sewage disposal functions of local authorities have been transferred to 9 water authorities in England and the Welsh Water Authority. Water authorities, however, are expected to make agreements whereby the new district councils discharge sewerage functions on an agency basis. Apart from these functions, the water authorities are responsible for water supply and conservation; river pollution control and river management; fisheries; land drainage; and use of water space for recreation and amenity purposes.

The personal health functions of local authorities were transferred in 1977 to area health authorities, whose areas were the same as non-metropolitan and Welsh counties and metropolitan districts. From April 1982 this two-tier structure was replaced by about 199 District Health Authorities. They work in close collaboration with local education, social services and environmental health authorities.

Residuary Bodies

Residuary bodies were set up in 1985 to deal with the business of the Greater London and Metropolitan County Councils which had not already devolved onto other bodies at the time of the Councils' abolition in 1986. Addresses and details of principal officers are given on page 579 (page 598 for Greater London).

Parishes

Parishes with 200 or more electors must generally have parish councils, and about three-quarters of the parishes have councils. A parish council comprises at least 5 members, the number being fixed by the district council. Elections are held every four years, in the year in which the local district councillor is elected. All parishes have parish meetings, comprising the electors of the parish. Where there is no council, the meeting must be held at least twice a year.

Parish council functions include: allotments; encouragement of arts and crafts; community halls, recreational facilities (e.g. open spaces, swimming pools), cemeteries and crematoria; and many minor functions. They must also be given an opportunity to comment on planning applications. They may, like county and district councils, spend limited sums for the general benefit of the parish. They precept on the district councils for their rate funds.

Civic Dignities

District councils may petition for a Royal Charter granting borough status to the district. In boroughs the chairman of the council is the mayor. The status "City" and the right to call the mayor "Lord Mayor" may also be granted by letters patent. Parish councils may call themselves "town councils", in which case their chairman is the "town mayor".

Charter trustees were established for those former boroughs which were too large to have parish councils when local government was reorganised in 1974 and they became part of districts without city or borough status. The charter trustees are the district councillors representing the area of the former borough and they elect a mayor, continue civic tradition, and look after the charters, insignia and civic plate of the former borough.

Local Commissioners for England and Wales

Commissioners for Local Administration in England and in Wales (*see* page 341) have been appointed with the duty of investigating complaints of maladministration in aspects of local government; they report to the local council concerned.

Wales

Since 1974 Wales, including the former Monmouthshire, has been divided into eight counties; Gwynedd; Clwyd; Powys; Dyfed; West, Mid and South Glamorgan; and Gwent. There are 37 districts in Wales, many of those in the less populated parts reflecting the areas of former Welsh counties.

The arrangements for Welsh counties and districts are generally similar to those for English non-metropolitan counties and districts. There are some differences in functions: Welsh district councils have refuse disposal as well as refuse collection functions and they may provide on-street as well as off-street car parks with the consent of the county council. A few districts have also been designated as library authorities.

In Wales parishes have been replaced by communities. Unlike England, where many areas are not in any parish, communities have been established for the whole of Wales; approximately 1,000 communities in all. Community meetings may be convened as and when desired. Community councils exist in about 770 communities and further councils may be established at the request of a community meeting. Community councils have broadly the same range of powers as English parish councils. Community councillors are elected *en bloc* on the same basis as parish councillors in England, i.e. at the same time as a district council election and for a term of four years.

Local Government Finance

Local government is financed from various sources.

(1) *Rates.*—Levied by district councils, and in London by the boroughs and City Corporation. Sums required by county and parish councils, and joint boards for police, fire and transport services in the metropolitan areas are included in the rates levied by the rating authorities. Rates are levied by a poundage tax on the rateable value of property in the area of the rating authority. The General Rate Act 1967 requires rating authorities to charge a lower rate (18½p less) in the pound on dwellings than on property generally in their area. Annual rental values on certain statutory assumptions are determined as at the date of the current valuation lists prepared by valuation officers of the Board of Inland Revenue, which came into force on April 1, 1973.

New property is added to the list and significant changes to existing property necessitate amendments to the rateable value. The lists remain in force until the next general revaluation. Certain types of property are exempt from rates, e.g. agricultural land and buildings, and places of public religious worship. Some charities and other non-profit-making organizations can receive full or partial exemption. Local authorities can rate specified classes of empty property, though these powers have been suspended in respect of empty industrial properties since April 1984 and empty warehouses since April 1985. The Social Security and Housing Benefits Act 1982 (administered by the D.H.S.S.) makes provision for rate rebates for domestic ratepayers, eligibility depending on income, rates payable and number of people in the household. The Rating (Disabled Persons) Act 1978 provides rate relief in respect of certain facilities needed by disabled persons.

The Rates Act, 1984 gives the Secretary of State for the Environment power to limit by law the rates or precepts some local councils can ask their ratepayers to pay. Twenty authorities were subject to rate limitation in 1987–88, and a further twenty (I.L.E.A. and 19 joint boards set up following the abolition of the G.L.C. and the metropolitan counties in 1986) have their precepts limited.

(2) *Government Grants.*—In addition to specific Government grants-in-aid of revenue expenditure on particular services, from April 1, 1981 grants known as rate support grants have been payable to local authorities. These grants consist of two elements: block grant and domestic rate relief grant. The block grant, which is a single grant payment, is payable to local authorities and joint boards established by the Local Government Act, 1985. The block grant is

intended to enable all authorities to provide comparable standards of service at the same poundage cost to local ratepayers. The domestic rate relief grant is payable to all rating authorities to reimburse them for the cost of giving the domestic rate relief prescribed for the year.

In order to arrive at the total amount of the rate support grants to local authorities in England for any year (the grant system provides for Wales to be administered separately), the aggregate of Exchequer grants to local authorities in respect of their relevant expenditure for the year is determined in advance (housing subsidies and specific grants towards expenditure on rate rebates and mandatory awards to students and trainee teachers are outside this aggregate amount) and from this is deducted the estimated amount of specific grants for the year in aid of revenue expenditure and the supplementary grants for transport purposes and in connection with national parks; the resulting balance is the amount of rate support grant.

Forecasts of local authority relevant expenditure for 1988–89 in England adopted by the Government for rate support grant purposes were as follows. The amounts given are at 1988–89 cash prices.

Service	£m
Education	13,420
School meals and milk	450
Libraries, museums and art galleries ..	480
Personal social services and port health............................	3,035
Police	3,350
Fire...............................	717
Other Home Office services	443
Local transport	1,950
Local environmental services.........	3,015
Agricultural services	137
Consumer protection and trading standards	76
Employment	103
Non-Housing Revenue Account housing	175
Housing benefits	187
Unallocated current expenditure	—
Total current expenditure	27,538
Rate fund revenue account contributions to capital outlay:	
Unallocated contributions to special funds, etc.	−483
Other	387
Loan charges (including leasing)......	2,757
Rate fund revenue account contributions to Housing Revenue Account..	279
Interest receipts	−632
Total relevant expenditure	29,846

The aggregate amount of Exchequer grants for 1988–89 was determined at £13,775 million. Of this, the specific grants and the transport and National Parks supplementary grants were estimated at £3,556 million, giving a total for rate support grants of £10,209 million, of which £9,482 million was in respect of the block grant and £727 million the domestic rate relief grant.

Rates and Rateable Values.—The total rateable value for England on April 1, 1987 was £7,729·5 million (figure for 1988 not yet available) and an estimate of the amount to be raised in rates, gross of rebates, in 1988–89 is £18,464 million.

Average Rates.—The estimated average rates levied in England in 1987–88 were: Inner London Boroughs, *domestic* rate 176·7p, *non-domestic* rate

181·9p; Outer London, 190·7p and 214·3p; Metropolitan Districts, 268·5p and 289·7p. The average rates levied in England were estimated at 228·9p (*domestic*) and 239·5p (*non-domestic*). In Wales the estimated average rates levied were, *domestic* rate 238·8p, *non-domestic* rate 257·6p.

SCOTLAND

Since 1975, mainland Scotland has been divided into nine regions within which there are 53 districts. Regional and district councils have separate responsibility for specific functions. In the three islands areas, Orkney, Shetland and the Western Isles, there are single tier Islands Councils responsible for most of the functions of both regional and district councils.

Local Government Electors.—In 1988 the Register shows 3,967,334 electors in Scotland. Elections are next due to take place in 1992 for district councils, and in 1990 for regional and island councils.

Functions

Regional Councils are responsible for education; social work; strategic planning; the provision of infrastructure such as roads, water and sewerage; consumer protection; flood prevention; coast protection; and valuation and rating. They also have responsibility for the police and fire services; civil defence; and electoral registration, and in relation to public transport and registration of births, deaths and marriages.

District Councils deal with more local matters such as housing; leisure and recreation, including tourism, parks, libraries, museums and galleries; development control and building control; environmental health, including cleansing, refuse collection and disposal, food hygiene, inspection of shops, offices and factories, clean air, markets and slaughterhouses, burial and cremation; licensing, including liquor, cinemas and theatres, taxis, street traders, betting and gaming, and charitable collections; allotments; public conveniences; the administration of district courts.

Community Councils—Unlike the parish councils of England or community councils of Wales, Scottish community councils are not local authorities. Their purpose as defined in statute is to ascertain and express the views of the communities which they represent, and to take in the interests of their communities such action as appears to be expedient or practicable. Schemes drawn up by district and islands councils provide for a possible total of 1,342 community councils, of which about 1,130 are in existence.

Rates

In 1986–87, the latest year for which final figures were available, a total of £1,893,800,000 was received from the general rates of local government in Scotland and £52,800,000 from domestic water rates. The rateable value on which rates were leviable was £3,190,000,000 on the general rates and £1,326,900,000 on the domestic water rates. The average general rate levied was 67·4p and the domestic water rate levied was 4·0p.

Provisional figures for 1987–88 show total receipts from general rates of £2,133,600,000 and £64,100,000 from domestic water rates. The average rate per £ levied for 1987–88 was 75·47p (general) and 4·78p (domestic water rate).

Domestic rates will be abolished with effect from April 1, 1989 and will be replaced by Community Charges.

Local Commissioner

The Commissioner for Local Administration in Scotland is responsible for investigating complaints from members of the public against local authorities (*see* page 341).

NORTHERN IRELAND

For the purpose of local government Northern Ireland has a system of 26 single-tier district councils. There are 566 members of the councils, elected for periods of four years at a time on the principle of proportional representation.

The district councils all have the same three main roles. These are:

(a) an executive role in which the councils are responsible for a wide range of local services including the provision of recreational, social, community, and cultural facilities; environmental health; consumer protection; the enforcement of building regulations; the promotion of tourist development schemes; gas supply; street cleansing; refuse collection and disposal; litter prevention; and miscellaneous

licensing and registration provisions, including dog control;

(b) a representative role in which they nominate representatives to sit as members of the various statutory bodies responsible for the administration of regional services such as education and libraries, health and personal social services, drainage, fire and electricity; and

(c) a consultative role in which they act as the media through which the views of local people are expressed on the operation in their area of other regional services notably planning, roads, and conservation (including water supply and sewerage services) provided by those departments of central government which have an obligation, either statutorily or otherwise, to consult the district councils about proposals affecting their areas.

PARTY REPRESENTATION IN LOCAL GOVERNMENT
(as at end May 1988)

Abbreviations: *A.* = Liberal/S.D.P. Alliance; *C.* = Conservative; *Com.* = Communist; *Ind.* = Independent; *Ind.C.* = Independent Conservative; *Ind.L.* = Independent Liberal; *Ind.Lab.* = Independent Labour; *Lab.* = Labour; *M.K.* = Mebyon Kernow; *N.P.* = Non-Political/Non-Party; *P.C.* = Plaid Cymru; *R.A.* = Ratepayers'/Residents' Associations; *S.D.P.* = Social Democratic Party; *S.L.D.* = Social and Liberal Democrat; *S.N.P.* = Scottish National Party.

ENGLAND

Counties

Avon .... *Lab.* 35, *C.* 31, *S.L.D.* 9, (1 Vac.).
Bedfordshire .... *C.* 30, *Lab.* 28, *S.L.D.* 11, *Ind. L.* 3, (1 Vac.).
Berkshire .... *C.* 41, *A.* 17, *Lab.* 17, *R.A.* 1.
Buckinghamshire ... *C.* 49, *Lab.* 12, *S.L.D.* 7, *Ind.* 1, *S.D.P.* 1, *Others* 1.
Cambridgeshire .... *C.* 31, *S.L.D.* 24, *Lab.* 21, *Ind.* 1.
Cheshire .... *Lab.* 32, *C.* 27, *S.L.D.* 11, *Ind. Lab.* 1.
Cleveland .... *Lab.* 51, *C.* 21, *S.L.D.* 5.
Cornwall .... *S.L.D.* 30, *Ind.* 25, *C.* 15, *Lab.* 6, *Others* 1, (2 Vac.).
Cumbria............ *Lab.* 40, *C.* 36, *Ind. L.* 5, *Ind.* 2.
Derbyshire .... *Lab.* 53, *C.* 26, *S.L.D.* 3, *Ind.* 2.
Devon.............. *C.* 39, *S.L.D.* 26, *Lab.* 10, *S.D.P.* 8, *Ind.* 2.
Dorset .... *C.* 42, *A.* 24, *Ind.* 7, *Lab.* 4.
Durham .... *Lab.* 49, *S.L.D.* 7, *C.* 6, *Ind.* 5, *Ind. Lab.* 1, *Others* 4.
Essex .... *C.* 44, *Lab.* 29, *A.* 24, *R.A.* 1.
Gloucestershire ..... *C.* 24, *S.L.D.* 23, *Lab.* 13, *Ind.* 2, *R.A.* 1.
Hampshire .... *C.* 50, *S.L.D.* 30, *Lab.* 18, *Ind.* 2, *S.D.P.* 2.
Hereford and   *C.* 39, *Lab.* 18, *S.L.D.* 13, *Ind.* 4,
Worcester .... *Ind. L.* 1, (1 Vac.).
Hertfordshire ...... *C.* 36, *Lab.* 27, *S.L.D.* 14.
Humberside .... *Lab.* 36, *C.* 35, *S.L.D.* 4.
Kent............... *C.* 57, *Lab.* 24, *S.L.D.* 18.

Lancashire .... *Lab.* 48, *C.* 42, *Ind.L.* 9.
Leicestershire ...... *C.* 42, *Lab.* 32, *S.L.D.* 10, *Ind.* 1.
Lincolnshire........ *C.* 38, *Lab.* 15, *S.L.D.* 14, *Ind. L.* 5, *Ind.* 2, *R.A.* 1, *S.D.P.* 1.
Norfolk .... *C.* 43, *Lab.* 25, *S.L.D.* 16.
Northampton-
shire.......... *C.* 34, *Lab.* 28, *Ind. L.* 4, *Ind.* 1, (1 Vac.).
Northumberland .... *Lab.* 32, *Ind. L.* 19, *C.* 12, *Ind.* 1, *S.D.P.* 1, (1 Vac.).
Nottinghamshire.... *Lab.* 46, *C.* 37, *A.* 4, *Ind. Lab.* 1.
Oxfordshire .... *C.* 31, *Lab.* 20, *S.L.D.* 18, *Ind.* 1.
Shropshire .... *C.* 27, *Lab.* 23, *S.L.D.* 9, *Ind.* 7.
Somerset .... *S.L.D.* 25, *C.* 24, *Lab.* 6, *S.D.P.* 2.
Staffordshire ...... *Lab.* 48, *C.* 29, *S.L.D.* 4, (1 Vac.).
Suffolk .... *C.* 50, *Lab.* 23, *Ind.* 4, *S.L.D.* 2, *Others* 1.
Surrey .... *C.* 49, *S.L.D.* 14, *Lab.* 7, *Ind.* 3, *R.A.* 2, *S.D.P.* 1.
Sussex, East .... *C.* 35, *S.L.D.* 21, *Lab.* 14.
Sussex, West........ *C.* 46, *S.L.D.* 17, *Lab.* 7, *Ind.* 1.
Warwickshire ...... *C.* 26, *Lab.* 23, *S.L.D.* 8, *S.D.P.* 2, *Ind.* 1, *R.A.* 1, (1 Vac.).
Wight, Isle of ...... *Ind. L.* 27, *C.* 13, *Ind.* 2, *R.A.* 1.
Wiltshire .... *C.* 31, *A.* 24, *Lab.* 17, *R.A.* 1, (1 Vac.).
Yorkshire, North ... *C.* 42, *S.L.D.* 27, *Lab.* 19, *Ind. C.* 8.

Metropolitan District Councils

GREATER MANCHESTER

Bolton .... *Ind. Lab.* 39, *C.* 16, *S.L.D.* 5.
Bury .... *Lab.* 26, *C.* 22.
Manchester........ *Lab.* 77, *C.* 13, *S.L.D.* 9.
Oldham .... *Lab.* 42, *S.L.D.* 13, *C.* 5.
Rochdale .... *Lab.* 36, *S.L.D.* 13, *C.* 11.
Salford .... *Lab.* 54, *C.* 5, *Ind. Lab.* 1.
Stockport .... *S.L.D.* 24, *C.* 22, *Lab.* 14, *R.A.* 3.
Tameside .... *Lab.* 45, *C.* 8, *Ind. L.* 4.

Trafford .... *C.* 32, *Lab.* 27, *S.L.D.* 4.
Wigan .... *Lab.* 63, *S.L.D.* 5, *C.* 3, *Ind. Lab.* 1.

MERSEYSIDE

Knowsley .... *Lab.* 60, *C.* 3, *Ind. Lab.* 1, *Ind. L.* 1, (1 Vac.).
Liverpool.......... *Lab.* 56, *S.L.D.* 39, *C.* 2, *S.D.P.* 2.

St. Helens ....*Lab.* 40, *C.* 8, *S.L.D.* 6.
Sefton.............*C.* 24, *Lab.* 24, *S.L.D.* 20, (1 Vac.).
Wirral ....*Lab.* 32, *C.* 24, *S.L.D.* 10.

SOUTH YORKSHIRE

Barnsley ....*Lab.* 62, *C.* 2, *Ind.* 1, *R.A.* 1.
Doncaster ....*Lab.* 54, *C.* 9.
Rotherham ....*Lab.* 60, *Ind. L.* 2, *C.* 1, *S.D.P.* 1, (2 Vac.).
Sheffield ....*Lab.* 66, *C.* 12, *S.L.D.* 9.

TYNE AND WEAR

Gateshead ....*Lab.* 58, *S.L.D.* 4, *C.* 3, *Ind. L.* 1.
Newcastle upon Tyne ....*Lab.* 60, *S.L.D.* 11, *C.* 6, *S.D.P.* 1.
North Tyneside .....*Lab.* 34, *C.* 16, *S.L.D.* 6, *S.D.P.* 3, *Ind. Lab.* 1.

South Tyneside .....*Lab.* 56, *C.* 3, *Others* 1.
Sunderland ....*Lab.* 62, *C.* 9, *S.L.D.* 3, (1 Vac.).

WEST MIDLANDS

Birmingham ....*Lab.* 67, *C.* 43, *S.L.D.* 6, *S.D.P.* 1.
Coventry ....*Lab.* 43, *C.* 10, *Ind. Lab.* 1.
Dudley ....*Lab.* 41, *C.* 31.
Sandwell ....*Lab.* 57, *C.* 13, *Ind. L.* 2.
Solihull ....*C.* 29, *Lab.* 14, *R.A.* 4, *S.L.D.* 4.
Walsall.............*Lab.* 32, *C.* 18, *Ind. L.* 8, *Ind.* 2.
Wolverhampton.....*Lab.* 31, *C.* 23, *Ind. Lab.* 6.

WEST YORKSHIRE

Bradford ....*Lab.* 44, *C.* 43, *S.L.D.* 2, (1 Vac.).
Calderdale.........*Lab.* 26, *C.* 18, *S.L.D.* 10.
Kirklees............*Lab.* 33, *C.* 23, *S.L.D.* 15, *Ind.* 1.
Leeds ....*Lab.* 59, *C.* 25, *S.L.D.* 14, *Ind.* 1.
Wakefield ....*Lab.* 56, *C.* 3, *S.L.D.* 2, *Ind. Lab.* 1.

Non-Metropolitan District Councils

(* one-third of councillors of Councils so denoted retire each year, except in those years when County Council elections are held)

*Adur..............*S.L.D.* 22, *C.* 15, *R.A.* 2.
Allerdale ....*Lab.* 24, *Ind.* 19, *C.* 12.
Alnwick...........*Ind. L.* 12, *C.* 3, *Ind.* 3, *Lab.* 2, *Ind. Lab.* 1, *S.L.D.* 1, *Others* 7.
*Amber Valley ......*C.* 25, *Lab.* 14, *Ind.* 3, *S.L.D.* 1.
Arun ....*C.* 51, *S.L.D.* 4, *Lab.* 1.
Ashfield ....*Lab.* 26, *C.* 4, *S.L.D.* 3.
Ashford ....*C.* 31, *S.L.D.* 10, *Lab.* 6, *Ind.* 1, *Others* 1.
Aylesbury Vale ....*C.* 33, *S.L.D.* 13, *Ind.* 8, *Lab.* 2, *S.D.P.* 1, (1 Vac.).
Babergh ....*C.* 18, *Ind.* 11, *A.* 4, *Lab.* 3, *Others* 6.
*Barrow-in-Furness ....*Lab.* 23, *C.* 14, *Ind.* 1.
*Basildon ....*Lab.* 20, *C.* 13, *S.L.D.* 9.
*Basingstoke and Deane............*C.* 33, *Lab.* 13, *S.L.D.* 9, *Ind.* 4.
*Bassetlaw ....*Lab.* 25, *C.* 19, *Ind.* 6.
*Bath ....*C.* 26, *S.L.D.* 14, *Lab.* 8.
Berwick upon Tweed ..........*S.L.D.* 13, *C.* 5, *Ind.* 3, *Lab.* 1, *Others* 6.
Beverley ....*C.* 34, *Ind. L.* 16, *Lab.* 2, *Ind.* 1.
Blaby ....*C.* 32, *Ind.* 3, *S.L.D.* 3, *Ind.* 1.
*Blackburn ....*Lab.* 31, *C.* 24, *S.L.D.* 4, *S.D.P.* 1.
Blackpool ....*C.* 23, *Lab.* 15, *S.L.D.* 6.
Blyth Valley ......*Lab.* 24, *S.L.D.* 20, *S.D.P.* 3.
Bolsover ....*Lab.* 30, *R.A.* 2, *S.L.D.* 2, *C.* 1, *Ind.* 1, *Others* 1.
Boothferry ....*C.* 17, *Lab.* 10, *Ind.* 8.
Boston ....*C.* 15, *Ind.* 8, *S.L.D.* 6, *Lab.* 5.
Bournemouth......*C.* 37, *S.L.D.* 13, *Lab.* 4, *Ind.* 3.
Bracknell Forest ...*C.* 39, (1 Vac.).
Braintree ....*C.* 30, *Lab.* 14, *Ind.* 7, *Ind. L.* 5, *R.A.* 3, (1 Vac.).
Breckland ....*C.* 33, *Lab.* 7, *Ind.* 6, *N.P.* 5, *S.L.D.* 2.
*Brentwood ....*C.* 23, *Ind. L.* 14, *Lab.* 2.
Bridgnorth ....*Ind.* 16, *C.* 11, *Ind. Lab.* 2, *Ind. L.* 2, *S.L.D.* 2.
*Brighton ....*Lab.* 27, *C.* 19, *S.L.D.* 2.
*Bristol ....*Lab.* 39, *C.* 24, *S.L.D.* 5.
*Broadland ....*C.* 35, *S.L.D.* 7, *Ind.* 6, *S.D.P.* 1, *S.L.D.* 1.
Bromsgrove ....*C.* 29, *Lab.* 7, *Ind. L.* 3, *R.A.* 1, *S.L.D.* 1.
*Broxbourne ....*C.* 36, *Lab.* 5, *S.L.D.* 1.
Broxtowe..........*C.* 32, *Lab.* 10, *S.L.D.* 6, *Ind.* 1.

*Burnley ....*Lab.* 40, *C.* 5, *S.L.D.* 5, *Ind. L.* 2, *Ind.* 1.
*Cambridge.........*Lab.* 22, *C.* 13, *S.D.P.* 7.
*Cannock Chase ....*Lab.* 25, *S.L.D.* 14, *C.* 3.
Canterbury........*C.* 33, *A.* 8, *Lab.* 5, *Ind. L.* 3.
Caradon ....*Ind.* 25, *S.L.D.* 7, *C.* 5, *R.A.* 3, *Lab.* 1.
*Carlisle ....*Lab.* 29, *C.* 19, *Lib.* 2, *Ind.* 1.
Carrick ...........*S.L.D.* 21, *C.* 15, *Ind.* 5, *Lab.* 4.
Castle Morpeth ....*S.L.D.* 12, *Ind.* 10, *C.* 5, *Lab.* 5, *Others* 2.
Castle Point ....*C.* 39.
Charnwood ....*C.* 39, *Lab.* 10, *S.L.D.* 3.
Chelmsford ........*S.L.D.* 28, *C.* 24, *Ind.* 3, *S.D.P.* 1.
*Cheltenham ....*C.* 16, *S.L.D.* 14, *Lab.* 2, *R.A.* 1.
*Cherwell ....*C.* 32, *Lab.* 14, *S.D.P.* 3, *S.L.D.* 2, *Ind.* C. 1.
*Chester ....*C.* 30, *Lab.* 19, *S.L.D.* 10, *Ind.* 1.
Chesterfield ....*Lab.* 35, *S.L.D.* 7, *C.* 5.
Chester-le-Street ...*Lab.* 24, *Ind.* 4, *Ind. L.* 4, *C.* 1.
Chichester ....*C.* 35, *A.* 12, *Ind.* 2, *R.A.* 1.
Chiltern...........*C.* 42, *A.* 6, *Lab.* 1, *R.A.* 1.
*Chorley ....*C.* 24, *Lab.* 20, *S.L.D.* 3, *Ind.* 1.
Christchurch ......*C.* 15, *Ind.* 6, *Lab.* 3, *S.L.D.* 1.
Cleethorpes........*S.L.D.* 15, *C.* 11, *Lab.* 11, *Ind.* 4.
*Colchester.........*C.* 24, *S.L.D.* 24, *Lab.* 8, *R.A.* 3, *Ind.* 1.
*Congleton .........*S.L.D.* 22, *C.* 16, *Lab.* 5, *S.D.P.* 2.
Copeland ....*Lab.* 26, *C.* 20, *Ind.* 3, *R.A.* 2.
Corby ....*Lab.* 23, *C.* 3, *Ind. Lab.* 1.
Cotswold ....*C.* 9, *Ind.* 6, *Ind. L.* 2, *Ind.* C. 1, *Lab.* 1, *Others* 26.
*Craven............*Ind. L.* 13, *C.* 12, *Ind.* 5, *Lab.* 3, *Ind. C.* 1.
*Crawley...........*Lab.* 21, *C.* 10, *S.L.D.* 1.
*Crewe and Nantwich ....*C.* 27, *Lab.* 26, *S.L.D.* 4.
Dacorum ....*C.* 40, *Lab.* 8, *S.L.D.* 7, *S.D.P.* 3.
Darlington ....*C.* 24, *Lab.* 24, *Ind.* 2, *Ind. Lab.* 2.
Dartford ....*C.* 29, *Lab.* 16, *R.A.* 2.
*Daventry..........*C.* 19, *Lab.* 9, *Ind.* 5, *S.L.D.* 1, (1 Vac.).
*Derby.............*C.* 24, *Lab.* 20.
Derbyshire Dales ...*C.* 24, *S.L.D.* 9, *Lab.* 3, *Ind.* 1, (2 Vac.).
Derwentside.......*Lab.* 43, *Ind.* 9, *C.* 3.
Dover ....*C.* 33, *Lab.* 19, *S.L.D.* 4.

Nottingham . . . . *C.* 28, *Lab.* 26, *Com.* 1.
*Nuneaton and
Bedworth . . . .*Lab.* 34, *C.* 9, (2 Vac.).
*Oadby & Wigston . .*C.* 18, *S.L.D.* 8.
Oswestry . . . .*N.P.* 13, *C.* 7, *Lab.* 5, *S.L.D.* 4.
*Oxford . . . .*Lab.* 30, *C.* 10, *S.L.D.* 5.
*Pendle . . . .*Ind. L.* 27, *Lab.* 19, *C.* 5.
*Penwith . . . .*C.* 14, *Ind.* 9, *Lab.* 7, *S.L.D.* 2,
M.K. 1, *S.D.P.* 1.
*Peterborough . . . . . .*Lab.* 22, *C.* 20, *Ind. L.* 6.
Plymouth . . . .*C.* 31, *Lab.* 20, *S.D.P.* 8, *Ind. L.*
1.
Poole . . . .*C.* 21, *S.L.D.* 15.
*Portsmouth . . . .*C.* 25, *Lab.* 8, *S.L.D.* 5, *Ind.* 1.
*Preston . . . .*Lab.* 36, *C.* 16, *Ind. L.* 5.
*Purbeck . . . .*C.* 10, *Ind.* 6, *S.L.D.* 5, *R.A.* 1.
*Reading . . . .*Lab.* 25, *C.* 13, *Ind. L.* 5, *Ind. C.*
2.
*Redditch . . . .*Lab.* 18, *C.* 9, *S.L.D.* 2.
*Reigate and
Banstead . . . . *C.* 32, *Lab.* 10, *S.L.D.* 3, *S.D.P.*
2, *Ind.* 1, *R.A.* 1.
Restormel . . . .*S.L.D.* 21, *N.P.* 10, *Ind.* 7, *C.* 4,
Ind. C. 1, *Lab.* 1.
Ribble Valley . . . . . .*C.* 33, *Lab.* 4, *Ind.* 1, *S.L.D.* 1.
Richmondshire . . . .*Ind.* 26, *S.D.P.* 6, *C.* 1, (1 Vac.).
Rochester upon
Medway . . . .*C.* 29, *Lab.* 15, *A.* 5, *Ind.* 1.
*Rochford . . . .*C.* 22, *Ind. L.* 13, *Lab.* 4, *Ind.* 1.
*Rossendale . . . .*Lab.* 22, *C.* 14.
Rother . . . .*C.* 29, *Ind.* 7, *R.A.* 3, *S.L.D.* 3,
Lab. 2, (1 Vac.).
*Rugby . . . .*C.* 25, *Lab.* 16, *R.A.* 5, *Ind.* 1,
Other 1.
*Runnymede . . . .*C.* 25, *Lab.* 8, *Ind.* 6, *S.L.D.* 2,
S.D.P. 1.
Rushcliffe . . . .*C.* 46, *S.L.D.* 6, *Lab.* 2.
*Rushmoor . . . .*C.* 32, *S.L.D.* 8, *Lab.* 5.
Rutland . . . .*C.* 9, *Ind.* 7, *Ind. L.* 3, (1 Vac.).
Ryedale . . . .*A.* 17, *Ind.* 16, *C.* 9.
*St. Albans . . . .*C.* 32, *S.L.D.* 17, *Lab.* 8.
St. Edmundsbury . . .*C.* 30, *Lab.* 8, *S.L.D.* 4, *Ind.* 2.
Salisbury . . . .*C.* 33, *Ind.* 9, *S.L.D.* 7, *R.A.* 5,
Lab. 2, *S.D.P.* 2.
Scarborough . . . .*C.* 20, *Ind.* 14, *Lab.* 8, *S.L.D.* 7.
*Scunthorpe . . . .*Lab.* 29, *C.* 7, *S.D.P.* 4.
Sedgefield . . . .*Lab.* 35, *S.L.D.* 7, *C.* 2, *Ind.* 2,
N.P. 2, (1 Vac.).
Sedgemoor . . . .*C.* 32, *S.L.D.* 7, *Lab.* 5, *Ind.* 4,
Ind. Lab. 1.
Selby . . . .*C.* 25, *Ind.* 11, *Lab.* 9, *S.L.D.* 5.
Sevenoaks . . . .*C.* 34, *Ind.* 12, *Ind. L.* 4, *S.D.P.*
3.
Shepway . . . .*S.L.D.* 27, *C.* 26, *Ind.* 3.
*Shrewsbury and
Atcham . . . .*C.* 19, *Lab.* 17, *S.L.D.* 9, *Ind.* 2,
S.D.P. 1.
*Slough . . . .*Lab.* 26, *C.* 8, *Ind. L.* 5.
*Southampton . . . . .*Lab.* 24, *C.* 17, *S.L.D.* 4.
*South Bedfordshire .*C.* 39, *Lab.* 8, *S.L.D.* 4, *R.A.* 2.
South Bucks. . . . . . .*C.* 30, *A.* 4, *R.A.* 4, *N.P.* 2, *Ind.*
1.
*South
Cambridgeshire . . .*Ind.* 29, *C.* 22, *Lab.* 3, *S.L.D.* 1.
South Derbyshire . .*Lab.* 18, *C.* 11, *Ind.* 4, *Ind. L.* 1.
*Southend-on-Sea . . .*S.L.D.* 18, *C.* 16, *Lab.* 5.
South Hams . . . .*C.* 27, *N.P.* 7, *Ind.* 6, *Ind. L.* 2,
Lab. 1, *S.L.D.* 1.
*S. Herefordshire . . .*N.P.* 17, *Ind.* 8, *C.* 5, *S.L.D.* 5.
South Holland . . . . .*C.* 13, *N.P.* 7, *Ind.* 5, *A.* 2, *Lab.*
1, *Others* 10.
South Kesteven . . . .*C.* 33, *Lab.* 10, *S.L.D.* 8, *Ind.* 5,
Ind. C. 1.
*South Lakeland . . . .*C.* 23, *S.L.D.* 10, *Lab.* 5, *Others*
13, (1 Vac.).
South Norfolk . . . . .*C.* 25, *S.L.D.* 17, *C.* 5.
South Northants. . .*C.* 28, *Ind.* 8, *Lab.* 2, *Others* 2.

South Oxfordshire .*C.* 36, *Lab.* 8, *Ind.* 6, *S.L.D.* 6.
South Ribble . . . .*C.* 37, *Lab.* 9, *Ind.* 7, (1 Vac.).
South Shropshire . .*Ind. L.* 8, *S.L.D.* 6, *C.* 5, *Ind.* 4,
Others 17.
South Somerset . . . .*S.L.D.* 34, *C.* 15, *Ind.* 11.
South Staffordshire *C.* 38, *Lab.* 4, *Ind. L.* 3, *Ind.* 2,
Others 3.
South Wight . . . .*C.* 13, *Ind.* 6, *Ind. L.* 4, *R.A.* 1.
Spelthorne . . . .*C.* 38, *Lab.* 2.
Stafford . . . .*C.* 31, *Lab.* 17, *A.* 12.
Staffordshire
Moorlands . . . .*C.* 34, *Lab.* 9, *R.A.* 6, *Ind.* 5,
S.L.D. 2.
*Stevenage . . . .*Lab.* 27, *S.L.D.* 10, *C.* 1, *Ind.*
Lab. 1.
Stockton-on-Tees . .*Lab.* 27, *C.* 18, *S.L.D.* 9, (1 Vac.).
*Stoke-on-Trent . . . .*Lab.* 54, *C.* 6.
*Stratford-on-
Avon. . . . .*C.* 35, *S.L.D.* 12, *Ind.* 6, *Lab.* 2.
*Stroud . . . .*C.* 22, *Lab.* 12, *S.L.D.* 12, *Ind.* 7,
Others 3.
Suffolk Coastal . . . . .*C.* 40, *S.L.D.* 6, *Ind.* 5, *Lab.* 1,
Others 3.
Surrey Heath . . . . . .*C.* 36.
*Swale . . . .*C.* 21, *S.L.D.* 14, *Lab.* 13, *S.D.P.*
1.
*Tamworth . . . .*C.* 15, *Lab.* 15.
*Tandridge . . . .*C.* 26, *S.L.D.* 11, *Lab.* 4, *Ind.* 1.
Taunton Deane . . . .*C.* 28, *S.L.D.* 8, *Lab.* 7, *S.D.P.* 7,
Ind. 3.
Teesdale . . . .*Ind.* 20, *Lab.* 5, *C.* 3, *Ind. Lab.*
1, *Ind. L.* 1, (1 Vac.).
Teignbridge . . . .*C.* 28, *N.P.* 24, *S.L.D.* 3, *Lab.* 2,
(1 Vac.).
Tendring . . . .*C.* 31, *S.L.D.* 15, *Lab.* 5, *R.A.* 5,
Ind. 1, *Ind. C.* 1, *Others* 2.
Test Valley . . . .*C.* 25, *S.L.D.* 14, *Ind.* 2, *N.P.* 2,
(1 Vac.).
Tewkesbury . . . .*C.* 17, *Ind.* 10, *N.P.* 9, *A.* 5, *Lab.*
1, *Others* 3.
*Thamesdown . . . . . .*Lab.* 36, *C.* 11, *S.L.D.* 6, *Ind.* 1.
Thanet . . . .*C.* 22, *Ind.* 13, *Lab.* 7, *S.D.P.* 7,
Ind. C. 3, *S.L.D.* 2.
*Three Rivers . . . . . .*S.L.D.* 24, *C.* 16, *Lab.* 7.
*Thurrock . . . .*Lab.* 29, *C.* 8, *Ind. Lab.* 2.
*Tonbridge and
Malling . . . .*C.* 32, *S.L.D.* 13, *Lab.* 6, *Ind.* 1.
*Torbay . . . .*C.* 26, *S.L.D.* 7, *Ind.* 2, *S.D.P.* 1.
Torridge . . . .*C.* 8, *Ind.* 6, *Lab.* 3, *S.L.D.* 3,
Others 16.
*Tunbridge Wells . . .*C.* 36, *S.L.D.* 10, *Lab.* 1, *Ind.* 1.
Tynedale . . . .*C.* 16, *S.L.D.* 13, *Lab.* 10, *Ind.* 8.
Uttlesford . . . .*C.* 25, *S.L.D.* 7, *Ind.* 6, *Ind. L.* 3,
Lab. 1.
Vale of White
Horse . . . .*C.* 41, *S.L.D.* 8, *Ind.* 1, *Lab.* 1.
Vale Royal . . . .*C.* 28, *Lab.* 24, *Ind.* 3, *S.L.D.* 3,
R.A. 1, (1 Vac.).
Wansbeck . . . .*Lab.* 39, *S.L.D.* 7.
Wansdyke . . . .*C.* 28, *Lab.* 16, *Ind.* 3.
Warrington . . . .*Lab.* 37, *C.* 15, *S.L.D.* 8.
Warwick . . . .*C.* 29, *Lab.* 7, *S.L.D.* 6, *R.A.* 3.
*Watford . . . .*Lab.* 16, *C.* 11, *Ind. Lab.* 6,
S.L.D. 3.
*Waveney . . . .*C.* 22, *Lab.* 20, *S.L.D.* 4, *Ind.* 1,
(1 Vac.).
Waverley . . . .*C.* 42, *S.L.D.* 9, *S.D.P.* 4, *Ind.* 2.
Wealden . . . .*C.* 49, *S.L.D.* 5, *R.A.* 4.
Wear Valley . . . .*Lab.* 26, *Ind.* 7, *C.* 3, *S.L.D.* 3,
Ind. Lab. 1.
Wellingborough . . . .*C.* 21, *Lab.* 9, *Ind.* 3, *Ind. L.* 1.
*Welwyn Hatfield . . .*Lab.* 22, *C.* 19, *S.L.D.* 2.
West Devon . . . .*C.* 11, *N.P.* 11, *Ind.* 6, *A.* 1, *Lab.*
1.
West Dorset . . . .*N.P.* 27, *C.* 11, *A.* 5, *Ind.* 4, *Ind.*
C. 3, *Lab.* 2.
*West Lancashire . . .*C.* 30, *Lab.* 23, *S.L.D.* 2.

*West Lindsey ...... *S.L.D.* 15, *C.* 12, *Ind.* 9, *Lab.* 1.
*West Oxfordshire .. *C.* 26, *Ind.* 10, *S.L.D.* 6, *Lab.* 4, *Ind. C.* 1, *Others* 2.
West Somerset ..... *N.P.* 23, *C.* 5, *Ind.* 4.
West Wiltshire..... *C.* 31, *A.* 7, *Lab.* 3, *Ind.* 1, *Ind. C.* 1.
*Weymouth and
  Portland .... *Lab.* 13, *C.* 12, *Ind. L.* 5, *Ind.* 4, *R.A.* 1.
*Winchester .... *C.* 26, *S.L.D.* 22, *Lab.* 5, *Ind.* 2.
Windsor and
  Maidenhead ...... *C.* 41, *S.L.D.* 10, *R.A.* 7.
*Woking .... *C.* 15, *S.L.D.* 14, *Lab.* 6.

*Wokingham .... *C.* 37, *A.* 15, *Lab.* 2.
Woodspring .... *C.* 45, *Lab.* 4, *Ind.* 3, *S.L.D.* 3, *S.D.P.* 2, *Ind. C.* 1, *Others* 1.
*Worcester .... *Lab.* 22, *C.* 14.
*Worthing .... *C.* 26, *S.L.D.* 10.
Wrekin .... *Lab.* 29, *C.* 11, *Ind.* 4, *A.* 2.
Wychavon......... *C.* 35, *S.L.D.* 8, *Ind.* 3, *Lab.* 3.
Wycombe......... *C.* 49, *Lab.* 4, *Ind.* 2, *S.L.D.* 2, *Ind. L.* 1, *S.D.P.* 1, (1 Vac.).
Wyre .... *C.* 43, *Lab.* 7, *Ind. L.* 4, *Ind. Lab.* 1, *R.A.* 1.
*Wyre Forest ...... *A.* 16, *C.* 13, *Lab.* 10, *Ind.* 3.
*York .... *Lab.* 29, *C.* 10, *S.L.D.* 6.

Greater London Boroughs

Barking .... *Lab.* 36, *S.L.D.* 5, *C.* 3, *R.A.* 3, (1 Vac.).
Barnet .... *C.* 39, *Lab.* 18, *S.L.D.* 3.
Bexley .... *C.* 37, *Lab.* 15, *S.L.D.* 10.
Brent .... *Lab.* 41, *C.* 21, *S.L.D.* 4.
Bromley.......... *C.* 44, *Lab.* 10, *S.L.D.* 6.
Camden .... *Lab.* 44, *C.* 13, *S.L.D.* 2.
Croydon .... *C.* 44, *Lab.* 24, (2 Vac.).
Ealing .... *Lab.* 47, *C.* 20, *S.L.D.* 3.
Enfield .... *C.* 40, *Lab.* 26.
Greenwich .... *Lab.* 42, *C.* 12, *S.L.D.* 8.
Hackney .... *Lab.* 48, *S.L.D.* 5, *C.* 4, (3 Vac.).
Hammersmith .... *Lab.* 40, *C.* 9, *Ind. L.* 1.
Haringey .... *Lab.* 41, *C.* 17, *Ind. L.* 1.
Harrow .... *C.* 31, *Ind. L.* 18, *Lab.* 8, *R.A.* 4, *Ind. C.* 1, *Ind. Lab.* 1.
Havering.......... *C.* 28, *Lab.* 20, *R.A.* 10, *S.L.D.* 5.
Hillingdon......... *Lab.* 34, *C.* 28, *S.L.D.* 7.
Hounslow .... *Lab.* 40, *C.* 17, *S.L.D.* 3.

Islington .... *Lab.* 36, *A.* 16.
Kensington and
  Chelsea .... *C.* 39, *Lab.* 14, *Ind. Lab.* 1.
Kingston-upon-
  Thames .... *C.* 26, *S.L.D.* 20, *Lab.* 4.
Lambeth .... *Lab.* 40, *C.* 21, *S.L.D.* 3.
Lewisham .... *Lab.* 48, *C.* 18, *S.D.P.* 1.
Merton........... *C.* 29, *Lab.* 25, *S.L.D.* 3.
Newham .... *Lab.* 59, *S.L.D.* 1.
Redbridge .... *C.* 45, *Lab.* 17, *S.L.D.* 1.
Richmond upon
  Thames .... *S.L.D.* 46, *C.* 4, *S.D.P.* 2.
Southwark .... *Lab.* 43, *S.L.D.* 11, *C.* 7.
Sutton .... *S.L.D.* 28, *C.* 21, *Lab.* 7.
Tower Hamlets .... *Ind. L.* 25, *Lab.* 24, *S.L.D.* 1.
Waltham Forest..... *Lab.* 29, *C.* 16, *S.L.D.* 11, (1 Vac.).
Wandsworth....... *C.* 31, *Lab.* 30.
Westminster ...... *C.* 32, *Lab.* 27, *Ind.* 1.

WALES
County Councils

Clwyd............. *Lab.* 25, *Ind.* 19, *C.* 15, *Others* 7.
Dyfed .... *Ind.* 34, *Lab.* 30, *Ind. L.* 7, *P.C.* 5, *Ind. Lab.* 1, *R.A.* 1, *S.D.P.* 1, (1 Vac.).
Gwent .... *Lab.* 67, *C.* 9, *Ind. L.* 1, *P.C.* 1.
Gwynedd.......... *Ind.* 40, *N.P.* 10, *Lab.* 6, *S.L.D.* 4, *C.* 3, *Ind. L.* 3.
Mid Glamorgan ..... *Lab.* 68, *P.C.* 7, *Ind.* 3, *A.* 1,

C. 1, *Com.* 1, *Ind. L.* 1, *R.A.* 1, *S.D.P.* 1, *Others* 1.
Powys............. *Ind.* 41, *Lab.* 8, *S.L.D.* 3, (1 Vac.).
South Glamorgan ... *Lab.* 34, *C.* 18, *S.L.D.* 5, *S.D.P.* 4, *P.C.* 1.
West Glamorgan .... *Lab.* 53, *C.* 7, *S.L.D.* 5, *R.A.* 2, *Ind.* 1, *N.P.* 1, (1 Vac.).

District Councils

Aberconwy .... *N.P.* 12, *A.* 11, *C.* 8, *Ind.* 5, *Lab.* 4, *P.C.* 1.
Alyn & Deeside .... *Lab.* 25, *C.* 8, *Ind.* 6, *S.L.D.* 4.
Arfon .... *Ind.* 14, *P.C.* 13, *Lab.* 11, *S.L.D.* 1.
Blaenau Gwent ..... *Lab.* 35, *R.A.* 4, *C.* 1, *Ind.* 1, *Ind. L.* 1, *Ind. Lab.* 1, *P.C.* 1.
Brecknock......... *Ind.* 30, *Lab.* 13, *Ind. L.* 1.
Cardiff .... *Lab.* 28, *C.* 24, *S.L.D.* 12, (1 Vac.).
Carmarthen .... *Ind.* 28, *Lab.* 4, *P.C.* 2, *R.A.* 2, *S.L.D.* 1.
Ceredigion .... *Ind.* 22, *A.* 16, *P.C.* 4, *Lab.* 2.
Colwyn .... *S.L.D.* 15, *Ind.* 11, *C.* 3, *R.A.* 3, *Lab.* 2.
Cynon Valley ...... *Lab.* 30, *P.C.* 5, *Ind.* 1, *Ind. Lab.* 1, *Com.* 1.
Delyn .... *Ind.* 19, *Lab.* 11, *S.L.D.* 5, *C.* 3, *Ind. Lab.* 3, *P.C.* 1.
Dinefwr........... *Lab.* 18, *Ind.* 11, *P.C.* 2, *Ind. Lab.* 1.
Dwyfor............ *P.C.* 6, *Others* 23.
Glyndwr .... *Ind.* 29, *Lab.* 3, *S.L.D.* 3.
Islwyn .... *Lab.* 23, *P.C.* 10, *S.D.P.* 1, (1 Vac.).

Llanelli .... *Lab.* 25, *S.L.D.* 3, *Ind.* 2, *Ind. Lab.* 1, *Others* 4.
Lliw Valley .... *Lab.* 24, *Ind.* 5, *P.C.* 3, *C.* 1.
Meirionnydd .... *N.P.* 27, *P.C.* 7, *Lab.* 6, *Ind.* 1.
Merthyr Tydfil ..... *Lab.* 22, *R.A.* 7, *Ind.* 3, *P.C.* 1.
Monmouth .... *C.* 26, *Lab.* 13, *Ind.* 1.
Montgomery-
  shire .... *N.P.* 39, *Ind.* 3, *Ind. L.* 2, *Lab.* 1, *P.C.* 1.
Neath .... *Lab.* 30, *S.D.P.* 2, *Com.* 1, *P.C.* 1.
Newport .... *Lab.* 40, *C.* 7.
Ogwr .... *Lab.* 30, *C.* 17, *Ind.* 2.
Port Talbot .... *Lab.* 24, *R.A.* 4, *Ind.* 1, *S.D.P.* 1, *S.L.D.* 1.
Preseli
  Pembrokeshire.... *Ind.* 36, *S.L.D.* 2, *C.* 1, *Lab.* 1.
Radnor............ *N.P.* 25, *R.A.* 4, *Ind.* 3, *Lab.* 1.
Rhondda .... *Lab.* 26, *R.A.* 4, *P.C.* 2, *Ind.* 1.
Rhuddlan .... *Ind.* 20, *C.* 6, *Lab.* 6.
Rhymney Valley .... *Lab.* 32, *P.C.* 7, *Ind. Lab.* 2, *R.A.* 2, *Ind.* 1, *Ind. L.* 1, *Others* 1.
S. Pembrokeshire.... *N.P.* 24, *Ind.* 2, *Lab.* 2, *P.C.* 1, *S.L.D.* 1.

Swansea............*Lab.* 29, *C.* 10, *S.L.D.* 7, *Ind.* 3, *R.A.* 2.
Taff-Ely ....*Lab.* 23, *P.C.* 10, *Ind.* 3, *R.A.* 3, *Ind. L.* 2, *S.L.D.* 1.
Torfaen ....*Lab.* 33, *Ind.* 6, *C.* 1, *Com.* 1, *Ind. Lab.* 1, *R.A.* 1, *S.D.P.* 1.

Vale of Glamorgan . . *C.* 26, *Lab.* 14, *P.C.* 4, *Ind.* 2.
Wrexham Maelor . . .*Lab.* 26, *C.* 9, *Ind.* 4, *A.* 3, *P.C.* 1, *Others* 2, (1 Vac.).
Ynys Môn ..........*N.P.* 29, *Lab.* 4, *P.C.* 3, *Ind.* 2, *C.* 1.

SCOTLAND
Scottish Regional Councils

Borders ....*Ind.* 10, *C.* 4, *A.* 4, *N.P.* 3, *S.N.P.* 1, (1 Vac.).
Central ....*Lab.* 23, *S.N.P.* 5, *C.* 4, *Ind.* 1, *A.* 1.
Dumfries &
  Galloway........*Lab.* 8, *S.N.P.* 5, *Ind.* 4, *A.* 3, *Others* 15.
Fife ....*Lab.* 28, *S.L.D.* 8, *C.* 3, *Ind.* 3, *S.N.P.* 3, *Com.* 1.
Grampian ....*Lab.* 16, *C.* 15, *S.L.D.* 12, *S.N.P.* 7, *Ind.* 4, *S.D.P.* 1, (2 Vac.).

Highland ...........*N.P.* 25, *Ind.* 13, *Lab.* 7, *Ind. L.* 3, *C.* 2, *S.N.P.* 2.
Lothian ....*Lab.* 32, *C.* 13, *S.L.D.* 3, *S.N.P.* 1.
Orkney ............*N.P.* 24.
Shetland ...........*N.P.* 25.
Strathclyde........*Lab.* 87, *C.* 6, *S.L.D.* 5, *S.N.P.* 3, *Ind.* 2.
Tayside ....*Lab.* 19, *C.* 14, *S.N.P.* 9, *Ind.* 2, *Ind. Lab.* 1, *S.L.D.* 1.
Western Isles .......*N.P.* 30.

Scottish District Councils

Aberdeen...........*Lab.* 28, *S.L.D.* 14, *C.* 9, *S.N.P.* 1.
Angus..............*S.N.P.* 13, *C.* 6, *Ind.* 1, *Others* 1.
Annandale
  & Eskdale ....*Ind. L.* 8, *Ind.* 6, *Lab.* 2.
Argyll & Bute......*Ind.* 9, *C.* 3, *S.L.D.* 3, *S.N.P.* 3, *Lab.* 1, *Others* 7.
Badenoch and
  Strathspey ....*Ind.* 10, *S.N.P.* 1.
Banff & Buchan .....*Ind.* 9, *S.N.P.* 9.
Bearsden and
  Milngavie ....*C.* 6, *S.L.D.* 2, *Ind.* 1, *Lab.* 1.
Berwickshire ....*C.* 9, *Ind.* 1, *S.L.D.* 1, (1 Vac.).
Caithness ..........*N.P.* 12, *Lab.* 2, *Ind.* 1, *Ind. L.* 1.
Clackmannan......*Lab.* 9, *C.* 1, *S.N.P.* 1, (1 Vac.).
Clydebank..........*Lab.* 11, *C.* 1.
Clydesdale.........*Lab.* 9, *S.N.P.* 4, *Ind.* 2, *C.* 1.
Cumbernauld
  & Kilsyth........*Lab.* 6, *S.N.P.* 6.
Cumnock and
  Doon Valley ......*Lab.* 8, *Ind. Lab.* 1, *S.D.P.* 1.
Cunninghame .....*Lab.* 24, *C.* 4, *Ind.* 2.
Dumbarton ....*Lab.* 7, *C.* 4, *S.N.P.* 3, *Ind.* 1, *N.P.* 1.
Dundee ....*Lab.* 29, *C.* 9, *S.N.P.* 5, *Ind. C.* 1.
Dunfermline.......*Lab.* 25, *C.* 3, *S.L.D.* 3, *S.N.P.* 3.
East Kilbride ......*Lab.* 14, *C.* 2..
East Lothian.......*Lab.* 12, *C.* 4, *Ind. Lab.* 1.
Eastwood...........*C.* 8, *R.A.* 2, *Lab.* 1, *S.L.D.* 1.
Edinburgh.........*Lab.* 33, *C.* 23, *S.L.D.* 4, *S.N.P.* 2.
Ettrick and   *Ind.* 4, *C.* 1, *Lab.* 1, *S.N.P.* 1,
  Lauderdale ....   *Others* 9.
Falkirk ....*Lab.* 20, *S.N.P.* 10, *C.* 3, *Ind.* 2, *Ind. Lab.* 1.
Glasgow............*Lab.* 60, *C.* 4, *S.L.D.* 2.
Gordon.............*S.L.D.* 10, *Ind.* 6.

Hamilton ....*Lab.* 15, *S.L.D.* 2, *C.* 1, *Ind. Lab.* 1, *S.N.P.* 1.
Inverclyde.........*Lab.* 12, *S.L.D.* 7, *C.* 1.
Inverness ....*Ind.* 14, *Lab.* 12, *Ind. L.* 2.
Kilmarnock and
  Loudoun ....*Lab.* 12, *C.* 3, *S.N.P.* 3.
Kincardine and
  Deeside ....*Ind.* 6, *S.L.D.* 3, *C.* 2, *S.N.P.* 1.
Kirkcaldy ....*Lab.* 33, *C.* 2, *Ind.* 2, *S.N.P.* 2, *S.L.D.* 1.
Kyle and Carrick....*Lab.* 16, *C.* 7, *Ind. C.* 1, *Ind. Lab.* 1.
Lochaber ....*Ind.* 7, *Lab.* 4, *Ind. Lab.* 3, *N.P.* 1.
Midlothian ....*Lab.* 14, *C.* 1.
Monklands ....*Lab.* 18, *S.N.P.* 2.
Moray .............*S.N.P.* 8, *N.P.* 5, *Ind.* 3, *Lab.* 2.
Motherwell ....*Lab.* 23, *S.N.P.* 3, *C.* 2, *Ind. Lab.* 1, *N.P.* 1.
Nairn ....*Ind.* 9, *C.* 1.
Nithsdale...........*Lab.* 12, *S.N.P.* 6, *C.* 4, *Ind.* 4, *Others* 2.
N.E. Fife ..........*S.L.D.* 12, *C.* 4, *Ind.* 2.
Perth and Kinross...*C.* 12, *S.N.P.* 8, *Lab.* 5, *Ind.* 2, *S.L.D.* 2.
Renfrew............*Lab.* 32, *C.* 6, *S.N.P.* 5, *Ind. L.* 1, *S.D.P.* 1.
Ross & Cromarty ....*Ind.* 18, *Lab.* 2, *C.* 1, *S.N.P.* 1.
Roxburgh ....*Ind.* 7, *N.P.* 4, *C.* 2, *S.N.P.* 2, *S.L.D.* 1.
Skye & Lochalsh ....*Ind.* 10, *S.L.D.* 1.
Stewartry ..........*N.P.* 9, *Ind.* 3.
Stirling ....*Lab.* 10, *C.* 10.
Strathkelvin.......*Lab.* 12, *C.* 2, *S.L.D.* 1.
Sutherland ....*Ind.* 13, (1 Vac.).
Tweeddale..........*Ind.* 7, *C.* 1, *Lab.* 1, *S.N.P.* 1.
West Lothian ....*Lab.* 14, *S.N.P.* 7, *Ind.* 3.
Wigtown ...........*N.P.* 9, *Ind.* 3, *Lab.* 1, *S.N.P.* 1.

REGIONAL WATER AUTHORITIES

THAMES WATER AUTHORITY, Nugent House, Vastern Road, Reading RG1 8DB.
SOUTHERN WATER AUTHORITY, Guildborne House, Worthing, Sussex.
SEVERN TRENT WATER AUTHORITY, Abelson House, 2297 Coventry Road, Sheldon, Birmingham.
WESSEX WATER AUTHORITY, Wessex House, Passage Street, Bristol.
ANGLIAN WATER AUTHORITY, Ambury House, Huntingdon.
SOUTH WEST WATER AUTHORITY, Peninsula House, Rydon Lane, Exeter EX2 7HR.

NORTHUMBRIAN WATER AUTHORITY, Northumbria House, Regent Centre, Gosforth, Newcastle-upon-Tyne.
NORTH WEST WATER AUTHORITY, Dawson House, Great Sankey, Warrington.
YORKSHIRE WATER AUTHORITY, West Riding House, 67 Albion Street, Leeds.
WELSH WATER AUTHORITY, Cambrian Way, Brecon, Powys.
THE WATER AUTHORITIES ASSOCIATION, 1 Queen Anne's Gate, SW1H 9BT [01-222 8111]—*Secretary*, M. Carney.

The Kingdom of England

Position and Extent.—The Kingdom of England lies between 55° 46′ and 49° 57′ 30″ N. latitude (from a few miles north of the mouth of the Tweed to the Lizard), and between 1° 46′ E. and 5° 43′ W. (from Lowestoft to Land's End). England is bounded on the north by the Cheviot Hills; on the south by the English Channel; on the east by the Straits of Dover (Pas de Calais) and the North Sea; and on the West by the Atlantic Ocean, Wales and the Irish Sea.

It has a total area of 50,363 sq. miles (land 50,070; inland water 293). The population (1981 Census) was 46,362,836 (males 22,520,723; females 23,842,113). The average density of the population in 1981 was 915 per square mile. The population, mid-1986 estimate, was 47,254,000.

Relief.—There is a marked division between the upland and lowland areas of England. In the extreme north the Cheviot Hills (highest point, *The Cheviot*, 2,674 ft.) form a natural boundary with the Kingdom of Scotland. Running south from the Cheviots, though divided from them by the Tyne Gap, is the Pennine range (highest point, *Cross Fell*, 2,930 ft.), the main orological feature of the country. The Pennines culminate in the Peak District of Derbyshire (*Kinder Scout*, 2,088 ft.). West of the Pennines are the Cumbrian mountains, which include *Scafell Pike* (3,210 ft.), the highest peak in England, and to the east are the Yorkshire Moors, their highest point being *Urra Moor* (1,490 ft.).

In the west, the foothills of the Welsh mountains extend into the bordering English counties of Shropshire (the *Wrekin*, 1,334 ft.; *Long Mynd*, 1,694 ft.) and Hereford and Worcester (the Malvern Hills—*Worcestershire Beacon*, 1,394 ft.). Extensive areas of high land and moorland are also to be found in the southwestern peninsula formed by Somerset, Devon and Cornwall: principally Exmoor (*Dunkery Beacon*, 1,704 ft.), Dartmoor (*High Willhays*, 2,038 ft.) and Bodmin Moor (*Brown Willy*, 1,377 ft.). Ranges of low, undulating hills run across the south of the country, including the Cotswolds in the Midlands and southwest, the Chilterns to the north of Greater London, and the North (Kent) and South (Sussex) Downs of the south-east coastal areas.

The lowlands of England lie in the Vale of York, East Anglia and the area around the Wash, the lowest lying being the Cambridgeshire Fens in the valleys of the Great Ouse and the River Nene, which are below sea-level in places; since the 17th century extensive drainage has brought much of the Fens under cultivation. The North Sea coast between the Thames and the Humber, low-lying and formed of sand and shingle for the most part, is subject to erosion and defences against further incursion have been built along many stretches.

Hydrography.—The *Severn* is the longest river in Great Britain, rising in the north-eastern slopes of Plinlimmon (Wales) and entering England in Shropshire with a total length of 220 miles from its source to its outflow into the Bristol Channel, where it receives on the east the Bristol Avon, and on the west the Wye, its other tributaries being the Vrynwy, Tern, Stour, Teme and Upper (or Warwickshire) Avon. The Severn is tidal below Gloucester, and a high bore or tidal wave sometimes reverses the flow as high as Tewkesbury (13½ miles above Gloucester). The scenery of the greater part of the river is very picturesque and beautiful, and the Severn is a noted salmon river, some of its tributaries being famous for trout. Navigation is assisted by the Gloucester and Berkeley Ship Canal (16¾ miles), which admits vessels of 350 tons to Gloucester. The *Severn Tunnel*, begun

in 1873 and completed in 1886 (at a cost of £2,000,000) after many difficulties from flooding, is 4 miles 628 yards in length (of which 2¼ miles are under the river). The Severn road bridge between Haysgate, Gwent, and Almondsbury, Glos., with a centre span of 3,240 ft. was opened in 1966.

The longest river wholly in England is the *Thames*, with a total length of 215 miles from its source in the Cotswold hills to the Nore, and is navigable by ocean-going ships to London Bridge. The Thames is tidal to Teddington (69 miles from its mouth) and forms county boundaries almost throughout its course; on its banks are situated London, Windsor Castle, the home of the Sovereign, Eton College, the first of the public schools, and Oxford, the oldest university in the kingdom.

Of the remaining English rivers those flowing into the North Sea are the Tyne, Wear, Tees, Ouse and Trent from the Pennine Range, the Great Ouse (160 miles) from Northamptonshire, and the Orwell and Stour from the hills of East Anglia. Flowing into the English Channel are the Sussex Ouse from the Weald, the Itchen from the Hampshire Hills, and the Axe, Teign, Dart, Tamar and Exe from the Devonian hills; and flowing into the Irish Sea are the Mersey, Ribble and Eden from the western slopes of the Pennines and the Derwent from the Cumbrian mountains. The English Lakes, noteworthy for their picturesque scenery and poetic associations, lie in Cumbria, the largest being *Windermere* (10 miles long), *Ullswater* and *Derwentwater*.

Islands.—The *Isle of Wight* is separated from Hampshire by the Solent; total area 147 sq. miles, population about 124,600. The climate is mild and healthy, making the island a popular holiday resort. Capital, Newport, at the head of the estuary of the Medina, Cowes (at the mouth) being the chief port; other centres are Ryde, Sandown, Shanklin, Ventnor, Freshwater, Yarmouth, Totland Bay, Seaview and Bembridge.

Lundy (= Puffin Island) 11 miles N.W. off Hartland Point, Devon, is about 2 miles long and about half a mile broad (average), with a total area of about 1,116 acres, and a population of about 20; it became the property of the National Trust in 1969 and is now principally a bird sanctuary.

(*See also* The Isles of Scilly, p. 624.)

Climate.—England has a generally mild and temperate climate. Because of the prevailing southwesterly winds, the weather day to day is variable, being affected mainly by depressions moving eastwards across the Atlantic Ocean. This maritime influence means that the west of the country tends to experience wetter but also milder weather than the east. Rainfall also increases with altitude, the mountainous areas of the north and west having more rain than the lowlands of the south and east. Rain is fairly well-distributed throughout the year in all areas but, on average, the driest months are March to June, and the wettest September to January.

The mean annual temperature reduced to sea-level varies from 11°C in the south-west to 9°C near Berwick-on-Tweed. In winter, temperatures tend to be higher in the south and west than in the east, while the warmest in summer are the south and inland areas. Latitude for latitude the mean annual temperature is lower in the east; the decrease of mean temperature with height is about 0·6°C per 100 metres.

EARLY INHABITANTS

Prehistoric Man.—Archaeological evidence suggests that England has been inhabited since at least the Palaeolithic period, though the extent of the various Palaeolithic cultures was dependent upon the degree of glaciation. The succeeding Neolithic and Bronze Age cultures have left abundant remains throughout the country, the best-known of these being the henges and stone circles of Stonehenge (10 miles north of Salisbury, Wilts.) and Avebury (Wilts.), both of which are believed to have been of religious significance. In the latter part of the Bronze Age the Goidels, a people of Celtic race, and in the Iron Age other Celtic races of Brythons and Belgae, invaded the country and brought with them Celtic civilization and dialects, place names in England bearing witness to the spread of the invasion over the whole kingdom.

The Roman Conquest.—The Roman conquest of Gaul (57–50 B.C.) brought Britain into close contact with Roman civilization, but although Julius Cæsar raided the south of Britain in 55 B.C., and 54 B.C., conquest was not undertaken until nearly 100 years later. In A.D. 43 the Emperor Claudius dispatched Aulus Plautius, with a well-equipped force of 40,000, and himself followed with reinforcements in the same year. Success was delayed by the resistance of Caratacus (Caractacus), the British leader from A.D. 48–51, who was finally captured and sent to Rome, and by a great revolt in A.D. 61 led by Boudicca (Boadicea), Queen of the Iceni; but the south of Britain was secured by A.D. 70, and Wales and the area north to the Tyne by about A.D. 80.

In A.D. 122, the Emperor Hadrian visited Britain and built a continuous rampart, since known as Hadrian's Wall, from Wallsend to Bowness (Tyne to Solway). The work was entrusted by the Emperor Hadrian to Aulus Platorius Nepos, legate of Britain from 122 to 126, and it was intended to form the northern frontier of the Roman Empire.

The Romans administered Britain as a Province under a Governor, with a well-defined system of local government, each Roman municipality ruling itself and surrounding territory, while London was the centre of the road system and the seat of the financial officials of the Province of Britain. Colchester, Lincoln, York, Gloucester and St. Albans stand on the sites of five Roman municipalities, and Wroxeter, Caerleon, Chester, Lincoln and York were at various times the sites of legionary fortresses. Well-preserved Roman towns have been uncovered at (or near) Silchester (*Calleva Atrebatum*), 10 miles south of Reading, Wroxeter (*Viroconium Cornoviorum*), near Shrewsbury, and St. Albans (*Verulamium*) in Hertfordshire.

Four main groups of roads radiated from London, and a fifth (the Fosse) ran obliquely from Lincoln through Leicester, Cirencester and Bath to Exeter. Of the four groups radiating from London one ran S.E. to Canterbury and the coast of Kent, a second to Silchester and thence to parts of Western Britain and South Wales, a third (later known as Watling Street) ran through Verulamium to Chester, with various branches, and the fourth reached Colchester, Lincoln, York and the eastern counties.

In the 4th century Britain was subject to raids along the east coast by Saxon pirates, which led to the establishment of a system of coast defence from the Wash to Southampton Water, with forts at Brancaster, Burgh Castle (Yarmouth), Walton (Felixstowe), Bradwell, Reculver, Richborough, Dover, Lympne, Pevensey and Porchester (Portsmouth). The Irish (Scoti) and Picts in the north were also becoming more aggressive; from about A.D. 350

incursions became more frequent and more formidable. As the Roman Empire came under attack increasingly towards the end of the 4th century many troops were removed from Britain for service in other parts of the Empire. The island was eventually cut off from Rome by the Teutonic conquest of Gaul, and with the withdrawal of the last Roman garrison early in the 5th century, the Romano-British were left to themselves.

According to legend, the British King Vortigern called in the Saxons to defend him against the Picts, the Saxon chieftains being Hengist and Horsa, who landed at Ebbsfleet, Kent, and established themselves in the Isle of Thanet; but the events during the one and a half centuries between the final break with Rome and the re-establishment of Christianity are unclear. However, it would appear that in the course of this period the raids turned into large-scale settlement by invaders traditionally known as Angles (England north of the Wash and East Anglia), Saxons (Essex and southern England) and Jutes (Kent and the Weald), which pushed the Romano-British into the mountainous areas of the north and west, Celtic culture outside Wales and Cornwall surviving only in topographical names. Various kingdoms were established at this time which attempted to claim overlordship of the whole country, hegemony finally being achieved by Wessex (capital, Winchester) in the 9th century. This century also saw the beginning of raids by the Vikings (Danes), which were resisted by Alfred the Great (871–899), the greatest of the Wessex kings, who fixed a limit to the advance of Danish settlement by the Treaty of Wedmore (878), giving them the area north and east of Watling Street, on condition they adopt Christianity.

In the 10th century the Kings of Wessex recovered the whole of England from the Danes, but subsequent rulers were unable to resist a second wave of invaders. England paid tribute (*Danegeld*) for many years, and was invaded in 1013 by the Danes and ruled by Danish Kings from 1016 until 1042, when Edward the Confessor was recalled from exile in Normandy. In 1066 Harold Godwinson (brother-in-law of Edward and son of Earl Godwin of Wessex) was chosen King of England. After defeating (at Stamford Bridge, Yorkshire, Sept. 25) an invading army under Harald Hadraada, King of Norway (aided by the outlawed Earl Tostig of Northumbria, Harold's brother), Harold was himself defeated at the Battle of Hastings on Oct. 14, 1066, and the Norman Conquest secured the throne of England for Duke William of Normandy, a cousin of Edward the Confessor.

Christianity reached the Roman province of Britain from Gaul in the 3rd century (or possibly earlier); Alban, traditionally Britain's first martyr, was put to death as a Christian during the persecution of Diocletian (June 22, 303), at his native town Verulamium; and the Bishops of Londinium, Eboracum (York), and Lindum (Lincoln) attended the Council of Arles in 314. However, the Anglo-Saxon invasions submerged the Christian religion in England until the 6th century when conversion was undertaken in the north from 563 by Celtic missionaries from Ireland led by St. Columba, and in the south by a mission sent from Rome in 597 which was led by St. Augustine, who became the first archbishop of Canterbury. England appears to have been converted again by the end of the 7th century and followed, after the Council of Whitby in 663, the practices of the Roman Church, which brought the country into the mainstream of European thought and culture.

ENGLISH COUNTIES AND SHIRES
LORD LIEUTENANTS AND HIGH SHERIFFS

County or Shire	Lord Lieutenant	*High Sheriff, 1988–89
Avon	Sir John Wills, Bt., T.D.	C. R. T. Laws
Bedfordshire	Lt. Col. H. C. Hanbury, L.V.O., M.C.	W. Powers, M.B.E.
Berkshire	Col. The Hon. G. W. N. Palmer, O.B.E., T.D.	D. A. W. Gardiner
Buckinghamshire	Cdr. The Hon. J. T. Fremantle, R.N.(*retd*)	Lt.-Col. A. F. M. Matthews, O.B.E.
Cambridgeshire	M. G. M. Bevan	M. J. Marshall
Cheshire	The Rt. Hon. The Viscount Leverhulme, T.D.	S. B. J. Z. de Ferranti
Cleveland	The Rt. Hon. The Lord Gisborough	Mrs. H. Bloom
Cornwall	The Rt. Hon. The Viscount Falmouth	Ms. D. E. Colville
Cumbria	Maj. Sir Charles Graham, Bt.	R. Brockbank
Derbyshire	Col. P. Hilton, M.C.	Mrs. M. H. Kenning, O.B.E.
Devon	Lt. Col. The Rt. Hon. The Earl of Morley	Sir Paul Studholme, Bt.
Dorset	The Rt. Hon. The Lord Digby	H. W. Plunkett-Ernle-Earle-Drax
Durham	D. J. Grant, C.B.E.	R. P. Thompson
Essex	Adm. Sir Andrew Lewis, K.C.B.	L. F. Ratcliff, D.S.O., D.F.C., A.F.C.
Gloucestershire	Col. M. St. J. V. Gibbs, C.B., D.S.O., T.D.	Capt. C. P. D. Berrill
Hampshire	Lt. Col. Sir James Scott, Bt.	Capt. A. W. Murdoch
Hereford and Worcester	T. R. Dunne	T. M. Berington
Hertfordshire	S. A. Bowes Lyon	J. L. Wood
Humberside	R. A. Bethell	Sir Ian Macdonald of Sleat, Bt.
Kent	The Rt. Hon. The Lord Robin Leigh-Pemberton	Lt.-Col. J. R. Yerburgh
Lancashire	S. Towneley	Col. J. F. Greenhough
Leicestershire	Col. Sir Robert Martin, K.C.V.O., O.B.E.	A. T. C. Heywood
Lincolnshire	Capt. H. N. Neville	J. N. Heneage
Greater London	Field Marshal the Lord Bramall, G.C.B., O.B.E., M.C.	R. M. Brew, C.B.E.
Greater Manchester	Col. J. B. Timmins, O.B.E., T.D.	A. W. Guest
Merseyside	Wg. Cdr. K. M. Stoddart, A.E.	Lt.-Col. F. J. K. Williams, C.B.E., T.D.
Norfolk	T. C. Colman	Capt. W. H. Bulwer-Long
Northamptonshire	J. L. Lowther, C.B.E.	C. G. V. Davidge, O.B.E.
Northumberland	The Rt. Hon. The Viscount Ridley, T.D.	C. J. R. Nicholl
Nottinghamshire	Sir Gordon Hobday	J. E. Madocks, C.B.E.
Oxfordshire	Sir Ashley Ponsonby, Bt., M.C.	H. J. L. Brunner
Shropshire	J. R. S. Dugdale	R. E. Angell-James
Somerset	Col. G. W. F. Luttrell, M.C.	W. A. C. Theed
Staffordshire	Sir Arthur Bryan	D. G. Stern
Suffolk	Sir Joshua Rowley, Bt.	R. J. Upton
Surrey	R. E. Thornton, O.B.E.	Maj. W. J. Hacket Pain
Sussex, East	The Most Hon. The Marquess of Abergavenny, K.G., O.B.E.	E. J. B. Hardcastle, T.D.
Sussex, West	Her Grace Lavinia, Duchess of Norfolk, C.B.E.	R. C. Langmead
Tyne and Wear	Sir Ralph Carr-Ellison, T.D.	R. I. Stewart, C.B.E.
Warwickshire	C. M. T. Smith-Ryland	Miss E. Creak
West Midlands	The Rt. Hon. The Earl of Aylesford	F. C. Graves, O.B.E.
Wight, Isle of	The Rt. Hon. The Lord Mottistone, C.B.E.	R. J. Westmore
Wiltshire	Col. Sir Hugh Brassey, K.C.V.O., O.B.E., M.C.	B. H. C. Sykes
Yorkshire, North	Sir Marcus Worsley, Bt.	Col. E. C. York
Yorkshire, South	J. H. Neill, C.B.E., T.D.	W. H. W. Ping
Yorkshire, West	The Rt. Hon. The Lord Ingrow, O.B.E., T.D.	J. R. M. Roscoe

* High Sheriffs are nominated by the Queen on November 12 and come into office after Hilary Term.

ENGLISH COUNTY COUNCILS
AREAS AND POPULATIONS

County	Administrative Headquarters	Area (hectares)	Population	Rateable Value 1988 £	Actual Rateable Value per head £
Avon	Avon House, The Haymarket, Bristol	134,614	946,600	132,339,688	139·10
Bedfordshire......	*Bedford	123,460	528,100	91,980,000	174·20
Berkshire	†Reading	125,890	750,100	143,596,371	191·44
Buckinghamshire .	*Aylesbury	188,284	628,700	114,113,000	181·51
Cambridgeshire ...	†Cambridge	340,892	632,800	99,371,000	157·03
Cheshire	*Chester	232,846	946,500	148,071,949	154·85
Cleveland	Municipal Buildings, Middlesbrough	58,308	554,700	80,446,000	145·03
Cornwall	*Truro	354,792‡	456,900	51,745,694	113·25
Cumbria..........	The Courts, Carlisle	681,012	487,700	54,098,744	110·93
Derbyshire	County Offices, Matlock	263,094	916,800	111,283,577°	121·97°
Devon............	*Exeter	671,088	1,011,000	124,142,366	122·80
Dorset	*Dorchester	265,375	638,200	95,467,158	200·03
Durham	*Durham	243,592	599,553	61,856,864	103·17
Essex	*Chelmsford	367,192	1,521,800	254,080,051	168·00
Gloucestershire ...	†Gloucester	264,266	517,100	71,856,409	138·96
Hampshire	The Castle, Winchester	377,698	1,573,320	225,936,570	148·26
Hereford and Worcester	*Worcester	392,650	654,500	95,235,875	145·51
Hertfordshire.....	*Hertford	163,415	996,200	183,211,000	183·91
Humberside	*Beverley, N. Humberside	351,212	848,500	103,464,506	121·94
Kent.............	*Maidstone	373,060	1,500,000	203,265,000	135·51
Lancashire	*Preston	306,346	1,383,100	154,787,597	111·91
Leicestershire	*Leicester	255,293	875,000	122,584,404	140·10
Lincolnshire......	County Offices, Lincoln	591,485	584,600	70,262,000	120·19
Norfolk	*Norwich	536,776	727,800	100,727,085	138·00
Northamptonshire	*Northampton	236,737	554,400	84,278,635	151·00
Northumberland ..	*Morpeth	503,165	304,150	35,647,621	117·20
Nottinghamshire..	*Nottingham	216,365	1,006,400	130,829,000	130·00
Oxfordshire	*Oxford	260,782	583,200	92,717,600	158·98
Shropshire	The Shirehall, Shrewsbury	349,014	392,700	49,429,310	122·81
Somerset	*Taunton	345,094	456,800	57,534,315	125·95
Staffordshire	County Buildings, Stafford	271,615	1,022,735	135,051,152	132·05
Suffolk	*Ipswich	379,663	628,600	87,327,632	138·92
Surrey	*Kingston upon Thames	167,924	1,011,400	184,247,964	181·76
Sussex, East	Pelham House, St. Andrew's Lane, Lewes	179,512	689,700	107,576,284	155·98
Sussex, West	*Chichester	198,935	691,650	110,803,687	160·20
Warwickshire	†Warwick	198,053	480,700	74,888,955	155·79
Wight, Isle of	*Newport, I.O.W.	38,066	126,500	14,886,970	117·68
Wiltshire.........	*Trowbridge	348,070	555,200	69,630,000	125·41
Yorkshire, North .	*Northallerton	830,865	709,000	85,548,294	120·66

* County Hall.   † Shire Hall.   ‡ Excluding Isles of Scilly.   ° 1987 figure.

CHIEF EXECUTIVES, TREASURERS AND CHAIRMEN

County or Shire	Chief Executive	County Treasurer	Chairman of County Council
Avon	N. J. L. Pearce	D. G. Morgan	W. Fowler
Bedfordshire........	J. W. Elven	V. F. Phillips	J. P. B. Kinchella
Berkshire	A. J. Allen	M. C. Beasley	F. G. R. Gimblett
Buckinghamshire ...	C. Garrett	H. Springthorpe	W. Rooke
Cambridgeshire	G. Lister	D. Prince	Mrs. B. L. Wrout
Cheshire	R. G. Wendt	J. E. H. Whiteoak	H. Tomlins
Cleveland	B. Stevenson	P. Riley	R. A. Dobson
Cornwall	G. K. Burgess	A. L. Wilkes	F. J. Williams, C.B.E.
Cumbria...........	J. R. Ford	R. Wirth	H. Little
Derbyshire	R. Race*	R. C. Beard	A. J. Hough
Devon..............	D. D. Macklin	B. J. Weston	Mrs. E. M. Stacey, M.B.E.
Dorset	K. A. Abel, C.B.E.	D. M. Gasson	Sir Stephen Hammick, Bt.
Durham	K. W. Smith°	J. Kirkby†	R. Pendlebury
Essex	R. W. Adcock	K. D. Neale	R. W. Dixon Smith
Gloucestershire	M. G. Bichard	J. R. Cockroft	E. J. Radley
Hampshire	A. R. Hodgson	J. E. Scotford	Mrs. S. M. Bartlet
Hereford and Worcester	G. A. Price	(vacant)	J. T. Arnett
Hertfordshire	M. J. Le Fleming	K. S. Cliff	F. Peacock
Humberside	D. G. Graham, C.B.E.	J. A. Parkes	D. A Southwick, O.B.E.
Kent	P. R. Sabin	P. Martin	W. J. McNeill, M.B.E.
Lancashire	B. Hill	D. Morgan	L. Proos
Leicestershire	S. Jones	R. Hale	N. R. Hangar
Lincolnshire........	R. J. D. Procter	D. G. Barrett	Mrs. Z. M. Scoley
Norfolk	B. J. Capon	C. A. Boar	J. A. Alston, C.B.E.
Northamptonshire ..	A. J. Greenwell	D. W. Cleggett	G. Pollard
Northumberland	C. B. Rodger	K. Morris	W. J. Nicholson
Nottinghamshire....	A. Sandford	G. S. Luff	A. Palmer
Oxfordshire	A. T. Brown, C.B.E.	J. T. Vokins	B. H. Duggan
Shropshire	M. Suter	M. N. Davis	J. Turner
Somerset	J. E. Whittaker	B. M. Tanner	R. B. Clark
Staffordshire	B. A. Price	B. Smith	F. A. Cholerton, C.B.E.
Suffolk	C. W. Smith	P. B. Atkinson	Sir Macdonald Miller of Glenlee, Bt.
Surrey	D. J. Thomas	R. Wolstenholme	D. Robertson
Sussex, East	R. M. Beechey	M. R. Hancock	N. P. Mackilligin
Sussex, West	J. R. Hooley	B. Fieldhouse	P. G. Shepherd
Warwickshire	I. G. Caulfield	J. P. Hunt	H. W. De'Ath
Wight, Isle of	J. S. Horsnell	J. Proctor	B. H. Drake
Wiltshire...........	I. A. Browning	A. F. Gould	J. B. Ainslie, O.B.E.
Yorkshire, North ...	H. J. Evans	D. Martin	L. Backhouse

* Director of Administration. ° Principal Executive Officer. †County Finance Officer.

Residuary Bodies

GREATER LONDON, (see page 598).

GREATER MANCHESTER, P.O. Box 440, 358 The Royal Exchange, Cross Street, Manchester M60 1RB (061 832 4495).
Chairman, J. P. B. Hadfield.
Chief Executive, P. D. Quick.

MERSEYSIDE, 3rd Floor, Steers House, Canning Place, Liverpool.
Chairman, N. G. Brodrick.
Chief Executive, A. A. Thompson.
Treasurer, J. R. Smith.

TYNE AND WEAR.—The residuary body is to be wound up in October 1988.

WEST MIDLANDS, 1 Lancaster Circus, Queensway, Birmingham B4 7DJ (021–300 5151).
Chairman, Dr. M. Skillicorn.
Chief Executive, K. E. Rose.

SOUTH YORKSHIRE, Britannic Assurance Building, Regent Street, Barnsley S70 2HG (0226–730002).
Chairman, B. E. Cotton, C.B.E..
Chief Executive, W. K. Irvine.
Treasurer, P. R. Appleyard.

WEST YORKSHIRE, P.O. Box 22, Pearl Assurance House, Queen Street, Wakefield, WF1 2QN (0924–367111).
Chairman, T. McDonald.
Chief Executive, P. Lodge.

MUNICIPAL DIRECTORY OF ENGLAND

A list of METROPOLITAN BOROUGH AND CITY COUNCILS. Those accorded CITY status are in SMALL CAPITALS.

Metropolitan Boroughs	Estimated Resident Population 1986	Rateable Value 1988 £	Chief Executive	Mayor †Lord Mayor *Chairman 1988–89
GREATER MANCHESTER	2,579,400			
Bolton	261,600	29,679,888	K. P. Bounds	B. M. Allanson
Bury	172,600	20,365,666	D. J. Burton	W. Johnson
MANCHESTER	451,400	80,892,234	P. Short (acting)	†P. Conquest
Oldham	220,000	23,821,692	C. Smith	H. Slack
Rochdale	206,600	22,248,663	J. F. D. Pierce	R. Taylor
SALFORD	239,300	32,837,078	R. C. Rees	J. Holt
Stockport	289,900	41,002,913	A. L. Wilson	J. M. Ashworth
Tameside	215,200	22,689,681	D. Spiers	M. Wareing
Trafford	216,300	40,736,031	W. A. Lewis	G. Marland
Wigan	306,600	32,980,624	P. Johnson	D. N. Caley
MERSEYSIDE	1,467,600			
Knowsley	163,800	21,517,746	R. Penn	F. J. Curran
LIVERPOOL	483,000	70,122,611	C. M. Reddington	*Ms. D. Gavin
St. Helens	187,900	23,769,716	(vacant)	W. Noctor
Sefton	298,000	37,825,499	A. G. Corless	Miss J. Goodwir Kemp, M.B.E.
Wirral	334,800	43,893,087	C. D. Darley	R. L. S. Cumpstey
SOUTH YORKSHIRE	1,297,000			
Barnsley	222,200	20,212,249	P. G. Thompson	B. G. Goddard
Doncaster	289,300	30,804,563	C. B. Jeynes	R. Gillies
Rotherham	252,100	24,525,374	J. Bell	M. F. Eagleton
SHEFFIELD	534,300	66,689,687	I. L. Podmore	†Mrs. P. Smith
TYNE AND WEAR	1,135,400			
Gateshead	207,300	22,135,624	L. N. Elton	S. E. Potter
NEWCASTLE UPON TYNE	281,400	43,002,661	G. N. Cook	†D. Webster
North Tyneside	192,300	21,837,509	E. B. Lincoln	N. Hunter
South Tyneside	156,900	15,702,735	S. Clark	D. Maidment
Sunderland	297,700	29,492,302	G. P. Key	L. Mann
WEST MIDLANDS	2,632,400			
BIRMINGHAM	1,004,100	168,019,394	R. M. W. Taylor	†H. C. Blumenthal
COVENTRY	310,400	45,271,869	B. V. Redknap (acting)	†A. J. Waugh (Jnr.)
Dudley	300,900	46,074,167	A. V. Astling	Mrs. C. Hough
Sandwell	301,100	50,407,032	G. A. Hadley	R. Whyley
Solihull	202,900	32,564,698	J. Scampion	R. S. Davies
Walsall	261,800	39,666,301	J. W. Hadley	B. S. Powell
Wolverhampton	251,900	43,522,584	M. T. Lyons	P. R. Richards
WEST YORKSHIRE	2,053,100			
BRADFORD	463,100	46,581,517	D. F. Holmes	†S. Midgley
Calderdale	193,100	17,870,414	M. Ellison	A. Berry
Kirklees	376,600	34,400,000	R. V. Hughes	J. Holt
LEEDS	710,900	94,900,000	D. Ansbro	†A. Vollans
WAKEFIELD	309,300	35,362,825	J. G. Stanbury	G. H. Parkinson

DISTRICT COUNCILS

A list of non-Metropolitan District Councils in England. Those accorded CITY status are in SMALL CAPITALS, those with Borough status are distinguished by having § prefixed.

District	Estimated Resident Population 1986	Rateable Value 1988 £	Chief Executive (*Clerk)	Chairman 1988–89 (a) Mayor (b) Lord Mayor
Adur, West Sussex	58,100	8,771,086	F. M. G. Staden	P. Shephard
Allerdale, Cumbria	95,800	9,503,817	A. G. Perry	L. G. Lytollis
Alnwick, Northumberland	29,800	3,168,000	A. G. A. Groome	A. Davidson
Amber Valley, Derbyshire	109,700	12,779,269	J. Ragsdale	Mrs. J. McKee
Arun, West Sussex	126,900	17,977,609	J. V. Midgley	F. C. Lyons
Ashfield, Nottinghamshire	106,700	10,837,370	S. Beedham	Mrs. G. Thierry
§Ashford, Kent	92,400	12,718,030	E. H. W. Mexter	(a) D. S. Madgett
Aylesbury Vale, Bucks.	142,500	21,951,012	B. J. Quoroll	B. M. Griffin

District	Estimated Resident Population 1986	Rateable Value 1988 £	Chief Executive (*Clerk)	Chairman 1988–89 (a) Mayor (b) Lord Mayor
Babergh, Suffolk	77,100	10,127,142	D. C. Bishop	T. M. Bailey-Smith
§Barrow in Furness, Cumbria	74,200	6,821,147	R. H. McCulloch	(a) J. E. Dick
Basildon, Essex	156,900	27,713,276	R. C. Mitchinson°	F. Tomlin
§Basingstoke and Deane, Hants.	137,900	23,136,618	D. W. Pilkington, R.D.	(a) H. G. D. Allerston
Bassetlaw, Notts.	104,906	17,139,877	R. D. Blair	Mrs. E. J. P. Bloomer
BATH, Avon	84,400	11,645,638	N. C. Abbott	(a) Cdr. J. J. Malloy
§Berwick-upon-Tweed, Northumberland	26,500	3,210,953	J. V. Picking	(a) G. E. Miller
§Beverley, Humberside	109,700	13,060,748	W. J. H. Thomas	(a) Mrs. E. Eaton
Blaby, Leics.	81,500	10,338,991	J. E. Meakin	Mrs. L. K. Woodhouse
§Blackburn, Lancs.	139,100	14,215,072	S. M. Jones	(a) G. P. Toole
§Blackpool, Lancs.	145,400	19,333,985	D. Wardman	(a) R. D. Crichton
§Blyth Valley, Northumberland	78,300	7,600,000	D. Crawford	(a) J. Bradshaw
§Bolsover, Derbys.	70,200	6,235,442	C. A. Tucker	G. Dale
§Boothferry, Humberside	61,900	5,695,111	J. W. Barber	(a) G. A. Barker
§Boston, Lincs.	51,900	6,730,941	R. E. Coley	(a) C. H. A. Allen
Bournemouth, Dorset	152,200	25,784,451	K. Lomas	(a) Mrs. J. C. Harris
Bracknell Forest, Berks.	93,200	16,767,424	A. J. Targett	(a) A. Cheney
Braintree, Essex	115,800	16,430,068	C. R. Daybell	E. J. R. McDowell
Breckland, Norfolk	101,900	12,658,078	J. B. Heath	Mrs. R. M. Butler-Stoney
Brentwood, Essex	70,900	13,974,040	C. P. Sivell	C. B. Colley
Bridgnorth, Salop	51,500	6,235,396	G. C. Nutley	C. D. Bache
§Brighton, East Sussex	141,900	25,847,893	T. J. Blake	(a) Ms. P. A. Hawkes
BRISTOL, Avon	391,500	62,500,000	W. G. Miller	(b) D. Tedder
Broadland, Norfolk	100,800	11,529,969	B. R. Grayling	K. T. M. A. Wintle
Bromsgrove, Hereford and Worcs.	89,200	12,557,076	R. P. Bradshaw	B. G. Green
§Broxbourne, Herts.	82,400	13,281,290	M. J. Walker	(a) R. E. Chaplon
§Broxtowe, Notts.	106,100	12,324,732	A. E. Hodder	(a) Mrs. S. Foster
§Burnley, Lancs.	88,200	8,561,314	B. Whittle	(a) K. McGeorge
CAMBRIDGE	99,800	23,589,088	G. G. Datson	(b) L. A. D. Hawes
Cannock Chase, Staffs.	85,100	11,531,330	C. E. Evans	A. B. Hill
CANTERBURY, Kent	127,700	16,224,263	C. Gay	(a) T. Steele
Caradon, Cornwall	72,700	7,421,903	J. O. Collins	A. Brooking
CARLISLE, Cumbria	101,400	11,840,259	R. Wilson	(a) C. F. Weber
Carrick, Cornwall	79,000	9,599,020	P. M. Talbot	F. A. Cheshire
§Castle Morpeth, Northumberland	50,700	6,808,212	M. Cole	(a) I. Hunter
Castle Point, Essex	85,900	12,150,620	A. R. Neighbour	J. M. Greenwood
§Charnwood, Leics.	144,900	20,597,942	D. L. Harris	(a) B. Henman
§Chelmsford, Essex	149,800	26,608,941	R. M. C. Hartley	(a) P. Firth
§Cheltenham, Glos.	86,700	15,788,000	B. N. Wynn	(a) Mrs. M. A. Stafford
Cherwell, Oxon.	121,500	18,161,921	A. M. Brace	A. W. A. Tallents
CHESTER, Cheshire	116,600	19,602,628	D. F. G. Burton	(a) W. G. G. Fair
§Chesterfield, Derbyshire	96,700	12,870,674	D. R. Shaw	(a) J. Smith
Chester-le-Street, Durham	52,900	4,808,722	A. Golightly	T. Pounder
Chichester, West Sussex	104,400	15,203,163	P. Ryan	Mrs. J. M. Illius
Chiltern, Bucks.	90,800	17,063,325	D. G. Sainsbury	A. J. H. Tate
§Chorley, Lancs.	94,500	9,685,770	J. W. Davies	(a) J. Livesey
§Christchurch, Dorset	41,100	7,061,250	C. H. Dewsnap	(a) Mrs. M. P. Pardy
§Cleethorpes, Humberside	68,600	9,107,240	R. W. Bull	(a) Mrs. G. E. Nuttall
§Colchester, Essex	145,100	20,968,559	J. Cobley	(a) G. F. D. Bober
§Congleton, Cheshire	84,700	11,309,716	A. Molyneux	(a) R. Domleo
§Copeland, Cumbria	71,400	9,031,058	P. N. Denson	(a) J. Close
Corby, Northants.	50,700	9,535,809	T. J. Simmons	J. Adamson
Cotswold, Glos.	72,700	10,177,429	D. A. Sketchley	P. A. Cutts
Craven, North Yorks	48,200	5,389,829	A. Howell*	Ms. K. C. Brooks, O.B.E.
§Crawley, West Sussex	83,800	20,368,959	M. D. Sander	(a) R. G. Rudd
§Crewe and Nantwich, Cheshire	96,500	13,613,582	R. Mather	(a) Mrs. A. A. M. Roberts
Dacorum, Herts.	132,600	24,918,768	R. H. Davis	(a) Mrs. H. Bassadone
§Darlington, Durham	99,200	13,429,809	H. R. C. Owen	(a) Mrs. H. I. Scott
§Dartford, Kent	76,100	13,125,592	J. D. Hehir	(a) A. J. Smith
Daventry, Northants.	61,200	9,527,075	R. J. Symons, R.D.	T. C. Matts
§DERBY	216,200	31,765,147	R. H. Cowlishaw	(a) L. J. Shepley
Derbyshire Dales	66,800	7,569,813	R. Bubb	K. C. Bull
Derwentside, Durham	86,100	7,797,791	N. F. Johnson	J. K. Pears

° Town Manager.

District	Estimated Resident Population 1986	Rateable Value 1988 £	Chief Executive (* Clerk)	Chairman 1988–89 (a) Mayor (b) Lord Mayor
Dover, Kent	103,800	12,374,853	J. P. Moir, T.D.	Mrs. A. M. Williamson
DURHAM......................	86,600	9,558,610	C. G. Firmin	(a) Ms. M. Brown
Easington, Durham...........	96,500	7,884,721	T. Robinson†	B. Quinn
§Eastbourne, East Sussex	80,700	14,763,823	C. A. Bloor	A. G. S. Enser
East Cambridgeshire	58,400	6,489,252	T. T. G. Hardy	A. N. Wright
East Devon	113,200	13,604,858	F. J. Vallender	R. L. Gigg
East Dorset	77,800	11,476,189	A. Breakwell	Mrs. D. J. Harrison
East Hampshire	97,800	13,695,777	H. S. Fry	Miss B. M. Jones
East Hertfordshire	118,100	18,670,500	D. J. Anstey	P. A. Ruffles
§Eastleigh, Hants.............	99,500	15,701,950	M. C. Brainsby	(a) G. Raymond, M.B.E.
East Lindsey, Lincs.	110,500	13,824,234	A. W. Silcox-Crowe	Mrs. R. Lindop
East Northamptonshire	64,200	7,446,935	R. K. Heath	J. A. Stott-Everett
East Staffordshire	93,900	13,623,162	F. W. Saunders	S. Deeming
§East Yorkshire, Humberside ...	79,200	7,750,256	J. H. Gibson	(a) Ms. M. R. Chapman
Eden, Cumbria	45,300	5,019,557	I. W. Bruce	J. M. Carlyle
§Ellesmere Port and Neston, Cheshire	80,200	17,326,341	S. Ewbank	(a) N. G. Williams
§Elmbridge, Surrey	110,300	23,987,722	D. W. L. Jenkins	(a) J. Trevena
Epping Forest, Essex	114,100	19,803,836	A. V. Hackman	Mrs. A. Miller
§Epsom and Ewell, Surrey	67,200	12,271,012	D. J. Smith	(a) Mrs. J. M. Stoker
§Erewash, Derbyshire..........	106,200	12,249,412	J. M. Parker	(a) S. W. Stevens
EXETER, Devon	99,300	16,036,647	B. Frowd	(a) M. J. O'Callaghan
§Fareham, Hants.	95,700	14,530,666	O. D. Ellis	(a) Mrs. H. K. Ekins
Fenland, Cambs.	70,000	8,470,641	E. S. Thompson	M. Cotterell
Forest Heath, Suffolk	55,700	7,079,797	J. F. Gale	H. M. Jackson
Forest of Dean, Glos...........	75,200	7,313,727	P. R. Starling	A. C. Cooper
§Fylde, Lancs.................	72,800	9,545,000	B. J. Smith	(a) J. M. Tavernor
§Gedling, Notts.	107,100	12,206,903	W. Brown	(a) P. G. Barnes
§Gillingham, Kent.............	95,900	11,250,902	Dr. R. Chilton	(a) G. W. Payne
§Glanford, Humberside	69,500	9,575,597	D. D. H. Cameron	(a) Mrs. S. M. Heseltine
GLOUCESTER	90,900	13,625,756	H. R. T. Shackleton	(a) D. K. Hartshorne
§Gosport, Hants.	77,500	10,132,621	W. D. Hooper	(a) Dr. H. A. B.. Nicholls
§Gravesham, Kent	93,800	13,126,103	E. V. J. Seager	(a) P. J. Hart
§Great Grimsby, Humberside	90,400	12,025,518	R. S. G. Bennett	(a) Mrs. S. C. Woodliff
§Great Yarmouth, Norfolk	85,600	12,214,752	K. G. Ward	(a) D. J. H. Maddeys
§Guildford, Surrey	125,100	21,032,575	D. T. Watts	(a) Mrs. E. M. Cobbett
§Halton, Cheshire	123,200	18,220,835	R. Turton	(a) A. Inett
Hambleton, North Yorks.	75,700	8,576,674	C. Spencer	B. Bosomworth
Harborough, Leics.	63,900	8,545,030	F. T. Berry	W. C. Hill
Harlow, Essex.................	74,000	14,657,780	H. Platt	Ms. J. McAlpine
§Harrogate, North Yorks.	145,200	18,113,566	J. V. Lovell	(a) J. W. Marhsall
Hart, Hants.	81,300	11,404,727	M. W. Tyler	J. G. York
§Hartlepool, Cleveland	90,700	12,066,065	N. D. Abram	(a) J. MacRae
§Hastings, East Sussex	81,100	10,515,955	R. A. Carrier	(a) Mrs. S. Barr
§Havant, Hants................	118,900	16,472,969	D. E. Ridley	(a) P. N. Osborne
HEREFORD	48,400	7,158,180	C. E. S. Willis	(a) B. C. Baldwin
§Hertsmere, Hertfordshire	88,100	16,896,632	J. N. Pearson	(a) M. O. Colne
High Peak, Derbyshire.	83,400	9,544,468	R. P. H. Brady	(a) Mrs D. M. Brennard
§Hinckley and Bosworth, Leics..	94,100	12,593,816	F. Shaw	(a) T. W. Lucas
§Holderness, Humberside	48,700	5,331,464	D. B. Law	(a) T. W. Graham
Horsham, West Sussex	105,800	15,818,395	M. J. Pearson	D. Hillard
§Hove, East Sussex	89,800	15,605,673	G. H. Longden	(a) J. M. Buttimer
§Huntingdonshire, Cambs.	141,700	17,972,465	T. J. Gee	Mrs. R. L. Mills
§Hyndburn, Lancs.	80,000	6,820,481	N. D. Macgregor	(a) C. Westell
§Ipswich, Suffolk	118,600	19,470,064	J. R. Savage	(a) W. A. Quinton
Kennet, Wilts.	67,400	7,012,972	P. L. Owens	A. V. Gray
Kerrier, Cornwall	85,800	9,012,681	J. G. Millward	R. G. Parker
§Kettering, Northants.	73,200	9,010,855	R. M. Eagland	(a) Mrs. J. M. Pearce
King's Lynn and W. Norfolk ...	128,300	17,450,630	A. E. Pask	(a) Maj. L. H. Dutton
KINGSTON UPON HULL, Humberside	258,000	29,732,156	A. B. Wood	(b) Mrs. M. Smelt
Kingswood, Avon	88,500	9,294,552	A. Smith	(a) A. W. Cuillimore
LANCASTER, Lancs.	130,000	15,813,554	W. Pearson*	(a) R. H. Carr
§Langbaurgh, Cleveland	146,800	23,154,787	K. Abigail	(a) D. W. Lane
LEICESTER	281,100	43,830,041	D. Mellor	(b) G. J. P. M. Collis
Leominster, Hereford and Worcs.	38,100	3,921,966	G. A. Robson	Mrs. P. B. Housden
Lewes, East Sussex	87,000	13,297,726	C. W. Mann	A. R. Deats, L.V.O.
LICHFIELD, Staffs.............	91,700	13,176,038	J. T. Thompson	Mrs. A. Hall

† Principal Officer.

District	Estimated Resident Population 1986	Rateable Value 1988 £	Chief Executive (* Clerk)	Chairman 1988–89 (a) Mayor (b) Lord Mayor
LINCOLN	79,000	11,546,010	C. J. Thomas	(a) N. S. L. McDonald
§Luton, Beds.	166,300	32,772,358	J. C. Southwell	(a) Mrs. A. Bush
§Macclesfield, Cheshire	151,800	24,493,157	B. W. Longden	(a) Mrs. S. L. Hardern
§Maidstone, Kent	133,700	18,525,544	J. D. Makepeace	(a) J. Hindle
Maldon, Essex	52,200	7,864,140	T. K. Griffin	R. L. Bass
Malvern Hills, Hereford and Worcs.	86,900	10,851,910	M. J. Jones	P. H. W. Sharpe-Neal
Mansfield, Notts.	100,300	10,562,659	R. P. Goad	Mrs. L. A. Carter
§Medina, Isle of Wight	70,700	8,504,931	P. Keith-Lucas	(a) N. J. H. Bartholomew
§Melton, Leics.	42,900	5,878,358	P. J. G. Herrick°	(a) B. B. Hart
Mendip, Somerset	93,500	10,895,552	G. Jeffs	R. Clark
Mid Bedfordshire	110,800	15,095,915	P. A. Freeman	R. O. Bennett
Mid Devon	61,400	5,975,057	R. C. Greensmith	E. F. Champion
§Middlesbrough, Cleveland	144,300	18,252,988	J. R. Foster	(a) B. Lonsbrough
Mid Suffolk	75,500	9,089,844	H. McFarlane	P. T. Chapman
Mid Sussex	119,900	17,922,152	B. J. Grimshaw	Mrs. J. Mackelden
§Milton Keynes, Bucks.	161,800	29,512,024	M. J. Murray	(a) S. T. Branson
Mole Valley, Surrey	77,600	13,579,738	A. A. Huggins	I. Lewis
Newark and Sherwood, Notts.	106,600	11,531,660	V. G. Crawley	D. R. Payne
Newbury, Berks.	134,100	22,615,269	P. E. McMahon	G. R. McGeachie
§Newcastle under Lyme, Staffs.	117,800	14,348,136	A. G. Owen	(a) H. Broad
§New Forest, Hants.	159,000	25,388,053	P. Bassett	A. Lee
§Northampton	172,500	30,909,563	R. J. B. Morris	(a) R. G. Liddington
Northavon, Avon	126,200	18,623,346	F. Maude	P. Arnold
§North Bedfordshire	134,900	22,267,403	J. F. Hayward	(a) Mrs. E. J. Luper
North Cornwall	69,800	7,943,748	I. Whiting	W. J. H. Burden
North Devon	81,600	8,600,000	R. D. Hall	F. Purcell
North Dorset	51,900	5,870,768	A. J. Bridgeman	Mrs. M. E. Cossins
North East Derbyshire	97,600	9,569,040	D. G. Hunt†	G. A. Shaw
North Hertfordshire	111,600	19,800,000	J. S. Philp	A. A. Evens
North Kesteven, Lincs.	82,900	8,750,128	Dr. G. J. Coady	A. Higgs
North Norfolk	90,200	11,433,982	T. V. Nolan	A. N. G. Duckworth-Chad
North Shropshire	53,100	5,311,252	K. Flood	W. Sinker
§North Warwickshire	59,700	8,962,203	D. Monks	(a) B. P. Moss
North West Leicestershire	78,900	10,999,523	J. E. White	W. H. Quelch
North Wiltshire	109,400	11,705,618	H. Miles	D. C. Hartley
NORWICH, Norfolk	121,600	23,976,947	(vacant)	(b) D. Bradford
NOTTINGHAM	277,800	43,938,629	M. H. F. Hammond	(b) M. W. Suthers, O.B.E.
§Nuneaton and Bedworth, Warwickshire	113,100	14,912,525	I. J. Clarke	(a) R. D. Walkden
§Oadby and Wigston, Leics.	52,000	7,197,108	J. B. Burton	(a) D. J. W. Evans
§Oswestry, Shropshire	31,500	3,349,276	D. A. Towers	(a) J. W. T. Davies
OXFORD	116,200	21,953,190	E. J. Patrick	(b) Mrs. N. D. Whorley
§Pendle, Lancs.	84,500	6,578,457	F. Wood	(a) Miss D. Riding
Penwith, Cornwall	56,600	6,361,189	J. Moore, M.B.E.	Miss B. Hicks
PETERBOROUGH, Cambs.	148,200	24,293,983	P. B. Sidebottom	(a) Mrs. C. M. Gray
PLYMOUTH, Devon	255,600	31,554,744	A. F. Watson	(b) G. A. Draper
§Poole, Dorset	126,400	21,991,578	I. K. D. Andrews	(a) K. P. J. Chaffey
PORTSMOUTH, Hants.	186,900	28,267,694	R. Trist	(b) K. Hale
§Preston, Lancs.	125,000	16,420,299	A. Owens	(a) J. Ward
Purbeck, Dorset	44,300	6,131,293	P. B. Croft	Mrs. T. A. Hunt
§Reading, Berks.	135,000	29,875,199	G. Filkin	(a) Mrs. K. M. Everett
§Redditch, Hereford and Worcs.	74,800	12,618,772	Miss A. Griffin	(a) C. Cheetham
§Reigate and Banstead, Surrey	115,800	20,516,434	C. T. Pollard	(a) Mrs. A. Fraser
§Restormel, Cornwall	82,400	10,937,749	D. Brown	(a) D. B. Harris
§Ribble Valley, Lancs.	51,900	5,859,137	M. Jackson	A. Atkinson
Richmondshire, North Yorks.	49,000	4,727,625	M. F. Tooze	J. T. L. Woodrow
ROCHESTER UPON MEDWAY, Kent	146,200	24,247,639	R. I. Gregory	(a) B. J. Reeves
Rochford, Essex	74,900	11,009,931	A. G. Cooke	R. Pearson
§Rossendale, Lancs.	64,200	5,526,553	J. S. Hartley‡	(a) P. Evans
Rother, East Sussex	81,600	11,875,814	D. F. Powell	S. A. Boyd
§Rugby, Warwicks.	84,900	13,472,000	J. S. R. Lawton	(a) J. Shera
§Runnymede, Surrey	71,300	12,739,906	J. M. A. Fabel, T.D.	(a) Mrs. B. L. Owen
§Rushcliffe, Notts.	96,900	13,562,586	J. Saxton	(a) M. E. Adlington
§Rushmoor, Hants.	79,100	12,984,485	D. Hartley	(a) D. M. Welch
Rutland, Leics.	35,600	4,295,342	A. S. Jowett	A. D. Makey

° Borough Secretary.   † Chief Officer.   ‡ Borough Director.

District	Esti-mated Resident Popula-tion 1986	Rateable Value 1988 £	Chief Executive (*Clerk)	Chairman 1988–89 (a) Mayor (b) Lord Mayor
Ryedale, North Yorks.	89,400	8,620,491	D. Cudworth	F. A. Wiggle
St. Albans, Herts.	128,700	24,159,286	R. H. Braddon	(a) K. Haywood
§St. Edmundsbury, Suffolk	91,500	13,144,313	G. R. N. Toft	(a) W. G. Elkins
Salisbury, Wilts.	103,400	13,880,176	D. R. J. Rawlinson	T. C. Cowie
§Scarborough, North Yorks.	103,700	11,594,305	J. M. Trebble	(a) Mrs. E. Mullineaux
§Scunthorpe, Humberside	62,500	12,443,222	(vacant)	(a) J. A. Pearson
Sedgefield, Durham	88,600	9,808,199	A. J. Roberts	W. Waters
Sedgemoor, Somerset	94,100	11,694,547	D. D. Tremlett	M. J. W. Tingley
Selby, North Yorks.	86,900	16,285,675	J. C. Edwards	J. A. Heppenstall
Sevenoaks, Kent	110,100	14,161,598	B. Cova	Mrs. E. F. Dick
Shepway, Kent	88,700	14,347,636	R. H. Summers	A. H. Deighton
§Shrewsbury and Atcham, Shropshire	91,300	12,816,623	D. M. Clarke	(a) V. T. Bushell
§Slough, Berks.	98,500	24,751,858	A. Bhattacharya*	(a) K. S. Parhar
Southampton, Hants.	200,500	32,566,000	E. A. Urquhart	(a) Mrs. P. Bear
South Bedfordshire	109,000	21,329,206	T. D. Rix	P. R. Rawcliffe
South Bucks.	61,100	14,619,093	S. R. Jobson	Mrs. R. K. Wingrove
South Cambridgeshire	117,200	18,427,894	B. J. Hancock	Mrs. D. S. K. Spink
South Derbyshire	70,100	9,969,151	I. F. Baylis	Mrs. E. Oakey
§Southend-on-Sea, Essex	159,900	28,010,522	D. Moulson	(a) J. Hugill
South Hams, Devon	71,800	8,435,000	F. G. Palmer	J. T. Pennington
South Herefordshire	48,700	5,409,695	D. T. Cole	S. I. Williams
South Holland, Lincs.	64,300	7,427,009	J. T. Brindley	J. R. Pearl
South Kesteven, Lincs.	101,600	13,311,000	K. R. Cann	D. Fletcher
South Lakeland, Cumbria	98,500	11,882,906	A. F. Winstanley	G. P. George
South Norfolk	99,400	11,464,727	A. G. T. Kellett	W. J. W. Hemmant
South Northamptonshire	67,500	8,437,102	P. A. Smithson (act-ing)	Mrs. S. A. Foulkes
South Oxfordshire	133,000	19,789,057	J. B. Chirnside	Miss N. L. Blackmore
§South Ribble, Lancs.	98,300	11,170,689	J. B. R. Leadbetter	(a) F. A. Cooper
South Shropshire	35,000	3,678,281	G. Kellet, M.B.E.	J. H. Meredith
South Somerset	139,000	16,810,349	D. J. Ashford	Mrs. J. P. Clark
South Staffordshire	104,900	13,545,874	G. J. Haywood	C. J. Wakeman
§South Wight, I.O.W.	53,900	6,334,938	D. W. Jaggar	(a) J. L. Hunter
§Spelthorne, Surrey	88,800	23,168,058	M. B. Taylor	(a) E. C. L. Baxter
§Stafford	118,000	17,241,827	J. K. M. Krawiec	(a) M. H. Guymer
Staffordshire Moorlands	96,900	10,321,703	A. W. Law	F. J. White
§Stevenage, Herts.	74,400	14,900,000	H. L. Miller	(a) A. C. Luhman
§Stockton-on-Tees, Cleveland . .	175,800	26,972,205	F. F. Theobalds*	(a) Mrs. W. Hodgson
Stoke-on-Trent, Staffs.	246,900	32,746,150	S. W. Titchener	(b) K. A. Edwards
Stratford-on-Avon, Warwicks. . .	105,700	17,283,910	T. J. W. Foy	Mrs. R. M. Styles
Stroud, Glos.	106,700	13,090,319	D. F. Collins	Mrs. V. Gardiner
Suffolk Coastal	105,700	15,902,757	D. L. Blay	D. E. Gooch
§Surrey Heath	80,100	14,910,860	M. F. Orlik	(a) R. C. Lilley
§Swale, Kent	110,900	13,256,835	W. Croydon	(a) L. T. Vaughan
§Tamworth, Staffs.	66,700	8,592,182	P. E. Thorpe	(a) J. A. Garner
Tandridge, Surrey	76,100	10,621,375	C. W. Rockall	(a) J. A. Rawling
§Taunton Deane, Somerset	91,300	11,996,393	P. F. Berman	(a) P. F. G. Horsford
Teesdale, Durham	24,800	2,313,287	C. E. Fell	W. McCrickard
Teignbridge, Devon	105,400	12,326,020	P. B. Young	Mrs. M. Stanton
Tendring, Essex	122,800	16,720,669	D. Mitchell-Gears	M. Page
§Test Valley, Hants.	99,300	15,385,914	G. Blythe	(a) Mrs. J. A. Fisher
§Tewkesbury, Glos.	84,900	12,696,110	R. A. Wheeler	(a) P. J. Randell
§Thamesdown, Wilts.	162,800	24,591,184	D. M. Kent	(a) J. R. Cordon
Thanet, Kent	123,600	15,782,265	I. G. Gill	W. H. Dawson
Three Rivers, Herts.	80,300	13,215,622	A. S. Potts	P. Goggins
§Thurrock, Essex	124,100	28,138,183	C. Ennis	(a) G. Watts
Tonbridge and Malling, Kent . . .	99,700	14,493,231	T. J. Shellard	G. Horne
§Torbay, Devon	117,300	17,686,367	D. P. Hudson	(a) D. J. Reid, v.r.d.
Torridge, Devon	50,000	4,299,954	R. K. Brasington	J. W. E. Cowle
§Tunbridge Wells, Kent	98,400	13,180,539	R. J. Stone	(a) A. F. Sayer
Tynedale, Northumberland	55,300	6,656,988	A. Baty	R. I. Johnson
Uttlesford, Essex	65,700	10,005,829	J. F. Vernon	R. P. Chambers
Vale of White Horse, Oxon.	110,400	19,743,600	J. C. Neville Wood	Mrs. E. Webb
Vale Royal, Cheshire	113,500	15,689,800	W. R. T. Woods	(a) O. Kendrick
Wansbeck, Northumberland	60,400	7,973,472	A. G. White	C. Morris
Wansdyke, Avon	78,200	9,214,958	P. May‡	A. E. Webb

‡ General Manager.

District	Estimated Resident Population 1986	Rateable Value 1988 £	Chief Executive (*Clerk)	Chairman 1988–89 (a) Mayor (b) Lord Mayor
§Warrington, Cheshire	180,000	27,865,720	W. H. Lawton	(a) G. Orange
Warwick	117,300	20,641,189	M. J. Ward	S. C. Harrison
§Watford, Herts.	76,200	17,512,839	R. B. McMillan	(a) P. A. Allan
Waveney, Suffolk	104,600	12,513,715	M. Berridge	P. D. Hunt
Waverley, Surrey	112,500	18,285,065	G. W. Nuttall	(a) A. A. Lazarus
Wealden, East Sussex	127,600	15,669,400	D. R. Holness	Col. J. D. Richards, O.B.E.
Wear Valley, Durham	65,000	6,194,684	F. A. Dobson†	Mrs. J. E. Lee
§Wellingborough, Northants.	65,100	9,600,409	W. B. Veal	(a) J. L. Jessop
Welwyn Hatfield, Herts.	93,300	19,582,617	D. Riddle	Mrs. U. G. Bennett
§West Devon	43,400	4,361,654	J. S. Ligo	(a) L. J. Reece
West Dorset	82,300	10,363,125	R. C. Rennison	E. H. King
West Lancashire	106,800	13,598,793	J. Cowdall	Mrs. M. E. Edwards
West Lindsey, Lincs.	77,110	8,596,015	A. W. Hancock	P. A. Addison
West Oxfordshire	93,600	11,496,482	N. J. B. Robson	Mrs. M. I. Frost
West Somerset	31,000	6,068,774	H. Close	D. F. Dyer
West Wiltshire	102,200	12,225,943	G. A. F. Garland	Mrs. K. M. Self
§Weymouth and Portland, Dorset	62,100	7,000,551	R. E. F. Norman	(a) L. H. Ames
WINCHESTER, Hants.	94,200	14,557,000	D. H. Cowan	(a) B. Hall, M.B.E.
§Windsor and Maidenhead, Berks.	132,400	27,634,088	G. Blacker	(a) R. Bennett
§Woking, Surrey	86,600	17,168,728	P. Russell	(a) A. N. Grayson
Wokingham, Berks.	140,900	21,937,656	N. E. Butler	Maj. D. G. Goddard
Woodspring, Avon	177,800	21,262,139	R. H. Moon	G. Jones
WORCESTER	76,600	13,972,693	R. G. Grant	(a) B. Neil
§Worthing, West Sussex	95,900	15,299,713	M. Ball	(a) J. W. Cotton
Wrekin, Shropshire	130,200	18,038,842	R. E. Paine	J. T. Hicks
Wychavon, Hereford	98,800	15,059,909	P. G. Rust, M.B.E.	Mrs. C. J. Brackston
Wycombe, Bucks.	156,700	31,030,305	L. Timms	E. Burrows
§Wyre, Lancs.	100,100	11,748,886	M. Brown	(a) R. C. Williamson
Wyre Forest, Hereford and Worcs.	93,000	13,691,956	A. S. Dick	M. M. G. Oborski
YORK, North Yorks.	101,600	12,343,392	J. Cairns	(b) R. Pulleyn

† Principal Officer.

THE PRINCIPAL ENGLISH CITIES

BIRMINGHAM

BIRMINGHAM (West Midlands) is Britain's second city and the largest metropolitan district in the country. It is a focal point in national communications networks with a rapidly expanding International Airport.

The generally accepted derivation of "Birmingham" is the *ham* or dwelling-place of the *ing* or the family of *Beorma*, presumed to have been a Saxon. During the Industrial Revolution the town grew into a major manufacturing centre. In 1889 Birmingham was granted City status.

Despite the decline in manufacturing, Birmingham is still a major hardware trade and motor component industry centre. Recent development includes the National Exhibition Centre and the Aston Science Park. An Urban Development Agency has been set up.

The principal buildings are the Town Hall, built in 1832–1834; the Council House (1879); Victoria Law Courts (1891); the University (1909); the 13th century Church of St. Martin (rebuilt 1873); the Cathedral (formerly St. Philip's Church) (1711) and the Roman Catholic Cathedral of St. Chad (1839–41).

BRADFORD

BRADFORD (West Yorkshire), 192 miles N.N.W. of London, is the administrative centre of the Metropolitan District of Bradford. The District covers an area of 91,444 acres and lies on the southern edge of the Yorkshire Dales National Park, including within its boundaries the village of Haworth, home of the Brontë sisters, and Ilkley Moor.

Originally a Saxon township, Bradford received a market charter in 1251 but developed only slowly until the industrialisation of the textile industry brought rapid growth during the 19th century. The prosperity of that period is reflected in much of the city's architecture, particularly the public buildings—City Hall (1873), Wool Exchange (1867), St George's Hall (Concert Hall, 1853), Cartwright Hall (Art Gallery, 1904) and Technical College (1882). Other chief buildings are the Cathedral (15th century) and Bolling Hall (14th century).

Textiles still play an important part in the city's economy but industry is now more broadly based, including engineering and micro-electronics. The city has a strong banking, insurance and building society sector, and a growing tourism industry.

BRISTOL

BRISTOL (Avon) is the largest non-metropolitan district in population in the country, and lies 119 miles W. of London. The present municipal area is 10,954 hectares.

Bristol's commercial port systems comprise the largest municipally owned port in the country. The Avonmouth dock complex, Royal Portbury Dock and

Portishead Dock handle import and export cargoes. Principal imports include cocoa, timber, metals, animal feeding stuffs, oil products, chemicals, vehicles and molasses. The Royal Portbury Dock, opened by H.M. the Queen in Aug. 1977, is capable of accommodating up to six vessels of 70,000 d.w.t.

The chief buildings include the 12th century Cathedral (with later additions), with Norman chapter house and gateway, the 14th century Church of St. Mary Redcliffe, Wesley's Chapel, Broadmead, the Merchant Venturers' Almshouses, the Council House (1956), Guildhall, Exchange (erected from the designs of John Wood in 1743), Cabot Tower, the University and Clifton College. The Roman Catholic Cathedral at Clifton was opened in 1973.

The Clifton Suspension Bridge, with a span of 702 feet over the Avon, was projected by Brunel in 1836 but was not completed until 1864. Brunel's *SS Great Britain*, the first ocean going propeller driven ship, is now being restored in the City Docks from where she was launched in 1843. The docks themselves have been extensively restored and redeveloped.

Bristol was a Royal Borough before the Norman Conquest. The earliest form of the name is *Bricgstow*. In 1373 it received from Edward III a charter granting it county status.

CAMBRIDGE

CAMBRIDGE, a settlement far older than its ancient University, lies on the Cam or Granta, 51 miles north of London. It has an area of 10,060 acres.

The city is a county town and regional headquarters. Its industries include electronics, flour milling, cement making and the manufacture of scientific instruments. Among its open spaces are Jesus Green, Sheep's Green, Coe Fen, Parker's Piece, Christ's Pieces, the University Botanic Garden, and the Backs, or lawns and gardens through which the Cam winds behind the principal line of college buildings. East of the Cam, King's Parade, upon which stand Great St. Mary's Church, Gibbs' Senate House and King's College Chapel with Wilkins' screen, joins Trumpington Street to form one of the most beautiful throughfares in Europe.

University and College buildings provide the outstanding features of Cambridge architecture but several churches (especially St. Benet's, the oldest building in the City, and St. Sepulchre's the Round Church) also are notable. The modern Guildhall (1939) stands on a site of which at least part has held municipal buildings since 1224.

CANTERBURY

CANTERBURY, the Metropolitan City of the Anglican Communion, has a history going back to prehistoric times. It was the Roman *Durovernum Cantiacorum* and the Saxon Cant-wara-byrig (stronghold of the men of Kent). Here in 597 St. Augustine began the conversion of the English to Christianity, when Ethelbert, King of Kent, was baptized.

Of the Benedictine St. Augustine's Abbey, burial place of the Jutish Kings of Kent (whose capital Canterbury was) only extensive ruins remain. St. Martin's Church, on the eastern outskirts of the City, is stated by Bede to have been the place of worship of Queen Bertha, the Christian wife of King Ethelbert, before the advent of St. Augustine.

In 1170 the rivalry of Church and State culminated in the murder in Canterbury Cathedral, by Henry II's knights, of Archbishop Thomas Becket, whose shrine became a great centre of pilgrimage as described by Chaucer in his *Canterbury Tales*. After the Reformation pilgrimages ceased, but the prosperity of the City was strengthened by an influx of Huguenot refugees, who introduced weaving. The

Elizabethan poet and playwright Christopher Marlowe was born and reared in Canterbury, and there are literary associations also with Defoe, Dickens, Joseph Conrad and Somerset Maugham.

The Cathedral, with architecture ranging from the 11th to 15th centuries, is world famous. Modern pilgrims are attracted particularly to the Martyrdom, The Black Prince's Tomb, the Warriors' Chapel and the many examples of medieval stained glass.

The medieval City Walls are built on Roman foundations and the 14th century West Gate is one of the finest buildings of its kind in the country.

The 1,000 seat Marlowe Theatre is the base for the Canterbury International Festival of the Arts each autumn.

CARLISLE

CARLISLE is situated at the confluence of the River Eden and River Caldew, 309 miles north west of London and a few miles from the Scottish border. It has an area of 254,955 acres, and was granted a charter in 1158.

The city stands at the western end of Hadrian's Wall and dates from the original Roman settlement of *Luguvalium*. Granted to Scotland in the 10th century, Carlisle is not included in the Doomsday Book. William Rufus reclaimed the area in 1092 and the Castle and city walls were built to guard Carlisle and the western border; the Citadel is a Tudor addition to protect the south of the city. Until the Union of the Crowns in 1603, Carlisle changed hands several times and was frequently besieged. During the Civil War the city remained Royalist; in 1745 it supported the Young Pretender.

The Cathedral, originally a 12th century Augustinian priory, was enlarged in the 13th and 14th centuries after the diocese was created in 1133. To the south is a restored Tithe Barn and nearby the 18th century church of St. Cuthbert, the third to stand on a site dating from the 7th century.

Carlisle is the major shopping, commercial and agricultural centre for the area, and industries include the manufacture of metal goods, biscuits and textiles. However, the largest employer is the services sector, notably in retailing and transport. The city has an important communications position at the centre of a network of major roads, as an important stage on the main west coast rail services and with its own airport at Crosby.

CHESTER

CHESTER is situated on the River Dee, 189 miles north west of London. The city administers an area of 173 square miles and was granted Borough and City status in 1974.

Chester's recorded history dates from the 1st century when the Romans founded the fortress of *Deva*. The city's name is derived from the Latin *castra* (a camp or encampment). During the Middle Ages, Chester was the principal port of north west England but declined with the silting of the Dee estuary and competition from Liverpool. The city was also an important military centre, notably during Edward I's Welsh campaigns and the Elizabethan Irish campaigns. During the Civil War, Chester supported the King and was besieged from 1643–46. Chester's first charter was granted c. 1175 and the city was incorporated in 1506. The office of Sheriff is the earliest created in the country (c. 1120's), and the Mayor also enjoys the title "Admiral of the Dee".

The city's architectural features include the city walls (an almost complete two mile circuit), the unique Rows (covered galleries above the street level shops), the Victorian Gothic Town Hall (1869), the

Castle (rebuilt 1788 and 1822) and numerous half-timbered buildings. The Cathedral was a Benedictine abbey until the Dissolution. Remaining monastic buildings include the chapter house, refectory and cloisters and there is a modern free-standing bell tower. The Norman church of St. John the Baptist was a Cathedral church in the early Middle Ages.

Chester is primarily a regional service centre and has considerable tourist appeal. In 1984 the city was awarded Development Area status which has attracted a range of nationally known companies to expand or locate in Chester.

COVENTRY

COVENTRY (West Midlands) is 92 miles N.W. of London, and an important industrial centre, producing cars, machine tools, agricultural machinery, man made fibres, composite materials and telecommunications equipment.

The city owes its beginning to Leofric, Earl of Mercia and his wife Godiva who, in 1043, founded a Benedictine monastery. The guildhall of St. Mary dates from the 14th century, three of the city's churches date from the 14th and 15th centuries and 16th century almshouses may still be seen. Coventry's first cathedral was destroyed at the Reformation, its second in the 1940 blitz (its walls and spire remain) and the new cathedral designed by Sir Basil Spence, consecrated in 1962, now draws innumerable visitors.

Coventry is the home of the University of Warwick and its Science Park, the rapidly-expanding Westwood Business Park and the Museum of British Transport.

DERBY

DERBY stands on the banks of the River Derwent, 127 miles N.N.W. of London, and covers an area of 30 square miles. The name Derby dates back to 880 when the Danes settled in the locality and changed the original Saxon name of "Northworthy" to "Deoraby".

Derby has a wide range of industries: its products include aero engines, lawn mowers, pipework, specialised mechanical engineering equipment, textiles, chemicals, plastics and the Royal Crown Derby porcelain. The city is an established railway centre, the site of British Rail's Technical Centre with its research laboratories.

Buildings of interest include St Peter's Church and the Old Abbey Building (14th century), the Cathedral (1525), St Mary's Roman Catholic Church (1839), the Industrial Museum, formerly the Old Silk Mill (1721). The traditional city centre is complemented by the new Eagle Centre and "out-of-centre" retail developments. In addition to the Derby Playhouse, the Assembly Rooms are a multi-purpose venue.

The first charter granting a Mayor and Aldermen was that of Charles I in 1637. Previous charters date back to 1154. It was granted City status in 1977.

DURHAM

The city of DURHAM is a district in the county of Durham and covers an area of 73 square miles. The city is a major tourist attraction in the county because of its prominent Norman Cathedral and Castle set high on a wooded peninsula overlooking the River Wear. The Cathedral was founded as a shrine for the body of St. Cuthbert in 995. The present building dates from 1093 and among its many treasures is the tomb of the Venerable Bede (673–735). Durham's Prince Bishops had unique powers up to 1836, being lay rulers as well as religious leaders. As a palatinate Durham could have its own army,

nobility, coinage and courts. The Castle was the main seat of the Prince Bishops for nearly 800 years; it is now used as a college by the University.

The University, founded on the initiative of Bishop William Van Mildert, is England's third oldest. Its students live in 14 colleges spread across the city.

Among other buildings of interest is the Guildhall in the Market Place which dates originally from the 14th century. Much work has been carried out to conserve this area, forming part of the city's major contribution to the Council of Europe's Urban Renaissance Campaign. Annual events include Durham's Regatta in June (claimed to be the oldest rowing event in Britain) and the Miners' Gala in July.

In the past 20 years the economy of Durham has undergone a significant change with the replacement of mining as the dominant feature by "white collar" employment. Although still a predominantly rural area, the industrial and commercial sector is growing and a wide range of manufacturing and service industries are based on industrial estates on and around the City area.

EXETER

EXETER lies on the River Exe 170 miles S.W. of London and 10 miles from the sea. It covers an area of 11,661 acres and was granted a Royal Charter by Henry II.

The Romans founded *Isca Dumnoniorum* in the 1st century A.D., and in the 3rd century a stone wall (most of which remains) was built, providing protection against Saxon, and then Danish invasions. After the Conquest, the city led resistance to William in the west, until reduced by siege. The Normans built the motte and bailey castle of Rougemont, the gatehouse and one tower of which remain, although the rest was pulled down in 1784. The first bridge across the Exe was built in the 13th century. The city's role as a port declined due to the silting of the river, but was somewhat restored by the construction in the 1560's of the first ship canal in England. Exeter was the Royalist headquarters in the West during the Civil War.

The diocese of Exeter was established by Edward the Confessor in 1050, although a church existed on the Cathedral site in the early 10th century. A new cathedral was built in the 12th century but the present building was begun c. 1275 in the Gothic style, although incorporating the Norman towers, and completed about a century later with the West Front. The Guildhall dates from the 12th century and there are many other medieval buildings in the city, as well as architecture in the Georgian and Regency styles (Custom House, The Quay). Damage suffered by bombing in 1942 led to the redevelopment of the city centre.

Exeter's prosperity from medieval times was based on trade in wool and woollen cloth (commemorated by Tuckers Hall), which remained at its height until the late 18th century when export trade was hit by the French Wars. Subsequently Exeter has developed as an administrative and commercial centre, notably in the distributive trades and light manufacturing industries.

KINGSTON UPON HULL

HULL (officially "Kingston upon Hull") lies in the mostly rural County of Humberside, at the junction of the River Hull with the Humber, 22 miles from the North Sea and 205 miles N. of London. The municipal area is 17,535 acres.

Hull is one of the great seaports of the United Kingdom. It has docks covering a water area of 172 acres, equipped to handle cargoes by unit-load techniques, and is a departure point for car ferry services to the continent. There is a great variety of industry and service industries, as well as increasing tourism and conference business.

The city, restored after very heavy air raid damage during World War II, has good office and administrative buildings, its municipal centre being the Guildhall, its educational centre the University of Hull and its religious centre the Parish Church of the Holy Trinity. The old Town area is being renovated and includes a new marina and plans for a shopping complex. Just west of the city is the Humber Bridge, the world's longest single span suspension bridge, which was officially opened by H.M. the Queen in July 1981.

Kingston upon Hull was so named by Edward I. City status was accorded in 1897 and the office of Mayor raised to the dignity of Lord Mayor in 1914.

LEEDS

LEEDS (West Yorkshire), a Metropolitan District from April 1, 1974, is a junction for road, rail, canal and air services and an important commercial centre, situated in the lower Aire Valley, 195 miles by road N.N.W. of London. The metropolitan area is 138,915 acres.

The main manufacturing industries are mechanical engineering, printing, publishing and clothing. However, 65 per cent of employment is in services, notably professional and scientific, particularly education and medicine, distributive trades, finance and banking.

The principal buildings are the Civic Hall (1933), the Town Hall (1858), the Municipal Buildings and Art Gallery (1884) with the Henry Moore Gallery (1982), the Corn Exchange (1863) and the University. The Parish Church (St. Peter's) was rebuilt in 1841; the 17th century St. John's Church has a fine interior with a famous English renaissance screen; the last remaining 18th century church is Holy Trinity, Boar Lane (1727). Kirkstall Abbey (about 3 miles from the centre of the city), founded by Henry de Lacy in 1152, is one of the most complete examples of Cistercian houses now remaining. Temple Newsam, birthplace of Lord Darnley, was acquired by the Council in 1922. The present house was largely re-built by Sir Arthur Ingram in about 1620. Adel Church, about 5 miles from the centre of the city, is a fine Norman structure.

Leeds was first incorporated by Charles I in 1626. The earliest forms of the name are *Loidis* or *Ledes*, the origins of which are obscure.

LEICESTER

LEICESTER is situated geographically in the centre of England, 100 miles N. of London. The City dates back to pre-Roman times and was one of the five Danish *Burhs*. In 1589 Queen Elizabeth I granted a Charter to the City and the ancient title was confirmed by Letters Patent in 1919. Under local government reorganization Leicester's area remained unchanged at 18,141 acres, and it retains its designation as a City.

The principal industries of the city are hosiery, and knitwear, footwear manufacturing and engineering. The growth of Leicester as a hosiery centre increased rapidly from the introduction there of the first stocking frame in 1670 and to-day it has some of the largest hosiery factories in the world,with much of the output being exported.

The principal buildings in the city are the Town Hall, the New Walk Centre, the University, Leicester Polytechnic, De Montfort Hall, one of the finest concert halls in the provinces seating over 2,750 persons, and the Granby Halls, a major indoor sports facility. The ancient Churches of St. Martin (now

Leicester Cathedral), St. Nicholas, St. Margaret, All Saints, St. Mary de Castro, and buildings such as the Guildhall, the 14th century Newarke Gate, the Castle and the Jewry Wall Roman site still exist. The Haymarket Theatre, an integral part of a large shopping and car-parking complex, was opened in 1973.

LINCOLN

Situated 143 miles N. of London and 40 miles inland on the River Witham, LINCOLN derives its name from a contraction of *Lindum Colonia*, the settlement founded in A.D. 48 by the Romans to command the crossing of Ermine Street and Fosse Way. Sections of the 3rd century Roman city wall can be seen, including an extant gateway (Newport Arch), and excavations have discovered traces of a sewerage system unique in Britain. The Romans also drained the surrounding fenland and created a canal system, laying the foundations of Lincoln's agricultural prosperity, and also of the city's importance in the medieval wool trade as a port and Staple town. As one of the Five Boroughs of the Danelaw, Lincoln was an important trading centre in the 9th and 10th centuries and medieval prosperity from the wool trade lasted until the 14th century, enabling local merchants to build parish churches (of which three survive), and attracting in the 12th century a Jewish community (Jew's House and Court, Aaron's House). However, the removal of the Staple to Boston in 1369 heralded a decline from which the city only recovered fully in the 19th century when improved fen drainage made Lincoln agriculturally important, and improved canal and rail links led to industrial development, mainly in the manufacture of machinery, components and engineering products.

The Castle was built shortly after the Conquest and is unusual in having two mounds; on one motte stands a Keep (Lucy's Tower) added in the 12th century. The Cathedral was begun *c.*1073 when the first Norman bishop moved the see of Lindsey to Lincoln, but was mostly destroyed by fire and earthquake in the 12th century. Rebuilding was begun by St. Hugh and completed over a century later. The Wren library contains manuscripts including one of the four surviving originals of the Magna Carta. Other notable architectural features of the city are the 12th century High Bridge, the oldest in Britain still to carry buildings, and the Guildhall situated above the 15–16th century Stonebow gateway.

LIVERPOOL

LIVERPOOL (Merseyside) on the right bank of the river Mersey, 3 miles from the Irish Sea and 210 miles N.W. of London, is the U.K.'s fourth most important port and the foremost for the Atlantic trade. The municipal area of 27,864 acres includes 2,840 acres in the bed of the river Mersey. Tunnels link Liverpool with Birkenhead and Wallasey.

There are 2,100 acres of dockland on both sides of the river and the Gladstone and Royal Seaforth Docks can accommodate the largest vessels afloat. Annual tonnage of cargo handled is approximately 10,500,000 tonnes. The main imports are crude oil, grain, ores, edible oils, timber, containers and break bulk cargo. Liverpool Free Port, Britain's largest, was opened in 1984.

Liverpool was created a free borough in 1207 and a city in 1880. From the early eighteenth century it expanded rapidly with the growth of industrialisation and Atlantic trade. Surviving buildings from this date include the Bluecoat Chambers (1717, formerly the Bluecoat School), the Town Hall (1754, rebuilt to the original design, 1795), and buildings in

Rodney Street, Canning Street and the suburbs. Notable from the 19th and 20th centuries are the Anglican Cathedral, built from the designs of Sir Giles Gilbert Scott (the foundation stone was laid in 1904, and the building was only completed in 1980), the Catholic Metropolitan Cathedral (designed by Sir Frederick Gibberd, consecrated 1967) and St. George's Hall, (1838–1854), regarded as one of the finest modern examples of classical architecture. In 1852 an Act was obtained for establishing a public library, museum and art gallery; as a result Liverpool had one of the first public libraries in the country. The Brown, Picton and Hornby libraries now form one of the country's major libraries. The Victoria Building of Liverpool University, the Royal Liver, Cunard and Mersey Docks & Harbour Company buildings at the Pier Head, the Municipal Buildings and the Philharmonic Hall are other examples of the City's fine buildings.

Britain's first International Garden Festival was held in Liverpool in 1984.

MANCHESTER

MANCHESTER (the *Mamucium* of the Romans, who occupied it in A.D. 78) is 189 miles N.W. of London and covers about 43 square miles.

Manchester is a commercial and industrial centre with a population engaged in engineering, chemical, clothing, food processing and textile industries. Banking and insurance are among the prime commercial activities. The city is connected with the sea by the Manchester Ship Canal, opened in 1894, 35½ miles long, and accommodating ships up to 15,000 tons. Manchester Airport handles more than 5 million passengers yearly.

The principal buildings are the Town Hall, erected in 1877 from the designs of Alfred Waterhouse, R.A., together with a large extension of 1938; the Royal Exchange (1869, enlarged 1921) the Central Library (1934); Heaton Hall; the 17th century Chetham Library; the Rylands Library (1899), which includes the Althorp collection; the University precinct; the 15th-century Cathedral (formerly the parish church) and the Free Trade Hall. Manchester is the home of the Hallé Orchestra, the Royal Northern College of Music, the Royal Exchange Theatre and seven public art galleries.

The town received its first charter of incorporation in 1838 and was created a city in 1853. The title of city was retained under local government reorganization.

NEWCASTLE UPON TYNE

NEWCASTLE UPON TYNE (Tyne and Wear) a Metropolitan District on the north bank of the River Tyne, is 8 miles from the North Sea, 272 miles N. of London and has an area of 27,640 acres. A Cathedral and University City, it is the administrative, commercial and cultural centre for north-east England and the principal port. It is an important manufacturing centre with a wide variety of industries.

The principal buildings include the Castle Keep (12th century), Black Gate (13th century), Blackfriars (13th century), West Walls (13th century), St. Nicholas's Cathedral (15th century, fine lantern tower), St. Andrew's Church (12th–14th century), St. John's (14th–15th century), All Saints (1786 by Stephenson), St. Mary's Roman Catholic Cathedral (1844), Trinity House (17th century), Sandhill (16th century houses), Guildhall (Georgian), Grey Street (1834–39), Central Station (1846–50), Laing Art Gallery (1904), University of Newcastle Physics Building (1962) and Medical Building (1985), Civic Centre (1963), Central Library (1969) and Eldon Square Development (1976). Open spaces include the Town Moor (927 acres) and

Jesmond Dene. Eight bridges span the Tyne at Newcastle.

The City derives its name from the "new castle" (1080) erected as a defence against the Scots. In 1400 it was made a County, and in 1882 a City.

NORWICH

NORWICH (Norfolk) is an ancient City 110 miles N.E. of London. It grew from an early Anglo-Saxon settlement near the confluence of the Rivers Yare and Wensum, and now serves as provincial capital for the predominantly agricultural region of East Anglia. The name is thought to relate to the most northerly of a group of Anglo-Saxon villages or "wics". The present City has an area of 9,655 acres. The City's first known Charter was granted in 1158 by Henry II.

Norwich serves its surrounding area as a market town and commercial centre, banking and insurance being prominent among the City's businesses. From the 14th century until the Industrial Revolution, Norwich was the regional centre of the woollen industry, but now the biggest single industry is financial services and principal trades are engineering, printing, shoemaking, double glazing, and the production of chemicals, clothing, confectionery and other foodstuffs. Norwich is accessible to seagoing vessels by means of the River Yare, entered at Great Yarmouth, 20 miles to the east.

Among many historic buildings are the Cathedral (completed in the twelfth century and surmounted by a fifteenth century spire 315 feet in height), the Keep of the Norman Castle (now a museum and art gallery), the fifteenth century flint-walled Guildhall (now a tourist information centre), some thirty medieval parish churches, St. Andrew's and Blackfriars' Halls, the Tudor houses preserved in Elm Hill and the Georgian Assembly House. The University of East Anglia has been established in Norwich on a spacious site at Earlham on the City's western boundary and received its first students in 1963.

NOTTINGHAM

NOTTINGHAM (Nottinghamshire) stands on the River Trent, 124 miles N.N.W. of London in one of the most valuable coalfields of the country connected by canal with the Atlantic and the North Sea. The municipal area is 18,364 acres.

The principal industries are hosiery, lace, bleaching, dyeing and spinning, tanning, engineering and cycle works, brewing and the manufacture of tobacco, chemicals, furniture, typewriters and mechanical products.

The chief buildings are the 17th century Nottingham Castle (restored in 1878, and now the City Museum and Gallery of Art), Wollaton Hall (1580–88) owned by the City Council and now a Natural History Museum, St. Mary's, St. Peter's, and St. Nicholas's Churches, the Roman Catholic Cathedral (Pugin, 1842–4), the Council House (1929), the Guildhall and Court House (1888), Shire Hall, Albert Hall, the University, Trent Polytechnic, Newstead Abbey, home of Lord Byron, the Theatre Royal (1865), the Playhouse (1963) and the Royal Concert Hall (1982).

Snotingaham or *Notingeham*, "the village or home of the sons of Snot" (the Wise), is the Anglo-Saxon name for the Celtic *Tuigogobauc*, "Cave Homes". The City possesses a Charter of Henry II, and was created a City in 1897. Under local government reorganization, the style of city was reaccorded from April, 1974.

OXFORD

OXFORD is a University City, an important industrial centre, and a market town, with an area of 8,785 acres. Industry played a minor part in Oxford until the motor industry was established in 1912.

It is for its architecture that Oxford is of most interest to the visitor, its oldest specimens being the reputed Saxon tower of St. Michael's church, the remains of the Norman castle and city walls and the Norman church at Iffley. It is chiefly famous however, for its Gothic buildings, such as the Divinity Schools, the Old Library at Merton College, William of Wykeham's New College, Magdalen College and Christ Church and many other college buildings. Later centuries are represented by the Laudian quadrangle at St. John's College, the Renaissance Sheldonian Theatre by Wren, Trinity College Chapel, and All Saints Church; Hawksmoor's mock-Gothic at All Souls College, and the eighteenth century Queens' College. In addition to individual buildings, High Street and Radcliffe Square, just off it, both form architectural compositions of great beauty. Most of the Colleges have gardens, those of Magdalen, New College, St. John's (designed by "Capability" Brown) and Worcester being the largest.

PLYMOUTH

PLYMOUTH is situated on the borders of Devon and Cornwall at the confluence of the Rivers Tamar and Plym, 210 miles from London, with an area of 19,572 acres. The city has a long maritime history; it was the home port of Sir Francis Drake and the starting point for his circumnavigation of the world, as well as the last port of call for the *Mayflower* when the Pilgrim Fathers sailed for the New World in 1620. Today Plymouth is host to many international yacht races. The Barbican harbour area has many Elizabethan buildings, and on Plymouth Hoe stands the first lighthouse to be built on the Eddystone Rocks, some miles offshore.

Following extensive war damage, the city centre, comprising a large shopping centre, municipal offices, law courts and public buildings, has been re-built. The main employment is provided by H.M.Dockyard, though many new industrial firms and service industries have become established in the post-war period and the city is a growing tourism centre. In 1982 the Theatre Royal was opened. In conjunction with the Cornwall County Council, the Tamar Bridge was constructed linking the City by road with Cornwall.

PORTSMOUTH

PORTSMOUTH occupies Portsea Island, Hampshire, with boundaries extending to the mainland. It has an area of 15½ sq. miles and is 70 miles from London.

Portsmouth is a centre of industry and commerce, including many high technology and manufacturing industries. It is the U.K. headquarters of a major computer company and two insurance companies. H.M. Naval Base still has a substantial work force, although this has decreased in recent years. The commercial port and Continental Ferry Port is owned and run by the City Council, and carries passengers and vehicles to France and the Channel Islands.

A major port since the 16th century, Portsmouth is also a thriving seaside resort catering for thousands of visitors and day-trippers annually. Among many historic attractions are Lord Nelson's flagship, H.M.S. *Victory*, the Tudor warship *Mary Rose*, Britain's first "ironclad", H.M.S. *Warrior*, the D-Day Museum, Charles Dickens' birthplace at 393 Old Commercial Road, the Royal Naval and Royal Marine museums, Southsea Castle (built by Henry VIII), the Round Tower and Point Battery, which for hundreds of years have guarded the entrance to Portsmouth Harbour, Fort Widley on Portsdown Hill and the Sealife Centre.

ST. ALBANS

Twenty-five miles north west of London and situated on the River Ver, ST. ALBANS' origins stem from the major Roman town of *Verulamium*. Named after the first Christian martyr in Britain, who was executed here, St. Albans has developed around the Norman Abbey and Cathedral Church (consecrated 1115), the second longest in Britain, built partly of materials from the old Roman city. The museums house Iron Age and Roman artifacts and the Roman Theatre, unique in Britain, has a stage as opposed to an amphitheatre. Archæological excavations in the city centre continue also to reveal evidence of pre-Roman, Saxon and medieval occupation.

The town's significance grew to the extent that it was a signatory and venue for the drafting of the Magna Carta. It was also the scene of major riots during the Peasants' Revolt; the French King John was imprisoned there after the Battle of Poitiers, and heavy fighting took place during the Wars of the Roses; but it is as a Roman town that it is best recognized.

Previously controlled by the Abbot, the town achieved a Royal Charter in 1553 and City status in 1877. The street market, first established in 1553, is still an important feature of the city, as are many hotels and inns which survive from the days when St. Albans was an important coach stop. Tourist attractions include historic churches and houses, and a fifteenth century clock tower.

The advent of the railway saw the gradual expansion of the city, and the area now contains a wide range of firms, with special emphasis on microtechnology and electronics, particularly in the medical field. In addition, it is the home of the Royal National Rose Society, and of Rothamsted Park, the agricultural research centre.

In 1974 the City and District of St. Albans was formed, taking in the town of Harpenden and many villages, and it now covers an area of 63 square miles.

SHEFFIELD

SHEFFIELD (South Yorkshire), the centre of the special steel and cutlery trades, is situated 159 miles N.N.W. of London, at the junction of the Sheaf, Porter, Rivelin and Loxley with the River Don.

Sheffield has an area of 91,000 acres (nearly 150 square miles), including 4,619 acres of publicly owned parks and woodland. Though its cutlery, silverware and plate have long been famous, Sheffield has other and now more important industries—special and alloy steels, engineering and tool-making. Research in glass, metallurgy, radiotherapy and other fields is carried on.

The parish church of St. Peter and St. Paul, founded in the twelfth century, became the Cathedral Church of the Diocese of Sheffield in 1914. The Roman Catholic Cathedral Church of St. Marie (founded 1847) was created Cathedral for the new diocese of Hallam in 1980. Parts of the present building date from about 1435. The principal buildings are the Town Hall (1897, 1923 and 1977), the Cutlers' Hall (1832), the University (1905 and recent extensions, including 19-storey Arts Tower), City Hall (1932), Graves Art Gallery (1934), Castle Market Building (1959), the retail market (1973), Mappin Art Gallery and the Crucible Theatre.

Sheffield was created a city in 1893 and on April 1, 1974 became a Metropolitan District Council incorporating Stocksbridge and most of the Wortley Rural area, and retained city status.

Master Cutler (1987–88) *of the Company of Cutlers in Hallamshire*, R. Walker.

SOUTHAMPTON

SOUTHAMPTON is the leading British deep sea port on the Channel and is situated on one of the finest natural harbours in the world. In 1984 a Free Trade Zone was established in the port. The first Charter was granted by Henry II and Southampton was created a county of itself in 1447. In February, 1964, Her Majesty the Queen granted city status by Royal Charter. The city has an area of 12,071 acres excluding tidal waters.

There have been Roman and Saxon settlements on the site of the city, which has been an important port since the time of the Conquest due to its natural deep-water harbour. The oldest church is St. Michael's (1070) which has a black tournai marble font and an unusually tall spire built in the eighteenth century as a landmark for navigators of Southampton Water. Other buildings and monuments within the city walls are the Tudor House, God's House Tower, Bargate Museum, the Tudor Merchants Hall, the Weigh-house, West Gate, King John's House, Long House, Wool House, the ruins of Holy Rood Church, St. Julien's Church and the Mayflower Memorial. The medieval town walls, built for artillery, are among the most complete in Europe. Public open spaces total over 1,000 acres in extent and comprise 9 per cent. of the city's area. The Common covers an area of 328 acres in the central district of the city and is mostly natural parkland.

STOKE-ON-TRENT

STOKE-ON-TRENT (Staffordshire), familiarly known as The Potteries, stands on the River Trent 157 miles N. of London. The present municipal area is 22,916 acres (36 square miles) and the city is the main centre of employment for the population of North Staffordshire. It is the largest clayware producer in the world (china, earthenware, sanitary goods, refractories, bricks and tiles) and has a considerable coal mining output drawn from one of the richest coalfields in Western Europe. The city has steelworks, foundries, chemical works, engineering plants, rubber works, paper mills, and a very wide range of manufactures. Extensive reconstruction has been carried on in recent years.

The City was formed by the federation in 1910 of the separate municipal authorities of Tunstall, Burslem, Hanley, Stoke-upon-Trent, Fenton, and Longton, all of which are now combined in the present City of Stoke-on-Trent.

WINCHESTER

WINCHESTER, the ancient capital of England, is situated on the River Itchen 65 miles S.W. of London and 12 miles N. of Southampton. Since local government reorganization in 1974, the style of City has been accorded to the whole of the new district of Winchester, which embraces an area of 162,921 acres of mid-Hampshire.

Winchester is rich in architecture of all types but the Cathedral takes pride of place. The longest Gothic cathedral in the world, it was built in 1079–1093 and exhibits examples of Norman, Early English and Perpendicular styles. Winchester College, founded in 1382, is one of the most famous public schools, the original building (of 1393) remaining unaltered. St. Cross Hospital, another great medieval foundation, lies 1 mile south of the city. The Almshouses were founded in 1136 by Bishop Henry de Blois, and Cardinal Henry Beaufort added a new Alms House of "Noble Poverty" in 1446. The Chapel and dwellings are of great architectural interest, and visitors may still receive the "Wayfarer's Dole" of bread and ale.

Recent excavations have done much to clarify the origins and development of Winchester. Part of the forum and several of the streets of the Roman town have been discovered; and excavations in the Cathedral Close have uncovered the entire site of the Anglo-Saxon cathedral (known as the Old Minster) and parts of the New Minster, built by Alfred's son Edward the Elder, and the burial place of the Alfredian dynasty. The original burial place of St. Swithun, before his remains were translated to a site in the present cathedral, was also uncovered.

Excavations in other parts of the City have thrown much light on Norman Winchester, notably on the site of the Royal Castle, adjacent to which the new Law Courts have been built, and in the grounds of Wolvesey Castle, where the great house built by Bishops Giffard and Henry of Blois in the twelfth century has been uncovered.

YORK

The City of YORK is a District in the County of North Yorkshire, and is an archiepiscopal seat. The City has an area of 7,295 acres.

The recorded history of York dates from A.D. 71, when the Roman Ninth Legion established a base under Petilius Cerealis which later became the fortress of *Eburacum*. In Anglo-Saxon times the city was the royal and ecclesiastical centre of Northumbria, and was captured by a Viking army in A.D. 866, after which it became the capital of the Viking kingdom of Jorvik. By the 14th century the city had become a great mercantile centre, chiefly owing to its control of the wool trade, and was used as the chief base against the Scots. Under the Tudors its fortunes declined, though Henry VIII made it the headquarters of the Council of the North. Recent excavations on many sites, including Coppergate, has greatly expanded knowledge of Roman, Viking and medieval urban life.

With its development as a railway centre in the 19th century the commercial life of York expanded and it is now a flourishing modern city. The principal industries are the manufacture of chocolate, railway coaches, scientific instruments, and sugar. The City is also an important tourist centre.

It is rich in examples of architecture of all periods. The earliest church (built, 627) was succeeded by several others until, in the 12th to the 15th centuries, the present Minster was built in a succession of styles. The finest features are the West front with its two towers, the spacious transepts and the stained glass. Other examples within the city are the medieval city walls and gateways, churches and guildhalls. Domestic architecture includes the Georgian mansions of The Mount, Micklegate and Bootham. Its museums are world-famous and include the Castle Museum, one of the best-known folk museums in Great Britain, the National Railway Museum, and the Jorvik Viking Centre.

THE CORPORATION OF LONDON

The City of London is the historic centre at the heart of London known as "the square mile" around which the vast metropolis has grown over the centuries. The City's residential population is 5,300 (1981 Census). The civic government is carried on by the Corporation of London through the Court of Common Council, a body consisting of the Lord Mayor, 24 other Aldermen and 132 Common Councilmen. The legal title of the Corporation is "the Mayor and Commonalty and Citizens of the City of London."

The City is the financial and business centre of London and includes the head offices of the principal banks, insurance companies and mercantile houses, in addition to buildings ranging from the historic interest of the Roman Wall and the 15th century Guildhall, to the massive splendour of St. Paul's Cathedral and the architectural beauty of Wren's spires.

The City of London was described by Tacitus in 62 A.D. as "a busy emporium for trade and traders". Under the Romans it became an important administration centre and hub of the road system. Little is known of London in Saxon times when it formed part of the kingdom of the East Saxons. In 886 Alfred recovered London from the Danes and reconstituted it a burgh under his son-in-law. In 1066 the citizens submitted to William the Conqueror who in 1067 granted them a charter, which is still preserved, establishing them in the rights and privileges they had hitherto enjoyed. The mayoralty was established on the recognition of the corporate unity of the citizens by Prince John in 1191, the first Mayor being Henry Fitz Ailwyn who filled the office for 21 years and was succeeded by Fitz Alan (1212–14). A new charter was granted by King John in 1215, directing the Mayor to be chosen annually, which has ever since been done, though in early times the same individual often held the office more than once. A familiar instance is that of "Whittington, thrice Lord Mayor of London" (in reality four times, 1397, 1398, 1406, 1419); and many modern cases have occurred. The earliest instance of the phrase "Lord Mayor" in English is in 1414. It was used more generally in the latter part of the 15th century and became invariable from 1535 onwards. At Michaelmas the Liverymen in Common Hall choose two Aldermen who have served the office of Sheriff for presentation to the Court of Aldermen, and one is chosen to be Lord Mayor for the ensuing mayoral year. The Lord Mayor is presented to the Lord Chief Justice at the Royal Courts of Justice on the second Saturday in November to make the final declaration of office, having been sworn in at Guildhall on the preceding day. The procession to the Royal Courts of Justice is popularly known as the *Lord Mayor's Show*.

Aldermen are mentioned in the 11th century and their office is of Saxon origin. They were elected annually between 1377 and 1394, when an Act of Parliament of Richard II directed them to be chosen for life. The *Common Council*, elected annually on the first Friday in December, was, at an early date, substituted for a popular assembly called the *Folk-mote*. At first only two representatives were sent from each ward, but the number has since been greatly increased.

Sheriffs were Saxon officers: their predecessors were the *wic-reeves* and *portreeves* of London and Middlesex. At first they were officers of the Crown, and were named by the Barons of the Exchequer; but Henry I (in 1132) gave the citizens permission to choose their own Sheriffs, and the annual election of Sheriffs became fully operative under King John's charter of 1199. The citizens lost this privilege, as far as the election of Sheriff of Middlesex was concerned, by the Local Government Act, 1888; but the Liverymen continue, as heretofore, to choose two Sheriffs of the City of London, who are appointed on Midsummer Day, and take office at Michaelmas.

Officers.—The Recorder was first appointed in 1298. The office of Chamberlain is an ancient one, the first contemporary record of which is 1237. The Town Clerk (or Common Clerk) is mentioned in 1274 and the Common Serjeant in 1291.

Activities.—The work is assigned to a number of committees which present reports to the Court of Common Council. These Committees are:—City Lands and Bridge House Estates, Policy and Resources, Coal, Corn and Rates Finance, Planning and Communications, Central Markets, Billingsgate and Leadenhall Markets, Spitalfields Market, Police, Port and City of London Health and Social Services, Library (Library, Records, Art Gallery), Boards of Governors of Schools, Music (Guildhall School of Music and Drama), Establishment, Housing, Gresham (City side), Epping Forest and Open Spaces, West Ham Park, Privileges, Barbican Residential and Barbican Centre (Barbican Arts and Conference Centre).

The Honourable the *Irish Society*, which manages the Corporation's Estates in Ulster, consists of a Governor and 5 other Aldermen, the Recorder, and 19 Common Councilmen, of whom one is elected Deputy Governor.

The *City's Estate*, in the possession of which the Corporation of London differs from other municipalities, is managed by the City Lands and Bridge House Estates Committee, the Chairmanship of which carries with it the title of "Chief Commoner."

The Right Honourable the Lord Mayor 1987–1988*

Sir Greville Douglas Spratt, G.B.E., T.D., *born* 1927; Alderman of *Castle Baynard*, 1978; *Sheriff of London*, 1984; *Lord Mayor*, 1987.

Secretary, Rear-Admiral A. J. Cooke, C.B.

Recorder, Sir James Miskin, Q.C., 1975; *Chamberlain*, Bernard Peter Harty, 1983; *Town Clerk*, Geoffrey William Rowley, 1982; *Common Serjeant*, Thomas Herbert Pigott, Q.C., 1984.

* The Lord Mayor for 1988–89 was elected on Michaelmas Day (*See* "Occurrences During Printing").

The Aldermen

Aldermen	Ward	Born	C.C.	Ald.	Shff.	Lord Mayor
Cdr. Sir Robin Danvers Penrose Gillett, Bt., G.B.E., R.D., R.N.R.	Bassishaw	1925	1965	1969	1973	1976
Sir Peter Drury Haggerston Gadsden, G.B.E.	Farringdon Wt.	1929	1969	1971	1970	1979
Sir Christopher Leaver, G.B.E.	Dowgate	1937	1973	1974	1979	1981
Dame Mary Donaldson, G.B.E.	Coleman St.	1921	1966	1975	1981	1983
Sir Alan Towers Traill, G.B.E.	Langbourn	1935	1970	1975	1982	1984
Sir William Allan Davis, G.B.E.	Cripplegate	1921	1971	1976	1982	1985
Sir David Kenneth Rowe-Ham, G.B.E.	Bridge	1935	....	1976	1984	1986
Sir Greville Douglas Spratt, G.B.E., T.D.	Castle Baynard	1927	....	1978	1984	1987
All the above have passed the Civic Chair						
Christopher Collett	Broad Street	1931	1973	1979	1985	....
Hugh Charles Philip Bidwell	Billingsgate	1934	....	1979	1986	....
Alexander Michael Graham	Queenhithe	1938	1978	1979	1986	....
Brian Garton Jenkins	Cordwainer	1935	....	1980	1987	....
Francis McWilliams	Aldersgate	1926	1978	1980	....	....
Paul Henry Newall, T.D.	Walbrook	1934	1980	1981	....	....
Christopher Rupert Walford	Farringdon Wn.	1935	....	1982	....	....
Roderic Neil Young	Bread Street	1933	1980	1982	....	....
Roger William Cork	Tower	1947	1978	1983	....	....
Brian Edward Toye	Lime Street	1938	....	1983	....	....
Richard Everard Nichols	Candlewick	1938	1983	1984	....	....
Peter Anthony Bull	Cheap	1937	1968	1984	....	....
Peter Keith Levene	Portsoken	1941	1983	1984	....	....
Leonard John Chalstrey	Vintry	1931	1981	1984	....	....
Clive Haydn Martin, O.B.E., T.D.	Aldgate	1935	....	1985	....	....
David Howarth Seymour Howard	Cornhill	1945	1972	1985	....	....
James Michael Yorrick Oliver	Bishopsgate	1940	1980	1986	....	....

The Sheriffs 1988–1989

Francis McWilliams (*see above*) and Simon Block (*see below*), *elected* June 24; *assumed office* September 28, 1988.

THE COMMON COUNCIL OF LONDON

Alexander, Mrs. M. (1987) .... Farringdon Wt.
Anstee, N. J. (1987) .... Aldersgate
Archibald, W. W. (1986) .... Cornhill
Ballard, K. A., M.C. (1969) .... Castle Baynard
Balls, *Deputy* H. D. (1970) ...... Cripplegate Wt.
Barker, J. A. (1981) .... Cripplegate Wt.
Barnes, H. M. F. (1986) .... Coleman Street
Beale, M. J. (1979) .... Lime Street
Bird, J. L. (1977) .... Bridge
Biroum-Smith, P. L. (1988) .... Dowgate
Block, S. A. A. (1983) .... Cheap
Boreham, B. P. (1986) .... Dowgate
Bramwell, F. M. (1983) .... Langbourn
Brighton, R. L. (1984) .... Portsoken
Brown, *Deputy* D. T. (1971) ...... Walbrook
Cassidy, *Deputy* M. J. (1980) .... Aldersgate
Catt, B. F. (1982) .... Farringdon Wn.
Challis, G. H. (1978) .... Langbourn
Chandler, *Deputy* E. G., C.B.E. (1982) . Cornhill
Clements, *Deputy* G. E. I. (1960) .... Farringdon Wt.
Cohen, Mrs. C. M. (1986) .... Lime Street
Cole, Lt.-Col., Sir Colin, K.C.V.O., T.D. (1964) .... Castle Baynard
Colover, D. (1975) .... Bishopsgate
Cope, Dr. J. (1963) .... Farringdon Wt.
Coven, *Deputy* Mrs. E. O., C.B.E. (1972) .... Dowgate
Currie, Miss S. E. M. (1985) ...... Cripplegate Wt.
David, C. P. (1984) .... Aldgate
Delderfield, D. W. (1982) .... Aldersgate
Denny, A. M. (1971) .... Billingsgate
de Silva, D., Q.C. (1980) .... Farringdon Wt.
Donnelly, T. A., M.B.E. (1982) .... Bread Street
Drummond, P. H. (1987) .... Walbrook
Duckworth, *Deputy* H., C.B.E. (1960) . Lime Street
Dunitz, A. A. (1984) .... Portsoken
Durnin, J. C. (1976) .... Cordwainer

Edwards, R. D. K. (1978) .... Bassishaw
Eskenzi, A. N. (1970) .... Farringdon Wn.
Evans, Mrs. J. (1975) .... Farringdon Wt.
Eve, R. A. (1980) .... Cheap
Everett, K. M. (1984) .... Candlewick
Falk, F. A., T.D. (1984) .... Farringdon Wt.
Farrow, M. W. W. (1987) .... Bishopsgate
Farthing, R. B. C. (1981) .... Aldgate
Fell, J. A. (1982) .... Queenhithe
FitzGerald, R. C. A. (1981) .... Bread Street
Floyd-Ewin, *Deputy* Sir David, L.V.O., O.B.E. (1963) .... Castle Baynard
Frappell, C. E. (1973) .... Bread Street
Fraser, W. B. (1981) .... Vintry
Frazer, C. M. (1986) .... Farringdon Wt.
Galloway, A. D. (1981) .... Broad Street
Gass, *Deputy* G. J. (1967) .... Coleman Street
Gold, R. (1965) .... Castle Baynard
Gordon, Miss C. F. (1978) .... Cripplegate Wn.
Graves, A. C. (1985) .... Bishopsgate
Gugan, K., PH.D. (1974) .... Dowgate
Harding, N. H. (1970) .... Farringdon Wn.
Hardwick, Dr. P. B. (1987) .... Aldgate
Hart, *Deputy* M. G. (1970) .... Bridge
Hatfield, A. F. R. (1968) .... Bishopsgate
Haynes, J. E. H. (1986) .... Cornhill
Henderson, *Deputy* J. S., O.B.E. (1975) Langbourn
Henderson-Begg, M. (1977) .... Coleman Street
Holland, *Deputy* J. (1972) .... Aldgate
Horlock, *Deputy* H. W. S. (1969) .... Farringdon Wn.
Humphrays, Mrs. R. (1976) .... Cripplegate Wt.
Ide, W. R. (1972) .... Castle Baynard
Jackson, L. St. J. T., (1978) ..... Bassishaw
James, A. J. (1973) .... Cordwainer
Keep, Mrs. B. (1987) .... Cripplegate Wn.
Kellett, Mrs. M. W. F. (1986) ..... Tower
Kemp, D. L. (1984) .... Coleman Street

Knowles, S. K. (1984) .... *Candlewick*
Lamport, J. C. (1987) .... *Cripplegate Wt.*
Langmead, A. D. G., T.D. (1982) ...... *Tower*
Lawrence, D. W. O., T.D. (1979) ...... *Bridge*
Lawson, G. C. H. (1971) .... *Portsoken*
McAuley, *Deputy*, C. (1957) .... *Bread Street*
McNeil, I. D. (1977) .... *Lime Street*
Malins, J. H. (1981) .... *Farringdon Wt.*
Martin, R. C. (1986) .... *Queenhithe*
Mayhew, Miss J. (1986) .... *Queenhithe*
Mills, A. P. (1969) .... *Bassishaw*
Minshull-Fogg, J., T.D. (1986) .... *Walbrook*
Mitchell, C. R. (1971) .... *Castle Baynard*
Mizen, *Deputy* D. H. (1979) .... *Broad Street*
Mobsby, D. J. L. (1985) .... *Billingsgate*
Morgan, *Deputy* B. L., C.B.E. (1963) .. *Bishopsgate*
Murkin, *Deputy* C. H., O.B.E. (1969) .. *Vintry*
Nash, Mrs. J. C. (1983) .... *Aldersgate*
Neary, J. E. (1982) .... *Aldgate*
Northall-Laurie, P. D. (1975) .... *Walbrook*
Olson, A. H. F. (1972) .... *Dowgate*
Owen, Mrs. J. (1975) .... *Langbourn*
Owen-Ward, J. R. (1983)............. *Bridge*
Packard, Brig. J. J. (1972) .... *Cripplegate Wn.*
Palmer, D. H. (1985)............... *Cripplegate Wn.*
Pembroke, *Deputy* Mrs. A. M. F.
   (1978) .... *Cheap*
Ponsonby of Shulbrede, The Lady
   (1981) .... *Farringdon Wt.*
Pulman, G. A. G. (1983) .... *Tower*
Ratner, R. A., T.D. (1981) .... *Broad Street*
Reed, *Deputy* J. L., M.B.E. (1967) ..... *Farringdon Wn.*

Revell-Smith, P. A. (1959) .... *Vintry*
Rigby, P. P. (1972) .... *Farringdon Wn.*
Rigg-Milner, Mrs. A. I. (1987) .... *Cripplegate Wn.*
Rodgers, Miss E. H. L. (1987) .... *Vintry*
Rodgers, S. C. (1969) .... *Farringdon Wt.*
Roney, *Deputy* E. P. T., C.B.E. (1974) . *Bishopsgate*
Samuel, *Deputy* Mrs. I. (1971) .... *Portsoken*
Saunders, *Deputy* R. (1975) .... *Candlewick*
Savory, M. B. (1980) .... *Broad Street*
Scriven, R. G. (1984) .... *Candlewick*
Scrivener, M. J. H. (1986)........... *Cripplegate Wn.*
Shalit, D. M. (1972) .... *Farringdon Wn.*
Sharp, *Deputy* Mrs. I. M. (1974) ..... *Queenhithe*
Shindler, *Deputy* A. B. (1966) ...... *Billingsgate*
Simpson, A. S. J. (1987)............. *Aldersgate*
Smithers, H. J. (1986) .... *Billingsgate*
Snyder, M. J. (1986)................ *Cordwainer*
Spanner, J. H., T.D. (1984).......... *Broad Street*
Stevenson, J. L. (1970) .... *Coleman Street*
Stitcher, *Deputy* G. M., C.B.E. (1966) . *Farringdon Wt.*
Swan, N. E. B. (1985) .... *Coleman Street*
Turner, *Deputy* R. L. (1973) .... *Tower*
Webb, C. J. (1986)................. *Bishopsgate*
White, J. W. (1986) .... *Cornhill*
Williams, G. M. E. (1985) .... *Aldersgate*
Willoughby, P. J. (1985) .... *Bishopsgate*
Wilmot, *Deputy* R. T. D. (1973) ..... *Cordwainer*
Wilson, A. B. (1984) .... *Cheap*
Wixley, *Deputy* G. R. A., C.B.E., T.D.
   (1964) .... *Bassishaw*
Woodward, *Deputy* C. D., O.B.E. (1972)*Cripplegate*
Wylie-Harris, W. H. (1957).......... *Farringdon Wn.*

Deputies.—In the preceding list each Common Councilman so described serves as *Deputy* to the Alderman of his Ward.

THE CITY GUILDS (LIVERY COMPANIES)

The Livery Companies of the City of London derive their name from the assumption of a distinctive dress or livery by their members in the 14th century.

The order of precedence (according to 2nd Report of Municipal Corporations' Commissioners, 1837, omitting extinct companies, is given in parentheses after the name of each Company.

About 22,500 Liverymen of the Guilds are entitled to vote at elections in *Common Hall.*

MERCERS (*1*). *Hall,* Ironmonger Lane, EC2V 8HE. *Livery,* 237.—*Clerk,* G. M. M. Wakeford; *Master,* B. M. Watney.

GROCERS (*2*). *Hall,* Princes Street, EC2R 8AD. *Livery,* 297.—*Clerk,* C. Mattingley, C.B.E.; *Master,* Dr. P. Massey.

DRAPERS (*3*). *Hall,* Throgmorton Street, EC2N 2DQ. *Livery,* 250.—*Clerk,* R. C. G. Strick; *Master,* F. M. W. R. Neville.

FISHMONGERS (*4*). *Hall,* London Bridge, EC4R 9EL. *Livery,* 320.—*Clerk,* M. R. T. O'Brien; *Prime Warden,* P. J. S. Lumsden.

GOLDSMITHS (*5*). *Hall,* Foster Lane, EC2V 6BN. *Livery,* 275.—*Clerk,* R. D. Buchanan-Dunlop, C.B.E.; *Prime Warden,* C. R. C. Aston, T.D.

MERCHANT TAYLORS (*6* and *7*). *Hall,* 30 Threadneedle Street, EC2R 8AY. *Livery* 330.—*Clerk,* Capt. D. A. Wallis, R.N.; *Master,* J. R. Perring

SKINNERS (*6* and *7*). *Hall,* 8 Dowgate Hill, EC4R 2SP. *Livery,* 360.—*Clerk,* M. H. Glover; *Master,* C. Harris, R.D.

HABERDASHERS (*8*). *Hall,* Staining Lane, EC2V 7DD. *Livery,* 320.—*Clerk,* Capt. M. E. Barrow, D.S.O., R.N.; *Master,* M. A. B. Jenks.

SALTERS (*9*). *Hall,* 4 Fore Street, EC2Y 5DE. *Livery,* 150.—*Clerk,* J. M. Montgomery; *Master,* R. Nichols.

IRONMONGERS (*10*). *Hall,* Barbican, EC2Y 8AA. *Freemen,* 183.—*Clerk,* R. B. Brayne, M.B.E.; *Master,* B. J. Livingston.

VINTNERS (*11*). *Hall,* 68½ Upper Thames Street, EC4V 3BE. *Livery,* 327.—*Clerk,* Brig. G. Read, C.B.E. *Master,* C. I. A. Matheson.

CLOTHWORKERS (*12*). *Hall,* Dunster Court, Mincing Lane, EC3R 7AH. *Livery,* 185.—*Clerk,* C. M. Mowll; *Master,* C. S. P. Rawson.

The above are the Twelve "Great" London Companies in order of Civic precedence.

ACCOUNTANTS, CHARTERED (86). *Livery*, 325.—*Clerk*, G. H. Kingsmill, The Grove, Hinton Parva, Swindon SN4 0DH; *Master*, The Hon. G. H. Wilson.

ACTUARIES (91). *Livery*, 148.—*Clerk*, A. K. Tudor, 8 Madgeways Close, Great Amwell, Herts., SG12 9RU; *Master*, P. E. Moody, C.B.E.

AIR PILOTS AND AIR NAVIGATORS, GUILD OF (81). *Livery*, 400.—*Grand Master*, H.R.H. the Prince Philip, Duke of Edinburgh, K.G., K.T.; *Clerk*, Capt. P. Wilson, 291 Gray's Inn Road, WC1X 8QF; *Master*, Capt. F. H. Dell.

APOTHECARIES, SOCIETY OF (58). *Hall*, Black Friars Lane, EC4V 6EJ. *Livery*, 1,125.—*Clerk*, Maj. J. C. O'Leary; *Master*, Col. F. G. Neild.

ARBITRATORS (93). *Livery*, 190.—*Clerk*, B. W. Vigrass, O.B.E., V.R.D., 75 Cannon Street, EC4N 5BH; *Master*, A. B. Shindler.

ARMOURERS AND BRASIERS (22). *Hall*, 81 Coleman Street, EC2R 5BJ. *Livery*, 120.—*Clerk*, Lt. Col. R. R. F. Cowe; *Master*, D. T. James.

BAKERS (19). *Hall*, Harp Lane, Lower Thames Street, EC3R 6DP. *Livery*, 400.—*Clerk*, P. F. Wilson, D.F.C.; *Master*, J. E. Kirby.

BARBERS (17). *Hall*, Monkwell Square, Wood Street, EC2Y 5BL. *Livery*, 200.—*Clerk*, Col. A. B. Harfield, C.B.E.; *Master*, J. H. Scrutton.

BASKETMAKERS (52). *Livery*, 500.—*Clerk*, D. J. Farrier, 5 The Spinney, Warren Road, Purley, Surrey CR2 1AB; *Prime Warden*, T. O. D. Craig.

BLACKSMITHS (40). *Livery*, 250.—*Clerk*, D. T. Dresch, Hill House, Branksome Park Road, Camberley, Surrey GU15 2AE; *Prime Warden*, R. Gabriel.

BOWYERS (38). *Livery*, 36.—*Clerk*, A. Black, 2 Serjeants' Inn, Fleet Street, EC4Y 1LL; *Master*, J. R. Bickford Smith, C.B., T.D.

BREWERS (14). *Hall*, Aldermanbury Square, EC2V 7HR. *Livery*, 84.—*Clerk*, Rear-Adm. M. L. T. Wemyss, C.B; *Master*, Sir Derrick Holden-Brown.

BRODERERS (48). *Livery*, 100.—*Clerk*, S. G. B. Underwood, 11a Bridge Road, East Molesey, Surrey KT8 9EY; *Master*, Maj. G. A. Charrington.

BUILDERS MERCHANTS (88). *Livery*, 210.—*Clerk*, A. G. P. Lincoln, 9 Little Trinity Lane, EC4V 2AD; *Master*, M. P. Vintner.

BUTCHERS (24). *Hall*, 87 Bartholomew Close, EC1A 7EB. *Livery*, 660.—*Clerk*, A. H. Emus; *Master*, R. W. Baker.

CARMEN (77). *Livery*, 457.—*Clerk*, Lt. Col. G. T. Pearce, M.B.E., St. Olave's Rectory, 8 Hart Street, EC3R 7NB; *Master*, Maj. D. R. Baker.

CARPENTERS (26). *Hall*, 1 Throgmorton Avenue, EC2N 2JJ. *Livery*, 150.—*Clerk*, Capt. K. G. Hamon, R.N.; *Master*, J. G. Ridley.

CHARTERED SECRETARIES AND ADMINISTRATORS (87). *Livery*, 226.—*Hon. Clerk*, G. H. Challis, The Irish Chamber, Guildhall Yard, EC2V 5AE; *Master*, D. H. Roberts.

CLOCKMAKERS (61). *Livery*, 281.—*Clerk*, Air Cdre. B. G. Frow, D.S.O., D.F.C., 2 Greycoat Place, SW1P 1SD; *Master*, Lord Murton of Lindisfarne.

COACHMAKERS AND COACH-HARNESS MAKERS (72). *Livery*, 400.—*Clerk*, Maj. W. H. Wharfe, R.M., 149 Banstead Road, Ewell, Epsom, Surrey KT17 3HL; *Master*, B. L. M. Brew, T.D.

COOKS (35). *Livery*, 75.—*Clerk*, H. J. Lavington, T.D. 49 Queen Victoria Street, EC4N 4SE; *Master*, Adm. Sir Lindsay Bryson, K.C.B.

COOPERS (36). *Hall*, 13 Devonshire Square, EC2M 4TH. *Livery*, 260.—*Clerk*, J. A. Newton; *Master*, B. Atchley.

CORDWAINERS (27). *Livery* 141.—*Clerk*, Capt. C. T. Codrington, C.B.E., R.N., Eldon Chambers, 30 Fleet Street, EC4Y 1AA; *Master*, R. D. Emerson.

CURRIERS (29). *Livery*, 92.—*Clerk*, I. R. McNeil, 43 Church Road, Hove, Sussex BN3 2BT; *Master*, A. McNeil.

CUTLERS (18). *Hall*, Warwick Lane, EC4M 7BR.

Livery, 100.—*Clerk*, K. S. G. Hinde, T.D.; *Master*, Dr. W. J. Herbert.

DISTILLERS (69). *Livery*, 275.—*Clerk*, B. Dehn, 60 Montford Place, Kennington Lane, SE11 5DF; *Master*, N. C. Burrough, C.B.E.

DYERS (13). *Hall*, Dowgate Hill, EC4R 2ST. *Livery*, 131.—*Clerk*, J. R. Chambers; *Prime Warden*, Dr. P. R. V. Tomson.

ENGINEERS (94). *Livery*, 270.—*Clerk*, Cdr. B. D. Gibson, R.N. (retd.), 1 Carlton House Terrace, SW1Y 5DB; *Master*, Rear-Adm. P. G. Hammersley, C.B., O.B.E.

ENVIRONMENTAL CLEANERS (97). *Hall*, Mark Lane, EC3. *Livery*, 164.—*Clerk*, S. J. Holt; *Master*, Dr. B. A. Smith.

FAN MAKERS (76). *Hall*, St. Botolph's Hall, Bishopsgate, EC2. *Livery*, 215.—*Clerk*, Lt. Col. I. R. P. Green; *Master*, P. G. Bird, T.D.

FARMERS (80). *Hall*, 3 Cloth Street, EC1A 7LD. *Livery*, 300.—*Clerk*, C. M. Taylor; *Master*, R. M. Older.

FARRIERS (55). *Livery*, 375.—*Clerk*, H. W. H. Ellis, 37 The Uplands, Loughton, Essex IG10 1NQ; *Master*, W. J. Alsford.

FELTMAKERS (63). *Livery*, 225.—*Clerk*, R. M. Peel, 10 Carteret Street, SW1H 9DR; *Master*, C. F. C. Simeons.

FLETCHERS (39). *Hall*, 3 Cloth Street, EC1A 7LD. *Livery*, 115—*Clerk*, J. R. Garnett; *Master*, C. A. Coward.

FOUNDERS (33). *Hall*, 1 Cloth Fair, EC1. *Livery*, 180.—*Clerk*, A. J. Gillett; *Master*, H. J. V. Williams.

FRAMEWORK KNITTERS (64). *Livery*, 225.—*Clerk*, C. J. Eldridge, Apothecaries' Hall, Black Friars Lane, EC4V 6EL; *Master*, M. C. Martin.

FRUITERERS (45). *Livery*, 237.—*Clerk*, Brig. R. Eccles, D.S.O., Church Leys, Buckland, Aylesbury, Bucks. HP22 5HX; *Master*, D. G. Hope-Mason.

FUELLERS (95). *Livery*, 250.—*Clerk*, H. C. F. Squire, 6 Farm Avenue, Horsham, W. Sussex RH12 2JY; *Master*, R. N. Horne.

FURNITURE MAKERS (83). *Livery*, 250.—*Clerk*, Wg. Cdr. G. Acklam, M.B.E., 30 Harcourt Street, W1H 2AA; *Master*, R. H. Richardson, R.D.

GARDENERS (66). *Livery*, 250.—*Clerk*, A. L. McGeachy, 14/15 Craven Street, WC2N 5AD; *Master*, E. G. Chandler, C.B.E.

GIRDLERS (23). *Hall*, Basinghall Avenue, EC2V 5DD. *Livery*, 80.—*Clerk*, T. J. Straker; *Master*, Dr. J. York Moore.

GLASS-SELLERS (71). *Livery*, 180.—*Clerk*, P. J. Willoughby, 25 New Street Square, EC4A 3LN; *Master*, M. C. Wallis.

GLAZIERS (53). *Hall*, 9 Montague Close, SE1 9DD. *Livery*, 277.—*Clerk*, P. H. Trollope; *Master*, Very Rev. P. C. Moore.

GLOVERS (62). *Livery*, 300.—*Clerk*, Gp. Capt. D. G. F. Palmer, O.B.E., Glovers, Tismans Common, Rudgwick, W. Sussex RH12 3DU; *Master*, K. D. Smith.

GOLD AND SILVER WYRE DRAWERS (74). *Livery*, 350. *Clerk*, J. R. Williams, 50 Cheyne Avenue, E18 2DR; *Master*, P. J. Nathan.

GUNMAKERS (73). *Livery*, 220.—*Clerk*, F. B. Brandt, The Proof House, 48/50 Commercial Road, E1 1LP; *Master*, The Hon. Sir Peter Vanneck, G.B.E., C.B., A.F.C.

HORNERS (54). *Livery*, 430.—*Clerk*, Dr. E. M. Hunt, 11 Hobart Place, SW1W 0HL; *Master*, R. E. Gill.

INNHOLDERS (32). *Hall*, College House, Dowgate Hill, EC4R 2SR. *Livery*, 120.—*Clerk*, J. R. Edwardes Jones; *Master*, S. Druce.

INSURERS (92). *Hall*, 20 Aldermanbury, EC2V 7HY. *Livery*, 325.—*Clerk*, V. D. Webb; *Master*, R. H. Peet.

JOINERS AND CEILERS (41). *Livery*, 124.—*Clerk*, D. A. Tate, Parkville House, Bridge Street, Pinner, Middx. HA5 3JD; *Master*, J. H. T. Brown.

LAUNDERERS *(89)*. *Hall*, London Bridge, SE1. *Livery*, 190.—*Clerk*, W. E. Kingsland; *Master*, J. C. H. Baker.

LEATHERSELLERS *(15)*. *Hall*, 15 St. Helen's Place, EC3A 6DQ. *Livery*, 150.—*Clerk*, Capt. N. MacEacharn, C.B.E., R.N.; *Master*, V. C. M. Lister.

LIGHTMONGERS *(96)*. *Livery*, 107.—*Clerk*, S. H. Birch, 53 Leithcote Gardens, SW16 2UX; *Master*, I. F. Davies.

LORINERS *(57)*. *Livery*, 350.—*Clerk*, J. R. Williams, 50 Cheyne Avenue, E18 2DR; *Master*, J. S. Walker-Arnott.

MARKETORS *(90)*. *Livery*, 158.—*Clerk*, B. F. Catt, 29 Queen Street, EC4R 1BH; *Master*, H. F. Druce.

MASONS *(30)*. *Livery*, 111.—*Clerk*, H. J. Maddocks, 9 New Square, WC2R 3QN; *Master*, Dr. R. J. Woodward.

MASTER MARINERS, HONOURABLE COMPANY OF *(78)*. H.Q.S. *Wellington*, Temple Stairs, WC2R 2PN. *Livery*, 300.—*Clerk*, D. H. W. Field; *Admiral*, H.R.H. the Duke of Edinburgh, K.G., K.T.; *Master*, H.R.H. the Prince of Wales.

MUSICIANS *(50)*. *Livery*, 263.—*Clerk*, M. J. G. Fletcher, 1 The Sanctuary, Westminster, SW1P 3JT; *Master*, W. R. I. Crewdson.

NEEDLEMAKERS *(65)*. *Livery*, 250.—*Clerk*, M. G. Cook, 17 Southampton Place, WC1A 2EH; *Master*, Sir Henry Warner, Bt.

PAINTER STAINERS *(28)*. *Hall*, 9 Little Trinity Lane, EC4V 2AD. *Livery*, 400.—*Clerk*, A. G. P. Lincoln, M.C., T.D.; *Master* J. G. Lightowler.

PATTENMAKERS *(70)*. *Livery*, 250.—*Clerk*, P. Merritt, 25 Wellesley Road, W4 4BU; *Master*, His Hon. Judge L. J. Verney, T.D.

PAVIORS *(56)*. *Hall*, Cutlers' Hall, Warwick Lane, EC4M 7BR. *Livery*, 275.—*Clerk*, R. F. Coe; *Master*, G. F. J. Goff.

PEWTERERS *(16)*. *Hall*, Oat Lane, EC2V 7DE. *Livery*, 110.—*Clerk*, Maj. J. M. Halford, R.M.; *Master*, J. S. Holden.

PLAISTERERS *(46)*. *Hall*, 1 London Wall, EC2Y 5JU. *Livery*, 203.—*Clerk*, H. Mott; *Master*, R. F. Beavis.

PLAYING CARDS, MAKERS OF *(75)*. *Livery*, 145.—*Clerk*, M. J. Smyth, 6 The Priory, Godstone, Surrey RH9 8NL; *Master*, B. G. Rigg.

PLUMBERS *(31)*. *Livery*, 310.—*Clerk*, Col. E. M. P. Hardy, 3rd Floor, 21 Fleet Street, EC4Y 1AA; *Master*, L. Hill.

POULTERS *(34)*. *Hall*, Armourers' Hall, 81 Coleman Street, EC2R 5BJ. *Livery*, 172.—*Clerk*, Lt-Col. R. F. Cowe; *Master*, P. Kemp, O.B.E.

SADDLERS *(25)*. *Hall*, 40 Gutter Lane, EC2V 6BR. *Livery*, 70.—*Clerk*, Gp. Capt. K. M. Oliver; *Master*, R. C. Gidden.

SCIENTIFIC INSTRUMENT MAKERS *(84)*. *Livery*, 230.—*Clerk*, Gp. Cpt. R. L. Smith, 9 Montague Close, SE1 9DD; *Master*, D. M. Read.

SCRIVENERS *(44)*. *Livery*, 183.—*Clerk*, H. J. W. Harman, Chancery House, 53/64 Chancery Lane, WC2A 1QU; *Master*, M. Maclagan.

SHIPWRIGHTS *(59)*. *Livery*, 500.—*Clerk*, Gp. Capt. R. C. Olding, C.B.E., D.S.C., Ironmongers' Hall, Barbican, EC2Y 8AA; *Permanent Master*, H.R.H. the Duke of Edinburgh, K.G., K.T.; *Prime Warden*, G. R. Newman.

SOLICITORS *(79)*. *Livery*, 413.—*Clerk*, Miss S. H. Robinson, T.D., 14 Charterhouse Square, EC1M 6AX; *Master*, K. S. G. Hinde, T.D.

SPECTACLE MAKERS *(60)*. *Livery*, 328.—*Clerk*, C. J. Eldridge, Apothecaries' Hall, Black Friars Lane, EC4V 6EL; *Master*, Prof. H. Dartnall.

STATIONERS AND NEWSPAPER MAKERS *(47)*. *Hall*, Ave Maria Lane, EC4M 7DD. *Livery*, 450.—*Clerk*, Capt. P. Hames, R.N.; *Master*, R. J. Leighton, T.D.

SURVEYORS, CHARTERED *(85)*. *Livery*, 320.—*Clerk*, Mrs. A. L. Jackson, 16 Mary-at-Hill, EC3R 8EE; *Master*, R. Steel, C.B.E.

TALLOW CHANDLERS *(21)*. *Hall*, 4 Dowgate Hill, EC4R 2SH. *Livery*, 175.—*Clerk*, Col. M. ff. Woodhead, O.B.E.; *Master*, Sir Christopher Laidlaw.

TIN PLATE WORKERS *(67)*. *Livery*, 154.—*Hon. Clerk*, R. G. Vincent, 14 Talbot House, 98 St. Martin's Lane, WC2N 4AX; *Master*, R. H. Boissier.

TOBACCO PIPE MAKERS AND TOBACCO BLENDERS *(82)*. *Livery*, 189.—*Clerk*, I. J. Kimmins, Bouverie House, 154 Fleet Street, EC4A 2HX; *Master*, D. P. C. Harris.

TURNERS *(51)*. *Livery*, 165.—*Clerk*, R. G. Woodwark, D.S.C., 33a Hill Avenue, Amersham, Bucks. HP6 5BX; *Master*, G. A. Todd.

TYLERS AND BRICKLAYERS *(37)*. *Livery*, 130.—*Clerk*, F. A. G. Rider, 6 Martin Lane, Cannon Street, EC4R 0DP; *Master*, D. W. Fuller.

UPHOLDERS *(49)*. *Livery*, 200.—*Clerk*, W. R. Wallis, Charrington House, The Causeway, Bishops Stortford CH23 2EW; *Master*, S. A. G. Rust.

WAX CHANDLERS *(20)*. *Hall*, Gresham Street, EC2V 7AD. *Livery*, 100.—*Clerk*, T. Wood; *Master*, R. Hamblin.

WEAVERS *(42)*. *Livery*, 125.—*Clerk*, J. G. Ouvry, 1 The Sanctuary, Westminster, SW1P 3JT; *Upper Bailiff*, M. A. C. Winterton, PH.D.

WHEELWRIGHTS *(68)*. *Livery*, 256.—*Clerk*, M. R. Francis, Greenup, Milton Avenue, Gerrards Cross, Bucks. SL9 8QW; *Master*, E. J. Macey.

WOOLMEN *(43)*. *Livery*, 150.—*Clerk*, D. R. L. Humble, R.D., Kingsmead House, 250 King's Road, SW3 5UE; *Master*, D. N. Ing, M.B.E.

PARISH CLERKS *(No livery)* *(Members*, 100).—*Clerk*, J. D. Hebblethwaite, General Synod Office, Church House, Great Smith Street, SW1P 3NZ; *Master*, H. V. Shooter.

WATERMEN AND LIGHTERMEN *(No livery)*. *(Craft Owning Freemen*, 300).—*Hall*, 18 St. Mary-at-Hill, EC3R 8EE.—*Clerk*, W. A. A. Wells, T.D.; *Master*, M. J. Turk.

NOTE.—In certain companies the election of Master or Prime Warden for the year does not take place till the autumn. In such cases the Master or Prime Warden for 1987–88 is given.

LONDON BOROUGHS

City or Borough (*Inner London Borough)	Municipal Offices	Estimated resident population 1986	Rateable Value 1988 £	Town Clerk (*Chief Executive)	Mayor or (a) Lord Mayor
GTR. LONDON .		6,775,200			
City of Westminster*	City Hall, Victoria Street, SW1E 6QP.	176,100	336,366,002	*R. G. Brooke	(a) Mrs. E. Flach
Barking and Dagenham	°Dagenham, RM10 7BN.	148,100	27,052,260	*D. C. J. Farr	P. Bradley
Barnet	†The Burroughs, Hendon, NW4 4BG.	304,600	63,521,106	E. M. Bennett	D. Goodman
Bexley	‡Bexleyheath, DA6 7LB.	220,100	32,106,114	*T. Musgrave	J. N. Harrington
Brent	†Forty Lane, Wembley, HA9 9HX.	255,700	52,250,000	C. Wood	H. S. Wadhwa
Bromley	°Bromley, BR1 3UH.	297,000	52,688,133	*N. T. Palk	Mrs. M. D. Moir
Camden*	†Euston Road, NW1 2RU.	183,300	124,215,812	*F. Nickson	B. Budd
Croydon........	Taberner House, Park Lane, Croydon.	319,300	73,180,890	F. S. H. Birch	D. Loughborough
Ealing	°Uxbridge Road, W5 2HL.	295,500	59,219,006	*Ms. J. Hunt	E. F. Dunckley
Enfield	°Enfield, EN1 3XA.	265,400	50,426,584	*B. McAndrew	H. Corpe
Greenwich*	†Wellington Street, SE18 6PW.	217,800	33,695,079	*C. Roberts	J. Austin-Walker
Hackney*	Mare St., E8 1EA.	187,100	40,077,676	*Ms. P. Gordon	M. Lewis
Hammersmith and Fulham* .	†King St., W6 9JU.	150,800	37,648,328	*T. Eddison	J. S. Mirwitch
Haringey.......	°Wood Green, N22 4LE.	196,100	37,368,018	(vacant)	V. King
Harrow	°Harrow, HA1 2UH.	201,900	36,389,203	*A. G. Redmond	R. J. Denney
Havering	†Romford, RM1 3BD.	238,100	39,149,941	*J. L. Guest	Mrs. L. G. Sinclair
Hillingdon......	°Uxbridge, UB8 1JN.	232,000	61,588,980	P. Johnson	E. Hales
Hounslow	°Lampton Rd., Hounslow, TW3 4DN.	194,900	52,923,427	*R. D. Jefferies	D. Mockeridge
Islington*	†Upper St., N1 2UD.	168,000	55,863,655	*E. W. Dear	V. James
Kensington and Chelsea (Royal Borough)*	†Hornton St., W8 7NX.	137,400	70,500,000	*R. S. Webber	E. P. Tomlin
Kingston upon Thames (Royal Borough).....	Guildhall, Kingston upon Thames.	133,800	30,104,433	*R. McCloy	Mrs. M. Hartfree
Lambeth*	†Brixton Hill, SW2 1RW.	245,000	63,168,286	*A. J. George	B. Houghting
Lewisham*	†Catford, SE6 4RU.	232,000	35,595,687	*J. W. Harwood	Ms. P. Fitzsimmons
Merton.........	Crown House, London Rd., Morden, SM4 5DX.	164,800	32,585,358	*W. A. McKee	A. Jones
Newham	†East Ham, E6 2RP.	205,200	36,746,938	*J. Samuel	J. Newstead
Redbridge	†Ilford, IG1 1DD.	227,900	37,365,722	*G. U. Price	K. E. Axon
Richmond upon Thames	York House, Twickenham, TW1 3AA.	162,000	33,995,682	R. L. Harbord (acting)	Mrs. A. M. Cornish
Southwark*	†Peckham Rd., SE5 8UB.	216,000	62,888,160	*Ms. A. Whyatt	Ms. R. Sergeant
Sutton	‡St. Nicholas Way, Sutton, SM1 1EA.	168,700	30,628,248	*A. Taylor	Ms. L. Sharp
Tower Hamlets*.	†Patriot Square, E2 9LN.	152,800	60,888,263	(vacant)	B. Duffy
Waltham Forest .	†Walthamstow, E17 4JF.	215,800	32,494,891	*L. G. Knox	J. J. Walsh
Wandsworth*...	†Wandsworth, SW18 2PU.	257,100	45,770,556	*S. K. Jones	J. Garrett

°Civic Centre.   ‡Civic Offices.   †Town Hall.

ABOLITION OF THE G.L.C.

The abolition of the Greater London Council on April 1, 1986, led to the bulk of its work being passed to the London Boroughs, Government Departments and Government-appointed bodies, and to joint boards and committees.

The London Residuary Body (L.R.B.) was established by the Local Government Act, 1985, which abolished the G.L.C. Its function is to wind up the affairs of the G.L.C. within a maximum life of five years. Its tasks have fallen mainly in three areas:

(i) to clear up functions of the G.L.C. which have not been transferred to other successor bodies. These include debt management, the preparation of the final (i.e. 1985–86) accounts of the G.L.C., and payment of compensation to former G.L.C. staff made redundant. These responsibilities have now been completely discharged.

(ii) to dispose of former G.L.C. properties, other than those such as fire stations, piers and refuse transfer stations passing to other successor bodies.

(iii) to manage former G.L.C. services until new homes have been found for them.

Properties.—One of the L.R.B.'s major duties is the sale of ex-G.L.C. buildings and properties, the proceeds being distributed among the London Boroughs. Amongst the more important are Thamesmead Town, Covent Garden, and County Hall, sold to a consortium for conversion to hotel, shop, office, residential and leisure accommodation.

Other property including shops, flats, commercial and industrial premises must be disposed of within the L.R.B.'s five year lifespan. With this aim a programme of sales and auctions is taking place. Management of mortgages granted by the G.L.C. has now been transferred to the London Borough of Richmond upon Thames.

Services.—Services which have now been successfully transferred include:

(i) Traffic control—to the Secretary of State for Transport.

(ii) Work on the North–South route.

(iii) The Research and Intelligence Unit, Central Computing Services and London Scientific Services.

(iv) Recreation, Parks, etc.—The arts facilities on the South Bank to the South Bank Board and the Arts Council. Responsibility for historic buildings, parks, open spaces, etc. to Borough Councils or bodies such as English Heritage.

(v) Land Drainage and Flood Prevention.—The Borough Councils and the Thames Water Authority.

Finance.—The boroughs and successor bodies finance the L.R.B. In Feb. 1988 the budget was £199,000,000, the boroughs meeting a £17,500,000 levy and the remainder coming from grants, mortgage repayments and rents, in addition to G.L.C. balances which were inherited at abolition. More than £300,000,000 has been distributed amongst the boroughs.

LONDON RESIDUARY BODY, St. Vincent House, 30 Orange Street, WC2H 7HH. (01-633 5000).
Chairman, Sir Godfrey Taylor.
Director of Administration, J. Howes.
Director of Finance, C. McArdle.

Education

The local education authority for an area corresponding with the area of the twelve inner London boroughs and the City of London is the Inner London Education Authority which took over responsibility for the education service from the G.L.C. on April 1, 1986. The first elections of the 58 members took place on May 8, 1986. The 20 outer London Borough Councils remain the education authorities for their Boroughs.

The total number of pupils on the rolls of the Authority's nursery, primary and secondary schools (including special schools for handicapped children) is 270,062. There are 946 schools, staffed by the equivalent of 18,647 full-time teachers. Vocational instruction, cultural studies and recreational activities for persons over compulsory school age are arranged at the various establishments for further education. The Authority maintains 25 colleges and makes grants to 5 polytechnics and 2 other institutions. Part-time classes are offered at 20 adult education and literary institutes, and 78 youth centres, including 2 drama centres.

Since the G.L.C.'s abolition, I.L.E.A. is solely responsible for the Geffrye and Horniman Museums.

I.L.E.A., County Hall, SE1 7PB (01-633 5000).

(The Government is proposing to abolish I.L.E.A. from April 1, 1990).

Transport

The G.L.C.'s responsibility, through the London Transport Executive, for transport services in London was transferred in June 1984 to the London Regional Transport board (*see* p. 341), which is responsible to the Secretary of State for Transport. Former G.L.C. responsibilities, including the maintenance of the Thames bridges, ferries and tunnels, have been passed to the Borough councils and to the Department of Transport.

Solid waste disposal

Responsibility for the disposal of London's household, commercial and civic amenity refuse lies with 16 Waste Disposal Authorities.

There are four statutory bodies—*West London Waste Authority* (Brent, Ealing, Harrow, Hillingdon, Hounslow, Richmond upon Thames), *North London Waste Authority* (Barnet, Camden, Enfield, Hackney, Haringey, Islington, Waltham Forest), *East London Waste Authority* (Barking and Dagenham, Havering, Newham, Redbridge) and *Western Riverside Waste Authority* (Hammersmith and Fulham, Kensington and Chelsea, Lambeth, Wandsworth).

Twelve boroughs are Waste Disposal Authorities in their own right and eleven of them have come together in voluntary groupings—*Central London Group* (City of London, City of Westminster, Tower Hamlets), *South London Group* (Bromley, Croydon, Kingston upon Thames, Merton, Sutton) and *South East London Group* (Greenwich, Lewisham, Southwark). The twelfth, Bexley, liaises with Kent County Council.

The London Waste Regulation Authority regulates and controls waste management activities in both the public and private sectors.

LONDON WASTE REGULATION AUTHORITY, County Hall, SE1 7PB (01-633 4149).

Fire Services

The successor authority for London's fire service is the London Fire and Civil Defence Authority (L.F.C.D.A.), with effect from April 1, 1986. The Fire Brigade is now organised into five Area Commands, which coincide with Borough boundaries. The L.F.C.D.A.'s responsibilities also include petroleum licensing.

LONDON FIRE AND CIVIL DEFENCE AUTHORITY, London Fire Brigade Headquarters, 8 Albert Embankment, SE1 7SD (01-582 3811).

LONDON AND ITS ENVIRONS

(For National Art Galleries and Museums in London and for London Cathedrals, Churches, etc. see Index.)

Adelphi, Strand, W.C.2.—Adelphi Terrace and district commemorate the four Adam brothers, James, John, Robert and William, who laid out the district (formerly Durham House) at the close of the 18th century, though few 18th century buildings now remain. Four of the streets were formerly called after the brothers but are now Adam Street, John Adam Street, Robert Street and Durham House Street. In the neighbourhood of the Adelphi was York House, built by the Duke of Buckingham in 1625 (the Water Gate of which still stands in Embankment Gardens), the commemorative streets being Charles Street, Villiers Street, Duke Street, Buckingham Street.

Alexandra Palace and Park, Wood Green, N22 4AY.—Set in 200 acres of parkland. The Victorian Palace was severely damaged by fire in 1980 but has been restored and developed and reopened in January 1988. Alexandra Palace provides modern facilities for exhibitions, sports, conferences and leisure activities. The Palace is a charitable trust administered by the London Borough of Haringey.

Baltic Exchange, St. Mary Axe, E.C.3.—The world market for the chartering of cargo ships. The present Exchange was built in 1903 and the new wing opened by H.M. The Queen on Nov. 21, 1956.

Bank of England, Threadneedle Street, E.C.2. (Not open to the public)—The Bank of England, founded in 1694, has always been closely connected with the Government. The present building, completed in 1940 to the designs of Sir Herbert Baker, incorporates features reminiscent of the earlier architects, Sampson (1734), Sir Robert Taylor (1765) and Sir John Soane (1788).

Banqueting House, Whitehall, S.W.1.—The only important building left of the great Palace of Whitehall. The previous banqueting house was burnt down in 1619, and replaced by the present structure designed by Inigo Jones. In 1635 it was enriched with Rubens' ceiling paintings. Charles I was executed on a scaffold set up just in front of the present entrance. Open Tues.–Sat. 10–5, Sun. 2–5. Closed Mon. Admission (1988) 80p, concessions 40p.

Barbican Centre, Silk Street, EC2Y 8DS.—Owned, funded and managed by the Corporation of London, the Barbican Centre was opened on March 3, 1982 by H.M. The Queen, and is the largest complex of its kind in Western Europe. It houses the 1,166 seat Barbican Theatre, now the London base of the Royal Shakespeare Company, along with a smaller 200 seat studio theatre (The Pit), and the 2,026 seat Barbican Hall, the home of the London Symphony Orchestra. There are also three cinemas, an art gallery, a sculpture court, a large lending library, facilities for trade exhibitions and conferences, and bars and restaurants.

Blackheath, S.E.10.—272 acres of parkland. Morden College, founded in 1695 as a home for "decayed Turkey merchants", is near the S.E. corner. The building was designed by Wren and its Chapel doors have carvings attributed to Grinling Gibbons. Concerts and poetry recitals are held at Rangers House, a villa built c. 1700 which houses the Suffolk collection of English portraits from Larkin to Lely, and the Dolmetsch Collection of musical instruments. Open daily 10–5 (Nov.–Jan. 10–4). Closed Good Friday, Dec. 24, 25. Admission free.

Bridges.—The bridges over the Thames (from East to West) are: *Tower Bridge* (built by the Corporation of London and opened in 1894), with its bascules, operated now by new electrically-run machinery, walkway, opened to the public in 1982, and museum, opened in 1983; *London Bridge* (opened after rebuilding in 1831 by Rennie; the new London Bridge was completed in 1973 and opened by H.M. The Queen on March 16, 1973); *Southwark Bridge* (opened in 1819, also by Rennie; rebuilt by the Corporation of London, 1922); *Blackfriars Bridge* (opened in 1769, rebuilt, 1869, and widened by the Corporation of London in 1909); *Waterloo Bridge* (Rennie), opened in 1817, commanding a fine view of western London, rebuilt by L.C.C. and reopened 1944; *Hungerford Bridge,* 1863 (railway bridge with a footbridge); *Westminster Bridge* (built in 1750 and then presenting a view that inspired Wordsworth's sonnet; rebuilt and re-opened in 1862; width, 84 ft.) with Thomas Thornycroft's *Boadicea* at the north-eastern end; this bridge leads from Westminster Abbey and the Houses of Parliament to the County Hall and St. Thomas' Hospital; *Lambeth Bridge* (built 1862, rebuilt 1932) leading from Lambeth Palace to Millbank; *Vauxhall Bridge* (built in 1811–16, rebuilt in 1906), leading to Kennington Oval; *Chelsea Bridge,* leading from Chelsea Hospital to Battersea Park (reconstructed and widened, 1937) and *Albert Bridge* (1873); *Battersea Bridge* (opened in 1890); *Wandsworth Bridge* (opened in 1873; rebuilt and re-opened in 1940); *Putney Bridge* (built 1729, rebuilt 1884, widened in 1933), where the Oxford and Cambridge Boat Race is started for Mortlake; *Hammersmith Bridge* (rebuilt 1887; for pedestrians only, 1933); *Barnes Bridge* (for pedestrians only, 1933); *Chiswick Bridge* (opened in 1933); *King Edward VII Bridge, Kew* (rebuilt in 1902, opened 1903), leading to the Royal Botanic Gardens, Kew; *Twickenham Lock Bridge; Twickenham Bridge* (opened 1933); *Richmond Bridge* (opened in 1777); *Kingston Bridge* (built 1828 and widened 1914) and *Hampton Court Bridge* (rebuilt, 1933).

Buckingham Palace, SW1A 1AA. (Not open to the public.)—Purchased by King George III in 1762 from the heir of the Duke of Buckingham, the Palace has been the London home of the Sovereign since Queen Victoria's accession in 1837. It was altered by Nash for King George IV, and refronted in stone (part of the Queen Victoria Memorial) by Sir Aston Webb in 1913.

The Queen's Gallery, containing a changing selection of the finest pictures and works of art from all parts of the royal collection, was opened to the public on July 25, 1962. Open Tues.–Sat. and Bank Holidays 10.30–5, Sun. 2–5. Admission charges are payable, entering from Buckingham Palace Road.

The Royal Mews is open to visitors on Wed. and Thurs. throughout the year (except in Ascot Week), 2–4. Admission charges, the net proceeds of which are devoted to charities, are payable at the entrance.

Canada House, Trafalgar Square, S.W.1.—Designed by Sir Robert Smirke and built in 1824–7, it underwent major alterations to incorporate the former Royal College of Physicians building, also by Smirke, between 1964–67. Certain interior features of the original building, now housing the Canadian High Commission, are preserved including the spacious, richly furnished room now occupied by the High Commissioner.

Canonbury Tower, N.1.—The largest remaining part of a 16th century house originally built by the Priors of St. Bartholomew, and since 1952 used as the headquarters of a non-professional theatre company. Contains the "Spencer" and "Compton" oak-panelled rooms. Other relics of Canonbury House can be seen nearby.

Carlyle's House, 24 Cheyne Row, Chelsea, SW3 5HL. The home of Thomas Carlyle for 47 years until his death in 1881, and containing many of his effects. Now the property of the National Trust. Open daily, April–Oct. Wed.–Sun. and Bank Holiday Mondays 11–5. Admission £1·60; concessions 80p.

Catholic Central Library, St. Francis Friary, 47 Francis Street, SW1P 1QR.—Founded as a private library in 1914, it was taken over in 1959 by the Franciscan Friars of the Atonement. It is an up-to-date lending and research library of over 55,000 volumes and 150 periodicals, for the general reader, student and ecumenist. Books are sent by post when required. Open Mon.-Fri. 10–5, Sat. 10–1.30.

Cemeteries.—In *Kensal Green Cemetery,* North Kensington, W.10 (70 acres), are tombs of Thackeray, Trollope, Sydney Smith, Wilkie Collins, Tom Hood, George Cruikshank, John Leech, Leigh Hunt, I. K. Brunel, Charles Kemble (actor). In *Highgate Cemetery,* N.6, are the tombs of George Eliot, Herbert Spencer, Faraday and Marx. In *Abney Park Cemetery,* Stoke Newington, N.16 are the tomb of General Booth, founder of the Salvation Army, and memorials to many Nonconformist Divines. In the *South Metropolitan Cemetery,* Norwood, S.E.27, are the tombs of Sir Henry Bessemer, Sir Hiram Maxim, Mrs. Beeton, Sir Henry Tate and Joseph Whitaker, F.S.A. (*Whitaker's Almanack*). In the churchyard of the former *Marylebone Chapel* are buried Charles Wesley and his son Samuel Wesley (musician). The chapel itself was demolished in 1949. **Crematoria.**—*Ilford* (City of London); *Norwood; Hendon; Streatham Park; Finchley* (St. Marylebone) and *Golders Green* (12 acres), near Hampstead Heath, with "Garden of Rest" and memorials to famous men and women.

Cenotaph, Whitehall, S.W.1.—(Literally "empty tomb"). Monument erected "To the Glorious Dead", as a memorial to all ranks of the Sea, Land and Air Forces who gave their lives in the service of the Empire during the First World War. Designed by Sir Edwin Lutyens. Erected as a temporary memorial in 1919 and replaced by a permament structure in 1920. Unveiled by King George V on Armistice Day, 1920. An additional inscription was added after the 1939–45 War to commemorate those who gave their lives in that conflict.

Charterhouse, Sutton's Hospital, Charterhouse Square, EC1M 6AN. (*Master,* E. E. Harrison, F.S.A.; *Registrar and Clerk to the Governors,* Lt. Col. I. Macdonald). A Carthusian monastery from 1371–1537, when it came into the possession of Sir Edward (later first Lord) North, who sold it in 1565 to the fourth Duke of Norfolk. After his execution in 1572, following the Ridolfi Plot, hatched at Charterhouse, it was eventually granted by Queen Elizabeth I, in 1587, to Norfolk's second son, Thomas Howard, later Earl of Suffolk. In 1611 he sold it to Thomas Sutton, who endowed it as a Hospital for aged men "of gentle birth" and a school for poor scholars (removed to Godalming in 1872). The buildings are partly 15th but mainly 16th and 17th century. Parts of the building were damaged by enemy action in 1941 but have been largely restored and now accommodate some 30 pensioners. Roger Williams, founder and governor of Rhode Island, was a scholar on the foundation. Among other famous pupils were John Wesley, Lord Baden-Powell, the poets and writers Crashaw, Lovelace and Thackeray, and more recently Lord Beveridge. Visitors are shown round on Wednesdays at 2.45 (April–July). Admission £1·50.

Chelsea Physic Garden, 66 Royal Hospital Road, SW3 4HS.—A garden of general botanical research, maintaining a wide range of rare and unusual plants. The garden was established in 1673 by the Society of Apothecaries. Open on Wed. and Sun. p.m. during summer months. All enquiries to the Curator at above address.

Chelsea, Royal Hospital, Royal Hospital Road, Chelsea, S.W.3. Founded by Charles II, in 1682, and built by Wren; opened in 1692 for old and disabled soldiers. Great Hall, Chapel and Museum open daily 10–12, 2–4 (Museum closed on Sunday afternoons Oct.–March). The extensive grounds include the former Ranelagh Gardens, and are the venue for the Chelsea Flower Show held each May by the Royal Horticultural Society. *Governor,* General Sir Roland Guy, G.C.B., C.B.E., D.S.O.; *Lieut-Governor and Secretary,* Major-Gen. A. L. Watson, C.B.

City Business Library (Corporation of London), 55 Basinghall Street, EC2V 5BX. Open Mon.-Fri. 9.30-5.00.

College of Arms or Heralds' College, Queen Victoria Street, E.C.4—Her Majesty's Officers of Arms (Kings, Heralds and Pursuivants of Arms) were first incorporated by Richard III, and granted Derby House on the site of the present College building by Philip and Mary. The building now in use dates from 1671–88. The powers vested by the Crown in the Earl Marshal (The Duke of Norfolk) with regard to State ceremonial are largely exercised through the College, which is also the official repository of English pedigrees and all Arms granted to subjects of the Queen (except in Scotland). Enquiry may be made to the Officer on duty in the Public Office, Mon.-Fri. 10–4.

The Heralds Museum at the Tower of London (admission charge included in the Tower's own charge) aims to explain what heraldry is about and traces its development over the centuries to its application and use in modern times. Open April–Sept.

Commonwealth Institute, Kensington High Street, W.8.—A cultural and educational centre opened on Nov. 6, 1962, by Her Majesty the Queen, replacing the former Imperial Institute opened in 1893 in S. Kensington. A distinctive feature of the building is its paraboloid copper-sheathed roof. The Institute contains, in 60,000 square feet arranged in 3 floors of circular galleries, a visual representation of the history, geography and ways of life of the Commonwealth countries and dependencies, as well as art galleries, a cinema, a theatre, a Teachers' Resource Centre, a restaurant and a bookshop.

Open Mon.–Sat. 10–5.30, Sun. 2–5. Admission free. Closed Christmas Eve, Christmas Day, Boxing Day, New Year's Day, Good Friday and May Day.

County Hall, Westminster Bridge, S.E.1.—Formerly the Headquarters of the Greater London Council, built on the Pedlar's Acre, Bishop's Acre, Four Acres and Float Mead, Lambeth, from the designs of Ralph Knott, with a river façade of 750 ft. The main building was completed in 1933. The North and South blocks were occupied in 1939 but not finally completed until 1963.

Courtauld Institute Galleries, University of London, Woburn Square, WC1.—The galleries of the University of London contain the Lee collection and the Gambier–Parry collections (14th century to 18th century old masters); the important Courtauld collection of Impressionist and Post-Impressionist paintings; the Roger Fry collection and the Witt and Spooner collections (old master drawings and English water-colours). A major new bequest, the Princes Gate collection of old master paintings and drawings, was opened to the public in July 1981. The Galleries will be moving to Somerset House during summer 1989. Open weekdays 10–5, Sun. 2–5. Admission £1·50, concessions 50p.

Custom House, Lower Thames Street, E.C.3.—Built 1813–17, with a wide quay on Thames. The Long Room is about 190 ft. long.

Dickens House, 48 Doughty Street, WC1N 2LF.—In this house Charles Dickens lived from 1837 to 1839, and here he completed *Pickwick Papers.* It is the headquarters of the Dickens Fellowship and contains many relics of the novelist. Open daily 10–5 (except Sundays and Bank Holidays). Admission £1·50, concessions 75p/50p, family ticket £3.

Downing Street.—Number 10 Downing Street, S.W.1, is the official town residence of the Prime Minister. No. 11 of the Chancellor of the Exchequer and No. 12 is the office of the Government Whips. The street was named after Sir George Downing, Bt. soldier and diplomatist, who was M.P. for Morpeth from 1660 to 1684.

Chequers, a Tudor mansion in the Chilterns, about 3 miles from Princes Risborough, was presented together with a maintenance endowment by Lord and Lady Lee of Fareham in 1917 to serve, from Jan. 1, 1921, as a country residence for the Prime Minister of the day, the Chequers estate of 700 acres being added to the gift by Lord Lee in 1921. The mansion contains a famous collection of Cromwellian portraits and relics.

Dr. Johnson's House, Gough Square, Fleet Street, E.C.4.—A tall late 17th century house in which Johnson (and his wife) lived between 1748 and 1759. His *Dictionary* was compiled here. The house is furnished with 18th century pieces and there is an excellent collection of Johnsoniana. Open daily (except Sundays and Bank Holidays) 11–5.30 (winter 11–5). Admission charge.

Dulwich, S.E.21.—Contains *Dulwich College* (founded by Edward Alleyn in 1619) and the *Dulwich Picture Gallery,* built by Sir John Soane to house the collection bequeathed by the artist Sir Francis Bourgeois. The gallery was damaged in the Second World War but rebuilt with the aid of a grant from the Pilgrim Trust and reopened in 1953. *Dulwich Village* retains many of the rural characteristics of the pre-suburban period.

Eltham, S.E.9.—Contains remains of 13th–15th century *Eltham Palace,* the birthplace of John of Eltham (1316), son of Edward II. The hall, built by Edward IV, has a hammer-beam roof of chestnut. In the churchyard of St. John the Baptist is the tomb of *Thomas Doggett,* the comedian and founder of the Thames Watermen's championship (Doggett's Coat and Badge).

Ely Place, Holborn Circus, E.C.1.—Previously the site of the London house of the Bishop of Ely, Ely Place is a private street (built in 1773) whose affairs are administered by Commissioners under a special Act of Parliament. The 14th century chapel, now St. Etheldreda's (R.C.) Church, is open daily until dusk.

Eton College.—The most famous of English public schools, founded by Henry VI in 1440. The buildings date from 1442.

Fulham Palace, Bishop's Avenue, Fulham, S.W.6.—The courtyard is 16th century, remainder 18th and 19th century. Former residence of the Bishop of London.

Geffrye Museum, Kingsland Road, E2 8EA.—Open on Tuesdays to Saturdays 10 to 5, Sundays 2 to 5. Closed on Christmas Eve, Christmas Day, Boxing Day and New Year's Day and on Mondays except Bank Holidays. Admission free.

The Museum is housed in a building erected originally as almshouses in 1713. The exhibits are displayed in a series of period rooms dating from 1600 to 1939, showing the development of decorative art and design. A display of woodworking tools focuses on furniture-making, and the museum has an interesting picture collection. Events and temporary exhibitions are held. Special arrangements exist for children visiting the Museum in school parties (which must be booked in advance) and in their leisure time. *Director,* D. Rodgers.

George Inn, Southwark.—Near London Bridge Station. Given to the National Trust in 1937. Last galleried inn in London, built in 1677. Open during licensed hours.

Greenwich, S.E.10.—*Greenwich Hospital* (since 1873, the Royal Naval College) was built by Charles II, largely from designs by John Webb, and by Queen Anne and William III, from designs by Wren, on the site of an ancient royal palace, and of the more recent *Palace of Placentia,* an enlarged edition of the palace, constructed by Humphrey, Duke of Gloucester (1391–1447), son of Henry IV. Henry VIII, Queen Mary I and Queen Elizabeth I were born in the Royal Palace (which reverted to the Crown in 1447) and King Edward VI died there. In the principal quadrangle is a marble statue of George II, by Rysbraeck. (For *National Maritime Museum,* see Index.) *Painted Hall* and *Chapel* open daily (except Thursdays) 2.30–5. Visitors are also admitted to Sunday Service in the Chapel at 11 a.m., summer and winter, except during College vacations. *Greenwich Park* (196½ acres) was enclosed by Humphrey, Duke of Gloucester, and laid out by Charles II, from the designs of Le Nôtre. *The Queen's House,* begun in 1616, was designed for Anne of Denmark by Inigo Jones (closed for repairs from Oct. 1984). On a hill in Greenwich Park is the former Royal Observatory (founded 1675). Part of its buildings at Greenwich have been taken over by the Maritime Museum and named *Flamsteed House,* after John Flamsteed (1646–1719), first Astronomer Royal. Astronomical and navigational equipment is exhibited, and the time ball and zero meridian of longitude can also be seen. The Parish church of Greenwich (*St. Alfege*) was rebuilt by Hawksmoor (Wren's pupil) in 1728, and restored after severe damage during the Second World War. General Wolfe and Thomas Tallis are buried in the church. Henry VIII was christened in the former church. *Charlton House,* built in the early 17th century (1607–1612) for Adam Newton, tutor to Prince Henry, brother to Charles I, is largely in the Jacobean style of architecture. *Cutty Sark,* the last of the famous tea clippers, which has been preserved as a memorial to ships and men of a past era is fully restored and re-rigged, with a museum of sail on board. Open weekdays 11–5 (summer 11–6), Sundays and Boxing Day 2.30–5. The yacht *Gipsy Moth IV* in which Sir Francis Chichester sailed single-handed round the world, 1966–67, is preserved alongside the *Cutty Sark.*

Guildhall, Gresham Street, City, E.C.2.—Scene of civic government for the City for more than a thousand years. Built c. 1440; façade built 1788–9; damaged in the Great Fire, 1666, and by incendiary bombs, 1940. The main hall and crypt (the most extensive medieval crypt in London) have been restored. Events in Guildhall include the annual election of Lord Mayor, election of Sheriffs, receptions in honour of Sovereigns and Heads of State, and the meetings of the Court of Common Council (*see* "Corporation of London"). Open weekdays 10–5, Sun. (May to Sept.) 10–4. Admission free. *Keeper of the Guildhall,* J. H. Lucioni.

The Guildhall (reference) Library and the Library and Museum of the Clockmakers' Company are housed in new premises. Library open Mon.–Sat. 9.30–5, Museum open Mon. to Fri. 9–6. Admission free (entrance in Aldermanbury). The Library contains

Plans of London, 1570; Deed of Sale with Shakespeare's signature; first, second and fourth folios of Shakespeare's plays etc. (*See also* City Business Library).

Ham House, Richmond.—A notable example of 17th century domestic architecture, long the home of the Tollemache family (Earls of Dysart). The contents were purchased for the Victoria and Albert Museum which now administers the house. Open Tues.–Sun. 11–5. Closed Mon. (except Bank Holidays), Christmas Eve, Christmas Day, Boxing Day, New Year's Day, Good Friday and May Day. Admission £2, concessions £1.

Hampton Court.—Sixteenth-century Palace built by Cardinal Wolsey, with additions by Sir Christopher Wren for William and Mary. Beautiful gardens with maze and grape vine (planted in 1769). State Apartments and collection of pictures. Tennis Court, built by King Henry VIII in 1530. Collection of Mantegna paintings. Gardens open daily 7–9 (or dusk), Maze March–Oct. Palace open mid March–mid Oct. daily 9.30–6, mid Oct.–Dec. 9.30–4.30. Admission prices vary for specific attractions: all-inclusive ticket £2·80. Gardens free.

Harrow.—Public school founded by John Lyon in 1571. The "Fourth Form Room" dates from 1608.

Holland Park, W.8.—55 acres including an open air theatre and concerts; floodlit gardens; King George VI Memorial Youth Hostel; restaurant.

Honourable Artillery Company's Headquarters, City Road, EC1Y 2BQ.—The H.A.C. (*Chief Exec.* Capt. G. C. Lloyd, C.B.E., R.N.) received its charter of incorporation from Henry VIII in 1537, and has occupied its present ground since 1641. The Armoury House dates from 1735. The present castellated barracks date from 1860. Four of its members who emigrated in the 17th century, founded in 1638 the Ancient and Honorable Artillery Company of Massachusetts. The H.A.C. is the senior regiment of the Territorial Army Volunteer Reserves, and maintains a Headquarters, four squadrons, a gun troop, and two companies of the Home Service Force.

Horniman Museum and Library, London Road, Forest Hill, S.E.23.—The Museum was presented in 1901 to the London County Council by the founder, Mr. F. J. Horniman, M.P. It is now administered by I.L.E.A. The Museum has three main departments, ethnography, musical instruments and natural history. In the ethnography department the large collections include exhibits illustrating man's progress in the arts and crafts from prehistoric times. The natural history department includes an aquarium. Reference library (except Mondays). Education Service (adults and schoolchildren). Free concerts and lectures (autumn and spring). Special exhibitions. *Director,* D. M. Boston, O.B.E. Open Mon.–Sat. 10.30–6, Sun. 2–6. Admission free.

Horse Guards, Whitehall, S.W.1.—Archway and offices built about 1753. The mounting of the guard (Life Guards, or the Blues and Royals) at 11 a.m. (10 a.m. on Sundays) and the dismounted inspection at 4 p.m. are picturesque ceremonies. Only those on the Lord Chamberlain's list may drive through the gates and archway into *Horse Guard's Parade* (230,000 sq. ft.), where the Colour is "trooped" on the Queen's Official Birthday.

The Houses of Parliament, Westminster, S.W.1.—An ordinance issued in the reign of Richard II stated that "Parliament shall be holden or kepid wheresoever it pleaseth the King" and at the present day the Sovereign summons Parliament to meet and prescribes the time and place of meeting. The royal palace of Westminster, originally built by Edward

the Confessor (Westminster Hall (*q.v.*) being added by William Rufus), was the normal place of Parliament from about 1340. St. Stephen's Chapel was used from about 1550 for the meetings of the House of Commons, which had previously been held in the Chapter House or Refectory of Westminster Abbey. The House of Lords met in an apartment of the royal palace.

The fire of 1834 destroyed much of the palace and the present Houses of Parliament were erected on the site from the designs of Sir Charles Barry and Augustus Welby Pugin between 1840 and 1867. The Chamber of the House of Commons was destroyed by enemy action in 1941 and a new Chamber designed by Sir Giles Gilbert Scott was used for the first time on Oct. 26, 1950.

The Victoria Tower of the House of Lords is about 330 ft. high, and when Parliament is sitting the Union Flag flies by day from its flagstaff. *The Clock Tower* of the House of Commons is about 320 ft. high and contains "Big Ben", the hour bell said to be named after Sir Benjamin Hall, First Commissioner of Works when the original bell was cast in 1856. This bell, which weighed 16 tons 11 cwt., was found to be cracked in 1857. The present bell (13½ tons) is a recasting of the original and was first brought into use in July, 1859. The dials of the clock are 23 ft. in diameter, the hands being 9 ft. and 14 ft. long (including balance piece). A light is displayed from the Clock Tower at night when Parliament is sitting.

For security reasons tours of the Houses of Parliament are available only to those who have made advance arrangements through a Member or Peer.

Admission to the Strangers' Gallery of the House of Lords is arranged by a Peer or by queue *via* St. Stephen's Entrance. Admission to the Strangers' Gallery of the House of Commons, is by Members' order (Members' orders should be sought several weeks in advance), or by queue *via* St. Stephen's Entrance. Queues are usually shorter after 6 p.m., Mon.–Thurs. Overseas visitors may obtain cards of introduction from their Embassy or High Commission.

Inns of Court.—The *Inner* and *Middle Temple,* S. of Fleet Street, E.C.4, and N. of Victoria Embankment, to which the gardens extend, have occupied (since early 14th century) the site of the buildings of the Order of Knights Templars. *Inner Temple Hall* (rebuilt in 1955 after bomb damage) is open Mon.–Fri. 10.30–11.30 and 3–4 on application to Treasurer's Office during law sittings. *Temple Church,* restored in 1958 after severe damage by bombing, is open on weekdays 9.30–4 and the public is admitted to Sunday services. *Middle Temple Hall* (1562–70) is open when not in use, Mon.–Fri. 10–12 and 3–4, Sat. when staff are available. Closed on Public Holidays. In Middle Temple Gardens (not open to the public) Shakespeare (Henry VI, Part I) places the incident which led to the "Wars of the Roses" (1455–85). *Lincoln's Inn,* from Chancery Lane to Lincoln's Inn Fields, W.C.2, occupies the site of the palace of a former Bishop of Chichester and of a Black Friars monastery. Records show the Society as being in existence in 1422. The Hall and Library Buildings are of 1845, although the Library is first mentioned in 1474, the old Hall early 16th century and the Chapel was rebuilt c. 1619–23. Halls open by appointment, Chapel and Gardens, Mon.–Fri. 12–2.30. Tours, weekdays mid March–mid Sept. 9.30–11.30, £2. Chapel services Sun. 11.30 a.m. during Law Terms. *Lincoln's Inn Fields* (7 acres). The Square, laid out by Inigo Jones, contains many fine old houses with handsome interiors. *Gray's Inn,* Holborn/Gray's Inn Road, W.C.1. Early 14th century. Hall (1556–60). Chapel (largely rebuilt in 1698). Services 11.15 a.m. (during Law Dining Terms only.)

Holy Communion 1st Sunday in every month except Aug.–Sept. Public welcome. Library (30,000 vols., mss. and printed books) may be viewed by appointment. Gardens open to the public May–Sept. 12–2.30. The Inn, although badly damaged during the last war, has been completely restored to its former beauty with gracious red brick buildings overlooking grass covered squares and gardens. Strong Elizabethan associations. No other "Inns" are active, but what remains of *Staple Inn* is worth visiting as a relic of Elizabethan London; though heavy damage was done by a flying-bomb, it retains a picturesque gabled front on Holborn (opposite Gray's Inn Road). *Clement's Inn* (near St. Clement Danes' Church), *Clifford's Inn*, Fleet Street, and *Thavies Inn*, Holborn Circus, are all rebuilt. *Serjeant's Inn*, Fleet Street (damaged by bombing) and another (demolished 1910) of the same name in Chancery Lane, were composed of Serjeants-at-Law, the last of whom died in 1922.

Jewish Museum, Woburn House, Tavistock Square, WC1H 0EP.—Opened in 1932, the Museum contains a rich collection of ceremonial art, portraits and antiquities, illustrating Jewish life, history and religion. Open Tues.–Thurs. and Sun. (and Fri. in summer) 10–4, Fri. in winter 10–12.45. Closed on Public and Jewish Holidays. Group visits by arrangement with Secretary.

Keats House, Keats Grove, Hampstead, NW3 2RR.—In two houses here, now made into one, John Keats lived at various times between 1818 and 1820. Restored 1974–75. Open April–Oct. Mon.–Fri. 2–6, Sat. 10–5, Sun. and Bank Hols. 2–5, Nov.–March, Mon.–Fri. 1–5, Sat. 10–5, Sun. 2–5. Closed on Christmas Day, Boxing Day, New Year's Day, Good Friday, Easter Eve and May Day. The Keats Memorial Library contains over 7,000 volumes.

Kensington Palace, W8 4PX.—The original house was bought by William III in 1689 and enlarged by Christoper Wren. The birthplace of Queen Victoria in 1819. The State Apartments contain pictures and furniture from the royal collections. A suite of rooms devoted to the memory of Queen Victoria is also shown. The *Court Dress Collection* is also open, and includes three restored rooms, the Red Saloon, the Teck Saloon and the room where Queen Victoria is said to have been born. Both open weekdays 9–5, Sun. 1–5. Admission £2·60, concessions £1·70; £1·30.

Kenwood, NW3 7JR.—Nearly 200 acres forming the northern part of Hampstead Heath. Open air symphony concerts each summer. The Iveagh Bequest, in an Adam villa, includes valuable paintings and furniture. Recitals and poetry readings in the Orangery. House open daily, except Good Friday and Dec. 24, 25. Times vary seasonally. Admission free.

Kew, Surrey.—A favourite home of the early Hanoverian monarchs. Kew House, the residence of Frederick, Prince of Wales, and later of his son, George III, was pulled down in 1803, but the earlier Dutch House, now known as Kew Palace, survives. It was built in 1631 and acquired by George III as an annexe to Kew House in 1781. The famous Kew Gardens (*see* Index) were originally laid out as a private garden for Kew House for George III's mother in 1759 and were much enlarged in the 19th century, notably by the inclusion of the grounds of the former Richmond Lodge.

Kneller Hall, Twickenham, TW2 7DU.—Royal Military School of Music. A band of up to 120 instrumentalists gives concerts in the grounds on Wednesdays throughout the summer, commencing at 8 p.m. Admission charge. Season tickets and party bookings available.

Lambeth Palace, S.E.1.—The official residence of the Archbishop of Canterbury, on south bank of Thames; the oldest part is 13th century, the house itself is early 19th century. For leave to visit the historical portions, applications should be made by letter to the Archbishop's Chaplain.

Livery Companies' Halls.—The Principal Companies (*see* Index) have magnificent halls but admission to view them has generally to be arranged beforehand. The following are among the finest or more interesting. *Goldsmiths' Hall,* Foster Lane. The present hall was completed in 1835, and contains some magnificent rooms. Exhibitions of plate have been shown here periodically in recent years. *Fishmongers' Hall,* London Bridge (built 1831–3), now admirably restored after severe bomb damage, also contains fine rooms. *Apothecaries' Hall,* Black Friars Lane, was rebuilt in 1670, after the Great Fire, and has library, hall and kitchen which are good examples of this period, together with a pleasant courtyard. *Vintners' Hall,* Upper Thames Street, was also rebuilt after the Great Fire, and its hall has very fine late 17th century panelling. The Watermen and Lightermen's Company is not, strictly speaking, a Livery Company, but its *Hall,* in St. Mary at Hill, is a good example of a smaller 18th century building, with pilastered façade. It was completed in 1780. *Stationers' Hall,* in Stationers' Hall Court, behind Ludgate Hill, another post-fire Hall, standing in its own court, has a particularly finely carved screen; its façade dates from 1800. *Barbers' Hall,* Monkwell Street, with a Hall attributed to Inigo Jones, was completely destroyed by bombing, but has now been rebuilt. The new hall was built some 30 ft. from the old site to enable one of the bastions and part of the wall of the Roman fort to remain exposed to view.

Lloyd's, Lime Street, EC3M 7HA.—Society of private underwriters which evolved during the 18th century from Lloyds Coffee House. Housed in the Royal Exchange for 150 years and in Leadenhall Street and Lime Street from 1928–1986. The present building was opened for business in May 1986, and houses the Lutine Bell. Underwriting is on four floors with a total area of 114,000 sq. ft. A visitors' gallery is open daily and incorporates an exhibition showing the history and operation of the insurance market at Lloyds.

London Planetarium, Marylebone Road, NW1 5LR.—Open daily (except Christmas Day), star shows 11–4.30. Admission charge.

London Transport Museum, Covent Garden, W.C.2.—Housed in the former Flower Market, the Museum contains a collection of buses, trams, trolleybuses, trains, working displays and London Transport paraphernalia. There is a research library and lecture theatre. Open daily 10–6 (except Dec. 24, 25, 26). Admission £2·40, concessions £1·10.

Lord's Cricket Ground, St. John's Wood Road, N.W.8.—The headquarters (since 1814) of the Marylebone Cricket Club (founded 1787), the premier cricket club in England, the scene of some of the principal matches of the season and Middlesex County headquarters. Real tennis court and squash courts in building behind members' pavilion.

The Cricket Memorial Gallery, a museum of cricket, open on match days (except Sun.) 10.30–5. Admission £1, concessions 50p. In winter and on non-match days admission is by prior arrangement with the Curator.

Madame Tussaud's Exhibition, Marylebone Road NW1 5LR.—Open daily (except Christmas Day) 10–5.30. Admission charge.

Mansion House, City, E.C.4.—(Built 1739–53, reconstructed 1930–31.) The official residence of the Lord Mayor; the Egyptian Hall and Ballroom are the chief attractions. Admission by order from the Lord Mayor's Secretary.

Marble Hill House, Twickenham, TW1 2NL (English Heritage).—Example of the English Palladian style, built 1724–9 for Henrietta Howard, Countess of Suffolk, mistress of George II. Houses fine collection of early 18th century paintings and furniture including original overmantel and overdoors by Panini. The house set in 66½ acres running down to the Thames open air theatre in June. Open daily (except Fri.) 10–5, Nov.–Jan. 10–4. Closed Good Friday and Dec. 24, 25. Admission free.

Markets.—The London markets (administered by the Corporation of the City of London) provide foodstuffs for 8,500,000 to 9,000,000 people. *Central Meat, Fish, Fruit, Vegetable, and Poultry Markets,* Smithfield (present buildings, 1866) the largest meat market in the world and site of St. Bartholomew's Fair from 9th to 19th century; *Leadenhall Market* (meat and poultry), built 1881, part recently demolished; *Billingsgate* (fish), Thames Street, built 1875, part recently demolished, a market site for over 1,000 years (moved to the Isle of Dogs in Jan. 1982); *Spitalfields,* E.1 (vegetables, fruit, etc.), enlarged 1928, and opened by Queen Mary; *London Fruit Exchange,* Brushfield Street, built by Corporation of London 1928–29, faces Spitalfields Market; *Covent Garden* (vegetables, fruit, flowers, etc.), (now moved to Nine Elms) established under a charter of Charles II, in 1661; *Borough Market,* S.E.1 (vegetables, fruit, flowers, etc.).

Marlborough House, Pall Mall, S.W.1.—Built by Wren for the first Duke of Marlborough and completed in 1711, the house finally reverted to the Crown in 1835. Prince Leopold lived there until 1831, and Queen Adelaide from 1837 until her death in 1849. In 1863 it became the London house of the Prince of Wales and was the London home of Queen Mary until her death in 1953. The Queen's Chapel, Marlborough Gate, begun in 1623 from the designs of Inigo Jones for the Infanta Maria of Spain, and completed for Queen Henrietta Maria, is open to the public for services on Sundays at 8.30 a.m. and 11.15 a.m. between Easter Day and end July (*see also* St. James's Palace for winter services in The Chapel Royal). In 1959 Marlborough House was given by the Queen as a centre for Commonwealth Government conferences and it was opened as such in March, 1962.

London Monument (commonly called "The Monument"), Monument Street, E.C.3.—Built from designs of Wren, 1671–77, to commemorate the *Great Fire of London,* which broke out in Pudding Lane, Sept. 2, 1666. The fluted Doric column is 120 ft. high (the moulded cylinder above the balcony supporting a flaming vase of gilt bronze is 42 ft. in addition), and is based on a square plinth 40 ft. high, with fine carvings on W. face (making a total height of 202 ft.). Splendid views of London from gallery at top of column (311 steps). Open Mon.–Fri. 9–2, 3–6 (Oct.–March 9–2, 3–4), Sat. 9–2, 3–4 (Oct.–March), Sat. and Sun. 2–6 (April–Sept.) Closed Christmas Day, Boxing Day and Good Friday. Admission charge.

Monuments.—*Albert Memorial,* South Kensington; *Royal Air Force,* Victoria Embankment; *Beaconsfield,* Parliament Square; *Beatty, Jellicoe* and *Cunningham,* Trafalgar Square; *Belgian Gratitude* (Reginald Blomfield), Victoria Embankment; *Boadicea* (or "Boudicca"), Queen of the Iceni, E. Anglia (Thomas Thornycroft), Westminster Bridge; *Brunel* (Marochetti), Victoria Embankment; *Burghers of Calais* (Rodin), Victoria Tower Gardens, Westminster; *Burns,* Embankment Gardens; *Carlyle* (Boehm), Cheyne Walk, Chelsea; *Cavalry,* Hyde Park; *Cavell* (Frampton), St. Martin's Place; *Cenotaph* (Lutyens),

Whitehall; *Charles I,* Trafalgar Square; *Charles II,* inside the Royal Exchange; *Churchill,* Parliament Square; *Cleopatra's Needle* (68½ ft. high *c.* 1500 B.C. erected on the Thames Embankment in 1877–8)—the Sphinxes are Victorian; *Clive,* Whitehall; *Captain Cook* (Brock), The Mall; *Crimean,* Broad Sanctuary; *Oliver Cromwell* (Thornycroft), outside Westminster Hall; *Duke of Cambridge,* Whitehall; *Duke of York* (124 ft.), Carlton House Terrace; *Edward VII* (Mackennal), Waterloo Place; *Elizabeth I* (1586, oldest outdoor statue in London) (from Ludgate), Fleet Street; *Eros* (Shaftesbury Memorial) (Gilbert), Piccadilly Circus; *Marechal Foch,* Grosvenor Gardens; *Charles James Fox,* Bloomsbury Square; *George III,* Cockspur Street; *George IV* (Chantrey), riding without stirrups, Trafalgar Square; *George V,* Old Palace Yard; *George VI,* Carlton Gardens; *Gladstone,* facing Australia House, Strand; *Guards'* (Crimea), Waterloo Place; (Great War), Horse Guards' Parade; *Haig* (Hardiman), Whitehall; *Irving* (Brock), N. side of National Portrait Gallery; *James II,* Trafalgar Square; *Samuel Johnson,* opposite St. Clement Danes; *Kitchener,* Horse Guards' Parade; *Abraham Lincoln,* Parliament Square; *Milton,* St. Giles, Cripplegate; *Monument, The* (*see above*); *Mountbatten,* Foreign Office Green; *Nelson* (170 ft. 2 in.), Trafalgar Square, with Lanseer's lions (cast from guns recovered from the wreck of the *Royal George*); *Florence Nightingale,* Waterloo Place; *Palmerston,* Parliament Square; *Peel,* Parliament Square; *Pitt* (Chantrey), Hanover Square ; *Portal,* Embankment Gardens; *Prince Consort,* Holborn Circus; *Raleigh,* Whitehall; *Richard Coeur de Lion* (Marochetti), Old Palace Yard; *Roberts,* Horse Guards' Parade; *Franklin D. Roosevelt* (Reid Dick), Grosvenor Square; *Royal Artillery* (South Africa), The Mall; (Great War), Hyde Park Corner; *Captain Scott* (Lady Scott), Waterloo Place; *Shackleton,* Kensington Gore; *Shakespeare,* Leicester Square; *Smuts* (Epstein), Parliament Square; *Sullivan,* Victoria Embankment; *Trenchard,* Victoria Embankment; *Victoria Memorial,* in front of Buckingham Palace; *George Washington* (Houdon copy), Trafalgar Square; *Wellington,* Hyde Park Corner; *Wellington* (Chantrey) riding without stirrups, Royal Exchange; *John Wesley,* City Road; *William III,* St. James's Square; *Wolseley,* Horse Guards' Parade.

Osterley Park, Osterley, Middx.—House and park of 140 acres given to the National Trust by the Earl of Jersey in 1949 and administered by the Victoria and Albert Museum. The Elizabethan house, built in 1577 for Sir Thomas Gresham, was largely remodelled by Robert Adam, and the staterooms are among the best examples of Adam decoration. Open daily (except Mondays) 11–5. Closed Mon. (except Bank Holidays), Christmas Eve, Christmas Day, Boxing Day, New Year's Day, Good Friday and May Day. Admission £2, concessions £1.

Percival David Foundation of Chinese Art, 53 Gordon Square, WC1H 0RD.—Set up in 1950, the Foundation contains the collection of Chinese ceramics formed by Sir Percival David and his important library of books on Chinese art. To these was added a gift from the Hon. Mountstuart Elphinstone of part of his collection of Chinese monochrome porcelains. The Foundation is administered on behalf of the University of London by the School of Oriental and African Studies. Galleries, Mon.–Fri. 10.30–5. Closed weekends and Bank Holidays. Library available to ticket holders only; applications in writing to the Curator, Miss R. Scott.

Port of London.—The Port of London covers the tidal portion of the River Thames from Teddington to the seaward limit (Tongue light vessel), a distance of 150 km. The governing body is the Port of London

Authority (P.L.A.), whose Head Office is at Europe House, World Trade Centre, E1 9AA. The enclosed dock at Tilbury is wholly-owned by the P.L.A. and is 40 km. below London Bridge. The docks have a comprehensive range of modern cargo-handling facilities and perform every type of cargo-handling operation. Tilbury is principally used by vessels to and from Australia, North and South America, India, Middle and Far East, Scandinavia, U.S.S.R. and the Continent.

Privately owned cargo-handling facilities along the River Thames are an important part of the Port of London, handling some 40 million tonnes of cargo a year, 60 per cent. of which is crude oil and refined products. The combination of P.L.A. and privately-owned facilities makes the Port of London the U.K.'s largest non-oil port.

Passenger vessels and cruise liners can be handled at moorings at Greenwich, near Tower Bridge and at Tilbury Passenger Landing Stage. The latter provides accommodation for liners at all states of the tide.

Prince Henry's Room, 17 Fleet Street, E.C.4.—Early 17th century timber-framed house containing fine room on first floor with panelling and moulded plaster ceiling. Includes an exhibition on Samuel Pepys and the London in which he lived. Open Mon.–Fri. 1.45–5, Sat 1.45–4.30. Closed Christmas Day, Good Friday and Bank Holidays. Admission free. Available for morning or evening lettings on application to The Town Clerk, Guildhall, E.C.2.

Richmond, Surrey. Contains the red brick gateway of *Richmond Palace* (Henry VII, 1485–1509) and buildings of the Jacobean, Queen Anne, and early Georgian periods, including *White Lodge* in Richmond Park, the former home of Queen Mary's mother (the Duke of Windsor was born there, June 23, 1894), and now the home of the Royal Ballet School. The *Star and Garter* Home for Disabled Soldiers, Sailors, and Airmen (the Women's Memorial of the Great War) was opened by Queen Mary in 1924. *Richmond Park* (2,469 acres) contains herds of fallow and red deer.

Roman London.—Although visible remains from this period are few, excavations carried out in the City on sites due for redevelopment often reveal Roman features. Sections of the City Wall are the most striking remains to be seen of Roman *Londinium,* although even these are largely medieval due to the Roman wall being rebuilt during the medieval period. Sections may be seen near the White Tower in the Tower of London; at Tower Hill; at Coopers' Row; at All Hallows, London Wall, its vestry being built on the remains of a semi-circular Roman bastion; at St. Alphage, London Wall, showing a striking succession of building repairs from Roman until the late medieval period, and at St. Giles Cripplegate. Excavations in the Cripplegate area have revealed that a Roman fort was built there in about A.D.100–120. It was later incorporated into the city wall when this was built about A.D.200.

The administrative centre of the Roman city was the great forum and basilica, more than 165 metres square, sections of which have been encountered during excavations in the area of Leadenhall, Gracechurch Street and Lombard Street. Excavations during the past few years have revealed Roman activity along the river. Traces of a massive riverside wall, built in the late Roman period, have been found and a succession of Roman timber quays have been excavated along Lower and Upper Thames Street helping to prove that Roman London was a thriving commercial centre.

Other major buildings found are the Provincial Governor's Palace in Cannon Street; remains of a bath-building, preserved in Lower Thames Street; and the Temple of Mithras in Walbrook. The fine sculptures from this temple are displayed in the Museum of London, where many other relics from the Roman City may be seen. There is also an Ordnance Survey map of Roman London.

Royal Albert Hall, Kensington Gore, SW7 2AP. The elliptical hall, one of the largest in the world, was completed in 1871, and since 1941 has been the venue each summer for the Promenade Concerts founded in 1895 by Sir Henry Wood. Also used for public meetings, concerts, sports and other entertainments. Guided tours are available in the summer months. *Gen. Manager,* D. C. McNicol.

Royal Exchange, EC3V 3LS. (founded by Sir Thomas Gresham, 1566, opened as "The Bourse" and proclaimed "The Royal Exchange" by Queen Elizabeth I, 1571, rebuilt 1667–69 and 1842–44). The building is occupied by the Guardian Royal Exchange Assurance Group and by the London International Financial Futures Exchange. It is administered by the Gresham Committee (*Clerk,* Mercers' Hall, Ironmonger Lane, E.C.2.).

Royal Geographical Society, Kensington Gore, SW7 2AR.—Map room open to public, admission free. Advice for scientific expeditions abroad, by appointment only.

Royal Opera House, Covent Garden, WC2E 7DD.—Home of The Royal Ballet (1931), The Royal Opera (1946) and Sadler's Wells Royal Ballet (1946) companies, the Royal Opera House is the third theatre to be built on the site, opening May 15, 1858: the first was opened Dec. 7, 1732. The season of the resident companies runs mid Sept.–Aug. *General Director,* J. Isaacs.

Runnymede.—A meadow of about 100 acres, on S. bank of Thames (part of the Crown Lands), between Windsor and Staines. From June 15 to 23, 1215, the hostile Barons encamped on this meadow during negotiations with King John, who rode over each day from Windsor. The 48 "Articles of the Barons" were accepted by the King on June 15, and were subsequently embodied in a charter, since known as *Magna Carta,* of which several copies were sealed on June 19. About half a mile N.E. of the meadow is *Magna Carta Island* (claimed as the actual site of the sealing), presented to the National Trust in 1930.

A memorial at *Cooper's Hill,* near Runnymede, to members of the Commonwealth air forces who lost their lives in the Second World War while serving from bases in the United Kingdom and north-western Europe and have no known grave, was unveiled by the Queen on October 17, 1953. Her Majesty on May 14, 1965, unveiled a memorial to the late President of the United States, John F. Kennedy, on ground nearby.

St. James's Palace, in Pall Mall, S.W.1.—(Closed to the public.) Built by Henry VIII; the Gatehouse and Presence Chamber remain, later alterations by Wren and Kent. The Chapel Royal is open for services on Sundays at 8.30 a.m. and 11.15 a.m. between beginning October and Good Friday (*see also* Marlborough House for summer services in The Queen's Chapel). Representatives of Foreign Powers are still accredited "to the Court of St. James's". *Clarence House* (1825) in the palace precinct is the home of H.M. The Queen Mother.

St. John's Gate, Clerkenwell, E.C.1.—Now the Chancery of the Order of St. John of Jerusalem, and formerly the entrance of the Priory of that Order, of which the gate house (early 16th century) and crypt of Church (12th century) alone survive. They may be inspected on application to the Curator.

Sir John Soane's Museum, 13 Lincoln's Inn Fields, WC2A 3BP. The house and galleries, built 1812–24, are the work of the founder, Sir John Soane (1753–1837) and contain his collections, arranged as he left them, in pursuance of an Act procured by him in 1833. Exhibits include the Sarcophagus of Seti 1 (c. 1290 B.C.), Classical vases and marbles, Hogarth's *Rake's Progress* and *Election* series, paintings by Canaletto, Reynolds, Turner, Lawrence, etc., and sculpture by Chantrey, Flaxman, etc. Soane's library of 8,000 vols, and collection of 40,000 architectural drawings are available for study by appointment. Open Tues.–Sat. 10–5. Closed Bank Holidays. Tours must be booked in advance. *Curator,* P. Thornton, F.S.A. *Assistant Curator,* Mrs M. Richardson.

Somerset House, Strand, W.C.2, and Victoria Embankment, W.C.2.—The beautiful river façade (600 ft. long) was built in 1776–86 from the designs of Sir W. Chambers; the eastern extension, which houses part of King's College, was built by Smirke in 1829. Somerset House was the property of Lord Protector Somerset, at whose attainder in 1552 the palace passed to the Crown, and it was a royal residence until 1692.

South Bank, S.E.1.—The arts complex on the south bank of the River Thames includes the South Bank Centre, owned and managed by the South Bank Board, and consisting of the 2,903-seat *Royal Festival Hall* (opened in 1951 for the Festival of Britain), a major venue for concert and ballet seasons, with the adjacent 1,056-seat *Queen Elizabeth Hall* and 368-seat *Purcell Room,* accommodating smaller-scale performances.

The *National Film Theatre* (opened 1958), administered by the British Film Institute, has two auditoria showing films, television and video of outstanding historical, artistic or technical merit. The London Film Festival is held here every November.

The *National Theatre* opened in 1976 and stages classical, modern, new and neglected plays in its three auditoria; the 1,160-seat Olivier theatre (apron stage), the 890-seat Lyttleton theatre (proscenium stage) and the experimental Cottesloe theatre, which holds up to 400.

The *Museum of the Moving Image* charts the history of the moving image in cinema and television from the earliest devices through to disc technology. Open Tues.–Sat. 10–8, Sun. and Bank Holidays 10–6. Admission £3·25, concessions £2·50.

Stock Exchange, E.C.2.—The market floor of the new Stock Exchange building in London opened for trading in June, 1973. A tower, 331 feet high, and the new Market replace the complex of buildings started in 1801 on the same site. The new building is the headquarters of The Stock Exchange, following the amalgamation of all the Stock Exchanges in Great Britain and Ireland on March 25, 1973.

The Visitors Gallery is open between 9.30 a.m. and 5.00 p.m. Monday to Friday. Admission free and without ticket. Film show, advance bookings are advisable via the Public Information Unit (01-588 2355).

Syon House, Brentford.—The summer home of the Duke of Northumberland. The House is built on the remains of the Nunnery of Syon, founded by order of Henry V in 1415. At the Dissolution of the Monasteries the estate reverted to the Crown. In 1594 it was granted to the 9th Earl of Northumberland, who altered and improved the property. In the eight years, 1762–1770, the interior was transformed and furnished by Robert Adam. Open April 1–Sept. 27 (Sun.–Thurs.), Oct. Sun. only, 12–5.

Thames Embankments.—The *Victoria Embank-ment,* on the N. side (from Westminster to Blackfriars), was constructed by Sir J. W. Bazalgette for the Metropolitan Board of Works, 1864–70 (the seats, of which the supports of some are a kneeling camel, laden with spicery, and of others a winged sphinx, were presented by the Grocers' Company, and by Rt. Hon. W. H. Smith, M.P., in 1874); the *Albert Embankment,* on the S. side (from Westminster Bridge to Vauxhall), 1866–69; the *Chelsea Embankment,* 1871–74. The total cost exceeded £2,000,000. Sir J. W. Bazalgette (1819–91) also inaugurated the London main drainage system, 1858–65. A medallion has been placed on a pier of the Victoria Embankment to commemorate the engineer of the Thames waterside improvements ("Flumini vincula posuit"). County Hall includes an embankment on the Surrey side.

Thames Flood Barrier.—Officially opened in May 1984, though first used in Feb. 1983, the Barrier consists of ten rising sector gates which span 570 yards from bank to bank of the Thames at Woolwich Reach. When not in use the gates lie horizontally, allowing shipping to navigate the river normally; when the Barrier is closed, the gates turn through 90 degrees to stand vertically more than 50 feet above the river bed. The Barrier took eight years to complete and can be raised within about 30 minutes.

Thames Tunnels.—The *Rotherhithe Tunnel,* constructed by the L.C.C. and opened in 1908, connects Commercial Road, E.14, with Lower Road, Rotherhithe; the total length is 1 mile 332 yards, of which 474 yards are under the river. The cost of the tunnel and its approaches was £1,506,914. The first *Blackwall Tunnel* (pedestrians and vehicles) was constructed by the L.C.C. and opened in 1897, connecting East India Dock Road, Poplar, with Blackwall Lane, East Greenwich. The cost of the tunnel with its approaches was about £1,323,663. A second tunnel (for southbound vehicles only) was opened in August, 1967, at a cost of about £9,750,000 and the old tunnel was improved at a cost of about £1,350,000 and made one-way northbound. Both tunnels are for vehicles only. The relative lengths of the tunnels measured from East India Dock Road to the Gate House on the south side are 6,215 ft. (old tunnel) and 6,152 feet. *Greenwich Tunnel* (pedestrians only), constructed by the L.C.C. and opened in 1902, connects the Isle of Dogs, Poplar, with Greenwich. The length of the subway is 406 yards, and the cost was about £180,000. The *Woolwich Tunnel* (pedestrians only), constructed by the L.C.C. and opened in 1912, connects North and South Woolwich below the passenger and vehicular ferry from North Woolwich Station, E.16, to High Street, Woolwich, S.E.18. The length of the subway is 552 yards, and its cost was about £86,000. The *Thames Tunnel* (1,300 feet) was opened in 1843 to connect Wapping with Rotherhithe. In 1866 it was closed to the public, and purchased by the East London Railway Company. The *Tower Subway* for pedestrians was opened in 1870, and has long been closed.

Tower Bridge Walkways and Museum, SE1 2UP.—Owned by the Bridge House Trust and open daily April–Oct. 10–6·30, Nov.–March 10–4·45. Admission £2, concessions £1. Attractions include exhibitions, videos, the observation platform and walkway, engine rooms, working models and souvenir gift shop.

Tower Hill, E.C.1 and E.C.3, was formerly the place of execution for condemned prisoners from the Tower, the site of the scaffold being marked in the gardens of Trinity Square.

Tower of London, E.C.3.—Admission to a general view of the Tower, the White Tower (Armouries), the History, Oriental, Ordnance and 18th–19th century Galleries, and the Wall Walk Phases I and II.

The White Tower is the oldest and central building in Her Majesty's Royal Palace and Fortress of the Tower of London. It was built at the order of William I and constructed by Gundulph, Bishop of Rochester, in the years 1078–98. The Inner Wall, with thirteen towers, was constructed by Henry III in the 12th century. The Moat was extended and completed by Richard I and the Wharf first mentioned in 1228. The Outer Wall was completed in the reign of Edward I and now incorporates six towers and two bastions. The last Monarch to reside in the Tower of London was James I. The Crown Jewels came to the Tower in the reign of Henry III. All coinage used in Great Britain was minted in the Outer Ward of the Tower of London until 1810 when the Royal Mint was formed. The Tower of London has had a military garrison since 1078. The Chapel Royal of St. John the Evangelist, within the White Tower (1080–1088) is the oldest Norman church in London. The chapel of St. Peter ad Vincula was built in the early 16th century.

Constable, Field Marshal Sir Roland Gibbs, G.C.B., C.B.E., D.S.O., M.C.; *Lieutenant*, Lieut. Gen. Sir Peter Hudson, K.C.B., C.B.E.; *Resident Governor and Keeper of the Jewel House*, Maj.-Gen. A. P. W. MacLellan, M.B.E.; *Master of the Armouries*, G. Wilson; *Chaplain at the Chapel Royal of St. Peter ad Vincula*, Rev. J. F. M. Llewellyn. Open weekdays March 1–Oct. 31, 9.30–5, Nov. 1–Feb. 28, 9.30–4; Sundays, March–Oct. 2–5. Tower closed Christmas Eve, Christmas Day, Boxing Day, New Year's Day and Good Friday. On Sundays throughout the year (except August) the public is admitted to Holy Communion, 9.15 a.m. and Morning Service, 11 a.m. Admission £4·50 (£3·50 when Jewel House closed for cleaning in Feb.); concessions £2.

Waltham Abbey (or Waltham Holy Cross), Essex EN9 1UQ.—The Abbey ruins, Harold's Bridge (14th century), the Nave of the former cruciform Abbey Church c. 1120 and the traditional burial place of King Harold II (1066), and a Guild Chapel of Edward II, with crypt below, which houses a visitors centre with permanent exhibition. New evidence of the position and style of several buildings, which once stood on the site of the Augustinian monastery, were revealed by the prolonged drought in the summer of 1933 and by subsequent excavations. Lee Valley Regional Park Authority has a country centre in the Abbey grounds. At Waltham Cross, one mile from the Abbey, is one of the crosses (partly restored) erected by Edward I to mark a resting place of the corpse of Queen Eleanor on its way to Westminster Abbey. (Ten crosses were erected, but only those at Geddington, Northampton and Waltham remain; "Charing" Cross originally stood near the spot now occupied by the statue of Charles I at Whitehall.)

Wellington Museum, Apsley House, 149 Picca-dilly, at Hyde Park Corner, W.1. Known as "No. 1 London", Apsley House was designed by Robert Adam for Lord Bathurst and built 1771–8. It was bought in 1817 by the Duke of Wellington, who in 1828–29 employed Benjamin Wyatt to enlarge it, face it with Bath stone and add the Corinthian portico. The museum contains many fine paintings, sculpture, services of porcelain and silver plate and personal relics of the 1st Duke of Wellington (1769–1852). The House was given to the Nation by the 7th Duke and was first opened to the public in 1952, under the administration of the Victoria and Albert Museum. Open daily 11–5. Closed Mon., Christmas Eve, Christmas Day, Boxing Day and New Year's Day. Admission £2, concessions £1.

Westminster Hall, SW1A 0AA.—The only part of the old Palace of Westminster to survive the fire of 1834, Westminster Hall is adjacent to and incorpo-rated in the Houses of Parliament. Westminster Hall was built by William Rufus from 1097–99 and altered by Richard II, 1394–99. It is about 240 ft. long, 68 ft. wide and 92 ft. high; the hammerbeam roof of carved oak dates from 1396–98. The Hall was the scene of the trial of Charles I. Westminster Hall is included on the route followed by those who have arranged a visit to the Houses of Parliament with their M.P.

Whitechapel Art Gallery, Whitechapel High Street, E1 7QX.—Opened in 1901; administered by a charitable trust. There is no permanent collection; temporary exhibitions, mainly of modern art, are presented, and community and educational projects are run. Open Tues.–Suns. 11–5; Weds. 11–8.

Wimbledon Lawn Tennis Museum, SW19 5AE.—Exhibits include fashion, trophies, re-plicas and memorabilia representing the history of lawn tennis and a theatre shows films of great matches. Open Tues.–Sat. 11–5, Sun. 2–5. Admission £1·50, concessions 75p.

Windsor Castle (begun by William the Conqueror, A.D. 1066–87).—The Castle Precincts are open daily. Admission free. When the Queen is not in official residence, the *State Apartments* of Windsor Castle are open on weekdays and Sunday afternoons during the summer months. Admission £1·80, concessions 80p. *Queen Mary's Doll's House, the Exhibition of Dolls, the Exhibition of Drawings by Holbein, Leon-ardo da Vinci and other artists and the Royal Mews Exhibition* can be seen on the same days as the State Apartments; admission 80p, concessions 40p. When the State Apartments are closed, Queen Mary's Doll's House, the Exhibition of Drawings and the Royal Mews Exhibition remain open to the public. The *Albert Memorial Chapel* is open throughout the year (closed on Sundays). Admission free. A fee is charged to visit *St. George's Chapel*. The *Curfew Tower* may be seen under the guidance of the Keeper to whom application must be made at the entrance.

The *Royal Mausoleum*, Frogmore Gardens, Home Park, is open annually on two days in early May in conjunction with the opening of Frogmore Gardens in aid of the National Garden Scheme. Also open on the Wednesday nearest to May 24 (Queen Victoria's birthday). Admission free.

Zoological Gardens, Regent's Park, N.W.1.—(Opened in 1828). Open daily (except Christmas Day) March–Oct. 9–6 or dusk (Bank Holidays and associ-ated Suns. Easter–Aug. and Suns. July 12–Sept. 13, 9–7). Oct.–March opens 10. Admission £3·90, conces-sions £3·10; £2. Aquarium and Children's Zoo free.

[London Visitor and Convention Bureau.—Tourist Information Centre, Victoria Station Forecourt, S.W.1. (01–730 3488).]

PARKS, SPACES AND GARDENS

The principal Parks and Open Spaces in the Metro-politan area are maintained as under:—

By the Crown

BUSHY PARK (1,099 acres).—Adjoining Hampton Court, contains avenue of horse-chestnuts enclosed in a four-fold avenue of limes planted by William III. "Chestnut Sunday" (when the trees are in full bloom with their "candles") is usually about May 1 to 15.

GREEN PARK (49 acres), W.1.—Between Piccadilly and St. James's Park with Constitution Hill, leading to Hyde Park Corner.

GREENWICH PARK (196½ acres), S.E.10.

HAMPTON COURT GARDENS (54 acres).

HAMPTON COURT GREEN (17 acres).

HAMPTON COURT PARK (622 acres).

HYDE PARK (341 acres).—From Park Lane, W.1, to Kensington Gardens, W.2 containing the Serpentine. Fine gateway at Hyde Park Corner, with Apsley House, the Achilles Statue, Rotten Row and the Ladies' Mile. To the north-east is the Marble Arch, originally erected by George IV at the entrance to Buckingham Palace and re-erected in present position in 1851.

KENSINGTON GARDENS (275 acres), W.2.—From western boundary of Hyde Park to Kensington Palace, containing the Albert Memorial.

KEW, ROYAL BOTANIC GARDENS *see* p. 431–2.

REGENT'S PARK and PRIMROSE HILL (464 acres), N.W.1.—From Marylebone Road to Primrose Hill surrounded by the Outer Circle and divided by the Broad Walk leading to the Zoological Gardens.

RICHMOND PARK (2,469 acres).

ST. JAMES'S PARK (93 acres), S.W.1.—From Whitehall to Buckingham Palace. Ornamental lake of 12 acres. The original suspension bridge built in 1857 was replaced in 1957. The Mall leads from the Admiralty Arch to the Queen Victoria Memorial and Buckingham Palace, Birdcage Walk from Storey's Gate, past Wellington Barracks, to Buckingham Palace.

By the Corporation of London

BURNHAM BEECHES and FLEET WOOD, Bucks. (510 acres).—Purchased by the Corporation for the benefit of the public in 1880, Fleet Wood (65 acres) being presented in 1921.

COULSDON COMMON, Surrey (133 acres).

EPPING FOREST (6,000 acres).—Purchased by the Corporation for £250,000 and thrown open to the public in 1882. The present forest is 12 miles long by 1 to 2 miles wide, about one-tenth of its original area.

FARTHINGDOWN, Surrey (121 acres).

HIGHGATE WOOD (70 acres).

KENLEY COMMON, Surrey (138 acres).

QUEEN'S PARK, Kilburn (30 acres).

RIDDLESDOWN, Surrey (90 acres).

SPRING PARK, West Wickham (51 acres).

WEST HAM PARK (77 acres).

WEST WICKHAM COMMON, Kent (25 acres).

With smaller open spaces within the City of London, including FINSBURY CIRCUS GARDENS.

Temporarily Maintained by the London Residuary Body

When the G.L.C. was abolished in April 1986 the responsibility for some of its parks and open spaces had already been transferred to other bodies (indicated where known). Negotiating the transfer of the remainder to individual Boroughs has been the responsibility of the London Residuary Body since abolition.

HAMPSTEAD HEATH (676 acres), N.W.3. including Golders Hill (36 acres) and Parliament Hill (271 acres), is to be transferred to the Corporation of the City of London from April 1, 1989.

SOUTH BANK (10 acres, including Jubilee Gardens), Belvedere Road, S.E.1, vested in the L.R.B. but to be managed by the South Bank Board.

ROMAN NAMES OF ENGLISH TOWNS AND CITIES

Bath	*Aquae Sulis*	Lincoln	*Lindum*
Canterbury	*Durovernum Cantiacorum*	London	*Londinium*
Carlisle	*Luguvalium*	Manchester	*Mamucium*
Chelmsford	*Caesaromagus*	Newcastle upon Tyne	*Pons Aelius*
Chester	*Deva*		
Chichester	*Noviomagus Regnensium*	Pevensey	*Anderitium*
Cirencester	*Corinium Dobunnorum*	Rochester	*Durobrivae*
Colchester	*Camulodunum*	St. Albans	*Verulamium*
Doncaster	*Danum*	Salisbury	*Sorviodunum*
Dorchester	*Durnovaria*	(Old Sarum)	
Dover	*Dubris*	Silchester	*Calleva Atrebatum*
Exeter	*Isca Dumnoniorum*	Winchester	*Venta Belgarum*
Gloucester	*Glevum*	Wroxeter	*Viroconium Cornoviorum*
Leicester	*Ratae Corieltauvorum*	York	*Eburacum*

The Principality of Wales

Position and extent.—Wales (Cymru) occupies the extreme west of the central southern portion of the island of Great Britain, with a total area of 8,018 sq. miles (land 7,908; inland water 50); it is bounded on the N. by the Irish Sea, on the S. by the Bristol Channel, on the E. by the English counties of Cheshire, Shropshire, Hereford and Worcester, and Gloucester, and on the W. by St. George's Channel. Across the Menai Straits is the Welsh island of *Anglesey* or Ynys Môn (276 sq. miles), communication with which is facilitated by the Menai Suspension Bridge (1,000 ft. long), built by Telford in 1826 and by the tubular railway bridge (1,100 ft. long) built by Stephenson in 1850. Holyhead harbour, on Holy Isle (N.W. of Anglesey), provides accommodation for ferry services to Dublin (70 miles).

Population.—The population at the Census of 1981 was 2,791,851 (males 1,352,639; females 1,439,212). The average density of population in 1981 was 343 per square mile. The population, mid 1986 estimate, was 2,821,000.

Relief.—Wales is a country of extensive tracts of high plateau and shorter stretches of mountain ranges deeply dissected by river valleys. Lower-lying ground is largely confined to the coastal belt and the lower parts of the valleys. The highest mountains are those of Snowdonia in the north-west (*Snowdon*, 3,559 ft.), Berwyn (*Aran Fawddwy*, 2,971 ft.), Cader Idris (*Pen y Gadair*, 2,928 ft.), Dyfed (*Plynlimon*, 2,467 ft.), and the Black Mountain, Brecon Beacons and Black Forest ranges in the south-east (*Carmarthen Van*, 2,630 ft., *Pen y Fan*, 2,906 ft., *Waun Fâch*, 2,660 ft.).

Hydrography.—The principal river of those rising in Wales is the *Severn* (*see* England), which flows from the slopes of Plynlimon to the English border. The *Wye* (130 miles) also rises in the slopes of Plynlimon. The *Usk* (56 miles) flows into the Bristol Channel, through Gwent. The *Dee* (70 miles) rises in Bala Lake and flows through the Vale of Llangollen, where an aqueduct (built by Telford in 1805) carries the Pontcysyllte branch of the Shropshire Union Canal across the valley. The estuary of the Dee is the navigable portion, 14 miles in length and about 5 miles in breadth, and the tide rushes in with dangerous speed over the "Sands of Dee". The *Towy* (68 miles), *Teifi* (50 miles), *Taff* (40 miles), *Dovey* (30 miles), *Taf* (25 miles), and *Conway* (24 miles), the last named broad and navigable, are wholly Welsh rivers.

The largest natural lake in Wales is *Bala* (Llyn Tegid) in Gwynedd, 4 miles long and about 1 mile wide; *Lake Vyrnwy* is an artificial reservoir, about the size of Bala, and forms the water supply of Liverpool, and Birmingham is supplied from a chain of reservoirs in the Elan and Clærwen valleys.

The Welsh Language.—According to the 1981 Census results, the percentage of persons of three years and over able to speak Welsh were:

Clwyd	18·7	Powys	20·2
Dyfed	46·3	S. Glamorgan	5·8
Gwent	2·5	W. Glamorgan	16·4
Gwynedd	61·2		
Mid Glamorgan	8·4	**Wales**	18·9

The 1981 figure represents a slight decline from 20·8 per cent in 1971 (1961, 26 per cent; 1951, 28·9 per cent).

Flag.—A red dragon on a green and white field (per fess argent and vert a dragon passant gules). The flag was augmented in 1953 by a royal badge on a shield encircled with a riband bearing the words *Ddraig Goch Ddyry Cychwyn* and imperially crowned. Only the unaugmented flag is flown on Government offices in Wales and, where appropriate, in London. Both flags continue to be used elsewhere.

EARLY HISTORY

Celts and Romans.—The earliest inhabitants of whom there is any record appear to have been subdued or exterminated by the *Goidels* (a people of Celtic race) in the Bronze Age, and a further invasion of Celtic *Brythons* and *Belgae* followed in the ensuing Iron Age. The *Roman* conquest of South Britain and Wales was for some time successfully opposed by *Caratacus* (Caractacus or Caradog), chieftain of the Catuvellauni and son of *Cunobelinus* (Cymbeline). South east Wales was subjugated and the legionary fortress at Caerleon-on-Usk established by about A.D. 75–77: the conquest of Wales was completed by Agricola about A.D. 78. Communications were opened up by the construction of military roads from Chester to Caerleon-on-Usk and Caerwent, and from Chester to Conway (and thence to Camarthen and Neath). *Christianity* was introduced (during the Roman occupation) in the 4th century.

The Anglo-Saxon Attacks.—The Anglo-Saxon invaders of South Britain drove the Celts into the mountain fastness of Wales, and into Strathclyde (Cumberland and S.W. Scotland) and Cornwall, giving them the name of *Waelisc*, or Welsh (= foreign). The West Saxons' victory of Deorham (577) isolated Wales from Cornwall and the battle of Chester (613) cut off communication with Strathclyde and northern Britain. In the 8th century the boundaries of the Welsh were further restricted by the annexations of Offa, King of Mercia, and counterattacks were largely prevented by the construction of an artificial boundary from the Dee to the Wye (Offa's Dyke). In the 9th century Rhodri Mawr (844–78) united the country and successfully resisted further incursions of the Saxons by land and raids of Norse and Danish pirates by sea, but at his death his three provinces of *Gwynedd* (N.), *Powys* (Mid.) and *Deheubarth* (S.) were divided among his three sons—Anarawd, Mervyn and Cadell. Cadell's son Hywel Dda ruled a large part of Wales and codified its laws but the provinces were not united again until the rule of Llewelyn ap Seisyllt (husband of the heiress of Gwynedd) from 1018 to 1023.

The Norman Conquest.—After the Norman conquest of England, William I created Palatine counties along the Welsh frontier, and the Norman barons began to make encroachments into Welsh territory. The Welsh princes recovered many of their losses, however, during the civil wars of Stephen's reign and in the early 13th century Owen Gruffydd, prince of Gwynedd was the dominant figure in Wales. Under Llewelyn ap Iorwerth (1194–1240) the Welsh united in powerful resistance to English incursions and Llywelyn's privileges and *de facto* independence were recognized in Magna Carta. His grandson, Llywelyn ap Gruffydd, was the last native prince: he was killed in 1282 during hostilities between the Welsh and English, allowing Edward I of England to establish his authority over the country. On Feb. 7, 1301, Edward of Caernarvon, son of Edward I, was created *Prince of Wales*, a title which has subsequently been borne by the eldest son of the sovereign.

Strong Welsh national feeling continued, expressed in the early 15th century in the rising led by Owain Glyndŵr, but the situation was altered by the accession to the English throne in 1485 of Henry VII of the Welsh House of Tudor. Wales was politically assimilated to England under the Act of Union of 1535, which extended English laws to the Principality and gave it parliamentary representation for the first time.

Eisteddfod.—The Welsh are a distinct nationality, with a language and literature of their own, and the national bardic festival (Eisteddfod), instituted by Prince Rhys ap Griffith in 1176, is annually maintained. These *Eisteddfodau* (sessions) form part of the *Gorsedd* (assembly), which is believed to date from the time of Prydian, a ruling prince in an age many centuries before the Christian era.

LORD LIEUTENANTS AND HIGH SHERIFFS

County	Lord Lieutenant	High Sheriff (1988–89)
Clwyd....................	Sir William Gladstone, BT.	H. S. Fetherstonhaugh
Dyfed	D. C. Mansel Lewis	G. B. Williams, M.B.E.
Gwent	R. Hanbury Tenison	Maj.-Gen. L. A. H. Napier, C.B., O.B.E., M.C.
Gwynedd.................	The Most Hon. The Marquess of Anglesey	O. M. Jonathan
Mid Glamorgan	D. G. Badham, C.B.E.	D. W. C. Morgan
Powys....................	M. L. Bourdillon	Maj. C. R. C. Inglis
South Glamorgan	Mrs. S. E. Williams, M.B.E.	D. H. Fisher
West Glamorgan	Lt.-Col. Sir Michael Llewllyn, Bt.	Dr. S. P. Jenkins

WELSH COUNTY COUNCILS
AREAS AND POPULATIONS

County	Administrative Headquarters	Area (*hectares*)	Population	Rateable Value 1988 £	Actual Rateable Value per head £
Clwyd............	Shire Hall, Mold	242,650	399,600	42,700,417	106·86
Dyfed	*Carmarthen	576,577	339,000	32,711,723	96·49
Gwent	*Cwmbran	137,599	441,800	47,703,734	107·98
Gwynedd.........	County Offices, Caernarfon	386,708	232,000	27,308,175	115·00
Mid Glamorgan ...	*Cardiff	101,867	530,800	41,892,055	78·92
Powys............	*Llandrindod Wells	507,741	112,373	10,604,085	94·37
South Glamorgan .	County Headquarters, Newport Road, Cardiff	41,629	398,300	55,627,395	139·66
West Glamorgan ..	*Swansea	81,657	363,400	39,804,303	109·53

* County Hall.

COUNTY OFFICIALS AND CHAIRMEN

County	Chief Executive	County Treasurer	Chairmen of C.C.
Clwyd............	M. H. Phillips	A. Dalby	R. W. Edwards, M.B.E.
Dyfed	D. H. Davies	D. C. Williams	D. J. Thomas
Gwent	M. J. Perry	R. Emmott	D. G. Price
Gwynedd.........	I. B. Rees	(vacant)	R. G. Roberts
Mid Glamorgan ...	D. H. Thomas*	L. D. Heycock	T. G. O'Brien
Powys............	M. J. Greenwood	M. J. Greenwood	Lt.-Col. J. D. Stephenson, M.B.E.
South Glamorgan .	M. Boyce	R. G. Tettenborn	W. P. Kitson
West Glamorgan ..	M. E. J. Rush	S. G. Dunster	D. T. Vernon Davies

* County Clerk.

MUNICIPAL DIRECTORY OF WALES

District Councils

Those accorded CITY Status are shown in SMALL CAPITALS; those with
Borough Status are distinguished by having § prefixed.

District	Estimated resident population 1986	Rateable Value 1988 £	Chief Executive	Chairman 1988–89 (a) Mayor (b) Lord Mayor
§Aberconwy, Gwynedd	52,600	5,750,567	J. E. Davies	(a) R. Ivor Thomas
Alyn and Deeside, Clwyd	72,200	8,769,646	W. E. Rogers	W. E. Barwell
§Arfon, Gwynedd	53,700	6,810,580	D. L. Jones	(a) A. Meurig Williams
§Blaenau Gwent, Gwent	77,600	5,963,187	R. Leadbeter	(a) P. J. Law
§Brecknock, Powys	40,600	3,531,297	R. O. Doylend	(a) G. J. Jones
CARDIFF, South Glamorgan	279,500	41,936,403	H. T. Crippin	(b) W. P. Herbert
Carmarthen, Dyfed	53,800	4,326,210	R. R. Morgan	T. W. Davies
Ceredigion, Dyfed	63,700	5,382,825	D. Morgan	W. R. Edwards
§Colwyn, Clwyd	51,600	5,626,121	O. Morris	(a) D. Hughes
§Cynon Valley, Mid Glamorgan ..	64,900	4,554,556	G. W. Hosgood	(a) Dr. S. M. Imtiaz
§Delyn, Clwyd	65,200	6,279,568	J. R. Packer	(a) G. B. Roberts
§Dinefwr, Dyfed...............	37,100	2,438,562	E. W. Harries	(a) T. Theophilus
Dwyfor, Gwynedd	26,400	2,748,963	E. Davies	R. Humphreys
Glyndwr, Clwyd	40,700	3,712,990	J. H. Parry	T. Clutton
§Islwyn, Gwent	65,700	4,723,479	B. Bird	(a) L. Gardiner
§Llanelli, Dyfed	73,900	6,317,768	A. B. Thomas	(a) W. M. Jones
§Lliw Valley, West Glamorgan...	60,900	4,777,812	J. C. Howells	(a) R. T. Daniel
Meirionnydd, Gwynedd.........	31,800	4,102,521	G. W. Hughes	G. Humphreys
§Merthyr Tydfil, Mid Glamorgan	58,500	1,820,499	R. V. Morris	(a) D. D. Games
Monmouth, Gwent	77,800	8,090,824	G. Cummings	Mrs. A. M. Palmer
Montgomeryshire, Powys	50,000	4,592,049	N. J. Bardsley	J. H. Evans
§Neath, West Glamorgan........	65,100	6,221,151	S. Penny	(a) J. Warman
§Newport, Gwent	129,800	19,573,245	C. Tapp	(a) Mrs. V. J. Brydon
§Ogwr, Mid Glamorgan	134,400	11,382,970	J. G. Cole	(a) V. Thomas
§Port Talbot, West Glamorgan...	50,000	8,416,041	C. A. Millward	(a) T. D. Morgans
Preseli Pembrokeshire, Dyfed....	70,600	7,038,842	I. W. R. David	W. L. Raymond
Radnor, Powys.................	21,700	2,369,756	G. C. Read	J. H. Lewis
§Rhondda, Mid Glamorgan	77,800	3,917,076	G. Evans	(a) Mrs. E. M. Evans
§Rhuddlan, Clwyd..............	55,200	6,222,963	E. O. Lake	(a) R. L. Williams
Rhymney Valley, Mid Glamorgan	104,100	7,873,355	P. A. Bennett	D. T. Davies
South Pembrokeshire, Dyfed	40,000	7,207,516	D. R. Jones	A. W. Edwards
SWANSEA, West Glamorgan	187,000	20,246,925	A. K. B. Boatswain	(b) H. J. Morgan
§Taff-Ely, Mid Glamorgan	94,800	9,386,164	D. Gethin	(a) E. Jones
§Torfaen, Gwent	90,900	9,379,999	M. B. Mehta	(a) Mrs. W. M. Howell
§Vale of Glamorgan, South Glamorgan	116,100	14,680,996	J. R. Gau	(a) J. George
§Wrexham Maelor, Clwyd	114,700	12,089,130	R. J. Dutton	(a) R. A. Matthews
§Ynys Môn (Isle of Anglesey), Gwynedd....................	70,100	7,827,434	E. L. Gibson	(a) E. Schofield

PRINCIPAL WELSH CITIES

CARDIFF

CARDIFF (South Glamorgan), at the mouth of the
rivers Taff, Rhymney and Ely, is the capital City of
Wales and one of Britain's major administrative,
commercial and office centres. It has many industries,
including steel works, cigars and a flourishing port
with a substantial and varied trade. There are many
fine buildings in the civic centre started early this
century which includes the City Hall, the National
Museum of Wales, University Buildings, Law Courts,
Welsh Office, County Hall, Police Headquarters and
the Temple of Peace and Health. Also in the city are
Llandaff Cathedral, the Welsh National Folk Museum
at St. Fagans, Cardiff Castle, the New Theatre, the
Sherman Theatre and the Cardiff College of Music
and Drama. New buildings include St. David's Hall,
a 2,000-seat concert and conference hall, and the
Welsh National Ice Rink.

SWANSEA

SWANSEA (in Welsh, Abertawe) is a City and a
seaport of West Glamorgan with its own municipal
airport. The beautiful Gower Peninsula was brought
within the City boundary under local government
reform on April 1, 1974. The trade of the port includes
coal, patent fuel, ores, and the import and export of
oil. The municipal area is 60,511 acres.

The principal buildings are the Norman Castle
(rebuilt in 1330), the Royal Institution of South
Wales, founded in 1835 (containing Museum and
Library), the University College at Singleton and the
Guildhall, containing the Brangwyn panels. New
buildings include the Industrial and Maritime Museum, the new Maritime Quarter and Marina and
the leisure centre. Swansea was chartered by the
Earl of Warwick, circa 1158–1184, and further charters were granted by King John, Henry III, Edward
II, Edward III and James II, 2 from Cromwell and 1
from Lord Marcher.

THE KINGDOM OF SCOTLAND

Position and Extent.—The Kingdom of Scotland occupies the northern portion of the main island of Great Britain and includes the Inner and Outer Hebrides, and the Orkney, Shetland, and many other islands. The Kingdom lies between 60° 51′ 30″ and 54° 38′ N. latitude and between 1° 45′ 32″ and 6° 14′ W. longitude, its southern neighbour being the Kingdom of England, with the Atlantic Ocean on the N. and W., and the North Sea on the E. The greatest length of the mainland (Cape Wrath to the Mull of Galloway) is 274 miles, and the greatest breadth (Buchan Ness to Applecross) is 154 miles. The customary measurement of the island of Great Britain is from the site of John o' Groats house, near Duncansby Head, Caithness (at the N.E. extremity of the island) to Land's End, Cornwall (at the S.W. extremity), a total distance of 603 miles in a straight line and (approximately) 900 by road.

The total area of the Kingdom is 30,414 square miles (land 29,761; inland water 653). The population (1981 Census) was 5,130,735 (males 2,466,437; females 2,664,298). The average density of the population in 1981 was 168 persons per square mile. The population, mid 1986 estimate, was 5,121,000.

Relief.—There are three natural orographic divisions of Scotland. The Southern Uplands have their highest points in Merrick (2,766 feet), Rhinns of Kells (2,669 feet), and Cairnsmuir of Carsphairn (2,614 feet), in the west; and the Tweedsmuir Hills in the east (*Hartfell* 2,651 ft., *Dollar Law* 2,682 ft., *Broad Law* 2,756 ft.). The Central Lowlands, formed by the valleys of the Clyde, Forth and Tay, divide the Southern Uplands from the heather-clad Northern Highlands, which extend almost from the extreme north of the mainland to the central lowlands, and are divided into a northern and southern system by the *Great Glen*. The Grampian Mountains, which entirely cover the southern Highland area, include in the west *Ben Nevis* (4,406 ft.), the highest point in the British Isles, and in the east the Cairngorm Mountains (*Cairn Gorm* 4,084 ft., *Braeriach* 4,248 ft., *Ben Macdui* 4,296 ft.). The north-western Highland area contains in the mountains of Wester and Eastern Ross *Carn Eige* (3,880 ft.) and *Sgurr na Lapaich* (3,775 ft.).

Created, like the Central Lowlands, by a major geological fault, the *Great Glen* (60 miles long) runs between Inverness and Fort William, and contains Loch Ness, Loch Oich and Loch Lochy. These are linked to each other and to the north-east and south-west coasts of Scotland by the Caledonian Canal, providing a navigable passage between the Moray Firth and the Inner Hebrides.

Hydrography.—The western coast of Scotland is fragmented by peninsulas and islands, and indented by fjords (sea-lochs), the longest of which is *Loch Fyne* (42 miles long) in Argyllshire. Although the east coast tends to be less fractured and lower, there are several great drowned inlets (firths), e.g. Firth of Forth, Firth of Tay, Moray Firth, as well as the Firth of Clyde in the west.

The lochs are the principal hydrographic feature of the Kingdom, both on the mainland and in many of the islands. The largest in the Kingdom and in Great Britain is *Loch Lomond* (27 square miles in area), in the Grampian valleys; the longest and deepest is *Loch Ness* (24 miles long and 800 feet deep), in the Great Glen; and Lochs Shin (20 miles) and Maree in the northern Highlands.

The longest river in Scotland is the *Tay* (117 miles), noted for its salmon. It flows into the North Sea, with Dundee on the estuary, which is spanned by the *Tay Bridge* (10,289 ft.) opened in 1887 and the *Tay Road Bridge* (7,365 ft.) opened in 1966. Other noted

salmon rivers are the *Dee* (90 miles) which flows into the North Sea at Aberdeen, and the *Spey* (110 miles), the swiftest flowing river in the British Isles, which flows into Moray Firth. The *Tweed*, which gave its name to the woollen cloth produced along its banks, marks in the lower stretches of its 96-mile course the border between Scotland and England.

The most important river commercially is the *Clyde* (106 miles), formed by the junction of the Daer and Portrait water, which flows through the city and port of Glasgow to the Firth of Clyde. During its course it passes over the picturesque Falls of Clyde, *Bonnington Linn* (30 ft.), *Corra Linn* (84 ft.), *Dundaff Linn* (10 ft.) and *Stonebyres Linn* (80 ft.), above and below Lanark. The *Forth* (66 miles), upon which stands Edinburgh, the capital, is spanned by the *Forth (Railway) Bridge* (1890), which is 5,330 feet long, and the *Forth (Road) Bridge* (1964), which has a total length of 6,156 ft. (over water) and a single span of 3,000 ft.

The highest waterfall in Scotland, and the British Isles, is *Eas a'Chùal Aluinn* with a total height of 658 ft., which falls from Glas Bheinn in Sutherland. The *Falls of Glomach*, on a head-stream of the Elchaig in Wester Ross, have a drop of 370 ft.

Gaelic Language.—According to the 1981 Census, 82,620 people, mainly in the Highlands and western coastal regions, were able to speak, read or write the Scottish form of Gaelic.

THE SCOTTISH ISLANDS

The Hebrides did not become part of the Kingdom of Scotland until 1266, when they were ceded to Alexander III by Magnus of Norway. Orkney and Shetland fell to the Scottish Crown as a pledge for the unpaid dowry of Margaret of Denmark, wife of James III, in 1468, the Danish claims to suzerainty being relinquished in 1590 when James VI married Anne of Denmark.

Orkney.—The Orkney Islands (total area 375½ square miles) lie about six miles north of the mainland, separated from it by the Pentland Firth. Of the 90 islands and islets (holms and skerries) in the group, about one-third are inhabited. The total population at the 1981 Census was 19,040; the 1981 populations of the islands shown here include those of smaller islands forming part of the same civil parish.

Mainland	14,299	Shapinsay	345
Eday	154	South Ronaldsay	1,188
Hoy and Graemsay	80	Stronsay	462
Papa Westray	94	Walls and Flotta	761
Rousay and Egilsay	264	Westray	741
Sanday and North Ronaldsay	652		

The islands are rich in Pictish and Scandinavian remains, the most notable being the Stone Age village of Skara Brae, the burial chamber of Maeshowe, the many brochs (Pictish towers) and St. Magnus Cathedral. Scapa Flow, between the Mainland and Hoy, was the war station of the British Grand Fleet from 1914–19 and the scene of the scuttling of the surrendered German High Seas Fleet (June 21, 1919).

Most of the islands are low-lying and fertile, and farming (principally beef cattle) is the main industry. Flotta, to the south of Scapa Flow, is now the site of the oil terminal for the Piper, Claymore and Tartan fields in the North Sea.

Capital.—Kirkwall (population 6,881) on Mainland.

Shetland.—The Shetland Islands (total area, 551 square miles; population (1981 Census) 27,271) lie about 50 miles north of the Orkneys, with Fair Isle about half way between the two groups. Out Stack, off Muckle Flugga, one mile north of Unst, is the most northern part of the British Isles (60° 51′ 30″ N. lat.). There are over 100 islands, of which 16 are inhabited.

Mainland	22,184	Muckle Roe	101
Bressay	335	Out Skerries	79
East and West Burra,		Papa Stour	29
and Trondra	930	Unst	1,206
Fair Isle	69	Whalsay	1,026
Fetlar	102	Yell	1,168
Foula	39		

Shetland's many archaeological sites include Jarlshof, Mousa and Clickhimin, and its long connection with Scandinavia has resulted in a strong Norse influence on its place names and dialect.

Industries include fishing, knitwear and farming. In addition to the fishing fleet there are fish processing factories, while the traditional handknitting of Fair Isle and Unst is supplemented now with machine knitted garments,. Farming is mainly crofting, with sheep being raised on the moorland and hills of the islands. Latterly the islands have become an important centre of the North Sea oil industry, with pipelines from the Brent and Ninian fields running to the terminal at Sullom Voe, the largest of its kind in Europe. Lerwick is the main centre for supply services for offshore oil exploration and development.

Capital.—Lerwick (population 7,901) on Mainland.

The Hebrides.—Until the closing years of the 13th century "The Hebrides" included other Scottish islands in the Firth of Clyde, the peninsula of Kintyre (Argyllshire), the Isle of Man, and the (Irish) Isle of Rathlin. The origin of the name is stated to be the Greek *Eboudai*, latinized as *Hebudes* by Pliny, and corrupted to its present form. The Norwegian name *Sudreyjar* (Southern Islands) was latinized as *Sodorenses*, a name that survives in the Anglican bishopric of Sodor and Man.

There are over 500 islands and islets, of which about 100 are inhabited, though mountainous terrain and extensive peat bogs mean that only a fraction of the total area is under cultivation. Stone, Bronze and Iron Age settlement has left many remains, including those at Callanish on Lewis, and Norse colonization has influenced language, customs and place-names. Occupations include farming (mostly crofting and stock-raising), fishing and the manufacture of tweeds and other woollens. Tourism is also an important factor in the economy.

The **Inner Hebrides** lie off the west coast of Scotland and relatively close to the mainland. The largest and best-known is *Skye* (area 643 sq. miles; pop. 8,139; chief town, Portree), which contains the Cuillin Hills (*Sgurr Alasdair* 3,257 feet), the Red Hills (*Beinn na Caillich* 2,403 feet) as well as *Bla Bheinn* (3,046 feet) and *The Storr* (2,358 feet). Skye is also famous as the refuge of the Young Pretender in 1746. Other islands in the Highland Region include *Raasay* (pop. 182) *Rum, Eigg* and *Muck*. Islands in the Strathclyde Region include *Arran* (pop. 4,726) containing *Goat Fell* (2,868 feet); *Coll and Tiree* (pop. 933); *Colonsay and Oronsay* (pop. 137); *Islay* (area 235 sq. miles; pop. 3,997; *Jura* (area 160 sq. miles; pop. 239) with a range of hills culminating in the Paps of Jura (*Beinn-an-Oir*, 2,576 feet, and *Beinn Chaolais*, 2,477 feet); *Mull* (area 367 sq. miles; pop. 2,605; chief town Tobermory) containing *Ben More* (3,171 feet).

The **Outer Hebrides**, separated from the mainland by the Minch, now form the Western Isles Islands Council area (area 1,119 sq. miles; pop. (1981 Census) 31,842). The main islands are *Lewis with Harris* (area 770 sq. miles, pop. 23,390), whose chief town, Stornoway (pop. 13,409), is the administrative headquarters; *North Uist* (pop. 1,454); *South Uist* (pop. 2,223); *Benbecula* (pop. 1,988) and *Barra* (pop. 1,232). Other inhabited islands include *Bernera* (292), *Berneray*

(134), *Eriskay* (219), *Grimsay* (206), *Scalpay* (461) and *Vatersay* (108).

EARLY HISTORY

Prehistoric Man.—The Picts, believed to be of non-Aryan origin, seem to have inhabited the whole of North Britain and to have spread over the north of Ireland. Remains are most frequent in Caithness and Sutherland and the Orkney Islands. Celts arrived from Belgic Gaul during the latter part of the Bronze Age and in the early Iron Age, and except in the extreme north of the mainland and in the islands, the civilization and speech of the people were definitely Celtic at the time of the Roman invasion of Britain.

The Roman Invasion.—In A.D. 79–80 Julius Agricola extended the Roman conquests in Britain by advancing into *Caledonia* and building a line of fortifications across the isthmus between the Forth and Clyde, but after a victory at *Mons Graupius* he was recalled. Hadrian's Wall, mostly complete by A.D. 130, marked the frontier until about A.D. 143 when the frontier moved north to the Forth-Clyde isthmus and was secured by the Antonine Wall. From about A.D. 155 the Antonine Wall was damaged by frequent attacks and by the close of the second century the northern limit of Roman Britain had receded to Hadrian's Wall.

The Scots.—After the withdrawal (or absorption) of the Roman garrison of Britain there were many years of tribal warfare between the Picts and Scots (the Gaelic tribe then dominant in Ireland), the Brythonic Waelisc (Welsh) of Strathclyde (southwest Scotland and Cumberland), and the Anglo-Saxons of Lothian. The Waelisc were isolated from their kinsmen in Wales by the victory of the West Saxons at Chester (613), and towards the close of the 9th century the Scots under *Kenneth Macalpine* became the dominant power in Caledonia. In the reign of Malcolm I (943–954) Strathclyde was brought into subjection, the English lowland kingdom (Lothian) being conquered by Malcolm II (1005–1034). From the late 11th century until the middle of the 16th there were constant wars between Scotland and England, the outstanding figures in the struggle being William Wallace, who defeated the English at Stirling Bridge (1297) and Robert Bruce, who won the victory of Bannockburn (1314). James IV and many of his nobles fell at the disastrous battle of Flodden (1513).

The Jacobite Revolts.—In 1603 James VI of Scotland succeeded Queen Elizabeth I on the throne of England (his mother, Mary Queen of Scots, was the great-granddaughter of Henry VII), his successors reigning as Sovereigns of Great Britain, although political union of the two countries did not occur until 1707. After the abdication (by flight) in 1688 of James VII and II, the crown devolved upon William III (grandson of Charles I) and Mary (daughter of James VII and II). In 1689 Graham of Claverhouse "roused the Highlands" on behalf of James VII and II, but died after a military success at Killiecrankie. After the death of Anne (second daughter of James VII and II) the throne devolved upon George I (great-grandson of James VI and I). In 1715, armed risings on behalf of James Stuart (the Old Pretender) led to the indecisive battle of Sheriffmuir, but the Jacobite movement died down until 1745, when Charles Stuart (the Young Pretender) defeated the Royalist troops at Prestonpans and advanced to Derby in England (1746). From Derby, the adherents of "James VIII and III" (the title claimed for his father by Charles Stuart) fell back on the defensive, and the movement was finally crushed at Culloden (April 16, 1746).

LORD LIEUTENANTS IN SCOTLAND

Region	Title	Name
Borders	Berwickshire	Lt. Col. Sir William Swan, K.C.V.O., C.B.E., T.D.
	Roxburgh, Ettrick and Lauderdale	The Duke of Buccleuch and Queensberry, K.T., V.R.D
	Tweeddale	Lt. Col. A. M. Sprot of Haystoun, M.C.
Central	Clackmannan	The Earl of Mar and Kellie
	Stirling and Falkirk	Lt. Col. J. Stirling of Garden, T.D.
Dumfries & Galloway	Dumfries	Capt. J. G. M. Home, T.D.
	The Stewartry of Kirkcudbright	The Lord Sinclair, M.V.O.
	Wigtown	Maj. H. J. Brewis
Fife	Fife	The Earl of Elgin and Kincardine, K.T.
Grampian	Aberdeenshire	Capt. C. A. Farquharson
	Banffshire	J. A. S. McPherson, C.B.E.
	Kincardineshire	The Viscount of Arbuthnott, D.S.C., F.R.S.E.
	Morayshire	Capt. Sir Iain Tennant, K.T.
Highland	Caithness	The Viscount Thurso
	Inverness	Lt. Comdr. L. R. D. Mackintosh of Mackintosh, O.B.E.
	Nairn	The Earl of Leven and Melville
	Ross and Cromarty	Capt. R. W. K. Stirling of Fairburn, T.D.
	Sutherland	Col. A. MacD. Gilmour, O.B.E., M.C.
Lothian	East Lothian	Sir Hew Hamilton-Dalrymple, Bt., K.V.C.O.
	Midlothian	Sir John Dutton Clerk of Penicuik, Bt., C.B.E., V.R.D.
	West Lothian	The Earl of Morton
Strathclyde	Argyll and Bute	The Lord Maclean, K.T., P.C., G.C.V.O., K.B.E.
	Ayr and Arran	Col. B. M. Knox, M.C., T.D.
	Dunbartonshire	Brig. A. S. Pearson, C.B., D.S.O., O.B.E., M.C., T.D.
	Lanarkshire	Col. The Lord Clydesmuir, K.T., C.B., M.B.E., T.D.
	Renfrewshire	Maj. J. D. M. Crichton Maitland
Tayside	Angus	The Earl of Dalhousie, K.T., G.C.V.O., G.B.E., M.C.
	Perth and Kinross	Maj. D. H. Butter, M.C.
Orkney	Orkney	Col. R. A. A. S. Macrae, M.B.E.
Shetland	Shetland	M. M. Shearer
Western Isles	Western Isles	The Earl Granville, M.C.

NOTE.—The Lord Provosts of the four city districts of Aberdeen, Dundee, Edinburgh and Glasgow are Lord Lieutenants for those districts *ex officio*.

PRECEDENCE IN SCOTLAND

The Sovereign.

The Prince Philip, Duke of Edinburgh.

The Lord High Commissioner to the General Assembly (while that Assembly *is sitting*).

The Duke of Rothesay (eldest son of the Sovereign). The Duke of York. The Prince Edward.

Nephews of the Sovereign.

Lords Lieutenant of Counties, Lord Provosts of Counties of Cities, and Sheriffs Principal (successively—within their own localities and during holding of office).

Lord Chancellor of Great Britain.

Moderator of the General Assembly of the Church of Scotland.

The Prime Minister.

Keepers of the Great Seal and of the Privy Seal (successively—if Peers).

Hereditary Lord High Constable of Scotland. Hereditary Master of the Household.

Dukes (successively) of England, Scotland, Great Britain and United Kingdom (including Ireland since date of Union).

Eldest sons of Dukes of the Blood Royal.

Marquesses, in same order as Dukes.

Dukes' eldest sons.

Earls, in order as Dukes.

Younger sons of Dukes of Blood Royal.

Marquesses' eldest sons.

Dukes' younger sons.

Keepers of the Great Seal and of the Privy Seal (successively—if not Peers).

Lord Justice General.

Lord Clerk Register.

Lord Advocate.

Lord Justice Clerk.

Viscounts, in order as Dukes.

Earls' eldest sons.

Marquesses' younger sons.

Lord-Barons, in order as Dukes.

Viscounts' eldest sons.

Earls' younger sons.

Lord-Barons' eldest sons.

Knights of the Garter.

Privy Counsellors not included in above ranks.

Senators of Coll. of Justice (Lords of Session).

Viscounts' younger sons.

Lord-Barons' younger sons.

Sons of Life Peers.

Baronets.

Knights of the Thistle.

Knights of other Orders as in England.

Solicitor-General for Scotland.

Lord Lyon King of Arms.

Sheriffs Principal (except as shown in column 1).

Knights Bachelor.

Sheriffs Substitute.

Companions of Orders as in England.

Commanders of Royal Victorian and British Empire Orders.

Eldest sons of younger sons of Peers.

Companions of Distinguished Service Order.

Lieutenants of Royal Victorian Order.

Officers of British Empire Order.

Baronets' eldest sons.

Knights' eldest sons successively (from Garter to Bachelor).

Members of Royal Victorian Order.

Members of British Empire Order.

Baronets' younger sons.

Knights' younger sons.

Queen's Counsel.

Barons-feudal.

Esquires.

Gentlemen.

SCOTTISH REGIONAL AND ISLANDS COUNCILS

AREA AND POPULATION

Region	Administrative Headquarters	Area (acres)	Population	Rateable Value 1988 £	Actual Rateable Value per head £
					p.
Borders	Newtown St. Boswells	1,154,366	102,141	50,725,201	494·41
Central	Stirling	1,015†	271,819	179,211,719	658·68
Dumfries and Galloway ..	Dumfries	1,574,074	145,139	76,481,592	526·94
Fife	Glenrothes	322,960	344,590	239,795,063	695·89
Grampian	Aberdeen	2,150,731	502,850	357,510,163	710·97
Highland	Inverness	10,091†	200,608	118,331,811	589·87
Lothian	Edinburgh	433,600	743,700	521,255,878	700·90
Orkney	Kirkwall	217,600	19,338	16,849,413	871·31
Shetland	Lerwick	551†	22,429	66,016,732	2,943·36
Strathclyde.............	Glasgow	5,348†	2,344,585	1,354,354,800	580·12
Tayside	Dundee	2,897†	393,762	228,074,938	579·22
Western Isles	Stornoway, Lewis	1,119†	31,048	10,002,169	115·33

† Sq. miles

CHIEF EXECUTIVES, DIRECTORS OF FINANCE AND CHAIRMEN

Region	Chief Executive	Director of Finance	Convener
Borders	K. J. Clark, C.B.E.	P. Jeary	T. Hunter, C.B.E.
Central	J. Broadfoot	S. C. Craig	C. Sneddon, O.B.E.
Dumfries and Galloway	N. W. D. McIntosh	J. C. Stewart	J. V. M. Jameson
Fife........................	Dr. J. A. Markland	A. E. Taylor	R. Gough
Grampian	J. D. Macnaughton	A. McLean	Dr. G. Hadley
Highland	R. H. Stevenson	J. W. Bremner	A. J. Russell
Lothian	G. M. Bowie	D. B. Chynoweth	J. Cook
Orkney	R. H. Gilbert	R. H. Gilbert	E. R. Eunson, O.B.E.
Shetland	M. A. Gerrard	M. E. Green	E. Thomason
Strathclyde.................	R. Calderwood	A. Gillespie	J. Jennings
Tayside	J. A. Wallace	I. B. McIver	R. M. Tosh
Western Isles	Dr. G. Macleod	D. G. Macleod	A. Matheson

PRINCIPAL SCOTTISH CITIES

ABERDEEN

ABERDEEN, 126 miles N.E. of Edinburgh, received its charter as a Royal Burgh from William the Lion in 1179. Scotland's third largest city, Aberdeen is the second largest Scottish fishing port and the main European centre for offshore oil exploration. It is also an ancient university town and distinguished research centre. Other industries include engineering, shipbuilding, food processing, textiles, paper manufacturing and chemicals. Places of interest: King's College, St. Machar's Cathedral, Brig o' Balgownie, the Kirk of St. Nicholas, Mercat Cross, Marischal College, Provost Skene's House, Art Gallery, James Dun's House (children's museum) and Provost Ross's House (maritime museum).

DUNDEE

DUNDEE, a Royal Burgh, is situated on the north bank of the Tay estuary. The city's port and dock installations are important to the offshore oil industry and the airport also provides servicing facilities. Principal industries include textiles, computers and other electronic industries, lasers, printing, tyre manufacture, food processing, carpets, engineering and clothing manufacture. Six sites have Enterprise Zone status, including the Technology Park, airport and port. The unique City Churches—three churches under one roof, together with the 15th century St. Mary's Tower—are the most prominent architectural feature.

EDINBURGH

EDINBURGH, the Capital of Scotland, has a municipal area of 100·6 sq. miles. The city is built on a group of hills and contains in Princes Street one of the most beautiful thoroughfares in the world. The principal buildings are the Castle, which includes St. Margaret's Chapel, the oldest building in Edinburgh, and near it, the Scottish National War Memorial; the Palace of Holyroodhouse; Parliament House, the present seat of the judicature; two universities (Edinburgh and Heriot-Watt); St. Giles' Cathedral (restored 1879–83); St. Mary's (Scottish Episcopal) Cathedral (Sir Gilbert Scott): the General Register House (Robert Adam): the National and the Signet Libraries; the National Gallery; the Royal Scottish Academy; and the National Portrait Gallery.

GLASGOW

GLASGOW, a Royal Burgh, is the principal commercial and industrial centre in Scotland. The city occupies the north and south banks of the Clyde, formerly one of the chief commercial estuaries in the world. The principal industries include engineering, aero and marine engines, chemicals, printing, etc. The city has also developed recently as a tourism and conference centre. The chief buildings are the 13th century Gothic Cathedral, the University (Sir Gilbert Scott), the City Chambers, Pollok House, the School of Art (Mackintosh), Kelvingrove Art Galleries, the Burrell Collection museum and the Mitchell Library. The city is home of the Scottish National Orchestra, Scottish Opera, Scottish Ballet, etc.

SCOTTISH DISTRICT COUNCILS

District	Administrative Headquarters	Population	Rateable Value 1988 £	Chief Executive	Chairman (a) Convener (b) Provost (c) Lord Provost
Aberdeen City (5)	Aberdeen	215,300	194,328,575	J. K. J. Smith‡	(c) R. A. Robertson
Angus (9)	Forfar	94,407	47,592,341	P. B. Regan	(b) B. M. C. Milne
Annandale and Eskdale (3)	Annan	35,945	18,473,409	J. A. Whitecross	(a) F. Park
Argyll and Bute (8) ...	Lochgilphead	65,737	36,044,965	M. A. J. Gossip	W. R. Hunter
Badenoch and Strathspey (6)	Kingussie	10,765	6,450,000	H. G. McCulloch	J. A. McCook
Banff and Buchan (5) .	Banff	84,650	54,383,278	R. W. Jackson†	(a) W. R. Cruickshank
Bearsden and Milngavie (8)	Bearsden	40,365	24,595,198	I. C. Laurie	(b) Mrs. J. Cameron
Berwickshire (1)	Duns	18,748	8,800,944	R. A. Christie	J. Evans
Caithness (6)	Wick	27,025	11,575,402	A. Beattie	(a) J. M. Young, O.B.E.
Clackmannan (2)	Alloa	47,412	27,631,441	I. F. Smith	(a) (vacant)
Clydebank (8)	Clydebank	48,573	24,900,000	J. T. McNally	(b) D. S. Grainger
Clydesdale (8)	Lanark	58,436	25,833,774	P. W. Daniels	(a) Mrs. E. Logan
Cumbernauld and Kilsyth (8)	Cumbernauld	62,503	30,185,000	J. Hutton	(b) Ms. M. McKenna
Cumnock and Doon Valley (8)	Cumnock	43,500	15,608,591	D. T. Hemmings O.B.E.	(a) J. Hodge, B.E.M.
Cunninghame (8).....	Irvine	137,376	79,630,009	B. Devine	(a) J. Carson
Dumbarton (8)	Dumbarton	79,100	48,379,795	L. MacKinnon	(b) W. Petrie
Dundee City (9)	Dundee	175,748	108,632,785	J. F. Hoey	(c) T. Mitchell
Dunfermline (4)	Dunfermline	129,210	102,317,492	G. Brown	(b) J. Cameron
East Kilbride (8)......	East Kilbride	81,718	52,765,000	D. Liddell	(b) Ms. H. Biggins
East Lothian (7)	Haddington	81,855	49,234,799	M. Duncan, O.B.E.	G. M. Wanless
Eastwood (8)	Giffnock	56,060	32,090,877	M. D. Henry	(b) Mrs. J. Macfie
Edinburgh City (7) ...	Edinburgh	438,232	359,538,963	A. Hepburn	(c) Rt. Hon. Eleanor T. McLaughlin
Ettrick and Lauderdale (1)	Galashiels	33,441	17,731,585	C. M. Anderson	(b) A. L. Tulley, M.B.E.
Falkirk (2)...........	Falkirk	144,361	98,529,104	J. P. H. Paton	(b) D. Goldie
Glasgow City (8)	Glasgow	718,823	485,388,593	S. F. Hamilton	(c) S. Baird
Gordon (5)...........	Inverurie	72,230	32,315,366	M. C. Barron	J. Lawrence
Hamilton (8)	Hamilton	106,945	52,515,956	A. Baird	(b) R. Gibb
Inverclyde (8)........	Greenock	96,382	50,162,751	I. C. Wilson	(b) F. A. McGlone
Inverness (6).........	Inverness	61,077	43,980,386	B. Wilson	A. G. Sellar
Kilmarnock and Loudoun (8)	Kilmarnock	81,186	39,323,104	R. W. Jenner	(b) J. Mills
Kincardine and Deeside (5).........	Stonehaven	48,402	26,150,248	T. Hyder	(a) D. J. Mackenzie M.B.E.
Kirkcaldy (4)	Kirkcaldy	148,193	98,200,233	{ J. M. Smith H. Wilson§	(a) R. King
Kyle and Carrick (8) ..	Ayr	113,081	65,484,114	I. R. D. Smillie	(b) D. MacNeill
Lochaber (6)	Fort William	19,369	10,901,000	D. A. B. Blair	D. P. MacFarlane
Midlothian (7)	Dalkeith	81,261	37,337,509	T. Muir	(a) D. Lennie
Monklands (8)	Coatbridge	106,187	50,730,000	M. V. P. Hart	(b) E. Cairns
Moray (5)............	Elgin	85,543	50,407,501	J. P. C. Bell	(a) E. Aldridge
Motherwell (8)	Motherwell	147,542	81,156,843	J. Bonomy	(b) J. Armstrong
Nairn (6)	Nairn	10,310	4,167,699	A. M. Kerr†	(b) S. A. Macarthur
Nithsdale (3)	Dumfries	57,293	33,070,733	W. W. Japp	(b) E. D. Gibson
North-East Fife (4) ...	Cupar	66,720	39,480,939	R. G. Brotherton	Dr. C. R. Sneddon
Perth and Kinross (9) .	Perth	123,607	71,685,000	J. E. D. Cormie	(b) A. Murray
Renfrew (8)	Paisley	203,220	116,616,229	Miss M. C. Thomson*	(b) G. Murray
Ross and Cromarty (6)	Dingwall	47,906	28,770,629	D. Sinclair	(a) G. D. Finlayson
Roxburgh (1).........	Hawick	35,225	16,589,000	K. W. Cramond	G. Yellowlees
Skye and Lochalsh (6).	Portree	11,500	4,238,277	D. H. Noble	J. F. Munro
Stewartry (3)	Kirkcudbright	23,292	11,312,800	J. C. Howie	(a) J. Nelson
Stirling (2)	Stirling	81,436	52,657,999	R. W. Black	(a) J. Hendry
Strathkelvin (8)	Kirkintilloch	89,274	37,383,900	C. Mallon	(b) R. M. Coyle
Sutherland (6)	Golspie	13,212	4,468,500	D. W. Martin	D. I. MacRae
Tweeddale (1)	Peebles	14,734	4,192,622	G. H. T. Garvie	M. A. R. Maher
West Lothian (7)	Bathgate	142,630	75,258,724	G. R. B. Blair†	(a) D. McCauley
Wigtown (3)	Stranraer	30,410	14,329,346	A. Geddes	J. Brown

‡ Town Clerk. † Director of Administration. § Joint Chief Officers. * District Administrator.
REGIONS.—(1) Borders; (2) Central; (3) Dumfries and Galloway; (4) Fife; (5) Grampian; (6) Highland; (7) Lothian; (8) Strathclyde; (9) Tayside.

CHIEFS OF CLANS AND NAMES IN SCOTLAND

THE ROYAL HOUSE: H.M. The Queen

AGNEW: Sir Crispin Agnew of Lochnaw, Bt., 6 Palmerston Road, Edinburgh.

ANSTRUTHER: Sir Ralph Anstruther of that Ilk, Bt., K.C.V.O., M.C., Balcaskie, Pittenweem, Fife.

ARBUTHNOTT: The Viscount of Arbuthnott, C.B.E., D.S.C., Arbuthnott House, Laurencekirk, Kincardineshire.

BARCLAY: Peter C. Barclay of that Ilk, Gatemans, Stratford St. Mary, Colchester, Essex.

BORTHWICK: The Lord Borthwick, T.D., Crookston, Heriot, Midlothian.

BOYD: The Lord Kilmarnock, Casa de Mondragon, Ronda (Malaga), Spain.

BOYLE: The Earl of Glasgow, Kelburn, Fairlie, Ayrshire.

BRODIE: Ninian Brodie of Brodie, Brodie Castle, Forres, Moray.

BRUCE: The Earl of Elgin and Kincardine, K.T., Broomhall, Dunfermline, Fife.

BUCHAN: David S. Buchan of Auchmacoy, Auchmacoy, Ellon, Aberdeenshire.

BURNETT: Dr. C. A. Burnett of Leys, Crathes Castle, Kincardineshire.

CAMERON: Col. Sir Donald Cameron of Lochiel, K.T., C.V.O., T.D., Achnacarry, Spean Bridge, Inverness.

CAMPBELL: The Duke of Argyll, Inveraray, Argyll.

CARMICHAEL: Richard J. Carmichael of Carmichael, Carmichael, Thankerton, Biggar, Lanarkshire.

CARNEGIE: The Earl of Southesk, K.C.V.O., Kinnaird Castle, Brechin.

CATHCART: Maj.-Gen. The Earl Cathcart, C.B., D.S.O., M.C., 2 Pembroke Gardens, W.8.

CHARTERIS: The Earl of Wemyss and March, K.T., Gosford House, Longniddry, East Lothian.

CLAN CHATTAN: M. K. Mackintosh of Clan Chattan, Maxwell Park, Gwelo, Zimbabwe.

CHISHOLM: Alastair Chisholm of Chisholm (*The Chisholm*), Silver Willows, Bury St. Edmunds.

COCHRANE: The Earl of Dundonald, Lochnell Castle, Ledaig, Argyllshire.

COLQUHOUN: Sir Ivar Colquhoun of Luss, Bt., Camstraddan, Luss, Dunbartonshire.

CRANSTOUN: Lt. Col. Alastair Cranstoun of that Ilk, M.C., Corehouse, Lanarkshire.

CRICHTON: Charles Crichton of that Ilk, Monzie, Perth.

DARROCH: Capt. Duncan Darroch of Gourock. The Red House, Branksome Park Rd., Camberley.

DRUMMOND: The Earl of Perth, P.C., Stobhall, Perth.

DUNBAR: Sir Jean Dunbar of Mochrum, Bt., 45/55 39th Street, Long Island City, New York.

DUNDAS: David D. Dundas of Dundas, 8 Derna Road, Kenwyn 7700, South Africa.

DURIE: Raymond V. D. Durie of Durie, Court House, Pewsey, Wilts.

ELIOTT: Sir Arthur Eliott of Stobs, Bt., Redheugh, Newcastleton, Roxburghshire.

ERSKINE: The Earl of Mar and Kellie, Claremont House, Alloa.

FARQUHARSON: Capt. A. A. C. Farquharson of Invercauld, M.C., Invercauld, Braemar.

FERGUSSON: Sir Charles Fergusson of Kilkerran, Bt., Kilkerran, Maybole, Ayrshire.

FORBES: The Lord Forbes, K.B.E., Balforbes, Alford, Aberdeenshire.

FORSYTH: Alistair Forsyth of that Ilk, Ethie Castle, by Arbroath, Angus.

FRASER: The Lady Saltoun, Cairnbulg Castle, Fraserburgh, Aberdeenshire.

FRASER (OF LOVAT)*: The Lord Lovat, D.S.O., M.C., T.D., Balblair House, Beauly, Inverness-shire.

GAYRE: Lt. Col. Robert Gayre of Gayre and Nigg, 1–3 Gloucester Lane, Edinburgh.

GORDON: The Marquess of Huntly, Aboyne Castle, Aberdeenshire.

GRAHAM: The Duke of Montrose, Auchmar, Drymen, Stirlingshire.

GRANT: The Lord Strathspey, 111 Elms Ride, West Wittering, W. Sussex.

HAIG: The Earl Haig, O.B.E., Bemersyde, Melrose, Roxburgh.

HALDANE: Alexander N. C. Haldane of Gleneagles, Auchterarder, Perthshire.

HANNAY: Ramsey W. R. Hannay of Kirkdale and of that Ilk, Cardoness House, Gatehouse-of-Fleet, Kirkcudbright.

HAY: The Earl of Erroll, Wolverton Farm, Wolverton, Basingstoke, Hants.

HENDERSON: John W. P. Henderson of Fordell, 7 Owen Street, Toowoomba, Queensland, Australia.

HUNTER: Neil A. Hunter of Hunterston, Tour d'Escas, Carretera d'Escas, La Massana, Andorra.

IRVINE OF DRUM: C. F. Irvine of Drum, 29 Forest Road, Hoylake, Wirral, Merseyside.

JARDINE: Sir Alexander Jardine of Applegirth, Bt., Denbie, Lockerbie, Dumfriesshire.

JOHNSTONE: The Earl of Annandale and Hartfell, Raehills, Lockerbie, Dumfriesshire.

KEITH: The Earl of Kintore, Glenton House, Rickarton, Stonehaven, Aberdeenshire.

KENNEDY: The Marquess of Ailsa, O.B.E., Blanefield, Kirkoswald, Ayrshire.

KERR: The Marquess of Lothian, K.C.V.O., Monteviot, Ancrum, Roxburgh.

KINCAID: Mrs. Heather V. Kincaid of Kincaid, 4a Bristol Gardens, Brighton, Sussex.

LAMONT: Peter N. Lamont of that Ilk, St. Patrick's College, Manley, N.S.W. 2095, Australia.

LEASK: Madam Leask of Leask, 1 Vincent Road, Sheringham, Norfolk.

LENNOX: Dennis P. H. Lennox of that Ilk, Pools Farm, Downton on the Rock, Ludlow, Shropshire.

LESLIE: The Earl of Rothes, Tanglewood, West Tytherley, Salisbury, Wilts.

LINDSAY: The Earl of Crawford and Balcarres, P.C., Balcarres, Colinsburgh, Fife.

LOCKHART: Angus H. Lockhart of the Lee, Newholme, Dunsyre, Lanark.

LUMSDEN: Gillem Lumsden of that Ilk and Blanerne, Kindersleigh, Bois Avenue, Chesham Bois, Amersham, Bucks.

McBAIN: J. H. McBain of McBain, 7025, North Finger Rock Place, Tucson, Arizona, U.S.A.

MALCOLM (MACCALLUM): Robin N. L. Malcolm of Poltalloch, Duntrune Castle, Lochgilphead, Argyll.

MACDONALD: The Lord Macdonald (*The Macdonald of Macdonald*), Ostaig House, Skye.

MACDONALD OF CLANRANALD*: Ranald A. Macdonald of Clanranald, 55 Compton Road, N.1.

MACDONALD OF SLEAT (CLAN HUSTEAIN)*: Sir Ian Bosville Macdonald of Sleat, Bt., Thorpe Hall, Rudston, Driffield, Yorks.

MACDONELL OF GLENGARRY*: Air Cdre. Aeneas R. MacDonell of Glengarry, C.B., D.F.C., Elonbank, Castle Street, Fortrose, Ross-shire.

MACDOUGALL: Madam Coline MacDougall of MacDougall, Dunollie, Argyll.

MACDOWELL: Fergus D. H. Macdowell of Garthland, 16 Tower Road, Nepean, Ontario, Canada.

MACGREGOR: Sir Gregor MacGregor of MacGregor, Bt., Bannatyne, Newtyle, Angus.

MACKAY: The Lord Reay, 11 Wilton Crescent, S.W.1.

MACKENZIE: The Earl of Cromartie, M.C., T.D., Castle Leod, Strathpeffer, Ross-shire.

MACKINNON: Madam Anne Mackinnon of Mackinnon, 16 Purleigh Road, Bridgewater, Somerset.

MACKINTOSH: The Mackintosh of Mackintosh, O.B.E., Moy Hall, Inverness.

MACLACHLAN: Madam Marjorie MacLachlan of MacLachlan, Castle Lachlan, Argyll.

MACLAREN: Donald MacLaren of MacLaren and Achleskine, British Military Government, Berlin (B.F.P.O. 45).

MACLEAN: The Lord Maclean, K.T., G.C.V.O., K.B.E., P.C., Duart Castle, Mull.

MACLENNAN: Ronald G. MacLennan of MacLennan, The Old Mill, Dores, Inverness.

MACLEOD: J. MacLeod of MacLeod, Dunvegan Castle, Skye.

MACMILLAN: George MacMillan of MacMillan, Finlaystone, Langbank, Renfrewshire.

MACNAB: J. C. Macnab of Macnab (*The Macnab*), Finlarig, Killin, Perthshire.

MACNAGHTEN: Sir Patrick Macnaghten of Macnaghten and Dundarave, Bt., Dundarave, Bushmills, Co. Antrim.

MACNEACAIL: Iain Macneacail of Macneacail and Scorrybreac, 12 Fox Street, Ballina, N.S.W., Australia.

MACNEIL OF BARRA: Ian R. Macneil of Barra (*The Macneil of Barra*), Kisimul Castle, Barra.

MACPHERSON: Hon. Sir William Macpherson of Cluny, T.D., Newtown Castle, Blairgowrie, Perthshire.

MACTHOMAS: Andrew P. C. MacThomas of Finegand, c/o The Clan MacThomas Society, 19 Warriston Avenue, Edinburgh 3.

MAITLAND: The Earl of Lauderdale, 12 St. Vincent Street, Edinburgh.

MAKGILL: The Viscount of Oxfuird, Hill House, St. Mary Bourne, Andover, Hants.

MAR: The Countess of Mar, St. Michael's Farm, Great Witley, Worcs.

MARJORIBANKS: William Marjoribanks of that Ilk, Kirklands of Forglen, Turriff, Aberdeenshire.

MATHESON: Sir Torquhil Matheson of Matheson, Bt., Sanderwick Court, Frome, Somerset.

MENZIES: David R. Menzies of Menzies, 20 Nardina Crescent, Dalkeith, Western Australia.

MOFFAT: Francis Moffat of that Ilk, Redacres, Moffat, Dumfriesshire.

MONCREIFFE: (vacant).

MONTGOMERIE: The Earl of Eglinton and Winton, The Dutch House, West Green, Hartley Wintney, Hants.

MORRISON: Dr. Iain M. Morrison of Ruchdi, Todhurst Farm, Lake Lane, Barnham, Sussex.

MUNRO: Patrick G. Munro of Foulis, T.D., Foulis Castle, Ross.

MURRAY: The Duke of Atholl, Blair Castle, Blair Atholl, Perthshire.

NICOLSON: The Lord Carnock, 90 Whitehall Court, London S.W.1.

OGILVY: The Earl of Airlie, K.T., G.C.V.O., P.C., Cortachy Castle, Kirriemuir, Angus.

RAMSAY: The Earl of Dalhousie, K.T., G.C.V.O., G.B.E., M.C., Brechin Castle, Angus.

RATTRAY: James S. Rattray of Rattray, Craighall, Rattray, Perthshire.

ROBERTSON: Alexander G. H. Robertson of Struan (*Struan-Robertson*), The Breach Farm, Goudhurst Road, Cranbrook, Kent.

ROLLO: The Lord Rollo, Pitcairns, Dunning, Perthshire.

ROSE: Miss Elizabeth Rose of Kilravock, Kilravock Castle, Croy, Inverness-shire.

ROSS: David C. Ross of that Ilk, The Old Schoolhouse, Fettercairn, Kincardineshire.

RUTHVEN: The Earl of Gowrie, P.C., Castlemartin, Kilcullen, Co. Kildare, Eire.

SCOTT: The Duke of Buccleuch and Queensberry, K.T., V.R.D., Bowhill, Selkirk.

SCRYMGEOUR: The Earl of Dundee, Birkhill, Cupar, Fife.

SEMPILL: The Lady Sempill, Druminnor Castle, Rhynie, Aberdeenshire.

SHAW: John Shaw of Tordarroch, Newhall, Balblair, By Conon Bridge, Ross-shire.

SINCLAIR: The Earl of Caithness, Finstock Manor, Finstock, Oxon.

STIRLING: Fraser J. Stirling of Cader, 17 Park Row, Farnham, Surrey.

SUTHERLAND: The Countess of Sutherland, House of Tongue, Brora, Sutherland.

SWINTON: W. F. H. Swinton of that Ilk, 23301 8th Avenue S.S., Calgary, Alberta, Canada.

URQUHART: Kenneth T. Urquhart of that Ilk, 4713 Orleans Boulevard, Jefferson, Louisiana, U.S.A.

WALLACE: Lt.-Col. M. R. Wallace of that Ilk, Hilton of Gask, Auchterarder, Perthshire.

WEDDERBURN OF THAT ILK: The Master of Dundee, Birkhill, Cupar, Fife.

WEMYSS: David Wemyss of that Ilk, Gosford House, Longniddry, East Lothian.

Only chiefs of *whole* Names or Clans are included (except certain special instances (marked *), who though not chiefs of a "whole name", were, or are, for some reason, (*e.g.* the Macdonald forfeiture), independent. Under decision (*Campbell-Gray*, 1950) that a bearer of a "double or triple-barrelled" surname cannot be held chief of a part of such, several others cannot be included in the list at present.

NEW TOWNS IN GREAT BRITAIN

Commission for the New Towns. Glen House, Stag Place, SW1E 5AJ.—The Commission was established under the New Towns Act, 1959, its remit is to (a) take over and, with a view to its eventual disposal, to hold, manage and turn to account the property of Development Corporations transferred to the Commission and (b) as soon as it considers it expedient to do so, to dispose of property so transferred and any other property held by it. In carrying out its remit the Commission must have due regard to the convenience and welfare of persons residing, working or carrying on business there and, until disposal, the maintenance and enhancement of the value of the land held and return obtained from it. The Commission has such responsibilities in Basildon, Bracknell, Central Lancashire, Corby, Crawley, Harlow, Hatfield, Hemel Hempstead, Northampton, Peterborough, Redditch, Skelmersdale, Stevenage, Washington and Welwyn Garden City. The Commission has minimal responsibilities (principally financial and litigation) in Aycliffe and Peterlee and Cwmbran following the wind-up of their Development Corporations in 1988.

Chairman, Sir Neil Shields, M.C.
Deputy Chairman, Sir Reginald Eyre.
Members, R. B. Caws, C.B.E.; W. J. Mackenzie, O.B.E.; P. M. Vine, C.B.E.; Sir Gordon Roberts, C.B.E.; The Lord Bellwin; E. G. Barratt; M. H. Mallinson; R. W. P. Luff.
Chief Executive, D. M. Woodhall.
Director of Estates and Technical Services, H. J. M. Thomas.
Director of Finance, Administrative and Legal Services, G. T. C. Probart.
Director of Promotion, J. Grafton.

BASILDON, Essex.—*Executive Officer,* H. Bacon. *Offices,* Gifford House, London Road, Bowers Gifford, Basildon SS13 2EX.
BRACKNELL, Berks.—Glen House, SW1E 5AJ.
CENTRAL LANCASHIRE, Lancs.—*Executive Officer,* B. Birtwistle. *Offices,* Cuerden Pavilion, Shady Lane, Bamber Bridge, Preston PR5 6AZ.
CORBY, Northants.—*Executive Officer,* J. G. Lloyd. *Offices,* Chisholm House, 9 Queen's Square, Corby NN17 1PA.
CRAWLEY, Sussex.—Glen House, SW1E 5AJ.
HARLOW, Essex.—Glen House, SW1E 5AJ.
HATFIELD, Herts.—Glen House, SW1E 5AJ.
HEMEL HEMPSTEAD, Herts.—Glen House, SW1E 5AJ.
NORTHAMPTON.—*Executive Officer,* W. A. Gray. *Offices,* 2/3 Market Square, Northampton NN1 2EN.
PETERBOROUGH, Cambs.—*Executive Officer,* P. Way. *Offices,* Stuart House, City Road, Peterborough PE1 1UJ.
REDDITCH, Worcs.—*Executive Officer,* I. McKay. *Offices,* Highfield House, Headless Cross Drive, Redditch B97 5EU.
SKELMERSDALE, Lancs.—*Executive Officer,* J. Leigh. *Offices,* Pennylands, Skelmersdale WN8 8AR.

STEVENAGE, Herts.—Glen House, SW1E 5AJ.
WASHINGTON, Tyne and Wear.— *Executive Officer,* J. Edwards. *Offices,* Usworth Hall, Stephenson, District 12, Washington NE37 3HS.
WELWYN GARDEN CITY, Herts.—Glen House, SW1E 5AJ.

DEVELOPMENT CORPORATIONS

England and Wales

MILTON KEYNES, Bucks.—Formed 1967. *Chairman,* Lord Chilver, F.R.S. *General Manager,* F. C. Henshaw. *Offices,* Saxon Court, 502 Avebury Boulevard, Central Milton Keynes MK9 3HS. Area, 22,000 acres. Population, 138,000. Estimated eventual population, 200,000.

TELFORD, Shropshire.—Formed 1963. *Chairman,* F. J. Jones. *General Manager,* M. D. Morgan. *Offices,* Priorslee Hall, Telford TF2 9NT. Area, 19,243 acres. Population, 112,901. Estimated eventual population, 130,000

WARRINGTON AND RUNCORN, Cheshire.—Amalgamated 1981 (Warrington formed 1968; Runcorn formed 1964). *Chairman,* Prof. A. Mercer. *General Manager,* D. J. Binns. *Offices,* P.O. Box 49, New Town House, Buttermarket Street, Warrington WA1 2LF. Area, Warrington 18,612 acres; Runcorn 7,234 acres. Population, Warrington 148,500; Runcorn 68,600.

DEVELOPMENT BOARD FOR RURAL WALES.—Formed 1977. *Chairman,* F. L. Morgan, C.B.E.. *Offices,* Ladywell House, Newtown, Powys, SY16 1JB.

Scotland

CUMBERNAULD, Strathclyde.—Formed 1956. *Chairman,* D. W. Mitchell, C.B.E.. *Chief Executive,* D. W. Anderson, C.B.E. *Headquarters,* Cumbernauld House, Cumbernauld G67 3JH. Area, 7,788 acres. Population, 49,200. Estimated eventual population, 55,000.

EAST KILBRIDE, Strathclyde.—Formed 1947. *Chairman,* J. A. Denholm. *Managing Director,* G. B. Young, C.B.E. *Offices,* Atholl House, East Kilbride G74 1LU. Area, 10,250 acres. Population, 69,700. Estimated eventual population not known.

GLENROTHES, Fife.—Formed 1948. *Chairman,* Prof. C. Blake. *Chief Executive,* W. M. Cracknell. *Offices,* Balbirnie House, Glenrothes KY7 6NR. Area, 5,763 acres. Population, 38,000. Estimated eventual population, 45,000.

IRVINE, Ayrshire.—Formed, 1966. *Chairman,* A. R. Belch, C.B.E. *Managing Director,* Brig. R. A. Rickets. *Offices,* Perceton House, Irvine KA12 2AL. Area, 12,409 acres. Population, 58,537. Estimated eventual population, 63,000.

LIVINGSTON, West Lothian.—Formed, 1962. *Chairman,* R. S. Watt. *Chief Executive,* J. A. Pollock. *Offices,* Sidlaw House, Almondvale, Livingston EH54 6QA. Area, 6,868 acres. Population, 41,000. Estimated eventual population, 70,000.

Northern Ireland

(For geographical, historical and judicial notes on Ireland, see Index)

The usually resident population of Northern Ireland, as revised, at the 1981 Census was 1,556,039 (males, 761,882; females, 794,157) compared with a total population of 1,536,065 at the Census of 1971. (N.B. This revised figure takes account of the population effect of non-enumerated households, estimated at 74,000 persons.) In 1981 the number of persons in the various religious denominations (expressed as percentages of the total usually resident population) were: Roman Catholic, 28·0; Presbyterian, 22·9; Church of Ireland, 19·0; Methodist, 4·0; others 7·6; not stated, 18·5. Northern Ireland has a total area of 5,452 sq. miles (land, 5,206 sq. miles; inland water and tideways, 246 sq. miles) with a density of population of 282 persons per sq. mile in 1981. The population, mid 1987 estimate, was 1,575,200.

CONSTITUTION AND GOVERNMENT

A separate parliament and executive Government was established for Northern Ireland in 1921 by the Government of Ireland Act. The Northern Ireland Constitution Act, 1973, abolished the post of Governor and Parliament of Northern Ireland and provided for the transfer of certain legislative functions to a Northern Ireland Assembly and Executive. Devolved Government came into operation with effect from January 1, 1974 but when the Executive collapsed the Northern Ireland Assembly was prorogued on May 29, 1974. The Northern Ireland Act, 1974, which became law in July 1974, made provision for temporary arrangements for the government of Northern Ireland by the Secretary of State for Northern Ireland and also provided for the holding of elections and a Constitutional Convention. Direct Rule continues in being under the terms of the Northern Ireland Act 1974.

Attempts have been made by successive governments to find a way of restoring devolved government to Northern Ireland. The most recent attempt failed when the Northern Ireland Assembly (elected on October 20, 1982) was dissolved on June 23, 1986.

FLAG.—The national flag is that of the United Kingdom.

THE PRIVY COUNCIL

R. J. Bailie (1971); D. W. Bleakley (1971); R. H. Bradford (1969); W. Craig (1963); J. Dobson (1969); W. K. Fitzsimmons (1965); Lt. Col. the Lord Glentoran (1953); Sir Edward Jones (1965); Mr. Justice Kelly (1969); H. V. Kirk (1962); Capt. W. J. Long (1966); Lord Lowry (1971); R. W. B. McConnell (1964); W. B. McIvor (1971); W. J. Morgan (1961); The Lord Moyola (1966); Sir Ivan Neill (1950); The Lord O'Neill of the Maine (1956); Sir Robert Porter, Q.C. (1969); Lord Rathcavan (1969); R. Simpson (1969); J. D. Taylor (1970); H. W. West (1960).

GOVERNMENT OFFICES

Department of Finance and Personnel

Permanent Secretary, J. L. Semple.
Under Secretaries, W. J. Hodges; J. M. Downdnall; P. J. Small; R. B. Spence.
Grade 4, D. W. Alexander; A. I. Devitt.
Assistant Secretaries:
 Resources Group, Miss J. O. M. Frame; Dr. J. J. M. Harbison; Miss J. A. Mills; W. G. Purdy; S. Quinn; Dr. D. G. Slattery; H. P. Simpson; J. F. Walker.
 Personnel and Finance Group, Mrs. D. A. Brown; J. R. Ingram; J. Maguire; H. Moore; R. G. Mussen; F. P. Smyth; P. J. Tweedale.
 Central Secretariat, N. Hamilton; R. Wilson.
Solicitor, R. F. Cole.
Commissioner of Valuation, B. T. Shiels.
First Legislative Draftsman, T. R. Erskine, C.B.
Director of Central Unit on Purchasing, D. J. Court.
Senior Principals, J. E. Henderson; T. Whiteside; R. E. Templeton; R. J. Jordon; E. F. Jardine.

Department of Education

Permanent Secretary, J. H. Parkes, C.B.
Under Secretaries, P. S. Holmes; R. D. Hill.
Senior Chief Inspector, I. H. N. Wallace.
Assistant Secretaries, A. M. Dodds; D. Woods; D. G. McNeill; K. H. Clark; J. S. Smith; T. Johnston; E. M. Power.
Deputy Senior Chief Inspector, N. Morrison.

Department of the Environment

Permanent Secretary, D. Barry, C.B..
Under Secretaries, W. E. C. Ford *(Personnel, Information Systems Unit, Solicitors Branch, Central Management, Local Government),* R. H. Mackenzie *(Conservation, Historic Monuments and Buildings, Environmental Protection, Works Service, Ordnance Survey, Land Registry, Registry of Deeds, Rates);* F. McCann *(Housing, Water);* G. F. Loughran *(Planning, Comprehensive Development, Lands Service);* J. A. G. Whitlaw *(Roads, Transport, Public Records Office).*
Director, Town and Country Planning Service, J. B. Davidson.
Director, Water Service, W. N. Smyth.
Director, Roads Service, I. W. Joiner.
Director, Works Services, J. Brennan.
Director, Conservation, J. B. Phillips.
Director, Environmental Protection, I. McQuiston.
Assistant Secretaries, W. Black; W. N. Campbell; H. E. Carson; J. Cowan; F. A. Dillon; T. Pearson; A. Miller; F. R. Rodgers; J. Kirk; J. M. Irvine; J. F. Russell; R. E. Aiken; E. J. Galway; D. B. McIldouh; Mrs. R. Brown.
Chief Local Government Auditor, S. J. Bailie.
Chief Engineer (Roads Service), Dr. W. M. C. Stevenson.
Chief Planning Officer, E. Hayes.
Chief Engineer (Water Service), S. T. Bratty.
Chief Quantity Surveyor, T. O'Hara.
Chief Survey Officer, M. J. D. Brand.
Chief Civil Engineer, C. E. Ronaldson.
Chief Architect, W. B. Sloan.
Chief Structural Engineer, K. Turkington.
Chief Alkali and Radiochemical Inspector, K. J. Ledgerwood.

Department of Health & Social Services

Permanent Secretary, F. A. Elliott.
Under Secretaries, G. Buchanan; R. F. Mills; Miss Z. Davies; J. G. Hunter.
Assistant Secretaries, A. N. Burns; C. McN. Davie; J. R. Kearney; J. Scott; J. A. Wylie; R. McMurray; A. S. Treacy; D. H. McNally; Dr. R. W. McQuiston; S. J. Peover; Miss J. Dixon; Miss M. McCann; Mr. H. Martin; Mr. P. Conliffe; Mr. P. Devlin.
Chief Medical Officer, Dr. J. F. McKenna.
Deputy Chief Medical Officers, Dr. W. D. Thornton; Dr. C. E. Hall.
Chief Inspector, Social Services Inspectorate, P. J. Armstrong.

Department of Economic Development

Permanent Secretary, D. Fell.
Under Secretaries, J. S. Crozier; D. Gibson; P. Carvill,
T. R. Copestake; D. C. Gowdy.
Assistant Secretaries, R. B. Gamble; R. J. O'Hara;
Miss S. Cooper; P. S. McDonnell; D. J. Alexander;
M. Warnock; J. E. Wolstencroft; R. H. Thompson;
M. P. Maxwell; L. Minnis; R. G. Smartt; Dr. J. G.
Hall; M. J. Briant; A. H. McAlister.
Director of Industrial Science Division, J. T. Mc-
Cullins.
Economic Adviser, Prof. W. Black.

Industrial Development Board

Chief Executive, A. S. Hopkins.
Deputy Chief Executives, F. A. Hewitt; J. M. Dowdall.
Executive Directors, P. T. Bill; J. H. Caldwell; J. J.
Monaghan; W. B. Robinson; I. Walters; H. G.
Thompson; S. L. Ross; M. J. M. Bohill; R. D. Lyon;
C. Harding; G. Wilson.
Corporate Finance, R. D. Lynn.

Department of Agriculture

Permanent Secretary, Dr. W. H. Jack, C.B.
Under Secretaries, J. C. Chalmers; D. M. Carson.
Chief Scientific Officer, Dr. C. H. McMurray.
Chief Agriculture Officer, T. A. Larmour.
Chief Veterinary Officer, E. W. Sullivan.
Chief Forest Officers, W. H. Forbes; W. J. Wright.
Assistant Secretaries, D. A. G. Hirrell; L. Sinclair; S.
R. Armstrong; N. E. Morrison; I. C. Henderson; K.
E. Brady; F. A. Dillon.

Head of Northern Ireland Civil Service and Central Secretariat

Head of Northern Ireland Civil Service, Sir Kenneth
Bloomfield, K.C.B.
Under Secretary, R. Spence.
Assistant Secretaries, N. Hamilton; R. Wilson.
Director of Information, A. Wood.

Northern Ireland Audit Office

Comptroller and Auditor General, L. V. D. Calvert,
C.B..
Secretary, J. G. W. McComish.
Directors of Audit, D. A. Kerr; K. G. McCormick; B.
H. Poulter; S. B. D. McConnell.

Northern Ireland Business Centre
11 Berkeley Street, W.1.

Senior Executive, F. G. Galbraith.
Executive, J. Hume.

FINANCE

Taxation in Northern Ireland is largely imposed
and collected by the United Kingdom Government.
After deducting the cost of collections and of
Northern Ireland's contributions to the European
Economic Community the balance, known as the
Attributed Share of Taxation, is paid over to the
Northern Ireland Consolidated Fund. Northern
Ireland's revenue is insufficient to meet its expendi-
ture and is supplemented by a grant in aid.

	1986–87*	1987–88**
	£	£
Public income.....	3,500,753,132	3,663,224,953
Public expenditure	3,500,648,309	3,663,124,953
	* Outturn	** Estimate

PRODUCTION

Industries.—The products of the engineering, shipbuilding and aircraft industries, which employed
29,000 persons, were valued at £823 million. The
textile industries, employing about 10,000 persons,

produced products valued at approximately £236
million. The food and drink industry, employing
about 20,000 persons, produced goods valued at £2,446
million.

Minerals.—1,310 persons were employed in mining
and quarrying operations in Northern Ireland in
1987 and the minerals raised (16,612,355 tonnes) were
valued at £29,160,136.

COMMUNICATIONS

Seaports.—The total tonnage handled by N. Irish
ports in 1987 was 13·7m. Regular ferry, freight and
container services operate to ports in Great Britain
and Europe from Belfast, Larne, Londonderry and
Warrenpoint.
Road and Rail Transport.—The Northern Ireland
Transport Holding Company is largely responsible
for the supervision of the subsidiary companies,
Ulsterbus and Citybus (which operate the public road
passenger services) and Northern Ireland Railways.
Road freight services are also provided by a large
number of hauliers operating competitively under
licence.
Air Transport.—Belfast International Airport is
run by Northern Ireland Airports Ltd., a subsidiary
of the Northern Ireland Transport Holding Company
and provides scheduled and chartered services on
domestic and international routes.
Scheduled services also operate from Belfast Harbour Airport to eleven British destinations and from
Eglinton, Co. Londonderry, to Blackpool, Glasgow
and Dublin.

BELFAST

BELFAST, the administrative centre of Northern
Ireland, is situated at the mouth of the River Lagan
at its entrance to Belfast Lough. It has a municipal
area of 16,017 acres, exclusive of tidal water (2,034)
and a population (mid-1987) of 303,800. The city grew,
owing to its easy access by sea to Scottish coal and
iron, to be a great industrial centre.
The principal buildings are of a relatively recent
date and include the Parliament Buildings at Stormont, the City Hall, the Law Courts, the Public
Library and the Museum and Art Gallery.
Belfast received its first charter of incorporation
in 1613 and was created a city in 1888; the title of
Lord Mayor was conferred in 1892.

LONDONDERRY

LONDONDERRY, situated on the River Foyle, has a
population (mid-1987) of 97,500 and was reputedly
founded in 546 by St. Columba. Londonderry (formerly *Derry*) has important associations with the
City of London. The Irish Society, under its royal
charter of 1613, fortified the city and was for long
closely associated with its administration.
Famous for the great siege of 1688–89, when for 105
days the town held out against the forces of James II
until relieved by sea, Londonderry was an important
naval base throughout the Second World War.
Interesting buildings are the Protestant Cathedral
of St. Columb's (1633) and the Guildhall reconstructed
in 1912 and containing a number of beautiful stained
glass windows, many of which were presented by the
livery companies of London. The famous Walls are
still intact and form a circuit of almost a mile around
the old city.

COUNTIES OF NORTHERN IRELAND

Counties and County Boroughs	Area* sq. miles	Lord Lieutenant	High Sheriff, 1988
Antrim....................	1,093	Capt. R. A. F. Dobbs	Sir Patrick Macnaughten, Bt.
Belfast County Borough	25	Sir Robin Kinahan, E.R.D.	(vacant)
Armagh	484	Capt. F. M. A. Torrens-Spence, D.S.O., D.S.C., A.F.C., R.N. (retd).	G. A. Forbes
Down	945	Col. W. N. Brann, O.B.E., E.R.D.	H. E. Henshall
Fermanagh	647	The Earl of Erne	J. S. Moffatt
Londonderry†	798	Col. M. W. McCorkell, O.B.E., T.D.	Dr. G. P. M. Marshall
Londonderry City	3·4	J. T. Eaton, T.D.	Maj. A. H. G. Gibbon, G.M.
Tyrone..................	1,211	The Duke of Abercorn	J. O'Dwyer, O.B.E.

* Excluding inland waters and tideways.   † Excluding the City of Londonderry.

MUNICIPAL DIRECTORY OF NORTHERN IRELAND

District and §Borough Councils	Population (June 30, 1987)	Net Annual Value	Council Clerk	Mayor (†) or Chairman 1988
		£		
§Antrim, Co. Antrim	46,600	6,187,649	S. J. Magee	†J. H. Allen, O.B.E.
§Ards, Co. Down	63,600	7,005,564	D. J. Fallows	†T. P. Benson
Armagh, Co. Armagh ...	50,700	4,563,290	D. R. D. Mitchell	S. Foster
§Ballymena, Co. Antrim .	56,100	7,379,867	J. S. McIlroy	†A. Spence, M.B.E.
§Ballymoney, Co. Antrim	23,800	2,341,678	W. J. Williamson	†C. J. Cousley
Banbridge, Co. Down ...	32,000	3,222,734	A. G. Waite (acting)	S. J. Cowan, O.B.E.
Belfast, Co. Antrim and Co. Down	303,800	50,605,570	C. Ward	N. A. Dodds (*Lord Mayor*)
§Carrickfergus, Co. Antrim...............	29,300	4,357,282	R. Boyd	†J. Brown
§Castlereagh, Co. Down ..	57,900	7,294,741	A. D. Nicol	†W. Abraham
§Coleraine, Co. Londonderry	47,700	7,015,869	W. E. Andrews	†W. J. Watt
Cookstown, Co. Tyrone .	27,700	2,766,598	W. A. Bownes	A. Kane
§Craigavon, Co Armagh..	76,600	9,753,690	E. A. McKinley	†S. Gardiner, M.B.E.
Down, Co. Down	56,400	5,256,985	S. Byrne	Mrs. A. Gallagher
Dungannon, Co. Tyrone	43,900	4,026,362	W. J. Beattie	G. N. Douglas
Fermanagh, Co. Fermanagh	50,300	4,667,363	G. Burns, M.B.E.	J. Canning
§Larne, Co. Antrim	28,700	3,637,364	G. McKinley	†J. Lunny
Limavady, Co. Londonderry	29,600	2,565,414	J. K. Stevenson	J. W. Fulton
§Lisburn, Co. Antrim and Co. Down	92,900	11,563,568	M. S. Fielding	†R. Cartwright
Londonderry, Co. Londonderry	97,500	10,713,397	C. M. Geary	†W. G. Bleakes
Magherafelt, Co. Londonderry	33,300	3,028,959	W. R. S. McMaster	Mrs. M. K. McSorley
Moyle, Co. Antrim	15,200	1,324,525	J. O'Kane	R. A. McIlroy
Newry and Mourne, Co. Down	87,100	7,121,027	K. O'Neill	E. Markey
§Newtownabbey, Co. Antrim...............	72,300	10,515,650	J. Campbell	†J. Smith
§North Down, Co. Down .	70,700	8,537,887	J. McKimm	†D. P. Hayes
Omagh, Co. Tyrone	45,800	3,886,309	J. P. McKinney	B. McGrath
Strabane, Co. Tyrone ...	35,700	2,725,852	J. T. Keanie	I. C. Barr
Northern Ireland	1,575,200	192,065,194		

NOTE.—Since the reorganisation of Local Government, rates in Northern Ireland are collected by the Department of Environment and consist of two rates, a regional rate made by the Department of Finance and a district rate made by individual District Councils.

THE ISLE OF MAN (ELLAN VANNIN)

An island in the Irish Sea, in lat. 54° 3′–54° 25′ N. and long. 4° 18′–4° 47′ W., nearly equidistant from England, Scotland, and Ireland. Although the early inhabitants were of Celtic origin, the Isle of Man was part of the Norwegian Kingdom of the Hebrides until 1266, when this was ceded to Scotland. Subsequently granted to the Stanleys (Earls of Derby) in the 15th century and later to the Dukes of Atholl, it was brought under the direct administration of the Crown in 1765. The island forms the bishopric of Sodor and Man.

The total land area is 141,263 acres (221 sq. miles). The report on the 1986 Census showed a resident population of 64,282 (males, 30,782; females, 33,500). In 1987 births numbered 729 and deaths 925. The main language in use is English. There are no remaining native speakers of Manx Gaelic but around 200 people are able to speak the language.

CAPITAL, ΨDouglas. Population (1986), 20,368; ΨCastletown (3,019) is the ancient capital; the other towns are ΨPeel (3,660), and ΨRamsey (5,778).

FLAG.—Three legs in white and gold armed conjoined on a red ground.

TYNWALD DAY.—July 5.

GOVERNMENT

The Isle of Man is a self-governing Crown dependency, having its own legal and administrative systems. The Lieutenant-Governor is the Queen's personal representative in the Island. The legislature, called the Tynwald, has two branches—the Legislative Council and the House of Keys. The Council consists of the Bishop of Sodor and Man, the Attorney-General and 8 members chosen by the House of Keys, one of whom is appointed President of the Council. The House of Keys, one of the most ancient legislative assemblies in the world, consists of 24 members, elected by the adult male and female population.

ECONOMY

Most of the income generated in the Island is earned in the services sector with financial and business services being considerably larger than the traditional industry of tourism. Manufacturing industry is also a major generator of income whilst the Island's other traditional industries of agriculture and fishing now play a minor role in the economy.

Under the terms of the Island's special relationship with the European Community the Island has free access to E.C. markets.

The Freeport at Ronaldsway Airport has been developed and will be opened in the near future.

The Island's unemployment rate is approximately 3 per cent and price inflation is around 5 per cent per annum.

FINANCE

The Island's Budget for 1988–89 provided for gross expenditure of £177,800,000. The principal sources of Government revenue are taxes on income and expenditure. Income tax is payable at a rate of 15 per cent. on the first £6,000 of taxable income of resident individuals and 20 per cent. on the balance. The rate of income tax is 20 per cent. on the whole taxable incomes of non-residents and companies. By agreement with the United Kingdom Government, the Island keeps most of its rates of indirect taxation (Value Added Tax and duties) the same as those in the United Kingdom, but this agreement may be terminated by either party. A reciprocal agreement on National Insurance benefits and pensions exists between the Governments of the Isle of Man and the United Kingdom. Taxes are also charged on property (rates), but these are comparatively low.

The major Government expenditure items are health, social security and education, which account for 61 per cent. of the Government budget. The Island makes a voluntary annual contribution to the United Kingdom for defence and other external services.

Although the Island has a special relationship with the European Community it neither contributes money to nor receives funds from the E.C. Budget.

Lieutenant-Governor, His Excellency Maj.-Gen. Laurence A. W. New, C.B., C.B.E.
A.D.C. to the Lieutenant-Governor, M. M. Wood.
President of the Legislative Council, J. C. Nivison, C.B.E.
Speaker, House of Keys, Sir Charles Kerruish, O.B.E.
His Honour the First Deemster and Clerk of the Rolls, J. W. Corrin.
Clerk of Tynwald and Secretary to the House of Keys, Prof. T. St. J. N. Bates.
Attorney-General, T. W. Cain.
Government Secretary, P. J. Hulme.
Chief Financial Officer, W. Dawson.

THE CHANNEL ISLANDS

The Channel Islands, situated off the north-west coast of France (at distances of from ten to thirty miles), are the only portions of the *Dukedom of Normandy* now belonging to the Crown, to which they have been attached ever since the Conquest. They consist of Jersey (28,717 acres), Guernsey (15,654 acres), and the dependencies of Guernsey—Alderney (1,962 acres), Brechou (74), Great Sark (1,035) Little Sark (239), Herm (320), Jethou (44) and Lihou (38)—a total of 48,083 acres, or 75 square miles. In 1986 the population of Jersey was 80,212; and of Guernsey, 54,380; Alderney, 2,000 and Sark, 604.

GOVERNMENT

The islands are Crown dependencies with their own legislative assemblies (the States in Jersey, Guernsey and Alderney, and the Court of Chief Pleas in Sark), and systems of local administration and of law, and their own courts. Acts passed by the States require the sanction of The Queen-in-Council. The British Government is responsible for defence and international relations.

In both Bailiwicks the Lieutenant-Governor and Commander-in-Chief, who is appointed by the Crown, is the personal representative of the Queen and the channel of communication between the Crown (via the Privy Council) and the insular government. The Bailiffs of Jersey and Guernsey, also appointed by the Crown, are President of the States and of the Royal Courts of their respective islands. The government of each Bailiwick is conducted by committees appointed by the States. Justice is administered by the

Royal Courts of Jersey and Guernsey, each consisting of the Bailiff and 12 elected Jurats.

Each Bailiwick constitutes a deanery under the jurisdiction of the Bishop of Winchester (*see* Index).

ECONOMY

A mild climate and good soil have led to the development of intensive systems of agriculture and horticulture, which form a significant part of the economy of the Channel Islands. Equally important are invisible earnings, principally from the tourist trade and from banking and finance, the low rate of income tax (20p. in the £ in Jersey and Guernsey; no tax of any kind in Sark) and the absence of super-tax and death duties making the Channel Islands a popular tax-haven. Principal exports are agricultural produce and flowers; imports are chiefly machinery, manufactured goods, food, fuel and chemicals. Trade with the U.K. is regarded as internal trade.

British currency is legal tender in the Channel Islands but each Bailiwick issues its own coins, and some notes, of the same values as those of the U.K. They also issue their own postage stamps; U.K. stamps are not valid.

LANGUAGE

The official languages are English and French, but French is gradually being supplanted by English, which is the language in daily use. In country districts of Jersey and Guernsey and throughout Sark a Norman-French *patois* is also in use, though to a declining extent.

CHIEF TOWNS, Ψ St. Helier on the south coast of Jersey; Ψ St. Peter Port, on the east coast of Guernsey, and St. Anne's on Alderney.

JERSEY

Lieutenant-Governor and Commander-in-Chief of Jersey, His Excellency Adm. Sir William Pillar, G.B.E., K.C.B. (1985).
Secretary and A.D.C., Comdr. D. M. L. Braybrooke, L.V.O., R.N.
Bailiff of Jersey, Sir Peter Crill, C.B.E.
Deputy Bailiff, V. A. Tomes
Attorney-General and Receiver-General, P. M. Bailhache

Solicitor-General, T. C. Sowden.
Greffier of the States, E. J. M. Potter.
States Treasurer, L. May.

Year to Dec. 31:	1986	1987
Revenue	£200,477,716	£234,061,396
Revenue Expenditure	154,065,104	177,041,020
Capital Expenditure ..	27,301,040	33,013,000
Public Debt	−1,650,055	−1,166,690

FLAG.—A white field charged with a red saltire, and coat of arms.

GUERNSEY AND DEPENDENCIES

Lieutenant-Governor and Commander-in-Chief of the Bailiwick of Guernsey and its Dependencies, His Excellency Lt.-Gen. Sir Alexander Boswell, K.C.B., C.B.E. (1985).
Secretary and A.D.C., Capt. D. P. L. Hodgetts.
Bailiff of Guernsey, Sir Charles Frossard.
Deputy Bailiff, G. M. Dorey.
H. M. Procureur and Receiver-General, de Vic G. Carey.
H. M. Comptroller, A. C. K. Day.
States Supervisor, F. N. Le Cheminant.

Year to Dec. 31:	1986	1987
Revenue	£90,603,226	£101,250,316
Expenditure	73,068,154	83,161,418

FLAG.—White, bearing a red cross of St. George, with an argent a cross gules superimposed on the cross.

Alderney

President of the States, J. Kay-Mouat.
Clerk of the States, D. V. Jenkins.
Clerk of the Court, P. Beer.

Sark

Le Seigneur of Sark, J. M. Beaumont.
The Seneschal, L. P. de Carteret.
The Greffier, J. P. Hamon.

Brechou, Lihou and Jethou are leased by the Crown. Herm is leased by the States of Guernsey.

THE ISLES OF SCILLY

There are about 140 islands and skerries in the Scillies group (total area, 6 square miles) situated 28 miles south-west of Land's End, of which only five are inhabited; St. Mary's, St. Agnes, Bryher, Tresco and St. Martin's. The population is 1,978. The entire group has been designated an Area of Outstanding Natural Beauty, and given National Nature Reserve status by the Nature Conservancy Council because of its unique flora and fauna. Tourism and the winter/spring flower trade for the home market form the basis of the economy of the Isles. The island group is a recognised rural development area.

The islands are administered by the Council of the Isles of Scilly, a 21-member non-political body, which combines the powers and duties of a County Council and a District Council under the Local Government

Act 1972 and the Isles of Scilly Orders 1978. Legislation is specifically applied to the Isles of Scilly by Special Order. The Council is responsible for education, fire services, highways, planning and social services, and Cornwall County Council provides other services on an agency basis: the police service is administered by the Devon and Cornwall Police Authority, of which the Council is a member. The Isles are part of the St. Ives electoral division.

Administrative Headquarters, Town Hall, St. Mary's, Isles of Scilly, TR21 0LW.
Chairman of the Council, H. R. Duncan.
Clerk, Chief Executive and Chief Financial Officer, L. W. Michell.
Chief Technical Officer, B. M. Lowen.

THE COMMONWEALTH

The Commonwealth is a free association of the 48 sovereign independent states listed below together with their associated states and dependencies.

ANTIGUA AND BARBUDA
AUSTRALIA
BAHAMAS
BANGLADESH
BARBADOS
BELIZE
BOTSWANA
BRUNEI
CANADA
CYPRUS
DOMINICA
GAMBIA, THE
GHANA
GREAT BRITAIN
GRENADA
GUYANA
INDIA
JAMAICA
KENYA
KIRIBATI
LESOTHO
MALAWI
MALAYSIA
MALDIVES
MALTA

MAURITIUS
NAURU
NEW ZEALAND
NIGERIA
PAPUA NEW GUINEA
SAINT CHRISTOPHER
   AND NEVIS
SAINT LUCIA
SAINT VINCENT AND THE
   GRENADINES
SEYCHELLES
SIERRA LEONE
SINGAPORE
SOLOMON ISLANDS
SRI LANKA
SWAZILAND
TANZANIA
TONGA
TRINIDAD AND TOBAGO
TUVALU
UGANDA
VANUATU
WESTERN SAMOA
ZAMBIA
ZIMBABWE

Area and Population.—The total area of the independent Commonwealth is estimated at over 19,500,000 sq. miles (50,504,000 sq. km.) (U.N. estimate 1985), over one third of the world total. The total population of the Commonwealth is estimated to be about one quarter of the world total. In 1985 this amounted to over 1,200,000,000 (U.N. estimate). Details of the areas and populations of the Member States and dependencies appear in the following pages.

History and Government.—The status and relationship of member nations was first defined by the Inter-Imperial Relations Committee of the 1926 Imperial Conference, under the chairmanship of Lord Balfour, in what came to be known as the "Balfour Declaration": "They are autonomous communities . . . equal in status, in no way subordinate one to another in any aspect of their domestic or external affairs, though united by a common allegiance to the Crown and freely associated as members of the British Commonwealth of Nations." This formula was given legal substance by the Statute of Westminster, 1931.

The concept of a group of countries owing allegiance to a single Crown changed in 1949 when India decided to become a republic, and her continued membership of the Commonwealth was agreed by the other members on the basis of her "acceptance of the King as the symbol of the free association of its independent member nations and as such the Head of the Commonwealth". Member nations agreed at the time of the accession of Queen Elizabeth II to recognize Her Majesty as the new Head of the Commonwealth. The position is not vested in the British Crown.

Most members of the Commonwealth are parliamentary democracies.

Queen Elizabeth II is Head of State of 17 member countries of the Commonwealth: Antigua and Barbuda, Australia, the Bahamas, Barbados, Belize, Britain, Canada, Grenada, Jamaica, Mauritius, New Zealand, Papua New Guinea, St. Christopher and Nevis, Saint Lucia, Saint Vincent and the Grenadines, Solomon Islands and Tuvalu. In each of these countries (except Britain) The Queen is personally represented by a Governor-General, who holds in all

essential respects the same position in relation to the administration of public affairs in the realm as is held by Her Majesty in Britain (with the exception of certain constitutional functions which are performed by The Queen personally). The Governor-General is appointed by The Queen on the advice of the Government of the country concerned.

Twenty-five member countries are republics: Bangladesh, Botswana, Cyprus, Dominica, The Gambia, Ghana, Guyana, India, Kenya, Kiribati, Malawi, The Maldives, Malta, Nauru, Nigeria, Seychelles, Sierra Leone, Singapore, Sri Lanka, Tanzania, Trinidad & Tobago, Uganda, Vanuatu, Zambia and Zimbabwe. In Malaysia, the Head of State is elected from among the nine hereditary Malay rulers and holds office for five years. Brunei, Lesotho, Tonga, and Swaziland have their own monarchs. Western Samoa has a Head of State whose functions are analogous to those of a constitutional monarch.

Membership of the Commonwealth is subject only to the approval of existing members. Two countries, Nauru and Tuvalu, are special members, with the right to participate in all functional Commonwealth meetings and activities, but not to attend Meetings of Commonwealth Heads of Government.

Consultation.—Commonwealth Heads of Government meet every two years to discuss international developments and to consider co-operation among members. These meetings, the successors to the pre-war Imperial Conferences, have grown in importance as they are the only regular forum of leaders from both developed and developing countries, constituting a broad sample of the world community. Decisions are reached by consensus, and the views of the meeting are set out in a communiqué.

In addition, there are annual meetings of Finance Ministers, and frequent meetings of Ministers and officials in the fields of trade, education, health, law, science, agriculture, labour and employment, and youth affairs.

Defence.—The Commonwealth is not a military alliance and members make their own defence arrangements in the light of their particular requirements. Some are parties to multi-lateral treaties, for example A.N.Z.U.S. and N.A.T.O. Various members of the Commonwealth co-operate with each other in combined exercises, joint research organizations and exchanges of personnel and training facilities.

Law.—English common law forms the basis of the legal system in many Commonwealth countries, although in most cases it has been radically adapted by statute to suit the individual needs and aspirations of a country, and there are countries where other systems have been adopted—for example, the law of Quebec Province and of Mauritius is founded on that of France, and Roman Dutch law forms the basis in Sri Lanka and Lesotho. Of the non-realms in the Commonwealth, Brunei, Dominica, The Gambia, Kiribati, Singapore, and Trinidad and Tobago retain the right of appeal to the Judicial Committee of the Privy Council in the United Kingdom, which also hears appeals from a number of realms (Antigua and Barbuda, the Bahamas, Barbados, Belize, Jamaica, Mauritius, New Zealand, St. Christopher and Nevis, St. Lucia, St. Vincent and the Grenadines, Tuvalu) and the dependent territories.

Citizenship and Nationality.—Each member of the Commonwealth defines the citizenship and nationality of its own people and determines the status of other Commonwealth nationals within its own boundaries. Members of the Commonwealth differentiate, to a greater or lesser degree, as regards the grant of privileges, between citizens of the Commonwealth and aliens. The Republic of Ireland, which in 1949 ceased to be a member of the Commonwealth, is not regarded by the other Commonwealth nations as a foreign country nor her citizens as foreigners.

Finance and Development.—Complete financial autonomy is enjoyed by all members of the Commonwealth. In some countries, customs tariffs are lower for merchandise of Commonwealth origin than for imports from foreign countries. Developing countries, including those in the Commonwealth, obtain preference for exports of industrial goods and some agricultural exports from the developed countries under the Generalised Scheme of Preferences (G.S.P.). Many smaller Commonwealth countries are also party to the Lomé Convention which accords preferential access to the European Community. Many former Commonwealth preferences have been replaced by these arrangements.

British aid for the development needs of the Commonwealth countries and dependent territories are dealt with under the provisions of the Overseas Aid Act 1966, administered by the Overseas Development Administration. This Act succeeds the former Colonial Development and Welfare Acts. Those countries which are party to the Lomé Convention also receive aid under that Convention from the European Community.

Commonwealth Secretariat. Marlborough House, Pall Mall, SW1Y 5HX [01-839 3411]. —This was established by decision of Commonwealth Heads of Government in 1965, and is the main agency for multi-lateral communication between Commonwealth Governments on issues relating to the Commonwealth as a whole. It promotes consultation and disseminates information on matters of common concern, organizes meetings and conferences, co-ordinates Commonwealth activities and provides technical assistance for economic and social development through the Commonwealth Fund for Technical Cooperation. *Secretary General*, Shridath S. Ramphal, Kt., C.M.G., Q.C.

Commonwealth Institute.—See p. 600.

Dependent Territories and Associated States. —Britain, Australia and New Zealand have a number of dependent territories. New Zealand also has two associated states: Cook Islands (since 1965) and Niue (since 1974).

Member States of the Commonwealth
(with dates of independence)

1867* Canada
1901* Australia
1907* New Zealand
1947   India (Republic, 1950)
1948   Sri Lanka (Republic, 1972)
1957   Ghana (Republic, 1960)
       Federation of Malaya (Federation of Malaysia since 1963—indigenous monarchy)
1960   Cyprus (Republic on independence; joined Commonwealth 1961)
       Nigeria (Republic, 1963)

1961   Sierra Leone (Republic, 1971)
       Tanganyika (Republic, 1962; united 1964 with Zanzibar as TANZANIA)
1962   Western Samoa (Republic on independence; joined Commonwealth 1970)
       Jamaica
       Trinidad and Tobago (Republic, 1976)
       Uganda (Republic, 1967)
1963   Kenya (Republic, 1964)
       Singapore (as State in Federation of Malaysia; seceded as Republic, 1965)
1964   Malawi (Republic, 1966)
       Malta (Republic, 1974)
       Zambia (Republic on independence)
1965   The Gambia (Republic, 1970)
       Maldives (Republic, 1968; joined Commonwealth as a Special Member 1982; full member 1985)
1966   Guyana (Republic, 1970)
       Botswana (Republic on independence)
       Lesotho (indigenous monarchy)
       Barbados
1968   Mauritius
       Nauru (Republic on independence—Special Member)
       Swaziland (indigenous monarchy)
1970   Tonga (indigenous monarchy)
       Fiji (membership lapsed 1987)
1971   Bangladesh (Republic on independence; joined Commonwealth 1972)
1973   Bahamas
1974   Grenada
1975   Papua New Guinea
1976   Seychelles (Republic on independence)
1978   Solomon Islands
       Tuvalu (Special Member)
       Dominica (Republic on independence)
1979   Saint Lucia
       Kiribati (Republic on independence)
       Saint Vincent and the Grenadines (Joined as a Special Member; became a full member 1985)
1980   Zimbabwe (Republic on independence)
       Vanuatu (Republic on independence)
1981   Belize
       Antigua and Barbuda
1983   Saint Christopher and Nevis
1984   Brunei (indigenous monarchy)

* These are the effective dates of independence, given legal effect by the Statute of Westminster, 1931.

(The above member states are Realms of Queen Elizabeth II unless otherwise stated.)

Associated States

The Cook Islands and Niue are self-governing states in association with New Zealand, which likewise remains responsible for their external affairs and defence.

Countries which have left the Commonwealth

1949   Republic of Ireland
1961   South Africa
1972   Pakistan

CANADA

AREA AND POPULATION

Provinces or Territories and Capitals (with official contractions)	Area (English Sq. Miles). Land and Water	Population	
		Census, 1981	Census, 1986
Alberta, *Alta.* (Edmonton)..................	255,285	2,237,724	2,365,825
British Columbia, *B.C.* (Victoria)	365,944	2,744,467	2,883,365
Manitoba, *Man.* (Winnipeg)	250,745	1,026,241	1,063,015
New Brunswick, *N.B.* (Fredericton)..........	28,355	696,403	709,440
Newfoundland and Labrador, *Nfld.* (St. John's).	156,648	567,681	568,350
Nova Scotia, *N.S.* (Halifax)	21,425	847,442	973,175
Ontario, *Ont.* (Toronto)	412,578	8,625,107	9,101,690
Prince Edward Island, *P.E.I.* (Charlottetown)..	2,185	122,506	126,645
Quebec, *Que.* (Quebec)	594,855	6,438,403	6,532,460
Saskatchewan, *Sask.* (Regina)	251,864	968,313	1,009,615
Yukon Territory, *Y.T.* (Whitehorse)	186,660	23,153	23,505
Northwest Territories, *N.W.T.* (Yellowknife) ..	1,322,900	45,741	52,240
Total..............	3,849,646	24,343,181	25,309,330

Of the total immigration of 152,098 in 1987, 7,967 were from the United States, 9,537 from the United Kingdom and Ireland, and 11,227 from the Caribbean.

Mother Tongues of the Population

	1981	1986
Sole Language		
English	14,684,365	15,334,085
French	6,127,530	6,159,740
Non-Official Languages	2,933,305	2,860,570
Native Indian Languages		
Cree	60,845	57,645
Inuktitut..	18,650	21,050
Ojibway	17,605	16,380
Bi/Multi-Lingual		
English and French	208,245	332,610
English and non-official language(s)	325,530	525,720
French and non-official language(s)	22,255	36,310
English, French and non-official language(s)	29,475	46,585
Non-official languages	12,485	13,715
Total Population...	24,343,180	25,309,330

PHYSIOGRAPHY

Canada was originally discovered by Cabot in 1497, but its history dates only from 1534, when the French took possession of the country. The first permanent settlement at Port Royal (now Annapolis), Nova Scotia, was founded in 1605, and Quebec was founded in 1608. In 1759 Quebec was captured by the British forces under General Wolfe, and in 1763 the whole territory of Canada became a possession of Great Britain by the Treaty of Paris of that year. Nova Scotia was ceded in 1713 by the Treaty of Utrecht, the Provinces of New Brunswick and Prince Edward Island being subsequently formed out of it. British Columbia was formed into a Crown colony in 1858, having previously been a part of the Hudson Bay Territory, and was united to Vancouver Island in 1866.

Canada occupies the whole of the northern part of the North American Continent (with the exception of Alaska), from 49° North latitude to the North Pole, and from the Pacific to the Atlantic Ocean. In Eastern Canada, the southernmost point is Middle Island in Lake Erie, at 41° 41'.

Relief.—The relief of Canada is dominated by the mountain ranges running north and south on the west side of the Continent, by the pre-Cambrian shield on the east, with, in between, the northern extension of the North American Plain. From the physiographic point of view Canada has six main divisions. These are: (1) Appalachian-Acadian Region, (2) the Canadian Shield, (3) the St. Lawrence-Great Lakes Lowland, (4) the Interior Plains, (5) the Cordilleran Region and (6) the Arctic Archipelago. The first region occupies all that part of Canada lying southeast of the St. Lawrence. In general, the relief is an alternation of highlands and lowlands and is hilly rather than mountainous. The great Canadian Shield comprises more than half the area. The interior as a whole is an undulating, low plateau (general level 1,000 to 1,500 feet), with the more rugged relief lying along the border between Northern Quebec and Labrador. Throughout the whole area water or muskeg-filled depressions separate irregular hills and ridges, 150 to 200 feet in elevation. Newfoundland, an outlying portion of the shield, consists of glaciated, low rolling terrain broken here and there by mountains.

The flat relief of the St. Lawrence-Great Lakes lowland varies from 500 feet in the east to 1,700 feet south of Georgian Bay. The most striking relief is provided by the eastward facing scarp of the Niagara escarpment (elevation 250 to 300 feet). The interior plains, comprising the Pacific Provinces, slope eastward and northward a few feet per mile. The descent from west to east is made from 5,000 feet to less than 1,000 feet in three distinct levels, with each new level being marked by an eastward facing *conteau* or scarp.

Five fairly well-developed topographic divisions mark out the Cordilleran region of western Canada. These are: (1) coastal ranges, largely above 5,000 feet with deep fjords and glaciated valleys, (2) the interior plateau, around 3,500 feet and comparatively level, (3) the Selkirk ranges, largely above 5,000 feet, (4) the Rocky Mountains with their chain of 10,000 to 12,000 feet peaks, and (5) the Peace River or Tramontane region with its rolling diversified country.

The Arctic Archipelago, with its plateau-like character has an elevation between 500 and 1,000 feet, though in Baffin Land and Ellesmere Island the mountain ranges rise to 8,500 and 9,500 feet. Two tremendous waterway systems, the St. Lawrence and the Mackenzie, providing thousands of miles of water highway, occupy a broad area of lowland with their dominant axis following the edge of the shield.

Climate.—The climate of the eastern and central portions presents greater extremes than in corresponding latitudes in Europe, but in the southwestern portion of the Prairie Region and the southern portions of the Pacific slope the climate is milder. Spring, summer, and autumn are of about seven to eight months' duration, and the winter four to five months.

GOVERNMENT

The Constitution of Canada had its source in the British North America Act of 1867 which formed a Dominion, under the name of Canada, of the four provinces: Ontario, Quebec, New Brunswick and Nova Scotia; to this Federation the other Provinces have subsequently been admitted. Under this Act Canada came into being on July 1, 1867 (Dominion Day), and under the Statute of Westminster, which received the royal assent on Dec. 11, 1931, Canada and the Provinces were exempted (in common with other self-governing Dominions of the Commonwealth of Nations) from the operation of the Colonial Laws Validity Act, the Statute of Westminster having removed all limitations with regard to the legislative autonomy of the Dominions, except that the British North America Act could be amended in important respects only by Acts of the British Parliament.

Provinces admitted since 1867 are: Manitoba (1870), British Columbia (1871), Prince Edward Island (1873), Alberta and Saskatchewan (1905) and Newfoundland (1949).

Agreement was reached in Nov. 1981 between the Federal and Provincial Governments (except Quebec) to patriate the Constitution so that it was amendable only in Canada. The inclusion in the Constitution of a Charter of Rights was also agreed. At the request of the Canadian Parliament, legislation was passed at Westminster and the Constitution formally patriated on 17th April 1982.

The Executive power is vested in a Governor-General appointed by the Sovereign on the advice of the Canadian Ministry, and aided by a Privy Council.
CURRENCY.—Canadian Dollar (C$) of 100 Cents.
FLAG.—Red maple leaf with 11 points on white square, flanked by vertical red bars one half the width of the square.
NATIONAL ANTHEM.—Oh Canada.
NATIONAL DAY.—July 1.

Governor General's Household

Governor General and Commander-in-Chief, Her Excellency The Rt. Hon. Jeanne Sauvé, C.C., C.M.M., C.D.
Secretary to the Governor-General and Sec. Gen. of Honours, L. Amyot.
Deputy Secretaries, A. Smyth; J. M. Sévigny.
Director, Chancellery, R. de C. Nantel, L.V.O., C.D.

Finance, Personnel and Administration Director, G. R. Brunet.
Cultural Advisor, J.-N. Tremblay.
Director, Information Services, Mlle. M. Bender.
Director, Programme Implementation, Health, Safety and Security Programme, C. A. Sangster, C.D.
Policy and Programme Director, Mrs. S. Orr.
Attaché, Miss L. Benoit.
Hospitality Director, Ms. L. D'Ascanio.
Director, Protocol and Ceremonial, L. Lemieux.
Aides-de-Camp, L. Maurice, C.D.; M. Phillips; D. Maybee.
Personal Asst. to the Governor General, Mlle. R. Langevin.

The Cabinet
(as at July 27, 1988)

Prime Minister, Rt. Hon. M. Brian Mulroney.
Veterans' Affairs, Hon. George H. Hees.
Secretary of State for External Affairs, Rt. Hon. C. Joseph Clark.
Communications, Hon. Flora I. MacDonald.
International Trade, Hon. John C. Crosbie.
Deputy P.M. and President of the Queen's Privy Council, Hon. Donald F. Mazankowski.
National Revenue, Hon. Elmer M. MacKay.
National Health and Welfare, Hon. A. Jacob Epp.
Agriculture, Hon. John Wise.
Justice and Attorney General, Hon. Ramon J. Hnatyshyn.
Regional Industrial Expansion and Minister of State for Science and Technology, Hon. Robert R. de Cotret.
National Defence, Hon. H. Perrin Beatty.
Finance, Hon. Michael H. Wilson.
Consumer and Corporate Affairs, Hon. Harvie Andre.
Supply and Services, Hon. Otto J. Jelinek.
Fisheries and Oceans, Hon. Thomas E. Siddon.
Minister of State, Grains and Oilseeds, Hon. Charles J. Mayer.
Indian Affairs and Northern Development, Hon. William H. McKnight.
Environment, Hon. Thomas M. McMillan.
President of the Treasury Board, Hon. Patricia Carney.
Transport, Hon. Benoit Bouchard.
Solicitor General, Hon. James F. Kelleher.
Energy, Mines and Resources, Hon. Marcel Masse.
Employment and Immigration, Hon. Barbara J. McDougall.
Minister of State, Forestry and Mines, Hon. Gerald S. Merrithew.
Minister of State, Employment and Immigration, Hon. Monique Vézina.
Public Works, Hon. Stewart D. McInnes.
Minister of State, Science and Technology, Hon. Frank Oberle.
Leader of Government in the Senate and Minister of State, Federal-Provincial Relations, Hon. Lowell Murray.
Associate Minister of National Defence, Hon. Paul W. Dick.
Labour, Hon Pierre H. Cadieux.
Minister of State, Youth and Fitness and Amateur Sport, Hon. Jean J. Charest.
Minister of State, Finance, Hon. Thomas Hockin.
External Relations, Hon. Monique Landry.
Ministers of State, Hon. Bernard Valcourt (*Small Businesses and Tourism; Indian Affairs and Northern Development*): Hon. Gerry Weiner (*Multiculturalism*); Hon. Douglas G. Lewis (*Treasury Board*); Hon. Pierre Blais (*Agriculture*); Hon. Gerry St. Germain (*Transport*).
Secretary of State of Canada, Hon. Lucien Bouchard.

The Prime Minister receives remuneration of $144,300; other ministers, each $122,200.

CANADIAN HIGH COMMISSION
Macdonald House, 1 Grosvenor Square, W1X 0AB.
[01–629 9492]
High Commissioner, His Excellency Donald Macdonald (1988).
Deputy High Commissioner, L. A. Delvoie.
Ministers, M. Phillips, L. J. Taylor (*Commercial/Economic*).
Minister-Counsellor, J. R. MacLachlan (*Immigration*).

BRITISH HIGH COMMISSION
80 Elgin Street, Ottawa
[Ottawa 237-1530]
High Commissioner, His Excellency Sir Alan Urwick, K.C.V.O., C.M.G.
Deputy High Commissioner, W. N. Wenban-Smith.
Counsellor, Miss C. S. Rycroft (*Economic and Commercial*).
Defence and Military Adviser, Brig. F. R. Maynard.
Naval Adviser, Cdr. J. J. Howard, M.B.E.
Air Adviser, Gp. Capt. M. A. Radnorth.
First Secretaries, D. J. Pugh, M.B.E. (*Administration*); A. N. Foggo; I. D. Kydd (*Commercial*); N. Penrhys-Evans; D. E. Donald (*Information*).
Cultural Affairs and British Council Representative, M. Evans.

THE LEGISLATURE

Parliament consists of a Senate and a House of Commons. The *Senate* consists of 104 members, nominated by the Governor General (age limit 75). They are distributed between the various provinces thus: 24 each for *Ontario* and *Quebec,* 10 each for *Nova Scotia* and *New Brunswick,* 6 each for *Newfoundland, British Columbia, Manitoba, Alberta,* and *Saskatchewan* and 4 for *Prince Edward Island,* 1 for *North West Territories* and 1 for *Yukon;* each Senator must be at least thirty years old, a resident in the province for which he is appointed, a natural-born or naturalized subject of the Queen, and the owner of a property qualification amounting to $4,000. The Speaker of the Senate is chosen by the Government of the day.

The *House of Commons* has 282 members and is elected every five years at longest. Representation by provinces is at present as follows: Newfoundland 7, Prince Edward Island 4, Nova Scotia 11, New Brunswick 10, Quebec 75, Ontario 95, Manitoba 14, Saskatchewan 14, Alberta 21, British Columbia 28, Yukon 1, Northwest Territories 2.

In every case—including the Prime Minister's—a sessional indemnity of $58,300 per annum is paid to members of the House of Commons. In addition, Ministers and members of the House of Commons receive an expense allowance. Certain Members of Parliament for large northern constituencies have larger expense allowances.

THE SENATE

The state of the parties in the Senate as of July 27, 1988, was *Liberal* 59, *Conservative* 31, *Independent* 5, *Independent Cons.* 1, (8 vacant).
Speaker of the Senate, Hon. Guy Chapbonneau, Q.C. $99,700
Clerk of the Senate & Clerk of the Parliaments, C. A. Lussier.

THE HOUSE OF COMMONS

The state of parties in the House of Commons as of July 27, 1988, was *Conservative* 207, *Liberals* 39, *N.D.P.* 32, *Independent* 3, (1 vacant).
Speaker of the House of Commons, Hon. John A. Fraser $122,200
Deputy Speaker, Marcel Danis $101,000
Clerk of the House of Commons, Robert Marleau.

THE JUDICATURE

The Judicature is administered by judges following the Civil Law in Quebec Province and Common Law in other Provinces. Each Province has its Court of Appeal. All Superior, County and District Court Judges are appointed by the Governor General, the others by the Lieutenant Governors of the Provinces.

The highest federal court is the Supreme Court of Canada, composed of a Chief Justice and eight puisne judges, which exercises general appellate jurisdiction throughout Canada in civil and criminal cases, and which usually holds three sessions each year. There is one other federally constituted Court, the Federal Court of Canada, which has jurisdiction on appeals from its Trial Division, from Federal Tribunals and reviews of decisions and references by Federal Boards and Commissions. The Trial Division has jurisdiction in claims by or against the Crown, its officers or servants or Federal bodies. It also deals with inter-Provincial and Federal-Provincial disputes.

SUPREME COURT OF CANADA

Chief Justice of Canada, Rt. Hon. Brian Dickson, P.C. $153,800
Puisne Judges, Hon. J. Beetz; Hon. W. R. McIntyre; Hon. A. Lamer; Hon. Bertha Wilson; Hon. G. Le Dain; Hon. G. V. LaForest; Hon. Claire L'Heureux-Dube; Hon. J. Sopinka. .... each $151,700

FEDERAL COURT OF CANADA

Chief Justice, Hon. A. L. Thurlow $139,700
Associate Chief Justice, Hon. J. A. Jerome. $139,700
Appeal Division Judges, Hon. L. Pratte; Hon. D. V. Heald; Hon. J. J. Urie; Hon. J. K. Hugessen; Hon. P. M. Mahoney, P.C.; Hon. L. Marceau; Hon. M. Mac-Guigan, P.C.; Hon. A. J. Stone; Hon. B. Lacombe; Hon. Alice Desjardins .. each $127,700
Trial Division Judges, Hon. J. E. Dubé; Hon. F. U. Collier; Hon. G. A. Addy; Hon. P. U. C. Rouleau; Hon. J. C. McNair; Hon. F. C. Muldoon; Hon. Barbara J. Reed; Hon. B. L. Strayer; Hon. Y. Pinard; Hon. L. M. Joyal; Hon. P. Denault; Hon. B. Cullen; Hon. L. A. Martin; Hon. M. A. Teitelbaum .... each $127,700

VITAL STATISTICS
BIRTHS, DEATHS AND MARRIAGES, 1986

Province	Births	Deaths	Marriages
Alberta	43,744	13,560	18,896
British Columbia .	41,976	21,213	21,826
Manitoba........	17,009	8,911	7,816
New Brunswick ..	9,788	5,458	4,962
Newfoundland ...	8,100	3,504	3,421
Nova Scotia	12,358	7,255	6,445
Ontario	133,882	67,865	70,839
P.E.I.	1,928	1,121	970
Quebec..........	84,634	46,892	33,083
Saskatchewan ...	17,513	8,061	6,820
Yukon	483	113	183
N. W. Territories	1,507	235	257
Total......	372,913	184,244	175,518

Canada's birth rate per 1,000 population (1986) 14·7; Death Rate 7·2; Marriage Rate 6·9. Divorces 78,160.

FINANCE

Federal Government gross general revenue and expenditure was ($ millions):—

	1986–87	1987–88
Total Revenue	90,229	96,758
Total Expenditure	116,643	125,046

DEBT ($ millions)

	1986–87	1987–88
Gross Public Debt	328,230	362,180
Net Public Debt	188,733	217,577

Banking.—There were 69 chartered banks on Dec. 31, 1987, with assets of $484,596 m. Deposits were $401,014 m. of which $149,331 m. were personal savings.

NATIONAL DEFENCE

The Minister of National Defence has the control and management of the Canadian Armed Forces and all matters relating to National Defence establishments and works for the defence of Canada.

The Canadian Forces are organized on a functional basis to reflect the major commitments assigned by the government and are formed into National Defence Headquarters and five major Commands reporting to the Chief of the Defence Staff. The roles of the five Commands are: *Mobile Command*—Provision of ground forces for the protection of Canadian territory, combat forces in Canada for support of overseas commitments, and forces for support of United Nations or other peace-keeping operations. *Maritime Command*—Provision of sea forces for the defence of Canada, anti-submarine defence in support of NATO. Maritime Command also has operational control of Maritime aircraft. *Air Command*—Provision of operationally ready air forces to national, continental and international commitments. *Canadian Forces Communication Command*—Manages, operates and maintains strategic communications for the Canadian Forces. *Canadian Forces Europe*—Canadian Forces allocated to support NATO in Europe consisting of land and air elements.

National Defence expenditure for the fiscal year 1987–88 was estimated at $10,644 million. Canadian Armed Forces strength at May 1988, 87,310 authorized force.

EDUCATION

Education is under the control of the Provincial Governments, the cost of the publicly controlled schools being met by local taxation, aided by provincial grants. In 1987–88 there were 15,533 publicly controlled elementary and secondary schools with 4,961,600 pupils. Of these, 1,294 were private schools with 226,000 pupils; 388 federal schools with 47,000 pupils and 21 special schools for the blind and deaf with 2,600 pupils.

In 1987–88 there were 68 degree-granting universities with a full-time enrolment of 474,820, as well as 320,550 students in 198 other post-secondary, non-university institutions.

CANADIAN PRODUCTION

Agriculture.—About 7 per cent. of the total land area of Canada is classified as farm land and approximately half of this is under cultivation, the remainder being woodland or suitable only for grazing purposes. More than three-quarters of the land now cultivated is found in the prairie region of Western Canada. Farm cash receipts from the sale of farm products in 1987 were $20,965,580,000. Livestock and animal products contributed $10,508,145,000; field crops $8,851,321,000.

Grain crop production ('000 tonnes)

	1986	1987
Wheat	31,377·9	26,342·1
Oats	3,251·1	2,995·2
Barley	14,633·6	14,382·1
Rye	609·0	492·6
Flaxseed	1,026·3	787·6
Canola	3,786·5	3,851·5
Total	54,684·4	48,851·1

Livestock.—In July 1987 the livestock included 11,745,900 cattle, 700,900 sheep, 10,493,000 hogs and 22,573,000 chickens (layers).

Fur Production.—Canada in 1986–87 produced pelts valued at $150,129,659. Wild life pelts made up 50·1 per cent of the total, with a value of $75,265,391.

Fisheries.—The marketed value of catches in 1987 was $3,287,020,000 (preliminary).

Forestry.—About 44 per cent. of the total land area is in forests. The shipment value of forest products in 1985 was: newsprint $4,982,928,000; paper (other than newsprint) $2,611,017,000; lumber $5,545,011,000; wood pulp $3,963,880,000.

Minerals.—Canada is the world's largest producer of zinc and the second largest of nickel, asbestos, potash, gypsum, uranium, elemental sulphur and titanium concentrates. The country is also rich in many other minerals, including gold, silver, iron, copper, cobalt and lead.

	1986	1987
	('000 tonnes)	
Copper	698·5	767·3
Nickel	163·6	187·8
Lead	334·3	390·5
Molybdenum	11·3	11·6
Zinc	988·2	1,329·4
Iron Ore	36,167·0	37,553·0
Asbestos	662·0	665·0
Gypsum	8,803·0	8,811·0
Cement	10,611·0	12,205·0
Lime	2,243·0	2,271·0
Salt	10,332·0	10,294·0
Potash	6,752·0	7,465·0

Production of gold was 117,834,000 grams in 1987 (102,899,000 in 1986) and of silver was 1,250,000 kg. (1,088,000 kg. in 1986). Uranium production in 1987 was 13,202,000 kilograms (11,502,000 kg. in 1986).

TRADE

Merchandise imports into Canada in 1987 were valued at $116,238,614,000 and merchandise exports (including re-exports) at $125,086,701,000. The main exports in 1987 were motor vehicles and parts, newsprint paper, wheat, crude petroleum, lumber, natural gas, woodpulp, petroleum and coal products, and television and telecommunication equipment. Trade with the U.S.A. accounts for 68 per cent of total trade in merchandise, although efforts are being made to develop alternative markets. Value of trade with Canada's largest trading partners in 1987 was as follows ($'000).

Country	Imports	Domestic Exports
United States	79,069,318	91,756,404
Japan	7,550,709	7,036,248
United Kingdom	4,339,184	2,849,882
Fed. Rep. of Germany	3,534,458	1,515,196
Republic of Korea	1,844,039	1,167,413
Taiwan	2,023,029	757,023
Italy	1,702,833	842,807
France	1,488,728	1,037,364
China	770,901	1,432,079
Netherlands	750,152	1,020,954
Benelux	618,951	1,137,151
Mexico	1,169,566	521,980
Hong Kong	1,137,618	480,055

COMMUNICATIONS

Railways.—The total track of railways in operation on Dec. 31, 1986, was 95,544 km.

	1986
Property Accounts	$16,324,743,403,000
Operating Revenues	7,570,483,000
Operating Expenses	6,787,364,000

In 1986 revenue freight was 244,783,844,635 tonne-kilometres.

Shipping.—The registered shipping on Jan. 1, 1986 including inland vessels, was 38,129 vessels with gross tonnage 5,776,882. The volume of international shipping handled at Canadian ports in 1986 was 144,560,692 metric tonnes loaded and 62,011,827 metric tonnes unloaded.

Canals.—The bulk of canal shipping in Canada is handled through the two sections of the St. Lawrence Seaway, which provide access to the Great Lakes for ocean-going ships. In 1987, transits on the Montreal-Lake Ontario section numbered 3,227 for a total of 39,968,615 cargo tonnes; transits in the Welland Canal section numbered 3,914 for a total of 42,724,755 cargo tonnes. Principal commodities carried were iron ore, wheat, corn, barley, soybeans, fuel oil, manufactured iron and steel, coal and coke.

Civil Aviation.—The number of passengers carried in 1986 (all major Canadian carriers) was 30,818,392. 1,202,882,196 tonne-km of freight were carried in 1986.

Motor Vehicles.—Total motor vehicle registrations numbered 15,227,311 in 1986.

Post.—There were over 8,000 postal facilities operating in Canada on March 31, 1987. Post office revenue in the fiscal year 1986–87 was $2,970 m.; total expenditure $3,099 m.

FEDERAL CAPITAL

OTTAWA, the federal capital, 111 miles west of Montreal and 247 miles north-east of Toronto, is a city on the south bank of the Ottawa river. The city was chosen as the capital of the Province of Canada in 1857 and was later selected as the site of the Dominion capital. Ottawa contains the Parliamentary Buildings, the Public Archives, Royal Mint, several national museums, the National Art Gallery and the Dominion Observatory.

Manufacturing is also carried on, medical advancement, high technology (communications, defence), printing and publishing being of greatest importance. Ottawa is connected with Lake Ontario by the Rideau Canal. The City population was 300,763 at the Census of 1986; and Metropolitan Ottawa 819,263.

YUKON TERRITORY

The Yukon Act, 1970, as amended, provides for the administration of the Territory by a Commissioner acting under instructions from time to time given by the Governor-in-Council or the Minister of Indian Affairs and Northern Development. Legislative powers, analogous to those of a provincial government, are exercised by a Legislative Assembly of 16 members elected from electoral districts in the Territory. The Executive Council of the Assembly consists of the government leader as chairman and four elected members. The area of the Territory is 186,660 sq. miles (483,450 sq. km.), with a population (1987) of 24,400. Minerals and tourism are the chief industries, followed closely by transport, communications and other utilities industry.

Seat of Government, Whitehorse. Pop. (1986) 15,199.
Commissioner, J. K. McKinnon.

NORTHWEST TERRITORIES

The Northwest Territories Act, 1979, as amended, provides for a Legislative Assembly of 24 elected members, of which the Executive Council under the chairmanship of the government leader is the senior decision-making body of the government in the Territory.

The Northwest Territories are subdivided into the districts of Mackenzie, Keewatin and Franklin.

The area of the Northwest Territories is 1,322,900 sq. miles (3,426,320 sq. km.), with a population (1987 estimate) of 51,700. The chief industry is mining, with a total value of $492,000,000 in 1985. Lead, zinc, gold, silver, oil exploration and natural gas contributed about 32 per cent. of the total activities in the Northwest Territories.

Seat of Government, Yellowknife. Pop. (1986) 11,753.
Commissioner, J. H. Parker.

PROVINCES OF CANADA

ALBERTA

Area and Population.—The Province of Alberta has an area of 255,285 sq. miles (661,185 sq. km.), including about 6,485 sq. miles of water (16,796 sq. km.), with a population (April 1988 estimate) of 2,391,700.

Government.—The Government is vested in a Lieutenant Governor and Legislative Assembly composed of 83 members, elected for five years, representing 83 electoral districts in the Province. At a provincial election held on May 8, 1986, the Progressive Conservative party took 61 seats, the New Democratic Party 16 seats, the Liberal Party 4 seats, and the Representative Party 2 seats.

Lt. Governor, Her Honour Helen Hunley.

EXECUTIVE

Premier, President of Executive Council, Hon. Don Getty $87,588*
Deputy Premier and Advanced Education, Hon. David Russell.
Municipal Affairs, Hon. Dennis Anderson.
Attorney General and Federal & Intergovernmental Affairs, Hon. Jim Horsman.

Economic Development & Trade, Hon. Larry Shaben.
Provincial Treasurer, Hon. Dick Johnston.
Energy, Hon. Neil Webber.
Technology, Research & Telecommunications and Government House Leader, Hon. Les Young.
Transportation and Utilities, Hon. Al Adair.
Hospitals and Medical Care, Hon. Marvin Moore.
Tourism, Hon. Don Sparrow.
Labour, Hon. Ian Reid.
Social Services, Hon. Connie Osterman.
Forestry, Lands & Wildlife, Hon. LeRoy Fjordbotten.
Environment, Hon. Ken Kowalski.
Public Works, Supply & Services, Hon. Ernie Isley.
Agriculture, Hon. Peter Elzinga.
Associate Minister of Agriculture, Hon. Shirley Cripps.
Culture and Multiculturalism, Hon. Greg Stevens.
Recreation & Parks, Hon. Norm Weiss.
Career Development and Employment, Hon. Rick Orman.
Education, Hon. Nancy Betkowski.
Solicitor General, Hon. Ken Rostad.
Consumer & Corporate Affairs, Hon. Elaine McCoy.
Community & Occupational Health, Hon. Jim Dinning.

Special Projects, Hon. Neil Crawford.

Speaker of the Legislative Assembly, Hon. D.
Carter $78,272*
London Office, Alberta House, 1, Mount Street, W1.
*Includes Legislative Assembly Members' Annuity
and Expense Allowances.

THE JUDICATURE

Court of Appeal of Alberta, Hon. J. H. Laycraft (*Chief
Justice*).
Justices, Hons. S. S. Lieberman; D. C. Prowse; W. J.
Haddad; J. W. McClung; A. M. Harradence; R. P.
Kerans; R. H. Belzil; W. A. Stevenson; M. M.
Hetherington; H. L. Irving; J. E. Cote; R. P. Foisy;
J. J. Stratton.
Court of Queen's Bench of Alberta, Hon. W. K. Moore
(*Chief Justice*); Hon. T. H. Miller (*Associate Chief
Justice*).

ECONOMY

The Gross Domestic Product at factor cost in 1986
was ($ millions):—

Agriculture, fishing and trapping	2,460
Forestry	125
Mining	9,736
Manufacturing	4,281
Construction	2,747
Transportation	4,049
Utilities	2,078
Trade.................................	5,019
Finance...............................	12,143
Services	10,320
Public Administration	3,336
Total G.D.P. at factor cost	55,933

Mineral Production 1987
(preliminary estimates)

	$ '000
Crude oil	10,003,912
Natural gas	3,843,639
Natural gas by-products..............	1,955,955
Coal	396,200
Sulphur (elemental)	604,805
Sand & gravel.......................	141,025
Cement	132,060
Other	70,496
Total............................	17,148,092

Manufacturing.—The total value of manufacturing
shipments (1987) was $16,620,858,000. Number of
industrial establishments 2,536 (1985), total employees 74,684 (1985). The leading industrial products are
refined petroleum and coal products, meat and meat
products, chemicals and chemical products, fabricated metal products, non-metallic mineral products
and primary metals.

GOVERNMENT FINANCE

Budgetary Estimates $ millions

	1987–88	1988–89
Revenue	8,627	9,819
Expenditure	10,556	10,654
Deficit	1,929	835

NOTE: The Budgetary revenue figure does not
include funds allocated to the Alberta Heritage
Savings Trust Fund.

CAPITAL.—Edmonton—city population (1986)
576,249, metropolitan area, 787,329. Other centres are
Calgary (647,285), Lethbridge (60,610), Red Deer
(54,309), Medicine Hat (41,804), St. Albert (37,008),
Fort McMurray (34,949).

BRITISH COLUMBIA

Area and Population.—British Columbia has a
total area estimated at 365,944 sq. miles (947,790 sq.
km.), with a population of 2,935,000 (April 1987).

Government.—The Government consists of a Lieutenant Governor and an Executive Council together
with a Legislative Assembly of 69 members.
Lt. Governor, His Honour Robert Gordon Rogers.

EXECUTIVE COUNCIL

Premier and President of the Council, Hon. William
N. Vander Zalm.
*Provincial Secretary and Minister of Government
Services*, Hon. Elwood Veitch.
Attorney-General, Hon. Brian R. D. Smith, Q.C.
Forests and Lands, Hon. David F. H. Parker.
Finance and Corporate Relations, Hon. Melville B.
Couvelier.
Agriculture and Fisheries, Hon. John Savage.
Energy, Mines and Petroleum Resources, Hon. John
Davis, P.C.
Education, Hon. Anthony J. Brummet.
Labour and Consumer Services, Hon. Lyall Hanson.
Economic Development, Hon. Grace M. McCarthy.
Municipal Affairs, Hon. Rita M. Johnston.
Health, Hon. Peter A. Dueck.
Social Services and Housing, Hon. Claude H. Rich-
mond.
Transportation and Highways, Hon. Clifford C.
Michael.
Environment and Parks, Hon. Bruce Strachan.
Intergovernmental Relations, Hon. C. Stephen Rogers.
Tourism, Recreation and Culture, Hon. William E.
Reid.
Advanced Education and Job Training, Hon. Stanley
Hagen.
(The Premier receives a total salary of $76,527:
Members of the Executive Council receive a total
salary of $71,330).
Speaker, Legislative Assembly, Hon. John D.
Reynolds $64,809

Agent-General in London, G. Gardom, Q.C., British
Columbia House, 1 Regent Street, SW1.

THE JUDICATURE

Court of Appeal—Chief Justice of British Columbia,
Hon. N. T. Nemetz.
Justices of Appeal, Hons. J. D. Taggart; P. D. Seaton;
A. B. B. Carrothers; E. E. Hinkson; W. A. Craig; J.
S. Aikins; J. D. Lambert; J. A. Macdonald; R. P.
Anderson; H. E. Hutcheon; A. B. Macfarlane; W.
A. Esson; B. M. McLachlin; W. J. Wallace; C. C.
Locke.
Supreme Court—Chief Justice, Hon. A. McEachern.
Puisne Judges, Hons. K. E. Meredith; A. A. Mackoff;
S. M. Toy; J. C. Bouck; L. G. McKenzie; G. L.
Murray; H. P. Legg; W. J. Trainor; P. M. Proud-
foot; H. A. Callaghan; A. G. MacKinnon; M. R.
Taylor; P. D. Dohm; R. M. P. Paris; D. B. Hinds; A.
A. W. Macdonell; J. E. Spencer; W. H. Davies; C.
R. Lander; B. D. Macdonald; K. M. Lysyk; L. S. G.
Finch; J. Wood; R. J. Gibbs; M. F. Southin; G. S.
Cumming; D. B. MacKinnon; W. T. Oppal; M. A.
Rowles; B. I. Cohen; C. M. Huddart; J. J. Gow; D.
W. Shaw; G. R. B. Coultas.

FINANCE

	1987–88	1988–89
Estimated Revenue	$10,322·0 m.	$11,440·0 m.
Estimated Expenditure ..	11,122·0 m.	11,835·0 m.
Net Guaranteed Debt	9,922·0 m.	9,418·7 m.

ECONOMY

Production and Industry.—Manufacturing activity is based largely on the processing of the output of
the logging, mineral, fishing and agriculture industries. The principal manufacturing centres are
Vancouver, New Westminster, Victoria, North Vancouver, Kelowna and Prince George. Forestry and
forest-based industries form the most important

economic activity, accounting for approximately 40 per cent of total production. British Columbia is the leading province of Canada in the quantity and value of its timber and sawmill products. Mining, the second most important non-service economic activity, is based on copper, zinc, lead, iron concentrates, molybdenum, coal, natural gas, crude petroleum, asbestos, gold and silver. Molybdenum production is approximately 99 per cent of the Canadian total.

The production levels for important industries were estimated for 1987 as follows:—

Lumber	37,455,600 cu. metres.
Paper	2,752,600 tonnes
Pulp	6,850,300 tonnes
Coal	21,964,200 tonnes
Natural Gas	9,281,300,000 cu. metres

Mineral production for 1987 was valued at $3,402·0 million.

The most important agricultural products are livestock, eggs and poultry, fruits and dairy products. Salmon accounts for approximately 60 per cent of the value of fisheries. Other species include halibut, herring, sole, cod, flounder, perch, tuna and shellfish. In 1987 farm cash receipts were valued at $1,056·3 million.

The economy is dependent upon markets outside the province for the disposal of most of the products of her industry. An estimated 55–60 per cent of production is exported to foreign markets. Manufacturing shipments in 1987 were valued at $23,008·5 million.

Transport.—The Province has deep water harbours which are well serviced by railways and modern highways. Vancouver is the base for regular scheduled air routes to other parts of Canada, the United States, Europe, Mexico, South America, Hawaii, Fiji, Australia, Japan, Hong Kong and the Middle East.

CAPITAL.—ψVictoria, Metropolitan population (1986) 265,385. ψVancouver metropolitan population (1986) 1,266,152, is the western terminus of the Canadian Pacific Railway and the Canadian National Railways (the C.N.R. also has a terminus at Prince Rupert) and the southern terminus of the British Columbia Railway, and possesses one of the finest natural harbours in the world, servicing a variety of vessels, including large bulk cargo carriers. Other principal cities are Prince George, Kamloops, Kelowna and Nanaimo.

MANITOBA

Area and Population.—Manitoba, originally the Red River settlement, is the central province of Canada. The Province has a considerable area of prairie land but is also a land of wide diversity combining 400 miles of sea-coast, large lakes and rivers covering an area of 30,225 sq. miles and precambrian rock which covers about three-fifths of the Province. The total area is 250,745 sq. miles (649,426 sq. km.), with a population (1987 estimate) of 1,082,800.

Government.—The Government is administered by a Lieutenant Governor, assisted by an Executive Council of Ministers, who are members of the Legislative Assembly of 57 members. Each member of the Legislative Assembly received an annual sessional indemnity totalling $37,521 for the year ending July 1, 1987.

The Progressive Conservatives formed a minority government after a General Election held on April 26, 1988. The standing in the House at May 1, 1988 was: Progressive Consevatives 25, Liberal 20, New Democratic Party 12.

Lt. Governor, His Honour George Johnson.

Premier, President of the Council and Minister of Federal-Provincial Relations, Hon. Gary A. Filmon.

Northern and Native Affairs, Hon. James E. Downey.
Health, Hon. Donald W. Orchard.
Highways and Transportation, and Government Services, Hon. Albert Driedger.
Finance, Hon. Clayton S. Manness.
Employment and Community Services, Economic Security, Hon. Charlotte L. Oleson.
Municipal Affairs, Hon. James G. Cummings.
Attorney-General, Minister of Consumer and Corporate Affairs, and Co-operate Development, Hon. James C. McCrae.
Labour, Environment and Workplace Safety and Health, Hon. Edward J. Connery.
Industry, Trade and Technology, Business Development and Tourism, Hon. James A. Ernst.
Agriculture, Hon. Glen M. Findlay.
Education, Hon. Leonard Derkach.
Urban Affairs and Housing, Hon. Gerald Ducharme.
Culture, Heritage and Recreation, Hon. Bonnie E. Mitchelson.
Natural Resources, Hon. John Penner.
Energy and Mines, Hon. Harold J. Neufeld.

THE JUDICATURE

Court of Appeal:—	
Chief Justice of Manitoba, Hon. A. M. Monnin	$117,900
Puisne Judges, Hons. G. C. Hall; J. F. O'Sullivan; C. R. Huband; A. R. Philp; A. K. Twaddle; S. R. Lyon	108,700
Queen's Bench, Chief Justice, Q.B.D. Hon. A. S. Dewar	117,900
Associate Chief Justice (Family Division), Hon. A. C. Hamilton	117,900

ECONOMY

Finance.—The revenue of the provincial government, 1987–88, is estimated at $3,773 million and the expenditure $4,188 million.

Agriculture.—The total land area in Manitoba is 135,342,565 acres, of which 19,126,517 acres are in occupied farms. The gross value of agriculture production in 1986 was estimated at $2,200 million.

Manufactures.—Manufacturing enterprises employed about 57,000 persons on average in 1986. The chief manufacturing centres are Winnipeg, Brandon, Selkirk and Portage la Prairie. The largest manufacturing industry is the food and beverage industry, followed by the machinery and metal fabricating industries.

CAPITAL.—Winnipeg, population 595,000. Other cities are Brandon (38,708), Thompson (14,701), Portage la Prairie (13,198) and Flin Flon (7,243).

NEW BRUNSWICK

Area and Population.—New Brunswick is situated between 45°–48° N. lat. and 63° 47′–69° W. long. and comprises an area of 28,355 sq. miles (73,439 sq. km.), with a population (June 1986 Census) of 710,422. It was first colonized by British subjects in 1761, and in 1783 by inhabitants of New England, who had been dispossessed of their property in consequence of their loyalty to the British Crown. New Brunswick entered Confederation in 1867.

Government.—Government is administered by a Lieutenant Governor, an Executive Council, and a Legislative Assembly of 58 members elected by the people. The present Legislative Assembly of the Province was elected on Oct. 13, 1987 and has 58 members, all of whom are from the Liberal Party.

Lt. Governor, His Honour Gilbert Finn.

Premier, Hon. Frank McKenna.
Justice, Hon. James Lockyer.

Transportation, Hon. Sheldon Lee.
Agriculture, Hon. Alan Graham.
Commerce and Technology, Hon. Al Lacey.
Health and Community Services, Hon. Raymond Frenette.
Education, Hon. Shirley Dysart.
Advanced Education and Training, Hon. Russell King.
Labour, Hon. Michael McKee.
Finance, Hon. Allan Maher.
Municipal Affairs and Environment, Hon. Vaughn Blaney.
Fisheries and Aquaculture, Hon. Douglas Young.
Tourism, Recreation and Heritage, Hon. Roland Beaulieu.
Chairman, Board of Management, Hon. Gérald Clavette.
Supply and Services, Hon. Bruce Smith.
Natural Resources, Hon. Morris Green.
Income Assistance, Hon. Laureen Jarrett.
Housing, Hon. Peter Trites.
Minister responsible for Intergovernmental Affairs, Hon Aldéa Landry.

Speaker of the House, Hon. Frank Branch.
Solicitor General, Hon. Joseph-Conrad Landry.

The Judicature
Court of Appeal
Chief Justice, Hon. S. G. Stratton.
Judges of Appeal, Hons. J. C. Angers; W. Hoyt; R. C. Rice; L. C. Ayles; P. A. A. Ryan.

Queen's Bench Division
Chief Justice, Hon. G. A. Richard.

Economy
Finance.—The estimated revenue for the year ending March 31, 1987, was $2,765,646,061 and ordinary expenditure, $2,837,964,380.

Manufactures.—New Brunswick's largest manufacturing group, in terms of shipments, is the paper and allied industries, followed by the food and wood industries. Together these industries accounted in 1987 for 54·8 per cent. of the total value of manufacturing shipments of $4,893·3 million. Saint John has a major ice-free port and is the principal manufacturing centre of the Province.

Agriculture.—Total land area 27,633 sq. miles; farms numbered 3,554 and averaged 284 acres each in 1986. Dairy products and potatoes are the leading agricultural products. Both industries together accounted for 44 per cent of total farm cash receipts in 1987. Farm cash receipts in 1987 totalled $242,481,000.

Fisheries.—Fishing is an important industry, employing about 7,500 fishermen. The chief commercial fish are lobsters, herring, tuna, crab and cod. Landings reached 131,562 tonnes valued at $101,010 in 1987.

Minerals.—Extensive zinc, lead and copper deposits are now being mined in the north-eastern part of the Province with New Brunswick being the third largest producer of zinc in Canada. A lead smelter, fertilizer plant and port facilities have been constructed at Belledune. Canada's only primary antimony producer is located at Lake George. There is exploration and development near Sussex and Salt Springs, where potash production continues to escalate. A potash terminal has been built at the port of St. John. Coal is mined at Grand Lake and exploration for other deposits is being undertaken. Total mineral production was valued at $700,709,000 in 1987.

Tourism is of increasing value to the economy.

Capital.—Fredericton: population (1986), 65,768. Other cities are ψSaint John (121,265); Moncton (102,084); Bathurst (34,895); Edmundston (22,614); Campbellton (17,418).

NEWFOUNDLAND AND LABRADOR
Area and Population.—The Island of Newfoundland is situated between 46° 37'–51° 37' N. latitude and 52° 44'–59° 30' W. longitude, on the north-east side of the Gulf of St. Lawrence, and is separated from the North American continent by the Straits of Belle Isle on the N.W. and by Cabot Strait on the S.W. The island is about 317 miles long and 316 miles broad and is triangular in shape. It comprises an area of 43,008 sq. miles (111,390 sq. km.), with a population (1986 Census) (inclusive of Labrador) of 568,349.

Labrador forms the most easterly part of the North American continent, and extends from Point St. Charles, at the northeast entrance to the Straits of Belle Isle, on the south, to Cape Chidley, at the eastern entrance to Hudson's Straits on the north. It has an area of 113,641 sq. miles (294,328 sq. km), with a population (1986 Census) of 28,741. Labrador is noted for its cod fisheries and also possesses valuable salmon, herring, trout and seal fisheries.

Government.—On March 31, 1949 Newfoundland became the 10th Province of the Dominion of Canada. The Government is administered by a Lieutenant Governor, aided by an Executive Council and a Legislative Assembly of 52 members elected for a term of five years. A General Election was held on April 12, 1985. The standings in the current House of Assembly are: 36 Progressive Conservatives, 15 Liberals, and 1 New Democrats.
Lt. Governor, His Honour James A. McGrath.

Executive
(as at June 9, 1988)
Premier and Minister of Energy, Hon. A. Brian Peckford.
Municipal Affairs, Hon. R. C. Brett.
Mines, Hon. J. W. Dinn.
Finance and Minister responsible for Newfoundland & Labrador Hydro, Hon. H. N. Windsor.
Deputy Premier and Minister of Health, Hon. Dr. J. Collins.
Rural, Agricultural and Northern Development, Hon. C. J. Power.
Consumer Affairs & Communications, Hon. H. Young.
Justice and Attorney General, Hon. Lynn Verge.
Intergovernmental Affairs, Hon. R. G. Dawe.
President of Treasury Board, President of the Executive Council and Government House Leader, Hon. L. A. Simms.
Transportation, Hon. N. E. Doyle.
Fisheries, Hon. T. G. Rideout.
Public Works & Services, Hon. Dr. H. M. Twomey.
Forest Resources, Hon. R. J. Alyward.
Environment and Lands, Hon. J. M. Russell.
Career Development and Advanced Studies, Hon. W. B. Matthews.
Education, Hon. W. L. Hearn.
Culture, Recreation and Youth, Hon. J. C. Butt.
Labour, Hon. T. A. Blanchard.
Development and Tourism, Hon. H. M. Barrett.
Social Services, Hon. G. Tobin.
Minister responsible for Newfoundland and Labrador Housing, Hon. M. Peach.
Northern Development, Hon. G. Warren.

Speaker of the House of Assembly, Hon. Dr. P. McNicholas.
Clerk of the Executive Council, H. M. Clarke.

Economy
Finance.—The estimated gross capital and current account revenues for 1988–89 were $2,664,144,000 and the gross current and capital account expenditures $2,925,583,000.

Production and Industry.—The main primary industries are fishing, forestry and mining. In 1984 shipments of fish products were valued at $450 million. In 1987 newsprint shipments from the three pulp and paper mills were valued at $516 million, mining plus structural materials shipments were estimated at $767·8 million, of which $685·4 million was from the two iron ore mines in Labrador. Manufacturing shipments with the exclusion of fish and paper products totalled approximately $630 million in 1987. The hydro-electric plant on the Churchill river is the largest underground plant in the world, with a capacity of 5,225,000 kw.

Petroleum and Natural Gas.—Over 129 wells have been drilled off Newfoundland since 1965. Discovery of oil was made in 1979 on the Grand Banks. Oil production is expected to begin in the 1990's, with a peak production of 110,000 barrels of oil a day. In 1987, offshore exploration expenditure was approximately $165 million

Transport.—The Province is connected to mainland Canada by a ferry service from North Sydney, Nova Scotia to Port aux Basques and Argentia. The main line of the railway extends from St. John's on the east coast to Port aux Basques on the west coast. Transport between various points on the island is by highway but the south coast and Labrador still rely on the coastal boat service.

CAPITAL.—ΨSt. John's (population 1986 Census, Greater St. John's 161,901) is North America's oldest city, and thus of historical interest and is the seat of the provincial legislature, the site of most provincial and federal government offices and the principal port for the island of Newfoundland. Newfoundland's second city of Corner Brook (population 1986 Census, 22,719) is situated on the west coast, its principal industry being its pulp and paper mill.

NOVA SCOTIA

Area and Population.—Nova Scotia is a peninsula between 43° 25′–47° N. lat. and 59° 40′–66° 25′ W. long., and is connected to New Brunswick by a low fertile isthmus about 17·5 miles wide. It comprises an area of 21,425 sq. miles (55,490 sq. km.), including 1,023 sq. miles of lakes and rivers and 6,479 miles of shoreline. No place is more than 35 miles from the Atlantic Ocean. Population (April 1988 estimate) 882,600.

Government.—The Government consists of a Lieutenant Governor and a 52-member elected Legislative Assembly, from which the Executive Council (Cabinet) is selected. The Lieutenant Governor represents the Queen and is appointed by the Governor-in-Council.

Lt. Governor, His Honour Alan R. Abraham.

EXECUTIVE COUNCIL

Premier, Hon. John M. Buchanan, P.C., Q.C.
Agriculture and Marketing, Hon. Roger S. Bacon.
Lands and Forests, Hon. John MacIsaac.
Mines and Energy, Hon. Kenneth Streatch.
Education, Hon. Ronald C. Giffin, Q.C.
Attorney General and Minister for Labour, Hon. Terence R. B. Donahoe, Q.C.
Community Services, Hon. Thomas J. McInnis.
Health and Fitness, Hon. Joel R. Matheson, Q.C.
Municipal Affairs, Hon. Laird Stirling.
Advanced Education and Job Training, Hon. Edmund Morris.
Solicitor General and Provincial Secretary, Hon. Ronald S. Russell.
Finance, Hon. Greg Kerr.
Government Services, Hon. Michael A. Laffin.
Fisheries, Hon. John G. Leefe.
Management Board, Hon. George C. Moody.
Housing, Hon. Milne C. Pickings.
Small Business Development, Hon. G. David Nantes.
Consumer Affairs, Hon. Maxine Cochran.

Transportation and Communications, Hon. Guy L. LeBlanc.
Tourism and Culture, Hon. Brian A. Young.
Industry, Trade and Technology, Hon. Donald W. Cameron.
Environment, Hon. Donald P. McInnes.

Speaker of the House of Assembly, Hon. Arthur R. Donahoe, Q.C.
Clerk of the Executive Council, H. F. G. Stevens, Q.C.

During the calendar year 1987, a Member of the House of Assembly was entitled to an Annual Indemnity of $27,860 together with an annual expense allowance of $10,550, a total basic remuneration of $38,410. In addition the Premier receives $42,510; a Minister having charge of a Department $32,950; and a Minister without Portfolio up to $32,950.

Agent-General in London, Donald M. Smith, 14 Pall Mall, SW1Y 5LU.

THE JUDICATURE

Supreme Court—Appeal Division
Chief Justice, Hon. L. O. Clarke $139,700
Judges, Hons. G. L. S. Hart; A. L. Macdonald; L. L. Pace; M. C. Jones; K. M. Matthews; A. G. Cooper; T. H. Coffin; D. R. Chipman. 127,700

Trial Division
Chief Justice, Hon. Constance R. Glube 139,700
Judges, Hons. A. M. MacIntosh; W. J. Grant; J. D. Hallett; K. P. Richard; C. Denne Burchell; R. M. Rogers; H. Nathanson; M. Nunn; R. B. Macdonald; F. B. W. Kelly; G. Tidman; J. M. Davison 127,700

ECONOMY

Finance.—The revenue for the fiscal year ending March 31, 1987, was $2,903,855,000 and expenditure was $3,093,046,000. The net direct debt was $3,503,671,000.

Manufacturing.—Manufacturing constitutes the most important goods producing sector of the economy. Shipments were worth $4,686 million in 1987 with a total added value estimated to be more than $1,600 million. Manufacturing plants provide employment for 45,000 or 13 per cent of the labour force. Capital expenditure in the manufacturing sector has increased from $380·1 million in 1987 to $563·6 million in 1988.

Utilities.—Electric power in Nova Scotia is supplied by the Nova Scotia Power Corporation, a Crown corporation. The Corporation's generating stations, which are predominantly coal fired have a nameplate capacity of 1,964,305 kilowatts. The Corporation's generating system is made up of seven thermal plants, three gas turbines, 33 hydro stations scattered throughout the Province and one tidal power station.

Petroleum Activity.—By mid-1988 a total of 125 wells had been completed off-shore since drilling began in 1967, the drilling being done by five major operations. There were no wells drilled onshore in 1985–86.

Mining.—The total value of mineral production in 1987 was estimated at $444,817,220. Dollar value of production for specific minerals was:—

Coal	$184,057,197
Sand and gravel	22,725,000
Salt	57,009,534
Limestone	1,412,044

Agriculture.—Farm cash receipts were about $290 million in 1987. About 3 per cent of the total area, or 390,000 acres, is classified as farm land. Dairy, horticulture, cattle, hogs, fur and poultry products form the largest sectors.

Fishing.—The value of fish landed in 1987 was $524,225,000. Products have been diversified and enlarged into a variety of processed foods that are increasing in number.

Forest Products.—The gross value of primary and secondary forestry was $743,947,000 in 1987. Forest lands total 10,800,000 acres or 84 per cent of the land area. About 75 per cent of forest land is privately owned. Forest based industries employ about 8,000.

Tourism.—Between May 15 and October 31, 1987, about 1·2 million visitors spent about $266 million in the Province.

CAPITAL.—ΨHalifax, including the neighbouring city of Dartmouth, has a population of 178,820. In addition to a container-handling terminal in South Halifax a new terminal at the north end of Halifax Harbour was opened in 1981. A 90-acre autoport has been built at Port Halifax to handle both the export and import of motor vehicles. A shipyard, with drydock, can build and repair the largest ocean-going liners. The harbour, ice-free the year round, is the main Atlantic winter port of Canada. Other cities and towns include ΨSydney (27,754), ΨGlace Bay (20,467), Amherst (9,671) and New Glasgow (10,022).

Cape Breton Island

This has been part of Nova Scotia since 1819. It is the centre of the steel manufacturing and coal mining industries, and is also noted for its lakes and coastal scenery, making it a tourist attraction in Canada.

ONTARIO

Area and Population.—The Province of Ontario contains a total area of 412,578 sq. miles (1,068,572 sq. km.), with a population (1986 Census) of 9,113,515.

Government.—The Government is vested in a Lieutenant Governor and a Legislative Assembly of 125 members elected for five years.

After the last election on Sept. 10, 1987, there were 95 Liberals, 19 New Democrats and 16 Progressive Conservatives.

Lt. Governor, His Honour Lincoln Alexander, P.C., Q.C.

EXECUTIVE COUNCIL

Premier and Minister of Intergovernmental Affairs, Hon David Peterson.

Deputy Premier, Minister of the Treasury, Economics and Financial Institutions, Hon. Robert Nixon.

Minister of Mines and Government House Leader, Hon. Sean Conway.

Environment, Hon. James Bradley.

Attorney General and Minister responsible for Native Affairs, Hon. Ian Scott.

Agriculture and Food, Hon. Jack Riddell.

Municipal Affairs, Hon. John Eakins.

Natural Resources, Hon. Vince Kerrio.

Tourism and Recreation, Hon. Hugh O'Neil.

Community and Social Services, Hon. John Sweeney.

Management Board, Chairman of Cabinet, Hon. Murray Elston.

Consumer and Commerical Relations, Hon. William Wrye.

Revenue and Francophone Affairs, Hon. Bernard Grandmaitre.

Skills Development, Hon. Alvin Curling.

Transportation, Hon. Edward Fulton.

Industry, Trade and Technology, Hon. Monte Kwinter.

Culture and Communications, Hon. Lily Munro.

Labour and Women's Issues, Hon. Gregory Sorbara.

Health, Hon. Elinor Caplan.

Northern Development, Hon. Rene Fontaine.

Correctional Services, Hon. David Ramsay.

Solicitor General, Hon. Joan Smith.

Education, Hon. Christopher Ward.

Housing, Hon. Chaviva Hosek.

Colleges and Universities, Hon. Lyn McLeod.

Governmental Services, Hon. Richard Patten.

Citizenship, Race Relations, Hon. Gerry Phillips.

Energy, Hon. Robert Wong.

Disabled Persons, Hon. Remo Mancini.

Senior Citizens, Hon. Mavis Wilson.

Secretary of the Cabinet and Clerk of the Executive Council, R. D. Caraman.

Speaker, Legislative Assembly, Hon. H. Edighoffer.

Agent-General in London, T. Wells, 13 Charles II Street, SW1.

JUDICATURE

Chief Justice of Ontario, Hon. W. G. C. Howland.

Chief Justice of the High Court, Hon. W. D. Pucker.

ECONOMY

Agriculture.—Ontario has the highest total of agricultural production in Canada with a gross value of $5,520,000,000 and a total net farm income of $5,460,000,000 in 1986.

Forestry.—Productive forested lands cover 377,000 sq. km. or 35·3 per cent of the land area of the Province. Paper and allied industries are by far the most important sector of Ontario's forest industry.

Minerals.—Ontario's natural resources include 15 basic minerals, such as copper, iron ore, zinc, sulphur, gold and platinum. The province has half the world's supply of nickel and the largest amount of uranium in the western world. Total value of the mineral production in 1986 was estimated at $4,800,000,000.

Energy.—Total electrical energy generated in Ontario in 1985 was 121,000 million kWh (34 per cent hydro, 40 per cent nuclear and 26 per cent other conventional fossil fuels).

Manufacture.—Ontario is the chief manufacturing province in Canada, producing 50 per cent of all manufactured goods. During 1985 Ontario's exports totalled $59,000 million, an increase in value of $4,000 million over 1984. A $4,200 million growth in the value of end products—the sector which contains the bulk of Ontario's manufactured exports—was also achieved.

CAPITAL.—ΨToronto (metropolitan population 1986, 2,192,721) has a wide range of manufacturing and service industries and is a centre of education, business and finance. Other major urban areas are: Ottawa, the national capital (300,763); ΨHamilton (306,140), with iron and steel industry, metal fabrication, machinery, electrical and chemical industries; London (269,140), a business and manufacturing centre; ΨWindsor (193,111); Kitchener (150,604) and Sudbury (88,717).

PRINCE EDWARD ISLAND

Area and Population.—Prince Edward Island lies in the southern part of the Gulf of St. Lawrence, between 46°–47° N. lat. and 62° 64° 30′ W. long. It is about 140 miles in length, and from 4 to 40 miles in breadth; its area is 2,185 sq. miles (5,659 sq. km.), and its population (1986) 126,645.

Government.—The Government is vested in a Lieutenant Governor and an Executive Council, and Legislative Assembly of 32 members elected for a term of up to 5 years, 16 as Councillors and 16 as Assemblymen. Party representation at July 1, 1987, was: Liberal 21; Progressive Conservative 10; Vacant 1.

Lt. Governor, His Honour Lloyd G. MacPhail $69,000
(and expense allowance)

EXECUTIVE

Premier and President of the Executive Council, Hon. Joseph A. Ghiz, Q.C.

Finance and Community and Cultural Affairs, Hon. Gilbert R. Clements.
Energy and Forestry, Hon. Allison Ellis.
Industry, Hon. Leonce Bernard.
Fisheries, Hon. Ross Young.
Transportation and Public Works, Hon. Robert Morrissey.
Education, Hon. Betty Jean Brown.
Agriculture, Hon. Tim Carroll.
Justice and Attorney General, and Labour, Hon. Wayne Cheverie, Q.C.
Tourism and Parks, Hon. Gordon MacInnis.
Health and Social Services, Hon. Keith Milligan.
Speaker of the Legislative Assembly Hon. Edward W. Clark.

Members of the Legislative Assembly received a salary of $18,000 per annum *plus* $9,000 expense allowance; in addition the Premier received $43,000 per annum; a Minister, $33,000 per annum; and the Speaker, $9,400 per annum, as at July 1, 1987.

SUPREME COURT

Chief Justice, Hon. Norman H. Carruthers $113,900
Associate Justices, Hon. G. Mitchell; Hon.
   C. R. McQuaid; Hon. K. R. MacDonald;
   Hon. A. B. Campbell; Hon. G. J. Mullally;
   Hon. G. R. McMahon .... each $105,000
Supernumary Justice, Hon. F. A. Large.

Finance.—The ordinary revenue in 1986–87 was $485·8 million and the expenditure was $511·3 million.
Education.—A university and a college of applied arts and technology were established in 1969, estimated full- and part-time enrolment for 1986–87 being 2,522 (University of Prince Edward Island), and 881 for the college of applied arts and technology (Holland College).
CAPITAL.—ΨCharlottetown (pop. July 1986 Census, 15,776), on the shore of Hillsborough Bay, which forms a good harbour.

QUEBEC

Area and Population.—The Province of Quebec contains an area estimated at 594,855 sq. miles (1,540,667 sq. km.) with a population (June, 1987 estimate) of 6,592,600.
Government.—The Government of the Province is vested in a Lieutenant Governor, a Council of ministers and a National Assembly of 122 members elected for five years. At May 1988, there were 99 Liberals, 20 Parti Quebecois, 1 Independent and 2 vacancies.
Lt. Governor, His Honour Gilles Lamontagne.

EXECUTIVE

Prime Minister, Hon. Robert Bourassa.
Deputy Prime Minister and Minister for Cultural Affairs, Hon. Lise Bacon.
Parliamentary Leader of the Government, Hon. Michel Gratton.
Municipal Affairs, Hon. André Boubeau.
Energy and Resources, Hon. John Ciaccia.
Transport and Regional Development, Hon. Marc-Yvan Côté.
Agriculture, Fisheries and Food, Hon. Michel Pagé.
Finance, Hon. Gérard D. Levesque.
Communications, Hon. Richard French.
Revenue, Hon. Yves Séguin.
Industry and Commerce, Hon. Daniel Johnson.
Supply and Services, Hon. Gilles Rocheleau.
Health and Social Services, Hon. Thérèse Lavoie-Roux.
Environment, Hon. Clifford Lincoln.
Foreign Trade and Technological Development, Hon. Pierre MacDonald.
Justice, Hon. Herbert Marx.

Manpower and Income Security, and Labour, Hon. Pierre Paradis.
Recreation, Fish and Game, Hon. Yvon Picotte.
International Relations, Hon. Gil Rémillard.
Cultural Communities and Immigration, Hon. Louise Robic.
Education, and Higher Education and Science, Hon. Claude Ryan.
President of the National Assembly, Hon. Pierre Lorrain.
Minister-Delegates, Hon. Albert Côté (*Forests*); Hon. Raymond Savoie (*Mines*); Hon. Robert Dutil (*Health and Social Services*); Hon. Pierre Fortier (*Finance and Privatization*); Hon. Monique Gagnon-Trembley (*Status of Women*); Hon. Paul Gobeil (*Administration/President, Treasury Board*); Hon. André Vallerand (*Small Businesses*).
Solicitor General, Hon. Gérard Latulippe.

Agent-General in London, Patrick Hyndmann, 59 Pall Mall, SW1Y 5JH.

JUDICATURE

Court of Appeal, Chief Justice of Quebec, Hon. Marcel Crête.
Superior Court, Chief Justice of Quebec (Montreal), Hon. Alan B. Gold.

ECONOMY

Finance.—The revenue for the year 1986–87 was $25,646,247,000; expenditure amounted to 28,465,454,000. The net debt (March 31, 1987) was $24,051,417,000.
Production and Industry.—The principal manufacturing centres are Montreal, Montreal East, Quebec, Trois-Rivières, Sherbrooke, Shawinigan Drummondville and Lachine. Forest lands cover 779,256 sq. km., of which 556,044 sq. km. are productive. Forest products in 1985 included wood pulp, 8,789,350 tonnes. Total estimated value of shipments in the manufacturing industries in 1987 was $65,564,385,000. Value of 1987 shipments in the chief industries:—

Food	$8,907,480,000
Beverages	1,391,768,000
Paper and allied industries	7,209,456,000
Petroleum and coal products	3,320,439,000
Primary metal industries	6,453,723,000
Transportation equipment industries	4,846,467,000

Agriculture and Fisheries.—In 1987 total farm receipts were:

Crops	$521,386,000
Livestock and livestock products	2,427,516,000
Other farm receipts.................	283,870,000

In 1987 95,469 tonnes of fish, to the value of $122,224,000 were landed.
Mineral Production.—Minerals to the value of $2,192,690,099 were mined in 1986. This included copper, $105,412,317; zinc, $45,108,362; asbestos, $178,035,832; and gold, $465,286,495.
CAPITAL.—ΨQuebec. Population (Census 1986), 164,580; historic city visited annually by thousands of tourists, and one of the great seaport towns of Canada. ΨMontreal (1,015,420) is the commercial metropolis. Other important cities are Laval (284,164); Verdun (60,246), Sherbrooke (74,438), Montreal-Nord (90,303) and La Salle (75,621).

SASKATCHEWAN

Area and Population.—The Province of Saskatchewan lies between Manitoba on the east and Alberta on the west and has an area of 251,864 sq. miles (652,324 sq. km.), (of which the land area is 220,182 sq. miles), with a population (estimated, 1987) of 1,014,000. Saskatchewan extends along the Canada–U.S.A. boundary for 393 miles and northwards for 761 miles. Its northern width is 276 miles.

Government.—The Government is vested in the Lieutenant Governor, with a Legislative Assembly of 64 members. There is an Executive Council of 16 members. The Legislative Assembly is elected for 5 years and the state of the parties in June 1988 was: Progressive Conservative 37; New Democratic Party 26; Liberal 1.

Lt. Governor, His Honour F. W. Johnson.

EXECUTIVE COUNCIL

Premier, President of the Council, and Minister of Agriculture, Hon. G. Devine.

Deputy Premier, Provincial Secretary, Hon. E. Berntson.

Attorney-General, Minister of Justice, Trade and Investment, Hon. R. Andrew.

Economic Development and Tourism, Hon. Joan Duncan.

Education, Hon. L. Hepworth.

Energy and Mines, Hon. Patricia Smith.

Environment and Public Safety, Hon. H. Swan.

Finance and Telecommunications, Hon. G. Lane.

Health, Hon. G. McLeod.

Highways and Transportation, Indian and Native Secretariat, Hon. G. Hodgins.

Human Resources, Labour and Employment, Hon. G. Schmidt.

Parks, Recreation and Culture, Hon. C. Maxwell.

Rural Development, Hon. N. Hardy.

Science and Technology, Consumer and Commercial Affairs, Hon. R. Meiklejohn.

Urban Affairs, Hon. J. Klein.

Premier, $72,867; Ministers, each $63,538.

Agent-General in London.—P. Rousseau, 21 Pall Mall, SW1.

Finance.—Combined* revenue for year ending March 1989 is $3,607,683,000 and combined* expenditure $3,935,896,000 (*Consolidated Fund and Heritage combined).

CAPITAL.—Regina. Population (Census 1986), 175,064. Other cities: Saskatoon (177,644), Moose Jaw (35,073); Prince Albert (33,686) and Yorkton (15,574).

THE COMMONWEALTH OF AUSTRALIA

AREA AND POPULATION

States and Capitals	Area (English Sq. Miles)	Estimated Resident Population		
		June 30, 1976 (a)	June 30, 1981 (a)	June 30, 1987 (a)
States				
New South Wales (Sydney)	309,433	4,959,600	5,234,900	5,612,244
Queensland (Brisbane)	667,000	2,092,400	2,345,200	2,676,765
South Australia (Adelaide)	380,070	1,274,100	1,318,800	1,394,154
Tasmania (Hobart)	26,383	412,300	427,200	447,941
Victoria (Melbourne)	87,884	3,810,400	3,946,900	4,208,946
Western Australia (Perth)	975,920	1,178,300	1,300,100	1,500,507
Territories				
Australian Capital Territory (Canberra)	939	207,700	227,600	266,088
Northern Territory (Darwin)	520,280	98,200	122,600	156,674
Total	2,967,909	14,033,100	14,923,300	16,263,319

Population of Aboriginal or Torres Strait Islander Origin (a)

	1976 number			1981 number		
	Aboriginal	T.S.I.	Total	Aboriginal	T.S.I.	Total
States						
New South Wales	37,688	2,763	40,451	33,414	1,953	35,367
Queensland	31,948	9,396	41,344	33,966	10,732	44,698
South Australia	9,940	774	10,714	9,476	349	9,825
Tasmania	2,522	421	2,943	2,334	354	2,688
Victoria	12,415	2,345	14,760	5,283	774	6,057
Western Australia	25,565	560	26,125	30,749	602	31,351
Territories						
Australian Capital Territory	769	59	828	763	60	823
Northern Territory	23,535	215	23,750	28,680	408	29,088
Total	144,382	16,533	160,915	144,665	15,232	159,897

Inter-Censal Increases, 1961–1986

Year of Census	Population at Census			Inter-Censal Increase	Net Immigration during Period	
	Males	Females	Total			
1961	5,333,185	5,215,082	10,548,267	(b) 1,521,656	1954–1961 ..	584,754
1966	5,841,588	5,757,910	11,599,498	1,051,231	1961–1966 ..	395,485
1971 (a)	6,567,936	6,499,329	13,067,265	(c) 1,156,140	1966–1971 ..	521,139
1976 (a)	7,032,034	7,001,049	14,033,083	965,818	1971–1976 ..	281,074
1981 (a)	7,448,267	7,474,993	14,923,260	890,177	1976–1981 ..	370,865
1986 (a)	8,000,187	8,018,163	16,018,350	1,095,090	1981–1986 ..	449,960

(a) Based on Census counts, place of usual residence, adjusted for under-enumeration, and including an estimate of Australian residents temporarily overseas on Census night.
(b) Excludes full-blood Aboriginals.
(c) Based on 1971 Census figure as enumerated.

Births, Deaths, Marriages and Divorces
(Year ended June 30)

	1985	1986	1987*
Births.........................	241,814	239,115	243,007
Deaths	114,197	116,069	116,180
Marriages	114,578	113,056	110,662
Divorces	39,830	39,417	39,548

*provisional

Migration
(Year ended June 30)

	1985	1986	1987
Permanent arrivals............	77,510	92,590	113,540
Permanent departures.........	20,380	18,100	19,930

PHYSICAL FEATURES

Australia, including Tasmania, comprises a land area of 7,682,300 square kilometres lying between latitudes 10°41′S (Cape York) and 43°39′S (South East Cape, Tasmania) and longitudes 113°09′E (Steep Point) and 153°39′E (Cape Byron). The latitudinal distance between Cape York and South East Cape is about 3,680 kilometres and the longitudinal distance between Steep Point and Cape Byron is about 4,000 kilometres. (The latitudinal distance between Cape York and the most southerly point on the mainland South Point, Wilson's Promontory, is about 3,180 kilometres.)

Australia has three major landforms: the western plateau, the interior lowlands and the eastern uplands. The western half of the continent consists mainly of a great plateau of altitude 300–600 metres. The interior lowland includes the channel country of southwest Queensland (drainage to Lake Eyre) and the Murray-Darling river system to the south. The eastern uplands consist of a broad belt of varied width extending from north Queensland to Tasmania and composed largely of tablelands, ranges and ridges with only limited mountain areas above 1,000 metres. The highest point is Mt. Kosciusko (2,228 m.) and the lowest, Lake Eyre (−15 m.).

Australia's large area and latitudinal range have resulted in climatic conditions ranging from the alpine to the tropical. Two thirds of the continent is arid or semi-arid although good rainfalls (over 800 mm annually) occur in the northern monsoonal belt under the influence of the Australian Asian Monsoon and along the eastern and southern highland regions under the influence of the great atmospheric depressions of the Southern Ocean. The effectiveness of the rainfall is greatly reduced by marked alternations of wet and dry seasons, unreliability from year to year, high temperatures and high potential evaporation.

Fifty per cent of the area of Australia has a medium rainfall of less than 300 mm per year and 80 per cent has less than 600 mm. Extreme minimum temperatures are not as low as those recorded in other continents because of the absence of extensive mountain masses and because of the expanse of ocean to the south. However, extreme maxima are comparatively high, reaching 50 C. over the inland, mainly due to the great east–west extent of the continent in the vicinity of the Tropic of Capricorn.

Only one third of the Australian land mass drains directly to the ocean, mainly on the coastal side of the Main Divide and inland with the Murray-Darling system. With the exception of the Murray-Darling system, most rivers draining to the ocean are comparatively short and account for the majority of the country's average annual discharge.

GOVERNMENT

The Commonwealth of Australia was constituted by an Act of the Imperial Parliament dated July 9, 1900, and was inaugurated Jan. 1, 1901. The Government is that of a Federal Commonwealth within the British Commonwealth of Nations, the executive power being vested in the Sovereign (through the Governor General), assisted by a Federal Ministry of twenty-seven Ministers of State. Under the Constitution the Federal Government has acquired and may acquire certain defined powers as surrendered by the States, residuary legislative power remaining

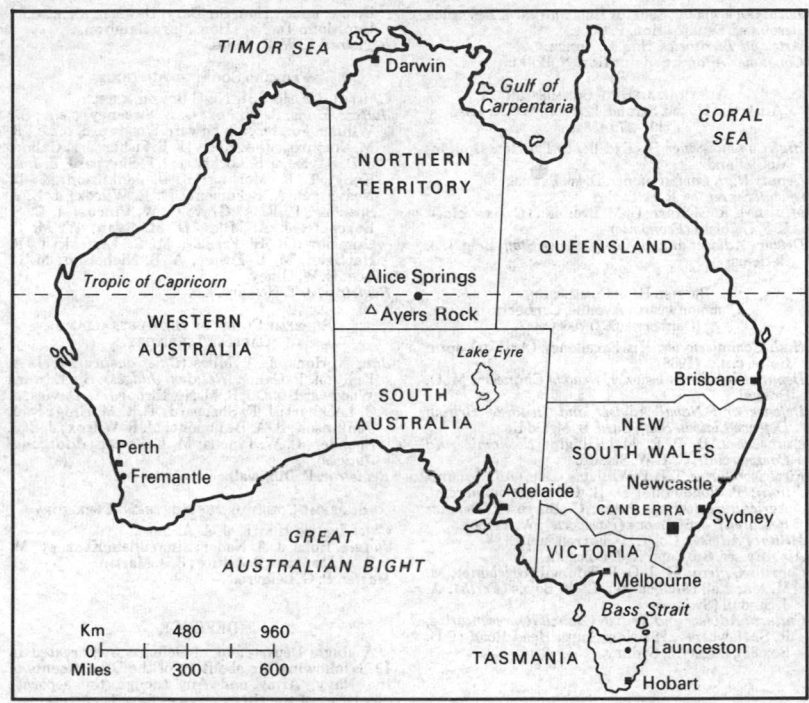

with the States. The right of a State to legislate on any matter is not abrogated except in connection with matters exclusively under Federal control, but where a State law is inconsistent with a law of the Commonwealth the latter prevails to the extent of the inconsistency.

CURRENCY.—Australian Dollar (A$) of 100 Cents.

FLAG.—The British Blue Ensign, consisting of a blue flag, with the Union Flag occupying the upper quarter next the staff, differenced by a large white star (representing the six States of Australia and the Territories of the Commonwealth) in the centre of the lower quarter next the staff and pointing direct to the centre of the St. George's Cross in the Union Flag and five white stars, representing the Southern Cross, in the fly.

NATIONAL ANTHEM.—Advance Australia Fair.

NATIONAL DAY.—January 26 (Australia Day).

Governor General and Staff

Governor General, His Excellency the Rt. Hon. Sir Ninian Stephen, G.C.M.G., G.C.V.O., K.B.E., *born* June 15, 1923; *assumed office* July 29, 1982.

Official Secretary, D. I. Smith, C.V.O.

Deputy Official Secretary, Mrs L. Lawless.

Cabinet

Prime Minister, Hon. Robert J. L. Hawke, A.C.

Deputy P.M. and Attorney-General, Hon. L. F. Bowen.

Industry, Technology and Commerce, Senator Hon. J. N. Button.

Transport and Communications, Senator Hon. G. Evans.

Treasurer, Hon. P. J. Keating.

Finance, Senator Hon. P. A. Walsh.

Foreign Affairs and Trade, Hon. W. G. Hayden.

Industrial Relations, Hon. R. Willis.

Employment, Education and Training, Hon. J. S. Dawkins.

Defence, Hon. K. C. Beazley.

Primary Industries and Energy, Hon. J. Kerin.

Social Security, Hon. B. Howe.

Administrative Services, Hon. S. West.

Community Services and Health, Hon. N. Blewett.

Trade Negotiations, Hon. M. Duffy.

Arts, Sport, the Environment, Tourism and Territories, Senator Hon. G. Richardson.

Immigration, Local Government, and Ethnic Affairs, Hon. A. C. Holding.

Junior Ministers

Transport and Communications Support, Hon. P. Morris.

Justice, Senator Hon. M. Tate.

Science, Customs and Small Business, Hon. B. Jones.

Veterans, Hon. B. Humphreys.

Aboriginal Affairs, Hon. G. Hand.

Home Affairs, Senator Hon. R. Ray.

Housing and Aged Care, Hon. P. Staples.

Employment and Education Services, Hon. P. Duncan.

Defence Science and Personnel, Hon. Roslyn Kelly.

Local Government, Senator Hon. Margaret Reynolds.
Resources, Senator Hon. P. Cook.
Arts and Territories, Hon. G. Punch.
Consumer Affairs, Senator Hon. N. Bolkus.

AUSTRALIAN HIGH COMMISSION

Australia House, Strand, London, WC2B 4LA.
[01–379 4334]

High Commissioner, His Excellency The Hon. Douglas McClelland.
Deputy High Commissioner, D. W. Evans.
Official Secretary, R. E. Taylor.
Ministers, R. G. Starr; G. M. Brennan (*Commercial*); E. F. Delofski (*Economic*).
Defence Adviser and Head of Defence Staff, Brig. I. J. C. Hearn.

BRITISH HIGH COMMISSION

Commonwealth Avenue, Canberra
[Canberra (062) 706666]

High Commissioner, His Excellency (Arthur) John Coles, C.M.G. (1988).
Deputy High Commissioner, Head of Chancery, M. G. Dougal
Defence and Naval Adviser and Head of British Defence Liaison Staff, Cdre. D. M. Oddie.
Counsellors, D. P. R. MacKilligin (*Economic and Commercial*); C. T. W. Skeate.
First Secretaries, T. E. F. Williams, O.B.E. (*Administration*); P. Reddicliffe; D. H. Cairns (*Commercial, Agriculture*); W. C. Patey; G. Burrows (*Defence Research*); J. Simmons (*Passports*); W. Talbot.
Military Adviser, Col. G. D. Farrell, M.B.E.
Air Adviser, Gp. Capt. R. J. Coleman.
Consuls-General, H. J. O. R. Tunnell (*Brisbane*); M. M. Marshall (*Melbourne*); L. W. Boyes (*Perth*); A. J. Sindall (*Sydney*).
Cultural Adviser and British Council Representative, R. S. Newberry, 203 New South Head Road (P.O. Box 88), Edgecliff, Sydney.

THE LEGISLATURE

Parliament consists of the Queen, the Senate and the House of Representatives. The Constitution provides that the number of members of the House of Representatives shall be, as nearly as practicable, twice the number of Senators. Members of the Senate are elected for six years by universal suffrage, half the members retiring every third year. Each of the six States returns an equal number of 10 Senators, and the Australian Capital Territory and the Northern Territory two each. The House of Representatives, similarly elected for a maximum of three years, contains members proportionate to the population, with a minimum of five members for each State. There are now 148 members in the House of Representatives, including one member for the Northern Territory and two for the Australian Capital Territory. Members of both Houses received $A46,065 per annum, plus allowances, with air and rail travel at Government expense while on parliamentary business.
President of the Senate, Senator Hon. K. Sibraa.
Speaker, House of Representatives, Hon. Joan Child.

THE JUDICATURE

HIGH COURT OF AUSTRALIA

Chief Justice, Hon. Sir Anthony Frank Mason, K.B.E.
Justices, Hon. Sir Ronald Wilson, K.B.E., C.M.G.; Hon. Sir Gerard Brennan, K.B.E.; Hon. Sir William Deane, K.B.E.; Hon. Sir Daryl Dawson, K.B.E., C.B.; Hon. John Toohey; Hon. Mary Gaudron.
Registrar, F. W. D. Jones.

FEDERAL COURT OF AUSTRALIA

Chief Judge, Hon. Sir Nigel Bowen, K.B.E.
Judges, Hons. R. W. Fox; C. A. Sweeney, C.B.E.; Sir William Forster; Sir Edward Woodward, O.B.E.; R. M. Northrop; J. A. Keely; F. R. Fisher; J. F. Gallop; J. D. Davies; J. S. Lockhart; I. F. Sheppard; J. J. A. Kelly; T. R. Morling; K. J. Jenkinson; A. R. Neaves; B. A. Beaumont; M. R. Wilcox; J. E. J. Spender; P. R. A. Gray; C. W. Pincus; J. C. S. Burchett; J. A. Miles; D. M. Ryan; W. M. C. Gummow; R. S. French; M. R. Einfeld; T. R. Hartigan; M. L. Foster; A. B. Nicholson; M. C. Lee; H. W. Olney.
Registrar, J. T. Howard, E.D.

SUPREME COURT OF THE AUSTRALIAN CAPITAL TERRITORY

Judges, Hons. J. A. Miles (*Chief Justice*); J. J. A. Kelly; J. F. Gallop (*Resident Judges*); Sir Edward Woodward, O.B.E.; R. M. Northrop; J. D. Davies; J. S. Lockhart; I. F. Sheppard; T. R. Morling; K. J. Jenkinson; B. A. Beaumont; M. R. Wilcox; J. E. J. Spender; C. W. Pincus; M. L. Foster (*Additional Judges*).
Registrar, P. Dingwall.

SUPREME COURT OF THE NORTHERN TERRITORY

Chief Justice, Hon. K. J. A. Asche.
Judges, Hons. J. A. Nader; Sir William Kearney; M. D. A. Maurice; P. J. Rice; B. J. Martin.
Master, P. G. Lefevre.

DEFENCE

A single Department of Defence was created in 1973, following the abolition of the Departments of the Navy, Army and Air, though the separate identities of the three services have been retained. The defence research and development elements of the former Department of Supply, along with other research groups on the three services, were incorporated in 1978 into the Defence, Science and Technology Organization. The Chief of Defence Force Staff is responsible for command of the Defence Force through the three Service Chiefs of Staff and is also the principal military adviser to the Minister.

The Secretary to the Department of Defence is responsible to the Minister for Defence for advice on policy, resources and organization.

Total defence expenditure was estimated at $A6,838,982,000 in 1985–86.

The personnel strengths of the Permanent Defence Force and the Reserve Forces at June 30, 1985 were:—

	P.D.F.	Reserves*
Navy	16,059	1,135
Army	32,460	23,846
Air Force	22,863	1,353
Total	71,382	26,334

(*Reserve components with training obligations.)

COMMONWEALTH GOVERNMENT FINANCE

Outlays and revenue of the Commonwealth Government were ($Amillion):

	1986–87	1987–88
Current outlays	70,934	75,965
Capital outlays	8,432	7,344
Revenue	74,264	80,831
Financing transactions	5,102	2,477

State	Outlay (current and capital)	Revenue and grants received	Financing trans-actions
N.S.W.	17,184·8	14,292·5	2,892·3
Victoria	13,358·8	11,129·5	2,229·3
Queensland	8,449·4	7,256·5	1,192·9
S. Australia	4,443·5	3,891·2	552·3
W. Australia ...	5,237·9	4,540·8	697·1
Tasmania	1,697·9	1,475·7	222·2
N.T.	1,208·6	1,050·1	158·5
Total	51,580·8	43,636·3	7,944·5

(p) preliminary

BANKING

In May 1986 the major trading banks had total liabilities of $A71,458 million including total deposits of $A44,735 million; and total assets of $A77,899 million, including $A7,400 million of liquid assets and Commonwealth Government securities.

PRODUCTION AND INDUSTRY

In 1985, 63·6 per cent of the Australian land area consisted of agricultural establishments, with the remainder being urban areas, State forests, mining leases and unoccupied land. Crop-growing areas constituted up to 4·32 per cent of the total agricultural establishments, emphasizing the relative importance of the livestock industries in Australia (sheep in the warm, temperate, semi-arid lands and beef cattle in the tropics).

The wide range of climatic and soil conditions over the agricultural regions of Australia has resulted in a diversity of crops being grown throughout the country. Generally, cereal crops (excluding rice and sorghum) are grown in all States over wide areas, while other crops are confined to specific locations in a few States. However, scanty or erratic rainfall, limited potential for irrigation and unsuitable soils or topography have restricted intensive agriculture.

The estimated gross values of agricultural commodities ($Am.):—

	1983–84	1984–85p
Crops	8,426·6	7,887·2
Livestock slaughterings ...	3,392·8	3,625·1
Livestock products	3,489·8	3,762·8
Total agriculture	15,309·1	15,276·1

p. provisional.

AGRICULTURAL PRODUCTION

The principal products (tonnes) were:—

	1984	1985p
Cereal crops		
Barley	4,890,000	5,559,000
Oats	2,296,000	1,395,000
Wheat	21,764,000	18,635,000
Rice	632,000	776,000
Crops for hay		
Barley	45,000	40,000
Oats	994,000	637,000
Wheat	209,000	171,000
Sugar-cane*	24,191,000	25,448,000
Fruit		
Oranges	392,000	439,000
Apples	267,000	n/a
Pears	122,000	n/a
Bananas..............	146,423,000	151,432,000
Pineapples............	115,056,000	135,267,000
Passion fruit	3,714,000	3,149,000
Strawberries..........	3,890,000	4,092,000
Wool (greasy basis)	728,898	799,961

* Cut for crushing.   (p) preliminary.

In 1984–85 (preliminary figures), gross value of wool production was $A2,398·8 million.

Livestock Numbers at March 31 (in thousands)

	1985	1986	1987
Sheep and lambs......	149,248	146,776	149,157
Cattle and calves	22,738	21,820	21,915
Pigs.................	2,463	2,512	2,611
Poultry	54,833	52,791	57,608

Mines and Minerals.—Significant mineral resources comprise bauxite, coal, copper, crude petroleum, gems, gold, ilmenite, iron ore, lead, limestone, manganese, nickel, rutile, salt, silver, tin, tungsten, uranium, zinc and zircon. Recently, geological exploration has significantly increased the mineral resources of the nation.

Australia now has fourteen oilfields in production: Alton, Bennett, Conloi, Kincora, Moonie and Trinidad in Queensland; Barracouta, Cobia, Halibut, Kingfish, Mackerel and Tuna in Victoria in the offshore Gippsland Basin and Dongara and Barrow Island in Western Australia.

In 1983–84, value added by the mining industry was $A8,825·4 million. Mine production of black coal was 116,346,000 tonnes, crude oil (incl. condensate) was 26,826 megalitres and natural gas 12,098 gigalitres. Production of principal metals was:—

Iron ore	76,478,000 tonnes
Copper	249,282 ,,
Lead-Zinc concentrate	37,932 ,,
Gold	33,881 kg.

Manufactures.—In 1983–84 there were in Australia 27,470 industrial establishments, employing 1,009,376 persons; wages paid amounted to $A17,461m; purchases, transfers in and selected expenses $A54,666m; value added by manufacture $A34,229m; and turnover $A88,632m.

Trade Unions.—On June 30, 1985, there were 323 reporting trade unions in Australia with a total membership of 3,154,200.

TRADE
Total external trade (including Bullion and Specie.)

	1985–86	1986–87
Imports	$A34,691,197,000	$A37,021,910,000
Exports	32,795,007,000	35,782,583,000

IMPORTS FROM ALL COUNTRIES, 1986–87
(by commodity classifications)

	$A'000
Food and live animals..................	1,611,975
Beverages and tobacco	326,823
Crude materials, inedible (except fuels) ..	1,083,281
Crude fertilizers, crude minerals (except coal, petroleum, precious stones)	224,207
Mineral fuels, lubricants, etc	1,749,220
Petroleum, petroleum products, etc ...	1,742,177
Animal and vegetable oils, fats and waxes	91,437
Chemical and related products, n.e.s.	3,472,036
Organic chemicals...................	880,624
Manufactured goods	6,185,759
Textile yarn, fabric, made-up articles, n.e.s., etc............................	1,831,296
Machinery and transport equipment	15,422,578
Road vehicles	2,720,006
Miscellaneous manufactured articles	5,184,816
Imports not classified elsewhere	1,893,984
TOTAL IMPORTS	37,021,910

EXPORTS 1986–87
(by commodity classifications)

	$A'000
Food and live animals	7,993,515
Meat and meat preparations	2,249,451
Cereal grains and preparations	2,800,645
Beverages and tobacco	151,558
Crude materials, inedible (except fuels)	9,903,965
Textile fibres and their wastes	3,871,492
Metalliferous ores and metal scrap	4,853,082
Mineral fuels, lubricants, etc	7,309,136
Coal, coke and briquettes	5,456,081
Animal and vegetable oils, fats and waxes	123,300
Chemical and related products, n.e.s.	663,367
Manufactured goods	3,834,748
Non-ferrous metals	2,307,831
Machinery and transport equipment	2,612,248
Miscellaneous manufactured articles	835,680
Exports not classified elsewhere	2,337,065
TOTAL EXPORTS	35,782,583

MAIN TRADING PARTNERS 1986–87

Imports from:—	Value ($Am.)	Percentage of total trade
U.S.A.	8,118·4	21·9
Japan	7,737·1	20·9
Germany, Fed. Rep.	2,732·1	7·5
U.K.	2,705·5	7·3
Taiwan	1,517·5	4·1
New Zealand	1,432·0	3·9
Italy	1,110·3	3·0
Korea, Rep. of	897·9	2·4

Exports to:—	Value ($Am.)	Percentage of total trade
Japan	9,088·0	25·4
U.S.A.	4,194·6	11·7
New Zealand	1,775·9	5·0
China	1,590·5	4·4
Korea, Rep. of	1,499·6	4·2
U.K.	1,374·9	3·8
Taiwan	1,227·6	3·4
Germany, Rep. of	1,101·1	3·1

FOOD EXPORTS TO U.K. 1986–87

	$A'000
Meat and meat preparations	66,922
Cereal and cereal preparations	23,146
Dairy products and birds' eggs	10,697
Vegetable and fruit	37,173
Sugar, sugar preparations and honey	4,490

COMMUNICATIONS

Railways.—There are six government owned railways systems, operated by the State Rail Authority of N.S.W., Victorian Railways, Queensland Government Railways, Western Australian Government Railways, the State Transport Authority of Southern Australia, and the Australian National Railways Commission. The A.N.R.C. incorporates the former Commonwealth Railways system, and the Tasmanian and non-metropolitan South Australian railways (urban rail services in Southern Australia remain the responsibility of the State Transport Authority). At June 30, 1984 there was a total of 39,251 route-kilometres open.

Gross earnings 1983–84 were:	$A'000
New South Wales	823,055
Victoria	305,283
Queensland	717,956
South Australia	50,277
Western Australia	228,339
A.N.R.C.	227,063
Total	2,351,973

Figures for all government rail services in the year 1983–84

Passenger journeys	403,456,000
Freight carried (tonnes)	142,183,000
Total gross earnings	$A2,351,973,000
Coaching	$A414,999,000
Freight	$A1,737,347,000
Total working expenses	$A3,374,398,000
Deficit at June 30, 1984	− 754,950,000

Shipping.—Total arrivals and departures (one arrival and one departure per voyage, irrespective of the number of ports visited) of vessels engaged in overseas trade at the various Australian ports in 1985–86 were: arrivals 6,824 (307,406,315 deadweight tonnes); departures 6,622 (304,839,309 deadweight tonnes).

Posts and Telegraphs.—In the year ended June 30, 1984, there were 4,790 post offices dealing with a total of 3,035,060 postal articles. Internal telegrams despatched numbered 3,668,907. At June 30, 1984, there were 53·6 telephones per 100 population.

Broadcasting and Television.—On June 30, 1984, the Australian Broadcasting Corporation operated 144 stations. Privately owned commercial broadcasting stations totalled 137. On June 30, 1984, 276 national and 152 commercial television and translator stations were in operation.

Motor Vehicles.—At June 30, 1985, there were 8,729,100 motor vehicles registered in Australia and 389,200 motor cycles. This represented 561·1 motor vehicles and 25·0 motor cycles per 1,000 population.

Civil Aviation.—At June 30, 1984, there were 441 licensed public aerodromes in the various States and Territories. Aircraft on the Australian Register at June 30, 1984, numbered 6,801.

FEDERAL CAPITAL

CANBERRA is the capital of Australia. It is situated in the Australian Capital Territory which has an area of 939 sq. miles (2,395 sq. km.) and was acquired from New South Wales in 1911. Canberra, which is the seat of the federal government, had a population (estimated) at June 30, 1985, of 273,600. Apart from Parliament House, the city also contains other national institutions, such as the Australian War Memorial, National Library, Royal Australian Mint and the Australian National University. Most Government departments have their headquarters in Canberra. An artificial lake is a central feature of this planned city, based on Walter Burley Griffin's design.

THE NORTHERN TERRITORY

The Northern Territory has a total area of 519,770 sq. miles (1,346,200 sq. km.), and lies between 129°–138° east longitude and 11°–26° south latitude. The estimated population in the Northern Territory at June 1986 was 170,000, of which about a quarter are Aboriginals.

The administration was taken over by the Commonwealth on January 1, 1911, from the government of the State of South Australia.

The Northern Territory (Self-Government) Act 1978 established the Northern Territory as a body politic as from 1 July 1978, with Ministers having control over and responsibility for Territory finances and the administration of the functions of government as specified by the Federal Government by regulations made pursuant to the Act. Proposed laws passed by the Legislative Assembly in relation to a transferred function require the assent of the Administrator. Proposed laws in all other cases may be assented to by the Administrator or reserved by the Administrator for the Governor General's pleasure.

The Governor General may disallow any laws assented to by the Administrator within six months of the Administrator's assent.

The Northern Territory has federal representation electing one member to the House of Representatives and two members to the Senate.

Administrator, His Hon. Commodore E. E. Johnston, A.M., O.B.E.

THE MINISTRY

Chief Minister, Hon. S. P. Hatton.

Deputy Chief Minister, Minister for Lands and Housing, Conservation and Tourism, Hon. R. A. Hanrahan.

Treasurer and Minister for Local Government, and Mines and Energy, Hon. B. F. Coulter.

Industries and Development, Hon. M. B. Perron.

Attorney-General, Minister for Education, Hon. D. W. Manzie.

Health and Community Services, Hon. D. F. Dale.

Labour and Administrative Services, Hon. T. R. McCarthy.

Transport and Works, F. A. Finch.

Various Aboriginal Land Trusts hold title to land previously called Reserves, totalling about one-fifth of the Northern Territory.

The Aboriginal Land Rights (N.T.) Act of 1976 provides for the investigation and determination of Aboriginal traditional claims to vacant Crown land or land already owned by or on behalf of Aboriginals. Successful land claims to date have increased Aboriginal ownership to 34 per cent of the Northern Territory whilst a further 13 per cent is the subject of claims.

A number of major Aboriginal communities previously administered by Church Mission Societies and the Federal Government are now controlled by the Aboriginal people themselves, through local Aboriginal Councils. A recent phenomenon is the voluntary movement of some Aboriginals to their traditional homeland areas where they feel that their culture will be better preserved.

ECONOMY

Northern Territory's economy is based on the exploitation of its natural resources of minerals, land, fisheries and tourist attractions. Following the introduction of a number of government measures designed to expand and diversify primary production, the Territory's agricultural and horticultural industries are also beginning to contribute an increasing amount to Territory rural output.

The beef cattle industry continues to be the major user of pastoral lands and cattle production in the financial year 1985–86 was valued at $109 million.

The buffalo population, estimated at 320,000 head is confined to the Darwin and Gulf districts. Live buffalos and buffalo meat products are an important export, currently valued at $6 million.

The Territory's six main crops are sorghum, maize, mung beans, soybeans, peanuts and rice. A total of 7,764 hectares was harvested in the 1985–86 season.

In 1986, 1,300 hectares were planted for horticulture in the Territory, yielding crops valued at $6 million. Crops include a wide range of temperate and tropical fruit and vegetables.

The annual gross value of production of the Northern Territory's fishing industry was approximately $30 million in 1986. The industry is based on barramundi and prawn fisheries. Other resources, such as mud crab, shark, mackerel and offshore reef fish are becoming increasingly important. A mooring basin for protection of the fleet from cyclonic conditions has been constructed.

Mining has played a major part in the development of the Northern Territory and in the calendar year 1986 the industry produced minerals with a value of $915 million. Four deposits of high-grade uranium have been located in the Alligator Rivers region. Of these, Ranger and Nabarlek are producing uranium oxide: their combined output in 1986 was 4,899 tonnes with a value of about $407 million. In 1986 1·86 million tonnes of manganese was sold, with a total value of about $88 million. Gold production for 1986 was valued at $97 million.

Tourism is of importance to the Territory's economy. It is a major growth industry and generates over $300 million annually.

COMMUNICATIONS

The Northern Territory has three main ports—Darwin, managed by the Darwin Port Authority; and the private mining ports of Gove, operated by Nabalco Pty. Ltd., and Groote Eylandt, operated by Groote Eylandt Mining Co. Pty. Ltd.

The new standard gauge rail link between Southern Australia and Alice Springs was officially opened in October, 1980. The link between Alice Springs and Darwin is provided by a fully co-ordinated rail-road service.

The main population centres are linked by the Stuart Highway, which connects Alice Springs to Darwin via Tennant Creek and Katherine. Of special interest to the Northern Territory is the operation of "road trains". These are basically massive trucks hauling two or three trailers, having a net capacity of about 100 tonnes and measuring up to 45 metres in length.

Darwin is a port of call for international air services between Australia and Asia, and New Zealand. Within Australia, there are flights from Darwin to all Australian capital cities by two major domestic carriers, Australian Airlines and Ansett Airlines of Australia. Internally, the main Territory centres of Katherine, Tennant Creek, Alice Springs, Ayers Rock, Nhulunbuy and Groote Eylandt are linked by Ansett N.T. All the major centres can take jet passenger traffic.

AUSTRALIAN EXTERNAL TERRITORIES

ASHMORE AND CARTIER ISLANDS

Ashmore Islands (known as Middle, East and West Islands) and Cartier Island are situated in the Indian Ocean some 850 km. and 790 km. west of Darwin respectively. The Islands lie at the outer edge of the continental shelf. They are small and low and are composed of coral and sand. Vegetation consists mainly of grass. Turtles are plentiful at certain times of the year and beche-de-mer is abundant. The Islands are uninhabited.

Great Britain took formal possession of the Ashmores in 1878 and Cartier was annexed in 1909. By Imperial Order in Council of July 23, 1931, the Islands were placed under the authority of the Commonwealth of Australia, and were accepted in 1933 under the name of the Territory of Ashmore and Cartier Islands. The Territory was annexed to the Northern Territory of Australia. With the granting of self-government to the Northern Territory on July 1, 1978, responsibility for the administration of Ashmore and Cartier Islands became a direct responsibility of the Commonwealth Government. In 1983 Ashmore Reef was declared a national nature reserve.

In accordance with an agreement between the governments of Indonesia and Australia, Indonesian fishermen who have traditionally plied the area may engage in limited fishing activity within the Territory but are prohibited from taking any products from the nature reserve. They can land to collect water at certain locations.

THE AUSTRALIAN ANTARCTIC TERRITORY

The *Australian Antarctic Territory* was established by an Order in Council, dated February 7, 1933, which placed under the government of the Commonwealth of Australia all the islands and territories, other than Adélie Land, which are situated south of the latitude 60° S. and lying between 160° E. longitude and 45° E. longitude. The Order came into force on August 24, 1936, after the passage of the Australian Antarctic Territory Acceptance Act, 1933. The boundaries of Terre Adélie were definitely fixed by a French Decree of April 1, 1938, as the islands and territories south of 60° S. latitude lying between 136° E. longitude and 142° E. longitude. The Australian Antarctic Territory Act, 1954 declared that the laws in force in the Australian Capital Territory are, so far as they are applicable, in force in the Australian Antarctic Territory. The Territory is administered by the Antarctic Division of the Department of Science, which, since its inception in 1947, has organized yearly expeditions to Antarctica, known as Australian National Antarctic Research Expeditions (ANARE).

On February 13, 1954, ANARE opened Mawson Station in Mac-Robertson Land at latitude 67° 36′ S. and longitude 62° 53′ E. Scientific research conducted at Mawson includes upper atmosphere physics, cosmic ray physics, meteorology, earth sciences, biology and medical science. Mawson is also a centre for coastal and inland exploration.

Davis Station was opened on the coast of Princess Elizabeth Land on January 13, 1957, at latitude 68° 35′ S. and longitude 77° 58′ E. Scientific programmes carried out at Davis include meteorology, biology, upper atmosphere physics, with field investigations in biology.

In February, 1959, the Australian Government accepted from the U.S. Government custody of Wilkes Station on the Budd Coast, Wilkes Land. The station was closed in February 1969, and activities were transferred to the nearby Casey Station at 66° 17′ S., 110° 32′ E. Scientific programmes carried out there include geophysics, meteorology with field programmes in glaciology, geology, etc.

Each of the stations on continental Antarctica are being replaced by new station buildings of advanced design, in a building programme which is expected to be completed in 1998.

Since 1948 ANARE has operated a station on Macquarie Island, a dependency of Tasmania, situated at 54° 30′ S. and 158° 57′ E., about 900 miles north of the Antarctic Continent.

Summer stations have been established in the Bunger Hills, 200 miles west of Casey, at Cape Denison in Commonwealth Bay, in the Larsemann Hills and on Heard Island.

CHRISTMAS ISLAND

Until the end of 1957 a part of the then Colony of Singapore, Christmas Island was administered as a separate colony until October 1, 1958, when it became an Australian territory. It is situated in the Indian Ocean about 224 miles S. of Java Head. Area 52 sq. miles. Population (estimated, June 30, 1988) is 1,100, consisting of former employees of the Phosphate Mining Corporation, and present employees of the Christmas Island Services Corporation, the Administration, and their families. There is no indigenous population.

The island is densely wooded and had extensive deposits of phosphates, the extraction of which has traditionally been the major economic activity. An Australian Government company, the Phosphate Mining Corporation of Christmas Island, which carried out the mining operations ceased operating on Dec. 31, 1987. Extensive deposits of low grade phosphate ore still remain but alternative economic development is being encouraged. The principal current development is a hotel complex.

The Administrator is responsible to the Australian Minister for Arts and Territories in Canberra. The second local elections were held in Oct. 1986 and nine members were elected to the Christmas Island Assembly. The Assembly is responsible for directing the operations of the Christmas Islands Services Corporation, which was established in 1984 to provide municipal functions and services.

Administrator, Hon. A. D. Taylor, O.B.E.

COCOS (KEELING) ISLANDS

The Cocos (Keeling) Islands were declared a British possession in 1857. In 1878 they were placed under the control of the Governor of Ceylon and were later annexed to the Straits Settlements and incorporated with the colony of Singapore. On Nov. 23, 1955, their administration was transferred to Australia. The Cocos (Keeling) Islands Act, 1955, provides the legal framework for the present political and administrative arrangements in the Territory. On April 6, 1984, the Cocos community, in an Act of Self-Determination observed by a U.N. mission, chose to integrate with Australia.

The Islands are two separate atolls (North Keeling Island and, 24 km. to the south, the main atoll) comprising some 27 small coral islands with a total area of about 14 sq. km., situated in the Indian Ocean in latitude 12° 5′ South and longitude 96° 53′ East. The main islands of the southern atoll are West Island (the largest, about 9 km. from north to south) on which are the administrative centre, the aerodrome, and the Australian-based employees of government departments; Home Island, where the Cocos Malay community lives; Direction Island, Horsburgh and South Island.

The Territory has no viable economic base at present. In 1986–87 the copra industry suffered severe losses and in 1987 ceased production. Tourism is being developed as a likely successor to the copra industry.

The climate is equable and pleasant, being usually under the influence of the south-east trade winds for about three-quarters of the year. A weekly air charter service operates between Perth, the Cocos (Keeling) Islands and Christmas Island. Population (June 30, 1986), 672. The islands are administered by the Australian Government through the Department of the Arts, Sport, the Environment, Tourism and Territories in Canberra. All proposed Ordinances, Regulations and By-laws for the Islands must be submitted to the Islands Council (est. 1979) for its consideration.

Acting Administrator, W. N. Syrette.

CORAL SEA ISLANDS TERRITORY

The Territory lies east of Queensland between the Great Barrier Reef and longitude 156° 06′ E., and between latitudes 12° and 24° S. It comprises scattered reefs and islands, often little more than sandbanks, spread over a sea area of 780,000 sq. km. The islands (or cays) are formed mainly of coral and sand. Some have grass or scrub cover but most are extremely small, with no permanent fresh water.

There is a manned metereological station in the Willis Group but the remaining islands and cays are uninhabited. Large populations of sea birds nest and breed in the area, and two national nature reserves were designated in the Territory in 1982.

The Australian Government bases its claim to the islands on numerous acts of sovereignty since early this century and enacted the Coral Sea Islands Act 1969 which declares the islands a Territory of the Commonwealth of Australia. The Department of the

Arts, Sport, the Environment, Tourism and Territories, Canberra, is responsible for the administration of the Territory.

HEARD ISLAND AND MCDONALD ISLANDS

The islands, about 4,100 km. south-west of Fremantle, comprise all the islands and rocks lying between 52° 30′ and 53° 30′ S. latitude and 72° and 74° 30′ E. longitude. Sovereignty over the islands was transferred by the U.K. to the Commonwealth of Australia in 1947. The Heard Island and McDonald Islands Act 1953 provides for the government of the islands as one Territory and under this Act the law operating there is that of the Australian Capital Territory. The Islands are administered by the Antarctic Division of the Department of Science.

NORFOLK ISLAND

The island is situated in the South Pacific Ocean at latitude 29° 02′ S. and longitude 167° 57′ E., being about 1,042 miles from Sydney and 400 miles north of New Zealand. It is about five miles in length by three in breadth, with an area of 8,528 acres. The climate is mild and sub tropical. Resident population at the 1986 Census was 1,977.

The island, discovered by Capt. Cook in 1774, served as a penal colony from 1788 to 1814 and 1825 to 1855.

In 1856, 194 descendants of the *Bounty* mutineers accepted an invitation to leave Pitcairn and settle on Norfolk Island, which led to Norfolk Island becoming a separate settlement under the jurisdiction of the Governor of N.S.W. In 1897 Norfolk Island became a dependency of N.S.W., and in 1914, pursuant to the Norfolk Island Act 1913, a territory of Australia. From that date, Norfolk Island has been regarded as an integral part of Australia.

In 1979 Norfolk Island gained a substantial degree of self-government, enabling the island to run its affairs to the greatest practical extent. Wide powers are exercised by a nine-member Legislative Assembly. The Act preserves the Commonwealth's responsibility for Norfolk Island as a Territory under its authority, with the Minister for the Arts and Territories as the responsible Minister. In 1985, responsibility for a range of matters was transferred, and the transference of more is proceeding.

The island is a popular tourist resort, and a large proportion of the population depends on tourism and its ancillaries for employment. In 1986–87 there were 29,085 tourist arrivals on the Island. Regular air services operate from mainland Australia and New Zealand.

Seat of Government and Administration Offices, Kingston.

Administrator, Cdre. J. A. Matthew, C.V.O., M.B.E.

STATES OF THE COMMONWEALTH OF AUSTRALIA

NEW SOUTH WALES

The State of New South Wales is situated entirely between the 28th and 38th parallels of S. lat. and 141st and 154th meridians of E. long., and comprises an area of 309,433 sq. miles (801,427 sq. km.) (exclusive of 939 sq. miles of Australian Capital Territory which lies within its borders).

POPULATION.—Preliminary estimated resident population at Dec. 31, 1987 was 5,660,500.

Births, deaths and marriages of usually resident population were:

	1986	1987
Births	84,531	86,060
Deaths	42,167	42,136
Marriages	41,319	40,650

Annual rate per 1,000 of estimated resident population in 1986:—Births, 15·3; Deaths, 7·6; Marriages, 7·5. Deaths under 1 year per 1,000 live births, 9·0.

Religions

The members of the Roman Catholic Church in New South Wales, according to the Census of 1986, numbered 1,529,176, Anglican Church 1,519,806, Uniting (including Methodist) 327,360, Presbyterian 227,663, Orthodox 165,659, Baptist 67,187, Lutheran 31,890, other Christian 288,865, Muslim 57,551, Hebrew 28,236 and other religions 57,079. The religion of 1,101,409 persons was either not stated in the census schedules or was stated as "none".

PHYSIOGRAPHY

Natural features divide the State into four main zones extending from north to south, viz., the Coastal Districts; the Tablelands, which form the Great Dividing Range between the coastal districts and the plains; the Western Slopes of the Dividing Range; and the Western Plains. The highest points are Mounts Kosciusko, 7,314 ft., and Townsend, 7,251 ft. The western portion of the State is watered by the rivers of the Murray-Darling system. The Darling, the major part of whose 1,712 miles is in N.S.W., and the Murrumbidgee, 981 miles, are both tributaries of the Murray, part of which forms the boundary between the States of New South Wales and Victoria.

Climate.—New South Wales is situated entirely in the Temperate Zone. The climate is generally mild and mostly free from extremes of heat and cold. At Sydney the average mean shade temperature is 18° C with a range of 11°C between the hottest and coldest months. Rainfall varies widely over the State diminishing from an annual average of about 2,000 mm. in parts of the north coast to about 200 mm. in the far north west.

GOVERNMENT

New South Wales was first colonized as a British possession in 1788, and after progressive settlement a partly elective legislature was established in 1843. In 1855 Responsible Government was granted, the present Constitution being founded on the Constitution Act of 1902. New South Wales federated with the other States of Australia in 1901. The executive authority of the State is vested in a Governor (appointed by the Crown), assisted by a Council of Ministers.

GOVERNOR

Governor of New South Wales, His Excellency Air Marshal Sir James Rowland, A.C., K.B.E., D.F.C., A.F.C., *assumed office* Jan. 20, 1981.

Lt. Governor, The Hon. Sir Laurence Whistler Street, K.C.M.G.

THE MINISTRY
(at June 8, 1988)

Premier, Treasurer and Minister for Ethnic Affairs, Hon. N. F. Greiner.

Deputy Premier, Minister for State Devlopment, and Public Works, Hon. W. T. J. Murray.

Health and Arts, Hon. P. E. J. Collins.

Agriculture and Rural Affairs, Hon. I. M. Armstrong, O.B.E.

Attorney General, Hon. J. R. A. Dowd.

Housing, Hon. J. J. Schipp.

Environment and Assistant Minister for Transport, Hon. T. J. Moore.

Chief Secretary and Minister for Tourism, Hon. G. B. West.

Police and Emergency Services, Vice-President of Executive Council, Hon. E. P. Pickering.

Sport, Recreation and Racing, Hon. R. B. R. Smith.

Family and Community Services, Hon. Virginia Chadwick.

Education and Youth Affairs, Hon. T. A. Metherell.

Transport, Hon. B. G. Baird.

Administrative Services and Assistant Minister for Transport, Hon. M. Singleton.

Business and Consumer Affairs, Hon. G. B. P. Peacocke.

Mineral Resources and Energy, Hon. N. E. W. Pickard.

Industrial Relations and Employment and Minister Assisting the Premier, Hon. J. J. Fahey.

Natural Resources, Hon. I. R. Causley.

Local Government and Planning, Hon. D. A. Hay.

Corrective Services, Hon. M. R. Yabsley.

The annual salaries of Ministers are: Premier, $A89,088; Deputy Premier, $A80,257; Leader of the Government members in the Legislative Council, $A81,155; (Deputy $A77,325); other Ministers $A75,808 each. Ministers also receive expense allowances and electoral allowances, and a special expense allowance is paid to Ministers who represent or reside in outlying electorates.

AGENT-GENERAL IN LONDON

Agent-General, Hon. K. J. Stewart, N.S.W. House, 66 Strand, WC2N 5LZ.

THE LEGISLATURE

The *Legislative Council* consists of 45 members, elected by popular vote and the *Legislative Assembly* consists of 109 members elected for a maximum period of 4 years. Party representation in the Council at June 8, 1988 was; Labor 21, Liberal 12, National 2, Australian Democrat 2, and Independent 3. Party representation in the Assembly at June 8, 1988 was: Liberal-National coalition 59 (Liberal 39, National 20), Labor 43, and Independent 7. The annual salary of members of the Legislative Council and Legislative Asssembly who are not Ministers is $A43,620. Members also receive expense and electoral allowances, and a special expense allowance is paid to members who reside in, or represent outlying electorates.

President of the Legislative Council, Hon. J. R. Johnson.

Speaker, Legislative Assembly, Hon. K. R. Rozzoli.

THE JUDICATURE

The judicial system includes a Supreme Court, Industrial Commission, District Court, Land and Environment Court, Compensation Court, and Local Courts (Magistrates).

Chief Justice, Supreme Court, Hon. Sir Laurence Street, K.C.M.G. (+ allce. $A7,465) $A113,603

President, Court of Appeal, Hon. Mr. Justice Kirby, C.M.G. (+ allce. $A6,019) $A107,147

GOVERNMENT FINANCES

State Government finances, for year ended June 30th, was:—

	1986 $A million	1987 $A million
Current outlays	11,621·7	13,318·2
Capital outlays	3,697·9	4,222·4
Revenue and grants .	13,269·3	14,886·2
Net financing	2,056·3	2,654·4

Banking, etc.—There were (March 1988) 29 trading banks with deposits of $A24,920 million. Savings

bank depositors' balances amounted to $A18,571 million, representing $A3,313 per head of the population.

EDUCATION

Education.—Education is compulsory between the ages of 6 and 15 years. It is non-sectarian and free at all government schools. The enrolment in July 1987 in 2,210 government schools was 755,084. In addition there were 852 non-government schools, with an enrolment of 275,940 students. The six universities had an enrolment of 69,726 students at April 30, 1987. In addition, there were 57,478 students enrolled in advanced education courses (predominantly in colleges of advanced education) in 1987. Students enrolled in technical and further education colleges in 1986 numbered 402,572. State Government recurrent expenditure on education was $A3,620 million in the year ended June 30, 1986.

PRODUCTION AND INDUSTRY

Local value of production in 1986–87 was ($A million):—

Agricultural commodities	$A4,280·8
Crops	1,718·9
Livestock products	1,406·9
Slaughterings....................	1,154·9
Value added ($A million)	
Mining and Quarrying (1985–86)	$A2,155·0
Manufacturing (1984–85).............	$A14,036·6

Crops.—Production in 1986–87 was (tonnes):

Wheat-grain	4,855,244
Wheat-hay	55,456
Barley	613,646
Oats	635,185
Rice	589,074
Cotton	499,356
Oilseed	156,452
Potatoes...........................	121,573
Sugar-cane, crushed	1,276,084

611,733 kg. of dried leaf tobacco and 79,478,200 kg. of bananas were obtained; almost every kind of fruit and vegetable is grown.

Livestock and Livestock Products.—A large area is suitable for sheep-raising, the principal breed of sheep being the merino, which was introduced in 1797. At March 31, 1987, there were 4,868,047 cattle, 52,191,792 sheep and lambs, and 829,833 pigs. In 1986–87, 229,711,693 kg. of wool (in the grease) were produced, 829 tonnes of butter, 13,411 tonnes of cheese, and 26,062 tonnes of bacon and ham.

Mining Industry.—The principal minerals are coal, lead, zinc, gold, rutile, copper and zircon. The total value of minerals extracted in 1986–87 was $A3,436,916,000, of which the value of output of the coal mining industry was $A2,611,741,000 and of the silver-lead-zinc industry, $A329,732,000 and the construction materials industry, including stone, gravel and sand, was $A304,845,000. The average number of persons employed in the mining industry during 1986–87 was 26,695. In 1986–87, 88,057,000 tonnes of coal were produced.

Manufacturing Industry.—At June 30, 1985, there were 10,238 manufacturing establishments (employing four of more persons). The average number of persons employed during 1984–85 was 364,847. Products include iron and steel, pipes, boilers, steel wire and wire netting, copper wire, copper and brass cables and tin-plate. Production of raw steel in 1986–87 was 5,080,000 tonnes.

OVERSEAS TRADE

	1987
Imports f.o.b......................	$16,131,220,000
Exports f.o.b......................	8,360,569,000

The chief exports in 1986–87 were coal and coke, wool, wheat, meat, non-ferrous metal and iron and steel. Chief imports were, office machines and data processing equipment, electrical machinery, road vehicles and general industrial machinery.

TRANSPORT AND COMMUNICATIONS

Shipping.—2,751 vessels entered the major ports of N.S.W. from overseas during the year ended June 30, 1987, the deadweight tonnage being 97,767,734. The shipping entries at Sydney were 1,185 vessels of 27,901,296 deadweight tonnage.

Roads and Bridges.—Expenditures by the State Government and the local authorities on road systems and regulation in 1986–87 was $A1,616·8 million.

Motor Vehicles.—At Dec. 31, 1987, there were 3,035,926 registered motor vehicles (cars, 1,910,986).

Railways.—The railways of New South Wales are controlled by the State Government. At June 30, 1987, the route kilometres of the State railways open for traffic was 9,909, revenue in the year 1986–87 being $A1,840·6 million.

Aviation.—Sydney is the principal overseas terminal in Australia. Overseas and local traffic at Sydney airport in 1987 were: passengers 9,889,680; freight 200,513 tonnes; aircraft, 110,477 (provisional figs.).

Postal and Telecommunication Services.—The postal and telecommunication services are administered by the Commonwealth Government.

Radio and Television.—At June 30, 1987, there were 33 Australian Broadcasting Corporation radio stations and 44 commercial radio stations operating under licence in N.S.W. There were also 30 licensed non-profit radio stations providing special interest services not catered for by the A.B.C. and commercial services. At June 30, 1987, there were 27 television stations (14 A.B.C., 13 commercial) in operation in the state.

TOWNS

ΨSydney, the State capital and the largest city in Australia, stands on the shores of Port Jackson. Sydney Harbour extends inland for 21 km.: the total area of water is about 55 sq. km.

The preliminary estimated resident population at June 30, 1987 of the Sydney Statistical Division was 3,525,850. The Newcastle and Wollongong Statistical subdivisions contain populations of 418,960 and 233,650 respectively.

The populations of principal municipalities located outside the boundaries of these statistical areas are: Albury 39,610, Dubbo 31,290, Greater Taree 36,960, Hastings 42,220, Lismore 38,130, Orange 32,520, Shoalhaven 59,470, Tamworth 33,830, Wagga Wagga 50,930.

LORD HOWE ISLAND

Lord Howe Island, which is part of New South Wales, is situated 702 kilometres north-east of Sydney. Lat. 31° 33′ 4″ S., Long. 159° 4′ 26″ E. Area 6·37 sq. miles (16·5 sq. km.). Pop. June 30, 1987, 290. The island is of volcanic origin with Mount Gower reaching an altitude of 866 m. The affairs of the Island are administered by the Lord Howe Island Board.

QUEENSLAND

This State, situated in lat. 10° 40′–29° S. and long. 138°–153° 30′ E., comprises the whole north-eastern portion of the Australian continent.

Queensland possesses an area of 666,798 sq. miles (1,727,000 sq. km.).

POPULATION.—At June 30, 1986, the resident population numbered 2,624,595.

Births, Deaths and Marriages were:

	1985	1986
Births	40,437	40,371
Deaths	18,629	17,861
Marriages	17,810	18,000

Annual rate per 1,000 of mean population in 1986; Births, 15·4; Deaths, 6·8; Marriages 6·9. Deaths under 1 year, 8·7 per 1,000 live births.

Religions

At the Census of 1986, there were 640,867 Anglican, 628,906 Catholics, 255,287 Uniting Church, 120,239 Presbyterians, 56,910 Lutherans, 30,089 Baptists, and 211,316 other Christians.

PHYSIOGRAPHY

The Great Dividing Range on the eastern coast of the continent produces a similar formation to that of New South Wales, the eastern side having a narrow slope to the coast and the western a long and gradual slope to the central plains, where the Selwyn and Kirby Ranges divide the land into a northern and southern watershed.

GOVERNMENT

Queensland was constituted a separate colony with responsible government in 1859, having previously formed part of New South Wales. The executive authority is vested in a Governor (appointed by the Crown), aided by an Executive Council of 18 members.

GOVERNOR

Governor of Queensland, His Excellency Sir Walter Benjamin Campbell, Q.C. $A74,000

EXECUTIVE COUNCIL.
(H.E. the Governor presides.)

Premier and Treasurer, and Minister for the Arts, Hon. M. J. Ahern $A96,821
Deputy Premier and Minister for Public Works, Main Roads, Expo and Police, Hon. W. A. M. Gunn $A83,293
Transport, Hon. I. J. Gibbs.
Land Management, Hon. W. H. Glasson.
Finance, Hon. B. D. Austin.
Education, Hon. L. W. Powell.
Employment, Training, and Industrial Affairs, Hon. V. P. Lester.
Mines and Energy, Hon. M. J. Tenni.
Primary Industries, Hon. N. J. Harper.
Environment, Conservation and Tourism, Hon. G. H. Muntz.
Family Services and Welfare Housing, Hon. P. R. McKechnie.
Northern Development, Community Services and Ethnic Affairs, Hon. R. C. Katter.
Water Resources and Maritime Services, Hon. D. M. Neal.
Justice and Attorney-General, Hon. P. J. Clauson.
Industry, Small Business, Communications and Technology, Hon. R. E. Borbidge.
Local Government and Racing, Hon. J. H. Randell.
Corrective Services and Administrative Services, Hon. T. R. Cooper.
Health, Hon. L. T. Harvey.
Education, Youth and Sport, Hon. B. G. Littleproud.

AGENT-GENERAL IN LONDON
Agent-General, D. T. McVeigh, 392–393 Strand, WC2.

THE LEGISLATURE

Parliament consists of a *Legislative Assembly* of 89 members, elected by all persons aged 18 years and over. Members of the Assembly receive $A47,315 per annum plus an electorate allowance. The Assembly, as elected on Nov. 1, 1986, was composed of: National

Party, 49; Liberal Party, 10; Australian Labor Party, 30.

Speaker, Hon. L. W. Powell $A69,163
Chairman of Committees, E. C. Row. $A58,572

THE JUDICATURE

There are a Supreme Court; District Courts; Children's Courts; an Industrial Court; a Land Court and a Medical Assessment Tribunal; a Local Government Court; the Industrial Conciliation and Arbitration Commission; Inferior Courts at all the principal towns, presided over by Stipendiary Magistrates; a Small Claims Tribunal; Small Debts Court; a Licensing Court and a Mining Warden's Court.

Chief Justice, Supreme Court, Hon.
Sir Dormer Andrews $A120,700
Senior Puisne Judge, Hon. J. L. Kelly.... $A107,550

EDUCATION

Education is compulsory between the ages of 6 and 15 years and is provided free in Government schools. At July 1987 the State administered 1,070 primary, 84 primary/secondary, and 166 secondary schools with 233,443 primary students, and 142,367 secondary students.

Post-secondary education involves technical and further education (TAFE), advanced education, and university education. During 1986, 158,516 students were enrolled in TAFE courses, including 52,319 enrolled in adult education courses. At April 30, 1987, there were 15,827 full-time, 7,247 part-time, and 8,339 external students enrolled in advanced education courses. The three universities had enrolments of 16,819 full-time students, 7,647 part-time, and 2,138 external students at April 30, 1987.

PRODUCTION AND INDUSTRY

Agriculture and Livestock.—The gross value of agricultural commodity production in 1986–87 was $A3,476,996,000 (including crops $A1,624,391,000, livestock disposals $A1,349,452,000, livestock products $A503,153,000).

The most important crops in 1986–87 were (tonnes):

Sugar (raw)......................... 3,209,365
Wheat 833,138
Maize 118,017
Sorghum 1,018,807
Barley 275,855

The livestock on March 31, 1987 included 9,011,497 cattle, 336,722 being dairy cattle, 14,626,881 sheep and 578,869 pigs.

Forestry.—Total Australian grown timber processed in 1986–87 amounted to 1,251,294 cubic metres (gross volume measure).

Minerals.—There are rich deposits of both metallic and non-metallic minerals. Coal is mined extensively in Central Queensland and on a lesser scale in North Queensland and Ipswich districts.

	$A'000
Bauxite	170,078
Coal	2,672,562
Copper concentrate................	295,456
Crude oil, natural gas, etc.	331,593
Gold (various forms)................	259,865
Lead concentrate	161,097
Mineral sands......................	85,200
Nickel ore	13,373
Scheelite and wolfram concentrate....	969
Tin concentrate....................	5,792
Zinc concentrate (incl. middlings).....	111,211
Other	237,979
Total..........................	4,345,175

Manufacturing.—In 1984–85 there were 3,392 establishments with four or more workers, employing 109,940 persons, and producing goods and services worth $A12,921 million. The value added was $A4,385 million. Much of the production was the processing of primary products, e.g. foodstuffs, timber and minerals. Included in other factory production were the products from engineering, transport equipment, basic and fabricated metal, chemical and fertilizer works, cement, paper and textile mills and oil refineries.

FINANCE

Government finance (Consolidated Revenue Fund) ($A'000) was:—

	1986	1987
Revenue	5,190,941	5,649,027
Expenditure	5,190,727	5,648,701
Gross Debt	2,459,161	2,477,500

Banking.—Advances made by Trading Banks (including the Commonwealth Trading Bank of Australia) at June 30, 1987, totalled $A7,136,652,000. The deposits at the same date amounted to $A7,949,839. Depositors' balances in Queensland savings banks at June 30, 1987, $A5,831,278,000, averaged $A2,222 for each inhabitant. There were 4,032,130 operative accounts.

OVERSEAS TRADE

	1985–86	1986–87
Imports	$A2,649,953,006	$A2,503,854,410
Exports	7,737,046,078	7,928,405,572

The chief overseas exports are coal, non-ferrous metals, meat, sugar, wool, and cereal grains.

COMMUNICATIONS

Road and Rail.—The State is served by 10,210 kilometres of railways. During 1986–87, 44,335,000 passengers and 75,169,000 tonnes of goods and livestock were carried. At June 30, 1987, there were 151,761 kilometres of formed roads in the State, and 1,575,300 motor vehicles were on the register.

Aviation.—Regular services operate between Brisbane, the main Queensland coastal and inland towns and the southern capitals. Brisbane, Townsville and Cairns are also ports of call on several international services.

Radio and Television.—On June 30, 1987, 11 national and 29 commercial sound broadcasting stations were operating in Queensland. There were seven public broadcasting stations.

CAPITAL.—ΨBrisbane, is situated on the Brisbane River, which is navigable by large vessels to the city, over 23 kilometres from Moreton Bay. The estimated resident population of the Brisbane Statistical Division at June 30, 1987 was 1,214,896. This area includes the cities of Brisbane (736,006), Ipswich (74,786), Logan (127,835) and Redcliffe (46,487).

Other cities with population over 30,000 at June 30, 1987, are: ΨTownsville, 82,253; Gold Coast, 122,780; Toowoomba, 79,100; ΨRockhampton, 57,794; ΨCairns, 40,323; ΨBundaberg, 32,428.

SOUTH AUSTRALIA

The State of South Australia is situated between 26° and 38° S. lat. and 129° and 141° E. long., the total area being 380,070 sq. miles (984,376 sq. km.).

POPULATION.—At June 30, 1987, the resident population was estimated to be 1,393,800.

Births, deaths and marriages were:

	1986	1987
Births.................	19,741	19,318
Deaths	10,328	10,565
Marriages	9,878	9,695

Religions

Religion is free and receives no State aid. At the Census, 1986, the persons belonging to the principal religious denominations were as follows: Catholic, 267,137; Anglican, 242,722; Uniting Church, 176,980; Lutheran, 64,851; Orthodox, 37,149; Baptist, 21,415; Presbyterian, 18,566; Church of Christ, 16,629; and Pentecostal, 14,997.

Physiography

The most important physical features of South Australia are broad plains, divided longitudinally by four great secondary features, which form barriers to east-west movement, and which have thus largely determined the direction of roads and railways, the sites of towns and villages and the manner of distribution of the population. These four barriers are Spencer Gulf, Gulf St. Vincent, the Mt. Lofty-Flinders Ranges and the River Murray.

The north-western portion of the State is mostly desert, while north of latitude 32° S. the country is unpromising by comparison with the fertile land which surrounds the hill country of the east. The Murray, which flows for some 400 miles through the south-eastern corner, is the only river of importance.

The lack of rivers and fresh-water lakes in the settled areas has necessitated the building of a number of reservoirs, which are supplemented by pipelines from the River Murray.

Climate.—The mean annual temperature at Adelaide is 17·1°C, the winter temperature (June-August) averaging 11·9°C, and the summer (Nov.-Mar.) 22·3°C. During the summer months the maximum temperature at times exceeds 40°C, but is associated with a relatively low humidity. The average annual rainfall at Adelaide is 21 inches.

Government

South Australia was proclaimed a British Province in 1836, and in 1851 a partially elective legislature was established. The present Constitution rests upon a Law of Oct. 24, 1856, the executive authority being vested in a Governor appointed by the Crown, aided by a Council of 13 Ministers.

Governor

Governor of South Australia, His Excellency Lt. Gen. Sir Donald B. Dunstan, K.B.E., C.B. (1982).
Lt. Governor, The Hon. Sir Condor Laucke, K.C.M.G. (1982).

The Ministry

Premier, Treasurer, and Minister for the Arts, Hon. J. C. Bannon.
Deputy Premier, Minister for Environment and Planning, Chief Secretary, Minister of Emergency Services and Water Resources, Hon. D. J. Hopgood.
Attorney-General, Minister of Consumer Affairs, Corporate Affairs, and Ethnic Affairs, Hon. C. J. Sumner.
Lands, Marine, Forests and Repatriation, Hon. R. K. Abbott.
Health and Community Welfare, Hon. J. R. Cornwall.
State Development and Technology, Employment, and Further Education, Hon. L. M. F. Arnold.
Transport, Hon. G. F. Keneally.
Mines and Energy, Hon. R. G. Payne.
Education, Children's Services, and Aboriginal Affairs, Hon. G. J. Crafter.
Housing and Construction, Public Works, Hon. T. H. Hemmings.
Labour, Correctional Services, Hon. F. T. Blevins.
Tourism, Local Government and Youth Affairs, Hon. Miss Barbara Wiese.
Agriculture, Fisheries, and Recreation and Sport, Hon. M. K. Mayes.

Agent-General in London

Agent-General, G. Walls, South Australia House, 50 Strand, WC2.

The Legislature

Parliament consists of a *Legislative Council* of 22 members elected for 8 years, one-half retiring every 4 years; and a *House of Assembly* of 47 members, elected for a maximum duration of 4 years. Election is by ballot, with universal adult suffrage for both the Legislative Council and the House of Assembly.

The representation in the House of Assembly is 27 Labor, 16 Liberals, 1 National Party and 3 Independent.

President of the Legislative Council, Hon. Anne Levy $A75,498
Speaker of the House of Assembly, Hon. J. P. Trainer $A75,498

The Judicature

Law and Justice.—The Supreme Court is presided over by the Chief Justice and 13 Puisne Judges.

Education

Education at the primary and secondary level is available at Government schools controlled by the Education Department and at non-government schools, most of which are denominational. In 1987 there were 717 Government schools with 187,388 students, and 177 independent schools with 53,959 students. Tertiary education is available through universities, colleges of advanced education, and technical and further education.

The two universities had, in 1986, a total enrolment of 13,971 full-time students.

Finance

Revenue and expenditure of the Consolidated Revenue Account and debt of South Australia (year ended June 30) was:—

	1986	1987
Revenue	3,468,164,000	3,788,253,000
Expenditure	3,457,064,000	3,778,336,000
Debt	n/a	n/a

Banking.—There are eleven trading banks in Adelaide, including the Commonwealth Trading Bank and the State Bank of South Australia, having total average deposits of $A3,783,796,000 in June 1987. The nine savings banks had deposits of $A3,389,934,000 at June 30, 1987.

Production and Industry

The gross value of primary production in 1986-87 was:—

Crops	$A1,030,753,000
Livestock products	496,724,000
Slaughterings...................	326,402,000
Fisheries	90,426,000

Agriculture.—Wheat harvest 1986-87 2,255,000 tonnes; barley, 1,592,000 tonnes. Oranges, lemons, apples, apricots, peaches, and all stone fruits and olives are successfully grown, and a quantity of this fruit is dried. In 1986-87, 194,362,000 litres of wine and 5,910 tonnes of sultanas, currants and raisins were produced. Considerable quantities of fruits (fresh and dried), wine and brandy, are annually sent to overseas countries, and to other Australian States. Some areas of the State, particularly near Adelaide, are also very suitable for growing all kinds of root crops and vegetables.

Livestock (March 31, 1988).—There were 17,969,000 sheep, 982,000 cattle, 436,000 pigs. Wool production (1987-88), 112,361,000 kg.

Minerals.—Iron, pyrite, gypsum, salt, coal, limestone, clay, oil and gas, etc., are found. The total mineral output was valued at $A1,107,382,000 in

1985–86, including oil and gas valued at $A864,179,000.

OVERSEAS TRADE

	1985–86	1986–87
Imports	1,736,757,000	1,501,827,000
Exports	1,988,233,000	2,047,147,000

The principal exports are wool, wheat, barley, meat, lead and lead alloys, silver, zinc, iron and steel, petroleum products, rock lobster and prawns.

TRANSPORT AND COMMUNICATIONS

The State Transport Authority operated (in 1987) 147 km. of railway and 1,033 km. of tram and bus routes in the metropolitan area. Australian National operated 5,420 km. of railway in country areas. There are 96,127 km. of roads.

There are a number of excellent harbours, of which Port Adelaide is the most important. The number of vessels (exceeding 200 net tonnage) entering South Australia from overseas during 1986–87 was 828 with 1,889,509 import tonnes and leaving with 6,381,640 export tonnes.

Civil Aviation.—There are 36 Government and licensed airports; the largest of these, Adelaide airport, recorded 2,063,521 passenger movements during 1986–87.

Motor Vehicles.—The registration on June 30, 1987, totalled 834,867.

Radio and Television (June 1988)—Broadcasting stations 44; Television stations 50 (including translator and satellite fed stations).

CAPITAL.—ΨAdelaide, the chief city and capital, estimated resident population on June 30, 1987, 1,012,782 inclusive of suburbs. Other centres (with 1987 populations) are: ΨWhyalla (28,175); ΨMt. Gambier (19,486); ΨPort Pirie (15,184); ΨPort Augusta (15,930); and ΨPort Lincoln (12,511).

TASMANIA

Tasmania is an island state of Australia situated in the Southern ocean off the south-eastern extremity of the mainland. It is separated from the Australian mainland by Bass Strait and incorporates King Island and the Furneaux group of islands which are in the Strait. It lies between 40° 38'–43° 39' S. lat. and 144° 36'–148° 23' E. long., and contains an area of 26,383 sq. miles (68,331 sq. km.).

POPULATION.—The estimated resident population at December 30, 1987 was 447,800.

Births, deaths and marriages were:

	1985	1986
Births..........................	7,249	6,950
Deaths	3,693	3,454
Marriages	3,520	3,302

Vital Statistics.—The birth rate in 1986 was 15·6, death rate 7·4, marriage rate 7·4 per 1,000. Infant mortality (1986) 10·6 per 1,000 births.

Religions

In 1986 there were 154,748 members of the Anglican Church of Australia, 80,479 Catholics, 36,724 Uniting Church of Australia, 12,084 Presbyterians and 8,092 Baptists.

PHYSIOGRAPHY

The surface of the country is generally hilly and wooded, with mountains from 1,500 to 5,300 ft. in height, and expanses of level, open plains. There are numerous rivers, the South Esk, Gordon, Derwent and Huon being the largest. At Hobart the mean maximum temperature ranges from about 12°C in winter to 21°C in summer, the mean minimum from

5°C to 11°C. The western side of the island is very wet, the eastern side being much drier.

GOVERNMENT

The island was first settled by a British party from New South Wales in 1803, becoming a separate colony in 1825. In 1851 a partly elective legislature was inaugurated, and in 1856 responsible government was established. In 1901 Tasmania became a State of the Australian Commonwealth. The State executive authority is vested in a Governor (appointed by the Crown), but is exercised by Cabinet Ministers responsible to the Legislature, of which they are members.

GOVERNOR

Governor of Tasmania, Gen. Sir Phillip Bennett, K.B.E.

THE MINISTRY

Premier, Treasurer, Minister for State Development, Small Businesses and Energy, Hon. R. T. Gray.
Deputy Premier, Minister for Tourism, Licensing, Police and Emergency Services, Road Safety and Gaming, Hon. G. A. Pearsall.
Attorney-General, Minister for Lands, Parks and Wildlife, Sport and Recreation, Hon. J. M. Bennett.
Employment and Training, Housing, Labour, and Industry and Consumer Affairs, Hon. R. J. Beswick.
Local Government, Main Roads, Water Resources and Racing, Hon. I. M. Braid.
Public Administration, Primary Industry and Transport, Hon. N. C. K. Evers.
Health, Community Welfare and the Elderly, Hon. F. R. Groom.
Forests, Mines, Sea Fisheries, Multicultural Affairs and Minister assisting the Premier, Hon. R. G. Groom.
Construction, Administrative Services, Environment and Inland Fisheries, Hon. P. C. L. Hodgman.
Education, the Arts, Industrial Relations, Deregulation and Technology, Hon. P. E. Rae.

THE LEGISLATURE

Parliament consists of two Houses, a *Legislative Council* of 19 members, elected for six years (3 retiring annually, in rotation, except in every sixth year, when four retire) and a *House of Assembly* of 35 members, elected by proportional representation for four years in five 7-member constituencies, the electors for both Houses being all Tasmanians of 18 years and over who have resided continuously in the State for at least 6 months. Elections for the Assembly are held every four years.

The election of Feb. 1986 resulted in the election of the Liberal Government. The state of the parties in the Legislative Council following the election was Independent 19. The state of parties in the House of Assembly in June 1988 was: Liberals 19, Labor 14, Independent 2.

President of the Legislative Council, Hon. A. J. Broadby.
Speaker of the House of Assembly, Hon. R. Cornish.

THE JUDICATURE

The Supreme Court of Tasmania, with civil, criminal ecclesiastical, admiralty and matrimonial jurisdiction, was established by Royal Charter on October 13, 1823.

Local Courts are held before Commissioners who are legal practitioners. Courts of General Sessions, constituted by a chairman who is a Justice of the Peace and at least one other Justice, are established in the municipalities and Courts of Petty Sessions are constituted by Magistrates sitting alone, or by two or more justices. A single justice may hear and determine certain matters.

Chief Justice, Supreme Court, Hon. Sir Guy Green, K.B.E.

EDUCATION

Government schools are of three main types: primary, secondary and secondary colleges. On July 1, 1987, there were 65,401 students enrolled in 261 Government schools. There were also 66 independent schools with an enrolment of 17,601. The University of Tasmania at Hobart, established 1890, had 3,457 full-time students and 1,750 part-time (including external) students in 1987. The Tasmanian State Institute of Technology, offering degree and diploma courses, was established in 1972. Enrolments in 1987 were 1,487 full-time students and 1,274 part-time students.

FINANCE

Revenue and expenditure of the Consolidated Revenue Fund and debt of Tasmania at current rates of exchange (June 30) was:—

	1986–87
Revenue	$A1,107,869,996
Expenditure	1,278,019,592
Debt	1,256,425,229

Banking.—The weekly average of depositors' balances at trading banks in December 1987 was $A734,000,000; the savings bank balances were $A1,651,000,000.

PRODUCTION AND INDUSTRY

Gross value of agricultural production in 1985–86 was $A390·2m. Total value added in manufacturing in 1984–85 was $A937·9m.; value added in mining was $A153m. in 1985–86.

Agriculture and Livestock.—The principal crops are apples, potatoes, green peas, oil poppies, hops, barley, beans and onions.

The livestock included (March 31, 1987) 534,800 cattle, 4,954,000 sheep and 46,000 pigs. The shorn wool production (1986–87) was 24,147 tonnes.

Electrical Energy.—Tasmania, the smallest Australian state, ranks fourth as a producer of electrical energy—most of it derived from water power, with a total installed generator capacity of 2,171,400 kW. By reason of its low-cost electrical energy, Tasmania has large plants producing ferro-manganese and newsprint. A large aluminium plant is situated at Bell Bay and Tasmania is the source of the bulk of Australian requirements of zinc and fine papers. The Hydro-Electric Commission has completed a network of 26 stations including a dual machine oil fired station at Bell Bay. Work is continuing on three hydro-electric developments in the remote western region of the State, which will increase the installed generator capacity to 2·54 million kW.

Forestry.—The quantity of timber (excluding firewood) of various species cut in 1986–87 was 4,797,400 cubic metres, including 3,970,400 cubic metres for woodchip and wood-pulp.

Minerals.—The chief ores mined are those containing copper, tin, iron, silver, zinc and lead.

Manufactures.—The chief manufactures for export are: refined metals, preserved fruit and vegetables, butter, cheese, textiles, paper, confectionery, wood chips and sawn timber. In 1984–85, 575 manufacturing establishments employed 24,494 persons, including working proprietors. Salaries and wages paid totalled $A443·0m.

OVERSEAS TRADE

	1985–86	1986–87
Imports	$A299,398,000	$A289,525,000
Exports	900,011,000	1,099,808,000

The principal overseas exports are ores and concentrates, refined metals, woodchips, greasy wool, meat, abalone, fresh fruit, cheese and hides and skins.

COMMUNICATIONS

Road and Rail.—Tasmania is served by a 1,067 mm. gauge Federal Government railway system of 856 route kms. An additional 134 route kms of the same gauge is privately operated. Regular passenger services no longer operate. At June 30, 1985 there were 22,406 kilometres of road normally open to traffic. Of this total 8,603 kilometres were sealed. Motor vehicles on the register at June 30, 1987 were: cars and station wagons, 207,000; commercial vehicles, 61,600 and motor cycles, 6,300.

Aviation.—Regular services operate between Tasmania and the other Australian States. During 1986–87 1,080,881 passengers were carried on these services. The main cities and towns in the State are served by regular internal services.

CAPITAL.—ΨHobart, founded 1804. Population (June 30, 1986), 127,106.

Other towns (with population at June 30, 1986) are ΨLaunceston (66,286), ΨDevonport (22,654), Burnie-Somerset (20,665), Ulverstone (10,055), Kingston-Blackmans Bay (10,932), New Norfolk (6,152).

VICTORIA

The State of Victoria comprises the south-east corner of Australia, at the part where its mainland territory projects farthest into the southern latitudes; it lies between 34°–39° S. latitude and 141°–150° E. longitude. Its extreme length from east to west is about 493 miles, its greatest breadth is about 290 miles, and its extent of coast-line is about 1,043 geographical miles, including the length around Port Phillip Bay, Western Port and Corner Inlet, the entire area being 87,876 sq. miles (227,597 sq. km.).

Population.—The estimated resident population at June 30, 1987 was 4,208,900.

Births, deaths and marriages were:

	1986	1987
Births	60,387	61,646
Deaths	30,062	31,481
Marriages	29,390	29,682

Annual rate per 1,000 of estimated resident population in 1987: Births, 14·65; Deaths, 7·50; Marriages, 7·05. Deaths under 1 year per 1,000 live births, 8·21.

Religions

At the Census in 1986, members of the Catholic Church numbered 1,104,044, Anglican, 715,414, Uniting (union of Presbyterian, Congregationalist and Methodist) 280,262, Presbyterian 138,000, Orthodox 177,565, and Baptist 39,784. The number of persons who did not state their religion was 589,132.

PHYSIOGRAPHY

The *Australian Alps* and the *Great Dividing Range* pass through the centre of the State, and divide it into a northern and southern watershed, the latter sloping down to the ocean and containing, especially in the south-east, well-wooded valleys. The length of the Murray River, which forms part of the northern boundary of Victoria, is about 1,196 miles along the Victorian bank. Melbourne, the capital city, stands upon the Yarra River, which rises in the southern slopes of the Dividing Range.

Climate.—The climate of Victoria is characterized by warm to hot summers and rather cold winters. The highest temperature ever recorded in the State is 50·8°C, the lowest being −12·8°C. Normally, rain falls at most places throughout the year, with a maximum in winter or spring. In Melbourne, the mean annual temperature is 14·8°C.

GOVERNMENT

Victoria was originally known as the Port Phillip District of New South Wales and was created a separate colony in 1851, with a partially elective legislature. In 1855 Responsible Government was conferred. The executive authority is vested in a Governor, appointed by the Crown, aided by an Executive Council of Ministers.

Governor of Victoria, His Excellency Rev. Dr. John Davis McCaughey, *assumed office* Feb. 18, 1986.
Lt. Governor, The Hon. Sir John McIntosh Young, K.C.M.G. (1974).

THE MINISTRY

Premier, Hon. J. Cain.
Deputy Premier and Minister of Industry, Technology and Resources, Hon. R. C. Fordham.
Arts, Hon. I. R. Cathie.
Labour, Hon. S. M. Crabb.
Treasurer, Hon. R. A. Jolly.
Community Services, Hon. C. R. T. Mathews.
Attorney General, Hon. A. McCutcheon.
Planning and Environment, and Consumer Affairs, Hon. T. W. Roper.
Local Government, Hon. J. L. Simmonds.
Property and Services, and Ethnic Affairs, Hon. P. C. Spyker.
Sport and Recreation, Hon. N. B. Trezise.
Housing and Construction, Hon. R. W. Walsh.
Water Resources and Tourism, Hon. F. N. Wilkes.
Agriculture and Rural Affairs, Hon. E. Walker.
Health, Hon. D. R. White.
Education, Hon. Caroline Hogg.
Transport, Hon. J. J. Kennan.
Conservation, Forests and Lands, Hon. Joan Kirner.

AGENT-GENERAL IN LONDON

Agent-General, Mr. K. Finnin, Victoria House, Melbourne Place, Strand, WC2B 4LG.

THE LEGISLATURE

Parliament consists of a *Legislative Council* of 44 members, elected for the 22 Provinces for 8 years, one-half retiring every 4 years; and a *Legislative Assembly* of 88 members, elected for a maximum duration of 4 years. Voting is compulsory.

President of the Legislative Council, Hon.
R. A. MacKenzie $A83,349
Speaker of the Legislative Assembly, Hon.
C. T. Edmunds 83,349

THE JUDICATURE

There is a Supreme Court with a Chief Justice and 21 Puisne Judges, a County Court and Magistrates' Courts.

Chief Justice, Supreme Court, Hon. Sir
John Young, K.C.M.G. $A112,996
Chief Judge, County Court, Hon. G. R. D.
Waldron $A100,077

EDUCATION

Primary education is compulsory, secular and free between the ages of 6 and 15. At July 1, 1987, there were 1,585 Government Primary Schools, 22 Primary–Secondary Schools and 399 Secondary Schools attended by 293,948 primary students and 238,824 secondary students. In addition there are technical and further education institutions and Colleges of Advanced Education.

At July 1, 1987, 253,086 pupils attended 729 non-Government schools, 502 of which were Roman Catholic.

There are four State-aided Universities.

FINANCE

Revenue and expenditure from the Consolidated Fund, and the debt of Victoria were:—

	1984–85	1985–86
Revenue	$A8,827,256,489	$A9,658,600,000
Expenditure	8,827,728,064	9,686,300,000
Debt	5,720,919,563	5,944,900,000

Banking, etc.—State Savings Bank deposits at June 30, 1986, amounted to $A8,059,400,000; in addition, deposits in the Commonwealth Savings Bank (in the State of Victoria) amounted to $A2,635,000,000, and in other savings banks $A5,891,300,000.

PRODUCTION AND INDUSTRY

The gross value of primary production (excluding mining and quarrying) in 1986–87 was $A4,020,600,000, crops $A1,494,600,000, livestock $A2,526,100,000. The local value of production of primary industries, excluding mining, was $A3,628,200,000. Wool, wheat, flour, butter, livestock, fruits, milk and cream, meats, poultry and eggs are staple products.

Livestock.—There were on establishments with agricultural activity on March 31, 1987, 28,102,000 sheep, 3,583,000 cattle, and 431,832 pigs. The quantity of wool produced in 1986–87 was valued at $A726,200,000.

Minerals.—Minerals raised include oil and natural gas, brown coal, limestone, clays and stone for construction material. Production of brown coal in 1985–86 amounted to 33,311,698 tonnes.

Crude Oil and Natural Gas.—In 1965 natural gas was first discovered in commercial quantities in the offshore waters of the Gippsland Basin in eastern Victoria and in 1966–67, three more valuable oilfields were located in the same general area. These fields are still the largest yet found in Australia. Following the development of the four fields, commercial gas and crude oil came on stream in October, 1969. Production from the Victorian fields during the financial year 1985–86 was: stabilized crude oil, 25,766 megalitres; treated natural gas, 5,506 gigalitres; commercial propane, 1,535 megalitres, and commercial ethane, 159 gigalitres.

Secondary Industry.—In 1984–85 there were 12,229 manufacturing establishments in which 256,230 males and 108,212 females were employed. Value added in the course of manufacture by all manufacturing establishments with four or more persons employed was $A13,179 million.

OVERSEAS TRADE

The export trade (excluding inter-state trade) consists largely of agricultural and mining products, machinery and transport equipment. The principal overseas imports of the State are apparel and textiles, electrical and other machines and machinery, motor vehicles and tractors, metals and metal manufactures, iron and steel, chemicals, petroleum and petroleum products, artificial resins and plastic materials.

	1985–86	1986–87
Imports	$A12,408,800,000	$A13,743,000,000
Exports	6,819,300,000	7,398,000,000

TRANSPORT

Motor Vehicle Registration.—The number of vehicles on the register at June 30, 1986, was: cars and stationwagons, 1,972,900; utilities and panel vans, 195,200; trucks and buses, 227,000, and motor cycles, 81,800.

CAPITAL.—ΨMelbourne, had a resident population at June 30, 1987, estimated at 2,964,800. Other urban centres are ΨGeelong, 149,310; Ballarat, 79,770; Bendigo, 66,840; Shepparton-Mooroopna, 39,100; ΨWarrnambool, 23,800; Wodonga, 23,620.

WESTERN AUSTRALIA

Includes all that portion of the continent west of 129° E. long., the most westerly point being in 113° 9′ E. long. and from 13° 44′ to 35° 8′ S. lat. Its extreme length is 1,480 miles, and 1,000 miles from east to west; total area 975,920 sq. miles (2,527,621 sq. km.).

POPULATION.—At June 1987, the estimated resident population was 1,500,507.

Births, deaths and marriages were:

	1986	1987p
Births	24,175	23,271
Deaths	9,315	8,889
Marriages	10,379	10,150

p = provisional

Religions

Census of 1986—Anglican Church 371,302, Roman Catholics 347,695, Uniting Church 82,876, and Presbyterians 31,641.

PHYSIOGRAPHY

Large areas of the State, for some hundreds of miles inland, are hilly and even mountainous, although the altitude, so far as ascertained, rises nowhere above that of Mount Meharry (4,097 ft.) in the northwest division or that of Bluff Knoll (3,640 ft.) in the Stirling Range in the south-west. The coastal regions are undulating, with an interior slope to the unsettled central portion of Australia. The Darling and Hamersley ranges of the west have a seaward slope to the Indian Ocean, into which flow many streams, notably the Preston, Collie, Murray, Swan, Murchison, Gascoyne, Ashburton, Fortescue and De Grey. In the north the Fitzroy flows from the King Leopold ranges into the Indian Ocean, and the Drysdale and Ord into the Timor Sea. The greater portion of the State may be described as an immense tableland, with an average elevation of 1,000 to 1,500 ft. above sealevel. The climate is one of the most temperate in the world. Of the total area two-thirds is suitable for pastoral purposes.

GOVERNMENT

Western Australia was first settled by the British in 1829, and in 1870 it was granted a partially elective legislature. In 1890 responsible government was granted, and the Administration vested in a Governor, a Legislative Council, and a Legislative Assembly. The present constitution rests upon the Constitution Act, 1889, the Constitution Acts Amendment Act, 1899, and amending Acts. The Executive is vested in a Governor appointed by the Crown and aided by a Council of responsible Ministers.

The Legislative Assembly (elected February, 1986) is composed of Australian Labor Party 32, Liberal Party 19, National Party of Australia 6.

Governor of Western Australia, His Excellency Prof. Gordon Reid.

Lt. Governor and Administrator, Hon. Sir Francis Burt, K.C.M.G.

THE MINISTRY

Premier, Treasurer, Minister for Productivity, Public Sector Management, Women's Interests, Hon. P. M. Dowding $A110,710
Deputy Premier, Minister for Economic Development and Trade, Hon. D. C. Parker $A98,775

Attorney General, Minister for Budget Management, Corrective Services, Leader of the Government in the Legislative Council, Hon. J. M. Berinson.
Community Services, The Family, Youth, The Aged, Minister assisting the Minister for Women's Interests, Deputy Leader of the Government in the Legislative Council, Hon. E. K. Hallahan.
Mines, Local Government, Regional Development, Hon. J. P. Carr.
Transport, Planning, Parliamentary and Electoral Reform, Intergovernmental Relations, Leader of the House in the Legislative Assembly, Hon. R. J. Pearce.
Conservation and Land Management, Environment, Waterways, Hon. B. J. Hodge.
Agriculture, the South West, Fisheries, Hon. J. F. Grill.
Health, Hon. K. J. Wilson.
Police and Emergency Services, Minister assisting the Treasurer, Hon. I. F. Taylor.
Housing, Tourism, Racing and Gaming, Hon. P. A. Beggs.
Labour, Works and Services, Minister assisting the Minister for Productivity and Public Sector Management, Hon. G. J. Troy.
Water Resources, Small Business, the North-West, Aboriginal Affairs, Hon. E. F. Bridge.
Employment and Training, Multicultural and Ethnic Affairs, Minister assisting the Minister for Education with Technical and Further Education, Hon. G. L. Hill.
Consumer Affairs, Sport and Recreation, Hon. G. J. Edwards.
Lands, The Arts, Hon. Y. D. Henderson.
Education, Hon. C. M. Lawrence.
Ministers each receive $A89,002–$A106,023, according to location of electorate.

Agent-General in London, R. Davies, Western Australia House, 115 Strand, WC2.

THE LEGISLATURE

Parliament consists of a *Legislative Council* and a *Legislative Assembly*, elected by adult suffrage subject to qualifications of residence and registration. The qualifying age for electors for both the Legislative Council and Legislative Assembly is 18 years. There are 34 members in the Legislative Council, two from each Province, for a period of 6 years, one member from each Province retiring triennially. The Legislative Assembly is composed of 57 members, who are elected for a term of 3 years.

President of the Legislative Council, Hon. C. E. Griffiths $A82,855
Speaker of the Legislative Assembly, Hon. M. Barnett 82,855

THE JUDICATURE

Chief Justice, Hon. D. K. Malcolm $A126,500
Senior Puisne Judge, Hon. A. R. A. Wallace 115,557
Puisne Judges, Hons. P. F. Brinsden; C. H. Smith; G. A. Kennedy; W. P. Pidgeon; B. W. Rowland; E. M. Franklyn; P. L. Seaman .... *each* 112,057

EDUCATION

In 1987 there were 731 government and 245 non-government primary and secondary school campuses with 208,078 and 62,662 students respectively. The total recurrent and capital outlay expended on education (by State authorities) during the year ended June 30, 1987, was $A1,221,700,000, including grants totalling $A108,263,000 to the University of Western Australia (9,625 enrolments in 1987), to Murdoch University (4,624 enrolments in 1987) and

Curtin University (12,669 enrolments in 1987). These amounts included Commonwealth monies.

PRODUCTION AND INDUSTRY

The gross value of agricultural production in 1986–87 was: crops $A1,363,267,000; livestock slaughterings, etc., $A409,427,000; livestock products $A806,196,000; fishing and gross value of fisheries was $A172,356,000.

Crops and Livestock.—The production of wheat for grain in 1986–87 was 5,377,000 tonnes. On March 31, 1987, the livestock included 1,660,000 cattle, 33,800,000 sheep, and 304,000 pigs. Wool production in 1985–86 was 175,500 tonnes in the grease.

Manufacturing Industries.—There were 3,902 manufacturing establishments operating in the State at June 30, 1985. The total number of persons employed (including working proprietors) by these establishments at the end of June, 1985 was 66,342.

Forestry.—The forests contain some of the finest hardwoods in the world. The total quantity of sawn timber produced during 1986–87 was 316,658 cubic metres.

Minerals.—The State has large deposits of a wide range of minerals, many of which are being mined or are under development for production. The ex-mine value of all minerals produced during 1985–86 was $A4,204,100,000.

Communications.—On June 30, 1987, there were 5,553 km. of State government railway open for

general and passenger traffic; and 731 km. (Kalgoorlie-W.A. border) of the Australian National Railway. In the year ended June 30, 1987, 2,580 vessels entered Western Australian ports direct from, and 2,571 were cleared direct to, overseas. The number of registered motor vehicles at June 30, 1987, was 906,100.

FINANCE

	1985–86	1986–87
	$A	$A
Revenue	3,099,411,391	3,284,233,136
Expenditure	3,099,044,981	3,277,526,154
Public Debt (June 30)	1,589,828,314	1,575,414,004

OVERSEAS TRADE

	1985–86	1986–87
Imports	$A2,063,186,000	$A2,545,141,255
Exports	6,513,174,000	6,667,948,670

Principal overseas exports in 1986–87 included iron ore and concentrates, wheat, wool, live sheep and lambs, petroleum and petroleum products, beef and veal, gold bullion, rock lobster tails.

CAPITAL.—ΨPerth. Estimated resident population (estimate for June 30, 1987) of Perth Statistical Division, including the port of ΨFremantle, 1,083,449.

Perth stands on the right bank of the Swan River estuary, 12 miles from Fremantle.

NEW ZEALAND

AREA AND POPULATION

Islands	Area (English) Sq. Miles	Population	
		Census Mar. 24, 1981†	Census Mar. 4, 1986†
(a) Exclusive of Island Territory:			
North Island	44,281	2,322,989	2,441,615
South Island	58,093	852,748	865,469
Stewart Island	670	600*	531*
Chatham Islands	372	751*	755*
Minor Islands:			
Inhabited—			
Kermadec Islands	13	5*	5**
Campbell Island	44	10*	10**
Uninhabited—			
Three Kings	3	..	..
Snares	1	..	..
Solander	⅓	..	..
Antipodes	24	..	..
Bounty	⅓	..	..
Auckland	234	..	..
Total exclusive of Island Territory	103,736	3,175,737	3,307,084
(b) Island Territory:			
Tokelau Islands	..	1,572‖	1,595§
(c) Niue island¶.............................	..	3,226§	3,002**
Cook Islands¶.................................	..	18,000‡	17,400**
Ross Dependency..............................	175,000	..	..

* Included in North Island and South Island totals.
† Excluding members of the Armed Forces overseas—979 in 1981; 1,247 in 1986.
¶ The Cook Islands have had complete internal self-government since Aug. 4, 1965, as has Niue since Oct. 19, 1974, but Cook Islanders and Niueans remain New Zealand citizens.
‖ Nov. 2, 1981.   § Oct. 1, 1983.   ‡ Dec. 31, 1980.   ** March 31, 1983.

Vital Statistics

Year	Births	Deaths	Natural Increase	Deaths of Infants under one year	Infant Mortality per 1,000 live births	Marriages
1980	50,542	26,676	23,866	650	12·86	22,981
1981	50,794	25,150	25,644	592	11·65	23,660
1982	49,938	25,532	24,406	587	11·75	25,537
1983	50,474	25,991	24,483	633	12·54	24,678
1984	51,636	25,378	26,258	597	11·56	25,272
1985	51,798	27,480	24,318	560	10·81	24,657
1986	52,824	27,045	25,779	592	11·21	24,037
1987	55,254	27,419	27,835	554	10·03	24,443

Inter-Censal Increases

Year	Results of Census			Numerical Increase	Net Inflow or Outflow from Total Migration
	Males	Females	Total		
1966	1,343,743	1,333,176	2,676,919	261,935	+ 12,950
1971	1,430,856	1,431,775	2,862,631	185,712	+ 8,481
1976	1,562,042	1,567,341	3,129,383	266,752	+ 6,567
1981	1,578,927	1,596,810	3,175,737	46,354	− 15,328
1986	1,616,004	1,645,782	3,261,786	131,347	− 18,518

Excluding 1,936 members of the Armed Forces overseas at the time of the 1966 Census, 1,482 at the 1971 Census, 1,333 at the 1976 Census, 979 at the 1981 Census and 1,247 at the 1986 Census.

Races and Religions

Races	1981	1986	Religions	1981	1986
				per cent	per cent
Europeans..............	2,696,568	2,612,958	Church of England	25·7	24·0
Maoris	279,084	294,201	Presbyterians............	16·7	18·0
Chinese	18,480	19,206	Roman Catholics	14·3	15·2
Polynesians (other than N.Z. Maoris)	88,827	90,612	Methodists	4·7	4·7
			Baptists	1·6	2·1

PHYSIOGRAPHY

New Zealand consists of a number of islands of varying size in the South Pacific Ocean, and has also administrative responsibility for a large tract in the Antarctic Ocean. The two larger and most important islands, the North and South Islands of New Zealand, are separated by only a relatively narrow strait. The remaining islands are very much smaller and, in general, are widely dispersed over a considerable expanse of ocean. The boundaries, inclusive of the most outlying islands and dependencies, range from 33° to 53° South latitude, and from 162° East longitude to 173° West longitude.

Geographical Features.—The two principal islands have a total length of 1,040 miles, and a combined area of 102,344 sq. miles, (265,069 sq. km.). A large proportion of the surface is mountainous in character. The principal range is that of the Southern Alps, extending over the entire length of the South Island and having its culminating point in Mount Cook (12,349 ft.). The North Island mountains include several volcanoes, two of which are active, others being dormant or extinct. Mt. Ruapehu (9,175 ft.) and Mt. Ngauruhoe (7,515 ft.) are the most important. Of the numerous glaciers in the South Island, the Tasman (18 miles long by 1¼ wide), the Franz Josef and the Fox are the best known. The North Island is noted for its hot springs and geysers. For the most part the rivers are too short and rapid for navigation. The more important include the Waikato (270 miles in length), Wanganui (180), and Clutha (210). Lakes (Taupo, 234 sq. miles in area; Wakatipu, 113; and Te Anau, 133) are abundant, many of them of great beauty.

Climate.—New Zealand has a moist-temperate marine climate, but with abundant sunshine. A very important feature is the small annual range of temperature which permits of some growth of vegetation, including pasture, all the year round. Very little snow falls on the low levels even in the South Island. The mean temperature ranges from 15° C. in the North to about 9° C. in the South. Rainfall over the more settled areas in the North Island ranges from 35 to 70 inches and in the South Island from 25 to 45 inches. The total range is from approximately 13 to over 250 inches.

GOVERNMENT

The discoverers and first colonists of New Zealand were Polynesian people, ancestors of the Maoris of today. Whether there was a single colonization, several, or many, is not known. By the 13th or 14th century early exploration was over and there were well established Maori settlements.

The first European to discover New Zealand was a Dutch navigator, Abel Tasman, who sighted the coast on December 13, 1642 but did not land. It was the British explorer James Cook who circumnavigated New Zealand and landed in 1769. Traders, whalers and sealers made up the majority of Europeans in New Zealand during the 18th century and until the late 1830s, when the proportion of permanent European settlers became significant.

Largely as a result of increased British emigration, the country was annexed by the British Government in 1840. The British Governor, William Hobson, R.N., proclaimed sovereignty over the North Island by virtue of the Treaty of Waitangi, signed by him and many Maori chiefs, and over the South Island and Stewart Island by right of discovery.

On May 3, 1841, New Zealand was, by letters patent, created a separate colony distinct from New South Wales. Organized colonization on a large scale commenced in 1840 with the New Zealand company's settlement at Wellington. On Sept. 26, 1907, the designation was changed to *The Dominion of New Zealand*. The Constitution rests upon the Imperial Act of 1852, and on the New Zealand Constitution (Amendment) Act of Dec. 10, 1947. The Statute of Westminster was formally adopted by New Zealand in 1947. The executive authority is entrusted to a Governor General appointed by the Crown and aided by an Executive Council, within a Legislature consisting of one chamber, the House of Representatives.

CAPITAL.—ΨWellington, in the North Island (estimated population March 1987, Wellington statistical division, 351,000).

Other large centres; ΨAuckland, 899,200; ΨChristchurch, 333,200; ΨDunedin, 113,300; Palmerston North, 93,700; Hamilton, 169,000; Ψ Napier-Hastings, 115,700.

CURRENCY.—New Zealand Dollar ($NZ) of 100 Cents.

FLAG.—Blue ground, with Union Jack in top left quarter, four five-pointed red stars with white borders on the fly. On June 20, 1968, a naval ensign bearing the Southern Cross was adopted, replacing the British white ensign.

NATIONAL ANTHEM.—God Save The Queen/God Defend New Zealand.

NATIONAL DAY.—February 6 (Waitangi Day).

Governor General and Staff

Governor General and Commander-in-Chief of New Zealand, His Excellency The Most Rev. Sir Paul Alfred Reeves, G.C.M.G., *sworn in*, Nov. 20, 1985.
Official Secretary, Paul Canham.

THE EXECUTIVE COUNCIL

His Excellency the GOVERNOR GENERAL

Prime Minister and Minister of Education, Hon. David Lange.
Deputy P.M., Attorney-General and Minister of Justice, Hon. Geoffrey Palmer.
Overseas Trade and Marketing, Tourism, Recreation and Sport, Hon. Michael Moore.
Finance, Hon. Roger Douglas.
State-Owned Enterprises, Postmaster General, Works and Development, Hon. Richard Prebble.
Maori Affairs, Hon. Koro Wetere.
Health, Trade and Industry, Hon. David Caygill.
Foreign Affairs, Disarmament and Arms Control, Hon. Russell Marshall.
Internal Affairs, Hon. Dr. Michael Bassett.
Minister of State and Leader of the House, Hon. Jonathan Hunt.
Defence, Hon. Bob Tizard.
Agriculture and Fisheries, Hon. Colin Moyle.
Labour and Immigration, Hon. Stan Rodger.
Employment, Hon. Phil Goff.
Women's Affairs, Consumer Affairs and Statistics, Hon. Mrs. Margaret Shields.
Police, Forestry and Lands, Hon. Peter Tapsell.
Housing and Conservation, Hon. Mrs. Helen Clark.
Social Welfare, Hon. Dr. Michael Cullen.
Transport and Civil Aviation, Hon. Bill Jeffries.
Energy and Regional Development, Hon. David Butcher.

The Prime Minister receives $141,550 per annum with an allowance of $23,400 for expenses of his office and the Ministerial residence. The salary of each Minister holding a portfolio is $98,800 with expense allowance of $9,600 and that of each Minister without portfolio $77,150, with $7,150 expense allowance.

NEW ZEALAND HIGH COMMISSION

New Zealand House, Haymarket, SW1Y 4TQ
[01-930 8422]

High Commissioner, His Excellency Bryce Harland (1985).
Deputy High Commissioner, R. A. Farrell.
Minister (Administration), P. K. Munn.
Minister (Commercial), R. J. Turnbull.
Head, Defence Liaison Staff, Brig. R. J. Andrews, O.B.E.

THE LEGISLATURE

Parliament consists of a House of Representatives consisting of 97 members elected for 3 years. There are four Maori electorates. Women have been entitled to vote since 1893, and to be elected Members of the House of Representatives since the passing of the Women's Parliamentary Rights Act, 1919. Following the General Election of August 15, 1987, the state of the parties in Parliament was Labour 58 and National Party 39.

Members of the House receive $NZ54,200 *per annum*, with an allowance of $NZ4,800 *per annum* for expenses, plus an electorate allowance. The Leader of the Opposition receives $NZ98,800 *per annum* and $NZ9,600 *per annum* for expenses, plus house and travelling allowances.

Speaker of the House of Representatives,
　Hon. T. K. Burke (*plus expense allowance and residential quarters in Parliament House*) $NZ91,600

THE JUDICATURE

The judicial system comprises a High Court and a Court of Appeal; also District Courts having both civil and criminal jurisdiction.

Chief Justice, Rt. Hon. Sir Ronald Davison, G.B.E., C.M.G. $NZ144,500
President, Court of Appeal, Rt. Hon. Sir Robin Cooke, K.B.E. 139,700
Judges, Rt. Hons. Sir Ivor Richardson; Sir Duncan McMullin; E. J. Somers; M. E. Casey; G. E. Bisson 134,900
High Court Puisne Judges, Hons. M. F. Chilwell; J. F. Jeffries; R. I. Barker; J. B. Sinclair; A. D. Holland; T. M. Thorp; L. M. Greig; M. Hardie-Boys; J. H. Wallace; J. T. Eichelbaum; P. G. Hillyer; R. G. Gallen; D. L. Tompkins; J. S. Henry; R. A. Heron; N. W. Williamson; A. A. T. Ellis; R. P. Smellie; R. E. Wylie; R. A. McGechan; J. A. Doogue; A. P. C. Tipping; N. C. Anderson; T. M. Gault; J. B. Robertson. 130,100
High Court Administrative Divn., Rt. Hon. Sir Ronald Davison (*Chief Justice*); Hons. M. F. Chilwell; J. F. Jeffries; A. D. Holland; L. M. Greig; D. L. Tompkins.
Chief Judge, Labour Court, J. R. P. Horn.

POLICE

On March 31, 1987 the strength of the New Zealand Police Force was 5,291 of all ranks, equivalent to 1 for every 627 of the population. Total police expenditure for the year 1986–87 was $NZ321,000,000.

DEFENCE

A unified Ministry of Defence which retained the three single services was set up in 1964. The Minister of Defence is responsible for national defence, and, with the other members of the Defence Council, commands and administers the three services:

The *Royal New Zealand Navy* consists of 2,626 officers and ratings as at March 31, 1987, as well as the Volunteer Reserve in four divisions. The strength is four frigates, one survey ship and one research vessel, as well as patrol and inshore survey craft.

The *New Zealand Army* consists of the Regular Force, the Territorial Force and the Army Reserve. The strength of the Regular Force at March 31, 1987 was 5,848, and of the Territorial Force and Army Reserve, 5,759. The Army is structured to provide a Regular Force battalion group which is available for rapid deployment on military operations or civil assistance tasks, as well as a framework of integrated Regular Force/Territorial Force Units as a basis for expansion when required. One infantry battalion is based in Singapore.

The *Royal New Zealand Air Force* had a Regular Force strength of 4,195 at March 31, 1987, with 1,016 Territorial and Reserve Forces. Operational units include fighter ground attack, maritime, medium and short-range transport, and helicopter squadrons, and flying training units. A helicopter support unit is based in Singapore.

FINANCE

Into the Consolidated Account (New Zealand's main public account) are paid the proceeds of income tax, sales tax, customs and excise duties and other taxes, also interest, profits from trading under-takings, and departmental receipts (departmental expenditure is included gross). Revenue from taxation is also paid into the National Roads Fund principally from a tax on motor spirits and registration and licence fees for motor vehicles.

Revenue and expenditure for year ended March 31 ($NZ'000):

	1986	1987
Revenue	18,317,591	32,039,492
Expenditure*	18,317,591	32,039,492

Revenue from taxation was ($NZ'000):

	1986	1987
Total...............	14,235,870	17,408,111
Consolidated Account........	13,812,265	16,989,095
National Roads Fund...........	423,605	419,016

*Includes ($NZ'000):

	1986	1987
Education	2,028,416	2,617,899
Social Welfare	5,363,389	6,175,123
Health	2,312,476	2,961,132
Development of Industry	1,697,287	11,531,500
Defence	870,456	1,095,961
Debt services	3,622,430	4,411,897
Law and order	458,872	622,022

DEBT

The gross *Public Debt* amounted on March 31, 1987, to $NZ42,478,877,000 of which $NZ5,872,091,000 was domiciled in Europe, $NZ8,968,997,000 in U.S.A. and $NZ6,055,083,000 in Japan; $NZ1,608,000 represented World Bank loans.

BANKING

There are four trading banks, two of which are predominantly New Zealand banks. At Dec. 24, 1986, assets of all trading banks in respect of New Zealand business amounted to $NZ19,478,700,000, liabilities, $NZ16,984,300,000; New Zealand's official overseas reserves at Dec. 1987, amounted to $NZ4,982,100,000.

The Reserve Bank of New Zealand notes are the legal tender. Value of notes in circulation on March 31, 1987 amounted to $NZ1,065,120,000.

EDUCATION

Schools are free and attendance is compulsory between the ages of 6 and 15. At July 1986 there were 429,611 pupils attending public primary schools, and 11,417 pupils attending registered private primary schools. The secondary education of boys and girls in the cities and large towns is carried on in 315 state secondary schools, and 21 private secondary schools. The total number of pupils receiving full-time secondary education in July 1986 was 231,012 and in addition there were 127,658 students attending technical classes including 33,598 receiving part-time tuition from the Technical Correspondence School. Almost all the students attending technical classes are part-time. There are six universities; the Lincoln university college of agriculture is associated with the University of Canterbury. The university system is co-ordinated by the University Grants Committee. The Universities had a total of 61,979 students in 1986.

The total expenditure on education out of public funds in 1986–87 is estimated at $NZ2,598,185.

PRODUCTION AND INDUSTRY

Gross Agricultural Production (Gross Output)

	Year ended March	
	1985–86	1986–87
	$NZ(million)	
Sheep	400	646
Wool	1,069	1,214
Cattle	779	974
Pigs	104	116
Dairy products	1,529	1,130
Crops and seeds	349	304
Fruit, nuts, oilseeds	424	621
Vegetables	266	364
Poultry products	176	170
Agricultural services	445	446
Other horticulture	173	208
Other products n.e.c.	151	179
Value of change in livestock	386	−34
Sales of live animals	630	607
Gross Output	6,878	6,945

Agricultural and Pastoral Production

	1986	1987
*Wheat, metric tons	379,700	336,800
*Wool, metric tons	n/a	n/a
†Butter, metric tons	299,600	n/a
†Cheese, metric tons	127,270	n/a
‡Stock Slaughtered—		
Lambs, No.	34,669,000	31,656,000
Sheep, No.	6,709,000	9,295,000
Cattle, No.	1,882,000	2,318,000
Calves, No.	952,000	857,000
Pigs, No.	843,000	774,000

* Year ended June 30.
† Year ended May 31.
‡ Year ended Sept. 30. Provisional.

Forestry.—The output of sawn timber for 1987 was 2,079,000 cubic metres, of which 1,966,000 cubic metres represented exotic varieties, mainly radiata pine.

Livestock.—Livestock on farms at June 30, 1987, included 3,195,000 dairy cattle (of which 2,551,000 were dairy cows in milk during season), 4,804,000 beef cattle (of which 1,586,000 were beef breeding cows), and 426,000 pigs. Sheep numbered 64,244,000.

Minerals.—Non-metallic minerals such as coal, clay, limestone and dolomite are both economically and industrially more important than metallic ones. Coal output in 1986 was 2,517,000 tonnes. Of the metals, the most important is ironsand, which is mined for export. Natural gas deposits in Taranaki are being used for electricity generation and as a premium fuel, piped to an increasing number of North Island centres.

TRADE

	1985–86	1986–87
Imports (v.f.d.)	NZ10,468,300,000	$NZ10,803,400,000
Exports (f.o.b.)	10,571,700,000	12,107,200,000

Trade with U.K.

	1986	1987
	('000)	('000)
Imports from U.K.	$NZ985,500	$NZ1,060,700
Exports to U.K.	933,900	1,125,100

New Zealand produce exported to the U.K. in the 12 months ending June, 1987, included butter, valued at $NZ232,481,000; beef ($NZ4,343,000); wool ($NZ160,972,000); lamb ($NZ309,523,000).

COMMUNICATIONS

Railways.—The national railway system is owned and operated by the New Zealand Railways Corporation. In March, 1987, there were 4,273 km. of Government railway in operation.

Motor Vehicles.—In the year ended June 30, 1986 there were 2,493,908 licensed motor vehicles. These included 1,558,307 cars and 143,165 motor and power cycles.

Shipping.—During 1987 the vessels entered from overseas ports numbered 3,060 (net tonnage 14,113,000) and those cleared for overseas 3,050 (net tonnage 14,107,000).

Civil Aviation—Figures are for scheduled services in the year to end Dec. 1985:

	Domestic Flights	International Flights
Kilometres flown	37,281	
Passengers carried	3,255	2,061
Freight carried (tonnes)	42,200	92,227
Mail carried (tonnes)	—	3,936

BRITISH HIGH COMMISSION
Reserve Bank of New Zealand Building,
2 The Terrace (P.O. Box 1812), Wellington, 1
[Wellington 726-049]

High Commissioner, His Excellency Ronald Archer Campbell Byatt, C.M.G. (1988).
Deputy High Commissioner, Head of Chancery, S. I. Soutar.
Defence Adviser, Gp. Capt. J. G. Sheldon.
First Secretaries, A. B. Cawthorn (*Agriculture and Food*); H. A. Payne (*Commercial*); J. R. Setterfield (*Chancery, Information*).
Second Secretaries, R. H. House (*Consular and Administration*); T. A. Torlot (*Chancery*).
Attaché, S. Bailey (*Consular*).

British Council Representative, A. C. Ramsay.

BRITISH CHAMBER OF COMMERCE FOR AUSTRALIA AND NEW ZEALAND, P.O. Box 141, Manuka, A.C.T. 2603, Australia; U.K. OFFICE, Suite 615, 6th Floor The Linen Hall, 162/8 Regent Street, W1R 5TB.

THE TERRITORIES OF NEW ZEALAND

In addition to North, South, Stewart and Chatham Islands:—

The Three Kings (discovered by Tasman on the Feast of the Epiphany), in 34° 9′ S. lat. and 172° 8′ 8″ E. long. *Auckland Islands*, about 290 miles south of Bluff Harbour, in 50° 32′ S. lat. and 166° 13′ E. long. *Antipodes Group*, 40° 41′ 15″ S. lat. and 178° 43′ E. long. *Bounty Islands*, 47° 4′ 43″ S. lat., 170° 0′ 30″ E. long. *Snares Islands and Solander*. All these islands are uninhabited.

The Kermadec Group (population normally 9 or 10) between 29° 10′ to 31° 30′ S. lat., and 177° 45′ to 179° W. long., includes Raoul or Sunday, Macauley, Curtis Islands, L'Esperance, and some islets. All the inhabitants are government employees at a meteorological station. *Campbell Island* (used as a weather station).

TOKELAU (OR UNION ISLANDS)

A group of atolls (Fakaofo, Nukunono and Atafu) (estimated population 1,627 at Oct. 1, 1984), proclaimed part of New Zealand as from Jan. 1, 1948.

THE ROSS DEPENDENCY

The *Ross Dependency*, placed under the jurisdiction of New Zealand by Order in Council dated July 30, 1923, and defined as all the islands and territories between 160° E. and 150° W. longitude which are situated south of the 60° S. parallel. The Ross Dependency includes Edward VII Land and portions of Victoria Land. For some years there have been permanent bases in the area, staffed by survey and scientific personnel.

ASSOCIATED STATES

COOK ISLANDS

Included in the boundaries of New Zealand since June, 1901, the group consists of the islands of Rarotonga, Aitutaki, Mangaia, Atiu, Mauke, Mitiaro, Manuae, Takutea, Palmerston, Penrhyn or Tongareva, Manihiki, Rakahanga, Suwarrow, Pukapuka or Danger and Nassau. The total population of the group was estimated at 18,000 (1985 U. N. estimate). The chief exports of the Cook Islands are fruit juice, clothing, copra, bananas, citrus fruit and pulp, and pearl shell. The trade is chiefly with New Zealand, Australia, Japan, the U.K. and the U.S.A. The New Zealand Government continues to give financial aid to the Cook Islands.

The High Commissioner of the Cook Islands is employed in a dual role, since he represents both the Queen and the New Zealand Government. Since Aug. 4, 1965, the Islands have enjoyed complete internal self-government, executive power being in the hands of a Cabinet consisting of the Premier and five other ministers. The new Constitution Act was passed by the New Zealand Parliament in November 1964, but did not come into force until it had been endorsed by the 22-member Legislative Assembly of the Cook Islands, elected in April 1965.

The New Zealand citizenship of the Cook Islanders is embodied in the Constitution, and assurances have been given that the changed status of the Islands will in no way affect the consideration of subsidies or the right of free entry into New Zealand for exports from the group.

New Zealand Representative, L. A. Beath.

NIUE

Geographically part of Cook Islands, but administered separately. Population (1985 U.N. estimate) of 3,000.

A New Zealand Representative is stationed at Niue, which since October 1974 has been self-governing in free association with New Zealand, which is responsible for external affairs and defence, and continues to give financial aid. Executive power is in the hands of a Premier and a Cabinet of 3 drawn from the Assembly of 20 members.

New Zealand Representative, M. J. Taylor.

ANTIGUA AND BARBUDA
(State of Antigua and Barbuda)

AREA, POPULATION, ETC.—Antigua and Barbuda comprises the islands of Antigua (108 sq. miles (279 sq. km.)), Barbuda (62 sq. miles (160 sq. km.)) 25 miles north of Antigua, and Redonda (⅓ square mile; 1·2 sq. km.) 25 miles south-west of Antigua. Antigua is part of the Leeward Islands in the Eastern Caribbean and lies 17° 3′ N. and 61° 48′ W. It is distinguished from the rest of the Leeward group by its absence of high hills and forest, and a drier climate than most of the W. Indies. Barbuda, formerly a possession of the Codrington family, is very flat with a large lagoon and well wooded in the north east. Antigua was first settled by the English in 1632, and was granted to

Lord Willoughby by Charles II. Antigua has a population of 80,000, (1985 U.N. estimate); Barbuda, 1,500, and Redonda is uninhabited.

CAPITAL.—VSt. John's. Population, 30,000. The town of Barbuda is Codrington.

CURRENCY.—East Caribbean Dollar (EC$) of 100 Cents.

FLAG.—Inverted triangle (centred on a red field) divided horizontally into three bands of black over blue over white; rising sun device in gold on black band.

NATIONAL ANTHEM.—"Fair Antigua and Barbuda".

NATIONAL DAY.—November 1 (Independence Day).

GOVERNMENT

Antigua became internally self-governing in 1967 and fully independent on Nov. 1, 1981, as a constitutional monarchy with H.M. The Queen as Head of State, represented by the Governor General. There is a Senate of 17 appointed members and a House of Representatives elected every 5 years. The Attorney-General may be appointed.

Governor General, Sir Wilfred Ebenezer Jacobs, G.C.M.G., G.C.V.O., O.B.E., Q.C.

Cabinet

Prime Minister, Defence, and Information, Rt. Hon. Vere C. Bird (Sr).
Deputy P.M. and Minister for Foreign Affairs, Economic Development, Tourism and Energy, Hon. Lester Bird.
Public Utilities and Aviation, Hon. Robin Yearwood.
Finance, Hon. John E. St. Luce.
Education, Culture and Youth Affairs and Sport, Hon. Reuben H. Harris.
Labour and Health, Hon. Adolphus Freeland.
Home Affairs, Hon. Christopher M. O'Mard.
Agriculture, Fisheries and Lands, Housing, Hon. Hilroy Humphreys.
Attorney General (apptd), Hon. Keith Ford.
Public Works, and Communications, Hon. V. C. Bird (Jnr).
Ministers within a Ministry:
　Foreign Affairs, Economic Development, Tourism and Energy, Hon. Hugh Marshall; Hon. Molwyn Joseph.
　Public Utilities and Aviation, Hon. Eustace Cochrane.
　Education, Culture and Youth Affairs, Hon. D. Christian.
　Finance and Port Authority, Hon. Henderson St. Clair Simon.

HIGH COMMISSION FOR
ANTIGUA AND BARBUDA
15 Thayer Street, W1M 5LD
[01 486 7073]

High Commissioner, His Excellency James Thomas (1987).

ECONOMY

Tourism is the main feature of the economy, with several hotels (and a number under construction) to take advantage of the many white sand beaches which made Antigua one of the first Caribbean islands to attract tourists.

For many years sugar was the dominant crop but is now produced primarily for local consumption. Areas of agricultural development include livestock, sea island cotton, corn (for cornmeal production) and improved vegetable and fruit production.

FINANCE

	1987	1988*
Revenue	EC$181,100,000	EC$217,000,000
Expenditure (recurrent) ...	214,400,000	231,700,000

*estimated

Trade with U.K.

	1986	1987
Imports from U.K.	£17,774,000	£19,334,000
Exports to U.K.	2,069,000	4,271,000

BRITISH HIGH COMMISSION
38 St. Mary's Street (P.O. 483), St. John's
[St. John's 462 0008/9]

High Commissioner, (resides at Bridgetown, Barbados).

Resident Representative, B. Taylor (*First Secretary*).

THE BAHAMAS
(The Commonwealth of The Bahamas)

AREA, POPULATION, ETC.—The Bahama Islands are an archipelago lying in the North Atlantic Ocean between 20° 55′–25° 42′ N. lat; 72° 35′–79° 35′ W. long. They extend from the coast of Florida on the northwest almost to Haiti on the south-east. The group consists of 700 islands, of which 30 are inhabited and 2,400 cays comprising an area of more than 5,380 sq. miles, (19,935 sq. km.). The population, at the census of 1980 was 237,090. The principal islands include: Abaco, Acklins, Andros, Berry Islands, Bimini, Cat Island, Crooked Island, Eleuthera, Exumas, Grand Bahama, Harbour Island, Inagua, Long Island, Mayaguana, New Providence (on which is located the capital, Nassau), Ragged Island, Rum Cay, San Salvador and Spanish Wells. San Salvador was the first landfall in the New World of Christopher Columbus on October 12, 1492.

The Bahamas were settled by British subjects when the islands were deserted. The ownership of The Bahamas was taken over in 1782 by the Spanish, but the Treaty of Versailles in 1783 restored them to the British.

CAPITAL.—ΨNassau. Population (1980 census), 135,437.

CURRENCY.—Bahamian Dollar of 100 Cents.

FLAG.—Horizontal stripes of aquamarine, gold and aquamarine, with a black equilateral triangle on the hoist.

NATIONAL ANTHEM.—March on, Bahamaland.

NATIONAL DAY.—July 10 (Independence Day).

GOVERNMENT

The Bahamas gained independence on July 10, 1973. The Head of State is H.M. Queen Elizabeth II, represented in the islands by a Governor General. There is a Senate of 16 members and an elected House of Assembly of 49 members.

Acting Governor General, His Excellency Sir Henry Milton Taylor (1988).

Cabinet

Prime Minister and Minister of Finance, Rt. Hon. Sir Lynden Pindling, K.C.M.G.

Deputy P.M., Foreign Affairs, Tourism, and Public Personnel, Hon. Clement T. Maynard.

Attorney General, Minister of Education and Government Leader in House of Assembly, Hon. Paul L. Adderley.

Works and Utilities, Hon. Darrell E. Rolle.

Employment and Immigration, Hon. Alfred T. Maycock.

Transport, and Local Government, Hon. Philip M. Bethel.

Health, Hon. Dr. Norman Gay.

Housing and National Insurance, Hon. George W. Mackey.

Agriculture, Trade and Industry, Hon. Ervin Knowles.

Youth, Sports and Community Affairs, Hon. Peter J. Bethell.

President of Court of Appeal, Kenneth C. Henry.

Chief Justice, Hon. Philip Telford-Georges.

BAHAMAS HIGH COMMISSION
Bahamas House, 10 Chesterfield Street, W1X 8AH
[01–408 4488]

High Commissioner, Her Excellency Dr. Patricia Rodgers (1988).

ECONOMY

Tourism is the economic mainstay of The Bahamas, employing about two-thirds of the labour force. It provides about two-thirds of Government revenue and about half the country's foreign exchange earnings. The second main industry is international banking and trust business, The Bahamas' absence of any direct taxation and internal stability enabling the country to become one of the world's leading financial centres.

Agricultural production is mainly of fresh vegetables, fruit, meat and eggs for the domestic market, and crawfish, mostly for export. There are large reserves of aragonite, and reserves of limestone and salt, all of which are being commercially exploited. Freeport is the country's leading industrial centre, with a chemicals and a pharmaceutical plant, an oil trans-shipment and storage terminal, and port and bunkering facilities. There are also a brewery and a rum distillery on New Providence.

EDUCATION

Education is compulsory between the ages of 5 and 14. More than 59,000 students are enrolled in Ministry of Education and Independent schools in New Providence and the Family Islands.

COMMUNICATIONS

The main ports are Nassau (New Providence), Freeport (Grand Bahama), Mathew Town (Inagua). International air services are operated from Abaco, Bimini, Eleuthera, Exuma, Grand Bahama and New Providence. About 50 smaller airports and landing strips facilitate services between the islands, the services being provided by Bahamasair, the national carrier. There are roads on the larger islands, and roads are under construction on the smaller islands. There are no railways. Wireless and telephone services are in operation to all parts of the world.

FINANCE AND TRADE

	1986	1987p.
Public revenue	B$381·1m	B$398·7m
Expenditure	399·7m	436·0m

p. provisional

Trade with U.K.

	1986	1987
Imports from U.K.	£95,816,000	£27,063,000
Exports to U.K.	10,266,000	15,943,000

The imports are chiefly foodstuffs, manufactured articles, building material, vehicles and machinery, chemicals and petroleum. The chief exports are rum, petroleum, hormones, salt, crawfish and aragonite.

BRITISH HIGH COMMISSION
Bitco Building, East St.
P.O. Box N7516, Nassau.
[Nassau 325-7471]

High Commissioner, His Excellency Colin Garth
Mays, C.M.G. (1986).
Deputy High Commissioner, P. H. Johnson (*Head of
Chancery*).

BANGLADESH
(Ghana Praja Tantri Bangladesh)

AREA, POPULATION, CLIMATE, ETC.—The People's
Republic of Bangladesh consists of the territory
which was formerly East Pakistan (the old province
of East Bengal and the Sylhet district of Assam),
covering an area of 55,598 sq. miles (143,998 sq. km.)
in the region of the Gangetic delta, and has a
population (1987 estimate) of just over 100 million.

The country is crossed by a network of navigable
rivers, including the eastern arms of the Ganges, the
Jamuna (Brahmaputra) and the Meghna, flowing
into the Bay of Bengal. The climate is tropical and
monsoon; hot and extremely humid during the
summer, and mild and dry during the short winter.
The rainfall is heavy, varying from 50 inches to 135
inches in different districts and the bulk of it falls
during monsoon season from June to September.

CAPITAL.—Dhaka. Population (1986 estimate),
4,047,000.

CURRENCY.—Taka of 100 Poisha.

FLAG.—Red circle on a bottle-green ground.

NATIONAL ANTHEM—Amar Sonar Bangla.

NATIONAL DAY.—March 26 (Independence Day).

GOVERNMENT

Prior to becoming East Pakistan, the territory had
been part of British India. It acceded to Pakistan in
October, 1947, which became a Republic on March 23,
1956.

By a proclamation of March 26, 1971, Bangladesh
purported to secede from the central government,
and a government-in-exile was set up in April in
Calcutta. The short war between India and Pakistan,
in both the East and the West, and India's overwhelm-
ing defeat of the Pakistani Army in the East, brought
about a *de facto* secession of the East wing. The Indo-
Pakistan war was concluded on December 16, 1971,
and Mr. Zulfiqar Ali Bhutto became President of
Pakistan on December 20. Sheikh Mujib was sworn
in as Prime Minister of Bangladesh on January 12,
1972. Pakistan and Bangladesh accorded one another
mutual recognition in Feb. 1974 and established
diplomatic relations in Jan. 1976.

From 1975 a non-political administration ran the
country under martial law. A Presidential election
was held on June 3, 1978, and President Zia was
elected by a considerable majority. Martial law was
subsequently lifted. Zia was assassinated in May 1981
in an unsuccessful coup, but the military, led by Lt.-
Gen. Ershad, took over in March 1982 and and martial
law was again imposed. Following elections in May
1986 a civilian Cabinet was appointed. Presidential
elections were held on Oct. 15, 1986 and Ershad
gained a substantial majority. Martial law was
subsequently lifted on Nov. 10 and the 1972 Constitution fully restored.

Parliament was dissolved by President Ershad on
December 6, 1987 amid growing political turmoil.
Parliamentary elections were held on March 3, 1988
and were boycotted by the country's main political
parties. In the new Parliament which convened on
April 25, the Jatiya Party of President Ershad had a
two-thirds majority. However, in July 1988 Ershad

prorogued Parliament and further elections seem
likely.

President, Hossain Mohammed Ershad.
Vice President, Justice A. K. M. Nurul Islam.

Council of Ministers
(as at July 6, 1988)

*Prime Minister and Minister for Industries, Law and
Justice,* Moudud Ahmed.
*Deputy P.M. and Minister for Home Affairs, Health
and Family Planning,* Prof. M. A. Matin.
Deputy P.M. and Political Adviser to the President,
Kazi Zafar Ahmed.
*Deputy P.M. and Minister for Local Government,
Rural Development and Co-operatives,* Shah Moa-
zeem Hossain.
Commerce, Lt.-Col. H. M. A. Ghaffar.
Finance, Maj.-Gen. M. A. Munim.
Energy and Mineral Resources, A. B. M. Gholam
Mostafa.
Foreign Affairs, Humayun Rasheed Chowdhury.
Information, Mahbubur Rahman.
Jute, Korban Ali.
Land, Mostafa Jamal Haider.
Communications, Anwar Hossain.
Civil Aviation and Tourism, A. Sattar.
Education and Establishment, Anisul Islam Mahmud.
Agriculture and Fisheries and Livestock, Maj.-Gen.
Mahmudul Hasan.
Food, Sardar Amzad Hossain.
Planning, Air Vice Marshal A. K. Khondaker.
Ports and Shipping, Mayeedul Islam.
Relief and Rehabilitation, Kazi Firoz Rasid.
Religious Affairs, Mufti Maulana Mohammad Wak-
kas.
Irrigation, Water Development and Flood Control,
Nazimuddin-al-Azad.
Labour and Manpower, Sirajul Hossain Khan.
Textiles, Zafar Imam.
Works, Sheikh Sahidul Islam.
Social Welfare and Women's Affairs, Rezwanul Huq
Chowdhury.
Youth and Sports, Sunil Gupta.
Posts and Telecommunications, Iqbal Hossain Chowd-
hury.
Cultural Affairs, Nur Muhammad Khan.
Tribal Affairs, Binoy Kumar Dewan.
Dhaka Municipal Corporation, Col. M. A. Malek.

BANGLADESH HIGH COMMISSION
28 Queen's Gate, SW7 5JA
[01–584 0081–4/589 4842–4]

High Commissioner, His Excellency Maj.-Gen. K. M.
Safiullah (1987).

RELIGION

The faith of over 90 per cent of the population is
Islam. Islam has been constitutionally declared the
state religion of Bangladesh.

LANGUAGE

The state language is Bengali. Use of Bengali is
compulsory in all government departments. English,
however, is understood and is used widely as an
unofficial second language.

EDUCATION

Primary education is free but not universal. Most
primary schools are under government management.
The majority of secondary schools and colleges are
privately managed, but many receive government
grants. There are six Universities. In 1981 literacy

was estimated at 23·8 per cent of the whole of Bangladesh; 31 per cent of the male population and 16 per cent of the female population.

TRANSPORT AND COMMUNICATIONS

Principal seaports are Chittagong and Mongla. The Bangladesh Shipping Corporation has been set up by the Government to operate the Bangladesh merchant fleet. The principal airports are Dhaka, (Zia International) and Chittagong. The international airline, Bangladesh Biman, serves Europe, the Middle East, South and South-East Asia, and an internal network.

There are about 6,880 miles of roads in Bangladesh; 4,724 miles are metalled. There are 2,798 miles of railway track.

Radio Bangladesh is the main national broadcasting service. A television service was introduced in 1965 and colour transmissions began in 1981.

ECONOMY

Bangladesh is a principal producer of raw jute. Other agricultural products are rice, tea, oil seeds, pulses, and sugar cane. The chief industries are jute, cotton, tea, leather, pharmaceuticals, fertilizer, sugar, fishing (prawns), natural gas and garment manufacture. Remittances sent home by Bangladeshi workers abroad have been of considerable support to the economy in recent years.

Aid

Bangladesh is a major recipient of bilateral and multilateral development aid. The total annual development plan for 1988–89 is budgeted at U.S. $1,423 million, of which U.S. $1,146 million will be financed from external sources as follows:

Project aid	U.S. $900 million
Commodity aid	445 million
Food aid	78 million

Trade with U.K.

	1986	1987
Imports from U.K.	£48,218,000	54,382,000
Exports to U.K.	34,117,000	35,454,000

BRITISH HIGH COMMISSION

Abu Bakr House, Plot 7, Road 84, Gulshan Dhaka, P.O. Box 6079
[Dhaka 600133/7]

High Commissioner, His Excellency Terence George Streeton, C.M.G, M.B.E. (1983).
Deputy High Commissioner, J. F. Holding.
British Council Representative, W. G. Harvey, 5 Fuller Road, (P.O. Box 161), Ramna, Dhaka 2.

BARBADOS

AREA, POPULATION, ETC.—Barbados, the most easterly of the Caribbean islands, is situated in latitude 13° 14′ N. and longitude 59° 37′ W. The island has a total area of 166 sq. miles, (430 sq. km.), the land rising in a series of tablelands marked by terraces to the highest point, Mt. Hillaby (1,116 ft.). It is nearly 21 miles long by 14 miles broad. The climate is equable with annual average temperature 26·6°C. (79·8°F.) and rainfall varying from a yearly average of 75 inches in the high central district to 50 inches in some of the low-lying coastal areas.

POPULATION.—The population of Barbados (1985 U.N. estimate) was 253,000. There are eleven adminis-trative areas (parishes); St. Michael; Christ Church; St. Andrews; St. George; St. James; St. John; St. Joseph; St. Lucy; St. Peter; St. Philip, and St. Thomas.

CAPITAL.—ΨBridgetown (population, estimated April, 1980, 7,466) in the parish of St. Michael. There are three other towns, Oistins in Christ Church, Holetown in St. James and Speightstown in St. Peter.

CURRENCY.—Barbados Dollar (B$) of 100 Cents.

FLAG.—Three vertical stripes, dark blue, gold and dark blue, with trident devises on gold stripe.

NATIONAL ANTHEM.—In Plenty and in Time of Need.

NATIONAL DAY.—November 30 (Independence Day).

GOVERNMENT

The first inhabitants of Barbados were Arawak Indians but the island was uninhabited when first settled by the British in 1627. It was a Crown Colony from 1652 until it became an independent state within the Commonwealth on November 30, 1966. The Legislature consists of the Governor General, a Senate and a House of Assembly. The Senate comprises 21 Senators appointed by the Governor General, of whom 12 are appointed on the advice of the Prime Minister, 2 on the advice of the Leader of the Opposition and 7 by the Governor General at his discretion to represent religious, economic or social interests in the Island or such other interests as the Governor General considers ought to be represented. The House of Assembly comprises 27 members elected every five years by adult suffrage. The last General Election took place on May 28, 1986 and, as a result, seats in the House of Assembly were distributed as follows: Democratic Labour Party 24, Barbados Labour Party 3.

Governor General, Sir Hugh Springer, G.C.M.G., G.C.V.O., C.B.E. (1984).

Cabinet

Prime Minister, Minister of Economic Affairs, Education, Culture, Information and Finance, Hon. L. Erskine Sandiford.
Deputy P.M., Minister of Transport, Works and Telecommunications, and Leader of the House, Hon. Philip M. Greaves, Q.C.
Attorney General and Minister of Legal Affairs, Hon. Maurice A. King, Q.C.
Agriculture, Food and Fisheries, Hon. Warwick O. Franklyn.
Employment, Labour Relations and Community Development, Hon. N. Keith Simmons.
Trade, Industry and Finance, Hon. E. Evelyn Greaves.
Foreign Affairs and Leader of the Senate, Senator Hon. Sir James Tudor, K.C.M.G.
Health, Hon. Branford M. Taitt.
Housing and Lands, Hon. Harold A. Blackman.
Tourism and Sport, Hon. Wesley W. Hall.
Minister of State for the Civil Service, Senator Hon. L. V. Harcourt Lewis.
Minister of State in the Ministry of Education and Culture, Hon. Cyril V. Walker.

President of the Senate, Senator Hon. Frank Walcott, O.B.E.
Speaker, House of Assembly, Hon. Lawson Weekes.

BARBADOS HIGH COMMISSION

1 Great Russell Street, WC1B 3NH
[01–631 4975]

High Commissioner, His Excellency Vernon O. Smith (1986).

JUDICATURE

There is a Supreme Court of Judicature consisting of a High Court and a Court of Appeal. In certain cases a further appeal lies to the Judicial Committee of H.M. Privy Council. The Chief Justice and Puisne Judges are appointed by the Governor General on the recommendation of the Prime Minister and after consultation with the Leader of the Opposition.

Chief Justice, The Hon. Sir Denys Ambrose Williams, K.B.

EDUCATION

Primary and secondary education is free in Government schools. There are 105 primary schools, 21 Government secondary schools and 15 approved Government secondary schools.

COMMUNICATIONS

Barbados has some 965 miles of roads, of which about 917 miles are asphalted. The Grantley Adams International airport is situated at Seawell, 12 miles from Bridgetown, and frequent scheduled services connect Barbados with the major world air routes. Bridgetown, the only port of entry, has a deep-water harbour with berths for 8 ships, but oil is pumped ashore at Spring Gardens and at an Esso installation on the West Coast. Barbados has a colour television service, three radio broadcasting services, and a wired broadcasting service.

FINANCE

	1987–88*
Current revenue	BDS$698,071,077
Current expenditure	711,636,404
Capital expenditure	176,518,229
* estimated.	

ECONOMY

The economy of the island is based on tourism, sugar and light manufacturing. In 1986, 369,770 tourists visited Barbados and 145,335 cruise ship passengers. Chief exports are sugar and its by-products (15·7 per cent of exports in 1986), electrical components (52·1 per cent) and clothing (8·4 per cent).

	1985	1986
	BDS$	BDS$
Total imports	1,221·5 m	1,181·0 m
Total exports	707·7 m	552·3 m

Trade with U.K.

	1986	1987
Imports from U.K.	£38,338,000	£33,067,000
Exports to U.K.	11,661,000	23,320,000

BRITISH HIGH COMMISSION
Lower Collymore Rock, P.O. Box 676,
Bridgetown
[Bridgetown 436 6694]

High Commissioner, His Excellency Kevin Francis Xavier Burns, C.M.G. (1986).

BELIZE

AREA, POPULATION, ETC.—Belize lies on the east coast of Central America, bounded on the north and north-west by Mexico, and on the west and south by Guatemala. The total area (including offshore islands) is about 8,867 sq. miles (22,965 sq. km.), with a length and breadth of 174 miles and 68 miles respectively. The climate is sub-tropical, with a mean annual temperature of 20°C, but is tempered by sea breezes. There are two dry seasons, the main one from March to May and the other (the Maugre season) from August to September. The country is occasionally affected by hurricanes.

The coastal areas are mostly flat and swampy but the country rises gradually towards the interior. The northern and western districts are hilly, and in the south the Maya Mountains and the Cockscombs form the backbone of the country, reaching a height of 3,800 feet at Victoria Peak.

The population is 166,000 (1985 U.N. estimate), of which the main racial groups are Creoles, Mestizos (Maya-Spanish) and Caribs, plus a number of East Indian and Spanish descent. The races are now heavily inter-mixed. The majority of the population is Christian, about 60 per cent Catholic and most of the remainder Protestant.

The early history of Belize is little known, although the numerous ruins in the area indicate that it was heavily populated by the Maya Indians. The first British settlement was established in 1638 but was subject to repeated attacks by the Spanish, who claimed sovereignty over the area, until the decline of Spanish power in the Americas in the 19th century. In 1862 the area was recognised by Britain as a Colony and called British Honduras. On June 1, 1973 the colony was officially renamed Belize, and was granted independence on September 21, 1981. The long-standing territorial dispute with Guatemala, which had delayed independence earlier, remains unresolved despite efforts to reach a settlement.

CAPITAL.—Belmopan (estimated population, 1980, 2,935). The largest city and the former capital is ΨBelize City (population, 1980 census, 39,771). Other towns are Corozal (6,899), San Ignacio (5,616), Dangriga (6,661), Orange Walk (8,439), Punta Gorda (2,396).

CURRENCY.—Belizean Dollar (BZ$) of 100 Cents.

FLAG.—Blue ground with red band along top and bottom edges, and in centre a white disc containing the coat of arms surrounded by a green garland.

NATIONAL ANTHEM.—Land of the Gods.

NATIONAL DAY.—September 21 (Independence Day).

GOVERNMENT

The Queen is Head of State, represented in Belize by a Governor General, who is a citizen of the country, appointed in consultation with the Prime Minister of Belize. There is a National Assembly, comprising a House of Representatives (28 members elected for 5 years) and a Senate (8 members appointed by the Governor General). Executive power is vested in the Cabinet, which is responsible to the National Assembly.

Governor General, Her Excellency Dame Minita Elvira Gordon, G.C.M.G.

The Cabinet

Prime Minister and Minister of Finance, Hon. Manuel Esquivel.
Deputy Prime Minister and Minister of Home Affairs, Hon. Curl Thompson.
Commerce, Industry and Tourism, Hon. Eduardo Juan (Jr.).
Education, Youth and Sports, Hon. Elodio Aragon.
Health, Hon. Israel Alpuche.
Natural Resources, Hon. Charles Wagner.
Foreign Affairs and Economic Development, Hon. Dean Barrow.
Electricity, Transport, and Communications, Hon. Derek Aikman.
Works and Housing, Hon. Hubert Elrington.

Agriculture, Hon. Dean Lindo.
Labour and Social Services, Hon. Philip Goldson.

BELIZE HIGH COMMISSION
15 Thayer Street,
WIM 5DL
[01–486 8381]
High Commissioner, His Excellency Sir Edney Cain,
O.B.E.

ECONOMY

About 42 per cent of the population is engaged in agriculture. Corn (maize), rice, red kidney beans, root crops and fruit are the main food crops, although main agricultural exports are sugar, bananas and citrus products. The country is more or less self-sufficient in fresh beef, pork and poultry, but processed meat and dairy products are imported. About 25 per cent of timber production (mostly mahogany) is exported, and there is a large U.S. market for lobster, conch and scale fish. Tourism is also a valuable source of income.

FINANCE

	1987–88	1988–89p
Revenue	BZ $114·2 m	BZ$132·2 m
Expenditure	134·6 m	131·3 m
Deficit	−20·4 m	0·9 m

p = provisional
The Belize dollar (BZ $) is tied to the U.S. dollar: BZ $2 = U.S. $1.

TRADE

	1986	1987
Total imports	BZ $243·9 m	BZ$285·9 m
Total exports	185·2 m	205·7 m

Trade with U.K.

	1986	1987
Imports from U.K.	£8,232,000	£7,543,000
Exports to U.K.	17,954,000	22,757,000

EDUCATION

Education is compulsory from 5 to 14 years of age. In 1985 primary education was provided by 225 schools, most of which are government aided. Enrolment totalled 38,512. Secondary education is provided by 29 secondary and post-secondary institutions with an enrolment of 7,441. Plans are underway for Ferris State College of Michigan, U.S.A., to establish an affiliate university in Belize. The Government also offers scholarships for students to go abroad. There is an extra-mural faculty of the University of the West Indies, with a resident tutor.

COMMUNICATIONS

There is a Government-operated radio service but no official television service in the country. An automatic telephone service operated by Belize Telecommunications Ltd. covers the whole country.

The principal airport is at Belize City and various airlines operate international flights to U.S. and other Central American states. The main port is also Belize City, where construction of deep water quays was recently completed. There are 1,865 miles of road, including four main highways, but there is no railway system.

BRITISH HIGH COMMISSION
P.O. Box 91, Belmopan.
[Belmopan 2146/7]
High Commissioner, His Excellency Peter Alexander Bremner Thomson, C.V.O. (1987).
Deputy High Commissioner, D. R. F. Flanagan.

BOTSWANA
(The Republic of Botswana)

AREA, POPULATION, ETC.—Botswana (formerly the British Protectorate of Bechuanaland) lies between latitudes 18° and 26° S. and longitudes 20° and 28° W. and is bounded by the Cape and Transvaal Provinces of South Africa on the south and east, by Zimbabwe, the Zambezi and Chobe (Linyanti) Rivers on the north and north-east and by South West Africa on the west. Botswana has a total area of 224,607 sq. miles (581,730 sq. km.). The climate of the country is generally sub-tropical, but varies considerably with latitude and altitude. A plateau at a height of about 4,000 feet divides Botswana into two main topographical regions. To the east of the plateau streams flow into the Marico, Notwani and Limpopo Rivers; to the west lies a flat region comprising the Kgalagadi Desert, the Okavango Swamps and the Northern State Lands area. Large areas of the country support only herds of game. Elephant numbers have been estimated at 15–30,000.

POPULATION.—Botswana has an estimated population (1986) of 1,127,880. The eight principal Botswana tribes are Bakgatla, Bakwena, Bangwaketse, Bamalete, Bamangwato, Barolong, Batawana and Batlokwa. The principal languages in use in Botswana are Setswana and English.

CAPITAL.—Gaborone, estimated population 103,000. Other centres are Francistown (47,000), Lobatse (25,000), and Selebi-Phikwe (45,000).

CURRENCY.—Pula of 100 Thebe. *P*1 = $US0·639 (Dec. 1987).

FLAG.—Horizontal bands of blue, white, blue, with a black stripe on the white band.

NATIONAL ANTHEM.—Fatshe La Rona.

NATIONAL DAY.—September 30.

GOVERNMENT

On September 30, 1966, Bechuanaland became a Republic within the Commonwealth under the name Botswana. The President of Botswana is Head of State and appoints as Vice President a member of the National Assembly who is his principal assistant and leader of Government business in the National Assembly. The Assembly consists of the President, 34 members elected on a basis of universal adult suffrage, 4 specially elected members, the Attorney-General (non-voting) and the Speaker. There is also a House of Chiefs.

President, His Excellency Dr. Q. K. J. Masire.

Cabinet

Vice President, Minister of Finance and Development Planning, Hon. P. S. Mmusi.
External Affairs, Hon. Dr. G. K. T. Chiepe, M.B.E.
Presidential Affairs and Public Administration, Hon. P. H. K. Kedikilwe.
Health, Hon. J. T. Mothibamele.
Agriculture, Hon. D. K. Kwelagobe.
Local Government and Lands, Hon. P. K. Balopi.
Works and Communications, Hon. C. J. Butale.
Commerce and Industry, Hon. M. P. K. Nwako.
Education, Hon. K. P. Morake.
Mineral Resources and Water Affairs, Hon. A. M. Mogwe, M.B.E.
Home Affairs, Hon. E. M. K. Kgabo.

Assistant Minister, Finance and Development Planning, Hon. I. O. Chilume.
Assistant Minister, Local Government and Lands, Hon. M. R. Tshipinare.
Assistant Minister, Agriculture, Hon. G. M. Oteng.

BOTSWANA HIGH COMMISSION
6 Stratford Place, WIN 9AE
[01–499 0031]

High Commissioner, His Excellency G. U. S. Matlhabaphiri (1986).

ECONOMY

Botswana is predominantly a pastoral country. The national herd is normally around 3 million cattle and 1 million sheep and goats but drought conditions during the past 6 years have reduced the number of cattle to around 2·3 million.

Cattle rearing accounts for about 85 per cent of agricultural output and livestock products, particularly beef, are a major source of foreign exchange earnings. The Government has a number of programmes to improve land use and cattle and crop production, and schemes to provide financial assistance for farmers.

Mineral extraction and processing is now the major source of income for the country following the opening of large mines for diamonds and copper-nickel. Botswana is one of the largest producers of diamonds in the world. Large deposits of coal have been discovered and are being mined on a small scale. Much of the country has yet to be fully prospected. Manufacturing industry is growing and will continue to do so as communications improve but it is still a small sector of the economy.

EDUCATION

There are over 500 primary schools (enrolment 230,890), 70 community junior secondary schools (enrolment 22,000) and 23 government and government-aided senior secondary schools (enrolment 7,000). The government embarked on a massive expansion of secondary education in January 1984 aimed at providing universal access to junior secondary education; over 50 more schools are being opened by 1990. There are 5 teacher training establishments (total enrolment 1,540) including one for secondary teachers (enrolment 340), one Polytechnic with 760 students and the University of Botswana with 1,800 undergraduates. Further expansion of the technical education system is planned via a network of vocational training centres.

COMMUNICATIONS

The railway from Cape Town to Zimbabwe passes through eastern Botswana. The main roads in the country are the north–south road, which closely follows the railway, and the road running east–west that links Francistown and Maun. A new road from Nata to Kazungula provides a direct link to Zambia from Botswana. Air services are provided on a scheduled basis between the main towns, linking with services from South Africa, Swaziland, Zambia and Zimbabwe.

FINANCE

	1985–86	1986–87
Actual Revenue (Recurrent and development)	*P*1,133 m	*P*1,548 m
Actual Expenditure	719 m	1,009 m

TRADE

Principal exports are diamonds, copper-nickel matte, and beef and beef products.

	1986	1987
Imports	*P*1,325·6 m	*P*1,642·0 m
Exports	1,449·6 m	2,482.4 m

Trade with U.K.

	1986	1987
Imports from U.K.	£8,629,000	£10,275,000
Exports to U.K.	16,652,000	11,836,000

BRITISH HIGH COMMISSION
Private Bag 0023, Gaborone
[Gaborone 352841]

High Commissioner, His Excellency Peter Albert Raftery, C.V.O., M.B.E. (1986).
British Council Representative, S. Moss, O.B.E.

BRUNEI
(Negara Brunei Darussalam)

Brunei is situated on the north-west coast of the island of Borneo, total area of 2,226 sq. miles (5,765 sq. km.), population (1986 estimate) 226,000 of whom 72 per cent are of Malay or other indigenous race and 20 per cent Chinese. The country has a humid tropical climate.

CAPITAL.—Bandar Seri Begawan, with a population of 58,000 (1981).
CURRENCY.—Brunei Dollar of 100 Sen. It is fully interchangeable with the currency of Singapore.
FLAG.—Yellow, with diagonal bands of white over narrow black band (from top by staff), with red device on diagonal bands.
NATIONAL ANTHEM.—Ya Allah Lanjutkan Lah Usia Duli Tuanku (Oh God, long live our Majesty the Sultan).
NATIONAL DAY.—February 23.

GOVERNMENT

In 1959, the Sultan of Brunei promulgated the first written Constitution, which provides for a Privy Council, a Council of Ministers and a Legislative Council. On January 1, 1984 Brunei resumed full independence. A ministerial system of government was established at independence, the seven Ministers being appointed by the Sultan and responsible to him. The Sultan presides over the Privy Council and the Council of Ministers. The Legislative Council was disbanded in Feb. 1984.

Sultan, H.M. Sir Muda Hassanal Bolkiah Mu'izzadin Waddaulah, G.C.M.G., *acceded* 1967, *crowned* Aug. 1, 1968.

The Government

Prime Minister, Minister of Defence, H.M. The Sultan.
Foreign Affairs, H.R.H. Prince Mohammed.
Finance, H.R.H. Prince Jefri.
Special Adviser to the Sultan and Minister for Home Affairs, Pehin Dato Haji Isa.
Communications, Pehin Dato Abdul Aziz.
Law, Pengiran Bahrin.
Education, Pehin Dato Abdul Rahman.
Religious Affairs, Pehin Dato Mohammed Zain.
Development, Pengiran Dato Dr. Ismail.
Culture, Youth and Sports, Pehin Dato Haji Hussein.
Health, Dato Dr. Johar.

BRUNEI HIGH COMMISSION
49 Cromwell Road, SW7 2ED
[01–581 0521]

High Commissioner, His Excellency Pengiran Setia
Raja Pengiran Haji Jaya (1984).

FINANCE

	1985 (forecast)
Revenue	*B*$4,500 million
Expenditure*	2,600 million

*Including development expenditure.

Trade with U.K.

	1986	1987
Imports from U.K.	£154,146,000	£204,129,000
Exports to U.K.	71,624,000	34,144,000

BRITISH HIGH COMMISSION
Hong Kong and Shanghai Bank
Building (3rd floor), Bandar
Seri Begawan.
[Bandar Seri Begawan 22231]

High Commissioner, His Excellency Roger Westbrook
(1986).

British Council Representative, D. Elliott, P.O. Box
3049, Bandar Seri Begawan.

CYPRUS
(Kypriaki Dimokratia/Kibris Cumhuriyeti)

AREA, CLIMATE AND POPULATION.—Cyprus with
an area of 3,572 sq. miles (9,251 sq. km.), is the third
largest island in the Mediterranean Sea. Its greatest
length is 140 miles and greatest breadth 60 miles,
situated at latitude 35°N. and longitude 33° 30′E. It
is about 40 miles distant from the nearest point of
Asia Minor, 60 miles from Syria and 240 miles from
Port Said.

Cyprus has a Mediterranean climate with a hot
dry summer and a variable warm winter, while the
intermediate seasons are short and transitional.

In 1985 the population (estimate) was 673,100.
There are two major communities, Greek Cypriots
(78 per cent) and Turkish Cypriots (18·2 per cent);
and minorities of Armenians, Maronites and others.

CAPITAL.—Nicosia, near the centre of the island,
with a population of 164,400 (in the Government
controlled area); the other principal towns are
ΨLimassol, ΨFamagusta, ΨLarnaca, Paphos and Kyr-
enia.

CURRENCY.—Cyprus Pound of 100 Cents.

FLAG.—Gold map of Cyprus on a white ground,
surmounting crossed olive branches (green).

NATIONAL ANTHEM.—Ode to Freedom.

NATIONAL DAY.—October 1 (Independence Day).

GOVERNMENT

Cyprus passed under British administration from
1878. Cyprus was formally annexed to Great Britain
on Nov. 5, 1914, on the outbreak of war with Turkey.
From 1925 to 1960 it was a Crown Colony administered by a Governor, assisted by an Executive Council
and also for a time by a partly-elected Legislative
Council. Following the launching in April 1955 of an
armed campaign by EOKA in support of union with
Greece, a state of emergency was declared in November, 1955, which lasted for four years. After a meeting
at Zürich between the Prime Ministers of Greece and
Turkey, a conference was held in London and an
agreement was signed on February 19, 1959, between
the United Kingdom, Greece, Turkey and the Greek

and Turkish Cypriots which provided that Cyprus
would be an independent Republic.

Under the Cyprus Act, 1960, the island became an
independent sovereign republic on August 16, 1960.
The constitution provided for a Greek Cypriot
President and a Turkish Cypriot Vice-President
elected for a five-year term by the Greek and Turkish
communities respectively. The House of Representatives, elected for five years by universal suffrage of
each community separately, was to consist of 35
Greek and 15 Turkish members. The 1960 Constitution proved unworkable in practice and led to
intercommunal troubles. The U.N. Peace Keeping
Force in Cyprus (UNFICYP) was set up in March
1964: its mandate was last renewed on June 13, 1986.

On July 15, 1974, mainland Greek officers of the
Greek Cypriot National Guard launched a *coup d'état*
against President Makarios and installed a former
EOKA member, Nikos Sampson, in his place. Turkey
reserved to itself the right to maintain constitutional
order and the independence and territorial integrity
of the island, invaded Northern Cyprus and occupied
over a third of the island. In Feb. 1975 a "Turkish
Federated State of Cyprus" under Mr. Rauf Denktash
was declared in this area, its constitution being
approved by referendum in July 1975. In Nov. 1983 a
"Declaration of Statehood" was issued which purported to establish the "Turkish Republic of Northern
Cyprus". The declaration was condemned by the
U.N. Security Council and only Turkey has recognized the new "state". In May 1985 a referendum in
the north of Cyprus approved a constitution for the
"Turkish Republic of Northern Cyprus": in June
1985 Mr. Denktash was elected President of the
"state" and a General Election was held.

Since 1974 attempts to reach a settlement have
focused on intercommunal talks under the auspices
of the U.N. The latest talks ended in Jan. 1985
without agreement, but the U.N. Secretary General
has continued his efforts to find a settlement.

A general election was held for the Greek House of
Representatives on Dec. 8, 1985, resulting in the
parties gaining the following number of seats:
Democratic Rally 19; Democratic Party (Centre) 16;
AKEL (Communist) 15; EDEK (Socialist) 6.

President, George Vassiliou, *elected* Feb. 21, 1988.

COUNCIL OF MINISTERS

Foreign Affairs, George Iacovou.
Interior, Christodoulos Veniamin.
Finance, George Syrimis.
Education, Andreas Philippou.
Justice, Christodoulos Chrysanthou.
Defence, Andreas Aloneftis.
Communications & Works, Nakos Protopapas.
Health, Panicos Papageorghiou.
Commerce and Industry, Takis Nemitsas.
Labour and Social Insurance, Takis Christofides.
Agriculture and Natural Resources, Andreas Gavrie-
    lides.

CYPRUS HIGH COMMISSION
93 Park Street, W1Y 4ET
[01-499 8272]

High Commissioner, His Excellency Tasos Panayides
(1979).

ECONOMY

Although agriculture still occupies a prime position
in the Cyprus economy it is unlikely to expand
further. Main products are citrus fruits, grapes and
vine products, potatoes and other vegetables. Manufacturing, construction, distribution and other service industries are other major employers. Tourism is
the main growth industry with over 1 million long-

stay tourists producing C£321 million in foreign exchange earnings in 1987. Some 4,700 foreign firms and individuals have registered as "offshore companies" in Cyprus, which supports Cyprus' claim to be a centre for Middle East trade.

Britain continues to be the country's most important trading partner, taking some 22·3 per cent of its exports in 1987 and supplying 14·3 per cent of its imports. Cyprus is seeking to diversify its export markets and until recently sold almost half its exports to the Middle East. However, these traditional markets are now drying up, and Cyprus is looking more towards Europe. A Customs Union between Cyprus and the E.C. came into force on Jan. 1, 1988.

There is a large visible trade deficit (C£413 million in 1987), which is offset by invisible earnings, particularly from tourism (C£321 million in 1987). The current account overall showed a surplus for the first time in 20 years amounting to C£51·5 million.

FINANCE

	1986	1987
Total Revenue	C£401·1 m	C£416·2 m
Ordinary Expenditure ...	530·6 m	581·4 m

TRADE

	1986	1987
Imports	C£659·1 m	C£711·4 m
Exports (including re-exports).............	260·2 m	297·9 m

Trade with U.K.

	1986	1987
Imports from U.K.	C£88·6 m	C£101·6 m
Exports to U.K.	58·9 m	66·5 m

BRITISH HIGH COMMISSION
Alexander Pallis Street (P.O. Box 1978)
Nicosia
[Nicosia 02-473131]

High Commissioner, His Excellency The Hon. Humphrey Maud, C.M.G. (1988).
British Council Representative, C. Mogford, P.O. Box 5654, 3 Museum Street, Nicosia.

BRITISH SOVEREIGN AREAS

The United Kingdom retained full sovereignty and jurisdiction over two areas of 99 square miles in all—Akrotiri–Episkopi–Paramali and Dhekelia–Pergamos–Ayios Nicolaos–Xylophagou—and use of roads and other facilities. The British Administrator of these areas is appointed by the Queen and is responsible to the Secretary of State for Defence.
Administrator of the British Sovereign Areas, Maj.-Gen. J. P. W. Friedberger, C.B.E.

DOMINICA
(The Commonwealth of Dominica)

AREA, POPULATION, ETC.—Dominica, the loftiest of the Lesser Antilles, lies in the Windward Group, between 15° 20′ and 15° 45′ N. lat. and 61° 13′ and 61° 30′ W. long., 95 miles S. of Antigua. It is about 29 miles long and 15 broad comprising an area of 290 sq. miles (751 sq. km.). The island is of volcanic origin and very mountainous, and the soil is very fertile. The temperature varies, according to the altitude, from 13°–29°C. The climate is healthy, and during the winter months is very pleasant. The population is 76,000 (1985 U.N. estimate).

CAPITAL.—ΨRoseau, on the south-west coast, population, 8,346. The other principal town is Portsmouth, population, 2,220.

CURRENCY.—East Caribbean Dollar (EC$) of 100 Cents.

FLAG.—Green ground with a cross overall of yellow, white and black stripes, and in the centre a red disc charged with a Sisserou parrot in natural colours within a ring of 11 green stars.

NATIONAL DAY.—November 3 (Independence Day).
NATIONAL ANTHEM.—Dominica Day Song.

GOVERNMENT

The island was discovered by Columbus in 1493, when it was a stronghold of the Caribs, who remained virtually the sole inhabitants until the French established settlements in the 18th century. It was captured by the British in 1759 but passed back and forth between France and Britain until 1805, after which British possession was not challenged. From 1871–1939 Dominica was part of the Leeward Islands Colony, then from 1940 the island was a unit of the Windward Islands group. Internal self-government from 1967 was followed on Nov. 3, 1978 by independence as a republic with the name The Commonwealth of Dominica. Executive authority is vested in the President, who is elected by the House of Assembly for not more than two terms of five years. Parliament consists of the President and the House of Assembly (representatives elected by universal adult suffrage) and nine Senators, who may be appointed by the President or elected. Parliament has a life of five years.

President, His Excellency Sir Clarence Seignoret, G.C.B., O.B.E.

Cabinet

Prime Minister and Minister for Finance, Economic Development, and Foreign Affairs, Hon. Mary Eugenia Charles.
Attorney General and Minister for Legal Affairs, and Labour, Hon. Brian Alleyne.
Agriculture, Lands, Trade, Industry and Tourism, Hon. Charles Maynard.
Communications and Works, Hon. Alleyne Carbon.
Education and Sports, Hon. Henry George.
Health, Hon. Ronan David.
Community Development, Housing and Social Affairs, Hon. Heskeith Alexander.

HONORARY CONSULTATE FOR THE COMMONWEALTH OF DOMINICA
1 Collingham Gardens, SW5 0HW
[01–370 5194/5]

High Commissioner, His Excellency M. A. D. Elwin (1988) (resident in Roseau).

FINANCE

	1985–86 revised	1986–87 estimated
Recurrent Revenue .	EC$83·6 m	EC$88·2 m
Recurrent Expenditure	81·1 m	91·6 m
Capital Revenue	37·9 m	49·3 m
Capital Expenditure .	45·3 m	57·2 m

ECONOMY

Agriculture is the principal occupation, with tropical and citrus fruits the main crops. Products for export are bananas, lime juice, lime oil, bay oil, copra and rum. Forestry and fisheries are being encouraged. The only commercially exploitable mineral is pumice, used chiefly for building purposes. Manufacturing consists largely of the processing of agricultural products.

TRADE

	1985
Imports	EC$149,376,000
Exports	76,766,000

Trade with U.K.

	1986	1987
Imports from U.K.	£8,780,000	£10,431,000
Exports to U.K.	26,612,000	37,083,000

BRITISH HIGH COMMISSION

High Commissioner, (resides at Bridgetown, Barbados).

THE GAMBIA
(The Republic of the Gambia)

AREA, POPULATION, ETC.—The Gambia takes its name from the Gambia River, which it straddles for over 200 miles inland from the west coast of Africa. It is a narrow strip, surrounded by the Republic of Senegal, except at the coast, lying between 13° 10'–13° 45' N. and 13° 90'–16° 50' W. The area is 4,361 sq. miles (11,295 sq. km.), of which one fifth is the river. The Gambia River basin was part of the region dominated in the 10th–16th centuries by the strong Songhai and Mali kingdoms centred on the upper Niger. The population comprises mainly Wolof, Mandinka and Fula peoples who originally migrated there from the north and east. Population (1983 Census) was 695,886.

The first recorded Europeans to reach the Gambia River were the Portuguese in 1447. In 1588 Queen Elizabeth I gave the first charter to English merchants to trade along the river. Merchants from France, Courland (now part of Latvia) and the Netherlands also established trading posts there. The English presence was strongly challenged by the French, who were dominant further north up the coast, but in 1783 the Treaty of Versailles acknowledged English rights. In 1816, after the Napoleonic Wars, and in order to enforce abolition of the slave trade, the British stationed a garrison on a low sandy island called Banjul at the river mouth. Renamed Bathurst, this became the capital of a small British-administered colony, initially under the Governor of Sierra Leone. Negotiations with France continued sporadically until 1889 when it was agreed that the British rights along the upper river should extend 10 km on either bank. British administration was extended from the Colony to this Protectorate. The Gambia became independent within the Commonwealth on February 18, 1965, and a Republic on April 24, 1970.

The Gambia's relationship with Senegal has always been an important factor in political and economic policy. Moves towards a closer association were accelerated after an abortive coup in The Gambia in July 1981 was put down with the help of Senegalese troops. In February 1982 the Senegambia Confederation was formally instituted based on certain joint institutions and integration of policies, but each country remains sovereign and independent.

Except during the rainy season from June to October, when it sometimes becomes uncomfortably humid, Banjul's climate is very pleasant. Rainfall is 32–40 inches a year.

CAPITAL.—ΨBanjul. Population (1983 Census) of island of Banjul was 44,536; and of adjacent Kombo St. Mary district 102,858. Total population of Banjul/Kombo St. Mary, 147,394.

CURRENCY.—Dalasi of 100 Butut.

FLAG.—Horizontal stripes of red, blue and green, separated by narrow white stripes.
NATIONAL ANTHEM.—For The Gambia, Our Homeland.
NATIONAL DAY.—February 18 (Independence Day).

GOVERNMENT

The constitution is democratic and Parliamentary, with an executive President elected for five years. The House of Representatives has 35 elected members, 5 elected Chiefs Representatives and up to 8 nominated members plus the Attorney-General (*ex-officio*). The Vice President and other Ministers are appointed by the President. Parliament must be dissolved after five years. The last general elections were held in March 1987. The present state of the parties for elected members is PPP (People's Progressive Party) 31; NCP (National Convention Party) 5.

President and Cabinet

President and Minister of Defence, His Excellency Alhaji Sir Dawda Kairaba Jawara, G.C.M.G.
Vice-President and Minister of Education, Youth, Sports and Culture, Hon. Bakary Bunja Darbo.
Attorney-General and Minister of Justice, Hon. Hassan B. Jallow.
Finance and Trade, Hon. Sheriff Saikouba Sisay.
External Affairs, Hon. Alhaji Omar Baru Sey.
Interior, Hon. Lamin Kiti Jabang.
Agriculture, Hon. Alhaji Saikou S. Sabally.
Local Government and Lands, Hon. Landing Jallow Sonko.
Water Resources, Forestry and Fisheries, Hon. Omar Amadou Jallow.
Health, Environment, Labour and Social Welfare, Hon. Mrs. Louise A. N'Jie.
Works and Communications, Hon. Alhaji Muhammadu Cadi Cham.
Economic Planning and Industrial Development, Hon. Mbemba Jatta.
Information and Tourism, Hon. Dr. Lamin Kebba Saho.

Chief Justice, Hon. E. O. Ayoola.
Speaker, Alhaji Hon. M. B. N'Jie.

GAMBIA HIGH COMMISSION
57 Kensington Court, W8 5DG
[01-937 6316–8]

High Commissioner, His Excellency Horace R. Monday (Jr.), (1987).

COMMUNICATIONS

There is an international airport at Yundum, 17 miles from Banjul, with scheduled services flying to other West African states and to the U.K. Banjul is the main port. Internal communication is by road and river. There is no railway system. There are two broadcasting stations and a U.H.F. telephone service linking Banjul with the principal towns in the provinces. There is no television service.

EDUCATION

There are 24 secondary schools (eight high and 16 technical) with a total enrolment of 15,635 students. Two High Schools provide 'A' level education. Gambia College provides post-secondary courses in education, agriculture, public health and nursing. There are seven vocational training institutions with a total enrolment of 1,400. Higher education and advanced training courses are taken outside The Gambia, currently by over 200 students.

PRODUCTION

Eighty-five per cent of the population depend for their livelihood on agriculture (40 per cent of G.D.P.). The chief product, groundnuts, is also the most important export item, forming over 90 per cent of all domestic exports. Other crops are rice, millet, sorghum, maize and cotton. Fishing and livestock industries are being developed. Thirty per cent of the country's basic food requirements are imported. There is no significant deposits of minerals. Manufactures are limited to groundnut processing, minor metal fabrications, paints, furniture, soap and bottling. Tourism is developing quickly, with 98,248 visitors in 1987–88. The entrepôt trade through The Gambia, re-exporting imported goods to neighbouring countries, is an important element in the national economy.

FINANCE

	1984–85	1985–86
Recurrent Revenue ...	D172,600,000	D218,000,000
Recurrent Expenditure	180,900,000	203,000,000

Over 80 per cent of capital expenditure comes from external aid grants and loans. The Five Year Development Plan 1981–86 envisaged an annual GDP growth rate of 5·1 per cent or 2·5 per cent per capita (at 1980–81 prices).

TRADE

	1986–87	1987–88
Total imports	D797,600,000	D844,900,000
Total exports	523,800,000	576,600,000

Trade with U.K.

	1986	1987
Imports from U.K.	£16,707,000	£19,765,000
Exports to U.K.	2,273,000	3,038,000

BRITISH HIGH COMMISSION
48 Atlantic Road, Fajara (P.O. Box 507), Banjul
[Banjul 95133]

High Commissioner, His Excellency Alec Ibbott, C.B.E. (1988).

GHANA
(The Republic of Ghana)

AREA AND POPULATION.—Ghana (formerly known as the Gold Coast) is situated on the Gulf of Guinea, between 3° 07′ W. long. and 1° 14′ E. long. (about 334 miles), and extends 441 miles north from Cape Three Points (4° 45′ N.) to 11° 11′ N. It is bounded on the north by Burkina, on the west by the Côte d'Ivoire, on the east by Togo, and on the south by the Atlantic Ocean. Although a tropical country, Ghana is cooler than many countries within similar latitudes.

Ghana has a total area of 92,099 sq. miles (238,537 sq. km.). The population at the Census of 1984 was 12,205,574. A 1985 U.N. estimate gave a figure of 13,588,000. Almost all Ghanaians are Sudanese Negroes, although Hamitic strains are common in Northern Ghana. The official language is English. The principal indigenous language group is Akan, of which Twi and Fanti are the most commonly used. Ga, Ewe and languages of the Mole–Dagbani group are common in certain regions.

CAPITAL.—ΨAccra. Population of the Greater Accra Region (including Tema) was (1984 Census) 1,420,066. Other towns are Kumasi, Tamale,

ΨSekondi-Takoradi, ΨCape Coast, Sunyani, Ho, Koforidua, Tarkwa and ΨWinneba.

CURRENCY.—Cedi of 100 Pesewas.

FLAG.—Equal horizontal bands of red over yellow over green; five-point black star on gold stripe.

NATIONAL ANTHEM.—Hail the Name of Ghana.

NATIONAL DAY.—March 6 (Independence Day).

GOVERNMENT

There is no recorded history of the Gold Coast region before the coming of Europeans in the fifteenth century. The constituent parts of the State came under British administration at various times, the original Gold Coast Colony (the coastal and Southern areas) being first constituted in 1874; Ashanti in 1901; and the Northern Territories Protectorate in 1901. The territory of Trans-Volta-Togoland, part of the former German colony of Togo, was mandated to Britain by the League of Nations after the First World War, and remained under British administration as a United Nations Trusteeship after the Second World War. After a plebiscite in May, 1956, under the auspices of the United Nations, the territory was integrated with the Gold Coast Colony.

The former Gold Coast Colony and associated territories became the independent state of Ghana and a member of the British Commonwealth on March 6, 1957 and adopted a Republican constitution on July 1, 1960. A coup in June 1979 led to the formation of an Armed Forces Revolutionary Council chaired by Flt.-Lt. Jerry Rawlings. Civilian rule was restored in Sept. 1979 but overthrown on Dec. 31, 1981, when another coup brought back into power Flt.-Lt. Rawlings.

Provisional National Defence Council

Chairman, Flt.-Lt. Jerry J. Rawlings.

Vice-Chairman, Justice Daniel Annan.

Members, Mrs. Aanaa Enin; Ebo Tawiah; Alhaji Mahama Iddrisu; P. V. Obeng; Capt. Kojo Tsikata (retd); Lt.-Gen. Arnold Quainoo; Maj.-Gen. W. M. Mensa-Wood.

P.N.D.C. Secretaries

Foreign Affairs, Obed Y. Asamoah.

Internal Affairs, Nii Okaija Adamafio.

Finance and Economic Planning, Dr. Kwesi Botchwey.

Defence, Alhaji Mahama Iddrisu.

Fuel and Power, Ato Ahwoi.

Trade and Tourism, Kofi Djin.

Local Government, K. Ahwoi.

Education and Culture, K. B. Asante.

Youth and Sports, K. Saarah-Mensah.

Transport and Communications, E. O. Donkor.

Works and Housing, E. Appiah-Korang.

Industries, Science and Technology, Dr. Francis Acquah.

Justice and Attorney-General, G. E. Aikins.

Agriculture, Cdre. Steve Obimpeh.

Information, Dr. M. Ben-Abdallah.

Lands and Natural Resources, Kwame Peprah.

Roads and Highways, Lt.-Col. Mensah Gbedemah.

Committee for the Defence of the Revolution, W. H. Yeboah.

Health, Nana A. Sarpong.

Mobilization and Productivity, Huudu Yahaya.

GHANA HIGH COMMISSION
13 Belgrave Square, SW1X 8PR
[01-235 4142]

High Commissioner, His Excellency Dr. J. L. S. Abbey (1986).

Production, etc.

Agriculture.—Agriculture forms the basis of Ghana's economy, employing 70 per cent. of the working population. Crops of the Forest Zone include cocoa, which is the largest single source of revenue, rice and a variety of other foodstuff crops grown on mixed-crop farms. Fruits such as avocado pears, oranges and pineapples are grown. Cassava is the most important crop of the Coastal Savannas Zone, of the lower Volta area. Production of pulses such as groundnuts is widespread. Near the Togo border oil palms, yams, maize, cassava, fruit and vegetables are produced. Livestock is raised in the uncultivated areas. The Northern Savanna Zone is Ghana's principal cattle rearing area and other livestock production there is important for home consumption. Corn and millet crops are produced in the far north and maize, yams, rice and groundnut crops in more southerly parts of the Zone.

Attempts are being made to diversify agricultural production, with cash crops being extensively cultivated for export and to provide raw materials for local industry.

Fisheries.—Fishing is important in coastal areas and in the Volta itself. However production cannot meet demand and there are considerable imports of fish products. About 80 per cent of home supply is obtained from sea fisheries, but production from the Volta Lake and other inland fisheries is increasing.

Mineral Production.—The area within a 60 mile radius of Dunkwa produces 90 per cent of Ghana's mineral exports. Manganese production from Nsuta ranks among the world's highest and gold, industrial diamonds and bauxite are also produced. Some 30,000 persons are employed by the mining companies.

Manufactures.—Examples of the small-scale traditional industries are tailoring, goldsmithing and carpentry. Priority has been given in recent years to the establishment of a number of "Pioneer Industries" including timber products, vehicle and refrigerator assembly, cigarettes, boatbuilding, food processing, cotton textiles, clothing, footwear, printing and other light industries. A modern industrial complex is growing in the Accra-Tema area.

Volta River Project.—Since 1966 the Volta Dam at Akosombo has generated hydro-electric power for the processing of bauxite and fed a power transmission network for the Accra-Kumasi-Takoradi area. Electricity is now also sent to Togo and Benin.

Communications

Accra Airport is an international airport and Ghana Airways Corporation is the national airline. There are also internal airports at Takoradi, Kumasi and Tamale.

There are 20,000 miles of motorable roads, of which 2,335 miles are bitumenated. There are 600 miles of railway, linking Accra and the principal ports of Takoradi and Tema with their hinterlands, and with each other.

Takoradi Harbour consists of seven quay berths—one is leased specially for manganese exports. Tema Harbour has 10 berths for larger ocean going vessels and the largest dry dock on the West African coast. An oil berth has also been built to serve the Ghaip refinery which has been constructed at Tema.

Trade with U.K.

	1986	1987
Imports from U.K.	£113,218,000	£138,081,000
Exports to U.K.	103,480,000	113,859,000

Principal exports are cocoa, timber and gold. Principal imports are road vehicles, manufacturing equipment, petroleum and raw materials.

British High Commission
P.O. Box 296, Osu Link, Accra
[Accra 221665]

High Commissioner, His Excellency Arthur Hope Wyatt, C.M.G. (1986).

British Council Representative, A. L. M. Russell, Liberia Road (P.O. Box 771), Accra, and an Office in *Kumasi.*

GRENADA
(The State of Grenada)

Area, Population.—Grenada is situated between the parallels of 12° 13′–11° 58′ N. lat. and 61° 20′–61° 35′ W. long., and is about 80 miles north of Trinidad, 68 miles S.S.W. of St. Vincent, and about 120 miles S.W. of Barbados. The island is about 21 miles in length and 12 miles in breadth, with an area of 133 sq. miles (344 sq. km.). Also included in the territory of Grenada are some of the Grenadines islets, the largest of which is Carriacou, 13 square miles in area. The population was estimated at 112,000 (1985 U.N. estimate). The country is mountainous and very picturesque, and the climate is healthy.

Capital.—ΨSt. George's (population 7,500) lies on the southwest coast, and possesses a good harbour.

Currency.—East Caribbean Dollar of 100 Cents.

Flag.—Rectangle formed of yellow triangles top and bottom, and green triangles at side, with yellow five-pointed star on red circle in centre, and a nutmeg in green triangle nearest the fly; all on a red ground with three yellow five-pointed stars at top and bottom.

National Day.—February 7 (Independence Day).

Government

Grenada was discovered by Columbus in 1498, and named Conception. It was originally colonized by the French, and was ceded to Great Britain by the Treaty of Versailles in 1783. It became an Associated State in 1967 and an independent nation on Feb. 7, 1974.

The government of Sir Eric Gairy was overthrown on March 13, 1979 by the New Jewel Movement and a People's Revolutionary Government was set up. Disagreements within the P.R.G. led, in Oct. 1983, to violence and the death of the Prime Minister, whose government was replaced by a Revolutionary Military Council. These events prompted the intervention of Caribbean and U.S. forces. The Governor General installed an advisory council in Nov. 1983 to act as an interim government until a General Election was held, on Dec. 3, 1984. The New National Party won 14 of the 15 seats in the House of Representatives and, following the dissolution of the advisory council, its leader, Mr. Herbert Blaize, was sworn in as Prime Minister. A phased withdrawal of U.S. forces was completed in June 1985.

Governor General, Sir Paul Scoon, G.C.M.G., G.C.V.O., O.B.E. (1978).

Cabinet
Prime Minister, National Security, Home Affairs, Carriacou and Petit Martinique Affairs, Information, Energy, Finance, Trade, Industry and Economic Planning, Rt. Hon. Herbert A. Blaize.

External Affairs, Agriculture, Lands, Forestry and Tourism, Hon. Benjamin Jones.

Attorney General, Legal Affairs, Health, Housing, Physical Planning, Hon. Daniel Williams.

Education, Social Security, Labour, Culture, Youth Affairs, Sport, Local Government, Fisheries, Hon. George McGuire.

Communications, Works, Public Utilities, Co-operatives, Community Development, Women's Affairs, Aviation, Hon. Dr. Keith Mitchell.

Ministers of State, Hon. Pauline Andrews (*Agriculture and Tourism*); Hon. Grace Duncan (*Women's Affairs and Community Development*); Hon. Alleyne Walker (*Works and Co-operatives*); Hon. Felix Alexander (*Information, Finance, Trade, Industry and Energy*); Senator the Hon. Lawrence Joseph (*Legal Affairs and National Security*); Senator the Hon. Ben Andrews (*Education, Culture, Youth Affairs and Fisheries*); Hon. Norton Noel (*Social Security, Local Government and Labour*).

GRENADA HIGH COMMISSION
1 Collingham Gardens, SW5 0HW
[01–373 7800/7808]

High Commissioner, His Excellency Oswald M. Gibbs, C.M.G. (1984).

ECONOMY

The economy is principally agrarian, with cocoa, nutmegs and bananas the major crops. Fruit and vegetables are grown and livestock raised for domestic consumption. The fishing industry is being developed. Manufacturing is mostly confined to processing agricultural products.

Tourism has prospered since the opening in 1984 of the Point Salines International Airport. British Airways began regular flights in April 1987. A hotel expansion programme is planned. The number of cruise ships visiting Grenada in 1986–87 was 236.

Total value of imports in 1986 was *EC*$225 million. Principal domestic exports for 1986 were cocoa (*EC*$10·6m), nutmeg (*EC*$26·1m), mace (*EC*$5·3m) and fruit (*EC*$15·3m).

Trade with U.K.

	1986	1987
Imports from U.K.	£8,628,000	£8,772,000
Exports to U.K.	7,011,000	6,302,000

BRITISH HIGH COMMISSION
14 Church Street, St. George's.
[St. George's 440-3222]

High Commissioner, (resides at Bridgetown, Barbados).
Resident Representative, G. Roberts (*First Secretary*).

GUYANA
(The Co-operative Republic of Guyana)

AREA, POPULATION, ETC.—Guyana, the former colony of British Guiana, which includes the Counties of Demerara, Essequibo and Berbice, is situated on the north-east coast of South America, bordering on Venezuela, Brazil and Suriname. It has a total area of 83,000 sq. miles (214,969 sq. km.). While the 1985 U.N. estimate puts the population at 790,000, 750,000 is generally considered to be a more representative figure. There are three distinct areas. (1) A narrow alluvial coastal belt 10 to 40 miles deep, the eastern part of which is intensively cultivated and contains some 90 per cent of the population. Much of this is below the level of the sea and is drained and irrigated by an intricate system of canals constructed by the Dutch. (2) A mountainous area of dense rain forest behind the coastland, still partly unexplored, which reaches its highest point at Mount Roraima (9,000 ft.) on the junction of the Guyana–Brazil–Venezuela borders. (3) The open savanna country of the Rupununi in the south-west where cattle ranching is practised and oil deposits have been discovered.

The entire country is intersected by numerous large rivers, though these are of limited navigational use because of rapids and waterfalls, the most notable of which are the *Kaieteur Fall* on the Potaro River with a sheer drop of 741 ft., the *Horse Shoe Falls* on the Essequibo and the *Marina Fall* on the Ipobe River.

Climate.—The two dry seasons normally last from mid February to end April, and from mid August to end November. In the Aug.–Oct. period it is hot. The mean temperature is 27°C., the usual extremes being 21°C and 32°C. In the interior the mean temperature is higher—28°C., its extremes ranging from 19°C to 40°C. The yearly rainfall is subject to marked variation, its mean on the coast lands averaging about 90 inches with an average of 58 inches on the savannas.

CAPITAL.—ΨGeorgetown. Estimated population, including environs, 185,000. Other towns are: Linden (population 29,000); ΨNew Amsterdam (population 23,000); Corriverton (population 17,000).

CURRENCY.—Guyana Dollar of 100 Cents.

FLAG.—Red triangle with black border, pointing from hoist to fly, on a yellow triangle with white border, all on a green field.

NATIONAL ANTHEM.—"Dear Land of Guyana".

NATIONAL DAYS.—May 26 (Independence Day); February 23 (Republic Day).

GOVERNMENT

Guyana became independent on May 26, 1966, with a Governor General appointed by the Queen. It became a Co-operative Republic on Feb. 23, 1970. Under the Independence Constitution the Prime Minister and Cabinet were responsible to a National Assembly elected by secret ballot every 5 years. The last election under this Constitution was in 1973 and the term of that Assembly was later extended to October 1980.

A new Constitution was passed into law in February 1980 and promulgated in October 1980. It provides for an Executive President, a National Assembly of 65 members, and also for a National Congress of Local Democratic Organs responsible for local government. The Supreme Congress of the People consists of all members of these two assemblies.

The electoral system is a Proportional Representation or "single list" system, each voter casting his vote for a party list of candidates. The voting age is 18.

Executive President, H. Desmond Hoyte, *took office* Aug. 1985, *sworn in* Dec. 12, 1985 for five-year term.

Cabinet

Executive President (*with responsibility for Home Affairs, Co-operatives, Regional Development*), H. D. Hoyte.
First Vice President and Prime Minister, Hamilton Green.
Vice President (*National Development*) *and Deputy P.M.*, Ranji Chandisingh.
Vice President (*Education and Social Development*) *and Deputy P.M.*, Mrs. Viola Burnham.
Attorney-General and Minister for Legal Affairs, Keith Massiah.
Deputy P.M. (*Public Utilities*), Robert H. O. Corbin.
Deputy P.M. (*Planning and Development*), William H. Parris.

SENIOR MINISTERS

Foreign Affairs, Rashleigh Jackson.
Finance, Carl Greenidge.
Labour and Co-operatives, Seeram Prashad.
Trade and Tourism, Winston Murray.

GUYANA HIGH COMMISSION
3 Palace Court, Bayswater Road, W2 4LP
[01-229 7684]

High Commissioner, His Excellency Mr. Cecil Stanley
Pilgrim (1986).

JUDICATURE

The Supreme Court of Judicature consists of a
Court of Appeal and a High Court. There are also
Courts of Summary Jurisdiction. The Court of
Appeal consists of the Chancellor as President, the
Chief Justice and such number of Justices of Appeal
as may be prescribed by Parliament.

The High Court consists of the Chief Justice, as
President, and nine Puisne Judges. It is a court with
unlimited jurisdiction in civil matters and exercises
exclusive jurisdiction in probate, divorce and admiralty, and certain other matters.

Chancellor, K. M. George.
Chief Justice, R. Harper.

PRODUCTION, ETC.

The economy is based almost entirely on the main
export items of sugar, rice, bauxite and alumina.
Diamonds and gold are also mined, timber and rum
are produced and there is some cattle ranching. The
fishing industry is being expanded. Industry is fairly
small-scale.

COMMUNICATIONS

Georgetown and New Amsterdam are the principal
ports, though bauxite ships also sail to Linden, on the
R. Demerara, and Everton, on the R. Berbice. There
are no public railways and the few roads are confined
mainly to the coastal areas. Air transport is the
easiest form of communication between the coast and
the interior. There is a state-owned radio broadcasting station which operates two channels; there is no
television service.

EDUCATION

The Government assumed total control of the
education system in September 1976 and made
education free from nursery to university level. The
Government trains teachers for primary and secondary schools at its own institutions. In 1982 there
were 368 nursery schools with 29,958 pupils, 423
primary schools with 130,003 pupils, and 414 secondary schools with 73,762 students.

Approximately 1,800 students were enrolled at the
University of Guyana in degree programmes and
certificate and diploma courses in 1986.

There are several technical and vocational institutions, as well as some 30 adult education schools
(with an enrolment of 13,500). There are also a
number of technical and vocational institutions not
under the aegis of the Ministry of Education.

Trade with U.K.

	1986	1987
Imports from U.K.	£13,737,000	£15,371,000
Exports to U.K.	55,535,000	58,502,000

BRITISH HIGH COMMISSION
44 Main Street (P.O. Box 10849),
Georgetown
[Georgetown 65881/4]

High Commissioner, His Excellency David Purvis
Small, C.M.G., M.B.E. (1987) (also Ambassador to
Suriname).

INDIA
(The Republic of India)

AREA AND POPULATION.—The Republic of India
has an area of 1,269,346 sq. miles (3,287,590 sq. km.),
composed of three well-defined regions: the mountain
range of the Himalayas; the Indo–Gangetic plain;
and the Southern Peninsula. The main mountain
ranges are the Himalayas in the north (over 29,000
feet) and the Western and Eastern Ghats (over 8,000
feet). Major rivers include the Ganges, Indus,
Krishna, Godavari and Mahanadi.

There are four seasons: the cold season (Dec.–
March); the hot season (April–May); the rainy season
(June–Sept.); and the season of the retreating S.W.
monsoon (Oct.–Nov.). Temperatures vary over the
whole country, between averages of about 10° C and
33° C, reaching over 38° C in some parts during the
hot season. There are similar variations in rainfall,
from only a few inches a year falling in the western
Thar Desert to over 400 inches in Meghalaya.

India is the second most populous country in the
world. The population at the 1981 Census was
685,184,692, of which slightly more than 20 per cent
was urban. A 1985 U.N. estimate gave a figure of
750,900,000. The majority of the population are Hindu
(82 per cent), the rest being Muslim (11 per cent),
Christian (2·5 per cent), Sikh (1·8 per cent), Buddhist
(0·7 per cent) and Jain (0·5 per cent). The official
languages are Hindi in the Devanagari script and
English, though 14 regional languages also are
recognized for adoption as official State languages.

HISTORY.—The Indus civilization was fully developed by c. 2,500 B.C. but collapsed c. 1,750 B.C.,
subsequently being replaced by an Aryan civilization
spread from the west. The first Arabic invasions of
the north west began in the seventh century and
Moslem, Hindu and Buddhist states developed until
the establishment of the Mogul dynasty in 1526. The
British East India Company established settlements
throughout the 17th century; clashes with the
French and native princes led to the British government taking control of the Company in 1784. The
separate dominions of India and Pakistan became
independent within the Commonwealth in 1947 and
India became a Republic in 1950.

CAPITAL.—Delhi (population in 1981 was 6,220,000).
Populations of other principal cities (1981 figures)
were ΨCalcutta, 9,166,000; ΨBombay (Mumbai),
8,202,000; ΨMadras, 4,277,000; Bangalore, 2,914,000;
Hyderabad, 2,566,000; Ahmedabad, 2,124,000; Kan-
pur, 1,685,000; Pune, 1,685,000; Lucknow, 1,007,000.

CURRENCY.—Indian Rupee of 100 Paisa.

FLAG.—The National Flag is a horizontal tricolour
with bands of deep saffron, white and dark green in
equal proportions. In the centre of the white band
appears an Asoka wheel in navy blue.

NATIONAL ANTHEM.—Jana-gana-mana.

NATIONAL DAY.—January 26 (Republic Day).

STATES AND TERRITORIES OF THE UNION

There are 25 States and seven Union Territories.
Each State is governed by a Governor appointed by
the President who holds office for five years, and a
Council of Ministers. All States have a Legislative
Assembly, and some have also a Legislative Council,
elected directly by adult suffrage for a maximum
period of five years. The judges of the High Court of
a State are appointed by the President.

The Union Territories are administered, except
where otherwise provided by Parliament, by the
President acting through an Administrator or Lieutenant Governor, or other authority appointed by
him.

States and Teritories (Capitals)	Area (sq. km.)	Population (1981 Census)	Governor	Chief Minister
STATES				
Andhra Pradesh (Hyderabad)...	275,100p	53,549,673	Miss K. Joshi	N. T. Rama Rao
Arunachal Pradesh (Itanagar)..	83,700p	631,839	B. N. Singh	Gegong Apang
Assam (Dispur)	78,400	19,896,843†	B. N. Singh	P. K. Mahanta
Bihar (Patna)	173,900p	69,914,734	G. N. Singh	B. J. Azad
Goa (Panaji)	3,701	1,000,000†	Dr. G. Singh	P. S. Rane
Gujurat (Gandhinagar)	196,000p	34,085,799	R. K. Trivedi	Amarsinh Chaudhary
Haryana (Chandigarh).........	44,200p	12,922,618	B. M. Brari	Devi Lal
Himachal Pradesh (Shimla)	55,700	4,280,818	Vice-Adm. (retd) R. K. S. Ghandi	Virbhadra Singh
Jammu and Kashmir* (Srinagar/Jammu)..........	222,200p	5,987,389	Jag Mohan	Dr. Farooq Abdullah
Karnataka (Bangalore)	191,800	37,135,714	P. Venkatasubbiah	(vacant)
Kerala (Trivandrum)	38,900p	25,453,680	Mrs. R. D. Sinha	E. K. Nayanar
Madhya Pradesh (Bhopal)......	443,500p	52,178,844	K. M. Chandy	Arjun Singh
Maharashtra (Bombay Mumbai)	307,700p	62,784,171	K. B. Reddy	S. B. Chavan
Manipur (Imphal)	22,300	1,420,953	Gen. K. V. Krishna Rao	R. K. Jaichandra Singh
Meghalaya (Shillong)	22,400p	1,335,819	B. N. Singh	P. A. Sangma
Mizoram (Aizawl)	21,100	493,757	H. Saikia	Laldenga
Nagaland (Kohima)	16,600	774,930	Gen. K. V. Krishna Rao	Hokishe Sema
Orissa (Bhubaneswar)	155,700	26,370,271	B. N. Pande	J. B. Patnaik
Punjab (Chandigarh)	50,400	16,788,915	S. S. Ray	(President's rule)
Rajasthan (Jaipur)	342,200	34,261,862	S. Prasad	S. C. Mathur
Sikkim (Gangtok)	7,100	316,385	T. V. Rajeshwar	Narbahadur Bhandari
Tamil Nadu (Madras)	130,100p	48,408,077	Dr. P. C. Alexander	(President's rule)
Tripura (Agartala)	10,500	2,053,058	Gen. K. V. Krishna Rao	S. R. Majumdar
Uttar Pradesh (Lucknow)	294,400p	110,862,013	M. Usman Arif	Birbahadur Singh
West Bengal (Calcutta)	88,800p	54,580,647	S. Nurul Hasan	Jyoti Basu
UNION TERRITORIES			*Lt. Governor*	
Andaman and Nicobar Is. (Port Blair)	8,200	188,741	Lt.-Gen. T. S. Oberoi	
Chandigarh	100	451,610	S. S. Ray‡	
Dadra and Nagar Haveli (Silvassa)..................	500	103,676	Dr. Gopal Singh‡	
Daman and Diu	112	51,602†	P. V. Jaikrishnan	
Delhi	1,500	6,220,406	A.V.M. (retd) H. Lal Kapur	
Lakshadweep (Kavaratti)	30	40,249	J. Sagar‡	
Pondicherry	500	604,471	T. P. Tewary	

p provisional figure   † estimated figure   ‡ Administrator

* Jammu and Kashmir is an area disputed between India, Pakistan and China, all three controlling a part of the territory. The area figure includes those parts occupied by Pakistan and China, which are claimed by India, but the population figure excludes the population of these areas, where the census was not taken. The state's capital is at Srinagar in winter and Jammu in summer.

GOVERNMENT

The Constitution of India came into force in 1950. Executive power is vested in the President, who is elected for a five year term by an electoral college consisting of the elected members of the Union and State Legislatures. He appoints the Prime Minister and, on the latter's advice, the Ministers, and can dismiss them. The Council of Ministers is collectively responsible to the *Lok Sabha* (Lower House). The Vice President is *ex-officio* chairman of the *Rajya Sabha* (Upper House).

Legislative power rests with the President, the *Rajya Sabha* (which has up to 250 members) and the *Lok Sabha* (which has up to 544 members). Twelve members of the *Rajya Sabha* are nominated by the President, the rest are indirectly elected representatives of the State and Union Territories. They hold office for six years. The 525 members of the *Lok Sabha* representing the States are directly elected by universal adult franchise, and 17 representatives of the Union Territories are chosen, for a maximum term of five years. Subject to the provisions of the Constitution, the Union Parliament can make laws for the whole of India and the State legislatures for their respective units.

The Supreme Court consists of the Chief Justice and not more than 17 other judges, appointed by the President. It is the highest court in respect of all constitutional matters and the final Court of Appeal.

President of the Republic of India, Ramaswami Venkataraman, *elected* July 16, 1987.
Vice-President, Shankar Dayal Sharma.

Cabinet

Prime Minister (also head of Ministries of Foreign Affairs; Personnel; Administrative Reforms; Planning; Science & Technology; Atomic Energy;

Electronics; Ocean Development; Space; Water Resources), Rajiv Gandhi.
Urban Development and Tourism, Mrs. Mohsina Kidwai.
Home Affairs, Buta Singh.
Parliamentary Affairs (and additional charge of Information and Broadcasting), H. K. L. Bhagat.
Steel and Mines, M. L. Fotedar.
Human Resources Development, P. V. Narasimha Rao
Power, Puroshottam Vasant Sathe.
Finance and Commerce, Narayan Dutt Tiwari.
Agriculture and Rural Development, Bhajan Lal.
Communications, Arjun Singh.
Defence, K. C. Pant.
Environment and Forests, Z. R. Ansari.
Industry, J. Vengal Rao.
Petroleum and Natural Gas, Brahm Dutt.
Health and Family Welfare, Motilal Vohra.

In addition to the members of the Council of Ministers there are six Ministers of State with independent charge, 32 Ministers of State and three Deputy Ministers in the Government.

INDIAN HIGH COMMISSION
India House, Aldwych, WC2B 4NA
[01-836 8484]

High Commissioner, His Excellency Maharaj Kishen Rasgotra (1988).
Deputy High Commissioner, S. S. Haider.

DEFENCE

The supreme command of the armed forces is vested in the President. Administrative and operational control resides in the Army, Navy and Air Headquarters under the supervision of the Ministry of Defence.

The *Army* has five Commands, Southern, Eastern, Northern, Western and Central.

The *Indian Navy* consists of two aircraft-carriers, a number of frigate squadrons, including some of the latest type of anti-submarine and anti-aircraft frigates, a squadron of anti-submarine patrol vessels, minesweeping squadrons, conventional type submarines and a submarine depot ship. A Naval aviation wing and a hydrographic office have also been set up. India has started building her own naval craft.

The *Indian Air Force* is organized in seven major formations, the Western, Eastern, Central, Southern and South Western Air Commands, and the Training and Maintenance Commands. Aircraft in use include SU-7, Hunter, Gnat, MiG 21 and MiG 23, Canberra bomber, Jaguar and Mirage-2000, helicopter and training planes.

PRODUCTION
Agriculture

Agriculture is the chief industry, supporting about 70 per cent of the population, and providing nearly 40 per cent of the Gross Domestic Product. The area under cultivation has been increased by irrigation schemes, but most holdings are less than five acres. Production has grown by three per cent each year since 1951, remaining slightly ahead of the two per cent increase necessary to keep pace with the rising population. Food crops occupy three-quarters of the total cropped area and production of food grains amounted to 144 million tonnes in 1986-87. The main food crops are rice, cereals (principally wheat), pulses, sugar cane, jute, cotton and tea. Other products include oil seeds, spices, groundnuts, tobacco, rubber and coffee. Livestock is raised, principally for dairy purposes or for the hides: cattle (181 million), goats (71 million), sheep (41 million) and pigs (9.9 million).

Industry

India's major industries are based on the exploitation and processing of her mineral resources, principally coal, oil and iron. The coal industry, nationalized in the early 1970s, reached an output in 1986-87 of 166 million tonnes. Production of crude oil, from the main fields in Assam and from offshore drilling was about 30.5 million tonnes in 1986-87. Steel production is mainly in the hands of the public sector, with five public and one private sector integrated steel plants producing 12.4 million tonnes of ingot steel in 1986-87. The engineering industry, heavy and light, is also primarily in the hands of the public sector. The manufacture of chemicals, fertilizers, petrochemicals, motor vehicles and commercial vehicles has been expanded.

Other principal manufactures are those derived from agricultural products, textiles, jute goods, sugar, leather, which along with tea, fish, and iron ore and concentrates, are India's major exports.

FINANCE

The budget estimates for 1988-89, placed expenditure (on revenue account) at *Rs*.526,400 million. Revenue (excluding States' shares) was estimated at *Rs*.416,200 million.

Trade with U.K.

	1986	1987
Imports from U.K.	£941,169,000	£1,090,146,000
Exports to U.K.	440,681,000	536,704,000

COMMUNICATIONS

Civil Aviation.—Four international airports—Palam (Delhi), Sahar (Bombay), Dum Dum (Calcutta), Meenambakkam (Madras)—are managed by the International Airports Authority. The other 87 aerodromes are controlled and operated by the Civil Aviation Department of the Government. The national airlines are Indian Airlines (internal) and Air India (international).

Railways.—The railways are grouped into nine administrative zones, Southern, Central, Western, Northern, North-Eastern, North-East Frontier, Eastern, South-Eastern and South-Central.

Gross Traffic Receipts (1986-87), crores of rupees, 7,505.66. Working expenses, 6,900.56. Net railway revenues, 680.84.

Ports.—The chief seaports are Bombay (Mumbai), Calcutta, Haldia, Madras, Mormugao, Cochin, Visakhapatnam, Kandla, Paradip, Mangalore and Tuticorin. There are 139 minor working ports with varying capacity.

Shipping.—On Nov. 30, 1986, 375 ships totalling 5,448,182 gross tons were on the Indian Register.

BRITISH HIGH COMMISSION
Chanakyapuri, New Delhi, 21, 1100-21.
[New Delhi 601371]

High Commissioner, His Excellency Sir David Goodall, K.C.M.G. (1987).
British Council Representative in India, R. Arbuthnott, AIFACS Building, Rafi Marg, New Delhi 110 001. Offices also at *Bombay, Madras* and *Calcutta*. There are British Council libraries at these four centres and British libraries at *Ahmedabad, Bangalore, Bhopal, Hyderabad, Lucknow, Patna, Pune, Ranchi* and *Trivandrum*.

JAMAICA

AREA, POPULATION, ETC.—Jamaica is situated in the Caribbean Sea south of the eastern extremity of Cuba and lies between latitudes 17° 43′ and 18° 32′ North, and longitude 76° 11′ and 78° 21′ West. Jamaica is 4,244 sq. miles (10,991 sq. km.) in area and is divided into three counties (Surrey, Middlesex and Cornwall) and 14 parishes. The greatest length from east to west (Morant Point to Negril Point) is 146 miles and the extreme breadth 51 miles.

The topography consists mainly of coastal plains, divided by the Blue Mountain Range in the east, and the hills and limestone plateaux which occupy the central and western areas of the interior. The central chain of high peaks of the Blue Mountains is over 6,000 feet above sea level, and the Blue Mountain Peak, the highest of these, reaches an elevation of 7,402 feet.

At Dec. 31, 1987 Jamaica's population was estimated to be 2,355,100. The island was discovered by Columbus on May 4, 1494, and occupied by the Spanish from 1509 until 1655 when a British expedition, sent out by Oliver Cromwell, under Admiral Penn and General Venables, attacked the island, which capitulated after a token resistance. In 1670 it was formally ceded to England by the Treaty of Madrid.

CAPITAL.—The seat of government is ΨKingston, the largest town and seaport (estimated population of the Corporate area of Kingston and St. Andrew in 1982, 696,300). Other towns are ΨMontego Bay, Spanish Town, Mandeville and May Pen.

CURRENCY.—Jamaican Dollar of 100 Cents.

FLAG.—Gold diagonal cross forming triangles of green at top and bottom, triangles of black at hoist and in fly.

NATIONAL DAY.—First Monday in August (Independence Day).

GOVERNMENT

Jamaica became an independent state within the Commonwealth on Aug. 6, 1962. The Legislature consists of a Senate of 21 nominated members and a House of Representatives consisting of 60 members elected by universal adult suffrage. The Senate has no power to delay money bills for longer than one month or other bills for longer than seven months against the wishes of the House of Representatives. The Constitution provides for a Leader of the Opposition.

At the General Election of Dec. 15, 1983, the Jamaica Labour Party won all 60 seats after the People's National Party decided not to contest the election.

Governor General, His Excellency Sir Florizel Glasspole, G.C.M.G., G.C.V.O.

Cabinet

Prime Minister and Minister of Finance and Planning, Rt. Hon. E. Seaga, P.C., M.P.
Deputy Prime Minister, Minister of Foreign Affairs, Trade and Industry, Rt. Hon. H. Shearer.
Construction and Electoral Affairs, Hon. B. Golding.
Agriculture, Hon. Dr. P. Broderick.
Justice and Attorney General, Senator Hon. O. Harding.
National Security, Hon. E. Anderson.
Local Government, Hon. N. B. Lewis.
Labour, Hon. J. A. G. Smith.
Public Utilities and Transport, Hon. P. Charles.
Education, Hon. Dr. N. Gallimore.
Public Service, Hon. C. Stone.
Youth and Community Development, Hon. E. C. Bartlett.

Mining, Energy and Tourism, Senator Hon. H. Hart.
Social Security and Consumer Affairs, Hon. Dr. Mavis Gilmour.
Ministers of State, Hon. Enid Bennett (*Social Security and Consumer Affairs*), Hon. H. Brown (*Tourism*); Hon. B. Lee (*Construction*); Hon. K. Sangster (*Youth and Community Development*); Hon. K. Samuda (*Health*); Hon. A. Johnson (*Agriculture*); Hon. M. Henry (*Office of Prime Minister*); Hon. R. Peralto (*National Security*); Hon. P. Stephens (*Public Utilities and Transport*); Hon. R. Marsh (*Construction*).

JAMAICAN HIGH COMMISSION
63 St. James's Street, SW1A 1LS
[01–499 8600]

High Commissioner, His Excellency H. S. Walker (1981).

JUDICATURE

Chief Justice and Keeper of Records, Hon. E. Zacca.
Judges of the Court of Appeal, Hon. I. D. Rowe (*President*); Hons. H. D. Carberry; J. S. Kerr; B. H. Carey; R. O. C. White; M. L. Wright; J. Campbell; D. Bingham.

COMMUNICATIONS

There are several excellent harbours, Kingston being the principal port. The island has 2,944 miles of main roads and over 7,000 miles of subsidiary roads. There are about 204 miles of railway. Telegraph stations and post offices are established in every town and in very many villages.

There are two international airports capable of handling the largest civil jet aircraft, the Norman Manley International Airport on the south coast serving Kingston, and Sangster Airport on the north coast serving the major tourist areas. In addition there are licensed aerodromes at Port Antonio, Ocho Rios, Mandeville and Negril. There are 16 privately owned, seven public and two military airstrips.

Air Jamaica, the national airline, operates international services; Trans-Jamaica Airlines operates scheduled internal services.

PRODUCTION

Agriculture.—Most of the staple products of tropical climates are grown; sugar, bananas, pimento, coffee and citrus fruit. Some of the sugar is used to produce rum and molasses. Main products exported in 1987 were sugar (US$74·1 million), bananas (US$19·1 million), citrus fruit and citrus products (US$6·1 million).

Industry.—Jamaica is the fourth largest producer of bauxite in the world; output for 1985 was 5,975,000 tonnes of which 1,513,000 tonnes were processed into alumina before being exported. In 1987 exports of bauxite and alumina were valued at US$336·5 million. Cement is manufactured locally, the output being 232,800 long tons in 1985.

In the last decade, manufacturing has grown from the processing of a few agricultural products into the production of a whole range of commodities such as textiles, clothing, footwear, and construction materials. Jamaica is a popular tourist resort, attracting visitors mainly from the U.S.A. In 1985 the total number of visitor arrivals was 846,716, and expenditure was estimated at US$406·8 million.

FINANCE

FINANCE

	1985–86*	1986–87**
Revenue	J$3,078·4m	J$3,942·9m
Expenditure	3,830·9m	4,688·5m
*provisional	**estimates	

National External Debt at Dec. 1985 US$1,841·3 million.

TRADE

	1986	1987
Total imports	J$5,322·2m	J$6,788·65m
Total exports	3,089·2m	3,896·20m

Trade with U.K.

	1986	1987
Imports from U.K......	£43,380,000	£54,644,000
Exports to U.K.	87,420,000	85,655,000

BRITISH HIGH COMMISSION
P.O. Box 575, Trafalgar Road, Kingston 10.
[Kingston 92-69050]

High Commissioner, His Excellency Alan Jeffrey Payne, C.M.G. (1987).

KENYA
(Jamhuri ya Kenya)

AREA, POPULATION, ETC.—Kenya is bisected by the equator and extends approximately from latitude 4° N. to latitude 4° S. and from longitude 34° E. to 41° E. From the coast of the Indian Ocean in the east, the borders of Kenya are with Somalia in the east and Ethiopia and Sudan in the north and north-west. To the west lie Uganda and Lake Victoria. On the south is Tanzania. The total area is 224,961 sq. miles (582,646 sq. km.), including 5,171 square miles of water. The country is divided into 7 Provinces (Nyanza, Rift Valley, Central, Coast, Western, Eastern and North-Eastern). The population is 20,333,000 (1985 U.N. estimate). The main tribal groups are the Kikuyu, Luhya, Luo, Kamba, Kalenjin and Masai. The official languages are Swahili, which is generally understood throughout Kenya, and English: numerous indigenous languages are also spoken.

CAPITAL.—Nairobi, population 1,103,554 (1984 estimate).

CURRENCY. Kenya Shilling of 100 Cents.

FLAG.—Three equal horizontal bands of black over red over green; red and white spears and shield device in centre.

NATIONAL ANTHEM.—Kenya, Land of the Lion.

NATIONAL DAY.—December 12 (Independence Day).

GOVERNMENT

Kenya became an independent state and a member of the British Commonwealth on December 12, 1963, after six months of internal self-government. Kenya became a Republic on Dec. 12, 1964. In 1982 the Government introduced amendments to the constitution and election law, making the country a one-party (K.A.N.U.) state. There is a uni-cameral National Assembly of 171 members, which will increase to 202 at the next General Election.

President, Hon. Daniel T. arap Moi, *took office,* Oct. 14, 1978.

Cabinet

Vice-President and Minister of Home Affairs, Hon. Dr. J. Karanja.

Finance and Planning, Hon. Prof. George Saitoti.
Co-operative Development, Hon. N. K. Ngala.
Agriculture, Hon. Elijah Mwangale.
Livestock, Hon. Maina Wanjigi.
Culture and Social Services, Hon. P. J. Ngei.
Information and Broadcasting, Hon. Waruru Kanja.
Foreign Affairs and International Co-operation, Dr. R. J. Ouko.
Water Development, Hon. Ndolo Ayah.
Local Government and Physical Planning, Hon. Moses Mudavadi.
Education, Hon. P. Oloo Aringo.
Tourism and Wildlife, Hon. George Muhoho.
Energy and Regional Development, Hon. Nicholas Biwott.
Commerce, Hon. K. K. Arap Sego.
Planning and National Development, Hon. Dr. Z. Onyonka.
Health, Hon. Mwai Kibaki.
Labour, Hon. Peter Okondo.
Industry, Hon. D. Otieno.
Transport and Communications, Hon. K. Matiba.
Research, Science and Technology, Hon. G. Ndotto.
Environment and Natural Resources, Hon. Jeremiah Nyagah.
Supplies and Marketing, Hon. W. ole Ntimama.
Lands and Housing, Hon. D. Mbela.
Technical Training and Applied Technology, Hon. Prof. S. K. Ongeri.
Manpower Development and Employment, Hon. A. K. Magugu.
National Guidance and Political Affairs, Hon. J. Njiru.
Regional Development, Hon. J. Okwanyo.
Ministers of State in the Office of the President, Hon. Jackson Angaine; Hon. B. Nabwera; Hon. H. Maalim; Hon L. Kitele.
Attorney-General, Hon. Matthew Guy Muli.

KENYA HIGH COMMISSION
24-25 New Bond Street, W1Y 9HD
[01–636 2371]

High Commissioner, Her Excellency Dr. Sally Jemng-Etich Kosgei (1987).

PRODUCTION

Agriculture provides about 52 per cent of total export earnings (excluding processed oil products). The great variation in altitude and ecology provide conditions under which a wide range of crops can be grown. These include wheat, barley, pyrethrum, coffee, tea, sisal, coconuts, cashew nuts, cotton, maize and a wide variety of tropical and temperate fruits and vegetables. The total area of well-farmed land on which concentrated mixed farming can be practised is small and the remainder is arid or semi-arid country but population pressure and the need to increase agricultural production for export has led to attempts to develop such areas.

Prospecting and mining are carried on in some parts of the country, the principal minerals produced being soda ash, salt and limestone.

Hydro-electric power has been developed, particularly on the Upper Tana River. Kenya is now almost self-sufficient in electric power generation but the connection with Owen Falls in Uganda is still in being.

There has been considerable industrial development over the last 15 years and Kenya has a wide variety of industries processing agricultural produce and manufacturing an increasing range of products from local and imported raw materials. New industries have recently come into being such as steel, textile mills, dehydrated vegetable processing and motor tyre manufacture as well as many smaller schemes which have added to the country's already considerable consumer goods. There is an oil refinery in Mombasa supplying both Kenya and Uganda, and a fuel pipeline now connects Mombasa and Nairobi.

COMMUNICATIONS

The Kenya Railways Corporation has 1,300 miles of railway open to traffic. There are also 31,000 miles of road, of which 2,700 are bitumen surfaced. Trans-border links with Tanzania were re-opened in 1985 with rail services for freight and steamer services for passengers and freight.

The principal port is Mombasa, operated by the Kenya Ports Authority.

International air services operate from airports at Nairobi and Mombasa.

TRADE

Principal exports are coffee and tea, which account for 33 per cent of total export earnings. Also exported are fruit, vegetables, and crude animal and vegetable material. Petroleum products account for about 37 per cent of imports; other imports are manufactured goods, particularly machinery, transport equipment, metals, pharmaceuticals and chemicals.

Trade with U.K.

	1986	1987
Imports from U.K.	£170,671,000	£199,059,000
Exports to U.K.	163,745,000	129,236,000

BRITISH HIGH COMMISSION
Bruce House, Standard Street, P.O. Box 30465
Nairobi
[Nairobi 335944]

High Commissioner, His Excellency Sir John Rodney Johnson, K.C.M.G. (1986).
British Council Representative, T. Edmundson, (P.O. Box 40751) ICEA Building, Kenyatta Avenue, Nairobi. There are offices at *Kisumu* and *Mombasa.*

KIRIBATI
(Ribaberikin Kiribati)

AREA, POPULATION, ETC.—Kiribati, the former Gilbert Islands, became an independent Republic in 1979. Kiribati comprises 36 islands—the Gilberts Group (17) including Banaba, formerly Ocean Island; the Phoenix Islands (8); and the Line Islands (11) (Jarvis, Palmyra and Kingman Islands are uninhabited dependencies of the U.S.A.)—situated in the South West Central Pacific around the point at which the International Date Line cuts the Equator. The total land area of 281 sq. miles (728 sq. km), is spread over some 2 million square miles of ocean. Few of the atolls are more than half a mile in width or more than 12 feet high. The vegetation consists mainly of coconut palms, breadfruit trees and pandanus. The population (1985 Census) was approx. 63,800. The population is predominantly Christian.

CAPITAL.—Tarawa (Population estimated at 24,400).
CURRENCY.—Kiribati uses the Australian Dollar.
FLAG.—Red, with blue and white wavy lines in base, and in the centre a gold rising sun and a flying frigate bird.
NATIONAL ANTHEM.—Teirake Kain Kiribati (Stand Kiribati).
NATIONAL DAY.—July 12 (Independence Day).

GOVERNMENT

The President is Head of State as well as Head of Government and is elected nationally. There is an elected House of Assembly (36 members); executive authority is vested in the Cabinet.

President and Minister of Foreign Affairs, Hon. Ieremia Tabai, G.C.M.G..
Vice-President and Minister of Finance, Hon. Teatao Teannaki.
Works and Energy, Hon. Ieruru Karotu.
Natural Resources Development, Hon. Taomati T. Iuta.
Home Affairs and Decentralization, Hon. Babera Kirata, O.B.E.
The Line and Phoenix Islands, Hon. Tekinaiti Kaiteie.
Trade, Industry and Labour, Hon. Raion Bataroma.
Transport and Communications, Hon. Uera Rabaua.
Health and Family Planning, Hon. Rotaria Ataia.
Education, Hon. Ataraoti Bwebwenibure.
Attorney-General, Hon. Michael N. Takabwebwe.
Chief Justice, Hon. V. Maxwell.

ECONOMY

Most people still practise a semi-subsistence economy, the main staples of their diet being coconuts and fish.

Estimated recurrent revenue for 1987 is $A18,381,940. United Kingdom budgetary assistance ceased in 1985. The principal imports are foodstuffs, consumer goods, machinery and transport equipment. The principal exports are copra, which earned $A459,000, and fish, income from which was around $A1,775,000 in 1986. Total value of exports in 1986 was $A2,495,833.

COMMUNICATIONS

Air communication exists between most of the islands, and is operated by Air Tungaru, a statutory corporation. Air Nauru flies weekly between Tarawa and Nauru. Air Marshall Islands operate a weekly service between Majuro/Tarawa/Funafuti and Nandi. Inter-island shipping is operated by a statutory corporation, the Shipping Corporation of Kiribati.

SOCIAL WELFARE

The Government maintains a teacher training college and a secondary school. Four junior secondary schools are maintained by missions. Throughout the Republic there are about a hundred primary schools. The total enrolment of children of school age is about 14,000. The Marine Training School at Tarawa trains seamen for service with overseas shipping lines. There is a general hospital at Tarawa. The other inhabited islands have dispensaries.

Trade with U.K.

	1986	1987
Imports from U.K.	£179,000	£301,000
Exports to U.K.	4,000	8,000

BRITISH HIGH COMMISSION
P.O. Box 61, Bairiki, Tarawa
[Bairiki 21327]

High Commissioner, His Excellency Charles Thompson (1983).

LESOTHO
('Muso oa Lesotho)

Lesotho is a landlocked mountainous state entirely surrounded by the Republic of South Africa. Of the total area of 11,720 sq. miles, (30,355 sq. km.), a belt between 20 and 40 miles in width lying across the western and southern boundaries and comprising about one-third of the total is classed as lowlands, being between 5,000 and 6,000 ft. above sea level. The remaining two-thirds are classed as foothills and highlands, rising to 11,425 ft. The population was 1,443,853 (1986 Census).

CAPITAL.—Maseru, population, (1986 Census) 288,951.

CURRENCY.—Maloti of 100 Lisente.

FLAG.—Diagonally white over blue over green with the white of double width, and an assegai and knobkerrie on a Basotho shield in brown in the upper hoist.

NATIONAL ANTHEM.—Pina ea Sechaba.

NATIONAL DAY.—October 4 (Independence Day).

GOVERNMENT

Lesotho became a constitutional monarchy within the Commonwealth on October 4, 1966. The independence constitution was suspended in January 1970, when the country was governed by a Council of Ministers, until the establishment of a nominated National Assembly in April 1974. The Government was overthrown in Jan. 1986: all legislative and executive authority is now vested in the King acting on advice from a Military Council and with the assistance of a Council of Ministers.

The country is divided into ten administrative districts. In each district there is a District Co-ordinator who co-ordinates all Government activity in the area, working in co-operation with hereditary chiefs.

Head of State, H.M. King Moshoeshoe II.

Military Council

Chairman, Maj. Gen. Justin Metsing Lekhanya.
Members, Col. Elias P. Ramaema; Col. Aloysieus K. Mosoeunyane; Col. Michael N. Ts'otetsi; Col. Thaabe S. Letsie; Col. J. Sekhobe N. Letsie.

Council of Ministers

Chairman, Minister of Defence and Internal Security, Public Service and Cabinet Office, H.E. Maj.-Gen. Justin Metsing Lekhanya.
Foreign Affairs, H.E. Col. Thaabe S. Letsie.
Law, Constitutional and Parliamentary Affairs, Hon. K. Sello.
Finance, Hon. E. R. Sekhonyana.
Works, Hon. L. D. Monyake.
Justice and Prisons, Hon. B. M. Khaketla.
Information and Broadcasting, Hon. V. M. Malebo.
Employment, Social Welfare and Pensions, Hon. M. M. Tiheli.
Planning, Economic and Manpower Development, Hon. Dr. M. M. Sefali.
Agriculture, Co-operatives and Marketing, Hon. Dr. D. R. Phororo.
Transport and Communications, Hon. Col. P. M. Mokhants'o.
Tourism, Sports and Culture, Hon. M. L. Mathealire.
Water, Energy and Mining, Hon. Col. A. L. Jane.
Highlands, Water and Energy Affairs, Hon. M. M. Lebotsa.
Interior and Chieftainship Affairs and Rural Development, Hon. Morena M. Seeiso.
Education, Hon. Prof. L. B. J. Machobane.

Trade and Industry, Hon. M. Mokoroane
Health, Hon. Dr. S. T. Makenete.
Ministers of State, Hon. Mrs. A. 'M. Hlalele (*Youth and Women's Affairs*); Hon. P. M. 'Mabathoana (*Interior, Chieftainship Affairs and Rural Development*); Hon. M. P. Molapo (*Military Council*).

JUDICIARY

The Lesotho Courts of Law consist of the Court of Appeal, the High Court, Magistrates' Courts, Judicial Commissioners' Court, Central and local Courts. Magistrates' and higher courts administer the laws of Lesotho. They also adjudicate appeals from the Judicial Commissioner's and Subordinate Courts.

Chief Justice, Hon. B. P. Cullinan.

LESOTHO HIGH COMMISSION
10 Collingham Road, SW5 0NR
[01–373 8581]

High Commissioner, His Excellency Dr. John Teboho Kolane (1986).

EDUCATION

Most schools are mission-controlled, the Government providing grants for salaries and buildings. There are over 1,000 primary and over 100 secondary schools; few areas lack a school and there is a high literacy rate of about 70 per cent. Increasing emphasis is being laid on agricultural and vocational education. The National University of Lesotho at Roma was established in 1975.

COMMUNICATIONS

A tarred road of 110 miles links Maseru to several of the main lowland towns, and this is being extended in the south of the country. The mountainous areas are linked by 1,300 miles of gravelled and earth roads and tracks. Roads link border towns in South Africa with the main towns in Lesotho. Maseru is connected by rail with the main Bloemfontein–Natal line of the South African Railways. Scheduled international air services are operated daily between Maseru and Johannesburg and other scheduled international flights are to Manzini and Maputo. There are around 30 airstrips. Internal scheduled services are operated by the Lesotho Airways Corporation.

The telephone network is fully automated in all urban centres. Radio telephone communication is used extensively in the remote rural areas.

PRODUCTION

The economy of Lesotho is based on agriculture and animal husbandry, and the adverse balance of trade (mainly consumer and capital goods) is offset by the earnings of the large numbers of the population who work in South Africa. Apart from some diamonds, Lesotho has few natural resources and only small-scale industrial development. The Lesotho National Development Corporation was set up to promote the development of industry, mining, trade and tourism. Work has commenced on the Highlands Water Scheme designed to provide water for the Vaal industrial zone in South Africa and hydro-electricity for Lesotho. Drilling is being carried out for oil. A National Park has been established at Sehlabathebe in the Maluti mountains. A number of light manufacturing and processing industries have recently been established.

FINANCE AND TRADE

The main sources of revenue are customs and excise duty. Estimates of expenditure and revenue (1986) are recurrent revenue M241·2 million; recurrent expenditure M265·3 million; capital revenue M144 million; capital expenditure M198 million.

Trade with U.K.

	1986	1987
Imports from U.K.	£2,128,000	£1,112,000
Exports to U.K.	277,000	486,000

BRITISH HIGH COMMISSION
P.O. Box 521, Maseru
[Maseru 31396l]

High Commissioner, His Excellency John Coates Edwards (1988).
British Council Representative, A. D. Bates, Hobson's Square, P.O. Box 429, Maseru, 100.

MALAWI
(Mfuko La Malawi)

AREA, POPULATION, ETC.—Malawi comprises Lake Malawi (formerly Lake Nyasa) and its western shore, with the high table-land separating it from the basin of the Luangwa River, the watershed forming the western frontier with Zambia; south of the lake, Malawi reaches almost to the Zambezi and is surrounded by Mozambique, the frontier lying on the west on the watershed of the Zambezi and Shire Rivers, and to the east on the Ruo, a tributary of the Shire, and Lakes Chiuta and Chirwa. This boundary reaches the eastern shore of Lake Malawi and extends up to the mid-point of the lake for about half its length where it returns to the eastern and northern shores to form a frontier with Tanzania. Malawi has a total area of 45,747 sq. miles (118,484 sq. km.). The population, according to the Census held in September 1977, is 5,547,460; a U.N. estimate put the figure at 7,059,000 in 1985. The official languages are Chichewa and English.

CAPITAL.—Lilongwe (population (1987) 175,000). The city of Blantyre in the Southern Region, incorporating Blantyre and Limbe (population (1987) 289,000), is the major commercial and industrial centre. Other main centres are: Mzuzu, Thyolo, Mulanje, Mangochi, Salima, Dedza and Zomba, the former capital.

CURRENCY.—Malawi Kwacha of 100 Tambala.

FLAG.—Horizontal stripes of black, red and green, with rising sun in the centre of the black stripe.

NATIONAL ANTHEM.—O God Bless Our Land of Malawi.

NATIONAL DAY.—July 6 (Independence Day).

GOVERNMENT

Malawi became a republic on July 6, 1966, having assumed internal self-government on February 1, 1963, and achieved independence on July 6, 1964. There is a Cabinet consisting of the Life President and other Ministers. The Parliament consists of 112 members, each elected by universal suffrage. Under the 1981 Amendment to the Constitution, the Life President has the power to nominate as many Members of Parliament as he wishes. Being a one-party State (the Malawi Congress Party), all elected members are required to be members of the Party. The Parliament, which usually meets three times a year, is presided over by a Speaker.

President, Minister of External Affairs, Agriculture, Justice, Works, Supplies, Dr. H. Kamuzu Banda, *elected* 1966, *sworn in as* President for Life, July 6, 1971.

Cabinet

Trade, Industry and Tourism, Hon. Robson Chirwa.
Transport and Communications, Hon. Dalton Katopola.
Health, Hon. Edward Bwanali.
Finance, Hon. Louis Chimango.
Labour, Wadson Bini Deleza.
Education and Culture, Hon. Michael Mlambala.
Community Services, Hon. E. C. Katola Phiri.
Forestry and Natural Resources, Hon. Stanford Demba.
Local Government, Hon. M. M. Mwakikunga.

JUDICIARY

Chief Justice, Hon. F. L. Makuta.

MALAWI HIGH COMMISSION
33 Grosvenor Street, W1X 0DE
[01–491 4172/7]

High Commissioner, His Excellency Mr. Bernard B. Mtawali (1987).

EDUCATION

Primary education is the responsibility of local authorities in both urban and rural areas, although policy, curricula and inspection are the responsibility of the Ministry of Education and Culture. The Ministry is also responsible for secondary schools, technical education and primary teacher training. Religious bodies, with Government assistance, still play an important part in these fields. The University of Malawi was opened in 1965 and has four constituent colleges.

COMMUNICATIONS

A single-track railway runs from Mchinji on the Zambian border, through Lilongwe and Salima on Lake Malawi (itself served by two passenger and a number of cargo boats) through Blantyre to the southern frontier into Mozambique, and connecting with the Mozambique port of Beira. There are 12,215 km. of roads in Malawi of which about 21·8 per cent are bituminised.

There is an international airport 26 km. from Lilongwe, which handles regional and inter-continental flights.

FINANCE

(excluding Development Account)

	1985–86	1986–87
Revenue	K483m	K512m
Expenditure	658m	547m

ECONOMY

The economy is largely agricultural, with maize the main subsistence crop. Tobacco, sugar, tea, groundnuts and cotton are the main cash crops and principal exports. There are two sugar mills and total production in 1987 was 167,925 tonnes. A number of light manufacturing industries have been established recently.

TRADE

	1985	1986
Imports	K492m	K478m
Exports	420m	462m

Trade with U.K.

	1986	1987
Imports from U.K.	£28,557,000	£18,069,000
Exports to U.K.	56,983,000	44,223,000

BRITISH HIGH COMMISSION
Lingadzi House (P.O. Box 30042),
Lilongwe 3
[Lilongwe 731544]

High Commissioner, His Excellency Dr. Denis Osborne (1987).
Deputy High Commissioner, J. Wilde.
British Council Representative, S. Newton, (P.O. Box 30222), Lilongwe. There is also a library at Blantyre.

MALAYSIA

(Persekutuan Tanah Malaysia)

AREA, POPULATION, ETC.—Malaysia, comprising the 11 states of peninsular Malaya plus Sabah and Sarawak, forms a crescent well over 1,000 miles long between latitudes 1° and 7° N. and longitudes 100° and 119° E. It occupies two distinct regions—the Malay peninsula which extends from the isthmus of Kra to the Singapore Strait and the north-west coastal area of the island of Borneo. Each is separated from the other by 400 miles of the South China Sea. The total area of Malaysia, including the Federal Territories of Kuala Lumpur and Labuan, is approx. 127,317 sq. miles, (329,749 sq. km.), containing a population of 16,544,000 (1986 Census). The principal racial groups are the Malays, the Chinese and those of Indian and Sri Lankan origin, as well as the indigenous races of Sarawak and Sabah. Bahasa Malaysia (Malay) is the sole official language, but English, various dialects of Chinese, and Tamil are also widely spoken. There are a few indigenous languages widely spoken in Sabah and Sarawak.

RELIGION.—Islam is the official religion of Malaysia, each Ruler being the head of religion in his State, though the Heads of State of Sabah and Sarawak are not heads of the Muslim religion in their States. The Yang di-Pertuan Agung is the head of religion in Malacca and Penang. The Constitution guarantees religious freedom.

CLIMATE.—The year is commonly divided into the Southwest and Northwest monsoon seasons. Rainfall averages about 100 inches throughout the year, though the annual fall varies from place to place. The average daily temperature throughout Malaysia varies from 21° C. to 32° C., though in higher areas temperatures are lower and vary widely.

CAPITAL—Kuala Lumpur was proclaimed Federal Territory on February 1, 1974. Its population is (1985) 1,103,200.

CURRENCY.—Malaysian Dollar (Ringgit) of 100 Sen.
FLAG.—Equal horizontal stripes of red (7) and white (7); 14 point yellow star and crescent in blue canton.
NATIONAL ANTHEM.—Negara-Ku.
NATIONAL DAY.—August 31 (*Hari Kebangsaan*).

STATES OF THE FEDERATION

The 13 States of the Federation of Malaysia (State capitals in brackets) and their populations at the 1986 Census are:

ψJohore (Johore Bahru)	1,867,333
Kedah (Alor Setar).................	1,263,155
Kelantan (Kota Bahru).............	1,048,420
ψMelaka (Melaka)...................	524,028
Negri Sembilan (Seremban)	647,159
ψPahang (Kuantan)	921,360
ψPenang (Georgetown)	1,049,282
Perak (Ipoh)......................	2,020,135
Perlis (Kangar)	166,948
ψSabah (Kota Kinabalu)	1,222,718
ψSarawak (Kuching)	1,477,428

ψSelangor (Shah Alam)	1,731,090
ψTerengganu (Kuala Terengganu)....	638,830
ψSeaport	

FEDERAL TERRITORIES

The two Federal Territories and their populations at the 1986 Census are:

Kuala Lumpur	1,103,200
Labuan............................	12,219*
* 1980 Census	

GOVERNMENT

The Federation of Malaya became an independent country within the Commonwealth on August 31, 1957, as a result of an agreement between H.M. the Queen and the Rulers of the Malay States. On Sept. 16, 1963, the Federation was enlarged by the accession of the states of Singapore, Sabah (formerly British North Borneo) and Sarawak, and the name of Malaysia was adopted from that date. On Aug. 9, 1965, Singapore seceded from the Federation.

The Constitution was designed to ensure the existence of a strong Federal Government and also a measure of autonomy for the State Governments. It provides for a constitutional Supreme Head of the Federation (H.M. the *Yang di-Pertuan Agung*) to be elected for a term of five years by the Rulers from among their number, and for a Deputy Supreme Head (H.R.H. *Timbalan Yang di-Pertuan Agung*) to be similarly elected. The Malay Rulers are either chosen or succeed to their position in accordance with the custom of the particular state. In other states of Malaysia choice of the Head of State is at the discretion of the *Yang di-Pertuan Agung* after consultation with the Chief Minister of the State.

The Federal Parliament consists of two houses, the Senate and the House of Representatives. The Senate (*Dewan Negara*) consists of 68 members, under a President (*Yang di-Pertua Dewan Negara*), 26 elected by the Legislative Assemblies of the States (2 from each) and 42 appointed by the *Yang di-Pertuan Agung*. The House of Representatives (*Dewan Rakyat*), consists of 177 members (Peninsular Malaysia, 134; Sarawak, 24; and Sabah, 20). Members are elected on the principle of universal adult suffrage with a common electoral roll.

The Constitution provides that each State shall have its own Constitution not inconsistent with the Federal Constitution, with the Ruler or Governor acting on the advice of an Executive Council appointed on the advice of the Chief Minister and a single chamber Legislative Assembly. The State Secretary, the State Legal Adviser and the State Financial Officer sit in the Executive Council as *ex-officio* members. The Legislative Assemblies are fully elected on the same basis as the Federal Parliament.

Supreme Head of State, H.M. Sultan Mahmood Iskandar Al-Haj ibni Al-Marhun Sultan Ismail (Sultan of Johore), *assumed office for a term of five years,* April 1984, *sworn in* Nov. 15, 1984.
Deputy Supreme Head of State, H.R.H. Raja Tun Azlan Shah (Sultan of Perak).

MINISTRY

Prime Minister and Minister of Home Affairs and Justice, Datuk Seri Dr. Mahathir Muhammad.
Deputy P.M. and Minister of National and Rural Development, Ghafar Baba.
Labour, Encik Lee Kim Sai.
Welfare Services, Encik Mustaffa Muhammad.
Youth and Sports, Datuk Najib Tun Razak.
Land and Regional Development, Datuk Sulaiman Daud.

Works, Datuk S. Samy Vellu.
Health, Datuk Chan Siang Sun.
Finance, Datu Paduka Daim Zainuddin.
Foreign Affairs, Datuk Haji Abu Hassan Omar.
Education, Anwar Ibrahim.
Information, Datuk Muhammad Rahmat.
Transport, Datuk Ling Liong Sik.
Trade and Industry, Datin Paduka Rafidah Aziz.
Defence, Tengku Ahmad Rithaudden.
Agriculture, Datuk Seri Sanusi Junid.
Public Enterprises, Datuk Napsiah Omar.
Primary Industries, Datuk Lim Kheng Yaik.
Science, Technology and Environment, Datuk Stephen Yong.
Energy, Telecommunications and Posts, Datuk Leo Moggie.
Housing and Local Government, Datuk Ng Cheng Kiat.
Tourism and Culture, Datuk Hj Sabaruddin Chik.
Ministers in Prime Minister's Department, Kasitah Gadam; Datuk Dr. Yusoff Noor.

NOTE.—The words "Tunku/Tengku", "Tun", "Tan Sri", and "Datuk" are titles. The word "Tunku/Tengku" is equivalent to "Prince". "Tun" denotes membership of a high Order of Malaysian Chivalry and "Tan Sri" and "Datuk" ("Datuk Seri" in Perak and "Datu" in Sabah) are each the equivalent of a knighthood. The wife of a "Tun" is styled "Toh Puan", that of a "Tan Sri" is styled "Puan Sri" and of a "Datuk" "Datin". The honorific "Tuan" or "Encik" is equivalent to "Mr." and the honorific "Puan" is equivalent to "Mrs.". The words "Al-Haj" or "Haji" indicate that the person so named has made the pilgrimage to Mecca.

MALAYSIAN HIGH COMMISSION
45 Belgrave Square, SW1X 8QT
[01–235 8033]

High Commissioner, His Excellency Dato Mon Jamaluddin (1988).

JUDICATURE

The Judicial System consists of a Supreme Court and two High Courts, one in Peninsular Malaysia and one for Sabah and Sarawak (sitting alternately in Kota Kinabalu and Kuching).

The Supreme Court comprises a President, the two Chief Justices of the High Courts and other judges. It possesses appellate, original and advisory jurisdiction.

Each of the High Courts consists of a Chief Justice and not less than 4 other judges. The Federal Constitution allows for a maximum of twelve such judges for Malaya and eight for Borneo. In Peninsular Malaysia the Subordinate Courts consist of the Sessions Courts and the Magistrates' Courts. In Sabah/Sarawak the Magistrates' Courts constitute the Subordinate Courts.

DEFENCE

The Malaysian Armed Forces consist of the Army, Navy and Air Force, together with volunteer forces for each arm. The defence of the country is largely borne by the army in its role of providing defence against external threat and counter-insurgency operations and also to assist the police in the performance of public order duties. The *Royal Malaysian Navy (RMN)* has the responsibility of defending the 3,000 miles of the country's coastline and maintaining constant patrol of 500 miles of the high seas that separate Sabah and Sarawak from the mainland. The *Royal Malaysian Air Force (RMAF)* is capable of providing close strategic and tactical support to the army and police in the defence and internal security of the country.

FINANCE

	1987	M$million 1988
Revenue	18,021	20,834
Expenditure	26,312	27,121

PRODUCTION AND TRADE

The agricultural sector continues to be the mainstay of the Malaysian economy. However, diversification of crops and rapid growth in the manufacturing sector has made Malaysia less vulnerable to fluctuations in the price of its primary crop, natural rubber.

Malaysia is the largest exporter of natural rubber, tin, palm oil and tropical hardwoods. Other major export commodities are manufactured and processed products, petroleum, oil, and other minerals, palm kernel oil, tea and pepper.

Exports of major commodities were (percentage of total exports):

	1986	1987
Primary commodities	27·9	31·9
Petroleum	19·9	15·2
Manufactured goods	40·5	44·2

Another commodity which is produced throughout Malaysia is rice, the staple food, and efforts are being made to achieve self-sufficiency.

Imports consist mainly of machinery and transport equipment, manufactured goods, foods, mineral fuels, chemicals and inedible crude materials for her growing population and to accelerate the pace of her economic growth and development.

	1986	M$million 1987
Imports	26,774	31,983
Exports	33,552	45,176

Trade with U.K.

	1986	1987
Imports from U.K.	£226,912,000	£257,970,000
Exports to U.K.	350,058,000	397,122,000

BRITISH HIGH COMMISSION
Wisma Damansara, Jalan Semantan
(P.O. Box 11030), 50732 Kuala Lumpur
[Kuala Lumpur 03–2541533]

High Commissioner, His Excellency John Nicholas Teague Spreckley, C.M.G. (1986).

British Council Representative, A. Johnson, Jalan Bukit Aman, 50480, Kuala Lumpur 10–01; offices at *Kota Kinabalu* (Sabah) and *Kuching* (Sarawak), and a library in Penang.

THE MALDIVES
(Divehi Jumhuriya)

AREA, POPULATION, ETC.—The Maldives are a chain of coral atolls, some 400 miles to the south-west of Sri Lanka, stretching from just south of the equator for about 600 miles to the north. There are about 20 coral atolls comprising over 1,200 islands, 202 of which are inhabited. Total area of the islands is 115 sq. miles (298 sq. km.). No point in the entire chain of islands is more than 8 feet above sea-level. The population of the islands (1986) is 189,400. The people are Sunni Moslems and the Maldivian language is akin to Elu or old Sinhalese.

CAPITAL.—ΨMalé (population, 1985, 46,334). There is an international airport at Malé.

CURRENCY.—Rufiyaa of 100 Laris.

FLAG.—Green field bearing a white crescent, with wide red border.

NATIONAL ANTHEM.—Qawmee Salaam.

NATIONAL DAY.—July 26.

GOVERNMENT

Until 1952 the islands were a Sultanate under the protection of the British Crown. Internal self-government was achieved in 1948 and full independence in 1965. In 1982 the Republic of the Maldives became a special member of the Commonwealth, and a full member in 1985.

The Maldives form a Republic which is elective. There is a Parliament (the *Citizens' Majlis*) with representatives elected from all the atolls. The life of the Majlis is 5 years. The Government consists of a Cabinet, which is responsible to the Majlis.

President, His Excellency Maumoon Abdul Gayoom, *elected* 1978, *re-elected* Sept. 30, 1983 (also *Minister of Defence and National Security*).

Cabinet

Foreign Affairs, Hon. Fathulla Jameel.
Justice, Hon. Abdulla Hameed (*acting*).
Home Affairs and Social Services, Hon. Umar Zahir.
Education, Hon. Mohamed Zahir Hussain.
Health, Hon. Abdulla Jameel.
Fisheries, Hon. Abdul Sattar.
Agriculture, (vacant).
Transport and Shipping, Hon. Ahmed Mujathaba.
Atolls Administration, Hon. Abdulla Hameed.
Trade and Industries, Hon. Ilyas Ibrahim.
Attorney General, Hon. Ahmed Zaki.
Speaker of Majlis, Hon. Ibrahim Shihab.
Chief Justice, Hon. Moosa Sathy.

PRODUCTION

The vegetation of the islands is coconut palms with some scrub. Hardly any cultivation of crops is possible and nearly all food to supplement the basic fish diet has to be imported. The principal industry is fishing and considerable quantities of fish are exported to Japan. Dried fish is exported to Sri Lanka, where it is a delicacy. The tourist industry is expanding very rapidly. Maldives Shipping Ltd. has a fleet of some 30 merchant ships.

Trade with U.K.

	1986	1987
Imports from U.K.	£1,321,000	£2,772,000
Exports to U.K.	276,000	440,000

BRITISH HIGH COMMISSION

High Commissioner, (*resident* at Colombo).

MALTA

(Repubblika Ta'Malta)

AREA, POPULATION, ETC.—Malta lies in the Mediterranean Sea, 58 miles from Sicily and about 180 miles from the African coast, about 17 miles in length and 9 in breadth, and having an area of 94·9 square miles. Malta includes also the adjoining island of *Gozo* (area 25·9 sq. miles); *Comino* and minor islets. The U.N. estimated population at 1985 was 383,000.

Maltese and English are the official languages of administration and Maltese is ordinarily the official language in all the courts of law and the language of general use in the islands.

Malta was in turn held by the Phoenicians, Greeks, Carthaginians, Romans and Arabs. In 1090 it was conquered by Count Roger of Normandy. In 1530 it was handed over to the Knights of St. John, who made of it a stronghold of Christianity. In 1565 it sustained the famous siege, when the last great effort of the Turks was successfully withstood by Grandmaster La Valette. The Knights expended large sums in fortifying the island and carrying out many magnificent works, until they were expelled by Napoleon in 1798. The Maltese rose against the French garrison soon afterwards, and the island was subsequently blockaded by the British fleet. The Maltese people freely requested the protection of the British Crown in 1802 on condition that their rights and privileges would be preserved and respected. The islands were finally annexed to the British Crown by the Treaty of Paris in 1814.

Malta was again closely besieged in the last war. From June, 1940, to the end of the war, 432 members of the garrison and 1,540 civilians were killed by enemy aircraft, and about 35,000 houses were destroyed or damaged. The island was awarded the George Cross in 1942.

CAPITAL.—Valletta. Population (estimated 1984), 14,013. Valletta Grand Harbour is one of the finest in the world; it is very deep, and large vessels can anchor alongside the shore. It is an important port of call and ship repairing centre for vessels, being half-way between Gibraltar and Port Said.

CURRENCY.— Maltese Lira of 100 Cents and 1,000 Mils.

FLAG.—Two equal vertical stripes, white at the hoists and red at the fly. A representation of the George Cross is carried edged in red in the top corner of the white stripe.

NATIONAL ANTHEM.—Lil Din I-Art Helwa.

NATIONAL DAY.—March 31.

GOVERNMENT

On Sept. 21, 1964, under the Malta Independence Order, 1964, Malta became an independent state within the Commonwealth; on December 13, 1974, Malta became a republic within the Commonwealth.

Elections are held every five years by a system of proportional representation. Seats are obtained by the highest number of votes in the respective districts. The party with the highest number of votes forms the government, with extra members being co-opted if necessary.

Acting President.—Paul Xuereb.

Cabinet

Prime Minister, Hon. Dr. Edward Fenech Adami.
Deputy P.M. and Minister of the Interior and Justice, Hon. Dr. Guido De Marco.
Foreign Affairs, Hon. Dr. Vincent Tabone.
Education, Hon. Dr. Ugo Mifsud Bonnici.
Social Policy, Hon. Dr. Louis Galea.
Finance, Hon. Dr. G. Bonello Du Puis.
Infrastructure Development, Hon. Michael Falzon.
Productive Development, Hon. Lawrence Gatt.
Tertiary Sector Development, Hon. Dr. Emmanuel Bonnici.
Gozo, Hon. Anton Tabone.
Health, Hon. Dr. George Hyzler.
Elderly, Hon. Dr. John Rizzo Naudi.
Housing, Hon. Dr. Joe Cassar.
Water, Electricity and Energy, Hon. Anthony Zammit.
Post and Telecommunications, Hon. Pierre Muscat.
Industry, Hon. John Dalli.
Tourism, Hon. Dr. Michael Refalo.
Maritime Affairs, Hon. Dr. Joe Fenech.

MALTA HIGH COMMISSION

16 Kensington Square, W8 5HH
[01–938 1712]

High Commissioner, His Excellency John A. Manduca (1987).

EDUCATION

In June 1986 there were 92 Government Primary Schools with 26,341 pupils and 43 Secondary Schools and new Lyceums, with a total of 13,813 pupils.

The Government also runs 24 Technical/Trade Schools (with an enrolment of 6,358 students). Schools of Art, Music, Secretarial Studies, Catering, Nursing and Dramatic Art are sponsored by the Government. Tertiary education is available at the University of Malta, which had 1,449 students in 1987.

A number of private schools offer more or less the same facilities that exist in Government schools. All state education is free.

The Maltese are mainly Roman Catholic. The Maltese language is of Semitic origin and held by some to be derived from the Carthaginian and Phoenician tongues.

AGRICULTURE

Agriculture plays a significant role in the economy. There are 2,518 full time farmers and about 12,274 part time farmers. The yearly crop production is about 104,270 tonnes consisting mainly of tomatoes, potatoes, onions, cabbages and cauliflowers, and some 6,576 tonnes of fruit. Grape is the largest fruit crop. Flowers and cuttings are produced for export markets.

INDUSTRY

The island's leading industry is the state-owned Malta Drydocks, employing about 5,000 people. The main port of Grand Harbour handled traffic (excluding mineral oils) of 2,243,524 tonnes in 1986.

At the end of 1986 manufacturing firms employed some 30,571 people. The wide range of produce includes food processing, textiles and clothing, plastics and chemical products, electronic equipment and components. The gross output of the manufacturing industry in 1986 was £M331·5 million, of which £M172·3 million were export sales.

Tourism has assumed primary importance, with over 574,189 tourists visiting the island in 1986, and there are plans to develop Marsamxett Harbour as a yachting centre. Gross income from this industry stood at £M79·4 million.

FINANCE

	1986	1987
Revenue	£M231,500,000	£M241,000,000
Expenditure	240,000,000	269,000,000

TRADE

The principal imports for home consumption are foodstuffs—mainly wheat, meat and bullocks, milk and fruit—fodder, beverages and tobacco, fuels, chemicals, textiles and machinery (industrial, agricultural and transport). The chief domestic exports are processed food, electronics, textiles, and other manufactures.

	1985	1986
Imports	£M354,000,000	£M347,909,000
Exports	186,000,000	194,668,000

Trade with U.K.

	1986	1987
Imports from U.K. ...	£101,877,000	£107,941,000
Exports from U.K. ...	49,197,000	52,105,000

BRITISH HIGH COMMISSION

7 St. Anne Street, Floriana, Malta
[233134/8]

High Commissioner, His Excellency Brian Hitch, C.M.G., C.V.O. (1988).

MAURITIUS

AREA, POPULATION, ETC.—Mauritius is an island group lying in the Indian Ocean, 550 miles east of Madagascar, between 57° 17′–57° 46′ E. long. and 19° 58′–20° 33′ S. lat., and comprising with its dependencies an area of 790 square miles (2,045 sq. km.). The population (1987 U.N. estimate) was 1,054,200 made up of Asiatic races (Hindus 52·6 per cent, Muslims 16·5 per cent), and persons of European (mainly French extraction), mixed and African descent (28·3 per cent).

English is the official language but French may be used in the Legislative Assembly and lower law courts. However, Creole is the mostly commonly used language.

CLIMATE.—Mauritius enjoys a sub-tropical maritime climate, with a wide range of rainfall and temperature resulting from the mountainous nature of the island. Humidity is rather high throughout the year and rainfall is sufficient to maintain a green cover of vegetation, except for a brief period in the driest districts.

CAPITAL.—ΨPort Louis, population (1985), 138,272; other centres are Beau Bassin-Rose Hill (93,059); Curepipe (64,072); Vacoas-Phoenix (55,330) and Quatre Bornes (65.405).

CURRENCY.—Mauritian Rupee of 100 cents.

FLAG.—Red, blue, yellow and green horizontal stripes.

NATIONAL ANTHEM.—Glory to the Motherland.

NATIONAL DAY.—March 12.

GOVERNMENT

Mauritius was discovered in 1511 by the Portuguese; the Dutch visited it in 1598, and named it Mauritius, after Prince Maurice of Nassau. From 1638 to 1710 it was held as a small Dutch colony and in 1715 the French took possession but did not settle it until 1721. Mauritius was taken by a British Force in 1810. A British garrison remained on the island until June 1960. The French language and French law were preserved under British rule.

A Crown Colony for 158 years, Mauritius became an independent state within the Commonwealth on March 12, 1968. The Constitution defined by Order in Council in 1964 was slightly altered in 1966 on the recommendation of the Banwell Commission, the effect being to increase the membership of the Legislative Assembly to 70, 62 elected by block voting in multi-member constituencies (including 2 members for Rodrigues) and 8 specially-elected members. Of the latter, 4 seats go to the "best loser" of whichever communities in the island are under-represented in the Assembly after the General Election and the four remaining seats are allocated on the basis of both party and community. The Constitution provides for the appointment of a Governor General who acts on the advice of the Council of Ministers, collectively responsible to the Legislative Assembly.

In the August 1987 General Election, the Mouvement Socialiste Militant, allied with the Labour Party and the Parti Mauricien Social Democrate, defeated the Mouvement Mauricien Militant and formed the Government, with a majority of 22 seats.

Governor General, His Excellency Sir Veerasamy Ringadoo, G.C.M.G., Q.C.

Council of Ministers

Prime Minister and Minister of Defence, Internal Security, External Communications, Information, Industry and of the Outer Islands, Rt. Hon. Sir Ancrood Jugnauth, K.C.M.G., Q.C.

Deputy P.M. and Minister of Employment and Tourism, Hon. Sir Gaetan Duval, Q.C.

Deputy P.M. and Attorney-General, Minister of Justice, External Affairs and Emigration, Hon. Sir Satcam Boolell, Q.C.

Deputy P.M. and Minister for Finance, Hon. Seetanah Lutchmeenaraidoo.

Economic Planning and Development, Dr. Hon. Beergoonath Ghurburrun.

Industry, Hon. Herve Duval.

Education, Arts and Culture, Hon. Armoogum Parsuramen.

Trade and Shipping, Hon. Dwarkanath Gungah.

Energy and Internal Communications, Hon. Mahyendrah Utchanah.

Social Security, National Solidarity and Reform Institutions, Dr. Hon. Dineshwar Ramjuttun.

Housing, Lands and the Environment, Hon. Sir Ramesh Jeewoolall.

Women's Rights and Family Affairs, Labour and Industrial Relations, Hon. Mrs. Sheilabai Bappoo.

Youth and Sports, Hon. Michael J. K. Glover.

Rodrigues, Hon. Serge Clair.

Co-operatives, Hon. Vishwanath Sajadah.

Health, Hon. Jagdishwar Goburdhun.

Agriculture, Fisheries and Natural Resources, Hon. Murlidas Dulloo.

Local Government, Hon. Clarel Malherbe.

Works, Hon. Ramduthsing Jaddoo.

MAURITIUS HIGH COMMISSION
32–33 Elvaston Place, SW7 5NN
[01–581 0294–7]

High Commissioner, His Excellency Soo Soobiah (1988).

EDUCATION

Primary education is free and in 1986 was provided for 138,765 children at 273 primary schools. Although education is not compulsory it is estimated that about 90 per cent of children of primary age attend school. At post-primary level there are a total of 68,604 students attending secondary schools: fees and teachers' salaries in the private secondary schools are paid by government. 168 students attend the Industrial Trade Training Centre. The College of Education trains primary school teachers. The Institute of Education is responsible for training secondary school teachers and for curriculum development. The University of Mauritius consists of Schools of Agriculture, of Administration and of Industrial Technology. Estimated expenditure on education in 1985–86 was *Rs* 604,600,000.

COMMUNICATIONS

Port Louis, on the N.W. coast, handles the bulk of the island's external trade. A bulk sugar terminal capable of handling the total crop began operating in 1980. The international airport is located at Plaisance in the southeast of the island about 5 miles from Mahébourg. There are 6 daily newspapers and 5 weeklies, mostly in French, and 2 Chinese daily papers and one weekly paper. The Mauritius Broadcasting Corporation has a monopoly of radio broadcasting in the country: television was introduced in 1965. There is a satellite communications ground station near Port Louis.

PRODUCTION

In 1987 the manufacturing sector employed 99,373, while the sugar industry employed 44,832.

About 55 per cent of the total sugar crop is produced on a plantation scale, while smaller owners (cultivating less than 10 acres) cultivate about 24 per cent of the land under cane. Tea and tobacco are also grown commercially but on a smaller scale than sugar.

	1986	1987
	tonnes	
Sugar	706,839	691,134
Tea (manufactured)	7,876	7,147
Tobacco (leaves)	982	912

In 1987 production of molasses, mainly for export, was 192,072 tonnes. Other products include alcohol, rum, denatured spirits, perfumed spirits and vinegar.

The bulk of the island's requirements in manufactured products still has to be imported. However, the Mauritius Export Processing Zone (M.E.P.Z.) scheme, introduced in 1971, has attracted investment from overseas and the number of export-orientated enterprises has risen from ten in 1971 to 531 at the end of 1987, employing 87,900 people. The biggest firms are in clothing manufacture, particularly woollen knitwear, but the range of goods produced includes toys, plastic products, leather goods, diamond cutting and polishing, watches, television sets and telephones.

Tourism is a major source of income for Mauritius, with 213,360 tourists in 1987. Earnings from tourism in 1987 are estimated to be *Rs*1,786 million (£85 million), compared with *Rs*1,175 million (£57 million) in 1986. The neighbouring French island of Réunion is the most important source of tourists, followed closely by mainland France.

FINANCE

The main sources of Government revenue are private and company income tax, customs and excise duties, mainly on imports, but also on sugar exports.

	1985–86	1986–87
Public revenue	*Rs*.4,130·5 m	*Rs*.5,008·7 m
Public expenditure	4,504·9 m	4,635·1 m

TRADE

Most foodstuffs and raw materials have to be imported from abroad. Apart from local consumption (about 36,500 tonnes per annum), the sugar produced is exported, mainly to Britain.

	1986	1987
Total imports	*Rs*.9,090·0 m	*Rs*.13,042 m
Total exports	9,400·5 m	12,034 m

Trade with U.K.

	1986	1987
Imports from U.K.	*Rs*.706 m	*Rs*. 1,058 m
Exports to U.K.	3,405 m	4,055 m

BRITISH HIGH COMMISSION
King George V Avenue, Floreal.
[Floreal 865795/9]

High Commissioner, His Excellency Richard Borman Crowson, C.M.G. (1985).

RODRIGUES AND DEPENDENCIES OF MAURITIUS

Rodrigues, formerly a dependency but now part of Mauritius, is about 350 miles east of Mauritius. Area, 40 square miles. Population (1985) 35,303. Cattle, salt fish, sheep, goats, pigs and onions are the principal exports. The island is administered by an Administrative Secretary.

Administrative Secretary, Claude Wong So.

The islands of Agalega and St. Brandon are dependencies of Mauritius. Other small islands, formerly Mauritian dependencies, have since 1965 constituted the British Indian Ocean Territory (*see* pp. 708–9).

REPUBLIC OF NAURU

The Republic of Nauru is an island of 8·2 sq. miles (21 sq. km.) in size, situated in 166° 55′ E. longitude and 0° 32′ S. of the Equator. It has a population (Census May 1983) of 8,042 (Nauruans 4,964; other Pacific Islanders 2,134; Asians 682; Caucasians 262). About 43 per cent of Nauruans are adherents of the Nauruan Protestant Church and there is a Roman Catholic Mission on the island.

CURRENCY.—Australian currency is legal tender.

FLAG.—Twelve-point star (representing the 12 original Nauruan tribes) below a gold bar (representing the Equator), all on a blue ground.

NATIONAL DAY.—January 31 (Independence Day).

GOVERNMENT

From 1888 until the First World War Nauru was administered by Germany, in 1920 becoming a British mandated territory under the League of Nations administered by Australia. A Trusteeship superceding the Mandate was approved in 1947 by the U.N. and Nauru continued to be administered by Australia until it became an Independent State on February 1, 1968. It was announced in November, 1968, that a limited form of membership of the Commonwealth had been devised for Nauru at the request of its Government.

Parliament has eighteen members including the Cabinet and Speaker. Voting is compulsory for all Nauruans over 20 years of age, except in certain specified instances. Elections are held every three years. The Cabinet is chosen by the President and comprises not fewer than five nor more than six members including the President.

President and Minister for External Affairs, Internal Affairs, Island Development and Industry, Civil Aviation Authority and the Public Service, His Excellency Hon. Hammer DeRoburt, G.C.M.G., O.B.E.

Cabinet
(as at December 1987)

Works and Community Services and Minister Assisting the President, Hon. R. B. Detundamo.
Finance, Hon. K. Clodumar.
Health and Education, Hon. R. Kun.
Justice, Hon. B. Dowiyogo.

JUDICIARY

A Supreme Court of Nauru is presided over by the Chief Justice. The District Court, which is subordinate to the Supreme Court, is presided over by a Resident Magistrate. Both the Supreme Court and the District Court are Courts of Record. The Supreme Court exercises both original and appellate jurisdiction.

EDUCATION AND WELFARE

Nauru has a hospital service and other medical and dental services. There is also a maternity and child welfare service. Education is available in 9 primary and 2 secondary schools on the island with a total enrolment of about 1,600 pupils receiving primary education and 500 secondary education.

PRODUCTION, ETC.

The only fertile areas are the narrow coastal belt and local requirements of fruit and vegetables are mostly met by imports. The economy is heavily dependent on the extraction of phosphate, of which the island has one of the world's richest deposits. About 2 million tonnes of phosphate are mined each year, providing employment for over 1,000 people. The industry has been run since 1970 by the Nauru Phosphate Corporation. Considerable investments have been made abroad with the royalties on phosphate exports to provide for a time when production declines.

The Nauru Pacific Line owns six ships: the Government-owned Air Nauru operates scheduled air services throughout the Pacific region and to Australia, New Zealand, Japan, Singapore and the Philippines.

Trade with U.K.

	1986	1987
Imports from U.K.	£1,239,000	£394,000
Exports to U.K.	148,000	674,000

British High Commissioner, (resident at Suva, Fiji).

NIGERIA
(Federal Republic of Nigeria)

AREA, POPULATION, ETC.—The Republic of Nigeria is situated on the west coast of Africa. It is bounded on the south by the Gulf of Guinea, on the west by the Republic of Benin, on the north by Niger and on the east by Cameroon. It has an area of 356,669 sq. miles (923,768 sq. km.), with a population presently estimated at around 100,000,000. The population is almost entirely African. The main ethnic groups are Hausa/Fulani, Yoruba and Ibo, and the principal languages are English, Hausa, Yoruba and Ibo. Over half the population are Muslim, these being concentrated in the north and west. In the southern areas in particular there are many Christians.

A belt of mangrove swamp forest 10–60 miles in width lies along the entire coastline. North of this there is a zone 50–100 miles wide of tropical rain forest and oil-palms. North of this the country rises and the vegetation changes to open woodland and savanna. In the extreme north the country is semi-desert. There are few mountains, but in Northern Nigeria the central plateau rises to an average level of 4,000 feet. The Niger, Benue, and Cross are the main rivers.

The climate varies with the types of country described above, but Nigeria lies entirely within the tropics and temperatures are high. The rainy season is from about April to October; rainfall varies from under 25 inches a year in the extreme north to 172 inches on the coast line. During the dry season the *harmattan* wind blows from the desert; it is cool and laden with fine particles of dust.

CAPITAL.—ΨLagos, estimated population, 3,000,000. Other important towns are Ibadan, Kaduna, Kano, Benin City, Enugu and Ψ Port Harcourt. Movement of Federal Ministries to a new capital at Abuja has begun.

CURRENCY.—Naira of 100 kobo.

FLAG.—Three equal vertical bands, green, white and green.

NATIONAL ANTHEM.—Arise, O Compatriots.

NATIONAL DAY.—October 1 (Republic Day).

GOVERNMENT

The Federation of Nigeria attained independence as a member of the Commonwealth on Oct. 1, 1960 and became a republic in 1963. On Jan. 15, 1966 the military took power, suspended the Constitution and dissolved the legislature. In 1979 civil rule was restored under a new constitution similar to that of the United States after elections at National and State level. After similar elections in 1983 the new administration was removed by the military on Dec. 31, this regime itself being overthrown in Aug. 1985. A 28-member Armed Forces Ruling Council was sworn in on Aug. 30. It is the country's most senior decision-making body. The Council of Ministers is the third most senior body after the A.F.R.C. and the National Council of States, which comprises the 21 State Governors.

Originally regional in structure the Federation was divided into 12 states in 1967. It was divided again into 19 states in 1976, and a further two states were created in 1987.

Head of State, Commander-in-Chief of the Armed Forces, Chairman of the Armed Forces Ruling Council, Maj.-Gen. Ibrahim Babangida.

Armed Forces Ruling Council

Chairman, General Ibrahim Badamasi Babangida. *Members,* Vice-Adm. A. Aikhomu; Lt.-Gen. D. Y. Bali; Lt.-Gen. S. Abacha; Vice-Adm. P. S. Koshoni; Air Marshal I. Alfa; A. M. A. Gambo; Maj.-Gen M. G. Nasko; Maj.-Gen. P. Omu; Air Vice-Marshal M. Yahaya; Maj.-Gen. P. Adomokai; Maj.-Gen. D. O. Ajayi; Maj.-Gen. A. B. Mamman; Maj.-Gen. S. O. Ifere; Maj.-Gen. G. Duba; Brig. O. Diya; Brig. J. N. Dogonyaro; Cdre. M. A. B. Elegbede; Cdre. N. Kanu; Cdre. S. Aluko; Rear-Adm. A. Nyako; Air Vice-Marshal N. Yusuf; Air Cdre. L. Koinyan; Air Vice-Marshal N. M. Imam; Col. J. N. Shagaya; Col. H. Akilu; Col. D. Mark; Maj.-Gen. Y. Y. Kure; Maj.-Gen. S. Sami.

Council of Ministers

Agriculture, Water Resources and Rural Development, Maj.-Gen. G. Nasko.
Communications, Col. D. Mark.
Defence, Maj.-Gen. D. Y. Bali.
Education, Prof. J. Aminu.
Employment, Labour and Productivity, A. A. Umar.
External Affairs, Maj.-Gen. I. O. S. Nwachukwu.
Federal Capital Territory, Abuja, Air Cdre. H. Abdullahi.
Finance and Economic Development, Dr. C. S. P. Okongwu.
Health, Prof. K. Ransome-Kuti.
Information and Culture, Prince Tony Momoh.
Internal Affairs, Col. J. N. Shagaya.
Industry, Lt.-Gen. A. I. Akinrinade.
Justice, Prince Bola Ajibola.
Mines, Power and Steel, Alhaji Bunu Sheriff Musa.
Petroleum Resources, Alhaji Rilwanu Lukman.
Science and Technology, Prof. E. Emovon.
Social Development, Youth and Sports, Air Cdre. B. Lawal.
Trade, Alhaji Samaila Mamman.
Transport, Dr. K. I. Kalu.
Aviation, Air Vice-Marshal T. Okpere.
Works and Housing, Brig. Kontagora.
Special Duties, Air Vice-Marshal A. I. Shekarri.

Nigeria High Commission
Nigeria House, 9 Northumberland Avenue,
WC2N 5BX
[01–839 1244]

High Commissioner, His Excellency Mr. George Dove-Edwin (1986).

Education

A programme was introduced in September 1976 intended to achieve universal primary education. Numbers of pupils in 1982–83 were: 15·4 million in primary schools, 3·5 million in secondary schools, 53,766 in polytechnics and 88,636 in universities. There are 24 universities.

Communications

The Nigerian railway system, which is controlled by the Nigerian Railway Corporation, is the most extensive in West Africa. There are 2,178 route miles of lines. The principal international airlines operating from Lagos, Kano and Port Harcourt bring Nigeria within about six hours of the Western European capitals. There are also services to other parts of Africa and to the United States. A network of internal air services connects the main centres. The principal seaports are served by a number of shipping lines, including the Nigerian National Line. A nationwide television and radio network is being developed, with each State eventually having its own television and radio station. There is a network of meteorological reporting stations.

Production and Industry

Nigeria was a predominantly agricultural country until the early 1970s with agriculture contributing over 60 per cent of export revenue and 45 per cent of G.N.P. Tin and calumbite mining on the Jos plateau, textiles and coal mining were also important. The major exports were ground nuts, palm products, tin, cocoa, rubber and timber. Recently oil has provided over 90 per cent of exports revenue and agricultural exports have greatly declined. Though agriculture still employs half the labour force it contributes only 20 per cent of G.N.P., exceeded by trading and oil. The construction sector is twice as large as the manufacturing sector and industries dependent on imported raw materials such as vehicle assembly have faltered recently. Three oil refineries are in operation at Port Harcourt, Warri and Kaduna. A steel plant has been opened near Warri and a larger one is being completed at Ajaokuta. Other projects include natural gas liquifaction, petro-chemicals, fertilizers and several power stations plus the Abuja Federal Capital. Several large irrigation schemes have been completed and more are planned.

Trade

Oil revenues have been falling since 1981 and are now restricted by an OPEC production quota and lower prices to half their peak level. In March 1982 imports curbs and payments restrictions were introduced but exchange reserves fell and debts increased. Austerity measures were introduced, and continue, while the present Government attempts to stimulate greater self-reliance in the economy by encouraging non-oil exports and the use of local rather than imported raw materials.

Trade with U.K.

	1986	1987
Imports from U.K.	£566,176,000	£481,568,000
Exports to U.K.	329,036,000	159,386,000

British High Commission
Eleke Crescent, Victoria Island, Lagos
[Lagos 619531]

High Commissioner, His Excellency Brian Leon Barder (1988).

British Council Representative, D. M. Waterhouse, 11 Kingsway Road, Ikoyi, (P.O. Box 3702), Lagos. Branch offices at Kano, Kaduna and Enugu.

PAPUA NEW GUINEA

AREA, POPULATION, ETC.—Papua New Guinea extends from the equator to Cape Baganowa in the Louisiade Archipelago at 11° S. latitude and from the border with Irian Jaya to 160° E. longitude. The total area of Papua New Guinea is 178,260 sq. miles, (461,691 sq. km.), of which approximately 152,420 sq. miles form the mainland, on the island of New Guinea. The country has many island groups, principally the Bismarck Archipelago, a portion of the Solomon Islands, the Trobriands, the D'Entrecasteaux Islands and the Louisade Archipelago. The main islands of the Bismarck Archipelago are New Britain, New Ireland and Manus. Bougainville is the largest of the Solomon Islands within Papua New Guinea.

Papua New Guinea lies within the tropics and has a typically monsoonal climate. Temperature and humidity are uniformly high throughout the year. The average rainfall is about 80 inches per year but there are wide variations—from 47 inches at Port Moresby to over 200 inches in mountainous western areas.

The estimated population in 1985 was 3,329,000. The inhabitants of the country comprise a great diversity of physical types and a large number of linguistic groups.

CAPITAL.—ΨPort Moresby. Estimated population (1985), 139,300. Other major towns are Lae, Rabaul, Madang, Wewak, Goroka and Mount Hagen.

CURRENCY.—Kina of 100 Toea.

FLAG.—A rectangle divided diagonally from the top of the hoist to the bottom of the fly, the upper segment scarlet and containing a soaring yellow bird of paradise. The lower segment is black charged with five white five-pointed stars representing the Southern Cross.

NATIONAL ANTHEM.—Arise All You Sons.

NATIONAL DAY.—September 16 (Independence Day).

GOVERNMENT

New Guinea was sighted by Portuguese and Spanish navigators in the early sixteenth century, but remained largely isolated from the rest of the world. In 1884, a British Protectorate was proclaimed over the southern coast of New Guinea (Papua) and the adjacent islands. British New Guinea, as the Protectorate was called, was annexed outright in 1888. In 1906 the Territory of British New Guinea was placed under the authority of the Commonwealth of Australia. Also in 1884 Germany had formally taken possession of certain northern areas, which later came to be known as the Trust Territory of New Guinea. In 1914 the German areas were occupied by Australian troops and remained under military administration until 1921, when the League of Nations conferred on Australia a mandate for their government.

New Guinea was administered under the Mandate and Papua under the Papua Act until the invasion by the Japanese in 1942 when the civil administration was suspended until the surrender of the Japanese in 1945.

The first House of Assembly for the whole country met in 1964 and included an elected majority and ten nominated official members. After 1970 there was a gradual assumption of powers by the Papua New Guinea Government, culminating in formal self-government in December 1973. Final reserve powers held by Australia over defence and foreign relations were relinquished to Papua New Guinea in March 1975, and Papua New Guinea achieved full independence on September 16, 1975.

Elections are held every five years. The Parliament comprises 109 elected Members, 20 from Regional electorates, the remainder from Open electorates.

There are 19 provinces, which have their own provincial governments with certain legislative and administrative powers.

Governor General, Sir Kingsford Dibela, G.C.M.G.

National Executive Council
(CABINET)

Prime Minister, Rabbie Namaliu.
Deputy P.M. and Minister for Trade and Industry, Rt. Hon. Sir Julius Chan, K.B.E.
Treasury, Michael Mel.
Transport, Roy Yaki.
Agriculture, Utula Samana.
Finance, Galeva Kwarara.
Forests, Tom Horick.
Lands, Albert Kipalan.
Public Services, Michael Ogio.
Labour and Employment, Masket Yangalio.
Defence, James Pokasui.
Police, Peter Kuman.
Education, Joseph Aoae.
Culture and Tourism, Albert Karo.
Environment and Conservation, Parry Zeipi.
Administrative Services, Johnson Maladina.
Housing, Bill Ninkama.
Fisheries, Thomas Negints.
Provincial Affairs, Jacob Lemeki.
Works, Aita Ivarato.
Minerals and Energy, Wiwa Korowi.
Justice, Kala Swokin.
Communications, Gabriel Ramoi.
Health, Ben Sabumei.
Civil Aviation, Hugo Berghuser, M.B.E.
Home Affairs, Eserom Burege.
Correctional Services, Allan Ebu.

PAPUA NEW GUINEA HIGH COMMISSION
3rd Floor, 14 Waterloo Place, SW1Y 4AR
[01–930 0922/6]

High Commissioner, His Excellency Mr. Ilinome F. Tarua, O.B.E. (1983).

COMMUNICATIONS

Road communications are very limited, the most important road being that linking Lae with the populous highlands.

Air Niugini (the national airline) and Qantas operate regular air services between Port Moresby and Australia. Air Niugini also operates services to Manila (Philippines), Honiara (Solomon Islands), Jayapura (Indonesia), Honolulu and Singapore. Internal air services are operated by Air Niugini, Douglas Airways, and Talair.

Several shipping companies operate cargo services between Papua New Guinea and Australia, Europe, the Far East and U.S.A. There are very limited cargo and passenger services between Papua New Guinea main ports, outports, plantations and missions.

Papua New Guinea is linked by international cable to Australia, Guam, Hong Kong, Kota Kinabalu, the Far East and U.S.A. Telecommunications are widely available.

ECONOMY

Until the 1970s the Papua New Guinea economy was based almost entirely on agriculture. At the beginning of the 20th century copra plantations formed the basis of the cash economy. Further crops which have been introduced over the years are cocoa, tea, coffee, palm oil, rubber, groundnuts, spices and timber. A variety of commercial agricultural developments now co-exist with the traditional informal rural economy. Government expenditure is still reliant on Australian budgetary support, to the extent of just under 30 per cent in 1983.

In 1972, Bougainville Copper Pty Ltd (BCL) began mining in the North Solomons Province, producing copper, silver and gold. There are extensive mineral deposits throughout Papua New Guinea, including nickel, chromite, bauxite and possibly commercial deposits of oil and gas. The most important new development is the exploitation of large copper and gold deposits on the Ok Tedi, in the Western Province.

In 1984 the Papua New Guinea economy was influenced by good prices for agricultural commodities, offset by low prices for copper and gold. New developments to promote export crops and increase employment, typically involving foreign investment, are planned for the future.

Industry includes processing of primary products, and brewing, bottling and packaging, paint, plywood, and metal manufacturing and the construction industries.

Although the formal economy is still dominated by non-Papua New Guineans, the participation of Papua New Guineans is increasing.

Trade with U.K.

	1986	1987
Imports from U.K.	£12,084,000	£16,693,000
Exports to U.K.	38,474,000	46,045,000

BRITISH HIGH COMMISSION
P.O. Box 4778, Boroko, Port Moresby
[Port Moresby 212500]

High Commissioner, His Excellency Michael Edward Howell, O.B.E. (1986).

ST. CHRISTOPHER AND NEVIS

(The Federation of St. Christopher and Nevis)

The State of St. Christopher and Nevis is located at the northern end of the Eastern Caribbean. It comprises the islands of St. Christopher (St. Kitts) (65 sq. miles: 168 sq. km.; population about 35,700) and Nevis (36 sq. miles: 93·2 sq. km.; population about 9,400).

St. Christopher, lat. 17° 18′ N. and long. 62° 48′ W. was the first island in the British West Indies to be colonized (1623). The central area of the island is forest-clad and mountainous, rising to the 3,792 ft. Mount Liamuiga.

CAPITAL—ΨBasseterre (estimated population, 15,000).

Nevis, lat. 17° 10′ N. and long. 62° 35′ W. is separated from the southern tip of St. Christopher by a strait two miles wide and is dominated by the central Nevis Peak, 3,232 ft. *Chief town*—ΨCharlestown (pop. 1,200), is a port of entry.

CURRENCY.—East Caribbean Dollar (EC$) of 100 cents.

FLAG.—Three diagonal bands, green, black and red; each colour separated by a stripe of yellow. Two white stars on the black band.

NATIONAL ANTHEM.—Our Land of Beauty.

NATIONAL DAY.—September 19 (Independence Day).

GOVERNMENT

The Territory of St. Kitts and Nevis became a State in Association with Britain on Feb. 27, 1967. The State of St. Kitts and Nevis became an independent nation on Sept. 19, 1983, with a new constitution under which Great Britain relinquished its responsibility for defence and external affairs. Under the new Constitution, H.M. The Queen is Head of State, represented in the islands by the Governor General. There is a central Cabinet Government with a

Ministerial system, the Head of which is the Prime Minister of St. Christopher and Nevis, and a National Assembly located on St. Kitts. On Nevis there is a Nevis Island Administration, the Head being styled Premier of Nevis, and a Nevis Island Assembly.

Governor General, His Excellency Sir Clement Athelston Arrindell, G.C.M.G. (1981).

Cabinet

Prime Minister and Minister of Finance, Home Affairs and Foreign Affairs,, Rt. Hon. Dr. K. A. Simmonds.
Deputy P.M. and Minister of Labour and Tourism, Rt. Hon. M. O. Powell.
Natural Resources and Environment, Hon. S. Daniel.
Education, Health and Community Affairs, Hon. S. E. Morris.
Communications, Works and Public Utilities, Hon. I. A. W. Stevens.
Agriculture, Lands, Housing and Development, Hon. H. C. Heyliger.
Women's Affairs, Hon. Constance Mitcham.
Trade and Industry, Hon. F. Jones.
In Ministry of Finance, Hon. R. Caines.
Without Portfolio, Hon. U. S. Swanston.
Attorney-General, Hon. S. W. T. Seaton.
Cabinet Secretary, C. Farier.

ST. KITTS HIGH COMMISSION
10 Kensington Court, W8 5DL
[01-937 9522]

High Commissioner for the Eastern Caribbean States, His Excellency Richard Gunn (1987).

FINANCE

	1986	1987
Revenue	EC$62,226,809	EC$72,927,410
Expenditure	58,854,228	69,456,759

ECONOMY

The economy of the islands has been based on sugar for over three centuries. Tourism and light industry are now being developed. The economy of Nevis centres on small peasant farmers, but a sea-island cotton industry is being developed for export.

COMMUNICATIONS

Basseterre is a port of registry and has deep water harbour facilities. Golden Rock airport, on St. Kitts, can take most large jet aircraft; Newcastle airstrip on Nevis can take small aircraft and has night landing facilities.

The sea ferry route from Basseterre to Charlestown is 11 miles.

Trade with U.K.

	1986	1987
Imports from U.K.	£6,008,000	£7,041,000
Exports to U.K.	4,429,000	4,677,000

ST. LUCIA

St. Lucia, the second largest of the Windward group, situated in 13° 54′ N. lat. and 60° 50′ W. long., at a distance of about 21 miles N. of St. Vincent, and 24 miles S. of Martinique, is 27 miles in length, with an extreme breadth of 14 miles. It comprises an area of 238 sq. miles (616 sq. km.), with an estimated population (1986) of 138,000. It possesses perhaps the most interesting history of all the smaller islands. Fights raged hotly around it, and it constantly changed hands between the English and the French. It is mountainous, its highest point being Mt. Gimie (3,145 feet) and for the most part it is covered with forest and tropical vegetation.

CAPITAL.—ΨCastries (estimated population 1984, 50,798) is recognized as being one of the finest ports in the West Indies on account of its reputation as a safe anchorage in the hurricane season.

CURRENCY.—East Caribbean Dollar (EC$) of 100 cents.

FLAG.—Blue, bearing in centre a device of yellow over black over white triangles having a common base.

NATIONAL ANTHEM.—"Sons and Daughters of Saint Lucia."

NATIONAL DAY.—February 22 (Independence Day).

GOVERNMENT

St. Lucia became independent within the Commonwealth on Feb. 22, 1979. The Head of State is H.M. The Queen, represented in the island by a St. Lucian Governor General, and there is a bicameral legislature. The Senate has 11 members, 6 appointed by the ruling party, 3 by the Opposition and 2 by the Governor General. The House of Assembly, which has a life of five years, has 17 elected Members and a Speaker, who may be elected from outside the House.

Acting Governor General, His Excellency Sir Vincent Floissac, C.M.G., Q.C.

Cabinet

Prime Minister, Minister of Finance, Foreign Affairs, Development and Home Affairs, Rt. Hon. John G. M. Compton.

Deputy P.M. and Minister of Trade, Industry and Tourism, Hon. George Mallet.

Communications, Works and Transport, Hon. Senator Desmond Fostin.

Health, Housing, Labour, Information and Broadcasting, Hon. Romanus Lansiquot.

Youth, Community Development, Social Affairs, Sport, Hon. Stephenson King.

Attorney General and Minister for Legal Affairs, Hon. Senator Parry Husbands.

Agriculture, Lands, Fisheries and Co-operatives, Hon. Ferdinand Henry.

Education and Culture, Hon. Louis George.

ST. LUCIA HIGH COMMISSION
10 Kensington Court, W8 5DL.
[01–937 9522]

High Commissioner for the Eastern Caribbean States, His Excellency Richard Gunn (1987).

ECONOMY

The economy is mainly agrarian, with manufacturing based on the processing of agricultural products. Principal crops are bananas, coconuts, cocoa, mangoes, avocado pears, breadfruit, spices, root crops such as cassava and yams, and citrus fruit. Attempts are being made to diversify the economy, in particular through greater industrialization; tourism is also of increasing importance, with 171,000 visiting the island in 1986.

The principal exports are bananas, coconut products (copra, edible oils, soap), cardboard boxes, beer, and textile manufactures. The chief imports are flour, meat, machinery, building materials, motor vehicles, cotton piece goods, petroleum and fertilizers.

Trade with U.K.

	1986	1987
Imports from U.K.	£12,441,000	£13,196,000
Exports to U.K.	59,855,000	40,908,000

OFFICE OF THE BRITISH HIGH COMMISSION
Columbus Square, P.O. Box 227, Castries.
[Castries 22484]

High Commissioner, (resides at Bridgetown, Barbados).

Resident Representative, C. H. Woodland.

ST. VINCENT AND THE GRENADINES

The territory of the State of St. Vincent includes certain of the Grenadines, a chain of small islands stretching 40 miles across the Caribbean Sea between Grenada and St. Vincent, some of the larger of which are Bequia, Canouan, Mayreau, Mustique, Union Island, Petit St. Vincent and Prune Island. The whole territory extends 150 sq. miles (388 sq. km.).

The main island, St. Vincent, is situated between 13° 6′ and 14° 35′ N. latitude and 61° 6′ and 61° 20′ W. longitude, approximately 21 miles south west of St. Lucia and 100 miles west of Barbados. The island is 18 miles long and 11 miles wide at its extremities comprising an area of 133 sq. miles (344 sq. km.), and a population (1985 U.N. estimate) of 104,000. St. Vincent was discovered by Christopher Columbus in 1498. It was granted by Charles I to the Earl of Carlisle in 1627 and after subsequent grants and a series of occupations alternately by the French and English, it was finally restored to Britain in 1783.

CAPITAL.—ΨKingstown, population approximately 33,694.

CURRENCY.—East Caribbean Dollar (EC$) of 100 cents.

FLAG.—Three vertical bands, of blue, yellow and green, with three green diamonds in the shape of a "V" mounted on the yellow band.

NATIONAL ANTHEM.—St. Vincent, Land So Beautiful.

NATIONAL DAY.—October 27 (Independence Day).

GOVERNMENT

St. Vincent and the Grenadines achieved full independence within the Commonwealth on Oct. 27, 1979.

St. Vincent has a constitution under which there is a Governor General who is Her Majesty's Representative. Except where otherwise provided, the Governor General is required to act in accordance with the advice of the Prime Minister.

The House of Assembly consists of 13 elected members and 6 Senators appointed by the Governor General. It is presided over by a Speaker elected by the House from within or without it.

Acting Governor General, His Excellency Henry Williams, *sworn in* Feb. 29, 1988.

Cabinet

Prime Minister, Minister of Finance and Foreign Affairs, Rt. Hon. James Mitchell.

Trade, Industry and Agriculture, Hon. M. P. DeFreitas.

Housing, Labour and Community Development, Hon. J. C. Scott.

Tourism, Aviation, Culture and Women's Affairs, Hon. B. B. Williams.

Education, Hon. J. C. A. Horne.

Health, Hon. D. E. Jack.

Communications and Works, Hon. A. C. Cruickshank.

Attorney General and Minister of Legal Affairs and Information, Hon. P. R. Campbell, C.V.O.

Ministers of State, Hon. H. B. Young (*Trade, Industry and Agriculture*).

Parliamentary Secretary, Hon. R. S. Nanton (*Office of the Prime Minister*).

ST. VINCENT AND THE GRENADINES
HIGH COMMISSION
10 Kensington Court, W8 5DL
[01-937 9522]

High Commissioner for the Eastern Caribbean States,
His Excellency Richard Gunn (1987).

ECONOMY

This is based mainly on agriculture but the tourist and manufacturing industries have been expanding. The main products are bananas, arrowroot, coconuts, sugar, cocoa, spices and various kinds of food crops. The main imports are foodstuffs (meat, rice, beverages), textiles, lumber, cement and other building materials, fertilizers, motor vehicles and fuel.

EDUCATION

Primary and secondary education in Government schools is free but not compulsory. In 1982 there were 24,651 enrolments in state primary schools and 5,501 enrolments in state secondary schools.

Trade with U.K.

	1986	1987
Imports from U.K.	£8,288,000	£8,529,000
Exports to U.K.	21,161,000	20,208,000

OFFICE OF THE BRITISH HIGH COMMISSION
Granby Street (P.O. Box 132), Kingstown.
[St Vincent 71701]

High Commissioner, (resides at Bridgetown, Barbados).
Resident Representative, G. Greaves.

SEYCHELLES

(The Republic of Seychelles)

The Republic of Seychelles, in the Indian Ocean, consists of 115 islands with a total land area of 108 sq. miles (280 sq. km.), spread over 400,000 square miles of ocean. There is a relatively compact granitic group, 32 islands in all, with high hills and mountains (highest point about 2,990 ft.), of which Mahé is the largest and most populated (90 per cent of the population live on Mahé): and the outlying coralline group, for the most part, only a little above sea-level. Although only 4° S. of the Equator, the climate is pleasant though tropical. The population was estimated (end 1984) to be 65,032.

CAPITAL.—ΨVictoria (population, 1982, 24,733), on the N.E. side of Mahé.

CURRENCY.—Seychelles Rupee of 100 cents.

FLAG.—Red over green, divided by wavy white band.

NATIONAL ANTHEM.—Fyer Seselwa (Proud Seychellois).

NATIONAL DAY.—June 5.

GOVERNMENT

Proclaimed as French territory in 1756, the Mahé group began to be settled as a dependency of Mauritius from 1770, was captured by a British ship in 1794, changed hands several times between 1803 and 1814, when it was finally assigned to Great Britain. By Letters Patent of September, 1903, these islands, together with the coralline group, were formed into a separate Colony. On June 29, 1976, the Islands became an independent republic within the Commonwealth. A coup d'état took place on June 5, 1977.

A new constitution making Seychelles a one-party state came into force in June 1979. The executive power lies with the President, who is elected by universal suffrage for a five year term. Legislative power lies with the President and the People's Assembly which has 23 elected members and two nominated by the President.

President, France Albert René, *assumed office* June 5, 1977; *elected* June 26, 1979; *re-elected* June 18, 1984.

Council of Ministers

Administration, Finance, Legal Affairs, Planning, External Relations and Defence, The President.
Education, Information and Youth, James Michel.
National Development, Jacques Hodoul.
Health and Social Services, Joseph Belmont.
Political Organization, Esme Jumeau.
Internal Affairs, Mrs. Rita Sinon.
Tourism and Transport, Ralph Adam.
Manpower, Jeremie Bonnelame.

SEYCHELLES HIGH COMMISSION
Box No. 4PE, 50 Conduit Street, W1A 4PE
[01–439 0405]

High Commissioner, His Excellency Robert F. Delpech (1987).

ECONOMY

The economy is based on tourism, fishing, small-scale agriculture and manufacturing, and the re-export of fuel for aircraft and ships. Copra and cinnamon bark have lost their importance as exports.

Deep sea tuna fishing by foreign fleets under licence, improved trans-shipment and other port facilities at Victoria, exports from a tuna canning factory opened in 1987 and the export of fresh and frozen fish, attract growing revenues.

TRADE

	1985	1986
Imports	Rs.718,700,000	Rs.686,600,000
Exports	19,500,000	14,500,000
Re-exports	177,200,000	94,200,000

The principal imports are foodstuffs, beverages, tobacco, mineral fuels, manufactured items, building materials, machinery and transport equipment.

Trade with U.K.

	1986	1987
Imports from U.K.	£9,639,000	£10,770,000
Exports to U.K.	938,000	880,000

BRITISH HIGH COMMISSION
Victoria House, P.O. Box 161,
Victoria, Mahé.
[Victoria 23055]

High Commissioner, His Excellency (Alexander Basil) Peter Smart (1986).

SIERRA LEONE

(The Republic of Sierra Leone)

AREA, POPULATION, ETC.—Sierra Leone, with a total land area of 27,699 sq. miles (71,740 sq. km.), is on the west coast of Africa, between Guinea and Liberia. A Census of December 1985 put the population at 3,700,000. The origins of the country date back to the late 18th century when a project was begun to settle destitute Africans from England on Freetown peninsula. In 1808 the settlement was declared a Crown Colony and became the main base in West Africa for enforcing the 1807 Act outlawing the slave trade. The Colony was also used as a settlement for Africans from North America and the West Indies, and great numbers of Africans rescued from slave ships, also settled there. Their descendants, known as Creoles, still live on Freetown peninsula. The southern half of Sierra Leone is inhabited by peoples whose languages fall into the Mende group; the northern half by the Temne, and smaller groups such as the Limba, Loko, Koranko and Susu.

CAPITAL.—ΨFreetown (population at 1985 Census, 470,000).

CURRENCY.—Leone of 100 cents.

FLAG.—Three horizontal stripes of leaf green, white and cobalt blue.

NATIONAL ANTHEM.—"High We Exalt Thee, Realm of the Free."

NATIONAL DAY.—April 27 (Independence Day).

GOVERNMENT

Sierra Leone became a fully independent state within the Commonwealth on April 27, 1961. On April 19, 1971 a Republican Constitution was adopted and Dr. Siaka Stevens became the first Executive President. In June 1978 Sierra Leone became a one-Party State, following approval by Parliament and a Referendum. The first General Election under the one party system was held on May 1, 1982. The Parliament now comprises 85 elected members and 12 Paramount Chiefs, plus nine nominated members, two of whom are the Army Commander and the Inspector General of Police.

President, His Excellency Maj.-Gen. Joseph Saidu Momoh, *sworn in* Nov. 28, 1985.

Cabinet

President and Minister of Defence with responsibility for Public Services, His Excellency Maj.-Gen. J. S. Momoh.

First Vice-President and Minister of Lands, Housing and Environment, Hon. A. B. Kamara.

Second Vice-President and Minister of State Enterprises, Hon. S. Jusu Sheriff.

Finance, Hon. H. Gbessay Kanu.

Attorney-General and Minister of Justice, Hon. Dr. Abdulai Conteh.

Foreign Affairs, Hon. Abdul Karim Koroma.

Economic Planning and National Development, Hon. Dr. Sheka Kanu.

Agriculture, Natural Resources and Forestry, (vacant).

Trade and Industry, Hon. J. Amara Bangali.

Education, Cultural Affairs and Sports, Hon. Dr. Moses Dumbuya.

Transport and Communications, Hon. Michael Abdulai.

Mines, Hon. Birch Conteh.

Health, Hon. Dr. Wiltshire Johnson.

Works and Labour, Hon. Prof. V. Mambu.

Energy and Power, Hon. Dr. Sheku Sesay.

Information and Broadcasting, Hon. Eya Mbayo.

Tourism, Hon. Abdul Iscandari.

Internal Affairs, Hon. M. L. Siddique.

Rural Development, Social Services and Youth, Hon. Alhaji Musa Kabia.

Ministers of State, Hon. Harry Williams (*Leader of the House*); Hon. Maj.-Gen. M. S. Tarawallie (*Force Cdr.*); Hon. Bambay Kamara (*Inspector General of Police*); Hon. E. T. Kamara (*Party Affairs*).

SIERRA LEONE HIGH COMMISSION
33 Portland Place, W1N 3AG
[01-636 6483-6]

High Commissioner, His Excellency Caleb B. Aubee (1987).

COMMUNICATIONS

Since the phasing out of the railway system in 1974 the road network has been developed considerably and there are now 5,000 miles of roads in the country, over 2,000 miles being surfaced. A bridge has been constructed over the Mano River linking Sierra Leone and Liberia.

The Freetown international airport is situated at Lungi, across the Sierra Leone River from Freetown. The main port is Freetown, which has one of the largest natural harbours in the world, and where there is a deep water quay providing about six berths for medium sized ships. There are smaller ports at Pepel, Bonthe and Niti.

Radio and television are operated by the Department of Broadcasting of the Sierra Leone Government. There are two shortwave transmitting and receiving stations in Freetown. Broadcasts are made in several of the more important indigenous languages in addition to English. There is also a weekly broadcast in French.

EDUCATION

In 1988 there were 1,952 primary schools in Sierra Leone and 213 secondary schools. Technical education is provided in the two Government Technical Institutes, situated in Freetown and Kenema, in two Trade Centres and in the technical training establishments of the mining companies. Teacher training is carried out at the university, six colleges in the Provinces and in the Milton Margai Training College near Freetown. The University of Sierra Leone (1967), consists of Fourah Bay College (1827) and Njala University College (1964).

PRODUCTION AND TRADE

On the Freetown peninsula, farming is largely confined to the production of cassava and garden crops, such as maize and vegetables, for local consumption. In the hinterland, the principal agricultural product is rice, which is the staple food of the country, and cash crops such as cocoa, coffee, palm kernels, and ginger.

The economy depends largely on mineral exports; mainly diamonds, gold, bauxite and rutile. Iron ore production recommenced in 1982. Diamond exports provided Le447m in 1986. Total imports for 1986 were Le2,022m and exports were Le2,001m.

Trade with U.K.

	1986	1987
Imports from U.K.	£17,403,000	£16,221,019
Exports to U.K.	11,599,000	12,678,907

BRITISH HIGH COMMISSION
Standard Bank of Sierra Leone Building
Lightfoot Boston Street, Freetown
[Freetown 23961/5]

High Commissioner, His Excellency Derek William Partridge, C.M.G. (1986).

British Council Representative, Theresa Harvey, P.O. Box 124, Tower Hill, Freetown.

SINGAPORE

AREA, POPULATION, ETC.—The Republic of Singapore consists of the island of Singapore and 57 smaller islands, covering a total area of 224 sq. miles (581 sq. km.). Singapore island is 26 miles long and 14 miles in breadth and is situated just north of the Equator off the southern extremity of the Malay Peninsula, from which it is separated by the Straits of Johore. A causeway, carrying a road, railway and a water pipeline, crosses the three-quarters of a mile to the mainland. The highest point of the island is 581 feet above sea level. The climate is hot and humid and there are no clearly defined seasons. Rainfall averages 240 cm. a year and temperature ranges from 24°–32° C (76°–89° F).

In June 1987, the population was 2,612,800. (Chinese, 1,988,600; Malays, 393,800; Indians, 169,100; others (Europeans, Eurasians, etc.), 61,300). Malay, Mandarin, Tamil and English are the official languages. At least 8 Chinese dialects are used.

CURRENCY.—Singapore Dollar (S$) of 100 cents.

FLAG.—Horizontal bands of red over white; crescent with five five-point stars on red band near staff.

NATIONAL ANTHEM.—Majulah Singapura.

NATIONAL DAY.—August 9.

GOVERNMENT

Singapore, where Sir Stamford Raffles had first established a trading post under the East India Company in 1819, was incorporated with Penang and Malacca to form the Straits Settlements in 1826. The Straits Settlements became a Crown Colony in 1867. Singapore fell into Japanese hands in 1942 and civil government was not restored until 1946, when it became a separate colony. Internal self-government and the title "State of Singapore" were introduced in 1959. Singapore became a state of Malaysia when the Federation was enlarged in September, 1963, but left Malaysia and became an independent sovereign state within the Commonwealth on August 9, 1965. Singapore adopted a Republican constitution from that date, the Yang di-Pertuan Negara being re-styled President. There is a Cabinet collectively responsible to a fully-elected Parliament of 79 members.

HEAD OF STATE

President, Wee Kim Wee, *elected* Aug. 30, 1985.

Cabinet

(as at end July 1988.)

Prime Minister, Lee Kuan Yew, G.C.M.G., C.H.
Senior Minister, S. Rajaratnam.
First Deputy P.M. and Minister for Defence, Goh Chok Tong.
Second Deputy P.M., Ong Teng Cheong.
Law, E. W. Barker.
Foreign Affairs and National Development, S. Dhanabalan.
Education, Dr. Tony Tan Keng Yam.
Environment, Dr. Ahmad Mattar.
Communications and Information, Dr. Yeo Ning Hong.
Home Affairs, Prof. S. Jayakumar.
Finance, Dr. Richard Hu Tsu Tau.
Labour, Lee Yock Suan.
Community Development, Wong Kan Seng.
Trade and Industry, Lee Hsien Loong.
Health (acting), Yeo Cheow Tong.

Speaker of Parliament, Dr. Yeoh Ghim Seng.
(Singapore's government was dissolved on Aug. 17, and a General Election called for Sept. 3, 1988.)

SINGAPORE HIGH COMMISSION
2 Wilton Crescent, SW1X 8RW
[01–235 8315–8]

High Commissioner, His Excellency Abdul Aziz Mahmood (1988).

COMMUNICATIONS

Singapore is one of the largest and busiest seaports in the world, with deep water wharves and ship repairing facilities. Ships also anchor in the roads, unloading into lighters. In 1987, 71,297,800 freight tonnes of seaborne cargo was discharged and 46,997,600 freight tonnes loaded. More than 500 shipping lines use the port, with over 30,000 foreign flagged ships calling annually. The international airport is at Changi, in the east of the island. There are 25·75 km. of metric gauge railway connected to the Malaysian rail system by the causeway across the Straits of Johore, and 2,686 kilometres of roads. There are both wireless and wired broadcasting services carrying commercial advertising. There are three television channels. The Singapore Broadcasting Authority Corporation was established in February 1980.

ECONOMY

Historically Singapore's economy was largely based on the sale and distribution of raw materials from surrounding countries and on entrepot trade in finished products. In the last decade, however, new manufacturing industries have been introduced, including ship building and repairing, iron and steel, textiles, footwear, wood products, micro-electronics, scientific instruments, detergents, confectionery, pharmaceuticals, petroleum products, etc. Singapore has also become a financial centre with 133 commercial banks and 62 merchant banks established in the Republic, and an oil-refining centre.

Projects now being undertaken include the construction of a Mass Rapid Transit Rail system (phase one opened in December 1987); expansion of Changi airport; the improvement of public utilities (electricity and gas supply, sewage system) and telecommunications, including a submarine telephone cable system; building projects; computerization in schools and government departments; and the construction of a new container terminal at Pulau Brani, an offshore island.

Finance (estimates)

	1987–88	1988–89
Revenue	S$12,582·6m	S$11,560·0m
Expenditure	15,270·9m	12,470·0m

Trade

	1986	1987
Total imports	S$55,545·4m	S$68,415·2m
Total exports	48,985·5m	60,265·7m

Trade with U.K.

	1986	1987
Imports from U.K.	£547,419,000	£602,627,000
Exports to U.K.	462,878,000	473,814,000

BRITISH HIGH COMMISSION
Tanglin Road, Singapore 1024
[Singapore 4739333]

High Commissioner, His Excellency Michael Edmund Pike, C.M.G. (1987).
British Council Representative, D. R. Howell, O.B.E., 30 Napier Road, Singapore 1024.

SOLOMON ISLANDS

Forming a scattered archipelago of mountainous islands and low-lying coral atolls, Solomon Islands stretches about 900 miles in a south-easterly direction from Bougainville, in Papua New Guinea, to the Santa Cruz islands. The archipelago covers an area of about 249,000 square nautical miles while the land area is 10,938 sq. miles (28,446 sq. km.). Solomon Islands lies between the east longitudes 155° 30′ and 170° 30′ and between south latitudes 5° 10′ and 12° 45′. The six biggest islands are: Choiseul, New Georgia, Santa Isabel, Guadalcanal, Malaita and Makira. They are characterised by precipitous, thickly-forested mountain ranges intersected by deep, narrow valleys, and vary between 90 to 120 miles in length and between 20 to 30 miles in width.

Distribution of population at the Census of 1986 was: Melanesian 268,536; Polynesian 10,661; Micronesian 3,929; European 1,107; Chinese 379; Others 564. Total 285,176.

CAPITAL.—ΨHoniara (population (1986), 30,499).

CURRENCY.—Solomon Islands Dollar of 100 cents.

FLAG.—Blue over green divided by a diagonal yellow band, with five white stars in the top left quarter.

NATIONAL ANTHEM.—God Bless our Solomon Islands.

NATIONAL DAY.—July 7 (Independence Day).

GOVERNMENT

The origin of the present Melanesian inhabitants is uncertain. European discovery of the islands began in the mid-16th century and continued intermittently for about 300 years, when the inauguration of sugar plantations in Queensland and Fiji (which created a need for labour) and the arrival of missionaries and traders led to increased European interest in the region. Great Britain declared a Protectorate in 1893 over the Southern Solomons, adding the Santa Cruz group in 1898 and 1899. The islands of the Shortland groups were transferred by treaty from Germany to Great Britain in 1900.

The Solomon Islands achieved internal self-government in 1976, and became independent in July 1978. The Solomon Islands is a constitutional monarchy, H.M. The Queen being represented locally by the Governor General. Legislative power is vested in a unicameral National Parliament of 38 members, elected for a four-year term. The executive authority is exercised by the Cabinet.

Governor General, His Excellency Sir George Lepping, G.C.M.G. (1988).

Cabinet

Prime Minister, Rt. Hon. Ezekiel Alebua.

Deputy P.M. and Minister of Foreign Affairs, Rt. Hon. Sir Peter Kenilorea, K.B.E.

Agriculture and Lands, Joini Tutua.

Economic Planning, Paul Tovua.

Education and Training, Daniel Sande.

Finance, George Kejoa.

Health and Medical Services, John Tepaika.

Home Affairs and Provincial Government, Andrew Nori.

Immigration and Labour, Jason Dorovolomo.

Natural Resources, Robert Bera.

Police and Justice, Swanson Konofilia.

Post and Communications, John Kaliuae.

Public Service, Alex Bartlett.

Trade, Commerce and Industry, Augustine Rose.

Transport, Works and Utilities, Alfred Maetia.

JUDICIARY

The High Court of Solomon Islands, constituted by the Solomon Islands Independence Order, consists of a Chief Justice and not fewer than two nor more than three Puisne Judges. The Court of Appeal Act was enacted on May 8, 1978.

FINANCE AND TRADE

Revenue (1985), SI$63,567,000.

The main imports are foodstuffs, consumer goods, machinery and transport materials. Principal exports are timber, fish, copra, and palm oil. Other exports include cocoa and marine shells.

Trade with U.K.

	1986	1987
Imports from U.K........	£1,618,000	£1,566,000
Exports to U.K.	4,074,000	4,461,000

COMMUNICATIONS

Solomon Islands Airways Ltd. serves 28 airstrips throughout the country, four of which are designated international airports. It also has combined services with Quantas making three flights each way weekly between Honiara and Brisbane and one each way between Honiara and Nadi. Air Niugini has a weekly combined service with Solomon Islands Airways.

There are about 52 miles of secondary and minor roads in the urban areas of Honiara, Auki and Gizo. About 18 miles of road in and around Honiara and one mile in Auki and Gizo are bitumen sealed, the remainder being coral or gravel surfaced. In the rural areas there are some 800 miles of road, including those in private plantations, forestry areas and roads built and maintained by councils. All main islands have transreceivers to maintain communications with Honiara and there is a telephone link between Honiara and Auki, Gizo and Tulagi.

Soltel, a company jointly owned by Cable and Wireless Limited and Solomon Islands Government operates the international telephone circuits from a ground station in Honiara via the Intelsat Pacific Ocean communication satellite.

BRITISH HIGH COMMISSION
Soltel House, Mendana Avenue,
Honiara.
[Honiara 21705]
High Commissioner, His Excellency Junor Young (1988).

SRI LANKA

(Sri Lanka Prajatantrika Samajawadi Janarajaya)

AREA, POPULATION, ETC.—Sri Lanka (formerly Ceylon) is an island in the Indian Ocean, off the southern tip of the peninsula of India and separated from it by a narrow strip of shallow water, the Palk Strait. Situated between 5° 55′–9° 50′ N. latitude and 79° 42′–81° 52′ E. longitude, it has an area of 25,332 sq. miles (65,610 sq. km.), including 33 square miles of inland water. Its greatest length is from north to south, 270 miles; and its greatest width 140 miles, no point in Sri Lanka being more than 80 miles from the sea.

The population at the 1981 census was 14,800,001. (A 1985 U.N. estimate gave a figure of 15,837,000.) Of these 74 per cent were Sinhalese, 12·6 per cent Sri Lankan Tamils, 5·6 per cent Indian Tamils, 7·1 per cent Sri Lankan Moors and 0·7 per cent Burghers, Malays and others. The religion of the great majority of inhabitants is Buddhism, introduced from India, according to ancient Sinhalese chronicles, in 247 B.C. After Buddhism (69·3 per cent), Hinduism has the largest following (15·5 per cent); 7·6 per cent of the population are Muslims and 7·5 per cent are Christians. The national languages are Sinhalese, Tamil and English.

Forests, jungle and scrub cover the greater part of the island, often being intermingled. In areas over 2,000 feet above sea level grasslands (*patanas* or *talawas*) are found. One of the highest peaks in the central massif is Adam's Peak (7,360 ft), a place of pilgrimage for Buddhists, Hindus and Moslems.

The climate of Sri Lanka is warm throughout the year, with a high relative humidity. In the hills the climate is more temperate. Temperatures average 27° C. in the lowlands, and 16° C. at elevations over 6,000 ft. Day humidity is over 70 per cent and night humidity over 85 per cent. Rainfall is generally heavy, with marked regional variations. The two main monsoon seasons are mid-May to September (south-west) and November to March (north-east).

CAPITAL.—ΨColombo, population (1981) 585,776. 1984 estimate 643,000. Other principal towns are ΨJaffna (118,215), Kandy (101,281), ΨGalle (77,183), ΨNegombo (51,376) and ΨTrincomalee (44,913).

CURRENCY.—Sri Lankan Rupee of 100 cents.

FLAG.—On a dark red field, within a golden border, a golden lion passant holding a sword in its right paw, and a representation of a *bo*-leaf, issuing from each corner; and to its right, two vertical stripes of saffron and green also placed within a golden border, to represent the minorities of the country.

NATIONAL ANTHEM.—Namo Namo Matha (We all stand together).

NATIONAL DAY.—February 4 (Independence Commemoration Day).

GOVERNMENT

Early in the sixteenth century the Portuguese landed in Ceylon and founded settlements, eventually conquering much of the country. Portuguese rule in Ceylon lasted 150 years, but in 1658, following a twenty-year period of decline, Portuguese rule gave place to that of the Dutch East India Company which was to exploit Ceylon with varying fortunes until 1796.

The Maritime Provinces of Ceylon were ceded by the Dutch to the British on February 16, 1798, becoming a British Crown Colony in 1802 under the terms of the Treaty of Amiens. With the annexation of the Kingdom of Kandy in 1815, all Ceylon came under British rule.

On February 4, 1948, Ceylon became a self-governing state and a member of the British Commonwealth of Nations. A republican Constitution was adopted on May 22, 1972, providing for a unicameral legislature, the National State Assembly, which has a six year term, and the country was renamed the Republic of Sri Lanka (meaning 'Resplendent Island'). On Sept. 5, 1978 a new Constitution introduced the title the Democratic Socialist Republic of Sri Lanka and a system of proportional representation. Legislative power is exercised by Parliament, the executive power being exercised by the President. A referendum in Dec. 1982 extended the life of the 1977 Parliament by six years from Aug. 1983.

Following increased Tamil guerilla activity throughout 1987 in northern and eastern Sri Lanka, an agreement was signed between President Jayewardene of Sri Lanka and the Prime Minister of India designed to merge the Northern and Eastern provinces. A ceasefire by Tamil guerrillas was agreed and arms surrendered. President Jayewardene promised that a referendum would be held before the end of 1988.

President, His Excellency Junius Jayewardene, *acceded,* Feb. 4, 1978, *elected* Oct. 20, 1982. (*also Minister of Defence, Plan Implementation, Janatha Estates Development, State Plantations, Power and Energy, Manpower Mobilization*).

Cabinet

Prime Minister, Minister of Local Government, Housing and Construction, Highways and of the Emergency Civil Administration, and Leader of the House of Parliament, Hon. R. Premadasa.

Public Administration and Plantation Industries, Hon. W. G. Montague Jayawickrema.

Social Services, Hon. N. H. Asoka Mahanama Karunaratne.

Cultural Affairs, Hon, E. L. B. Hurulle.

Transport, Transport Boards and Security of Commercial and Industrial Establishments, Hon. M. H. Mohamed.

Rural Development, Hon. Wimala Kannangara.

Textile Industries, Hon. Wijayapala Mendis.

Agricultural Development and Research and Food, Hon. Gamani N. Jayasuriya.

Foreign Affairs, Hon. A. C. S. Hameed.

Home Affairs, Hon. K. W. Devanayagam.

Posts and Telecommunications, Hon. D. B.Wijetunge.

Finance and Planning, Hon. M. H. M. Naina Marikar.

Lands and Land Development and Mahaweli Development, Hon. L. Gamini Dissanayake.

Parliamentary Affairs and Sports, (vacant).

National Security, Hon. Lalith W. Athulathmudali.

Justice, Hon. Nissanka P. Wijeyeratna.

Fisheries, Hon. M. Festus W. Perara.

Rural Industrial Development, Hon. S. Thondaman.

Youth Affairs and Employment and Education, Hon. Ranil Wickremasinghe.

Minister of State, Hon. Anandatissa de Alwis.

Regional Development, Hon. C. Rajadurai.

Health, Hon. Ranjith Atapattu.

Women's Affairs and Teaching Hospitals, Hon. Sunethra Ranasinghe.

Without Portfolio, Hon. M. A. B. M. Bakeer Markar.

Trade and Shipping, Hon. M. S. Amarasiri.

Industries and Scientific Affairs, Hon. Denzil Fernande.

Labour, Hon. P. C. Imbulana.

Co-operatives, Hon. Dr. W. Dahanayake.

SRI LANKA HIGH COMMISSION
13 Hyde Park Gardens, W2 2LU
[01–262 1841]

High Commissioner, His Excellency Chandra Monerawela (1984).

THE JUDICATURE

The Judicial System provides for a Supreme Court, a Court of Appeal, a High Court and other Courts of First Instance.

PRODUCTION

Agriculture.—The staple products of the island are tea, rubber, copra, spices and gems. There is increasing emphasis on local production of food, especially rice, and plans for the large-scale production of sugar cane, cotton and citrus fruits.

Industry.—Factories are established for the manufacture or processing of ceramic ware, vegetable oils and by-products, paper, tobacco, tanning and leather goods, plywood, cement, chemicals, sugar, flour, salt, textiles, ilmenite, tiles, tyres, fertilizers, clothing, jewellery and hardware and there is a petroleum refinery.

Trade with U.K.

	1986	1987
Imports from U.K.	£83,316,000	£84,680,000
Exports to U.K.	51,860,000	53,817,000

COMMUNICATIONS

There are over 15,660 miles of motorable roads in Sri Lanka and a government-run railway system with 984 miles of lines.

There is a satellite earth station at Padukka, in south-west Sri Lanka, which provides telecommunication links *via* satellite with any part of the globe.

The principal airports are at Katunayake, 19 miles north of Colombo, and Ratmalana, nine miles south of the capital. Air Lanka operates on 76 flights weekly to the Gulf States, the Maldives, Western Europe and throughout the Far East.

BRITISH HIGH COMMISSION
Galle Road, Kollupitiya (P.O. Box 1433),
Colombo 3
[Colombo 27611/9]

High Commissioner, His Excellency David Arthur Steuart Gladstone, C.M.G. (1987).

British Council Representative, R. A. K. Baker, 49 Alfred House Gardens, Colombo 3. Office also in Kandy.

SWAZILAND

(Umbuso we Swatini)

AREA, POPULATION, ETC.—Surrounded by South Africa on its northern, western and southern borders and by Mozambique to the east, this small land-locked country is geographically and climatically divided into three principal areas. The broken mountainous Highveld along the western border with an average altitude of 4,000 feet is densely forested mainly with conifers and eucalyptus; the Middleveld, averaging about 2,000 feet, is a mixed farming area including cotton and pineapples; and the Lowveld in the east, which was mainly scrubland until the introduction of large sugar cane plantations west of the Lubombo mountain range and the Mozambique border. Four rivers, the Komati, Usutu, Mbuluzi and Ngwavuma, flow from west to east. The total area of Swaziland is 6,704 sq. miles (17,363 sq. km.), and the population is estimated at some 647,000.

CAPITAL.—Mbabane (population, estimated 30,000), the headquarters of the Government, is situated at an average altitude of 3,800 ft. Other main townships are: Manzini (population, estimated, 30,000), Big Bend, Mhlambanyati, Mhlume, Nhlangano, Pigg's Peak and Simunye.

CURRENCY.—Lilangeni of 100 cents.

FLAG.—Five horizontal bands, crimson, bearing shield and spears device, bordered by narrow yellow bands; blue bands at top and foot.

NATIONAL ANTHEM.—Elwatini.

NATIONAL DAY.—September 6 (Independence Day).

GOVERNMENT

The Kingdom of Swaziland came into being on April 25, 1967, under a new internal self-government constitution and became an independent kingdom, headed by H.M. Sobhuza II, in membership of the Commonwealth on September 6, 1968.

A new electoral law was introduced in 1978, under which each of the 40 traditional Tinkhundla elect two members to the electoral college who elect 40 members to the House of Assembly. The King nominates 10 members to the House of Assembly, making 50 in all, who then elect 10 members (not of their own number) to the Senate. To these are added 10 senators nominated by the King, bringing the full membership of the Senate to 20. Under the Establishment of the Parliament of Swaziland Order, 1978, the Head of State, advised by the Swazi National Council, continues to reserve a large measure of executive, legislative and judicial authority.

Head of State, H.M. King Mswati III, *inaugurated* April 25, 1986.

Cabinet

Prime Minister, H. E. the Hon. Sotsha E. Dlamini.
Foreign Affairs, Hon. Senator George Mamba, G.C.V.O.
Labour and Public Service, Hon. Ben Nsibandze.
Defence and Youth, (vacant).
Justice, Hon. Reginald Dhladhla.
Education, Hon. Chief Sipho Shongwe.
Agriculture and Co-operatives, Hon. Sipho Hezekiel Mamba.
Finance, Hon. Barnabas Sibusiso Dlamini.
Commerce, Industry, Mines and Tourism, Hon. Nkomeni Douglas Ntiwane.
Natural Resources, Land Utilisation and Energy, H.R.H. the Hon. Prince Nqaba Dlamini.
Interior and Immigration, Hon. Mrs. Enzenjani Enoch Shabalala.
Health, Hon. Dr. Fanie Friedman.
Works and Communications, Hon. Wilson Mkhonta.

SWAZILAND HIGH COMMISSION
58 Pont Street, SW1X 0AE
[01–581 4976/8]

High Commissioner, His Excellency Mboni N. Dlamini (1988).

EDUCATION

In 1982, there were 125,303 pupils enrolled at 470 primary schools and 26,576 at 86 secondary schools. The University of Swaziland was founded in 1976.

COMMUNICATIONS

Swaziland's railway is about 150 miles long and runs from Ngwenya in the west to the Mozambique border near Goba in the east, and thence to the Mozambique port of Maputo. A southern link from Phuzumoya in central Swaziland joins up with the South African railway network to Richards Bay. A rail link from Mpaka in central Swaziland to the north-west border opened in 1986 and provides a link to Komatipoort.

Most passenger and goods traffic is carried by privately-owned motor transport services. There are daily scheduled air services by Royal Swazi National Airways to Johannesburg and scheduled routes to Durban, Harare, Lusaka, Gaborone, Nairobi and Dar es Salaam. International telecommunications and television services are provided through a satellite earth station opened in 1983. There is also a national telephone network through a series of microwave links.

FINANCE

Government revenue for 1987–88 is estimated at £284,783,000, of which £134,928,000 (or 47·4 per cent) is anticipated revenue from the South African Common Customs Union with South Africa, Botswana and Lesotho. A local sales tax introduced from Sept. 1984 is expected to yield £38,412,000 in 1987–88. Total Government-financed recurrent and capital expenditure in 1987–88 is estimated at £295,857,000.

Swaziland is a member of the Common Monetary Area and its unit of currency *Emalangeni* (singular *Lilangeni*) has a par value with the South African Rand.

Trade with U.K.

	1986	1987
Imports from U.K.	£3,922,262	£2,257,000
Exports to U.K.	48,194,218	36,901,000

BRITISH HIGH COMMISSION
Allister Miller Street, Mbabane
[Mbabane 42581/6]

High Commissioner, His Excellency John Gerrard Flynn (1987).

TANZANIA

(Jamhuri ya Mwungano wa Tanzania)

AREA, POPULATION, ETC.—Tanganyika, the mainland part of the United Republic of Tanzania (Tanganyika and Zanzibar), occupies the east-central portion of the African continent, between 1°–11° 45′ S. lat. and 29° 20′–40° 38′ E. long. It is bounded on the N. by Kenya and Uganda; on the S.W. by Lake Malawi, Malawi and Zambia; on the S. by Mozambique; on the W. it is bounded by Rwanda, Burundi and Zaire; on the E. the boundary is the Indian Ocean. Tanzania has an area of 364,900 sq. miles (945,087 sq. km.). The greater part of the country is occupied by the Central African plateau from which rise, among others, Mt. Kilimanjaro (19,340 ft.), the highest point on the continent of Africa, and Mt.

Meru (14,974 ft.). The Serengeti National Park, which covers an area of 6,000 sq. miles in the Arusha, Mwanza and Mara Regions, is famous for its variety and number of species of game.

The African population consists mostly of tribes of mixed Bantu race. The total population of Tanzania at the Census held in August, 1978 was 17,551,925; a 1985 estimate put the figure at 21,733,000. Africans form a very large majority, while Europeans, Asians, and other non-Africans form a small minority. Swahili is the national and official language. The use of English is widespread both for educational and government purposes.

Zanzibar.—Formerly ruled by the Sultan of Zanzibar, and a British Protectorate until Dec. 10, 1963. Zanzibar consists of the islands of Zanzibar, Pemba and Latham.

CAPITAL.—ΨDar es Salaam (population 1,096,000 1985 estimate). Other towns (1978 population) are ΨTanga (103,409); Mwanza (110,611); Arusha (55,281); Moshi (52,223); Morogoro (61,890); Dodoma (45,703); Tabora (67,392) and ΨMtwara (48,510). ΨZanzibar (population, 110,669) is the chief town and seaport of the island.

CURRENCY.—Tanzanian Shilling of 100 cents.

FLAG.—Green (above) and blue; divided by diagonal black stripe bordered by gold, running from bottom (next staff) to top (in fly).

NATIONAL ANTHEM.—Mungu Ibariki Afrika (God Bless Africa).

NATIONAL DAY.—April 26 (Union Day).

GOVERNMENT

Tanganyika became an independent state and a member of the British Commonwealth on December 9, 1961, and a Republic, within the Commonwealth, on December 9, 1962, with an executive President, elected by universal suffrage as the Head of State and Head of the Government. On Dec. 10, 1963, Zanzibar became an independent state within the Commonwealth and on April 26, 1964, Tanganyika united with Zanzibar to form the United Republic of Tanzania.

Tanzania became a one-party state on July 10, 1965 but with the Tanganyika African National Union (TANU) and the Afro-Shirazi Party (ASP) remaining the ruling parties in Tanganyika and Zanzibar respectively. On Feb. 5, 1977 these two parties merged to form the Chama Cha Mapinduzi (CCM) (Revolutionary Party).

A new constitution was introduced on April 26, 1977 and revised in Oct. 1984. There is a President and two Vice-Presidents, one the President of Zanzibar and the other the Prime Minister. The President may only serve two five year terms and if he comes from Zanzibar the Prime Minister will be the First Vice-President and must come from Tanganyika. If the President comes from Tanganyika the President of Zanzibar will be the First Vice President. In a Presidential election a single Presidential candidate nominated by the C.C.M. has to obtain an affirmative majority of the votes cast, failing which a fresh candidate must be nominated. The National Assembly contains 243 members, of whom 118 are elected from mainland constituencies and 50 from Zanzibar, 25 are ex-officio, 15 nominated and 35 indirectly elected. The Speaker may either be elected from among the members or be an additional member. Constituency members are elected by popular vote at a general election held at a maximum of five-yearly intervals in which the C.C.M. nominates two candidates to contest each seat.

A new constitution was also approved in 1984 for Zanzibar providing for an elected President and House of Representatives. Although Zanzibar has its own government and Chief Minister, Tanganyika is governed by the government of the Union. Overall policy is decided by the C.C.M. whose chairman, Julius Nyerere, was re-elected in 1987 by the Party National Conference for a 5 year term.

President of the United Republic, H.E. Hon. Ali Hassan Mwinyi, *b.* 1925; *elected* Oct. 27, 1985; *sworn in* Nov. 5, 1985.

First Vice-President of the United Republic and Prime Minister, Hon. Joseph Sinde Warioba.

Second Vice-President of the United Republic and President of Zanzibar, H.E. Idris Abdul Wakil.

Cabinet

Deputy Prime Minister and Minister of Defence, Hon. Salim Ahmed Salim.

Without Portfolio, Hon. Rashidi Kawawa; Hon. Gertrude Mongella.

Foreign Affairs, Hon. Benjamin Mkapa.

Finance, Economic Affairs and Planning, Hon. Cleopa Msuya.

Communications and Works, Hon. Mustafa Nyang'anyi.

Local Government Co-operatives and Marketing, Hon. Paul Bomani.

Agriculture and Livestock Development, Hon. Jackson Makwetta.

Labour and Manpower Development, Hon. Christian Kisanji.

Home Affairs, Hon. Brig. Muhidin Kimario.

Energy and Minerals, Hon. Al-Noor Kassum.

Lands, Natural Resources and Tourism, Hon. Arcado Ntagazwa.

Industry and Trade, Hon. Joseph Rwegasira.

Education, Hon. Kighoma Malima.

Health and Social Welfare, Hon. Aaron Chiduo.

Justice, and Attorney-General, Hon. Damian Lubuva.

Water, Hon. Pius Ng'wandu.

Community Development, Culture, Youth and Sport, Hon. Fatima Saidi Ali.

TANZANIA HIGH COMMISSION
43 Hertford Street, W1Y 7TF
[01-499 8951]

High Commissioner, His Excellency Anthony B. Nyakyi (1981).

EDUCATION

Education, almost entirely under state control, is characterised by official insistence that education must serve the aims of overall Government policy and planning. All Tanzanian secondary schools are expected to include practical subjects in the basic course. All who receive secondary (or equivalent) education are called up for a period of National Service. The school system is administered in Swahili but the Government is making efforts to improve English standards for the purposes of secondary and higher education. For higher education Tanzanian students go to the University of Dar es Salaam, Sokoine University of Agriculture in Morogoro, other East African universities, or to universities and colleges outside East Africa, including Britain.

COMMUNICATIONS

The main port is Dar es Salaam, and there are other ports on the coast at Tanga, Mtwara, Zanzibar, Mkoani and Wete, in addition to Mwanza, Musoma and Bukoba on Lake Victoria and Kigoma on Lake Tanganyika. Coastal shipping services connect the mainland to Zanzibar, and lake services are operated on Lake Tanganyika and Lake Malawi with neighbouring countries.

The principal international airports are Dar es Salaam and Kilimanjaro. Other airports include Zanzibar, Arusha, Mwanza and Tanga.

There are two railway systems; one connecting Dar es Salaam to Zambia; and the second having two main lines running from Dar es Salaam, one to northern Tanzania and Kenya and the other to Lake Tanganyika and Victoria.

PRODUCTION AND TRADE

The economy is based mainly on the production and export of primary produce and the growing of foodstuffs for local consumption. The islands of Zanzibar and Pemba produce a large part of the world's supply of cloves and clove oil; and coconuts, coconut oil and copra are also produced. The mainland's chief export crops are coffee, cotton, sisal, tea, tobacco, cashew nuts and diamonds. The most important minerals are diamonds. Hides and skins are another valuable export. Industry is at present largely concerned with the processing of raw material for either export or local consumption. There are also secondary manufacturing industries, including factories for the manufacture of leather and rubber footwear, knitwear, razor blades, cigarettes and textiles, and a wheat flour mill.

Trade with U.K.

	1986	1987
Imports from U.K........	£62,870,000	£91,874,000
Exports to U.K.	40,270,000	26,400,000

BRITISH HIGH COMMISSION
Hifadhi House, Samora Avenue (P.O. Box 9200), Dar es Salaam.
[Dar es Salaam 29601]

High Commissioner, His Excellency Colin Henry Imray, C.M.G. (1985).
British Council Representative, J. Mayatt, Samora Avenue, (P.O. Box 9100), Dar es Salaam.

TONGA

(Kingdom of Tonga)

Tonga, or the Friendly Islands, comprises a group of islands situated in the Southern Pacific some 450 miles to the E.S.E. of Fiji, with an area of 270 sq. miles (699 sq. km.), and population (1985 U.N. estimate) of 97,000. The largest island, Tongatapu, was discovered by Tasman in 1643. Most of the islands are of coral formation, but some are volcanic (Tofua, Kao and Niuafoou or "Tin Can" Island). The limits of the group are between 15° and 23° 30′ S., and 173° and 177° W.

CAPITAL.—ΨNuku'alofa (28,899), on Tongatapu.
CURRENCY.—Pa'anga of 100 Seniti.
FLAG.—Truncated red cross on rectangular white ground (next staff) on a red field.
NATIONAL ANTHEM.—E, 'Otua Mafimafi (Oh, Almighty God Above).
NATIONAL DAY.—June 4 (Independence Day).

GOVERNMENT

The Kingdom of Tonga is an independent constitutional monarchy within the Commonwealth. Prior to June 4, 1970 it had been a British-protected state for 70 years. The constitution provides for a Government consisting of the Sovereign, a privy council and cabinet, a legislative assembly and a judiciary. The legislative assembly has 29 members, with a Speaker, and includes the Ministers of the Crown, the two Governors of Island groups, and the representatives of the Nobles and of the people (nine of each), who are elected triennially.

Head of State, H.M. King Taufa'ahau Tupou IV, G.C.M.G., G.C.V.O., K.B.E., *acceded* Dec. 16, 1965.
Heir, H.R.H. Crown Prince Tupouto'a.

Cabinet

Prime Minister and Minister of Agriculture, H.R.H. Prince Fatafehi Tu'ipelehake, K.B.E.
Deputy Prime Minister, Minister of Lands, Hon. Baron Tuita, C.B.E.
Health, Hon. Dr. S. Tapa.
Finance, Hon. J. C. Cocker.
Education, Works and Civil Aviation, Hon. Dr. S. L. Kavaliku.
Police, Hon. 'Akau'ola.
Labour, Commerce and Industries, Baron Vaea.
Foreign Affairs and Defence, H.R.H. Crown Prince Tupouto'a.
Justice, and Attorney General, Hon. Tevita Tupou.
Governor of Vava'u, Hon. Dr. Ma'afu Tupou.
Governor of Ha'apai, Hon. Fakafanua.

TONGA HIGH COMMISSION
New Zealand House, Haymarket, SW1Y 4TE
[01–839 3287]

High Commissioner, His Excellency Mr. S. T. 'Aho (1986).

ECONOMY

The economy is primarily agricultural; the main crops are coconuts, bananas, vanilla, yams, taro, cassava, groundnuts and other fruits. Fish is an important staple food though recent shortfalls have led to canned fish being imported. Industry is based on the processing of agricultural produce, and the manufacture of foodstuffs, clothing and sports equipment. The principal exports are copra, other coconut products, tropical root crops and bananas.

Trade

	1984	1985
Total imports	T$46,614,000	T$58,900,000
Total exports	9,995,000	7,700,000

Trade with U.K.

	1986	1987
Imports from U.K........	£936,000	£2,013,000
Exports to U.K.	86,000	100,000

BRITISH HIGH COMMISSION
P.O. Box 56, Nuku'alofa
[Nuku'alofa 21020]

High Commissioner, His Excellency (Andrew) Paul Fabian (1987).

TRINIDAD AND TOBAGO

(The Republic of Trinidad and Tobago)

AREA, POPULATION, ETC.—*Trinidad*, the most southerly of the West Indian islands, lies close to the north coast of S. America, the nearest point being Venezuela, 7 miles distant. The island is situated between 10° 2′–11° 12′ N. lat. and 60° 30′–61° 56′ W. long., and is about 50 miles in length by 37 miles in width, with an area of 1,864 sq. miles (4,827 sq. km.). Two mountain systems, the Northern and Southern Ranges, stretch across almost its entire width and a third, the Central Range, lies diagonally across its middle portion; otherwise the island is mostly flat. The climate is tropical with temperatures averaging 82° F. (27.8° C) by day and 74° F. (23.3° C) by night, and a rainfall averaging 82 inches a year. There is a well-marked dry season from January to May, and a wet season from June to December broken by a short dry season (the Petite Careme) in September and October. The island was discovered by Columbus in 1498, was colonized in 1532 by the Spaniards, capitulated to the British under Abercromby in 1797, and was ceded to Britain under the Treaty of Amiens (March 25, 1802).

Tobago lies between 11° 9′ and 11° 21′ N. lat. and between 60° 30′ and 60° 50′ W. long., 19 miles northeast of Trinidad. The island is 32 miles long at its widest point, and 11 wide, and has an area of 116 sq. miles (300 sq. km.). It is a popular tourist resort. It was ceded to the British Crown in 1814 and amalgamated with Trinidad in 1888.

In 1985 the population of Trinidad and Tobago was estimated at 1,185,000.

Other Islands.—Corozal Point and Icacos Point, the N.W. and S.W. extremities of Trinidad, enclose the Gulf of Paria. West of Corozal Point lie several islands, of which Chacachacare, Huevos, Monos and Gaspar Grande are the most important.

CAPITAL.—ΨPort-of-Spain (population approximately 59,649 in 1985) is the administrative centre of the islands. About 33 miles south of the capital is San Fernando (population approximately 34,300 in 1985), a town of growing importance which is emerging as the industrial centre of Trinidad, and which is in close proximity to a number of large industrial plants. The main town of Tobago is ΨScarborough.

CURRENCY.—Trinidad and Tobago Dollar of 100 cents.

FLAG.—Black diagonal stripe bordered with white stripes, running from top by staff, all on a red field.

NATIONAL DAYS.—August 31 (Independence Day); September 24 (Republic Day).

GOVERNMENT

The Territory of Trinidad and Tobago became an independent state and a member of the British Commonwealth on August 31, 1962, and a Republic in 1976. The President is elected for 5 years by all members of the Senate and the House of Representatives. The House of Representatives has 36 members, elected by universal adult suffrage, and the Senate has 31, of whom 16 are appointed on the advice of the Prime Minister, 6 on the advice of the Leader of the Opposition and 9 at the discretion of the President. Legislation was passed in Sept. 1980 which afforded Tobago a degree of self-administration through the 12-member Tobago House of Assembly.

President, His Excellency Noor Mohammed Hassanali.

Cabinet

Prime Minister, Minister of Finance and The Economy, Hon. Arthur Robinson.
Food Production, Marine Exploitation and Forestry, Hon. Lincoln Myers.
Education, Hon. Clive Pantin.
External Affairs and International Trade, Hon. Dr. Sahadeo Basdeo.
Health, Hon. Dr. Emmanuel Hosein.
Industry, Enterprise and Tourism, Hon. Kenneth Gordon.
Energy, Labour, Employment and Manpower Resources, Hon. Dr. Albert Atwell.
Planning and Reconstruction, Hon. Winston Dookeran.
Youth, Sport, Culture and Creative Arts, Hon. Jennifer Johnson.
Works, Hon. Dr. Carson Charles.
Attorney General and Legal Affairs, Hon. Selwyn Richardson.
Community Development, Welfare and Status of Women, Hon. Gloria Henry.
Settlements and Public Utilities, Hon. Pamela Nicholson.
Local Government Improvement and Decentralization, Hon. Dr. Brinsley Samaroo.
Without Portfolio, Hon. Dr. Bau Tewari.

TRINIDAD AND TOBAGO HIGH COMMISSION
42 Belgrave Square, SW1X 8NT
[01–245 9351]

High Commissioner, His Excellency Mervyn I. Assam (1987).

EDUCATION

The education system provides for free education at all state-owned and government-assisted denominational schools and certain faculties at the University of the West Indies. In addition there are various private teaching establishments. Attendance is compulsory for children aged 6–12 years, after which attendance at free secondary schools is determined by success in the common entrance examination at 11 years. There are three technical institutes, two teachers' training colleges, and one of the three branches of the University of the West Indies is located in Trinidad, at the St. Augustine campus. A medical teaching complex was built at Mt. Hope, and operates in collaboration with the University of the West Indies.

COMMUNICATIONS

There are some 6,436 km. of all-weather roads in Trinidad and Tobago. The only general cargo port is Port-of-Spain but there are specialized port facilities elsewhere for landing crude oil, loading refinery products and sugar, and for storing and transmitting bauxite and cement. Regular shipping services call here and many inter-island craft use the port. Another, rapidly growing, port is at Port Lisas where new industries powered by local natural gas are located.

International scheduled airlines, including the national airline, Trinidad and Tobago Airways (BWIA) Corporation, use Piarco International Airport outside Port-of-Spain. The airline also flies between Piarco and Crown Point Airport in Tobago.

Two commercial broadcasting stations and one commercial television station operate in Trinidad and Tobago. The internal telephone system and the external telephone and telegraph connections are operated by state-owned companies.

PRODUCTION

Trinidad and Tobago's main source of revenue is from oil. Production of domestic crude in 1985 was 10·2 million cu. metres. The two major oil refineries increased production in 1985 to an average throughput of 12,538 cu. metres per day, and refined both local and imported crude. Trinidad has large reserves of natural gas, estimated at 18,000,000 million cu. feet, and in 1985 production was 7,413 million cu. metres. An integrated steel plant, an anhydrous ammonia plant and a methanol plant have been constructed at Point Lisas.

Fertilizers, tyres, clothing, soap, furniture and foodstuffs are manufactured locally while motor vehicles, radios, TV sets, and electro-domestic equipment are assembled from parts, mainly from Japan.

Finance

	1985	1986
Revenue	TT$6,766·7m	TT$5,239·9m
Expenditure	7,684·1m	8,004·4m
Gross public debt	3,640·7m	3,605·4m

TRADE

	1985	1986
Imports	TT$3,739·0m	TT$4,207·2m
Exports	5,247·1m	4,249·8m

In Jan. 1987, the exchange rate was unified at TT$1·00 = US$0·27778.

Trade with U.K.

	1986	1987
Imports from U.K.	£79,029,000	£57,016,000
Exports to U.K.	41,622,000	38,600,000

BRITISH HIGH COMMISSION
Furness House, 90 Independence Square
(P.O. Box 778) Port of Spain
[Port of Spain 62528616]

High Commissioner, His Excellency Martin Seymour Berthoud, C.M.G.

TUVALU

Tuvalu, formerly the Ellice Islands, formed part of the Gilbert and Ellice Islands Colony until October 1, 1975, when separate constitutions came into force. Separation from the Gilbert Islands was implemented on January 1, 1976.

Tuvalu comprises nine coral atolls situated in the South West Pacific around the point at which the International Date Line cuts the Equator. The total land area is only about 10 sq. miles. Few of the atolls are more than 12 ft above sea level or more than half a mile in width. The vegetation consists mainly of coconut palms. The resident population in 1985 was 8,229, but it is estimated that about 1,500 Tuvaluans work overseas, mostly in Nauru, or as seamen. The people are almost entirely Polynesian. The principal languages are Tuvaluan and English. The entire population is Christian and is predominantly Protestant.

CAPITAL.—ΨFunafuti. Estimated population 2,856. The capital has a grass strip airfield from which a service operates regularly to Fiji and Kiribati, and is also the only port.

CURRENCY.—Australian currency is legal tender.

FLAG.—Blue ground with Union Jack in top left quarter and nine five-pointed gold stars in the fly.

NATIONAL ANTHEM.—Tuvalu Mo Te Atua (Tuvalu for the Almighty).

NATIONAL DAY.—October 1 (Independence Day).

GOVERNMENT

On October 1, 1978, Tuvalu became fully independent as a sovereign state within the Commonwealth. The Constitution provides for a Prime Minister and four other Ministers who must be members of the 12-member elected Parliament. The Prime Minister presides at meetings of the Cabinet, which consists of the five Ministers, and is attended by the Attorney General. Local Government services are provided by elected Island Councils.

Governor General, His Excellency Sir Tupua Leupena, G.C.M.G., M.B.E., *sworn in* March 1, 1986.

Cabinet

Prime Minister, Rt. Hon. Dr. Tomasi Puapua.
Minister for Finance, Hon. Kitiseni Lopati.
Commerce and Natural Resources, Hon. Lale Seluka.
Works and Communications, Hon. Metia Tealofi.
Social Services, Hon. Telava Tevasa.
Secretary to Government (acting), Silinga Kofe.
Attorney-General, Robin Webster.

EDUCATION AND WELFARE

There are eight primary schools in Tuvalu and a church secondary school run jointly with the Government. The total of enrolled children of school age in 1985 was 1,300. A Maritime Training School started in 1979 now caters for 60 boys per annum.

There is a 30-bed hospital at Funafuti. All islands are served by a dispensary and a primary school.

ECONOMY

Most people still practise a subsistence economy, the main staples of their diet being coconuts and fish. The main imports are foodstuffs, consumer goods and building materials. The only export is copra (333 tons in 1985), but philatelic sales provide a major source of revenue and handicraft sales are increasing. The unit of currency is the Australian dollar. In addition there are Tuvalu dollar and cent coins in circulation.

Trade

	1984
Imports	A$3,954,000
Exports	307,917

Trade with U.K.

	1986	1987
Imports from U.K.	£78,000	£106,000
Exports to U.K.	88,000	2,000

UGANDA
(Republic of Uganda)

AREA, POPULATION, ETC.—Situated in Eastern Africa, Uganda is flanked by Zaire, the Sudan, Kenya and on the south by Tanzania and Rwanda. Large parts of Lakes Victoria, Edward and Albert (Mobuto) are within its boundaries, as are Lakes Kyoga, Kwania, George and Bisina (formerly Salisbury) and the course of the River Nile from its outlet from Lake Victoria to the Sudan frontier post at Nimule. Uganda has an area of 91,259 sq. miles (236,036 sq. km.) (water and swamp 16,400 sq. miles) and population (1985 U.N. estimate) of 15,477,000. The official language of Uganda is English. The main local vernaculars are of Bantu, Nilotic and Hamitic origins. Ki-Swahili is generally understood in trading centres.

Despite its tropical location, the climate is tempered by its situation some 3,000 ft. above sea level, and well over that altitude in the highlands of the Western and Eastern Regions. In South Uganda, temperatures seldom rise above 85° F. (29° C.) or fall below 60° F. (15° C.). The rainfall averages about 50 inches a year. Uganda has three National Parks and a fourth (Lake Mburo) has been designated.

CAPITAL.—Kampala (population of Greater Kampala, 460,000). Other principal towns are Jinja (45,000), Mbale (28,000) and Masaka (29,000).

CURRENCY.—Uganda Shilling of 100 cents.

FLAG.—Six horizontal stripes of black, yellow and red (repeated) with a crested crane emblem on a white orb in the centre.

NATIONAL ANTHEM.—"Oh Uganda".

NATIONAL DAY.—October 9 (Independence Day).

GOVERNMENT

Uganda became an independent state and a member of the Commonwealth on October 9, 1962, after some 70 years of British rule. A Republic was instituted on September 8, 1967, under an executive President, assisted by a Cabinet of Ministers.

Early in 1971 an army coup took place and Maj.-Gen. Idi Amin, the Army Commander, proclaimed himself Head of State. In 1979, following risings and military intervention by Tanzania, President Amin was overthrown. Following elections in 1980, Dr. Milton Obote became President. A military coup on July 27, 1985 ousted Dr. Obote and installed a military council which attempted to negotiate a power-sharing agreement with the National Resistance Movement led by Yoweri Museveni. However, the National Resistance Army captured Kampala in late Jan. 1986, securing control of the rest of the country in the following few months. Yoweri Museveni was sworn in as President on Jan. 29, 1986; subsequently the Prime Minister and a 24-member National Resistance Council were appointed, and a government was formed.

President, H. E. Yoweri Museveni, *sworn in* Jan. 29, 1986.

Cabinet

President and Minister of Defence, Lt.-Gen. Yoweri Museveni.
Prime Minister, Dr. Samson Kisseka.
1st Deputy P.M., Eriya Kategaya.
2nd Deputy P.M. and Minister for Foreign Affairs, Paul Ssemogerere.
3rd Deputy P.M., Abu Bakar Mayanja.
Internal Affairs, Ibrahim Mukiibi.
Finance, Dr. Crispus Kiyonga.
Planning and Economic Development, Prof. Yoweri Kyesimira.
Agriculture, Mrs. Victoria Ssekitoleko.
Industry, Prof. Stanley Tumwine.
Commerce, Dr. George Kanyeihamba.
Local Government, Amanya Mushega.
Animal Industries and Fisheries, Prof. George Mondo Kagonyera.
Youth, Culture and Sports, Dr. Edward Kakonge.
Public Services and Cabinet Affairs, Tom Rubale.
Regional Co-operation, Paul Etiang.
Information and Broadcasting, Ali Kirunda Kivejinja.
Education, Joshua Mayanja-Nkangi.
Land and Surveys, Ben Luwum.
Minerals and Water Development, Robert Kitariko.
Justice, Joseph Mulenga.
Constitutional Affairs, Sam Njuba.
Co-operatives and Marketing, John Ssebaana-Kizito.
Labour, Stanislaus Okurut.
Transport and Communications, Dr. Ruhakana-Rugunda.
Energy, Jaberi Bidandi-Ssali.
Tourism and Wildlife, Brig. Moses Ali.
Works, Daniel Kigozi.
Health, Dr. Adoko Nekyon.
Housing and Urban Development, James Wapakabulo.
Environment, Joseph Okune.
Relief and Social Rehabilitation, B. Chango-Machyo.

UGANDA HIGH COMMISSION
Uganda House, 58–59 Trafalgar Square, WC2N 5DX
[01–839 5783]
High Commissioner, His Excellency William S. K. Matovu (1988).

EDUCATION

Education is a joint undertaking by the Government, local authorities and, to some extent, voluntary agencies. In 1981 Uganda had 4,276 primary schools with an enrolment of 1,421,615 children. Secondary schools numbered 199 with 78,727 students enrolled; and 4,979 students in various technical training institutions.

The National University is Makerere University, Kampala, founded as a trade school in 1921 and becoming an independent University in 1970.

COMMUNICATIONS

There is an international airport at Entebbe, with direct flights to destinations in Africa and Europe. There are 8 other airfields in Uganda. Having no sea coast, Uganda is heavily dependent upon rail and road links to Mombasa for her trade. There are 2,226 kilometres of bituminized and 25,310 kilometres of gravel roads. Roads are poor but many are being rebitumenized. A railway network joins the capital to the western, eastern and northern centres.

TRADE, ETC.

The principal export earner is coffee (over 90 per cent of all exports), which earned $397 million in 1986. Attempts are being made to increase production of cotton and tea for export. Hydro-electricity is produced from the Owen Falls power station which generated 539 KW in 1987, 217 KW of which was exported to Kenya. The principal food crops are plantains, bananas, cassava, sweet potatoes, potatoes and sorghum.

Trade with U.K.

	1986	1987
Imports from U.K.	£26,046,000	£38,500,000
Exports to U.K.	50,870,000	37,100,000

BRITISH HIGH COMMISSION
10/12 Parliament Avenue, P.O. Box 7070, Kampala
[Kampala 57054/9]
High Commissioner, His Excellency Sir Derek March, K.B.E. (1986).
British Council Representative, T. L. G. Mullen.

VANUATU
(Ripablik Blang Vanuatu)

AREA, POPULATION, ETC.—Vanuatu, the former Anglo-French Condominium of the New Hebrides, is situated in the South Pacific Ocean, between 13° and 21° S. and 166° and 170° E. It includes 13 large and some 70 small islands, of coral and volcanic origin, including the Banks and Torres Islands in the North, and has a total land area of 5,700 sq. miles (14,763 sq. km.). The principal islands are Vanua Lava, Espiritu Santo, Maewo, Pentecost, Aoba, Malekula, Ambrym, Epi, Efate, Erromango, Tanna and Aneityum. Most islands are mountainous and there are active volcanoes on several. The climate is oceanic tropical, moderated by the south-east trade winds which blow between May and October. At other times winds are variable and cyclones may occur. Temperatures range between 17° C. and 28° C, with annual rainfall averaging 90 in. in the south and 155 in. in the north.

A 1986 estimate showed a population of 140,154. About 95 per cent of the population are Melanesian, the rest being made up largely of Micronesians, Polynesians and Europeans. The national language is Bislama, but English and French are also official languages.

SEAT OF ADMINISTRATION—ΨVila, Efate, population (1986), 14,184. The only other town is Luganville (population, 1986, 5,621), on Espiritu Santo.

CURRENCY.—Vatu of 100 Centimes.

FLAG.—Red over green with a black triangle in the hoist, the three parts being divided by fimbriations of black and yellow, and in the centre of the black triangle a boar's tusk overlaid by two crossed fern leaves.

NATIONAL ANTHEM.—"Nasimal Sing sing long Vanuatu."

NATIONAL DAY.—July 30 (Independence Day).

GOVERNMENT

The Condominium of the New Hebrides became an independent republic within the Commonwealth under the name of Vanuatu on July 30, 1980.

President, His Excellency Ati George Sokomanu, M.B.E., *elected* 1980, *re-elected* 1984.

Council of Ministers

Prime Minister and Minister of Planning, Hon. Father Walter Lini, C.B.E.
Education, Hon. S. J. Regenvanu.

Finance and Housing, Hon. S. Molisa.
Lands, Minerals and Fisheries, Hon. W. Mahit.
Foreign Affairs and Judicial Services, Hon. D. Kalpokas.
Health, Hon. F. Timakata.
Agriculture, Livestock and Forestry, Hon. J. Hopa.
Home Affairs, Hon. I. Abbil.
Civil Aviation, Tourism, Telecommunications and Energy, Hon. H. Qualo.
Trade, Commerce, Industry, Labour and Co-operatives, Hon. E. Natapei.
Public Works and Water Supply, Hon. J. M. Chilia.
Chief Justice, Hon. Mr. Justice F. G. Cooke.
Attorney-General, S. Hakwa.

ECONOMY

Most of the population is employed on plantations or in subsistence agriculture. Subsistence crops include yams, taro, manioc, sweet potato and breadfruit; principal cash crops are copra, cocoa and coffee. Large numbers of cattle are kept on the plantations and beef is the second largest export after copra.

Principal exports are copra, meat (frozen, tinned and chilled), timber and cocoa.

Tourism is an important revenue earner, and the absence of direct taxation has led to growth in the finance and associated industries.

Trade with U.K.

	1986	1987
Imports from U.K.	£1,037,000	£1,058,000
Exports to U.K.	62,000	15,000

BRITISH HIGH COMMISSION
Melitco House, Rue Pasteur, Vila.
[Vila 3100]
High Commissioner, His Excellency John Thompson, M.B.E. (1988).

WESTERN SAMOA

(Malotuto'atasi o Samoa i Sisifo)

Western Samoa lies in the south Pacific Ocean between latitudes 13° and 15° S. and 171° and 173° W. It consists of the islands of Savai'i (662 sq. miles) and of Upolu, which, with seven other islands (Apolima, Manono, Fanuatapu, Namua, Nuutele, Nuulua and Nuusafee) has an area of 435 sq. miles (1,714 sq. km.). All the islands are mountainous. Upolu, the most fertile, contains the harbours of ΨApia and ΨSaluafata, and Savai'i the harbour of ΨAsau. The population at the 1981 census was 158,130, the largest numbers being on Upolu (114,980) and Savai'i (43,150): a 1985 U.N. estimate put the figure at 163,000. The Samoans are a Polynesian people, though the population also includes other Pacific Islanders, Euronesians, Chinese and Europeans. The main languages spoken are Samoan and English. The islanders are Christians of different denominations.

CAPITAL.—ΨApia, on Upolu (population (1981 census) 33,100). Robert Louis Stevenson died and was buried at Apia in 1894.
CURRENCY.—Tala of 100 sene.
FLAG.—Five white stars (depicting the Southern Cross) on a quarter royal blue at top next staff, and three quarters red.
NATIONAL ANTHEM.—The Banner of Freedom.
NATIONAL DAY.—January 1 (Independence Day).

GOVERNMENT

Formerly administered by New Zealand (latterly with internal self-government), Western Samoa became, on January 1, 1962, the first fully-independent Polynesian State. The State was treated as a member country of the Commonwealth until its formal admission on August 28, 1970.

The 1962 Constitution provides for a Head of State to be elected by the Legislative Assembly for a five year term. However, it was decided that initially two of the four Paramount chiefs should jointly hold the office of Head of State for life. When one of the chiefs died in April 1963, Malietoa Tanumafili II became the holder of the office of Head of State for life. The Head of State's functions are analogous to those of a constitutional monarch. Executive government is carried out by a Cabinet of Ministers.

Head of State, H. H. Malietoa Tanumafili II, G.C.M.G., C.B.E. (April 15, 1963).
Deputy Head of State, Hon. Mataafa Faasuamaleaui Puela.

Cabinet

Prime Minister and Minister of Foreign Affairs, Internal Affairs, Immigration, Police and Prisons, Hon. Vaai Kolone.
Deputy P.M. and Minister of Public Works, Hon. Tupuola Efi.
Finance, Hon. Faasootauloa Semu Saili.
Agriculture, Forestries and Fisheries, Hon. Fuimaono Mimio.
Economic Development, Telecommunications and Broadcasting, Hon. Le Tagaloa Pita.
Lands and Survey, Parks and Recreation, Hon. Faumuina Anapapa.
Education, Sports, Youth and Culture, Hon. Le Mamea Ropati Mualia.
Health and Transport, Hon. Toeolesulusulu Siueva.
Justice and Labour, Hon. George M. Lober.

ECONOMY

Agriculture is the basis of Western Samoa's economy, the principal cash crops (and exports) being coconuts (copra), cocoa and bananas. Other agricultural exports include coffee, timber, tropical fruits and seeds. Efforts are being made to develop fishing on a commercial scale. Manufacturing is very small in scope and concerned largely with processing agricultural products, but is being encouraged by the Government. Tourism is increasing rapidly.

Trade with U.K.

	1985	1986
Imports from U.K.	£619,000	£433,000
Exports to U.K.	292,000	622,000

BRITISH HIGH COMMISSION (*see* New Zealand)

ZAMBIA

(Republic of Zambia)

AREA, POPULATION, ETC.—The Republic of Zambia lies on the plateau of Central Africa between the longitudes 22° E. and 33° 33′ E. and between the latitudes 8° 15′ S. and 18° S. It has an area of 290,586 sq. miles (752,614 sq. km.) within boundaries 3,515 miles in length and a population (U.N. estimate, 1985) of 6,666,000, including about 50,000 non-Africans.

With the exception of the valleys of the Zambezi, the Luapula, the Kafue and the Luangwa Rivers, and the Luano valley, elevations vary from 3,000 to 5,000 feet above sea level, but in the north-east the plateau rises to occasional altitudes of over 6,000 feet.

Although Zambia lies within the tropics, and fairly centrally in the African land mass, its elevation relieves it from extremely high temperatures and humidity.

CAPITAL.—Lusaka, situated in the Central Province. Population (estimated, 1980), 641,000. Other centres are Livingstone, Kabwe, Chipata, Mazabuka, Mbala, Kasama, Solwezi, Mongu, Mansa, Ndola, Luanshya, Mufulira, Chingola, Chililabombwe, Kalulushi and Kitwe, the last six towns being the main centres on the Copperbelt.

CURRENCY.—Zambian Kwacha of 100 Ngwee.

FLAG.—Green with three small vertical stripes, red, black and orange (next fly); eagle device on green above stripes.

NATIONAL ANTHEM.—Stand and Sing of Zambia, Proud and Free.

NATIONAL DAY.—October 24 (Independence Day).

GOVERNMENT

At the dissolution of the Federation of Rhodesia and Nyasaland, on December 31, 1963, Northern Rhodesia (as Zambia was then known) achieved internal self-government under a new constitution. Zambia became an independent republic within the Commonwealth on October 24, 1964—75 years after coming under British rule and nine months after achieving internal self-government.

In July 1973, a new Constitution was introduced, making the United National Independence Party (U.N.I.P.) the only party.

President, Dr. Kenneth David Kaunda, *assumed office* Oct. 24, 1964; *re-elected,* Dec. 1973, Dec. 1978 and Oct. 1983.

Cabinet

Prime Minister, K. Musokotwane.
General Education and Culture, B. Kabwe.
Defence, Gen. M. Masheke.
Secretary of State for Defence, A. Shapi.
Foreign Affairs, L. Mwananshiku.
Finance, and National Commission for Development Planning, G. Chigaga.
Legal Affairs (Attorney-General), F. M. Chomba.
Higher Education, Prof. L. Goma.
Health, R. Sakuhuka.
Commerce and Industry, J. K. M. Kalaluka.
Home Affairs, P. Malukutila.
Mines, P. S. Chitambala.
Agriculture and Water Development, F. Chuula.
Power, Transport and Communications, Gen. G. K. Chinkuli.
Works and Supply, H. Mwale.
Labour and Social Services, U. G. Mwila.
Tourism, L. S. Subulwa.
National Guidance, Information and Broadcasting Services, J. C. M. Punabantu.
Youth and Sports, F. Hapunda.
Lands and Natural Resources, B. Kakoma.
Co-operatives, J. Mukanda.
Decentralization, R. Kunda.
Presidential Affairs, A. K. Simuchimba.

Sec. Gen., U.N.I.P., A. G. Zulu.

ZAMBIA HIGH COMMISSION
2 Palace Gate, W8 5LS
[01–589 6655]

High Commissioner, His Excellency Wilted Phiri (1986).

JUDICATURE

There is a Chief Justice appointed by the President, all other judges being appointed on the recommendation of the Judicial Service Commission consisting of the Chief Justice, the chairman of the Public Service Commission, a senior Justice of Appeal and one Presidential nominee.

PRODUCTION

Principal products are maize, sugar, groundnuts, cotton, livestock, vegetables and tobacco.

Mineral production was valued at K8,390,765,000 in 1987, of which copper production (of 483,100 tonnes) accounted for K6,870,386,000.

FINANCE AND TRADE

Gross Domestic Product (current prices) was K6,332·1m in 1985. G.D.P. per capita (current prices) was K942·3.

	1986	1987
Imports	K4,447,687	K6,627,473
Exports	3,074,357	8,058,595

Trade with U.K.

	1986	1987
Imports from U.K. ...	£77,840,000	£75,178,000
Exports to U.K.	27,260,000	30,310,000

BRITISH HIGH COMMISSION
Independence Avenue (P.O. Box 50050), Lusaka
[Lusaka 216770]

High Commissioner, His Excellency John Michael Willson, C.M.G. (1988).

British Council Representative, J. Mulholland, O.B.E., Heroes Place, Cairo Road, (P.O. Box 34571), Lusaka. There is also a library in Ndola.

ZIMBABWE

(Republic of Zimbabwe)

AREA, POPULATION, ETC.—Zimbabwe, the former Southern Rhodesia (named after Cecil Rhodes) comprising eight provinces (Manicaland, Masvingo, Matabeleland North, Matabeleland South, Midlands, Mashonaland West, Central and East), lies south of the Zambezi river. The political neighbours are Zambia and Mozambique on the N. South Africa and Botswana on the S. and W., and Mozambique on the E. It has a total area of 150,804 sq. miles (390,580 sq. km.), and a population (estimated 1987) of 8,660,000.

CAPITAL.—Harare (formerly Salisbury) situated on the Mashonaland plateau, population (August 1982) 658,364. Bulawayo—the largest town in Matabeleland, population (August 1982) 495,317. Other centres are, Chitungwiza, Mutare, Gweru, Kadoma, Kwe Kwe, Masvingo and Hwange.

CURRENCY.—Zimbabwe Dollar of 100 cents.

FLAG.—Seven horizontal stripes (green, gold, red, black, red, gold, green) with white triangle at the hoist containing the Zimbabwe bird superimposed on red five-point star.

NATIONAL ANTHEM.—Ishe Komborerai Africa.

NATIONAL DAY.—April 18 (Independence Day).

GOVERNMENT

Southern Rhodesia was granted responsible government in 1923. An illegal declaration of independence on November 11, 1965 was finally terminated on December 12, 1979. Following elections in February 1980 the country obtained independence on April 18, 1980 as the Republic of Zimbabwe, a member of the British Commonwealth. The Parliament consists of a House of Assembly of 100 members and a Senate of 40 Senators and has a maximum life of five years. A Constitutional Amendment Bill designed to replace the 20 reserved white seats with nominated members from any race, was approved in Sept. 1987.

On Oct. 30, 1987 a Constitutional Amendment Bill was passed providing for the creation of an executive presidency. On Dec. 30, 1987 Mr. Robert Mugabe was elected by M.P.s and Senators as the first President. The Bill provides for a President to be popularly elected every six years. The President has the power to appoint a Cabinet and to veto parliamentary bills.

A merger agreement between the ZANU (PF) and ZAPU parties was signed on Dec. 22, 1987 which will lead to the eventual creation of a one-party state. The new party is known as ZANU-PF.

Executive President, Hon. Robert Gabriel Mugabe, *elected* Dec. 30, 1987.

Cabinet

President, Robert Mugabe.

Vice President, Simon Muzenda.

Ministers in the President's Office, Joshua Nkomo; Maurice Nyagumbo (*Political Affairs*); Dr. Bernard Chidzero (*Finance, Economic Planning and Development*).

Foreign Affairs, Dr. Nathan Shamuyarira.

Telecommunications, Dr. Witness Mangwende.

Higher Education, Dr. Dzingai Mutumbuka.

Primary and Secondary Education, Fay Chung.

Industry and Technology, Dr. Callistus Ndlovu.

Trade and Commerce, Oliver Munyaradzi.

Transport, Simbarashe Mumbengegwi.

Construction and National Housing, Joseph Msika.

Mines, Richard Hove.

Defence, Enos Nkala.

Lands, Agriculture and Rural Settlement, David Karimanzira.

Youth, Sport and Culture, David Kwidini.

Community Development, Co-operatives and Women's Affairs, Joyce Wachuru.

Justice, Legal and Parliamentary Affairs, Emmerson Munangagwa.

National Supplies, Simbi Mubako.

Health, Brig. Felix Muchemwa.

Energy, Water Resources and Development, Kumbirai Kangai.

Labour, Manpower Planning and Social Welfare, John Nkomo.

Home Affairs, Moven Mahachi.

Natural Resources and Tourism, Victoria Chitepo.

Local Government, Rural and Urban Development, Enos Chikowore.

Ministers of State in the President's Office, Christopher Anderson (*Public Service*); Dr. Sydney Sekeremayi (*National Security*); Joseph Culverwell (*National Scholarships*).

ZIMBABWE HIGH COMMISSION
Zimbabwe House, 429 Strand, WC2R 0SA
[01-836 7755]

High Commissioner, His Excellency Dr. Herbert M. Murerwa (1984).

EDUCATION

Since independence, a policy of free primary education and accelerated expansion at secondary level has resulted in rapidly expanding enrolment. In 1986 there were 2,260,367 primary school and 545,841 secondary school pupils in both Government and Government aid schools. Over 80 per cent of schools are privately run; they receive grants for materials. Other schools are government-owned and run. The University of Zimbabwe was founded in 1955.

ECONOMY

The country is endowed with minerals, water, forests, wildlife and other resources. The agricultural sector is well developed with both commercial and communal farmers. Tobacco remains the most important crop in terms of export and maize the most important for domestic consumption. Other crops include wheat, cotton, and sugar. Good quality beef is exported to the E.C. Production can be severely affected by drought.

The manufacturing sector has a high degree of inter-dependency and many industries depend on the agricultural sector for their raw materials. Industry is dependent on vital imports e.g. fuel oil, steel products and chemicals, as well as heavy machinery and items of transport. The mining sector, although contributing a relatively small portion to G.D.P. (7·6 per cent in 1984) is important to the economy as a foreign exchange earner (26 per cent of total in 1984). Almost all mineral production is exported. Gold is the most important mineral, others are asbestos, silver, nickel, copper, chrome ore, tin, iron ore and cobalt. There is a successful ferro-chrome industry and a substantial steel works which has been heavily subsidized by Government.

A high domestic budget deficit combining with a high external debt service ratio has put the economy into decline. The 1986–87 drought made this worse.

GOVERNMENT FINANCE

	1984-85	1985–86
Revenue	Z$2,212·3m	Z$2,616·2m
Expenditure	2,923·0m	3,307·8m

Trade with U.K.

	1986	1987
Imports from U.K.	£61,937,000	£63,181,000
Exports to U.K.	80,702,000	79,771,000

BRITISH HIGH COMMISSION
Stanley House, Stanley Avenue,
(PO Box 4490), Harare
[Harare 793781]

High Commissioner, His Excellency Michael Ramsay Melhuish, C.M.G. (1985).

British Council Representative, N. M. Ross, 23 Stanley Avenue, (P.O. Box 664), Harare.

Dependent Territories, etc.

ANGUILLA

Anguilla is a flat coralline island, about 16 miles in length, 3¼ miles in breadth at its widest point and its area is about 35 sq. miles (91 sq. km.). It lies approximately 18° N. latitude and 63° W longitude, to the north of the Leeward Islands group.

The island is covered with low scrub and fringed with some of the finest white coral-sand beaches in the Caribbean. The climate is pleasant and healthy with temperatures in the range of 24-30° C. throughout the year. The population (U.N. 1985 estimate) is about 7,000.

CAPITAL.—The Valley (population 500).

CURRENCY.—East Caribbean Dollar (EC$) of 100 cents.

GOVERNMENT

Anguilla has been a British colony since 1650. For most of its history it has been linked administratively with St. Christopher, but three months after the Associated State of Saint Christopher (St. Kitts)-Nevis-Anguilla came into being in 1967 the Anguillans repudiated government from St. Kitts. A Commissioner was installed in 1969 and in 1976 Anguilla was given a new status and separate constitution. Final separation from St. Kitts and Nevis was effected on Dec. 19, 1980 and Anguilla reverted to a British Dependency. A new Constitution was introduced in 1982, providing for a Governor, an Executive Council comprising four elected Ministers and two *ex-officio* members (Attorney General and Permanent Secretary, Finance), and an 11-member legislative House of Assembly presided over by a Speaker.

Governor, His Excellency Mr. G. O. Whittaker, O.B.E. (1987).

Executive Council

Chief Minister and Minister of Home Affairs, Tourism and Economic Development, Hon. Emile Gumbs.
Lands, Agriculture and Fisheries, Health and Prisons, Hon. Eric Reid.
Communications, Public Utilities and Works, Hon. Nashville Webster.
Finance, Education, Community Development, Osbourne Fleming.
Permanent Secretary (Finance), Hon. Franklin Connor, O.B.E.
Attorney-General, Hon. R. Whitehead.

ECONOMY

Low rainfall limits agricultural output and export earnings are mainly from sales of lobsters. Tourism has developed rapidly in recent years and accounts for most of the islands economic activity. In 1987 there were 21,000 tourists and a further 50,500 day visitors.

FINANCE

	1987	1988*
Revenue	EC$20,000,000	EC$22,700,000
Expenditure	18,227,000	20,840,000
Capital Expenditure	1,453,000	2,982,000

*estimate

Trade with U.K.

	1986	1987
Imports from U.K.	£1,136,000	£1,328,000
Exports to U.K.	60,000	188,000

ASCENSION
See ST. HELENA

BERMUDA

The Bermudas, or Somers Islands, are a cluster of about 100 small islands (about 20 only of which are inhabited) situated in the west of the Atlantic Ocean, in 32° 18′ N. lat. and 64° 46′ W. long., the nearest point of the mainland being Cape Hatteras in North Carolina, about 570 miles distant. The colony derives its name from Juan Bermudez, a Spaniard, who sighted it before 1515, but no settlement was made until 1609, when Sir George Somers, who was shipwrecked here on his way to Virginia, colonized the islands.

The total area is approximately 20·59 sq. miles (53 sq. km.), which includes 2·3 sq. miles leased to the U.S.A. The civil population was 56,000 in 1985 (U.N. estimate).

CAPITAL.—ΨHamilton (population, 1984, 1,669).
CURRENCY.—The Bermudan Dollar (Bd$) of 100 cents.

GOVERNMENT

Internal self-government was introduced on June 8, 1968. There is a Senate of 11 Members and an elected House of Assembly of 40 Members. The Governor retains responsibility for external affairs, defence, internal security and the police, although administrative matters for the Police Service have been delegated to the Minister of Home Affairs.

Governor and Commander-in-Chief, His Excellency Sir (Henry) Desmond (Allen) Langley, K.C.V.O., M.B.E. (1988).
Deputy Governor, B. Canty, O.B.E.

Cabinet

Premier, Hon. J. W. Swan.
Deputy Premier and Minister of Finance, Dr. Hon. C. James.
Tourism, Hon. J. Irving Pearman.
Education, Hon. G. D. E. Simons.
Works and Housing, Hon. Q. L. Edness.
Health and Social Services, Hon. A. F. Cartwright DeCouto.
Transport, Hon. S. Stallard.
Environment, Hon. T. H. Davis.
Labour and Home Affairs, Hon. Sir John Sharpe.
Community and Cultural Affairs, Hon. R. Barritt.
Youth, Sport and Recreation, Hon. M. A. Burgess.
Legislative Affairs, with responsibility for Telecommunications, Sen. Hon. C. T. M. Collis.

President of the Senate, Hon. A. S. Jackson, M.B.E.
Speaker of the House of Assembly, Hon. F. J. Barritt, C.B.E.
Chief Justice, Hon. Sir James R. Astwood.
Puisne Judges, Hon. L. Austin Ward, Q.C.; Hon. M. Ward; Hon. D. Hull.

ECONOMY

Locally manufactured concentrates and pharmaceuticals are now the colony's leading exports. Little food is produced except vegetables and fish, other foodstuffs being imported.

The Islands' economic structure is based on tourism, the major industry, and international company business, attracted by the low level of taxation and sophisticated telecommunications system. In 1987 a total of 613,628 visitors arrived by air and cruise ship. Cruise ships dock at Hamilton, Somerset and St. George's.

Free elementary education was introduced in 1949. Free secondary education was introduced in 1965 for those children in the aided and maintained schools who were below the upper limit of the statutory school age of 16 (from 1969 onwards).

There are 5 radio and one television station, one daily and 2 weekly newspapers and overseas telephone and telegraph services are maintained.

FINANCE

	1987–88	1988–89
Public revenue	$251,550,300	$279,639,200
Public expenditure	220,172,000	245,542,700

THE BRITISH ANTARCTIC TERRITORY

The British Antarctic Territory was designated in 1962 and consists of the areas south of 60°S. latitude which were previously included in the Falkland Islands Dependencies. The territory lies between longitudes 20° and 80°W., south of latitude 60°S. and includes the South Orkney Islands, the South Shetland Islands, the mountainous Antarctic Peninsula (highest point *Mount Jackson*, 13,620ft, in Palmer Land) and all adjacent islands, and the land mass extending to the South Pole. The territory has no indigenous inhabitants and the British population consists of the scientists and technicians who man the British Antarctic Survey stations. The number averages about 60 to 70 in winter, but increases considerably in the summer months with the arrival of field workers; Argentina, Brazil, Chile, China, Poland, U.S.A., U.S.S.R. and Uruguay also have scientific stations in the territory.

The first two British Antarctic Survey stations were established in the South Shetland Islands in 1944, and by 1956 the number of stations had risen to twelve. Due to the completion of field work in some areas and increased mobility, the number has now been reduced to five. These are Signy (Signy Island, S. Orkney Islands), Faraday (Argentine Islands, Graham Coast), Rothera (Adelaide Island), Halley (Caird Coast) and, in summer only, Fossil Bluff (George VI Sound). Fifteen other stations have been established but are at present unoccupied.

The territory is administered by a High Commissioner, resident in the Falkland Islands.

High Commissioner, His Excellency William Hugh Fullerton (1988).

(*see also index for* the Antarctic)

THE BRITISH INDIAN OCEAN TERRITORY

The British Indian Ocean Territory was established by an Order in Council in 1965 and included islands formerly administered by Mauritius and the Seychelles. After the independence of both, the territory was redefined in 1976 as comprising only the islands of the Chagos Archipelago.

The Chagos Archipelago consists of six main groups of islands situated on the Great Chagos Bank and covering some 21,000 sq. miles (54,389 sq. km.). The largest and most southerly of the Chagos Islands is *Diego Garcia*, a sand cay with a land area of about 17 square miles approximately 1,100 miles east of Mahe, used as a joint naval support facility by Britain and U.S.A.

The other main island groups of the archipelago, *Peros Banhos* (29 islands with a total land area of 4 sq. miles) and *Salomon* (11 islands with a total land area of 2 sq. miles) are uninhabited. The islands have a typical tropical maritime climate, with average temperatures between 25° C and 29° C in Diego Garcia, and rainfall in the whole archipelago of 90–100 inches a year.

Commissioner, R. Edis.
Administrator, R. Crompton.

THE BRITISH VIRGIN ISLANDS

The Virgin Islands are a group of islands at the eastern extremity of the Greater Antilles, divided between Great Britain and the U.S.A. Those of the group which are British number 46, of which 11 are inhabited, and have a total area of about 59 sq. miles, (153 sq. km.). The principal are Tortola, the largest (situated in 18° 27′ N. lat. and 64° 40′ W. long., area, 21 sq. miles), Virgin Gorda (8½ sq. miles), Anegada (15 sq.miles) and Jost Van Dyke (3¼ sq. miles). The 1980 Census showed a total population of 10,985 (Tortola (9,119); Virgin Gorda (1,443); Anegada (169); Jost Van Dyke (136); and other islands (82). A 1985 U.N. estimate gave a figure of 13,000. Apart from Anegada, which is a flat coral island, the British Virgin Islands are hilly, being an extension of the Puerto Rico and the U.S. Virgin Islands archipelago. The highest point is Sage Mountain on Tortola which rises to a height of 1,780 feet. Tourism is the main industry, but there is some cattle raising and fishing. Other products are vegetables, fruit, charcoal and rum.

The islands lie within the Trade Winds belt and possess a pleasant and healthy sub-tropical climate. The average temperature varies from 22°–28° C. in winter and 26°–31° C. in summer. The summer heat is tempered by sea breezes and the temperature usually falls by about 6° C. at night. Average rainfall is 53 inches.

CAPITAL.—ΨRoad Town, on the south-east of Tortola. Population, 2,479.

GOVERNMENT

Under the 1977 Constitution, the Governor, appointed by the Crown, remains responsible for defence and internal security, external affairs and the civil service but in other matters acts in accordance with the advice of the Executive Council. The Executive Council consists of the Governor as Chairman, one *ex officio* member (the Attorney-General), the Chief Minister and three other ministers. The Legislative Council consists of a Speaker chosen from outside the Council, one *ex officio* member (the Attorney-General), and nine elected members returned from nine one-member electoral districts.

Governor, His Excellency (John) Mark (Ambrose) Herdman, L.V.O. (1986).
Deputy Governor, E. Georges.
Financial Secretary, R. Mathavious.

The Executive Council

Chairman, The Governor.
Chief Minister and Minister of Finance, Hon. H. Lavity Stoutt.
Natural Resources and Labour, Hon. Omar Hodge.
Communications and Works, Hon. Oliver Cills.
Health, Education and Welfare, Hon. Louis Walters, M.B.E.
Attorney-General, Hon. Karl S. Atterbury.

Puisne Judge (resident), Hon. Miss Sylvia Bertrand.

FINANCE

	1985	1986
Revenue	U.S.$21,370,000	U.S.$23,195,000
Expenditure	20,123,100	21,213,097

ECONOMY

Tourism is the main industry but other industries include a rum distillery, three stone-crushing plants and factories manufacturing concrete blocks and paint. The major export items are fresh fish, gravel, sand, fruits and vegetables: exports are largely confined to the U.S. Virgin Islands. Chief imports are building materials, machinery, cars and beverages.

Trade with U.K.

	1986	1987
Imports from U.K........	£3,491,000	£3,310,000
Exports to U.K.	267,000	752,000

COMMUNICATIONS

The principal airport is on Beef Island, linked by bridge to Tortola, and an extended runway of 3,600 feet enables larger aircraft to call. There is a second airfield on Virgin Gorda and a third on Anegada. There are direct shipping services to the United Kingdom and the United States and fast passenger services connect the main islands by ferry.

THE CAYMAN ISLANDS

The Cayman Islands, between 79° 44' and 81° 26' W. and 19° 15' and 19° 46' N., consist of three islands, Grand Cayman, Cayman Brac, and Little Cayman, with a total area of 100 sq. miles (259 sq. km.). Population (1987 estimate), 23,400.

CAPITAL.—ΨGeorge Town, in Grand Cayman, population (1987) 10,000.

GOVERNMENT

The constitution provides for a Governor, Legislative Assembly and an Executive Council, and effectively allows a large measure of self-government. Unless there are exceptional reasons, the Governor must take the advice of the Executive Council, which comprises three official members and four others elected from the 12 elected members of the Assembly. The Governor retains control over the police, civil service, defence and external affairs. He presides over the Assembly, in which the three official members also sit, though there is provision for the appointment of a Speaker if the members request it. The normal life of the Assembly is four years, with a general election next due on November 16, 1988.

Governor, His Excellency Alan James Scott, C.V.O., C.B.E.

Executive Council

President, The Governor.
Financial Secretary, Hon. T. C. Jefferson, O.B.E.
Administrative Secretary, Hon. J. L. Hurlston.
Attorney-General, Hon. R. W. Ground, Q.C.
Member for Health, Education and Social Services, Hon. B. O. Ebanks, O.B.E.
Member for Communications, Works and District Administration, Hon. Capt. C. Kirkconnell.
Member for Tourism, Aviation and Trade, Hon. W. N. Bodden, O.B.E.
Member for Development and Natural Resources, Hon. V. Johnson, C.B.E.

LONDON OFFICE

Cayman Islands Government Office, 100 Brompton Road, SW3 1EX.
[01–581 9418]

Government Representative, T. Russell, C.M.G., C.B.E.

ECONOMY

Based on a complete absence of direct taxation, the Cayman Islands have been successfully promoted over the past 25 years as an offshore financial centre. At the end of 1987 there were 515 banks and trust companies and 360 insurance companies licensed, and over 16,500 companies registered. Promotion of tourism, with an emphasis on scuba diving, has also

been successful, and there were 209,044 visitors by air and 271,740 cruise ship callers in 1987. The two industries support a heavy imbalance in trade resulting from the need to import most of what is consumed and used on the Islands. Import duty and fees from financial centre operations have provided revenue enabling the government to undertake heavy investment in education, health and other social programmes.

FINANCE

	1987	1988*
Revenue	CI$75·5m	CI$79·62m
Expenditure	71·8m	84·16m
*estimated		

At end 1987, public debt totalled CI$18·17 million, compared to CI$12·95 million at end 1986.

TRADE

	1985	1986
Total imports	CI$122m	CI$134m
Total exports	1·5m	2·2m

Trade with U.K.

	1986	1987
Imports from U.K........	£11,403,000	£6,442,000
Exports to U.K.	2,422,000	1,318,000

FALKLAND ISLANDS

The Falkland Islands, the only considerable group in the South Atlantic, lie about 300 miles east of the Straits of Magellan, between 52° 15'–53° S. lat. and 57° 40'–62° W. long. They consist of East Falkland (area 2,610 sq. miles; 6,759 sq. km.), West Falkland (2,090 sq. miles; 5,413 sq. km.) and upwards of 100 small islands in the aggregate. Mount Usborne (E. Falkland), the loftiest peak, rises 2,312 feet above the level of the sea.

The climate is cool. At Stanley the mean monthly temperature varies between 9° C. in January and 2° C. in July. The islands are chiefly moorland.

The Falklands were sighted first by Davis in 1592, and by Hawkins in 1594: the first known landing was by Strong in 1690. A settlement was made by France in 1764; this was subsequently sold to Spain, but the latter country recognized Great Britain's title to a part at least of the group in 1771. The settlement was destroyed by the Americans in 1831. In 1833 occupation was resumed by the British for the protection of the seal-fisheries, and the islands were permanently colonized as the most southerly organized colony of the British Empire. Argentina has long claimed sovereignty over the Islands (known to them as las Islas Malvinas), and in pursuance of this claim invaded the Islands on April 2, 1982 and also occupied South Georgia. A Task Force despatched from Great Britain recaptured South Georgia on April 25, and after landing at San Carlos Bay on May 21, recaptured the Islands from the Argentines, who surrendered on June 14, 1982. A British naval and military presence remains in the area.

The population was 1,916 at Dec. 31, 1986 and is almost totally British.

CHIEF TOWN.—ΨStanley, population 1,231 (1986). Stanley is distant from England about 8,103 miles.

GOVERNMENT

Under the 1985 Constitution, the Governor is advised by an Executive Council consisting of three elected members of the Legislative Council and two *ex-officio* members, the Chief Executive and the Financial Secretary. The Legislative Council consists of eight elected members and the same two *ex-officio* members.

Governor, His Excellency William Hugh Fullerton (1988).

Commander, British Forces, Falkland Islands, Air Vice-Marshal D. O. Crwys-Williams.

Acting Chief Executive, D. G. P. Taylor.

Financial Secretary, H. T. Rowlands, C.B.E.

Attorney General, D. G. Lang, Q.C.

FINANCE

	1987–88*	1988–89*
Public Revenue	£39,762,000	£35,761,000
Expenditure	24,592,000	28,646,000

*Estimated.

ECONOMY

The economy was formerly based solely on agriculture, principally sheep-farming with a little dairy farming for domestic requirements and crops for winter fodder. Since the establishment of an interim conservation and management zone around the Islands and the consequent introduction on Feb. 1, 1987 of a licensing regime for vessels fishing within the zone the economy has diversified and income from the associated fishing activities is now the largest source of revenue. Chief imports are provisions, alcoholic beverages, timber, clothing and hardware.

Trade with U.K.

	1986	1987
Imports from U.K.	£11,135,000	£7,353,000
Exports to U.K.	14,286,000	8,148,000

GIBRALTAR

Gibraltar is a rocky promontory, 2¾ miles in length, three-quarters of a mile in breadth and 1,396 ft. high at its greatest elevation, near the southern extremity of Spain, with which it is connected by a low isthmus. It is about 14 miles distant from the opposite coast of Africa. In a total area of 2¼ sq. miles (6 sq. km.), the population at the census of Nov. 1981 was 28,719. At the end of 1987, it stood at 29,692.

Gibraltar is a naval base of strategic importance to Great Britain. It was captured in 1704, during the war of the Spanish Succession, by a combined Dutch and English force, under Sir George Rooke, and was ceded to Great Britain by the Treaty of Utrecht, 1713. Several attempts have been made to retake it, the most celebrated being the great siege, 1779–83, when General Eliott, afterwards Lord Heathfield, held it for three years and seven months against a combined French and Spanish force. The town stands at the foot of the promontory on the W. side.

GOVERNMENT

The Constitution of Gibraltar, approved in 1969, made formal provision for certain domestic matters to devolve on Ministers appointed from among elected members of the House of Assembly then set up to replace the former Legislative Council. The House of Assembly consists of an independent Speaker, 15 elected members, the Attorney-General and the Financial and Development Secretary.

Governor and Commander-in-Chief, His Excellency Air Chief Marshal Sir Peter Terry, G.C.B., A.F.C.

Flag Officer, Gibraltar, and Admiral Supr., H.M. Naval Base, Gibraltar, Rear-Adm. N. J. Hill Norton.

Deputy Governor, W. E. Quantrill £34,000

Financial and Development Secretary, B. Traynor

£30,344

Attorney-General, E. Thistlethwaite £30,344

Chief Justice, A. Kneller £34,000

Chief Minister, J. Bossano.

Speaker, Sir Alfred Vasquez, C.B.E., Q.C.

ECONOMY

Gibraltar enjoys the advantages of an extensive shipping trade and is a popular shopping centre. The chief sources of revenue are the port dues, the rent of the Crown estate in the town, and duties on consumer items. The free port tradition of Gibraltar is still reflected in the low rates of import duty. The gradual change from a fortress city to a holiday centre has led to a flourishing tourist trade.

A total of 2,601 merchant ships (35,651,314 gross registered tons aggregate) entered the port during 1987. Of these 1,921 were deep-sea ships (35,490,934 gross registered tons aggregate). In addition 5,071 yachts (113,088 gross registered tons) called at the port. There are 26·75 miles of roads.

Education is compulsory and free for children between the ages of 4 and 15 whose parents are ordinarily resident in Gibraltar. Scholarships are available for higher education in Britain. The total enrolment in Government schools was 4,538 in Dec. 1987.

Finance and Trade

	1985–86	1986–87
Revenue	£64,500,000	£74,216,000
Expenditure	61,054,000	71,051,000

	1985–86	1986–87
Total imports	£111,651,000	£140,962,000
Total exports	44,323,000	51,731,000

Trade with U.K.

	1986	1987
Imports from U.K.	£46,200,000	£49,986,000
Exports to U.K.	6,021,000	3,367,000

HONG KONG

Hong Kong, consisting of a number of islands and of a portion of the mainland (Kowloon and the New Territories), on the south-eastern coast of China, is situated at the eastern side of the mouth of the Pearl River, between 22° 9′ and 22° 37′ N. lat. and 113° 52′– 114° 30′ E. long. The total area of the territory (including recent reclamation) is 413 sq. miles (1,071 sq. km.) with a population which at the end of 1987 was 5,600,000.

The island of Hong Kong is about 11 miles long and from two to five miles broad, with a total area of 29 sq. miles; at the eastern entrance to the harbour it is separated from the mainland by a narrow strait. The island was first occupied by Great Britain in January, 1841, and formally ceded by the Treaty of Nanking in 1842; Kowloon was subsequently acquired by the Peking Convention of 1860; and the New Territories, consisting of a peninsula in the southern part of the Guangdong province, together with adjacent islands, by a 99-year lease signed June 9, 1898.

Climate.—Hong Kong enjoys unusually varied weather for a tropical area. The mean monthly temperature ranges from 15° C. to 29° C., though summer temperatures can exceed 33° C and winter temperatures drop below 10° C. The average annual rainfall is 2,225 mm., of which nearly 80 per cent falls between May and September. Tropical cyclones passing at various distances from Hong Kong occur between July and September, causing high winds and heavy rain.

CAPITAL.—ΨVictoria, situated on the island of Hong Kong, is about 81 miles S.E. of Canton and 40 miles E. of the Portuguese province of Macao at the other side of the Pearl River. It lies along the northern shore of the island and faces the mainland; the harbour (23 sq. miles water area) lies between the city and the mainland.

GOVERNMENT

Hong Kong is administered by the Hong Kong Government, at the head of which is the Governor, and its administration has developed from the basic pattern applied to all British-governed territories overseas. Under the terms of the Joint Declaration of the British and Chinese Governments, which entered into force on May 27, 1985, Hong Kong will become with effect from July 1, 1997, a Special Administrative Region of the People's Republic of China. However, the social and economic systems in the S.A.R. will remain unchanged for 50 years.

The Governor governs aided by an Executive Council, consisting of four *ex-officio* and nine appointed members, and a Legislative Council, which consists of three *ex-officio* and seven official members, 22 appointed members and 24 elected members.

There is also an Urban Council which provides services relating to public health and sanitation, culture and recreation in the urban area. A Regional Council was also set up in 1986 to provide similar services in the New Territories. Both Councils are financially autonomous.

Governor, His Excellency Sir David Wilson, K.C.M.G. (1987).
Chief Secretary, Hon. Sir David Ford, K.B.E., L.V.O.
Commander, British Forces, Maj.-Gen. G. D. Johnson, O.B.E., M.C.
Financial Secretary, Hon. P. Jacobs, O.B.E.
Attorney-General, Hon. J. F. Mathews.
Secretary for Trade and Industry, N. W. H. Macleod.
Secretary for District Administration, Hon. D. Liao, C.B.E.
Secretary for Economic Services, Mrs. Anson Chan.
Secretary for Security, Hon. G. T. Barnes.
Secretary for Lands and Works, Hon. G. Barnes, C.B.E.
Secretary for Education and Manpower, Hon. R. G. B. Bridge, O.B.E.
Secretary for Health and Welfare, Hon. J. W. Chambers, O.B.E.
Secretary for Administrative Services and Information, Hon. P. K. Y. Tsao, C.P.M.
Secretary for Housing, Hon. J. R. Todd, C.V.O., O.B.E.
Secretary for Transport, Hon. M. Leung.
Secretary for Monetary Affairs, D. A. C. Nendick.
Secretary for the Civil Service, H. S. Grewal, E.D.
Secretary for Municipal Services, A. K. Chui.
Secretary (General Duties), E. B. Wiggham.
Chief Justice, Hon. Sir Ti Liang Yang, K.B.E.
British Council Representative, J. Davey, Easey Commercial Building, 225 Hennessy Road, Hong Kong.

HONG KONG GOVERNMENT OFFICE IN LONDON
6 Grafton Street, W1X 3LB
[01-499 9821]
Commissioner, Mr. Selwyn Alleyne, C.B.E.

COMMUNICATIONS

Hong Kong, one of the world's finest natural harbours, possesses excellent wharves. The Kwai Chung container terminal has six berths which can accommodate six "third-generation" container ships simultaneously. An ocean terminal pier with an overall length of 381 m. can accommodate large liners and cargo vessels. Other vessels up to 305 metres length and 14·6 metres draught can be berthed. Mooring buoys in the harbour are available to vessels of up to 11·2 metres draught. Excellent dockyard facilities are available and include five floating drydocks, the largest of which has a lifting capacity of over 40,000 tonnes. In 1987 some 15,170 ocean-going vessels and 86,490 river-trade vessels called at Hong Kong and loaded and discharged more than 70 million tonnes of cargo.

Hong Kong International Airport, Kai Tak, situated on the north shore of Kowloon Bay, is an important link on the main air routes of the Far East. It is regularly used by over 38 international airlines, providing some 1,000 frequent scheduled passenger and cargo services each week between Hong Kong and the United Kingdom, the People's Republic of China, North and South America, Europe, East and South Africa, the Middle East, Australasia, the South Pacific region, and Asian countries. In addition, several other airlines operate about 90 non-scheduled services a week.

During 1987, 73,370 aircraft on international flights arrived and departed, carrying 12·7 million passengers and 611,000 tonnes of freight.

EDUCATION

In 1987 there were 2,602 schools with 1,380,293 pupils. Free education for children up to the age of 15 was made compulsory in 1979. Post-secondary education is provided by two universities, two polytechnics, the Hong Kong Baptist College and two approved post-secondary colleges. The Hong Kong Polytechnic and City Polytechnic of Hong Kong have about 9,540 and 2,740 full-time students respectively. There are also five technical institutes and four teacher-training colleges.

FINANCE

	1985–86	1986–87
Public revenue	HK$43,695m	HK$48,602m
Public expenditure	40,692m	42,702m

TRADE AND INDUSTRY

The manufacturing sector is the mainstay of Hong Kong's economy, contributing about 22 per cent to the G.D.P. and accounting for about 35 per cent of total employment. Up to 90 per cent of Hong Kong's manufacturing output is eventually exported.

Hong Kong's manufacturing industries produce mainly light consumer goods. In the past ten years or so, industries like electronics, plastics, electrical products, and watches and clocks have grown significantly—they accounted for 39 per cent of Hong Kong's total domestic exports in 1987. The corresponding share of textiles and clothing, Hong Kong's traditional leading industries, increased to 42 per cent in 1987.

Diversification in terms of products and markets continues to be the main feature of recent industrial development, as are industrial partnerships with overseas companies. It is the world's largest exporter of toys and games, fur clothing and imitation jewellery in value terms. The economy of Hong Kong is based on export rather than the domestic market. In 1987, the total value of visible trade (including domestic exports, re-exports and imports) amounted to 210 per cent of the G.D.P. Hong Kong's visible trade account attained in 1987 a surplus of HK$87 million. Taking visible and invisible trade together, there was a combined surplus of HK$21,383 million, compared with HK$15,260 million in 1986. In 1987, Hong Kong's principal customers for its domestic products, in order of value of trade, were U.S.A.,

China, the Federal Republic of Germany, the United Kingdom, Japan, Canada and the Netherlands. China was its principal supplier.

	1986 HK$	1987 HK$
Total Exports	276,530m	378,034m
Total Imports	275,955m	377,948m

Trade with U.K.

	1986	1987
Imports from U.K....	£960,956,000	£1,013,038,000
Exports to U.K.	1,530,786,000	1,531,681,000

MONTSERRAT

Situated in 16° 45′ N. lat. and 61° 15′ W. long., 27 miles S.W. of Antigua, the island is about 11 miles long and seven wide, with an area of 38 sq. miles (98 sq. km.), and a population (1988), of 11,900. Discovered by Columbus in 1493, it was settled by Irishmen in 1632, conquered and held by the French for some time, and finally assigned to Great Britain in 1783. Fertile and green, it is volcanic with several hot springs. About two-thirds of the island is mountainous, the rest capable of cultivation.

CHIEF TOWN.—ΨPlymouth. Population 3,000.

GOVERNMENT

A Ministerial system was introduced in Montserrat in 1960. The Executive Council is presided over by the Governor and is composed of four elected members (the Chief and three other Ministers) and two *ex-officio* members (the Attorney-General and the Financial Secretary). The four Ministers are appointed from the members of the political party holding the majority in the Legislative Council. The Legislative Council consists of the Speaker, two *ex-officio* members (the Attorney General and the Financial Secretary), two nominated unofficial members and seven elected members.

Governor, His Excellency Christopher John Turner, O.B.E. (1987).

(Executive Council

President, The Governor.
Chief Minister and Minister of Finance, Hon. J. A. Osborne.
Communications and Works, Hon. J. B. Chalmers.
Education, Health and Community Services, Hon. V. K. Jeffers.
Agriculture, Trade, Lands and Housing, Hon. N. Tuitt.
Attorney-General, Hon. O. Adams.
Acting Financial Secretary, Hon. C. T. John.

Speaker of the Legislative Council, Hon. H. A. Fergus, O.B.E.

ECONOMY

The economy is dominated by tourism, related construction activities and offshore business services. The chief export in 1987 was electronic components assembled on the island, but attempts are being made to expand sea island cotton, agriculture, data processing and some other island-based exports. The island has also established a computer centre to reinforce its position as a regional information technology, telecommunications and media communications base.

FINANCE

	1986	1987
Revenue	EC$25,843,338	EC$27,734,100
Expenditure	25,156,090	27,241,000

Trade with U.K.

	1986	1987
Imports from U.K....	EC$8,000,000	EC$12,649,238
Exports to U.K.	182,000	126,580

PITCAIRN ISLANDS

Pitcairn, a small volcanic island, 1·9 sq. miles (5 sq. km.), in area, is the chief of a group of Islands situated about midway between New Zealand and Panama in the South Pacific Ocean at longitude 130° 06′ W. and latitude 25° 04′ S.

The island rises in cliffs to a height of 1,100 feet and access from the sea is possible only at Bounty Bay, a small rocky cove, and then only by surf boats. Mean monthly temperatures vary between 66° F. in August and 75° F. in February and the average annual rainfall is 80 inches. With an equable climate, the island is very fertile and produces both tropical and sub-tropical trees and crops.

The small community, numbering 57 (1987), are descendants of the Bounty mutineers and their Tahitian companions who did not wish to remain on Norfolk Island when the entire community was transferred there in 1856, and returned to Pitcairn three years later.

Pitcairn became a British Settlement under the British Settlement Act, 1887, and was administered by the Governor of Fiji from 1952 until 1970, when the administration was transferred to the British High Commission in New Zealand and the British High Commissioner was appointed Governor. The local Government Ordinance of 1964 provides for a Council of ten members of whom four are elected.

Governor of Pitcairn, Henderson, Ducie and Oeno Islands, His Excellency R. A. C. Byatt, C.M.G. (*British High Commissioner to New Zealand*).
Island Magistrate and Chairman of Island Council, B. Young.
Education Officer and Government Adviser, L. Buckley.

The Islanders live by subsistence gardening and fishing, and their limited monetary needs are satisfied by the manufacture of wood carvings and other handicrafts which are sold to passing ships and to a few overseas customers. Other than small fees charged for gun and driving licences there are no taxes and Government revenue is derived almost solely from the sale of postage stamps. Communication with the outside world is maintained by cargo vessels travelling between New Zealand and Panama which call at irregular intervals; and by means of telephone telegraphic links with New Zealand.

The New Zealand Education Department provides assistance in recruiting a teacher for the sole-charge school. Education is compulsory between the ages of five and fifteen. Secondary education in New Zealand is encouraged by the Administration which provides scholarships and bursaries for the purpose. Medical care is provided by a registered nurse when a doctor is not present. Since 1887 the islanders have all been adherents of the Seventh Day Adventist Church.

The other three islands of the group (Henderson lying 105 miles E.N.E. of Pitcairn, Oeno lying 75 miles N.W. and Ducie lying 293 miles E.) are all uninhabited. Henderson Island is occasionally visited by the Pitcairn Islanders to obtain supplies of "miro" wood which is used for their carvings. Oeno is visited for excursions of about a week's duration every two years or so.

ST. HELENA

Probably the best known of all the solitary islands in the world, St. Helena is situated in the South Atlantic Ocean, 955 miles S. of the Equator, 702 S.E. of Ascension, 1,140 from the nearest point of the African Continent, 1,800 from the coast of S. America, 1,694 from Cape Town and 4,477 from Southampton (transit 5 days and 16 days respectively), in 15° 55′ S. lat. and 5° 42′ W. longitude. It is 10½ miles long, 6½ broad, and encloses an area of 47 sq. miles (122 sq. km.), with a population of 5,564 (end 1987).

St. Helena is of volcanic origin, and consists of numerous rugged mountains, the highest rising to 2,700 feet, interspersed with picturesque ravines. Although within the tropics, the south-east "trades" keep the temperature mild and equable. St. Helena was discovered by the Portuguese navigator, Juan da Nova Castella, in 1502 (probably on St. Helena's Day) and remained unknown to other European nations until 1588. It was used as a port of call for vessels of all nations trading to the East until it was annexed by the Dutch in 1633. It was never occupied by them, however, and the English East India Company seized it in 1659. In 1834 it was ceded to the Crown. During the period 1815 to 1821 the island was lent to the British Government as a place of exile for the Emperor Napoleon Bonaparte who died in St. Helena on May 5, 1821. It was formerly an important station on the route to India, but its prosperity decreased after the construction of the Suez Canal. Since the collapse of the New Zealand flax industry in 1965, there have been no significant exports, but a second five year development plan, launched in 1979, sought primarily to increase the island's productivity in its limited land and sea resources. ΨSt. James's Bay, on the north-west of the Island, possesses a good anchorage. There is no airport or airstrip.

CAPITAL.—ΨJamestown. Population (1987), 1,330.

GOVERNMENT

The government of St. Helena is administered by a Governor, with the aid of a Legislative Council, consisting of the Governor, two *ex-officio* members (Government Secretary and Treasurer) and twelve elected members. Six committees of the Legislative Council are reponsible for general oversight of the activities of Government Departments and have in addition a wide range of statutory and administrative functions. The Governor is also assisted by an Executive Council of the two *ex-officio* members and the Chairmen of the Council committees.

Governor, His Excellency Francis E. Baker, C.B.E. (1984).
Government Secretary, E. C. Brooks, O.B.E.
Treasurer and Development Secretary, P. C. Knights, M.B.E.
Senior Medical Officer, Dr. S. J. Woolterton.
Agricultural and Forestry Officer, M. D. Holland.
Education Officer, B. A. George.

FINANCE AND TRADE

	1984	1985
Public revenue........	£8,296,154	£8,484,825
Expenditure.........	7,721,940	7,370,155
Total imports........	3,219,960	4,090,516
Imports from U.K.	1,820,782	2,452,129

Figures include development aid, shipping subsidy and grant-in-aid.

ASCENSION

The small island of Ascension lies in the South Atlantic (7° 56′ S., 14° 22′ W.) some 700 miles north-west of the island of St. Helena. It is a rocky peak of purely volcanic origin, the highest point (Green Mountain) some 2,817 ft. is covered with lush vegetation. B.B.C. (Ascension Island Services) operate a farm of some 10 acres on the mountain, permitting the production of vegetables and live-stock. The island is famous for turtles, which land on the beaches from January to May to lay their eggs. It is also a breeding area for the sooty tern, or wideawake, large numbers of which settle on the south-western coastal section every eighth month to hatch their eggs. Other wild life on the island includes feral donkeys and cats, rabbits and francolin partridge. All wild life except rabbits and cats is protected by law. The ocean surrounding the island abounds with shark, barracuda, tuna, bonito and many other fish.

Ascension is said to have been discovered by Juan da Nova Castella, on Ascension Day, 1501, and two years later was visited by Alphonse d'Albuquerque, who gave the island its present name. It was uninhabited until the arrival of Napoleon in St. Helena in 1815 when a small British naval garrison was stationed on the island. It remained under the supervision of the Board of Admiralty until 1922, when it was made a dependency of St. Helena by Royal Letters Patent.

The British Foreign Secretary appoints the Administrator. There is a small Police Force and Post Office. The British organizations provide and operate various common services for the island (school, hospital, public works etc).

Ascension Island is a main relay point of the coaxial submarine cable system laid between South Africa, Portugal and the United Kingdom, which is operated by the South Atlantic Cable Company. Cable & Wireless Ltd operates the international telephone and cable services, maintains an internal telephone service, and also operates an Earth Station on behalf of N.A.S.A. The B.B.C. opened its Atlantic relay station broadcasting to Africa and South America in 1967.

The resident population in March 1988 totalled 1,155, of whom 729 were from St. Helena, 210 from the U.K., 193 from the U.S.A. and 13 from the Republic of South Africa. The residents consist of the employees and families of the British organizations, of the contractors for the U.S. Air Force and N.A.S.A. (Pan American Airways, Radio Corporation of America and Bendix Field Engineering Corporation) and of the St. Helena Government.

British forces returned to the island in April 1982 in support of operations in the Falkland Islands. At present there are about 160 R.A.F. personnel on the island supporting the air link to the Falklands.

Capital, Georgetown
Administrator, M. T. Blick.

TRISTAN DA CUNHA

Tristan da Cunha is the chief of a group of islands of volcanic origin lying in lat. 37° 6′ S. and long. 12° 2′ W., discovered in 1506 by a Portuguese admiral (Tristão da Cunha), after whom they are named. They have a total area of 40 sq. miles (104 sq. km.). Population (1988) 311. The main island, with a peak rising to 6,760 ft., is about 1,500 miles W. of the Cape of Good Hope, 3,600 miles N.E. of Cape Horn, and about 1,320 miles S.S.W. of St. Helena. It was the resort of British and American sealers from the middle of the 18th century, and in 1760 a British naval officer visited the group and gave his name to

Nightingale Island. On August 14, 1816, the group was annexed to the British Crown and a garrison was placed on Tristan da Cunha, but this force was withdrawn in 1817, William Glass, a corporal of artillery (*died* 1853), remaining at his own request, with his wife and two children. This party, with five others, formed a settlement. In 1827 five women from St. Helena, and afterwards others from Cape Colony, joined the party.

The islands form a dependency of St. Helena, being administered by the Foreign and Commonwealth Office through a resident Administrator, with headquarters at the settlement of Edinburgh. Under a new constitution introduced in 1969, he is advised by an elected Island Council of 8 members of whom one must be a woman, and three appointed members, with universal suffrage at 18. The population numbered 294 persons in 1986, plus five expatriate Government officers and their families, and a resident chaplain.

In October, 1961, a volcano, believed to have been extinct for thousands of years, erupted and the danger of further volcanic activity led to the evacuation of inhabitants to the United Kingdom. An advance party returned to Tristan da Cunha in the spring of 1963, and subsequently the main body of the islanders returned to the island.

A boat harbour was completed in 1967. The first freezing factory was re-established in 1966. There are no taxes on Tristan, income being derived from royalties paid by the fishing company and from the sale of stamps and handicrafts. The Camogli Hospital was opened early in 1971 and a new school in 1975.

Capital, Edinburgh.
Administrator, R. Perry.

INACCESSIBLE ISLAND is a lofty mass of rock with sides 2 miles in length; the island is the resort of penguins and sea-fowl. Cultivation was started in 1937, but has been abandoned.

THE NIGHTINGALE ISLANDS are three in number, of which the largest is 1 mile long and ¾ mile wide, and rises in two peaks, 960 and 1,105 ft. above sea-level respectively. The smaller islands, Stoltenhoff and Middle Isle, are little more than huge rocks. Seals, innumerable penguins, and vast numbers of sea-fowl visit these islands.

GOUGH ISLAND (or Diego Alvarez), in 40° 20′ S. and 9° 44′ W., lies about 250 miles S.S.E. of Tristan da Cunha. The island is about 8 miles long and 4 miles broad, with a total area of 40 square miles, and has been a British possession since 1816. The island is the resort of penguins and sea-elephants and has valuable guano deposits. There is no permanent population, but there is a meteorological station maintained on the island by the South African Government and manned by South Africans.

SOUTH GEORGIA AND THE SOUTH SANDWICH ISLANDS

South Georgia is an island 800 miles east-south-east of the Falkland group, with an area of 1,450 sq. miles. The population comprises an army unit at King Edward Point, and staff of the British Antarctic Survey at Bird Island, in the north-west of S. Georgia.

The South Sandwich Islands lie some 470 miles S.E. of South Georgia. The group is a chain of uninhabited, actively volcanic islands about 150 miles long, with a wholly Antarctic climate.

The present constitution came into effect on Oct. 3, 1985. It provides for a Commissioner who, for the time being, shall be the officer administering the Government of the Falkland Islands.

Commissioner for South Georgia and the South Sandwich Islands, William Hugh Fullerton (1988).

TURKS AND CAICOS ISLANDS

The Turks and Caicos Islands are situated between 21° and 22° N. latitude and 71° and 72° W. longitude, about 100 miles north of the Dominican Republic and 50 miles south-east of the Bahamas of which they are geographically an extension. There are over 30 islands of which eight are inhabited covering an estimated area of 166 sq. miles (430 sq. km.). The principal is Grand Turk. The population in 1988 was estimated to be 14,000 (Grand Turk 3,146).

The Islands lie in the Trade Wind but with an excellent climate. The average temperature varies from 24°–27° C. in the winter and 29°–32° C. in the summer and humidity is generally low. Average rainfall is 21 inches per annum.

GOVERNMENT

A new Constitution was introduced in 1988, providing for an enlarged Executive Council and Legislative Council. The Executive Council is presided over by the Governor and comprises the Chief Minister and four elected Ministers, together with the Chief Secretary, the Attorney General and the Financial Secretary *ex-officio*.

Governor, His Excellency Michael John Bradley, Q.C. (1987).

Executive Council

President, The Governor.
Chief Secretary, Hon. A. N. Hoole.
Attorney-General, Hon. I. S. Lamb.
Financial Secretary, Hon. A. Robinson, M.B.E.
Members, Hon. O. O. Skippings (*Chief Minister*); Hon. L. N. A. Handfield; Hon. W. L. Swann; Hon. S. I. Harvey; Hon. D. H. Taylor.

The principal airports are on the islands of Grand Turk, Providenciales and South Caicos. There are direct shipping services to the U.S.A. (Miami). There is an air service between Miami, Providenciales and Grand Turk, and between South Caicos and the Bahamas. An internal air service provides a twice daily service between the principal islands. A comprehensive telephone and telex service is provided by Cable and Wireless (W.I.) Ltd.

The most important industries are fishing, tourism and offshore finance.

FINANCE

	1986–87	1987–88
Local Revenue	U.S.$10,895,915	U.S.$12,992,896
Expenditure	13,269,795	14,770,808
Budgetary Aid	3,016,000	2,022,000

Trade with U.K.

	1986	1987
Imports	£1,025,000	£496,000
Exports	86,000	31,000

VIRGIN ISLANDS,
see BRITISH

FOREIGN EXCHANGE RATES

Country	Denomination	1939 Average Rate to £ (approx.)	September 1, 1988 Middle Rate

A. London Market Rates

Country	Denomination	1939 Average Rate to £ (approx.)	September 1, 1988 Middle Rate
Austria	Schilling	—	22·1589
Belgium	Franc	26·49 *Belgas*	66·03
Canada	Canadian Dollar	4·545	2·0761
Denmark	Krone	22·26	12·1079
Finland	Markka	217¼	7·4794
France	Franc	176·10	10·7017
Germany, Federal Rep.	Deutsche Mark	—	3·1519
Greece	Drachma	545	254·54
Italy	Lira	85	2,345·70
Japan	Yen	½d	229·29
Netherlands	Guilder	8·34	3·5594
Netherlands Antilles	Antillian Guilder	8·34	3·02
Norway	Krone	19·45	11·6398
Portugal	Escudo	110·07	258·73
Spain	Peseta	42·45	208·76
Sweden	Krona	18·59	10·8753
Switzerland	Franc	19·87	2·6563
U.S.A.	Dollar	4·485	1·6770

B. Former Scheduled Territories

Country	Denomination	1939 Average Rate to £ (approx.)	September 1, 1988 Middle Rate
Australia	Australian Dollar	A£1·2525	2·1094
Bahamas	Bahamas Dollar	—	1·6900
Barbados	Barbados Dollar	—	3·3931
Belize	Belize Dollar	—	3·3740
Bermuda	Bermuda Dollar	—	1·6900
Cyprus	Cyprus £	—	0·8145
Ghana	New Cedi	—	383·07
Hong Kong	Hong Kong Dollar	—	13·0944
Iceland	Króna	—	78·82
India	Rupee	13·38	24·1172
Jamaica	Jamaica Dollar	—	9·1150
Jordan	Dinar	Par	0·6360
Kenya	Shilling	—	30·80
Kuwait	Dinar	—	0·47875
Libya	Dinar	—	0·4992
Malawi	Kwacha	—	4·5050
Malaysia	Malaysian Dollar	—	4·4963
Malta	Maltese Lira	—	0·5743
New Zealand	New Zealand Dollar	£1·2425	2·7842
Nigeria	Naira	—	7·7167
Pakistan	Rupee	—	30·5116
South Africa	Rand	S.A.£1	4·1090
Tanzania	Shilling	—	176·00
Trinidad	Trinidad and Tobago $	—	7·1698
Uganda	Shilling	—	251·11
Yemen, North	Riyal	—	17·29
Zambia	Kwacha	—	13·10

C. Other Rates

Country	Denomination	1939 Average Rate to £ (approx.)	September 1, 1988 Middle Rate
Algeria	Dinar	—	10·91
Argentina	Austral	19	20·1705
Bolivia	Peso	141·50	4·25
Brazil	Cruzado	—	475·45
Bulgaria	Lev	375	1·4461
Burma	Kyat	13·38	11·2754
Chile	Peso	116½	415·47
China	Renminbi (Yuan)	4½	6·2939
Colombia	Peso	7·59	523·29
Costa Rica	Colon	25·16	129·81
Cuba	Peso	4·386	1·2848
Czechoslovakia	Koruna	—	9·2419
Ecuador	Sucre	66	420·78
Egypt	Egyptian £	97½ (per £100 London)	3·9000
Ethiopia	Birr	—	3·4678
German Democratic Rep.	Ostmark	—	3·1400

Country	Denomination	1939 Average Rate to £ (approx.)	September 1, 1988 Middle Rate
Guatemala	Quetzal	4·386	1·6900
Guinea	Franc Guineen	—	506·10
Haiti	Gourde	22·4	8·4350
Honduras	Lempira	8¾	3·3730
Hungary	Forint	20½	91·6637
Indonesia	Rupiah	—	2,887·23
Iran	Rial	80·50 (Persian)	120·50
Iraq	Dinar	Par	0·5247
Israel	Shekel	—	2·780
Lebanon	Lebanese £	9·65	621·42
Madagascar	Franc M. G.	17 (F. Fr.)	2,110·00
Mexico	Peso	—	3,681·04
Morocco	Dirham	176·10 (F. Fr.)	14·1050
Nicaragua	Córdoba	24	134·92
Paraguay	Guarani	—	539·68
Peru	Inti	24¼	55·65
Philippines	Peso	—	34·40
Poland	Zloty	23½	786·59
Romania	Leu	655	14·781
Salvador, El	Colon	11·20	8·4325
Saudi Arabia	Riyal	—	6·2914
Sudan	Sudan £	97½ (per 100)	7·5915
Syria	Syrian £	—	35·427
Thailand	Baht	10·91	42·70
Tunisia	Tunisian Dinar	—	1·5319
Turkey	Turkish Lira	—	2,585·17
Uruguay	New Peso	9	641·71
U.S.S.R.	Rouble	23·75	1·0377
Venezuela	Bolivar	14·15	59·3986
Vietnam	Dông	—	620·82
Yugoslavia	Yugoslav Dinar	197½ (YD)	4,700·20
Zaire	Zaïre	—	339·984

FOREIGN COUNTRIES

The following articles have been revised under the direction of the various Governments or of the British Representatives at foreign capitals and by the Foreign and Commonwealth Office in London, whom the Editor warmly thanks. The Editor is also greatly indebted to the Embassies and Consulates-General in London for various corrections and additions.

AFGHANISTAN
(Da Afghanistan Jamhuriat)

President of the Republic of Afghanistan, Dr. Najib.
Vice Presidents, Abdul Rahim Hatif; Col.-Gen. Mohammad Rafie; Abdul Hamid Mohtat; Abdul Wahid Sorabi.

COUNCIL OF MINISTERS
(as at June 4, 1988)

Prime Minister, Dr. Mohammad Hassan Sharq.
Deputy Prime Ministers, Sayed Amanuddin Amin; Mohammad Sarwar Mangal; Mahbubullah Koshani.
Finance, Hamidullah Tarzi.
Interior, Gen. Sayed Mohammad Gulabzoi.
Higher and Vocational Education, Noor Ahmad Barets.
State Security, Gen. Ghulam Faruq Yaqubi.
Public Health, Dr. Abdul Fatah Najum.
Foreign Affairs, Abdul Wakil.
Commerce, Mohammad Khan Jalalar.
Planning, Sultan Hussain.
Agriculture and Land Reform, Mohammad Ghafran.
Tribal Affairs, Sulaiman Laeq.
Repatriates, Abdul Ghafar Farahi.
Education, Dr. Ghulum Rasul Rasuli.
Civil Aviation, Pachar Gul Wafadar.
Transport, Mohammad Aziz.
Mines and Industries, Mohammad Ishaq Kawa.
Water and Power, Raz Mohammad Paktin.
Construction, Nazar Mohammad.
Communications, Mohammad Aslam Watanjar.
Rehabilitation and Rural Development, Mohammad Asif Zahir.
Light Industry and Foodstuffs, Dost Mohammad Fazl.
Justice, Mohammad Bashir Baghlani.
Information and Culture, Ahmad Bashir Roigar.
Without Portfolio, Nehmat ullah Pazhwak; Sarjang Zazi; Faqir Mohammad Yaqubi; Fazil-ul-Haq Khalikyar; Shah Mohammad Dost.
Chairman of National Assembly, Khalil Ahmad Abawi.
Chairman of Senate, Mahmoud Habibi.

PEOPLE'S DEMOCRATIC PARTY OF AFGHANISTAN

Politburo:
Secretary General, Dr. Najib.
Secretary, Sultan Ali Keshtmand.
Full Members, Noor Ahmad Noor; Saleh Mohammad Zeary; Gen. Mohammad Rafie; Mohammad Aslam Watanjar; Sulaiman Laeq; Gen. Ghulam Faruq Yaqubi; Abdul Zohur Razmjo; Abdul Wakil; Gen. Sayed Mohammad Gulabzoi; Najmuddin Kawyani; Niaz Mohammad Mohmand; Haider Massoud.
Alternate Members, Nazar Mohammad; Mir Saheb Karwal; Farid Ahmad Mazdak; Lt. Gen. Shahnawaz Tanai.
Central Committee Secretariat, Noor Ahmad Noor; Saleh Mohammad Zeary; Niaz Mohammad Mohmand; Mir Saheb Karwal; Najmuddin Kawyani; Haider Massoud; Mohammad Daoud Razmyar; Abdul Zohur Razmjo.

EMBASSY OF THE REPUBLIC OF AFGHANISTAN
31 Prince's Gate, SW7 1QQ
[01–589 8891/2]

Chargé d'Affaires, Ahmad Sarwar.

Afghanistan lies to the N. and W. of Pakistan. Its ancient name was Aryana, by which title it is referred to by Strabo, the Greek geographer who lived in the 1st century B.C. The estimated area is 250,000 sq. miles (647,497 sq. km.), and the population 18,136,000 (1985 U.N. estimate), although it is estimated that over four million have become refugees in Pakistan and over one million in Iran since the Soviet invasion. The population is very mixed. The most numerous race is the Pushtoons who predominate in the South and West, the Tadjiks, a Persian-speaking people mainly cultivators and small traders, Uzbeks and Turkomen in the North, Hazaras in the centre, Baluchis in the South-West and Nuristanis, who live near the Chitral border. All are Sunni Moslems, except the Hazaras and Kizilbashes, who belong to the Shia sect.

Afghanistan is bounded on the W. by Iran, on the S. by Pakistan, on the N. by the U.S.S.R., and on the E. by Pakistan and China.

Mountains, chief among which are the Hindu Kush, cover three-quarters of the country, the elevation being generally over 4,000 feet. There are three great river basins, the Oxus, Helmand, and Kabul. The climate is dry, with extreme temperatures.

Government.—The constitutional monarchy, introduced by the 1964 Constitution, was overthrown by a coup on July 17, 1973. The country was ruled by Presidential decree until February 1977 when a constitution was approved by a Loya Jirgah (Grand Assembly). Mohammad Daoud was elected President of the Republic but was overthrown on April 27, 1978, by the Armed Forces and power handed to the People's Democratic Party of Afghanistan (PDPA). In December 1979 Soviet troops invaded Afghanistan and installed Babrak Karmal as Secretary-General of the PDPA, President of the Revolutionary Council and Head of State. Karmal was replaced as General Secretary of the PDPA by Dr. Najib in May 1986. A peace agreement in April 1988 led to the withdrawal of Soviet troops from May 15. In June Dr. Mohammad Hassan Sharq became Prime Minister.

A new Constitution, approved in Nov. 1987, provides for a President, a Council of Ministers, a National Assembly and a Senate.

Afghanistan is divided into 30 provinces each under a centrally appointed governor.

Judiciary.—The Constitution introduced in 1965 provided for the creation of a legal code, and for a new structure of courts, consisting of a lower court in each *woleswali* (sub province), and a court of appeal in each province, with a Supreme Court in Kabul. The complete separation of executive and judiciary in this constitution was abolished by Presidential Decree in July, 1973. In late 1976 and early 1977 new Penal and Civil Codes were published. The new Constitution leaves the judicial system largely untouched.

Defence.—The Army, which numbered about 80,000 before the Soviet invasion, has been greatly depleted by desertions. Men between the ages of 18 and 40 are liable to four years' military service. A military academy and military colleges are located in Kabul; some regular officers are trained in the U.S.S.R. A small Air Force is maintained. All military and air force equipment is now of Russian pattern.

Production.—Agriculture and sheep raising are the principal industries. There are generally two crops a year, one of wheat (the staple food), barley, or lentils, the other of rice, millet, maize, and dal. Sugar beet and cotton are grown. Afghanistan is rich in fruits. Sheep, including the Karakuli, and transport animals are bred. Silk, woollen and hair cloths and carpets are manufactured. Salt, silver, copper, coal, iron, lead, rubies, lapis lazuli, gold, chrome, barite, uranium, and talc are found.

Main roads run from Kabul to Kandahar, Herat, Maimana via Mazari-Sharif and Faizabad via Khanabad. The road from Kabul to the North was shortened by the completion in 1964 of the Salang pass. Roads cross the border with Pakistan at Chaman and via the Khyber Pass, and there are roads from Herat to the Russian and Iranian borders. A network of minor roads fit for motor traffic in fine weather links up all important towns and districts.

In 1982 the Afghan and Soviet shores of the River Oxus were linked by a road and rail bridge which joins the Afghan port of Hairatan and the Soviet port of Termez. A network of internal air services operates between the main towns.

Language and Literature.—The principal languages of the country are Dari (a form of Persian) and Pushtu, although a number of minority languages are also spoken in various provinces. All schoolchildren learn both Persian and Pushtu. Education is free and nominally compulsory, elementary schools having been established in most centres; there are secondary schools in large urban areas and two universities, one in Kabul (established 1932) and one in Jalalabad (established early 1970's).

Trade with U.K.

	1986	1987
Imports from U.K.	£11,444,000	£10,735,000
Exports to U.K.	11,913,000	11,289,000

Exports are mainly Persian lambskins (Karakul), dried fruits, nuts, cotton, raw wool, carpets, spice and natural gas, while the imports are chiefly oil, cotton yarn and piece goods, tea, sugar, machinery and transport equipment.

CAPITAL, Kabul (about 2,000,000). The chief commercial centres are Kabul and Kandahar (185,000). Other provincial capitals are Herat (145,000), Mazar-i-Sharif (105,000), Jalalabad (55,000).

CURRENCY.—Afghani (Af) of 100 puls.

FLAG.—Black, red and green horizontal stripes with a device in top left-hand corner.

NATIONAL ANTHEM.—Soroud-e-Melli.

NATIONAL DAY.—April 27.

BRITISH EMBASSY
Karte Parwan, Kabul
[Kabul 30511/3]

Chargé d'Affaires a.i., I. W. Mackley.

ALBANIA
(Republika Popullore Socialiste e Shqipërisë)

Chairman of the Presidium of the People's Assembly (i.e. Head of State), Ramiz Alia, *assumed office,* Nov. 22, 1982; *re-elected,* Feb. 19, 1987.

COUNCIL OF MINISTERS

Chairman, Adil Çarçani.
Deputy Chairmen, Manush Myftiu; Besnik Bekteshi; Vangjel Cerrava; Farudin Hoxha.
Deputy Chairman, and Minister of the Interior, Hekuran Isai.

Agriculture, Mrs. Themie Thomai.
Transport, Luan Babamento.
Construction, Ismail Ahmeti.
People's Defence, Prokop Murra.
Education, Skenda Gjinushi.
Energy, Lavdosh Hametaj.
Finance, Andrea Nako.
Foreign Affairs, Reis Malile.
Foreign Trade, Shane Korbeci.
Health Service, Ahmet Kamberi.
Food Industry, Jovan Bardhi.
Industry and Mining, Llambi Gegprifti.
Chairman of State Planning Commission, Niko Gjyzari.
Chairman of State Control Commission, Enver Halili.
Public Services, Xhemal Tafaj.
Minister to the Presidium of the Council of Ministers, Farudin Hoxha.

Albanian Party of Labour

Politbureau of the Central Committee, R. Alia; M. Asllani; A. Carcani; H. Celiku; H. Isai; R. Marko; P. Miska; M. Myftiu; L. Cuko; S. Stefani; B. Bekteshi; F. Cami; P. Murra (*full members*); L. Gegprifti; Q. Mihali; K. Mustaqi; P. Kondi; V. Cerava (*candidate members*).
Secretariat of the Central Committee, R. Alia (*First Secretary*); F. Çami; H. Celiku; L. Cuko; S. Stefani.

Situated on the Adriatic Sea, Albania is bounded on the north and east by Yugoslavia and on the south by Greece. The area of the Republic is estimated at 11,099 sq. miles (28,748 sq. km.), with a population (1986 estimate) of about 3 million.

Albania was under Turkish suzerainty from 1468 until 1912, when independence was declared. After a period of unrest, a republic was declared in 1925, and in 1928 a monarchy. The King went into exile in 1939 when the country was occupied by the Italians: Albania was liberated in Nov. 1944. Elections in Dec. 1945 resulted in a Communist-controlled Assembly: the King was deposed in absentia and a republic declared in Jan. 1946. United Kingdom diplomatic relations with Albania ceased due to the invasion in 1939 and although U.K. recognized the provisional government of Enver Hoxha in 1945, relations were broken off in 1946 after a mine sunk a British warship in Albanian waters. They have so far not been restored.

Much of the country is mountainous and nearly a half is covered by forest. There are fertile areas along the Adriatic coast and the Koritza Basin and there have been land reclamation and irrigation programmes. The main crops are wheat, maize, sugarbeet, potatoes and fruit.

All industry is nationalized. The principal industries are agricultural product processing, textiles, oil products and cement. Output is small at present but the chemical and engineering industries are being built up and the country's considerable mineral resources are being increasingly exploited.

Exports include crude oil, minerals (bitumen, chrome, nickel, copper), tobacco, fruit and vegetables.

Trade with U.K.

	1986	1987
Imports from U.K.	£2,887,000	£2,565,000
Exports to U.K.	129,000	91,000

CAPITAL, Tirana, pop. 210,757 (1984).

CURRENCY.—Lek (Lk) of 100 Qindarka.

FLAG.—Black-two-headed eagle surmounted by yellow outline star, all on a red field.

NATIONAL DAY.—January 11.

ALGERIA
(Al-Jumhuriya al-Jazairiya ad-Dimuqratiya ash-Shabiya)

President of State, Secretary-General of the Party, Bendjedid Chadli, *elected*, Feb. 1979, *re-elected*, Jan. 1984.

Ministers

Prime Minister, Abdelhamid Brahimi.
Foreign Affairs, Dr. Ahmed Taleb Ibrahimi.
Interior and Collectives, El Hadj Hedi Khediri.
Finance, Abdelaziz Khellef.
Justice, Mohamed Cherif Kherroubi.
Agriculture, Mohamed Rouighi.
Information, Bachir Rouis.
Posts and Telecommunications, Mostefa Benzaza.
Transport, Rachid Benyelles.
Energy, Chemical and Petro-Chemical Industries, Belkacem Nabi.
Heavy Industry, Faycal Boudraa.
Light Industry, Zitouni Messaoudi.
Trade, Mohand Amokrane Cherifi.
Hydraulics, Ahmed Benfreha.
Education and Training, Motefa Benamar.
Higher Education, Aboubakr Belkaid.
Labour and Social Affairs, Mohamed Nabi.
Youth and Sports, Abdelhak Rafik Brerhi.
Public Health, Abdellah Khalef dit Kasdi Merbah.
Ex-combatants, Mohamed Djeghaba.
Public Works, Aissa Abdellaoui.
Town Planning, Construction and Housing, Abdelmalek Nourani.
Religious Affairs, Boualem Bessaih.
Minister of State at the Presidency, Mohamed Benahmed Abdelghani.

ALGERIAN EMBASSY IN LONDON
54 Holland Park, W11 3RS
[01–221 7800]

Ambassador Extraordinary and Plenipotentiary, (new appointment awaited).

Algeria lies between 8° 45′ W. to 12° E. longitude 27° 6′ N. to a southern limit about 19° N. Area, 919,595 sq. miles (U.N. estimate). The population (1987 Census) totals 22,971,558.

Government.—Algiers surrendered to a French force on July 5, 1830, and Algeria was annexed to France in Feb. 1842. From 1881 the three northern departments of Algiers, Oran and Constantine formed an integral part of France. The Southern Territories of the Sahara, formerly a separate colony, became an integral part of Algeria on the attainment of independence. An armed rebellion led by the Moslem *Front de Liberation Nationale (F.L.N.)* against French rule broke out on Nov. 1, 1954. French control of Algeria came to an end when President de Gaulle declared Algeria independent on July 3, 1962; by October, 1963, all agricultural land held by foreigners had been expropriated and by 1965 more than 80 per cent. of the French population had left Algeria.

Ben Bella was elected President of the Republic in Sept., 1963, but was deposed and a Council of the Revolution presided over by Col. Boumediène assumed power on June 19,1965.

A new constitution was established by referendum on Nov. 19, 1976, and on Dec. 10, 1976 President Boumediène was elected for a six-year term of office. Elections for a national popular assembly were held in Feb. 1977. Following President Boumediène's death in December 1978, M. Bendjedid Chadli was elected President in February 1979.

Development in Algeria is regulated by a series of national development plans. The 1970–73 Plan placed emphasis on industrial development, and the 1974–77 Plan on infrastructure development and social services. The 1980–84 Plan concentrated on housing,

water supply and agriculture. The 1985–89 Plan continues with these objectives and also includes food and processing industries.

Algeria's main industry is the hydrocarbons industry. Oil and natural gas are pumped from the Sahara to terminals on the coast before being exported; the gas is first liquefied at liquefaction plants at Skikda and Arzew.

Other major industries being developed include a steel industry, motor vehicles, building materials, paper making, chemical products and metal manufactures. All major industrial enterprises are now under State control.

Trade with U.K.

	1986	1987
Imports from U.K.	£129,624,000	£73,115,000
Exports to U.K.	140,860,000	172,927,000

Algeria's main exports are crude oil and liquefied natural gas. Principal imports from the United Kingdom are capital plant, equipment for industrial use and foodstuffs.

Algeria has a rapidly expanding network of roads and railways. Considerable sums are also being spent on the development of the State airline, the national shipping company and telecommunications.

CAPITAL.—ΨAlgiers, population 3,250,000 (approx). It is one of the principal ports of the Mediterranean as well as an important industrial centre. Other towns include ΨOran; Constantine; ΨAnnaba; Blida; Setif; Sidi-Bel-Abbès; Tlemcen; ΨMostaganem; ΨSkikda; ΨBejaia and Tizi Ouzou.

CURRENCY.—Algerian Dinar of 100 Centimes.

FLAG.—Red crescent and star on vertically divided green and white background.

NATIONAL ANTHEM.—Qassaman.

NATIONAL DAY.—November 1.

BRITISH EMBASSY
Résidence Cassiopée, 7 Chemin de Glycines, Algiers.
[Algiers 605601]

Ambassador Extraordinary and Plenipotentiary, His Excellency Patrick Howard Caines Eyers, C.M.G., L.V.O.

Counsellor, Head of Chancery and Consul General, J. Illman.

Cultural Attaché, British Council Representative, W. M. Jefferson, O.B.E., 6 Avenue Souidani Boudjemaa, Algiers. There is a British Council library in Algiers.

ANDORRA
(Principat d'Andorra)

Viguier Français, M. Louis Deblé.
Viguier Episcopal, Sr. Francesc Badia.
Head of Government, Sr. Josep Pintat Solens.

A small, neutral principality (formed by a treaty in 1278), situated on the southern slopes of the Pyrenees between Spain and France, with an approximate area of 175 sq. miles (453 sq. km.), and population of about 40,000, less than one fifth of whom are native Andorrans. It is surrounded by mountains of 6,500 to 10,000 feet. Andorra is divided into seven Parishes, each of which has four Councillors elected by vote to the Valleys of Andorra Council of twenty-eight. The Council appoints the head of the executive government, who designates the members of his government. Constitutionally, the sovereignty of Andorra is vested in two "Co-Princes", the President of the French Republic and the Spanish Bishop of Urgel. These two "co-princes" can veto certain decisions of the Council of the Valleys but cannot impose their own decisions without the consent of the Council. They are represented by Permanent Delegates of whom one is the French Prefect of the Pyrenees Orientales Department at Perpignan and the other is the Spanish Vicar-General of the Diocese of Urgel. They are in turn represented in Andorra la Vella by two resident "Viguiers" known as the Viguier Français and the Viguier Episcopal, who have a joint responsibility for law and order and overall administration policy, together with judicial powers as members of the Supreme Court.

The language of the country is Catalan, but French and Spanish (Castilian) are also spoken. Spanish pesetas and French francs are the accepted currency and the Budget is expressed in pesetas. The estimated national revenue (1985) was US$457 million, with a per capita income of $10,255. The climate is cold for six months, but mild in spring and summer. Potatoes are produced in the highlands and tobacco in the valleys. The mountain slopes have been developed for skiing, and it is estimated that 10,000,000 tourists visit the Valleys during the year. The economy is largely based on tourism, commerce, tobacco, construction and forestry; a third of the country is classified as forest in which pine, fir, oak, birch and box-tree predominate.

A good road into the Valleys from Spain is open all year round, and that from France is closed only occasionally in winter. An airport at Seo d'Urgell just outside Andorra provides daily air connections with Barcelona. There are two radio stations in Andorra, one privately-owned and one operated by a French Government corporation. Both pay dues to the Council of the Valleys.

Trade with U.K.

	1986	1987
Imports from U.K.	£13,174,000	£10,976,000
Exports to U.K.	40,000	200,000

CAPITAL: Andorra la Vella (population 16,000).
CURRENCY.—French Francs and Spanish Pesetas are both in use.
FLAG.—Three vertical bands, blue, yellow, red; Andorran coat of arms frequently imposed on central (yellow) band but not essential.
NATIONAL DAY.—September 8.

H.M. Consul-General, J. C. Church, C.M.G., M.B.E. *(resident at Barcelona)* (Tel. 3–322 2151).

ANGOLA
(República Popular de Angola)

President, Jose Eduardo Dos Santos.

COUNCIL OF MINISTERS

Interior, Gen. Manuel Rodrigues.
State Security, (vacant).
Defence, Col. Gen. Pedro Tonha.
Foreign Affairs, Afonso van Dunem.
Planning, Antonio Henriques da Silva.
Internal Trade, Adriano Pereira dos Santos.
External Trade, Ismael Gaspar Martins.
Justice, Fernando Franca van Dunem.
Petroleum and Energy, Col. Pedro Van Dunen.
Industry, Henrique de Carvalho Santos.
Health, Antonio Ferreira Neto.
Labour and Social Security, Diogo Jorge de Jesus.
Construction and Housing, Joac Garcia de Carvalho.
Fisheries, Emilio Guerra.
Agriculture, Col. Evaristo Domingos.
Transport and Communications, Carlos Antonio Femandes.
Education, Augusto Teixeira.
Finance Augusto Teixeira de Matos.
Ministers of State, Mrs. M. Mambo Café (*Economic and Social Sphere*); K. Paihama (*Inspection and Control*); Pedro van Dumem (*Productive Sector*).

ANGOLAN EMBASSY IN LONDON
87 Jermyn Street, SW1.
[01–839 5743]

Ambassador Extraordinary and Plenipotentiary, His Excellency Elisio de Figueiredo (1984).

Angola, which has an area of 481,354 sq. miles (1,246,700 sq. km.), lies on the western coast of Africa; its population in 1985 was estimated at 8,754,000.

After a Portuguese presence of at least four centuries, and an anti-colonial war since 1961, Angola became independent on Nov. 11, 1975 in the midst of civil war. Soviet-Cuban military assistance to the Popular Movement for the Liberation of Angola (M.P.L.A.) enabled it to defeat its rivals early in 1976. However, the M.P.L.A. government remains under pressure from the U.N.I.T.A. guerrilla movement (led by Dr. Jonas Savimbi) which now controls up to one-third of the country and operates freely in another third. On Aug. 8, 1988 it was announced that a ceasefire between South African, Cuban and Angolan forces had taken place pending talks on withdrawal from Angola. The ceasefire agreement was signed, and came into effect, on Aug. 22.

The M.P.L.A., a Marxist-Leninist party, is the sole legal party. The Constitution provides for an executive President, who appoints a Council of Ministers to assist him, and a National People's Assembly.

Angola has valuable oil and diamond deposits and exports of these two commodities account for 70–80 per cent of total exports.

Principal agricultural crops are cassava, maize, bananas, coffee, palm oil and kernals, cotton and sisal. Coffee, sisal, maize and palm oil are exported: exports also include mahogany and other hardwoods from the tropical rain forests in the north of the country.

Trade with U.K.

	1986	1987
Imports from U.K.	£30,896,000	£29,573,000
Exports to U.K.	43,147,000	2,312,000

CAPITAL.—ΨLuanda (Est. over 1 million in 1984).
CURRENCY.—Kwanza of 100 Lwei.
FLAG.—Red and black with a yellow star, machete and cog-wheel.
NATIONAL ANTHEM.—Angola Avante.
NATIONAL DAY.—November 11. (Independence Day).

BRITISH EMBASSY
Rua Diogo Cao 4 (Caixa Postal 1244), Luanda.
[Luanda 334582/3]

Ambassador Extraordinary and Plentipotentiary, His Excellency Michael John Carlisle Glaze, C.M.G., (1987).

ARGENTINE REPUBLIC
(República Argentina)

President, Dr. Rául Alfonsín, *took office* Dec. 10, 1983.

Vice President, Dr. Víctor Martínez.

CABINET

Interior, Sr. Enrique Nosiglia.
Foreign Affairs, Sr. Dante Caputo.
Labour, Sr. Ideler Tonelli.
Economy, Sr. Juan Sourouille.
Education and Justice, Sr. Jorge Sábato.
Defence, Dr. Horacio Juan Jaunarena.
Health and Social Welfare, Dr. Ricardo Barrios Arrechea.
Public Works, Sr. Rodolfo Terragno.

EMBASSY IN LONDON

The Embassy closed after the Argentine invasion of the Falkland Islands. Argentine interests in Great Britain are currently handled by the Brazilian Embassy.

Argentina is a wedge-shaped country, occupying the greater portion of the southern part of the South American Continent, and extending from Bolivia to Cape Horn, a total distance of nearly 2,300 miles; its greatest breadth is about 930 miles. It is bounded on the north by Bolivia, on the north-east by Paraguay, Brazil and Uruguay, on the south-east and south by the Atlantic, and on the west by Chile, from which Republic it is separated by the Cordillera de los Andes. On the west the mountainous Cordilleras, with their plateaux, extend from the northern to the southern boundaries: on the east are the great plains.

The Republic consists of 22 provinces, one territory (Tierra del Fuego) and one federal district (Buenos Aires), comprising in all an area of 1,068,302 sq. miles (2,766,889 sq. km.), with a population of 30,564,000 (1985, U.N. estimate).

Government.—The estuary of La Plata was discovered in 1515 by Juan Díaz de Solís, but it was not until 1534 that Pedro de Mendoza founded Buenos Aires. This city was abandoned and later re-founded by Don Juan de Garay in 1580. In 1810 (May 25) Spanish rule was defied, and in 1816 (July 9), after a long campaign of liberation conducted by General José de San Martín, the independence of Argentina was declared by the Congress of Tucumán.

In 1946 Juan Domingo Perón became President until overthrown in 1955. There followed eighteen years of political and economic instability, and eventually in 1973, Perón was recalled from exile. Elected President he died within a year and was succeeded by his widow, Vice President María Estela Martínez de Perón. However, warring factions in the Perónist movement and increasing terrorist activity eventually led to a bloodless coup by the armed forces on March 24, 1976. A Junta, consisting of the three commanders of the Armed Forces, was established with one of their number as President. Following the Falkland Islands defeat in 1982 the President, Gen. Galtieri, resigned and the Army appointed Gen. Bignone as President. The Navy and Air Force withdrew from the Junta but this was reconstituted shortly afterwards. Elections for a civilian government to replace the military one were held on October 30, 1983 and the Radical Party's candidate, Raúl Alfonsín, was elected President. There will be Presidential elections in May 1989.

Agriculture.—Of a total land area of approximately 700 million acres, farms occupy about 425 million. About 60 per cent. of the farmland is pasture, 10 per cent. annual crops, 5 per cent. permanent crops and the remaining 25 per cent. forest and wasteland. A large proportion of the land is still held in large estates devoted to cattle raising but the number of small farms is increasing. The principal crops are wheat, maize, oats, barley, rye, linseed, sunflower seed, alfalfa, sugar, fruit and cotton. Argentina is pre-eminent in the production of beef, mutton and wool, and pastoral and agricultural products provide about 85 per cent. of Argentina's exports.

Mineral Production.—Oil is found in various parts of the Republic and the production of oil is of first importance to her industries and, to some extent, to her economic and financial development. Total petroleum output for 1986 was 450,000 b.p.d. There is a refinery in San Lorenzo (Santa Fé province). Natural gas is also produced in a number of provinces.

Coal, lead, zinc, tungsten, iron ore, sulphur, mica and salt are the other chief minerals being exploited. There are small worked deposits of beryllium, manganese, bismuth, uranium, antimony, copper, kaolin, arsenate, gold, silver and tin. Coal production in 1984 was 500,000 tonnes, this is produced at the Rio Turbio mine in the province of Santa Cruz. The output of other materials is not large but greater attention is now being paid to the development of these natural resources, especially copper for which the Government and private companies are carrying out exploration.

Industries.—Meat-packing is one of the principal industries; flour-milling, sugar-refining, and the wine industry are also important. In recent years great strides have been made by the textile, plastic and machine tool industries and engineering, especially in the production of motor vehicles and steel manufactures.

Communications.—There are 25,386 miles of railways, which are State property. Plans are in hand for complete re-organization of the railways in order to improve their operating efficiency and reduce a very large financial deficit. The combined national and provincial road network totals approximately 137,000 miles of which 23,180 miles are surfaced. There are air services between Argentina and all the neighbouring republics, Europe, Asia, Canada, the U.S.A. and South Africa. Total tonnage entering Argentine ports in 1979 was 13,879,391.

Defence.—The Army consists of four corps organized into 12 brigades, including mountain, jungle, airborne and armoured troops. It numbers about 47,000, consisting of 20,000 officers and N.C.O.s and 27,000 conscripts who serve for between 6 months and 1 year.

The Navy consists of 1 aircraft carrier, 6 destroyers, 6 corvettes, 4 submarines, 6 minesweepers and ancillary craft. Strength is about 27,000, consisting of 19,500 officers and N.C.O.s and 7,500 conscripts.

The Air Force consists of 9 brigades and a training force, with a strength of 12,000, consisting of 6,900 officers and N.C.O.s and 5,100 conscripts.

Education—Primary and Secondary. The government is formulating a new education policy. At the moment, education is compulsory for the 7 grades of primary school (6 to 13). Secondary schools (14 to 17+) are available in and around Buenos Aires and in most of the important towns in the interior of the country. Most secondary schools are administered by the Central Ministry of Education in Buenos Aires, while primary schools are administered by the Central Ministry or by Provincial Ministries of

Education. Private schools, of which there are many, are also loosely controlled by the Central Ministry. Teacher training now takes place at post school level, courses lasting from 2 to 5 years. Many new universities have been created in recent years. The total is now over 50 with 24 national, 25 private and a small number of provincial universities.

Language and Literature.—Spanish is the language of the Republic and the literature of Spain is accepted as an inheritance by the people. There is little indigenous literature before the break from Spain, but all branches have flourished since the latter half of the nineteenth century. About 450 daily newspapers are published in Argentina, including 7 major ones in the city of Buenos Aires. The English language newspaper is the *Buenos Aires Herald* (daily). There are several other foreign language newspapers.

Trade with U.K.

	1986	1987
Imports from U.K.	£10,115,000	£10,267,000
Exports to U.K.	28,635,000	64,595,000

CAPITAL.—ΨBuenos Aires, Pop. (1988), Metropolitan area 3,323,000; with suburbs, 9,677,200. Other large towns are: ΨRosario de Santa Fé (798,292), Córdoba (798,663), ΨLa Plata (408,300), ΨMar del Plata (317,444), San Miguel de Tucuman (326,000), ΨSanta Fé (312,427) and Mendoza (118,568).

CURRENCY.—Austral (A) of 100 Centavos or 1,000 Pesos.

FLAG.—Horizontal bands of blue, white, blue; gold sun in centre of white band.

NATIONAL ANTHEM.—Oid Mortales! El Grito Sagrado, Libertad (Hear, oh mortals! The sacred cry, freedom).

NATIONAL DAY.—May 25.

BRITISH EMBASSY

The British Embassy was closed after the Argentine invasion of the Falkland Islands. British interests are currently handled by a section at the Swiss Embassy, Dr. Luis Agote 2412 52, 1425, Buenos Aires.
BRITISH CHAMBER OF COMMERCE, Av. Corrientes 457, 10 piso, 1043 Buenos Aires.

AUSTRIA
(Republik Österreich)

President of the Republic of Austria, Dr. Kurt Waldheim, *born* 1918; *elected* June 8, 1986.

CABINET

Chancellor, Dr. Franz Vranitzky (*SPÖ*).
Vice-Chancellor and Minister for Foreign Affairs, Dr. Alois Mock (*ÖVP*).
Interior, Karl Blecha (*SPÖ*).
Justice, Dr. Egmont Foregger (*Ind.*).
Finance, Ferdinand Lacina (*SPÖ*).
Nationalized Industries and Transport, Dr. Rudolf Streicher (*SPÖ*).
Agriculture and Forestry, Josef Riegler (*ÖVP*).
Defence, Dr. Robert Lichal (*ÖVP*).
Science and Research, Prof. Dr. Hans Tuppy (*ÖVP*).
Employment and Social Affairs, Alfred Dallinger (*SPÖ*).
Education, Arts and Sports, Dr. Hilde Hawlicek (*SPÖ*).
Economic Affairs, Robert Graf (*ÖVP*).
Environment, Youth and Family, Dr. Marilies Flemming (*ÖVP*).
Ministers at Federal Chancellery, Dr. Franz Loweschnack (*SPÖ*) (*Civil Servants and Health*); Dr. Heinrich Neisser (*ÖVP*) (*Reforms, Constitution, Federalism*); Johanna Dohnal (*SPÖ*) (*Women's Affairs*).
SPÖ: Socialists; *ÖVP*: People's Party (Conservatives); *FPÖ*: Freedom Party (Liberals).

AUSTRIAN EMBASSY IN LONDON
18 Belgrave Mews, SW1X 8HU
[01–235 3731]

Ambassador Extraordinary and Plenipotentiary, His Excellency Dr. Walter F. Magrutsch (1987).

Austria is a country of Central Europe bounded on the north by Czechoslovakia, on the south by Italy and Yugoslavia, on the east by Hungary, on the north-west by Germany and on the west by Switzerland and Liechtenstein. Its area is 32,374 sq. miles (83,849, sq. km.), and its population is 7,566,000 (1986, estimate).

Government.—The Republic of Austria comprises nine provinces (Vienna, Lower Austria, Upper Austria, Salzburg, Tyrol, Vorarlberg, Carinthia, Styria and Burgenland) and was established in 1918 on the break-up of the Austro-Hungarian Empire. In March 13, 1938, as a result of the *Anschluss*, Austria (*Österreich*) was incorporated into the *Deutsches Reich* under the name *Ostmark*. After the liberation of Vienna in 1945, the Republic of Austria was reconstituted within the frontiers of 1937 and a freely-elected Government took office on December 20, 1945. The country was divided at this time into four zones occupied respectively by the U.K., U.S.A., U.S.S.R. and France, while Vienna was jointly occupied by the four Powers. On May 15, 1955, the Austrian State Treaty was signed in Vienna by the Foreign Ministers of the four Powers and of Austria. This Treaty recognized the re-establishment of Austria as a sovereign, independent and democratic state, having the same frontiers as on January 1, 1938.

There is a national assembly of 183 Deputies. After the elections of Nov. 1986, the Socialists formed a coalition with the People's Party.

The state of the parties in the Nationalrat (Lower House) in Nov. 1986, was:

Socialist Party (Social Democrat)	80
People's Party (Conservative)	77
Freedom Party (Liberal)	18
Green Party	8

In the Bundesrat (Upper House) in March 1988 the People's Party held 32 seats, the Socialist Party, 30 and the Liberal Party 1 seat.

Religion and Education.—The predominant religion is Roman Catholic. Education is free and compulsory between the ages of 6 and 15 and there are good facilities for secondary, technical and professional education. There are 12 state-maintained Universities and six colleges of art.

Language and Literature.—The language of Austria is German, but the rights of the Slovene- and Croat-speaking minorities in Carinthia, Styria and Burgenland are protected. The press is free.

Communications.—Internal communications in Austria are partly restricted because of the mountainous nature of the country, although there has been an extensive programme to increase the number of motorways, many of which are tunnelled through the mountains. There were, in 1985, 37,501 km. of roads, including a network of *autobahn* between major cities which also links up with the West German and Italian networks. The railways in Austria are state-owned and in 1985 had 5,766 km. of track, over half of which is electrified. Of the 425 km. of waterways, 355 km. are navigable and there is considerable trade through the Danube ports by both local and foreign shipping. There are six commercial airports catering for 4,872,922 passengers in 1985.

Tourism.—In 1986, 15,092,200 tourists visited Austria. Foreign exchange receipts from tourism were 101,555 million Schilling—a major contribution to the balance of payments.

PRODUCTION AND INDUSTRY

The origin of Gross Domestic Product in 1986 was as follows (in per cent.):

Agriculture and forestry	4·7
Mining and material goods production	30·8
Energy and water supply	3·2
Construction	6·3
Commerce, hotels, restaurants	16·4
Transport and communications	6·4
Asset management	12·6
Other services and producers	16·7
Import duties and other items	2·9

The value of G.D.P. in 1986 (at current prices) was S1,441,100 million: G.D.P. per capita (at current prices) was S190,627.

Agriculture.—The arable land produces wheat, rye, barley, oats, maize, potatoes, sugar beet, turnips, and miscellaneous crops. Many varieties of fruit trees flourish and the vineyards produce excellent wine. The pastures support horses, cattle and pigs. Timber forms a valuable source of Austria's indigenous wealth, about 40·7 per cent. of the total land area consisting of forest areas. Coniferous species predominate (75 per cent. of afforested area).

Energy.—Energy production in 1986 was:—

Crude oil		
—production	1,116,000 tonnes	
—imports	6,188,000	„
(from Libya	2,113,202	„)
(from Algeria	838,647	„)
Natural gas		
—production	1,112m. cu. metres	
—imports	4,055m. cu. metres	
(from U.S.S.R.	3,956m. cu. metres)	

Electric power	
—output	44,652m. kWh.
—imports	5,962m. kWh.
—exports	7,426m. kWh.

A 700 mw nuclear power station had already been constructed when in November 1978 the Austrian people decided by a very small margin in a national referendum not to allow the introduction of nuclear power stations in Austria.

Mining.—Production was (tonnes):—

	1985	1986
Lignite	3,081,071	2,968,978
Iron/manganese ore	3,270,000	3,120,000
Raw magnesite	1,255,043	1,084,360
Lead/zinc ore	643,255	400,246
Crystal salt	437,584	485,513
Graphite	30,764	36,167

In addition 2,306,706 cu. metres of brine was produced in 1985 and 2,335,067 cu. metres in 1986.

Industry.—Heavy industry production in 1986 included pig iron 3,348,600 tonnes, raw steel 4,291,895 tonnes and rolled steel 3,461,545 tonnes. In addition, petroleum, non-ferrous metals and chemicals are processed in quantity and construction materials, industrial machinery, vehicles, paper and textiles are produced.

FINANCE

	1985	1986
	Schilling, million	
Federal Budget:		
Revenue	372,841	391,675
Expenditure	464,482	498,380
Gross Budget Deficit...	91,641	106,715

Federal Budget expenditure (S million):—

	1985	1986
Agriculture, forestry	12,493·0	13,622·0
Defence	17,147·3	18,495·0
Education	39,733·6	42,452·0
Internal security, justice	14,583·4	15,365·0
Public services	7,892·8	6,479·0
Roads	15,927·8	16,682·0
Science and research	14,110·8	17,162·0
Health and Social welfare	113,686·3	119,949·0
Transportation	89,369·4	97,668·0
Expenditure on debts	69,654·0	75,707·0
Other purposes	69,883·6	74,782·0

TRADE

Main exports are processed goods (iron and steel, textiles, paper and cardboard products), machinery and transport equipment, other finished goods (including clothing) raw materials and foodstuffs. Main imports are machinery and transport equipment, processed goods, chemical products, foodstuffs, fuel and energy.

	1986	1987
	Schilling, million	
Imports	407,954	411,859
Exports	342,479	342,433

Over 80 per cent. of all trade is with other European countries, E.C. countries accounting for about 60 per cent., Eastern Europe for about 9 per cent. and E.F.T.A. members for 9 per cent.

Trade with U.K.

	1986	1987
Imports from U.K.	$9,356 m	$9,887 m
Exports to U.K.	15,297 m	15,650 m

CAPITAL, Vienna, on the Danube, population 1,531,346. Other towns are Graz (243,166), Linz (199,910), Innsbruck (117,287), Salzburg (139,426), and Klagenfurt (87,321).

CURRENCY.—Schilling (S) of 100 Groschen.
FLAG.—Horizontal stripes of red, white, red, with eagle crest on white stripe.
NATIONAL ANTHEM.—Land der Berge, Land am Strome (Land of mountains, land of streams).
NATIONAL DAY.—October 26.

BRITISH EMBASSY
Jauresgasse 12, 1030 Vienna
[Vienna 7131575]

Ambassador Extraordinary and Plenipotentiary, His Excellency Robert James O'Neill, C.M.G. (1986).
Counsellor, Consul General and Head of Chancery, R. P. Nash, L.V.O.
Counsellor, D. H. Cecil.
1st Secretaries, R. G. Bowen; Miss D. M. Symes (*Commercial*); J. Moorby, M.B.E. (*H.M. Consul*); A. N. King, L.V.O. (*Administration*).
Defence Attaché, Lt.-Col. M. Ledger.
There is a British Consular Office at *Vienna*, and Honorary Consulates at *Bregenz, Innsbruck, Graz and Salzburg*.
British Council Representative, T. Sandell, Schenkenstrasse 4, A-1010 Vienna.

BAHRAIN
(Dawlet al-Bahrein)

Amir, H.H. Shaikh Isa bin Sulman Al Khalifa, G.C.M.G., *born* 1932; *acceded* Dec. 16, 1961.
Crown Prince and C.-in-C., Bahrain Defence Force, H.E. Shaikh Hamad bin Isa Al Khalifa, K.C.M.G.

CABINET

Prime Minister, H.E. Shaikh Khalifa bin Sulman Al-Khalifa.
Foreign Affairs, Shaikh Mohammed bin Mubarak Al-Khalifa.
Defence, Maj.-Gen. Shaikh Khalifa bin Ahmed Al Khalifa.
Justice and Islamic Affairs, Shaikh Abdullah bin Khalid Al-Khalifa.
Development and Industry, and Cabinet Affairs, Yusuf Ahmad Shirawi.
Education, Dr. Ali Fakhroo.
Health, Jawad Salim Al-Arayyed.
Transportation, Ibrahim Mohammed Humaidan.
Interior, Shaikh Mohammed bin Khalifa Al-Khalifa.
Information, Tariq Abdulrahman Al Moayed.
Labour and Social Affairs, Shaikh Khalifa bin Sulman bin Mohammed Al-Khalifa.
Works, Power and Water, Majid Jawad Al-Jishi.
Housing, Shaikh Khalid bin Abdullah Al-Khalifa.
Finance and National Economy, Ibrahim Abdulkarim Mohammed.
Commerce and Agriculture, Habib Ahmed Kassim.
Minister of State, Legal Affairs, Dr. Hussain Al-Baharna.

BAHRAIN EMBASSY IN LONDON
98 Gloucester Road, SW7 4AU
[01–370 5132]

Ambassador Extraordinary and Plenipotentiary, His Excellency Salman Abdul Wahab Al Sabbagh (1984).

Area and Population.—Bahrain consists of a group of low-lying islands situated about half-way down the Gulf, some 20 miles off the east coast of Arabia. The largest of these, Bahrain island itself, is about 30 miles long and 10 miles wide at its broadest. The capital, Manama, is situated on the north shore of this island. The next largest, Muharraq, with the town and Bahrain International Airport, is connected to Manama by a causeway 1½ miles long.

The population (1985 estimate) is 417,210, of whom 151,831 are foreign. About 35 per cent. of the Bahrainis are Sunni Moslems, the remaining 65 per cent. being Shias; the ruling family and many of the most prominent merchants are Sunnis.
Climate.—The climate is humid all the year round, with rainfall of about 3 in. concentrated in the mild winter months, December to March; in summer, May to October, temperatures can exceed 110° F. (44°C).
Government.—Bahrain has been a fully independent state since 1971. Government takes the form of a constitutional monarchy, in which traditional consultative procedures continue to play an important role.
Economy.—The largest sources of revenue are oil production and refining. The Bahrain field, discovered in 1932, is wholly owned by the Bahrain National Oil Co. Production in 1986 stood at about 42,000 b.p.d. The Sitra refinery derives about 70 per cent. of its crude oil by submarine pipeline from Saudi Arabia. Bahrain also has a half share with Saudi Arabia in the profits of the offshore Abu Sa'afa field. A reservoir of unassociated gas has recently been developed on Bahrain island.
Heavy industry is currently limited to the Aluminium Bahrain (ALBA) smelter, producing 170,000 tonnes p.a.; the Gulf Petrochemical Industries Co. (GPIC) producing 150,000 tonnes p.a. of ammonia and methanol, the Gulf Aluminium Rolling Mill (GARMCO), and the Arab Shipbuilding and Repair Yard (ASRY), operating dry dock facilities up to 500,000 tons.
There are a number of small to medium sized industrial units.
The state has developed as a financial centre. Apart from commercial banks, led by the National Bank of Bahrain, the Standard Chartered Bank, the British Bank of the Middle East and the Bank of Bahrain and Kuwait, many international banks have been licensed as "offshore banking units"; there are also money brokers and merchant banks.

Trade with U.K.

	1986	1987
Imports from U.K.	£130,991,000	£125,189,000
Exports to U.K.	19,732,000	60,687,000

Communications.—Bahrain International airport is the main air traffic centre of the Gulf; it is the headquarters of Gulf Air, and a stopping point on routes between Europe and Australia and the Far East for other airlines. A causeway linking Bahrain to Saudi Arabia was opened in Nov. 1986.
A world-wide telephone and telex service, by satellite and cable, is operated by Bahrain Telecommunications Company.
CAPITAL.—ΨManama; population (1981 Census), 121,986.
CURRENCY.—Bahrain Dinar of 1,000 Fils.
FLAG.—Red, with vertical serrated white bar next to staff.
NATIONAL DAY.—December 16.

BRITISH EMBASSY
21 Government Avenue,
Manama 306, P.O. Box 114
[Manama 254002]

Ambassador Extraordinary and Plenipotentiary, His Excellency John Alan Shepherd (1988).
1st Secretaries, W. I. Rae, M.B.E. (*Commercial and Head of Chancery*); S. P. Muir.
2nd Secretary, D. Leith (*Commercial*).
British Council Representative, D. R. Thomas, 21 Government Avenue (P.O. Box 452), Manama 306.

BELGIUM
(Royaume de Belgique)

King of the Belgians, H.M. King Baudouin, K.G., *born* Sept. 7, 1930; *succeeded* July 17, 1951, on the abdication of his father, King Leopold III, after having acted as Head of the State since August 11, 1950; *married* Dec. 15, 1960, Doña Fabiola de Mora y Aragòn.

Heir Presumptive, H.R.H. Prince Albert, *born* June 6, 1934, *brother* of the King; *married* July 2, 1959, Donna Paola Ruffo di Calabria, and has *issue* Prince Philippe Léopold Louis Marie, *b.* April 15, 1960; Princess Astrid Josephine-Charlotte Fabrizia Elisabeth Paola Marie, *b.* June 5, 1962; Prince Laurent, *b.* Oct. 20, 1963.

Cabinet

Prime Minister, Dr. Wilfried Martens (*CVP*).
Deputy P.M. and Minister for the Brussels Region, and Institutional Reform, Philippe Moureaux (*PS*).
Deputy P.M. and Minister for Economic Affairs and Planning, and National Education (Flemish Sector), Willy Claes (*SP*).
Deputy P.M. and Minister of Communications, and Institutional Reform, Jean-Luc Dehaene (*CVP*).
Deputy P.M. and Minister of Justice, and the Middle Classes, Melchior Wathelet (*PSC*).
Deputy P.M. and Minister for the Budget and Scientific Policy, Hugo Schiltz (*VU*).
Foreign Affairs, Leo Tindemans (*CVP*).
Finance, Philippe Maystadt (*PSC*).
Foreign Trade, Robert Urbain (*PS*).
Public Affairs, Michel Hansenne (*PSC*).
Posts and Telecommunications, Freddy Willockx (*SP*).
Social Affairs, Philippe Busquin (*PS*).
Defence, Guy Coëme (*PS*).
Public Works, Paula D'Hondt-Van Opdenbosch (*CVP*).
Interior, Modernization of Public Services and National Scientific and Cultural Institutions, Louis Tobback (*SP*).
National Education (French Sector), Yvan Ylieff (*PS*).
Co-operation and Development, André Geens (*VU*).
Pensions, Alain Van Der Biest (*PS*).
Employment and Work, Luc Vanden Brande (*CVP*).

CVP—Christian Social Party (Flemish); *PS*—Socialist Party (Francophone); *SP*—Socialist Party (Flemish); *PSC*—Christian Social Party (Francophone); *VU*—Flemish Peoples' Union.

Belgian Embassy in London
103 Eaton Square, SW1W 9AB
[01-235 5422]

Ambassador Extraordinary and Plenipotentiary, His Excellency Jean-Paul van Bellinghen (1984)
Minister Plenipotentiary, L. Willems.
Minister Counsellor, R. Vandemeulebroucke (*Economic*).
Military, Naval and Air Attaché, Capt. W. Cornelis.

A Kingdom of Western Europe, with a total area of 11,781 sq. miles (30,513 sq. km.), and a population, (1986) of 9,858,895 (Greater Brussels, 976,536; Flanders, 5,676,194; Wallonia, 3,206,165, of whom 66,445 are German-speaking). The majority of Belgians are Roman Catholics. The Kingdom of Belgium is bounded on the N. by the Kingdom of the Netherlands, on the S. by France, on the E. by W. Germany and Luxembourg, and on the W. by the North Sea.

Belgium has a frontier of 898 miles, and a seaboard of 41 miles. The Meuse and its tributary, the Sambre, divide it into two distinct regions, that in the west

being generally level and fertile, while the table-land of the Ardennes, in the east, has for the most part a poor soil. The polders, near the coast, which are protected by dykes against floods, cover an area of 193 sq. miles. The highest hill, Signal de Botranges, rises to a height of 2,276 feet, but the mean elevation of the whole country does not exceed 526 feet. The principal rivers are the Scheldt and the Meuse.

Government.—The kingdom formed part of the "Low Countries" (Netherlands) from 1815 until Oct. 14, 1830, when a National Congress proclaimed its independence, and on June 4, 1831, Prince Leopold of Coburg was chosen hereditary king. The separation from the Netherlands and the neutrality and inviolability of Belgium were guaranteed by a Conference of the European Powers, and by the *Treaty of London* (April 19, 1839), the famous "Scrap of Paper," signed by Austria, France, Great Britain, Prussia, The Netherlands, and Russia. On Aug. 4, 1914, The Germans invaded Belgium, in violation of the terms of the treaty. The Kingdom was again invaded by Germany on May 10, 1940. The whole Kingdom eventually fell and was occupied by Nazi troops until liberated by the Allies in September 1944.

According to the Constitution of 1831 the form of government is a constitutional representative and hereditary monarchy with a bicameral legislature, consisting of the King, the Senate and the Chamber of Deputies. The parliamentary term is four years.

The last general election was held on December 13, 1987. The results were as follows (seats):

Chamber of Deputies: CVP, 43; PS, 40; SP, 32; PVV (Flemish Freedom and Progress Party), 25; PRL (Liberal Reform Party (Francophone)), 23; PSC, 19; VU, 16; Agalev (Flemish Environmental Party), 6; Ecolo (Francophone Ecology Party), 3; FDF (Francophone Democratic Front), 3; Vlaams Blok (Flemish Nationalist Party), 2.

Senate: CVP, 25; PS, 18; SP, 16; PRL, 13; PVV, 11; PSC, 10; VU, 8; Ecologists, 4; FDF, 1. Besides these directly elected representatives the Senate also includes 51 members who are elected by the Provincial Councils and 26 who are co-opted in the proportions of the directly elected seats. H.R.H. Prince Albert is a "sénateur de droit".

Regional Governments.—The 1980 regionalization law made provision for the establishment of three Regional Community Parliaments (Assemblies) with executive councils which were set up in November 1981 and became effective in January 1982. The executives are autonomous from the central government, and their members are elected by the members of the Assemblies to whom they are responsible. They prepare Bills within the limits of their regional/ community competences, and once these Bills have been passed by the regional assembly and published in the *Moniteur Belge*, they have the force of law.

The Flemish Regional Assembly (182 members) and Executive (a President and 8 Regional Ministers) covers the provinces of Antwerp, East and West Flanders, Limbourg and the Flemish *arrondissements* (Halle, Vilvoorde, Leuven) in the province of Brabant, and is also responsible for the Flemish population of Brussels. The Walloon Regional Assembly (106 members) and Executive (a President and 5 Regional Ministers) covers the provinces of Hainaut, Liege, Luxembourg and Namur, and the *arrondissement* of Nivelles in the province of Brabant. The French Community Assembly (137 members) and Executive (a President and 2 Community Ministers) has no fixed territory but is responsbile for the francophone population of Brussels and, in concert with the Walloon Regional Assembly, deals with certain Walloon regional affairs. The German-speaking community (about 66,000) also has an Assembly, which gained autonomy in 1984. It is based in Eupen.

Although the regionalization laws defined the City of Brussels as a region, there is no autonomous regional parliament for the City and its affairs are handled by a Brussels Executive within the national government.

An Arbitration Court was set up in 1984 to resolve conflicts between laws made by the various legislative bodies.

Language and Literature.—Belgium is divided between those who speak Dutch (the Flemings) and those who speak French (the Walloons). Dutch is spoken in the provinces of West Flanders, East Flanders, Antwerp, Limburg, and the northern half of Brabant, and French in the provinces of Hainault, Namur, Luxembourg, Liège and the southern half of Brabant. Dutch is recognized as the official language in the northern areas and French in the southern (Walloon) area and there are guarantees for the respective linguistic minorities. Brussels is officially bi-lingual. There is a small German-speaking area (Eupen and Malmedy) along the German border, east of Liège.

The literature of France and the Netherlands is supplemented by an indigenous Belgian literary activity, in both French and Dutch. Maurice Maeterlinck (1862–1949) was awarded the Nobel Prize for Literature in 1911. Emile Verhaeren (1855–1916) was a poet of international standing. Of contemporary Belgian writers, perhaps the most celebrated is Georges Simenon (*born* at Liège in 1903). There are 39 daily newspapers in Belgium (23 in French, 15 in Dutch and 1 in German).

Education.—The nursery schools provide free education for the 2½ to 6 age group. There are over 8,000 primary schools (6 to 12 years) of which approximately 5,000 are administered by the State, province or commune and the remainder are free institutions (predominantly Roman Catholic). There are more than 1,100 secondary schools offering a general academic education slightly over half of which are free institutions (predominantly Roman Catholic but subsidized by the State) and the remainder official institutions. The official school leaving age is 18.

Production.—Belgium is a manufacturing country. With no natural resources except coal, annual production of which was approximately 6 million tonnes in 1986, industry is based largely on the processing for re-export of imported raw materials. Gross National Product per capita in 1986 was B.Fr.439,992. Principal industries are steel and metal products, chemicals and petrochemicals, textiles, glass, and foodstuffs.

FINANCE

Budget	1985	1986
	B. Fr. (millions)	
Consolidated revenue....	2,363,800	2,434,200
Consolidated expenditure	2,918,300	3,007,300

External trade figures relate to Luxembourg as well as Belgium since the two countries formed an Economic Union in 1921.

TRADE

	1985	1986
	B. Fr. (millions)	
Total Imports	3,315,468	2,990,700
Total Exports	3,163,724	3,060,200

Trade with U.K. (Belgium and Luxembourg)

	1986	1987
Imports from U.K...	£3,832,605,000	£9,713,881,000
Exports to U.K.	4,083,883,000	11,510,499,000

Communications.—In 1983, there were 3,920 kilometres of normal gauge railways operated by the Belgian National Railways, of which 1,763 kilometres were electrified. The Belgian National Light Railways (SNCV) also operated 27,671 kilometres of regular bus routes. In 1984 there were 2,930,000 telephone subscribers in Belgium.

Ship canals include *Ghent-Terneuzen* (18 miles, of which half is in Belgium and half in the Netherlands) which permits the passage to Ghent of ships up to 60,000 tons; the Canal of *Willebroek Rupel-Brussels* (20 miles, by which ships drawing 18 ft reach Brussels from the sea; opened in 1922); and *Bruges* (from Zeebrugge on the North Sea to Bruges, 6½ miles). The *Albert Canal* (79 miles), links Liège with Antwerp; it was completed in 1939 and accommodates barges up to 1,350 tons. The modernization of the port of Antwerp is well advanced. Inland waterway approaches to Antwerp are also to be improved. The river Meuse from the Dutch to the French frontiers, the river Sambre between Namur and Monceau, the river Scheldt from Antwerp-Ghent and the Brussels-Charleroi Canal are being widened or deepened to take barges up to 1,350 tons. Most of the maritime trade of Belgium is carried in foreign shipping.

In 1986 there were 14,260 km. of trunk roads of which about 1,550 km. are motorways.

The Belgian National Airline *Sabena* operates regular services between Brussels and London, and many continental centres, as well as overseas services to Northern and Central America, Africa, Middle East, Far East, etc. Many foreign airlines call at Brussels.

THE CAPITAL, Brussels, has a population (1986) of 976,536. Other towns are ΨAntwerp, the chief port (918,963); ΨGhent (484,295); Liège (592,732); Charleroi (430,767); Bruges (258,917); ΨOstend (134,215); Malines (293,050).

CURRENCY.—Belgian Franc (B.Fr.) of 100 Centimes.

FLAG.—Three vertical bands, black, yellow, red.

NATIONAL ANTHEM.—La Brabançonne.

NATIONAL DAY.—July 21 (Accession of King Leopold I, 1831).

BRITISH EMBASSY.
Britannia House, 28 rue Joseph II,
1040 Brussels.
[Brussels 2179000]

Ambassador Extraordinary and Plenipotentiary, His Excellency Sir Peter Petrie, Bt., C.M.G., (1985).
Counsellors, M. G. D. Evans (*Head of Chancery*); B. Attewell (*Commercial*).

Defence and Military Attaché, Col. P. M. Beaumont, M.B.E.

Naval and Air Attaché, Wing Cdr. J. N. Landeryou, R.A.F.

There are British Consular Offices at *Brussels, Antwerp* and *Liège.*

British Council Representative to Belgium and Luxembourg, K. McGuinness, 30 rue Joseph II, 1040 Brussels (Council Library at *Brussels*).

BRITISH CHAMBER OF COMMERCE FOR BELGIUM AND LUXEMBOURG (INC.), 30 rue Joseph II, 1040 Brussels.

BENIN
(République Populaire du Benin)

President of the Military Revolutionary Government and Head of State, Brig.-Gen. Ahmed Mathieu Kerekou; *assumed office,* Oct. 26, 1972, *re-elected,* July 31, 1984.

NATIONAL EXECUTIVE COUNCIL
(as at Feb. 13, 1987)

President of the Council and Minister of Defence, Brig.-Gen. Ahmed Mathieu Kerekou.

Minister-Delegate to the Presidency (Interior, Security, Territorial Administration), Maj. Edouard Zodehougan.

Minister-Delegate to the Presidency (Planning, Statistics), Ibrahim Souradjou.

Rural Development and Co-operative Action, Maj. Martin Dohou Azonhiho.

Equipment and Transport, Soule Dankoro.

Finance and Economy, Barnabe Bidouzo.

Commerce, Crafts and Tourism, Girigissou Gado.

Primary Education, Capt. Philippe Akpo.

Secondary and Higher Education, Vincent Guedzodje.

Culture, Youth and Sports, Ousmane Batoko.

Labour and Social Affairs, Lt. Col. Nathanael Mensah.

Public Health, André Atchade.

Information and Communications, Houdou Ali.

Foreign Affairs and Co-operation, Guy Landry Hazoume.

Justice, and Inspection of Parastatal Enterprises, Saliou Abdoudou.

A republic situated in West Africa, between 2° and 3° W. and 6° and 12° N., Benin (formerly known as Dahomey) has a short coastline of 78 miles on the Gulf of Guinea but extends northwards inland for 437 miles. It is flanked on the west by Togo, on the north by Burkina Faso and Niger and on the east by Nigeria. It has an area of 43,484 sq. miles (122,622 sq. km.), and a population of 3,932,000 (1985, U.N. estimate). Although poor in resources, Benin is one of the most heavily populated areas in West Africa, with a high standard of education. It is divided into four main regions running horizontally: a narrow sandy coastal strip, a succession of inter-communicating lagoons, a clay belt and a sandy plateau in the north.

Government.—The first treaty with France was signed by one of the kings of Abomey in 1851 but the country was not placed under French administration until 1892. Benin became an independent republic within the French Community on Dec. 4, 1958; full independence outside the Community was proclaimed on August 1, 1960. In October, 1963, a popular revolution led to the fall of the government and the Army held power until a civilian government was formed. The government's life was very short, however, and in the subsequent 8–9 years successive governments were overthrown by the military after only a short term in office until a *coup d'état* of October 26, 1972 brought to power a Military Revolutionary Government, headed by Lt.-Col. Kerekou. Although now a one party state, a general election was held in Nov. 1979, and a new Constitution and National Assembly were established.

Benin is a member of the *Conseil de l'Entente,* the *Organisation Commune Africaine et Malgache* (OCAM), the Organization of African Unity (O.A.U.) and the Economic Community of West African States (ECOWAS). The official language is French.

Trade.—The principal exports are cotton, palm products, ground nuts, shea-nuts, and coffee. Small deposits of gold, iron and chrome have been found; oil production started in 1983.

Trade with U.K.

	1986	1987
Imports from U.K.	£6,728,000	£7,207,000
Exports to U.K.	4,910,000	2,930,000

CAPITAL.—ΨPorto Novo (population (1982 estimate) 208,258). Political capital and principal commercial town and port, ΨCotonou (popn. (1982) 487,020).

CURRENCY.—Franc C.F.A. of 100 Centimes.

FLAG.—Green, with five pointed red star in the top left corner.

NATIONAL DAY.—November 30.

British Embassy (see Lagos, Nigeria).

BHUTAN
(Druk-yul)

King of Bhutan, H.M. Jigme Singye Wangchuck, *born* Nov. 11, 1955; *succeeded his father,* July, 1972; *crowned,* June 2, 1974.

COUNCIL OF MINISTERS

H.M. Representative in the Ministry of Finance, H.R.H. Ashi S. C. Wangchuk.

H.M. Representative in the Ministry of Agriculture, H.R.H. Ashi D. W. Wangchuk.

Home Affairs, Trade, Industry and Forests, H.R.H. Namgyel Wangchuk.

Foreign Affairs, Lyonpo Dawa Tshering.

Social Services, Lyonpo Sangye Penjor.

Communications, Tourism and Social Services, Lyonpo Dr. T. Tobgyal.

Deputy Minister of Defence, Maj.-Gen. Lam Dorji.

Speaker of the National Assembly, Lyonpo Tamji Jagar.

Bhutan is a small Himalayan Kingdom situated between Tibet (to the north) and India (to the west, south and east). The total area is about 18,147 sq. miles (47,000 sq. km.), with a mountainous northern region which is infertile and sparsely populated, a central zone of upland valleys where most of the population and cultivated land is found, and in the south the densely forested foothills of the Himalayas, which are mainly inhabited by Nepalese settlers and indigenous tribespeople.

The population of Bhutan is estimated at 1,417,000 (1985, U.N. estimate), about three-quarters of whom are Buddhists. The remainder (mostly the Nepali Bhutanese) are Hindu. The official language, for administrative and religious purposes, is Dzongkha, a variant of Tibetan, which functions as a *lingua franca* amongst a variety of languages and dialects. It is government policy to make the study of Dzongkha compulsory in schools, although English is the medium of instruction and has become widely used within the administration.

In 1949, a treaty was concluded with the Government of India under which the Kingdom of Bhutan agreed to be guided by the Government of India in regard to its external relations, but it still retains independence, issues its own passports, has its own diplomatic representatives and is a member of the U.N. and other international and regional organizations. It also receives from the Government of India an annual payment of *Rs*.500,000 as compensation for portions of its territory annexed by the British Government in India in 1864.

Government.—Bhutan has a 150-member National Assembly which meets twice a year. The ten-member Royal Advisory Council, nominated by the King and the National Assembly, acts as a consultative body when the National Assembly is not in session. The King is also assisted by a Council of Ministers.

Economy.—The sixth 5-year Plan (1987–92) has a projected expenditure of Nu 9,485m. Economic emphasis is on the infrastructure, especially roads and telecommunications. The economy is based on agriculture and animal husbandry, which engage over 90 per cent of the workforce in what is largely a self-sufficient rural society. The principal food crops are rice, wheat, maize and barley. Vegetables and fruit are also produced. Bhutan is the world's largest producer of cardamon, which forms its principal export to countries other than India. Mineral resources include dolomite and small amounts of coal, which are exported to India. A modest industrial base is being developed. A distillery and cement, chemicals and food processing plants are in production: a forestry industries complex is being expanded. Tourism and postage stamps are increasingly important sources of foreign exchange. Over 90 per cent of foreign trade is with India. Principal exports are agricultural products, timber, cement and coal; main imports are textiles, cereals and consumer goods. Bhutan's airline, Druk Air, flies between Paro and Calcutta.

Trade with U.K.

	1986	1987
Imports from U.K.	£76,000	£411,000
Exports to U.K.	—	14,000

CAPITAL.—Thimphu (Population estimate 1977, 8,922).

CURRENCY.—Ngultrum of 100 Chetrums. Indian currency is also legal tender.

FLAG.—Saffron yellow and orange-red divided diagonally, with dragon device in centre.

NATIONAL DAY.—December 17.

BOLIVIA
(República de Bolivia)

President of the Republic, Sr. Victor Paz Estenssoro, inaugurated, Aug. 6, 1985.
Vice President, Sr. Julio Garret Ayllón.

CABINET

Foreign Affairs, Guillermo Bedregal.
Interior, Dr. Juan Carlos Duran Saucedo.
Defence, Alfonso Revollo Thenier.
Finance, Juan Cariaga Osorio.
Planning, Gonzalo Sanchez de Lozada.
Education, Enrique Ipiña Melgar.
Transport and Communications, Andrés Petricevic.
Industry and Commerce, Fernando Moscoso.
Labour, Dr. Alfredo Franco Guachalla.
Health, Dr. Carlos Perez Guzman.
Mines and Metallurgy, Jaime Villalobos.
Agriculture, José Guillermo Justiniano.
Energy and Hydrocarbons, Fernando Illánes.
Housing, Franklin Anaya.
Information, Herman Antelo Louckling.
Aeronautics, Gen. Jaime Cevada Hurtado.

Secretary General, Dr. Walter Zuleta Roncal.
Secretary to the Presidency, Eduardo O. Lopez Muñoz.

BOLIVIAN EMBASSY IN LONDON
106 Eaton Square, SW1W 9AD
[01–235 2257/4248]

Ambassador Extraordinary and Plenipotentiary, His Excellency Eduardo Arauco-Paz (1985).
Minister Counsellor, J. Loayza.
1st Secretary, Srta. Marta Bosacoma Bonel.

The land-locked Republic of Bolivia extends between lat. 10° and 23° S. and long. 57° 30′ and 69° 45′ W. It has an area estimated at 424,165 sq. miles (1,098,581 sq. km.), with a population (1985 U.N. estimate) of 6,429,000. The Republic derives its name from its liberator, Simon Bolivar (1783–1830).

The chief topographical feature is the great central plateau (65,000 square miles) over 500 miles in length, at an average altitude of 12,500 feet above sea level, between the two great chains of the Andes, which traverse the country from south to north. The total length of the navigable streams is about 12,000 miles, the principal rivers being the Itenez, Beni, Mamore and Madre de Dios.

Language and Literature.—The official language of the country is Spanish, but many of the Indian inhabitants (about two-thirds of the population) speak Quechua or Aymará, the two linguistic groups being more or less equal in numbers.

The Roman Catholic religion was disestablished in 1961 but relations between it and the State are good. Elementary education is compulsory and free and there are secondary schools in urban centres. Provision is also made for higher education; in addition to St. Francisco Xavier's University at Sucre, founded in 1624, there are six other universities, the largest being the University of San Andres at La Paz. There are nine principal daily newspapers in Bolivia.

Production.—Mining, natural gas, petroleum and agriculture are the principal industries. The ancient silver mines of Potosí are now worked chiefly for tin, but gold, partly dug and partly washed, is obtained on the Eastern Cordillera of the Andes; the tin output is one of the largest in the world, and together with other minerals (copper, antimony, lead, zinc, asbestos, wolfram, bismuth salt and sulphur), provides over half of Bolivia's exports.

In 1982 Bolivia produced 1·4 million cubic metres of oil, sufficient for internal consumption. Gas (currently providing about a quarter of Bolivia's export income) is piped to Argentina and there are plans to build a pipeline to Sao Paulo, Brazil, by 1988. Bolivia's agricultural produce consists chiefly of rice, barley, oats, wheat, sugar-cane, maize, cotton, indigo, rubber, cacao, potatoes, cinchona bark, medicinal herbs, brazil nuts etc.

Transport and Communications.—There are 2,200 miles of railways in operation including the lines from Corumbá to Santa Cruz (312 miles). There are about 10,950 miles of telegraphs, and microwave telephone communications between La Paz, Santa Cruz, Cochabamba, Oruro and Sucre. Most other towns of any size have radio/telephone communication with the main cities. There is direct railway communication to the sea at Antofagasta (32 hours), Arica (10 hours), and Mollendo (2 days), and also to Buenos Aires (3¼ days). Communication with Peru is by road from La Paz via Copacabana and thence to the railhead at Puno.

Commercial aviation in Bolivia is conducted by the national airline, Lloyd Aereo Boliviano and Transporte Aereo Militar between the major towns, and Lloyd Aereo Boliviano and a number of foreign airlines provide international flights to the U.S.A., South and Central America and Europe.

Bolivia is without a coastline, having been deprived of the ports of Tocopilla, Cobija, Mejillones and Antofagasta by the "Pacific War" of 1879–1884.

FINANCE

The economy has deteriorated since 1977, with disappointing petroleum reserves, a large external debt, and the collapse of world tin prices (Oct. 1985). The peso was replaced in Jan. 1987 with the Boliviano of 1,000,000 old pesos in an effort to stem inflation. The inflation rate in 1985 was about 11,750 per cent. Total exports (c.i.f.) in 1985 were U.S. $672·5 million.

Trade with U.K.

	1986	1987
Imports from U.K.	£3,663,000	£3,658,000
Exports to U.K.	10,225,000	14,799,000

Mineral exports represent about 94 per cent of these totals. A large part of Bolivia's minerals were shipped to U.K. for smelting and re-export, but Bolivia is now developing her own smelters and will in future be exporting metals. The chief imports are wheat and flour, iron and steel products, machinery, vehicles and textiles.

CAPITAL.—La Paz (Population, 1,000,000). Other large centres are Cochabamba (250,000), Oruro (180,000), Santa Cruz (380,000), Potosí (90,000), Sucre, the legal capital and seat of the judiciary (80,000) and Tarija (45,000).

CURRENCY.—Bolivian Peso of 100 Centavos.

FLAG.—Three horizontal bands; red, yellow, green.

NATIONAL ANTHEM.—"Bolivianos, El Hado Propicio" (Oh Bolivia, our long-felt desires).

NATIONAL DAY.—August 6 (Independence Day).

BRITISH EMBASSY
Avenida Arce 2732–2754,
(Casilla 694) La Paz.
[La Paz 329401/3]

Ambassador Extraordinary and Plenipotentiary, His Excellency Colum John Sharkey, C.M.G., M.B.E., (1987).
First Secretary, T. J. Duggin (*Commercial and Head of Chancery*).

BRITISH CONSULAR OFFICES

There is a British Consulate at *Santa Cruz.*

BRAZIL
(República Federativa do Brasil)

President, José Sarney, *inaugurated*, April 22, 1985.

CABINET

Chief Minister Civil Staff, Ronaldo Costa Couto.
Chief Minister Military Staff, Gen. Rubens Bayma Denys.
Justice, Paulo Brossard.
Navy, Adm. Henrique Sabóia.
External Relations, Roberto Abreu Sodré.
Army, Gen. Leônidas Pires Gonçalves.
Finance, Mailson da Nobrega.
Transport, José Reinaldo C. Tavares.
Agriculture, Iris Rezende.
Education, Hugo Napoleão.
Labour, Almir Pazzianotto.
Air Force, Brig. Octavio J. Moreira Lima.
Health, Luiz Carlos Borges da Silveira.
Industry and Commerce, José Hugo Castelo Branco.
Mines and Energy, A. Aureliano Chaves.
Planning, João Batista de Abreu.
Interior, João Alves Filho.

Communications, Antonio Carlos Magalhães.
Social Security, Renato Archer.
National Information Service, Gen. Ivan de Souza Mendes.
Armed Forces General Staff, Adm. Valbert Lisieux Medeiros de Figueiredo.
Land Reform and Development, Jader Barbalho.
Science and Technology, Luiz Henrique da Silveira.
Culture, Celso M. Furtado.
Housing, Urban Planning and Environment, L. H. Prisco Viana.
Administration, Aluízio Alves.

BRAZILIAN EMBASSY IN LONDON
32 Green Street, W1Y 4AT
[01–499 0877]

Ambassador Extraordinary and Plenipotentiary, His Excellency Senhor Celso de Souza e Silva (1986).

There are also a Brazilian Consulate-General in *London* and honorary consular offices at *Cardiff* and *Glasgow.*

Area and Population.—Brazil, discovered in 1500 by Portuguese navigator Pedro Alvares Cabral, is bounded on the north by the Atlantic Ocean, the Guianas, Colombia and Venezuela; on the west by Peru, Bolivia, Paraguay, and Argentina; on the south by Uruguay; and on the east by the Atlantic Ocean. Brazil extends between lat. 5° 16′ N. and 33° 45′ S. and long. 34° 45′ and 73° 59′22″ W. The Republic comprises an area of 3,286,488 sq. miles (8,511,965 sq. km.), with a population (1985 U.N. estimate) of 135,564,000.

The northern States of Amazonas and Pará are mainly wide, low-lying, forest-clad plains. The central states of Mato Grosso are principally plateau land and the eastern and southern States are traversed by successive mountain ranges interspersed with fertile valleys. The principal ranges are *Serra do Mar*, the *Serra da Mantiqueira* and the *Serra do Espinhaco* along the east coast. The River *Amazon* with a total length of some 4,000 miles has tributaries which are themselves great rivers, and flows from the Peruvian Andes to the Atlantic. Its principal northern tributaries are the *Rio Branco, Rio Negro,* and *Japurá*; its southern tributaries are the *Juruá, Purus, Madeira* and *Tapajós,* while the *Xingú* meets it within 200 miles of its outflow into the Atlantic. The *Tocantins* and *Araguaia* flow northwards from Mato Grosso and Goiás to the Gulf of Pará. The *Parnaiba* flows from Piaui into the Atlantic. The *São Francisco* rises in the South of Minas Gerais and flows to the eastern coast. The *Paraguai*, rising in the south-west of Mato Grosso, flows through Paraguay to its confluence with the *Paraná*, which rises in the mountains of that name and divides Brazil from Paraguay.

Government.—Brazil was colonized by Portugal in the early part of the sixteenth century, and in 1822 became an independent empire under Dom Pedro, son of the refugee King Joao VI of Portugal. On Nov. 15, 1889, Dom Pedro II, second of the line, was dethroned and a republic was proclaimed.

The Federative Republic of Brazil is made up of the Federal District, 23 States and 3 Territories (the most under-developed frontier regions). The constitution of January 1967 draws on the same conceptual basis as that of the United States, and envisages an equal distribution of power between the executive, the legislature and the judiciary. Under the existing constitutional provisions the President, who heads the executive, is indirectly elected for a five-year term.

The Congress consists of a Senate (3 Senators per State elected for an 8-year term) and a Chamber of Deputies which is re-elected every 4 years. (The number of Deputies per State depends upon the

State's population). Each State has a Governor, and a Legislative Assembly with a 4-year term.

The Congress has been sitting as the Constituent Assembly since February 1, 1987, in order to rewrite the Constitution. The new Brazilian Constitution will be promulgated after its approval by the Constituent Assembly in 1988.

Production.—There are large and valuable mineral deposits including among others, iron ore (hematite), manganese, bauxite, beryllium, chrome, nickel, tungsten, cassiterite, lead, gold, monazite (containing rare earths and thorium) and zirconium. Diamonds and precious and semi-precious stones are also found. The mineral wealth is being exploited to an increasing extent. The iron ore deposits of Minas Gerais are exceeded by those of the Amazon region, principally in the Carajás areas where deposits are estimated at 35,000 million tonnes. Mining operations began in Feb. 1985.

Electric power production in 1987 was 202,287 Gwh. In the same year, the total output of steel was 22,227 million tonnes. Production of oil was 566,000 b.p.d. Of these 487,000 b.p.d. were produced from offshore fields.

Agriculture production was (tonnes):

	1986	1987
Black Beans	2,221,000	2,019,000
Cassava	25,542,000	23,399,000
Cocoa	459,000	337,000
Coffee	2,007,000	4,220,000
Cotton	2,314,000	1,672,000
Maize	20,510,000	26,787,000
Peanuts	216,000	196,000
Potatoes	1,834,000	2,343,000
Rice	10,399,000	10,422,000
Soya	13,335,000	16,814,000
Tobacco	386,000	398,000
Wheat	5,433,000	5,889,000

Defence.—The peace-time strength of the Army is 192,000. The Navy consists of 1 aircraft carrier, 7 submarines, 10 destroyers, 6 frigates, 9 patrol vessels, 5 river patrol ships, 1 river monitor, 1 river transport, 6 coastal mine sweepers, 7 survey ships, and 29 other vessels. The strength of the Navy is 49,000. The Air Force, with a strength of 45,000, has 680 aircraft, of which 151 are fast-jet.

Education.—Primary education is compulsory and is the responsibility of State governments and municipalities. At this level approximately 10 per cent. attend private schools. Secondary education is largely the responsibility of State and municipal governments, although a small number of very old foundations (the Pedro II Schools) remain under direct federal control. Over 50 per cent. of all pupils at this level attend private schools. Higher education is available in Federal, State, municipal and private universities and faculties.

Language and Literature.—Portuguese is the language of the country, but Italian, Spanish, German, Japanese and Arabic are spoken by immigrant minorities, and newspapers of considerable circulation are produced in those languages. English and French are currently spoken by educated Brazilians.

Public libraries have been established in urban centres and there is a flourishing national press with widely circulated daily and weekly newspapers.

Communications. In 1983 there were 1,552,463 km. of highways. The route-length of railways in 1980 was 35,100 km. Internal air services are highly developed. There are 21,944 miles of navigable inland waterways. During 1982, 9,574 vessels entered Rio de Janeiro and Santos, the two leading ports.

FINANCE

	1986	1987
	Cruzados	
Revenue	394,036 m.	1,203,001 m.
Expenditure	500,178 m.	1,392,120 m.

At Dec. 1987 Brazil's foreign debt stood at U.S.$121,264 million. Reserves in Dec. 1987 were $6,799 million.

TRADE

	1985	1986
Total imports	US$13,168 m.	US$12,866 m.
Total exports	25,639 m.	22,393 m.

Trade with U.K.

	1986	1987
Imports from U.K.	£295,152,000	£347,916,000
Exports to U.K.	552,259,000	636,675,000

Principal imports are fuel and lubricants, machinery, chemicals, wheat, metals and metal manufactures. Principal exports are coffee, iron ore, soya, meat, steel and orange juice. In 1987 the Brazilian automobile industry produced 920,300 vehicles. Of these, 339,900 vehicles were exported.

CAPITAL.—Brasilia (inaugurated on April 21, 1960). Population (1985 estimate), 1,576,657. Other important centres (1980 Census) are São Paulo (8,490,763); the former capital ΨRio de Janeiro (5,094,396); Belo Horizonte (1,774,712); ΨRecife (1,204,794); ΨSalvador (1,017,591); ΨPorto Alegre (1,125,091); ΨFortaleza (1,308,859); and Belem (934,330).

CURRENCY.—Cruzado (CZ$) of 1,000 Cruzeiros.

FLAG.—Green, with yellow lozenge in centre; blue sphere with white band and stars in centre of lozenge.

NATIONAL ANTHEM.—Ouviram do Ipirangas Margens (From peaceful Ypiranga's banks).

NATIONAL DAY.—September 7 (Independence Day).

BRITISH EMBASSY
Setor de Embaixadus Sul, Quadra 801, Conjunto K, 70.408 Brasilia, D.F.
[Brasilia 225–2710]

Ambassador Extraordinary and Plenipotentiary, His Excellency Michael John Newington, C.M.G. (1987).

There are British Consulates-General at Rio de Janeiro and São Paulo.

British Council Representative, J. Lawrence, SCRN 708/9-BLF Nos 1/3 (Caixa Postal 6104), 70,740 Brasilia D.F. Tel. 270–3060. Regional Directors in *Rio de Janeiro, Recife* and *São Paulo*.

BRITISH AND COMMONWEALTH CHAMBER OF COMMERCE IN SÃO PAULO, Rua Barão de Itapetininga 275, 7th Floor, 01042, São Paulo (*Postal Address*, P.O. Box 1621, 01000 Sao Paulo) and Rua Real Grandeza 99, 22281 Rio de Janeiro.

BULGARIA
(Narodna Republika Bulgaria)
COUNCIL OF STATE

Chairman of the Council of State, Todor Zhivkov, elected, July 7, 1971; re-elected, June 1981 and June 1986 (*Head of State*).
First Deputy Chairman, Petur Tanchev.
Deputy Chairmen, Georgi Dzhagarov; Yaroslav Radev.
Secretary, Nikola Manolov.

COUNCIL OF MINISTERS

Chairman (Prime Minister), Georgi Atanasov.
Deputy Chairman, Grigor Stoichkov.
Culture, Science and Education, Georgi Yordanov.
Economy and Planning, Stoyan Ovcharov.
Agriculture and Forests, Aleksi Ivanov.
Foreign Economic Relations, Andrei Lukanov.
Foreign Affairs, Petur Mladenov.
Internal Affairs, Col. Gen. Dimitur Stoyanov.
Justice, Mrs. Svetla Daskalova.
National Defence, Gen. Dobri Dzhurov
Health and Social Welfare, Radoy Popivanov.
Transport, Vasil Tsanov.
Without Portfolio, Georgi Pankov.
Chairman, Committee on State and People's Control, Georgi Georgiev.

THE COMMUNIST PARTY

Politbureau of the Central Committee, T. Zhivkov; P. Kubadinski; G. Filipov; O. Doynov; D. Dzhurov; P. Mladenov; M. Balev; Y. Yotov; G. Atanasov (*full members*); A. Lukanov; G. Yordanov; P. Dyulgerov; G. Stoichkov; D. Stoyanov; S. Markov (*candidate members*).
Secretariat of the Central Committee, Todor Zhivkov (*Secretary General*); D. Stanishev; S. Mikhaylov; M. Balev; V. Tsanov; E. Khristov; Č. Aleksandrov; G. Filipov; Y. Yotov.

BULGARIAN EMBASSY AND CONSULATE IN LONDON
186–188 Queen's Gate Gardens, SW7 5HL
[01–584 9400/9433]

Ambassador Extraordinary and Plenipotentiary, His Excellency Dimitar Zhulev (1987).

The Republic of Bulgaria is bounded on the north by Romania, on the west by Yugoslavia, on the east by the Black Sea, and on the south by Greece and Turkey. The total area is 42,823 sq. miles (110,912 sq. km.), with a population at the Dec. 1985 Census of 8,948,388. The largest religion of the Bulgarians is the Bulgarian Orthodox Church.

A Principality of Bulgaria was created by the *Treaty of Berlin* (July 13, 1878) and in 1885 Eastern Roumelia was added to the newly-created principality. In 1908 the country was declared to be an independent kingdom. In 1912–13 a successful war of the *Balkan League* against Turkey increased the size of the kingdom, but in August, 1913, a short campaign against the remaining members of the League reduced the acquired area, and led to the surrender of Southern Dobrudja to Romania. On Oct. 12, 1915,

Bulgaria entered the War on the side of the Central Powers by declaring war on Serbia. She thus became involved in the defeats of 1918, and on Sept. 29, 1918, made an unconditional surrender to the Allied Powers. On Nov. 29, 1919, she signed the *Treaty of Neuilly*, which ceded to the Allies her Thracian territories (later handed over to Greece) and some territory on the western frontier to Yugoslavia.

Nazi troops entered the country on March 3, 1941, and occupied Black Sea ports, but Bulgaria was not at war with the Soviet Union. On August 26, 1944, the government declared Bulgaria to be "neutral in the Russo-German war" and sought terms of peace from Great Britain and the United States. The Soviet Union refused to recognize the so-called "neutrality" and called upon Bulgaria to declare war against Germany, and no satisfactory reply being received on Sept. 5, 1944, the U.S.S.R. declared war on Bulgaria. Bulgaria then asked for an armistice and on Sept. 7 declared war on Germany, hostilities with U.S.S.R. ending on Sept. 10. The armistice with the Allies was signed in Moscow, Oct. 28, 1944. The Peace Treaty with Bulgaria was signed on Feb. 22, 1947, and came into force on Sept. 15, 1947. It recognized the return of Southern Dobrudja to Bulgaria.

On Sept. 9, 1944 a coup d'état gave power to the Fatherland Front, a coalition of Communists, Agrarians, Social Democrats and officers and intellectuals. In August, 1945, the main body of Agrarians and Social Democrats left the Government. On Sept. 8, 1946, a referendum was held, which led to the abolition of the Monarchy and the setting up of a Republic. On Oct. 27, 1946, a general election to a Grand National Assembly (with power to make a constitution) was held; the Opposition won 101 seats out of 465. The opposition Agrarian Party was suppressed in 1947, but its remnant was later revived as the Agrarian Union which now constitutionally shares power with the Communist Party.

A new Constitution was adopted in 1971 according to which the legislature is a single chamber National Assembly or *Subranie* elected by adult suffrage for a maximum term of 5 years and consisting of 400 deputies representing constituencies of equal size. This Constitution also established the Council of State, being the supreme permanent body of the National Assembly with both legislative and executive functions.

Production.—Until 1939 Bulgaria was a predominantly agricultural country, but has since pursued an elaborate programme of industrialization. About 90 per cent of the country's agriculture has been turned over to co-operatives, and a smaller proportion mechanized. The principal crops are wheat, maize, beet, tomatoes, tobacco, oleaginous seeds, fruit, vegetables and cotton. The livestock includes cattle, sheep, goats, pigs, horses, asses, mules and water buffaloes.

There is now a substantial engineering industry which accounts for about two-thirds of Bulgaria's exports; and considerable production of ferrous and non-ferrous metals. In 1985 production of electricity was 41,621 million kilowatt-hours, of steel 2,926,000 tons and of coal 32,450,000 tons (of which about one-quarter was soft coal).

There are mineral deposits of varying importance. Bulgaria's heavy industry includes the Kremikovtsi Steel Plant near Sofia and the Lenin steel mill at Pernik, the chemical complex at Devnia, the petrochemical plant at Bourgas and various other chemical and metallurgical works situated around the country. The Soviet-designed nuclear power station at Kozlodui has four reactors, each with a capability of producing 800 million kilowatt/hours.

Defence.—Under the Peace Treaty signed between Bulgaria and the Allies, the Bulgarian Army is limited to 55,000 men, but it is believed at present to be at least 152,000 strong.

Education.—Free basic education is compulsory for children from 7 to 15 years inclusive. The Bulgarian educational system was reorganized on Soviet lines in September, 1950, providing kindergartens and educational establishments for primary and secondary education including vocational, technical and other specialized schools for secondary age pupils. There are three Universities (at Sofia, Plovdiv and Veliko Turnovo) and 21 higher educational establishments.

Language and Literature.—Bulgarian is a Southern Slavonic tongue, closely allied to Serbo-Croat and Russian with local admixtures of modern Greek, Albanian and Turkish words. There is a modern literature, chiefly educational and popular. The alphabet is Cyrillic. In 1983 there were 8 daily newspapers in Sofia.

Finance.—Planned budget revenue for 1987 is 20,672,800,000 *leva*, expenditure 20,662,800,000 *leva*.

TRADE

The principal imports are industrial and agricultural machinery, industrial raw materials, machine tools, chemicals, dyestuffs, pharmaceuticals, rubber, paper. The principal exports are non-ferrous metals, electric trucks and motors, pumps, ships, accumulators and machine tools, cereals, tobacco, fruit, vegetables, oil seeds, fats, textiles, eggs, chemicals and oils including attar of roses. In 1986, 79·2 per cent of Bulgaria's foreign trade was within the C.M.E.A., including 59·2 per cent with the Soviet Union.

Trade with U.K.

	1986	1987
Imports from U.K.	£80,504,000	£88,761,000
Exports to U.K.	32,459,000	24,249,000

CAPITAL.—Sofia, Pop. (1985), 1,114,759, at the foot of the Vitosha Range, the capital and commercial centre is on the main railway line to Istanbul, 338 miles from the Black Sea port of ΨVarna (302,211) and 125 miles from Lom (32,121), on the Danube; ΨBourgas (182,549) is also a Black Sea Port. Other important trading and industrial centres are Plovdiv (342,131), Rousse (183,746), Pleven (129,766), Stara Zagora (150,803), Pernik (94,758), Sliven (102,423), Yambol (90,215), Khaskovo (97,763) and Tolbukhin (109,066).

CURRENCY.—Lev of 100 Stotinki.

FLAG.—3 horizontal bands, white, green, red; national emblem on white stripe near hoist.

NATIONAL DAY.—September 9 (Day of Freedom).

BRITISH EMBASSY
Boulevard Marshal Tolbukhin, 65–67, Sofia.
[Sofia 885361/2]

Ambassador Extraordinary and Plenipotentiary, His Excellency John Harold Fawcett C.M.G. (1986).
First Secretaries, M. E. Frost, L.V.O. (*Consul and Head of Chancery*); B. W. Cross (*Commercial*); J. B. Macpherson (*Chancery/Information*).
Cultural Attaché and British Council Representative, P. Lyner.

BURKINA
(**République Démocratique Populaire de Burkina Faso**)

President of the Popular Front and Head of State, Capt. Blaise Compaoré, *assumed office*, October 1987.

COUNCIL OF MINISTERS

Defence and Security, Cmdt. Boukari Jean-Baptiste Lengani.
Economic Promotion, Capt. Henri Zongo.
Foreign Affairs, Jean Marc Palm.
Health and Social Work, Alain Zoubga.
Higher Education, Clement Oumaroo Ouedraogo.
Planning and Co-operation, Issouf Ouedraogo.
National Education, Philippe Some.
Peasants' Affairs, Jean Leonard Compaore.
Information and Culture, Serge Theophile Balima.
Environment and Tourism, Beatrice Damiba.
Trade and Supply, Frederic Konsaga.
Transport and Communications, Issa Konate.
Territorial Administration, Leopold Ouedraogo.
Justice, Salif Sampebogo.
Equipment, Balao Badiel.
Sport, Kilimite Hien.
Labour, Social Security and Public Works, Albert D. Millogo.
Finance, Guy Some.
Agriculture and Livestock, Albert Guigma.
Water, Alfred Nombre.
Secretaries of State, Celestin Tiendrebeogo (*Budget*); Alimata Salembere (*Culture*); Jean Yado Toe (*Mines*); Alice Tiendrebeogo (*Social Work*); Amadou Guia (*Livestock*).
Secretary General, Prosper Vokouma.

Burkina is an inland savanna state in West Africa, situated between 9° and 15°N. and 2°E. and 5°W. with an area of 105,869 sq. miles (274,200 sq. km.), and a population of 8,846,929 (1985 estimate). It has common boundaries with Mali on the west, Niger and Benin on the east and Togo, Ghana and the Côte d'Ivoire on the south. The largest tribe is the Mossi whose king, the Moro Naba, still wields a certain moral influence.

Burkina was annexed by France in 1896 and between 1932 and 1947 was administered as part of the Colony of the Ivory Coast. It decided on December 11, 1958, to remain an autonomous republic within the French Community; full independence outside the Community was proclaimed on August 5, 1960. The official language is French.

The 1960 constitution provided for a presidential form of government with a single chamber National Assembly, but in January, 1966, the Army assumed power. A new constitution allowing for a partial return to civilian rule but with the Army still in effective control was adopted in 1970, but in 1974 this was suspended. Full legislative and presidential elections were held again in 1978. In a military coup in Nov. 1980, Col. Zerbo assumed power. He was overthrown in Nov. 1982 by Maj. Ouedraogo, who was himself overthrown in Aug. 1983 by radical Army officers led by Capt. Sankara. On Oct. 15, 1987 Capt. Sankara was overthrown and killed in a military coup led by his former Minister of Justice, Capt. Blaise Compaoré. The present government is a broad-based coalition (the Popular Front). New constitutional proposals are being considered for 1989.

On 4 Aug. 1984, Upper Volta changed its name to Burkina.

Trade.—The 1988 Budget totalled *Francs CFA* 90,300 million.

The principal industry is the rearing of cattle and sheep and the chief exports are livestock, groundnuts, shea-nuts and cotton. Small deposits of gold, manganese, copper, bauxite and graphite have been found. Trade in 1985 was valued at Imports, *CFA* 95,158 m. Exports, *CFA* 23,065 m.

Trade with U.K.

	1986	1987
Imports from U.K.	£3,104,000	£4,168,000
Exports to U.K.	1,369,000	462,000

CAPITAL.—Ouagadougou (375,001). Other principal towns; Bobo-Dioulasso (211,538) and Kouddougou (52,431).

CURRENCY.—Franc C.F.A. of 100 Centimes.

FLAG.—Equal bands of red over green, with a yellow star in centre.

NATIONAL DAY.—August 4.

BRITISH REPRESENTATION

British Ambassador (resident in Abidjan, Côte d'Ivoire).

BURMA
(Pyidaungsu Socialist Thammada Myanma Naingngandaw)

Government of the Union
(as at June 1988)

*President, San Yu, *elected* Nov. 9, 1981, *re-elected* Nov 4, 1985.

COUNCIL OF MINISTERS

*Prime Minister, Maung Maung Kha.
*Deputy Prime Minister and Planning and Finance, Thura Tun Tin.
Deputy Prime Minister and Defence, Thura Kyaw Htin.
Home and Religious Affairs, Brig. Gen. Pe Myaing.
Agriculture and Forests, Than Nyunt.
Industry I, Tint Swe.
Education, Dr. Kyaw Sein.
Industry II, Maung Cho.
Trade, Khin Maung Gyi.
Co-operatives, Than Hlaing.
Livestock and Fisheries, Maung Maung Win.
Labour and Social Welfare, Ohn Kyaw.
Foreign Affairs, Ye Gaung.
Culture and Information, Aung Kyaw Myint.
Construction, Myint Lwin.
Transport and Communications, Sein Ya.
Health, Tun Wai.
Mines, Than Tin.
Energy, Sein Tun.

* On July 27, Gen. Sein Lwin was elected President and Tun Tin was elected Prime Minister. Following civil disturbances, in which over 1,000 were killed, President Sein Lwin left office and was replaced by Dr. Maung Maung on August 19, 1988.

BURMESE EMBASSY AND CONSULATE
19a Charles St., Berkeley Square, W1X 8ER
[01–499 8841]

Ambassador Extraordinary and Plenipotentiary, His Excellency U Tin Tun (1985).

Area and Population.—Burma forms the western portion of the Indo-Chinese district of the continent of Asia, lying between 9° 58′ and 28° N. latitude and 92° 11′ and 101° 9′ E. longitude, with an extreme length of approximately 1,200 miles and an extreme width of 575 miles. It has a sea coast on the Bay of Bengal to the south and west and a frontier with Bangladesh along the Naaf River (defined in 1964) and India to the north-west (defined in 1967). In the north and east the frontier with China was determined by a treaty with the People's Republic in October, 1960, and has since been demarcated; there is a short frontier with Laos in the east, while the long finger of Tenasserim stretches southward along the west coast of the Malay Peninsula, forming a frontier with Thailand to the east. The total area of the Union is 261,218 sq. miles (676,552 sq. km.), with a population of 37,153,000 (1985 U.N. estimate).

Physical Features.—Burma falls into four natural divisions. Arakan (with the Chin Hills region), the

Irrawaddy basin, Tenasserim, including the Salween basin and extending southwards to the Burma-Thailand peninsula, and the elevated plateau on the east. Mountains enclose Burma on three sides, the highest point being Hka-kabo Razi (19,296 ft.) in the northern Kachin hills. Mt. Popa, 4,981 ft., in the Myingyan district is an extinct volcano and a well-known landmark in Central Burma. The principal river systems are the Kaladan-Lemro in Arakan, the Irrawaddy-Chindwin and the Sittang in Central Burma, and the Salween which flows through the Shan Plateau.

Races, Language and Religions.—The indigenous inhabitants who entered Burma from the north and east are of similar racial types and speak languages of the Tibeto-Burman, Mon-Khmer and Thai groups. The three important non-indigenous elements are Indians, Chinese and those from the former East Pakistan. Burmese is the official language, but minority languages include Shan, Karen, Chin, Kayah and the various Kachin dialects. English is spoken in educated circles. Buddhism is the religion of 85 per cent of the people, with 5 per cent Animists, 4 per cent Moslems, 4 per cent Hindus and less than 3 per cent Christians.

Government.—Burma became an independent republic outside the British Commonwealth on January 4, 1948, and remained a parliamentary democracy for 14 years. On March 2, 1962 the army took power, and suspended the parliamentary Constitution. A Revolutionary Council of senior officers under General Ne Win took measures to create a Socialist State.

In January 1974 a new Constitution was adopted under which the highest authority is the People's Assembly (476 representatives) which meets twice a year. When the Assembly is not in session the Council of State (29 members) is vested with wide powers. The senior executive body is the Council of Ministers. The Chairman of the Council of State is also President of the Socialist Republic of the Union of Burma. The Burmese Socialist Programme Party is the only legal political party. Riots in Burma during the summer of 1988 led to the declaration of martial law on Aug. 3.

Political Divisions.—Burma is comprised of seven States (Chin, Kachin, Karen, Kayah, Mon, Rakhine, Shan) and seven Divisions (Irrawaddy, Magwe, Mandalay, Pegu, Rangoon, Sagaing, Tenasserim).

Education.—The literacy rate is high compared with other Asian countries, there is no caste system and women engage freely in social intercourse and play an important part in agriculture and retail trade.

Most Burmese children attend primary school, and about four million are currently enrolled; in middle and high schools, 11 million. There are two universities, at Rangoon and Mandalay, and in 1986–87 the numbers graduating were 9,981. A number of autonomous institutes of university standard award their own degrees. Under the two universities are three affiliated Degree Colleges and the Workers' College, Rangoon. There are also 14 two-year colleges affiliated to the universities, spread throughout the country.

There are three Teachers' Training Institutes for middle and primary schools, and 13 Teachers' Training Schools for primary only. Seven Government Technical Institutes offer post-secondary technical training courses and 14 Technical High Schools train semi-skilled tradesmen. Six Agricultural Institutes offer training courses in agriculture and veterinary science; nine Agricultural High Schools train semi-skilled agriculturists. There are 34 Vocational Schools for weaving, handicrafts, etc.

Finance.—The chief sources of revenue are profits on state trading, income-tax, customs duties, commercial taxes and excise duties; the chief heads of expenditure are general administration, defence, education, police and development. The budget estimates for 1987–88 were: Revenue, *K*45,421,000,000; Expenditure, *K*63,226,000,000.

Production, Industry and Commerce.—Three-quarters of the population depend on agriculture; the chief products are rice, oilseeds (sesamum and groundnut), maize, millet, cotton, beans, wheat, grain, tea, sugarcane, Virginia and Burmese tobacco, jute and rubber. Rice has traditionally been the mainstay of Burma's economy and the quantity of rice and by-products available for export was 900,000 tons in 1986–87. The principal export after rice is teak, of which 190,000 cubic tons was exported in 1986–87.

Burma is rich in minerals, including petroleum, lead, silver, tungsten, zinc, tin, wolfram and gemstones. Of these, petroleum products are the most important. Oil is now being produced from oilfields in Myanaung, Prome and Shwepyitha and at Chauk, Yenangyaung, Mann, and Letpando. Production of crude oil in 1986–87 totalled 10,103,000 U.S. barrels. There is a refinery at the main oilfield, Chauk, another at Syriam near Rangoon and a third is being built at Mann. There has been a slight decline in Burma's oil production in recent years and the country is no longer self-sufficient. Onshore exploration continues. There has also been some offshore oil exploration on a small scale. Major reserves of natural gas have been discovered in the Martaban Gulf, which Burma is hoping to develop.

All industrial activity of any size is in the public sector. Under development plans, projects completed or under construction with overseas financial and technical assistance include the production of cement, bricks and tiles, sheet glass, steel sections, jute bags and twine, cotton yarns, cotton and cotton mixture cloth, pharmaceuticals, sugar, paper, plywood, urea fertilizers, soda ash, tractors and tyres; also a hydro-electric scheme and various irrigation works. Japan continues to be the major individual donor of soft loans and grant aid in the industrial and agricultural sectors. West Germany has also been an important contributor of soft loans.

Loans amounting to US $450 million have been extended by the World Bank. As a member of the Colombo Plan since 1952 Burma continues to receive technical assistance from a number of countries and international agencies. Faced with a serious foreign exchange shortage, Burma has applied for Least Developed Country status (LLDC) at the U.N.

Trade with U.K.

	1986	1987
Imports from U.K.	£10,835,000	£24,715,000
Exports to U.K.	6,092,000	3,826,000

Communications.—The Irrawaddy and its chief tributary, the Chindwin, form important waterways, the main stream being navigable beyond Bhamo (900 miles from its mouth) and carrying much traffic.

The chief seaports are Rangoon, Moulmein, Akyab and Bassein.

The Burma Railways network covers 2,764 route miles, extending to Myitkyina, on the Upper Irrawaddy. There were 2,452 miles of Union highways and 11,767 miles of other main roads in 1982–83. The airport at Mingaladon, about 13 miles north of Rangoon, only handles limited international air traffic.

CAPITAL.—The chief city of Lower Burma, and the seat of the government of the Union is ΨRangoon, on the left bank of the Rangoon river, about 21 miles from the sea. The city contains the Shwe Dagon pagoda, much venerated by Burmese Buddhists. Population (1983): Rangoon District, 3,973,872; city population, 2,458,712.

Mandalay is the chief city of Upper Burma, population (1983): Mandalay district, 4,580,923; city, 532,985; Moulmein of 219,991 and Bassein of 144,092. Pagan, on the Irrawaddy, S.W. of Mandalay, contains many sacred buildings.

CURRENCY.—Kyat of 100 Pyas.

FLAG.—The Union flag is red, with a canton of dark blue, inside which are a cogwheel and two rice ears surrounded by 14 white stars.

NATIONAL DAY.—January 4.

BRITISH EMBASSY
80 Strand Road (Box No. 638), Rangoon
[Rangoon 81700]

Ambassador Extraordinary and Plenipotentiary, His Excellency Martin Robert Morland C.M.G. (1986).

First Secretaries, D. G. Alexander, M.B.E. (*Head of Chancery and Consul*); F. A. Wilson, M.B.E. (*Commercial*).

Cultural Attaché and British Council Representative, T. C. White, M.B.E.

BURUNDI
(République de Burundi)

President, Major Pierre Buyoya, *elected* Sept. 9, 1987, *sworn in* Oct. 2, 1987.

COUNCIL OF MINISTERS

Defence, The President.
Foreign Affairs and Co-operation, Cyprien Mbonimpa.
Agriculture and Livestock, Jumaine Hussein.
Finance, Pierre Binoba.
Rural Development, Gabriel Toyi.
Justice, Evariste Niyonkuru.
Interior, Lt.-Col. Aloys Kadoyi.
Commerce and Industry, Bonaventure Kidwingira.
National Education, Lt. Col. Jean-Claude Ndiyo.
Transport, Posts and Telecommunications, Maj. Simon Rusuka.
Public Works and Urban Development, Evariste Simbarakiye.
Energy and Mines, Victor Ciza.
Public Health, Tharcisse Nyunguka.
Civil Service, Charles Karikurubu.
Employment and Professional Training, Gamaliel Ndaruzaniye.
Family and Women's Affairs, Dorothée Cishahayo.
Social Affairs, Pia Ndayiragije.
Information, Frederick Ngenzebuhoro.
Youth, Sport and Culture, Adolphe Nahayo.

Formerly a Belgian trusteeship under the United Nations, Burundi was proclaimed an independent State on July 1, 1962. Situated on the east side of Lake Tanganyika, the State has an area of 10,747 sq. miles (27,834 sq. km.) and a population (1985 U.N. estimate) of 4,718,000. The majority of the population are of the Bahutu ethnic group, but power rests in the hands of the minority Batutsi ethnic group.

Burundi became independent as a constitutional monarchy but this was overthrown on November 28, 1966 and the country became a republic. On Nov. 1, 1976, the government of President Micombero was overthrown and a Supreme Revolutionary Council led by Col. Jean-Baptiste Bagaza took power. In 1980 the S.R.C. was replaced by a political bureau and central committee as part of a process of political normalization, which continued with elections to the National Assembly, a 65-member legislature. On Sept. 3, 1987 the government of President Bagaza was overthrown by a Military Committee of National Redemption led by Major Pierre Buyoya.

The chief crop is coffee, representing about 80 per cent of Burundi's export earnings. Cotton is the second most important crop. Minerals, tea, hides and skins exports are also important.

Trade with U.K.

	1986	1987
Imports from U.K.	£2,324,000	£2,867,000
Exports to U.K.	3,074,000	1,330,000

CAPITAL.—Bujumbura (*formerly* Usumbura), with about 150,000 inhabitants. Kitega (18,000 inhabitants) is the only other sizeable town. Official languages are Kirundi, a Bantu language, and French. Kiswahili is also used.

CURRENCY.—Burundi Franc of 100 Centimes.

FLAG.—White diagonal cross on green and red quarters, with a circular white panel in the centre.

NATIONAL DAY.—July 1.

British Ambassador (*see* Kinshasa, Zaire).

CAMEROON
(République Unie du Cameroun)

President, Head of State, Government and Commander in Chief of the Armed Forces, His Excellency Paul Biya, *acceded* Nov. 6, 1982, *elected* Jan. 14, 1984, *re-elected* April 24, 1988, *sworn in* May 13, 1988.

MINISTRY

At the Presidency, Paul Tessa (*Secretary General*); Emmanuel Zoa Oloa, Laurent Esso (*Asst. Secretary Generals*); Prof. Titus Edzoa (*Special Adviser*); Adolphe Moudiki (*Dir. of Civil Cabinet*); Jean Baptiste Baskouda (*Asst. Dir. of Civil Cabinet*).

Ministers:
Defence, Michel Meva'A M'Eboutou.
Territorial Administration, Ibrahim Mbombo Njoya.
Women's Affairs and Social Welfare, Aissatou Yaou.
Agriculture, John Niba Ngu.
Special Functions at the Presidency, Ogork Ebot Ntui.
Industrial and Commercial Development, Joseph Tsanga Abanda.
National Education, Prof. Georges Ngango.
Animal Husbandry, Fisheries and Animal Industries, Hamadjoda Abjoudji.
Higher Education, Scientific Research and Computer Services, Abdoulaye Babale.
Finance, Sadou Hayatou.
Public Service and State Control, Prof. Joseph Owono.
Information and Culture, Henri Bandolo.
Youth and Sports, Dr. Joseph Fofe.
Justice, Benjamin Itoe.
Mines, Water and Energy, Francis Wainchom Nkwain.
Planning and Territorial Development, Elisabeth Tankeu.
Posts and Telecommunications, Sanda Oumarou.
External Relations, Jacques Roger Booh Booh.
Public Health, Prof. Joseph Mbedi.
Public Works and Transport, Claude Tchepannou.
Labour and Social Insurance, Jean Baptiste Bokam.
Town Planning and Housing, Ferdinand Leopold Oyono.

CAMEROON EMBASSY
84 Holland Park, W11 3SB
[01–727 0771]

Ambassador Extraordinary and Plenipotentiary, His Excellency Dr. Gibering Bol-Alima (1987).

The Republic of Cameroon lies on the Gulf of Guinea between Nigeria to the west, Chad and the Central African Republic to the east and Congo and Gabon and Equatorial Guinea to the south. It has an area of 183,569 sq. miles, (475,442 sq. km.) and a population of 10,106,000 (1985 U.N. estimate).

The whole territory was administered by Germany from 1884 to 1916. From 1916 to 1959, the former East Cameroon was administered by France as a League of Nations (later U.N.) trusteeship. On Jan. 1, 1960 it became independent as the Republic of Cameroon. The Republic was joined on October 1, 1961, by the former British administered trust territory of the Southern Cameroons, after a plebiscite held under United Nations auspices. Cameroon became a Federal Republic with separate East and West Cameroon state governments. Subsequently, after plebiscite held in May, 1972, Cameroon became a United Republic.

Cameroon is the only country in Africa where French and English are both official languages enjoying equal status, and the government's declared long-term objective is to achieve complete "bilingualism" and "biculturalism".

The main economic emphasis is on agricultural development, both through encouraging small-scale peasant agriculture, and through the development of large-scale agro-industrial complexes, with the aim of making the country agriculturally self-sufficient and a major food exporter.

Principal products are cocoa, coffee, bananas, cotton, timber, ground-nuts, aluminium, rubber and palm products. There is an aluminium smelting plant at Edéa with an annual capacity of 50,000 tons. Oil is now also one of Cameroon's principal products with an estimated production of 9·2m. tonnes during 1984-5.

TRADE

	1985	1986
	FCFA million	
Total imports	£508,756	£590,439
Total exports	321,751	£271,639

Trade with U.K.

	1986	1987
Imports from U.K.	£34,368,000	£28,057,000
Exports to U.K.	7,634,000	14,201,000

CAPITAL.—Yaoundé (1984 estimate, 522,000). ΨDouala (1984 estimate, 763,000) is the commercial centre.

CURRENCY.—Franc C.F.A. of 100 Centimes.

FLAG.—Vertical stripes of green, red and yellow with single five-pointed yellow star in centre of red stripe.

NATIONAL ANTHEM.—O Cameroun, Berceau de Nos Ancêtres (O Cameroon, cradle of our forefathers).

NATIONAL DAY.—May 20.

BRITISH EMBASSY
Avenue Winston Churchill, B.P. 547
Yaoundé
[Yaoundé 220545]

Ambassador Extraordinary and Plenipotentiary, His Excellency Martin Reith (1987).
First Secretary, R. P. Osborne (Head of Chancery and Consul).
Second Secretaries, R. O. Arrowsmith; W. N. C. Paterson (Commercial/Aid); R. W. Hyde, M.B.E. (Administration and Vice Consul).
British Council Representative, P. Ellwood, Les Galéries, Avenue J. F. Kennedy, (B.P. 818), Yaoundé. Tel. 223172.

CAPE VERDE ISLANDS
(República de Cabo Verde)

President, Aristides Pereira born 1924, assumed office, July 5, 1975, re-elected, Jan. 13, 1986.

COUNCIL OF MINISTERS

Prime Minister, Minister of Co-operation and Planning, and Minister for Finance, M. Pedro Pires.
Justice, Dr. José E. F. Araujo.
Foreign Affairs, Col. Silvino M. Da Luz.
Civil Aeronatics, Tourism and Communications, Maj. Osvaldo L. da Silva.
Armed Forces and Security, Maj. Julio de Carvalho.
Agriculture and Fisheries, Maj. João P. Silva.
Education, André C. Tolentino.
Local Government and Town Planning, Tito L. S. de O. Ramos.
Information, Culture and Sport, Dr. David H. Almada.
Health, Labour and Social Services, Dr. Irineu Gomes.
Industry and Energy, Adão Rocha.
Public Works, Adriano de O. Lima.

The Cape Verde Islands, off the west coast of Africa, consist of two groups of islands, Windward (Santo Antão, São Vicente, Santa Luzia, São Nicolau, Boa Vista and Sal) and Leeward (Maio, São Tiago, Fogo and Brava) with a total area of 1,557 sq. miles, (4,033 sq. km.). The population (1985 U.N. estimate) was 326,000, the majority of whom are Roman Catholic.

The Islands, colonized in c. 1460, achieved independence from Portugal on July 5, 1975, under the nationalist party of Guinea Bissau and Cape Verde. A federation of the islands with Guinea Bissau was planned (till 1879 Guinea-Bissau and the Islands were a single administrative unit) but this was dropped following the 1980 coup in Guinea Bissau.

The Republic is a one-party (the P.A.I.C.V.) state with a President elected by the National Assembly. He has a mandate of 5 years, as do Assembly deputies, who are elected by universal adult suffrage.

The islands have had little rain since 1969, and agriculture is mostly confined to irrigated inland valleys, the chief products being bananas and coffee (for export), maize, sugarcane and nuts. Fish and shellfish are important exports. Salt is obtained on Sal, Boa Vista and Maio; volcanic rock is also mined for export. The main ports are Praia and Mindelo, and there is an international airport on Sal.

Trade with U.K.

	1986	1987
Imports from U.K.	£1,618,000	£1,207,526
Exports to U.K.	426,000	300,905

CAPITAL, ΨPraia (1980, 57,748).
CURRENCY.—Escudo Caboverdiano of 100 Centavos.
FLAG.—Horizontal band of yellow over green, with a vertical red band in the hoist charged with a black star over a garland of maize sheaves, two corn cobs and a clam shell.
NATIONAL DAY.—July 5. (Independence Day).
British Ambassador (resident at Dakar, Senegal.)

CENTRAL AFRICAN REPUBLIC
(République Centrafricaine)

Head of State, Gen. Andre Kolingba, assumed office Sept. 1, 1981, re-elected Nov. 21, 1986.

COUNCIL OF MINISTERS

President, Prime Minister, Minister of Defence, Gen. André Kolingba.
Economy, Finance, Planning and International Co-operation, Dieudonné Wazoua.
Foreign Affairs, Jean-Louis Psimhis.
Rural Development, Theodore Bagua-Yambo.
Public Health and Social Affairs, Jean Willybiro-Sako.

Interior and Territorial Administration, Christophe Grelombe.
Justice, Michel Gbezera-Eria.
Public Works and Territorial Planning, Jacques Kithe.
Education, Pierre Samy-Mackfoy.
Post Office and Telecommunications, Thomas Mapouka.
Transport and Civil Aviation, Pierre Gonifei Gaibonanou.
Trade and Industry, and Small and Medium Enterprises, Thimothée Marboua.
Civil Service, Labour, Social Security and Professional Training, Daniel Sehoulia.
Tourism, Water, Forests, Hunting and Fishing, Raymond Mbetikon.
Energy, Mines and Hydraulics, Michel Salle.
Information, Arts and Culture, David N'Guindo.

The Republic lies just north of the Equator between the Cameroon Republic, the Republic of Chad, the southern part of Sudan and Zaire. The Republic has an area of 240,535 sq. miles, (622,984 sq. km.), and a population (1985 U.N. estimate) of 2,608,000.

On December 1, 1958, the French colony of Ubanghi Shari elected to remain within the French Community and adopted the title of the Central African Republic. It became fully independent on August 17, 1960. The first President of the Central African Republic, M. David Dacko, held office from 1960 until Jan. 1, 1966, when he was replaced by the then Col. Bokassa after a coup d'état. On Dec. 4, 1976, President Bokassa proclaimed himself Emperor and a new constitution (Parliamentary Monarchy) was introduced, the country being known as the Central African Empire. On Sept. 20, 1979, Emperor Bokassa was deposed by M. David Dacko in a bloodless coup and the country reverted to a Republic. President Dacko surrendered power on 1st September 1981 to army commander Gen. Andre Kolingba in a bloodless coup. On Sept. 21, 1985 President Kolingba dissolved the Military Committee for National Recovery (C.M.R.N.) and appointed a civilian-dominated cabinet. Moves towards democratization have been made and on Nov. 21, 1986, a referendum was held whereby voters approved a new Constitution and the establishment of a one-party state. Legislative elections are to be held in the near future.

Economy.—A programme of economic reconstruction is under way, concentrating on agricultural production and private investment. Cotton, diamonds, coffee and timber are the major exports.

Trade with U.K.

	1986	1987
Imports from U.K.	£787,000	£1,127,000
Exports to U.K.	1,452,000	233,000

CAPITAL.—Bangui, near the border with Zaire, 473,817 (1984 est.).
CURRENCY.—Franc C.F.A. of 100 Centimes.
FLAG.—Four horizontal stripes, blue, white, green, yellow, crossed by central vertical red stripe with a yellow five-pointed star in top left-hand corner.
NATIONAL DAY.—December 1.
British Ambassador, (resident at Yaoundé, Cameroon).

CHAD REPUBLIC
(Republique du Tchad)

Head of State, Hissène Habré, *took office* June 1982.

COUNCIL OF MINISTERS

President and Minister of Defence, Veterans and War Victims, Hissène Habré.

Minister of State, Djidingar Dono Ngardoum.
Foreign Affairs and Co-operation, Goura Lassou.
Interior, and Administrative Reform, Ibrahim Mahamat Itno.
Justice, Kassire Delwa Coumakoye.
National Education, Mahamat Senoussir.
Finance and Data Processing, Mbailem Bana Ngarnyal.
Transport and Civil Aviation, Djibril Negue Djogo.
Civil Service, Oudalbaye Naham.
Livestock and Water Resources, Ibn Oumar Mahamat Salet.
Agriculture and Rural Development, Yoyama Baniara.
Mines and Energy, Mohammed Senoussi Khatir.
Public Health, Alphonse Kotiga Guerina.
Public Works, Housing & Town Planning, Abdoulaye Douto.
Social Affairs & Womens' Advancement, Mme. Yomite Romba.
Labour, Employment and Vocational Training, Capt. Rotouang Yoma Galom.
Food, Security and Disaster Relief, Seid Bauche.
Post and Telecommunications, Assilec Halata.
Tourism and Environment, M'Bailaou Naimbaye Lossimian.
Planning (Minister Delegate at the Presidency), Mahamat Soumaila.
Culture, Youth and Sport, Djibrine Grinky,
Trade and Industry, Haroun Abdoulaye.
Presidential Advisor, Ouang Monching Homsala.

Situated in north-central Africa, the Chad Republic extends from 23° N. latitude to 7° N. latitude and is flanked by the Republics of Niger and Cameroon on the west, by Libya in the north, by the Sudan on the east and by the Central African Republic on the south. It has an area of 495,755 sq. miles, (1,284,000 sq. km.) and a population (1985 U.N. estimate) of 5,018,000.

Chad became a member state of the French Community on Nov. 28, 1958, and was proclaimed fully independent on August 11, 1960. On April 14, 1962, a new Constitution was adopted involving a presidential-type regime. This was suspended on April 13, 1975 when President Tombalbaye was killed in a military coup. The country was run by a Supreme Military Council, under General Felix Malloum until his overthrow in February 1979. A Transitional Government of National Unity, headed by Goukouni Oueddei, was replaced in June 1982 by the government of Hissène Habre. A ceasefire between Chad and Libya was agreed in Sept. 1987. In May 1988, Libya's Col. Gadaffi formally recognized the government of Habre and offered to help in the reconstruction of northern Chad.

About 90 per cent of the workforce is occupied in agriculture, fishing and forestry. There is an oilfield in Kanem and salt is mined around Lake Chad, but the most important activities are cotton growing (mostly in the south) and animal husbandry (in central areas). Raw cotton and meat are the main exports.

Trade with U.K.

	1986	1987
Imports from U.K	£1,250,000	£1,006,000
Exports to U.K.	2,806,000	1,101,000

CAPITAL.—Ndjaména (formerly known as Fort Lamy) south of Lake Chad (402,000).
CURRENCY.—Franc C.F.A. of 100 Centimes.
FLAG.—Vertical stripes, blue, yellow and red.
NATIONAL DAY.— April 13.
British Ambassador (resident in London).

CHILE
(República de Chile)

Head of State, Army Commander-in-Chief and President of the Republic, General Augusto Pinochet (Ugarte), *born*, November 25, 1915.
Junta Members, Adm. José T. Merino, C.-in-C. Navy; Gen. Fernando Matthei, C.-in-C. Air Force; Gen. Rodolfo Stange, Dir.-Gen. of Carabineros; Lt.-Gen. Humberto Gordon (Army).

CABINET
(as at June 30, 1988)

Foreign Affairs, Ricardo García.
Interior, Sergio Fernández.
Defence, Vice Adm. Patricio Carvajal.
Education, Juan Antonio Guzman.
Mines, Samuel Lira.
Finance, Hernán Büchi.
Justice, Hugo Rosende.
Public Works, Brig.-Gen. Bruno Siebert.
Transport, Gen. Jorge Massa.
Agriculture, Jorge Prado Aranguiz.
National Patrimony, Gen. Jorge Veloso.
Labour and Social Security, Alfonso Márquez de la Plata.
Health, Juan Giaconi.
Housing, Miguel Angel Poduje.
Economy, Manuel Concha.
Planning, Gen. Sergio Valenzuela.
Energy, Gen. Hernan Brady.
Secretary General of the Government, Orlando Poblete.

CHILEAN EMBASSY AND CONSULATE IN LONDON
12 Devonshire Street, W1N 2FS
[01–580 6392/4]

Ambassador Extraordinary and Plenipotentiary, His Excellency Juan Carlos Delano (1987).

A State of South America lying between the Andes and the shores of the South Pacific, Chile extends coastwise from just north of Arica to Cape Horn south, between lat. 17° 15′ and 55° 59′ S. and long. 66° 30′ and 75° 48′ W. Extreme length of the country is about 2,800 miles, with an average breadth, north of 41°, of 100 miles. The great chain of the Andes runs along its eastern limit, with a general elevation of 5,000 to 15,000 feet above the level of the sea; but numerous summits attain a greater height. The chain, however, lowers considerably towards its southern extremity. The Andes form a boundary with Argentina, and at the head of the pass where the international road from Chile to Argentina crosses the frontier, has been erected a statue of *Christ the Redeemer*, 26 feet high, made of bronze from old cannon, to commemorate the peaceful settlement of a boundary dispute in 1902. There are no rivers of great size, and none of them is of much service as a navigable highway. In the north the country is arid. The total area of the Republic is 292,258 sq. miles, (756,945 sq. km.), with a population (1985 U.N. estimate) of 12,074,000.

Among the island possessions of Chile are the *Juan Fernandez group* (3 islands) about 360 miles distant from Valparaiso. One of these islands is the reputed scene of Alexander Selkirk's (Robinson Crusoe) shipwreck. *Easter Island* (27° 8′ S. and 109° 28′ W.), about 2,000 miles distant in the South Pacific Ocean, contains stone platforms and hundreds of stone figures, the origin of which has not yet been determined. The area of the island is about 45 sq. miles, (116·5 sq. km.).

Chile is divided into 12 regions and the Metropolitan Area. The disputed boundary with Argentina in the Beagle Channel was settled by a treaty ratified in May 1985.

The Chilean population has four main sources: (*a*) indigenous Araucanian Indians, Fuegians, and Changos; (*b*) Spanish settlers and their descendants; (*c*) mixed Spanish Indians; and (*d*) European immigrants. Only the few remaining indigenous Indians and some originally Bolivian Indians in the north are racially separate. Following extensive intermarriage there is no effective distinction among the remainder.

Government.—Chile was discovered by Spanish adventurers in the 16th century and remained under Spanish rule until 1810, when a revolutionary war, culminating in the Battle of Maipu (April 5, 1818), achieved the independence of the nation.

At a general election held on Sept. 4, 1970, the Marxist candidate Dr. Allende was elected President by a narrow margin. After severe industrial unrest and widespread violent incidents, Allende was overthrown on September 11, 1973, in a coup carried out by leaders of the Armed Forces and National Police. President Allende was said to have committed suicide.

After a national plebiscite, the Constitution of 1925 was replaced early in 1981 and Gen. Pinochet was sworn in as President, to serve until 1989. Economically, the regime is pursuing a free-market economy and the level of inflation has been reduced, from 1,000 per cent in 1973 to about 20 per cent in 1987.

Production.—Cereals, legumes, sugar beet, vegetables, fruit, tobacco, hemp and vines are grown extensively (especially in the central zone) and livestock accounts for nearly 40 per cent of agricultural production. Sheep farming predominates in the extreme south (Province of Magallanes). There are large timber tracts in the central and southern zones of Chile, some types of which are exported, along with wood derivatives such as cellulose and pulp. Industrial-scale fishing, which exceeds 5·5 million tonnes p.a., makes Chile the third largest nation in terms of catch. The principal end product is fish meal.

The mineral wealth is considerable, the country being particularly rich in copper-ore, iron-ore and nitrate. Chile also produces iodine, manganese ore, coal, mercury, molybdenum, zinc, lead and a small quantity of gold. Uranium is also said to have been discovered in small quantities. The rainless north is the scene of the only commercial production of nitrate of soda (Chile saltpetre) from natural resources in the world. The country has also large deposits of high grade sulphur, but mostly around high extinct volcanoes in the Andes Cordillera, difficult of access. Oil was struck in Magallanes (Tierra del Fuego) in December, 1945, and oil and natural gas are produced in the Magallanes area from on- and off-shore wells. This domestic production, despite declining, covers approximately 50 per cent of total oil requirement, and imported crude oil is refined at Concon and San Vicente in the central part of the country. There is a steel plant at Huachipato, near Concepción.

Production figures for 1987 were:

Copper (tonnes)	1,398,263
Potassium and sodium nitrate (tonnes)	795,268
Coal (tonnes)	1,515,604
Steel ingots (tonnes)	744,468
Crude oil (cu. metres)	1,736,500
Natural gas (cu. metres)	4,352,600,000

Industry is based on the processing of mineral, forestry, fish and agricultural products, and the manufacture of consumer goods.

Communications.—Chilean ships have a virtual monopoly in the coastwide trade, though, with the improvement of the roads, an increasing share of internal transportation is moving by road and rail. The Chilean mercantile marine numbers 57 vessels (of over 100 tons gross) with a total deadweight tonnage of 1,125,200 (1987).

There are 6,575 miles of railway track. A metre-gauge line (the *Longitudinál*) runs from La Calera, just north of Santiago, to Iquique: however, road transport has caused a reduction in rail traffic along this route. The wide gauge railway runs from Valparaiso through La Calera, 60 miles inland, and after passing through Santiago ends at Puerto Montt.

With the completion of a section of 435 miles from Corumba, Brazil, to Santa Cruz, Bolivia, the Trans-Continental Line will link the Chilean Pacific port of Arica with Rio de Janeiro on the Atlantic. Another line from Antofagasta to Salta (Argentine) was opened in 1948. Further south, the Trans-Andine Railway connects Valparaiso on the Pacific with Buenos Aires, crossing the Andes at 11,500 ft. However services have now been suspended due to financial difficulties.

Chile is served by about 20 international airlines. The domestic traffic is carried by the State-owned Linea Aerea Nacional and the privately-owned LADECO, which also operate internationally, and smaller regional carriers.

Chile's road system is about 65,000 kilometres in length, but only an estimated 7,000 kilometres are first-class paved highways.

Defence.—Military service is compulsory, but not all those who are liable are required. Recruitment for the Navy is mostly voluntary, but there are some conscripts. The Navy consists of 1 cruiser, 10 destroyers, frigates and escorts, 6 patrol vessels and FPBs and 4 submarines. There is a support force of transports, tankers, 1 submarine depot ship and ancillary small craft. The strength of the Navy is 28,000 (3,000 conscripts) including men of the Marine Force. The Army's total strength is 53,000, which includes 3,000 officers and 30,000 conscripts (2 years). In addition there is a police force of "Carabineros" of 28,000 officers and men. The Air Force total strength is 15,000 with a strength of 120 aircraft.

Education.—Elementary education is free, and has been compulsory since 1920. There are 8 Universities (3 in Santiago, 2 in Valparaiso, 1 in Antofagasta, 1 in Concepción and 1 in Valdivia). The religion is Roman Catholic.

Language and Literature.—Spanish is the language of the country, with admixtures of local words of Indian origin. Recent efforts have reduced illiteracy and have thus afforded access to the literature of Spain, to supplement the vigorous national output. The Nobel Prize for Literature was awarded in 1945 to Señorita Gabriela Mistral, for Chilean verse and prose, and in 1971 to the poet Pablo Neruda. There are over 100 newspapers and a large number of periodicals.

FINANCE

	1986
Total revenue..................	US$3,841·4 m.
Total expenditure	4,232·0 m.

Foreign debt at December 31, 1987 was provisionally quoted at U.S. $19,100 million.

EXTERNAL TRADE
($U.S. ,000)

	1986	1987
Total imports	3,156,900	4,023,300
Total exports	4,222,400	5,101,900

Trade with U.K.

	1986	1987
Imports from U.K........	£67,459,000	£105,838,000
Exports to U.K.	128,007,000	112,843,000

The principal exports are metallic and non-metallic minerals (copper represented 41 per cent. of total export earnings in 1987), sawn timber, cellulose and other wood derivatives, some metal products, fish products, vegetables, fruit and wool. The principal imports are sugar and other food products, industrial raw materials, machinery, equipment and spares, oil fuels, lubricants and transportation equipment.

CAPITAL, Santiago, 4,132,293 (Greater Santiago), Other large towns are:—ΨValparaiso (500,000), Concepción (170,000), Temuco (110,000), ΨAntofagasta (110,000), Chillán (79,461), ΨTalcahuano (75,643), Talca (75,354); ΨValdivia (70,000), ΨIquique (50,000), ΨPunta Arenas (50,000). Punta Arenas on the Straits of Magellan, is the southernmost city in the world.

CURRENCY.—Chilean Peso of 100 Centavos.

FLAG.—Two horizontal bands, white, red; in top sixth a white star on blue square, next staff.

NATIONAL ANTHEM.—Canción Nacional de Chile.

NATIONAL DAY.—September 18 (National Anniversary).

BRITISH EMBASSY
Avenida La Concepción 177, Santiago 9
(Casilla 72-D)
[Santiago 2239166]

Ambassador Extraordinary and Plenipotentiary, His Excellency Alan White, C.M.G., O.B.E. (1987).
Counsellor, Head of Chancery and Consul-General, G. M. Baker.
Defence Attaché, Capt. T. Leland, R.N.

BRITISH CONSULAR OFFICES

There are British Consular Offices at *Santiago, Arica, Valparaiso* and *Punta Arenas.*

BRITISH COUNCIL

Cultural Attaché and British Council Representative, W. Campbell, Eliodoro Yañez 832, Santiago (Casilla 15-T). The Council supplies books to the libraries of the *Instituto Chileno-Britanico* in *Santiago, Viña del Mar/Valparaiso* and *Concepción.*

BRITISH-CHILEAN CHAMBER OF COMMERCE
Luis Thayer Ojeda 0115 O.F. 3021 Santiago
(*Postal Address*, Casilla 536, Santiago).

CHINA
(Zhonghua Renmin Gongheguo—
The People's Republic of China.)

President of the People's Republic of China, Yang Shangkun, *elected* April 1988.
Vice President, Wang Zhen.
Chairman of the Standing Committee of the Seventh National People's Congress, Wan Li.
Chairman of the Central Military Commission, Deng Xiaoping.

STATE COUNCIL

Premier, Li Peng.
Vice-Premiers, Yao Yilin; Tian Jiyun; Wu Xueqian.
State Councillors, Li Tieying; Qin Jiwei; Wang Bingqian; Song Jian; Wang Fang; Zou Jiahua; Li Guixian; Chen Xitong; Chen Junsheng.

Ministers:
Aeronautics and Astronautics Industry, Lin Zongtang.
Agriculture, He Kang.
Chemical Industry, Qin Zhongda.
Civil Affairs, Cui Naifu.
Commerce, Hu Ping.
Communications, Qian Yongchang.
Construction, Lin Hanxiong.
Culture, Wang Meng.
Energy Resources, Huang Yicheng.

Finance, Wang Bingqian.
Foreign Affairs, Qian Qichen.
Foreign Economic Relations and Trade, Zheng Tuobin.
Forestry, Gao Dezhan.
Geology and Mineral Resources, Zhu Xun.
Justice, Cai Cheng.
Labour, Luo Gan.
Light Industry, Zeng Xianlin.
Machine Building and Electronics Industry, Zou Jiahua.
Metallurgical Industry, Qi Yuanjing.
National Defence, Qin Jiwei.
Personnel, Zhao Dongwan.
Posts and Telecommunications, Yang Taifang.
Public Health, Chen Minzhang.
Public Security, Wang Fang.
Radio, Film and Television, Ai Zhisheng.
Railways, Li Senmao.
State Security, Jia Chunwang.
Supervision, Wei Jianxing.
Textile Industry, Wu Wenying.
Water Resources, Yang Zhenhuai.

MINISTERS IN CHARGE OF STATE COMMISSIONS

Education, Li Tieying.
Family Planning, Peng Peiyun.
Nationalities Affairs, Ismail Amat.
Physical Culture and Sports, Li Menghua.
Planning, Yao Yiling.
Restructuring Economy, Li Peng.
Science, Technology and Industry for National Defence, Ding Henggao.
Science and Technology, Song Jian.
Auditor General, Lu Peijian.
Secretary General, Chen Junsheng.

President of the People's Bank of China, Li Guixian.

THE CHINESE COMMUNIST PARTY

General Secretary, Zhao Ziyang.
The Politburo Standing Committee, Zhao Ziyang; Li Peng; Qiao Shi; Hu Qili; Yao Yilin.
The Politburo of the Central Committee, Wan Li; Tian Jiyun; Qiao Shi; Jiang Zemin; Li Tieying; Li Ruihuan; Li Ximing; Yang Rudai; Yang Shangkun; Wu Xueqian; Song Ping; Zhao Ziyang; Hu Qili; Hu Yaobang; Yao Yilin; Qin Jiwei; Li Peng (*full members*); Ding Guangen (*alternate member*).
The Secretariat of the Central Committee, Hu Qili; Qiao Shi; Rui Xingwen; Yan Mingfu (*full members*); Wen Jiabao (*alternate member*).
The Advisory Commission, Chen Yun (*Chairman*); Bo Yibo; Song Renqiong; (*Vice Chairmen*).
The Discipline Inspection Commission, Secretary, Qiao Shi; *Deputy Secretaries*, Chen Zuolin; Li Zhengting; Xiao Hongda.
Membership, 42,000,000.

EMBASSY IN LONDON
49–51 Portland Place, W1N 3AH
[01-636 9375]

Ambassador Extraordinary and Plenipotentiary, His Excellency Ji Chaozhu (1987).

AREA AND POPULATION.—The area of China is 3,705,408 sq. miles, (9,596,961 sq. km.). A nationwide census (the third) was held in July 1982, which recorded a total population of 1,008,175,288. According to the P.R.C. State Statistical Bureau, the population at the end of 1987 was 1,080,000,000. China is anxious to control the growth of the population and has introduced stringent policies intended to result in a population of 1,200 million by the year 2000. About 6 per cent of the population belong to around 55 ethnic minorities. Among the largest are

the Zhuang of Guangxi, the Uygurs of Xinjiang, the Tibetans and the Mongols.

THE PROVINCES OF CHINA

1982 census results were:

Anhui	49,665,724
Beijing	9,230,687
Fujian	25,931,106
Gansu	19,569,261
Guangdong	59,299,220
Guangxi Zhuang Autonomous Region	36,420,960
Guizhou	28,552,997
Hebei	53,005,875
Heilongjiang	32,665,546
Henan	74,422,739
Hubei	47,804,150
Hunan	54,008,851
Jiangsu	60,521,114
Jiangxi	33,184,827
Liaoning	35,721,693
Nei Monggol Autonomous Region	19,274,279
Ningxia Hui Autonomous Region	3,895,578
Qinghai	3,895,706
Shaanxi	28,904,423
Shandong	74,419,054
Shanghai	11,859,748
Shanxi	25,291,389
Sichuan	99,713,310
(Taiwan	18,270,749)
Tianjin	7,764,141
Tibet Autonomous Region	1,892,392
Xinjiang Uygur Autonomous Region	13,081,681
Yunnan	32,553,817
Zhejiang	38,884,603
Armed Forces	4,238,210

Government.—On October 10, 1911, the party of reform forced the Imperial dynasty to a "voluntary" abdication, and a Republic was proclaimed at Wuchang.

On September 30, 1949, the Chinese People's Political Consultative Conference (C.P.P.C.C) met in Peking and appointed the National People's Government Council under the Chairmanship of Mao Zedong (Mao Tse-Tung). On October 1, Mao proclaimed the inauguration of the Chinese People's Republic.

The régime was recognized by all the Communist bloc countries in quick succession, and soon after by the Asian countries of the Commonwealth, the United Kingdom and by a number of other countries. Others, led by the United States, continued to recognize the Chiang Kai-shek régime on Taiwan as the rightful Government of China. In 1971 the People's Republic won acceptance into the United Nations on the expulsion of Taiwan. Since then many more countries have accorded recognition.

A new Constitution was adopted in December 1982, under which the National People's Congress is the highest organ of state power. It is elected for a term of five years and is supposed to hold one session a year. It is empowered to amend the Constitution, make laws, select the President and Vice-President and other leading officials of the state, approve the national economic plan, the state budget and the final state accounts, and to decide on questions of war and peace. The State Council is the highest organ of the state administration. It is composed of the Premier, the Vice Premiers, the State Councillors, heads of Ministries and Commissions, the Auditor General and the Secretary General. Command over the armed forces is vested in the Central Military Commission, of which Deng Xiaoping is the Chairman.

Deputies to congresses at the primary level are "directly elected" by the voters "through a secret ballot after democratic consultation". This is now being extended to county level. These Congresses elect the Deputies to the Congress at the next higher level. Deputies to the National People's Congress are elected by the People's Congresses of the provinces, autonomous regions and municipalities directly under the Central Government, and by the armed forces.

Local government is conducted through People's Governments at provincial, municipal and county levels. Autonomous regions, prefectures and counties exist for national minorities and are described as self-governing. The system prevailing is that found elsewhere, i.e. People's Congresses and People's Governments. Beijing, Shanghai and Tianjin continue to come directly under the central government.

Following the deaths of Mao Zedong and Zhou Enlai in 1976 the disgraced Vice-Premier Deng Xiaoping was recalled. At the 11th Party Congress in 1977 Deng was elected Vice-Chairman and has since become the dominant force within the Party by eliminating leftist influence, rehabilitating fallen leaders and adjusting Maoist policies to meet the needs of a developing economy. Deng's policies were reaffirmed at the 12th Congress in 1982. The Congress also elected a new Party leadership dominated by Deng and his supporters. The post of Chairman of the Party was abolished. The Party leader now holds the post of General Secretary. The 13th Party Congress in 1987 reaffirmed open-door policies. Most of the old revolutionary generation were removed, in elections, from the top posts.

Armed Forces.—All three military arms in China are parts of the People's Liberation Army (P.L.A.) The size of this body has not been formally given, but it is estimated that China has approximately 3·5 million men under arms, with a further 12 million (or perhaps many more) reserves who take part in militia activities. In June 1985 a planned reduction of over 1 million in the course of a year was officially announced. In 1955 compulsory military service was introduced for all men between the ages of 18 and 40. This service was on a selective basis. The present length of service for those conscripted is three years in the Army, four years in the Air Force and five years in the Navy. With effect from June 1, 1965, the rank structure was abolished, together with all marks of distinction of branch of service. Both are expected to be reinstated.

China exploded her first experimental nuclear device on Oct. 16, 1964 and made further tests in 1965 and in May, Oct. and Dec., 1966. Her first hydrogen bomb was tested in June, 1967. Further tests of nuclear devices and hydrogen bombs have since been announced, though China no longer conducts atmospheric nuclear tests. China embarked on a programme of earth-satellite launchings in April 1970, the latest being made in January 1978. A long-range I.C.B.M. was tested in 1980, and a submarine-launched ballistic missile in 1982.

Religion.—The indigenous religions of China are Confucianism (which includes ancestor worship), Taoism (originally a philosophy rather than a religion) and, since its introduction in the first century of the Christian era, Buddhism. There are also Chinese Moslems (officially estimated at about 12 million) and Christians (unofficially estimated at about 50 million). Religious freedoms, severely curtailed during the Cultural Revolution, are reviving slightly under more liberal policies.

Education.—The Cultural Revolution caused considerable disruption to the educational system and since 1976 attempts have been made to raise academic standards. Primary education now lasts five years, and has a claimed enrolment of 146,000,000 pupils. Secondary education lasts five years (three years in Junior Middle School and two years in Senior Middle School). There were 47,000,000 Middle School pupils in 1986. The proportion of illiterates and semi-illiterates in 1982 was 23·5 per cent, but efforts are being made to expand secondary education, particularly in the rural areas. Particular attention is being paid to higher education where there are over 1,000 universities, colleges and institutes with an enrolment of 1,700,000 students. In May 1985 the Central Committee of the Party announced the abolition of free higher education except for teacher training, and the aim of providing all children with junior secondary education within 10 years.

Language and Literature.—The Chinese language has many dialects, notably Cantonese, Hakka, Amoy, Foochow, Changsha, Nanchang, Wu (Shanghai) and the northern dialect. The Common Speech or *Putonghua* (often referred to as "Mandarin") which is being taught throughout the country is based on the northern dialect. The Communists have promoted it as the national language and made intensive efforts to propagate it throughout the country. Since the most important aspect of this policy is the use of the spoken language in writing, the old literary style and ideographic form of writing has fallen into disuse.

In 1956, after some 4 years of study, the Government decided to introduce 230 simplified characters with a view to making reading and writing easier. The list was enlarged and there are now over 2,000 simplified characters in use. In Jan. 1956, all Chinese newspapers and most books began to appear with the characters printed horizontally from left to right, instead of vertically reading from right to left, as previously.

In Feb. 1958 The National People's Congress adopted a system of Romanization, known as pinyin, using 25 of the letters of the Latin alphabet (not v). This has been used within the country largely for assisting school children and others to learn the pronunciation of characters in *Putonghua*, and is now used for Chinese names in foreign-language publications.

Chinese literature is one of the richest in the world. Paper has been employed for writing and printing for nearly 2,000 years. The Confucian classics which formed the basis of the traditional Chinese culture date from the Warring States period (4th–3rd centuries B.C.) as do the earliest texts of the rival tradition, Taoism. Histories, philosophical and scientific works, poetry, literary and art criticism, novels and romances survive from most periods. Many have been translated into English. In the past all this considerable literature was available only to a very small class of *literati*, but with the spread of literacy in the 20th century, a process which has received enormous impetus since the Communists took over in 1950, the old traditional literature has been largely superseded by modern works of a popular kind and by the classics of Marxism and modern developments from them.

The most important among the newspapers and magazines are the People's Daily and the twice-monthly Red Flag, the communist party organs.

Production and Industry.—China is essentially an agricultural and pastoral country: peasants constitute about 80 per cent of the population. People's communes gave way to townships as the basic level of State administration in rural districts under the 1982 Constitution.

New agricultural policies, designed to give greater incentives to the rural population, have meant that the responsibility for agricultural production has been devolved down to individual households, whereas previously work was generally assigned on a collective basis.

Wheat, barley, maize, millet and other cereals, with peas and beans, are grown in the northern provinces, and rice and sugar in the south. Rice is the staple food of the inhabitants. Cotton (mostly in valleys of the Yangtze and Yellow Rivers), tea (in the west and

south), with hemp, jute and flax, are the most important crops.

Livestock is raised in large numbers. Silkworm culture is one of the oldest industries. Cottons, woollens and silks are manufactured in large quantities. The mineral wealth of the country is very great. Coal of excellent quality is produced. Iron ore, tin, antimony, wolfram, bismuth and molybdenum are also abundant. Oil is produced in several northern provinces, particularly in Heilongjiang and Shandong, and off-shore deposits are being sought in co-operation with Western and Japanese companies.

The Chinese State Statistical Bureau issues production figures annually. The following are of note for 1987:

Grain (tons)	402,410,000
Pork, beef, mutton (tons)	19,210,000
Tea (tons)	497,000
Cotton (tons)	4,190,000
Timber (cu. metres)	68,430,000
Crude oil (tons)	134,000,000
Steel (tons)	56,020,000
Electric power (KWh)	496 billion
Machine tools	146,000
Motor vehicles	472,000

The State Statistical Bureau valued the national income for 1987 at Yuan 915·3 billion, an increase of 9·3 per cent over 1986. The Gross National Product in 1987 was Yuan 1,092 billion, a 9·3 per cent. increase over 1986. The total value of agricultural output rose by 4·7 per cent. over the 1986 figure to Yuan 444·7 billion. The total value of industrial output rose by 16·5 per cent. to Yuan 1,378 billion.

In 1982 China set itself the aim of quadrupling the 1980 gross agricultural and industrial output value by the year 2000. The focus of its reform programme was switched to industry in 1984. Wide-ranging reforms have been introduced to make the industrial sector more efficient by narrowing the scope of central planning and broadening enterprise decision-making, material incentives and the role of the market.

Foreign trade and external economic relations have expanded quickly since the open-door policy, adopted in the late 1970's. The principal articles of export are animals and animal products; oil; textiles; ores, metals, tea and manufactured goods. The principal imports are motor vehicles; machinery; chemical fertilizer plants; aircraft; books, paper and paper-making materials; chemicals; metals and ores; and dyes.

Trade with U.K.

	1986	1987
Imports from U.K.	£535,943,000	£416,012,000
Exports to U.K.	327,032,000	391,766,000

Communications.—Of the total area of China over half consists of tableland and mountainous areas where communications and travel are generally difficult. The country has more than 52,000 kilometres of railway trunk and branch lines and some 926,746 kilometres of highway. In addition, internal civil aviation has been developed, with routes now totalling more than 340,000 kilometres. As a result the communications network now covers most of the country.

In the past where roads did not exist the principal means of communication east to west was provided by the rivers, the most important of which are the Yangtze (Changjiang) (3,400 miles long), the Yellow River (Huanghe) (2,600 miles long) and the West River (Xihe) (1,650 miles). These, together with the network of canals connecting them are still much used, but their overall importance is less than it was. Coastal port facilities are being improved and the merchant fleet expanded. In the past 10 years great

progress has been made in developing postal services and telecommunications. It is now claimed that 95 per cent of all rural communes are on the telephone and that postal routes reach practically every production brigade headquarters.

CAPITAL.—Beijing (Peking), population (1986), 5,970,000.

Population of major cities in 1986:

Shanghai	7,100,000	Harbin	2,670,000
Tianjin	5,460,000	Chengdu	2,640,000
Shenyang	4,290,000	Xian	2,390,000
Wuhan	3,490,000	Nanjing	2,290,000
Guangzhou		Taiyuan	1,930,000
(Canton)	3,360,000	Kunming	1,520,000
Chongqing	2,700,000	Lanzhou	1,390,000

CURRENCY.—Yuan of 10 Jiao or 100 Fen.

FLAG.—Red, with large gold five-point star and four small gold stars in crescent, all in upper quarter next staff.

NATIONAL ANTHEM.—March of the Volunteers.

NATIONAL DAY.—October 1 (Founding of People's Republic).

BRITISH EMBASSY
11 Guang Hua Lu,
Jian Guo Men Wai, Peking.
[Peking 521961/5]

Ambassador, His Excellency Sir Alan Ewen Donald, K.C.M.G. (1988).
Counsellors, Miss A. J. K. Bailes; J. K. Chapman *(Commercial);* D. Marler, O.B.E. *(Cultural, and British Council Representative).*
Defence Attaché, Col. W. H. Clements.
First Secretaries, Dr. J. E. Hoare *(Head of Chancery);* P. G. Wood; D. Harris; P. Davies; P. Clark; Ms. P. M. Barnsley; S. Prince; C. O. Piggott; S. S. Calder; I. A. Seaton; J. P. Eyres.
There is also a Consulate-General in *Shanghai.*

TIBET

Tibet is a plateau seldom lower than 10,000 feet, which forms the northern frontier of India (boundary imperfectly demarcated), from Kashmir to Burma, but is separated therefrom by the Himalayas. The area is estimated at 463,000 square miles with a population of 1,892,392 in 1982.

From 1911 to 1950, Tibet was virtually an independent country though its status was never officially so recognized. In October 1950, Chinese Communist forces invaded Eastern Tibet. On May 23, 1951, an agreement was reached whereby the Chinese army was allowed entry into Tibet. A Communist military and administrative headquarters was set up. In 1954 the Government of India recognized that Tibet was an integral part of China, in return for the right to maintain trade and consular representation there.

A series of revolts against Chinese rule over several years culminated on March 17, 1959, in a rising in Lhasa. Heavy fighting continued for several days before the rebellion was suppressed by Chinese troops and military rule imposed. The Dalai Lama fled to India where he and his followers were granted political asylum. On March 28, 1959, the Chinese Premier issued an order dissolving the Tibetan Government. In its place the 16-member Preparatory Committee for the Tibetan Autonomous Region, originally set up in 1955 with the Dalai Lama as Chairman, was to administer Tibet under the State Council. The Preparatory Committee was to have the Panchen Lama as Acting Chairman and also to include 4 Chinese Officials. Elections were held to choose local People's Congresses in Tibet, thus indicating that the government organization there no longer differed significantly from that of any ordinary province in China.

In December, 1964, the Dalai Lama was declared to be a traitor, and both he and the Panchen Lama were dismissed. The position of Acting Chairman of the Preparatory Committee was assumed by Ngapoi Ngawang Jigmi, who had long been the most prominent secular figure in Tibet. This move marked the end of the period of co-operation by the Chinese Government with the traditional religious authorities, and the eclipse of the latter. The Preparatory Committee completed its work with the setting up of Tibet as an Autonomous Region of China on Sept. 9, 1965. The Panchen Lama is now rehabilitated as an official of the C.P.P.C.C., and the Chinese have invited the Dalai Lama to return from exile.

TAIWAN
(Ta Chung-Hwa Min-Kwo)

President, Lee Teng-hui, *elected,* Jan. 13, 1988.
Vice-President, (vacant).
Premier, Yu Kuo-hwa (May 20, 1984).

An island of some 13,800 sq. miles, (35,742 sq. km.), in the China Sea, Taiwan, formerly Formosa, lies 90 miles east of the Chinese mainland in latitude 21° 45′N.—25° 38′N. The population (19,135,254 in 1985), is almost entirely Chinese in origin and includes about 2,000,000 mainlanders who came to the island with Chiang Kai-shek in 1947–49. The territories administered by the Chinese Nationalists include the Pescadores Islands (50 sq. miles), some 35 miles west of Taiwan, as well as Quemoy (68 sq. miles) and Matsu (11 sq. miles) which are only a few miles from the mainland. Settled for centuries by the Chinese, the island was administered by Japan from 1895 to 1945. General Chiang Kai-shek withdrew to Taiwan in 1949, towards the end of the war against the Communist régime, accompanied by 500,000 Nationalist troops, after which the territory continued under his presidency until his death on April 5, 1975. A mutual defence treaty between the United States and Taiwan Governments was signed in 1954 but this was terminated when the United States recognized the People's Republic of China on January 1, 1979. Martial law was lifted in July 1987, after 38 years. Chiang Kai-shek's son Chiang Ching-kuo died in Jan. 1988 and was succeeded by Vice President Lee Teng-hui, a native Taiwanese.

The eastern part of the main island is mountainous and forest covered. Mt. Morrison (Yu Shan) (13,035 ft.) and Mt. Sylvia (Tz'ukaoshan) (12,972 ft.) are the highest peaks. The western plains are watered by many rivers and the soil is very fertile, producing sugar, rice, sweet potatoes, tea, bananas, pineapples and tobacco. Coal, sulphur, iron, petroleum, copper and gold are mined. There are important fisheries. The principal seaports ψKeelung and ψKaohsiung are situated in the northern and southern sections of the island.

Trade with U.K.

	1986	1987
Imports from U.K.	£192,492,000	£292,275,000
Exports to U.K.	705,775,000	1,006,880,000

CAPITAL.—Taipei (population 1985, 2,507,620). Other towns are ψKaohsiung (1,314,364); Tainan (572,590); Taichung (585,205); and ψKeelung (345,392).

CURRENCY.—New Taiwan Dollar of 100 Cents.

FLAG.—Red, with blue quarter at top next staff, bearing a twelve-point white sun.
NATIONAL DAY.—October 10.

COLOMBIA
(República de Colombia)

President, Dr. Virgilio Barco Vargas, *assumed office,* August 7, 1986.

CABINET

Home Affairs, César Gaviria Trujillo.
Foreign Affairs, Julio Londoño Paredes.
Finance, Luis Fernando Alarcón Mantilla.
National Defence, Rafael Samudio Molina.
Public Works, Luis Fernando Jaramillo Correa.
Justice, Guillermo Plazas Alcid.
Labour, Juan Martín Caicedo Ferrer.
Agriculture, Gabriel Rosas Vega.
Health, Luis H. Arraut.
Mines, Oscar Mejía.
Communications, Pedro Martín Leyes.
Education, Manuel Francisco Becerra.
Development, Carlos Arturo Marulanda Ramírez.

COLOMBIAN EMBASSY IN LONDON
3 Hans Crescent, SW1X 0LR
[01–589 9177]

Ambassador Extraordinary and Plenipotentiary, His Excellency Dr. Fernando Cepeda (1988).
Chargé d'Affaires, Dr. Ricardo Samper.
There are *Consulates-General* in *London* and *Liverpool.*

The Republic of Colombia lies in the extreme north-west of South America, having a coastline on both the Caribbean Sea and Pacific Ocean. It is situated between 4° 13′ S. to 12° 30′ N. lat. and 68° to 79° W. long., with an area of 439,737 sq. miles (1,138,914 sq. km.), and a population (census 1985) of 26,525,670.

The country is divided into a narrow coastal strip in the west and extensive plains in the east by the Cordillera de los Andes. The Eastern Cordillera consists of a series of vast tablelands. This temperate region is the most densely peopled portion of the Republic. The principal rivers are the Magdalena, Guaviare, Cauca, Atrato, Caquetá, Putumayo and Patia.

Government.—The Colombian coast was visited in 1502 by Christopher Columbus, and in 1536 a Spanish expedition under Jiménez de Quesada penetrated to the interior and established on the site of the present capital a government which continued under Spanish rule until the revolt of the Spanish–American colonies of 1811–1824. In 1819 Simón Bolívar (1783–1831) established the Republic of Colombia, consisting of the territories now known as Colombia, Panama, Venezuela and Ecuador. In 1829–1830 Venezuela and Ecuador withdrew from the association of provinces, and in 1831 the remaining territories were formed into the Republic of New Granada. In 1858 the name was changed to the Granadine Confederation and in 1861 to the United States of Colombia. In 1866 the present title was adopted. In 1903 Panama seceded from Colombia, and became a separate Republic.

During the early nineteen-fifties Colombia suffered a period of virtual civil war between the supporters of the traditional political parties, the Conservatives and the Liberals. From 1957–1974 the country was governed under the "National Front" agreement with the presidency alternating between the two parties every four years and ministerial posts being shared equally by the parties. The alternation of the presidency was ended in 1974 and parity in appointments in 1978. Thereafter, the constitution lays down that Government portfolios and Administrative appointments shall be divided among the two majority parties in Congress in an "adequate and equitable" manner. However, after a General Election in 1986, the Liberal Party won a large majority. The Liberals are now known as the majority and the Conservaties, the Opposition.

Defence.—The Army peace effective strength is 60,000; war effective, approx. 400,000. The Navy, with 9,000 personnel including approximately 5,000 marines, has four corvettes, one destroyer, one frigate, one sail training ship, two submarines and a number of patrol boats. The Air Force, with 6,000 personnel, is equipped with Mirage fighters, 837B's, C47's and a number of support helicopters.

Production.—Much of Colombia's natural resources in coal, natural gas and hydro-electricity remain largely unexploited. Development of coal is being given priority but no new hydro projects are likely to be started for the next 4–5 years. Annual coal production is increasing from the recent peak of 5·5 million tonnes now that the Cerrejón Norte coalfield is being fully worked. This is essentially for export. Proven coal reserves stand at 16,000 million tonnes. Estimated natural gas reserves are 3,788,000 million cu. ft., with daily use at 381,772 million B.t.u. Proven crude oil reserves stand at 1,300 million barrels. Colombia is again a net exporter of oil. In 1987 exports averaged 152,000 b.p.d. and are expected to rise to 282,000 b.p.d. by 1989.

The hydrocarbon sector accounts for over half of the mining output with precious metals (gold, platinum and silver) and iron ore accounting for the remainder. Iron ore production in 1982 was 450,000 tons. Other mineral deposits include nickel (a processing plant started operating in 1982), bauxite, copper, gypsum, limestone, phosphates, sulphur and uranium. Colombia is also the world's largest producer of emeralds and has deposits of other precious and semi-precious stones.

Because of the range of climate, a wide variety of crops can be grown, and the country is close to self-suffiency in food. The principal agriculture products are coffee (Colombia is second only to Brazil as the world's largest coffee producer) and other major cash crops are sugar, bananas, cut flowers and cotton. Cattle are raised in large numbers, and meat and cured skins and hides are also exported.

Industry.—The Government has encouraged diversification to reduce dependence on coffee as the major export and this has led to the growth of new export-orientated industries, particularly textiles, paper products and leather goods. Stimulus to the economy has been provided by large loans from the World Bank and IADB for project development, particularly in the power sector (in which hydroelectric projects have predominated) and for telecommunications.

Communications.—The massive ranges of the Andes make surface transport difficult therefore air transport is used extensively. There are daily passenger and cargo air services between Bogotá and all the principal towns, as well as daily services to the U.S.A., frequent services to other countries in South America, and to Europe. The "Atlantic Railway" links the departmental lines running down to the river, and completes the connection between Bogotá and Santa Marta. Although the railways generally are in a poor state there are about 2,600 miles of rail in use at present. The total road network (1985) consists of 105,201 km. of roads of all types, of which 21,800 km. are classified as main trunk and transversal roads.

Large appropriations have been made for modernization of the country's telecommunication system. There are 485 radio stations (1983) and two national television channels with several regional ones.

Language and Literature.—Spanish is the language of the country and education has been free since 1870. Great efforts have been made in reducing illiteracy and estimates (1980) put the literacy rate at 77·6 per cent of those over 10 years of age. In addition to the National University with headquarters at Bogotá there are 26 other universities. There is a flourishing press in urban areas and a national literature supplements the rich inheritance from the time of Spanish rule.

Roman Catholicism is the established religion.

TRADE

Colombia's principal export is still coffee although other products, principally bananas, cut flowers, clothing and textiles, ferro-nickel and coal are important exports.

	1984	1985
	$U.S.	$U.S.
Total imports (c.i.f.)	4,492m.	4,688m.
Total exports (f.o.b.)	3,483m.	3,763m.

Trade with U.K.

	1986	1987
Imports from U.K.	£58,084,000	£61,385,000
Exports to U.K.	94,112,000	65,331,000

CAPITAL, Bogotá, population (census, 1985) 3,967,988. Bogotá is an inland city in the Eastern Cordilleras, at an elevation of 8,600 to 9,000 ft. above sea level. Other centres are Medellín (1,500,000); Cali (1,350,000); ΨBarranquilla (900,000); ΨCartagena (530,000); Bucaramanga (350,000); ΨBuenaventura (130,000) is the country's major port.

CURRENCY.—Colombian Peso of 100 Centavos.

FLAG.—Broad yellow band in upper half, surmounting equal bands of blue and red.

NATIONAL ANTHEM.—"Oh gloria inmarcesible".

NATIONAL DAY.—July 20 (National Independence Day).

BRITISH EMBASSY
Torre Propaganda Sancho, Calle 98, No. 9–03, Piso 4, Bogotá
[Bogota 2185111]

Ambassador Extraordinary and Plenipotentiary, His Excellency Richard A. Neilson, C.M.G., L.V.O. (1987). There are British Consular Offices at *Bogotá*, *Barranquilla* and *Cali*.
British Council Representative, J. Coope, Calle 87, No. 12–79, Bogotá D.E.

COLOMBO-BRITISH CHAMBER OF COMMERCE, Apartado Aereo 54 728, CVA. 13 No. 82-20, Bogotá D.E.

THE COMOROS
(Republique Fédérale Islamique des Comores)

Head of State, President Ahmed Abdallah Abdermane, *took office* May 1978; *elected*, Oct. 22, 1978; *re-elected*, Sept. 30, 1984.
Prime Minister, Ahmed Abdallah Abdermane.
Director of the President's Office, Ali Nassor.
Secretary General of the Presidency and Government, Said Ahmed Cheikh.

MINISTERS

Interior, Information and Press, Omar Tamou.
Vocational Training, Culture, Youth and Sports, Education, Salim Idarousse.
Production, Industry, Economy and Trade, Tourism and Crafts, Mohamed Ali.
Economics and Trade, Management, Control of State Companies, Commercial and Public Organisations, Said Ahmed Said Ali.
Environment, Urban Planning, Housing, Mikidache Abdourahim.
Foreign Affairs and Co-operation, Said Kafe.
Finance and Budget, Said Ahmed Ali.
Public Health and Population, Ali Hassan Ali.
Justice, Civil Service, Employment and Professional Training, Dr. Ben Ali Bacar.

The Comoro archipelago includes the islands of Great Comoro, Anjouan, Mayotte and Moheli and certain islets in the Indian Ocean with an area of 838 sq. miles (2,171 sq. km.) and a population (1985 U.N. estimate) of 444,000, most of whom are Muslim. The islanders voted for independence from France in December 1974 and three islands became independent on July 6, 1975. (The island of Mayotte was against independence and has remained under French administration.) On October 1, 1978 the three islands voted in a referendum to adopt a new Constitution which provides for a President, directly elected for a six year term. The Council of Government, consisting of a Prime Minister and up to nine other Ministers, is appointed by the President. There is a 39-member Federal Assembly elected for 5 years. Each island is administered by a Governor, assisted by up to four Commissioners whom he appoints, and has an elected Legislative Council.
The most important products are vanilla, copra, cloves and essential oils, which are the principal exports; cacao, sisal and coffee are also cultivated. Great Comoro is well forested and produces some timber.

Trade with U.K.

	1986	1987
Imports from U.K.	£307,000	£527,000
Exports to U.K.	—	91,000

CAPITAL.—Moroni, on Great Comoro. (Pop. 17,267).
CURRENCY.—Comorian Franc of 100 Centimes. The Comoros also use the Franc C.F.A.
FLAG.—Green ground with a crescent and four stars all in white in the half by the hoist.
NATIONAL DAY.—July 6. (Independence Day).
British Ambassador, (resident in Mauritius).

CONGO
(République Populaire du Congo)

President, Col. Denis Sassou-Nguesso, *appointed* 1979, *re-elected,* July 30, 1984 (*also holds Defence and Security Portfolios*).

COUNCIL OF MINISTERS

Prime Minister, A. E. Poungui.
Rural Development, I. O. Lekoundzou.
Territorial Administration and Local Government, R. D. Ngollo.
Transport and Civil Aviation, H. Mount.
Planning and the Economy, P. Moussa.
Foreign Affairs and Co-operation, A. Ndinga Oba.
Health and Social Affairs, B. Combo Matsiona.
Public Works, Construction, Town Planning and Housing, B. Moundele Ngollo.

Higher Education, Culture and the Arts, J. B. Tati Loutard.
Industry, Fisheries and Workers, A. Noumazalay.
Minister at the Presidency in charge of Defence and Security, E. Elenga.
Mines and Energy, R. Adada.
Primary Education and Literacy, P. D. Boussoukou Boumba.
Labour, Social Security and Justice, D. Kimbembe.
Trade, and Small and Medium Enterprises, A. Poaty Souchlaty.
Forestries, O. Douniam.
Scientific Research and the Environment, C. Bouramoue.
Information, Posts and Telecommunications, C. G. Bembet.
Tourism, Sport and Recreation, J. C. Ganga.

The Republic lies on the Equator between Gabon on the west and Zaire on the east, the River Congo and its tributary the Ubanghi forming most of the eastern boundary of the state. The Congo has a short Atlantic coastline. Area of the Republic of Congo is 132,047 sq. miles (342,000 sq. km.), with a population of 1,740,000 (1985 U.N. estimate). Formerly the French colony of Middle Congo, it became a member state of the French Community on November 28, 1958, and was proclaimed fully independent on August 17, 1960.
In 1968, conduct of affairs was assumed by a National Council of Army officers. The Parti Congolais du Travail (*PCT*) was created by the Congress of December 29–31, 1969 and the People's Republic of the Congo was established. Under the present Constitution, approved by referendum in 1979, executive power is vested in the President, who is elected by the Congress of the P.C.T. (the only legal party). The Council of Ministers is appointed and led by the President.
Congo has its own oil deposits, producing about 6 million tonnes annually. It also produces lead, zinc and gold. The principal agricultural products are timber, cassava, sugar cane and yams. Imports are mainly of machinery.

Trade with U.K.

	1986	1987
Imports from U.K.	£9,165,243	£19,218,901
Exports to U.K.	2,443,964	1,930,030

CAPITAL.—Brazzaville (600,000); Ψ Pointe Noire (350,000).
CURRENCY.—Franc C.F.A. of 100 Centimes.
FLAG.—Red, with hammer and hoe in wreath of leaves in top corner.
NATIONAL DAY.—August 15.

BRITISH EMBASSY
B.P. 1038, Brazzaville
[Brazzaville 834944]

Ambassador Extraordinary and Plenipotentiary, His Excellency Thomas Clive Almond (1987).

COSTA RICA
(República de Costa Rica)

President, Dr. Oscar Arias Sánchez, *took office,* May 8, 1986.

MINISTERS

Vice Presidents, J. Manuel Dengo; Sra. V Garrón de Doryan.
Minister for the Presidency, R. Arias Sánchez.
Foreign Affairs and Worship, R. Madrigal Nieto.
Interior and Police, R. Ramirez Paniagua.
Justice, L. Paulino Mora.

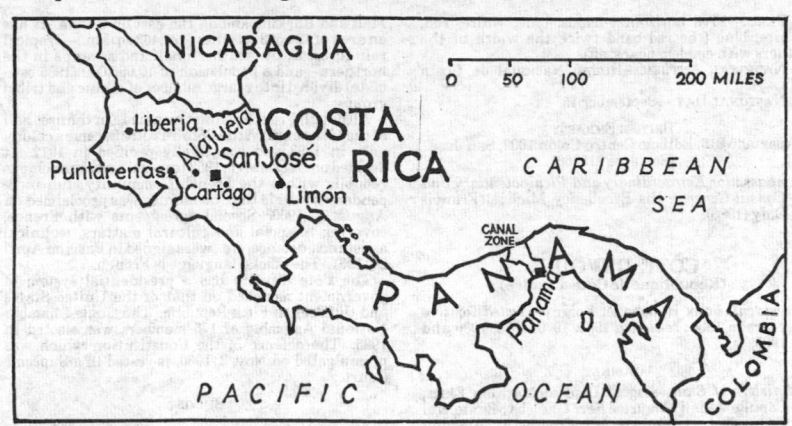

Public Security, H. Garrón Salazar.
Finance, Dr. F. Naranjo Villalobos.
Agriculture, A. Alvarez Desanti.
Economy, Industry and Commerce, L. D. Escalante Vargas.
Natural Resources, Energy and Mines, Dr. A. Umaña.
Public Works and Transport, Dr. G. Constenla Umaña.
Education, F. Antonio Pacheco.
Health, Dr. E. Mohs Villalta.
Culture, Youth and Sports, C. Echeverría Salgado.
Labour and Social Security, E. León Villalobos.
Planning, O. Solís Fallas.
Housing and Urban Development, Dr. F. Zumbado Jiménez.
Foreign Trade, J. M. Figueres.
Science and Technology, R. Zeledón Araya.
Information, G. Fernandez Saborio.

COSTA RICAN EMBASSY
Flat 1, 14 Lancaster Gate, W2 3LH
[01–723 1772/9630]

Ambassador Extraordinary and Plenipotentiary, new appointment awaited.

The Republic of Costa Rica in Central America extends across the isthmus between 8° 17′ and 11° 10′ N. lat. and from 82° 30′ to 85° 45′ W. long., has an area of 19,575 sq. miles (50,700 sq. km.), and a population (1988 estimate) of 2,816,558. The population is basically of European stock, in which Costa Rica differs from most Latin American countries. The Republic lies between Nicaragua and Panama and between the Caribbean Sea and the Pacific Ocean. The coastal lowlands by the Caribbean Sea and Pacific have a tropical climate but the interior plateau, with a mean elevation of 4,000 feet, enjoys a temperate climate.

For nearly three centuries (1530–1821) Costa Rica formed part of the Spanish-American dominions, the seat of government being at Cartago. In 1821 the country obtained its independence, although from 1824 to 1839 it was one of the United States of Central America.

On Dec. 1, 1948, the Army was abolished, the President declaring it unnecessary, as the country loved peace.

Economy.—Agriculture is the chief industry and the principal products are coffee, bananas, sugar and cattle (for meat), all of which are important exports. Other crops are cocoa, rice, maize, potatoes and hemp. Industrial activity is principally in the manufacturing sector and manufactured goods are the largest category of exports. The main goods are foodstuffs, textiles and clothing, plastic goods, pharmaceuticals, fertilizers and electrical equipment.

Communications.—The chief ports are Limón, on the Atlantic coast, through which passes most of the coffee exported, and Caldera on the Pacific coast, currently under construction with Japanese aid. In 1982, 1,236 ships entered Costa Rican ports handling imports and exports of approximately 2,666,386,811 tons of goods. The railway system is nationalized. About 500 miles of railroad are open. LACSA is the national airline, operating flights throughout Central and South America, the Caribbean and U.S.A., besides internal flights to local airports by SANSA.

Language, etc.—Spanish is the language of the country. Education is compulsory and free. The literacy rate is the highest in Latin America.

FINANCE

	1987
	Colones
Revenue	35,665·3m.
Expenditure	42,500·6m.

TRADE

The chief exports were manufactured goods and other products, coffee, bananas, cocoa and sugar. The chief imports were machinery, including transport equipment, manufactures, chemicals, fuel and mineral oils and foodstuffs.

	1986	1987
	(US$ '000)	
Total imports	1,163	1,385
Total exports	1,085	1,113

Trade with U.K.

	1986	1987
Imports from U.K.	£12,007,000	£14,407,000
Exports to U.K.	30,318,000	16,752,000

CAPITAL.—San José pop. (estimate 1988) 1,031,102; Alajuela (499,623); Cartago (316,379); Heredia (197,575); Guanacaste (227,950); ΨPuntarenas (313,541); ΨLimón (200,638). (Populations shown are of provinces, cantons and districts).
CURRENCY.—Costa Rican Colón of 100 Céntimos.

FLAG.—Five horizontal bands, blue, white, red, white, blue (the red band twice the width of the others with emblem near staff).

NATIONAL ANTHEM.—Himno Nacional de Costa Rica.

NATIONAL DAY.—September 15.

BRITISH EMBASSY
Apartado 815, Edificio Centro Colon 1007, San José.
[San José 215566]

Ambassador Extraordinary and Plenipotentiary and Consul-General, His Excellency Michael Francis Daly (1986).

CÔTE D'IVOIRE
(République de Côte d'Ivoire)

President, Félix Houphouët-Boigny, *elected* for five years in 1960; *re-elected* 1965, 1970, 1975, 1980 and 1985.

CABINET

Ministers of State, August Denise; Mathieu Ekra; Camille Alliali; Maurice Séri Gnoléba; Emile Kei Boguinard; Lazéni N. P. Coulibaly; Amadou Thiam; Paul Gui Dibo; Lamine Diabaté.

Ministers:
Defence and the Navy, Jean Konan Banny.
Foreign Affairs, Siméon Aké.
Information, Culture, Youth and Sports, Laurent Dona Fologo.
Interior, Léon Konan Koffi.
Economy and Finance, Abdoulayé Koné.
Agriculture and Rural Development, Denis Bra Kanon.
Technical Education and Vocational Training A. F. Barry-Battesti.
Public Works and Transport, Aoussou Koffi.
Secondary and Higher Education, Balla Keita.
Justice, Noël Nemin.
Labour, Albert Vanié Bi Tra.
Internal Security, Oumar N'Daw.
Industry, Bernard K. Ehui.
Health and Population, Mady Alphonse Djédjé.
Women's Affairs, Hortense Aka Anghui.
Commerce, Angba Nicolas Kouandi.
Public Service, Jean-Jacques Béchio.
Tourism, Duon Sadia.
Social Affairs, Yaya Ouattara.
National Assembly, Emile Brou.
Planning, Oumar Diarra
Construction and Town Planning, Vamoussa Bamba.
Scientific Research, Alhassane N'Diaye.
Budget, Moïse Koumoué Koffi.
Pre-School and Primary Education, Odette Kouamé N'Guessan.
Mines, Yed Esaïe Angoran.
Posts and Telecommunications, Vincent Tieko Djedje.
Animal Production, Christophe Gboho.
Water Resources and Forests, Vincent-Pierre Lokrou.
President of the National Assembly, Henri Konan Bédie.
President of the Economic and Social Council, Philippe Yacé

CÔTE D'IVOIRE EMBASSY IN LONDON
2 Upper Belgrave Street, SW1X 8BJ
[01-235 6991]

Ambassador Extraordinary and Plenipotentiary, His Excellency Mr. Theodore de Mel (1986).

First Counsellor, G. G. Ballou.

The Côte d'Ivoire is situated on the Gulf of Guinea between 5° and 10° N. and 3° and 8° W. and is flanked on the west by Guinea and Liberia, on the north by Mali and Burkina and on the east by Ghana. It has an area of 124,503 sq. miles (322,463 sq. km.)—tropical rain forest in the southern half and savanna in the northern—and a population of 10,056,000 (1985 estimate) divided into a large number of ethnic and tribal groups.

Although French contact was made in the first half of the 19th century, the Côte d'Ivoire became a colony only in 1893 and was finally pacified in 1912. It decided on December 5, 1958 to remain an autonomous republic within the French Community; full independence outside the Community was proclaimed on August 7, 1960. Special agreements with France, covering financial and cultural matters, technical assistance, defence, etc., were signed in Paris on April 24, 1961. The official language is French.

The Côte d'Ivoire has a presidential system of government modelled on that of the United States and the French Fifth Republic. The single Chamber National Assembly of 175 members was elected in 1985. The defence of the Constitution which was promulgated on Nov. 3, 1960, is vested in a Supreme Court.

BUDGET

	1988
Current Expenditure	CFA493,500m.
Investment and Equipment.......	143,600m.

Trade.—The principal exports are coffee, cocoa, timber, palm oil, pineapples, bananas, and cotton. Diamonds are exported. There are a few deposits of minerals including manganese and iron.

TRADE

	1985	1986
Imports	CFA772,987m.	CFA709,040m.
Exports	1,318,059m.	1,160,400m.

Trade with U.K.

	1986	1987
Imports from U.K..	£34,270,000	£26,834,000
Exports to U.K. ...	117,058,000	90,246,000

CAPITAL, ΨAbidjan (population, 2,000,000) which is also the main port. In March 1983 the National Assembly ratified a decision to transfer the political and administrative capital from Abidjan to Yamoussoukro, but the date of the transfer is not yet known.

CURRENCY.—Franc C.F.A. of 100 Centimes.

FLAG.—Three vertical stripes, orange, white and green.

NATIONAL ANTHEM.—L'Abidjanaise.

NATIONAL DAY.—December 7.

BRITISH EMBASSY
Immeuble Les Harmonies, 01 B.P. 2581,
Abidjan 01.
[Abidjan 226850]

Ambassador Extraordinary and Plenipotentiary, Her Excellency Veronica Evelyn Sutherland, C.M.G. (1987).

Head of Chancery and Consul, P. W. Chandley, M.V.O.

First Secretary (Education) and British Council Representative, C. Hickey.

BRITISH CHAMBER OF COMMERCE, c/o Price Waterhouse & Co., Boite Postale 2921, Abidjan 01.

CUBA
(Republica de Cuba)

President of Council of State and Head of Government, Dr. Fidel Castro Ruz, *appointed* Nov. 2, 1976.

COUNCIL OF STATE

President, Dr. Fidel Castro Ruz.

First Vice-President, Raúl Castro Ruz.

Vice-Presidents, Juan Almeida Bosque; Osmany Cienfuegos Gorriarán; José Ramón Machado Ventura; Pedro Miret Prieto; Carlos Rafael Rodríguez.

Secretary, José M. Miyar Barrueco.

COUNCIL OF MINISTERS

President, Dr. Fidel Castro Ruz.

First Vice-President, Raúl Castro Ruz.

Vice-Presidents, Dr. Carlos Rafael Rodríguez; Pedro Miret Prieto; Diocles Torralba González; José Ramón Fernández Alvarez; José A. López Moreno; Osmany Cienfuegos Gorriarán; Antonio Esquivel Yedra; Raul Cabrera Nunez; Joel Domenech Benítez; Antonio Rodriguez Maurell.

Secretary, Osmany Cienfuegos Gorriarán.

Presidents of State Committees: Jose A. Lopez Moreno *(Central Planning Board);* Hector Rodriguez Llompart *(National Bank);* Levi Farah Balmaseda *(Construction Materials Industry);* Ernesto Melendez Bachs *(Economic Co-operation);* Rodrigo J. Garcia Leon *(Finance);* Francisco Linares Calvo *(Labour and Social Security);* Sonia Rodriguez Cardona *(Material and Technical Supply);* Arturo Guzman Pascual *(Prices);* Ramón Darias Rodés *(Standardization);* Fidel Emilio Vascos Gonzalez *(Statistics).*

Ministers, Adolfo Diaz Suarez *(Agriculture);* Marcos J. Portal Leon *(Basic Industry);* Manuel Castillo Rabasa *(Communications);* Homero Crabb *(Construction);* Levi Farah Balmaseda *(Construction Materials Industry);* Armando Enrique Hart Davalos *(Culture);* Manuel Vila Sosa *(Domestic Trade);* José Ramon Fernandez Alvarez *(Education);* Jorge A. Fernandez Cuervo-Vinent *(Fishing);* Alejandro Roca Iglesias *(Food Industry);* Isidoro Octavio Malmierca Peoli *(Foreign Relations);* Ricardo Cabrisas Ruiz *(Foreign Trade);* Fernando Vecino Alegret *(Higher Education);* José Abrantes Fernández *(Interior);* Juan Escalona Reguera *(Justice);* Antonio Esquivel Yedra *(Light Industry);* Julio Jesus Teja Pérez *(Public Health);* Raul Castro Ruz *(Revolutionary Armed Forces);* Marcos Lage Coello *(Steel Industry);* Juan Ramon Herrera Machado *(Sugar Industry);* Diocles Torralba Gonzalez *(Transport);* Jose Alberto Naranjo Morales; Raul Cabrera Nunez *(Ministers without Portfolio).*

CUBAN EMBASSY IN LONDON
167 High Holborn, WC1
[01–240 2488]

Ambassador Extraordinary and Plenipotentiary, His Excellency Dr. Oscar Fernández-Mell (1987).

Cuba, the largest island in the Caribbean, lies between 74° and 85° W. long., and 19° and 23° N. lat., with a total area of 42,804 sq. miles (110,861 sq. km.). The country is divided into 14 provinces. The estimated total population in 1987 was 10,356,400.

The island of Cuba was visited by Christopher Columbus during his first voyage, on Oct. 27, 1492, and was then believed to be part of the western mainland of India. Early in the 16th century the island was conquered by the Spanish, to be used later as a base of operations for the conquest of Mexico and Central America, and for almost four centuries Cuba remained under a Spanish Captain-General. [The island was under British rule for one year, 1762–1763, when it was returned to Spain in exchange for Florida.] Separatist agitation culminated in the closing years of the 19th century in open warfare. In 1898 the government of the United States intervened and on April 20, 1898, demanded the evacuation of Cuba by the Spanish forces. A short Spanish–American war led to the abandonment of the island,

which was occupied by U.S. troops. Cuba was under U.S. military rule from Jan. 1, 1899 until May 20, 1902, when an autonomous government was inaugurated with an elected President, and a legislature of two houses. The island was, however, again the prey of revolution from Aug. to Sept., 1906, when the U.S. Government resumed control. On Jan. 28, 1909, a republican government was again inaugurated.

A revolution led by Dr. Fidel Castro overthrew the Government of General Batista on January 1, 1959. In October, 1965, the Communist Party of Cuba was formed to succeed the United Party of the Socialist Revolution. It is the only authorized political party. The new Socialist Constitution came into force on February 24, 1976 and indirect elections to the National Assembly of People's Power were subsequently held.

Production.—The Government has carried out programmes of land and urban reform and of nationalization; by March, 1968, virtually all industrial and commercial enterprises were nationalized. About 85 per cent of the cultivated land is in state farms or State-controlled co-operatives. Private smallholders, who own the remainder, have to sell all their produce to the state.

Although efforts are being made to diversify the economy, sugar is still its mainstay and principal source of foreign exchange. In 1986–87 the harvest was 7·2 million tons. Cuba's other main exports are oil, nickel, seafood, citrus fruits, tobacco and rum.

Despite increased trade with Western Europe and Japan, the Communist countries, particularly the Soviet Union, form Cuba's main trading partners, covering about 86 per cent of imports and exports. In addition, the U.S.S.R. offers substantial aid through a system of subsidies which has recently been estimated to amount to $4,500 million.

There are 12,700 kms. of railway track, of which 5,000 kms. are in public service. In 1986 there were 13,247 kms. of road. At present scheduled international air services run to North, Central and South American countries and Europe.

Language and Literature.—Spanish is the language of the island. English, formerly widely understood, is now spoken less. Education is compulsory and free. In 1964 illiteracy was officially declared to be completely eliminated. The press and broadcasting and television are under the control of the Government.

	1986	1987
	Pesos, million	
Imports	7,569·0	7,611·5
Exports	5,325·0	5,401·0

Trade with U.K.

	1986	1987
Imports from U.K.	£58,760,000	£41,510,000
Exports to U.K.	8,550,000	12,776,000

CAPITAL.— ΨHavana (pop., est. 1986), 2,100,000; other towns are ΨSantiago (429,800), Santa Clara (198,800), Camagüey (279,800), Holguín (254,300), and ΨCienfuegos (124,600).

CURRENCY.—Cuban Peso of 100 Centavos.

FLAG.—Five horizontal bands, blue and white (blue at top and bottom) with red triangle, close to staff, charged with 5-point star.

NATIONAL ANTHEM.—"Al Combate, Corred Bayameses" (To battle, men of Bayamo).

NATIONAL DAY.—January 1 (Day of Liberation).

BRITISH EMBASSY
Edificio Bolívar, Cárcel 101–103
e Morro y Prado, Apartado 1069, Havana.
[Havana 615681/4]

Ambassador Extraordinary and Plenipotentiary, His Excellency Andrew E. Palmer, C.M.G., C.V.O. (1986).

Counsellor, A. R. F. Burgess, c.v.o. (*Head of Chancery*).
First Secretary, G. C. Livesey, m.b.e. (*Commercial and H.M. Consul*).

CZECHOSLOVAKIA
(Československá Socialistická Republika)

President, Gustáv Husák, *born* Jan. 10, 1913; *elected* May 29, 1975, *re-elected*, May, 1980, 1985.

Federal Government

Prime Minister, Lubomír Štrougal.
First Deputy Prime Minister, Rudolf Rohlíček.
Deputy Prime Ministers, Ladislav Adamec; Peter Colotka; Matej Lúčan; Svatopluk Potač; Jaromír Obzina.

Ministers

Agriculture and Food, Miroslav Toman.
Finance, Jaromír Zák.
Foreign Affairs, Bohuslav Chňoupek.
Foreign Trade, Jan Štěrba.
Fuel and Power, Vlastimil Ehrenberger.
Interior, Vratislav Vajnar.
Labour and Social Affairs, Miroslav Boda.
National Defence, Col. Gen. Milan Václavík.
Transport and Communications, Vladimir Blažek.
People's Control, František Ondřich.
Prices, Pavel Hrivnak.
Metallurgy, Engineering and Electrical Engineering, Ladislav Gerle.
Without Portfolio, Marian Čalfe.
Chairman of State Planning Commission, Svatopluk Potač.

Prime Minister of the Czech Socialist Republic, Ladislav Adamec.
Prime Minister of the Slovak Socialist Republic, Dr. Peter Colotka.

Czechoslovak Communist Party

Presidium of the Central Committee, G. Husák; L. Adamec; V. Bilak; P. Colotka; K. Hoffman; A. Indra; M. Jakeš; J. Kempný; J. Lenárt; L. Štrougal; J. Fojtík; I. Janák (*full members*); M. Hruškovič; J. Haman; V. Herman; F. Pitra; M. Hruškovič; M. Zavadil (*candidate members*).
Secretariat of the Central Committee, Miloš Jakeš (*General Secretary*); M. Beňo; V. Bilak; J. Fojtík; F. Pitra; F. Hanus; K. Hoffmann; J. Lehart (*secretaries*); M. Kabrhelová; Z. Hoření; V. Mohorita; J. Poledník; M. Štěpán (*members*).

Czechoslovak Embassy
25 Kensington Palace Gardens, W8 4QY
[01–229 1255]

Ambassador Extraordinary and Plenipotentiary, His Excellency Jan Fidler (1986).
Counsellor, R. Hronek.
Commercial Counsellor, S. Žiak.
Military and Air Attaché, Col. Jaromír Široký.
Commercial Attachés, J. Slánský; J. Navara.
Assistant Military and Air Attaché, Maj. B. Kramář.
Press Secretary, J. Pavlíček.

Area and Population.—Czechoslovakia, formerly part of the Austro-Hungarian Empire, declared its independence on Oct. 28, 1918 (Czechoslovak Independence Day). It has an area of 49,370 sq. miles (127,869 sq. km.). The population of Czechoslovakia (1985 U.N. estimate) was 15,500,000.
Government.—The Communist Party came to power in Czechoslovakia in February, 1948, and Communist control of the country is now unqualified.

On July 11, 1960, a new constitution was proclaimed, replacing that of 1948 and the official title of the State was accordingly changed to "The Czechoslovak Socialist Republic".
In January, 1968, pressures for reform of the system led to the proposal of new legislation, which envisaged the democratization of the country's political life, greater guarantees of fundamental liberties and the establishment of a federal system.
The implications for the internal development of the other communist regimes in Eastern Europe and the Soviet Union, as well as for the system of alliances among these countries, alarmed the Soviet Union. On the night of August 20, Czechoslovakia was invaded by Soviet, Polish, East German, Hungarian and Bulgarian troops, the capital and all major towns being occupied. The Czechoslovak leadership was forced to modify its policies and to legalize the presence of Soviet troops on Czechoslovak territory. With the exception of the Federal system of government, the reforms of 1968 were abandoned when Gustáv Husák became leader of the Communist party in April 1969.
Czechoslovakia now consists of the Czech Socialist Republic and the Slovak Socialist Republic, each of which has its own government responsible to its legislative body—the National Council. Areas such as the constitution, defence, foreign affairs, state material reserves and currency are the responsibility of the Federal Administration. The Federal Government is responsible to the Federal Assembly, which is composed of two Chambers, the Chamber of the People, whose deputies are elected throughout the Federation, and the Chamber of the Nations, consisting of an equal number of Czech and Slovak Deputies. The federal system was not extended to the organization of the Communist Party.
The Economic System.—Under the present political system industry is state-owned, and nearly all agricultural land is cultivated by state or co-operative farms. Economic planning is centralized, and state economic plans have the force of law. In Jan. 1987 a programme of "reconstruction" was announced, aimed at increasing the efficiency of the economy by a measure of decentralization and relaxation of controls.
Czechoslovakia is not rich in minerals, although significant quantities of coal, brown coal and lignite are mined. Principal agricultural products are sugar-beet, potatoes and cereal crops; the timber industry is also very important. The country has long been highly industrialized, and machinery, industrial consumer goods and raw materials are major exports. The 8th Five Year Plan (1986–90) aims to raise national income by 18–19 per cent over the five years.
Language and Literature.—Czech and Slovak are the official languages, each having its own literature. The Reformation gave a wide-spread impulse to Czech literature, the writings of Jan Hus (martyred in 1415 as a religious and social reformer) familiarizing the people with Wyclif's teaching. This impulse endured to the close of the 17th century when Jan Amos Komensky or Comenius (1592–1670) was expelled from the country. Under Austrian rule and with the persistent pursuit of Germanization, there was a period of stagnation until the national revival in the first half of the 19th century. Authors of international reputation include Jaroslav Hašek (1883–1923), Jaroslav Seifert (1901–1986, Nobel Prize for Literature, 1985), Václav Havel (b. 1936) and Milan Kundera (b. 1929). Many of the best Czechoslovak authors are either in exile or in disfavour at home.
Education.—Education is compulsory and free for all children from the ages of 6 to 16. The number of pupils in basic nine-year schools is 1,992,000 (1983). There are 175,198 students in the secondary grammar schools and the number given for technical schools

of all kinds is 290,038. There are five universities in Czechoslovakia of which the most famous is Charles University in Prague (founded 1348), the others being situated at Bratislava, Brno, Olomouc and Košice. In addition there are a considerable number of other institutions of university standing, technical colleges, agricultural colleges, etc.

Trade with U.K.

	1986	1987
Imports from U.K.	£108,836,000	£114,101,000
Exports to U.K.	125,366,000	141,472,000

CAPITAL.—Prague (Praha), on the Vltava (Moldau), the former capital of Bohemia with a population (1985) of 1,190,576. Other towns are Brno (Brünn), capital of Moravia (381,000), Bratislava (Pressburg), capital of Slovakia (401,000), Ostrava (324,000), Košiče (214,000) and Plzen (Pilsen) (174,000).

CURRENCY.—Koruna (Kcs) or Czechoslovak Crown of 100 Haléru (Heller).

FLAG.—Two equal horizontal stripes, white (above) and red; a blue triangle next to staff.

NATIONAL ANTHEM.—Kde Domov Můj (Where is my Motherland).

NATIONAL DAY.—May 9.

BRITISH EMBASSY
Thunovská 14, 11800 Prague 1.
[Prague 533347]

Ambassador Extraordinary and Plenipotentiary, His Excellency Stephen Jeremy Barrett, C.M.G.
Counsellor, J. M. Macgregor (*Head of Chancery*).
Defence and Military Attaché, Col. R. J. M. Drummond, O.B.E.
Air Attaché, Wing-Cdr. C. A. S. Maynard.
Cultural Attaché, J. R. Potts (*British Council Representative*).

DENMARK
(Kongeriget Danmark)

Queen, Margrethe II, eldest daughter of King Frederik IX, *born* April 16, 1940, *succeeded* Jan. 14, 1972, *married* June 10, 1967, Count Henri de Monpezat (Prince Henrik of Denmark) and *has issue* Crown Prince Frederik *born* May 26, 1968; and Prince Joachim, *born* June 7, 1969.

CABINET
(as at June 1988)

Prime Minister, Poul Schlüter (*C*).
Foreign Affairs, Uffe Ellemann-Jensen (*V*).
Finance, Palle Simonsen (*C*).
Justice, Erik Ninn-Hansen (*C*).
Economy, Niels Helveg Petersen (*RL*).
Environment, Lone Dybkjaer (*RL*).
Education and Research, Bertel Haarder (*V*).
Social Affairs, Aase Olesen (*RL*).
Ecclesiastical Affairs, Torben Rechendorff (*C*).
Energy, Jens Bilgrav-Nielsen (*RL*).
Fisheries, Lars Gammelgaard (*C*).
Labour, Henning Dyremose (*C*).
Interior and Nordic Co-operation, Thor Pedersen (*V*).
Culture, Ole Vig Jensen (*RL*).
Industry, Nils Wilhjelm (*C*).
Traffic and Communications, Hans Peter Clausen (*C*).
Taxation, Anders Fogh Rasmussen (*V*).
Health, Elsebeth Kock-Petersen (*V*).
Agriculture, Laurits Toernaes (*V*).
Defence, Knud Enggaard (*V*).
Housing, Agnete Laustsen (*C*).

C, Conservative Party; *V*, Venstre (Liberals); *RL*, Radical Liberal Party.

ROYAL DANISH EMBASSY IN LONDON
55 Sloane Street, SW1X 9SR
[01–235 1255]

Ambassador Extraordinary and Plenipotentiary, His Excellency Potor Dyvig (1086).
Minister Counsellors, H. M. Kofoed-Hansen; P. Essemann (*Commercial*); J. Anker Nielsen (*Press and Culture*); S. R. Nielsen (*Economic and Consular Affairs*).
Defence Attaché, Col. F. Tingleff.

Area and Population.—A Kingdom of Northern Europe, consisting of the islands of Zeeland, Funen, Lolland, etc., the peninsula of Jutland, and the outlying island of Bornholm in the Baltic, the Faroes and Greenland. Denmark is situated between 54° 34′–57° 45′ N. lat., 8° 5′–15° E. 12′ long., with an area of 16,629 sq. miles (43,069 sq. km.), and a population estimated (1987) of 5,124,794.

Government.—Under the Constitution of the Kingdom of Denmark Act of June 5, 1953, the legislature consists of one chamber, the *Folketing*, of not more than 179 members, including 2 for the Faröes and 2 for Greenland. The voting age is 18.

The new Coalition government of Mr. Poul Schluter was formed in June 1988 after the General Election on May 10.

Education is free and compulsory. Special schools are numerous, commercial, technical and agricultural predominating. There are Universities at Copenhagen (founded in 1479), Aarhus (1933), Odense (1966), Roskilde (1972) and Aalborg (1974). A further University at Esbjerg is planned.

Language and Literature.—The Danish language is akin to Swedish and Norwegian. Danish literature, ancient and modern, embraces all forms of expression, familiar names being Hans Christian Andersen (1805–1875), Sören Kierkegaard (1813–1855) and Karen Blixen (1885–1962). Some 48 newspapers are published in Denmark; 10 daily papers are published in Copenhagen.

Production and Industry.—Of the labour force, in 1985, 6·9 per cent was engaged in agriculture, fishing, forestry, etc.; 27·3 per cent. in manufacturing, building and construction; 11·3 per cent. in commerce and 53·7 per cent. in administration, transport, financial services, the liberal professions, etc. The chief agricultural products are pigs, cattle, dairy products, poultry and eggs, seeds, cereals and sugar beet; manufactures are mostly based on imported raw material but there are also considerable imports of finished goods.

Communications.—Mercantile marine (ships above 100 gross tonnage) at end of 1985, totalled 598 ships, with a gross tonnage of 4,339,757. In 1984 there was 2,471 km. of railway.

FINANCE (BUDGET ESTIMATES)

	1985	1986
Revenue	*Kr.* 204,100m.	*Kr.* 185,955m.
Expenditure	240,600m.	185,437m.

Denmark's balance of payments on current account showed a deficit for 1986 of *Kr.*34,545 million (1985, *Kr.* 28,400 million).

MERCHANDISE TRADE

The principal imports are petroleum and its products, machinery, raw materials, vehicles and textile products. The chief exports are agricultural and dairy products and machinery.

	1985	1986
	Kr. million	
Total Imports	191,371	185,955
Total Exports	179,339	185,437

Trade with U.K.

	1986	1987
Imports from U.K.	£1,211,637,000	£1,231,097,000
Exports to U.K.	1,752,174,000	1,873,495,000

CAPITAL.—Ψ Copenhagen, pop. (1987), 469,706; Greater Copenhagen, 1,716,237. Other centres are: Ψ Aarhus, 255,932; Ψ Odense 173,331; Ψ Aalborg, 154,853; Ψ Esbjerg, 80,825; Ψ Randers, 61,094; Helsingør, 56,618; Ψ Kolding, 57,148; Ψ Horsens, 54,676; Roskilde, 48,862; Ψ Vejle, 50,492; Ψ Fredericia, 45,935.

CURRENCY.—Danish Krone (Kr.) of 100 Øre.

FLAG.—Red, with white cross.

NATIONAL ANTHEM.—Kong Kristian.

NATIONAL DAY.—April 16 (The Queen's Birthday).

BRITISH EMBASSY

36–40 Kastelsvej, DK-2100 Copenhagen.
[Copenhagen 264600]

Ambassador Extraordinary and Plenipotentiary, His Excellency Nigel Christopher Ransome Williams, C.M.G. (1989).

Counsellors, J. W. Hodge (*Head of Chancery*); P. Longworth (*Commercial*).

Defence Attaché, Cmdr. T. Goetz, R.N.

There are Consulates at *Aabenraa, Aalborg, Aarhus, Esbjerg, Fredericia, Odense* and at *Tórshavn* (Faröe Islands).

British Council Representative and Cultural Attaché, J. A. A. H. Moore, Møntergade 1, Copenhagen.

Outlying Parts of the Kingdom

THE FARÖES, or Sheep Islands (540 sq. miles; 1,399 sq. km.; pop. (1985) 46,000), capital, Thorshavn, are governed by a *Lagting* of 26 members, a *Landsstyre* of 4 members which deals with special Faröes affairs, and send 2 representatives to the *Folketing* at Copenhagen. On Sept. 14, 1946, the *Lagting,* with the consent of the Danish Government, for its own guidance held a plebiscite on the Faröes. About one-third of the electors did not, however, take part in the voting: of the rest a little more than half the votes cast were in favour of separation from Denmark and the establishment of a republic. At subsequent general election for the *Lagting* a great majority voted in favour of remaining part of the Kingdom of

Denmark with a certain measure of home rule and in 1948 the Faröes received this. The Faröes are not part of the E.C.

Prime Minister, Atli Dam.

GREENLAND (ice-free portion about 132,000 sq. m., total area about 840,000 sq. m., population (1985) 52,940) is divided into 3 provinces (West, North and East). Greenland (capital, Nuuk (Godthåb)) has a *Landsraad* of 17 members and sends 2 representatives to the *Folketing* at Copenhagen. Greenland attained a status of internal autonomy on May 1, 1979. The trade of Greenland is mainly under the management of the Royal Greenland Trade Department. Following a plebiscite Greenland negotiated its withdrawal from the E.C., but without discontinuing relations with Denmark, and left in Feb. 1, 1985. Mineral and oil prospecting revealed deposits of lead, zinc, iron ore, oil, gas and uranium. Commercial exploitation of these resources has already begun. The United States of America has acquired certain rights to maintain air bases in Greenland.

Premier, Jonathan Motzfeldt.

DJIBOUTI
(Jumhouriyya Djibouti)

President, Hassan Gouled Aptidon.

CABINET

Prime Minister and Minister for Port Affairs, Barkat Gourad Hamadou.

Justice, Omar Kamil Warsama.

Foreign Affairs and Co-operation, Moumin Bahdon Farah.

Interior, Posts and Telecommunications, Youssouf Ali Chirdon.

Defence, Moussa Boúraleh Robleh.

Finance, Mohamed Djaha Elabeh.

Commerce, Transport and Tourism, Moussa Bouraleh Robleh.

Education, Youth and Sports, Souleiman Farah Lodon.

Public Health, Mohamed Adabo Kako.

Labour, Mohamed Del Waiss.

Civil Service and Administrative Reform, Helem Houmed.

Public Works, Town Planning and Housing, Bourhan Ali Warki.

Industry, Salem Abdou Yaya.

Rural Development, Ahmed Hassan Liban.

Formerly known as French Somaliland and then the French Territory of the Afars and the Issas, the country became independent on June 27, 1977. Djibouti is situated on the north-east coast of Africa (i.e. the Horn of Africa) and has an area of 8,494 sq. miles (22,000 sq. km.). It has an estimated population (1985) of 430,000. The climate is harsh and much of the country is semi-arid desert. The French continue to maintain army, navy and air force bases. Djibouti has an excellent port, international airport and a railway line runs to Addis Ababa.

Trade with U.K.

	1986	1987
Imports from U.K.	£12,537,000	£12,501,000
Exports to U.K.	53,000	175,000

CAPITAL.—Ψ Djibouti (1985, 200,000).

CURRENCY.—Djibouti Franc of 100 Centimes.

FLAG.—Blue over green with white triangle in the hoist containing a red star.

NATIONAL DAY.—June 27 (Independence Day).

BRITISH CONSULATE

P.O. Box 81/9–11, Rue de Geneve, Djibouti.

Honorary Consul, G. G. D. Cattle.

DOMINICAN REPUBLIC
(República Dominicana)

President, Dr. Joaquin Balaguer, *took office,* Aug. 16. 1986.
Vice-President, Carlos Morales Troncoso.

CABINET

Armed Forces, (vacant).
Interior and Police, Juan Cotes Morales.
Secretary for the Presidency, Rafael Bello Andino.
Administrative Secretary of the Presidency, Luis Toral.
Secretary of the Presidency (Technical), Guillermo Caram.
External Relations, Dr. Donald Reid Cabral.
Finance, Roberto Martinez Villanueva.
Education, Dr. Pedro C. Pichardo.
Agriculture, Agronomo Manuel Amezquita.
Public Works and Communications, A. Subero Sajuin.
Labour, Dr. José Carlos Isaias.
Public Health, Dr. Ney Arias Lora.
Industry and Commerce, Rafael Conrado Marion-Landais.
Sport, Temiztocle Metz.
Tourism, Fernando Rainieri.
Sec. of State without Portfolio, Simon Tomás Fernandéz.

HONORARY CONSULATE
6 Queen's Mansions, Brook Green, W6 7EB
[01–602 1885]
Honorary Consul, Mrs. J. De Wardener.
There are also Consular Offices at *Liverpool, Birmingham, Manchester, Grimsby, Southampton, Cardiff* and *Plymouth.*

The Dominican Republic, formerly the Spanish portion of the island of Hispaniola, is the oldest settlement of European origin in America. The western part of the island forms the Republic of Haiti. The island lies between Cuba on the west and Puerto Rico on the east and the Republic covers an area of 18,816 sq. miles (48,734 sq. km.), with a population (1984 Census) of 6,416,000. The climate is tropical in the lowlands and semi-tropical to temperate in the higher altitudes.

Spanish is the language of the Republic.

Government.—Santo Domingo was discovered by Christopher Columbus in December, 1492, and remained a Spanish Colony until 1821. In 1822 it was subjugated by the neighbouring Haitians who remained in control until 1844 when the Dominican Republic was proclaimed. The country was occupied by American marines from 1916 until the adoption of a new Constitution in 1924. From 1930 until May 30, 1961 (when he was assassinated) Generalissimo Rafael Trujillo ruled the country.

President Juan Bosch held office from Dec. 1962 to Sept. 1963, when he was deposed by a military junta. A revolt in favour of ex-President Bosch in April, 1965, developed into civil war lasting until September the same year when a provisional President was elected. On June 1, 1966, Dr. Joaquin Balaguer was elected President and in Nov. 1966 a new Constitution was introduced.

Executive power is vested in the President, who is elected by direct vote and serves for four years. The President forms his cabinet without reference to the Congress.

Legislative power is exercised by the Congress, which has a term of four years concurrent with the Presidency. The Upper Chamber is the Senate of 27 senators, one for each province and one for Santo Domingo. The lower is the Chamber of Deputies which has 120 members, one for each 50,000 inhabitants in each province, with the provision that no province has less than two members. Judicial power is exercised by the Supreme Court of Justice.

Communications.—According to local classification there are 2,932 miles of first class and 1,392 miles of second class and inter-communal roads in the Republic. There is a direct road from Santo Domingo to Port-au-Prince, the capital of Haiti, but that part of it in the border area has fallen into disuse. The frontier has been closed since Sept., 1967, except for that section crossed by the main road linking the two capitals. A telephone system connects practically all the principal towns of the republic and there is a telegraph service with all parts of the world. There are more than 90 commercial broadcasting stations and six television stations.

The Republic is served by two national and six foreign airlines, and an international airport 18 miles to the east of the capital is in operation. Another has been built near Puerto Plata on the north coast.

Economy.—Sugar, coffee, cocoa, and tobacco are the most important crops. Other products are peanuts, maize, rice, bananas, molasses, salt, cement, ferro-nickel, gold, silver, cattle, sisal products, honey and chocolate. There is a growing number of light industries producing beer, tinned foodstuffs, glass products, textiles, soap, cigarettes, construction materials, plastic articles, shoes, papers, paint, rum, matches, peanut oil and other products.

FINANCE

	1983	1984 (est.)
Budget		
Revenue	RD$999,300,000	RD$1,345,751,270

TRADE

The chief imports are machinery, food stuffs, iron and steel, cotton textiles and yarns, mineral oils (including petrol), cars and other motor vehicles, chemical and pharmaceutical products, electrical equipment and accessories, construction material, paper and paper products, and rubber and rubber products. The chief exports are sugar, coffee, cocoa, tobacco, chocolate, molasses, bauxite, ferro-nickel and gold. Tobacco and tobacco manufactures are the principal exports to the U.K.

	1983	1984
Imports	RD$1,279,019,958	RD$1,459,000,000
Exports	811,054,942	1,211,100,000

Trade with U.K.

	1986	1987
Imports from U.K.	£15,178,000	£23,887,000
Exports to U.K.	7,599,000	8,637,000

CAPITAL.—Ψ Santo Domingo, population of the Capital District (1981 census), 1,313,172. Other centres, with populations (1981 census); Santiago de los Caballeros (550,372); La Vega (385,043); San Francisco De Macoris (235,544); San Juan (239,957); San Cristóbal (446,132).

CURRENCY.—Dominican Republic Peso of 100 Centavos.

FLAG.—Red and blue, with white cross bearing an emblem at centre.

NATIONAL ANTHEM.—"Quisqueyanos Valientes, Alcemos" (Brave men of Quisqueya, let's raise our song).

NATIONAL DAY.—February 27 (Independence Day, 1844).

BRITISH AMBASSADOR, (resident at Caracas, Venezuela).

ECUADOR
(Republica del Ecuador)

President, Rodrigo Borja Cevallos, *took office* Aug. 10, 1988.

CABINET

Interior, Andrés Vallejo.
Foreign Affairs, Diego Cordovéz.
Education, Alfredo Vera.
Social Welfare, Raul Baca.
Health, Plutarco Naranjo.
Agriculture and Livestock, Enrique Delgado.
Public Works, Juan Neira.
Finance, Jorge Gallardo.
Industry and Commerce, Juan José Pons.
Energy and Mines, Diego Tamariz.
Employment, César Verduga.
Defence, Gen. Jorge Félix.

EMBASSY AND CONSULATE
Flat 3b, 3 Hans Crescent, SW1X 0LS
[01–584 1367/2648]

Ambassador Extraordinary and Plenipotentiary, His
Excellency Rafael Pérez y Reyna (1987).

Area and Population.—Ecuador is an equatorial
state of South America, the mainland extending from
lat. 1° 38′ N. to 4° 50′ S., and between 75° 20′ and 81°
W. long., comprising an area reduced by boundary
settlements with Peru (Jan. 29, 1942) to about 109,484
sq. miles (283,561 sq. km.).

The Republic of Ecuador is divided into 20 provinces. It has a population (1985 U.N. estimate) of
approximately 9,378,000, mostly descendants of the
Spanish, aboriginal Indians, and Mestizoes. The
territory of the Republic extends across the Western
Andes, the highest peaks in Ecuador being Chimbor-
azo (20,408 ft.) and Ilinza (17,405 ft.) in the Western
Cordillera; and Cotopaxi (19,612 ft.) and Cayambe
(19,160 ft.) in the Eastern Cordillera. Ecuador is
watered by the Upper Amazon, and by the rivers
Guayas, Mira, Santiago, Chone, and Esmeraldas on
the Pacific coast. There are extensive forests.

Government.—The former *Kingdom of Quito* was
conquered by the Incas of Peru in the latter part of
the 15th century. Early in the 16th century Pizarro's
conquests led to the inclusion of the present territory
of Ecuador in the Spanish Vice-royalty of Peru. The
independence of the country was achieved in a
revolutionary war which culminated in the battle of
Mount Pichincha (May 24, 1822).

After seven years of military rule, Ecuador returned to democracy in 1979. The present constitution, introduced in 1978, provides for an elected
President and Vice-President who serve for a four
year term. (Neither may stand for re-election.) There
is a Chamber of Representatives with 71 members
elected every four years, 12 of whom are elected on a
national basis and the rest by the provinces. The
Chamber meets for two months every year (Aug.–
Oct.) but can be convoked at any time for extraordinary sessions. Four Legislative Commissions meet
through the year.

Voting is compulsory for all literate and (since
1980) voluntary for all illiterate citizens over the age
of 18. Sixteen political parties took part in the 1988
elections.

Agriculture and Industry.—Agriculture is the most
important sector of the economy, supporting nearly
50 per cent of the population (particularly the poorest)
and contributing 14·5 per cent of the Gross Domestic
Product and 19·5 per cent of exports. The main
products for export are fish (mainly shrimps, tuna
and sardines), which had become the largest agricultural export by early 1982; bananas, which provide a
third of agricultural exports; cocoa and coffee. Other
important crops are sugar, corn, soya, rice, cotton,
African palm (for oil), vegetables, fruit and timber,
the temperate crops being produced mostly in the
highlands.

The economy was transformed by the discovery in
1972 of major oil fields in the Oriente area, and oil

accounted for two thirds of 1981 export earnings.
The economy grew rapidly in the 1970s but is now
faced with reduced growth, due mainly to the fall in
the price of oil. The oil deposits in the Oriente are
estimated at between 10–15,000 million barrels, and
further exploration and development is taking place.
The oil is evacuated by a trans-Andean pipeline to
the port of Balao (near Esmeraldes).

Communications.—There are 23,256 km. of permanent roads and 5,044 km. of roads which are only
open during the dry season. There are about 750
miles of railway, including the railway from Quito to
Guayaquil. Ten commercial airlines operate international flights, linking Ecuador with major foreign
cities and there are internal services between all
important towns.

Defence.—The standing Army has a strength of
about 38,000. There is an Air Force of some 120
aircraft of various kinds and 4,800 personnel. The
Navy is 4,500 strong.

Language, etc.—Spanish is the principal language
of the country but Quechua is also a recognized
language and is spoken by the majority of the Indian
population. As a result of an intensive national
education programme more than 75 per cent of the
population are now literate. Elementary education
is free and compulsory. There are 9 Universities, at
Quito (2), Guayaquil (3), Cuenca, Machala, Loja and
Portoviejo, Polytechnic Schools at Quito and Guayaquil and 8 technical colleges in other provincial
capitals. 2 daily newspapers are published at Quito
and 4 at Guayaquil.

Finance.—The estimated government budget at
Jan. 1985 was 144,151 million *sucres* (53,600 million
sucres in 1981). The balance of payments deficit
stands at U.S.$25 million, and foreign exchange
reserves at U.S.$195 million.

TRADE
Import licences are required for all merchandise
and these are issued by the Central Bank of Ecuador.

	1985
Imports	U.S.$1,614·5m.
Exports	2,904·6m.

Trade with U.K.

	1986	1987
Imports from U.K.	£46,673,000	£37,934,000
Exports to U.K.	11,339,000	14,002,000

Manufactured goods and machinery are the main
imports.

CAPITAL.—Quito. Population (1985 estimate),
1,003,875; Ψ Guayaquil (1,000,000) is the chief port;
Cuenca (110,000).

CURRENCY.—Sucre of 100 Centavos.

FLAG.—Three horizontal bands, yellow, blue and
red (the yellow band twice the width of the others);
emblem in centre.

NATIONAL DAY.—August 10 (*Independence Day*).

BRITISH EMBASSY
Calle Gonzalez Suarez, 111 (Casilla 314),
Quito.
[Quito 560669]

Ambassador Extraordinary and Plenipotentiary, His
Excellency Michael William Atkinson, C.M.G.,
M.B.E. (1985).

There is a British Consular Office at Guayaquil.

British Council Representative, J. T. Wright, O.B.E.,
Av. Amazonas 1646 (Casilla 8829), Quito.

The GALÁPAGOS (Giant Tortoise) ISLANDS forming
the province of the Archipelago de Colón, were
annexed by Ecuador in 1832. The archipelago lies in
the Pacific, about 500 miles from Saint Elena penin-

sula, the most westerly point of the mainland. There are 12 large and several hundred smaller islands with a total area of about 3,000 sq. miles and an estimated population (1982) of 6,119. The capital is San Cristobal, on Chatham Island. Although the archipelago lies on the equator, the temperature of the surrounding water is well below equatorial average owing to the *Antarctic Humboldt Current*. The province consists for the most part of National Park Territory, where unique marine birds, iguanas, and the giant tortoises are conserved. There is some local subsistence farming; the main industry, apart from tourism, is tuna and lobster fishing.

EGYPT
(Al-Jumhuriyat Misr al-Arabiya)

President, Muhammad Hosni Mubarak, *elected,* Oct. 14, 1981 *re-elected,* 1987.

COUNCIL OF MINISTERS

Prime Minister, Dr. Atef Muhammad Naguib Sidqi.
Deputy P.M. and Minister of Defence and Military Production, F. M. Muhammad Abdul Halim Abu Ghazala.
Deputy P.M. and Foreign Minister, Dr. Ahmed Ismat Abdul Magid.
Deputy P.M. and Minister of Planning and International Co-operation, Dr. Kamal Ahmed al-Ganzuri.
Deputy P.M. and Minister of Agriculture and Land Reclamation, Dr. Yussif Amin Wali.
Economy and Foreign Trade, Dr. Yussri Ali Mustafa.
Finance, Dr. Muhammad Ahmed el-Razzaz.
Interior, Maj.-Gen. Zaki Badr.
Oil and Mineral Wealth, Abdul-Hadi Muhammad Qandil.
Tourism and Civil Aviation, Fouad Abdul Latif Sultan.
Justice, Farouq Saif al-Nasr.
Culture, Farouq Hosni.
Industry, Muhammad Mahmoud Abdul Wahhab.
Parliamentary and Shura Council Affairs, Dr. Ahmed Salama.
Supply and Internal Trade, Dr. Mohammed Galaleddin Abdul-Dahab.
Public Works and Water Resources, 'Issam Abdul Hamid Radi.
Manpower and Vocational Training, Assem Abdul Haq.
Education, Dr. Ahmed Fathi Sorour.
Transport, Communications and Marine Transport, Suliman Metwalli Suliman.
Scientific Research, Dr. Adel Abul-Hamid 'Ezz.
Health, Dr. Mohammed Ragheb Dawidar.
Information, Muhammad Safwat al-Sharif.
Cabinet Affairs and Administrative Development, Dr. 'Atif Mohammad 'Ebeid.
Religious Affairs (Waqfs), Dr. Muhammad Ali Mahgoub.
Social Affairs and Social Insurance, Dr. Amal Abdul Rahim Osman.
Electricity and Energy, Mohammad Mahir Osman Abaza.
Housing, New Communities and Public Utilities, Hasaballah Mohammad al-Kafrawi.
Ministers of State, Dr. Boutros Yussef Boutros-Ghali (*Foreign Affairs*); Gamal al-Sayyid Ibrahim (*Military Production*); Dr. Fouad Iskander (*Immigration and Egyptians living abroad*); Dr. Mouris Makramallah (*International Co-operation*).

EGYPTIAN EMBASSY
26 South Street, W1Y 8EL
[01–499 2401]

Ambassador Extraordinary and Plenipotentiary, His Excellency Yousef Sharara (1984).

AREA AND POPULATION.—The total area of Egypt is 386,662 sq. miles (1,001,449 sq. km.), only three per cent of which is cultivated land, with a population now officially estimated (1987) at 52,000,000.

There are three distinct elements in the native population. The largest, or "Egyptian" element, is a Hamito-Semite race, known in the rural districts as *Fellahin (fellâh*—ploughman, or tiller of the soil). A second element is the *Bedouin,* or nomadic Arabs of the Western and Arabian deserts, of whom about one-seventh are real nomads, and the remainder semi-sedentary tent-dwellers on the outskirts of the cultivated end of the Nile Valley and the Fayûm. The third element is the *Nubian* of the Nile Valley between Aswân and Wadi-Halfa of mixed Arab and Negro blood. Over 90 per cent of the population are Moslems of the Sunnî denomination, and most of the rest Coptic Christians.

The territory of Egypt comprises (1) Egypt Proper, forming the N.E. corner of the African continent, divisible into (*a*) the valley and delta of the Nile, (*b*) the Western Desert, and (*c*) the Arabian or Eastern Desert; (2) The Peninsula of Sinai, forming part of the continent of Asia; and (3) a number of Islands in the Gulf of Suez and Red Sea, of which the principal are Jubal, Shadwan, Gafatin and Zeberged (or St. John's Island). This territory lies between 22° and 32° N. lat. and 24° and 37° E. long. The northern boundary is the Mediterranean, and in the south Egypt is conterminous with the Sudan. The western boundary runs from a point on the coast 10 kilometres N.W. of Sollûm to the latitude of Siwa and thence due S. along the 25th meridian. The E. boundary follows a line drawn from Rafa on the Mediterranean (34° 15′ E. long.) to the head of the Gulf of 'Aqaba.

Physical Features.—The country is mainly flat but there are mountainous areas in the south-west, along the Red Sea coast and in the south of the Sinai peninsula, rising in some places to peaks of over 6,000 ft. The highest mountain in Egypt is Mt. Catherina (8,668 ft). Most of the land is desert but the Nile valley and delta are covered by silt 20–30 feet deep, and areas of desert are increasingly being reclaimed by irrigation and fertilization.

The Nile has a total length of 4,145 miles. In the 960 miles of its course through Egypt it receives not a single tributary stream. The river formerly had a regular yearly rise and fall of about 13 feet at Cairo, but since the completion of the Aswan High Dam in 1965, there has been no flood downstream of the dam and the water level remains almost constant throughout the year. The area of fertile land, a 5–15 mile wide strip in the Nile valley and some 6,000 square miles of the Nile delta, has been increased by the opening of the Aswan Dam. This has allowed the reclamation of about 1,300,000 acres, and a further 700,000 acres have been converted from basin to perennial irrigation. Westward from the Nile Valley stretches the Western desert, containing some depressions, whose springs irrigate small areas known as *Oases*, of which the principal, from S.E. to N.W., are known as Kharga, Dakhla, Farafra, Baharia and Siwa.

In the Eastern Desert between the Nile and the mountains along the Red Sea coast, are plateaux of sandstones and limestones, dissected by *wadis* (dry water-courses), often of great length and depth, with some wild vegetation and occasional wells and springs.

History.—The unification of the Kingdoms of Lower and Upper Egypt under the Pharaohs in *c.* 3,100 B.C. marked the establishment of the Egyptian state, with Memphis as its capital. Egypt was ruled for nearly 2,800 years by a succession of Pharaonic dynasties (31 in all), which built the pyramids at Gizeh. The oldest of these is that of Zoser, built *c.* 2,700 B.C., and the highest the Great Pyramid of Cheops, at 451 feet; nearby is the Sphinx, 189 feet long. A period of Hellenic rule began in 332 B.C., after the conquest of Egypt by Alexander the Great, followed by a period of rule by Rome (30 B.C. to A.D. 324) and then by the Byzantine Empire. In A.D. 640 Egypt was subjugated by Arab Muslim invaders, becoming a province of the Eastern Caliphate. In 1517 the country was incorporated in the Ottoman Empire under which it remained until early in the 19th century.

A British Protectorate over Egypt declared on Dec. 18, 1914, lasted until Feb. 28, 1922, when Sultan Ahmed Fuad was proclaimed King of Egypt. In July, 1952, following a military coup d'état, King Farouk abdicated in favour of his infant son, who became King Ahmed Fuad II. In June, 1953, however, Gen. Neguib's military council deposed the young king, and Egypt became a Republic.

In 1956, as a result of Egypt's trade agreements with Communist countries, Britain and U.S.A. withdrew offers of financial aid and in retaliation Pres. Nasser seized the assets of the Suez Canal Company. An Egyptian invasion of the Canal Zone while repulsing an Israeli attack provoked military action by Britain and France in support of their Suez Canal Company interests. A ceasefire and Anglo-French withdrawal were negotiated by the U.N.

The Israeli invasion of 1956 overran the Sinai peninsula but six months later Israel withdrew and a U.N. peace-keeping force was established in the area. However, mounting tension culminated in a second invasion of Sinai (the Six Day War of June 1967) and occupation of the peninsula by Israel. Egypt's attempt to recapture the territory (the Yom Kippur War of October 1973) was unsuccessful but Sinai was returned to Egypt in April 1982, under the treaty of 1979 which resulted from the Camp David talks between Pres. Sadat and Mr. Begin and formally terminated a 31-year old state of war between the two countries. Pres. Hosni Mubarak came to power on Oct. 6, 1981 after the assassination of Pres. Sadat by Moslem fundamentalists.

Government.—The Constitution of 1971 provides for an executive President who appoints Ministers to the Cabinet. The President determines policy which the Cabinet implements and Ministers are responsible to him. The Legislature consists of the People's Assembly (458 members, 448 of whom are elected, the remaining 10 nominated by the President); the Shura Council, or Consultative Assembly (210 members) has an advisory role. The Constitution guarantees also the independence of the Judiciary. Religious courts were abolished in 1956 and their functions transferred to the national court system. Freedom of the press is guaranteed under the Constitution.

Agriculture.—Despite increasing industrialization, agriculture remains the most important economic activity, employing over 45 per cent of the labour force and contributing to 17 per cent. of the country's exports. Agricultural output has been increased as a result of land reclamation programmes and the introduction of more efficient methods, e.g. the change from basin to perennial irrigation which yields 2–3 crops per year instead of one, the pivotal sprinkling irrigation system which uses water more efficiently, and the increasing mechanization and use of fertilizers. Egypt is still a net importer of foodstuffs, especially grain, and a food security programme has been set up with the aim of achieving self-sufficiency through the use of more advanced technology. Estimates suggest that an additional 3 million acres of land could be reclaimed by the end of the century.

The main cash crop is cotton, of which Egypt is one of the world's main producers. Production in 1986 was 403,000 tons. Other important summer crops are (1986 figures) maize 2,908,000 tons, rice 2,445,000 tons, and sugar cane 9,684,000 tons. Important winter crops are wheat 1,929,000 tons, and beans 382,000 tons. Citrus fruit and other fruits and vegetables are also grown.

Energy.—With its considerable reserves of petroleum and natural gas in Sinai, the Nile Delta and the Western Desert, and the hydro-electric power produced by the Aswan and High Dams, Egypt is self-sufficient in energy. Electricity has been provided to almost all of the country and there are plans to extend the natural gas network to all major cities.

Industry.—The production of petroleum provides Egypt with its major export (60–65 per cent. of total exports), and supports a growing refining industry. Steel production is another important heavy industry. The major manufacturing industries are in food processing, motor cars and electrical goods, chemical products and yarns and textiles.

FINANCE

	1986–87	1987–88
Estimated revenue ..	£E12·4m.	£E14·2m.
Total expenditure ...	19·9m.	21·7m.

TRADE

The main imports are wheat and flour, wood and trucks. The main exports are crude petroleum, cotton, cotton yarn, oranges, rice and cotton textiles.

	1986–87
Imports	£E7·8m.
Exports	2·6m.

Trade with U.K.

	1986	1987
Imports from U.K.	£371,007,000	£342,195,000
Exports to U.K.	328,053,000	127,261,000

Communications.—The road and rail networks link the Nile Valley and Delta with the main development areas to east and west of the river.

The Suez Canal was re-opened in 1975 and a two-stage development project begun to widen and deepen the canal to allow the passage of larger shipping and to permit two-way traffic. Port Said and Suez have been reconstructed and the port of Alexandria is being improved.

CAPITAL.—Cairo (population, estimated in 1986 at 14,000,000), stands on the E. bank of the Nile, about

14 miles from the head of the Delta. Its oldest part is the fortress of Babylon in old Cairo, with its Roman bastions and Coptic churches. The earliest Arab building is the Mosque of 'Amr, dating from A.D. 643, and the most conspicuous is the Citadel, built by Saladin towards the end of the 12th century and containing in its walls the Mosque of Mohamed Ali built in the 19th century.

ΨAlexandria (estimated population in 1986 of 5,000,000), founded 332 B.C. by Alexander the Great, was for over 1,000 years the capital of Egypt and a centre of Hellenic culture which vied with Athens herself. Its great *pharos* (lighthouse), 480 feet high, with a lantern burning resinous wood, was one of the "Seven Wonders of the World". Other towns are: Ismailia (400,000); ΨPort Said (285,000); Mansura (120,000); Asyût (300,000); Faiyûm (180,000); Tanta (150,000); Mahalla el Kubra (130,000); ΨSuez; ΨDamietta (100,000).

CURRENCY.—Egyptian Pound (£E) of 100 Piastres and 1,000 Millièmes.

FLAG.—Horizontal bands of red, white and black, with an eagle in the centre of the white band.

NATIONAL DAY.—July 23 (Anniversary of Revolution in 1952).

BRITISH EMBASSY
Ahmed Ragheb Street, Garden City, Cairo
[Cairo 354–0850]

Ambassador Extraordinary and Plenipotentiary, His Excellency (William) James Adams, C.M.G. (1987).
British Council Representative, G. Tindale, 192 Sharia el Nil, Agouza, Cairo. There is also a library in Alexandria.

EQUATORIAL GUINEA
(República de Guinea Ecuatorial)

President, Col. Teodoro Obiang Nguema Mbasogo, *took office,* Aug. 1979.

MINISTERS

Minister of Defence, Security and Political Affairs, The President.
Prime Minister and Minister for Health, C. Seriche Bioko.
Deputy P.M., Minister of Territorial Administration and National Security, Monsuy Andeme.
Public Works, Housing, Town Planning, Alejandro Envoro Ovono.
Economic Planning, Hilario Nsue Alene.
Education and Sport, Fortunato Nzambi Michinde.
Information and Tourism, Leandro Mbomio Nsue.
Labour, Anacleto Ejapa Bolekia.
Communications and Transport, Demetrio Elo Ndongo Nsefumu.
Agriculture, Alfredo Abero Nvono.
Industry and Commerce, Francisco Pascual Obama Eyegue.
Justice and Religion, Angel Ndong Micha.
Civil Service, Massoko Mecheba Ikaka.
Secretary-General to the Presidency, Martin Mka Esono.
Territorial Administration, Isidoro Eyi Monsuy Andeme.
Energy, Juan Olo Mba Nseng.
Water Resources and Forestry, Angel Alogo Nchama.
Foreign Affairs, Marcelino Nguema Ongueme.
Finance, Felipe Inestroca Ikaka.
Relations with the House of Reps, Eloy Elo Nve Mbengono.
Deputy Minister of Defence, Maj. Melanio Ebendeng Nsomo.

Equatorial Guinea (formerly Spanish Guinea) consists of the island of Biogo (formerly Macias

Nguema), in the Bight of Biafra about 20 miles from the west coast of Africa, Pagalu Island (formerly Annobon) in the Gulf of Guinea, the Corisco Islands (Corisco, Elobey Grande and Elobey Chico) and Rio Muni, a mainland area between Cameroon and Gabon. It has a total area of 10,830 sq. miles (28,051 sq. km.), and a population (1985 U.N. estimate) of 392,000.

Government.—Formerly colonies of Spain, the territories now forming the Republic of Equatorial Guinea were constituted as two provinces of Metropolitan Spain, in 1960, became autonomous in 1964 and fully independent in 1968. Serious disorders in Rio Muni early in 1969 caused many of the Spanish community to leave. Following Nigerian allegations of continuing mistreatment, most of the Nigerian labour force, on whom cocoa production largely depended, were repatriated in late 1975 and early 1976.

In Aug. 1979, President Macias was deposed by a revolutionary military council headed by his nephew Col. T. Obiang Nguema. The first parliamentary elections since 1968 were held on Aug. 28, 1983, under a new constitution approved by a referendum in Aug. 1982. Forty-one representatives were elected to the National Assembly for a five-year term.

Economy.—The chief products are cocoa, coffee and wood (which is exported almost entirely from Rio Muni). Production has declined and except for cocoa, there is little commercial agriculture and the economy is now heavily dependent on outside aid, principally from Spain. Equatorial Guinea entered the 'Franc zone' in 1985.

TRADE

	1984
Total Imports	US$18·7m.
Total Exports	30·0m.

Trade with U.K.

	1986	1987
Imports from U.K.	£633,000	£1,572,000
Exports to U.K.	1,000	—

CAPITAL.—ΨMalabo on the island of Bioco (population 1983 estimate, 34,980). ΨBata is the principal town and port of Rio Muni.

CURRENCY.— Franc C.F.A. of 100 Centimes.

FLAG.—Three horizontal bands, green over white over red; blue triangle next staff; coat of arms in centre of white band.

NATIONAL DAY.—October 12.

British Ambassador, (resides at Yaoundé).

ETHIOPIA
(Hebretesebawit Ityopia)

President of the People's Democratic Republic, Mengistu Haile Mariam, *elected* Sept. 10, 1987.
Vice President, Lt.-Col. Fisseha Desta.

STATE COUNCIL

Vice Presidents, Emanuel Amde-Mikhail; Debela Dinsa; Yusuf Ahmed.
Secretary, Embibe Ayele.
Members, Capt. Fikre Selassie Wogderesse; Lt.-Gen. Tesfaye Gebre Kidan; Lt.-Col. Berhanu Bayeh; Addis Tedla; Hailu Yimenu; Alemu Agebe; Fasika Sidelil; Tesfaye Dinka; Shewandagn Belete; Endalle Tessema; Ashagre Yigletu; Tefera Wonde; Kasaye Aragaw; Tadese Tamirat; Abdela Sonesa; Haile Gabriel Dagne; Asegedech Bizuneh; Getachew Robele.

COUNCIL OF MINISTERS

Prime Minister, Capt. Fikre Selassie Wogderesse.
Agriculture, Geremew Debele.
Coffee and Tea Development, Tekola Dejene.
Construction, Kassa Gebre.
Culture, Youth and Sports, Maj. Girma Yilma.
Defence, Maj.-Gen. Haile Giorgis Haile Mariam.
Domestic Trade, Mersha Wodajo.
Education, Dr. Yaherad Kitaw.
Finance, Wole Chekol.
Foreign Affairs, Lt.-Col. Berhanu Bayeh.
Foreign Trade, Tadesse Gebre Kidan.
Health, Brig.-Gen. Gizaw Tsehai.
Industry, Maj.-Gen. Fanta Belai.
Information and National Guidance, Abdul Hafis Yusuf.
Internal Affairs, Col. Tesfaye Wolde Selassie.
Labour and Social Affairs, Shimelis Adugna.
Law and Justice, Wondayen Mehretu.
Mines, Energy and Water Resources, Tekeze Shoa Autenfesu.
State Farms, Yoseph Muleta.
Transport and Communications, Asegid Wolde Amanuel.
Urban Development and Housing, Tesfaye Maru.
Ministers in President's Office, Dr. Feleke Gedle-Ghiorgis *(Foreign Relations);* Maj.-Gen. Kefelegn Yibza *(Chief Inspector of Military Affairs);* Neguse Wolde Mikael *(Chief Inspector of Economic, Social and Administrative Affairs);* Maj.-Gen. Seyoum Mekonen *(Chief of Defence and Security).*

EMBASSY IN LONDON
17 Prince's Gate, SW7 1PZ
[01-589 7212]

Ambassador Extraordinary and Plenipotentiary, His Excellency Ato Teferra Haile-Selassie (1985).

Position and Extent.—Ethiopia is in North-Eastern Africa, bounded on the north-west by the Sudan; on the south by Kenya; on the east by Djibouti and the Republic of Somalia: and on the north-east by the Red Sea. The area is 471,778 sq. miles (1,221,900 sq. km.), with a population (1985) of 43,350,000. About one-third are of the dominant race of Semitic origin (Amharas and Tigreans) and the remainder mainly Gallas (about 40 per cent of the population), Somalis and Afar.

Ethiopia has a large central plateau (average height, 6,000–7,000 ft.) which rises to nearly 15,000 ft.

at Ras Dashan in the north. The plateau drops to the Nile basin in the west and the Red Sea in the east. To the north (Eritrea) and east (Ogaden) the land is mostly desert. The chief river is the Blue Nile, issuing from Lake Tana; the Atbara and many other tributaries of the Nile also rise in the Ethiopian highlands.

Those of Semitic origin (Amharas and Tigreans), and many of the Gallas, are Christians of the Ethiopian Orthodox Church, which was formerly led by the head of the Coptic Church, the Patriarch at Alexandria. Since 1959, however, the Ethiopian Church has been autocephalous and the new Patriarch, Abuna Tekle Haimanot, was enthroned in 1976. The Afar people, who inhabit lowland Eritrea, Wollo, Hararghe and Bale provinces, and the Somalis, in the south-east, are Moslem. The Falashas, to be found principally in Gandar and Tigre provinces, practise Judaism. Between autumn 1984 and February 1985 a secret airlift ("Operation Moses") took 7,000 of the estimated 25,000 Falashas to Israel, via Sudan.

History.—The basic Hamitic culture was heavily influenced by Semitic immigration from Arabia in the centuries about the time of Christ. Christianity was introduced in the 4th century. The empire expanded sporadically, attaining a zenith in the 6th century under the Axum rulers, but subsequently checked by Islamic expansion from the east. Modern Ethiopia dates from 1855 when Theodore succeeded in establishing supremacy over the various tribes. The last Emperor was Haile Selassie who reigned from 1930, though in exile from 1936–1941 during the Italian occupation. After considerable military and civil unrest the armed forces assumed power in Sept. 1972 and deposed the Emperor. A Worker's Party on the Soviet model was formed in Sept. 1984, with Mengistu as General-Secretary.

The civilian government of the People's Democratic Republic of Ethiopia was established in Sept. 1987 with Lt.-Col. Mengistu being elected the first President. A new constitution was established and provides for the *Shengo* (National Assembly) of 835 seats. The *Shengo* votes on the membership of the 24-member State Council.

Eritrea was administered by Great Britain from the end of the Second World War until September 15, 1952, when it was federated with Ethiopia. It was incorporated as a province of Ethiopia in 1962. An armed campaign for independence started in 1962 and has intensified since the early 1970's.

Due to the lack of spring rains both the harvests of 1983 and 1984 failed. A famine relief programme launched in October 1984 drew world-wide attention to the problem, and airlifts of food began almost immediately. In two of the worst hit areas, the provinces of Tigre and Eritrea, the situation was exacerbated by the difficulty of supplying food and other aid to areas experiencing guerrilla activity.

In July 1977, Somalia, claiming the Ogaden region of Ethiopia in support of Western Somalia Liberation Front guerrillas, invaded the region. Ethiopia, with Soviet arms, and the aid of Cuban troops, was able to defeat the Somalis. The Somali regular army withdrew in March 1978, but guerrilla activity by the Western Somalia Liberation Front continues.

The Tigrean province, which lies south of Eritrea, seeks to establish greater autonomy: the activities of the Tigrean People's Liberation Front have escalated since the early 1980s, and the T.P.L.F. claims to control and administer large areas of the province.

Production and Industry.—The principal pursuit is agriculture, which accounts for approximately 50 per cent. of G.D.P., 90 per cent. of exports and 85 per cent. of total employment. Land was nationalized in 1975 and tenants given rights of use to the land they had tilled: large private holdings became state farms. The major food crops are teff, maize, barley, sorghum, wheat, pulses and oil seeds. Coffee, the principal export crop generates over 60 per cent. of the country's export earnings.

Manufacturing industry accounts for 10 per cent. of G.D.P. and is heavily dependent on agriculture. Ethiopia's known, but as yet largely unexploited, natural resources include gold, platinum, copper and potash. Traces of oil and natural gas have been found.

Communications.—With the aid of loans from the IBRD and the International Development Agency, a network of roads has been built linking the major cities with each other, and with the Sudanese and Kenyan borders and the Red Sea coast. There is a railway link from Addis Ababa to Djibouti, though this is vulnerable to guerrilla activity. The narrow gauge line in Eritrea has been closed by conflict. The Ethiopian Air Lines maintain regular services from Addis Ababa to many provincial towns. External services are operated throughout Africa and to Europe and the Middle and Far East.

Defence.—Under the Ministry of Defence the armed forces comprise the Army, the Air Force and the Navy. The Army strength totals 210,000 personnel (including a People's Militia) divided into 23 divisions.

The Air Force comprises a transport squadron, a bomber squadron, three fighter squadrons, a training squadron, a jet conversion squadron, and an elementary training unit. There are 120 fighter planes, mostly of Russian manufacture, and a few F.5.s. The Air Force headquarters is situated at Debre Zeit.

The Navy has a headquarters in Addis Ababa with a main base at Massawa and a smaller one at Assab.

National Military Service was established on May 4, 1983 and came into effect in May 1984.

Education.—Elementary education is provided without religious discrimination by Government schools in the main centres of population; there are also Mission schools, and cadet-schools for the Army, Navy, Air Force, and Police. Government secondary schools are found mainly in Addis Ababa, but also in most of the provincial capitals. The National University (founded 1961) co-ordinates the institutions of higher education (University College, Engineering, Building and Theological Colleges in Addis Ababa, Agricultural College at Alemaya, near Harar, and Public Health Centre in Gondar, etc.). It is intended to develop the provincial colleges to university level and status. Amharic is the official language of instruction, with English as the first foreign language and main language of instruction from secondary level upwards. Arabic is taught in Koran Schools; and Ge'ez (the ancient Ethiopic) in Christian Church Schools, which abound.

FINANCE

	1984
Revenue	US$1,062·8m.
Expenditure	1,449·3m.

Trade.—The chief imports by value are machinery and transport equipment, manufactured goods and chemicals (from U.K.); the principal exports by value being coffee, oilseeds, hides and skins, and pulses.

TRADE

	1984
Total Imports	US$917·8m.
Total Exports	402·8m.

Trade with U.K.

	1986	1987
Imports from U.K.	£50,049,000	£46,146,000
Exports to U.K.	22,343,000	12,875,000

CAPITAL.— Addis Ababa (population, 1985 estimate 1,464,901), also capital of the province of Shoa; Asmara (population 250,000) is the capital of the

Province of Eritrea. Dire Dawa is the most important commercial centre after Addis Ababa and Asmara, ΨMassawa and ΨAssab (recently enlarged) are the two main ports. There are ancient architectural remains at Aksum, Gondar, Lalibela and elsewhere.

CURRENCY.—Ethiopian Birr of 100 Cents.

FLAG.—Three horizontal bands; green, yellow, red.

NATIONAL ANTHEM.—Ityopya, Ityopya Kidemi.

NATIONAL DAY.—September 12 (People's Revolution Day).

BRITISH EMBASSY
Fikre Mariam Abatechan Street (P.O. Box 858), Addis Ababa
[Addis Ababa 182354]

Ambassador Extraordinary and Plenipotentiary, His Excellency Harold Berners Walker, C.M.G. (1986).

There is a British Consular Office at *Addis Ababa.*

British Council Representative, N. O. Hudson, O.B.E., Artistic Building, Adwa Avenue (P.O. Box 1043), Addis Ababa. There is also a library in Asmara.

FIJI
(Matanitu Ko Fiti)

President, Ratu Sir Penaia Ganilau, G.C.M.G., K.V.C.O., K.B.E., D.S.O., *apptd.* Dec. 5, 1987.

Cabinet
(as at January 1988)

Prime Minister and Foreign Affairs, Ratu Sir Kamisese Mara, G.C.M.G., K.B.E.

Home Affairs, National Youth Service and Auxiliary Army Services, Brig. Sitiveni Rabuka.

Fijian Affairs, Col. Vatiliai Navunisaravi.

Finance and Economic Planning, Josefata Kamikamica.

Education, Felipe Bole.

Primary Industry, Viliame Gonelevu.

Trade and Commerce, Berenado Vunibobo.

Health, Apenisa Kurusiqila.

Communications, Works and Transport, Apisai Tora.

Attorney-General and Justice, Sailosi Kepa.

Tourism, Civil Aviation and Energy, David Pickering.

Youth and Sport, Col. Ilaisa Kacisolome.

Rural Development, and Rural Housing, Col. Apolosi Buivakaloloma.

Indian Affairs, Mrs. Irene Jai Narayan.

Forestry, Ratu Sir Josaia Tavaiqila, K.B.E.

Employment and Industrial Relations, Taniela Veitara.

Co-operatives and National Marketing Authority, Iswari Bajpai.

Women's Affairs and Social Welfare, Ms. Finau Tabakaucoro.

Housing and Urban Development, Tomasi Vakatora.

Lands and Mineral Resources, Ratu William Tonganivalu.

Information, Charles Walter.

FIJI EMBASSY
34 Hyde Park Gate, SW7 5BN
[01-584 3661/2]

Ambassador Extraordinary and Plenipotentiary, His Excellency Brig. Ratu Epeli Nailatikau, L.V.O., O.B.E. (1988).

Area, Population, etc.—Fiji is made up of about 332 islands and over 500 islets (including numerous atolls and reefs) in the South Pacific Ocean, about 1,100 miles north of New Zealand. About 100 islands are permanently inhabited. The gross area of the group, which extends 300 miles from east to west, and 300 north to south, between 15° 45′—21° 10′ S. lat. and

176° E.—178° W. long. is 7,055 sq. miles (18,274 sq. km.). The International Date Line has been diverted to the east of the island group. The largest islands are Viti Levu and Vanua Levu. The main groups of islands are Lomaiviti, Lau and Yasawas. Most of the larger islands are mountainous with sharp peaks and crags, but also have conspicuous areas of flat land and many of the rivers have built extensive deltas. The climate is tropical, without extremes of heat and temperatures rarely exceed 32°C. and seldom fall below 15°C.

The population (Census 1986) was 715,373 comprising 48·6 per cent. Indians, 46·2 per cent. Fijians, and 5·2 per cent. other races.

Government.—Fiji was a British colony from 1874 until October 10, 1970, when it became an independent state and a member of the Commonwealth.

A coalition of the left under Dr. Timoci Bavadra defeated the Alliance Party of Ratu Sir Kamisese Mara in a General Election on April 12, 1987. The new Government, drawing its support mainly from the Indian population, was overthrown in a military coup on May 14 by Lt.-Col. Sitiveni Rabuka. In the wake of the constitutional crisis an Advisory Council of 19 members was set up by the Governor General as an interim government to consider constitutional reform.

A second coup occurred on Sept. 25, 1987. On Oct. 7 Rabuka declared Fiji to be a republic; the Governor General resigned on Oct. 15 and Fiji's Commonwealth membership lapsed. An Executive Council of Ministers, with Rabuka at its head, assumed control until Dec. 5 when Ratu Sir Ganilau was appointed President. The President called upon Ratu Sir Kamisese Mara to form another interim administration to work for a resolution to the political crisis.

FINANCE

	1983	1984
Public Income	$296,405,000	$337,658,000
Public Expenditure	304,100,000	344,407,000

Economy.—The economy is primarily agrarian, with about 600,000 acres under cultivation. The principal cash crop is sugar cane, which is the main export, followed by coconuts, ginger and copra. A variety of other fruit, vegetables and root crops are also grown, and self-sufficiency in rice is a major aim. Forestry, fishing and beef production are being encouraged in order to diversify the economy. The processing of agricultural, marine and timber products are the main industries, along with gold mining.

Tourism is also a major factor in the economy, second only to sugar as a money-earner.

TRADE

	1984	1985
Total Imports	$487,105,000	$508,191,000
Total Exports (including Re-exports)	279,418,000	263,887,000

Trade with U.K.

	1986	1987
Imports from U.K.	£8,775,000	£7,381,000
Exports to U.K.	66,500,000	53,062,000

The chief imports are foodstuffs, machinery, mineral fuels, chemicals, beverages, tobacco and manufactured articles. Chief exports are sugar, coconut oil, gold, lumber, molasses, ginger and canned fish.

Communications.—Fiji is one of the main aerial crossroads in the Pacific, providing services to New Zealand, Australia, Tonga, Western Samoa, Vanuatu, the Solomon Islands, Kiribati, Tuvalu, New Caledonia and American Samoa.

Fiji has three ports of entry, at Suva, Lautoka and Levuka.

CAPITAL.—ΨSuva, in the island of Viti Levu. Population (1985) 75,000.

CURRENCY.—Fiji Dollar of 100 Cents.

FLAG.—Light blue ground with Union flag in top left quarter and the shield of Fiji in the fly.

NATIONAL ANTHEM.—Hail to Fiji.

NATIONAL DAY.—October 10 (Dominion Day).

BRITISH HIGH COMMISSION
Victoria House, 47 Gladstone Road,
P.O. Box 1355, Suva
[Suva 311033]

Ambassador Extraordinary and Plenipotentiary, His Excellency Roger Arnold Rowlandson Barltrop, C.V.O. (1982).

FINLAND
(Suomen Tasavalta)

President, Dr. Mauno Koivisto, *born*, 1923, *elected*, Jan 26, 1982, *re-elected*, March 1, 1988.

CABINET

Prime Minister, Harri Holkeri (*NCP*).
Foreign Affairs, Kalevi Sorsa (*SDP*).
Cabinet, Ilkka Kanerva (*NCP*).
Foreign Trade, Pertti Salolainen (*NCP*).
Justice, Matti Louekoski (*SDP*).
Interior, Jarmo Rantanen (*SDP*).
Defence, Ole Norrback (*SPP*).
Finance, Erkki Liikanen (*SDP*).
Deputy Minister of Finance, Ms. Ulla Puolanne (*NCP*).
Education, Christoffer Taxell (*SPP*).
Deputy Minister of Education, Ms. Anna-Liisa Piipari (*SDP*).
Agriculture and Forestry, Toivo T. Pohjola (*NCP*).
Transport and Communications, Pekka Vennamo (*FRP*).
Trade and Industry, Ilkka Suominen (*NCP*).
Social Affairs and Health, Ms. Helena Pesola (*NCP*).
Deputy Minister of Social Affairs and Health, Ms. Tarja Halonen (*SDP*).
Labour, Matti Puhakka (*SDP*).
Environment, Kaj Bärlund (*SDP*).

(*NCP*=National Coalition Party, *SDP*=Social Democratic Party, *SPP*=Swedish People's Party of Finland, *FRP*=Finnish Rural Party).

FINNISH EMBASSY AND CONSULATE
38 Chesham Place, SW1X 8HW
[01-235 9531]

Ambassador Extraordinary and Plenipotentiary, His Excellency Ilkka Pastinen, K.C.M.G. (1983).
Minister Counsellor, Seppo Kauppila.
Counsellors, Asko Numminen; J. Leino.
Press Counsellor, Lasse Lehtinen.
Defence Attaché, Col. T. Aaltonen.

Area and Population.—A country situated on the Gulfs of Finland and Bothnia, with a total area of 137,851 sq. miles (337,032 sq. km.), of which 65 per cent. is forest, 8 per cent. cultivated, 9 per cent. lakes and 18 per cent. waste and other land. The population (December, 1985) was 4,908,000, of whom 90·3 per cent. are Lutheran, 1·1 per cent. Greek Orthodox and 8·4 per cent. others.

The Aland Archipelago (Ahvenanmaa), a group of small islands at the entrance to the Gulf of Bothnia, covers about 572 square miles, with a population (December, 1985) of 23,600 (95·2 per cent. Swedish-speaking). The islands have a semi-autonomous status.

Government.—Under the Constitution there is a single Chamber (*Eduskunta*) composed of 200 members, elected by universal suffrage. The legislative power is vested in the Chamber and the President. The highest executive power is held by the President who is elected for a period of 6 years.

The present government came into office on April 30, 1987. The four parties in the coalition are the National Coalition Party (conservative), the Social Democratic Party, the Swedish People's Party of Finland, and the Finnish Rural Party.

Defence.—By the terms of the Peace Treaty (Feb. 10, 1947) with U.K. and U.S.S.R., the Army is limited to a force not exceeding 34,400. The Navy is limited to a total of 10,000 tons displacement with personnel not exceeding 4,500. The Air Force, including naval air arm, is limited to 60 machines with a personnel not exceeding 3,000. Bombers or aircraft with bomb-carrying facilities are expressly forbidden. The Defence Forces contain a cadre of regular officers and N.C.O.'s, but their bulk is provided by conscripts who serve for 8–11 months. Total strength of trained and equipped reserves is over 700,000, 16,500 of whom have served in the U.N. peacekeeping force.

Education.—Primary education (co-educational comprehensive school) is compulsory for children from 7 to 16 years, and free of charge. In the autumn of 1985, there were 685,052 in comprehensive schools (374,413 at basic stage and 310,639 at upper stage), and 115,000 in vocational institutions of senior level. There are 21 universities or other schools of academic level, and enrolment was (1985) 92,230.

Language and Literature.—There are two official languages in Finland. 93·5 per cent of the population speak Finnish as their first language, 6·3 Swedish (1979). The remaining 0·2 per cent. speak other languages (mainly Lapps who number about 2,500 and live in the Far North). Both Finnish and Swedish are used for administration and education; newspapers, books, plays and films appear in both languages. There is a vigorous modern literature. F. E. Sillanpää, who died in 1964, was awarded the Nobel prize for

Literature. Best known among the living authors are Väinö Linna, Veijo Meri and Paavo Haavikko. There are 99 daily newspapers in Finland which appear on 4 or more days per week (12 Swedish).

Production and Industry.—Finland is a highly industrialized country producing a wide range of capital and consumer goods. Timber and the products of the forest-based industries remain the backbone of the economy, accounting for 40 per cent. of her export earnings, but the importance of the metal-working, shipbuilding and engineering industries has been growing. This sector in 1986 accounted for 30 per cent. of Finland's exports. The textile industry is well developed and Finland's glass, ceramics and furniture industries enjoy international reputations. Other important industries are rubber, plastics, chemicals and pharmaceuticals, footwear, foodstuffs and electronic equipment.

Communications.—There are 9,000 kilometres of railroad, a railway connection with Sweden and U.S.S.R., passenger boat connection with Sweden, West Germany, Poland and U.S.S.R. Vessels on the London to Leningrad route call at Helsinki. There are also passenger/cargo services between Britain and Helsinki, Kotka and other Finnish ports. External civil air services are maintained by most European airlines. The merchant fleet at the end of Dec. 1986 totalled 1,900,000 tons gross.

FINANCE

	1983	1984
	Finnmarks	*Finnmarks*
Revenue (*Budget*) ...	64,938,000	75,395,000
Expenditure (*Budget*)	76,590,000	86,095,000

TRADE

The principal imports are raw materials, machinery and manufactured goods. The exports are principally the output of the paper and other forest industries, engineering, metal industry (*e.g.* paper-working machinery and ships) and chemicals.

	1983	1984
	Finnmarks	*Finnmarks*
Total Imports	71,519,000	74,684,000
Total Exports	69,751,000	80,922,000

Trade with U.K.

	1986	1987
Imports from U.K. ...	£664,461,000	£797,236,000
Exports to U.K.	1,346,058,000	1,539,011,000

CAPITAL.—ΨHelsinki (Helsingfors). Population (Jan. 1986), 485,626; other towns are Tampere (Tammerfors), 169,153; ΨTurku (Åbo), 161,508; Espoo (Esbo), 156,851; Vantaa (Vanda), 143,986; ΨOulu (Uleåborg), 97,329; Lahti (Lahtis), 94,467; ΨPori (Björneborg), 78,365.

CURRENCY.—Markka of 100 Penniä.

FLAG.—White with blue cross.

NATIONAL DAY.—December 6 (Day of Independence).

BRITISH EMBASSY
Uudenmaankatu 16–20
00120 Helsinki 12
[Helsinki 647922]

Ambassador Extraordinary and Plenipotentiary, His Excellency (Hubert Anthony) Justin Staples, C.M.G. (1986).
Counsellor (*Commercial*), B. Rose.
First Secretaries, G. S. Hand (*Head of Chancery*); A. J. Marlowe; A. R. Powell.
Defence, Naval, Military and Air Attaché, Lt.-Col. W. J. Collings, M.B.E.
There are British Consular offices at *Helsinki, Tampere, Turku, Pori, Kotka, Oulu, Vaasa, Jyväskylä* and *Kuopio.*

British Council Representative, M. B. L. Nightingale,
Erottajankatu 7B, 00130 Helsinki 13.

FRANCE
(La République Française)

President of the French Republic, Francois Mitterrand, *elected* May 10, 1981, *re-elected* May 8, 1988.

CABINET
(as at end June 1988)

Prime Minister, Michel Rocard (*PS*).
National Education, Research and Sport, Lionel
Jospin (*PS*).
Economy, Finance and Budget, Pierre Bérégovoy
(*PS*).
Equipment and Housing, Maurice Faure (*MRG*).
Foreign Affairs, Roland Dumas (*PS*).
Justice, Pierre Arpaillange.
Defence, Jean-Pierre Chevènement (*PS*).
Interior, Pierre Joxe (*PS*).
Industry and Territorial Development, Roger Faroux.
European Affairs, Edith Cresson (*PS*).
Transport, Michel Delebarre (*PS*).
Civil Service and Administrative Reform, Michel
Durafour (*UDF*).
Labour and Employment, Jean-Pierre Soisson.
Co-operation and Development, Jacques Pelletier
(*UDF*).
*Culture and Communications, Major Public Works,
and Bicentenary,* Jack Lang (*PS*).
Overseas Departments and Territories, Louis Le
Pensec (*PS*).

Agriculture and Forests, Henri Nallet (*PS*).
Posts and Telecommunications, and Space, Paul
Quilès (*PS*).
Relations with Parliament, Jean Poperen (*PS*).
*Solidarity, Health, Social Protection, Government
Spokesman,* Claude Evin (*PS*).
Research and Technology, Hubert Curien (*PS*).
Foreign Trade, Jean-Marie Rausch.

(*PS,* Parti socialiste; *UDF,* Union pour la démocratie
française; *MRG,* Mouvement des radicaux de
gauche.)

In presidential elections held on April 24 and May
8, 1988 Francois Mitterrand was re-elected. M.
Michel Rocard was appointed Prime Minister, after
the resignation of M. Jacques Chirac, and appointed
a socialist-dominated cabinet. However, as the socialists did not have a majority in the National
Assembly, the Assembly was dissolved and elections
followed in June. A hung parliament resulted, but
with the support of the Communist Party the socialist
Laurent Fabius was elected President of the National
Assembly. Michel Rocard formed his second cabinet
on June 28.

FRENCH EMBASSY IN LONDON
58 Knightsbridge, SW1X 7JT
[01–235 8080].

Ambassador Extraordinary and Plenipotentiary, His
Excellency Vicomte Luc de La Barre de Nanteuil
(1986).

Area and Population.—The largest state in Central
Europe, extending from 42° 20' to 51° 5' N. lat., and
from 7° 85' E. to 4° 45' W. long. Its area is estimated

at 211,208 sq. miles (547,026 sq. km.), divided into 95 departments, including the island of Corsica, in the Mediterranean, off the west coast of Italy. The population of France in 1986 was 55,279,100.

POPULATION OF THE REGIONS 1986
(Names of Departments in brackets)

Alsace (Bas-Rhin, Haut-Rhin)	1,599,800
Aquitaine (Dordogne, Gironde, Landes, Lot-et-Garonne, Pyrénées-Atlantiques)	2,718,200
Auvergne (Allier, Cantal, Haute-Loire, Puy-de-Dôme)	1,334,400
Basse-Normandie (Calvados, Manche, Orne)	1,373,400
Bourgogne (Côte-d'Or, Nièvre, Saône-et-Loire, Yonne)	1,607,200
Bretagne (Côtes du Nord, Finistère, Ille-et-Vilaine, Morbihan)	2,764,200
Centre (Cher, Eure-et-Loir, Indre, Indre-et-Loire, Loir-et-Cher, Loiret)	2,324,400
Champagne-Ardenne (Ardennes, Aube, Marne, Haute-Marne)	1,352,500
Corse (Corse-du-Sud, Haute-Corse)	248,700
Franche-Comté (Doubs, Haute-Saône, Jura, Territoire-de-Belfort)	1,085,900
Haute-Normandie (Eure, Seine-Maritime)	1,692,800
Ile-de-France (Essone, Haute-de-Seine, Seine-et-Marne, Seine-St. Denis, Val-de Marne, Val-d'Oise, Ville de Paris, Yvelines)	10,250,900
Languedoc-Roussillon (Aude, Gard, Hérault, Lozère, Pyrénées-Orientales)	2,011,900
Limousin (Corrèze, Creuse, Haute-Vienne)	735,800
Lorraine (Meurthe-et-Moselle, Meuse, Moselle, Vosges)	2,313,200
Midi-Pyrénées (Ariège, Aveyron, Haute-Garonne, Gers, Lot, Hautes-Pyrénées, Tarn, Tarn-et-Garonne)	2,355,100
Nord (Nord, Pas-de-Calais)	3,923,200
Pays-de-la Loire (Loire-Atlantique, Maine-et-Loire, Mayenne, Sarthe, Vendee)	3,017,700
Picardie (Aisne, Oise, Somme)	1,774,000
Poitou-Charentes (Charente, Charente-Maritime, Deux-Sèvres, Vienne)	1,583,600
Provence-Alpes-Côte d'Azur (Alpes-de-Haute Provence, Alpes-Maritime, Bouches-du-Rhône, Haute-Alpes, Var, Vaucluse)	4,058,800
Rhône-Alpes (Ain, Ardèche, Drôme, Isère, Loire, Rhône, Savoie, Haute-Savoie)	5,153,600

Archaeology, etc.—There are dolmens and menhirs in Brittany, prehistoric remains and cave drawings in Dordogne and Ariège, and throughout France various megalithic monuments erected by primitive tribes, predecessors of Iberian invaders from Spain (now represented by the Basques), Ligurians from northern Italy and Celts or Gauls from the valley of the Danube. Julius Cæsar found Gaul "divided into three parts" and described three political groups—Aquitanians south of the Garonne, Celts between the Garonne and the Seine and Marne, and Belgae from the Seine to the Rhine. Roman remains are plentiful throughout France in the form of aqueducts, arenas, triumphal arches, etc., and the celebrated Norman and Gothic Cathedrals, including Notre Dame in Paris, and those of Chartres, Reims, Amiens (where Peter the Hermit preached the First Crusade for the recovery of the Holy Sepulchre), Bourges, Beauvais, Rouen, etc., have survived invasions and bombardments, with only partial damage, and many of the renaissance and the seventeenth and eighteenth century châteaux survived the French Revolution.

Language and Literature.—French is the universal language of France and of a large proportion of the people of Belgium, Luxembourg, Switzerland, North and West Africa, and the Province of Quebec, Canada. The work of the *French Academy*, founded by Richelieu in 1635, has established *le bon usage*, equivalent to "The Queen's English" in Great Britain. French authors have been awarded the Nobel Prize for Literature on 12 occasions, including R.F.A. Sully-Prudhomme (1901), Anatole France (1921), André Gide (1947), François Mauriac (1952), Albert Camus (1957), Jean Paul Sartre (1964) and Claude Simon (1985).

GOVERNMENT

Parliament consists of the National Assembly and the Senate. The normal session of Parliament is confined to 5½ months each year and it may also meet in extraordinary session for 12 days at the request of the Prime Minister or a majority of the Assembly.

The Prime Minister is appointed by the President, as is the Cabinet on the Prime Minister's recommendation. They are responsible to Parliament, but as the executive is constitutionally separate from the legislature Ministers may not sit in Parliament.

A Constitutional Council is responsible for supervising all elections and referenda and must be consulted on all constitutional matters and before the President of the Republic assumes emergency powers.

DEFENCE

The personnel of the Defence Forces in 1985 totalled 464,000. National nuclear forces include medium-range ballistic missiles, submarine-launched ballistic missiles and *Mirage* IV medium bombers. The Army has a variety of new French-made equipment in service, including medium tanks, field and anti-aircraft SP guns, trucks and radio equipment. Defence Budget for 1987, 169,200 million francs.

EDUCATION

The educational system is highly centralized and is administered by the Ministry of National Education. Local Administration comprises 25 Territorial Academies, with inspecting staff for all grades, and Departmental Councils presided over by the *Préfet*, and charged especially with primary education.

Primary and secondary education are compulsory, free and secular, the school age being from 6 to 16. Schools may be single-sex or co-educational. Primary education is given in nursery schools, primary schools and *collèges d'enseignement général* (4-year secondary modern course); secondary education in *collèges d'enseignement technique, collèges d'enseignement secondaire* and *lycées* (7-year course leading to one of the five *baccalauréats*). Special schools are numerous.

There are many *Grandes Ecoles* in France which award diplomas in many subjects not taught at university, especially applied science and engineering. Most of them are State institutions but have a competitive system of entry, unlike the universities. There are universities in twenty-four towns in France, two or three in some major provincial towns and thirteen in Paris and the immediate surrounding district.

In 1985–86 enrolment in primary schools was 5,666,840; in secondary schools 4,224,480, and in post-secondary education 1,108,685 (of which university students accounted for 960,533).

COMMUNICATIONS

Roads.—The length of roads in use at the end of 1986 was 34,276 km. of which 6,019 km. were motorways.

Railways.—The system of railroads in France is very extensive. The length of lines open for traffic at the end of 1986 was 34,640 km., of which 11,584 km. were electrified.

Shipping.—The French mercantile marine consisted in Jan. 1987, of 283 ships of over 100 tons gross, of which 26 were passenger vessels (173,000 tons gross), 66 tankers (2,614,000 tons gross) and 191 cargo vessels (2,175,000 tons gross). The principal rivers of France are the Seine, Loire, Garonne, and Rhône.

ECONOMY

Budget.—Government expenditure (ordinary and capital) by function, as provided for in the 1986 general Budget, was:

	F million
Agriculture	35,679
Commerce, Working Classes and Tourism	1,016
Culture	8,403
Defence	154,908
Economy, Finance and Budget	469,722
Education	163,761
Environment	749
Foreign Affairs	16,610
Health, Labour, Employment and Social Services	111,268
Industry and Research	78,440
Interior	47,432
Justice	10,839
Overseas Departments	1,872
Planning and Development	2,267
Prime Ministerial	2,468
Town Planning and Housing	35,280
Transport	54,493
Veterans	26,866
Other	5,728
Total	1,225,806

PRODUCTION

Agriculture.—Approximately 31,513,000 hectares of land is used for agricultural purposes, 14,389,000 hectares is forested. Production in 1985 included wheat, 29,011,840 tonnes, and sugar-beet, 28,684,280 tonnes. Value of production in 1983 was crops *F*119,400 million and livestock *F*113,100 million.

The vine is extensively cultivated, regions famous for their wines including Bordeaux, Burgundy and Champagne. Production of wine in 1985 was 15,918,121 hectolitres. Cognac, liqueurs and cider are also important products.

Energy.—France produces its own oil, the greater part coming from fields in the Landes area, but is a net importer of crude oil, for processing by its important oil-refining industry. Natural gas is produced in the foothills of the Pyrenees. Electricity production was 328,600 GWh in 1985, of which 19·3 per cent. was hydro-electric and 64·9 per cent. nuclear power.

Industry.—France's heavy industries include oil-refining and the production of iron and steel, and aluminium. In 1986 production of steel was 17,900,000 tonnes, cement 22,500,000 tonnes and paper products 5,600,000 tonnes. Other important industries produce chemicals, tyres, aluminium, textiles, and processed food. Engineering products include motor vehicles, and television and radio sets.

TRADE

The principal imports are raw materials for the heavy and manufacturing industries (e.g. oil, minerals, chemicals), machinery and precision instruments, agricultural products and vehicles. Raw materials, semi-manufactured and manufactured goods are also France's principal exports. Other member countries of the E.E.C. are France's main trading partners.

TOTAL TRADE

	1985	1986
	Francs	*Francs*
Imports	962,746 m.	887,502 m.
Exports	870,812 m.	825,417 m.

Trade with U.K.

	1986	1987
Imports from U.K.	£6,210,216,000	£7,781,546,000
Exports to U.K.	7,348,574,000	8,381,984,000

CAPITAL.—Paris, on the Seine. Population (census, 1982), 2,188,918 (town); 8,707,000 (incl. suburbs).

The largest conurbations (populations, 1982) are ΨMarseilles (1,111,000); Lyons (1,221,000); Toulouse (541,000); Lille (936,000) and ΨBordeaux (640,000).

The chief towns of Corsica are ΨAjaccio (55,279) and ΨBastia (45,081).

CURRENCY.—French Franc of 100 Centimes.

FLAG.—The "tricolour", three vertical bands, blue, white, red (blue next to flagstaff).

NATIONAL ANTHEM.—La Marseillaise.

NATIONAL DAY.—July 14 (Bastille Day).

BRITISH EMBASSY

35 rue du Faubourg St. Honoré, 75383 Paris Cedex 08 [Paris 42 66 91 42]

Ambassador Extraordinary and Plenipotentiary, His Excellency Sir Ewan Alastair John Fergusson, K.C.M.G. (1987).

Minister, M. J. Llewellyn Smith.

Defence and Air Attaché, Air Cdre. B. N. J. Speed, O.B.E.

Counsellor and Head of Chancery, J. Q. Greenstock.

Consul-General, J. Daly.

BRITISH CONSULAR OFFICES

There are British Consulates-General in Metropolitan France at *Paris, Bordeaux, Lille, Lyons, Marseilles.*

BRITISH COUNCIL

Representative in Paris, P. J. Prescott, 9 rue de Constantine, 75007 Paris.

There are British Council libraries at *Paris, Bordeaux, Lille, Lyons* and *Marseilles.*

FRANCO-BRITISH CHAMBER OF COMMERCE

8 rue Cimarosa, 75116 Paris

President, R. Mitchell.
Vice-Presidents, R. Lyon; R. King.

OVERSEAS DEPARTMENTS

Legislation passed in Dec. 1982 by the French Parliament granted greater powers of self-government to four of the five overseas departments—French Guiana, Guadeloupe, Martinique and Réunion. These former colonies had enjoyed departmental status since 1947 and the status of regions of France since 1974. Elections to their new directly-elected Assemblies were held in each department in Feb. 1983 and the Assemblies will operate in parallel with the existing, indirectly constituted Regional Councils.

French Guiana.—Situated on the north-eastern coast of South America, French Guiana is flanked by Suriname on the west and by Brazil on the south and east. Area, 34,749 sq. miles (90,000 sq. km.). Population (1985 U.N. estimate), 82,000. Capital, ΨCayenne (38,135). Under the administration of French Guiana is a group of islands (St. Joseph, Ile Royal and Ile du Diable), known as Iles du Salut. On Devil's Isle, Captain Dreyfus was imprisoned from 1894 to 1899.

Guadeloupe.—A number of islands in the Leeward Islands group of the West Indies, consisting of the two main islands of Guadeloupe (or Basse-Terre) and

Grande-Terre, with the adjacent islands of Marie-Galante, La Désirade and Îles des Saintes, and the islands of St. Martin and St. Barthélemy over 150 miles to the north-west. Area, 687 sq. miles (1,779 sq. km.). Population (1985 U.N. estimate), 334,000. Capital ΨBasse Terre (15,778) in Guadeloupe. Other towns are ΨPointe à Pitre (23,889) on Grande-Terre and ΨGrand Bourg (6,611) in Marie Galante.

Martinique.—An island situated in the Windward Islands group of the West Indies, between Dominica in the north and St. Lucia in the south. Area, 425 sq. miles (1,102 sq. km.). Population (1985), 328,566. Capital ΨFort de France (100,576). Other towns are ΨTrinité (11,214) and ΨMarin (6,104).

Réunion.—Réunion, which became a French possession in 1638, lies in the Indian Ocean, about 569 miles east of Madagascar and 110 miles S.W. of Mauritius. Area, 969 sq. miles (2,510 sq. km.). Population (1985 U.N. estimate), 531,000. Capital, St. Denis (109,072).

Also lying in the Indian Ocean adjacent to Madagascar are the smaller, uninhabited islands of Bassas da India, Europa, Îles Glorieuses, Juan de Nova and Tromelin, which are administered from Réunion.

TERRITORIAL COLLECTIVITIES

Mayotte.—Area, 144 sq. miles (372 sq. km.). Population (1985 estimate), 67,000. Capital, Mamoundzou (12,000). Part of the Comoros Islands group, Mayotte remained a French dependency when the other 3 islands became independent as the Comoros Republic in 1975. Since 1976 the island has been a *collectivité territoriale*, an intermediate status between Overseas Department and Overseas Territory.

St. Pierre and Miquelon—Area, 93 sq. miles (242 sq. km.). Population (1987), 6,500. Two small groups of islands off the coast of Newfoundland. Became a *collectivité territoriale* in June 1985.

OVERSEAS TERRITORIES

French Polynesia.—Five archipelagos in the south Pacific, comprising the Society Islands (Windward Islands group includes Tahiti, Moorea, Makatea, Mehetia, Tetiaoro, Tubai Manu, etc: Leeward Islands group includes Huahine, Raiatea, Tahaa, Bora-Bora, Maupiti, etc.), the Tuamotu Islands (Rangiroa, Hao, Turéia, etc.), the Gambier Islands (Mangareva, etc.), the Tubuai Islands (Rimatara, Rurutu, Tubuai, Raivavae, Rapa, etc.) and the Marquesas Islands (Nuku-Hiva, Hiva-Oa, Fatu-Hiva, Tahuata, Ua Huka, etc.). Area, 1,544 sq. miles (4,000 sq. km.). Population (1985 estimate) 176,400. Capital, ΨPapeete (22,967) in Tahiti. Economy based on tourism and exports of copra, coffee, vanilla, citrus fruits and cultured pearls.

New Caledonia.—A large island in the Western Pacific, 700 miles E. of Queensland. Dependencies are the Isles of Pines, the Loyalty Islands (Mahé, Lifou, Urea, etc.), the Bélep Archipelago, the Chesterfield Islands, the Huon Islands and Walpole. New Caledonia was discovered in 1774 and annexed by France in 1854; from 1871 to 1896 it was a convict settlement. A referendum in 1987 on the question of independence for New Caledonia was boycotted by the indigenous Kanaks, and New Caledonia therefore voted to remain French. However, a new independence referendum has been promised for 1998. Area, 7,358 sq. miles (19,058 sq. km.). Population (1985 U.N. estimate), 153,000. Capital ΨNoumea (60,112). It is one of the world's largest producers of nickel.

Southern and Antarctic Territories.—Created in 1955 from the former Réunion dependencies, the territory comprises the islands of New Amsterdam (25 sq. miles) and St. Paul (2·7 sq. miles), the Kerguelen

Islands (2,700 sq. miles) and Crozet Islands (116 sq. miles) archipelagos and Adélie Land (116,800 sq. miles) in the Antarctic continent. The only population are members of staff of the scientific stations.

Wallis and Futuna Islands.—Two groups of islands (the Wallis Archipelago and the Îles du Hooru) in the central Pacific, N.E. of Fiji. Area, 106 sq. miles (274 sq. km.). Population (estimate 1985) 13,100. Capital, Mata-Utu on Urea, the main island of the Wallis group.

THE FRENCH COMMUNITY

The Constitution of the fifth French Republic promulgated on Oct. 6, 1958, envisaged the establishment of a French Community of States closely linked with common institutions. A number of the former French States in Africa have seceded from the Community but for all practical purposes continue to enjoy the same close links with France as those that remain formally members of the French Community. The Community Institutions in fact never operated as envisaged. Nevertheless, with the exception of Guinea, which opted out of the Community in the 1958 referendum, all the former French African colonies are closely linked to France by a series of financial, technical and economic agreements.

FRANCOPHONE COUNTRIES

In the following countries French is either the official or national language or the language of instruction; where there is another national language the name of it is shown after the name of the country:—Algeria (*Arabic*); Belgium (*Flemish*); Benin; Burkina Faso; Burundi (*Kirundi*); Cameroon (*English*); parts of Canada (in Quebec, parts of Ontario and New Brunswick) (*English*); Central African Republic (*Sangho*); Chad; Congo; Côte d'Ivoire; France; Gabon; Guinea; Haiti (*Creole*); Kampuchea (*Khmer*); Laos (*Laotian*); Lebanon (*Arabic*); Luxembourg (*German and Letzeburgesch*); Madagascar (*Malagasy*); Mali; Morocco (*Arabic*); Mauritania (*Arabic*); Niger; Rwanda (*Kinyarwanda*); Senegal; Switzerland (1,000,000 French speaking); Togo; Tunisia (*Arabic*); Vietnam (*Vietnamese*); Zaire. French is also spoken in the Overseas Departments (*see* above).

GABON
(République Gabonaise)

President, El Hadj Omar Bongo, *assumed office,* Dec. 1967, *re-elected,* Feb. 1973, Dec. 1979 and Nov. 1986.

MINISTERS

Prime Minister, L. Mébiame.
First Deputy P.M., Minister for Transport, Water, Forests and Social Communications, G. Rawiri.
Second Deputy P.M., Minister for Mines and Hydrocarbons, E.-G. Mouvagha Tchioba.
Third Deputy P.M., Minister for the Civil Service and Administrative Reform, E. Kassa Mapsi.
Fourth Deputy P.M., Minister for Housing and Town Planning, S. Essimengane.
Foreign Affairs and Co-operation, M. Bongo.
Public Lands and Registration, and Law of the Sea, H. Minko.
Secretary General to the Presidency, R. R. Coniquet.
Higher Education and Scientific Research, J. B. Ogouliguende.
Industry and Consumer Affairs, E. Moussirou.
Territorial Administration, Local Collectives and Immigration, R. Nguema Bekale.

Commerce, Technology Transfer and Rationalization, J.-F. Ntoutoume-Emane.

Culture and Arts, F. Owono-Nguema.

Defence, Veterans' Affairs and Public Security, J. Mpouho-Epigat.

Justice, Mrs. S. Ngwamassana.

Information, Post and Telecommunications, Z. Myboto.

Finance, Budget and State Shareholdings, J.-P. Lemboumba-Le-Pandou.

Public Works and Construction, Gen. J.-B. Assele.

Planning and Economy, P. Nze.

Agriculture, Livestock and Rural Development, M. Anchouey.

Education, G. Nzouba.

Labour and Employment, L.-G. Mayila.

Civil and Commercial Aviation, M. Essonghe.

Public Health and Population, J.-P. Okias.

Social Affairs, Natural Disasters and Social Security, S. Oyouomi.

Youth and Sports, V. Afene.

State Control, E. Mbot.

Professional Training and Handicrafts, J.-J. Amiar Nganga.

Energy and Water Resources, D. Di Dinge.

Small and Medium-Sized Enterprises, E. Nze-Bekale.

Environment and Conservation, Dr. H. Moutsinga.

Tourism, A. Sambat.

EMBASSY IN LONDON
48 Kensington Court, W8 5DB
[01–937 5285/9]

Ambassador Extraordinary and Plenipotentiary, His Excellency Charles Mamadou Diop (1986).

Gabon lies on the Atlantic coast of Africa at the Equator and is flanked on the north by Equatorial Guinea and Cameroon and on the east and south by the People's Republic of Congo. It has an area of 103,347 sq. miles (267,667 sq. km.) and a population (1985 U.N. estimate) of 1,151,000. Gabon elected on Nov. 28, 1958, to remain an autonomous republic within the French Community and was proclaimed fully independent on August 17, 1960.

The Constitution provides for an Executive President directly elected for a seven-year term, who appoints the Council of Ministers. There is a unicameral National Assembly comprising 84 members directly elected for a five-year term and nine members nominated by the President. The sole legal party is the *Parti democratique gabonais*.

Gabon's economy remains heavily dependent on oil, and, to a much lesser extent, other mineral resources, including manganese and uranium. Gabon has considerable timber reserves (particularly Okoumé) although production in this industry has stagnated in recent years.

The economy, which experienced considerable growth in real terms from the mid-1970s onwards, has since 1986 been adversely affected by the fall in oil prices. As a result government spending is expected to remain at a reduced level until 1989.

Gabon is a full member of OPEC.

Trade with U.K.

	1986	1987
Imports from U.K.	£16,627,000	£11,962,000
Exports to U.K.	36,642,000	5,357,000

CAPITAL.—ΨLibreville (251,000).

CURRENCY.—Franc C.F.A. of 100 Centimes.

FLAG.—Horizontal bands, green, yellow and blue.

NATIONAL ANTHEM.—"La Concorde".

NATIONAL DAY.—August 17.

BRITISH EMBASSY
B.P. 476, Libreville
[Libreville 72 29 85]

Ambassador Extraordinary and Plenipotentiary, His Excellency Mark Aubrey Goodfellow (1986).

Second Secretary, I. M. Thom.

GERMANY
* Deutsches Reich (German Realm)

The term "deutsch" (German) probably began to be used in the 8th century and initially described the language spoken in the eastern part of the Frankish realm which reached its apogee in Charlemagne's reign, subsequently being divided into an eastern and western realm whose political and linguistic borders coincided. Then the term was transferred from the language to its speakers, and ultimately to the region they lived in. The first German realm was the Holy Roman Empire, established in A.D. 962 when Otto I of Saxony was crowned Emperor. The Empire endured until 1806, but from as early as the 12th century the achievement of a national state was prevented by territorial fragmentation into small principalities and dukedoms, the gradually increasing autonomy of their rulers weakening the central power.

The Holy Roman Empire was replaced by a loose association of the individual sovereign states known as the German Confederation, which survived until 1866 when it was dissolved and replaced by the Prussian-dominated North German Federation. Prussia, directed by its Prime Minister (later Chancellor) Otto von Bismarck, had translated its earlier economic predominance amongst the German states into political hegemony by the annexation of the duchies of Schleswig and Holstein from Denmark in 1864 and a decisive defeat of Austria in 1866 (the Seven Weeks' War) which ended Austrian influence over German politics. After the Franco-Prussian War of 1870–71 resulted in the defeat of France and the cession to Prussia of Alsace and Lorraine, the south German principalities united with the northern federation to form a second German Empire, the King of Prussia being proclaimed Emperor at Versailles on Jan. 18, 1871.

Germany's defeat in the 1914–18 War led to the abdication of the Emperor and the princes, and the country became a Republic. The 1919 Treaty of Versailles returned Alsace and Lorraine to France, large areas in the east of the country were lost to the newly created state of Poland, and all German colonies placed under the administration of other countries. The world economic crisis of 1929 led to the collapse of the Weimar Republic and the subsequent rise to power of the National Socialist movement of Adolf Hitler, who became Chancellor in 1933.

THE WAR OF 1939–1945.—After concluding a Treaty of Non-Aggression with Soviet Russia (Aug. 24, 1939), Germany invaded Poland (Sept. 1, 1939), thus precipitating war with France and Great Britain, which had (March 31) given a pledge to support Poland against aggression.

Hitler committed suicide on April 30, 1945. On May 8, 1945, the unconditional surrender of all German forces was accepted by representatives of the Western Allied and Soviet Supreme Commanders.

THE POST WAR PERIOD.—After the surrender the Allied Powers exercised supreme authority in Germany on lines laid down in the Potsdam agreement

---

* Nazi historians referred to the National Socialist régime as *Drittes Reich*.

(August 1945) between the U.K., U.S.A. and U.S.S.R. Power was exercised by the Commanders-in-Chief, each in his own zone of occupation and jointly in matters affecting Germany as a whole through a Control Council. Berlin was governed jointly by the four occupying powers. The agreement also provided for the total disarmament and demilitarization of Germany, the destruction of the National Socialist German Workers' Party, the decentralization of the economy and the construction of a democratic constitution. No central German government was permitted but central German administration was established in the fields of finance, industry, foreign trade, transport and communications as support organs for the Control Council. The Potsdam agreement was to have been confirmed or revised by a peace treaty but no treaty has been drawn up. Some provisions of the Potsdam agreement were carried out but differences in interpretation among the Allies made it impossible to implement in full and the system of quadripartite control broke down when the Russians withdrew from the Control Council in March 1948.

FEDERAL REPUBLIC OF GERMANY
(Bundesrepublik Deutschland)

Federal President, Dr. Richard von Weizsäcker, *born* 1920, *elected* May 22, 1984, *sworn in*, July 1, 1984, *for five years.*

CABINET

Federal Chancellor, Dr. Helmut Kohl (*CDU*).
Foreign Minister and Vice-Chancellor, Hans Dietrich Genscher (*FDP*).
Interior, Dr. Friedrich Zimmerman (*CSU*).
Justice, Hans Engelhard (*FDP*).
Finance, Dr. Gerhard Stoltenberg (*CDU*).
Economics, Dr. Martin Bangemann (*FDP*).
Food, Agriculture and Forestry, Ignaz Kiechle (*CSU*).
Intra-German Relations, Dr. Dorothee Wilms (*CDU*).
Labour and Social Affairs, Dr. Norbert Blüm (*CDU*).
Defence, Prof. Rupert Scholz (*CDU*).
Youth, Family Affairs, Women and Health, Prof. Dr. Rita Süssmuth (*CDU*).
Transport, Dr. Jürgen Warnke (*CSU*).
Environment, Nature Conservation and Reactor Safety, Prof. Klaus Töpfer (*CDU*).
Posts and Telecommunications, Dr. Christian Schwarz-Schilling (*CDU*).
Regional Planning, Building and Urban Development, Dr. Oscar Schneider (*CSU*).
Research and Technology, Dr. Heinz Riesenhuber (*CDU*).
Education and Science, Jürgen Möllemann (*FDP*).
Economic Co-operation, Dr. Hans Klein (*CSU*).
Federal Minister at the Chancellery, Dr. Wolfgang Schäuble (*CDU*)
CDU = Christian Democratic Union; *CSU* = Christian Social Union; *FDP* = Free Democratic Party.

EMBASSY IN LONDON
23 Belgrave Square, SW1X 8PZ
[01–235 5033]

Ambassador Extraordinary and Plenipotentiary, His Excellency Baron Rüdiger von Wechmar, G.C.V.O. (1984).
Minister Plenipotentiary, Helmut Wegner.
Minister-Counsellor, Dr.Klaus-Peter Klaiber, C.M.G.
First Counsellors, Dr. Otto Roever (*Head of Economic Dept.*); G. H. von Neubronner, C.V.O. (*Cultural*); Dr. W. Hoffman (*Scientific Affairs*); Dr. R. Peters (*Agriculture*).

NOTE.—Except where otherwise indicated statistical data on the Federal Republic of Germany include Berlin (West).
Area and Population.—The area of the Federal Republic is approximately 95,976 sq. miles (248,577 sq. km.). Total population of the Federal Republic at April 1987 was 61,149,000. Distribution of the population among the *Länder* at end 1987 was:

Baden-Württemberg	9,327,000
Bavaria	11,026,000
Berlin (West)	1,879,000
Bremen	654,000
Hamburg	1,571,000
Hesse	5,544,000
Lower Saxony	7,196,000
North Rhine Westphalia	16,677,000
Rhineland Palatinate	3,611,000
Saarland	1,042,000
Schleswig-Holstein	2,613,000

Vital Statistics.—There were 10·5 live births per 1,000 inhabitants in the Federal Republic in 1987.
Government.—The Federal Republic grew out of the fusion of the three western zones. The economic union of the U.K. and U.S. zones was later joined by the French zone and in 1948–49 Parliamentary Council, elected by the parliaments of the *Länder* in the three zones, drafted a provisional democratic federal constitution for Germany. This Basic Law came into force in the three western zones on May 23, 1949. When the Federal Government took office the Allied Military Governors were replaced by High Commissioners. In 1952 a contractual agreement was signed between the Federal Republic and the western Allies, whereby the Republic, in return for certain promises regarding a defence contribution, a foreign debt settlement, and the continuation of allied policies concerning decartelization, democratization, restitution, etc., regained virtual sovereignty in May, 1955, after ratification by all the parties concerned. The High Commissioners then became Ambassadors.
The Basic Law provides for a President, elected for a five-year term, a Lower House (*Bundestag*), with a four-year term of office, elected by direct universal suffrage, and an Upper House (*Bundesrat*) composed of 45 delegates of the *Länder*, without a fixed term of office.
The results of the elections held for the lower House (*Bundestag*) on Jan. 25, 1987, were as follows:

Party	Numbers
Social Democrats	186
Christian Democratic Union	174
Christian Social Union	49
Free Democrats	46
The Greens	42

with an additional 22 representatives of Berlin elected by the House of Representatives of Berlin (CDU 11; SPD 7; FDP 2; Alternative Liste 2).
The Prime Ministers of the *Länder* governments in July 1988, were:

Ministers-President
Baden-Württemberg.—Lothar Späth.
Bavaria.—Franz Josef Strauss.
Berlin.—Eberhard Diepgen (*Governing Mayor*).
Bremen.—Klaus Wedemeier (*Mayor*).
Hamburg.—Henning Voscherau (*First Mayor*).
Hesse.—Dr. Walter Wallmann.
Lower Saxony.—Dr. Ernst Albrecht.
North Rhine-Westphalia.—Johannes Rau.
Rhineland-Palatinate.—Dr. Bernhard Vogel.
Saarland.—Oskar Lafontaine.
Schleswig-Holstein.—Björn Engholm.

Law and Justice

Law and Justice.—Judicial authority is exercised by the Federal Constitutional Court, the Federal courts provided for in the Basic Law and the courts of the Länder.

The death sentence has been abolished.

ECONOMY

Despite the difficulties arising from the division of Germany, which cut off from the Federal Republic the main food producing areas of Eastern Germany and some of the principal centres of light industry, Germany has regained her position as the main industrial power on the Continent, and is the most economically powerful member of the European Community. The Gross National Product at current prices in 1987 was estimated at *DM*2,023,200 million, an increase of 3·8 per cent over 1986. In real terms GNP grew by 1·7 per cent, after a 2·5 per cent growth in 1986. Forecasts for real growth in 1988 range from 1·5 to 2·0 per cent.

Agriculture.—In 1986 total area of farmland was 11,999,700 hectares, of which 7,251,300 hectares were arable land. Forest areas cover 7,360,000 hectares.

Crop yields were (tonnes):

	1985	1986
Rye	1,821,400	1,768,300
Wheat	9,865,900	10,406,200
Maslin	55,100	49,400
Barley	9,690,500	9,377,100
Oats	2,806,500	2,276,000
Potatoes	7,905,300	7,390,300
Sugar beet	20,813,000	20,260,000
Colza and rape	802,800	968,900
Fruit	2,548,515	3,478,527

Milk production in 1986 was 26,350,000 tonnes. Total yield of fisheries was 161,280 tonnes, valued at DM.237,531,000.

Industrial Production.—The Federal Republic has a predominantly industrial economy. Principal industries are coal mining, iron and steel production, machine construction, the electrical industry, the manufacture of steel and metal products, chemicals and textiles, and the processing of foodstuffs. The index of industrial net production adjusted for irregularities of the calendar (1985 = 100) is as follows:

	1986	1987
Mining	95·9	91·6
Manufacturing industry	102·4	102·6
(i) Basic materials	99·4	99·3
(ii) Capital goods	104·4	104·8
(iii) Consumer goods	102·2	103·2
(iv) Foodstuffs	101·5	100·3
Power (electricity and gas)	99·2	103·0
Construction	106·1	105·7
Total industry	102·3	102·6

Annual production figures were:

	1986	1987
	Tonnes '000	
Hard coal	80,801	76,300
Brown coal	114,310	108,799
Crude petroleum	4,017	3,800
Pig iron	27,622	27,333
Raw steel	36,370	35,916
Rolled steel	27,524	27,440
Fuel oils	34,208	31,757
Petrol, special and testing benzines	19,200	18,598
Chemical fibres	952	985
Cement	26,639	25,243
	Number	
Passenger cars	3,953,000	4,008,000
Televisions	3,866,000	3,454,000

Labour.—Labour figures, in annual averages, were:

	1986	1987
Employment	25,794,000	25,971,000
Unemployed	2,228,000	2,228,800
Men	1,200,000	1,207,000
Foreign Workers	1,570,000	1,611,000*

*August 1987

FINANCE

Receipts.—As from January 1, 1979, the distribution of taxes in the Fed. Rep. of Germany between Federation, Länder, communities and local authorities has been regulated by the Basic Law (Constitution).

Expenditure.—Figures of budgetary expenditure are:

	1987	Draft 1988
	DM billion	
Total expenditure	269·1	275·0
Agriculture	7·9	8·4
Defence	50·6	51·6
Social Welfare	77·9	79·4
Transport	25·6	25·7

TRADE

	1986	1987
	DM million	
Total imports	413,744·4	409,470·3
Total exports	526,363·0	527,018·2

Of imports, 12·7 per cent were foodstuffs and 6·8 per cent industrial raw materials in 1987. Main trading partners in 1987 were (figures shown as percentage of total trade):

	Imports	Exports
Netherlands	11·0	8·7
France	11·6	12·1
U.K.	7·1	8·8
Italy	9·6	8·7
U.S.A.	6·3	9·5
Japan	6·2	2·0

Trade with U.K.

	1986	1987
Imports from U.K	£8,542,196,000	£9,404,257,000
Exports to U.K.	14,139,097,000	15,783,904,000

The U.K. is currently the largest supplier to the Federal Republic of petroleum and petroleum products (1987: £1,266,054,000).

Communications.—At the end of 1985 the state-owned railways of the Federal Republic (*Deutsche Bundesbahn*) measured 27,649 kilometres of which 11,388 kilometres were electrified, and the privately owned railways 2,919 kilometres, a total of 30,568 kilometres. Railway rolling stock included, in 1985, 2,632 electric locomotives, 4,404 diesel locomotives and 260,136 goods waggons; in 1985 the railways handled 321,283,000 tonnes of goods. Classified roads measured 173,240 kilometres in 1985, of which motorways were 8,350 kilometres. On Jan 1, 1988, there were 28,304,184 cars registered, 1,379,078 commercial vehicles and 1,664,532 tractors. Ocean-going shipping under the German flag in Dec., 1985, amounted to 5,627,000 tons gross. Inland waterways handled 222,408,000 tonnes of goods in 1985.

Social Welfare.—There is compulsory insurance against sickness, accident, old age and unemployment. Children's allowances are payable in respect of the second and subsequent children. Pension schemes for widows and orphans of public servants are in operation. Public assistance is given to persons unable to earn their living, or with insufficient income to maintain a decent standard of living.

Education.—School attendance is compulsory for all children and juveniles between the ages of 6 and 18 and comprises 9 years full-time compulsory education at primary and main schools (*Grund und Hauptschulen*) and 3 years of compulsory vocational education on a part-time basis. In autumn, 1985, there were in the Federal Republic 19,280 primary and main schools (*Grund und Hauptschulen*) with 3,827,875 pupils. Secondary modern schools (*Realschulen*) numbered 2,617 with 1,049,010 pupils. There were 2,800 other general secondary schools (*Gymnasien* including *Gesamtschulen*) with 1,967,838 pupils.

There were also 2,826 special schools (*Sonderschulen*) for retarded, physically and mentally handicapped and socially maladjusted children in the Federal Republic with 271,424 pupils.

The secondary school leaving examination (*Abitur*) entitles the holder to a place of study at a university or another institution of higher education.

Children below the age of 18 who are not attending a general secondary or a full-time vocational school are obliged to take a three-year course (part-time) at a vocational school. In November, 1985, there were 1,549 full and part-time vocational schools (*Berufsschulen*) and 333 vocational extension schools (*Berufsaufbauschulen*) with 2,014,506 pupils, 2,326 full-time vocational schools (*Berufsfachschulen*) with 392,477 pupils, 940 schools for secondary technical studies (*Fachoberschulen/Fachgymnasien*) with 135,511 students.

Results for the winter term 1986–87 show a total of 1,367,699 students at institutions of higher education, of whom 931,348 were attending universities. The largest universities were in Munich, Berlin, Hamburg, Bonn and Cologne.

Language and Literature.—Modern (or New High) German has developed from the time of the Reformation to the present day, with differences of dialect in

Austria and Alsace and in the German-speaking cantons of Switzerland. The literary language is usually regarded as having become fixed by Luther and Zwingli at the Reformation, since which time many great names occur in all branches, notably philosophy, from Leibnitz (1646–1716) to Kant (1724–1804), Fichte (1762–1814), Schelling (1775–1854) and Hegel (1770–1831); the drama from Goethe (1749–1832) and Schiller (1759–1805) to Gerhart Hauptmann (1862–1946); and in poetry, Heine (1797–1856). German authors have received the Nobel Prize for Literature on seven occasions—Theodor Mommsen (1902), R. Eucken (1908), P. Heyse (1909), Gerhart Hauptmann (1912), Thomas Mann (1929), N. Sachs (1966) and Heinrich Böll (1972). In 1985 there were 382 daily papers.

Religion.—In 1970 there were 29,696,571 Protestants in the Republic, 27,060,826 Roman Catholics, 31,684 Jews and 3,861,518 others.

CAPITAL.—Bonn, in North Rhine Westphalia, 15 miles distant from Cologne. Population 290,800 (end June 1986).

The population of the principal cities and towns in the Federal Republic at end June 1986, was:

Berlin (West)	1,868,700	Dortmund	569,800
ΨHamburg ...	1,575,700	Stuttgart	564,500
Munich	1,269,400	Düsseldorf....	561,200
Cologne	914,000	ΨBremen	524,700
Essen	617,700	Duisburg	516,600
Frankfurt am		Hanover	506,400
Main.......	593,400	Nuremberg ...	466,500

CURRENCY.—Deutsche Mark (DM) of 100 Pfennig.
FLAG.—Horizontal bars of black, red and gold.
NATIONAL ANTHEM.—"Einigkeit und Recht und Freiheit" (Unity, right and freedom).
NATIONAL DAY.—May 23.

BRITISH EMBASSY
Friedrich-Ebert-Allee 77, 5300 Bonn 1
[Bonn 23 40 61]

Ambassador Extraordinary and Plenipotentiary, His Excellency Sir Christopher Leslie George Mallaby, K.C.M.G. (1988).
Minister, Miss L. P. Neville Jones, C.M.G.
Counsellors, A. St. J. Figgis (*Head of Chancery*); R. P. Flower; Miss A. Walker (*Defence Supply*); A. C. Thorpe (*Economic*); Dr. J. K. Duxbury (*Science and Technology*); A. L. Free-Gore (*Administration*); Mrs. A. Le Sage (*Labour*).
First Secretaries, D. M. Bell; A. Noble; R. E. Brinkley; R. W. Barnett; R. Weaver; V. Evans; P. Elliott; M. Uden; I. Woods; E. Jenkinson; M. Evans; P. Cunningham; R. Sands.
Legal Advisor, J. O. Hill.
Defence and Military Attaché, Brig. A. P. Sims.
Asst. Military Attaché, Lt. Col. J. D. Colson.
Naval Attaché, Capt. W. K. Hutchinson, R.N.
Asst. Naval Attaché, Lt. Cdr. T. J. Lankester.
Air Attaché, Air Cdre. B. T. Sills.
Head of Visa Section (*Düsseldorf*), P. Faulkner.
Chaplain, Rev. J. Newsome.

There are British Consulates-General at *Berlin, Hamburg, Düsseldorf, Frankfurt* and *Munich.*

BRITISH COUNCIL

Representative, T. Rutter, O.B.E., Hahnenstrasse 6, 5000 Cologne 1. Offices at *Berlin, Hamburg* and *Munich* and British Council libraries at all four centres.

BRITISH CHAMBER OF COMMERCE
Neumarkt 14, D-5000 Cologne 1.

Director, J. Parr.

BERLIN
G.O.C. *British Sector*, Maj.-Gen. P. G. Brooking, M.B.E.
Minister and Deputy Commandant, M. St. E. Burton, C.V.O.
Counsellor, R. H. Smith (*Political Adviser and Head of Chancery*).

GERMAN DEMOCRATIC REPUBLIC
(Deutsche Demokratische Republik)

COUNCIL OF STATE
Chairman, Erich Honecker.
Deputy Chairmen, Dr. Manfred Gerlach; Günter Maleuda; Gerald Götting; Prof. Heinrich Homann; Horst Sindermann; Willi Stoph; Egon Krenz; Günter Mittag.
Members, W. Felfe; Prof. K. Hager; Frau B. Hanke; F. Kind; Prof. L. Kolditz; Frau M. Müller; A. Pisnik; B. Quandt; Dr. K. Sorgenicht; P. Strauss; Frau I. Thiele; H. Tisch; Prof. J. Töpfer; Frau R. Walther; K. Anclam; W. Seifert.
Secretary, H. Eichler.
Head of the Chairman's Chancery, F.-J. Herrmann.

COUNCIL OF MINISTERS
Chairman, Willi Stoph.
Deputy Chairmen, Werner Krolikowski; Alfred Neumann (*First Deputy Chairmen*); M. Flegel; H-J. Heusinger; G. Kleiber; W. Rauchfuss; Dr. H. Reichelt; G. Schürer; R. Schulze; H. Sölle; Dr. H. Weiz.
Total membership of the Council is 45.

SOCIALIST UNITY PARTY OF GERMANY
Politbureau of the Central Committee, H. Axen; H.-J. Böhme; H. Dohlus; W. Eberlein; W. Felfe; Prof. K. Hager; J. Herrmann; E. Honecker; W. Jarowinsky; Gen. H. Kessler; G. Kleiber; E. Krenz; W. Krolikowski; S. Lorenz; E. Mielke; G. Mittag; E. Mückenberger; A. Neumann; G. Schabowski; H. Sindermann; W. Stoph; H. Tisch (*full members*); Frau I. Lange; G. Müller; Frau M. Müller; G. Schürer; W. Walde (*candidate members*).
Secretariat of the Central Committee, E. Honecker (*General Secretary*); H. Axen; H. Dohlus; W. Felfe; Prof. K. Hager; J. Herrmann; W. Jarowinsky; E. Krenz; I. Lange; G. Mittag; G. Schabowski (*secretaries*).

EMBASSY OF THE G.D.R.
34 Belgrave Square, SW1X 8QB
[01–235 9941]

Ambassador Extraordinary and Plenipotentiary, His Excellency Dr. Gerhard Lindner (1984).
Counsellors, H. Bock; H. Vorpahl (*Commercial*); Dr. G. Schaller.
First Secretaries, H. Kopp; M. Rudolph, Dr. H. Kluge; J. Döring.

Area and Population.—The German Democratic Republic comprises the five former German *Länder* of Brandenburg, Mecklenburg, Saxony, Saxony-Anhalt and Thuringia (an area of 41,768 sq. miles; 108,178 sq. km.). The seat of Government is the Soviet sector of Berlin (eastern part of Berlin) (156 sq. miles). The population of the Republic, including East Berlin (end of 1985) was 16,644,000. In 1952 the former *Länder* were replaced by fourteen *Bezirke* (regions): Potsdam, Cottbus and Frankfurt (*formerly* Brandenburg); Rostock, Schwerin and Neubrandenburg (*formerly* Mecklenburg); Karl-Marx-Stadt, Dresden and

Leipzig (*formerly* Saxony); Halle and Magdeburg (*formerly* Saxony-Anhalt); Erfurt, Gera and Suhl (*formerly* Thuringia.)

Government.—The present Constitution, which defines the G.D.R. as a Socialist state, came into force on April 9, 1968 after endorsement by a referendum. It replaced the first Constitution of October 7, 1949. The supreme organ of State power is the *Volkskammer*, which has power to elect and dismiss the Council of State, the Council of Ministers, the Chairman of the National Defence Council, the Supreme Court and the Procurator-General. The Council of State retains the presidential powers which it has exercised since the abolition of the office of President on September 12, 1960, together with responsibility for the organization of defence with the help of the National Defence Council. The Council of Ministers is responsible to the *Volkskammer* for the conduct of State policy. The present *Volkskammer* is that elected in April 1986.

As with other communist countries, effective power lies with the ruling Marxist-Leninist Party, in this case the Socialist Unity Party of Germany (SED). The other parties and mass organizations are members of the SED-controlled National Front.

ECONOMY

The G.D.R. economy, including the control of industry and foreign trade, is centrally planned and administered. The State Planning Commission, which is subordinate to the Council of Ministers, is responsible for drawing up the 5- and 1-Year Plans. The 5-Year Plans determine the future development and structure of the economy; the 1-Year Plans have to achieve these aims. The implementation of these plans is the responsibility of the State Production Enterprises under the supervision of the economic and industrial Ministries. The economy is very closely integrated with those of other member countries of C.M.E.A. and particularly with the U.S.S.R.

The Budget for 1986 was: revenue, *M*263,750·7 million; expenditure, *M*263,590·9 million.

Agriculture.—Land is cultivated mostly on state or collective farms, though some is cultivated independently. Crop yields in 1985 were: potatoes 12,350,000 tonnes; sugar-beet 7,397,000 tonnes; corn (green and silage) 12,884,000 tonnes; grain 11,640,000 tonnes, and oilseeds 396,000 tonnes.

Industry.—Almost all industry is nationally or co-operatively owned with less than 2 per cent. of the working population engaged in private enterprise. G.D.R. is the leading world producer of lignite, production in 1985 was 312,000,000 tonnes, and the iron and steel industry is also important. Other highly developed industries include basic chemicals and petro-chemicals, machine tools and industrial plant, ship-building and transport equipment, electronic and engineering equipment, precision tools and optical instruments.

Trade with U.K.

	1986	1987
Imports from U.K. . . .	£81,276,000	£81,489,000
Exports to U.K.	195,513,000	180,299,000

Principal cities and towns (population, 1985): East Berlin (1,202,895); Leipzig (554,595); Dresden (519,860); Karl-Marx-Stadt (316,361); Magdeburg (288,914); Rostock (242,729); Halle (Saale) (235,858); Erfurt (215,499); Potsdam (138,737).

CURRENCY.—Mark der Deutschen Demokratischen Republik of 100 Pfennig.

FLAG.—Horizontal bands of black, red, gold; hammer, compasses and corn device at centre.

NATIONAL ANTHEM.—Auferstanden Aus Ruinen (Risen from ruins).
NATIONAL DAY.—October 7.

BRITISH EMBASSY
108 Berlin, Unter den Linden 32/34
[Berlin 220–2431]

Ambassador Extraordinary and Plenipotentiary, His Excellency Nigel Hugh Robert Allen Broomfield, C.M.G. (1988).
Counsellor, C. Munro.
First Secretaries, D. B. Merry (*Head of Chancery*); G. Deane (*Information*); D. J. Young (*Commercial*).
Second Secretaries, A. R. Weeks (*Administration and Consul*); J. W. Lawson.
Third Secretary, R. C. Morton.
Cultural Attaché, M. G. Holcroft (*British Council Representative*).

GREECE
(Elliniki Dimokratia)

President of the Hellenic Republic, Christos Sartzetakis, *born* 1927, *elected* March 29, 1985.

CABINET
(as at May 9, 1988)

Prime Minister, Andreas Papandreou.
Deputy P.M. and Defence Minister, Ioannis Haralambopoulos.
Deputy P.M. and Justice Minister, Agamemnon Koutsoyiorgas.
Minister in Charge of P.M.'s office, Apostolos Kaklamanis.
Minister of State for the Media, Dimitris Maroudas.
Foreign Affairs, Karolos Papoulias.
E.C. Affairs, Theodoros Pangalos.
Alternate Foreign Minister, Ioannis Kapsis.
Interior, Akis Tsohatzopoulos.
National Economy, Panayotis Roumeliotis.
Tourism and Air Transport, Nikos Skoulas.
Finance, Dimitris Tsovolas.
Health and Welfare, Ioannis Floros.
Education, George Papandreou.
Culture, Melina Mercouri.
Public Order, Tasos Sehiotis.
Northern Greece, Stelios Papathemelis.
Aegean, Petros Valvis.
Agriculture, Ioannis Pottakis.
Environment, Evanghelos Kouloumbis.
Industry, Anastasios Peponis.
Labour, George Yennimatas.
Commerce, Nikos Akritidis.
Transport, George Petsos.
Merchant Marine, Evanghelos Yiannopoulos.

GREEK EMBASSY IN LONDON
1a Holland Park, W11 3TP
[01–727 8040]

Ambassador Extraordinary and Plenipotentiary, His Excellency Stephanos G. Stathatos (1986).
Defence Attaché, Capt. H. N. George Beserianos.
Counsellors, D. Vidouris; E. Clis; A. Mitsialis (*Consular Affairs*); G. Protonotarios (*Economic and Commercial*); I. Staikos (*Education*); A. Xerikos (*Labour*); G. Arzoglou (*Press*).
Tourist Adviser, P. Analytis.

There are Honorary Consulates at *Belfast, Birmingham, Edinburgh, Falmouth, Glasgow, Leeds* and *Southampton*.

A maritime State in the south-east of Europe, bounded on the N. by Albania, Yugoslavia and

GREECE

MILES

0   100   200

Bulgaria, on the S. and W. by the Ionian and Mediterranean seas, and on the E. by Turkey, with an estimated area of 50,944 sq. miles (131,944 sq. km.). Population (1985 U.N. estimate) is given as 9,935,000.

The main areas of Greece are: *Macedonia* (which includes Mt. Athos and the island of Thasos), *Thrace* (including the island of Samothrace), *Epirus, Thessaly, Continental Greece* (which includes the island of Euboea and the Sporades or "scattered islands" of which the largest is Skyros), the *Peloponnese* (or *Morea*), the *Dodecanese* or *Southern Sporades* (12 islands occupied by Italy in 1911 during the Italo-Turkish War and ceded to Greece by Italy in 1947) consisting of Rhodes, Astypalaia, Karpathos, Kassos, Nisyros, Kalymnos, Leros, Patmos, Kos, Symi, Khalki and Tilos, the *Cyclades* (a circular group numbering about 200, with a total area of 923 sq. miles; the chief islands are Syros, Andros, Tinos, Naxos, Paros, Santorini, Milos and Serifos), the *Ionian Islands* (Corfu, Paxos, Levkas, Ithaca, Cephalonia, Zante and Cerigo), the *Aegean Islands* (Chios, Lesbos, Limnos and Samos). In *Crete* there was for over 1,500 years (3000 to 1400 B.C.) a flourishing civilization which spread its influence far and wide throughout the Aegean, and the ruins of the palace of Minos at Knossos afford evidence of astonishing comfort and luxury. Greek civilization emerged about 1300 B.C. and the poems of Homer, the blind poet of Chios, which were probably current about 800 B.C., record the 10-year struggle between the Achaeans of Greece and the Phrygians of Troy (1194–1184 B.C.).

Language and Literature.—The spoken language of modern Greece is descended by a process of natural development from the "Common Greek" of Alexander's empire. *Katharevousa*, a conservative literary dialect evolved by Adamantios Corais (Diamant Coray), who lived and died in Paris (1748–1833) and used for official and technical matters, is to be phased out over the next few years. Novels and poetry are mostly composed in *dimotiki*, a progressive literary dialect which owes much to John Psycharis (1854–1929). The poets Solomos, Palamas, Cavafis, Sikelianos, Seferis and Elytis have won a European reputation.

Religion.—Over 97 per cent of the people are adherents of the Greek Orthodox Church, which is the State religion, all others being tolerated and free from interference. The Church of Greece recognizes the spiritual primacy of the Œcumenical Patriarch of Constantinople, but is otherwise a self-governing

body administered by the Holy Synod under the Presidency of the Archbishop of Athens and All Greece. It has no jurisdiction over the Church of Crete, which has a degree of autonomy under the Œcumenical Patriarch, nor over the Monastic Community of Mount Athos and the Church in the Dodecanese, both of which come directly under the Œcumenical Patriarch.

Government.—A military coup on April 21, 1967, suspended parliamentary government and, following an unsuccessful royal counter coup on December 13, 1967, King Constantine went into voluntary exile in Rome. On June 1, 1973 the monarchy was abolished and a republic established under the Presidency of Mr. George Papadopoulos.

The overthrow of Archbishop Makarios, President of Cyprus, on July 15, 1974, by a military coup led by Greek officers of the Cypriot National Guard caused an international crisis, in the wake of which the heads of the Greek armed forces decided, on July 23, to relinquish power. Mr. Konstantinos Karamanlis, Prime Minister between 1955 and 1963, returned from his self-imposed exile in Paris to form a provisional Government, and the first elections for ten years were held on November 17, 1974.

The constitutional position of the King, who was still in exile, remained unsettled until December 8, when by a referendum, the Greek people rejected "crowned democracy" by 69·2 per cent to 30·8 per cent and Greece became a republic. A new constitution came into force on June 11, 1975.

The Socialist Movement under Andreas Papandreou came into office following the General Election of Oct. 1981, and remained in power after winning the 1985 General Election.

Defence.—The strength of the Army is 130,000 backed up by some 50,000 in the National Guard. The Navy consists of 19,500 men and is equipped with a fleet of destroyers, submarines, patrol boats and amphibious warfare vessels, mostly of U.S., French, Dutch and German origin. The Air Force consists of 25,000 men and is equipped with aircraft disposed in 14 combat squadrons supported by the necessary transport, training, helicopter and reconnaissance squadrons. National service is 2 years on average.

Communications.—The 2,650 kilometres of Greek railways are State-owned with the exception of the Athens–Piraeus Electric Railway. Greek roads total somewhat over 35,500 kilometres, of which about 25 per cent are classified as national highways and just under 30,000 km. are classified as provincial roads. The road connection with Albania was reopened in 1985.

On Dec. 31, 1986, the Greek Mercantile fleet numbered 2,138 ships with a total tonnage of 24,792,516 tons gross. On the same day Greek-owned ships registered under foreign flags numbered 276 with a total tonnage of 5,176,347 tons gross. (N.B. These figures exclude Greek-owned vessels under 100 tons gross). Athens has direct airline links with Australasia, North America, most countries in Europe, Africa and the Middle East.

Education is free and compulsory from the age of 6 to 15 and is maintained by State grants. There are six Universities, Athens, Salonika, Patras, Thrace, Ioannina and Crete. There are several other institutes of higher learning, mostly in Athens.

Production.—Though there has in recent years been a substantial measure of industrialization, agriculture still employs about a quarter of the working population. The most important agricultural products are tobacco, wheat, cotton, sugar and rice. The most important of the fruit trees are the olive, peach, vine, orange, lemon, fig, almond and currant-vine, and now exports of Greek fresh fruit and vegetables have established themselves as an important contributor to the economy and have considerable growth potential. Currants, grown mainly around Patras, remain one of Greece's main exports, the United Kingdom being the principal purchaser.

The principal minerals mined in Greece are nickel, bauxite, iron ore, iron pyrites, manganese magnesite, chrome, lead, zinc and emery, and prospecting for petroleum is being carried on. Oil refineries are in operation near Athens and at Salonika, where there is also a petro-chemical plant. The chief industries are textiles (cotton, woollen and synthetics), chemicals, cement, glass, metallurgy, shipbuilding, domestic electrical equipment and footwear. In recent years new factories have been opened for the production of aluminium, nickel, iron and steel products, tyres, chemicals fertilizers and sugar (from locally-grown beet). Food processing and ancillary industries have also grown up throughout the country. The development of the country's electric power resources, irrigation and land reclamation schemes and the exploitation of Greece's lignite resources for fuel and industrial purposes are also being carried out. Tourism has developed rapidly, but is now slowing down.

TRADE

	1985	1986
Total imports ...	Drs 1,412,797·3m.	Drs 1,587,214·0m.
Total exports ...	629,188·3m.	789,994·6m.

Trade with U.K.

	1986	1987
Imports from U.K.	£356,020,000	£444,500,000
Exports to U.K.	308,644,000	355,320,000

CAPITAL.—Athens. Population (including ΨPiraeus and suburbs), 3,027,331 (1981 Census). Other large towns are ΨSalonika (706,180); ΨPatras (154,596), ΨVolos (107,407); Larissa (102,426); and ΨKavalla (56,705); in Crete—ΨHeraklion or Candia (102,398), ΨCanea (47,451), and ΨRethymnon (18,190); in the Ionian Islands—ΨCorfu (36,901); in the Dodecanese—ΨRhodes (41,425); in the Cyclades— ΨSyros Hermoupolis (13,877); in Lesbos—ΨMytilene (24,991); in Chios—ΨChios (24,070).

CURRENCY.—Drachma of 100 Lepta.

FLAG.—Blue and white stripes with a white cross on a blue field in the canton.

NATIONAL ANTHEM.—Imnos Eis Tin Eleftherian (Hymn to Freedom).

NATIONAL DAY.—March 25 (Independence Day).

BRITISH EMBASSY
1 Ploutarchou Street, 10675 Athens.
[Athens 7236–211/9]

Ambassador Extraordinary and Plenipotentiary, His Excellency Sir Jeremy Cashel Thomas, K.C.M.G. (1985).

Counsellors, J. B. Donnelly (*Political and Consul-General*); B. S. T. Eastwood (*Economic and Commercial*); W. V. Fell.

Defence and Military Attaché, Brig. G. R. A. Evans.

Naval and Air Attaché, Capt. R. Evans, L.V.O.

Embassy Chaplain, Rev. J. F. Maddock-Lyon.

Hon. Attaché, H. W. Catling, O.B.E., D.Phil. (*Director, British School of Archaeology*).

BRITISH CONSULAR OFFICES

There are British Consular Offices at *Athens, Corfu, Samos, Rhodes, Salonika, Heraklion* (Crete) and *Patras*.

BRITISH COUNCIL
17 Plateia Philikis Etairias (P.O. Box 3488), 10673 Athens.

Representative, Dr. R. T. Taylor.

There is also an office at *Salonika* and British Council libraries at both centres.

BRITISH-HELLENIC CHAMBER OF COMMERCE
4 Valaoritou Street, GR-10671 Athens.

GUATEMALA
(República de Guatemala)

Head of State, President Marco Vinicio Cerezo, *inaugurated*, Jan. 14, 1986.

CABINET

Vice President, Roberto Carpio Nicolle.
Minister of Government, Juan Jose Rodil Peralta.
Foreign Affairs, Alfonso Cabrera Hidalgo.
National Defence, Gen. Héctor Alejandro Gramajo.
Finance, Dr. Rudolfo Paiz Andrade.
Communications, Eduardo Goyzeuta Weissbach.
Education, Ricardo Gómez.
Agriculture, Rodolfo Augusto Estrada.
Economy, Lizardo Arturo Sosa Lopez.
Public Health and Social Welfare, Carlos Gehelert Matta.
Labour and Social Insurance, Rodolfo Maldonado.
Energy and Mines, Roland Castillo Contoux.
Special Affairs, (vacant).
Urban and Rural Development, Rene Armando De-Léon Schlotter.
Culture and Sport, (vacant).

EMBASSY OF GUATEMALA
13 Fawcett Street, SW10 9HN
[01–351 3042]

Ambassador Extraordinary and Plenipotentiary, His Excellency Dr. Erwin Blandon (1987).

Guatemala, in Central America, is situated in N. lat. from 13° 45′ to 17° 49′, and in W. long. from 88° 12′ 49″ to 92°13′ 43″, and has an area of 42,042 sq. miles (108,889 sq. km.), and a population (1985 U.N. estimate) of 7,963,000.

The Republic is divided into 22 departments, and is traversed from W. to E. by an elevated mountain chain, containing several volcanic summits rising to 13,000 feet above sea level; earthquakes are frequent. The country is well watered by numerous rivers; the climate is hot and malarial near the coast, temperate in the higher regions. The rainfall in the capital averages 57 in. per annum. The chief seaports are San José de Guatemala and Champerico on the Pacific and Santo Tomás de Castilla and Puerto Barrios on the Atlantic side.

Language and Literature.—Spanish is the language of the country, but 40 per cent. of the population speak an Indian language. Since the establishment of the University in the capital, education has received a marked impulse and the high figure of illiteracy is being reduced. The National library contains about 80,000 volumes in Spanish

Government.—The constitutionally elected president, Gen. Miguel Ydigoras Fuentes, was overthrown on March 31, 1963, by the Army, which handed executive and legislative powers to the Minister of Defence, Col. Enrique Peralta Azurdia. Important changes were included in a new constitution promulgated on Sept. 15, 1965, and elections for a new Congress and for President and Vice-President took place on March 6, 1966. The constitution was suspended "for as long as the situation demands" following a military coup in March 1982. An amnesty for guerrillas was unsuccessful and the Army was fully occupied dealing with the proliferating subversive groups throughout the country.

Elections for a Constituent Assembly were held on July 1, 1984, as promised by Gen. Mejía Víctores when he overthrew Gen. Rios Montt in 1983. The Assembly drew up a new Constitution, promulgated in June 1985, and a new electoral law, paving the way for Presidential, Governmental and Municipal elections which took place on Nov. 3 and Dec. 8, 1985. The elections were won by the Christian Democratic party and Vinicio Cerezo was elected President.

Finance.—The Central Government revenue in 1985 was *Quetzales* 865 million, and expenditure *Quetzales* 1,076 million.

TRADE

	1985	1986
Imports (c.i.f.) ...	U.S.$1,755 m.	U.S.$1,261 m.
Exports (f.o.b.) ..	1,112 m.	1,210 m.

Trade with U.K.

	1986	1987
Imports from U.K.	£9,288,000	£13,926,000
Exports to U.K.	8,098,000	7,536,000

The principal export is coffee, other articles being manufactured goods, sugar, bananas, cotton, beef and essential oils. The chief imports are petroleum, vehicles, machinery and foodstuffs.

CAPITAL.—Guatemala City. Population: 1,300,000. Quezaltenango has a pop. of over 100,000. Other towns are ΨPuerto Barrios (23,000), Mazatenango (21,000), and Antigua (30,000).

CURRENCY.—Quetzal of 100 Centavos.

FLAG.—Three vertical bands, blue, white, blue; coat of arms on white stripe.

NATIONAL ANTHEM.—Guatemala Feliz (Guatemala be praised).

NATIONAL DAY.—September 15.

BRITISH EMBASSY

Centro Financiero Torre II (7th Floor), Seventh Avenue 5–10 Zone 4, Guatemala City.
[Guatemala City 321601]

Ambassador Extraordinary and Plenipotentiary, His Excellency Bernard Everett.

GUINEA
(République de Guinée)

President, Brig. Gen. Lansana Conté, *took power*, April 3, 1984.

COUNCIL OF MINISTERS

Ministers of the Presidency, Cmdt. Babacar N'Diaye (*Defence*); Zainoul Abidine Sanoussi (*Information, Culture and Tourism*); Kemoko Keita (*Economy and Finance*); Capt. Abdourahamane Diallo (*Special Missions*).
Justice, Bassirou Barry.
Foreign Affairs, Cmdt. Jean Traore.
Economy and Finance, Cmdt. Lamine Bolivogui.
Agriculture and Animal Resources, Cmdt. Alhousseiny Fofana.
Industry, Trade and Handicrafts, Cmdt. Ousmane Sow.
Administrative Reform and Civil Service, Mamouna Bangoura.
Social Affairs and Employment, Cmdt. Jean Kolipé Lama.
Natural Resources and Environment, Dr. Ousmane Sylla.
Town Planning and Housing, Dr. Bana Sidibe.
Education, Saliou Coumbassa.
Public Health and Population, Dr. M. Pathé Diallo.
Religious Affairs, El Hadj Abdourahmane Bah.
Transport and Public Works, Cmdt. Facinet Toure.
Post and Telecommunications, Hervé-Vincent Bangoura.
Interior and Decentralization, Cmdt. Henri Tofani.

Planning and International Co-operation, Edouard Benjamin.
Regional Ministers, Capt. Gbago Zoumanigui (*Maritime Guinea: Kindia*); Lt.-Col. Sory Doumbouya (*Middle Guinea: Labe*); Cmdt. Kerfalla Camara (*Upper Guinea: Kankan*); Cmdt. Mamadou Baldet (*Forest Region: Nzerekore*).

Formerly part of French West Africa, Guinea has a coastline on the Atlantic Ocean between Guinea-Bissau and Sierra Leone and in the interior is adjacent to Senegal, Mali, Côte d'Ivoire, Liberia and Sierra Leone. Area, 94,926 sq. miles (245,857 sq. km.). The population (1985 U.N. estimate) was 6,075,000, mostly the Fullah, Malinké and Soussou tribes.

Government.—Guinea was separated from Senegal in 1891 and administered by France as a separate colony until 1958. In a referendum held in Sept. 1958, Guinea rejected the new French Constitution and on Oct. 2, 1958, became an independent republic governed by a Constituent Assembly. M. Sékou Touré, Prime Minister in the Territorial Assembly, assumed office as head of the new Government.

Under a provisional constitution, adopted on Nov. 12, 1958, powers of government are exercised by a president assisted by the Cabinet. The President, eligible for a term of 7 years and for re-election, is head of state and of the armed forces. M. Sékou Touré was elected President of the Republic in January, 1961. Pres. Sékou Touré died in March 1984: a few days later there was a military coup. Guinea is now ruled by a military government, which is directed by a Military Committee for National Recovery (C.M.R.N.). The country's foreign policy is one of non-alignment.

Guinea withdrew from the Franc Zone on March 1, 1960, and established her own currency. Guinea is in receipt of economic aid and technical assistance from a number of countries, including the United States, Canada, Federal Republic of Germany, Yugoslavia, the Soviet Union and China.

Production, etc.—The principal products of Guinea are bauxite, alumina, iron-ore, palm kernels, millet, rice, coffee, bananas, pineapples and rubber. At Sangaredi in the mountainous hinterland, where the rivers Senegal, Gambia and Niger have their sources, large deposits of bauxite are mined. Deposits of iron ore, gold, diamonds and uranium have also been discovered. Principal imports are cotton goods, manufactured goods, tobacco, petroleum products, sugar, rice, flour and salt; exports, bauxite, alumina, iron-ore, diamonds, coffee, hides, bananas, palm kernels and pineapples.

Trade with U.K.

	1986	1987
Imports from U.K.	£10,679,000	£10,675,000
Exports to U.K.	23,892,000	19,538,000

CAPITAL.—ΨConakry (763,000). Other towns are Kankan, which is connected with Conakry by a railway, Kindia, N'Zérékoré, Mamou, Siguiri and Labé.

CURRENCY.—Guinea Franc of 100 Centimes.

FLAG.—Three vertical stripes of red, yellow and green.

NATIONAL DAY.—October 2 (Anniversary of Proclamation of Independence).

BRITISH EMBASSY

British Ambassador (resident at Dakar, Senegal).

GUINEA-BISSAU
(República da Guiné-Bissau)

President of the Council of State (*Head of State*), Gen. João Bernardo Vieira, *took power*, Nov. 1980.

Minister of State for the Armed Forces, Col. Iafai Camara.

Minister of State at the Presidency, Tiago Aleluia Lopes.

Rural Development and Fisheries, Carlos Correia.

Education, Culture and Sports, Fidelis Cabral d'Almada.

Commerce and Tourism, Manuel Maria Santos.

National Security and Public Order, José Pereira.

Minister for the Northern Province, Mario Cabral.

Natural Resources and Industry, Filinto Barros.

Foreign Affairs, Julio Semedo.

Public Health, Alexandre Nunes Correia.

Minister for the Eastern Province, Malan Bacai Sanha.

Minister for the Southern Province, Luis Oliveira Sanca.

Justice, Nicandro Pereira Barreto.

Finance, Victor Freire Monteiro.

Governor of the National Bank, Pedro Godinho Gomes.

Information and Telecommunications, Musa Djassi.

Planning, Bartolomeu S. Pereira.

Public Works, Avito José Da Silva.

Civil Service, Labour and Social Security, Henriqueta Godinho Gomes.

Guinea-Bissau, formerly Portuguese Guinea, lies in Western Africa, between Senegal and Guinea; it has an area of 13,948 sq. miles (36,125 sq. km.), and had a population (1985 U.N. estimate) of 890,000. The main ethnic groups are the Balante, Malinké, Fulani, Mandjako and Pepel.

Guinea-Bissau achieved independence on Sept. 10, 1974. Sr. Luis Cabral was ousted in a coup led by Maj. (now Gen.) Vieira in November, 1980. Following the coup the Assembly was suspended, and a Revolutionary Council was established. Under a new constitution adopted in April 1984 the Revolutionary Council became a 15-member Council of State, and a parliament was set up. An attempted coup to overthrow President Vieira was defeated in November 1985.

Economy.—The country produces rice, coconuts, ground-nuts and palm oil products. Cattle are raised, and there are bauxite deposits in the south.

Trade with U.K.

	1986	1987
Imports from U.K....	£1,319,000	£1,152,043
Exports to U.K.	214,000	16,660

CAPITAL.—ΨBissau (census 1979, 109,486), also the chief port.

CURRENCY.—Guinea-Bissau Peso of 100 Centavos.

FLAG.—Horizontal bands of yellow over green with vertical red band in the hoist charged with a black star.

NATIONAL DAY.—September 24 (Independence Day).

BRITISH EMBASSY
British Ambassador, (resident at Dakar, Senegal).

HAITI
(République d'Haiti)

President of the Military Government, Lt. Gen. Henri Namphy.

CABINET
(as at June 1988)

Interior and Defence, Maj.-Gen. Williams Regala.
Foreign Affairs, Gen. Herard Abraham.
Information and Co-ordination, Col. Acedius Saint Louis.
Economy and Finance, Col. Andre Jean Pierre.
Justice, Gen. Fritz Antoine.
Public Health and Population, Lt.-Col. Jean Verly.
Public Works, Transport and Communications, Lt.Col. Alphonse Desulme.
Agriculture, National Resources and Rural Development, Lt.-Col. Damax Signeus.
Education, Youth and Sports, Gen. Cecilio Dorce.
Social Affairs, Col. Phede Desir.
Trade and Industry, Col. Eric Brunel Lamour.

The London Embassy of the Republic of Haiti closed on March 30, 1987.

The Republic of Haiti occupies the western third of the island of Hispaniola, which, after Cuba, is the largest island in the West Indies.

The area of the Republic, including off-shore islands, is 10,714 sq. miles (27,750 sq. km.) (of which about three-quarters is mountainous), with a population (1985 U.N. estimate) of 6,585,000, 85 per cent of whom live in rural areas. The people are mainly negroes but there are numbers of mulattoes and others with some admixture of European blood.

Climate.—The climate is tropical with comparatively little difference in the temperatures between the summer (March–Oct.) and the winter (Nov.–Feb.). Humidity is high, especially in the autumn.

Language.—Following the new constitution of March 1987 both French and Creole are regarded as the official languages of Haiti. French is the language of the government and the press, but it is only spoken by the educated minority. The usual language of the people is Creole.

Haiti was a French colony under the name of Saint-Domingue from 1697. The slave population, estimated at 500,000, revolted in 1791 under the leadership of Toussaint L'Ouverture, who was born a slave and

made himself Governor General of the colony. He capitulated to the French in 1802 and died in captivity in 1803. Resistance was continued by Jean Jacques Dessalines, also a former negro slave, who, on January 1, 1804, declared the former French colony to be an independent state. It was at this time that the name Haiti, an aboriginal word meaning mountainous, was adopted. Dessalines became Emperor of Haiti, but was assassinated in 1806. In 1915, following a period of political upheaval, the country was occupied by a force of U.S. marines. The occupation came to an end in 1934, and U.S. control of the revenue of Haiti officially ended on October 1, 1947.

Dr. Duvalier was installed as President in 1957 and held the position until his death in 1971. He was succeeded as President for life on the same day by his son, Jean Claude Duvalier, whom he had nominated as his successor. President Duvalier fled to France on Feb. 7, 1986 in the face of sustained popular unrest, and a council headed by Gen. Henri Namphy assumed power. In March 1987, by popular referendum, a new Constitution was agreed and Presidential elections scheduled for Nov. 29. These elections were aborted following violence in the capital. The elections held on Jan. 17, 1988, were boycotted by a number of leading candidates but Leslie Manigat eventually won after a very low turnout. President Manigat was inaugurated on Feb. 7, 1988, but he and his government were ousted on June 19 by Gen. Henri Namphy. Manigat was deported to the Dominican Republic and Namphy set up a military government.

Production.—In recent years measures for agricultural rehabilitation have been taken with the aim of a gradual restoration of productivity, which had declined after the ending of the colonial plantation system. The main project is a scheme for the irrigation of more than 70,000 acres of the Artibonite valley.

Coffee accounts for about 32 per cent of total exports, worth approximately U.S.$55 million in 1986. Cocoa is the second largest export earner at U.S.$4·5 million. Corn, 110,000 tonnes (1985), sorghum, 108,000 tonnes (1985), and rice are also grown. Increased production of tropical fruits and vegetables is being encouraged.

Industry.—Export assembly industries account for about 30 per cent of the total manufacturing industry in Haiti, employing an estimated 40,000 people. Items such as leather goods, textiles, electronic components and sports equipment are manufactured, using imported raw materials, for re-export, primarily to the U.S.A. Principal imports are raw materials for the export assembly sector, foodstuffs, machinery, vehicles, mineral oils and textiles.

Communications.—The main roads are asphalted and secondary roads are fair. Internal air services are maintained between the capital and the principal provincial towns. International air-services connect Port-au-Prince with the U.S.A. and other Caribbean and South American cities. The principal towns and villages are connected by telephone and/or telegraph. The telephone company is state owned (51 per cent.) and the service both in Port-au-Prince and Interurban has been greatly improved. External telegraph, telephone and postal services are normal. There are several commercial radio stations and two television stations at Port-au-Prince.

Regular passenger liner services to New York have ceased, but cruise ships call occasionally. Freight sailings are frequent for the U.S.A., Canada, Europe, Latin America (except Cuba) and the main Caribbean ports.

Education.—Education is free but estimates of illiteracy are as high as 85 per cent.

Trade.—Value of imports 1984 U.S.$ 474·1 million; exports 1984 U.S.$ 219·4 million.

ATLANTIC OCEAN

CUBA

Port de Paix   Cap Haitien   P. Plata

HAITI
Gonaives / St Marc   Santiago

Jérémie   Port-au-Prince   Santo Domingo   S. Cristóbal

Les Cayes   Jacmel   DOMINICAN REPUBLIC

CARIBBEAN SEA

0   50   100 MILES

Trade with U.K.

	1986	1987
Imports from U.K.	£5,147,000	£5,327,000
Exports to U.K.	899,000	621,000

CAPITAL.—Ψ Port-au-Prince. Population estimated at about 1 million. Other centres are: Ψ Cap Haitien (54,691); Gonaives (36,736); Les Cayes (27,222); Jérémie (25,117); St. Marc (20,504); Jacmel (16,449); Ψ Port de Paix (21,733).

CURRENCY.—Gourde of 100 Centimes.

FLAG.—Horizontal blue over red with national arms on a white square in the centre.

NATIONAL ANTHEM.—La Dessalinienne.

NATIONAL DAY.—January 1.

British Ambassador, (resident at Kingston, Jamaica).

HOLY SEE
(see, VATICAN CITY STATE)

HONDURAS
(Republica de Honduras)

President of the Republic, José Azcona del Hoyo, *assumed office,* 27 Jan. 1986.

CABINET

Interior and Justice, Raúl Elvir Colindres.
Foreign Affairs, Carlos López Contreras.

Defence, Col. Luiz Alonzo Cardona.
Education, Elisa Valle de Martinez.
Finance, Efraín Bú Girón.
Economy, Reginaldo Panting.
Communications, Public Works and Transport, Juan Fernando López.
Health, Dr. Rubén Villeda Bermúdez.
Labour and Social Security, Adalberto Discua.
Natural Resources, Rodrigo Castilla.
Culture and Tourism, Dr. Arturo Rendón Pineda.
Economic Planning, Francisco Figueroa.
Director of National Agrarian Institute, Marlo Espinal Zelaya.
Minister for the Presidency, Celeo Arias Moncada.

HONDURAS EMBASSY IN LONDON
47 Manchester Street, W1M 5PB
[01–486 3380]

Ambassador Extraordinary and Plenipotentiary, His Excellency Sr. Max Velásquez-Diaz (1984).

Honduras, in Central America, lies between lat. 13° and 16° 30′ N. and long. 83° and 89° 41′ W. with a seaboard of about 375 miles on the Caribbean Sea and an outlet, consisting of a small strip of coast 63 miles in length on the Pacific. Its frontiers are contiguous with those of Guatemala, Nicaragua and El Salvador.

The Republic contains a total area of approximately 43,277 sq. miles (112,088 sq. km.) and is very mountainous, being traversed by the Cordilleras, with peaks rising to 1,500 and 2,400 metres above sea level. Most of the soil is poor and acid, except for the coastal plains of the north and some areas of the interior.

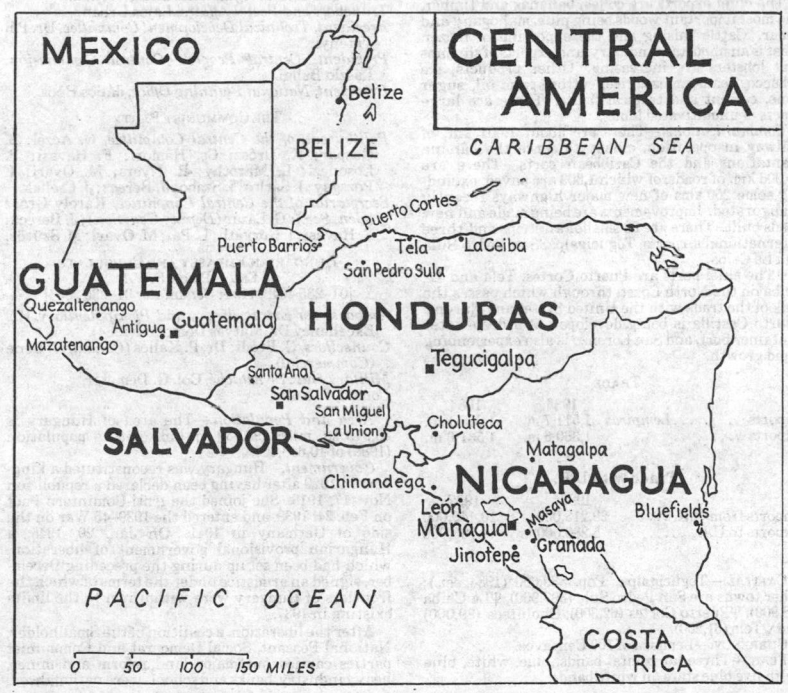

Rainfall is seasonal, May to October being wet and November to April dry. Three-quarters of the territory is covered by pine forests which contribute to much of the country's wealth in natural resources. The population (1985 U.N. estimate) of 4,372,000 is of mixed Spanish and Indian blood. There is a negro (West Indian) element in Northern Honduras who are known as Garifunas.

The language of the country is Spanish, although English is the first language of many in the islands and on the North coast. Primary and secondary education is free, primary education being compulsory, and the Government have launched a campaign to eradicate illiteracy.

Government.—Originally discovered and settled by the Spanish at the beginning of the sixteenth century Honduras formed part of the Spanish American Dominions for nearly three centuries until 1821 when independence was proclaimed. Under military government from 1972–81, the present Liberal government was elected in Nov. 1985 and took office in Jan. 1986.

The Republic is divided into 18 departments, the newest of which, Gracias a Dios, formed in Feb. 1957, is now the home of thousands of Miskito Indian refugees from Nicaragua.

Production.—Agriculture is mainly confined to the large and fertile valleys on the wide Caribbean plain, and the extensive valleys found in the Comayagua and Olancho regions of the interior. Reaching inland from the Caribbean towards the eastern border with Nicaragua a vast tropical forest area called the Mosquitia provides valuable reserves of timber. Lead, zinc and silver are mined on a small scale.

The chief exports are coffee, bananas and timber, the most important woods being pine, mahogany and cedar. Cattle raising and the exporting of frozen meat is an important industry, and exports of shrimps and lobsters are increasing. Other products are tobacco, beans, maize, rice, cotton, palm oil, sugar cane, cement and tropical fruits. There are large tracts of uncultivated land.

Communications.—There are about 1,004 km. of railway in operation, chiefly to serve the banana plantations and the Caribbean ports. There are 15,006 km. of roads, of which 1,809 are paved, excluding some 250 kms of new major highways recently inaugurated. Improvements are being made and new roads built. There are 33 smaller airstrips and three international airports, Tegucigalpa, San Pedro Sula and La Ceiba.

Ψ The chief ports are Puerto Cortes, Tela and La Ceiba on the North Coast, through which passes the bulk of the trade with the United States and Europe. Peurto Castilla is being developed as a deep-water container port, and San Lorenzo is also experiencing rapid growth.

TRADE

	1983	1984
Imports .... *Lempiras*	1,511·7 m.	1,688·1 m.
Exports .... „	1,360·6 m.	1,531·6 m.

Trade with U.K.

	1986	1987
Imports from U.K. ...	£9,213,000	£10,449,000
Exports to U.K.	5,280,000	4,703,000

CAPITAL.—Tegucigalpa. Pop. 539,600 (1984 est.); other towns are San Pedro Sula (397,900), ΨLa Ceiba (68,900), ΨPuerto Cortes (62,300), Choluteca (89,000) and ΨTela (61,200).

CURRENCY.—Lempira of 100 Centavos.

FLAG.—Three horizontal bands, blue, white, blue (with five blue stars on white band).

NATIONAL ANTHEM.—Tu Bandera Es Un Lampo De Cielo (Your flag is a heavenly light).
NATIONAL DAY.—September 15.

BRITISH EMBASSY
Apartado Postal 290, Tegucigalpa.
[Tegucigalpa 32–5480]
Ambassador Extraordinary and Plenipotentiary, His Excellency David Joy, C.B.E. (1987).

HUNGARY
(Magyar Népköztársaság)

President of the Presidential Council of the Republic, Bruno Ferenc Straub, *elected* June 1988.

COUNCIL OF MINISTERS

Prime Minister, Károly Grósz.
Deputy P.M. and Minister for Trade, József Marjai.
Deputy P.M. and Chairman of Planning and Economic Committee, Péter Medgyessy.
Agriculture and Food, Jenö Váncsa.
Construction and Urban Development, Lászlo Somogyi.
Culture and Education, Tibor Czibere.
Defence, Lt.-Gen. Ferenc Kárpáti.
Environment and Water, Dr Lászlo Maróthy.
Finance Miklós Villányi.
Foreign Affairs, Péter Várkonyi.
Industry, Frigyes Berecz.
Interior, István Horváth.
Justice, Kálman Kulcsar.
Social and Health Affairs, Dr. Judit Csehák.
Transport and Postal Affairs, Lajos Urbán.
President, Technical Development Committee, Dr. Pál Tétényi.
President, Central People's Control Commission, Lászlo Ballai.
President, National Planning Office, János Hoos.

THE COMMUNIST PARTY

Politbureau of the Central Committee, G. Aczél; S. Gáspár; K. Grósz; Cs. Hámori; F. Havasi; P. Losonczi; L. Maróthy; R. Nyers; M. Ovári; I. Pozsgay; I. Sárlos; I. Szabó; J. Berecz; J. Csehak.
Secretariat of the Central Committee, Károly Grósz *(Gen. Sec.);* G. Lázár *(Deputy Gen. Sec.);* J. Berecz; F. Havasi; I. Horváth; L. Pál; M. Ovári; M. Szürös.

HUNGARIAN EMBASSY AND CONSULATE
35 Eaton Place, S.W.1.
[01–235 4048, 7191; *Consulate:* 01–235 2664]
Ambassador Extraordinary and Plenipotentiary, His Excellency Dr. Mátyás Domokos (1984).
Counsellors, G. Bródi; Dr. P. Kallós *(Consul);* I. Bene *(Commercial).*
Military and Air Attaché, Col. G. Demeter.
Consul, P. Kallo.

Area and Population.—The area of Hungary is 35,919 sq. miles (93,030 sq. km.) with a population (1985) of 10,658,000.

Government.—Hungary was reconstituted a kingdom in 1920 after having been declared a republic on Nov. 17, 1918. She joined the Anti-Comintern Pact on Feb. 24, 1939, and entered the 1939–45 War on the side of Germany in 1941. On Jan. 20, 1945, a Hungarian provisional government of liberation, which had been set up during the preceding December, signed an armistice under the terms of which the frontiers of Hungary were withdrawn to the limits existing in 1937.

After the liberation, a coalition of the Smallholder, National Peasant, Social Democrat and Communist parties carried out major land reform and mines, heavy industry, banks and schools were nationalised.

By 1949 the Communists had succeeded in gaining a monopoly of power. A campaign was opened to collectivize agriculture and by 1952 practically the entire economy had been "socialized". The Party formulates policy and the function of the Government is mainly executive.

The period from July 1956 to the outbreak of the national revolution on Oct. 23 was marked by growing ferment in intellectual circles and increased discord within the Party. The withdrawal of Soviet troops from the country and free elections were among the demands put forward. Fighting broke out on the night of Oct. 23 between demonstrators, who had been joined by large numbers of factory workers, and the State Security Police (A.V.H.). Soviet forces intervened in strength early the next morning. By Oct. 30 Soviet troops had withdrawn from Budapest and on Nov. 3 an all-party coalition government under Imre Nagy was formed. This government was overthrown and the revolution suppressed as the result of a renewed attack by Soviet forces on Budapest in the early hours of Nov. 4. Simultaneously the formation of a new Hungarian Revolutionary Worker Peasant Government under the leadership of Mr. Kádár was announced.

Economy.—Since 1968 the Hungarian economy has been run according to a system which allows more decentralized decision-making than in some other Eastern European countries, although central control in vital areas such as the allocation of fuels and raw materials has remained. Industrialization has made considerable progress in the last decade and now produces 68 per cent of national income. Industry is mainly based on imported raw materials but Hungary has her own coal (mostly brown), bauxite, considerable deposits of natural gas (some not yet under full exploitation), some iron ore and oil. Output figures in 1985 (1,000 tons), coal, 24,042; bauxite, 2,815; rolled steel 2,860; crude oil, 2,000; cement, 3,678. Natural gas production totalled 7,441 million cubic metres.

Agriculture still occupies an important place in the Hungarian economy. Ten and a half per cent. of the entire land area is owned by State farms and a further 63·8 per cent is within co-operative farms. Production in 1986 was (tons):

Wheat	5,744,000
Rye	169,000
Barley	845,000
Maize	7,024,000
Oats	121,000
Sugar beet	3,764,000

In 1983, national income grew by only 0·5 per cent. Consumption and, particularly, investment continued to be squeezed by the adjustment measures necessitated by Hungary's hard currency debts. Retail prices rose by just under 8 per cent, whilst real incomes stagnated.

Religion and Education.—About two-thirds of the population are Roman Catholics, and the remainder mostly Calvinist. There are five types of schools under the Ministry of Education—kindergartens 3–6, general schools 6–14 (compulsory), vocational schools (15–18), secondary schools (15–18), universities and adult training schools (over 18).

Language and Literature.—Magyar, or Hungarian, is one of the Finno-Ugrian languages. Hungarian literature began to flourish in the second half of the sixteenth century. Among the greatest writers of the nineteenth and twentieth centuries are Mihály Vörösmarty (1800–1855), Sándor Petőfi (1823–1849), János Arany (1817–1882), Imre Madach (1823–1864), Kálmán Mikszáth (1847–1910), Endre Ady (1877–1918), Attila József (1905–1937), Mihály Babits (1883–1941) and Dezső Kosztolányi (1885–1936).

Finance.—The budget estimates for the year 1986 were: Revenue, *Forints* 681,000 million; Expenditure, *Forints* 706,000 million.

TRADE

	1985	
	Non-convertible trade (*roubles*)	Convertible trade U.S.$
Imports	4,620·8 m.	6,734·8 m.
Exports	4,741·7 m.	7,041·5 m.

(1 *rouble* = 26 forints: 1 U.S.$ = 48·05 forints)

Trade with U.K.

	1986	1987
Imports from U.K. ...	£101,557,000	£101,300,000
Exports to U.K.	77,228,000	83,267,000

CAPITAL.—Budapest, on the Danube; population (1985), 2,072,000. Other large towns are: Miskolc (212,000); Debrecen (210,000); Szeged (181,000) and Pecs (175,000).

CURRENCY.—Forint of 100 Fillér.

FLAG.—Red, white, green (horizontally).

NATIONAL ANTHEM.—Isten Aldd Meg A Magyart (God Bless the Hungarians).

NATIONAL DAY.—April 4 (Anniversary of Liberation, 1945).

BRITISH EMBASSY
Harmincad Utca 6, Budapest V
[Budapest 182–888]

Ambassador Extraordinary and Plenipotentiary, His Excellency Leonard Vincent Appleyard, C.M.G. (1986).

Counsellor, P. G. Harborne (*Head of Chancery*).

Defence and Military Attaché, Col. F. N. J. Davies.

Air Attaché, Wg.-Cdr. O. J. A. Knight.

First Secretary and British Council Representative, D. J. Harvey.

Consul, J. W. P. Bradley

ICELAND
(Island)

President, Vigdís Finnbogadóttir, *born* 1930, *elected* June 29, 1980, *re-elected,* July 1984.

CABINET

Prime Minister, Thorsteinn Pálsson (*I.*).
Foreign Affairs, Steingrímur Hermannsson (*Pr.*).
Finance, Jón Baldvin Hannibalsson (*SDP*).
Industry, Fridrik Sóphusson (*I.*).
Fisheries, Halldór Asgrímsson (*Pr.*).
Commerce and Justice, Jón Sigurdsson (*SDP*).
Communications, Matthías A. Mathiesen (*I.*).
Health, Gudmundur Bjarnason (*Pr.*).
Education, Birgir I. Gunnarsson (*I.*).
Agriculture, Jón Helgason (*Pr.*).
Social Affairs, Jóhanna Sigurdardóttir (*SDP*).
(*I.*—Independence Party; *Pr.*—Progressive Party; *SDP*—Social Democrat Party.)

EMBASSY IN LONDON
1 Eaton Terrace, SW1W 8EY
[01–730 5131]

Ambassador Extraordinary and Plenipotentiary, His Excellency Ólafur Egilsson (1986).

Minister Counsellor, T. Karlsson.

Iceland is a large volcanic island in the North Atlantic Ocean, extending from 63° 23′ to 66° 33′ N. lat., and from 13° 22′ to 24° 35′ W. long., with an estimated area of 39,768 sq. miles (103,000 sq. km.). The population was 247,024 on Dec. 1, 1987.

Iceland was uninhabited before the ninth century, when settlers came from Norway. For several

ICELAND

FAEROES

centuries a form of republican government prevailed, with an annual assembly of leading men called the *Althing*, but in 1241 Iceland became subject to Norway, and later to Denmark. During the colonial period, Iceland maintained its cultural integrity but a deterioration in the climate, together with frequent volcanic eruptions and outbreaks of disease led to a serious fall in the standard of living and to a decline in the population to little more than 40,000. In the nineteenth century a struggle for independence began which led first to home rule for Iceland under the Danish Crown (1918), and later to complete independence under a republican form of rule in 1944.

Government.—The parliamentary (*Althing*) elections in April 1987 gave the Independence Party 18 seats, Progressives 13, Social Democratic Party 10, People's Alliance 8, Citizens' Party 7, Women's Alliance 6 and 1 Independent.

Language and Literature.—The ancient Norraena (or Northern tongue) presents close affinities to Anglo-Saxon and as spoken and written in Iceland today differs little from that introduced into the island in the ninth century. There is a rich literature with two distinct periods of development, from the mid-11th to the late 13th century and from the early 19th century to the present.

Production.—Iceland has considerable resources of hydro-electric and geothermal energy. It is estimated that exploited water power (4,000 Gigawatt hours/a) represents only about 9 per cent of that economically exploitable, whereas only 5 per cent of the estimated 80,000 Gigawatt hours/a of available geothermal power has so far been harnessed. Energy-intensive heavy industry includes an aluminium smelter, a nitrogen fertilizer factory, a diatomite plant and a ferro-silicone plant.

The principal exports are frozen fish fillets, salt fish, stock fish, fresh fish on ice, frozen scampi, fishmeal and oil, skins and aluminium; the imports consist of almost all the necessities of life, the chief items being petroleum products, transport equipment, textiles, foodstuffs, animal feeds, timber, and alumina.

At January 1, 1988, the mercantile marine consisted of 639 vessels of under 100 gross tons and 398 ships of 100 gross tons and over; a total of 1,037 vessels (187,829 gross tons), of which 899 (117,452 gross tons) are decked fishing vessels. There are regular shipping services between Reykjavík and Felixstowe, Humber ports and the Continent.

A regular air service is maintained between Glasgow and London and Reykjavík. There are also air services from the island to Scandinavia, U.S.A., Germany, France and Luxembourg.

Road communications are adequate in summer but greatly restricted by snow in winter. Only roads in town centres and key highways are metalled the rest being of gravel, sand and lava dust. The climate and terrain make first-class surfaces for highways out of the question. There are no railways.

FINANCE

	1986	1987
	Krónur (millions)	
Revenue	38,235	48,963
Expenditure	40,111	51,668

TRADE

	1986	1987
	Krónur (millions)	
Exports	44,968	53,053
Imports	45,910	61,237

Trade with U.K.

	1986	1987
Imports from U.K.	£73,640,000	£84,866,000
Exports to U.K.	173,140,000	178,314,000

CAPITAL: ΨReykjavík. Population (Dec. 1, 1987), 93,270.

Other centres in approximate order of importance are ΨAkureyri, Kópavogur, ΨHafnarfjördur, Keflavík, Westmann Islands, Akranes, Isafjördur and ΨSiglufjördur.

CURRENCY.—Icelandic Króna of 100 Aurar.

FLAG.—Blue, with white-bordered red cross.

NATIONAL ANTHEM.—O Gud Vors Lands. (Our Country's God).

NATIONAL DAY.—June 17.

BRITISH EMBASSY
Laufásvegur 49, Reykjavik
[Reykjavik 15883/4]

Ambassador Extraordinary and Plenipotentiary and Consul-General, His Excellency Mark Fenger Chapman, C.V.O. (1986).

First Secretary, Head of Chancery and Consul, S. C. Parris.

Vice Consul and Attaché (Commercial), J. N. L. Burgess.

BRITISH CONSULAR OFFICES

There are Consular Offices at *Reykjavík* and *Akureyri.*

INDONESIA
(Republik Indonesia)

President, General Suharto, *born* June 9, 1921. *Acting President,* March 12, 1967; *confirmed as President,* Mar. 28, 1968, *re-elected for a term of 5 years,* March, 1973, March 1978, March 1983 and March 1988.

Vice-President, Lt.-Gen. Sudharmono, *elected* March 1988.

CABINET

Co-ordinating Ministers, Adm. Sudomo (*Political and Security Affairs*); Dr. Radius Prawiro (*Economy, Finance, Industry and Development Supervision*); Gen. Supardjo Rustam (*Public Welfare*).

Ministers, Gen. Rudini (*Internal Affairs*); Ali Alatas (*Foreign Affairs*); Gen. L. B. Murdani (*Defence and Security*); Lt.-Gen. Ismail Saleh (*Justice*); Mr. Harmoko (*Information*); Dr. J. B. Sumarlin (*Finance*); Dr. Arifin Siregar (*Trade*); Mr. Hartarto (*Industry*); Mr. Wardoyo (*Agriculture*); Air Vice

Marshal Ginandjar Kartasasmita (*Mines and Energy*); Radinal Mochtar (*Public Works*); Maj.-Gen. Azwar Anas (*Communications*); Maj.-Gen. Bustanil Arifin (*Co-operatives*); Cosmas Batubara (*Manpower*); Lt. Gen. Sugiarto (*Transmigration*); Gen. Susilo Sudarman (*Tourism, Posts and Telecommunications*); Prof. Fuad Hassan (*Education and Culture*); Dr. Adhyatma (*Health*); Haji Munawir Sjadzali (*Religious Affairs*); Prof. Haryati Subadio (*Social Affairs*); Hasjrul Harahap (*Forestry*).

Ministers of State, Maj.-Gen. Murdiono (*State Secretary*); Dr. Saleh Afif (*National Development Planning*); Siswono Judo Husodo (*Housing*); Prof. Emil Salim (*Population and Environment*); Sarwono Kusumaatmadja (*Administrative Reform*); Prof. B. J. Habibie (*Research and Technology*); Mrs. A. Sulasikin Murpratomo (*Women's Affairs*); Akbar Tandjung (*Sport and Youth Affairs*).

INDONESIAN EMBASSY
157 Edgware Road, W2 2HR
[01–499 7661]

Ambassador Extraordinary and Plenipotentiary, His Excellency S. Suhartoyo (1986).

Minister, Hidayat Soemo (*Deputy Chief of Mission*).

Situated between latitudes 6° North and 11° South and between longitudes 95° and 141° East, Indonesia comprises the islands of *Java*, *Madura*, and *Sumatra*, the *Riouw-Lingga Archipelago* (which with Karimon, Anambas, Natuna Islands, Tambelan, and part of Sumatra, forms the province of Riau), the islands of *Bangka* and *Billiton*, part of the island of *Borneo* (Kalimantan), *Sulawesi* (*formerly Celebes*) *Island*, the *Molucca Islands* (Ternate, Tidore, Halmahera, Buru, Seram, Banda, Timor-Laut, Larat, Bachiam, Obi, Kei, Aru, Babar, Leti and Wetar), the island of *Bali* and the islands of *Lombok, Sumbawa, Sumba, Flores, Timor* and others comprising the provinces of East and West *Nusa Tenggara* and the western half of the island of New Guinea (*Irian Jaya*), with a total area of 735,358 sq. miles (1,904,569 sq. km.), and a population (1985) of about 165,030,000.

From the early part of the 17th century much of the Indonesian Archipelago was under Netherlands rule. Following the World War 1939–45, during which the Archipelago was occupied by the Japanese, a strong nationalistic movement manifested itself and after sporadic fighting the formal transfer of sovereignty by the Netherlands of all the former Dutch East Indies except W. New Guinea took place on December 27, 1949.

Western New Guinea became part of Indonesia in 1963 under the name West Irian (now Irian Jaya), this interpretation being confirmed in an "Act of Free Choice" in July, 1969, of which the United Nations took note in November 1969. Following a unilateral declaration of independence by the Fretilin, Indonesia took over the former Portuguese colony of East Timor, which in July 1976 was declared the 27th province of Indonesia.

Following a three-week period of unrest and violent student demonstrations the Minister of the Army, General Suharto, took over effective political power in March, 1966.

General Suharto was made Acting President with full powers, on March 11, 1967, and on March 28, 1968, appointed full President for a period of five years.

In the general election of April 1987, Golkar obtained 299 seats, the Moslem United Development Party 61 seats and the Indonesian Democratic Party 40 seats.

Production.—Nearly 70 per cent. of the population of Indonesia is engaged in agriculture and related production. Copra, kapok, nutmeg, pepper and cloves are produced, mainly by smallholders; palm oil, sugar, fibres and cinchona are produced by large estates. Rubber, tea, coffee and tobacco are also produced by both in large quantities. Rice is a traditional staple food for the people of Indonesia and the islands of Java, Sulawesi and Sumatra are important producers. Production has risen rapidly in recent years to 25 million tons and the country is now self sufficient.

Oil and LNG are the most important assets, the export of which in 1985–86 earned about U.S. $11,000 million (about 80 per cent. of Indonesia's exports), but more recent developments have underscored the vulnerability of the economy to depressed international markets and weak oil prices. Timber is the second largest foreign exchange earner after oil.

Indonesia is rich in minerals, particularly tin, of which the country is the world's third biggest producer; petroleum, coal, nickel and bauxite are the other principal products; there are also considerable deposits of gold, silver, manganese phosphates and sulphur. Aid to Indonesia is channelled through the Inter-Governmental Group on Indonesia (IGGI), which has pledged U.S. $2,500,000 for 1986–7.

Indonesia's Fourth Development Programme started in 1984 and its main objectives are the elimination of poverty, agricultural and urban problems, and the continued growth of installed power generation.

Finance.—The drop in oil prices led in March 1983 to the rupiah being devalued by 27 per cent, and a rescheduling of major projects was undertaken. More recently an increase in foreign reserves has meant that several of these projects could be re-instated.

Trade with U.K.

	1986	1987
Direct Imports from U.K.	£196,629,000	£236,027,000
Exports to U.K.	141,242,000	144,819,000

Principal exports to the United Kingdom are rubber, timber, non-ferrous metals, tea, coffee, spices, and crude oil for refinement. Imports from the United Kingdom are mainly of machinery, transport equipment and electrical equipment.

Transport.—In Java a main line connects Jakarta with Surabaya in the East of Java and there are several branches. In Sumatra the important towns of Medan, Padang and Palembang are the centres of short railway systems.

Sea communications in the archipelago are maintained by the State-run shipping companies Djakarta-Lloyd (ocean-going) and Pelni (coastal and inter-island) and other small concerns. Transport by small craft on the rivers of the larger islands plays an important part in trade. Air services in Indonesia are operated by Garuda Indonesian Airways and other local airlines, and Jakarta is served by various international services. There are approximately 50,000 miles of roads.

CAPITAL.—ψ Jakarta (population 6,503,449). Other important centres are: (Java) ψ Surabaya (2,027,913), ψ Semarang (1,026,671), Bandung (1,462,637); (Sumatra) Palembang (787,187), Medan (1,378,955); (Sulawesi), ψ Ujung Pandang (*formerly Makassar*) (709,038); (Kalimantan) Banjarmasin (381,286), ψ Pontianak (304,778), ψ Balikpapan (280,675); (Moluccas) Ambon (208,898); (Bali) Denpasar, Singaraja (for whole island 2,174,105); (Nusa Tenggara) Kupang (329,371); (Irian Jaya) Jayapura (107,164).

CURRENCY.—Rupiah of 100 Sen.

FLAG.—Equal bands of red over white.

NATIONAL ANTHEM.—Indonesia Raya (Great Indonesia).

NATIONAL DAY.—August 17 (Anniversary of Proclamation of Independence).

BRITISH EMBASSY
Jalan M. H. Thamrin 75, Jakarta
[Jakarta 330904]

Ambassador Extraordinary and Plenipotentiary, His Excellency (William) Kelvin (Kennedy) White, C.M.G. (1988).

BRITISH CONSULAR OFFICES

There are British Consular Offices at *Jakarta* and *Medan*.

British Council Representative, Dr. J. C. Blackwell, C.B.E., S Widjojo Centre, Jalan Jendral Sudirman, 71, Jakarta. There are also libraries at *Bandung* and *Medan*.

INDONESIA BRITAIN ASSOCIATION

c/o Mr. R. A. M. Ramsay, Sarinah Building, 13th Floor, J1. M. H. Thamrin 11, Jakarta.

IRAN
(Jomhori-e-Islami-e-Iran)

Leader of the Islamic Revolution, Ayatollah Ruhollah Khomeini, *born* 1902; *assumed power*, Feb., 1979.
President, Hojatoleslam Seyed Ali Khamene'i, *elected* Oct. 2, 1981, *re-elected* Aug. 16, 1985.
Prime Minister, Mir Hossein Moussavi.
Foreign Affairs, Dr. Ali Akbar Velayati.
Education, Seyed Kazem Akrami.
Commerce, Hassan Abedi Jaafari.
Health, Dr. Ali Reza Marandi.
Justice, Dr. Hassan Ebrahim Habibi.
Defence, Col. Mohammad Hussein Jalali.
Oil, Gholamreza Aqazadeh.
Energy, (vacant).
Agriculture, Dr. Abbas Ali Zali.
Economics and Finance, Mohammad Javad Iravani.
Interior, Ali Akbar Mohtashami.
Labour, Abol Hassan Sarhadi-Zadeh.
Housing, Serajeddin Kazeruni.
Mining and Metals, Mohammad Reza Ayatollahi.
Industry, Gholamreza Shafei.
Heavy Industry, Behzad Nabavi.
Islamic Guidance, Seyed Mohammed Khatami.
Culture and Higher Education, Mohammad Farhadi.
Intelligence, Mohammad Mohammadi Reyshahri.
Roads and Transport, Mohammad Saeedi Kia.
Construction Crusade, Bijan Namdar Zanganeh.
Islamic Revolutionary Guard, Mohsen Rafiqdust.

EMBASSY OF THE ISLAMIC REPUBLIC OF IRAN
27 Prince's Gate, SW7 1PX
[01–584 8101–8]

Chargé d'Affaires, Mr. Mohammad Mehdi Akhoond Zadeh Basti.

Area and Population.—Iran has an area of 636,296 sq. miles (1,648,000 sq. km.), with a population (1986 estimate) of 49,765,000. It is mostly an arid tableland, encircled, except in the east, by mountains, the highest in the north rising to 18,934 ft. The central and eastern portion is a vast salt desert.

The Iranians are mostly Shi'ah Moslems but among them are Zoroastrians, Bahais, Sunni Moslems and Armenian and Assyrian Christians. Emigration has much reduced the once substantial Jewish community.

Language and Literature.—Persian, or Farsi, the language of Iran, and of some other areas formerly under Persian rule, is an Indo-European tongue with many Arabic elements added; the alphabet is mainly Arabic, with writing from right to left. Among the great names in Persian literature are those of Abu'l Kásim Mansúr, of Firdausi (A.D. 939–1020), Omar Khayyám, the astronomer-poet (died A.D. 1122), Muslihu'd-Din, known as Sa'di (born A.D. 1184) and Shems-ed-Din Muhammad, or Hafiz (died A.D. 1389).

Government.—Iran was ruled from the end of the 18th century by Shahs of the Qajar Dynasty. A nationalist movement became active in Dec., 1905, and in Aug., 1906, the Shah, Muzaffer-ud-Din, admitting the need for reforms, granted a Constitution. After the war of 1914–18, the subsequent troubles and the signature of the Soviet-Iranian Treaty of 1921, a vigorous Prime Minister, Reza Khan re-established general order. On Oct. 31, 1925, the last representative of the Qajar Dynasty, Sultan Ahmed Shah was deposed in his absence by the National Assembly, which handed over the government to the Prime Minister, Reza Khan, who was elected Shah on Dec. 13, 1925, by the Constituent Assembly, and took the title Reza Shah Pahlavi. On September 16, 1941, Reza Shah abdicated in favour of the Crown Prince, who ascended the throne under the title of Mohammed Reza Shah Pahlavi.

Following widespread and persistent opposition to his regime, the Shah departed from Iran in January, 1979. Ayatollah Khomeini, the main spiritual leader of the Shi'ah Moslems, returned to Iran from exile on February 1. Following a national referendum, Iran was declared an Islamic Republic by Ayatollah Khomeini on April 1, 1979. A new constitution, providing for a President, Prime Minister and Consultative Assembly, and also for overall leadership by Khomeini, was approved by referendum in December 1979. The government's severe measures suppressed violent opposition. In 1982 an Assembly of Experts was constituted to decide the eventual succession to Ayatollah Khomeini and in 1985 it designated Grand Ayatollah Montazeri.

Iran was at war with Iraq following the Iraqi invasion of Iran in Sept. 1980. Both sides carried out attacks on neutral shipping in the Gulf and in 1987 several foreign navies entered the Gulf to escort neutral merchant shipping. International efforts to end the fighting focused on United Nations Security Council Resolution 598 of July 1987, and a ceasefire came into effect on Aug. 20, 1988. A U.N. Observer Peace-Keeping Force was sent to the Gulf to monitor the ceasefire whilst peace talks continued.

Defence.—The Army has a strength of about 150,000 men, in 4 armoured divisions, 4 infantry divisions and one airborne division. The Air Force has a strength of about 35,000, with some 70 combat aircraft. The Navy has a strength of about 20,000 and consists of 3 destroyers, 3 frigates, 4 corvettes, 5 minesweepers, and patrol boats, support ships, landing craft and hovercraft. The Islamic Revolutionary Guards Corps numbers about 500,000 men. Total armed forces personnel including paramilitary forces number over one million.

Education.—Since 1943 primary education has been compulsory and free, but there is large scale absenteeism, particularly outside the towns. There are in Iran 22 universities (8 in Tehran, 14 in the provinces). The educational system has been reformed following the revolution.

Finance.—The budget for the Iranian year beginning March 21, 1988, was revenue *Rials.* 9,800,290 million; expenditure *Rials.* 9,800,290 million.

Agriculture.—While petroleum is the principal product and by far the greatest export, Iran is otherwise largely an agricultural and pastoral country. After the 1979 revolution the Government announced its intention of giving greater emphasis to the development of agriculture with a view to reducing Iran's dependence on food imports, but it has so far had only limited success. Some redistribution of land has taken place, but agreement has not been reached on basic land reform.

Wheat is the principal crop; other important crops are barley, rice, cotton, sugar beet, fruit, nuts and vegetables. Wool is also a major product. There are extensive forests in the north and west, the conservation of which is a continuing problem.

Industry.—Under the Shah, great emphasis was given to the development of industry. Apart from oil, the principal industrial products are carpets, textiles, sugar, cement and other construction materials, ginned cotton, vegetable oil and other food products, leather and shoes, metal manufactures, pharmaceuticals, motor vehicles, fertilizers and plastics. Industrial output was severely curtailed by the 1979 revolution, as a result of which many industrialists left the country. In July 1979 the Government nationalized a wide range of major industrial concerns, having nationalized the banks and the insurance companies the previous month. Foreign trade is controlled by the State, although formal legislation to this effect has yet to be passed and the private sector plays an increasingly important role.

Energy.—The oilfields, which lie in South Western Iran, were nationalized in 1951. From 1957 until the 1979 revolution a consortium of eight oil companies (one British, one French, one Dutch, and five U.S.) was responsible for the production, refining and sale of oil. In July 1979 the National Iranian Oil Company assumed full control of the oil industry. In addition to that extracted from the onshore wells, oil is also produced from a number of off-shore oilfields. Oil production by June 1979 had reached an average of 3·5 million b.p.d., but is now approximately 2·2 million b.p.d., of which some 1·5 million b.p.d. is exported. Iran is a member of O.P.E.C.

Communications.—Tehran is at the centre of a network of highways linking the capital with other major towns, the ports and the frontiers with Turkey, U.S.S.R., Afghanistan and Pakistan, and with the Caspian Sea. The Trans-Iranian Railway runs from Bandar Turcoman, on the Caspian Sea, via Tehran to Bandar Khomeini, on the Persian Gulf. Other lines link Tehran with Tabriz and with Mashad. There are also railways from Tabriz to Julfa and from

Zahedan to Quetta, and a branch line from Ahwaz to Khorramshahr. An extension from Qom to Yazd via Kashan is now in operation, as is one from Bandar Turcoman to Gorgan. An extension from Yazd to Kerman is partially complete. The Iranian rail system is linked to the Turkish system via Van. There is an international airport at Tehran (Mehrabad), and airports at all the major provincial centres. The national airline, Iranair, is government-owned and operates international and domestic routes.

TRADE

Imports to Iran declined dramatically at the beginning of 1979 as a result of the economic disruption caused by the revolution. Iran's aggressive oil sales policy during 1982 enabled foreign exchange reserves to recover from the 1981 low level and made possible increased imports. However, the drop in world oil prices in 1986 again affected Iran's foreign exchange earnings, and her level of imports declined.

Imports into Iran consist mainly of industrial and agricultural machinery, motor vehicles and motor vehicle components for assembly, iron and steel (including manufactures), electrical machinery and goods, meat, various other foods, and certain textile fabrics and yarns. The principal exports, apart from oil, are cotton, carpets, dried fruit, nuts, hides and skins, mineral ores, wool, gums, caviare, cumin seed and spices. Federal Republic of Germany, Japan and the U.K. are Iran's leading suppliers.

	1984	1985
Imports	US$15,343 m.	US$11,145 m.
Exports	15,136 m.	13,952 m.

Trade with U.K.

	1986	1987
Imports from U.K. ...	£399,373,000	£307,853,000
Exports to U.K.	100,303,000	187,572,000

CAPITAL: Tehran, population (1986 estimate) over 6 million. Other large towns are Tabriz (853,296), Isfahan (1,000,000) Meshed (500,000), Shiraz (300,000), Resht (150,000), Kerman (100,000), Hamadan (130,000), Yazd (70,000), Kermanshah (152,000), Ahwaz (175,000).

CURRENCY.—Iranian Rial of 100 Dinars.

FLAG.—Equal horizontal bands of green, white and red; with an emblem of the Islamic Republic.

NATIONAL ANTHEM.—Sorood-e Jomhoori-e Eslami.

NATIONAL DAY.—February 11.

BRITISH DIPLOMATIC REPRESENTATION

(The Embassy was closed on September 9, 1980, and British interests are handled by the Swedish Embassy.)

IRAQ
(Al-Jumhouriya al-'Iraqia)

REVOLUTIONARY COMMAND COUNCIL

Chairman, President of the Republic, and *Supreme Commander of the Armed Forces,* Saddam Hussain, *assumed office* July 16, 1979.

Members, Izzat Ibrahim (*RCC Vice-Chairman*); Taha Muhiddin Ma'aruf (*Vice-President of the Republic*); Taha Yasin Ramadhan (*First Deputy Prime Minister*); Dr. Sa'doun Hammadi (*Speaker of National Assembly*); Tariq 'Aziz (*Deputy Prime Minister and Foreign Minister*); General Adnan Khairallah (*Deputy Prime Minister and Minister of Defence*); Sa'doun Shakir; Hassan Ali; Khalid Abdul Mun'im Rasheed (*acting Secretary-General*).

In addition to those members of the R.C.C. holding departmental portfolios listed above, there are 17 other Ministers and 4 Ministers of State.

EMBASSY OF THE REPUBLIC OF IRAQ
21 Queen's Gate, SW7 5JG
[01-584 7141/6]

Ambassador Extraordinary and Plenipotentiary, His Excellency Dr. Mohammed Sadiq Al-Mashat (1987).

Area, etc.—Traversed by the Rivers Euphrates and Tigris, Iraq extends from Turkey on N. and N.E. to the Gulf on the S. and S.E. and from Iran on E. to Syria and Arabian Desert on W., the approximate position being between 37¼° to 48¼° E. long., and from 37¼° to 30° N. lat. (*see* MAP, p. 781). The area of Iraq is 167,925 sq. miles (434,924 sq. km.), of which 37 per cent. is desert land. About 35 to 40 per cent. of the remainder is potentially cultivable either by rainfall or by irrigation.

The *Euphrates* (which has a total length of 1,700 miles from its source to its outflow in the Persian Gulf) is formed by two arms, of which the Murad Su (415 miles) rises in eastern Erzurum, and flows westwards to a junction with the Kara Su, or Frat Su (275 miles); the other arm rises in the north-west of Erzurum in the Dumlu Dagh. The *Tigris* has a total length of 1,150 miles from its source to its junction with the Euphrates at Qurna, 70 miles from the Gulf, and rises in two arms south of the Taurus mountains, in Kurdistan, uniting at Til, where the boundaries of the districts of Diarbekir, Van and Bitlis conjoin.

Population.—At the Census of October 1987 Iraq had a total population of 16,278,316.

Language.—The language is mainly Arabic and English is widely used in commerce, science and the arts.

Antiquities.—In 1944 excavations at Tell Hassuna, near Shura (on the Tigris in North Iraq) unearthed abundant traces of culture dating back to 5000 B.C. Excavations in 1948 at Tel Abu Shahrain, south of "Ur of the Chaldees," confirm Eridu's claim to be the most ancient city of the Sumerian world. Hillah, the ancient city on the left bank of the Shatt el Hillah, a branch of the Euphrates, about 70 miles south of Baghdad, is near the site of Babylon and of the "house of the lofty-head" or "gate of the god" (Tower of Babel). Mosul Governorate covers a great part of the ancient kingdom of *Assyria,* the ruins of Nineveh, the Assyrian capital, being visible on the banks of the Tigris, opposite Mosul. Qurna, at the junction of the Tigris and Euphrates, is traditionally supposed to be the site of the *Garden of Eden.*

Government.—Under the Treaty of Lausanne (1923), Turkey renounced sovereignty over Mesopotamia. A provisional Arab Government was set up in Nov., 1920, and in Aug., 1921, the Emir Faisal was elected King of Iraq. The country was a monarchy until July, 1958, when King Faisal II was assassinated. From 1958 Iraq has been under Presidential rule. The ruling Party is the Arab Ba'ath Socialist Party, which came to power on July 17, 1968.

Iraq has been engaged in hostilities with Iran since September 1980, originally over control of the Shatt-al-Arab waterway. In July 1982 Iranian forces moved across the border into Iraq, and since that time a series of inconclusive battles have been fought along the borders. Both sides carried out attacks on neutral shipping and in the summer of 1987 foreign navies entered the Gulf to escort neutral merchant shipping.

International efforts to end the fighting focused on United Nations Security Council Resolution 598 of July 1987, and a ceasefire came into effect on Aug. 20, 1988. A U.N. Observer Peace-Keeping Force was sent to the Gulf to monitor the ceasefire whilst peace talks continued.

Communications and Trade.—New roads are being rapidly built, and communications between Baghdad and the provincial capitals are being improved and secured. Facilities at the port of Basra have been improved but the port has not been used since the outbreak of hostilities with Iran in Sept. 1980. Continuous dredging of the Shatt-al-Arab has also been suspended by hostilities and the channel has seriously silted. The port of Um Qasr near the Kuwaiti border has been developed for freight and sulphur handling and a container terminal is ready for operation but not in use due to the port's proximity to the war zone. Road routes from Turkey and the Mediterranean are well used, and carry through traffic to Kuwait and the south. The border between Syria and Iraq was closed in late 1977, reopened in November, 1978 and closed again in April 1982.

There is an international airport at Baghdad. Iraqi Airways provide flights between Baghdad and London, and other international airlines operate to Europe. Iraqi Republican Railways provide regular passenger and goods services between Basra, Baghdad and Mosul, and links up through Syria and Turkey with the Mediterranean and the Bosphorus, though no through traffic has used the line since the Syrian government cut the rail link in April 1982. There is also a metre gauge line connecting Baghdad with Khanaqin, Kirkuk and Arbil.

Agriculture and Industry.—Apart from the valuable revenues to be derived from oil, agricultural development makes a valuable contribution to the wealth of the country and two harvests can usually be gathered in the year. Production fluctuates from year to year according to rainfall. The Government's concern with agricultural development is shown in the large financial allocations made to the sector. Salinity and soil erosion, caused by a high water table, inadequate irrigation and drainage and traditional farming methods, are the major problems now being addressed by development planners.

Increasing industrialization is taking place. Since 1987 the Government has been encouraging increased private and mixed sector involvement in the economy. Priority is being given to petro-chemicals, food industries, construction industries and engineering. Existing industries include cement, building materials, steel fabrications, food processing and the manufacture of consumer goods, as well as the development of mineral resources.

Iraq's major industry is oil production. It was nationalized on June 1, 1972 and accounts for approximately 98 per cent. of the total government revenue and 45 per cent. of the Gross National Product. Production was some 3·5 million barrels per day in 1979 but the effects of war damage on the Basra terminals and the closure of the trans-Syria pipeline reduced production until new pipelines were built via Turkey and Saudi Arabia. Total revenues from oil are estimated at $11,000–14,000 million in 1988, although they are difficult to calculate due to fluctuations in price.

FINANCE

	1981*
Total revenue	*ID*19,434,856,809
Total expenditure	19,250,261,450

* Estimates.

TRADE

	1984
Total Imports	$11,260,000
Total Exports	11,720,000

Trade with U.K.

	1986	1987
Imports from U.K.	£443,890,000	£271,655,000
Exports to U.K.	66,129,000	33,871,000

The principal imports are iron and steel, cement and other building materials, mechanical and electrical machinery, motor vehicles, textiles and clothing, essential foodstuffs, grain, tinned foods and raw industrial materials. The chief exports are crude petroleum, dates, raw wool, raw hides and skins and raw cotton.

CAPITAL.—Baghdad. Population of the governorate (Census 1977) 3,205,645. Other towns of importance are Ψ Basra, Mosul and Kirkuk.

CURRENCY.—Iraqi Dinar of 1,000 Fils.

FLAG.—Horizontal stripes of red, white and black, with three green stars on the white stripe.

NATIONAL DAY.—July 17 (Revolution Day).

BRITISH EMBASSY
Zukaq 12, Mahala 218,
Hai Al Khelood, Baghdad
[Baghdad 5372121/5]

Ambassador Extraordinary and Plenipotentiary, His Excellency Terence Joseph Clark, C.M.G., C.V.O. (1985).

Counsellor, R. A. Kealy (*Head of Chancery and Consul General*).

First Secretary, A. R. Brown, C.V.O. (*Commercial*).

Defence Attaché, Col. B. Aldridge, O.B.E.

British Council Representative, P. Elborn, Waziriya, 301, Street 3, (P.O. Box 298), Baghdad.

IRELAND

Position and Extent.—Ireland lies in the Atlantic Ocean, to the W. of Great Britain, and is separated from Scotland by the North Channel and from Wales by the Irish Sea and St. George's Channel. The area of the island is 32,588 sq. miles (84,402 sq. km.), and its geographical position between 51° 26′ and 55° 21′ N. latitude and from 5° 25′ to 10° 30′ W. longitude. The greatest length of the island, from N.E. to S.W. (Torr Head to Mizen Head), is 302 miles, and the greatest breadth, from E. to W. (Dundrum Bay to Annagh Head), is 174 miles. On the N. Coast of *Achill Island* (Co. Mayo) are the highest cliffs in the British Isles, 2,000 feet sheer above the sea. Ireland is occupied for the greater part of its area by the *Central Plain*, with an elevation 50 to 350 ft. above mean sea level, with isolated mountain ranges near the coastline. The principal mountains, with their highest points, are the *Sperrin Mountains* (Sawel 2,240 ft.) of County Tyrone; the *Mountains of Mourne* (Slieve Donard 2,796 ft.) of County Down, and the *Wicklow Mountains* (Lugnaquilla 3,039 ft.); the *Derryveagh Mountains* (Errigal, 2,466 ft.) of County Donegal; the *Connemara Mountains* (Twelve Pins 2,695 ft.) of County Galway; *Macgillicuddy's Reeks* (Carrantuohill 3,414 ft., the highest point in Ireland); and the *Galtee Mountains* (3,018 ft.) of County Tipperary, and the *Knockmealdown* (2,609 ft.) and *Comeragh Mountains* (2,470 ft.) of County Waterford. The principal river of Ireland (and the longest in the British Isles) is the *Shannon* (240 miles), rising in County Cavan and draining the central plain; the Shannon flows through a chain of loughs to the city of Limerick, and thence to an estuary on the western Atlantic seaboard. The *Slaney* flows into Wexford Harbour, the *Liffey* to Dublin Bay, the *Boyne* to Drogheda, the *Lee* to Cork Harbour, the *Blackwater* to Youghal Harbour, and the *Suir, Barrow* and *Nore,* to Waterford Harbour. As in Scotland, the principal hydrographic feature is the *Loughs,* of which Lough *Neagh* (150 sq. miles) in the north-east is the largest in Ireland and the British Isles, others being the Shannon Chain of *Allen, Boderg, Forbes, Ree* and *Derg,* and the Erne Chain of *Gowna, Oughter, Lower Erne,* and *Erne; Melvin, Gill, Gara* and *Conn* in the north-west; and *Corrib* and *Mask* (joined by a hidden channel) in the west. In County Kerry, to the east of

Macgillicuddy's Reeks, are the famous *lakes of Killarney*.

Primitive Man.—Although little is known concerning the earliest inhabitants of Ireland, there are many traces of neolithic man throughout the island; a grave containing a polished stone axehead assigned to 2,500 B.C. was found at Linkardstown, Co. Carlow, in 1944, and the use of bronze implements appears to have become known about the middle of the 17th century B.C. In the later Bronze Age a Celtic race of *Goidels* appears to have invaded the island, and in the early Iron Age *Brythons* from South Britain are believed to have effected settlements in the south-east, while *Picts* from North Britain established similar settlements in the north. Towards the close of the Roman occupation of Britain, the dominant tribe in the island was that of the *Scoti*, who afterwards established themselves in Scotland.

History.—According to Irish legends, the island of Ierne was settled by a Milesian race, who came from Scythia by way of Spain, and established the *Kingdom of Tara*, about 500 B.C. The supremacy of the *Ardri* (high king) of Tara was acknowledged by eight lesser kingdoms (Munster, Connaught, Ailech, Oriel, Ulidia, Meath, Leinster and Ossory) ruled by descendants of the eight sons of Miled. The basalt columns on the coast of Antrim, eight miles from Portrush, known as the *Giant's Causeway*, are connected with the legendary history of Ireland as the remnants of a bridge built in the time of Finn M'Coul (Fingal) to connect Antrim with Scotland (Staffa).

Hibernia was visited by Roman merchants but never by Roman legions, and little is known of the history of the country until the invasions of *Northmen* (Norwegians and Danes) towards the close of the 8th century A.D. The Norwegians were distinguished as Findgaill (White Strangers) and the Danes as Dubgaill (Black Strangers), names which survive in "Fingall," "MacDougall" and "MacDowell," while the name of the island itself is held to be derived from the Scandinavian *Ira-land* (land of the Irish), the names of the Provinces being survivals of Norse dialect forms (Ulaids-tir, Laiginstir, Mumans-tir and Kunnak-tir). The outstanding events in the encounters with the Northmen are the *Battle of Tara* (980), at which the Hy Neill king Maelsechlainn II defeated the Scandinavians of Dublin and the Hebrides under the king Amlaib Cuarán; and the *Battle of Clontarf* (1014) by which the Scandinavian power was completely broken. After Clontarf the supreme power was disputed by the O'Briens of Munster, the O'Neills of Ulster, and the O'Connors of Connaught, with varying fortunes. In 1152 Dermod MacMurrough (Diarmit MacMurchada), the deposed king of Leinster, sought assistance in his struggle with Rauidhri O'Connor (the high king of Ireland), and visited Henry II, the Norman king of England. Henry authorized him to obtain armed support in England for the recovery of his kingdom, and Dermod enlisted the services of Richard de Clare, the Norman Earl of Pembroke, afterwards known as *Strongbow*, who landed at Waterford (Aug. 23, 1170) with 200 knights and 1,000 other troops for the reconquest of Leinster, where he eventually settled, after marriage with Dermod's daughter. In 1172 (Oct. 18) Henry II himself landed in Ireland. He received homage from the Irish kings and established his capital at Dublin. The invaders subsequently conquered most of the island and a feudal government was created. In the 14th and 15th centuries, the Irish recovered most of their lands, while many Anglo-Irish lords became virtually independent, royal authority being confined to the "Pale," a small district round Dublin. Though, under Henry VII, Sir Edward Poynings, as Lord Deputy, had passed at the *Parliament of Drogheda* (1494) the act later known as *Poynings' Law*, subordinating the Irish Legislature to the Crown, the Earls of Kildare

retained effective power until, in 1534, Henry VIII began the reconquest of Ireland. Parliament in 1541 recognized him as King of Ireland and by 1603 English authority was supreme.

Christianity.—Christianity did not become general until the advent of St. Patrick. *St. Patrick* was born in Britain about 389, and was taken to Ireland as a slave about sixteen years later escaping to Gaul at the age of 22. In 432 he was consecrated Bishop of Auxerre and landed in Wicklow to establish and organize the Christian religion throughout the island.

REPUBLIC OF IRELAND
(Poblacht Na L'Eireann)

Uachtarán-na-hÉireann (President), Patrick J. Hillery, *born* 1923, *assumed office*, Dec. 3, 1976, *sworn in for 2nd term*, Dec. 3, 1983.

MEMBERS OF THE GOVERNMENT

Taoiseach and Minister for the Gaeltacht, Charles J. Haughey.

Tánaiste and Minister for Foreign Affairs, Brian Lenihan.

Finance, Ray MacSharry.

Justice, Gerard Collins.

Tourism and Transport, John P. Wilson.

Agriculture and Food, Michael O'Kennedy.

Social Welfare, Michael Woods.

Industry and Commerce, Albert Reynolds.

Energy and Communications, Ray Burke.

Marine, Brendan Daly.

Environment, Pádraig Flynn.

Labour, Bertie Ahern.

Health, Rory O'Hanlon.

Defence, Michael J. Noonan.

Education, Mary O'Rourke.

The present Government was formed by the Fianna Fail Party following a general election on Feb. 17, 1987.

EMBASSY IN LONDON
17 Grosvenor Place, SW1X 7HR
[01-235 2171]

Ambassador Extraordinary and Plenipotentiary, His Excellency Andrew O'Rourke (1987).

Area and Population.—The Republic has a land area of 27,136 sq. miles (70,283 sq. km.), divided into the four Provinces of *Leinster* (Carlow, Dublin, Kildare, Kilkenny, Laoighis, Longford, Louth, Meath, Offaly, Westmeath, Wexford and Wicklow); *Munster* (Clare, Cork, Kerry, Limerick, Tipperary and Waterford); *Connacht* (Galway, Leitrim, Mayo, Roscommon and Sligo); and part of *Ulster* (Cavan, Donegal and Monaghan).

Total population of the Republic at the Census held on April 13, 1986, was 3,540,643. Figures also showed 62,388 births, 18,791 marriages and 33,213 deaths in the year 1986.

GOVERNMENT

The Constitution.—The constitution, approved by a plebiscite on July 1, 1937, came into operation on December 29, 1937. The Constitution declares the national territory to be the whole island of Ireland, its islands and the territorial seas. Pending the reintegration of the national territory, and without prejudice to the right of the Parliament and the Government established by the Constitution to exercise jurisdiction over the whole of the national territory, the laws enacted by that Parliament shall have the like area and extent of application as those of the Irish Free State, which did not include the six counties of Northern Ireland.

The Irish language, being the national language, is the first official language. The English language is recognized as a second official language.

The President (*Uachtarán na hEireann*) is elected by direct vote of the people for a period of seven years. A former or retiring President is eligible for a second term. The President summons and dissolves Dáil Éireann on the advice of the *Taoiseach* (Head of the Government). He signs and promulgates laws. The supreme command of the Defence forces is vested in him, its exercise being regulated by law. He has the power of pardon. The President, in the exercise and performance of certain of his constitutional powers and functions, is aided and advised by a Council of State.

The National Parliament (*Oireachtas*) consists of the President and two Houses: a House of Representatives (*Dáil Éireann*) and a Senate (*Seanad Éireann*).

Dáil Éireann is composed of 166 members elected by adult suffrage on a basis of proportional representation by means of the single transferable vote. All citizens, and such other persons in the state as may be determined by law, who have reached the age of 18 years and are not disqualified by law have the right to vote. Each Dáil may continue for a period not exceeding five years from the date of election.

Seanad Éireann is composed of 60 members, of whom 11 are nominated by the Taoiseach and 49 are elected; six by institutions of higher education, and 43 from panels of candidates, established on a vocational basis.

Members of Dáil Éireann are paid an allowance of IR£19,713 per annum (and members of Seanad Éireann IR£10,991). They are allowed travelling facilities between Dublin and their constituencies and are, subject to certain restrictions, granted free telephone and postal facilities from Leinster House and allowances for overnight stays in Dublin.

The executive authority is exercised by the Government subject to the Constitution. The Government is responsible to Dáil Éireann, meets and acts as a collective authority, and is collectively responsible for the Departments of State administered by the Ministers.

The Taoiseach is appointed by the President on the nomination of Dáil Éireann. The other members of the government are appointed by the President on the nomination of the Taoiseach with the previous approval of Dáil Éireann. The Taoiseach appoints a member of the Government to be the *Tánaiste* who acts for all purposes in the place of the Taoiseach in the event of the death, permanent incapacitation, or temporary absence of the Taoiseach. The Taoiseach, the Tánaiste and the Minister for Finance must be members of Dáil Éireann. The other members of the Goverment must be members of Dáil Éireann or Seanad Éireann, but not more than two may be members of Seanad Éireann.

The result of the general election on Feb. 17, 1987 was as follows: *Fianna Fáil*, 81; *Fine Gael*, 51; *Progressive Democrats*, 14; *Labour*, 12; *Workers' Party*, 4; *Independent*, 4. Total membership including the *Ceann Comhairle* (Chairman), 166.

JUDICIAL SYSTEM

The Judicial system comprises Courts of First Instance and a Court of Final Appeal called the Supreme Court (*Cúirt Uachtarach*). The Courts of First Instance include a High Court (*Ard-Chúirt*) and Courts of local and limited jurisdiction, with a right of appeal as determined by law. The High Court alone has original jurisdiction to consider the question of the validity of any law having regard to the provisions of the Constitution. The Supreme Court has appellate jurisdiction from all decisions of the High Court, with such exceptions and subject to such regulations as may be prescribed by law.

Chief Justice, Hon. Thomas A. Finlay	IR£53,171
President of the High Court, Hon. Liam Hamilton	IR£46,130
Judges, Supreme Court, Hon. Brian Walsh; Hon. Seamus Henchy; Hon. Francis Griffin; Hon. Anthony Hederman; Hon. Niall J. McCarthy	IR£43,490
Judges, High Court, Hon. Donal Barrington; Hon. John M. Gannon; Hon. Rory O'Hanlon; Hon. Declan Costello; Hon. Ronan Keane; Hon. Ms. Mella Carroll; Hon. Henry D. Barron; Hon. Francis D. Murphy; Hon. Kevin Lynch; Hon. Seamus Egan; Hon. Robert Barr; Hon. Gerard Lardner; Hon. John J. Blayney; Hon. John P. McKenzie; Hon. Richard Johnson; Hon. Thomas F. Roe (*ex officio*)	IR£39,089

Attorney-General, John Murray.

RELIGION
(Census of 1981)

Catholic	3,204,476
Church of Ireland	95,366
Presbyterians	14,255
Methodists	5,790
Others	123,518
Total	3,443,405

DEFENCE

Establishments provide at present for a Permanent Defence Force of approximately 17,980 all ranks, including the Air Corps and the Naval Service. Recruitment is on a voluntary basis. Minimum term of enlistment is three years in the Permanent Defence Force followed by six years in the Reserve Defence Force. Establishments also provide for a Reserve Defence Force of 22,214 all ranks. Recruitment is also on a voluntary basis; minimum term of enlistment is three years. The Defence Estimate for the year ending Dec. 31, 1988 provides for an expenditure of IR£252,144,000.

FINANCE

	1987 (*Provisional Out-Turn*)	1988 (*Post-Budget Estimate*)
	IR£m.	IR£m.
Total Current Revenue	7,151	7,035
Total Current Expenditure	8,326	8,183
Current Revenue		
Customs	88	95
Excise Duties	1,391	1,412
Capital Taxes	40	40
Stamp Duties	169	186
Income Tax	2,713	2,706
Income Levy	3	—
Corporation Tax	257	280
Value-Added Tax	1,585	1,666
Agricultural Levies (E.E.C.)	11	13
Motor Vehicle Duties	139	140
Employment and Training Levy*	97	97
Total Tax Revenue	6,493	6,635
Non-Tax Revenue	658	400
Total Current Revenue	7,151	7,035

*Formerly Youth Employment Levy.

	1987 (Provisional Out-turn) IR£m.	1988 (Post-Budget Estimate) IR£m.
Current Expenditure		
Debt Service	2,118	2,173
Industry and Labour	217	215
Agriculture	288	240
Fisheries	14	13
Forestry	11	10
Tourism	25	23
Roads	31	30
Sanitary Services	3	2
Transport	1	1
Health	1,043	1,020
Education	1,064	1,072
Social Welfare	1,667	1,698
Housing	36	38
Subsidies	174	174
Defence	287	292
Garda	267	275
Prisons	51	52
Legal, etc.	43	43
Other	684	812
Total (excluding Local Loans Fund Subsidies)*	8,024	8,183
Add back:		
Local Loans Fund Subsidies	302	—
Total (including Local Loans Fund Subsidies)	8,326	8,183

Note: The figures do not take account of Departmental balances.

*The 1988 Estimate takes account of changes in the Local Loans Fund Subsidy arrangements which had the effect of reducing expenditure by £317 million below the abridged Estimates Volume allocations. For comparability purposes, the 1987 figures have seen similarly adjusted and the adjustment is shown separately.

The Gross Debt at end 1986 was IR£24,416,485,279 and capital assets were IR£5,936,113,768.

EDUCATION

Primary education is directed by the State, with the exception of 63 private primary schools with an enrolment of 8,734 in 1986–87.

There were 3,385 State-aided primary schools with an enrolment of 567,272.

In 1986-87 there were 503 recognized secondary schools with 215,618 pupils under private management (mainly religious orders), and 252 vocational schools with 83,182 pupils. Vocational schools are controlled by 38 statutory local Vocational Education Committees. There were 15 State comprehensive schools in 1986–87 with a total enrolment of 8,941 students, and 44 community schools with an enrolment of 30,455 students. There were also other miscellaneous second-level schools and the total full-time enrolment at second-level for 1986–87 was 341,681.

Third-level education is catered for by five University Colleges, two National Institutes for Higher Education, and also by third-level courses offered by the Technical Colleges and Regional Technical Colleges and other miscellaneous third-level institutions. There were 56,504 full-time third-level students in 1986–87, of whom 26,822 were attending university courses.

The estimated State expenditure on education in 1988, excluding administration and inspection, is first-level education IR£405,524,000; second-level education IR£422,862,000. The vote for third-level education amounted to IR£214,440,000.

MINERALS AND FISHERIES

Minerals.—264 persons were employed in the coal mines in 1987 and 45,200 tons of coal were produced.

Sea Fisheries.—An estimated 7,750 persons were employed in the fisheries in 1986. Total value of all fish landed in 1986 was IR£64,400,000.

COMMUNICATIONS

Railways.—In the year ended Dec. 31, 1986, there were 1,944 kms of railway; 21,735,000 passengers and 3,126,000 tonnes of merchandise were conveyed; the receipts were IR£135,936,000 and expenditure IR£133,011,000. These figures are in respect of railway working by *Coras Iompair Eireann*.

Road Motor Services.—In 1986 road motor vehicles carried 231,903,404 passengers, the gross receipts being IR£128,245,949.

Shipping.—In 1986 the number of ships with cargo which arrived at Irish ports was 11,344 (20,915,000 net registered tons); of these 2,378 (5,489,000 net registered tons) were of Irish nationality.

CIVIL AVIATION

Shannon Airport, 15 miles W. of Limerick, is on the main transatlantic air route. In 1987 the airport handled 1,246,206 passengers.

Dublin Airport, 6 miles N. of Dublin, serves the cross-channel and European services operated by the Irish national airline *Aer Lingus* and other airlines. In 1987 the airport handled 3,551,032 passengers.

Cork Airport, 5 miles S. of Cork serves the cross Channel and European services operated by *Aer Lingus* and other airlines. In 1987 the airport handled 441,336 passengers.

Trade with U.K.

	1986 IR£	1987 IR£
Imports from U.K.	3,587,779,363	3,815,916,879
Exports to U.K.	3,201,368,304	3,662,629,824

OVERSEAS TRADE

	1986 IR£	1987 IR£
Imports	8,621,291,016	9,155,206,863
Exports	9,374,310,355	10,723,497,879
Trade balance	753,019,339	1,568,291,016

PRINCIPAL ARTICLES

Principal imports in 1987 were:

	IR£
Live animals	64,523,518
Food, drink and tobacco	1,025,331,161
Petrol and petroleum products	551,739,352
Chemicals	1,126,241,468
Machinery	2,555,585,415
Transport equipment	509,749,884
Metal and manufactures	543,696,256
Textiles and clothing	782,327,078
Paper, paperboard and manufactures	298,763,424
Professional, scientific etc. goods	199,116,545

Principal exports in 1987 were:

	IR£
Live animals	173,893,047
Meat and meat preparations	763,031,172
Other food, drink and tobacco	1,976,023,709
Machinery and transport equipment	3,364,527,973
Clothing, headgear and footwear	223,230,050
Textiles	379,823,145

Metal ores and scrap	152,232,485
Metal and manufactures	290,996,448
Non-metallic mineral manufactures .	138,196,167
Chemicals	1,307,169,062
Professional, scientific etc., goods ...	421,952,722

CAPITAL.—ΨDublin (*Baile Atha Cliath*) is a City and County Borough on the River Liffey at the head of Dublin Bay. In April 1986 the population was (1986 Census) was 502,749.

Other cities and towns with their populations at the Census of 1986 are ΨCork (133,271); ΨLimerick (56,279); ΨDun Laoghaire (54,715); ΨWaterford (39,529); Ψ Galway (47,104); and ΨDundalk (26,669).

CURRENCY.—Irish Pound (Punt) (IR£) of 100 Pence.

FLAG.—Equal vertical stripes of green, white and orange.

NATIONAL ANTHEM.—Amhrán na BhFiann (The Soldier's Song).

NATIONAL DAY.—March 17 (St. Patrick's Day).

BRITISH EMBASSY
31 Merrion Road, Dublin 4
[Dublin 695211]

Ambassador Extraordinary and Plenipotentiary, His Excellency Nicholas Maxted Fenn, C.M.G. (1986).
Counsellor and Head of Chancery, J. Thorpe.
First Secretaries, D. L. S. Coombe (*Commercial*); W. M. L. Dickinson; J. C. Radcliffe, M.V.O.; G. Ferguson; Miss B. M. Pugh; P. M. Innes.

ISRAEL
(Medinat Israel)

President of Israel, Chaim Herzog, *born* 1918, *elected* 1983, *re-elected* Feb. 20, 1988, *inaugurated*, May 8, 1988.

CABINET
*Prime Minister, Yitzhak Shamir (*L.H.*).
*Vice-Premier and Foreign Minister, Shimon Peres (*Lab.*).
*Deputy P.M. and Education and Culture, Yitzhak Navon (*Lab.*).
*Deputy P.M. and Construction and Housing, David Levy (*L.H.*).
Agriculture, Arieh Nehamkin (*Lab.*).
*Commerce and Industry, Ariel Sharon (*L.H.*).
Communications, Gad Yaacobi (*Lab.*).
*Defence, Yitzhak Rabin (*Lab.*).
Economy and Planning, Gad Yaacobi (*Lab.*).
Energy and Infrastructure, Moshe Shahal (*Lab.*).
Justice, Avraham Sharir (*L.L.*).
Health, Shoshana Arbeli Almoslino (*Lab.*).
Immigration and Absorption, Yaakov Tsur (*Lab.*).
*Finance, Moshe Nissim (*L.L.*).
Labour and Social Affairs, Moshe Katzav (*L.H.*).
*Police, Haim Bar-Lev (*Lab.*).
Science and Development, Gideon Patt (*L.L.*).
Tourism, Avraham Sharir (*L.L.*).
Transportation, Haim Corfu (*L.H.*).
Interior, Yitzhak Shamir (*acting*).
Religious Affairs, Zevulun Hammer (*National Religious Party*).
*In Prime Minister's Office, Ezer Weizman (*Lab.*).
Without Portfolio, Moshe Arens (*L.H.*); Yosef Shapira (*Morasha*); Yigal Hurwitz (*Ometz*); Rabbi Yitzak Peretz (*Shas*); Mordehai Gur (*Lab.*); *Yitzhak Modai (*L.L.*).

Lab. = Labour Party; L.H. = Likud Party—Herut faction; L.L. = Likud Party—Liberal faction.
* Member of Inner Cabinet.
(Under the agreement by which the Government of National Unity was formed, Mr. Peres gave up the Premiership in Oct. 1986 to Mr. Shamir.)

2 Palace Green, Kensington, W8 4QB
[01–937 8050]

Ambassador Extraordinary and Plenipotentiary, His Excellency Yoav Biran (1988).

Area and Population.—Israel lies on the western edge of the continent of Asia at the eastern extremity of the Mediterranean Sea, between lat. 29° 30'–33° 15' N. and longitude 34° 15'–35° 40' E. Its political neighbours are Lebanon on the North, Syria on the North and East, Jordan on the East and the Egyptian province of Sinai on the South-West.

The area is estimated at 8,019 sq. miles (20,770 sq. km.). The population was estimated at the end of 1987 at 4,404,000. During the upheavals of 1948–49 a large number of Arabs left the country as refugees and settled in neighbouring countries.

Hebrew and Arabic are the official languages of Israel. Arabs are entitled to transact all official business with Government Departments in Arabic, and provision is made in the *Knesset* for the simultaneous translation of all speeches into Arabic.

Physical Features.—Israel comprises four main regions: (*a*) the hill country of Galilee and Judea and Samaria, rising in places to heights of nearly 4,000 ft.; (*b*) the coastal plain from the Gaza strip to North of Acre, including the plain of Esdraelon running from Haifa Bay to the south-east, and cutting in two the hill region; (*c*) the Negev, a semi-desert triangular-shaped region, extending from a base south of Beersheba, to an apex at the head of the Gulf of 'Aqaba; and (*d*) parts of the Jordan valley, including the Hula Region, Tiberias and the south-western extremity of the Dead Sea. The principal river is the Jordan, which rises from three main sources in Israel, the Lebanon and Syria, and flows through the Hula valley and the canals which have replaced Lake Hula, drained in 1958. Between Hulata and Tiberias (Sea of Galilee) the river falls 926 ft. in 11 miles and becomes a turbulent stream. Lake Tiberias is 696 ft. below sea-level and liable to sudden storms. Between it and the Dead Sea the Jordan falls 591 ft. The other principal rivers are the Yarkon and Kishon. The largest lake is the *Dead Sea* (shared between Israel and Jordan); area 393 sq. miles, 1,286 feet below sea-level, 51·5 miles long, with a maximum width of 11 miles and a maximum depth of 1,309 ft.; it receives the waters of the Jordan and of six other streams, and has no outlet, the surplus being carried off by evaporation. The water contains an extraordinarily high concentration of mineral substances. The highest mountain peak is Mount Meron, 3,962 ft. above sea-level, near Safad, Upper Galilee.

Climate.—The climate is variable, similar to that of Lower Egypt, but modified by altitude and distance from the sea. The summer is hot but tempered in most parts by daily winds from the Mediterranean. The winter is the rainy season lasting from November to April, the period of maximum rainfall being January and February.

Antiquities.—The following are among the principal historic sites in Israel: *Jerusalem*: the Church of the Holy Sepulchre: the Al Aqsa Mosque and Dome of the Rock, standing on the remains of the Temple Mount of Herod the Great, of which the Western (wailing) Wall is a fragment; the Church of the Dormition and the Coenaculum on Mount Zion; Ein Karem: Church of the Visitation, Church of St. John the Baptist. *Galilee*: The Sea; Church and Mount of the Beatitudes, ruins of Capernaum and other sites connected with the life of Christ. *Mount Tabor*: Church of the Transfiguration. *Nazareth*: Church of the Annunciation and other Christian shrines associated with the childhood of Christ. There are also numerous sites dating from biblical and medieval days, such as Ascalon, Caesarea, Atlit, Massada,

Megiddo and Hazor. Other antiquities in the West Bank of Jordan and the Golan Heights at present occupied by Israel can now be visited from Israel. In accordance with the terms of the peace treaty signed between Egypt and Israel on March 26, 1979, Israel withdrew in April 1982 to the pre-1967 boundary, returning the Sinai area to Egyptian sovereignty.

Government.—There is a Cabinet and a single-chamber Parliament (*Knesset*) of 120 members. A general election is held at least once every four years. The last General Election was held on July 23, 1984; the result was inconclusive. After about six weeks of negotiations between political parties a Government of National Unity was formed.

Immigration.—The Declaration of Independence of May 14, 1948, laid down that "the State of Israel will be open to the immigration of Jews from all countries of their dispersion." The Law of Return, passed by the *Knesset* on July 5, 1950, provides that an immigrant visa shall be granted to every Jew who expresses his desire to settle in Israel. From the establishment of the State until April 1978, about 1·7 million immigrants had entered Israel from over 100 different countries.

Education.—Elementary education for all children from 5 to 15 years is free, though secondary education is not compulsory. The law also provides for working youth, age 15–18 who for some reason have not completed their primary education, to be exempted from work in order to do so.

In 1985–86 enrolment in all educational establish-ments was 1,383,838: kindergartens 277,200; elementary education, 622,056; secondary education, 348,262; post-secondary, 98,420.

Finance.—Government expenditure in 1986 was 25,399,234,000 new Shekels at market prices. GNP at market prices was 40,354,955,000 new Shekels.

COMMUNICATIONS

Railways and Roads.—Israel State Railways started operating in August 1949. Towns now served are Haifa, Tel Aviv, Jerusalem, Lod, Nahariya, Beersheba, Dimona, Ashdod and intermediate stations. In 1986 the total railway network amounted to 528 km. There were 12,823 km. of paved road and in 1986 819,102 licensed vehicles.

Shipping.—Israel's merchant marine had reached a total of 2,805,000 tons deadweight by December, 1985.

The chief ports are Haifa, a modern harbour, with a depth of 30 ft. alongside the main quay; the harbour on the Red Sea at Eilat, inaugurated in September 1965, has a capacity of 10,000 tons a day; Acre has an anchorage for small vessels; the deep-water port at Ashdod, 20 miles south of Tel Aviv, which started operations at the end of 1965, handled 8,006,000 tons of cargo in 1986. In the same year Israel's three main ports handled 17,048,000 tons of cargo.

Civil Aviation.—In 1986, 3,098,000 passengers passed through Ben Gurion airport, of which 230,146 arrived by charter flight.

PRODUCTION AND INDUSTRY

Agriculture.—The country is generally fertile and climatic conditions vary so widely that a large variety of crops can be grown, ranging from temperate crops, such as wheat and cherries, to subtropical crops such as sorghum, millet and mangoes. The famous "Jaffa" orange is produced in large quantities mostly in the coastal plain for export: high-profit export crops such as strawberries and cut flowers are increasingly important. The citrus yield during the 1985–86 season was 1,308,700 tons. Specialized glasshouse crops for export, such as flowers, tomatoes and strawberries, are becoming increasingly popular and exports of flowers in 1985 earned U.S.$75,454,000. Olives are cultivated, mainly for the production of oil used for edible purposes and for the manufacture of soap. The main winter crops are wheat and barley and various kinds of pulses, while in summer sorghum, millet, maize, sesame and summer pulses are grown. Large areas of seasonal vegetables are planted. Beef, cattle and poultry farming have been developed and the production of mixed vegetables and dairy produce has greatly increased. Tobacco and medium staple cotton are now grown. Fishing production (mostly from fish farms) was 14,958 tons in 1985–86. All kinds of summer fruits such as figs, grapes, plums and apples are produced in increasing quantities for local consumption. Water supply for irrigation is the principal limiting factor to greater production. The area under cultivation is 4,370,000 dunams, of which 2,370,000 is under irrigation. The Israel land measure is the *dunam*, equivalent to 1,000 square metres (approximately a quarter of an acre).

Industry.—In value polished diamonds account for about one quarter of Israel's total exports. Amongst the most important of her exporting industries are textiles, foodstuffs, chemicals (mainly fertilizers and pharmaceuticals). Her metal-working and science-based industries are highly sophisticated and technologically advanced. These include the aircraft and military industries. Other important manufacturing industries include plastics, rubber, cement, glass, paper and oil refining.

TRADE

The principal imports are foodstuffs, crude oil, machinery and vehicles, iron, steel and manufactures thereof, and chemicals. The principal exports are citrus fruits and by-products, polished diamonds, plywood, cement, tyres, minerals, finished and semi-finished textiles.

	1986	1987
Imports	U.S.$9,275·4 m.	U.S.$11,451·0 m.
Exports	6,914·2 m.	8,222·4 m.

Trade with U.K.

	1986	1987
Imports from U.K.	£462,407,000	£523,591,000
Exports to U.K.	385,164,000	437,014,000

CAPITAL.—Most of the Government departments are in Jerusalem (population, 1984, 506,200). A resolution proclaiming Jerusalem as the capital of Israel was adopted by the Israel parliament on Jan. 23, 1950. It is not, however, recognized as the capital by the United Nations. Other principal towns (1986) were ΨTel Aviv and district (1,624,100); ΨHaifa and district (393,000) and Beersheba and district (115,000).

CURRENCY.—Shekel of 100 Agora.

FLAG.—White, with two horizontal blue stripes, the Shield of David in the centre.

NATIONAL ANTHEM.—Hatikvah (The Hope).

JERUSALEM

Until 1967 Jerusalem was divided between Israel and Jordan, two of the 36 recognized Christian Holy Places (in the New City) being under Jewish administration, the remainder under Arab administration in the Old City. At the conclusion of hostilities between Israel and the surrounding Arab countries in 1967 the entire city was under Israeli control.

BRITISH EMBASSY
192 Hayarkon Street, Tel Aviv.
[Tel Aviv 249171/5]

Ambassador Extraordinary and Plenipotentiary, His Excellency Mark Elliott, C.M.G.
Counsellor, S. W. J. Fuller (*Head of Chancery, Consul-General and Counsellor*).
Defence Attaché, Col. R. McCrum, M.V.O.

British Council Representative, P. Sandiford, 140 Hayarkon Street, (P.O. Box 3302), Tel Aviv. There is a library in *Tel Aviv* and in *West Jerusalem.*
ISRAEL-BRITISH CHAMBER OF COMMERCE, 76 IBN Guirol Street, Tel Aviv 64162.

ITALY
(Repubblica Italiana)

President of the Italian Republic, Francesco Cossiga, *born* 1928, *sworn in,* July 3, 1985.

COUNCIL OF MINISTERS

Prime Minister, Ciriaco de Mita (*DC*).
Deputy P.M., Gianni de Michelio (*PSI*).
Foreign Affairs, Giulio Andreotti (*DC*).
Internal Affairs, Antonio Gava (*DC*).
Justice, Prof. Giuliano Vassalli (*PSI*).
Budget, Amintore Fanfani (*DC*).
Finance, Emilio Colombo (*DC*).
Treasury, Giuliano Amato (*PSI*).
Defence, Valerio Zanone (*PLI*).
Education, Giovanni Galloni (*DC*).
Public Works, Dr. Enrico Ferri (*PSDI*).
Agriculture, Calogero Mannino (*DC*).
Transport, Giorgio Santuz (*DC*).
Posts and Telecommunications, Oscar Mammi' (*PRI*).
Industry, Adolfo Battaglia (*PRI*).
Labour, Rino Formica (*PSI*).
Foreign Trade, Renato Ruggiero (*PSI*).
Merchant Navy, Giovanni Prandini (*DC*).
State Holdings, Carlo Fracanzani (*DC*).
Health, Carlo Donat Cattin (*DC*).
Tourism and Entertainment, Dr. Franco Carraro (*PSI*).
Environment, Prof. Giorgio Ruffolo (*PSI*).
Culture, Vincenza Bono Parrino (*PSDI*).
Ministers without portfolio, Remo Gaspari (*DC*) (*The South*); Prof. Antonio Ruberti (*PSI*) (*Scientific Research and Higher Education*); Paulo Cirino Pomicino (*DC*) (*Public Administration*); Sergio Mattarella (*DC*) (*Relations with Parliament*); Dr. Antonio Maccanico (*PRI*) (*Regions and Reform of Institutions*); Prof. Antonio La Pergola (*PSDI*) (*E.C. Policy*); Vito Lattanzio (*DC*) (*Civil Protection*); Carlo Tognoli (*PSI*) (*Urban Affairs*), Rosa Russo Jervolino (*DC*) (*Social Affairs*).

DC—Christian Democrat Party; PSI—Socialist Party; PLI—Liberal Party; PSDI—Social Democratic Party; PRI—Republican Party.

ITALIAN EMBASSY IN LONDON
14 Three Kings Yard, Davies Street, W1Y 2EH
[01–629 8200]

Ambassador Extraordinary and Plenipotentiary, Boris Biancheri (1987).
Minister-Counsellor, Livio Muzi-Falconi.
First Counsellors, Mario Fugazzola; Enrico Augelli; Fabio Pigliapoco; Roberto Di Leo (*Consular Affairs*).

Italy is a Republic in the south of Europe, consisting of a peninsula, the large islands of Sicily and Sardinia, the island of Elba and about 70 other small islands. Italy is bounded on the N. by Switzerland and Austria, on the S. by the Mediterranean, on the E. by the Adriatic and Yugoslavia, and on the W. by France and the Ligurian and Tyrrhenian Seas. The total area is about 116,304 sq. miles (301,225 sq. km.).

The peninsula is for the most part mountainous, but between the Apennines, which form its spine, and the East coastline are two large fertile plains: of Emilia/Romagna in the north and of Apulia in the south. The Alps form the northern limit of Italy, dividing it from France, Switzerland, Austria and Yugoslavia. *Mont Blanc* (15,771 ft.), the highest peak, is in the French Pennine Alps, but partly within the Italian borders are Monte Rosa (15,217 ft.), Matterhorn (14,780 ft.) and several peaks from 12,000 to 14,000 ft.

The chief rivers are the Po (405 miles), which flows through Piedmont, Lombardy and the Veneto, and the Adige (Trentino and Veneto) in the north, the Arno (Florentine Plain) and the Tiber (flowing through Rome to Ostia). The *Rubicon*, a small stream flowing into the Adriatic near Rimini formed the boundary between Italy and Cisalpine Gaul: "crossing the Rubicon" (as Caesar did in 49 B.C., thus "invading" Italy in arms) is used to indicate definite committal to some course of action.

Population.—In Feb. 1986 Italy's population was 57,193,708. The annual rate of population increase between 1981 and 1985 was 0·3 per cent.

Government.—Italian unity was accomplished under the House of Savoy, after a struggle from 1848 to 1870, in which Mazzini (1805–72), Garibaldi (1807–82) and Cavour (1810–61) were the principal figures. It was completed when Lombardy was ceded by Austria in 1859 and Venice in 1866, and through the evacuation of Rome by the French in 1870. In 1871 the King of Italy entered Rome, and that city was declared to be the capital.

Benito Mussolini, known as *Il Duce* (The Leader) was continuously in office as Prime Minister from Oct. 30, 1922, until July 25, 1943, when the Fascist régime was abolished. He was captured by Italian partisans while attempting to escape across the Swiss frontier and was put to death on April 28, 1945.

In fulfilment of a promise given in April, 1944, that he would retire when the Allies entered Rome, a decree was signed on June 5, 1944, by the late King

Victor Emmanuel III under which Prince Umberto, the King's son, became "Lieutenant General of the Realm." The King remained head of the House of Savoy and retained the title King of Italy until his abdication on May 9, 1946, when he was succeeded by the Crown Prince.

A general election was held on June 2, 1946, together with a referendum on the future of the monarchy. The result showed a majority in favour of replacing the monarchy with a Republic. The Royal Family left the country on June 13, and on June 28, 1946, a Provisional President was elected.

Constitution.—The constitution of the Republic of Italy, approved by the Constituent Assembly on December 22, 1947, provides for the election of the President by an electoral college which consists of the two Houses of Parliament (the Chamber of Deputies and the Senate) sitting in joint session together with three delegates from each region (one in the case of the Valle d'Aosta). The President, who must be over 50 years of age, holds office for 7 years. He has numerous carefully defined powers, the main one of which is the right to dissolve one or both Houses of Parliament, after consultation with the Speakers.

Defence.—The Armed Forces are largely manned by conscripts, who serve for 12 months. The Army has approx. 295,000 men, of whom 40,000 are regular officers and N.C.O.s. In addition, the elite paramilitary *Carabinieri* force, which is part of the Army, has over 96,000 men, most of whom are regulars. The Army, which has three Corps concentrated in the North, is equipped with Leopard 1 and M60 tanks and M113 armoured personnel carriers. There is also a parachute brigade, 5 alpine brigades, a missile brigade, and a Light Aviation Arm with over 300 helicopters. The Navy consists of one helicopter carrier, 3 cruisers, 4 destroyers, 9 submarines, 24 frigates and corvettes and 24 mine warfare ships. Manpower strength is approx. 45,000. The Air Force has 70,000 men and 347 combat aircraft. It is largely a tactical airforce, equipped with Tornado, F104 and G91 aircraft, but also has transport, anti-submarine and helicopter search and rescue units. There is a large Reserve Force of ex-conscripts under the age of 35.

REGIONS OF ITALY

Rome and Central Italy.—Rome was founded, according to legend, by Romulus in the year now known as 753 B.C. It was the focal point of Latin civilization and dominion under the Republic and afterwards under the Roman Empire, and became the capital of Italy when the Kingdom was established in 1871. The capital is concerned mainly with tourism and government, but its importance as a business centre is steadily increasing, and it is reportedly the third largest industrial centre in the country.

Lombardy and Milan.—In the Lombardy region are to be found some 15·7 per cent of Italy's commercial and banking services and some 21·9 per cent of her manufacturing industry. The whole range of Italian industry is represented, most important being the steel, machine tool and motor car factories.

Turin and Piedmont.—Turin between 1861 and 1865 was Italy's first capital as the home of the Piedmontese Royal Family. Now it is the headquarters of Europe's largest manufacturer of motor cars, produces 75 per cent. of Italy's motor vehicles and over 80 per cent. of its roller bearings. Turin is also Italy's second largest steel producing city. Piedmont is the centre of the Italian textile industry based mainly on Biella.

Genoa and the Ligurian Riviera.—Genoa has been one of Europe's major ports since the Middle Ages, and handles one-third of Italy's foreign trade. About 80 per cent. of the goods handled are imports.

Venice and the North-East.—Venice is primarily a tourist attraction of unique beauty. It was founded in the middle of the 5th century by refugees from the mainland fleeing attacks, and by the 16th century it was one of the strongest and richest states of Europe, dominating Eastern Mediterranean trade. It lost its independence in 1797 when Napoleon handed it over to Austria. Industry (paper and stationery, mechanical equipment, consumer goods, electrical appliances, woollens) is now developing in the Venice area, particularly on the autostrada linking Venice with her historical and now developing rivals, Verona, Vicenza, Padua and in the areas around Treviso and Pordenone. Near Trieste, is the modern Monfalcone shipyard.

Tuscany, Emilia and Romagna.—Florence, the capital of Tuscany, was one of the greatest cities in Europe from the 11th to the 16th centuries, and the cradle of the Renaissance. Under the Medici family in the 15th century flourished many of the greatest names in Italian art, including Filippo Lippi, Botticelli, Donatello and Brunelleschi and in the 16th century great Florentine artists like Michelangelo and Leonardo da Vinci. These regions were the agricultural centre of Italy but the post-war period has seen the development of large industrial centres at Bologna, Florence, Modena, Pistoia and Ravenna. Most of the new firms are small or medium-sized. The footwear industry is based in Florence, textiles in Prato, reproduction furniture at Cascina and Poggibonsi, ceramics at Sassuolo, and glass and pottery at Empoli and Montelupo. Bologna is an important centre for the food industry.

Naples and the Toe of Italy.—Naples, formerly the capital and administrative centre of the Kingdom of Naples and Sicily, remains the dominant city in the area, but it is beset with great problems of unemployment and the need for modernization. Around it, however, helped by Government incentives, industry is slowly developing, northwards to Caserta, southwards to Salerno and eastwards to Benevento.

Puglia.—Bari has always been a commercial centre and now industrial development is also taking place in the areas of Taranto, Brindisi and Foggia. At Taranto there are a highly-mechanized steel-works and a modern oil refinery. The Bari industrial zone has factories producing electronic and pneumatic valves, specialized vehicle bodies and tyres, etc. The main industry of Brindisi is a petro-chemical plant. At Foggia there is a textile factory.

Sicily.—The main source of income is agriculture, particularly citrus fruits, almonds and tomatoes, but this faces severe competition. Oil in small quantities has been found off the southern shore of the island and drilling continues, while onshore there are growing oil-refining, natural gas and petrochemical industries. Small and medium sized industries, benefiting from the Government's incentives, are developing, and tourism is bringing an increasing amount of revenue to the island.

Sardinia.—Sardinia is an autonomous region, with its capital at Cagliari. Six main industrial development areas have been officially designated. The major industries are aluminium production (there is a smelting plant at Porto Vesme), petrochemicals, lead and zinc mining; and the tourist industry is flourishing.

THE ECONOMY

Italian gross domestic product in 1986 was *L*894,362,000 million. The economy has recovered from the setbacks of the early seventies, reversing the balance of payments and halving inflation, but this was accompanied by stagnation and increasing unemployment. The rate of inflation for 1985–86 was 5·9 per cent.

Industry.—The general index of industrial production (1980 = 100) stood at +2·7 per cent in 1985–86. The State-owned sector of Italian industry is important, dominated by the holding companies IRI (mechanical, steel, airlines), ENI (petro-chemicals) and ENEL (electricity).

Mineral Production.—Italy is generally poor in mineral resources but since the war deposits of natural methane gas and small deposits of oil have been discovered and rapidly exploited. Production of lignite has also increased. Other minerals produced in significant quantities include iron ores and pyrites, mercury (over one-quarter of the world production), lead, zinc and aluminium. Marble is a traditional product of the Massa Carrara district.

Agriculture.—Agriculture accounted for 5·2 per cent. of gross domestic product in 1984. The agricultural labour force was 2,242,000 in 1986.

Tourist Traffic.—In 1986 an estimated 18 million foreign tourists visited Italy, and in 1986 foreigners spent an estimated L14,691,000 million. The net balance on tourism was about L10,579,000 million.

Communications.—The main railway system is State-run by the *Ferrovia dello Stato.* A network of motorways (*autostrade*) covers the country, built and operated mainly by the IRI State-holding company and ANAS the State highway authority. The autostrada network covered 5,176 kms. in 1974. *Alitalia,* the principal international and domestic airline, is also State-controlled by the IRI group. Other smaller companies, including ATI (an *Alitalia* subsidiary) and Air Mediterranea operate on domestic routes. The Italian mercantile marine totalled 7,587,117 tons in December, 1985.

FOREIGN TRADE

The balance of trade in 1987 showed a deficit of 11,138 billion lire, compared with 3,722 billion lira in 1986.

The main markets for Italian exports in 1987 were the O.E.C.D. countries, which accounted for almost 80 per cent. of the total, and the E. C. markets with 56 per cent. of the total. Imports came principally from West Germany, France and the U.S.A.

Trade with U.K.

	1986	1987
Imports from U.K. .	£3,472,364,000	£4,145,659,000
Exports to U.K. . . .	4,658,036,000	5,216,751,000

Language and Literature.—Italian is a Romance language derived from Latin. It is spoken in its purest form in Tuscany, but there are numerous dialects, showing variously French, German, Spanish and Arabic influences. Sard, the dialect of Sardinia, is accorded by some authorities the status of a distinct Romance language. Italian literature (in addition to Latin literature, which is the common inheritance of Western Europe) is one of the richest in Europe, particularly in its golden age (Dante, 1265–1321; Petrarch, 1304–1374; Boccaccio, 1313–1375) and in the renaissance (Ariosto, 1474–1533; Machiavelli, 1469–1527; Tasso, 1544–1595). Modern Italian literature has many noted names in prose and verse, notably Manzoni (1785–1873), Carducci (1835–1907) and Gabriele d'Annunzio (1864–1938). The Nobel Prize for Literature has been awarded to Italian authors on five occasions—G. Carducci (1906), Signora G. Deledda (1926), Luigi Pirandello (1934), Salvatore Quasimodo (1959) and Eugenio Montale (1975). In 1985, there were 48 daily newspapers published in Italy, of which 6 were published in Rome and 7 in Milan.

Education.—Education is free and compulsory between the ages of 6 and 14; this comprises five years

at primary school and three in the "middle school", of which there are about 8,000. Pupils who obtain the middle school certificate may seek admission to any "senior secondary school", which may be a lyceum with a classical or scientific or artistic bias, or an institute directed at technology (of which there are eight different types), trade or industry (including vocational schools), or teacher-training. Courses at the lyceums and technical institutes usually last for five years and success in the final examination qualifies for admission to university. There are 35 State and 14 private universities, some of ancient foundation; those at Bologna, Modena, Parma and Padua were started in the 12th century. University education is not free, but entrants with higher qualifications are charged reduced fees according to a sliding scale. In general, schools, lyceums and universities are financed by local taxation and central government grants.

ISLANDS.—*Pantelleria Island* (part of Trapani Province) in the Sicilian Narrows, has an area of 31 sq. miles and a population of 9,601. The *Pelagian Islands* (Lampedusa, Linosa and Lampione) are part of the Province of Agrigento and have an area of 8 sq. miles, pop. 4,811. The Tuscan Archipelago (including Elba), area 293 sq. km., pop. 31,861; Pontine Archipelago (including Ponza, area 10 sq. km., pop. 2,515); Flegrean Islands (including Ischia, area 60 sq. km., pop. 51,883); Capri; Eolian Islands (including Lipari, area 116 sq. km., pop. 18,636); Tremiti Islands (area 3 sq. km., pop. 426).

CAPITAL.—Rome. Population of the commune (1986) 2,821,420.

1986 estimates of the population of the communes of the principal cities and towns are Milan, 1,511,193; Ψ Naples, 1,204,959; Turin, 1,034,007; Ψ Genoa, 733,990; Bologna, 436,570; Florence, 429,865; *Sicily,* Ψ Palermo, 719,960; *Sardinia,* Ψ Cagliari, 223,021.

CURRENCY.—Lira of 100 Centesimi.

FLAG.—Vertical stripes of green, white and red.

NATIONAL ANTHEM.—"Inno di Mameli".

NATIONAL DAY.—June 2.

BRITISH EMBASSY
Via XX Settembre 80a, 00187 Rome
[Rome 475–5441]

Ambassador Extraordinary and Plenipotentiary, His Excellency Sir Derek Morison David Thomas, K.C.M.G. (1987).

Ministers, G. E. Fitzherbert, C.M.G.; R. F. R. Deane (*FAO*); J. R. Goldsack.

Minister, R. F. R. Deare (*FAO*).

Defence and Military Attaché, Brig. M. J. Hague.

Naval Attaché, Capt. N. Harris, R.N.

Air Attaché, Group-Capt. R. J. M. David, R.A.F.

Counsellors, M. J. Williams, C.V.O., O.B.E. (*Head of Chancery*); G. Tantum, O.B.E.; M. Perceval (*Commercial*).

First Secretaries, A. McGuffog (*Labour*); N. E. Cole, O.B.E. (*Administration*); Miss C. M. T. Elmes (*Economic*); R. Godfrey (*Consul*); M. Adams (*Commercial*); D. B. A. Evans (*Agriculture*); Miss K. Coombs (*Information*); A. C. Tutton; N. Martin.

Chaplain, Rev. B. Wardrobe.

There are British Consular Offices at *Milan, Rome, Naples, Genoa, Florence, Venice, Trieste* and *Cagliari* and a trade representative at *Turin.*

British Council Representative, D. T. Ricks, O.B.E., Palazzo del Drago, Via Quattro Fontane 20, 00184, Rome.

There are *British Council Offices* at Milan and Naples, each with a library.

BRITISH CHAMBER OF COMMERCE, Via San Paolo 7, 20121 Milan.

JAPAN
(Nihon Koku—Land of the Rising Sun)

Emperor of Japan, His Majesty Hirohito, *born* April 29, 1901; *succeeded* Dec. 25, 1926; *married* (1924) Princess Nagako (*born* March 6, 1903), daughter of the late Prince Kuniyoshi Kuni, and has issue two sons and four daughters.

Heir-Apparent, His Imperial Highness Prince Akihito, *Crown Prince, born* Dec. 23, 1933; *married* April 10, 1959, Miss Michiko Shoda and has issue Prince Naruhito Hironomiya, *born* Feb. 23, 1960, Prince Fumihito, *born* Nov. 30, 1965 and Princess Sayako, *born* April 18, 1969.

THE CABINET

Prime Minister, Noboru Takeshita.
Deputy P. M. and Finance, Kiichi Miyazawa.
Justice, Yukio Hayashida.
Foreign Affairs, Sosuke Uno.
Education, Gentaro Nakajima.
Health and Welfare, Takao Fujimoto.
Agriculture, Forestry and Fisheries, Takashi Sato.
International Trade and Industry, Hajime Tamura.
Transport, Shintaro Ishihara.
Posts and Telecommunications, Masaaki Nakayama.
Labour, Taro Nakamura.
Construction, Ihei Ochi.
Home Affairs, Seiroku Kajiyama.
Management and Co-ordination, Osamu Takatori.
Hokkaido Development Agency and National Land Agency, Shigeru Kasuya.
Defence, Tsutomu Kawara.
Economic Planning, Eiichi Nakao.
Science and Technology, Soichiro Ito.
Environment, Toshio Horiuchi.
Okinawa Development Agency, Shigeru Kasuya.
Chief Cabinet Secretary, Keizo Obuchi.
National Land Agency, Hideo Utsumi.

JAPANESE EMBASSY AND CONSULATE
46 Grosvenor Street, W1X 0BA
Information Centre: 9 Grosvenor Square, W1X 9LB
[01–493 6030]

Ambassador Extraordinary and Plenipotentiary, His Excellency Kazuo Chiba (1988).
Ministers, Katsumi Sezaki; Mikio Shibata (*Commercial*); Hiroshi Hashimoto; Shotaro Miyake (*Financial*).
Counsellors, T. Ito (*Economic*); Dr. N. Tode (*Medical Attaché*); G. Kano (*Information*); I. Fujisaki (*Political*); T. Sugiyama; A. Suda (*Political*); S. Shiga (*Financial*).
Defence Attaché, Capt. Isamu Kyoda.

Area and Population.—Japan consists of 4 large and many small islands situated in the North Pacific Ocean between longitude 128° 6′ East and 145° 49′ East and between latitude 26° 59′ and 45° 31′ N., with a total area of 145,834 sq. miles (377,708 sq. km.), and a population (1986) of 121,740,000. In 1985 the birth rate was 11·9 per 1,000, and the death rate 6·3 per 1,000.

Japan Proper consists of *Honshū* (or Mainland), 230,448 sq. km. (88,839 sq. m.), *Shikoku*, 18,757 sq. km. (7,231 sq. m.), *Kyūshū*, 42,079 sq. km. (16,170 sq. m.), *Hokkaido*, 78,508 sq. km. (30,265 sq. m.).

Physiography.—The coastline exceeds 17,000 miles and is deeply indented, so that few places are far from the sea. The interior is very mountainous, and crossing the mainland from the Sea of Japan to the Pacific is a group of volcanoes, mainly extinct or dormant. Mount Fuji, the loftiest and most sacred mountain of Japan, about 60 miles from Tokyo, is 12,370 ft. high and has been dormant since 1707, but there are other volcanoes which are active, including Mount Aso in Kyūshū. There are frequent earthquakes, mainly along the Pacific coast near the Bay of Tokyo. Japan proper extends from sub-tropical in the south to cool temperate in the north. Heavy snowfalls are frequent on the western slopes of Hokkaidō and Honshū, but the Pacific coasts are warmed by the Japan current. There is a plentiful rainfall and the rivers are short and swift-flowing offering abundant opportunities for the supply of hydro-electric power.

Government.—According to Japanese tradition, Jimmu, the First Emperor of Japan, ascended the throne on Feb. 11, 660 B.C. Under the *Meiji* constitution of Feb. 11, 1889, the monarchy was hereditary in the male heirs of the Imperial house.

After the unconditional surrender to the Allied Nations (Aug. 14, 1945), Japan was occupied by Allied forces under General MacArthur (Sept. 15, 1945). A Japanese peace treaty conference opened at San Francisco on Sept. 4, 1951, and on Sept. 8, 48 nations signed the treaty, which became effective on April 28, 1952. Japan then resumed her status as an independent power.

A new constitution came into force on May 3, 1947. Legislative authority rests with *The Diet*, which is bicameral, consisting of a *House of Representatives* and a *House of Councillors*, both Houses being composed of elected members. Executive authority is vested in the Cabinet which is responsible to the Legislature.

The conservatives have governed Japan almost without interruption since World War II. Since 1955, when it was formed, the Liberal Democratic Party has maintained an absolute majority in the House of Representatives. In June 1987 the strength of the Parties was: Liberal Democratic Party, 303; Japan Socialist Party, 87; Komeito, 57; Democratic Socialist, 29; Japan Communist Party, 27; Independents, 5. (Four vacant seats).

The House of Councillors whose powers are subordinate to the House of Representatives, re-elects half of its members every three years. In June, 1987, the strength of the Parties was: Liberal Democratic Party, 142; Japan Socialist Party, 42; Komeito, 24; Japan Communist Party, 16; Democratic Socialist Party, 12; Shimsei Club, 4; Niim Club, 4; Salaryman Party, 3; Independents, 4. (Two vacant seats).

Agriculture and Livestock.—Owing to the mountainous nature of the country not more than one-sixth of its area is available for cultivation. The forest land includes Cryptomeria japonica, Pinus massoniana, Zeikowaskeaki, and Paulownia imperialis, in addition to camphor trees, mulberry, vegetable wax tree and a lacquer tree which furnishes the celebrated lacquer of Japan. The soil is only moderately fertile, but intensive cultivation secures good crops. Tobacco, tea, potato, rice, wheat and other cereals are all cultivated: rice is the staple food of the people, about 11,500,000 tonnes being produced in 1986. Fruit is abundant, including the mandarin, persimmon, loquat and peach; European fruits such as apples, strawberries, pears, grapes and figs are also produced. There is a small-scale beef industry and pigs and chickens are widely reared.

Minerals.—The country has mineral resources, including gold and silver, and copper, lead, zinc, iron chromite, white arsenic, coal, sulphur, petroleum, salt and uranium, but iron ore, coal and crude oil are among the principal post-war imports to supply deficiencies at home.

Industry.—Japan is the most highly industrialized nation in the Far East, with the whole range of modern light and heavy industries, including automobiles, electronics, metals, machinery, chemicals, textiles (cotton, silk, wool and synthetics), cement, pottery, glass, rubber, lumber, paper, oil refining and shipbuilding. The labour force of Japan in 1985 (average) was 59,630,000, of which around 2·6 per cent

(1,560,000) are permanently unemployed. Of the total labour force, over 15 per cent are over 65 and this rate is increasing. Industrial, manufacturing and services workers numbered 53,430,000 and agricultural, forestries and fisheries workers 5,090,000 in 1985.

Communications.—There were 1,120,051 km. of road and 44,297 km. of rail road (steam and electric) in 1984. Also new Shinkansen (bullet train) tracks are currently being expanded. Japan National Railways was privatized on April 1, 1987 and is known as Japan Railways (JR). There are six regional companies and one goods company. The merchant fleet (oceangoing ships over 100 tons gross) totalled an aggregate of 64·16m. tons in 1985. The opening in 1988 of the Seikan rail tunnel and the Seto Osashi rail bridge means that the four major islands are now linked for the first time.

Armed Forces.—After the unconditional surrender of August, 1945, the Imperial Army and Navy were disarmed and disbanded.

Although the Constitution of Japan prohibits the maintenance of armed forces, internal security forces came into being in 1950, and 1952. In July, 1954, the mission of the forces was extended to include the defence of Japan against direct and indirect aggression.

The defence budget allocated for the fiscal year 1986–87 amounted to *Yen* 3,343,549 million, equivalent to 6·18 per cent of the General Account budget. The authorized uniformed strength was: Ground Self-Defence Force (GSDF) 180,000 (Reserve 43,000); Maritime Self-Defence Force (MSDF) 43,897 (Reserve 600); Air Self-Defence Force (ASDF) 46,204. Actual strengths of all three services are slightly below their authorised figure.

The GSDF is organized into five regional Armies, totalling thirteen Divisions, one of which is an Armoured Division. Major equipment includes tanks, APC's, towed and SP guns and rocket launchers, Hawk AA missiles, and 425 aircraft. Equipment is now largely manufactured in Japan.

The MSDF has 164 warships and auxiliaries including four DDH, four TARTAR-equipped GMDs, 42 destroyers, 14 submarines and 99 others, 205 fixed-wing aircraft and 97 helicopters.

The ASDF has 820 aircraft including 375 trainers; 43 transports and 75 support aircraft including helicopters). There are 6 groups of Nike SAM missiles and one training unit of Patriot.

Religion.—All religions are tolerated. The principal religions of Japan are Mahayana Buddhism and Shinto. About 1 per cent of Japanese are Christians. The Roman Catholic Church has 2 archbishops and 16 bishops. The Nippon Seikokai (Holy Catholic Church of Japan) has 11 Japanese bishops (1987) and is an autonomous branch of the Anglican communion. There is also a United Protestant Church.

Education.—Under the Education Law of 1948 education at elementary (6 year course) and lower secondary (3 year course) schools is free, compulsory and co-educational. The (3 year) upper secondary schools are attended by 93 per cent of the age group. They have courses in general, agricultural, commercial, technical, mercantile marine, radio-communication and home-economics education, etc. 33 per cent of the population aged between 18 and 21 were enrolled in higher education in 1984. There are 2 or 3 year junior colleges and 4 year universities. Some of the 4 year universities have graduate schools. In 1983 there were 989 universities and junior colleges, the vast majority of which are privately maintained. The most prominent universities are the seven State Universities of Tokyo, Kyoto, Tohoku (Sendai), Hokkaido (Sapporo), Kyushu (Fukuoka), Osaka and Nagoya, and the two private universities, Keio and Waseda.

Language and Literature. Japanese is said to be one of the Uro-Altaic group of languages and remained a spoken tongue until the fifth–seventh centuries A.D., when Chinese characters came into use. Japanese who have received school education (99·8 per cent of the population) can read and write the Chinese characters in current use (about 1,800 characters) and also the syllabary characters called Kana. English is the best known foreign language. It is taught in all middle and high schools and universities. There are 125 daily newspapers in Japan.

FINANCE

The Budget for the financial year 1988 for revenue and expenditure on the general account was *Yen*56,690,000 million.

PRODUCTION AND TRADE

Being deficient in natural resources, Japan has had to develop a complex foreign trade. Principal imports in 1984 consisted of mineral oils (44·4 per cent), raw materials (14·3 per cent) e.g. metal ores and scrap, 4·8 per cent, timber, 2·9 per cent, foodstuffs (11·7 per cent) (e.g. wheat and sugar), machinery (8·8 per cent), chemicals (6·1 per cent) and textiles (2·8 per cent).

Principal exports consist of steel (8·1 per cent), ships (4·3 per cent), automobiles (17·5 per cent), electric machinery and appliances (17·2 per cent), non-electric machinery (16·4 per cent), chemicals (4·5 per cent) and textile goods (4·0 per cent).

FOREIGN TRADE

	1985	1986
	($1,000)	($1,000)
Total imports	129,538,747	126,407,786
Total exports	175,637,772	209,151,151

Trade with U.K.

	1986	1987
Imports from U.K. .	£1,193,933,000	£1,495,111,000
Exports to U.K. ...	4,932,497,000	5,463,116,000

CAPITAL.—Tokyo. Population, 11,806,729. The other chief cities had the following populations: ΨOsaka (2,629,135); ΨNagoya (2,103,460); ΨYokohama (2,925,877); Kyoto, the ancient capital (1,486,873); ΨKobé (1,401,928); Kita-Kyushu (1,060,470); Sapporo (1,515,582); ΨKawasaki (1,076,673); ΨFukuoka (1,144,802).

CURRENCY.—Yen of 100 Sen.

FLAG.—White, charged with sun (red).

NATIONAL ANTHEM.—"Kimigayo."

NATIONAL DAY.—April 29.

BRITISH EMBASSY

No. 1 Ichiban-cho, Chiyoda-ku, Tokyo 102
[Tokyo 265–5511]

Ambassador Extraordinary and Plenipotentiary, His Excellency Sir John Stainton Whitehead, K.C.M.G., C.V.O. (1986).

Minister, E. J. Field

Counsellors, S. J. Gomersall (*Economic*); M. R. J. Guest (*Commercial*); D. G. Raikes (*Financial*); J. A. Barnett, C.B.E., (*Cultural*); A. N. R. Millington (*Head of Chancery*); Dr. C. C. Bradley (*Science and Technology*); R. Mrowicki (*Atomic Energy*); D. L. Brown (*Administration*); J. R. H. Walker.

First Secretaries, S. D. M. Jack; R. R. Hoggard; D. J. Fitton; D. F. Middleton (*Economic*); G. Williams; N. K. Hook (*Commercial*); K. J. Pocknell (*Science and Technology*); E. Hewlett (*Consul*); C. E. J. Wilton; P. Sprunt; A. T. MacDermott (*Information*).

Defence and Air Attaché, Gp. Capt. A. Terrett.

Naval Attaché, Capt. N. Tobin, R.N.

Air Attaché, Gp. Capt. D. I. Oakden, R.A.F.

There is a British Consulate-General at *Osaka* and an Honorary Consulate at *Fukuoka*.

British Council Representative, J. A. Barnett, C.B.E., 2 Kagurazaka, 1-Chome, Shinjuku-ku, Tokyo 162. There is also an office and library in Kyoto.

BRITISH CHAMBER OF COMMERCE

World Import Mart Branch 7th Floor, 1–3 Higashi-Ikebukuro 3-Chome, Toshima-ku, Tokyo 170; (*Postal Address*, P.O. Box 2145, World Import Mart Branch, Toshima-ku, Tokyo 170).

JORDAN
(Al-Mamlaka al Urduniya al-Hashemiyah)

King of the Jordan, Hussein, G.C.V.O., *born* November 14, 1935, *succeeded* on the deposition of his father, King Talal, Aug. 11, 1952, *assumed constitutional powers*, May 2, 1953, on coming of age.

Crown Prince, Prince Hassan, third son of King Talal of Jordan, *born* 1948, *appointed Crown Prince*, April 1, 1965.

CABINET

Prime Minister and Minister for Defence, Zaid Rifa'i.

Deputy P.M. and Minister of Education, Dr. Thoukan Al Hindawi.

Minister of State for Parliamentary Affairs, Dr. Sami Joudeh.

Agriculture, Dr. Marwan Hmoud.

Awqaf and Islamic Affairs, Sheikh Aboul Aziz Khayyat.

Higher Education, Dr. Nasreddin Al Asad.

Energy and Mineral Resources, Dr. Hisham Al Khatib.

Finance, Dr. Hanna Odeh.

Foreign Affairs, Taher al Masri.

Health, Dr. Zaid Hamzeh.

Interior, Rajai Dajani.

Justice, Riyad Al Shakaa.

Municipal and Rural Affairs and the Environment, Yousef Hamdan Al Jaber.

Occupied Territories Affairs, Marwan Dudin.

Planning, Dr. Taher Kanaan.

Information, Dr. Hani Khasawneh.

Labour and Social Development, Rashid Ureikat.

Tourism, Zuhair Ajlouni.

Culture and Heritage, Dr. Mohammad Hammouri.

Youth, Dr. Awad Khleifat.

Water and Irrigation, Ahmad Dakhqan.

Public Works and Housing, Shafiq Zawaideh.

Industry, Trade and Supply, Hamdi Tabbaa.

Minister of State for Prime Ministry Affairs, Dr. Fayez Tarawneh.
Communications and Transport, Khaled Al Haj Hassan.

JORDANIAN EMBASSY
6 Upper Phillimore Gardens, W8 7HB
[01-937 3685/7]
Ambassador Extraordinary and Plenipotentiary, His Excellency Dr. Albert Butros.
Counsellor, Dr. Issa Dabbah.
Defence Attaché, Brig. Ahmed Suleiman Nawawi.
Service Office: 16 Upper Phillimore Gardens, W8. (01-937-9611).

Area and Population.—The Hashemite Kingdom of the Jordan, which covers 37,738 sq. miles (97,740 sq. km.), is bounded on the north by Syria, on the west by Israel, on the south by Saudi Arabia and on the east by Iraq. Since the hostilities of June, 1967, that part of the country lying to the west of the Jordan River has been under Israeli occupation. The majority of the population are Sunni Moslems and Islam is the religion of the State, freedom of belief is, however, guaranteed by the Constitution. Total population on the East Bank of the Jordan was estimated (1987) to be 2,670,000.

History.—After the defeat of Turkey in the First World War the Amirate of Transjordan was established in the area east of the River Jordan as a state under British mandate. The mandate was terminated after the Second World War and the Amirate, still ruled by its founder, the Amir Abdullah, became the Hashemite Kingdom of Jordan. Following the 1948 war between Israel and the Arab States, that part of Palestine remaining in Arab hands (but excluding Gaza) was incorporated into the Hashemite Kingdom. King Abdullah was assassinated in 1951; his son Talal ruled briefly but abdicated in favour of the present King, Hussein, in 1952. All of Jordan west of the River has been under Israeli occupation since 1967. As a result of the wars of 1948 and 1967 there are about 991,000 refugees and displaced persons living in East Jordan, about 200,000 of whom live in refugee and displaced persons camps established by the U.N. Relief and Works Agency (UNRWA). In addition there are some 300,000 entirely self-supporting Palestinian members of the East Jordanian community.

Government.—The present constitution of the Kingdom came into force in 1952. It provides for a senate of 30 members (all appointed by the King) and an elected House of Representatives of 60 persons. (New legislation has been passed to more than double the size of both houses at the next general election). Half of the constituencies of the latter are on the West Bank and since the Israeli occupation of this area in 1967 it has not been possible to hold elections there. For a time membership of the House continued on the basis of pre-1967 membership but was eventually suspended in 1974. The Lower House was recalled in January 1984. By-elections were held in March 1984 to fill East Bank seats which had become vacant as a result of the death of deputies elected in 1967, and the House appointed new West Bank members to bring itself up to full strength. The King himself appoints the members of the Council of Ministers. Crown Prince Hassan normally acts as Regent when King Hussein is away from Jordan. Following the Arab summit meeting at Rabat in October 1974, and the U.N. General Assembly in November, at which the Palestinian Liberation Organization achieved recognition as the sole legitimate representative of the Palestinian people, King Hussein took measures to amend the 1952 constitution to take account of the resultant change in the status of the West Bank in relation to the administration of Jordan east of the river.

Production and Industry.—West Jordan is fertile, though many areas have suffered from soil erosion. In East Jordan the main agricultural areas are the east part of the Jordan Valley, the hills overlooking the Valley and the flatter country to the south of Amman and around Madaba and Irbid. The rest of the country is desert and semi-desert. The principal crops are wheat, barley, vegetables, olives and fruit (mainly grapes and citrus fruits). Agricultural production in the Jordan Valley has increased considerably in recent years due to the extension of the East Ghor Canal and the King Talal Dam. The only important industrial products are raw phosphates (production 1987: 6,800,000 tons) and potash, most of which is exported. There are schemes under construction for the production of potash and phosphate fertilizers. The Trans-Arabian oil pipeline (Tapline) runs through North Jordan on its way from the eastern province of Saudi Arabia to the Lebanese coast of Sidon. A branch pipeline feeds a refinery at Zerqa (production 1987: 2,404,533 tons) which meets most of Jordan's requirements for refined petroleum products.

Tourism has recovered steadily since the Israeli occupation of the West Bank in 1967. International-class hotels have been built to cater for businessmen, and for tourists visiting the archaeological sites of East Jordan and the resort of Aqaba.

Communications.—The trunk road system is good. Amman is linked to Damascus, Baghdad and Jeddah by tarred roads which are of considerable importance in the overland trade of the Middle East. The former Hejaz Railway enters Jordan east of Ramtha and runs through Zerqa and Amman to Ma'an with a spur to the top of the Ras al-Naqb escarpment. The formerly abandoned section from Ma'an to Medina in Saudi Arabia is being studied and redesigned by consultants. A total of 2,555 vessels called at Aqaba in 1987 and 20,015,371 tons of cargo were handled. The Royal Jordanian Airline operates from Amman Airport to other cities in the Middle East and Gulf area, to most major European cities, to five destinations in North America, and to Bangkok in the Far East. There is also a service to the airport at Aqaba.

FINANCE

	1986	1987
	JD (Thousands)	
Revenue	937,100	804,170
Expenditure	1,002,600	1,008,750
Surplus/Deficit...........	−65,500	−204,580

Trade with U.K.

	1986	1987
Imports from U.K.	£130,385,000	£188,998,000
Exports to U.K.	49,766,000	29,285,000

CAPITAL.—Amman. Population, 1,100,000 (1988 estimate).
CURRENCY.—Jordanian Dinar of 1,000 Fils.
FLAG.—Black, white and green horizontal stripes, surcharged with white seven-point star on red triangle.
NATIONAL ANTHEM.—Long Live the King.
NATIONAL DAY.—May 25 (Independence Day).

BRITISH EMBASSY
Abdoun (P.O. Box 87),
Amman
[Amman 823100]
Ambassador Extraordinary and Plenipotentiary, His Excellency Anthony Reeve, C.M.G. (1988).
Counsellors, H. N. H. Synnott (*Head of Chancery and Consul-General*); P. J. F. Mansley.
Defence Attaché, Col. A. E. Cornick.
Air Attaché, Wing-Cdr. P. W. Mayes.

First Secretaries, M. Thomas (*Commercial*); D. H. Whitbread (*Information*); R. Kay M.B.E. (*Consul and Administration*).
Second Secretaries, M. Ives (*Development*); N. S. Archer; W. Hamilton (*Commercial*).

British Council Representative, D. A. M. Latta, Rainbow Street, (P.O. Box 634), Jebel Amman, Amman.

KAMPUCHEA

COALITION GOVERNMENT OF
DEMOCRATIC KAMPUCHEA

President, Prince Norodom Sihanouk (*resigned* July 1988).
Vice-President responsible for Foreign Affairs, Khieu Samphan.
Prime Minister and Defence Minister, Tie Banh.

PEOPLE'S REPUBLIC OF KAMPUCHEA

Head of State, Heng Samrin.
Chairman of Council of Ministers and Foreign Minister, Hun Sen.

Area and Population.—Situated between Thailand and the south of Vietnam and extending from the border with Laos on the north to the Gulf of Thailand, Cambodia covers an area of 69,898 sq. miles, (181,035 sq. km.). It has a population (1985 U.N. estimate) of 7,284,000. The climate is tropical monsoon with a rainy season from May to October.

Fifty per cent. of the total land area is forest or jungle. Around the Tonlé Sap lake in the centre of the country and along the Mekong river, which traverses the country, there is ample fertile land for the support of the population in times of peace.

History.—Once a powerful kingdom, which, as the Khmer Empire, flourished between the tenth and fourteenth centuries, Cambodia became a French protectorate in 1863 and was granted independence within the French Union as an Associate State in 1949. Full independence was proclaimed on November 9, 1953, and the process was completed when, in January, 1955, the Kingdom of Cambodia became financially and economically independent not only of France but also of Laos and Vietnam. For the next fifteen years the political life of the country was dominated by Prince Norodom Sihanouk, first as King, then as Head of Government after he had abdicated in favour of his father and finally (following his father's death in 1960) as Head of State.

On March 18, 1970, during his absence from the country, Prince Sihanouk was deposed as Head of State by a vote of the National Assembly. A Republic was declared on October 9, 1970, and the name of the country changed to the Khmer Republic.

In April 1970 widespread fighting developed between communist insurgents and government forces which gradually developed into a general civil war. In April 1975 Phnom-Penh fell to the North Vietnamese-backed Khmer Rouge. Prince Sihanouk returned to Cambodia on September 9, as nominal Head of State. However, a new Constitution was promulgated in Jan. 1976 and elections to a People's Representative Assembly were held in March. Prince Sihanouk resigned as Head of State in April, and Khieu Samphan was elected President of the State Presidium. A Government led by Pol Pot, the leader of the Khmer Rouge (Communist) party, was appointed; during the years of Khmer Rouge rule thousands of Cambodians died or fled into exile. Relations between the Khmer Rouge regime and their Vietnamese backers deteriorated sharply, and on Dec. 25, 1978

Vietnamese troops invaded Cambodia in support of an uprising. The Cambodian capital, Phnom-Penh, fell on Jan. 7, 1979. The following day the Cambodian National United Front for National Salvation established a People's Revolutionary Council, recognized by Vietnam, U.S.S.R. and by other, chiefly Soviet-aligned, countries. The P.R.K. Government, backed by an occupation army of some 120,000 Vietnamese troops, more or less controls Kampuchea, but is challenged by the guerrilla forces of the Coalition Government of Democratic Kampuchea, which was formed in June 1982 by the Khmer Rouge and non-communist groups. Talks intended to end the conflict in Kampuchea continued throughout 1988. In the meantime the Vietnamese continued to withdraw their forces from the country. The C.G.D.K. occupies Kampuchea's seat at the U.N.

Economy.—Kampuchea has an economy based on agriculture, fishing and forestry, the bulk of its people being rice-growing farmers. In addition to rice, which is the staple crop, the major products are rubber, livestock, maize, timber, pepper, palm sugar, fresh and dried fish, kapok, beans, soya and tobacco. Rice and rubber used to be the main exports though production was brought to a standstill by the hostilities. Following the Khmer Rouge victory, the populations of Phnom-Penh and other towns were forcibly evacuated to the country to work on the land, and re-establish the plantations producing such crops as cotton, rubber and bananas. Following the Vietnamese invasion of 1978 the towns were repopulated and commerce revived; currency was reintroduced. Factories, in particular textile mills, iron smelting works and cement works were put back in production.

Trade with U.K.

	1986	1987
Imports from U.K.	£217,000	£435,000
Exports to U.K.	58,000	268,000

Communications.—The country had over 5,000 kilometres of roads, of which nearly half were hard-surfaced and passable in the rainy season, although now in a state of disrepair. There are two railways, one from Phnom-Penh to the Thai border; the other from Phnom-Penh to Kampot and Kompong Som, but operations and repairs are hindered by the continuing fighting. Phnom-Penh is on a river capable of receiving ships of up to 2,500 tons all the year round. The deep water port at Kompong Som on the Gulf of Thailand can receive ships up to 10,000 tons. The port is linked to Phnom-Penh by a modern highway.

Religion and Education.—The state religion was Buddhism of the "Little Vehicle". The new constitution guaranteed religious freedom, but in practice Buddhism was suppressed by the Khmer Rouge. There has been some revival recently. There were also small Muslim and Christian communities, but many members of them died or fled the country during Khmer Rouge rule. The national language is Khmer. In the years preceding the civil war considerable efforts were devoted to the development of education and new schools, colleges and technical institutes had been established. Until April 1975 there was a Buddhist University in Phnom-Penh, and several residential teachers' training colleges were in operation. However, most of the country's educated elite died under the Khmer Rouge regime, which closed all institutions of higher education. The University was re-opened in 1988.

CAPITAL.—Phnom-Penh.
CURRENCY.—Riel of 100 Sen.
FLAG.—(C.G.D.K.) Red, with a yellow three-towered temple in the middle. (P.R.K.) Red with a yellow five-towered temple in the middle.
NATIONAL DAY.—April 17.

KOREA

Korea is situated between 124° 11″ and 130° 57′ E. long., and between 33° 7′ and 43° 1″ N. lat. It has an area of 84,565 sq. miles (219,022 sq. km.), with an estimated population of approx. 62 million, of whom about 42 million live south of the present dividing line. The southern and western coasts are fringed with innumerable islands, of which the largest, forming a province of its own, is Cheju.

History.—The last native dynasty (Yi) ruled from 1392 until 1910, in which year Japan formally annexed Korea. The country remained an integral part of the Japanese Empire until the defeat of Japan in 1945, when it was occupied by troops of the U.S.A. and the U.S.S.R., the 38th parallel being fixed as the boundary between the two zones of occupation. The U.S. Government endeavoured to reach agreement with the Soviet Government for the creation of a Korean Government for the whole country and the withdrawal of all Russian and American troops. These efforts met with no success, and in September, 1947, the U.S. Government laid the whole question of the future of Korea before the General Assembly of the United Nations. The Assembly in November, 1947, resolved that elections should be held in Korea for a National Assembly under the supervision of a temporary Commission formed for that purpose by the United Nations and that the National Assembly when elected should set up a Government. The Soviet Government refused to allow the Commission to visit the Russian Occupied Zone and in consequence it was only able to discharge its function in that part of Korea which lies to the south of the 38th parallel.

A general election was held on May 10, 1948, and the first National Assembly met in Seoul on May 31. The Assembly passed a constitution on July 12, and on July 20 elected Dr. Syngman Rhee as the first President of the Republic of Korea. On August 15, 1948, the Republic was formerly inaugurated and American Military Government came to an end.

Meanwhile in the Russian-occupied zone north of the 38th parallel the Democratic People's Republic had been set up with its capital at Pyongyang; a Supreme People's Soviet was elected in September 1948, and a Soviet-style Constitution adopted.

The Korean War.—The country remained effectively divided into two along the line of 38th parallel until the aggression of June 25, 1950, when the North Korean forces invaded South Korea. An emergency meeting of the U.N. Security Council adopted a Resolution calling for an immediate cease fire and the withdrawal of North Korean forces. This was ignored and the communist advance continued. In response to Security Council recommendations that United Nations members should furnish assistance to repel the attack, 16 nations including the U.S.A. and the U.K. came to the aid of the Republic of Korea. However the communist advance could not be contained until eventually a front was established around Pusan. Later, following a successful U.S. marine landing at Inchon, the communist forces were driven beyond the 38th parallel. At this point the Chinese "volunteers" joined the campaign and although the U.N. forces were initially driven back beyond Seoul they regrouped and threw the communist forces back to approximately the old dividing line. The fighting was ended by an Armistice Agreement signed by the U.N. Commander-in-Chief and the Commander of the North Korean army and the Chinese People's "volunteers" on July 27, 1953. By this Agreement (which was not signed by the representatives of the Republic of Korea) the line of division between North and South Korea remained in the neighbourhood of the 38th parallel. The Geneva Conference discussed Korea in 1954, but failed to agree on measures for re-unifying the country. Talks between North and South Korea on the reunification of the country have taken place intermittently.

Language and Literature.—Despite the great cultural influence of the Chinese, Koreans have developed and preserved their own cultural heritage. The Korean language is of the Ural-Altaic Group. Its script, Hangul, was invented in the 15th century; prior to this Chinese characters alone were used. Also invented around this time was the first metal movable printing type. The first works translated into Hangul were Buddhist, Confucian and other classics and it was only in the late 19th century that the European influence first began to be felt.

REPUBLIC OF KOREA
(Daehan minkuk)

President, Roh Tae Woo (February 24, 1988).

CABINET

Prime Minister, Lee Hyun Jae.
Deputy P.M. and Head of the Economic Planning Board, Rha Woong Bae.
Foreign Affairs, Choi Kwang Soo.
Home Affairs, Lee Chun Koo.
Finance, Sakong Il.
Justice, Chung Hae Chang.
Defence, Oh Ja Bok.
Education, Kim Young Shik.
Sports, Cho Sang Ho.
Agriculture and Fisheries, Yun Kum Kwan.
Energy and Resources, Lee Bong Soo.
Construction, Choi Dong Sup.
Health and Social Affairs, Kwon Ei Hyuck.
Labour, Choi Myon Hyon.
Transportation, Lee Bom Jun.
Communication, Oh Myong.
Culture and Information, Chung Han Mo.
Government Administration, Kim Yong Gap.
Science and Technology, Lee Kwan.
Unification, Lee Kong Gi.
Political Affairs I, Kim Yun Hwan.
Political Affairs II, Cho Kyong Hui.
Legal Affairs, Hyon Hong Choo.
Veterans' Affairs, Chon Sok Hong.
Dir. of National Security Planning Agency, Bae Mung In.

KOREAN EMBASSY
4 Palace Gate, W8 5NF
[01–581 0247]

Ambassador Extraordinary and Plenipotentiary, His Excellency Jay Hee Oh (1987).
Minister, Ri Hoon Hur.

The Republic of Korea has been officially recognized by the Governments of the United States, France, United Kingdom, and most other countries except the communist bloc.

President Syngman Rhee was overthrown by a popular rising in 1960. After a year of unstable government a new regime was set up on May 16, 1961 by an army officers' coup led by Major General Park Chung Hee. On March 22, 1962 he took over as acting President. He was elected President in December 1963 and again in 1967, 1971, 1972 and 1978, but was assassinated on October 26, 1979. The country was placed under partial martial law. The then Prime Minister Choi Kyu Hah was elected President that December but resigned in August 1980 to be succeeded by Gen. Chun Doo Hwan. The constitution was revised and new elections held. President Chun was re-elected and his Democratic Justice Party gained a majority in the National Assembly after elections in

March 1981. Following extensive political unrest a new constitution was agreed in October 1987. Roh Tae Woo became President in Feb. 1988. In elections to the new 299-seat National Assembly the largest number of seats (125) were won by the Democratic Justice Party but it failed to achieve an overall majority.

Constitution.—The President, who is Head of State, Chief of the Executive and Commander-in-Chief of the Armed Forces, is directly elected for a single term of five years. He appoints the Prime Minister with the consent of the National Assembly, and members of the State Council on the recommendation of the Prime Minister. The President is also empowered to take wide-ranging measures in an emergency, including the declaration of martial law, but must obtain the agreement of the National Assembly. The National Assembly is directly elected for a four-year term.

Armed Forces.—The Republic of Korea has an army of about 520,000, a small navy mostly for coastal patrol and protection duties, an air force with over 500 combat aircraft and a marine corps which is incorporated in the navy. About six per cent of the nation's G.N.P. is currently spent on defence.

Education and Religion.—Primary education is compulsory for six years from the age of seven. Secondary and higher education is extensive. The national illiteracy rate is among the lowest in Asia. There is freedom of religion. Buddhism has the most followers (13 million) followed by Protestantism (8 million) and Confucianism (4·7 million). Catholics number 2·2 million.

Agriculture and Fisheries.—The soil is fertile but the arable land is limited by the mountainous nature of the country. Staple agricultural products are rice, barley and other cereals, beans, tobacco and hemp. Fruit growing and sericulture are also practised. Ginseng, a medicinal root much used by both the Chinese and Koreans, forms a useful source of revenue. The Korean fishing industry is a major contributor to both food supply and exports.

Minerals.—The Republic of Korea is deficient in mineral resources, except for deposits of coal on the East Coast and tungsten. There are some prospects of discovering oil in the sea between Korea and Japan.

Finance.—The budget for 1986 totals about U.S.$15,500 million.

Trade and Industry.—Since the beginning of 1962 a series of successful five-year plans resulted in real economic growth averaging around 10 per cent a year. The 6th economic development plan (1987–91) envisages a growth rate of 7·5 per cent. Annual per capita G.N.P. is U.S.$2,094.

Since the 1960s the Republic of Korea has industrialized rapidly on the basis of greatly expanded exports. Important exports include cars, electrical and electronic equipment, footwear, ships, railway rolling stock and iron and steel products.

TRADE

	1984	1985
Imports	U.S.$30,796 m.	U.S.$31,132 m.
Exports	28,090 m.	30,273 m.

Trade with U.K.

	1986	1987
Imports from U.K.	£288,421,000	£427,229,000
Exports to U.K.	£661,975,000	936,038,000

Communications and Transport.—In 1980 there were 15,599 km. of paved road. Seoul has a subway system and there are national railway and airline systems. Korean Air operates regular flights to Europe, the United States, the Middle East and South East Asia. Pusan and Inchon are the major ports

with Pusan serving the industrial areas of the southeast. Inchon, 28 miles from Seoul, serves the capital, but development and operation at Inchon are hampered by a tidal variation of 9–10 metres.

CAPITAL.—Seoul, population (1988), 10,000,000. Other main centres are ΨPusan (pop. 3,160,000), Taegu (pop. 1,607,000) and ΨInchon (pop. 1,084,000).

CURRENCY.—Won of 100 Jeon.

FLAG.—White, with red over blue device in centre, three black parallel bars, some broken, in each quarter.

NATIONAL ANTHEM.—"Aegukka".

NATIONAL DAY.—August 15 (Independence Day).

BRITISH EMBASSY
No. 4, Chung-Dong, Chung-Ku, Seoul 100
[Seoul 735–7341/3]

Ambassador Extraordinary and Plenipotentiary, His Excellency Lawrence John Middleton, C.M.G. (1986).

Counsellor, R. M. Jackson, C.V.O. *(Commercial).*

Defence and Military Attaché, Brig. D. S. Williams.

First Secretaries, W. Morris *(Head of Chancery and Consul);* A. V. Hill *(Commercial/ Information).*

Cultural Attaché and British Council Representative, D. G. Rogers, Room 401 Anglican Church Annex, 3/7 Chung Dong, Chung-ku, Seoul.

There is an Honorary British Consul at Pusan.

BRITISH CHAMBER OF COMMERCE, c/o Chartered Bank, 1st and 2nd Floors, Samsung Building, 50, 1-Ka Ulchi Ro, Chung-Ku, Seoul.

DEMOCRATIC PEOPLE'S REPUBLIC OF KOREA
(Chosun Minchu-chui Inmin Kongwa-guk)

Politburo of the Central Committee, Kim Il-sung; Kim Chong-il; O Chin-u *(full members and members of the presidium);* Pak Song-chol; Yim Chun-chu; So Chol; Kim Yong-nam; Yon Hyong-muk; O Kuk-yol; Kang Song-san; So Yun-sok; Ho Tam; Yi Chong-ok; Yi Kun-mo; Hong Song-nam; Kyu Ung-tae *(full members).* Choe Kwang; Cho Se-ung; Chong Chun-ki; Hyon Mu-kwang; Kang Huiwon; Chon Pyong-ho; Kim Pok-sin; Hong Si-hak; Yi Son-sil *(alternate members).*

Secretariat of the Central Committee, Kim Il-sung *(General Secretary);* Kim Chong-il; Yon Hyong-muk; Hwang Chang-yop; Ho Chong-suk; So Kwan-hui; Ho Tam; Kye Ung-tae; Kang Song-san; Chon Pyong-ho; Choe Tae-pok.

The area of North Korea is 46,540 sq. miles (120,538 sq. km.), with a population of about 20,385,000 (1985 U.N. estimate). North Korea is rich in minerals and industry has been developed, but the economy has stagnated in recent years because of poor planning and a shortage of foreign exchange. The armed forces are believed to number about 750,000 men.

Government.—The Constitution of the Democratic People's Republic of Korea provides for a Supreme People's Assembly, presently consisting of 615 deputies, which is elected every four years by universal suffrage. The Assembly elects a President, and the Central People's Committee. In turn, the Central People's Committee directs the Administrative Council which implements the policy formulated by the Committee. The Administrative Council (31 members), formally the government of N. Korea, includes the Prime Minister and various ministers. In practice, however, the country is ruled by the Communist Party which elects a Central Committee; this in turn appoints a Politburo. The Senior Ministers of the

Administrative Council are all members of the Communist Central Committee and the majority are also members of the Politburo.

Trade with U.K.

	1986	1987
Imports from U.K........	£3,331,000	£2,198,000
Exports to U.K.	1,374,000	641,000

CAPITAL.—Pyongyang (population, approx. 1,500,000).

CURRENCY.—Won of 100 Chon.

FLAG.—Broad red horizontal band bordered by white lines bearing a five-point red star on a white disc in centre; blue horizontal bands at top and bottom.

NATIONAL DAY.—September 8.

NATIONAL ANTHEM.—A Chi Mun Bin No Ra I Gang San (Shine bright, oh dawn, on this land so fair).

KUWAIT
(Dowlat al- Kuwait)

Amir, H. H. Sheikh Jaber Al Ahmad Al Sabah, *born* 1928; acceded Jan. 1, 1978.

CABINET

Prime Minister, H.H. Crown Prince, Sheikh Saad Al-Abdullah.

Deputy Premier and Minister of Foreign Affairs, Sheikh Sabah Al-Ahmed Al Jaber.

Education, Anwar Abdulla Al Nouri.

Social Affairs, and Labour, Sheikh Jaber Mubarak Al Hamad.

Finance, Jasem Mohammed Al Khorafi.

Awqaf and Islamic Affairs, Khalid Ahmed Al Jassar.

Communications, Abdul Mohsen Al-Sharahan.

Minister of State for Cabinet, Rashed Abdul Aziz Al Rashed.

Defence, Sheikh Nawaf Al Ahmen Al Jaber.

Minister of State for Foreign Affairs, Saoud Mohammed Al Osaimi.

Justice and Legal Affairs, Dhari Abdulla Al Othman.

Public Works, Abdul Rahman Ibrahim Al Houti.

Minister of State for Municipality Affairs, Abdul Rahman Khalid Al Ghunaim.

Public Health, Abdul Razzaq Youssef.

Oil, Sheikh Ali Al-Khalifa Al-Athbi.

Minister of State for Services Affairs, Issa Mohammed Al Mazeidi.

Commerce and Industry, Faisal Abdul Razaq Al Khalid.

Planning, Mohammed Soleiman Sayed Ali.

Electricity and Water, Hamoud Abdulla Al-Raqba.

Interior, Sheikh Salem Sabah Al Salem.

Minister of State for Housing Affairs, Naser Abdulla Al Rodhan.

Information, Sheikh Nasser Mohammed Al Ahmed.

KUWAIT EMBASSY IN LONDON
45–46 Queen's Gate, SW7.
[01–589 4533]

Ambassador Extraordinary and Plenipotentiary, His Excellency Ghazi M. A. Al-Rayes (1980).

Area and Population.—Kuwait extends along the shore of the Persian Gulf from Iraq to Saudi Arabia, with an area of 6,880 sq. miles (17,818 sq. km.). Kuwait has a dry, desert climate with a summer season extending from April to September. The mean temperature varies between 29–45° C. in summer, and 8–18° C. in winter. Humidity rarely exceeds 60 per cent except in July and August. The population is 1,695,128 (census 1985), of which about 42 per cent are Kuwaiti citizens, the remainder being large numbers of other Arab peoples, Iranians, Indians and Pakistanis. The total European and American population is about 12,500. The gross population growth rate is 6·4 per cent, a growth rate of 3·5 per cent for Kuwaiti citizens.

The official language is Arabic, and English is widely spoken as a second language. Islam is the official religion, though religious freedom is constitutionally guaranteed.

Government.—Although Kuwait had been independent for some years, the "exclusive agreement" of 1899 between the Sheikh of Kuwait and the British Government was formally abrogated by an exchange of letters dated June 19, 1961. This exchange was immediately followed by Iraqi claims to sovereignty over Kuwait, but on Oct. 4, 1963, Iraq recognized Kuwait's independence although the Kuwait-Iraqi border has not yet been determined formally. Under the Constitution legislative power is vested in the Amir and the 50-member National Assembly, and executive power in the Amir and the Cabinet. The sixth National Assembly was elected for a four year term in March 1985.

Education, etc.—As a result of the very considerable oil revenues, the Kuwait Government embarked on a large scale development scheme and plans for social services. Education and medical treatment are free. New hospitals and schools continue to be built. Kuwait University was opened in 1966, and in 1985 had 16,000 students. In 1983 there were over 433,000 pupils at government and private schools.

Public Utilities.—Kuwait has a domestic water supply from water distillation plants which operate on natural gas from the oil fields. These plants can produce over 118,000,000 gallons of fresh water daily. Total water storage capacity, in reservoirs and water towers, amounts to over 1,201 million gallons. A natural source of fresh water, discovered at Raudhatain in the north of the State, has been developed to produce up to 3,000,000 gallons per day for at least 20 years and a pipeline has been built to carry the water to Kuwait town.

Electricity is produced by four power stations in Kuwait. Production in 1985 was 18,694 million Kwh.

Communications.—Ships of British, Dutch, Kuwaiti and other lines make regular calls at Kuwait. Several international and Middle Eastern airlines operate regular air services, and other companies make non-scheduled flights to Kuwait under charter. There is a network of dual-carriageway roads and more are under construction. Telecommunications and postal services are conducted by the Kuwait Government, which has built an earth satellite station.

Finance.— Revenue for the financial year 1985–86 was *KD*3,120 m and expenditure was *KD*4,200 m. Oil revenues constitute 91·8 per cent. of total revenue. There are a large number of investment banks in some of which the Government holds equity. The banking system is controlled by the Central Bank of Kuwait.

Production.—The G.N.P. of Kuwait in 1983 was estimated at *KD*7,593 million.

Despite the desert terrain, 8·4 per cent of land is under cultivation, fruit and vegetables being the main crops. Shrimp fishing is becoming important.

The Government of Kuwait began to participate in the ownership of the British- and American-owned Kuwait Oil Company in 1974 and an agreement was signed in November 1975 which brought 100 per cent government ownership. After a reorganization of the national oil industry in 1980, all the business was taken over by the Kuwait Petroleum Corporation.

The centre of Kuwait oil production is at Burgan, south of Kuwait City. Oil is also lifted in the Kuwait/Saudi Arabia Partitioned Zone (Wafra) south of the State. Oil is exported through a specially constructed port at Mina al Ahmadi. Production of crude oil in

1984 was approximately 1,115 million barrels per day. About 3,000 people are employed, including Kuwaitis, British, Americans, Indians, Pakistanis and citizens of other Arab countries.

Trade.—Oil exports constitute about 88 per cent. of Kuwait's total exports. Non-oil exports include chemical fertilizers, ammonia and other chemicals, metal pipes, shrimps and building materials; re-exports accounted for 73 per cent. of non-oil exports in 1982. Major trading partners are Asian countries, followed by E.C. countries and Arab states.

	1984
Imports	KD2,780m
Exports	3,500m

Trade with U.K.

	1986	1987
Imports from U.K.	£300,586,000	£225,168,000
Exports to U.K.	58,517,000	81,530,000

CAPITAL.— Ψ Kuwait (population, excluding suburbs, 400,000).

CURRENCY.—Kuwaiti Dinar of 1,000 Fils.

FLAG.—Three horizontal stripes of green, white and red, with black trapezoid next to staff.

NATIONAL DAY.—February 25.

BRITISH EMBASSY
P.O. Box Safat 2,
Arabian Gulf Street, Kuwait
[Kuwait 2432046/9]

Ambassador Extraordinary and Plenipotentiary, His Excellency Peter Robert Mossom Hinchcliffe, C.M.G., C.V.O. (1987).

Counsellor, D. R. MacLennan.

First Secretaries, T. Millson (*Financial and Economic, and Head of Chancery*); L. Banks (*Consul*); A. R. Michael (*Commercial*); J. Brand; M. J. Reynolds (*Chancery*); A. Young.

British Council Representative, D. Brown, O.B.E., P.O. Box 345, 2 al Arabi Street, Mansouriyah. There is a library in *Kuwait.*

LAOS
(Sathalamalid Pasathu' Paait)

President, Phoumi Vongvichit (*acting*).

President of the Supreme People's Assembly, Sisomphone Lovansay (*acting*).

Deputy President, Khamsouk Keola.

COUNCIL OF MINISTERS

Prime Minister, Kaysone Phomvihane.

First Deputy P.M., Nouhak Phoumsavan (*responsibility for economic matters*).

Deputy P.M.s, Phoun Sipaseut (*Minister, Foreign Affairs*); Khamtai Siphandone (*Minister of Defence*); Sali Vongkhamsao (*Chairman, State Planning Committee*).

Ministers attached to the P.M.'s Office, Ma Khaikhamphithoun. (*Special Affairs*); Souli Nanthavong (*Chairman, State Commission for Science and Technology*); Thongchanh Ouplavan (*Prices*); Soth Phetrasi (*Mapping and Frontiers*).

Agriculture, Irrigation and Agricultural Co-operatives, Inkong Mahavong.

Construction, Khemphon Phouipaseut.

Culture, Thongsing Thammavong.

Education, Bountiam Phitsamai.

Finance, Yao Phonvantha.

Health, Khamlien Pholsena.

Industry, Handicrafts and Forestry, Maysouk Saysompheng.

Chairman, Information, Press, Radio and Television Committee, Interior, Sisavath Keobounphan.

Justice, Kou Souvannamethi.

Materials and Technology, Thongsouk Saisangkhi.

Chairman, National Bank, Bousbong Souvannavong.

Chairman, Nationalities Committee, Nhiaveu Lobliayao.

Chairman, Social Welfare and Veterans Committee, Meun Somvichit.

Trade, Vanthong Sengmuong.

Transport, Posts and Telecommunications, Phao Bounnaphon.

Position and Extent.—The People's Democratic Republic of Laos is in the northerly part of Indo-China, lying between China and Vietnam, on the north and east, and Burma and Thailand on the west. Laos has a common boundary with Kampuchea to the south. The area of the country is 91,429 sq. miles (231,800 sq. km.), with a population (1985 U.N. estimate) of 4,117,000.

History.—The Kingdom of Lane Xang, the Land of a Million Elephants, was founded in the 14th century, but broke up at the beginning of the 15th century into the separate kingdoms of Luang Prabang and Vientiane and the Principality of Champassac, which together came under French protection in 1893. In 1945 the Japanese executed a coup and suppressed the French administration. Under a Constitution of 1947 Laos became a constitutional monarchy under King Sisvang Vong of the House of Luang Prabang, and an independent sovereign state in 1949. The next twenty-five years in Laos were marked by power struggles and civil war.

After the fall of Saigon in April 1975, internal resistance to the *Pathet Lao* (communists) crumbled; Communist troops occupied the whole country and, though still paying lip-service to the 1973 ceasefire agreement and maintaining a facade of coalition, the *Pathet Lao* took over the government and began to implement an authoritarian regime with policies of austerity and economic self-sufficiency. On December 2, 1975, following the abdication of the King, Laos was declared a People's Democratic Republic and the *Pathet Lao* assumed full charge of the country.

Economy.—There is no significant industrial base in Laos, an estimated 85 per cent. of the work force being engaged in agriculture, largely concerned with rice cultivation. Rice production in 1984 amounted to 1·3 million tonnes, thus rendering the country theoretically self-sufficient in this staple food. In 1983, however, the authorities stated that due to late rains there was an overall shortfall of about 100,000 tons.

In 1984, exports amounted to US$36·2 m. and imports to US$98·4 m. Hydro-electric power was 88·3 per cent. of exports, timber 8·5 per cent. and coffee 1·2 per cent. Clearing agreements have been signed with certain socialist countries and the trade gap is largely financed by foreign aid, of which some 60 per cent. is provided by socialist countries.

Laos' economic performance so far has been poor and shows no signs of early recovery, the free market rate for the dollar is much higher than the official rate and prices of consumer items continue to increase.

Currency.—In January 1980 a "new" *Kip* replaced the former currency. In July 1983 the non-commercial rate of exchange was rectified by the State Bank.

Trade with U.K.

	1986	1987
Imports from U.K.	£1,460,000	£1,742,000
Exports to U.K.	150,000	621,000

CAPITAL.—Vientiane, population (estimated 1984) 120,000.

CURRENCY.—Kip of 100 At.

FLAG.—Blue background with a central white circle, framed by 2 horizontal red stripes.
NATIONAL DAY.—December 2.

BRITISH AMBASSADOR, *resides at* Bangkok, Thailand.

LEBANON
(Al-Jumhouriya al-Lubnaniya)

President of the Republic of Lebanon, Amin Gemayel, *elected,* Sept. 21, 1982.
Prime Minister, Selim Hoss (*acting*).

LEBANESE EMBASSY IN LONDON
21 Kensington Palace Gardens, W8 4QM
[01–229 7265/8485]

Ambassador Extraordinary and Plenipotentiary, His Excellency Gen. Ahmed El-Hajj (1983).
First Secretaries, Michel El-Khoury; Mohammed Dib.
Consular Section, 15 Palace Gardens Mews, W8 (01–727 6696)

Area and Population.—Lebanon forms a strip about 120 miles in length and varying in width from 30 to 35 miles, along the Mediterranean littoral, and extending from the Israel frontier on the south to the Nahr al Kebir (15 miles north of Tripoli) on the north; its eastern boundary runs down the Anti-Lebanon range and then down the Great Central depression, the *Beqaa,* from which flow the rivers Orontes and Litani. It is divided into 5 districts, North Lebanon, Mount Lebanon, Beirut, South Lebanon and Beqaa. The seaward slopes of the mountains have a Mediterranean climate and vegetation. The inland range of Anti-Lebanon has the characteristics of steppe country. There is a mixed Arabic-speaking population of Christians, Moslems and Druses. The total area of Lebanon is 4,015 sq. miles, (10,400 sq. km.), population (1985 U.N. estimate), 2,668,000.

Government.—Lebanon became an independent State on Sept. 1, 1920, administered under French Mandate until Nov. 22, 1943. Powers were transferred to the Lebanese Government from Jan. 1, 1944, and French troops were withdrawn in 1946.

In April 1975, serious fighting broke out in Beirut between members of the predominantly Christian Phalangist Party and mainly Moslem militias later supported by Palestinian guerrillas based in Lebanon. The fighting continued and increased throughout 1975 and 1976. In the autumn of 1976 the Arab Deterrent Forces composed mainly of Syrian troops, imposed an effective ceasefire. In March 1978, Israeli forces invaded but withdrew some months later, handing over their positions, except for a belt in the south, to the U.N. Interim Force in Lebanon (UNIFIL). Major bouts of fighting took place in October 1978 and April/May 1981, interspersed with regular clashes on a smaller scale. In the summer of 1982 Israeli forces again invaded the country, penetrating as far as Beirut. Following negotiations, Palestine Liberation Organization guerrillas left Beirut for various Arab countries.

The north-east of the country is currently occupied by Syrian and Palestinian forces. Although the bulk of Israeli troops withdrew from southern Lebanon in 1985, a buffer zone controlled by Israeli-backed Christian militias has been established along the Israeli-Lebanon border.

Reconciliation talks in Geneva and Lausanne, Switzerland, in March 1984, failed to produce any lasting agreement. Attempts to impose a Syrian-brokered accord in December 1985 failed when the main Christian militia overthrew the leadership which had signed it.

Production.—Fruits are the most important products and include citrus fruit, apples, grapes, bananas and olives. There is some light industry, mostly for the production of consumer goods, but most factories have been adversely affected by the instability of the past thirteen years. There is little remaining of the famous cedars of Lebanon.

Communications.—A railway runs from Beirut to Damascus, connecting at Rayak with a branch line which runs from Tripoli through Homs, Hama and Aleppo to the Turkish frontier, from Nusaybin to the Iraq frontier at Tel Kotchek. A railway also runs up the coast from Nakowia to Tripoli. The railways are not functioning as a result of the civil war. There is an international airport at Beirut, served by the national carrier MEA and a few others from East Europe. Operations can be disrupted by fighting in the city.

Archaeology, etc.—Lebanon has some important historical remains, notably Baalbek (Heliopolis) which contains the ruins of first to third century Roman temples and Jubail (Biblos), one of the oldest continuously inhabited towns in the world, and ancient Tyre.

Language and Literature.—Arabic is the official language, and French and English are also widely used.

Education.—There are six universities in Beirut, the American and the French (R.C.) Universities established in the last century, and the Lebanese National University, the Beirut University College, the Kaskik Saint Esprit University and the Arab University which are recent foundations in the early stages of development. There are several institutions for vocational training, some of which have been rendered inoperative by the civil war, and there is a good provision throughout the country of primary and secondary schools, among which are a great number of private schools.

Finance.—No reliable statistics have been published for some time. The country is known to have a deficit, and the Lebanese £ has lost much of its value against foreign currencies.

Trade.—Principal imports are gold and precious metals, machinery and electrical equipment, textiles and yarns, vegetable products, iron and steel goods, and motor vehicles. There has been a gradual decline in the overall amount of imports, as a result of continued instability.

Principal exports include gold and precious metals, fruits and vegetables, textiles, building materials, furniture, plastic goods, foodstuffs, tobacco and wine.

At one time there was a considerable transit trade through Beirut into the Arab hinterland. Lebanon is the terminal for two oil pipe lines, one formerly belonging to the Iraq Petroleum Company, debouching at Tripoli, the other belonging to the Trans Arabian Pipeline Company, at Sidon. These lines have not functioned for some years, for political/security considerations.

Trade with U.K.

	1986	1987
Imports from U.K.	£55,867,000	£40,707,000
Exports to U.K.	9,845,000	9,528,000

CAPITAL.— ΨBeirut (population, 702,000). Other towns are ΨTripoli (175,000), Zahlé (46,800), ΨSidon (24,740), ΨTyre (14,000).
CURRENCY.—Lebanese Pound (£L) of 100 Piastres.
FLAG.—Horizontal bands of red, white and red with a green cedar of Lebanon in the centre of the white band.
NATIONAL ANTHEM.—Kulluna Lil Watan Lil'ula Lil'alam (We all belong to the home land).
NATIONAL DAY.—November 22.

BRITISH EMBASSY
Shamma Building, Raouché, Ras Beirut, Beirut
[Beirut 417007]

Ambassador Extraordinary and Plenipotentiary, His
Excellency Allan John Ramsay (1988).

LIBERIA
(Republic of Liberia)

President and Commander-in-Chief, Samuel K. Doe.

CABINET

Defence, Maj. Gen. Gray D. Allison.
Finance, David Fahrat.
Justice, Jenkins Scott.
Internal Affairs, Edward Sackor.
Public Works, Yudu Gray.
Posts and Telecommunications, Morris Dukuly.
Planning and Economic Affairs, Dr. Elijah Taylor.
Agriculture, Scott Gblorzuo Toweh.
Health and Social Welfare, Martha Sandolo Belleh.
Commerce and Industry, Wisseh McClain.
Lands, Mines and Energy, William Freeman.
Minister of State for Presidential Affairs, Alvin Jones.
Rural Development, Samuel Brownell.
Youth and Sports, Haven Grigsby.
Education, Othello Gonga.
Foreign Affairs, Rudolph Johnson.
Information, Culture and Tourism, Emmanuel Bowier.
Labour, Peter Naigow.
National Security, Patrick Minikon.
Transport, Mcleod Darpoh.
Minister of State without Portfolio, John Beh.
Director General of the Cabinet, Momolu Getaweh.

LIBERIAN EMBASSY IN LONDON
2 Pembridge Place, W2 4XB
[01–221 1036]

Ambassador Extraordinary and Plenipotentiary, His
Excellency Willie A. Givens (1985).

An independent republic of West Africa, occupying
that part of the coast between Sierra Leone and the
Côte d'Ivoire, which is between the rivers Mano in
the N.W. and Cavalla in the S.E., a distance of about
350 miles, with an area of about 43,000 sq. miles
(111,369 sq. km.), and extending to the interior to
latitude 8° 50', a distance of 150 miles from the
seaboard. It was founded by the American Colonization Society in 1822, and has been recognized since
1847 as an independent State. The population at the
Census of 1974 was 1,481,524; a 1985 U.N. estimate
put the figure at 2,189,000.

William V. S. Tubman, President of Liberia since
1944, died on July 23, 1971, and was succeeded by Dr.
Tolbert. The Constitution was suspended following
a military coup on April 12, 1980 led by M/Sgt. Samuel
K. Doe, who then became Head of State. Executive
power is now vested in the Head of State assisted by
an appointed Cabinet. A new Constitution was
endorsed by a referendum on July 3, 1984 and on July
22 the People's Redemptive Council was dissolved
and replaced by an interim National Assembly,
comprising the Council and 35 civilian members,
which will oversee the country's return to civilian
rule. Presidential and legislative elections were held
in Oct. 1985; and on Jan. 6, 1986 the Interim Assembly
was dissolved and replaced by a legislative Assembly.

The Army of Liberia consists of one division of 2
brigades of militia, three regular infantry battalions,
one engineer battalion and a small coastguard.

The artificial harbour and free port of Monrovia
was opened on July 26, 1948. There are 9 ports of
entry, including 3 river ports. International and

African airlines call at Robertsfield, 35 miles from
Monrovia. Spriggs Payne airfield, on the outskirts of
Monrovia, is used by Air Liberia for internal flights.

Liberia is receiving assistance from a number of
countries, including the United Kingdom, and from
the E.C. and various international agencies. This aid
is mainly directed towards the implementation of
Liberia's National Socio-Economic Development
Plan.

FINANCE

	1984	1985
Revenue	\$183,000,000	\$192,000,000
Expenditure	241,600,000	172,000,000
	\$ = U.S. Dollar	

TRADE

The principal exports are iron ore, crude rubber,
timber, uncut diamonds, palm kernels, cocoa and
coffee. The chief imports are manufactured goods of
all kinds, transport and iron-ore mining equipment
and foodstuffs.

	1985	1986
Imports	\$284,377,000	\$259,037,900
Exports	435,570,000	408,374,099

Trade with U.K.

	1986	1987
Imports from U.K.	£22,056,000	£13,538,000
Exports to U.K.	7,574,000	7,284,000

The language of the Republic is English. American
weights and measures are used.

CAPITAL, Ψ Monrovia. Est. Pop. (1984) 425,000.
Other ports are Ψ Buchanan, Ψ Greenville (Sinoe) and
Ψ Harper (Cape Palmas).

CURRENCY.—Liberian Dollar (L\$) of 100 Cents.

FLAG.—Alternate horizontal stripes (5 white, 6
red), with 5-pointed white star on blue field in upper
corner next to flagstaff.

NATIONAL ANTHEM.—All Hail, Liberia, Hail.

NATIONAL DAY.—July 26.

BRITISH EMBASSY
Mamba Point (P.O. Box 120), Monrovia
[Monrovia 221055]

*Ambassador Extraordinary and Plenipotentiary, and
Consul-General*, His Excellency Michael Edward
John Gore (1988).

First Secretary and Consul, R. Daly (*Commercial*).

LIBYA
(Al-Jamahiriya Al-Arabiya
Al-Libya Al-Shabiya Al-Ishtirakiya)

Leader of the Revolution, Col. Muammar al-Gadaffi.

Secretary of the General People's Committee, Umar al-
Muntasir.

GENERAL PEOPLE'S COMMITTEE

Sec. of External Relations, Jadallah Azzuz al-Talhi.
Sec. of Public Service, Fawzi al-Shashuki.
Sec. of Communications and Maritime Transport,
Mubarak al-Shamikh.
Sec. of Education and Scientific Research, Ahmad
Ibrahim.
Sec. of Economy and Foreign Trade, Farhat Sharnana.
Sec. of Planning, Muhammad Lufti Farhat.
Sec. of Health, Mustafa Muhammad al-Zaydi.
Sec. of Industry, Fathi Ahmad Bin Shatwan.
Sec. of Treasury, Muhammad al-Madani al-Bukhari.
Sec. of Information and Culture, Rajab Miftah Abu
Dabbus.
Sec. of Marine Wealth, Miftah Muhammad Ku'aybah.

Sec. of Vocational Training, Ma'tuq Muhammad Ma'tuq.

Sec. of Mass Mobilization and Revolutionary Guidance, Ali al-Sha'iri.

LIBYAN DIPLOMATIC MISSION IN LONDON

Following the break of diplomatic relations with Libya in April 1984, the Royal Embassy of Saudi Arabia has handled Libyan interests in Britain.

Libya, on the Mediterranean coast of Africa, is bounded on the East by Egypt and the Sudan, on the South by the Republics of Chad and Niger, and on the West by Algeria and Tunisia. It consists of the three former provinces of Tripolitania, Cyrenaica and the Fezzan, with a combined area of 679,362 sq. miles (1,759,540 sq. km) and a population (1985 estimate) of 3,800,000. The people of Libya are principally Arab with some Berbers in the West and aboriginal tribes in the Fezzan. Islam is the official religion of Libya, but other religions are tolerated. The official language is Arabic.

Vast sand and rock deserts, almost completely barren, occupy the greater part of Libya. The southern part of the country lies within the Sahara Desert. There are no rivers, and, as rainfall is irregular good harvests are rare. The ancient ruins in Cyrenaica, at Cyrene, Ptolemais (Tolmeta) and Apollonia, are outstanding, as are those at Leptis Magna near Homs, 70 miles from Tripoli and at Sabratha, 40 miles west of Tripoli. An Italian expedition found in the S.W. of the Fezzan a series of rock-paintings more than 5,000 years old.

Production and Industry.—Agriculture is confined mainly to the coastal areas of Tripolitania and Cyrenaica, where barley, wheat, olives, almonds, citrus fruits and dates are produced, and to the areas of the oases, many of which are well supplied with springs supporting small fertile areas. Among the important oases are Jaghbub, Ghadames, Jofra, Sebha, Murzuq, Brak, Ghat, Jalo and the Kufra group in the South-East. The main industry is oil and gas production. There are pipelines from Zelten to the terminal at Mersa Brega, from Dahra to Ras-es-Sider, from Amal to Ras Lanuf and from the Intisar field to Zuetina. Since 1984 average production of crude oil has been about 1 million barrels per day. A major petrochemical complex is under construction at Ras Lanuf where a refinery and ethylene plant began operations in early 1985. The construction of an iron and steel plant at Misurata is under way, though its completion has been slower than expected. Economic constraints have delayed some projects, particularly since Libya decided in 1983 to go ahead with a major irrigation scheme, the "Great Man-Made River".

Exports from Libya are dominated by crude oil, but some wool, cattle, sheep and horses, olive oil, and hides and skins are also exported. Principal imports are foodstuffs, including sugar, tea and coffee and most constructional materials and consumer goods. In recent years the private sector has been virtually eliminated and Libya is now a state trading country with imports controlled by state monopolies. In early 1988, however, reforms were proposed which may allow a small private sector to be re-established.

Communications in Libya are good. Besides the coastal road running from the Tunisian frontier through Tripoli to Benghazi, Tobruk and the Egyptian border, which serves the main population centres, main roads now link the provincial centres, and the oil-producing areas of the south with the coastal towns. There are airports at Tripoli and Benghazi (Benina), Tobruk, Mersa Brega, Sebha, Ghadames and Kufra regularly used by commercial airlines, and military airfields near Tobruk, near Tripoli and at Al Watiya, south of Zuara.

Government.—Libya was occupied by Italy in 1911–12 in the course of the Italo-Turkish War, and under the Treaty of Ouchy (Oct. 1912) the sovereignty of the province was transferred by Turkey to Italy. In 1939 the four Provinces of Libya (Tripoli, Misurata, Benghazi and Derna) were incorporated in the national territory of Italy as *Libia Italiana*. After the Second World War Tripolitania and Cyrenaica were placed provisionally under British and the Fezzan under French administration, and in conformity with a resolution of the U.N. General Assembly on Nov. 21, 1949, Libya became on Dec. 24, 1951, the first independent state to be created by the United Nations. The monarchy was overthrown by a revolution on Sept. 1, 1969, and the country was declared a republic. It was ruled by the Revolutionary Command Council (RCC) under the leadership of Colonel Muammar Gadaffi.

In March 1977 a new form of direct democracy, the "Jamahiriya" (state of the masses) was promulgated and the official name of the country was changed to Socialist People's Libyan Arab Jamahiriya. At local level authority is now vested in about 1,500 Basic and 14 Municipal People's Congresses which appoint Popular Committees to execute policy. Officials of these Congresses and Committees, together with representatives from unions and other organizations, form the General People's Congress, which normally meets for about a week early each year. This is the highest policy-making body in the country. The General People's Congress appoints its own General Secretariat and the General People's Committee, whose members head the 13 government departments which execute policy at national level. The Secretary of the General People's Committee has functions similar to those of a Prime Minister.

Since a reorganization in March 1979 neither Col. Gadaffi nor his former RCC colleagues have held formal posts in the administration. Gadaffi continues to hold the ceremonial title "Leader of the Revolution".

Libya has technical assistance agreements with a number of countries, and also employs large numbers of foreign labourers and experts.

Trade with U.K.

	1986	1987
Imports from U.K.	£260,529,000	£220,626,000
Exports to U.K.	136,390,000	133,649,000

CAPITAL.—ΨTripoli, pop. 1981, about 1,000,000. The principal towns are: ΨBenghazi (500,000); ΨMisurata (194,047).

CURRENCY.—Libyan Dinar of 1,000 Dirhams.

FLAG.—Libya uses a plain emerald green flag.

NATIONAL DAY.—September 1.

BRITISH EMBASSY

Diplomatic relations between the U.K. and Libya were broken in April 1984. British interests are currently handled by a section at the Italian Embassy, 1 Sharia Oran, Tripoli.

LIECHTENSTEIN
(Fürstentum Liechtenstein)

Prince, Franz Josef II., *b.* Aug. 16, 1906; *suc.* July 26, 1938; *married* March 7, 1943, Countess Gina von Wilczek.

Heir, Crown Prince Hans Adam, *b.* Feb. 14, 1945; *married* July 30, 1967, Countess Marie Kinsky; and has issue, Prince Alois, *b.* June 11, 1968; Prince Maximilian, *b.* May 16, 1969; Prince Constantin, *b.* March 15, 1972; Princess Tatjana, *b.* April 10, 1973.

From Aug. 26, 1984, Prince Hans Adam took over official duties and executive authority; Prince Franz Josef II remains titular Head of State.

MINISTRY

Prime Minister, Hans Brunhart *(Foreign Affairs, Education, Finance, Construction).*

Deputy P.M., Dr. Herbert Wille *(Interior, Agriculture, Forestry and Environment, Culture, Youth and Sport, Justice).*

Government Councillors, René Ritter *(Economy),* Dr. Peter Wolff *(Social and Health Services),* Wilfried Büchel *(Communications).*

Liechtenstein is represented in diplomatic and consular matters in the United Kingdom by the Swiss Embassy, *q.v.*

Liechtenstein is a Principality on the Upper Rhine, between Vorarlberg (Austria) and Switzerland, with an area of 61 sq. miles (157 sq. km.), and a population in 1987 of 27,714. The language of the Principality is German.

At the General Election on Feb. 2, 1986, the Patriotic Union Party won 8 seats and Progressive Citizens Party 7.

The main industries are high and ultra-high vacuum engineering, semi-conductor industry, roller bearings, fastenings and securing systems, artificial teeth, heating and hot water equipment, synthetic fibres, woollen and homespun fabrics.

FINANCE

	1986	1987
Revenue	*F*313,333,018	*F*318,401,301
Expenditure	320,263,293	308,306,099
	(F = Swiss *francs)*	

CAPITAL, Vaduz. Pop. (1987), 4,890.

CURRENCY.—Swiss currency is legal tender.

FLAG.—Equal horizontal bands of blue over red; gold crown on blue band near staff.

NATIONAL ANTHEM.—Oben Am Jungen Rhein (High on the Rhine).

NATIONAL DAY.—August 15.

British Consul General, Anthony Hugh Morgan *(office* at Dufourstrasse 56, 8008 Zürich).

LUXEMBOURG
(Grand-Duché de Luxembourg)

Grand Duke, H.R.H. Jean, *b.* Jan. 5, 1921, *married,* April 9, 1953, Princess Joséphine-Charlotte of Belgium, and has issue, 3 sons and 2 daughters; *succeeded* (on the abdication of his mother) Nov. 12, 1964.

Heir Apparent, Prince Henri, *b.* April 16, 1955, *married* February 14, 1981, Maria Teresa Mestre, and *has issue,* Prince Guillaume, *b.* Nov. 11, 1981; Prince Felix, *b.* June 3, 1984; Prince Louis, *b.* Aug. 1986.

CABINET

Christian Socialists:

Minister of State, President of the Government, Minister of Finance, National Development, Posts, Telecommunications and Information Technology, M. Jacques Santer.

Interior, the Family, Housing, Social Solidarity, M. Jean Spautz.

Education and Tourism, M. Fernand Boden.

Labour and Minister-Delegate for Finance, M. Jean-Claude Juncker.

Defence, Agriculture, Sport and the Civil Service, M. Marc Fischbach.

State Sec. for Agriculture and Viticulture, M. Rene Steichen.

Social Democrats:

Vice-President of the Government, Minister of the Economy, Foreign Affairs, Foreign Trade and Co-operation, Middle Classes and Treasury, M. Jacques Poos.

Public Health and Social Security, M. Benny Berg.

Justice, Cultural Affairs and the Environment, M. Robert Krieps.

Energy, Transport and Public Works, M. Marcel Schlechter.

State Secretary for Foreign Affairs, Foreign Trade and Co-operation and the Middle Classes, M. Robert Goebbels.

State Secretary for the Economy, M. Johny Lahure.

EMBASSY AND CONSULATE
27 Wilton Crescent, SW1X 8SD
[01–235 6961]

Ambassador Extraordinary and Plenipotentiary, His Excellency Jean Wagner (1986).

Luxembourg is a Grand Duchy in Western Europe, bounded by the Federal Republic of Germany, Belgium, and France. The area is 998 sq. miles (2,586 sq. km.), the population (Dec. 1984) 365,900, nearly all Roman Catholics. The country is well wooded, with many deer and wild boar. The language is Letzeburgesch but French is the official language; most speak German and many English.

Established as an independent State under the sovereignty of the King of the Netherlands as Grand Duke by the Congress of Vienna in 1815, it formed part of the Germanic Confederation, 1815–66, and was included in the German "Zollverein". In 1867 the Treaty of London declared it a neutral territory. On the death of the King of the Netherlands in 1890 it passed to the Duke of Nassau. The territory was invaded and overrun by the Germans at the beginning of the war in 1914, but was liberated in 1918. By the Treaty of Versailles, 1919, Germany renounced her former agreements with Luxembourg in respect of the customs union, etc., and in 1921 an economic union was made with Belgium. The Grand Duchy was again invaded and occupied by Germany on May 10, 1940. The constitution of the Grand Duchy was modified on April 28, 1948, and the stipulation of permanent neutrality was then abandoned. Luxembourg is now a fully effective member of the Western association of powers and a signatory of the Brussels and North Atlantic Treaties, and also a member of the European Communities. Luxembourg is a member of the Belgium–Netherlands–Luxembourg Customs Union (Benelux, 1960).

The Court of the European Communities has its seat in Luxembourg, as does the Secretariat of the European Parliament, the European Investment Bank, the European Audit Court and the European Monetary Co-operation fund.

There is a Chamber of 64 Deputies, elected by universal suffrage for 5 years. Legislation is submitted to the Council of State.

The Grand Duchy was rich in iron-ore and possesses an important iron and steel industry with an annual productive capacity over 5,700,000 tons. Government revenue for 1987 was estimated at *L.F.* 79,600 million, expenditure *L.F.* 79,700 million. The Luxembourg *franc* has at present the same value as the Belgian *franc.*

There are 170 miles of railway.

Trade with U.K.

	1985	1986
Imports from U.K.	£62,217,000	£58,507,000
Exports to U.K.	133,450,000	148,811,000

CAPITAL.—Luxembourg, pop. (1987), 77,500, is a dismantled fortress.

CURRENCY.—Luxembourg Franc of 100 Centimes. Belgian currency is also legal tender.
FLAG.—Three horizontal bands, red, white and blue.
NATIONAL ANTHEM.—Ons Hémécht (Our homeland).
NATIONAL DAY.—June 23.

BRITISH EMBASSY
14 Boulevard F. D. Roosevelt, L-2450, Luxembourg
[Luxembourg 29864]
Ambassador Extraordinary and Plenipotentiary, Her Excellency Juliet Jeanne Campbell, C.M.G. (1988).

MADAGASCAR
(Repoblika Demokratika n'i Madagaskar)

President, Didier Ratsiraka, *took office* 1975, *re-elected* Nov. 7, 1982 for a seven-year term.

COUNCIL OF MINISTERS

Prime Minister, Lt.-Col. Victor Ramahatra.
Finance and Economy, Pascal Rakotomavo.
Agricultural Production, Jose Michel Andrianoelison.
Animal Production, Water and Forests, Joseph Randrianasolo.
Trade, Georges Solofoson.
Industry, Energy and Mines, Jose Rakotomavo.
Population and Social Condition, Youth and Sports, Jean André Ndremanjary.
Revolutionary Art and Culture, Gisèle Rabesahala.
Posts and Telecommunications, Rakotovoa Andriantiana.
Justice, Joseph Bedo.
Transport, Meteorology and Tourism, Cmdt. Jean Emile Tsaranazy.
Civil Service and Labour, Georges Ruphin.
Defence, Gen. Mahasampa Raveloson.
Health, Dr. Jean-Jacques Séraphin.
Interior, Ampy Portos.
Primary and Secondary Education, Charles Zeny.
Higher Education, Ignace Rakoto.
Scientific Research, Antoine Zafera.
Information, Pierre Simon.
Foreign Affairs, Jean Bemananjara.
Public Works, Andrianaivomanana Razafindramisa.

Madagascar lies 240 miles off the east coast of Africa and is the fourth largest island in the world. It has an area of 226,669 sq. miles (587,041 sq. km.), and a population (1987 estimate) of 11,000,000. The people are of mixed Polynesian, Arab and Negro origin. The languages spoken are Malagasy and French. There are sizeable French, Chinese and Indian communities.

Government.—It became a French protectorate in 1895, and a French colony in 1896 when the former queen was exiled. Republican status was adopted on October 14, 1958, and independence was proclaimed on June 26, 1960.

The post-independence civilian government was replaced by a military government in Jan. 1975 and the following month martial law was declared. A Supreme Council of the Revolution of 18 members under Capitaine de Frégate (now Admiral) Didier Ratsiraka was established on June 15, 1975.

In December 1975 a new constitution was approved in a referendum, which vested executive power in the President. He appoints a Council of Ministers to assist him, with the guidance of the Revolutionary Supreme Council. There is a 137-member National People's Assembly elected for a 5-year term by universal suffrage.

Revised agreements with France, signed on June 4, 1973, provided for the withdrawal of the French forces stationed in the country after independence. The French naval base at Diégo Suarez was turned into a civilian ship repair yard. Madagascar also withdrew from the Franc Zone and announced a claim to the Islands of Juan de Nova, Glorieuses, Isle de l'Europe, Bassa da India and Tromelin which had remained integral parts of the French Republic after independence.

The island's economy is still largely based on agriculture, which accounts for three-quarters of its exports. Development plans have placed emphasis on increasing agricultural and livestock production, the improvement of communications, the exploitation of mineral deposits and the creation of small industries.

TRADE

	1985	1986
Imports	$U.S. 400·54 m.	$U.S. 441·54 m.
Exports	274·23 m.	351·18 m.

Trade with U.K.

	1986	1987
Imports from U.K.	£6,872,000	£6,382,000
Exports to U.K.	6,432,000	6,925,000

CAPITAL.—Antananarivo (population about 1,000,000). Other main towns are the chief port ΨToamasina (55,000); Ψ Mahajanga (50,000); Fianarantsoa (47,000); Ψ Antsiranana (41,000).
CURRENCY.—Franc Malgache (Malagasy Franc) (F.M.G.) of 100 Centimes.
FLAG.—Equal horizontal bands of red (above) and green, with vertical white band by staff.
NATIONAL DAY.—June 26 (Independence Day).

BRITISH EMBASSY
(BP 167, Antananarivo)
[Antananarivo 277 49]
Ambassador Extraordinary and Plenipotentiary, His Excellency Anthony Victor Hayday (1987).
Second Secretary, J. MacAdie.
Vice-Consul (Commercial), A. J. Marcelin.

MALI
(République du Mali)

Secretary-General of the U.D.P.M., President of the Government, and Minister of Defence, Gen. Moussa Traore, *born* 1937, *assumed office* Nov. 20, 1968, *elected* June 19, 1979, *re-elected* June 9, 1985.

GOVERNMENT MINISTERS

Public Health and Social Affairs, Prof. Mamadou Dembele.
Education, Gen. Sékou Ly.
Foreign Affairs and International Co-operation, Modibo Keita.
Territorial Administration and Basic Development, Col. Issa Ongoiba.
Industry, Hydraulics and Energy, Drissa Keita.
Justice, Oumar Issaka Ba.
Information, Sidibe Aissata Cisse.
Sport, Art and Culture, Bakary Traore.
Public Works, Urbanism and Construction, Cheick Oumar Doumbia.
Planning, Anthioumane N'Diaye.
Transport, Telecommunications and Tourism, Mohamed Alhousseyni Toure.
Agriculture, Moulaye Mohamed Haidara.
Finance and Trade, Tiénan Coulibaly.
Environment and Farming, Morifing Kone.
Employment and Civil Service, Diallo Lalla Sy.
Minister delegate to the Ministry of Defence, Gen. Abdoulaye Ouologuem.

The Republic of Mali, an inland state in north-west Africa has an area of 478,791 sq. miles (1,240,000 sq.

km.), and a population (1985 U.N. estimate) of 8,206,000. The principal rivers are the Niger and the Senegal.

Formerly the French colony of Soudan, the territory elected on Nov. 24, 1958, to remain as an autonomous republic within the French Community. It associated with Senegal in the Federation of Mali which was granted full independence on June 20, 1960. The Federation was effectively dissolved on August 22 by the secession of Senegal. The title of the Republic of Mali was adopted on Sept. 22, 1960.

Government.—The regime of Modibo Keita was overthrown on Nov. 19, 1968, by a group of Army officers who formed a National Liberation Committee and appointed a Prime Minister. Moussa Traore assumed the functions of Head of State. A new civil constitution came into being in 1979. The new government formed on May 4, 1978 contained a majority of civilians. On June 19, 1979, elections were held for an 82-member National Assembly. Presidential elections held on the same day confirmed Traore as President.

Economy.—Mali's principal exports are groundnuts (raw and processed), cotton fibres, meat and dried fish. The Republic rejoined the CFA franc zone on June 1, 1984 when measures were taken to convert the *Franc Malien* at the rate of 2*FM* : 1 *Franc CFA*.

Trade with UK.

	1986	1987
Imports from UK.	£4,121,000	£5,573,000
Exports to U.K.	8,282,000	6,937,000

CAPITAL.—Bamako (600,000). Other towns are Gao, Kayes, Mopti, Sikasso, Segou and Timbuktu (all regional capitals).

CURRENCY.—Franc C.F.A. of 100 Centimes.

FLAG.—Vertical stripes of green (by staff), yellow and red.

NATIONAL DAY.—September 22.

BRITISH EMBASSY

British Ambassador (resident at Dakar, Senegal).

MAURITANIA
(République Islamique de Mauritanie)

President, Col. Maaouya Ould Sid' Ahmed Taya, *took power* Dec. 12, 1984 (*also holds portfolios of Prime Minister and Defence*).

GOVERNMENT MINISTERS
(as at March 20, 1988)

Foreign Affairs and Co-operation, Mohamed Lemine Ould N'Diayane.

Justice, Mouhamed Salem Ould Mohamed Lemine.

Interior, Post and Telecommunications, Lt.-Col. Djibril Ould Abdallahi.

Economy and Finance, Dr. Cherif Ahmed Mahmoud Cheikh Ould Ahmed Louly.

Fisheries and Marine Economy, Khattry Ould Seguane Dah Ould Cheikh.

Industry and Mining, M'Barek Ould Maoulou Khadijetou Abderahmane.

Equipment, Lt.-Col. Oumar Dieng Harouna.

National and Higher Education, Ba Aliou Ibra Hasni Ould Didi.

Civil Service, Employment, Youth and Sport, Mohammed Ould Haimer.

Hydraulics and Energy, Mohamed Lemine Ould Abdi Soumare Oumar.

Rural Development, Hamoud Ould Ely.

Health and Social Affairs, Cmdt. N'Diaye Kane.

Trade and Transport, Hamdi Samba Diop.

Information, Fall Oumar Haibetna Ould Sidy Haiba.

Culture and Islamization, Sidi Ould Benahi Mohamed Saloum Ould Abdel Weddoud.

State Security, Ethmane Sid'Ahmed Yessa.

Secretary General, Barro Abdoulaye.

Asst. Sec. Gen., Ba Alassane Yero.

Culture and Literacy, Isselmou Ould Mohamed.

Controller General, Boullaha Ould Mogueya Ethmane Ould Yessa.

Mauritania lies on the north-west coast of Africa immediately to the north of Senegal. It is bounded on the east by the Republic of Mali. To the north it is bounded by Morocco and the Western Sahara. Mauritania and Morocco took possession of that territory in February 1976 when Spain formally relinquished all right to it and in April 1976 agreed on a new frontier dividing the territory between them. In August 1979, Mauritania relinquished all claim to the southern sector of the Western Sahara after a three-year war against the Polisario front guerrilla army. Area 397,955 sq. miles (1,030,700 sq. km.). The population was estimated at 1,888,000 in 1985. The Republic of Mauritania elected on November 28, 1958, to remain within the French Community as an autonomous republic. It became fully independent on Nov. 28, 1960. In 1972 Mauritania broke with the franc zone and established its own unit of currency, the *Ouguiya*, equal in value to 5 *francs CFA*.

Mauritania's main source of potential wealth lies in rich deposits of iron ore around Zouérate, in the north of the country. Exports began in 1963, via a railway laid for the purpose from the mine to the port of Nouadhibou. The deposits are being exploited under the aegis of the *Société Nationale Industrielle Miniere* following the nationalization in 1974 of the internationally based company MIFERMA. There are copper deposits at Akjoujt which are being exploited by SOMIMA, a company nationalized on Feb. 25, 1975; the mine was closed in 1978, but reopened in 1981.

Trade with U.K.

	1986	1987
Imports from U.K.	£2,496,000	£3,862,000
Exports to U.K.	2,184,000	8,724,000

CAPITAL.—Nouakchott (500,000).

CURRENCY.—Ouguiya of 5 Khoums.

FLAG.—Yellow star and crescent on green ground.

NATIONAL DAY.—November 28.

British Ambassador, (Resident at *Dakar, Senegal*).

MEXICO
(Estados Unidos Mexicanos)

President (1982–88), Lic. Miguel de la Madrid Hurtado, *elected,* 4 July 1982, *took office,* 1 Dec. 1982.

President-elect (takes office Dec. 1, 1988), Sr. Carlos Salinas de Gortari.

THE CABINET
(as at June 1988)

Interior, Sr. Manuel Bartlett Diaz.

Foreign Affairs, Sr. Bernardo Sepúlveda Amor.

Finance and Public Credit, Sr. Gustavo Petricioli Iturbide.

Defence, Gen. Juan José Arévalo Gardoqui.

Navy, Adm. Miguel Angel Gómez Ortega.

Budget and Planning, Sr. Pedro Aspe Armella.

Energy, Mines and Parastatal Industries, Sr. Fernando Hiriart Balderrama.

Trade and Industrial Development, Sr. Héctor Hernández Cervantes.

Agriculture and Water Resources, Sr. Eduardo Pesqueira Olea.

Communications and Transport, Sr. Daniel Diaz Diaz.

Education, Sr. José Miguel González Avelar.
Urban Development and Ecology, Sr. Manuel Camacho Solis.
Health, Dr. Guillermo Soberón Acevedo.
Labour and Social Security, Sr. Arsenio Farell Cubillas.
Agrarian Reform, Sr. Rafael Rodríguez Barrera.
Tourism, Sr. Antonio Enríquez Savignac.
Fisheries, Sr. Pedro Ojeda Paullada.
Attorney-General, Sr. Sergio Garcia Ramírez.
Attorney-General of Federal District, Sr. Renato Sales Gasque.
Comptroller-General, Sr. Ignacio Pichardo Pagaza.
Mayor of Mexico City, Sr. C. P. Ramón Aguirre Velázquez.

MEXICAN EMBASSY IN LONDON
8 Halkin St., SW1X 7DW
[01–235 6393]

Ambassador Extraordinary and Plenipotentiary, His Excellency Jorge Eduardo Navarrete (1986).

Area and Population.—Mexico occupies the southern part of the continent of North America, with an extensive seaboard to both the Atlantic and Pacific Oceans, extending from 14° 33' to 32° 43' N. lat. and 86° 46' to 117° 08' W. long., and comprising one of the most varied zones in the world. It contains 31 states and the federal district of Mexico, making in all 32 political divisions, covering an area of 761,605 sq. miles (1,972,547 sq. km.). At the 1980 Mexican General Census, the total population was 67,383,000, but a 1985 U.N. estimate gives a figure of 78,524,000.

The two great ranges of North America, the Sierra Nevada and Rocky Mountains, are prolonged from the north to a convergence towards the narrowing isthmus of Tehuantepec, their course being parallel to the west and east coasts. The surface of the interior consists of an elevated plateau between the two ranges, with steep slopes both to the Pacific and Atlantic (Gulf of Mexico). In the west is the peninsula of Lower California, with a mountainous surface, separated from the mainland by the Gulf of California. The Sierra Nevada, known in Mexico as the *Sierra Madre*, terminates in a transverse series of volcanic peaks, from Colima on the west to Citlaltepetl ("El Pico de Orizaba") on the east. The low-lying lands of the coasts form the *Tierra Caliente*, or tropical regions (below 3,000 ft.), the higher levels form the *Tierra Templada*, or temperate region (from 3,000 to 6,000 ft.), and the summit of the plateau with its peaks is known as *Tierra Fria*, or cold region (above 6,000 ft.). The only considerable rivers are the *Rio Grande del Norte* which forms part of the northern boundary, and is navigable for about 70 miles from its mouth in the Gulf of Mexico, and the *Rio Grande de Santiago*, the *Rio Balsas* and *Rio Papaloapan*. The largest fresh-water lakes are *Chapala* (70 miles long and 20 miles wide), and *Pátzcuaro*.

History and Archaeology.—The present Mexico and Guatemala were once the centre of a remarkable indigenous civilization, which had unknown beginnings in the centuries before Christ, flowered in the periods from A.D. 500 to 1100 and A.D. 1300 to 1500 and collapsed before the little army of Spanish adventurers under Hernán Cortés in the years following 1519. Pre-Columbian Mexico was divided between different but connected Indian cultures, each of which has left distinctive archaeological remains: the best-known of these are Chichén Itzá, Uxmal, Bonampak and Palenque, in Yucatán and Chiapas (Maya); Teotihuacon, renowned for the Pyramid of the Sun (216 feet high) in the Valley of Mexico (Teotihuacáno); Monte Albán and Mitla, near Oaxaca (Zapotec); El Tajín in the State of Veracruz (Totonac); and Tula in the State of Hidalgo (Toltec). The last and most famous Indian culture of all, the Aztec, based on Tenochitlán suffered more than the others from the Spanish and only very few Aztec monuments remain.

A few years after the Conquest, the Spanish built Mexico City on the ruins of Tenochitlán, and appointed a Viceroy to rule their new dominions, which they called New Spain. The country was largely converted to Christianity, and a distinctive colonial civilization, representing a marriage of Indian and Spanish traditions, developed and flourished, notably in architecture and sculpture. In 1810 a revolt began against Spanish rule. This was finally successful in 1821, when a precarious independence was proclaimed. Friction with the United States in Texas led to the war of 1845–48, at the end of which Mexico was forced to cede the northern provinces of Texas, California and New Mexico. In 1862 Mexican insolvency led to invasion by French forces which installed Archduke Maximilian of Austria as Emperor. The empire collapsed with the execution of the Emperor in 1867 and the austere reformer, Juárez, restored the republic. Juárez's death was followed by the dictatorship of Porfirio Diaz, which saw an enormous increase of foreign, particularly British and United States, investment in the country. In 1910 began the Mexican Revolution which reformed the social structure and the land system, curbed the power of foreign companies and ushered in the independent industrial Mexico of today.

Government.—Under the Constitution of Feb. 5, 1917 (as subsequently amended), Congress consists of a Senate of 64 members, elected for six years, and of a Chamber of Deputies, at present numbering 400, elected for three years. Presidents, who wield full executive powers, are elected for six years; they cannot be re-elected.

There are nine political parties registered in Mexico, of which by far the largest and most influential is the *Partido Revolucionario Institucional* (P.R.I.) which has for many years constituted the governing party. The Mexican Communists allied with several like-minded smaller parties to form the Mexican United Socialist Party (P.S.U.M.) in 1982.

Communications.—Veracruz, Tampico and Coatzacoalcos are the chief ports of the Atlantic, and Guaymas, Mazatlán, Puerto Lázaro Cárdenas, Acapulco, Salina Cruz and Puerto Madero on the Pacific. Work is proceeding on the reorganization and re-equipment of the whole system; help in this has been forthcoming from the World Bank, the Export-Import Bank and private sources in the United States. The railways were completely nationalized in 1970.

Mexico City may be reached by at least three highways (with 14 entry points) from the United States, and work is complete on roads southward from Mexico City to Yucatán as well as on two principal highways to the Guatemalan border (with three entry points).

International telegraph services to the United States frontier are provided by the government-owned Mexican Telegraph Company and then through the United States to Canada and Europe.

Teléfonos de México, a state-controlled company, controls about 98 per cent of all telephone services. Satélite Latinoamericano, S.A. (SATELAT) is a joint government/private sector venture disseminating television programmes to Latin America through Intelstat IV satellite facilities leased by the Mexican Government.

There is a good national and international network of air services. There are 1,113 airports and landing fields in Mexico, of which eighteen are equipped to handle long-distance flights. There are 166 airline companies, including two of the major national airlines—*Mexicana de Aviación* and *Aeroméxico*. Passenger traffic is growing by about 14 per cent yearly, while cargo is increasing by a similar percentage.

Production.—The principal agricultural crops are maize, beans, rice, wheat, sugar cane, coffee, cotton, tomatoes, chili, tobacco, chick-peas, groundnuts, sesame, alfalfa, vanilla, cocoa and many kinds of fruit, both tropical and temperate. The maguey, or Mexican cactus, yields several fermented drinks, mezcal and tequila (distilled) and pulque (undistilled). Another species of the same plant supplies sisal-hemp (henequen). The forests abound in mahogany, rosewood, ebony and chicle trees. Agriculture employs an estimated 30 per cent of the working population.

The principal industries are mining and petroleum, but over the last twenty years there has been very considerable expansion of both light and heavy industries. Exports of manufactured goods now average about 20 per cent of total exports. The steel industry expanded steadily until recently and current production is around 6·5 m. tons. The mineral wealth is great, and principal minerals are gold, silver, copper, lead, zinc, quicksilver, iron and sulphur. Substantial reserves of uranium have been found. In the non-metals sector, Mexico continues to produce 25 per cent of the world's supply of fluorspar.

The total proven petroleum reserves were 72 billion barrels in 1983. Crude oil production is currently about 2,600,000 barrels. Daily production of natural gas is approximately 3 billion cubic feet. Oil reserves have increased substantially due to important discoveries in the Gulf of Campeche. A new refinery at Tula, State of Hidalgo is the nation's largest; and new refineries in Monterrey, State of Nuevo Leon, and Salina Cruz, State of Oaxaca, are under construction.

Textile production is led by the artificial fibres sector, which comprised 66 per cent of the industry's output in 1983.

Defence.—Supreme command is vested in the President, exercised through the Ministries of Defence (for Army and Air Force) and Marine.

The country is divided into 36 zones in which the regular army (106,000) and part-time conscripts (250,000) are trained. The Army in 1985 had three HQ Brigades, five Artillery Regiments, 26 mechanized and one Horse Cavalry Regiments, Transport, Engineering and Signals Regiments, and 78 Infantry Battalions. In addition, there is a Rural Defence Militia of some 12,000 men.

The Navy has a strength of about 38,500 officers and men including the Naval Air Force and Marines. It is equipped with three destroyers, five frigates, six OPVs, 19 corvettes, 17 minesweepers, 31 coastal craft patrol, 12 inshore and river patrol boats, 13 transports and tugs, and one sail training ship. Many vessels are non-operational. The Marine Infantry has 10 battalions (4,300 officers and men). The Naval Air Force consists of four squadrons and 49 aircraft.

The Air Force has an approximate strength of 5,500 officers and men and 298 aircraft, including tactical/training aircraft, reconnaissance aircraft/helicopters and transport aircraft. There is a Parachute Brigade consisting of three Parachute battalions (approx. 2,000 men).

Language and Literature.—Spanish is the official language of Mexico and is spoken by about 95 per cent of the population. In addition to Spanish, there are five basic groups of Indian languages spoken in Mexico. The 1970 Census showed that of the 3,111,415 inhabitants speaking an Indian language, 25·7 per cent spoke Náhuatl; 14·6 per cent Maya; 9·1 per cent Zapotec; 7·1 per cent Otomí; 7·5 per cent Mixtec and 36 per cent one or other of the 59 dialects derived from these basic languages.

Education.—Education is divided into primary, secondary, preparatory and university. Primary education is free, secular and nominally compulsory.

Trade with U.K.

	1986	1987
Imports from U.K.	£162,328,000	£198,992,000
Exports to U.K.	116,078,000	244,719,000

Imports consist largely of transport, sound-recording and power-generating equipment, chemicals, industrial machinery, pharmaceuticals and special ized appliances. Principal exports are oil, fertilizers, minerals, metallic ores and scrap, sugar, honey, textiles and power-generating equipment.

CAPITAL.—Mexico City, metropolitan area 18,748,000 (est. pop. 1986). Other cities (est. pop. 1986) are:

Guadalajara	2,587,000	Puebla	1,217,600
Monterrey	2,335,000	León	946,800
Torréon	729,800	Ciudad	
San Luis		Juarez	595,700
Potosì	601,900	Mérida	580,300

CURRENCY.—Mexican Peso of 100 Centavos.

FLAG.—Three vertical bands in green, white, red, with the Mexican emblem (an eagle on a cactus devouring a snake) in the centre.

NATIONAL ANTHEM.—Mexicanos, Al Grito De Guerra (Mexicans, to the war cry).

NATIONAL DAY.—September 16 (Proclamation of Independence).

BRITISH EMBASSY
Calle Rio Lerma 71, Colonia Cuauhtémoc,
06500 Mexico City, D.F.
[Mexico City 207 20 89]

Ambassador Extraordinary and Plenipotentiary, His Excellency John Albert Leigh Morgan, C.M.G. (1986).

There are British Consular Offices at *Mexico City, Acapulco, Guadalajara, Mérida, Monterrey, Tampico* and *Cuidad Juarez.*

British Council Representative.—R. Watkins, Maestro Antonio Caso 127, Col. San Rafael (P.O. Box 30-588), Mexico 06470, D.F.

BRITISH CHAMBER OF COMMERCE, British Trade Centre, Rio Tiber 103–60, Mexico 5 D.F.—*Manager*, J. Carral.

MONACO
(Principauté de Monaco)

Sovereign Prince, H.S.H. Rainier III-Louis-Henri-Maxence Bertrand, *born* May 31, 1923, *succeeded his grandfather* (H.S.H. Prince Louis II), May 9, 1949; *married* April 19, 1956, Miss Grace Patricia Kelly (died Sept. 14, 1982) and *has issue* Prince

Albert Alexandre Louis Pierre, *born* March 14, 1958, Princess Caroline Louise Marguerite, *born* January 23, 1957; and Princess Stephanie Marie Elisabeth, *born* Feb. 1, 1965.
President of the Crown Council, M. Jean-Charles Marquet.
President of the National Council, M. Jean-Charles Rey.

Minister of State, Jean Ausseil, *appointed* 1985.

CONSULATE-GENERAL IN LONDON
4 Audley Square, W1Y 5DR
[01–629 0734]
Consul-General, I. S. Ivanovic.

A small Principality on the Mediterranean, with land frontiers joining France at every point, and consisting of the old town of Monaco, La Condamine, Fontvielle and Monte Carlo, the location of the famous casino. The Principality comprises a narrow strip of country about 2 miles long (area approx. 467 acres), with approximately 28,000 inhabitants (1983) and a yearly average of over 250,000 visitors.

The principality, ruled by the Grimaldi family since the late 13th century, was abolished during the French Revolution and re-established in 1815 under the protection of the Kingdom of Sardinia. In 1861 Monaco came under French protection. The 1962 Constitution, which can be modified only with the approval of the National Council, maintains the traditional hereditary monarchy and guarantees freedom of association, trade union freedom and the right to strike. Legislative power is held jointly by the Prince and a uni-cameral, 18 member National Council elected by universal suffrage. Executive power is exercised by the Prince and a four-member Council of Government, headed by a Minister of State. The judicial code is based on that of France.

The whole available ground is built over, so that there is no cultivation, though there are some notable public and private gardens. Monaco has a small harbour (30 ft. alongside quay) and the import duties are the same as in France.

CAPITAL.—Monaco-ville (1,443).
CURRENCY.—French currency is legal tender.
FLAG.—Two equal horizontal stripes, red over white.
NATIONAL ANTHEM.—Hymne Monegasque.
NATIONAL DAY.—November 19.
H.M. Consul-General, T. E. J. Mound, C.V.O., O.B.E. (*Resident at Marseilles*).

MONGOLIA
(Mongolian People's Republic—
Bugd Nairamdakh Mongol Ard Uls)

President: J. Batmunkh.
Prime Minister: D. Sodnom.

**Mongolian People's Revolutionary
(= *Communist*) Party**

Politburo of the Central Committee, J. Batmunkh; D. Sodnom; D. Molomjamts; B. Dejid; B. Altangerel; B. Lamjav (*full members*); N. Jagaval; S. Luvsangombo; P. Damdin (*candidate members*).
Secretariat of the Central Committee, J. Batmunkh (*General Secretary*); D. Molomjamts; Ts. Namsrai; B. Dejid; P. Damdin; Ts. Balkhaajav.
Chairman, Council of Ministers, D. Sodnom.
First Deputy Chairman, (vacant).
Deputy Chairmen, B. Altangerel; S. Luvsangombo; Ch. Suren; M. Peljee; P. Jasrai.

MONGOLIAN EMBASSY
7 Kensington Court, W8 5DL
[01–937 0150]
Ambassador Extraordinary and Plenipotentiary, His Excellency Ishetsogyin Ochirbal (1987).
Third Secretary, C. Battomor.
Attaché, T. O. Munkhsaikhan.

Area and Population.—The Mongolian People's Republic (Mongolia) is a large and sparsely populated country to the north of China. Its area is 604,250 sq. miles (1,565,000 sq. km.). Its population (Dec. 1985) is about 1,900,000. However, this total constitutes only part of the Mongolians of Asia, a number of whom are to be found in China and in the neighbouring regions of the Soviet Union (especially the Mongolian Buryat Autonomous Region). This country, which is almost nowhere below 1,000 metres above sea level, forms part of the Central Asiatic Plateau and rises towards the west in the high mountains of the Mongolian Altai and Khanggai Ranges. The Khentai Mountain Range, situated to the north-east of the capital Ulan Bator, is less high. The Gobi region covers much of the southern half of the country. It contains some sand deserts, but between these less hospitable areas there is semi-desert which provides pasture for great numbers of sheep, goats, camels and horses (the latter is still the characteristic means of transport for the rural population) and some cattle. In the steppe areas to the north pasturage is better and livestock more abundant. Even further north, in the better watered provinces, grain, fodder and vegetable crops are increasingly grown. There are several long rivers and many lakes, but good water is scarce since much of the lake water is salty. The climate is harsh, with a short mild summer giving way to a long winter when temperatures can drop as low as minus 50° C.

History.—Mongolia, under Genghis Khan the conqueror of China and much of Asia, was for many years a buffer state between Tsarist Russia and China, although it was under general Chinese suzerainty. The outbreak of the Chinese Revolution in 1911 led to a declaration of autonomy under Chinese suzerainty which was confirmed by the Sino-Russian Treaty of Kiakhta (1915), but cancelled by a unilateral Chinese declaration in 1919. Later the country became a battleground of the Russian Civil War, and Soviet and Mongolian troops occupied Ulan Bator in 1921: this was followed by another declaration of independence. However, in 1924 the Soviet Union in a Treaty with China again recognized the latter's sovereignty over Mongolia; but this was never properly exercised because of China's pre-occupation with internal affairs, and later by the anti-Japanese war. The Mongolian People's Republic was formally established in 1924. Under the Yalta Agreement, Chiang Kai-shek agreed to a plebiscite, held in 1945, in which the Mongolians declared their desire for independence and this was formally recognized by Nationalist China. The country entered the United Nations in 1961. The heroes of Mongolian history during the earlier part of the century were Sukhebator, who died in 1923, and the Communist Choibalsan (died 1952), who did much to turn the country into the Communist state it is today, and carried out a systematic destruction of the power of the Lamas and the old princely houses which had previously been the dominant force in both the economy and the government.

Production, etc.—The total of Mongolia's livestock was 23 million in 1984. Traditionally the Mongolian is a herdsman, tending his flock of sheep, goats and horses, cows and camels and leading a totally nomadic life. With the coming of the Communist régime (under the Mongolian People's Revolutionary Party) and especially since 1952, great efforts have been made to settle the population, but a large proportion still live nomadically or semi-nomadically in the traditional *ger* (circular tent). The pastoral population was collectivized at the end of the 1950s into huge *negdels* (co-operatives) and State farms which have hastened the process of settlement, but within these the herdsmen and their families still move with their *gers* from pasture to pasture as the seasons change. The country, and three city districts (Ulan Bator, Darkhan and Erdenet), is today divided into 18 *aimaks* (provinces) and beneath these into 258 *somons* (districts), and these form the basis of the State organization of the country, parallel with which runs the apparatus of the Revolutionary Party.

Membership of the Communist bloc has brought Mongolia considerable quantities of aid from other Socialist countries, especially Czech, Polish and East German aid to supplement the massive assistance from the Soviet Union. Soviet and Bloc aid is hastening the process of industrialization; for although the economy remains predominantly based on the herds of animals, and the principal exports of the country are still animal by-products (especially wool, hides and furs) and cattle, factories serving the needs of the country have been started up and the coal and electricity industries are being developed to provide an industrial base. A joint Mongolian/Soviet enterprise for copper and molybdenum mining was opened in 1978, at Erdenet in northern Mongolia. It is now in full production and processes 16 million tonnes of ore annually. A major geological survey is being carried out by the CMEA countries, in order to prepare for the extraction of the considerable mineral deposits known to exist in Mongolia. Coal production in 1980 was 4·5 million tons and was expected to rise to 6·8 million tons by 1985.

Ulan Bator, which contains over a quarter of the country's population, is the main seat of industry. The second largest industrial centre is at Darkhan (pop. 60,000), north of the capital, near the Soviet frontier. Its industries include lime, cement and building materials, a flour mill and a power station. Choibalsan, in the east, is also being developed industrially. Agriculture, formerly little practised, is now being extended. Average cereal production for 1976–80 was 347,000 tons, but by 1983 had risen to 800,000 tonnes. Communication is still difficult in the country as there are very few tarmac roads. The trans-Mongolian railway, following the line of the old north-south trade route, was opened in 1955 and links Mongolia with both China and Russia. Mongolia's fundamental difficulty is its very small population and labour force.

Foreign trade is dominated by the Soviet Union, with the eastern European countries taking most of what is left. Trade with western countries and Japan is developing slowly.

Trade with U.K.

	1986	1987
Imports from U.K.	£1,031,000	£941,000
Exports to U.K.	4,750,000	3,847,000

CAPITAL.—Ulan Bator. (Pop. 480,000.)

CURRENCY.—Tugrik of 100 Mongo.

FLAG.—Vertical tri-colour red, blue, red and in the hoist the traditional Soyombo symbol in gold.

NATIONAL DAY.—July 11 (Anniversary of the Mongolian People's Republic).

BRITISH EMBASSY
30 Enkh Taivny Gudamzh (P.O. Box 703)
Ulan Bator 13
[Ulan Bator 51033/4]

Ambassador Extraordinary and Plenipotentiary, His Excellency Guy William Pulbrook Hart, O.B.E. (1987).

Second Secretary, D. A. Slinn (*Head of Chancery*).
Attachés, I. Grant; S. G. McDonald.

MOROCCO
(Al-Mamlaka Al-Maghrebia)

King, H.M. King Hassan II (Moulay Hassan Ben Mohammed), *born* July 9, 1929; *acceded* February 26, 1961, *on the death of his father,* King Mohammad V. *Heir,* Crown Prince Sidi Mohamed, *b.* August 21, 1963.

MINISTERS

Prime Minister, Azeddine Laraki
Ministers of State, Hadj M'hamid Bahnini; Moulay Ahmed Alaoui.
Justice, Moulay Mustapha Belarbi Alaoui.
Interior and Information, Driss Basri.
Foreign Affairs and Co-operation, Abdellatif Filali.
National Education, Mohamed Hilali.
Health, Tayeb Bencheikh.
Religious Endowments and Islamic Affairs, Abdelkebir Alaoui M'Daghri.
Equipment, Training of Cadres and Professional Training, Mohamed Kabbaj.
Finance, Mohamed Berrada.
Tourism, Moussa Saadi.
Traditional Industry and Social Affairs, Mohamed Labied.
Transport, Mohamed Bouamoud.
Energy and Mines, Mohamed Fettah.
Youth and Sport, Abdellatif Semlali.
Fisheries and Merchant Shipping, Bensalem Smili.
Secretary General of the Government, Abbès Kaissi.
Culture, Mohamed Benaissa.
Environment, Abderrahmane Boufettass.
Posts and Telecommunications, Mohamed Laensar.
Agriculture and Agricultural Reform, Othman Demnati.
Trade and Industry, Abdellah Al Azmani.
Employment, Hassan Abbadi.
Prime Minister's Office, Moulay Zine Zahidi (*Economic Affairs*); Khali Hanna Ould Errachid (*Development of the Sahara Provinces*); Rachidi Ghazouani (*the Plan*); Abdeslem Baraka (*Relations with Parliament*); Abderrahim Ben Abdeljalil (*Administrative Affairs*).

EMBASSY OF THE KINGDOM OF MOROCCO
49 Queen's Gate Gardens, SW7 5NE
[01–581 5001–4]

Ambassador Extraordinary and Plenipotentiary, His Excellency Abdeslam Zenined, G.C.V.O. (1987).
Military, Naval and Air Attaché, Col. Mustapha Jabrane.

Area and Population.—Morocco is situated in the north-western corner of the African continent between latitude 27° 40′–36° N. and longitude 1°–13° W. with an area estimated at 172,414 sq. miles (446,550 sq. km.), and a population (1985 U.N. estimate) of 23,602,000. It is traversed in the north by the Rif mountains and in a general S.W. to N.E. direction, by the Middle Atlas, the High Atlas, the Anti-Atlas and the Sarrho ranges. The northern flanks of the Middle and High Atlas mountains are well wooded but their southern slopes, exposed to the dry desert winds, are generally arid and desolate. The north-westerly point of Morocco is the peninsula of Tangier which is separated from the continent of Europe by the narrow strait of Gibraltar. The Jebel Mousa dominates the promontory and, with the rocky eminence of Gibraltar, was known to the ancients as the *Pillars of Hercules,* the western gateway of the Mediterranean.

Western Sahara.—Formerly the Spanish Sahara, the territory was split between Morocco and Mauritania in 1976 after Spain withdrew in Dec. 1975. In 1979 Mauritania renounced its claim to its share of the territory, which was added by Morocco to its area. Morocco's annexation has been opposed by Polisario guerrillas, who want the territory to become an independent state. On August 30, 1988, Morocco and the Polisario Front accepted a U.N. peace plan. Under the plan a ceasefire will come into effect, probably by the end of 1988, and a referendum to determine the future of the area will be held.

Climate.—The climate of Morocco is generally good and healthy, especially on the Atlantic coast, (where a high degree of humidity is, however, prevalent) the country being partially sheltered by the Atlas mountains from the hot winds of the Sahara. The rainy season may last from November to April. The plains of the interior are intensely hot in summer. Average summer and winter temperatures for Rabat are 27° C. and 7° C.

Government.—Morocco became an independent sovereign state in 1956, following joint declarations made with France on March 2, 1956, and with Spain on April 7, 1956. The Sultan of Morocco, Sidi Mohammad ben Youssef, adopted the title of King Mohammad V.

Following serious disturbances in Casablanca in March, 1965, attempts were made by King Hassan, in consultation with all political parties, to form a government of national union. These efforts were unsuccessful and on June 7, 1965, the King proclaimed a "state of exception" and suspended Parliament. Assuming himself the office of Prime Minister, he announced the formation of a new government and indicated that constitutional changes were to follow. A revised Constitution was approved by a national referendum on July 24, 1970 and brought into effect soon after. It was superseded by another constitution, also approved by a national referendum, on March 1, 1972. This provides that not only political parties, but trade unions, chambers of commerce and professional bodies will participate in the organization of the State and representation of the people; specifies that the King is the supreme representative of the people; makes changes in the composition of the Regency Council and the Sovereign's rights and establishes a unicameral legislature. The Chamber has 306 members, 204 elected by direct universal suffrage (including 5 representing overseas workers) and 102 members elected by electoral colleges representing local government, industry, agriculture and working class groups. There were elections in Sept.-Oct 1984 and the new Parliament began its 6 year term on Oct. 12. A new government was named in April 1985 which included members of three political parties, though over half the portfolios went to non-political appointees.

Defence.—The Moroccan army, formed in 1956, is about 140,000 strong. A Moroccan air force was formed in 1959 and a navy in 1960. Their strengths are about 13,000 and 6,000 respectively. The armed forces possess quantities of French and American equipment, including aircraft, as well as Soviet-supplied hardware.

Production and Trade.—Morocco's main sources of wealth are agricultural and mineral. The Five Year Plan (1981–85) for economic development placed particular emphasis on social improvement. Other priority sectors were industrial development, fisheries, agriculture and tourism. The next development plan (1987 onwards) is similar to the last. The world recession and high energy prices, coupled with a fall in the price of phosphates and poor harvests due to low rainfall have created problems for the economy since the end of the 1970's. However, rains in the winter of 1985–6 ended the long drought and the 1986 harvest was good with the 1988 harvest expected to be even better. Similarly the fall in oil prices, the value of the dollar and interest rates have helped.

Agriculture employs more than 40 per cent. of the working population and accounts for about 36 per cent. of Morocco's exports. The main agricultural exports are fruit and vegetables. Cork and wood-pulp are the most important commercial forest products. Esparto grass is also produced. There is a fishing industry and substantial quantities of canned fish, mainly sardines and fishmeal, are exported. Manufacturing industries are centred in Casablanca, Fez, Tangier and Safi.

Morocco's mineral exports are phosphates, fluorite, barite, manganese, iron ore, lead, zinc, cobalt, copper and antimony. Morocco possesses nearly three-quarters of the world's estimated reserves of phosphates. There are oil refineries at Mohammedia and Sidi Kacem handling about four million tonnes of crude oil per year, but no significant quantities of hydrocarbons have been found.

Tourism is of increasing importance to the Moroccan economy with development concentrated in Agadir and Marrakesh.

Morocco's main import requirements are petroleum products, motor vehicles, building materials, agricultural and other machinery, chemical products, sugar, green tea and other foodstuffs.

The trade of Morocco is chiefly with France, U.S.A., Saudi Arabia, the Federal Republic of Germany, Italy, the United Kingdom and Spain.

	1985	1986
Imports	DH 78,376m.	DH 78,686m.
Exports	48,132m.	50,718m.

Trade with U.K.

	1986	1987
Imports from U.K.	£84,510,000	£94,486,589
Exports to U.K.	65,419,000	61,108,450

Communications.—The railway runs south from Tangier to Sidi Kacem. From this junction, one line runs eastwards through Fez to Oujda, and another continues southwards, through Rabat and Casablanca, to Marrakesh. A line running due south from Oujda skirts the Morocco-Algeria frontier and reaches Bouarfa. Moroccan railroads cover 1,250 miles and traction is electric or diesel. An extensive network of well-surfaced roads covers all the main towns in the kingdom.

British Airways and Royal-Air-Maroc operates services between Casablanca and London. There are air services between Tangier, Agadir (seasonal), Marrakesh and London, and also between Tangier and Gibraltar connecting with London. Royal Air Inter operates internal services. There are also regular services by many airlines with many parts of the world.

Language.—Arabic is the official language. Berber is the vernacular mainly in the mountain regions. French and Spanish are also spoken mainly in the towns. The national daily press consists of 6 Arabic and 5 French newspapers.

Education.—There are government primary, secondary and technical schools. At Fez there is a theological university of great repute in the Moslem world. There is a secular university at Rabat. Schools for special denominations, Jewish and Catholic, are permitted and may receive government grants.

CAPITAL.—ΨRabat (population 893,402). Regional capitals, with municipal population figures as at 1982, are: ΨCasablanca (2,139,204); Marrakesh (439,728); Fez (448,823); Oujda (260,082); Meknes (319,783); Ψ Agadir (110,479). The towns of Fez, Marrakesh and Meknes were capitals at various times in Morocco's history.

CURRENCY.—Dirham of 100 Centimes.

FLAG.—Red, with green pentagram (the Seal of Solomon).

NATIONAL DAY.—March 3 (Anniversary of the Throne).

Ambassador Extraordinary and Plenipotentiary, His Excellency John William Richmond Shakespeare, C.M.G., L.V.O. (1987).

First Secretary, S. R. H. Pease (*Head of Chancery/ Commercial, and Consul*).

Defence Attaché, Lt.-Col. R. Chetwyn-Stapylton.

Vice Consul (Tangier), W. A. T. Pulleyblank, O.B.E.

There is a British Consular/Commercial Office at Casablanca.

British Council Representative, P. Taylor, (P.O. Box 427), 22 Avenue Moulay Youssef, Rabat.

BRITISH CHAMBER OF COMMERCE, 291 Boulevard Mohamed V, Casablanca.

MOZAMBIQUE
(República Popular de Moçambique)

President, Joaquim Alberto Chissano, *sworn in,* November 1986.

COUNCIL OF MINISTERS

Prime Minister, Mario da Graca Machungo.

Foreign Affairs, Pascoal Mocumbi.

National Defence, Alberto Joaquim Chipande.

Chief of Staff of the Armed Forces, Lt.-Gen. Antonio Hama Thai.

Co-operation, Jacinto Veloso.

Planning, Mario Machungo.

Minister in the Presidency, Feliciano Gundana.

State Administration, Jose Oscar Montaire.

Education, Graca Machel.

Interior, Manuel Antonio.

Security, Mariano de Araujo Matsinha.

Transport and Communications, Armando Emilio Guebuza.

Finance, Abdul Magid Osman.

Health, Dr. Leonardo Simao.

Information, Teodato Hunguana.

Construction and Water, Joao Salomao.

Trade, Aranda da Silva.

Agriculture, Alexandre Jose Zandamela.

Industry and Energy, Antonio Branco.

Mineral Resources, John Kachamila.

Justice, Ossumane Ali Dauto.

Area and Population.—The People's Republic of Mozambique lies on the east coast of Africa, and is bounded by Swaziland in the south, South Africa in the south and west, Zimbabwe in the west, Zambia and Malawi in the north-west and Tanzania in the north. It has an area of 309,495 sq. miles (801,590 sq. km.), with a population estimated at 14,000,000 (1986). The official language is Portuguese.

Government.—Mozambique, discovered by Vasco de Gama in 1498, and colonized by Portugal, achieved complete independence from Portugal on June 25, 1975. The date had been agreed in September 1974 by Portugal and *Frelimo* (*Frente de Libertação de Moçambique*), the Marxist liberation movement.

Constitution.—The country is governed by a Council of Ministers and by the Permanent Political Committee of the *Frelimo* Party; membership of these two bodies virtually overlaps. No other political parties are permitted. The principal legislative body, the People's Assembly, consists of 216 members nominated by *Frelimo*.

The basis of the economy is subsistence agriculture, but there is an industrial sector based mainly in Beira and Maputo. After giving priority to the development of collective farms and state enterprises in all sectors, the government is now encouraging the private sector and foreign investment, particularly in agriculture and consumer goods production. Main exports are sugar, cashew nuts, copra, cotton, tea and sisal. There are substantial coal deposits in Tete province. Mozambique has a range of aid and co-operation agreements with a number of countries in Eastern Europe and in the West. An agreement of non-aggression and good neighbourliness with South Africa was signed on March 16, 1984 (the Nkomati Accord).

Trade with U.K.

	1986	1987
Imports from U.K.	£13,175,000	£21,168,000
Exports to U.K.	1,335,000	6,580,000

CAPITAL.—Ψ Maputo (pop. 1,000,000). Other main ports are Ψ Beira and Ψ Nacala.

CURRENCY.—Metical of 100 Centavos.

FLAG.—From top, three lateral bands of green, black and yellow separated by white stripes, and red half diamond pointing to centre of flag over which is superimposed a yellow star, book, and crossed rifle and hoe.

NATIONAL DAY.—June 25 (Independence Day).

Ambassador Extraordinary and Plenipotentiary, His Excellency James Nicholas Allan, C.B.E. (1986).

First Secretary, D. S. Gordon-MacLeod (*Head of Chancery and Consul*); J. M. Winter (*Aid/Commercial*); C. A. Pagett (*Chancery*).

Second Secretary, Miss E. A. Rose, M.B.E.

NEPAL
(Sri Nepala Sarkar)

Sovereign, H.M. King Birendra Bir Bikram Shah Dev, *born* Dec. 28, 1945; *succeeded* Jan. 31, 1972; *crowned* Feb. 24, 1975; *married,* Feb. 1970, H.M. Queen Aishwara Rajya Laxmi Devi Shah. *Heir,* H.R.H. Crown Prince Dipendra Bir Bikram Shah Dev, *born,* June 27, 1971.

COUNCIL OF MINISTERS

Prime Minister, Royal Palace and Defence, Rt. Hon. Marich Man Singh Shrestha.

Foreign Affairs, Rt. Hon. Shailendra Kumar Upadhaya.

Supplies, Rt. Hon. Dill Bahadur Shrestha.

Communications, Rt. Hon. Hari Bahadur Basnet.

Land Reforms and Management, Rt. Hon. Padma Sundar Lawati.

Panchayat and Local Development, Rt. Hon. Pashupati Shumsher J. B. Rana.

Industry, Rt. Hon. Balaram Gharti Magar.

Water Resources, Rt. Hon. Yadav Prasad Pant.

Housing and Physical Planning, Rt. Hon. Dr. Prakash Chandra Lohani.

Commerce, Labour and Social Welfare, Rt. Hon. Parsu Narayan Chaudhari.

Health, Rt. Hon. Mrs. Sushila Thapa.

Education and Culture, (vacant).

Finance, Rt. Hon. Bharat Bahadur Pradhan.

Tourism, Rt. Hon. Dr. Mohammed Mohsin.

ROYAL NEPALESE EMBASSY IN LONDON
12a, Kensington Palace Gardens, W8 4QU
[01–229 1594/6231]

Ambassador Extraordinary and Plenipotentiary, His
Excellency Maj.-Gen. Bharat Kesher Simha (1988).
Chargé d'Affairs, Badri Prasad Khanal.
Military Attaché, Lt.-Col. C. B. Gurung.
Attachés, Baikuntha Prasad Aryal; Ghanashyam
Lall Joshi; Rameswor Paudel.

Area and Population.—Nepal lies between India
and the Tibet Autonomous Region of China on the
slopes of the Himalayas, and includes Mount Everest
(29,028 ft). It has a total area of 54,342 sq. miles
(140,747 sq. km.), and a population estimated (1987) at
about 17·5 million. The country comprises three
distinct horizontal formations. In the south, joining
the Indian plains, is the Terai, a fair proportion of
which was covered with jungle. It has recently been
more widely cultivated but wild life is preserved in
parts. The region represents 10 per cent of the total
land area and nearly 40 per cent of the population
live there. The central belt of the country is hilly,
but with many fertile valleys, leading up to the
snowline at about 14,000 feet. The hills account for
60 per cent of the area of the country and about 50
per cent of the population. The remainder of the
country consists of high mountains which are
sparsely inhabited. The country is drained by three
great river systems rising within and beyond the
Himalayan mountain ranges and eventually flowing
into the Ganges in India.

The inhabitants are of mixed stock, with Mongolian
characteristics prevailing in the North and Indian
in the south. The official religion is Hinduism but
there is also a strong Buddhist adherence. Gautama
Buddha was born in Nepal.

History and Government.—The country was originally divided into numerous hill clans and petty
principalities, but Nepal emerged as a nation in the
middle of the 18th Century when its component parts
were unified by the warrior Raja of Gorkha, Prithvi
Narayan Shah, who founded the present Nepalese
dynasty. In 1846 power was seized by Jung Bahadur
Rana after a massacre of nobles, and he was the first
of a line of hereditary Rana Prime Ministers who
ruled Nepal for 104 years. During this time the role
of the Monarchs was mainly ceremonial.

In 1950–51 a revolutionary movement achieved its
aim of breaking the hereditary power of the Ranas
and restoring the Monarchy to its former position.
After 10 years, during which various parties and
individuals tried their hand at government, the late
King Mahendra proscribed all political parties and
assumed direct powers on December 16, 1960, with
the object of leading a united country to democracy.
In 1962 he introduced a new Constitution embodying
a tiered, partyless system of panchayat (council)
democracy, under which there were elected councils
at village level which in turn elect members to district
council and thence to zonal councils; a referendum
in May 1980 decided in favour of retaining the
panchayat system, with some reforms; namely, election to the Rastriaya Panchayat (National Parliament) by universal adult franchise (over 21 years
old); selection of the Prime Minister by the Rastriaya
Panchayat and responsibility of his government to
that body. The King retains certain reserve powers.
In a general election in May 1986, 112 members were
elected from the 75 districts of Nepal. The King
appoints 28 other members, making a total of 140.

Economy.—Nepal exports carpets, textile yarn,
fabrics, clothing, jute, rice and other grains, hides,
oil seeds, ghi, cattle, timber, etc., and imports cotton
goods and yarns, sugar, salt, spices, petrol, metals,
etc. Foreign aid supports 60 per cent of the development budget of the Kingdom and tourism is the single

largest commercial earner of foreign exchange
(U.S.$55·9 million in 1986–87).

Revenue for the fiscal year 1987–88 is estimated at
N Rps. 7,355·75m; foreign aid *N Rps.* 6,601·99m; and
internal borrowing *N Rps.* 1,230m.

Trade with U.K.

	1986	1987
Imports from U.K.	£4,670,000	£8,707,000
Exports to U.K.	6,960,000	8,331,000

A State Bank was inaugurated on April 26, 1956,
to issue bank notes, regulate the Nepalese currency,
fix foreign exchange rates and help in the preparation
of a national budget. There are three commercial
banks with branches throughout Nepal and three
further banks, based only in Kathmandu, established
since 1984 with approximately 49 per cent foreign
bank participation.

Communications.—Kathmandu is connected with
India by a road, the mountain section of which was
built by India under the Colombo Plan, and to Tibet
by a road to Kodari on the border which was built by
the Chinese and opened on May 26, 1967. The Indian-
aided Sunauli-Pokhara road (128 miles) was inaugurated in April 1972, and a road between Pokhara and
Kathmandu, constructed by the Chinese, was opened
in 1973. A link road between Mugling and Nary-
anghat, completed by the Chinese in 1981, has further
improved communications between Kathmandu and
the Terai. The East–West Highway (Mahendra Raj
Marg) to run the length of the country, is almost
complete. Work is in progress from Butwal westwards. Sections of the highway have been built, with
aid from India, United Kingdom, U.S.S.R., U.S.A. and
the Asian Development Bank. British assistance has
included major road projects, rural development in
the Koshi Hills, and extensive educational and
technical training.

There are daily flights from Kathmandu to New
Delhi, and frequent flights to Calcutta and Patna.
There are also daily flights to Bangkok, a twice
weekly direct flight to Dhaka, and regular flights to
to Rangoon, Colombo, Hong Kong, Karachi, Lhasa
and Dubai. A weekly flight to Frankfurt was
scheduled to start in Autumn 1987.

CAPITAL.—Kathmandu, population (1981) 235,000.
Other towns of importance are Biratnagar (94,000),
Lalitpur (81,000) and Bhaktapur (50,500) and Pokhara
(48,500).

CURRENCY.—Nepalese Rupee of 100 Paisa.

FLAG.—Double pennant of crimson with blue
border on peaks; white moon with rays in centre of
top peak; white quarter sun, recumbent in centre of
bottom peak.

NATIONAL ANTHEM.—May Glory Crown Our Illus-
trious Sovereign.

NATIONAL DAY.—December 28.

BRITISH EMBASSY
(Lainchaur Kathmandu, P.O. Box 106)
[Kathmandu 411589]

Ambassador Extraordinary and Plenipotentiary, His
Excellency Richard Eagleson Gordon Burges Wat-
son, C.M.G. (1987).
First Secretary, A. MacLean (*Head of Chancery and
Consul*).
Defence and Military Attaché, Lt.-Col. F. D. Scotson.
Vice-Consul, B. Mason.

British Council Representative, P. Moss, (P.O. Box
640), Kanti Path, Kathmandu.

NETHERLANDS (or HOLLAND)
(Koninkrijk der Nederlanden)

Queen of the Netherlands, Her Majesty Queen Beatrix Wilhelmina Armgard, G.C.V.O., *born* Jan. 31, 1938; *married* March 10, 1966, H.R.H. Prince Claus George Willem Otto Frederik Geert of the Netherlands, Jonkheer van Amsberg; *and has issue*, Prince Willem Alexander, *b.* April 27, 1967; Prince Johan Friso, *b.* Sept, 25, 1968; Prince Constantijn Christof, *b.* Oct. 11, 1969; *succeeded*, April 30, 1980, upon the abdication of her mother Queen Juliana.

CABINET

Prime Minister and Minister of General Affairs, Ruud Lubbers (*C.D.A.*).
Deputy P.M. and Minister for Economic Affairs, Dr. Rudolf de Korte (*V.V.D.*).
Social Affairs and Employment, and Netherlands Antillean and Aruban Affairs, Dr. Jan de Koning (*C.D.A.*).
Defence, Dr. Wim van Eekelen (*V.V.D.*).
Finance, Dr. Herman Ruding (*C.D.A.*).
Transport and Waterways, Mrs. Neelie Smit-Kroes (*V.V.D.*).
Education and Science, Dr. Wim Deetman (C.D.A.).
Welfare, Public Health and Culture, Elco Brinkman (*C.D.A.*).
Development Co-operation, Piet Buckman (*C.D.A.*).
Agriculture and Fisheries, Gerrit Braks (*C.D.A.*).
Housing, Physical Planning and Environment, Ed Nijpels (*V.V.D.*).
Justice, Frits Korthals Altes, (*V.V.D.*).
Home Affairs, Cees van Dijk, (*C.D.A.*).
Foreign Affairs, Hans van den Broek (*C.D.A.*).
(*C.D.A.* = Christian Democrats; *V.V.D.* = Liberals.)

ROYAL NETHERLANDS EMBASSY IN LONDON
38 Hyde Park Gate, SW7 5DP
[01–584 5040]

Ambassador Extraordinary and Plenipotentiary, His Excellency Hans Jonkman, G.C.V.O.
Ministers Plenipotentiary, E. J. P. Roberts; R. R. Smit.
Counsellors, A. J. van der Stadt; D. Vries; A. D. H. Simonsz; A. E. Moses; A. Verduyn.
1st Secretaries, Baroness H. J. C. M. van Lynden; A. C. Brouwer; R. G. de Vos.
Defence, Naval and Air Attaché, Capt. A. H. A. G. Remmen.
Military Attaché, Col. J. Smit.

Area and Population.—The Kingdom of the Netherlands is a maritime country of Western Europe, situated on the North Sea, in lat. 50° 46'–53° 34' N. and long. 3° 22'–7° 14' E., consisting of 12 provinces (Eastern and Southern Flevoland being amalgamated to form the twelfth province) and containing a total area of 15,770 sq. miles (40,844 sq. km). The population (1987 estimate) is 14,615,000. The live birth rate in Jan., 1984 was 12·1 per 1,000 of the population, and the death-rate was 8·3.

The land is generally flat and low, intersected by numerous canals and connecting rivers—in fact, a network of water courses. The principal rivers are the Rhine, Maas, Yssel and Scheldt.

Language and Literature.—Dutch is a West-Germanic language of Saxon origin, closely akin to Old English and Low German. It is spoken in the Netherlands and the northern part of Belgium. It is also used in the Netherlands Antilles. Afrikaans, one of the two South African languages, has Dutch as its origin, but differs from it in grammar and pronunciation. There are six national papers, four of which are morning papers, and there are many regional daily papers.

Government.—In 1815 the Netherlands became a constitutional Kingdom under King William I, a Prince of Orange-Nassau, a descendant of the house which had taken a leading part in the destiny of the nation since the 16th century. The States-General consists of the *Eerste Kamer* (First Chamber) of 75 members, elected for 4 years by the Provincial Council; and the *Tweede Kamer* (Second Chamber) of 150 members, elected for 4 years by voters of 18 years and upwards. Members of the *Tweede Kamer* are paid.

Production. The chief agricultural products are potatoes, wheat, rye, barley, sugar beet, cattle, pigs, milk and milk products, cheese, butter, poultry, eggs, beans, peas, vegetables, fruit, flower bulbs, plants and cut flowers and there is an important fishing industry. Among the principal industries are engineering, both mechanical and electrical, electronics, nuclear energy, petro-chemicals and plastics, road vehicles, aircraft and defence equipment, shipbuilding repair, steel, textiles of all types, electrical appliances, metal ware, furniture, paper, cigars, sugar, liqueurs, beer, clothing etc.

In 1985 the production of crude oil was 3,729 million kgs and refined oil products 61,000 million kgs; steel (1984) 5,739 million kgs, and natural gas 80,721 million cubic metres.

Defence.—The armed forces are almost entirely committed to NATO. All ground and air units are assigned to the NATO Central Region, and naval forces to the Atlantic and Channel commands. Total armed forces number 106,183, which includes 48,720 conscripts and 1,495 women. In addition there are over 176,000 reservists. There is compulsory military service of 14–17 months.

Education.—Primary and secondary education is given in both denominational and State schools, the denominational schools being eligible for State assistance on equal terms with the State schools. Attendance at primary school is compulsory. The principal Universities are at Leiden, Utrecht, Groningen, Amsterdam (2), Nijmegen (R.C.) and Rotterdam, and there are technical Universities at Delft (polytechnic); Eindhoven (polytechnic), Enschede (polytechnic) Wageningen (agriculture). Illiteracy is practically non-existent.

Communications.—The total extent of navigable rivers including canals, was 4,845 km. at Jan. 1, 1985, and of metalled roads 97,189 km. In 1985 the total length of the railway system amounted to 2,867 km., of which 1,810 km. were electrified. The mercantile marine in January 1985 consisted of 550 ships of total 3,461,000 gross registered tons. The total length of air routes covered by K.L.M. (Royal Dutch Airlines) in 1985 was 370,640 km.

FINANCE

	1986
Budget Revenue	D.fl. 175,610 m.
Budget Expenditure	194,493 m.

TRADE

The Dutch are traditionally a trading nation. Entrepôt trade, banking and shipping are of particular importance to the economy. The geographical position of the Netherlands, at the mouths of the Rhine, Meuse and Scheldt, brings a large volume of transit trade to and from the interior of Europe to Dutch ports.

Principal trading partners are the Federal Republic of Germany and Belgium/Luxembourg. U.K. supplied 10 per cent of Netherlands imports in 1985 and took 9·5 per cent of Netherlands exports.

Excluding the building industry, the index of industrial production in the Netherlands (1980 = 100) was 101 in 1984 and the index of industrial production per worker (1980 = 100) was 122 in 1984.

	1984	1985
Imports	D.fl. 198,922 m.	D.fl. 215,467 m.
Exports	210,691 m.	225,568 m.

Trade with U.K.

	1985	1986
Imports from U.K.	£7,344,681,000	£5,442,503,000
Exports to U.K.	6,550,735,000	6,615,581,000

CAPITAL.—ΨAmsterdam, 1,031,000 (urban agglomeration). SEAT OF GOVERNMENT, The Hague (Den Haag or, in full, 's-Gravenhage). Pop. 443,456. Other principal cities; ΨRotterdam, 571,081; Utrecht, 229,969; Eindhoven, 191,675; Haarlem, 151,025; Groningen, 168,119; Tilburg, 153,812.

CURRENCY.—Netherlands Guilder or Florin of 100 Cents.

FLAG.—Three horizontal bands of red, white and blue.

NATIONAL ANTHEM.—"Wilhelmus".

BRITISH EMBASSY
Lange Voorhout, 10, The Hague, 2514 ED
[The Hague 64 58 00]

Ambassador Extraordinary and Plenipotentiary, His Excellency Michael Romilly Heald Jenkins, C.M.G. (1988).

Counsellors, G. Archer; L. G. Faulkner (*Commercial/Agriculture*).

Defence and Naval Attaché, Capt. R. N. Blair, R.N.

Military and Air Attaché, Lt. Col. R. H. Paterson, O.B.E.

First Secretary and Head of Chancery, P. J. Sullivan.

British Council Representative, J. Andrews, Keizersgracht 343, Amsterdam (Library).

NETHERLANDS-BRITISH CHAMBER OF COMMERCE, The Dutch House, 307–308 High Holborn, WC1V 7LS; U.K. OFFICE, Holland Trade House, Bezuidenhoutseweg 181, 2594 AH The Hague.

OVERSEAS TERRITORIES

Aruba covers an area of 75 sq. miles (193 sq. km.). The island of Aruba was from 1828 part of the Dutch West Indies and from 1845 part of the Netherlands Antilles. On Jan. 1, 1986 it became a separate territory within the Kingdom of the Netherlands. The 1983 Constitutional Conference agreed that Aruba's separate status would last for ten years from 1986, after which the island would become fully independent.

The economy of Aruba is based largely on tourism. In 1986 there were over 180,000 tourists.

Governor, F. B. Tromp.
Prime Minister, J. Henny Eman.

Trade with U.K.

	1986	1987
Imports from U.K.	£6,972,000	£5,652,000
Exports to U.K.	576,000	296,000

CAPITAL.—ΨOranjestad (pop. 17,000); and Sint Nicolaas (17,000).

Netherlands Antilles comprise certain islands in the West Indies (Curaçao, Bonaire, part of St. Martin, St. Eustatius, and Saba). The Islands cover an area of 308 sq. miles (800 sq. km.). The Netherland Antilles (which have a federal parliament) are largely self-governing under the terms of the Realm Statute which took effect on December 29, 1954.

The economy of the Netherlands Antilles is based on small manufacturing industries. The soil is too poor to permit large-scale agriculture and most products for consumption, and industrial raw materials must be imported.

Governor, Dr. R. A. Römer (1983).
Prime Minister, Don Martina.

Trade with U.K.

	1986	1987
Imports from U.K.	£17,260,000	£19,635,000
Exports to U.K.	78,509,000	5,133,000

CAPITAL.—ΨWillemstad (on Curaçao) (pop. 50,000).

NICARAGUA
(República de Nicaragua)

President, Cmdt. Daniel Ortega Saavedra, *inaugurated*, Jan. 10, 1985.
Vice-President, Dr. Sergio Ramírez Mercado.

MINISTERS

Foreign, Fr. Miguel d'Escoto.
Defence, Gen. Humberto Ortega.
Minister of the Interior, Cmdt. Tomás Borge.
External Co-operation, Cmdt. Henry Ruiz.
Agriculture, Cmdt. Jaime Wheelock.
Economy, Industry and Commerce, Cmdt. Luis Carrión.
Minister of the Presidency, René Núñez Téllez.
Vice Minister of the Presidency, Cmdt. Mónica Baltodano.
Secretariat of Planning and Budgeting, Dr. Alejandro Martínez.
Finance, William Hupper.
Construction, Transport and Housing, Cmdt. Mauricio Valenzuala.
Health, Cmdt. Dora María Téllez.
Education and Culture, Fr. Fernando Cardenal.
Justice, Dr. Rodrigo Reyes.
Labour, Benedicto Meneses.

NICARAGUAN EMBASSY IN LONDON
8 Gloucester Road, SW7 4PP
[01–584 4365]

Ambassador Extraordinary and Plenipotentiary, His Excellency Señor Francisco José d'Escoto (1981).

Nicaragua is the largest State of Central America, with a long seaboard on both the Atlantic and Pacific Oceans, situated between 10° 45′–15° N. lat. and 83° 40′–87° 38′ W. long., containing an area of 50,193 sq. miles (130,000 sq. km.). It has a population (1985 U.N. estimate) of 3,272,000, of whom about three-quarters are of mixed blood. Another 15 per cent are white, mostly of pure Spanish descent and the remaining 10 per cent are Indians or negroes. The latter group includes the Mosquitos, who live on the Atlantic coast and were formerly under British protection.

Government.—The eastern coast of Nicaragua was touched by Columbus in 1502, and in 1518 was overrun by Spanish forces under Davila, and formed part of the Spanish Captaincy-General of Guatemala until 1821, when its independence was secured. In 1927, Augusto Cesar Sandino began a guerrilla war against the occupation of Nicaragua by U.S. Marines, which continued until they were expelled in 1933. Sandino was assassinated by Anastasio Somoza, Director of the National Guard, and in 1936 Somoza assumed the Presidency. He was succeeded in power by his sons Luis and Anastasio Somoza, until 1979 when the family and the National Guard were overthrown by guerrillas of the Sandinista National Liberation Front. A Junta of National Reconstruction subsequently took power.

Elections for President, Vice-President and a National Assembly were held on Nov. 4, 1984, and on Jan. 10, 1985 they replaced the Junta and the Council of State. Distribution of seats in the National Assembly was: Sandinista National Liberation Front 61; Democratic Conservative Party 14; Independent Liberal Party 9; People's Christian Social Party 6; Communist Party 2; Socialist Party 2; Marxist-Leninist Popular Action Movement 2.

On Jan. 9, 1987, President Ortega signed the new constitution but almost immediately re-introduced the state of emergency.

Agriculture and Industry.—The country is mainly agricultural. The major crops are cotton, coffee (30 per cent of total export earnings), sugar cane, tobacco, sesame and bananas. Beans, rice, maize and ipeca-cuanha, livestock and timber production are also important. However, fishing, forestry, grain and cattle production have been hit by the civil war in the main growing areas. Nicaragua possesses deposits of gold and silver.

Communications.—There are 252 miles of railway, all on the Pacific side and approximately 5,500 miles of telegraph. There are 51 radio stations and two television stations in Managua. An automatic telephone system has been installed in the capital and extended to all major cities. A ground station for satellite communication was inaugurated in 1973. Transport except on the Pacific slope, is still attended with difficulty but many new roads have either been opened or are under construction. The Inter-American Highway runs from the Honduras frontier in the north to the Costa Rican border in the south; the interoceanic highway runs from the Corinto on the Pacific coast via Managua to Rama, where there is a natural waterway to Bluefields on the Atlantic. The country's main airport is at Managua. The chief port is Corinto on the Pacific.

Language and Literature.—The official language of the country is Spanish and the majority profess Catholicism, although the English language and the Moravian Church are widespread on the Atlantic coast. There are 3 daily newspapers published at Managua, apart from the official Gazette (*La Gaceta*). A national literacy campaign in 1980 has reduced illiteracy to 12 per cent. There are universities at León and Managua.

Trade with U.K.

	1986	1987
Imports from U.K.	£7,349,000	£7,883,000
Exports to U.K.	1,307,000	717,000

Considerable quantities of foodstuffs are imported as well as cotton goods, jute, iron and steel, machinery and petroleum products. The chief exports are cotton, coffee, beef, gold, sugar, cottonseed and bananas.

CAPITAL.—Managua, population 615,000. The centre was almost totally destroyed in the earthquake of December 1972. León, 158,577; Granada, 72,640; Masaya, 78,308; Chinandega, 144,291.

CURRENCY.—Córdoba of 100 Centavos.

FLAG.—Horizontal stripes of blue, white and blue, with the Nicaraguan coats of arms in the centre of the white stripe.

NATIONAL DAY.—September 15.

NATIONAL ANTHEM.—Salve A Ti Nicaragua (Hail, Nicaragua).

BRITISH EMBASSY
P.O. Box A-169, Reparto Los Robles, Primera Etapa, De la entrada principal, la 4ᵉ casa a mano derecha, Managua, Nicaragua.
[Managua 70034]

British Ambassador and Consul-General, (resides at San José, Costa Rica).

NIGER
(République du Niger)

President, Col. Ali Saibou (*also holds Defence and Interior portfolios*).

MINISTERS

Prime Minister, Hamid Algabid.
Finance, Beidari Mamadou.
Public Health and Social Affairs, Bare Mainassara Ibrahim.
Public Works and Housing, Oumarou Coulibali.
Post and Telecommunications, Issa Amsa.
Transport and Tourism, Amadou Moussa Gros.
Youth, Sport and Culture, Abdourahamane Seydou.
Higher Education and Technical Research, Yahaya Tounkara.
Minister delegate for Interior, Amadou Fiti Maiga.
Mines and Energy, Allele Elhadj Habibou.
Planning, Almoustapha Soumaila.
Foreign Affairs and Co-operation, Sani Bako.
Public Establishments, State Enterprises, and Parastatals, Maina Boukar Moussa.
National Education, Amadou Madougou.
Labour, Aboubacar Abdou.
Trade, Industry and Workers, Madou Mahamadou.
Agriculture and Environment, Amadou Mamadou.
Information, Sahidou Alou.
Animal Resources and Hydraulics, Mahamadou Danda.
Justice, Soli Abdourahamane.

Situated in West Central Africa, between 12° and 24° N. and 0° and 16° E., Niger has common boundaries with Algeria and Libya in the north, Chad, Nigeria, Benin, Mali and Burkina.

It has an area of about 489,191 sq. miles (1,267,000 sq. km.), with a population (estimate, 1985) of 6,317,550. Apart from a small region along the Niger Valley in the south-west near the capital the country is entirely savannah or desert. The main ethnic groups are the Hausa (54 per cent.) in the south, the Songhai and

Djerma in the south-west, the Fulani, the Beriberi–Manga, and the nomadic Tuareg in the north. The official language is French.

The first French expedition arrived in 1891 and the country was fully occupied by 1914. It decided on December 18, 1958, to remain an autonomous republic within the French Community; full independence outside the Community was proclaimed on August 3, 1960. Special agreements with France, covering financial and cultural matters, technical assistance, defence, etc., were signed in Paris on April 24, 1961. These are now being revised.

The constitution of Niger, adopted on November 8, 1960, provided for a presidential system of government, modelled on that of the United States and the French Fifth Republic, and a single Chamber National Assembly. In April 1974 Lt.-Col. Seyni Kountché seized power, suspended the Constitution, dissolved the National Assembly, and suppressed all political organizations. He then set up a Supreme Military Council with himself as President. President Kountché died on Nov. 10, 1987 and was succeeded peacefully by his cousin, Col. Ali Saibou.

Finance,—The 1987 General Budget allocation was *CFA* 198,100 million.

Trade.—The cultivation of ground-nuts and the production of livestock are the main industries and provide two of the main exports. A company formed by the Government, the French Atomic Energy Authority and private interests is exploiting uranium deposits at Arlit, and this is the main export. Value of imports in 1985 was *CFA* 123,977 m.; exports was *CFA* 77,940 m.

Trade with U.K.

	1986	1987
Imports from U.K.	£10,370,000	£7,026,000
Exports to U.K.	850,000	10,556,000

CAPITAL.—Niamey (399,100).

CURRENCY.—Franc C.F.A. of 100 Centimes.

FLAG.—Three horizontal stripes, orange, white and green with an orange disc in the middle of the white stripe.

NATIONAL DAY.—December 18.

British Ambassador, (resident at Abidjan, Côte d'I-voire).

NORWAY
(Kongeriket Norge)

King, Olav V, K.G., K.T., G.C.B., G.C.V.O., *b.* July 2, 1903; *succeeded,* Sept. 21, 1957, on death of his father King Haakon VII; *married* March 21, 1929, Princess Märtha of Sweden (*born* March 28, 1901; *died* April 5, 1954); having issue, Harald (*see below*) and two daughters.

Heir-Apparent, H.R.H. Prince Harald, G.C.V.O., *b.* Feb. 21, 1937; *m.* Aug. 29, 1968, Sonja Haraldsen, and has issue Princess Märtha Louise, *b.*Sept. 22, 1971; and Prince Haakon Magnus, *b.* July 20, 1973.

CABINET

Prime Minister, Ms. Gro Harlem Brundtland.
Foreign Affairs, Thorvald Stoltenberg.
Cultural and Scientific Affairs, Hallvard Bakke.
Environment, Ms. Sissel Rønbeck.
Industry, Finn Kristensen.
Petroleum and Energy, Arne Øien.
Local Government and Labour, Kjell Borgen.
Development Co-operation, Ms. Kirsti Kolle Grøndahl.
Trade, Kurt Mosbakk.
Fisheries, Bjarne Mørk Eidem.

Defence, Johan Jørgen Holst.
Transport and Communications, William Engseth.
Justice, Ms. Helen Bøsterud.
Finance, Gunnar Berge.
Church and Education, Ms. Mary Kvidal.
Health and Social Affairs, Ms. Tove Strand Gerhard-sen.
Agriculture, Ms. Gunhild Øyangen.
Consumer Affairs and Government Administration, Ms. Einfrid Halvorsen.

ROYAL NORWEGIAN EMBASSY IN LONDON
Offices: 25 Belgrave Square, SW1X 8QD
[01–235 7151]

Ambassador Extraordinary and Plenipotentiary, His Excellency Rolf Busch (1982).
Minister-Counsellor, Haakon B. Hjelde.
Counsellors, Jan Flatla (*Press and Cultural*); Viggo Jan Olsen (*Fisheries*); Eva Bugge (*Economic*); Viggo Smestad (*Commercial*).
First Secretaries, Kjell Harald Dalen (*Political*); Øistein Bergh (*Consul*); Rune Aasheim (*Economic*).
Second Secretaries, Anna Rikter-Svendsen (*Press, Information and Cultural*).

Area and Population.—Norway ("The Northern Way"), a kingdom in the northern and western portion of the Scandinavian peninsula, was founded in 872. It is 1,752 km. in length, its greatest width about 430 km. The length of the coastline is 2,542 km., and the frontier between Norway and the neighbouring countries is 2,542 km. (Sweden 1,619 km., Finland 727 km. and U.S.S.R. 196 km.). It is divided into 19 counties (*fylker*) and comprises an area of 149,282 sq. miles (386,638 sq. km.), of which Svalbard and Jan Mayen have a combined area of 24,101 sq. km., with a population (estimated, Jan. 1987) of 4,198,637.

The Norwegian coastline is extensive, deeply indented with numerous fjords, and fringed with an immense number of rocky islands. The surface is mountainous, consisting of elevated and barren tablelands, separated by deep and narrow valleys. At the North Cape the sun does not appear to set from the second week in May to the last week in July, causing the phenomenon known as the *Midnight Sun*; conversely, there is no apparent sunrise from about Nov. 18 to Jan. 23. During the long winter nights are seen the multiple coloured *Northern Lights* or *Aurora Borealis,* which have a maximum intensity in a line crossing North America from Alaska to Labrador and Northern Europe to the Arctic coast and Siberia.

Language and Literature.—Old Norse literature is among the most ancient and richest in Europe. Norwegian in both its present forms is closely related to other Scandinavian languages. Independence from Denmark (1814) and resurgent nationalism led to the development of "new Norwegian" based on dialects, which now has equal official standing with "bokmål", in which Danish influence is more obvious. This was formed in the time of the Reformation, and Ludvig Holberg (1684–1754) is regarded as the father of Norwegian literature, though the modern period begins with the patriotic and romantic writings of Henrik Wergeland (1808–1845). Some of the famous names are Henrik Ibsen (1828–1906), Bjørnstjerne Bjørnson (1832–1910), Nobel Prizewinner in 1903, and the novelists Jonas Lie (1833–1908), Alexander Kielland (1849–1906), Knut Hamsun (1859–1952) and Sigrid Undset (1882–1949), the latter two both Nobel Prizewinners, and the latter a champion of Norwegian womanhood. In 1988 there were 157 daily newspapers.

Government.—From 1397 to 1814 Norway was united with Denmark, and from Nov. 4, 1814, with Sweden, under a personal union which was dissolved on June 7, 1905, when Norway regained complete independence. Under the constitution of May 17, 1814, the *Storting* (Parliament) itself elects one-quarter of its members to constitute the *Lagting* (Upper Chamber), the other three-quarters forming the *Odelsting* (Lower Chamber). Legislative questions alone are dealt with by both parts in separate sittings.

The three-party coalition government fell on May 1, 1986, when it lost a vote of confidence, and was succeeded by a minority Labour government which took office on May 9, 1986.

Production.—The cultivated area is about 8,636 sq. km. (2·3 per cent of total surface area); forests cover nearly 25 per cent; the rest consists of highland pastures or uninhabitable mountains.

The *Gulf Stream* pours from 140 to 170 million cubic feet of warm water per second into the sea around Norway and causes the temperature to be higher than the average for the latitude. It brings shoals of herring and cod into the fishing grounds and causes a warm current of air over the west coast, making it possible to cultivate potatoes and barley in latitudes which in other countries are perpetually frozen. In normal years the quantity of fish caught by Norwegian fishing vessels is greater than that of any other European country except U.S.S.R. In 1987 the total catch amounted to 1,867,720 tonnes.

The chief industries are manufactures, agriculture and forestry, fisheries, mining, production of metals and ferro-alloys and shipping. Also in recent years industries providing both manufactured products and services for the development of North Sea oil and gas resources have assumed growing importance. In 1987, the total workforce was 2,126,000 of which 352,000 persons were employed in Norwegian industry. Manufactures are aided by great resources of hydro-electric power. Actual production in 1987 amounted to 104,283 Gwh.

Defence.—Norway is a member of the North Atlantic Treaty Organization, and the Headquarters of Allied Forces, Northern Europe, is situated near Oslo. The period of compulsory national service is 15 months (without refresher training) in the Navy and Air Force, and 12 months (with refresher training) in the Army. In March 1978 Norway committed an infantry battalion with additional support to the U.N. Interim Force in the Lebanon.

Education from 7 to 16 is free and compulsory in the "basic schools" maintained by the municipalities with State grants-in-aid. The majority of the pupils receive post-compulsory schooling at "upper secondary" schools, colleges of education (19) regional colleges akin to polytechnics (12), universities (4) and other university-level specialist institutions.

Communications.—The total length of railways open at the end of 1987 was 4,218 km., excluding private lines. There are 86,805 km. of public roads in Norway (including urban streets). At the end of 1987, 2,865,462 road motor vehicles were registered.

Scheduled internal air services are operated by Scandinavian Airlines System (SAS) on behalf of Det Norske Luftfartselskap (DNL), by Braathens South American and Far East Airtransport (SAFE), and by Wideróes Flyveselskap A.S.

The Mercantile Marine, 1987, consisted of 1,195 vessels of 7,197,036 gross tons (vessels above 100 gross tons, excluding fishing boats, floating whaling factories, tugs, salvage vessels, icebreakers and similar types of vessel).

FINANCE

	1986	1987
Total Revenue	*K*240,905,920	*K*321,677,000
Total Expenditure	228,340,220	282,648,000

TRADE

	1986	1987
	million *Kroner*	
Total imports	211,054	211,794
Total exports	194,047	199,731

Trade with U.K.

	1986	1987
Imports from U.K.	£1,147,790	£1,220,844,000
Exports to U.K.	3,265,157	3,290,339,000

The chief imports are raw materials, motor vehicles, chemicals, motor spirit, fuel and other oils; coal, ships and machinery; together with manufactures of silk, cotton and wool. The exports consist chiefly of crude oil and gas, manufactured goods, fish and products of fish (as canned fish, whale oils), pulp, paper, iron ore and pyrites, nitrate of lime, stone, calcium carbide, aluminium, ferro-alloys, zinc, nickel, cyanamide, etc.

CAPITAL.—ΨOslo (incl. Aker). Pop. (Jan. 1987), 450,808. Other towns are ΨTrondheim, 135,542; ΨBergen, 209,912; ΨStavanger, 96,316; ΨKristiansand, 63,637; ΨDrammen, 55,180; ΨTromsø, 49,358.

FLAG.—Red, with white-bordered blue cross.

NATIONAL ANTHEM.—Ja, Vi Elsker Dette Landet (Yes, we love this country).

NATIONAL DAY.—May 17 (Constitution Day).

BRITISH EMBASSY
Thomas Heftyesgate 8,0264 Oslo 2.
[Oslo 55 24 00]

Ambassador Extraordinary and Plenipotentiary, His Excellency John Adam Robson, C.M.G. (1987).
Counsellors, R. G. Short, M.V.O. (*Head of Chancery and Consul General*); C. P. Burdess, (*Economic*).
First Secretaries, J. Venning; D. O. Hay-Edie.
Defence and Air Attaché, Wg. Cdr. S. Wrigley, R.A.F.
Naval Attaché, Cdr. H. L. Foxworthy, R.N.
Military Attaché, Lt. Col. R. A. Gamble.

BRITISH CONSULAR OFFICES

There is a British Consular Office at *Oslo* and Honorary Consulates at *Bergen, Tromsø, Alesund, Kristiansund, Stavanger, Trondheim, Kristiansand, Haugesund* and *Harstad.*

British Council Representative, P. A. Thompson, Fridtjof Nansens Plass 5,0160, Oslo 1.

SVALBARD
(Spitsbergen and Bear Island)

By Treaty (Feb. 9, 1920) the sovereignty of Norway over the Spitsbergen ("Pointed Mountain") Archipelago was recognized by the Great Powers and other interested nations, and on Aug. 14, 1925, Norway assumed sovereignty. In September, 1941, Allied forces (British, Canadian and Norwegian) landed on the main island. After destruction of the accumulated stocks of coal and dismantling of mining machinery and the wireless installation, the Norwegian inhabitants (about 600) were evacuated to a British port and the Russians (about 1,500) to the U.S.S.R. After the war the Norwegian mining plants were rebuilt. 288,000 metric tons of coal were extracted from Norwegian mines in Svalbard in 1980.

The Svalbard Archipelago lies between 74°–81° N. lat. and between 10°–35° E. long., with an estimated area of 24,295 square miles. The archipelago consists of a main island, known as Spitsbergen (15,200 sq. miles); North East Land, closely adjoining and separated by Hinlopen Strait; the Wiche Islands, separated from the mainland by Olga Strait; Barents and Edge Islands, separated from the mainland by Stor Fjord (or Wybe Jansz Water); Prince Charles Foreland, to the W.; Hope Island, to the S.E.; Bear Island (68 square miles) 127 miles to the S.; with many similar islands in the neighbourhood of the main group. In addition to those engaged in coal-mining, the archipelago is also visited by hunters for seals, foxes and polar bears.

South Cape is 355 miles from the Norwegian Coast. Ice Fjord is 520 miles from Tromsø, 650 miles from Murmansk, and 1,300 miles from Aberdeen. Transit from Tromsø to Green Harbour 2 to 3 days; from Aberdeen 5 to 6 days.

JAN MAYEN, an island in the Arctic Ocean (70° 49′–71° 9′ N. lat. and 7° 53′–9° 5′ W. long.) was joined to Norway by law of Feb. 27, 1930.

Norwegian Antarctic

BOUVET ISLAND (54° 26′ S. lat. and 3° 24′ E. long.) was declared a dependency of Norway by law of Feb. 27, 1930.

PETER THE FIRST ISLAND (68° 48′ S. lat. and 90° 35′ W. long.), was declared a dependency of Norway by resolution of Government, May 1, 1931.

PRINCESS RAGNHILD LAND (from 70° 30′ to 68° 40′ S. lat. and 24° 15′ to 33° 30′ E. long.) has been claimed as Norwegian since Feb. 17, 1931.

QUEEN MAUD LAND.—On Jan. 14, 1939, the Norwegian Government declared the area between 20° W. and 45° E., adjacent to Australian Antarctica, to be Norwegian territory.

OMAN
(The Sultanate of Oman)

Sultan, Qaboos Bin-Said, *succeeded* on deposition of Sultan Said bin Taimur, July 23, 1970.
(The Sultan acts as his own Prime Minister, Minister of Foreign Affairs, Defence and Finance.)

COUNCIL OF MINISTERS

Agriculture and Fisheries, H.E. Muhammad bin Abdullah bin Zahir al Hinai.

Commerce and Industry, H.E. Col. Salim bin Abdullah al Ghazali.
Communications, H.E. Hamoud bin Abdullah al Harthi.
Deputy P.M., Security and Defence, H.H. Sayyid Fahr bin Taimur Al Said.
Minister of State for Defence, H.E. Brig. Sayyid al Mutassim bin Hamoud Al Bu Saidi.
Office of the Personal Representative of H.M. The Sultan, H.H. Sayyid Thuwaini bin Shihab Al Said.
Education and Youth Affairs, H.E. Yahya bin Mahfuth al Manthari.
Electricity and Water, H.E. Khalfan bin Nasr al Wahaibi.
Environment and Water Resources, H.H. Sayyid Shabib bin Taimur Al Said.
Deputy P.M., Financial and Economic Affairs, H.E. Qais bin Abdul Munim al Zawawi.
Minister of State for Foreign Affairs, H.E. Yusuf bin Alawi bin Abdullah.
Health, H.E. Dr. Mubarak bin Salih al Khaduri.
Housing, H.E. Sayyid Abdullah bin Hamad bin Saif Al Busaidi.
Information, H.E. Abdul Aziz bin Muhammad al Rowas.
Interior, H.E. Sayyid Badr bin Saud bin Harib al Bu Saidi.
Justice, Awqaf and Islamic Affairs, H.E. Sayyid Hilal Bin Saud bin Hamad Al Bu Saidi.
Deputy Prime Minister for Legal Affairs, H.H. Sayyid Fahd bin Mahmoud Al Said.
National Heritage and Culture, H.H. Sayyid Faisal bin Ali Al Said.
Petroleum and Minerals, H.E. Said bin Ahmad bin Said al Shanfari.
Posts, Telegraphs and Telephones, H.E. Ahmid bin Suwaidan al Balushi.
Regional Municipalities, H.E. Sheikh Muhammad bin Ali al Qutbi.
Special Adviser to H.M. The Sultan, H.E. Sayyid Hamad bin Hamoud Al Said.
Social Affairs and Labour, H.E. Sheikh Mustahail bin Ahmad al Mashani.
President, Consultative Council of the State, H.E. Sheikh Abdullah Bin Ali Bin Muhammad Al Qutbi.
Office of the Minister of State and Wali of Dhofar, H.E. Sayyid Musallim Bin Ali Al Bu Saidi.
President, Diwan of Royal Court Affairs, H.E. Sayyid Saif bin Hamad bin Saud.
First ADC to H.M. The Sultan and President of the Palace Office, H.E. Maj. Gen. Ali bin Majid al Mamari.
Civil Service, H. E. Ahmad Bin Abdul Nabi Macki.
Secretary to the Council of Ministers, H.E. Sayyid Hamoud bin Faisal Al Bu Saidi.

OMAN EMBASSY IN LONDON
44a/b Montpelier Square, SW7 1JJ
[01–589 6782/3/4]

Ambassador, His Excellency Hussain bin Mohamed bin Ali (1984).

The independent Sultanate of Oman lies at the eastern corner of the Arabian Peninsula. Its seaboard is nearly 1,000 miles long and extends from near Tibat on the west coast of the Musandam Peninsula round to Ras Darbat Ali, with the exception of the stretch between Dibba and Kalba on the east coast which belongs to Sharjah and Fujairah of the United Arab Emirates. Ras Darbat Ali marks the boundary between the Sultanate and the People's Democratic Republic of Yemen. The Sultanate extends inland to the borders of the Rub al Khali, or "Empty Quarter" of the Arabian Desert.

The area of Oman has been estimated at 82,030 sq. miles (212,457 sq. km.), and the population at 1,500,000 (1986). The inhabitants of the North are for the most part Arab but along the coast there is a strong infusion of negro blood, while in the Capital Area which stretches from Muscat to Seeb there are large communities of Hindus, Khojas and Baluch, in addition to Zanzibaris of Omani origin. In Dhofar there is also an infusion of negro blood around Salalah, but in the mountains the inhabitants are either of pure Arab descent or belong to tribes of pre-Arab origin, the Qarra and Mahra, who speak their own dialects of semitic origin.

Physically and historically modern Oman can be split into two main parts, the North and the South, divided by a large tract of desert. *Northern Oman* has three main sections. The *Batinah*, the coastal plain, varies in width from 30 miles in the neighbourhood of Suwaiq to almost nothing at Muscat where the mountains descend abruptly to the sea. The plain is fertile, with date gardens extending over its full length of 150 miles. The *Hajjar*, a mountain spine running from north west to south east, reaching nearly 10,000 feet in height on Jebal Akhdar. For the most part the mountains are barren, but numerous valleys penetrate the central massif of Jabal Akhdar and in these there is considerable cultivation irrigated by wells or a system of underground canals called *falajs* which tap the water table. The two plateaus leading from the western slopes of the mountains, the *Dhahirah*, in the north and the *Sharqia* in the south east also have centres of settlements and cultivation. They fall from an average height of 1,000 feet into the sands of the Empty Quarter. The north is separated from the south by nearly 400 miles of inhospitable country crossed by one trunk road, the only land link. *Dhofar*, the southern province, is the only part of the Arabian Peninsula to be touched by the south west monsoon. Temperatures are more moderate than in the north and sugar cane and coconuts are grown on the coastal plain, while cattle are bred on the mountains.

Government.—A Consultative Council for the State was established by Sultanic decree on October 18, 1981. The Council is a nominated body consisting of 55 members (36 representing the public and 19 representing the government). The Council's jurisdiction is confined to economic affairs and social development.

Commerce and Trade.—Trade is mainly with the United Kingdom, Japan, the Netherlands, U.S., West Germany, France and India. Total imports for the year 1987 were *OR* 700,730,000. Chief imports were machinery, cars, building materials, refined petroleum and food and telecommunications equipment.

Trade with U.K.

	1986	1987
Imports from U.K.	£399,600,000	£249,916,000
Exports to U.K.	87,200,000	3,951,000

Production.—Petroleum Development (Oman) Ltd. (owned 60 per cent by Oman Government and 34 per cent by Shell) began exporting oil in 1967. Concessions (off and on shore) are held by several major international companies. The current level of oil production is about 600,000 barrels per day.

Development.—For many years the Sultanate was a poor country with a total annual income of less than £1,000,000. The advent of oil revenues since 1967 and the change of régime in 1970 led to the initiation of a wide-ranging development programme, especially concerned with health, education and communications. New hospitals have been completed in the main provincial centres and there are now 40 hospitals with 2,861 beds, and 696 schools, with 272,018 pupils, were in operation in 1987. A gas turbine power station operates at Rusail, where there is also a 200 plot industrial estate. There is a

desalination plant near Muscat and flour, animal feed, cement and copper production facilities.

Communications.—Since 1972 ships have been using Port Qaboos at Matrah, where eight deep water berths have been constructed as part of the new harbour facilities.

The telegraph office, an automatic telephone service in Muscat and Matrah and an international telephone service are operated by the General Telecommunications Organization. There are now good tarmac roads linking most main population centres of the country with the coast and with the towns of the U.A.E. There is now over 4,000 km. of asphalted road in the Sultanate.

CAPITAL.—Ψ Muscat, population (estimated), 400,000. The commercial centre has grown around Mutrah, 3 miles away and the main port, and Ruwi. The main towns on the northern coast are ΨSur, ΨBarka and ΨSohar. The main town of Dhofar is Salalah.

CURRENCY.—Rial Omani of 1,000 Baiza.

FLAG.—Red, green and white with crossed daggers in red sector.

NATIONAL DAY.—November 18.

BRITISH EMBASSY
P.O. Box 300, Muscat
[Muscat 738501/5]

Ambassador Extraordinary and Plenipotentiary, His Excellency Robert John Alston, C.M.G. (1986).
Counsellor, A. M. Layden (*Head of Chancery*).
Defence Attaché, Brig. M. J. Smith.
Naval and Air Attaché, Cdr. A. R. W. Ogilvy, A.F.C., R.N
First Secretaries, D. S. Watson; B. Baldwin.
British Council Representative, E. K. Jones, P.O. Box 7090, Jibroo, Oman.

PAKISTAN
(Islami Jamhuriya-e-Pakistan)

*President, Gen. Mohammad Zia-ul-Haq, *assumed power*, July 1977; *elected*, Dec. 19, 1984.

CABINET MINISTERS
(as at June 1988)

Prime Minister, Communications and Chairman, Provincial Co-ordination Committee, Mohammad Aslam Khan Khattak.
Interior, Kashmir Affairs and Northern Affairs Division, Malik Naseem Ahmad Aheer.
Industries, Chaudhry Shujaat Hussain.
Justice and Parliamentary Affairs, Wasim Ahmad Sajjad.
Petroleum and Natural Resources, Science and Technology, Chaudhry Nisar Ali Khan.
Commerce, Finance and Economic Affairs, and Planning and Development, Dr. Mahbubul Haq.
Foreign Affairs, Sahabzada Yaqub Khan.
Food, Agriculture and Co-operatives and Local and Rural Development, Sartaj Aziz.
Production, Mir Afzal Khan.
Culture and Tourism, Haji Malik Faridullah Khan.
Defence and States and Frontier Regions Division, Mahmood A. Haroon.
Information and Broadcasting, Water and Power, Illahi Bakhsh Soomro.
Health, Special Education and Social Welfare, Housing and Works, Mir Hazar Khan Bijarani.

* President Zia was killed in a plane crash on Aug. 17, 1988 and a state of emergency was declared. Ghulum Ishaq Khan became acting President, pending democratic elections in November.

Religious and Minority Affairs, Maulana Wasi Mazhar Nadvi.
Education, Sardar Wazir Ahmad Jogezai.
Railways, Mir Zafarullah Khan Jamali.
Labour, Manpower and Overseas Pakistanis, Mir Ahmad Nawaz Bugti.

PAKISTAN EMBASSY
35 Lowndes Square, SW1X 9JN
[01–235 2044]

Ambassador Extraordinary and Plenipotentiary, His Excellency Shaharyar M. Khan (1987).
Ministers, Karam Elahi (*Deputy Head of Mission*); Nawabzada Mehboob Ali Khan (*Political*); Zubair Ali (*Information*).
Defence Attaché, Cdre N. M. Siddiqui.

Area and Population.—The Islamic Republic of Pakistan consists of country situated to the northwest of the Indian sub-continent, bordered by Iran, Afghanistan, the disputed territory of Kashmir, and India. It covers a total area of 307,374 sq. miles (746,045 sq. km.). The Government of Pakistan census in 1981 showed a population figure of 83,780,000 (1985 U.N. estimate, 96,180,000). Of these, about 95 per cent are Moslems, about 1 per cent Hindus, about 3·5 per cent Christians, and 0·5 per cent Buddhists.

Running through Pakistan are five great rivers, the Indus, Jhelum, Chenab, Ravi and Sutlej. The upper reaches of these rivers are in Kashmir, and their sources in the Himalayas.

Government.—Pakistan was constituted as a Dominion under the Indian Independence Act, 1947, which received Royal Assent on July 18, 1947. In terms of the Act the Dominion of Pakistan consisted of former territories of British India. The States of Bahawalpur and Khairpur (in Punjab and Sind), with a Muslim population of almost 80 per cent and with Muslim rulers, acceded to Pakistan in October, 1947. The following States also acceded to Pakistan: the Baluchistan States of Kalat, Mekran, Las Bela and Kharan, and the North-West Frontier States of Amb, Chitral, Dir and Swat. (The States of Junagadh and Manavadar which had acceded to Pakistan were occupied by India on November 8, 1947.) Boundaries of the Provinces of East Bengal and of Punjab (West Punjab) were defined by a Boundary Commission. Thus, until 1972, when East Pakistan seceded Pakistan consisted of two geographical units, West and East Pakistan, which were separated by about 1,100 miles of Indian territory.

Pakistan became a Republic on March 23, 1956, when a Parliamentary Constitution came into force. On October 7, 1958, however, this Constitution was abrogated and Pakistan came under martial law.

The first general elections ever held in Pakistan on a basis of "one man, one vote", were held in Dec. 1970 and Jan. 1971. The Awami League in East Pakistan, led by Shiekh Mujibur Rahman, and the Pakistan People's Party in West Pakistan, led by Zulfikar Ali Bhutto, won large majorities. Following the elections there was total disagreement between the two main parties on the question of a new Constitution for Pakistan, Sheikh Mujib insisting on complete autonomy for East Pakistan. The proposed opening of the National Assembly at Dacca on March 25, 1971, was postponed and civil war broke out. East Pakistan seceded by unilateral declaration the following day. Fighting continued until Dec. 1971 when a ceasefire was arranged, and "The Democratic Government of Bangladesh" was formally proclaimed on April 17, 1972.

Following general elections in March 1977 and allegations of vote-rigging the Armed Forces under Gen. Zia-ul-Haq assumed power on July 5, 1977 and imposed martial law throughout the country. The military government scheduled new general elections

for October 1977, but these were postponed. Gen. Zia declared himself President on Sept. 16, 1978. In Dec. 1984 Gen Zia got a five-year mandate as a civilian President through a national referendum. There was a general election to a National Assembly on Feb. 25, 1985. In March 1985 President Zia nominated Mohammad Khan Junejo as Prime Minister who received a vote of confidence by the National Assembly. Martial law was lifted on Dec. 30, 1985. On May 29, 1988, Zia dissolved the National Assembly and the Cabinet and announced fresh elections. A caretaker cabinet was announced on June 9. Zia was killed in a plane crash on Aug. 17, 1988.

Education.—Formal education in Pakistan is organized into five stages. These are five years of primary education (5–9 years), three years of middle or lower secondary (general or vocational), two years of upper secondary, two years of higher secondary (intermediate) and two to five years of higher education in colleges and universities. Education is free to upper secondary level. It was anticipated that primary education would become universal for boys by mid-1985 and for girls by mid-1988.

At primary level enrolment had increased to 6·5 million in 1984–85, and the number of schools to 75,000. At the middle level enrolment had increased to 1·7 million in 1984–85, and the number of schools to 6,200. At the upper secondary level enrolment increased to 570,000 in 1984–85.

Provincial Governments are responsible for the total financial support of the government institutions and for grants to non-government institutions. But policy making is authorized by the national Government, which makes annual grants. In 1986, 24 per cent of adults were estimated as being literate.

Production.—Pakistan's economy is chiefly based on agriculture. The principal crops are cotton, rice, wheat, sugar cane, maize and tobacco. There are large deposits of rock salt. Pakistan has one of the longest irrigation systems in the world. The total area irrigated is 33 million acres.

Pakistan also produces hides and skins, leather, wool, fertilizers, paints and varnishes, soda ash, paper, cement, fish, carpets, sports goods, surgical appliances and engineering goods, including switchgear, transformers, cables and wires.

Trade.—Pakistan imported manufactured goods and raw materials to the value of US$5,792 million in 1986–87 and exported mainly agricultural products valued at US$3,498 million. Principal imports are listed as: petroleum products, machinery, fertilizers, transport equipment, edible oils, chemicals and ferrous metals. Principal exports are raw cotton, cotton yarn and cloth, carpets, rice, petroleum products, synthetic textiles, leather, and fish.

Trade with U.K.

	1986	1987
Imports from U.K.	£228,384,000	£252,978,000
Exports to U.K.	131,333,000	167,315,000

Finance.—The 1988–89 Budget anticipated net federal revenues of *Rs*.140,905·5 million and current expenditure (excluding development expenditure) of some *Rs*.131,830·9 million.

Communications.—The main seaport is Karachi. The main airport at Karachi occupies an important position on international trunk routes and is equipped with modern facilities and equipment. Pakistan International Airlines (P.I.A.) operates air services between the principal cities within the country as well as abroad.

Post and telegraph facilities are available to every country in the world.

CAPITAL.—Islamabad, pop. 350,000. ΨKarachi (pop. est. 6,500,000) is the largest city and seaport; Lahore has a population of about 3,500,000.

CURRENCY.—Pakistani Rupee of 100 Paisa.

FLAG.—Dark green ground, with white vertical stripes at the mast, the green portion bearing a white crescent in the centre and a five-pointed heraldic star.

NATIONAL ANTHEM.—"Quami Tarana."

NATIONAL DAYS.—March 23 (Pakistan Day), August 14 (Independence Day).

BRITISH EMBASSY
Diplomatic Enclave, Ramna 5,
P.O. Box 1122, Islamabad.
[Islamabad 822131/5]

Ambassador Extraordinary and Plenipotentiary, His Excellency Nicholas John Barrington, C.M.G., C.V.O. (1987).

There is a British Consulate-General at *Karachi.*

British Council Representative, R. F. Budd, P.O. Box 1135, Islamabad. There are regional offices at Karachi and Lahore, and a library in Peshawar.

PANAMA
(República de Panama)

Minister in Charge of the Presidency, Manuel Solís Palma, *apptd.* Feb. 26, 1988.

MINISTERS OF STATE

Government and Justice, Rodolfo Chiari de León.
Foreign Affairs, Dr. Jorge Eduardo Ritter.
Treasury and Finance, Dr. Orville Goodin.
Agricultural Development, Darisnel Espino.
Public Works, René Bultrón.
Commerce and Industry, Mario Rognoni.
Labour and Social Welfare, Dr. César Martans.
Health, Dr. Francisco Sánchez Cárdenas.
Housing, Ricardo Bermúdez.
Planning and Economic Policy, Gustavo González.
Education, Dr. Rolando Murgas.
Presidency, Nander Pitty Velásquez.

PANAMANIAN EMBASSY IN LONDON
119 Crawford Street, SW1
[01–487 5633]

Ambassador Extraordinary and Plenipotentiary, His Excellency Lic. Guillermo Vega (1984).
Minister-Counsellor, Prof. Dionisio Johnson.

CONSULATE
24 Tudor Street, EC4Y 0JD
[01–353 4792/3].

There are also Consular Offices of the Republic at *Glasgow* and *Liverpool.*

Panama lies on the isthmus of that name which connects N. and S. America. The area of the Republic is 29,762 sq. miles (77,082 sq. km.), the population (1986 estimate) 2,227,254. After a revolt (Nov. 3, 1903) it declared its independence from Colombia and established a separate Government.

After 1968 control of Panama was increasingly taken over by Gen. Omar Torrijos, Commander of the National Guard, following a military coup. On October 11, 1972, at an assembly of representatives from the 505 electoral districts, the President and Vice-President were installed for a six-year term, and General Torrijos was designated as "Leader of the Revolution" with wide overriding powers. In October 1978 he withdrew from government, and Dr. Aristides Royo was elected President by the Assembly of Representatives. In a Presidential election in May 1984, Dr. Nicolas Barletta was elected president and took office in Nov. 1984. However, he resigned in

Sept. 1985 after disagreements with military leaders and was succeeded by his Vice-President, Eric Arturo Delvalle. An attempt in Feb. 1988 by President Delvalle to remove Gen. Noriega as Commander of the Defence Forces failed. Noriega, using the legislative body dominated by his supporters, ousted Delvalle and replaced him with Manuel Solis Palma. The U.S. Government continues to recognize President Delvalle and has imposed economic sanctions against Panama.

The Panama Canal Zone.—With effect from Oct. 1, 1979 the Canal Zone (647 sq. miles) was disestablished, with all areas of land and water within the Zone reverting to Panama. By the 1977 treaty with the U.S.A., the U.S.A. is allowed the use of operating bases for the Panama Canal, together with several military bases, but the Republic of Panama is sovereign in all such areas. Control of the Canal will revert to Panama in the year 2000.

The soil is moderately fertile, but nearly one-half of the land is uncultivated. The chief crops are bananas, sugar, coconuts, cacao, coffee and cereals. The shrimping industry plays an important role in the Panamanian economy. A railway 47 miles in length joins the Atlantic and Pacific oceans.

Education is compulsory and free from 7 to 15 years.

Language and Literature.—The official language is Spanish. There are five Spanish language and one English language newspapers published daily in the capital but in 1988 the opposition press was banned.

TRADE

Republic of Panama	1987
Imports	U.S.$1,211 million
Exports	338 million
Colon Free Zone	1987
Imports	U.S.$2,044 million
Exports	2,285 million

Trade with U.K.†

	1986	1987
Imports from U.K.	£44,975,000	£40,020,000
Exports to U.K.	4,950,000	4,919,000

† Including Colon Free Zone.

The imports are mostly manufactured goods, machinery, lubricants, chemicals and foodstuffs; exports are bananas, petroleum products, shrimps, sugar, meat and fishmeal.

CAPITAL, ΨPanama City. Population (1985 est.), 608,890.

CURRENCY.—Balboa of 100 Centésimos. U.S. notes are also in circulation.

FLAG.—Four quarters; white with blue star (top, next staff), red (in fly), blue (below, next staff) and white with red star.

NATIONAL ANTHEM.—"Alcanzamos Por Fin La Victoria" ("Victory is ours at last).

NATIONAL DAY. November 3.

Dependencies of Panama.—Taboga Island (area 4 sq. miles) is a popular tourist resort of some 12 miles from the Pacific entrance to the Panama Canal. Tourist facilities have also been developed in the Las Perlas Archipelago in the Gulf of Panama, particularly on the island of Contadora. There is a penal settlement at Guardia on the island of Coiba (area 19 sq. miles) in the Gulf of Chiriqui.

BRITISH EMBASSY
120 Via España, Panama
[Panama City 23–0451/3]

Ambassador Extraordinary and Plenipotentiary, Her Excellency Mrs. Margaret Bryan, C.M.G. (1986).
First Secretary and Consul, N. J. Bown.

There is a British consular office at *Panama City.*

PARAGUAY
(República del Paraguay)

President, General Alfredo Stroessner, *inaugurated* Aug. 15, 1954, *re-elected* 1958, 1963, 1968, 1973, 1978, 1983 and 1988.

Foreign Affairs, Dr. Carlos Augustus Saldívar.

Finance, (vacant).

Interior, Dr. Sabino A. Montanero.

Defence, General Gaspar Germán Martínez.

Justice and Labour, Dr. José Eugenio Jacquet.

Education and Worship, Dr. Carlos Ortíz Ramirez.

Public Works and Communications, General de División Juan A. Cáceres.

Agriculture and Livestock, Ing. Hernando Bertoni.

Industry and Commerce, Dr. Delfin Ugarte Centurión.

Public Health and Social Welfare, Dr. Adán Godoy Jiménez.

President of Central Bank, Dr. César Romero Acosta.

PARAGUAYAN EMBASSY AND CONSULATE IN LONDON
Braemer Lodge, Cornwall Gardens, SW7 4AQ
[01–937 1253; *Consulate:* 01-937 6629]

Ambassador Extraordinary and Plenipotentiary, His Excellency Antonio Zuccolillo (1981).

Counsellor and Consul General, Rubén Alvarenga-Cabañas.

Area and Population.—Paraguay is an inland subtropical state of South America, situated between Argentina, Bolivia and Brazil.

The area is estimated at 157,048 sq. miles (406,752 sq. km.), with a population (1987 estimate) of 3,930,000.

Paraguay is a country of grassy plains and dense forest, the soil being marshy in many parts and liable to floods; while the hills are covered for the most part with immense forests. The streams flowing into the Alto Paraná descend precipitously into that river. In the angle formed by the Paraná-Paraguay confluence are extensive marshes, one of which, known as "Neembucú," or "endless," is drained by *Lake Ypoa*, a large lagoon, south-east of the capital. The *Chaco*, lying between the rivers Paraguay and Pilcomayo and bounded on the north by Bolivia, formed the subject of a long-standing dispute with that country and led to war between Paraguay and Bolivia from 1932 to 1935. The Chaco is a flat plain, rising uniformly towards its western boundary to a height of 1,140 feet; it suffers much from floods and still more from drought, but the building of dams and reservoirs has converted part of it into good pasture for cattle raising.

Government.—In 1535 Paraguay was settled as a Spanish possession. In 1811 it declared its independence of Spain.

The constitution provides for a two-chamber parliament consisting of a 36-member Senate and a 72-member Chamber of Deputies. Two-thirds of the seats in each chamber are allocated to the majority party and the remaining one-third shared among the minority parties in proportion to the votes cast. Voting is compulsory for all citizens over 18.

The President is elected for 5 years and may be re-elected for a further term. He appoints the Cabinet, which exercises all the functions of government. During parliamentary recess it can govern by decree through the Council of State, the members of which are representative of the Government, the armed forces and various other bodies. The state of siege, in force since 1947, was lifted on April 8, 1987.

Production.—About three-quarters of the population are engaged in agriculture and cattle raising. Cotton, soya beans, tobacco, edible and essential oils, sugar, coffee and timber are the main exports. The forests contain many varieties of timber which find a good market abroad. Paraguay's hydroelectric power station at Acaray produced in 1985, 1,118 Kwh. of which a surplus is exported to Argentina and Brazil.

At Itaipú the largest hydroelectric dam in the world, a joint project by Paraguay and Brazil, was inaugurated in 1982. It is expected to be completed in 1990 when it will have a capacity of over 12 million k.w. Work is also under way on a hydroelectric project with Argentina at Yacyretá which it is hoped will be in operation by the end of the decade.

Communications.—A railway, 985 miles in length, connects Asunción with Buenos Aires. The journey takes 55 hours. Train ferries enable the run to be accomplished without break of bulk. River steamers also connect Buenos Aires and Asunción (3 to 5 days). This service is liable to cancellation without warning when the river is low or in flood. There are direct shipping services to Asunción from England, Western Europe and the U.S.A. Eight airlines operate services from Asunción.

There are 1,176 km. of asphalted roads in Paraguay, connecting Asunción with São Paulo (26 hrs.) via the Bridge of Friendship and Foz de Yguazú and with Buenos Aires (24 hrs.) via Puerto Pilcomayo, and about 4,050 miles of earth roads in fairly good condition, but liable to be closed or to become impassable in wet weather. A 1,000 km. road, of which 300 km. are paved, links Asunción with the Bolivian border. There are services to Buenos Aires, São Paulo and Paranagua, a port on the Brazilian coast.

Defence.—There is a permanent military force of about 25,000 all ranks, most of whom are conscripts doing their military service; and about 6,500 armed police (again mostly conscripts). Three gunboats and a number of small armed launches patrol inland waters.

Language and Literature.—Spanish is the official language of the country but outside the larger towns *Guarani*, the language of the largest single unit of original Indian inhabitants, is widely spoken. Four daily, one weekly and one bi-weekly newspapers are published in Asunción. There are 48 AM, 15 FM and three TV stations in the country.

Education.—Education is free and compulsory. In 1984 there were 3,209 government primary schools and 587 private schools with 559,080 pupils and 22,091 teachers. There are 713 secondary schools with 149,019 pupils and 2,448 teachers. The National University in Asunción had in 1984 20,343 students. The Catholic University had 10,971 students.

BUDGET 1988
(in million guaranies)

	Central Government	Decentralized Bodies
Expenditure	250·8	608·5

Trade.—Total value of imports (U.S.$) in 1987 was $592,302,000. The chief imports were machinery ($151,951,000); fuels and lubricants ($102,773,000); transport and accessories ($47,869,000); and drinks and tobacco ($41,626,000). Total value of exports in 1987 was $353,377,000. The chief exports were soya bean ($122,783,000); cotton fibres ($100,957,000); sawn wood ($25,084,000); and processed meat.

Trade with U.K.

	1986	1987
Imports from U.K.	£31,010,000	£25,409,000
Exports to U.K.	1,455,000	1,409,000

CAPITAL, Asunción, about 1,000 miles up the River Paraguay from Buenos Aires. Pop. (census, 1985), 729,307; other centres being Ciudad Presidente Stroessner, 98,491; Encarnación, 31,445; Concepción, 25,607; P. Juan Caballero, 41,475.

CURRENCY.—Guarani of 100 Céntimos.

FLAG.—Three horizontal bands, red, white, blue

with the National seal on the obverse white band and the Treasury seal on the reverse white band.

NATIONAL ANTHEM.—"Paraguayos, Republica O Muerte" (Paraguayans, republic or death).

NATIONAL DAY.—May 14.

BRITISH EMBASSY
Calle Presidente Franco 706,
(PO Box 404)
[Asuncíon 444472]

Ambassador Extraordinary and Plenipotentiary and Consul-General, His Excellency John Grant MacDonald, C.M.G., M.B.E. (1986).

PERU
(República del Peru)

President, Sr. Alan García Pérez, *assumed office*, July 28, 1985.

CABINET

President of the Council of Ministers and Minister of the Presidency, Armando Villanueva del Campo.
Foreign Affairs, Dr. Luiz Gonzáles.
Interior, Adm. Juan Soria Diaz (*retd*).
Agriculture, Remigio Morales Bermúdez Pedraglio.
Defence, López Albújar Trint.
Economy and Finance, Cesar Robles Freyre.
Education, Mercedes Cabanillasde Llanos de la Mata.
Energy and Mines, Abel Salinas Izaguirre.
Health, Dr. Luis Pinillos Ashton.
Housing and Construction, Luis Bedoya Vélez.
Industry, Internal Commerce, Tourism and Integration, Guillermo Arteaga Ralston.
Justice, Dr. Camilo Carrillo Gómez.
Labour and Social Development, Dr. Orestes Rodriguez Campos.
Fisheries, Dr. Rómulo León Alegria.
Transport and Communications, Francisco Maury López.

PERUVIAN EMBASSY AND CONSULATE
52 Sloane Street, SW1X 9SP
[01–235 1917/2545]

Ambassador Extraordinary and Plenipotentiary, Dr. Carlos A. Raffo (1986).
Minister, Counsellor, Jose Augusto Tenorio.
Naval Attaché, Rear Adm. Francisco Rolando Rabines.
Air and Military Attaché, Maj. Gen. Oscar German Carrera.

Area and Population.—Peru is a maritime Republic of South America, situated between 0° 00′ 48″ and 18° 21′ 00″ S. latitude and between 68° 39′ 27″ and 81° 20′ 13″ W. longitude. The area of the Republic is 496,225 sq. miles (1,285,216 sq. km.), with a population estimated (1985) at 19,700,000.

Physical Features.—The country is traversed throughout its length by the Andes, running parallel to the Pacific coast, the highest points in Peru being *Huascaran* (22,211 ft), *Huandoy* (20,855 ft), *Ausangate* (20,235 feet), *Misti* volcano (18,364 ft), *Hualcan* (20,000 ft), *Chachani* (19,037 ft), *Antajasha* (18,020 ft), *Pichu-pichu* (17,724 ft), and *Mount Meiggs* (17,583 ft).

There are three main regions, the *Costa*, west of the Andes, the *Sierra* or mountain ranges of the Andes, which include the *Punas* or mountainous wastes below the region of perpetual snow and the *Montaña*, or *Selva*, which is the vast area of jungle stretching from the eastern foothills of the Andes to the eastern frontiers of Peru. The coastal area, lying upon and near the Pacific, is not tropical, though close to the Equator, being cooled by the Humboldt Current. It contains the capital, Lima, and most of the white population.

In the mountains, where most of the Indians live, are to be found minerals in great richness and variety, and cattle, sheep, llamas and alpacas are bred there.

Language and Literature.—Spanish, the language of the original Spanish stock from which the governing and professional classes are mainly recruited, was formerly the only official language of the country. However, in May 1975, the Quechua language was declared the second official tongue. Quechua and Aymará are widely spoken by more than half the population of the country. Before the arrival of Pizarro, the Incas had attained a high state of culture, some traces of which survived three centuries of Spanish rule. Modern Peruvian literature includes a national drama in the Spanish tongue and many Peruvian writers have attained international fame.

Government.—Peru was conquered in the early 16th century by Francisco Pizarro (born 1478, died 1541). He subjugated the Incas (the ruling caste of the Quechua Indians), who had started their rise to power some 500 years earlier, and for nearly three centuries Peru remained under Spanish rule. A revolutionary war of 1821–1824 established its independence, declared on July 28, 1821. The constitution rests upon the fundamental law of Oct. 18, 1856, and is that of a democratic Republic. A new constitution was drawn up and approved in July 1979.

Production.—The chief products of the coastal belt are cotton, sugar and petroleum. There are large tracts of land suitable for cultivation and stock raising on the eastern slopes of the Andes, and in the mountain valleys maize, potatoes and wheat are grown. The jungle area is a source of timber and petroleum. Other major crops are fruit, vegetables, rice, barley, grapes and coffee. Mineral exports include lead, zinc, copper, iron ore and silver. Peru is normally the world's largest exporter of fishmeal.

Communications.—In recent years the coastal and sierra zones have been opened up by means of roads and air routes and there is air communication, as well as communication by protracted land routes, with the tropical and little known eastern zones, which lie east of the Andes towards the borders of Brazil. The completion in 1944 of the trunk road of the Andean Highway from the Pacific port of Callao, via Lima to Pucallpa, the river port on the Ucayali, forms a link between the Pacific, the Amazon and the Atlantic.

The first railway was opened in 1850 and the 2,400 miles of track are now administered by the Government. There is also steam navigation on the Ucayali and Huallaga, and in the south on Lake Titicaca. Air services are maintained throughout Peru, and many international services call at Lima.

Defence.—The Army is recruited by voluntary enlistment, supplemented by conscription (2 years), and numbers about 45,000 of all ranks. Armoured units are equipped with American, Russian and French vehicles. Engineer units are employed on the construction of roadways in Peru using American equipment. The main Naval base is in Callao and supports all ships of the Fleet. There are training establishments in Callao and La Punta. The Naval Air Arm consists of U.S. and French helicopters; U.S. anti-submarine aircraft and DC3's. The Air Force is equipped with British, U.S. and French aircraft and U.S. and French helicopters. There are military airfields at Talara, Piura, Chiclayo, Lima, Pisco, Joya, Iquitos and Arequipa plus a seaplane base at Iquitos. There are also a Civil Guard and a Republican Guard whose members number respectively 30,000 and 5,000.

Education.—Education is compulsory and free for both sexes between the ages of 6 and 15.

Trade.—Import trade of Peru in 1987 totalled U.S.$2,520 million and exports U.S.$2,605 million.

Trade with U.K.

	1986	1987
Imports from U.K.	£48,275,000	£49,324,000
Exports to U.K.	82,141,000	91,689,000

The principal imports are machinery and chemicals and pharmaceutical products. The chief exports are minerals and metals, fishmeal, sugar, cotton and coffee.

CAPITAL.—Metropolitan Lima (including ΨCallao), population (1983) 5,258,600. Other major cities (with pop. census, 1981) are: Arequipa (561,338) Iquitos (540,560), ΨChiclayo (533,266).

CURRENCY.—Inti of 100 Céntimos.

FLAG.—Three vertical bands, red, white, red; coat of arms on white band.

NATIONAL ANTHEM.—Samos Libres, Seamoslo Siempre (We are free, let us remain so forever).

NATIONAL DAY.—July 28 (Anniversary of Independence).

BRITISH EMBASSY

Natalio Sánchez 125 Piso 12, Sanata Beatriz, (P.O. Box 854), Lima 100.

[Lima 334738]

Ambassador Extraordinary and Plenipotentiary, His Excellency Adrian John Beamish, C.M.G. (1987).

First Secretaries, B. B. Low (*Head of Chancery and Consul*); T. H. Malcolmson (*Commercial*); D. J. Logan; J. Blount (*Chancery and Economic*).

Defence Attaché, Col. P. R. Rostron, M.B.E.

There are British Consular Offices at *Lima Arequipa.*

British Council Representative, A. Moore, P.O. Box No. 14.0114, Calle Alberto Lynch 110, San Isidro, Lima 1.

THE PHILIPPINES
(República ng Pilipinas)

President, Corazon C. Aquino *b.* 1933, *elected* Feb. 7, 1986, *assumed office* Feb. 25, 1986.

CABINET SECRETARIES

Foreign Affairs, Raul Manglapus.
Finance, Vicente Jayme.
Justice, Sedfrey Ordonez.

Agriculture, Carlos Dominguez.
Public Works and Highways, Juanito Ferrer.
Education, Culture and Sports, Lourdes Quisumbing.
Labour, Franklin Drilon.
Health, Alfredo Bengzon.
Trade and Industry, Jose Concepcion.
Social Services and Development, Mita Pardo de Tavera.
Economic Planning, Solita Monsod.
Agrarian Reform, Philip Ella Juico.
Special Counsel, Teodoro Locsin Jr.
Local Government, Luis Santos.
Tourism, Jose Antonio Gonzalez.
Natural Resources, Fulgenio Factóran.
Budget, Guillermo Carague.
Transportation and Communications, Rainerio Reyes.
National Defence, Fidel Ramos.
Executive Secretary, Catalino Macaraig Jr.
Muslim Affairs and Cultural Communities, Jiamil Dianalan.
Chairman, Presidential Commission on Good Government, Ramon Diaz.
Science and Technology, Antonio Arrizabal.
Presidential Press Secretary, Teodoro Benigno.
Presidential Adviser on National Security, Emanuel Soriano.
Cabinet Secretary, Jose de Jesus.

PHILIPPINE EMBASSY

9a Palace Green, W8 4QE
[01–937 1600/9]

Ambassador Extraordinary and Plenipotentiary, His Excellency Juan T. Quimson (1986).

Minister-Counsellor and Consul General, Edmundo Libid.

Commercial Counsellor, Peregrino Sales.

Area and Population.—The Philippines are situated between 21° 20'–4° 30' N. Lat. and 116° 55'–126° 36' E. long., and are distant about 500 miles from the south-east coast of the continent of Asia. (For MAP, see p. 780).

The total land area of the country is 115,831 sq. miles (300,000 sq. km.). There are eleven larger islands and 7,079 other islands.

The principal islands are:—

Name	sq. miles	Name	sq. miles
Luzon	40,422	Mindoro	3,759
Mindanao	36,538	Leyte	2,786
Samar	5,050	Cebu	1,703
Negros	4,906	Bohol	1,492
Palawan	4,550	Masbate	1,262
Panay	4,446		

Other groups in the Republic are the Sulu islands (Capital, Jolo), Babuyanes and Batanes; the Catanduanes; and Culion Islands.

The population of the Philippines was estimated (1987) at 57,000,000.

The inhabitants, known as Filipinos, are basically all of Malay stock, with a considerable admixture of Spanish and Chinese blood in many localities, and about 90 per cent of them are Christians, predominantly Roman Catholics. Most of the remainder are Moslems, in the south, and animists and pagans, mainly in the north. There is a Chinese minority estimated at 500,000, and other much smaller foreign communities, notably Spanish, American and Indian.

History.—The Portuguese navigator Magellan came to the Philippines in 1521 and was slain by the natives of Mactan, a small island near Cebu. In 1565 Spain undertook the conquest of the country which was named "Filipinas", after the son of the King of Spain, and in 1571 the city of Manila was begun by the conquistador Legaspi, who subdued the inhabitants of almost all the islands, their conversion being undertaken by the Augustinian friars in Legaspi's train. In 1762 Manila was occupied by a British force, but in 1764 it was restored to Spain. In the Spanish-American War of 1898, Manila was captured by American troops with the help of Filipinos and the Islands were ceded to the United States by the *Treaty of Paris* of Dec. 10, 1898. Despite a rebellion against the U.S. government between 1899 and 1902, the Americans remained in control of the country until 1946.

The Republic of the Philippines came into existence on July 4, 1946 with a presidential form of government based on the American system.

Martial law was imposed on September 21, 1972. This was lifted, except in two southern provinces, on January 17, 1981.

The assassination on Aug. 21, 1983 of Marcos' main political opponent, Benigno Aquino, and a subsequent financial crisis caused a weakening in Marcos' position. Although Marcos gained a majority of votes in the official count of a Presidential election in Feb. 1986, the election was marred by widespread electoral abuse and his rival, Mrs Corazon Aquino, launched a series of non-violent civil disturbance actions.

On Feb. 22, Defence Minister Enrile and Vice Chief of Staff Ramos broke away from the Marcos government and declared their support for Mrs. Aquino. Thousands of people took to the streets to support their revolt and they were joined by a large section of the Armed Forces. On Feb. 25, Marcos, his family and aides left for Hawaii. Mrs Aquino took over as President. On March 25, she abolished the Batasan (legislature) and promulgated a Freedom (Provisional) Constitution.

An appointed Constitutional Convention drafted a new Constitution with a Congressional system of government, having a senate of 24 members and a House of Representatives with 250 members. This was overwhelmingly approved by a referendum in Feb. 1987. Elections to the Congress were held in May and the new Constitution came into force on July 27, 1987.

There is unrest in many of the islands due to insurgency. Muslim insurgents, the Moro National Liberation Front, operate in western Mindanao and the Sula archipelago. Most of the current activity is due to the Communist New People's Army, which is strongest in eastern Mindanao, Negros, Samar, Bicol, the mountains of northern Luzon, and Bataan. As of June 1987 the ceasefire agreed between the Government and the Moro National Liberation Front was still holding, unlike the ceasefire with the Communists which ended in Feb. 1987.

Language and Literature.—The official languages are Filipino and English. Filipino, the national language, is based on Tagalog, one of the Malay-Polynesian languages and the language of the part of Luzon surrounding Metro Manilla. Filipino is spoken by 29·66 per cent of the total number of households, but local languages and dialects are strong and Cebuano is spoken by 24·20 per cent. of total households. English, which is the language of government and of instruction in secondary and university education, is spoken by at least 44 per cent of the population. Spanish, which ceased to be an official language in 1973, is now spoken by a very small minority. 89 per cent of the population are literate.

Education.—Secondary and higher education is extensive and there are 37 private universities recognized by the Government, including the Dominican University of Santo Tomas (founded in 1611); there are also 296 State-supported colleges and universities, including the University of the Philippines, founded 1908. Students at private and state colleges and universities in 1984–85 numbered 13,814,359.

Roads and Railways.—The highway system covered 157,709 kilometres in 1985 and there was a total of 1,120,172 registered road vehicles. The Philippine National Railway operate 740 km. of track on Luzon Island.

Shipping.—There are 94 ports of entry in the Philippines and 164,404 vessels of various types totalling 50,467,000 tons, are engaged in inter-island traffic.

Civil Aviation.—There 82 national airports and 137 privately operated airports. Philippine Air Lines have regular flights throughout the Far East, to the U.S.A. and Europe, in addition to inter-island services.

TRADE

	1985	1986
Total imports	$5,110,673,000	$5,043,597,000
Total exports	4,628,954,000	4,841,780,000

Trade with U.K.

	1986	1987
Imports from U.K.	£79,809,000	£113,784,000
Exports to U.K.	182,852,000	202,707,000

The Philippines is a predominantly agricultural country, the chief products being rice, coconuts, maize, sugar-cane, abaca (manila hemp), fruits, tobacco and lumber. There is, however, an increasing number of manufacturing industries and it is the policy of the Government to diversify its economy.

Principal exports are sugar, coconut oil, copper concentrate, lumber and copra.

CAPITAL.—ΨManila, in the island of Luzon: population (1980): City area, 1,630,485; Manila with suburbs (incl. Quezon City, Pasay City, Caloocan City, Makati, Parañaque, San Juan Mandaluyong and Navotas), 6,720,050. The next largest cities are ΨCebu (490,281), ΨDavao (610,375), ΨIloilo (244,027), ΨZamboanga (343,722), and Bacolod (262,415).

CURRENCY.—Philippine Peso of 100 Centavos.

FLAG.—Equal horizontal bands of blue (above) and red; gold sun with three stars on a white triangle next staff.

NATIONAL ANTHEM.—"Pambansang Awit".

NATIONAL DAY.—June 12 (Independence Day).

BRITISH EMBASSY
(P.O. Box 1970 MCC), Manila
[Manila 853002/9]

Ambassador Extraordinary and Plenipotentiary, His Excellency Keith Gordon MacInnes, C.M.G. (1987).
Counsellor, P. J. Priestley.
Defence Attaché, Col. P. D. Pettigrew.
First Secretaries, A. E. Huckle (*Head of Chancery*); K. R. Gosling.
Second Secretaries, J. R. Albright (*Commercial*); P. J. Karmy (*Consul*).
Third Secretary, A. E. Conroy (*Information/Aid*).
Cultural Attaché, H. Salmon (*British Council Representative*).

POLAND
(Polska Rzeczpospolita Ludowa)

COUNCIL OF STATE

Chairman (i.e. Head of State), Gen. Wojciech Jaruzelski.
Deputy Chairmen, T. Mlynczak; K. Barcikowski; Z. Komender; T. Szelachowski.

COUNCIL OF MINISTERS

Prime Minister, Zbigniew Messner.
Deputy Prime Minister and Chairman, Planning Commission, Zdzislaw Sadowski.

Deputy Prime Ministers, Josef Koziol; Zbigniew Szalajda.
Chairman, Supreme Chamber of Control, Tadeusz Hupalowski.
Interior, Lt.-Gen. Czeslaw Kiszczak.
Foreign Affairs, Tadeusz Olechowski.
Defence, Gen. Florian Siwicki.
Finance, Bazyli Samojlik.
Foreign Economic Co-operation, Wladyslaw Gwiazda.
Justice, Lech Domeradzki.
National Education, Henryk Bednarski.
Health and Social Welfare, Janusz Komender.
Labour, Ireneusz Sekula.
Culture and Art, Alexsander Krawczuk.
Metallurgical and Engineering Industries, Janusz Maciejewicz.
Agriculture, Forestry and Food Industry, Stanislaw Zieba.
Industry, Jerzy Bilip.
Transport, Navigation and Communications, Jan Kaminski.
Environmental Protection and Water Economy, Waldemar Michna.
Land Management and the Construction Industry, Bogumil Ferensztajn.
Head of Office for Scientific and Technical Progress, Konrad Tott.
Government Spokesman, Jerzy Urban.
Head of Office of Council of Ministers, Michal Janiszewski.
Youth Affairs, Aleksander Kwasniewski.

POLISH UNITED WORKERS' PARTY

Politburo, W. Baka; K. Barcikowski; J. Baryla; J. Czyrek; J. Glowczyk; W. Jaruzelski; C. Kiszczak; Z. Messner; A. Miodowicz; Z. Muranski; M. Orzechowski; T. Porebski; M. Rakowski; F. Siwicki; Z. Stepien; (full Members); S. Ciosek; M. Gorywoda; J. Kubasiewicz; Z. Michalek; G. Rembisz (candidate members).
Secretariat, W. Baka; K. Cypryniak; J. Czyrek; J. Glowczyk; B. Kolodziejczak; M. Orzechowski; M. Rakowski; A. Wasilewski.

POLISH EMBASSY IN LONDON
47 Portland Place, W1N 3AG
[01–580 4324]

Ambassador Extraordinary and Plenipotentiary, His Excellency Dr. Zbigniew Gertych (1987).

Area and Population.—Poland adjoins East Germany in the west, the boundary being formed by the rivers Oder and Neisse, Czechoslovakia in the south, and the U.S.S.R. in the east. (The present frontiers were established at the end of the Second World War.) To the north is the Baltic Sea. The country has an area of 120,725 sq. miles (312,677 sq. km.), and a population (1985 U.N. estimate) of 37,203,000. Roman Catholicism is the religion of 95 per cent. of the inhabitants.

Government.—The Polish Commonwealth had ceased to exist in 1795 after three successive partitions in 1772, 1793 and 1795, in which Prussia, Russia and Austria shared. The Republic of Poland (reconstituted within the limits of the old Polish Commonwealth) was proclaimed at Warsaw in November, 1918, and its independence guaranteed by the signatories of the Treaty of Versailles.

German forces invaded Poland on Sept. 1, 1939; on Sept. 17, Russian forces invaded eastern Poland, and on September 21, 1939, Poland was declared by Germany and Russia to have ceased to exist. A line of demarcation was established between the areas occupied by German and Russian forces. At the end of the war a Coalition Government was formed in which the Polish Workers' Party played a large part. In December, 1948, the Polish Workers' Party and

the Polish Socialist Party fused in the new Polish United Workers' Party. This is a Communist Party which closely controls every branch of State activity. A new Constitution modelled on the Soviet Constitution of 1936 was adopted on July 22, 1952, and was modified in February 1976. It changed the title of the country to the Polish People's Republic (Polska Rzeczpospolita Ludowa). It made no provision for a President of the Republic, whose functions were to be jointly exercised by a Council of State. Private ownership of land and freedom of religion were recognized. Church and State were to be separate.

Despite the guarantee of religious freedom in the Constitution, a campaign of encroachment in 1953 culminated in the arrest of the Primate of the Roman Catholic Church, and dissatisfaction with the régime and conditions of life have led periodically to unrest. The expression of severe popular discontent in December 1970 led to the ousting of Gomulka, and substantial Government and Party changes followed. In July 1980 steep rises in food prices but static wages led to widespread strikes. The strikes continued throughout August, causing a major government reshuffle and obliging the government to agree to allow independent trade unions, the right to strike, the easing of censorship and other political and economic demands. The independent trade union movement, Solidarity, led by Lech Walesa, became a powerful force but many of its leaders, including Walesa, were detained and union activity suspended when martial law was declared on Dec. 13, 1981. Initially there was some passive resistance to martial law, which was suspended on Dec. 31, 1982, and finally lifted in July 1983.

Education.—Elementary education (ages 7–15) is compulsory and free. Secondary education is optional and free. There are universities at Kraków, Warsaw, Poznan, Lódź, Wroclaw, Lublin and Toruń and a considerable number of other towns.

Language and Literature.—Polish is a western Slavonic tongue (see U.S.S.R.), the Latin alphabet being used. Polish literature developed rapidly after the foundation of the University of Krakow (a printing press was established there in 1474 and there Copernicus died in 1543). A national school of poetry and drama survived the dismemberment and the former era of romanticism, whose chief Polish exponent was Adam Mickiewicz, was followed by realistic and historical fiction, including the works of Henryk Sienkiewicz (1846–1916), Nobel Prize-winner for

Literature in 1905, Boleslaw Prus (1847–1912), and Stanislaw Reymont (1868–1925), Nobel Prize-winner in 1924.

Production and Industry.—On January 3, 1946, a decree was issued to provide for the nationalization of mines, petroleum resources, water, gas and electricity services, banks, textile factories and large retail stores. At present over 99 per cent of Polish industry is stated to be "socialized", but 68 per cent of agricultural land is privately farmed.

Trade with U.K.

	1986	1987
Imports from U.K.	£182,841,000	£181,451,000
Exports to U.K.	309,746,000	303,418,000

CAPITAL.—Warsaw, on the Vistula, pop. (1984) 1,644,626. Other large towns are Lódz (849,000); Kraków (735,000); Wroclaw (632,000); Poznan (571,000); Gdansk (464,000); Szczecin (389,000); Katowice (361,000); Bydgoszcz (358,000).

CURRENCY.—Zloty of 100 Groszy.

FLAG.—Equal horizontal stripes of white (above) and red.

NATIONAL ANTHEM.—Jeszcze Polska Nie Zginela (Poland has not yet been destroyed).

NATIONAL DAY.—July 22.

BRITISH EMBASSY
No. 1 Aleja Róz, 00-556 Warsaw
[Warsaw 281001]

Ambassador Extraordinary and Plenipotentiary, His Excellency Stephen Jeremy Barrett, C.M.G. (1988).
Counsellor, N. J. Thorpe (*Head of Chancery*).
Defence and Air Attaché, Gp.-Capt. M. R. Killick.
Naval and Military Attaché, Lt.-Col. R. C. Eyres.
British Council Representative, R. H. Alford, O.B.E., Al. Jerozolimskie 59, 00–697 Warsaw.

PORTUGAL
(República Portuguesa)

President of the Republic, Dr. Mario A. Nombre Lopes Soares, *elected,* February 16, 1986.

Prime Minister, Prof. Anibal Cavaco Silva.
Deputy P.M. and Defence, Eurico de Melo.
Minister at the P.M.'s Office and Minister for Justice, Dr. Fernando Nogueira.
Parliamentary Affairs, Dr, Antonio Capucho.
Finance, Dr. Miguel Ribeiro Cadilhe.
Planning and Territorial Administration, Prof. Luis Valente de Oliveira.
Internal Administration, Dr. José Silveira Godinho.
Foreign, Prof. João de Deus Pinheiro.
Agriculture, Fisheries and Food, Alvaro Barreto.
Industry and Energy, Luis Mira Amaral.
Education, Dr. Roberto Carneiro.
Public Works, Transport and Communications, João Oliveira Martins.
Health, Leonor Beleza.
Employment and Social Security, Dr. José Silva Peneda.
Trade and Tourism, Joaquim Ferreira do Amaral.
Youth, Antonio Couto dos Santos.

EMBASSY IN LONDON
11 Belgrave Square, SW1X 8PP
[01–235 5331]

Ambassador Extraordinary and Plenipotentiary, His Excellency João Hall Themido, G.C.V.O. (1984).
Minister Counsellor, Sr. Manuel Corte Real, C.B.E.
First Secretary, Sra Ana Barata, O.B.E.

Area and Population.—Continental Portugal occupies the western part of the Iberian Peninsula, covering an area of 34,317 sq. miles (88,880 sq. km.). It lies between 36° 58′–42° 12″ N. lat. and 6° 11′ 48″–9° 29′ 45″ W. long., being 362 miles in length from N. to S., and averaging about 117 in breadth from E. to W. The population (including the Azores and Madeira) was estimated at 10,229,000 in 1985.

Language and Literature.—Portuguese is a Romance language with admixtures of Arabic and other idioms. It is the language of Portugal and Brazil, and is the *lingua franca* of Angola, Mozambique and Guinea-Bissau.

Portuguese language and literature reached the culminating point of their development in the *Lusiadas* (dealing with the voyage of Vasco da Gama) and other works of Camoens (Camões) (1524–1580).

Government.—From the eleventh century until 1910 the government of Portugal was a monarchy, and for many centuries included the Vice-Royalty of Brazil, which declared its independence in 1822. In 1910 an armed rising in Lisbon drove King Manuel II and the Royal family into exile, and the National Assembly of Aug. 21, 1911, sanctioned a Republican form of government. A period of great political instability ensued until eventually the military stepped in. The Constitution of 1933 gave formal expression to the corporative "Estado Novo" (New State) which was personified by Dr. Salazar, Prime Minister from 1932–68. Dr. Caetano succeeded Salazar as Prime Minister in 1968 but his failure to liberalize the régime or to conclude the wars in the African colonies resulted in his government's overthrow by a military coup on April 25, 1974. The next two years were characterized by great political turmoil with no fewer than 6 provisional governments between April 1974 and July 1976 but with the failure of an attempted coup by the extreme left in November 1975 the situation began to become more stable.

Constitutional reforms introduced in Aug. 1982 have reduced the President's scope for day-to-day intervention in government but the decision to dissolve the Assembly is still largely the President's. The revisions also ended the military's capacity for political interference, and created two new organs of state, the Constitutional Tribunal and the Council of State, to advise the President.

In the General Election held on July 19, 1987, the Social Democratic Party (*P.S.D.*) won 148 of the 250 seats; the Socialist Party (*P.S.*) 60 seats; the Communist Party (*P.C.P.*) 31 seats, The Democratic Renewal Party (*P.R.D.*) 7 seats and the Christian Democrats (*C.D.S.*) 4 seats.

Defence.—Most physically fit males are liable for military service but conscription is becoming increasingly selective as the armed forces were greatly reduced following the end of the colonial wars, and reorganized and re-equipped for a conventional national defence role. The present strength of the Army is about 41,000. One brigade is earmarked for N.A.T.O. service. The Navy consists of about 14,800 officers and men, including 2,500 marines, manning about 60 craft of various types, many of which are obsolete. The present serving strength of the Air Force is about 12,600, (including 2,200 paratroops) and about 80 combat aircraft plus helicopters and transport and training aircraft.

Education is free and compulsory for eight years from the age of 7. Secondary education is mainly conducted in State lyceums, commercial and industrial schools, but there are also private schools. There are also military, naval, technical and other special schools. There are old established Universities at Coimbra (founded in 1290), Oporto and Lisbon. New Universities have been established at Lisbon, Braga, Aveiro and in the Azores; a University at Faro was expected to open in 1987.

Newspapers and Broadcasting.—There are now

five morning and three evening daily newspapers in Lisbon and 3 morning papers in Oporto, and 5 main weekly newspapers. There are 2 TV channels (broadcasting in colour) and 4 radio stations (3 state controlled) broadcasting nationwide.

Civil aviation is controlled by the Administração Nacional Aeronaútica. There is an international airport at Portela, about 5 miles from Lisbon, and the airport of Pedras Rubras near Oporto is also used for scheduled international services. There are direct flights between London and Faro in the Algarve.

Agriculture.—The chief agricultural products are cork, cereals, rice, vegetables, olives, figs, citrus fruits, almonds, timber, port wine and table wines. There are extensive forests of pine, cork, eucalyptus and chestnut covering about 20 per cent of the total area of the country.

Minerals.—The principal mineral products are pyrites, wolfram, tin, iron ores, copper and sodium and calcium minerals.

Industry.—The country is so far only moderately industrialized, but is fairly rapidly extending its industries. The principal manufactures, some of which are still protected by high tariffs, are textiles, clothing and footwear, machinery (including electric machinery and transport equipment), foodstuffs (tomato concentrates and canned fish), chemicals, fertilizers, wood, cork, furniture, cement, glassware and pottery. There is a modern steelworks, and two modern and very large shipbuilding and repair yards at Lisbon and Setúbal working mainly for foreign ship-owners. There are several hydro-electric power stations and a new thermal power station.

Finance.—Portugal is a member of the European Monetary Agreement, the World Bank, the International Monetary Fund and the International Finance Corporation. The country has substantial, but declining, gold and foreign exchange reserves.

Trade.—Portugal joined the E.E.C. on January 1, 1986.

The principal imports are cereals, meat, raw and semi-manufactured iron and steel, industrial machinery, chemicals, crude oil, motor vehicles and raw materials for textiles.

The principal exports are textiles, footwear, timber, cork, electrical and other machinery, and chemicals.

	1986	1987
Total imports	£1,412,579 m.	£3,500,000 m.
Total exports	1,076,079 m.	2,600,000 m.

Trade with U.K.

	1986	1987
Imports from U.K..	£472,078,000	£699,915,000
Exports to U.K. ...	768,470,000	847,980,000

The British share of the Portuguese market was 8·3 per cent in 1987 and the U.K. was the fifth largest market for Portuguese exports.

CAPITAL.—ΨLisbon. Population (estimated, 1984) 807,937. ΨOporto 327,368; ΨSetubal 77,885.

CURRENCY.—Escudo of 100 Centavos.

FLAG.—Vertical band of green (next staff) and square of red, bearing arms of the Republic, framed.

NATIONAL ANTHEM.—A Portuguesa.

NATIONAL DAY.—June 10.

BRITISH EMBASSY
35–37 Rua de S. Domingos à Lapa,
1200 Lisbon
[Lisbon 661191]

Ambassador Extraordinary and Plenipotentiary, His Excellency Michael Keith Orlebar Simpson-Orlebar, C.M.G. (1986).

There are British Consulates in *Oporto*, *Portimão*, *Funchal* (Madeira) and *Ponta Delgada* (Azores).

British Council Representative, J. Mallon, O.B.E., The British Institute, Rua Cecilio de Sousa 65, 1294 Lisbon.

BRITISH PORTUGUESE CHAMBER OF COMMERCE, Rua da Estrela 8, 1200 Lisbon and Rua Sa de Bandeira 784–20E, Frente, 4000 Oporto.

MADEIRA AND THE AZORES

Madeira and The Azores are two administratively autonomous regions of Portugal, having locally elected Assemblies and Governments.

Madeira is a group of islands in the Atlantic Ocean about 520 miles south-west of Lisbon, and consist of Madeira, Porto, Santo and 3 uninhabited islands (Desertas). The total area is 314 sq. miles (813 sq. km.), with a population of 264,800 (1984). ΨFunchal in Madeira, the largest island (270 square miles), is the capital, with a population of 44,111; Machico (10,905).

The Azores are a group of 9 islands (Flores, Corvo, Terceira, São Jorge, Pico, Faial, Graciosa, São Miguel and Santa Maria) in the Atlantic Ocean, with a total area of 922 sq. miles (2,387 sq. km.), and a population of 250,700 (1984). ΨPonta Delgada, on São Miguel, is the capital of the group; population is 21,347. Other ports are ΨAngra, in Terceira, (16,476) and ΨHorta (2,509).

MACAO

Macao, situated at the mouth of the Pearl River, comprises a peninsula and the islands of Coloane and Taipa, having an area of six sq. miles (15·5 sq. km.), with a population 1984 estimate of 343,000. Portuguese trade with China began early in the 16th century and Macao became a Portuguese colony in 1557: in a Sino-Portuguese treaty of Dec. 1887 China recognised Portugal's sovereignty over, and government of, Macao. In 1974 Portugal changed Macao's status from that of an Overseas Province to "a territory under Portuguese administration". Following the Sino-British Joint Declaration on Hong Kong in 1984, Sino-Portuguese negotiations on the transfer of administration began on June 30, 1986. The agreement on the transfer of the Administration of Macao to the Chinese authorities was signed on April 13, 1987. Macao will become a 'special administrative region' of China when transferred on Dec. 20, 1999.

Macao is subject to Portuguese constitutional law but otherwise enjoys administrative, economic and financial autonomy. The Governor is appointed by the Portuguese President and since 1976 there has been a 17 member legislative assembly, which has a three year term. The assembly comprises 12 elected deputies appointed by the Governor. A new electoral system which came into effect February 28th 1984, gave equal voting rights to all residents, thus enfranchising the Chinese population.

Macao's major industry is textile manufacturing which accounts for 62 per cent. of all exports. Port Macao is served by British, Portuguese and Dutch shipping lines and has regular services to Hong Kong, some 35 miles away.

Governor, Carlos Melancia.

Trade with U.K.

	1986	1987
Imports from U.K....	£9,109,131	£5,617,000
Exports to U.K.	52,981,000	45,896,000

QATAR
(Dawlat Qatar)

Amir of Qatar, H.H. Sheikh Khalifa Bin Hamad Al-Thani, G.C.M.G.; *assumed power* February 22, 1972 (*also Prime Minister*).

COUNCIL OF MINISTERS

Heir Apparent, Minister of Defence and Commander-in Chief of the Qatar Armed Forces, H.H. Sheikh Hamad Bin Khalifa Al-Thani, K.C.M.G.
Education, H.E. Shaikh Mohammad Bin Hamad Al-Thani.
Foreign, (vacant).
Finance and Petroleum Affairs, H.E. Shaikh Abdul Aziz Bin Khalifa Al-Thani.
Municipal Affairs, (vacant).
Economy and Commerce, (vacant).
Justice (vacant).
Electricity and Water, H.E. Shaikh Jasem Bin Moh'd Al-Thani.
Interior, H.E. Shaikh Khalid Bin Hamad Al-Thani.
Industry and Agriculture, H.E. Shaikh Faisal Bin Thani Al-Thani.
Public Health, H.E. Sayed Khalid Bin Mohammed al-Mana.
Public Works, H.E. Sayed Khaled Bin Abdullah al-Attiyah.
Labour and Social Welfare Affairs, H.E. Sayed Ali Bin Ahmed Al-Ansari.
Communications and Transport, H.E. Sayed Abdullah Bin Naser al-Suwaidi.
Information, H.E. Sayed Issa Ghanim al-Kawari.
Minister of State for Foreign Affairs, H.E. Shaikh Ahmed bin Saif Al-Thani.
Adviser to H.H. The Amir, Dr. Hassan Kamel.

EMBASSY IN LONDON
27 Chesham Place, SW1X 8HG
[01–235 0851/4]

Ambassador Extraordinary and Plenipotentiary, His Excellency Sherida Sa'ad Jubran Al-Ka'abi, G.C.V.O. (1981).

The state of Qatar covers the peninsula of Qatar from approximately the northern shore of Khor al Odaid to the eastern shore of Khor al Salwa. The area is about 4,247 sq. miles (11,000 sq. km.), with a population estimated in 1985 at about 315,000. The great majority of the population is concentrated in the urban district of the capital Doha. Only a small minority still pursue the traditional life of the semi nomadic tribesmen and fisherfolk.

Until 1971, Qatar was one of the nine independent Emirates in the Arabian Gulf in special treaty relations with the U.K. In that year, with the withdrawal of H.M. Forces from the area, these special treaty relations were terminated. On April 2, 1970 a Provisional Constitution for Qatar was proclaimed, providing for the establishment of a Council of Ministers and for the formation of a Consultative Council to assist the Council of Ministers in running the affairs of the State. The first Cabinet was formed of 10 members on May 29, 1970. Qatar is a member of the Arab League as well as of the United Nations.

Production.—Although Qatar is a desert country, there are gardens and smallholdings near Doha and to the north and encouragement is being given to the development of agriculture.

The Qatar General Petroleum Corporation is the state-owned company controlling Qatar's interests in oil, gas and petrochemicals. The corporation is responsible for Qatar's oil production onshore and offshore. The production level for Qatar agreed in O.P.E.C. is currently 299,000 b.p.d. Explorations continue for further oil. The large reserves of natural gas in the North Field are expected to come into production by 1991. A 50,000 b.p.d. oil refinery was commissioned in 1984 to increase domestic refinery capacity.

Current industries include a steel mill, a fertilizer plant, a cement factory, a petrochemical complex and two natural gas liquids plants. With the exception of the cement works, which is at Umm Bab, all these industries are at Umm Said, about 30 miles south of Doha. There are tentative plans for new industry, including an aluminium smelter and a second ammonia plant, downstream of the North Field. Qatar is also expanding its infrastructure including electrical generation and water distillation, roads, houses, and Government buildings, although reduced demand for crude oil in international markets has led to a downturn in the economy and a slower rate of development than hitherto.

Communications.—Doha is an expanding town with an airport built to international standards. Regular air services connect Qatar with Bahrain and the United Arab Emirates, Kuwait, Muscat, Saudi Arabia, Jordan, Syria, Lebanon, Egypt, the Indian sub-continent, Africa and Europe. The Qatar Broadcasting Service transmits on medium, shortwave, and V.H.F. Regular television transmissions in colour began in 1974 and a second channel opened in 1982.

Trade with U.K.

	1986	1987
Imports from U.K.	£112,000,000	£105,087,000
Exports to U.K.	30,000,000	13,765,000

CAPITAL.—ΨDoha. Population (estimated) 220,000. Other towns include Khor, Dukhan, Wakra and ΨUmm Said.
CURRENCY.—Qatar Riyal of 100 Dirhams.
FLAG.—White and maroon, white portion nearer the mast; vertical indented line comprising 17 angles divides the colours.
NATIONAL DAY.—September 3.

BRITISH EMBASSY
P.O. Box 3, Doha
[Doha 421991]

Ambassador Extraordinary and Plenipotentiary, His Excellency Patrick Michael Nixon, O.B.E. (1987).
First Secretary, K. N. Johnson, M.B.E. (*Commercial*).
Second Secretary, G. Fairhurst (*Consul and Administration*).
Third Secretary, C. A. R. Forester-Bennett.
Attaché, C. D. Wright (*Commercial*).
Vice Consul, R. J. Clark.
British Council Representative, W. S. Beniston, Ras Abu Aboud Road (P.O. Box 2992), Doha.

ROMANIA
(Republica Socialistă România)

President of the Republic, Nicolae Ceauşescu, *first elected,* 1967; *latest re-election,* March 28, 1985.
State Council, N. Ceauşescu (*President*); Manea Mănescu; Gheorghe Rădulescu; Maria Ghitulica; Árpád Páll (*Vice-Presidents*); Dumitru Apostolu (*Secretary*).

COUNCIL OF MINISTERS

Prime Minister, Constantin Dascalescu.
1st Deputy Prime Ministers, Elena Ceauşescu; Ion Dinca; Gheorghe Oprea.
Deputy Prime Ministers, Gheorghe Petrescu; Ludovic Fazekas; Neculai Ibanescu, Cornel Pacoste; Stefan Andrei; Lina Ciobanu; Constantin Radu.

Agriculture, Gheorghe David.
Chemical and Petrochemical Industry, Ion M. Nicolae.
Education and Instruction, Ion Teoreanu.
Finance, Gheorghe Paraschiv.
Food Industry, Paula Prioteasa.
Foreign Affairs, Ioan Totu.
Foreign Trade and International Economic Co-operation, Ilie Vaduva.
Forestry Administration, Eugen Tarhon.
Geology, Ioan Folea.
Health, Victor Ciobanu.
Industrial Construction, Alexandru Dimitriu.
Internal Affairs, Tudor Postelnicu.
Internal Trade, Ana Muresan.
Justice, Maria Bobu.
Labour, Maxim Berghianu.
Light Industry, Maria Flucsa.
Heavy Equipment Industry, Radu Paul Panescu.
Machine-Building Industry, Serban Teodorescu.
Electrical Engineering Industry, Nicolae Vaidescu.
Metallurgical Industry, Marin Enache.
National Defence, Col. Gen. Vasile Milea.
Technical and Material Supply and Control of Fixed Assets, Gheorghe Stoica.
Tourism, Ion Stanescu.
Transportation and Communications, Pavel Aron.
Timber and Building Materials, Gheorghe Constantinescu.
Youth, Ioan Toma.
Acquisition of Farm Produce, Constantin Zanfir.
Electricity, Petre Fluture.
Mining, Marin Stefanache.
Oil, Nicolae Amza.

Minister, Chairmen of Central Bodies, Gheorghe Pana (*Committee of People's Councils' Affairs*); Decebal Urdea (*State Prices Committee*); Cornel Mihulecea (*State Committee for Nuclear Power*); Stefan Birlea (*State Planning Committee*); Miu Dobrescu (*Central Council of General Confederation of Trade Unions*); (vacant) (*1st Vice-Chairman, Council of Economic and Social Organisations*); Suzana Gadea (*Council for Socialist Culture and Education*); Elena Ceausescu (*National Council of Science and Technology*); Ioan Ursu (*1st Vice-Chairman, National Council of Science and Technology*); Ion Badea (*National Council for Water Resources*); Ana Muresan (*National Council of Women*); Traian Girba (*National Union of Agricultural Production Co-operatives*).

Minister, Secretaries of State, Col. Gen. I. Vlad (*Internal Affairs, and Chief of State Security Dept.*); A. Duma (*Foreign Affairs*); I. Ceausescu (*1st Vice-Chair, State Planning Committee*); (vacant) (*State Planning Committee*); D. Bejan (*Technical and Material Supply and Control of Fixed Assets*); C. Panzaru; C. Stanca (*Foreign Trade*); F. Nagy; F. Gruia (*Agriculture*); M. Florescu, E. Dobrescu (*National Council for Science and Technology*).

THE COMMUNIST PARTY

Political Executive Committee, N. Ceauşescu; E. Bobu; V. Cazacu; E. Ceauşescu; L. Ciobanu; I. Coman; N. Constantin; C. Dascalescu; I. Dinca; M. Dobrescu; L. Fazekąs; M. Mănescu; P. Niculescu; C. Olteanu; G. Oprea; G. Pana; I. Pătan; D. Popescu; G. Rădulescu (*full members*); S. Andrei; S. Birlea; N. Ceausescu; G. David; S. Gadea; M. Gere; M. Ghitulica; N. Giosan; I. Moga; A. Mureşan; E. Nae; C. Pacoste; T. Postelnicu; I. Radu; I. Stoian; I. Szasz; I. Totu; I. Ursu; R. Winter; M. Marina; I. Matei; V. Milea; N. Ibanescu (*candidate members*).

Permanent Bureau of the Political Executive Committee, N. Ceauşescu; E. Bobu; E. Ceauşescu; C. Dascalescu; M. Mănescu; G. Oprea; G. Rădulescu.

Secretariat of the Central Committee, N. Ceauşescu (*Secretary General*); I. Coman; E. Bobu; S. Curti-

ceanu; I. Stoian; V. Barbulescu; C. Mitea; G. Tanase; R. Balan; I. Radu.

ROMANIAN EMBASSY IN LONDON

4 Palace Green, W8 4QD
[01–937 9666]

Ambassador Extraordinary and Plenipotentiary, His Excellency Mr. Stan Soare (1986).

Area and Population.—Romania is a republic of South-Eastern Europe, formerly the classical *Dacia* and *Scythia Pontica*, having its origin in the union of the Danubian principalities of *Wallachia* and *Moldavia* under the *Treaty of Paris* (April, 1856). The area of Romania is 91,699 sq. miles (237,500 sq. km.) and the population (1986 estimate) is 22,823,500.

Government.—The principalities remained separate entities under Turkish suzerainty until 1859, when Prince Alexandru Ion Cuza was elected Prince of both, still under the suzerainty of Turkey. Prince Cuza abdicated in 1866 and was succeeded by Prince Charles of Hohenzollern-Sigmaringen, in whose successors the crown was vested. By the *Treaty of Berlin* (July 13, 1878) the Principality was recognized as an independent State, and part of the *Dobrudja* (which had been occupied by the Romanians) was incorporated. On March 27, 1881, it was recognized as a Kingdom.

The outcome of the War of 1914–18 added Bessarabia, the Bukovina, Transylvania, The Banat and Crisana-Maramures, these additions of territory being confirmed in the Treaty of St. Germain, 1919, and the Treaty of Petit Trianon, 1920.

On June 27, 1940, in compliance with an ultimatum from U.S.S.R., Bessarabia and Northern Bukovina were ceded to the Soviet Government, and in August, 1940, Romania ceded to Bulgaria the portion of Southern Dobrudja taken from Bulgaria in 1913.

Romania became "The Romanian People's Republic" in December, 1947, on the abdication of King Michael. A new Constitution, modelled on the Soviet Constitution of 1936, was adopted unanimously on September 24, 1952, by the Grand National Assembly. The Assembly was later dissolved and elections were held for a new Grand National Assembly on November 30, 1952; in each constituency there was only one candidate for election, representing the People's Democratic Front, now the Socialist and Democratic Unity Front (S.D.U.F.) A new Constitution was approved by the Grand National Assembly in 1965 when the name of the state was changed to The Socialist Republic of Romania. The Constitution states (Art. 3) that the leading political force of the whole society is the Romanian Communist Party. The Constitution was modified in March, 1974.

Agriculture.—Wallachia, Moldavia and Transylvania are potentially among the most fertile areas in Europe, and agriculture and sheep and cattle raising are the principal industries of Romania, although the intense winter cold and summer heat, and fierce summer drought sometimes have adverse effects on crops. These are principally cereal crops, legumes and other vegetables, flax and hemp. Vines and fruits are also grown. The forests of the mountainous regions are extensive, and the timber industry is important.

Socialization of agriculture was completed when collectivization was achieved in the spring of 1962.

Natural Resources and Industry.—Before the war petroleum and agriculture were the backbone of the Romanian economy but rapid industrialization since 1948 has meant that they no longer hold the same dominant position. There are plentiful supplies of natural gas, together with various mineral deposits including coal, iron ore, bauxite, lead, zinc, copper and uranium in quantities which allow a substantial part of the requirements of industry to be met from local resources. Production of crude oil was put at about 10,125,000 tonnes in 1986.

The economy has faced increasing problems since the late 1970s, the result of over investment in energy-intensive heavy industry and neglect of agriculture, which has led to food shortages. The effects of these policies were aggravated by the international recession and by high interest rates, and Romania was severely in debt by the early 1980s. The government has sought to alleviate the situation by reducing borrowing and cutting imports. The economy is centrally organized on the basis of Five-Year Plans which cover all branches of national activity including investment and production.

Language and Literature.—Romanian is a Romance language with many archaic forms and with admixtures of Slavonic, Turkish, Magyar and French words. The folk-songs and folklore, transmitted orally through many centuries and collected in the 19th century, form one of the most interesting of such collections. The publication of all books and reviews is controlled and authorized by the Council for Socialist Culture and Education, which has the status of a Ministry. The leading religion is that of the Romanian Orthodox Church; the Roman Catholics and some Protestant denominations are of importance numerically. The Jewish community has declined through emigration.

Education is free and nominally compulsory. There are Universities at Bucharest, Iasi, Cluj, Timisoara, Craiova and Brasov, polytechnics at Bucharest, Timisoara, Cluj, Brasov, Galati and Iasi, two commercial academies at Bucharest and Brasov, and agricultural colleges at Bucharest, Iasi, Cluj, Craiova and Timisoara.

Communications.—In 1979 there were 11,113 km. of railway open for traffic. The mercantile marine had a gross tonnage of 13,220,000 tons in 1979. The principal ports are Constanta (on the Black Sea), Sulina (on the Danube Estuary), Galati, Braila, Giurgiu and Turnu Severin. The Danube and the Black Sea are linked by a canal completed in 1984. Romania is a member of the Danube Commission whose seat is at Budapest.

In 1986 combined imports and exports totalled *Lei* 300·6 billion, compared with *Lei* 340·7 billion in 1985.

Imports are chiefly semi-manufactured goods, raw materials, machinery and metals; export consists principally of maize, wheat, barley, oats, petroleum, timber, cattle, machines and industrial equipment.

Trade with U.K.

	1986	1987
Imports from U.K......	£81,986,000	£55,688,000
Exports to U.K.	86,730,000	92,526,000

CAPITAL, Bucharest, on the Dimbovita, population 1,961,189 Other large towns are:

Brasov 290,722	Ψ Galati 254,636
Constanţa 284,801	Craiova 243,117
Cluj-Napoca ...270,820	Ploiesti.......215,500
Iasi 265,176	Ψ Brăila 214,561
Timişoara 261,950	

CURRENCY.—Leu of 100 Bani.
FLAG.—Three vertical bands, blue, yellow, red, with the emblem of the Republic in the centre band.
NATIONAL ANTHEM.—Trei Culori (Three colours).
NATIONAL DAY.—August 23 (Liberation Day, 1944).

24 Strada Jules Michelet, Bucharest
[Bucharest 111634/6]

Ambassador Extraordinary and Plenipotentiary, His Excellency Hugh James Arbuthnott, C.M.G. (1987).

Counsellor, A. R. Clark (*Head of Chancery*).
Defence, Naval and Military Attaché, Lt.-Col. W. J. Chesshyre.
Cultural Attaché and British Council Representative, Λ. Pattison.

RWANDA
(Republika y'u Rwanda)

President, Maj. Gen. Juvénal Habyarimana, *assumed office,* July 5, 1973, *elected,* Dec. 24, 1978, *re-elected,* Dec. 19, 1983.

Minister of Defence, The President.
Sec. Gen. of the National Revolutionary Movement for Development, Bonaventure Habimana.
President of the National Council for Development, Maurice Ntahobari.
Minister at the Presidency, Simeon Nteziryayo.
Institutional Relations, Edouard Karemera.
Interior and Community Development, Thomas Habanabakize.
Justice, Jean-Marie-Vianney Mugemana.
Civil Service, François Habiyakare.
Finance and Economy, Vincent Ruhamanya.
Mines and Industry, Juvénal Uwilingiyimana.
Agriculture, Husbandry and Forests, Anastase Nteziryayo.
Planning, Ambroise Mulindangabo.
Public Works and Energy, Joseph Nzirorera.
Transport and Communications, Andre Ntageruru.
Primary and Secondary Education, Col. Aloys Nsekalije.
Higher Education and Scientific Research, Charles Nyandwi.
Youth, Lt.-Col. Augustin Ndindiliyimana.
Foreign Affairs and Co-operation, François Ngarukiyintwali.
Public Health and Social Welfare, Dr. Casimir Bizimungu.

Rwanda, formerly part of the Belgian-administered trusteeship of Ruanda-Urundi, has an area of 10,169 sq. miles (26,338 sq. km.), and a population (1985 U.N. estimate) of 6,070,000, mainly of the Bahutu tribe, with Batutsi and Batwa minorities.

A referendum held in September, 1961, showed the majority of the population were opposed to the retention of the monarchy which was accordingly abolished on Oct. 2, 1961. Rwanda became an independent Republic on July 1, 1962, with Gregoire Kayibanda as Head of State and Head of the Government. He was deposed in 1973, and replaced by a military government under Maj.-Gen. Juvénal Habyarimana.

Coffee (the chief cash crop), tea and sugar are grown. Tin, hides, bark of quinine and extract of pyrethrum flowers are also exported.

The National University of Rwanda is situated at two campuses, Butare and Ruhengeri.

In 1983 total imports were valued at *Rw.Fr.*25,267 m.; total exports, *Rw.Fr.*7,427 m.

Trade with U.K.

	1986	1987
Imports from U.K........	£1,681,000	£2,526,000
Exports to U.K.	7,487,000	4,291,000

CAPITAL.—Kigali (156,000).
CURRENCY.—Rwanda Franc of 100 Centimes.
FLAG.—Three vertical bands, red, yellow and green with letter R on yellow band.
NATIONAL DAY.—July 1.

British Ambassador (resident at *Kinshasa,* Zaire).

EL SALVADOR
(República de El Salvador)

President, José Napoleon Duarte, *elected* March 25, 1984, *assumed office*, June 1, 1984.

CABINET

Vice-President and Foreign Minister, Ricardo Acebeoto Peralta.
Minister of the Presidency, Dr. Jorge E. Tenorio.
Culture and Communications, Julio A. Rey Prendes.
Planning and Co-ordination of Economic and Social Development, Dr. Fidel Chávez Mena.
Justice, Dr. Julio A. Samayoa.
Finance, Ricardo J. López.
Trade, Julio Rivas Gallont.
Economy, Dr. Ricardo Gonzalez Camacho.
Education, Prof. Alberto Buendía Flores.
Defence and Public Security, Gen. Carlos E. Vides Casanova.
Labour and Social Security, Dr. Miguel A. Gallegos.
Agriculture, Carlos A. Duarte Funes.
Public Works, Roberto Mueza.
Health, Dr. Benjamin Valdés.

SALVADOREAN EMBASSY AND CONSULATE
9 Welbeck House, 62 Welbeck Street, W1
[01-486 8182]

Ambassador Extraordinary and Plenipotentiary, His Excellency Dr. Maurico Rosales-Rivera.
First Secretary and Consul, Snrta Carolina Calderón.

Area and Population.—The Republic of El Salvador extends along the Pacific coast of Central America for 160 miles with a general breadth of about 50 miles, and contains an area of 8,124 sq. miles (21,041 sq. km.), with a population (1985 estimate) of 5,480,000. It is divided into 14 Departments.

The surface of the country is very mountainous, many of the peaks being extinct volcanoes. The highest are the Santa Ana volcano (7,700 ft.) and the San Vicente volcano (7,200 ft.). Much of the interior has an average altitude of 2,000 feet. The lowlands along the coast are generally hot, but towards the interior the altitude tempers the severity of the heat. There is a wet season from May to October, and a dry season from November to April. Earthquakes have been frequent in the history of El Salvador, the most recent being that of May 3, 1965, when considerable damage was done to San Salvador.

The principal river is the Rio Lempa. There is a large volcanic lake (Ilopango) a few miles to the east of the capital, while farther away and to the west lies the smaller lake of Coatepeque, which appears to have been formed in a vast crater flanked by the Santa Ana volcano.

Government.—El Salvador was conquered in 1526 by Pedro de Alvarado, and formed part of the Spanish vice-royalty of Guatemala until 1821.

After two years of government by a Junta headed by José Napoleon Duarte, elections for a Constituent Assembly were held in March 1982. The Assembly has completed its principal task of adopting a new Constitution. Presidential elections, although boycotted by the guerrilla movement, were held in March 1984 and in the run-off between the two largest parties, Sr. Duarte, the Christian Democrat leader, won with a 54 per cent. majority over the ARENA candidate, Roberto d'Aubuisson. Assembly and municipal elections took place in March 1988.

Agriculture.—The principal cash crops are coffee, which is grown principally on the slopes of the volcanoes, cotton, which is cultivated on the coastal plains, and sugarcane. (However, cotton and sugar production have decreased as a result of the civil war.) Also cultivated are maize, sesame, indigo, rice, balsam, etc. In the lower altitudes towards the east,

sisal is produced and used in the manufacture of coffee and cereal bags. Land reforms, announced in March 1980, are being undertaken. The Salvadorean Coffee Company, sugar exports and the banking system are nationalised.

Industry.—Existing factories make textiles, constructional steel, furniture, cement and household items. El Salvador is a member of the Central American Common Market. The first trade zone was inaugurated in November 1974 and the National Assembly approved a new Export Development Law.

Education.—The illiteracy rate is about 30·5 per cent (1980). Primary education is nominally compulsory, but the number of schools and teachers available is too small to enable education to be given to all children of school age. In recent Budgets, however, a high percentage of the national revenue has been devoted to education and great efforts are being made to eliminate the existing shortage of schools and teachers.

Language and Literature.—The language of the country is Spanish. Indigenous literature has not yet produced work of international repute. There are 4 daily newspapers published at the capital, and 4 in the provinces.

Communications.—The Executive Autonomous Port Commission (CEPA) which administers the previously foreign-owned port of Cutuco, at La Union and the principal port of Acajutla, and the railways under the new railroad organization, FENADESAL. There is continuous railway communication between San Salvador and Guatemala City and Puerto Barrios on the Caribbean coast. The roads are paved and in good condition but bridges are frequently dynamited. There are good roads between Port Acajutla and the capital (60 miles), and between the capital and Guatemala City. The Pan-American Highway from the Guatemalan frontier follows this route and continues to the Honduran frontier. The El Salvador international airport can receive jet aircraft and many international airlines fly to San Salvador.

There are post and telegraph offices throughout the country. There are 40 broadcasting stations and six television stations.

BUDGET

	1985
	Colones '000
Revenue	2,391,010
Expenditure	2,276,052

Trade with U.K.

	1986	1987
Imports from U.K.	£6,917,000	£9,595,000
Exports to U.K.	1,323,000	1,890,000

There is strict foreign exchange control.

Other exports are sugar, shrimps, sisal (in the form of bags used for exporting coffee, sugar, etc.), balsam, meat, towels, hides and skins. The chief imports are chemicals, fertilizers, pharmaceutical goods, petroleum, manufactured goods, industrial and electronic machinery and equipment.

CAPITAL.—San Salvador. Population, (est. 1980) 425,119. Other towns are Santa Ana (204,570), San Miguel (157,838), Ψ La Union (Cutuco), Ψ La Libertad and Ψ Acajutia.

CURRENCY.—El Salvador Colón of 100 Centavos.

FLAG.—Three horizontal bands light blue, white, light blue; coat of arms on white band.

NATIONAL ANTHEM.—Saludemos La Patria Orgullosos (Let us proudly hail the Fatherland).

NATIONAL DAY.—September 15.

BRITISH EMBASSY
P.O. Box 1591, San Salvador

British Ambassador, (resident at Tegucigalpa, Honduras).
Chargé d'Affaires a.i., D. F. C. Ridgway *(First Secretary).*

SAN MARINO
(Repubblica di San Marino)

Regents, Two "Capitani Reggenti".

CONSULATE GENERAL IN LONDON
166 High Holborn, WC1V 6TT
[01-836 7744]
Consul-General, The Lord Forte.

A small Republic in the hills near Rimini, on the Adriatic, founded, it is stated, by a pious stonecutter of Dalmatia in the 4th century. The Republic always resisted the Papal claims, and those of neighbouring dukedoms, during the 15th–18th centuries, and its integrity and sovereignty is recognized and respected by Italy. The Republic is governed by a State Congress of 10 members, under the Presidency of two Heads of State, who are elected at six-monthly intervals. The Great and General Council, a legislative body of 60 members, is elected by a universal suffrage for a term of 5 years. A Council of Twelve forms in certain cases a Supreme Court of Justice. The area is approximately 23 sq. miles (61 sq. km.), the population (April 30, 1985) was 22,361. The city of San Marino, on the slope of Monte Titano, has three towers, a fine church and Government palace, a theatre and museums. The principal products are wine, cereals, and cattle, and the main industries are tourism, ceramics, lime, concrete, cotton yarns, colour and paints. A Treaty of Extradition between the Governments of Great Britain and the Republic of San Marino has been in force since 1899.

CURRENCY.—Italian currency is in circulation.
FLAG.—Two horizontal bands, white, blue (with coat of arms of the Republic in centre).
NATIONAL DAY.—September 3.

BRITISH CONSULATE-GENERAL
Consul-General, Miss M. L. Croll (resides at Florence).

SÃO TOMÉ AND PRÍNCIPE
(República Democrática de São Tomé e Príncipe)

President, Dr. Manuel Pinto da Costa.

COUNCIL OF MINISTERS

Prime Minister, Celestino Rocha da Costa.
Defence and Internal Security, Raul Braganca Neto.
Foreign Affairs, Carlos da Graca.
Justice and Public Affairs, Francesco Fortunato Pires.
Planning and Trade, Teotonio d'Alva Torres.
Agriculture and Fisheries, Oscar Aguiar Sacramento e Sousa.
Co-operation, Guillermo Posser da Costa.
Education and Culture, Ligia do Espirito Santo Costa.
Health, Labour and Social Security, Armindo Vaz de Almeida.
Equipment, Environment, Transport and Communications, Carlos Ferreira.
Ministers Delegate, Manuel Quaresma Costa *(Príncipe Islands);* Manuel Vaz Alfonso Fernades *(Secretary General).*

The islands of São Tomé and Príncipe are situated in the gulf of Guinea, off the west coast of Africa. They have an area of 372 sq. miles (964 sq. km.), and a population (1985 U.N. estimate) of 108,000.

Following Portugal's decision to grant independence, a transitional government was installed on Dec. 21, 1974, and the islands became an independent democratic republic on July 12, 1975.

Cacao is the main product.

Trade with U.K.

	1986	1987
Imports from U.K.	£455,000	£329,000
Exports to U.K.	327,000	205,000

CAPITAL.—ΨSão Tomé (25,000).
CURRENCY.—Dobra of 100 Centavos.
FLAG.—Horizontal stripes of green, yellow, green, the yellow of double width and bearing two black stars; and a red triangle in the hoist.
NATIONAL DAY.—July 12 (Independence Day).

British Ambassador (resident in *Luanda,* Angola).

SAUDI ARABIA
(Al Mamlaka al Arabiya as-Sa'udiyya)

Custodian of the Two Holy Mosques and King of Saudi Arabia, H.M. King Fahd bin Abdul Aziz, *born,* 1921, *ascended the throne* June 1, 1982.
Crown Prince, H.R.H. Amir Abdullah bin Abdul Aziz.

COUNCIL OF MINISTERS

Prime Minister, H.M. King Fahd bin Abdul Aziz.
First Deputy Prime Minister and Commander of the National Guard, H.R.H. Prince Abdullah bin Abdul Aziz.
Second Deputy Prime Minister, Defence and Aviation, H.R.H. Prince Sultan bin Abdul Aziz.
Public Works and Housing, H.R.H. Prince Mit'ab bin Abdul Aziz.
Interior, H.R.H. Prince Naif bin Abdul Aziz.
Foreign Affairs, H.R.H. Prince Saud al-Faisal bin Abdul Aziz.
Finance and National Economy, Muhammad Aba al-Khail.
Agriculture and Water, Dr. Abdul Rahman bin Abdul Aziz bin Hassan Al al-Shaikh.
Municipal and Rural Affairs, Ibrahim bin Abdullah al-Angari.
Commerce, Dr Sulaiman al-Solaim.
Communications, Dr. Hussain Mansouri.
Petroleum and Mineral Resources, Hisham Nazer *(and acting Minister of Planning).*
Justice, Ibrahim bin Mohammed Al al-Shaikh.
Labour and Social Affairs, Dr. Mohamed Ali al-Faiz.
Information, Ali Sha'er.
Health, Faisal bin Abdul Aziz al Hejailan.
Pilgrimage and Endowments, Abdul Wahhab Ahmed Abdul Wasi.
Education, Dr. Abdul Aziz Al-Abdullah al-Khuwaiter *(and acting Minister of Higher Education).*
Posts, Telegraphs and Telephones, Dr. Alawi Darwish Kayyal.
Industry and Electricity, Abdul Aziz al-Zamil.
Ministers of State, Muhammad Ibrahim Mas'oud; Dr. Muhammad Abdul Latif al-Melhem; Omar Abdul Qader Faqih; Dr. Fayez Ibrahim Badr; Turki bin Khalid Al Sudairi; Mohammed bin Abdulaziz Bin Zar'a; Mohammed bin Ibrahim Bin Jubeir.

ROYAL SAUDI ARABIAN EMBASSY
30 Belgrave Square, SW1X 8QB
[01-235 0831]

Ambassador Extraordinary and Plenipotentiary, His Excellency Sheikh Nasser Almanqour, G.C.V.O. (1980).

Ministers Plenipotentiary, Ibrahim M. Mosly; Saud Ahmed M. Alyahya, L.V.O.

The Kingdom of Saudi Arabia is a personal union of two countries, the Sultan of Nejd becoming also King of the Hejaz. Great Britain recognized Abdul Aziz Ibn Saud as an independent ruler, King of the Hejaz and of Nejd and its Dependencies, by the Treaty of Jeddah (May 20, 1927). The name was changed to the Kingdom of Saudi Arabia in Sept 1932.

The total area of the Kingdom is about 830,000 sq. miles (2,149,640 sq. km.), with a population (1985 est.) of 12,400,000, of whom perhaps 3 million are non-Saudis. Islam is the established and only permitted religion.

In the 18th century Nejd was an independent state governed from Diriya (now in ruins, 25 km. from Riyadh) and the stronghold of the Wahhabis, a puritanical Islamic sect. It subsequently fell under the Turkish yoke, but in 1913 Abdul Aziz Ibn Saud threw off Turkish rule and captured the Turkish province of Al Hasa. In 1920 he captured the Asir, and in 1921, by force of arms, he added to his dominions the Jebel Shammar territory of the Rashid family. In 1925 he completed the conquest of the Hejaz.

Saudi Arabia comprises almost the whole of the Arabian peninsula, with the exception of the small states in the extreme south (N. and S. Yemen), south-east (Oman and the U.A.E.) and east (Qatar). In the north-west it borders Jordan and in the north-east Iraq and Kuwait, while to the west lies the Red Sea and to the east the Gulf. The Nejd ("Plateau"), now the Central Province, extends over the centre of the peninsula, including the Nafud and Dahna deserts. The Hejaz ("the Boundary") now the Western Province, extends along the Red Sea coast to Asir and contains the holy towns of Mecca and Medina. The former, about 60 km. east of Jeddah, is the birthplace of the Prophet Mohammed, and contains the Great Mosque, within which is the Kaaba or sacred shrine of the Muslim religion. This is the focus of the annual Hajj ("Pilgrimage") performed by 3·4 million in 1986. The latter, Medina Al Munawwarah ("The City of Light") some 300 km. north of Mecca, is celebrated as the first city to embrace Islam and as the Prophet Mohammed's burial place (he died there on Rabia 12, 11 AH, corresponding to June 7, 632 AD).

Asir ("Inaccessible") is named for its mountainous terrain, and, with the coastal plain of the Tihama, lies along the southern Red Sea coast from Hejaz to the border with Yemen. It is the only region to enjoy substantial rainfall. Water supplies are, however, supplemented by dams and irrigation. The east and south-east of the country are lower-lying and largely desert. Outside the manufacturing centres which have grown up around some of the towns, most of the population are engaged in agriculture. The productivity of traditional dryland farming is increasingly supplemented by irrigation.

Industry.—Oil was first found in commercial quantities in Dhahran, near Dammam, in 1938. Total production of crude oil peaked at 9·9 m.b.d. in 1980, and in 1986 was 4·8 m.b.d. About 97 per cent of the total is extracted by the Arabian–American Oil Company. Recoverable reserves stood at about 167 billion barrels at the end of 1986, equivalent to about 95 years' production at the 1986 rate. Aramco's 66-year lease will terminate in 1999 but the company was effectively nationalized in 1980. Aramco operates a deepwater oil terminal at Ras Tanura.

The Government actively encourages the establishment of manufacturing industries in the country. The policy includes the provision of industrial estates and loans covering 50 per cent of capital investment. By the end of 1984 3,310 private industrial licences

had been granted, and 650 were in production. These establishments were concentrated in the fields of construction materials, metal fabrication, simple machinery and electrical equipment, food and beverages, chemicals and plastics. The Government is trying to encourage future investment in industrial gases, intermediate petrochemicals, light engineering, machinery and all kinds of spare parts. A new pharmaceutical plant is scheduled for completion by 1989.

The Government has also established two industrial poles at Jubail and Yanbu, financed by the state agency Saudi Arabian Basic Industries Corp., to be the focus of heavy industrial development. Linked by gas and oil pipelines, both are to have petrochemical complexes producing, initially, ethylene and methanol, six of the seven plants now on-stream are joint ventures with American and Japanese companies. In addition an integrated steel complex and a urea fertilizer factory are in production in Jubail with West German and Taiwanese partners. Complete new cities are being built at each pole: Jubail will eventually house 300,000 and Yanbu 190,000. The state agency Petromin operates three domestic refineries and two lubricant plants and the last of three joint-venture export refineries came on-stream in 1986. Total refining capacity is now approximately 1,950,000 b.p.d.

Communications.—The railway from the port of Dammam to the oilfields at Abqaiq and through Hofuf to Riyadh was opened in 1951, and a direct Dammam-Riyadh line opened in 1985. An extension to Jeddah via Medina and the reopening of the Hejaz railway are planned. Metalled roads connect all the cities and main towns: the network consisted of 28,500 km. in 1985. The principal port of the Gulf is Dammam which has 39 berths and an annual capacity of 9·1 million tons. Jeddah is the centre of commercial traffic on the Red Sea and has 51 piers, giving an annual capacity of 17 million tons. The Government-owned Saudi Arabian Airlines (Saudia) operate scheduled services to 19 domestic airports. There are international class airports at Dhahran, Jeddah and Riyadh. Work has begun on the new King Fahd International Airport in Eastern Province, due to be completed in 1990. Saudia have an extensive overseas operation, and a large number of international airlines operate into the country. Telecommunications are being rapidly expanded. By the end of 1985 60,000 telex and 1,216,000 telephone lines were installed; telephone and telex exchanges will be able to handle 2·25 million lines by 1990. The Government is a major participant in the Arab Satellite Communications Organization.

Education.—With the exception of a few schools for expatriate children, all schools are government supervised and segregated for boys and girls. By mid-1985 there were a total of 1,692,300 schoolchildren in 5,323 primary and 1,219 intermediate and 418 second ary schools. There are Universities in Jeddah, Mecca, Riyadh (branches in Abha and Qassim), Dammam (branch at Hofuf) and Dhahran, and there are Islamic universities in Medina and Riyadh. In addition there is great emphasis on vocational training, provided at 24 literacy and artisan skill training centres and 21 more advanced industrial, commercial and agricultural education institutes. Education in government-owned institutes is free at all levels.

Finance and Trade.—Oil remains the main source of receipts in the balance of payments. As a result, Government revenues have been markedly affected by oil prices and volume of production, and fell away from a peak of SR368,000 million in 1981–82 to SR133,600 million in 1985–86. The 1987 budget provided for expenditure of SR170,000 million. There is no public debt. There are no restrictions on foreign exchange transactions. The currency is strong, backed by gold and foreign exchange reserves, and maintained on a close parity to the U.S. dollar.

There is a total ban on the importation of alcohol, pork products, firearms and items regarded as non-Islamic or pornographic. The Arab boycott list also applies. In addition, certain chemicals now require import licences and fresh food items require radiation-free certificates. The leading suppliers of imports are U.S.A., Japan, West Germany, the U.K., Italy and France and the chief customers for exports are Japan, France, U.S.A. and Singapore.

	1985	1986
Total imports	SR99,645m.	SR75,000m.
Total exports	85,500m.	70,800m.

Trade with U.K.

	1986	1987
Imports from U.K....	£1,507,000,000	£1,978,440,000
Exports to U.K.	435,000,000	383,143,000

CAPITAL.—Riyadh, population about 1 million. Other major centres are Jeddah (pop. approx. 1 million), Damman, Buraydah, Hofuf and Tabuk.

CURRENCY.—Saudi Riyal of 20 Qursh or 100 Halala.

FLAG.—Green oblong, white Arabic device in centre: "There is no God but God, Muhammad is the Prophet of God," and a white scimitar beneath the lettering.

NATIONAL ANTHEM.—"Long live our beloved King".

BRITISH EMBASSY
P.O. Box 94351, Riyadh 11693.
[Riyadh 488 0077]

Ambassador Extraordinary and Plenipotentiary, His Excellency Sir Stephen Egerton, K.C.M.G. (1986).

Counsellors, D. J. Plumbly (*Head of Chancery and Consul-General*); P. W. Ford (*Commercial*).

Defence and Military Attaché, Brig. P. Sincock, M.B.E.

Air Attaché, Wing-Cdr. R. Springett.

Naval Attaché, Cdr. N. Kerr.

First Secretaries, M. J. Crawford (*Chancery*); D. E. Lyscom (*Economic*); H. Formstone (*Commercial*); J. B. Midgley (*Consul General*); S. R. Bonde (*Commercial*).

Consul General, Jeddah, G. P. Lockton, M.B.E., P.O. Box 393, Jeddah 21411.

British Council Representative, W. L. Radford, Mura'aba, P.O. Box 2701, Riyadh 11461. There is also an office in Jeddah.

SENEGAL
(République du Sénégal)

President and Head of Government, Abdou Diouf, installed, Jan. 1, 1981, elected for 5 year term, Feb. 27, 1983; re-elected Feb. 28, 1988.

MINISTERS

Minister of State and Secretary General of the Presidency, Jean Collin.

Armed Forces, Médoune Fall.

Justice, Seydou Madani Sy.

Foreign Affairs, Ibrahima Fall.

Interior, André Sonko.

Economy and Finance, Serigne Lamine Diop.

Planning and Co-operation, Djibo Ka.

Communications, Robert Sagna.

Higher Education, Sakhir Thiam.

National Education, Ibrahima Niang.

Equipment, Alassane Dialy Ndiaye.

Rural Development, Cheikh Abdoul Khadre Cissokho.

Industrial Development and Handicrafts, Famara Ibrahima Sagna.

Trade, Seydina Oumar Sy.

Hydraulics, Samba Yela Diop.

Public Health, Mme. Thérèse King.

Youth and Sport, Abdoulaye Makhtar Diop.

Civil Service and Employment, Moussa Ndoye.

Tourism, El-Hadji Malick Sy.

Culture, Moustapha Ka.

Social Development, Mme. Ndioro Ndiaye.

Urban Affairs and Housing, Mamadou Abbas Ba.

Ministers Delegate, Mme. Fatou Ndongo Dieng (*Emigration*); Farba Lo (*Relations with National Assembly*); Moussa Toure (*Economy and Finance*); Mbaye Diouf (*Rural Development and Animal Resources*); Moctar Kebe (*Rural Development and Environmental Protection*).

SENEGAL EMBASSY IN LONDON
11 Phillimore Gardens, W8 7QG
[01–937 0925/6, 3139]

Ambassador Extraordinary and Plenipotentiary, His Excellency Gen. Idrissa Fall, M.B.E. (1984).

Senegal lies on the west coast of Africa between Mauritania in the north, Mali in the east, and Guinea-Bissau and Guinea in the south. The Gambia lies entirely within Senegal, except for its sea-coast. (*For* MAP, *see* index.) It has an area of 75,750 sq. miles (196,192 sq. km.), and a population (1985 estimate) of 6,540,000.

Formerly a French colony, Senegal elected on Nov. 25, 1958, to remain within the French Community as an autonomous republic. In March, 1963 (after an attempted coup d'état by the then Prime Minister in the previous December) a new constitution was approved giving executive powers to the President, on the lines of the present French constitution. The process of political liberalization continued; there are now 16 political parties officially recognized. Six parties contested the General Election in Feb. 1988. The P.S. took 103 seats and the P.D.S. 17.

In Feb. 1982, after an attempted coup in The Gambia in July 1981 had been put down with the aid of Senegalese troops, the Senegambia Confederation was established, based on certain joint institutions and the integration of defence, security and some other matters. Each country remains sovereign and independent. The President of Senegal is President of the Confederation and the President of The Gambia is Confederal Vice-President.

Senegal's principal exports are groundnuts (raw and processed) and phosphates. Tourism is also of growing importance as a revenue earner.

Trade with U.K.

	1986	1987
Imports from U.K.	£12,328,000	£11,877,708
Exports to U.K.	13,881,000	11,307,022

CAPITAL—ΨDakar (1,000,000).

CURRENCY.—Franc C.F.A. of 100 Centimes.

FLAG.—Three vertical bands, green, yellow and red; a green star on the yellow band.

NATIONAL DAY.—April 4.

BRITISH EMBASSY
B.P. 6025, Dakar.
[Dakar 217392]

Ambassador Extraordinary and Plenipotentiary, His Excellency John Esmond Campbell Macrae, C.M.G. (1985).

First Secretary, R. S. Dewar (*Head of Chancery*).

Second Secretaries, B. Williams (*Consul*); Miss J. M. Pearce.

Cultural Attaché (British Council Representative), Dr. M. Cooper.

SOMALIA
(Jamhuuriyadda Diimoqraadiga ee Soomaaliya)

President and Sec. Gen. of Somali Revolutionary Socialist Party, Maj.-Gen. Mohamed Siad Barre, *assumed office* Oct. 21, 1969.

Prime Minister, Lt.-Gen. M. A. Samantar.

Deputy P.M., Economic Affairs, Maj.-Gen. H. K. Afrah.

Deputy P.M., Social and Security Affairs, Brig.-Gen. A. S. Abdullah.

Deputy P.M., Political Affairs, Col. A. M. Farah.

Defence, Maj.-Gen. A. A. Noor.

Foreign Affairs (acting), M. A. Hamud.

Interior, M. A. Ba'adleh.

Finance and Revenues, Dr. A. J. Barre.

Industry and Commerce, H. A. Alasow.

Agriculture, A. M. Abubakar.

Education, A. M. Mireh.

Livestock, Forestry and Range, Col. B. R. Guleid.

Information and Tourism, Dr. A. S. Ahmed.

National Planning and Juba Valley Development, H. A. Habib.

Land, Air, Marine Transport and Fisheries, A. M. Ali.

Minerals and Water Development, A. M. Hersi.

Health, Dr. M. A. Munassar.

Posts and Telecommunications, Y. H. Elmi.

Public Works and Housing, Col. M. R. Ghod.

Labour, Sports and Social Affairs, Col. M. A. Jama.

There are also nine Ministers in the Presidency.

Chairman, People's Assembly, Brig.-Gen. M. I. Ahmed.

SOMALI EMBASSY
60 Portland Place, W1N 3DG
[01–580 7148]

Ambassador Extraordinary and Plenipotentiary, (new appointment awaited).

The Somali Democratic Republic occupies part of the north-east horn of Africa, with a coast-line on the Indian Ocean extending from the boundary with Kenya (2° South latitude) to Cape Guardafui (12° N.); and on the Gulf of Aden to the boundary with Djibouti. Somalia is bounded on the west by Djibouti, Ethiopia and Kenya and covers an area of approximately 246,201 sq. miles (637,657 sq. km.). The population, of which a large proportion is nomadic, is estimated (1987) at 5,800,000.

Government.—The Somali Democratic Republic, consisting of the former British Somaliland Protectorate and the former Italian trust territory of Somalia, was established on July 1, 1960. British rule in Somaliland lasted from 1887 until 1960 except for a short period in 1940–41 when the Protectorate was occupied by Italian forces. Somalia, formerly an Italian colony, was occupied by British forces in 1941. In 1950 it was placed under Italian administration by a resolution of the U.N.; this trusteeship lasted until independence. Following the assassination of President Shermake on October 15, 1969, the armed forces, assisted by the police, took over the Government without resistance and a Revolutionary Council under Siad Barre assumed control of the country. A new constitution was introduced following a referendum in 1979. This provides for an elected People's Assembly of 171 seats. The Assembly met for the first time in January 1980. Following a dispute with Ethiopia over territory, which lasted many years, a peace agreement between the two countries was signed on April 3 in Mogadishu.

Livestock raising is the main occupation in Somalia and there is a modest export trade in livestock on the hoof, skins and hides. Italy, the Gulf States and Saudi Arabia import the bulk of the banana crop, the second biggest export.

Trade with U.K.

	1986	1987
Imports from U.K.	£9,140,000	£11,417,000
Exports to U.K.	740,000	825,000

CAPITAL.—ΨMogadishu, population (estimated 1987), 1,000,000. Other towns are Hargeisa (150,000), ΨKisimayu (30,000), Ψ Berbera (60,000) and Burao (15,000).

CURRENCY.—Somali Shilling of 100 Cents.

FLAG.—Five-pointed white star on blue ground.

NATIONAL DAY.—October 21.

BRITISH EMBASSY
(PO Box No. 1036) Mogadishu
[Mogadishu 20288/9]

Ambassador Extraordinary and Plenipotentiary, His Excellency Jeremy Richard Lovering Grosvenor Varcoe (1987).

First Secretary and Consul, R. C. Huxley (*Head of Chancery*).

SOUTH AFRICA
(Republiek van Suid-Afrika)

State President, Pieter Willem Botha, *sworn in,* Sept. 14, 1984.

CABINET

Constitutional Development and Planning, J. C. Heunis.

Foreign Affairs, R. F. (Pik) Botha.

National Education, F. W. de Klerk.

Education and Development Aid, Dr. G. Van N. Viljoen.

Defence, Gen. M. A. de M. Malan.

Manpower, Public Works and Land Affairs, P. T. C. du Plessis.

Administration and Privatization, Dr. D. J. de Villiers.

Justice, H. J. Coetsee.

Agriculture, J. J. G. Wentzel.

Economic Affairs and Technology, D. W. Steyn.

Finance, B. J. du Plessis.

Home Affairs and Communications, J. C. G. Botha.

Transport Affairs, E. van der M. Louw.

Chairman of the Minister' Council of the House of Delegates, A. Rajbansi.

National Health and Population Development, Dr. W. A. Van Niekerk.

Law and Order, A. J. Vlok.
Environment Affairs and Water Affairs, G. J. Kotze.
Information, Broadcasting Services and the Film
Industry, Dr. C. J. van der Merwe.

EMBASSY AND CONSULATE
South Africa House, Trafalgar Square, WC2N 5DP
[01–930 4488]
Ambassador Extraordinary and Plenipotentiary, His
Excellency P. R. (Rae) Killen (1987).
Minister, J. De Goede.
Counsellor (Press & Information), R. Ballard-Tre-
meer.
Minister (Commercial), P. Lategan.

There is a consulate-general at Golden Cross House,
8 Duncannon Street, W.C.2. [01–839 2211]

Area and Population.—The Republic, comprising
the Provinces of the Cape of Good Hope, Natal, the
Transvaal and the Orange Free State, occupies the
southernmost part of the African continent from the
courses of the Limpopo, Molopo and Orange Rivers
(34° 50′ 22″ South latitude) to the Cape of Good Hope,
with the exception of Lesotho, Botswana and Swaziland, and part of Mozambique. It has a total area of
471,445 sq. miles (1,221,031 sq. km.) and a total population (U.N. estimate, 1985) of 32,392,000 (of which
approx. 18 per cent are white).

The southernmost province contains many parallel
ranges, which rise in steps towards the interior. The
south-western peninsula contains the famous *Table
Mountain* (3,582 ft.), while the *Great Swartberg* and
Langeberg run in parallel lines from west to east of
the Cape Province. Between these two ranges lie
the *Roggeveld* and *Nuweveld* ranges to the north is
the Great Karoo Plateau, which is bounded on the
east by the *Sneeuberg*, containing the highest summit
in the province (Kompasberg, 7,800 ft.). In the east
are ranges which join the *Drakensberg* (11,000 ft.)
between Natal and the Orange Free State.

The Orange Free State presents a succession of
undulating grassy plains with occasional hills or
kopjes. The Transvaal is also mainly an elevated
plateau with parallel ridges in the *Magaliesberg* and
Waterberg ranges of no great height. The eastern
province of Natal has pastoral lowlands and rich
agriculture land between the slopes of the Drakensberg and the coast, the interior rising in terraces as
in the southern provinces. The *Orange*, with its
tributary the *Vaal*, is the principal river of the south,
rising in the Drakensberg and flowing into the
Atlantic between Namibia and the Cape Province.
The *Limpopo*, or Crocodile River, in the north, rises
in the Transvaal and flows into the Indian Ocean
through Mozambique. Most of the remaining rivers
are furious torrents after rain, with partially dry
beds at other seasons.

Government.—The self-governing colonies of the
Cape of Good Hope, Natal, the Transvaal and the
Orange River Colony became united on May 31, 1910,
under the South Africa Act, 1909, in a legislative
union under the name of the Union of South Africa,
the four colonies becoming Provinces of the Union.
The Union of South Africa continued as a member of
the British Commonwealth until 1961. After a
referendum held among white voters on October 5,
1960, the Union of South Africa became a republic on
May 31, 1961, and withdrew from the Commonwealth.

A new Constitution came into effect on Sept. 30,
1984, which provided for an executive President and
a three-chamber Parliament; the House of Assembly
(178 members) representing Whites, the House of
Representatives (85 members) representing Col-
oureds, and the House of Delegates (45 members)
representing Indians. The black population has no
representation. There is joint parliamentary responsibility for "general" affairs (foreign policy, defence,

finance, law and order, justice, transport, manpower,
commerce and industry, agriculture), and each chamber has separate responsibility for the "own" affairs
of the population group it represents (housing, social
welfare, health, education, local government and
some aspects of agriculture). Disputes between the
chambers may be referred by the President to the
President's Council (60 members—20 White, 10 Coloured, 5 Indian elected by their respective chambers,
15 nominated by the President, 10 nominated by
Opposition parties).

The President is chosen by an 88-member electoral
college (in the proportion 4 White : 2 Coloured : 1
Indian) of the majority parties of the three chambers.
The President appoints the Cabinet from all three
communities, and also appoints each community's
ministerial council for "own" affairs.

Elections to the House of Representatives and
House of Delegates took place in Aug. 1984. The
Coloured Labour Party (led by the Rev. H. J.
Hendrickse) and the Indian National Peoples Party
(led by Mr. A. Rajbansi) won the majority of seats
respectively.

Elections to the House of Assembly took place on
May 6, 1987 and the results were: National Party, 133
seats; Conservative Party, 23; Progressive Federal
Party, 20; New Republic Party, 1; Independent, 1.

The promulgation of the new Constitution on Sept.
3, 1984 coincided with rioting in the black townships
and the continuing unrest led to the declaration on
July 20, 1985 of a State of Emergency in 36 districts.

A nationwide State of Emergency was declared on
June 12, 1986; it was renewed in June 1987 and
extended again for up to a further twelve months in
June 1988.

In April 1988 President Botha announced proposals
for black representation in the cabinet and in the
electoral college. Constitutional amendments to
effect these changes and to adjust the numbers of
seats in each chamber are expected before the next
General Election, which must be held before March
1990.

The Black Homelands.—The homelands are areas
set aside for occupation by blacks. Six areas—
Gazankulu, Lebowa, KwaNdbele, KaNgwane,
Qwaqwa and KwaZulu—are designated self-governing "national states." A further four areas—Bophu-
thatswana, Ciskei, Transkei and Venda—are
regarded as independent republics by the South
African government but they are not recognized as
such by the United Nations.

Education.—The Provinces have been relieved of
all vocational education (technical and industrial),
and the Department of National Education under the
Minister is concerned with universities, technical
colleges, schools of industries, reformatories and

State technical, housecraft and commercial high schools, State-aided vocational schools and State and State-aided special schools for the physically handicapped.

Communications.—The State-owned and controlled South African Transport Services operates the national railway system, the principal harbours, most long-distance passenger and freight road transport services, the South African Airways airline and a network of pipelines for petroleum products.

There are international airports at Johannesburg (Jan Smuts), Durban (Louis Botha) and Cape Town (D. F. Malan), with another under construction at La Mercy, Natal. South African Airways operates international services to Europe, North and South America, Australia, the Far East and the Middle East, as well as to neighbouring countries, and it is the principal operator of domestic flights.

The largest sea-port is Durban, Natal. Other major ports are Cape Town, Port Elizabeth, East London, Saldanha Bay and Mossel Bay in Cape Province and Richards Bay, Natal.

Production.—Mining is of the greatest importance to the South African economy, contributing 14·3 per cent to G.D.P. in 1982 (of which gold mining accounted for 10 per cent). Principal minerals produced are: gold, coal, iron ore, diamonds, copper, manganese, lime and limestone and asbestos.

Agriculture, forestry and fishing accounts for 6·2 per cent of G.D.P. Over 50 per cent of land is pasture so livestock farming is widespread with meat and wool important products. Principal crops are maize, sugar-cane, fruits and vegetables, wheat, sorghum, sunflower seed and groundnuts. Cotton is widely grown because of its suitability to the climate, and viticulture is also widespread.

Industries, concentrated most heavily around Johannesburg, Pretoria and the major ports, process foodstuffs, metals and non-metallic mineral products, and also produce beverages and tobacco, motor vehicles, chemicals and chemical products, machinery, textiles and clothing, and paper and paper products.

Trade.—Principal exports are: gold, base metals and metal products, diamonds, food (especially fruit), chemicals, machinery and transport equipment, and wool. Principal imports are: machinery, chemicals, motor vehicles, metals and metal products, food, inedible raw materials and textiles.

Trade with U.K.

	1986	1987
Imports from U.K.	£849,557,000	£948,584,000
Exports to U.K.	829,305,000	£658,162,000

Finance.—Estimated revenue for 1985–86 was R29,851 million, and estimated expenditure was R33,026 million.

CAPITAL.—The administrative seat of the Government is Pretoria, Transvaal; population (1985 estimate), 822,925; the seat of the Legislature is ΨCape Town, population (1985) 1,911,521. Other large towns (1985 figures) are Johannesburg, Transvaal (1,609,408); ΨDurban, Natal, the largest seaport (634,301); Ψ Port Elizabeth, Cape (651,993); Bloemfontein, capital of Orange ∴ree State (232,984); ΨEast London, Cape (167,992); and Pietermaritzburg, capital of Natal (192,417).

CURRENCY.—Rand of 100 Cents.

FLAG.—Three horizontal stripes of equal width; from top to bottom, orange, white, blue; in the centre of the white stripe, the old Orange Free State flag hanging vertical, towards the pole the Union Flag horizontal, away from the pole the old Transvaal Vierkleur, all spread full.

NATIONAL ANTHEM.—Die Stem Van Suid-Afrika (The Call of South Africa).

NATIONAL DAY.—May 31.

BRITISH EMBASSY
255 Hill Street, Pretoria
[Pretoria 433121]
91 Parliament Street, Cape Town (Jan.–June)
[Cape Town 4617220]

Ambassador Extraordinary and Plenipotentiary, His Excellency Robin William Renwick, C.M.G. (1987).
Minister, P. G. Wallis.
Counsellors, J. R. James (*Head of Chancery*); M. G. Thickett.
First Secretaries, R. J. Sawers (*Labour*); C. G. Crawford (*Political*); A. E. Lewis (*Economic*); A. P. S. Gibbs (*Press*); A. E. Gay (*Administration*).
Cultural Attaché and British Council Representative, R. E. Underwood, 4th Flr. Federated Building, 38 Ameshoff St., (P.O. Box 30637), Braamfontein 2017, Johannesburg.

There are British Consular Offices at *Cape Town, Johannesburg* and *Durban*; and Honorary Consuls at *Port Elizabeth* and *East London.*

NAMIBIA

Administrator General, Louis Pienaar.

CABINET

Mining, Conservation, Tourism and Commerce, Andreas Zack Shipanga.
Agriculture, Water Affairs, and Sea Fisheries, Kosie Pretorius.
Justice, Information, Posts and Telecommunications, Fanuel Jariretundu Kozonguizi.
National Health, Welfare and Manpower, Moses Ngesuako Katjiuongua.
Local Government and Civic Affairs, Hans Diergaardt.
Education, Andrew Nick Matjila.
Finance and Governmental Affairs, Dirk Frederik Mudge.
Transport Services, Harry Booysen.

Namibia (South West Africa) stretches from the southern border of Angola (lat. 17° 23′ S.) to part of the northern (Orange River) and north-western borders of the Cape Province of the Republic of South Africa; and from the Atlantic Ocean in the west to Botswana in the east. The average rainfall over 70 per cent of the Territory is below 400 mm. per annum.

The territory has an area of 318,261 sq. miles (824,292 sq. km.), including the area of Walvis Bay (434 sq. miles) which is claimed by South Africa. The population was estimated at 1,184,000 in 1986 and the main population groups are: Ovambo (587,000), Whites (78,000), Damara (89,000), Kavango (110,000), Herero (89,000), Nama (57,000), Coloured (48,000), Caprivians (44,000), Bushmen (34,000), Rehoboth Baster (29,000), Tswana (7,000).

Government.—A German protectorate from 1880 to 1915, South West Africa was administered until the end of 1920 by the Union of South Africa. In terms of the Treaty of Versailles the Territory was entrusted to South Africa with full powers of administration and legislation over the Territory. After the dissolution of the League of Nations and in the absence of a trusteeship agreement, South Africa informed the United Nations that she would continue to administer South West Africa in the spirit of the Mandate. Since the establishment of the United Nations, South West Africa has been the subject of dispute.

On June 21, 1971, the International Court of Justice at The Hague delivered an advisory opinion as requested by the U.N. Security Council on the legal consequences for States of the continued presence of South Africa in "Namibia" (South West Africa). The Court decided by 13 votes to 2, that (*inter alia*) "the continued presence of South Africa being illegal, South Africa is under obligation to withdraw its administration from Namibia immediately and thus put an end to its occupation of the Territory". The South African Government rejected this opinion, but accepted the principle that the territory should attain independence. In September 1975 constitutional talks (known as the Turnhalle Conference) were begun in Windhoek between delegates from the 11 ethnic groups of the territory in order to determine the future of South West Africa. But their representative nature was contested by, *inter alia*, SWAPO, a liberation movement with substantial international support and when, in April 1977, it became clear that independence based on the Turnhalle would not solve the problem, the Five Western members of the U.N. Security Council at that time drew up a plan, later incorporated into Security Council Resolution 435, for a peaceful settlement. The plan involves free and fair elections under U.N. supervision leading to independence. The plan has been accepted by all the parties to the Namibia question and attempts to implement the plan are continuing.

Meanwhile, the South African Government appointed an Administrator-General in 1977 to establish a central administration there for those functions previously administered from Pretoria. In December 1978, the South Africans organized an election for a constituent assembly which SWAPO and most of the internal political parties boycotted. The resultant assembly was transformed into a National Assembly with legislative powers in May 1979, and a Council of Ministers was established in 1980 but both were abolished in Jan. 1983 and the territory again came under direct rule. However, in May 1985 legislative powers and executive authority were restored under a Transitional Government of National Utility intended to hold office while South Africa and the U.N. negotiate Namibia's independence. In accordance with U.N. Resolution 435 South African troops are to be gradually withdrawn from Namibia to pave the way for talks on independence.

Production.—Mining, agriculture and fisheries are important. Animal husbandry accounts for 99 per cent of the total gross output of commercial agriculture.

Trade with U.K.

	1986	1987
Imports from U.K.	£2,915,000	£3,909,000
Exports to U.K.	6,826,000	7,681,000

CAPTIAL.—Windhoek (population, 1970 census, 61,260). The only port of any size is Ψ Walvis Bay.
CURRENCY.—South African Rand.

SPAIN
(España)

Head of the Spanish State, King Juan Carlos I de Borbón y Borbón, *born* Jan. 5, 1938, *acceded to the throne,* Nov. 22, 1975, *married* May 14, 1962, Princess Sophie of Greece *and has issue,* Infante Felipe Juan Pablo Alfonso Todos Los Santos (Prince of Asturias, *and heir to the throne) born* Jan. 30, 1968; Infanta Elena Maria Isabel Dominica, *born* Dec. 20, 1963; and Infanta Christina Frederica Victoria, *born* June 13, 1965.

CABINET

Prime Minister, Felipe González.
Deputy P.M., Alfonso Guerra.
Foreign Affairs, Francisco Fernández Ordóñez.
Justice, Enrique Múgica.
Defence, Narcis Serra Serra.
Economy and Finance, Carlos Solchaga.
Interior, José Luis Corcuera.

Transport, Tourism and Communications, José Barrionuevo.
Public Works and Urban Planning, Javier Sáenz de Coscullela.
Education and Science, Javier Solana.
Labour and Social Security, Manuel Chaves.
Industry and Energy, José Claudio Aranzadi.
Agriculture, Fisheries and Food, Carlos Romero Herrera.
Public Administration, Joaquín Almunia.
Culture, Jorge Semprún.
Health and Consumer Affairs, Julián García Vargas.
Cabinet Secretary and Parliamentary Relations, Virgilio Zapatero.
Social Welfare, Matilde Fernández.
Chief Government Spokeswoman, Rosa Conde.

SPANISH EMBASSY IN LONDON
24 Belgrave Square, SW1X 8QA
[01-235 5555]

Ambassador Extraordinary and Plenipotentiary, His Excellency José Joaquin Puig de la Bellacasa, G.C.V.O. (1983).
Minister-Counsellor, Sr. D. J. I. Carbajal, C.V.O.

Area and Population.—Situated in the south-west of Europe, between 36°–43° 45′ N. lat. and 4° 25′ E.–9° 20′ W. long., Spain is bounded on the south and east by the Mediterranean, on the west by the Atlantic and Portugal, and on the north by the Bay of Biscay and France, from which it is separated by the Pyrenees. Continental Spain occupies about eleven-thirteenths of the Iberian peninsula, the remaining portion forming the Republic of Portugal. Its coast-line extends 1,317 miles—712 formed by the Mediterranean and 605 by the Atlantic—and it comprises a total area of 194,897 sq. miles (504,782 sq. km.), with a population (1986 estimate) of 38,818,355.

Physical Features.—The interior of the Iberian Peninsula consists of an elevated tableland surrounded and traversed by mountain ranges—the Pyrenees, the Cantabrian Mountains, the Sierra Guadarrama, Sierra Morena, Sierra Nevada, Montes de Toledo, etc. The principal rivers are the Duero, the Tajo, the Guadiana, the Guadalquivir, the Ebro and the Miño.

Government.—Spain was a monarchy until April 1931, when King Alfonso XIII left the country and a Republic was proclaimed and a Provisional Government, drawn from the various Republican and Socialist parties, was formed. On July 18, 1936, a counter-revolution broke out in many military garrisons in Spanish Morocco and spread rapidly throughout Spain. The principal leader was General Francisco Franco Bahamonde, formerly Governor of the Canary Islands. The struggle, in its later phases, threatened to embroil other European countries, those of Nazi-Fascist tendency lending aid to General Franco (leader of the Military-Fascist fusion, or *Falange)* while those of Communist views supported the Azaña (*Popular Front)* government. In October, 1938, many of the supporting troops were withdrawn, and on March 29, 1939, the Civil War was declared to have ended, the Popular Front Governments in Madrid and Barcelona surrendering to the *Nationalists* (as General Franco's followers were then named). On June 5, 1939, the Grand Council of the *Falange Española Tradicionalista y de las Juntas Ofensivas Nacional-Sindicalistas,* met at Burgos to legislate for the reorganization of the country under the Presidency of General Franco, who had assumed the title of *Caudillo (Leader) of Spain and Chief of the State.* In the Civil War of 1936–39 over 1,000,000 lives were lost.

On July 22, 1969, General Franco nominated Prince Juan Carlos (Alfonso) of Bourbon (grandson of the late King Alfonso XIII) to succeed him as head of state at his death or retirement. The nomination was approved in the *Cortes* by a large majority. Following the death of General Franco, on November 20, 1975, Juan Carlos acceded to the throne on Nov. 22, 1975.

Under the Constitution drawn up in 1977–78 there is a bi-cameral *Cortes* comprising a 350-member Congress of Deputies elected for 4 years by universal adult suffrage, and a Senate consisting of directly elected representatives of the provinces, islands, autonomous regions and Ceuta and Melilla.

In the regional and municipal elections of May 1983, the P.S.O.E. won the majority of the votes. In elections held in the Basque country in February, and in Cataluña in April 1984, local nationalist parties (P.N.V. and C.I.U.) retained their majorities and formed autonomous governments. At the General Election on June 22, 1986, P.S.O.E. won 184 seats; C.P., 105; C.D.S., 19; and I.U., 7 seats.

Regions.—Since the promulgation of the 1978 Constitution, 17 autonomous regions have been established, with their own parliaments and governments. These are Andalucia, Aragon, Asturias, Balaerics, the Basque country, Canaries, Castilla-La Mancha, Castilla-Leon, Cantabria, Cataluña, Extremadura, Galicia, Madrid, Murcia, Navarre, La Rioja and Valencia.

Defence.—*Army:* There are in Spain 1 armoured, 1 mechanized, 1 motorized and 2 mountain divisions; 1 artillery brigade, 2 cavalry brigades, 1 air-transportable brigade, 1 helicopter brigade, 1 coastal artillery brigade. The *Guardia Civil* operates as a gendarmerie in the rural areas under the control of the Ministry of Defence.

The active Spanish *Navy* consists of 1 aircraft carrier, 9 destroyers, 12 frigates and corvettes, 12 minesweepers, 6 major amphibious vessels, 8 submarines, 12 fast patrol craft, 6 hydrographic vessels, 1 tanker, and many smaller patrol craft and auxiliaries. The Navy also has 50 helicopters and 10 Harrier aircraft.

The *Air Force* is divided geographically into 3 Regions covering Spain plus an Air Zone for the Canaries. There are also separate functional Combat, Tactical and Transport Commands. The Air Force consists of 4 attack squadrons, 6 air defence squadrons, 1 maritime squadron, 9 transport squadrons, 3 search and rescue squadrons, 9 training squadrons and 1 firefighting squadron.

Spain became a member of N.A.T.O. in May 1982. Her continued membership (linked to non-military integration) was confirmed in a referendum in March 1986. The present government has also initiated reorganization of the military structure.

Education.—Under the Education Law 1985 free education for all children aged 6 to 15 is guaranteed. Under the new law, private schools (30 per cent of primary and 60 per cent of secondary schools) will have to fulfill certain criteria to receive government maintenance grants.

There are 29 state universities, the oldest of which, Salamanca, was founded in 1230. Other ancient foundations are Valencia (1245), Oviedo (1317), Valladolid (1346), Barcelona (1450), Zaragoza (1474), Santiago (1501), Seville (1502), Granada (1526), and Madrid (1590). Private universities are Deusto in Bilbao, and Navarra in Pamplona. Student numbers in the universities have risen to over 700,000.

Language and Literature.—Castilian is the language of more than three-quarters of the population of Spain. Basque, reported to have been the original language of Iberia, is spoken in the rural districts of Vizcaya, Guipuzcoa and Alava. Catalan is spoken in Provençal Spain, and Galician, spoken in the northwestern provinces, is akin to Portuguese; the governments of these regions actively encourage use of their local languages.

The literature of Spain is one of the oldest and richest in the world, the *Poem of the Cid*, the earliest and best of the heroic songs of Spain, having been written about A.D. 1140. The outstanding writings of its golden age are those of Miguel de Cervantes Saavedra (1547–1616), Lope Felix de Vega Carpio (1562–1635) and Pedro Calderón de la Barca (1600–1681). The Nobel Prize for Literature has four times been awarded to Spanish authors—J. Echegaray (1904), J. Benavente (1922), Juan Ramón Jimenez (1956) and Vicente Aleixandre (1977).

Production and Industry.—The country is generally fertile, and well adapted to agriculture and the cultivation of heat-loving fruits—olives, oranges, lemons, almonds, pomegranates, bananas, apricots, tomatoes, peppers, cucumbers and grapes. The agricultural products include wheat, barley, oats, rice, hemp and flax. The orange crop is exported mainly to Germany, France and the United Kingdom. The vine is cultivated widely; in the south-west, Jerez, the well-known sherry and tent wines are produced. The fishing industry is important.

Spain's mineral resources of coal, iron, wolfram, copper, zinc, lead and iron ores are variously exploited. Many of the richer and more easily worked deposits have been exhausted, but the authorities are actively engaged in stimulating the exploitation of hitherto unworked or lower grade deposits. Output of coal in 1985 was 29·4 million tonnes; output of iron ore (1985) was 6·5 million tonnes and of steel (1986) 13 million tonnes.

The principal goods produced are cars, steel, ships, manufactured goods, textiles, chemical products, footwear and other leather goods, ceramics, sewing machines and bicycles. In 1985 an estimated 47,400,000 tourists visited Spain.

TRADE

	1985	1986
	million pesetas	
Imports	5,073,239·1	4,890,768·0
Exports	4,093,208·6	3,800,225·0

The balance of payments on current account showed a surplus of $4,963m. in 1986 and reserves stood at $17,327 million at the end of the year.

Trade with U.K.
(inc. Canary Islands)

	1986	1987
Imports from U.K.	£1,975,200,000	£2,164,221,000
Exports to U.K.	1,840,800,000	2,099,139,000

The principal imports are cotton, tobacco, cellulose, timber, coffee and cocoa, food products, fertilizers, dyes, machinery, motor vehicles and agricultural tractors, wool and petroleum products. The principal exports include cars, petroleum products, iron ore, cork, salt, vegetables, fruits, wines, olive oil, potash, mercury, pyrites, tinned fruit and fish, tomatoes and footwear.

CAPITAL, Madrid. Population (1982) 3,188,297. Other large cities are ΨBarcelona (1,754,900), ΨValencia (751,734), Seville (653,833), Zaragoza (590,750), ΨMálaga (503,251), Bilbao (433,030); Murcia (288,631).

CURRENCY.—Spanish Peseta of 100 Céntimos.

FLAG.—Three horizontal bands, red, yellow and red, with coat of arms on yellow band.

NATIONAL ANTHEM.—"Marcha Real Española".

NATIONAL DAY.—October 12.

BRITISH EMBASSY
Calle Fernando el Santo, 16, Madrid 4
[Madrid 419 0200]

Ambassador Extraordinary and Plenipotentiary, His Excellency Lord Nicholas Gordon Lennox, K.C.M.G., L.V.O. (1984).

Minister, D. C. Walker, L.V.O.

Counsellor, D. R. Christopher (*Commercial*).

Defence and Military Attaché, Brig. A. D. Morland, M.B.E.

Head of Chancery, R. H. T. Gozney.
There are Consulates General in *Barcelona, Bilbao;* Consulates in *Tenerife, Alicante, Seville, Malaga, Palma de Mallorca, Las Palmas, Santander, Tarragona, Vigo* and *Lanzarote,* and Vice Consulates in *Algeciras, Ibiza* and *Menorca.*

British Council Representative, R. T. Joscelyne, Plaza de Santa Barbara 10, Madrid 28004. There is also a regional office in Seville and offices with English language institutes in Bilbao, Granada, Palma de Mallorca, Las Palmas and Vigo.

BRITISH CHAMBER OF COMMERCE, Marques de Valdeiglesias 3, Madrid 4 also Paseo de Gracia 11, Barcelona 7 and Alameda de Mazarredo 5, Bilbao 1.

The BALEARIC ISLES form an archipelago off the east coast of Spain. There are four large islands (Majorca, Minorca, Ibiza and Formentera), and seven smaller (Aire, Aucanada, Botafoch, Cabrera, Dragonera, Pinto and El Rey). The islands were occupied by the Romans after the destruction of Carthage and provided contingents of the celebrated Balearic slingers. The total area is 1,935 sq. miles (5,011 sq. km.), with a population of 685,088. The archipelago forms a province of Spain, the capital being ΨPalma in Majorca, pop. 304,422; ΨMahon (Minorca), pop. 22,926.

The CANARY ISLANDS are an archipelago in the Atlantic, off the African coast, consisting of 7 islands and 6 mostly uninhabited islets. The total area is 2,807 sq. miles (7,270 sq. km.), with a population of 1,444,626. The Canary Islands form two Provinces of Spain.—*Las Palmas* (Gran Canaria, Lanzarote (38,500), Fuerteventura (19,500) and the islets of Alegranza, Roque del Este, Roque del Oeste, Graciosa, Montaña Clara and Lobos), with seat of administration at ΨLas Palmas (pop. 366,454) in Gran Canaria, where major oil companies have installations for refueling shipping; and *Santa Cruz de Tenerife* (Tenerife, La Palma (76,000), Gomera (31,829), and Hierro (10,000)), with seat of administration at ΨSanta Cruz in Tenerife, pop. 190,784.

ISLA DE FAISANES is an uninhabited Franco-Spanish condominium, at the mouth of the Bidassoa in La Higuera bay.

ΨCEUTA is a fortified post on the Moroccan coast, opposite Gibraltar. The total area is 5 sq. miles (13 sq. km.), with a population of 70,864.

ΨMELILLA is a town on a rocky promontory of the Rif coast, connected with the mainland by a narrow isthmus. Melilla has been in Spanish possession since 1492. Population 58,449. Ceuta and Melilla are parts of Metropolitan Spain.

OVERSEAS TERRITORIES
Spanish settlements on the Moroccan seaboard are:—

Peñon de Alhucemas, the bay of that name includes six islands: population 366.

Peñon de la Gomera (or *Peñon de Velez*) is a fortified rocky islet about 40 miles west of Alhucemas Bay; population 450.

The Chaffarinas (or Zaffarines) are a group of three islands near the Algerian frontier, about 2 miles north of Cape del Agua; population 610.

The former provinces of Spanish Guinea, Fernando Póo and Rio Muni achieved independence on October 12, 1968, under the title of Equatorial Guinea.

The protectorate of Spanish Morocco was incorporated in Morocco on the latter's independence in 1956. Ifni, the former enclave in Morocco, was incorporated by treaty, on June 30, 1969, and the Spanish Sahara came under joint Moroccan and Mauritanian control in November 1975.

SUDAN
(Al-Jamhuryat es-Sudan Al-Democratia)

President, Ahmed Ali Al Mirghani (D.U.P.).

SOVEREIGNTY COUNCIL

The President; Mirghani Al Nasri (Ind/Umma); Idris Abdalla Al Banna (Umma); Ali Hassan Taj Al Din (Umma); Pacifico Lado Lolik (S.A.P.C.O.).

CABINET

Prime Minister, Al Sadiq Al Mahdi (*Umma*).

Defence, Abdul Magid Hamid Khalil (*Umma*).

Cabinet Affairs, Salah Abdul Salam Al Khalifa (*Umma*).

Irrigation, Mahmoud Beshir Gamaa (*Umma*).

Finance, Omer Nur Al Daim (*Umma*).

Economy and Foreign Trade, Mubarak Abdalla Al Fadl (*Umma*).

Energy and Mining, Bakri Ahmed Adil (*Umma*).

Animal Wealth, Ismael Abbaker (*Umma*).

Education, Al Sheikh Mahgoub (*Umma*).

Culture and Information, Abdulla Mohammed Ahmed (*Umma*).

Public Service and Reform, Fadlalla Ali Fadlalla (*Umma*).

Foreign Affairs, Hussein Suleiman Abu Salih (*D.U.P.*).

Agriculture, Al Fatih Al Tigani (*D.U.P.*).

Health, Awhaj Mohammed Musa (*D.U.P.*).

Works and Housing Planning, Osman Omer Ali (*D.U.P.*).

Refugees and Relief Affairs, Hassan Ali Shibbu (*D.U.P.*).

Religious Affairs, Abdul Malik Al Gali (*D.U.P.*).

Internal Commerce, Co-operation and Supply, Ali Al Haj (*N.I.F.*).

Industry, Abdel Wahab Osman (*N.I.F.*).

Communications, Taj El Sir Mustafa Abdul Salam (*N.I.F.*).

Attorney General, Hassan Abdulla Al Turabi (*N.I.F.*).

Social Welfare and Zakat, Ahmed Abdul Rahman Mohammed (*N.I.F.*).

Tourism and Hotels, Amin Beshir Fellin (*National*).

Regional Co-ordinator for Planning and Local Government, Richard Makubi (*Southern*).

Transport and Deputy Premier, Aldo Ajo Deng (*Southern*).

Labour and Social Insurance, Mathew Abor (*Southern*).

Chairman of the South Council, Anglo Beida (*Southern*).

SUDANESE EMBASSY IN LONDON
3 Cleveland Row, SW1A 1DD
[01-839 8080]

Ambassador Extraordinary and Plenipotentiary, His Excellency Sayed Ibrahim Mohamed Ali (1985).

Area and Population.—The Sudan extends from the southern boundary of Egypt, 22° N. lat., to the northern boundary of Uganda, 3° 36′ N. lat., and reaches from the Republic of Chad about 21° 49′ E. (at 12° 45′ N.) to the north-west boundary of Ethiopia in 38° 35′ E. (at 18° N.). On the east lie the Red Sea and Ethiopia; on the south lie Kenya, Uganda and Zaire; and on the west the Central African Republic, Chad, and Libya. The greatest length from north to south is approximately 1,300 miles, and east to west 950 miles.

The *White Nile* enters from Uganda at Nimule as the *Bahr el Jebel,* and leaves the Sudan at Wadi Halfa. The *Blue Nile* flows from Lake Tana on the Ethiopian Plateau. Its course in the Sudan is nearly 500 miles long, before it joins the White Nile at Khartoum. The next confluence of importance is at Atbara where the main Nile is joined by the River Atbara. Between Khartoum and Wadi Halfa lie five of the six *Cataracts.*

The estimated area is about 967,500 sq. miles (2,505,813 sq. km.), with a population of 21,550,000, partly Arabs, partly Negros, and partly of mixed Arab-Negro blood, with a small foreign element. The Arabs are mostly Moslems. The Nilotics of the Bahr el Ghazal and Upper Nile Valleys are generally animists, but some have been converted to Christianity and others are Moslems. There are some 1 million refugees in the Sudan.

Government.—The Anglo-Egyptian Condominium over the Sudan which had been established in 1899 ended when the Sudan House of Representatives, on Dec. 19, 1955, voted unanimously a declaration that the Sudan was a fully independent sovereign state. A Republic was proclaimed on Jan. 1, 1956, and was recognized by Great Britain and Egypt, a Supreme Commission being sworn in to take over sovereignty. The Sudan was under military rule from Nov., 1958, until 1964 when a new civilian Cabinet was appointed. Government of the country was taken over on May

25, 1969, by a ten-man revolutionary council headed by Col. Gaafar Mohamed El Nimeri. In February 1972 an agreement was signed at Addis Ababa which brought to an end nearly 17 years of insurrection and civil war in the six southern provinces, and which recognized southern regional autonomy within a unified Sudanese State. Insurrection broke out again in 1983. In April 1985 the Army command assumed power after popular demonstrations, deposed Nimeiri and appointed transitional government which undertook to hand over power to a democratically elected government. Elections were held in April 1986 and a new government formed, a coalition of Umma and D.U.P. members. A new broad-based coalition was formed in May 1988 with representatives from the Umma, D.U.P., National Islamic Front and Southern parties. The Umma party won 100 seats, the Democratic Unionist Party, 63 seats, and National Islamic Front, 51 seats; Progressive Peoples' Party, 10 seats; S. Sudanese Political Association, 8 seats; Sudanese National Party 8 seats; Sudan African Peoples Congress, 7 seats and others 13.

Education.—School education is free for most children, but not compulsory, beginning with six years primary education, followed by three years secondary education at general secondary schools, the more academic higher secondary schools or vocational schools. The medium of instruction is Arabic. English is taught as the principal foreign language in all schools.

Khartoum University has 10 faculties. There is a branch of Cairo University in Khartoum, an Islamic University at Omdurman and a Universities at Wad Medani and Juba.

In addition to the universities there are various technical post-secondary institutes as well as professional and vocational training establishments.

Production.—The principal grain crops are *dura* (great millet) and wheat, the staple food of the people in the Sudan. Sesame and ground-nuts are other important food crops, which also yield an exportable surplus and a promising start has been made with castor seed. The principal export crop is cotton. Traditionally a major producer of long-staple cotton, Sudan has in recent years grown more short and medium-staple cotton. These grades now account for more than half total production. Production in 1987–88 is estimated to have been around 837,000 bales. The Sudan also produces the bulk of the world's supply of gum arabic. Sugar is an increasingly important crop. The Sudan still has to achieve self sufficiency in sugar production. Livestock is the mainstay of the nomadic Arab tribes of the desert and the negro tribes of the swamp and wooded grassland country in the South. Production has, however, been affected by drought, famine and flooding.

Sudan's agriculture production provided employment for over 60 per cent. of the labour force and contributed 37 per cent. to G.D.P. in 1986–87. It is based on large and medium sized public sector irrigation projects with small scale private irrigation schemes providing mostly fruit and vegetables. Mechanised and traditional agriculture is practiced in areas of sufficient rainfall.

The manufacturing sector contributed less than 8 per cent. to G.D.P. in 1986–87 and provided employment for 4 per cent. of the work force. The main manufacturing enterprises are concentrated in the areas of food processing, textiles, shoes, cigarettes and batteries.

Communications.—The railway system has a route length of about 3,200 miles, linking Khartoum with Wadi Halfa, Karima, Port Sudan, Wad Medani, Sennar, El Damazin, Kosti, El Obeid and Nyala. A line branches out southwards to Wau from the Sennar/Nyala western line. Nile river services between Khartoum and Juba have been interrupted by the southern insurrection. ΨPort Sudan is a well-equipped modern seaport. Sudan Airways fly services from Khartoum to many parts of the Sudan and to other African states, Europe and the Middle East.

FINANCE

	1986–87
Revenue	£S 2,741·1 m.
Expenditure	6,100·7 m.
Deficit	2,527·6 m.
Deficit financing	2,527·6 m.

TRADE

	1985–86*	1986–87*
Total Imports ...	US$1,055·2 m.	US$832·3 m.
Total Exports ...	497·2 m.	481·6 m.
*Estimates		

Trade with U.K.

	1986	1987
Imports from U.K. ...	£83,300,000	£75,322,000
Exports to U.K.	12,800,000	18,850,000

The principal exports are cotton, livestock, gum arabic and other agricultural produce. The chief imports are petroleum goods and other raw materials, machinery and equipment, transport and equipment, medicines and chemicals.

CAPITAL, Khartoum. The town contains many mosques, a Catholic cathedral and an Anglican cathedral, and the University with extensive government buildings. The combined population of Khartoum, Khartoum North and Omdurman (excluding refugees and displaced people) is just over 2,000,000.

CURRENCY.—Sudanese Pound (£S) of 100 Piastres and 1,000 Millièmes.

FLAG.—Three horizontal stripes of red, white and black with a green triangle next to the hoist.

NATIONAL ANTHEM.— "Nahnu Djundullah" (We are the army of God).

NATIONAL DAY.—January 1 (Independence Day).

BRITISH EMBASSY
(P.O. Box 801)
Khartoum
[Khartoum 70760/7]

Ambassador Extraordinary and Plenipotentiary, His Excellency John Lewis Beaven, C.M.G., C.V.O. (1987).
Counsellor, D. I. Lewty (*Head of Chancery*).
Defence and Military Attaché, Col. R.J.M. Carson, O.B.E.
British Council Representative, P. B. M. Early, P.O. Box 1253, Khartoum. The British Council has a sub-office in Juba and there are libraries at *El Obeid*, and *Omdurman*.

SURINAME
(Nieuwe Republick van Suriname)

President, Ramsewak Shankar, *sworn in* Jan. 25, 1988.
Head of the National Military Council, Cmdr. Desi Bouterse.

COUNCIL OF MINISTERS

Vice President, Chairman of Council of Ministers, Henk A. E. Arron.
Foreign Affairs, Dr. E. Sedoc.
Finance and Planning, Subhes Chandra Mungra.
Natural Resources and Energy, Pretaapnarian Radhakishun.
Home Affairs, District Administration and Mobilization, Evelyn Alexander-Vanenburg.
Public Works, Telecommunications and Construction, H. Jankipersadsing.
Health, Henk Ali Mahumed.

Education, Science, Culture, Sport and Youth Affairs, Roland Venetiann.
Transport, Trade and Industry, W. Grep.
Labour, Romeo Van Russel.
Agriculture, Livestock, Fisheries and Forestry, S. Redjosenpono.
Housing and Social Affairs, Willy Soemita.
Justice and Police, J. Adjodhia.
Army, Maj. A. Sheikkariem.

Suriname is situated on the north coast of South America and is bounded by French Guyana in the east, Brazil in the south and Guyana in the west. It has an area of 63,037 sq. miles (163,265 sq. km.), with a population (1985 U.N. estimate) of 375,000.

Formerly known as Dutch Guiana, Suriname remained part of the Netherlands West Indies until November 25, 1975, when it achieved complete independence. Suriname had received autonomy in domestic affairs under the Realm Statute which took effect on December 29, 1954. The civilian government was ousted by the military in Feb. 1980, who appointed the predominantly civilian Cabinet. A National Assembly of 31 members was appointed on Jan. 1, 1985 to draft a new constitution. A referendum held on Sept. 30, 1987 voted for the new constitution and in elections held on Nov. 25 a coalition of three opposition parties won a landslide victory over Cmdr. Bouterse's N.D.P. party. President Shankar and Vice-President Arron were sworn in on Jan. 25, 1988, and a new Council of Ministers was installed on Jan. 26.

Suriname has large timber resources. Rice and sugar cane are the main crops. Bauxite is mined, and is the principal export.

TRADE

	1985
Imports	U.S.$ 359·5 m
Exports	337·3 m

Trade with U.K.

	1986	1987
Imports from U.K.	£9,743,000	£7,974,000
Exports to U.K.	15,554,000	12,488,000

CAPITAL.—ΨParamaribo (population, 1971, 110,000).

CURRENCY.—Suriname Guilder of 100 Cents.

FLAG.—Horizontal stripes of green, white, red, white, green, with a five pointed yellow star in the centre.

NATIONAL DAY.—November 25.

British Ambassador (resides at *Georgetown*, Guyana).
British Consulate, c/o V.S.H. United Buildings, Van't Hogerhuystraat, P.O. Box 1300, Paramaribo.
Honorary Consul, J. J. Healy, M.B.E.

SWEDEN
(Konungariket Sverige)

King of Sweden, Carl XVI Gustaf, *born* April 30, 1946, *succeeded* September 15, 1973, *married* June 19, 1976 Fräulein Silvia Renate Sommerlath *and has issue*, Crown Princess Victoria Ingrid Alice Désirée, Duchess of Västergötland, *born* July 14, 1977; Prince Carl Philip Edmund Bertil, Duke of Värmland, *born* May 13, 1979; Princess Madeleine Thérèse Amelie Josephine, Duchess of Hälsingland and Gästrikland, *born* June 10, 1982.

COUNCIL OF MINISTERS

Prime Minister, Ingvar Carlsson.
Justice, Thage Peterson (*temp.*).
Foreign Affairs, Sten Andersson.
Agriculture, Mats Hellström.
Finance, Kjell-Olof Feldt.

Housing, Hans Gustafsson.
Labour, Ingela Thalen.
Education, Lennart Bodström.
Industry, Thage Peterson.
Health and Social Affairs, Gertrud Sigurdsen.
Culture, Bengt Göransson.
Equality and Immigration, Georg Andersson.
Energy and the Environment, Birgitta Dahl.
Public Sector, Bo Holmberg.
Foreign Trade, Anita Gradin.
Defence, Roine Carlsson.
Health and Social Affairs (Deputy Minister), Bengt Lindqvist.
Communications, Sven Hulterström.
Aid, Lena Hjelm-Wallén.
Wages and Salaries, Bengt Johansson.
Sport, Youth and Tourism, Ulf Lönnqvist.

SWEDISH EMBASSY IN LONDON
11 Montagu Place, W1H 2AL
[01-724 2101]

Ambassador Extraordinary and Plenipotentiary, His Excellency Leif Leifland, G.C.V.O. (1982).
Minister Plenipotentiary, H. Granqvist.
Counsellors, A. A. E. Alsterdal (*Press*); P. Bruce (*Commodities*); H. Leo. (*Consular and Administration*); N. Daag (*Political*).
Defence and Air Attaché, Gp. Capt. B. Lennhammar.
Military and Naval Attaché, Col. G. De Geer.
Trade Commissioner, M. Nilsson (73 Welbeck Street, W1M 8AN.).

Area and Population.—Sweden occupies the eastern area of the Scandinavian peninsula in N.W. Europe and comprises 24 local government districts, "*Län*", with a total area of 173,732 sq. miles (449,964 sq. km.), and population Dec. 31, 1985 of 8,358,139. In 1985 the birth rate was 11·79 per 1,000 inhabitants, the death rate 11·26 per 1,000 inhabitants and infant mortality rate was 6·8 per 1,000 live births.

Government.—Under the Act of Succession of June 6, 1809 (with amendments) the throne is hereditary in the House of Bernadotte. (A 1979 amendment vested the succession in the monarch's eldest child, irrespective of sex.) Jean-Baptiste Jules Bernadotte, Prince of Ponte Corvo, a Marshal of France, was invited to accept the title of Crown Prince, with succession to the throne. He succeeded Charles XIII in 1818. There is a unicameral Diet (*Riksdag*) of 349 members elected for 3 years. The Council of Ministers (*Statsråd*) is responsible to the *Riksdag*.

Production and Industry.—The country's industrial prosperity is based on an abundance of natural resources in the form of forests, mineral deposits and water power. The forests are extensive, covering about half the total land surface, and sustain flourishing timber, pulp and paper milling industries. The mineral resources include iron ore, lead, zinc, sulphur, granite, marble, precious and heavy metals (the latter not exploited) and extensive deposits of low grade uranium ore. Industries based on mining, principally iron and steel, aluminium and copper are important but it is the general engineering industry that provides the basis of Sweden's exports. Growth areas are largely in the specialized machinery and systems and chemical industries. The relative importance of agriculture has declined and in 1983 only 5·4 per cent of the population was engaged in farming.

Apart from water power Sweden has no significant indigenous resources of conventional hydrocarbon fuels and relies to a high degree upon imported oil. Much of Sweden's electricity is generated by nuclear power but as a result of a referendum in 1980 the nuclear programme is to be discontinued by 2010. Small supplies of natural gas are imported from Denmark into southern Sweden, with the pipeline being extended to Gothenburg.

Communications.—The total length of Swedish railroads is 11,745 km. The number of passenger cars in use on December 31, 1985 was 3,151,195.

The Mercantile Marine amounted on December 31, 1985 to 2,619,625 gross tonnage. The Board of Civil Aviation under the control of the Ministry of Communications handles civil aviation matters. Regular domestic air traffic is maintained by the Scandinavian Airlines System and by A. B. Linjeflyg. Regular European and inter-continental air traffic is maintained by the Scandinavian Airlines System.

Defence.—Based on the policy of non-alignment in peace leading to neutrality in war Sweden maintains a Total Defence intended to make any attack on her costly. Total Defence includes peacetime organizations for civil, economic and psychological defence as well as compulsory national service for all acceptable males. Some 50,000 National Servicemen are called up for 7–15 months training each year and all are recalled every fourth year for refresher training. On mobilization the Army strength totals 4 armoured brigades, 1 mechanized brigade and 23 infantry and winter warfare brigades. The Navy has 12 submarines, 48 fast attack craft, a number of minor craft and auxiliaries and 5 coast artillery units. The Air Force has modern supersonic aircraft of Swedish manufacture forming a standing force of 220 air defence, 150 attack and 55 reconnaissance with support aircraft and a modern air defence radar system. Facilities exist for rapid dispersal from main bases in war.

Religion.—The State religion is Lutheran Protestant, to which over 95 per cent of the people officially adhere.

Language and Literature.—Swedish belongs, with Danish and Norwegian, to the North Germanic language group. Swedish literature dates back to King Magnus Eriksson, who codified the old Swedish provincial laws in 1350. With his translation of the Bible, Olaus Petri (1493–1552) formed the basis for the modern Swedish language. Literature flourished during the reign of Gustavus III, who founded the Swedish Academy in 1786. Swedish literature is studded with names such as Almquist (1795–1866), Strindberg (1849–1912) and Lagerlöf (1858–1940), Nobel Prize Winner in 1909. Contemporary authors include Lagerquist (1891–1974), Nobel Laureate in 1951, Martinson (1904–1978) and Johnson (1900–1976), Nobel Laureates jointly in 1974. The Swedish scientist Alfred Nobel (1833–1896) founded the Nobel Prizes for Literature, Science and Peace.

Education.—Tuition within the State system, which is maintained by the State and by local taxation, is free. It provides 9 years' compulsory schooling from the age of 7 to 16 in the comprehensive elementary schools; further education of 2, 3 or 4 years in the upper secondary schools; a unified higher education system administered in 6 regional areas containing one of the universities—Uppsala (founded 1477); Lund (1668); Stockholm (1878); Gothenburg (1887); Umeå (1963) and Linköping (1967). At present there are 33 institutions of higher education including three technical universities in Stockholm, Gothenburg and Luleå, and the Karolinska Institute in Stockholm, which specializes in medicine and dentistry.

FINANCE

	1985–86	1986–87
	Kronor million	*Kronor* million
Revenue	275,638	293,190
Expenditure	327,177	336,392

TRADE

	1985	1986
	Kronor million	*Kronor* million
Imports	243,974·4	231,444·9
Exports	259,985·1	265,039·7

Trade with U.K.

	1986	1987
Imports from U.K...	£2,307,900,000	£2,322,235,000
Exports to U.K.	2,756,536,000	2,952,453,000

Sweden's main imports from Britain are crude oil and petroleum products, machinery and parts, road vehicles and components, clothing and textiles and steel. Britain's main imports from Sweden are paper and board, road vehicles, machinery, wood, steel and pulp.

CAPITAL.—ΨStockholm. Population (1985): City 659,030; Greater Stockholm, 1,435,474; ΨGothenburg (Göteborg) (425,495); ΨMalmö (229,936); Uppsala (154,859)

CURRENCY.—Swedish Krona of 100 Øre.

FLAG.—Yellow cross on a blue ground.

NATIONAL ANTHEM.—"Du Gamla, Du Fria" (Thou ancient, thou freeborn).

NATIONAL DAY.—June 6 (Day of the Swedish Flag).

BRITISH EMBASSY

Skarpögatan 6–8, 115 27 Stockholm
[Stockholm 670140]

Ambassador Extraordinary and Plenipotentiary, His Excellency Sir John Ure, K.C.M.G., L.V.O. (1987).
British Council Representative, J. R. Day.

BRITISH CONSULAR OFFICE

There is a British Consular Office at *Stockholm*.
BRITISH-SWEDISH CHAMBER OF COMMERCE, Grevgatan 34, 11453 Stockholm.

SWITZERLAND
(Schweizerische Eidgenossenschaft—
Confédération Suisse—Confederazione
Svizzera.)

FEDERAL COUNCIL

President of the Swiss Confederation (1988) *and Head of Finance*, Otto Stich.
Vice-President (1988) *and Head of Public Economy*, Jean-Pascal Delamuraz.
Military, Arnold Koller.
Justice and Police, Mrs. Elizabeth Kopp.
Transport, Energy and Communications, Adolf Ogi.
Foreign Affairs, René Felber.
Interior, Flavio Cotti.

SWISS EMBASSY IN LONDON

16–18 Montagu Place, W1H 2BQ
[01–723 0701]

Ambassador Extraordinary and Plenipotentiary, His Excellency François-Charles Pictet (1984).
Ministers, C. M. W. Faessler; Milan J. A. Lusser (*Economic and Financial*).
Counsellor, H. Hofer (*Commodities and Agriculture*).
Defence, Military, Naval and Air Attaché, Maj.-Gen. G. de Loës.
Consul and Head of Administration, A. Mehr.

There is a Swiss Consulate-General in *Manchester*.

Area and Population.—The Helvetia of the Romans, a Federal Republic of Central Europe, situated between 45° 50'–47° 48' N. lat. and 5° 58'–10° 3' E. long. It is composed of 23 Cantons, 3 subdivided, making 26 in all, and comprises a total area of 15,943 sq. miles (41,293 sq. km.), with a population (Dec. 31, 1986) of 6,532,400. In 1986 there were 76,320 live births, 60,105 deaths and 40,234 marriages. Of the total population in 1980, 44·3 per cent of the population was Protestant, 47·6 per cent Roman Catholic and 0·3 per cent Jewish.

Physical Features.—Switzerland is the most mountainous country in all Europe. The Alps, covered with perennial snow and from 5,000 to 15,217 feet in height, occupy its southern and eastern frontiers,

and the chief part of its interior; and the Jura mountains rise in the north-west. The Alps occupy 61 per cent, and the Jura mountains 12 per cent, of the country. The *Alps* are a crescent-shaped mountain system situated in France, Italy, Switzerland, Bavaria and Austria, covering an area of 80,000 square miles from the Mediterranean to the Danube (600 miles). The highest peak, Mont Blanc, Pennine Alps (15,782 ft.) is partly in France and Italy; Monte Rosa (15,217 ft.) and Matterhorn (14,780 ft.) are partly in Switzerland and partly in Italy. The highest wholly Swiss peaks are Dufourspitze (15,203 ft.), Finsteraarhorn (14,026), Aletschhorn (13,711), Jungfrau (13,671), Mönch (13,456), Eiger (13,040), Schreckhorn (13,385), and Wetterhorn (12,150) in the Bernese Alps, and Dom (14,918), Weisshorn (14,803) and Breithorn (13,685).

The Swiss lakes are famous for their beauty and include Lakes Maggiore, Zürich, Lucerne, Neuchâtel, Geneva, Constance, Thun, Zug, Lugano, Brienz and the Walensee. There are also many artificial lakes.

Government.—The legislative power is vested in a Parliament, consisting of two Chambers, a National Council (*Nationalrat*) of 200 members, and a States Council (*Ständerat*) of 46 members; both Chambers united are called the Federal Assembly, and the members of the National Council are elected for four years, an election taking place in October. The executive power is in the hands of a Federal Council (*Bundesrat*) of seven members, elected for four years by the Federal Assembly and presided over by the President of the Confederation. Each year the Federal Assembly elects from the Federal Council the President and the Vice-President. Not more than one of the same canton may be elected member of the Federal Council; on the other hand, there is a tradition that Italian and French-speaking areas should between them be represented on the Federal Council by at least two members.

Defence.—All Swiss males must undertake military service in the Army or the Air Force, which is part of the Army. Swiss Army equipment includes some British items, such as Centurion tanks, Bloodhound missiles, Vampire and Hunter aircraft and the Medium Girder Bridge. The Rapier guided missile system is being delivered.

Production and Industry.—Agriculture is followed chiefly in the valleys and all over the Mittelland, where cereals, flax, hemp, and tobacco are produced, and nearly all temperate zone fruits and vegetables as well as grapes are grown. Dairying and stock-raising are the principal industries, about 3,000,000 acres being under grass for hay and 2,000,000 acres pasturage. The forests cover about one-quarter of the whole surface. The chief manufacturing industries comprise engineering and electrical engineering, metal-working, chemicals and pharmaceuticals, textiles, watchmaking, woodworking, foodstuffs and footwear. Banking, insurance and tourism are major industries.

Communications.—There are 4,997 km of railway tracks (Swiss Federal Railways, 2,946 km; Swiss privately owned railways 2,951 km). At the end of 1985 the number of telephones amounted to 5,435,800 and the network was fully automatic throughout the country. At the same time there were 2,467,200 licensed radio receivers and 2,186,500 television receivers.

At the end of 1982 the total length of motorways was 1,288 km. The number of motor vehicles licensed in 1986 was 3,306,000.

A merchant marine, established in 1940, consisted at the end of 1985 of 39 vessels with a total gross tonnage of 225,434 tonnes. In 1982, goods handled at Basle Rhine ports amounted to 9,423,093 tonnes. In 1982 151 lake vessels transported 9,146,000 passengers and 2,640 tonnes of freight. Swiss airlines have a network covering 314,762 km and in 1985 carried 7,498,000 passengers. Swissair, the State airline, which owned 51 aircraft in 1983, flies to and from the Swiss airports at Zürich, Geneva and Basle.

Education.—Control by cantonal and communal authorities. No central organization. Illiteracy practically unknown. (i) *Primary*: Free and compulsory. School age varies, generally 7 to 14. (ii) *Secondary*: Age 12–15 for boys and girls. Schools numerous and well-attended, and there are many private institutions. (iii) *Special schools* make a feature of commercial and technical instruction. (iv) *Universities*: Basle (founded 1460), Berne (1834), Fribourg (1889), Geneva (1873), Lausanne (1890), Zürich (1832), and Neuchâtel (1909), and the technical Universities of Lausanne and Zürich and commercial University of St. Gall.

Language and Literature.—There are three official languages: French, German and Italian. In addition Romansch is recognized as a national, but not an official language. German is the dominating language in 19 of the 26 cantons; French in Fribourg, Jura, Geneva, Neuchâtel, Valais and Vaud; Italian in Ticino, and Romansch in parts of the Grisons.

Many modern authors, alike in the German school and in the Suisse Romande, have achieved international fame. Karl Spitteler (1845–1924) and Hermann Hesse (1877–1962) were awarded the Nobel Prize for Literature, the former in 1919, the latter in 1946.

FINANCE

	1986	1987
	Sw. Frs.	*Sw. Frs.*
Revenue	25,144m.	24,396m.
Expenditure	23,176m.	24,225m.

TRADE

	1985	1986
	Sw. Frs.	*Sw. Frs.*
Total Imports	74,785m.	73,512m.
Total Exports	66,624m.	67,004m.

Trade with U.K.
(including Liechtenstein)

	1986	1987
Imports from U.K.	£1,575,247,000	£1,835,851,000
Exports to U.K.	2,989,112,000	3,298,009,000

The principal imports are machinery, electrical and electronic equipment, textiles, motor vehicles, non-ferrous metals, chemical elements, clothing, food, medicinal and pharmaceutical products. The principal exports are machinery, chemical elements, non-ferrous metals, watches, electrical and electronic

equipment, textiles, dyeing, tanning and colouring equipment. Switzerland is a member of E.F.T.A.

CAPITAL.—Berne. Population, 301,100 (urban agglomeration). Other large towns are Zürich (840,000), Basle (363,600), Geneva (382,000), Lausanne (260,200), Winterthur (107,400), St. Gallen (125,400), Lucerne (160,000).

CURRENCY.—Swiss Franc of 100 Rappen or Centimes.

FLAG.—Red, with white cross.

NATIONAL ANTHEM.—Trittst im Morgenrot Daher (Radiant in the morning sky).

NATIONAL DAY.—August 1.

BRITISH EMBASSY
Thunstrasse 50, 3000 Berne 15
[Berne 445021]

Ambassador Extraordinary and Plenipotentiary, His Excellency Christopher William Long, C.M.G. (1988).

Counsellors, M. L. H. Hope; C. W. Wainwright.

First Secretary, P. Cole.

Second Secretary, A. M. M. McDermott; I. N. Hughes.

Defence, Naval and Military Attaché, Lt.-Col. J. Bolton-Clark.

Air Attaché, Wing. Cdr. J. L. Bishop.

Attaché, P. C. Albrecht (*Commercial*).

BRITISH CONSULAR OFFICES

There is a Consular Section at H.M. Embassy, Berne; *Consulates-General* at *Zürich* and *Geneva* and Consular offices at *Lugano* and *Montreux*. The Directorate of British Export Promotion in Switzerland is in the Consulate-General Office in *Zürich*.

BRITISH-SWISS CHAMBER OF COMMERCE, Freiestrasse 155, 8032 Zürich.

SWISS-BRITISH SOCIETIES:
Berne.—*President*, Dr. H. Beriger.
Zürich.—*President*, J.-P. Müller.
Basle.—*President*, G. Simons.

SYRIA
(Al-Jamhouriya Al-Arabia as-Souriya)

President, Lt.-Gen. Hafez el Assad, *b.* 1930, *assumed office* March 14, 1971, *re-elected*, Feb. 1978, March 13, 1985.

Vice-Presidents, Abdul Halim Khaddam, Rifaat Al Assad, Zuhair Mashariqa.

Prime Minister, Mahmoud Al Zubi.

Deputy Prime Minister and Minister for Defence, Gen. Mustafa Tlass.

Deputy Prime Minister for Public Services, Mahmoud Qaddur.

Deputy Prime Minister for Economic Affairs, Dr. Salim Yassin.

SYRIAN EMBASSY IN LONDON

The Syrian Embassy has been closed since Oct. 31, 1986, when Syria and the U.K. broke off diplomatic relations.

Area and Population.—Syria is in the Levant, covering a portion of the former Ottoman Empire, with an estimated area of 71,498 sq. miles (185,180 sq. km.), and a population (1985 U.N. estimate) of 10,267,000, most of whom are Arabic-speaking and Muslim. The Orontes flows northwards from the Lebanon range across the northern boundary to Antakya (Antioch, Turkey). The Euphrates crosses the northern boundary near Jerablus and flows through north-eastern Syria to the boundary of Iraq.

Archaeology, etc.—The region is rich in historical remains. Damascus (*Dimishq ash-Sham*) is said to be the oldest continuously inhabited city in the world (although Aleppo disputes this claim), having an existence as a city for over 4,000 years. It is situated on the river Barada, in an oasis at the eastern foot of the Anti-Lebanon, and at the edge of the wide sandy desert which stretches to the Euphrates. The city contains the Omayed Mosque, the Tomb of Saladin, and the "Street Called Straight" (Acts ix. 11), while to the North-East is the Roman outpost of Dmeir and further east is Palmyra.

On the Mediterranean coast at Amrit are ruins of the Phoenician town of Marath, where the well has been found and is being excavated and also ruins of Crusaders' fortresses at Markab, Sahyoun, and Krak des Chevaliers. At Tartous (also on the coast) the cathedral of Our Lady of Syria, built by the Knights Templars in the 12th and 13th centuries has been restored as a museum. One of the oldest alphabets in the world has been discovered at Ugarit (Ras Shamra), a Phoenician village near the port of Latakia.

Hittite cities dating from 2,000 to 1,500 B.C., have recently been explored on the west bank of the Euphrates at Jerablus and Kadesh.

Government.—Syria, which had been under French mandate since the 1914–18 war, became an independent Republic during the 1939–45 war. The first independently elected Parliament met on August 17, 1943, but foreign troops were in part occupation until April, 1946. Syria remained an independent Republic until February, 1958, when it became part of the United Arab Republic. It seceded from the United Arab Republic on Sept. 28, 1961.

A new Constitution was promulgated in March 1973; this declared that Syria is a "democratic, popular socialist State", and that the Ba'ath Party, which has been the ruling party since 1963, is "the leading party in the State and society". Elections to the 195-seat Peoples' Council in February 1986 resulted in a large majority for the Ba'ath Party, who had 129 seats, Arab Socialist Union 9, Socialist Unionist Movement 8, Arab Socialist Party 5, Syrian Communist Party 9, and Independents 35.

Production and Industry.—Agriculture is the principal source of production; wheat and barley are the main cereal crops, but the cotton crop is the highest in value. Tobacco is grown in the maritime plain in Sahel, the Sahyoun and the Djebleh district of Lattakia. Large new areas are coming under irrigation and cultivation in the north-east of the country as a result of the Thawra dam. Skins and hides, leather goods, wool and silk, textiles, cement, vegetable oil, glass, soap, sugar, plastics and copper and brass utensils are produced. There are an increasing number of light assembly plants as Syria's industrialization programme develops. Oil has been found at Karachuk and other parts in the north-eastern corner of the country and production of high quality reserves is proceeding in the region of Deir ez Zor. Syria produces about 12 million tons of oil per year at present. A pipeline has been built to the Mediterranean port of Banias, via Homs. Two oil refineries are in production at Homs and Banias. Revenue is derived from the pipeline from the oilfields of Saudi Arabia to Sidon in Lebanon (Tapline). Another pipeline from the Iraq oilfields was closed in April 1982. Syria also has deposits of phosphate and rock salt, and produces asphalt.

Language and Literature.—Arabic is the principal language, but Kurdish, Turkish and Armenian are spoken among significant minorities and a few villages still speak Aramaic, the language spoken by Christ and the Apostles. There are 3 daily newspapers and several periodicals in Arabic published in Damascus, and also a daily newspaper in English. English has taken over from French as the main foreign language, especially among the young.

Education.—Education in Syria is under State control and, although a few of the schools are privately owned, they all follow a common system and syllabus. Elementary education is free at State Schools, and is compulsory from the age of seven. Secondary education is not compulsory and is free only at the State Schools. Because of the shortage of places, entry to these State Schools is competitive. Damascus University, founded in 1924, has nine faculties and a Higher Teachers' Training College. The number of students has risen to over 60,000. There are also about 20,000 students at Aleppo University (founded 1961), over 10,000 at Tishrin University, Latakia (founded 1975) and 6,000 at Ba'ath University, Homs. Approximately 10 per cent of all students receive scholarships, and at the present time Palestinian refugees are admitted free. The rest pay fees.

Communications.—Although railway lines run from Damascus to both Beirut and Amman, train services go only as far as the border towns. A track has been opened connecting Homs with Damascus. A track links Homs, Hamah, Aleppo and Qamishliye to the Iraq frontier. Branch lines connect the ports of Tartous and Latakia to the system and another line runs from Aleppo down Euphrates valley to Deir ez Zor and thence north to Qamishliye, with a branch going to the Euphrates Dam. All the principal towns in the country are connected by roads which vary from modern dual carriageways to narrow country lanes. An internal air service operates between all major towns. The main International Airport is at Damascus and there are also flights to Eastern Europe, Turkey, Greece and Armenia from Aleppo.

Trade.—The principal imports are foodstuffs (fruit, vegetables, cereals, meat and dairy products, tea, coffee and sugar), mineral and petroleum products, yarn and textiles, iron and steel manufactures, machinery, chemicals, pharmaceuticals, fertilizers and timber. Raw cotton, oil, cereals, fruit, phosphates, livestock and dairy products, other foodstuffs, textiles and raw wool.

Trade with U.K.

	1986	1987
Imports from U.K.	£55,511,000	£34,053,000
Exports to U.K.	31,298,000	24,937,000

CAPITAL.—Damascus (population (estimated) 2,250,000). Other important towns are Aleppo, Homs and Hama, and the principal port is ΨLatakia.

CURRENCY.—Syrian Pound of 100 Piastres.

FLAG.—Red over white over black horizontal bands, with two green stars on central white band.

NATIONAL DAY.—April 17.

BRITISH INTERESTS SECTION
Quartier Malki, 11 rue Mohammad Kurd Ali, Imm. Kotob, Damascus.
[Damascus 712561]

Following the break in diplomatic relations with Syria in October 1986, Australia has been protecting British interests in Syria.

THAILAND
(Prathes Thai)

King, His Majesty Bhumibol Adulyadej, *born* 1927; *succeeded his brother*, June 9, 1946; *married* Princess Sirikit Kitiyakara, April 28, 1950; *crowned* May 5, 1950; *and has issue*, Princess Ubolratana, *born*, April 6, 1951; Crown Prince Vajiralongkorn, *born*, July 28, 1952; Princess Sirindhorn, *born*, April 2, 1955; Princess Chulabhorn *born*, July 4, 1957.

CABINET

Prime Minister, Gen. Prem Tinsulanonda.
Deputy Prime Ministers, Bhichai Rattakul; Maj.-

Gen. Chatichai Choonhavan; Pong Sarasin; Gen. Thienchai Sirisamphan; Adm. Sontee Boonyachai.

Ministers attached to the Prime Minister's Office, Vichit Saengtong; Amnuay Suwankhiri; Chaisiri Ruangkarnchanaset; Meechai Ruchupan; Ft.-Lt. Suli Mahasantana; Chirayu Isarangkun Na Ayuthaya.

Defence, Air Chief Marshal Panieng Kantarat.

Foreign Affairs, Air Chief Marshal Panieng Siddhi Savetsila.

Finance, Suthee Singhasaneh.

Interior, Gen. Prachuab Suntrangkoon.

Agriculture and Co-operatives, Gen. Harn Leenanonda.

Commerce, Montri Pongpanit.

Industry, Pramual Sapavasu.

Communications, Banharn Silpa-archa.

Education, Marut Bunnag.

Public Health, Tirdpong Jayanandana.

Science, Technology and Energy, Banyat Bantadtan.

Justice, Sa-ard Piyawan.

University Affairs, Subin Pinkayan.

N.B. A General Election was held on July 24, 1988 and the leader of the winning party, Maj.-Gen. Chatichai Choonhavan, was endorsed as Prime Minister. A new cabinet had still to be announced at the time of going to press.

ROYAL THAI EMBASSY IN LONDON
30 Queen's Gate, SW7 5JB
[01–589 0173]

Ambassador Extraordinary and Plenipotentiary, His Excellency Mr. Sudhee Prasasvinitchai (1986).

Area and Population.—The Kingdom of Thailand, formerly known as Siam, has an area of 198,457 sq. miles (514,000 sq. km.), with a population (estimated 1986) of 52,970,000. The population growth rate averages 2·4 per cent. per year. It has a common boundary with Malaysia in the south, is bounded on the west by Burma and on the north-east and east by Laos and Kampuchea. Although there is no common boundary between Thailand and China, the Chinese province of Yunnan is separated from the Thai northern border only by a narrow stretch of Burmese and Laotian territory.

The capital, Bangkok, is situated in the south of the central plain area. To the north-east there is a plateau area and to the north-west mountains. The south of Thailand consists of a narrow mountainous peninsula. The principal rivers are the Chao Phraya in the central plains, and the Mekong on the northern and north-eastern borders.

Language and Religion.—Thai is basically a monosyllabic, tonal language, a branch of the Indo-Chinese linguistic family, but its vocabulary especially has been strongly influenced by Sanskrit and Pali. It is written in an alphabetic script derived from ancient Indian scripts. The principal religion is Buddhism. In 1985 94·95 per cent of the population were Buddhists, 3·91 per cent Moslems, 0·53 per cent Christians and 0·61 per cent other religions.

Government.—Thailand became a Constitutional Monarchy in 1932. The Constitution promulgated in December 1978 provides for a National Assembly consisting of a Senate appointed by the King and a House of Representatives elected by universal adult suffrage. There are 260 Senate seats and 347 House seats. Each senator is appointed for six years and each M.P. for four years.

A General Election was held in July 1986, following the dissolution of the House after three years. Sixteen political parties entered the contest. The results were: Democrat, 100 seats; Chart Thai, 63; Social Action 51; United Democracy, 38; Prachakorn Thai, 24; Ruam Thai, 19; Rassadorn, 18; Community Action, 15; Progressive, 9; Chart Prachatipatai, 3;

Mass, 3; Puang Chon Chao Thai, 1; New Force, 1; Democratic Labour, 1; Liberal, 1; and Rak Thai, 0.

Education.—Primary education is compulsory and free and secondary education in Government Schools is free. In 1983 there were 35,846 schools and training colleges, with a total of 10,058,295 pupils and 539,680 teachers. Private universities and colleges are playing an increasing role in higher education. In 1984 the Government agreed to upgrade four private colleges to universities. Out of 29 universities and other similar higher institutes of learning, 11 are private and attended by some 25,000 students. In 1984 their total enrolment was 668,810 students. The two open universities, Ramkamhaeng and Sukhothaithammathirat, had an enrolment of 409,686 and 73,000 students respectively.

Agriculture and Industry.—The agricultural sector provides just under half the national income and employs 67·5 per cent of the labour force, which in 1985 was estimated at 26·8 million. Rice remains the most important crop, accounting for 60 per cent of the area planted. After rice the main crops are sugar, maize, rubber, tobacco, kenaf and jute. In recent years the production of livestock and poultry, especially pigs and chickens for export, has gained importance. There is a large fishing industry with more than 20,000 vessels registered. Fish farming is popular in many inland areas. A ban on hardwood export has resulted in the decline of the forestry industry.

The discovery of onshore oil and offshore gas in the late 1970s ushered in a new economic era. Crude production which began in 1983 stood at around 20,000 barrels per day in mid-1985, or about 10 per cent of the country's need. At the same time gas and condensate output stood at over 350 million cubic feet per day. It was estimated that by the end of 1985 indigenous oil and gas supplies should account for about half of Thailand's petroleum demand. The predicted surplus of natural gas has led the Government to designate an area on the east coast as the future centre of the petrochemical industry. Another energy resource becoming more important is lignite which is found mainly in the north and is being used increasingly for electricity production.

Mineral resources are mainly tin, tungsten, lead, antimony and iron. Among these, tin is the most important, with exports totalling 18,455 tons in 1984. In addition, about 60,000 tons of zinc ingots a year are expected to be produced by a zinc refinery which was opened in early 1984.

Industry is divided into two main categories: service and manufacturing. Since 1982 tourism has replaced rice as the country's top foreign exchange earner. There were 3·5 million overseas visitors in 1987, an increase of 22 per cent. over 1986, generating an estimated 45,000 million baht for the country. The banking system is large and contributes much to the economy, especially employment. There are over 1,800 bank branches in the country employing some 72,000 workers.

Since 1960 the Government has actively promoted industrial investments by means of tax relief and other incentives to local and foreign investors; in 1985, 74·6 per cent. of this investment was in Thai projects. Most of the industries established under this scheme in early years were import-substituting. However, there has been an increasing shift to export-oriented industries, taking advantages of low-wage labour and available domestic resources. Manufacturing now accounts for about 21·8 per cent of the national income. Crops contribute 12·1 per cent. of G.D.P.

Communications.—The importance of rivers and canals as the traditional mode of transportation has been replaced by highways and roads. The existing road and highway network, totalling 34,701 kilometres in 1984, reaches all parts of the country. Most of the smaller towns and bigger villages are now served by paved roads.

Navigable waterways have a length of about 1,100 km. in the dry season and 1,600 km. in the wet season. About 3,825 km of State-owned railways were open to traffic in 1984. Main lines run from Bangkok to Aranya Prathet on the Kampuchean border via Korat to Ubon and to Nong Khai, the ferry terminal on the River Mekong opposite Vientiane, capital of Laos; to Chiang Mai and to Hat Yai, whence lines go down the eastern and western sides of the Malay peninsula, via Sungei Galok and Penang respectively, to Singapore. A new line to Sattahip on the east coast is being constructed.

Bangkok is an important international air centre and has direct flights to most of the world's major cities. The airports at Chiang Mai, Phuket and Hat Yai also receive international flights. Most major provincial towns have airports. Thai International and Thai Airways merged in April 1988. Now named THAI, the airline is state-owned.

Thailand has an extensive network of telecommunications services, and the telephone service though still poor is being improved. All major cities and towns are linked by direct long-distance calls. Thailand has two mobile telephone networks, AMPS (urban), and NMT (rural) presently covering only the central area but expanding rapidly.

There are two important ports in the country. Bangkok, which is a river port, can serve vessels up to 27 ft. draught. The deep-sea port at Sattahip caters for larger vessels. Phuket and Songkhla deep water ports have just been completed and will be the first to be managed privately under a ten-year concession. Construction of Laem Chabang deep water port started in 1988.

TRADE

Thailand's main exports are rice, tapioca and tapioca products, garments, rubber, integrated circuit boards, precious stones, pearls and other ornaments, maize, canned sea food, fabrics, sugar and tin. Main imports are crude oil, chemicals and pharmaceuticals, electrical and non-electrical machinery and spare parts, industrial machinery, iron and steel, diesel oil and other fuel oil, vehicle and transport equipment.

	1986	1987p
	millions of *Baht*	
Total imports	245·9	337·0
Total exports	231·5	291·0

p = preliminary.

Trade with U.K.

	1986	1987
Imports from U.K.	£182,756,079	£206,571,000
Exports to U.K.	158,194,823	239,430,000

CAPITAL.—ΨBangkok (population 5,400,000 (1985)); at the mouth of the River Chao Phraya. Other centres are Chiang Mai, Phitsanuloke, Chon Buri, Korat, Khon Kaen, Surat Thani, Hat Yai and ΨPhuket but none approaches Bangkok in size or importance.

CURRENCY.—Baht of 100 Stang.

FLAG.—Five horizontal bands, red, white, dark blue, white, red (the blue band twice the width of the others).

NATIONAL ANTHEM.—"Sanrasern Pra Barami".

NATIONAL DAY.—December 5 (The King's Birthday).

BRITISH EMBASSY
Wireless Road, Bangkok
[Bangkok 253 0191]

Ambassador Extraordinary and Plenipotentiary, His Excellency Derek Tonkin, C.M.G. (1985).

British Council Representative, E. C. Pugh, 428 Rama 1 Road, Siam Square, Bangkok 10500.

BRITISH CHAMBER OF COMMERCE, 302 Silom Road, Bangkok 10500

TOGO
(République Togolaise)

President and Minister of Defence, Gen. Gnassingbé Eyadéma, *born* 1937, *assumed office,* April 14, 1967; *re-elected for seven-year term,* Dec. 23, 1986.

Interior, Komla Agbetiafa.
Planning and Mines, Barry Moussa Barque.
Rural Development, Koffi Walla.
Minister Delegate to the Presidency (Information), Gbegnon Amegboh.
Equipment, Posts and Telecommunications, Nassirou Ayeva.
National Education and Scientific Research, Tchaa-Kozah Tchalim.
Public Health, Social and Women's Affairs, Aissah Agbetra.
Commerce and Transport, N'Souwoudji Kawo Ehe.
Youth, Sports and Culture, Komla Dometo Gnémégna.
Foreign Affairs and Co-operation, Yaovi Adodo.
Industry and State Enterprises, Koffi Djondo.
Technical Instruction and Professional Training, Koffi Edoh.
Economy and Finance, Komla Alipui.
Environment and Tourism, Yao Komlavi.
Labour and Civil Service, Bitokotipou Yagninim.
Justice, Kpotivi Tevi Djidjogbe Lacle.

EMBASSY IN LONDON
30 Sloane Street, SW1.
[01–235 0147/9]

Ambassador Extraordinary and Plenipotentiary, His Excellency Assiongbon Agbenou (1986).
Counsellor, Djibril Akanga.

The Republic is situated in West Africa between 0°–2° W. and 6°–11° N., with a coastline only 35 miles long on the Gulf of Guinea, and extends northward inland for 350 miles. It is flanked on the west by Ghana, on the north by Burkina Faso and in the east by Benin. It has an area of 21,925 sq. miles (56,785 sq. km.), and a population (estimate, 1985) of 3,030,000, including people of several African races. The official language is French.

The first President of Togo, Sylvanus Olympio, assassinated on January 13, 1963, was succeeded by Nicolas Grunitzky, who was himself overthrown by an army coup d'état on January 13, 1967. On April 14, 1967, the Commander-in-Chief of the Togolese army, Lt. Colonel (later promoted General) Eyadéma named himself President.

Production and Trade.—Although the economy of Togo remains largely agricultural, exports of phosphates have superseded agricultural products as the main source of export earnings. Other exports include palm kernels, copra and manioc. The production of phosphates entirely for export was taken over completely by the government in February 1974.

Trade with U.K.

	1986	1987
Imports from U.K.	£17,490,000	£15,431,000
Exports to U.K.	5,001,000	2,579,000

CAPITAL.—ΨLomé, population (1983), 366,476.

CURRENCY.—Franc C.F.A. of 100 Centimes.

FLAG.—Five alternating green and yellow horizontal stripes; a quarter in red at top next staff bearing a white star.

NATIONAL DAY.—January 13 (National Liberation Day).

BRITISH EMBASSY
British Ambassador, (resides at *Accra, Ghana*).

TUNISIA
(Al-Djoumhouria Attunusia)

President, Zine el-Abidine Ben Ali *took office* Nov. 7, 1987.

CABINET

Prime Minister, Hédi Baccouche.
Minister of State for Justice, Slaheddine Baly.
Foreign Affairs, Mahmoud Mestiri.
Interior, Habib Ammar.
Minister Delegate for Planning, Mohamed Ghannouchi.
Minister Delegate to the Prime Minister, Hamed Karoui.
Information, Abdelwaheb Abdallah.
National Economy, Slaheddine Ben M'Barek.
Finance, Nouri Zorgati.
National Education, Hédi Khelil.
Higher Education and Scientific Research, Abdessalem M'Seddi.
Supplies and Housing, Sadok Ben Jemaa.
Transport and Tourism, Abderrazak Kefi.
Social Affairs, Taoufik Cheikhrouhou.
Public Health, Souad Lyagoubi.
Agriculture, Lassaâd Ben Osman.
Culture, Abdelmalek Laarif.
Youth and Sports, Abdelhamid Escheikh.
Communications, Brahim Khouaja.
Governor of the Central Bank, Ismail Khelil.
Secretary General to the Minister of Defence, Abdallah Kallel.

TUNISIAN EMBASSY IN LONDON
29 Prince's Gate, SW7 1QG
[01–584 8117]

Ambassador Extraordinary and Plenipotentiary, His Excellency Hamadi Khouini, C.B.E. (1987).

Area and Population.—Tunisia lies between Algeria and Libya and extends southwards to the Sahara Desert, with a total area of 63,170 sq. miles (163,610 sq. km.), and an estimated population in 1985 of 7,205,106.

Government.—A French Protectorate from 1881 to 1956, Tunisia became an independent sovereign State with the signing on March 20, 1956, of an agreement whereby France recognized Tunisia's independence and right to conduct her own foreign policy and to form a Tunisian Army.

Following a first general election held on March 25, 1956, a Constituent Assembly met for the first time on April 8. On July 25, 1957, the Constituent Assembly deposed the Bey, abolished the monarchy and elected M. Bourguiba first President of the Republic. On June 1, 1959, the Constitution was promulgated and on December 7, 1959, the National Assembly held its first session. In March 1975 the National Assembly proclaimed M. Bourguiba as President for life. On Nov. 7, 1987 M. Bourguiba was deposed and succeeded by President Zine el-Abidine Ben Ali.

The country is divided into 22 regions (*gouvernorats*) each administered by a Governor.

Production, Trade, etc.—The valleys of the northern region support large flocks and herds, and contain rich agricultural areas, in which wheat, barley, and oats are grown. The vine and olive are extensively cultivated.

The chief exports are crude oil, phosphates, olive oil, finished textiles, and fruit. The chief imports are machinery and equipment, foodstuffs, petroleum products, and textiles. Some oil has been discovered and production reached an annual rate of 5 million tons in 1987. Gas has also been discovered off the east coast but exploitation is not viable at present. Tourists numbered almost 1·8 million in 1987.

	1986	1987
Total Imports	TD2,294,400	TD2,509,100
Total Exports	1,403,600	1,770,700

France remains the main trading partner, supplying 27·6 per cent of the country's imports and purchasing 22·9 per cent of Tunisia's exports.

Trade with U.K.

	1986	1987
Imports from U.K.	£39,824,358	£24,942,830
Exports to U.K.	17,291,779	14,713,628

Tunisia became an associate member of the E.C. early in 1969, and signed a new agreement with the E.C. in 1976. In 1977 the introduction of import quota measures by the E.C. on some textile goods resulted in a reduction of growth in this important sector of the Tunisian market. The quotas for some textile products was renegotiated and increased in 1982.

CAPITAL.—Ψ Tunis, connected by canal with La Goulette on the coast, had a population (1984) of 1,394,749. The ruins of ancient Carthage lie a few miles from the city. Other towns of importance are: Ψ Sfax (577,992); Ψ Sousse (322,491); Ψ Bizerta (394,670); Kairouan; Gabes; Menzel Bourguiba.

CURRENCY.—Tunisian Dinar of 1,000 Millimes.

FLAG.—Red crescent and star in a white orb, all on a red ground.

NATIONAL ANTHEM.—"Himat Al Hima".

NATIONAL DAY.—March 20.

BRITISH EMBASSY
Place de la Victoire, Tunis
[Tunis 245100]

Ambassador Extraordinary and Plenipotentiary and Consul-General, His Excellency Stephen Peter Day (1987).

First Secretary, B. E. Stewart (*Head of Chancery*).
Second Secretary, C. Innes-Hopkins (*Commercial and Consul*).
British Council Representative, D. Handforth.
There is a British Council Library in *Tunis*.

TURKEY
(Türkiye Cumhuriyeti)

President, Gen. Kenan Evren, *assumed power*, Sept. 12, 1980; *elected for 7-year term*, Nov. 1982.

GOVERNMENT

Prime Minister, Turgut Özal.
Deputy Prime Minister, Kaya Erdem.
Ministers of State, Kazim Oksay; Brig.-Gen. Abdullah Tenekeci; Kamran Inan; Prof. Ali Bozer; Yusuf Bozkurt Özal; Adnan Kahveci; Mehmet Yazar; Cemil Cicek; Nihat Kitapci.
Justice, Mehmet Topac.
National Defence, Ecran Vuralhan.
Interior, Mustafa Kalemli.
Foreign Affairs, Mesut Yilmaz.
Finance and Customs, Ahmet Kurtcebe Alptemocin.
Education, Youth and Sports, Hasan Celal Guzel.
Public Works and Housing, Safa Giray.
Health and Social Welfare, (vacant).
Communications and Transport, Ekrem Pakdemirli.
Agriculture, Forestry and Rural Affairs, Hüsnü Dogan.
Labour and Social Security, Imren Aykut.
Industry and Commerce, Sukru Yurur.
Energy and Natural Resources, Fahrettin Kurt.
Culture and Tourism, Mustafa Tinaz Titiz.

TURKISH EMBASSY IN LONDON
Chancery: 43 Belgrave Square, SW1X 8PA
[01–235 5252]

Ambassador Extraordinary and Plenipotentiary, His Excellency Rahmi Gümrükcüoğlu (1981).

Area and Population.—People of Turkic stock are to be found scattered throughout a wide belt extending from China through the Soviet Union, Afghanistan and Iran to the present day Turkish State, and into Bulgaria.

Turkey itself extends from Edirne (Adrianople) to Transcaucasia and Iran, and from the Black Sea to the Mediterranean, Syria and Iraq. Total population at the Census of 1985 was 51,428,514, of which 6,942,780 were in Europe and 44,485,734 in Asia.

Turkey in Europe consists of Eastern Thrace, including the cities of Istanbul and Edirne, and is separated from Asia by the Bosphorus at Istanbul and by the Dardanelles—about 40 miles in length with a width varying from 1 to 4 miles—the political neighbours being Greece and Bulgaria on the west.

Turkey in Asia comprises the whole of Asia Minor or Anatolia and extends from the Aegean Sea to the western boundaries of Georgia, Soviet Armenia and Iran, and from the Black Sea to the Mediterranean and the northern boundaries of Syria and Iraq.

Government.—On October 29, 1923, the National Assembly declared Turkey a Republic and elected Gazi Mustafa Kemal (later known as Kemal Ataturk) President. In 1945 a multi-party system was introduced but in 1960 the government was overthrown by the Turkish Armed Forces which ruled through the Committee of National Union, a body of military officers. A new constitution was adopted in July 1961 and in Oct., after a general election, a civilian government took office. Civilian governments remained in power until Sept. 1980 when mounting problems with the economy and terrorism led the military to assume legislative powers. A civilian technocratic government was appointed later that month.

A new Constitution, extending the powers of the President, was approved by a referendum on Nov. 7, 1982. It provided for the separation of powers between the legislature, executive and judiciary, and the holding of free elections to the unicameral Grand National Assembly, which has 400 members elected every five years. Following the General Election on Nov. 6, 1983 the military leadership handed over power to a newly elected civilian government.

Party representation in the newly enlarged 450-seat Assembly, December 1987 was: Motherland Party, 292 seats; Social Democrat Populist Party, 99; Correct Way Party, 59.

Turkey is divided for administrative purposes into 67 *il* with subdivisions into *kaza* and *nahiye*. Each *il* has a governor (*vali*) and elective council.

Religion and Education.—On April 10, 1928, the Grand National Assembly passed a law in virtue of which Islam ceased to be the State religion of the Republic. However, 98·99 per cent of the population are Moslems. The main religious minorities, which are concentrated in Istanbul and on the Syrian frontier, are: Greek Orthodox, 10,000; Armenians, 42,000; Syriani Christians, 42,000; Others, 6,000. (Total Christians, 100,000); Jewish, 44,000. Education is free, secular and compulsory at primary level. There are elementary, secondary and vocational schools.

There are 27 universities in Turkey, including four in Istanbul, four in Ankara, two in Izmir, and one each in Erzurum and Trabzon.

The expenditure allocated to education in the 4th Five Year Plan (1979–83) was *TL*76,000,000,000, compared with *TL*14,000,000,000 in the 3rd Five Year Plan (1973–77).

Language and Literature.—Until 1926, Turkish was written in Arabic script, but in that year the Roman alphabet was substituted for use in official correspondence and in 1928 for universal use, with Arabic numerals as used throughout Europe. Ancient Turkish literature aped the Arabic manner, but

the revolution of 1908 led to the introduction of a native literature free from foreign influences and adapted to the understanding of the people. The leading Turkish newspapers are centred in Istanbul and Ankara, although most provincial towns have their own daily papers. There are foreign language papers in French, Greek, Armenian and English and numerous magazines and weeklies on various subjects, but few trade commercial publications.

Agricultural Production.—In 1985 agricultural production accounted for some 16 per cent of the gross domestic product at constant factor prices. About 50 per cent of the working population are in the rural sector. Estimated production figures for the principal crops in 1986 were ('000 tons):

Wheat	19,000	Olives	600
Barley	7,000	Tea (wet leaves)	690
Rice	165	Hazelnuts	300
Tobacco	170	Oranges	750
Sugar	1,429	Grapes	3,000

With the important exception of wheat, which is mostly grown on the arid Central Anatolian Plateau, most of the crops are grown on the fertile littoral. Tobacco, sultana and fig cultivation is centred around Izmir, where substantial quantities of cotton are also grown. The main cotton area is in the Cukurova Plain around Adana. The forests which lie between the littoral plain and the Anatolian Plateau, contain beech, pine, oak, elm, chestnut, lime, plane, alder, box, poplar and maple. During recent years the Government has attempted, so far not altogether successfully, to combat the depredations of peasant and goat which threaten to destroy the existing forests within the next 25 years.

Industry.—After agriculture, Turkey's second most important industry is based on her considerable mineral wealth which is, however, as yet comparatively unexploited. The main export minerals are chromite and boron. Production in 1984 was (tons):

Coal	7,103,000
Lignite	27,199,000
Iron ore	4,049,000
Chrome ore	689,000
Copper	2,466,000
Boron minerals	1,411,000

The progress made in the manufacture of sugar, cotton, woollen and silk textiles, and cement, has been such that the bulk of the country's requirements can now be produced locally, while other industries contributing substantially to local needs include vehicle assembly, paper, glass and glassware, iron and steel, leather and leather goods, sulphur refining, canning and rubber goods, soaps and cosmetics, pharmaceutical products, prepared foodstuffs and a host of minor industries.

In common with other developing countries, Turkey's economy was adversely affected by the steep rises in oil prices from 1973 onwards. This led to a succession of economic crises and high inflation culminating in Jan. 1980 in the introduction of an economic stability programme. Exports have since risen dramatically, topping $8,000 million in 1985. Inflation, however, remains high (43 per cent. in 1985) and as a result investment is low. Turkey's current account deficit has been reduced to about $1,000 million. G.N.P. growth for 1985 was about 5 per cent. and unemployment remains high.

COMMUNICATIONS

Railways.—The complete network became the property of the State Railways Administration in 1948. The total length of lines in operation is 8,193 kilometres.

Roads.—At the end of 1985 there were 59,300 km. of national roads (55,296 of which were macadamized).

The estimated number of vehicles in 1984 was 2,159,417.

The Bosporus is spanned by a single bridge, opened in 1973. Work on a second bridge began in 1985 and plans are being drawn up for a third fixed link between the two continents.

Shipping.—In August 1980 there were 343 merchants ships over 300 gross tons, 79 passenger ships and 73 tankers, giving a total draft weight of 1,545,062 tons.

Civil Aviation.—The State airlines (T.H.Y.) operate all internal services and have services to Europe and the Middle East. Most of the leading European airlines, including British Airways, operate services to Istanbul and some also to Ankara.

FINANCE

	1985–86 TLmillion
Estimated Expenditure	4,173,510
Estimated Revenue	5,766,727

TRADE

	1985	1986
Total imports ...	US$11,343·6 m.	US$11,105·0 m.
Total exports ...	7,558·1 m.	7,457·0 m.

Most imports are no longer subject to licence. The main imports are machinery, crude oil and petroleum products, iron and steel, vehicles, medicines and dyes, chemicals, fertilizers and electrical appliances. Agricultural commodities (cotton, tobacco, fruits, nuts, livestock) represent 47 per cent of total exports. Other exports are minerals, textiles, glass and cement.

Trade with U.K.

	1986	1987
Imports from U.K.	£433,753,000	£513,479,000
Exports to U.K.	406,605,000	579,366,000

CAPITAL.—Ankara (Angora), an inland town of Asia Minor, about 275 miles E.S.E. of Istanbul, with a population (1980) of 3,196,460. Ankara (or Ancyra) was the capital of the Roman Province of *Galatia Prima*, and a marble temple (now in ruins), dedicated to Augustus, contains the *Monumentum (Marmor) Ancyranum*, inscribed with a record of the reign of Augustus Cæsar. ΨIstanbul (4,870,747), the former capital, was the Roman city of Byzantium. It was selected by Constantine the Great as the capital of the Roman Empire about A.D. 328 and renamed Constantinople. Istanbul contains the celebrated church of St. Sophia, which, after becoming a mosque, was made a museum in 1934; it also contains Topkapi, former Palace of the Ottoman Sultans, which is also a museum. Other cities are ΨIzmir (1,968,614); Adana (1,467,346); Bursa (1,161,553); Gaziantep (387,093); and Eskişehir (543,733).

CURRENCY.—Turkish Lira of 100 Kurus.

FLAG.—Red, with white crescent and star.

NATIONAL ANTHEM.—"Istikâl Marşi" (The Independence March).

NATIONAL DAY.—October 29 (Republic Day).

BRITISH EMBASSY

Sehit Ersan Caddesi 46/A, Cankaya, Ankara [Ankara 274310/4]

Ambassador Extraordinary and Plenipotentiary, His Excellency Timothy Lewis Achilles Daunt, C.M.G. (1986).

Counsellor, C. T. Humfrey.

First Secretaries, P. J. Westmacott (*Head of Chancery*); N. J. Morley (*Consul*); I. C. Sloan (*Economic and Commercial*); Ms. C. M. Street (*Cultural Affairs*); M. R. Willson (*Cultural and Science Affairs*); J. M. Brown (*Administration*).

Defence and Military Attaché, Brig. S. T. Anderson, O.B.E., M.C.

Naval and Air Attaché, Cmdr. B. Jones, O.B.E.

BRITISH CONSULAR OFFICES

There is a British Consulate-General at *Istanbul*, a Vice-Consulate at *Izmir* and an Hon. British Consulate at *Iskenderun*.

British Council Representative, E. Marsden, Kirklangic Sokak 9, Gazi Osman Pasa, Ankara 06700.— There is also a centre and library at *Istanbul* and a library at *Ankara*.

BRITISH CHAMBER OF COMMERCE OF TURKEY INC., Mesrutiyet Caddessi No. 34, Tepebasi Beyoğlu, Istanbul (Postal Address, P.O. Box 190 Karaköy, Istanbul).

UNION OF SOVIET SOCIALIST REPUBLICS
(Soyuz Sovetskikh Sotsialisticheskikh Respublik)

THE COMMUNIST PARTY OF THE SOVIET UNION
(K.P.S.S. = Kommunisticheskaya Partiya Sovetskogo Soyuza)

Politbureau, V. M. Chebrikov; M. S. Gorbachev; A. A. Gromyko; E. K. Ligachev; V. P. Nikonov; N. I. Ryzhkov; V. V. Shcherbitsky; E. A. Shevardnadze; N. N. Slyunkov; M. S. Solomentsev; V. I. Vorotnikov; A. N. Yakovlev; L. N. Zaikov (*full members*); P. N. Demichev; V. I. Dolgikh; Yu. D. Maslyukov; G. P. Razumovsky; Yu. F. Soloviev; N. V. Talyzin; D. T. Yazov (*candidate members*).

Secretariat, Mikhail Sergevich Gorbachev (*General Secretary since* March 11, 1985); O. D. Baklanov; A. P. Biryukova; A. F. Dobrynin; V. I. Dolgikh; E. K. Ligachev; A. I. Lukyanov; V. A. Medvedev; V. P. Nikonov; G. P. Razumovsky; N . N. Slyunkov; A. N. Yakovlev; L. N. Zaikov.

Committee of Party Control, M. S. Solomentsev (*Chairman*).

Komsomol (*Young Communist League*) V. I. Mironenko (*First Secretary*).

GOVERNMENT OF THE U.S.S.R.

The Presidium of the Supreme Soviet of the U.S.S.R.

Chairman (= *President of the U.S.S.R.*), Andrei A. Gromyko, *since* July 2, 1985.

Secretary, T. N. Menteshashvili.

The Supreme Soviet (= Parliament) consists of two chambers.

Chairman (= *Speaker) of the Council of the Union,* Yu. N. Khristoradnov.

Chairman (= *Speaker) of the Council of Nationalities,* A. E. Voss.

The Council of Ministers of the U.S.S.R.

Chairman (= *Prime Minister),* Nikolai Ryzhkov *since* Sept. 27, 1985.

First Vice-Chairmen, Yu. D. Maslyukov; V. S. Murakhovsky; N. V. Talyzin.

Vice-Chairmen, A. K. Antonov; B. E. Shcherbina; Yu. P. Batalin; V. K. Gusev; V. M. Kamentsev; I. S. Silaev; B. L. Tolstykh; G. G. Vedernikov; L. A. Voronin; I. S. Belousov.

Five Buros/State Commissions of the Council of Ministers have been set up since March 1985:
Chemical-Wood Complex, (no published chairman).
Fuel and Energy Complex, B. E. Shcherbina.
Machine Building, I. S. Silaev.
Social Development, G. A. Aliev.
State Foreign Economic Commission, V. M. Kamentsev.

Ministries.—There are three groups of departmental ministries, with a total of 79 ministers—40 All Union Ministries, *i.e.* federal ministries, 15 Union Republican Ministries (co-ordinating ministries of individual republics) and 24 State Committees whose Chairmen rank as Ministers. The Prime Ministers of the 15 constituent republics belong to the Council *ex officio.*

FEDERAL MINISTRIES

Atomic Energy, N. F. Lukonin.
Automobile Industry, N. A. Pugin.
Aviation Industry, A. S. Systsov.
Chemical Industry, Yu. A. Bespalov.
Chemical and Oil Machine Building, V. M. Lukyanenko.
Civil Aviation, A. N. Volkov.
Coal Industry, M. I. Shchadov.
Communications Equipment Industry, E. K. Pervyshin.
Construction, Road and Municipal Machine Building, E. A. Varnachev.
Construction in Eastern Regions, A. A. Babenko.
Construction in Northern and Western Regions, V. I. Reshetilov.
Construction in Southern Regions, A. N. Shchepetilnikov.
Construction in Regions of Urals and Western Siberia, S. V. Bashilov.
Construction Materials Industry, S. F. Voenushkin.
Defence, Marshal D. T. Yazov.
Defence Industry, P. V. Finogenov.
Electronics Industry, V. G. Kolesnikov.
Electrical Engineering Industry, O. G. Anfimov.
Ferrous Metallurgy, S. V. Kolpakov.
Foreign Economic Relations, K. F. Katushev.
Gas Industry, V. S. Chernomyrdin.
General Machine Building, V. Kh. Doguzhiev.
Geology, E. A. Kozlovsky.
Heavy, Power and Transport, Machine Building, V. M. Velichko.
Instrument-Making, Automation and Control Systems, M. S. Shkabardnya.
Machine Building, B. M. Belousov.
Machine-Tool Building and Tool Industry, N. A. Panichev.
Medical and Micro-biological Industry, V. A. Bykov.
Medium Machine Building, L. D. Ryabev.
Merchant Marine, Yu. M. Volmer.
Non-Ferrous Metallurgy, V. A. Durasov.
Oil Industry, V. A. Dinkov.
Oil Processing and Petrochemical Industry, N. V. Lemaev.
Petroleum and Gas Industry Enterprises Construction, V. G. Chirskov.
Production of Mineral Fertilizers, N. M. Olshansky.
Radio Industry, V. I. Shimko.
Railways, N. S. Konarev.
Ship Building Industry, I. V. Koksanov.
Tractor and Agricultural Machine Building, A. A. Ezhevsky.
Transport Construction, V. A. Brezhnev.

Among the more important Union Republican Ministries are:
Finance, B. I. Gostev.
Foreign Affairs, E. A. Shevardnadze.
Health, E. I. Chazov.
Internal Affairs, A. V. Vlasov.
Justice, B. Kravtsov.

ALL-UNION STATE COMMITTEES

Computer and Information Technology, N. V. Gorshkov.
Hydrometeorology, Yu. A. Izrael.
Inventions and Discoveries, I. S. Nayashkov.
Material Reserves, F. I. Loshchenkov.
Science and Technology, B. L. Tolstykh.

Standards, G. D. Kolmogorov.
Supervision of Atomic Energy Industry Safety, V. M. Malyshev.

EMBASSY OF THE U.S.S.R. IN LONDON
13 Kensington Palace Gardens, W8 4QX
[01–229 3628]
Ambassador Extraordinary and Plenipotentiary, His Excellency Leonid M. Zamyatin (1986).

AREA AND POPULATION

The total area of the U.S.S.R. is 8,649,461 sq. miles (22,402,000 sq. km.); the total population: (Jan. 1, 1987) 281,700,000.

Area and population (January, 1987) of the constituent Republics of the U.S.S.R. with their capitals:—

Republic (Capital)	Sq. miles	Population
I. R.S.F.S.R.		
(Moscow)........	6,593,391	145,300,000
II. Ukraine (Kiev)......	252,046	51,200,000
III. Belorussia (Minsk) .	80,300	10,078,000
IV. Uzbekistan		
(Tashkent)	157,181*	19,026,000
V. Kazakhstan		
(Alma-Ata)	1,064,980*	16,244,000
VI. Georgia (Tbilisi) ...	26,911	5,266,000
VII. Azerbaidjan (Baku).	33,436	6,811,000
VIII. Lithuania (Vilnius)	26,173	3,641,000
IX. Moldavia (Kishinev)	13,912	4,185,000
X. Latvia (Riga)	24,695	2,647,000
XI. Kirghizia (Frunze) .	76,642	4,143,000
XII. Tadjikistan		
(Dushanbe)	54,019	4,807,000
XIII. Armenia (Erevan)..	11,306	3,412,000
XIV. Turkmenistan		
(Ashkhabad)	188,417	3,361,000
XV. Estonia (Tallinn) ...	17,413	1,556,000

* (Adjusted to include transfer of 3 border regions—888 sq. miles and 162,000 inhabitants—by Uzbek S.S.R., Kazakh S.S.R. and U.S.S.R. decrees of May–June 1971.)

In 1987 66 per cent of the population lived in urban areas.

The proportion of women to men is 53 to 47. In 1985 the birth-rate was 19·4 and the mortality rate, 10·6.

Before the outbreak of the Second World War (1941–45 in U.S.S.R.), the U.S.S.R. consisted of 14 Republics. In August 1940, the major part of *Bessarabia* ceded by Romania in June was joined to the Moldavian A.S.S.R. to form a Moldavian S.S.R. The same month, the three independent Baltic States, *Estonia, Latvia* and *Lithuania,* were forcibly incorporated into the Soviet Union. In October, 1944, *Tannu-Tuva,* until the Second World War a nominally independent state lying to the N.W. of Outer Mongolia, became the autonomous province of *Tuva* and, in 1961, the Autonomous Republic of Tuva, within the R.S.F.S.R.

In July, 1956, the Karelo-Finnish Republic (formed in 1940 from the Karelian A.S.S.R. and land ceded by Finland) reverted to the status of an Autonomous (*Karelian*) Republic within the R.S.F.S.R.

Main Nationalities
(1979 Census)

The most numerous national groups of U.S.S.R. are: Russian, 137 m. and Ukrainian, 42 m. There are between 6 and 12 million Kazakhs, Tatars, Belorussians, and Uzbeks respectively. Azerbaidjani, Armenians and Georgians number between 3·5 and 5·5 million each group. There are some 1·9 to 2·9 million Lithuanians, Kirghizians, Turkmens, Germans, Moldavians and Tadjiks. In each of the following nationality groups the population numbers between 1·02 and 1·8 millions: Chuvashes, Latvians, Poles,

Mordovians, Bashkirs, Estonians, Dagestanis and Jews.

The 1979 census revealed a marked difference between the growth rates of individual nationalities: while the Slav nations showed an annual increase of under one per cent, certain Central Asian and Caucasian (mostly Moslem) nations recorded an annual net growth of 2·5 to 3·5 per cent.

Chronological System.—On February 14, 1918, the Soviet Government adopted the Gregorian (Western) Calendar. In 1981 Summer Time was introduced between April 1 and October 1, but there are some geographical anomalies in its application. The country is divided into 11 time zones (Moscow time is 3 hours ahead of G.M.T.).

LANGUAGE, LITERATURE AND ARTS

Language and Literature.—Russian is a branch of the Slavonic family of languages which is divided into the following groups: *Eastern,* including Russian, Ukrainian and White Russian; *Western,* including Polish, Czech, Slovak and Sorbish (or Lusatian Wendish); and *Southern,* including Serbo-Croat, Slovene, Macedonian and Bulgarian. The Western group and part of the Southern group are written in the Latin alphabet, the others in the Cyrillic, said to have been instituted by SS. Cyril and Methodius in the ninth century, and largely based on the Greek alphabet. Before the Westernization of Russia under Peter the Great (1682–1725), Russian literature consisted mainly of folk ballads (*byliny*), epic songs, chronicles and works of moral theology. The eighteenth and particularly the nineteenth centuries saw a brilliant development of Russian poetry and fiction. Romantic poetry reached its zenith with Alexander Pushkin (1799–1837) and Mikhail Lermontov (1814–1841). The 20th century produced great poets like Alexander Blok (1880–1921), the 1958 Nobel Prize laureate Boris Pasternak (1890–1960), Vladimir Mayakovsky (1893–1930) and Anna Akhmatova (1888–1966). Realistic fiction is associated with the names of Nikolai Gogol (1809–1852), Ivan Turgenev (1818–1883), Fedor Dostoyevsky (1821–1881) and Leo Tolstoy (1828–1910), and later with Anton Chekhov (1860–1904), Maxim Gorky (1868–1936), Ivan Bunin (1870–1953) and Alexander Solzhenitsyn (b. 1918).

Great names in music include Glinka (1804–1857), Borodin (1833–87), Mussorgsky (1839–1881), Rimsky-Korsakov (1844–1908), Rubinstein (1829–1894), Tchaikovsky (1840–1893), Rakhmaninov (1873–1943), Skriabin (1872–1915), Prokofiev (1891–1953), Stravinsky (1882–1971) and Shostakovich (1906–1975). Performers include Igor Oistrakh, M. Rostropovich, S. Richter and the famous conductor G. Rozhdestvensky.

THE CONSTITUTION

On October 7, 1977 a new Constitution was adopted to replace the 1936 ("Stalin") Constitution.

The Constitution is divided into a preamble and 9 Sections. The preamble describes the Soviet Union as a "developed Socialist society", which is said to be a logical stage on the road to communism. The highest aim of the Soviet state is said to be the building of a classless communist society.

Section I covers the *bases of the social-political and economic system.* The economic system is based on "socialist ownership of the means of production" (Article 9). The economy is managed on the basis of state plans (Article 15).

This section also contains chapters on *social development and culture, foreign policy,* and the *defence of the socialist Fatherland.* The foreign policy of the U.S.S.R. is said to be "directed to ensuring favourable international conditions for the building of communism in the U.S.S.R." (Article 28).

Section II is devoted to the *state and the individual.* This includes a long chapter on the basic rights, freedoms and duties of citizens of the U.S.S.R., all of which are subject to the proviso that "exercise by citizens of rights and freedoms must not injure the interests of society and state, and the rights of other citizens" (Article 39). The rights are listed in Articles 40–50. Freedom to profess or not profess a religion, and Church-State relations are dealt with in Article 52. Section II also includes a list of obligations (Articles 59–68).

Section III on the *national-state structure of the U.S.S.R.* describes it as a "unitary federal multinational state, formed as a result of the free self-determination of nations and the voluntary union of equal Soviet Socialist Republics (Article 69). "Each Union Republic shall retain the right freely to secede from the U.S.S.R." (Article 71).

Section IV on the *Soviets of people's deputies and the procedure for electing them* provides for the Supreme Soviet of the U.S.S.R. and the Supreme Soviets of Union and Republics to be elected for a term of 5 years and for local Soviets to be elected for 2½ years (Article 89). The minimum voting age and minimum age for deputies in all Soviets is 18 (Article 95).

Under Section V, *the higher organs of State power and administration of the U.S.S.R.,* the Supreme Soviet of the U.S.S.R. is the highest organ of State power (Article 106). It consists of two chambers, a Council of the Union and Council of Nationalities, which consist of the same number of deputies (Articles 107 and 108). Sessions of the Supreme Soviet are convoked twice a year (Article 110); between sessions the Supreme Soviet is represented by its Presidium, (Articles 117 and 118).

The highest executive organ of the State is the Council of Ministers of the U.S.S.R. (Article 127), consisting of the Chairman, his Deputies, U.S.S.R. Ministers and Chairmen of State Committees, Chairmen of the Councils of Ministers of Union Republics *ex officio* and others (Article 128). The Council of Ministers is accountable to the Supreme Soviet (Article 129). A smaller body, the Presidium of the Council of Ministers, acts as the permanent organ of the Council of Ministers (Article 131).

Section VI covers the bases of the structure of organs of state power and administration in Union Republics. Section VII deals with justice, arbitration and supervision by the Procuracy. Section VIII deals with the arms, flag, anthem and capital of the U.S.S.R. Section IX is on the procedure for bringing the Constitution into effect and amending it.

Constitutionally, the highest executive organ of the C.P.S.U. is its *Central Committee,* as elected by the *Party Congress.* The Central Committee elected at the XXVIIth Party Congress in March, 1986 consisted of 307 full members and 170 candidate members with a consultative voice; another 83 were elected members of the *Central Revision Commission.* The real power in the Party is vested, however, in the *Politbureau,* the *Secretariat* and the permanent Departments of the Central Committee.

DEFENCE

Defence expenditure in the U.S.S.R. for 1988 is set officially at 20,244,000,000 roubles (or 4·6 per cent of total budget). It has been admitted that this covers only manpower costs, not weapon procurement, etc. Despite the I.N.F. Treaty with the U.S.A. of December 1987, which will eliminate a whole class of land-based nuclear weapons, and progress towards a START accord, there is a continuing reliance on nuclear weapons while improving the levels and capabilities of conventional arms.

The basic military service is two years in the Army

and Air Force and two to three years in the Navy and Border Guards.

The total size of the Soviet regular forces is now estimated to be about 5,130,000, excluding some 1,135,000 Border Guard, internal security, railway and construction troops (mainly uniformed civilians), but including some 1,500,000 command and general support troops not otherwise listed.

Operational ICBMs, i.e. Inter-Continental Ballistic Missiles, now total about 1,400. SLBMs number 983. The number of MRBMs and IRBMs deployed is 553. The operational personnel of the Strategic Rocket Forces totals 298,000 (not including 112,000 assigned from Air and Navy).

The total strength of all Soviet air elements (including helicopters) is some 19,000. Of these, 10,000 can be classified as combat aircraft. The total strength of the Air Forces, excluding the Naval Air Force (68,000) and the bomber forces of the Aviation Armies (100,000), is about 450,000 men. The total personnel of the separate Air Defence Command, now merged with the Air Defence Troops of the Ground Forces, is estimated at 630,000 men.

The total size of the Soviet Army is estimated at 1,991,000. It is thought to be organized in 194 divisions, distributed as follows: 30 divisions in Central and Eastern Europe, 63 in European U.S.S.R., 30 in Southern Theatre, 53 in Far Eastern Theatre, and 18 in the Central Strategic Reserve.

The total strength of the Soviet Navy and Naval Air Force is 451,000 men. In total tonnage, it is the second largest navy in the world, and its main strength lies in the submarine fleet. There are now 277 cruise missile and attack submarines, (118 nuclear-powered, 145 diesel-powered submarines), with a further 14 converting to other roles including SSN, and 84 attack submarines in reserve.

The Soviet Navy now has 269 major surface combat vessels, including five aircraft carriers, 36 cruisers and 61 destroyers and some 180 frigates. The landbased Naval Air Force comprises about 915 combat aircraft, 395 of which are bombers, and some 300 helicopters.

The para-military forces number 570,000, including 230,000 border troops and 340,000 internal security troops. There are also DOSAAF members (claimed active membership, 80 million) who participate in such activities as athletics, flight training, shooting, parachuting and pre-military training.

Minister of Defence, Gen. D. T. Yazov.
Chief of General Staff, Marshal S. F. Akhromeyev.
Chief, Political Administration, Soviet Army and Navy, Army Gen. A. D. Lizichev.

On May 14, 1955, a Treaty of Friendship, Mutual Assistance and Co-operation was signed in Warsaw between the Soviet Union and its European associates (Bulgaria, East Germany, Hungary, Poland, Romania, and Czechoslovakia) (and Albania which left the Pact in Sept. 1968) to serve as a counterpoise to NATO. A united military command was set up in Moscow, *C.-in-C.,* Marshal V. G. Kulikov; *Chief of Staff,* Army General A. I. Gribkov. The Treaty (Warsaw Pact), due to have expired in June 1985, was extended by Protocol in its existing form for a further 20 years, with provision for a further 10 year extension thereafter, at a meeting of Pact leaders in Warsaw on April 26, 1985. The Pact came into force on May 31, 1985.

INDUSTRY AND AGRICULTURE

One of the most remarkable aspects of the Soviet economy has been the transformation of an essentially agricultural country into the second-strongest industrial power in the world. The 1987 output amounted to 162 million tonnes of steel, 114 million tonnes of rolled metal, 760 million tonnes of coal, 624 million tonnes of crude oil, 137 million tonnes of cement, 1,665,000 million kW/h of electricity and 1,300,000 cars.

Agricultural development has been slower, mainly owing to lack of incentives among peasants organized in *kolkhozy* (collective farms). Repeated droughts, such as in 1980-81, were a contributing factor to a shortage of grain. The 1987 harvest was 211·3 million tonnes. Stock breeding has also suffered from the general mismanagement of farming, and from shortages of fodder in recent years. The livestock at Jan. 1, 1988 included 42,000,000 cows, 77,300,000 pigs and 147,000,000 sheep and goats. Besides *kolkhozy* (collective farms) and *sovkhozy* (state farms) a significant contribution to agricultural production is made by the private plots cultivated by individual peasants. The cultivation of these plots is encouraged by the Soviet authorities. The level of productivity remains very low. Forests cover nearly 40 per cent of the whole area of the Union and form a considerable source of wealth.

Trade with U.K.

	1986	1987
Imports from U.K.	£539,368,000	£491,615,000
Exports to U.K.	694,624,000	875,431,000

COMMUNICATIONS

European Russia is relatively well served by railways, Leningrad and Moscow being the two main focal points of rail routes. The centre and south have a good system of north-south and east-west lines, but the eastern part (the Volga lands), traversed as it is by trunk lines between Europe and Asia which enter Siberia via Sverdlovsk, Chelyabinsk, Magnitogorsk and Ufa, lacks north-south routes. In Asia, there are still large areas of the U.S.S.R., notably in the Far North and Siberia, with few or no railways. Railways built since 1928 include the Turkestan-Siberian line (*Turksib*) which has made possible a large-scale industrial exploitation of Kazakhstan, a number of lines within the system of the *Trans-Siberian Railway* (Magnitogorsk-Kartaly-Troitsk, Sverdlovsk-Kurgan, Novosibirsk-Proyektnaya, etc.), which are of great importance for the industrial development in the east, the Petropavlovsk-Karaganda-Balkhash line which has made possible the development of the Karaganda coal basin and of the Balkhash copper mines, and the Moscow-Donbass trunk line. In the northern part of European Russia, the North Pechora Railway has been completed, while in the Far East a recently completed second Trans-Siberian line (the Baikal-Amur Railway) is partially in use; it follows a more northerly alignment than the earlier Trans-Siberian and terminates in the Pacific port of Sovetskaya Gavan.

Sea Ports and Inland Waterways.—The most important ports (Odessa, Nikolayev, Batumi, Taganrog, Rostov, Kerch, Sevastopol and Novorossiisk) lie around the Black Sea and the Sea of Azov. The northern ports (Leningrad, Murmansk and Archangel) are, with the exception of Murmansk, icebound during winter. Several ports have been built along the Arctic Sea route between Murmansk and Vladivostok and are in regular use every summer. The great Far Eastern port of Vladivostok, the Pacific naval base of the U.S.S.R., is kept open by icebreakers all the year round. Inland waterways, both natural and artificial, are of great importance in the country, although some of them are icebound in winter (from 2½ months in the south to 6 months in the north). The great rivers of European Russia flow outwards from the centre, linking all parts of the plain with the chief ports, an immense system of navigable waterways which carried about 632,600,000 tons of freight in 1985. They are supplemented by a system of canals which provide a through traffic between the

White, Baltic, Black and Caspian Seas. The most notable of them are the *White Sea-Baltic Canal*, the *Moscow-Volga Canal* and the *Volga-Don Canal* linking the Baltic and the White Seas in the north to the Caspian, the Black Sea and the Sea of Azov in the south.

CURRENCY.—Rouble of 100 Kopeks.

FLAG.—Red, with five-pointed star above hammer and sickle.

NATIONAL DAY.—November 7 (Commemorating the October Bolshevik Revolution of 1917).

NATIONAL ANTHEM.—Soyuz Nerushimy Respublik Svobodnykh (All the republics of the Soviet Union).

BRITISH EMBASSY
(Naberezhnaya Morisa Toreza 14, Moscow)
[Moscow 2318511]

Ambassador Extraordinary and Plenipotentiary, His Excellency Sir Rodric Braithwaite, K.C.M.G. (1988).
Minister, N. H. Marshall, C.M.G.

There is a Consular Section attached to the Embassy.

I.—R.S.F.S.R.

(The Russian Soviet Federal Socialist Republic)

Chairman of the Presidium of the Supreme Soviet, V. P. Orlov.

Chairman of the Council of Ministers, V. I. Vorotnikov.

The R.S.F.S.R. has no central Communist Party organization of its own.

The R.S.F.S.R., the largest and the most important of the Republics, occupies the major half of the European part of the U.S.S.R. and the major northern portion of its Asiatic part and makes up 77 per cent of the total territory of the U.S.S.R. with 53 per cent of the total population. (About 83 per cent of the population are Russians.) It consists of 16 Autonomous Republics (the Bashkir, Buryat, Checheno-Ingush, Chuvash, Daghestan, Kabardin-Balkar, Kalmyk, Karelian, Komi, Mari, Mordovian, North-Ossetian, Tatar, Tuva, Udmurt and Yakut, A.S.S.R.s); 6 regions (Altai, Khabarovsk, Krasnodar, Krasnoyarsk, Maritime and Stavropol) containing in their turn 5 autonomous provinces; 49 provinces (Amur, Archangel, Astrakhan, Belgorod, Bryansk, Chelyabinsk, Chita, Gorky, Irkutsk, Ivanovo, Kalinin, Kaliningrad, Kaluga, Kamchatka, Kemerovo, Kirov, Kostroma, Kuibyshev, Kurgan, Kursk, Leningrad, Lipetsk, Magadan, Moscow, Murmansk, Novgorod, Novosibirsk, Omsk, Orel, Orenburg, Penza, Perm, Pskov, Rostov, Ryazan, Sakhalin, Saratov, Smolensk, Sverdlovsk, Tambov, Tomsk, Tula, Tyumen, Ulyanovsk, Vladimir, Volgograd, Vologda, Voronezh and Yaroslavl).

There are three principal geographic areas: a low-lying flat Western part stretching eastwards up to the Yenisei and divided in two by the Ural ridge; an eastern part, between the Yenisei and the Pacific, consisting of a number of tablelands and ridges, and a southern mountainous part. Climatically, the R.S.F.S.R. extends from arctic and tundra belts to the sub-tropical in the south. It has a very long coastline, including the longest Arctic coast-line in the world (about 17,000 miles). The most important rivers are the Volga, the Northern Dvina and the Pechora, the Neva, the Don and the Kuban in the European part, and in the Asiatic part, the Ob, the Irtysh, the Yenisei, the Lena and the Amur, and, further north, Khatanga, Olenek, Yana, Indigirka, Kolyma and Anadyr. Lakes are abundant, particularly in the north-west. The huge Baikal Lake in Eastern Siberia is the deepest lake in the world. There are also two large artificial water reservoirs within the Greater Volga canal system, the Moscow and Rybinsk "Seas".

Minerals.—The Republic has some of the richest mineral deposits in the world. Coal is mined in the Kuznetsk area, in the Urals, south of Moscow, in the Donets basin (its Eastern part lies in the R.S.F.S.R.) and in the Pechora area in the North. Oil is produced in the Northern Caucasus, in the area between the Volga and the Ural and in Western Siberia, which also has large deposits of natural gas. Coal and gas deposits in Siberia and the Far East (especially Yakutia) are currently being developed, now that some deposits in the western parts of the U.S.S.R. are approaching exhaustion. The Ural mountains contain a unique assortment of minerals—high-quality iron ore, manganese, copper, aluminium, gold, platinum, precious stones, salt, asbestos, pyrites, coal, oil, etc. Iron ore is also mined near Kursk, Tula, Lipetsk, in several areas in Siberia and in the Kola Peninsula. Non-ferrous metals are found in the Altai, in Eastern Siberia, in the Northern Caucasus, in the Kuznetsk-Basin, in the Far East and in the Far North. Nine-tenths of all U.S.S.R. forests are located in the R.S.F.S.R.

Production and Industry.—The vastness of the territory of the Republic and the great variety in climatic conditions cause great differences in the structure of agriculture from north to south and from west to east. In the far north reindeer breeding, hunting and fishing are predominant. Further south, timber industry is combined with grain growing. In the southern half of the forest zone and in the adjacent forest-steppe zone, the acreage under grain crops is far larger and the structure of agriculture more complex. An extensive programme of land improvement mainly involving this zone aims to double its total agricultural output by 1990. In the eastern part of this zone, between the Volga and the Urals, cericulture is predominant (particularly summer wheat), with cattle breeding next. Beyond the Urals is another important grain-growing and stock-breeding area in the southern part of the Western-Siberian plain. The southern steppe zone is the main wheat granary of the U.S.S.R., containing also large acreages under barley, maize and sunflower. In the extreme south cotton is now cultivated. Vine, tobacco and other southern crops are grown on the Black Sea shore of the Caucasus.

Industrially, the R.S.F.S.R. occupies the first place among the Soviet Republics. Moscow and Leningrad are still the two largest industrial centres in the country, but new industrial areas are being developed in the Urals, the Kuznetsk basin, and more recently in Siberia and the Far East. Most of the oil produced in the U.S.S.R. now comes from the R.S.F.S.R., half annual output comes from Tyumen Oblast in Western Siberia. All industries are represented in the R.S.F.S.R., including iron and steel and engineering.

CAPITAL.—Moscow. Population 8,815,000 (Jan. 1, 1987). Moscow, founded about A.D. 1147 by Yuri Dolgoruki, became first the centre of the rising Moscow principality and in the 15th century, the capital of the whole of Russia (Muscovy). In 1325, it became the seat of the Metropolitan of Russia. In 1703 Peter the Great transferred the capital to the newly built St. Petersburg, but on March 14, 1918, Moscow was again designated as the capital. ΨLeningrad (before the First World War "St. Petersburg" and from 1914–1924 "Petrograd") has a population of 4,948,000 (Jan. 1, 1987).

Other towns with populations exceeding 1,000,000 are:—

Gorky (Nizhny-Novogorod)	1,425,000
Novosibirsk (Novonikolayevsk)	1,423,000
Sverdlovsk (Yekaterinburg)	1,331,000
Kuibyshev (Samara)	1,280,000
Omsk	1,134,000
Chelyabinsk	1,119,000

Ufa	1,092,000
Perm (Molotov)	1,075,000
Kazan	1,068,000
Rostov-on-Don	1,004,000

II.—UKRAINE

First Secretary of the Party Central Committee, V. V. Shcherbitsky.

Chairman of the Presidium of the Supreme Soviet, V. S. Shevchenko.

Chairman of the Council of Ministers, V. A. Masol.

This Republic, second largest in population, lying in the south-western part of the European half of the U.S.S.R., was formed in December, 1917. Ukrainians make up nearly 75 per cent. of the population, with 21 per cent. Russians. It consists of 25 provinces—Cherkassy, Chernigov, Chernovtsy, Crimea, Dnepropetrovsk, Donetsk, Ivano-Frankovsk, Kharkov, Kherson, Khmelnitsky, Kiev, Kirovograd, Lvov, Nikolayev, Odessa, Poltava, Rovno, Sumy, Ternopol, Transcarpathia, Vinnitsa, Volhynia, Voroshilovgrad, Zaporozhye and Zhitomir.

Physical Features.—The larger part of the Ukraine forms a plain with small elevations. The Carpathian mountains lie in the south-western part of the Republic. The climate is moderate, with relatively mild winters (particularly in the south-west) and hot summers. The main rivers are the Dnieper with its tributaries, the Southern Bug and the Northern Donets (a tributary of the Don).

Production and Industry.—The main centre of Soviet coal mining and iron and steel industry is situated in the southern part of the Ukraine. In 1980, the Ukraine provided 36 per cent of the total Soviet steel, 51 per cent of iron ore and 27 per cent of coal. The engineering and chemical industries are also of importance. The central forest-steppe region (mainly on the right bank of the Dnieper) is the greatest sugar-producing area in the U.S.S.R. The Ukraine also leads in grain-growing and stock-raising.

There are large deposits of coal and salt in the Donets Basin, of iron ore in Krivoy Rog and near Kerch in the Crimea, of manganese in Nikopol, and of quicksilver in Nikitovka.

CAPITAL (since 1934), Kiev, one of the oldest cities in the U.S.S.R., founded in the 6th–7th century A.D., was the capital of the Russian State from 865 to 1240. Population (Jan. 1, 1987), 2,558,000. Other towns are:—

Kharkov	1,587,000
Dnepropetrovsk (Yekaterinoslav)	1,182,000
Ψ Odessa	1,141,000
Donetsk (Stalino; Yuzovka, i.e. Hughesovka)	1,090,000

III.—BELORUSSIA
(White Russia)

First Secretary of the Party Central Committee, E. E. Sokolov.

Chairman of the Presidium of the Supreme Soviet, G. S. Tarazevich.

Chairman of the Council of Ministers, M. V. Kovalev.

The Belorussian S.S.R., lying in the western part of the European area of the U.S.S.R., was formed early in 1919. It now consists of six provinces (Brest, Gomel, Grodno, Minsk, Mogilev and Vitebsk). Belorussians make up four-fifths of the population, with Russians and Poles coming next. It is largely a plain with many lakes, swamps and marshy land. Before the revolution of 1917 the area was one of the most backward parts of European Russia. Since then, agriculture has been greatly developed, thanks to draining of swamps. Most of the Republic's industry is also of recent growth. Woodworking is of great importance, but engineering has also been greatly extended with several major plants built in Gomel and Minsk.

The main rivers are the upper reaches of the Dnieper, of the Nieman and of the Western Dvina.

CAPITAL, Minsk. Population 1,566,000 (Jan. 1, 1987).

IV.—UZBEKISTAN

First Secretary of the Party Central Committee, R. N. Nishanov.

Chairman of the Presidium of the Supreme Soviet, P. K. Khabibullaev.

Chairman of the Council of Ministers, G. Kh. Kadyrov.

The Uzbek S.S.R. was formed in 1924 and consists of the Kara-Kalpak A.S.S.R. and of 12 provinces (Andizhan, Bokhara, Dzhizak, Ferghana, Kashkadarya, Khorezm, Namangan, Navoi, Samarkand, Surkhan-darya, Syr-darya and Tashkent). It lies between the high Tienshan Mountains and the Pamir highlands in the east and south-east and sandy lowlands in the west and north-west. The major part of the territory is a plain with huge waterless deserts and several large oases, which form the main centres of population and economic life. The largest is the Ferghana valley, watered by the Syr-Darya. Other oases include Tashkent, Samarkand, Bokhara and Khorezm. The climate is continental and dry. Minerals include gold, natural gas, oil, copper, lead, zinc and coal.

The Uzbeks, a Turkic people, make up 68·7 per cent of the population, the Russians (10·8 per cent), Tatars (4·2 per cent) and Kazakhs (4 per cent) come next.

There are major agricultural and textile machinery plants and several chemical combines. Uzbekistan is the main cotton-growing area of the U.S.S.R. producing more than 60 per cent of all Soviet cotton. Irrigation has always been of decisive importance in this area, and the Soviet Government has done much in this field, including the construction of the Great Ferghana Canal (230 miles).

CAPITAL, Tashkent. Population 2,131,000 (Jan. 1, 1987). Samarkand (population (1987), 388,000) contains the Gur-Emir (Tamerlane's Mausoleum), completed A.D. 1400 by Ulugbek, Tamerlane's astronomer-grandson, and a 15th-century observatory.

V.—KAZAKHSTAN

First Secretary of the Party Central Committee, G. V. Kolbin.

Chairman of the Presidium of Supreme Soviet, Z. K. Kamalidenov.

Chairman of the Council of Ministers, N. A. Nazarbaev.

The Kazakh S.S.R., the second-largest Union-Republic, stretching from the lower reaches of the Volga and the Caspian in the west to the Altai and Tienshan in the east, and bordering on China, was formed in 1920 as an autonomous republic (under the name of the Kazakh A.S.S.R.) within the R.S.F.S.R., and was constituted a Union Republic in 1936. It consists of 17 Provinces: Aktyubinsk, Alma-Ata, Chimkent, Dzhambul, Dzhezkazgan, East-Kazakhstan, Guryev, Karaganda, Kokchetav, Kustanay, Kzyl-Orda, North-Kazakhstan, Pavlodar, Semipalatinsk, Taldy-Kurgan, Tselinograd and Uralsk.

Kazakhstan is a country of arid steppes and semi-deserts, flat in the west, hilly in the east and mountainous in the south-east (Southern Altai and Tienshan). The climate is continental and very dry. The main rivers are the (Upper) Irtysh, the Ural, the Syr-Darya and the Ili. Kazakhstan is very rich in minerals: copper in Kounrad and Dzhezkazgan, lead and zinc in the Altai and Karatau mountains, iron ore in Radryg and Lisakovsk, coal in Ekibastuz and Karaganda and oil and natural gas in the Mangyshlak peninsula. Major centres of metal industry exist in the Altai Mountains, in Chimkent, north of the Balkhash Lake and in Central Kazakhstan. Stock-raising is highly developed, particularly in the central and south-western parts of the Republic. Grain is grown in the north and north-east and cotton in the south and south-east.

The Kazakhs (a Turkic people) are in a minority in the Republic named after them; they constitute only 36 per cent of its population, Russian settlers make up 41 per cent and Ukrainians 6 per cent.

CAPITAL, Alma-Ata (formerly Verny). Population 1,113,000 (Jan. 1, 1987). Karaganda, a major mining centre, has a population of 633,000 (Jan. 1, 1987).

VI.—GEORGIA

First Secretary of the Party Central Committee, Dzh. I. Patiashvili.
Chairman of the Presidium of the Supreme Soviet, P. G. Gilashvili.
Chairman of the Council of Ministers, O. E. Cherke-ziya.

The Georgian, S.S.R., occupying the north-western part of Transcaucasia, lies on the shore of the Black Sea and borders in the south-east on Turkey. It was formed in 1921; in 1922 it joined the Transcaucasian Federation which, in its turn, adhered to the U.S.S.R. in the same year. After the liquidation of the Transcaucasian S.F.S.R. in 1936 Georgia became a Union Republic. It contains two Autonomous Republics (Abkhazia and Adjaria) and the South-Osetian Autonomous Province. Georgia is a country of mountains, with the Greater Caucasus in the north and the Lesser Caucasus in the south. A relatively low-lying land between these two ridges is divided into two parts by the Surz Ridge: Western Georgia with a mild and damp climate and Eastern Georgia with a more continental and dry climate. The Black Sea shore and the Rioni lowland are subtropical in their climatic character. The most important mineral deposits are manganese (Chia-tura), coal (Tkibuli and Tkvarcheli) and oil (Kakhe-tia). Georgia is a leading producer of manganese in the U.S.S.R. There are also many oil refineries. viniculture, tea and tobacco-growing are the three main agricultural industries. The Black Sea har-bours many famous holiday resorts. Georgians make up 68·8 per cent of the population, the remainder being largely composed of Armenians (9 per cent.), Russians, Azerbaidjanis and Osetians.

CAPITAL, Tbilisi (Tiflis), population 1,197,000 (Jan. 1, 1987).

VII.—AZERBAIDJAN

First Secretary of the Party Central Committee, A. Kh. Vezirov.
Chairman of the Presidium of the Supreme Soviet, S. B. Tatliov.
Chairman of the Council of Ministers, G. N. Seidov.

The Azerbaidjan S.S.R. occupies the eastern part of Transcaucasia, on the shore of the Caspian Sea, and borders on Iran. It was formed in 1920. Between 1922 and 1936 it formed part of the Transcaucasian Federation. In 1936 it became a Union Republic. It includes the Nakhichevan Autonomous Republic and the Nagorno-Karabakh Autonomous Province.

The north-eastern part of the Republic is taken up by the south-eastern end of the main Caucasus ridge, its south-western part by the smaller Caucasus hills, and its south-eastern corner by the spurs of the Talysh Ridge. Its central part is a depression irrigated by the Kura and by the lower reaches of its tributary Araks. Sheltered by the mountains from the humid west winds blowing from the Black Sea, Azerbaidjan

has a continental climate. The land requires artificial irrigation. Industry is dominated by oil and natural gas extraction and related chemical and engineering industries centred on Baku and Sumgait. A large power station on the Araks was completed in 1969, in conjunction with Iran. Azerbaidjan is also important as a cotton growing area. The Azerbaidjani (Turkic) make up more than three-quarters of the population of the Republic, Armenians, about 8 per cent, and Russians, 8 per cent.

CAPITAL, Ψ Baku. Population 1,741,000 (Jan. 1, 1987).

VIII.—LITHUANIA

First Secretary of the Party Central Committee, R.-B. I. Songaila.
Chairman of the Presidium of the Supreme Soviet, V. S. Astrauskas.
Chairman of the Council of Ministers, V. V. Sakalaus-kas.

Lithuania, formerly a Province of the Russian Empire, was declared an independent Republic at Vilna in 1918 and was incorporated into the U.S.S.R. in August, 1940. The Republic forms a plain with a large number of lakes and swamps. The forests occupy 19 per cent of the whole area. The main river is the Niemen with its tributaries.

The chief industries are agriculture and forestry, the chief products being rye, oats, wheat, barley, flax, sugar-beet and potatoes.

The Lithuanians make up four-fifths of the popu-lation, Russians and Poles, 7–9 per cent each.

CAPITAL, Vilnius (Vilna). Population 566,000 (Jan. 1, 1987).

IX.—MOLDAVIA

First Secretary of the Party Central Committee, S. K. Grossu.
Chairman of the Presidium of the Supreme Soviet, A. A. Mokanu.
Chairman of the Council of Ministers, I. P. Kalin.

Moldavia, occupying the south-western corner of the U.S.S.R., borders in the west on Romania with the Pruth forming the frontier. In 1918, Romania seized the Russian Province of Bessarabia, but in 1940 the U.S.S.R. forced Romania to give back Bessarabia, the major part of which was merged with the Moldavian A.S.S.R. (formed in 1924) to create the Moldavian S.S.R.

The northern part of the Republic consists of flat steppe lands, now all under plough. Some forests skirt the Dniester. Further south, around Kishinev, there are woody hills and further south again, low-lying steppe lands. The climate is moderate. The main river is the Dniester, navigable along the whole course.

The main industry is agriculture (viniculture, fruit-growing and market-gardening). Industry is insignificant in both parts of Moldavia, but the Republic has the densest population in the U.S.S.R. Moldavians make up 64 per cent of the population, with Ukrainians (14·2 per cent.), and Russians (12·8 per cent.) next.

CAPITAL, Kishinev (Chisinau). Population, 672,000 (Jan. 1, 1987).

X.—LATVIA

First Secretary of the Party Central Committee, B. K. Pugo.
Chairman of the Presidium of the Supreme Soviet, Ya. Ya. Vagris.
Chairman of the Council of Ministers, Yu. Ya. Ruben.

The Latvian S.S.R., lying on the shores of the

Baltic and of the Gulf of Riga, was formerly a Baltic Province of the Russian Empire. It was proclaimed an independent state in 1918 and was forcibly incorporated into the U.S.S.R. in August 1940.

The surface of the country is generally flat, interspersed by occasional chains of hills. The climate is moderately continental. The main rivers are the lower reaches of the Western Dvina and its tributaries. Forests occupy 20 per cent of the total territory. The Latvians make up 53·7 per cent of the Republic's population, Russians 32·8 per cent.

Latvian industry was always highly developed, with shipbuilding, engineering, chemical industry, textile industry, wood-working and dairying being the chief occupations. Both Riga and Liepaja (Libava, Libau) are important sea-ports.

CAPITAL, Ψ Riga. Population, 900,000 (Jan. 1, 1987).

XI.—KIRGHIZIA

First Secretary of the Party Central Committee, A. M. Masaliev.
Chairman of the Presidium of the Supreme Soviet, T. Akmatov.
Chairman of the Council of Ministers, A. Dzhumagulov.

The Kirghiz S.S.R. occupies the north-eastern part of Soviet Central Asia and borders in the south-east on China. In 1924, a Kara-Kirghiz Autonomous Province was formed within the R.S.F.S.R. In 1926 it became a Kirghiz Autonomous Republic, and in 1936 a Union Republic. It contains three provinces, Issyk-Kul, Naryn and Osh. The Kirghiz Republic is a mountainous country, the major part being covered by the ridge of the Central Tienshan, while mountains of the Pamir-Altai system occupy its southern part. There are a number of spacious mountain valleys, the Alai, Susamyr, the Issyk-Kul lake and others. The majority of the population is concentrated in plains, lying at the foot of mountains—Chu, Talass, part of the Ferghana Valley where agriculture prospers. Crops include sugar beet and cotton, and sheep are important in the mountains. Industry is being developed and some mining is done. The Kirghiz constitute 47·9 per cent of the population, the Russians 25·9 per cent. The Uzbeks (in Eastern Ferghana) amount to 12·1 per cent.

CAPITAL, Frunze (formerly Pishpek). Population, 641,000 (Jan. 1, 1987).

XII.—TADJIKSTAN

First Secretary of the Party Central Committee, K. Makhkamov.
Chairman of the Presidium of the Supreme Soviet, G. Pallaev.
Chairman of the Council of Ministers, I. Khaeev.

The Tadjik S.S.R. lies in the extreme south-east of Soviet Central Asia and borders in the south on Afghanistan and in the east on China. It was originally formed in 1924 as an Autonomous Republic within the Uzbek S.S.R. and became a Union Republic in 1929. It includes the Gorno-Badakhshan Autonomous Province and the Kulyab and Leninabad Provinces.

The country is mountainous: in the east lie the Pamir highlands with the highest point in the U.S.S.R., Pik Kommunizma (24,590 feet), in the centre the high ridges of the Pamir-Altai system. Plains are formed by wide stretches of the Syr-Darya valley in the north and of the Amu-Darya in the south.

Like the other Central-Asiatic Republics, Tadjikistan is a cotton-growing country. Its climatic conditions favour the cultivation of Egyptian cotton. Irrigation is of great importance. Of the population 58·8 per cent are Tadjiks (linguistically and culturally akin to the Persians), 23 per cent Uzbeks, the rest Russians and others.

CAPITAL, Dushanbe (formerly Stalinabad; Dyushambe). Population, 591,000 (Jan. 1, 1987).

XIII.—ARMENIA

First Secretary of the Party Central Committee, S. G. Arutyunyan.
Chairman of the Presidium of the Supreme Soviet, G. M. Voskanyan.
Chairman of the Council of Ministers, F. T. Sarkisyan.

The Armenian S.S.R. occupies the south-western part of Transcaucasia: it was formed in 1920. In 1922 it joined the Transcaucasian Federation, and on its liquidation in 1936 became a Union Republic. In the south it borders on Turkey. It is a mountainous country consisting of several vast table lands surrounded by ridges. The population and the economic life are concentrated in the low-lying part of Armenia, the Aras valley and the Erevan hollow; the climate is continental, dry and cold, but the Araks valley has a long, hot and dry summer. Irrigation is essential for agriculture. Industrial and fruit crops are grown in the low-lying districts, grain in the hills. Armenia is traditionally noted for her wine. There are large copper ore and molybdenum deposits and other minerals. The Armenian Church centred in Etchmiadzin is the oldest established Christian Church, Christianity having been recognized as the State religion in A.D. 300.

Nearly 90 per cent of the population is Armenian.

CAPITAL, Erevan. Population, 1,185,000 (Jan. 1, 1987).

XIV.—TURKMENISTAN

First Secretary of the Party Committee, S. A. Niyazov.
Chairman of the Presidium of the Supreme Soviet, B. Yazkuliev.
Chairman of the Council of Ministers, A. Khodzhamuradov.

Turkmenia occupies the extreme south of Soviet Central Asia, between the Caspian and the Amu-Darya, and borders in the south on Iran and Afghanistan. It was formed in 1924 and contains five Provinces: Ashkhabad, Chardjou, Krasnovodsk, Mary and Tashauz. The country is a low-lying plain, fringed by hills in the south. Ninety per cent of the plain is taken up by the arid Kara-Kum desert. Of all Central-Asiatic Republics, Turkmenia is the lowest and driest. The cultivation of cotton, stock-raising and mineral extraction are the principal industries. The republic produces about 16 per cent of the Soviet Union's natural gas, as well as astrakhan furs and carpets. Most of the land under plough is artificially irrigated. The oil and silk industries are of old standing. There are also some fisheries in the Caspian.

Turkmens make up 68·4 per cent of the population, Russians 12·6 per cent, and Uzbeks 8·5 per cent.

CAPITAL, Ashkhabad (formerly Askhabad, Poltoratsk). Population, 386,000 (Jan. 1, 1987).

XV.—ESTONIA

First Secretary of the Party Central Committee, V. Vaelaes.
Chairman of the Presidium of the Supreme Soviet, A. F. Ryuitel.
Chairman of the Council of Ministers, B. E. Saul.

Estonia, formerly a Baltic province of the Russian Empire, was proclaimed an independent Republic in 1918. In 1940, it was forcibly incorporated into the U.S.S.R. It lies on the shores of the Baltic and of the Finnish Gulf in the north and of the Gulf of Riga in the south-west. Some 800 islands, among them Dagö and Ösel, form part of Estonian territory.

The country forms a low-lying plain with many lakes, among them the Chud (or Pskov) Lake, on the border with the R.S.F.S.R. Forests take up about one-fifth of the territory. Agriculture and dairy-farming are the chief industries, rye, oats, barley, flax and potatoes being the chief crops, and butter, bacon and eggs the chief products of dairy farming. There are important manufactures, including textiles, engineering, shipbuilding, woodworking, etc.

The population consists of Estonians (64·7 per cent) and Russians (27·9 per cent).

CAPITAL, Ψ Tallinn (formerly Reval). Population, 494,000 (Jan. 1, 1987).

UNITED ARAB EMIRATES
(Al Imarat Al-Arabiya Al-Muttahida)

President, Shaikh Zaid bin Sultan al Nahayyan (*Abu Dhabi*).

Vice-President and Prime Minister, Shaikh Rashid bin Said al Maktum.

Deputy Prime Ministers, Shaikh Maktum bin Rashid al Maktum; Shaikh Hamdan bin Muhammad al Nahayyan.

Interior, Shaikh Mubarak bin Muhammad al Nahayyan.

Finance and Industry, Shaikh Hamdan bin Rashid al Maktum.

Defence, Shaikh Muhammad bin Rashid al Maktum.

Minister of State for Foreign Affairs, Sayyid Rashid Abdullah al Nu'aimi.

Petroleum and Mineral Resources, Dr. Mana Said al Otaiba.

Economy and Commerce, Sayyid Saif al Jarwan.

Information and Culture, Shaikh Ahmad bin Hamid bin Butti.

Communications, Sayyid Muhammad Said al Mulla.

Public Works and Housing, Sayyid Muhammad Khalifa al Kindi.

Education, Sayyid Faraj Fadel al Mazroui.

Planning, (vacant).

Justice, Sayyid Abdullah Humaid al Mazroni.

Islamic Affairs and Awqaf, Shaikh Mohammad bin Hassan al Khazraji.

Agriculture and Fisheries, Sayyid Said al Raqabani.

Water and Electricity, Sayyid Humaid Nasser al Owais.

Labour and Social Affairs, Sayyid Khalfan al Roumi.

Health, Sayyid Hamad Abdul Rahman al Madfa.

EMBASSY IN LONDON
30 Prince's Gate, SW7 1PT
[01-581 1281]

Ambassador Extraordinary and Plenipotentiary, new appointment awaited.

Chargé d'Affaires, Ali Mubarak Ahmed Al Mansoori.

Area and Population. The approximate area of the U.A.E. is 32,278 sq. miles (83,600 sq. km.), and the population in 1985 was estimated at about 1·6 million.

The United Arab Emirates (formerly the Trucial States) is composed of seven Emirates (Abu Dhabi, Ajman, Dubai, Fujeirah, Ras al Khaimah, Sharjah and Umm al Qaiwain) which came together as an independent state on December 2, 1971, when they ended their individual special treaty relationships with the British Government (Ras al Khaimah joined the other six on February 10, 1972).

The British Government, by virtue of a treaty made in 1892, had been responsible for the external affairs of the states through the British Political Resident in the Persian Gulf and the British Political Agents in each state, but on independence the Union Government assumed full responsibility for all internal and external affairs apart from some internal

matters that remained the prerogative of the individual Emirates. Six of the Emirates lie on the shore of the Gulf between the Musandam peninsula in the East and the Qatar peninsula in the West while the seventh, Fujeirah, lies on the gulf of Oman.

Security in the area is maintained by the U.A.E. Armed Forces. The Ministry of Defence is located in Dubai with a General Headquarters in Abu Dhabi. Most of the separate police forces have also been merged.

Revenue is chiefly derived from oil, re-exports and customs dues on imports. A substantial amount is spent on overseas aid, where commitments in 1980 totalled £154·8 million, doubling those of 1979.

Trade with U.K.

	1986	1987
Imports from U.K.	£581,762,000	£478,997,000
Exports to U.K.	74,012,000	94,989,000

CURRENCY.—U.A.E. Dirham of 100 Fils.

FLAG.—Horizontal stripes of green over white over black with vertical red stripe in the hoist.

NATIONAL DAY.—December 2.

Abu Dhabi

Abu Dhabi is the largest Emirate of the U.A.E. in area, stretching from Khor al Odaid in the west to the borders with Dubai in the Jebel Ali area. It includes six villages in the Buraimi oasis, the other three being part of the Sultanate of Oman, and a number of settlements in the Liwa Oasis system. Following negotiations with Saudi Arabia, some adjustment of the border has now been made in the Khor al Odaid region, but the agreement has not yet been ratified. The population of the Emirate is now about 670,000

The Abu Dhabi Government controls oil, gas and petrochemical operations in the Emirate through the Abu Dhabi National Oil Company (ADNOC) which has majority shareholdings in the several oil operating and gas treatment companies. ADNOC also has majority shareholdings in oil industry-related companies covering drilling, refining, distribution, chemical manufacture and investment. Offshore production began in 1962, the most important fields being Umm Shaif and Lower Zakum, near Das Island, site of a large associated gas liquefaction plant. The Upper Zakum field came on stream in late 1982, and four other offshore fields are being developed, one near Abu Dhabi city and three near Delma. Production of oil onshore began in 1963 from the Murban field. A large onshore associated gas liquefaction project based at Ruwais started production in 1981. Other large natural gas finds in recent years will consolidate Abu Dhabi's position as a holder of some of the largest reserves of natural gas in the world. Abu Dhabi's crude oil production in 1987 was approximately 1 million barrels per day.

With its oil wealth the Emirate has seen a decade of growth (which is currently slowing down), not only at Abu Dhabi, now a modern city of about 450,000 people, but also at Al Ain in the Buraimi Oasis and at the new petro-chemical city at Ruwais. An international airport opened in 1982 at Abu Dhabi and another is under construction at Al Ain. There are airfields at Das Island and Jebel Dhanna. The port and harbour on Abu Dhabi island are now completed and there are port facilities at Ruwais.

Ajman and Umm al Qaiwain

Ajman and Umm al Qaiwain are the smallest Emirates, having populations of approx. 64,000 and 29,000 respectively. Both lie on the Gulf coast although Ajman has two inland enclaves at Manama and Masfut. Exploration work continues in both

Emirates for oil and gas but so far only Umm Al Qaiwain has experienced any success, with the offshore discovery of natural gas, but the field has yet to be commercially developed. The discovery of onshore gas in nearby Sharjah has increased hopes of similar discoveries in both Ajman and Umm Al Qaiwain.

Dubai

Dubai is the second largest Emirate both in size and in population, which is now about 419,000. The town of Dubai is the main port for the import of goods into the U.A.E. and has a wide re-export trade to the other Gulf States. Dubai's prosperity was established by this trade long before the discovery of oil. Oil was discovered in 1966 and production began in September 1969. The producer in Dubai's offshore oilfields is Dubai Petroleum Company, operated by CONOCO. Production is in excess of 350,000 b.p.d. In 1982 an ARCO-Britoil joint venture discovered an extensive gas and condensate field onshore. A small amount of condensate is produced from the onshore Margam field.

Oil income has been used to finance Dubai's infrastructure and major construction projects include an international airport, a dry dock complex and an international trade and exhibition centre. There is also a 66 berth port at Jebel Ali, forming the heart of an industrial complex which includes an aluminium smelter with an associated de-salination plant and a gas processing plant. The port and its immediate area is a free trade zone which is expected to attract more industry.

Fujeirah

Fujeirah, with a population of 40,000, is the most remote of the seven Emirates lying on the Gulf of Oman coast, and only connected by a metal road to the rest of the country since the end of 1975. Largely agricultural, its population is spread between the slopes of the inland Hajar mountain range and the town of Fujeirah itself, together with a number of smaller settlements on the comparatively fertile plain on the coast. Although exploration work continues, there have been no hydrocarbon discoveries in the Emirate. However, there are some chrome and other mineral deposits. Fujeirah has a new general cargo port.

Ras al Khaimah

Ras al Khaimah has a population of 116,000 of whom more than half live in the town. An ancient sea-port, near to which archaeological remains have been found, Ras al Khaimah is developing as the most agricultural of the Emirates, producing vegetables, dates, fruit and tobacco. In 1982 Ras al Khaimah announced the discovery of oil and gas offshore and this field currently produces approximately 5,000 b.p.d. An industrial area has been developed to the north of the Emirate, which includes 2 cement works. Ras al-Khaimah has an international airport and has also expanded its port. A new international airport is nearing completion. A new trade centre has just been completed and it is hoped that more industry will be attracted to the emirate.

Sharjah

Sharjah, with a present population of approx. 269,000, has declined from its position 50 years ago as principal town in the area. It became the third oil producing Emirate in the summer of 1974, following the discovery of oil offshore. The field declined over the years and by 1982 was yielding less than 6,000 b.p.d. However, new oil and gas discoveries were made in 1982 in the northern emirates and production now stands at about 50,000 b.p.d. Sharjah is well connected by metalled roads to all the other Northern Emirates. It experienced a construction boom in the mid-1970's including an ambitious layout of roads and flyovers within the town. A new container port has been constructed on the Gulf of Oman at Khor Fakkan. The international airport was officially opened in 1979.

BRITISH EMBASSY
P.O. Box 248, Abu Dhabi
[Dubai 326600]

Ambassador Extraordinary and Plenipotentiary, His Excellency Michael Logan Tait, C.M.G., L.V.O. (1986).
British Council Representative, Dr. P. Clark, P.O. Box 248, Abu Dhabi.

(Dubai)
Counsellor and Consul General, J. C. Kay.
British Council Representative, A. Swales, P.O. Box 1636, Dubai.

UNITED STATES OF AMERICA

PHYSIOGRAPHY

The conterminous States of the Republic occupy nearly all that portion of the North American Continent between the Atlantic and Pacific Oceans, in latitude 25° 07'–49° 23' North and longitude 66° 57'–124° 44' West, its northern boundary being Canada and the southern boundary Mexico. The separate State of Alaska reaches a latitude of 71' 23° N., at Point Barrow (2,502 miles from the U.S. geographic centre).

The general coastline of the 50 States has a length of about 2,069 miles on the Atlantic, 7,623 miles on the Pacific, 1,060 miles on the Arctic, and 1,631 miles on the Gulf of Mexico.

The principal river is the mighty Mississippi-Missouri-Red, traversing the whole country from north to south, and having a course of 3,710 miles to its mouth in the Gulf of Mexico, with many large affluents, the chief of which are the Yellowstone, Platte, Arkansas, and Ohio, Rivers. The rivers

flowing into the Atlantic and Pacific Oceans are comparatively small; among the former may be noticed the Hudson, Delaware, Susquehanna, Potomac, James, Roanoke and Savannah; of the latter, the Columbia-Snake, Sacramento, and Colorado. The Nueces, Brazos, Trinity, Pearl, Mobile-Tombigbee-Alabama, Apalachicola-Chattahoochee, Suwannee and Colorado of Texas fall into the Gulf of Mexico, also the Rio Grande, a long river partly forming the boundary with Mexico. The areas of the water-basins have been estimated as follows:—Rivers flowing to the Pacific, 647,300 square miles; to the Atlantic, 488,877; and to the Gulf of Mexico, 1,683,325 square miles, of which 1,234,600 are drained by the Mississippi-Missouri-Red. The chain of the Rocky Mountains separates the western portion of the country from the remainder, communications being carried on over certain elevated passes, several of which are now traversed by railroads and major highways; west of these, bordering the Pacific coast, the Cascade Mountains and Sierra Nevada form the outer edge of a high tableland, consisting in part of stony and sandy desert and partly of grazing land and forested mountains, and including the Great Salt Lake, which extends to the Rocky Mountains. In the Eastern States (which form the more settled and most thickly inhabited portion of the country) large forests of valuable timber, as beech, birch, maple, oak, pine, spruce, elm, ash, walnut; and in the south, live oak, water-oak, magnolia, palmetto, pine, tulip-tree, cypress, etc., still exist, the remnants of the forests which formerly extended over all the Atlantic slope, but into which great inroads have been made by the advance of civilization. The mineral kingdom produces ore of iron, copper, lead, zinc, and aluminium, the non-metallic minerals include large quantities of coal, petroleum, stone, phosphate rock, and salt. The highest point is Mount McKinley (Alaska), 20,320 ft. above sea level and the lowest point of dry land is in Death Valley (Inyo, California), 282 ft. below sea-level.

AREA AND POPULATION

	Area, 1980 (sq. miles)		Population	
	Total	Land	Census 1970	Census 1980
The United States (a)	3,618,770	3,539,289	203,302,031*	226,545,805
Puerto Rico..........................	3,515	3,459	2,712,033	3,196,520
Outlying areas under U.S. jurisdiction	1,176	1,176	314,657*	368,856
Territories	459	459	179,519**	235,927
Guam	209	209	84,996	105,979
Virgin Islands of U.S.	132	132	62,468	96,569
American Samoa	77	77	27,159	32,297
Midway Islands	2	2	2,220	453
Wake Island	3	3	1,647	302
Canton Island and Enderbury Island........................	27	27	—	—
Johnston Atoll (b)	0·5	0·5	1,007	327
Other (c)	9	9	—	—
Pacific Islands Trust Territory (excluding N. Mariana Is.)........	533	533	81,300	116,149
N. Mariana Islands	184	184	9,640	16,780
Population abroad (d)			1,737,836†	995,546
Armed Forces.....................			1,057,776	515,408
Total	3,543,924	3,623,461	208,066,557	231,106,727

(a) The 50 States and the Federal District of Columbia.
(b) Formerly listed as Johnston and Sand Island. Sand Island uninhabited at time of enumeration.
(c) Navassa, Baker, Howland and Jarvis Islands, Kingman Reef, and Palmyra Atoll.
(d) Excludes U.S. citizens temporarily abroad on private business.
* Includes population of Swan Islands (22) and Panama Canal Zone (44,198). Jurisdiction over the Swan Islands was transferrred to Honduras in 1972. Due to the 1978 Treaty, the Census is no longer conducted in the Canal Zone.
** Includes population of Swan Islands (22).
† Includes U.S. citizens abroad for long periods who were not connected with the U.S. government (236,336) and crews of U.S. merchant vessels (15,910).

Resident Population by Race 1980
(in thousands)

White	188,372	Filipino	774·7	Vietnamese	261·7	Puerto Rican ..	2,014
Black..........	26,495	Japanese	701	Spanish origin**	14,609	Other Spanish .	3,051
American Indian*.......	1,420·4	Asian Indian	361·5	Cuban	803	All other races...	6,999·2
		Korean	354·6	Mexican	8,740	Total	226,546
Chinese	806						

*Includes Eskimo and Aleut.
** Persons of Spanish origin may be of any race.

1 New York
2 Philadelphia
3 Baltimore
4 Nashville
5 Memphis
6 Jacksonville
7 New Orleans
8 Cleveland
9 Columbus
10 Indianapolis
11 Detroit
12 Milwaukee
13 Chicago

Immigrants, by Place of Birth, 1951–87
(1951–76, year ends June 30: from 1977, year ends Sept. 30)

Place of Birth	1951–60	1961–70	1971–80	1987
Europe	1,492,200	1,238,600	801,300	61,174
Asia	159,000	445,300	1,633,800	257,684
North America	769,200	1,351,100	1,645,000	216,550
Canada	274,900	286,700	114,800	11,876
Mexico	319,300	443,300	637,200	72,351
West Indies	122,900	519,600	759,800	102,899
Central America	44,600	97,700	132,400	29,296
South America	72,200	228,300	284,400	44,385
Africa	14,800	39,300	91,500	17,724
Australia	4,600	9,800	14,300	1,253
New Zealand	1,700	3,700	5,300	591
Other countries	1,800	5,500	17,700	2,155
TOTAL	3,277,200	3,321,700	4,493,300	601,516

From 1820 to 1986, 53,122,000 immigrants were admitted to the United States.

REGISTERED BIRTHS AND DEATHS

Cal-endar Year	Live Births		Deaths	
	Number	Rate per 1,000	Number	Rate per 1,000
1982	3,680,537	15·9	1,974,797	8·5
1983	3,638,933	15·5	2,019,201	8·6
1984	3,669,141	15·5	2,039,369	8·6
1985	3,760,561	15·8	2,086,440	8·7
1986*	3,731,000	15·5	2,099,000	8·7
1987*	3,829,000	15·7	2,127,000	8·7

For 1981–84 births based on 100 per cent. sample in most states and 50 per cent. sample in remaining states. For 1985 sample base was 100 per cent.

Note.—Figures tabulated are for the United States. Deaths exclude foetal deaths. Rates are based on the population as estimated on July 1.
* Provisional.

MARRIAGE AND DIVORCE

Laws of marriage and of divorce are within the exclusive jurisdiction of each State. Each State legislature enacts its own laws prescribing rules and qualifications pertaining to marriage and its dissolution.

Year	Marriages	Per 1,000 Pop.§	Estimated Divorces	Per 1,000 Pop.§
1982	2,456,278	10·6	1,170,000	5·0
1983	2,445,604	10·5	1,158,000	4·9
1984	2,477,192	10·5	1,169,000	5·0
1985	2,412,625	10·1	1,190,000	5·0
1986*	2,400,000	10·0	1,159,000	4·8
1987*	2,421,000	9·9	1,157,000	4·8

§ Population as estimated on July 1.
* Provisional.

Largest Cities 1986 (estimated populations)

ᴪ New York, N.Y.	7,262,700
ᴪ Los Angeles, California	3,259,340
ᴪ Chicago, Illinois	3,009,530
ᴪ Houston, Texas	1,728,910
ᴪ Philadelphia, Pennsylvania	1,642,900
ᴪ Detroit, Michigan	1,086,220
ᴪ San Diego, California	1,015,190
Dallas, Texas	1,003,520
San Antonio, Texas	914,350
Phoenix, Arizona	894,070
ᴪ Baltimore, Maryland	752,800
ᴪ San Francisco, California	749,000
ᴪ Indianapolis, Indiana	719,820
San Jose, California	712,080
Memphis, Tennessee	652,640
Washington, D.C.	626,000
Jacksonville, Florida	609,860
ᴪ Milwaukee, Wisconsin	605,090
ᴪ Boston, Massachusetts	573,600
Columbus, Ohio	566,030
ᴪ New Orleans, Louisiana	554,500
ᴪ Cleveland, Ohio	535,830
Denver, Colorado	505,000
El Paso, Texas	491,800
ᴪ Seattle, Washington	486,200

ᴪ Seaport

THE UNITED STATES

State (with date and *order* of admission)	Land Area Sq. M.	Population, (1986 estimates)	Capital	Governor (term of office in years, and expiry year)
Alabama (Ala.) (1819) (*22*)	50,708	4,053,000	Montgomery..	Harold G. Hunt (*R*) ...... (4—1991)
Alaska (1959) (*49*)	570,833	534,000	Juneau........	Steven Cowper (*D*) ...... (4—1990)
Arizona (Ariz.) (1912) (*48*)	113,417	3,317,000	Phoenix	Rose Mofford* (*D*) .... (4—1991)
Arkansas (Ark.) (1836) (*25*)	51,945	2,372,000	Little Rock ...	Bill Clinton (*D*) .... (4—1991)
California (Calif.) (1850) (*31*)	156,361	26,981,000	Sacramento..	George Deukmejian (*R*) .. (4—1991)
Colorado (Colo.) (1876) (*38*)	103,766	3,267,000	Denver.......	Roy Romer (*D*) .... (4—1991)
Connecticut (Conn.)§(1788) (*5*) .	4,862	3,189,000	Hartford	William O'Neill (*D*)....... (4—1991)
Delaware (Del.) § (1787) (*1*)....	1,982	633,000	Dover	Michael N. Castle (*R*) .... (4—1989)
Florida (Fla.) (1845) (*27*)	54,136	11,675,000	Tallahassee ..	Bob Martinez (*R*) .... (4—1991)
Georgia (Ga.) § (1788) (*4*).......	58,073	5,975,000	Atlanta	Joe F. Harris (*D*) .... (4—1991)
Hawaii (1959) (*50*).............	6,425	1,062,000	Honolulu	John D. Waihee III (*D*)... (4—1990)
Idaho (1890) (*43*)...............	82,677	1,003,000	Boise........	Cecil D. Andrus (*D*) ..... (4—1991)
Illinois (Ill.) (1818) (*21*)	55,748	11,553,000	Springfield ...	James R. Thompson (*R*) .. (4—1991)
Indiana (Ind.) (1816) (*19*)	36,097	5,504,000	Indianapolis ..	Robert D. Orr (*R*)........ (4—1989)
Iowa (1846) (*29*)................	55,941	2,851,000	Des Moines ...	Terry Branstad (*R*) ...... (4—1991)
Kansas (Kan.) (1861) (*34*)	81,787	2,461,000	Topeka	Mike Hayden (*R*) .... (4—1991)
Kentucky (Ky.) (1792) (*15*)	39,650	3,728,000	Frankfort	Wallace G. Wilkinson (*D*) (4—1992)
Louisiana (La.) (1812) (*18*)	44,930	4,501,000	Baton Rouge..	Buddy Roemer (*D*) ...... (4—1992)
Maine (Me.) (1820) (*23*)	30,920	1,174,000	Augusta	John R. McKernan, Jr. (*R*) (4—1991)
Maryland (Md.)§ (1788) (*7*)	9,891	4,463,000	Annapolis	William D. Schaefer (*D*) .. (4—1991)
Massachusetts (Mass.)§(1788)(*6*)	7,826	5,832,000	Boston	Michael S. Dukakis (*D*) .. (4—1991)
Michigan (Mich.) (1837) (*26*) ...	56,817	9,145,000	Lansing	James J. Blanchard (*D*) .. (4—1991)
Minnesota (Minn.) (1858) (*32*) .	79,289	4,214,000	St. Paul	Rudy Perpich (*DFL*) ..... (4—1991)
Mississippi (Miss.) (1817) (*20*)..	47,296	2,625,000	Jackson	Ray Mabus (*D*) .... (4—1992)
Missouri (Mo.) (1821) (*24*)	68,995	5,066,000	Jefferson City.	John Ashcroft (*R*) .... (4—1989)
Montana (Mont.) (1889) (*41*) ...	145,587	819,000	Helena	Ted Schwinden (*D*) ...... (4—1989)
Nebraska (Neb.) (1867) (*37*).....	76,483	1,598,000	Lincoln	Kay A. Orr (*R*) .... (4—1991)
Nevada (Nev.) (1864) (*36*)	109,889	963,000	Carson City ..	Richard H. Bryan (*D*) .... (4—1991)
New Hampshire (N.H.)§(1788)(*9*)	9,027	1,027,000	Concord	John H. Sununu (*R*) ..... (2—1989)
New Jersey (N.J.)§ (1787) (*3*) ...	7,521	7,620,000	Trenton	Thomas H. Kean (*R*) ..... (4—1990)
New Mexico (N.M.) (1912) (*47*) .	121,412	1,479,000	Santa Fé	Garry E. Carruthers (*R*) . (4—1991)
New York (N.Y.)§ (1788) (*11*) ...	47,831	17,772,000	Albany	Mario M. Cuomo (*D*) ..... (4—1991)
North Carolina (N.C.)§(1789)(*12*)	48,798	6,331,000	Raleigh	James G. Martin (*R*) ..... (4—1989)
North Dakota (N.D.) (1889) (*39*)	69,273	679,000	Bismarck	George A. Sinner (*D*) .... (4—1989)
Ohio (1803) (*17*)................	40,975	10,752,000	Columbus	Richard F. Celeste (*D*) ... (4—1991)
Oklahoma (Okla.) (1907) (*46*) ...	68,782	3,305,000	Oklahoma City	Henry Bellmon (*R*) ...... (4—1991)
Oregon (Ore.) (1859) (*33*).......	96,184	2,698,000	Salem	Neil Goldschmidt (*D*) .... (4—1991)
Pennsylvania (Pa.)§ (1787) (*2*) ..	44,966	11,889,000	Harrisburg ...	Robert P. Casey (*D*)...... (4—1991)
Rhode Island (R.I.)§ (1790) (*13*) .	1,049	975,000	Providence ...	Edward D. Di Prete (*R*) .. (2—1989)
South Carolina (S.C.)§ (1788) (*8*)	37,000	3,378,000	Columbia	Carroll A. Campbell, Jr.(*R*) (4—1991)
South Dakota (S.D.) (1889) (*40*) .	75,955	708,000	Pierre........	George S. Mickelson (*R*).. (4—1991)
Tennessee (Tenn.) (1796) (*16*)..	41,155	4,803,000	Nashville	Ned R. McWherter (*D*) ... (4—1991)
Texas (1845) (*28*)..............	262,134	16,682,000	Austin	William P. Clements, Jr. (*R*)........... (4—1991)
Utah (1896) (*45*)...............	82,073	1,665,000	Salt Lake City	Norman H. Bangerter (*R*) (4—1989)
Vermont (Vt.) (1791) (*14*)	9,267	541,000	Montpelier ...	Madeleine M. Kunin (*D*) . (2—1989)
Virginia (Va.)§ (1788) (*10*)	39,780	5,787,000	Richmond	Gerald L. Baliles (*D*) ..... (4—1990)
Washington (Wash.) (1889) (*42*)	66,570	4,463,000	Olympia	Booth Gardner (*D*) ...... (4—1989)
West Virginia (W.Va.) (1863)(*35*)	24,070	1,919,000	Charleston ...	Arch A. Moore, Jr.(*R*) ... (4—1989)
Wisconsin (Wis.) (1848) (*30*) ...	54,464	4,785,000	Madison......	Tommy Thompson (*R*) ... (4—1991)
Wyoming (Wyo.) (1890) (*44*)	97,023	507,000	Cheyenne	Michael Sullivan (*D*) .... (4—1991)
Dist. of Columbia (D.C.) (1791)..	67	626,000	..	†
OUTLYING TERRITORIES AND POSSESSIONS				
American Samoa	76	34,500	Pago Pago	A. P. Lutali (*D*) .... (4—1989)
Guam	209	120,977	Agaña	Joseph Ada (*R*).......... (4—1991)
Marshall Is.	70	35,000	Majuro.......	..
Fed. States of Micronesia	271	73,160	Kolonia	..
North Mariana Is.	184	22,000	Saipan	Pedro P. Tenorio (*R*) ..... (4—1990)
Palau.......................	191	14,000	Koror	..
Puerto Rico	3,421	3,451,000	San Juan	R. Hernandez-Colon (*PDP*)............... (4—1989)
Virgin Is.	132	108,000	Charlotte Amalie	Alexander Farrelly (*D*) .. (4—1991)

D.—Democratic Party. *DFL.*—Democrat-Farmer-Labor. *R.*—Republican Party. *I.*—Independent.
PDP.—Popular Democratic party. § The 13 Original States.
† The capital territory is governed by Congress through a Commissioner and City Council.
* Succeeded to governor's office April 1988, after her predecessor's impeachment.

THE PRESIDENTS OF THE UNITED STATES OF AMERICA

Name (*with Native State*)	Party	Born	Inaug.	Died	Age
George Washington, *Va.*	Fed.	1732, Feb. 22	1789	1799, Dec. 14	67
John Adams, *Mass.*	„	1735, Oct. 30	1797	1826, July 4	90
Thomas Jefferson, *Va.*	Rep.	1743, April 13	1801	1826, July 4	83
James Madison, *Va.*	„	1751, Mar. 16	1809	1836, June 28	85
James Monroe, *Va.*	„	1758, April 28	1817	1831, July 4	73
John Quincy Adams, *Mass.*	„	1767, July 11	1825	1848, Feb 23	80
Andrew Jackson, *S.C.*	Dem.	1767, Mar. 15	1829	1845, June, 8	78
Martin Van Buren, *N.Y.*	„	1782, Dec. 5	1837	1862, July 24	79
William Henry Harrison†, *Va.*	Whig.	1773, Feb. 9	1841	1841, April 4	68
John Tyler (*a*), *Va.*	„	1790, Mar. 29	1841	1862, Jan. 17	71
James Knox Polk, *N.C.*	Dem.	1795, Nov. 2	1845	1849, June 15	53
Zachary Taylor† *Va.*	Whig.	1784, Nov. 24	1849	1850, July 9	65
Millard Fillmore (*a*), *N.Y.*	„	1800, Jan. 7	1850	1874, Mar. 8	74
Franklin Pierce, *N.H.*	Dem.	1804, Nov. 23	1853	1869, Oct. 8	64
James Buchanan, *Pa.*	„	1791, April 23	1857	1868, June 1	77
Abraham Lincoln†§, *Ky.*	Rep.	1809, Feb. 12	1861	1865, April 15	56
Andrew Johnson (*a*), *N.C.*	„	1808, Dec. 29	1865	1875, July 31	66
Ulysses Simpson Grant, *Ohio*	„	1822, April 27	1869	1885, July 23	63
Rutherford Birchard Hayes, *Ohio*	„	1822, Oct. 4	1877	1893, Jan. 17	70
James Abram Garfield†§, *Ohio*	„	1831, Nov. 19	1881	1881, Sept. 19	49
Chester Alan Arthur (*a*), *Vt.*	„	1830, Oct. 5	1881	1886, Nov. 18	56
Grover Cleveland, *N.J.*	Dem.	1837, Mar. 18	1885	1908, June 24	71
Benjamin Harrison, *Ohio*	Rep.	1833, Aug. 20	1889	1901, Mar. 13	67
Grover Cleveland, *N.J.*	Dem.	1837, Mar. 18	1893	1908, June 24	71
William McKinley†§, *Ohio*	Rep.	1843, Jan. 29	1897	1901, Sept. 14	58
Theodore Roosevelt (*a*), *N.Y.*	„	1858, Oct. 27	1901	1919, Jan. 6	60
William Howard Taft, *Ohio*	„	1857, Sept. 15	1909	1930, Mar. 8	72
Woodrow Wilson, *Va.*	Dem.	1856, Dec. 28	1913	1924, Feb. 3	67
Warren Gamaliel Harding†, *Ohio*	Rep.	1865, Nov. 2	1921	1923, Aug. 2	57
Calvin Coolidge (*a*), *Vt.*	„	1872, July 4	1923	1933, Jan. 5	60
Herbert Clark Hoover, *Iowa.*	„	1874, Aug. 10	1929	1964, Oct. 20	90
Franklin Delano Roosevelt†‡, *N.Y.*	Dem.	1882, Jan. 30	1933	1945, April 12	63
Harry S. Truman (*a*), *Missouri*	„	1884, May 8	1945	1972, Dec. 26	88
Dwight David Eisenhower, *Texas*	Rep.	1890, Oct. 14	1953	1969, Mar. 28	78
John Fitzgerald Kennedy, *Mass.*†§	Dem.	1917, May 29	1961	1963, Nov. 22	46
Lyndon Baines Johnson (*a*), *Texas*	„	1908, Aug. 27	1963	1973, Jan. 22	64
Richard Milhous Nixon, *California*	Rep.	1913, Jan. 9	1969	..	..
Gerald Rudolph Ford (*a*), *Nebraska*	„	1913, July 14	1974	..	..
James Earl Carter, *Georgia*	Dem.	1924, Oct. 1	1977	..	..
Ronald Wilson Reagan, *Illinois*	Rep.	1911, Feb. 6	1981	..	..

† Died in office.   § Assassinated.   (*a*) Elected as Vice-President.
‡ Re-elected Nov. 5, 1940, the first case of a third term; re-elected for a fourth term Nov. 7, 1944.

GOVERNMENT

The United States of America is a Federal Republic consisting of 50 States and 1 Federal District (of which 13 are Original States, 7 were admitted without previous organization as Territories, and 30 were admitted after such organization), and of organized Territories. Hawaii formally entered the Union as the 50th State on Aug. 21, 1959, from which date the flag of the United States has 13 stripes and 50 stars in 9 horizontal rows of six and five alternatively.

NATIONAL ANTHEM.—The Star-Spangled Banner.
NATIONAL DAY.—July 4 (Independence Day).

THE CONSTITUTION.—By the Constitution of Sept. 17, 1787 (to which ten amendments were added on Dec. 15, 1791 and eleventh to twenty-sixth, Jan. 8, 1798, Sept. 25, 1804, Dec. 18, 1865, July 28, 1868, March 30, 1870, Feb. 25, 1913, May 31, 1913, Jan. 16, 1920, Aug. 26, 1920, Feb. 6, 1933, Dec. 5, 1933, Feb. 26, 1951, March 29, 1961, Jan. 23, 1964, Feb. 10, 1967 and June 30, 1971), the government of the United States is entrusted to three separate authorities—the Executive, the Legislative, and the Judicial.

THE EXECUTIVE

THE *Executive* power is vested in a President, who is elected every four years. The mode of electing the President is as follows:—Each State elects (on the first Tuesday after the first Monday in November of the year preceding the year in which the Presidential term expires), a number of electors, equal to the whole number of Senators and Representatives to which the State may be entitled in the Congress; but no Senator or Representative, or anyone holding office under Government, shall be appointed an elector. The electors for each State meet in their respective States on the *first Monday after the second Wednesday in December* following, and there vote for a President by ballot. The ballots are then sent to Washington, and opened on the *sixth day of January* by the President of Senate in presence of Congress, and the candidate who has received a majority of the whole number of electoral votes cast is declared President for the ensuing term. If no one has a majority, then from the highest on the list (not exceeding three) the House of Representatives elects a President, the votes being taken by States, the representation from each State having one vote. There is also a Vice-President, who, on the death of the President, becomes President for the remainder of the term. Under the XXth Amendment to the Constitution the terms of the President and Vice-President end at noon on the 20th day of January of the years in which such terms would have ended if the Amendment had not been ratified, and the terms of their successors then begin. In case of the removal or death of both President and

Vice-President, a statute provides for the succession. Under the XXIInd Amendment to the Constitution, the tenure of the Presidency is limited to two terms.

Executive duties:—(1) He is Commander-in-Chief of the Army and of the Navy (and of the Militias when they are in Federal service), and he commissions all officers therein. (2) With the consent of the Senate, he appoints the Cabinet officers and all the chief (and many minor) officials. (3) He exercises a general supervision over the whole Federal Administration and sees that the Federal Laws are duly carried out. Should disorder arise in any state which the authorities thereof are unable to suppress, the aid of the President is invoked. (4) He conducts the foreign policy of the Republic, and has power, "by and with the Advice and Consent of the Senate, to make Treaties, provided two thirds of the senators present concur." The declaration of war rests with Congress. (5) He makes recommendation of a general nature to Congress, and when laws are passed by Congress he may return them to Congress with a veto. But if a measure so vetoed is again passed by both Houses of Congress by two-thirds majority in each House, it becomes law, notwithstanding the objection of the President. The President must be at least 35 years of age and a native citizen of the United States. He receives a taxable salary of $200,000 with a taxable expense allowance of $50,000 and a nontaxable travelling allowance not exceeding $100,000.

President of the United States, RONALD WILSON REAGAN, *born* Feb. 6, 1911, *sworn in* January 20, 1981; *for a second term* January 20, 1985. Republican.

Vice-President, George Herbert Walker Bush, *born* June 12, 1924, *sworn in* Jan. 20, 1981; *for a second term* Jan. 20, 1985.

THE CABINET

Secretary of State, George Shultz.
Secretary of the Treasury, Nicholas Brady.
Secretary of Defence, Frank Carlucci.
Attorney-General, Richard Thornburgh.
Secretary of the Interior, Donald P. Hodel.
Secretary of Agriculture, Richard E. Lyng.
Secretary of Commerce, William Verity.
Secretary of Labour, Ann McLaughlin.
Secretary of Health and Human Services, Otis R. Bowen.
Secretary of Housing and Urban Development, Samuel J. Pierce, Jr.
Secretary of Transportation, James H. Burnley IV.
Secretary of Energy, John S. Herrington.
Secretary of Education, Dr. Lauro Cavazos.

UNITED STATES EMBASSY
24 Grosvenor Square W1A 1AE
[01-499 9000]

Ambassador Extraordinary and Plenipotentiary, His Excellency Charles H. Price II (1983).
Minister, Hon. Raymond G. H. Seitz.
Minister for Economic Affairs, Richard M. Ogden.
Counsellors, Edward Kreuser (*Consular Affairs*); Lawrence D. Russell (*Administrative Affairs*); David K. Diebold (*Commercial Affairs*); James B. Devine (*Scientific and Technological Affairs*); Robert J. Korengold (*Public Affairs*); Rolland E. Anderson (*Agricultural Affairs*); Miles S. Pendleton (*Political Affairs*); Lawrence P. Taylor (*Economic Affairs*); William J. Graver (*Programme Coordinator*).
Defence Attaché, Col. Keith N. Lacey II.
Army Attaché, Col. James T. Hennessey, Jr.
Naval Attaché, Cpt. Joseph R. McCleary.

CAPITAL OF THE UNITED STATES

In 1790 Congress ratified the cession of 100 sq. miles by the States of Maryland and Virginia as a site for a Federal City to be the national capital of the United States. In 1791 it was decided to name the capital *Washington* and in 1793 the foundation-stone of the Capitol building was laid. In 1800 the seat of Government was removed to Washington, which was chartered as a city in 1802. In 1846 the Virginia portion was retroceded and the present area of the *District of Columbia* (with which the City of Washington is considered co-extensive) is 67 sq. miles, with a resident population (mid-1986 estimate) of 626,000.

The District of Columbia is governed by an elected mayor and City Council.

The *City of Washington* is situated on the west central edge of Maryland, opposite the State of Virginia, on the left bank of the Potomac at its confluence with the Anacostia. The population of the metropolitan area in 1986 was estimated at 3,563,000.

THE CONGRESS

The Legislative power is vested in two Houses, the Senate and the House of Representatives, the President having a *veto* power, which may be overcome by a two-thirds vote of each House. The Senate is composed of two Senators from each State, elected by the people thereof for the term of six years, and each Senator has one vote. Representatives are chosen in each State, by popular vote, for two years. The average number of persons represented by each Congressman is 1 for 550,000. The *Senate* consists of 100 members. The salary of a Senator is $89,500 per annum. The *House of Representatives* consists of 435 Representatives, a resident commissioner from Puerto Rico and a delegate from American Samoa, the District of Columbia, Guam and the Virgin Islands. The salary of a Representative is $89,500 per annum. By the XIXth Amendment, sex is no disqualification for the franchise. The Bureau of the Census estimated that there were 182,628,000 persons of voting age, excluding members of the armed forces overseas as of November 1988.

THE HUNDRETH CONGRESS

President of the Senate, George Bush (*Vice President of the United States*).
Speaker of the House of Representatives, James C. Wright, Jr., *Texas*.
Secretary of the Senate, Walter J. Stewart, *Dist. of Columbia*.
Clerk of the House of Representatives, Donnald K. Anderson, *California*.
Members of the 100th Congress were elected on Nov. 4, 1986.
The 100th Congress is constituted as follows:
Senate.—Democrats 54; Republicans, 46; Total, 100.
House of Representatives.—Democrats, 254; Republicans, 178; Vacancies, 3. Total, 435 (May 26, 1988).

THE JUDICATURE

The *Federal Judiciary* consists of three sets of Federal Courts: (1) The *Supreme Court* at Washington, D.C., consisting of a Chief Justice and eight Associate Justices, with original jurisdiction in cases affecting Ambassadors, etc., or where a State is a party to the suit, and with appellate jurisdiction from inferior Federal Courts and from the judgments of the highest Courts of the States. (2) The *United States Courts of Appeals*, dealing with appeals from District Courts and from certain federal administrative agencies, and consisting of all the Circuit Judges within the circuit. (3) The 94 *United States District Courts* served by 700 District Court Judges.

THE SUPREME COURT
(U.S. Supreme Court Building, Washington, D.C.,
20543)

Chief Justice, William H. Rehnquist, *Ariz.*, born Oct.
1, 1924, *appointed* 1986.

ASSOCIATE JUSTICES

Name	Born	Apptd
William J. Brennan, Jr., *N.J.*	1906	1956
Byron R. White, *Colo.*	1917	1962
Thurgood Marshall, *N.Y.*	1908	1967
Harry Blackmun, *Minn.*	1908	1970
John Paul Stevens, *Ill.*	1920	1975
Sandra Day O'Connor, *Ariz.*	1930	1981
Antonin Scalia, *Va.*	1936	1986
Anthony M. Kennedy, *Calif.*	1936	1988

Clerk of the Supreme Court, Joseph F. Spaniol, Jr.

CRIMINAL STATISTICS, U.S.

Crime	No. of offences 1986	1987
Murder and Non-negligent Manslaughter	20,613	20,096
Rape	91,459	91,111
Robbery	542,775	517,704
Aggravated Assault	834,322	855,088
Burglary	3,241,410	3,236,184
Larceny—Theft	7,257,153	7,499,851
Thefts of Motor Vehicles	1,224,137	1,288,674
Total	13,211,869	13,508,708

DEFENCE

Department of Defence

Secretary of Defence (in the Cabinet), Frank C.
Carlucci.
Secretary of the Army, John O. Marsh, Jr.
Secretary of the Navy, William L. Ball III.
Secretary of the Air Force, Edward Aldridge.
Chairman, Joint Chiefs of Staff, Adm. William Crowe.

The Department of Defence includes the Secretary
of Defence as its head, the Deputy Secretary of
Defence, the Defence staff offices, the Joint Chiefs of
Staff and the Joint Staff, the three military departments and the military services within those departments, the unified and specified commands, and other
Department of Defence agencies as the Secretary of
Defence establishes to meet specific requirements.
The Defence staff offices and the joint Chiefs of Staff,
although separately organized, function in full coor-
dination and cooperation. They include the offices of
the Director of Defence Research and Engineering,
the Assistant Secretaries of Defence, the General
Counsel of the Department of Defence and such other
staff offices as the Secretary of Defence may establish.
The Joint Chiefs of Staff, as a group, are directly
responsible to the Secretary of Defence for the
functions assigned to them. Each member of the
Joint Chiefs of Staff, other than the Chairman and
Vice Chairman, is responsible for keeping the Secretary of his military department fully informed on
matters considered or acted upon by the Joint Chiefs
of Staff.

Each military department is separately organized
under its own Secretary and functions under the
direction, authority and control of the Secretary of
Defence.

The Department of Defence maintains and employs
armed forces: (1) to support and defend the Constitution of the United States against all enemies,
foreign and domestic; (2) to insure, by timely and
effective military action, the security of the United
States, its possessions, and areas vital to its interests;
(3) to uphold and advance the national policies and
interest of the United States; and (4) to safeguard
the internal security of the United States. All
functions in the Department of Defence and its
component agencies are performed under the direction, authority and control of the Secretary of
Defence.

Commanders of unified and specified commands are
responsible to the President and the Secretary of
Defence for the accomplishment of military missions
assigned to them.

Unified Defence Commands

COMMANDERS-IN-CHIEF

U.S. European Command, Brussels.—Gen. John R.
Galvin (*U.S. Army*) (concurrently *N.A.T.O. Su-
preme Allied Commander*).
*U.S. Southern Command, Quarry Heights, Panama
Canal Zone.*—Lt.-Gen. Frederick F. Woerner (*U.S.
Army*).
U.S. Atlantic Command, Norfolk, Virginia.—Adm.
Lee Baggett, Jr. (*U.S. Navy*) (concurrently
N.A.T.O. Supreme Allied Commander, Atlantic).
U.S. Pacific Command, Hawaii.—Adm. Ronald J.
Hays (*U.S. Navy*).
U.S. Space Command, Gen. John L. Piotrowski
(*U.S.A.F.*).
Strategic Air Command, Omaha.—Gen. John T.
Chain (*U.S.A.F.*).
U.S. Transportation Command, Gen. Duane H.
Cassidy (*U.S.A.F.*).
*U.S. Special Operations Command, MacDill A.F.B.,
Florida.*—Gen. James J. Lindsay (*U.S. Army*).
U.S. Central Command, Gen. George B. Crist (*U.S.
Marine Corps*).
* A Specified Command.

Army.—The U.S. Army had a strength on March
31, 1988, of 764,247. Stationed in Germany were four
divisions.
Chief of the Staff of the Army, Gen. Carl E. Vuono.
Navy.—The strength of the Navy (including Ma-
rine Corps) on Sept. 30, 1987 was 786,300 active duty
personnel.
The U.S. Navy had in service at Sept. 30, 1987, 568
active fleet ships (Surface vessels, 429; Submarines,
139).
Chief of Naval Operations, Adm. Carlisle A. H. Trost.
Marine Corps.—Established 1775. Strength on
Sept. 30, 1987 was 199,500 active duty personnel.
Commandant, Gen. Alfred M. Gray.
Air.—The United States Air Force was established
as a separate organization on September 18, 1947. On
Sept. 30, 1987, there were 606,900 officers and airmen
on active duty, with 264,330 civilian employees. Air
Force Reserve and Air National Guard numbered
264,330.
The Air Force has up to 30 per cent of the strategic
bomber and tanker forces maintaining constant alert
as well as 1,000 inter-continental ballistic missiles in
silos. In addition, the Air Force maintains the
capability to carry out limited war and special
warfare operations, with more than 9,300 strategic,
tactical and support aircraft. In March, 1961, the Air
Force was assigned primary responsibility for the
Department of Defence space development programmes and projects.
Chief of Staff of the U.S. Air Force, Larry D. Welch.

THE UNITED STATES BUDGET
(fiscal year; in millions of dollars)

Receipts by Source	1987 (actual)	1988 (estimated)
Individual income taxes	364,000	
Corporation income taxes	104,800	
Social insurance taxes and contributions	301,500	
Excise taxes	32,600	n/a
Estate and gift taxes	6,000	
Customs duties	14,400	
Miscellaneous	19,100	
Total	842,400	
Outlays by Function		
National defence	281,999	285,423
International affairs	11,649	9,926
General science, space, and technology	9,216	10,903
Energy	4,115	2,713
Natural resources and environment	13,363	15,139
Agriculture	27,356	22,352
Commerce and housing credit	6,182	12,364
Transportation	26,228	27,237
Community and regional development	5,051	6,321
Education, training, employment, and social services	29,724	33,652
Health	39,968	44,479
Social security and medicare	282,473	298,574
Income security	123,250	129,560
Veterans' benefits and services	26,782	27,748
Administration of justice	7,548	8,970
General government	7,569	8,796
General purpose fiscal assistance	1,621	1,804
Interest	138,570	147,871
Undistributed offsetting receipts	−36,455	−36,123
Total	1,004,586	1,055,904

FINANCE
SOCIAL WELFARE EXPENDITURE

Total expenditure by programme was (millions):

	1984	1985
Social insurance	342,264	372,582
Education	152,045	166,362
Public aid	89,871	95,965
Health and medical	37,090	39,955
Veterans' programmes	26,127	27,171
Other social welfare	13,177	13,946
Housing	10,374	11,878
TOTAL	670,945	727,861

Expenditure per capita was ($):

	1984	1985
Social insurance	1,424	1,528
Education	635	685
Public aid	375	395
Health and medical	155	165
Veterans' programmes	108	111
Other social welfare	56	57
Housing	43	49
TOTAL	2,800	2,991

PUBLIC DEBT

At the end Sept 1987 the total gross *Federal Debt* of the United States stood at $2,355,280 million.

COST OF LIVING IN U.S.A.

The Consumer Price Index for all urban consumers (CPI-U) with prices collected in 91 areas across the U.S.A. was measured for the year 1987 at 112·5 (1982–84 = 100), a rise of 3·6 per cent. over the 1986 figure.

GROSS NATIONAL PRODUCT

Gross National Product by industry in 1987 was ($ million):—

All industries, total	4,461,200
Agriculture, forestry, fisheries	98,800
Mining	95,300
Construction	208,700
Manufacturing	861,200
Transportation and public utilities	406,900
Trade	740,600
Finance, insurance, real estate	755,100
Services	757,900
Government and government enterprises	541,200
Rest of the world	27,400

G.N.P., national and personal income in 1987 were ($ million):—

Gross national product	3,821,000
Net national product	3,362,300
National income	3,045,700
Corporate profits	304,700
Net interest	337,100
Personal income	3,746,500
Personal tax and non-tax payments	564,800
Disposable personal income	3,181,700
Personal outlays	3,062,700
Personal saving	119,000

Personal consumption expenditure in 1987 was $2,497,200 million, of which durable goods accounted for $388,200 million, non-durable goods $878,100 million and services $1,230,900 million. Gross private domestic investment in 1986 was $671,000 million.

UNITED STATES STOCK OF CURRENCY AND COIN

The U.S. unit of currency is the Dollar ($) of 100 Cents.

U.S. stock of currency and coin at March 31, 1988 was:—

	$ million
Gold	11,062·5
Dollars	340·1
Subsidiary Coin	93·8
Minor Coin	20·7
Silver Certificates	198·6
U.S. Notes	322·5
Federal Reserve Notes	255,200·3
TOTAL	267,238·5

AGRICULTURE AND LIVESTOCK

The total number of farms in 1987 was 2,173,000, with a total area of land in farms of 1,002,000,000 acres, and an average acreage per farm of 461 acres. The total number of people employed on farms during the week of July 6–12, 1986 was 3,469,000, of whom 1,971,000 were unpaid workers, 1,233,000 hired workers and 265,000 agricultural service workers.

Principal crops are corn for grain, soybeans, wheat hay, cotton, tobacco, grain sorghums, potatoes, oranges and barley.

Livestock on farms on Jan. 1, 1986 and 1987 (*Dec. 1985 and 1986) was:—

	1986 (000's)	1987 (000's)
All cattle	105,468	102,031
Milk cows	11,177	10,547
Sheep and lambs	9,983	10,328
Hogs and pigs*	52,313	51,160
Chickens*	386,548	368,681

Gross income from farming in 1986 was $159,500 million, of which cash receipts from marketing were $135,200 million and Government payments $11,800 million. Cash income from all crops in 1986 was $63,600 million and from livestock and livestock products $71,600 million.

NONFUEL MINERALS

The value of nonfuel raw mineral production in the United States in 1986 totalled an estimated $23,480 million compared with $23,233 million in 1985.

Trading Figures

	1984	1985
Imports	$31,500 m	$29,500 m
Exports	14,000 m	13,000 m

Production Figures
('000 tonnes)

	1986	1987p
Aluminium*	3,348	3,685
Iron Ore†	38,825	47,053
Phosphate rock	40,320	40,954
Zinc Ore	221	233
Refined Copper	1,479	1,560
Refined Lead	975	1,070

* measured in short tons
† measured in long tons
p=preliminary.

ENERGY

Energy Summary
(Quadrillion (10¹⁵) Btu)

	1985	1986	1987
Production	64·76	64·24	64·53
Consumption	73·94	74·26	76·04
Imports	12·09	14·43	15·41
Exports	4·23	4·05	3·87

Breakdown of Production and Consumption
(Quadrillion (10¹⁵) Btu)

	1986	1987
Production		
Crude Oil	18·37	17·59
Coal	19·51	20·12
Natural Gas (dry)	16·47	16·82
Natural Gas Plant Liquids	2·14	2·22
Hydroelectric	3·03	2·60
Nuclear	4·47	4·92
Other*	0·23	0·24
Total	64·24	64·53
Consumption		
Petroleum	32·19	32·62
Natural Gas (dry)	16·70	17·18
Coal	17·26	18·02
Hydroelectric	3·40	3·04
Nuclear	4·47	4·92
Other*	0·21	0·25
Total	74·26	76·04

* Includes geothermal power, photovoltaic solar power and electricity produced from wood and waste.

During 1987 oil and gas drilling rigs in operation averaged 936 and the number of well completions in 1987 totalled 33,430. Seismic exploration work in progress involved a total (average) of 176 crews, 24 in offshore areas and 153 on shore. Domestic crude oil production in 1987 averaged 8,311,000 barrels per day and total petroleum imports averaged 6,541,000 barrels per day. Production of dry natural gas in 1987 was 16,334 billion cubic feet (Bcf). Stocks of gas available for withdrawal were estimated at 1,981 Bcf in 1987. Production of coal in 1987 was 916,851,000 short tons with domestic consumption requiring 836,941,000 short tons. In 1987 U.S. nuclear power generators produced 455,270 million net kilowatt-hours of electricity, accounting for 17·7 per cent of domestic electricity generation. Operable reactors at end Dec. 1987 totalled 107, with a net summer capacity of 93·7 million net kilowatts.

LABOUR

Organized Labour.—Approximately 17·0 per cent. of the employed wage and salary workers in the United States were members of labour organizations in 1987.

Work Stoppages.—There were 46 stoppages involving 1,000 or more workers in 1987. They resulted in 4,481,000 man-days of idleness, representing 0·02 per cent. of estimated working time of all non-agricultural workers.

Employment and Unemployment.—The civilian labour force (working population) was 120,978,000 in May 1988. This includes self-employed wage and salary-earners, and unpaid family workers, employed and unemployed. Unemployment was estimated at 6,783,000 in May 1988 (5·6 per cent.) (it was 6·3 per cent. in May 1987).

Wages.—In March 1988, gross average weekly

earnings in industry ranged from $711·47 per week in malt beverage industry (42·4 hours and $16·78 average hourly earnings) to $113·85 in eating and drinking places (25·3 hours and $4·50 average hourly earnings). The average for all manufacturing was $411·86 compared with $403·27 in March 1987.

On Jan. 1, 1981, the minimum wage set by federal law became $3·35. The law requires at least time and a half of an employee's regular rate of pay for all hours over 40 a week for most covered workers.

The Fair Labour Standards Act covers all employees of certain enterprises having workers engaged in interstate commerce, producing goods for interstate commerce, or handling, selling, or otherwise working on goods or materials that have been moved in or produced for such commerce by any person.

There are certain exemptions from these requirements in specific occupations and industries.

In addition to cash wages, almost all workers are covered by legally required social security, unemployment insurance and workers' compensation insurance. Also though not required by law, most workers receive some type of "fringe" benefits—the most common forms being paid vacations, and public holidays, various types of retirement plans, insurance and health benefits financed by the employer or by employer and employees jointly.

EXTERNAL TRADE OF THE UNITED STATES

	1986	1987
	\$ million	
General Imports:		
c.i.f. value	387,082·0	424,082·3
customs value	369,961·0	405,900·6
Exports and re-exports:		
f.a.s. value†	217,292·0	252,852·7
Trade balance:		
f.a.s. exports : c.i.f.		
imports	−169,790·0	−171,229·6
f.a.s. exports : customs		
imports	−152,669·0	−153,048·0

† Excluding military aid.

EXPORTS BY PRINCIPAL COMMODITIES OF DOMESTIC ORIGIN, 1987

Commodity	Value
	\$ (million)
Food and Live Animals	19,178·8
Grain and cereal preparations	8,058·1
Beverages and Tobacco	3,666·7
Crude materials (inedible) except fuel .	20,416·3
Raw cotton	1,630·8
Metal ores, concentrates, scrap	3,018·3
Mineral fuels, lubricants, etc.........	7,713·1
Coal (bituminous)	3,322·7
Oils and Fats (animal and vegetable) ..	961·4
Chemicals and products	26,380·9
Machinery and Transport Equipment .	108,596·0
Electronic computers, parts, etc.	17,494·8
Electrical machinery, appliances, etc.	16,637·2
Motor vehicles and parts	20,878·8
Other Manufactured Goods	19,409·0
Unclassified Commodities	20,380·7

U.S. IMPORTS BY PRINCIPAL COMMODITIES, 1987

Commodity	Value
	\$ (million)
Food and Live Animals	20,547·1
Fish and fish preparations..........	5,590·0
Vegetables and fruit	4,475·9
Coffee–crude.....................	2,705·8

Beverages and Tobacco	4,104·9
Crude materials (inedible), except fuels	11,525·7
Mineral fuels, lubricants, etc.........	64,219·5
Crude petroleum	29,320·5
Petroleum products	12,208·9
Oils and Fats (animal and vegetable) ..	568·1
Chemicals and products	16,213·4
Machinery and Transport Equipment .	177,808·7
Telecommunications, sound recording apparatus	20,820·5
Electrical machinery, parts.........	24,428·3
Motor vehicles	57,023·8
Other Manufactured Goods	66,183·1
Unclassified Commodities	12,373·4

U.S. FOREIGN TRADE BY ECONOMIC CLASS 1987

	\$ million	
Class	Imports	Exports*
Crude Materials...	38,645	11,973
Crude Foodstuffs ..	10,123	10,197
Manufactured Foods	14,225	10,312
Semi-manufactures	44,820	41,594
Finished Manufactures...	298,088	167,323
Total..........	405,901	241,399

*Excluding the total military grant-aid of $228,280 million.

U.S. FOREIGN TRADE BY PRINCIPAL AREAS AND COUNTRIES, 1986

Area/Country	Exports and Re-exports to	General Imports from
	\$ million	
Africa...................	5,978·2	11,056·8
Asia	64,531·8	162,667·8
Japan	26,881·6	85,456·7
Saudi Arabia	3,448·8	4,054·3
Taiwan	5,524·2	21,251·5
Korea, Rep. of	6,354·9	13,497·0
Hong Kong	3,030·1	9,473·6
Oceania	6,658·5	4,080·3
Australia	5,551·2	2,872·6
Europe	64,269·8	97,267·5
West Germany	10,560·5	26,128·1
U.K.	11,418·2	16,032·5
Other E.C.	31,175·3	79,520·2
Other O.E.C.D.	7,849·4	14,011·2
Communist bloc	1,989·2	2,205·6
N. & Central America....	121,004·0	92,664·2
Canada	45,332·6	68,662·4
Mexico	12,391·6	17,558·3
S. America	11,788·1	19,803·9

COMMUNICATIONS

RAILWAYS

Data on Class I line-haul railroads (*dollars in thousands*)

	1985	1986
Operating Revenues		
Freight	26,687,652	25,343,911
Passenger	103,205	107,717
Total.......	27,586,441	26,204,122

Total operating expenses	25,225,295	24,896,015
Net working capital	1,083,524	742,739
Average number of employees	301,879	275,817

ROADS

In 1986 there were 3·88 million miles of public roads and streets in the United States, of which 3·18 million miles were in rural areas and 701,000 miles were in urban areas. Surfaced roads and streets account for 3·50 million miles, or 90·2 per cent, of the total; 375,000 miles, or 9·8 per cent, were unimproved or graded and drained.

An estimated total of $58,934 million was spent in 1986 for roads and streets in the United States. Capital outlay accounts for 49·0 per cent of the total expenditure; 29·4 per cent was spent for maintenance, and 7·8 per cent for administration; 9·5 per cent for highway police and safety; and 4·3 per cent for interest on highway bonds.

Motor Vehicles and Taxation.—The number of motor vehicles registered in 1986 in the United States was 176,191,339, an increase of 2·4 per cent over the 1985 total of 171,688,878. In 1986 the State governments received $24,258,000,000 in State Highway-User Tax Receipts, including road and crossing tolls, and $12,777,000,000 in Federal Highway-User Tax Receipts.

Accidents.—In 1986 there were 46,056 deaths caused by motor vehicle accidents. The death rate per 100,000,000 vehicle-miles of travel was 2·51 in 1986 compared with 2·47 in 1985.

SHIPPING

The ocean-going Merchant Marine of the U.S. on April 1, 1988, consisted of 699 vessels of 1,000 gross tons and over, of which 437 were privately owned and 262 were government-owned ships. Of the 437 privately owned vessels, 382 were active including 2 combination passenger and cargo ships, 35 freighters, 23 bulk carriers, 176 tankers, 14 tug-barge units, 10 liquefied natural gas carriers and 122 intermodal ships. There were 249 ships in the National Defence Reserve Fleet of inactive government-owned vessels, of which 8 were to be sold for scrap.

AIR TRANSPORT

United States domestic and international scheduled airlines in 1984 carried 344,460,600 passengers over 304,987,288,000 revenue passenger miles. Cargo revenue ton-miles totalled 8,200,000,000, an increase of 8·0 per cent over 1983. Air cargo ton-miles were distributed as follows: freight 6,500,000,000 (up 7·7 per cent); express 64,400,000 (up 2·8 per cent); and air mail 1,600,000,000 (up 9·3 per cent).

Total operating revenues of all U.S. scheduled airlines were $43,800,000,000 in 1984, an increase of 13·5 per cent from 1983.

Total operating expenses rose to $41,700,000,000 in 1984, a 9·0 per cent increase over 1983. Scheduled operations showed a net operating profit of $2,100,000,000 in 1984, compared with a net operating profit of $361,700,000 in 1983.

Three principal classes of commercial air carriers have been established in the United States based on annual operating revenues. They are: Majors, with annual operating revenues of over $1,000 million; Nationals, with annual operating revenues of $75–1,000 million; and Regionals, with annual operating revenues of up to $75,999,000.

U.S. SCHEDULED AIRLINE INDUSTRY STATISTICS, 1984 (Thousands)

	Majors	Nationals	Regionals	System
Revenue Passenger Carried	250,150	80,337	13,974	344,461
Revenue Passengers Miles	252,295,400	43,820,182	8,871,706	304,987,288
Air Mail Ton Miles	1,402,063	199,028	15,841	1,616,932
Express Ton Miles	60,255	2,024	131	62,410
Freight Ton Miles	3,905,550	2,445,897	145,714	6,497,161
Revenue Ton Miles	30,597,429	7,028,968	1,048,857	38,675,254
Revenue Plane Miles	2,391,806	579,533	159,890	3,131,229

EDUCATION
State School Systems

All the 50 States and the District of Columbia have compulsory school attendance laws. In general, children are obliged to attend school from 7 to 16 years of age. Officers of local administrative units, usually known as truant or attendance officers, are charged with enforcing the compulsory attendance laws.

In the autumn of 1987, 45,900,000 children were enrolled in regular elementary and secondary day schools in the United States, of whom 5·7 million or 12·4 per cent attended private schools.

The following percentages of the school-age population were estimated to be enrolled in school in the autumn of 1986; of 5- and 6-year-olds, 95 per cent; of 7- to 13-year-olds, 99 per cent; of 14- to 17-year-olds, 95 per cent; and of 18- to 24-year-olds, 32 per cent.

During the 1986–87 school year, the average daily attendance in regular public elementary and secondary day schools was 36,951,000. In the 1986–87 school year 2,428,000 students graduated from regular public high schools, 265,000 graduated from private high

school. In addition some 25,000 graduated from evening schools and adult education programmes, and an estimated 400,000 received high school equivalency certificates. Public school teachers numbered 2,423,000, with an average salary of $26,534.

Most of the revenue for public elementary and secondary school purposes comes from the Federal, State, and local governments. Less than ½ per cent comes from gifts from tuition and transportation fees. Estimated revenue receipts during 1986–87 amounted to $162,453,000,000; 6·6 per cent from the Federal Government, 49·6 per cent from State governments, and 43·8 per cent from local sources. Estimated current expenditure in the 1986–87 school year was $149,099 million; for sites, buildings, furniture and equipment expenditures, $9,210 million; for interest in school debt $2,956 million.

Institutions of Higher Education

In the autumn of 1986, total enrolment in universities, colleges, professional schools, and two-year schools numbered 12,501,000.

Degrees conferred during the academic years 1985–86 and 1986–87 were:—

Degree	1985–86	1986–87
Bachelor's	987,823	987,000
First-Professional	73,910	73,000
Master's...................	288,567	291,000
Doctorates	33,653	34,200

During 1985–86 the major fields for bachelor's degrees were business and management (238,160), engineering (95,953) and social sciences (93,703). First-profession degrees in law (35,844) and medicine (15,938) predominated. Master's degrees were heavily concentrated in education (76,353) and business and management (67,137). The most popular fields of study for doctorates were education (7,110) and life sciences (3,358).

During the 1986–87 academic year, the 3,406 colleges and universities employed about 717,000 (full-time equivalent) instructional faculty. Total expenditures for colleges and universities during the 1986–87 academic year were $115,900 million.

Particulars of some of the Universities (with opening autumn enrolment figures, 1985) are: *Harvard* (20,711 students, including 7,747 women), founded at Cambridge, Mass. on Oct. 28, 1636, and named after John Harvard of Emmanuel College, Cambridge, England, who bequeathed to it his library and a sum of money in 1638; *Yale* (10,809 students, including 4,740 women), founded at New Haven, Connecticut, in 1701; *Bowdoin*, Brunswick, Me. (founded 1794; 1,446 students including 626 women); *Brown*, Providence, R.I. (founded 1764; 7,277 students, including 3,398 women); *Columbia*, New York, N.Y. (founded 1754; 23,556 students, including 12,393 women); *Cornell* (founded at Ithaca, N.Y., 1865; 19,680 students, including 8,626 women); *Dartmouth*, Hanover, N.H. (founded 1769, 4,519 students, including 1,826 women); *Georgetown*, Washington, D.C. (founded 1789; 11,985 students, including 5,484 women); *North Carolina*, Chapel Hill, N.C. (founded in 1789; 22,066 students, including 12,504 women); *Pennsylvania*, Philadelphia, Pa. (founded 1740; 21,870 students, including 9,926 women); *Princeton*, N.J. (founded 1746; 6,293 students and 2,215 women); and *William and Mary*, Williamsburg, Va. (founded 1693; 6,676 students, including 3,448 women).

WEIGHTS AND MEASURES

The weights and measures in common use in the United States are of British origin, and date back to the American Revolution when practically all the standards were intended to be equivalent to those used in England at that period. Divergencies in these weights and measures were, however, quite common, due no doubt to the fact that the system of weights and measures in England was not itself well established, and hence the copies brought to the United States were often adjusted to different standards. Because of these discrepancies, the system of weights and measures in the United States (U.S. inch-pound system) is not identical with the British system.

The U.S. ton (short) = 2,000 pounds (British Imperial ton = 2,240 pounds, or 1 U.S. long ton). The U.S. gallon = 231 cubic inches (277·42 cubic inches in U.K.) or 128 fluid ounces (160 fluid ounces in U.K.). In the British system the units of dry measure are the same as those of liquid measure. In the United States these two are not the same, the gallon and its subdivisions being used in the measurement of liquids, while the bushel, with its subdivisions, is used in the measurement of certain dry commodities. The U.S. gallon is divided into 4 liquid quarts and the U.S. bushel into 32 dry quarts.

The International System of Units—officially abbreviated SI—is a modernized version of the metric system. It was established by international agreement to provide a logical and interconnected framework for all measurements in science, industry and commerce.

In 1971, a study recommended a concerted, coordinated, but voluntary national effort to make the SI the predominant form of measurement in the United States. In December 1975, legislation was passed which established the United States Metric Board to coordinate voluntary conversion to the metric system. Since 1982 this function has been assumed by the Office of Metric Programmes of the U.S. Department of Commerce.

TERRITORIES, ETC. OF THE UNITED STATES

The territories and the principal islands and island groups under the sovereignty of the United States of America comprise the Commonwealth of Puerto Rico, the Commonwealth of the Northern Mariana Islands, and the following territories: Guam; American Samoa; U.S. Virgin Islands; Johnston Atoll; Midway Islands; Wake Islands.

Johnston Atoll (formerly Johnston and Sand Islands) comprises two small islands, less than 1 sq. mile in area, to the south-west of Hawaii which are administered by the U.S. Air Force. The two Midway Islands (area, 2 sq. miles; population (1970), 2,200), at the western end of the Hawaiian chain, are administered by the U.S. Navy. The Wake Islands have an area of about 3 sq. miles and a population (1979) of 300. They lie about 2,300 miles west of Hawaii and are administered by the U.S. Air Force.

Under the terms of a Treaty of Friendship between the United States and Kiribati, signed in 1979 and subsequently ratified by the U.S. Senate, the United States renounced its claim to Canton and Enderbury Islands.

There are certain small guano islands, rocks, or keys which, in pursuance of action taken under the Act of Congress, August 18, 1856, subsequently embodied in Sections 5570–5578 of the Revised Statutes are considered as appertaining to the United States. Responsibility for territorial affairs generally is centred in the Office of the Assistant Secretary, Territorial and International Affairs, Dept. of the Interior, Washington, D.C. Puerto Rico was removed from the Department of the Interior's administrative jurisdiction with the acquisition of Commonwealth status in 1952.

THE COMMONWEALTH OF PUERTO RICO

Puerto Rico (Rich Port) is an island of the Greater Antilles group in the West Indies, and lies between 17° 50′–18° 30′ N. lat. and 65° 30′–67° 15′ W. long., with a total area of 3,421 sq. miles (8,860 sq. km.), and an estimated population (1985) of 3,451,000. The majority of the inhabitants are of Spanish descent and Spanish and English are the official languages. The island is about 111 miles from west to east, and 36 miles from north to south. The capital is 1,600 miles distant from New York, and 1,000 miles from Miami.

Puerto Rico was discovered in 1493 by Christopher Columbus and explored by Ponce de Léon in 1508. It continued as a Spanish possession until Oct. 18, 1898, when the United States took formal possession as a result of the Spanish-American War. It was ceded by Spain to the United States by the Treaty ratified on April 11, 1899.

The Constitution approved by the Congress and

the President of the United States, which came into force on July 25, 1952, establishes the Commonwealth of Puerto Rico with full powers of local government. Legislative functions are vested in the Legislative Assembly, which consists of 2 elected houses; the Senate of 27 members (2 from each of 8 senatorial districts and 11 at large) and the House of Representatives of 51 members (1 from each of 40 representative districts and 11 at large). Membership of each house may be increased slightly to accommodate minority representatives. The term of the Legislative Assembly is 4 years. The selection of the Secretary of State must be approved also by the House of Representatives.

The Governor is popularly elected for a term of 4 years. A Supreme Court of 7 members is appointed by the Governor, with the advice and consent of the Senate. The Governor appoints all Judges. Residents of Puerto Rico are U.S. citizens. Puerto Rico is represented in Congress by a Resident Commissioner, elected for a term of 4 years, who has a seat in the House of Representatives, but not a vote, although he has a right to vote on those committees of which he is a member.

Preliminary 1983 figures for the Commonwealth Government's budget were Receipts, $4,948 million (of which $1,180 million were transfers from the Federal Government) and Expenditures, $4,111 million (including payments of $135 million to the Federal Government). Manufacturing added $5,765 million to net Commonwealth income in 1983 (preliminary figures), trade $1,743 million, finance, insurance and real estate $1,841 million and agriculture $435 million. Principal crops are sugar cane, coffee, vegetables, fruits and tobacco. Most valuable areas of manufacturing are chemicals and allied products, metal products and machinery. Public and private schools are established throughout—enrolment in 1985–86 was 686,914. Enrolment in private colleges and universities for 1985–86 was 98,402.

CAPITAL.—ΨSan Juan, population of the municipality, 1,816,300; Other major towns are: ΨPonce (188,500); Bayamón (205,800); ΨMayagüez (99,800); and ΨArecibo (83,300).

Governor, Rafael Hernández Colón.
Secretary of State, Hector Luis Acevedo.
Resident Commissioner, Jaime Fuster.
Chief Justice, Victor Pons.

TRADE

	1985	1986
Total Imports	$10,113 m.	$10,108 m.
Total Exports	10,543 m.	11,588 m.

Trade with U.K.

	1986	1987
Imports from U.K.	£49,620,000	£39,405,000
Exports to U.K.	81,131,000	76,347,000

GUAM

Guam, the largest of the Ladrone or Mariana Islands in the North Pacific Ocean, lies in 13° 26′ N. lat. and 144° 39′ E. long., at a distance of about 1,506 miles east of Manila. The area of the island is estimated at 209 sq. miles (541 sq. km.), with an estimated population (1985) of 120,977.

The Guamanians are of Chamorro stock mingled with Filipino and Spanish blood. The Chamorro language belongs to the Malayo-Polynesian family, but has had considerable admixture of Spanish. English is the language used throughout the island, although Chamorro is also used in Guamanian homes.

Guam was occupied by the Japanese in Dec. 1941 but was recaptured and occupied throughout by U.S. forces before the end of July, 1944. Under the Organic Act of Guam of August 1, 1950 (Public Law 630 of the 81st Congress), Guam has statutory powers of self-government, and Guamanians are United States citizens. A 21-member unicameral legislature is elected biennially. The Governor and Lieutenant Governor are popularly elected. A non-voting Delegate is elected to serve in the U.S. House of Representatives. There is also a District Court of Guam, with original jurisdiction in cases under federal law.

CAPITAL.—Agaña. Port of entry, ΨApra.

Governor, Joseph Ada.

AMERICAN SAMOA

American Samoa consists of the island of Tutuila, Anu'u, Ofu, Olesega, Ta'u, Rose and Swains Islands, with a total area of 76 sq. miles (197 sq. km.) and an estimated population of 34,500 in 1986.

Tutuila, the largest of the group, has an area of 52 square miles and contains a magnificent harbour at ΨPago Pago. The remaining islands have an area of about 24 square miles. Tuna and copra are the chief exports.

American Samoans are U.S. nationals, but some have acquired citizenship through service in the United States armed forces or other naturalization procedure.

The 1960 Constitution grants American Samoa a measure of self-government, with certain powers reserved to the U.S. Secretary of the Interior. There is a bicameral legislature with popularly elected Representatives and Governors, and a popularly-elected Governor. A non-voting Delegate is elected to serve in the U.S. House of Representatives.

The constitution of American Samoa designates the village of Fagatogo as the seat of government.

Governor, A. P. Lutali, *elected* Nov. 1984.
Lt. Governor, Eni F. Hunkin, Jr.

VIRGIN ISLANDS

Purchased by the United States from Denmark for the sum of $25 million, and proclaimed, January 25, 1917. The total area of the islands is 132 sq. miles (342 sq. km.), with an estimated population (1984) of 108,000. There are three main islands, St. Thomas (28 sq. miles), St. Croix (84 sq. miles), St. John (20 sq. miles) and about 50 small islets or cays, mostly uninhabited.

The government of the Virgin Islands is organized under the provisions of the Revised Organic Act of the Virgin Islands, enacted by the Congress of the United States on July 22, 1954. Legislative power is vested in the Legislature of the Virgin Islands, a unicameral body composed of 15 senators popularly elected for two-year terms. Virgin Islanders are citizens of the United States. From the elections of November, 1970, the Governor has been popularly elected. A non-voting Delegate is elected to serve in the U.S. House of Representatives. The Virgin Islands are now a favourite tourist area in the Caribbean. The climate of the islands is delightful at all times, and particularly so during the winter months.

CAPITAL.—ΨCharlotte Amalie on St. Thomas.

Governor, Alexander Farrelly.
Lt. Governor, Julio Bradley.

NORTHERN MARIANA ISLANDS

The land area of the Northern Mariana Islands is 184 sq. miles (476 sq. km.) with an estimated population (1987) of 22,000.

A law enacted by Congress on March 24, 1976

provides a Covenant to establish a Commonwealth of the Northern Mariana Islands. The provisions of the Covenant became fully effective upon termination of the Trusteeship Agreement on Nov. 3, 1986. Most of the residents became U.S. citizens. There is a popularly elected bicameral legislature and a popularly elected Governor.

Governor, Pedro P. Tenorio.
Lt. Governor, Pedro A. Tenario.

MARSHALL ISLANDS

The land area of the Marshall Islands is 70 sq. miles (181 sq. km.), with an estimated population of 35,000. The capital is Majuro with 14,500 inhabitants.

In May 1979 Constitutional Government was installed in the Marshall Islands which provides for a bicameral legislature comprising a Senate and a House of Assembly. A Compact of Free Association with the United States was signed on June 25, 1983, becoming law on Jan. 14, 1986. This allows the Marshall Islands self government and vests in the United States full responsibility for the defence of the Marshall Islands for 15 years.

President, Amata Kabua.

FEDERATED STATES OF MICRONESIA

The Federated States of Micronesia comprise the four states of Kosrae, Pohnpei, Truk and Yap, which have a combined area of 271 sq. miles (701 sq. km.) and an estimated population of 88,000. The capital is Kolonia, on Pohnpei, with an estimated population of 6,000.

Constitutional government was installed in the Federated States of Micronesia in May 1979 and provides for a unicameral 14-member National Congress comprising members from the four states. Each state also elects its own Governor and legislature.

A Compact of Free Association with the United States was signed on Oct. 1, 1982, becoming law on Jan. 14, 1986. The Federated States enjoy full self-government and the responsibility for their defence is vested fully in the United States for 15 years.

President of the Federated States of Micronesia, John R. Haglelgam.

REPUBLIC OF PALAU

Palau consists of more than 200 Pacific Ocean islands of which eight are permanently inhabited. The Palau archipelago stretches over 400 miles. The land area is 191 sq. miles (494 sq. km.), with an estimated population of 14,000. The major island is Koror with a population of 6,500.

Palau and the U.S.A. signed a Compact of Free Association on Aug. 26, 1982, which, when approved by the U.S. Congress, will recognize the Republic of Palau to be a self-governing state. The U.S.A. is responsible for financial support, and for the defence of Palau for 50 years.

Constitutional government was installed in Palau in Jan. 1981 and provides for a bicameral legislature. The President and Vice President are directly elected.

Acting President, Thomas Remengesau.

THE PANAMA CANAL

As a result of the Panama Canal Treaty, 1977, the Canal Zone was disestablished, with all areas of land and water within the former Canal Zone reverting to Panama with effect from October 1, 1979. Under the treaty, the United States is allowed the use of operating areas for the Panama Canal, together with several military bases, although the Republic of Panama is sovereign in all such areas. The Panama Canal Commission, an arm of the U.S. Government, will continue to operate the canal until the year 2000.

TOTAL OCEAN GOING TRAFFIC

Fiscal Year	No. of Transits	Canal, Net Tons	Cargo Tons
1980	13,507	182,063,175	167,214,955
1981	13,884	188,656,491	171,221,762
1982	14,009	202,884,207	185,452,332
1983	11,707	169,503,918	145,590,759
1984	11,384	163,469,927	140,800,425
1985	11,654	170,091,933	138,903,287
1986	12,023	183,750,972	140,125,818
1987	12,230	186,405,525	148,690,380

The canal is fifty statute miles long (44·08 nautical miles), and the channel is from 500 to 1,000 feet wide at the bottom. It contains 12 locks in twin flights; 3 steps at Gatun on the Atlantic side, 1 step at Pedro Miguel and 2 at Miraflores on the Pacific side. Each lock chamber is 1,000 feet long and 110 feet wide. Transit from sea to sea takes on average 8 to 10 hours. The least width is in Gaillard Cut, and the greatest in Gatun Lake.

BRITISH EMBASSY
3100 Massachusetts Avenue, N.W.
Washington, D.C. 20008
[Washington D.C. 462 1340]

Ambassador Extraordinary and Plenipotentiary, His Excellency Sir Antony Acland, G.C.M.G., K.C.V.O., (1986).
Ministers, T. Lankester (*Economic*); J. S. Shrimplin (*Defence Equipment*); B. L. Crowe, C.M.G. (*Commercial*); B. J. P. Fall, C.M.G.; R. J. Harding, C.M.G. (Defence Material).
Head of British Defence Staff and Defence Attaché, Maj.-Gen. E. H. A. Beckett, C.B., M.B.E.
Naval Attaché, Rear Adm. M. C. Cole.
Military Attaché, Brig. R. D. Grist, O.B.E.
Air Attaché, Air Cdre. R. G. Peters, R.A.F.
Counsellors and Attachés, R. B. Bone (*Head of Chancery*); A. Pover (*Admin. and H.M. Consul-General*); R. C. Pratt (*Economic*); D. J. Hall (*Commercial*); J. A. L. Faint (*Overseas Development*); P. Lo (*Hong Kong Commercial Affairs*); Mrs. S. S. Lee-Birch (*Hong Kong Commercial Affairs*); A. J. Hunt (*Civil Aviation and Shipping*); M. Parkes (*Civil Aviation Air Traffic Systems*); P. Meiklem (*Civil Aviation, Safety*); A. W. R. Allcock (*Science and Technology*); Dr. M. F. Steeden (*Defence*); M. Hall (*Technical Works Group*); J. D. Gutteridge (*Defence Supply*); Dr. D. I. Kirkpatrick (*Defence Equipment*); D. Johnson (*Defence Equipment*); J. Platt (*Defence Equipment*); H. J. Muir (*Defence Equipment*); R. F. Cornish, L.V.O. (*Information*); M. E. Pellew, L.V.O.; D. Stuart; M. L. H. Doyle; J. D. Hansen; S. Band.
Cultural Attaché and British Council Representative, J. W. Daniel.

There are British Consulates General in Atlanta, Boston, Chicago, Cleveland, Houston, Los Angeles, Miami, New York and San Francisco.

BRITISH-AMERICAN CHAMBER OF COMMERCE, 275 Madison Avenue, New York 10016; U.K. OFFICE, Suite 201, High Holborn, WCIV 6RR.

URUGUAY
(República Oriental del Uruguay)

President, Dr. Julio María Sanguinetti, *took office*, March 1, 1985.
Vice President, Sr. Enrique Tarigo.

CABINET

Interior, Dr. Antonio Marchesano.
Foreign Affairs, Dr. Luis Barrios Tassano.
Economy and Finance, Cr. Ricardo Zerbino.
Transport and Public Works, Sr. Jorge Sanguinetti.
Public Health, Dr. Raúl M. Ugarte.
Labour and Social Security, Sr. Hugo Fernández Faingold.
Agriculture and Fisheries, Sr. Pedro Bonino.
Education, Culture and Justice, Dra. Adela Reta.
National Defence, Hugo Medina.
Industry and Energy, Dr. Jorge Presno.
Planning and Budget Office, Cr. Ariel Davrieux.
Tourism, Sr. José Villar.

URUGUAYAN EMBASSY AND CONSULATE
48 Lennox Gardens, SW1X 0DL
[01–589 8835; *Consulate* 01–589 8735]

Ambassador Extraordinary and Plenipotentiary, His Excellency Dr. Luis Alberto Solé-Romeo (1987).

Area and Population.—The smallest Republic in South America, on the east coast of the Rio de la Plata situated in lat. 30°–35° S. and long. 53° 15′–57° 42′ W., with an area of 68,037 sq. miles (176,215 sq. km.), and an estimated population (1985) of 3,012,000, almost entirely white and predominantly of Spanish and Italian descent. Many Uruguayans are Roman Catholics. There is complete freedom of religion and no church is established by the State.

Physical Features.—The country consists mainly of undulating grassy plains. The principal chains of hills are the Cuchilla del Haedo, which cross the Brazilian boundary and extend southwards to the Cuchilla Grande of the south and east. In no case do the peaks exceed 2,000 feet.

The principal river is the *Rio Negro* (with its tributary the Yi), flowing from north-east to south-west into the *Rio Uruguay*. The boundary river *Uruguay* is navigable from its estuary to Salto, about 200 miles north, and the Negro is also navigable for a considerable distance. Smaller rivers are the Cuareim, Yaguaron, Santa Lucia, Queguay and the Cebollati.

The climate is reasonably healthy. The summer is warm, but the heat is often tempered by the breezes of the Atlantic. The winter is, on the whole, mild, but cold spells, characterized by winds from the South Polar regions, are experienced in June, July and August. Rainfall is regular throughout the year, but there are occasional droughts. Floods also occur.

Government.—Uruguay—or the *Banda Oriental*, as this territory lying on the eastern bank of the Uruguay River was then called—resisted all attempted invasions of the Portuguese and Spanish until the beginning of the 17th century, and 100 years later the Portuguese settlements were captured by the Spanish. From 1726 to 1814 the country formed part of Spanish South America and underwent many vicissitudes during the Wars of Independence. In 1814 the armies of the Argentine Confederation captured the capital and annexed the province, and it was afterwards annexed by Portugal and became a province of Brazil. In 1825, the country threw off the Brazilian yoke. This action led to war between Argentina and Brazil which was settled by the mediation of the United Kingdom, Uruguay being declared an independent state in 1828. In 1830 a Republic was inaugurated.

According to the Constitution the President ap-

points a council of 11 ministers and a Secretary (Planning and Budget Office), and the Vice-President presides over Congress. The legislature consists of a Chamber of 99 deputies and a Senate of 30 members (plus the Vice-President), elected for five years by a system of proportional representation. Voting is obligatory and extends to all citizens of good repute and certain long standing residents who are not citizens, from the age of 18. General elections held in Nov. 1984 marked the return to democracy after 11 years of presidential rule with military support. The new government took office on March 1, 1985 and the provisions of the 1967 Constitution now prevail.

The Republic is divided into 19 Departments each with a chief of police and a Departmental Council.

Production and Industry.—Wheat, barley, maize, linseed, sunflower seed and rice are cultivated. The wealth of the country is obtained from its pasturage, which supports large herds of cattle and sheep, the wool of which is of excellent quality. There are just over 9 million cattle and just under 24 million sheep. In addition to meat packing, other foodstuffs, (citrus, wine, beer), fishing and textile industries are of importance.

The development of local industry continues and, in addition to the greatly augmented textile industry, marked expansion in local production is notable in respect of tyres, sheet-glass, three-ply wood, cement, leather-curing, beet sugar, plastics, household consumer goods, edible oils and the refining of petroleum and petroleum products.

Mineral Deposits.—There are some ferrous minerals, not extracted at present. Non-ferrous exploited minerals include clinker, dolomite, marble and granite.

Communications.—There are about 9,899 km. of national highways, and about 12,083 km. of telegraph and 48,375 miles of telephone communications.

There are about 2,987 km. of standard gauge railway in use in Uruguay. A State Autonomous Entity was formed to administer the railway systems purchased by the Government from four British companies in 1948.

An airline, PLUNA, which is owned by the State, runs daily services to southern Brazil, Paraguay and Argentina, and two flights a week to Madrid. The principal capitals of the interior and a limited freight service are connected to Montevideo by TAMU, another State owned airline, using principally military aircraft and personnel. International passenger and freight services are maintained by American, South American and European airlines. The international airport of Carrasco lies 12 miles outside Montevideo.

Education and Social Services.—Uruguay is one of the most advanced of the South American states, with old-age pensions, maternity and child welfare centres, accident insurance, etc. Primary education is compulsory and free, and technical and trade schools and evening courses for adult education are state controlled. There are about 322,053 pupils in the 2,362 state schools. The University at Montevideo (founded in 1849) has about 18,000 students enrolled in its ten faculties.

Language and Literature.—Spanish is the language of the Republic. Modern literature has provided some authors with international reputations and the literature of Spain is accessible in all public libraries. Five daily newspapers are published in Montevideo with an estimated total circulation of 150,000. Most of them are distributed throughout the country.

FINANCE

	1986	1987
Revenue	N$149,851·6 m.	N$270,939·2 m.
Expenditure	161,170·4 m.	292,987·7 m.

The external debt at Dec. 1987 was U.S.$5,887·5 million. Central Bank reserves (Dec., 1987) were US$865·2 million.

TRADE

	1986	1987
Total exports .	US$1,087,600,000	US$1,189,100,000
Total imports .	838,800,000	1,141,900,000

The major exports are meat and by-products, wool and by-products, hides and bristle and agricultural products. The principal imports are raw materials, construction materials, oils and lubricants, automotive vehicles, kits and machinery.

Trade with U.K.

	1986	1987
Imports from U.K. . . .	£26,465,000	£26,484,000
Exports to U.K.	41,366,000	40,474,000

The principal export items to the U.K. are wool and beef, the main imports are chemicals, kits, machinery, raw materials and metals.

CAPITAL.—ΨMontevideo. Population (1984) 1,355,312. Other centres (with 1967 estimates) are Salto (60,000), ΨPaysandu (60,000), Mercedes (34,000), Minas (34,000), Melo (30,000), and Rivera (40,000).

CURRENCY.—New Uruguayan Peso of 100 Centésimos.

FLAG.—Four blue and five white horizontal stripes surcharged with sun on a white ground in the top corner, next flagstaff.

NATIONAL ANTHEM.—Orientales, La Patria O La Tumba (Uruguayans, the fatherland or death).

NATIONAL DAY.—August 25 (Declaration of Independence, 1825).

BRITISH EMBASSY
Calle Marco Bruto 1073 Montevideo
[Montevideo 723533]

Ambassador Extraordinary and Plenipotentiary, His Excellency Eric Victor Vines, C.M.G., O.B.E. (1986)
First Secretary, P. Hunt (*Head of Chancery and Consul*).
Second Secretaries, B. McIntyre (*Commercial*); W. A. Allan; R. Graham; R. S. Dillow.
Defence Attaché, Capt. J. W. Porter.

BRITISH CONSULAR OFFICES
There is a British Consular Office at *Montevideo.*

ANGLO-URUGUAYAN CULTURAL INSTITUTE, San José 1426, Montevideo. There are branch Institutes throughout Uruguay.

BRITISH-URUGUAYAN CHAMBER OF COMMERCE, Avenida Labertador Brig. Gen., Lavalleja 1641, P2-OF 201, Montevideo.

THE VATICAN CITY STATE
(Stato della Città del Vaticano)

Sovereign Pontiff, His Holiness Pope John Paul II (Karol Wojtyla), *born* at Wadowice (Krakow, Poland), May 18, 1920, *elected* Pope (in succession to Pope John Paul I), Oct. 16, 1978.
Secretary of State, Cardinal Agostino Casaroli, *appointed* April, 1979.

APOSTOLIC NUNCIATURE IN LONDON
54 Parkside, SW19 5NF
[01–946 1410]

Apostolic Pro Nuncio, His Excellency Archbishop Luigi Barbarito (1986).
Counsellor, Mons. Rino Passigato.

The office of the ecclesiastical head of the Roman Catholic Church (Holy See) is vested in the Pope, the Sovereign Pontiff. For many centuries the Sovereign Pontiff exercised temporal power, but by 1870 the Papal States had become part of unified Italy. The temporal power of the Pope was in suspense until the treaty of Feb. 11, 1929, which recognized the full and independent sovereignty of the Holy See in the City of the Vatican. The area of the Vatican City is 108 acres and its population in 1985 was 1,000.

CURRENCY.—Italian currency is legal tender.

FLAG.—Square flag; equal vertical bands of yellow (next staff) and white; crossed keys and triple crown device on white band.

NATIONAL DAY.—October 22 (Inauguration of present Pontiff).

BRITISH EMBASSY TO THE HOLY SEE
91 Via Condotti, 00187 Rome
[Rome 678 9462]

Ambassador Extraordinary and Plenipotentiary, His Excellency John Keith Elliott Broadley, C.M.G. (1988).
First Secretary, P. J. McCormick.

VENEZUELA
(La Republica de Venezuela)

President, Dr. Jaime Lusinchi, *elected* Dec. 4, 1983, *assumed office* Feb. 2, 1984.

COUNCIL OF MINISTERS

Interior, Jose Angel Ciliberto.
Foreign Affairs, German Nava Carrillo.
Finance, Dr. Hector Hurtado Navarro.
Defence, Gen. Eliodoro Guerrero Gomez.
Development, Dr. Hector Meneses.
Education, Pedro Cabello Poleo.
Health and Social Welfare, Dr. Francisco Montbrun.
Agriculture and Livestock, Wenceslao Mantilla.
Labour, Jose Arnaldo Puigbo Morales.
Transport and Communications, Vincente Perez Cagena.
Justice, Pedro Torres Agudo.
Mines and Energy, Dr. Arturo Hernández Grisanti.
Planning, Modesto Freitas.
Environment and Natural Resources, Guillermo Colmenares Fimol.
Urban Development, Cesar Quintana.
Youth, Dra. Virginia Olivo de Celli.
Secretariat of the Presidency, Dr. Carmello Lauria Lesseur.
Ministers of State, Adolfo Ramirez Torres (*Governor of Caracas*); Leopoldo Sucre Figarella (*Venezuela-Guyana Corporation*); Tulio Arends (*Science and Technology*); Dr. Carlos Croes (*Dir. of Central Information Office*); Herberto Urdaneta (*Venezuelan Investment Fund*); Francisco Sucre Figarella (*Culture*); Mauricio Garcia Araujo (*Central Bank President*).

VENEZUELAN EMBASSY IN LONDON
1 Cromwell Road, SW7 2HW
[01–584 4206/7]

Ambassador Extraordinary and Plenipotentiary, His Excellency Dr. Francisco Kerdel-Vegas (1988).
Minister Counsellor, E. González-Urrutia.

There is also a Consulate-General at *Liverpool.*

Area and Population.—A South American Republic, situated approximately between 0° 45′ S. lat. and 12° 12′ N. lat. and 59° 45′–73° 09′ W. long. It consists of one Federal District, 20 states and 2 territories. Venezuela has a total area of 352,144 sq. miles (912,050 sq. km.) and a population (1985) of 17,323,000.

Venezuela lies on the north of the South American continent, and is bounded on the north by the Caribbean Sea, west by the Republic of Colombia, east by Guyana, and south by Brazil. Included in the area of the Republic are 72 islands off the coast, with a total area of about 14,650 square miles, the largest being *Margarita*, which is politically associated with Tortuga, Cubagua and Coche to form the State of *Nueva Esparta*. Margarita has an area of about 400 square miles.

Physical Features.—The Eastern Andes from the south-west cross the border and reach to the Caribbean Coast, where they are prolonged by the Maritime Andes of Venezuela to the Gulf of Paria on the north-east. The main range is known as the Sierra Nevada de Merida, and contains the highest peaks in the country in Pico Bolivar (16,411 feet) and Picacho de la Sierra (15,420 feet). Near the Brazilian border the Sierras Parima and Pacaraima, and on the eastern border the Sierras de Rincote and de Usupamo, enclose the republic with parallel northward spurs, between which are valleys of the Orinoco tributaries. The slopes of the mountains and foothills are covered with dense forests, but the basin of the Orinoco is mainly *llanos*, or level stretches of open prairie, with occasional woods.

The principal river is the *Orinoco*, with innumerable affluents, the main river exceeding 1,600 miles in length from its rise in the southern highlands of the republic to its outflow in the deltaic region of the north-east. The Orinoco is navigable for large steamers from its mouth for 700 miles, and by smaller vessels as far as the Maipures Cataract, some 200 miles farther up-stream. Dredging operations have opened the Orinoco to ocean-going ships, of up to 40 ft. draft, as far as Ciudad Guayana (about 150 miles up-stream). Among the many tributaries of the main stream are the Ventuari, Apure (with its tributary the Portuguesa), Arauca, Meta, and Guaviare from the west, the Meta and Guaviare being principally Colombian rivers. The upper waters of the Orinoco are united with those of the Rio Negro (a Brazilian tributary of the Amazon) by a natural river or canal, known as the *Casiquiare*.

The coastal regions of Venezuela are much indented and contain many lagoons and lakes, of which *Maracaibo*, with an area of 8,296 square miles, is the largest lake in South America. Other lakes are Zulia (290 square miles), south-west of Maracaibo, and Valencia (216 square miles) about 1,400 ft. above sea-level in the Maritime Andes.

The climate is tropical and, except where modified by altitude or tempered by sea breezes, is unhealthy, particularly in the coastal regions and in the neighbourhood of lowland streams and lagoons. The hot, wet season lasts from April to October, the dry, cooler season from November to March.

Language and Literature.—Spanish is the language of the country. There are 61 daily newspapers in Venezuela, of which ten are published in Caracas, and about 60 to 70 weekly news magazines. There are also a large number of fortnightly, monthly and quarterly publications.

Education is free and compulsory between the ages of 7 and 13. There are ten universities in Venezuela, five in Caracas and the others in Maracaibo, Mérida, Valencia, Cumaná and Barquisimeto.

Production and Industry.—Products of the tropical forest region include: orchids, wild rubber, timber, mangrove bark, balata gum and tonka beans: of agricultural areas, cocoa beans, coffee, cotton, rice, maize, sugar, sesame, groundnuts, potatoes, tomatoes, other vegetables, sisal and tobacco. There is an extensive beef and dairy farming industry. Despite substantial improvements in agriculture, Venezuela is heavily reliant upon food imports, which constitute about 60 per cent of total consumption.

The principal industry is that of petroleum, which in 1986 contributed 83 per cent of Venezuela's foreign exchange income. Daily production in the oilfields (nationalized 1976) has steadily declined since 1973 in line with Venezuela's conservation policies, reaching 1·7 mbd in 1986 (1973—3·366 mbd). There are refineries at Punta Cardon, Amuay, Caripitó, San Lorenzo, Puerto La Cruz, Tucupeido, El Chaure and El Palito. Development of the Orinoco heavy oil belt is now moving ahead with the inauguration of the Lagovén continuous steam injection pilot plant at El Jobo in southern Monagas. It has been estimated conservatively that there might exist recoverable resources of 70,000 million barrels in the Orinoco region, but the initial aim of the Lagovén project is the production of 125,000 and 500,000 bpd of upgraded crude by 1988 and 2000 respectively.

Aluminium is the second highest source of foreign exchange after petroleum. The Venezuelan state now holds the majority stake in both the principal producing companies, Venalum and Alcasa, and is moving towards a consolidation of the aluminium industry, with both companies sharing their resources and adopting general policies of marketing and procurement of supplies. Output in 1980 was 222,160 tons, with 151,250 tons exported.

Rich iron ore deposits in Eastern Venezuela have been developed. Secondary processes for pelletizing and briqueting ore for export have been installed. The government-owned steel mill at Matanzas in the Guayana uses local iron ore and obtains its electric power from hydro-electric installations on the Caroni River. It produces seamless steel tubes, billets, wire and profiles. The production of more steel products is planned over the next few years. A mill at Ciudad Guayana for the production of centrifugally-cast iron pipe came into operation at the end of 1970, with an annual capacity of 30,000 tons.

Other industries include petrochemicals, gold, diamonds and asbestos; textiles, clothing and footwear; plastics; manufacture or preparation of foodstuffs, alcoholic and non-alcoholic beverages; manufacture of paper, cement, glass, tyres, cigarettes, soap, animal feeding concentrates, simple steel products, tins, jewellery, rope, furniture, sacks, paint and motor-vehicle assembly; preparation of pharmaceutical goods; pearl fishing, sanitary ware, electric home appliances, pumps, toys, agricultural machinery, bicycles, electronic components, cosmetics and many others.

Communications.—There are about 62,449 km. of roads, 22,975 km. of them paved. The State has now acquired all but a very few of the railway lines, whose total length is only some 372 kilometres. Road and river communications have made railways of negligibile importance in Venezuela except for carrying iron ore in the south-east. However, the government is restoring the Puerto Cabello-Barquisimeto line and expanding it to Turén in the agricultural heartland of Venezuela. A new line connecting Caracas with La Guaira and the Litoral is planned, and in 1983 the Caracas Metro came into operation. British, U.S. and European airlines provide Venezuela with a wide range of services. There are three Venezuelan airlines (two of them state-owned) which between them have a comprehensive network of internal lines and also connect Caracas with the United States, Central and South America, the Caribbean and Europe. Foreign vessels are not permitted to engage in the coast trade. The telegraph, radio-telegraph and radio-telephone services are state-owned. There are two government-controlled, 150 commercial and one cultural, FM, broadcasting stations. There are four television stations in Venezuela, all in Caracas. Two are government controlled.

TRADE

	1985	1986
Total imports	US$7,388 m	US$7,600 m
Total exports	14,178 m	8,880 m

Trade with U.K.

	1986	1987
Imports from U.K.	£170,101,000	£157,760,000
Exports to U.K.	96,339,000	91,749,000

CAPITAL.—Caracas, population (1981), 1,816,901. Other principal towns are Ψ Maracaibo (870,000), Barquisimeto (495,000), Valencia (495,000), Maracay (322,000), San Cristobal (164,000), Cumaná (135,000) and Ciudad Guayana (250,000).

CURRENCY.—Bolivar of 100 Céntimos.

FLAG.—Three horizontal bands, yellow, blue, red (with seven white stars on blue band and coat of arms next to staff on yellow band).

NATIONAL ANTHEM.—Gloria Al Bravo Pueblo (Glory to the brave people).

NATIONAL DAY.—July 5.

BRITISH EMBASSY
Apartado 1246, Caracas 1010-A.

[Caracas 911255]

Ambassador Extraordinary and Plenipotentiary, His Excellency Giles Eden FiztHerbert, C.M.G. (1987).
Counsellor, A. R. Murray *(Head of Chancery)*.
Defence Attaché, Capt. J. B. Lean, R.N.

BRITISH CONSULAR OFFICES

There are British Consular Offices at *Caracas, Maracaibo, Puerto La Cruz* and *Valencia.*

British Council Representative, Dr. V. A. Atkinson, Aparto 1246, Caracas 1010-A.

BRITISH-VENEZUELAN CHAMBER OF COMMERCE, Apartado 5713 Edificio Blandin, Piso I Oficina I-C, Plaza Chacaito, Caracas.

VIETNAM
(Công Hòa Xã Hôi Chu Nghĩa Viêt Nam)

COUNCIL OF STATE
Chairman, Vo Chi Cong.
Deputy Chairmen, Nguyen Huu Tho; Huynh Tan Phat; Le Quang Dao; Nguyen Quyet; Dam Quang Trung; Mrs. Nguyen Thi Dinh.

Gen. Secretary, Nguyen Viet Dung.
Members, Y Ngong Niet Dam; Pham The Duyet; Tran Do; Nguyen Xuan Huu; Vu Mao; Hoang Bich Son; Nguyen Dinh Tu.

COUNCIL OF MINISTERS
Chairman, Do Muoi.
Vice Chairmen, Vo Van Kiet; Nguyen Co Thach; Dong Sy Nguyen; Vo Nguyen Giap; Nguyen Khanh; Tran Duc Luong.
Members, all Ministers, and Chairmen of most State Committees (around 35 in all).

VIETNAMESE COMMUNIST PARTY
Politburo of the Central Committee, Nguyen Van Linh (*General Secretary*); Vo Chi Cong; Do Muoi; Vo Van Kiet; Le Duc Anh; Nguyen Duc Tam; Nguyen Co Thach; Dong Sy Nguyen; Tran Xuan Bach; Nguyen Thanh Binh; Doan Khue; Mai Chi Tho; Dao Duy Tung *(full members)*.

EMBASSY IN LONDON
12–14 Victoria Road, W8 5RD
[01–937 1912–8564]

Ambassador Extraordinary and Plenipotentiary, His Excellency Tran Van Hung (1986).
Third Secretary, Ngo Ngoc Phieu.

Vietnam, with an area of 127,242 sq. miles (329,556 sq. km.), and an estimated population (1987) of 62,300,000, is bordered on the north by China and the west by Laos and Kampuchea.

Government.—Following the end of the war in Vietnam in 1975, and the establishment of a Provisional Revolutionary Government to administer South Vietnam, a National Assembly representing the whole of Vietnam was elected on April 25, 1976. The Assembly met in Hanoi on June 24, and on July 2 approved the reunification of North and South Vietnam under the name of the Socialist Republic of Vietnam. The national flag, anthem and capital of North Vietnam were unanimously adopted for the Socialist Republic, and Saigon was renamed Ho Chi Minh City.

Effective power lies with the ruling Party, the Vietnamese Communist Party (*V.C.P.*), its highest executive body being the Central Committee, elected by a Party Congress on a national basis.

The Sixth Party Congress of the V.C.P. in December 1986 elected a new Central Committee. It is the Politburo and the Secretariat of the Central Committee which exercises real power and rules Vietnam.

Economy.—During the last nine years, Vietnam's economy has faced considerable problems. These include serious agricultural losses because of adverse weather, major reductions in Western aid (as a result of Vietnam's invasion and occupation of neighbouring Kampuchea), border hostilities with China, and the continued allocation of resources to military expenditure. Efforts to integrate the economies of the North and South have not been very successful.

Although food production has substantially increased (over 18 million tonnes of grain in 1985) as has G.D.P. in general, Vietnam's overall economic position at the end of 1985 was not good. Food production has stagnated in the last three years. There was little foreign exchange because of minimal exports to hard currency areas. Vietnam was in default of repayments to the international banking world from the I.M.F. to major commercial and merchant banks and therefore received very few long term credits. Some attempted reforms of the economic system in 1985, including devaluation and a currency change, were implemented disastrously and inflation increased rapidly in late 1985 and early 1986. Despite massive assistance from the Soviet Union (estimated at US$2·3 billion p.a. in 1987) and other member countries of C.M.E.A. (of which Vietnam is a member), Vietnam's economy continued to decline. Economic reforms were instituted in the wake of the sixth Party Congress.

Trade with U.K.

	1986	1987
Imports from U.K.	£1,288,000	£2,598,000
Exports to U.K.	1,200,000	357,000

CAPITAL.—Hanoi (population (1984), City, 925,000; Province, 2,800,000).

CURRENCY.—Dông of 10 Hao and 100 Xu.

FLAG.—Red, with yellow five-point star in centre.

NATIONAL ANTHEM.—Tien Quan Ca (The troops are advancing).

NATIONAL DAY.—September 2.

BRITISH EMBASSY
16 Pho Ly Thuong Kiet, Hanoi
[Hanoi 52349]

Ambassador Extraordinary and Plenipotentiary, His Excellency Emrys Thomas Davies, C.M.G. (1987).
First Secretary, C. D. Partridge.

YEMEN (North)
(Al-Jamhuriya Al-Arabiya Al-Yamaniya)

President and Commander of the Armed Forces, Col. Ali Abdullah Saleh, *elected* July 19, 1978, *re-elected* May 23, 1983.

Prime Minister, Abdul Aziz Abdul Ghani.

Deputy Premiers, Dr. Hassan Mohammed Makki; Dr. Abdul Karim Aliryani (*Foreign Affairs*); Dr. Mohamed Saeed Alattar (*Development, and Chairman of Central Planning Organization*); Lt.-Col. Mujahid Abu Sha'warib (*Internal Affairs*).

Public Works and President of Supreme Council for Reconstruction of Earthquake Affected Areas, Abdullah Al Kurshumi.

Awqaf and Guidance, Qadi Ali Al Samman.

Economy, Supply and Trade, Mohammed Al Khadim Al Wajih.

Social Affairs and Labour, Lt. Col. Mohsin Mohammed al Ulafi.

Agriculture and Fisheries, Dr. Hussein Abdullah Al Amri.

Civil Service & Administrative Reform, Ismail Ahmed Al Wazir.

Finance, Alwi Saleh as Salami.

Communications and Transport, Ahmed Al Anisi.

Interior, Lt. Col. Abdullah Hussein Barakat.

Information and Culture, Hassan Al Lawzi.

Municipalities and Planning, Mohammed Ahmed Luqman.

Oil and Mineral Resources, Ahmed Ali Al Mohanni.

Health, Dr. Mohammed Al Kabab.

Electricity, Water and Sewerage, Mohammed Hassan Sabra.

Minister of State and Sec. Gen. of Council for Youth and Sports, Abdullah Nasir Al Dhorafi.

Education, Mohammed Abdullah Al Jaifi.

Justice, Qadi Ahmed Mohammed Al Jawbi.

Minister of State for Prime Ministerial Affairs, Ahmed Saleh Al Roueni.

Minister of State for Unity Affairs, Yahya Hussein Al Arashi.

YEMEN EMBASSY
41 South Street, W1Y 5PD
[01–629 9905/8]

Ambassador Extraordinary and Plenipotentiary, His Excellency Ahmed Daifellah Alazeib (1981).

Yemen, the *Arabia Felix* of the ancients, occupies the S.W. corner of Arabia between the kingdom of Saudi Arabia and the People's Democratic Republic of Yemen, with an estimated area of 75,290 sq. miles (195,000 sq. km.). The highlands and central plateau of Yemen, and the highest portions of the maritime range, form the most fertile part of Arabia, with an abundant but irregular rainfall. The ruins of Marib, the ancient Sabæan capital, and its dam are in the Yemen.

The population is (1987 Census) 9,250,000.

Government.—A General Popular Conference was established in Aug. 1982, consisting of 700 elected members and 300 appointed members. It agreed a new National Charter and elected a Permanent Council of 75 members (50 elected, 25 appointed), with a General Council and four sub-committees (economic; political; administrative and public works; cultural and reform).

The General Popular Conference meets every two years and is re-elected every four. The Permanent Council meets regularly for two months, followed by a two-month break. The General Council and sub-committees meet regularly. In 1986 the total membership of the General Popular Conference was expanded to 22,250, comprising elected and appointed members.

Economy.—The main exports are cotton, coffee, hides and skins. Oil has been produced at Marib since Dec. 1987. Production averages 150,000 b.p.d.

Trade with U.K.

	1986	1987
Imports from U.K.	£58,149,000	£55,334,000
Exports to U.K.	2,106,000	2,306,000

CAPITAL.—Sana'a (pop. 427,185). Other main cities are Taiz (178,043), Hodeida (155,110), Ibb (48,806) and Dhamar (47,733).

CURRENCY.—Yemeni Riyal of 100 Fils.

FLAG.—Horizontal bands of red, white and black, with 5-point green star in centre of white band.

NATIONAL DAY.—September 26.

BRITISH EMBASSY
P.O. Box 1287, Sana'a
[Sana'a 215630/3]

Ambassador Extraordinary and Plenipotentiary, His Excellency Mark Anthony Marshal (1987).
First Secretaries, B. C. Seddon (*Head of Chancery and Aid*); J. D. Orr (*Commercial*).
British Council Representative, J. McGrath, Beit Al-Mottahar, Al-Bonia Street, Harat Handhal (P.O. Box 2157), Sana'a.

YEMEN (South)
(Al-Jumhurijah Al-Yemen Al-Dimugratiyah Al Sha'abiyah)

President, Haider Abubaker Al-Attas, *assumed power* January 1986, *elected* Nov. 6, 1986 *for a 5-year term.*
Prime Minister, Dr. Yassin Saeed No'man.

EMBASSY OF THE PEOPLE'S DEMOCRATIC REPUBLIC OF YEMEN
57 Cromwell Road, SW7 2ED
[01–584 6607/9]

Ambassador Extraordinary and Plenipotentiary, His Excellency Ahmed Abdo Rageh (1987).

Area and Population.—The Democratic Republic of Yemen lies at the southern end of the Arabian peninsula, having a frontier with the Yemen Arab Republic, Saudi Arabia and the Sultanate of Oman, and a coastline extending 700 miles from the Red Sea eastwards along the Gulf of Aden. The area is largely composed of mountains and desert. Rainfall is generally scarce and unpredictable. The population outside Aden is concentrated in the fertile districts. In the more extensive desert and near-desert areas nomadic communities depend on their livestock for a livelihood.

Included in the State are the offshore islands of Perim (in the Bab al-Mandeb Straits) and Socotra. Sovereignty over the island of Kamaran (area 70 sq. miles) in the Red Sea is under dispute following its occupation by forces of the Yemen Arab Republic during border conflicts in October, 1972. The area of the People's Democratic Republic is 128,560 sq. miles (332,968 sq. km.), with a population (1985 estimate) of 2,500,000.

Government.—The People's Republic of South Yemen was set up on Nov. 30, 1967 when the British government ceded power to the National Liberation Front, thus bringing to an end 129 years of British rule in Aden and some years of protectorate status in the hinterland. Its name was changed to People's Democratic Republic of Yemen on Nov. 30, 1970. Territory of the Republic is that of the former Federation of South Arabia and the Aden Protectorates, consisting of the State of Aden and some 17 sultanates and emirates. It is now divided into six Governorates. Under a constitution promulgated on Nov. 30, 1970, there is a Supreme People's Council of 101 members and an 11-member Presidium. The Chairman of the Presidium is head of state.

In Jan. 1986, severe rivalries within the régime led to a fierce outbreak of fighting in Aden and the temporary evacuation of the foreign community. The President, Ali Nasser Mohammed, escaped abroad and a new government was set up continuing the existing Marxist régime.

The Government receives substantial development from the World Bank, Kuwait and Abu Dhabi (Arab Development Funds). Other aid is provided by China, the E.C., U.S.S.R. (including military aid) and other Socialist Bloc countries.

Production.—Agriculture is the main occupation of the inhabitants outside Aden. This is largely of a subsistence nature, sorghum, sesame and millets being the chief crops, with wheat and barley widely grown at the higher elevations. Disastrous floods in 1983 caused major damage to the principal agricultural areas.

Yemen is not an oil producing country but significant traces of hydrocarbons were found during exploration activities offshore in 1982. The Aden Refinery Company has a refining capacity of 8 m. tons per annum but for a number of years output has not exceeded a rate equivalent to 5 m. tons annually. Several Western companies are now involved in oil exploration and production is expected to begin in late 1988. The exact reserves and estimated production levels are unknown.

Under the Five Year Development Plan 1974–79 much importance was attached to the development of agricultural and fisheries projects. Under the second Five Year Plan (1981–85) emphasis shifted to industrial development, which was allocated 29 per cent of the total investment budget (YD508m); agricultural development was allocated 12 per cent. Light industries are being established which will replace imports and use locally produced raw materials.

Expenditure in 1986 was severely affected by the January fighting and had to be diverted to repair the considerable material damage.

Communications.—Following the closure of the Suez Canal in 1967 the once prosperous trading economy of Aden fell into a steady decline, which has not been reversed by the re-opening of the Canal. In the main harbour, cargo handling for larger vessels is by lighter, but wharves at Maalla can accommodate alongside vessels up to 300 feet in length and 18 feet in draught.

There are no railways in the Republic. Yemen has 760 miles of good roads and construction of a further 300 miles is in hand. A system of undeveloped but motorable roads links the towns and villages outside Aden. There is an international airport at Aden (Khormaksar) into which a limited number of international airlines operate.

FINANCE

	1986	1987
G.D.P.	YD 204·6m	YD215·6m
Per capita income	YD92·27	YD94·5

Trade with U.K.

	1986	1987
Imports from U.K.	£23,928,000	£28,271,000
Exports to U.K.	4,848,000	1,056,000

CAPITAL.—Ψ Aden (population, 270,000). Other towns are Ψ Mukalla, Seiyoun, Shabwa, Beihan, Lawdar, Shuqra, Dhala and Lahes.

CURRENCY.—Yemeni Dinar (YD) of 1,000 Fils.

FLAG.—A tricolour, red, white and black horizontal bands, with a triangle of light blue at the hoist pointing towards the fly and charged with a five pointed red star.

NATIONAL DAYS.—November 30 (Independence Day); October 14 (Revolution Day).

BRITISH EMBASSY
Khormaksar, Aden.

[Aden 32711/6]

Ambassador Extraordinary and Plenipotentiary, His Excellency Arthur Stirling-Maxwell Marshall, C.B.E. (1986).

Second Secretary, M. S. T. Morgan (*Vice-Consul*).

YUGOSLAVIA
(Socijalistička Federativna Republika Jugoslavije)

President of the Presidency (1988–89), Raif Dizdarević (*Bosnia/Hercegovina*).

Vice-President of the Presidency (1988–89), Stane Dolanc (*Slovenia*).

Members of the Presidency, Raif Dizdarević (*Bosnia/Hercegovina*); Stane Dolanc (*Slovenia*); Nikola Ljubičić (*Serbia*); Josip Vrhovec (*Croatia*); Veselin Djuranović (*Montenegro*); Radovan Vlajković (*Vojvodina*); Stipe Šuvar (*L.C.Y.*).

FEDERAL EXECUTIVE COUNCIL

President, Branko Mikulić.

Vice-Presidents, Miloš Milosavijević; Janez Zemljarič.

Foreign Affairs, Budimir Lončar.

National Defence, Veljko Kadijević.

Internal Affairs, Dobroslav Ćulafić.

Finance, Svetozar Rikanović.

Foreign Trade, Nenad Krekić.

Trade and General Economic Affairs, Šarac Milehko.

Justice and Organization of Federal Administration, Petar Vajović.

Information, Svetozar Durutović.

Federal Committee Presidents:—

Agriculture, Sava Vujkov.

Transport and Communications, Mustafa Pljakić.

Labour, Health and Social Security, Janko Obočki.

Questions concerning War Veterans and Disabled Veterans, Sesuja Milan.

Scientific and Technological Development, Božidar Matić.

Tourism, Franc Horvat.

Other F.E.C. members, Dragi Danev; Francka Herga; Oskar Kovač; Radoje Kontić; Radovan Makić; Nevenka Meralić-Milivojević; Muhamet Mustafa; Tibor Salma; Ibrahim Tabaković; Momčilo Vučinić; Egon Padovan; Mito Pejovski.

President of the SFRY Assembly, Dušan Popoyski.
President of the Socialist Alliance of the Working People, Dr. Božidar Čolakovic.

LEAGUE OF COMMUNISTS OF YUGOSLAVIA

Presidency of the Central Committee
President of the Presidency, Dr. Stipe Šuvar *(elected for one year in June* 1988).
Secretary, Stefan Korošec *(elected for two years in June* 1988).
Members, Ivan Brigić; Dušan Čkrebić; V. Kadijević; Štefan Korošec; Ivica Račan; Milanko Renovica; Franc Šetinc; Stipe Šuvar; V. Tupurkovski; V. Žarković.

YUGOSLAV EMBASSY IN LONDON
5–7 Lexham Gardens W8 5JJ
[01–370 6105]

Ambassador Extraordinary and Plenipotentiary, His Excellency Mitko Čalovski (1985).
Minister Counsellors, Branko Brankovic; Predrag Mitic *(Economic).*
Counsellor, Mario Mikolic *(Press and Culture).*
Defence Attaché, Col. Dragoljub Milovanovic.

Area and Population.—Yugoslavia is a Federation comprising the Socialist Republics of Serbia, Croatia, Slovenia, Montenegro, Bosnia and Hercegovina, and Macedonia. Serbia includes the Socialist Autonomous Provinces of Vojvodina and Kosovo. The area of Yugoslavia is estimated at 98,766 sq. miles (255,804 sq. km.). The population was estimated (1985) at 23,123,000; the latest Census (April 1981) broke down the population into 8,140,000 Serbs, 4,430,000 Croats, 1,750,000 Slovenes, 1,730,000 Albanians, 1,341,000 Macedonians and 1,220,000 "Yugoslavs", as well as a variety of other minorities.

Government.—On Nov. 29, 1945, the Constituent Assembly of Yugoslavia at a joint session of the Skupština and the House of Nationalities, proclaimed Yugoslavia a Republic.

The official name of the country, "The Socialist Federal Republic of Yugoslavia", was adopted by the 1963 Constitution.

Several amendments to the Constitution were made in 1971. The most important formed a new ruling body called the Presidency, which has 8 members, one from each Republic and Autonomous Province. Since the death of President Tito in May 1980, its members take it in turns according to a fixed order of succession to become President of the Presidency of the Republic for a period of 12 months each. A new Constitution was proclaimed in 1974 followed by the reconstitution of the Federal Assembly into two chambers consisting of the Federal Chamber (220 delegates) and the Republican/Provincial Chamber (88 delegates). A new Federal Executive Council (i.e. government) was also formed. The current Council was elected in May 1986 with a 2 year renewable mandate. The first election of the S.F.R.Y. Presidency since Pres. Tito's death took place in May 1984; each new member has a five-year mandate.

There is only one political party in Yugoslavia, the "League of Communists of Yugoslavia" (within which each Republic and Province has its own separate L.C.Y. organization) but there is a formal separation of State and Party; no-one may hold a post in the Federal or Republican/Provincial governments and a paid L.C.Y. post simultaneously. Political and economic decisions on many issues are devolved from Federal to Republican/Provincial level. Yugoslavia has a "self-management" form of industrial organi-

zation under which the workforce have the constitutional right to own and control their own enterprises.

Defence.—The Army, Navy and Air Force on a peace footing consist of 250,000 officers and men.

Religion and Education.—The three main religions are the Orthodox, Catholic and Islamic, and freedom to practice is constitutionally guaranteed. Religion is separated from the State and no religious instruction is allowed in state schools.

Education.—Eight years' elementary education is compulsory and all education is free. There are 18 universities.

Language and Literature.—The language mainly used throughout Yugoslavia and in the Federal Government is Serbo-Croat but Slovenian and Macedonian (also South-Slav tongues) and Albanian, Bulgarian, Romanian, Italian, Slovak, Ruthenian, Hungarian and Turkish are also spoken in certain areas. There is, however, no official language since all are constitutionally equal, except in the Armed Forces where Serbo Croat is obligatory. In Serbia, Macedonia and Montenegro the Cyrillic script is used and in the rest of the country the Latin. There are 4 Serbian daily newspapers in Belgrade, 2 Slovene dailies in Ljubljana, 2 Croat dailies in Zagreb, and many other dailies published in other towns. There are also many local newspapers and radio programmes in the different "minority" languages.

Production and Industry.—The share of industry in Gross Domestic Product (average annual rate in real terms of 6·5 per cent in 1981) is now 40 per cent, while agriculture is 14 per cent. In industry the high level of investment of recent years is being cut back and present efforts are directed towards development of high priority areas such as mining, energy resources and transport and communications. Agricultural policy is directed towards substantially increased production, to make the country self-sufficient and to provide significant exports of foodstuffs. Some 80 per cent of land is still privately owned.

The main crops are wheat, maize, sugar beet, sunflower and soya. Yields in 1985 were (tons): wheat, 4·9 m; maize, 9·9 m; sugar beet, 6·2 m. According to Yugoslav official estimates, the livestock population in 1985 was approximately as follows: cattle, 5,199,000; sheep, 7,678,000; pigs, 8,673,000; poultry, 70,453,000.

Minerals are an important source of wealth particularly in the central and south eastern regions. Production in 1985 included the following (tons):—

Coal	69,000,000
Coke	3,538,000
Iron ore	5,444,000
Pig iron	3,199,000
Steel	4,463,000
Crude oil	4,144,000

Smaller quantities of copper, zinc and mercury are produced.

Communications.—In 1984 there were 9,279 kms of standard and narrow gauge railway and approximately 116,600 kms of classified roads. In 1984 there were 3,031,000 telephones in use in the country. The principal ports on the long Adriatic seaboard of Yugoslavia are Rijeka, Bakar, Šibenik, Split, Zadar, Kardeljeva (formerly Ploče), Dubrovnik, Bar, Kotor (Cattaro) and Koper. The Danube forms a great commercial highway and the tributary rivers Sava and Tisa provide other shipping routes.

FINANCE

	1983 million *Dinars*	1984 million *Dinars*
Revenue	1,140,000	374,000
Expenditure	1,140,000	374,000

The rate of exchange is variable. On June 6, 1980 the *dinar* was devalued against all convertible currencies and there have been several devaluations since then. (*See also* p. 716.)

Trade with U.K.

	1986	1987
Imports from U.K.	£188,330,000	£206,932,000
Exports to U.K.	144,800,000	175,301,000

CAPITAL.—Belgrade, population (1981) 1,455,000. Other towns are Zagreb (763,000); Skopje (503,000); Ljubljana (253,000); Sarajevo (447,000); Novi Sad (169,000); Priština (1971) (153,000); Ψ Split (152,000); Ψ Rijeka (133,000); Titograd (95,000).

CURRENCY.—Yugoslav Dinar of 100 Paras.

FLAG.—Five-point red star outlined by narrow yellow stripe, on a ground of three horizontal bars, blue, white and red.

NATIONAL ANTHEM.—Hej, Slaveni, Jošte Živi Reč Naših Dedova (Oh! Slavs, our ancestors' words still live).

NATIONAL DAY.—November 29.

BRITISH EMBASSY
General Ždanova 46, Belgrade.

[Belgrade 645055]

Ambassador Extraordinary and Plenipotentiary, His Excellency Andrew Marley Wood, C.M.G., (1985).

Counsellor, D. C. A. Madden.

Defence and Military Attaché, Col. A. E. F. Cowan, O.B.E.

Naval and Air Attaché, Wg. Cdr. M. B. M. Canavan.

First Secretaries, R. J. Campbell (*Economic*); F. B. Holroyd, O.B.E. (*Admin. and Consular*); J. D. Clark (*Commercial*).

Second Secretary, R. J. A. Huxter (*Chancery and Information*).

BRITISH CONSULAR OFFICES

There are British Consular Offices at *Belgrade, Zagreb* and *Split*.

British Council Representative, D. Gunton, O.B.E. Generala Ždanova 34, (P.O. Box 248), 11001 Belgrade. British Council Reading Room, Knez Mihajlova 45, Belgrade. There are also a centre and library at *Zagreb*.

ZAIRE
(République du Zaïre)

President of the Republic and National Security, Marshal Mobutu Sésé Séko, born Oct. 30, 1930; *assumed office* November 25, 1965; *elected* Nov. 5, 1970; *re-elected for third term*, July 28, 1984.

EXECUTIVE COUNCIL

Prime Minister, Sambwa Pida N'Bagui.

Deputy P.M. charged with Political, Administrative and Social Affairs and State Commissioner for Human Rights, Me Nimy Mayidika Ngimbi.

Deputy P.M. charged with Economic, Fiscal and Monetary Affairs and State Commissioner for Agriculture, Nyembo Shabani.

Territorial Administration and Decentralization, Mandungu Bula Nyati.

Foreign Affairs and International Co-operation, Nguza Karl-I-Bond.

Information and Press, Ekila Liyonda.

Planning, Kasereka Kasai.

Finance, Kamitatu Massamba.

Budget, Prof. Kinzonzi Mvutukidi Ngindu Kagbia.

Economy and Industry, Mokonda Bonza.

Parastatals, Prof. Mulumba Lukoji.

Foreign Trade, Kanumubadi Badibanga Mbakese.

Rural Development, Kayinga Onsi Ndal.

Mines and Energy, Kisanga Kabongelo.

Public Works and Regional Development, Mokolo wa Mpombo.

Transport and Communications, Sampassa Kaweta Milombe.

Land, Environment and Conservation, Pendje Demodetdo.

Higher Education, Universities and Scientific Research, Luhahi a Niami.

Primary and Secondary Education, Nzege Alaziambina.

Public Health, Dr. Ngandu Kabeya.

Town Planning and Housing, Kibangula Kia Makonga.

Social Affairs, Maduka Inyanza.

Labour and Social Security, Kisolokele Wamba.

Civil Service, Mwando Nsimba.

Post and Telecommunications, Ileo Itambala.

Sport and Leisure, Tshimbombo Mukuna.

Culture, Arts and Tourism, Beyeye Djema.

President of the Judicial Council, N'Singa Undjuu Ongwankebi Untumbe.

ZAIRE EMBASSY
26 Chesham Place, SW1X 8HH
[01–235 6137]

Ambassador Extraordinary and Plenipotentiary, His Excellency Citoyen Kitshodi Nzekele (1987).

The State of the Congo, founded in 1885, became a Belgian Colony on Nov. 15, 1908, and was administered by Belgium until 1960, when it became the Democratic Republic of the Congo. In October 1971 the name changed to the Republic of Zaire. Situated between long. 12°–31° E. and lat. 5° N.–13° S., the Republic of Zaire comprises an area of 905,567 sq. miles (2,345,409 sq. km.), with a population (1985 Census) of 34,671,607.

Climate.—Apart from the coastal district in the West which is fairly dry, the rainfall averages between 60 and 80 inches. The average temperature is about 27°C., but in the South the winter temperature can fall nearly to freezing point. Extensive forest covers the central districts.

Government.—On June 30, 1960, the Belgian Congo became an independent unitary state under the Presidency of M. Kasavubu with a provisional constitution drawn up by the metropolitan Belgian Parliament. On July 11, M. Moïse Tshombe announced the independence of the State of Katanga although he failed to obtain international recognition. Katanga did not come under the Government at Leopoldville until January 14, 1963.

The constitutional and political situation remained unsettled, the United Nations having mixed forces in the country until 1964. By the middle of 1965, the Congolese Government formed by M. Tshombe in July, 1964, had succeeded in gaining control of all the towns from the rebels and depriving them of military aid from outside the Congo. Gen. Joseph-Désiré Mobutu, Commander-in-Chief of the Congolese National Army, announced on November 25, 1965 that he had assumed the Presidency.

A Presidential régime was instituted by the 1967 Constitution, subsequently amended in 1974 and totally revised in Feb. 1978. The Mouvement Populaire de la Révolution is the sole political party. The President changed his name to Mobutu Sésé Séko Kuku Ngbendu Wa Za Banga in 1972, but is usually known by the first three of these names only.

Provinces.—There are 9 regions, each under a Governor and provincial administration (names of capitals in brackets) Bas-Zaire (*Matadi*); Bandundu (*Bandundu*); Equateur (*Mbandaka*); Haut-Zaire (*Kisangani*); Kinshasa (*Kinshasa*); Kivu (*Bukavu*);

Shaba, *formerly* Katanga *(Lubumbashi)*; East Kasai *(Mbuji-Mayi)*; West Kasai *(Kananga)*.

Language, Religion and Education.—The people are mainly of Bantu-Negro stock, divided into semi-autonomous tribes, each speaking a Bantu tongue. Swahili, a Bantu dialect with an admixture of Arabic, is the nearest approach to a common language in the East and South, while Lingala is the language of a large area along the river and in the north, and Kikongo of the region between Kinshasa and the sea. French is the language of administration. It is estimated there are 9,500,000 African Christians in the Republic (Roman Catholic 5,800,000, Protestant 1,600,000). The local Kimbanguist religion has over two million adherents. The National University of Zaire has campuses in Kinshasa, Kisangani and Lubumbashi, with approximately 28,000 students (1978–79).

Production.—The cultivation of oil palms is widespread, palm oil being the most important agricultural cash product though it is no longer exported. Coffee, rubber, cocoa and timber are the most important agricultural exports. The production of cotton, pyrethrum and copal fell sharply on independence but is now increasing. The country is rich in minerals, particularly Shaba (ex-Katanga) province. Copper is widely exploited, and industrial diamonds and cobalt are also produced. Oil deposits are exploited off the Zaire estuary and reef-gold is mined in the north-east of the country.

There is a wide variety of small secondary industries, the main products being: cotton fabrics, blankets, sacks, footwear, beer, cigarettes, cement, paint, sugar, furniture, metal goods and tyres, and local assembly of motor vehicles. There are very large reserves of hydro-electric power and the huge Inga dam on the river Zaire is now supplying electricity to Matadi, Kinshasa and Shaba.

The chief exports are copper, crude oil, coffee, diamonds, rubber, cobalt, gold, cassiterite, zinc and other metals.

Communications. There are approximately 20,500 km of roads (earth-surfaced) of national importance, and 6,000 km of railways. The country has two international and 40 principal airports.

Trade with U.K.

	1986	1987
Imports from U.K.....	£34,220,000	£26,142,000
Exports to U.K.	17,190,000	8,544,000

CAPITAL.—Kinshasa (formerly Leopoldville), population (Census, 1985) 2,778,281. Principal towns, Lubumbashi (formerly Elisabethville) (403,623); Kisangani (formerly Stanleyville) (310,705); Likasi (146,394); Kananga (601,239); Ψ Matadi (143,598); and Mbandaka (134,495).

CURRENCY.—Zaïre of 100 Makuta and 10,000 Sengi.

FLAG.—Dark brown hand and torch with red flame in yellow roundel on green background.

NATIONAL DAY.—November 24.

BRITISH EMBASSY
B.P. 8049, Kinshasa.

[Kinshasa 23483/6]

Ambassador Extraordinary and Plenipotentiary, His Excellency Robert Linklater Burke Cormack, C.M.G. (1987).

First Secretaries, T. I. Hay-Campbell; (*Head of Chancery and H.M. Consul*); F. Geere (*Commercial*).

Second Secretary, A. D. B. Newton.

CURRENCIES OF THE WORLD

For Antigua and Barbuda, Dominica, Grenada, St. Christopher and Nevis, St. Lucia, and St. Vincent and the Grenadines, *see* East Caribbean Territories.

Country	Monetary Unit	Denomination in Circulation	
		Notes	Coins
Afghanistan	*Afghani* of 100 *Puls*	*Afghanis* 1,000, 500, 100, 50, 20, 10	*Afghanis* 5, 2, 1; *Puls* 50, 25
Albania	*Lek* of 100 *Qindarka*	*Leks* 100, 50, 25, 10, 5, 3, 1	*Lek* 1: *Qindarka* 50, 20, 10, 5
Algeria...........	*Dinar* of 100 *Centimes*	*Dinars* 200, 100, 50, 20, 10	*Dinars* 5, 1; *Centimes* 50, 20, 10, 5, 2, 1
Andorra..........	French and Spanish currencies are legal tender	—	—
Angola	*Kwanza* of 100 *Lwei*	*Kwanzas* 1,000, 500, 100, 50, 20	*Kwanzas* 20, 10, 5, 2, 1; *Lwei* 50
Argentina	*Austral* of 100 *Centavos*	*Australes* 100, 50, 10, 5, 1	*Centavos* 50, 10, 5, 1, ½
Australia	*Australian Dollar* of 100 *Cents*	$A 100, 50, 20, 10, 5, 2	$A 200, 10, 1; *Cents* 50, 20, 10, 5, 2, 1
Austria	*Schilling* of 100 *Groschen*	*Schillings* 1,000, 500, 100, 50, 20	*Schillings* 1,000, 500, 100, 50, 25, 20, 10, 5, 1; *Groschen* 50, 10, 5, 2, 1
Bahamas	*Bahamian Dollar* of 100 *Cents*	B$ 100, 50, 20, 10, 5, 3, 1; *Cents* 50	B$ 5, 2, 1; *Cents* 50, 25, 15, 5, 1
Bahrain	*Dinar* of 1,000 *Fils*	*Dinars* 20, 10, 5, 1, ½	*Fils* 100, 50, 25, 10, 5
Bangladesh	*Taka* of 100 *Paisas*	*Taka* 500, 100, 50, 20, 10, 1	*Taka* 1; *Paisa* 50, 25, 10, 5, 1
Barbados	*Barbados Dollar* of 100 *Cents*	BDS$100, 20, 10, 5, 2, 1	BDS$1; *Cents* 25, 10, 5, 1
Belgium	*Belgian Franc* of 100 *Centimes*	Frs. 5,000, 1,000, 500, 100	Frs. 500, 20, 5, 1; *Centimes* 50
Belize	*Belize Dollar* of 100 *Cents*	$100, 20, 10, 5, 1	*Cents* 50, 25, 10, 5, 1
Benin	*Franc C.F.A.*	Frs. 10,000, 5,000, 1,000, 500, 100, 50	Frs. 100, 50, 25, 10, 5, 2, 1
Bermuda	*Bermuda Dollar* of 100 *Cents*	$100, 50, 20, 10, 5, 1	$5, 1; *Cents* 50, 25, 10, 5, 1
Bhutan	*Ngultrum* of 100 *Chetrums**	Nu 100, 50, 20, 10, 5, 2, 1	Nu 1; *Ch* 50, 25, 10, 5
Bolivia	*Boliviano* of 1,000,000 *Pesos* of 100 *Centavos*	*Pesos* 100,000, 50,000, 10,000, 5,000, 1,000, 500, 100, 50, 20, 10, 5, 1	*Peso* 1; *Centavos* 50, 25, 20, 10, 5
Botswana	*Pula* of 100 *Thebe*	*Pula* 20, 10, 5, 2, 1	*Pula* 1; *Thebe* 50, 25, 10, 5, 2, 1
Brazil	*Cruzado* (= 1,000 old *Cruzeiros*) of 100 *Centavos*	CZ$500,100, 50, 10; *Cruzeiros* 100,000, 10,000, 5,000, 1,000, 500, 200, 100	CZ$1; *Centavos* 50, 20, 10; *Cruzeiros* 200, 100, 50
Brunei	*Brunei Dollar* of 100 *Sen†*	$1,000, 500, 100, 50, 10, 5, 1	*Sen* 50, 20, 10, 5, 1
Bulgaria	*Lev* of 100 *Stotinki*	*Léva* 20, 10, 5, 2, 1	*Léva* 2, 1; *Stotinki* 50, 20, 10, 5, 2, 1
Burkina..........	*Franc C.F.A.*	Frs. 10,000, 5,000, 1,000, 500, 100, 50	Frs. 100, 50, 25, 10, 5, 2, 1
Burma	*Kyat* of 100 *Pyas*	*Kyats* 100, 25, 10, 5, 1	*Kyat* 1; *Pyas* 50, 25, 10, 5, 1
Burundi..........	*Burundi Franc*	Frs. 5,000, 1,000, 500, 100, 50, 20, 10	Frs. 10, 5, 1
Cameroon	*Franc C.F.A.*	Frs. 10,000, 5,000, 1,000, 500, 100	Frs. 500, 100, 50, 25, 10, 5, 2, 1
Canada...........	*Dollar* of 100 *Cents*	$1,000, 100, 50, 20, 10, 5, 2, 1	$1; *Cents* 50, 25, 10, 5, 1
Cape Verde Is.	*Escudo* of 100 *Centavos*	*Escs.* 1,000, 500, 100	*Escs.* 50, 20, 10, 2·50, 1, *Centavos* $50, $20
Cayman Islands ...	*Cayman Is. Dollar* of 100 *Cents*	$100, 50, 25, 10, 5, 1	*Cents* 25, 10, 5, 1
Central African Republic	*Franc C.F.A.*	Frs. 10,000, 5,000, 1,000, 500, 100	Frs. 500, 100, 50, 25, 10, 5, 2, 1
Chad.............	*Franc C.F.A.*	Frs. 10,000, 5,000, 1,000, 500, 100	Frs. 500, 100, 50, 25, 10, 5, 2, 1
Chile.............	*New Peso* of 100 *Centavos*	*Pesos* 5,000, 1,000, 500	*Pesos* 100, 50, 10, 5, 1
China	*Renminbi* or *Yuan* of 10 *Jiao* or 100 *Fen*	*Yuan* 10, 5, 2, 1; *Jiao* 5, 2, 1; *Fen* 5, 2, 1	*Yuan* 1; *Jiao* 5, 2, 1; *Fen* 5, 2, 1
Colombia	*Peso* of 100 *Centavos*	*Pesos* 5,000, 2,000, 1,000, 500, 200, 100	*Pesos* 50, 20, 10, 5, 2, 1; *Centavos* 50, 25, 20, 10
Comoros..........	*Franc KMF* (*Comorian Franc*)	Frs. 5,000, 1,000, 500	

* Indian currency is also legal tender.   † Singaporean currency also negotiable at par.

Country	Monetary Unit	Denomination in Circulation	
		Notes	Coins
Congo............	*Franc C.F.A.*	*Frs.* 10,000, 5,000, 1,000, 500, 100	*Frs.* 500, 100, 50, 25, 10, 5, 2, 1
Costa Rica........	*Colon* of 100 *Céntimos*	*Colones* 1,000, 500, 100, 50, 20, 10, 5	*Colones* 25, 20, 10, 5, 2, 1; *Céntimos* 50, 25, 10, 5
Côte d'Ivoire......	*Franc C.F.A.*	*Frs.* 10,000, 5,000, 1,000, 500, 100, 50	*Frs.* 100, 50, 25, 10, 5, 2, 1
Cuba.............	*Peso* of 100 *Centavos*	*Pesos* $100, 50, 20, 10, 5, 1	*Cents.* 40, 20, 5, 3, 2, 1
Cyprus...........	*Cyprus Pound* of 100 *Cents*	£10, 5, 1; *Cents* 50	*Cents* 20, 10, 5, 2, 1, ½
Czechoslovakia ...	*Koruna* (*Crown*) of 100 *Haléru* (*Heller*)	*Kcs.* 1,000, 500, 100, 50, 20, 10	*Kcs.* 5, 2, 1; *Heller* 50, 20, 10, 5, 1
Denmark.........	*Krone* of 100 *Øre*	*Kroner* 1,000, 500, 100, 50, 20	*Kroner* 10, 5, 1; *Øre* 25, 10, 5
Djibouti..........	*Djibouti Franc*	*Francs* 5,000, 1,000, 500	*Francs* 100, 50, 20, 10, 5, 2, 1
Dominican Republic	*Dominican Republic Peso* of 100 *Centavos*	*RD*$1,000, 500, 100, 50, 20, 10, 5, 1	*RD*$1; *Centavos* 50, 25, 10, 5, 1
East Caribbean Territories	*E. C. Dollar* of 100 *Cents*	$100, 20, 5, 1	*Cents* 50, 25, 10, 5, 2, 1
Ecuador..........	*Sucre* of 100 *Centavos*	*Sucres* 1,000, 500, 100, 50, 20, 10, 5	*Sucre* 1; *Centavos* 50, 20, 10
Egypt............	*Egyptian Pound* of 100 *Piastres*	£E.100, 20, 10, 5, 1, ½, ¼; *Piastres* 10, 5	£E.5, 1; *Piastres* 20, 10, 5, 2, 1
Equatorial Guinea	*Franc C.F.A.*	*Frs.* 10,000, 5,000, 1000, 500, 100	*Frs.* 500, 100, 50, 25, 10, 5, 1
Ethiopia..........	*Ethiopian Birr* of 100 *Cents*	*Eth. Birr* 100, 50, 10, 5, 1	*Cents* 50, 25, 10, 5, 1
Falkland Islands ..	*Pound* of 100 *Pence*	£20, 10, 5, 1	£1; *Pence* 50, 20, 10, 5, 2, 1. U.K. coins are also in circulation.
Fiji..............	*Fiji Dollar* of 100 *Cents*	$20, 10, 5, 2, 1	*Cents* 50, 20, 10, 5, 2, 1
Finland..........	*Markka* of 100 *Penniä*	*Mk.* 1,000, 500, 100, 50, 10	*Mk.* 5, 1; *P.* 50, 20, 10, 5
France...........	*Franc* of 100 *Centimes*	*Francs* 500, 200, 100, 50, 20	*Francs* 10, 5, 2, 1, ½; *Centimes* 20, 10, 5
French Polynesia .	*Franc C.F.P.*	*C.F.P. Frs.* 10,000, 5,000, 1,000, 500	*C.F.P. Frs.* 100, 50, 20, 10, 5, 2, 1
Gabon............	*Franc C.F.A.*	*Frs.* 10,000, 5,000, 1,000, 500, 100	*Frs.* 500, 100, 50, 25, 10, 5, 2, 1
Gambia..........	*Dalasi* of 100 *Bututs*	*Dalasis* 25, 10, 5, 1	*Dalasi* 1; *Bututs* 50, 25, 10, 5, 1
German Democratic Republic (East)	*Mark der Deutschen Demokratischen Republik* of 100 *Pfennig*	*M.* 100, 50, 20, 10, 5	*M.* 20, 10, 5, 2, 1; *Pfennig* 50, 20, 10, 5, 1
Germany, Federal Republic of (West)	*Deutsche Mark* of 100 *Pfennig*	*D.M.* 1,000, 500, 100, 50, 20, 10, 5	*D.M.* 10, 5, 2, 1; *Pfennig* 50, 10, 5, 2, 1
Ghana...........	*Cedi* of 100 *Pesewas*	*Cedis* 200, 100, 50, 20, 10, 5, 2, 1	*Cedis* 5, 1; *Pesewas* 50, 20, 10, 5, 2½, 1, ½
Gibraltar.........	*Pound* of 100 *Pence*	£20, 10, 5, 1	As in U.K.
Greece...........	*Drachma* of 100 *Lepta*	*Drachmae* 5,000, 1,000, 500, 100, 50	*Drachmae* 50, 20, 10, 5, 2, 1; *Lepta* 50
Guatemala	*Quetzal* of 100 *Centavos*	*Quetzales* 100, 50, 20, 10, 5, 1; *Centavos* 50	*Centavos* 25, 10, 5, 1
Guinea...........	*Franc Guineen* of 100 *Centimes*	*Francs Guineen* 5,000, 1,000, 500, 100, 50, 25	—
Guinea-Bissau	*Guinean Peso* of 100 *Centavos*	*P.G.* 1,000, 500, 100, 50	*P.G.* 20, 5, 2, 1; *Centavos* 50
Guyana..........	*Guyana Dollar* of 100 *Cents*	*Dollars* 20, 10, 5, 1	*Cents* 100, 50, 25, 10, 5, 1
Haiti.............	*Gourde* of 100 *Centimes*	*Gourdes* 500, 250, 100, 50, 10, 5, 2, 1*	*Gourdes* 1,000, 200, 100, 50, 25, 20, 10, 5; *Centimes* 50, 20, 10, 5
Honduras	*Lempira* of 100 *Centavos*	*Lempiras* 100, 50, 20, 10, 5, 2, 1	*Centavos* 50, 20, 10, 5, 2, 1
Hong Kong	*Hong Kong Dollar* of 100 *Cents*	*HK Dollars* 1,000, 500, 100, 50, 20, 10; *Cent* 1	*HK Dollars* 5, 2, 1; *Cents* 50, 20, 10, 5
Hungary	*Forint* of 100 *Fillér*	*Forints* 1,000, 500, 100, 50, 20, 10	*Forints* 500, 100, 20, 10, 5, 2, 1; *Fillér* 50, 20, 10, 5, 2
Iceland...........	*Króna* of 100 *Aurar*	*Kr.* 5,000, 1,000, 500, 100, 50, 10	*Kr.* 5, 1; *Aurar* 50, 10, 5
India.............	*Rupee* of 100 *Paise*	*Rs.* 100, 50, 20, 10, 5, 2, 1	*Rs.* 5, 2, 1; *Paise* 50, 25, 20, 10, 5
Indonesia	*Rupiah* of 100 *Sen*	*Rupiahs* 10,000, 5,000, 1,000, 500, 100; *Sen* 50, 25, 10, 5, 1	*Rupiahs* 100, 50, 25, 10, 5, 2, 1
Iran	*Rial* of 100 *Dinars*	*Rials* 10,000, 5,000, 1,000, 500, 200, 100	*Rials* 50, 20, 10, 5, 2, 1

* U.S. $ notes also circulate.

Country	Monetary Unit	Denomination in Circulation	
		Notes	Coins
Iraq..............	*Iraqi Dinar* of 1000 *Fils*	*Dinars* 25, 10, 5, 1, ½, ¼	*Fils* 100, 50, 25, 10, 5, 1
Ireland, Republic of	*Irish Pound* of 100 *Pence*	£50, 20, 10, 5, 1	*Pence* 50, 20, 10, 5, 2, 1
Israel	*New Israel Shekel* of 100 *Agora*	*NIS* 100, 50, 10, 5, 1	*Shekel* 1, ½; *Agora* 10, 5, 1
Italy	*Lira* of 100 *Centesimi*	*Lire* 100,000, 50,000, 10,000, 5,000, 2,000, 1,000	*Lire* 1,000, 500, 200, 100, 50, 20, 10, 5
Jamaica	*Jamaican Dollar* of 100 *Cents*	$100, 20, 10, 5, 2, 1	$1, *Cents* 50, 25, 20, 10, 5, 1
Japan	*Yen*	*Yen* 10,000, 5,000, 1,000, 500	*Yen* 500, 100, 50, 10, 5, 1
Jordan	*Jordanian Dinar* of 1,000 *Fils*	*J. D.* 20, 10, 5, 1; *Fils* 500	*Fils* 250, 100, 50, 25, 20, 10, 5, 1
Kampuchea.......	*Riel* of 100 *Sen*	*Riel* 50, 20, 10, 5, 1; *Sen* 50, 20, 10	*Sen* 5
Kenya	*Kenya Shilling* of 100 *Cents*	*Shillings* 100, 50, 20, 10, 5	*Shillings* 1; *Cents* 50, 10, 5
Kiribati	Australian currency is legal tender	—	—
Korea, Democratic People's Republic of (North)	*Won* of 100 *Chon*	*Won* 100, 50, 10, 5, 1	*Chon* 50, 10, 5, 1
Korea, Republic of (South).........	*Won* of 100 *Jeon*	*Won* 10,000, 5,000, 1,000, 500	*Won* 500, 100, 50, 10, 5, 1
Kuwait	*Kuwaiti Dinar* of 1,000 *Fils*	*Dinars* 20, 10, 5, 1, ½, ¼	*Fils* 100, 50, 20, 10, 5, 1
Laos	*Kip* of 100 *Ats*	*Kips* 500, 200, 50, 20, 10	—
Lebanon.........	*Lebanese Pound* of 100 *Piastres*	*LL.* 250, 100, 50, 25, 10, 5, 1	*LL.* 1; *Piastres* 50, 25, 10, 5, 2½, 1
Lesotho	*Loti* (plural *Maloti*) of 100 *Lisente* (singular *Sente*)	*Maloti* 20, 10, 5, 2	*Loti* 1; *Lisente* 50, 20, 10, 5, 2, 1
Liberia	*Liberian $* of 100 *Cents*	$20, 10, 5, 1 (U.S. notes)	$5, 1; *Cents* 50, 25, 10, 5, 1*
Libya	*Libyan Dinar* of 1,000 *Dirhams*	*LD.* 10, 5, 1, ½, ¼	*Dirham* 100, 50, 20, 10, 5, 1
Liechtenstein.....	Swiss currency is legal tender		
Luxembourg	*Franc*†	*Francs* 1000, 100	*Francs* 20, 5, 1, ½
Macao	*Pataca* of 100 *Avos*	*Patacas* 500, 100, 50, 10, 5	*Patacas* 5, 1; *Avos* 50, 20, 10
Madagascar	*Franc Malgache* (*F.M.G.*)	*Frs.* 10,000, 5,000, 1,000, 500, 100, 50	*Frs.* 100, 50, 20, 10, 5, 2, 1
Malawi...........	*Kwacha* of 100 *Tambala*	*K.* 20, 10, 5, 1; *Tambala* 50	*Tambala* 20, 10, 5, 2, 1
Malaysia	*Malaysian Dollar* (*Ringgit*) of 100 *Cents* (*Sen*)	*Dollars* 1,000, 500, 100, 50, 20, 10, 5, 1	*Dollar* 1; *Cents* 50, 20, 10, 5, 1
Maldives	*Rufiyaa* of 100 *Laris*	*Rupees* 100, 50, 10, 5, 2, 1, ½	—
Mali	*Franc C.F.A.*	*Frs.* 10,000, 5,000, 1,000, 500, 100, 50	*Frs.* 100, 50, 25, 10, 5, 2, 1
Malta	*Maltese Lira* of 100 *Cents* or 1,000 *Mils*	*Lm* 20, 10, 5, 2	*Lm* 100, 50, 25, 20, 10, 5, 4, 2, 1; *Cents* 50, 25, 10, 5, 2, 1; *Mils* 5, 3, 2
Mauritania	*Ouguiya* of 5 *Khoums*	*UM* 1,000, 500, 200, 100	*UM* 20, 10, 5, 1, ⅕
Mauritius	*Rupee* of 100 *Cents*	*Rs.* 200, 100, 50, 25, 10, 5	*Rupee* 1; *Cents* 50, 25, 10, 5, 2, 1
Mexico	*Peso ($)* of 100 *Centavos*	*Pesos* 10,000, 5,000, 2,000, 1,000, 500, 100, 50, 20	*Pesos* 10, 5, 1; *Centavos* 50, 20, 10
Monaco	*Franc*	As in France	*Francs* 50, 10, 5, 1, ½, 0·20, 0·10
Mongolia	*Tugrik* of 100 *Mongo*	*Tugriks* 100, 50, 25, 20, 10, 5, 3, 1	*Tugrik* 1; *Mongo* 50, 20, 15, 10, 5, 2, 1
Morocco..........	*Dirham* of 100 *Centimes*	*DH.* 100, 50, 10, 5	*DH.* 5, 1, ½; *Centimes* 20, 10, 5
Mozambique	*Metical* of 100 *Centavos*	*MT.* 1,000, 500, 100, 50	*MT.* 20, 10, 5, 2½, 1, ½
Nauru	Australian currency is legal tender	—	—
Nepal	*Rupee* of 100 *Paisa*	*Rupees* 1,000, 500, 100, 50, 20, 10, 5, 2, 1	*Rupee* 100, 50, 25, 20, 10, 5, 2, 1; *Paisa* 50, 25, 20, 10, 5, 2, 1
Netherlands	*Florin (Guilder)* of 100 *Cents*	*Florins* 1,000, 250, 100, 50, 25, 10, 5	*Florins* 10, 2·50, 1; *Cents* 25, 10, 5
Netherlands Antilles	*Netherlands Antilles Guilder* of 100 *Cents*	*Guilders* 250, 100, 50, 25, 10, 5, 2½, 1	*Guilders* 2½, 1, ¼, 1/10; *Cents* 5, 2½, 1
New Caledonia....	*Franc C.F.P.*	*Frs.* 5,000, 1,000, 500, 100	*Frs.* 100, 50, 20, 10, 5, 2, 1; *Centimes* 50
New Zealand......	*New Zealand Dollar* of 100 *Cents*	*N.Z.$* 100, 50, 20, 10, 5, 2, 1	*Cents* 50, 20, 10, 5, 2, 1
Nicaragua	*Córdoba* of 100 *Centavos*	*Córdobas* 1,000, 500, 100, 50, 20, 10, 5, 2, 1	*Cordobas* 5, 1; *Centavos* 50, 25, 10, 5

* U.S. coins also circulate. † Belgian currency is also legal tender.

Country	Monetary Unit	Denomination in Circulation	
		Notes	Coins
Niger	*Franc C.F.A.*	*Frs. C.F.A.* 10,000, 5,000, 1,000, 500, 100, 50	*Frs. C.F.A.* 100, 50, 25, 10, 5, 2, 1
Nigeria	*Naira* of 100 *kobo*	*N* 20, 10, 5, 1, *k.* 50	*k* 25, 10, 5, 1, ½
Norway	*Krone* of 100 *Öre*	*Kroner* 1,000, 500, 100, 50	*Kroner* 10, 5, 1; *Öre* 50, 10
Oman	*Rial Omani* of 1,000 *Baiza*	*Rial Omani* 50, 20, 10, 5, 1, ½, ¼; *Baiza* 200, 100	*Baiza* 500, 250, 100, 50, 25, 10, 5, 2
Pakistan	*Rupee* of 100 *Paisa*	*Rs.* 500, 100, 50, 10, 5, 2, 1	*Re.* 1, ½, ¼; *Paisa* 50, 25, 10, 5, 2, 1
Panama	*Balboa* of 100 *Cents* (= U.S.$1)	As in U.S.A.	*Balboa* 500, 150, 100, 5, 1, ½, ¼, ¹⁄₁₀, ¹⁄₂₀; *Cent* 1*.
Papua New Guinea	*Kina* of 100 *Toea*	*K.* 20, 10, 5, 2	*K.* 1; *T.* 50, 20, 10, 5, 2, 1
Paraguay.........	*Guarani* of 100 *Céntimos*	*Guaranies* 10,000, 5,000, 1,000, 500, 100, 50, 10, 5, 1	——
Peru	*Inti* of 100 *Centimos*	*Intis* 100, 50, 10, 5	—
Philippines	*Philippine Peso* of 100 *Centavos*	*Pesos* 100, 50, 20, 10, 5, 2	*Peso* 1; *Centavos* 50, 25, 10, 5, 1
Poland	*Zloty* of 100 *Groszy*	*Zlotys* 10,000, 5,000, 2,000, 1,000, 500, 200, 100, 50, 20, 10	*Zlotys* 10,000, 2,000, 1,000, 500, 200, 100, 50, 20, 10, 5, 2, 1
Portugal	*Escudo* of 100 *Centavos*	*Esc.* 5,000, 1,000, 500, 100	*Esc.* 50, 25, 20, 10, 5, 2·50, 1; *Centavos* 50
Qatar	*Qatar Riyal* of 100 *Dirhams*	*Qatar Riyals* 500, 100, 50, 10, 5, 1	*Dirhams* 50, 25, 10, 5, 1
Romania	*Leu* of 100 *Bani*	*Lei* 100, 50, 25, 10, 5, 3, 1	*Lei* 5, 3, 1; *Bani* 25, 15, 10, 5, 3, 1
Rwanda	*Rwanda Franc*	*Frs.* 5,000, 1,000, 500, 100	*Frs.* 50, 20, 10, 5, 1
St. Helena	*St. Helena Pound* of 100 *Pence*	*St. Hel.* £10, 5	*St. Hel.* £1; *Pence* 50, 10, 5, 2, 1
El Salvador	*Colon* of 100 *Centavos*	*Colones* 100, 50, 25, 10, 5, 2, 1	*Centavos* 50, 25, 10, 5, 3, 2, 1
San Marino.......	Italian currency circulates		
Sao Tomé and Principé	*Dobra* of 100 *Cêntimos*	*Dobras* 1,000, 500, 100, 50	*Dobras* 20, 10, 5, 2, 1; *Cêntimos* 50
Saudi Arabia	*Riyal* of 20 *Qursh* or 100 *Halala*	*Riyals* 500, 100, 50, 10, 5, 1	*Halala* 100, 50, 25, 10, 5, 1
Senegal	*Franc C.F.A.*	*Frs.* 10,000, 5,000, 1,000, 500, 100, 50	*Frs.* 100, 50, 25, 10, 5, 2, 1
Seychelles	*Rupee* of 100 *Cents*	*SR* 100, 50, 25, 10	*Rupees* 1,500, 1,000, 500, 100, 50, 25, 10, 5, 1; *Cents* 25, 10, 5, 1
Sierra Leone......	*Leone* of 100 *Cents*	*Le.* 20, 10, 5, 2, 1; *Cents* 50	*Cents* 50, 20, 10, 5, 1, ½
Singapore	*Singapore Dollar* of 100 *Cents†*	*Dollars* 10,000, 1,000, 500, 100, 50, 20, 10, 5, 1	*Dollar* 1; *Cents* 50, 20, 10, 5, 1
Solomon Islands...	*Solomon Islands Dollar* of 100 *Cents*	*SI.*$50, 20, 10, 5, 2	*SI.*$ 1; *Cents* 20, 10, 5, 2, 1
Somalia	*Somali Shilling* of 100 *Cents*	*Som. Sh.* 100, 20, 10, 5	*Som. Sh.* 1, ½; *Cents* 10, 5, 1
South Africa......	*Rand* of 100 *Cents*	*R* 50, 20, 10, 5, 2	*R* 1; *Cents* 50, 20, 10, 5, 2, 1
Spain	*Peseta* of 100 *Céntimos*	*Pesetas* 10,000, 5,000, 2,000, 1,000, 500, 200, 100	*Pesetas* 100, 50, 25, 5, 1; *Céntimos* 50
Sri Lanka	*Rupee* of 100 *Cents*	*Rs.* 1,000, 500, 100, 50, 20, 10, 5, 2	*Rs.* 1; *Cents* 50, 25, 10, 5, 2, 1
Sudan............	*Sudanese Pound* of 100 *Piastres* or 1,000 *Milliemes*	*£S.* 50, 20, 10, 5, 1; *Piastres* 50, 25	*Piastres* 50, 10, 5, 2; *Milliemes* 10, 5, 2, 1
Suriname.........	*Guilder (Sf.)* of 100 *Cents*	*Sf.* 500, 100, 25, 10, 5, 2·50, 1	*Guilder* 1; *Cents* 25, 10, 5, 1
Swaziland	*Lilangeni* (plural *Emalangeni*) of 100 *Cents*	*E* 20, 10, 5, 2, 1	*E* 2, 1; *Cents* 50, 20, 10, 5, 2, 1
Sweden	*Krona* of 100 *Öre*	*Kronor* 10,000, 1,000, 500, 100, 50, 10, 2·5	*Kronor* 5, 2, 1; *Öre* 50, 10
Switzerland	*Franc* of 100 *Centimes*	*Frs.* 1,000, 500, 100, 50, 20, 10	*Frs.* 5, 2, 1; *Centimes* 50, 20, 10, 5, 1
Syria.............	*Syrian Pound* of 100 *Piastres*	*S. Pounds* 500, 100, 50, 25, 10, 5, 1	*Pound* 1, ½; *Piastres* 50, 25, 10, 5, 2½
Taiwan	*New Taiwan Dollar* of 100 *Cents*	*NT*$ 1,000, 500, 100, 50, 10, 5, 1	*NT*$10, 5, 1; *Cents* 50, 10
Tanzania	*Tanzanian Shilling* of 100 *Cents*	*Shillings* 200, 100, 50, 20, 10	*Shilling* 10, 5, 1; *Cents* 50, 20, 10, 5
Thailand	*Baht* of 100 *Satangs*	*Bahts* 500, 100, 20, 10, 5, 1; *Satangs* 50	*Baht* 5, 1; *Satangs* 50, 25, 10, 5, 1

* U.S. coins also circulate.   † Brunei currency also negotiable at par.

Country	Monetary Unit	Denomination in Circulation	
		Notes	Coins
Togo	*Franc C.F.A.*	*Frs.* 10,000, 5,000, 1,000, 500, 100, 50	*Frs.* 500, 100, 50, 25, 10, 5, 2, 1
Tonga............	*Pa'anga (T$)* of 100 *Seniti*	*T$* 20, 10, 5, 2, 1	*T$* 2, 1; *Seniti* 50, 20, 10, 5, 2, 1
Trinidad and Tobago	*Trinidad and Tobago Dollar* of 100 *Cents*	*Dollars* 100, 20, 10, 5, 1	*Dollar* 1; *Cents* 50, 25, 10, 5, 1
Tunisia	*Tunisian Dinar* of 1,000 *Millimes*	*Dinars* 20, 10, 5, 1, ½	*Dinars* 5, 1, ½; *Millimes* 100, 50, 20, 10, 5, 2, 1
Turkey..........	*Turkish Lira* of 100 *Kurus*	*TL.* 10,000, 5,000, 1,000, 500, 100	*TL.* 100, 50, 25, 20, 10, 5, 1
Tuvalu	Australian notes and coins are legal tender with Tuvalu coinage	—	*Dollars* 5, 1; *Cents* 50, 20, 10, 5, 2, 1
Uganda	*Uganda New Shilling* (= 100 old *Shillings*) of 100 *Cents*	*Shillings* 100, 50, 20, 10	*Shillings* 5, 2, 1; *Cents* 50, 20, 10, 5
U.S.S.R.	*Rouble* of 100 *Kopecks*	*Roubles* 100, 50, 25, 10, 5, 3, 1	*Rouble* 1; *Kopecks* 50, 20, 15, 10, 5, 3, 2, 1
United Arab Emirates	*Dirham* of 100 *Fils*	*Dirhams* 1,000, 100, 50, 10, 5, 1	*Dirham* 1; *Fils* 50, 25, 10, 5, 1
United Kingdom ..	*Pound Sterling* of 100 *Pence*	£50, £20, £10, £5	£1; *Pence* 50, 20, 10, 5, 2, 1; 2*s.* (10p), 1*s.* (5p)
U.S.A............	*Dollar* of 100 *Cents*	$100, 50, 20, 10, 5, 2, 1	$1; *Cents* 50, 25, 10, 5, 1
Uruguay	*New Peso* (= 1,000 old *Pesos*) of 100 *Centésimos*	*New Pesos* 10,000, 5,000, 1,000, 500, 200, 100, 50	*Pesos* 20,000, 2,000; *New Pesos* 10, 5, 2, 1; *Centésimos* 50, 20, 10
Vanuatu	*Vatu* of 100 *Centimes*	*Vatu* 1,000, 500, 100	*Vatu* 50, 20, 10, 5, 2, 1
Vatican	Italian currency circulates	—	*Lire* 500, 100, 50, 20, 10, 5
Venezuela	*Bolívar* of 100 *Céntimos*	*Bolívares* 500, 100, 50, 20, 10, 5	*Bolívares* 100, 20, 10, 5, 2, 1, 0·50, 0·25, 0·10, 0·05; *Cents* 1, ⅛, ¼, 0·05
Vietnam	*Dông* of 10 *Hào* or 100 *Xu*	*Dông* 10, 5, 2, 1; *Hào* 5, 2, 1; *Xu* 5	*Xu* 5, 2, 1
Western Samoa ...	*Tala (WS$)* of 100 *Sene*	*Tala* 20, 10, 5, 2	*Sene* 50, 20, 10, 5, 2, 1
Yemen, Arab Republic (North)	*Riyal* of 100 *Fils*	*Riyals* 100, 50, 20, 10, 5, 1	*Fils* 50, 25, 10, 5, 1
Yemen, People's Democratic Republic (South)	*Yemeni Dinar* of 1,000 *Fils*	*YD* 10, 5, 1; *Fils* 500, 250	*Fils* 50, 25, 5, 2·20, 1
Yugoslavia	*Dinar* of 100 *Paras*	*Dinars* 5,000, 1,000, 500, 100, 50, 20, 10, 5	*Dinars* 100, 50, 20, 10, 5, 2, 1
Zaïre	*Zaïre* of 100 *Makuta* or 10,000 *Sengi*	*Zaïres* 1,000, 500, 100, 50, 10, 5, 1; *Makuta* 50	*Makuta* 20, 10, 5, 1; *Sengi* 10
Zambia	*Kwacha* of 100 *Ngwee*	*Kwacha* 20, 10, 5, 2, 1	*Ngwee* 50, 20, 10, 5, 2, 1
Zimbabwe	*Dollar* of 100 *Cents*	*Z.$* 20, 10, 5, 2, 1	*Z.$* 1, *Cents* 50, 20, 10, 5, 1

INTERNATIONAL ORGANIZATIONS

THE UNITED NATIONS

The foundations of the Charter of the United Nations were laid at the Conference of Foreign Ministers in Moscow in 1943, and upon those foundations a structure was built at the meetings at Dumbarton Oaks, Washington, D.C., from Aug. 21 to Oct. 7, 1944. The design was discussed and criticized at San Francisco from April 25 to June 26, 1945, on which date representatives of 50 Allied Nations appended their signatures to the Charter.

The United Nations formally came into existence on October 24, 1945. It was later decided that its seat should be in the United States. Permanent headquarters have been erected at Manhattan, New York. October 24 has been designated "United Nations Day".

The following 159 states are members of the United Nations:—

Afghanistan
Albania
Algeria
Angola
Antigua and Barbuda
*Argentina
*Australia
Austria
Bahamas
Bahrain
Bangladesh
Barbados
*Belgium
Belize
Benin
Bhutan
*Bolivia
Botswana
*Brazil
Brunei
Bulgaria
Burkina Faso
Burma
Burundi
*Byelorussian S.S.R.
Cameroon
*Canada
Cape Verde
Central African Rep.
Chad
*Chile
*China
*Colombia
Comoros
Congo
*Costa Rica
Côte d'Ivoire
*Cuba
Cyprus
*Czechoslovakia
*Denmark
Djibouti
Dominica
*Dominican Rep.
*Ecuador
*Egypt
Equatorial Guinea
*Ethiopia
Fiji
Finland
*France
Gabon
Gambia
German Democratic Rep.
Germany, Federal Rep. of
Ghana
*Greece
Grenada

*Guatemala
Guinea
Guinea-Bissau
Guyana
*Haiti
*Honduras
Hungary
Iceland
*India
Indonesia
*Iran
*Iraq
Ireland, Rep. of
Israel
Italy
Jamaica
Japan
Jordan
Kampuchea
Kenya
Kuwait
Laos
*Lebanon
Lesotho
*Liberia
Libya
*Luxembourg
Madagascar
Malawi
Malaysia
Maldives
Mali
Malta
Mauritania
Mauritius
*Mexico
Mongolia
Morocco
Mozambique
Nepal
*Netherlands
*New Zealand
*Nicaragua
Niger
Nigeria
*Norway
Oman
Pakistan
*Panama
Papua New Guinea
*Paraguay
*Peru
*Philippines
*Poland
Portugal
Qatar
Romania
Rwanda
St. Christopher and Nevis

St. Lucia
St. Vincent and the Grenadines
*El Salvador
São Tomé and Príncipe
*Saudi Arabia
Senegal
Seychelles
Sierra Leone
Singapore
Solomon Is.
Somalia
*South Africa
Spain
Sri Lanka
Sudan
Suriname
Swaziland
Sweden
*Syria
Tanzania
Thailand
Togo

Trinidad and Tobago
Tunisia
*Turkey
Uganda
*Ukrainian S.S.R.
*Union of Soviet Socialist Republics
United Arab Emirates
*United Kingdom
*United States of America
*Uruguay
Vanuatu
*Venezuela
Vietnam
Western Samoa
Yemen Arab Rep.
Yemen, People's Dem. Rep. of
*Yugoslavia
Zaire
Zambia
Zimbabwe

*Original member (i.e. from 1945). (From October 25, 1971, "China" was taken to mean the People's Republic of China.)

The principal organs of the United Nations are:— (1) The General Assembly; (2) The Security Council; (3) The Economic and Social Council; (4) The Trusteeship Council; (5) The International Court of Justice; (6) The Secretariat.

1. The General Assembly

The General Assembly consists of all the Members of the United Nations. Each Member is entitled to be represented at its meetings by five representatives, but has only one vote. The General Assembly meets once a year in regular session beginning on the third Tuesday in September. A new President is elected by the General Assembly at the start of every annual session. Special Sessions may also be held.

The work of the General Assembly is divided among seven Main Committees, on each of which every Member has the right to be represented:—(1) Disarmament and related security questions; (2) Economic and Financial; (3) Social, Humanitarian and Cultural; (4) Decolonization (including Non-Self Governing Territories); (5) Administrative and Budgetary; (6) Legal. There is also a Special Political Committee, to relieve the burden on the first Committee.

The Main Committees consider items referred to them by the General Assembly and recommend draft resolutions for submission to the Assembly's plenary meetings.

The Assembly has two procedural committees—a General Committee and a Credentials Committee; and three standing committees—an Advisory Committee on Administrative and Budgetary Questions, a Committee on Contributions and a Disarmament Commission.

The General Assembly appoints such ad hoc committees as may be required from time to time for special purposes. The Assembly is also assisted in its work by subsidiary bodies such as the Board of Auditors, the Committee on Conferences, the International Law Commission, etc. In 1964 the General

Assembly set up the United Nations Conference on Trade and Development (UNCTAD) as a permanent body.

The United Nations Industrial Development Organization was set up on Jan. 1, 1967, to promote industrialization and co-ordinate United Nations activities in this field.

President of the United Nations General Assembly, Peter Florin (*G.D.R.*) (1987).

2. The Security Council

The Security Council consists of fifteen Members, each of which has one representative and one vote. There are five permanent Members and ten non-permanent Members elected for a two-year term.

The Security Council bears the primary responsibility for the maintenance of peace and security. Decisions on procedural questions are made by an affirmative vote of nine Members. On all other matters the affirmative vote of nine Members must include the concurring votes of the permanent Members, and it is this clause which makes the Veto possible.

The General Assembly, any member of the United Nations, or the Secretary-General, can bring to the Council's attention any matter considered to threaten international peace and security. A non-member State can bring a dispute before the Council provided it accepts in advance the U.N. Charter obligations for peaceful settlement.

The Security Council also establishes ad hoc committees and commissions which may be required from time to time for special purposes.

The five permanent Members are China, France, U.K., U.S.A., and U.S.S.R. The present ten non-permanent Members are: Argentina, Federal Republic of Germany, Italy, Japan and Zambia (*elected in 1986*): Algeria, Brazil, Nepal, Senegal and Yugoslavia (*elected in 1987*).

3. The Economic and Social Council

This body is responsible under the General Assembly for carrying out the functions of the United Nations with regard to international economic, social, cultural, educational, health and related matters.

The Council has 54 members who are elected for three-year terms by the General Assembly.

It has established the following Commissions: Statistical, Human Rights, Social Development, Status of Women, Narcotic Drugs, Population, Regional Economic Commissions for Europe, Asia and the Pacific, Western Asia, Latin America and Africa. The Council also makes recommendations for the co-ordination of the policies and activities of 15 specialized agencies and other organizations in the U.N. system.

4. Trusteeship Council

The Trusteeship Council now consists of five members: the U.S.A. (administering authority of Micronesia, the only remaining trust Territory of the original 11), and the other four permanent members of the Security Council, China, France, U.K. and U.S.S.R.

The Trusteeship Council considers reports from administering authorities; examines petitions in consultation with the administering authority; makes periodic inspection visits; and checks conditions with an annual questionnaire on the political, economic, social, and educational advancement of the inhabitants of trust territories.

5. International Court of Justice

The International Court of Justice is the principal judicial organ of the United Nations. The Statute of the court is an integral part of the Charter and all

Members of the United Nations are *ipso facto* parties to it. The Court is composed of 15 judges, no two of whom may be nationals of the same State and each serves a term of nine years. The Court is based at The Hague.

If any party to a case fails to adhere to the judgment of the Court, the other party may have recourse to the Security Council.

President, Nagendra Singh (*India*) (1991).
Vice-President, K. Mbaye (*Senegal*) (1991).
Judges, M. Lachs (*Poland*) (1994); J. M. Ruda (*Argentina*) (1991); T. O. Elias (*Nigeria*) (1994); S. Oda (*Japan*) (1994); R. Ago (*Italy*) (1997); M. Shahabuddeen (*Guyana*) (1997); S. Schwebel (*U.S.A.*) (1997); Sir Robert Jennings (*U.K.*) (1991); K. Mbaye (*Senegal*) (1991); M. Bedjaoui (*Algeria*) (1997); Ni Zhengyu (*China*) (1994); J. Evensen (*Norway*) (1994); N. K. Tarasov (*U.S.S.R.*) (1997); G. Guillaume (*France*) (1991).
(The judges are listed in order of precedence with date of expiry of office in parentheses.)

THE SECRETARIAT

Secretary General, Javier Pérez de Cuellar (*Peru*).
Director General, Development and International Economic Co-operation, Jean Ripert (*France*).

U.N. Office and Information Centre, Ship House, 20 Buckingham Gate, SW1.

OTHER ORGANS

The U.N. Centre for Human Settlements (Habitat), Nairobi; U.N. Children's Fund (UNICEF), New York; U.N. Conference on Trade and Development (UNCTAD), Geneva; U.N. Development Programme (UNDP), New York; U.N. Disaster Relief Office (UNDRO), Geneva; U.N. Environment Programme (UNEP), Nairobi; U.N. Fund for Population Activities (UNFPA), New York; U.N. High Commissioner for Refugees (UNHCR), Geneva; U.N. Institute for Training and Research (UNITAR), New York; International Research and Training Institute for the Advancement of Women (INSTRAW); U.N. Relief and Works Agency for Palestine Refugees in the Near East (UNRWA), Vienna; U.N. University (UNU), Tokyo; World Food Council (WFC), Rome; World Food Programme (WFP), Rome.

These programmes are supported by voluntary contributions from governments, non-governmental organizations and individuals. The U.N. programmes receiving the largest total contributions in 1983 were: the U.N. Development Programme (UNDP.—$714m); the U.N. Children's Fund (UNICEF.—$297m), and the U.N. Fund for Population Activities (UNFPA.—$310m). The World Food Programme (WFP), jointly administered by the U.N. and FAO, provided aid worth $900m in 1983.

BUDGET OF THE UNITED NATIONS

The budget adopted at the 42nd session for the biennium 1988–89 was slightly over U.S.$1,769,000,000. However, talks on the budget continued in 1988. The scale of assessment contributions of 78 U.N. members is set at 0·01 per cent., that of a further 11 at 0·02 per cent., and a further five at 0·03 per cent. The ten largest assessments are as follows: U.S.A., 25 per cent.; U.S.S.R., 11·82 per cent.; Japan, 10·84 per cent.; West Germany, 8·26 per cent.; France, 6·37 per cent.; U.K., 4·67 per cent.; Italy, 3·79 per cent.; Canada, 3·06 per cent.; Spain, 2·03 per cent. and Netherlands, 1·74 per cent.

U.K. MISSION TO THE UNITED NATIONS
845 Third Avenue, New York, NY 10022

Permanent Representative to the United Nations and Representative on the Security Council, Sir Crispin Tickell, K.C.V.O. (1987).
Deputy Permanent Representative, J. A. Birch, C.M.G.
Counsellors, D. E. S. Blatherwick, O.B.E. (*Head of Chancery*); A. I. Aust (*Legal Adviser*); J. F. R. Martin (*Economic and Social Affairs*); R. C. Tutt; J. R. Leeland (*Administration*).

U.K. MISSION TO THE U.N. AND OTHER INTERNATIONAL ORGANIZATIONS IN GENEVA
37–39 rue de Vermont, 1211 Geneva 20

Ambassador, Permanent U.K. Representative, John Anthony Sankey, C.M.G. (1985).
Deputy Permanent Representatives, G. W. Hewitt; P. W. M. Vereker (*Economic Affairs*).

SPECIALIZED AGENCIES

Sixteen other independent international organizations, each with its own membership, budget and headquarters, carry out their responsibilities in co-ordination with the U.N. under agreements made with the Economic and Social Council. These agencies set standards and provide technical assistance in economic, social and cultural and technical fields.

Food and Agriculture Organization of the United Nations (FAO), Via delle Terme di Caracalla, 00100 Rome.—Established on October 16, 1945, to raise levels of nutrition and standards of living, to secure improvements in the efficiency of the production and distribution of all food and agricultural products and to better the condition of rural populations, thus contributing to the expansion of world economy and ensuring man's freedom from hunger. Among its many activities the Organization promotes the global exchange of information in the fields of agriculture, forestry and fisheries, facilitates international agreement in these fields and provides technical assistance in such subjects as nutrition and food management, soil erosion control, re-afforestation, the establishment of paper industries, irrigation engineering, control of infestation of stored foods, production of fertilizers, control of crop pests and diseases, and improvement of fishing vessels, fish distribution and marketing. The 1987 session of the FAO governing Conference approved a budget of $492,000,000 for the two years 1986–87. In addition FAO is carrying out field programmes involving annual expenditure of about $310,000,000 under the U.N. Development Programme and other aid programmes including trust funds. Through its co-operative programme with the World Bank it is helping to increase international investment in agriculture and allied fields.

The policy of the Organization is directed by a two-yearly Conference of the 158 member countries. A council (49 members) acts for the Conference between its sessions.
Director General, Edouard Saouma (*Lebanon*).
Permanent U.K. Representative, R. F. R. Deare.

International Bank for Reconstruction and Development (IBRD), Washington, D.C. 20433; *European office,* 66 Ave. d'Iéna, 75116, Paris, France; *Tokyo office,* Kokusai Building 1–1, Marunouchi 3-Chome, Chiyoda-ku, Tokyo 100.—(Together with IDA known as the World Bank) Established on Dec. 27, 1945, to help raise standards of living in developing countries by the provision of financial resources through loans made for productive purposes to a government, or guaranteed by the government concerned. Loans are directed towards developing countries at more advanced stages of economic and social growth.

The Bank, which is owned by the governments of 151 countries and whose capital is subscribed by its member countries, finances its lending operations primarily from its own borrowing in the world capital markets, and derives a substantial contribution to its resources from its retained earnings and the repayment of loans. The interest rate on its loans is calculated in relation to its cost of borrowing; loans generally have a grace period of five years and are repayable over 20 years or less. The loans made by the Bank since its inception to June 30, 1987, totalled $140,286,800,000 to 110 countries. Subscribed capital, $77,526,969,000.

The Board of Governors consists of one Governor and one alternate appointed by each of the member countries. Twenty-two Executive Directors exercise all powers of the Bank except those reserved to the Board of Governors. The President, selected by the Executive Directors, conducts the business of the Bank, with the assistance of an international staff.
President, B. B. Conable (*U.S.A.*).
U.K. Executive Director, T. P. Lankester.

International Civil Aviation Organization (ICAO), 1,000 Sherbrooke Street, W., Montreal, Quebec, Canada H3A 2R2.—ICAO was established on April 4, 1947, to study problems of international civil aviation to establish international standards and recommended practices for civil aviation in areas such as airworthiness, personnel licensing, aeronautical charts, rules of the air, etc., ICAO encourages the use of safety measures, uniform regulations or operation, and simpler procedures at international airports. It promotes the use of new technical methods and equipment. With the co-operation of members, it has evolved a pattern for meteorological services, traffic control, telecommunications, search and rescue organization, and other facilities required for safe international flight. It has secured much simplification of government customs, immigration, and public health regulations as they apply to international air transport. 158 states are now members of ICAO.

An Assembly of delegates from member states meets at least once every three years. A Council of 33 members is elected by the Assembly, taking into account the countries of chief importance in air transport: countries which make the largest contribution to the provision of facilities for international civil air transport and those ensuring representation of the main geographical areas of the world. The Council is the executive body, working through subsidiary committees.
President of Council, Dr. Assad Kotaite (*Lebanon*).
Secretary General, Dr. Shivinder Singh Sidhu (*India*).

International Development Association (IDA), Washington, D.C. 20433; *European office,* 66 Ave. d'Iéna, 75116 Paris, France; *Tokyo office,* Kokusai Building 1–1, Marunouchi 3-Chome, Chiyoda-ku, Tokyo 100.—The IDA is an affiliate of the IBRD (the two together comprising the World Bank) and was established in September 1960 to provide assistance for the same purposes as the IBRD but primarily in the poorer developing countries and on terms that bear less heavily on their balance of payments than IBRD loans. Assistance is concentrated on the very poor countries, i.e. those with an annual per capita GNP of less than $835 (in 1986 dollars); more than 50 countries are eligible.

Membership is open to all members of IBRD and

135 have joined to date. Funds, called credits to distinguish them from IBRD loans, come mostly in the form of subscriptions, general replenishments and special contributions by IDA's richer members, and transfers from the net earnings of the IBRD. The term of IDA credits, which are made to governments only, are ten-year grace periods, 35 or 40 year maturities, and no interest. By June 30, 1987, IDA had extended development credits totalling $43,308,000,000 in 95 countries.

Although legally and financially distinct from the IBRD, IDA is administered by the same staff, and the Board of Governors and Executive Directors are the same as those holding equivalent positions in the IBRD.

International Finance Corporation (IFC), 1818 H Street, Washington, D.C. 20433; *European representative*, New Zealand House, Haymarket, SW1.— The IFC was established in 1956 as an affiliate of the World Bank to assist developing member countries by promoting the growth of the private sector of their economies and helping to mobilize domestic and foreign capital for this purpose. Membership of the IBRD is a prerequisite for membership in the IFC, which has 133 members. Legally and financially the IFC and IBRD are separate entities; the Corporation has its own operating and legal staff, but draws upon the Bank for administrative and other services. IFC's subscribed share capital was $1,300,000,000 at June 30, 1987, and it is also empowered to borrow up to four times the amount of its unimpaired subscribed capital and accumulated earnings for use in its lending programme. At the end of June 1987, IFC had made approved investments totalling more than $9,200,000,000 in over 90 countries.
President, B. B. Conable (*U.S.A*).

International Fund for Agricultural Development (IFAD), 107 Via del Serafico, 00142 Rome, Italy.—The establishment of the Fund was proposed by the 1974 World Food Conference and it began operations in December 1977. The Fund's purpose is to mobilize additional funds for agricultural and rural development in developing countries through projects and programmes directly benefiting the poorest rural populations.

The Fund's operations are directed by the Governing Council, consisting of the entire membership. It has an 18-member Executive Board. Its governing structure provides for equal voting rights among the three groups of member countries, namely, the developed countries, the oil-exporting developing countries and other developing countries.
President, Idriss Jazairy (*Algeria*).

International Labour Organization (ILO) Geneva (*London Branch Office*, Vincent House, Vincent Square, SW1P 2NB). Established with the League of Nations in 1919 under the Treaty of Versailles, the ILO became in 1946 the first specialized agency associated with the United Nations. In May, 1988 the Organization had 150 member States. The aim of the ILO is to promote lasting peace through social justice, and to this end it works for better economic and social conditions everywhere. It was awarded the Nobel Peace Prize in 1969.

The ILO establishes international labour standards, which set guidelines for improving working conditions and protecting basic human rights; runs a world-wide programme of technical assistance to developing countries; conducts research and disseminates information on the human aspects of economic activity, with a view to improving social and economic well-being. Through its World Employment Programme, the ILO is attacking unemployment and its associated ills by aiding national and international efforts to provide productive work for the world's fast-growing population. It is also developing an international programme for the improvement of working conditions and the working environment.

The ILO is financed by contributions from its member states. A proportion of its budget is devoted to its technical assistance programme, but this is financed mainly by funds from UNDP and other sources. The I.L.O. budget for 1986–87 amounted to U.S.$324,860,000.

The International Labour Conference, composed of national delegations of two government delegates, one worker delegate and one employer delegate, meets annually. It formulates international labour standards and broad policies of the Organization, provides a forum for discussion of world labour and social problems, and approves the ILO's work programme and budget, which is financed by member States.

A 56-member Governing Body, composed of 28 government members, 14 worker members and 14 employer members, acts as the Organization's executive council. Ten governments hold seats on the Governing Body because of their industrial importance.

The International Labour Office, the secretariat of the Organization, collects and distributes information, assists governments on request in drafting legislation on the basis of international labour standards, directs technical co-operation activities, and issues publications.
Director General, Francis Blanchard (*France*).

International Maritime Organization (IMO), Albert Embankment, SE1. A United Nations Specialized Agency established on March 17, 1958, to provide means for co-operation and exchange of information among governments on technical matters related to international shipping, especially with regard to safety at sea and preventing marine pollution caused by ships. IMO is responsible for calling maritime conferences and drafting maritime agreements. It has produced numerous technical codes relating to the carriage of various types of cargo such as chemicals, ores, and dangerous goods and to the construction and equipment of ships, e.g., gas and chemical carriers. In June, 1988, 131 nations were in membership. Budget, 1988–89, $21,627,200. (The Organization changed its name from the Inter-Governmental Maritime Consultative Organization (IMCO) on May 22, 1982.)
Secretary General, C. P. Srivastava (*India*).

International Monetary Fund (IMF), 700 19th Street N.W., Washington, D.C. 20431 Established on Dec. 27, 1945, the Fund exists to promote international monetary co-operation and the expansion of international trade; to promote exchange stability; maintain orderly exchange arrangements and avoid competitive exchange depreciations; and to assist in the establishment of a multilateral system of payments in respect of current transactions between members and in the elimination of foreign exchange restrictions which hamper world trade. 151 countries were in membership of the Fund in June, 1988.

The Fund's financial assistance takes the form of a foreign exchange transaction. The member pays to the Fund an amount of its own money equivalent to the amount of foreign currency it wishes to purchase. The member is expected to "repurchase" its own currency from the Fund, usually within three to five years, with a payment of SDRs (Special Drawing Rights) or dollars or usable currency acceptable to the Fund. These arrangements are subject to certain charges.

Currencies drawn from the Fund may be used in a

flexible way to relieve the member's payments difficulty, and usually the member is expected to undertake policy changes, where needed, to correct the payment imbalance.

Each member of the Fund is assigned a quota which determines its voting power and the amount of resources that it may draw from the Fund. The subscription of each member is equal to its quota, and is payable in the member's own currency and SDRs.
Managing Director, Michel Camdessus *(France)*.
U.K. Executive Director, F. Cassell.

International Telecommunication Union (ITU), Place des Nations, Geneva.—Founded at Paris in 1865 as the International Telegraph Union. ITU became a U.N. Specialized Agency in 1947 and as from Jan. 1, 1984, is governed by the Convention adopted by the Torremolinos Convention held in Nairobi in 1982. ITU exists to set up international regulations for telegraph, telephone and radio services to further their development and extend their utilization by the public, at the lowest possible rates; to promote international co-operation for the improvement and rational use of telecommunications of all kinds; the development of technical facilities and their most efficient operation. ITU allocates the radio frequency spectrum and registers radio frequency assignments. It studies, recommends, collects and publishes information on telecommunication matters, including space radio communications. The Budget for 1988 is S. Fr. 125,967,000.
Secretary General, R. E. Butler *(Australia)*.

United Nations Educational, Scientific and Cultural Organization (UNESCO), 7 Place de Fontenoy, Paris 75700.—Under its constitution, the Organization makes its contribution to peace and security by promoting collaboration among its Member States in the fields of education, science, culture and communication. It aims at furthering a universal respect for justice, for the rule of law and for human rights, without distinction of race, sex, language or religion, in accordance with the Charter of the United Nations.

The Organization is composed of three organs: (i) the *General Conference*, consisting of representatives of Member States, which meets biennially to decide the programme and budget; (ii) the *Executive Board*, composed of 51 members elected by the General Conference to supervise the execution of the approved programme and (iii) the *Secretariat*, which is responsible for Unesco's day-to-day functioning and the execution of the programme. In most Member States National Commissions serve as a link with Unesco and help to carry out the programme. Member States in June 1986, 158 and three Associate Members (British Eastern Caribbean group, Netherlands Antilles and the British Virgin Islands).

The U.K. withdrew from Unesco on Dec. 31, 1985. At its 124th session the Executive Board of Unesco decided to grant to the U.K. the observer facilities requested.
Director General, Federico Mayor Zaragoza *(Spain)*.

United Nations Industrial Development Organization (UNIDO), Wagramerstrasse 5, P.O. Box 300, 1400 Vienna, Austria.—Established as an organ of the U.N. General Assembly in Nov. 1966, as an action-oriented body, replacing the Centre for Industrial Development, which had been operating since July 1961. It became a U.N. specialized agency on Jan. 1, 1986, with the aim of promoting the industrialization of developing countries, with special emphasis upon the mobilization of the manufacturing sector. UNIDO provides help on formulation of planning policies, and technical advice and assistance to Third World countries. UNIDO's principal policy-making body is the Industrial Development Board, with 53 members each serving a four year term.
Director General, Domingo Siazon *(Philippines)*.

Universal Postal Union (UPU), Weltpoststrasse 4, 3000 Berne 15.—Established on October 9, 1874, by the postal Convention of Berne and in operation from July 1, 1875, UPU exists to form a single postal territory of all the countries, members of the Union, for the reciprocal exchange of correspondence in order to secure the organization and improvement of the various postal services and to promote in this sphere the development of international collaboration. Every member agrees to transmit the mail of all other members by the best means used for its own mail. The Union includes almost all the countries of the world. Budget, 1988, S.Fr. 22,487,630. A Universal Postal Congress meets at five-yearly intervals. The last was held in Hamburg in June-July 1984, and the next is scheduled to take place in Washington in the autumn of 1989.
Director General, A.C. Botto de Barros *(Brazil)*.

World Bank (see International Bank for Reconstruction and Development and International Development Association).

World Health Organization (WHO), 1211 Geneva 27. Established on April 7, 1948, the aim of the World Health Organization is the attainment by all peoples of the highest possible level of health. It co-operates with its member governments in their efforts to develop health manpower, streamline health services, control communicable diseases, promote family health including mother and child care, family planning, nutrition and health education—and strengthen environmental health. It promotes biomedical and health services research through some 850 collaborating research centres in different parts of the world. Its other services include the International Pharmacopoeia, drug evaluation and monitoring, biological standardization, epidemiological surveillance and scientific publications. Approved budget for 1988 and 1989, $633,980,000. Membership (May 1988), 166.

Organs are a World Health Assembly meeting annually to frame policy, an Executive Board (31 members), meeting at least twice a year, and a Secretariat.
Director General, Dr. H. Nakajima *(Japan)*.

World Intellectual Property Organization (WIPO), 34 chemin des Colombettes, 1211 Geneva 20, Switzerland.—Established by a 1967 convention to succeed the United International Bureau for the Protection of Intellectual Property. Became a specialized agency of the United Nations in 1974, and has 121 members. The World Intellectual Property Organization is the United Nations specialized agency for intergovernmental co-operation in "industrial property" (patents and other rights in technological inventions, rights in trademarks, industrial designs, appellations of origin, etc.) and "copyright and neighbouring rights" (in literary, musical and artistic works, in films, performances of performing artists, phonograms, etc.). WIPO carries out a substantial programme of activities to promote creative intellectual activity and to facilitate the transfer of technology, especially to and among developing countries.

The Conference and the General Assembly control the International Bureau (or secretariat). The Bureau provides the necessary documentation and other services for meetings and carries out projects for the promotion of increased international co-operation among member states.
Director General: Arpad Bogsch *(U.S.A.)*

World Meteorological Organization (WMO), Geneva.—Came into existence in 1951. The present membership is 155 States and 5 Territories. WMO exists to facilitate world-wide co-operation in establishing networks of stations making observations related to meteorology and hydrology, and to promote the establishment and maintenance of centres providing meteorological and related services; to promote the establishment of systems for the rapid exchange of weather information; to promote standardization of meteorological observations and to ensure their uniform publication; to further the application of meteorology to aviation, shipping, water problems, agriculture, and other human activities; to promote activities in operational hydrology and to further close co-operation between meteorological and hydrological services; to encourage research and training in meteorology and to co-ordinate their international aspects. Budget (1988–91), S. Fr. 170,000,000. A World Meteorological Congress meets at least once every four years. An Executive Council (36 members), meeting at least annually, carries out the resolutions of the Congress, initiates studies and makes recommendations on matters requiring international action. Other organs are six Regional Meteorological Associations (Africa, Asia, S. America, N. and Central America, Europe and South-West Pacific), eight technical commissions and a Secretariat.

Secretary General, G. O. P. Obasi (*Nigeria*).

RELATED ORGANIZATIONS

International Atomic Energy Agency, Vienna International Centre, P.O. Box 100, A–1400, Vienna. Set up on July 29, 1957, to accelerate and enlarge the contribution of atomic energy to peace, health and prosperity throughout the world and to ensure that assistance provided by it or under its supervision is not used to further any military purpose. Agreements have been reached concerning the Agency's working relationship with the United Nations and some of the specialized agencies. In June, 1988, 113 states were members.

A General Conference of all members meets in regular annual session and in such special session as may be necessary. A Board of Governors (35 members) carries out the functions of the Agency and meets usually four times a year. The Regular Budget for 1988 amounted to $137,337,000.

Director General, Hans Blix (*Sweden*).
Permanent U.K. Representative, G. E. Clark.

General Agreement on Tariffs and Trade (GATT), Centre William Rappard, Rue de Lausanne 154, CH-1211 Geneva 21. A multilateral treaty, in operation since 1948, to which 96 countries are party, and one acceded provisionally; a further 28 countries apply GATT de facto. Its rules thus govern nearly 90 per cent of world trade. Objectives of GATT are to expand international trade and promote economic development. GATT provides a permanent forum for discussion and solution of particular international trade problems, and for multilateral negotiations to reduce tariffs and other obstacles to the expansion of international trade. Special attention is given to trade problems of developing countries. In November 1979, participating countries concluded the Tokyo Round of multilateral trade negotiations with agreements covering tariff reductions, non-tariff measures, an improved legal framework for the conduct of international trade, bovine meat, dairy products, tropical products, civil aircraft, and a revised GATT anti-dumping code. The Uruguay Round of multilateral trade negotiations was launched in October 1986 and is expected to last four years. The 105 participating countries in the eighth GATT Round are conducting negotiations on tariffs, non-tariff measures, tropical products, textiles, agriculture, subsidies, safeguards, etc. An International Trade Centre, set up by GATT in 1964 to aid developing countries in export promotion, is now operated jointly by GATT and UNCTAD.

Director General, A. Dunkel (*Switzerland*).

EUROPEAN COMMUNITY

The twelve member states: Belgium, Denmark, France, Federal Republic of Germany, Greece, Republic of Ireland, Italy, Luxembourg, The Netherlands, Portugal, Spain, the United Kingdom.

The beginnings of the European Community date from May 9, 1950, when Robert Schuman, France's Foreign Minister, proposed that France and Germany should pool their coal and steel industries under an independent ("supranational") High Authority, in a Community open to the membership of any other European country wishing to join. Not only West Germany, but also Italy, Belgium, the Netherlands, and Luxembourg accepted this invitation.

The Coal and Steel Community (E.C.S.C.), European Economic Community and Euratom share a single institutional framework : a Commission, Council of Ministers, Parliament and Court of Justice. The core of the Community policymaking process is the "dialogue" between the Commission, which initiates and implements policy, and the Council of Ministers, which takes major policy decisions. The beginnings of democratic control are exercised by the European Parliament, while the Court of Justice ensures the rule of law and is the final arbiter in all matters arising from the Community Treaties.

Since the start of the European Economic Community and Euratom in 1958, the Parliament and Court of Justice have been common to all three Communities. Up to July, 1967, each Community had its own executive body (the E.E.C. and Euratom Commis-sions, and the E.C.S.C. High Authority) and its own Council of Ministers.

In April, 1965, the Six signed a treaty providing for the merger of the three executive bodies in a single Commission and the three Councils in a single Council, with a view to the eventual merger of the three Communities themselves. The merger treaty came into force on July 1, 1967; the single Commission and single Council then took office. They enjoy the same powers under the three Community Treaties as did their predecessors.

On December 1 and 2, 1969, the Heads of State or Government of the Six met at the Hague and decided on the completion, strengthening, and, provided that other European countries wished to accept the Treaties of Rome, enlargement of the Community. They instructed the Commission to draw up a plan for economic and monetary union, and the Foreign Ministers to report by the end of July on possible moves towards political unification. They also resolved to intensify the co-ordination of research and development programmes.

In accordance with the Hague decisions the Council of Ministers agreed in April, 1970, that as from 1975 the Community would have its own revenue, independent of national contributions. The

Foreign Ministers agreed (May, 1970) to hold formal political consultations twice a year.

In June, 1970, the Six invited Britain, the Irish Republic, Denmark and Norway to open negotiations on June 30 at Luxembourg on their applications to join the Community. Negotiations continued in 1971 and were concluded with the United Kingdom Government for all major questions by the end of June; on July 8, H.M. Government issued a White Paper on the results. On Jan. 22, 1972, the four applicant countries signed the Treaty of Accession in Brussels. Norway conducted a referendum on its Common Market entry and as a result withdrew its application. The enlarged Community of the Nine came into existence on Jan. 1, 1973.

With the advent of a Labour Government in the U.K. in 1974, there followed a period of renegotiation of the terms of Britain's entry into the Community, culminating in a referendum on June 5, 1975, as to whether or not the country should remain a member of the E.C. The result of the referendum showed two to one in favour of staying in. British Labour Party representatives who had hitherto boycotted the European Parliament then took up their 18 allotted seats.

In January 1976 the European Parliament approved a Report urging direct elections to the Parliament in 1978. On July 12–13, 1976, the Heads of Government or State, meeting in European Council, decided to approve a 410 member Parliament with Britain, France, West Germany and Italy allocated 81 seats each; the Netherlands 25, Belgium 24, Denmark 16, Ireland 15 and Luxembourg 6. Because some countries (including Britain) had not passed the relevant legislation in time, the date of European Elections was postponed until June 1979. When Greece joined the E.C. in January 1981, she was allocated 24 seats in the Parliament, bringing the total number to 434. When Spain and Portugal became members in 1986, they took an additional 84 seats; Spain taking 60 and Portugal 24 making the total 518.

The "European Council", an addition to the institutionalized meetings provided under the Treaties, evolved from the "summit" conference of December 1974, when the Heads of Government decided to meet at least three times a year in order to discuss Community problems and matters requiring political co-operation.

Office of the United Kingdom Permanent Representative to the European Communities
Rond-point Robert Schuman 6, 1040 Brussels

Ambassador and U.K. Permanent Representative, Sir David Hannay, K.C.M.G. (1985).

The Commission

On July 1, 1970, the Commission was reduced from 14 members to nine, two each from Germany, France and Italy, and one each from Belgium, the Netherlands and Luxembourg. Following the 1973 enlargement, the number rose to 13, with two seats each from Britain, France, Germany, and Italy and one each for the other members. The admission of Greece in 1981, with 1 seat, brought the total to 14 Commissioners. When the Community was again enlarged in 1986, the total number of Commissioners grew to 17, two being appointed from Spain and one from Portugal.

The members of the Commission are appointed by agreement among the twelve member governments for a four-year renewable term; the president and vice-presidents are appointed from among the members for a two-year term, also renewable.

The members of the Commission are pledged to independence of the governments and of national or other particular interests. They accept joint respon-

sibility for their decisions, which are taken by majority vote.

In addition to being the initiator of Community action and having specific powers, the Commission acts as a mediator between the member governments in Community affairs and is the guardian of the Community Treaties.

Commission of the European Communities
200 Rue de la Loi, 1049 Brussels

President, Jacques Delors (France).

Vice-Presidents, Frans Andriessen (Netherlands), Henning Christophersen (Denmark), Lord Cockfield (U.K.), Manuel Marin (Spain), Karl-Heinz Narjes (Federal Republic of Germany), Lorenzo Natali (Italy).

Members, Claude Cheysson (France), Antonio José Baptista Cardoso e Cunha (Portugal), Stanley Clinton Davis (U.K.), Willy de Clercq (Belgium), Abel Matutes (Spain), Nicolas Mosar (Luxembourg), Alois Pfeiffer (Federal Republic of Germany), Carlo Ripa di Meana (Italy), Peter Sutherland (Ireland), Grigoris Varfis (Greece).

The Rt. Hon. Leon Brittan and the Rt. Hon. Bruce Millan will replace Lord Cockfield and Stanley Clinton Davis as the U.K. Commissioners from January 1989.

Secretary General, D. Williamson (U.K.).

The Commission maintains information offices in London (8 Storey's Gate, SWIP 3AT), Edinburgh (7 Alva Street EH2 4PH), Cardiff (4 Cathedral Road), Belfast (Windsor House, 9/15 Bedford Street), Dublin (39 Molesworth Street), Washington (2100 M. Street, N.W. (Suite 707), Washington, D.C. 20037), New York (1 Dag Hammarskjöld Plaza, 245 East 47th Street, New York, N.Y. 10017), Ottawa (Inn of the Provinces, Office Tower (Suite 1110), 350 Sparks Street, Ontario, KIR 7S8), and other cities.

The Council of the European Communities
170 Rue de la Loi, 1048 Brussels

This consists of ministers from the governments of each of the twelve member states, the ministers concerned depending on the subject under discussion. A single Council exists for the three European Communities. It is the main decision-taking body within the Community legislative process. The Council acts, in almost all cases, on the basis of proposals submitted by the Commission, which is present at Council sessions to participate in the shaping of the measures taken. Before examining Commission proposals the Council normally obtains the opinions of the European Parliament and the Economic and Social Committee on them.

As prescribed by the E.C. treaty, under which the great majority of the Council's business falls, decisions are taken by majority vote, qualified majority vote (a system in which the members' votes are weighted) or by unanimity. The Council acts under the E.C. treaty by issuing (a) "regulations" which are binding in their entirety and directly applicable in all member states; (b) "directives" which are binding as to the result to be achieved but leave open to national governments the method of attaining this result; (c) "decisions" which bind those addressed; (d) "recommendations" and (e) "opinions", which have no binding force. The Euratom treaty has the same system of voting and taking action; the E.C.S.C. system differs in certain respects.

The Presidency of the Council is held in rotation for periods of six months. The sessions of the Council are prepared by a Committee of Permanent Representatives of the member states. The Council and its committees are serviced by a general secretariat.

European Parliament

Secretariat: Centre Européen, Kirchberg, Luxembourg.

U.K. Information Office, 2 Queen Anne's Gate, SW1H 9AA.

The first direct elections to the European Parliament were held in mid-1979, the second five years later. Of 518 seats, the United Kingdom, France, Germany and Italy have 81 each, Spain 60, the Netherlands 25, Belgium, Greece, and Portugal 24, Denmark 16, Ireland 15 and Luxembourg 6. The Parliament meets in Strasbourg and its Committees in Brussels. The pre-1979 Parliament consisted of 198 members nominated by their national Parliaments— the United Kingdom, France, Germany and Italy had 36 seats each, Belgium and the Netherlands 14 each, Denmark and Ireland 10 each and Luxembourg 6. Set up in 1952 under the European Coal and Steel Community Treaty of 1951, the Parliament's authority was extended by the 1957 Convention on Common Institutions to cover the European Economic Community and Euratom. It must be consulted on all major issues and has the right to dismiss the Commission by a vote of censure. Apart from general powers of supervision and consultation, it questions the Commission and the Council of Ministers and has a measure of control over the Community's annual budget including its final adoption. It can reject the budget as a whole and can amend items of non-obligatory expenditure (i.e. expenditure not specified in the original treaties or derived legislation— amounting to some 27 per cent. of the total budget). The Members of the Parliament serve on specialized committees and sit in political groups—Socialists, Christian Democrats, Liberals and Democrats, European Democrats, European Progressive Democrats and Communists. There are also a number of Independents in the Parliament.

President, Lord Plumb (*U.K.*).

European Court of Justice
L–2925 Luxembourg

The European Court superseded the Court of Justice of E.C.S.C. and is common to the three European Communities. It exists to safeguard the law in the interpretation and application of the Community treaties, to decide on the legality of decisions of the Council of Ministers or the Commission and to determine violations of the Treaties. Cases may be brought to it by the member States, the Community institutions, firms or individuals. Its decisions are directly binding in the member countries. The thirteen judges and six advocates-general of the Court are appointed for renewable six-year terms by the member Governments in concert. During 1987, 395 new cases were lodged at the court and 208 judgments were delivered.

Judges, Hon. Lord Mackenzie Stuart (*President*); G. Bosco (*President of 1st and 5th Chambers*); O Due (*President of 2nd and 6th Chambers*); J. C. Moitinho de Almeida (*President of 3rd Chamber*); G. C. Rodriguez Iglesias (*President of 4th Chamber*); T. Koopmans; U. Everling; K. Bahlmann; Y. Galmot; C. N. Kakouris; R. Joliet; T. F. O'Higgins; F. A. Schockweiler.
Advocates-General, M. Darmon (*1st Advocate-General*); Sir Gordon Slynn; G. F. Mancini; C. O. Lenz; J. Mischo; J. L. da Cruz Vilaça.
Registrar, J.-G. Giraud.

The European Investment Bank
100 Boulevard Konrad Adenauer,
L–2950 Luxembourg

The European Investment Bank (E.I.B.) was set up in 1958 under the terms of the Treaty of Rome to finance capital investment projects promoting the balanced development of the European Community.

It grants long-term loans to private enterprises, public authorities and financial institutions, to finance projects which further: the economic development of less advanced regions (Assisted Areas); improve communication systems between Member States; environmental protection; attainment of the Communities energy policy objectives; modernization of enterprises; and co-operation between undertakings in the different Member States.

E.I.B. activities have also been extended outside member countries under the terms of different association or cooperation agreements with twelve countries in the Mediterranean region and, under the Lomé Conventions, 66 in Africa, the Caribbean and the Pacific.

The Bank's total financing operations in 1987 amounted to 7,843 million E.C.U.,* of which 7,450 million (including 447 million from the resources of the New Community Instrument for borrowing and lending) were for investments in the European Community and 392 million for outside the Community. Between 1973 and 1986 the E.I.B. had made available a total of £5,845 million E.C.U. for investment in the U.K.

The members of the European Investment Bank are the twelve member states of the Community, who have all subscribed to the Bank's capital, of 28,000 million E.C.U. (of which 2,596 E.C.U. is the paid in or due to be paid in portion). The bulk of the funds required by the Bank to carry out its tasks are borrowed on the capital markets of the Community and non-member countries, and on the international market.

As it operates on a non-profit-making basis, the interest rates charged by the E.I.B. reflect the cost of the Bank's borrowings and closely follow conditions on world capital markets.

The Board of Governors of the European Investment Bank consists of one Minister nominated by each of the member countries, usually the Finance Minister, who lay down general directives on the policy of the Bank and appoint members to the Board of Directors (21 nominated by the member states, 1 by the Commission of the European Communities), which takes decisions on the granting and raising of loans and the fixing of interest rates. A Management Committee, also appointed by the Board of Governors, is responsible for the day-to-day operations of the Bank.

President, Ernst-Günther Bröder.
Vice-Presidents, C. Richard Ross; Lucio Izzo; Alain Prate; Miguel A. Arnedo Orbañanos; Erling Jørgensen; Ludovicus Meulemans.
(The President and Vice-Presidents also preside as Chairman and Vice-Chairmen at meetings of the Board of Directors.)

U.K. Office: 68 Pall Mall, SW1Y 5ES.

EUROPEAN COAL AND STEEL COMMUNITY

This, the first of the European Communities, was established in 1952. Since then, for coal, iron ore and scrap, it has abolished customs duties, quantitative restrictions, the dual pricing system whereby prices charged on exported coal or steel differed from those

----

* The financial statements of the European Investment Bank are drawn up in E.C.U. which at June 30, 1988 equalled ± £0·67, U.S.$1·14.

charged to home consumers, currency restrictions and discrimination in transport rates based on the nationality of customers and the special frontier charges which made international transport of these goods within the Community dearer than transport within national frontiers. It has applied rules for fair competition and a harmonized external tariff for the whole Community.

THE TREATY OF ROME

Discussions were held at Messina, Sicily, in 1955 between the foreign ministers of the six member states of E.C.S.C. (Belgium, France, Federal Republic of Germany, Italy, Luxembourg and The Netherlands) on proposals for further advances towards economic integration in Europe, and after intensive study of these proposals, a treaty was signed at Rome on March 25, 1957, setting up the European Economic Community.

The Treaty aimed to lay the foundations of an enduring and closer union between the European peoples by gradually removing the economic effects of their political frontiers. The Treaty provides for the elimination of customs duties and quotas in trade between member states; the establishment of a common customs tariff and a common trade policy towards third countries; the abolition of the obstacles to free movement of persons, services and capital between member states; the inauguration of common policies for agriculture and transport; the establishment of a system ensuring that competition shall not be distorted in the Common Market; the co-ordination of economic policies; the harmonization of social and economic legislation to the extent necessary in order to enable the Common Market to work; the creation of a European Social Fund in order to improve the possibilities of employment for workers and to contribute to the raising of their standard of living; the establishment of an Economic and Social Committee which must be consulted on major proposals, consisting of representatives of employers, workers, consumers and other groups; the establishment of a European Investment Bank intended to aid investment in underdeveloped areas and help to finance modernization; and the association of overseas countries and territories with the Community with a view to increasing trade and to pursuing jointly their effort towards economic and social development.

ENLARGEMENT OF THE COMMUNITY

The question of possible enlargement of the Community played an important part in its development from the autumn of 1961 when Britain, the Irish Republic, Denmark and Norway first sought membership, and Austria, Sweden, Switzerland, Spain and Cyprus sought association with the Community. The negotiations were vetoed by France in January, 1963.

In May, 1967, Britain, the Irish Republic and Denmark formally submitted applications for Community membership. In July Norway followed suit and Sweden announced that it would seek to participate in the enlargement of the Community on terms compatible with its neutrality. These applications made very slow progress and appeared to come to a standstill when in December, 1967, France declared that Britain's economy would have to be strengthened before negotiations could begin. But shortly after taking office as President of France, Georges Pompidou stated in July, 1969, that there was no objection in principle to the admission of Britain to the Community. At the Hague "summit" meeting in December, 1969, the Six decided that provided that the completion of the Community was not prejudiced, and provided that the Community was strengthened to provide for enlargement, then the entry of other European countries would be desirable. After deciding on a common negotiating position, the Six invited Britain and the other applicants to begin negotiations for membership.

A single overall transitional period of five years, during which the Three were to adopt Community rules and regulations, started on January 1, 1973, giving time for the gradual integration of the economies of the Three with the Six by the end of 1977.

The first 40 per cent alignment on the Community's Common External Tariff (C.E.T.)—i.e. 40 per cent of the difference between the new members' tariffs and the C.E.T.—was made at the beginning of 1974, and three further alignments of 20 per cent each followed.

Negotiations with Greece were concluded and the Treaty of Accession signed on May 28, 1979. Greece became the tenth member of the Community on January 1, 1981. Portugal and Spain applied to join the Community and became the eleventh and twelfth members on January 1, 1986.

Following a plebiscite, Greenland negotiated its withdrawal from the E.C. (but without discontinuing relations with Denmark) and formally left on February 1, 1986.

EUROPEAN ATOMIC ENERGY COMMUNITY (EURATOM)

A second treaty, arising from the Messina discussions between the E.C.S.C. powers on additional means of co-operation, was signed in Rome on March 25, 1957, setting up the European Atomic Energy Community. The task of Euratom, defined in detail in the Treaty, is to create within a short period the technical and industrial conditions necessary to utilize nuclear discoveries and especially to produce nuclear energy on a large scale. The United Kingdom, Denmark and Ireland joined Euratom on Jan. 1, 1973, Greece on Jan. 1, 1981, and Spain and Portugal on Jan. 1, 1986.

OTHER INTERNATIONAL ORGANIZATIONS

ASIAN DEVELOPMENT BANK

2330 Roxas Boulevard, 1300 Metropolitan Manila
Philippines

The Asian Development Bank began operations in December 1966. It has 47 member countries, 32 countries from the Asia–Pacific region and 15 from Europe and North America.

The aim of the Bank is to promote the economic and social progress of its developing member countries. It makes loans and equity investments; provides technical assistance for development programmes and advisory services; promotes public and private investment in development schemes; and co-ordinates development plans and policies.

The Bank's highest policy-making body is the board of Governors, which meets annually. Each member country appoints one governor and one alternate governor. The President, who is elected by the Board of Governors for a term of five years, acts as the

Chairman of the Board of Directors. The twelve-man Board of Directors is responsible for the direction of the Bank's operations.
President, Masao Fujioka (*Japan*).

ASSOCIATION OF SOUTH EAST ASIAN NATIONS (A.S.E.A.N.)

Jakarta, Indonesia

Formed in 1967, the main aims of the Association are the acceleration of economic growth, social progress and cultural development, the promotion of collaboration and mutual assistance in matters of common interest, and the continuing stability of the South East Asian region.

The Heads of Government of the member countries are the highest authority and give directions to A.S.E.A.N. as and when necessary. The main policy-making body is the annual meeting of foreign ministers of the member countries. The members of the Association are Brunei, Indonesia, Malaysia, the Philippines, Singapore and Thailand.
Sec. Gen., Roderick Yong (*Brunei*).

BANK FOR INTERNATIONAL SETTLEMENTS

(1930), Centrebahnplatz 2, 4002 Basle, Switzerland

The objectives of the Bank are to promote the co-operation of central banks; to provide facilities for international financial operations; and to act as trustee or agent in international financial settlements entrusted to it. The London agent is the Bank of England, and the Governor of the Bank of England is a member of the Board of Directors, in which administrative control is vested.
Chairman of the Board of Directors and President of the Bank for International Settlement, Dr. W. S. Duisberg (*Netherlands*), from Jan. 1, 1988.

C.A.B. INTERNATIONAL

Wallingford, Oxon. OX10 8DE
[0491-32111]

C.A.B. International (formerly the Commonwealth Agricultural Bureaux) was founded in 1929. It consists of four Institutes and eleven Bureaux under the control of an Executive Council comprising representatives of the countries which contribute to its funds. The functions of C.A.B.I. are to provide a scientific information service, identification of pests, biological control services and mutual assistance. Each Institute and Bureau acts as an effective clearing house for the collection, collation and dissemination of information in its particular branch of agricultural science.
Director General, D. Mentz.

CARIBBEAN COMMUNITY AND COMMON MARKET (CARICOM)

P.O. Box 10827, Georgetown, Guyana

CARICOM was established on 1973 with three objectives: economic co-operation through the Caribbean Common Market; the co-ordination of foreign policy among the independent member states; the provision of common services and co-operation in functional matters such as health, education and culture, communications and industrial relations. The principal organs are the Conference of Heads of Government, which determines policy, and the Common Market Council of Ministers, consisting of Ministers of Government (usually Ministers of Trade)

designated by each member state, which is responsible for the development and smooth running of the Common Market and for the settlement of any problems arising out of its functioning. The principal administrative arm is the Secretariat, based in Guyana.

The 13 member states are Antigua and Barbuda, The Bahamas (which is not a member of the Common Market), Barbados, Belize, Dominica, Grenada, Guyana, Jamaica, Montserrat, St. Christopher and Nevis, St. Lucia, St. Vincent and the Grenadines and Trinidad and Tobago. The Dominican Republic, Suriname and Haiti have observer status.
Sec. Gen., Roderick Rainford (*Jamaica*).

CONFERENCE ON DISARMAMENT

Palais des Nations, CH-1211, Geneva 10, Switzerland

The Conference on Disarmament (C.D.) was founded in its original form as the 18-nation Committee on Disarmament in 1962. The present title of the organization was adopted in 1984. The membership stood at 40 nations in June 1988.

The Conference holds two regular sessions per year, Feb.–April and June–August. The work of the Conference is conducted both in plenary session and in ad hoc committees set up with the consent of all members to deal with specific items of the agenda. Currently on the agenda are negotiations towards a global ban on chemical weapons.

The Conference on Disarmament is accepted by the U.N. as the single multilateral disarmament negotiating body.
Secretary General, His Excellency Miljan Komatina.
U.K. Delegation to the Conference on Disarmament, 37–39 rue de Vermont, 1211 Geneva 20, Switzerland.—*Leader of U.K. Delegation*, Miss T. A. H. Solesby, C.M.G.

COUNCIL FOR MUTUAL ECONOMIC ASSISTANCE (C.M.E.A. OR COMECON)

56 Kalinin Avenue, Moscow G–205, U.S.S.R

Established in 1949, the Council's aim is to promote the development of the national economies of the member states and the development of socialist economic integration, through the co-operation of members in the most rational use of resources and the acceleration of economic and technical progress, industrialisation and productivity. The highest body is the Session of the Council, which consists of delegations from all member states, usually led by the heads of government. The Executive Committee consists of representatives of member states at the level of deputy heads of government, and is responsible for the implementation of the tasks set by the Session of the Council and for directing the work of the Committees, Standing Commissions, Secretariat and other bodies. In 1988 the C.M.E.A. established official relations with the E.C.

The member countries are Bulgaria, Cuba, Czechoslovakia, German Democratic Republic, Hungary, Mongolia, Poland, Romania, U.S.S.R. and Vietnam. Yugoslavia participates in the work of some C.M.E.A. bodies. There are also co-operation agreements with Afghanistan, Angola, Ethiopia, Finland, Iraq, Mexico, Mozambique, Nicaragua, the People's Democratic Republic of Yemen, and Yugoslavia.
Secretary, V. Sytchev (U.S.S.R.).

THE COUNCIL OF EUROPE

67006 Strasbourg, France

A European organization founded in 1949 whose aim is to achieve greater unity between its members to safeguard their European heritage and to facilitate their economic and social progress through discussion and common action in economic, social, cultural, educational, scientific, legal and administrative matters and in the maintenance and furtherance of human rights and fundamental freedoms.

The 21 members are Austria, Belgium, Cyprus, Denmark, France, the Federal Republic of Germany, Greece, Iceland, the Republic of Ireland, Italy, Liechtenstein, Luxembourg, Malta, Netherlands, Norway, Portugal, Spain, Sweden, Switzerland, Turkey and the U.K.

The organs are the Committee of Ministers, consisting of the Foreign Ministers of member countries, who meet twice yearly, and the Parliamentary Assembly of 170 members, elected or chosen by the national parliaments of member countries in proportion to the relative strength of political parties. There is also a Joint Committee of Ministers and Representatives of the Parliamentary Assembly.

The Committee of Ministers is the executive organ of the Council. The majority of its conclusions take the form of international agreements (known as European Conventions) or recommendations to governments. Decisions of the Ministers may also be embodied in partial agreements to which a limited number of member governments are party. Member governments accredit Permanent Representatives to the Council in Strasbourg, who are also the Ministers' Deputies. The Committee of Deputies meets every month to transact business and to take decisions on behalf of Ministers.

The Parliamentary Assembly holds three week-long sessions a year. It debates reports on, *inter alia*, political, economic, agricultural, social, educational, legal and regional planning affairs, and also reports received annually from the O.E.C.D., other European organizations and certain specialized agencies of the United Nations. Its 13 permanent committees meet, normally in private, once or twice between each public plenary session of the Assembly. The Standing Conference of Local and Regional Authorities of Europe each year brings together mayors and municipal councillors in the same numbers as the members of the Parliamentary Assembly.

One of the principal achievements of the Council of Europe is the European Convention of Human Rights (1950) under which was established the European Commission and the European Court of Human Rights. 128 other conventions and agreements have now been concluded. They include the European Social Charter, the European Social Security Code, and conventions on extradition, the legal status of migrant workers, conservation, and the transfer of sentenced prisoners.

Non-member states take part in certain Council of Europe activities on a regular or ad hoc basis; thus Finland, San Marino, the Holy See and Yugoslavia participate in all the educational, cultural and sports activities. The European Youth Foundation funds events in both Eastern and Western European countries and in some outside Europe, while nationals of these countries attend courses and seminars at the European Youth Centre.

Secretary General, Marcelino Oreja (*Spain*).
Permanent U.K. Representative, His Excellency Colin McLean, C.M.G., M.B.E.

EUROPEAN FREE TRADE ASSOCIATION (E.F.T.A.)

The members of the European Free Trade Association, which was established on May 3, 1960, are Austria, Finland (an associate from 1960 to 1985 and a member since Jan. 1, 1986), Iceland (since March 1, 1970), Norway, Sweden and Switzerland.

In 1973 all the E.F.T.A. Member States entered into a new relationship with the E.C. Two—Denmark and the United Kingdom—withdrew from E.F.T.A. at the end of December 1972 to become members of the E.C. on January 1, 1973. Agreements establishing industrial free trade between all other E.F.T.A. Member States and the enlarged E.C. came into force on that same date. Similar agreements with Norway and Finland came into force on July 1, 1973, and Jan. 1, 1974, respectively. On Jan. 1, 1986 Portugal became a member of the E.C. The free trade agreements therefore now apply to trade between the six countries remaining in E.F.T.A. and Portugal.

E.F.T.A.'s first objective was free trade between its original members and this was realized at the end of 1966. Its second objective was the creation of a single market to include all Western European countries, achieved through the free trade agreements.

The final abolition of tariffs on E.F.T.A.–E.C. trade was marked by a meeting in Luxembourg in April 1984 when ministers from all E.F.T.A. and E.C. countries met. They agreed on general guidelines for greatly increased co-operation between their countries. The emphasis was on the removal of technical barriers to trade and the simplification of the origin rules which determine which products may be traded free of duty. A start was made towards multilateral co-operation in research and development as a means of strengthening the industrial potential of Western Europe, and multilateral efforts to protect the environment are under discussion.

All E.F.T.A. and E.C. countries have co-operated in a successful attempt to simplify border formalities for trade in goods in Western Europe: new multilateral conventions provide for the use of a single administrative document for customs purposes and for the introduction of a common transit procedure.

The Council of E.F.T.A. meets every two weeks at the level of the heads of the permanent national delegations to E.F.T.A. and usually twice a year at the level of ministers. Each state has a single vote and recommendations must normally be unanimous. Decisions of the Council are binding on member countries.

Secretary General, Georg Reisch (*Austria*) 9–11 Rue de Varembé, 1211 Geneva 20.

EUROPEAN SPACE AGENCY

8–10 rue Mario Nikis, 75738 Paris, France

The European Space Agency (E.S.A.) was set up on May 31, 1975. It was formed from two earlier space organizations—the European Space Research Organization (E.S.R.O.) and the Euroean Launcher Development Organization (E.L.D.O.). Its aims include the advancement of space research and technology, the implementation of a long-term European space policy and the co-ordination of national space programmes.

The member countries are Austria, Belgium, Denmark, France, Federal Republic of Germany, Republic of Ireland, Italy, Netherlands, Norway, Spain, Sweden, Switzerland and the United Kingdom. Finland is an associate member and Canada a co-operating state.

The agency is directed by a Council composed of the representatives of the member states, and its chief officer is the Director General.

Director General, Prof. Dr. Reimar Lüst.

INTERNATIONAL CONFEDERATION OF FREE TRADE UNIONS

37/41 rue Montagne aux Herbes Potageres, 1000 Brussels, Belgium

Formed in 1949 the International Confederation of Free Trade Unions (I.C.F.T.U.) was created to promote free trade unionism worldwide. It aims to establish, maintain and develop free trade unions, particularly in economically under-developed countries.

Affiliated to the I.C.F.T.U. are 141 individual unions and representative bodies in 97 countries and territories: on Dec. 16, 1987 there were over 87 million members.

The supreme authority of the organization is the Congress which convenes at least every four years. It is composed of delegates from the affiliated trade organizations. The Congress elects an Executive Board of 35 members which meets at least twice a year. The Board establishes the budget and receives suggestions and proposals from affiliates as well as acting on behalf of the Confederation. The Congress also elects the General Secretary.

General Secretary, John Vanderveken.
U.K. Affiliate, T.U.C., Congress House, 23–28 Great Russell Street, WC1B 3LS.

INTERNATIONAL CRIMINAL POLICE ORGANIZATION (INTERPOL)

26 rue Armengaud, 92210 Saint-Cloud, France

The International Criminal Police Commission was set up in 1923 to establish an international criminal records office and to harmonize extradition procedures. In 1956 a revised Constitution was adopted and the organization adopted its present name. On Jan. 1, 1988 the organization comprised 146 member states.

INTERPOL's aims are to ensure and promote mutual assistance between all criminal police authorities, and to support government agencies concerned with combatting crime, whilst respecting the national sovereignty of members. INTERPOL is financed by annual contributions from the governments of member states.

INTERPOL's policy is decided by the General Assembly which meets annually: it is composed of delegates appointed by the member states. The 13-member Executive Committee is elected by the General Assembly from among the member states' delegates, and is chaired by the President, who has a four-year term of office. The permanent administrative organ is the General Secretariat, headed by the Secretary General, who is appointed by the General Assembly.
President, Jolly Bugarin.
U.K. Office, Criminal Investigation Department, New Scotland Yard, SW1H 0BG.—*U.K. Representative,* H. N. Annesley.

INTERNATIONAL ENERGY AGENCY

Chateau de la Muette, 2 rue Andre-Pascal, 75775 Paris, France

The International Energy Agency (I.E.A.), founded in November 1974, is an autonomous agency within the framework of the Organization for Economic Co-operation and Development (O.E.C.D.). The I.E.A. had 21 member countries at September 1987.

The I.E.A.'s objectives include improvement of energy supply and demand worldwide, increased efficiency, development of alternative energy sources and the promotion of relations between oil producing and oil consuming countries. The I.E.A. also maintains an emergency system to alleviate the effects of severe oil supply disruptions.

The main decision-making body is the Governing Board composed of senior energy officials from member countries. Various standing groups and special committees exist to facilitate the work of the Board. The I.E.A. Secretariat, with a staff of energy experts, carries out the work of the Governing Board

and its subordinate bodies. The Executive Director is appointed by the Board.
Executive Director, Mrs. Helga Steeg (*Federal Rep. of Germany*).

INTERNATIONAL MARITIME SATELLITE ORGANIZATION

40 Melton Street, NW1 2EQ

The International Maritime Satellite Organization (INMARSAT) was founded in July 1978 and began operations on Feb. 1, 1982. INMARSAT operates a system of satellites to provide telephone, telex, data and facsimile transmission, as well as distress and safety communication services to the world's shipping, aviation and offshore industries.

INMARSAT comprises three bodies: The Assembly is composed of representatives of all member countries, each with one vote. It meets every two years to review activities and objectives, to make recommendations to the Council. The Council consists of representatives of the 18 members with the largest investment shares, and four others who represent the interests of developing countries. The Council meets at least three times a year and oversees the activities of the Directorate, the permanent staff of INMARSAT.

As at April 30, 1988 there were 52 member countries.
Director General, Olof Lundberg.

INTERNATIONAL RED CROSS AND RED CRESCENT MOVEMENT

17 avenue de la Paix, 1202 Geneva, Switzerland

The International Red Cross and Red Crescent Movement is composed of three elements. The International Committee of the Red Cross (I.C.R.C.) is the founding body of the Red Cross and was formed in 1863. It is a neutral intermediary negotiating between warring parties. It also ensures the application of the Geneva Conventions with regard to prisoners of war and internees.

The League of Red Cross and Red Crescent Societies, founded in 1919, is the international federation which exists to contribute to humanitarian activities such as co-ordinating relief work, caring for refugees, training personnel and furthering medical research. There are also national Red Cross and Red Crescent Societies in 146 countries with a global membership of 250 million.

The International Red Cross meets every four years at the International Red Cross Conference, which is also attended by nations bound by the Geneva Conventions.
President of the I.C.R.C., Cornelio Sommaruga.
British Red Cross Society, 9 Grosvenor Crescent, SW1X 7EJ.—*Director,* J. C. Burke-Gaffney.

INTERNATIONAL TELECOMMUNICATIONS SATELLITE ORGANIZATION

3400 International Drive, N.W., Washington D.C. 20008–3098, U.S.A.

Formed in 1964, the International Telecommunications Satellite Organization (INTELSAT) owns and operates the world-wide commercial communications satellite system. The system is composed of a network of thirteen satellites and more than 700 antennas which link together over 165 member and non-member users.

INTELSAT provides an international telephony service; an international television service; the Intelsat Business Service (I.B.S.); Intelnet (a digital service designed for data collection and distribution);

domestic telecommunications services and the Vista service providing telecommunications to remote communities.

Each of the 115 national signatories contributed to the capital costs of the organization in proportion to its investment share. The investment share is based on the relative usage of the system by member countries.

There is a four-tier hierarchy: the Assembly of Parties to the agreement meets every two years to consider long-term objectives. It is composed of representatives of the member governments: the Meeting of Signatories consider annually the financial, technical and operational aspects of the system: the Board of Governors, which has 28 members: the Executive Organ is the permanent staff of Intelsat and is headed by a Director General who reports to the Board of Governors.

LEAGUE OF ARAB STATES

37 Av. Khereddine Pacha, Tunis, Tunisia

The purpose of the League of Arab States (founded 1945) is to ensure co-operation among member states and protect their independence and sovereignty, to supervise the affairs and interests of Arab countries and to control the execution of agreements concluded among the member states. The League considers itself a regional organization and is an observer at the United Nations.

Member states are Algeria, Bahrain, Djibouti, Iraq, Jordan, Kuwait, Lebanon, Libya, Mauritania, Morocco, Oman, Palestine, Qatar, Saudi Arabia, Somalia, Sudan, Syria, Tunisia, United Arab Emirates, Arab Republic of Yemen and Democratic Republic of Yemen. (The membership of Egypt, a founder state, was suspended in 1979.)

Secretary General, Chedli Klibi *(Tunisia)*.

U.K. Office—Arab Information Centre, 52 Green Street, WIY 3RH.

NORTH ATLANTIC TREATY ORGANIZATION

Brussels 1110, Belgium.

The North Atlantic Treaty was signed on April 4, 1949, by the Foreign Ministers of twelve nations. The twelve are Belgium, Canada, Denmark, France, Iceland, Italy, Luxembourg, the Netherlands, Norway, Portugal, the United Kingdom and United States. Greece and Turkey acceded to the Treaty in 1952, the Federal Republic of Germany in 1955, and Spain in 1982. The North Atlantic Council, chaired by the Secretary General, is the highest authority of the Alliance and is composed of permanent representatives of the sixteen member countries. It meets at ministerial level (Foreign Ministers) at least twice per year. The permanent representatives (Ambassadors) head national delegations of advisers and experts.

Defence matters are dealt with in the Defence Planning Committee (D.P.C.), composed of representatives of all member countries, except France. Within the specialized field of defence, the D.P.C. has the same functions and authority as the Council. Like the Council it meets regularly at ambassador level and twice a year in ministerial sessions, when the nations are represented by their Defence Ministers.

The Council/D.P.C., as a unique forum for confidential and constant inter-governmental consultation and as the main decision-making body within the North Atlantic Alliance, is assisted by an International Staff, divided into five divisions: Political

Affairs; Defence Planning and Policy; Defence Support; Infrastructure, Logistics and Civil Emergency Planning; Scientific Affairs.

U.K. Permanent Representative, His Excellency Sir Michael Alexander, K.C.M.G.

The senior military authority in N.A.T.O., under the Council and D.P.C., is the Military Committee composed of the Chief of Defence of each member country except France and Iceland. The Military Committee, which is assisted by an international military staff, functions in permanent session with permanent military representatives and is responsible for making recommendations to the Council and Defence Planning Committee on measures considered necessary for the common defence of the N.A.T.O. area and for supplying guidance on military matters to the major N.A.T.O. Commanders.

Chairman of the Military Committee, Gen. Wolfgang Altenburg *(Federal Republic of Germany)*.

The strategic area covered by the North Atlantic Treaty is divided among three Commands (European, Atlantic and Channel) and a Regional Planning Group (Canada and the United States).

The Major N.A.T.O Commanders are responsible for the development of defence plans for their respective areas, for the determination of force requirements and for the deployment and exercise of the forces under their command. The Major N.A.T.O. Commanders report to the Military Committee.

The three Major N.A.T.O Commanders are:

Supreme Allied Commander, Europe, Gen. John R. Galvin *(U.S.)*.

Supreme Allied Commander, Atlantic, Adm. Lee Baggett, Jr. *(U.S.)*.

Commander-in-Chief, Channel, Adm. Sir Julian Oswald *(U.K.)*.

Secretary General, Manfred Wörner *(Federal Rep. of Germany)*.

ORGANIZATION FOR ECONOMIC CO-OPERATION AND DEVELOPMENT

2, rue André-Pascal, 75116 Paris

Formed on September 30, 1961, the O.E.C.D. replaced the Organization for European Economic Co-operation (O.E.E.C). The O.E.C.D. is the instrument for international co-operation among industrialized member countries on economic and social policies. Its objectives are to assist its member governments in the formulation and co-ordination of policies designed to achieve high, sustained economic growth while maintaining financial stability, to contribute to world trade on a multilateral basis and to stimulate members' aid to developing countries.

The following countries belong to the O.E.C.D.: Australia, Austria, Belgium, Canada, Denmark, Federal Republic of Germany, Finland, France, Greece, Iceland, Republic of Ireland, Italy, Japan, Luxembourg, the Netherlands, New Zealand, Norway, Portugal, Spain, Sweden, Switzerland, Turkey, U.K. and U.S.A. (Yugoslavia participates with a special status).

The Council is the supreme body of the Organization. Composed of one representative for each member country, it meets at Permanent Representative level under the Chairmanship of the Secretary General, or at Ministerial level (usually once a year) under the Chairmanship of a Minister elected annually. Decisions and recommendations are adopted by mutual agreement of all members of the Council. Fourteen members of the Council are chosen annually to form an Executive Committee to assist the Council. However, most of the O.E.C.D.'s work is undertaken in over 200 specialized committees and working parties. Five autonomous or semi-autonomous bodies are related in varying degrees to the Organization: the Nuclear Energy Agency, the International Energy Agency, the Development Centre, the Centre for Educational Research and Innovation, and the European Conference of Ministers of Transport. These bodies, the committees and the Council are serviced by an international Secretariat headed by the Secretary General of the Organization.

Secretary General, Jean-Claude Paye (*France*).

U.K. Permanent Representative, John Walton David Gray, C.M.G., 19 rue de Franqueville, Paris 75116.

ORGANIZATION OF AFRICAN UNITY (O.A.U.)

P.O. Box 3243, Addis Ababa, Ethiopia

The Organization of African Unity was established in 1963 and has 50 members. It aims to further African unity and solidarity, to co-ordinate political, economic, social and defence policies, and to eliminate colonialism in Africa.

The chief organs are the Assembly of heads of state or government and the Council of Foreign Ministers. The main administrative body is the Secretariat, based in Addis Ababa.

Sec. Gen., Ide Oumarou (*Niger*).

ORGANIZATION OF AMERICAN STATES (O.A.S.)

17th Street and Constitution Ave. N.W., Washington D.C. 20006, U.S.A.

Originally founded in 1890 for largely commercial purposes, the O.A.S adopted its present name and charter in 1948. Its aims are to strengthen the peace and security of the continent; to prevent possible causes of difficulties and to ensure the pacific settlement of disputes that may arise among the member states; to provide for common action on the part of those states in the event of aggression; to seek the solution of political, judicial and economic problems that may arise among them; and to promote, by co-operative action, their economic, social and cultural development. The O.A.S. is a regional organization within the United Nations.

Policy is determined by the annual General Assembly. Meetings of Ministers of Foreign Affairs consider urgent problems, and advise in cases of armed attack and threats to peace.

The 32 member states are Antigua and Barbuda, Argentina, Bahamas, Barbados, Bolivia, Brazil, Chile, Colombia, Costa Rica, Cuba, Dominica, Dominican Republic, Ecuador, Grenada, Guatemala, Haiti, Honduras, Jamaica, Mexico, Nicaragua, Panama, Paraguay, Peru, St. Christopher and Nevis, St. Lucia, St. Vincent and the Grenadines, El Salvador, Suriname, Trinidad and Tobago, U.S.A., Uruguay and Venezuela.

Secretary General, João Clemente Baena Soares (*Brazil*).

ORGANIZATION OF ARAB PETROLEUM EXPORTING COUNTRIES

P.O. Box 20501 Safat, 13066 Kuwait

The Organization of Arab Petroleum and Exporting Countries (O.A.P.E.C.) was founded in Jan. 1968. The objectives of the organization are to promote co-operation in economic activities; to safeguard members' interests; to unite efforts to ensure the flow of

oil to consumer markets; and to create a favourable climate for the investment of capital and expertise.

The Ministerial Council is composed of oil ministers from the member countries and meets twice a year to determine policy, to direct activities and to approve the budgets and accounts of the General Secretariat and the Judicial Tribunal. The Judicial Tribunal is composed of nine part-time judges who rule on disputes between member nations and disputes between nations and oil companies. The executive organ of O.A.P.E.C. is the General Secretariat.

The member countries of O.A.P.E.C. are Algeria, Bahrain, Iraq, Kuwait, Libya, Qatar, Saudi Arabia, Syria and the United Arab Emirates (The membership of Egypt was suspended in 1979).

Acting Secretary General, Abdelaziz Alwattari.

ORGANIZATION OF THE PETROLEUM EXPORTING COUNTRIES (O.P.E.C.)

Obere Donaustrasse 93, A-1020 Vienna, Austria

The Organization of the Petroleum Exporting Countries was created in 1960 as a permanent intergovernmental organization with the aims of unifying and co-ordinating the pertroleum policies of members and determining the best means of protecting their interests, individually and collectively.

The supreme authority is the Conference of Ministers of Oil, Mines and Energy of member countries which meets at least twice a year and formulates policy. The Board of Governors, nominated by member countries, directs the management of O.P.E.C. and implements Conference resolutions. The Secretariat, based in Vienna, carries out executive functions under the direction of the Board of Governors.

The 13 member countries are Algeria, Ecuador, Gabon, Indonesia, Iran, Iraq, Kuwait, Libya, Nigeria, Qatar, Saudi Arabia, U.A.E. and Venezuela.

SOUTH PACIFIC COMMISSION

Anse Vata, Noumea, New Caledonia

The South Pacific Commission is a technical assistance agency with an advisory and consultative role in such fields as marine resources, rural management and technology, and community and education services. The management committee is involved with the day-to-day running of the organization and is headed by the Secretary General. The other members are the Director and the Deputy Director of Programmes.

The South Pacific Commission was established in February 1947 following the signing of the Canberra Agreement by the governments of Australia, France, the Netherlands, New Zealand, the U.K. and the U.S.A. The aim was to promote the economic and social stability of the islands in the region.

Following the 23rd Conference of member nations in 1983 the independent island governments in the region were given equal and full membership: by 1987, there were 27 members of the Conference, including five of the original signatories (the Netherlands withdrew in 1962). Since 1967 the Conference has met annually to discuss the future policy of the Commission, to adopt the budget and to nominate the officers of the Commission.

Secretary General, Palauni M. Tuiasospo (*American Samoa*).

Director of Programmes, Jon Jonasson (*Cook Is.*).

Deputy Director of Programmes, Helene Courte (*New Caledonia*).

THE WORLD COUNCIL OF CHURCHES

150 route de Ferney, CH–1211 Geneva 20, Switzerland

The World Council of Churches was constituted in Amsterdam in 1948 to promote unity among the many different Christian churches. The 307 member churches of the W.C.C. have adherents in more than 100 countries. With the exception of Roman Catholicism, virtually all Christian traditions are included in the W.C.C. membership.

The policies of the Council are determined by delegates of the member churches meeting in Assembly, about every 10 years, the last Assembly being in Vancouver in 1983. More detailed decisions are taken by a 150-member Central Committee which is elected by the Assembly and meets, with the seven W.C.C. Presidents, annually. The Central Committee in turn appoints a smaller Executive Committee and also nominates commissions and working groups, to guide the various programmes. The implementation of the policies laid down by the churches and the co-ordination of the 14 programmes are the responsibility of the General Secretariat.

General Secretary, Dr. Emilio Castro (*Uruguay*).
British Council of Churches, 35–41 Lower Marsh, SE1 7RL.

WORLD FEDERATION OF TRADE UNIONS

Vinohradska 10, 12147 Prague 2, Czechoslovakia

The World Federation of Trade Unions (W.F.T.U.) was founded in October 1945. In Jan. 1949 a number of members withdrew and founded the International Confederation of Free Trade Unions. The W.F.T.U. now has 94 affiliated federations with 214 million members, mainly in Eastern Europe and the developing nations.

The Congress, which is comprised of delegates from member nations, meets every four years to review W.F.T.U.'s work and to elect the General Council and Bureau. The General Council is elected from members of national federations and meets once a year. Each affiliated organization has one member and one deputy. The Bureau of 40 members is elected by the General Council and carries out the executive work of the W.F.T.U.

General Secretary, Ibrahim Zakaria (*Sudan*).

BROADCASTING

BRITISH BROADCASTING CORPORATION
(*see also* entry on pages 304–5)

Radio

BBC Radio broadcasts four national services to the United Kingdom, Isle of Man and the Channel Islands plus a fifth tier consisting of national regional services in Wales, Scotland and Northern Ireland and local radio services in England and the Channel Islands. In Wales there are two regional services based on the Welsh and English languages respectively.

The four national services are:

Radio 1: ("Pop" and "rock" network)—Mon. to Fri. 5.30 a.m.–12 midnight. Sat. and Sun. 6 a.m.–12 midnight. Frequencies: MW 1053 kHz/285m and 1089 kHz/275m, plus two local fillers giving population coverage 96% (day) and 57% (night); VHF-FM 88–91 MHz (shared with Radio 2), coverage 97%.

Radio 2: (Light music, entertainment and sport)—24 hours a day. Frequencies: MW 693 kHz/433m and 909 kHz/330m, plus three local fillers giving population coverage 98% (day) and 65% (night); VHF-FM 88–91 MHz (shared with Radio 1), coverage 97%.

Radio 3: (Serious music, drama and documentaries, poetry, and cricket in season)—6.55 a.m.–12 midnight daily. Frequencies: VHF-FM 90·2–92·5 MHz, population coverage 97%. MW (Main centres of population only), 1215 kHz/247m, plus four local fillers on 1197 kHz/251m, coverage 87% (day) and 38% (night).

Radio 4: (News, documentaries, drama and entertainment)—6 a.m. to 12.15 a.m. daily. Frequencies: LW 200 kHz/1500m (from Feb. 1988, 198kHz/1515m), plus eight local fillers on MW giving population coverage 98% (day) and 91% (night); VHF-FM (England, C.I. and I.O.M. plus part of South Wales, S.W. Scotland) 92–95 MHz, coverage 97%.

The national regional services are:

Radio Scotland: Frequencies: MW 810 kHz/370m plus two local fillers, coverage 95% (day) and 87% (night); VHF-FM 92–95 MHz, coverage 94%.

Local programmes on VHF-FM 92–95 MHz: *Radio Aberdeen* (also MW 990 kHz/303m); *Radio Highland; Radio nan Eilean; Radio nan Gaidheal; Radio Orkney; Radio Shetland; Radio Solway* (also MW 585 kHz/513m); *Radio Tweed.*

Radio Ulster: Frequencies: MW 1341 kHz/224m, plus one local filler, coverage 96% (day) and 80% (night); VHF-FM 92–95 MHz, coverage 97%.

Radio Foyle: Frequencies: MW 792 kHz/379m; VHF-FM 92–95 MHz.

Radio Wales: Frequency: MW 882 kHz/340m and 1125 kHz plus two local fillers giving coverage 96% (day) and 63% (night).

Radio Clwyd: Frequency: MW 657 kHz/457m.

Radio Cymru (Welsh-language): Frequencies: VHF-FM 92–95 MHz, coverage 91%.

Local Radio: There are 32 local stations serving England and the Channel Islands (*see* below).

Television

The BBC's experiments in television broadcasting started in 1929 and in 1936 the BBC began the world's first public service of high-definition television from Alexandra Palace.

The BBC broadcasts two national television services, BBC 1 (BBC Wales in Wales, BBC Scotland in Scotland, BBC Northern Ireland in Northern Ireland) and BBC 2. These are broadcast in colour on 625-lines and UHF from a network of transmitting stations planned and built jointly with the Independent Broadcasting Authority. All stations (with a few exceptions) carry four channels including the two IBA channels.

Transmissions from 50 main stations and more than 800 relays are available to more than 99 per cent of the population.

World Service

The World Service broadcasts over 700 hours of programmes a week in 37 languages including the English Service. Ninety-nine transmitters are used, 48 of them in the U.K. and 51 at relay stations overseas. In addition the World Service supplies many recorded programmes to other radio stations.

World Service in English, 24 hours a day, directed to all parts of the world, and with additional streams of programmes specially designated for audiences in Africa and South Asia at appropriate peak listening times.

African Service, which broadcasts in Swahili, Somali and Hausa.

Arabic Service, on the air for 9 hours a day to Middle East and North Africa.

Eastern Service, which broadcasts in Bengali, Burmese, Hindi, Nepali, Pashto, Persian, Tamil and Urdu.

Far Eastern Service, in Chinese (Cantonese and Standard Chinese), Indonesian, Japanese, Malay, Thai and Vietnamese.

Latin American Service, in Spanish and Portuguese.

French and Portuguese Service, directed to Europe and Africa.

German Service, directed to West and East Germany, Austria, and German-speaking Switzerland.

Central European Service, in Czech and Slovak, Hungarian, Polish and Finnish.

Russian Service, on the air for 6½ hours a day in Russian to the U.S.S.R.

South-East European Service, in Bulgarian, Romanian, Serbo-Croat, Slovene, Greek and Turkish.

South European Service, in Greek, Portuguese to Europe and Africa, and Turkish.

Topical Tapes provides a variety of programmes on tape for overseas radio stations and produces the twice-weekly 'Calling the Falklands' programme.

BBC English by Radio and Television teaches English to learners outside Britain through radio, television and a wide range of published courses.

Transcription Service produces and sells to overseas radio stations recorded programmes drawn from the whole range of BBC Radio.

Monitoring Service provides regional summaries and a teleprinted news service from the output of overseas radio stations.

BBC Local Radio Stations

BEDFORDSHIRE, P.O. Box 476, Hastings Street, Luton LU1 5BA. (Tel: 0582-459111). *Wavelengths:* 258/476m, 1161/630 kHz, 95·5/103·8 VHF-FM.

BRISTOL, 3 Tyndalls Park Road, Bristol BS8 1PP. (Tel: 0272-741111). *Wavelengths:* 194/227m, 1548/1323 kHz, 94·9/95·5/104·6 VHF-FM.

CAMBRIDGESHIRE, Broadcasting House, Hills Road, Cambridge CB2 1LD. (Tel: 0223-315970). *Wave-*

lengths: 207/292m, 1449/1026 kHz, 96·0/95·7 VHF-FM.

CLEVELAND, PO Box 1548, Broadcasting House, Newport Road, Middlesbrough, Cleveland TS1 5DG. (Tel: 0642-225211). *Wavelengths*: 194m, 1548 kHz, 95·0/95·8 VHF-FM.

CORNWALL, Phoenix Wharf, Truro, Cornwall TR1 1UA. (Tel: 0872-75421). *Wavelengths*: 476/457m, 630/657 kHz, 95·2/96·0/103·9 VHF-FM.

CUMBRIA, Hilltop Heights, London Road, Carlisle, Cumbria CA1 2NA. (Tel: 0228-31661). *Wavelengths*: 397/206/358m, 756/1458/837 kHz, 95·2/95·6/96·1/104·2 VHF-FM.

DERBY, 56 St. Helen's Street, Derby DE1 3HY. (Tel: 0332-361111). *Wavelengths*: 269m, 1116 kHz, 104·5/94·2/95·3 VHF-FM.

DEVON, P.O. Box 100, St. David's Hill, Exeter, Devon EX4 4DB. (Tel: 0392-215651). *Wavelengths*: 351/303/206/375m, 855/990/1458/801 kHz, 103·4/97·0/96·0/94·8 VHF-FM.

ESSEX, 198 New London Road, Chelmsford, Essex CM2 9AB. (Tel: 0245-262393). *Wavelengths*: 392/196/412m, 765/729/1530 kHz, 103·5/95·3 VHF-FM.

GLOUCESTERSHIRE, London Road, Gloucester GL1 1SW. (Tel: 0452-307091). *Wavelengths*: 603 kHz, 95·0/104·7 VHF-FM.

HUMBERSIDE, 63 Jameson Street, Hull HU1 3NU. (Tel: 0482-23232). *Wavelengths*: 202m, 1485 kHz, 95·9 VHF-FM.

KENT, Sun Pier, Chatham, Kent ME4 4EZ. (Tel: 0634-46284). *Wavelengths*: 290/388/187m, 1035/774/1602 kHz, 96·7/104·2 VHF-FM.

LANCASHIRE, King Street, Blackburn, Lancs. BB2 2EA. (Tel: 0254-62411). *Wavelengths*: 351/193m, 855/1557 kHz, 95·5/104·5/103·9 VHF-FM.

LEEDS, Broadcasting House, Woodhouse Lane, Leeds LS2 9PN. (Tel: 0532-442131). *Wavelengths*: 388m, 774 kHz, 92·4/195·3 VHF-FM.

LEICESTER, Epic House, Charles Street, Leicester LE1 3SH. (Tel: 0533-27113). *Wavelengths*: 358m, 837 kHz, 95·1 VHF-FM.

LINCOLNSHIRE, Radion Buildings, P.O. Box 219, Newport, Lincoln LN1 3XY. (Tel: 0522-40011). *Wavelengths*: 219m, 1368 kHz, 94·9 VHF-FM.

LONDON, 35a Marylebone High Street, London W1A 4LG. (Tel: 01-486 7611). *Wavelengths*: 206m, 1458 kHz, 94·9 VHF-FM.

MANCHESTER, New Broadcasting House, Oxford Road, Manchester M60 1SJ. (Tel: 061-228 3434). *Wavelengths*: 206m, 1458 kHz, 95·1 VHF-FM.

MERSEYSIDE, 55 Paradise Street, Liverpool L1 3BP. (Tel: 051-708 5500). *Wavelengths*: 202m, 1485 kHz, 95·8 VHF-FM.

NEWCASTLE, Broadcasting Centre, Barrack Road, Fenham, Newcastle upon Tyne NE99 1RN. (Tel: 091-232 4141). *Wavelengths*: 206m, 1458 kHz, 95·4/104·4/96·0 VHF-FM.

NORFOLK, Norfolk Tower, Surrey Street, Norwich NR1 3PA. (Tel: 0603-617411). *Wavelengths*: 351/344m, 855/873 kHz, 95·1/104·4 VHF-FM.

NORTHAMPTON, PO Box 1107, Abington Street, Northampton NN1 2BE. (Tel: 0604-20621). *Wavelengths*: 271m, 1107 kHz, 104·2/103·6 VHF-FM.

NOTTINGHAM, York House, Mansfield Road, Nottingham NG1 3JB. (Tel: 0602-415161). *Wavelengths*: 197/189m, 1521/1584 kHz, 103·8/95·5 VHF-FM.

OXFORD, 242/254 Banbury Road, Oxford OX2 7DW. (Tel: 0865-53411). *Wavelengths*: 202m, 1485 kHz, 95·2 VHF-FM.

SHEFFIELD, Ashdell Grove, 60 Westbourne Road, Sheffield S10 2QU. (Tel: 0742-686185). *Wavelengths*: 290m, 1035 kHz, 104·1/88·6 VHF-FM.

SHROPSHIRE, 2–4 Boscobel Drive, Shrewsbury, Shropshire SY1 3TT. (Tel: 0743-248484). *Wavelengths*: 189/397m, 1584/756 kHz, 95·0/96·0 VHF-FM.

SOLENT, South Western House, Canute Road, Southampton SO9 4PJ. (Tel: 0703-631311). *Wave-*

lengths: 300m, 999 kHz, 96·1 VHF-FM, 221m, 1359 kHz.

STOKE ON TRENT, Conway House, Cheapside, Hanley, Stoke-on-Trent, Staffs. ST1 1JJ. (Tel: 0782-208080). *Wavelengths*: 200m, 1503 kHz, 94·6 VHF-FM.

SUSSEX, Marlborough Place, Brighton, Sussex BN1 1TU (Tel: 0273-680231). *Wavelengths*: 202/258/219m, 1485/1161/1368 kHz, 95·3/104·5/104·0 VHF-FM.

WM (WEST MIDLANDS), PO Box 206, Pebble Mill Road, Birmingham B5 7SD. (Tel: 021-472 5141). *Wavelengths*: 206/362m, 1458/828 kHz, 95·6 VHF-FM.

YORK, 20 Bootham Row, York YO3 7BR. (Tel: 0904-641351). *Wavelengths*: 450/238m, 666/1260 kHz, 103·7/104·3/95·5 VHF-FM.

Two Stations outside the UK:—

GUERNSEY, Commerce House, Les Banques, St. Peter Port, Guernsey. (Tel: 0481-28977). *Wavelengths*: 269m, 1116 kHz, 93·2 VHF-FM.

JERSEY, Broadcasting House, Rouge Bouillon, St. Helier, Jersey. (Tel: 0534-70000). *Wavelengths*: 292m, 1026 kHz, 88·8 VHF-FM.

INDEPENDENT BROADCASTING AUTHORITY

(*see also* entry on pages 334–5)

Independent Television Programme Companies, etc.

ANGLIA TELEVISION (*East of England*), Anglia House, Norwich. (Tel: 0603-615151).

BORDER TELEVISION (*The Borders*), Television Centre, Carlisle. (Tel: 0228-25101).

CENTRAL INDEPENDENT TELEVISION (*East and West Midlands*), Central House, Broad Street, Birmingham. (Tel: 021-643 9898).

CHANNEL TELEVISION (*Channel Islands*), The Television Centre, St. Helier, Jersey. (Tel: 0534-73999).

GRAMPIAN TELEVISION (*North Scotland*), Queen's Cross, Aberdeen. (Tel: 0224-646464).

GRANADA TELEVISION (*North-West England*), Granada TV Centre, Manchester. (Tel: 061-832 7211).

HTV (*Wales and West of England*), HTV Wales, Television Centre, Cardiff CF5 6XJ. (Tel: 0222-590590).

LONDON WEEKEND TELEVISION (*London* [*weekends*]), South Bank Television Centre, Kent House, Upper Ground, London S.E.1. (Tel: 01-261 3434).

SCOTTISH TELEVISION (*Central Scotland*), Cowcaddens, Glasgow. (Tel: 041-332 9999).

THAMES TELEVISION (*London* [*weekdays*]), Thames Television House, 306–316 Euston Road, London N.W.1. (Tel: 01-387 9494).

TSW (TELEVISION SOUTH WEST) (*South-West England*), Derry's Cross, Plymouth. (Tel: 0752-663322).

TVS (TELEVISION SOUTH) (*South and South-East England*), Television Centre, Southampton. (Tel: 0703-34211).

TYNE TEES TELEVISION (*North-East England*), The Television Centre, City Road, Newcastle upon Tyne. (Tel: 091-261 0181).

ULSTER TELEVISION (*Northern Ireland*), Havelock House, Ormeau Road, Belfast. (Tel: 0232-228122).

YORKSHIRE TELEVISION (*Yorkshire*), The Television Centre, Leeds. (Tel: 0532-438283).

TV-AM, Hawley Crescent, London N.W.1. (Tel: 01-267 4300).

CHANNEL FOUR TELEVISION COMPANY LTD, 60 Charlotte Street, London W.1. (Tel: 01-631 4444).

WELSH FOURTH CHANNEL AUTHORITY (Sianel Pedwar Cymru), Sophia Close, Cardiff CF1 9XY. (Tel: 0222-43421).

INDEPENDENT TELEVISION COMPANIES ASSOCIATION LTD., Knighton House, 56 Mortimer Street, London W.1. (Tel: 01-636 6866).

INDEPENDENT TELEVISION NEWS LTD, ITN House, 48 Wells Street, London W.1. (Tel: 01-637 2424).

ORACLE TELETEXT LTD., Craven House, 25–32 Marshall Street, London W.1. (Tel: 01-434 3121).

[NOTE: It has only been possible to give one address for each of the Programme Companies].

Independent Local Radio Stations

LBC (London Broadcasting Company Ltd.), Communications House, Gough Square, London E.C.4. (Tel: 01-353 1010). *Wavelengths*: 261m, 1152 kHz, 97·3 VHF-FM.

CAPITAL RADIO P.L.C., Euston Tower, London NW1. (Tel: 01-388 1288). *Wavelengths*: 194m, 1548 kHz, 95·8 VHF-FM.

RADIO CLYDE LTD., Clydebank Business Park, Clydebank, Glasgow. (Tel: 041-941 1111). *Wavelengths*: 261m, 1152 kHz, 95·1 VHF-FM.

BRMB RADIO, (Birmingham Broadcasting Ltd.), PO Box 555, Radio House, Aston Road North, Aston, Birmingham. (Tel: 021-359 4481/9). *Wavelengths*: 261m, 1152 kHz, 96·4 VHF-FM.

PICCADILLY RADIO LTD., 127/131 The Piazza, Piccadilly Plaza, Manchester. (Tel: 061-236 9913). *Wavelengths*: 261m, 1152 kHz, 103·0 VHF-FM.

METRO RADIO (North East Broadcasting Company Ltd.), Radio House, Long Rigg, Swalwell, Newcastle upon Tyne. (Tel: 091-488 3131). *Wavelengths*: 261m, 1152 kHz, 97·1 VHF-FM.

SWANSEA SOUND LTD., Victoria Road, Gowerton, Swansea. (Tel: 0792-893751). *Wavelengths*: 257m, 1170 kHz, 95·1 VHF-FM.

RADIO HALLAM LTD., PO Box 194, Hartshead, Sheffield. (Tel: 0742-71188). *Wavelengths*: 194m, 1548 kHz, 96·1 VHF-FM (Rotherham), 97·4 VHF-FM (Sheffield), 302m, 990 kHz, 103·4 VHF-FM. (Doncaster).

RADIO CITY (Sound of Merseyside Ltd.), PO Box 194, 8–10 Stanley Street, Liverpool. (Tel: 051-227 5100). *Wavelengths*: 194m, 1548 kHz, 96·7 VHF-FM.

RADIO FORTH LTD., Forth House, Forth Street, Edinburgh. (Tel: 031-556 9255). *Wavelengths*: 194m, 1548 kHz, 97·3 VHF-FM.

PLYMOUTH SOUND LTD., Earl's Acre, Alma Road, Plymouth. (Tel: 0752-27272). *Wavelengths*: 261m, 1152 kHz, 96·0 VHF-FM.

RADIO TFM (Sound Broadcasting (Teesside) Ltd.), 74 Dovecot Street, Stockton-on-Tees, Cleveland. (Tel: 0642-615111). *Wavelengths*: 257m, 1170 kHz, 96·6 VHF-FM.

RADIO TRENT LTD., 29–31 Castle Gate, Nottingham. (Tel: 0602-581731). *Wavelengths*: 301m, 999 kHz, 96·2 VHF-FM.

PENNINE RADIO, (Bradford Community Radio Ltd.), PO Box 235, Pennine House, Forster Square, Bradford. (Tel: 0274-390417). *Wavelengths*: 235/196m, 1278/1530 kHz, 97·5 VHF-FM (Bradford, Huddersfield, Halifax) 102·5 VHF-FM.

OCEAN SOUND LTD., 43–44 Bedford Place, Southampton. *Wavelengths*: 257m, 1170 kHz, 103·2 VHF-FM (Southampton), 97·5 VHF-FM (Portsmouth).

RADIO ORWELL LTD., Electric House, Lloyds Avenue, Ipswich. (Tel: 0473-216971). *Wavelengths*: 257m, 1170 kHz, 97·1 VHF-FM.

RADIO 210 THAMES VALLEY (Thames Valley Broadcasting Ltd.), PO Box 210, Reading, Berkshire. (Tel: 0734-413131). *Wavelengths*: 210m, 1431 kHz, 97·0 VHF-FM.

DOWNTOWN RADIO (Community Radio Services Ltd.), PO Box 293, Kiltonga Industrial Estate, Newtownards, Northern Ireland. (Tel: 0247-815555). *Wavelengths*: 293m, 1026 kHz, 97·4 VHF-FM.

BEACON RADIO (Beacon Broadcasting Ltd.), PO Box 303, 267 Tettenhall Road, Wolverhampton. (Tel: 0902-757211). *Wavelengths*: 303m, 990 kHz, 97·2 VHF-FM.

MERCIA SOUND (Midland Community Radio Ltd.), Hertford Place, Coventry. (Tel: 0203-28451). *Wavelengths*: 220m, 1359 kHz, 95·9 VHF-FM.

HEREWARD RADIO LTD., PO Box 225. 114 Bridge Street, Peterborough. (Tel: 0733-46225). *Wavelengths*: 225m, 1332 kHz, 102·7 VHF-FM.

TWO COUNTIES RADIO LTD., 5–7 Southcote Road, Bournemouth. (Tel: 0202-294881). *Wavelengths*: 362m, 828 kHz, 97·2 VHF-FM.

RADIO TAY (Tay Sound Broadcasting Ltd.), PO Box 123, Dundee. (Tel: 0382-29551). *Wavelengths*: 258m, 1161 kHz, 95·8 VHF-FM (Dundee); 189m, 1584 kHz, 96·4 VHF-FM (Perth).

SEVERN SOUND (Gloucestershire Broadcasting Company Ltd.), PO Box 388, Old Talbot House, 67 Southgate Street, Gloucester. (Tel: 0452-423791). *Wavelengths*: 388m, 774 kHz, 102·4 VHF-FM.

NORTH SOUND (North of Scotland Radio Ltd.), 45 Kings Gate, Aberdeen. (Tel: 0224-632234). *Wavelengths*: 290m, 1035 kHz, 96·9 VHF-FM.

RADIO AIRE (West Yorkshire Broadcasting P.L.C.), PO Box 362, 51 Burley Road, Leeds. (Tel: 0532-452299). *Wavelengths*: 362m, 828 kHz, 96·3 VHF-FM.

ESSEX RADIO P.L.C., Radio House, Clifftown Road, Southend-on-Sea, Essex. (Tel: 0702-333711). *Wavelengths*: 210m, 1431 kHz, 96·3 VHF-FM (Southend), 220m, 1359 kHz, 102·6 VHF-FM (Chelmsford).

CHILTERN RADIO P.L.C., Chiltern Radio, Dunstable, Bedfordshire. (Tel: 0582-666001). *Wavelengths*: 362m, 828 kHz, 97·6 VHF-FM (Luton), 379m, 792 kHz, 96·9 VHF-FM (Bedford).

WEST SOUND (Radio Ayrshire Limited), Radio House, 54 Holmston Road, Ayr. (Tel: 0292-283662). *Wavelengths*: 290m, 1035 kHz, 96·7 VHF-FM (Ayr), 97·1 97·5 VHF-FM (Girvan).

GWR RADIO WEST P.L.C., PO Box 963, Watershed, Canons Road, Bristol. (Tel: 0272-279900). *Wavelengths*: 238m, 1260 kHz, 96·3 VHF-FM.

MORAY FIRTH RADIO LTD., PO Box 271, Inverness. (Tel: 0463-224433). *Wavelengths*: 271m, 1107 kHz, 97·4 VHF-FM.

RADIO WYVERN P.L.C., 5/6 Barbourne Terrace, Worcester. (Tel: 0905-612212). *Wavelengths*: 314m, 954 kHz, 97·6 VHF-FM (Hereford), 196m, 1530 kHz, 102·8 VHF-FM (Worcester).

RED ROSE RADIO P.L.C., PO Box 301, St. Paul's Square, Preston, Lancashire. (Tel: 0772-556301). *Wavelengths*: 301m, 999 kHz, 97·3 VHF-FM.

GWR (Wiltshire Radio) P.L.C., Old Lime Kiln, High Street, Wootton Bassett, Swindon, Wiltshire. (Tel: 0793-853222). *Wavelengths*: 258m, 1161 kHz, 97·2 VHF-FM (Swindon), 321m, 936 kHz, 102·6 VHF-FM (West Wiltshire).

SAXON RADIO LTD. IN ASSOCIATION WITH RADIO ORWELL LTD., Long Brackland, Bury St. Edmunds, Suffolk. (Tel: 0284-701511). *Wavelengths*: 240m, 1251 kHz, 96·4 VHF-FM.

COUNTY SOUND P.L.C., The Friary, Guildford. (Tel: 0483-505566). *Wavelengths*: 203m, 1476 kHz, 96·4 VHF-FM.

RED DRAGON RADIO, Radio House, West Canal Wharf, Cardiff. (Tel: 0222-384041). *Wavelengths*: 230m, 1305 kHz, 97·4 VHF-FM.

SOUTHERN SOUND P.L.C., Radio House, Franklin Road, Portslade. (Tel: 0273-422288). *Wavelengths*: 225m, 1332 kHz, 103·4 MHz.

MARCHER SOUND/SAIN-Y-GORORAU, The Studios, Mold Road, Gwersyllt, Wrexham, Clwyd. (Tel: 0978-752202). *Wavelengths*: 238m, 1260 kHz, 95·4 VHF-FM.

SIGNAL RADIO, 67–73 Stoke Road, Stoke-on-Trent, Staffordshire. (Tel: 0782-417111). *Wavelengths*: 257m, 1170 kHz, 102·6 VHF-FM.

VIKING RADIO LTD., Commercial Road, Hull. (Tel: 0482-25141). *Wavelengths*: 258m, 1161 kHz, 96·9 VHF-FM.

RADIO MERCURY, Broadfield House, Brighton Road,

Crawley, W. Sussex. (Tel: 0293-519161). *Wavelengths*: 197m, 1521 kHz, 102·7, 97·5 VHF-FM (Horsham).

INVICTA RADIO P.L.C. (incorporating Northdown Radio), 15 Station Road East, Canterbury, Kent. (Tel: 0227-58761). *Wavelengths*: 242m, 1242 kHz, 103·1 VHF-FM.

INVICTA RADIO P.L.C. (incorporating Network East Kent), 15 Station Road East, Canterbury, Kent.

(Tel: 0227-58761). *Wavelengths*: 497m, 603 kHz, 97·0 VHF-FM (Dover), 95·9 VHF-FM (Thanet), 102·8 VHF-FM (Canterbury), 96·1 MHz (Ashford).

RADIO BROADLAND, PO Box 260, Norwich. (Tel: 0603-660926). *Wavelengths*: 260m, 1152 kHz, 97·6 MHz.

NORTHANTS 96 (Hereward Radio) P.L.C., PO Box 193, 73 Abington Street, Northampton. (Tel: 0733-46225). *Wavelengths*: 193m, 1557 kHz, 96·6 VHF-FM.

SERVICES SOUND AND VISION CORPORATION
(Incorporating B.F.B.S.)
Chalfont Grove, Gerrards Cross, Bucks. SL9 8TN
[02407-4461]

The Services Sound and Vision Corporation (S.S.V.C.) is the official organization charged by the Ministry of Defence with providing radio and television broadcasting, training support and entertainment for British armed forces. The S.S.V.C. is a financially self-supporting private company and registered charity with 1,200 employees worldwide and an annual turnover approaching £40 million; financial surpluses are donated to Services' welfare.

S.S.V.C. radio (the British Forces Broadcasting Service) operates stations for British Forces in West Germany, Gibraltar, Cyprus, the Falklands, Belize and in Hong Kong, Nepal and Brunei. B.F.B.S. London provides all stations except Nepal and Brunei with a 24-hour news, sport and information service by satellite, and also by landline and microwave stereo link to West Germany. Every week more than 60 hours of programmes are recorded and syndicated to overseas stations and Royal Navy ships.

S.S.V.C. television broadcasts its own, B.B.C. and I.T.V. programmes in West Germany, Cyprus and the Falklands Islands. Each week some 40 garrisons and ships receive U.K. television programmes.

Live entertainment is provided through the Combined Services Entertainment division of S.S.V.C.; venues include Cyprus, the Falkland Islands, West Germany and Northern Ireland. Cinemas are provided and maintained in the U.K., West Germany, Cyprus and Hong Kong.

Audio-visual rentals and sales are provided through S.S.V.C.'s Sound and Vision Centre shops in Europe and S.S.V.C.'s wholly-owned subsidiary provides similar services to non M.o.D. or H.M. Forces customers.

S.S.V.C. produces training and educational films and videos for the three Armed Services, and maintains and distributes worldwide the Royal Navy, Army and Royal Air Force training film library material. It is the sole agent for the sale of M.o.D. films and videos.

Managing Director, S.S.V.C., A. Protheroe.

PRINCIPAL NEWSPAPERS

DAILY NEWSPAPERS

National

Daily Express, 121–128 Fleet Street, EC4P 4JT.

Daily Mail, Northcliffe House, EC4 0JA.

Daily Mirror, Holborn Circus, EC1P 1DQ.

Daily Telegraph, 181 Marsh Wall, E14 9SR.

Financial Times, Bracken House, 10 Cannon Street, EC4P 4BY.

The Guardian, 119 Farringdon Road, EC1R 3ER.

The Independent, 40 City Road, EC1Y 2DB.

Morning Star, 74 Luke Street, EC2A 4EJ.

Racing Post, 120 Combe Lane, Raynes Park, SW20 0BA.

Sporting Life, Alexander House, 81–89 Farringdon Road, EC1M 3LH.

The Star, Great Ancoats Street, Manchester M60 4HB.

The Sun, Virginia Street, E1 9BD.

The Times, 1 Pennington Street, E1 9XN.

Today, 70 Vauxhall Bridge Road, SW1V 2RP.

ABERDEEN—Press and Journal, and Evening Express, P.O. Box 43, Lang Stracht, Mastrick, AB9 8AF.

BARROW—North-Western Evening Mail, Newspaper House, Abbey Road, LA14 5QS.

BATH—Bath and West Evening Chronicle, 33–34 Westgate Street, BA1 1EW.

BELFAST—Belfast Telegraph, 124–144 Royal Avenue, BT1 1EB; Irish News and Belfast Morning News, 113–117 Donegall Street, BT1 2GE; News Letter, 51–59 Donegall Street, BT1 2GB.

BIRMINGHAM—The Birmingham Post, and Birmingham Evening Mail, P.O. Box 18, 28 Colmore Circus, Queensway, B4 6AX (Birmingham Evening Mail B4 6AY).

BLACKBURN—Lancashire Evening Telegraph, Telegraph House, High Street, BB1 1HT.

BLACKPOOL—West Lancashire Evening Gazette, P.O. Box 20, FY4 4AU.

BOLTON—Bolton Evening News, Newspaper House, Mealhouse Lane, Churchgate, BL1 1DE.

BOURNEMOUTH—Evening Echo, Richmond Hill, BH2 6HH.

BRADFORD—Telegraph and Argus, P.O. Box 234, Hall Ings, BD1 1JR.

BRIGHTON—Evening Argus, 89 North Road, BN1 4AU.

BRISTOL—Bristol Evening Post, and Western Daily Press, Temple Way, BS99 7HD.

BURTON—Burton Mail, 65–68 High Street, DE14 1LE.

CAMBRIDGE—Cambridge Evening News, 51 Newmarket Road, CB5 8EJ.

CARDIFF—South Wales Echo, and Western Mail, Thomson House, Havelock Street, CF1 1WR.

CHATHAM—Kent Evening Post, New Hythe Lane, Larkfield, ME20 6SG.

CHELTENHAM—Gloucestershire Echo, 1 Clarence Parade, GL50 3NZ.

COLCHESTER—Evening Gazette, Oriel House, 43–44 North Hill, CO1 1TZ.

COVENTRY—Coventry Evening Telegraph, Corporation Street, CV1 1FP.

DARLINGTON—Northern Echo, Priestgate, DL1 1NP.

DERBY—Derby Evening Telegraph, Northcliffe House, Meadow Road, DE1 2DW.

DUNDEE—Courier and Advertiser, and Evening Telegraph and Post, 7 Bank Street, DD1 9HU.

EDINBURGH—The Scotsman, and Evening News, 20 North Bridge, EH1 1YT.

EXETER—Express and Echo, Sidwell House, Sidwell Street, EX4 6RS.

GLASGOW—Daily Record, 40 Anderston Quay, G3 8DA; Glasgow Herald, and Evening Times, 195 Albion Street, G1 1QP.

GLOUCESTER—The Citizen, St. John's Lane, GL1 2AY.

GREENOCK—Greenock Telegraph, 2 Crawfurd Street, PA15 1LH.

GRIMSBY—Grimsby Evening Telegraph, 80 Cleethorpe Road, DN31 3EH.

GUERNSEY—Guernsey Evening Press and Star, P.O. Box 57, Braye Road, Vale.

HALIFAX—Evening Courier, P.O. Box 19, Courier Buildings, HX1 2SF.

HARTLEPOOL—The Mail, Pennywell Industrial Estate, Sunderland, SR4 9ER.

HUDDERSFIELD—Huddersfield Daily Examiner, Ramsden Street, HD1 2TD.

HULL—Hull Daily Mail, 84–86 Jameson Street, HU1 3LF.

IPSWICH—East Anglian Daily Times, and Evening Star, 30 Lower Brook Street, IP4 1AN.

JERSEY—Jersey Evening Post, P.O. Box 582, Five Oaks, St. Saviour.

KETTERING—Northamptonshire Evening Telegraph, Northfield Avenue, NN16 9JN.

LEAMINGTON SPA—Leamington & District Morning News, P.O. Box 45, Tachbrook Road, CV31 3EP.

LEEDS—Yorkshire Evening Post, and Yorkshire Post, Wellington Street, LS1 1RF.

LEICESTER—Leicester Mercury, St. George Street, LE1 9FQ.

LINCOLN—Lincolnshire Echo, Brayford Wharf East, LN5 7AT.

LIVERPOOL—Daily Post, and Liverpool Echo, P.O. Box 48, Old Hall Street, L69 3EB.

LONDON—The London Evening Standard, 118 Fleet Street, EC4P 4JT.

MANCHESTER—Manchester Evening News, 164 Deansgate, M60 2RD.

MIDDLESBROUGH—Evening Gazette, Gazette Building, Borough Road, TS1 3AZ.

NEWCASTLE UPON TYNE—Evening Chronicle, and The Journal, Thomson House, Groat Market, NE1 1ED.

NEWPORT—South Wales Argus, Cardiff Road, Maesglas, NP9 1QW.

NORTHAMPTON—Chronicle and Echo, Upper Mounts, NN1 3HR.

NORWICH—Eastern Daily Press, and Eastern Evening News, Prospect House, Rouen Road, NR1 1RE.

NOTTINGHAM—Evening Post, Forman Street, NG1 4AB.

NUNEATON—Nuneaton Evening Tribune, Watling House, Whitacre Road, CV11 6BJ.

OLDHAM—Evening Chronicle, 172 Union Street, OL1 1EQ.

OXFORD—Oxford Mail, Newspaper House, Osney Mead, OX2 0EJ.

PAISLEY—Paisley Daily Express, Hellenic House, 87–97 Bath Street, Glasgow, G2 2DZ.

PETERBOROUGH—Peterborough Evening Telegraph, Telegraph House, Priestgate, PE1 1JW.

PLYMOUTH—Western Morning News, and Western Evening Herald, 65 New George Street, PL1 1RE.

PORTSMOUTH—The News, The News Centre, Hilsea, PO2 9SX.

PRESTON—Lancashire Evening Post, 127 Fishergate, PR1 2DN.

READING—Evening Post, 8 Tessa Road, RG1 8NS.

SCARBOROUGH—Scarborough Evening News, 17–23 Aberdeen Walk, YO11 1BB.

SCUNTHORPE—Scunthorpe Evening Telegraph, Telegraph House, Doncaster Road, DN15 7RE.

SHEFFIELD—The Star, York Street, S1 1PU.

SOUTH SHIELDS—Shields Gazette, Chapter Row, NE33 1BL.

SOUTHAMPTON—Southern Evening Echo, 45 Above Bar, SO9 7BA.

STOKE-ON-TRENT—Evening Sentinel, Sentinel House, Etruria, ST1 5SS.

SUNDERLAND—Sunderland Echo, Pennywell Industrial Estate, SR4 9ER.

SWANSEA—South Wales Evening Post, Adelaide Street, SA1 1QT.

SWINDON—Evening Advertiser, Newspaper House, 100 Victoria Road, SN1 3BE.

TELFORD—Shropshire Star, Ketley, TF1 4HU.

TORQUAY—Herald Express, Harmsworth House, Barton Hill Road, TQ2 8JN.

WEYMOUTH—Dorset Evening Echo, 57 St. Thomas Street, DT4 8EU.

WOLVERHAMPTON—Express and Star, 51–53 Queen Street, WV1 3BU.

WORCESTER—Evening News, Berrows House, Hylton Road, WR2 5JX.

YORK—Yorkshire Evening Press, 15 Coney Street, YO1 1YN.

The Friend—Drayton House, 30 Gordon Street, WC1H 0BQ. *W.*

The Inquirer—1–6 Essex Street, WC2R 3HY. *Alt. W.*

Jewish Chronicle—25 Furnival Street, EC4A 1JT. *W.*

Jewish Gazette—18 Cheetham Parade, Manchester M8 6DJ. *W.*

Jewish Telegraph—Telegraph House, 11 Park Hill, Bury Old Road, Prestwich, Manchester M25 8HH. *W.*

Leadership Today—37 Elm Road, New Malden, Surrey KT3 3HB. *M.*

Life and Work—Church of Scotland, 121 George Street, Edinburgh EH2 4QS. *M.*

Methodist Recorder—122 Golden Lane, EC1Y 0TL. *W.*

Orthodox News—64 Prebend Gardens, W6 0XU. *M.*

Reform—86 Tavistock Place, WC1H 9RT. *M.*

The Tablet—48 Great Peter Street, SW1P 2HB. *W.*

The Universe—33–39 Bowling Green Lane, EC1R 0AB. *W.*

The War Cry—101 Queen Victoria Street, EC4P 4EP. *W.*

SUNDAY NEWSPAPERS

The Mail on Sunday—Northcliffe House, EC4Y 0JA.

News of the World—1 Pennington Street, E1 9BH.

The Observer—Chelsea Bridge House, Queenstown Road, SW8 4NN.

The People—Holborn Circus, EC1P 1DQ.

Sunday Express—121–128 Fleet Street, EC4P 4JT.

Sunday Mail—40 Anderston Quay, Glasgow G3 8DA.

Sunday Mirror—Holborn Circus, EC1P 1DQ.

Sunday News—51–59 Donegall Street, Belfast BT1 2GB.

Sunday Post—Courier Place, Dundee DD1 9QJ.

Sunday Sport—50 Eagle Wharf Road, N1 7ED.

Sunday Telegraph—Peterborough Court at South Quay, 181 Marsh Wall, E14 9SR.

The Sunday Times—1 Pennington Street, E1 9XW.

RELIGIOUS PAPERS

[*W.* = Weekly; *M.* = Monthly; *Q.* = Quarterly]

Baptist Times—4 Southampton Row, WC1B 4AB. *W.*

Catholic Herald—Herald House, Lambs Passage, Bunhill Row, EC1Y 8TQ. *W.*

Challenge—the Good News Paper—Revenue Buildings, Chapel Road, Worthing, West Sussex BN11 1BQ. *M.*

Christian Herald—96 Dominion Road, Worthing, West Sussex BN14 8JP. *W.*

Christian Week—11 Carteret Street, SW1H 9DJ. *W.*

Church of England Newspaper—11 Carteret Street, SW1H 9DJ. *W.*

Church of Ireland Gazette—48 Bachelor's Walk, Lisburn, Co. Antrim. *W.*

Church Times—7 Portugal Street, WC2A 2HP. *W.*

English Churchman & St. James's Chronicle—Mill Lane House, Mill Lane, Margate, Kent CT9 1ND. *Alt. W.*

PERIODICALS, MAGAZINES AND REVIEWS

[*Alt.* = Alternate; *M.* = Monthly; *Q.* = Quarterly; *W.* = Weekly]

Amateur Gardening—Westover House, West Quay Road, Poole, Dorset BH15 1JG. *W.*

Amateur Photographer—Prospect House, 9–13 Ewell Road, Cheam, Surrey SM1 4QQ. *W.*

Angler's Mail—King's Reach Tower, Stamford Street, SE1 9LS. *W.*

Antiquaries Journal—Oxford University Press, Walton Street, Oxford OX2 6DP. *Three times a year.*

The Antique Collector—National Magazine House, 72 Broadwick Street, W1V 2BP. *M.*

Apollo Magazine—22 Davies Street, W1Y 1LH. *M.*

The Artist—102 High Street, Tenterden, Kent TN30 6HT. *M.*

Autocar—38–42 Hampton Road, Teddington, Middlesex TW11 0JE. *W.*

Bella—2nd Floor, Shirley House, 25–27 Camden Road, NW1 9LL. *W.*

Best—Portland House, Stag Place, SW1E 5AU. *W.*

Books—43 Museum Street, WC1A 1LY. *M.*

Boxing News—P.O. Box 94, W4 2ER. *W.*

Brain—Oxford University Press, Walton Street, Oxford OX2 6DP. *Alt. M.*

Brides & Setting up Home—Vogue House, Hanover Square, W1R 0AD. *Alt. M.*

British Birds—Fountains, Park Lane, Blunham, Bedford MK44 3NJ. *M.*

British Book News—The British Council, 65 Davies Street, W1Y 2AA. *M.*

Bunty—2 Albert Square, Dundee DD1 9QJ. *W.*

The Burlington Magazine—6 Bloomsbury Square, WC1A 2LP. *M.*

Buses—Coombelands House, Addlestone, Surrey KT15 1HY. *M.*

Cage and Aviary Birds—Prospect House, 9–13 Ewell Road, Cheam, Surrey SM1 4QQ. *W.*

Camper—38–42 Hampton Road, Teddington, Middlesex TW11 0JE. *M.*

Caravan Magazine—Link House, Dingwall Avenue, Croydon, Surrey CR9 2TA. *M.*

Classical Quarterly—Oxford University Press, Walton Street, Oxford OX2 6DP. *Twice a Year.*

Classical Review—Oxford University Press, Walton Street, Oxford OX2 6DP. *Twice a Year.*

Coal News—Hobart House, Grosvenor Place, SW1X 7AE. *M.*

Country Living—72 Broadwick Street, W1V 2BP. *Alt. M.*

Coin and Medal News—Crossways Road, Grayshott, Hindhead, Surrey GU26 6HF. *M.*

Coin Monthly—Sovereign House, Brentwood, Essex CM14 4SE. *M.*

Company—72 Broadwick Street, W1V 2BP. *M.*

Contemporary Review—61 Carey Street, WC2A 2JG. *M.*

Cosmopolitan—72 Broadwick Street, W1V 2BP. *M.*

Country Homes and Interiors—25 Newman Street, W1P 3HA. *M.*

Country Life—King's Reach Tower, Stamford Street, SE1 9LS. *M.*

The Countryman—23–27 Tudor Street, EC4Y 0HR. *Q.*

Cricketer International—Beech Hangar, Ashurst, Tunbridge Wells, Kent TN3 9ST. *M.*

Criminologist—Little London, Chichester, West Sussex PO19 1PG. *Q.*

Cycling Weekly—Prospect House, 9–13 Ewell Road, Cheam, Surrey SM1 4QQ. *W.*

Daltons Weekly—Apex Tower, High Street, New Malden, Surrey KT3 4EE. *W.*

Dance and Dancers—Cloister Court, 22–26 Farringdon Lane, EC1R 6HU. *M.*

Dancing Times—Clerkenwell House, 45–47 Clerkenwell Green, EC1R 0BE. *M.*

Dog World—9 Tufton Street, Ashford, Kent TN23 1QN. *W.*

Do It Yourself—Link House, Dingwall Avenue, Croydon CR9 2TA. *M.*

Drama—British Theatre Association, Regent's College, Inner Circle, Regent's Park, NW1 4NW. *Q.*

Drive and Trail—Automobile Association, Fanum House, Basingstoke, Hants RG21 2EA. *M.*

Economic Journal—108 Cowley Road, Oxford OX4 1JF. *Q.*

Economica—London School of Economics and Political Science, Houghton Street, WC2A 2AE. *Q.*

The Economist—25 St. James's Street, SW1A 1HG. *W.*

Edinburgh Gazette (*Official*)—H.M.S.O., St. Crispins, Duke Street, Norwich NR3 1PD. *Twice a week.*

Elle—Rex House, 4–12 Lower Regent Street, SW1Y 4PE. *M.*

Encounter—44 Great Windmill Street, W1V 7PA. *Ten times a year.*

The English Historical Review—Longman House, Burnt Mill, Harlow, Essex CM20 2JE. *Q.*

Essentials—King's Reach Tower, Stamford Street, SE1 9LS. *M.*

Everywoman—34A Islington Green, N1 8DU. *M.*

Exchange and Mart—25 West Street, Poole, Dorset BH15 1LL. *W.*

Family Circle—38 Hans Crescent, SW1X 0LZ. *Thirteen times a year.*

The Field—Carmelite House, Carmelite Street, EC4Y 0JA.. *W.*

Garden News—Bushfield House, Orton Centre, Peterborough PE2 0UW. *W.*

Geographical Magazine, 1 Kensington Gore, SW7 2AR. *M.*

Golf Illustrated—47 Dartford Road, Sevenoaks, Kent TN13 3TE. *Alt. W.*

Golf Monthly—King's Reach Tower, Stamford Street, SE1 9LS. *M.*

Good Housekeeping—72 Broadwick Street, W1V 2BP. *M.*

Good Motoring—352 Lewisham High Street, SE13 6LE. *Alt. M.*

Gramophone—177–179 Kenton Road, Harrow, Middx. HA3 0HA. *M.*

Granta—44A Hobson Street, Cambridge, CB1 1NL. *Q.*

Greece and Rome—Oxford University Press, Walton Street, Oxford OX2 6DP. *Twice a year.*

Guiding—17–19 Buckingham Palace Road, SW1W 0PT. *M.*

Harpers and Queen—72 Broadwick Street, W1V 2BP. *M.*

High Magazine—Springfield House, The Parade, Oadby, Leics. LE2 5BF. *Six times a year.*

History—59A Kennington Park Road, SE11 4JH. *Three times a year.*

History Today—83–84 Berwick Street, W1V 3PJ. *M.*

Homes and Gardens—King's Reach Tower, Stamford Street, SE1 9LS. *M.*

Homoeopathy—27A Devonshire Street, W1N 1RJ. *Alt. M.*

Horse and Hound—King's Reach Tower, Stamford Street, SE1 9LS. *W.*

House and Garden—Vogue House, Hanover Square, W1R 0AD. *M.*

Ideal Home—King's Reach Tower, Stamford Street, SE1 9LS. *M.*

Illustrated London News—20 Upper Ground, SE1 9PF. *M.*

In Britain—B.T.A., Thames Tower, Black's Road, W6 9EL. *M.*

International Affairs—P.O. Box 63, Westbury House, Bury Street, Guildford GU2 5BH. *Q.*

Jazz Journal International—35 Great Russell Street, WC1B 3PP. *M.*

Kennel Gazette—1 Clarges Street, W1Y 8AB. *M.*

Labour Research— 78 Blackfriars Road, SE1 8HF. *M.*

The Lady—39–40 Bedford Street, WC2E 9ER. *W.*

Land and Liberty—177 Vauxhall Bridge Road, SW1V 1EU. *Alt. M.*

Light—16 Queensberry Place, SW7 2EB. *Three times a year.*

The Listener—35 Marylebone High Street, W1M 4AA. *W.*

Living—38 Hans Crescent, SW1X 0LZ. *Thirteen times a year.*

Local Government Chronicle—122 Minories Road, EC3N 1NT. *W.*

London Gazette (*Official*)—H.M.S.O., P.O. Box 276, SW8 5DT. *Four times a week.*

London Review of Books—Tavistock House South, Tavistock Square, WC1H 9JZ. *Alt. W.*

London Weekly Diary of Social Events—10 College Approach, Greenwich, SE10 9HY. *W.*

Look Now—25 Newman Street, W1P 3PE. *M.*

Melody Maker (MM)—King's Reach Tower, Stamford Street, SE1 9LS. *W.*

Meteorological Magazine—H.M.S.O., St. Crispins, Duke Street, Norwich NR3 1PD. *M.*

Mind—Oxford University Press, Walton Street, Oxford OX2 6DP. *Q.*

Model Boats—P.O. Box 35, Wolsey House, Wolsey Road, Hemel Hempstead, Herts. HP2 4SS *M.*

Model Railway Constructor—Coombelands House, Addlestone, Surrey KT15 1HY. *M.*

Modern Languages—10 Holt Park Way, Leeds LS16 7QR. *Q.*

Month—114 Mount Street, W1Y 6AH. *M.*

Monthly Digest of Statistics (*Official*)—H.M.S.O., P.O. Box 276, SW8 5DT. *M.*

Mother—12–18 Paul Street, EC2A 4JS. *M.*

Motor Cycle News—P.O. Box 11, Huxloe Place, High Street, Kettering, Northamptonshire NN16 8SS. *W.*

Municipal Review and AMA News—35 Great Smith Street, SW1P 3BJ. *Ten times a year.*

Museums Bulletin—34 Bloomsbury Way, WC1A 2SF. *M.*

Music and Letters—Oxford University Press, Walton Street, Oxford OX2 6DP. *Q.*

My Weekly—80 Kingsway East, Dundee DD4 8SL. *W.*

Nature—4 Little Essex Street, WC2R 3LF. *W.*

Nautical Magazine—4–10 Darnley Street, Glasgow G41 2SD. *M.*

Navy International—Hunters Moon, Hogspudding Lane, Newdigate, Dorking, Surrey RH5 5DS. *M.*

N.M.E.—King's Reach Tower, Stamford Street, SE1 9LS. *W.*

New Scientist—Commonwealth House, 1–19 New Oxford Street, WC1A 1NG. *W.*

New Statesman and Society—Foundation House, Perseverance Works, 38 Kingsland Road, E2 8DQ. *W.*

19—King's Reach Tower, Stamford Street, SE1 9LS. *M.*

Notes and Queries—Oxford University Press, Walton Street, Oxford OX2 6DP. *Q.*

Nursery World—24–25 Cowcross Street, EC1M 6DQ. *Alt. W.*

Opera—1A Mountgrove Road, N5 2LU. *M.*

Options—25 Newman Street, W1P 3PE. *M.*

Our Dogs—5 Oxford Road, Station Approach, Manchester M60 1SX. *W.*

Over 21—Greater London House, Hampstead Road, NW1 7QZ. *M.*

Parents—Victory House, Leicester Place, WC2H 7NB. *M.*

Parliamentary Debates (Lords) (Hansard)—H.M.S.O., P.O. Box 276, SW8 5DT. *Daily or weekly during Session.*

Parliamentary Debates (Commons) (Hansard)—H.M.S.O., P.O. Box 276, SW8 5DT. *Daily or weekly during Session.*

People's Friend—80 Kingsway East, Dundee DD4 8SL. *W.*

Philosophy—Cambridge University Press, The Edinburgh Building, Shaftesbury Road, Cambridge CB2 2RU. *Q.*

Pins and Needles—Milford House, 6–10 Kirby Street, EC1N 8TS. *M.*

Plays and Players—248 High Street, Croydon CR0 1NF. *M.*

Poetry Review—21 Earl's Court Square, SW5 9DE. *Q.*

Political Quarterly—108 Cowley Road, Oxford OX4 1JF. *Q.*

Pony—104 Ash Road, Sutton, Surrey SM3 9LD. *M.*

Poultry World—Carew House, Wallington, Surrey SM6 0DX. *M.*

Practical Boat Owner—Westover House, West Quay Road, Poole, Dorset BH15 1JG. *M.*

Practical Caravan—38–42 Hampton Road, Teddington, Middx. TW11 0JE. *M.*

Practical Gardening—Bushfield House, Orton Centre, Peterborough PE2 0UW. *M.*

Practical Householder—Greater London House, Hampstead Road NW1 7QP. *M.*

Prima—Portland House, Stag Place, SW1E 5AU. *M.*

Progress (*Braille Type*)—338–346 Goswell Road, EC1V 7JE. *M.*

Punch—23–27 Tudor Street, EC4 0HR. *W.*

Racing Calendar—42 Portman Square, W1H 0EN. *W.*

Radio Control Models and Electronics—Wolsey House, Wolsey Road, Hemel Hempstead, Herts. HP2 4SS. *M.*

Radio Times—35 Marylebone High Street, W1M 4AA. *W.*

Railway Magazine—Prospect House, 9–13 Ewell Road, Cheam, Surrey SM1 4QQ. *M.*

Railway World—Coombelands House, Addlestone, Surrey KT15 1HY. *M.*

Reader's Digest—25 Berkeley Square, W1X 6AB. *M.*

Riding—8 Stamford Hill, N16 6XZ. *M.*

Ritz Newspaper—35 Britannia Row, N1 8QH. *M.*

Scots Independent—51 Cowans Street, Stirling. *M.*

Scottish Field—Ravenseft House, 302 St. Vincent Street, Glasgow G2 5NL. *M.*

Scouting—Baden-Powell House, Queen's Gate, SW7 5JS. *M.*

The Seafarer—202 Lambeth Road, SE1 7JW. *Q.*

She—72 Broadwick Street, W1V 2BP. *M.*

Shoot—King's Reach Tower, Stamford Street, SE1 9LS. *W.*

Shooting Times and Country Magazine—10 Sheet Street, Windsor SL4 1BG. *W.*

Social and Liberal Democrat News—4 Cowley Street, SW1P 3NB. *W.*

Sociological Review—11 New Fetter Lane, EC4P 4EE. *Q.*

Spare Rib—27 Clerkenwell Close, EC1R 0AT. *M.*

The Spectator—56 Doughty Street, WC1N 2LL. *W.*

The Strad—8 Lower James Street, W1R 4DN. *M.*

Studio International—Tower House, Southampton Street, WC2E 7LS. *Q.*

Tatler—Vogue House, Hanover Square, W1R 0AD. *M.*

Tennis World—184 High Street, Berkhamsted, Herts. HP4 3AP. *M.*

This England—Alma House, Rodney Road, Cheltenham, Glos. GL50 1YQ. *Q.*

Time—Time and Life Building, New Bond Street, W1Y 0AA. *W.*

The Times Educational Supplement—Priory House, St. John's Lane, EC1M 4BX. *W.*

The Times Higher Education Supplement—Priory House, St. John's Lane, EC1M 4BX. *W.*

The Times Literary Supplement—Priory House, St. John's Lane, EC1M 4BX. *W.*

Tribune—308 Gray's Inn Road, WC1X 8DY. *W.*

Trout and Salmon—Bretton Court, Bretton, Peterborough PE3 8DZ. *M.*

True Romances—12–18 Paul Street, EC2A 4JS. *M.*

True Story—12–18 Paul Street, EC2A 4JS. *M.*

TV Times—247 Tottenham Court Road, W1P 0AU. *W.*

Vacher's Parliamentary Companion—113 High Street, Berkhamsted, Herts. HP4 2DJ. *Q.*

Vogue—Vogue House, Hanover Square, W1R 0AD. *M.*

Weather—James Glaisher House, Grenville Place, Bracknell, Berks. RG12 1BX. *M.*

Weekend—Carmelite House, Carmelite Street, EC4Y 0JA. *W.*

Welsh Nation—51 Cathedral Road, Cardiff CF1 9HD. *M.*

West Africa—Cambridge House, 373–375 Euston Road, NW1 3AR. *W.*

Woman—King's Reach Tower, Stamford Street, SE1 9LS. *W.*

Woman and Home—King's Reach Tower, Stamford Street, SE1 9LS. *M.*

Woman's Journal—King's Reach Tower, Stamford Street, SE1 9LS. *M.*

Woman's Own—King's Reach Tower, Stamford Street, SE1 9LS. *W.*

Woman's Realm—King's Reach Tower, Stamford Street, SE1 9LS. *W.*

Woman's Weekly—King's Reach Tower, Stamford Street, SE1 9LS. *W.*

Woman's World—25 Newman Street, W1P 3HA. *M.*

The World Today—Chatham House, 10 St. James's Square, SW1Y 4LE. *M.*

Yachting Monthly—King's Reach Tower, Stamford Street, SE1 9LS. *M.*

Yachting World—Prospect House, 9–13 Ewell Road, Cheam, Surrey SM1 4QQ. *M.*

Yachts and Yachting—196 Eastern Esplanade, Southend-on-Sea, Essex SS1 3AB. *Alt. W.*

Your Model Railway—P.O. Box 35, Wolsey House, Wolsey Road, Hemel Hempstead, Herts. HP2 4SS. *M.*

TRADE, PROFESSIONAL AND BUSINESS JOURNALS

[*W.* = Weekly; *M.* = Monthly; *Q.* = Quarterly]

Accountancy—40 Bernard Street, WC1N 1LD. *M.*

The Accountant—Axe & Bottle Court, 70 Newcomen Street, SE1 1YT.

Accountants' Magazine—27 Queen Street, Edinburgh EH2 1LA. *M.*

Administrator—2nd Floor, Caxton House, Wellesley Road, Ashford, Kent. *M.*

Agriculture International—Yew Tree House, Horne, Horley, Surrey RH6 9JP. *M.*

Anti-Corrosion Methods and Materials—127 Stanstead Road, SE23 1JE. *M.*

Antique Dealer and Collectors' Guide—King's Reach Tower, Stamford Street, SE1 9LS. *M.*

Architects' Journal—9 Queen Anne's Gate, SW1H 9BY. *W.*

Architectural Review—9 Queen Anne's Gate, SW1H 9BY. *M.*

The Author—84 Drayton Gardens, SW10 9SB. *Q.*

Bakers' Review—Penn House, Penn Place, Rickmansworth, Herts. WD3 1SN. *M.*

The Banker—102–108 Clerkenwell Road, EC1M 5SA. *M.*

Banking World—Athene House, 66–73 Shoe Lane, EC4P 4AB. *M.*

The Bookseller—12 Dyott Street, WC1A 1DF. *W.*

Brewers' Guardian—209 Central Markets, Smithfield, EC1A 9LH. *M.*

British Baker—P.O. Box 109, Maclaren House, 19 Scarbrook Road, Croydon, Surrey CR9 1QH. *W.*

British Business—D.T.I., 11th Floor, Millbank Tower, SW1P 4QU. *W.*

British Clothing Manufacturer—100 Avenue Road, NW3 3TP. *Q.*

British Dental Journal—B.M.A. House, Tavistock Square, WC1H 9JR. *Alt. W.*

British Food Journal—Peterson House, Northbank, Berryhill Industrial Estate, Droitwich, Worcs. WR9 9BL. *Alt. M.*

British Jeweller—St. Dunstan's House, Carey Lane, EC2V 8AA. *M.*

British Journal for the Philosophy of Science—Headington Hill Hall, Oxford OX3 0BW. *Q.*

British Journal of Photography—244–249 Temple Chambers, Temple Avenue, EC4Y 0DT. *W.*

British Medical Journal—B.M.A. House, Tavistock Square, WC1H 9JR. *W.*

British Printer—Maclean Hunter House, Chalk Lane, Cockfosters Road, Barnet, Herts. EN4 0BU. *M.*

British Sugar Beet Review—P.O. Box 26, Oundle Road, Peterborough PE2 9QU. *Q.*

British Tax Review—11 New Fetter Lane, EC4P 4EE. *Alt. M.*

British Veterinary Journal—1 Vincent Square, SW1P 2PN. *Alt. M.*

Builders Merchants Journal—Sovereign Way, Tonbridge, Kent TN9 1RW. *Twenty times a year.*

Building—Builder House, 1 Pemberton Row, EC4P 4HL. *W.*

Cabinet Maker and Retail Furnisher—Sovereign Way, Tonbridge, Kent TN9 1RW. *W.*

Campaign—22 Lancaster Gate, W2 3LY. *W.*

Carpet and Floorcoverings Review—Sovereign Way, Tonbridge, Kent TN9 1RW. *Alt. W.*

Caterer and Hotelkeeper—Quadrant House, The Quadrant, Sutton, Surrey SM2 5AS. *W.*

Chemist and Druggist—Sovereign Way, Tonbridge, Kent TN9 1RW. *W.*

Chemistry and Industry—14 Belgrave Square, SW1X 8PS. *Alt. W.*

Chemistry in Britain—Burlington House, Piccadilly, W1V 0BN. *M.*

Child Education—Marlborough House, Holly Walk, Leamington Spa, Warwickshire CV32 4LS. *M.*

Chiropodist—53 Welbeck Street, W1M 7HE. *M.*

Civil Engineering—Morgan-Grampian House, 30 Calderwood Street, SE18 6QH. *M.*

Club Mirror—Maclaren House, Scarbrook Road, Croydon, Surrey CR9 1QH. *M.*

Colliery Guardian—Queensway House, 2 Queensway, Redhill, Surrey RH1 1QS. *M.*

Commercial Motor—Quadrant House, The Quadrant, Sutton, Surrey SM2 5AS. *W.*

Computer Survey—U.T.P. House, 33–35 Bowling Green Lane, EC1R 0DA. *Alt. M.*

Concrete—11 Grosvenor Crescent, SW1X 7EE. *M.*

Containerisation International—72 Broadwick Street, W1V 2BP. *M.*

Contract Journal—Carew House, Wallington, Surrey SM6 0DX. *W.*

Control and Instrumentation—Morgan-Grampian House, 30 Calderwood Street, SE18 6QH. *M.*

C.S.E. News (Camping and Sports Equipment)—Exhibition House, 4 Spring Street, W2 3RB. *M.*

Dairy Farmer—Wharfedale Road, Ipswich IP1 4LG. *M.*

Dairy Industries International—U.T.P. House, 33–35 Bowling Green Lane, EC1R 0DA. *M.*

Design—The Design Centre, 28 Haymarket, SW1Y 4SU. *M.*

Director—10 Belgrave Square, SW1X 8PH. *M.*

Dock and Harbour Authority—19 Harcourt Street, W1H 2AX. *M.*

Drapers Record—100 Avenue Road, NW3 3TP. *W.*

Education—21–27 Lamb's Conduit Street, WC1N 3NJ. *W.*

Education Equipment—Sovereign Way, Tonbridge, Kent TN9 1RW. *M.*

Electrical & Electronic Trader—Quadrant House, The Quadrant, Sutton, Surrey SM2 5AS. *W.*

Electrical and Radio Trading—Quadrant House, The Quadrant, Sutton, Surrey SM2 5AS. *W.*

Electrical Review—Quadrant House, The Quadrant, Sutton, Surrey SM2 5AS. *W.*

Electrical Times—Quadrant House, The Quadrant, Sutton, Surrey SM2 5AS. *M.*

Electronic Engineering—Morgan-Grampian House, 30 Calderwood Street, SE18 6QH. *M.*

Electronics Weekly—Quadrant House, The Quadrant, Sutton, Surrey SM2 5AS. *W.*

Embroidery—P.O. Box 42B, East Molesey, Surrey KT8 9BB. *Q.*

The Engineer—Morgan-Grampian House, 30 Calderwood Street, SE18 6QH. *W.*

Engineering—28 Haymarket, SW1Y 4SU. *M.*

Engineer's Digest—Catalyst House, 159–160 High Street, Clapham, SW4 7SS. *Ten times a year.*

Estates Gazette—151 Wardour Street, W1V 4BN. *W.*

Fairplay International Shipping Weekly—52–54 Southwark Street, SE1 1UJ. *W.*

Farmers Weekly—Carew House, Wallington, Surrey SM6 0DX. *W.*

Fire—Queensway House, 2 Queensway, Redhill, Surrey RH1 1QS. *M.*

Fire and Security Protection—Stanley House, 9 West Street, Epsom, Surrey KT18 7RL. *M.*

Fish Friers Review—289 Dewsbury Road, Leeds LS11 5HW. *M.*

Fish Trader—Queensway House, 2 Queensway, Redhill, Surrey RH1 1QS. *W.*

Flight International—Quadrant House, The Quadrant, Sutton, Surrey SM2 5AS. *W.*

Food Trade Review—29 High Street, Green Street Green, Orpington, Kent BR6 6LS. *M.*

Forestry and British Timber—Sovereign Way, Tonbridge, Kent TN9 1RW. *M.*

Foundry Trade Journal—Queensway House, 2 Queensway, Redhill, Surrey RH1 1QS. *Alt. W.*

Frozen and Chilled Foods—Queensway House, 2 Queensway, Redhill, Surrey RH1 1QS. *M.*

Fuel—P.O. Box 63, Westbury House, Bury Street, Guildford GU2 5BH. *M.*

Funeral Service Journal—Press House, Rockingham Road, Uxbridge, Middx. UB8 2YW. *M.*

Fur Weekly News—4 Great Saint Thomas Apostle, EC4V 2BH. *W.*

Gas Marketing—Sovereign Way, Tonbridge, Kent TN9 1RW. *M.*

Gas World—Sovereign Way, Tonbridge, Kent TN9 1RW. *M.*

Gifts International—Sovereign Way, Tonbridge, Kent TN9 1RW. *M.*

Glass—Queensway House, 2 Queensway, Redhill, Surrey RH1 1QS. *M.*

The Grocer—5–7 Southwark Street, SE1 1RQ. *W.*

The Grower—50 Doughty Street, WC1N 2LP. *W.*

Hair and Beauty—Quadrant House, The Quadrant, Sutton, Surrey SM2 5AS. *M.*

Hairdressers' Journal International—Quadrant House, The Quadrant, Sutton, Surrey SM2 5AS. *W.*

Handy Shipping Guide—230–234 Long Lane, SE1 4QE. *W.*

Hardware Trade Journal—Sovereign Way, Tonbridge, Kent TN9 1RW. *W.*

Harpers Sports & Leisure—Unit 1, Mill Hill Industrial Estate, Flower Lane, NW7 2HU. *Every three weeks.*

Harpers Wine and Spirit Gazette—Harling House, 47–51 Great Suffolk Street, SE1 0BS. *W.*

Health Visitor—BMA House, Tavistock Square, WC1H 9JR. *M.*

Heating and Ventilating Engineer—177 Hagden Lane, Watford, Herts. WD1 8LW. *Alt. M.*

Hospital and Health Services Review—6th Floor, Westgate House, The High, Harlow, Essex CM20 1NE. *Alt. M.*

Ice Cream and Frozen Confectionery—90–94 Gray's Inn Road, WC1X 8AH. *M.*

Industrial Society—Peter Runge House, 3 Carlton House Terrace, SW1Y 5DG. *Q.*

Insurance Mail—Mitre House, 44 Fleet Street, EC4Y 1BS. *M.*

Investors Chronicle—Greystoke Place, Fetter Lane, EC4A 1ND. *W.*

Journal of The Chemical Society—Burlington House, Piccadilly, W1V 0BN. *In six parts* (each *M*).

The Journalist—Acorn House, 314 Gray's Inn Rd., WC1X 8DP. *M.*

Justice of the Peace—East Row, Little London, Chichester, W. Sussex PO19 1PG. *W.*

Knitting and Haberdashery Review—80A South Street, Romford, Essex RM1 1RX. *Alt. M.*

The Lancet—7 Adam Street, WC2N 6AD. *W.*

Law Quarterly Review—11 New Fetter Lane, EC4P 4EE. *Q.*

The Law Reports—3 Stone Buildings, Lincoln's Inn, WC2A 3XN. *M.*

Law Society's Gazette—113 Chancery Lane, WC2A 1PL. *W.*

Leather—Sovereign Way, Tonbridge, Kent TN9 1RW. *M.*

The Legal Executive—Kempston Manor, Kempston, Beds. MK42 7AB. *M.*

Library Review—302 St. Vincent Street, Glasgow G2 5NL. *Q.*

Litho Week—38–42 Hampton Road, Teddington, Middx. TW11 0JE. *W.*

Lloyd's Loading List—Sheepen Place, Colchester, Essex CO3 3LP. *W.*

Locomotive Journal—9 Arkwright Road, NW3 6AB. *M.*

London Corn Circular—54 Wentworth Crescent, Ash Vale, Aldershot, Hants. GU12 5LF. *W.*

Machinery and Production Engineering—Franks Hall, Franks Lane, Horton Kirby, Dartford, Kent DA4 9LL. *Alt. W.*

Machinery Market—6 Blyth Road, Bromley, Kent BR1 3RX. *W.*

Management Accounting—63 Portland Place, W1N 4AB. *M.*

Management Decision—62 Toller Lane, Bradford BD8 9BY. *Alt. M.*

Management Today—30 Lancaster Gate, W2 3LP. *M.*

Manufacturing Chemist—Morgan-Grampian House, 30 Calderwood Street, SE18 6QH. *M.*

Marketing—22 Lancaster Gate, W2 3LY. *W.*

Materials Reclamation Weekly—Maclaren House, 19 Scarbrook Road, Croydon CR9 1QH. *W.*

Meat Trades' Journal—100 Avenue Road, NW3 3TP. *W.*

Medico-Legal Journal—5 New Square, Lincoln's Inn, WC2A 3RJ. *Q.*

Men's Wear—100 Avenue Road, NW3 3TP. *W.*

Metal Bulletin—Park House, Park Terrace, Worcester Park, Surrey KT4 7HY. *Twice a week.*

Metallurgia—Queensway House, 2 Queensway, Redhill, Surrey RH1 1QS. *M.*

Metals and Minerals International—5 Pond Street, NW3 2PN. *Q.*

Milk Industry—19 Cornwall Terrace, NW1 4QP. *M.*

Mining Journal—60 Worship Street, EC2A 2HD. *W.*

Mining Magazine—60 Worship Street, EC2A 2HD. *M.*

Model Engineer—P.O. Box 35, Wolsey House, Wolsey Road, Hemel Hempstead, Herts. HP2 4SS. *Alt. W.*

Modern Law Review—11 New Fetter Lane, EC4P 4EE. *Alt. M.*

Modern Railways—Coombelands House, Addlestone, Surrey KT15 1HY. *M.*

Motor—Prospect House, 9–13 Ewell Road, Cheam, Surrey SM1 4QQ. *W.*

Motor Boat and Yachting—Prospect House, 9–13 Ewell Road, Cheam, Surrey SM1 4QQ. *M.*

Motorcycle Trader—177 Hagden Lane, Watford, Herts. WD1 8LW. *M.*

Motor Trader—Quadrant House, The Quadrant, Sutton, Surrey SM2 5AS. *W.*

Motor Transport—Quadrant House, The Quadrant, Sutton, Surrey SM2 5AS. *W.*

The Musical Times—8 Lower James Street, W1R 4DN. *M.*

National Builder—82 New Cavendish Street, W1M 8AD. *M.*

Natural Gas—Sovereign Way, Tonbridge, Kent TN9 1RW. *Alt. M.*

New Law Journal—9–12 Bell Yard, WC2A 2JR. *W.*

Nuclear Engineering International—Quadrant House, The Quadrant, Sutton, Surrey SM2 5AS. *M.*

Nurseryman & Garden Centre—Monchelsea Farm, Boughton Monchelsea, Maidstone, Kent ME17 4JD. *Alt. W.*

Nursing Times & Nursing Mirror—4 Little Essex Street, WC2R 3LF. *W.*

Off-Licence News—5–7 Southwark Street, SE1 1RQ. *W.*

Optician, The—Quadrant House, The Quadrant, Sutton, Surrey SM2 5AS. *W.*

Optometry Today—233–234 Blackfriars Road, SE1 8NW. *Alt. W.*

Packaging—177 Hagden Lane, Watford, Herts. WD1 8LW. *M.*

Packaging Week—Sovereign Way, Tonbridge, Kent TN9 1RW. *W.*

Paint & Resin—177 Hagden Lane, Watford, Herts. WD1 8LW. *M.*

Painting and Decorating Journal—177 Hagden Lane, Watford, Herts. WD1 8LW. *Eight times a year.*

Paper—Sovereign Way, Tonbridge, Kent TN9 1RW. *Alt. W.*

Personnel Management—1 Hills Place, W1R 1AG. *M.*

Pharmaceutical Journal, The—1 Lambeth High Street, SE1 7JN. *W.*

The Photographer—1 Gayford Road, W12 9BY. *M.*

Physics Bulletin—Techno House, Redcliffe Way, Bristol BS1 6NX. *M.*

Physics Education—Techno House, Redcliffe Way, Bristol BS1 6NX. *Seven times a year.*

Physics in Technology—Techno House, Redcliffe Way, Bristol BS1 6NX. *Alt. M.*

Plumbing and Heating Equipment News—Peterson House, Northbank, Berryhill Industrial Estate, Droitwich, Worcs. WR9 9BL. *M.*

Police Review—14 St. Cross Street, EC1N 8FE. *W.*

Power Farming—Carew House, Wallington, Surrey SM6 0DX. *M.*

Practical Wireless—Enefco House, The Quay, Poole, Dorset B15 1PP. *M.*

Practical Woodworking—King's Reach Tower, Stamford Street, SE1 9LS. *M.*

The Practitioner—Morgan-Grampian House, 30 Calderwood Street, SE18 6QH. *M.*

Precision Toolmaker—Queensway House, 2 Queensway, Redhill, Surrey RH1 1QS. *M.*

Printing World—Sovereign Way, Tonbridge, Kent TN9 1RW. *W.*

Product Finishing—127 Stanstead Road, SE23 1JE. *M.*

Public Law—11 New Fetter Lane, EC4P 4EE. *Q.*

Public Ledger, The—12 Greycaine Road, Watford, Herts. WD2 4JP. *Daily* and *W.*

Public Service—1 Mabledon Place, WC1H 9AJ. *M.*

Quarry Management—7 Regent Street, Nottingham NG1 5BY. *M.*

Quarterly Journal of Experimental Psychology— Cambridge University Press, The Edinburgh Building, Shaftesbury Road, Cambridge CB2 2RU. *Q.*

Quarterly Journal of Medicine—Oxford University Press, Walton Street, Oxford OX2 6DP. *M.*

Railway Gazette International—Quadrant House, The Quadrant, Sutton, Surrey SM2 5AS. *M.*

Rating & Valuation Reporter—2 Paper Buildings, Temple, EC4. *M.*

Resale Weekly—1–23 Queen's Road West, E13 0PE. *W.*

Retail Jeweller—100 Avenue Road, NW3 3TP. *Alt. W.*

Retail Newsagent Tobacconist Confectioner—60–66 Saffron Hill, EC1N 8QX. *W.*

The Review: Worldwide Reinsurance—U.T.P. House, 33–35 Bowling Green Lane, EC1R 0DA. *Twenty-two times a year.*

Review of English Studies—Oxford University Press, Walton Street, Oxford OX2 6DP. *Q.*

Safety at Sea—Queensway House, 2 Queensway, Redhill, Surrey RH1 1QS. *M.*

The Scottish Farmer—302–304 St. Vincent Street, Glasgow G2 5NL. *W.*

Scottish Grocer—36 North Frederick Street, Glasgow G1 2BT. *M.*

Service Station—1A Dunvegan Road, Eltham, SE9 1RZ. *M.*

Sheet Metal Industries—Queensway House, 2 Queensway, Redhill, Surrey RH1 1QS. *M.*

Shipping World & Shipbuilder—4 Hubbard Road, Houndsmill, Basingstoke, Hants. RG21 2UH. *M.*

Shoe & Leather News—84–88 Great Eastern Street, EC2A 3ED. *W.*

Soap, Perfumery and Cosmetics—U.T.P. House, 33–35 Bowling Green Lane, EC1R 0DA. *M.*

Solicitors' Journal—21–27 Lamb's Conduit Street, WC1N 3NJ. *W.*

Sports Retailing—Sovereign Way, Tonbridge, Kent TN9 1RW. *Alt. W.*

The Stage—47 Bermondsey Street, SE1 3XT. *W.*

Stamp News—6 London Street, W2 1HR. *Alt. W.*

Structural Engineer—11 Upper Belgrave Street, SW1X 8BH. *M. (Part A), Q. (Part B).*

Surveyor—Public Works Weekly—Carew House, Wallington, Surrey SM6 0DX. *W.*

Tableware International—Queensway House, 2 Queensway, Redhill, Surrey RH1 1QS. *M.*

Taxation—17 Scarbrook Road, Croydon, Surrey CR0 1SQ. *W.*

The Teacher—Derbyshire House, Lower Street, Kettering, Northants. NN16 8BB. *W.*

Teaching History—59A Kennington Park Road, SE11 4JH. *Three times a year.*

Television—King's Reach Tower, Stamford Street, SE1 9LS. *M.*

Textile Horizons—10 Blackfriars Street, Manchester M3 5DR. *M.*

Textile Month—Cainden House, Canal Road, Timperley, Altrincham, Cheshire WA14 1TD. *M.*

Timber Trades Journal & Wood Processing—Sovereign Way, Tonbridge, Kent TN9 1RW. *W.*

Tobacco—Queensway House, 2 Queensway, Redhill, Surrey RH1 1QS. *M.*

Town and Country Planning—17 Carlton House Terrace, SW1Y 5AH. *M.*

Town Planning Review—Liverpool University Press, P.O. Box 147, Liverpool L69 3BX. *Q.*

Toy Trader—177 Hagden Lane, Watford, Herts. WD1 8LW. *M.*

Trade Marks Journal—25 Southampton Buildings, WC2A 1AY. *W.*

Traffic Engineering and Control—29 Newman Street, W1P 3PE. *M.*

U.K. Press Gazette—244–249 Temple Chambers, Temple Avenue, EC4Y 0DT. *W.*

Ultrasonics—P.O. Box 63, Westbury House, Bury Street, Guildford, Surrey GU2 5BH. *Alt. M.*

Weekly Law Reports—3 Stone Buildings, Lincoln's Inn, WC2A 3XN. *W.*

Welding and Metal Fabrication—Queensway House, 2 Queensway, Redhill, Surrey RH1 1QS. *Five times a year.*

Which?—14 Buckingham Street, WC2N 6DS. *M.*

Whitaker's Books of the Month and Books to Come—12 Dyott Street, WC1A 1DF. *M.*

Whitaker's Classified Monthly Book List—12 Dyott Street, WC1A 1DF. *M.*

Wire Industry—110–112 Station Road East, Oxted, Surrey RH8 0QA. *M.*

Woodworker—1 Golden Square, W1R 3AB. *M.*

World's Fair—2 Daltry Street, Oldham OL1 4BB. *W.*

REPORTING AND NEWS AGENCIES IN LONDON

THE ASSOCIATED PRESS LTD., 12 Norwich Street, EC4A 4BP. 01–353 1515.

BRENARD PRESS LTD., Building 221, Heathrow Airport, Hounslow, Middx. TW6 2BU. 01–759 1235.

CENTRAL PRESS FEATURES LTD., 131 Aldersgate Street, Barbican, EC1A 4JA.

THE EXCHANGE TELEGRAPH CO. LTD., Extel House, East Harding Street, EC4P 4HB. 01–353 1080.

HAYTERS 4–5 Gough Square, EC4A 3DE. 01–353 0971.

PARLIAMENTARY AND COMMON MARKET NEWS SERVICES, 19 Kingsdowne Road, Surbiton, Surrey KT6 6JZ. 01–399 2049.

PRESS ASSOCIATION LTD., 85 Fleet Street, EC4P 4BE. 01–353 7440.

REUTERS LTD., 85 Fleet Street, EC4P 4AJ. 01–250 1122.

UNITED PRESS INTERNATIONAL (U.K.) LTD., 8 Bouverie Street, EC4Y 8BB. 01–353 2282.

UNIVERSAL NEWS SERVICE, LTD., Communications House, Gough Square, Fleet Street, EC4 4DP. 01–353 5200.

PRINCIPAL BOOK PUBLISHERS AND THEIR ADDRESSES

More than 10,000 firms, individuals and societies have published one or more books in recent years. The list which follows is a selective one comprising, in the main, those firms whose names are most familiar to the general public. An interleaved list containing some 2,500 names and addresses is issued annually in April by the publishers of *Whitaker's Almanack*.

Abelard-Schuman, 7 Leicester Place, WC2H 7BP.
Allan (Ian), Coombelands House, Addlestone, Weybridge, Surrey KT15 1HY.
Allen (J. A.), 1 Lower Grosvenor Place, SW1W 0EL.
Allen (W. H.), 44 Hill Street, W1X 8LB.
Angus & Robertson, 16 Golden Square, W1R 4BN.
Apple Press, 79 Great Titchfield Street, W1P 7FN.
Argus Books, Wolsey House, Wolsey Road, Hemel Hempstead HP2 4SS.
Arlington Books, 15 King Street, SW1Y 6QU.
Armada Books, 8 Grafton Street. W1X 3LA.
Arms & Armour Press, 3 Fleets Lane, Poole BH15 3AJ.
Arnold (Edward), 41 Bedford Square, WC1B 3DQ.
Arnold (E. J.) & Son, Parkside Lane, Leeds LS11 5TD.
Arrow Books, 62 Chandos Place, WC2N 4NW.
Athlone Press, 44 Bedford Row, WC1R 4LY.
B.B.C. Books, 80 Wood Lane, W12 0TT.
Baillière, Tindall, 24 Oval Road, NW1 7DX.
Bantam Bks., 61 Uxbridge Road, W5 5SA.
Barker (Arthur), 91 Clapham High Street, SW4 9TA.
Barrie & Jenkins, 289 Westbourne Grove, W11 2QA.
Bartholomew & Son, 12 Duncan Street, Edinburgh EH9 1TA.
Batsford, 4 Fitzhardinge Street, W1H 0AH.
Benn (Ernest), 35 Bedford Row, WC1R 4JH.
Bingley (Clive), 7 Ridgmount Street, WC1E 7AE.
Black (A. & C.), 35 Bedford Row, WC1R 4JH.
Blackie, Bishopbriggs, Glasgow G64 2NZ.
Blackwell (Basil), 108 Cowley Rd., Oxford OX4 1JF.
Blackwood Pillans & Wilson, 61 North Castle Street, Edinburgh 2.
Blandford Press, Artillery House, Artillery Row, SW1P 1RT.
Blond (Anthony), 62 Chandos Place, WC2N 4NW.
Bloomsbury Publishing, 2 Soho Square, W1V 5DE.
Bodley Head, 32 Bedford Square, WC1B 3EL.
Boxtree, 36 Tavistock Street, WC2E 7PB.
Boyars (Marion), 24 Lacy Road, SW15 1NL.
Bracken Books, 50 Eastcastle Street, W1N 7AP.
British Museum, 46 Bloomsbury Street, WC1B 3QQ.
Brown, Son & Ferguson, 4 Darnley Street, Glasgow G41 2SD.
Burke Pub. Co., 116 Golden Lane, EC1Y 0TL.
Butterworth & Co., Borough Green, Sevenoaks TN15 8PH.
Calder (John), 18 Brewer Street, W1R 4AS.
Cambridge Univ. Press, Shaftesbury Road, Cambridge CB2 2RU.
Cape (Jonathan), 32 Bedford Square, WC1B 3EL.
Cassell, Artillery House, Artillery Row, SW1P 1RT.
Centaur Press, Fontwell, Arundel, Sussex BN18 0TA.
Century Hutchinson, 62 Chandos Place, WC2N 4NW.
Century Publishing Co., *see* Century Hutchinson
Chambers (W. & R.), 43 Annandale Street, Edinburgh EH7 4AZ.
Chapman & Hall, 11 New Fetter Lane, EC4P 4EE.
Chapman (Geoffrey), Artillery House, Artillery Row, SW1P 1RT.
Chatto & Windus, 30 Bedford Square, WC1B 3RP.
Church House Publishing, Dean's Yard, SW1P 3NZ.
Churchill Livingstone, 1–3 Baxter's Place, Leith Walk, Edinburgh EH1 3AF.
Collins (William), 8 Grafton Street, W1X 3LA.
Constable & Co., 10 Orange Street, WC2H 7EG.
Consumers' Assn., Marylebone Road, NW1 4DX.
Corgi Books, 61 Uxbridge Road, W5 5SA.
Darton, Longman & Todd, 89 Lillie Road, SW6 1UD.
David & Charles, Brunel House, Newton Abbot, Devon TQ12 4PU.
Dean & Son, *see* Hamlyn.

Dent (J. M.) & Sons, 91 Clapham High Street, SW4 9TA.
Deutsch (A.), 105 Gt. Russell Street, WC1B 3LJ.
Dobson Books, Brancepeth Castle, Durham DH7 8DF.
Dorling Kindersley, 9 Henrietta Street, WC2E 8PS.
Duckworth & Co., 43 Gloucester Crescent, NW1 7DY.
Elliot Right Way Books, Kingswood Bldg., Kingswood, Tadworth, Surrey KT20 6TD.
Encyclopædia Britannica, Carew House, Station Approach, Wallington, Surrey SM6 0DA.
Epworth Press, 1 Central Bldgs., SW1H 9NR.
Evans Bros., 2A Portman Mansions, Chiltern Street, W1M 1LE.
Eyre & Spottiswoode, North Way, Andover, Hants. SP10 5BE.
Faber & Faber, 3 Queen Square, WC1N 3AU.
Fontana, 8 Grafton Street, W1X 3LA.
Foulis (G. T.), Sparkford, Yeovil, Somerset BA22 7JJ.
Foulsham & Co., Yeovil Rd., Slough SL14 4JH.
Fountain Press, 45 The Broadway, Tolworth, Surbiton, Surrey KT6 7DW.
French (Samuel), 52 Fitzroy Street, W1P 6JR.
Futura, *see* Macdonald & Co.
Gee & Co., 7 Swallow Place, W1R 8AB.
Geographia, 12 Duncan Street, Edinburgh EH9 1TA.
Gibbons (Stanley), 5 Parkside, Christchurch Road, Ringwood, Hants. BH24 3SH.
Gibson (Robert), 17 Fitzroy Place, Glasgow G3 7SF.
Ginn & Co., Prebendal House, Parson's Fee, Aylesbury, Bucks. HP20 2QZ.
Glasgow (Mary), 131 Holland Park Avenue, W11 4UT.
Gollancz (Victor), 14 Henrietta Street, WC2E 8QJ.
Gower Publishing Co., Croft Road, Aldershot, Hants. GU11 3HR
Grafton Books, 8 Grafton Street, W1X 3LA.
Graham (Frank), 6 Queen's Terrace, Newcastle NE2 2PL.
Green (W.), 2 St. Giles Street, Edinburgh EH1 1PU.
Griffin (Charles), 41 Bedford Square, WC1B 3DQ.
Guinness Publishing, 33 London Road, Enfield, Middx. EN2 6DJ.
H.M. Stationery Office, 51 Nine Elms Lane, SW8 5DR.
Hale (Robert), 45 Clerkenwell Green, EC1R 0HT.
Hamilton (Hamish), 27 Wright's Lane, W8 5TZ.
Hamlyn, 81 Fulham Road, SW3 6RB.
Harcourt Brace Jovanovich, 24 Oval Road, NW1 7DX.
Harlequin, 18 Paradise Rd., Richmond, Surrey TW9 1SR.
Harper & Row, 34 Cleveland Street, W1P 5FB.
Harrap, 19 Ludgate Hill, EC4M 7PD.
Hart-Davis, 8 Grafton Street, W1X 3LA.
Harvester Wheatsheaf, Wolsey House, Wolsey Road, Hemel Hempstead HP2 4SS.
Haynes (J. H.), Sparkford, Yeovil, Som. BA22 7TJ.
Headline Book Publishing, 79 Great Titchfield Street, W1P 7FN.
Heinemann (Wm.), 81 Fulham Road, SW3 6RB.
Hodder & Stoughton, 47 Bedford Square, WC1B 3DP.
Hodge & Co., 34 N. Frederick St., Glasgow G1 2BT.
Hogarth Press, 30 Bedford Square, WC1B 3RP.
Holmes McDougall, 137 Leith Walk, Edinburgh EH6 8NS.
Hutchinson, 62 Chandos Place, WC2N 4NW.
Jane's Publishing Co., 163 Brighton Road, Coulsdon CR3 2NX.
Jarrold Colour, Barrack Street, Norwich NR3 1TR.
Johnston & Bacon, P. O. Box 1, Stirling.
Jordan & Sons, 21 St. Thomas Street, Bristol BS1 6JS.
Joseph (Michael), 27 Wright's Lane, W8 5TZ.
Kaye & Ward, 81 Fulham Road, SW3 6RB.

Kegan Paul Internat., 11 New Fetter Lane, EC4P 4EE.

Kelly's Directories, East Grinstead House, East Grinstead, Sussex RH19 1XB.

Kimber (Wm.), Denington Estate, Wellingborough NN8 2QD.

Kimpton Medical, 205 Great Portland Street, W1N 6LR.

Kingsway Publications, Lottbridge Drove, Eastbourne BN23 6NT.

Kogan Page, 120 Pentonville Road, N1 9JN.

Ladybird, Beeches Road, Loughborough LE11 2NQ.

Lawrence & Wishart, 39 Museum Street, WC1A 1LQ.

Letts (Charles), 77 Borough Road, SE1 1DW.

Lewis (H. K.), 136 Gower Street, WC1E 6BS.

Lion Publishing, Icknield Way, Tring, Herts. HP23 4LE.

Longman Group, Burnt Mill, Harlow, Essex CM20 2JE.

Lund Humphries, 16 Pembridge Road, W11 3HL.

Lutterworth Press, P.O. Box 60, Cambridge CB1 2NT.

Macdonald & Co., Greater London House, Hampstead Road, NW1 7QX.

Macdonald & Evans, 128 Long Acre, WC2E 9AN.

McGraw-Hill, Shoppenhangers Road, Maidenhead, Berks. SL6 2QL.

Macmillan Publishers, 4 Little Essex Street, WC2R 3LF.

Marshall Cavendish, 58 Old Compton Street, W1V 5PA.

Marshall Pickering, 3 Beggarwood Lane, Basingstoke, Hants. RG23 7LP.

Mayflower, 8 Grafton Street, W1X 3LA.

Methodist Publishing, 20 Ivatt Way, Peterborough PE3 7PG.

Methuen London, 81 Fulham Road, SW3 6RB.

Mills & Boon, 18 Paradise Rd., Richmond, Surrey TW9 1SR.

Mitchell Beazley, 14 Manette Street, W1V 5LB.

Mowbray, St. Thomas Ho., Becket Street, Oxford OX1 1SJ.

Muller (Frederick), 62 Chandos Place, WC2N 4NW.

Murray (John), 50 Albemarle Street, W1X 4BD.

National Christian Education Council, Robert Denholm Ho., Nutfield, Redhill RH1 4HW.

Nelson (T.), Mayfield Rd., Walton-on-Thames KT12 5PL.

New English Library, 47 Bedford Square, WC1B 3DP.

Nisbet & Co., 78 Tilehouse St., Hitchin, Herts. SG5 2DY.

Nonesuch Library, 32 Bedford Square, WC1B 3EL.

Novello & Co., Borough Green, Sevenoaks, Kent.

Octopus Books, 81 Fulham Road, SW3 6RB.

Oliver & Boyd, 1–3 Baxter's Place, Leith Walk, Edinburgh EH1 3BB.

O'Mara (Michael) Books, 20 Queen Anne Street, W1N 9FB.

Owen (Peter), 73 Kenway Road, SW5 0RE.

Oxford Univ. Press, Walton Street, Oxford OX2 6DP.

Paladin Books, 8 Grafton Street, W1X 3LA.

Pan Books, 18 Cavaye Place, SW10 9PG.

Panther, 8 Grafton Street, W1X 3LA.

Paul (Stanley), 62 Chandos Place, WC2N 4NW.

Pelham Books, 27 Wright's Lane, W8 5TZ.

Penguin Books, Harmondsworth, Middx. UB7 0DA.

Pergamon Press, Headington Hill Hall, Oxford OX3 0BW.

Phaidon Press, St. Ebbes Street, Oxford OX1 1SQ.

Pharmaceutical Press, 1 Lambeth High Street, SE1 7JN.

Philip (George), 59 Grosvenor Street, W1X 9DA.

Piatkus Books, 5 Windmill Street, W1P 1HF.

Piccadilly Press, 5 Canfield Place, NW6 3BT.

Pitkins, North Way, Andover, Hants. SP10 5BE.

Pitman Publishing, 128 Long Acre, WC2E 9AN.

Putnam & Co., 24 Bride Lane, EC4Y 8DR.

Quartet Books, 27 Goodge Street, W1P 1FD.

Quiller Press, 50 Albemarle Street, W1X 4BD.

Random House, 30 Bedford Square, WC1B 3SG.

Reader's Digest, 25 Berkeley Square, W1X 6AB.

Religious & Moral Education Press, Hennock Rd., Exeter EX2 8RP.

Rider & Co., 62 Chandos Place, WC2N 4NW.

Routledge, 11 New Fetter Lane, EC4P 4EE.

S.C.M. Press, 26 Tottenham Road, N1 4BZ.

S.P.C.K., Holy Trinity Church, Marylebone Road, NW1 4DU.

St. Andrew Press, 121 George Street, Edinburgh EH2 4YN.

Scripture Union, 130 City Road, EC1V 2NJ.

Secker & Warburg, 81 Fulham Road, SW3 6RB.

Severn House, 40 William IV Street, WC2N 4DF.

Sheed & Ward, 2 Creechurch Lane, EC3A 5AQ.

Sheldon Press, Holy Trinity Church, Marylebone Road, NW1 4DU.

Sidgwick & Jackson, 1 Tavistock Chambers, WC1A 2SG.

Simon & Schuster, Wolsey House, Wolsey Road, Hemel Hempstead HP2 4SS.

Smith (M. Temple), Gower House, Croft Road, Aldershot, Hants. GU11 3HR.

Smythe (Colin), P.O. Box 6, Gerrards Cross, Bucks. SL9 8XA.

Souvenir Press, 43 Great Russell Street, WC1B 3PA.

Sphere Books, 27 Wright's Lane, W8 5TZ.

Spon (E. & F. N.), 11 New Fetter Lane, EC4P 4EE.

Stanford Maritime, 59 Grosvenor Street, W1X 9DA.

Stephens (Patrick), Denington Estate, Wellingborough, Northants. NN8 2QD.

Stevens & Sons, 11 New Fetter Lane, EC4P 4EE.

Sweet & Maxwell, 11 New Fetter Lane, EC4P 4EE.

Technical Press, Gower House, Croft Road, Aldershot, Hants. GU11 3HR.

Thames & Hudson, 30 Bloomsbury Street, WC1B 3QP.

Thorsons, Denington Estate, Wellingborough, Northants. NN8 2RQ.

Times Books, 16 Golden Square, W1R 4BN.

Turnstone Books, Denington Estate, Wellingborough, Northants. NN8 2RQ.

University of Wales Press, Gwennyth Street, Cardiff CF2 4YD.

Unwin Hyman, 15 Broadwick Street, W1V 1FP.

Vallentine Mitchell, 11 Gainsborough Road, E11 1RS.

Viking, 27 Wright's Lane, W8 5TZ.

Virago Press, 20–23 Mandela Street, NW1 0HQ.

Walker Books, 87 Vauxhall Walk, SE11 5HJ.

Ward Lock, 8 Clifford Street, W1X 1RB.

Ward Lock Educational Co., 47 Marylebone Lane, W1M 6AX.

Warne, 27 Wright's Lane, W8 5TZ.

Webb & Bower, 9 Colleton Crescent, Exeter EX2 4BY.

Weidenfeld & Nicolson, 91 Clapham High Street, SW4 9TA.

Wheaton (A.), Hennock Road, Exeter EX2 8RP.

Whitaker (J.), 12 Dyott Street, WC1A 1DF.

Wildwood House, Gower Ho., Croft Rd., Aldershot, Hants. GU11 3HR.

Wisden (John), Station Road, Robertsbridge TN32 5DH.

Witherby (H. F. & G.), 14 Henrietta Street, WC2E 8QJ.

Wolfe Publishing, 2 Torrington Place, WC1E 7LT.

World's Work, see Heinemann (Wm.).

Wright (John), P.O. Box 63, Guildford GU2 5BH.

Zomba Books, 165 High Rd., NW10 2SG.

BOOKS PUBLISHED IN GREAT BRITAIN IN 1987

This table shows the books published in 1987 with the number of new editions, translations and limited editions. Books and pamphlets priced at less than 12p have been omitted, as are also all Government publications except the more important issued by H.M. Stationery Office.

Classification	Total	Reprints and New Editions	Translations	Limited Editions
Aeronautics	269	59	2	—
Agriculture and Forestry	456	101	2	—
Architecture	408	84	8	—
Art	1,573	246	40	8
Astronomy	133	34	3	—
Bibliography and Library Economy	628	127	1	—
Biography	1,880	578	86	2
Chemistry and Physics	811	163	18	—
Children's Books	5,014	1,187	183	2
Commerce	1,898	484	4	—
Customs, Costumes, Folklore	167	37	9	—
Domestic Science	837	217	4	—
Education	1,226	188	5	1
Engineering	1,604	365	23	—
Entertainment	627	130	27	—
Fiction	6,389	3,107	252	11
General	1,032	171	8	—
Geography and Archaeology	596	198	3	2
Geology and Meteorology	270	33	3	—
History	2,015	428	73	1
Humour	260	50	—	—
Industry	460	121	3	—
Language	700	205	8	1
Law and Public Administration	1,904	394	20	—
Literature	1,412	224	75	2
Mathematics	929	194	22	—
Medical Science	3,345	671	24	—
Military Science	277	52	9	—
Music	394	92	18	—
Natural Sciences	1,254	173	16	—
Occultism	451	137	15	—
Philosophy	578	118	75	—
Photography	189	31	3	—
Plays	358	89	55	—
Poetry	758	93	70	21
Political Science and Economics	4,451	789	109	1
Psychology	812	170	17	—
Religion and Theology	2,028	322	142	1
School Textbooks	1,881	237	5	—
Science, General	78	14	5	—
Sociology	1,118	144	23	—
Sports and Outdoor Games	919	217	8	2
Stockbreeding	354	80	1	—
Trade	454	124	2	—
Travel and Guidebooks	1,355	568	40	2
Wireless and Television	194	50	2	—
Totals	54,746	13,296	1,521	57

COPYRIGHT

The Government Department dealing with Copyright is the *Industrial Property and Copyright Dept., Department of Trade and Industry*, Patent Office, State House, 66–71 High Holborn, WC1R 4TP.

Subject to the provisions of the Copyright Act, 1956, copyright subsists automatically in every original literary, dramatic, musical and artistic work and continues to subsist until the end of the period of fifty years from the end of the calendar year in which the author died, and shall then expire. *No registration nor other formalities are required in order to obtain the protection of the Act.* Protection is conferred not only against reproduction but also against the public performance of a work without permission. Copyright may also subsist in sound recordings, cinematograph films (including video recordings) and television, sound broadcasts and cable programmes. (In 1988 a new Copyright Bill was presented to Parliament.) Libraries entitled, under a provision still in force of the Copyright Act, 1911, to receive free copies of books published in the United Kingdom are the British Library, the Bodleian Library, Oxford, University Library, Cambridge, the National Library of Wales, the National Library of Scotland and Trinity College, Dublin.

As the U.K. is a party to both the Berne Copyright Convention and the Universal Copyright Convention, a work originating in this country is automatically protected in all the other countries which are members of these Conventions.

Voluntary Registration at Stationers' Hall.—Compulsory registration at Stationers' Hall was terminated by the Copyright Act of 1911, but in 1924 the Stationers' Company established a *new* Register, in which Books and Fine Arts can be registered, to help establish ownership of copyright.

ANNUAL REFERENCE BOOKS

Advertiser's Annual.—East Grinstead House, East Grinstead, W. Sussex RH19 1XE. £49·00.

Allied Dunbar Investment Guide.—Fourth Avenue, Harlow, Essex CM19 5AA. £13·50.

Allied Dunbar Tax Guide.—Fourth Avenue, Harlow, Essex CM19 5AA. £13·50.

Annual Register of World Events.—Fourth Avenue, Harlow, Essex, CM19 5AA. £95·00.

Antique Shops of Britain, Guide to the.—5 Church Street, Woodbridge, Suffolk IP12 1DS. £9·95.

Art Sales Index.—1 Thames Street, Weybridge, Surrey KT1 8JG. £87·00.

Astronomical Almanac.—H.M.S.O., 51 Nine Elms Lane, SW8 5DR. (Aug.) £18·00.

Automobile Year.—Unit 6, Pilton Estate, Croydon, Surrey CR0 3RY. £22·95.

Baily's Hunting Directory.—1 Lower Grosvenor Place, SW1W 0EL. (Oct.) £22·00.

Banker's Almanac & Year Book.—East Grinstead House, East Grinstead, W. Sussex RH19 1XE. (Feb.) 2 v. £125·00.

Benedictine Year Book.—Ampleforth Abbey, York YO6 4EN. £1·00.

Benn's Direct Marketing Services.—P.O. Box 20, Sovereign Way, Tonbridge, Kent TN9 1RQ. £80·00.

Benn's Hardware & Do-it-Yourself Buyer's Guide.—P.O. Box 20, Sovereign Way, Tonbridge, Kent TN9 1RQ. £26·00.

Benn's Media Directory.—P.O. Box 20, Sovereign Way, Tonbridge, Kent TN9 1RQ. 2v. ea £60·00.

"Birmingham Post & Mail" Year Book & Who's Who.—Colmore Circus, Birmingham B4 6AX. (July) £13·25.

British Art & Antiques Directory.—72 Broadwick Street, W1V 2BP. £9·50.

British Clothing Industry Year Book.—Westbury House, 701–705 Warwick Road, Solihull B91 3DA. £28·00.

British Music Year Book.—241 Shaftesbury Avenue, WC2H 8EH. £10·95.

British Plastics & Rubber Directory.—Catalyst House, 159 Clapham High Street, SW4 7SS. £10·00.

Brown's Nautical Almanack.—4–10 Darnley Street, Glasgow G41 2SD. (Sept.) £24·00.

Building Societies Who's Who.—7 Swallow Place, WIR 8AB. £32·00.

Building Societies Year Book.—7 Swallow Place, WIR 8AB. £31·50.

Buses Yearbook.—Coombelands House, Addlestone, Weybridge, Surrey KT15 1HY. £7·00.

Carpet Annual. P.O. Box 20, Sovereign Way, Tonbridge, Kent TN9 1RQ. £45·00.

Catholic Directory.—18 Crosby Road North, Liverpool L22 4QF. £17·50.

Charities Digest.—501–5 Kingsland Road, E8 4AU. £8·95.

Chemical Industry Directory.—P.O. Box 20, Sovereign Way, Tonbridge, Kent TN9 1RQ. £60·00.

"Chemist & Druggist" Directory.—P.O. Box 20, Sovereign Way, Tonbridge, Kent TN9 1RQ. £55·00.

Christies' Review of the Season.—Littlegate House, St. Ebbe's Street, Oxford OX1 1SQ. (Dec.) £30·00.

Church of England Year Book.—Church House, Dean's Yard, Westminster, SW1P 3NZ. (Jan.) £13·50.

Church of Scotland Year Book.—121 George Street, Edinburgh EH2 4YN. (Apr.) £8·25.

City of London Directory & Livery Companies Guide.—Fairfax House, Causton Road, Colchester CO1 1RJ. £17·00, £15·00.

Civil Aviation Review.—Coombelands House, Addlestone, Weybridge, Surrey KT15 1HY. £7·00.

Civil Service Year Book.—H.M.S.O., 51 Nine Elms Lane, SW8 5DR. (Feb.) £14·75.

Commonwealth Universities Year Book.—36 Gordon Square, WC1H 0PF. (Sept.) £83·00.

Commonwealth Year Book.—H.M.S.O., 51 Nine Elms Lane, SW8 5DR. (May) £17.50.

Computer Users' Year Book.—32–34 Broadwick Street, W1A 2HG. £94·50.

Concrete Year Book.—11 Grosvenor Crescent, SW1X 7EE. £35·00.

Consulting Engineers Who's Who & Year Book.—178–202 Great Portland Street, W1N 6NH. £28·00.

"Containerization International" Year Book.—72 Broadwick Street, W1V 2BP. (Mar.) £102·00.

Coventry Evening Telegraph Year Book and Who's Who.—Coventry Newspapers Ltd, Corporation Street, Coventry CV1 1FP. (Nov.) £8·50.

Current Law Year Book.—11 New Fetter Lane, EC4P 4EE. £55·00.

"Daily Mail" Year Book.—Carmelite House, Fleet Street, EC4Y 0JA. (Dec.) £3·95.

Diplomatic Service List.—H.M.S.O., 51 Nine Elms Lane, SW8 5DR. (April) £16·95.

Directory of Directors.—East Grinstead House, East Grinstead, W. Sussex RH19 1XE. (Apr.) £75·00.

Directory of Official Architecture & Planning.—Fourth Avenue, Harlow, Essex CM19 5AA. £40·00.

Directory of Opportunities for Graduates.—Newpoint House, St. James's Lane, N10 3DF. 7v. each £7·95.

Dod's Parliamentary Companion.—Hurst Green, Etchingham, E. Sussex TN19 7PX. £48·00.

Education Authorities' Directory and Annual.—Derby House, Bletchingley Road, Merstham, Surrey RH1 3DN. (Jan.) £40·00.

Education Year Book.—Fourth Avenue, Harlow, Essex CM19 5AA. £43·00.

Electrical & Electronics Trades Directory.—P.O. Box 26, Station House, Nightingale Road, Hitchin, Herts SG5 1SA. (Feb.) £47·00.

Electricity Supply Handbook.—Quadrant House, The Quadrant, Sutton, Surrey SM2 5AS. (Feb.) £13·75.

"Engineer" Buyers' Guide.—30 Calderwood Street, SE18 6QH. £30·00.

Europa Year Book.—18 Bedford Square, WC1B 3JN. 2 v. £155·00.

European Glass Directory & Buyer's Guide.—2 Queensway, Redhill, Surrey RH1 1QS. £35·00.

Fairplay World Shipping Year Book.—P.O. Box 96, Coulsdon, Surrey CR3 2TE. £25·00.

Farm and Garden Equipment Data Book.—63 Ulcombe Gardens, Canterbury, Kent CT2 7QZ. £10·95.

Fire Protection Directory.—Stanley House, 9 West Street, Epsom, Surrey KT18 7RL. (Nov.) £14·50.

"Flight International" Directory of British Aviation.—Quadrant House, The Quadrant, Sutton, Surrey SM2 5AS. £30·00.

Food Industry Directory.—48 Poland St., WIV 4PP. £29·00.

Frozen & Chilled Foods Year Book.—2 Queensway, Redhill, Surrey RH1 1QS. £29·00.

Furnishing Trade, Directory to the.—P.O. Box 20, Sovereign Way, Tonbridge, Kent TN9 1RQ. £60·00.

Gas Directory.—P.O. Box 20, Sovereign Way, Tonbridge, Kent TN9 1RQ. (Jan.) £45·00.

Gibbons' Stamps of the World Catalogue.—5 Parkside, Christchurch Road, Ringwood, Hants BH24 3SH.(Oct.) 2v. each £17·50.

Good Food Guide.—P.O. Box 6, Mill Road, Dunton Green, Sevenoaks, Kent TN13 2XX. £10·95.

Good Hotel Guide.—P.O. Box 6, Mill Road, Dunton Green, Sevenoaks, Kent TN13 2XX. £10·95.

Government & Municipal Contractors Register.—55 High Street, Epsom, Surrey KT19 8DW. (Jan.) £30·00.

Guinness Book of Records.—33 London Road, Enfield EN2 6DJ. (Oct.) £9·95.

Historic Houses, Castles and Gardens in Great Britain and Ireland.—East Grinstead House, East Grinstead, W. Sussex RH19 1XA. (Jan.) £3·50.

Hollis Press and P.R. Annual.—Contact House, Lower Hampton Road, Sunbury-on-Thames, TW16 5HG. (Oct.) £35·50.

Hospitals & Health Services Yearbook & Directory of Hospital Suppliers.—75 Portland Place, W1N 4AN. £51·60.

Hotel, Restaurant & Catering Supplies.—55 High Street, Epsom, Surrey KT19 8DW. £30·00.

Hutchins' Priced Schedules.—33 Station Road, Bexhill-on-Sea. £26·00.

Independent Schools Year Book.—35 Bedford Row, WC1R 4JH. 2v. £13·50, £8·95.

Insurance Directory & Yearbook.—The Butts, Half Acre, Brentford TW8 8BN. £55·00.

International Yearbook & Statesman's Who's Who.—East Grinstead House, East Grinstead, W. Sussex RH19 1XE. (Apr.) £90·00.

Jane's All The World's Aircraft.—Sentinel House, 163 Brighton Road, Coulsdon, Surrey CR3 2NX. (Oct.) £85·00.

Jane's Armour & Artillery.—Sentinel House, 163 Brighton Road, Coulsdon, Surrey CR3 2NX. (Nov.) £80·00.

Jane's Containerisation Direct.—Sentinel House, 163 Brighton Road, Coulsdon, Surrey CR3 2NX. (Nov.) £60·00.

Jane's Fighting Ships.—Sentinel House, 163 Brighton Road, Coulsdon, Surrey CR3 2NX. £85·00.

Jane's High Speed Marine Craft & Air Cushion Vehicles.—Sentinel House, 163 Brighton Road, Coulsdon, Surrey CR3 2NX. £85·00.

Jane's Infantry Weapons.—Sentinel House, 163 Brighton Road, Coulsdon, Surrey CR3 2NX. (Aug.) £85·00.

Jane's Weapon Systems.—Sentinel House, 163 Brighton Road, Coulsdon, Surrey CR3 2NX. £95·00.

Jane's World Railways.—Sentinel House, 163 Brighton Road, Coulsdon, Surrey CR3 2NX. £85·00.

Jewish Year Book.—25 Furnival Street, EC4A 1JT. (Jan.) £10·95.

Kelly's Business Directory.—East Grinstead House, East Grinstead, W. Sussex RH19 1XB. £90·00.

Kelly's Post Office London Business Directory.—East Grinstead House, East Grinstead, W. Sussex RH19 1XB. 2v, £95·00.

Kelly's U.K. Exports.—East Grinstead House, East Grinstead, W. Sussex RH19 1XB. £50·00.

Kempe's Engineers Year Book.—30 Calderwood Street, SE18 6QH. £65·00.

Kemp's International Film & T.V. Year Book.—Westbury House, 701–705 Warwick Road, Solihull B91 3DA. (May) £35·00.

Kemp's International Music & Recording Industry Year Book.—Westbury House, 701–705 Warwick Road, Solihull B91 3DA. £19·00.

Kemp's Property Industry Year Book.—Westbury House, 701–705 Warwick Road, Solihull B91 3DA. (Feb.) £17·50.

Kime's International Law Directory.—P.O. Box 67, Carlisle CA4 9DE. (June) £22·00.

Laxton's National Building Price Book.—East Grinstead House, East Grinstead, W. Sussex RH19 1XE. £44·00.

Library Association Yearbook.—7 Ridgmount Street, WC1E 7AE. (May) £22·50.

Lloyd's List of Shipowners.—71 Fenchurch Street, EC3M 4BS. (Sept.) £60·00.

Lloyd's Maritime Directory.—Sheepen Place, Colchester CO3 3LP. (Jan.) £90·00.

Lloyd's Nautical Year Book.—Sheepen Place, Colchester CO3 3LP. (Sept.) £18·00.

Lloyd's Register of Ships.—71 Fenchurch Street, EC3M 4BS. (July). £265·00.

London Chamber of Commerce and Industry Directory.—3rd Floor, Albany House, Hurst Street, Birmingham B5 4BD. (Sept.) £45·00.

Lyle's Official Antiques Review, Glenmayne, Galashiels TD1 3NR. £14·95.

Lyle's Official Arts Review, Glenmayne, Galashiels TD1 3NR. £14·95.

Macmillan & Silk Cut Nautical Almanack.—Little Essex Street, WC2R 3LF. £14·95.

Magistrates' Court Guide.—Borough Green, Sevenoaks, Kent TN15 8PH. £15·95.

Medical Annual.—P.O. Box 63, Westbury House, Bury Street, Guildford, Surrey GU2 5BH. (July). £25·00.

Medical Directory.—Fourth Avenue, Harlow, Essex CM19 5AA. (Apr.) 2v, £95·00.

Medical Register.—44 Hallam Street, W1N 6AE. (Mar.) £57·00.

Middle East & North Africa.—18 Bedford Square, WC1B 3JN. (Oct.) £70·00.

Military Aviation Review.—Coombelands House, Addlestone, Weybridge, Surrey KT15 1HY. £7·00.

Miller's Antiques Price Guide.—Sissinghurst Court, Sissinghurst, Kent TN17 2JA. £14·95.

"Mining" Annual Review.—P.O. Box 10, Edenbridge, Kent TN8 5NE. £35·00.

Mining International Year Book.—Fourth Avenue, Harlow, Essex CM19 5AA. (June) £75·00.

Motor Industry of Great Britain World Automotive Statistics.—Forbes House, Halkin Street, SW1X 7DS. (Oct.) £45·00.

Municipal Yearbook & Public Services Directory, 178 Great Portland Street, W1N 6NH. (Dec.) £65·00.

Museums and Galleries in Great Britain and Ireland.—East Grinstead House, East Grinstead, W. Sussex RH19 1XA. (Nov.) £2·95.

Nautical Almanac.—H.M.S.O., 51 Nine Elms Lane, SW8 5DR. (Oct.) £10·95.

Offshore Oil & Gas Year Book.—Tolley House, 17 Scarbrook Road, Croydon CR0 1SQ. £50·00.

Old Moore's Almanac.—Yeovil Road, Slough, Bucks. SL1 4JH. (July) £0·65.

Owen's Africa Business Directory.—18 Farndon Road, Oxford OX6 2RT. £60·00.

Owen's Arabian Year Book.—18 Farndon Road, Oxford OX6 2RT. £80·00.

Packaging Industry Review Directory.—P.O. Box 20, Sovereign Way, Tonbridge, Kent TN9 1RQ. £40·00.

Paper Trade Directory, Phillips'.—P.O. Box 20, Sovereign Way, Tonbridge, Kent TN9 1RQ. £65·00.

Pears Cyclopedia.—27 Wright's Lane, W8 5TZ. £10·95.

Personnel Yearbook.—120 Pentonville Road, N1 9JN. £25·00.

Photography Year Book.—45 The Broadway, Tolworth, Surbiton, Surrey KT6 7DW. £16·95.

Polymers, Paint & Colour Year Book.—2 Queensway, Redhill, Surrey RH1 1QS. £33·50.

Ports of the World.—Sheepen Place, Colchester, Essex CO3 3LP. £75·00.

Printers' Year Book.—11 Bedford Row, WC1R 4DX. £40·00.

Printing Trades Directory.—P. O. Box 20, Sovereign Way, Tonbridge, Kent TN9 1RQ. £60·00.

Publishing, Directory of.—Artillery House, Artillery Row, SW1P 1RT. (Oct.) £26·00.

R.A.C. Continental Hotel Guide.—P.O. Box 100, RAC House, Lansdowne Rd., Croydon CR9 2JA. (Jan.) £5·25.

R.A.C. Hotel & Touring Guide.—P.O. Box 100, RAC House, Lansdowne Rd., Croydon CR9 2JA. (Apr.) £4·95.

R.U.S.I. & Brassey's Defence Year Book.—Headington Hill Hall, Oxford OX3 0BW. £34·00, £18·50.

Railway Directory & Year Book.—Quadrant House, The Quadrant, Sutton, Surrey SM2 5AS. (Dec.) £34·00.

"Railway World" Year Book.—Coombelands House, Addlestone, Weybridge, Surrey KT15 1HY. £7·00.

Reed's Nautical Almanac & Tide Tables.—80 Coombe Road, New Malden, Sutton KT3 4QS. (Oct.) £14·95.

RIBA Directory of Practices.—Royal Institute of British Architects, 39 Moreland Street, EC1V 8BB. (Oct.) £35·00.

Royal Society Year Book.—6 Carlton House Terrace, SW1Y 5AG. (Feb.) £11·00.

Ruff's Guide to the Turf & "Sporting Life" Annual.—3rd Floor, Greater London House, Hampstead Road, NW1 7RQ. (Dec.) £50·00.

Salvation Army Year Book.—117–121 Judd Street, WC1H 9NN. (Apr.) £6 95, £3 50.

Scottish Current Law Year Book.—2 St. Giles Street, Edinburgh EH1 1PU. £87·00.

Scottish Law Directory.—34–36 North Frederick Street, Glasgow G1 2BT. £23·00.

"Screen International" Film & Television Year Book.—6 Great Chapel Street, W.1. £31·00.

Screen World.—Brookmount House, 62–65 Chandos Place, WC1N 4NW. £16·95.

Sell's Aviation Europe.—55 High Street, Epsom, Surrey KT19 8DW. £35·00.

Sell's British Exporters.—55 High Street, Epsom, Surrey KT19 8DW. £30·00.

Sell's Building Index.—55 High Street, Epsom, Surrey KT 19 8DW. £30·00.

Sell's Directory of Products and Services.—55 High Street, Epsom, Surrey KT19 8DW. (July) £40·00.

Sell's Health Service Buyers Guide.—55 High Street, Epsom, Surrey, KT19 8DW. £30·00.

Sheet Metal Industries Year Book.—2 Queensway, Redhill, Surrey RH1 1QS. £35·00.

Shipowners, Shipbuilders & Marine Engineers, Directory of.—Quadrant House, The Quadrant, Sutton, Surrey SM2 5AS. £45·00.

Solicitors & Barristers Directory.—P.O. Box 55, Oyez House, 27 Crimscott Street, SE1 5TS. £30·00.

Specification.—9–13 Queen Anne's Gate, SW1H 9BY. (May) 6v. £68·00.

Spon's Architects' & Builders' Price Book.—11 New Fetter Lane, EC4P 4EE. £37·50.

Spon's Mechanical & Electrical Services Prices Book.—11 New Fetter Lane, EC4P 4EE. £37·50.

Statesman's Yearbook.—4 Little Essex Street, WC2R 3LF. (Aug.) £28·50.

Stock Exchange Official Year Book.—4 Little Essex Street, WC2R 3LF. £115·00.

Stone's Justices' Manual.—Borough Green, Sevenoaks, Kent TN15 8PH. 3v. (May) £102·00.

Stores, Shops, Hypermarkets Retail Directory.—48 Poland Street, W1V 4PP. £78·00.

T.V. & Radio: Guide to Independent Television.—247 Tottenham Court Road, W1P 0AU. £5·90.

Tanker Register.—12 Camomile Street, EC3A 7BP. (May) £110·00.

"Timber Trades Journal" Telephone Address Book.—Sovereign Way, Tonbridge, Kent TN9 1RQ. £29·00.

Travel Trade Directory.—30 Calderwood Street, SE18 6QH. (July) £30·00.

U.K. Kompass Register of British Industry & Commerce.—East Grinstead House, East Grinstead, W. Sussex RH19 1XD. v. 1–3, £165·00, v. 4, £100·00.

Unit Trust Year Book.—7th Floor, 50–64 Broadway, SW1H 0DB. (Mar.) £25·00.

United Reformed Church Year Book.—86 Tavistock Place, WC1H 9RT. (Sept.) £7·00.

Veterinary Annual.—P.O. Box 63, Westbury House, Bury Street, Guildford GU2 5BH. £30·00.

Water Services Year Book.—2 Queensway, Redhill, Surrey RH1 1QS. (Oct.) £30·00.

Whitaker's Almanack.—12 Dyott Street, WC1A 1DF. (Nov.) £27·75, £16·50, £8·50.

Whitaker's Books in Print.—12 Dyott Street, WC1A 1DF. (Sept.) £115·00.

Whitaker's Publishers in the United Kingdom and their Addresses.—12 Dyott Street, WC1A 1DF. (Mar.) £4·25.

Who Owns Whom?—26–32 Clifton Street, EC2P 2LY. 2v. £189·00.

Who's Who.—35 Bedford Row, WC1R 4JH. £58·00.

Who's Who, International.—18 Bedford Square, WC1R 4JH. (Sept.) £75·00.

Willing's Press Guide.—East Grinstead House, East Grinstead, W. Sussex RH19 1XE. (Feb.) £49·00.

Wisden Cricketers' Almanack.—13–14 Eldon Way, Lineside Estate, Littlehampton BN17 7HE. £16·50; £14·50.

World Advertising Review: Modern Publicity.—Artillery House, Artillery Row, SW1P 1RT. £40·00.

World Hotel Directory.—Fourth Avenue, Harlow, Essex CM19 5AA. £49·00.

World Insurance Year Book.—Fourth Avenue, Harlow, Essex CM19 5AA. £80.00.

World of Learning.—18 Bedford Square, WC1B 3JN. (Jan.) 2v. £95·00.

Writers' & Artists' Year Book.—35 Bedford Row, WC1R 4JH. (Jan.) £5·95.

BOOK PRODUCTION AND BOOK EXPORTS

These figures for book production and exports are issued by the Department of Trade and Industry. The totals for the years 1972 to 1987 are shown below:

Year	Total value of Books produced in U.K. £ million	Total value of Books exported from U.K. £ million	Year	Total value of Books produced in U.K. £ million	Total value of Books exported from U.K. £ million
1972	205·3	81·2	1980	666·9	213·7
1973	230·1	95·9	1981	738·0	234·5
1974	281·5	119·4	1982	759·1	232·8
1975	342·4	138·6	1983	831·9	261·1
1976	408·3	175·8	1984	937·2	307·3
1977	467·0	203·9	1985	1044·0	340·9
1978	521·4	211·8	1986	1068·3	315·4
1979	580·4	215·3	1987 (provisional)	1194·0	343·1

THE PRESS COUNCIL
1 Salisbury Square, EC4Y 8AE
[01–353 1248]

In April, 1947, a Royal Commission was appointed to enquire into the control, management and ownership, etc., of the Press and news agencies and to make recommendations thereon. The Commission, in its report of June, 1949, recommended *inter alia* that a voluntary Press Council be formed.

A constitution ultimately set up provided for the establishment of such a council on July 1, 1953. This constitution was materially amended in 1963 by the introduction of an independent chairman and up to 20 per cent. lay membership. In 1973, the Council was increased to 30 (excluding the Chairman) of whom one-third were lay members. Following a recommendation of the third Royal Commission on the Press made in 1977, the size of the Council was increased in 1978 to 36 (excluding the Chairman) of which half are press members and half non-press members. The objects of the Council are (1) to preserve the established freedom of the British Press; (2) to maintain the character of the British Press in accordance with the highest professional and commercial standards; (3) to consider complaints about the conduct of the Press or the conduct of persons and organizations towards the Press; to deal with these complaints in whatever manner might seem practical and appropriate and record resultant action; (4) to keep under review developments likely to restrict the supply of information of public interest and importance; (5) to report publicly on developments that may tend towards greater concentration or monopoly in the Press (including changes in ownership, control and growth of Press undertakings) and to publish statistical information relating thereto; (6) to make representations on appropriate occasions to the Government, organs of the United Nations and Press organizations abroad; and (7) to publish periodical reports recording the Council's work and to review, from time to time, developments in the Press and the factors affecting them.

The constitution of the Council provides for 18 Press members who are editorial and managerial nominees of The Newspaper Publishers Association Ltd. (3), The Newspaper Society (3), The Periodical Publishers Association Ltd. (2), The Scottish Daily Newspaper Society (1), Scottish Newspaper Proprietors' Association (1), The Guild of British Newspaper Editors (2), The National Union of Journalists (4), The Institute of Journalists (2) plus 18 public members appointed by the Press Council Appointments Commission. In addition each constituent body nominates one official as a non-voting member.

Chairman, L. Blom-Cooper, Q.C.
Director, K. Morgan, O.B.E.

SYMBOLS FOR CORRECTING PROOFS

Supplied by WILLIAM CLOWES LTD, Beccles, Suffolk, Printers of "WHITAKER'S ALMANACK"

Letter(s) or word(s) requiring alteration should be struck through IN INK in the text, and the substitution should be written in the nearest margin followed by / (the symbol used to denote that the marginal mark is concluded). Insertions should be indicated by / or ∧ at the conclusion of the marginal mark *and* at the desired place in the text.

Alteration required	Mark in margin	Mark in text	Alteration required	Mark in margin	Mark in text
Delete (take out)	ϑ or ϑ/	/ or ——— Vertical stroke to delete one or two letters; horizontal line to delete more	Take letter(s) or word(s) from beginning of one line to end of preceding line	(back) or (take back)	⌐
Delete and close up	ϑ or ϑ/	⊥ Strike out letter(s) not required and add "close up" mark above and below	Begin a new paragraph	n.p.	⌐ before first word of new paragraph
Close up: delete space between letters	◡	◡ linking letters or words	No new para. here or run on with previous matter with later matter	run on	⌐ between paras. or other matter
Use ligature (fi, fl, ffl, etc.) or diphthong (æ, œ)	◡ *enclosing ligature or diphthong required*	◡ enclosing letters to be altered	Spell out in full the abbreviation, contraction, or figure	spell out	Encircle words, etc., or figures concerned
Insert space between letters or words	#∧	∧	Insert omitted portion of copy	out-see copy	∧ Attach the relevant copy to the proof, indicating omitted portion
Leave as printed (i.e. a cancellation of previous marking)	*stet*	.... under letter(s) or word(s) crossed out but to be retained	Inserted or substituted letter(s), figure(s), or sign(s) under which this is placed to be superscript (i.e. high alignment)[1]	⌐ *(see footnote)*	∧ for insertions For substitutions encircle letter(s). figure(s). or sign(s) to be altered
Invert type (of letter(s) upside down)	☺	Encircle letter(s) to be altered	Inserted or substituted letter(s), figure(s), or sign(s) over which this is placed to be subscript (low alignment)[2]	⌐ *(see footnote)*	∧ for insertions For substitutions encircle letter(s), figure(s), etc., to be altered
"Battered" letter(s) to be replaced by similar but undamaged characters	✕	Encircle letter(s) or word(s) to be replaced and write the correct letter(s) in the margin	Change to lower case	l.c.	Encircle letter(s) to be altered
Push down space or "high" letter(s) or word(s)	⊥	Encircle space, letter(s), or word(s) affected	Replace "wrong fount" by letter(s) of correct fount	w.f.	Encircle letter(s) or word(s) to be altered
Transpose	tr. or trs.	⌐⌐ between letters or words, numbered when necessary	Change to capital letters	caps.	≡ under letter(s) or word(s) to be altered
Take letter(s) or word(s) from end of one line to beginning of next line	take over or over	⌐	Change to small capitals	s.c.	= under letter(s) or word(s) to be altered

⌐ indicates a superior (superscript) figure one   ⌐[2] indicates an inferior (subscript) figure two

Alteration required	Mark in margin	Mark in text	Alteration required	Mark in margin	Mark in text
Use capital letters for initial letter(s) (as desired) and small capitals for rest of word(s)	*caps & s.c.*	under initial letter(s) and under the remainder of the word(s)	Move lines to the left		at right side of group of lines to be moved (indicating approx. position)
Change to bold type	*bold*	Draw wavy line under letter(s) or word(s) to be altered	Move portion of matter so that it is positioned as indicated	[ ]	at limits of required position
Change to roman type	*rom.*	Encircle letter(s) or word(s) to be altered	Raise lines	*raise*	over lines to be raised
Change to italic type	*italic*	Draw this straight line under letter(s) or word(s) to be altered	Lower lines	*lower*	under lines to be lowered
Letter(s) or word(s) to be underlined	*underline*	under letter(s), word(s), etc., to be underlined	Correct the vertical alignment	‖	‖
			Straighten lines		through lines to be straightened
Equalize space between words	*eq.* #	between words	Insert parentheses (round-shaped brackets)	⟨/⟩ *or* ⟨/⟩/	‖
Reduce space	*less* #	between words	Insert [square] brackets	[/] *or* [/]/	‖
Space to be inserted between lines or paragraphs	#>	*Amount of space should be indicated*	Insert hyphen	/-/	ʌ
To be placed in centre of line, etc.	*centre*	Position to be indicated by	Insert en (= half-em) rule (*see above*)	*en*/	ʌ
Indent one en (approx. space occupied by n of type in use)	*en*	indicating approximate position	Insert one-em rule (*see above*)	*em*/	ʌ
Indent one em (approx. space occupied by M of type in use)	*em*	Ditto	Insert two-em rule (*see above*)	2-*em*/	ʌ
Indent two ems (approx. space occupied by MM of type in use)		Ditto	Insert apostrophe	ʼ	ʌ
Move to the left		Ditto	Insert single quotation marks	ʻ ʼ	ʌ ʌ
Move to the right		Ditto	Insert double quotation marks	ʻʻ ʼʼ	ʌ ʌ
Move lines to the right		at left side of group of lines to be moved (indicating approx. position)	Insert ellipsis	... /	ʌ
			Insert leader (*visual guide to alignment in contents pages, etc.*)	⋯ ⋰ ⋅	(*three, two, or one dot*)
			Insert oblique stroke	/	ʌ

Punctuation	ʌ/	,/	;ʌ	;/	⊙	⊙	?ʌ	?/	!ʌ	!/	

PRINCIPAL LONDON CLUBS

ALPINE (1857), 74 South Audley Street, W1Y 5FF.—*Hon. Sec.*, S. W. Town.

AMERICAN (1919), 95 Piccadilly, W1V 0BS.—*Sec.*, A. M. Cook.

AMERICAN WOMEN'S (1899), 95 Piccadilly, W1V 0BS.—*Sec.*, Ms. M. Dougan.

ANGLO-BELGIAN (1955), 60 Knightsbridge, SW1X 7LF.—*Hon. Sec.*, Baron de Gerlache de Gomery, L.V.O.

ARMY AND NAVY (1837), 36–39 Pall Mall, SW1Y 5JN.—*Sec.*, Col. D. O. O'Reilly.

ARTS (1863), 40 Dover Street, W1X 3RB.—*Sec.*, C. Miers.

ARTS THEATRE (1927), 7 Great Newport Street, W.C.2.—*Sec.*, Miss C. Dowling.

THE ATHENAEUM (1824), 107 Pall Mall, SW1Y 5ER.—*Sec.*, R. R. T. Smith.

AUTHOR'S (1892), 40 Dover Street, W1X 3RB.—*Sec.*, Mrs. H. Ridgway.

BEEFSTEAK (1876), 9 Irving Street, WC2H 7AT.—*Sec.*, E. Pool, M.C.

BOODLE'S (1762), 28 St. James's Street, S.W.1.—*Sec.*, R. J. Edmonds.

BROOKS'S (1764), St. James's Street, SW1A 1LN.—*Sec.*, M. A. Roberts.

BUCK'S (1919), 18 Clifford Street, New Bond Street, W1X 1RG.—*Sec.*, R. C. Eggleshaw.

CALEDONIAN (1891), 9 Halkin Street, SW1X 7DR.—*Sec.*, P. J. Varney.

CANNING (1910), 42 Half Moon Street, W1Y 8DS.—*Sec.*, T. M. Harrington.

CARLTON (1832), 69 St. James's Street, SW1A 1PJ.—*Sec.*, R. N. Linsley.

CAVALRY AND GUARDS (1893), 127 Piccadilly, W1V 0PX.—*Sec.*, L. D. de Pinna.

CHALLONER (1949), 59/61 Pont Street, SW1 0BG—*Gen. Manager*, G. W. Jago.

CHELSEA ARTS (1891), 143 Old Church Street, SW3 6EB.—*Sec.*, D. Winterbottom.

CITY LIVERY (1914), Sion College, Victoria Embankment, EC4Y 0DN.—*Hon. Sec.*, B. L. Morgan, C.B.E.

CITY OF LONDON (1832), 19 Old Broad Street, EC2N 1DS.—*Sec.*, G. S. Chisholm.

CITY UNIVERSITY (1895), 50 Cornhill, EC3V 3PD.—*Sec.*, Miss R. C. Graham.

EAST INDIA (1849), 16 St. James's Square, SW1Y 4LH.—*Sec.*, J. G. F. Stoy.

FARMERS (1842), 3 Whitehall Court, SW1A 2EL.—*Sec.*, Lt. Col. J. L. S. Andrews, O.B.E.

FLYFISHERS' (1884), 24a Old Burlington Street, W1X 1RG.—*Sec.*, Cdr. N. T. Fuller, R.N. (retd.).

GARRICK (1831), 15 Garrick Street, WC2E 9AY.—*Sec.*, M. J. Harvey.

GREEN ROOM (1877), 9 Adam Street, WC2N 6AA.—*Hon. Sec.*, J. Booth.

GRESHAM (1843), 15 Abchurch Lane, EC4N 7BB.—*Sec.*, Mrs. J. Downing.

GROUCHO (1985), 45 Dean Street, W1V 5AP.—*Gen. Manager*, L. Carson.

HURLINGHAM (1869), Ranelagh Gardens, SW6 3PR.—*Chief Exec.*, P. H. Covell.

KEMPTON PARK (1878), Kempton Park Racecourse, Sunbury-on-Thames, Middx., TW16 5AQ.—*Sec.*, Miss S. Bainbridge.

KENNEL (1873), 1 Clarges Street, W1Y 8AB.—*Sec.*, Maj. Gen. M. H. Sinnatt, O.D.

LANSDOWNE (1934), 9 Fitzmaurice Place, Berkeley Square, W1X 6JD.—*Sec.*, Lt. Cdr. T. P. Havers.

LONDON ROWING (1856), Embankment, Putney, SW15 1LB.—*Hon. Sec.*, N. A. Smith.

LONDON THAMES FENCING (1848), 83 Perham Road, W14 9SY.—*Hon. Sec.*, G. Morrison.

MARYLEBONE CRICKET CLUB (M.C.C.) (1787), Lord's Cricket Ground, NW8 8QN.—*Sec.*, Lt.-Col. J. R. Stephenson, O.B.E.

MINING (1910), 3 London Wall Buildings, E.C.2.—*Sec.*, Miss P. Warner.

NATIONAL (1845), c/o Carlton Club (q.v.).—*Sec.*, I. E. Nash.

NATIONAL LIBERAL (1882), Whitehall Place, SW1A 2HE.—*Sec.*, G. Snell.

NAVAL (1946), 38 Hill Street, W1X 8DP.—*Gen. Sec.*, Cdr. C. R. Parkes, R.D., R.N.R.

NAVAL AND MILITARY (1862), 94 Piccadilly, W1V 0BP.—*Gen. Manager*, A. Hickey.

ORIENTAL (1824), Stratford House, Stratford Place, W1N 0ES.—*Sec.*, S. C. Doble.

PORTLAND (1816), 42 Half Moon Street, W1Y 7RD.—*Sec.*, R. B. Little.

PRATT'S (1841), 14 Park Place, SW1A 1LP.—*Sec.*, Capt. P. W. E. Parry, M.B.E.

QUEEN'S (1886), Palliser Road, W14 9EQ.—*Sec.*, J. A. S. Edwardes.

RAILWAY (1899), Keen House, 4 Calshot Street, N1 9DA.—*Hon. Sec.*, N. C. Farebrother.

REFORM (1836), 104–105 Pall Mall, SW1Y 5EW.—*Sec.*, R. A. M. Forrest.

ROEHAMPTON (1901), Roehampton Lane, SW15 5LR.—*Sec.*, R. W. Varley.

ROYAL AIR FORCE (1918), 128 Piccadilly, W1V 0PY.—*Sec.*, Sqn. Ldr. J. Swaffield.

ROYAL AUTOMOBILE (1897), 89–91 Pall Mall, S.W.1.—*Sec.*, J. N. Cranfield.

ROYAL COMMONWEALTH SOCIETY (1868), 18 Northumberland Avenue, WC2N 5BJ.—*Sec. Gen.*, Sir Michael Scott, K.C.V.O., C.M.G.

ROYAL OCEAN RACING (1925), 20 St. James's Place, SW1A 1NN.—*Sec.*, E. A. Green.

ROYAL OVER-SEAS LEAGUE (1910), Over-Seas House, Park Place, St. James's Street, SW1A 1LR.—*Gen. Manager*, R. F. Newell.

ROYAL THAMES YACHT (1775), 60 Knightsbridge, SW1X 7LF.—*Sec.*, Capt. A. R. Ward, C.B.E., R.N.

ST. STEPHEN's CONSTITUTIONAL (1870), 34 Queen Anne's Gate, SW1H 9AB.—*Sec.*, L. D. Mawby.

SAVAGE (1857), 9 Fitzmaurice Place, W1X 5DE.—*Hon. Sec.*, D. Coomber, O.B.E.

SAVILE (1868), 69 Brook Street, W1Y 2ER.—*Sec.*, P. Aldersley.

SKI CLUB OF GREAT BRITAIN (1903), 118 Eaton Square, SW1W 9AF.—*Sec.*, Air Vice-Marshal J. M. Jones, C.B. (retd).

THAMES ROWING (1860), Embankment, Putney, SW15 1LB.—*Hon. Sec.*, F. S. Beardmore.

TRAVELLERS' (1819), 106 Pall Mall, SW1Y 5EP.—*Sec.*, M. S. Allcock.

TURF (1868), 5 Carlton House Terrace, SW1Y 5AQ.—*Sec.*, Col. J. G. B. Rigby, O.B.E.

UNITED NURSING SERVICES (1921), 40 South Street, W.1.—*Sec.*, W. Oakes.

UNITED OXFORD AND CAMBRIDGE UNIVERSITY (1972), 71 Pall Mall, SW1Y 5HD.—*Gen. Sec.*, D. McDougall.

UNIVERSITY WOMEN'S (1886), 2 Audley Square, W1Y 6DB.—*Sec.*, Mrs. P. J. Gray.

V.A.D. (1920), 44 Great Cumberland Place, W1H 8BS.—*Sec.*, G. Maylett.

VICTORIA (1863), 1 North Court, Great Peter Street, SW1P 3LL.—*Sec.*, Ms. H. David.

VICTORY SERVICES (1907), 63–79 Seymour Street, W2 2HL.—*Gen. Manager*, Capt. G. F. Taylor.

WHITE'S (1693), 37–38 St. James's Street, SW1A 1JG.—*Sec.*, W. H. West.

WIG AND PEN (1908), 229–230 Strand, WC2R 1BA.—*Sec.*, J. Reynolds.

PRINCIPAL CLUBS OUTSIDE LONDON

Aldershot.—ROYAL ALDERSHOT OFFICERS CLUB (1856), Farnborough Road, Aldershot, Hants.—*Sec.*, Lt. Col. A. F. J. Channon, M.B.E.

Bath.—BATH AND COUNTY CLUB (1865), Queens Parade, Bath, BA1 2NJ.—*Sec.*, Mrs. G. M. Jones.

Birmingham.—BIRMINGHAM CLUB (1872), Winston Churchill House, 8 Ethel Street, Birmingham B2 4BG.—*Hon. Sec.*, T. R. Pepper.

ST. PAUL'S CLUB (1859), 34 St. Paul's Square, Birmingham B3 1QZ.—*Hon. Sec.*, J. S. Scott, T.D.

Bishop Auckland.—THE CLUB (1868), 1 Victoria Avenue, Bishop Auckland, Co. Durham DL14 7JH.—*Hon. Sec.*, L. Cooke.

Bristol.—BEAUFORT CLUB (1885), Marsh Street, Bristol BS1 4BG.—*Sec.*, M. Lansdell.

CLIFTON CLUB (1882), 22 The Mall, Clifton, Bristol BS8 4DS.—*Hon. Sec.*, H. Walder.

Cambridge.—AMATEUR DRAMATIC CLUB (1855), A.D.C. Theatre, Park Street, Cambridge.—*Hon. Sec.*, B. Ball.

HAWKS CLUB (1874), Jesus Lane, Cambridge.—*Hon. Sec.*, J. D. Barton.

THE UNION (1815), Bridge Street, Cambridge CB2 1UB.—*Chief Clerk*, B. Thoday.

Canterbury.—KENT AND CANTERBURY CLUB (1868), 17 Old Dover Road, Canterbury CT1 3JB.—*Sec.*, F. T. Bedingham.

Cardiff.—CARDIFF AND COUNTY CLUB (1866), Westgate Street, Cardiff CF1 1DA.—*Hon. Sec.*, A. G. Robertson.

Cheltenham.—NEW CLUB (1874), Montpellier Parade, Cheltenham GL5O 1UD.—*Hon. Sec.*, J. A. Warhurst, O.B.E.

Chester.—CITY CLUB (1807), St. Peter's Churchyard, Chester CH1 2AG.—*Sec.*, C. Hodkinson.

GROSVENOR CLUB (1866), Vicars Lane, Chester CH1 1QX.—*Hon. Sec.*, Maj. U. C. E. Farr.

Chichester.—WEST SUSSEX COUNTY CLUB (1872), 5 Stirling Road, Chichester, W. Sussex.—*Sec.*, J. S. Winny.

Colchester.—THE CLUB (1874), 3–5 Culver Street West, Colchester, Essex.—*Sec.*, N. Duncan.

Devizes.—DEVIZES AND DISTRICT CLUB (1932), 27 St. John Street, Devizes, Wilts. SN10 1BN.—*Sec.*, D. J. J. Cox.

Durham.—COUNTY CLUB (1890), 52 Old Elvet, Durham.—*Sec.*, Mrs. C. Arnot.

Eastbourne.—DEVONSHIRE CLUB (1872), Hartington Place, Eastbourne, Sussex BN21 3RN.—*Hon. Sec.*, D. G. Matthews.

Exeter.—EXETER AND COUNTY CLUB (1871), 5 Cathedral Close, Exeter, Devon EX1 1EZ.—*Sec.*, F. W. Taylor.

Guildford.—COUNTY CLUB, 158 High Street, Guildford GU1 3HF.—*Hon. Sec.*, R. W. D. Hemingway.

Harrogate.—THE CLUB (1857), 36 Victoria Avenue, Harrogate, N. Yorks.—*Hon. Sec.*, C. L. Leslie.

Henley-on-Thames.—LEANDER CLUB (1818), Henley-on-Thames, Oxon. RG9 2LP.—*Hon. Sec.*, J. D. Randall.

PHYLLIS COURT CLUB (1906), Marlow Road, Henley, Oxon. RG9 2HT.—*Sec.*, R. I. Bulloch.

Hove.—HOVE CLUB (1882), 28 Fourth Avenue, Hove, Sussex BN3 2PJ.—*Sec.*, Sqn. Ldr. G. A. Inverarity, D.F.C.

Jersey.—VICTORIA CLUB (1853), Beresford Street, St. Helier, Jersey.—*Sec.*, Gp. Capt. J. W. E. Holmes, D.F.C., A.F.C.

Leamington.—TENNIS COURT CLUB (1846), 50 Bedford Street, Leamington, Warwicks. CV32 5DT.—*Hon. Sec.*, O. D. R. Dixon.

Leeds.—LEEDS CLUB (1850), 3 Albion Place, Leeds LS1 6JL.—*Administrator*, Mrs. D. Kavanagh.

Leicester.—LEICESTERSHIRE CLUB (1873), 9 Welford Place, Leicester LE1 6ZH.—*Manager*, J. A. Evans.

Liverpool.—THE ATHENAEUM (1797), Church Alley, Liverpool L1 3DD.—*Hon. Sec.*, D. Gee, T.D.

Manchester.—ST. JAMES'S CLUB, St. James's House, Charlotte Street, Manchester M1 4DZ.—*Hon. Sec.*, C. A. Hadfield.

Newcastle upon Tyne.—NORTHERN CONSTITUTIONAL CLUB (1882), 37 Pilgrim Street, Newcastle upon Tyne NE1 6QE.—*Hon. Sec.*, J. L. Browne.

Northampton.—NORTHAMPTON AND COUNTY CLUB (1873), George Row, Northampton NN1 1DF.—*Sec.*, Maj. G. D. Denholm, B.E.M.

Norwich.—NORFOLK CLUB (1770), 17 Upper King Street, Norwich NR3 1RB.—*Sec.*, A. J. M. Williamson.

Nottingham.—NOTTINGHAM AND NOTTS. UNITED SERVICES CLUB (1920), Newdigate House, Castle Gate, Nottingham NG1 6AF.—*Hon. Sec.*, A. C. Ready.

Oxford.—FREWEN CLUB (1869), 98 St. Aldate's, Oxford OX1 1BT.—*Hon. Sec.*, W. H. Miller, B.E.M.

OXFORD UNION SOCIETY (1823), Frewin Court, Oxford OX1 3JB.—*Sec.*, S. Green.

VINCENT CLUB (1863), 1A King Edward Street, Oxford OX1 4HS.—*Sec.*, M. Lawson-Statham.

Paignton.—PAIGNTON CLUB (1882), The Esplanade, Paignton, Devon TQ4 6ED.—*Hon. Sec.* P. Grafton.

Peterborough.—CITY AND COUNTIES CLUB (1867), Priestgate, Peterborough PE6 7LT.—*Sec.*, J. R. Fillingham.

Reading.—BERKSHIRE ATHENAEUM CLUB (1972), 53 Blagrave Street, Reading, Berks.—*Hon. Sec.*, W. J. Stuck.

Rye.—DORMY HOUSE CLUB (1896), Rye, Sussex TN31 7LD.—*Hon. Sec.*, J. O'Brien.

St. Leonards on Sea.—EAST SUSSEX CLUB (1893), 1 Warrior Square, St. Leonards on Sea, E. Sussex.—*Hon. Sec.*, E. J. Morris.

Shrewsbury.—SALOP CLUB (1974), The Old House, Dogpole, Shrewsbury SY1 1EP.—*Hon. Sec.*, T. P. Roberts.

Teddington.—ROYAL CANOE CLUB (1866), Trowlock Island, Teddington, Middx.—*Hon. Sec.*, Mrs. J. Williams.

Worcester.—UNION AND COUNTY CLUB (1861), 40 Foregate Street, Worcester.—*Sec.*, M. G. Maton.

York.—YORKSHIRE CLUB (1839), 17 Museum Street, York YO1 2DW.—*Hon. Sec.*, D. Laughton.

CITY CLUB (1976), 4 Museum Street, York.—*Hon. Sec.*, C. H. Copeland.

Scotland

Ayr.—COUNTY CLUB (1872), 24 Sandgate, Ayr KA7 1BP.—*Hon. Sec.*, W. W. McHarg.

Edinburgh.—CALEDONIAN CLUB (1825), 32 Abercromby Place, Edinburgh EH3 6QE.—*Sec.*, I. Harvey.

NEW CLUB (1787), 86 Princes Street, Edinburgh EH2 2BB.—*Sec.*, Cdr. G. J. T. Creedy, L.V.O., R.N.

Glasgow.—ART CLUB (1867), 185 Bath Street, Glasgow G2 4HU.—*Sec.*, L. J. McIntyre.

ROYAL SCOTTISH AUTOMOBILE CLUB (1899), 11 Blythswood Square, Glasgow G2 4AG.—*Sec.*, H. Dewar.

WESTERN CLUB (1825), 32 Royal Exchange Square, Glasgow G1 3AB.—*Sec.*, D. H. Gifford.

Ireland

Belfast.—ULSTER REFORM CLUB (1885), 4 Royal Avenue, Belfast BT1 1DA.—*Sec.*, Miss M. P. Mackintosh.

Dublin.—STEPHEN'S GREEN CLUB (1840), 9 St. Stephen's Green, Dublin 2.—*Hon. Sec.*, D. H. O'Neill.

Enniskillen.—FERMANAGH COUNTY CLUB (1883), 20 Church Street, Enniskillen, N. Ireland BT74 6DF.—*Hon. Sec.*, P. Little.

YACHT CLUBS

Beaumaris.—ROYAL ANGLESEY YACHT CLUB (1802), 6-7 Green Edge, Beaumaris, Gwynedd LL58 8AL.—*Hon. Sec.*, V. G. Keep.

Bembridge.—BEMBRIDGE SAILING CLUB (1886), Embankment Road, Bembridge, I.o.W. PO35 5NR.—*Sec.*, N. McLean.

Birkenhead.—ROYAL MERSEY YACHT CLUB (1844), Bedford Road East, Rock Ferry, Birkenhead, Merseyside L42 1LS.—*Hon. Sec.*, C. P. Broad.

Bridlington.—ROYAL YORKSHIRE YACHT CLUB (1847), 1 Windsor Crescent, Bridlington, Yorks. YO15 3HX.—*Sec.*, I. Harness.

Burnham-on-Crouch.—ROYAL CORINTHIAN YACHT CLUB (1872), Burnham-on-Crouch, Essex CM0 8AX.—*Sec.*, N. R. Wynn.

Caernarvon.—ROYAL WELSH YACHT CLUB (1847), Porth-Yr-Aur, Caernarvon, Gwynned LL55 1SW.—*Hon. Sec.*, J. N. L. Thomas.

Cowes.—ROYAL YACHT SQUADRON (1815), The Castle, Cowes, I.o.W. PO31 7QT.—*Sec.*, Maj. R. P. Rising, R.M.

ROYAL LONDON YACHT CLUB (1838), The Parade, Cowes, I. o. W. PO31 7QS.—*Sec.*, A. J. Clarke.

Dover.—ROYAL CINQUE PORTS YACHT CLUB (1872), 5 Waterloo Crescent, Dover CT16 1LA.—*Hon. Sec.*, G. M. Cartwright.

Fishbourne.—ROYAL VICTORIA YACHT CLUB (1844), Fishbourne Lane, Ryde, I. o. W. PO33 4EU.—*Hon. Sec.*, R. M. Young.

Fowey.—ROYAL FOWEY YACHT CLUB (1881), Fowey, Cornwall PL23 1BH.—*Hon. Sec.*, E. P. Warren.

Harwich.—ROYAL HARWICH YACHT CLUB (1843), Woolverstone, Ipswich IP9 1AT.—*Sec.*, G. M. Ward, D.S.C.

Jersey.—ROYAL CHANNEL ISLANDS YACHT CLUB (1862), Le Boulevard, Bulwarks, St. Aubin, Jersey.—*Hon. Sec.*, A. K. Jackson.

Kingswear.—ROYAL DART YACHT CLUB (1866), Priory Street, Kingswear, S. Devon TQ6 0AB.—*Hon. Sec.*, P. Youd.

Leigh-on-Sea.—ESSEX YACHT CLUB (1890), H.Q.S. Bembridge, Foreshore, Leigh-on-Sea, Essex.—*Hon. Sec.*, A. Manning.

London.—THE CRUISING ASSOCIATION (1908), Ivory House, St. Katharine Dock, E1 9AT.—*Gen. Sec.*, Miss L. Nunn.

ROYAL CRUISING CLUB (1880), c/o Naval and Military Club.—*Hon. Sec.*, E. Bourne.

Lowestoft.—ROYAL NORFOLK AND SUFFOLK YACHT CLUB (1859), Royal Plain, Lowestoft, Suffolk NR33 0AQ.—*Sec.*, Lt.-Cdr. M. Dowsett (*retd*).

Lymington.—ROYAL LYMINGTON YACHT CLUB (1922), Bath Road, Lymington, Hants. SO41 9SE.—*Sec.*, Gp. Capt. J. D. Hutchinson (*retd*).

Penarth.—PENARTH YACHT CLUB (1880). The Esplanade, Penarth, S. Glamorgan CF6 2AU.—*Hon. Sec.*, W. H. Jones.

Plymouth.—ROYAL WESTERN YACHT CLUB (1827), 9 Grand Parade, Plymouth PL1 3DG.—*Sec.*, A. Miller.

ROYAL PLYMOUTH CORINTHIAN YACHT CLUB (1877), 1 Elford Crescent, Colebrook, Plympton, Plymouth PL7 4BT.—*Hon. Sec.*, A. R. Trim.

Poole.—EAST DORSET SAILING CLUB (1875), 352 Sandbanks Road, Poole, Dorset BH14 8HY.—*Hon. Sec.*, R. W. Howard.

PARKSTONE YACHT CLUB (1895), Pearce Avenue, Parkstone, Poole, Dorset BH14 8EH.—*Sec.*, Brig. H. J. Goodson, O.B.E.

POOLE HARBOUR YACHT CLUB (1949), 38 Salterns Way, Lilliput, Poole, Dorset BH14 8JR.—*Sec.*, J. N. J. Smith.

POOLE YACHT CLUB (1865), New Harbour Road West, Hamworthy, Poole, Dorset BH15 4AQ.—*Sec.*, Miss L. Clark.

Portsmouth.—ROYAL NAVAL CLUB AND ROYAL ALBERT YACHT CLUB (1867), 17 Pembroke Road, Portsmouth, Hants. PO1 2NT.—*Sec.*, Cdr. T. C. C. Greaves, O.B.E., R.N. (*retd*).

Ramsgate.—ROYAL TEMPLE YACHT CLUB (1857), 6 Westcliff Mansions, Ramsgate, Kent CT11 9HY.—*Hon. Sec.*, G. F. Randell.

Southampton.—ROYAL AIR FORCE YACHT CLUB (1932), Riverside House, Rope Walk, Hamble, Southampton SO3 5HD.—*Sec.*, Mrs. J. Hill.

ROYAL SOUTHAMPTON YACHT CLUB, Ocean Village, Southampton.—*Sec.*, Mrs. J. Cox.

ROYAL SOUTHERN YACHT CLUB (1837), Hamble, Hants. SO3 5HB.—*Sec.*, Mrs. W. J. F. Clampett.

Southend.—ALEXANDRA YACHT CLUB (1873), Clifton Terrace, Southend-on-Sea, Essex SS2 4PP.—*Hon. Sec.*, Lt.-Cdr. I. H. Bufton, R.N.R.

Swansea.—BRISTOL CHANNEL YACHT CLUB (1875), 744 Mumbles Road, Mumbles, Swansea SA3 4EL.— *Hon. Sec.*, R. L. Burrell.

Westcliff-on-Sea.—THAMES ESTUARY YACHT CLUB (1895), 3 The Leas, Westcliff-on-Sea, Essex SS0 7ST.—*Hon. Sec.*, J. G. Davison.

Weymouth.—ROYAL DORSET YACHT CLUB (1875), 11 Custom House Quay, Weymouth, Dorset DT4 8BG.—*Sec.*, Mrs. J. B. Cannon.

Windermere.—ROYAL WINDERMERE YACHT CLUB (1860), Fallbarrow Road, Bowness-on-Windermere, Cumbria LA23 3DJ.—*Hon. Sec.*, C. H. Peters.

Yarmouth.—ROYAL SOLENT YACHT CLUB (1878), Yarmouth, I. o. W. PO41 0NS.—*Sec.*, G. L. Bartlett.

Edinburgh.—ROYAL FORTH YACHT CLUB (1868), Middle Pier, Granton Harbour, Edinburgh, EH5 1HF.— *Hon. Sec.*, A. R. Woods.

Glasgow.—ROYAL WESTERN YACHT CLUB (1875), 42 Methil Street, Glasgow G14 0AN.—*Hon. Sec.*, Mrs. N. Simpson.

Oban.—ROYAL HIGHLAND YACHT CLUB (1881), Whins, 8 Grianach Gardens, Oban, Argyllshire PA34 4LZ.—*Sec.*, M. Bolton.

Rhu.—ROYAL NORTHERN AND CLYDE YACHT CLUB (1978), Rhu, By Helensburgh, Dunbartonshire G84 8NG.—*Hon. Sec.*, Dr. J. A. Ritchie.

Scotland

Dundee.—ROYAL TAY YACHT CLUB (1885), 34 Dundee Road, Broughty Ferry, Dundee DD5 1LX.—*Hon. Sec.*, T. Black.

Northern Ireland

Bangor.—ROYAL ULSTER YACHT CLUB (1866), 101 Clifton Road, Bangor, Co. Down BT20 5HY.—*Hon. Sec.*, T. O'Hara.

PRINCIPAL BRITISH AND IRISH SOCIETIES
AND INSTITUTIONS

THE ROYAL ACADEMY OF ARTS (1768), Burlington House W1V 0DS—*President*, Roger de Grey, P.R.A., (1984); *Keeper*, Prof. N. Adams, R.A.; *Treas.*, Sir Philip Powell, C.H., O.B.E., R.A.; *Sec.* Piers Rodgers.

1977 Sutton, Philip	1980 Whishaw,
1983 Symons, Patrick	Anthony
1985 Tilson, Joe	1983 Wragg, John
1986 Titchell, John	

Royal Academicians

1972 Adams, Norman
1988*Agar, Eileen
1956*Bawden, Edward, C.B.E.
1976 Blackadder, Elizabeth, O.B.E.
1981 Blake, Peter, C.B.E.
1975 Blamey, Norman
1978 Blow, Sandra
1975 Bowey, Olwyn
1981 Bowyer, William
1971 Bratby, John R.
1972 Brown, Ralph
1956 Buhler, Robert
1972 Butler, James
1975 Cadbury-Brown, H. T., O.B.E.
1984 Camp, Jeffery
1970*Casson, Sir Hugh, C.H., K.C.V.O.
1976 Clarke, Geoffrey
1973 Clatworthy, Robert
1972 Coker, Peter
1988*Collins, Cecil
1972 Cooke, Jean E.
1974 Cuming, Frederick
1983 Dannatt, Trevor
1969 de Grey, Roger
1976 Dickson, Jennifer
1985 Dowson, Sir Philip, C.B.E.
1955*Dring, William
1968 Dunstan, Bernard
1953*Eurich, Richard, O.B.E.
1986 Eyton, Anthony
1985 Fraser, Donald Hamilton
1977 Frink, Dame Elisabeth, D.D.E.
1972 Gore, Frederick, C.B.E.
1977 Green, Anthony
1960*Greenham, Peter, C.B.E.
1981 Harpley, Sydney
1970 Hayes, Colin

1961*Hepple, Norman
1984 Hogarth, Paul
1986 Jones, Allen
1986 Kenny, Michael
1988 King, Phillip, C.B.E.
1974 Kneale, Bryan
1986*Lessore, Helen
1986 Levene, Ben
1963 McFall, David
1956 Machin, Arnold, O.B.E.
1979 Manasseh, Leonard, O.B.E.
1985*Martin, Sir Leslie
1985*Medley, Robert
1979*Moynihan, Rodrigo, C.B.E.
1979 Paolozzi, Eduardo, C.B.E.
1983*Pasmore, Victor, C.H., C.B.E.
1981 Philipson, Sir Robin
1977 Powell, Sir Philip, C.H., O.B.E.
1973 Roberts-Jones, Ivor, C.B.E.
1984 Rogers, Richard
1969 Rosoman, Leonard, O.B.E.
1983*Rothenstein, Michael
1961*Sanders, Christopher C.
1984 Scott, William, C.B.E.
1969*Soukop, Willi
1954*Spear, Ruskin, C.B.E.
1986 Stephenson, Ian
1979 Swanwick, Betty
1979 Tindle, David
1965 Ward, John S., C.B.E.
1965*Weight, Carel, C.B.E.
1974 Williams, Kyffin, O.B.E.

Associates

1988 Ackroyd, Norman
1978 Aitchison, Craigie
1982 Ayres, Gillian, O.B.E.
1986 Bellany, John
1980 Christopher, Ann
1982 Crosby, Theo
1987 Flanagan, Barry
1983 Foster, Norman
1978 Gowing, Sir Lawrence, C.B.E.
1985 Hockney, David
1983 Howard, Ken

1983 Hoyland, John
1987 Huxley, Paul
1984 Kitaj, R. B.
1986 Koralek, Paul, C.B.E.
1982 Lawson, Sonia
1987 McComb, Leonard
1987 Nolan, Sir Sidney
1980 Partridge, John, C.B.E.
1984 Phillips, Tom
1982 Sandle, Michael
1985 Stirling, James

* Senior.

Former Presidents of the Royal Academy

Sir J. Reynolds, 1768	Sir F. Dicksee, 1924
Benjamin West, 1792	Sir W. Llewellyn, 1928
James Wyatt, 1805	Sir E. Lutyens, 1938
Benjamin West, 1806	Sir A. J. Munnings, 1944
Sir T. Lawrence, 1820	
Sir M. A. Shee, 1830	Sir G. F. Kelly, 1949
Sir C. Eastlake, 1850	Sir A. E. Richardson, 1954
Sir F. Grant, 1866	
Lord Leighton, 1878	Sir C. Wheeler, 1956
Sir J. Millais, 1896	Sir T. Monnington, 1966
Sir E. Poynter, 1896	
Sir A. Webb, 1919	Sir Hugh Casson, 1976

THE ROYAL CAMBRIAN ACADEMY OF ART (1882), Plas Mawr, High Street, Conwy, Gwynedd LL32 8DE—*Pres.*, R. Fields; *Hon. Sec.*, Ms. A. Hind; *Curator and Sec.*, L. H. S. Mercer.

THE ROYAL SCOTTISH ACADEMY (1826), Princes Street, Edinburgh EH2 2EL—*Pres.*, Sir Anthony Wheeler, O.B.E., R.S.A.; *Sec.*, R. R. Steedman, R.S.A.; *Treas.*, W. J. L. Baillie, R.S.A.; *Librarian*, P. Collins, R.S.A.; *Admin. Sec.*, W. T. Meikle.

Hon. Retired Academicians:

1958 Armour, Mrs. M.	1981 Glover, J. Hardie, O.B.E.
1966 Johnston, Ninian	
1967 Lorimer, Hew	1966 Peploe, Denis
1977 Whiston, Peter	

Royal Scottish Academicians

1979 Baillie, W. J. L.
1972 Blackadder, Elizabeth
1986 Bushe, Fred
1977 Butler, Vincent
1971 Cameron, Gordon S.
1981 Campbell, Alex
1974 Collins, Peter
1974 Crosbie, William
1970 Cumming, James
1962 Donaldson, David A.
1956 Fleming, Ian
1067 Gordon, Esmé
1972 Houston, John
1979 Knox, John
1973 Littlejohn, W.
1971 McClure, David
1976 Malcolm, Ellen

1972 Michie, David
1963 Morocco, Alberto
1957 Patrick, J. McIntosh
1962 Philipson, Sir Robin
1976 Reeves, Philip
1986 Reiach, Alan
1977 Robertson, R. Ross
1984 Scott, Bill
1987 Smith, Ian McKenzie
1985 Snowden, Michael (*elect.*)
1979 Steedman, R. R.
1975 Wheeler, Sir Anthony, O.B.E.
1982 Walker, Frances

Associates

Arnott, Ian
Balmer, Barbara
Boys, John
Brotherston, William
Brown, Neil Dallas
Bryce, Gordon
Buchan, Dennis
Busby, John
Cairns, Joyce
Campbell, A. Buchanan

Clifford, J. G.
Cocker, Douglas
Crowe, Victoria
Dean, Fiona
Docherty, Michael
Donald, George
Evans, David
Fairgrieve, James
Fraser, Alexander
Gasson, Barry

The Earl Haig
Harvey, Jake
Howard, Ian
Johnstone, John
Law, Graham C.
Low, Bet
McIntosh, Iain R.
Maclean, William J.
MacMillan, Andrew
MacPherson, George
Main, Kirkland
Merrylees, Andrew
Metzstein, Isi
Mooney, John
Morris, James
Morrison, James

Onwin, Glen
Pelly, Frances
Pottinger, Frank
Rae, Barbara
Renton, James S., O.B.E.
Richards, John, C.B.E.
Robertson, James D.
Ross, Alastair
Shanks, Duncan F.
Smart, Alastair
Squire, Geoffrey
Stenhouse, Andrew
Stiven, Fred
Watson, Arthur
Wedgwood, Roland

Non-Resident Associates, Charles Pulsford; Peter Womersley, Leon Morrocco.

ROYAL IRISH ACADEMY (1786), 19 Dawson Street, Dublin 2.—*Pres.*, Prof. J. C. I. Dooge; *Treas.*, Prof. A. F. Hegarty; *Sec.*, Prof. J. O. Scanlan.

ABBEYFIELD SOCIETY, 186–192 Darkes Lane, Potters Bar, Herts. EN6 1AB—Housing for elderly people. 1,000 homes nationwide.—*Chief Exec.*, B. Palmer.

ACCOUNTANTS, INSTITUTE OF CHARTERED, IN ENGLAND AND WALES (1880), P.O. Box 433, Chartered Accountants' Hall, Moorgate Place, EC2P 2BJ.

ACCOUNTANTS, CHARTERED ASSOCIATION OF CERTIFIED (1904), 29 Lincoln's Inn Fields, WC2A 3EE—*Sec.*, A. W. Sansom.

ACCOUNTANTS OF SCOTLAND, THE INSTITUTE OF CHARTERED (1854), 27 Queen Street, Edinburgh EH2 1LA—*Sec.*, E. Tait, M.B.E.

ACCOUNTANTS IN IRELAND, INSTITUTE OF CHARTERED (1888), Chartered Accountants House, 87–89 Pembroke Road, Dublin 4.—*Dir.*, R. F. Hussey.

ACCOUNTANTS, SOCIETY OF COMPANY AND COMMERCIAL (1974), 40 Tyndalls Park Road, Bristol BS8 1PL—*Sec. Gen.*, B. T. Banks.

ACCOUNTING TECHNICIANS, ASSOCIATION OF (1980), 154 Clerkenwell Road, EC1R 5AD—*Sec.*, J. Hanson.

ACTION RESEARCH FOR THE CRIPPLED CHILD (1952), Vincent House, North Parade, Horsham, West Sussex RH12 2DA—*Dir.*, Col. A. N. Brearley-Smith, O.B.E.

ACTORS' BENEVOLENT FUND (1882), 6 Adam Street, WC2N 6AA—*Gen. Sec.*, Mrs. R. Stevens.

ACTORS' CHARITABLE TRUST, 19–20 Euston Centre, NW1 3JH—*Admin. Sec.*, Ms. A. Stewart.

ACTORS' CHURCH UNION (1899), St. Paul's Church, Bedford Street, WC2E 9ED—*Senior Chaplain*, Rev. M. Hurst-Bannister.

ACTUARIES IN SCOTLAND, THE FACULTY OF (1856), 23 St. Andrew Square, Edinburgh EH2 1AQ—*Sec.*, W. W. Mair.

ACTUARIES, INSTITUTE OF (1848), Staple Inn Hall, High Holborn, WC1V 7QJ—*Sec.-Gen.*, C. D. A. Mackie.

ADDICTION (TO ALCOHOL AND OTHER DRUGS), SOCIETY FOR THE STUDY OF (1884).—*Sec.*, Mrs. N. C. Blackburn, 3 Oakfield Gardens, Dulwich Wood Avenue, SE19 1HF.

ADMINISTRATIVE ACCOUNTANTS, INSTITUTE OF (1916), Burford House, 44 London Road, Sevenoaks, Kent TN13 1AS.—*Dir.-Gen.*, D. W. Bradley, F.C.I.S.

ADMINISTRATIVE MANAGEMENT, INSTITUTE OF (1915), 40 Chatsworth Parade, Petts Wood, Orpington, Kent BR5 1RW—*Sec.-Gen.*, M. J. Ainsworth.

ADULT SCHOOL ORGANIZATION, NATIONAL (1899),

Norfolk House, Smallbrook Queensway, Birmingham B5 4LJ—*Gen. Sec.*, W. J. Scarle.

ADVERTISING BENEVOLENT SOCIETY, NATIONAL (1913), 3 Crawford Place, W1H 1JB—*Dir.*, Mrs. D. Larkin.

ADVERTISING, INSTITUTE OF PRACTITIONERS IN, 44 Belgrave Square, SW1X 8QS—*Dir. Gen.*, D. Wheeler.

ADVERTISING STANDARDS AUTHORITY (1962), Brook House, 2–16 Torrington Place, WC1E 7HN—*Director General*, P. Thomson.

AERONAUTICAL SOCIETY, ROYAL (1866), 4 Hamilton Place, W1V 0BQ—*Sec.*, G. C. May.

AFRICAN INSTITUTE, INTERNATIONAL (1926), Lionel Robbins Building, 10 Portugal Street, WC2A 2HD.—*Hon. Dir.*, Prof. I. M. Lewis.

AFRICAN MEDICAL AND RESEARCH FOUNDATION, London House, 68 Upper Richmond Road, SW15 2RP—*Exec. Dir.*, Mrs. E. Young.

AGE CONCERN ENGLAND, Bernard Sunley House, 60 Pitcairn Road, Mitcham, Surrey, CR4 3LL.—*Dir.*, Ms. S. Greengross.

AGE CONCERN NORTHERN IRELAND, 6 Lower Crescent, Belfast, BT2 7BG—*Dir.*, J. A. O'Neill.

AGE CONCERN SCOTLAND, 33 Castle Street, Edinburgh EH2 3DN—*Dir.*, Ms. M. Marshall.

AGE CONCERN WALES, 4th Floor, 1 Cathedral Road, Cardiff, CF1 9SD—*Chief Officer*, D. Haydn Thomas.

AGED POOR SOCIETY (1708), St. Joseph's House, 42 Brook Green, W6 7BW—*Sec.*, Flt. Lt. W. Watson (retd).

AGEING, CENTRE FOR POLICY ON, 25–31 Ironmonger Row, EC1V 3QP—*Dir.*, Dr. E. Midwinter, D.Phil.

AGEING, RESEARCH INTO (1978), 49 Queen Victoria Street, EC4N 4SA—*Dir.*, J. Allfrey.

AGRICULTURAL BENEVOLENT INSTITUTION, ROYAL, Shaw House, 27 West Way, Oxford OX2 0QH—*Chief Exec.*, Maj. Gen. P. L. Spurgeon, C.B.

AGRICULTURAL BENEVOLENT INSTITUTION, ROYAL SCOTTISH (1897), Ingliston, Edinburgh, EH28 8NB—*Org. Sec.*, I. G. Cumming, T.D.

AGRICULTURAL SOCIETY, EAST OF ENGLAND, East of England Showground, Peterborough PE2 0XE—*Sec.*, R. W. Bird, M.B.E..

AGRICULTURAL SOCIETY OF ENGLAND, ROYAL (1838), National Agricultural Centre, Stoneleigh, Kenilworth, Warwicks, CV8 2LZ—*Chief Exec.*, J. D. M. Hearth, C.B.E.

AGRICULTURAL SOCIETY OF THE COMMONWEALTH, ROYAL (1957), 55 Sleaford Street, SW8 5AB—*Hon. Sec.*, F. R. Francis, L.V.O., M.B.E.

AGRICULTURAL SOCIETY, ROYAL ULSTER (1826), The King's Hall, Balmoral Show Grounds, Belfast BT9 6GW—*Chief Exec.*, W. H. Yarr.

AGRICULTURE, ASSOCIATION OF (1947), Victoria Chambers, 16–20 Strutton Ground, SW1P 2HP—*Gen. Sec.*, Miss J. H. D. Bostock, M.B.E.

AIR LEAGUE, THE (1909), 4 Hamilton Place, W1V 0BQ—*Chairman*, Air Marshal Sir Charles Ness, K.C.B., C.B.E.; *Sec. Gen.*, Air Comm. C. A. Alldis, C.B.E., D.F.C., A.F.C.

ALCOHOLICS ANONYMOUS, P.O. Box 1, Stonebow House, Stonebow, York YO1 2NJ.

ALEXANDRA ROSE DAY FUND, 1 Castelnau, Barnes, SW13 9RP—*Nat. Organiser and Administrator*, Mrs. L. Weston.

ALLOTMENT AND LEISURE GARDENERS LIMITED, NATIONAL SOCIETY OF, Hunters Road, Corby, Northants., NN17 1JE—*Sec.*, (vacant).

ALMSHOUSES, NATIONAL ASSOCIATION OF, Billingbear Lodge, Wokingham, Berks. RG11 5RU—*Dir.*, D. M. Scott.

ANAESTHETISTS OF GREAT BRITAIN AND IRELAND, ASSOCIATION OF (1932), 9 Bedford Square, WC1B 3RA—*Hon. Sec.*, Dr. W. L. M. Baird.

ANCIENT BUILDINGS, SOCIETY FOR THE PROTECTION OF (1877), 37 Spital Square, E1 6DY—*Sec.*, P. Venning.

ANCIENT MONUMENTS SOCIETY (1924), St. Andrew-by-the-Wardrobe, Queen Victoria Street, EC4V 5DE—*Sec.*, M. Saunders.

ANGLO-ARAB ASSOCIATION (1961), The Arab British Centre, 21 Collingham Road, SW5 0NU—*Exec. Dir.*, D. R. Collard, O.B.E.

ANGLO-BELGIAN SOCIETY, 46 Belgrave Manor, Brooklyn Road, Woking, Surrey GU22 7TW—*Hon. Sec.*, Mrs. S. G. Ault.

ANGLO-BRAZILIAN SOCIETY (1943), 32 Green Street, W1Y 3FD—*Sec.*, Mrs. M. J. Fyfe.

ANGLO-DANISH SOCIETY (1924), 25 New Street Square, EC4A 3LN—*Chairman*, Sir Andrew Stark, K.C.M.G., C.V.O.

ANGLO-NORSE SOCIETY, 25 Belgrave Square, SW1X 8QD—*Chairman*, Mrs. A. Dixon.

ANGLO-POLISH SOCIETY (1832), London H.Q., c/o S.P.C.K., 238–246 King Street, W6 0RF—*Hon. Sec.*, Mrs. K. Szymaniak.

ANGLO-THAI SOCIETY (1962).—*Hon. Sec.*, Lt. Col. H. Docherty, O.B.E., 22 Ulster Court, Albany Park Road, Kingbaston, Surrey KT2 5SS.

ANIMAL CONCERN (SCOTLAND), 121 West Regent Street, Glasgow G2 2SD—*Organising Sec.*, J. F. Robins.

ANIMAL HEALTH TRUST, Lanwades Hall, Kennett, Newmarket, Suffolk CB8 7PN—*Dir.*, A. J. Higgins, PH.D.

ANTHROPOLOGICAL INSTITUTE, ROYAL (1843), 50 Fitzroy Street, W1P 5HS—*Dir.*, J. C. M. Benthall.

ANTHROPOSOPHICAL SOCIETY IN GREAT BRITAIN, Rudolf Steiner House, 35 Park Road, NW1 6XT—*Gen. Sec.*, N. C. Thomas.

ANTI-COMMON MARKET CAMPAIGN, BRITISH (1976), 81 Ashmole Street, SW8 1NF—*Hon. Sec.*, Sir Robin Williams, Bt.

ANTIQUARIES, SOCIETY OF (1717), Burlington House, Piccadilly, W1V 0HS—*Dir.*, G. J. Wainwright, PH.D.

ANTIQUARIES OF SCOTLAND, SOCIETY OF (1780), Royal Museum of Scotland, Queen Street, Edinburgh EH2 1JD—*Sec.*, Miss C. Wickham-Jones.

ANTI-SLAVERY SOCIETY FOR THE PROTECTION OF HUMAN RIGHTS (1839), 180 Brixton Road, SW9 6AT—*Dir.*, P. D. Lowes.

ANTI-VIVISECTION: BRITISH UNION FOR THE ABOLITION OF VIVISECTION (1898), 16a Crane Grove, N7 8LB—*Sec.*, A. Cheeseman.

ANTI-VIVISECTION SOCIETY, THE NATIONAL (1875), 51 Harley Street, W1N 1DD—*Gen. Sec.*, Ms. J. Creamer.

APOSTLESHIP OF THE SEA (1920), Stella Maris, Atlantic House, New Strand, Bootle, Merseyside L20 4TQ—For active seafarers. *Nat. Dir.*, Very Rev. Mgr. A. Stringfellow.

APOTHECARIES OF LONDON, SOCIETY OF (1617), Black Friars Lane, EC4V 6EJ—*Clerk*, Maj. J. C. O'Leary; *Registrar*, D. H. C. Barrie.

APPLIED BIOLOGISTS, ASSOCIATION OF, Hill Farming Research Organisation, Bush Estate, Penicuik, Midlothian EH26 0PY—*Hon. Gen. Sec.*, Dr. P. Newbould.

ARBITRATORS, THE CHARTERED INSTITUTE OF, 75 Cannon Street, EC4N 5BH—*Sec.*, K. R. K. Harding.

ARCHÆOLOGICAL ASSOCIATION, BRITISH (1843), 61 Old Park Ridings, Winchmore Hill, N21 2ET—*Hon. Asst. Treas. and Sec.*, Miss I. B. McClure.

ARCHÆOLOGICAL ASSOCIATION, CAMBRIAN (1846), Lleifior, 60 Dan-y-Coed, Aberystwyth, Dyfed SY23 2HA—*Gen.Sec.*, G. L. Jones.

ARCHÆOLOGICAL INSTITUTE, ROYAL (1843), c/o Society of Antiquaries of London, Burlington House, Piccadilly, W1V 0HS—*Sec.*, J. G. Coad.

ARCHÆOLOGY, COUNCIL FOR BRITISH (1944), 112 Kennington Road, SE11 6RE—*Dir.*, Dr. H. F. Cleere.

ARCHITECTS, THE ROYAL INSTITUTE OF BRITISH (1834), 66 Portland Place, W1N 4AD—*Pres.*, R. Hackney, PH.D.; *Dir.-Gen.*, The Rt. Hon. W. Rodgers.

ARCHITECTS REGISTRATION COUNCIL OF THE UNITED KINGDOM, 73 Hallam Street, W1N 6EE—*Chairman*, Prof. J. Tarn; *Registrar*, K. J. Forder.

ARCHITECTS AND SURVEYORS, INCORPORATED ASSOCIATION OF (1925), Jubilee House, Billing Brook Road, Weston Favell, Northampton NN3 4NW—*Hon. Sec.*, W. A. Black.

ARCHITECTS AND SURVEYORS, THE FACULTY OF, 15 St. Mary Street, Chippenham, Wilts. SN15 3JN—*Sec.*, Mrs. J. E. Allen.

ARCHITECTS BENEVOLENT SOCIETY (1850), 66 Portland Place, W1N 4AD—*Hon. Sec.*, R. P. B. Roth.

ARCHITECTS IN SCOTLAND, ROYAL INCORPORATION OF (1922), 15 Rutland Square, Edinburgh EH1 2BE—*Sec.*, C. A. McKean, F.R.S.A.

ARCHITECTURAL ASSOCIATION (INC.) (1847), 34–36 Bedford Square, W.C.1.—*Sec.*, E. Le Maistre.

ARCHITECTURAL HERITAGE FUND, THE (1976), 17 Carlton House Terrace, SW1Y 5AW.—*Sec.*, Lady Weir.

ARCHIVISTS, SOCIETY OF (1947), Suffolk Record Office, County Hall, Ipswich IP4 2JS—*Hon. Sec.*, Ms. A. J. E. Arrowsmith.

ARMY BENEVOLENT FUND (1944), 41 Queen's Gate, SW7 5HR—*Controller*, Maj.-Gen. G. M. G. Swindells, C.B.

ARMY CADET FORCE ASSOCIATION (1930), Cheltenham Terrace, SW3 4RR—*Gen. Sec.*, Brigadier R. B. MacGregor-Oakford, C.B.E., M.C.

ART-COLLECTIONS FUND, NATIONAL (1903), 20 John Islip Street, SW1P 4JX—*Dir.*, Sir Peter Wakefield, K.B.E., C.M.G.

ART LIBRARIES SOCIETY (ARLIS) (1969).—Central School of Art and Design, Southampton Row WC1B 4AP—*Sec.*, S. M. Price.

ART WORKERS' GUILD (1884), 6 Queen Square, WC1N 3AR—*Sec.*, D. G. Pullen.

ARTHRITIS AND RHEUMATISM COUNCIL FOR RESEARCH, 41 Eagle Street, WC1R 4AR—*Gen. Sec.*, J. Norton.

ARTHRITIS CARE, 6 Grosvenor Crescent, SW1X 7ER—*Sec.*, R. M. Sorsbie.

ARTISTS, FEDERATION OF BRITISH, 17 Carlton House Terrace, SW1Y 5BD—*Pres.*, D. Poole; *Chief Exec.*, O. Warman.

ARTISTS' GENERAL BENEVOLENT INSTITUTION (1814) AND ARTISTS' ORPHAN FUND (1871), Burlington House, Piccadilly, W1V 0DJ—*Sec.*, T. Maloss.

ARTISTS, ROYAL SOCIETY OF BRITISH, 17 Carlton House Terrace, SW1Y 5BD—*President*, T. Coates; *Sec.*, R. Morgan.

ASLIB (1924). (The Association for Information Management), Information House, 26–27 Boswell Street, WC1N 3JZ—*Dir.*, Dr. D. A. Lewis.

ASSISTANT MASTERS AND MISTRESSES ASSOCIATION, 7 Northumberland Street, WC2N 5DA—*Secs.*, Miss J. E. L. Baird; P. Smith.

ASTHMA RESEARCH COUNCIL, 300 Upper Street, N1 2XX—*Chairman*, Sir Dennis Walters, M.B.E., M.P.

ASTRONOMICAL ASSOCIATION, BRITISH.—*Office*, Burlington House, Piccadilly, W1V 0NL. Meetings at 23 Savile Row, W.1.—*President*, S. R. Dunlop; *Sec.*, M. de Faubert Maunder; *Asst. Sec.*, E. Watson Jones.

ASTRONOMICAL SOCIETY, ROYAL (1820), Burlington House, Piccadilly, W1V 0NL—*Pres.*, Prof. R. D. Davies; *Secs.*, Dr. C. Jordan; Dr. B. A. Hobbs; Prof. D. A. Williams.

A.T.S. and W.R.A.C. BENEVOLENT FUNDS (1964), Queen Elizabeth Park, Guildford, Surrey GU2 6QH—*Sec.*, Mrs. K. E. Laurence-Smith.

AUDIT BUREAU OF CIRCULATIONS LTD., 13 Wimpole Street, W1M 7AB—*Dir.*, J. G. Holmes.

AUTHORS, THE SOCIETY OF, 84 Drayton Gardens, SW10 9SB—*Gen. Sec.*, M. Le Fanu.

AUTOMOBILE ASSOCIATION (1905), Fanum House, Basingstoke, Hants.,—*Dir. Gen.*, S. Dyer.

AVICULTURAL SOCIETY (1894), Warren Hill, Hulford's Lane, Hartley Wintney, Hampshire RG27 8AG.— *Hon. Sec.*, H. J. Horswell.

AYRSHIRE CATTLE SOCIETY OF GREAT BRITAIN AND IRELAND (1877), P.O. Box 8, 1 Racecourse Road, Ayr KA7 2DE.—*Gen. Sec.*, S. J. Thomson.

BALTIC AIR CHARTER ASSOCIATION, The Baltic Exchange, St. Mary Axe, EC3A 8BU—*Hon. Exec.*, D. Shepherd.

BALTIC EXCHANGE LTD. (1903), 14–20 St. Mary Axe, EC3A 8BU—*Sec.*, D. J. Walker.

BALTIC EXCHANGE CHARITABLE SOCIETY (1978), 14–20 St. Mary Axe, EC3A 8BU—*Sec.*, R. T. Wheelans.

BALZAN FOUNDATION 'PRIZE', INTERNATIONAL (1956), Piazzetta U. Giordano 4, Milan, Italy. (Awards prizes for Literature, Moral Sciences and the Arts, Physical, Mathematical and Natural Sciences, Medicine, Humanity, Peace and Brotherhood).— *Sec. Gen.*, F. M. Tedeschi.

BANKERS, THE CHARTERED INSTITUTE OF (1879), 10 Lombard Street, EC3V 9AS—*Sec. Gen.*, E. Glover.

BANKERS IN SCOTLAND, THE INSTITUTE OF (1875), 20 Rutland Square, Edinburgh EH1 2DE—*Sec.*, C. W. Munn.

BAPTIST MISSIONARY SOCIETY (1792), 93–97 Gloucester Place, W1H 4AA—*Gen. Sec.*, Rev. R. G. S. Harvey.

BAR ASSOCIATION FOR LOCAL GOVERNMENT AND THE PUBLIC SERVICE, 23 Wentworth Way, Bletchley, Milton Keynes MK3 7RW—*Chairman*, P. G. Stivadoros.

(DR.) BARNARDO'S (1866), Tanners Lane, Barkingside, Essex IG6 1QG. Helps over 22,000 children and young people each year, many of them with special needs, in the United Kingdom, Republic of Ireland, Australia and New Zealand.—*Senior Dir.*, R. Singleton.

BARONETAGE, STANDING COUNCIL OF THE (1898), The College of Arms, Queen Victoria Street, EC4V 4BT.—*Sec.*, H. Bedingfeld, Rouge Croix Pursuivant of Arms.

BARRISTERS' BENEVOLENT ASSOCIATION, THE (1873), 14 Gray's Inn Square, WC1R 5JP—*Sec.*, Miss K. M. Hopper.

BEECHAM TRUST, SIR THOMAS, Denton House, Denton, Harleston, Norfolk IP20 0AA—*Sec.*, Shirley, Lady Beecham.

BEE-KEEPERS' ASSOCIATION, BRITISH (1874), National Agricultural Centre, Stoneleigh, Kenilworth, Warwicks. CV8 2LZ—*Gen.Sec.*, M. H. Solley.

BIBLE CHURCHMEN'S MISSIONARY SOCIETY (1922), 251 Lewisham Way, SE4 1XF—*Gen. Sec.*, Rev. Canon J. M. Ball.

BIBLE SOCIETY, BRITISH AND FOREIGN (1804), Stonehill Green, Westlea, Swindon, Wilts. SN5 7DG—*Exec. Dir.*, R. Worthing Davies.

BIBLIOGRAPHICAL SOCIETY (1892), British Library, Humanities and Social Sciences, Great Russell Street, WC1B 3DG—*Hon. Sec.*, Dr. M. M. Foot.

BIBLIOGRAPHICAL SOCIETY, EDINBURGH (1890), c/o National Library of Scotland, George IV Bridge, Edinburgh EH1 1EW—*Hon. Sec.*, I. C. Cunningham.

BIOCHEMICAL SOCIETY (1911), 7 Warwick Court, High Holborn, WC1R 5DP—*Exec. Sec.*, G. D. Jones.

BIOLOGICAL COUNCIL, THE, c/o Institute of Biology, 20 Queensberry Place, SW7 2DZ—*Hon. Sec.*, Prof. M. Sandler.

BIOLOGICAL ENGINEERING SOCIETY.—c/o Royal College of Surgeons, Lincoln's Inn Fields, WC2A 3PN—*Hon. Sec.*, Dr. R. E. Trotman.

BIOLOGY, THE INSTITUTE OF, 20 Queensberry Place, SW7 2DZ—*Gen. Sec.*, P. N. O'Donoghue.

BIRD PRESERVATION, INTERNATIONAL COUNCIL FOR (BRITISH SECTION), c/o Flora and Fauna Preservation Society, 8–12 Camden High Street, NW1 0JH— *Exec. Sec.* J. R. Wilson.

BIRMINGHAM AND MIDLAND INSTITUTE (1854) and PRIESTLEY LIBRARY (1779), Margaret Street, Birmingham B3 3BS—*Admin.* J. Hunt.

BIRTHDAY TRUST FUND, NATIONAL (1928), 57 Lower Belgrave Street, SW1W 0LR. For extension of maternity services.—*Sec.*, Mrs. M. C. Matthews.

BLIND, GUIDE DOGS FOR THE, ASSOCIATION, Alexandra House, 9 Park Street, Windsor, Berks. SL4 1JR— *Dir. Gen.*, Maj.-Gen. J. P. Groom, C.B., C.B.E.

BLIND, INCORPORATED ASSOCIATION FOR PROMOTING THE GENERAL WELFARE OF THE (1854), 37–55 Ashburton Grove, N7 7DW—*Chief Exec.*, G. P. Robinson; *Sec.*, A. W. Cairns.

BLIND, LONDON ASSOCIATION FOR THE (1857), 14–16 Verney Road, SE16 3DZ—*Dir.*, P. Holland.

BLIND, NATIONAL LIBRARY FOR THE (1882), Cromwell Road, Bredbury, Stockport, Cheshire SK6 2SG. Over 400,000 volumes available.—*Dir. Gen.*, A. Leach.

BLIND, ROYAL COMMONWEALTH SOCIETY FOR THE (1950), Commonwealth House, Heath Road, Haywards Heath, West Sussex RH16 3AZ—*Exec. Dir.*, A. W. Johns, O.B.E.

BLIND, ROYAL LONDON SOCIETY FOR THE (1838), 105–9 Salusbury Road, Kilburn, NW6 6RH—*Sec. Gen.*, R. J. Pocock.

BLIND, ROYAL NATIONAL COLLEGE (1872), College Road, Hereford HR1 1EB——*Principal*, L. Marshall.

BLIND, ROYAL NATIONAL INSTITUTE FOR THE (1868), 224 Great Portland Street, W1N 6AA—*Dir. Gen.*, I. Bruce.

BLIND, ROYAL SCHOOL FOR THE (1799), Leatherhead, Surrey KT22 8NR—*Dir.*, B. A. Coote.

BLOOD TRANFUSION ASSOCIATION, SCOTTISH NATIONAL (1940), 29 Abercromby Place, Edinburgh EH3 6UE—*Sec.*, P. C. Taylor.

BLUE CROSS, THE (Incorporating Our Dumb Friends' League) (1897), Animals' Hospital, Hugh Street, Victoria, SW1V 1QQ—*Sec.*, P. Hannon.

BODLEIAN, FRIENDS OF THE, Bodleian Library, Oxford OX1 3BG—*Sec.*, G. Groom.

BOOKSELLERS ASSOCIATION OF GREAT BRITAIN AND IRELAND (1895), 154 Buckingham Palace Road, SW1W 9TZ—*Dir.*, T. E. Godfray.

BOOK TRADE BENEVOLENT SOCIETY (1967), Dillon Lodge, The Booksellers Retreat, Kings Langley, Herts. WD4 8LT—*Exec. Sec.*, Mrs. A. R. Brown.

BOOK TRUST, Book House, 45 East Hill, SW18 2QZ—*Chief Exec.*, K. McWilliams.

BOTANICAL SOCIETY OF THE BRITISH ISLES (1836), British Museum (Natural History), Cromwell Road, SW7 5BD—*Hon. Gen. Sec.*, Mrs. M. Briggs, M.B.E.

BOTANICAL SOCIETY OF EDINBURGH, Royal Botanic Garden, Inverleith Row, Edinburgh EH3 5LR—*Hon. Gen. Sec.*, Dr. I. Edwards.

BOY SCOUTS ASSOCIATION, *see* SCOUT ASSOCIATION, THE.

BOYS' BRIGADE, THE (1883), 1 Kings Terrace, Galena Road, Hammersmith, W6 0LT. Membership worldwide: 400,000 in 60 countries—*Brigade Sec.*, S. Jones.

BOYS' CLUBS, NATIONAL ASSOCIATION OF (1925), 369 Kennington Lane, SE11 5QY. Has affiliated to it 2,000 clubs—*Nat. Dir.*, D. P. Harris.

BOYS' CLUBS, NORTHERN IRELAND ASSOCIATION OF (1940), Bryson House, 28 Bedford Street, Belfast BT2 7FE—*Gen. Sec.*, C. E. Larmour, M.B.E.

BREWING, INSTITUTE OF (1886), 33 Clarges Street, W1Y 8EE—*Sec.*, Capt. K. A. Leppard, C.B.E., R.N.

BRIDEWELL ROYAL HOSPITAL (1553), Wormley Hill, Godalming, Surrey GU8 5SG—*Clerk to the Governors*, Mrs. A. C. R. Mitchell.

BRITAIN-NEPAL SOCIETY (1960), *Hon. Sec.*, Mrs. C. Brown, 1 Allen Mansions, Allen Street, W8 6UY.

BRITISH ACADEMY, THE (1901), 20–21 Cornwall Terrace, NW1 4QP—*President*, Sir Randolph Quirk, C.B.E.; *Sec.*, P. W. H. Brown.

BRITISH AND FOREIGN SCHOOL SOCIETY (1808), Richard Mayo Hall, Eden Street, Kingston upon Thames, Surrey KT1 1HZ—*Sec.*, S. M. A. Banister.

BRITISH ATLANTIC COMMITTEE, 5 St. James's Place, SW1A 1NP—*Dir.*, Maj.-Gen. C. J. Popham, C.B.

BRITISH INSTITUTE IN EASTERN AFRICA, 1 Kensington Gore, SW7 2AR—*London Sec.*, Mrs. J. Moyo.

BRITISH INSTITUTE OF ARCHÆOLOGY AT ANKARA, c/o The British Academy, 20–21 Cornwall Terrace, NW1 4QP—*London Sec.*, Ms. F. Chapman-Purchas.

BRITISH INSTITUTE OF PERSIAN STUDIES (1961), 13 Cambrian Road, Richmond, Surrey TW10 6JQ—*Sec.*, Mrs. M. E. Gueritz, M.B.E.

BRITISH INTERPLANETARY SOCIETY (1933), 27–29 South Lambeth Road, SW8 1SZ—*Exec. Sec.*, L. J. Carter.

BRITISH ISRAEL WORLD FEDERATION (1919), 6 Buckingham Gate, SW1E 6JP—*Sec.*, R. B. H. Hall.

BRITISH LEGION, ROYAL, 48 Pall Mall, SW1Y 5JY—*Gen. Sec.*, Lt.-Col. P. C. E. Creasy.

BRITISH LEGION SCOTLAND, ROYAL, New Haig House, Logie Green Road, Edinburgh EH7 4HR—*Sec.*, Brig. R. W. Riddle, O.B.E.

BRITISH MEDICAL ASSOCIATION (1832), B.M.A. House, Tavistock Square, WC1H 9JP—*President*, Sir David Innes Williams, M.D.; *Sec.*, J. D. J. Havard, M.D.

BRITISH SCHOOL OF ARCHÆOLOGY IN JERUSALEM (1919), The British Academy, 20 Cornwall Terrace, N.W.1.—*Pres.*, The Rev. Prof. H. Chadwick, D.D., F.B.A. *Dir.*, Dr. R. Harper.

BRUSH MANUFACTURERS' ASSOCIATION, BRITISH, 6a East Street, Epsom, Surrey KT17 1HH—*Sec.*, J. A. Snellgrove.

BUDDHIST SOCIETY, THE (1924), 58 Eccleston Square, SW1V 1PH—*Gen. Sec.*, R. C. Maddox.

BUDGERIGAR SOCIETY, THE (1925), 49–53 Hazelwood Road, Northampton NN1 1LG—*Gen. Sec.*, A. C. Crook.

BUILDING, CHARTERED INSTITUTE OF (1834), Englemere, Kings Ride, Ascot, Berks. SL5 8BJ—*Chief Exec.*, K. Banbury.

BUILDING SERVICES ENGINEERS, CHARTERED INSTITUTION OF (1897), Delta House, 222 Balham High Road, SW12 9BS—*Sec.*, A. V. Ramsay.

BUILDING SOCIETIES ASSOCIATION, 3 Savile Row, W1X 1AF—*Dir.-Gen.*, M. J. Boléat.

BUILDING SOCIETIES INSTITUTE, THE CHARTERED, 19 Baldock Street, Ware, Herts. SG12 9DH—*Sec.*, R. D. Crerar.

BUSINESS AND PROFESSIONAL WOMEN, UNITED KINGDOM FEDERATION OF (1938), 23 Ansdell Street, W8 5BN—*Sec.*, Mrs. R. Bangle.

BUSINESS ARCHIVES COUNCIL, 185 Tower Bridge Road, SE1 2UF—*Sec. Gen.*, S. Kelly.

BUTCHERS' AND DROVERS' CHARITABLE INSTITUTION (1828), 61 West Smithfield, EC1A 9EA—*Sec.*, J. A. Fordyce.

CADET FORCE ASSOCIATION, COMBINED, (1952), Cheltenham Terrace, SW3 4RR—*Sec.*, Brig. R. B. MacGregor-Oakford, C.B.E., M.C.

CALOUSTE GULBENKIAN FOUNDATION, (1956), 98 Portland Place, W1N 4ET—*Dir.*, B. Whitaker.

CAMBRIDGE PRESERVATION SOCIETY (1929), Wandlebury Ring, Gog Magog Hills, Babraham, Cambridge CB2 4AE—*Sec.*, Mrs. K. Wright.

CAMERA CLUB, THE (1885), 8 Great Newport Street, WC2H 7JA—*Sec.*, D. Pincham.

CAMERON FUND, THE, (1971), Tavistock House North, Tavistock Square, WC1H 9JP—*Sec.*, Mrs. J. Martin.

CAMPAIGN FOR NUCLEAR DISARMAMENT (CND) (1958), 22–24 Underwood Street, N1 7JG—*Gen. Sec.*, Meg Beresford.

CANCER RESEARCH CAMPAIGN, 2 Carlton House Terrace, SW1Y 5AR—*Dir. Gen.*, D. de Peyer.

CANCER RELIEF, NATIONAL SOCIETY FOR (MACMILLAN FUND) (1911), Anchor House, 15–19 Britten Street, SW3 3TZ—*Dir. and Gen. Sec.*, D. Scott.

CANCER RESEARCH FUND, IMPERIAL (1902), P.O. Box 123, Lincoln's Inn Fields, WC2A 3PX—*Sec.*, Maj.-Gen. A. W. Dennis, C.B., O.B.E.

CANCER RESEARCH, THE INSTITUTE OF: Royal Cancer Hospital, 17A Onslow Gardens, SW7 3AL—*Sec.*, J. Defries.

CAREER TEACHERS, ASSOCIATION OF, Hillsboro., Castledine Street, Loughborough, Leics. LE11 2DX—*Gen. Sec.*, Miss R. Yaffé.

CARNEGIE DUNFERMLINE TRUST (1903). (Social and cultural purposes in Dunfermline). Abbey Park House, Dunfermline KY12 7PB—*Sec.*, F. Mann.

CARNEGIE HERO FUND TRUST (1908). Makes grants and allowances to people injured or the dependants of people killed in saving human life within the British Isles and territorial waters. Abbey Park House, Dunfermline KY12 7PB—*Sec.*, F. Mann.

CARNEGIE UNITED KINGDOM TRUST (1913). Comely Park House, Dunfermline, KY12 7EJ—*Sec.*, G. Lord.

CATHEDRALS ADVISORY COMMISSION FOR ENGLAND, 83 London Wall, EC2M 5NA—*Sec.*, P. A. T. Burman.

CATHOLIC MARRIAGE ADVISORY COUNCIL, Clitherow House, 1 Blythe Mews, Blythe Road, W14 0NW—*Chief Exec.*, Mrs. J. Judge.

CATHOLIC RECORD SOCIETY (1904). c/o 114 Mount Street, W1Y 6AH—*Hon. Sec.*, Miss R. Rendel.

CATHOLIC TRUTH SOCIETY (1868), 38–40 Eccleston Square, SW1V 1PD—*Gen. Sec.*, D. Murphy.

CATHOLIC UNION OF GREAT BRITAIN, St. Maximilian Kolbe House, 63 Jeddo Road, W12 9EE—*Pres.*, The Duke of Norfolk, K.G., G.C.V.O., C.B., C.B.E., M.C.; *Hon. Sec.*, Mrs. J. Stuyt, M.B.E.

CATTLE BREEDERS' ASSOCIATION, NATIONAL, 24 Courtenay Park, Newton Abbot, Devon TQ12 2HB—*Sec.*, J. H. Pappin.

CATTLE BREEDER'S CLUB, LTD., Lavenders, Isfield, Uckfield, Sussex TN22 5TX—*Sec.*, C. R. Stains.

CECIL HOUSES (Inc.) (Housing Association), 2 Priory Road, Kew, Richmond, Surrey TW9 3DG—*Sec.*, D. S. Cottrell.

CENTRAL BUREAU (for educational visits and exchanges) (1948), Seymour Mews House, Seymour Mews, W1H 9PE—*Dir.* A. H. Male.

CERAMICS, INSTITUTE OF (1955), Shelton House, Stoke Road, Shelton, Stoke-on-Trent, Staffs., ST4 2DR—*Pres.*, Dr. D. Taylor.

CHADWICK TRUST (1895) (for the promotion of health and prevention of disease).—Department of Civil Engineering, University College London, Gower Street, WC1E 6BT—*Sec.*, D. Kasher.

CHANTREY BEQUEST (1875), Royal Academy of Arts, Burlington House, Piccadilly, W1V 0DS—*Sec.*, P. Rodgers.

CHARTERED SECRETARIES AND ADMINISTRATORS, INSTITUTE OF (1891), 16 Park Crescent, W1N 4AH—*Sec.*, B. Barker, M.B.E.

CHEMICAL ENGINEERS, INSTITUTION OF (1922), George E. Davis Building, 165–171 Railway Terrace, Rugby, Warks. CV21 3HQ—*Gen. Sec.*, Dr. T. J. Evans.

CHEMICAL INDUSTRY, SOCIETY OF, 14–15 Belgrave Square, SW1X 8PS—*Pres.*, Dr. L. Fernandez; *Gen. Sec.*, Dr. P. P. King, F.R.S.C.

CHEMISTRY, THE ROYAL SOCIETY OF, Burlington House, Piccadilly, W1V 0BN—*Pres.*, Prof. J. M Ward; *Sec. Gen.*, Dr. J. S. Gow, F.R.S.E.

(LEONARD) CHESHIRE FOUNDATION (1955), 26–29 Maunsel Street, SW1P 2QN. 78 homes and 23 family support services in U.K. and affiliated to a further 165 world-wide.—*Dir.*, A. L. Bennett.

CHESS FEDERATION, BRITISH, 9A Grand Parade, St. Leonards-on-Sea, East Sussex TN38 0DD—*Gen. Sec.*, G. Lee.

CHEST, HEART AND STROKE ASSOCIATION (1899), Tavistock House North, Tavistock Square, WC1H 9JE—*Dir. Gen.*, Sir David Atkinson, K.B.E.

CHILDBIRTH TRUST, NATIONAL (1956), Alexandra House, Oldham Terrace, Acton, W3 6NH—*Nat. Sec.*, Mrs. H. Corbishley.

CHILDREN'S HOME, NATIONAL (1869), 85 Highbury Park, N5 1UD. Supports over 10,000 disadvantaged

and disabled children and their parents annually in Great Britain and the Third World—*Principal*, Rev. M. Newman.

CHILDREN'S SOCIETY, THE, (1881), Edward Rudolf House, Margery Street, WC1X 0JL—*Dir.*, I. Sparks.

CHINA ASSOCIATION (1889), Swire House, 59 Buckingham Gate., SW1E 6AJ—*Exec. Dir.*, Brig. B. G. Hickey, O.B.E., M.C.

CHIROPODISTS, SOCIETY OF, 53 Welbeck Street, W1M 7HE—*Gen. Sec.*, J. G. C. Trouncer.

CHOIRS SCHOOLS ASSOCIATION (1921), Ambrosden Avenue, SW1P 1QH—*Hon. Sec.*, P. Hannigan.

CHRISTIAN ACTION, St. Peter's House, 308 Kennington Lane, SE11 5HY—*Dir.*, Canon E. James.

CHRISTIAN AID (1945), P.O. Box 100, SE1 7RT—*Dir.*, Rev. M. H. Taylor.

CHRISTIAN EDUCATION COUNCIL, NATIONAL, Robert Denholm House, Nutfield, Redhill, Surrey RH1 4HW—*Exec. Officer*, E. A. Thorn.

CHRISTIAN EDUCATION MOVEMENT (1965), Lancaster House, Borough Road, Isleworth, Middx. TW7 5DU. *Gen. Sec.*, Rev. Dr. S. Orchard.

CHRISTIAN EVIDENCE SOCIETY (1870), St. Stephen's House, St. Stephen's Crescent, Brentwood, Essex CM13 2AT—*Hon. Sec.*, Mrs. G. M. Ryeland.

CHRISTIAN KNOWLEDGE, SOCIETY FOR PROMOTING (S.P.C.K.) (1698), Holy Trinity Church, Marylebone Road, NW1 4DU—*Gen. Sec.*, P. N. G. Gilbert.

CHRISTIANS AND JEWS, COUNCIL OF (1942), 1 Dennington Park Road, West End Lane, NW6 1AX—*Exec. Dir.*, (vacant).

CHURCH ARMY, Independents Road, Blackheath, SE3 9LG.—*Chief Sec.*, Rev. M. Rees.

CHURCH BUILDING SOCIETY, INCORPORATED (1818), Fulham Palace, SW6 6EA—*Sec.*, Maj. R. I. Radford, M.B.E.

CHURCH EDUCATION CORPORATION, Bedgebury School, Goudhurst, Cranbrook, Kent TN17 2SH.—*Sec.*, R. P. Gilbert.

CHURCH HOUSE, THE CORPORATION OF (1888), Dean's Yard, SW1P 3NZ—*Sec.*, Capt. P. W. E. Parry, M.B.E.

CHURCH LADS' AND CHURCH GIRLS' BRIGADE, 2 Barnsley Road, Wath upon Dearne, S. Yorks. S63 9PY—*Gen. Sec.*, Rev. C. Grice, M.B.E.

CHURCH MISSIONARY SOCIETY (1799), Partnership House, 157 Waterloo Road, SE1 8UU—*Gen. Sec.*, Rt. Rev. H. W. Moore.

CHURCH MUSIC, ROYAL SCHOOL OF, Addington Place, Croydon, Surrey CR9 5AD—*Sec.*, V. Waterhouse.

CHURCH OF ENGLAND PENSIONS BOARD (1926), 53 Tufton Street, SW1P 3QP—*Sec.*, R. G. Radford.

CHURCH OF ENGLAND SOLDIERS', SAILORS' AND AIRMEN'S CLUBS (1891), 1 Shakespeare Terrace, 126 High Street, Portsmouth PO1 2RH. *Chairman*, Rear-Adm. A. G. Watson, C.B.

CHURCH UNION (1859), Faith House, 7 Tufton Street, SW1P 3QN—*Gen. Sec.*, Father R. E. Thompson.

CHURCHES, BRITISH COUNCIL OF (1942), Inter-Church House, 35–41 Lower Marsh, SE1 7RL—*Gen. Sec.*, Rev. Dr. P. Morgan.

CHURCHES, COUNCIL FOR THE CARE OF, 83 London Wall, EC2M 5NA.—*Sec.*, P. A. T. Burman.

CHURCHES, FRIENDLESS, FRIENDS OF (1957), 12 Edwardes Square, W8 6HG—*Hon. Sec.*, L. E. Jones.

CHURCHES MAIN COMMITTEE (1941), Fielden House, Little College Street, SW1P 3JZ—*Sec.*, B. M. Thimont, C.B.

CITIZENS' ADVICE BUREAUX, NATIONAL ASSOCIATION OF (1931), Myddelton House, 115–123 Pentonville Road, N1 9LZ—*Chief Exec. Officer*, Ms. E. Filkin.

CITY PAROCHIAL FOUNDATION, 10 Fleet Street, EC4Y 1AU—*Clerk*, T. Cook.

CIVIL DEFENCE, INSTITUTE OF (1938), Bell Court House, 11 Blomfield Street, EC2M 7AY—*Hon. Gen. Sec.*, T. B. Schofield.

CIVIL ENGINEERS, INSTITUTION OF (1818), Great George Street, SW1P 3AA—*Sec.*, J. C. McKenzie.

CIVIL LIBERTIES, NATIONAL COUNCIL FOR (1934), 21 Tabard Street, SE1 4LA—*Gen. Sec.*, Ms. S. Spencer.

CLASSICAL ASSOCIATION (1903).—*Hon. Treas.*, R. Wallace, Dept. of Classics, University of Keele, Keele, Staffs. ST5 5BG.

CLASSICAL TEACHERS, JOINT ASSOCIATION OF (1962), 31–34 Gordon Square, WC1H 0PY—*Exec. Sec.*, Mrs. L. Kellett.

CLEAN AIR, NATIONAL SOCIETY FOR (1899), 136 North Street, Brighton BN1 1RG—*Sec. Gen.*, J. Langston, C.B.E..

CLERGY ORPHAN CORPORATION (1749), 57b Tufton Street, SW1P 3QL—*Sec.*, J. Buncher.

CLERKS OF WORKS OF GREAT BRITAIN, INSTITUTE OF (1882), 41 The Mall, Ealing, W5 3TJ—*Sec.*, A. P. Macnamara.

COACHING CLUB (1871), 8 Parthenia Road, SW6 4BD—*Sec.*, D. H. Clarke.

COMMERCE, ASSOCIATION OF BRITISH CHAMBERS OF (1860), Sovereign House, 212a Shaftesbury Avenue, WC2H 8EW.—*Dir. Gen.*, R. G. Taylor, C.B.E.

COMMERCE, ASSOCIATION OF SCOTTISH CHAMBERS OF, 30 George Square, Glasgow G2 1EQ—*Sec.*, E. Marwick.

COMMERCE AND INDUSTRY, LONDON CHAMBER OF (1881), 69 Cannon Street, EC4N 5AB—*Dir.*, A. M. W. Platt.

COMMERCE AND MANUFACTURES, EDINBURGH CHAMBER OF (1786), 3 Randolph Crescent, Edinburgh EH3 7UD—*Chief Exec.*, D. M. Mowat.

COMMERCE, CANADA UNITED KINGDOM CHAMBER OF, 3 Regent Street, SW1Y 4NZ—*Exec. Dir.*, G. F. Bacon.

COMMERCE, GLASGOW CHAMBER OF (1783), 30 George Square, Glasgow G2 1EQ—*Sec.*, E. Marwick.

COMMERCIAL AND INDUSTRIAL EDUCATION, BRITISH ASSOCIATION FOR (BACIE), 16 Park Crescent, W1N 4AP—*Dir.*, B. V. Murphy.

COMMERCIAL TRAVELLERS' BENEVOLENT INSTITUTION (1849), *Sec.*, M. N. Bown, Gable End, Mill Hill Road, Arnesby, Leics. LE8 3WG.

COMMISSIONAIRES, THE CORPS OF (1859), provides employment for ex-members of H.M. forces and ex-police, fire service and merchant navy men and prison officers, *Headquarters*, 3 Crane Court, Fleet Street, EC4A 2EJ. Divisions in Belfast, Birmingham, Bristol, Edinburgh, Glasgow, Leeds, Liverpool, London, Manchester, Newcastle upon Tyne. Total strength, 2,800—*Commandant*, Col. R. B. Robertson; *Deputy Commandant*, Brig. The Hon. H. E. C. Willoughby.

COMPLEMENTARY MEDICINE, INSTITUTE FOR (1856), 21 Portland Place, W1N 3AF—*Dir.*, A. Baird.

COMPOSERS' GUILD OF GREAT BRITAIN, THE (1945), 34 Hanway Street, W1P 9DE—*Gen. Sec.*, Ms. E. Yeoman.

COMPUTER SOCIETY, BRITISH (1957), 13 Mansfield Street, W1M 0BP—*Chief Exec.*, J. R. Brookes.

CONSERVATION OF HISTORIC AND ARTISTIC WORKS, INTERNATIONAL INSTITUTE FOR, 6 Buckingham Street, WC2N 6BA— *Sec. Gen.*, Prof. H. W. M. Hodges.

CONSERVATION VOLUNTEERS, BRITISH TRUST FOR (1970), 36 St. Mary's Street, Wallingford, Oxon. OX10 0EU—*Dir.*, I. Branton, O.B.E.

CONSTRUCTION SURVEYORS' INSTITUTE (1952), Wellington House, 203 Lordship Lane, SE22 8HA—*Exec. Officer*, A. Hunt.

CONSULTING ECONOMISTS' ASSOCIATION, INTERNATIONAL (1986), 363 Upper Richmond Road West, SW14 7NX—*Chairman*, Hon. Maureen Hadfield.

CONSULTING ENGINEERS, ASSOCIATION OF (1913), Alliance House, 12 Caxton Street, SW1H 0QL—*Sec.*, Brig. H. Woodrow.

CONSULTING SCIENTISTS, ASSOCIATION OF, 11 Rosemont Road, NW3 6NG—*Hon. Sec.*, W. G. Simpson.

CONSUMERS' ASSOCIATION, 2 Marylebone Road, NW1 4DX—*Dir.*, J. Beishon.

CONTEMPORARY APPLIED ARTS, 43 Earlham Street, WC2H 9LD—*Dir.*, Ms. T. Marsden.

CONVEYANCERS, COUNCIL FOR LICENSED (1986), Golden Cross House, Duncannon Street, WC2N 4JF—*Sec.*, N. R. Osner.

CO OPERATIVE SOCIETIES AND ASSOCIATIONS:—

Co-operative Party, 158 Buckingham Palace Road, SW1W 9UB—*Sec.*, D. Wise, O.B.E.

Co-operative Union Ltd. (1869), Holyoake House, Hanover Street, Manchester M60 0AS—*Chief Exec. and Gen. Sec.*, D. L. Wilkinson.

Co-operative Wholesale Society (C.W.S.) (1863), P.O. Box 53, New Century House, Manchester M60 4ES—*Chief Exec.*, Sir Dennis Landau.

Co-operative Women's Guild, 342 Hoe Street, Walthamstow, E17 9PX—*Nat. Officer.*, Ms D. Paskin.

Fisheries Organization Society, Ltd. (1914), Lancastrian House, Derry's Cross, Plymouth PL1 2SG—*Sec.*, W. Williams, M.B.E.

Plunkett Foundation for Co-operative Studies (1919), 31 St. Giles, Oxford OX1 3LF—*Dir.*, E. Parnell.

COPYRIGHT COUNCIL, BRITISH (1953), 29–33 Berners Street, W1P 4AA—*Sec.*, G. V. Adams.

CORONERS' SOCIETY OF ENGLAND AND WALES (1846)— *Hon. Sec.*, Dr. J. D. K. Burton, C.B.E., 7 Orchard Rise, Richmond, Surrey TW10 5BX.

CORPORATE TREASURERS, ASSOCIATION OF, 16 Park Crescent, W1N 4AH—*Sec.*, R. Plastow.

CORPORATE TRUSTEES, ASSOCIATION OF, 2 Withdean Rise, Brighton BN1 6YN.—*Sec.*, L. C. Howes.

CORRESPONDENCE COLLEGES, ASSOCIATION OF BRITISH (1955), 6 Francis Grove, SW19 4DT—*Sec.*, Mrs. M. Coren.

COTTON GROWING ASSOCIATION, BRITISH (1904), 3 Shortlands, Hammersmith, W6 8RT—*Man. Dir.*, M. T. G. Davies.

COUNSEL AND CARE FOR THE ELDERLY, 16 Bonny Street, NW1 9LR—*Gen. Sec.*, J. Hobart.

COUNTRY HOUSES ASSOCIATION LTD. (1955), 41 Kingsway, WC2B 6UB—*Chief Exec.*, R. D. Bratby.

COUNTRY LANDOWNERS' ASSOCIATION (1907), 16 Belgrave Square, SW1X 8PQ—*Dir. Gen.*, J. M. Douglas, C.B.E.

COUNTY CHIEF EXECUTIVES, ASSOCIATION OF—*Hon. Sec.*, R. W. Adcock, County Hall, Chelmsford, Essex CM1 1LX.

COUNTY COUNCILS, ASSOCIATION OF, Eaton House, 66a Eaton Square, SW1W 9BH—*Sec.*, Sir P. Newsam.

COUNTY EMERGENCY PLANNING OFFICERS' SOCIETY—*Hon. Sec.*, J. A. M. Holloway, Hampton House, 20 Albert Embankment, SE1 7SS.

COUNTY SECRETARIES, SOCIETY OF—*Hon. Sec.*, J. R. Gregory, County Buildings, Stafford, ST16 2LH.

COUNTY SURVEYORS' SOCIETY (1884)—*Hon. Sec.*, J. J. Stansfield, Suffolk County Council, St. Edmunds House, Rope Walk, Ipswich IP4 1LZ.

COUNTY TREASURERS, SOCIETY OF (1903)—*President*, J. A. Parkes; *Hon. Sec.*, D. G. Barrett, County Offices, Newland, Lincoln, Lincolnshire LN1 1YG.

CRUELTY TO ANIMALS, ROYAL SOCIETY FOR THE PREVENTION OF. See "ROYAL" and "SCOTTISH SOCIETY."

CRUELTY TO CHILDREN. See "NATIONAL" and "ROYAL SCOTTISH."

CULTURAL EXCHANGE, ASSOCIATION FOR (1958), Babraham, Cambridge CB2 4AP—*Gen. Sec.*, P. B. Barnes.

CURWEN INSTITUTE, 17 Primrose Avenue, Romford, Essex RM6 4QB—*Gen. Sec.*, H. Jones.

CWMNI URDD GOBAITH CYMRU, Swyddfa'r Urdd, Aberystwyth, Dyfed SY23 1EN—*Dir.*, J. E. Williams.

CYCLISTS' TOURING CLUB (1878), Cotterell House, 69 Meadrow, Godalming, Surrey GU7 3HS—*Sec.*, A. J. Leng.

CYMMRODORION, THE HONOURABLE SOCIETY OF (1751), 30 Eastcastle Street, W1N 7PD—*Hon. Sec.*, Mrs. J. Gruffydd.

CYSTIC FIBROSIS RESEARCH TRUST (1964), Alexandra House, 5 Blyth Road, Bromley, Kent BR1 3RS—*Dir.*, Mrs. B. Bentley.

DAIRY ASSOCIATION, UNITED KINGDOM (1950), Giggs Hill Green, Thames Ditton, Surrey KT7 0EL—*Sec.*, Mrs. J. M. Newton.

DAIRY FARMERS, ROYAL ASSOCIATION OF BRITISH (1876) 55 Sleaford Street, SW8 5AB—*Chief Exec.*, F. R. Francis, L.V.O., M.B.E.

DAIRY TECHNOLOGY, SOCIETY OF (1943), 72 Ermine Street, Huntingdon, Cambs. PE18 6EZ—*Nat. Sec.*, P. H. F. Lee.

D-DAY AND NORMANDY FELLOWSHIP.—*Hon. Sec.*, Mrs. L. R. Reed, 9 South Parade, Southsea, Hants. PO5 2JB.

DEAF ASSOCIATION, BRITISH (1890 *formerly* BRITISH DEAF AND DUMB ASSOCIATION), 38 Victoria Place, Carlisle CA1 1HU—*Gen. Sec.*, A. W. Verney.

DEAF CHILDREN, ROYAL SCHOOL FOR (1792), Victoria Road, Margate, Kent CT9 1NB—*Sec.*, D. E. Downs.

DEAF, COMMONWEALTH SOCIETY FOR THE (1959), 105 Gower Street, WC1E 6AH—*Chairman*, C. Holborow, T.D., M.D.

DEAF, ROYAL NATIONAL INSTITUTE FOR THE (1911), 105 Gower Street, WC1E 6AH—*Chief Exec.*, M. Whitlam.

DEAF PEOPLE, ROYAL ASSOCIATION IN AID OF, 27 Old Oak Road, W3 7HN—*Chief Exec.*, Ms. R. Brotherweed.

DEAF WOMEN, FOLEY HOUSE RESIDENTIAL HOME FOR, Foley House, 115 High Garrett, Braintree, Essex CM7 5NU—*Dir.*, Mrs. N. Hartard.

DEER MANAGEMENT SOCIETIES, THE FEDERATION OF (1975)—*Hon. Sec.*, R. Young, Easters, Sandhills, Cattistock, Dorchester DT2 0HQ.

DEER SOCIETY, BRITISH, Church Farm, Lower Basildon, Reading, Berks. RG8 9NH.

DEFENCE STUDIES, ROYAL UNITED SERVICES INSTITUTE FOR, Whitehall, SW1A 2ET—*Dir.*, Gp. Capt. D. Bolton (*retd*).

DENTAL ASSOCIATION, BRITISH (1880), 64 Wimpole Street, W1M 8AL—*Sec.*, N. H. Whitehouse.

DENTAL COUNCIL, GENERAL, 37 Wimpole Street W1M 8DQ—*Registrar*, N. T. Davies, M.B.E.

DENTAL HOSPITALS OF THE UNITED KINGDOM, ASSOCIATION OF (1942).—*Hon. Sec.*, Mrs. P. Harrington, St. Chad's Queensway, Birmingham B4 6NN.

DESIGN AND INDUSTRIES ASSOCIATION (1915), 29 Bedford Square, WC1B 3EG—*Hon. Dir.*, P. Guilmant.

DESIGNERS FOR INDUSTRY, FACULTY OF ROYAL (1936), John Adam Street, WC2N 6EZ—*Sec.*, C. Lucas.

DESIGNERS, THE CHARTERED SOCIETY OF (1930), 29 Bedford Square, WC1B 3EG—*Dir.*, Ms. P. Rees Cummings.

DEVON AND CORNWALL RECORD SOCIETY (1904), c/o Devon and Exeter Institution, 7 The Close, Exeter EX1 1EZ.—*Hon. Sec.*, J. D. Brunton.

DIABETIC ASSOCIATION, BRITISH (1934), 10 Queen Anne Street, W1M 0BD—*Sec. Gen.*, Capt. D. G. Armytage, C.B.E., R.N.

DICKENS FELLOWSHIP, Dickens House, 48 Doughty Street, WC1N 2LF—*Hon. Gen. Sec.*, A. S. Watts.

DIRECTORS, INSTITUTE OF, 116 Pall Mall, SW1Y 5ED—*Dir. Gen.*, Sir John Hoskyns.

DISABILITY AND REHABILITATION, ROYAL ASSOCIATION FOR, 25 Mortimer Street, W1N 8AB—*Dir.*, G. Wilson, C.B.E.

DISPENSING OPTICIANS, ASSOCIATION OF BRITISH (1925), 22 Nottingham Place, W1M 4AT—*Sec.*, J. W. Roskill.

DISTRESSED GENTLEFOLKS' AID ASSOCIATION (1897), Vicarage Gate House, Vicarage Gate, W8 4AQ—*Gen. Sec.*, J. A. Marshall, C.B.

DISTRICT COUNCILS, ASSOCIATION OF (1974), 9 Buckingham Gate, SW1E 6LE—*Sec.*, G. McCartney.

DISTRICT MEDICAL OFFICERS, ASSOCIATION OF (1982). *Hon. Sec.*, Dr. D. Cullen, Mount Gould Hospital, Mount Gould Road, Plymouth PL4 7QD.

DISTRICT SECRETARIES, ASSOCIATION OF, 9 Margaret Road, Bishopsworth, Bristol BS13 9DQ—*Hon. Sec.*, D. C. Lunn.

DITCHLEY FOUNDATION, Ditchley Park, Enstone, Oxford OX7 4ER—*Dir.*, Sir John Graham, Bt., G.C.M.G.

DOCKLAND SETTLEMENTS, 197 East Ferry Road, Isle of Dogs, E14 9AB—*Chief Exec.*, M. S. Stribling.

DOMESTIC SERVANTS' BENEVOLENT INSTITUTION (1846), Royal Bank of Scotland P.L.C., 7 Burlington Gardens, W1A 3DD—*Sec.*, A. J. Gibson.

DOWSERS, BRITISH SOCIETY OF—*Sec.*, M. D. Rust, Sycamore Cottage, Tamley Lane, Hastingleigh, Ashford, Kent TN25 5HW.

DRAINAGE AUTHORITIES, ASSOCIATION OF (1937).—*Sec.*, D. Noble, The Mews, 3 Royal Oak Passage, High Street, Huntingdon, Cambs. PE18 6EA.

DRINKING FOUNTAIN AND CATTLE TROUGH ASSOCIATION, METROPOLITAN (1859)—*Sec.* D. R. W. Randall, 105 Wansunt Road, Bexley, Kent DA5 2DN.

DRIVING SOCIETY, BRITISH, 27 Dugard Place, Barford, Nr. Warwick CV35 8DX—*Sec.*, Mrs. J. M. Dillon.

DRUG DEPENDENCE, INSTITUTE FOR THE STUDY OF, 1–4 Hatton Place, EC1N 8ND—*Dir.*, J. Woodcock, O.B.E.

DUKE OF EDINBURGH'S AWARD SCHEME. 57,355 awards gained world-wide. 5 Prince of Wales Terrace, W8 5PG—*Dir.*, Maj.-Gen. M. F. Hobbs, C.B.E.

DYERS AND COLOURISTS, SOCIETY OF (1884), Perkin House, P.O. Box 244, 82 Grattan Road, Bradford BD1 2JB—*Gen. Sec.*, M. Tordoff, PH.D.

EARL HAIG'S (BRITISH LEGION) APPEAL FUND. *See* "BRITISH LEGION."

EARLY CHILDHOOD EDUCATION, BRITISH ASSOCIATION FOR, Studio 3:2, 140 Tabernacle Street, EC2A 4SD—*Sec.*, Mrs. B. Boon.

ECCLESIASTICAL HISTORY SOCIETY—*Sec.*, Dr. V. G. Davies, Dept. of History, Westfield College, NW3 7ST.

ECCLESIOLOGICAL SOCIETY—*Hon. Sec.*, S. C. Humphrey, 1 Cornish House, Otto Street, SE17 3PE.

EDUCATION IN ART AND DESIGN, NATIONAL SOCIETY FOR (1888), 7a High Street, Corsham, Wilts. SN13 0ES—*Gen. Sec.*, J. Steers.

EDUCATION OFFICERS, SOCIETY OF, 21–27 Lambs Conduit Street, WC1N 3NJ—*Gen. Sec.*, R. P. Harding, C.B.E.

EDUCATION OFFICERS' SOCIETY, COUNTY—*Hon. Sec.*, N. J. Fitton, County Hall, Chester CH1 1SQ.

EDUCATIONAL CENTRES ASSOCIATION, Chequer Centre, Chequer Street, EC1Y 8PL—*Sec.*, D. Delahunt.

EDUCATIONAL INSTITUTE OF DESIGN, CRAFT AND TECHNOLOGY, 852 Melton Road, Thurmaston, Leicester LE7 8BW—*Administrator*, C. Grimes.

EDUCATIONAL MANAGEMENT AND ADMINISTRATION SOCIETY, BRITISH (1977)—*Sec.*, Miss M. E. Hewitt, Buxton Girls' School, Buxton, Derbys. SK17 6RB.

EDUCATIONAL RESEARCH IN ENGLAND AND WALES, NATIONAL FOUNDATION FOR, The Mere, Upton Park, Slough, Berks. SL1 2DQ—*Dir.*, Dr. Clare Burstall.

EGYPT EXPLORATION SOCIETY (1882), 3 Doughty Mews, WC1N 2PG—*Sec.*, Dr. Patricia A. Spencer.

ELECTORAL REFORM SOCIETY OF GREAT BRITAIN AND IRELAND, 6 Chancel Street, SE1 0UU—*Pres.*, Lord Blake, F.B.A..

ELECTRICAL ENGINEERS, INSTITUTION OF (1871), Savoy Place, WC2R 0BL—*Sec.*, H. H. W. Losty.

ELECTRICITY CONSUMERS' COUNCIL, Brook House, 2 16 Torrington Place, WC1E 7LL—*Dir.*, T. Boorman.

ELGAR FOUNDATION, Elgar's Birthplace, Crown East Lane, Lower Broadheath, Worcester WR2 6RH—*Hon. Sec.*, B. Edgington.

ELGAR SOCIETY (1951)—*Sec.*, Mrs. C. Holt, 20 Geraldine Road, Malvern, Worcs. WR14 3PA.

ENERGY, INSTITUTE OF (1927), 18 Devonshire Street, Portland Place, W1N 2AU—*Sec.*, C. Rigg.

ENGINEERING COUNCIL, THE, 10 Maltravers Street, WC2R 3ER—*Sec.*, J. Carlill, O.B.E.

ENGINEERING DESIGNERS, INSTITUTION OF (1945), Courtleigh, Westbury Leigh, Westbury, Wilts. BA13 3TA—*Sec.*, M. J. Osborne.

ENGINEERING, FELLOWSHIP OF (1976), 2 Little Smith Street, SW1P 3DL—*Exec. Sec.*, V. J. Osola, C.B.E.

ENGINEERING INDUSTRIES ASSOCIATION, 16 Dartmouth Street, SW1H 9BL—*Dir.*, Col. W. T. Williams.

ENGINEERS AND SHIPBUILDERS IN SCOTLAND, INSTITUTION OF (1857), Charing Cross Tower, 10 Elmbank Gardens, Glasgow, G2 4HT—*Sec.*, G. V. Dare.

ENGINEERS AND SHIPBUILDERS, N.E. COAST INSTITU-TION OF (1884), 12 Windsor Terrace, Jesmond, Newcastle upon Tyne, NE2 4HE—*Sec.*, Mrs. A. J. Rainsford.

ENGINEERS, INSTITUTION OF BRITISH (1928), Royal Liver Building, 6 Hampton Place, Brighton, BN1 3DD—*Sec.*, Mrs. D. Henry.

ENGINEERS, SOCIETY OF (1854), Parsifal College, 527 Finchley Road, NW3 7BG—*Sec.*, P. A. Lancaster.

ENGLISH ASSOCIATION, THE (1906), The Vicarage, Priory Gardens, W4 1TT—*Sec.*, Dr. Ruth Fairbanks-Joseph.

ENGLISH FOLK DANCE AND SONG SOCIETY (1932), Cecil Sharp House, 2 Regent's Park Road, NW1 7AY—*Hon. Dir.*, S. A. Mathews.

ENGLISH PLACE-NAME SURVEY (1923)—*Hon. Director*, Prof. K. Cameron, C.B.E., F.B.A., The University, Nottingham NG7 2RD.

ENGLISH-SPEAKING UNION OF THE COMMONWEALTH (1918), 37 Charles Street, W1X 8AB—*Dir. Gen.*, Rear-Adm. R. Heaslip, C.B.

ENTOMOLOGICAL SOCIETY OF LONDON, ROYAL (1833), 41 Queen's Gate, SW7 5HU—*Registrar*, G. G. Bentley.

ENVIRONMENTAL CONSERVATION, COUNCIL FOR (1969), London Ecology Centre, 80 York Way, N1 9AG—*Sec.*, D. Hughes.

ENVIRONMENTAL HEALTH OFFICERS, INSTITUTION OF, Chadwick House, Rushworth Street, SE1 0QT—*Sec.*, A. M. Tanner.

EPILEPSY ASSOCIATION, BRITISH, Anstey House, 40 Hanover Square, Leeds LS3 1BE—*Chief Exec.*, A. Aspinall.

EPILEPSY, THE NATIONAL SOCIETY FOR (1892), Chalfont Centre for Epilepsy, Chalfont St. Peter, Gerrards Cross, Bucks. SL9 0RJ—*Chief Exec.*, Col. D. W. Eking.

EQUESTRIAN FEDERATION, BRITISH, British Equestrian Centre, Kenilworth, Warwicks. CV8 2LR—*Dir. Gen.*, M. C. R. Wallace.

ESPERANTO ASSOCIATION OF BRITAIN (1977), 140 Holland Park Avenue, W11 4UF—*Hon. Sec.*, W. Green.

ESTATE AGENTS, NATIONAL ASSOCIATION OF, (1962), Arbon House, 21 Jury Street, Warwick CV34 4EH—*Gen. Sec.*, A. B. Clark.

EUGENICS SOCIETY (1907), 19 Northfields Prospect, Northfields, SW18 1PE—*Gen. Sec.*, Mrs. L. Brooks.

EVANGELICAL ALLIANCE (1846), 186 Kennington Park Road, SE11 4BT—*Gen. Sec.*, Rev. C. Calver.

EVANGELICAL LIBRARY, THE, 78a Chiltern Street, W1M 2HB—*Librarian*, Miss F. S. Wright.

EXAMINERS UNDER SOLICITORS (SCOTLAND) ACT (1980), Law Society's Hall, 26 Drumsheugh Gardens, Edinburgh EH3 7YR—*Clerk*, K. W. Pritchard.

EXECUTIVES ASSOCIATION OF GREAT BRITAIN, Suite 87–89, The Hop Exchange, 24 Southwark Street, SE1 1TY—*Sec.*, J. J. Langdon-Mudge.

EXPORT-FINANCE ADVISORY COUNCIL, BRITISH (1981), 1 Grosvenor Place, SW1X 7JB—*Chairman*, C. D. Hankes-Drielsma.

EXPORT, INSTITUTE OF, Export House, 64 Clifton Street, EC2A 4HB—*Sec.*, D. J. Langham.

EX-SERVICES LEAGUE, BRITISH COMMONWEALTH, 48 Pall Mall, SW1Y 5JG—*Sec. Gen.*, Brig. M. J. Doyle, M.B.E.

EX-SERVICES MENTAL WELFARE SOCIETY, Broadway House, The Broadway, Wimbledon, SW19 1RL—*Gen. Sec.*, Brig. A. K. Dixon.

FABIAN SOCIETY (1884), 11 Dartmouth Street, SW1H 9BN—*Gen. Sec.*, J. Willman.

FAIRBRIDGE SOCIETY (1909), 119–126 Bush House (N.E.), Aldwych, WC2B 4PY—*Dir. and Sec.*, Mrs. C. P. MacGregor.

FAIR ISLE BIRD OBSERVATORY TRUST, 21 Regent Terrace, Edinburgh EH7 5BT—*Hon. Sec.*, V. M. Thorn.

FAMILY CONCILIATION COUNCIL, NATIONAL (1982), 34 Milton Road, Swindon, Wilts. SN1 5JA—*Chairman*, Mrs. T. Fisher.

FAMILY HISTORY SOCIETIES, FEDERATION OF (1974)—*Administrator*, Mrs. P. Saul, c/o The Benson Room, Birmingham and Midland Institution, Margaret Street, B3 3BS.

FAMILY PLANNING ASSOCIATION, 27–35 Mortimer Street, W1N 7RJ—*Gen. Sec.*, A. Service.

FAMILY WELFARE ASSOCIATION (1869) 501–5 Kingsland Road, E8 4AU—*Dir.*, R. E. Morley.

FAUNA AND FLORA PRESERVATION SOCIETY (1903)—c/o Zoological Society of London, Regent's Park, NW1 4RY—*Exec. Sec.*, J. A. Burton.

FELLOWSHIP HOUSES TRUST (1937), Clock House, Byfleet, Weybridge, Surrey KT14 7RN—*Sec.*, L. P. Leech.

FIELD SPORTS SOCIETY, BRITISH (1930), 59 Kennington Road, SE1 7PZ—*Dir.*, Maj.-Gen. J. Hopkinson, C.B.

FIELD STUDIES COUNCIL (1943), Preston Montford, Montford Bridge, Shrewsbury SY4 1HW—*Dir.*, A. D. Thomas.

FILM CLASSIFICATION, BRITISH BOARD OF, 3 Soho Square, W1V 5DE—*Dir.*, J. Ferman.

FILM INSTITUTE, BRITISH (1933), 21 Stephen Street, W1P 1PL—*Dir.*, W. Stevenson; *Controller, National Film Theatre*, L. Hardcastle, O.B.E.

FIRE ENGINEERS, INSTITUTION OF, 148 New Walk, Leicester LE1 7QB—*Gen. Sec.*, Mrs. C. E. Mackwood.

FIRE PROTECTION ASSOCIATION, 140 Aldersgate Street, EC1A 4HX—*Dir.*, C. D. Woodward.

FIRE SERVICES ASSOCIATION, THE BRITISH, 86 London Road, Leicester LE2 0QR—*Gen. Sec.*, T. A. Plummer.

FIRE SERVICES NATIONAL BENEVOLENT FUND (1943), Marine Court, Fitzalan Road, Littlehampton, W. Sussex BN17 5NF—*Gen. Man.*, R. A. Spackman.

FLEET AIR ARM OFFICERS ASSOCIATION (1957), 94 Piccadilly, W1V 0BP—*Chairman*, W. J. Hanks.

FOLKLORE SOCIETY, c/o University College London, Gower Street, WC1E 6BT—*Hon. Sec.*, A. R. Vickery.

FOOD SCIENCE AND TECHNOLOGY, INSTITUTE OF, 5 Cambridge Court, 210 Shepherd's Bush Road, W6 7NL.—*Exec. Sec.*, Ms. H. G. Wild.

FOOD FROM BRITAIN, 301–344 Market Towers, New Covent Garden Market, SW8 5NQ—*Chairman*, B. Law.

FORCES HELP SOCIETY AND LORD ROBERTS WORKSHOPS (1899), 122 Brompton Road, SW3 1JE—*Comptroller and Sec.*, Col. A. W. Davis, M.B.E.

FOREIGN BONDHOLDERS, COUNCIL OF (1873), 35 High Street, Bromley, Kent BR1 1LE—*Manager*, E. J. French.

FOREIGN PRESS ASSOCIATION IN LONDON, 11 Carlton House Terrace, SW1Y 5AJ—*Sec.* Mrs D. Crole.

FORENSIC SCIENCES, BRITISH ACADEMY OF (1959)—*Sec.-Gen.*, Dr. Patricia J. Flynn, Anaesthetic Unit, The London Hospital Medical College, Turner Street, E1 2AD.

FORESTERS, INSTITUTE OF CHARTERED (1982), 22 Walker Street, Edinburgh EH3 7HR—*Sec.*, Mrs. M. W. Dick.

FORESTRY ASSOCIATION, COMMONWEALTH (1921), c/o Oxford Forestry Institute, South Parks Road, Oxford OX1 3RB—*Sec.*, M. T. Rogers.

FORESTRY SOCIETY OF ENGLAND, WALES AND NORTHERN IRELAND, ROYAL (1882), 102 High Street, Tring, Herts. HP23 4AH—*Dir.*, E. H. M. Harris.

FORESTRY SOCIETY, ROYAL SCOTTISH (1854), 11 Atholl Crescent, Edinburgh EH3 8HE—*Sec.* W. B. C. Walker.

FOUNDRYMEN, INSTITUTE OF BRITISH (1904), Bridge House, 121 Smallbrook Queensway, Birmingham B5 4JP—*Sec.*, G. A. Schofield.

FRANCO-BRITISH SOCIETY, Room 636, Linen Hall, 162–168 Regent Street, W1R 5TB—*Exec. Sec.*, Mrs. M. Clarke.

FREE CHURCH FEDERAL COUNCIL, 27 Tavistock Square, WC1H 9HH—*Gen. Sec.*, Rev. D. Staple.

FREEDOM ASSOCIATION (1975), Avon House, 360–366 Oxford Street, W1N 0AA—*Executive Officer*, Cdr. C. J. Paterson.

FREEMASONS, GRAND LODGE OF ANTIENT FREE AND ACCEPTED MASONS OF SCOTLAND (1736), Freemasons' Hall, 96 George Street, Edinburgh EH2 3DH—*Grand Master Mason of Scotland*, J. M. Marcus Humphrey of Dinnet; *Grand Sec.*, A. O. Hazel.

FREEMASONS, UNITED GRAND LODGE OF ENGLAND, Freemasons' Hall, Great Queen Street, WC2B 5AZ—*Grand Master*, H.R.H. the Duke of Kent, K.G., G.C.M.G., G.C.V.O.; *Grand Sec.*, Cdr. M. B. S. Higham, R.N.

FREEMEN OF ENGLAND (1966), *Sec.*, E. T. Ellis, Gardener's Cottage, Saxby All Saints, Brigg, S. Humberside DN20 0QF.

FREEMEN'S GUILDS:—
Freemen's Guild of Berwick upon Tweed, 9 Church Street, Berwick upon Tweed TD15 1EF—*Clerk*, J. R. Reay.
Freemen and Guilds of the City of Chester, The Guildhall, Chester.
City of Coventry Freemen's Guild—*Hon. Sec.*, H. J. McCranor, 89 Brinklow Road, Binley, Coventry CV3 2JB—*Hon. Clerk*, H. J. McCranor.
Guild of Freemen of the City of London, P.O. Box 153, 40a Ludgate Hill, EC4M 7DE—*Clerk*, Col. D. Ivy.
Gild of Freemen of the City of Newcastle upon Tyne—*Hon. Sec.*, F. P. M. Cook, 79 Holly Avenue, Jesmond, Newcastle upon Tyne NE2 7QB.
Gild of Freemen of the City of York—*Hon. Clerk*, R. Lee, 29 Albemarle Road, York YO2 1EW.

FRESHWATER BIOLOGICAL ASSOCIATION (1929), The Ferry House, Ambleside, Cumbria LA22 0LP—*Sec. and Director of Laboratories*, Prof. J. Gwynfryn Jones, D.SC.

FRIENDLY SOCIETIES, NATIONAL CONFERENCE OF, Room 313, Victoria House, Vernon Place, WC1B 4DP—*Sec.*, P. M. Madders.

FRIENDS OF CATHEDRAL MUSIC (1956), c/o Addington Palace, Croydon, Surrey CR9 5AD.—*Hon. Gen. Sec.*, N. T. Barnes.

FRIENDS OF THE CLERGY CORPORATION, THE, 27 Medway Street, SW1P 2BD—*Sec.*, J. M. Greany.

FRIENDS OF THE NATIONAL LIBRARIES, The British Library, WC1B 3DG—*Hon. Sec.*, J. F. Fuggles.

FRIENDS OF THE ELDERLY & GENTLEFOLK'S HELP, 42 Ebury Street, SW1W 0LZ—*Gen. Sec.*, Rev. J. Schofield.

FURNITURE HISTORY SOCIETY (1964), c/o Dept. of Furniture and Interior Design, Victoria and Albert Museum, SW7 2RL—*Hon. Sec.*, Dr. B. Austen.

GALLIPOLI ASSOCIATION (1915)—*Hon. Sec.*, J. C. Watson Smith, Berry Cottage, Nuptown, Warfield, Berks. RG12 6HP.

GAME CONSERVANCY, THE, Fordingbridge, Hants. SP6 1EF—*Dir.*, R. M. Van Oss.

GARDEN HISTORY SOCIETY (1965), 5 The Knoll, Hereford HR1 1RU—*Hon. Membership Sec.*, Mrs. A. Richards.

GARDENERS' ASSOCIATION, THE GOOD, Two Mile Lane, Higham, Glos. GL2 8DW—*Hon. Dir.*, J. D. Wilkin.

GARDENERS' ROYAL BENEVOLENT SOCIETY (1839), Bridge House, 139 Kingston Road, Leatherhead, Surrey KT22 7NT—*Sec-Administrator*, C. R. C. Bunce.

GAS CONSUMERS COUNCIL, 6th Floor, Abford House, 15 Wilton Road, SW1V 1LT—*Dir.*, I. W. Powe.

GAS ENGINEERS, INSTITUTION OF (1863), 17 Grosvenor Crescent, SW1X 7ES—*Sec.*, D. J. Chapman.

GEMMOLOGICAL ASSOCIATION OF GREAT BRITAIN (1931), St. Dunstan's House, Carey Lane, EC2V 8AB—*Sec.*, J. P. Brown.

GENEALOGICAL RESEARCH SOCIETY, IRISH—*Sec.*, Miss Z. A. M. Kelly, 11 Lyric Road, SW13 9QA

GENEALOGISTS AND RECORD AGENTS, ASSOCIATION OF (1968), 1 Woodside Close, Caterham, Surrey CR3 6AU—*Sec.*, Mrs. J. Tooke.

GENEALOGISTS, SOCIETY OF (1911), 14 Charterhouse Buildings, Goswell Road, EC1M 7BA—*Dir.*, A. J. Camp.

GENERAL PRACTITIONERS, ROYAL COLLEGE OF (1952), 14 Princes Gate, Hyde Park, SW7 1PU—*Gen. Administrator*, Mrs. S. Irvine.

GENTLEPEOPLE, GUILD OF AID FOR (1904), 10 St. Christopher's Place, W1M 6HY—*Sec.*, Mrs. G. A. Burgess.

GEOGRAPHICAL ASSOCIATION, 343 Fulwood Road, Sheffield S10 3BP—*Joint Hon. Secs.*, Dr. J. A. Binns; P. S. Fox.

GEOGRAPHICAL SOCIETY, ROYAL (1830), 1 Kensington Gore, SW7 2AR—*Pres.*, Lord Chorley.

GEOGRAPHICAL SOCIETY, ROYAL SCOTTISH (1884), 10 Randolph Crescent, Edinburgh EH3 7TU—*Sec.*, A. B. Cruickshank.

GEOLOGICAL SOCIETY (1807), Burlington House, Piccadilly, W1V 0JU—*Pres.*, Prof. D. J. Blundell; *Exec. Sec.*, R. M. Bateman.

GEOLOGISTS' ASSOCIATION, Burlington House, Piccadilly, W1V 9AG—*Hon. Gen. Sec.*, Dr. Mrs. S. M. Dellow.

GEOLOGISTS, THE INSTITUTION OF (1977), Burlington House, Piccadilly, W1V 0AG—*Sec.*, Dr. J. A. Seymour.

GEORGIAN GROUP (1937), 37 Spital Square, E1 6DY—*Sec.*, R. White.

GIFTED CHILDREN, NATIONAL ASSOCIATION FOR (1966), 1 South Audley Street, W1Y 5DQ—*Dir.*, J. Welch.

GILBERT AND SULLIVAN SOCIETY, 273 Northfield Avenue, W5 4UA.

GIRL GUIDES ASSOCIATION (1910), 17–19 Buckingham Palace Road, SW1W 0PT. In 1987 the total membership in the United Kingdom was 749,362.—*Chief Commissioner*, Dr. June Paterson-Brown; *Gen. Sec.*, Miss M. W. Hayter.

GIRLS' BRIGADE, THE, Girls' Brigade House, 62 Foxhall Road, Didcot, Oxon. OX11 7BQ—*Brigade Sec. for Eng. & Wales*, Miss D. M. Cosser.

GIRLS' FRIENDLY SOCIETY AND TOWNSEND FELLOWSHIP (1875), 126 Queens Gate, SW7 5LQ—*Gen. Sec.*, Miss H. G. Smith.

GIRLS OF THE REALM GUILD (1900) Educational grants and loans towards professional training.—*Sec.*, Mrs. B. Hayward, 2 Watchoak, Blackham, Tunbridge Wells, Kent TN3 9TP.

GIRLS' VENTURE CORPS AIR CADETS, Redhill Aerodrome, Kings Mill Lane, Redhill, Surrey RH1 5JY—*Sec. Gen.*, Miss H. P. Prosper.

GLASS ENGRAVERS, THE GUILD OF, Unit 27d, Thames House, South Bank Business Centre, 140 Battersea Park Road, SW11 4NB—*Sec.*, Miss M. Methven.

GLASS TECHNOLOGY, SOCIETY OF (1916), 20 Hallam Gate Road, Sheffield S10 5BT—*Hon. Sec.*, W. Simpson.

GLIDING ASSOCIATION, BRITISH (1930), Kimberley House, Vaughan Way, Leicester LE1 4SE—*Gen. Sec.*, B. Rolfe.

GOAT SOCIETY, BRITISH (1879), 34–36 Fore Street, Bovey Tracey, Newton Abbot, Devon TQ13 9AD—*Sec.*, S. Knowles.

GRAPHIC FINE ART, SOCIETY OF (1919), 9 Newburgh Street, W1V 1LH—*Sec.*, Miss L. A. Robinson.

GRAPHOLOGISTS, THE BRITISH INSTITUTE OF (1983), Bell Court House, 11 Blomfield Street, EC2M 7AY—*Chairman*, J. E. Blomfield.

GREATER LONDON PLAYING FIELDS ASSOCIATION (1926), 147 Church Street, W2 1NA.

GREEK INSTITUTE (1969), 34 Bush Hill Road, N21 2DS—*Dir.*, Dr. K. Tofallis.

GREEN PARTY, THE (1973), 10 Station Parade, Balham High Road, SW12 9AZ—*Gen. Manager*, J. Bishop.

GROCERS ASSOCIATION, BRITISH INDEPENDENT, 17 Farnborough Street, Farnborough, Hants. GU14 8AG—*Nat. Sec.*, I. A. McKee.

GULBENKIAN FOUNDATION, *see* CALOUSTE.

HAKLUYT SOCIETY (1846), c/o Map Library, The British Library, Great Russell Street, WC1B 3DG—*Joint Hon. Secs.*, Dr. T. E. Armstrong; Mrs. S. Tyacke.

HANSARD SOCIETY FOR PARLIAMENTARY GOVERNMENT (1944), 16 Gower Street, WC1E 6DP—*Dir.*, Ms. M. Goudie.

HARD OF HEARING, BRITISH ASSOCIATION OF THE, 7–11 Armstrong Road, W3 7JL—*Chairman*, E. Trinder.

HARVEIAN SOCIETY OF EDINBURGH (1782), Dept. of Medicine, The Royal Infirmary, Edinburgh EH3 9YW—*Joint Secs.*, Dr. A. D. Toft, A. B. MacGregor.

HARVEIAN SOCIETY OF LONDON, 11 Chandos Street, Cavendish Square, W1M 0EB—*Exec. Sec.*, Maj. T. Tudor-Williams.

HEAD TEACHERS, NATIONAL ASSOCIATION OF—*Gen. Sec.*, D. M. Hart, Holly House, 6 Paddockhall Road, Haywards Heath, West Sussex RH16 1RG.

HEALTH AUTHORITIES, NATIONAL ASSOCIATION OF (1974), Garth House, 47 Edgbaston Park Road, Birmingham B15 2RS—*Dir.*, P. Hunt.

HEALTH CARE ASSOCIATION, BRITISH, 41 St. Paul's Street, Leeds LS1 2JL—*Nat. Sec.*, G. K. Waite.

HEALTH EDUCATION, INSTITUTE OF—*Hon. Sec.*, Dr. L. Baric, 14 High Elm Road, Hale Barns, Altrincham, Cheshire WA15 0HS.

HEALTH, GUILD OF (1904), Edward Wilson House, 26 Queen Anne Street, W1M 9LB—*Sec.*, Ms. T. F. Parker.

HEALTH SERVICES MANAGEMENT, INSTITUTE OF (1902), 75 Portland Place, W1N 4AN—*Dir.*, Ms. M. Dixon, PH.D.

HEART FOUNDATION, BRITISH (1963), 102 Gloucester Place, W1H 4DH—*Dir. Gen.*, Brig. P. G. S. Tower, C.B.E.

HEDGEHOG PRESERVATION SOCIETY, BRITISH (1982), Knowbury House, Ludlow, Shropshire SY8 3LQ— *Sec.*, Mrs. A. Jenkins.

HELLENIC STUDIES, SOCIETY FOR THE PROMOTION OF (1879), 31–34 Gordon Square, WC1H 0PP—*Hon. Sec.*, Dr. Lyn Rodley.

HENRY GEORGE FOUNDATION, 177 Vauxhall Bridge Road, SW1V 1EU—*Company Sec.*, Mrs. B. P. Sobrielo.

HERALDIC AND GENEALOGICAL STUDIES, INSTITUTE OF (1961), 79–82 Northgate, Canterbury, Kent CT1 1BA—*Sec.*, C. H. Schofield.

HERALDRY SOCIETY, THE (1947)—*Sec.*, Marian Miles, M.B.E., Magpie Cottage, Pondwood Lane, Shottesbrooke, Nr. Maidenhead, Berks. SL6 3SS.

HERALDRY SOCIETY OF SCOTLAND (1977)—*Sec.*, Dr. M. C. Stanton, 9 Priestden Park, St. Andrews, Fife KY16 8DL.

HERPETOLOGICAL SOCIETY, BRITISH (1947), c/o Zoological Society of London, Regent's Park, NW1 4RY— *Sec.*, Mrs. M. Green.

HIGHWAYS AND TRANSPORTATION, INSTITUTION OF (1930), 3 Lygon Place, Ebury Street, SW1W 0JS— *Sec.*, Miss P. A. Steel.

HISPANIC AND LUSO BRAZILIAN COUNCIL, Canning House, 2 Belgrave Square, SW1X 8PJ—*Dir. Gen.*, Sir Kenneth James, K.C.M.G.

HISTORICAL ASSOCIATION, THE (1906), 59a Kennington Park Road, SE11 4JH—*Sec.*, Mrs. M. Stiles.

HISTORICAL SOCIETY, ROYAL (1868), University College London, Gower Street, WC1E 6BT—*Pres.*, Dr. G. E. Aylmer; *Exec. Sec.*, Mrs. J. N. McCarthy.

HOMEOPATHIC ASSOCIATION, BRITISH (1902), 27a Devonshire Street, W1N 1RJ—*Gen. Sec.*, Mrs. E. Segall.

HONG KONG ASSOCIATION, THE (1961), Swire House, 59 Buckingham Gate, SW1E 6AJ—*Exec. Dir.*, Brig. B. G. Hickey, O.B.E., M.C.

HORATIAN SOCIETY (1933), 4 Stone Buildings, Lincolns Inn, WC2A 3XT—*Hon. Sec.*, C. P. Sydenham.

HOROLOGICAL INSTITUTE, BRITISH (1858), Upton Hall, Upton, Newark, Notts. NG23 5TE—*Sec.*, W. M. G. Evans.

HOROLOGICAL SOCIETY, ANTIQUARIAN (1953), New House, High Street, Ticehurst, Wadhurst, E. Sussex TN5 7AL—*Acting Sec.*, Mrs. M. Janes.

HORSE SOCIETY, BRITISH (incorporating THE PONY CLUB), British Equestrian Centre, Kenilworth, Warwicks, CV8 2LR—*Dir.*, Col. N. F. Grove-White.

HOSPITAL FEDERATION, INTERNATIONAL (1947), 2 St. Andrew's Place, NW1 4LB—*Dir. Gen.*, Dr. E. N. Pickering.

HOSPITAL SATURDAY FUND, THE (1873), 192–198 Vauxhall Bridge Road, SW1V 1EE—*Acting Sec.*, Miss I. Gleeson.

HOSPITAL SAVING ASSOCIATION, THE, Hambleden House, Andover, Hants. SP10 1LQ—*Gen. Sec.*, J. A. Young.

HOTEL CATERING AND INSTITUTIONAL MANAGEMENT ASSOCIATION, 191 Trinity Road, SW17 7HN—*Dir.*, Miss E. Gadsby.

HOTELS, RESTAURANTS AND CATERERS ASSOCIATION, BRITISH (1907), 40 Duke Street, W1M 6HR—*Chief Exec.*, R. Lees, C.B., M.B.E.

HOUSE OF HOSPITALITY LTD., Holy Cross Priory, Cross-in-Hand, Heathfield, Sussex. Homes (28) for old people.—*Dir.*, Mother Mary Garson.

HOUSE OF ST. BARNABAS IN SOHO (for Homeless Women in London) (1846), 1 Greek Street, W1V 6NQ—*Dir.*, Gp. Capt. H. A. Lax.

HOUSING, INSTITUTE OF, 9 White Lion Street, N1 9XJ—*Dir.*, P. McGurk.

HOUSING AID SOCIETY, CATHOLIC (1956), 189A Old Brompton Road, SW5 0AR—*Dir.*, Ms. R. Rafferty.

HOUSING AND TOWN PLANNING COUNCIL, NATIONAL (1900), 14–18 Old Street, EC1V 9AB—*Dir.*, R. Walker.

HOUSING ASSOCIATION FOR OFFICERS' FAMILIES (1916), Alban Dobson House, Green Lane, Morden, Surrey SM4 5NS—*Gen. Sec.*, J. B. Holt.

HOVERCRAFT SOCIETY, THE (1971), 24 Jellicoe Avenue, Alverstoke, Gosport, Hants. PO12 2PE—*Chairman*, B. J. Russell.

HOWARD LEAGUE FOR PENAL REFORM, THE (1866), 322 Kennington Park Road, SE11 4PP—*Dir.*, Ms. F. Crook.

HUGUENOT SOCIETY OF GREAT BRITAIN AND IRELAND (1885), The Huguenot Library, University College, Gower Street, WC1E 6BT—*Sec.*, Mrs. M. Bayliss.

HUMANE RESEARCH TRUST, THE (1974), Brook House, 29 Bramhall Lane South, Bramhall, Cheshire SK7 2DN—*Chairman*, R. MacAlastair Brown.

HYDROGRAPHIC SOCIETY (1972), North East London Polytechnic, Longbridge Road, Dagenham, Essex RM8 2AS—*Hon. Sec.*, Dr. R. C. Britton.

HYMN SOCIETY OF GREAT BRITAIN AND IRELAND (1936)—*Sec.*, Rev. M. Garland, The Vicarage, 51 Overgreen Drive, Birmingham B37 6EY.

INDEPENDENT SCHOOL BURSARS' ASSOCIATION, *Sec.*, D. J. Bird, Woodlands, Closewood Road, Denmead, Hants. PO7 6JD.

INDEPENDENT SCHOOLS CAREERS ORGANIZATION, 12a-18a Princess Way, Camberley, Surrey GU15 3SP— *Dir.* G. W. Searle.

INDEPENDENT SCHOOLS INFORMATION SERVICE (I.S.I.S.) (1972), 56 Buckingham Gate, SW1E 6AG— *Dir.*, D. J. Woodhead.

INDEPENDENT SCHOOLS JOINT COUNCIL, 25 Victoria Street, SW1H 0EX—*Gen. Sec.*, Dr. A. G. Hearnden.

INDEXERS, SOCIETY OF—*Sec.*, Mrs. C. Troughton, 16 Green Road, Birchington, Kent CT7 9JZ.

INDUSTRIAL CHRISTIAN FELLOWSHIP (1877), St. Katharine Cree Church, 86 Leadenhall Street EC3A 3DH—*Dir.*, D. Arthur.

INDUSTRIAL MANAGERS, INSTITUTION OF, Rochester House, 66 Little Ealing Lane, W5 4XX—*Chief Exec.*, Brig. P. V. Crooks.

INDUSTRIAL MARKETING RESEARCH ASSOCIATION— *Dir. Gen.*, E. Barnsley, 11 Bird Street, Lichfield, Staffs. WS13 6PW.

INDUSTRIAL PARTICIPATION ASSOCIATION (1884), 85 Tooley Street, SE1 2QZ—*Dir.*, B. C. Stevens.

INDUSTRIAL SOCIETY, THE (1918), Peter Runge House, 3 Carlton House Terrace, SW1Y 5DG—*Dir.*, A. Graham; *Sec.*, M. R. Hyde.

INDUSTRY AND PARLIAMENT TRUST, 25 Victoria Street, SW1H 0EX. Aims to bridge the gap in understanding between industry and parliament.—*Dir.*, F. R. Hyde-Chambers.

INFANT DEATHS, THE FOUNDATION FOR THE STUDY OF (1971), 15 Belgrave Square, SW1X 8PS—*Administrative Sec.*, (vacant).

INFORMATION SCIENTISTS, INSTITUTE OF (1958), 44 Museum Street, WC1A 1LY—*Exec. Sec.*, Mrs. S. A. Carter.

INNER WHEEL CLUBS IN GREAT BRITAIN AND IRELAND, ASSOCIATION OF (1934), 51 Warwick Square, SW1V 2AT—*Gen. Sec.*, Miss J. Dobson.

INSURANCE AND INVESTMENT BROKERS' ASSOCIATION, BRITISH, BIIBA House, 14 Bevis Marks, EC3A 7NT—*Dir. Gen.*, J. C. T. Hackett.

INSURANCE BROKERS REGISTRATION COUNCIL, 15 St. Helen's Place, EC3A 6DS—*Registrar,* Miss E. J. Rees.

INSURANCE INSTITUTE, CHARTERED (1897), 20 Aldermanbury, EC2V 7HY—*Sec. Gen.*, P. V. Saxton.

INSURERS, ASSOCIATION OF BRITISH, Aldermary House, Queen Street, EC4N 1TT—*Chief Exec.*, M. A. Jones.

INTERCONTINENTAL CHURCH SOCIETY, 175 Tower Bridge Road, SE1 2AQ—*Gen. Sec.*, Rev. Canon D. R. Irving.

INTERIOR DESIGN, BRITISH INSTITUTE OF (1899), 1c Devonshire Avenue, Beeston, Nottingham NG9 1BS—*Administrator*, N. Parker.

INTERNATIONAL AFFAIRS, ROYAL INSTITUTE OF (1920), Chatham House, 10 St. James's Square, SW1Y 4LE—*Dir.*, Adm. Sir James Eberle, G.C.B.

INTERNATIONAL FRIENDSHIP LEAGUE (1931), 3 Creswick Road, W3 9HE—*Sec.*, Mrs. B. Macdonald.

INTERNATIONAL LAW ASSOCIATION (1873), 3 Paper Buildings, Temple, EC4Y 7EU—*Hon. Sec. Gen.*, B. Mauleverer, Q.C..

INTERNATIONAL POLICE ASSOCIATION (British Section)—1 Fox Road, West Bridgford, Nottingham NG2 6AJ—*Chief Exec. Officer,* K. H. Robinson.

INTERNATIONAL SHIPPING FEDERATION (1909), 30–32 St. Mary Axe, EC3A 8ET—*Sec.*, D. A. Dearsley.

INTERNATIONAL STUDENTS TRUST (1962), 229 Great Portland Street, W1N 5HD—*Sec.*, G. D. Rates.

INTERNATIONAL TIN RESEARCH INSTITUTE (1932)—*Dir.*, Dr. B. T. K. Barry, Kingston Lane, Uxbridge, Middx. UB8 3PJ.

INTERNATIONAL VOLUNTARY SERVICE (1920), 162 Upper New Walk, Leicester LE1 7QA—*Sec.*, P. Ticher.

INTERSERVE (formerly B.M.M.F.) (1852), Whitefield House, 186 Kennington Park Road, SE11 4BT—*Gen. Sec.*, A. M. S. Pont.

INTER-VARSITY CLUBS, ASSOCIATION OF (1946), 26 Chesswood Road, Worthing, W. Sussex BN11 2AD—*Sec.*, M. A. Rooke-Matthews.

INVALID CHILDREN'S AID NATIONWIDE (I CAN) (1888), Allen Graham House, 198 City Road, EC1V 2PH—*Dir.*, J. McKinnon.

INVALIDS-AT-HOME (1966) Helps seriously disabled people living at home—*Hon. Sec.*, Mrs. E. Pierce, 23 Farm Avenue, NW2 2BJ.

INVISIBLE EXPORTS COUNCIL, BRITISH (1983), Winsor House, 39 King Street, EC2V 8DQ—*Dir. Gen.*, D. Thomson.

IRAN SOCIETY (1936), 2 Belgrave Square, SW1X 8PJ—*Hon. Sec.*, K. Bradford.

IRISH SOCIETY, THE HONOURABLE THE (1613), Irish Chamber, Guildhall Yard, EC2V 5AE—*Sec.*, B. E. Manning; *Representative (Ireland)*, Cmdr. P. C. D. Campbell, M.V.O.

JAPAN ASSOCIATION (1950), Swire House, 59 Buckingham Gate, SW1E 6AJ—*Exec. Dir.*, Brig. B. G. Hickey, O.B.E., M.C.

JERUSALEM AND THE MIDDLE EAST CHURCH ASSOCIATION, THE (1887)—*Gen. Sec.*, Ven. R. H. Roberts,

C.B., The Old Gatehouse, Castle Hill, Farnham, Surrey GU9 0AE.

JEWISH WELFARE BOARD (1859)—*Exec. Dir.*, M. I. Carlowe, 221 Golders Green Road, NW11 9DW.

JEWISH HISTORICAL SOCIETY OF ENGLAND, 33 Seymour Place, W1H 5AP—*Hon. Sec.*, C. M. Drukker.

JEWISH YOUTH, ASSOCIATION FOR (1899), A.J.Y. House, 50 Lindley Street, E1 3AX—*Exec. Dir.*, A. Greenbat.

JEWS, CHURCH'S MINISTRY AMONG THE, 30c Clarence Road, St. Albans, Herts. AL1 4JJ—*Gen. Dir.*, Rev. J. M. V. Drummond.

JOHN INNES INSTITUTE (1910), Colney Lane, Norwich NR4 7UH—*Dir.*, Prof. R. B. Flavell, PH.D.

JOURNALISTS, THE INSTITUTE OF, Suite 2, Dock Offices, Surrey Quays, Lower Road, SE16 2XL—*Gen. Sec.*, J. R. Hart.

JUSTICE (British Section of the International Commission of Jurists) (1957), 95a Chancery Lane, WC2A 1DT—*Dir.*, Ms. L. Levin.

JUSTICES' CLERKS' SOCIETY (1839).—*Hon. Sec.*, A. R. Heath, The Court House, Homer Road, Solihull, W. Midlands B91 3RD.

KEEP BRITAIN TIDY GROUP, Bostel House, 37 West Street, Brighton, Sussex BN1 2RE—*Dir. Gen.*, D. J. Lowis.

KING EDWARD'S HOSPITAL FUND FOR LONDON (1897), 14 Palace Court, W2 4HT—Makes grants to hospitals and related organizations both within and outside the N.H.S. in the Greater London area.—*Secretary*, R. J. Maxwell, PH.D.

KING GEORGE'S FUND FOR SAILORS (1917), 1 Chesham Street, SW1X 8NF. Supports all seafarers or their dependants in need. Distributes over £1,300,000 in grants annually.—*Dir. Gen.*, Hon. H. Lawson.

KIPLING SOCIETY, THE (1927), 18 Northumberland Avenue, WC2N 5BJ—*Hon. Sec.*, N. Entract.

LADIES IN REDUCED CIRCUMSTANCES, SOCIETY FOR THE ASSISTANCE OF (1886), Lancaster House, 25 Hornyold Road, Malvern, Worcs. WR14 1QQ.

LANCASTRIANS IN LONDON, ASSOCIATION OF (1892), Burnley House, 129 Kingsway, WC2B 6NJ—*Hon. Sec.*, J. D. Dwyer.

LANDSCAPE INSTITUTE 12 Carlton House Terrace, SW1Y 5AH.—*Registrar*, P. R. Broadbent, O.R.F.

LAND VALUE TAXATION AND FREE TRADE, INTERNATIONAL UNION FOR, 177 Vauxhall Bridge Road, SW1V 1EU—*Sec.*, Mrs. B. Sobrielo.

LAND-VALUE TAXATION LEAGUE, 177 Vauxhall Bridge Road, SW1V 1EU—*Pres.*, V. G. Saldji.

LAW REPORTING FOR ENGLAND AND WALES, INCORPORATED COUNCIL OF (1865), 3 Stone Buildings, Lincoln's Inn, WC2A 3XN—*Sec.* R. H. Pettit.

LEAGUE OF THE HELPING HAND, Baileys, Church Street, Charlbury, Oxford OX7 3PR—*Sec.*, Mrs. D. R. Colvin.

LEAGUE OF WELLDOERS (1893), 119–121 Limekiln Lane, Liverpool L5 8SN—*Warden and Sec.*, K. H. Stanton.

LEATHER AND HIDE TRADES' BENEVOLENT INSTITUTION (1860), 60 Wickham Hill, Hurstpierpoint, Hassocks, Sussex BN6 9NP—*Sec.*, Mrs. G. M. Stapleton, M.B.E.

LEGAL EXECUTIVES, INSTITUTE OF, Kempston Manor, Kempston, Bedford MK42 7AB—*Sec. Gen.*, L. A. Evans.

LEPROSY MISSION, THE (England and Wales) (1874), 50 Portland Place, W1N 3DG—*Chairman*, D. G. Selley; *Exec. Dir.*, The Rev. R. J. Findlay.

LEUKAEMIA RESEARCH FUND (1962), 43 Great Ormond Street, WC1N 3JJ—*Dir.*, G. J. Piller, O.B.E.

LIBRARY ASSOCIATION (1877), 7 Ridgmount Street, WC1E 7AE—*Chief Exec.*, G. Cunningham.

LIFEBOATS. See "ROYAL NATIONAL."

LIGHT HORSE BREEDING SOCIETY, NATIONAL (1885), 96 High Street, Edenbridge, Kent TN8 5AR—*Sec.*, G. W. Evans.

LINGUISTS, INSTITUTE OF (1910), 24a Highbury Grove, N5 2EA—*Gen. Sec.*, A. Root.

LINNEAN SOCIETY OF LONDON (1788), Burlington House, Piccadilly, W1V 0LQ—*Pres.*, M. F. Claridge; *Exec. Sec.*, J. H. Fiddian-Green.

LIONS CLUBS INTERNATIONAL (British Isles & Ireland) (1949).—*Gen. Sec.*, T. L. Packer, 22 Craddock Street, Swansea SA1 3HE.

LLOYD'S, Lime Street, EC3M 7HL—*Chief Exec.*, A. Lord, C.B.

LLOYD'S PATRIOTIC FUND (1803), Lloyd's, Lime Street, EC3M 7HA—*Sec.*, Mrs. J. H. Bright.

LLOYD'S REGISTER OF SHIPPING (1760), 71 Fenchurch Street, EC3M 4BS—*Sec.*, W. T. Leadbetter.

LOCAL AUTHORITIES, INTERNATIONAL UNION OF (British Section) (1913), (*also* COUNCIL OF EUROPEAN MUNICIPALITIES AND REGIONS (British Section) (1951)), 35 Great Smith Street, SW1P 3BJ—*Sec. Gen.*, P. N. Bongers.

LOCAL AUTHORITY CHIEF EXECUTIVES, SOCIETY OF— *Hon. Sec.*, S. Jones, County Hall, Glenfield, Leicester, LE3 8RA.

LOCAL COUNCILS, NATIONAL ASSOCIATION OF (1947), 108 Great Russell Street, WC1B 3LD—*Sec.*, J. Clark.

LONDON APPRECIATION SOCIETY (1932), 17 Manson Mews, SW7 5AF—*Hon. Sec.*, B. Peers, PH.D.

LONDON BOROUGHS ASSOCIATION (1964), Westminster City Hall, Victoria Street, SW1E 6QP—*Hon. Sec.*, R. G. Brooke.

LONDON CITY MISSION (1835), 175 Tower Bridge Road, SE1 2AH—*Gen. Sec.*, Rev. D. M. Whyte.

LONDON CORNISH ASSOCIATION (1898), *Hon. Gen. Sec.*, N. S. Bunney, 119 Warwick Road, N11 2SR.

LONDON COURT OF INTERNATIONAL ARBITRATION (1892), 75 Cannon Street, EC4N 5BH—*Pres.*, The Rt. Hon. Sir Michael Kerr; *Registrar*, B. W. Vigrass, O.B.E., V.R.D.

LONDON FLOTILLA (Association of Reserve and Retired Officers of The Royal Navy).—*Hon. Sec.*, Lt. Cdr. P. A. G. Norman R.D., R.N.R., Marden Rise, 81 Lower Road, Fetcham, Surrey KT22 9HG.

LONDON LIBRARY, THE (1841), 14 St. James's Square, SW1Y 4LG—*Librarian*, D. Matthews.

LONDON MAGISTRATES' CLERKS' ASSOCIATION (1889), *Hon. Sec.*, Miss C. Glenn, Horseferry Road Magistrates Court, 70 Horseferry Road, SW1P 2AX.

"LONDON OVER THE BORDER" CHURCH FUND (1878), 53 New Street, Chelmsford, Essex CM1 1NG—*Sec.*, J. C. Reddington.

LONDON PLAYING FIELDS SOCIETY, THE (1890), Boston Manor Playing Field, Boston Gardens, Brentford, Middx. TW8 9LR—*Sec.*, D. C. Northwood.

LONDON SOCIETY, THE, Room U722, The City University, Northampton Square, EC1V 0HB—*Hon. Sec.*, Mrs. J. E. Vernau.

LORD'S DAY OBSERVANCE SOCIETY (1831), 5 Victory Avenue, Morden, Surrey SM4 6DL—*Gen. Sec.*, J. G. Roberts.

LORD'S TAVERNERS, THE, 1 Chester Street, SW1X 7HP—*Dir.*, Capt. J. A. R. Swainson, O.B.E.

LOTTERIES COUNCIL, THE, 81 Mansel Street, Swansea SA1 5TT—*Hon. Sec.* J. H. Solly.

MAGISTRATES' ASSOCIATION, THE (1920), 28 Fitzroy Square, W1P 6DD—*Sec.*, T. R. P. Rudin.

MAIL USERS' ASSOCIATION, 6 Whitgift Street, Croydon, Surrey CR0 1DH—*Chairman*, J. Blackwell.

MALAYSIA, SINGAPORE AND BRUNEI ASSOCIATION (1955), 90 Fenchurch Street, EC3M 4BY—*Sec.*, Mrs. J. Taylor.

MALAYSIAN RUBBER PRODUCERS' RESEARCH ASSOCIATION (1938), Tun Abdul Razak Laboratory, Brickendonbury, Hertford SG13 8NL—*Dir.*, C. S. L. Baker.

MALCOLM SARGENT CANCER FUND FOR CHILDREN— *Gen. Administrator*, Miss S. Darley, O.B.E., 14 Abingdon Road, W8 6AF.

MALONE SOCIETY (for the publication of scholarly editions and facsimiles of early English dramatic texts).—*Hon. Sec.*, Dr. Lois Potter, Dept. of English, University of Leicester LE1 7RH.

MANAGEMENT, BRITISH INSTITUTE OF, Management House, Parker Street, WC2B 5PT—*Dir. Gen.*, Dr. J. Constable.

MANAGEMENT CONSULTANCIES ASSOCIATION (1956), 11 West Halkin Street, SW1X 8JL—*Exec. Dir.*, B. O'Rorke.

MANAGEMENT AND PROFESSIONAL STAFFS, ASSOCIATION OF, Parkgates, Bury New Road, Prestwich, Manchester M25 8JX—*Exec. Sec.*, Mr. A. J. Casey.

MANAGEMENT SERVICES, INSTITUTE OF, 1 Cecil Court, London Road, Enfield, Middx. EN2 6DD—*Dir. and Gen. Sec.*, E. A. King.

MANORIAL SOCIETY OF GREAT BRITAIN (1906), 104 Kennington Road, SE11 6RE—*Hon. Chairman*, R. A. Smith.

MANPOWER SOCIETY, THE, Freepost, Headington, Oxford OX3 0BR—*Hon. Sec.*, Mrs. B. Hurley.

MARIE CURIE CANCER CARE (Marie Curie Memorial Foundation), 28 Belgrave Square, SW1X 8QG— *Dir. Gen.*, Maj. Gen. M. E. Carleton-Smith, C.B.E. *Scottish Office*, 21 Rutland Street, Edinburgh EH1 2AH.

MARINE ARTISTS, ROYAL SOCIETY OF (1939), 17 Carlton House Terrace, SW1V 4DG—*Sec.*, M. Myers.

MARINE BIOLOGICAL ASSOCIATION OF THE U.K. (1884), The Laboratory, Citadel Hill, Plymouth PL1 2PB— *Sec. to Council and Director of Plymouth Laboratory*, Dr. M. Whitfield.

MARINE BIOLOGICAL SOCIETY, SCOTTISH (1914), Dunstaffnage Marine Research Laboratory, P.O. Box 3, Oban, Argyll PA34 4AD—*Dir. and Sec.*, Prof. J. B. L. Matthews.

MARINE ENGINEERS, INSTITUTE OF (1889), 76 Mark Lane, EC3R 7JN—*Sec.*, J. E. Sloggett.

MARINE SOCIETY, THE (1756), 202 Lambeth Road, SE1 7JW—*Gen. Sec.*, Lt. Cdr. R. M. Frampton, R.N.

MARIO LANZA EDUCATIONAL FOUNDATION (for singers)—*Hon. Sec.*, Miss P. Franklin, Flat 21, Chiswick House, 210 Bell Barn Road, Edgbaston, Birmingham B15 2AB.

MARKET AUTHORITIES, NATIONAL ASSOCIATION OF BRITISH—*Sec.*, B. Ormshaw, 19 Derwent Avenue, Milnrow, Rochdale, Lancs. OL16 3UD.

MARKETING, INSTITUTE OF (1911), Moor Hall, Cookham, Maidenhead, Berks. SL6 9QH—*Dir. Gen.*, T. McBurnie.

MARKET TRADERS' FEDERATION, NATIONAL (1899), Hampton House, Hawshaw Lane, Hoyland, Barnsley S74 0HA—*Gen. Sec.*, R. J. Toller.

MARK MASTER MASONS, GRAND LODGE OF (1856), Mark Masons' Hall, 86 St. James's Street, SW1A 1PL—*Grand Master*, H.R.H. Prince Michael of Kent; *Grand Sec.*, P. G. Williams.

MARRIAGE GUIDANCE *see* RELATE.

MASONIC BENEVOLENT INSTITUTION, ROYAL (1842), 20 Great Queen Street, WC2B 5BG—*Sec.*, N. A. Grout.

MASONIC BENEVOLENT INSTITUTIONS IN IRELAND—*Sec.*, R. J. Clinton, 17–19 Molesworth Street, Dublin 2.

MASONIC TRUST FOR GIRLS AND BOYS (1985), 31 Great Queen Street, WC2B 5AG—*Sec.*, Col. R. K. Hind.

MASTER BUILDERS, FEDERATION OF, Gordon Fisher House, 33 John Street, WC1 2BB—*Dir. Gen.*, W. S. Hilton.

MASTERS OF FOXHOUNDS ASSOCIATION (1881)—*Sec.*, A. H. B. Hart, Parsloes Cottage, Bagendon, Cirencester, Glos. GL7 7DU.

MASTERS OF WINE, THE INSTITUTE OF (1955), Five Kings House, Kennet Wharf Lane, EC4V 3BH—*Exec. Dir.*, D. F. Stevens.

MATERNAL AND CHILD WELFARE, NATIONAL ASSOCIATION FOR (1911), 1 South Audley Street, W1Y 6JS—*Gen. Sec.*, W. Rice.

MATHEMATICAL ASSOCIATION (1871), 259 London Road, Leicester LE2 3BE—*Exec. Sec.*, F. A. Wood.

MATHEMATICS AND ITS APPLICATIONS, INSTITUTE OF (1964), Maitland House, Warrior Square, Southend-on-Sea, Essex SS1 2JY—*Sec. and Registrar*, Miss C. M. Richards.

MEASUREMENT AND CONTROL, INSTITUTE OF (1944), 87 Gower Street, WC1E 6AA—*Sec. and Chief Exec.*, M. J. Yates.

MECHANICAL ENGINEERS, INSTITUTION OF, 1 Birdcage Walk, SW1H 9JJ—*Sec.*, R. Mellor.

MEDIC ALERT FOUNDATION. For the protection, in emergencies, of those with a hidden medical disability or allergy. 11–13 Clifton Terrace, N4 3JP—*Sec. Gen.*, Mrs. M. L. Stanton.

MEDICAL COUNCIL, GENERAL, 44 Hallam Street, W1N 6AE—*Registrar*, P. L. Towers.

MEDICAL SOCIETY OF LONDON (1773), 11 Chandos Street, W1M 0EB—*Registrar*, Maj. T. Tudor-Williams.

MEDICAL WOMEN'S FEDERATION (1917), Tavistock House North, Tavistock Square, WC1H 9HX—*Hon. Sec.*, Dr. Patricia Price.

MEDIEVAL ARCHAEOLOGY, SOCIETY FOR (1957)—*Hon. Sec.*, A. Vince, PH.D., C.L.A.U., The Sessions House, Lindum Road, Lincoln LN2 1PB.

MEN OF THE TREES (1922), Turners Hill Road, Crawley Down, Crawley, Sussex RH10 4HL—*Exec. Sec.*, Mrs. E. Sandwell.

MENTAL AFTER CARE ASSOCIATION (1879), Bainbridge House, Bainbridge Street, WC1A 1HP.—*Dir.*, B. G. Garner.

MENTAL HEALTH FOUNDATION, THE (1949), 8 Hallam Street, W1N 6DH—*Dir.*, Maj. Gen. R. B. Loudoun, C.B., O.B.E.

MERCHANT NAVY WELFARE BOARD, 19–21 Lancaster Gate, W2 3LN—*Gen. Sec.*, J. I. K. Walker.

METALS, THE INSTITUTE OF (1985), 1 Carlton House Terrace, SW1Y 5DB—*Sec.*, Dr. J. A. Catterall.

METAL TRADES BENEVOLENT SOCIETY, ROYAL (1843), Kelvin House, 1 Totteridge Avenue, High Wycombe, Bucks. HP13 6XG—*Sec.*, A Whittle, M.B.E..

METEOROLOGICAL SOCIETY, ROYAL (1850), James Glaisher House, Grenville Place, Bracknell, Berks. RG12 1BX—*Exec. Sec.*, D. R. Grant.

METROPOLITAN AND CITY POLICE ORPHANS FUND (1870), 30 Hazlewell Road, SW15 6LH—*Sec.*, R. Duff-Cole, B.E.M.

METROPOLITAN AUTHORITIES, ASSOCIATION OF (1974), 35 Great Smith Street, SW1P 3BJ—*Sec.*, A. Gronow.

METROPOLITAN HOSPITAL-SUNDAY FUND (1872), 40 High Street, Teddington, Middx. TW11 8EW. In 1986, £35,816 was distributed to N.H.S. hospitals. £158,780 was distributed to hospitals outside the N.H.S., and £40,900 to other medical charities.—*Sec.*, D. A. B. Lynch.

METROPOLITAN PUBLIC GARDENS ASSOCIATION (1882)—*Sec.*, Mrs. J. Bellamy, 3 Mayfield Road, Thornton Heath, Croydon CR4 6DN.

MIDDLE EAST ASSOCIATION, THE (1961), Bury House, 33 Bury Street, SW1Y 6AX—*Dir.-Gen.*, Sir James Craig, G.C.M.G..

MIDWIVES, ROYAL COLLEGE OF (1881), 15 Mansfield Street, W1M 0BE—*Gen. Sec.*, Miss R. M. Ashton.

MIGRAINE ASSOCIATION, BRITISH, 178a High Road, Byfleet, Weybridge, Surrey KT14 7ED—*Hon. Sec.*, Mrs. J. Liddell.

MIGRAINE TRUST (1965), 45 Great Ormond Street, WC1N 3HD—*Dir.*, Cdr. O. Wright.

MILITARY HISTORICAL SOCIETY, National Army Museum, Royal Hospital Road, SW3 4HT, *Hon. Sec.*, J. Gaylor.

MIND (National Association for Mental Health), 22 Harley Street, W1N 2ED—*Dir.*, C. Heginbotham.

MINERALOGICAL SOCIETY (1876), 41 Queen's Gate, SW7 5HR—*Hon. Gen. Sec.*, Dr. M. G. Bown.

MINES OF GREAT BRITAIN, FEDERATION OF SMALL, Northcote Chambers, 13a King Street, Newcastle-under-Lyme, Staffs. ST5 1ER—*Sec.*, R. W. Bladen.

MINIATURE PAINTERS, SCULPTORS AND GRAVERS, ROYAL SOCIETY OF (1895)—*Exec. Sec.*, Mrs. S. M. Burton, 15 Union Street, Wells, Somerset BA5 2PU.

MINIATURISTS, SOCIETY OF (1895), Castle Gallery, Castle Hill, Ilkley, West Yorks. LS29 9DT—*Dir.*, L. Simpson.

MINING INSTITUTE OF SCOTLAND, c/o British Coal Corporation, Green Park, Greenend, Edinburgh, EH17 7PZ—*Sec.*, E. R. Rodger.

MISSION TO DEEP SEA FISHERMEN, ROYAL NATIONAL (1881), 43 Nottingham Place, W1M 4BX—*Sec.*, B. O. Clampton.

MISSIONS TO SEAMEN, THE, St. Michael Paternoster Royal, College Hill, EC4R 2RL—*Gen. Sec.*, Rev. Canon W. J. D. Down.

MODERN CHURCHPEOPLE'S UNION (1898), for the advancement of liberal religious thought—*Hon. Sec.*, Rev. R. C. Truss, The Rectory, Church Square, Shepperton, Middx. TW17 9JY.

MODERN LANGUAGE ASSOCIATION, Regent's College, Inner Circle, Regent's Park, NW1 4NS—*Gen. Sec.*, Miss E. H. Ingham.

MONUMENTAL BRASS SOCIETY (1887), *Hon. Sec.*, W. Mendelsson, 57 Leeside Crescent, NW11 0HA.

MORAVIAN MISSIONS, LONDON ASSOCIATION IN AID OF (1817), Moravian Church House, 5–7 Muswell Hill, N10 3TJ—*Sec.*, Rev. F. J. C. Smith.

MOTOR INDUSTRY, THE INSTITUTE OF THE, Fanshaws, Brickendon, Hertford SG13 8PQ—*Sec.*, F. W. Janes.

MOUNTBATTEN MEMORIAL TRUST (1979), 18 Northumberland Avenue, WC2N 5BJ—*Dir. and Sec.*, Mrs. S. Barnett, O.B.E.

MOUNTBATTEN TRUST, THE EDWINA 1 Grosvenor Crescent, SW1X 7EF—*Sec.*, J. Boyd-Brent.

MULTIPLE SCLEROSIS SOCIETY, 25 Effie Road, SW6 1EE—*Gen. Sec.*, J. Walford.

MUNICIPAL ENGINEERS, ASSOCIATION OF, 1/7 Great George Street, SW1P 3AA—*Dir.*, K. J. Marchant.

MUSEUMS ASSOCIATION (1889), 34 Bloomsbury Way, WC1A 2SF—*Dir. Gen.*, G. Farnell.

MUSIC HALL SOCIETY, BRITISH (1963), 68 Drury Lane, WC2B 5SP—*Hon. Sec.*, Mrs. D. Masterton.

MUSICIANS BENEVOLENT FUND, 16 Ogle Street W1P 7LG—*Sec.*, M. B. M. Williams.

MUSICIANS, INCORPORATED SOCIETY OF (1882) 10 Stratford Place, W1N 9AE—*Gen. Sec.*, D. E. Padgett-Chandler.

MUSICIANS OF GREAT BRITAIN, ROYAL SOCIETY OF (1738), 10 Stratford Place, W1N 9AE—*Sec.*, Mrs. M. E. Gleed, M.B.E.

MUSIC INFORMATION CENTRE, BRITISH, 10 Stratford Place, W1N 9AE—*Centre Mgrs.*, T. Morgan, M. Greenall.

MUSIC SOCIETIES, NATIONAL FEDERATION OF (1935), Francis House, Francis Street, SW1P 1DE—*Administrator*, R. Jones.

MYALGIC ENCEPHALOMYELITIS ASSOCIATION (1976), P.O. Box 8, Stanford-le-Hope, Essex SS17 8EX—*Dir.*, P. M. Blackman.

NATIONAL AND UNIVERSITY LIBRARIES, STANDING CONFERENCE OF (SCONUL) (1950), 102 Euston Street, NW1 2HA—*Sec.*, A. J. Loveday.

NATIONAL BENEVOLENT INSTITUTION (1812), 61 Bayswater Road, W2 3PG—*Sec.*, Gp. Capt. D. St. J. Homer.

NATIONAL COUNCIL FOR VOLUNTARY ORGANIZATIONS, 26 Bedford Square, WC1B 3HU—*Dir.*, Ms. U. Prashar.

NATIONAL COUNCIL OF WOMEN OF GREAT BRITAIN (1895)—*Sec.*, Mrs. J. D. Norman, 36 Danbury Street, Islington, N1 8JU.

NATIONAL SOCIETY, THE, (1811), for promoting religious education. Church House, Great Smith Street, SW1P 3NZ—*Gen. Sec.*, C. Alves.

NATIONAL SOCIETY FOR THE PREVENTION OF CRUELTY TO CHILDREN (1884), 67 Saffron Hill, EC1N 8RS—*Dir.*, Dr. A. Gilmour, C.B.E.

NATIONAL UNION OF STUDENTS, Nelson Mandela House, 461 Holloway Road N7 6LJ—*Nat. Sec.*, M. Carlisle.

NATIONAL VIEWERS' AND LISTENERS' ASSOCIATION—*President*, Mrs. M. Whitehouse, C.B.E, Ardleigh, Colchester, Essex CO7 7RH.

NATION'S FUND FOR NURSES, 57 Lower Belgrave Street, SW1W 0LP—*Administrator*, P. E. Starr.

NATURALISTS' ASSOCIATION, BRITISH (1905), *Hon. Mem. Sec.*, Mrs. Y. H. Griffiths, 23 Oak Hill Close, Woodford Green, Essex IG8 9PH.

NATURE CONSERVATION, ROYAL SOCIETY FOR (1912).—*Gen. Sec.*, Dr. F. H. Perring, The Green, Nettleham, Lincoln LN2 2NR.

NAUTICAL RESEARCH, SOCIETY FOR (1911), c/o National Maritime Museum, Greenwich, SE10 9NF—*Hon. Sec.*, Lt. Cdr. L. Phillipps.

NAVAL, MILITARY AND AIR FORCE BIBLE SOCIETY (1780), Radstock House, 3 Eccleston Street, SW1W 9LZ—*Gen. Sec.*, R. Kennedy.

NAVAL ARCHITECTS, ROYAL INSTITUTION OF (1860), 10 Upper Belgrave Street, SW1X 8BQ—*Sec.*, P. W. Ayling.

NAVIGATION, ROYAL INSTITUTE OF, c/o The Royal Geographical Society, 1 Kensington Gore, SW7 2AT. *Dir.*, Rear Adm. R. M. Burgoyne, C.B.

NAVY RECORDS SOCIETY, Public Record Office, Chancery Lane, WC2A 1LR—*Hon. Sec.*, Dr. N. A. M. Rodger.

NEEDLEWORK, ROYAL SCHOOL OF (1872), 5 King Street, Covent Garden, WC2 8HN—*Dir. of Ed.*, Mrs. J. Fitzgerald Bond.

NEWCOMEN SOCIETY (1920), for the study of the history of engineering and technology, Science Museum, SW7 2DD—*Exec. Sec.*, A. Smith.

NEW ENGLISH ART CLUB (1886), 17 Carlton House Terrace, SW1Y 5BD—*Sec.*, W. Bowyer, R.A.

NEWSAGENTS, NATIONAL FEDERATION OF RETAIL, Yeoman House, Sekforde Street, Clerkenwell Green, EC1R 0HD—*Chief Exec.*, K. E. J. Peters.

NEWSPAPER EDITORS, GUILD OF BRITISH (1946), Bloomsbury House, Bloomsbury Square, 74–77 Great Russell Street, WC1B 3DA—*Sec.*, C. Gordon Page.

NEWSPAPER PRESS FUND (1864), Dickens House, 35 Wathen Road, Dorking, Surrey RH4 1JY—*Dir.*, P. W. Evans.

NEWSPAPER SOCIETY (1836), Bloomsbury House, Bloomsbury Square, 74–77 Great Russell Street, WC1B 3DA—*Dir.*, D. Nisbet-Smith.

NEWSVENDORS' BENEVOLENT INSTITUTION (1839), P.O. Box 306, Dunmow, Essex CM6 1HY—*Dir.*, C. S. Jones.

NOISE ABATEMENT SOCIETY, P.O. Box 8, Bromley, Kent BR2 0UH—*Chairman*, J. Connell.

NON-SMOKERS, NATIONAL SOCIETY OF (1926), Latimer House, 40–48 Hanson Street, W1P 7DE—*Hon. Sec.*, T. W. Hurst.

NORTHERN IRELAND TOURIST BOARD, River House, 48 High Street, Belfast BT1 2DS—*Chief Exec.*, S. B. Belford.

NORWOOD CHILD CARE (1795) (Jewish welfare organization for Jewish children), Stuart Young House, 221 Golders Green Road, NW11 9DL—*Exec. Dir.*, S. Brier.

NUCLEAR ENERGY SOCIETY, BRITISH (1962), 1–7 Great George Street, SW1P 3AA—*Exec. Officer*, P. Bacos.

NUFFIELD FOUNDATION (1943), 28 Bedford Square, WC1B 3EG—*Dir.*, J. Cornford.

NUFFIELD PROVINCIAL HOSPITALS TRUST (1939), 3 Prince Albert Road, NW1 7SP—*Gen. Sec.*, Dr. M. Ashley-Miller.

NUMISMATIC SOCIETY, BRITISH—*Hon. Sec.*, W. Slayter, 63 West Way, Edgware, Middx. HA8 9LA.

NUMISMATIC SOCIETY, ROYAL, c/o Dept. of Coins and Medals, The British Museum, Great Russell Street, WC1B 3DG—*Hon. Sec.*, J. E. Cribb.

NURSES ASSOCIATION, ROYAL BRITISH, 94 Upper Tollington Park, N4 4NB—*Hon. Sec.*, Mrs. H. M. Vorstermans, M.B.E.

NURSES', RETIRED, NATIONAL HOME, Riverside Avenue, Bournemouth BH7 7EE—*Chairman*, Dr. R. E. Chaplin.

NURSES, ROYAL NATIONAL PENSION FUND FOR, 15 Buckingham Street, WC2—*General Manager and Actuary*, V. G. West.

NURSING, MIDWIFERY AND HEALTH VISITING, U.K. CENTRAL COUNCIL FOR, 23 Portland Place, W1N 3AF—*Registrar and Chief Exec.*, C. Ralph.

England.—Victory House, 170 Tottenham Court Road, W1P 0HA.

Wales.—Floor 13, Pearl Assurance House, Greyfriars Road, Cardiff CF1 3AG.

Scotland.—22 Queen Street, Edinburgh EH2 1JX.

N.Ireland—R.A.C House, 79 Chichester Street, Belfast BT1 4JE.

NURSING, ROYAL COLLEGE OF, 20 Cavendish Square, W1M 0AB.

NUTRITION FOUNDATION, BRITISH (1967), 15 Belgrave Square, SW1X 8PS—*Dir. Gen.* Prof. D. M. Conning.

NUTRITION SOCIETY (1941)—*Hon. Sec.*, Dr. Margaret Ashwell, Grosvenor Gardens House, 35–37 Grosvenor Gardens, SW1W 0BS.

OBSTETRICIANS AND GYNAECOLOGISTS, ROYAL COLLEGE OF (1929), 27 Sussex Place, NW1 4RG—*Pres.*, G. Pinker, C.V.O.; *Sec.*, P. Barnett.

OCCUPATIONAL SAFETY AND HEALTH, INSTITUTION OF, 222 Uppingham Road, Leicester LE5 0QG—*Sec.*, J. R. Barrell.

OFFICERS' ASSOCIATION, THE (1920), 48 Pall Mall, SW1Y 5JU. Assists former officers of the Armed Forces, their widows and dependants.—*Gen. Sec.*, Brig. P. D. Johnson.

OFFICERS' FAMILIES FUND (1899), 48 Pall Mall, SW1Y 5JY—*Sec*, Mrs. I. C. Riley.

OFFICERS' PENSIONS SOCIETY, LTD., 15 Buckingham Gate, SW1E 6NS—*Gen. Sec.*, Maj. Gen. L. W. A. Gingell, C.B., O.B.E.

OIL PAINTERS, ROYAL INSTITUTE OF (1883)—*Sec.*, Mrs. J. Easterling, 76 Coniston Road, Bromley, Kent BR1 4JB.

OILSEED, OIL AND FEEDINGSTUFFS TRADES BENEVOLENT ASSOCIATION, 14–20 St. Mary Axe, EC3A 8BU—*Sec.*, R. T. Wheelans.

ONE PARENT FAMILIES, NATIONAL COUNCIL FOR, 255 Kentish Town Road, NW5 2LX—*Dir.*, Miss S. Slipman.

OPEN-AIR MISSION, THE (1853), 19 John Street, WC1N 2DL—*Sec.*, A. J. Greenbank.

OPEN SPACES SOCIETY (COMMONS, OPEN SPACES AND FOOTPATHS PRESERVATION SOCIETY) (1865), 25a Bell Street, Henley-on-Thames, Oxon RG9 2BA—*Gen. Sec.*, Miss K. Ashbrook.

OPERATIC AND DRAMATIC ASSOCIATION, NATIONAL (1899), NODA House, 1 Crestfield Street, WC1H 8AU—*Gen. Administrator*, B. Clarke.

OPTICAL COUNCIL, GENERAL, 41 Harley Street, W1N 2DJ—*Registrar*, R. Wilshin.

OPTOMETRISTS, BRITISH COLLEGE OF, 10 Knaresborough Place, SW5 0TG—*Gen. Sec.*, T. H. Collingridge.

ORDERS AND MEDALS RESEARCH SOCIETY—*Gen. Sec.*, N. G. Gooding, 123 Turnpike Link, Croydon CR0 5NU.

ORIENTAL CERAMIC SOCIETY (1921), 31b Torrington Square, WC1E 7LJ—*Sec.*, Vice-Adm. Sir John Gray, K.B.E., C.B.

ORNITHOLOGISTS' CLUB, SCOTTISH, 21 Regent Terrace, Edinburgh EH7 5BT—*Sec.*, J. C. Davies.

ORNITHOLOGISTS' UNION, BRITISH, c/o British Museum (Natural History), Sub-dept. of Ornithology, Tring, Herts. HP23 6AP—*Hon. Sec.*, Mrs. G. Bonham.

ORNITHOLOGY, BRITISH TRUST FOR (1932), Beech Grove, Tring, Herts. HP23 5NR—*Administrator*, J. C. G. Wolf.

ORTHOPÆDIC ASSOCIATION, BRITISH (1918), c/o The

Royal College of Surgeons, 35–43 Lincoln's Inn Fields, WC2A 3PN—*Hon. Sec.*, C. E. Ackroyd.

OSTEOPATHIC MEDICINE, LONDON COLLEGE OF, 8–10 Boston Place, NW1 6QH.

OUTWARD BOUND TRUST, Chestnut Field, Regent Place, Rugby CV21 2PJ—*Dir.*, I. L. Fothergill.

OVERSEAS DEVELOPMENT INSTITUTE (1960), Regent's College, Inner Circle, Regent's Park, NW1 4NS.

OVERSEAS SERVICE PENSIONERS' ASSOCIATION (1960), 63 Church Road, Hove, Sussex BN3 2BD—*Sec.*, C. D. Stenton.

OVERSEAS SETTLEMENT, CHURCH OF ENGLAND BOARD FOR SOCIAL RESPONSIBILITY (1925), Church House, Great Smith Street, SW1P 3NZ—*Admin. Sec.*, Miss P. J. Hallett.

OXFAM (1942), 274 Banbury Road, Oxford OX2 7DZ—*Dir.*, F. Judd.

OXFORD PRESERVATION TRUST (1927), 10 Turn Again Lane, St. Ebbes, Oxford OX1 1QL—*Sec.*, Mrs. H. E. Turner.

OXFORD SOCIETY (1932), 8 Wellington Square, Oxford OX1 2HY—*Sec.*, Dr. H. A. Hurren.

PAEDIATRIC ASSOCIATION, BRITISH, 5 St. Andrews Place, NW1 4LB—*Hon. Sec.*, Dr. T. L. Chambers.

PAINTER-ETCHERS AND ENGRAVERS, ROYAL SOCIETY OF (1880), Bankside Gallery, 48 Hopton Street, SE1 9JH—*Sec.*, M. Spender.

PAINTERS IN WATER COLOURS, ROYAL INSTITUTE OF (1831), 17 Carlton House Terrace, S.W.1.—*Sec.*, R. Spurrier.

PAINTERS IN WATER COLOURS, ROYAL SOCIETY OF (1804), Bankside Gallery, 48 Hopton Street, SE1 9JH—*Sec.*, M. Spender.

PALÆONTOGRAPHICAL SOCIETY (1847) c/o British Geological Survey, Keyworth, Nottingham NG12 5GG—*Sec.*, S. P. Tunnicliff.

PALÆONTOLOGICAL ASSOCIATION (1957)—Dr. P. Wallace, The Croft Barn, Church Street, East Hendred, Oxon. OX12 8LA.

PARKINSON'S DISEASE SOCIETY (1969), 36 Portland Place, W1N 3DG—*Exec. Dir.*, C. A. A. Kilmister.

PARLIAMENTARY AND SCIENTIFIC COMMITTEE, 30 Farringdon Street, EC4A 4EA—*Sec.*, A. Butler.

PASTORAL PSYCHOLOGY, GUILD OF (1936)—*Hon. Sec.*, Mrs. M. Ditchfield, 37 Hogarth Hill, NW11 6AY.

PATENT AGENTS, CHARTERED INSTITUTE OF (1882), Staple Inn Buildings, High Holborn, WC1V 7PZ—*Sec. and Registrar*, Miss M. E. Poole.

PATENTEES AND INVENTORS, INSTITUTE OF (1919), Triumph House, 189 Regent Street, W1R 7WF—*Sec.*, J. R. Kay.

PATHOLOGISTS, ROYAL COLLEGE OF, 2 Carlton House Terrace, SW1Y 5AF—*Sec.*, K. Lockyer.

PATIENTS ASSOCIATION (1963), Room 33, 18 Charing Cross Road, WC2H 0HR—*Chairman*, Rabbi Julia Neuberger.

PEACE COUNCIL, NATIONAL (1908), 29 Great James Street, WC1N 3ES—*Co-ordinator*, A. L. McLeod.

PEAK AND NORTHERN FOOTPATHS SOCIETY (1894)—*Hon. Gen. Sec.*, D. Taylor, 15 Parkfield Drive, Tyldesley, Manchester M29 8NR.

PEARSON'S HOLIDAY FUND, 2a Amity Grove, Raynes Park, SW20 0LH—*Gen. Sec.*, G. P. Holloway.

PEDESTRIANS' ASSOCIATION, 1 Wandsworth Road, SW8 2XX—*Chairman*, C. Myerscough.

P.E.N. INTERNATIONAL (1921), 38 King Street, WC2E 8JT. World association of writers.—*International Sec.*, A. Blokh.

PENSION FUNDS, NATIONAL ASSOCIATION OF, LTD (1923), 12–18 Grosvenor Gardens, SW1W 0DH—*Dir. Gen.*, M. A. Elton.

PEOPLE'S DISPENSARY FOR SICK ANIMALS (1917), PDSA House, South Street, Dorking, Surrey RH4 2LB—*Gen. Sec.*, M. R. Curtis, M.B.E.

PERFORMING RIGHT SOCIETY LTD. (1914), 29–33 Berners Street, W1P 4AA—*Chief Exec.*, M. J. Freegard.

PERIODICAL PUBLISHERS ASSOCATION LTD., Imperial House, 15–19 Kingsway, WC2B 6UN.

PESTALOZZI CHILDREN'S VILLAGE TRUST, Sedlescombe, Battle, E. Sussex TN33 0RR—*Warden*, A. G. Hatter.

PETROLEUM, INSTITUTE OF, 61 New Cavendish Street, W1M 8AR—*Dir. Gen.*, A. E. H. Williams.

PHARMACEUTICAL SOCIETY OF GREAT BRITAIN, ROYAL, 1 Lambeth High Street, SE1 7JN—*Sec. and Registrar*, J. Ferguson.

PHARMACOLOGICAL SOCIETY, BRITISH.—*Hon. Gen. Sec.*, Dr. G. N. Woodruff, Merck Sharp and Dohme Research Laboratories, Neuroscience Research Centre, Terlings Park, Eastwick Road, Harlow, Essex CM20 2QR.

PHILOLOGICAL SOCIETY (1842).—*Hon. Sec.*, Prof. Theodora Bynon, School of Oriental and African Studies, University of London, Malet Street, WC1E 7HP.

PHILOSOPHY, ROYAL INSTITUTE OF, 14 Gordon Square, WC1H 0AG—*Director*, Prof. A. Phillips Griffiths.

PHOTOGRAMMETRIC SOCIETY (1952)—*Hon. Sec.*, Dr. A. S. Walker, Kern Instruments Ltd., Kern House, Faraday Court, Faraday Road, Crawley, W. Sussex RH10 2PU.

PHOTOGRAPHY, BRITISH INSTITUTE OF PROFESSIONAL (1901), Amwell End, Ware, Herts. SG12 9HN—*Sec.*, R. C. Reece.

PHYSICAL EDUCATION ASSOCIATION OF GREAT BRITAIN AND N. IRELAND, 162 King's Cross Road, WC1X 9DH—*Gen. Sec.*, (vacant).

PHYSICAL RECREATION, CENTRAL COUNCIL OF (1935), Francis House, Francis Street, SW1P 1DE—*Gen. Sec.*, P. Lawson.

PHYSICIANS, ROYAL COLLEGE OF (1518), 11 St. Andrew's Place, NW1 4LE—*Registrar*, D. A. Pyke, C.B.E., M.D.

PHYSICIANS AND SURGEONS, ROYAL COLLEGE OF (Glasgow) (1599), 234–243 St. Vincent Street, Glasgow G2 5RJ—*Hon. Sec.*, Dr. A. D. Beattie.

PHYSICIANS OF EDINBURGH, ROYAL COLLEGE OF (1681), 9 Queen Street, Edinburgh EH2 1JQ—*Sec.*, Dr. J. L. Anderton.

PHYSICS, INSTITUTE OF (1874), 47 Belgrave Square, SW1X 8QX—*Sec.*, L. Cohen, PH.D.

PHYSIOLOGICAL SOCIETY (1876)—*Hon. Sec.*, Prof. R. A. Chapman, Dept. of Physiology, School of Veterinary Science, Park Row, Bristol BS1 5LS.

PHYSIOTHERAPY, THE CHARTERED SOCIETY OF (1894), 14 Bedford Row, WC1R 4ED—*Sec.*, T. Simon.

PIG BREEDERS ASSOCIATION, NATIONAL (1884), 7 Rickmansworth Road, Watford, Herts. WD1 7HE—*Chief Exec.*, G. E. Welsh.

PILGRIM TRUST, THE (1930), Fielden House, Little College Street, SW1P 3SH—*Sec.*, Hon. A. H. Millar.

PILGRIMS OF GREAT BRITAIN, THE (1902), Savoy Hotel WC2—*Hon. Sec.*, Lt. Col. S. W. Chant-Sempill, O.B.E., M.C.

PLANT ENGINEERS, INSTITUTION OF, 138 Buckingham Palace Road, SW1W 9SG—*Sec. Gen.*, J. K. Bennett.

PLASTICS AND RUBBER INSTITUTE, THE (1921), 11 Hobart Place, SW1W 0HL—*Sec. Gen.* G. W. Stockdale.

PLAYING CARD SOCIETY, THE INTERNATIONAL (1972), 188 Sheen Lane, SW14 8LF—*Sec.*, F. M. Collett.

PLAYING FIELDS ASSOCIATION, NATIONAL (1925), 25 Ovington Square, SW3 1LQ—*Dir.*, A. M. Watson.

P.N.E.U., WORLD-WIDE EDUCATION SERVICE OF THE (1888), Strode House, 44/50 Osnaburgh Street, NW1 3NN—*Dir.*, H. Boulter.

POETRY SOCIETY (1909), 21 Earl's Court Square, SW5 9DE—*Dir. and Gen. Sec.*, P. Ralph.

POLICY STUDIES INSTITUTE, 100 Park Village East, NW1 3SR—*Dir.*, W. W. Daniel

POLIO FELLOWSHIP, BRITISH (1939), Bell Close, West End Road, Ruislip, Middx. HA4 6LP—*Gen. Sec.*, L. P. Jackson.

POLYTECHNICS, COMMITTEE OF DIRECTORS OF, Kirkman House, 12–14 Whitfield Street, W1P 6AX—*Chairman*, Prof. G. T. Fowler; *Sec.*, Dr. M. S. Lewis.

POLYTECHNIC TEACHERS, ASSOCIATION OF (1973), Caxton Chambers, 81 Albert Road, Southsea, Hants. PO5 2SG—*Chief Exec.*, M. Douglass.

PORTRAIT PAINTERS, ROYAL SOCIETY OF (1891), 17 Carlton House Terrace, SW1Y 5BD—*President*, D. Poole.

POST OFFICE USERS' NATIONAL COUNCIL (1970), Waterloo Bridge House, Waterloo Road, SE1 8UA—*Sec.*, B. R. Jones.

POULTRY CLUB OF GREAT BRITAIN, THE (1877) *Sec.*, Mrs. M. A. Carefoot, Cliveden, Sandy Bank Farm, Chipping, Preston, Lancs. PR3 2GA.

PRAYER BOOK SOCIETY, THE (1975), St. James Garlickhythe, Garlick Hill, EC4 2AL—*Hon. Sec.*, M. Thompson.

PRECEPTORS, COLLEGE OF, Coppice Row, Theydon Bois, Epping, Essex CM16 7DN. Membership is open to practising educationalists.—*Chief Admin. Officer*, P. R. Daniels.

PREPARATORY SCHOOLS, INCORPORATED ASSOCIATION OF, 138 Kensington Church Street, W8 4BN—*Sec.*, J. M. C. Coates.

PRE-SCHOOL PLAYGROUPS ASSOCIATION—61–63 Kings Cross Road, WC1X 9LL—*Nat. Administrator*, Ms. M. Lochrie.

PRESS ASSOCIATION (1868), 85 Fleet Street EC4P 4BE—*Sec.*, E. G. Rhodes.

PRESS UNION, COMMONWEALTH (1909), Studio House, 184 Fleet Street, EC4A 2DU—*Dir.*, J. Rajepakse.

PREVENTION OF ACCIDENTS, ROYAL SOCIETY FOR THE, Cannon House, Priory Queensway, Birmingham B4 6BS—*Dir. Gen.*, R. M. Warburton.

PRINCESS LOUISE SCOTTISH HOSPITAL (Erskine Hospital) for disabled ex-servicemen and women (1916), Bishopton, Renfrewshire PA7 5PU—*Commandant*, Col. W. K. Shepherd.

PRINTERS' CHARITABLE CORPORATION (1827), 20 West Street, Reigate, Surrey RH2 9BS—*Dir. & Sec.*, Cpt. D. J. Bradby, R.N. (*retd*).

PRINTING HISTORICAL SOCIETY (1964), St. Bride Institute, Bride Lane, EC4Y 8EE—*Hon. Sec.*, C. L. Hicks.

PRINTING, INSTITUTE OF (1961), 8 Lonsdale Gardens, Tunbridge Wells, Kent TN1 1NU—*Sec.*, C. F. Partridge.

PRISON VISITORS, NATIONAL ASSOCIATION OF (1922), 46b Hartington Street, Bedford MK41 7RP—*Gen. Sec.*, Mrs. A. G. McKenna.

PRIVATE LIBRARIES ASSOCIATION (1957)—*Hon. Sec.*, F. Broomhead, Ravelston, South View Road, Pinner, Middx. HA5 3YD.

PROCURATORS IN GLASGOW, ROYAL FACULTY OF (1000), 12 Nelson Mandela Place, Glasgow G2 1BT—*Clerk*, J. H. Sinclair.

PRODUCTION CONTROL, INSTITUTE OF, Elmcroft House, Tiddington Road, Tiddington, Stratford upon Avon, Warwicks. CV37 7AQ—*Gen. Sec.*, K. Roberts.

PRODUCTION ENGINEERS, INSTITUTION OF, Rochester House, 66 Little Ealing Lane, W5 4XX—*Sec.*, Brig. P. V. Crooks.

PROFESSIONAL CLASSES AID COUNCIL, 10 St. Christopher's Place, W1M 6HY—*Sec.*, Mrs. G. A. Burgess.

PROFESSIONAL ENGINEERS, U.K. ASSOCIATION OF, Hayes Court, West Common Road, Bromley, Kent BR2 7AU—*Sec.*, C. K. Hickling.

PROFESSIONAL FOOTBALLERS' ASSOCIATION, 2 Oxford Court, Bishopsgate, Lower Moseley Street, Manchester M2 3WQ—*Sec.*, G. Taylor.

PROFESSIONS SUPPLEMENTARY TO MEDICINE, COUNCIL FOR, Park House, 184 Kennington Park Road, SE11 4BU—*Registrar*, F. Whitehill.

PROPAGATION OF THE GOSPEL, UNITED SOCIETY FOR THE (U.S.P.G.), Partnership House, 157 Waterloo Road, SE1 8XA—*Sec.*, Rev. Canon H. V. Taylor.

PROTESTANT ALLIANCE, THE (1845), 112 Colin Gardens, NW9 6ER—*Gen. Sec.*, Rev. A. G. Ashdown.

PROVINCIAL NOTARIES SOCIETY (1907), P.O. Box 102, Amersham, Bucks. HP7 0QB—*Sec.*, P. D. Leonard.

PSORIASIS ASSOCIATION (1968), 7 Milton Street, Northampton NN2 7JG—*Nat. Sec.*, Mrs. L. Henley.

PSYCHIATRISTS, ROYAL COLLEGE OF (1971) 17 Belgrave Square, SW1X 8PG—*Sec.*, Mrs. V. Cameron.

PSYCHICAL RESEARCH, SOCIETY FOR (1882), 1 Adam and Eve Mews, W8 6UG—*Pres.*, Prof. I. D. Stevenson, M.D.

PSYCHOLOGICAL SOCIETY, THE BRITISH (1901), St. Andrew's House, 48 Princess Road East, Leicester LE1 7DR—*Exec. Sec.*, C. V. Newman, PH.D.

PUBLIC ADMINISTRATION, ROYAL INSTITUTE OF (1922), 3 Birdcage Walk, SW1H 9JH—*Dir.-Gen.*, D. Falcon.

PUBLIC FINANCE AND ACCOUNTANCY, CHARTERED INSTITUTE OF (1885), 3 Robert Street, WC2N 6BH—*Dir.*, N. P. Hepworth, O.B.E.

PUBLIC HEALTH AND HYGIENE, THE ROYAL INSTITUTE OF (1937), 28 Portland Place, W1N 4DE—*Sec.*, Rear-Adm. W. A. Waddell, C.B., O.B.E.

PUBLIC HEALTH ENGINEERS, INSTITUTION OF (1895), *see* WATER AND ENVIRONMENTAL MANAGEMENT.

PUBLIC RELATIONS, INSTITUTE OF (1948), Gate House, St. John's Square, EC1M 4DH—*Exec. Dir.*, J. B. Lavelle.

PUBLIC TEACHERS OF LAW, SOCIETY OF (1908)—*Hon. Sec.*, Prof. D. B. Casson, University of Buckingham, MK18 1EG.

PURCHASING AND SUPPLY, INSTITUTE OF (1967), Easton House, Easton on the Hill, Stamford, Lincs. PE9 3NZ—*Dir.-Gen.*, I. G. S. Groundwater.

PURE WATER ASSOCIATION, NATIONAL—*Sec.*, N. Brugge, Bank Farm, Aston Pigott, Westbury, Shrewsbury SY5 9HH.

QUALITY ASSURANCE, INSTITUTE OF, 10 Grosvenor Gardens, SW1 0DQ—*Sec.-Gen.*, Dr. J. Davies.

QUARRIER'S HOMES (1871), Bridge of Weir, Renfrewshire PA11 3SA—*Chief Exec.*, Dr. J. R. Minto, O.B.E.

QUARRYING, INSTITUTE OF (1917), 7 Regent Street, Nottingham NG1 5BY—*Sec.*, R. Oates.

QUEEN ELIZABETH'S FOUNDATION FOR THE DISABLED (1967), Leatherhead, Surrey KT22 0BN—*Dir.*, M. B. Clark, PH.D.

QUEEN VICTORIA CLERGY FUND (1897), Church House, Dean's Yard, SW1P 3NZ—*Sec.*, Capt. P. W. E. Parry, M.B.E.

QUEEN VICTORIA SCHOOL, Dunblane, Perthshire FK15 0JY—*Headmaster*, J. D. Hankinson.

QUEEN'S ENGLISH SOCIETY, THE—*Hon. Sec.*, A. I. Thompson, 2 South Side, Pulborough, Sussex RH20 2DH.

QUEEN'S NURSING INSTITUTE (1887), 57 Lower Belgrave Street, SW1W 0LP—*Dir.*, P. E. Starr.

QUEKETT MICROSCOPICAL CLUB—*Hon. Business Sec.*, A. V. Dodge, 61 Pewley Way, Guildford GU1 3PZ.

RADIOLOGISTS, ROYAL COLLEGE OF (1934), 38 Portland Place, W1N 3DG—*Sec.*, A. J. Cowles.

RADIOLOGY, BRITISH INSTITUTE OF, 36 Portland Place, W1N 4AT—*Sec. Gen.*, Miss S. M. Johnstone.

RAILWAY AND CANAL HISTORICAL SOCIETY, THE.—*Hon. Sec.*, R. E. Kilsby, Banestree, Jacobs Well Road, Guildford, Surrey GU4 7PA.

RAILWAY BENEVOLENT INSTITUTION (1858), 67 Ashbourne Road, Derby DE3 3FY—*Exec. Officer and Gen. Sec.*, W. W. K. Humphreys.

RAINER FOUNDATION, 227–239 Tooley Street, SE1 2JX. Helps young people at risk or in need: administers the Intermediate Treatment Fund on behalf of the government—*Dir.*, R. Kay.

RAMBLERS' ASSOCIATION (1935), 1–5 Wandsworth Road, SW8 2XX—*Dir.*, A. Mattingly.

RATEPAYERS' ASSOCIATIONS, NATIONAL UNION OF, 4 Eysham Court, Station Road, New Barnet, Herts. EN5 1PS—*Hon. Gen. Sec.*, Mrs. D. E. Pannell.

RATING AND VALUATION ASSOCIATION (1882), 41 Doughty Street, WC1N 2LF—*Dir.*, C. Farrington.

RECORD SOCIETY, SCOTTISH, Dept. of Scottish History, University of Glasgow, Glasgow G12 8QQ—*Hon. Sec.*, Dr. J. Kirk.

RECORDS ASSOCIATION, BRITISH (1932)—*Sec.*, 18 Padbury Court, E2 7EH.

RED CROSS SOCIETY, BRITISH (1870), 9 Grosvenor Crescent, SW1X 7EJ—*Dir. Gen.*, J. C. Burke-Gaffney.

RED POLL CATTLE SOCIETY, 6 Church Street, Woodbridge, Suffolk IP12 1DH—*Sec.*, P. Ryder-Davies.

REFRIGERATION, INSTITUTE OF (1899), Kelvin House, 76 Mill Lane, Carshalton, Surrey SM5 2JR—*Sec.*, M. J. Horlick.

REFUGEE COUNCIL, BRITISH (1981), Bondway House, 3–9 Bondway, SW8 1SJ—*Dir.*, M. Barbor, PH.D.

REGIONAL STUDIES ASSOCIATION, 29 Great James Street, WC1N 3ES—*Exec. Sec.*, Ms. S. J. Parkinson.

REGULAR FORCES EMPLOYMENT ASSOCIATION (1885), 25 Bloomsbury Square, WC1A 2LN. Finds employment for non-commissioned ex-Regulars.—*General Manager*, Maj.-Gen. D. T. Crabtree, C.B.

REINDEER COUNCIL OF THE UNITED KINGDOM (1949), Newton Road, Harston, Cambridge CB2 5NZ—*Hon. Sec.*, (vacant).

RELATE: NATIONAL MARRIAGE GUIDANCE, Herbert Gray College, Little Church Street, Rugby, Warwicks, CV21 3AP—*Dir.*, D. French.

RELIGION AND MEDICINE, INSTITUTE OF (1964).—*Organising Sec.*, C. H. Sinclair, St. Marylebone Parish Church, Marylebone Road, NW1 5LT.

RENT OFFICERS, INSTITUTE OF.—*Hon. Sec.*, M. R. Webber, Musgrave House, Musgrave Row, Exeter, EX4 3TW.

RESEARCH DEFENCE SOCIETY, Grosvenor Gardens House, Grosvenor Gardens, SW1W 0BS—*Gen. Sec.*, Miss M. H. Franklin.

RETAIL BOOK, STATIONERY AND ALLIED TRADES EMPLOYEES' ASSOCIATION, 8–9 Commercial Road, Swindon, Wilts. SN1 5RB—*Gen. Sec.*, D. A. Williamson.

RETIREMENT PENSIONS ASSOCIATIONS, NATIONAL FEDERATION OF, 14 St. Peter Street, Blackburn, Lancs. BB2 2HD—*Sec.*, G. Dunn.

RICHARD III SOCIETY, 4 Oakley Street, SW3 5NN—*Sec.*, Miss E. M. Nokes.

ROAD SAFETY OFFICERS, INSTITUTE OF (1971)—*Nat. Sec.*, E. M. Marsh, 31 Dyers Close, West Buckland, Somerset TA21 9JU.

ROAD TRANSPORT ENGINEERS, INSTITUTE OF (1945), 1 Cromwell Place, SW7 2JF—*Sec. and Chief Exec.*, D. M. Ivison.

ROMAN STUDIES, SOCIETY FOR PROMOTION OF, 31–34 Gordon Square, WC1H 0PP—*Sec.*, Mrs. P. Gilbert.

ROTARY INTERNATIONAL IN GREAT BRITAIN AND IRELAND (1914), Kinwarton Road, Alcester, Warwickshire B49 6BP—*Sec.*, J. H. Jackson.

ROUND TABLES OF GREAT BRITAIN AND IRELAND, NATIONAL ASSOCIATION OF (1927), Marchesi House, 15 Park Road, N.W.1.—*Gen. Sec.*, P. W. Tipton.

ROYAL AFRICAN SOCIETY (1901), 18 Northumberland Avenue, WC2N 5BJ—*Sec.*, (vacant).

ROYAL AIR FORCE BENEVOLENT FUND (1919), 67 Portland Place, W1N 4AR—*Controller*, Air Chief Marshal Sir Thomas Kennedy, G.C.B., A.F.C.

ROYAL AIR FORCES ASSOCIATION, 43 Grove Park Road, W4 3RX—*Sec. Gen.*, M. G. Tomkins, M.B.E.

ROYAL ALEXANDRA AND ALBERT SCHOOL (1758), Gatton Park, Reigate, Surrey RH2 0TW—*Sec.*, Capt. A. J. Walsh, R.N.

ROYAL ALFRED SEAFARERS' SOCIETY (1865), Weston Acres, Woodmansterne Lane, Banstead, Surrey SM7 3HB—*Gen. Sec.*, J. H. Moore.

ROYAL ARMOURED CORPS WAR MEMORIAL BENEVOLENT FUND, R.H.Q. R.T.R., Bovington Camp, Dorset BH20 6JA—*Sec.*, Maj. R. Clooney (*retd*).

ROYAL ARTILLERY ASSOCIATION, Artillery House, Connaught Barracks, Grand Depot Road, SE18 6SL—*Gen. Sec.*, Col. R. H. Haynes, M.B.E.

ROYAL ASIATIC SOCIETY OF GREAT BRITAIN AND IRELAND (1823), 60 Queen's Gardens, W2 3AF—*Dir.*, Dr. D. J. Duncanson, O.B.E.

ROYAL CALEDONIAN SCHOOLS (1815), Bushey, Herts. WD2 3TS—*The Master*, Capt. R. E. Wilson, C.B.E., D.F.C., R.N.

ROYAL CELTIC SOCIETY (1820), 23 Rutland Street, Edinburgh EH1 2RN—*Sec.*, J. G. S. Cameron.

ROYAL CHORAL SOCIETY (1871), Royal Albert Hall, SW7 2AP—*Gen. Man.*, M. Heyland.

ROYAL COMMONWEALTH SOCIETY (1868), Northumberland Avenue, WC2N 5BJ—*Sec.-Gen.*, (vacant).

ROYAL ENGINEERS ASSOCIATION, R.H.Q. Royal Engineers, Brompton Barracks, Chatham, Kent ME4 4UG—*Controller*, Maj. C. F. Cooper, M.B.E., (*retd*).

ROYAL ENGINEERS, THE INSTITUTION OF (1875), Brompton Barracks, Chatham, Kent ME4 4UG—*Sec.*, Col. G. W. A. Napier.

ROYAL HIGHLAND AND AGRICULTURAL SOCIETY OF SCOTLAND (1784), Edinburgh Exhibition and Trade Centre, Ingliston, Midlothian EH28 8NF—*Sec.*, J. R. Good.

ROYAL HORTICULTURAL SOCIETY (1804), P.O. Box 313, 80 Vincent Square, SW1P 2PE—*Sec.*, J. R. Cowell.

ROYAL HOSPITAL AND HOME, PUTNEY (1854), West Hill, SW15 3SW—*Chief Exec.*, Col. B. E. Blunt.

ROYAL HUMANE SOCIETY (1774), Brettenham House, Lancaster Place, WC2E 7EP. Gives bravery awards for saving and attempting to save human life.—*Sec.*, Maj. A. J. Dickinson.

ROYAL INSTITUTION, THE (1799), 21 Albemarle Street, W1X 4BS—*Pres.*, H.R.H. The Duke of Kent, K.G., G.C.M.G., G.C.V.O.; *Dir.*, Prof. J. M. Thomas, F.R.S.; *Sec.*, Prof. D. C. Bradley, F.R.S.

ROYAL LIFE SAVING SOCIETY, U.K. (1891), Mountbatten House, Studley, Warwicks. B80 7NN—*Dir.*, K. H. Sach.

ROYAL LITERARY FUND (1790), 144 Temple Chambers, Temple Avenue, EC4Y 0DT. Grants to necessitous authors of some published work of approved literary merit or to their immediate dependants.—*Sec.*, Mrs. F. M. Clark.

ROYAL MEDICAL BENEVOLENT FUND (1836), 24 King's Road, Wimbledon, SW19 8QN—*Sec.*, P. G. Gordon-Smith.

ROYAL MEDICAL SOCIETY (1737), Students Centre, 5/5 Bristo Square, Edinburgh EH8 9AL—*Sec.*, G. Clarke.

ROYAL MICROSCOPICAL SOCIETY, 37–38 St. Clements, Oxford OX4 1AJ—*Administrator*, Lt. Col. P. G. Fleming.

ROYAL MUSICAL ASSOCIATION—*Sec.*, P. Owens, 135 Purves Road, NW10 5TH.

ROYAL NATIONAL LIFEBOAT INSTITUTION, (1824)—261 lifeboats are maintained on the coasts of Great Britain and Ireland. In 1987 the lifeboats launched 3,706 times and saved 1,474 lives. The net cost of running the RNLI in 1988 is over £31m. *Offices*, West Quay Road, Poole, Dorset BH15 1HZ—*Chairman*, The Duke of Atholl.

ROYAL NAVAL AND ROYAL MARINES CHILDREN'S TRUST (1834), H.M.S. *Nelson*, Portsmouth, Hants, PO1 3HH—*Sec.*, Mrs. M. Bateman.

ROYAL NAVAL ASSOCIATION (1950), 82 Chelsea Manor Street, SW3 5QJ—*Gen. Sec.*, Capt. J. W. Rayner.

ROYAL NAVAL BENEVOLENT SOCIETY (1739), 1 Fleet Street, EC4Y 1BD—*Sec.*, Capt. M. Murray, R.N., (*retd*).

ROYAL NAVAL BENEVOLENT TRUST (1922), 1 High Street, Brompton, Gillingham, Kent ME7 5QZ—*Gen. Sec.*, Lt.-Cdr. D. C. Lawrence, R.N. (*retd.*).

ROYAL NAVY OFFICERS, ASSOCIATION OF, 70 Porchester Terrace, W2 3TP—*Sec.*, Lt.-Cdr. J. V. Watson, M.B.E., R.N.

ROYAL OVER-SEAS LEAGUE (1910), Over-Seas House, Park Place, St. James's Street, SW1A 1LR—*Dir. Gen.*, Capt. J. B. Rumble, R.N.

ROYAL PATRIOTIC FUND CORPORATION (1854), Golden Cross House, Duncannon Street, WC2 4JR. Administers funds for the benefit of widows, children and other dependants of deceased officers and servicemen of the Armed Forces.—*Sec.*, Brig. D. C. Blomfield-Smith, M.B.E.

ROYAL PHILHARMONIC SOCIETY (1813), 10 Stratford Place, W1N 9AE—*Hon. Sec.*, E. Thompson, O.B.E.

ROYAL PHOTOGRAPHIC SOCIETY (1853), The Octagon, Milsom Street, Bath BA1 1DN—*Sec.*, K. R. Warr.

ROYAL PINNER SCHOOL FOUNDATION, 110 Old Brompton Road, SW7 3RB. Assists in the education of children of sales representatives.—*Sec.*, S. Thurtell.

"ROYAL SAILORS' RESTS" (1876), 2a South Street, Gosport, Hants. PO12 1ES—*Sec.*, A. A. Lockwood.

ROYAL SCOTTISH SOCIETY FOR PREVENTION OF CRUELTY TO CHILDREN (1884), Melville House, 41 Polwarth Terrace, Edinburgh EH11 1NU—*Gen. Sec.*, A. M. M. Wood, O.B.E.

ROYAL SIGNALS INSTITUTION (1950), 56 Regency Street, SW1P 4AD—*Sec.*, Col. A. N. de Bretton-Gordon.

ROYAL SOCIETY, THE (1660), 6 Carlton House Terrace, SW1Y 5AG—*Pres.*, Sir George Porter; *Treas. and Vice-Pres.*, Prof. R. W. K. Honeycombe; *Secretaries and Vice-Presidents*, Prof. R. J. Elliott, Prof. B. K. Follett, Prof. M. A. Epstein; *Executive Sec.*, Dr. P. T. Warren.

ROYAL SOCIETY FOR ASIAN AFFAIRS (1901), 2 Belgrave Square, SW1X 8PJ—*Sec.*, Miss M. FitzSimons.

ROYAL SOCIETY FOR THE ENCOURAGEMENT OF ARTS, MANUFACTURES AND COMMERCE (Royal Society of Arts) (1754), 8 John Adam Street, WC2N 6EZ—*Chairman*, Prof. C. B. Handy.

ROYAL SOCIETY FOR THE PREVENTION OF CRUELTY TO ANIMALS (1824), Causeway, Horsham, Sussex RH12 1HG—*Exec. Dir.*, A. Richmond, C.B.

ROYAL SOCIETY FOR THE PROTECTION OF BIRDS (1889), The Lodge, Sandy, Beds. SG19 2DL—*Dir. Gen.*, I. Prestt, C.B.E.

ROYAL SOCIETY OF EDINBURGH (1783), 22–24 George Street, Edinburgh EH2 2PQ—*Pres.*, Prof. C. Kemball; *Gen. Sec.*, Dr. C. D. Waterston.

ROYAL SOCIETY OF HEALTH, THE (1876), R.S.H. House, 38a St. George's Drive, SW1V 4BH—*Sec.*, D. Goad.

ROYAL SOCIETY OF LITERATURE (1823), 1 Hyde Park Gardens, W2 2LT—*Sec.*, Mrs. P. M. Schute.

ROYAL SOCIETY OF MEDICINE (1805), 1 Wimpole Street, W1M 8AE—*Exec. Dir.*, R. N. Thomson.

ROYAL SOCIETY OF ST. GEORGE, (1894), Dartmouth House, 37 Charles Street, W1X 8AB—*Gen. Sec.*, Lt. Col. J. A. Williams (*retd*).

ROYAL STAR AND GARTER HOME FOR DISABLED EX-SERVICEMEN (1916), Richmond, Surrey TW10 6RR—*Commandant*, Col. R. N. Harris, M.B.E.

ROYAL STATISTICAL SOCIETY (1834), 25 Enford Street, W1H 2BH—*Exec. Sec.*, D. W. Harding.

ROYAL TANK REGIMENT BENEVOLENT FUND, R.H.Q. R.T.R. Centre, Bovington Camp, Dorset BH20 6JA—*Regimental Sec.*, Maj. R. Clooney (*retd*).

ROYAL TELEVISION SOCIETY, Tavistock House East, Tavistock Square, WC1H 9HR—*Hon. Sec.*, A. Pilgrim.

ROYAL UNITED KINGDOM BENEFICENT ASSOCIATION (1863), 6 Avonmore Road, W14 8RL—*Dir.*, Rear-Adm. B. C. Perowne, C.B.

RURAL ENGLAND, COUNCIL FOR THE PROTECTION OF (1926), 4 Hobart Place, SW1W 0HY—*Dir.*, A. Purkis.

RURAL SCOTLAND, ASSOCIATION FOR THE PROTECTION OF (1926), 14a Napier Road, Edinburgh EH10 5AY—*Dir.*, R. L. Smith, O.B.E.

RURAL WALES, COUNCIL FOR THE PROTECTION OF, Ty Gwyn, 31 High Street, Welshpool, Powys SY21 7JP—*Dir.*, Dr. N. Caldwell.

SAILORS' CHILDREN'S SOCIETY, THE (1821), Newland, Hull HU6 7RJ. Cares for seamen and their children.—*Gen. Sec.*, Lt.-Cdr. C. G. R. Streatfeild-James, R.N.

SAILORS' SOCIETY, BRITISH (1818), 406–410 Eastern Avenue, Ilford, Essex, IG2 6NG—*Gen. Sec.*, G. Chambers.

ST. DEINIOL'S LIBRARY (1902), Hawarden, Deeside, Clwyd CH5 3DF—*Warden and Chief Librarian*, Rev. Dr. P. J. Jagger.

ST. DUNSTAN'S, P.O. Box 4XB, 12–14 Harcourt Street, W1A 4XB. For men and women blinded on war service.—*Sec.*, W. C. Weisblatt.

ST. JOHN AMBULANCE, 1 Grosvenor Crescent, SW1X 7EF. Voluntary unpaid body providing first-aid cover at public events and first aid training for industry and the public. *Brigade Strength* (U.K. 1987), 80,000.—*Chief Sec.*, Brig. R. C. Middleton, O.B.E.

SALES AND MARKETING MANAGEMENT, INSTITUTE OF—*Chief Exec.*, D. Waller, Georgian House, 31 Upper George Street, Luton, Beds. LU1 2RD.

SALMON AND TROUT ASSOCIATION (1903), Fishmongers' Hall, London Bridge, EC4R 9EL—*Dir.*, Col. J. Ferguson.

SALTIRE SOCIETY (1936), 9 Fountain Close, Edinburgh EH1 1TF—*Sec.*, Miss K. Austin.

SAMARITANS, THE (to help the suicidal and despairing. Tel. numbers in local telephone directories).—*Gen. Sec.*, D. Evans, 17 Uxbridge Road, Slough, Berks. SL1 1SN.

SAMUEL PEPYS CLUB—*Sec.*, R. H. Adams, T.D., F.S.A., 14 Dale Close, Oxford OX1 1TU.

SAVE THE CHILDREN FUND, THE (1919), Mary Datchelor House, 17 Grove Lane, SE5 8RD—*Dir. Gen.*, N. Hinton, C.B.E.

SCHOOL LIBRARY ASSOCIATION, Liden Library, Barrington Close, Liden, Swindon, Wilts. SN3 6HF—*Exec. Sec.*, Ms. V. Fea.

SCHOOL NATURAL SCIENCE SOCIETY—*Hon. Gen. Sec.*, Miss D. S. Jackson, 153 Fernside Avenue, Hanworth, Middx. TW13 7BQ.

SCHOOLMASTERS, SOCIETY OF (1798) (for the relief of necessitous schoolmasters and their dependants)—*Sec.*, Mrs. M. S. Freeburn, Hall Farm Dairy, Wood Norton, Dereham, Norfolk NR20 5AR.

SCHOOLMISTRESSES AND GOVERNESSES BENEVOLENT INSTITUTION, Queen Mary House, Manor Park Road, Chislehurst, Kent BR7 5PY.—*Dir.*, R. W. Hayward.

SCIENCE AND LEARNING, SOCIETY FOR THE PROTECTION OF, 20–21 Compton Terrace, NI 2UN—*Sec.*, Ms. E. Fraser.

SCIENCE, BRITISH ASSOCIATION FOR THE ADVANCEMENT OF (1831), Fortress House, 23 Savile Row, W1X 1AB—*Exec. Sec.*, Dr. D. Morley.

SCIENCE EDUCATION, ASSOCIATION FOR, College Lane, Hatfield, Herts. AL10 9AA—*Gen. Sec.*, B. G. Atwood, O.B.E.

SCOTCH WHISKY ASSOCIATION, 20 Atholl Crescent, Edinburgh EH3 8HF.—*Dir. Gen.*, Col. H. F. O. Bewsher, O.B.E.

SCOTTISH CHURCH HISTORY SOCIETY (1922)—*Hon. Sec.*, Rev. C. G. F. Brockie, Grange Manse, 51 Portland Road, Kilmarnock KA1 2EQ.

SCOTTISH CORPORATION, THE ROYAL (1611), 37 King Street, WC2E 8JS—*Chief Exec.*, Wg. Cdr. A. Robertson.

SCOTTISH COUNTRY DANCE SOCIETY, ROYAL (1923), 12 Coates Crescent, Edinburgh EH3 7AF—*Sec.*, Mrs. J. Moore.

SCOTTISH GENEALOGY SOCIETY (1953)—*Hon. Sec.*, Miss J. P. S. Ferguson, 21 Howard Place, Edinburgh EH3 5JY.

SCOTTISH HISTORY SOCIETY (1886)—*Hon. Sec.*, Dr. N. MacDougall, Dept. of Scottish History, St. Salvator's College, University of St. Andrews, Fife KY16 9AJ.

SCOTTISH LANDOWNERS' FEDERATION (1906), 18 Abercromby Place, Edinburgh EH3 6TY—*Dir.*, D. J. Hughes Hallett.

SCOTTISH LAW AGENTS SOCIETY, 33–34 Charlotte Square, Edinburgh EH2 4HF—*Sec.*, G. F. Davidson.

SCOTTISH LIFE OFFICES, ASSOCIATED (1841), 23 St. Andrew Square, Edinburgh EH2 1AQ—*Sec.*, W. W. Mair.

SCOTTISH NATIONAL INSTITUTION FOR THE WAR BLINDED, P.O. Box 500, Gillespie Crescent, Edinburgh EH10 4HZ—*Sec. and Treas.*, J. B. M. Munro.

SCOTTISH NATIONAL WAR MEMORIAL (1927), The Castle, Edinburgh EH1 2YT—*Sec.*, T. C. Barker.

SCOTTISH SECONDARY TEACHERS' ASSOCIATION, 15 Dundas Street, Edinburgh EH3 6QG—*Gen. Sec.*, A. A. Stanley.

SCOTTISH SOCIETY FOR THE PREVENTION OF CRUELTY TO ANIMALS (1950), 19 Melville Street, Edinburgh EH3 7PL—*Chief Exec.*, Sir Cameron Rusby, K.C.B., L.V.O.

SCOTTISH SOCIETY FOR THE PROTECTION OF WILD BIRDS (1927), Foremount House, Kilbarchan, Renfrewshire PA10 2EZ—*Sec.*, Dr. J. A. Gibson.

SCOTTISH TOURIST BOARD (1969), 23 Ravelston Terrace, Edinburgh EH4 3EU—*Chief Exec.*, T. M. Band.

SCOTTISH WILDLIFE TRUST (1964), 25 Johnston Terrace, Edinburgh EH1 2NH—*Chief Exec.*, J. R. Baldwin.

SCOUT ASSOCIATION, THE, Baden-Powell House, Queen's Gate, SW7 5JS—*Chief Scout*, W. Garth Morrison, *Chief Exec. Commissioner*, A. E. N. Black, O.B.E. Membership in U.K. (1987), 658,499; World Membership over 16,000,000 in over 150 countries and territories.

SCRIBES AND ILLUMINATORS, THE SOCIETY OF—*Hon. Sec.*, Mrs. S. Cavendish, 54 Boileau Road, SW13 9BL.

SCRIPTURE GIFT MISSION INCORPORATED (1888), Radstock House, 3 Eccleston Street, SW1W 9LZ—*Gen. Sec.*, R. Kennedy.

SCRIPTURE UNION (1867), 130 City Road, EC1V 2NJ—*Gen. Dir.*, Rev. D. M. S. Cohen.

SCULPTORS, ROYAL SOCIETY OF BRITISH (1904), 108 Old Brompton Road, SW7 3RA—*President*, J. E. Ravera; *Sec.*, Miss M. O'Connor.

SEA CADETS, 202 Lambeth Road, SE1 7JF—*Gen. Sec.*, Cmdr. P. J. Everett, O.B.E., R.N.

SEAMEN'S BOYS' HOME, BRITISH, Grenville House, Brixham, Devon TQ5 9AF—*Sec.*, Capt. E. M. Marks, R.D., R.N.R.

SEAMEN'S CHRISTIAN FRIEND SOCIETY (1846), 26 Davyhulme Road East, Stretford, Manchester M32 0DW—*Gen. Sec.*, G. D. Cartwright.

SEAMEN'S PENSION FUND, ROYAL (1919), 65 High Street, Ewell, Epsom, Surrey KT17 1RX—*Sec.*, D. Barker.

SECONDARY HEADS ASSOCIATION, 130 Regent Road, Leicester LE1 7PG—*Gen. Sec.*, J. Sutton.

SECULAR SOCIETY, NATIONAL (1866), 702 Holloway Road, N19 3NL—*Gen. Sec.*, T. Mullins.

SELDEN SOCIETY (1887), Faculty of Laws, Queen Mary College, Mile End Road, E1 4NS To advance the study of the history of English Law.—*Sec.*, V. Tunkel.

SELF EMPLOYED AND SMALL BUSINESSES, NATIONAL FEDERATION OF (1974), 32 St. Annes Road West, Lytham St. Annes, Lancs., FY8 1NY—*Nat. Chairman*, B. A. Prime.

SHAFTESBURY HOMES AND *Arethusa* (1843), 3 Rectory Grove, SW4 0EG—*Gen. Sec.*, Maj. R. P. A. de Berniere-Smart.

SHAFTESBURY SOCIETY, THE (1844), 2a Amity Grove, Raynes Park, SW20 0LJ. Cares for physically and mentally handicapped, the elderly and socially deprived. —*Dir.*, G. Holloway.

SHEEP ASSOCIATION, NATIONAL, 106 High Street, Tring, Herts. HP23 4AF—*Sec.*, J. Thorley.

SHELLFISH ASSOCIATION OF GREAT BRITAIN, Fishmongers' Hall, London Bridge, EC4R 9EL—*Dir.*, Dr. E. Edwards.

SHELTER, 88 Old Street, EC1V 9HU—*Dir.*, Miss S. McKechnie.

SHERLOCK HOLMES SOCIETY OF LONDON (1951)—*Hon. Sec.*, Cdr. G. S. Stavert, M.B.E., R.N. (retd), 3 Outram Road, Southsea, Hants. PO5 1PQ.

SHIPBROKERS, INSTITUTE OF CHARTERED (1911), 24 St. Mary Axe, EC3A 8DE—*Sec.*, J. H. Parker.

SHIRE HORSE SOCIETY (1878), East of England Showground, Peterborough PE2 0XE—*Chief Exec.*, R. W. Bird, M.B.E.

SHRIEVALTY ASSOCIATION, 14 Clumber Street, Nottingham NG1 3DS—*Sec.*, R. Bullock.

SIMPLIFIED SPELLING SOCIETY (1908)—*Chairman*, C. J. H. Jolly, Clare Hall, Chapel Lane, Chigwell, Essex IG7 6JJ.

SIR OSWALD STOLL FOUNDATION, 446 Fulham Road, SW6 1DT—*Dir.*, R. Brunwin.

SMALL FARMERS ASSOCIATION, THE (1979), P.O. Box 6, Ludlow, Shropshire SY8 1ZZ—*Hon. Sec.*, Miss V. Minet.

SOCIAL RESPONSIBILITY AND EDUCATION, QUAKER, Friends House, Euston Road, NW1 2BJ—*Gen. Sec.*, T. Jaggar.

SOCIAL WORKERS, BRITISH ASSOCIATION OF (1970), 16 Kent Street, Birmingham B5 6RD—*Gen. Sec.*, D. N. Jones.

SOCIALIST PARTY OF GREAT BRITAIN (1904), 52 Clapham High Street, SW4 7UN—*Gen. Sec.*, P. Hope.

SOLDIERS' AND AIRMEN'S SCRIPTURE READERS ASSOCIATION, THE (1838), Havelock House, Barrack Road, Aldershot, Hants. GU11 3NP—*Gen. Sec.*, Lt. Col. K. W. Sear.

SOLDIERS', SAILORS' AND AIRMEN'S FAMILIES ASSOCIATION (1885), 16–18 Old Queen Street, SW1H 9HP—*Chairman*, Adm. Sir Peter Herbert, K.C.B., O.B.E.; *Controller*, Maj. Gen. C. B. Grey, C.B.; *Sec.*, Capt. W. Stuart.

SOLDIERS, SAILORS AND AIRMEN'S HELP SOCIETY (Incorporated) (1899), *See* FORCES HELP SOCIETY.

SOLDIERS' WIDOWS, ROYAL CAMBRIDGE HOME FOR, 82–84 Hurst Road, East Molesey, Surrey KT8 9AH—*Superintendent*, Mrs. A. M. Webb.

SOLICITORS BENEVOLENT ASSOCIATION (1858), Lonsdale Chambers, 27 Chancery Lane, WC2A 1NF—*Sec.*, Lt. Col. D. G. Martin, O.B.E.

SOLICITORS IN THE SUPREME COURTS OF SCOTLAND, SOCIETY OF—*Sec.*, A. R. Brownlie, 2 Abercromby Place, Edinburgh EH3 6JZ.

SOROPTIMIST INTERNATIONAL OF GREAT BRITAIN AND IRELAND (1923), 63 Bayswater Road, W2 3PJ—*Administrative Officer*, J. E. Tuson.

S.O.S. SOCIETY, THE (1929), 38 Kensington Park Road, W11 3BU. Old people's homes (5), Mental Rehabilitation homes (3).—*Chief Exec.*, Lt.-Col. P. Rew.

SOUTH AMERICAN MISSIONARY SOCIETY, Allen Gardiner House, Pembury Road, Tunbridge Wells, Kent TN2 3QU—*Gen. Sec.*, Rt. Rev. J. W. H. Flagg.

SOUTH WALES INSTITUTE OF ENGINEERS (1857), Coal House, Ty Glas Avenue, Llanishen, Cardiff CF4 5YS—*Hon. Sec.*, R. E. Lindsay.

SPASTICS SOCIETY, THE (1952), 12 Park Crescent, W1N 4EQ—*Sec.*, Sir John Cox, K.C.B.

SPEAKERS CLUBS, THE ASSOCIATION OF (1971), 93, Revidge Road, Blackburn BB2 6JH—*Sec.*, B. A. Driscoll.

SPINA BIFIDA AND HYDROCEPHALUS, ASSOCIATION FOR (ASBAH), 22 Upper Woburn Place, WC1H 0EP—*Exec. Dir.*, Miss M. P. Gilbertson.

SPORTS MEDICINE, INSTITUTE OF (1963), c/o Faculty of Engineering & Science, Polytechnic of Central London, 115 New Cavendish Street, W1M 8JS—*Hon. Sec.*, P. Sebastian.

SPURGEON'S CHILD CARE (1867), 30 Mill Street, Bedford MK40 3HD.

STATISTICIANS, INSTITUTE OF (1948), 36 Churchgate Street, Bury St. Edmunds, Suffolk IP33 1RD—*Sec.*, D. A. Holland.

STATUTE LAW SOCIETY (1968), 186 City Road, EC1V 2NU—*Hon. Sec.*, C. E. Shanbury.

STEWART SOCIETY (1899), 48 Castle Street, Edinburgh EH2 3LX—*Hon. Sec.*, Mrs. M. Walker.

STRATEGIC PLANNING SOCIETY, THE (1967), 15 Belgrave Square, SW1X 8PU *Exec. Sec.*, Miss C. E. Langan.

STRATEGIC STUDIES, THE INTERNATIONAL INSTITUTE FOR (1958), 23 Tavistock Street, WC2E 7NQ—*Dir.*, F. Heisbourg.

STRUCTURAL ENGINEERS, INSTITUTION OF (1908), 11 Upper Belgrave Street, SW1X 8BH—*Sec.*, D. J. Clark.

STUDENT CHRISTIAN MOVEMENT (1889), 186 St. Paul's Road, Balsall Heath, Birmingham B12 8LZ—*Gen. Sec.*, Rev. T. E. McClure.

SUFFOLK HORSE SOCIETY, 6 Church Street, Woodbridge, Suffolk IP12 1DH—*Sec.*, P. Ryder-Davies.

SURGEONS OF ENGLAND, ROYAL COLLEGE OF (1800), Lincoln's Inn Fields, WC2A 3PN—*Pres.*, I. P. Todd, M.D.; *Sec.*, R. S. Johnson-Gilbert, O.B.E.

SURGEONS OF EDINBURGH, ROYAL COLLEGE OF (1505), Nicolson Street, Edinburgh EH8 9DW—*Sec.*, Dr. A. G. D. Maran.

SURVEYORS, ROYAL INSTITUTION OF CHARTERED (incorporating the Institute of Quantity Surveyors) (1868), 12 Great George Street, SW1P 3AD—*Sec. Gen.*, M. Pattison.

SUSSEX CATTLE SOCIETY (1887), Station Road, Robertsbridge, E. Sussex TN32 5DG—*Manager*, Miss S. G. Kennedy.

SWEDENBORG SOCIETY (1810), 20–21 Bloomsbury Way, WC1A 2TH—*Sec.*, Ms. M. G. Waters.

TALKING BOOKS FOR THE HANDICAPPED (National Listening Library), 12 Lant Street, SE1 1QH—*Exec. Dir.*, D. J. Roskilly.

TAVISTOCK INSTITUTE OF HUMAN RELATIONS, The Tavistock Centre, Belsize Lane, NW3 5BA—*Sec.*, P. M. Foster, D.F.C.

TAXATION, INSTITUTE OF (1930), 12 Upper Belgrave Street, SW1X 8BB—*Sec.*, R. J. Ison.

TAX PAYERS' SOCIETY, 22 Wheatsheaf House, 4 Carmelite Street, EC4Y 0BN—*Dir.*, D. J. Bryant.

TEACHERS IN COMMERCE LTD., FACULTY OF, 141 Bedford Road, Sutton Coldfield, West Midlands B75 6DB—*Sec.*, J. Snowdon.

TEACHERS OF HOME ECONOMICS LTD., NATIONAL ASSOCIATION OF, Hamilton House, Mabledon Place, WC1H 9BJ—*Gen. Man.*, P. G. Higgins.

TEACHERS OF MATHEMATICS, ASSOCIATION OF, 7 Shaftesbury Avenue, Derby DE3 8YB—*Hon. Sec.*, Ms. G. M. Hatch.

TEACHERS OF THE DEAF, BRITISH ASSOCIATION OF—*Sec.*, Miss S. Dowe, Icknield High School H.I.U., Riddy Lane, Luton, Beds. LU3 2AH.

TEACHERS' UNION, ULSTER (1919), 94 Malone Road, Belfast BT9 5HP—*Gen. Sec.*, D. Allen.

TELECOMMUNICATIONS USERS' ASSOCIATION, 48 Percy Road, N12 8BU—*Dir.*, M. Elwes.

TEMPERANCE SOCIETIES:—

British National Temperance League (1834), Room 4, Shirley House, 31 Psalter Lane, Sheffield S11 8YL—*Sec.*, L. Swales.

British Women's Temperance Association (1876), 8 North Bank Street, Edinburgh EH1 2LP—*Hon. Sec.*, Miss J. E. H. Gillon.

Church of England National Council for Social Aid, 38 Ebury Street, SW1W 0LU *Gen. Sec.*, Rev. E. W. F. Agar.

Churches Council on Alcohol and Drugs (1915), 4 Southampton Row, WC1B 4AA—*Gen. Sec.*, Mrs. B. Smith.

Division of Social Responsibility of the Methodist Church, 1 Central Buildings, Westminster, SW1H 9NH—*Gen. Sec.*, Rev. B. Duckworth.

National United Temperance Council, 123 Regent Street, W1R 7HA—*Gen. Sec.*, Rev. B. Kinman.

Order of the Sons of Temperance, 5 Ashbourne Road, Derby, DE3 3FQ—*Sec.*, D. Newbury.

Royal Naval Temperance Society (auxiliary of Royal Sailors' Rests), 2a South Street, Gosport, Hants. PO12 1ES—*Sec.*, A. A. Lockwood.

Social Responsibility Dept., General Assembly of Unitarian and Free Christian Churches, Essex Hall, 1–6 Essex Street, WC2R 3HY—*Hon. Sec.*, C. Shute.

United Kingdom Alliance, Alliance House, 123 Regent Street W1R 7HA—*Gen. Sec.*, Rev. B. Kinman.

TEMPLETON FOUNDATION, 16 Kingfisher Lane, Turners Hill, Crawley, Sussex RH10 4QP—*U.K. Rep.*, Mrs. N. Pearse.

TERRITORIAL, AUXILIARY AND VOLUNTEER RESERVE ASSOCIATIONS, COUNCIL OF (1908), Centre Block, Duke of York's Headquarters, SW3 4SG—*Sec.*, Maj.-Gen. M. Matthews, C.B.

TEXTILE INSTITUTE, THE (1910), International Headquarters, 10 Blackfriars Street, Manchester M3 5DR—*Gen. Sec.*, R. G. Denyer.

THEATRE ASSOCIATION, BRITISH (1919), Darwin Infill Building, Regent's College, Inner Circle, Regent's Park, NW1 4NW—*Dir.*, Ms. S. Meades.

THEATRE RESEARCH, SOCIETY FOR (1948), c/o The Theatre Museum, 1e Tavistock Street, WC2E 7PA—*Hon. Sec.*, D. Forbes.

THEATRICAL FUND, ROYAL (1839), 11 Garrick Street, WC2E 9AR—*Sec.*, J. Berkeley.

THEATRICAL LADIES' GUILD OF CHARITY (1892)—*Admin. Sec.*, Mrs. K. Nichols, 60 York Way, N1 9AB.

THEOSOPHICAL SOCIETY IN ENGLAND (1875), 50 Gloucester Place, W1H 3HJ—*Gen. Sec.*, Dr. H. Gray.

THISTLE FOUNDATION, THE (1945), 27a Walker Street, Edinburgh EH3 7HX—*Dir.*, P. Croft.

THOMAS CORAM FOUNDATION FOR CHILDREN (1739), 40 Brunswick Square, WC1N 1AZ—*Dir. and Sec.*, C. Masters.

TIDY BRITAIN GROUP, The Pier, Wigan WN3 4EX—*Dir. Gen.*, Prof. G. Ashworth, C.B.E.

TOC H (1915), 1 Forest Close, Wendover, Aylesbury, Bucks. HP22 6BT—*Gen. Sec.*, Dr. J. M. A. Kilburn.

TOWN AND COUNTRY PLANNING ASSOCIATION, 17 Carlton House Terrace, SW1Y 5AS—*Dir.*, D. Hall.

TOWN PLANNING INSTITUTE, ROYAL (1914), 26 Portland Place, W1N 4BE.

TOWNSWOMEN'S GUILDS, NATIONAL UNION OF (1929), 75 Harborne Road, Edgbaston, Birmingham B15 3DA—*Nat. Sec.*, Mrs. J. R. Campbell-Tanner.

TOYNBEE HALL, The Universities' Settlement in East London, 28 Commercial Street, Whitechapel, E1 6LS—*Warden and Chief Exec.*, A. L. Williams, O.B.E.

TRADE MARK AGENTS, INSTITUTE OF (1934), Canterbury House, 2–6 Sydenham Road, Croydon, Surrey CR0 9XE—*Sec.*, Mrs. M. J. Tyler.

TRADE, NATIONAL CHAMBER OF (1897), Enterprise House, Henley-upon-Thames, Oxon. RG9 1TU—*Chief Exec.*, B. Tennant.

TRADING STANDARDS ADMINISTRATION, THE INSTITUTE OF, Thamesgate House, 37 Victoria Avenue, Southend-on-Sea, Essex SS2 6BU—*Dir. of Admin. and P.R*, Mrs. G. Jordan.

TRANSPORT ADMINISTRATION, INSTITUTE OF (1944), 32 Palmerston Road, Southampton SO1 1LL—*Dir.*, Wg. Cdr. P. F. Green (*retd*).

TRANSPORT, CHARTERED INSTITUTE OF (1919), 80 Portland Place, W1N 4DP—*Dir. Gen.*, J. C. F. Cameron.

TRANSPORT CONSULTATIVE COMMITTEE, CENTRAL (1948), 1st Floor, Golden Cross House, Duncannon Street, WC2N 4JF—*Sec.*, M. Patterson.

TRAVEL AGENTS, ASSOCIATION OF BRITISH (1950), 55–57 Newman Street, W1P 4AH—*Dir. Gen.*, D. Epstein.

TROPICAL MEDICINE AND HYGIENE, ROYAL SOCIETY OF (1907), Manson House, 26 Portland Place, W1N 4EY.

TURNER SOCIETY, BCM Box Turner, WC1N 3XX—*Chairman*, S. Warburton.

UFAW (Universities Federation for Animal Welfare) (1926), 8 Hamilton Close, South Mimms, Potters Bar, Herts. EN6 3QD—*Sec.*, Lt.-Col. T. J. Reynolds.

UNIT TRUST ASSOCIATION (1959), 65 Kingsway, WC2B 6TD—*Chief Exec.*, A. C. Smith.

UNITED NATIONS ASSOCIATION OF GREAT BRITAIN AND NORTHERN IRELAND (1945), 3 Whitehall Court, SW1A 2EL—*Dir.*, M. C. Harper.

UNITED REFORMED CHURCH HISTORY SOCIETY, 86 Tavistock Place, WC1H 9RT—*Hon. Sec.*, Rev. Dr. S. Orchard.

UNITED SOCIETY FOR CHRISTIAN LITERATURE, Robertson House, Leas Road, Guildford, Surrey GU14 4QW—*Gen. Sec.*, Rev. A. Gilmore.

UNIVERSITIES CENTRAL COUNCIL ON ADMISSIONS (1961), P.O. Box 28, Cheltenham, Glos. GL50 1HY—*Gen. Sec.*, P. A. Oakley, M.B.E.

UNIVERSITY WOMEN, BRITISH FEDERATION OF (1907), Crosby Hall, Cheyne Walk, SW3 5BA—*Sec.*, Mrs. C. Ellis.

VALUERS AND AUCTIONEERS, INCORPORATED SOCIETY OF, 3 Cadogan Gate, SW1X 0AS—*Sec.*, M. Astbury.

VEGAN SOCIETY, THE (1944), 33–35 George Street, Oxford OX1 2AY—*Gen. Sec.*, B. Kew.

VEGETARIAN SOCIETY OF THE UNITED KINGDOM LTD., Parkdale, Dunham Road, Altrincham, Cheshire WA14 4QG—*Gen. Manager*, Ms. P. McGlashan.

VENEREAL DISEASES, MEDICAL SOCIETY FOR THE STUDY OF—*Hon. Sec.*, Dr. M. A. Waugh, Dept. of Genito-Urinary Medicine, Leeds General Infirmary, Great George Street, Leeds LS1 3EX.

VERNACULAR ARCHITECTURE GROUP (1953), 18 Portland Place, Leamington Spa, Warwicks. CV32 5EU—*Hon. Sec.*, Dr. N. W. Alcock.

VETERINARY ASSOCIATION, BRITISH (1881), 7 Mansfield Street, W1M 0AT—*Chief Exec.*, J. H. Baird.

VETERINARY SURGEONS, ROYAL COLLEGE OF, 32 Belgrave Square, SW1X 8QP—*President*, Prof. L. C. Vaughan; *Registrar*, A. R. W. Porter, C.B.E.

VICE-CHANCELLORS AND PRINCIPALS OF THE UNIVERSITIES OF THE UNITED KINGDOM, COMMITTEE OF, 29 Tavistock Square, WC1H 9EZ—*Chairman*, Prof. Sir Mark Richmond, F.R.S.

VICTORIA CROSS AND GEORGE CROSS ASSOCIATION, Room 04, Archway Block South, Old Admiralty Building, SW1A 2BE—*Chairman*, Rear-Adm. B. C. G. Place, V.C., C.B., D.S.C.

VICTORIA INSTITUTE, THE (Philosophical Society of Great Britain), 29 Queen Street, EC4R 1BH—*Hon. Treas.*, B. H. T. Weller.

VICTORIAN SOCIETY (1958), 1 Priory Gardens, Bedford Park, W4 1TT—*Sec.*, Ms. T. Sladen.

VICTORY (SERVICES) ASSOCIATION LTD. AND CLUB, 63–79 Seymour Street, W2 2HF—*General Manager*, Capt. G. F. Taylor.

VIKING SOCIETY FOR NORTHERN RESEARCH, University College London, Gower Street, WC1E 6BT—*Joint Hon. Secs.*, Mrs. U. Dronke; Prof. M. P. Barnes.

VITREOUS ENAMELLERS, INSTITUTE OF, Ripley, Derby DE5 3EB—*Sec.*, J. D. Gardom.

V.S.O. (Voluntary Service Overseas) (1958), 9 Belgrave Square, SW1X 8PW—*Dir.*, N. McIntosh.

WAR ON WANT (1952), 37–39 Great Guildford Street, SE1 0ES—*Gen. Sec.* (vacant).

WATER AND ENVIRONMENTAL MANAGEMENT, INSTITUTION OF, 15 John Street, WC1N 2EB—*Exec. Dir.*, H. R. Evans.

WELDING INSTITUTE, THE, Abington Hall, Cambridge CB1 6AL—*Chief Exec.*, A. B. M. Braithwaite.

WELFARE OFFICERS, INSTITUTE OF, 254 The Corn Exchange, Hanging Ditch, Manchester, M4 3ES—*Sec.*, Mrs. M. Heywood.

WELLCOME TRUST (1936), 1 Park Square West, NW1 4LJ—*Dir.*, Dr. P. O. Williams.

WELLS, H. G., SOCIETY, Polytechnic of North London, Prince of Wales Road, NW5 3LB—*Sec.*, C. Rolfe.

WESLEY HISTORICAL SOCIETY (1893)—*Gen. Sec.*, Dr. E. D. Graham, 34 Spiceland Road, Northfield, Birmingham B31 1NJ.

WEST AFRICA COMMITTEE (1956), 315 Oxford Street, W1R 2BQ—*Secs.*, L. J. Walters; G. W. House.

WEST INDIA COMMITTEE (1750), 48 Albemarle Street, W1X 4AR—*Dir.*, D. A. Jessop.

WEST LONDON MISSION (1887), 19 Thayer Street, W1M 5LJ—*Supt.*, Rev. L. J. Griffiths, PH.D.

WILDLIFE ARTISTS, SOCIETY OF (1962), 17 Carlton House Terrace, S.W.1.—*Hon. Sec.*, K. J. Wood.

WILLIAM MORRIS SOCIETY AND KELMSCOTT FELLOWSHIP (1918), Kelmscott House, 26 Upper Mall, W6 9TA—*Hon. Sec.*, P. Preston.

WINE AND SPIRIT ASSOCIATION OF GREAT BRITAIN AND NORTHERN IRELAND, Five Kings House, Upper Thames Street, EC4V 3BH—*Dir.*, R. H. Insoll.

WOMEN ARTISTS, SOCIETY OF (1855)—*Sec.*, Ms. B. Carruthers-Jones, Orchard House, Adam and Eve Mews, 167–169 Kensington High Street, W8 6SH.

WOMEN, NATIONAL ADVISORY CENTRE ON CAREERS FOR (1933), 8th Floor, Artillery House, Artillery Row, SW1P 1RT—*Dir.*, Miss K. M. Menon.

WOMEN, SOCIETY FOR PROMOTING THE TRAINING OF (1859), The Dean Cottages, Hedgerley, Bucks. SL2 3UY. Interest-free loan training fund for women students in higher education—*Sec.*, Mrs. W. M. Golding.

WOMEN'S ENGINEERING SOCIETY (1920), Imperial College of Science and Technology, Dept. of Civil Engineering, Imperial College Road, SW7 2BU—*Sec.*, Miss G. Maxwell.

WOMEN'S INSTITUTES, NATIONAL FEDERATION OF (1915), 39 Eccleston Street, SW1W 9NT—*Gen. Sec.*, Mrs. A. Ballard.

WOMEN'S INTERNATIONAL LEAGUE FOR PEACE AND FREEDOM (British Section) (1915), 29 Great James Street, WC1N 3ES—*Chair*, Ms. M. Miller.

WOMEN'S NATIONAL CANCER CONTROL CAMPAIGN, 1 South Audley Street, W1Y 5DQ—*Dir.*, Ms. S. McKenzie.

WOMEN'S ROYAL NAVAL SERVICE BENEVOLENT TRUST, 1a Chesham Street, SW1X 8NL—*Sec.*, Mrs. J. Y. Ellis.

WOMEN'S ROYAL VOLUNTARY SERVICE (WRVS) (1938), 17 Old Park Lane, W1Y 4AJ—*National Chairman*, Dame Barbara Shenfield, D.B.E.

WOMEN'S RURAL INSTITUTES, SCOTTISH (1917), 42 Heriot Row, Edinburgh EH3 6ES—*Gen. Sec.*, Mrs E. Nicol.

WOMEN'S TRANSPORT SERVICE (FANY) (1907), FANY H.Q. (E Block), Duke of York's H.Q., SW3 4SJ—*Corps Commander*, Mrs. S. Y. Parkinson, O.B.E.

WOODLAND TRUST, THE (1972), Autumn Park, Dysart Road, Grantham, Lincs. NG31 6LL—*Exec. Dir.*, J. D. James.

WOOD PRESERVING ASSOCIATION, BRITISH, 6 The Office Village, 4 Romford Road, Stratford, E15 4EA—*Dir.*, D. Scorbie.

WORCESTERSHIRE ASSOCIATION (1926).—*Hon. Sec.*, D. M. Alexander, 8 Sansome Walk, Worcester WR1 1LW.

WORKERS' EDUCATIONAL ASSOCIATION, Temple House, 9 Upper Berkeley Street, W1H 8BY—*Gen. Sec.*, R. Lochrie.

WORLD EDUCATION FELLOWSHIP (1921), 33 Kinnaird Avenue, W4 3SH—*Gen. Sec.*, Mrs. R. Crommelin.

WORLD ENERGY CONFERENCE (1924), 34 St. James's Street, SW1A 1HD—*Sec. Gen.*, I. D. Lindsay.

WORLD MISSION, COUNCIL FOR (1977), Livingstone House, 11 Carteret Street, SW1H 9DL——*Gen. Sec.*, Rev. Dr. C. Duraisingh.

WORLD SHIP SOCIETY (1946)—*Sec.*, S. J. F. Miller, 35 Wickham Way, Haywards Heath, W. Sussex RH16 1UJ.

WORLD SOCIETY FOR THE PROTECTION OF ANIMALS, 106 Jermyn Street, SW1Y 6EE—*Dir. Gen.*, G. Walwyn, C.V.O.

WORLD WIDE FUND FOR NATURE (1961), Panda House, 11–13 Ockford Road, Godalming, Surrey GU7 1QU—*Dir.*, G. J. Medley.

WRITERS TO H.M. SIGNET, SOCIETY OF, 16 Hill Street, Edinburgh EH2 3LD—*Deputy Keeper of the Signet*, P. C. Millar, O.B.E.; *Sub-Keeper and Clerk*, A. M. Kerr.

YEOMANRY BENEVOLENT FUND, 10 Stone Buildings, Lincoln's Inn, WC2A 3TG—*Sec.*, Mrs. C. W. Chrystie.

YORKSHIRE AGRICULTURAL SOCIETY (1837), Great Yorkshire Showground, Hookstone Oval, Harrogate HG2 8PW—*Sec.-Gen.*, Lt.-Col. M. G. A. Young.

YORKSHIRE SOCIETY, THE (1812), 27 Kensington Park, Milford-on-Sea, Hants. SO41 0WD. Educational trust making grants to students of all ages.—*Sec.*, G. G. Prince, T.D.

YOUNG FARMERS' CLUBS, NATIONAL FEDERATION OF, The Y.F.C. Centre, National Agricultural Centre, Kenilworth, Warwicks. CV8 2LG—*Sec.*, F. E. Shields.

YOUNG MEN'S CHRISTIAN ASSOCIATION, National Council of YMCS's, 640 Forest Road, E17 3DZ—*Nat. Sec.*, C. J. Naylor.

YOUNG WOMEN'S CHRISTIAN ASSOCIATION OF GREAT BRITAIN (YWCA) (1855), Clarendon House, 52 Cornmarket Street, Oxford OX1 3EJ—*Exec. Dir.*, Miss F. E. Sharples.

YOUTH CLUBS U.K., 30 Peacock Lane, Leicester LE1 5NY—*Chief Exec.*, J. Holt.

YOUTH CLUBS, NORTHERN IRELAND ASSOCIATION OF, Hampton, Glenmachan Park, Belfast BT4 2PJ—*Dir.*, G. Johnston.

YOUTH HOSTELS ASSOCIATION (ENGLAND AND WALES) (1930), Trevelyan House, 8 St. Stephens Hill, St. Albans, Herts. AL1 2DY—*Chief Exec.*, A. G. F. Chinneck.

YOUTH HOSTELS ASSOCIATION, SCOTTISH (1931), 7 Glebe Crescent, Stirling FK8 2JA—*Gen. Sec.*, J. Martin.

YOUTH HOSTELS ASSOCIATION OF NORTHERN IRELAND (1931), Bradbury Buildings, 56 Bradbury Place, Belfast BT7 1RU—*Hon. Sec.*, E. R. Henderson.

ZOOLOGICAL SOCIETY OF LONDON, Regent's Park, NW1 4RY—*Pres.*, Sir William Henderson, F.R.S.; *Man. Dir.*, A. Grant. Attendances (1987), Regent's Park 1,303,797; Whipsnade 382,134.

ZOOLOGICAL SOCIETY OF SCOTLAND, ROYAL, Scottish National Zoological Park, Murrayfield, Edinburgh EH12 6TS—*Dir.*, R. J. Wheater, F.R.S.E.

LOCAL HISTORY AND ARCHAEOLOGICAL SOCIETIES

England and Wales

Bedfordshire.—SOUTH BEDFORDSHIRE ARCHAEO-LOGICAL SOCIETY. *Hon. Sec.* D. H. Kennett, 27 Lords Lane, Bradwell, Great Yarmouth, Norfolk NR31 8NY.

Berkshire.—BERKSHIRE ARCHAEOLOGICAL SOCIETY. *Hon. Sec.,* L. J. Over, 43 Laburnham Road, Maidenhead, Berks. SL6 4DE.

NEWBURY DISTRICT FIELD CLUB. *Hon. Sec.,* Mrs. D. E. Hawkes, 22 Westgate Road, Newbury, Berks. RG14 6AX.

Buckinghamshire.—BUCKS. ARCHAEOLOGICAL SO-CIETY. *Hon. Sec.,* Dr. R. P. Hagerty, County Museum, Church Street, Aylesbury, Bucks. HP20 2QP.

Cambridgeshire.—CAMBRIDGE ANTIQUARIAN SO-CIETY. *Sec.,* Miss A. S. Bendall, Emmanuel College, Cambridge CB2 3AP.

Cheshire.—CHESTER ARCHAEOLOGICAL SOCIETY. *Sec.,* G. R. Coppack, Chamonix, Station Lane, Mickle Trafford, Chester CH2 4EH. *See also under Lancashire.*

Cornwall.—CORNWALL ARCHAEOLOGICAL SOCIETY, County Museum and Art Gallery, Truro TR1 2SJ. *Hon. Sec.,* Miss D. Harris.

Cumberland and Westmorland.—CUMBERLAND AND WESTMORLAND ANTIQUARIAN AND ARCHAEOLOGI-CAL SOCIETY. *Hon. Sec.,* R. Hall, 2 High Tenterfell, Kendal, Cumbria LA9 4PG.

Derbyshire.—DERBYSHIRE ARCHAEOLOGICAL SOCIETY. *Hon. Sec.,* M. E. Burrows, 12 Wilne Road, Draycott, Derby DE7 3NG.

Devonshire.—DEVON ARCHAEOLOGICAL SOCIETY. *Hon. Sec.,* Mrs. D. Butler, 19 Pool Anthony Drive, Tiverton.

Dorset.—DORSET NATURAL HISTORY AND ARCHAEO-LOGICAL SOCIETY, Dorset County Museum, Dorchester DT1 1XA. *Curator and Sec.,* R. N. R. Peers.

Durham.—DURHAM AND NORTHUMBERLAND ARCHI-TECTURAL AND ARCHAEOLOGICAL SOCIETY. *Hon. Sec.,* Dr. M. J. Millett, 46 Saddler Street, Durham DH1 3NU.

Dyfed.—CEREDIGION ANTIQUARIAN SOCIETY. *Hon. Sec.,* I. M. Jones, Dolau-gwyn Dole, Bow Street, Dyfed SY24 5AE.

Essex.—ESSEX SOCIETY FOR ARCHAEOLOGY AND HIS-TORY, Hollytrees Museum, High Street, Colchester CO1 1UG. *Sec.,* V. W. Gray.

Gloucestershire.—BRISTOL AND GLOUCESTERSHIRE ARCHAEOLOGICAL SOCIETY, *Hon. Sec.,* D. J. H. Smith, 22 Beaumont Road, Gloucester GL2 0EJ.

Gwynedd.—ANGLESEY ANTIQUARIAN SOCIETY. *Hon. Sec.,* S. C. G. Caffell, 1 Fronheulog Sling, Tregarth, Bangor LL57 4RD.

Hampshire.—HAMPSHIRE FIELD CLUB AND ARCHAEO-LOGICAL SOCIETY. *Hon. Sec.,* Dr. M. A. Hicks, King Alfred's College, Winchester, Hants. SO22 4NR.

Herefordshire.—WOOLHOPE NATURALISTS' FIELD CLUB. *Hon. Sec.,* J. W. Tonkin, F.S.A., Chy an Whyloryon, Wigmore, Leominster, Herefordshire HR6 9UD.

Hertfordshire.—EAST HERTFORDSHIRE ARCHAEOLOG-ICAL SOCIETY. *Hon. Sec.,* Mrs. M. C. Readman, 1 Marsh Lane, Stanstead Abbots, Ware, Herts. SG12 8HH.

ST. ALBANS AND HERTFORDSHIRE ARCHITEC-TURAL AND ARCHAEOLOGICAL SOCIETY. *Hon. Sec.,* F. I. Kilvington, 122 Marshalswick Lane, St. Albans AL1 4XD.

Kent.—KENT ARCHAEOLOGICAL SOCIETY. *Gen. Sec.,* A. C. Harrison, F.S.A., Prings Cottage, Pilgrims Road, Upper Halling, Rochester ME2 1HR.

Lancashire.— HISTORIC SOCIETY OF LANCASHIRE AND CHESHIRE. *Hon. Sec.,* Dr. J. E. Hollinshead, Liverpool Institute of H.E., Stand Park Road, Liverpool L16 9JD.

Leicestershire.—LEICESTERSHIRE ARCHAEOLOGICAL AND HISTORICAL SOCIETY. *Hon. Sec.,* Dr. A. D. McWhirr. The Guildhall, Leicester LE1 5FQ.

London and Middlesex.—CITY OF LONDON ARCHAE-OLOGICAL SOCIETY. *Hon. Sec.,* D. R. Lewis, 11 Chatsworth Avenue, Wimbledon Chase, SW20 8JZ.

LONDON AND MIDDLESEX ARCHAEOLOGICAL SO-CIETY. *Hon. Sec.,* Miss J. Macdonald, 3 Cedar Drive, Pinner, Middx. HA5 4DD.

Norfolk.—NORFOLK AND NORWICH ARCHAEOLOGICAL SOCIETY. *Hon. Gen. Sec.,* R. Bellinger, 30 Brettingham Avenue, Cringleford, Norwich NR4 6XG.

Northumberland and Tyne and Wear.—SOCIETY OF ANTIQUARIES OF NEWCASTLE UPON TYNE. *Sec.,* Dr. C. M. Fraser, c/o Centre for Continuing Education, University of Newcastle upon Tyne, NE1 7RU.

SUNDERLAND ANTIQUARIAN SOCIETY. *Hon. Sec.,* Ms. V. M. Stevens, 16 Grizedale Court, Seaburn Dene, Sunderland SR6 8JP.

Nottinghamshire.—THOROTON SOCIETY OF NOT-TINGHAMSHIRE, Bromley House, Angel Row, Nottingham NG1 6HL. *Hon. Sec.,* J. S. Childs, F.R.S.A.

Oxfordshire.—OXFORDSHIRE ARCHITECTURAL AND HISTORICAL SOCIETY. *Hon. Sec.,* Miss J. M. Cook, Ashmolean Museum, Oxford OX1 2PH.

Powys.—POWYSLAND CLUB. *Hon. Sec.,* W. G. J. Hughes, The Library, Brook Street, Welshpool, Powys SY21 7PH.

RADNORSHIRE SOCIETY. *Hon. Sec.,* A. Batley, c/o Radnor College of F.E., Llandrindod Wells, Powys LD1 5ES.

Shropshire.—SHROPSHIRE ARCHAEOLOGICAL SOCIETY. *Chairman,* J. B. Lawson, Westcott Farm, Habberley, Pontesbury, Shropshire SY5 0SQ.

Somerset.—SOMERSET ARCHAEOLOGICAL AND NATU-RAL HISTORY SOCIETY, Taunton Castle, Taunton TA1 4AD. *Hon. Sec.,* J. Reynolds.

Staffordshire.—CITY OF STOKE-ON-TRENT MUSEUM ARCHAEOLOGICAL SOCIETY, City Museum and Art Gallery, Hanley, Stoke-on-Trent. *Chairman,* E. E. Royle.

Suffolk.—SUFFOLK INSTITUTE OF ARCHAEOLOGY AND HISTORY. *Hon. Sec.,* E. A. Martin, Oak Tree Farm, Finborough Road, Hitcham, Ipswich IP7 7LS.

Surrey.—SURREY ARCHAEOLOGICAL SOCIETY, Castle Arch, Guildford GU1 3SX. *Hon. Secs.,* Mr. and Mrs. K. D. Graham.

Sussex.—SUSSEX ARCHAEOLOGICAL SOCIETY, Barbican House, High Street, Lewes, E. Sussex BN7 3BS. *Exec. Sec.,* J. Houghton.

Warwickshire.—BIRMINGHAM AND WARWICKSHIRE ARCHAEOLOGICAL SOCIETY, c/o Birmingham and Midland Institute, Margaret Street, Birmingham B3 3BS. *Hon. Sec.,* A. J. Wilson.

Wight.—ISLE OF WIGHT NATURAL HISTORY AND ARCHAEOLOGICAL SOCIETY. *Hon. Sec.,* Mrs. T. Goodley, Ivy Cottage, New Barn Lane, Shorwell, Isle of Wight PO30 3JQ.

Wiltshire.—WILTSHIRE ARCHAEOLOGICAL AND NATU-RAL HISTORY SOCIETY, The Museum, 41 Long Street, Devizes SN10 1NS. *Sec.,* M. Cowan.

Worcestershire.—WORCESTERSHIRE ARCHAEOLOGICAL
SOCIETY. *Hon. Sec.*, Mrs. G. Grice, 91 Hallow Road,
Worcester WR2 6DF.

Yorkshire.—YORKSHIRE ARCHAEOLOGICAL SOCIETY.
Hon. Sec., P. B. Davidson, Claremont, 23 Clarendon
Road, Leeds LS2 9NZ.

HALIFAX ANTIQUARIAN SOCIETY. *Hon. Sec.*, J.
Hargreaves, 7 Hyde Park Gardens, Haugh Shaw
Road, Halifax HX1 3AH.

THORESBY SOCIETY. *Hon. Sec.*, D. M. Watson.
Claremont, 23 Clarendon Road, Leeds LS2 9NZ.

Channel Islands

SOCIETE JERSIAISE, Archaeological Section, The Jersey Museum, Pier Road, St. Helier, Jersey. *Hon. Sec.*, Ms. T. Tilling.

Scotland

AYRSHIRE ARCHAEOLOGICAL AND NATURAL HISTORY
SOCIETY. *Hon. Sec.*, Dr. T. Mathews, 10 Longlands
Park, Ayr KA7 4RJ.

DUMFRIESSHIRE AND GALLOWAY NATURAL HISTORY
AND ANTIQUARIAN SOCIETY. *Hon. Sec.*, R. H.
McEwen, Seaforth, 13 Douglas Terrace, Lockerbie,
Dumfries DG11 2DZ.

HAWICK ARCHAEOLOGICAL SOCIETY. *Hon. Sec.*, I. W.
Landles, Orrock House, Stirches Road, Hawick,
Borders TD9 7HF.

INVERNESS FIELD CLUB. *Hon. Sec.*, Mrs. E. H. L.
Macaskill, 9 Dores Road, Inverness IV2 4QX.

THE CIVIC TRUST
17 Carlton House Terrace, SW1Y 5AW
[01–930 0914]

The Civic Trust founded in 1957, is a registered charity whose object is to stimulate interest in, and action for, the improvement of the environment throughout the U.K. The Trust is supported by voluntary contributions. It has no individual membership and owns no land but works in close co-operation with over a 1,000 local amenity societies. It acts as a spokesman on issues of national concern.

The Trust is regularly consulted by Government about new legislation concerning the environment. (It inspired the Civic Amenities Act, 1967 which created Conservation Areas.)

On behalf of the Department of the Environment, the Trust runs the Civic Trust Education Group which aims to stimulate environmental education at all levels, but particularly in schools. The Trust is also a founder member of the Government's UK2000 initiative. It organizes annually National Environment Week.

There are Associate Trusts in the North East and North West of England, in Scotland and in Wales.—*Dir.*, M. C. Bradshaw.

NATIONAL TRUST
36 Queen Anne's Gate, SW1H 9AS
[01–222 9251]

The National Trust was founded in 1895 by Miss Octavia Hill, Sir Robert Hunter and Canon Rawnsley, their object being to preserve as much as possible the history and beauty of their country for its people. It became an organization incorporated by Act of Parliament (1907) to ensure the preservation of lands and buildings of historic interest or natural beauty for public access and benefit. It is independent of the state and relies on the voluntary support of private individuals for working funds. The Trust has now some 1,530,000 members paying an annual subscription. Rents, admission fees, legacies and gifts are other important sources of support and income.

The Trust protects more than 610,000 acres, much of it in the National Parks. The Trust also owns and opens to the public some 291 country houses, other buildings and gardens and preserves villages, nature reserves, archaeological sites and many farms. Through Enterprise Neptune, launched 1965, the Trust now protects 500 miles of coastline.

The policy of the Trust is determined by the governing body, the Council. Half of its members are appointed by national institutions, such as the British Museum, the National Gallery, the Ramblers' Association and the Royal Horticultural Society; the other half are elected by Trust members at the annual general meeting. The Council appoints the Executive Committee, which in turn has established Regional Committees responsible for the management of the Trust's properties.
Chairman, Dame Jennifer Jenkins; *Dir. Gen.*, A. Stirling.

NATIONAL TRUST FOR SCOTLAND
5 Charlotte Square, Edinburgh EH2 4DU

The National Trust for Scotland was founded in 1931, and its objects are similar to those of the National Trust. Like that organization, it is incorporated by Act of Parliament and is dependent for finance upon legacies, donations and the subscriptions of its members.

The Trust administers over 100 properties covering some 100,000 acres. These include several noteworthy gardens, some associated with the great houses.

Among the mountainous country owned by the Trust is the Pass of Glen Coe and the mountain group "The Five Sisters of Kintail" and the estate of Torridon in Wester Ross, and Ben Lomond.

Islands in the Trust's care include the St. Kilda group, Staffa, Fair Isle, Iona and Canna (St. Kilda was designated by UNESCO in 1987 as Scotland's first World Heritage site). At Bannockburn, Killiecrankie, Glenfinnan and Culloden, the Trust owns sites associated with Scottish history.

The Trust also administers the Little Houses Improvement Scheme, under which properties are bought, restored and re-sold. Since its inception over 200 houses reflecting the vernacular architecture of Scotland have been restored throughout the country.

962

PRINCIPAL CHARITABLE BEQUESTS OF THE YEAR

The alphabetical list below represents some of the principal charitable bequests from wills published since the last edition. Exact amounts available from residuary bequests is not usually known, as prior legacies, testamentary expenses and inheritance tax are all deductible from the net value of estates.

Sir David Robinson, who during his lifetime gave away over £25 million, including £18 million to found the Cambridge College bearing his name, still left over £1 million. The residue of this was left to the R.N.L.I. on the death of his wife, who in fact died six days after him. The R.S.P.C.A. received the whole of the £2·7 million estate of Dorothy Walker, easily their highest ever bequest, and they also shared with the P.D.S.A. the residue of the £3·3 million estate of Amy Bell. Dorset stockbroker Victor Robson left over £2 million, with six sevenths of the residue being left to the Imperial Cancer Research Fund and the other seventh to the International Spinal Research Trust. Cecil Lock, a well-known town centre planner, left over £1 million, three sevenths of the residue being shared between six environmental charities and a seventh for such charitable purposes as his trustees determined. One of the largest single "environmental" bequests was the bulk of the £449,479 estate of George Lowe-Willetts, which was left to Greenpeace.

Violet Green, a former proprietor of the *West Sussex County Times* at Horsham, left a large part of the residue of her £1·4 million estate for private old people's homes within the circulation area of that newspaper, and Norah Jervis left the income from the residue of her £1·3 million estate to King's School, Canterbury, so long as it remained outside Government control. The Hon. Joane Dutton left £100,000 to the National Trust for the upkeep of the estate already left to them by her late brother Lord Sherborne, and the residue of her £1·1 million estate to the Hampshire and Isle of Wight Naturalists Trust. The R.N.L.I. received two large residues—from Amy Anthony and Doris Mann both of whom left just under £1 million. The R.N.L.I. also shared the residue of the £1·5 million estate of Sarah Harrop with the Imperial Cancer Research Fund.

Great Ormond Street Hospital received two large bequests—the residue of the £2 million estate of Lady McAlpine and £385,254 left by Ada Stanley. Bryony Coate, left over £1 million with the residue going to Dr. Spittals Cancer Research Fund at Middlesex Hospital and three other charities. Elsie Sykes also left large bequests for hospitals. She was a local benefactor from Harrogate and left over £4 million, with most of it going to various local health authorities for medical equipment and other purposes. St. Mark's Hospital, London, received the residue of the estate of Joseph King, and Marjorie Lewis-Manning left the residue of her estate to the Lewis-Manning Cancer Trust—they both left nearly £1 million.

The National Trust received most of the £612,068 estate of solicitor David Jenkins and nearly all the £536,483 estate of retired company director Harold Judd, who directed it be used solely for the maintenance of further acquisition of gardens and woodlands. Several prominent personalities left large residues for charity, including Sir Douglas Howard, former Minister to the Holy See; Doris Butler, a high school headmistress from the West Midlands; and Dame Elizabeth Ackroyd, the first director of the Consumer Council.

The list includes several other large estates left entirely to charity—in descending order they are Anne Crutchley (£526,546) to Dr. Barnardo's and the R.N.I.B.; Joy Lowe (£524,974) to the R.N.I.D.; Louise Davidson (£473,000) to the R.S.P.B.; Marcus Staple-

ton Martin (£462,413) to the National Trust; Charles Crowson (£462,358) to the Cancer Research Campaign; Werner Feig (£373,615) to the Association of Jewish Refugees Charitable Trust; Christina Dawson (£365,665) to the Salvation Army; and retired army officer Oliver Evans (£338,963) to the Regiments Fund of the South Wales Borderers and Monmouthshire Regiment.

William Burndred, a retired union official, left nearly all his £539,722 estate to the Salvation Army, mostly for its work in India and Africa, and Myrtle Solomon left the bulk of her £376,702 estate to War Resisters International. Evelyn Elmitt left most of her £724,354 estate to the Scout Association "because we think that young people can be the hope of the world". May Laws left nearly all her £302,006 estate to her local Rotary Club in Retford, Notts., and Rosemary Rooke left the residue of her £595,007 estate to the Helpers League of her local hospital at Newbury. The most remarkable bequest is not included in the list and was made by Muriel Jones to Ancoats Hospital, Manchester, in thanks for treatment received "some years ago". She died in May 1987 and the will was made in December 1931, making this probably the longest interval between the making of a charitable bequest and its fulfilment.

Dame Elizabeth **Ackroyd**, D.B.E., of St. James's Street, London SW1 .... £535,858
(The residue equally between Help the Aged, National Association for Mental Health and the National Old People's Welfare Council)

Mr. Reginald **Alsop**, of Cambridge £616,973
(£20,000 and one quarter of the residue to the Cambridge 99 Rowing Club, and one quarter of the residue each to the Save the Children Fund, Imperial Cancer Research Fund and Multiple Sclerosis Society)

Miss Dorothy Jane **Ambrose**, of Deal, Kent £431,008
(Half the residue to R.U.K.B.A., and half equally between the Deal Centre for the Retired, Dr. Barnardo's, Lord Roberts Workshops, Missions to Seamen, Cancer Research Campaign, and Gifford House, Worthing)

Mr. George Snowdon **Anderson**, of Ripon, North Yorks. £424,746
(The residue to his trustees for distribution between national and local charities which help the elderly, infirm and blind)

Amy **Anthony**, of Colwyn Bay, Clwyd... £906,844
(The residue to the R.N.L.I., for a lifeboat)

Miss Ethel Beatrice **Ashby**, of Boscombe, Dorset £456,915
(The residue equally between King George's Fund for Sailors, the R.A.F. Benevolent Fund and the Army Benevolent Fund)

Miss Elen Elaine **Austin**, of Bromley, Kent £1,252,866
(Four fifths of the residue to the Gables Charitable Trust and one fifth to the National Trust)

Mrs. Enid Dorothy **Barff**, of Thames Ditton, Surrey £402,406
(The residue equally between the Distressed Gentlefolk's Aid Association, the P.D.S.A. and Animal Health Trust)

Annette Jacqueline Kate **Barrett**, of Pagham, West Sussex £497,776
(The residue equally between the Imperial Cancer Research Fund, Muscular Dystrophy Group and Dr. Barnardo's)

Mrs. Wilhelmina **Bayliss**, of Hove, East Sussex £299,030
(The residue to the Royal Masonic Hospital)

Amy **Bell**, of Eaton Square, London SW1 .... £3,381,496
(The residue equally between the R.S.P.C.A. and P.D.S.A.)

Phyllis **Boland**, of Northwood, Middx. ... £501,317
(The residue equally between the League of Friends of Northwick Park Hospital, Harrow, and Imperial Cancer Research Fund)

Miss Daphne Elizabeth **Braggins**, of Bedford £1,108,984
(Half the residue to Bedford General Hospital, and one quarter each to the Guide Dogs for the Blind Association, and Elizabeth Garrett Anderson Hospital, London NW1)

Mr. Albert George **Brailey**, of Churston Ferrers, Devon £929,162
(Two thirds of the residue to the Salvation Army, and one third to the National Trust, for houses in Devon)

Enid Mary **Brewis**, of Edstone, Warwicks. £551,048
(The residue equally between the Cancer Research Campaign and the British Rheumatism and Arthritis Association)

Prof. George Leslie **Brook**, of Grange-over-Sands, Cumbria £722,574
(The residue equally between Help the Aged and Age Concern England)

Mr. Donald Masters **Brown**, of Wolverhampton £522,980
(The residue equally between the Royal College of Surgeons and the World Wildlife Fund)

Mrs. Annie Muriel **Bullivant**, of Minehead, Somerset £1,809,426
(The residue equally between St. Margaret's Somerset Hospice, Taunton, the Somerset Trust for Nature Conservation, United Cambridge Hospitals, N.S.P.C.C., P.D.S.A., R.S.P.B., R.S.P.C.A. and World Wildlife Fund)

Mr. William **Burndred**, of Hanley, Staffs. £539,722
(The residue to the Salvation Army, for work in India and Africa)

Janet Muriel **Burrell**, of Ewell, Surrey .. £399,927
(The residue equally between the Marie Curie Memorial Foundation and Help the Aged)

Miss Doris Audrey **Butler**, of Old Swinford, West Midlands £750,798
(The residue equally between the R.N.I.B., Imperial Cancer Research Fund, Methodist Homes for the Aged, R.U.K.B.A., Wireless for the Blind Fund and the Inter Church Aid and Refugee Service)

Mr. Frederick **Cahn**, of Keats Close, London NW3 .... £2,300,714
(One quarter of the residue to the Jewish Welfare Board)

Mrs. Kathleen Margaret **Carr**, of Ettington, Warwicks. £584,262
(The residue equally between St. Peter's Church, Wellesbourne, the North Lancashire and Lakeland Continuing Care Trust and the World Wildlife Fund)

Mrs. Ivy Florence Rosina **Cleak**, of Hayes, Kent £394,413
(The residue equally between the P.D.S.A., Dr. Barnardo's and the "Kidney Research Aid Fund")

Bryony Jane **Coate**, of East Sheen, London SW14 .... £1,169,258
(Forty per cent. of the residue each to Dr. Spittals Cancer Research Fund of the Radiotherapy Department at Middlesex Hospital, and Imperial Cancer Research Fund and 10 per cent. each to the Marie Curie Memorial Foundation and Malcolm Sargent Cancer Fund for Children)

Mrs. Doris Mabel **Cowan**, of Littlehampton, West Sussex £354,487
(The residue for charitable institutions as her executor selects)

Muriel Maud **Craiggy**, of East Preston, West Sussex £486,941
(The residue equally between the R.S.P.C.A., World Wildlife Fund and the People's Trust for Endangered Species)

Mr. Charles William **Crowson**, of Peakirk, Peterborough £462,358
(His entire estate to the Cancer Research Campaign)

Miss Anne Frances **Crutchley**, of Claverdon, Warwicks. £526,546
(Her entire estate equally between Dr. Barnardo's and R.N.I.B.)

Louise **Davidson**, of Sunningdale, Berks. £473,000
(Her entire estate to the R.S.P.B.)

Mr. Percival Charles **Davis**, of Bishops Waltham, Hants. £387,735
(The residue for charitable institutions as his executors decide, other than animal charities)

Christina Isabella **Dawson**, of Kingswinford, West Midlands £365,665
(Her entire estate to the Salvation Army)

Mr. Cyril Frank **Derrick**, of Sanderstead, Surrey £752,699
(The residue equally between the National Trust, Royal Star and Garter Home, Richmond, Gardeners Royal Benevolent Society and Shaftesbury Homes)

Kathleen Vasey **Doxford**, of Lanchester, Co. Durham £336,658
(The residue to the Imperial Cancer Research Fund)

Ethel Muriel **Dunkley**, of Bury, West Sussex £625,984
(The residue equally between the Cancer Research Campaign, Multiple Sclerosis Society, R.N.L.I., Salvation Army, Tear Fund, and St. Barnabas Home, Worthing)

Mr. Arthur George **Dunn**, of Epsom, Surrey £368,200
(The residue to the National Trust)

Hon. Miss Joane **Dutton**, of West Meon, Hants. £1,159,557
(The residue to the Hampshire and Isle of Wight Naturalists Trust)

Mr. Charles William **Edmans**, of North Harrow, Middx. £339,841
(The residue to the Wood Green Animal Shelter)

Mrs. Evelyn Hannah **Elmitt**, of Leigh-on-Sea, Essex £724,354
(The residue to the Scout Association)

Mr. Oliver Aneurin **Evans**, of Frognal Gardens, London NW3 .... £338,963
(His entire estate to the Regiments Fund of the South Wales Borderers and Monmouthshire Regiment)

Mr. Werner **Feig**, of Leeside Crescent, London NW11 .... £373,615
(His entire estate to the Association of Jewish Refugees Charitable Trust)

Miss Laura Pleasants **Gilpin**, of Mold, Clwyd £440,968
(Two thirds of the residue to John Hopkins University, Maryland, U.S.A., and one third to Goucher College, Towson, Maryland)

Mrs. Violet Evelyn Ivy Suzanne **Green**, of Buxted, East Sussex £1,417,625
(Twenty per cent. of the residue—less £2,000—for such private old people's homes within the circulation area of the *West Sussex County Times* as her trustees decide)

Mrs. Sarah Emily **Harrop**, of Harrogate, North Yorks. £1,508,793
(The residue equally between the R.N.L.I. and Imperial Cancer Research Fund)

Mrs. Madeline Constance **Hedges**, M.B.E., of Paignton, Devon £586,460
(The residue equally between the Imperial Cancer

Research Fund and the Voluntary and Christian Service Trust Help the Aged Appeal)

Sir Douglas **Howard**, K.C.M.G., M.C., of Clophill, Beds. .... £630,306 (The residue equally between the Cheshire Home, Ampthill, R.N.I.D., R.N.I.B., R.N.L.I. and Dr. Barnardo's)

Mrs Helen Kemp **Huggett**, of Beaumont Street, London W1 .... £723,423 (£100,000 to Help the Aged and the residue to the Royal Society of London)

Mrs Marjorie Denson **Hutchinson**, of East Preston, West Sussex .... £560,927 (The residue for charities in the U.K. as her executors choose)

Mr. Leonard Percival **Jackson**, of Illetas, Majorca .... £1,641,162 (One seventh of the residue and £10,000 each to Norwood Children's Orphanage, Home for Aged Jews, London SW12, and Jewish Blind Society, and one seventh each to the Jewish Home and Hospital, Tottenham, Jewish Welfare Board, Marie Curie Memorial Foundation, and the Home for Handicapped Children, London)

Barbara Morison **Jeakes**, of Henley-on-Thames, Oxon. .... £899,000 (The residue equally between the N.S.P.C.C., R.S.P.C.A. and Church Army)

Mr. David Caldicott Heald **Jenkins**, of Mansfield Street, London W1 .... £612,068 (The residue to the National Trust)

Miss Norah Elizabeth **Jervis**, of Ospringe, Faversham, Kent .... £1,350,455 (The residue to the King's School, Canterbury)

Mrs. Hilda **Johnson**, of Canford Cliffs, Poole, Dorset .... £665,439 (£2,000 and one quarter of the residue to the Imperial Cancer Research Fund, £1,000 and one quarter each to the R.N.L.I. and Missions to Seamen, and £500 and one quarter to the R.S.P.C.A.)

Mr. Harold Bartlett **Judd**, of Earls Court Gardens, London SW5 .... £536,483 (The residue to the National Trust, for acquisition of gardens and woodlands)

Mr. Joseph **King**, M.B.E., of Snaresbrook, London E18 .... £948,512 (The residue to St. Mark's Hospital, London EC1)

Mrs. May **Laws**, of Newark, Notts. ...... £302,006 (The residue to Retford Rotary Club)

Mrs. Grace Frances **Lee**, of Camden Town, London NW1 .... £345,684 (The residue to the Imperial Cancer Research Fund)

Lilly Helen **Le Grand**, of Corfe Mullen, Dorset .... £349,845 (Three quarters of her estate to Action Research for the Crippled Child)

Mrs. Marjorie **Lewis-Manning**, of Lilliput, Poole, Dorset .... £985,788 (The residue to the Lewis-Manning Cancer Trust)

Miss Edith Mary **Loader**, of Penywern Road, London SW5 .... £1,000,883 (£1,000 and one quarter of the residue to the National Benevolent Association, and one quarter each to John Groom's Association, Guide Dogs for the Blind Association and British Red Cross Society)

Mr. Cecil Max **Lock**, of Victoria Square, London SW1 .... £1,074,115 (One seventh of the residue for charitable purposes as his trustees determine, and three sevenths equally between the World Wildlife Fund, Friends of the Earth, Greenpeace, Woodland Trust, Peoples Trust for Endangered Species and Cornwall Trust for Nature Conservation)

Joy Cunninghame Erskine **Lowe**, of Wadhurst,

East Sussex .... £524,974 (Her entire estate to the R.N.I.D.)

Mr. George Edward **Lowe-Willetts**, of Weymouth, Dorset .... £449,479 (The residue to the Greenpeace Organization)

Mrs. Katie Brazier Emily **Luff**, of Sunningdale, Berks. .... £520,549 (The residue to the British Heart Foundation)

Mr. Charles Augustus **Main**, of Northam, Devon. .... £449,413 (The residue equally between the Imperial Cancer Research Fund and St. Dunstan's)

Miss Doris May **Mann**, of Ampthill, Beds. £953,827 (The residue to the R.N.L.I., for a lifeboat for the Norfolk or Essex coast)

Mr. Marcus Beresford Busfeild Stapleton **Martin**, of Norbury, Derbys. .... £462,413 (His entire estate to the National Trust)

Mr. Fred **Maude**, of Keighley, West Yorks. .... £502,520 (The residue to the Sue Ryder Foundation, for Manorlands Home, Oxenhope)

Lady (Philippa) **McAlpine**, of Bernard Street, London WC1 .... £2,089,126 (The residue to the Great Ormond Street Hospital for Sick Children, London)

Mr. Frederick Alexander **Moffat**, of Shamley Green, Surrey .... £1,918,310 (One sixth of the residue to charities selected by his trustees)

Mr. Valentine George **Moore**, of Redcliffe Road, London SW10 .... £403,580 (The residue to the Marie Curie Memorial Foundation)

Niobe Ulrica Wilhelmina **Murdoch**, of Hove, East Sussex .... £548,057 (The residue equally between the R.N.L.I. and Pestalozzi Children's Village Trust)

Lt. Comdr. Robert George Iltyd **Nicholl**, R.N. (retd.), of Grundisburgh, Suffolk .... £968,910 (The residue equally between King Edward VII Hospital for Officers, London, Distressed Gentlefolk's Aid Association, R.U.K.B.A. and Cheshire Foundation)

Mrs. Emma Elsie Gladys **Norwood**, of Harrogate, North Yorks. .... £1,201,680 (The residue equally between St. George's Home for the Disabled, Harrogate, St. Gemma's Hospice, Leeds, National Deaf Children's Society, Malcolm Sargent Cancer Fund for Children, Treloar Trust, Save the Children Fund, Henshaw's Society for the Blind, Children's Society, Cheshire Foundation, Brooke Hospital for Animals, P.D.S.A., R.N.I.D., N.S.P.C.C., R.S.P.C.A., Salvation Army, R.N.I.B., National Children's Home, Spastics Society, Leukaemia Research Fund, Guide Dogs for the Blind Association and Blue Cross)

Mr. Herbert Charles **Otton**, of Budleigh Salterton, Devon. .... £634,794 (The residue equally between the National Society for Cancer Relief, R.N.I.B. and Invalid Children's Aid Association)

Mr. Charles William **Payne**, of Wellingborough, Northants. .... £451,419 (The residue to the Gardeners Royal Benevolent Society)

Mr. Roy **Perkins**, of Northwood, Middx. . £417,779 (Half the residue to the R.A.F. Benevolent Fund)

Mrs Euphemia Mill **Peters**, of Somerset Road, London SW19 .... £715,694 (Seven tenths of the residue to the Arthritis and Rheumatism Council and one tenth each to the Guide Dogs for the Blind Association, the R.S.P.C.A. and P.D.S.A.)

Mrs. Margot **Pottlitzer**, of Wedderburn Road, London NW3 .... £755,187 (Seventy-five per cent. of the residue to the Central

British Fund for World Jewish Relief and twenty-five per cent. to the Children and Youth Aliyah)

Sir David **Robinson**, of Newmarket, Suffolk £1,366,114
(The residue, on the death of his wife, to the R.N.L.I.)

Mr. Victor Charles **Robson**, of Canford Cliffs, Poole, Dorset £2,131,267
(Six sevenths of the residue to the Imperial Cancer Research Fund and one seventh to the International Spinal Research Trust)

Miss Rosemary **Rooke**, of Washwater, Newbury, Berks. £595,007
(The residue to Newbury Hospital Helpers League)

Miss Kathleen Dorothy **Rouse**, of West Byfleet, Surrey £1,011,130
(The residue equally between Lloyds Benevolent Fund, National Trust, Oxfam, Children's Society, N.S.P.C.C., London Association for the Blind, "Greater London Fund for the Blind", Guide Dogs for the Blind, Royal Association for the Deaf and Dumb, Cancer Research Campaign, Spastics Society, National Society for Cancer Relief, "British Rheumatism Association", Mission to Lepers, British Red Cross Society, Salvation Army, Actors Benevolent Fund, Gardeners Royal Benevolent Society, R.S.P.C.A., Battersea Dogs Home, Blue Cross, Friends of the Clergy Corporation, Architects Benevolent Society, Distressed Gentlefolk's Aid Association, British Sailors Society, Metropolitan and City Police Orphans Fund and British Heart Foundation)

Mrs Annie Dorothy **Sennitt**, of Leicester £801,479
(The residue to Cambridge University, to assist post-graduate students in medicine research)

Bessie Laura **Shillabeer**, of Teigngrace, Devon £314,068
(The residue to the R.S.P.C.A.)

Myrtle Ariege **Solomon**, of Rockford, Ringwood, Hants. £376,702
(The residue to War Resisters International)

Mrs. Norah **Spencer**, of Mytholmroyd, West Yorks. £498,147
(The residue equally between the Children's Society, R.N.L.I and Salvation Army)

Miss Ada **Stanley**, of Ruislip, Middx. £385,254
(The residue to Great Ormond Street Hospital for Sick Children)

Mr. George Stupples **Stickells**, of Ash, Canterbury £871,513
(The residue equally between the R.N.I.B., Cancer Research Campaign and Imperial Cancer Research Fund)

Mrs. Elsie May **Sykes**, O.B.E., of Harrogate, North Yorks. £4,057,839
(Five sixteenths of the residue to the Charles Sykes

Trust, three sixteenths to Leeds Eastern Health Authority, one eighth to Leeds Western Health Authority and one sixteenth each to York and Bradford Health Authorities, all for medical equipment, one eighth to Harrogate Health Authority, for the Elsie Sykes Endowment Fund, and one sixteenth each to the Brain Research Trust and Skin Disease Research Fund)

Mr. Alec Arthur **Symonds**, of Hinton St. George, Somerset £524,841
(The residue equally between Emmanuel College, Cambridge, Papworth Village Industries, R.N.I.B., Oxfam, King Edward VII Hospital, London, Guy's Hospital, London, and the R.S.P.C.A.)

Mr. Edward Hardy **Taylor**, of Newark, Notts. £593,656
(The residue equally between the League of Friends of Newark Hospital, Save the Children Fund, N.S.P.C.C., Spastics Society, British Red Cross Society, St. John Ambulance Brigade, Age Concern England, King George's Fund for Sailors, Royal British Legion, Salvation Army, R.A.F. Benevolent Fund and R.N.L.I.)

Jean Smith **Thomson**, of Woking, Surrey £538,542
(Three fifths of her estate to the Imperial Cancer Research Fund and two fifths to the Scottish Corporation, London)

Mr. John Harold **Tidmarsh**, of Hove, East Sussex £958,828
(The residue equally between the Salvation Army and Dr. Barnardo's)

Frederika, Countess **Von Waldburg zu Wolfegg Waldsee**, of Menelik Road, London NW2 £1,082,585
(The residue to her trustees for charities concerned with the work of Mother Teresa in India, cancer research and treatment, welfare of the disabled and care of the aged at their discretion)

Mrs. Dorothy Rose **Walker**, of Richmond, Surrey £2,765,043
(Her entire estate to the R.S.P.C.A.)

Miss Margaret Marian **Wethered**, of Liverpool £556,115
(The residue for charities in England as her executor selects)

Mrs. Jessie Westworth **Whitfield**, of St. Helens, Merseyside £560,972
(The residue equally between the Abbeyfield St. Helens Society, P.D.S.A., Cancer Research Campaign, R.S.P.B. and British Diabetic Association)

Ethel Alice **Woolf**, of Brockley, Avon ... £338,995
(The residue to Bristol Royal Infirmary, for diabetes research)

Mrs. Bertha Lyndall **Workman**, of Petts Wood, Kent £492,809
(The residue equally between the National Trust and R.S.P.C.A.)

CONFEDERATION OF BRITISH INDUSTRY

Centre Point, 103 New Oxford Street, London WC1A 1DU

[01-379 7400]

The Confederation of British Industry was founded in August 1965 and is an independent non-party political body financed by industry and commerce. It exists primarily to ensure that the Government understands the intentions, needs and problems of British business. It is the recognized spokesman for the business viewpoint and is consulted as such by the Government.

The C.B.I. represents, directly and indirectly, some 250,000 companies. All the major nationalized industries are in membership and thereby able to work with the C.B.I. on problems that are the concern of all management.

The governing body of the C.B.I. is the 400-strong Council, which meets monthly in London under the chairmanship of the President. It is assisted by some 27 expert standing committees which advise on the main aspects of policy. There are 13 Regional Councils and offices covering the administrative regions of England, Scotland, Wales and Northern Ireland.

President, Sir Trevor Holdsworth.
Director-General, J. Banham.
Secretary, M. W. Hunt.

NATIONAL ASSOCIATION OF INDUSTRIES FOR THE BLIND AND DISABLED INC.

Triton House, 43a High Street South,

Dunstable, Beds. LU6 3RZ

[0582–606796]

The National Association of Industries for the Blind and Disabled Inc. was established in 1929 and incorporated in 1936; it is registered as a charity.

The Association acts in the nature of a trade association providing facilities for consultation and co-operation between its members who operate workshops employing blind and disabled people and it represents their interests in discussions with, and

representations to, other organisations (e.g. government departments and local authorities) concerned with sheltered employment. It does not own or operate any of the workshops, which are run by local authorities or voluntary organisations acting as their agents.

Chairman (1988–89), R. J. Pocock.
Hon. Secretary, G. J. Entwistle.

EMPLOYERS' AND TRADE BODIES

ADVERTISING ASSOCIATION, Abford House, 15 Wilton Road, SW1V 1NJ.—*Dir. Gen.,* R. Underhill, O.B.E.

AEROSPACE COMPANIES LTD., SOCIETY OF BRITISH, 29 King Street, SW1Y 6RD.—*Dir.,* Air Marshal Sir John Curtiss, K.C.B., K.B.E.

BAKERS, FEDERATION OF, 20 Bedford Square, WC1B 3HF.—*Dir.,* A. Casdagli, C.B.E.

BANKERS' ASSOCIATION, BRITISH, 10 Lombard Street, EC3V 9EL.—*Sec.-Gen.,* The Hon. R. C. R. Hoyer Millar.

BREWERS' SOCIETY, 42 Portman Square, W1H 0BB.—*Dir.,* Maj. Gen. W. D. Mangham, C.B.

BUILDING EMPLOYERS' CONFEDERATION, 82 New Cavendish Street, W1M 8AD.—*Dir. Gen.,* J. A. Newby.

BUILDING MATERIAL PRODUCERS, NATIONAL COUNCIL OF, 10 Great George Street, SW1P 3AE.—*Dir. Gen.,* N. M. Chaldecott.

BUS AND COACH COUNCIL, Sardinia House, 52 Lincoln's Inn Fields, WC2A 3LZ.—*Dir. Gen.,* D. R. Quin.

CHEMICAL INDUSTRIES ASSOCIATION LTD., Alembic House, 93 Albert Embankment, SE1 7TU.—*Dir. Gen.,* J. C. L. Cox.

CLOTHING INDUSTRY ASSOCIATION LTD., BRITISH, British Apparel Centre, 7 Swallow Place, W1R 7AA.—*Dir.* J. R. Wilson.

DAIRY TRADE FEDERATION, 19 Cornwall Terrace, NW1 4QP.—*Dir. Gen.,* J. P. Price.

ELECTROTECHNICAL AND ALLIED MANUFACTURERS' ASSOCIATIONS, FEDERATION OF BRITISH (BEAMA), Leicester House, 8 Leicester Street, WC2H 7BN.—*Dir. Gen.,* J. G. Gaddes.

ENGINEERING EMPLOYERS' FEDERATION, Broadway House, Tothill Street, SW1H 9NQ.—*Dir. Gen.,* Dr. J. S. McFarlane, C.B.E.

FARMERS' UNION, NATIONAL (NFU), Agriculture House, Knightsbridge, SW1X 7NJ. *Dir. Gen.,* D. Evans.

FARMERS' UNION OF SCOTLAND, NATIONAL, 17 Grosvenor Crescent, Edinburgh EH12 5EN.—*Dir.,* D. S. Johnston.

FARMERS' UNION, ULSTER, Dunedin, 475–477 Antrim Road, Belfast BT15 3DA.—*Gen. Sec.,* J. V. Smyth.

FINANCE HOUSES ASSOCIATION, 18 Upper Grosvenor Street, W1X 9PB.—*Dir.,* N. A. D. Grant.

FOOD AND DRINK FEDERATION, 6 Catherine Street, WC2B 5JJ.—*Dir. Gen.,* M. P. Mackenzie.

FREIGHT TRANSPORT ASSOCIATION LTD., Hermes House, 157 St. John's Road, Tunbridge Wells, Kent TN4 9UZ.—*Dir.-Gen.,* G. Turvey.

INSURERS, ASSOCIATION OF BRITISH, Aldermary House, Queen Street, EC4N 1TT.—*Chief Exec.,* M. A. Jones.

KNITTING INDUSTRIES FEDERATION LTD., 7 Gregory Boulevard, Nottingham NG7 6NB.—*Sec.,* C. J. Moye.

LEATHER CONFEDERATION, BRITISH, Leather Trade House, Kings Park Road, Moulton Park, Northampton NN3 1JD.—*Dir.*, R. L. Sykes, O.B.E., PH.D.

LEATHER PRODUCERS' ASSOCIATION, Leather Trade House, Kings Park Road, Moulton Park, Northampton NN3 1JD.—*Nat. Sec.*, J. Purvis.

MAN-MADE FIBRES FEDERATION, BRITISH, 24 Buckingham Gate, SW1E 6LB.

MARINE INDUSTRIES FEDERATION, BRITISH, Boating Industry House, Vale Road, Oatlands Park, Weybridge, Surrey KT13 9NS.—*Chief Exec.*, P. V. Wagstaffe.

MOTOR MANUFACTURERS AND TRADERS LTD., SOCIETY OF, Forbes House, Halkin Street, SW1X 7DS.—*Dir.*, S. Foster.

NEWSPAPER PUBLISHERS ASSOCIATION LTD., 34 Southwark Bridge Road, SE1 9EU.—*Dir.*, J. E. Lepage.

OFFICE SYSTEMS AND STATIONERY FEDERATION, BRITISH, 6 Wimpole Street, W1M 8AS.—*Dir.*, D. F. Hall.

PAPER AND BOARD INDUSTRY FEDERATION, BRITISH, Papermakers House, Rivenhall Road, Westlea, Swindon, Wilts. SN5 7BE.—*Dir.-Gen.*, W. J. Bartlett.

PLASTICS FEDERATION, BRITISH, 5 Belgrave Square, SW1X 8PD.—*Dir.*, D. R. Jones.

PORT EMPLOYERS, NATIONAL ASSOCIATION OF, Commonwealth House, 1–19 New Oxford Street, WC1A 1DZ.—*Dir.*, N. H. Finney.

PORTS FEDERATION, BRITISH, Commonwealth House, 1–19 New Oxford Street, WC1A 1DZ.—*Man. Dir.* N. H. Finney.

PRINTING INDUSTRIES FEDERATION, BRITISH, 11 Bedford Row, WC1R 4DX.—*Dir. Gen.*, S. W. Bradley.

PUBLISHERS ASSOCIATION, THE, 19 Bedford Square, WC1B 3HJ.—*Chief Exec.*, C. Bradley.

RADIO CONTRACTORS LTD., ASSOCIATION OF INDEPENDENT, Radio House, 46 Westbourne Grove, W2 5SH.—*Dir.*, B. West.

RETAIL CONSORTIUM, THE, Commonwealth House, 1–19 New Oxford Street, WC1A 1PA.—*Dir. Gen.*, R. S. Weir.

ROAD FEDERATION, BRITISH, Cowdray House, 6 Portugal Street, WC2A 2HG.—*Dir.*, P. Witt.

ROAD HAULAGE ASSOCIATION LTD., Roadway House, 104 New Kings Road, SW6 4LN.—*Dir.-Gen.*, D. B. H. Colley, C.B.E.

RUBBER MANUFACTURERS' ASSOCIATION LTD., BRITISH, 90–91 Tottenham Court Road, W1P 0BR.—*Dir.*, G. C. Gullan.

SHIPPING, GENERAL COUNCIL OF BRITISH, 30–32 St. Mary Axe, EC3A 8ET.—*Dir.-Gen.*, P. Le Cheminant, C.B.

SPORT AND ALLIED INDUSTRIES FEDERATION LTD., BRITISH, Prudential House, Wellesley Road, Croydon, Surrey CR0 9XY.—*Chief Exec.*, L. F. Standen.

TELEVISION ASSOCIATION LTD., INDEPENDENT, Knighton House, 56 Mortimer Street, W1N 8AN.—*Dir.*, D. Shaw.

TEXTILE CONFEDERATION, BRITISH, 24 Buckingham Gate, SW1E 6LB.—*Dir.*, I. MacArthur, OBE.

TIMBER GROWERS' UNITED KINGDOM, Agriculture House, Knightsbridge, SW1X 7NJ.—*Chief Exec.*, A. R. Williams.

TIMBER MERCHANTS' ASSOCIATION, BRITISH, Ridgeway House, 6 Ridgeway Road, Long Ashton, Bristol BS18 9EU.—*Sec.*, H. B. Roberts.

TIMBER TRADE FEDERATION, THE, Clareville House, 26–27 Oxenden Street, SW1Y 4EL.—*Dir. Gen.*, A. A. Lockyer, L.V.O.

U.K. OFFSHORE OPERATORS ASSOCIATION LTD., 3 Hans Crescent, SW1X 0LN.—*Dir.*, G. C. Band.

U.K. PETROLEUM INDUSTRY ASSOCIATION LTD., 9 Kingsway, WC2B 6XH.—*Dir. Gen.*, Dr. I. D. G. Berwick.

WHOLESALE AND INDUSTRIAL DISTRIBUTORS, FEDERATION OF, The Old Post Office, Dunchideock, Exeter EX2 9TU.—*Dir.*, J. Hussey.

CAR PRODUCTION IN MAIN PRODUCING COUNTRIES (thousands)

	1978	1979	1980	1981	1982	1983	1984	1985	1986	1987
United Kingdom	1,223	1,070	924	955	888	1,045	909	1,048	1,019	1,143
France	3,111	3,220	2,939	2,612	2,777	2,961	2,713	2,632	2,773	3,052
W. Germany	3,890	3,933	3,521	3,578	3,761	3,878	3,790	4,167	4,311	4,374
Italy	1,509	1,481	1,445	1,257	1,297	1,396	1,439	1,389	1,652	1,713
Sweden	254	297	235	258	295	362	373	401	421	432
Japan	5,748	6,176	7,038	6,974	6,882	7,152	7,073	7,647	7,810	7,891
U.S.A.	9,176	8,434	6,376	6,253	5,073	6,781	7,774	8,185	7,829	7,099
Canada	1,143	988	847	803	808	969	1,021	1,078	1,061	803
Total	26,054	25,599	23,325	22,690	21,785	24,527	25,072	26,547	26,876	26,507
UK % of total	5	4	4	4	4	4	4	4	4	4

BRITISH MOTOR VEHICLE PRODUCTION AND EXPORTS

Year	Weeks	Passenger Cars (including taxis)			Commercial Road Vehicles		
		For Export*	Total	Weekly average	For Export*	Total	Weekly average
1981.......	...52...	304,678	954,650	18,359	113,862	229,555	4,416
1982.......	...52...	225,865	887,679	17,070	92,510	268,798	5,169
1983.......	...53...	237,376	1,044,597	19,709	62,801	244,514	4,613
1984.......	...52...	192,213	908,906	17,479	49,808	224,825	4,323
1985.......	...52...	207,671	1,047,973	20,153	65,756	265,973	5,115
1986.......	...52...	187,556	1,018,962	19,595	49,776	228,685	4,398
1987.......	...52...	226,197	1,142,985	21,980	60,736	246,727	4,745

*Export Allocation

TRADES UNION CONGRESS (T.U.C.)

Congress House, 23–28 Great Russell Street, WC1B 3LS
[01–636–4030]

The Trades Union Congress, founded in 1868, is a voluntary association of Trade Unions, the representatives of which meet annually to consider matters of common concern to their members. The Congress has met annually since 1871 and in recent years has met normally on the first Monday in September, its sessions extending through the succeeding four days. Congress is constituted by delegates of the affiliated unions on the basis of one delegate for every 5,000 members, or fraction thereof, on whose behalf affiliation fees are paid. Affiliated unions (in 1987–88) totalled 83 with an aggregate membership of 9,126,911.

The main business of the annual Congress is to consider the report of its General Council dealing with the activities of the Congress year, along with motions from affiliated societies on questions of policy and organization.

The Standing Committees of the General Council are serviced by a full time staff appointed by the General Secretary, who is himself elected by Congress and who remains in office until the age of 65, subject to decision of Congress or the General Council.

Through the General Council and its committees the trade union movement maintains systematic relations with the Government and Government Departments, with the Confederation of British Industry and with a large number of other bodies. It is represented on the National Economic Development Council, the Training Commission, the Health and Safety Commission, the Council of the Advisory Conciliation and Arbitration Service and a number of other bodies.

Among powers vested in the General Council by consent of the unions in Congress is the responsibility of intervening in disputes and differences between affiliated organizations; if possible this is done through informal conciliation meetings under T.U.C. auspices but where necessary a Disputes Committee is formed consisting of one member of the General Council and two senior officials of unions not involved in the dispute. This investigates the matter concerned and issues its findings.

Unions retain full control of their own affairs and the only sanctions which Congress can apply are suspension or exclusion from membership.

Chairman (1988–89), A. M. G. Christopher, C.B.E. (*Inland Revenue Staff Federation*).
General Secretary, N. D. Willis.

SCOTTISH TRADES UNION CONGRESS

16 Woodlands Terrace, Glasgow G3 6DF
[041-332 4946]

The Congress was formed in 1897 and acts as a national centre for the trade union movement in Scotland. In 1987 it consisted of 61 unions with a membership of 910,942 and 49 directly affiliated Trades Councils. The majority of the unions organize throughout Britain and affiliate on their membership in Scotland.

The Annual Congress in April elects a 26-member General Council on the basis of 13 industrial sections. Congress has been prominent in pressing for economic expansion and full employment in Scotland and the development of the social services, most of which are separately organized in Scotland.

Chairperson R. R. Webster.
General Secretary, C. Christie.

TRADES UNIONS AFFILIATED TO T.U.C.

A list of the Trades Unions affiliated to the Trades Union Congress at Sept. 1, 1988 (*see also* **Occurrences during Printing**). The number of members of each Union is shown in parentheses.

AMALGAMATED ASSOCIATION OF BEAMERS, TWISTERS AND DRAWERS (HAND AND MACHINE), THE (470), 27 Every Street, Nelson, Lancs. BB9 7NE—*Gen. Sec.*, A. H. Edmondson.

AMALGAMATED ENGINEERING UNION (A.E.U.) (815,000), 110 Peckham Road, SE15 5EL—*Gen. Sec.*, G. H. Laird, C.B.E.

AMALGAMATED SOCIETY OF TEXTILE WORKERS AND KINDRED TRADES (2,838), Foxlowe, Market Place, Leek, Staffs. ST13 6AD—*Gen. Sec.*, A. Hitchmough.

AMALGAMATED UNION OF ASPHALT WORKERS, THE (amalgamated with T.G.W.U. since Jan. 1988).

ASSOCIATED SOCIETY OF LOCOMOTIVE ENGINEERS AND FIREMEN (A.S.L.E.F.) (20,000), 9 Arkwright Road, Hampstead, NW3 6AB—*Sec.*, N. Milligan.

ASSOCIATION OF CINEMATOGRAPH, TELEVISION AND ALLIED TECHNICIANS (29,000), 111 Wardour Street, W1V 4AY—*Gen. Sec.*, A. Sapper.

ASSOCIATION OF FIRST DIVISION CIVIL SERVANTS (9,386), 2 Caxton Street, SW1H 0QH—*Gen. Sec.*, J. Ward.

ASSOCIATION OF PROFESSIONAL, EXECUTIVE, CLERICAL AND COMPUTER STAFF (APEX) (80,000), 22 Worple Road, SW19 4DF—*Gen. Sec.*, R. Grantham.

ASSOCIATION OF SCIENTIFIC, TECHNICAL AND MANAGERIAL STAFFS (A.S.T.M.S.) (amalgamated with T.A.S.S. to form Manufacturing, Science and Finance).

ASSOCIATION OF UNIVERSITY TEACHERS (30,000), United House, 1 Pembridge Road, W11 3HJ—*Gen. Sec.*, Ms. D. Warwick.

BAKERS, FOOD AND ALLIED WORKERS' UNION (35,000), Stanborough House, Great North Road, Stanborough, Welwyn Garden City, Herts. AL8 7TA—*Gen. Sec.*, J. R. Marino.

BANKING, INSURANCE AND FINANCE UNION, THE (165,839), Sheffield House, 1b Amity Grove, SW20 0LG—*Gen. Sec.*, L. Mills.

BRITISH ACTORS' EQUITY ASSOCIATION (36,000), 8 Harley Street, W1N 2AB—*Gen. Sec.*, P. Plouviez.

BRITISH AIR LINE PILOTS ASSOCIATION, THE (4,000), 81 New Road, Harlington, Hayes, Middlesex UB3 5BG—*Gen. Sec.*, M. Young.

BRITISH ASSOCIATION OF COLLIERY MANAGEMENT, THE (11,000), BACM House, 317 Nottingham Road, Old Basford, Nottingham NG7 7DP—*Gen. Sec.*, A. Wilson.

BROADCASTING AND ENTERTAINMENT TRADES ALLIANCE (30,000), 181–185 Wardour Street, W1V 4BE—*Gen. Sec.*, D. A. Hearn.

CARD SETTING MACHINE TENTERS' SOCIETY (100), 36 Greenton Avenue, Scholes, Cleckheaton, W. Yorks. BD19 6DT—*Sec.*, G. Priestley.

CERAMIC AND ALLIED TRADES UNION, THE (29,957), Hillcrest House, Garth Street, Hanley, Stoke-on-Trent ST1 2AB—*Gen. Sec.*, A. W. Clowes.

CIVIL AND PUBLIC SERVICES ASSOCIATION, THE (149,500), 160 Falcon Road, SW11 2LN—*Gen. Sec.*, J. N. Ellis.

CIVIL SERVICE UNION (amalgamated with Society of Civil and Public Servants to form National Union of Civil and Public Servants).

COMMUNICATION MANAGERS' ASSOCIATION (19,600), Hughes House, Ruscombe Business Park, Twyford, Reading RG10 9JD—*Gen. Sec.*, R. J. Cowley.

CONFEDERATION OF HEALTH SERVICE EMPLOYEES (C.O.H.S.E.) (208,000), Glen House, High Street, Banstead, Surrey SM7 2LH—*Gen. Sec.*, H. Mac-Kenzie.

EDUCATIONAL INSTITUTE OF SCOTLAND, THE (43,886), 46 Moray Place, Edinburgh EH3 6BH—*Gen. Sec.*, J. Martin.

ELECTRICAL, ELECTRONIC, TELECOMMUNICATION AND PLUMBING UNION (E.E.T.P.U.) (330,000), Hayes Court, West Common Road, Bromley, Kent BR2 7AU—*Gen. Sec.*, E. A. B. Hammond, O.B.E.

ENGINEERS' AND MANAGERS' ASSOCIATION (40,506), Station House, Fox Lane North, Chertsey, Surrey KT16 9HW—*Gen. Sec.*, J. Lyons.

FILM ARTISTES' ASSOCIATION (2,000), 61 Marloes Road, W8 6LE—*Sec.*, M. Reynel.

FIRE BRIGADES UNION, THE (45,503), Bradley House, 68 Coombe Road, Kingston upon Thames, Surrey KT2 7AE—*Gen. Sec.*, K. Cameron.

FURNITURE, TIMBER AND ALLIED TRADES UNION (47,000), Fairfields, Roe Green, Kingsbury, NW9 0PT—*Gen. Sec.*, C. A. Christopher.

GENERAL, MUNICIPAL, BOILERMAKERS AND ALLIED TRADES UNION (G.M.W.) (803,000), Thorne House, Claygate, Esher, Surrey KT10 0TL—*Gen. Sec.*, J. Edmonds.

GENERAL UNION OF ASSOCIATIONS OF LOOM OVER-LOOKERS, THE (1,175), Overlookers Institute, Jude Street, Nelson, Lancs. BB9 7NP—*Pres.*, E. Macro.

GREATER LONDON STAFF ASSOCIATION, THE (12,240), Room 151, North Block, County Hall, SE1 7PB—*Gen. Sec.*, A. Capelin.

HEALTH VISITORS' ASSOCIATION (16,700), 50 South-wark Street, SE1 1UN—*Gen. Sec.*, Ms. S. Goodwin.

HOSPITAL CONSULTANTS AND SPECIALISTS ASSOCIA-TION, THE (2,400), The Old Court House, London Road, Ascot, Berks. SL5 7EN—*Chief Exec.*, S. Charkham.

INLAND REVENUE STAFF FEDERATION (53,000), Doug-las Houghton House, 231 Vauxhall Bridge Road, SW1V 1EH—*Gen. Sec.*, A. M. G. Christopher, C.B.E.

INSTITUTION OF PROFESSIONAL CIVIL SERVANTS, THE (90,750), 75–79 York Road, SE1 7AQ—*Gen. Sec.*, W. McCall.

IRON AND STEEL TRADES CONFEDERATION, THE (43,000), Swinton House, 324 Gray's Inn Road, WC1X 8DD—*Gen. Sec.*, R. L. Evans.

MANUFACTURING, SCIENCE AND FINANCE (650,000) 79 Camden Road, NW1 9ES—*Joint Gen. Secs.*, K. Gill; C. Jenkins.

MILITARY AND ORCHESTRAL MUSICAL INSTRUMENT MAKERS' TRADE SOCIETY (41), 2 Whitehorse Ave-nue, Boreham Wood, Herts. WD6 1HD—*Gen. Sec.*, F. McKenzie.

MUSICIANS' UNION (40,000), 60–62 Clapham Road, SW9 0JJ—*Gen. Sec.*, J. Morton.

NATIONAL AND LOCAL GOVERNMENT OFFICERS' AS-SOCIATION (N.A.L.G.O.) (758,780), 1 Mabledon Place, WC1H 9AJ—*Gen. Sec.*, J. D. Daly.

NATIONAL ASSOCIATION OF COLLIERY OVERMEN, DEPUTIES AND SHOTFIRERS (9,000), Simpson House, 48 Nether Hall Road, Doncaster, S. Yorks. DN1 2PZ—*Sec.*, P. McNestry.

NATIONAL ASSOCIATION OF CO-OPERATIVE OFFICIALS (4,400), Saxone House, 56 Market Street, Manches-ter M1 1PW—*Gen. Sec.*, L. W. Ewing.

NATIONAL ASSOCIATION OF LICENSED HOUSE MAN-AGERS (14,000), 9 Coombe Lane, Raynes Park, SW20 8NE—*Gen. Sec.*, J. Madden.

NATIONAL ASSOCIATION OF PROBATION OFFICERS (6,310), 3–4 Chivalry Road, Battersea, SW11 1HT—*Sec.*, W. L. Beaumont.

NATIONAL ASSOCIATION OF SCHOOLMASTERS/UNION OF WOMEN TEACHERS (N.A.S./U.W.T.) (121,000), Hills-court Education Centre, Rose Hill, Rednal, Bir-mingham B45 8RS—*Gen. Sec.*, F. A. Smithies.

NATIONAL ASSOCIATION OF TEACHERS IN FURTHER AND HIGHER EDUCATION (78,000), 27 Britannia Street, WC1X 9JP—*Gen. Sec.*, J. P. Dawson.

NATIONAL COMMUNICATIONS UNION (147,105), Grey-stoke House, 150 Brunswick Road, W5 1AW—*Gen. Sec.*, E. C. George (*acting*).

NATIONAL GRAPHICAL ASSOCIATION 1982 (N.G.A. '82) (130,000), Graphic House, 63–67 Bromham Road, Bedford MK40 2AG—*Sec.*, A. D. Dubbins.

NATIONAL LEAGUE OF THE BLIND AND DISABLED, THE (3,000), 2 Tenterden Road, N17 8BE—*Sec.*, M. A. Barrett.

NATIONAL UNION OF CIVIL AND PUBLIC SERVANTS (N.U.C.P.S.) (120,000), 124–130 Southwark Street, SE1 0TU—*Gen. Sec.*, L. Christie.

NATIONAL UNION OF DOMESTIC APPLIANCES AND GENERAL OPERATIVES, THE (3,100), 6–8 Imperial Buildings, Corporation Street, Rotherham, S. Yorks. S60 1PB—*Gen. Sec.*, R. D. Preston.

NATIONAL UNION OF HOSIERY AND KNITWEAR WORK-ERS, THE (47,238), 55 New Walk, Leicester LE1 7EB—*Gen. Sec.*, T. Kirk.

NATIONAL UNION OF INSURANCE WORKERS (18,131), 27 Old Gloucester Street, WC1N 3AF—*Gen. Sec.*, R. Main.

NATIONAL UNION OF JOURNALISTS (N.U.J.) (32,000), Acorn House, 314–320 Gray's Inn Road, WC1X 8DP—*Gen. Sec.*, H. Conroy.

NATIONAL UNION OF LOCK AND METAL WORKERS (5,400), Bellamy House, Wilkes Street, Willenhall, West Midlands WV13 2BS—*Gen. Sec.*, M. Bradley.

NATIONAL UNION OF MARINE, AVIATION AND SHIPPING TRANSPORT OFFICERS, THE (21,201), Oceanair House, 750–760 High Road, Leytonstone, E11 3BB—*Gen. Sec.*, E. Nevin.

NATIONAL UNION OF MINEWORKERS (N.U.M.) (91,000), St. James' House, Vicar Lane, Sheffield S1 2EX—*Sec.*, P. E. Heathfield.

NATIONAL UNION OF PUBLIC EMPLOYEES (N.U.P.E.) (650,000), Civic House, 20 Grand Depot Road, SE18 6SF—*Sec.*, R. K. Bickerstaffe.

NATIONAL UNION OF RAILWAYMEN (N.U.R.) (117,594), Unity House, Euston Road, NW1 2BL—*Gen. Sec.*, J. Knapp.

NATIONAL UNION OF SCALEMAKERS (935), Queensway House, 57 Livery Street, Birmingham B3 1HA—*Gen. Sec.*, A. F. Smith.

NATIONAL UNION OF SEAMEN (N.U.S.) (24,000), Mari-time House, Old Town, Clapham, SW4 0JP—*Gen. Sec.*, S. McCluskie.

NATIONAL UNION OF TAILORS AND GARMENT WORK-ERS (78,000), 16 Charles Square, N1 6HP—*Gen. Sec.*, A. Smith.

NATIONAL UNION OF TEACHERS (N.U.T.) (179,000), Hamilton House, Mabledon Place, WC1H 9BD—*Gen. Sec.*, F. F. Jarvis.

NATIONAL UNION OF THE FOOTWEAR, LEATHER AND ALLIED TRADES (35,000), The Grange, 108 Northampton Road, Earls Barton, Northampton NN6 0JH—*Gen. Sec.*, G. F. Browett.

NORTHERN CARPET TRADES' UNION (842), 22 Clare Road, Halifax HX1 2HX—*Gen. Sec.*, K. Edmondson.

PATTERN WEAVERS' SOCIETY (62), 38, St. Paul's Road, Kirkheaton, Huddersfield HD5 0EY—*Gen. Sec.*, K. K. Bradley.

POWER LOOM CARPET WEAVERS' AND TEXTILE WORKERS' UNION, THE (3,500), Callows Lane, Kidderminster, Worcs. DY10 2JG—*Gen. Sec.*, B. C. Moule.

PRISON OFFICERS' ASSOCIATION, THE (24,358), Cronin House, 245 Church Street, Edmonton, N9 9HW—*Gen. Sec.*, D. Evans.

ROSSENDALE UNION OF BOOT, SHOE AND SLIPPER OPERATIVES, THE (4,457), Taylor House, 7 Tenterfield Street, Waterfoot, Rossendale, Lancs. BB4 7BA.—*Gen. Sec.*, M. Murray.

SCOTTISH PRISON OFFICERS' ASSOCIATION (3,405), 21 Calder Road, Edinburgh EH11 3PF—*Gen. Sec.*, J. Renton, M.B.E.

SCOTTISH UNION OF POWER-LOOM OVERLOOKERS (60), 3 Napier Terrace, Dundee, Tayside.—*Sec.*, J. Reilly.

SCREW, NUT, BOLT AND RIVET TRADE UNION (400), 368 Dudley Road, Birmingham B18 4HH—*Gen. Sec.*, W. J. Redmond.

SHEFFIELD WOOL SHEAR WORKERS' UNION (17), 50 Bankfield Road, Malin Bridge, Sheffield S6 4RD—*Sec.*, J. H. R. Cutler.

SOCIETY OF CIVIL AND PUBLIC SERVANTS (amalgamated with Civil Service Union to form National Union of Civil and Public Servants).

SOCIETY OF GRAPHICAL AND ALLIED TRADES 1982 (SOGAT '82) (192,000), Sogat House, 274–288 London Road, Hadleigh, Benfleet, Essex SS7 2DE—*Gen. Sec.*, Ms. B. Dean.

SOCIETY OF SHUTTLEMAKERS (41), 211 Burnley Road, Colne, Lancs. BB8 8JD—*Gen. Sec.*, L. Illingworth.

SOCIETY OF TELECOM EXECUTIVES (28,834), 1 Park Road, Teddington, Middx. TW11 0AR—*Gen. Sec.*, S. Petch.

SPRING TRAPMAKERS' SOCIETY (dissolved in March 1988).

TECHNICAL, ADMINISTRATIVE AND SUPERVISORY SECTION (T.A.S.S.) (amalgamated with A.S.T.M.S. to form Manufacturing, Science and Finance).

TOBACCO MECHANICS ASSOCIATION (110), 30 Battson Road, Stockswood, Bristol BS14 8FN—*Sec.*, G. Dart.

TRANSPORT AND GENERAL WORKERS' UNION (T.G.W.U.) (1,338,000), Transport House, Smith Square, Westminster, SW1P 3JB—*Gen. Sec.*, R. Todd.

TRANSPORT SALARIED STAFFS' ASSOCIATION (41,977), Walkden House, 10 Melton Street, NW1 2EJ—*Gen. Sec.*, C. A. Lyons.

UNION OF COMMUNICATION WORKERS, THE (198,000), U.C.W. House, Crescent Lane, SW4 9RN—*Gen. Sec.*, A. D. Tuffin.

UNION OF CONSTRUCTION, ALLIED TRADES AND TECHNICIANS (U.C.A.T.T.) (255,226), UCATT House, 177 Abbeville Road, Clapham, SW4 9RL—*Sec.*, A. Williams.

UNION OF SHOP, DISTRIBUTIVE AND ALLIED WORKERS (U.S.D.A.W.) (399,000), Oakley, 188 Wilmslow Road, Fallowfield, Manchester M14 6LJ—*Sec.*, G. Davies.

UNITED ROAD TRANSPORT UNION (21,000), 76 High Lane, Chorlton, Manchester M21 1FD—*Gen. Sec.*, F. Griffin.

WIRE WORKERS' UNION (5,103), Prospect House, Alma Street, Sheffield S3 8SA—*Gen. Sec.*, A. M. Ardron.

WRITERS' GUILD OF GREAT BRITAIN, THE (1,600), 430 Edgware Road, W2 1EH—*Gen. Sec.*, W. J. Jeffrey.

YORKSHIRE ASSOCIATION OF POWER LOOM OVERLOOKERS (561), 20 Hallfield Road, Bradford, BD1 3RQ—*Gen. Sec.*, A. D. Barrow.

LABOUR STATISTICS

Industrial Stoppages (thousands)

	Workers beginning in period	Total working days lost						
		All industries and services	Coal, coke, mineral oil and natural gas	Metals, engineering and vehicles	Textiles, footwear and clothing	Construction	Transport and communication	All other industries and services
1982	2,101	5,313	380	1,457	61	41	1,675	1,699
1983	573	3,754	591	1,420	32	68	295	1,348
1984	1,436	27,135	22,484	2,055	66	334	666	1,530
1985	643	6,402	4,143	590	31	50	197	1,391
1986	538	1,920	143	895	38	33	190	622
1987	884	3,546	217	458	50	22	1,705	1,095
1988 January	39	96	35	21	6	2	9	24
February	162	704	183	380	1	1	55	84
March	29	254	6	141	5	—	55	47
April	12	84	—	9	—	3	62	10
May	35	103	—	19	33	—	32	19

INDUSTRIAL RESEARCH ASSOCIATIONS

The following are members of the Association of Independent Research and Technology Organizations (A.I.R.T.O.), c/o Helliar & Co., 15 Church Street, Ilchester, Yeovil, Somerset BA22 8LN.

AIRCRAFT RESEARCH ASSOCIATION LTD., Manton Lane, Bedford MK41 7PF.

ADVANCED MANUFACTURING TECHNOLOGY RESEARCH INSTITUTE (*Machine tools and other machinery*), Hulley Road, Macclesfield, Cheshire SK10 2NE.

BCIRA (*Foundry and associated industries*), Alvechurch, Birmingham B48 7QB.

BHRA (BRITISH HYDROMECHANICS RESEARCH ASSOCIATION), The Fluid Engineering Centre, Wharley End, Cranfield, Bedford MK43 0AJ.

BICERI (THE BRITISH INTERNAL COMBUSTION ENGINE RESEARCH INSTITUTE LTD.), 111–112 Buckingham Avenue, Slough SL1 4PH.

BNF METALS TECHNOLOGY CENTRE, Denchworth Road, Wantage, Oxon., OX12 9BJ.

BRITISH CERAMIC RESEARCH LTD., Queen's Road, Penkhull, Stoke-on-Trent ST4 7LQ.

BRITISH GLASS INDUSTRY RESEARCH ASSOCIATION, Northumberland Road, Sheffield S10 2UA.

BRITISH LEATHER CONFEDERATION, Leather Trade House, Kings Park Road, Moulton Park, Northampton NN3 1JD.

BRITISH MARITIME TECHNOLOGY LTD., Faggs Road, Feltham, Middx., TW14 0LQ.

BUILDING SERVICES RESEARCH INFORMATION ASSOCIATION, Old Bracknell Lane West, Bracknell, Berks., RG12 4AH.

CAMBRIDGE CONSULTANTS LTD. (*Product design and process development*), Science Park, Milton Road, Cambridge CB4 4DW.

CIRIA (CONSTRUCTION INDUSTRY RESEARCH AND INFORMATION ASSOCIATION), 6 Storey's Gate, SW1P 3AU.

CUTLERY AND ALLIED TRADES RESEARCH ASSOCIATION, Henry Street, Sheffield S3 7EQ.

ERA TECHNOLOGY LTD. (*Electronic and electrical engineering*), Cleeve Road, Leatherhead, Surrey KT22 7SA.

FABRIC CARE RESEARCH ASSOCIATION, Forest House Laboratories, Knaresborough Road, Harrogate, N. Yorks., HG2 7LZ.

FULMER LTD. (*New materials development*), Hollybush Hill, Stoke Poges, Slough SL2 4QD.

FURNITURE INDUSTRY RESEARCH ASSOCIATION, Maxwell Road, Stevenage, Herts., SG1 2EW.

HATRA (HOSIERY AND ALLIED TRADES RESEARCH ASSOCIATION), 7 Gregory Boulevard, Nottingham NG7 6LD.

HAZLETON UK (*Agro-chemical, chemical and pharmaceutical product development*), Otley Road, Harrogate, N. Yorks., HG3 1PY.

HYDRAULICS RESEARCH LTD., Howbery Park, Wallingford, Oxon., OX10 8BA.

INVERESK RESEARCH INTERNATIONAL LTD. (*Pharmaceutical, veterinary, agricultural and chemical product evaluation*), Musselburgh EH21 7UB.

LAMBEG INDUSTRIAL RESEARCH ASSOCIATION (*Linen textiles*), The Research Institute, Lisburn, Co. Antrim, N. Ireland BT27 4RG.

LIFE SCIENCE RESEARCH LTD., Eye, Suffolk IP23 7PX.

MOTOR INDUSTRY RESEARCH ASSOCIATION, Watling Street, Nuneaton, Warwicks., CV10 0TU.

NATIONAL COMPUTING CENTRE LTD., Oxford Road, Manchester M1 7ED.

NEI INTERNATIONAL RESEARCH AND DEVELOPMENT COMPANY LTD., (*Electronics and engineering*), Fossway, Newcastle upon Tyne NE6 2YD.

PAINT RESEARCH ASSOCIATION, 8 Waldegrave Road, Teddington, Middx., TW11 8LD.

PERA (PRODUCTION ENGINEERING RESEARCH ASSOCIATION) (*Advanced manufacturing technology*), Melton Mowbray, Leics. LE13 0PB.

PIRA (*Paper and board, printing and packaging research*), Randalls Road, Leatherhead, Surrey KT22 7RU.

RAPRA TECHNOLOGY LTD. (*Polymer materials*), Shawbury, Shrewsbury, Shropshire SY4 4NR.

RICARDO CONSULTING ENGINEERS P.L.C., Bridge Works, Shoreham by Sea, W. Sussex BN4 5FG.

SATRA FOOTWEAR TECHNOLOGY CENTRE, Satra House, Rockingham Road, Kettering, Northants., NN16 9JH.

SHIPOWNERS REFRIGERATED CARGO RESEARCH ASSOCIATION, 140 Newmarket Road, Cambridge CB5 8HE.

SHIRLEY INSTITUTE (*Textiles and related industries*), Wilmslow Road, Didsbury, Manchester M20 8RX.

SIRA LTD. (*Instrumentation and systems technology*), South Hill, Chislehurst, Kent BR7 5EH.

SMITH ASSOCIATES LTD., (*Electronic, optical, mechanical and software systems*), Surrey Research Park, Guildford GU2 5YP.

SPRING RESEARCH AND MANUFACTURERS' ASSOCIATION, Henry Street, Sheffield S3 7EQ.

STEEL CASTINGS RESEARCH AND TRADE ASSOCIATION, 5 East Bank Road, Sheffield S2 3PT.

TIMBER RESEARCH AND DEVELOPMENT ASSOCIATION, Stocking Lane, Hughenden Valley, High Wycombe, Bucks., HP14 4ND.

TOXICOL LABORATORIES LTD., Bromyard Road, Ledbury, Hereford., HR8 1LG.

WATER RESEARCH CENTRE, Henley Road, Medmenham, Marlow, Bucks., SL7 2HD.

THE WELDING INSTITUTE, Abington Hall, Abington, Cambridge CB1 6AL.

WIRA TECHNOLOGY GROUP (*Wool textile processes and products*), Wira House, West Park Ring Road, Leeds LS16 6QL.

AGRICULTURAL AND FOOD RESEARCH INSTITUTES AND UNITS

A.F.R.C. Institute for Animal Health
Director of Research: Prof. F. J. Bourne, PH.D., Compton, Nr. Newbury, Berks., RG16 0NN.

Compton Laboratory, Compton, Nr. Newbury, Berks., RG16 0NN.—*Head of Lab. (Acting)*, J. M. Rutter, PH.D.

Houghton Laboratory, Houghton, Huntingdon, Cambs., PE17 2DA.—*Head of Lab. (Acting)*, L. N. Payne, PH.D., D.SC.

Pirbright Laboratory, Ash Road, Woking, Surrey GU24 0NF.—*Head of Lab.*, Prof. B. W. J. Mahy, PH.D., SC.D.

AFRC and MRC Neuropathogenesis Unit, Ogston Building, West Mains Road, Edinburgh EH9 3JF.—*Dir (Acting)*, J. Hope, PH.D.

A.F.R.C. Institute of Animal Physiology and Genetics Research
Dir. of Research, B. A. Cross, C.B.E., PH.D., SC.D., F.R.S., Babraham Hall, Babraham, Cambridge CB2 4AT.

Cambridge Research Station, Babraham, Cambridge CB2 4AT.—*Head of Station*, R. B. Heap, PH.D., SC.D.

Edinburgh Research Station, Roslin, Midlothian EH25 9PS.—*Head of Station (Acting)*, P. E. Lake, PH.D.

Edinburgh Research Station, King's Buildings, West Mains Road, Edinburgh EH9 3JQ.

Dryden Laboratory, Roslin, Midlothian EH25 9PS.

A.F.R.C. Institute of Arable Crops Research
Dir. of Research, Prof. K. J. Treharne, PhD. Rothamsted Experimental Station, Harpenden, Herts., AL5 2JQ.

Long Ashton Research Station, Long Ashton, Bristol BS18 9AF.—*Dir.*, (vacant).

Rothamsted Experimental Station, Harpenden, Herts., AL5 2JQ.—*Head of Station*, T. Lewis, PH.D., D.SC.

Broom's Barn Experimental Station, Higham, Bury St. Edmunds, Suffolk IP28 6NP.—*Head of Station*, T. H. Thomas, PH.D., D.SC.

Unit of Insect Neurophysiology and Pharmacology, Department of Zoology, University of Cambridge, Downing Street, Cambridge CB2 3EJ.—*Hon. Dir.*, J. E. Treherne, PH.D., SC.D.

A.F.R.C. Institute of Engineering Research
Director of Research, Prof. J. Matthews, Wrest Park, Silsoe, Bedford MK45 4HS.

A.F.R.C. Institute of Food Research
Director of Research, D. L. Georgala, C.B.E., PH.D., Shinfield, Reading RG2 9AT.

Bristol Laboratory, Langford, Bristol BS18 7DY.—*Head of Lab.* Prof. A. J. Bailey, SC.D.

Norwich Laboratory, Colney Lane, Norwich NR4 7UA.—*Head of Lab.*, Prof. P. Richmond, D.SC.

Reading Laboratory, Shinfield, Reading RG2 9AT.—*Head of Lab.*, Prof. B. E. B. Moseley, PH.D.

A.F.R.C. Institute for Grassland and Animal Production
Director of Research, Prof. J. L. Stoddart, PH.D., D.SC., Hurley, Maidenhead, Berks., SL6 5LR.

Plant Science and Plant Breeding Division:
Welsh Plant Breeding Station, Plas Gogerddan, Aberystwyth, Dyfed SY23 3EB.—*Dir. (Acting) and Head of Division (Acting)*, D. Wilson, PH.D.

Grassland and Ruminant Division:
Hurley Research Station, Maidenhead, Berks., SL6 5LR.—*Deputy Head of Division*, R. D. Baker.

North Wyke Research Station, Okehampton, Devon EX20 2SB.—*Head of Division*, R. J. Wilkins, PH.D.

Pig and Poultry Division:
Shinfield Research Station (Pig Dept.), Church Lane, Shinfield, Reading RG2 9AQ.—*Deputy Head of Division*, D. Lister, PH.D.

Roslin Research Station (Poultry Dept.), Roslin, Midlothian EH25 9PS.—*Head of Division*, C. Fisher, PH.D.

A.F.R.C. Institute of Horticultural Research
Director of Research, Prof. T. R. Swinburne, D.SC., PH.D. Bradbourne House, East Malling, Maidstone, Kent ME19 6BJ.

I.H.R. East Malling, East Malling, Maidstone, Kent ME19 6BJ.—*Head of Station*, C. C. Payne.

I.H.R. Littlehampton, Worthing Road, Littlehampton, West Sussex BN17 6LP.—*Head of Station*, R. S. Fraser, PH.D., D.SC.

I.H.R. Wellesbourne, Wellesbourne, Warwick CV35 9EF.—*Head of Station*, H. G. Jones, PH.D.

I.H.R. Department of Hop Research, Wye College, Wye, Ashford, Kent TN25 5AH.—*Head of Station*, R. E. Gunn.

A.F.R.C. Institute of Plant Science Research
Dir. of Research, Prof. H. W. Woolhouse, John Innes Institute, Colney Lane, Norwich NR4 7UH.

John Innes Institute, Colney Lane, Norwich NR4 7UH.—*Dir.*, Prof. R. B. Flavell.

I.P.S.R Cambridge Laboratory, Maris Lane, Trumpington, Cambridge CB2 2LQ.—*Head*, C. N. Law, PH.D.

I.P.S.R. Nitrogen Fixation Laboratory, University of Sussex, Brighton BN1 9RQ.—*Head*, B. E. Smith, PH.D.

A.F.R.C. Computing Division, West Common, Harpenden, Herts., AL5 2JE.—*Dir.*, P. Chandler.

SCOTTISH AGRICULTURAL RESEARCH INSTITUTES

Hannah Research Institute, Ayr KA6 5HL.—*Dir.*, Prof. M. Peaker.

Macaulay Land Use Research Institute, Craigiebuckler, Aberdeen AB9 2QJ; Bush Estate, Penicuik, Midlothian EH26 0PY.—*Dir.*, Prof. T. J. Maxwell, PH.D.

Moredun Research Institute, 408 Gilmerton Road, Edinburgh EH17 7JH.—*Dir.*, I. D. Aitken, PH.D.

Rowett Research Institute, Greenburn Road, Bucksburn, Aberdeen AB2 9SB.—*Dir.*, Prof. W. P. T. James.

Scottish Crop Research Institute, Invergowrie, Dundee DD2 5DA; Pentlandfield, Roslin, Midlothian, EH25 9RF.—*Dir.*, Prof. J. Hillman, PH.D., F.L.S., F.R.S.E.

Scottish Agricultural Statistics Service, University of Edinburgh, James Clerk Maxwell Building, The King's Buildings, Mayfield Road, Edinburgh EH9 3JZ.—*Dir.*, R. A. Kempton.

C.A.B. INTERNATIONAL

Each Institute and Bureau of C.A.B. International (Commonwealth Agricultural Bureaux International) acts as a clearing house for the collection, collation and dissemination of information in its particular branch of agricultural science.

Institutes

C.A.B.I. Institute of Entomology, 56 Queen's Gate, S.W.7. *Director*, K. M. Harris, Ph.D.

C.A.B.I. Mycological Institute, Ferry Lane, Kew, Richmond, Surrey. *Director*, D. L. Hawksworth, Ph.D.

C.A.B.I. Institute of Biological Control, Imperial College, Silwood Park, Ascot, Berks., SL5 7PY. *Director*, D. J. Greathead, Ph.D.

C.A.B.I. Institute of Parasitology, 395A Hatfield Road, St. Albans, Herts. *Director*, R. L. J. Muller, Ph.D.

C.A.B. International Bureaux
Wallingford, Oxon. OX10 8DE.

Agricultural Economics Bureau.
Animal Breeding and Genetics Bureau.
Animal Health Bureau.
Crop Protection Bureau.
Dairy Science and Technology Bureau.
Forestry Bureau.
Horticulture and Plantation Crops Bureau.
Nutrition Bureau.
Pastures and Field Crops Bureau.
Plant Breeding and Genetics Bureau.
Soils Bureau.

COST OF RESEARCH AND DEVELOPMENT

(excluding social science research)

Work performed within each sector

	1978		1981		1983		1985	
	£ million	Per cent	£ million	Per cent	£ million	Per cent	£ million	Per cent
Sector carrying out the work								
Central government								
Defence	331·0	9·4	557·7	9·4	654·9	9·9	752·7	9·5
Civil:								
Research councils	152·3	4·3	250·2	4·2	279·0	4·2	313·0	4·0
Other	271·8	7·7	526·5	8·9	552·9	8·4	537·2	6·8
Local government	3·0	0·1	5·0	0·1	7·0	0·1	8·1	1·1
Total	758·1	21·6	1,339·4	22·6	1,493·8	22·7	1,611·0	20·3
Universities and further								
education establishments	317·3	9·0	629·6	10·6	749·5	11·4	906·2	11·4
Public corporations	212·5	6·1	384·8	6·5⎫	526·2	8·0⎫		
Research associations	50·8	1·4	88·1	1·5⎭		⎭	5,145·8	65·0
Private industry	2,061·0	58·7	3,319·5	56·1	3,637·1	55·2⎭		
Other	110·6	3·2	159·6	2·7	176·4	2·7	256·2	3·2
Total cost of research and								
development performed	3,510·3	100·0	5,921·1	100·0	6,583·0	100·0	7,919·2	100·0

Finance provided by each sector

	1978		1981		1983		1985	
	£ million	Per cent	£ million	Per cent	£ million	Per cent	£ million	Per cent
Sector providing the funds								
Central government								
Defence	949·8	25·4	1,666·7	24·8	1,884·3	25·7	2,263·7	21·8
Civil:								
Research councils	186·2	4·9	363·5	5·4	408·3	5·6	553·8	5·3
Other	610·9	16·4	1,161·3	17·3	1,265·4	17·3	1,534·0	14·8
Local government	10·0	0·3	20·0	0·3	25·5	0·3	27·0	0·3
Total as returned by								
Government	1,756·9	47·0	3,211·5	47·7	3,583·5	48·9	4,378·5	42·2
Total as returned by sectors								
carrying out work	1,651·4	47·0	2,825·9	47·7	3,217·9	48·9	3,340·4	42·2
Universities	28·4	0·8	58·0	1·0	25·0	0·4	35·0	0·4
Public corporations	259·7	7·4	449·2	7·6⎫				
Private industry*	1,292·4	36·8	2,080·1	35·1⎭	2,869·4	43·6	3,752·4	47·4
Overseas	222·6	6·3	411·4	6·9	347·9	5·3	647·1	8·2
Other	55·8	1·6	96·6	1·6	122·8	1·9	144·3	1·8
Total	3,510·3	100·0	5,921·1	100·0	6,583·0	100·0	7,919·2	100·0

*Including research associations.

THE QUEEN'S AWARDS FOR EXPORT AND TECHNOLOGY

The Queen's Award for Export Achievement and The Queen's Award for Technological Achievement were instituted by Royal Warrant in 1976, the two separate Awards taking the place of The Queen's Award to Industry which had been instituted in 1965.

The Awards are designed to recognize and encourage outstanding achievements in exporting goods or services from the United Kingdom and in advancing process or product technology. They differ from a personal Royal honour in that they are given to a unit as a whole—management and employees working as a team.

They may be applied for by any organization within the United Kingdom, the Channel Islands or the Isle of Man producing goods or services which meet the criteria for the Awards. Eligibility is not influenced in any way by the particular activities of the unit applying, its location, or size. Units or agencies of central and local government with industrial functions, as well as research associations, educational institutions and bodies of a similar character, are also eligible, provided that they can show they have contributed to industrial efficiency.

The criteria on which recommendations for the Awards are based are:

1. Export Achievement

A substantial and sustained increase in export earnings to a level which is outstanding for the products or services concerned and for the size of the applicant unit's operations. Account will be taken of any special market factors described in the application. Applicants for the Award will be expected to explain the basis of the achievement (e.g. improved marketing organization or new initiative to cater for export markets) and this will be taken into consideration. Export earnings considered will include receipts by the applicant unit in this country from the export of goods produced in this country, and the provision of services to non-residents. Account will be taken of the overseas expenses incurred other than marketing expenses. Income from profits (after overseas tax) remitted to this country from the applicant unit's direct investments in its overseas branches, subsidiaries or associates in the same general line of business will be taken into account, but not receipts from profits on other overseas investments or by interest on overseas loans or credits.

2. Technological Achievement

A significant advance, leading to increased efficiency, in the application of technology to a production or development process in British industry or the production for sale of goods which incorporate new and advanced technological qualities.

Each award is formally conferred by a Grant of Appointment and is symbolized by a representation of its emblem cast in stainless steel and encapsulated in a transparent acrylic block.

Awards are held for five years and holders are entitled to fly the appropriate Award flag and to display the emblem on the packaging of goods produced in this country, on the goods themselves, on the unit's stationery, in advertising and on certain articles used by employees: units may also display the emblem of any previous current Awards during the 5 years.

Awards are announced on April 21 (the actual birthday of Her Majesty the Queen) and published formally in a special supplement to the London Gazette. All enquiries about the scheme and requests for application forms—completed forms must be returned by October 31—should be made to: The Secretary, The Queen's Awards Office, Dean Bradley House, 52 Horseferry Road, London SW1P 2AG. Telephone: 01-222 2277.

Awards for Export Achievement

In 1988, the Queen's Award for Export Achievement was conferred on the following concerns:

ABI Caravans Ltd., Beverley, Humberside; AFE Displays Ltd., Sutton Coldfield; Abbeycraft Furniture Ltd., Clacton-on-Sea, Essex; BCB International Ltd., Cardiff; Edward Baker Ltd., Sudbury, Suffolk; Baring Securities Ltd., London E.1; Bemac Engineering Ltd., Lisburn Co. Antrim; Bennett Opie Ltd., Sittingbourne, Kent; Berghaus Ltd., Newcastle upon Tyne; Biwater Pipes & Castings Ltd., Clay Cross, Derbys.; Black Clawson International Ltd., Newport, Gwent; The Hatfield Unit of the Civil Aircraft Division of British Aerospace PLC., Hatfield, Herts.; The On Line Inspection Centre of British Gas PLC, Cramlington, Northumberland; Brush Electrical Machines Ltd., Loughborough; Burleigh Marine International Ltd., Brentford, Middx.; Sericol Group Ltd. Division of Burmah Oil Trading Ltd., Broadstairs, Kent; Cape Contracts International Ltd., Watford, Herts.; Casburt Pharmaceutical Equipment Ltd., Longton, Stoke-on-Trent, Staffs.; Chemical Design Ltd., Oxford; Churchill Tableware Ltd., Longton, Stoke-on-Trent; City Technology Ltd., London E.C.1; Cleveland Potash Ltd., Loftus, Cleveland; The Vascutek Division of Coats Viyella Medical Ltd., Inchinnan, Renfrewshire; Cobden Chadwick Ltd., Oldham; Colloids Ltd., Widnes, Cheshire; Consort Hotels Ltd., York; Cotswold Pig Development Company Ltd., Rothwell, Lincoln; Davy McKee (Stockton) Ltd., Stockton-on-Tees, Cleveland; Dearden Davies Associates Ltd., Hounslow, Middx.; Derwent Publications Ltd., London W.C.1; Donner Underwriting Agencies Ltd., London E.C.3; Dow Corning Ltd., Barry, S. Glamorgan; F. Drake & Company of Golcar Ltd., Golcar, W. Yorks; Durmech Engineering Ltd., Pensett, W. Midlands; Dynapert Precima Ltd., Colchester; Eclipse Blinds Ltd., Glasgow; Enterprise Computer Services PLC., Aldermaston, Berks.; Eurocast Bar Ltd., Loughborough; Euro-Magnetic Products Ltd., Salfords, Surrey; Europa Manor Engineers Ltd., Chipping Warden, Oxon.; Fastnet Fish (Exports) Ltd., Grimsby; Filtronic Components Ltd., Shipley, W. Yorks.; Flight Equipment & Engineering Ltd., Chesham Bucks.; Forest & Sawmill Equipments (Engineers) Ltd., Whitchurch, Hants.; The Great Scottish and Western Railway Company Ltd., London S.W.11; H.P. Bulmer Pectin Ltd., Hereford; Hawker Siddeley Power Engineering Ltd., Burton on the Wolds, Leics.; Hepworth & Grandage Ltd., Bradford; Herga Electric Ltd., Bury St. Edmunds, Suffolk; Hilden Manufacturing Co. Ltd., Oswaldtwistle, Lancs.; John Hine Ltd., Bordon, Hants; Homark Associates Ltd., Parkstone, Dorset; Hunting Precision Components Ltd., Tonbridge, Kent; Husky Computers Ltd., Coventry; Doncasters Blaenavon Division of INCO Engineered Products Ltd., Blaenavon, Gwent; Ingersoll-Rand Company Ltd., Gateshead; JCB Sales Ltd., Rocester, Staffs.; I & M Kindler Ltd., Crewe; The Lafferty Group Ltd., London S.E.1; Lilliput Lane Ltd., Skirsgill, Cumbria; The Electric Actuator Division of Lucas Aerospace Ltd., Bradford; Macallan-Glenlivet PLC., Craigellachie, Banffshire; Malvern Instruments Ltd., Malvern, Worcs.; Marine

Projects (Plymouth) Ltd., Plymouth; The Winnersh Site of Mars Electronics International, Wokingham, Berks.; Monocon Refractories Ltd., Old Denaby, S. Yorks.; Northern Engineering Industries PLC., Newcastle upon Tyne.; Oxford Medical Ltd., Abingdon, Oxon.; Pitney Bowes PLC., Harlow, Essex; Polaroid (UK) Ltd., Dumbarton; Sortaweigh Division of Portals Engineering Ltd., Aldershot, Hants.; Pro-Micro Ltd., London N.W.6; Queenborough Rolling Mill Co. Ltd., Queenborough, Kent; Queensgate Instruments Ltd., Ascot, Berks.; Rediffusion Simulation Ltd., Crawley, W. Sussex; The Regent Belt Company Ltd., Walgrave-St.-Peters, Northants.; The Elan Division of the Reiss Engineering Co. Ltd., Binley, W. Midlands; Rexodan Ltd., Widnes, Cheshire; Reynolds Medical Ltd., Hertford; Rolls Royce PLC., London S.W.1; Optical Devices Division of STC Defence Systems, Paignton, Devon; Sco-Fro Foods Ltd., Glasgow; Seabourne Express Ltd., Barking, Essex; Seawheel Ltd., Ipswich; Serono Diagnostics Ltd., Woking, Surrey; Shorko Films, Swindon; Sigmex Ltd., Horsham, W. Sussex; Daniel Smith Ltd., Wolverhampton; Sperrin Metal Products Ltd., Draperstown, Co. Londonderry; Pressing & Assembly Division of Stadco Ltd., Shrewsbury; Technophone Ltd., Camberley, Surrey; Tiphook Group PLC., Bromley, Kent; Triplex Aircraft & Special Products Ltd., Kings Norton, Birmingham; Varian-TEM Ltd., Crawley, W. Sussex; Verson Wilkins Ltd., Darlaston, W. Midlands; Vickers Instruments, York; Walkers Shortbread Ltd., Aberlour on Spey; Wardley Export Finance Ltd., London E.C.2; The Mostyn Unit of Warwick International Ltd., Mostyn, Holywell, Clwyd; The Wedgwood Hotelware Division of Josiah Wedgwood & Sons Ltd., Barlaston, Staffs.; A. R. Wilmshurst Ltd. T/A Soundwave, Witham, Essex; Wilson Jones & Company, Basford, Nottingham.

Awards for Technological Achievement 1988

In 1988 the Queen's Award for Technological Achievement was conferred on the following concerns:

AES Engineering Ltd., Rotheram (*Development of mechanical shaft seals*); Airopak Division of Air Products Ltd., Crewe (*Development of solvent resistant polythene containers*); The Filton Unit of the Civil Aircraft Division of British Aerospace PLC., Bristol (*Development of wings for the Airbus A320 Airliner (jointly with the Aerodynamics Department of the Royal Aircraft Establishment)*); The Speciality and Aerospace Division of British Alcan Aluminium PLC., Gerrards Cross, Bucks. (*Development of lightweight aluminium alloys for aerospace applications (jointly with The Materials & Structures Department of the Royal Aircraft Establishment)*); The Headquarters Technical Department of British Coal Corporation, Stanhope Bretby, Staffs. (*Development of an in-seam seismic method for detecting geological faults in coal seams*); The On Line Inspection Centre of British Gas PLC., Cramlington, Northumberland (*Development of a high performance on-line pipline inspection system*); The Research & Development Department of British Gypsum Ltd, East Leake, Leics. (*Development of an improved kettle for the calcination of gypsum*); John Brown Automation Ltd., Coventry (*Development of an automatic system for automotive clutches*); The Vascutek Division of Coats Viyella Medical Ltd., Inchinnan, Renfrewshire (*Development of a non-porous vascular prosthesis*); Cosrol Ltd., Holmfield, W. Yorks. (*Development of high-perfor-*

mance carding machine); Cybrid Ltd., Leighton Buzzard, Beds. (*Development of an automated pattern-scanning and nesting system for the garment industry*); The Aerodynamics Department of the Royal Aircraft Establishment (M.o.D.), Farnborough, Hants. (*Development of wings for the Airbus A320 Airliner (jointly with the Filton Unit of British Aerospace plc.)*); The Materials & Structures Department of the Royal Aircraft Establishment (M.o.D.), Farnborough, Hants. (*Development of lightweight aluminium alloys for aerospace applications (jointly with the Speciality and Aerospace Division of British Alcan Aluminium PLC.)*); Dowty Meco Ltd., Worcester (*Development of heavy-duty armoured flexible conveyors for longwall coal mining*); Dowty Filtration Technology Division of Dowty Mining Equipment Ltd., Ashchurch, Glos. (*Development of an automatic self-cleaning filtration system*); Eley Ltd., Witton, W. Midlands (*Development of a safer method of producing percussion-type primers for ammunition*); The Instrument Systems Division of GEC Avionics Ltd., Rochester, Kent (*Development of Standard Central Air Data Computers for aircraft*); GKN Composites Ltd., Telford and GKN Technology Ltd., Wolverhampton (*jointly, development of vehicle leaf springs made from glass fibre and epoxy resin*); Graseby Ionics Ltd., Watford, Herts. (*Development of a hand-held Chemical Agent Monitor*); Herga Electric Ltd., Bury St. Edmunds, Suffolk (*Development of fibre optic sensors*); Hydraroll Ltd., Gaerwen, Isle of Anglesey (*Development of a shipchain and roller track system for transfer of pallets*); IBM United Kingdom Laboratories Ltd., Portsmouth (*Development of the IBM 9335 high-density magnetic storage sub-system*); The Systems Engineering and Development Unit of ICL Mainframe Systems of International Computers Ltd., West Gorton, Manchester (*Design and application of nodal architecture in the development of the ICL Series 39 "multiprocessor" computer systems*); IMI Titanium Ltd., Witton, W. Midlands (*Development of high-temperature creep-resistant titanium alloys for aircraft gas turbines*); The Automotive Group of ICI Paints Division of Imperial Chemical Industries PLC., Slough (*Development of low-emission surface coatings for automotive vehicles*); Itek Colour Graphics Ltd., Cheltenham, Glos. (*Development of electronic colour separation scanners for the printing industry*); Materials Technology Group of the Laboratory of The Government Chemist, London S.E.1 (*Development of glass-ionomer cements for dentistry*); Malvern Instruments Ltd., Malvern, Worcs. (*Development of an instrument to determine particle sizes using laser light diffraction*); K. S. Paul Products Ltd., London N.18 (*Development of PolyButylCuprysil, an advanced lubricant with anti-seize and anti-corrooion properties*); Quantel Ltd., Newbury, Berks. (*Development of a digital video recording, editing, processing and compositing system*); Queensgate Instruments Ltd., Ascot, Berks. (*Development of servo-stabilised scanning interferometers*); Racal Marine Systems Ltd., New Malden, Surrey (*Development of the "MICRO-FIX" microwave electronic positioning system*); Response Company Ltd., Winchester (*Development of solid state electricity meters and energy audit systems*); Reynolds Medical Ltd., Hertford (*Development of the PATHFINDER 3 SYSTEM for high-speed analysis of long-term electrocardiograms*); The Tay Project of Rolls-Royce PLC., Derby (*Development of the Tay engine*); Safecom Ltd., Ashbourne, Derbys. (*Development of an electronic communications and safety system for use in mine shaft cages*); Sigmex Ltd.,

Horsham, W. Sussex (*Development of the 6000 series of computergraphic terminals and generators*); Technophone Ltd., Camberley, Surrey (*Development of the PC105 POCKETPHONE pocket cellular telephone*); Thurne Engineering Company Ltd., Norwich (*Development of a versatile high-speed industrial food slicer*); Tunnel Refineries Ltd., London, S.E.10 (*Production of vital gluten and glucose syrups from British Wheat*); Varian-TEM Ltd., Crawley, W. Sussex (*Development of the Ximatron C series of radiotherapy simulators*); Vickers Instruments, York (*Development of a fully automated optical measuring instrument*).

DISTANCES FROM LONDON BY AIR

A list of the distances in statute miles from London, Heathrow, to various places abroad. They have been supplied by the publishers of *IATA/IAL Air Distances Manual*, Southall, Middx.

To	Miles	To	Miles	To	Miles
Abidjan	3,197	Detroit	3,754	Munich	588
Abu Dhabi	3,425	Dhaka	4,976	Nairobi	4,248
Addis Ababa	3,675	Doha	3,253	Naples	1,011
Aden	3,670	Dubai	3,414	Nassau	4,333
Algiers	1,035	Dublin	279	New York (J. F. Kennedy)	3,440
Amman	2,287	Durban	5,937	Nice	645
Amsterdam	230	Düsseldorf	310	Oporto	806
Ankara	1,770	Entebbe	4,033	Oslo (Fornebu)	723
Athens	1,500	Frankfurt	406	Ottawa	3,321
Auckland	11,404	Freetown	3,046	Palma, Majorca	836
Baghdad	2,551	Geneva	468	Paris	215; (Orly 227)
Bahrain	3,163	Gibraltar	1,084	Perth, Australia	9,008
Bangkok	5,928	Gothenburg (Landvetter)	664	Port of Spain, Trinidad	4,405
Barbados	4,193	Hamburg	463	Prague	649
Barcelona	712	Harare	5,156	Rangoon	5,582
Basle	447	Havana	4,647	Reykjavik	1,167
Beijing (Peking)	5,063	Helsinki (Vantaa)	1,147	Rhodes	1,743
Beirut	2,161	Hong Kong	5,990	Rio de Janeiro	5,745
Belfast	325	Honolulu	7,220	Riyadh	3,067
Belgrade	1,056	Istanbul	1,560	Rome (Fiumicino)	895
Berlin (Tegel)	588	Jeddah	2,947	Salzburg	651
Bermuda	3,428	Johannesburg	5,634	San Francisco	5,351
Berne	476	Karachi	3,935	Seoul	5,507
Bombay	4,478	Khartoum	3,071	Shannon	369
Brasilia	5,452	Kingston, Jamaica	4,668	Singapore	6,756
Brisbane	10,273	Kuala Lumpur	6,557	Sofia	1,266
Brussels	217	Kuwait	2,903	Stockholm (Arlanda)	908
Bucharest	1,307	Lagos	3,107	Sydney, Australia	10,568
Budapest	923	Larnaca, Cyprus	2,036	Tangier	1,120
Buenos Aires	6,915	Leningrad	1,314	Teheran	2,741
Cairo	2,194	Lima	6,303	Tel Aviv	2,227
Calcutta	4,958	Lisbon	972	Tokyo (Narita)	5,956
Canberra	10,563	Lomé	3,129	Toronto	3,545
Cape Town	6,011	Los Angeles	5,439	Tripoli	1,468
Caracas	4,639	Madrid	773	Tunis	4,524
Casablanca	1,300	Malta	1,305	Turin (Caselle)	570
Chicago (O'Hare)	3,941	Manila	6,685	Valencia	826
Cologne	331	Marseilles	614	Vancouver	4,707
Colombo	5,411	Mauritius	6,075	Venice (Tessera)	715
Copenhagen	608	Mexico City	5,529	Vienna (Schwechat)	790
Dakar	2,706	Milan	609	Warsaw	912
Damascus	2,223	Montego Bay	4,687	Washington	3,665
Dar-es-Salaam	4,662	Montevideo	6,841	Wellington	11,692
Darwin	8,613	Montreal (Mirabel)	3,241	Zagreb	848
Delhi	4,180	Moscow (Sheremetievo)	1,557	Zürich	490

BRITISH MONETARY UNITS

COIN

Gold Coins	Nickel-Brass(Copper/
†One Hundred Pounds £100	Nickel/Zinc) Coins
†Fifty Pounds £50	Two Pounds £2
†Twenty-five Pounds £25	One Pound £1
†Ten Pounds £10	
Five Pounds £5	
Two Pounds £2	
Sovereign £1	
Half-Sovereign 50p	

Silver Coins	Cupro-Nickel Coins
Crown 25p	50 Pence 50p
Maundy Money‡	Crown 25p
Fourpence 4p	20 Pence 20p
Threepence 3p	10 Pence 10p
Twopence 2p	5 Pence 5p
Penny 1p	

Bronze Coins
2 Pence 2p
1 Penny 1p

†Britannia gold bullion coins, introduced in October 1987.

‡Gifts of special money distributed by the Sovereign annually on Maundy Thursday to the number of aged poor men and women corresponding to the Sovereign's own age.

Gold Coin.—Gold ceased to circulate during the First World War. An Order of April 27, 1966, made it illegal for U.K. residents to continue holding more than four gold coins minted after 1837, or to acquire such coins unless they had been licensed as genuine collectors by the Bank of England. This Order was revoked on April 1, 1971, by the Exchange Control (Gold Coins Exemption) Order, 1971, whereby residents of the United Kingdom, Channel Islands and the Isle of Man may freely buy and sell and hold gold coins.

The 1971 Order was revoked on April 15, 1975, by the Exchange Control (Gold Coins Exemption) Order, 1975. Under this Order Section 1 of the Exchange Control Act 1947 (which prohibits dealings in gold or foreign currency except with Treasury permission) was exempted for gold coins minted in or before 1837. The import of gold coins minted after 1837 was prohibited except by authorised dealers in gold with individual import licences from the Department of Trade, and dealing between other U.K. residents was restricted to coins already held in the U.K.

Under an amendment, dated December 16, 1977, the exemptions contained in the 1975 Order were extended to cover gold coins minted in or before 1937.

The 1975 controls over the import of and dealing in gold coins were abolished on June 13, 1979 under the Exchange Control (Gold Coins Exemption) Order 1979, and gold coins, with certain exceptions,* may now be imported and exported without restriction.

On April 1, 1982 the Government introduced VAT (currently 15 per cent) on sales of all gold coin.

Silver Coin.—Prior to 1920 our silver coins were struck from standard silver—an alloy of which 925 parts in 1,000 were silver. In 1920 the proportion of silver was reduced to 500 parts. From January 1, 1947 all "silver" coins, except Maundy money, have been struck from cupro-nickel—an alloy of copper 75 parts and nickel 25 parts, except for the 20p, composed of copper 84 parts, nickel 16 parts. Maundy coins since 1947 have been struck from standard silver.

Bronze Coin.—Bronze, introduced in 1860 to replace copper, is currently an alloy of copper 97 parts, zinc 2½ parts and tin ½ part. These proportions have been subject to slight variations in the past.

The "Remedy" is the amount of variation from standard permitted in weight and fineness of coins when first issued from the Mint.

Legal tender of coin.—Gold, dated 1838 onwards, if not below least current weight, is legal tender to any amount. £2 and £1 coins are legal tender to any amount. 50p and 20p coins are legal tender up to £10; 10p and 5p coins are legal tender up to £5 and bronze coins are legal tender for amounts up to 20p. Farthings ceased to be legal tender on December 31, 1960, the halfpenny on August 1, 1969, the halfcrown on January 1, 1970, the threepence and penny on August 31, 1971, the sixpence on June 30, 1980 and the decimal halfpenny on December 31, 1984.

The decimal system was introduced on Feb. 15, 1971. Since 1982 the word "new" in "new pence" displayed on decimal coins has been dropped.

---

* Gold coins which are more than fifty years old and valued at a sum in excess of £8,000 cannot be exported without specific authorization from the Department of Trade and Industry.

Denomination	Metal	Standard Weight (grams)	Standard Diameter (centimetres)
Penny	bronze	3·56400	2·0320
2 pence	bronze	7·12800	2·5910
5 pence	cupro-nickel	5·65518	2·3595
10 pence	cupro-nickel	11·31036	2·8500
20 pence	cupro-nickel	5·0	2·14
25p Crown	silver	28·27590	3·8608
25p Crown	cupro-nickel	28·27590	3·8608
50 pence	cupro-nickel	13·5	3·0
£1	copper/nickel/zinc	9·5	2·25
£2	copper/nickel/zinc	15·98	2·84

BANK NOTES

Bank of England notes are currently issued in denominations of £5, £10, £20 and £50 for the amount of the Fiduciary Note Issue, and are legal tender in England and Wales.

The old white notes for £10, £20, £50, £100, £500 and £1,000, which were issued until April 22, 1943, ceased to be legal tender in May 1945.

The old white £5 issued between October 1945 and September 1956, the £5 notes issued between 1957 and 1963, bearing a portrait of Britannia and the first series to bear a portrait of the Queen, issued between 1963 and 1971, ceased to be legal tender on March 14, 1961, June 27, 1967 and September 1, 1973 respectively. The series of £1 notes issued during the years 1928 to 1960 and the 10s. notes of the same type issued from 1928 to 1961—those without the royal portrait—ceased to be legal tender on May 29 and October 30, 1962 respectively. The £1 note first issued in March 1960 (bearing on the back a representation of Britannia) and the £10 note first issued in February 1964 (bearing a lion on the back) both bearing a portrait of the Queen on the front ceased to be legal tender on June 1, 1979. The 10s. note was replaced by the 50p coin in October 1969, and ceased to be legal tender on November 21, 1970. Bank notes which are no longer legal tender are payable when presented at the Head Office of the Bank of England in London.

The first of the current series of Bank notes was a £20 note issued on July 9, 1970. This was followed by the £5 note on November 11, 1971, £10 note on February 20, 1975, £1 note on February 9, 1978 and £50 note on March 20, 1981. The £1 coin was introduced on April 21, 1983 and the £1 denomination note ceased to be legal tender on March 11, 1988. The predominant identifying feature of each note is the portrayal on the back of a prominent figure from Britain's history namely, £5: The Duke of Wellington; £10: Florence Nightingale; £20: William Shakespeare; and £50: Sir Christopher Wren.

Note Circulation.—Note circulation is highest at the two peak spending periods of the year—around Christmas and during the summer holiday period. A peak of £15,278 million was reached immediately prior to Christmas 1987, a 3·9 per cent increase on the previous year.

The proportion of the total value of notes in circulation of £1 and £5 notes at end-February 1988 compared with the previous year, fell from 0·9 per cent and 15·8 per cent to 0·8 per cent and 14·3 per cent respectively. £10 notes fell from 43·9 per cent to 43·7 per cent, as did £20 notes, from 20·3 per cent to 20·0 per cent. However, £50 notes increased from 11·5 per cent to 13·3 per cent.

On February 29, 1988 the values of notes in circulation were: £1: £107,728,496; £5: £1,896,164,954; £10: £5,810,057,500; £20: £2,932,334,920; £50: £1,755,115,450.

OTHER BANK NOTES

Scotland.—Bank notes are issued by three Scottish banks. The Royal Bank of Scotland and the Bank of Scotland issue notes for £1, £5, £10, £20 and £100. The Clydesdale Bank issues notes for £1, £5, £10, £20, £50, £100. Scottish notes are not legal tender, but in Scotland they enjoy a status equal to that of the Bank of England note.

Channel Islands and the Isle of Man.—The states of Jersey and Guernsey issue notes for £1, £5, £10 and £20. The Government of the Isle of Man issues notes for 50p, £1, £5, £10 and £20. These are legal tender only in their respective islands.

Although none of the series of notes specified above is legal tender in the United Kingdom they are generally accepted by the banks irrespective of their place of issue. At one time the banks made a commission charge for handling Scottish and Irish notes but this was abolished some years ago.

The Channel Islands and the Isle of Man also issue their own coinage. The states of Jersey and Guernsey issue coins for ½p, 1p, 2p, 5p, 10p, 20p, 50p and £1. The Isle of Man issues coins for ½p, 1p, 2p, 5p, 10p, 20p, 50p and £1.

EXPECTATION OF LIFE

(Interim figures)

Age	England and Wales		Scotland		Northern Ireland	
	Life Table, 1983–85		Life Table, 1983–85		Life Table, 1983–85	
	Males	Females	Males	Females	Males	Females
0	71·8	77·6	69·9	75·8	70·1	76·3
5	67·7	73·3	65·8	71·6	66·2	72·2
10	62·8	68·4	60·9	66·7	61·3	67·3
15	57·8	63·5	56·0	61·7	56·4	62·4
20	53·0	58·6	51·2	56·8	51·6	57·4
25	48·2	53·6	46·4	51·9	46·9	52·6
30	43·4	48·7	41·6	47·0	42·2	47·7
35	38·6	43·9	36·9	42·2	37·5	42·8
40	33·8	39·1	32·2	37·4	32·7	38·0
45	29·2	34·3	27·6	32·7	28·2	33·3
50	24·7	29·7	23·3	28·2	23·8	28·7
55	20·5	25·3	19·3	23·9	19·8	24·3
60	16·7	21·2	15·7	20·0	16·0	20·3
65	13·3	17·3	12·5	16·3	12·8	16·4
70	10·4	13·7	9·8	12·9	9·9	12·9
75	7·9	10·5	7·5	9·9	7·4	9·7
80	5·9	7·7	5·7	7·3	5·5	7·1
85	4·4	5·5	4·3	5·2	4·2	5·1

THE STOCK EXCHANGE

The International Stock Exchange of the United Kingdom and Republic of Ireland Ltd. serves the needs of government, industry and investors by providing facilities for raising capital and a central market place for securities trading. There are over 7,000 securities listed on the International Stock Exchange, which have a value of over £1,359,142·2 million. Last year, shares worth some £961,000,000 million changed hands. This central market place covers not only government stocks (called gilts) and U.K. and overseas company shares (called equities and fixed interest stocks) but other investment instruments such as traded options on equities, currencies and indices.

During 1986 the International Stock Exchange went through the greatest period of change in its two hundred year history. In March 1986 it opened its doors for the first time to overseas and corporate membership of the Exchange, allowing banks, insurance companies and overseas securities houses to become Members of The Exchange and to buy existing Member Firms. On October 27, 1986, three major reforms took place, changes which became known as "Big Bang":

(i) abolition of scales of minimum commissions, allowing clients to negotiate freely with their brokers about the charge for their services

(ii) abolition of the separation of member firms into brokers and jobbers. Under the new system, Firms are broker/dealers, able to act as agents on behalf of clients; to act as principals buying and selling shares for their own account; and to become registered market makers, making continuous buying and selling prices in specific securities

(iii) the introduction of the Stock Exchange Automated Quotations (S.E.A.Q.) system. Market makers input their buying and selling prices into S.E.A.Q., which displays the competing quotations on a composite page on-screen. For the largest and most frequently traded company shares ("Alpha"), e.g. Marks and Spencer or BP, volumes and last trade prices are also updated continuously throughout the day.

Of all these changes, the implementation of S.E.A.Q. has had perhaps the most visible effect. Dealing in stocks and shares now takes place via the telephone in the Firms' own dealing rooms, rather than face to face on the floor of the Exchange. The new systems also provide increased investor protection. All deals taking place via the Exchange's S.E.A.Q. system are recorded on a database which can be used to resolve disputes or to carry out investigations.

Members of the International Stock Exchange buy and sell shares on behalf of the public, as well as institutions such as pension funds or insurance companies. In return for transacting the deal, the broker will charge a commission, which is usually based upon the value of the transaction. The market makers, or wholesalers, in each security do not charge a commission for their services, but will quote the broker two prices, a price at which they will buy and a price at which they will sell. It is the middle of these two prices which is published in lists of Stock Exchange prices in newspapers.

On November 12, 1986 Members of the Exchange agreed to merge with members of the international broking community in London, based outside the Exchange, in order to form two new bodies—the International Stock Exchange of the United Kingdom and Republic of Ireland Ltd. and the Securities Association Ltd. These two regulatory bodies have been formed under the provisions of the Financial Services Act, which requires investment businesses to be authorised and regulated by a Self Regulating Organisation (S.R.O.) of which the Securities Association is one. The Act also requires business to be conducted through a Registered Investment Exchange (R.I.E.). The International Stock Exchange is an R.I.E., regulating four main markets. U.K. equities, foreign equities, gilts and options.

As well as advising and dealing on behalf of investors, stockbrokers provide a range of services to industry from the raising of initial capital and future, additional, funds to advice on mergers and acquisitions. For a company entering the market for the first time there are three possible Stock Exchange markets, depending upon the size, history and requirements of the company. The first is the listed market, on which the shares of over 2,500 companies are traded. For entry to this market, the company must have an audited trading history of at least five years, and place 25 per cent of its shares in public hands. The second type of market is for smaller, less established companies and is called the Unlisted Securities Market (U.S.M.). In January, 1986, the International Stock Exchange established a third tier called simply the Third Market. This is for very new and small companies incorporated in the U.K. or Ireland. Once admitted to the Exchange, all companies are obliged to keep their shareholders informed of their progress, making announcements of a price-sensitive nature through the Exchange's company announcements department.

The International Stock Exchange has its headquarters in London, and also administrative centres around the U.K. and the Republic of Ireland. At present there are some 5,300 individual Members grouped into about 360 Member Firms.

Chairman, Sir Nicholas Goodison (until end 1988).

BALANCE OF PAYMENTS OF THE UNITED KINGDOM (£ million)

	1981	1982	1983	1984	1985	1986
Current account						
Visible trade						
Exports (fob)	50,977	55,565	60,776	70,367	78,111	72,843
Imports (fob)	47,617	53,234	61,611	74,751	80,289	81,306
Visible balance	3,360	2,331	−835	−4,384	−2,178	−8,463
Invisibles						
Credits	56,740	64,718	65,269	77,061	79,784	76,188
Debits	53,788	63,014	61,096	71,203	74,687	68,581
Invisibles balance	2,952	1,704	4,173	5,858	5,097	7,607
of which:						
Services balance	*3,693*	*2,435*	*3,437*	*3,481*	*5,381*	*5,114*
Interest, profits and dividends balance	*945*	*1,078*	*2,479*	*4,216*	*2,992*	*4,686*
Transfers balance	*−1,686*	*−1,809*	*−1,743*	*−1,839*	*−3,276*	*−2,193*
Current balance	6,321	4,035	3,338	1,474	2,919	−856
Transactions in external assets and liabilities*						
Investment overseas by U.K. residents						
Direct	−6,005	−4,090	−5,369	−6,086	−8,821	−11,386
Portfolio	−4,300	−6,710	−6,510	−9,550	−17,830	−22,870
Total U.K. investment overseas	−10,305	−10,800	−11,879	−15,636	−26,651	−34,256
Investment in the U.K. by overseas residents						
Direct	2,932	3,027	3,386	−181	4,421	5,420
Portfolio	323	225	1,888	1,419	7,079	8,202
Total overseas investment in U.K.	3,255	3,252	5,274	1,238	11,500	13,622
Foreign currency lending abroad by U.K. banks	−37,164	−16,539	−16,100	−9,134	−20,406	−47,945
Foreign currency borrowing abroad by U.K. banks	36,763	19,904	17,192	18,648	25,306	58,439
Net foreign currency transactions of U.K. banks	−401	3,365	1,092	9,514	4,900	10,494
Sterling lending abroad by U.K. banks	−2,987	−4,019	−2,232	−4,933	−1,637	−5,953
Sterling borrowing and deposit liabilities abroad of U.K. banks	2,497	4,421	3,945	6,149	4,150	5,610
Net sterling transactions of U.K. banks	−490	402	1,713	1,216	2,513	−343
Deposits with and lending to banks abroad by U.K. non-bank private sector	−494	−908	−648	−3,126	−748	−2,642
Borrowing from banks abroad by:						
U.K. non-bank private sector	716	504	380	−2,274	2,323	3,407
Public corporations	−178	−35	−35	−47	64	−30
General government	−192	57	77	48	87	100
Official reserves (additions to − drawings on +)	2,419	1,421	607	908	−1,758	−2,891
Other external assets of:						
U.K. non-bank private sector and public corporations	−1,037	175	−120	+1,626	+629	+1,992
General government	93	−161	−478	−743	−730	−535
Other external liabilities of:						
U.K. non-bank private sector and public corporations	224	116	−64	+449	517	267
General government	−14	350	−661	−88	−67	+67
Net transactions in assets and liabilities	−6,404	−2,262	−4,742	−6,916	−7,421	−10,747
Allocation of special drawing rights	158	—	—	—	—	—
Balancing item	−66	−1,773	1,404	5,442	4,502	11,603

* Assets: increase −/decrease +. Liabilities: increase +/decrease−.

U.K. TRADE OVERSEAS (£'000)

	1986		1987	
	Imports	Exports	Imports	Exports
Benelux*	10,699,734	9,275,108	11,510,499	9,713,881
Denmark	1,752,174	1,211,637	1,873,495	1,231,097
France	7,348,574	6,210,216	8,381,984	7,781,546
Germany, Fed. Rep. of	14,139,097	8,542,196	15,783,904	9,404,257
Greece	308,644	356,020	355,320	444,500
Ireland, Republic of	3,053,807	3,558,372	3,488,406	3,831,737
Italy	4,658,036	3,472,364	5,216,751	4,145,659
Portugal	768,470	472,078	847,980	699,915
Spain	1,777,341	1,905,479	2,099,139	2,164,221
E.C.—TOTAL	44,505,877	35,003,470	49,557,478	39,416,813
Afghanistan	11,913	11,444	11,289	10,735
Albania	129	2,887	91	2,565
Algeria	140,860	129,624	172,927	73,115
Andorra	40	13,174	200	10,976
Angola	43,147	30,896	2,312	29,573
Anguilla	60	1,136	188	1,328
Antigua and Barbuda	2,069	17,774	4,271	19,334
Argentina	28,635	10,115	64,595	10,267
Aruba	576	6,972	296	5,652
Australia	643,238	1,227,647	673,837	1,223,613
Austria	705,732	403,000	781,986	463,187
Bahamas	10,266	95,816	15,943	27,063
Bahrain	19,732	130,991	60,687	125,189
Bangladesh	34,117	48,218	35,454	54,382
Barbados	11,661	38,338	23,320	33,067
Belize	17,954	8,232	22,757	7,543
Benin	4,910	6,728	2,930	7,207
Bermuda	1,262	26,180	1,208	25,383
Bhutan	—	76	14	411
Bolivia	10,225	3,663	14,799	3,658
Botswana	16,652	8,629	11,836	10,275
Brazil	552,259	295,152	636,675	347,916
Brit. Indian Ocean Terr.	54	817	9	320
Brunei	71,624	154,146	34,144	204,129
Bulgaria	32,459	80,504	24,249	88,761
Burkina	1,369	3,104	462	4,168
Burma	6,092	10,835	3,826	24,715
Burundi	3,074	2,324	1,330	2,867
Cameroon	7,634	34,368	14,201	28,057
Canada	1,499,600	1,698,372	1,568,305	1,938,237
Canary Is.	63,529	66,949	77,191	86,185
Cape Verde	426	1,618	301	1,208
Cayman Is.	2,422	11,403	1,318	6,442
Central African Republic	1,452	787	233	1,127
Ceuta & Melilla	44	2,762	—	3,831
Chad	2,806	1,250	1,101	1,006
Chile	128,007	67,459	112,843	105,838
China	327,032	535,943	391,766	416,012
Colombia	94,112	58,084	65,331	61,385
The Comoros	—	307	91	527
Congo	2,444	9,165	1,930	19,219
Cook Is.	46	279	167	194
Costa Rica	30,318	12,007	16,752	14,407
Côte d'Ivoire	117,058	34,266	90,246	26,834
Cuba	8,555	58,760	12,776	41,510
Curaçao	78,509	17,260	5,133	19,635
Cyprus	124,198	140,387	118,250	141,129
Czechoslovakia	125,399	108,841	141,472	114,101
Djibouti	53	12,537	175	12,501
Dominica	26,612	8,780	37,083	10,431
Dominican Republic	7,599	15,178	8,637	23,887
Ecuador	11,339	46,673	14,002	37,934
Egypt	328,053	371,007	127,261	342,195
Equatorial Guinea	1	633	—	1,572
Ethiopia	22,343	50,049	12,875	46,146
Falkland Is.	14,286	11,135	8,148	7,353
Faroe Islands	21,380	5,709	19,239	7,165

* Belgium, Luxembourg and the Netherlands

	1986		1987	
	Imports	Exports	Imports	Exports
Fiji	66,500	8,775	53,062	7,381
Finland	1,346,058	664,461	1,539,011	797,236
French Guiana	55	1,052	380	1,134
French Polynesia	95	4,890	18	5,275
Gabon	36,642	16,627	5,357	11,962
Gambia	2,273	16,707	3,038	19,765
German Democratic Rep.	195,513	81,276	180,299	81,489
Ghana	103,480	113,218	113,859	138,081
Gibraltar	6,021	46,200	3,367	49,986
Greenland	4,789	452	838	735
Grenada	7,011	8,628	6,302	8,772
Guadeloupe	1,711	3,477	459	4,063
Guatemala	8,098	9,288	7,536	13,926
Guinea	23,892	10,679	19,538	10,675
Guinea-Bissau	214	1,319	17	1,152
Guyana	55,535	13,737	58,502	15,371
Haiti	899	5,147	621	5,327
Honduras	5,280	9,213	4,703	10,449
Hong Kong	1,530,786	960,956	1,531,681	1,013,038
Hungary	77,228	101,557	83,267	101,300
Iceland	173,140	73,640	178,314	84,866
India	440,681	941,169	536,704	1,090,146
Indonesia	141,242	196,629	144,819	236,027
Iran	100,303	399,373	187,572	307,853
Iraq	66,129	443,890	33,871	271,655
Israel	385,164	462,407	437,014	523,591
Jamaica	87,416	43,378	85,655	54,644
Japan	4,932,497	1,193,933	5,463,116	1,495,111
Jordan	49,766	130,385	29,285	188,998
Kampuchea	58	217	268	435
Kenya	163,745	170,671	129,236	199,059
Kiribati	4	179	8	301
Korea, Democratic Rep. of	1,374	3,331	641	2,198
Korea, Republic of	661,975	288,421	936,038	427,229
Kuwait	58,517	300,586	81,530	225,168
Laos	150	1,460	621	1,742
Lebanon	9,845	55,867	9,528	40,707
Lesotho	277	2,128	486	1,112
Liberia	7,574	22,056	7,284	13,538
Libya	136,390	260,529	133,649	220,626
Macao	45,286	6,522	45,896	5,617
Madagascar	6,432	6,872	6,925	6,382
Malawi	56,983	28,557	44,223	18,069
Malaysia	350,058	226,912	397,122	257,970
Maldives	276	1,321	440	2,772
Mali	8,282	4,121	6,937	5,573
Malta	49,197	101,877	52,105	107,941
Martinique	14	21,230	712	10,705
Mauritania	2,184	2,496	8,724	3,862
Mauritius	153,271	32,087	163,271	44,395
Mayotte	9	506	185	2,352
Mexico	116,078	162,328	244,719	198,992
Mongolia	4,750	1,031	3,847	941
Montserrat	358	3,926	139	2,432
Morocco	65,419	84,510	61,108	94,487
Mozambique	1,335	13,175	6,580	21,168
Namibia	6,826	2,915	7,681	3,909
Nauru	148	1,239	674	394
Nepal	6,966	4,672	8,331	8,707
New Caledonia	45	3,520	618	4,806
New Zealand	455,694	343,145	487,332	378,368
Nicaragua	1,307	7,349	717	7,883
Niger	848	10,367	10,556	7,026
Nigeria	329,036	566,176	159,386	481,568
Niue & Tokelau	236	327	154	206
Norway	3,265,157	1,147,790	3,290,339	1,220,844
Oceania, Australian	524	488	41	529
Oceania, U.S.	287	3,154	178	5,809
Oman	87,236	399,647	3,951	249,916
Pakistan	131,296	227,064	167,315	252,978
Panama	4,950	44,975	4,919	40,020
Papua New Guinea	38,474	12,084	46,045	16,693

	1986		1987	
	Imports	Exports	Imports	Exports
Paraguay	1,455	31,010	1,409	25,409
Peru	82,141	48,275	91,689	49,324
Philippines	182,852	79,809	202,707	113,784
Pitcairn Is.	459	912	86	378
Poland	309,746	182,841	303,418	181,451
Polar Regions	43	674	137	1,199
Puerto Rico	81,131	49,620	76,347	39,405
Qatar	29,587	112,143	13,765	105,087
Réunion	12,259	4,225	1,056	8,624
Romania	86,730	82,011	92,526	55,688
Rwanda	7,487	1,681	4,291	2,526
St. Christopher and Nevis	4,429	6,008	4,677	7,041
St. Helena	380	8,196	189	8,065
St. Lucia	59,855	12,441	40,908	13,196
St. Pierre & Miquelon	474	367	77	604
St. Vincent	21,161	8,288	20,208	8,529
El Salvador	1,323	6,917	1,890	9,595
Sao Tomé & Príncipé	327	455	205	329
Saudi Arabia	435,930	1,507,062	383,143	1,978,440
Senegal	13,881	12,328	11,307	11,878
Seychelles	938	9,639	884	10,770
Sierra Leone	11,599	17,403	12,679	16,221
Singapore	462,878	547,419	473,814	602,627
Solomon Is.	4,074	1,618	4,461	1,566
Somalia	740	9,139	825	11,417
South Africa	829,305	849,557	658,162	948,584
Sri Lanka	51,860	83,316	53,817	84,680
Sudan	12,826	83,335	18,850	75,322
Suriname	15,554	9,743	12,488	7,974
Swaziland	48,194	3,922	36,901	2,257
Sweden	2,756,536	2,307,900	2,952,453	2,322,235
Switzerland	2,989,112	1,575,247	3,298,009	1,835,851
Syria	31,298	55,511	24,937	34,053
Taiwan	705,775	192,492	1,006,880	292,275
Tanzania	40,268	62,869	26,400	91,874
Thailand	182,756	158,195	239,430	206,571
Tonga	86	936	100	2,013
Togo	5,008	17,488	2,579	15,431
Trinidad & Tobago	41,622	79,029	38,600	57,016
Tunisia	17,292	39,824	14,714	24,943
Turkey	406,605	433,753	579,366	513,479
Turks & Caicos Is.	86	1,025	31	496
Tuvalu	88	78	2	106
Uganda	50,870	26,046	37,076	38,545
U.A.E.	74,012	581,762	94,989	478,997
U.S.A.	8,468,160	10,379,585	9,136,016	11,014,242
U.S.S.R.	694,624	539,368	875,431	491,615
Uruguay	41,366	24,465	40,474	26,484
Vanuatu	62	1,037	15	1,058
Vatican City	76	1,099	31	813
Venezuela	96,339	170,101	91,749	157,760
Vietnam	1,200	1,288	357	2,598
Virgin Is., British	267	3,491	752	3,310
Virgin Is., U.S.	5,455	5,955	2,674	6,503
Wallis & Futuna	—	—	—	53
Western Samoa	531	1,650	531	1,650
Yemen, Arab Rep.	2,106	58,149	2,306	55,334
Yemen, People's Dem. Rep.	4,848	23,928	1,056	28,271
Yugoslavia	145,127	188,390	175,301	206,932
Zaire	17,192	34,217	8,544	26,142
Zambia	27,260	77,840	30,310	75,178
Zimbabwe	80,702	61,937	79,771	63,181

LIFE ASSURANCE AND GENERAL INSURANCE

BRITISH INSURANCE COMPANIES IN 1987

The following Insurance Company figures refer to members of the Association of British Insurers, and also to certain non-members who represent about 4 per cent of the total long-term business and about 6 per cent of the general business figures given.

Worldwide General Business Trading Result

	1985 £m	1986 £m	1987 £m
Net Written Premiums	15,795	18,817	19,706
Underwriting Profit/Loss for 1 year Account Business			
Motor	−736	−638	−477
Fire & Accident	−1,054	−524	−470
Transfer to Profit and Loss Account for Other Business			
Marine, Aviation, Transport	−56	−6	+52
Other	−366	−252	−235
Total Underwriting Result	−2,212	−1,420	−1,130
Investment Income	2,213	2,514	2,631
Overall Trading Profit	1	1,094	1,501
Profit as a % of Premium Income	0·0	+5·8	+7·6

Worldwide General Business Underwriting Result

	1986				1987			
	U.K.	U.S.A.	Other	Total	U.K.	U.S.A.	Other	Total
Fire & Accident								
Premiums (£m)	5,328	2,059	2,570	9,957	6,097	1,829	2,331	10,257
Profit/Loss (£m)	−161·9	−132·8	−223·0	−517·7	−407·7	−79·1	+1·4	−485·4
% of Premiums	−3·0	−6·4	−8·7	−5·2	−6·7	−4·3	+0·1	−4·7
Motor								
Premiums (£m)	2,666	1,258	1,595	5,519	3,410	1,135	1,607	6,152
Profit/Loss (£m)	−369·8	−76·6	−192·0	−638·4	−198·4	−56·6	−160·4	−415·4
% of Premiums	−13·9	−6·1	−12·0	−11·6	−5·8	−5·0	−10·0	−6·8

Net Premium Income by Territory 1987

	U.K. £m	Other E.C. countries £m	U.S.A. £m	Other overseas £m	Total (world-wide) £m
Fire and Accident (non-motor)	6,603 (+15·4%)	994 (+0·7%)	1,876 (+11·8%)	2,681 (+10·5%)	12,154 (+2·7%)
Motor	3,437 (+27·7%)	717 (+3·6%)	1,135 (−10·1%)	902 (−1·8%)	6,191 (+11·2%)
Marine, Aviation and Transport	1,023 (−9·9%)	—	—	341 (−6·1%)	1,364 (−8·9%)
Total General Business	11,063 (+15·8%)	1,711 (+1·9%)	3,011 (−11·2%)	3,924 (−8·3%)	19,709 (+4·3%)
Ordinary Long-Term	20,334 (+19·7%)	1,360 (+14·0%)	864 (+329·9%)	1,752 (−2·0%)	24,310 (+20·5%)
Industrial Long-Term	1,301 (+4·2%)	—	—	—	1,301 (+4·2%)
Total Long-Term Business	21,635 (+18·6%)	1,360 (+14·0%)	864 (+329·9%)	1,752 (−2·0%)	25,611 (+19·5%)
TOTAL	32,698 (+17·7%)	3,071 (+6·9%)	3,875 (+7·9%)	5,676 (−6·4%)	45,320 (+12·4%)

(The figures in brackets show the percentage increase (+) or decrease (−) of the 1987 figures over those for 1986).

Insurance Company Investments

	1985 £m	1986 £m	1987 £m
Invested Funds			
Long-Term	142,596	174,633	190,371
General	28,805	36,833	36,857
Net Income from Investments			
Long-Term	8,854	10,018	11,021
General	2,213	2,526	2,625

Premium Income for Worldwide Long-Term Insurance Business

	1985 £m	1986 £m	1987 £m
Ordinary Branch:			
Yearly premiums for life insurances, annuities and pensions in the U.K.	8,570	9,501	10,640 (+12·0%)
Single premiums for life insurances, annuities and pensions in the U.K.	4,998	7,323	9,495 (+29·7%)
Premiums for permanent health and other long-term insurances in the U.K.	143	169	199 (+17·8%)
Overseas premium income	2,341	3,183	3,976 (+24·9%)
Industrial Branch:			
Premium Income (U.K. only)	1,198	1,248	1,301 (+4·2%)

Worldwide Long-Term Insurance Business—Outgo 1985 & 1986

	1985 £m	1986 £m	1987 £m
Ordinary Branch:			
Total payments made to U.K. policyholders	9,019	11,213	13,418 (+19·7%)
Total payments made to overseas policyholders	1,399	1,973	1,874 (−5·0%)
Industrial Branch:			
Total payments made to U.K. policyholders	1,071	1,177	1,287 (+9·3%)

NOTE: Payments to policyholders includes death claims, maturities, annuities, surrenders (including planned cashing in of linked and other similar savings policies and surrenders of bonus and bonuses in cash), refunds under pension schemes and payments under P.H.I. and other long-term contracts.

LLOYD'S OF LONDON

Lloyd's of London is an incorporated society of private underwriters who provide an international market for almost any type of insurance. Ships, aircraft, oil rigs, cargo of all descriptions, motor cars, civil engineering projects, fire, personal accident and third party liability are a few random examples of the everyday risks placed at Lloyd's which currently bring over £8,000 million of premiums to underwriters each year. Three-quarters of this business comes from outside Great Britain and makes a valuable contribution to the country's balance of payments.

Today, as it was three centuries ago, a policy is subscribed at Lloyd's by private individuals with unlimited liability. Now that Lloyd's members are numbered in their thousands, however, the method of underwriting is the same only in principle. The merchant of the past, signing policies in a coffee house as a sideline to his main business, has long since given way to the specialist underwriter who accepts risks at Lloyd's on behalf of members (often referred to as "names") grouped in a syndicate. There are currently over 30,000 members in over 350 syndicates of varying sizes, some with over two thousand names and each managed by an underwriting agent approved by the Council of Lloyd's.

Lloyd's membership today is drawn from many sources. Industry, commerce and the professions are strongly represented while many members work at Lloyd's either for brokerage firms or for underwriting agencies.

Underwriting membership of Lloyd's is open to men and women of any nationality provided that they meet the stringent financial requirements of the Society, or Corporation, of Lloyd's. Assets of up to £500,000 have to be shown and a deposit lodged with the Corporation as security for underwriting liabilities. This deposit, which must be in the form of approved securities, is determined at a percentage of the member's annual premium income, ranging from 25 per cent for an "external" member resident in the United Kingdom, to 50 per cent for a name working in the Lloyd's market and showing nominal means.

Lloyd's is incorporated by Act of Parliament (Lloyd's Acts 1871–1982) and governed by a Council of 28 members, twelve of whom are elected from and by underwriting members working at Lloyd's and eight from and by the external membership. Eight Council members are nominated by the Council subject to confirmation by the Governor of the Bank of England.

The Council is a legislative body responsible for deciding on major policy matters, for regulating the Lloyd's market, for the election of new underwriting members, and for establishing the requirements of membership and the rules governing the financial security to be provided by those doing business at Lloyd's.

The Council's "working" members form the Committee of Lloyd's, an executive body which is responsible for putting the Council's directives into effect, managing the Society's affairs, and administering the Lloyd's market on a day-to-day basis.

The Corporation is a non-profit-making body chiefly financed by its members' subscriptions. It provides the premises, administrative staff and services enabling Lloyd's underwriting syndicates to conduct their business. It does not, however, assume corporate liability for the risks accepted by its members, who remain responsible to the full extent of their personal means for their underwriting affairs.

Lloyd's syndicates have no direct contact with the public. All business is transacted through some 260 firms of insurance brokers accredited by the Corporation of Lloyd's. In addition, non-Lloyd's brokers in the United Kingdom when guaranteed by Lloyd's brokers, are able to deal directly with Lloyd's motor syndicates, a facility which has made the Lloyd's market more accessible to the insuring public.

Lloyd's also provides the most comprehensive shipping intelligence service available in the world. The enormous volume of shipping and other information received from Lloyd's Agents, shipowners, news agencies and other sources throughout the world, is collated and distributed to newspapers, radio and television services, as well as to the maritime and commercial communities in general.

This information is compiled, edited and published by a subsidiary company, Lloyd's of London Press Ltd., and distributed worldwide. "Lloyd's List" is London's oldest daily newspaper and contains news of general commercial interest as well as shipping information. "Lloyd's Shipping Index" also published daily, lists some 20,000 ocean-going vessels in alphabetical order and gives the latest known report of each.

LLOYD'S THREE YEAR BUSINESS SUMMARY

	Premiums	Underwriting profit	Investment income and appreciation
	£m	£m	£m
Short Term Life			
1981	1·95	0·50	0·27
1982	2·23	0·68	0·25
1983	2·89	1·03	0·26
Accident & Health			
1981	108·35	11·06	11·63
1982	169·75	(6·20)	13·96
1983	188·38	13·06	14·00
Motor Vehicle Damage & Liability			
1981	265·21	52·06	33·42
1982	273·59	40·13	29·29
1983	283·44	34·60	25·51
Ships, Aircraft Damage & Liability & Transit			
1981	1,110·89	7·48	141·04
1982	1,446·75	138·81	191·95
1983	1,211·42	187·79	184·25
All Other Insurance Business		(loss)	
1981	771·85	(114·62)	175·04
1982	1,000·16	(361·36)	206·53
1983	883·51	(351·17)	192·87

LLOYD'S MEMBERSHIP SYNDICATES AND BROKERS 1981–1988

	1981	1982	1983	1984	1985	1986	1987	1988
Membership	19,136	20,145	21,601	23,438	26,050	28,944	31,484	33,532
Including: Brokers	270	266	272	265	261	258	258	275

LLOYD'S GLOBAL UNDERWRITING ACCOUNTS

Net Premium Income

	1983 A/C	1984 A/C	1985 A/C
	£m	£m	£m
Life	2·886	4·030	3·833
Accident & Health	188·383	155·452	86·009
Motor Vehicle Damage & Liability	283·439	325·868	346·313
Ships, Aircraft Damage & Liability and Transit	1,211·427	1,372·845	1,085·716
All Other Insurance Business	883·502	1,106·419	988·491
TOTAL	2,569·637	2,964·614	2,310·362

DIRECTORY OF INSURANCE COMPANIES

The class of Insurance undertaken is shown in the second column as follows: A—Accident (which includes Motor, Employers' Liability, etc.); F—Fire (including Burglary); L—Life; and M—Marine. A number of offices are now included in a Group—the initials of which appear after the name. The main Groups are as follows—E.S.—Eagle Star; C.U.—Commercial Union; G.R.E.—Guardian Royal Exchange; G.A.—General Accident; N.U.—Norwich Union; R—Royal; S.A.—Sun Alliance & London.

Est'd.	Nature of Business	Name of Company	Address
1961	L	Abbey Life	Holdenhurst Rd., Bournemouth.
1951	AFM	Albion	Plantation House, 31/35 Fenchurch St., E.C.3.
1824	AFM	Alliance .................S.A.	1 Bartholomew Lane, E.C.2.
1965	L	Allied Dunbar	Allied Dunbar Centre, Swindon.
1921	L	American Life	2–8 Altyre Road, Croydon.
1960	AFLM	Ansvar	St. Leonards Rd., Eastbourne.
1808	ALFM	Atlas.................G.R.E.	Royal Exchange, E.C.3.
1849	L	Australian Mutual Provident ..	A.M.P. Ho., Dingwall Rd., Croydon.
1925	AFL	Avon	Tiddington Road, Stratford-upon-Avon.
1905	AFM	Baptist	4 Southampton Row, W.C.1.
1965	L	Barclays	94 St Paul's Churchyard, E.C.4.
1883	AFM	Beacon .................S.A.	1 Bartholomew Lane, E.C.2.
1894	AFM	Bedford General	Zurich House, Stanhope Rd., Portsmouth.
1925	AFM	Black Sea and Baltic	65 Fenchurch St., E.C.3.
1959	AFLM	Bradford	North Park, Halifax.
1866	AFL	Britannic	Moor Green, Moseley, Birmingham.
1863	M	British & Foreign Marine....R.	New Hall Place, Liverpool.
1878	Machinery	British Engine, &c ....R.	Longridge House, Manchester 4.
1854	AFL	British Equitable........G.R.E.	Royal Exchange, E.C.3.
1904	AFM	British General .........C.U.	St. Helen's, 1 Undershaft, E.C.3.
1888	AFM	British Law .............S.A.	1 Bartholomew Lane, E.C.2.
1896	L	British Life	Reliance House, Tunbridge Wells, Kent.
1008	AFM	British Oak ............G.R.E.	Royal Exchange, E.C.3.
1881	A	Builders' Accident	31 & 32 Bedford St., Strand, W.C.2.
1805	AFLM	Caledonian .............G.R.E.	Royal Exchange, E.C.3.
1934	AFM	Cambrian .............G.R.E.	Royal Exchange, E.C.3.
1847	AL	Canada Life	Canada Life House, Potters Bar, Herts.
1963	L	Cannon Lincoln	1 Olympic Way, Wembley.
1903	AFM	Car & General .........G.R.E.	Royal Exchange, E.C.3.
1885	AFM	Century.................S.A.	1 Bartholomew Lane, E.C.2.
1922	AFMex-motor	Chemists' Mutual	321 Chase Rd., Southgate, N.14.
1920	L	Citicorp British National	Perrymount Road, Haywards Heath, W. Sussex.
1862	L	City of Glasgow Friendly	200 Bath Street, Glasgow G.2.
1824	L	Clerical, Medical & Gen.	Narrow Plain, Bristol.
1873	L & Pers. Acc.	Colonial Mutual	24 Ludgate Hill, E.C.4.
1919	AFM	Comrcl. Ins. Co. of Ireland	5 Donegall Square, S., Belfast.
1861	AFLM	Commercial Union	St. Helen's, 1 Undershaft, E.C.3.
1871	L	Confederation	Lyttan Way, Stevenage, Herts.
1891	AF	Congregational	21–22 Apsley Crescent, Bradford 8.
1867	AFLM	Co-operative	Miller St., Manchester.
1905	AFLM	Cornhill	32 Cornhill, E.C.3.
1900	L	Crown Financial Management .	Crown House, Crown Square, Woking, Surrey.
1899	AFLM	Crusader	Woodhatch, Reigate, Surrey.
1908	AFM	Dominion	92/94 Gracechurch St., E.C.3.
1904	AFLM	Eagle Star	1 Threadneedle St., E.C.2.
1887	AFL	Ecclesiastical	Beaufort House, Brunswick Rd., Gloucester.
1901	AFLM	Economic	Economic House, London Road, Sittingbourne.
1823	AFM	Edinburgh.............C.U.	St. Helen's, 1 Undershaft, E.C.3.
1880	AFM	Employers' Liability ......C.U.	St. Helen's, 1 Undershaft, E.C.3.
1932	Animal Ins.	Equine and Livestock	610–616 Chiswick High Rd, W.4.
1762	L	Equitable Life	4 Coleman St., E.C.2.
1844	L	Equity & Law	Amersham Road, High Wycombe, Bucks.
1802	AF	Essex & Suffolk .........G.R.E.	Royal Exchange, E.C.3.
1894	AFM	Excess	13 Fenchurch Avenue, E.C.3.
1925	AFL	Federation Mutual	29 Linkfield Lane, Redhill, Surrey.
1890	AF	Fine Art & General .......C.U.	St. Helen's, 1 Undershaft, E.C.3.
1832	L	Friends' Prov	Pixham End, Dorking, Surrey.
1899	L	FS Assurance	190 West George St., Glasgow.
1885	AFM	General Accident	General Buildings, Perth, Scotland.
1837	L	General Accident Life	2 Rougier St., York.
1848	L	Gresham Life	2–6 Prince of Wales Rd., Bournemouth.
1910	AFM	Gresham Fire & Accident	11 Queen Victoria St., E.C.4.
1840	AFM	Guarantee Society .......G.A.	36–37 Old Jewry, E.C.2.
1821	ALFM	Guardian..............G.R.E.	68 King William Street, E.C.4.

Est'd.	Nature of Business	Name of Company	Address
1908	AFM	Hibernian	Haddington Road, Dublin, 4.
1960	L	Hill Samuel	NLA Tower, Addiscombe Rd., Croydon.
1966	AF	Household & General ...... S.A.	1 Bartholomew Lane, E.C.2.
1932	FL	Ideal	Pitmaston, Birmingham, 13.
1896	L	Imperial Life of Canada	Petrofina House, London Road, Gloucester.
1935	L	Insurance Corporation of Ireland (Life)	Burlington Road, Dublin 4.
1939	L	Irish Life	Lr. Abbey St., Dublin 2.
1880	A	Iron Trades Employers'	Iron Trades Ho., 21–24 Grosvenor Pl., S.W.1.
1838	L	LAS Group	10 George St., Edinburgh.
1845	AF	Law Fire ..................S.A.	1 Bartholomew Lane, E.C.2.
1806	AFM	Law Union & Rock ....R.	1 North John St., Liverpool, 2.
1907	AFM	Legal ....R.	1 North John St., Liverpool, 2.
1836	AFLM	Legal and General	Temple Court, 11 Queen Victoria St., E.C.4.
1970	L	Liberty Life	Liberty House, Station Rd., New Barnet.
1890	AFLM	Licenses & General	14 Bonhill Street, E.C.2.
1836	AFM	L'pool & London & Globe. ....R.	New Hall Place, Liverpool.
1918	AFM	Liverpool Marine & General....	4–5 King William St., E.C.4.
1843	L	Liverpool Victoria Friendly	Victoria House, Southampton Row., W.C.1.
1890	AFM	Local Government Guarantee G.R.E.	Royal Exchange, E.C.3
1836	AFM	Lombard Continental Insurance	Plantation House, 31–35 Fenchurch St., E.C.3.
1720	AFLM	London Assurance ........S.A.	1 Bartholomew Lane, E.C.2.
1869	AFM	London Guar. & Reinsurance...	Kings Orchard, 1 Queen St., Bristol.
1919	AFM	London & Lancashire..........	New Hall Place, Liverpool.
1806	L	London Life	100 Temple St., Bristol.
1869	AFL	London & Manchester	Winslade Park, Exeter, Devon.
1860	AFM	London & Provincial Marine G.A.	Lloyd's Building, Lime St., E.C.3.
1862	AFM	London & Scottish .... C.U.	St. Helen's, 1 Undershaft, E.C.3.
1961	L	M & G Assurance	M & G House, Victoria Rd., Chelmsford
1887	L	Manufacturers Life	St. George's Way, Stevenage.
1836	M	Marine.....................R.	34–36 Lime St., E.C.3.
1852	L	Marine & General	MGM House, Heene Rd., Worthing.
1864	M	Maritime .... N.U.	Surrey St., Norwich.
1884	L Sickness A	Med., Sickness, Ann. and Life...	7–10 Chandos St., Cavendish Sq., W.1.
1907	Reinsurance	Mercantile & General..........	Moorfields House, Moorfields, E.C.2.
1970	L	Merchant Investors	High Street, Croydon.
1871	M	Merchants' Marine .... C.U.	St. Helen's, 1 Undershaft, E.C.3.
1872	AF	Methodist	Brazennose House, Brazennose St., Manchester.
1940	AFM	Minster	Minster House, Arthur St., E.C.4.
1906	AFM	Motor Union ...........G.R.E.	Royal Exchange, E.C.3.
1903	AF	Municipal Mutual	25–27 Old Queen St., Westminster, S.W.1.
1890	AFL	Nalgo Insurance Association ...	1 Mabledon Place, W.C.1.
1935	L	NEL Britannia Group of Companies.................	Milton Court, Dorking, Surrey.
1914	AFM	National Employers' Mutual ...	N.E.M. House, Mitre Sq., E.C.3.
1910	AFL	National Farmers' Union	Tiddington Rd., Stratford-upon-Avon.
1863	Fidelity Guar.	Natl. Guaran. & Suretyship C.U.	St. Helen's, 1 Undershaft, E.C.3.
1894	AF	National Ins. & Guarantee Cor. .	Heron House, 145 City Rd., E.C.1.
1830	L	National Mutual Life	The Priory, Priory Park, Hitchin, Herts.
1835	L	National Provident Institution .	N.P. House, Tunbridge Wells, Kent
1854	Plate Glass	National Provincial .....G.R.E.	Royal Exchange, E.C.3.
1864	Machinery	National Vulcan Eng. Ins. Group.................S.A.	Empire House, St. Martin's-le-Grand, E.C.1.
1921	Naval Officers risks, etc.	Navigators & General ..... E.S.	1 Threadneedle St., E.C.2.
1924	L	New Ireland	11/12 Dawson St., Dublin, 2.
1869	L	N.M. Schroder Life Assurance ..	N.M. House, Seldown, Poole, Dorset.
1809	AFLM	North British & Mercantile C.U.	St. Helen's, 1 Undershaft, E.C.3.
1862	FM	North Pacific ...........G.R.E.	Royal Exchange, E.C.3.
1836	AFLM	Northern .... C.U.	St. Helen's, 1 Undershaft, E.C.3.
1797	AFM	Norwich Union Fire...........	Surrey Street, Norwich.
1808	L	Norwich Union Life	Surrey Street, Norwich.
1871	AFM	Ocean Accident .... C.U.	St. Helen's, 1 Undershaft, E.C.3.
1859	M	Ocean Marine .... C.U.	4 Fenchurch Ave., E.C.3.
1931	AFM	Orion	Orion House, Bouverie Road West, Folkestone, Kent.
1886	AF	Palatine......................	77 Leadenhall St., E.C.3.
1864	AFLM	Pearl.........................	High Holborn, W.C.1.
1958	Sickness A	Permanent	7–10 Chandos Street, Cavendish Sq., W.1.
1782	AFLM	Phoenix	see Sun Alliance

Est'd.	Nature of Business	Name of Company	Address
1891	L	Pioneer Mutual	16 Crosby Rd. N., Liverpool.
1920	AFM	Planet Assurance ...........S.A.	1 Bartholomew Lane, E.C.2.
1969	L	Property Growth..............	Leon House, High St., Croydon
1877	L	Prov. Life Assocn.	Provident Way, Basingstoke, Hampshire.
1840	L	Provident Mutual Life.........	25/31 Moorgate, London E.C.2.
1903	AFM	Provincial...................	Stramongate, Kendal, Cumbria.
1848	AFLM	Prudential...................	142 Holborn Bars, E.C.1.
1849	AF	Railway Passengers ...... C.U.	St. Helen's, 1 Undershaft, E.C.3.
1864	AFL	Refuge	Refuge House, Alderley Road, Wilmslow, Cheshire.
1911	L	Reliance Mutual	Reliance House, Tunbridge Wells, Kent.
1906	AF	Reliance Fire & Accident	Reliance House, Tunbridge Wells, Kent.
1881	AFM	Reliance Marine ........G.R.E.	Royal Exchange, E.C.3.
1823	Reversions	Reversionary Interest Society. .	4 Coleman St., E.C.2.
1918	AF	Road Transport & General G.A.	77 Upper Richmond Rd., S.W.15.
1845	L	Royal Life	New Hall Place, Liverpool.
1720	AFL	Royal Exchange...............	Royal Exchange, E.C.3.
1971	L	Royal Heritage Life	Bretton Way, Peterborough.
1850	L	Royal Liver Friendly	Royal Liver Building, Liverpool 3.
1861	AFL	Royal London.................	Royal London House, Middleborough, Colchester.
1887	L	Royal Nat. Pension Fund for Nurses	15 Buckingham St., W.C.2.
1909	AFM	Salvation Army	117–121 Judd St., W.C.1.
1963	L	Save and Prosper..............	1 Finsbury Ave., London E.C.2.
1826	L	Scottish Amicable.............	150 St. Vincent St., Glasgow.
1881	FM	Scottish Boiler .... G.A.	100 West Nile Street, Glasgow.
1831	L	Scottish Equitable............	28 St. Andrew Square, Edinburgh.
1919	AFM	Scottish General .... G.A.	100 West Nile St., Glasgow, G.2.
1852	L	Scottish Legal	95 Bothwell St., Glasgow, G.2.
1881	L	Scottish Life.................	19 St. Andrew Square, Edinburgh, 2.
1876	AF	Scottish Metropolitan .... C.U.	St. Helen's, 1 Undershaft, E.C.3.
1883	AL	Scottish Mutual..............	109 St. Vincent Street, Glasgow, G.2.
1837	L	Scottish Provident Institution .	6 St. Andrew Square, Edinburgh.
1824	AFLM	Scottish Union & National N.U.	Surrey St., Norwich.
1815	L	Scottish Widows'..............	15 Dalkeith Rd., Edinburgh.
1875	AFM	Sea ......................S.A.	1 Bartholomew Lane, E.C.2.
1904	AFL	Sentinel.....................	2 Eyre Street Hill, E.C.1.
1964	L	Stalwart Assurance	Tuition Hse., St. George's Rd., Wimbledon.
1825	L	Standard Life.................	3 George Street, Edinburgh.
1891	AFM	State....................G.R.E.	Royal Exchange, E.C.3.
1710	AFM	Sun ......................S.A.	1 Bartholomew Lane, E.C.2.
*	AFLM	Sun Alliance & London and Phoenix....................	1 Bartholomew Lane, E.C.2.
1810	L	Sun Life Assurance Group	107 Cheapside, E.C.2.
1865	L	Sun Life of Canada	2, 3 & 4 Cockspur St., S.W.1.
1936	FL	Teacher's Assurance	12 Christchurch Rd., Bournemouth.
1969	L	Trident	London Road, Gloucester.
1869	L	Tunstall & District	Station Chambers, Tunstall, Stoke on Trent.
1867	M	Ulster Marine .... G.A.	5 Donegall Sq., S., Belfast.
1714	AFM	Union Assurance.......... C.U.	St. Helen's, 1 Undershaft, E.C.3.
1835	AFM	Union Ins. Soc. of Canton G.R.E.	Royal Exchange, E.C.3.
1863	M	Union Marine	4–5 King William St., E.C.4.
1915	AFM	United British ...........G.R.E.	Royal Exchange, E.C.3.
1908	AFL	United Friendly..............	42 Southwark Bridge Road, S.E.1.
1963	L	UK Life Assurance	Royal Albert House, Windsor.
1825	L	University	4 Coleman St., E.C.2.
1974	L	Vanbrugh	41–43 Maddox St., W.1.
1919	Reinsurance	Victory Reinsurance	Castle Hill Ave., Folkestone, Kent
1875	AFM	Warden ....R.	1 North John St., Liverpool.
1911	AF	Welsh Insurance Corpn. ... C.U.	St. Helen's, 1 Undershaft, E.C.3.
1841	AFL	Wesleyan & General	Colmore Circus, Queensway, Birmingham 4.
1886	AF	West of Scotland .... C.U.	26 George St., Edinburgh 2.
1851	AFM	Western Assurance..........R.	New Hall Place, Liverpool.
1912	AFLM	Western Australian	Swan Court, Mansel Rd., Wimbledon, S.W.19.
1717	AF	Westminster Fire .........S.A.	1 Bartholomew Lane, E.C.2.
1865	AF	White Cross .... C.U.	St. Helen's, 1 Undershaft, E.C.3.
1963	L	Windsor Life	Royal Albert House, Windsor.
1894	AFM	World Marine & General .. C.U.	Dunster House, Mark Lane, E.C.3.
1872	AF	Zurich	P.O. Box, Stanhope Rd., Portsmouth.

* Sun Alliance & London—Incorporating Funds established 1710, 1720, 1782 and 1824.

FRIENDLY SOCIETIES—GREAT BRITAIN

Acts 1974–1984

Friendly societies are voluntary mutual organizations the main purposes of which are the provision of relief or maintenance during sickness, unemployment or retirement, and the provision of life assurance. Many of the older traditional societies complement their business activities by social activity and a general care for individual members in ways normally outside the scope of a purely commercial organization. There are three main categories of friendly societies—societies with separately registered branches, commonly called orders, centralized societies, which conduct business directly with members (having no separately registered branches), and collecting societies. Collecting societies conduct industrial assurance business and are subject to the requirements of the Industrial Assurance Acts in addition to the Friendly Societies Acts. Industrial assurance is life assurance, the premiums in respect of which are payable at intervals of less than two months and are received by means of collectors who make house-to-house visits for the purpose.

At the end of 1987 there were 21 orders with 2,796 branches, 375 centralized societies, and 32 collecting societies.

Long before the term "Friendly Society" came into use, the seeds of voluntary mutual insurance had been sown in the ancient religious and trade "Guilds". As is evident from the many extant parchment returns detailing their rules and possessions under a decree of Richard II, Guilds had become widespread in Britain by the 14th century. By then, the purely charitable character of the original Guilds had largely changed with the emergence of numerous small institutions adopting primitive mutual insurance methods of a regular flat rate contribution to insure relief when sick or in old age and a payment to the widow in the event of death.

The present register of Friendly Societies includes several societies which have been in existence for upwards of 200 years, the oldest, operating in Scotland, being the "Incorporation of Carters in Leith" established as long ago as 1555.

The first Act for the encouragement and protection of "Friendly Societies" in this country was not passed until 1793, but various amending Acts were put on the Statute Book during the next century as the result of the recommendations of successive Select Committees (including a Royal Commission in 1871). For example, it was not until the 1829 Act that all registered Friendly Societies were required to keep proper records of individual sickness and mortality amongst their members, which data enabled the construction of standard actuarial tables showing the expected (average) duration of sickness at successive ages, and also (with data from the Census) the corresponding mortality rates.

The rules and other documents of societies deposited with local justices passed into the custody of the Registrar following the Act of 1846 and are of considerable interest to social historians. Those relating to some societies no longer on the register have been transferred to the Public Record Office for permanent preservation.

The Friendly Societies Act 1974, which came into force in April, 1975, consolidated the nine Acts which comprised the Friendly Societies Acts 1896 to 1971 and a few other minor enactments relating to societies to which those Acts applied. The Act allows various specific classes other than "Friendly Societies" to be registered thereunder, but tax exemption (irrespective of the extent of interest income) is enjoyed only by registered "Friendly Societies". Removal of the £750 sum assured limit for tax exempt business was announced in the March 1987 Budget and enacted in the Finance Act 1987. It was replaced by a more flexible limit applied to premiums—up to £100 per annum.

The Friendly Societies Act 1984 abolished the limits on the size of taxable life and annuity business societies could write.

In addition to Friendly Societies there are three other main classes of society which may be registered under the Friendly Societies Act 1974: benevolent societies, working men's clubs and specially authorized societies. Benevolent societies are established for any charitable or benevolent purpose, to provide the same type of benefits as would be permissible for a friendly society, but in contrast the benefits must be for persons who are not members instead of, or in addition to, members. Working men's clubs provide social and recreational facilities for members. Specially authorized societies are registered for any purpose authorized by the Treasury as a purpose to which some or all of the provisions of the 1974 Act ought to be extended. Examples are societies for the promotion of science, literature and the fine arts, or to enable members to pursue an interest in sports and games. At the end of 1987 there were 87 benevolent societies, 2,408 working men's clubs, and 150 specially authorized societies.

The principal statistics at the end of 1986 are given in the table below.

	Friendly Societies (a)	Collecting Societies	Benevolent Societies	Working Men's Clubs	Special Authorized Societies		Other
					Loan	Others	
Number of Societies	3,350	33	88	2,427	9	141	2
Number of Members 000's	3,005	16,343 (b)	322	2,078 (c)	13	123	3
Total Benefits Paid £000's	113,319	138,748	5,541	Not applicable	Not applicable	28	54
Total Funds £000's	1,371,653	1,613,759	18,633	141,877 (c)	480	13,400	507

(a) Centralized societies, orders and branches of orders
(b) Assurances

(c) 1985 figures

INDUSTRIAL AND PROVIDENT SOCIETIES—GREAT BRITAIN

Acts 1965–1979

The familiar "Co-op" societies are amongst the wide variety which are registered under the Industrial and Provident Societies Act 1965. This consolidating Act, which like the Friendly and the Building Societies Act is administered by the Chief Registrar of Friendly Societies, provides for the registration of societies and lays down the broad framework within which they must operate. Internal relations of societies are governed by their registered rules.

Registration under the Act confers upon a society corporate status by its registered name with perpetual succession and a common seal, and limited liability. A society qualifies for registration if it is carrying on an industry, business or trade, and it satisfies the Registrar that either (a) it is a bona fide co-operative society or (b) in view of the fact that its business is being, or is intended to be, conducted for the benefit of the community there are special reasons why it

should be registered under the Act rather than as a company under the Companies Act.

The Credit Unions Act 1979 added a new class of society registerable under the 1965 Act. The Act also lays down provision for supervision of these savings and loan bodies. A similar framework of law for credit unions has existed in Northern Ireland since 1969.

During 1986 the number of registered societies increased by 279 to 10,486. The largest single group was the 3,903 housing societies. The largest group in terms of turnover was that consisting of the retail societies which includes those trading under the familiar "Co-op" sign, with sales (in 1986) of £3,989 million. Sales of wholesale and productive societies amounted to £3,007 million in 1986. The principal statistics at the end of 1986 are given in the table below.

	Retail	Wholesale and Productive	Agricultural	Fishing	Social and Recreational Clubs	General Service	Housing	Credit Unions	Total
Number of Societies	213	234	1,081	107	3,757	1,035	3,686	94	10,207
Number of Members 000's	7,805	53	383	8	2,948	513	149	24	11,883
Funds of Members £000's	684,582	357,510	191,567	3,025	177,580	2,761,392	5,782,383	5,168	9,963,206
Total Assets £000's	1,339,138	893,978	466,835	11,368	344,260	3,240,591	9,343,714	5,424	15,645,308

BUILDING SOCIETIES—UNITED KINGDOM

Act 1986

The most significant event for the building societies in recent times was the passage of the Building Societies Act 1986, which received the Royal Assent on July 25, 1986. Most of the provisions of the Act came into effect on January 1, 1987. The Act gave building societies a completely new legal framework, the first since the initial comprehensive building society legislation in 1874. The new Act replaces both the 1962 Act and the 1967 Act covering Northern Ireland, and therefore applies to societies based throughout the United Kingdom.

The number of building societies in Great Britain declined from 151 at the end of 1986 to 138 at the end of 1987. There were 13 mergers in 1987 and one small society had its registration cancelled.

The 1986 Act makes provision for a Building Societies Commission to promote the protection of shareholders and depositors, the financial stability of societies, and to administer the system of regulation of building societies provided under the Act. Much of the Act is concerned with the powers of control of the Commission and provision in relation to the

management of societies, accounts, audit and so on. But the greatest impact and the most visible changes so far as the general public is concerned flow from the new powers which societies may adopt, leading to an increased range of services which they may provide. There are also some interesting changes in relation to members' rights.

Under the 1962 Act raising funds to make loans was the only purpose for which a building society could exist. Under the 1986 Act that has only to be its principal purpose. The constitutional provisions include the right of members to have access to the register of members, entitlement to have notices of meetings and to vote, and the right of members to have a resolution circulated.

In addition to traditional mortgage business, the power of societies to lend in respect of shared ownership, index-linked and equity-linked schemes is given. Societies may also lend the deposit, lend on registered land before the borrower is registered as the owner and on other equitable interests which may be prescribed by order. Provision is also made

BUILDING SOCIETIES, GREAT BRITAIN, 1977–1987

Year	1 Number of Societies	2 Number of Share Holders 000's	3 Number of Depositors 000's	4 Number of Borrowers 000's	5 Share Balances £m	6 Deposit Balances £m
1977	339	22,536	760	4,836	31,110	1,224
1978	316	24,999	781	5,108	36,186	1,254
1979	287	27,878	797	5,251	42,023	1,281
1980	273	30,636	915	5,383	48,915	1,742
1981	253	33,388	995	5,490	55,463	2,539
1982	227	36,609	1,094	5,643	64,977	3,447
1983	206	37,713	1,202	5,928	75,180	5,610
1984	190	39,385	1,550	6,317	88,078	8,426
1985	167	39,997	2,150	6,659	102,331	10,751
1986	151	40,563	2,850	7,025	115,538	16,864
1987	138	41,953	3,648	7,182	129,948	20,575

Year	7 Mortgage Balances £m	8 Total Assets £m	9 Number 000's	10 Amount £m	11 Average Mortgage Rate %	12 Average Share Rate %
			Advances during year			
1977	26,427	34,288	946	6,745	11·05	6·98
1978	31,598	39,538	1,184	8,808	9·55	6·46
1979	36,801	45,789	1,040	9,002	11·94	8·45
1980	42,437	53,793	936	9,503	14·92	10·34
1981	48,875	61,815	1,096	12,005	14·01	9·19
1982	56,691	73,033	1,320	14,971	13·32	8·77
1983	67,490	85,868	1,513	19,357	11·05	7·26
1984	81,879	102,688	1,657	23,767	11·83	7·71
1985	96,751	120,764	1,678	26,508	13·46	8·65
1986	115,644	140,603	2,058	35,885	12·07	7·75
1987	130,905	160,098	1,889	35,848	11·64	7·42

for power to be given, by statutory instrument, for societies to make advances secured on land outside the United Kingdom. Larger societies may, for the first time, make unsecured loans. The power to lend on overdraft is specifically provided for. These societies may also make loans on mobile homes.

Under the 1962 Act building societies could only hold land for the purposes of running their business. Section 17 of the 1986 Act gives building societies power to hold and develop land as a commercial asset. However, the land has to be primarily for residential purposes, or adjoining land, or for purposes incidental to the holding of residential land.

Detailed provisions are contained in the Act for an Investor Protection Scheme similar to those in the Banking Act of 1979. The level of protection given is 90 per cent of accounts up to £10,000.

Societies were also empowered to offer for the first time the following services:—

(a) Money transmission services
(b) Foreign exchange services
(c) Making or receiving of payments as agents
(d) Management, as agents, of mortgage investments
(e) Management, as agents, of land (larger societies only)
(f) Arranging for the provision of services relating to the acquisition or disposal of investments for individuals.
(g) Establishment and management of personal equity plans.
(h) Arranging for the provision of credit to individuals.

(i) Establishment and management of unit trust schemes for the provision of pensions (through a subsidiary).
(j) Establishment and administration of pension schemes.
(k) Arranging for the provision of insurance of any description.
(l) Giving advice on insurance of any description.
(m) Estate agency service (through a subsidiary).
(n) Surveys and valuations of land.
(o) Conveyancing services.

There emerged a number of technical problems in relation to these services, for example concerning the introduction of credit cards, and in October 1987 a review of the powers was announced by the Government. In February 1988 it was announced that societies would have the power to own up to 100 per cent of a life assurance company, 15 per cent of a general insurance company, 100 per cent of a stockbroking company and to offer an additional range of financial services including executorship and trusteeship, hire purchase and leasing and safe deposit facilities.

Societies must belong to an "Ombudsman" scheme for the investigation of complaints. Matters to be covered by the scheme include operation of share and deposit accounts, loans (but not the making of new loans), money transmission services, foreign exchange services, agency payments and receipts, and the provision of credit. Grounds for complaint include breach of the Act or contract, unfair treatment or maladministration, and where the complainant has suffered pecuniary loss or expense or inconvenience. A society must agree to be bound by decisions of the adjudicator unless it agrees to give notice to its members and the public of its reasons for not doing so. For address of the Building Societies Ombudsman Scheme, *see* Index.

On mergers, the main difference is that borrowers will have a vote. For a merger to be approved at least 50 per cent of borrowers who exercise their right to

vote must vote in favour, as well as 75 per cent of qualifying share investors who vote. Provision is also made for a society to convert to company status.

At the end of 1987 the six largest societies again accounted for about 66 per cent of the assets of all building societies. The 15 largest societies accounted for about 86 per cent. Details of all societies with assets exceeding £1m. at the end of 1987 are given in the following list.

SOCIETIES WITH TOTAL ASSETS EXCEEDING £1 MILLION AT END OF FINANCIAL YEAR 1986

Year Estab- lished	* Name of Society (abbreviated) Head Office	Share Investors	Assets Total £'000
1849	Abbey National, Abbey House, 27 Baker St., London NW1 6XL	7,532,400	26,411,206
1885	Aid to Thrift, 38 Finsbury Sq., London EC2	1,166	3,809
1985	Alliance and Leicester, 49 Park Lane, London W1Y 4EQ	2,145,122	9,286,612
1853	Barnsley, Regent St., Barnsley, South Yorks	25,228	104,516
1953	Bath Investment and Bldg. Soc., 20 Charles St., Bath	10,702	26,464
1879	Bedford, 65 Midland Rd., Bedford	10,410	40,282
1881	Bedford Crown, 117 Midland Rd., Bedford	3,179	10,505
1866	Beverley, 57 Market Place, Beverley, Yorks	5,622	15,730
1914	Bexhill-on-Sea, 2 Devonshire Sq., Bexhill-on-Sea, Sussex	3,030	10,830
1889	Birmingham Midshires, 42/44 Waterloo Street, Birmingham	684,961	2,243,122
1864	Bolton, 235–237 Baker St., London NW1	6,225	93,238
1851	Bradford and Bingley, P.O. Box 2, Bingley, West Yorks.	1,779,775	4,950,961
1850	Bristol and West, Broad Quay, Bristol	715,219	2,925,002
1856	Britannia, Cheadle Rd., Newton House, Leek, Staffs.	1,077,495	4,657,931
1907	Buckinghamshire, High St., Chalfont St. Giles, Bucks.	5,602	24,702
1866	Bury St. Edmunds, 8 Guildhall St., Bury St. Edmunds	4,124	20,720
1850	Cambridge, 32 St. Andrew's St., Cambridge	33,605	160,044
1960	Catholic, 7 Strutton Ground, London SW1	2,850	12,757
1899	Century, 21–23 Albany St., Edinburgh	1,291	6,723
1875	Chelsea, Thirlestaine Hall, Thirlestaine Rd., Cheltenham, Glos.	170,115	1,013,158
1850	Cheltenham and Gloucester, 37–43 Clarence St., Cheltenham, Glos.	805,764	4,472,110
1845	Chesham, 12 Market Sq., Chesham, Bucks.	7,986	33,561
1870	Cheshire, Castle St., Macclesfield	207,114	542,768
1861	Cheshunt, 100 Crossbrook St., Waltham Cross, Herts.	48,317	232,764
1859	Chorley and Dt., 51 St. Thomas's Rd., Chorley, Lancs.	6,390	27,784
1946	City and Metropolitan, 37 Ludgate Hill, London EC4	11,182	56,630
1862	City of London, 54/60 Gresham Street, London EC2V 7LL	25,218	180,261
1859	Clay Cross Benefit, 42 Thanet St., Clay Cross, Chesterfield	3,254	8,836
1884	Coventry, P.O. Box 9, High Street, Coventry	346,990	1,072,451
1850	Cumberland, 38 Fisher St., Carlisle	94,025	253,622
1946	Darlington, Tubwell Row, Market Pl., Darlington, Co. Durham	37,384	143,538
1859	Derbyshire, Duffield Hall, Duffield, Derby	264,492	804,031
1858	Dudley, Dudley Hse., Stone St., Dudley, Worcs.	14,209	42,953
1869	Dunfermline, 12 East Port, Dunfermline, Fife.	87,300	349,925
1857	Earl Shilton, 22 The Hollow, Earl Shilton, Leicester	8,939	30,635
1877	Eastbourne Mut., Eastbourne Hse., 22 Gildredge Rd., Eastbourne, Sussex	54,640	236,556
1980	Ecology, 8A Main St., Cross Hills, Keighley, West Yorks BD20 8TT	1,089	2,376
1847	Essex Eq., 11 Orsett Rd., Grays, Essex	5,014	27,780
1860	Frome Selwood P., 3 Market Pl., Frome, Som.	13,272	37,711
1865	Furness, 51–55 Duke Street, Barrow-in-Furness	56,543	166,497
1911	Gainsborough, 26 Lord St., Gainsborough, Lincs.	3,630	9,897
1924	Gateway, 223–227 Regent St., London W1R 8AR	463,048	1,939,017
1852	Greenwich, 279–283 Greenwich High Rd., London SE10	29,599	106,158
1871	Guardian, Guardian Hse., 120 High Holborn, London WC1	65,953	960,043
1853	Halifax, Trinity Rd., Halifax, West Yorks	8,280,797	33,039,500
1866	Hampshire, Anchor Hse., Kingston Crescent, Portsmouth	14,944	72,175
1854	Hanley Econ., 42 Cheapside, Hanley, Stoke-on-Trent, Staffs.	31,121	92,552
1953	Harpenden, 14 Station Rd., Harpenden, Herts.	6,818	25,322
1890	Haywards Heath and Dt., 33 The Broadway, Haywards Heath, West Sussex	19,552	88,901
1863	Heart of England, 22–26 Jury St., Warwick	132,903	428,517
1926	Hendon, 9 Central Circus, Hendon, London NW4	3,557	23,501
1888	Herts. and Essex, 4 Market Sq., Bishop's Stortford, Herts.	3,906	16,719
1865	Hinckley, and Rugby, Upper Bond St., Hinckley, Leics.	35,773	136,922

* P. = Permanent; B. = Benefit. The words "Building Society" are the last words in every society's name.

Year Established	Name of Society (abbreviated) Head Office	Share Investors	Assets Total £'000
1855	Holmesdale B., 43 Church St., Reigate, Surrey	3,115	34,864
1853	Ilkeston P., 24–26 South Street, Ilkeston, Derby	3,883	10,309
1849	Ipswich, 44 Upper Brook St., Ipswich	30,151	95,355
1888	Kent Reliance, Reliance Hse, Manor Rd, Chatham, Kent	46,228	142,252
1852	Lambeth, 118–120 Westminster Bridge Rd., London SE1	53,093	406,662
1872	Lancastrian, Sadler St., Middleton, Manchester	46,214	164,841
1853	Leamington Spa, Leamington House, Milverton Hill, Leamington Spa, Warws.	131,300	823,586
1875	Leeds and Holbeck, 105 Albion St., Leeds	218,340	967,584
1848	Leeds P., Permanent Hse., The Headrow, Leeds	2,960,535	8,828,341
1863	Leek United and Midlands, 50 St. Edward St., Leek, Staffs.	44,703	163,001
1876	Londonderry Provident, 7 Castle Street, Londonderry BT48 6HQ	930	3,398
1867	Loughborough P., 6 High St., Loughborough, Leics.	9,265	42,626
1877	Louth, Mablethorpe and Sutton P.B., 3 Eastgate, Louth, Lincs.	1,446	4,934
1922	Manchester, 18–20 Bridge St., Manchester	7,681	36,784
1870	Mansfield, Regent Hse., Regent St., Mansfield, Notts.	15,190	61,352
1870	Market Harborough, Welland Hse., The Sq., Market Harborough, Leics.	27,730	104,940
1860	Marsden, 6–20 Russell St., Nelson, Lancs.	30,045	147,222
1874	Melton Mowbray, 39 Nottingham St., Melton Mowbray, Leics.	28,449	110,595
1966	Mercantile, 75 Howard St., North Shields, Tyne and Wear	15,274	70,683
1880	Mid-Sussex, Mid-Sussex Hse., 66 Church Rd., Burgess Hill, Sussex	5,817	20,368
1869	Monmouthshire, John Frost Sq., Newport, Gwent	13,503	67,342
1866	Mornington, 158 Kentish Town Rd., London NW5	19,095	140,326
1869	National and Provincial, Provincial Hse., Bradford	1,377,271	6,734,456
1896	National Counties, Waterloo Hse., 147–153 High St., Epsom, Surrey	23,134	223,872
1884	Nationwide Anglia, Chesterfield Hse., Bloomsbury Way, London WC1	5,566,750	21,060,900
1856	Newbury, 17–20 Bartholomew St., Newbury, Berks.	25,381	112,322
1863	Newcastle, Grainger Chambers, Hood Street, Newcastle upon Tyne	109,199	524,560
1877	North of England, 57 Fawcett St., Sunderland	202,103	536,430
1983	North Wilts Ridgeway, 18 and 19 Commercial Rd., Swindon, Wilts.	8,579	48,691
1850	Northern Rock, Northern Rock Hse., Gosforth, Newcastle upon Tyne	589,823	2,016,215
1852	Norwich and Peterborough, St. Andrew's Hse., St. Andrew St., Norwich, Norfolk	181,860	623,356
1850	Nottingham, 5–13 Upper Parliament St., Nottingham	123,535	311,506
1935	Nottingham Imperial, Imperial Bldg., 29 Bridgeford Rd., West Bridgeford, Nottingham	5,392	16,558
1879	Peckham Graylaw Hse., 1 Copers Cope Rd, Beckenham, Kent BR3 1MB	10,764	53,269
1877	Penrith, 7 King St., Penrith, Cumb.	7,792	28,923
1881	Portman, 40 Portman Sq., London W1	138,816	571,756
1896	Portsmouth, Churchill Hse., Winston Churchill Ave., Portsmouth	79,116	570,395
1860	Principality, Principality Bldgs., Queen St., Cardiff	192,339	536,185
1914	Progressive, 33–37 Wellington Place, Belfast BT1 6HH	25,306	121,812
1872	Regency, 130 Western Road, Hove, East Sussex BN3 1DR	72,500	426,158
1888	Rowley Regis, 223 Halesowen Rd., Cradley Heath, Warley, Worcs	30,065	82,065
1849	Saffron Walden and Essex, Market Place, Saffron Walden, Essex	26,382	101,366
1937	St. Pancras, 200 Finchley Rd., London NW3	9,698	64,782
1955	St. Stephens, 70 Chepstow Road, London W2	385	1,481
1846	Scarborough, Prospect House, 442/444 Scalby Road, Scarborough, Yorks.	42,499	157,531
1848	Scottish, 2 York Place, Edinburgh.	13,163	51,783
1935	Sheffield, 66 Campo Lane, Sheffield, Yorks.	3,852	13,814
1879	Shepshed, Bull Ring, Shepshed, Loughborough, Leics.	5,888	18,965
1853	Skipton, 59 High St., Skipton, Yorks.	160,146	1,004,904
1877	Stafford Railway, 4 Market Sq., Stafford	7,304	25,171
1902	Staffordshire, Jubilee Hse., P.O. Box 66, 84 Salop St., Wolverhampton	145,210	464,390
1875	Standard, 64 Church Way, North Shields, Tyne and Wear	2,347	9,645
1850	Stroud and Swindon, 7 Russell St., Stroud, Glos.	59,271	215,106
1903	Surrey, 54 Station Rd., Redhill, Surrey RH1 1PH	10,380	61,198
1870	Sussex County, 40/42 Friars Walk, Lewes, East Sussex	86,578	344,006
1923	Swansea, 11 Cradock St., Swansea	3,183	14,488
1966	Teachers, Allenview Hse., Wimborne, Dorset	9,724	80,391
1901	Tipton and Coseley, 57–60 High St., Tipton, Staffs.	14,182	40,254
1853	Town and Country, 215 Strand, London WC2	202,612	1,424,387
1855	Tynemouth, 53–55 Howard St., North Shields, Tyne and Wear	5,480	27,436
1863	Universal, 41 Pilgrim St., Newcastle upon Tyne	22,947	100,580
1924	Vernon, 26 St. Petersgate, Stockport, Chesh.	15,823	54,174
1877	Walthamstow, 869 Forest Rd., Walthamstow, London E17	42,515	212,394
1949	Wessex, 115 Old Christchurch Rd., Bournemouth, Hants.	34,767	177,950
1849	West Bromwich, 374 High St., West Bromwich, Staffs.	267,185	856,940
1882	West Cumbria, Cumbria Hse., Murray Rd., Workington	6,402	22,972
1846	West of England, 25 High Street, Marlborough, Wilts SN8 1NF	140,901	507,202
1847	Woolwich Eq., Equitable Hse., London SE18	2,221,855	9,261,844
1885	Yorkshire, Yorkshire House, Westgate, Bradford	617,314	2,373,222

INTEREST RATES – MORTGAGE AND SHARE

The interest rates prevailing on mortgage lending and share investment vary to a degree from society to society and in relation to the type or amount of loan or investment. The system whereby the Building Societies Association advised specific rates ceased in November 1984 and in April 1986 collective discussion, leading to a statement that a reduction or increase of a certain order was appropriate, was discontinued. General rate changes, however, continue in response to market conditions and the predominant rates in each of the last 3 years, with the dates of change, are given below.

	Jan. 1985	March 1985	Aug. 1985	March 1986	June 1986	Nov. 1986	May 1987
Mortgages	12·75–13·00	13·75–14·00	12·75	12·00	11·00	12·25–12·375	11·25
Ordinary Shares	7·50	8·25	7·00	6·00	5·25	6·00	5·00

THE COST OF LIVING

The first cost-of-living index to be calculated in Great Britain was the one which took July, 1914, as 100 and was based on the pattern of expenditure of working class families in 1904. Since 1947 the Index of Retail Prices has superseded the cost-of-living index, although the older term is still often popularly applied to it. This index is designed to reflect the month-by-month changes in the average level of retail prices of goods and services purchased by the "majority" of households in the United Kingdom, including practically all wage-earners and most small and medium salary-earners. For spending coming within the scope of the index, a representative list of items is selected and the prices actually charged for these items are collected at regular intervals. In working out the index figure, the price changes are "weighted"—that is, given different degrees of importance—in accordance with the pattern of consumption of the average family.

A more widely used guide when considering changes in the average level of prices of all consumer goods and services, particularly over a number of years, is the consumer price index, now renamed the consumers' expenditure deflator. This index, which has been calculated back to 1938, covers the expenditure of all consumers as defined for national income purposes, and compares the price of goods and services actually purchased in a given year with the prices of the same goods and services in a base year.

During 1973 the Central Statistical Office constructed an annual index of prices of consumer goods and services over the period 1914 to 1972. This index has been constructed by linking together the pre-war cost of living index for the period 1914–1938, the consumers' expenditure deflator for the period 1938 and 1946–62* and the General Index of Retail Prices for the period 1962–1972.

In August 1979, the tax and price index (TPI) was introduced in order to provide a statistic which incorporates the effects of direct and indirect taxation, as well as prices, on taxpayers. The TPI is not directly concerned with the purchasing power of money, however, but with the purchasing power of pre-tax income. The General Index of Retail Prices thus retains its function of measuring the changes in the prices of goods and services purchased by households (from their post-tax income), and therefore as an indicator of the purchasing power of money.

	Long Term Index of Retail Prices Jan. 1974 = 100 Annual averages	Comparable Purchasing Power of £1 in 1987
1914............	11·1	36·20
1915............	13·7	29·33
1920............	27·7	14·50
1925............	19·6	20·50
1930............	17·6	22·83
1935............	15·9	25·20
1938............	17·4	23·09
1946............	29·4	13·67
1950............	35·6	11·28
1955............	44·1	9·11
1960............	49·6	8·10
1965............	58·4	6·88
1970............	73·1	5·49
1971............	80·0	5·02
1972............	85·7	4·68
1973............	93·5	4·29
1974............	108·5	3·70
1975............	134·8	2·98
1976............	157·1	2·55
1977............	182·0	2·20
1978............	197·1	2·03
1979............	223·5	1·79
1980............	263·7	1·52
1981............	295·0	1·36
1982............	320·4	1·25
1983............	335·1	1·19
1984............	351·8	1·14
1985............	373·2	1·07
1986............	385·9	1·04
1987............	401·9	1·00

By employing this table an annual purchasing power of the pound index may be derived by taking the inverse of the price index. So, for example, if the purchasing power of the pound is taken to be 100p in 1972, then its comparable purchasing power in 1987 would be:

$$100 \times \frac{85 \cdot 7}{401 \cdot 9} = 21 \cdot 3p$$

It should be noted that these figures can only be approximate.

* There are no official figures for 1939–45.

BANKING IN BRITAIN

The main institutions within the British banking system are the Bank of England (the central bank, see p. 303), the clearing banks (the major retail banks), the merchant banks, the overseas banks and the discount houses.

The clearing banks are Bank of Scotland, Barclays, Clydesdale, Co-operative, Coutts, Girobank, Lloyds, Midland, National Westminster, Royal Bank of Scotland, the T.S.B. and the Yorkshire Bank.

Deposit-taking institutions may be broadly divided into the monetary sector which is predominantly banks and is supervised by the Bank of England, and those institutions outside the monetary sector of which the most important are the building societies and the National Savings Bank. The Banking Act 1987 established a single category of authorized institutions eligible to carry out banking business. There follows a list of authorized institutions as at August 1, 1988.

Authorized Institutions

U.K.—INCORPORATED
(Including partnerships formed under the law of any part of the U.K.)

A1 Credit P.L.C.
A.N.Z. Merchant Bank Ltd.
Adam & Company P.L.C.
Afghan National Credit & Finance Ltd.
Airdrie Savings Bank
Aitken Hume Ltd.
Ak International Bank Ltd.
Albaraka International Bank Ltd.
Alliance Trust (Finance) Ltd.
Allied Arab Bank Ltd.
Anglo-Romanian Bank Ltd.
Anglo Yugoslav Bank Ltd.
Henry Ansbacher & Co. Ltd.
Arbuthnot Latham Bank Ltd.
Argonaut Securities Ltd.
Assemblies of God Property Trust
Associated Credits Ltd.
Associated Japanese Bank (International) Ltd.
Associates Capital Corporation Ltd.
Atlanta Trust Ltd.
Auban Finance Ltd.
Authority Bank Ltd.
Avco Trust Ltd.

B.A.I.I. P.L.C.
B.C. Finance Ltd.
B.N.L. Investment Bank P.L.C.
Banco Hispano Americano Ltd.
Bank in Liechtenstein (U.K.) Ltd.
Bank Leumi (U.K.) P.L.C.
Bank of America International Ltd.
Bank of Boston Ltd.
Bank of Cyprus (London) Ltd.
Bank of Scotland
Bank of Tokyo International Ltd.
Bank of Wales P.L.C.
Bankers Trust International Ltd.
Banque Belge Ltd.
Banque de la Méditerranée (U.K.) Ltd.
Banque Nationale de Paris P.L.C.
The Baptist Union Corporation Ltd.
Barclays Bank P.L.C.
Barclays de Zoete Wedd Ltd.
Barclays Bank Trust Company Ltd.
Baring Brothers & Co. Ltd.
Benchmark Bank P.L.C.
Beneficial Trust Ltd.
Boston Safe Deposit and Trust Company (U.K.) Ltd.
Bradford Investments P.L.C.
British and Commonwealth Merchant Bank P.L.C.
The British Bank of the Middle East
British Credit Trust Ltd.
The British Linen Bank Ltd.
British Railways Savings Company Ltd.
Brown, Shipley & Co. Ltd.
Bunge Finance Ltd.
Burns-Anderson Trust Company Ltd.
Business Mortgages Trust P.L.C.

C.L.-Alexanders Discount P.L.C.
Canadian Laurentian Bank Ltd.
James Capel Bankers Ltd.
Cater Allen Ltd.
Central Capital Mortgage Corporation Ltd.
Chancery Securities P.L.C.
The Charities Aid Foundation Money Management Company Ltd.
Charter Consolidated Financial Services Ltd.
Chartered Trust P.L.C.
Charterhouse Bank Ltd.
Chase Investment Bank Ltd.
Chesterfield Street Trust Ltd.
Citibank Trust Ltd.
Citicorp Investment Bank Ltd.
City Merchants Bank Ltd.
City Trust Ltd.
Clive Discount Company Ltd.
Close Brothers Ltd.
Clydesdale Bank P.L.C.
Clydesdale Bank Finance Corporation Ltd.
Combined Capital Ltd.
The Commerical Bank of the Near East P.L.C.
Consolidated Credits Bank Ltd.
Co-operative Bank P.L.C.
Coutts & Co.
Coutts Finance Co.
Craneheath Securities Ltd.
Credito Italiano International Ltd.
Credit Suisse First Boston Ltd.
Cyprus Finance Corporation (London) Ltd.

Daiwa Europe Bank P.L.C.
Dalbeattie Finance Co. Ltd.
Darlington Merchant Credits Ltd.
Dartington & Co. Ltd.
Deacon Hoare & Co. Ltd.
Den norske Creditbank P.L.C.
The Dorset, Somerset & Wilts Investment Society Ltd.
Dryfield Finance Ltd.
Dunbar Bank P.L.C.
Duncan Lawrie Ltd.

E.B.C. Amro Bank Ltd.
E.T. Trust Ltd.
Eagil Trust Co. Ltd.
East Anglican Securities Trust Ltd.
East Midlands Finance Co. Ltd.
Eccles Savings and Loans Ltd.
Edington P.L.C.
Enskilda Securities-Skandinaviska Enskilda Ltd.
Equatorial Bank P.L.C.
Euro-Latinamerican Bank P.L.C.
European Brazilian Bank P.L.C.
Everett Chettle Associates
Exeter Trust Ltd.

F.I.B.I. Bank (U.K.) Ltd.

Fairmount Trust Ltd.
Family Finance Ltd.
Federated Trust Corporation Ltd.
FennoScandia Bank Ltd.
Financial & General Bank P.L.C.
James Finlay Bank Ltd.
First Indemnity Credit Ltd.
First Interstate Capital Markets Ltd.
First National Bank P.L.C.
First National Commerical Bank P.L.C.
Robert Fleming & Co. Ltd.
Ford Financial Trust Ltd.
Ford Motor Credit Co. Ltd.
Foreign & Colonial Management Ltd.
Forward Trust Ltd.
Robert Fraser & Partners Ltd.
Frizzell Banking Services Ltd.

Gartmore Money Management Ltd.
Gerrard & National Ltd.
Girobank P.L.C.
Goldman Sachs Ltd.
Goode Durrant Trust P.L.C.
Granville Trust Ltd.
Gresham Trust P.L.C.
Greyhound Guaranty Ltd.
Grindlays Bank Ltd.
Guinness Mahon & Co Ltd.
Gulf Guarantee Trust Ltd.

H.F.C. Bank P.L.C.
Habibsons Bank Ltd.
Hambros Bank Ltd.
Hampshire Trust P.L.C.
The Hardware Federation Finance Co. Ltd.
Harrods Bank Ltd.
Harton Securities Ltd.
Havana International Bank Ltd.
The Heritable & General Investment Bank P.L.C.
Hill Samuel & Co. Ltd.
Hill Samuel Personal Finance Ltd.
C. Hoare & Co.
Julian Hodge Bank Ltd.
Holdenhurst Securities P.L.C.
Humberclyde Finance Group Ltd.
Hungarian International Bank Ltd.

3i P.L.C.
3i Group P.L.C.
I.B.J. International Ltd.
Industrial Funding Trust Ltd.
International Commercial Bank P.L.C.
International Mexican Bank Ltd.
International Westminster Bank P.L.C.
Iran Overseas Investment Bank Ltd.
Itab Bank Ltd.
Italian International Bank P.L.C.

Jabac Finances Ltd.
Japan International Bank Ltd.
Jordan International Bank P.L.C.
Leopold Joseph & Sons Ltd.

King & Shaxson Ltd.
Kleinwort Benson Ltd.

Lazard Brothers & Co. Ltd.
Libra Bank P.L.C.
Little Lakes Finance Ltd.
Lloyds Bank P.L.C.
Lloyds Bank (B.L.S.A.) Ltd.
Lloyds Bank (France) Ltd.
Lloyds Bowmaker Ltd.
Lloyds Merchant Bank Ltd.
Lombard Bank Ltd.
Lombard & Ulster Ltd.
Lombard North Central P.L.C.
London Arab Investment Bank Ltd.
London & Continental Bankers Ltd.
London Law Securities Ltd.

London Scottish Bank P.L.C.
Lordsvale Finance P.L.C.

M.L.A. Bank Ltd.
McDonnell Douglas Bank Ltd.
McNeill Pearson Ltd.
Manchester Exchange and Investment Bank Ltd.
W.M. Mann & Co. (Investments) Ltd.
Manufacturers Hanover Ltd.
The Mardun Investment Co. Ltd.
Marks and Spencer Financial Services Ltd.
Mase Westpac Ltd.
Matheson Bank Ltd.
Medens Trust Ltd.
Meghraj Bank Ltd.
Mercantile Credit Company Ltd.
Mercury Provident P.L.C.
Merrill Lynch International Bank Ltd.
The Methodist Chapel Aid Association Ltd.
Midland Bank P.L.C.
Midland Bank Finance Corporation Ltd.
Midland Bank Trust Company Ltd.
Minories Finance Ltd.
Minster Trust Ltd.
Moneycare Ltd.
Samuel Montagu & Co. Ltd.
Moorgate Mercantile Holdings P.L.C.
Morgan Grenfell & Co. Ltd.
Moscow Narodny Bank Ltd.
Mount Banking Corporation Ltd.
Mutual Trust and Savings Ltd.
Mynshul Trust Ltd.

N.I.I.B. Group Ltd.
National Guardian Finance Corporation Ltd.
National Westminster Bank P.L.C.
NatWest Investment Bank Ltd.
The Nikko Bank (U.K.) P.L.C.
Noble Grossart Ltd.
Nomura Bank International P.L.C.
Northern Bank Ltd.
Northern Bank Executor & Trustee Company Ltd.
Norwich General Trust Ltd.
North West Securities Ltd.

Omega Trust Co. Ltd.
Orion Royal Bank Ltd.

P.K. English Trust Company Ltd.
PaineWebber International Bank Ltd.
Panmure Gordon Bankers Ltd.
The People's Trust & Savings Ltd.
Philadelphia National Ltd.
Phillips & Drew Trust Ltd.
Pointon York Ltd.
Postipankki (U.K.) Ltd.
Prestwick Investment Trust P.L.C.
Privatbanken Ltd.
Provincial Bank Ltd.

Quin Cope Ltd.

Ralli Investment Company Ltd.
R. Raphael & Sons P.L.C.
Rathbone Bros & Co.
Rea Brothers Ltd.
Reliance Bank Ltd.
Riggs A. P. Bank Ltd.
N. M. Rothschild & Sons Ltd.
Roxburghe Guarantee Corporation Ltd.
The Royal Bank of Scotland P.L.C.
Royal Trust Bank
RoyScot Trust P.L.C.

S.B.C.I. Swiss Bank Corporation Investment
    Banking Ltd.
S.D.S. Bank Ltd.
S.F.E. Bank Ltd.
S.P. Finance Ltd.
Sangster Trust Corporation

Saudi International Bank (Al-Bank Al-Saudi Al-Alami Ltd.)
Scandinavian Bank Group P.L.C.
Schroder Leasing Ltd.
J. Henry Schroder Wagg & Co. Ltd.
Scotiabank (U.K.) Ltd.
Scottish Amicable Money Managers Ltd.
Seccombe Marshall & Campion P.L.C.
Secure Homes Ltd.
Security Pacific Trust Ltd.
Shire Trust Ltd.
Singer & Friedlander Ltd.
Smith & Williamson Securities
Société Générale Merchant Bank P.L.C.
Southsea Mortgage & Investment Co. Ltd.
Spry Finance Ltd.
Standard Chartered Bank
Standard Chartered Bank Africa P.L.C.
Standard Chartered Merchant Bank Ltd.
Standard Property Investment P.L.C.
Sterling Bank & Trust Ltd.
Svenska International P.L.C.

T.S.B. England & Wales P.L.C.
T.S.B. Northern Ireland P.L.C.
T.S.B. Scotland P.L.C.

Thorncliffe Finance Ltd.
Treloan Ltd.
Trucanda Trusts Ltd.
Tyndall & Co. Ltd.

U.B.A.F. Bank Ltd.
U.C.B. Bank P.L.C.

Ulster Bank Ltd.
Ulster Bank Trust Company
Union Discount Company Ltd.
The United Bank of Kuwait P.L.C.
Union Dominions Trust Ltd.
Unity Trust Bank P.L.C.

Wagon Finance Ltd.
Wallace, Smith Trust Co. Ltd.
S. G. Warburg & Co. Ltd.
Welbeck Finance P.L.C.
Western Trust & Savings Ltd.
Whiteaway Laidlaw Bank Ltd.
Wimbledon & South West Finance Co. Ltd.
Wintrust Securities Ltd.

Yamaichi Bank (U.K.) P.L.C.
Yorkshire Bank P.L.C.
H.F. Young & Co. Ltd.

INCORPORATED OUTSIDE THE U.K.

(Including partnerships or other unincorporated associations formed under the law of any member State of the European Community other than the U.K.)

African Continental Bank Ltd.
Algemene Bank Nederland N.V.
Allied Bank of Pakistan Ltd.
Allied Banking Corporation
Allied Irish Finance Co. Ltd.
Allied Irish Banks P.L.C.
Allied Irish Investment Bank P.L.C.
Al Saudi Banque S.A.
American Express Bank Ltd.
Amsterdam-Rotterdam Bank N.V.
Arab African International Bank
Arab Bank Ltd.
Arab Banking Corporation B.S.C.
Australia & New Zealand Banking Group Ltd.

Badische Kommunale Landesbank Girozentrale
Banca Commerciale Italiana
Banca della Svizzera Italiana
Banca Nazionale dell'Agricoltura SpA
Banca Nazionale del Lavoro
Banca Serfin S.N.C.
Banco Central, S.A.
Banco de Bilbao, S.A.
Banco de la Nación Argentina
Banco de Sabadell
Banco de Santander, S.A.
Banco de Vizcaya, S.A.
Banco di Napoli
Banco di Roma SpA
Banco di Santo Spirito
Banco di Sicilia
Banco do Brasil S.A.
Banco do Estado de São Paulo S.A.
Banco Espirito Santo e Commercial de Lisboa
Banco Exterior—U.K. S.A.
Banco Mercantil de São Paulo S.A.
Banco Nacional de México S.N.C.
Banco Português do Atlântico
Banco Real S.A.
Banco Totta & Açores E.P.
Bancomer S.N.C.
Bangkok Bank Ltd.
Bank Julius Baer & Co. Ltd.
Bank Bumiputra Malaysia Berhad
Bank für Gemeinwirtschaft A.G.

Bank Handlowy w Warszawie S.A.
Bank Hapoalim B.M.
Bank Mees & Hope N.V.
Bank Mellat
Bank Melli Iran
Bank Negara Indonesia 1946
Bank of America N.T. & S.A.
Bank of Baroda
The Bank of California N.A.
Bank of Ceylon
Bank of China
Bank of Credit and Commerce International S.A.
Bank of India
The Bank of Ireland
Bank of Montreal
Bank of New England N.A.
The Bank of New York
Bank of New Zealand
The Bank of Nova Scotia
Bank of Oman Ltd.
Bank of Seoul
The Bank of Tokyo Ltd.
The Bank of Yokohama Ltd.
Bank Saderat Iran
Bank Sepah-Iran
Bank Tejarat
Bankers Trust Company
Banque Belgo-Zairoise S.A.
Banque Bruxelles Lambert S.A.
Banque du Liban et d'Outre-Mer S.A.L.
Banque Francaise du Commerce Extérieur
Bank Indosuez
Banque Internationale à Luxembourg S.A.
Banque Internationale pour L'Afrique Occidentale S.A.
Banque Nationale de Paris
Banque Paribas
Banque Worms
Barbados National Bank
Bayerische Hypotheken-und Wechsel-Bank A.G.
Bayerische Landesbank Girozentrale
Bayerische Vereinsbank
Beirut Riyad Bank S.A.L.
Bergen Bank A/S.
Berliner Bank A.G.

Berliner Handels-und Frankfurter Bank
Byblos Bank S.A.L.

C.I.C.-Union Européenne, International et Cie
Caisse Nationale de Crédit Agricole
Canadian Imperial Bank of Commerce
Canara Bank
Cassa di Risparmio delle Provincie Lombarde
The Chase Manhattan Bank N.A.
Chemical Bank
Cho Hung Bank
Christiania Bank og Kreditkasse
The Chuo Trust & Banking Co. Ltd.
Citibank N.A.
Commercial Bank of Korea Ltd.
Commerzbank A.G.
Commonwealth Bank of Australia
Confederacion Española de Cajas de Ahorros
Continental Illinois National Bank and Trust Company of Chicago
Copenhagen Handelsbank A/S
Crédit Commercial de France
Crédit du Nord
Crédit Lyonnais
Crédit Lyonnais Bank Nederland N.V.
Crédit Suisse
Creditanstalt-Bankverein
Credito Italiano
Cyprus Credit Bank Ltd.
The Cyprus Popular Bank

The Dai-Ichi Kangyo Bank Ltd.
The Daiwa Bank Ltd.
Den Danske Bank af 1871 Aktieselskab
Deutsche Bank A.G.
Deutsche Genossenschaftsbank
The Development Bank of Singapore Ltd.
Discount Bank and Trust Company
Dresdner Bank A.G.

Fidelity Bank N.A.
First Bank National Association
First Bank of Nigeria Ltd.
First City National Bank of Houston
First Commercial Bank
First Interstate Bank of California
The First National Bank of Boston
The First National Bank of Chicago
First Republic Bank Dallas N.A.
First Wisconsin National Bank of Milwaukee
Fleet National Bank
French Bank of Southern Africa Ltd.
The Fuji Bank Ltd.

Generale Bank
Ghana Commercial Bank
Girozentrale und Bank der österreichischen Sparkassen A.G.
Götabanken
Gulf International Bank B.S.C.

Habib Bank A.G. Zurich
Habib Bank Ltd.
Hanil Bank
Harris Trust and Savings Bank
Hessische Landesbank-Girozentrale
The Hokkaido Takushoku Bank Ltd.
The Hongkong and Shanghai Banking Corporation

The Industrial Bank of Japan Ltd.
The Investment Bank of Ireland Ltd.
Irving Trust Company
Istituto Bancario San Paolo di Torino

Jyske Bank

Kansallis-Osake-Pankki
Keesler Federal Credit Union
Korea Exchange Bank
Korea First Bank
Kredietbank N.V.

The Kyowa Bank Ltd.

Landesbank Stuttgart Girozentrale
The Long-Term Credit Bank of Japan Ltd.

Malayan Banking Berhad
Manufacturers Hanover Trust Company
Mellon Bank N.A.
Middle East Bank Ltd.
The Mitsubishi Bank Ltd.
The Mitsubishi Trust and Banking Corporation
The Mitsui Bank Ltd.
The Mitsui Trust & Banking Co. Ltd.
Morgan Guaranty Trust Company of New York
Multibanco Comermex S.N.C.
Muslim Commercial Bank Ltd.

N.C.N.B. National Bank of North Carolina
National Australia Bank Ltd.
National Bank of Abu Dhabi
National Bank of Canada
National Bank of Detroit
The National Bank of Dubai Ltd.
National Bank of Egypt
National Bank of Greece S.A.
The National Bank of Kuwait S.A.K.
The National Bank of New Zealand Ltd.
National Bank of Nigeria Ltd.
The National Commercial Bank
National Bank of Pakistan
Nedbank Ltd.
Nederlandsche Middenstandsbank N.V.
New Nigeria Bank Ltd.
The Nippon Credit Bank Ltd.
Norddeutsche Landesbank Girozentrale
The Northern Trust Company

Österreichische Länderbank A.G.
Oversea-Chinese Banking Corporation Ltd.
Overseas Trust Bank Ltd.
Overseas Union Bank Ltd.

Philadelphia National Bank
Philippine National Bank

Qatar National Bank S.A.Q.

Rabobank Nederland (Coöperatieve Centrale Raiffeisen-Boerenleenbank B.A.)
Rafidain Bank
Republic National Bank of New York
Reserve Bank of Australia
The Riggs National Bank of Washington D.C.
Riyad Bank
The Royal Bank of Canada
The Rural and Industries Bank of Western Australia

The Saitama Bank Ltd.
The Sanwa Bank Ltd.
Saudi American Bank
Seattle—First National Bank
Security Pacific National Bank
Shanghai Commercial Bank Ltd.
The Siam Commercial Bank Ltd.
Skandinaviska Enskilda Banken
Société Générale
Sonali Bank
State Bank of India
State Bank of New South Wales
State Bank of South Australia
State Bank of Victoria
State Street Bank and Trust Company
The Sumitomo Bank Ltd.
The Sumitomo Trust & Banking Co. Ltd.
Svenska Handelsbanken
Swiss Bank Corporation
Swiss Cantobank (International)
Swiss Volksbank
Sydicate Bank

T.C. Ziraat Bankasi

T.D.B. American Express Bank
The Taiyo Kobe Bank Ltd.
The Thai Farmers Bank Ltd.
The Tokai Bank P.L.C.
The Toronto-Dominion Bank
The Toyo Trust & Banking Company Ltd.
The Trust Bank of Africa Ltd.
Turkish Bank Ltd.
Türkiye İş Bankasi A.S.

Uco Bank
Ulster Investment Bank Ltd.
Union Bank of Finland Ltd.
Union Bank of Nigeria Ltd.
Union Bank of Norway

Union Bank of Switzerland
United Bank Ltd.
United Mizrahi Bank Ltd.
United Overseas Bank (Banque Unie pour les Pays d'Outre Mer)
United Overseas Bank Ltd.

Volkskas Ltd.

Westdeutsche Landesbank Girozentrale
Westpac Banking Corporation

The Yasuda Trust & Banking Co. Ltd.

Zambia National Commerical Bank Ltd.
Zivnostenská Banka National Corporation

BANKING HOURS

England and Wales.—Mon.–Fri. 9.30–3.30*; *City of London town clearers*, 9.30–3.00; Saturdays (selected branches open); Barclays, 9.30–12.00; Lloyds, 9.30–12.30 or 10.00–3.00; Midland and National Westminster, 9.30–12.30; T.S.B., 9.30–4.00.

Scotland.—Banking hours in Scotland are: Mon.–Wed., 9.30–12.30; 1.30–3.30; Thursday, 9.30–12.30; 1.30–3.30; 4.30–6 p.m.; Fri. 9.30–3.30; Saturday, *closed*.

Northern Ireland.—Mon.–Fri. 10.00–3.30; 9.30 opening two mornings per week. Open until 5.00 one summer evening per week.

* Still the minimum banking hours but many banks are experimenting with longer hours (usually 9.15–4.30). The Co-operative Bank remains open until 5.00.

FINANCIAL FIGURES, ETC. FOR THE "BIG FOUR" BANKS, 1987

Bank Group	Profit/loss before taxation £m	Profit/loss after taxation £m	Total Asssets £m	Number of U.K. branches
Barclays	339 (895)	191 (618)	87,786 (78,952)	3,000
Lloyds	—248 (700)	—224 (470)	44,910 (47,829)	2,189
Midland....................	—506 (434)	—447 (262)	48,450 (53,169)	2,080
National Westminster	704 (1,011)	442 (614)	87,027 (83,325)	3,200

1986 figures in parentheses.

GIROBANK

Girobank provides a broad range of corporate and personal banking facilities. It operates through 20,0000 U.K. post offices. Girobank is expected to be privatized at the end of 1988.

OPERATING STATISTICS	1986–87	1987–88
Number of accounts at year end, thousands	2,005	2,134
Pre-tax profit, £m	23·1	23·5

BANKING SERVICES

Association for Payment Clearing Services (APACS)
Mercury House, Triton Court, 14 Finsbury Square, EC2A 1BR.

APACS was set up by the banks in 1985 to manage the payment clearing systems and oversee money transmission in the U.K.

Three operational clearing companies operate under the aegis of APACS. They are:

B.A.C.S. LTD., De Havilland Road, Edgware, Middx. HA8 5QA.—Provides an automated service for inter-bank clearing of payment and collection transactions in the U.K. (e.g. standing orders, direct debits). *Chief Exec.*, G. R. Simpson.

CHEQUE AND CREDIT CLEARING CO. LTD., Mercury House, Triton Court, 14 Finsbury Square, EC2A 1BR.—Operates bulk clearing systems for inter-bank cheques and paper credit items. *Chief Inspector*, E. W. Stubbs.

C.H.A.P.S. AND TOWN CLEARING CO. LTD., Mercury House, Triton Court, 14 Finsbury Square, EC2A 1BR.—Provides same-day clearing for high value cheques and electronic funds transfer. *Chief Inspector*, E. W. Stubbs.

In addition, EftPos U.K. Ltd. is a company within the APACS structure set up to develop a national scheme for electronic funds transfer at the point of sale. APACS also oversees the London Dollar Clearing, the London Currency Settlement Scheme and the Cheque Card and eurocheque schemes in the U.K.

Membership of APACS and the operational clearing companies is open to any appropriately regulated institution providing payment services and meeting the relevant membership criteria.
Chief Executive, R. I. L. Allen.

Committee of London and Scottish Bankers
10 Lombard Street, EC3V 9AP
[01-283 8866]

The Committee is the successor to the Committee of London Clearing Bankers. It consists of the Chairmen of Barclays, Lloyds, Midland, National Westminster, Standard Chartered, Bank of Scotland, Royal Bank of Scotland and the T.S.B. Group, and meets regularly to discuss matters of common interest. It is the body through which the Bank of England communicates official policy to the banks and through which the banks may present their views to the Bank of England and the Treasury.
Secretary-General, The Hon. R. C. R. Hoyer Millar.

FINANCIAL OMBUDSMEN

The following Ombudsmen schemes are non-statutory.

The Office of the Banking Ombudsman
Citadel House, 5–11 Fetter Lane, EC4A 1BR
[01-583 1395]

The purpose of the Banking Ombudsman Scheme is to investigate complaints from bank customers dissatisfied with the banking services of member banks. The Scheme was set up in 1985, becoming operational on Jan. 1, 1986, by 19 banks and it is funded by contributions from the member banks (19 banks and 17 designated associates). There is a seven-member Council who appoint the Ombudsman, give guidance in the performance of his duties, monitor his terms of reference, prepare the budget and approve the annual report. The Ombudsman and his staff are responsible to the Council.
The Banking Ombudsman, I. Edwards-Jones, Q.C.

The Office of the Building Societies Ombudsman
Grosvenor Gardens House, 35–37 Grosvenor Gardens, SW1X 7AW
[01-931 0044]

The purpose of the Building Societies Ombudsman Scheme, which came into operation on July 1, 1987, is to investigate complaints from building society customers about the services of building societies belonging to the Scheme. All building societies belong to the Scheme and it is funded by contributions from the members. The Ombudsman is appointed by and responsible to an independent Ombudsman Council.
The Building Society Ombudsman, S. Edell.

The Insurance Ombudsman Bureau
31 Southampton Row, WC1B 5HJ
[01-242 8613]

The purpose of the Insurance Ombudsman Scheme is to settle disputes between insurance policyholders and member insurance companies. The Scheme came into operation in March 1981 and is funded by contributions from the member companies. Over 200 companies are members of the Scheme. An independent Council appoints and supervises the work of the Ombudsman.

The Insurance Ombudsman Bureau also runs the Unit Trusts Ombudsman Scheme, the purpose of which is to settle disputes between personal unit trust holders and member unit trust management companies. The first Unit Trusts Ombudsman took up his position in October 1988.
The Insurance Ombudsman, J. Haswell, O.B.E. (until end Jan. 1989).
The Unit Trusts Ombudsman, Lt.-Col. C. Rice.

THE NATIONAL DEBT

Net central government borrowing each year represents an addition to the National Debt. At the end of March 1987 the National Debt amounted to some £186,000 million of which about £6,000 million was in currencies other than sterling. Of the £180,000 million sterling debt, £137,000 million consisted of gilt-edged stock; of this, 30 per cent had a maturity of up to five years, 41 per cent a maturity of over five years and up to 15 years and 29 per cent a maturity of over 15 years or undated. The remaining sterling debt was made up mainly of national savings (£27,000 million), certificates of tax deposits, Treasury bills, and Ways and Means advances (very short-term internal government borrowing).

NATIONAL SAVINGS

PREMIUM BONDS

Premium Bonds are a Government security which were first introduced on November 1, 1956. Premium Bonds enable savers to enter a regular draw for tax-free prizes, whilst retaining the right to get their money back. A sum equivalent to interest on each bond is put into a prize fund and distributed by weekly and monthly prize draws. (The rate of interest is 6·5 per cent. a year from July 1, 1988.) The prizes are drawn by ERNIE (electronic random number indicator equipment) and are free of all U.K. income tax and capital gains tax.

Bonds are in units of £1, with a minimum purchase of £10; above this, purchases must be in multiples of £5, up to a maximum holding limit of £10,000 per person. Bonds can only be held in the name of an individual and not by organizations.

Bonds become eligible for prizes once they have been held for three clear calendar months following the month of purchase. Each £1 unit can win only one prize per draw, but it will be awarded the highest for which it is drawn. Bonds remain eligible for prizes until they are repaid. When a holder dies, bonds remain eligible for prizes up to and including the twelfth monthly draw after the month in which the holder dies.

By April 1988 bonds to the value of £4,207 million had been sold. Of these £2,101 million had been cashed, leaving £2,106 million still invested. By the April 1988 prize draw, 30 million prizes totalling £1,749 million had been distributed since the first prize draw in June 1957.

INCOME BONDS

National Savings Income Bonds were introduced in 1982. They are particularly suitable for those who want to receive regular monthly payments of interest while preserving the full cash value of their capital. The Bonds are sold in multiples of £1,000. The minimum holding is £2,000 and the maximum £100,000.

Interest is calculated on a day-to-day basis and paid monthly. Interest is taxable, but is paid without deduction of tax at source. The Bonds have a guaranteed life of ten years, but may be repaid at par before maturity on giving three months' notice. If repayment of a bond is made within the first year of purchase, interest from the date of purchase to the date of repayment is earned at half rate. If the sole or sole surviving holder dies, however, no formal period of notice is required and there is no loss of interest for repayment made within the first year.

Net investment in National Savings Income Bonds was £7,081,814,000 at the end of April 1988.

INDEXED INCOME BONDS

Indexed Income Bonds were withdrawn from sale on August 28, 1987. Existing holders will continue to receive monthly income in accordance with the prospectus.

ORDINARY AND INVESTMENT ACCOUNTS

National Savings Bank.—On May 31, 1988, there were about 15,619,000 active accounts with the sum of approximately £1,670,000,000 due to depositors in Ordinary accounts and about 4,103,000 active accounts with the sum of approximately £7,313,000,000 due to depositors in Investment accounts.

Interest is earned at 5 per cent per year on each Ordinary account for every complete calendar month in which the balance is £500 or more provided the account is kept open for the whole of 1988 (December 31, 1987—January 1, 1989); and at 2·5 per cent per year for all other Ordinary accounts. The minimum deposit is £1; maximum balance £10,000 plus interest credited. On May 31, 1988 the average amount held in Ordinary accounts was approximately £107.

The Investment account pays a higher rate of interest (the current rate can be ascertained at any Savings Bank Post Office). The minimum deposit is £5; maximum balance £100,000 plus interest credited. On May 31, 1988 the average amount held in Investment accounts was approximately £1,782.

DEPOSIT BONDS

National Savings Deposit Bonds were introduced on October 17, 1983. They offer a premium rate of interest on lump sum savings and are best suited for money not needed in less than a year. The minimum purchase is £100, larger purchases can be made in multiples of £50 and the maximum holding is £100,000 plus interest credited.

Interest is taxable, but tax is not deducted at source. The interest rate is variable but is kept competitive. Interest is calculated on a daily basis and credited on the anniversary of purchase. Minimum amount of repayment is £50 and three months notice is required. Any amount repaid within a year of purchase earns interest at half the published rate. No interest is lost once a Bond has been held for a full year. Net investment in National Savings Deposit Bonds was £839,900,000 at May 31, 1988.

YEARLY PLAN

The National Savings "Yearly Plan" was introduced on July 2, 1984. It offers a guaranteed tax-free return. Applicants agree to make 12 monthly payments, leading to the issue of a Yearly Plan Certificate. The maximum guaranteed rate of interest is earned if the Certificate is held for a full four years. Applications may be made by any individuals aged 7 or over; in the name of children under 7; and by not more than two trustees for a sole beneficiary.

Payments must be made on the same date every month by standing order from a bank or other acceptable account. Only one payment may be made in any one month and must be in multiples of £5. Minimum monthly contribution is £20, maximum £200. Net investment in National Savings Yearly Plan was £430,596,657 at May 31, 1988.

On receipt of an application the applicant is sent an Offer Letter telling him the interest rates he will receive on his agreement if he accepts. The Certificate is sent at the end of the first year. It shows the total value of the payments made and the value of the Certificate if held for four years. The Certificate earns interest compounded annually on the anniversaries of the Certificate Date. Maximum interest is earned if the Certificate is held for the full four years. At the end of each year, providing at least seven payments have been made during that year, the applicant is given the option to take up a subsequent agreement, leading to the issue of a further Certificate.

GILTS ON THE NATIONAL SAVINGS STOCK REGISTER

Government Stock or "Gilts" are stock Exchange Securities issued by the Government. They usually have a life of between 5 and 20 years and most pay a guaranteed fixed rate of interest twice a year throughout this period. When they reach the end of this period they are "redeemed" (which means repaid) at their face value. There are also a few "undated" Gilts with no set date for redemption and some Index-

Linked Gilts, which have both the interest and the value of the capital on redemption increased in line with inflation.

The National Savings Stock Register offers investors an alternative to the main Bank of England Register and is run by National Savings from their Blackpool office. It enables customers to buy and sell Gilts by post. It is now possible to have most new issues of Gilts registered on the National Savings Stock Register. Interest on Gilts held on the National Savings Stock Register, although taxable, is paid in full without deduction of tax at source.

NATIONAL SAVINGS CERTIFICATES

The amount, including accrued interest, index-linked increase or bonus remaining to the credit of investors in National Savings Certificates on March 31, 1988 was approximately £16,615·9m. In 1987–88, approx. £653·5m was subscribed and £1,659·1m (excluding interest, index-linked increase or bonus) was repaid. Interest, index-linked increase, bonus or other sum payable is free of United Kingdom income tax (including investment income surcharge) and capital gains tax. The 1st–14th and 16th issues continue to attract interest.

Issue and Maximum Holding (in units)	Unit Cost £	Value after		Interest Per Unit
		Years	£ p	
Index-Linked Retirement Issue (June 2, 1975–Nov. 15, 1980) (120)	10			Unlike conventional issues where interest is accrued periodically the repayment value of Index-Linked Certificates, subject to their being held a year, is related to the movement of the U.K. General Index of Retail Prices.** N.B. Certificates of the Retirement Issue were on sale only to men aged 65 years and over and women aged 60 years and over, but may now be transferred to anyone.
Eighteenth . . . . (Jan. 29, 1979–Feb. 2, 1980) (150)	10	5	15·00	After 1 year, 50p is added, during 2nd year, 25p per completed 4 months, during 3rd year, 33p per completed 4 months, during 4th year, 42p per completed 4 months, during 5th year, 50p per completed 4 months.†
Nineteenth . . . . (Feb. 4, 1980–May 9, 1981) (500)	10	5	16·35	After 1 year 50p is added, during 2nd year 30p per completed 4 months, during 3rd year 35p per completed 4 months, during 4th year 55p per completed 4 months and during 5th year 75p per completed 4 months.†
2nd Index-Linked Issue (Nov. 17, 1980–June 26, 1985) (1,000)	10			Like Retirement Issue, the repayment value of 2nd Index-Linked Issue Certificates, subject to their being held a year, is related to the movement of the U.K. General Index of Retail Prices.** N.B. Certificates of the 2nd Index-Linked Issue were made available to anyone, regardless of age, from September 7, 1981.
Twenty-First . . . . Issue (May 11, 1981–Nov. 7, 1981) (500)	10	5	15·40	After 1 year, 75p is added, during 2nd year, 28p per completed 4 months, during 3rd year, 33p per completed 4 months, during 4th year, 40p per completed 4 months and during 5th year 54p per completed 4 months.†
Twenty-Third . . . . . . (Nov. 9, 1981– March 10, 1982) (200)	25	5	41·20	After 1 year, £2·25 is added, during 2nd year, 87p per completed 4 months, during 3rd year, £1·02 per completed 4 months, during 4th year, £1·23 per completed 4 months and during 5th year £1·53 per completed 4 months.†
Twenty-Fourth . . . . . (April 19, 1982–Nov. 4, 1982) (200)	25	5	38·32	After 1 year, £1·80 is added, during 2nd year, 53p per completed 3 months, during 3rd year, 63p per completed 3 months, during 4th year, 77p per completed 3 months and during 5th year 95p per completed 3 months.†
Twenty-Fifth . . . . (Nov. 17, 1982–Aug. 13, 1983) (200)	25	5	35·90	After 1 year, £1·50 is added, during 2nd year, 43p per completed 3 months, during 3rd year, 51p per completed 3 months, during 4th year, 62p per completed 3 months and during 5th year 79p per completed 3 months.*
Twenty-Sixth . . . . (Aug. 15, 1983–Mar. 19, 1984) (200)	25	5	37·17	After 1 year, £1·53 is added, during 2nd year, 47p per completed 3 months, during 3rd year, 58p per completed 3 months, during 4th year, 72p per completed 3 months and during 5th year 89p per completed 3 months.*
Twenty-Seventh . . . . (April 5, 1984–Aug. 7, 1984) (200)	25	5	35·48	After 1 year, £1·32 is added, during 2nd year, 41p per completed 3 months, during 3rd year, 50p per completed 3 months, during 4th year, 62p per completed 3 months and during 5th year 76p per completed 3 months.*

Issue and Maximum Holding (in units)	Unit Cost £	Value after		Interest Per Unit
		Years	£ p	
Twenty-Eighth ..... (Aug. 8, 1984–Sept. 11, 1984) (200)	25	5	38·47	After 1 year, £1·63 is added, during 2nd year, 51p per completed 3 months, during 3rd year, 64p per completed 3 months, during 4th year, 80p per completed 3 months and during 5th year £1·01 per completed 3 months.*
Twenty-Ninth ...... (Oct. 15, 1984–Feb. 12, 1985) (200)	25	5	36·74	After 1 year, £1·50 is added, during 2nd year, 46p per completed 3 months, during 3rd year, 56p per completed 3 months, during 4th year, 69p per completed 3 months and during 5th year 85p per completed 3 months.*
Thirtieth .... (Feb. 13, 1985–Sept. 9, 1985) (200)	25	5	38·21	After 1 year, £1·69 is added, during 2nd year, 50p per completed 3 months, during 3rd year, 62p per completed 3 months, during 4th year, 78p per completed 3 months and during 5th year 98p per completed 3 months.*
3rd Index-Linked Issue (July 1, 1985– July 31, 1986) (200)	25			Like 2nd Issue Index-Linked Certificates, the repayment value of 3rd Issue Index-Linked Certificates, subject to their being held for one year, is related to the movement of the U.K. General Index of Retail Prices.** In addition, there is guaranteed extra interest of 2·5 per cent for the 1st year, 2·75 per cent for the 2nd year, 3·25 per cent for the 3rd year, 4·0 per cent for the 4th year and 5·25 per cent for the 5th year. This interest is worth 3·54 per cent compound over a full five years.
Thirty-First .... (Sept. 26, 1985–Nov. 11, 1986) (200)	25	5	36·48	After 1 year, £1·44 is added, during 2nd year, 44p per completed 3 months, during 3rd year, 55p per completed 3 months, during 4th year, 68p per completed 3 months and during 5th year, 84p per completed 3 months.*
4th Index-Linked Issue (Aug. 1, 1986–) (200)	25			Like 3rd Issue Index-Linked Certificates, the repayment value of 4th Issue Index-Linked Certificates, subject to their being held for one year, is related to the movement of the U.K. General Index of Retail Prices.** In addition, there is guaranteed extra interest of 3·0 per cent for the 1st year, 3·25 per cent for the 2nd year, 3·5 per cent for the 3rd year, 4·5 per cent for the 4th year, and 6·0 per cent for the 5th year. This interest is worth 4·04 per cent compound over a full five years.
Thirty-Second ...... (Nov. 12, 1986– March 10, 1987) (200)	25	5	38·03	After 1 year, £1·63 is added, during 2nd year, 50p per completed 3 months, during 3rd year, 62p per completed 3 months, during 4th year, 77p per completed 3 months and during 5th year, 96p per completed 3 months.*
Thirty-Third .... (May 1, 1987–) (40, plus special facilities to hold up to a further 200)	25	5	35·06	After 1 year, the repayment value increases by 5·5 per cent for ordinarily held 33rd Issue. However, 33rd Reinvestment Certificates earn interest during the 1st year at the rate of 5·5 per cent per annum for each 3 month period. Thereafter all 33rd Issue earn 5·75 per cent after 2 years, 6·0 per cent after 3 years, 6·5 per cent after 4 years and 7·0 per cent after 5 years.*

* As announced by the Treasury.

† From June 1982, savings certificates of the 7th to 14th, 16th, 18th, 19th, 21st, 23rd, 24th and 25th Issues will be extended on General Extension Rates as they reach the end of their existing extension periods. The percentage interest rate is determined by the Treasury and any change in this General Extension Rate will be applicable from the 1st of the month following its announcement.

Under the new system, a certificate earns interest for each complete period of three months beyond the expiry of the previous extension terms. Within each three month period interest is calculated separately for each month at the rate applicable from the beginning of that month. The interest for each month is one twelfth of the annual rate (i.e. it does not vary with the number of days in the month) and is capitalised annually on the anniversary of the date of purchase. The current rate of interest under the General Extension Rate is displayed on special posters at most post offices.

** Index-linked certificates are eligible for an annual supplement of 3 per cent for the year to August 1, 1988. There have been five previous annual supplements of 2·4 per cent for 1982–83 and 1983–84 and 3 per cent for 1984–85, 1985–86 and 1986–87. At the 5th anniversary there is a bonus of 4 per cent of the purchase price and at the 10th anniversary there is a second bonus of 4 per cent of the full 5th anniversary value. All supplements and bonuses are fully index-linked once earned.

TAXATION

INCOME TAX

Income tax is charged on the total income of individuals for a year of assessment commencing on April 6 and ending on the following April 5. The rates of tax and the calculation of liability will frequently differ, sometimes substantially, as between one year of assessment and another. The following information is confined to the year of assessment 1988–89, ending on April 5, 1989.

Liability is determined by establishing the taxable income for a year of assessment. The income will be reduced by an individual's personal allowances and other reliefs. The first £19,300 of taxable income remaining is assessable to income tax at the basic rate of 25 per cent, with any excess over this amount taxable at the higher rate of 40 per cent. Unlike the position for previous years, there is now only one higher rate.

The two rates apply to the assessment of both earned and investment income. Indeed there is little distinction between the two classes, although the receipt of earned income may produce an entitlement to some allowances not available against investment income.

The tables on the following pages show the income tax payable for 1988–89 by an individual on the amount of income specified, after deducting the personal allowance and age allowance. Elderly persons over the age of eighty years may suffer less tax. The taxpayer may also be entitled to further reliefs and allowances which reduce the tax payable below the amount shown in the tables.

The special rules for taxing income derived by a husband and wife are examined later.

Trustees administering settled property are chargeable to income tax at the basic rate of 25 per cent. Where the trustees retain discretionary powers, or income is accumulated, there will also be liability to the additional rate of 10 per cent. Companies residing in the United Kingdom are not liable to income tax but suffer corporation tax on income, profits and gains.

The charge to income tax broadly arises on all taxable income accruing from sources in the United Kingdom. Individuals who are resident in this territory may also become liable on income arising overseas. An individual is resident in the United Kingdom if he or she normally resides here. Persons not normally residing in the United Kingdom may become resident if they visit this territory for periods which average three months or more throughout a period of years, or are present for at least 183 days in a particular year. The existence of a place of abode in the United Kingdom may be sufficient to indicate residence if visits of any duration are made during the year of assessment.

Income arising overseas will often incur liability to foreign taxation. If that income is also chargeable to United Kingdom income tax, excessive liability may well arise. The United Kingdom has concluded Double Taxation Agreements with many overseas territories which ensure that the same slice of income is not doubly assessed. In the absence of such an agreement, foreign tax suffered can usually be relieved when calculating liability to United Kingdom income tax.

INCOME TAXABLE

Income tax is assessed and collected under several Schedules. Each Schedule determines the extent of liability and establishes the amount to be included in taxable income. In some instances the actual income arising in a year of assessment will be charged to income tax for that year. A different basis of assessment may arise for income taxable under Cases I to V of Schedule D. Frequently, income assessable under these Cases will be that arising in a previous year or period but there are special rules where a new source is acquired or an existing source discontinued. The contents of the various Schedules are shown below:

Schedule A.—Tax is charged on annual profits from the ownership or occupation of land in the United Kingdom. This will include rents, ground rents and other income arising from land. Expenditure incurred by the landlord on maintenance, repairs, insurance and management can be subtracted from the annual profits. This Schedule does not include profits from farming, market gardening or woodlands, nor does it extend to mineral rents and royalties. Premiums arising on the grant of a lease for a period not exceeding fifty years are assessed to income tax. However, the amount of the taxable premium may be reduced by 2 per cent for each complete year, after the first year, of the leasing period. Income from furnished lettings is assessable under Case VI of Schedule D, unless an option is exercised for such income to be assessed under Schedule A. Where income arises from furnished holiday lettings additional expenditure may be included in calculating income chargeable to tax. Income of this nature is treated as earned income.

Schedule B.—Assessment under this schedule was confined to woodlands in the United Kingdom managed on a commercial basis and with a view to the realisation of profits, with liability based on one-third of an assumed annual value. The occupier of woodlands retained the option of being assessed under Case I of Schedule D on profits arising from management. Schedule B was abolished on April 6, 1988, and no new options for assessment under Schedule D can now be made.

Schedule C.—This Schedule is confined to interest or dividends on Government or public authority funds and certain payments made out of the public revenues of overseas countries.

Schedule D.—This Schedule is divided into six Cases as follows:

Cases I and II.—Profits arising from trades, professions and vocations, including farming and market gardening. Capital expenditure incurred on assets used for business purposes will often produce an entitlement to capital allowances which reduce the profits chargeable. These profits may also be reduced following the submission of claims for loss relief and other matters.

Case III.—Interest on Government Stocks not taxed at source (e.g. War Loan and British Savings Bonds), interest on National Savings Bank deposits and discounts. Interest up to £70 on ordinary National Savings Bank deposits is exempt from income tax. The exemption applies to both husband and wife separately. Interest on National Savings Bank Special Investment Accounts is not exempt.

Cases IV and V.—Interest from overseas securities, rents, dividends and all other income accruing outside the United Kingdom. Assessment is based on

(1) SINGLE PERSONS

Income	Persons under 65		Persons 65 or over*	
	Income Tax	Average Rate	Income Tax	Average Rate
£	£	per cent	£	per cent
3,000	99	3·3	—	—
4,000	349	8·7	205	5·1
5,000	599	12·0	455	9·1
6,000	849	14·2	705	11·8
7,000	1,099	15·7	955	13·6
8,000	1,349	16·9	1,205	15·1
9,000	1,599	17·8	1,455	16·2
10,000	1,849	18·5	1,705	17·0
12,000	2,349	19·6	2,349	19·6
14,000	2,849	20·4	2,849	20·4
16,000	3,349	20·9	3,349	20·9
18,000	3,849	21·4	3,849	21·4
20,000	4,349	21·7	4,349	21·7
25,000	6,063	24·3	6,063	24·3
30,000	8,063	26·9	8,063	26·9
40,000	12,063	30·2	12,063	30·2
50,000	16,063	32·1	16,063	32·1
100,000	36,063	36·1	36,063	36·1

* Persons aged 80 or over suffer rather less tax on income falling below £12,000.

the full amount of income arising, whether remitted to the United Kingdom or retained overseas, but individuals who are either not domiciled in the United Kingdom or who are ordinarily resident overseas may apply the remittance basis. Overseas pensions are taxable but the amount arising may be reduced by 10 per cent for assessment purposes.

Case VI.—Sundry profits and annual receipts not assessed under any other Case or Schedule. These may include insurance commissions, post-cessation receipts and numerous other receipts specifically charged under Case VI.

Schedule E.—All emoluments from an office or employment are assessable under this Schedule. There are three Cases as follows:

Case I.—This applies to all emoluments of an individual resident and ordinarily resident in the United Kingdom.

Case II.—Of application where the individual is not resident or not ordinarily resident and extends to emoluments for duties undertaken in the United Kingdom.

Case III.—Applies in rare situations to other emoluments remitted to the United Kingdom.

Special rules apply to emoluments received by non-domiciled employees employed by non-resident employers. In general, where the duties are performed in the United Kingdom such earnings will be assessable subject to a percentage deduction. This deduction, which is gradually being withdrawn, applies at different rates which are governed by personal circumstances.

Although foreign earnings may be assessable under Case I where the employee is resident and ordinarily resident in the United Kingdom, a deduction of 100 per cent may be available for 1988–89. This deduction can be obtained where duties are performed overseas for a continuous period reaching or exceeding 365 days and is confined to earnings from the overseas activity.

The emoluments assessable under Schedule E include all salaries, wages, director's fees and other

money sums. In addition, there are a wide range of benefits which must also be added to taxable emoluments. These include the provision of living accommodation on advantageous terms and advantages arising from the use of vouchers.

Further taxable benefits accrue to directors and employees receiving emoluments of £8,500 or more in the year of assessment. These benefits include the reimbursement of expenses, the availability of motor cars for private motoring, the provision of petrol or other fuel for private motoring, the provision of interest free loans, and other benefits provided at the employer's expense.

In arriving at the amount to be assessed under Schedule E all expenses incurred wholly, exclusively and necessarily in the performance of the duties may be deducted. This includes fees and subscriptions paid to certain professional bodies and learned societies.

Compensation for loss of office and other sums received on the termination of an office or employment are assessable to tax. However, the first £30,000 may be excluded and only the balance remains chargeable, subject to some reduction in the amount of tax payable.

A part, not exceeding one half, of earnings received from an approved profit-related pay scheme is exempt from income tax.

Schedule F.—This Schedule is concerned with company dividends and distributions. A United Kingdom resident company paying a dividend or distribution must account to the Inland Revenue for advance corporation tax at the rate of one-third calculated on the amount paid in 1988–89. A shareholder residing in the United Kingdom receives the dividend or distribution, together with a tax credit equal to the amount of advance corporation tax. The dividend or distribution is regarded as having suffered income tax, equal to the tax credit, at the basic rate, and where the shareholder is not liable, or fully liable, at this rate a repayment can be obtained. Individuals liable at the higher rate of 40 per cent will incur further liability. Some payments made by

(2) MARRIED COUPLES

Income	Couples under 65		Couples 65 or over*	
	Income Tax	Average Rate	Income Tax	Average Rate
£	£	per cent	£	per cent
5,000	226	4·5	—	—
6,000	476	7·9	241	4·0
7,000	726	10·4	491	7·0
8,000	976	12·2	741	9·3
9,000	1,226	13·6	991	11·0
10,000	1,476	14·8	1,241	12·4
12,000	1,976	16·5	1,975	16·5
14,000	2,476	17·7	2,476	17·7
16,000	2,976	18·6	2,976	18·6
18,000	3,476	19·3	3,476	19·3
20,000	3,976	19·9	3,976	19·9
25,000	5,467	21·9	5,467	21·9
30,000	7,467	24·9	7,467	24·9
40,000	11,467	28·7	11,467	28·7
50,000	15,467	30·9	15,467	30·9
100,000	35,467	35·5	35,467	35·5

* Persons aged 80 or over suffer rather less tax on income falling below £12,000.

an unquoted trading company to redeem or purchase its own shares will not be treated as distributions.

Building society interest and bank interest. A special composite rate tax scheme applies to payments of building society interest and most payments of bank interest made to individuals. Interest of this nature incurs no liability to basic rate income tax in the hands of the depositor, nor can tax be recovered by a depositor not liable to income tax. The actual interest received must be "grossed up" at the rate of one third to establish the amount of total income received by a depositor liable at the higher rate of 40 per cent.

INCOME NOT TAXABLE

This includes interest on National Savings Certificates, most scholarship income, bounty payments to members of the armed services and annuities payable to the holders of certain awards. Dividend income arising from investments in personal equity plans may be exempt from tax, if the investment is not withdrawn for a complete calendar year. Income received under most maintenance agreements and court orders made after June 30, 1988 will not be liable to tax. Nor will payments made under many deeds of covenant executed after March 14, 1988 be recognized for tax purposes, unless the recipient is a charity.

SOCIAL SECURITY BENEFITS

Many Social Security benefits are not liable to income tax. These include family income supplement, long term sickness benefit, child benefit, war widow's pension, mobility allowance and numerous others. Among the limited range of benefits which are taxable is the retirement pension, widow's allowance, widowed mother's allowance, and unemployment benefits. Short-term sickness benefit and maternity pay payable by an employer is also chargeable to tax.

PAY AS YOU EARN

The Pay As You Earn system is not an independent form of taxation but has been designed to collect income tax by deduction from most emoluments. When paying emoluments to employees an employer is usually required to deduct income tax and account for that tax to the Inland Revenue. In many cases this deduction procedure will fully exhaust the individual's liability to income tax, unless there is other income.

PERSONAL ALLOWANCES

The following personal allowances are available to individuals and may be subtracted when calculating income chargeable to income tax. The list no longer includes the dependent relatives allowance, son's or daughter's Services allowance or the housekeeper allowance, all of which were withdrawn on April 6, 1988).

Personal Allowance.—A single person is entitled to a personal allowance of £2,605. This is increased to £4,095 for a married man whose wife is living with or maintained by him. For the year of marriage the increased allowance will only be available if marriage occurs before May 6. The increased allowance is then reduced by one-twelfth of £1,490 (£4,095 less £2,605) for each complete month preceding the marriage date.

The increased married man's allowance may be withdrawn where a wife's earning election is made (see "Husband and Wife" below).

Age Allowance.—A single person who has attained the age of 65 years and is in receipt of income not exceeding £10,600 receives an age allowance of £3,180. This is increased to £5,035 where a married man, or his wife living with him, has reached 65. If the income exceeds £10,600 the allowance is reduced by two-thirds of the amount of the excess. This reduction continues until the age allowance is reduced to the amount of the normal personal allowance. The age allowance is increased to £3,310, or £5,205 for a married couple, where the taxpayer or his wife has reached the age of 80 years. These increased amounts are also subject to restriction where income exceeds £10,600. Age allowance is in substitution for, and not in addition to, the personal allowance.

Wife's Earned Income Allowance.—An allowance equal to the wife's earned income, but limited to a maximum of £2,605, may be obtained. This allowance is not granted in the year of marriage or where a wife's earnings election is in operation (see "Husband and Wife" below).

Additional Personal Allowance.

An allowance of £1,490 is available to a single person who has a qualifying child resident with him or her in the year of assessment. The allowance can also be obtained by a married man whose wife is totally incapacitated by physical or mental infirmity throughout the year and a child is similarly resident.

A "qualifying child" for 1988–89 must be born during the year, be under the age of 16 years at the commencement of the year, or over the age of 16 years at the commencement of the year and either receiving full-time instruction at a university, college, school or other educational establishment or undergoing training for a trade, profession or vocation throughout a minimum period of two years. It is also necessary that the child is the claimant's own or, if not such a child, was either born during 1988–89 or under the age of 18 years at the commencement of the year and maintained by the claimant at his or her own expense during the whole of the succeeding twelve month period.

It is possible for an unmarried couple residing together and having two or more children to each obtain the additional personal allowance. This will no longer be possible after April 5, 1989, as only one allowance will be due.

Blind Person's Allowance.

An allowance of £540 is available to a single person if at any time during the year ending on April 5, 1989, that person was registered as blind on a register maintained by a local authority. The allowance will also be available to a married man if either he or his wife living with him is similarly registered. An increased allowance of £1,080 will be available if both husband and wife are registered blind persons.

Widow's Bereavement Allowance.

For the year of assessment in which a husband dies his surviving widow may obtain a widow's bereavement allowance of £1,490. It is a necessary requirement that the parties were living together immediately before death. A similar allowance will be available in the year following death, unless the widow remarried in the year of death. The special widow's bereavement allowance is available only for the year of death and the following year. It cannot be obtained in subsequent years.

Life Assurance Relief.

Life assurance deduction relief is limited to premiums paid on policies made before March 14, 1984. No relief is available for policies issued after this date. Where the terms of a policy made before March 14, 1984 are subsequently varied or extended to produce increased benefits, future premiums paid may no longer qualify for relief.

When paying premiums under a qualifying policy made before March 14, 1984 the payer will deduct and retain income tax at the rate of 15 per cent. The ability to retain deductions made in this manner is not affected by the payer's liability to income tax on taxable income. No restriction to the deduction procedure arises if aggregate premiums paid during a year of assessment do not exceed £1,500 (calculated before deducting tax). Should premiums exceed this amount, relief will be confined to £1,500 or one-sixth of total income, whichever is the greater. Where sums deducted exceed the maximum limit, the excess must be accounted for to the Inland Revenue.

The deduction rate will be reduced from 15 to 12·5 per cent for payments made after April 5, 1989.

OTHER DEDUCTIONS

In addition to personal allowances, which reduce taxable income, other eligible deductions may be available to an individual. These include payments of interest.

In some instances interest paid by a business proprietor may be relieved when calculating profits chargeable to income tax under Case I or Case II of Schedule D. Many private individuals cannot obtain relief in this manner and must satisfy stringent requirements before relief will be forthcoming. In general terms, before interest can qualify for relief it must be annual, as opposed to short, interest or paid to a bank, stockbroker or discount house. Relief will not be available to the extent that interest exceeds a reasonable commercial rate and no relief will be forthcoming for interest on an overdraft.

For 1988–89 relief will be available on the following payments:

(i) Interest on a loan to purchase, develop or improve an interest in land owned by the individual and used as the only or main residence or similarly used by a dependent relative or a former or separated spouse. "Land" includes large houseboats and also caravans used for a similar purpose. No relief is available for interest on loans applied after April 5, 1988 for the development or improvement of land, unless the work involves the construction of a new building. Nor can relief be obtained for interest on loans applied after this date for the purchase of property occupied by a dependent relative, spouse or former spouse. Relief may, however, be forthcoming for interest on a loan used to acquire some other property, perhaps to be used as the only or main residence on retirement, by an individual who is compelled to occupy property by reason of his or her work. If the loan, or aggregate of several loans, exceeds £30,000 relief is restricted to that amount. Where two or more persons apply loans after July 31, 1988 to acquire interests in a single building, those persons cannot, collectively, obtain relief for interest on more than £30,000 in relation to that building.

(ii) Interest on a loan to purchase or improve an interest in land which is let or available for letting at a commercial rent. This interest is only capable of being deducted from rental income.

(iii) Interest on a loan made to acquire an interest in a close company or in a partnership.

(iv) Interest on a loan to a member of a partnership to acquire machinery or plant for use in the partnership business.

(v) Interest on a loan to an employed person to acquire machinery or plant for the purposes of his employment.

(vi) Interest on a loan made for the purpose of contributing capital to an industrial co-operative.

(vii) Interest on a loan applied for investment in an employee-controlled company.

(viii) Interest on a loan made to elderly persons for the purchase of an annuity where the loan is secured on land. If the loan exceeds

£30,000 relief is limited to interest on this amount.

(ix) Interest on a loan to personal representatives for the payment of capital transfer tax or inheritance tax.

Relief for many payments of mortgage interest is obtained through a special scheme known as MIRAS (mortgage interest relief at source). This applies to interest paid to a building society, bank, insurance company and certain other persons. When making payments of this nature the payer will deduct and retain income tax at the basic rate. This will provide the payer with full relief at the basic rate and no other relief will be necessary, unless the payer is liable at the higher rate of 40 per cent. Qualifying payments of interest outside the MIRAS scheme continue to produce relief by deduction from income chargeable to income tax.

Many employees pay contributions to an approved occupational pension scheme. The amount of their contributions may be deducted when establishing emoluments assessable under Schedule E. Relief should also be available for any additional voluntary contributions paid.

Self-employed individuals and those receiving earnings not covered by an occupational pension scheme may contribute under personal pension scheme arrangements. These schemes were introduced on July 1, 1988 to replace the previous retirement annuity schemes. Contributions paid may obtain income tax relief, subject to maximum limits.

Subject to a maximum of £40,000 in any one year the cost of subscribing for shares in an unquoted company may qualify as a deduction from taxable income under the Business Expansion Scheme. Many requirements must be satisfied before this relief can be obtained.

HUSBAND AND WIFE

It is a general rule that the income of a married woman living with her husband must be aggregated with his income for the purpose of charging income tax. Aggregation does not, however, apply for the year of assessment in which the parties marry. For that year the husband will receive the personal allowance appropriate to a married man, although the amount of this allowance may require some restriction if marriage takes place after May 5. The wife will be taxed for the year of marriage as if she were a single person and no wife's earned income allowance can be obtained by the husband.

For subsequent years of assessment the incomes of husband and wife will be aggregated and if the husband does not satisfy the total tax liability the Inland Revenue may require the wife to pay the tax appropriate to her income.

Husband and wife may, however, claim to be separately assessed. This claim does not affect the total amount of income tax payable but allocates the liability between the parties. A quite different election may be made for separate assessment of wife's earnings. The effect of such an election is that the husband will be assessed on his income and on the wife's investment income and will receive the personal allowance appropriate to a single man. The wife will be separately assessed on her earned income and receive allowances as a single person. The wife's earnings election may be of advantage where the saving in higher rate tax on the wife's income is greater than the increased tax resulting from the loss of the married personal allowance.

This system for taxing husband and wife will cease to apply after April 5, 1990, following the introduction of independent taxation. Each spouse will be separately assessed and receive his or her own personal allowance. In addition, there will be a married couples allowance, initially given to the husband, but any unused balance will be transferred to the wife.

CAPITAL GAINS TAX

A person is chargeable to capital gains tax on chargeable gains which accrue to him or her during a year of assessment ending on April 5. The application of the tax has been amended substantially in recent years and the following information is confined to the year of assessment 1988–89, ending on April 5 1989.

Liability extends to persons who are either resident or ordinarily resident for the year but special rules apply where a person permanently leaves the United Kingdom or comes to this territory for the purpose of acquiring residence. Non-residents are not liable to capital gains tax unless, exceptionally, they carry on a business in the United Kingdom through a branch or agency.

Chargeable gains accruing to companies are assessable to corporation tax and not to capital gains tax.

Capital gains tax is chargeable on the total of chargeable gains which accrue to a person in a year of assessment, after subtracting allowable losses arising in the same year. Unused allowable losses brought forward from some earlier year may be offset against current chargeable gains but in the case of individuals this must not reduce the net chargeable gains for 1988–89 below £5,000.

RATE OF TAX

Where the net chargeable gains accruing to an individual during 1988–89 do not exceed £5,000 there will be no liability to capital gains tax. If the net gains exceed £5,000 the excess is chargeable at the taxpayers marginal rate of income tax. This is achieved by adding to the amount of revenue chargeable to income tax the net chargeable gains. The rate attributable to this top slice will disclose the rate of capital gains tax payable, which may be at 25 per cent, 40 per cent or a combination of the two. Although income tax rates are used, capital gains tax remains a separate tax.

Capital gains tax for 1988–89 normally falls due for payment on or before December 1, 1989. If the return or other information recording chargeable gains is delayed, interest may become chargeable.

HUSBAND AND WIFE

In the year of marriage chargeable gains accruing to husband and wife are separately assessed. Each party may independently obtain the £5,000 exemption for 1988–89 and there is no aggregation. For subsequent years, however, chargeable gains arising to a married woman living with her husband are assessed and charged on the husband, unless an election for separate assessment is made. This election will not reduce the aggregate tax payable but merely apportions liability between the spouses on an equitable basis. This treatment of a married woman's gains will be discontinued following the introduction of independent taxation on April 6, 1990.

DISPOSAL OF ASSETS

Before liability to capital gains tax can arise a disposal, or deemed disposal, of an asset must take place. This occurs not only where assets are sold or exchanged but applies on the making of a gift. There is also a disposal of assets where any capital sum is derived from assets, for example, where compensation is received for loss or damage to an asset.

The date on which a disposal must be treated as having taken place will determine the year of assessment in which the chargeable gain or allowable loss falls. In those cases where a disposal is made under an unconditional contract, the time of disposal will be that when the contract was entered into and not the subsequent date of conveyance or transfer. A disposal under a conditional contract or option is treated as taking place when the contract becomes unconditional or the option is exercised. Disposals by way of gift are undertaken when the gift becomes effective.

VALUATION OF ASSETS

The amount actually received as consideration for the disposal of an asset will be the sum from which very limited outgoings must be deducted for the purpose of establishing the gain or loss. In some cases, however, the consideration passing will not accurately reflect the value of the asset and a different basis must be used. This applies, in particular, where an asset is transferred by way of gift or otherwise than by a bargain made at arm's length. Such transactions are deemed to take place for a consideration representing market value, which will determine both the disposal proceeds accruing to the transferor and the cost of acquisition to the transferee.

Market value represents the price which an asset might reasonably be expected to fetch on a sale in the open market. In the case of unquoted shares or securities it is to be assumed that the hypothetical purchaser in the open market would have available all the information which a prudent prospective purchaser of shares or securities might reasonably require if he were proposing to purchase them from a willing vendor by private treaty and at arm's length. This is an important consideration as the amount of information deemed to be available to a hypothetical purchaser may materially affect the price "reasonably" offered in an open market situation. The market value of unquoted shares or securities will usually be established following negotiations with the Shares Valuation Division of the Capital Taxes Office.

Special rules apply to determine the market value of shares quoted on the Stock Exchange.

DEDUCTION FOR OUTGOINGS

Once the actual or notional disposal proceeds have been determined it only remains to subtract eligible outgoings for the purpose of computing the gain or loss. There is the general rule that any outgoings deducted, or which are available to be deducted, when calculating income tax liability must be ignored. Subject to this, deductions will usually be limited to—

(a) the cost of acquiring the asset, together with incidental costs wholly and exclusively incurred in connection with the acquisition;

(b) expenditure incurred wholly and exclusively on the asset in enhancing its value, being expenditure reflected in the state or nature of the asset at the time of the disposal, and any other expenditure wholly and exclusively incurred in establishing, preserving or defending title to, or a right over, the asset; and

(c) the incidental costs of making the disposal.

Where the disposal concerns a leasehold interest having less than 50 years to run, any expenditure falling under (a) and (b) must be written off throughout the duration of the lease. This recognises that a lease is a wasting asset which, at the termination of the leasing period, will retain no value.

INDEXATION ALLOWANCE

An indexation allowance will be available when calculating the chargeable gain or allowable loss. This allowance is based on percentage increases in the retail prices index between the month of March 1982, or if later the month in which expenditure is incurred, and the month of disposal. The increase is applied to the items of expenditure in (a) and (b) above to determine the amount of the indexation allowance. However, if the asset was acquired before March 31, 1982 and the disposal occurs after April 5, 1988, the allowance will be based on market value on that date.

The amount of the indexation allowance will be subtracted from the gain, or added to the loss, to calculate the chargeable gain or allowable loss arising on disposal.

ASSETS HELD ON MARCH 31, 1988

Where the disposal of assets held on March 31, 1988, takes place after April 5, 1988, the actual cost of acquisition will not usually enter into the calculation of gain. It is to be assumed that such assets were acquired on March 31, 1988, for a consideration representing market value on that date. The increase in value, if any, occurring before March 31, 1988, will not be assessable to capital gains tax.

EXEMPTIONS

There is a general exemption from liability to capital gains tax where the net gains of an individual for 1988–89 do not exceed £5,000.

The disposal of many assets will not give rise to chargeable gains or allowable losses and these include—

(a) private motor cars;

(b) Government securities.

(c) Loan stock and other securities (but not shares) quoted on a United Kingdom stock exchange or dealt in on the Unlisted Securities Market.

(d) Options and contracts relating to securities within (b) and (c).

(e) National Savings Certificates, Premium Bonds, Defence Bonds and National Development Bonds;

(f) currency of any description acquired for personal expenditure outside the United Kingdom;

(g) decorations awarded for valour;

(h) betting wins and pools, lottery or games prizes;

(i) compensation or damages for any wrong or injury suffered by an individual in his person or in his profession or vocation;

(j) life assurance and deferred annuity contracts where the person making the disposal is the original beneficial owner;

(k) dwelling-houses and land enjoyed with the residence which is an individual's only or main residence;

(l) tangible movable property, the consideration for the disposal of which does not exceed £3,000;

(m) certain tangible movable property which is a wasting asset having a life not exceeding 50 years;

(n) assets transferred to charities and other bodies;

(o) works of art, historic buildings and similar assets;

(p) assets used to provide maintenance funds for historic buildings;

(q) assets transferred to trustees for the benefit of employees.

DWELLING-HOUSES

Exemption from capital gains tax will usually be available for any gain which accrues to an individual from the disposal of, or of an interest in, a dwelling-house or part of a dwelling-house which has been his only or main residence. The exemption extends to land which has been occupied and enjoyed with the residence as its garden or grounds. Some restriction may be necessary where the land exceeds one acre.

The gain will not be chargeable to capital gains tax if the dwelling-house, or part, has been the individual's only or main residence throughout the period of ownership, or throughout the entire period except for all or any part of the last two years. A proportionate part of the gain will be exempt if the dwelling-house has been the individual's only or main residence for part only of the period of ownership.

Where part of the dwelling-house has been used exclusively for business purposes, part of the gain arising on disposal will not be exempt. It will be comparatively unusual for any part to be used exclusively for such a purpose, except perhaps in the case of doctors' or dentists' surgeries.

In those cases where part of a qualifying dwelling-house has been used to provide rented accommodation this non-personal use may frequently be ignored when calculating exemption from capital gains tax, unless relatively substantial sums are involved.

Dwellings occupied by dependent relatives or separated or divorced former spouses, may also qualify for the exemption, but only where occupation commenced before April 6, 1988.

ROLL-OVER RELIEF

Persons carrying on business will often undertake the disposal of an asset and use the proceeds to finance the acquisition of a replacement asset. Where this situation arises a claim for roll-over relief may be made. The broad effect of such a claim is that all or part of the gain arising on the disposal of the old assset may be disregarded. The gain or part is then subtracted from the cost of acquiring the replacement asset. As this cost is reduced, any gain arising from the future disposal of the replacement asset will be correspondingly increased, unless of course a further roll-over situation then develops.

It remains a requirement that both the old and the replacement asset must be used for the purpose of the taxpayer's business. Relief will only be available if the acquisition of the replacement asset takes place within a period commencing twelve months before, and ending three years after, the disposal of the old asset, although the Board of Inland Revenue retain a discretion to extend this period where the circumstances were such that it was impossible for the taxpayer to acquire the replacement asset before the expiration of the normal time limit.

Whilst many business assets qualify for roll-over relief there are exceptions.

GIFTS

Although the gift of an asset is deemed to be a disposal made for a consideration representing market value, a claim for hold-over can frequently be made to avoid capital gains tax liability. This claim applies to the gift of assets by one individual to a second individual, by an individual to trustees, by trustees to an individual, or between trustees, residing in the United Kingdom. The effect of the claim is similar to that arising following a claim for roll-over relief and the cost to the transferee will be reduced. Adjustments will be necessary where a transaction undertaken, otherwise than by way of bargain made at arm's length, involves some inadequate consideration.

A limited claim may also be made on the disposal of assets by an individual to some other person, perhaps a company. This claim is confined to the disposal of business assets, including shares in certain companies.

RETIREMENT RELIEF

Retirement relief is available to an individual who disposes by way of sale or gift of the whole or part of a business. It does not necessarily follow that the isolated disposal of assets will represent the disposal of the whole or part of a business. The main condition for granting this relief is that throughout a period of at least one year the business has been owned either by the individual or by a trading company in which the individual retained a sufficient shareholding interest. The relief extends also to cases where an individual disposes by way of sale or gift of shares or securities of a company. It must be demonstrated that the company was a trading company, the individual retained a sufficient shareholding interest, and he was engaged as a full-time working director.

An individual who has attained the age of 60 years at the time of a disposal may obtain maximum retirement relief exceeding £300,000 for disposals taking place after April 5, 1988. The amount of this relief must be reduced if the conditions have not been satisfied throughout a ten year period. With a single exception no retirement relief can be obtained if the disposal occurs before the individuals 60th birthday. This exception arises where an individual is compelled to retire early on the grounds of ill-health. The normal retirement relief may then be obtained. Any retirement relief must be subtracted from the net gains arising on disposal, leaving the balance remaining, if any, chargeable to capital gains tax in the normal manner.

DEATH

No capital gains tax is chargeable on the value of assets retained at the time of death. However, the personal representatives administering the deceased's estate are deemed to acquire those assets for a consideration representing market value on death. This ensures that any increase in value occurring before the date of death will not be chargeable to capital gains tax. If a legatee or other person acquires an asset under a will or intestacy no chargeable gain will accrue to the personal representatives, and the person taking the asset will also be treated as having acquired it at the time of death for its then market value.

INHERITANCE TAX

Throughout a period of some 90 years estate duty was payable on the value of an individual's estate at the time of death. Liability did not extend to lifetime gifts other than those made shortly before death and a limited range of further gifts where the donor continued to retain some benefit from the assets gifted. Estate duty ceased to apply for deaths occurring after March 12, 1975 following the introduction of capital transfer tax. This tax was not limited to the value of an estate at the time of death but applied to many gifts made during lifetime. Although the broad framework of capital transfer tax remains, very substantial changes were introduced for events occurring after March 17, 1986. In recognition of these changes the tax was renamed inheritance tax and now bears many characteristics of the former estate duty.

The nature and scope of inheritance tax is outlined below, but the comments made have little application to events occurring before 18 March 1986 when capital transfer tax applied.

Liability to inheritance tax may arise on a limited range of lifetime gifts and other dispositions and also on the value of assets retained, or deemed to be retained, at the time of death. An individual's domicile at the time of any gift or on death is an important matter. Domicile will generally be determined by applying normal rules, but special considerations may be necessary where an individual was previously domiciled in the United Kingdom but subsequently acquired a domicile of choice overseas. Where a person was domiciled in the United Kingdom at the time of a disposition or on death the location of assets is immaterial and full liability to inheritance tax arises. Individuals domiciled outside the United Kindom are, however, chargeable to inheritance tax only on transactions affecting assets located in the United Kingdom.

The assets of husband and wife are not merged for inheritance tax purposes. Each spouse is treated as a separate individual entitled to receive the benefit of his or her exemptions, reliefs and rates of tax. Where husband and wife retain similar assets, special "related property" provisions may require the merger of those assets for valuation purposes only.

LIFETIME GIFTS AND DISPOSITIONS

Gifts and dispositions made during lifetime fall under four broad headings, namely:

(a) dispositions which are not transfers of value;
(b) exempt transfers;
(c) potentially exempt transfers; and
(d) chargeable transfers.

Dispositions which are not transfers of value.— Several lifetime transactions are not treated as transfers of value and may be disregarded for inheritance tax purposes. These include transactions not undertaken to confer gratuitous benefit, the provision of family maintenance, the waiver of the right to receive remuneration or dividends, and the grant of agricultural tenancies for full consideration.

Exempt transfers.—Certain other transfers are treated as "exempt transfers" and incur no liability to inheritance tax. The main exempt transfers are listed below:

Transfers Between Spouses.—Transfers between husband and wife are usually exempt. However, if the transferor is, but the transferee spouse is not, domiciled in the United Kingdom transfers will be exempt only to the extent that the total does not exceed £55,000. Unlike the requirement used for income tax and capital gains tax purposes, it is immaterial whether husband and wife are "living together".

Annual exemption.—The first £3,000 of gifts and other dispositions made in a year ending on April 5 is exempt. If the exemption is not used, or not wholly used, in any year the balance may be carried forward to the following year only. The annual exemption will only be available for a potentially exempt transfer (see below) if that transfer subsequently becomes chargeable by reason of the donor's death.

Small Gifts.—Outright gifts of £250 or less to any person in one year ending April 5 are exempt.

Normal Expenditure.—A transfer made during lifetime and comprising normal expenditure is exempt. To obtain this exemption it must be shown that:

(a) the transfer was made as part of the normal expenditure of the transferor;
(b) taking one year with another, the transfer was made out of income; and
(c) after allowing for all transfers of value forming part of normal expenditure the transferor was left with sufficient income to maintain his or her usual standard of living.

Gifts in Consideration of Marriage.—These are exempt if they satisfy certain requirements. The amount allowed will be governed by the relationship between the donor and a party to the marriage. The allowable amounts comprise—

(a) gifts by a parent—£5,000
(b) gifts by a grandparent—£2,500
(c) gifts by a party to the marriage—£2,500
(d) gifts by other persons—£1,000

Gifts to Charities.—Gifts to charities are exempt from liability.

Gifts to Political Parties.—Gifts to political parties which satisfy certain requirements are generally exempt.

Gifts for National Purposes.—Gifts made to an extensive list of bodies are exempt from liability. These include, among others,—

(a) The National Gallery;
(b) The British Museum;
(c) The National Trust for Places of Historic Interest or Natural Beauty;
(d) The National Art Collections Fund;
(e) The Nature Conservancy Council;
(f) The Historic Buildings and Monuments Commission for England;
(g) Any local authority;
(h) Any university or university college in the United Kingdom.

A number of other gifts made for the public benefit are also exempt.

Potentially Exempt Transfers.—Lifetime gifts and dispositions which are neither to be ignored nor comprise exempt transfers incur possible liability to inheritance tax. However, relief is available for a range of potentially exempt transfers. These comprise gifts made by an individual to—

(a) a second individual;
(b) trustees administering an accumulation and maintenance trust; or
(c) trustees administering a disabled person's trust.

The accumulation and maintenance trust mentioned in (b) must provide that on reaching a specified age, not exceeding twenty-five years, a beneficiary will become absolutely entitled to trust assets or obtain an interest in possession in those assets.

Further additions were made to the list of potentially exempt transfers for transactions taking place after March 16, 1987. These affect settled property administered by trustees where an individual, or individuals, retain an interest in possession. The transfer of assets to, the removal of assets from, or the rearrangement of interests in such property now comprise potentially exempt transfers if the person transferring an interest and the person benefitting from the transfer are both individuals.

No immediate liability to inheritance tax will arise on the making of a potentially exempt transfer. Should the donor survive for a period of seven years, immunity from liability will be confirmed. However, the donor's death within the seven-year *inter vivos* period produces liability, as explained later, if the amounts involved are sufficiently substantial.

Chargeable Transfers.—Any remaining lifetime gifts or dispositions which are neither to be ignored, represent exempt transfers or potentially exempt transfers incur liability to inheritance tax. The range of such chargeable transfers is severely limited and is broadly confined to transfers made to or affecting certain trusts, transfers to non-individuals and transfers involving companies.

GIFTS WITH RESERVATION

A lifetime gift of assets made at any time after March 17, 1986, may incur additional liability to inheritance tax if the donor retains some interest in the subject matter of the gift. This may arise, for example, where a parent transfers a dwelling-house to a son or daughter and continues to occupy the property or to enjoy some benefit from that property. The retention of a benefit may be ignored where it is enjoyed in return for full consideration, perhaps a commercial rent, or the benefit arises from changed circumstances which could not have been foreseen at the time of the original gift. The gift with reservation provisions will not usually apply to most exempt transfers.

There are three possibilities which may arise where the donor reserves or enjoys some benefit from the subject matter of a previous gift and subsequently dies, namely:

(a) If no benefit is enjoyed within a period of seven years before death there can be no further liability.
(b) If the benefit ceased to be enjoyed within a period of seven years before the date of death the original donor is deemed to have made a potentially exempt transfer representing the value of the asset at the time of cessation.

(c) If the benefit is enjoyed at the time of death the value of the asset must be included in the value of the deceased's estate on death.

It must be emphasised that the existence of a benefit enjoyed at any time within a period of seven years before death will establish liability on gifts with reservation, notwithstanding that the gift may have been made many years earlier, providing it was undertaken after March 17, 1986.

DEATH

Immediately before the time of death an individual is deemed to make a transfer of value. This transfer will comprise the value of assets forming part of the deceased's estate after subtracting most liabilities. Any exempt transfers may, however, be excluded. These include transfers for the benefit of a surviving spouse, a charity and a qualifying political party together with bequests to approved bodies and for national purposes.

Death may also trigger three additional liabilities, namely:

(a) A potentially exempt transfer made within the period of seven years ending on death loses its potential status and becomes chargeable to inheritance tax.
(b) The value of gifts made with reservation may incur liability if any benefit was enjoyed within a period of seven years preceding death.
(c) Additional tax may become payable for chargeable lifetime transfers made within seven years before death.

VALUATIONS

The valuation of assets is an important matter as this will establish the value transferred for lifetime dispositions and also the value of a person's estate at the time of death. The value of property will represent the price which might reasonably be expected from a sale in the open market. This price cannot be reduced on the grounds that the whole property is placed on the market simultaneously and may therefore depress values.

In some cases it may be necessary to incorporate the value of "related property". This will include property comprised in the estate of the transferor's spouse and certain property previously transferred to charities. The purpose of the related property valuation rules is not to add the value of the property to the estate of the transferor. Related property must be merged to establish the aggregate value of the respective interests and this value is then apportioned, usually on a *pro rata* basis, to the separate interests.

The value of shares and securities quoted on the Stock Exchange will be determined by extracting figures from the daily list of official prices.

Where quoted shares and securities are sold within a period of twelve months following the date of death a claim may be made to substitute the proceeds for the value on death. This claim will only be beneficial if the gross proceeds realized are lower than market value on death. A similar claim may be available for interests in land sold within a period of three years following death.

RELIEF FOR ASSETS

Special relief is made available for certain assets, notably woodlands, agricultural property and business property. The effect of this relief is summarized below:

Woodlands.—Where woodlands pass on death the value will usually be included in the deceased's estate.

However, an election may be made in respect of land in the United Kingdom on which trees or underwood is growing to delete the value of those assets. Relief is confined to the value of trees or underwood and does not extend to the land on which they are growing. Liability to inheritance tax will arise if and when the trees or underwood are sold on a future occasion.

Agricultural Property.—Relief is available for the agricultural value of agricultural property. Such property must be occupied and used for agricultural purposes and relief is confined to the agricultural value.

The value transferred, either on a lifetime gift or on death, must be determined. This value may then be reduced by a percentage. A higher 50 per cent deduction will be available if the transferor retained vacant possession or could have obtained that possession within a period of twelve months following the transfer. The increased deduction of 50 per cent may also be available for certain agricultural property held on March 9, 1981. In other cases, notably including land let to tenants, a lower deduction of 30 per cent is available.

It remains a requirement that the agricultural property was either occupied by the transferor for the purposes of agriculture throughout a two-year period ending on the date of the transfer, or was owned by him throughout a period of seven years ending on that date and occupied for agricultural purposes.

Business Property.—Where value transferred is attributable to relevant business property that value may be reduced by a percentage. The reduction in value applies to—

(a) property consisting of a business or an interest in a business;

(b) shares or securities of a company, whether quoted or unquoted, which, provided the transferor with control of the company immediately before the transfer. Control for this purpose may include that created by related property;

(c) unquoted shares or securities not falling within (b) which provided the transferor with more than 25 per cent of voting rights;

(d) other unquoted shares or securities not falling within (c);

(e) any land, building, machinery or plant which, immediately before the transfer, was used wholly or mainly for the purposes of a business carried on by a company of which the transferor had control;

(f) any land, building, machinery or plant which, immediately before the transfer, was used wholly or mainly for the purposes of a business carried on by a partnership of which the transferor was a partner; and

(g) any land, building, machinery or plant which, immediately before the transfer, was used wholly or mainly for the purposes of a business carried on by the transferor and was then settled property in which he retained an interest in possession.

For property falling within (a) or (b) the deduction is 50 per cent. A similar deduction is available for property in (c), if the event occurs after March 16, 1987. A reduced deduction of 30 per cent applies to property in (d) to (g).

It is a general requirement that the property must have been retained for a period of two years before the transfer or death and restrictions may be necessary if the property has not been used wholly for business purposes. The same slice of property cannot obtain both business property relief and the relief available for agricultural property.

CALCULATION OF TAX PAYABLE

The calculation of inheritance tax payable adopts the use of a cumulative total. Each chargeable lifetime transfer is added to the total with a final addition made on death. The top slice added to the total for the current event determines the rate at which inheritance tax must be paid. However, the cumulative total will only include transfers made within a period of seven years before the current event and those undertaken outside this period must be excluded. Although inheritance tax was only introduced on March 18, 1986, the seven-year cumulative total will include chargeable lifetime gifts made before that date, subject to the seven-year limitation.

Lifetime transfers.—The limited range of lifetime transfers must be added to the seven-year cumulative total to calculate the amount of inheritance tax due. The tax is imposed at one-half of the rate shown below. However, if the donor dies within a period of seven years from the date of the chargeable lifetime transfer, additional tax may be due. This is calculated by applying tax at the full rate (in substitution for the one-half rate previously used). The amount of tax is then reduced to a percentage by applying tapering relief. This percentage is governed by the number of years from the date of the lifetime gift to the date of death and is as follows:

Period of years before death	Percentage
Not more than 3	100
More than 3 but not more than 4	80
More than 4 but not more than 5	60
More than 5 but not more than 6	40
More than 6 but not more than 7	20

Should this exercise produce liability greater than that previously paid at the one-half rate on the lifetime transfer, additional tax, representing the difference, must be paid. Where the calculation shows an amount falling below tax paid on the lifetime transfer, no additional liability can arise nor will the deficiency become repayable.

Potentially exempt transfers.—Where a potentially exempt transfer loses immunity from liability, due to the donor's death within the seven-year *inter vivos* period, the value transferred becomes liable to inheritance tax. Liability is calculated by applying the full rate shown below, reduced to the percentage governed by tapering relief if the original transfer occurred more than three years before death.

Death.—The final addition to the seven-year cumulative total will comprise the value of an estate on death. Inheritance tax will be calculated by applying the full rate shown below. No tapering relief can be obtained.

RATES OF TAX

In earlier times there were several rates of inheritance tax which progressively increased as the value transferred grew in size. However, for events taking place after March 14, 1988, a nil rate applies to the first £110,000 of value. Any excess is charged at the single positive rate of 40 per cent.

Only one-half of the 40 per cent rate (namely 20 per cent) will be applicable for chargeable lifetime transfers.

It must be anticipated that the above rate and rateband will be amended on future occasions.

PAYMENT OF TAX

Inheritance tax usually falls due for payment six months after the end of the month in which the chargeable transaction takes place. Where a transfer, other than that made on death, occurs after April 5 and before the folllowing October 1, tax falls due on the following April 30, although there are some exceptions to this general rule.

Inheritance tax attributable to the transfer of certain land, controlling shareholding interests, unquoted shares, businesses and interests in businesses, together with agricultural property, may usually be satisfied by instalments spread over ten years. No liability to interest arises where tax is paid on the due date. In other cases, delay in the payment of tax may incur liability to interest.

SETTLED PROPERTY

Complex rules apply to establish inheritance tax liability on settled property. Where a person is beneficially entitled to an interest in possession, that person is effectively deemed to "own" the property in which the interest subsists. It follows that where the interest comes to an end during the beneficiary's lifetime and some other person becomes entitled to the property or interest, the beneficiary is treated as having made a transfer of value. However, for events taking place after March 16, 1987 this will usually comprise a potentially exempt transfer. No liability will arise, however, where the property vests in the absolute ownership of the previous beneficiary. The death of a person entitled to an interest in possession will require the value of the underlying property to be added to the value of the deceased's estate.

In the case of other settled property where there is no interest in possession (e.g. discretionary trusts), liability to tax will arise on each ten-year anniversary of the trust. There will also be liability if property ceases to be held on discretionary trusts before the first ten-year anniversary date is reached or between anniversaries. The rate of tax suffered will be governed by several considerations, including previous dispositions made by the settlor, transactions concluded by the trustees, and the period throughout which property has been held in trust.

Accumulation and maintenance settlements which require assets to be distributed not later than a beneficiary's twenty-fifth birthday may be exempt from any liability to inheritance tax.

CORPORATION TAX

Profits, gains and income accruing to companies resident in the United Kingdom incur liability to corporation tax. Non-resident companies are immune from this tax unless they carry on a trade in the United Kingdom through a permanent establishment, branch or office. Companies residing outside the United Kingdom may be liable to income tax at the basic rate on other income arising in the United Kingdom, perhaps from letting property. The following comments are confined to companies resident in the United Kingdom and have little application to those residing overseas.

Liability to corporation tax is governed by the profits, gains or income for an accounting period. This is the period for which financial accounts are made up, and in the case of companies preparing accounts to the same accounting date annually will comprise successive periods of twelve months.

RATE OF TAX

The amount of profits or income for an accounting period must be determined on normal taxation principles. The special rules which apply to individuals where a source of income is acquired or discontinued are ignored and consideration is confined to the actual profits or income for an accounting period.

The rate of corporation tax is fixed for a financial year ending on March 31. Where the accounting period of a company overlaps this date and there is a change in the rate of corporation tax, profits and income must be apportioned.

For earlier years the full rate of corporation tax was 52 per cent but this rate was progressively reduced as follows:

Financial year	Per cent
12 months ending March 31, 1984	50
12 months ending March 31, 1985	45
12 months ending March 31, 1986	40
12 months ending March 31, 1987, 1988 and 1989	35

The progressive reduction in the rate of corporation tax was made to compensate companies for the loss of stock relief and the withdrawal of certain allowances for capital expenditure which increased the amount of profits and income chargeable to that tax.

SMALL COMPANIES RATE

Where the profits of a company do not exceed stated limits corporation tax becomes payable at the small companies rate. It is the amount of profits and not the size of the company which governs the application of this rate.

The level of profits which a company may derive without losing the benefit of the small companies rate has been frequently changed. However, in recent years the following small companies rate applies where profits do not exceed £100,000:

Financial year	Per cent
12 months ending March 31, 1984	38
12 months ending March 31, 1985 and 1986	30
12 months ending March 31, 1987	29
12 months ending March 31, 1988	27
12 months ending March 31, 1989	25

If profits do exceed £100,000 but fall below £500,000 marginal small companies rate relief applies. The broad effect of marginal relief is that the first £100,000 of profits is taxed at the appropriate small companies rate. Profits falling in the margin exceeding £100,000 then incur liability at the following marginal rates:

Financial year	Per cent
12 months ending March 31, 1984	55
12 months ending March 31, 1985	48·75
12 months ending March 31, 1986	42·5
12 months ending March 31, 1987	36·5
12 months ending March 31, 1988	37
12 months ending March 31, 1989	37·5

If the accounting period of a company overlaps March 31, profits must be apportioned to establish the appropriate rate for each part of those profits.

The lower limit of £100,000 and the upper limit of £500,000 applies for a period of twelve months in duration and must be proportionately reduced for shorter periods. Some restriction in the small companies rate and the marginal rate may be necessary if there are two or more "associated companies", namely companies under common control.

CAPITAL GAINS

Chargeable gains arising to a company are calculated in a manner similar to that used for individuals. However, companies cannot obtain the annual exemption of £5,000, nor are they assessed to capital gains tax. In place of this tax companies suffer liability to corporation tax on chargeable gains.

For disposals taking place before March 17, 1987 only a fraction of the chargeable gain was assessable to corporation tax at the full rate. The fraction selected ensured that companies effectively suffered corporation tax at the rate of 30 per cent on the full chargeable gain. A different approach is adopted for disposals taking place after this date. The full chargeable gain, and not a fraction, is assessable to corporation tax. However, unlike the previous system, the chargeable gain is treated as ordinary profit, thereby obtaining the benefit of the small companies rate where figures are sufficiently low.

DISTRIBUTIONS

Dividends and other qualifying distributions made by a United Kingdom resident company are not satisfied after deduction of income tax. However, when making a distribution a company is required to account to the Inland Revenue for an amount of advance corporation tax. For distributions made in the year ending April 5, 1989, the amount of advance corporation tax will represent one-third of the distribution. Thus a cash dividend of £75 paid to a shareholder will also require satisfaction of advance corporation tax amounting to £25.

Advance corporation tax accounted for in this manner for distributions made in an accounting period may usually be set against a company's corporation tax liability for the same period. Some restrictions are imposed on the amount which can be offset but any surplus can be carried forward, or carried backwards, and set against corporation tax due for other accounting periods.

A United Kingdom resident shareholder receiving a qualifying distribution also obtains a tax credit, which for the year ending April 5, 1989, is equal to one-third of the distribution made. Therefore the total income of the individual comprises the aggre-

gate of the distribution and the tax credit. If the individual is not liable, or not fully liable, to income tax at the basic rate, all or part of the tax credit can be refunded by the Inland Revenue. Individuals with substantial income incur liability to income tax at the higher rate of 40 per cent on the aggregate of the distribution and the tax credit.

PAYMENT OF TAX

Corporation tax, less any relief for advance corporation tax, usually falls due for payment nine months following the end of the accounting period to which the tax relates. Companies who were carrying on business before 1966 may have a later due and payable date, but this is gradually being amended to achieve a common nine month period for all companies.

INTEREST

On making many payments of interest a company is required to deduct income tax at the basic rate and account for the tax deducted to the Inland Revenue. The gross amount of interest paid will usually comprise a charge on income to be offset against profits on which corporation tax becomes payable.

GROUPS OF COMPANIES

Each company within a group is separately charged to corporation tax on profits, gains and income. However, where one group member realizes a loss, other than a capital loss, a claim may be made to offset the deficiency against profits of some other member of the same group.

Claims are also available to avoid the payment of advance corporation tax on distributions, or the deduction of income tax on the payment of interest, for transactions between members of a group of companies. The transfer of capital assets from one member of a group to a fellow member will incur no liability to tax on chargeable gains.

VALUE ADDED TAX

Unlike income tax, capital gains tax, inheritance tax and corporation tax, which are collected and administered by the Inland Revenue, value added tax is the responsibility of Customs and Excise. Value added tax is charged on the value of supplies made in the United Kingdom by a registered trader and extends both to the supply of goods and to the supply of services. Liability also arises on the value of goods imported into the United Kingdom.

REGISTRATION

All traders, including professional men and women, together with companies, making taxable supplies of a value exceeding stated limits are required to register for value added tax purposes. Taxable supplies represent the supply of goods and services potentially chargeable with value added tax. The limits which govern mandatory registration are amended annually but from March 16, 1988, an unregistered trader must register—

(a) at any time, if there are reasonable grounds for believing that the value of taxable supplies in the year then beginning will exceed £22,100, or

(b) at the end of any quarter, namely March 31, June 30, September 30 or December 31, if the total amount of taxable supplies has exceeded either £7,500 in the last quarter or £22,100 in the last four quarters. Registration will not be mandatory if it can be shown that the value of taxable supplies in the last quarter and the next three quarters is not expected to exceed £22,100.

Where the limits governing mandatory registration have been exceeded it is necessary for the trader to notify Customs and Excise. Failure to provide prompt notification may have unfortunate results as the person concerned will be required to account for value added tax from the proper registration date. In some situations a trader whose taxable supplies do not reach the mandatory registration limits may apply for voluntary registration.

A registered trader may submit an application for de-registration if the value of taxable supplies subsequently falls. From June 1, 1988, an application for de-registration can be made if the value of taxable supplies for the year beginning on the application date is not expected to exceed £21,100. De-registration can also be achieved if the value of taxable supplies in each of the two previous years did not exceed £22,100 and is unlikely to exceed this threshold in the following twelve-month period.

INPUT TAX

A registered trader will both suffer tax (input tax) when obtaining goods or services for the purposes of his business and also become liable to account for tax (output tax) on the value of goods and services which he supplies. Relief can usually be obtained for input tax suffered, either by setting that tax against output tax due or by repayment. Most items of input tax can be relieved in this manner but there are exceptions including the prohibition of relief for the cost of business entertaining. Where a registered trader makes both exempt supplies and also taxable supplies to his customers or clients there may be some restriction in the amount of input tax which can be recovered.

OUTPUT TAX

When making a taxable supply of goods or services a registered trader must account for output tax, if any, on the value of the supply. Usually the price charged by the registered trader will be increased by adding value added tax but failure to make the required addition will not remove liability to account for output tax.

EXEMPT SUPPLIES

No value added tax is chargeable on the supply of goods or services which are treated as exempt supplies. These include the provision of burial and cremation facilities, insurance, finance and education. The granting of a lease to occupy land will usually comprise an exempt supply, but there are numerous exceptions.

Exempt supplies do not enter into the value of taxable supplies which governs liability to mandatory registration. Such supplies made by a registered trader may however limit the amount of input tax which can be relieved.

RATES OF TAX

Two rates of value added tax have applied since June 18, 1979, namely:

(a) a zero, or nil, rate; and

(b) a standard rate of 15 per cent.

Although no tax is due on a zero-rated supply, this does comprise a taxable supply which must be included in the calculation governing liability to register.

ZERO-RATING

A large number of supplies are zero-rated, including the following, among others—

(a) the supply of many items of food and drink for human consumption. This does not include ice creams, chocolates, sweets, potato crisps and alcoholic drinks. Nor does it extend to supplies made in the course of catering, for example, at a wedding reception or other social function,

or to items supplied for consumption in a restaurant or cafe. Whilst the supply of "cold" items, for example sandwiches, for consumption away from the suppliers premises, is zero rated, the supply of "hot" food, for example fish and chips, is not.

(b) animal feeding stuffs;

(c) sewerage and water;

(d) books, brochures, pamphlets, leaflets, newspapers, maps and charts;

(e) talking books for the blind and handicapped and wireless sets for the blind;

(f) electricity, gas and coal;

(g) supplies made in the construction of a building. Zero-rating extends to the construction of a new building, the construction of a garage in conjunction with the construction of a new dwelling and the installation of working surfaces in the kitchen of a new building. Alterations to our existing building are not zero-rated, unless they relate to a listed building;

(h) the transportation of persons in a vehicle, ship or aircraft designed to carry not less than twelve persons;

(i) supplies of drugs, medicines and other aids for the handicapped;

(j) supplies of clothing and footwear for young persons;

(k) exports.

This list is not exhaustive but indicates the wide range of supplies which may be zero-rated. Some of these items will shortly cease to be zero rated following a decision by the European Court.

COLLECTION OF TAX

Registered traders submit value added tax returns for accounting periods. Each accounting period is for three months in duration but arrangements can be made to submit returns on a monthly basis. The return will show both the output tax due for supplies made by the trader in the accounting period and also the input tax for which relief is claimed. If the output tax exceeds input tax the balance must be remitted with the value added tax return. Where input tax suffered exceeds the output tax due the registered trader may claim recovery of the excess from Customs and Excise.

This basis for collecting tax explains the structure of value added tax. Where supplies are made between registered traders the supplier will account for an amount of tax which will usually be identical to the tax recovered by the person to whom the supply is made. However, where the supply is made to a person who is not a registered trader there can be no recovery of input tax and it is on this person that the final burden of value added tax eventually falls.

Tax on imports into the United Kingdom must be satisfied at the time of importation or perhaps later where special arrangements have been agreed.

An optional scheme will be made available for registered traders having an annual turnover of taxable supplies not exceeding £250,000. Such traders may, if they wish, render returns annually. Nine equal payments of value added tax will be paid on account, with a final balancing payment accompanying submission of the return.

BAD DEBTS

Many retailers operate special retail schemes for calculating the amount of value added tax due. These schemes are, broadly, based on the volume of consideration received in an accounting period. Should a customer fail to pay for goods or services supplied, there will be no consideration on which value added tax falls to be calculated. In other cases, where the special retailers' schemes do not apply, output tax falls due on the value of the supply and liability is not affected by failure to receive consideration. This implies that there will be no relief for the value added tax element in bad debts. However, relief for this element may be obtained where the debtor becomes insolvent.

To avoid the problem of bad debts incurred by traders not operating a special retail scheme, an optional system of cash accounting is available. This scheme, confined to traders with annual taxable supplies not exceeding £250,000, enables returns to be made on a cash basis, in substitution for the normal supply basis. Traders using such a scheme will not, of course, include bad debts in the calculation of cash receipts.

OTHER SPECIAL SCHEMES

In addition to the schemes for retailers, there are several special schemes applied to calculate the amount of value added tax due and which also limit the ability to recover input tax. These schemes apply to the supply of second-hand motor cars, motor cycles, caravans, boats, electronic organs, aircraft and firearms, together with works of art, antiques and collectors' pieces.

OTHER TAXES AND STAMP DUTIES

The Commissioners as a general rule allow deeds, etc., to be stamped after execution:—

WITHOUT PENALTY, ON PAYMENT OF DUTY ONLY.
Deeds and instruments not otherwise excepted, within 30 days of *first* execution.
NOTE.—Where wholly executed *abroad,* the period begins to run from the date of arrival here.

PENALTIES ENFORCEABLE ON STAMPING IN ADDITION TO DUTY:—
Instruments presented after the proper time (subject to special provisions in some cases and subject to the commissioner's power to mitigate) a penalty equal to the duty   . £10

AGREEMENT for Lease, *see* LEASES.
AGREEMENT FOR SALE OF PROPERTY—charged with *ad val.* duty as if an actual conveyance on sale with certain exceptions, *e.g.* agreements for the sale of land, stocks and shares, goods, wares or merchandise, or a ship (*see* s. 59 (1), Stamp Act 1891). If *ad val.* duty is paid on an agreement in accordance with this provision, the subsequent conveyance or transfer is not chargeable with any *ad val.* duty and the Commissioners will upon application either place a denoting stamp on such conveyance or transfer or will transfer the *ad val.* duty thereto. Further, if such an agreement is rescinded, not performed, etc., the Commissioners will return the *ad val.* duty paid.
AGREEMENT under seal subject to exemptions.   50p
ASSIGNMENT:
By way of sale—*see* Conveyance.
By way of gift—*see* Voluntary Disposition.
ASSURANCE—*see* Insurance Policies.
BEARER INSTRUMENT:
Inland bearer instrument, *i.e.* share warrant, stock certificate to bearer or any other instrument to bearer by which stock can be transferred, issued by a company or body formed or established in U.K. ......   1½%.
Overseas bearer instrument, *i.e.,* such an instrument issued in G.B. by a company formed out of the U.K. ....   1½%.
BILL OF SALE, Absolute, *see* CONVEYANCE ON SALE.
CAPITAL DUTY.—This was charged at 1 per cent. on every £100 or fraction of £100 of the actual value of assets contributed by the members of a company provided the place of effective management of the company was in G.B. or its registered office was in G.B. but the place of its effective management was outside the E.C. (Finance Act 1973).
The tax was abolished by the Finance Act 1988 in respect of transactions entered into on or after March 16, 1988.

CONTRACT, *see* AGREEMENT.

CONTRACT OR GRANT FOR PAYMENT OF A SUPERANNUATION ANNUITY: for every £10 or fractional part of £10 ....   5p

CONVEYANCE OR TRANSFER ON SALE (in the case of a Voluntary Disposition, *see* below) of any property (*except* stock or marketable securities), where the Conveyance or Transfer contains a certificate of value certifying that the transaction does not form part of a larger transaction or a series of transactions in respect of which the aggregate amount or value of the consideration exceeds £30,000..   nil
Exceeds £30,000 (for every £100 or fraction of £100) £1
If the Conveyance or Transfer on Sale does not contain the appropriate statement duty at the full rate of £1 for every £100 or fraction of £100 will be payable whatever the amount of the consideration.
However, if the consideration does not exceed £500, and the instrument does not contain a certificate of value, there are graduated duties ranging from 50p to £5.
Conveyances to charities are exempt from duty under this head provided the instrument is stamped with a denoting stamp.

CONVEYANCE OR TRANSFER of any other kind .... fixed duty   50p

However, under the Stamp Duty (Exempt Instruments) Regulations, 1987, instruments which would otherwise fall under this head are exempt from stamp duty provided that the document is duly certified. The certificate must contain a sufficient description of the category into which the instrument falls, and must be signed by the transferor, his solicitor or agent. "I/We hereby certify that this instrument falls within category ... in the Schedule to the Stamp Duty (Exempt Instruments) Regulations, 1987."

COVENANT—For original creation and sale of any annuity, *see* CONVEYANCE.

DECLARATION OF TRUST, not being a Will or Settlement 50p

DEMISE, *see* LEASE

DUPLICATE OR COUNTERPART
Same duty as original, but not to exceed ... 50p

GIFT (*see* VOLUNTARY DISPOSITION).

GUARANTEE:
If under seal 50p

INHERITANCE TAX
Inheritance Tax was introduced by the Finance Act, 1986, to replace Capital Transfer Tax. The most radical change is to take outside the charge to tax many (but not all) lifetime gifts made more than seven years before the death of the donor.

Lifetime transfers made before March 18, 1986, may be subject to capital transfer tax and are broadly unaffected by the new regime. Thus, subject to exemptions and rate bands, capital transfer tax is payable on such tranfers at the lifetime rate with an additional charge to tax at the death rate if the donor dies within three years of the transfer, but no additional charge if the donor survives three years but dies within seven years of the gift.

If the gift is made on or after March 18, 1986, and comes within the definition of what is known as a potentially exempt transfer (for details, see page 1013), tax is not payable at the time of the gift and will not be payable if the donor survives the gift for seven years. If the donor does not survive for three years, the rate of tax payable on death for the year 1988–89 (based on the value of the property at the date of the gift) is shown in the following table—

Value transferred		Rate of tax
Lower limit £	Upper limit £	Per cent
0	110,000	*Nil*
over 110,000	—	40

If the donor survives the gift by more than three but less than seven years, tapering relief is given as follows.

Years between gift and death	*Percentage of full charge*
0–3	100
3–4	80
4–5	60
5–6	40
6–7	20

If the gift does not come within the definition of a potentially exempt transfer e.g., the creation of a discretionary trust, it is taxed at the time of transfer at half the full rate, with an additional charge to tax if the donor dies within seven years.

Among the exemptions and reliefs given are the following:

(a) Transfers between spouses.
(b) The first £3,000 of gifts made in each tax year. There is provision for carry forward of this relief for one year only, in so far as it has not been used in the previous year.
(c) Gifts which are normal expenditure out of income.

(d) Gifts in consideration of marriage are exempt up to £5,000 if made by a parent; £2,500 if made by a grandparent or some other lineal ancestor, or by one party to another; and £1,000 in any other case.
(e) Gifts to charities and certain other bodies.
(f) Certain relief is given for agricultural and business property where a charge to inheritance tax arises on the donor's death within seven years, to the extent that the recipient still owns the property transferred or it has been replaced by similar property qualifying for relief.

INSURANCE POLICIES:
Life:—
Exc. £50 and not exc. £1,000, for every £100 or part of £100 .... 5p
Exc. £1,000, for every £1,000 or any fractional part of £1,000 .... 50p
Made after 1 August 1966 for period not exceeding 2 years..................... 5p

LEASES:—Lease or tack for any definite term less than a year of any furnished dwelling-house or apartments where the rent for such term exceeds £500, £1; of any lands, tenements, etc., in consideration of any rent, according to the following table:—

Annual rent not exceeding	*Term not exceeding			Term exceeding 100 years
	7 years	35 years	100 years	
£	£ p	£ p	£ p	£ p
5	*Nil*	0·10	0·60	1·20
10	*Nil*	0·20	1·20	2·40
15	*Nil*	0·30	1·80	3·60
20	*Nil*	0·40	2·40	4·80
25	*Nil*	0·50	3·00	6·00
50	*Nil*	1·00	6·00	12·00
75	*Nil*	1·50	9·00	18·00
100	*Nil*	2·00	12·00	24·00
150	*Nil*	3·00	18·00	36·00
200	*Nil*	4·00	24·00	48·00
250	*Nil*	5·00	30·00	60·00
300	*Nil*	6·00	36·00	72·00
350	*Nil*	7·00	42·00	84·00
400	*Nil*	8·00	48·00	96·00
450	*Nil*	9·00	54·00	108·00
500	*Nil*	10·00	60·00	120·00
Exceeding £500 for every £50 or fraction of £50	0·50	1·00	6·00	12·00

*If the term is indefinite the same duty is payable as if the term did not exceed 7 years.

Agreement for lease, same as actual lease.

Where a consideration other than rent is payable, the same rule applies where the consideration does not exceed £30,000 as under Conveyance or Transfer on Sale (except stock or marketable securities), provided that any rent payable does not exceed £300 a year and a certificate of value is included in the Conveyance or Transfer.

Leases to charities are exempt from duty under this head provided the instrument is stamped with a denoting stamp.

MORTGAGES are exempt.

RECEIPTS FOR SALARIES, Wages and Superannuation, and other like allowances are exempt.

TRANSFER OF STOCK AND SHARES by way of gift
or sale................................... ½%

UNIT TRUST INSTRUMENT—Any trust instrument of a unit trust scheme—For every £100, and also for any fractional part of £100, of the amount or value of the property subject to the trusts created or recorded by the instrument........................ 25p

VOLUNTARY DISPOSITION *inter vivos:*— 50p

LEGAL NOTES

IMPORTANT

The purpose of these notes is to outline some of the more common parts of the law as they may affect the average person, and they are, of course, believed to be correct at the time of going to press. The law is constantly developing and changing, however, and it is dangerous for the layman to seek to be his own lawyer—he may not have access to completely up to date books and his case may, because of its special facts, come within an exception to the general rules set out herein.

It is always best to take expert advice, and if you have a solicitor who has acted for you in the past you should take any legal problems you have to him. If you do not have a solicitor a friend may be able to recommend one. Failing this your local Citizens' Advice Bureau (whose address can be obtained from the telephone directory or from any Post Office or Town Hall) has a list of solicitors in your area who deal with that particular type of problem which you have. If you are not able to find a solicitor in any of these ways you should ask for help in doing so from The Law Society, 113 Chancery Lane, London, W.C.2 or The Law Society of Scotland at 26 Drumsheugh Gardens, Edinburgh.

The Legal Aid and Legal Advice and Assistance schemes exist to make the help of the trained lawyer available to everyone whatever their means as of right. The best policy is if in doubt go to a solicitor without delay—timely advice will set your mind at rest but sitting on your rights can mean that you lose them.

Remember also that it is not necessary for a dispute to have arisen before you go to a solicitor—the Legal Advice and Assistance Scheme enables him to advise you on your rights say under a tenancy agreement, the estate of a deceased person or in connection with matrimonial and consumer matters, and to write letters or take other steps on your behalf. He can also act for you where there is no question of a dispute at all, e.g. in the making of a will.

Your entitlement to take advantage of the scheme depends on your means (see below) but a solicitor or Citizens' Advice Bureau will be able to tell you whether you are covered by it.

BRITISH CITIZENSHIP

Types of citizenship.—There are three types of citizenship known as "British Citizenship", "Citizenship of the British Dependent Territories", and "British Overseas Citizenship".

Acquisition of citizenship on change of law.—The British Nationality Act 1981 which came into force on 1st January 1983 made substantial changes to the law of citizenship (which before that date did not distinguish between the three types of citizenship referred to above). Almost all persons who were then both citizens of the U.K. and Colonies and who had a right of abode in the U.K. became British Citizens when the Act came into force. Most U.K. and Colonies Citizens who did not have a right of abode in the U.K. became Citizens of the British Dependent Territories. This type of citizenship was, broadly speaking, conferred on citizens of the U.K. and Colonies by birth, naturalisation or registration in dependent territories. Dependent territories include Hong Kong, Gibraltar, the Falkland Islands, and St Helena and its dependencies. Any U.K. and Colonies Citizen who, on 1st Jan. 1983, did not acquire either British or British Dependent Territories' Citizenship became a British Overseas Citizen.

Later acquisition of British Citizenship.—British Citizenship is acquired automatically by those born in the U.K. (including, for this purpose, the Channel Islands and the Isle of Man) who have a parent who is a British Citizen or a parent who is settled in the U.K. Certain other categories of children born in the U.K. also acquire this type of citizenship i.e. foundlings, those whose parents subsequently settle in the U.K., those who live in the U.K. for 10 years from birth and those adopted in the U.K.

A person born outside the U.K. may acquire British Citizenship in the following ways:—

(i) if one of his parents is a British Citizen otherwise than by descent (e.g. parent was born in the U.K.).

(ii) if one of his parents is a British Citizen serving the Crown overseas.

(iii) if the Secretary of State consents to his registration while he is a minor.

(iv) if he is a Citizen of the British Dependent Territories, a British Overseas Citizen, a British Subject or a British Protected Person (these last two are residual categories of people who have not acquired one of the 3 new types of citizenship) and has been lawfully resident in the U.K. for 5 years without any time restriction.

(v) if he is a British Dependent Territories Citizen who is a national of the U.K. for the purposes of the E.C. (i.e. a Gibraltarian).

(vi) if he is naturalized. Naturalization may be applied for only by adults and the Secretary of State has a discretion whether to permit it. The basic requirements are five years' residence, good character, sufficient knowledge of the English or Welsh language, and an intention to reside in the U.K. permanently. The requirements are somewhat less restrictive in the case of an applicant who is married to a British Citizen.

Acquisition of British Dependent Territories and British Overseas Citizenship after the Act.—These citizenships are intended for persons connected with certain Commonwealth countries other than the U.K. In the case of Dependent Territories the rules are very similar to those for acquiring British Citizenship except that the connection is with the Dependent Territory rather than with the U.K. British Overseas Citizenship may be acquired by the minor children and wives of British Overseas Citizens in certain circumstances.

Retention of nationality by persons born in or who are citizens of the Republic of Ireland.—By the Ireland Act 1949, a person who was born before December 6th, 1922, in what is now the Republic of Ireland (Eire) and was a British subject immediately before January 1st, 1949, is not deemed to have ceased to be a British subject unless either (i) he was domiciled in the Irish Free State on December 6th, 1922 or (ii) was on or after April 10th, 1935, and before January 1st, 1949, permanently resident there, or (iii) had before January 1st, 1949, been registered as a citizen of Eire under the laws of that country.

In addition, by the British Nationality Act 1948, any citizen of Eire who immediately before January 1st, 1949, was also a British subject can retain that status by submitting at any time a claim to the Home Secretary on any of the following grounds:

(a) he has been in the service of the United Kingdom Government;

(b) he holds a British passport issued in the United Kingdom or in any colony, protectorate, United Kingdom mandated or trust territory;

(c) he has associations by way of descent, residence or otherwise with any such place; or on complying with similar legislation in any of the "dominions".

The British Nationality Act 1981 provides that persons who have made a claim may continue to be British subjects. Any citizen of Éire who was a British subject before January 1st, 1949, who has not yet made a claim may do so provided that:

(a) he is or has been in Crown Service under the government of the United Kingdom; or

(b) he has associations by way of descent, residence or otherwise with the United Kingdom or any dependent territory.

Renunciation and Resumption.—A person may cease to be a British Citizen by renouncing his citizenship (with the consent of the Secretary of State in wartime). The renunciation is required to be registered with the Secretary of State and will be revoked if no new citizenship or nationality is acquired within six months. Once renounced, citizenship may be reacquired if the renunciation was necessary to retain or acquire some other citizenship or nationality. Similar rules as to renunciation and reacquisition apply in the case of British Dependent Territories Citizenships and of renunciation (but not reacquisition) in the case of British Overseas Citizenship.

Status of Aliens.—Property may be held by an alien in the same manner as by a natural-born British subject, but he may not hold public office, exercise the franchise or own a British ship or aircraft. The Republic of Ireland Act 1949 declares that the Republic, though not part of H.M. Dominions, is not a foreign country, and any reference in an Act of Parliament to foreigners, aliens, foreign countries, etc., shall be construed accordingly.

CONSUMER LAW

1. THE SUPPLY OF GOODS AND SERVICES

(a) The Sale of Goods Act 1979 provides protection to the purchaser of goods, by implying certain terms into every contract for the Sale of Goods. These implied terms are:

(i) A condition that the seller will pass good title to the buyer (unless the seller agrees to transfer only such title as he or his principal has) and warranties that the goods will be free from undisclosed encumbrances, and that the buyer will enjoy quiet possession of the goods.

(ii) Where there is a sale of goods by description, a condition that the goods will correspond with that description, and where the sale is by sample and description, a condition that the bulk of the goods shall correspond with both sample and description.

(iii) Where the seller sells goods in the course of a business, a condition that the goods will be of merchantable quality, unless before the contract is made, the buyer has examined the goods and ought to have noticed the defect, bearing in mind the purchaser's knowledge of the goods and the extent of the examination, or the seller has specifically drawn the attention of the buyer to the defect. Merchantable quality means fit for the purpose for which goods of the kind are commonly bought, taking into account any

description applied to them, the price and other relevant circumstances.

(iv) A condition that where the seller sells goods in the course of a business, the goods are reasonably fit for any purpose made known to the seller by the buyer, unless the buyer does not rely on the seller's skill and judgment, or it would be unreasonable for him to do so.

(v) Where there is a sale of goods by sample, conditions that the bulk of the goods shall correspond with the sample in quality, that the buyer will have a reasonable opportunity of comparing the bulk with the sample, and that the goods are free from any defect rendering them unmerchantable, which would not be apparent from the sample.

For these purposes, the broad difference between a condition and a warranty is that the remedy for a breach of an implied condition may enable the buyer to reject the goods and recover damages if he has suffered loss whereas the remedy for a breach of warranty will only enable the buyer to recover damages.

It is possible for a seller to exclude some of the above terms from a contract, subject to restrictions imposed by the Unfair Contract Terms Act 1977 as given below. These restrictions give more protection ... where the buyer "deals as consumer". In a contract of sale of goods, a buyer "deals as consumer" where there is ... a sale by a seller in the course of a business, the goods are of a type ordinarily bought for private use or consumption, and are sold to a person who does not buy or hold himself out as buying them in the course of a business. A buyer in a sale by auction or competitive tender never "deals as consumer".

The 1977 Act prohibits the exclusion of the implied terms given in (ii) to (v) above, where the buyer "deals as consumer". In sales where the buyer does not "deal as consumer", terms purporting to exclude these implied terms, may be relied upon only to the extent that it would be reasonable to allow reliance. The Act provides guidelines for determining whether it would be reasonable to allow reliance. The implied terms in (i) above cannot be excluded whether the buyer "deals as consumer" or not.

(b) Similar terms to those implied in contracts of sale of goods are implied into contracts of hire-purchase by the Supply of Goods (Implied Terms) Act, 1973 and the 1977 Act limits the exclusion of these implied terms in a similar manner.

(c) Under the Supply of Goods and Services Act 1982, terms similar to those in the Sale of Goods Act relating to quiet possession, compliance with description, merchantable quality, fitness for purpose and correspondence with sample are implied into other types of contract under which ownership of goods passes (e.g. a contract for "work and materials" such as a supply of new parts during the servicing of a motor car) and also into contracts for the hire of goods. In the case of contracts under which ownership of goods is to pass, there is also an implied condition as to title.

The 1977 Act limits the exclusion of these implied terms in a similar manner to the implied terms in the Sale of Goods Act.

(d) The Supply of Goods and Services Act 1982 also implies into a contract for the supply of services, terms that the supplier will use reasonable care and skill, carry out the service within a reasonable time (unless the time is agreed) and charge a reasonable charge (unless the charge is agreed).

(e) The Trade Descriptions Act 1968 provides that it is a criminal offence for a trader or business-man to apply a false trade description to any goods, or to supply or offer to supply any goods to which a false trade description has been applied. A trade description includes a description as to quantity, size, method, place and date of manufacture, other history, composition, other physical characteristics, fitness for purpose, behaviour or accuracy, testing or approval. It is also an offence to give a false indication as to the price of goods. Prosecutions are brought by trading standards inspectors.

(f) The Fair Trading Act 1973 is also designed to protect the consumer. It provides for the appointment of a Director General of Fair Trading, whose duties include keeping under review commercial activities in the U.K. relating to the supply of goods or services to consumers, and to collect information to discover practices that may adversely affect the economic interests of the consumer. He may refer certain consumer trade practices to the Consumer Protection Advisory Committee, or, of his own initiative take proceedings against firms that are trading unfairly. He may also publish information and advice to consumers. Examples of practices which have been prohibited by virtue of references made under this Act, include the use of certain void exclusion clauses in contracts for the sale of goods and hire-purchase, and advertisements by traders appearing to sell as private persons.

(g) The Consumer Protection Act 1987 makes the producer of a product liable for any damage caused by a defect in that product, subject to certain defences. (This provision is expected to be brought into force during 1988).

(h) The Consumer Protection (Cancellation of Contracts Concluded away from Business Premises) Regulations, 1987 allow consumers a seven day period in which to cancel most contracts for supply of goods or services exceeding £35 in cost, where these contracts have been made following an unsolicited visit to the consumer's home or workplace.

Scotland

The Sale of Goods Act, 1979, a consolidating Act, applies with some modification to Scotland. For example, it is not necessary in Scotland to distinguish between the words condition and warranty. The remedies of the buyer in both cases are the same, that is, he can either within a reasonable time reject the goods and treat the contract as repudiated, or retain the goods and treat the failure to perform such material part as a breach which may give rise to a claim for compensation or damages.

2. CONSUMER CREDIT
England and Wales

The Consumer Credit Act 1974 is now fully in force. It provides a system for the protection of the consumer, of licensing and control of all matters relating to the provision of credit, or the supply of goods on hire or hire-purchase, administered by the Director-General of Fair Trading. A licence is required to carry on a consumer credit or consumer hire business, or to deal in credit brokerage, debt adjusting, counselling or collecting, for which group licences are available. Any "fit person" may apply to the Director of Fair Trading for a licence which is

normally renewable after 10 years. A licence is not necessary if such types of business are only transacted "occasionally" or if exempt agreements only are involved.

For the Act's provisions to apply the agreement must be "regulated", i.e. be to individuals or partnerships only; must not be exempt, e.g. certain loans by local authorities or building societies; and the total credit must not exceed £15,000. The terms of a regulated agreement can be varied by the creditor, but only if the agreement gives him the right to do so, and the debtor receives notice in the prescribed form.

To be enforceable the agreement must be properly executed, and the specified information must be given during the antecedent negotiations for the contract. These are conducted by the creditor, credit broker or supplier (these being the creditor's agents) and begin when the parties first begin discussions.

The agreement must state certain information such as the amount of credit, the annual percentage rate of interest and the amount and timing of repayments.

An agreement is cancellable under the Act if oral representations were made in the debtor's presence during antecedent negotiations and the debtor signed the agreement other than at the creditor's (or credit-broker's or negotiator's) place of business. Time for cancellation expires five clear days after the debtor receives a second copy of the agreement. The agreement must inform the debtor of his right to cancel and how to cancel.

Where there are arrangements or connections between the creditor and supplier the former is generally liable for any misrepresentation or breach of contract by the latter, and will thus be liable to indemnify the debtor.

If the debtor is in arrears or is otherwise in breach of the agreement, the creditor may not enforce the agreement, e.g. by repossessing goods, without serving a default notice on the debtor. This notice will give the debtor a chance to remedy the default. Even if the default is not remedied by the debtor, if the agreement is a hire-purchase or conditional sale agreement, the creditor cannot repossess the goods without an order of the court, if the debtor has paid one-third of the total price of the goods.

Where the agreement requires the debtor to make grossly exorbitant payments or is contrary to the ordinary principles of fair dealing the Court can reopen it either at the debtor's request or during enforcement proceedings and (inter alia) alter the terms of the contract or set aside any obligations it imposes so as to do justice between the parties. Whether an agreement is such an extortionate credit bargain is decided by reference (inter alia) to interest rates prevailing at the date of agreement, the pressure for finance the debtor was under, etc.

If a credit reference agency was used to check the debtor's financial standing the creditor must give the agency's name to the debtor who is entitled to see the agency's file on him on payment of a fee of £1.

Scotland

The Consumer Credit Act (see above) also extends to Scotland and goes far in assimilating the Scots Law on this topic with English Law. The Supply of Goods (Implied Terms) Act 1973 also applies to Scotland. Parts II and III only of the Unfair Contract Terms Act 1977 apply to Scotland. The Sale of Goods Act, 1979, applies with some modification to Scotland.

3. RECEIPTS

The law on receipts in Scotland is governed by the Prescription and Limitations (Scotland) Act 1973, which for this purpose came into force on July 25, 1976. Now, receipts need only be kept for a period of five years and if a creditor does not make a relevant claim within that period no action can be raised.

CROWN—PROCEEDINGS AGAINST

Before 1947 proceedings against the Crown were generally possible only by a procedure known as a petition of right, which placed the litigant at a considerable disadvantage and which was not normally available at all in cases of tort (i.e., civil wrongs other than breach of contract). Thus, no proceedings would normally lie against the Government if a subject were injured by the negligent driving of a Government vehicle (although the driver could be sued) or if a Government employee were injured by the defective condition of the Crown premises on which he worked. Now however, by the Crown Proceedings Act 1947, which came into operation on Jan. 1, 1948, the Crown, in its public capacity, is largely placed in the same position as a subject, although some procedural disadvantages remain.

Scotland.—The Act as amended extends to Scotland and has the effect of bringing the practice of the two countries as closely together as the different legal systems will permit. While formerly actions against the Crown, when permissible, were confined to the Court of Session, proceedings may now be brought in the Sheriff Court.

The Act lays down that arrestment of money in the hands of the Crown or of a Government Department is competent in any case where arrestment in the hands of a subject would have been competent, but an exception is made in respect of National Savings Bank deposits. Section 2 (1) of the Law Reform (Miscellaneous Provisions) (Scotland) Act 1966 removes the privilege whereby the wages of Crown servants, other than serving members of the armed forces, are exempt from arrestment in execution.

DEATHS

REGISTRATION, BURIAL AND CREMATION

REGISTRATION

(For Certificates, *see* under FAMILY LAW—CERTIFICATES)

In England and Wales.—When a death takes place, information of it must be given in person to the local Registrar of Births and Deaths, and the register signed in his presence, by one of the following persons: (1) a relative of the deceased present at the death, or in attendance during the last illness. (2) Some other relative of the deceased. In default of any relatives (3) a person present at the death; or, the occupier of the house in which the death happened. (4) An inmate of the house. A person (other than a relative) registering the death must be causing the disposal of the body. The registration must be made within five days of the death, or within the same time written notice of the death must be sent to the Registrar. If the deceased was attended during his last illness by a registered medical practitioner, a certificate of cause of death must be sent by the doctor to the Registrar. The doctor must give to the informant of the death a written notice of the signing of the certificate, which must be delivered to the Registrar. It is essential that a certificate for disposal should be obtained from the Registrar before the funeral and delivered to the clergyman or other person in charge of the churchyard or cemetery. No fee is chargeable for this certificate. If the death is not registered within five days (or fourteen days if written notice of the occurrence of the death is sent

to him) the Registrar may require any one of the above-mentioned persons to attend to register at a stated time and place. Failure to comply involves a penalty of ten pounds. The registration of a death is free of charge. After twelve months no death can be registered without the Registrar General's consent.

Whenever the death of a child is registered, particulars of the name and occupation of the mother are to be entered in the register.

A body must not be disposed of until (1) either the Registrar has given a certificate to the effect that he has registered or received notice of the death, or (2) until the Coroner has made a disposal order (Births and Deaths Registration Act 1926, s. 1).

A person disposing of a body must within ninety-six hours deliver to the Registrar a notification as to the date, place, and means of the disposal of the body (*ib.*, S. 3).

"Still-born" child (*see* under Births (Registration) *below*).

Death at Sea.—The master of a British ship must record any death on board and send particulars to the Registrar General of Shipping.

Death Abroad.—Consular Officers are authorized to register deaths of British subjects occurring abroad. Certificates are procurable at the Registrar General's Office, London. If the deceased was of Scottish domicile, particulars are sent to the Registrar General for Scotland.

With regard to the registration of deaths of members of the armed forces, and deaths occurring on H.M. ships and aircraft, *see* the Registration of Births, etc. Act 1957.

Deaths (Registration) in Scotland.—The Registration of Births, Deaths and Marriages (Scotland) Act 1965 supersedes provisions in former Acts.

Personal notification within 8 days must be given to the registrar of (*a*) the registration district in which the death took place or (*b*) any registration district in which the deceased was ordinarily resident immediately before his death, and (*c*) when a body is found and the place of death is not known, either the registration district in which the body was found or any other registration district appropriate by virtue of the preceding paragraph. When a person dies (in or out of Scotland) in a ship, aircraft or land vehicle during a journey and the body is conveyed therein to any place in Scotland the death shall, unless the Registrar General otherwise directs, be deemed to have occurred at that place.

The register must be signed in the presence of the registrar by one of the following: (*a*) any relative of the deceased; (*b*) any person present at the death; (*c*) the deceased's executor or other legal representative; (*d*) the occupier, at the time of the death, of the premises where the death took place; (*e*) if these fail, any other person having knowledge of the particulars to be registered. Failure to comply involves a penalty not exceeding £50.

The medical practitioner who attended the deceased during the last illness must sign a certificate of the cause of death within 7 days. If there is no such medical practitioner, any medical practitioner who is able to do so, may sign the certificate. At the time of registering the death the registrar shall, without charge, give the informant a certificate of registration, and the person to whom the certificate is given must hand it to the undertaker previous to cremation. A body may, however, be interred before the death is registered, in which case the undertaker must deliver a certificate of burial to the Registrar within three days.

The mandatory death grant was abolished in April 1987 but assistance may be obtained from the

Department of Health and Social Security by those who are unable to meet funeral expenses.

BURIAL

The duty of burial is incumbent on the deceased person's executors (if any appointed); it is also a recognized obligation of the husband of a woman, and the parent of a child, also of a householder where the body lies. Funeral expenses of a reasonable amount will be repayable out of deceased's estate in priority to any other claims. Directions as to place and mode of burial are frequently contained in the deceased's will or in some memorandum placed with private papers, or may have been communicated verbally to a relative. Consequently steps should immediately be taken to ascertain the deceased's wishes from the above sources. If the wishes are considered objectionable, they are not necessarily enforceable; legal advice should be taken. A person may legally leave directions for the anatomical examination of his body. As to the place of burial—unless closed by Order in Council—the parish churchyard is the normal burying place for parishioners, or any person dying in the Parish, but nowadays this will apply only in villages and the smaller towns. In populous districts cemeteries and crematoria have been established either by the local council, or a private company, and burials will take place there in accordance with the regulations. For an exclusive right to a burial space in the churchyard a faculty is required from the Ecclesiastical Court. Poor persons may be buried at the public expense by the local authority. As to the necessity for obtaining a registrar's certificate or authority from the Coroner for disposal, *see* above.

CREMATION

Under the Cremation Acts, 1902 and 1952, regulations are made by the Home Secretary dealing fully with the cremation of a body, disposal of ashes, etc., and containing numerous essential safeguards.

If Cremation is desired it is advisable for instructions to be left in writing to that effect. However, in Scotland, even if the deceased wished his body to be cremated or anatomically dissected, relatives can still veto his or her wishes.

To arrange for Cremation the Executor or near relative should instruct the undertaker to that effect and obtain from him the Statutory Forms required as given in the Cremation Regulations issued in 1930 (Statutory Rules and Orders, 1930, No. 1016), as amended by the Cremation Regulations 1965 (No. 1146) and the Cremation (Amendment) Regulations 1985 (No. 153).

INTESTACY

ENGLAND AND WALES

As regards deaths on or after March 15, 1977, the position is governed by the Administration of Estates Act, 1925, as amended by the Intestates' Estates Act, 1952, the Family Provision Act, 1966 and Orders made thereunder. If the intestate leaves a spouse and issue, the spouse takes (i) the "personal chattels"; (ii) £75,000 with interest at 6 per cent. from death until payment; and (iii) a life interest in half of the rest of the estate. This life interest can be capitalized at the option of the spouse. "Personal chattels" are articles of household use or ornament (including motor-cars), not used for business purposes. The rest of the estate goes to the issue. If the intestate leaves a spouse and no issue, but leaves a parent or brother or sister of the whole blood or issue of such brothers and sisters the spouse takes (i) the "personal chattels"; (ii) £125,000 with interest at 6 per cent. from death until payment, and (iii) half of the rest of the estate

absolutely. The other half of the rest of the estate goes to the parents, equally if more than one, or, if none, to the brothers and sisters of the whole blood or issue of such brothers and sisters. If the intestate leaves a spouse, but no issue, no parents and no brothers or sisters of the whole blood or their issue, the spouse takes the whole estate absolutely. If resident therein at the intestate's death, the surviving spouse may generally require the personal representatives to appropriate the interest of the intestate in the matrimonial home in or towards satisfaction of any absolute interest of the spouse, including the capitalized value of a life interest. In certain cases, leave of Court is required. On a partial intestacy any benefit (other than personal chattels specifically bequeathed) received by the surviving spouse under the will must be brought into account against the statutory legacy of £75,000 or £125,000, as the case may be. If there is no surviving spouse, the estate is distributed among those who survive the intestate in the following order (those entitled under earlier numbers taking to the exclusion of those entitled under later numbers):—(1) children; (2) father or mother (equally, if both alive); (3) brothers and sisters of the whole blood; (4) brothers and sisters of the half blood; (5) grandparents (equally, if more than one alive); (6) uncles and aunts of the whole blood; (7) uncles and aunts of the half blood; (8) the Crown.

In cases (1), (3), (4), (6) and (7) the persons entitled lose their interests unless they or their issue not only survive the intestate, but also attain eighteen or marry under that age, their shares going to the persons (if any) within the same group who do attain eighteen or marry. Moreover, in the same cases, succession is not *per capita*, but *per stirpes*, i.e., by stocks or families. Thus, if the intestate leaves one child and two grandchildren, being the children of a child of the intestate, who pre-deceased the intestate, the two grandchildren represent their deceased parent and take between them one-half of the issue's share, the remaining half going to the surviving child. Similarly, nephews and nieces represent a deceased brother, and so on.

When the deceased died partially intestate (i.e., leaving a will which disposed of only part of his property), the above rules apply to the intestate part.

Children must bring into account (hotchpot) any substantial advances received from the intestate during his lifetime before claiming any further share under the intestacy. Special hotchpot provisions apply to partial intestacy.

In respect of deaths occurring on or after April 4, 1988, Section 18 of the Family Law Reform Act 1987 provides that references to any relationship between two persons shall, unless the contrary intention appears, be construed without regard to whether or not the father and mother of either of them, or the father and mother of any person through whom the relationship is deduced, have or had been married to each other at any time.

In respect of deaths after March 1976 the provisions of the Inheritance (Provision for Family and Dependants) Act 1975 may allow other persons to claim provision out of the estate. See *post* under "Wills".

For personal application for Letters of Administration—*see below*.

SCOTLAND

The Succession (Scotland) Act, 1964, provides that the whole estate of any person dying intestate shall devolve without distinction between heritable and moveable property. By that Act the surviving spouse of an intestate may, as a prior right (in addition to legal rights, *see* below), claim the matrimonial home to a maximum of £65,000, or a choice of one matrimonial home if more than one (or in certain circumstances the value thereof), with its furniture and plenishings not exceeding £12,000 in value, plus the sum of £21,000 if the deceased left issue or, if no issue, the sum of £35,000. These figures apply from 1st August 1981 and may be increased from time to time by order of the Secretary of State.

The Act has been modified by the Law Reform (Miscellaneous Provisions) (Scotland) Act, 1968, which provided that an illegitimate child had exactly the same rights of succession in the estate of his parents as a legitimate child. However, the position still remains that an illegitimate child has no succession rights in the estate of a grandparent even though such would have fallen to his predeceasing parent.

Legal rights, referred to above, are:—

Jus relicti (œ): the right of a surviving spouse to one half of the deceased's net moveable estate after satisfaction of prior rights if there are no surviving children, or to one third if there are any surviving children.

Legitim: right of surviving children to one-half of the net moveable estate of deceased parents if no surviving spouse, or one-third of the net moveable estate of deceased parents after satisfaction of prior rights where there is a surviving spouse.

There are no legal rights in heritage.

In general, the lines of succession are: (1) descendants; (2) collaterals; (3) ascendants and their collaterals, and so on in the ascending scale. The Crown is *ultimus haeres.* The right of representation, *i.e.,* the right of the issue of a person, who would have succeeded if he had survived the intestate, is open to any line of succession where previously it was limited to apply only when there were next of kin or the issue of predeceasing next of kin. The surviving mother of an intestate now has equal rights of succession with the surviving father, where formerly these were restricted. The intestate's maternal relations, who prior to the Act had no rights of succession, are now on an equal footing with his paternal relations. Where the intestate is survived only by parents, and by brothers and sisters (collaterals) half of the estate is taken by the parents and the other half by the brothers and sisters, those of the whole blood being preferred to those of the half blood; where, however, succession opens to collaterals—(which expression can include the brothers and sisters of an ancestor of the intestate)—of the half blood, they shall rank equally amongst themselves, whether related to the intestate (or his ancestor) through their father or their mother.

WILLS

IMPORTANT NOTE.—The following notes and those on Intestacy must be read subject to the provisions of the Inheritance (Provision for Family and Dependants) Act 1975 which can affect the estate of anyone dying domiciled in England and Wales after March 1976. Very broadly a spouse, former spouse who has not remarried, a child of the deceased himself or one treated by him as a child of his family, or any person maintained by him at his death may apply to the Court under the Act. If the Court thinks that the will or the law of intestacy or both do not make reasonable provision for the applicant it may order payment out of the net estate of maintenance or a lump sum. It may also order the transfer of property, vary certain trusts and the powers can affect property disposed of by the deceased in his lifetime intending to defeat the Act. It is up to the applicant to take the initiative, and the application must generally be made within six months of the grant of Probate or Letters of Administration.

REASONS FOR MAKING A WILL.—Every person over the age of 18 should make a will. However small the estate the rules of Intestacy (see above) may not reflect a person's wishes as to his property; in any case a will can do more than just deal with property—it can in particular appoint executors, give directions as to the disposal of the body and appoint guardians to take care of children in the event of the parents' death. For the wealthier person an appropriately drawn will can operate to reduce the burden of Inheritance Tax.

It is considered desirable for a will to be properly drawn up by a Solicitor, and the making of a will is one of the services which he can provide under the Legal Advice and Assistance Scheme (see below).

In no circumstances should one person prepare a Will for another person where the former is to take any benefit under it—this can easily lead to a suggestion of undue influence which may cause the will to be held bad.

Assuming a lawyer is not employed, a person having resolved to make a will must remember that it is only after a person is dead, and cannot explain his meaning, that his will can be open to dispute. It is the more necessary, therefore, to express what is meant in language of the utmost clearness, avoiding the use of any word or expression that admits of another meaning than the one intended. Avoid the use of "legal terms," such as "heirs" and "issue," when the same thing may be expressed in plain language. If in writing the will a mistake be made, it is better to rewrite the whole. Before a will is executed (*see below*) an alteration may be made by striking through the words with a pen, but opposite to such alteration the testator and witnesses should write their names or place their initials. Never scratch out a word with a knife or other instrument, and no alteration of any kind whatever must be made after the will is executed. If the testator afterwards wishes to change the disposition of his estate, it is best to make a new will, revoking the old one. The use of *codicils* should be left to the lawyer. A will should be written in ink and very legibly, on a single sheet of paper. Although, of course, forms of wills must vary to suit different cases, the following forms may be found useful to those who, in cases of emergency, are called upon to draw up wills, either for themselves or others.

Nothing more complicated should be attempted. The forms should be studied in conjunction with the notes following.

This is the last will and testament of me [*Thomas Smith*] of [*Vine Cottage, Silver Street, Reading, Berks*] which I make this [*thirteenth*] day of [*February,* 1989] and whereby I revoke all previous wills and testamentary dispositions.

1. I hereby appoint [*John Green of* —— *and Richard Brown of* ——] to be the executor(s) of this my will.

2. I give all my property real and personal to [*my wife Mary* or *my sons Raymond and David equally* or as the case may be].

Signed by the testator in the presence of us both present at the same time who, at his request, in his presence and in the presence of each other have hereunto set our names as witnesses.

    Thomas Smith
    Signature of Testator;

William Jones (*signed*) of Green Gables, South Street, Reading, tailor.

Henry Morgan (*signed*) of 16, North Street, Reading, butcher.

Should it be desired to give legacies and/or gifts of specific property, instead of giving the whole estate to one or more persons, the form above should be used with the substitution for clause 2 of the following clauses:

2. I give to —— of —— the sum of £—— and to — —— of —— the sum of £—— and to —— of —— all my books (*or as the case may require*).

3. All the residue of my property real and personal I give to —— of ——.

TERMS.—Real property includes freehold land and houses; while personal property includes debts due, arrears of rents, money, leasehold property, house furniture, goods, assurance policies, stocks and shares in companies, and the like. The words "my money," apart from the context, will normally only include actual real money. The expression "goods and chattels" should not be used. In giving particular property, ordinary language is sufficient, e.g., "my house, Vine Cottage, Silver Street, Reading, Berks." Such specific gifts fail if not owned by the testator at his death.

RESIDUARY LEGATEES.—It is well in all cases where legacies or specific gifts are made, to leave to some person or persons "the residue of my property," although it may be thought that the whole of the property has been disposed of in legacies, etc., already mentioned in the will. It should be remembered that a will operates on property owned at the time it is made or acquired after it has been made.

EXECUTION OF A WILL, AND WITNESSES.—The testator should sign his name at the foot or end of the will, in the presence of two witnesses, who will immediately afterwards sign their names in his and in each other's presence. A person who has been left any gift or share of residue in the will, or whose wife or husband has been left such a gift, should not be an attesting witness. Their attestation would be good, but they would forfeit the gift. It is better that a person named as executor should not be a witness. Husband and wife may both be witnesses, provided neither is a legatee. If a solicitor be appointed executor, it is lawful to direct that his ordinary fees and charges shall be paid; but in this case he (as an interested party) must not be a witness to the will.

It is desirable that the witnesses should be fully described, as they may possibly be wanted at some future time. If the testator should be too ill to sign, even by a mark, another person may sign the testator's name to the will for him, in his presence and by his direction, and in this case it should be shown that the testator knew the contents of the document. The attestation clause should therefore be worded: "Signed by Thomas Brown, by the direction and in the presence of the testator, Thomas Smith, in the joint presence of us, who thereupon signed our names in his presence and in the presence of each other, the will having been first read over to the testator, who appeared fully to understand the same."

Where there is any suspicion that the Testator is not, by reason of age or infirmity, fully in command of his faculties it is desirable to ask his Doctor to act as a witness (see Testamentary capacity below).

A *blind person* may make a will in Braille. If the testator be blind the will should be read aloud to him in the presence of the witnesses, and the fact mentioned in the attestation clause. A blind person cannot witness a will.

If by inadvertence the testator should have signed his will without the witnesses being present, then the attestation should be:—"The testator acknowledged his signature already made as his signature to his last will and testament, in the joint presence,"

etc. Any omission in the observance of these details may invalidate the will. The stringency of the law as to signature and witnessing of a will is only relaxed in favour of soldiers, sailors and airmen in certain circumstances.

EXECUTORS.—It is usual to appoint two executors, although one is sufficient; any number up to and including four may be appointed. The name and address of each executor should be given in full. An executor may be a legatee. Thus a child of full age or wife to whom the whole or a portion of the estate is left may be appointed sole executor, or one of two executors. The addresses of the executors are not essential; but it is desirable here as elsewhere, to avoid ambiguity or vagueness.

LAPSED LEGACIES.—If a legatee dies in the lifetime of the testator, the legacy generally lapses and falls into the residue. Where a residuary legatee predeceases the testator, his share of the residuary estate will not generally pass to the other residuary legatees, but will pass to the persons entitled on the deceased's intestacy. In all such cases it is desirable to make a new will.

An important exception to the general rule of lapse stated above is contained in the Administration of Justice Act 1982, where there is a gift to a child or remoter issue of the testator who dies before the testator leaving issue who survive the testator.

TESTAMENTARY CAPACITY.—A person under the age of 18 cannot make a will (except for soldiers, sailors and airmen and then only in exceptional circumstances).

So far as mental capacity is concerned the Testator must be able to understand and appreciate the nature and effect of making a will, the property of which he can dispose and the claims to which he ought to give effect. If a person is not mentally able to make a will provision exists (under the Mental Health Act, 1983) for the Court to do this for him.

REVOCATION.—A later will revokes an earlier will if it expressly says so, or is completely inconsistent with it. Otherwise the earlier one is only revoked insofar as it is inconsistent with the later one. A will may also be revoked by burning, tearing or otherwise *destroying* the will with the intention of revoking it. Such destruction must either be by the testator or by some other person in his presence and at his direction. It is not sufficient to obliterate the will with a pen. Marriage in every case acts as the revocation of a will, except that under the Administration of Justice Act 1982, there is a provision to the effect that if it appears from a will that at the time it was made the testator was expecting to be married to a particular person and that he intended that the will (or a disposition in the will) should not be revoked by the marriage to that person, the will will not be revoked by marriage to that person. The Act also provides that where after a testator has made a will the testator's marriage is terminated by a decree of divorce or nullity, any gift to a spouse shall lapse and any appointment of the spouse as executor shall be omitted from the will unless the will shows a contrary intention.

PERSONAL APPLICATION FOR PROBATE OR LETTERS OF ADMINISTRATION

Application for probate or for letters of administration may be made in person at the Personal Application Dept. of the Principal Registry of the Family Division, a district probate registry or sub-registry, or a probate office by the executors or persons entitled to a grant of administration. Applicants should bring (1) the will, if any; (2) a certificate of death; (3) particulars of all property and assets left by the deceased; and (4) a list of debts and funeral expenses.

Intending applicants, before attending at a registry or probate office, should write or telephone to the nearest probate registry or sub-registry for the necessary forms. Postal or telephone applications cannot be dealt with at the local probate offices, which are part-time only.

Certain property can be disposed of on death without a grant of probate or administration, or in pursuance of a nomination made by the deceased, provided the amount involved does not exceed £5,000. *See* the Administration of Estates (Small Payments) Act, 1965.

WHERE TO FIND A PROVED WILL

A will proved since 1858 must have been proved either at the Principal Registry at Somerset House, or a District Registry. In the former case the original will itself is carefully preserved at Somerset House, the copy of which probate has been granted is in the hands of the executors who proved the will, and another copy for Parliament is bound up in a folio volume of wills made by testators of that initial and date; the indices to these volumes fill a room of considerable size at Somerset House, where the indices may be examined and a copy of any will read. In the latter case, the original will proved in the District Registry, is kept there, and may be seen or a *copy* obtained, but a copy is sent to and filed at Somerset House, where also it may be seen. A general index of grants, both probates and administrations, is prepared and printed annually in lexicographical form, and may be seen at either the Principal or a District Registry. This index is usually ready by about October of the following year.

RECENT DEATHS.—A system introduced in 1975 enables a person to discover when a grant of Probate or Letters of Administration is made which may be invaluable to a creditor of the deceased or applicant under the Inheritance (Provision for Family and Dependants) Act 1975—*see above.* A "standing search" may be made by sending a request in the form set out below to the Record Keeper at the Principal Registry of the Family Division with a small fee. The searcher will receive particulars of any grant made in the previous 12 months or the following 6 months, including names and addresses of the executors or administrators and the Registry in which the grant was made.

FORM OF SEARCH

In the High Court of Justice
Family Division
The Principal Registry (Probate)
I/We apply for the entry of a standing search so that there shall be sent to me/us an office copy of every grant of representation in England & Wales in the estate of:—
Full name of deceased:
Alternative or alias name
Full address
Exact date of death
Which either has issued not more than 12 months before the entry of this application or issues within 6 months hereafter
Sgd.—(full address).

SCOTS LAW OF WILLS

A domiciled Scotsman, unlike a domiciled Englishman, cannot in certain circumstances dispose effectively of the entirety of his estate. If he leave a widow and children, the widow is entitled to a one-third share in the whole of the moveable estate (her *jus relictae*), and the children are entitled to another one-third share equally between them (their *legitim*). If he leave a widow but no children—or children but

no widow—the *jus relictae* or *legitim* is increased to a one-half share of the net moveable estate. The remaining portion is known as the *dead's part.* A surviving husband and children have comparable rights (*jus relicti* and *legitim*) in the wife's estate. The dead's part is the only portion of which the testator can freely dispose. Legacies and bequests are payable only out of the dead's part. All debts are payable out of the whole estate before any division. Pupils, i.e. a girl up to the age of twelve or a boy up to the age of fourteen, cannot make wills. Formerly a minor could dispose only of movables but since the passing of the Succession (Scotland) Act, 1964 he has a like capacity to test on heritable property. A will must be in writing and may be typewritten or even in pencil. A will may be either (1) *holograph*, i.e. written, dated and subscribed by the testator himself, in which case no witnesses are necessary; a printed form filled up by the testator or a typewritten document is not necessarily a holograph but may become so if the testator writes, in hand, at the foot of the form or document the words "*adopted as holograph*" followed by his signature and the date. Words written on erasure or marginal additions or interlineations in holograph writings, if proved to be in the handwriting of the maker of the deed, are valid; (2) *attested*, i.e. signed in presence of two witnesses. It is not necessary that these witnesses should sign in presence of one another, or even that they should see the testator signing so long as the testator acknowledges his signature to the witnesses. The Conveyancing and Feudal Reform (Scotland) Act, 1970 whilst altering generally the rules for the subscription of deeds, specifically (s. 44 (2)) makes no change in the rules applying to wills which must still be signed by the testator on every page. If the testator cannot write, or is blind, his will may be authenticated by a law agent, notary public or justice of the peace and two witnesses. It is better that the will be not witnessed by a beneficiary thereunder, although this circumstance will not invalidate the attestation of the will or (as it would in England) the gift. A parish minister may act as a notary for the purpose of subscribing a will in his own parish. Wills may be registered in the Books of the Sheriffdom in which the deceased died domiciled, or in the Books of Council and Session, H.M. General Register House, Edinburgh. The original deed may be inspected on payment of a small fee and a certified official copy may be obtained. A Scottish will is not revoked by the subsequent marriage of the testator. The subsequent birth of a child, no testamentary provision having been made for him, may revoke a will. A will may be revoked by a subsequent will, either expressly or by implication; but in so far as the two can be read together both wills have effect. If a subsequent will is revoked, the earlier will is revived.

"Confirmation", the Scottish equivalent of Probate, is obtained in the Sheriff Court of the Sheriffdom in which the deceased was domiciled at the date of his death or, where he had no fixed domicile or died abroad, in the commissariot of Edinburgh. Executors are either "nominate" or "dative". An Executor nominate is one nominated by the deceased in his will or, where such person has predeceased the testator, by the residuary beneficiary. An Executor dative is one appointed by the Court in the case of intestacy or where the deceased had failed to name an executor in his will and there is no residuary beneficiary. In the former case the deceased's next-of-kin are all entitled to be declared executors dative. An inventory of the deceased's estate and a schedule of debts, together with an affidavit, must first be given up. In estates under £13,000 gross, confirmation is obtained under a simplified procedure at reduced fees.

Presumption of Survivorship.—The Succession (Scotland) Act, 1964, referred to above provides, by s. 31, that where two persons die in circumstances indicating that they died simultaneously or if it is uncertain which was the survivor, the younger will be deemed to have survived the elder unless the elder person left testamentary provision in favour of the younger, whom failing in favour of a third person, the younger person having died intestate (partially or wholly); but if the persons so dying were husband and wife, neither shall be presumed to have survived the other.

EMPLOYMENT
WAGES AND SICK PAY

The Wages Act 1986 has repealed the Truck Acts. Under this Act, subject to certain exceptions, employers may not make deductions from an employee's wages unless authorised by statute or contract or with the employee's prior written consent. There is an upper limit of one-tenth of gross pay for deductions from retail workers' wages on account of cash or stock shortages.

Under the Social Security and Housing Benefits Act 1982 as amended, an employee absent from work due to illness or injury is entitled to receive Statutory Sick Pay from the employer for a maximum period of 28 weeks in any year. No payment is made for the first three days of any period of illness. The employer can recoup the payments from his National Insurance contributions.

The Equal Pay Act 1970, which extends to Scotland, and which came into force on December 29, 1975, prevents discrimination, as regards terms and conditions of employment between men and women employed on like work in the same employment.

PARTICULARS OF TERMS OF EMPLOYMENT

Under the Employment Protection (Consolidation) Act 1978, an employer must give each full-time employee within 13 weeks of the beginning of the employment a written statement containing the following particulars of the contract between them:

(1) the date when the employment began (when continuous employment began if previous work counts as continuous with this job);
(2) the rate of remuneration (or how it is calculated);
(3) the intervals at which wages are paid;
(4) the hours of work;
(5) the employee's entitlement to holidays (including public holidays) and holiday pay;
(6) the title of the employee's job;
(7) terms relating to sickness, injury and sick pay;
(8) details of any pension scheme;
(9) the length of notice which the employee should give and receive in order to terminate the contract.

In addition, the written particulars must specify any disciplinary rules; and also must identify the person to whom the employee can apply if he is dissatisfied with any disciplinary decision or to seek redress of any grievance and what further steps may ensue.

TERMINATION OF EMPLOYMENT

An employee may be dismissed without notice if he is guilty of gross breach of contract, such as disobedience to a lawful order or dishonesty. He is then only entitled to wages accrued due at the date of dismissal.

In other cases, the employee is entitled to reasonable notice which, under the Employment Protection (Consolidation) Act 1978, must not be less than one week if he has been continuously employed for four weeks, but less than two years; after two years it is two weeks' notice increasing by one week's notice for each further full year worked up to a maximum of 12 weeks' notice after 12 years' service.

An employer who wrongfully dismisses an employee (i.e. with less than the length of notice to which he is entitled) is generally liable to pay wages for the period of proper notice.

An employee who has a fixed term contract has no claim against his employer for wrongful dismissal if his contract is not renewed when it expires. He may, however, have a claim for a redundancy payment or compensation for unfair dismissal. If he is wrongfully dismissed before his contract expires, he is generally entitled to remuneration payable over the full period of the contract.

An employee may be entitled to a redundancy payment or to compensation for unfair dismissal if the employment has been terminated by the employer (with or without proper notice) or he has a fixed term contract which expires without being renewed or the employment has been terminated by the employee by reason of the employer's breach of contract.

Under the Employment Protection (Consolidation) Act 1978, an employee who satisfies the foregoing conditions and has been continuously employed for two years and who is dismissed by reason of redundancy may be entitled to a redundancy payment calculated by reference to his age, pay and length of service.

The Employment Protection (Consolidation) Act 1978 also enables an employee who is unfairly dismissed to complain to an Industrial Tribunal (generally within 3 months of dismissal). The onus will then be on the employer to prove that the dismissal was due to capability, conduct, redundancy, illegality or some other substantial reason justifying dismissal. The tribunal must then decide whether the employer acted reasonably in dismissing the employee. If the employer fails to prove that the dismissal was due to one or more of the above five reasons, or the tribunal decides that the employer did not act reasonably in dismissing the employee, the dismissal will be unfair, in which case the tribunal can

(a) order re-engagement or reinstatement or
(b) award compensation consisting of a basic and a compensatory award.

For an employee to bring himself within the unfair dismissal provisions, he must have been continuously employed for a period of two years.

All complaints of unfair dismissal are referred to a conciliation officer or the Department of Employment and a very high proportion of complaints are disposed of in this way.

FAMILY LAW
ADOPTION OF CHILDREN

In England and Wales this is now mainly governed by the Children Act 1975 and the Adoption Act 1976. A court order is necessary to legalise the adoption, which, when completed, has the effect of making the adopted child the child of the adopter as if he or she had been born to the adopter in lawful wedlock, and the original rights and duties of the natural parents are thereby cut. The adopter has full rights as to custody, education etc. and the child is treated as his for the purpose of any devolution of property on an intestacy occurring or under any disposition made after the adoption order. The application may be made to the High Court (Family Division) or to a County Court or Magistrates' Court.

Orders may be made in favour of married couples, single, widowed or divorced persons, but not of one party to a marriage alone unless the other spouse cannot be found, is physically or mentally incapable of making an application, or they are separated in circumstances likely to be permanent. A person aged under 21 cannot adopt.

The child's parents or guardians must consent unconditionally to the making of the order unless the court dispenses with the consent, which it may do if the parent cannot be found or is incapable of giving his consent, is withholding his consent unreasonably, or has neglected or ill-treated the child.

Restrictions are placed on societies which may arrange adoptions.

An adopted person aged over 18 may apply to the Registrar General for information to enable him to obtain a full certificate of his birth, but before being supplied with the information he will be informed that counselling services are available to him.

An adopter and the adopted child are within the prohibited degrees for the purposes of marriage to one another.

All Adoptions in Great Britain are registered in the Registers of Adopted Children kept by the Registrars General in London and Edinburgh respectively. Certificates from these registers including short certificates which contain no reference to adoptions, can be obtained on conditions similar to those relating to birth certificates, (*see below.*)

Scotland.—The Law is consolidated in the Adoption (Scotland) Act 1978 which is now fully in force. The Law relating to fostering is consolidated in the Foster Children(s) Act 1984. A petition for adoption is presented either to the Sheriff Court or the Court of Session. As in England the petitioner(s) must be 21 or over and may be a married couple or one person who, if married, is living apart permanently from his or her spouse. The consent of the child's natural parents/guardians is required unless dispensed with, or the child is already free for adoption.

The Succession (Scotland) Act 1964, gives the adopted child the same rights of succession as a child born to the adopter in wedlock but deprives him of any such rights in the estates of his natural parents.

BIRTHS (REGISTRATION)

When a birth takes place, personal information of it must be given to the Registrar of Births and Deaths for the sub-district in which the birth occurred, and the register signed in his presence, by one of the following persons:—

1. The father or mother of the child. If they fail; 2. the occupier of the house in which the birth happened; 3. a person present at the birth; or, 4. the person having charge of the child. The duty of attending to the registration therefore rests firstly on the parents. The mother is responsible for the registration of the birth of an illegitimate child. The registration is required to be made within 42 days of the birth. Failure to do this, without reasonable cause, involves liability to a penalty of twenty pounds. The registration of a birth is free. In England or Wales, the informant, instead of attending before the registrar of the sub-district where the birth occurred, may make a declaration of the particulars required to be registered in the presence of any registrar. Under the Public Health Act 1936, notice of every birth must be given by the father, or person in attendance on the mother, to the district medical officer of health by post within 36 hours of the birth. This is in addition to the registration already mentioned.

A "Stillbirth" must be registered and a certificate signed by the doctor or midwife who was present at the birth or has examined the body of the child must be produced to the registrar. The certificate must, where possible, state the cause of death and the estimated duration of the pregnancy. A stillbirth may only be registered within 3 months of the birth.

The re-registration of the birth of a person legitimated by the subsequent marriage of the parents is provided for in the Births and Deaths Registration Act 1953. Special provisions apply to the registration and re-registration of births of abandoned children, and the re-registration of births of illegitimate children showing the father's name; the mother must normally be party to the latter application.

Birth at Sea: The master of a British ship must record any birth on board and send particulars to the Registrar General of Shipping.

Birth Abroad: Consular Officers are authorized to register births of British subjects occurring abroad. Certificates are procurable in due course at Registrar General's Office, London.

The registration of births occurring out of the United Kingdom among members of the armed forces, or occurring on board H.M. ships and aircraft, is provided for by the Registration of Births, Deaths and Marriages (Special Provisions) Act 1957, applicable also to Scotland.

SCOTLAND

The Registration of Births, Deaths and Marriages (Scotland) Act 1965, supersedes former Acts. Personal notification within 21 days of any birth, must be given to the registrar of (*a*) the registration district in which the birth took place, or (*b*) any registration district in which the mother of the child was ordinarily resident at the time of the birth and (*c*) in the case of a foundling child, dead or alive, when the place of birth is not known, the registration district in which the child, or the body, was found, within two months from the date on which the child was found. When a child is born (in or out of Scotland) in a ship, aircraft or land vehicle during a journey and the child is conveyed therein to any place in Scotland, the birth shall, unless the Registrar General otherwise directs, be deemed to have occurred at that place.

The register must be signed in the presence of the registrar by the father or mother of the child, and if they fail, by one of the following: (*a*) any relative of either parent who has knowledge of the birth; (*b*) the occupier of the premises in which the child was, to the knowledge of that occupier, born; (*c*) any person present at the birth; (*d*) any person having charge of the child. Failure without reasonable cause involves a penalty not exceeding £50.

The name of the father of a child born out of wedlock may be entered in the register of births at the time of registration if jointly requested by the mother and father, and the latter's name may also be recorded at a later date on declaration by both parents. A free abbreviated certificate of birth will be issued to the informant at the time of registration. Provision is made for the re-registration of the birth of a person made legitimate by the subsequent marriage of the parents or whose birth entry is affected by any matter respecting status or paternity, or has been so made as to imply that he is a foundling.

A still-birth must be registered and a certificate, signed by the doctor or certified midwife present at the birth or who has examined the body of the child, must be produced.

CERTIFICATES OF BIRTHS, MARRIAGES, OR DEATHS

England and Wales.—Certificates of Births, Deaths, or Marriages can be obtained at the Office of Population Censuses and Surveys, St. Catherine's House, 10 Kingsway, WC2B 6JP or from the Superintendent Registrar having the legal custody of the register containing the entry of which a certificate is required. Certificates of marriage can also be obtained from the incumbent of the church in which the marriage took place; or from the Nonconformist minister (or other "authorized person") where the marriage takes place in a registered building (*see, post,* under Marriage).

It is considered desirable when a certificate is required to consult the nearest Register Office who, if told the exact or approximate date and place of registration, will be able to advise on the best way of obtaining it, and any fees payable, which vary according to the type of certificate required and other factors.

English Registers.—Records of births, deaths and marriages registered in England and Wales since 1837 are kept at the Office of Population Censuses and Surveys, St. Catherine's House, 10 Kingsway, WC2B 6JP. *The Society of Genealogists,* 14 Charterhouse Buildings, Goswell Road, EC1M 7BA, possess many records of Baptisms, Marriages and Deaths prior to 1837, including copies, in whole or in part of about 4,000 Parish Registers.

Scottish Registers of Births, Deaths, Marriages and Divorces.—Certificates of births, deaths or marriages registered from 1855 when compulsory registration commenced in Scotland can be obtained personally at the General Register Office, New Register House, Edinburgh, or from the appropriate local Registrar, on payment of the fee of £5·50 for a full extract entry of birth, death, or marriage, and £4·00 for an abbreviated certificate of birth. An abbreviated certificate of registration of deaths is issued free of charge for National Insurance purposes in certain cases. A Register of Divorces (which includes decrees of declaration of nullity of marriage) is kept by the Registrar General at the General Register Office. The fee for an extract decree is £5.50.

There are also available at the General Register Office old parish registers of the date prior to 1855, which were formerly kept under the administration of the Established Church of Scotland. An extract of an entry in these registers may be obtained on payment of the appropriate fee. A fee of £9·00 per day is payable for a general search of all the Scottish registers.

Registration of Presumed Deaths. (Prescription of Particulars) (Scotland) Regulations 1978 as read with Presumption of Death (Scotland) Act 1977 prescribe the particulars to be notified by the Clerk of Court to the Registrar General after a decree or variation order has been granted in an action of declarator of death of a missing person.

DIVORCE, SEPARATION AND ANCILLARY MATTERS

Preliminary—Matrimonial Suits may be conveniently divided into two classes, viz. (1) those in which it is sought to annul the marriage because of some defect; and (2) those in which the marriage being admitted, it is sought to end the marriage or the duties arising from it. By virtue of the Matrimonial and Family Proceedings Act 1984, all matrimonial

causes are commenced in one of the divorce county courts designated by the Lord Chancellor or in the Divorce Registry in London. If the suit becomes defended, it may be transferred to the High Court.

(1) *Nullity of Marriage.*—This is now mainly governed as to England and Wales by the Matrimonial Causes Act 1973. A marriage is void *ab initio* if the parties were within the prohibited degrees of affinity, or were not male and female, or if it was bigamous or if one of the parties was under the age of consent, i.e. 16, or in the case of a polygamous marriage entered into outside England and Wales, that either party was at the time of the marriage domiciled in England and Wales. Where the formalities of the marriage were defective, the marriage is generally void if both parties knew of the defect (e.g., where marriage took place otherwise than in an authorized building). But absence of the consent of parents or guardians (or of the Court or other authority, in lieu thereof) in the case of minors does not invalidate the marriage.

A marriage is voidable (i.e. a decree of nullity may be obtained but until such time the marriage remains valid) on the following grounds—(a) incapacity of either party to consummate; (b) respondent's wilful refusal to consummate; (c) that either party did not validly consent to the marriage, whether in consequence of duress, mistake, unsoundness of mind or otherwise, (d) that either party at the time of marriage was a mentally disordered person; (e) that at the time of marriage the respondent was suffering from communicable venereal disease; (f) that at the time of the marriage the respondent was pregnant by another man. In cases (e) and (f) the petitioner must have been ignorant of the grounds at the date of the marriage and in (c), (d), (e) and (f) proceedings must be instituted within 3 years of the marriage, although leave may be obtained to petition outside this period in the case of certain persons suffering from mental illness. In all cases the court shall not grant a decree where the petitioner has led the respondent to believe that he would not seek a decree and it would be unjust for it to be granted.

The 1973 Act provides that a decree of nullity in a voidable marriage only annuls the marriage from the date of the decree. The marriage remains valid until the decree, and any children of the marriage are legitimate. Children of a void marriage are illegitimate unless the father was domiciled in England and Wales at the child's birth (or father's death, if earlier) and at the time of conception (or marriage if later) both or either of the parents reasonably believed the marriage was valid.

A spouse's insistence upon the use of contraceptives will not constitute wilful refusal to consummate within (b) above, even though there has been no normal intercourse, but it may in certain circumstances constitute unreasonable behaviour for the purpose of divorce (as to which *see below*). Further it has been allowed as a defence to a charge of desertion against the aggrieved party.

(2) *Judicial Separation and Divorce.*—The second class of suit includes a suit for judicial separation (which does not dissolve a marriage) and a suit for divorce (which, if successful, dissolves the marriage altogether and leaves the parties at liberty to marry again). Either spouse may petition for judicial separation. It is not necessary to prove that the marriage has broken down irretrievably and the five facts listed (a) to (e) under divorce (below) are grounds for judicial separation.

Divorce.—The sole ground on which a divorce is obtained by either husband or wife is the irretrievable breakdown of the marriage. However, the court is precluded from holding that a marriage has irretrievably broken down unless it is satisfied of one or more of the following facts: (a) that the respondent has committed adultery since the marriage and the petitioner finds it intolerable to live with the respondent; (b) that the respondent has behaved in such a way that the petitioner cannot reasonably be expected to continue co-habitation; (c) desertion by the respondent for 2 years immediately before the petition; (d) 5 years separation immediately before the petition (but only 2 years where the respondent consents to the decree). Matrimonial Causes Act 1973.

The foregoing is subject to a clause prohibiting any petition for divorce (but not for judicial separation) before the lapse of one year from the date of the marriage.

Desertion may be defined as a voluntary withdrawal from cohabitation by one spouse without just cause and against the wishes of the other. Where one spouse is guilty of conduct of a serious nature which forces the other to leave, the party at fault is said to be guilty of constructive desertion.

Provisions designed to encourage reconciliation.— The 1973 Act requires the solicitor for the petitioner to certify whether he has or has not discussed the possibility of a reconciliation and whether or not he has given the petitioner the names and addresses of persons qualified to help effect a reconciliation.

A total period of less than six months during which the parties have resumed living together is to be disregarded in determining whether the prescribed period of desertion or separation has been continuous. Similar provision for effecting a reconciliation exists in relation to the other proofs of break-down, but a petitioner cannot rely on an act of adultery by the other party if they have lived together for more than six months after discovery of that act of adultery.

Obtaining the Decree Nisi. Where the suit is defended, i.e. the respondent opposes the dissolution or the fact/ground on which the petitioner seeks it— the petition will be heard by a Judge in open court, the parties giving oral evidence. Where the suit is undefended, the evidence will normally take the form of a sworn written statement made by the petitioner which will be sent to the Court and read over by the Registrar. If he is satisfied that he or she has proved the contents of the petition, he will simply fix a date for a Judge to pronounce the decree nisi, it being unnecessary for either party to attend. Only if the Registrar is not satisfied as above will he order that the petition be heard formally by the Judge.

Children.—Subject to exceptions, the decree nisi cannot be made absolute unless a Judge by order declares that he is satisfied with the proposed arrangements for the welfare of any child of the family who is under 16 or under 18 and receiving education or vocational training. If there is no dispute as to the children between the parties and the proposed arrangements for residence, education etc. are specific, an appointment will be made for the Judge to interview one or both parents informally and if satisfied he will make an order to that effect (this will usually be on the same day as the decree nisi is pronounced). If not the Registrar may inform the parties that it is up to them to seek a hearing before the Judge to resolve the matters in dispute.

Decree Absolute.—Every decree of divorce or nullity is in the first instance a decree nisi, and the marriage subsists until the decree is made absolute, usually six weeks after decree nisi on the petitioner's application. After the decree absolute either party is free to remarry.

Maintenance, etc.—The court has wide powers to order either party to the marriage to make financial provision (e.g. periodical payments, a lump sum, the transfer of property) for the other party or any child of the family, having regard to the party's means, the recipient's needs and all the important aspects of the case. These so-called 'ancillary matters' often present more difficulty than the divorce itself especially affecting the home, and may go on long after the marriage is dissolved. There is, however, nothing to stop financial matters being negotiated by the parties through their solicitors before the divorce goes through.

The court may, where the husband has wilfully neglected to provide reasonable maintenance for the wife or children, order the husband to make provision for them, even though no matrimonial suit is pending between the parties to the marriage, and while such an order is in force the court may also deal with custody of and access to the children.

CUSTODY OF CHILDREN ETC.

The Court may make orders in respect of access to and the custody, maintenance and education of children in connection with a suit for divorce, nullity or judicial separation (above) or with an application to the Magistrates (below) whether the suit succeeds or not. In addition, if there is no other matrimonial suit involved a parent may apply for custody under the Guardianship of Minors Acts 1971, and any person may apply to the High Court for the child to be made a ward of court.

In all cases the welfare of the child is the first and paramount consideration. The categories of child who may be covered by any particular type of proceedings differ according to the nature of those proceedings and to the nature of the particular relief sought, but it should be borne in mind that in connection with divorce, nullity and judicial separation a child which has been treated by the spouses as a child of the family may be included as a 'child of the family' as well as the children of the spouses themselves. This also applies to most maintenance cases in the magistrate's court—*see below.*

Under the Children Act 1975 a new procedure called "Custodianship" has been introduced, basically allowing long term foster parents to apply for custody of the foster child.

Any dispute relating to the above matters should be placed in the hands of a Solicitor without delay (see Legal Aid, etc. below) and in particular it should be borne in mind that where there is financial need (because of, e.g. continuing education or disability) maintenance may be ordered for children even beyond the age of majority.

SEPARATION BY AGREEMENT

Husband and wife may enter into an agreement to separate and live apart, but the agreement, to be valid, must be followed by an immediate separation. It is most desirable to consult a solicitor in every such case, who will often advise obtaining a court order by consent.

MAGISTRATES' CUSTODY AND MAINTENANCE ORDERS

For many years the law relating to domestic proceedings in magistrates' courts was out of line with the divorce law which was reformed in 1969. The Domestic Proceedings and Magistrates' Courts Act 1978 took effect in early 1981 and now contains the relevant law.

A husband or wife can apply to a magistrates' court for a matrimonial order on the grounds that the other spouse (a) has failed to pay reasonable maintenance for the applicant or (b) has failed to make a proper contribution towards the reasonable maintenance of a child of the family or (c) has deserted the applicant or (d) has behaved in such a way that the applicant cannot reasonably be expected to live with the respondent. If the case is proved the court can order (a) periodical payments for the applicant (b) periodical payments for a child of the family (c) a lump sum (not exceeding £1,000) for the benefit of the applicant and for any child of the family. In deciding what orders (if any) to make the magistrates must consider a number of guidelines which are similar to those governing financial orders on divorce. There are also special provisions relating to consent orders and separation by agreement. The court also has powers to make orders relating to the legal custody of a child of the family and these orders together with orders for child maintenance can be made even though the court makes no order for spouse maintenance. Legal custody can only be granted to one person but the court may order that the other party shall retain certain parental rights and exercise them jointly with the person who is awarded legal custody. Other provisions of the Act relate to access by grandparents, interim orders, and variation, discharge and revival of orders. An order may be enforceable even though the parties are living together, but in some cases it will cease to have effect if they continue to do so for six months. The hearing of matrimonial disputes is separate from ordinary court business, and the public are not admitted.

DOMESTIC VIOLENCE

The Domestic Violence and Matrimonial Proceedings Act 1976, the Domestic Proceedings and Magistrates' Courts Act 1978 (the former not being applicable to Scotland and the latter only to a limited extent; but see note below) and the Matrimonial Homes Act 1983 have made it easier for one spouse who has been subjected to violence by the other to obtain an order to restrain further violence and if need be to have the other excluded from the home. Such orders can be obtained very quickly, and a person disobeying them is liable to be imprisoned for contempt of court. There are some differences of detail between the three Acts; in particular the 1976 Act also applies to unmarried couples. Such orders may also be obtained in the course of suits for divorce and judicial separation.

SCOTLAND
Divorce

Actions of divorce could formerly only be raised in the Court of Session, having jurisdiction to entertain such actions only if either of the parties to the marriage in question (a) is domiciled in Scotland on the date when the action is begun; or (b) was habitually resident in Scotland throughout the period of one year ending with that date. As from May 1, 1984, however, when the Divorce Jurisdiction, Court Fees and Legal Aid (Scotland) Act 1983 came into force, actions of divorce may also be raised in the Sheriff Courts provided the above conditions (a) and (b) are complied with, and provided either party to the marriage was resident in the Sheriffdom for a period of forty days ending with the date the action was begun, or was resident in the Sheriffdom for a period of not less than forty days ending not more than forty days before the date the action was begun.

The Scots Law of Divorce is now governed by the Divorce (Scotland) Act 1976, which for the purposes of divorce came into force on January 1, 1977. The sole ground of divorce is now irretrievable breakdown of the marriage. This can only be established in one of the following ways:

(a) The defending spouse has committed adultery since the date of the marriage. Here it is not necessary for the pursuing spouse to prove that the fact of

adultery made it intolerable to live with the defending spouse.

(b) The defending spouse has behaved in such a way that the pursuing spouse cannot reasonably be expected to cohabit with him or her. It is immaterial whether or not the conduct founded upon is active or passive.

(c) The defending spouse has deserted the pursuing spouse for a continuous period of two years. There must be no question of the pursuing spouse having refused a genuine and reasonable offer to adhere. Nor is irretrievable breakdown established if cohabitation is resumed for a period of more than three months, after the two year period has expired.

(d) There has been no cohabitation at any time during a continuous period of two years immediately preceding the action between the parties to the action, and the defending spouse consents to the divorce being granted.

(e) There has been no cohabitation at any time during a continuous period of five years, as in (d) *supra*, except that on the expiry of the five year period, the consent of the defending spouse is not required.

The facts of desertion and separation are not interrupted by the parties cohabiting for a period or periods not exceeding six months. However such a period or periods of cohabitation would not be included in the calculation of the two-year or five-year periods.

Encouragement of Reconciliation. The burden of promoting a reconciliation between spouses in a divorce action in Scotland falls upon the Court by virtue of the 1976 Act. Where an action of divorce has been raised, it may be postponed by the Court to enable the parties to seek to effect a reconciliation, if the Court feels that there may be a reasonable prospect of such reconciliation. If the parties do cohabit during such postponement, no account shall be taken of such cohabitation if the action later proceeds.

Maintenance, etc.—The 1976 Act also provides that either party to a marriage can apply to the Court at any time prior to decree being granted for (a) an order for interim custody of all or some of the children of the marriage under 16 years of age (b) an order for access to all or some of the children of the marriage under 16 years of age in the custody of the other party.

The financial provisions on divorce in the 1976 Act have been superseded by the Family Law (Scotland) Act 1985 which allows either party to the marriage to apply to the court for an order for payment of a capital sum or for a periodical allowance or for an incidental order. The Act sets out principles to be applied by the Court, one of these being that the financial provisions awarded to a party who has been dependant for financial support on the other party should be given over a period of not more than three years.

The Act also defines the rights and obligations of aliment between parents and children thereby excluding aliment between grandparents and grandchildren and of children to parents and provides that a child is entitled to aliment up to the age of eighteen or to twenty five if in full time further education and for the claiming of aliment whether in connection with an action of divorce etc. or independently.

Nullity of Marriage.—A declaration of nullity of marriage may be obtained on the ground of any impediment, viz., consanguinity and affinity, subsistence of a previous marriage, non-age of one of the parties, incapacity or insanity of one of the parties, or by the absence of genuine consent. The financial provisions on divorce contained in the Family Law (Scotland) Act 1985 also apply to an action for declaration of nullity of marriage.

Procedure.—Appearance in Court at a Proof in an undefended Divorce Action has been rendered unnecessary since April, 1978. A full Proof is still necessary if the action is defended in any respect. In place of court appearance Affidavits (Statements sworn before a Notary Public) by the pursuer and any witnesses are lodged in the Court together with a Minute by the solicitor craving Decree.

A new simplified procedure for "do-it-yourself divorce" was introduced in January 1983 for certain divorces. Thus, if the action is based on (d) or (e) above and will not be opposed, there are no children under 16 and no financial claims, then the applicant can write directly to the Court of Session, Divorce Section (SP), Parliament House, Edinburgh or the local Sheriff Court for the appropriate forms to enable him or her to proceed. The fee is £40 unless the applicant receives Income Support, Family Credit or legal advice and assistance in which case there is no fee.

Separation

Under the Divorce (Scotland) Act 1976 *supra*, a decree of Judicial Separation can be obtained by proof of the same facts necessary to obtain decree of divorce—except that for the principle of irretrievable breakdown there is substituted that of grounds justifying separation. This type of action is competent in both the Court of Session and the Sheriff Court.

Custody of Children

In actions for divorce and separation, the Court has a discretion in awarding the custody of the children of the parties. The welfare of the children is the paramount consideration, and the mere fact that a spouse, by reason of his or her behaviour, brought about the breakdown of the marriage does not of itself preclude him or her from being awarded custody. The Children Act 1975 (*supra*) also applies to Scotland.

Domestic Violence

The Matrimonial Homes (Family Protection) (Scotland) Act 1981, as amended, provides that one spouse—whether or not he or she has title to the matrimonial home—can obtain an exclusion order suspending the other spouse's occupancy rights in the matrimonial home. The Court (either Court of Session or Sheriff Court) is empowered to make such an order if satisfied that it is necessary to protect the applicant or any child of the family from any conduct, actual or threatened or reasonably apprehended of the other spouse which would be injurious to the physical or mental health of the applicant or child. In making the order the Court may include a warrant for the summary ejection of the non-applicant spouse from the matrimonial home and for an interdict prohibiting him/her from entering it.

ILLEGITIMACY AND LEGITIMATION

ENGLAND AND WALES

The former provisions of the Affiliation Proceedings Act 1957, under which a man could be summoned to petty sessions on the application of the mother of an illegitimate child, or by the Supplementary Benefits Commission where benefit has been paid for the requirements of the child, and the Justices, on his being proved to be the father of the child, could make an order requiring him to pay for its maintenance and education a sum in their discretion, have been replaced by extensive provisions relating to

parental rights and duties in Part II of the Family Law Reform Act 1987. *Prima facie* every child born of a married woman during a marriage is legitimate; and this presumption can only be rebutted by strong evidence. However, under the Family Law Reform Act 1969, any presumption of law as to the legitimacy (or illegitimacy) of any person may in civil proceedings be rebutted by evidence showing that it is more probable than not that the person is illegitimate (or legitimate) and in any proceedings where paternity is in question, blood tests may be ordered. If however the husband and wife are separated under an Order of the Court, a child conceived by the wife during such separation is presumed not to be the husband's child.

LEGITIMATION.—The Legitimacy Act 1976 consolidates earlier legislation dating back to January 1, 1927. Where the parents of an illegitimate person marry, or have married, whether before or after that date, the marriage, if the father is at the date thereof domiciled in England or Wales, renders that person, if living, legitimate as from Jan. 1, 1927, or from the date of the marriage, whichever last happens. Marriage legitimates a person even though the father or mother was married to a third person at the time when the illegitimate person was born. It is the duty of the parents to supply to the Registrar-General information for re-registration of the birth of a legitimate child.

Declarations of Legitimacy.—A person claiming that he, his parents, or any remoter ancestor has become legitimated, may petition the High Court or the County Court for the necessary declaration.

Rights and Duties of Legitimated Persons.—A legitimated person, his spouse or issue may take property under an intestacy occurring after the date of legitimation, or under any disposition (e.g., a will) coming into operation after such date, as if he had been legitimate.

He must maintain all persons whom he would be bound to maintain had he been born legitimate, and he is entitled to the benefit of any Act of Parliament which confers rights on legitimate persons to recover damages or compensation. The Act specially provides that nothing therein contained is to render any person capable of succeeding to or transmitting a right to any dignity or title.

Property Rights of Illegitimate Children.—By the Family Law Reform Act 1969 the rights of an illegitimate child on an intestacy were broadly equated with those of a legitimate child, and in any disposition made after December 31, 1969, any reference to "children" or other relatives was, unless the contrary intention appears, to be construed as including any person who is illegitimate or who is related through another person who is illegitimate. However, these provisions of the 1969 Act have been replaced by the general provision of the Family Law Reform Act 1987 (*see* p. 1026).

SCOTLAND

The Law Reform (Parent & Child) Scotland Act 1986 implements the Scottish Law Commission's Report on Illegitimacy. The act contains a general provision granting equality status to all persons whatever the marital status of their parents. The mother of an illegitimate child may raise an action of affiliation and aliment against the father, either in the Court of Session or, more usually, in the Sheriff Court. Where in any such action the Court finds that the defender is the father of the child, the Court shall, in awarding inlying expenses, or aliment, have regard to the means of the parties, and the whole circumstances of the case. The Court may, upon application by the mother or by the father of any illegitimate child, or in any action for aliment for an illegitimate child, make such order as it may think fit regarding the custody of such child and the right of access thereto of either parent, having regard to the welfare of the child and to the conduct of the parents and to the wishes as well of the mother as of the father and may on the application of either parent recall or vary such order. The obligation of the mother and of the father of an illegitimate child to provide aliment for such child shall (without prejudice to any obligation attaching at common law) endure until the child attains the age of sixteen.

By Scots Law an illegitimate child is legitimated by and on the date of the subsequent marriage of its parents and there is no objection to there having been an impediment to the marriage of the parents at the time of the child's conception—*see* the Legitimation (Scotland) Act 1968, which came into operation on June 8, 1968, on which date thousands of existing illegitimate children were regarded as legitimated. By the Registration of Births, Deaths and Marriages (Scotland) Act 1965, a child so legitimated, who has already been registered as illegitimate, may be re-registered as legitimate. The consent of the father of an illegitimate child to its adoption is not required unless he has been awarded parental rights by the court.

The Law Reform (Miscellaneous Provisions) (Scotland) Act 1968, gives an illegitimate child full rights of succession (including legitim) in the estate of both parents, while the father and mother share equally in the estate of their illegitimate child. Unless expressly excluded, a reference in a deed executed on or after November 25, 1968, to a relationship, *e.g.*, "issue" or "children" is presumed to include illegitimate children.

MARRIAGE

A.—MARRIAGE ACCORDING TO RITES OF THE CHURCH OF ENGLAND

1. MARRIAGE BY BANNS.—The Marriage Act 1949, prescribes audible publication according to the rubric, on three Sundays preceding the ceremony during morning service or, if there is no morning service on a Sunday on which the banns are to be published, during evening service. Where the parties reside in different parishes, the banns must be published in both. Under the Act, banns may be published and the marriage solemnized in the parish church, which is the usual place of worship of the persons to be married or either of them, although neither of such persons dwells in such parish; but this publication of banns is in addition to any other publication required by law and does not apply if the church or the residence of either party is in Wales. The Act provides specially for the case where one of the parties resides in Scotland and the other in England, the publication being then in the parish in England in which one party resides, and, according to the law and custom in Scotland, in the place where the other party resides. After the lapse of three months from the last time of publication, the banns become useless, and the parties must either obtain a licence (*see below*), or submit to the republication of banns.

2. MARRIAGE BY LICENCE.—Marriage licences are of two kinds:—

   (i) *A Common Licence*, dispensing with the necessity for banns, granted by the Archbishops and Bishops through their Surrogates, for marriages in any church or chapel duly licensed for marriages. A Common Licence can be obtained in London by application at the Faculty Office (1 The Sanctuary, Westminster, S.W.1) and (for marriages in London) at the Bishop of London's Diocesan Registry (1 The

Sanctuary, S.W.1), by one of the parties about to be married. In the country they may be obtained at the offices of the Bishop's Registrars, but licences obtained at the Bishop's Diocesan Registry only enable the parties to be married in the diocese in which they are issued; those procured at the Faculty Office are available for all England and Wales. No instructions, either verbal or in writing, can be received, except from one of the parties. Affidavits are prepared from the personal instructions of one of the parties about to be married, and the licence is delivered to the party upon payment of fees amounting to six pounds. No previous notice is required and the licence is available as soon as it is issued. Before a licence can be granted one of the parties must make an affidavit that there is no legal impediment to the intended marriage; and also that one of such parties has had his or her usual place of abode for the space of fifteen days immediately preceding the issuing of the licence within the parish or ecclesiastical district of the church in which the marriage is to be solemnized, *or* the church in which the marriage is to be solemnized is the usual place of worship of the parties or one of them. In the country there may generally be found a parochial clergyman (Surrogate) before whom the affidavit may be taken, and whose office it is to deliver the licence personally to the applicant. (In some dioceses it is necessary for the Surrogate to procure the licence from the Bishop's Registry.) The licence continues in force for three months from its date.

   (ii) *A Special Licence* granted by the Archbishop of Canterbury, under special circumstances, for marriage at any place with or without previous residence in the district, or at any time, etc.; but the reasons assigned must meet with his Grace's approval. Application must be made to the Faculty Office. Fees for licence, etc., £25.

3. MARRIAGE UNDER SUPERINTENDENT REGISTRAR'S CERTIFICATE.—A marriage may be performed in church on the Superintendent Registrar's Certificate (as to which see below) without banns, provided that the incumbent's consent is obtained. One of the parties must be resident within the ecclesiastical parish of the church in which the marriage is to take place unless the church is the usual place of worship of the parties or one of them.

MARRIAGE FEES.—The Church Commissioners settle tables of fees for all parishes. The usual fees are paid although a stranger-clergyman may be invited to perform the service.

B. MARRIAGE UNDER SUPERINTENDENT REGISTRAR'S CERTIFICATE

The following marriages may be solemnized on the authority of a Superintendent Registrar's Certificate (either with or without a licence):—

   (*a*) A marriage in a registered building (*e.g.*, a nonconformist church registered for the solemnization of marriages therein).
   (*b*) A marriage in a register office.
   (*c*) A marriage according to the usages of the Society of Friends (commonly called Quakers).
   (*d*) A marriage between two persons professing the Jewish religion according to the usages of the Jews.
   (*e*) A marriage according to the rites of the Church of England (*see* above—in this case the marriage can only be without licence).

NOTICE.—Notice of the intended marriage must be given as follows:—

(i) Marriage by certificate (without licence)—if both parties reside in the same registration district, they must both have resided there for seven days before the notice can be given. It may then be given by either party. If the parties reside in different registration districts, notice must be given by each to the Superintendent Registrar of the district in which he or she resides, and the preliminary residential qualification of seven days must be fulfilled by each before either notice can be given.

(ii) Marriage by certificate (with licence)—one notice only is necessary, whether the parties live in the same or in different registration districts. Either party may give the notice, which must be given to the Superintendent Registrar of any registration district in which one of the parties has resided for the period of fifteen days immediately preceding the giving of notice, but both parties must be resident in England or Wales on the day notice is given.

The notice (in either case) must be in the prescribed form and must contain particulars as to names, marital status, occupation, residence, length of residence, and the building in which the marriage is to take place. The notice must also contain or have added at the foot thereof a solemn declaration that there is no legal impediment to the marriage, and, in the case of minors, that the consent of the person whose consent to the marriage is required by law (*see below*) has been duly given, and that the residential qualifications (mentioned above) have been complied with. A person making a false declaration renders himself or herself liable to prosecution for perjury. The notice is entered in the marriage notice book.

ISSUE OF CERTIFICATE:

(i) *Without licence.*—The notice (or an exact copy thereof) is affixed in some conspicuous place in the Superintendent Registrar's office for 21 days next after the notice was entered in the marriage notice book. After the lapse of this period the Superintendent Registrar may, provided no impediment is shown, issue his certificate for the marriage which can then take place at any time within three months from the date of the entry of the notice.

(ii) *With licence.*—The notice in this case is not affixed in the office of the Superintendent Registrar. After the lapse of one whole day (other than a Sunday, Christmas Day or Good Friday) from the date of entry of the notice, the Superintendent Registrar may, provided no impediment is shown, issue his certificate and licence for the marriage, which can then take place on any day within three months from the date of entry of the notice.

SOLEMNIZATION OF THE MARRIAGE:

(i) *In a Registered Building.*—The marriage must generally take place at a building within the district of residence of one of the parties, but if the usual place of worship of either is outside the district of his or her residence, it may take place in such usual place of worship. Further, if there is not within the district of residence of one of the parties a registered building within which marriages are solemnized according to the rites and ceremonies which the parties desire to adopt in solemnizing their marriage, it may take place in an appropriate registered building in the nearest district.

The presence of a Registrar of Marriages is not necessary at marriages at registered buildings which have adopted the provisions of section 43 of the Marriage Act 1949. This section provides for the appointment of an "authorized person" (a person, usually the minister or an official of the building, certified by the trustees or governing body as having been duly authorized for the purpose) who must be present and must register the marriage.

The marriage must be solemnized between the hours of 8 a.m. and 6 p.m., with open doors in the presence of two or more witnesses. The parties must at some time during the ceremony make the following declaration—"I do solemnly declare that I know not of any lawful impediment why I, A. B., may not be joined in matrimony to C. D." Also each of the parties must say to the other: "I call upon these persons here present to witness that I, A. B., do take thee, C. D., to be my lawful wedded wife [or husband]," *or*, if the marriage is solemnized in the presence of an authorized person without the presence of a Registrar, each party may say in lieu thereof: "I, A. B., do take thee, C. D., to be my wedded wife [or husband]."

(ii) *In a Register Office.*—The marriage may be solemnized in the office of the Superintendent Registrar to whom notice of the marriage has been given. The marriage must be solemnized between the hours of 8 a.m. and 6 p.m., with open doors in the presence of the Superintendent Registrar or a Registrar of the registration district of that Superintendent Registrar, and in the presence of two witnesses. The parties must make the following declaration: "I do solemnly declare that I know not of any lawful impediment why I, A. B., may not be joined in matrimony to C. D.," and each party must say to the other: "I call upon these persons here present to witness that I, A. B., do take thee, C. D., to be my lawful wedded wife [or husband]." No religious ceremony may take place in the Register Office, though the parties may, on production of their marriage certificate, go through a subsequent religious ceremony in any church or persuasion of which they are members.

(iii) *Other Cases.*—If both parties are members of the Society of Friends (Quakers), or if, not being in membership, they have been authorized by the Society of Friends to solemnize their marriage in accordance with its usages, they may be married in a Friends' meeting-house. The marriage must be registered by the registering officer of the Society appointed to act for the district in which the meeting house is situated. The presence of a Registrar of Marriages is not necessary.

If both parties are Jews they may marry according to their usages in a synagogue, which has a certified marriage secretary, or private dwelling-house at any hour; the building may be situated within or without the district of residence. The marriage must be registered by the secretary of the synagogue of which the man is a member. The presence of a Registrar of Marriages is not necessary.

C.—MARRIAGE UNDER REGISTRAR GENERAL'S LICENCE

The main purpose of the Marriage (Registrar General's Licence) Act, 1970, which came into force on January 1, 1971, is to enable non-Anglicans to be married in unregistered premises where one of the persons to be married is seriously ill, is not expected to recover and cannot be moved to registered premises. A fee of £15 is payable to the Registrar General for the licence, though he has power to remit this in whole or in part to avoid hardship.

D.—DETAINED AND HOUSE-BOUND PERSONS

The Marriage Act 1983 (which does not extend to Scotland) enables marriages of detained persons and house-bound persons to be solemnized at their place of residence. The Act came into operation on May 1, 1984.

MISCELLANEOUS NOTES

Consanguinity and Affinity.—A marriage between persons within the prohibited degrees of consanguinity or affinity is void. Relaxations have, however, been made by various statutes which have now been replaced by the Marriage Act 1949 (see the 1st Schedule to the Act) and the Marriage (Enabling) Act 1960. It is now permitted to contract a marriage with:—

Sister, aunt or niece of a former wife (whether living or not). Former wife of brother, uncle or nephew (whether living or not).

No clergyman can be compelled to solemnize any of the foregoing marriages, but he may allow his church to be used for the purpose by another minister.

The Marriage (Prohibited Degrees of Relationship) Act 1986 makes further provision with regard to the marriage of persons related by affinity e.g. after section 1 of the Act comes into force a marriage between a man and the daughter or grand-daughter of his former wife will not be void by reason only of that relationship if both parties have attained 21 at the time of the marriage and the younger party has not at any time before attaining 18 been a child of the family in relation to the other party.

Minors.—Persons under 18 years of age are generally required to obtain the consent of certain persons (see Marriage Act 1949, section 3 and 2nd Schedule as amended by the Family Law Reform Act 1969). Where both parents are living, both must consent, where one is dead, the survivor, or, if there is a guardian appointed by the deceased parent, the guardian and the survivor. (For the position where the parents of the child were not married to each other at the time of the birth, see section 9 of the Family Law Reform Act 1987.) No consent is required in the case of an infant's second marriage. In certain exceptional cases consent may be dispensed with, e.g., the insanity of a parent. If consent is refused the Court may, on application being made, consent to the marriage; application can be made for this purpose to the High Court, the County Court, or a Court of Summary Jurisdiction. The Act prohibits any marriage where either party is under 16 years of age.

E.—MARRIAGE IN ENGLAND OR WALES WHEN ONE PARTY LIVES IN SCOTLAND OR NORTHERN IRELAND

Notice for a marriage by a Superintendent Registrar's certificate in a register office or registered building may be given in the usual way by the party resident in England. As regards Scotland, the party there should give notice of intention to marry to the registrar; as regards Northern Ireland, the party there, after a residence of seven days, must give notice to the District Registrar of Marriages. Notice cannot be given for such marriages to take place by Certificate with licence of the Superintendent Registrar.

Marriage of such parties may take place in a church of the Church of England after the publication of banns, or by Ecclesiastical licence.

MARRIAGES IN SCOTLAND

According to the law of Scotland, marriage is a contract which is completed by the mutual consent of parties. The Marriage (Scotland) Act 1977, which came into force on January 1, 1978, states or restates the law in convenient form. References in this section are to that Act.

Impediments to Marriage: These are (a) nonage, i.e., where either party is under the age of 16. (b) forbidden degrees of relationship (Section 2) as amended by the Marriage Prohibited Degrees of Relationship Act 1986. (c) subsisting previous marriage. (d) incapacity to understand the nature of the contract. (e) both parties of the same sex. (f) non-residence, i.e., if the requirements of prior residence of one or other of the parties in Scotland have not been complied with. The Act also states the grounds on which certain marriages may be declared void but this is amended by the Law Reform (Miscellaneous Provisions) (Scotland) Act 1980 which prevents a marriage being rendered void solely due to the failure to comply with certain formalities, provided the particulars of that marriage are entered in a register of marriages by or at the behest of an appropriate registrar.

Marriages may be regular or irregular, thus:—

REGULAR MARRIAGES

A regular marriage is one which is celebrated by a Minister of Religion or authorised Registrar or other celebrant specified in the Act. The parties must submit to the District Registrar a statutory notice of intention to marry the fee for which is £5·00 each. The Registrar will then enter the parties' names and particulars in the Marriage Notice Book which must also show the intended date of the marriage. He must then display the notice of intention to marry in a prominent public place until the intended date, and any person claiming an interest may lodge written objections thereto with the Registrar (Section 5). The Registrar, after fourteen days of receipt of the Marriage Notice and on being satisfied that there are no legal impediments to the marriage, will issue to either or both parties a Marriage Schedule. The fourteen day period may be shortened under exceptional circumstances. The Marriage Schedule must be produced to the celebrant of the marriage. The fee for the solemnization ceremony in a Registry Office is £12. After the ceremony the marriage must be registered with the Registrar General for inclusion in the Register of Births, Deaths and Marriages, within three days. Within one month of the ceremony, the fee for an extract marriage certificate is £3; thereafter it is £5·50.

IRREGULAR MARRIAGES

Since the Marriage (Scotland) Act 1939 the only form of irregular marriage to be recognised by law—viz., marriage by habit and repute, remains competent under the 1977 Act. If the parties live together constantly as husband and wife and are held to be such by the general repute of the neighbourhood and among their friends and relations, then there may arise a presumption from which marriage can be inferred. Before such a marriage can be registered, however, a decree of declarator of marriage must be obtained from the Deputy Principal Clerk of the Court of Session. It is the duty of the Deputy Principal Clerk to register the decree as soon as it is granted.

JURY SERVICE

Every local or parliamentary elector between the ages of eighteen and sixty-five who has resided in the United Kingdom, Channel Islands or Isle of Man for at least five years since he attained the age of thirteen will be qualified to serve on a jury unless he is "ineligible" or "disqualified".

Ineligible persons include those who have at any time been judges, magistrates and certain senior court officials, those who within the previous ten years have been concerned with the law (such as barristers and solicitors and their clerks, court officers, coroners, police, prison and probation officers); priests of any religion and vowed members of religious communities; and certain sufferers from mental illness.

Disqualified persons are those who have at any time been sentenced by a Court in the United Kingdom, Channel Islands or Isle of Man, to a term of imprisonment of five years or more, or a person who in the last ten years has (a) served any part of a sentence of imprisonment, youth custody or dentention; or (b) been detained in a Borstal institution; or (c) had passed on him or made in respect of him a suspended sentence of imprisonment or order for detention; or (d) had made in respect of him a community service order. A person who at any time in the last five years has been placed on probation is also disqualified.

Some others are excusable as of right. These include members and officers of the Houses of Parliament, full-time serving members of the forces (including Women's forces) and registered and practising members of the medical, dental, nursing, veterinary and pharmaceutical professions and any person who has served on a jury in the two years before he is summoned. In other cases the court may excuse a juror at its discretion (e.g., where the service would be a hardship to the juror).

If a person serves on a jury knowing himself to be disqualified or ineligible he is liable to be fined up to £400 or £100 respectively.

A juror is entitled to subsistence and travelling expenses, compensation for other expenses incurred in consequence of attendance for jury service, loss of earnings and loss of national insurance benefits, but certain maximum figures (which are revised from time to time) are laid down.

A verdict of a jury must normally be unanimous but after two hours consideration (or such longer period as the Court thinks reasonable), a majority verdict is acceptable if ten jurors agree to it (or nine if the size of the jury has been reduced to ten, e.g., by illness during the trial).

Jury trial is now very unusual in civil cases but a person charged with any but the least serious crimes is entitled to be tried by a jury. The defendant may object to any juror if he can show that that juror ought not to be on the jury (e.g., because he is ineligible or is biased against him) and may object to three jurors without giving any reason.

The Coroners' Juries Act 1983 (which does not extend to Scotland) makes new provision in relation to qualification to serve on coroners' juries.

JURY SERVICE IN SCOTLAND

It is the duty of the sheriff principal of each sheriffdom, in respect of each sheriff court district in his sheriffdom, to maintain a book, known as the "general jury book", containing the names and designations of persons within the district who are qualified and liable to serve as jurors. The book, which is compiled from information which every householder is required to provide, is kept open for the inspection by any person, upon payment of a nominal fee, at the sheriff clerk's office for the district. Part II of the Juries Act 1949 (amended by regulations following thereon and by the Law Reform (Miscellaneous Provisions) (Scotland) Act 1980) applies only to Scotland and provides, *inter alia*, for the payment of travelling expenses and subsistence allowances to jurors and for loss of earnings.

The number of a jury in a civil cause in the Court of Session is twelve and in the Sheriff Court seven. In a criminal trial the number is fifteen.

QUALIFICATIONS

Under S.1 of the Law Reform (Miscellaneous Provisions) (Scotland) Act 1980, every man or woman between the ages of 18 and 65 who is for the time being registered as a parliamentary or local government elector and who has been ordinarily resident in the United Kingdom, the Channel Islands or the Isle of Man for any period of at least five years since attaining the age of 13 years, is qualified to serve on a jury.

Ineligible persons include those who at any time within the past ten years have been judges of the supreme courts, sheriffs and certain other senior court officials, those who at any time within the past five years have been concerned with the administration of justice (such as advocates and their clerks, solicitors, court staff, police officers, prison officers, sheriff officers, procurator fiscals, and members of parole boards and children's panels), and certain sufferers from mental illness.

The same rules for disqualified persons operate in Scotland as in England. Those excusable as of right are members and officers of the Houses of Parliament, full time serving members of H.M. naval, army and air forces, registered and practising members of the medical, dental, nursing, veterinary and pharmaceutical professions, ministers of religion and other persons in holy orders, and any person who has attended for jury service in the past five years.

If a person serves on a jury knowing himself to be disqualified or ineligible, he is liable to be fined up to £2,000 or £400 respectively. Jurors failing to attend without good cause are liable to a maximum fine of £400.

LANDLORD AND TENANT

ENGLAND AND WALES

Although basically the relationship between the parties to a lease is governed by the lease itself, the position is complicated by numerous statutory provisions. The few points dealt with may show the desirability of seeking professional assistance in these matters. Important provisions include:—

(1) As to agricultural holdings—the Agricultural Holdings Act 1986. Among other things, the Act regulates the length of notice necessary to determine an agricultural tenancy, the tenant's right to remove fixtures on the land, his right to compensation for damage done by game, for improvements and for disturbance, and his right to require the consent of the Agricultural Land Tribunal to the operation of a notice to quit.

(2) As to business premises—the Landlord and Tenant Acts 1927 and 1954, and the Law of Property Act 1969, Pt. I. Part II of the 1954 Act gives security of tenure to the tenant of most business premises, and in effect he can only be ousted on one or more of the seven grounds set out in the Act. In some cases, where the landlord can resume possession, the tenant is entitled to compensation.

(3) As to dwelling houses—the complicated mass of legislation is embodied in the Rent Act 1977, which does not extend to Scotland or Northern Ireland. If the house is within the Act, a tenant has a personal right to reside there, and he may only be ousted on certain grounds.

A number of amendments to the 1977 Act have been made by the Housing Acts 1980 and 1988.

Tenancies with full Rent Act protection are known as regulated tenancies. The maximum rent recoverable under such a tenancy is the rent agreed between the landlord and tenant, unless a fair rent has been registered, in which case that is the maximum rent recoverable. Application for the registration of a fair rent may be made by either the landlord or tenant, to the Local Rent Officer, and appeal against his decision lies to the Rent Assessment Committee.

When the Housing Act 1988 comes into force, no new regulated tenancies can be created, although the above protection remains for existing regulated tenancies. Tenancies granted after the 1988 Act comes into force will be known as assured tenancies provided they satisfy certain conditions, which are broadly the same as those for regulated tenancies under the 1977 Act. However, the rent payable by an assured tenant will be either that agreed with the landlord or the open market rent fixed by the Rent Assessment Committee.

(4) As to dwelling houses with resident landlords—the Rent Act 1974 gave tenants of dwellings let furnished the same security of tenure as those of unfurnished dwellings unless the landlord lived in part of the house. In the latter case, and in the case of a tenancy of a dwelling granted by a resident landlord after August 13, 1974, the tenancy will usually be outside full Rent Act protection, but may fall within the restricted contract provisions of the Rent Act 1977. In this event, the landlord or the tenant may apply to the Rent Tribunal for a reasonable rent to be registered, and once registered, this is the maximum rent recoverable. No new restricted contracts can be created after the Housing Act 1988 comes into force.

(5) The Protection from Eviction Act 1977, as amended by the Housing Act 1988, provides that if any person with intent to cause the residential occupier of any premises to give up the occupation thereof does any act calculated to interfere with the peace or comfort of the residential occupier or members of his household, he shall be guilty of an offence. A further provision prevents a landlord enforcing a right to possession against a tenant (who is not protected by any security of tenure legislation) without a court order, and there are special rules in such cases relating to agricultural employees.

(6) A notice to quit any dwellinghouse must be given at least four weeks before it is to take effect, and must be in writing and in the prescribed statutory form.

(7) Part I of the Landlord and Tenant Act 1954, applies to most tenancies of houses for over twenty-one years at a ground rent. Where it applies, the contractual tenancy is continued until brought to an end in the manner prescribed by the Act, and in effect the landlord can only get possession on limited grounds.

Further, under the Leasehold Reform Act 1967, tenants of houses under leases for over twenty-one years at a rent less than two-thirds of the rateable value of the house are in most cases given a right to purchase the freehold or to take an extended lease for a term of fifty years, provided the tenant at the time when he seeks to exercise the right has been occupying the house as his residence for the last three years or for periods amounting to three years in the last ten years.

(8) Full Rent Act protection is available only if a house is let on a tenancy, so that if the occupier of a house has a mere licence to occupy, he does not have Rent Act protection. Further, even if he has a tenancy, he will not be Rent Act protected if the rent payable is less than two-thirds of the rateable value of the house. For these reasons, many occupants of houses owned by farmers and occupied by farm workers did not enjoy full security of tenure. The Rent (Agriculture) Act 1976 contains detailed provisions conferring security of tenure on certain agricultural workers housed by their employers and on their successors on death.

(9) Under the Landlord and Tenant Act 1985 (which does not extend to Scotland), in a lease of a dwelling-house granted after October 24, 1961, for a term of less than 7 years, there is implied a covenant by the landlord (a) to keep in repair the structure and exterior of the house and (b) to keep in repair and proper working order the installations in the house (i) for the supply of water, gas and electricity, and for sanitation, and (ii) for space heating or heating water.

(10) The Housing Act 1985 gives security of tenure to many tenants of local authorities and certain other bodies. Further, and subject to certain conditions, such tenants may have the right to purchase their houses or to take a long lease of their flats.

(11) Tenants of flats are given a number of special rights by the Landlord and Tenant Act 1987.

SCOTLAND

A Lease is a Contract, the relationship of the parties being governed by the terms thereof. As is also the case in England (see the foregoing Section) legislation has played an important part in regulating that relationship. Thus, what at Common Law was an Agreement binding only the parties to the deed, becomes in virtue of the Leases Act 1449, a contract binding the landlord's successors, as purchasers or creditors, provided the following four conditions are observed; (1) the lease, if for more than one year, must be in writing, (2) there must be a rent, (3) there must be a term of expiry, and (4) the tenant must have entered into possession.

It would be impracticable in a brief section of these Notes to enter upon a general discussion of this branch of the law and, accordingly, the plan adopted in the preceding Section of quoting a few important Statutes is followed here.

The Agricultural Holdings (Scotland) Act 1949 (amended by the Agriculture Act 1958), which is a consolidating Act applicable to Scotland, contains provisions similar to those in the English Act, alluded to in the preceding Section. It cannot here be analysed in detail.

It is of interest to note that the Small Landholders Act, 1911, provided for the setting up of the Land Court which has jurisdiction over a large proportion of agricultural and pastoral land in Scotland.

In Scotland business premises are not controlled by Statute to so great an extent as in England, but the Tenancy of Shops (Scotland) Act, 1949 gives a measure of security to tenants of shops. This Act enables the tenant of a shop who is threatened with eviction to apply to the Sheriff for a renewal of the tenancy. If the landlord has offered to sell the subjects to the tenant at an agreed price the application for a renewal of the tenancy may be dismissed. Reference should be made to Section 1 (3) of the 1949 Act for particulars of other circumstances under which the Sheriff has a discretion to dismiss an application. The Act extends to premises held by the Crown or Government Departments, either as landlord or tenant.

The Rent (Scotland) Act 1984, a consolidating statute, defines regulated tenancies which may be either furnished or unfurnished and lays down the system by which a landlord or tenant may obtain from the Rent Office registration of a fair rent. The act gives to tenants of either furnished or unfurnished lets a substantial degree of security of tenure. There are, however, certain exceptions thus: they do not apply to tenancies where the interest belongs to the Crown or to a government department or to a local authority, a development corporation of a new town or a housing corporation. There must be a true tenancy for the Act to apply. It does not apply to licencees such as lodgers or persons allowed to occupy houses on a grace and favour basis or to services occupiers. The Act regulates the short tenancy, a category of let under which on compliance with certain conditions the landlord can be assured of recovering possession on the expiry of the stipulated period of let. The Act defines the circumstances under which generally a landlord may apply for increased rent as a consequence of having carried improvements to his property and also lays down the system of phasing such rent increases. On the death of a statutory successor to a tenancy, the tenancy may pass for a second time to a member of the family or a relative who has been in residence of the house for a period of at least 6 months. The Act further lays down the duties and functions of Rent Officers and Rent Assessment Committees with regard to unfurnished accommodation and of rent tribunals for furnished accommodation.

The Housing (Scotland) Act 1987 consolidates previous legislation in regard to the extensive powers and duties to Local Authorities in relation to housing. Included therein is the general provision regarding the rights of public sector tenants to purchase the houses which they occupy and the restrictions regarding this right in certain circumstances where the house has been designed or adapted for occupation by the elderly. This Act also makes provision for secure tenancies for public sector tenants.

LEGAL AID

LEGAL AID IN CIVIL PROCEEDINGS

The Legal Aid Act 1974 (as amended) is designed to make legal aid and advice more readily available for persons of small and moderate means. The main structure of the service is contained in the Act itself and the Regulations made thereunder, administered by the Law Society.

Legal aid is available for proceedings (including matrimonial causes) in the House of Lords, Court of Appeal, High Court, County Courts, Lands Tribunal, Restrictive Practices Court, before the Commons Commissioners, and civil proceedings in Magistrates' Courts. In any event, an application for legal aid will not be approved if it appears that the applicant would gain only a trivial advantage from the proceedings. Further, proceedings wholly or partly in respect of defamation are excepted from the scheme, as are also relator actions and election petitions. It is generally not available for obtaining the decree in undefended

divorce and judicial separation, although the Legal Advice and Assistance Scheme (*see* below) will be, and Legal Aid is still available to deal with property, custody disputes etc., arising in the suit.

Where a person is concerned in proceedings only in a representative, fiduciary or official capacity, his personal resources are not to be taken into account in considering eligibility for legal aid. Apart from this, eligibility in civil proceedings depends upon an applicant's "disposable income" and "disposable capital". The figures change frequently; particulars can be obtained from a solicitor, the Law Society or a Citizens' Advice Bureau. Disposable income is calculated by making deductions from gross income in respect of certain matters such as dependants, interest on loans, income tax, rates, rent and other matters for which the applicant must or reasonably may provide. Disposable capital is calculated by excluding from gross capital part of the value of the house in which the applicant resides, of furniture and household possessions; allowances are made in respect of dependants. Except in cases where the spouses are living apart, or have a contrary interest, any resources of a person's wife or husband are to be treated as that person's resources. These figures will be assessed by the Department of Social Security, and will be referred to The Law Society, who will determine whether reasonable grounds exist for the grant of a civil aid certificate. Appeal from refusal of a certificate lies to an Area Committee. A person resident in England or Wales desiring legal aid should apply for a certificate to the appropriate Area Director for the area in which s/he resides; if resident elsewhere application should be made to an Area Director in London. If a certificate is granted, the applicant may select his solicitor, and, if necessary, counsel from a panel. The costs of the assisted person's solicitor and counsel will be paid out of the legal aid fund. When, however, damages or property are recovered or preserved by the assisted person the legal aid fund has a charge over them in respect of these costs less any contribution towards costs recovered from the unsuccessful party. In matrimonial cases, maintenance is exempt, as is the first £2,500 of any property settlement. The court may order that the costs of a successful unassisted party shall be paid out of the legal aid fund.

In an urgent case, say of domestic violence, or to restrain the kidnapping abroad of a child, Legal Aid may be granted without the applicant's means being fully investigated beforehand. If on a full examination later he is found financially ineligible he is liable to pay all the costs incurred on his behalf, if he does not attend for an examination.

LEGAL ADVICE AND ASSISTANCE

The Scheme is governed by the Legal Aid Act 1974 (as amended).

Under this legal advice and assistance scheme a client may obtain such advice or assistance as is normally provided by a solicitor and if necessary the advice of a barrister may be obtained, but, with the exception of domestic proceedings in a magistrates' court and certain other proceedings (*see* below) the scheme does not extend to taking any step in any proceedings before any court or tribunal. Where legal aid is available for civil proceedings (see above) or in criminal cases (*see* below) the scheme covers work done in making application for such legal aid.

A person (other than one receiving advice and assistance at a police station or from a Duty Solicitor) is eligible for advice or assistance under the scheme provided his disposable capital and his disposable income do not exceed limits in force from time to time or if he is eligible for Income Support or Family Credit. For a married man or person with children or other dependants deductions will be made from gross income and capital and allowances are made in respect of income tax, National Insurance contributions, etc. It is intended that the financial limits shall approximate to those applying for legal aid in civil proceedings (see above). Except when they are separated or have conflicting interests the means of husband and wife will be aggregated for the purpose of determining financial eligibility. As in the case of Legal Aid, depending on his means, a person may be called upon to pay a contribution towards the costs of work done for him. Particulars may again be obtained from a solicitor, the Law Society or a Citizens' Advice Bureau.

Solicitor's costs and expenses, which should not together exceed £50 (V.A.T. exclusive), or £90 in the case of divorce etc. (not applicable to Scotland, where the £50 limit still applies) without leave of the Area Legal Aid Committee, will be paid out of the client's contribution and any monies recovered in respect of costs or damages from another party (although this may be waived by leave of the Area Committee in cases of hardship) and the balance will be paid by the Legal Aid Fund.

The Act also extends the scheme to cover the costs of a solicitor who is present within the precincts of a magistrates' court or county court and is requested by the court to advise or represent a person who is in need of help.

In April 1980 the Scheme was enlarged to cover the cost of representation in domestic proceedings in a magistrates' court. It has since been extended to cover the representation of parents and children in proceedings under the Child Care Act, 1980, and of patients before Mental Health Review Tribunals. Subject to financial eligibility limits, application is made to the area or local committee for "approval of assistance by way of representation" which will replace legal aid for such proceedings. However the £50 costs limit referred to above will not apply. An applicant who is outside the financial limits but eligible for legal aid will still have to apply for a legal aid certificate as before. Free advice and assistance, and assistance by way of representation from a Duty Solicitor is also available in limited circumstances to persons appearing before a magistrates' court charged with a criminal offence.

In January, 1986 the scheme was further extended to provide free advice and assistance to all suspects detained at a police station whether arrested or merely "helping police with their enquiries", and free representation for all arrested persons who are the subject of an application for a warrant of further detention under the Police and Criminal Evidence Act, 1984. Such persons may instruct a solicitor of their choice or take advantage of the Duty Solicitor Scheme which has now been extended to cover police stations.

LEGAL AID IN CRIMINAL CASES

The Legal Aid Act 1974 Part II and Legal Aid Act 1982 provide for legal aid in criminal proceedings, and for children and parents in care proceedings and related applications under the Children and Young Persons Act, 1969. A criminal court (e.g. magistrates' court, Crown Court) has power to order legal aid to be granted where it appears desirable to do so in the interests of justice. The court shall make an order in certain cases, e.g., where a person is committed for trial on a charge of murder. However, the court may not make an order unless it appears to the court that the person's disposable income and capital are such that he requires assistance in meeting the costs of the particular proceedings in question. Application should be made to the appropriate court where proceedings are to take place.

An applicant shall be required to make a contribution towards the costs of his case if his disposable income and capital exceed certain prescribed limits. Persons in receipt of Income Support are automatically exempt. In order to ascertain the amount of this contribution he will have to produce written evidence of his means. Investigation of means will be carried out by the court. Any person who falls into arrears with the payment of contribution is liable to have the order revoked.

Any practising barrister or solicitor may act for a legally aided person in criminal proceedings unless excluded by reason of misconduct. In general where legal aid is given it will normally include representation by both counsel and solicitor. However, in connection with magistrates' courts, representation will be by solicitor alone unless it is a serious offence.

Where any doubt arises about the grant of a legal aid order that doubt is to be resolved in favour of the applicant. The court also has power to amend or revoke a legal aid order. Legal aid may also be granted in connection with appellate proceedings, e.g., on appeal to the Criminal Division of the Court of Appeal under the Criminal Appeal Act 1968.

SCOTLAND
CIVIL PROCEEDINGS

Legal Aid in Scotland is now governed by the Legal Aid (Scotland) Act 1986 and the Regulations made thereunder. This Act established the Scottish Legal Board which has the general function of securing that Legal Aid and Legal Advice and Assistance are available in accordance with the Act, and of administering the Scottish Legal Aid Fund. The Board comprises not less than eleven and not more than fifteen members with one member appointed as Chairman. The members are appointed by the Secretary of State for Scotland. Civil Legal Aid is available in relation to civil proceedings in the House of Lords in Appeals from the Court of Session, in the Court of Session, the Lands Valuation Appeal Court, the Scottish Land Court, the Sheriff Court, the Lands Tribunal for Scotland, the Employment Appeals Tribunal and to the European Court of Human Rights. Civil Legal Aid is granted if on application to the Board, the Board is satisfied that there is *probabilis causa litigendi* and it is reasonable on the particular circumstances of the case that Legal Aid should be awarded. As in England eligibility and any contribution required from an applicant is dependent on their disposable income and disposable capital. Information on current financial limits can be obtained from the Scottish Legal Board (44 Drumsheugh Gardens, Edinburgh), a solicitor, or a Citizens' Advice Bureau. A person believing himself to be eligible may instruct any solicitor of his own choice. If a court action is not immediately contemplated application will be made for Legal Advice & Assistance which operates in a similar manner to the Legal Advice Assistance Scheme in England. If proceedings are contemplated then a formal application for Civil Legal Aid will be made and there are special provisions for emergency applications in appropriate circumstances.

If proceedings are decided against a person in receipt of Legal Aid the court shall determine a reasonable sum in the circumstances as an appropriate award of expenses to be made against the applicant. The court may only make an award out of the fund if proceedings were instituted by the legally assisted person and the court is satisfied that the resisting party would suffer severe financial hardship unless the order is made and the court is satisfied that in all the circumstances it is just and equitable that an award be made. If monies are recovered by a legally assisted person these fall to be paid to the Scottish Legal Board who will then determine the appropriate level of contribution from the sums received which should be made to the expenses of their litigation.

CRIMINAL PROCEEDINGS

Legal Aid in criminal causes is also administered under the Legal Aid (Scotland) Act 1986. The procedure for application for Criminal Legal Aid is dependent on the circumstances of each case. In serious cases heard before a jury under solemn procedure it is for the court to decide whether to grant Legal Aid. Applications for Legal Aid must normally be made on the prescribed forms to the clerk of court in question and an applicant is required to provide therein particulars of the merits of his case and his financial circumstances. In summary criminal causes however the procedure is dependent on whether the applicant is in custody: if so then he is entitled to automatic free Legal Aid from the Duty Solicitor. If the applicant is not in custody and wishes to plead guilty he is ineligible for full Legal Aid but may be entitled to Criminal Legal Advice & Assistance and in some circumstances may qualify for Assistance by way of Representation which will enable his solicitor to appear and make a plea in mitigation on his behalf. If he is not in custody and wishes to plead not guilty he can apply to the Scottish Legal Aid Board for Criminal Legal Aid on the prescribed form not later than fourteen days after the first court appearance at which he made the plea and Legal Aid shall only be granted if the Board is satisfied that the accused cannot meet the expenses of the case without undue hardship and that it is in the interest of justice as defined by the 1986 Act.

TOWN AND COUNTRY PLANNING

The Town and Country Planning Act 1971 (consolidating earlier Acts) contains very far-reaching provisions affecting the liberty of an owner of land to develop and use it as he will. A person has generally to get planning permission from the Local Planning Authority before carrying out any development on his land.

What is Development:—

(a) Carrying out of building, engineering, mining or other operations.

(b) Making a material change in use.

It is expressly provided that if one dwelling-house is converted into two or more dwelling-houses, this involves a material change in use.

Examples of what is not deemed Development:—

(a) Maintaining, improving or altering the interior of a building (except works for making good war damage), provided there is no material change to the exterior, with the exception that since December 5, 1968, any expansion, or works begun for the expansion, of a building below ground level constitutes development.

(b) Change of use of property within the curtilage of a dwelling-house for a purpose incidental to the use of the dwelling-house as such. (It will, however, be development if building operations are carried out.)

Application can be made to the Local Planning Authority to determine whether or not an operation or change of use constitutes development.

Planning Permission.—Application for such permission is not always necessary, as the Secretary of State may make Development Orders giving general permission for a specified type of development. Thus a General Development Order of 1987 specifies a number of types of development for which no permission is usually required, e.g., enlargement of a dwelling-house (including erection of a garage), so long as the cubic content of the original dwelling (external measurement) is not exceeded by more than 70 cubic metres or 15 per cent, whichever is greater, subject to a maximum of 115 cubic metres. However, in the case of a terraced house, the limitation is 50 cubic metres or 10 per cent, whichever is the greater, subject to the maximum of 115 cubic metres.

Appeal against refusal of permission lies to the Secretary of State and from his decision, in limited circumstances, to the High Court. If the result of the appeal is unsatisfactory, an applicant may in certain circumstances require the Council to purchase the land.

SCOTLAND

The Town and Country Planning (Scotland) Act 1972 consolidates the statute law relating to town and country planning in Scotland.

The Act contains provisions for an appeal to the Secretary of State against the refusal of planning permission. The decision of the Secretary of State is final.

Sections 87 and 92 of the Local Government, Planning and Land Act 1980 contain important provisions on planning applications and, unlike certain parts of this Act, extend to Scotland.

VOTERS' QUALIFICATIONS

The franchise is governed by the Representation of the People Acts 1983 and 1985. Those entitled to vote as electors at a parliamentary election in any constituency are all persons resident there on the qualifying date who, at that date and on the date of the poll are Commonwealth citizens or citizens of the Republic of Ireland and not subject to any legal incapacity to vote and who on the date of the poll are at least 18 years of age. However, a person is not entitled to vote at a parliamentary election in any constituency in Northern Ireland unless he was resident in Northern Ireland during the whole of the period of three months ending on the qualifying date for that election. Also, no person can use his vote unless he is on the Register of electors kept for the constituency. A person who is of voting age on the date of the poll at a parliamentary or local government election is entitled to vote, whether or not he was of voting age on the qualifying date. Accordingly, a qualified person will be entitled to be registered in a register of parliamentary electors or a register of local government electors if he will attain voting age within twelve months from the date on which the register is required to be published. Subject to certain conditions, the 1985 Act extends the franchise to British citizens overseas.

The Register is prepared by the Registration Officer in each constituency in Great Britain. It is the registration officer's duty to have a house to house or other official inquiry made as to the persons entitled to be registered and to publish preliminary electors lists showing the persons appearing to him to be entitled to be registered. Any person whose name is omitted may claim registration, and any person on the list may object to the inclusion therein of other persons' names: the registration officer determines the claims and objections.

Voters at a parliamentary or local government election must generally vote in person at the allotted polling station, except for those entitled to vote by post or at any polling station, and those for whom proxies have been appointed. Certain people can apply to be treated as absent voters at a parliamentary election and thus able to vote by post—among these are registered service voters, those unable by reason of blindness or other physical incapacity to go in person to the polling station, and those unable to go in person from their qualifying address to the polling station without making a journey by air or sea.

Unless entitled to vote by post, a person registered as a service voter may vote by proxy at a parliamentary or local government election. A proxy may also be appointed by a registered elector, where the registration officer is satisfied that the applicant's circumstances on the date of the poll are likely to be such that he cannot reasonably be expected to vote in person at the polling station allotted to him. The appointment of a person to vote as proxy at parliamentary elections has effect also for the purposes of local government elections.

THE PROBATION SERVICE

The Probation Service is employed in each county by an independent committee of justices and it provides a professional social work agency in the courts, with responsibility for a wide range of duties which include: (a) a social enquiry service for the criminal courts; (b) provision of a range of noncustodial measures involving the supervision of offenders in the community; (c) supervisory aftercare for offenders released from custody, together with social work in penal establishments and help for the families of those serving sentences; (d) an enquiry, conciliation and supervision service in the divorce and domestic courts; (e) support for and promotion of preventive and containment measures in the

community designed to reduce the level of crime and domestic breakdown. It is a direct grant service funded 80 per cent from the Home Office and 20 per cent from the relevant local authority.

Its national representative bodies are: (i) The Central Council of Probation Committees, 38 Belgrave Square, London SW1X 8NT—Tel: 01-245 9364 (*Secretary*, I. Miles); (ii) The Association of Chief Officers of Probation, 20-30 Lawefield Lane, Wakefield WF2 8SP—Tel: 0924-361156 (*Secretary*, W. R. Weston); (iii) The National Association of Probation Officers, 3-4 Chivalry Road, Battersea, London SW11 1HT—Tel: 01-223 4887 (*Gen. Secretary*, W. Beaumont).

NATIONAL INSURANCE AND RELATED CASH BENEFITS

The State insurance and assistance schemes, comprising schemes of national insurance and industrial injuries insurance, national assistance, and non-contributory old age pensions came into force from July 5, 1948. The Ministry of Social Security Act, 1966, replaced national assistance and non-contributory old age pensions with a scheme of non-contributory benefits, termed supplementary allowances and pensions. These, and subsequent measures relating to social security provision in Great Britain, were consolidated by the Social Security Act, 1975; the Social Security (Consequential Provisions) Act, 1975; and the Industrial Injuries and Diseases (Old Cases) Act, 1975: corresponding measures were passed for Northern Ireland. The Social Security Pensions Act, 1975, introduced a new State pensions scheme, which came into force on April 6, 1978, and the graduated pension scheme 1961–1975 has been wound up, existing rights being preserved. The Pensioners' Payments and Social Security Act, 1979, provided for a £10 bonus for pensioners in 1979 and also for the payment of a bonus in succeeding years at levels then to be determined. The Child Benefit Act, 1975, replaced family allowances (introduced 1946) with child benefit and one parent benefit.

Some of the above legislation has been superceded by the provisions of the Social Security Act, 1986, passed in July 1986 and introduced at various dates since.

NATIONAL INSURANCE SCHEME

The National Insurance scheme operates under the Social Security Acts, 1975 to 1980, and orders and regulations made thereunder. The scheme is financed by contributions payable by earners, employers and others (such as non-employed persons, paying voluntary contributions), together with the Treasury supplement. It provides the funds required for paying benefits payable under the Social Security Acts out of the National Insurance Fund and not out of other public money; for the making of payments towards the cost of the National Health Service and into the Redundancy and Maternity Pay Funds; and for paying benefit under the Industrial Injuries and Diseases (Old Cases) Act, 1975.

From April 6, 1987, the yearly Treasury supplement to the National Insurance Fund is equal to 7 per cent of all contributions (calculated so as to include those that would have been received if there had been no contracting out or statutory sick pay) after deducting the allocations to the National Health Service and the Redundancy and Maternity Pay Funds.

CONTRIBUTIONS

Contributions are of four classes:

Class 1 contributions are earnings-related, based on a percentage of the employee's earnings.

(a) *primary Class 1* contributions are payable by employed earners and office-holders over age 16 with gross earnings at or above the lower earnings limit of £41·00 per week. For those with gross earnings at or above this level, contributions are payable on *all* earnings up to an upper limit of £305 per week. "Gross earnings" include overtime pay, commission, bonus, etc., without deduction of any super-annuation contributions.

Women who marry for the first time no longer have a right to elect not to pay the full contribution rate. Married women and widows who before May 12, 1977, elected not to pay contributions at the full rate retain the right to pay a reduced rate over the same earnings range, which covers industrial injuries benefits and a contribution to the National Health Service. They lose this right if, after April 5, 1978, there are two consecutive tax years in which they have no earnings on which primary Class 1 contributions are payable and in which they have not been at any time self-employed earners. No primary contributions are due on earnings paid for a period on or after the employee's pension age, even when retirement is deferred.

(b) *secondary Class 1* contributions are payable by employers of employed earners, and by the appropriate authorities in the case of office-holders. On Oct. 6, 1985, the upper earnings limit for employers' contributions was abolished and secondary contributions are payable on *all* the employee's earnings if they reach or exceed £41·00 per week.

Primary contributions are deducted from earnings by the employer, and are paid, together with the employer's contributions, to the Inland Revenue along with income tax collected under the PAYE system, so dispensing with contribution cards for employed earners. On Oct. 6, 1985 several lower percentage rates of contribution for lower paid employees and their employers were introduced.

Class 2 contributions are flat-rate, paid weekly by self-employed earners over age 16. Those with earnings below £2,250 a year for the tax year 1988–89 can apply for exception from liability to pay Class 2 contributions. People who while self-employed are excepted from liability to pay contributions on the grounds of small earnings may pay either Class 2 or Class 3 contributions voluntarily. Self-employed earners (whether or not they pay Class 2 contributions) may also be liable to pay Class 4 contributions based on profits or gains within certain limits. There are special rules for those who are concurrently employed and self-employed. Married women and widows can no longer choose not to pay Class 2 contributions. Those who elected not to pay Class 2 contributions before May 12, 1977, retain the right until there is a period of two consecutive tax years after April 5, 1978 in which they were not at any time either self-employed earners or had earnings on which primary Class 1 contributions were payable.

Class 2 contributions may be paid by direct debit through a bank or National Giro account or by stamping a contribution card.

Class 3 contributions are voluntary flat-rate contributions payable by persons over school-leaving age who would otherwise be unable to qualify for retirement pension and certain other benefits because they have an insufficient record of Class 1 or Class 2 contributions. Married women and widows who on or before May 11, 1977, elected not to pay Class 1 (full rate) or Class 2 contributions cannot pay Class 3 contributions while they retain this right.

Payment may be made by stamping a contribution card or by direct debit through a bank Giro account.

Class 4 contributions are payable by self-employed earners, whether or not they pay Class 2 contributions, on annual profits or gains from a trade, profession or vocation chargeable to income tax under Schedule D, where these fall between £4,750 and £15,860 a year. The maximum Class 4 contribution, payable on profits or gains of £15,860 or more, is £699·93.

Class 4 contributions are generally assessed and collected by the Inland Revenue along with Schedule D income tax. Self-employed persons under 16, or who at the beginning of a tax year are over pension age even where retirement is deferred, are not liable to pay Class 4 contributions. There are special rules for people who have more than one job, or who pay Class 1 contributions on earnings which are chargeable to income tax under Schedule D.

Regulations state the cases in which earners may be excepted from liability to pay contributions, and the conditions upon which contributions are credited to persons who are excepted. Leaflet NI 208 is obtainable from local social security offices.

The Secretary of State for Social Services is empowered by the Social Security Acts to alter certain rates of contributions by order approved by both Houses of Parliament, and is required by the same enactments to make annual reviews of the general level of earnings in order to determine whether such an order should be made.

For the period April 6, 1988 to April 5, 1989 the earnings brackets determining Class 1 contributions are:

	Weekly earnings £
a	0 — 41·00
b	41·00— 69·99
c	70·00—104·99
d	105·00—154·99
e	155·00—305·00
f	over 305·00

Contribution rates for the period April 6, 1988 to April 5, 1989 are:

Class 1 contributions—not contracted out

Earnings bracket	Percentage of reckonable income		
	Employee's rate standard reduced		Employer's rate
a	0	0	0
b	5	3·85	5
c	7	3·85	7
d	9	3·85	9
e	9	3·85	10·45
f	9*	3·85*	10·45

* to a maximum of £305 per week.

Class 1 contributions—contracted out (see also p. 1046)

Employee's rates

Earnings bracket	On first £41·00		On earnings from £41·00–£305·00	
	standard	reduced	standard	reduced
a	0	0	0	0
b	5	3·85	3·00	3·85
c	7	3·85	5·00	3·85
d, e, f.	9	3·85	7·00	3·85

Employer's rates

Earnings bracket	On first £41·00	On earnings from £41·00–£305·00	On any earnings over £305·00
a	0	0	0
b	5	1·2	0
c	7	3·2	0
d	9	5·2	0
e	10·45	6·65	0
f	10·45	6·65	10·45

	Weekly flat rate
Class 2 contributions	£3·85
Class 3 contributions	£3·75

	Percentage of profits or gains
Class 4 contributions	6·3

THE STATE EARNINGS RELATED PENSION SCHEME

The Social Security Pensions Act, 1975, which came into force in April, 1978, aims to reduce reliance upon means-tested supplementary benefit in old age, in widowhood and in chronic ill-health by providing better pensions; to ensure that occupational pension schemes which are contracted out of part of the State scheme fulfil the conditions of a good scheme; that pensions are adequately protected against inflation; and that in both the State and occupational schemes men and women are treated equally. Retirement, widow's and invalidity pensions under the new scheme started in April 1979. Since April 6, 1979, flat-rate retirement and other State pensions have been augmented for employed earners by additional pensions related to earnings, but it will be twenty years before these additional pensions become payable at the full rate.

Under the scheme retirement, invalidity and widow's pensions for employees are related to the earnings on which national insurance contributions have been paid. For employees of either sex with a complete insurance record the scheme provides a category A retirement pension in two parts, a basic and an additional component. The basic pension corresponds to the old personal flat-rate national insurance pension. The additional component is 1·25 per cent of average earnings between the lower weekly earnings limit for Class 1 contribution liability and the upper earnings limit for each year of such earnings under the scheme, and will thus build up to 25 per cent in twenty years. When the number of years exceeds twenty, pensions will be based on contributors' twenty best years of earnings between age 16 and pension age (65 for men, 60 for women). Actual earnings are to be revalued in terms of the earnings level current in the last complete tax year before pension age (or death or incapacity). Both components of pensions in payment will be uprated annually in line with the movement of prices. Graduated retirement pensions in payment, and rights to such pensions earned by people who are still working, will be brought into the annual review of benefits.

Self-employed persons pay contributions towards the basic pension. The non-employed and employees with earnings below the lower limit may contribute voluntarily for basic pension. Although no primary Class 1 contributions or Class 2 or Class 4 contributions are payable by persons who work beyond pension age (65 for men, 60 for women), the employer's liability for secondary Class 1 contributions continues if earnings are at or above the lower earnings limit. Class 4 contributions are still payable up to the end of the tax year during which pension age is reached.

Widows will get the whole or part of additional pensions earned by their husbands with their widowed mother's allowances or widow's pensions; and can add to the retirement pensions earned by their own contributions any additional pensions earned by their husbands up to the maximum payable on one person's contributions. Men whose wives die when they are both over pension age can add together their own and their wives' pension rights in the same way as widows. Among the steps taken to give women equal treatment in benefit provision the State scheme permits years of home responsibilities to count towards satisfying the contribution conditions for retirement pension, widowed mother's allowance and widow's pension (and the "half-test" by which a married woman who married before age 55 could not qualify for a Category A retirement pension unless she had contributed on earnings at the basic level in at least half the years between marriage and pension age has been abolished with effect from Dec. 22, 1984). The range of short-term social security benefits and industrial injury benefits under the Social Security Act, 1975, continues with only minor changes.

Contracted-Out and Personal Pension Schemes.— Members of occupational pension schemes which meet the standards laid down in the Social Security Pensions Act, 1975, can be contracted-out of the earnings related part of the state scheme relating to retirement and widows' benefits. Regulations made under the Act require employers to consult employees and their organisations and inform them of their intention to contract out. (Leaflets relating to pensions and guidance for employers about contracting-out are available from local social security offices.) The Act also contains provisions ensuring equal access to membership of schemes for men and women.

Until April 6, 1988, occupational pension schemes can only contract out if they promise a pension that is related to earnings. These are known as contracted-out salary related schemes. They must provide a pension that is not less than the guaranteed minimum pension (G.M.P.), which is broadly equivalent to the state earnings related pension. However, new options have been introduced by the Social Security Act, 1986. From April 6, 1988, occupational pension schemes which promise a minimum level of contributions will also be able to contract out. These are known as contracted-out money purchase schemes. They provide a pension based on the value of the fund built up in the scheme.

In addition, from July 1988 employees whose employers do not provide a pension scheme will be able to start their own personal pension instead of staying in the state earnings related pension scheme. From April 6, 1988, this choice will be open to all employees even if their employer does have a pension scheme. A personal pension, like a contracted-out money purchase scheme, provides a pension based on the value of the fund built up in the scheme.

The decision on whether or not an occupational pension scheme may become contracted-out lies with the Occupational Pension Board, an independent statutory body who have a general responsibility for supervising contracting-out. They also consider and approve personal pension schemes which can be used instead of state additional pension.

The State earnings related pension payable to a member of a contracted-out salary related scheme, or his widow, will be reduced by the amount of G.M.P. payable (which in the case of a widow must be at least half of the late husband's G.M.P. entitlement). Members of contracted-out money purchase schemes and personal pension schemes, or their widows, have no G.M.P. entitlement as such. But the state earnings related pension payable will be reduced by an amount equivalent to a G.M.P. (or widow's G.M.P.).

From April 6, 1988 contracted-out salary related schemes must also provide a widower's G.M.P. which must be at least half of the late wife's G.M.P. entitlement built up from April 6, 1988. (A scheme need not provide entitlement to a G.M.P. for widowers of earners dying before April 1989.) Contracted-out money purchase schemes and personal pension schemes must provide half-rate widower's benefit.

In contracted-out schemes, both the employee and the employer pay the full ordinary rate of contribution on the first £41·00 (1988–89 figure) of earnings but earnings above that amount attract a lower rate of contribution from the employee, and from the employer where the employee's earnings are under £305·00 (1988–89 figure): where the employee's earnings exceed this amount, the full ordinary rate of contribution is payable only by the employer, the

employee has no liability for contributions on these earnings (*see also* p. 1045).

An employee who chooses a personal pension in place of S.E.R.P.S. or their employer's pension scheme must pay National Insurance contributions at the full ordinary rate (the employer's share must also be paid at the same rate). The D.o.S.S. pays the difference between the lower contracted-out rate and the full ordinary rate for the personal pension scheme.

BENEFITS

The benefits payable under the Social Security Acts are as follows:

(1) Contributory Benefits:
   Unemployment benefit.
   Sickness benefit.
   Invalidity pension and allowance.
   Maternity allowance.
   Widow's benefit, comprising widow's payment, widowed mother's allowance and widow's pension.
   Retirement pensions, categories A and B.

(2) Non-contributory Benefits:
   Child benefit.
   One parent benefit.
   Guardian's allowance.
   Invalid care allowance.
   Attendance allowance.
   Severe disablement allowance.
   Mobility allowance.
   Retirement pensions, categories C and D.
   Income Support.
   Family Credit.

(3) Benefits for Industrial Injuries and Diseases.

Leaflets relating to the various benefits are obtainable from local social security offices.

The Social Security Acts empower the Secretary of State to increase certain rates of benefit by order approved by both Houses of Parliament, and require him to increase certain rates by such an order if an annual review shows that they have not retained their value in relation to the general level of prices obtaining in Great Britain.

The latest order providing for increases in benefit rates took effect from the week commencing April 11, 1988.

CONTRIBUTORY BENEFITS

Entitlement to the contributory benefits depends on contribution conditions being satisfied either by the claimant or by some other person (depending on the kind of benefit). The class or classes of contribution which for this purpose are relevant to each benefit are as follows:

Short-term benefits

Unemployment benefit	Class 1
Sickness benefit	Class 1 or 2
Maternity allowance	Class 1 or 2
Widow's payment	Class 1, 2 or 3

Other benefits

Widowed mother's allowance	
Widow's pension	
Category A retirement pension	Class 1, 2 or 3
Category B retirement pension	
Invalidity benefit	Class 1 or 2

The system of contribution conditions relates to yearly levels of earnings on which contributions have been paid. The contribution conditions for different benefits are set out in summary form in leaflets available at local social security offices.

Unemployment Benefit

Benefit is payable in a period of interruption of employment for up to 312 days (a year, excluding Sundays). Spells of unemployment and sickness not separated by more than 8 weeks count as one period of interruption of employment. A person who has exhausted benefit requalifies when he has again worked as an employed earner for at least 16 hours a week for 13 weeks. These weeks need not be consecutive nor fall within the same year.

Disqualifications.—There are disqualifications from receiving benefit, e.g. for a period not exceeding 26 weeks if a person has lost his employment through his misconduct, or has voluntarily left his employment without just cause, or has, without good cause, refused an offer of suitable employment or training.

Sickness Benefit

Sickness benefit is payable for up to 28 weeks of sickness in a period of interruption of employment and is then replaced by invalidity benefit (*see* below).

Disqualifications.—There are disqualifications from receiving sickness or invalidity benefit for a period not exceeding six weeks if a person has become incapable of work through his own misconduct or if he fails without good cause to attend for or submit himself to prescribed medical or other examination or treatment, or observe prescribed rules of behaviour.

Since April 6, 1986, employers are responsible for paying Statutory Sick Pay (S.S.P.) to their employees for up to 28 weeks of sickness in any period of incapacity for work. S.S.P. replaces the employee's entitlement to State Sickness Benefit which is not payable as long as any S.S.P. liability remains. S.S.P. is subject to P.A.Y.E. and to N.I. deductions. Employers can recover the S.S.P. they have paid out and can also withhold an extra amount to compensate themselves for the N.I. contributions they have paid on S.S.P. from the payments of N.I. they make each month to the Collector of Taxes. Employees who cannot get S.S.P. can claim State Sickness Benefit instead.

Invalidity Benefit

Normally, after 28 weeks of sickness, sickness benefit, or S.S.P. where the underlying conditions for sickness benefit are satisfied, is replaced by an invalidity pension. In addition an invalidity allowance is payable if incapacity for work begins more than five years before pension age. The allowance varies according to the age on falling sick, and if still in payment at pension age will continue as an addition to retirement pension. From Sept. 16, 1985 invalidity allowance has been reduced or withdrawn completely if there is entitlement to an additional earnings-related pension and/or a guaranteed minimum pension.

Maternity Benefit

Statutory maternity pay (S.M.P.) is administered by employers but there is still a state maternity allowance scheme for women who are self-employed or otherwise do not qualify for S.M.P.

In general, employers pay S.M.P. to pregnant women who have been employed by them for at least six months and earned at least the lower earnings limit for the payment of N.I. contributions. For those who have been employed for at least two years, payment of S.M.P. for the first six weeks is related to earnings, followed by up to twelve weeks at a standard rate of £34·25. Those who have been employed for at least six months but less than two years receive payment at standard rate only for the 18 weeks. Part-time working women also qualify for the earnings-related element if employed for at least five years.

Women have some choice in deciding when to begin maternity leave but S.M.P. is not payable for any week in which work is done.

A woman may qualify for maternity allowance (M.A.) if she has been working and paying contributions at the full rate for at least 26 weeks in the 52-week period which ends 15 weeks before the baby is due. She also has an element of choice in deciding when to stop work and receive M.A., which is not payable for any period she works.

Widow's Benefits

Only the late husband's contributions of any class count for widow's benefit in any of its three forms.

Widow's Payment.—May be received by a woman who at her husband's death is under 60, or whose husband was not entitled to a Category A retirement pension when he died.

Widowed Mother's Allowance.—Payable to a widow if she is receiving child benefit for one of her children; if her husband was receiving child benefit; or if she is expecting her husband's baby.

Widow's Pension.—A widow may receive this pension if aged 45 or over at the time of her husband's death or when her widowed mother's allowance ends. If aged 55 or over she will receive the full widow's pension rate.

Widow's benefit of any form ceases upon remarriage.

Retirement Pension
Categories A and B

A *Category A pension* is payable for life to men or women on their own contributions if (a) they are over pension age (65 for a man and 60 for a woman), and (b) they have retired from regular employment. Men aged 70 or over and women aged 65 or over are not required to satisfy condition (b).

Where a person does not retire at 65 (60 for a woman) or later cancels retirement, and does not draw a Category A pension, the weekly rate of pension is increased, when he or she finally retires or reaches the age of 70 (65 for a woman), in respect of weeks when pension is foregone during the five years after reaching minimum pension age. Details of the increase in the rate of pension due to deferred retirement are given in leaflet NP32, available at social security offices. A married man can also earn extra pension for his wife.

A *Category B pension* is normally payable for life to a woman on her husband's contributions when he has retired, or is over 70, and has qualified for his own Category A pension, and she has reached 60 and retired from regular work or has reached 65. It is also payable on widowhood after 60 whether or not the late husband had retired and qualified for his own pension. The weekly pension is payable at the rate of the increase for a wife while the husband is alive, and at the single person's rate on widowhood after 60. Where a woman is widowed before she reaches 60, a Category B pension is paid to her on reaching 60 at the same weekly rate as her widow's pension if she retires. If a woman qualifies for a pension of each category she receives whichever pension is the larger. Details of the increase in the rate of pension due to deferred retirement are given in leaflet NP32A, available at social security offices.

A man aged 65 to 70, or a woman aged 60 to 65, who has qualified for pension will have it reduced if he or she earns more than a certain amount. Where an adult dependant is living with the claimant, an Adult Dependents Allowance will only be payable if the dependent's earning do not exceed the standard rate of unemployment benefit for a single person under pensionable age (*see* below). For the purpose of the dependency rule only, earnings will include payments by way of occupational pension. The earnings of a separated spouse affect the increase of retirement pension if they exceed £23·75 a week.

Unemployment, sickness or invalidity benefit is payable to men between 65 and 70 and women between 60 and 65 who have not retired from regular work and who would have been entitled to a retirement pension if they had retired at pension age. This applies in the case of sickness and invalidity benefit if incapacity for work is the result of an industrial accident or prescribed disease. These rates of benefit for people over pension age are shown in leaflet N.I. 196. A retirement pension will be increased by the amount of any invalidity allowance the pensioner was getting within the period of 8 weeks and one day before reaching minimum pension age. An age addition of 25p per week is payable if a retirement pensioner is aged 80 or over. (For attendance allowance and invalidity care allowance, *see* Non-contributory Benefits).

Graduated Pension

The graduated pension scheme under which national insurance contributions and retirement pensions were graduated within specified limits, according to earnings, was discontinued in April, 1975, under the Social Security Act, 1975. Any graduated pension which an employed person over 18 and under 70 (65 for a woman) had earned by paying graduated contributions between April 6, 1961, when the scheme started and April 5, 1975, will be paid when the contributor retires, or at 70 (65 for a woman), in addition to any retirement pension for which he or she qualifies.

Graduated pension is at the rate of 5·39p a week for each "unit" of graduated contributions paid by the employee (half a unit or more counts as a whole unit). A unit of contributions is £7·50 for men, and £9·00 for women, of graduated contributions paid.

A wife can get a graduated pension in return for her own graduated contributions, but not for her husband's. A widow gets a graduated addition to her retirement pension equal to half of any graduated additions earned by her late husband, plus any additions earned by her own graduated contributions. If a person defers retirement beyond 65 (60 for a woman), entitlement may be increased by one seventh of a penny per £1 of its weekly rate for each complete week of deferred retirement, as long as retirement is deferred for a minimum of seven weeks.

Rates of Benefits
(from week commencing April 11, 1988)

Benefit	Weekly rate £
Unemployment Benefit—standard rate	
Person under pension age	32·75
Increase for wife/other adult dependent	20·20
Person over pension age*	41·15
Increase for wife/other adult dependent	24·75
Sickness Benefit—standard rate	
Person under pension age	31·30
Increase for wife/other adult dependent	19·40
Person over pension age*	39·45
Increase for wife/other adult dependent	23·65
Invalidity Pension*	
Person (under or over pension age)	41·15
Increase for wife or adult dependent	24·75
Invalidity Allowance (maximum amounts payable)	
higher rate	8·65

middle rate	5·50
lower rate	2·75
Maternity Allowance	31·30
Widow's Payment*	57·65
Widowed Mother's Allowance* and Widow's Pension*	41·15
Retirement pension*—*categories A and B*	
Single person	41·15
Increase for wife or adult dependent	24·75
Earnings limit for retirement pensioners......................	75·00

* These benefits attract an increase for each dependent child (in addition to child benefit) of £8·40.

NON-CONTRIBUTORY BENEFITS
Child Benefit

Child benefit is payable for all children in a family within the age limits, including the first or only child. There is an additional payment for the first or only child in certain one-parent families.

Guardian's Allowance

Where the parents of a child are dead, the person who has the child in his family may claim a guardian's allowance in addition to child benefit. The allowance in exceptional circumstances, is payable on the death of only one parent.

Invalid Care Allowance

Invalid care allowance is payable to persons of working age, who are not gainfully employed because they are regularly and substantially engaged in caring for a severely disabled person who is receiving attendance allowance or constant attendance allowance with either a war or services pension, industrial disablement workman's compensation, or an allowance under the Pneumoconiosis, Byssinosis and Miscellaneous Diseases Benefit Scheme.

Mobility Allowance

The allowance is, subject to certain conditions, payable to persons who are suffering from such physical disablement that they are unable to walk or virtually unable to walk, and this condition is likely to last for at least a year. It can be claimed by persons over the age of 5 and under 65 (for this purpose a claim may be made up to 12 months from that birthday) and may be retained to age 75.

Severe Disablement Allowance

Persons of working age who have been continuously incapable of work for a period of at least 28 weeks but who do not qualify for a contributory invalidity pension may be entitled to severe disablement allowance. People who first become incapable of work after their 20th birthday must be at least 80 per cent disabled.

Attendance Allowance

Attendance allowance is payable to the severely disabled. Entitlement is determined by the Attendance Allowance Board or by a doctor acting on the Board's behalf. The full rate is paid to those in need of a great deal of attention or supervision both by day and by night. The allowance is paid at the lower rate to those whose need for attention or supervision arises either by day or by night. There is a six-month qualifying period.

Non-contributory Retirement Pension
Categories C and D

A *Category C pension* is provided, subject to a residence test, for persons who were over pensionable age on July 5, 1948, and for women whose husbands are so entitled if they are over pension age and have retired from regular work, with increases for adult and child dependents. A *Category D pension* is provided for others when they reach 80 if they are not already getting a retirement pension of any category or if they are getting that pension at less than these rates. An age addition of 25p per week is payable if persons entitled to retirement pension or their dependants are aged 80 or over.

Rates of Benefits
(from week commencing April 11, 1988)

Benefit	Weekly rate £
Child Benefit (per child)	7·25
One Parent Benefit	
First or only child of certain lone parents	4·90
Guardian's Allowance	8·40
Severe Disablement Allowance*	24·75
Increase for wife/other adult dependent	14·80
Mobility Allowance	23·05
Invalid Care Allowance*	24·75
Increase for wife/other adult dependent	14·80
Attendance Allowance	
higher rate	32·95
lower rate	22·00
Retirement Pension—Categories C* and D.	
Single person	23·75
Increase for wife/other adult dependent	14·20
(not payable with Category D pension)	

*These benefits attract an increase for each dependent child (in addition to child benefit) of £8·40.

INCOME SUPPORT

Income Support is a benefit for those whose income is inadequate and who are unemployed; over 60; bringing up children alone; unable to work or working only part-time through sickness or disability; or staying at home to care for a disabled relative. Except in special cases Income Support is not available to those who work for more than 24 hours per week or who have a partner who works for more than 24 hours per week. Income Support is not payable if the claimant, or claimant and partner, have capital or savings in excess of £6,000. The rate of benefits is affected by possession of capital or savings in excess of £3,000 and may be affected by a claimant's earnings. Sums payable depend on fixed allowances laid down by law for people in different circumstances. Special rates apply for people living in board and lodging, hostels, residential care or nursing homes. Details are available from local social security offices. Income Support is payable via post offices, either by order book or, for the unemployed, by girocheque. Applications for Income Support are made on form SB1, available from post offices; Income Support claim forms, available from social security offices; or on form B1 (for the unemployed), available from unemployment benefit offices. If both partners are entitled to Income Support, either may claim it. People receiving Income Support will be able to receive Housing Benefit, help with mortgage or home loan interest and help with health care. They may also be eligible for help with exceptional expenses,

from the Social Fund. Leaflet SB20 gives a detailed explanation of Income Support.

INCOME SUPPORT PREMIUMS

Income Support Premiums are additional weekly payments for those with special needs. People qualifying for more than one premium will normally only receive the highest single premium for which they qualify. However Family Premium, Disabled Child's Premium and Severe Disability Premium are payable in addition to other premiums.

People with children qualify for a Family Premium if they have at least one child; a Disabled Child's Premium if they have a child who receives Attendance Allowance or Mobility Allowance or is registered blind; or a Lone Parent Premium if they are bringing up one or more children alone.

Long-term sick or disabled people qualify for a Disability Premium if they or their partner are receiving certain benefits because they are disabled or cannot work; are registered blind; or have been sending in doctor's statements for at least 28 weeks stating inability to work through sickness. If they are in receipt of Attendance Allowance, without anyone receiving Invalid Care Allowance for looking after them, they qualify for a Severe Disability Premium in addition to a Disability Premium.

People qualify for a Pensioner Premium if they or their partner are aged between 60 and 79, and for a Higher Pensioner Premium if they or their partner are aged 80 or over. A Higher Pensioner Premium is also payable to people aged between 60 and 79 who receive Attendance Allowance, Mobility Allowance, Invalidity Benefit or Severe Disablement Allowance, or who are registered blind. A Higher Pensioner Premium may be paid as well as a Severe Disability Premium.

Rates of Benefit
(from week commencing April 11, 1988)

	Weekly rate £
INCOME SUPPORT	
Single people	
aged 16–17	19·40
aged 18–24	26·05
aged 25 and over	33·40
aged 18 and over and a single parent.	33·40
Couples	
both under 18	38·80
one or both aged 18 or over	51·45
For each child in a family	
under 11	10·75
aged 11–15	16·10
aged 16–17*	19·40
aged 18 and over*	26·05

*if in full-time education up to A level or O.N.D. standard.

Premiums	
Family Premium	6·15
Disabled Child's Premium	6·15
Lone Parent Premium	3·70
Disability Premium	
Single	13·05
Couple	18·60
Severe Disability Premium	
Single	24·75
Couple (one person qualified)	24·75
Couple (both qualified)	49·50
Pensioner Premium	
Single	10·65
Couple	16·25
Higher Pensioner Premium	
Single	13·05
Couple	18·60

FAMILY CREDIT

Family Credit is a tax-free benefit for working families with children. It is not a loan and need not be repaid. To qualify, a family must include at least one child under 16 (under 19 if in full-time education up to A level or O.N.D. standard), and the claimant, or partner, must be working for at least 24 hours per week. It does not matter which partner is working and they may be employed or self-employed. The right to Family Credit does not depend on N.I. contributions and the same rates of benefit are paid to one and two parent families. Family Credit is not payable if the claimant, or claimant and partner, have capital or savings in excess of £6,000 and the rate of benefits is affected if capital or savings in excess of £3,000 are held. The sums payable depend upon the claimant's (and partner's) income, number of children, and children's ages. Family Credit is normally paid for 26 weeks and the amount payable will usually remain constant throughout this period, regardless of change of circumstances. Payment is made via post offices or directly into a bank or building society account. Applications for Family Credit are made on form FC1, obtainable at a post office or social security office. In two parent families the woman should claim.

Rates of Benefit
(from week commencing April 11, 1988)

	Weekly rate £
Likely to be payable where "family income" (*see* form FC1) after tax and N.I. is less than £96·50	
plus for each child aged:	
under 11	8·50
11–15	16·00
16–17	21·00
18	30·50

The maximum amount will be payable where net income is less than £51·45 per week. The maximum rate consists of:

Adult credit (for one or two parents)	32·10
plus for each child aged:	
under 11	6·05
11–15	11·40
16–17	14·70
18	21·35

DETERMINATION OF CLAIMS AND QUESTIONS

With a few exceptions, claims and questions relating to Social Security benefits are decided by statutory authorities who act independently of the Department of Social Security and Department of Employment. The first of the statutory authorities, the Adjudication Officer, determines entitlement to benefit. A claimant who is dissatisfied with that decision has the right of appeal to a Social Security Appeal Tribunal. There is a further right of appeal to a Social Security Commissioner against the Tribunal's decision but leave to appeal must first be obtained. Appeals to the Commissioner must be on a point of law. Provision is also made for the determination of certain questions by the Secretary of State for Social Services.

Disablement questions are decided by adjudicating medical authorities or Medical Appeal Tribunals. Appeal to the Commissioner against a tribunal's decision is with leave and on a point of law only.

Leaflet NI 246 which is available from social security offices, explains how to appeal and leaflet NI260 is a guide to reviews and appeals.

INDUSTRIAL INJURIES AND DISEASES BENEFITS

The Industrial Injuries scheme, administered under the Social Security Act 1975 and subsequent Acts and Regulations, provides a range of benefits designed to compensate for disablement resulting from an industrial accident (i.e. an accident arising out of and in the course of an employed earner's employment) or from a prescribed disease due to the nature of a person's employment. Rates of benefit are increased periodically.

Determination of Claims and Questions.—Provision is made for the determination of certain questions by the Secretary of State for Social Security, and of "disablement questions" by a medical board (or a single doctor) or, on appeal, by a medical appeal tribunal. An appeal on a point of law against a medical appeal tribunal decision is determined by the Social Security Commissioner. Claims for benefit and certain questions arising in connection with a claim for or award of benefit (e.g. whether the accident arose out of and in the course of the employment) are determined by an adjudication officer appointed by the Secretary of State, or a Social Security Appeal Tribunal, or in certain circumstances, on further appeal, by the Commissioners.

Special schemes under the Industrial Injuries and Diseases (Old Cases) Act 1975 provide supplementary allowances to those entitled to receive weekly payments of workmen's compensation for loss of earnings due to injury at work, or disease contracted during employment before July 5, 1948 when the Industrial Injuries scheme was introduced. Other schemes under the Act provide allowances to those who contracted slowly developing diseases during employment before July 1948 where neither workmen's compensation nor Industrial Injuries Benefits are payable. A lump sum death benefit of up to £300 may also be payable to a dependant of such a person.

Benefits

Disablement Benefit is normally payable 15 weeks (90 days) after the date of accident or onset of disease if the employed earner suffers from loss of physical or mental faculty such that the resulting disablement is assessed at not less than 14 per cent. The amount of disablement benefit payable varies according to the degree of disablement (in the form of a percentage) assessed by an adjudicating medical authority or medical appeal tribunal.

Disablement assessed at less than 14 per cent. does not normally attract basic benefit except for certain progressive chest diseases. A weekly pension is payable where the assessment of disablement is between 14 and 100 per cent. (assessments of 14 to 19 per cent are payable at the 20 per cent rate). Payment can be made for a limited period or for life.

The basic rates are applicable to adults and to juveniles entitled to an increase for a child or adult dependent; other juveniles receive lower rates.

Basic rates of pension are not related to the pensioner's loss of earning power, and are payable whether he is in work or not. If disablement is assessed at one per cent. or more, loss of earnings may be compensated by a reduced earnings allowance. This may be paid even if basic disablement pension is not paid because disablement is assessed at less than 14 per cent. There is provision also for increases of pension if the pensioner requires constant attendance or if his disablement is exceptionally severe. A pensioner may draw S.S.P., sickness or invalidity benefit as appropriate, in addition to disablement pension, during spells of incapacity for work.

Death Benefit, in the form of a pension, is available for women widowed before April 11, 1988. The amount of pension depends on the widow's circumstances at the date of death and not upon the deceased's earnings.

Regulations impose certain obligations on claimants and beneficiaries and on employers, including, in the case of claimants for disablement benefit, that of submitting to medical examination.

Rates of Benefits
(from April 11, 1988)

	Weekly rate £
Disablement Benefit/Pension	
Degree of disablement—100 per cent.	67·20
90	60·48
80	53·76
70	47·04
60	40·32
50	33·60
40	26·88
30	20·16
20	13·44
Unemployability supplement*	41·15
Addition for adult dependent (subject to earnings rule)	24·75
Reduced earnings allowance (maximum)	26·88
Constant Attendance allowance (normal maximum rate)	26·90
Exceptionally severe disablement allowance	26·90
Industrial death benefit widow's pension*	
Higher permanent rate	41·15
Lower permanent rate	12·35

* These benefits attract an increase for each dependent child (in addition to child benefit) of £8·40.

FINANCE

The National Insurance Fund receives all social security contributions (less only the National Health Service and Redundancy Fund and Maternity Pay Fund allocations and the National Insurance Surcharge for taxation purposes) together with the Consolidated Fund supplement; and it bears the cost of all contributory benefits provided by the Social Security Acts and the cost of administration.

Approximate receipts and payments of the National Insurance Fund for the year ended March 31, 1987, were as follows:

Receipts	£'000
Balance, April 1, 1986	5,293,024
Contributions under the Social Security Acts (net of S.S.P.)	22,315,571
Consolidated Fund Supplement	2,412,000
Income from Investments	610,328
Other receipts	1,987
	30,632,910

Payments	£'000	£'000
Benefit:—		
Unemployment benefit.	1,733,537	
Sickness benefit	178,954	
Invalidity benefit	2,647,129	
Maternity allowance	168,824	
Widow's benefit	827,620	
Guardian's allowance and child's special allowance	1,181	
Retirement pension	17,817,145	
Death grant	18,439	
Industrial injuries benefits	—	
Disablement benefits	439,618	
Death benefit	61,214	
Other industrial injury benefits	4,428	
Pensioners lump sum payments	107,000	
Payments in lieu of benefit forgone	—	
		24,005,107
Transfers to Northern Ireland		175,000
Administration		738,055
Other payments		7,782
Write offs		—
Balance, March 31, 1986		5,706,966
		30,632,910

WAR PENSIONS

War pensions are awarded under The Naval, Military and Air Forces, Etc. (Disablement and Death) Service Pensions Order 1983, which was a consolidation of the previous Royal Warrants, Orders in Council and Orders by Her Majesty.

The D.o.S.S. award war pensions in respect of the periods Aug. 4, 1914 to Sept. 30, 1921 and subsequent to Sept. 3, 1939 (including present members of the armed forces). The D.o.S.S. also have special schemes for the Merchant Navy, Naval Auxiliary personnel, civil defence, civilians, Home Guard, Polish armed forces under British command and Polish resettlement forces.

War pensions for the period Oct. 1, 1921 to Sept. 2, 1939 are dealt with by the Ministry of Defence who are also responsible for the Armed Forces Pension Scheme.

ELIGIBILITY

War disablement pension is awarded for the disabling effects of any injury, wound or disease which is attributable to, or aggravated by, conditions of service in the armed forces. It cannot be paid until the serviceman has left the armed forces.

War widows pension is awarded where death occurs as a result of service. Where a war disablement pensioner was receiving constant attendance allowance at the time of his death, or would have been receiving it if he were not in hospital, his widow has automatic entitlement to a war widow's pension, regardless of the cause of death.

Claims.—Where a claim is made no later than 7 years after the termination of service, the claimant does not have to prove that the disablement or death on which the claim is based is related to service and receives the benefit of any reasonable doubt. Where a claim is made more than 7 years after the termination of service the claimant has to show that disablement or death is related to service. However, the claim succeeds if reliable evidence is produced which raises a reasonable doubt whether disablement or death is related to service. There is no time limit for making a claim for war pension.

Payment.—Rank additions are normally paid with war pensions where the rank held was above that of private (or equivalent).

When a war disablement pensioner is sick, unemployed or retired, the appropriate social security benefits are paid in addition to the war pension. Any sickness, invalidity or unemployment benefit or retirement pension for which a war widow qualifies on her own contributions, and any graduated retirement benefit, can be paid in addition to her war pension or temporary allowance. A war pensioner or war widow who claims Income Support has the first £5 of pension disregarded. A similar provision operates for housing benefit but the local authority may, at its discretion, disregard any or all of the balance. A special tax free Christmas bonus of £10.00 is payable to war disablement pensioners who are in receipt of unemployability supplement, constant attendance allowance, have retired, or are aged over 70 (65 for women); and to all war widows.

A reduced weekly rate is payable to war widows below the rank of Lieutenant-Colonel who are under the age of 40, without children and capable of maintaining themselves. This is increased to the standard rate at age 40.

The D.o.S.S. is responsible for the payment of war pensions, and provision of necessary treatment for accepted disablement, to pensioners who reside overseas. They receive the same pension rates as war pensioners in this country and benefit from the same annual upratings.

BASIC DISABLEMENT PENSION

Disablement is assessed by comparison of the disabled person's condition with that of a normal, healthy person of the same age and sex, without taking into account the disabled person's earnings or occupation, and is expressed on a percentage scale up to 100 per cent. Disablement above 20 per cent is assessed in steps of 10 per cent. For assessment of less than 20 per cent a lump sum is payable. Maximum assessment does not necessarily imply total incapacity.

A 100 per cent disabled pensioner may receive an allowance of 60p a week for his dependent. Where disablement is less than 100 per cent the allowance is proportionate to the degree of disablement. The allowance is no longer paid under the social security scheme, but it still being paid to war pensioners.

SUPPLEMENTARY ALLOWANCES

A number of supplementary allowances may be awarded to a war pensioner which are intended to meet the various needs which may result from disablement or death and take account of its particular effect on the pensioner. Decisions on supplementary allowances are made on a discretionary basis on behalf of the Secretary of State and there is no provision for a statutory right of appeal against them. However, war pensioners may have any aspect of their pension position discussed by their local War Pensions Committees, which may be able to arrange help or make representations to the war pensions branch of the D.o.S.S.

Unemployability supplement, with additional allowances for dependants, may be paid to a war pensioner who is so seriously disabled as to be unemployable. In addition, an invalidity allowance may be payable if the incapacity for work began more than 5 years before normal retirement age.

Allowance for lowered standard of occupation may be awarded to a partially disabled pensioner whose pensioned disablement permanently prevents him from following his pre-service occupation and from doing another job of equivalent financial standard. The allowance, together with the basic war disablement pension, must not exceed pension at the 100 per cent rate.

Constant attendance allowance may be awarded to a war pensioner who is so severely handicapped by the nature of his pensioned disablement, assessed at not less than 80 per cent, that he must depend to a greater or lesser extent upon the attendance of some other person. There are four rates of the allowance and these vary according to the amount of time attendance is needed.

Exceptionally severe disablement allowance is paid to pensioners who are receiving constant attendance allowance on a permanent basis at either of the two highest rates.

Severe disablement occupational allowance is paid to those pensioners who qualify for constant attendance allowance at either of the two highest rates and who, despite their handicap, are normally in employment. This allowance is not payable if the pensioner is in receipt of unemployability supplement.

Comforts allowance is payable at one of two rates. The higher rate is paid to those pensioners who are receiving both constant attendance allowance and unemployability supplement. When only one of these allowances is in payment the lower rate of comforts allowance is normally paid, but the higher rate can be paid under certain conditions where only constant attendance allowance is in payment.

Clothing allowance may be awarded where the pensioned disablement causes exceptional wear and tear of clothing. It is payable at two rates, depending on the degree of wear and tear caused.

Mobility supplement is intended to help those war pensioners who have problems in walking caused wholly or mainly by their pensioned disablement.

Treatment allowance may be paid to a pensioner receiving medical treatment in hospital or at home if the treatment is for the pensioned disablement, is necessary because of the continuing effects of service, and is of a kind which prevents the pensioner from working for more than seven days. The allowance replaces the disablement pension and is paid at the 100 per cent rate.

Age allowance may be awarded to those war pensioners aged 65 or over whose war disablement is assessed at 40 per cent or more. It is payable at four rates, depending on the degree of disablement.

Widows age allowance is paid at three different rates according to age (65–69, 70–79 and over 80).

Widows child's allowance may be paid in addition to child benefit.

Rent allowance may be paid to a widow who receives a war widows pension and maintains a home for a child eligible for an allowance.

Education allowance may be payable to a war disablement pensioner or war widow in respect of a dependent child if the D.o.S.S. is satisfied that the education is suitable for the child and that the family circumstances are such as to require an allowance.

Temporary allowance for widows may be payable in the form of a special allowance for the first 26 weeks of widowhood for widows of war pensioners who received constant attendance allowance or unemployability supplement. After 26 weeks the widow will get any war widows pension or national insurance widows benefit to which she is entitled.

Funeral grant may be payable where the pensioner dies as a result of his pensioned disablement. Claims should be made within three months of the funeral.

PENSIONS APPEAL TRIBUNALS

There are independent Pensions Appeal Tribunals which hear appeals against the decisions of the D.o.S.S. on entitlement, and assessment of disablement, in respect of 1939 War and subsequent service cases. There are now no rights of appeal in the 1914 War disablement cases, the great majority of which were given final assessment in the 1920s with a 12 months right of appeal at the time. An appeal by a

1914 war widow must be made within twelve months of the date on which the rejection of the claim is notified.

WAR PENSIONERS WELFARE SERVICE

The D.o.S.S. operates a war pensioners welfare service to advise and assist war pensioners and their widows on any matters affecting their welfare. Welfare officers are attached to War Pensioners' Welfare Offices located in the major towns, and work closely with central and local Government agencies as well as the various ex-service organisations. The service is available on call to any war pensioner or widow who needs it. In addition the service takes the initiative in arranging regular visits in certain cases.

Rates of Pensions and Allowances
(from week commencing April 11, 1988)

	Weekly rates £
Disablement pension	
(for Private or equivalent rank)	
Degree of disablement—	
100 per cent	67.20
90 per cent	60.48
80 per cent	53.76
70 per cent	47.04
60 per cent	40.32
50 per cent	33.60
40 per cent	26.88
30 per cent	20.16
20 per cent	13.44

Unemployability supplement	
Personal allowance	45.70
Increase for wife/other adult dependent	24.75
Increase for child	8.40
Allowance for lowered standard of	
occupation (maximum)	26.88
Constant attendance allowance	
Exceptional rate	53.80
Intermediate rate	40.35
Normal maximum	26.90
Half and quarter day	13.45
Exceptionally severe disablement	
allowance	26.90
Severe disablement occupational allowance	13.45
Comforts allowance	
Higher rate	11.60
Lower rate	5.80
Clothing allowance (per annum)	
Higher rate	92.00
Lower rate	58.00
Mobility supplement	25.60
Age allowance	
Disablement assessment—	
40–50 per cent	4.70
50–70 per cent	7.30
70–90 per cent	10.45
over 90 per cent	14.60
Widow's pension	
(widow of Private or equivalent rank)	
Standard rate	53.50
Childless widow under 40	12.35
Widow's age allowance	
Age—65–69	5.75
70–79	11.50
80 and over	14.45
Rent allowance (maximum)	20.35

NATIONAL HEALTH SERVICE

(and Local Authority Personal Social Services)

The National Health Service came into being on July 5, 1948, as a result of the National Health Service Act 1946. The Act placed a duty on the Secretary of State for Social Services to promote the establishment in England and Wales of a comprehensive Health Service designed to secure improvement in the mental and physical health of the people and the prevention, diagnosis and treatment of illness. The Secretary of State for Wales administers the National Health Service in Wales. There are separate Acts for Scotland and Northern Ireland, where the Health Services are run on very similar lines and the respective Secretaries of State are responsible to Parliament.

The National Health Service covers a comprehensive range of hospital, specialist, family practitioner (medical, dental, ophthalmic and pharmaceutical), artificial limb and appliance, ambulance, and community health services. Everyone normally resident in this country is entitled to use any of these services, there are no contribution conditions and the charges made (except those for amenity beds) are reduced or waived in cases of hardship. In addition the Secretary of State for Social Services is responsible under the Local Authority Social Services Act 1970 for the provision by local authorities of social services for the elderly, the disabled, those with mental disorders and for families and children.

The 1980 Health Services Act led to major changes in the structure of the Health Service. Since April 1982, District Health Authorities (DHAs) are responsible for the operational management of health services and for planning within regional and national strategic guidelines. There are 190 DHAs in England and nine in Wales and they are generally coterminous with the local authorities, which provide complementary personal social services. Each DHA is required to arrange its services into units of management at hospital and community services level, and as many decisions as possible are delegated to unit level. Four of the London postgraduate teaching hospitals are now managed by DHAs (and eight are managed by special health authorities). Arrangements for the Family Practitioner Service are administered by Family Practitioner Committees (FPCs)—90 in England and eight in Wales. FPCs also contribute to the planning of health services.

The 14 Regional Health Authorities (RHAs) in England are responsible for regional planning, the allocation of resources to District Authorities, and the promotion of national policies and priorities. Performance review meetings are held annually between each hospital unit and its DHA, each DHA and its RHA, and between each RHA and Department of Health Ministers, thereby strengthening Authorities' accountability to Parliament, whilst respecting the essentially locally-based nature of decision making. Professional advisory machinery incorporated within the structure ensures that Health Authorities and their staffs make decisions in the full knowledge of expert opinion.

The NHS is financed mainly from taxation and the cost met from moneys voted by Parliament. In the U.K. this will amount to £23·5 billion in 1988–89. The Department of Health makes capital and revenue allocations to the RHAs and from these the RHAs meet the cost of their own services and make allocations to DHAs as well as funding Community Health Councils.

THE HEALTH SERVICES

Family Doctor Service

In England and Wales the Family Doctor Service (or General Medical Services) is organized by 98 Family Practitioner Committees which also organize the general dental, pharmaceutical and ophthalmic services for their areas. There is a Family Practitioner Committee for one or more District Health Authorities. Under the Health and Social Security Act 1984, FPCs became employing authorities in their own right on April 1, 1985, and all the members and the chairmen (31 in all) are appointed by the Secretary of State. Fifteen of the appointments are made from nominations received from committees, representing local doctors (8), dentists (3), pharmacists (2), ophthalmic opticians (1) and from among all four professions (1). Of the fifteen lay members, four each are appointed from nominations received from District Health Authorities and Local Authorities. The remainder (7) are appointed after such consultations as the Secretary of State considers appropriate. One member must be a qualified district nurse, midwife or health visitor with recent community nursing experience.

Any doctor may take part in the Family Doctor Scheme, provided the area in which he wishes to practise has not already an adequate number of doctors, and about 25,000 general practitioners in England and Wales do so. They may at the same time have private fee-paying patients. Family doctors are paid for their Health Service work in accordance with a scheme of remuneration which includes *inter alia* a basic practice allowance, capitation fees, reimbursement of certain practice expenses and payments for "out of hours" work.

Everyone aged 16 or over can choose their doctor (parents or guardians choose for children under 16) and the doctor is also free to accept a person or not as he or she chooses. A person may change their doctor if they wish, either at once if they have changed address or obtained permission from the doctor on whose list they are, or by informing the Family Practitioner Committee (in which case 14 days must elapse before the other doctor can accept them). When people are away from home they can still use the Family Doctor Service if they ask to be treated as "temporary residents", and in an emergency, if a person's own doctor is not available, any doctor in the service will give treatment and advice.

Patients are treated either in the Doctor's surgery or, when necessary, at home. Doctors may prescribe for their patients all drugs and medicines which are medically necessary for their treatment and also a certain number of surgical appliances (the more elaborate being provided through the hospitals).

Dental Service

Dentists, like doctors, may take part in the Service and may also have private patients. About 14,500 of the dentists available for general practice in England provide NHS general dental services. They are responsible to the Family Practitioner Committees in whose areas they provide services.

Patients are free to go to any dentist taking part in the Service and willing to accept them. Dentists receive payment for items of treatment for individual patients, instead of the capitation fee received by doctors.

Patients are asked to pay three-quarters of the cost of NHS dental treatment and about three-quarters of the cost of standard bridges and dentures. The maximum charge for a course of treatment is £150. There is no charge for arrest of bleeding, repairs to dentures, home visits by the dentist or re-opening a surgery in an emergency (in these two cases you will have to pay for treatment given in the normal way) or clinical examinations (though the Government has announced proposals to charge for examinations subject to the approval of Parliament). The following are exempt from dental charges:

children under 16;
young people aged 16–18 (though dentures and bridges must be paid for);
full time students under 19;
expectant mothers who were pregnant when accepted for treatment;
women who have had a child in the previous 12 months.

People receiving Income Support or Family Credit, and members of the same family as someone receiving Income Support or Family Credit, are automatically entitled to full remission of charges.

Leaflet AB11 available from post offices and leaflet D11 available from local social security offices explain how other people on a low income can, depending on their financial circumstances, get free treatment or help with charges.

Pharmaceutical Service

Patients may obtain medicines, appliances and oral contraceptives prescribed under the NHS from any pharmacy whose owner has entered into arrangements with the Family Practitioner Committee to provide this service. Almost all pharmacy owners have done so and display notices that they dispense under the NHS: the number of these pharmacies in England and Wales at the end of 1986 was about 10,400. There are also some appliance suppliers who only provide special appliances. In country areas where access to a pharmacy may be difficult patients may be able to obtain medicines etc. from their doctor.

Except for contraceptives (for which there is no charge), a charge of £2·60 is payable for each item supplied unless the patient is exempt and the declaration on the back of the prescription form is completed. Exemptions cover children under 16, men aged 65 and over and women aged 60 and over, pregnant women and mothers who have had a baby within the last 12 months, people suffering from certain medical conditions, people who receive Income Support or Family Credit, people on low income and war pensioners (for their accepted disablements). In addition, prepayment certificates may be purchased by those patients not entitled to exemption who require frequent prescriptions. Further information about the exemption and prepayment arrangements is given in leaflet P.11.

General Ophthalmic Services

General Ophthalmic Services, which are administered by Family Practitioner Committees, form part of the ophthalmic services available under the National Health Service and provide for the testing of sight and, for children, full-time students under the age of 19 and people on a low income, help towards the cost of glasses under the NHS voucher scheme. Diagnosis and specialist treatment of eye conditions is available through the Hospital Eye Service as well as the provision of glasses of a special type. Testing of sight may be carried out by any ophthalmic medical practitioner or ophthalmic optician. The optician must hand the prescription, and a voucher if eligible,

to the patient who can take this to any supplier of glasses of his choice to have dispensed. However, only registered opticians can supply glasses to children, and people registered as blind or partially sighted.

The NHS sight test remains free. Certain groups are automatically entitled to help with the purchase of glasses under an NHS voucher scheme: children under 16; full-time students under 19; people who are themselves or whose partners, are in receipt of Income Support or Family Credit, and people wearing certain complex lenses. The value of the voucher depends on the lenses required. Vouchers may be used to help pay for the glasses or contact lenses of the patient's choice. People with a low income may claim help on form AG1. Glasses or contact lenses should not be purchased until the result of a claim is known as no refunds can be given. Leaflet G11 gives further details.

Primary Health Care Services

Primary health care services include the general medical, dental, ophthalmic and pharmaceutical services, health centres and clinics, family planning outside the hospital service and preventive activities in the community including vaccination, immunization and fluoridation. The district nursing and health visiting services include community psychiatric nursing for mentally ill people living outside hospital, and school nursing for the health surveillance of school children of all ages; much ante- and post-natal care and chiropody are also an integral part of the primary health care service.

Community Child Health Services

Pre-school services, usually at child health clinics, provide regular surveillance of children's physical, mental and emotional health and development, and advice to parents on their children's health and welfare. The School Health Service provides for the medical and dental examination of school-children, and advises the local education authority, the school, the parents and the pupil of any health factors which may require special consideration during the pupil's school life.

Hospitals and Other Services

The Secretary of State for Health has a duty to provide, to such extent as he/she considers necessary to meet all reasonable requirements, hospital and other accommodation; medical, dental, nursing and ambulance services; other facilities for the care of expectant and nursing mothers and young children, facilities for the prevention of illness, and the care and after-care of persons suffering from illness and such other services as are required for the diagnosis and treatment of illness. Rehabilitation services (occupational therapy, physiotherapy and speech therapy) may also be provided for those who need it and surgical and medical appliances are supplied in appropriate cases.

Specialists and consultants who take part in the Service can engage in private practice, including the treatment of their private patients in NHS hospitals.

In a number of hospitals accommodation is available for the treatment of private in-patients who undertake to pay the full costs of hospital accommodation and services and (usually) separate medical fees to a specialist as well. The amount of the medical fees is a matter for agreement between doctor and patient. Hospital charges for private resident patients are determined by District Health Authorities either on a local basis or in line with a central "model" list.

Certain hospitals have accommodation in single

rooms or small wards which, if not required for patients who need privacy for medical reasons, may be made available to patients who desire it as an amenity. In such cases the patients are treated in every other respect as National Health patients.

There is no charge for drugs supplied to National Health hospital in-patients but out-patients pay £2·60 per item unless they are exempt.

With certain exceptions, hospital out-patients have to pay fixed charges for dentures, glasses and certain appliances. The charge for glasses will be related to

the type of lens prescribed; and for dentures will be up to a maximum charge of £62·00.

Local Authority Personal Social Services

Local authorities are responsible for the organization, management and administration of the personal social services and each authority has a Director of Social Services and a Social Services Committee responsible for the social services functions placed upon them by the Local Authority Social Services Act 1970.

POSTAL AND TELECOMMUNICATIONS INFORMATION

STAMPS

POSTAGE STAMPS are sold in values of 1p, 2p, 3p, 4p, 5p, 10p, 14p, 19p, 20p, 23p, 27p, 28p, 32p, 35p, 50p, 75p, £1, £1·50 and £2.

Books of stamps costing 50p and £1 are available from electronic vending machines at some main post offices. At all other vending machines, books to the value of 50p are available. At post office counters, books are sold containing 10 stamps at 19p (£1·90) and 10 at 14p (£1·40). Rolls of 14p and 19p stamps are sold: mixed value rolls are only available on special order from post offices.

REGISTERED LETTER ENVELOPES printed with a £1·59 stamp (£1·40 for registration and 19p for postage) are in three sizes: G, 156 mm × 95 mm, £1·70 each; H, 203 mm × 120 mm, £1·75 each; K, 292 mm × 152 mm, £1·85 each.

FORCES AEROGRAMMES, 14p.

AEROGRAMMES to all destinations, 27p.

Printed postage stamps cut out of envelopes, postcards, lettercards, air letter forms or newspaper-wrappers may be used as adhesive stamps in payment of postage or telegrams provided they are not imperfect, mutilated or defaced in any way.

POSTAL ORDERS

Postal Orders (British pattern) are issued and paid at nearly all post offices in the United Kingdom during the ordinary hours of business on weekdays. They are also issued and/or paid in many countries overseas. These countries are listed in the Post Office Guide which may be seen at any post office transacting postal order business. Transmission of postal orders to any other country is prohibited except to members of H.M. Forces. British postal orders are paid and issued in the Channel Islands and the Isle of Man and paid in the Irish Republic. They are printed, with a counterfoil, for denominations of 25p, 30p, 40p, 50p, 60p, 70p, 80p, 90p and £1, followed by £1 steps to £10 and £20. Adhesive unmarked British Postage Stamps not exceeding two in number, if affixed in the space provided, may increase the value of an order by not more than 9p. Fees: 25p on each order up to £1, 38p on each order £2–£10, and 58p on £20. The name of the payee must be inserted. If not presented within six months of the last day of the month of issue orders must be sent to the local Head Postmaster or, in London, to the District Postmaster, to ascertain whether the order may still be paid.

GENERAL POSTAL REGULATIONS

Export Restrictions.—Under Department of Trade and Industry regulations the exportation of some goods by post is prohibited except under Department of Trade licence. Enquiries in the matter should be addressed to the Export Data Branch, Overseas Trade Divisions, Department of Trade and Industry, 1 Victoria Street, London, SW1H 0ET. Tel. 01–215 7877.

Prohibited Articles.—Among prohibitions are offensive or dangerous things, packets likely to impede the P.O. sorters, and certain kinds of advertisement.

Certificate of Posting.—Issued free on request at the time of posting.

Recorded Delivery (inland). Charge: 24p.—This service provides for a record of posting and delivery and is available for inland letters. Advice of delivery, a further 25p at time of posting. No compensation is payable in respect of money or jewellery sent by this service.

Unpaid Mail.—All unpaid or underpaid letters are treated as second class mail. The recipient will be charged the amount of underpayment plus 11p per item. The same rates apply to unpaid or underpaid parcels.

Undelivered Mail.—Undelivered mail is returned to the sender without charge provided the return address is indicated either on the outside of the envelope or inside. If the sender's address is not available, items not containing property are destroyed; however, if the packet contains something of intrinsic value, it is retained for up to three months pending reclaim before being disposed of. Perishable items within this category are dealt with as requisite. Exceptionally, items in the minimum weight step on which a rebate of postage has been allowed are destroyed unopened unless there is a return address shown on the outside of the cover. In addition, undeliverable second class mail in the minimum weight step, which, upon opening, is found to consist only of newspapers, magazines or commercial advertising material is also destroyed. *British packets undelivered abroad*: instructions for disposal are required if parcel is undeliverable and must be given at the time of posting. A parcel which cannot be delivered will be returned to sender at his expense.

International Reply Coupons, for the purpose of prepaying replies to letters, are exchangeable abroad for stamps representing the minimum surface mail letter rate from the country concerned to the U.K. Cost: 60p each.

Poste Restante (solely for the convenience of travellers, and for three months only in any one town).—A packet may be addressed as a rule to any post office except town sub-offices, and should have the words "Poste Restante" or "to be called for" in the address. If addressed to initials, fictitious names, or Christian name only, it is treated as undeliverable. Applicants must furnish sufficient particulars to ensure delivery to the proper person. Redirection from a Poste Restante is undertaken for up to three months. Letters at a seaport for an expected ship are kept 2 months; otherwise letters are kept for 2 weeks—or for 1 month if originating from abroad—at the end of which time they are treated as undeliverable, unless bearing a request for return at or before the end of the period.

Redirection.—(1) By agent of addressee: *Packets other than parcels, business reply and Freepost items* may be reposted free not later than the day after delivery (not counting Sundays and public holidays) if unopened and not tampered with, and if original addressee's name is unobscured. *Parcels* may be redirected free of charge within the same time limits, only if the original and the substituted address are both within the same local parcel delivery area (or within the London Postal Area). *Registered packets*, which must be taken to a post office, are *re-registered* free only up to day after delivery. (2) By the Post Office: Requests for redirection of *letters*, etc., should be on printed forms, obtainable from any post office, and must be signed by the person to whom the letters are to be addressed. The fees for redirection are as follows:—redirection for an initial period of up to one calendar month, £2·75; redirection for a period of up to three calendar months, commencing before the first anniversary of redirection, £6·25; redirection for a period of up to twelve calendar months, commencing before the first anniversary of redirection, £15; redirection for a period of up to 12 calendar months where redirection has already been in operation for 12 months or more, £51. A fee is payable for each different surname on the application form.

Additional postage is generally due on redirected parcels (*see* above).

Registration, Inland (First Class letters only).— All packets intended for registration must be handed to an officer of the Post Office, and a certificate of posting obtained. The fees for registration (exclusive of first class postage) are: £1·40 covering compensation up to £650; £1·55, £1,350; £1·70, £1,850 (maximum). (No legal right to compensation exists in respect of registered letters sent to and from Irish Republic or the Channel Islands.) Compensation Fee (C.F.) parcels, fees: 30p up to £60 compensation; 40p up to £125; 60p up to £225; 75p up to £350. Advice of delivery, a further 25p at time of posting, 65p after time of posting.

Compensation in respect of money of any kind (coin, notes, orders, cheques, stamps, etc.) is only given if the money is sent by registered letter post in one of the special envelopes sold officially. Compensation cannot be paid for loss or damage in the case of any packet containing anything not legally transmissible by post; and for fragile articles only if they have been adequately packed. No compensation is paid for deterioration due to delay of perishable articles or for damage to exceptionally fragile articles, liquids or semi-liquids sent by letter or parcel post to or from Irish Republic, whether registered or not.

Compensation, Inland.—The ordinary mail services are not designed as compensation services. However, compensation up to a maximum limit of £20·00 may be paid where it can be shown that a letter or parcel was damaged or lost in the post. The onus of making up properly any packet sent by post and of packing adequately any article or articles enclosed therein lies on the sender, and the Post Office does not accept any responsibility for loss arising from faulty or inadequate packing. No compensation may be claimed for consequential injury or damage arising in respect of anything sent by post unless the item is registered and covered by Consequential Loss Insurance. This special insurance is arranged with certain Lloyds underwriters. Ask for details at the post office. The service is available only to U.K. addresses. *Recorded delivery packets:* maximum compensation £20 provided no contents inadmissible. Fee 24p.

Registration, Overseas (except for parcels and printed paper items posted in bulk), is in force to all countries with the exception of British Indian Ocean Territory or Republic of Maldives. No compensation is payable for the loss of or damage to valuable articles or other items sent in an unregistered letter. Fee £1·40. If claimed within a year compensation is paid to the sender for entire loss of registered packets while in the custody of a country in the Universal Postal Union, subject to certain conditions. Compensation is also payable for the partial or complete loss of or damage to the contents of registered items in the service with certain countries (*see* Post Office Guide for list).

Insurance, Overseas, may be effected on packets to many countries at the following rates:—£1·40 for up to £140 cover; 20p for each additional £100 up to £3·20 for £1,400. For H.M. Ships abroad and also members of H.M. Army and Air Force overseas using closed Forces addresses (e.g. British Forces Post Office followed by a number) only parcels are insurable, up to £140. Fee £1·20. Packets containing valuable papers, (banknotes, etc.), documents (press, etc.) and, in some cases, valuable articles such as jewellery, can be insured as letters, or as parcels if the country of destination does not accept dutiable goods in the letter post.

The Post Office Guide should be consulted for details of the conditions of Insurance.

Compensation up to a maximum of £13·00 for parcels up to 5 kg. in weight, £20·00 for parcels up to 10 kg., £25·00 for parcels up to 15 kg. and £30·00 for parcels up to 20 kg may be given for loss or damage in the U.K. to uninsured parcels to or from most overseas countries, if certificate of posting is produced.

No compensation will be paid for any loss or damage due to the act of the Queen's Enemies.

Cash on Delivery Service, Inland (not to or from Irish Republic, nor to H.M. Ships).—A sum (Trade Charge) up to £350 can, under certain conditions, be collected from addresses and remitted to sender of a parcel containing an invoice. Invoice values over £50 are only collected at Post Office premises. Fee (extra to normal postage and registration charges): 75p for customers under contract; £1·00 for other customers. C.O.D. enquiry fee: 75p.

Cash on Delivery, Overseas.—Applicable to parcels only, but not all countries, nor to H.M. Naval and Military Forces and R.A.F. serving overseas. A fee, starting at £2.50 per parcel, must be prepaid in addition to the postage for outward parcels. For inward parcels the delivery fee is 70p. The Trade Charge (amount to be collected) may not exceed £1,500, but to most non-European countries the limit is lower. Addressee has also to pay on delivery, besides Customs, if any, a further fee (£1 in U.K.) not prepayable. If Trade Charge cannot be collected, special rules for undeliverable C.O.D. parcels apply.

Datapost.—A guaranteed service for the delivery of important documents and packages. Datapost Sameday provides same day collection and delivery in many areas. Datapost Overnight offers next day delivery nationwide. Items may be collected or handed in at post offices. Contractual arrangements may be made for regular consignments. There are also equally reliable and secure Datapost links with a number of overseas countries. Further details are available at local Head Post Offices or on 0800 884422.

Swiftair.—Express delivery of air mail letters and packets anywhere in the world. Items normally arrive at least one day in advance of normal air mail. Items should be handed in at a post office counter. Cost: normal postage plus £1·65.

Intelpost.—A public facsimile transmission service linking many towns and cities in the U.K. and also with international connections. Documents up to A4 size can be transmitted and received within minutes and the service can be used with hand delivery and collection services. Further details are available at local Head Post Offices or on Freephone Intelpost.

Royal Mail Special Delivery.—Offers special messenger treatment where necessary to ensure next day delivery of first class letters and packets. Special fee of £1·65 refunded if next working day delivery is not achieved provided items are posted before latest recommended posting times.

Express Delivery.—This service from the office of delivery by special messenger is available to or from certain countries. In some countries the service is restricted to certain towns. Fee payable in addition to postage, £1·65.

Business Reply and Freepost (Inland, excluding Irish Republic).—These services enable a person or firm to receive replies to advertisements, letters from clients, etc. without prepayment of postage, the addressee paying the postage together with a handling charge per item delivered. A licence must be obtained to use either service and these are available from Head Postmasters who will also provide any further information required.

Postage Forward Parcel Service.—This service enables a person or firm to receive parcels from clients without prepayment of postage, the addressee pays a fee of 10p on each parcel in addition to postage. A special label is used for this service. A licence to use the service must first be obtained from the local Head Postmaster.

Articles for the Blind (Inland, including Irish Republic).—Books, papers, literature and specified articles specially adapted for the use of the blind are admissible subject to certain conditions. A packet should bear on the outside the indication "Articles for the Blind" and the name and address of the sender. Packets must be capable of easy examination in the post. Postage free up to a maximum weight of 7 kg.

Blind Literature, Overseas (in other respects treated as Printed Papers).—Papers, periodicals and books, if printed in special type (also plates for embossing blind literature, and voice recordings and special paper intended solely for the use of the blind) subject to certain conditions of posting, marked outside "Literature for the Blind (Cécogrammes)", with name and address of sender. Packets must be capable of easy examination in the post. They may be sent post free up to 7 kg by surface route to all parts and free by air mail up to 1 kg to Europe; the air mail charge to other countries is 1p per 50 g up to 7 kg.

Small Packets Post, Overseas.—For the transmission of goods (including trade samples) in the same mails as Printed Papers up to 1 kg. Must be packed so that they can easily be opened for examination unless permission for sealing has been obtained from the Post Office. Registration is allowed; not insurance. Available to all countries, but to some countries there is a limit of 500 g. A customs declaration is required.

Newspaper Post, Inland.—For newspapers "registered at the P.O.".

Copies of registered newspapers may be posted by the publishers or their agents in wrappers open at both ends, in unsealed envelopes approved by the Post Office for the purpose or without covers and tied with string which can be removed without cutting. Wrappers and envelopes must be prominently marked Newspaper Post in the top left-hand corner and be easily removable for the purpose of examination. No writing or additional printing is permitted, other than the words "with compliments", name and address of sender, request for return if undeliverable and a reference to a page. Items receive first class letter service.

Newspapers posted by the public or supplements to registered newspapers despatched apart from their ordinary publications are transmitted under the conditions governing the first or second class letter services.

INLAND TELEPHONES

The quarterly rental for an exclusive business exchange line is £22·55 and £13·95 for a residential exclusive exchange line. For shared service, in which two subscribers share one line but have practically the same facilities as those provided by individual lines, each customer pays £1·20 per quarter less than for exclusive line service. Full self-dialling (STD) facilities are provided on all exchanges. Local and dialled national calls from these exchanges are charged in 4·4p units when made from ordinary lines, in 10p units when made from payphones and 10p minimum charge from press-button payphones with 2p incremental units. All charges except those from payphones, which are VAT inclusive, are subject to VAT. VAT on call charges from ordinary lines is charged as a percentage of the total on quarterly bills and VAT on calls from payphones is included in the unit fee. The length of time per unit depends on the distance of the call and time of day, from six minutes

for a cheap rate local call to 18 seconds for distances over 56 kilometres at peak rate. All direct dialled inland calls are cheaper if made before 8 a.m., after 6 p.m. or at weekends.

Operator-connected calls from ordinary lines have a three minute minimum charge (and thereafter by the minute) which varies with distance and time of day, but those from payphones are charged in 3 minute periods at the payphone tariff. For calls that have to be passed through the operator because a dialled call had failed, the charge is equivalent to the dialled rate, subject normally to the three minute minimum. Generally higher charges apply to other operator connected calls including special services calls and those to mobile phones, the Irish Republic and the Channel Isles. Personal calls (to specified person) £1·75 extra from ordinary lines and £2·10 from payphones, if the person cannot be found nothing further is charged. For fuller information *see* Preface to Phone Book or Dialling Code Booklet.

INTERNATIONAL TELEPHONES

The charges are the same for calls originating in any part of Great Britain, Northern Ireland and the Isle of Man. All U.K. customers have had access to International Direct Dialling from this country since 1982 and can dial direct to numbers on most exchanges in over 180 countries worldwide. The number of places abroad to which calls may be dialled direct is still increasing. Callers should consult their dialling codes booklets or International Telephone Guide for information on how to make calls.

Directly dialled calls are charged in units of time costing 5·06p, including VAT. Countries fall under one of eight charge bands. Cheaper rates are available at certain times for all calls except those in Charge Band G. Further details of international call charges and services may be found in the International Telephone Guide, available from British Telecom District Offices, or by dialling 100 and asking for Freefone BTI.

TELEX SERVICE

There are now 211 countries that can be reached by Telex from the UK; over 200 of them by Direct Dial.

For most customers Direct Dialled calls to all international destinations are charged in six second units costing between 2·3p and 13·2p depending upon the country called. Calls via the operator are charged in one minute steps with a three minute minimum, plus a surcharge of £1·30 per call.

Calls made via British Telecom's Telex Plus store and forward facility attract normal Telex charges plus a surcharge of 10p for inland delivered messages and 20p for international delivered messages.

TELEMESSAGE

Telemessages can be sent by telephone or telex to anywhere in the UK for 'hard copy' delivery the next working day, including Saturdays. To achieve this, a Telemessage must be telephoned/telexed before 10 p.m. Monday to Saturday (7 p.m. Sundays and Bank Holidays). Dial 100 (190 in London) and ask for the Telemessage Service or see the telex directory for dialling codes.

A Telemessage costs £5 for the first 50 words and £2·75 for each subsequent group of 50 words—the name and address are free. A sender's copy costs 85p. A selection of cards is available for special occasions at 80p per card. All prices are subject to VAT. Telemessage has a number of services for businesses. Details are available on 0800 282298 (free).

Telemessage is also available to the U.S.A. For next working day delivery in America a Telemessage must be filed by 10 p.m. U.K. time Monday to Saturday (7 p.m. Sundays and Bank Holidays). U.S. addresses must include the ZIP code. Charges are £7·25 for the first 50 words and £3·60 for each subsequent group of 50 words—the name and address are free. All charges are subject to VAT.

INTERNATIONAL TELEGRAMS

International Telegrams are available to most countries. Dial 0800 282298 (free) for full details and tariffs.

MARITIME COMMUNICATIONS

British Telecom International provides world-wide communication services for shipping, aircraft, oil and gas platforms and some remote land stations. HF, MF and VHF radio frequency bands are used as well as satellite. Services include telephone, telex, morse telegraphy and data transmission.

RADIOTELEGRAMS

To Ship.—Telegrams can be accepted by telex or telephone. *Telex.*—Call 46441 BTGKA G and provide the name of the vessel, call-sign, and, if known, name of the radio station through which the message should be delivered. *Telephone.*—Call the 100 operator and ask for Ships Radiotelegram Service. If known, the name and telephone number of the Coast Station through which the call is to be made should be given. If the ship's position or the appropriate radio station is unknown, callers should ask for Portishead Radio (0278-781111).

From Ship.—Long-range communications by H.F. are handled by Portishead Radio, medium-range W.T. communications by M.F. by a series of Coast Stations. On V.H.F. telegrams are dictated by Radiotelephone.

Voicebank.—A vessel may call Portishead, by H.F. radio, from where the message is dictated into the customer's Voicebank.

Charges.—(per word excl. VAT). To ship from the U.K.: 44p per word plus £2.00 per message. From ship to U.K.: 50p per word (minimum 7 words).

Further information is available from 0278-781111 (long-range services) or 01-583 9418 (medium range).

RADIOTELEPHONE SERVICE

To Ship.—Calls are made through the 100 operator and callers should ask for the Ships Radio-Telephone Service adding, if known, the telephone number and name of the Coast Station through which the call should be made. If the name of the Coast Station or the ship's position is not known, the caller should ask for Portishead Radio. Portishead Radio may be dialled direct 0278-781111 for the price of an inland call. When connected to the Coast Station Radio Officer, the caller should ask for a Ship's Telephone Call stating name and position of ship, and name or title of person being called.

From Ship.—Long range H.F. communications are handled by Portishead Radio. Medium/short range services are available through a series of Coast Stations on M.F. and V.H.F.

Charges.—(per min. excluding VAT). To ship from U.K.: V.H.F. 84p; M.F. £1·26; H.F. £1·87 (three mins. minimum).

From ship to U.K.: V.H.F. 84p; M.F. 96p; H.F. £1·87.

Further information and prices of calls from ship to other countries and from ship to ship via Coast Radio Stations available from 0278-781111 (long range) or 01-583 9416 (short and medium range).

RADIOTELEX

To Ship.—All short- and long-range radio telex services are controlled by Portishead Radio. For access to the fully automatic equipment, use telex 46116 (answerback 46116 BTGKA G). For two-way conversation, use telex 46300 (answerback 46300

BTGKA G) and follow the given prompts. To obtain ship or aircraft call-signs, etc., use telex 463000 BTGKA G and respond to first prompt with "SNF+". For Phonetex messages, dial the operator and ask for Portishead Radio, or dial direct 0278-781111.

From Ship.—The automatic system allows ships direct access to national and international telex routes. Voicebank, Telex Letter and Multitelex are also available.

Charges.—(per min. excluding VAT). To and from ship for the U.K.: M.F. £1·30; H.F. £1·80 (six second minimum). Prices for manually connected calls, and other facilities are available on request. For further information on Radiotelex services, dial 0278-78111.

INMARSAT

The Inmarsat service provides telephone, telex and other facilities for suitably equipped ships via its Coast Earth Station at Goonhilly which covers the Atlantic Ocean Region, while reciprocal arrangements with Norway and Singapore provide access to the Indian and Pacific Ocean Regions respectively.

Further information and details of charges are available from 01-492 4996.

AERONAUTICAL RADIO SERVICE

British Telecom International provides a public air-to-ground telephone service from suitably equipped aircraft through Portishead Radio. Portishead also accepts messages from aircraft for onward transmission via the SITA or telex network, and selected aircraft may be paged. Further details are available from 0278 781111.

Charges.—From aircraft to U.K.: £2.30 per min. (one min. minimum).

INTERNATIONAL DATA TRANSMISSION SERVICES

Public Switched Telephone Network.—BTI International Business Services offer data transmission over the public switched telephone network using International Direct Dialling (IDD). Calls are charged at the same rate as for telephone calls.

BTI has reached agreement with 70 countries for such use of the telephone network.

Analogue Private Circuits.—International private circuits are available for data transmission and are provided in accordance with the recommendations of the International Telephone & Telegraph Consultative Committee (CCITT).

International Packet Switching Service.—IPSS provides service with over 100 networks in more than 70 countries in Australasia, Europe, North and South America, the Caribbean and the Middle and Far East.

PRESTEL

Prestel, British Telecommunications' public videotex service, links adapted television screens to computers through ordinary telephone lines so information and two-way services can be delivered directly into offices and homes. Over 99 per cent of the U.K. telephone population can now use Prestel at local call rates, and about 80,000 terminals are attached to the network. Information on Prestel (from over 1,200 different sources) can be updated by the minute and is available 24 hours a day.

In addition, by using "Gateways", private computers can be linked to Prestel sets via Prestel computers. This facility makes possible services such as home banking, and for travel agents confirmed reservations of airline tickets.

Because the system is two-way, all customers can send messages, make bookings or request information at the touch of a button. There are over 330,000 frames (or "pages") of information available.

WEATHER INFORMATION AND FORECASTS

Recorded weather forecasts for the areas listed below are available by telephoning the numbers shown:

Herts, Beds and Inland Essex	Bedford 8091	N.W. England	051–246 8091
	Cambridge 8091		061–246 8091
	01–246 8099		Blackburn 8091
	Luton 8091		Blackpool 8091
Northern Ireland	Belfast 8091		Southport 8091
	Bangor 8091	West Yorkshire	Bradford 8091
West Midlands and Warwickshire	021–246 8091		Huddersfield 8091
	Coventry 8091		Leeds 8091
Avon and Somerset	Bristol 8091	Greater London	01–246 8091
	Swindon 8091		Tunbridge Wells 8091
Glamorgan, Gwent and South Dyfed	Cardiff 8091		Guildford 8091
	Newport 8091	East Anglia	Cambridge 8092
	Swansea 8091		Norwich 8091
Devon and Cornwall	Exeter 8091		Ipswich 8091
	Plymouth 8091		Lowestoft 8091
	Torquay 8091		Peterborough 8091
Dundee, Tayside and Fife	Dundee 8091	North East England (incl. N. Yorks)	
			Middlesbrough 8091
Edinburgh, S. Fife and Borders	031–246 8091		Newcastle upon Tyne 8091
Glasgow area	041–246 8091	Lincs & Humberside	Grimsby 8091
Grampian	Aberdeen 8091		Lincoln 8091
N. Kent and S. Essex Coast	01–246 8096	East Midlands	Nottingham 8091
	Canterbury 8091		Leicester 8091
	Medway 8091		Derby 8091
	Chelmsford 8091		Northampton 8091
	Colchester 8091	S. Yorkshire and Peak District	Sheffield 8091
	Southend 8091		Doncaster 8091

Dorset and Hants Coast (including I.O.W.)	
	Bournemouth 8091
	Portsmouth 8091
	Southampton 8091
Gloucestershire, Hereford and Worcester	
	Cheltenham 8091
	Gloucester 8091
	Hereford 8091
Sussex and S. Kent Coast	01–246 8097
	Brighton 8091
	Hastings 8091
	Canterbury 8092
Oxon, Berks and Bucks	01–246 8090
	High Wycombe 8091
	Oxford 8091
	Reading 8091
North Downs and the Weald	01–246 8092
Staffs and Shropshire	
	Stoke-on-Trent 8091
	Shrewsbury 8091
Lake District	Carlisle 8092
	Kendal 8092
	Leeds 8092
Wiltshire, N. Dorset and Hampshire	Swindon 8092
	Andover 8092

BASIC RATE OF INLAND LETTER POST

1840	1d	Sept. 1975	8½p
1918	1½d	June 1977	9p
1940	2½d	Aug. 1979	10p
1957	3d	Feb. 1980	12p
1965	4d	Jan. 1981	14p
1968*	5d	Feb. 1982	15½p
1971	3p	April 1983	16p
1973	3½p	Sept. 1984	17p
1974	4½p	Oct. 1986	18p
1975	7p	Sept. 1988	19p

(*Two tier postal system introduced—subsequent figures are for 1st class letter post)

BRITISH PASSPORT REGULATIONS

Applications for United Kingdom Passports must be made on the forms obtainable at any of the Passport Offices (addresses given below) or at any main Post Office (except in Northern Ireland).

London.—Clive House, 70–78 Petty France, SW1H 9HD.

Liverpool.—India Buildings, Water Street, Liverpool L2 0QZ.

Newport.—Olympia House, Upper Dock Street, Newport, Gwent NPT 1XA.

Peterborough.—Passport Office, 55 Westfield Road, Peterborough PE3 6TG.

Glasgow.—3 Northgate, 96 Milton Street, Cowcaddens, Glasgow G4 0BT.

Belfast.—Passport Office, Hampton House, 47–53 High Street, Belfast BT1 2QS.

Hours. The above offices are open Mon.-Fri. 9 a.m. to 4.30 p.m. The Passport Office, London, is also open for cases of special emergency (e.g. death or serious illness) arising outside normal office hours between 4.30 p.m. and 6.00 p.m. and on Saturdays between 10 a.m. and noon.

Completed forms of application should be sent to one of the six Passport Offices, with photographs, supporting documents and the fee of £15 (£22·50 if particulars of spouse included), in the form of a cheque or postal order which should be crossed and made payable to the Passport Office.

A passport cannot be issued or extended on behalf of a person already abroad; such person should apply to the nearest British High Commission or Consulate.

United Kingdom Passports are granted to:—
  (i) British Citizens.
  (ii) British Dependent Territories Citizens.
  (iii) British Nationals (overseas).
  (iv) British Overseas Citizens.
  (v) British Subjects.
  (vi) British Protected Persons.

A passport granted to a child under 16 will normally be valid for an initial period of five years, after which it may be extended for a further five years with no extra charge. A passport granted to a person over 16 will normally be valid for 10 years and will not be renewable. Thereafter, or if at any time the passport contains no further space for visas, a new passport must be obtained.

A passport including particulars of the holder's spouse is not available for his/her use when he/she is travelling alone. A spouse's particulars may only be added at the time of issue of a passport.

Children who have reached the age of sixteen years require separate passports. Their applications must be signed by one of their parents.

Completed passport applications should be countersigned by a Member of Parliament, Justice of the Peace, Minister of Religion, a professionally qualified person (e.g. doctor, engineer, lawyer, teacher), bank officer, established Civil Servant, police officer or a person of similar standing who has personally known the applicant for at least two years, and who is either a British citizen, a British Dependent Territories citizen, British overseas citizen, a British subject or a citizen of a Commonwealth country. A relative must not countersign the application. The applicant's birth certificate or previous British passport, and other evidence in support of the statements made in the application must be produced.

In the case of children under the age of 16 requiring a separate passport, an application should be made by one of the parents on Form B.

If the applicant for a passport is a British national by naturalization or registration, the Certificate of Naturalization or registration must be produced with the application, unless the applicant holds a previous United Kingdom Passport issued after registration or naturalization.

United Kingdom Passports are generally available for travel to all countries. The possession of a passport does not, however, exempt the holder from compliance with any immigration regulations in force in British or foreign countries, or from the necessity of obtaining a visa where required.

Photographs

Duplicate unmounted photographs of applicant (and wife/husband, if to be included in the passport) must be sent. These photographs should be printed on normal thin photographic paper. They should measure 45 mm. by 35 mm. (1·77 in. by 1·38 in.) and should be taken full face without a hat. One photograph should be certified as a true likeness of the applicant by the person who countersigns the application form.

Extension of Passports

Applications for the extension of United Kingdom passports which have been valid for less than ten years must be made on Form D.

94-Page Passports

In 1973, a new type of passport became available. Intended to meet the needs of frequent travellers who fill standard passports well before the ten-year validity has expired, it contains 94 pages, is valid for ten years and costs £30 (£45 if particulars of spouse included).

British Visitors' Passports

A simplified form of travel document is available for British Citizens, British Dependent Territories Citizens or British Overseas Citizens wishing to pay short visits (not exceeding three months) to the following foreign countries:

Andorra; Austria; Belgium; Bermuda; Denmark; Finland; France (incl. Corsica); Greece (& the Greek islands); W. Germany (incl. West Berlin by air only); Gibraltar; Iceland; Italy; Liechtenstein; Luxembourg; Malta; Monaco; Netherlands; Norway; Portugal (incl. Madeira & Azores); San Marino; Spain (incl. Balearic & Canary Islands); Sweden; Switzerland; Tunisia; Turkey.

A fee of £7·50 (£11·25 if particulars of spouse included) is charged for the issue of a British Visitors' Passport, which is valid for 12 months, cannot be amended and is not renewable; on expiry application should be made for a new passport if required. Particulars of an applicant's spouse and/or children under 16 years can be included at the time of issue only. A child of 8 years of age and over is eligible to hold a British Visitors' Passport. Applications for, or including, a person under 18 years of age (unless married or serving in H.M. Forces) must be countersigned by the legal guardian.

British Visitors' Passports are obtainable by application on Form VP (from any main Post Office except in Northern Ireland). Applicants in England, Scotland and Wales should take the completed form in person to any main Post Office which will normally issue the passport without further delay; applicants in Northern Ireland to the Passport Office, Belfast from whom application forms may be obtained. British Visitors' Passports are not obtainable from Passport Offices other than Belfast.

Two recent passport photographs will be required of the applicant and of his/her spouse, if to be included; photographs of children are not required. Size of photographs must be 50 mm. by 38 mm (2 in. × 1½ in.). They should be unmounted and must be printed on normal thin photographic paper. No visas are required on British Visitors' Passports. Applicants must also produce for the purpose of identification a N.H.S. Medical Card, birth certificate, driving licence or retirement pension book.

VISAS

Visa regulations are liable to change and enquiries should be made at the Consulate or Embassy concerned (addresses and telephone numbers are given in the Commonwealth and Foreign Countries sections).

For entry into the following countries a visa or permit may be required: Afghanistan; Albania; Algeria; Angola; Antigua; Argentina; Austria; Bahrain; Benin; Bermuda; Bolivia; Brazil; Brunei; Bulgaria; Burkina; Burma; Burundi; Cameroon Republic; Cape Verde; Central African Republic; Chad; Chile; China; Colombia; Congo; Costa Rica; Côte d'Ivoire; Cuba; Czechoslovakia; Djibouti; Dominica; Dominican Republic; Ecuador; Egypt; El Salvador; Equatorial Guinea; Ethiopia; Finland; Gabon; German Democratic Republic; Federal Republic of Germany; Gibraltar; Grenada; Guatemala; Guinea; Guinea Bissau; Haiti; Honduras; Hong Kong; Hungary; Indonesia; Iran; Iraq; Israel; Japan; Jordan; Korea; Kuwait; Laos; Lebanon; Liberia; Libya; Madagascar; Mali; Mauritania; Mexico; Mongolia; Morocco; Mozambique; Nepal; Nicaragua; Niger; Oman; Pakistan; Panama; Paraguay; Peru; Philippines; Poland; Qatar; Romania; Rwanda; St. Lucia; St. Vincent and the Grenadines; Saudi Arabia; Senegal; Somali Democratic Republic; South Africa; Sudan; Sweden; Switzerland; Syria; Thailand; Togo; Tunisia; Turkey; United Arab Emirates; Uruguay; U.S.S.R.; Venezuela; Vietnam; Yemen Arab Republic; People's Democratic Republic of Yemen; Yugoslavia; Zaire.

WORK AND BUSINESS OVERSEAS

A passport issued after December 31, 1982 showing the holder's national status as British citizen will secure for the holder the right to take employment or to establish himself in business or other self-employed activity in another member state of the European Community (except Spain and Portugal). A passport bearing the endorsement "holder has the right of abode in the United Kingdom" where the holder so qualifies will also secure the same right. Employment permits are required in most other countries, even for casual labour. The nearest representative of the country concerned should be consulted. Local Employment Offices have a booklet entitled "Working abroad".

Those planning to travel abroad on export business are advised to contact the British Overseas Trade Board, 1 Victoria Street, London SW1H 0ET or its Regional Offices in London SW1W 8QD, Birmingham, Bristol, Leeds, Manchester, Newcastle upon Tyne and Nottingham. *Wales:* Welsh Office Industry Department, New Crown Building, Cathays Park, Cardiff; *Scotland:* Scottish Export Office, Alhambra House, 45 Waterloo Street, Glasgow; *Northern Ireland:* Industrial Development Board for Northern Ireland, I.D.B. House, 64 Chichester Street, Belfast. These offices will send advance notification of the visit to the Commercial Section of the relevant Consulate or Embassy, and can offer advice and information about the markets to be visited.

VACCINATION

In very general terms vaccination for protection against cholera, typhoid and polio are recommended for all countries outside Europe, except North America, Australia and New Zealand. Protection, in the form of tablets, is advised for malaria similarly.

Vaccination against yellow fever is essential for entry into Angola, Benin, Burkina, Cameroon, Central African Republic, Chad, Congo, Côte d'Ivoire, French Guiana, Gambia, Ghana, Mali, Mauritania, Niger, Nigeria, Panama, Rwanda, São Tomé and Principé, Senegal, Sierra Leone, Togo and Uganda, and is recommended for most other African and South American countries. Fuller details are set out in D.H.S.S. leaflet SA 35 "Protect your health abroad". For up-to-date information about vaccination requirements, contact one of the following health departments: *England*—International Relations Division, Department of Health, Alexander Fleming House, Elephant and Castle, London SE1 6BY (01-407 5522 ext. 6749), Communicable Disease Surveillance Centre, 61 Colindale Avenue, London NW9 5EQ (01-200 4400); *Wales*—Welsh Office, Cathays Park, Cardiff CF1 3NQ (0222-825111 ext. 3336); *Scotland*—Scottish Home and Health Department, St. Andrew's House, Edinburgh EH1 3DE (031-5568501 ext. 2438) Communicable Diseases (Scotland) Unit, Ruchill Hospital, Bilsland Drive, Glasgow G20 9NB (041-946 7120); *Northern Ireland*—D.H.S.S., Dundonald House, Upper Newtownards Road, Belfast BT4 3SF (0232-63939 ext. 2593).

Your doctor should be consulted at least eight weeks before departure, and will advise you and arrange vaccinations. If children will be travelling outside Europe, North America, Australia and New Zealand the doctor should be informed, especially if they have not completed their full course of childhood immunization.

Details of free or reduced cost medical treatment when visiting other European countries, Hong Kong or New Zealand are set out in leaflet SA 30 "Medical costs abroad", available from some travel agents, local D.o.S.S. offices or the Leaflets Unit, P.O. Box 21, Stanmore, Middx. HA7 1AY.

WHITE PAPERS

PROMOTING BETTER HEALTH

For the first time since the National Health Service was founded in 1948, a review of primary health care services has been undertaken. The Government's objectives were first set out in a discussion document in April 1986. When responses to this and the report on primary health care by the House of Commons select committee on social services had been considered, the Government published a White Paper *Promoting Better Health*. This was presented to Parliament in November 1987 by the Secretaries of State for Social Services, Wales, Northern Ireland and Scotland.

A major theme of the White Paper is the need to shift the emphasis in primary health care from the treatment of illness to the promotion of health and the prevention of disease. Another theme is the Government's wish to improve value for money and to relate financial rewards for health professionals more closely to their performance.

The Government's objectives are: to make services more responsive to the consumer; to raise standards of care; to promote health and prevent illness; to give patients the widest range of choice in primary care services; to improve value for money; and to enable clearer priorities to be set for Family Practitioner Services in relation to the rest of the health service.

The Government believes that no opportunity should be lost to increase fair and open competition between those providing Family Practitioner Services. To that end, it wishes consumers to have readier access to more information about the services provided, and wishes the remuneration of practitioners to be more directly linked than at present to the level of their performance.

Some of the Government's intentions require legislation and the Government brought the Health and Medicines Bill before Parliament in the 1987–88 session.

Resources

The primary health care services are used on an average working day by over 1·2 million people. They cost over £5,000 million a year. Over the next three years gross expenditure on the Family Practitioner Services in the U.K. is expected to grow by 11 per cent in real terms (or £570 million at 1987–88 prices).

In addition, the Government is prepared to invest extra resources where most needed. The exact amount for each service will depend on the outcome of negotiations with the profession concerned. Timing of the introduction of changes will depend on when resources become available.

In order to help finance these developments, the Government intends to take powers so that those who can afford it will in future pay: the cost of a sight test; a small charge for dental examinations; dental charges which relate more directly to the treatment a patient receives.

Children, adults on low income and some other groups will continue to obtain N.H.S. dental and sight-testing services free of charge.

The Government intends to make the N.H.S. contract with family doctors more sensitive to the range of services provided. It intends therefore to raise from 47 per cent to at least 50 per cent, in the first instance, the proportion of a doctor's income represented by capitation fees.

Family Doctors

Family doctors are well placed to promote good health and prevent ill-health. The Government wishes to strengthen this role by:

(i) paying a special fee to encourage doctors to provide a health check and any necessary follow-up to patients registering for the first time with an N.H.S. doctor;

(ii) considering incentives to achieve specified target levels of vaccination and immunization and of screening, as well as to meet the cost of call and recall systems;

(iii) considering amendments to doctors' terms of service to clarify their role in the provision of health promotion services and prevention of ill-health.

The Government believes that there should be explicit recognition in remuneration for the provision of high standards of care, as shown by such factors as personal availability to patients and the provision of a wide range of services. Surveys show that some doctors appear to do no more than the minimum requirement. The Government therefore intends to tighten the qualifying criteria for receipt of the full basic practice allowance, at present £7,850. Currently, entitlement depends on a minimum list of 1,000 patients and the provision of an average 20 hours per week of direct services to patients in surgery consultations and home visits. Both criteria will be increased and, in addition, payment should depend on a doctor carrying out health promotion and prevention work.

Other measures intended to improve standards of care are:

(i) changing the remuneration system to encourage doctors to provide comprehensive regular care for elderly people;

(ii) developing the contribution of suitably-trained family doctors to the medical aspect of child health surveillance;

(iii) considering incentives for doctors carrying out minor surgery;

(iv) encouraging the continued development of information and communication technology and computerization in primary care;

(v) examining the scope for measures to reduce the isolation of some doctors in rural areas.

Primary health care teams

The Government is committed to the continued development of primary health care teams. It will therefore remove the restrictions on the types and number of staff whom family doctors may employ through the direct reimbursement scheme, whereby they recover part of the costs. The Government will also provide additional resources to extend the scheme under locally-controlled arrangements.

A major objective of policy is to improve practice premises, especially in deprived areas. The Government therefore proposes to:

(i) increase the financial support to doctors to improve their premises, for example through improvement grants. These will be targeted on premises needing greatest improvement;

(ii) consider introducing regional variations in the cost limits for the "cost rent scheme", which gives financial support to doctors investing in premises improvements, to take account of variations in building costs;

(iii) review its minimum standards for premises;

(iv) change the constitution of the General Practice Finance Corporation—which lends money for practice purchase and improvement—so that maximum use can be made of private sector funds.

Choice and Information

The Government will pursue a number of measures to give consumers more information about doctors and services and to encourage greater competition. Family Practitioner Committees and Health Boards will be required to provide more information about local medical practices, such as opening hours and services provided. This information should be made more widely available locally. The Government will also encourage the wider provision of factual leaflets for the public about doctors and their services and will discuss with the General Medical Council the removal of restraints on advertising, subject to proper safeguards.

It will be made easier to change doctor and arrangements for the handling of complaints will be simplified and streamlined. Steps will be taken to ensure that the public's comments are sought on local services and their views on proposed changes fully taken into account. The feasibility of requiring family doctor practices to submit annual reports to Family Practitioner Committees and Health Boards will be examined.

Doctors

Better information for consumers will be of less effect if there is an inadequate supply of doctors. So the Government plans to introduce a new allowance for those working in deprived areas. It will discuss with the Medical Practices Committee and its counterparts in Scotland and Northern Ireland how to take more account of local information about need in determining the distribution of doctors, and seek new opportunities to encourage more women to enter and remain in general practice, for example through part-time working and job sharing.

The Government recognizes the importance of continuing training and education. It plans to introduce a new postgraduate educational allowance to replace the current vocational training and postgraduate training allowances. Doctors will qualify for the new allowance by maintaining a regular programme of education and training throughout their careers.

It is also important that other members of primary health care teams are properly trained and kept up-to-date. The Government will arrange for the training costs of professional staff employed by family doctors to be directly reimbursed.

It is not reasonable to expect doctors to work past the age at which they can be expected to carry out properly the exacting responsibilities of a principal in general practice. The Government will therefore introduce a compulsory retirement age of 70 for family doctors and end the practice known as 24 hour retirement (whereby doctors aged 65 or over can retire, draw their pension and return to practice a day later without abatement of pay or pension). However, the Family Practitioner Committee or Health Board may exceptionally continue to contract with a doctor over 70 where his retirement would adversely affect services.

Dentists

The dental health and patterns of attendance of both adults and children has improved markedly since 1948. The Government proposes to secure this continued improvement by:

(i) increasing the funds for water fluoridation schemes;

(ii) launching a further initiative to promote dental awareness amongst the young, especially in deprived areas;

(iii) changing the responsibilities of the community dental services to place greater emphasis on prevention and health education;

(iv) negotiating changes in the dentists' N.H.S. contract to place greater emphasis on prevention;

(v) evaluating a study designed to encourage prevention whereby dentists are paid a lump sum for maintaining the oral health of children rather than a fee for each item of service. If successful, the new arrangements will be made available nationally.

The Government will enter into negotiations with the profession with a view to amending the dentists' remuneration system to encourage quality and a greater commitment to the N.H.S.

Monitoring of the general dental service will be stepped up by introducing advisers in a number of Family Practitioner Committee areas to provide a support role for practitioners. The Dental Estimates Boards will be given new powers to deal with dentists suspected or providing unnecessary treatment. Controls will, however, be relaxed in a number of areas, enabling dentists to treat their patients without undue delays.

Measures to provide wider choice and information for patients in relation to dentists are:

(i) new means of influencing the distribution of dentists through financial assistance towards the cost of establishing practices in designated areas;

(ii) improved information on dental lists and encouragement of dental practice leaflets;

(iii) the Dental Estimates Boards will be included among those bodies which the Health Service Commissioner may investigate.

The Government will provide substantial extra resources to expand vocational training places for newly-qualified dentists, for postgraduate training and, for the first time, to pay an allowance to offset lost income to encourage attendance at approved training courses.

To create more opportunities for young dentists, and in the light of a projected national over-supply, the Government has decided that, as with doctors, it will take powers to establish a compulsory age of retirement.

Opticians

The Government welcomes the favourable response to its existing policy of increasing competition for ophthalmic services whilst providing adequate safeguards for consumers. It proposes to extend this principle to sight testing. Except for children and young people in full-time education, those on low incomes and the registered blind and partially sighted, the Government will seek powers so that other patients will no longer get a free N.H.S. sight test but will in future obtain their sight tests privately just as they obtain their spectacles.

Consumer's rights will be strengthened. Powers will be sought to give consumers whose sight is tested the right to receive a prescription or a statement that no prescription is necessary. Opticians will not be able to charge for sight tests or glasses until this is done. They will be prohibited from offering sight tests only on condition that any spectacles are purchased from them.

Existing vouchers will be made available for contact lens purchase in addition to those already available for clinical reasons in the Hospital Eye Service. The Government will pay special attention to the partially sighted in deciding the new voucher values to apply from April 1988. The voucher scheme will be extended to help adults whose spectacles are damaged because of physical or mental disability.

The Government will discuss with the profession the payment of a fee for the provision of a domiciliary sight testing service for the housebound who remain entitled to an N.H.S. test.

Pharmacists

The Government will review the new pharmacists' contract in the light of experience to consider whether more competition is needed. In addition, to improve standards of care the Government proposes to:

(i) introduce an allowance for pharmacy contractors who provide pharmaceutical supervision of the supply and safekeeping of medicines in residential homes;

(ii) introduce an allowance for those pharmacies who maintain a substantial number of records relating to medicines used by patients who are either elderly or confused and who are on long-term medication;

(iii) enter into negotiations with the profession with a view to establishing a fund to attract and improve pharmacies in deprived areas;

(iv) provide on prescription blood glucose testing strips for diabetics as soon as the necessary arrangements can be made and, when resources permit, a new range of wound care products;

(v) when resources permit, fund a co-ordination centre to foster local liaison with doctors on achieving effective and economic use of medicines. Similar arrangements will be made in Scotland;

(vi) in due course fund research into pharmacy practice.

The Government will, as soon as resources permit, make funds available to assist in the provision of health education and health promotion material for display in pharmacies.

The changing role of pharmacists will require new skills and up-to-date knowledge. At an appropriate time, extra funds will be made available for continuing education and in-service training.

Community Nursing Services

A report "Neighbourhood Nursing—A Focus for Care" was published in England in 1986. Following on from this, the Government intends to issue a circular inviting Health Authorities in England to review the way in which their community nursing services are managed. It is for local health authorities to organize services but a neighbourhood approach based on local geography may commend itself in some areas, particularly inner cities.

The Government also plans to look further at the legal status, functions and qualifications for employment of nurse practitioners and consult the Professional Standing Advisory Committees with a view to their producing guidance on giving nurses more freedom to prescribe or supply certain items. It intends to support the development of training courses for practice nurses and to examine the most appropriate arrangements for Scotland, Wales and Northern Ireland in the light of consultations on the community nursing reviews undertaken in each country.

Complaints

Giving consumers more power requires straightforward procedures for making complaints. In order to simplify and streamline the procedures, the Government has decided to: allow oral complaints to be investigated, subject to conditions to safeguard impartiality; require complaints to be accepted as proper if received by a Regional or District Health Authority within the time limits; extend the period for registering a complaint from eight to thirteen weeks; make other changes to the complaints machinery, including the operation of appeal time limits and the membership of the Family Practitioner Committees hearing appeals.

All Family Practitioner Committees will be required to operate an informal complaints procedure and to extend it to all those providing services under Family Practitioner Service arrangements. The F.P.C.s will also be required to send the report into a complaint (and their decision thereon) to any Member of either House of Parliament on the request of a party to the investigation.

Similar changes will be introduced in Scotland and Northern Ireland.

Inner Cities

The Government is committed to improving primary care in inner cities and other deprived areas, where the quantity and quality of services if often poorer than elsewhere. Many proposals in the White Paper will have an important impact in such areas. For example, the proposal to introduce a "deprived areas allowance" will support doctors who work in such areas. The Government will create a special fund to help attract pharmacies to, or improve services in, inner city and other deprived areas.

Family Practitioner Committees

Family Practitioner Committees became independent authorities in April 1985. This was partly to allow them to be more active in planning the organization and development of primary health care services, and to enable them to collaborate on equal terms with other agencies. To take this forward the Government now proposes to encourage effective collaboration with other agencies in Family Practitioner Committee areas where it remains weak, and to encourage voluntary initiatives to review collaboration between Health Authorities and Family Practitioner Committees.

Family Practitioner Committees' responsibilities for the Family Practitioner Service will be extended and their management role strengthened, for example by developing policies for improving premises' standards.

These proposals will increase Family Practitioner Committees' workload. The Government recognizes this and will increase the funds available to them to carry out their responsibilities. In addition, it will set aside further sums to finance a range of national and local developments, such as experiments in service delivery. The Government will discuss with Health Boards and the professions the implementation of these proposals in Scotland.

The Government concludes by expressing its belief that the policies set out in the White Paper and the accompanying legislation will achieve important improvements in the provision of primary health care services in the U.K. It is hoped that these will benefit the consumer through the provision of better services, the professions by relating financial rewards more closely to performance, and the taxpayer by more cost-effective targeting of the resources available.

TRAINING FOR EMPLOYMENT

The White Paper *Training for Employment* (Cm. 316) was presented to Parliament by the Secretary of State for Employment (Mr. Norman Fowler) on February 16, 1988. The previous 18 months had seen a sustained fall in unemployment and a growth in the number of jobs available. Because of this trend most people who become unemployed are able to find another job quite quickly. But some people remain unemployed and find it progressively more difficult to obtain work. The White Paper described a number of steps the Government intends to take to help unemployed people, particularly the longer-term unemployed.

The White Paper identifies the problems of the unemployed as a growing pessimism about their job prospects, leading to financial and psychological adjustment to unemployment, and the widening gap between the skills unemployed people have and the skills required for the jobs that are available. It states that the Government's aim is to offer unemployed people a route back to work, by re-establishing and maintaining personal contact with each individual who is unemployed; by offering opportunities to acquire skills; and by giving improved access to information, advice and other practical assistance.

The Employment Service

At the centre of the Government's plans for helping unemployed people find work is the Employment Service. (This was established in October 1987 when the Jobcentre network previously run by the Manpower Services Commission was brought together with the Department of Employment's network of Unemployment Benefit Offices.)

The Government intends to concentrate the resources of the Employment Service primarily on placing unemployed people in jobs and on reaching and remotivating those who may have given up looking for jobs. In particular, the Government intends to build on the success of the Restart courses, which help unemployed people to rebuild their confidence and motivation, to reassess their strengths and skills, and to decide what action to take to get a job.

From April 1988 the Government guarantees that every unemployed person will be invited to a Restart interview and offered the full range of opportunities available through Restart every six months for as long as they remain unemployed. Every Restart interview will be based on detailed information about each unemployed person's experience, qualifications and job requirements based on a questionnaire completed before the interview.

The Employment Service is also pursuing a number of initiatives to ensure that its services are available to unemployed people in the areas where they live, including council estates which may be some distance from Jobcentres.

Training

Over the years the Department of Employment has introduced and developed a range of programmes to help unemployed people over the age of 18. However, the Government came to feel that none of these programmes met fully all the needs of longer-term unemployed people, and decided to concentrate the resources previously spread over the range of programmes.

From September 1988 the Government is bringing together all existing programmes to help unemployed adults into a single, unified training programme to be run by the Training Commission (formerly the Manpower Services Commission). This new programme will be able to provide training for some 600,000 people a year. Its emphasis will be on practical training to help people get back into employment and the training will range from basic working skills, including numeracy and literacy, to training at craft and technician level.

Training will be provided both with employers and through projects. The Government regards it as important that voluntary organizations and other parties which have an established role in the Community Programme should make a contribution to the new programme. Accordingly, the new programme will provide at least 170,000 places for project based training.

The Government considers it important that unemployed people should have a financial incentive to join the programme. Every trainee in the programme will receive a payment of £10 more than his or her weekly benefit entitlement, or a slightly higher payment if entitled to Income Support: entitlement to Housing Benefit or to free school meals for trainees' children will be unaffected. Payments to trainees will not be liable to National Insurance contributions or income tax, and certain expenses incurred during training will be reimbursed.

Incentives to Work

Some unemployed people want to work but believe they are better off living on benefits. Many are unaware of the value or even the existence of "in work" benefits. These include the Jobstart allowance for those in lower-paid jobs, the Enterprise Allowance Scheme for unemployed people who want to set up in business, and Income Support and Family Credit.

The Government will seek to ensure that unemployed people are aware that they will be financially better off in employment by doing much more to explain the facts about "in work" benefits. In addition, the number of Claimant Advisers will be increased so that unemployed people can be advised individually about the precise level of their net income in employment.

The White Paper also deals with the extent to which people are claiming benefit when they are not available for work. New measures are announced:

(i) to ensure that all new claims for benefit are handled by more senior staff who will be able to carry out a thorough check on the entitlement to benefit of each claimant and also ensure all claimants are fully aware of the jobs, training, "in work" benefits and other help available to them;

(ii) to test the availability for work of all benefit recipients automatically at regular intervals for as long as they remain unemployed;

(iii) to expand and strengthen resources devoted to combating benefit fraud.

Training for the Future

The other theme of the White Paper is the long-term problems of adjusting to radical changes in the pattern of employment, in the nature of the skills the economy will require and in the supply of people entering the labour force. The available evidence and projections point to a time of profound and continuing rapid change in the labour market. The changes are expected to include an increase in employment in professional, managerial, office, sales, technical, craft and skilled manual occupations; an increase in employment in the service sector; and a general high demand for highly motivated and adaptable employees, with improved basic, occupational and personal skills.

We are also living in a time of profound demographic change. Between 1988 and 1991 the population of 16 year-olds will fall by 18 per cent and that of 17 year-olds by 11 per cent. Employers who have become used to recruiting 16 and 17 year-olds will find it increasingly difficult to do so. If employers are to fill their vacancies, they will need to turn their attention increasingly towards the training and retraining of older people.

The Government's objective is to open up more opportunities for adults to train, retrain, acquire additional skills or upgrade those they already have, throughout their working lives. There are major questions of access to training and the relevance and responsiveness of provision. It will also be important to establish the organizational backup that will be needed for a vocational education and training system capable of providing for the country's needs in the next decade. The White Paper concludes by stating that the Government will continue to keep the whole area of vocational education and training under review.

SUMMARY OF SPORT 1987-88

THE WINTER OLYMPIC GAMES

Calgary, Canada. February 13-28, 1988

Alpine Skiing (Men)

Downhill.—P. Zurbriggen (Switz.).
Slalom.—A. Tomba (Italy).
Giant Slalom.—A. Tomba (Italy).
Super Giant Slalom.—F. Piccard (France).
Alpine Combination.—H. Strolz (Austria).

Alpine Skiing (Women)

Downhill.—M. Kiehl (F.R.G.).
Slalom.—V. Schneider (Switz.).
Giant Slalom.—V. Schneider (Switz.).
Super Giant Slalom.—S. Wolf (Austria).
Alpine Combination.—A. Wachter (Austria).

Bobsledding

Two-man.—J. Kipurs and V. Kozlov (U.S.S.R.).
Four-man.—Switzerland.

Figure Skating

Men's Singles.—B. Boitano (U.S.A.).
Women's Singles.—K. Witt (G.D.R.).
Pairs.—E. Gordeyeva and S. Grinkov (U.S.S.R.).
Ice Dance.—N. Bestemianova and A. Bukin (U.S.S.R.).

Ice Hockey

Winners.—U.S.S.R.

Lugeing

Men's Singles.—J. Müller (G.D.R.).
Men's Doubles.—J. Hoffmann and J. Pietsch (G.D.R.).
Women's Singles.—S. Walter (G.D.R.).

Nordic Skiing (Men)

15,000 metres Cross-Country. M. Deviatyarov (U.S.S.R.).
30,000 metres Cross-Country.—A. Prokourorov (U.S.S.R.).
50,000 metres Cross-Country.—G. Svan (Sweden).
4 × 10,000 metres Relay.—Sweden.
10,000 metres Biathlon.—F-P. Roetsch (G.D.R.).
20,000 metres Biathlon.—F-P. Roetsch (G.D.R.).
4 × 7,500 metres Biathlon Relay.—U.S.S.R.
Nordic Combination, Individual.—H. Kempf (Switz.).
Nordic Combination, Team.—W. Germany.
70 metres Jump, Individual.—M. Nykaenen (Finland).

90 metres Jump, Individual.—M. Nykaenen (Finland).
90 metres Jump, Team.—Finland.

Nordic Skiing (Women)

5,000 metres Cross-Country.—M. Matikainen (Finland).
10,000 metres Cross-Country.—V. Ventsene (U.S.S.R.).
20,000 metres Cross-Country.—T. Tikhonova (U.S.S.R.).
4 × 5,000 metres Relay.—U.S.S.R.

Speed Skating (Men)

500 metres.—J-U. Mey (G.D.R.).
1,000 metres.—N. Gulyayev (U.S.S.R.).
1,500 metres.—A. Hoffmann (G.D.R.).
5,000 metres.—T. Gustafson (Sweden).
10,000 metres.—T. Gustafson (Sweden).

Speed Skating (Women)

500 metres.—B. Blair (U.S.A.).
1,000 metres.—C. Rothenburger (G.D.R.).
1,500 metres.—Y. Van Gennip (Netherlands).
3,000 metres.—Y. Van Gennip (Netherlands).
5,000 metres.—Y. Van Gennip (Netherlands).

MEDAL TABLE

	Gold	Silver	Bronze	Total
U.S.S.R.	11	9	9	29
E. Germany (G.D.R.)	9	10	6	25
Switzerland	5	5	5	15
Finland	4	1	2	7
Sweden	4	0	2	6
Austria	3	5	2	10
Netherlands	3	2	2	7
W. Germany (F.R.G.)	2	4	2	8
U.S.A.	2	1	3	6
Italy	2	1	2	5
France	1	0	1	2
Norway	0	3	2	5
Canada	0	2	3	5
Yugoslavia	0	2	1	3
Czechoslovakia	0	1	2	3
Japan	0	0	1	1
Liechtenstein	0	0	1	1
	46	46	46	138

(For results of Olympic Games in Seoul, *see* pp. 1224-6)

ATHLETICS
WORLD RECORDS
(as at Aug. 31, 1988)

(All the world records given below have been accepted by the International Amateur Athletic Federation except those marked with an asterisk* which are awaiting homologation.)

Fully automatic timing to 1/100th second is mandatory up to and including 400 metres. For distances up to and including 10,000 metres records will be accepted to 1/100th second if timed automatically, and to 1/10th if hand timing is used.

MEN'S EVENTS
Running

Distances	hr.	min.	Time sec.	Name	Nation	Year
100 metres			9·83	B. Johnson	Canada	1987
200 metres			19·72	P. Mennea	Italy	1979
400 metres			43·29*	H.Reynolds	U.S.A.	1988
800 metres	1		41·73	S. Coe	G.B.	1981
1,000 metres	2		12·18	S. Coe	G.B.	1981
1,500 metres	3		29·46	S. Aouita	Morocco	1985
1 mile	3		46·32	S. Cram	G.B.	1985
2,000 metres	4		50·81	S. Aouita	Morocco	1987
3,000 metres	7		32·1	H. Rono	Kenya	1978
5,000 metres	12		58·39	S. Aouita	Morocco	1987
10,000 metres	27		13·81	F. Mamede	Portugal	1984
20,000 metres	57		24·2	J. Hermens	Netherlands	1976
20,944 metres (13 miles 24 yards 2 feet)	1	00	00·0	J. Hermens	Netherlands	1976
25,000 metres	1	13	55·8	T. Seko	Japan	1981
30,000 metres	1	29	18·8	T. Seko	Japan	1981
110 metres hurdles (3 ft. 6 in.)			12·93	R. Nehemiah	U.S.A.	1981
400 metres hurdles (3 ft. 0 in.)			47·02	E. Moses	U.S.A.	1983
3,000 metres steeplechase	8		05·4	H. Rono	Kenya	1978

Relay Racing

Distance	min.	Time sec.	Nation	Year
4 × 100 metres		37·83	U.S.A.	1984
4 × 200 metres	1	20·26	Univ. of S. Calif.	1978
4 × 400 metres	2	56·16	U.S.A.	1977
4 × 800 metres	7	03·89	G.B.	1982
4 × 1,500 metres	14	38·8	F.R.G.	1977

Jumping and Throwing

	ft.	in.	metres	Name	Nation	Year
High Jump	7	11¼	2·42	P. Sjöberg	Sweden	1987
Pole Vault	19	10¾	6·06*	S. Bubka	U.S.S.R.	1988
Long Jump	29	2½	8·90	R. Beamon	U.S.A.	1968
Triple Jump	58	11¼	17·97	W. Banks	U.S.A.	1985
Shot	75	8	23·06*	U. Timmermann	G.D.R.	1988
Discus	243	0	74·08	J. Schult	G.D.R.	1986
Hammer	284	7	86·74	Y. Sedykh	U.S.S.R.	1986
Javelin†	287	7	87·66	T. Zelezny	Czechoslovakia	1987
Decathlon‡			8,847 pts.°	D. Thompson	G.B.	1984

° Scored with new scoring tables.
† New type of javelin now in force
‡ Ten events comprising 100 m, long jump, shot, high jump, 400 m, 110 m hurdles, discus, pole vault, javelin, 1500 m.

Walking (Track)

Distance	hr.	min.	Time sec.	Name	Nation	Year
20,000 metres	1	18	40	E. Canto	Mexico	1984
28,565 metres (17 miles 1319 yards)	2	00	00·0	M. Damilano	Italy	1985
30,000 metres	2	06	07·3	M. Damilano	Italy	1985
50,000 metres	3	41	39·00	R. Gonzalez	Mexico	1979

WOMEN'S EVENTS
Running

Distance	min.	Time sec.	Name	Nation	Year
100 metres		10·49*	F. Griffith-Joyner	U.S.A.	1988
200 metres		21·71	M. Koch	G.D.R.	1979
		21·71	H. Drechsler	G.D.R.	1986
400 metres		47·60	M. Koch	G.D.R.	1985
800 metres	1	53·28	J. Kratochvilova	Czechoslovakia	1983
1,500 metres	3	52·47	T. Kazankina	U.S.S.R.	1980
1 mile	4	16·71	M. Slaney	U.S.A.	1985

Distance	Time		Name	Nation	Year
	min.	sec.			
3,000 metres	8	22·62	T. Kazankina	U.S.S.R.	1984
5,000 metres	14	37·33	I. Kristiansen	Norway	1986
10,000 metres	30	13·74	I. Kristiansen	Norway	1986
100 metres hurdles (2 ft. 9 in.)		12·21*	Y. Donkova	Bulgaria	1988
400 metres hurdles (2 ft. 6 in.)		52·94	M. Stepanova	U.S.S.R.	1986

Relays

Distance	Time		Nation	Year
	min.	sec.		
4 × 100 metres		41·37	G.D.R.	1985
4 × 200 metres	1	28·15	G.D.R.	1980
4 × 400 metres	3	15·92	G.D.R.	1984
4 × 800 metres	7	50·17	U.S.S.R.	1984

Women's Jumping and Throwing

	ft.	in.	metres	Name	Nation	Year
High Jump	6	10¼	2·09	S. Kostadinova	Bulgaria	1987
Long Jump	24	8¼	7·52*	G. Chistiakova	U.S.S.R.	1988
Shot	74	3	22·63	N. Lisovskaya	U.S.S.R.	1987
Discus	252	0	76·80*	G. Reinsch	G.D.R.	1988
Javelin	258	10	78·90	P. Felke	G.D.R.	1987
Heptathlon†	7,215* pts.			J. Joyner–Kersee	U.S.A.	1988

† Seven events comprising 100 m hurdles, shot, high jump, 200 m, long jump, javelin, 800 m.

UNITED KINGDOM (NATIONAL) RECORDS
(as at Aug. 31 1988)
(Records made anywhere by athletes eligible to represent Great Britain and Northern Ireland)

Men

100 *metres*—10·03 sec. (L. Christie, 1987).
200 *metres*—20·18 sec. (J. Regis, 1987).
400 *metres*—44·50 sec. (D. Redmond, 1987).
800 *metres*—1 min. 41·73 (S. Coe, 1981).
1,000 *metres*—2 min. 12·18 sec. (S. Coe, 1981).
1,500 *metres*—3 min. 29·67 sec. (S. Cram, 1985).
1 *mile*—3 min. 46·32 sec. (S. Cram, 1985).
2,000 *metres*—4 min. 51·39 sec. (S. Cram, 1985).
3,000 *metres*—7 min. 32·79 sec. (D. Moorcroft, 1982).
5,000 *metres*—13 min. 00·41 sec. (D. Moorcroft, 1982).
10,000 *metres*—27 min. 23·06 sec. (E. Martin, 1988).
20,000 *metres*—58 min. 39·0 sec. (R. Hill, 1968).
12 *miles* 1,268 *yards*—1 hr. (R. Hill, 1968).
25,000 *metres*—1 hr. 15 min. 22·6 sec. (R. Hill, 1965).
30,000 *metres*—1 hr. 31 min. 30·4 sec. (J. Alder, 1970).
3,000 *metres Steeplechase*—8 min. 12·11 sec. (C. Reitz, 1986).
110 *metres Hurdles*—13·11 sec. (C. Jackson, 1988).
400 *metres Hurdles*—48·12 sec. (D. P. Hemery, 1968).
4 × 100 *metres Relay*—38·62 (G.B. Team, 1980).
4 × 200 *metres*—1 min. 22·42 sec. (G.B. Team, 1988).
4 × 400 *metres*—2 min. 58·86 sec. (G.B. Team, 1987).
4 × 800 *metres*—7 min. 03·89 sec. (G.B. Team, 1982).
4 × 1,500 *metres*—14 min. 56·8 sec. (G.B. Team, 1979).
High Jump—2·29 m., 7 ft. 6 in. (D. Grant, 1988).
Pole Vault—5·65 m., 18 ft. 6¼ in. (K. Stock, 1981).
Long Jump—8·23 m., 27 ft. 0 in. (L. Davies, 1968).
Triple Jump—17·57 m., 57 ft. 7¼ in. (K. Connor, 1982).
Shot—21·68 m., 71 ft. 1¼ in. (G. Capes, 1980).
Discus—64·32 m., 211 ft. 0 in. (W. Tancred, 1974).
Hammer—77·54 m., 254 ft. 5 in. (M. Girvan, 1984).
Javelin—85·24 m., 279 ft. 8 in. (M. Hill, 1987).
Decathlon—8,847 pts.° (D. Thompson, 1984).
  ° Scored with new scoring tables.
Walking (Track)
20,000 *metres*—1 hr. 26 min. 07·6 sec. (P. Vesty, 1984).
2 *Hours*—16 miles 315 yds. (R. Wallwork, 1971).
30,000 *metres*—2 hr. 19 min. 18 sec. (C. Maddocks, 1984).
50,000 *metres*—4 hr. 05 min. 48 sec. (C. Maddocks, 1984).

Women

100 *metres*—11·10 sec. (K. Cook (née Smallwood), 1981).
200 *metres*—22·10 sec. (K. Cook (née Smallwood), 1984).
400 *metres*—49·43 sec. (K. Cook (née Smallwood), 1984).
800 *metres*—1 min. 57·42 sec. (K. Wade (née McDermott), 1985).
1,500 *metres*—3 min. 59·96 sec. (Z. Budd, 1985).
1 *mile*—4 min. 17·57 sec. (Z. Budd, 1985).
3,000 *metres*—8 min. 28·83 sec. (Z. Budd, 1985).
5,000 *metres*—14 min. 48·07 sec. (Z. Budd, 1985)
10,000 *metres*—31 min. 06·99 sec. (E. McColgan (née Lynch), 1988).
100 *metres Hurdles*—12·82 sec. (S. Gunnell, 1988).
400 *metres Hurdles*—55·00 sec. (S. Gunnell, 1988).
4 × 100 *metres Relay*—42·43 sec. (G.B. Team, 1980).
4 × 200 *metres Relay*—1 min. 31·57 sec. (G.B. Team, 1977).
4 × 400 *metres Relay*—3 min. 25·51 sec. (G.B. Team, 1984).
4 × 800 *metres Relay*—8 min. 23·8 sec. (G.B. Team, 1971).
High Jump—1·95 m., 6 ft. 4¼ in. (D. Elliott, 1982).
Long Jump—6·90 m., 22 ft. 7¾ in. (B. Kinch, 1983).
Shot—19·36 m., 63 ft. 6¼ in. (J. Oakes, 1988).
Discus—67·48 m., 221 ft. 5 in. (M. Ritchie, 1981).
Javelin—77·44 m., 254 ft. 1 in. (F. Whitbread, 1986).
Heptathlon—6,623 pts. (J. Simpson (née Livermore), 1986).

A.A.A./W.A.A.A. Indoor Championships

Held at Cosford, January 22–23, 1988
Men's Events

Metres	min.	sec.
60—L. Asquith (Birchfield)		6·62
200—L. Christie (T.V.H.)		21·36

400—M. Thomas (Wolverhampton &
  B.) .... 47·34
800—A. Morrell (Wolverhampton & B.) 1 49·70
1,500—G. Brown (unattached) .... 3 56·12
3,000—M. McLeod (Elswick) .... 8 06·07
60 *Hurdles*—J. Ridgeon (Achilles) ..... 7·68

	metres
High Jump—G. Parsons (London)	2·27
Pole Vault—A. Ashurst (Sale)	5·10
Long Jump—J. King (Wolverhampton & B.)	7·65
Triple Jump—E. McCalla (Birchfield) .	16·06
Shot—P. Edwards (Walton)	17·78

Women's Events

Metres	min.	sec.
60—P. Dunn (Stretford)		7·29
200—R. Kirby (Hounslow)		24·89
400—S. Gunnell (Essex Ladies)		53·28
800—D. Gandy (Hounslow)	2	05·62
1,500—B. Nicholson (Sale)	4	25·74
3,000[1]—W. Sly (Hounslow)	8	55·49
60 *Hurdles*—K. Robin-Millerchip (Birchfield)		8·29

	metres
High Jump—D. McDowell (Belfast) ...	1·88
Long Jump—K. Hagger (Essex Ladies)	6·17
Shot—J. Oakes (Croydon)	18·19

[1] Held at Cosford, January 9, 1988

United Kingdom v. France (Indoors)

Held at Glasgow, February 6, 1988

Men's Events

Metres	min.	sec.
60—L. Christie (U.K.)		6·67
200—L. Christie (U.K.)		21·11
400—B. Whittle (U.K.)		47·03
800—A. Morrell (U.K.)	1	51·48
1,500—G. Brown (U.K.)	3	45·09
60 *Hurdles*—J. Ridgeon (U.K.)		7·65
4 × 200 *Relay*—United Kingdom	1	23·93

	metres
High Jump—D. Grant (U.K.)	2·21
Pole Vault—P. Collet (France)	5·60
Long Jump—N. Brige (France)	7·77
Triple Jump—J. Herbert (U.K.)	16·49
Shot—P. Edwards (U.K.)	17·89

U.K. 73 pts., France 54.

Women's Events

Metres	min.	sec.
60—L Bily (France)		7·31
200—N. Simon (France)		23·82
400—S. Gunnell (U.K.)		52·81
800—J. Bell (U.K.)	2	04·77
1,500—B. Nicholson (U.K.)	4	18·27
60 *Hurdles*—M. Ewanje-Epee (France) .		8·24
4 × 200 *Relay*—France	1	34·69

	metres
High Jump—D. Davies (U.K.)	1·85
Long Jump—K. Hagger (U.K.)	6·38
Shot—J. Oakes (U.K.)	18·56

U.K. 57½ pts., France 48½.

National Cross-Country Championships (Women)

Held at Leeds, February 13, 1988

Senior Race (5,765 m)	min.	sec.
1. H. Titterington (Leicester)	20	57
2. J. Shields (Sheffield)	21	13
3. A. Pain (Leeds)	21	18

Team result:
1. Birchfield	41 pts.
2. Sale	94 pts.
3. Leeds	124 pts.

Intermediate Race (4,375 m)	min.	sec.
1. J. Adkin (Tonbridge)	16	12
2. S. Willicombe (G.E.C. Avionics)	16	19
3. A. Whitcombe (Parkside)	16	24

Team result:
1. Leicester	97 pts.
2. Norfolk O.	104 pts.
3. Oldham & Rochdale	129 pts.

Junior Race (3,500 m)	min.	sec.
1. C. Maycock (Rockingham)	13	04
2. P. Radcliffe (Bedford)	13	06
3. C. Holdcroft (City of Stoke)	13	10

Team result:
1. Bedford	57 pts.
2. City of Stoke	68 pts.
3. Liverpool H	174 pts.

Girl's Race (3,500 m)	min.	sec.
1. C. Whitley (Liverpool H.)	13	29
2. A. Foster (Morpeth)	13	40
3. C. Allen (Leicester)	13	43

Team result:
1. Bedford	57 pts.
2. Darlington	168 pts.
3. Bolton	168 pts.

United Kingdom v. Belgium v. Netherlands

Held at Ghent, Belgium, February 14, 1988

Men's Events

Metres	min.	sec.
60—D. Kirton (U.K.)		6·72
200—D. Reid (U.K.)		21·24
400—I. Delrue (Belgium)		47·15
800—A. Morrell (U.K.)	1	48·60
1,500—R. Druppers (Neth.)	3	45·17
3,000—M. Hawkins (U.K.)	7	58·37
60 *Hurdles*—J. Ridgeon (U.K.)		7·69
4 × 200 *Relay*—United Kingdom	1	27·12

	metres
High Jump—D. Grant (U.K.)	2·24
Pole Vault—D. Ledgen (Belgium)	5·30
Long Jump—E. Mellaard (Neth.)	7·87
Triple Jump—J. Herbert (U.K.)	16·66
Shot—P. Edwards (U.K.)	16·82

U.K. 119 pts., Belgium 73, Netherlands 70.

Women's Events

Metres	min.	sec.
60—E. Vader (Neth.)		7·34
200—M. Martinot (Neth.)		24·12
400—A. Piggford (U.K.)		54·65
800—J. Bell (U.K.)	2	02·80
1,500—C. Toonstra (Neth.)	4	13·79
3,000—A.-M. Richards (U.K.)	9	16·04
60 *Hurdles*—M. Olijslager (Neth.)		8·18
4 × 200 *Relay*—Belgium		N.T.

	metres
High Jump—D. Davies (U.K.)	1·89
Long Jump—J. Oladapo (U.K.)	6·33
Shot—J. Oakes (U.K.)	18·74

U.K. 96 pts., Netherlands 75, Belgium 48.

National Cross-Country Championships (Men)

Held at Newark, February 20, 1988

Senior Race (9 miles)	min.	sec.
1. D. Clarke (Hercules-Wimbledon)	44	14
2. D. Lewis (Rossendale)	45	00
3. C. Mochrie (Leicester)	45	12

Team result:
1. Birchfield .... 248 pts.
2. Tipton .... 369 pts.
3. Blackheath .... 516 pts.

Junior Race (6 miles)

	min.	sec.
1. S. Mugglestone (Westbury)	31	13
2. D. Mead (Thetford)	32	08
3. S. Brooks (Bingley)	32	21

Team result:
1. Aldershot, Farnham & District . 135 pts.
2. Westbury .... 154 pts.
3. Newham & Essex .... 177 pts.

Youth Race (4 miles)

	min.	sec.
1. J. Brown (Hallamshire)........	22	27
2. M. Campbell (Winchester)	22	45
3. J. Maycock (Rockingham)	23	02

Team result:
1. Chester-le-Street .... 113 pts.
2. Wirral .... 207 pts.
3. Leicester C. .... 249 pts.

European Indoor Championships

Held at Budapest, Hungary, March 5–6, 1988

Men's Events

Metres	min.	sec.
60—L. Christie (U.K.)................		6·57
200—N. Razgonov (U.S.S.R.).........		20·62
400—J. Carlowitz (G.D.R.)		45·63
800—D. Sharpe (U.K.)	1	49·17
1,500—A. Suhonen (Finland)	3	45·72
3,000—J.-L. Gonzalez (Spain)	7	55·29
60 *Hurdles*—A. Hoffer (Czechoslovakia)		7·56
5,000 *Walk*—J. Pribilinec (Czechoslovakia)	18	44·40

	metres
High Jump—P. Sjöberg (Sweden)	2·39
Pole Vault—R. Gataullin (U.S.S.R.) ...	5·75
Long Jump—F. Mass (Netherlands) ..	8·06
Triple Jump—O. Sakirkin (U.S.S.R.) ..	17·30
Shot—R. Machura (Czechoslovakia)...	21·42

Women's Events

Metres	min.	sec.
60—N. Cooman (Netherlands)		7·04
200—E. Kasprzyk (Poland)		22·69
400—P. Müller (G.D.R.)		50·28
800—S. Zweiner (F.R.G.)	2	01·19
1,500—D. Melinte (Romania)	4	05·77
3,000—E. Van Hulst (Netherlands)	8	44·50
60 *Hurdles*—C. Oschkenat (G.D.R.)....		7·77
3,000 *Walk*—R. Sobrino (Spain)	12	48·99

	metres
High Jump—S. Kostadinova (Bulgaria)	2·04
Long Jump—H. Drechsler (G.D.R.)	7·30
Shot—C. Losch (F.R.G.)	20·39

R.W.A. National 10 Mile Walk

Held at Dronfield, March 12, 1988

	min.	sec.
1. I. McCombie (Cambridge H.)	67	22
2. L. Morton (Sheffield)	70	20
3. M. Bell (Splott)	70	53

Team result:
1. Splott .... 51 pts.
2. Sheffield .... 73 pts.
3. Coventry .... 88 pts.

I.A.A.F. World 15 km. Road Race Championship (Women)

Held at Adelaide, Australia, March 20, 1988

	min.	sec.
1. I. Kristiansen (Norway)	48	24
2. X. Wang (China)...................	50	18
3. Z. Ivanova (U.S.S.R.)	50	28

Team result:
1. U.S.S.R. .... 21 pts.
2. China .... 31 pts.
3. Portugal .... 37 pts.

I.A.A.F. Cross-Country Championship

Held at Auckland, New Zealand, March 26, 1988

Men (12,000 m.)

	min.	sec.
1. J. Ngugi (Kenya)	34	32
2. P. Kipkoech (Kenya)	34	54
3. K. Koskei (Kenya)	35	07

Team result:
1. Kenya .... 23 pts.
2. Ethiopia .... 103 pts.
3. France .... 134 pts.

Women (6,000 m.)

	min.	sec.
1. I. Kristiansen (Norway)	19	04
2. A. Tooby (Great Britain)	19	23
3. A. Sergent (France)	19	29

Team result:
1. U.S.S.R. .... 51 pts.
2. Great Britain .... 61 pts.
3. France .... 72 pts.

Juniors (8,000 m.)

	min.	sec.
1. W. Kirochi (Kenya)	23	25
2. C. Ndeti (Kenya)..............	23	31
3. C. Muindi (Kenya)	23	39

Team result:
1. Kenya .... 11 pts.
2. Ethiopia .... 37 pts.
3. Spain .... 65 pts.

R.W.A. National 20 km. Walk

Held at Hoddesdon, May 21, 1988

	hr.	min.	sec.
1. I. McCombie (Cambridge H.)......................	1	23	31
2. D. Stone (Steyning)	1	27	02
3. A. Penn (Coventry)	1	28	17

United Kingdom Championships

Held at Derby, June 5–6, 1988

Men's Events

Metres	min.	sec.
100—J. Regis (Belgrave.)		10·65
200—L. Christie (T.V.H.)		20·75
400—B. Whittle (Haringey)		46·08
800—P. Herbert (Shaftesbury)	1	45·64
1,500—R. McDonnell (Haringey)	3	48·02
5,000—M. Harris (Portsmouth)	13	50·63
10,000—D. Lewis (Rossendale)	28	08·44
3,000 *Steeplechase*—N. Smart (Sutton) .	8	37·37
10,000 *Walk*—I. McCombie (Cambridge H.)	40	39·77
110 *Hurdles*—A. Jarrett (Haringey) ...		13·97
400 *Hurdles*—P. Harries (Derby & Co) .		50·01

	metres
High Jump—G. Parsons (London A.C.)	2·25
Pole Vault—A. Ashurst (Sale)	5·10
Long Jump—D. Brown (Haringey)	7·91
Triple Jump—R. Cameron (T.V.H.)....	16·20
Shot—G. Savory (Blackheath)	17·95

Discus—P. Mardle (Wolverhampton).. 59·42
Hammer—D. Smith (Hull Spartan)..... 70·66
Javelin—S. Backley (Cambridge H.) ... 79·50

Women's Events

Metres	min.	sec.
100—P. Dunn (Stretford).............		11·49
200—P. Dunn (Stretford).............		23·46
400—L. Keough (Basingstoke)		52·25
800—C. Cahill (Gateshead)	2	02·71
1,500—B. Nicholson (Sale)............	4	15·13
3,000—M. Watson (Swindon)	9	04·85
5,000—E. McColgan (Dundee)	15	10·17
5,000 *Walk*—B. Sworowski (Sheffield Utd.)............................	24	03·38
100 *Hurdles*—L. Green (Hallamshire)..		13·71
400 *Hurdles*—E. McLaughlin (Edinburgh S.H.)		56·22

	metres
High Jump—D. Davies (Leicester)	1·88
Long Jump—M. Berkeley (Croydon) ..	6·53
Shot—J. Oakes (Croydon)	18·76
Discus—V. Head (Cardiff)	53·66
Javelin—F. Whitbread (Thurrock)	70·10

R.W.A. National 35 km. Walk

Held at Leicester, June 11, 1988

	hr.	min.	sec.
1. E. Maddocks (Plymouth)...	2	45	09
2. D. Stone (Steyning)	2	51	27
3. C. Berwick (Leicester).....	2	58	21
Team result: Leicester 27 pts.			

United Kingdom v. U.S.S.R. v. France

Held at Portsmouth, June 19, 1988

Men's Events

Metres	min.	sec.
100—L. Christie (U.K.)................		10·21
200—L. Christie (U.K.)................		20·78
400—B. Whittle (U.K.)		45·45
800—S. Coe (U.K.)	1	48·63
1,500—S. Crabb (U.K.)	3	42·42
3,000—P. Thiebaut (France)	7	58·63
5,000—E. Martin (U.K.)	13	41·33
3,000 *Steeplechase*—R. Pannier (France)........................	8	29·16
110 *Hurdles*—C. Jackson (U.K.)		13·45
400 *Hurdles*—A. Bazarov (U.S.S.R.) ...		50·19
4 × 100 *Relay*—United Kingdom		38·86
4 × 400 *Relay*—U.S.S.R.	3	03·10
10,000 *Walk*—M. Shennikov (U.S.S.R.)	39	27·59

	metres
High Jump—D. Grant (U.K.)	2·29
Pole Vault—S. Ferreira (France)......	5·60
Long Jump—N. Brige (France)	8·12
Triple Jump—V. Inozemtsev (U.S.S.R)	16·60
Shot—L. Viudes (France)	18·92
Discus—R. Ubartas (U.S.S.R.)	67·72
Hammer—D. Smith (U.K.)	73·22
Javelin—V. Yevsyukov (U.S.S.R.).....	80·94

U.K. 156 pts., U.S.S.R. 149, France 136.

Women's Events

Metres	min.	sec.
100—P. Dunn (U.K.)		11·36
200—P. Dunn (U.K.)		23·26
400—O. Bryzgina (U.S.S.R.)		50·79
800—T. Samolenko (U.S.S.R.)	1	58·86
1,500—K. Wade (U.K.)	4	05·33
3,000—A. Tooby (U.K.)	8	50·10
100 *Hurdles*—L. Narozhilenko (U.S.S.R.).........................		12·99

Discus—I. Khval (U.S.S.R.)........... 62·74
Javelin—T. Sanderson (U.K.)......... 68·10

400 *Hurdles*—H. Huart (France) ...... 55·60
4 × 100 *Relay*—France .... 43·41
4 × 400 *Relay*—U.S.S.R. .... 3 26·01
5,000 *Walk*—Y. Nikolayeva (U.S.S.R.) . 21 08·65

	metres
High Jump—O. Turchak (U.S.S.R.) ...	1·95
Long Jump—Y. Belovskaya (U.S.S.R.) .	6·98
Shot—N. Lisovskaya (U.S.S.R.)	21·73
Discus—I. Khval (U.S.S.R.)...........	62·74
Javelin—T. Sanderson (U.K.).........	68·10

U.S.S.R. 143 pts., U.K. 112, France 77.

R.W.A. National 50 km. Walk

Held at York, July 10, 1988

	hr.	min.	sec.
1. L. Morton (Sheffield)	4	17	05
2. G. Vale (Boundary)	4	26	54
3. C. Berwick (Leicester)....	4	30	06
Team result: York.			

A.A.A./W.A.A.A. Championships

Held at Birmingham, August 5–7, 1988

Men's Events

Metres	min.	sec.
100—L. Christie (T.V.H.)		10·15
200—L. Christie (T.V.H.)		20·46
400—K. Akabusi (Team Solent)		44·93
800—S. Cram (Jarrow)	1	44·16
1,500—P. Elliott (Rotherham)	3	44·48
5,000—E. Martin (Basildon)	13	50·03
10,000—S. Binns (Bingley)	28	40·14
3,000 *Steeplechase*—M. Rowland (Phoenix)........................	8	32·60
110 *Hurdles*—C. Jackson (Cardiff)		13·29
400 *Hurdles*—M. Robertson (Wolverhampton)		50·23
10,000 *Walk*—I. McCombie (Cambridge H.)................................	41	36·51

	metres
High Jump—G. Parsons (London A.C.)	2·28
Pole Vault—S. Arkell (Australia)	5·10
Long Jump—S. Faulkner (Birchfield) .	7·98
Triple Jump—J. Herbert (Haringey) ..	17·12
Shot—S. Williams (Enfield)	17·78
Discus—P. Mardle (Wolverhampton)..	58·06
Hammer—D. Smith (Hull)	72·08
Javelin—D. Ottley (Telford)	80·34

Women's Events

Metres	min.	sec.
100—P. Dunn (Stretford)		11·26
200—S. Jacobs (Reading)		23·37
400—L. Keough (Basingstoke)		51·65
800—K. Wade (Blaydon)	2	01·52
1,500—C. Cahill (Gateshead)...........	4	08·26
3,000—Y. Murray (Edinburgh)........	8	47·34
10,000—A. Tooby (Cardiff)............	33	13·95
100 *Hurdles*—S. Gunnell (Essex Ladies)		13·02
400 *Hurdles*—S. Gunnell (Essex Ladies)		55·40
5,000 *Walk*—B. Sworowski (Sheffield)..	24	24·32

	metres
High Jump—J. Boyle (Belfast)	1·91
Long Jump—N. Boegman (Australia) .	6·82
Shot—J. Oakes (Croydon)	18·76
Discus—J. McKernan (Lisburn)	51·80
Javelin—S. Gibson (Nottingham)	57·32

A.A.A. Decathlon/W.A.A.A. Heptathlon

Held at Stoke, July 23–24, 1988

Decathlon—E. Gilkes (Newham) .... 7,529 pts.
Heptathlon—J. Mulliner (Wolverhampton) 5,728 pts.

United Kingdom v. Hungary v. International Select

Held at Gateshead, August 14, 1988

Men's Events

Metres		min.	sec.
100—E. Bunney (U.K.)			10·98
200—A. Carrott (U.K.)			20·10
400—D. Redmond (U.K.)			45·33
800—D. Sharpe (U.K.)		1	48·66
1 Mile—A. Passey (U.K.)		4	02·02
3,000—D. Moorcroft (U.K.)		8	04·48
2,000 *Steeplechase*—T. Hanlon (Guest)		5	26·62
110 *Hurdles*—C. Jackson (U.K.)			13·36
400 *Hurdles*—E. Moses (I.S./U.S.A.)			48·67
4 × 100 *Relay*—United Kingdom			39·36
4 × 400 *Relay*—United Kingdom		3	04·52
			metres
High Jump—D. Grant (U.K.)			2·27
Pole Vault—K. Tarpenning (I.S./ U.S.A.)			5·60
Long Jump—S. Faulkner (U.K.)			7·85
Triple Jump—J. Taiwo (I.S./Nigeria)			16·77
Shot—Z. Ladanyi (Hungary)			19·04
Discus—A. Horvath (Hungary)			63·82
Hammer—T. Gecsek (Hungary)			75·42
Javelin—R. Bradstock (U.K.)			76·04

U.K. 169 pts., I.S. 130, Hungary 95.

Women's Events

Metres		min.	sec.
100—F. Griffith-Joyner (I.S./U.S.A.)			11·54
200—K. Johnson (I.S./Australia)			23·56
400—M. Holland (I.S./Australia)			51·83
800—C. Cahill (U.K.)		2	01·99
1,500—B. Nicholson (U.K.)		4	11·99
3,000—J. Perkins (Guest/Australia)		9	01·88
100 *Hurdles*—X. Siska (Hungary)			13·59
400 *Hurdles*—E. McLaughlin (U.K.)			56·74
4 × 100 *Relay*—United Kingdom			44·55
4 × 400 *Relay*—United Kingdom		3	30·85
			metres
High Jump—S. Hutchings (I.S./U.K.)			1·86
Long Jump—N. Boegman (I.S./ Australia)			6·87
Shot—J. Oakes (U.K.)			19·36
Discus—A. Herczeg (Hungary)			60·60
Javelin—F. Whitbread (U.K.)			66·90

U.K. 132 pts., I.S. 102, Hungary 79.

THE OLYMPIC GAMES

The modern Olympic Games have been held as follows:

I	Athens	1896
II	Paris	1900
III	St. Louis	1904
IV	London	1908
V	Stockholm	1912
VII	Antwerp	1920
VIII	Paris	1924
IX	Amsterdam	1928
X	Los Angeles	1932
XI	Berlin	1936
XIV	London	1948
XV	Helsinki	1952
XVI	Melbourne	1956
XVII	Rome	1960
XVIII	Tokyo	1964
XIX	Mexico City	1968
XX	Munich	1972
XXI	Montreal	1976
XXII	Moscow	1980
XXIII	Los Angeles	1984
XXIV	Seoul	1988
XXV	Barcelona	1992

The following Games were scheduled but did not take place owing to World Wars:

VI	Berlin	1916
XII	Tokyo, then Helsinki	1940
XIII	London	1944

WINTER OLYMPIC GAMES

I	Chamonix (France)	1924
II	St. Moritz (Switzerland)	1928
III	Lake Placid (U.S.A.)	1932
IV	Garmisch-Partenkirchen (Germany)	1936
V	St. Moritz (Switzerland)	1948
VI	Oslo (Norway)	1952
VII	Cortina d'Ampezzo (Italy)	1956
VIII	Squaw Valley (U.S.A.)	1960
IX	Innsbruck (Austria)	1964
X	Grenoble (France)	1968
XI	Sapporo (Japan)	1972
XII	Innsbruck (Austria)	1976
XIII	Lake Placid (U.S.A.)	1980
XIV	Sarajevo (Yugoslavia)	1984
XV	Calgary (Canada)	1988
XVI	Albertville (France)	1992

THE TURF

Horseracing in Great Britain is under the control of THE JOCKEY CLUB.

The Jockey Club (incorporating the National Hunt Committee), 42 Portman Square, London, W1H 0EN. Stewards are: The Lord Fairhaven (*Senior Steward*); Viscount Chelsea (*Deputy Senior Steward*); A. T. A. Wates; Lord Vestey; Col. A. H. Parker Bowles; Sir John Barlow.

Winning Owners, 1987

Sheikh Mohammed	£1,232,255
L. Freedman ...	741,042
R. E. Sangster .	468,274
K. Abdulla	348,561
A. Clore	334,628
Hamdan Al-Maktoum ...	302,596
Sheikh A. Al Maktoum ...	256,739
Helena Springfield ..	229,332
F. Salman	225,516
H. H. Aga Khan	191,976

Winning Trainers, 1987

H. Cecil	£1,882,314
M. Stoute....	1,070,056
L. Cumani....	530,225
B. Hills	509,732
J. Dunlop ...	402,690
A. Stewart	397,655
G. Harwood ...	343,185
P. Biancone ...	293,748
P. Cole	270,832
J. Tree	227,172

Leading Breeders, 1987

	Value
Cliveden Stud..........................	£762,643
N. Bunker Hunt and E. Stephenson	265,308
J. Weinfeld	243,993
Juddmonte Farms	212,276
Swettenham Stud	210,619
H. H. Aga Khan	191,657
R. C. Wilson, Jnr.	182,381
J. L. Moore	180,271
E. Loder	176,449
Kinderhill/Aron Assoc. & Kinderhill Farm...............................	152,800

Winning Sires, 1987

	Races Horses won	Value
Mill Reef (USA) (1968), by Never Bend............	11 17	£947,129
Riverman (USA) (1969), by Never Bend............	9 17	407,936

	1st	2nd	3rd
Nureyev (USA) (1977), by Northern Dancer........	14	21	352,882
Busted (1963), by Crepello ..	10	22	305,136
Kris (1976), by Sharpen Up .	16	25	239,987
Known Fact (USA) (1977), by In Reality............	23	38	236,472
Mummy's Pet (1968), by Sing Sing	23	43	227,636
Be My Guest (USA) (1974), by Northern Dancer	11	20	204,726
Northern Dancer (1961), by Nearctic	7	10	199,947
Try My Best (USA) (1975), by Northern Dancer	11	26	196,256

Winning Flat Jockeys, 1987

	1st	2nd	3rd	Unpl.	Total Mts.
S. Cauthen	197	119	103	423	842
P. Eddery	195	153	126	522	996
R. Cochrane....	111	88	76	462	737
W. Carson	100	130	85	467	782
W. Swinburn...	93	76	67	342	578
M. Birch	92	72	58	366	588
J. Reid	81	77	64	438	660
M. Hills	75	55	57	304	491
M. Roberts	74	66	70	344	554
T. Ives	70	76	70	407	623

Winning National Hunt Jockeys 1987–88

	1st	2nd	3rd	Unpl.	Total Mts.
P. Scudamore ..	132	92	58	275	557
C. Grant	80	69	61	274	484
R. Dunwoody ..	79	60	86	357	582
M. Dwyer......	73	67	45	213	398
P. Tuck	71	48	41	206	366
G. McCourt	68	51	38	247	404
R. Rowe	64	48	34	212	358
M. Hammond...	63	32	28	124	247
S. Sherwood ...	55	51	41	183	330
P. Croucher	51	36	26	166	279

(The above statistics are the copyright of *The Sporting Life*.)

THE DERBY, 1985–88

For particulars of the Derby from 1780–1984 see 1921–88 editions.

The distance of the Derby course at Epsom is 1½ miles. First winner was Sir Charles Bunbury's Diomed in 1780. Lord Egremont won the Derby in 1782, 1804, 5, 7, 26 (also, 5 Oaks); Duke of Grafton, 1802, 9, 10, 15 (also, 9 Oaks); Mr. Bowes, 1835, 43, 52, 3; Sir J. Hawley, 1851, 58, 59, 68; the 1st Duke of Westminster, 1880, 82, 86, 99; Sir Victor Sassoon, 1953, 57, 58, 60. By winning his 5th Derby, in 1952, the late Aga Khan equalled Lord Egremont's record. He also won 2 Oaks.

The Derby was run at Newmarket from 1915–18 and again from 1940–45.

Year	Owner and Name of Winner	Betting	Jockey	Trainer	No. of Run'rs
1985	Lord H. de Walden's Slip Anchor	9–4 F.	S. Cauthen	H. Cecil	14
1986	H. H. Aga Khan's Shahrastani	11–2	W. Swinburn ...	M. Stoute.....	17
1987	Mr. L. Freedman's Reference Point	6–4 F.	S. Cauthen	H. Cecil	19
1988	H. H. Aga Khan's Kahyasi	11–1	R. Cochrane	L. Cumani	14

Record times: 2 min. 33·8 sec. by Mahmoud in 1936; 2 min. 33·84 sec. by Kahyasi in 1988 and 2 min. 33·9 sec. by Reference Point in 1987.

ONE THOUSAND GUINEAS. 1814. Rowley Mile. Newmarket. Fillies. 9st.

Year	Owner and Name of Winner	Betting	Jockey	Trainer	No. of Run'rs
1984	Capt. M. Lemos's Pebbles	8 to 1	P. Robinson	C. Brittain	15
1985	Sheikh Mohammed's Oh So Sharp	2 to 1 F.	S. Cauthen	H. Cecil	17
1986	H. Ranier's Midway Lady	10 to 1	R. Cochrane	B. Hanbury	15
1987	Mr. S. Niarchos's Miesque	15 to 8 F.	F. Head	F. Boutin	14
1988	E. Aland's Ravinella	4 to 5 F.	G. Moore	Mrs. C. Head	12

TWO THOUSAND GUINEAS. First Run, 1809. Rowley Mile. Newmarket. 9st.

Year	Owner and Name of Winner	Betting	Jockey	Trainer	No. of Run'rs
1984	Mr. R. Sangster's El Gran Senor	15 to 8 F.	P. Eddery	M. V. O'Brien	9
1985	Maktoum Al Maktoum's Shadeed	4 to 5 F.	L. Piggott	M. Stoute	14
1986	K. Abdulla's Dancing Brave	15 to 8 F.	G. Starkey	G. Harwood	15
1987	Mr. J. Horgan's Don't Forget Me	9 to 1	W. Carson	R. Hannon	13
1988	H. H. Aga Khan's Doyoun	4 to 5 F.	W. Swinburn	M. Stoute	9

OAKS. 1779. Epsom. 1½ Mile. Fillies. 9 st.

Year	Owner and Name of Winner	Betting	Jockey	Trainer	No. of Run'rs
1984	Sir Robin McAlpine's Circus Plume	4 to 1	L. Piggott	J. Dunlop	15
1985	Sheikh Mohammed's Oh So Sharp	6 to 4 F.	S. Cauthen	H. Cecil	12
1986	H. Ranier's Midway Lady	15 to 8 F.	R. Cochrane	B. Hanbury	15
1987	Sheikh Mohammed's Unite	11 to 1	W. Swinburn	M. Stoute	11
1988	Sheikh Mohammed's Diminuendo	7 to 4 F.	S. Cauthen	H. Cecil	11

ST. LEGER. 1776(8). Doncaster. 1¾ mile, 127 yards.

Year	Owner and Name of Winner	Betting	Jockey	Trainer	No. of Run'rs
1984	Mr. I. Allan's Commanche Run	7 to 4 F.	L. Piggott	L. Cumani	11
1985	Sheikh Mohammed's Oh So Sharp	8 to 11 F.	S. Cauthen	H. Cecil	6
1986	Lavinia Duchess of Norfolk's Moon Madness	9 to 2	P. Eddery	J. Dunlop	8
1987	Mr. L. Freedman's Reference Point	4 to 11 F.	S. Cauthen	H. Cecil	7
1988	Lady Beaverbrook's Minster Son	15 to 2	W. Carson	N. Graham	6

	Cheltenham Gold Cup* abt. 3¼ m.	Lincoln Handicap Doncaster—1 mile	Grand National* Liverpool—4½ m.	European Free Handicap Newmarket—3 yrs.—7 f.
1985	Forgive 'N Forget 8y 12st	Cataldi 4y 8st 10lb	Last Suspect 11y 10st 5lb	Over the Ocean 8st 11lb
1986	Dawn Run 8y 11st 9lb	K-Battery 5y 8st 4lb	West Tip 9y 10st 11lb	Green Desert 9st 7lb
1987	The Thinker 9y 12st	Star of a Gunner 7y 8st 8lb	Maori Venture 11y 10st 13lb	Noble Minstrel 9st 7lb
1988	Charter Party 10y 12st	Cuvee Charlie 4y 7st 13lb	Rhyme 'N' Reason 9y 11st	Lapierre 9st 1lb

	Irish Grand National* Fairyhouse—3 miles	Jockey Club Stakes Newmarket—1½ miles	Chester Cup Chester—2¼ m. 77 yd.	Coronation Cup Epsom—1½ miles
1985	Rhyme 'N' Reason 6y 10st 6lb	Kirmann 4y 8st 7lb	Morgan's Choice 8y 7st 11lb	Rainbow Quest 4y 9st
1986	Inauro 8y 9st 11lb	Phardante 4y 8st 7lb	Western Dancer 8y 9st	Saint Estephe 4y 9st
1987	Brittany Boy 8y 10st 10lb	Phardante 5y 8st 12lb	Just David 4y 9st 8lb	Triptych 5y 8st 11lb
1988	Perris Valley 7y 10st	Almaarad 4y 8st 5lb	Old Hubert 7y 7st 8lb	Triptych 6y 8st 11lb

	Coventry Stakes Ascot—2 yrs—5 furlongs	Gold Cup Ascot—2½ miles	Irish Sweeps Derby Curragh—3 yrs—1½ miles	Eclipse Stakes Sandown Park—1¼m.
1985	Sure Blade 8st 11lb	Gildoran 5y 9st	Law Society	Pebbles 4y 9st 4lb
1986	Cutting Blade 8st 11lb	Longboat 5y 9st	Shahrastani	Dancing Brave 3y 8st 8lb
1987	Always Fair 8st 13lb	Paean 4y 9st	Sir Harry Lewis	Mtoto 4y 9st 7lb
1988	High Estate 8st 13lb	Sadeem 6y 9st	Kahyasi 9st	Mtoto 5y 9st 7lb

	King George VI and Queen Elizabeth Stakes Ascot—1½ miles	Goodwood Cup 2 m. 5 f.	Gimcrack Stakes York—2 yrs.—6 Furlongs.	Middle Park Stakes Newmarket—2 yrs.—6 f.
1985	Petoski 3y 8st 8lb	Valuable Witness 5y 9st	Stalker 9st	Stalker 9st
1986	Dancing Brave 3y 8st 8lb	Longboat 5y 9st 7lb	Rich Charlie 9st 5lb	Mister Majestic 9st
1987	Reference Point 3y 8st 8lb	Sergeyevich 3y 7st	Reprimand 9st	Gallic League 9st
1988	Mtoto 5y 9st 7lb	Sadeem 5y 9st 7lb	Sharp 'N' Early 9st	Mon Tresor 9st

	Cambridgeshire Handicap Newmarket—9 f.	Prix de L'Arc de Triomphe Longchamp—1½ m.	Champion Stakes Newmarket—1¼ m.	Cesarewitch Newmarket—2¼ m.
1985	Tremblant 4y 9st 8lb	Rainbow Quest 4y 9st 4lb	Pebbles 4y 9st	Kayudee 5y 7st 11lb
1986	Dallas 3st 6lb	Dancing Brave 3y 8st 11lb	Triptych 4y 9st	Orange Hill 4y 7st 9lb
1987	Balthus 8st 1lb	Trempolino 3y 8st 11lb	Triptych 5y 9st	Private Audition 5y 7st 7lb
1988	Quinlan Terry 3y 8st 5lb	Tony Bin 5y 9st 4lb	Indian Skimmer 4y 9st	Nomadic Way 3y 7st 9lb

*National Hunt

CRICKET

TEST MATCHES
Pakistan v. England, 1987

First Test.—(Lahore, Nov. 25–28). Pakistan won by an innings and 87 runs. England 175 and 130; Pakistan 392.

Second Test.—(Faisalabad, Dec. 7–12). Drawn, England 292 and 137 for 6 dec.; Pakistan 191 and 51 for 1.

Third Test.—(Karachi, Dec. 16–21). Drawn, England 294 and 258 for 9; Pakistan 353.

India v. West Indies, 1987–88

First Test.—(Delhi, Nov. 25–29). West Indies won by five wickets. India 75 and 327; West Indies 127 and 276 for 5.

Second Test.—(Bombay, Dec. 13–16). Drawn. India 281 and 173; West Indies 337 and 4 for 1.

Third Test.—(Calcutta, Dec. 26–31). Drawn. West Indies 530 for 5 dec. and 157 for 2; India 565.

Fourth Test.—(Madras, Jan. 11–15). India won by 255 runs. India 382 and 217 for 8 dec.; West Indies 184 and 160.

Australia v. New Zealand, 1987

First Test.—(Brisbane, Dec. 4–7). Australia won by nine wickets. New Zealand 186 and 212; Australia 305 and 97 for 1.

Second Test.—(Adelaide, Dec. 11–15). Drawn. New Zealand 485 for 9 dec. and 182 for 7; Australia 496.

Third Test.—(Melbourne, Dec. 26–30). Drawn. New Zealand 317 and 286; Australia 357 and 230 for 9.

New Zealand v. England, 1988

First Test.—(Christchurch, Feb. 12–17). Drawn. England 319 and 152; New Zealand 168 and 130 for 4.

Second Test.—(Auckland, Feb. 25–29). Drawn. New Zealand 301 and 350 for 7 dec.; England 323.

Third Test.—(Wellington, March 3–7). Drawn. New Zealand 512 for 6 dec.; England 183 for 2. (match abandoned).

Australia v. Sri Lanka, 1988

Test.—(Perth, Feb. 12–15). Australia won by an innings and 108 runs. Australia 455; Sri Lanka 194 and 153.

West Indies v. Pakistan, 1988

First Test.—(Georgetown, April 2–7). Pakistan won by nine wickets. West Indies 292 and 172; Pakistan 435 and 32 for 1.

Second Test.—(Port of Spain, April 14–19). Drawn. West Indies 174 and 391; Pakistan 194 and 341 for 9.

Third Test.—(Bridgetown, April 22–27). West Indies won by two wickets. Pakistan 309 and 262; West Indies 306 and 268 for 8.

England v. West Indies, 1988

First Test.—(Trent Bridge, June 2–7). Drawn. England 245 and 301 for 3; West Indies 448 for 9 dec.

Second Test.—(Lord's, June 16–21). West Indies won by 134 runs. West Indies 209 and 397; England 165 and 307.

Third Test.—(Old Trafford, June 30–July 5). West Indies won by an innings and 156 runs. England 135 and 93; West Indies 384 for 7 dec.

Fourth Test.—(Headingley, July 21–26). West Indies won by ten wickets. England 201 and 138; West Indies 275 and 67 for 0.

Fifth Test.—(Oval, August 4–8). West Indies won by two wickets. England 205 and 202; West Indies 183 and 226 for 2.

England v. Sri Lanka

Test.—(Lord's, Aug. 25–30). England won by seven wickets. Sri Lanka 194 and 331; England 429 and 100 for 3.

OTHER INTERNATIONAL MATCHES

Reliance World Cup, 1987

Group A	P	W	L	Pts.
India	6	5	1	20
Australia	6	5	1	20
New Zealand	6	2	4	8
Zimbabwe	6	0	6	0
Group B	P	W	L	Pts.
Pakistan	6	5	1	20
England	6	4	2	16
West Indies	6	3	3	12
Sri Lanka	6	0	6	0

Semi-Finals.—1st. (Lahore, Pakistan, Nov. 4). Australia beat Pakistan by 18 runs. Australia 267 for 8; Pakistan 249 all out.

—2nd. (Bombay, India, Nov. 5). England beat India by 35 runs. England 254 for 6; India 219 all out.

Final.—(Calcutta, India, Nov. 8). Australia beat England by 7 runs. Australia 253 for 5; England 246 for 8.

ONE-DAY INTERNATIONALS
Pakistan v. England, 1987

Lahore, Nov. 18.—England bt. Pakistan by two wkts. Pakistan 166 all out; England 167 for 8.

Karachi, Nov. 20.—England bt. Pakistan by 23 runs. England 263 for 6; Pakistan 240 for 8.

Peshawar, Nov. 22.—England bt. Pakistan by 98 runs. England 236 for 8; Pakistan 138 all out.

New Zealand v. England, 1988

Dunedin, March 9.—England bt. New Zealand by five wkts. New Zealand 204; England 207 for 5.

Christchurch, March 12.—England bt. New Zealand by six wkts. New Zealand 186 for 8; England 188 for 4.

Napier, March 16.—New Zealand bt. England by seven wkts. England 219; New Zealand 223 for 3.

Auckland, March 19.—New Zealand bt. England by four wkts. England 208; New Zealand 211 for 6.

England v. West Indies, 1988

Edgbaston, May 19.—England won by six wkts. West Indies 217; England 219 for 4.

Headingley, May 21.—England won by 47 runs. England 186 for 8; West Indies 139.

Lord's, May 23–4.—England won by seven wkts. West Indies 178 for 7; England 180 for 3.

England v. Sri Lanka

Oval, Sept. 4.—England beat Sri Lanka by 5 wkts. Sri Lanka 242 for 7; England 245 for 5.

World Series Cup

Final.—1st Match (Melbourne, Jan. 22). Australia beat New Zealand by eight wickets.

2nd Match (Sydney, Jan. 24). Australia beat New Zealand by six wickets.

Australian Bicentenary Test

Sydney, Jan. 29–Feb. 2.—Drawn. England 425; Australia 214 and 328 for 2.

One Day Match

Melbourne, Feb. 4.—Australia won by 22 runs. Australia 235 for 6; England 213 for 8.

Pakistan v. England, 1987 (Averages)

PAKISTAN BATTING

Batsmen	I	NO	R	HS	Av.
Aamir Malik	2	1	103	98*	103·00
Salim Malik	4	1	143	60	47·66
Abdul Qadir	3	0	137	61	45.66
Wasim Akram ...	2	0	77	40	38.50
Ramiz Raja	4	1	110	50	36.66
Mudassar Nazar ..	4	0	131	120	32.75
Javed Miandad ...	3	0	88	65	29.33
Ijaz Ahmed	3	0	55	44	18.33
Iqbal Qasim	3	0	36	24	12.00
Ashraf Ali	3	0	23	12	7.66
Asif Mujtabe......	1	0	7	7	7.00
Shoaib Mohammad	1	0	0	0	0.00
Salim Jaffer.......	1	0	0	0	0.00
Tausif Ahmed.....	2	2	10	5*	—

*Not Out.

BOWLING

Bowlers	O	M	R	W	Av.
Abdul Qadir	234.4	68	437	30	14.56
Salim Malik	12	4	23	1	23.00
Tausif Ahmed.....	71.2	25	128	5	25.60
Iqbal Qasim	114.2	33	268	10	26.80
Mudasser Nazar...	26	8	56	2	28.00
Salim Jaffer......	65.5	15	153	5	30.60
Wasim Akram	40.1	7	102	2	51.00
Aamir Malik......	10	0	46	0	—
Shoaib Mohammad	1	1	0	0	—

ENGLAND BATTING

Batsmen	I	NO	R	HS	Av.
J. E. Emburey	6	3	207	74*	69.00
G. A. Gooch........	6	0	225	83	37.50
B. C. Broad	6	0	204	116	34.00
M. W. Gatting	6	0	128	79	21.33
D. J. Capel	6	0	125	98	20.83
B. N. French	5	1	80	38*	20.00
C. W. J. Athey	6	0	92	27	15.33
N. A. Foster	4	0	40	39	10.00
P. A. J. DeFreitas .	4	0	38	15	9.50
N. G. B. Cook	5	0	33	14	6.60
R. T. Robinson	4	1	16	7*	5.33
N. H. Fairbrother .	2	0	4	3	2.00
E. E. Hemmings ...	1	1	1	1*	—
G. R. Dilley	2	2	0	0*	—

*Not Out.

BOWLING

Bowlers	O	M	R	W	Av.
N. A. Foster	44	10	104	6	17.33
N. G. B. Cook	93.3	35	195	7	27.85
P. A. J. DeFreitas .	52.5	10	170	6	28.33
J. E. Emburey	124	48	251	7	35.85
E. E. Hemmings ..	25	8	51	1	51.00
D. J. Capel	13	1	59	1	59.00
G. R. Dilley	21	2	102	1	102.00
B. C. Broad	1	0	4	0	—
G. A. Gooch........	2	1	4	0	—

England v. West Indies, 1988 (Averages)

ENGLAND BATTING

Batsmen	I	NO	R	HS	Av.
G. A. Gooch........	10	0	459	146	45.90
A. J. Lamb........	8	2	254	113	42.33
D. I. Gower	8	1	211	88*	30.14
R. A. Smith	4	0	106	57	26.50
P. R. Downton	5	1	84	27	21.00
P. W. Jarvis	3	1	42	29*	21.00
B. C. Broad	4	0	71	54	17.75
T. S. Curtis	4	0	69	30	17.25
N. A. Foster	4	1	49	34	16.33
M. D. Moxon......	4	0	55	26	13.75
G. R. Dilley	7	1	58	28	9.66
M. W. Gatting	4	0	38	29	9.50
J. E. Emburey	5	0	46	30	9.20
D. R. Pringle	7	0	52	39	7.42
D. J. Capel	4	0	29	16	7.25
P. A. J. DeFreitas .	5	0	36	18	7.20
C. J. Richards.....	4	0	13	8	3.25
J. H. Childs	4	4	2	2*	—

Also batted: C. W. J. Athey, 16, 11; R. J. Bailey, 43, 3; C. S. Cowdrey, 0, 5; M. P. Maynard, 3, 10; G. C. Small, 5*, 7.
* Not Out.

BOWLING

Bowlers	O	M	R	W	Av.
G. R. Dilley	136.1	26	403	15	26.86
N. A. Foster	73.2	12	250	9	27.77
D. R. Pringle	119	33	326	11	29.63
G. C. Small	37.5	6	140	4	35.00
P. W. Jarvis	57.1	6	17	6	36.16
J. H. Childs	86	29	183	3	61.00
J. E. Emburey	62	14	228	3	76.00
P. A. J. DeFreitas .	92	16	253	3	84.33

WEST INDIES BATTING

Batsmen	I	NO	R	HS	Av.
A. L. Logie	7	2	364	95*	72.80
P. J. L. Dujon	7	1	305	67	50.83
R. A. Harper	3	0	147	74	49.00
C. G. Greenidge ...	6	0	282	103	47.00
D. L. Haynes	7	2	235	77*	47.00
I. V. A. Richards ..	6	0	223	80	37.16
M. D. Marshall	6	1	13	72	27.00
C. L. Hooper	7	0	166	84	23.71
C. E. L. Ambrose ..	6	2	75	43	18.75
R. B. Richardson ..	4	0	71	28	17.75
C. A. Walsh	5	3	26	9*	13.00
W. K. M. Benjamin	2	0	9	9	4.50
B. P. Patterson	2	0	2	2	1.00

Also batted: K. L. T. Arthurton, 27.
* Not Out.

BOWLING

Bowlers	O	M	R	W	Av.
W. K. M. Benjamin	67	17	151	12	12.58
R. A. Harper	89	11	63	5	12.60
M. D. Marshall	203.1	49	443	35	12.65
C. E. L. Ambrose ..	203.1	56	445	22	20.22
C. A. Walsh	157.2	40	412	12	34.33
B. P. Patterson	74.5	13	270	4	67.50

Also bowled: C. L. Hooper, 24-3-57-0; I. V. A. Richards, 10-1-28-0.

ENGLAND BATTING

Batsmen	I	NO	R	HS	Av.
M. D. Moxon	4	1	208	99	69·33
B. C. Broad	4	0	204	114	51·00
J. E. Emburey	3	0	106	45	35·33
M. W. Gatting	4	1	106	42	35·33
R. T. Robinson	4	0	126	70	31·50
C. W. J. Athey	2	0	41	22	20·50
G. R. Dilley	3	2	17	8*	17·00
P. W. Jarvis	3	1	34	14	17·00
P. A. J. DeFreitas ...	2	0	20	16	10·00
N. V. Radford	1	0	8	8	8·00
B. N. French	3	0	23	13	7·66
D. J. Capel	3	0	16	11	5·33
N. H. Fairbrother ...	1	0	1	1	1·00

BOWLING

Bowlers	O	M	R	W	Av.
G. R. Dilley	104·5	33	210	15	14·00
M. W. Gatting	6	1	21	1	21·00
P. W. Jarvis	98	31	201	6	33·50
P. A. J. DeFreitas .	91·1	33	175	4	43·75
D. J. Capel	109·2	22	274	5	54·80
J. E. Emburey	133·5	48	236	3	78·66
N. V. Radford	50	8	132	1	132·00
N. H. Fairbrother .	2	0	9	0	—
E. E. Hemmings ...	45	15	107	0	—
M. D. Moxon	2	0	3	0	—

New Zealand v. England, 1988 (Averages)

NEW ZEALAND BATTING

Batsmen	I	NO	R	HS	Av.
M. J. Greatbatch	3	1	186	107*	93·00
K. R. Rutherford	3	1	138	107*	69·00
R. H. Vance	1	0	47	47	47·00
I. D. S. Smith	4	2	92	33*	46·00
M. D. Crowe	5	0	227	143	45·40
J. G. Wright	5	0	221	103	44·20
J. G. Bracewell	5	1	152	54	38·00
R. J. Hadlee	1	0	37	37	37·00
A. H. Jones	2	0	62	54	31·00
T. J. Franklin	5	0	125	62	25·00
D. K. Morrison	2	1	14	14*	14·00
M. C. Snedden	3	0	34	20	11·33
E. J. Chatfield	2	1	10	10	10·00
J. J. Crowe	4	0	40	28	10·00

BOWLING

Bowlers	O	M	R	W	Av.
E. J. Chatfield	126·1	51	198	13	15·23
D. K. Morrison	80·2	14	269	8	33·62
M. C. Snedden	90	35	203	6	33·83
J. G. Bracewell	68	18	148	3	49·33
S. L. Boock	26	9	44	0	—
R. J. Hadlee	18	3	50	0	—
K. R. Rutherford ..	6	1	9	0	—

BATTING AND BOWLING AVERAGES
† Figures do not include averages for the West Indian and Sri Lankan tourists.

English Batting Averages, 1988†

Batsmen	I	NO	R	HS	Av.
G. A. Hick	37	2	2,713	405*	77·51
S. R. Waugh	24	6	1,314	161	73·00
C. W. J. Athey	22	6	1,064	168*	66·50
G. A. Gooch	37	1	2,324	275	64·55
M. D. Crowe	9	1	487	136*	60·87
A. R. Border	32	8	1,393	169*	58.04
K. J. Barnett	30	2	1,623	239*	57·96
A. J. Lamb	27	5	1,163	155	52·86
M. A. Atherton	27	4	1,121	152*	48·73
N. Hussain	13	3	486	165*	48·60
D. M. Smith.........	18	5	630	157*	48·46
M. W. Gatting	33	2	1,469	210	47·38
M. R. Ramprakash ...	13	4	421	68*	46·77
P. D. Bowler	42	5	1,726	159*	46·64
W. N. Slack	32	5	1,228	163*	45·48
G. S. Clinton	29	5	1,054	158	43·91
R. C. Ontong	25	8	734	120*	43·17
J. G. Wright	20	1	815	154*	42·89
C. J. Tavare	36	2	1,429	138*	42·02
N. G. Cowley	7	3	168	55	42·00

* Denotes not out.

English Bowling Averages, 1988†

Bowlers	O	M	R	W	Av.
O. H. Mortensen ..	233·3	73	464	34	13·64
S. T. Clarke	396·4	108	913	63	14·49
N. S. Williams	178·3	33	511	30	17·03
P. W. Jarvis	233·2	52	651	37	17·59
N. G. Cowans	492·0	124	1,290	71	18·16
F. D. Stephenson..	819·1	195	2,289	125	18·31
G. J. Parsons	228·0	69	553	29	19·06
A. R. C. Fraser ...	696·5	195	1,550	80	19·37
P. J. Newport	600·3	127	1,844	93	19·82
G. C. Small	628·1	170	1,605	80	20·06
A. A. Donald	180·4	40	534	26	20·53
P. J. W. Allott ...	590·2	159	1,378	67	20·56
A. Sidebottom ...	511·2	136	1,303	63	20·68
N. A. Mallender..	433·3	111	1,037	50	20·74
K. M. Curran	414·2	86	1,385	65	21·30
Wasim Akram	291·4	76	666	31	21·48
K. E. Cooper	816·0	220	2,179	101	21·57
A. P. Igglesden ...	234·3	46	805	37	21·75
K. D. James	298·5	72	763	35	21·80
R. K. Illingworth .	597·4	189	1,274	58	21·96

County Championship Table, 1988

Order for 1987 in brackets	Played	Won	Lost	Drawn	Bonus Btg.	Bonus Blng.	Points
Worcestershire (9)	22	10	3	9	55	75	290
Kent (14)................	22	10	5	7	57	72	289
Essex (12)	22	9	5	8	61	69	282
Surrey (4)	22	7	5	10	57	72	241
Nottinghamshire (1) ...	22	8	8	6	34	71	229
Warwickshire (15)	22	6	8	8	48	74	218
Middlesex (16)	22	7	3	12	49	54	215
Leicestershire (3)	22	6	3	13	56	63	215
Lancashire (2)	22	6	7	9	41	67	212
Gloucestershire (10)....	22	6	7	9	52	59	207
Somerset (11)...........	22	5	6	11	48	65	201
Northamptonshire (7) ..	22	5	7	10	48	71	199
Yorkshire (8)	22	4	6	12	48	65	177
Derbyshire (6)	22	4	3	15	53	54	171
Hampshire (5)	22	4	6	12	33	69	166
Sussex (17).............	22	3	11	8	37	65	150
Glamorgan (13)	22	1	8	13	42	53	111

Other Results, 1988

NatWest Trophy.—Middlesex beat Worcestershire by three wickets. Worcestershire 161 for 9; Middlesex 162 for 7.

Benson and Hedges Cup Final.—Hampshire beat Derbyshire by seven wickets. Derbyshire 117; Hampshire 118 for 3.

Refuge Assurance Sunday League Champions.—Worcestershire.

Refuge Assurance Cup.—Lancashire beat Worcestershire by 52 runs. Lancashire 201 for 5; Worcestershire 149.

Universities.—Match abandoned.

Village Cricket Final.—Goatacre (Wilts.) beat Himley (W. Midlands) by four wickets. Himley 192; Goatacre 193 for 6.

National Club Championship.—Enfield beat Wolverhampton by nine wickets. Wolverhampton 164; Enfield 165 for 1.

BOWLS, 1987–88

National Championships
(Worthing)

Fours.—Final: Somertown (Oxon.) beat Paddington (Middx.) 15–14.

Triples.—Final: Belgrave (Leics.) beat Clevedon (Somerset) 17–11.

Pairs.—Final: Belgrave (Leics.) beat Plessey (Notts.) 17–14.

Singles.—Final: R. C. Bray (Stanlees, Cornwall) beat I. Middlemast (Bath, Somerset) 21–12.

World Indoor Championship, H. Duff.

World Indoor Pairs Championship.—J. Yates and I. Schuback (Aus.).

National Indoor Singles Championship, A. Allcock.

World Fours Champions.—Ireland.

World Singles Champion.—D. Bryant (England).

Inter-County Championship (Middleton Cup).—Final: Northumberland beat Lincolnshire 126–117.

SNOOKER AND BILLIARDS, 1987–88

World Professional Snooker Championship.—S. Davis beat T. Griffiths by 18–11.

Benson and Hedges Masters Snooker Tournament.—S. Davis beat M. Hallett by 9–0.

U.K. Professional Snooker Championship.—S. Davis beat J. White by 16–14.

World Doubles Snooker Championship.—M. Hallett and S. Hendry beat C. Thorburn and D. Taylor by 12–8.

English Professional Snooker Championship.—D. Reynolds beat N. Foulds by 9–5.

British Open Snooker Championship.—S. Hendry beat M. Hallett by 13–2.

Mercantile Credit Classic.—S. Davis beat J. Parrott by 13–11.

World Team Cup.—England beat Australia by 9–7.

Rothmans Matchroom League.—S. Davis.

World Professional Billiards Championship.—N. Dagley beat E. Charlton by 7–4.

World Amateur Snooker Championship.—D. Morgan (Wales) beat J. Grech (Malta) by 11–4.

Women's World Snooker Championship.—A.-M. Farren beat S. Hillyard by 5–1.

GYMNASTICS, 1987

MEN'S

British Men's Champion, A. Morris.

British Men's Individual Apparatus Champions:
Floor, T. Bartlett.
Pommel Horse, A. Morris.
Rings, R. Edwards; C. Benyon.
Vault, T. Bartlett.
Parallel Bars, A. Morris.
High Bar, T. Bartlett.

British Men's Team Champions (Adam Shield), Bush Harlow 'A'.

WOMEN'S

British Women's Champion, L. Elliott.

British Women's Individual Apparatus Champions:
Vault, K. Hargate.
Asymmetric Bars, L. Thomas; J. Prescott.
Beam, K. Hargate.
Floor, K. Hargate.

British Rhythmics Champion, L. Black.

British Women's Open Club Team Champions, Heathrow.

RUGBY FOOTBALL
RUGBY UNION

International Matches 1987–88

1987
Nov. 7 Cardiff: Wales, 46 U.S. Eagles 0
1988
Jan. 16 Dublin: Ireland 22, Scotland 18
Paris: France 10, England 9
Feb. 6 Edinburgh: Scotland 23, France 12
Twickenham: England 3, Wales 11
Feb. 20 Cardiff: Wales 25, Scotland 20
Paris: France 25, Ireland 6
Mar. 5 Edinburgh: Scotland 6, England 9
Dublin: Ireland 9, Wales 12
Mar. 19 Cardiff: Wales 9, France 10
Twickenham: England 35, Ireland 3
Apr. 23 Dublin: Ireland 10, England 21
May 28 Christchurch: New Zealand 52, Wales 3
May 29 Brisbane: Australia 22, England 16
June 11 Auckland: New Zealand 59, Wales 9
June 12 Sydney: Australia 28, England 8

International Union Table, 1988

	P	W	D	L	Pts.		Total
					F	A	
Wales	4	3	0	1	57	42	6
France	4	3	0	1	57	47	6
England	4	2	0	2	56	30	4
Scotland	4	1	0	3	67	68	2
Ireland	4	1	0	3	40	90	2

County Championship Final

Lancashire beat Warwickshire 23–18

Other Chief Matches, 1987–88

Universities. 1987. Cambridge beat Oxford by 15–10 pts.
Services Championship.—Army beat Royal Navy 35–3; Army beat R.A.F. 26–3; R.A.F. beat Royal Navy 10–7.
John Player Special Cup Final: April 30 (Twickenham)—Harlequins beat Bristol 28–22 pts.
Hospitals' Cup Final.—St. Mary's beat Royal Free 32–0.
Middlesex Sevens.—Harlequins.
Division 1 Clubs Champions.—Leicester.
Division 2 Clubs Champions.—Rosslyn Park.
Division 3 Clubs Champions.—Wakefield.

RUGBY FOOTBALL LEAGUE
(Est. 1895)

International Matches

1987
Oct. 25 Wigan: Gt. Britain 42, Papua New Guinea 0.
1988
Jan. 24 Avignon: France 14, Gt. Britain 28.
Feb. 6 Leeds: Gt. Britain 30, France 12.
May. 22 Port Moresby: Papua New Guinea 22, Gt. Britain 42.
June 11 Sydney: Australia 17, Gt. Britain 6.
June 28 Brisbane: Australia 34, Gt. Britain 14.

July 9 Sydney: Australia 12, Gt. Britain 26*.
July 16 Christchurch: New Zealand 12, Gt. Britain 10*.
*World Cup match
Rugby League Challenge Cup Final: April 30 (Wembley)—Wigan beat Halifax 32–12 pts.
Premiership Trophy Final: May 15 (Old Trafford)—Widnes beat St. Helens 38–14 pts.
Stones Bitter Champions.—Widnes.
Second Division Champions.—Oldham.
Yorkshire Cup.—Bradford Northern and Castleford drew 1–1. Bradford Northern won 11–2 after a replay.
Lancashire Cup.—Wigan beat Warrington 28–16 pts.
John Player Special Trophy Final.—St. Helens beat Leeds 15–14 pts.

AMATEUR RUGBY LEAGUE 1987–88

County Championship.—Yorkshire.
National Inter-League Shield.—Copeland beat Humberside 20–10 pts.
National Cup.—St. Patricks beat Elland 28–8 pts.
National League Champions.—Milford.
National League Challenge Cup.—Leigh M.W. beat Milford 15–0 pts.

HOCKEY, 1987–88
MEN'S HOCKEY

Champions Trophy. West Germany.
Home Countries Indoor. England.
County Championship Final. Middlesex beat Worcestershire 1–0.
National Club Championship Final. Southgate beat Hounslow 2–1.
National Indoor Club Championship Final. St. Albans beat East Grinstead 4–3.
Universities. Cambridge beat Oxford 2–0.

WOMEN'S HOCKEY

Tipp-Ex Trophy.—England beat Spain, 3–1.
Home Countries Championship. England beat Scotland 2–0 and 2–1; England drew with Ireland 0–0; England beat Wales 3–0.
County Championship Final. Kent beat Staffordshire 2–1.

CHESS, 1988

British Championship. J. Mestel.
Ladies. C. Forbes.
Under-18 (Men). I. MacKay.
Under-18 (Women). N. Regan.

GREYHOUND RACING, 1988

Television Trophy (Birmingham).—Minnies Siren.
Grand National (Birmingham).—Breeks Rocket.
Greyhound Derby (Wimbledon).—Hit the Lid.
Scurry Gold Cup (Catford).—Francombe Black.

ASSOCIATION FOOTBALL

Div. I.—Champions: Liverpool, 90 pts. *Runners-up:* Manchester United, 81 pts. *Relegated:* Portsmouth, 35 pts.; Oxford, 32 pts.; Watford, 31 pts.
Div. II.—Champions: Millwall, 82 pts.; *Promoted:* Aston Villa, 78 pts. *Relegated:* Reading, 42 pts.; Huddersfield, 28 pts.
Div. III.—Champions: Sunderland, 93 pts. *Promoted:* Brighton, 84 pts. *Relegated:* Grimsby, 50 pts.; York, 33 pts.; Doncaster, 33 pts.
Div. IV.—Champions: Wolverhampton, 90 pts. *Promoted:* Cardiff, 85 pts.; Bolton, 78 pts. *Relegated to G.M. Vauxhall Conference:* Newport County, 25 pts.
G.M. Vauxhall Conference.—Champions and Promoted: Lincoln City, 82 pts.

END OF SEASON PLAY-OFFS.

Divisions 1 and 2: S.F.—Chelsea beat *Blackburn Rovers 6–1 on agg.; Middlesbrough beat *Bradford City 3–2 on agg.
Final.—*Middlesbrough beat Chelsea 2–1 on agg.
Divisions 2 and 3: S.F.—*Bristol City beat Sheffield United 2–1 on agg.; Walsall beat *Notts. County 4–2 on agg.
Final—Walsall 3, *Bristol City 3 on agg. Walsall won 4–0 after a replay.
Divisions 3 and 4: S.F.—*Swansea City beat Rotherham 2–1 on agg.; *Torquay United beat Scunthorpe United 3–1 on agg.
Final—*Swansea beat Torquay 5–4 on agg.

*Indicates home team in first match.

As a result of the end-of-season play-offs Chelsea were relegated to Division 2 and Middlesbrough promoted to Division 1. Sheffield United were relegated to Division 3 and Walsall promoted to Division 2. Rotherham were relegated to Division 4 and Swansea were promoted to Division 3.

SCOTTISH LEAGUE

Premier Div.—Champions: Celtic, 72 pts. *Runners-up:* Hearts, 62 pts. *Relegated:* Falkirk, 31 pts.; Dunfermline, 26 pts.; Morton, 16 pts.
Div. I.—Champions: Hamilton, 56 pts. *Relegated:* East Fife, 36 pts.; Dumbarton, 36 pts.
Div. II.—Champions: Ayr, 61 pts. *Promoted:* St. Johnstone, 59 pts.

CUP COMPETITIONS, 1987–88

F.A. CUP.—*S.F.*: (White Hart Lane), Wimbledon beat Luton Town, 2–1; (Hillsborough), Liverpool beat Nottingham Forest, 2–1.
Final: May 14 (Wembley Stadium), Wimbledon beat Liverpool, 1–0.
LITTLEWOODS CUP (formerly the *Milk Cup*).—*Final:* Luton Town beat Arsenal, 3–2.
SIMOD CUP.—*Final:* Reading beat Luton Town, 4–1.
SHERPA VAN TROPHY.—*Final:* Wolverhampton Wanderers beat Burnley, 2–0.
F.A. VASE.—*Final:* Colne Dynamoes beat Emley, 1–0 a.e.t.
F.A. TROPHY.—*Final:* Enfield 0, Telford 0. Enfield won 3–2 after a replay.
F.A. YOUTH CUP.—*Winners:* Arsenal.
ARTHUR DUNN CUP.—*Final:* Old Cholmeleians beat Old Brentwoods, 2–1.
SCOTTISH F.A. CUP.—*Final:* May 14 (Hampden Park), Celtic beat Dundee United, 2–1.
SKOL CUP.—*Final:* Rangers and Aberdeen drew 3–3 a.e.t. Rangers won 5–3 on penalties.
ROUS CUP.—*Winners:* England.

Scotland 0	Colombia 0		
England 1	Scotland 0		
England 1	Colombia 1		

EUROPEAN CUP.—*Final:* Benfica 0, P.S.V. Eindhoven

0. P.S.V. Eindhoven won 6–5 on penalties in Stuttgart.
EUROPEAN CUP-WINNERS' CUP—*Final:* Mechelen beat Ajax Amsterdam 1–0 in Strasbourg.
U.E.F.A. CUP.—*Final:* Bayer Leverkusen drew with Espanol 3–3 on agg. Leverkusen won 3–2 on penalties.

INTERNATIONALS

1987				
Sept. 9	Hampden:	Scotland	2	Hungary	0
	Düsseldorf:	W. Germany	3	England	1
1988				
Feb. 17	Riyadh:	Saudi Arabia	2	Scotland	2
	Tel Aviv:	Israel	0	England	0
	Athens:	Greece	3	N. Ireland	2
Mar. 22	Valletta:	Malta	1	Scotland	1
Mar. 23	Wembley:	England	2	Netherlands	2
	Belfast:	N. Ireland	1	Poland	1
	Swansea:	Wales	1	Yugoslavia	2
Apr. 27	Budapest:	Hungary	0	England	0
	Belfast:	N. Ireland	0	France	0
	Madrid:	Spain	0	Scotland	0
	Solna:	Sweden	4	Wales	1
May 28	Lausanne:	Switzerland	0	England	1
June 1	Valletta:	Malta	2	Wales	3
4	Brescia:	Italy	0	Wales	1

EUROPEAN CHAMPIONSHIP

Qualifying Rounds 1987

England, Northern Ireland (*Group 4*); Wales (*Group 6*); Scotland (*Group 7*).

Sept. 9	Cardiff:	Wales	1	Denmark	0
Oct. 14	Hampden:	Scotland	2	Belgium	0
	Wembley:	England	8	Turkey	0
	Sarajevo:	Yugoslavia	3	N. Ireland	0
	Copen-hagen:	Denmark	1	Wales	0
Nov. 11	Belgrade:	Yugoslavia	1	England	4
	Prague:	Czecho-slovakia	2	Wales	0
	Sofia:	Bulgaria	0	Scotland	1
	Belfast:	N. Ireland	1	Turkey	0
Dec. 2	Luxem-bourg:	Luxem-bourg	0	Scotland	0

Finals

(West Germany: June 10–25, 1988)

Group One: West Germany 1 Italy 1; Denmark 2 Spain 3; West Germany 2 Denmark 0; Italy 1 Spain 0; Italy 2 Denmark 0; West Germany 2 Spain 0.
Group Two: England 0 Rep. of Ireland 1; Netherlands 0 Soviet Union 1; England 1 Netherlands 3; Rep. of Ireland 1 Soviet Union 1; England 1 Soviet Union 3; Rep. of Ireland 0 Netherlands 1.
Semi-Finals: June 21 Hamburg: Netherlands beat West Germany, 2–1. June 22 Stuttgart: Soviet Union beat Italy, 2–0.
Final: June 25 Munich: Netherlands beat Soviet Union, 2–0.

PAST WORLD CUP WINNERS

1930	(*Played in Uruguay*)	Uruguay
1934	(*Italy*)	Italy
1938	(*France*)	Italy
1950	(*Brazil*)	Uruguay
1954	(*Switzerland*)	West Germany
1958	(*Sweden*)	Brazil
1962	(*Chile*)	Brazil
1966	(*England*)	England
1970	(*Mexico*)	Brazil
1974	(*West Germany*)	West Germany
1978	(*Argentina*)	Argentina
1982	(*Spain*)	Italy
1986	(*Mexico*)	Argentina

GOLF, 1987–88

MAJOR CHAMPIONSHIPS 1988

THE OPEN (Royal Lytham, July 14–18)
S. Ballesteros (*Spain*), 273.
THE U.S. OPEN (Brookline, Mass., June 16–20)
C. Strange (*U.S.A.*), 278.
THE MASTERS (Augusta, Georgia, April 7–10)
A. Lyle (*G.B.*), 281.
THE U.S. P.G.A. (Oklahoma City, Aug. 11–14)
J. Sluman (*U.S.A.*), 272.

TEAM EVENTS

RYDER CUP (Muirfield Village, Ohio, Sept. 25–27, 1987)
Great Britain and Europe beat U.S.A. by 15 to 13.
WALKER CUP (Sunningdale, May 27–28, 1987)
U.S.A. beat Great Britain and Ireland by 16½ to 7½.
CURTIS CUP (Sandwich, June 10–11, 1988)
Great Britain and Ireland beat U.S.A. by 11 to 7.
WORLD CUP (Hawaii)
Winners: Wales.

EUROPEAN P.G.A. TOUR, 1988

Majorca Open.—S. Ballesteros (Spain), 272.
Barcelona Open.—D. Whelan (G.B.), 276.
Biarritz Open.—D. Llewellyn (G.B.), 258.
Cannes Open.—M. McNulty (Zimbabwe), 279.
Madrid Open.—D. Cooper (G.B.), 275.
Portuguese Open.—M. Harwood (Aus.), 280.
Epson Grand Prix.—B. Langer (W. Germany).
Spanish Open.—M. James (G.B.), 262.
Italian Open.—G. Norman (Aus.), 270.
P. G. A. Championship.—I. Woosnam (G.B.), 274.
Dunhill British Masters.—A. Lyle (G.B.), 273.
National Pro-Celebrity Tournament.—R. Davis (Australia), 275.
Belgian Open.—J.-M. Olazabal (Spain), 269.
French Open.—N. Faldo (G.B.), 274.
Monte Carlo Open.—J. Rivero (Spain), 261.
Scottish Open.—B. Lane (G.B.), 271.
Dutch Open.—M. Mouland (G.B.), 274.
Scandinavian Enterprise Open.—S. Ballesteros (Spain), 270.
Benson and Hedges International.—P. Baker (G.B.), 271.
PLM Open.—F. Nobilo (N.Z.), 270.
Irish Open.—I. Woosnam (G.B.), 278.
German Open.—S. Ballesteros (Spain), 263.
Ebel European Open.—C. Moody (G.B.), 268.
Panasonic European Open.—I. Woosnam (G.B.), 260.
Lancôme Trophy.—S. Ballesteros (Spain), 269.
German Masters.—J.-M. Olazabal (Spain), 279.

WOMEN'S CHAMPIONSHIPS

U.S. Women's Open.—L. Neumann (Sweden), 277.
European Women's Open.—D. Reid (G.B.), 283.
British Women's Open.—C. Dibnah (Australia), 295.
British Women's Amateur Championship.—J. Furby.
European Ladies Amateur Team Championship (1987).—Sweden.
English Girls Open Championship.—H. Dobson.
British Girls Open Championship.—A. MacDonald.

MEN'S AMATEUR CHAMPIONSHIPS

Amateur Championship.—C. Hardin (Sweden).
English Championship.—R. Claydon.
British Youths Open Championship.—C. Cevaer, 275.
Boys Amateur Championship.—S. Pardoe.
Halford Hewitt (for schools).—Stowe.
Lytham Trophy.—P. Broadhurst.
Brabazon Trophy.—R. Eggo, 289.
Berkshire Trophy.—R. Claydon, 276.
Carris Trophy.—P. Page, 281.
President's Putter.—G. Wuollet (U.S.A.).

Championships

OPEN (Instituted 1860)	
1980 T. Watson (U.S.A.), 271.	1982 M. Thompson.
1981 W. Rogers (U.S.A.), 276.	1983 P. Parkin.
1982 T. Watson (U.S.A.), 284.	1984 J.-M. Olazabal (Spain).
1983 T. Watson (U.S.A.), 275.	1985 G. McGimpsey.
1984 S. Ballesteros (Spain), 276.	1986 D. Curry.
1985 S. Lyle (G.B.), 282.	1987 P. Mayo.
1986 G. Norman (Australia), 280.	1988 C. Hardin (Sweden).
1987 N. Faldo (G.B.), 279.	
1988 S. Ballesteros (Spain), 273.	

LADIES AMATEUR (1893)

1980 Mrs. A. Sander (U.S.A.).
1981 Mrs. B. Robertson.
1982 Miss K. Douglas.
1983 Mrs. J. Thornhill.
1984 Miss J. Rosenthal (U.S.A.).
1985 Miss L. Behan.
1986 Miss M. McGuire (N.Z.).
1987 Miss J. Furby.
1988 Miss J. Furby.

AMATEUR (1885)

1980 D. Evans.
1981 P. Ploujoux (France).

POLO, 1988

Queen's Cup.—NCP Broncus beat Tramontana, 10–9.
Cowdray Park Gold Cup.—Tramontana beat Hildon House, 15–8.
Royal Windsor Cup.—Parc beat Wings, 8–6½.
Coronation Cup.—England beat N. America, 8–7.
Silver Jubilee Cup.—France beat The Prince of Wales' Team, 4½–4.
Warwickshire Cup.—Black Bear beat Hildon House, 9–8.

WEIGHTLIFTING

WORLD WEIGHTLIFTING RECORDS (TOTALS)
(as at August 31, 1988)

Class	Kg		
52 kg	269·5	He-Zhuoqiang (China)	1988
56 kg	300	N. Shalamanov (Bulgaria)	1984
60 kg	335	N. Shalamanov (Bulgaria)	1986
67·5 kg	352·5	A.Behm (G.D.R.)	1984
75 kg	382·5	A. Varbanov (Bulgaria)	1988
82·5 kg	405	Y. Vardanyan (U.S.S.R.)	1984
90 kg	422·5	V. Solodov (U.S.S.R.)	1984
100 kg	440	Y. Zakharevich (U.S.S.R.)	1983
110 kg	452·5	Y. Zakharevich (U.S.S.R.)	1988
Over 110 kg	472·5	L. Taranenko (U.S.S.R.)	1987

LAWN TENNIS, 1987-88

THE ALL ENGLAND CHAMPIONSHIPS (WIMBLEDON) 1988

Men's Singles.—S. Edberg (Sweden) beat B. Becker (W. Germany), 4–6, 7–6, 6–4, 6–2.

Women's Singles.—Miss S. Graf (W. Germany) beat Miss M. Navratilova (U.S.A.), 5–7, 6–2, 6–1.

Men's Doubles.—K. Flach and R. Seguso (U.S.A.) beat J. Fitzgerald (Australia) and A. Jarryd (Sweden), 6–4, 2–6, 6–4, 7–6.

Women's Doubles.—Miss S. Graf (W. Germany) and Miss G. Sabatini (Argentina) beat Miss L. Savchenko and Miss N. Zvereva (U.S.S.R.), 6–3, 1–6, 12–10.

Mixed Doubles.—S. E. Stewart and Miss Z. Garrison (U.S.A.) beat K. Jones and Mrs. S. Magers (U.S.A.), 6–1, 7–6.

Australian Championships:
Men's Singles.—M. Wilander (Sweden).
Women's Singles.—Miss S. Graf (W. Germany).
Men's Doubles.—R. Leach and J. Pugh (U.S.A.).
Women's Doubles.—Miss M. Navratilova and Miss P. Shriver (U.S.A.).
Mixed Doubles.—J. Pugh (U.S.A.) and Miss J. Novotna (Czechoslovakia).

U.S.A. Championships:
Men's Singles.—M. Wilander (Sweden).
Women's Singles.—Miss S. Graf (W. Germany).
Men's Doubles.—S. Cascal and E. Sanchez (Spain).
Women's Doubles.—Miss G. Fernandez and Miss R. White (U.S.A.).
Mixed Doubles.—J. Pugh (U.S.A.) and Miss J. Novotna (Czechoslovakia).

French Championships:
Men's Singles.—M. Wilander (Sweden).
Women's Singles.—Miss S. Graf (W. Germany).
Men's Doubles.—A. Gomez (Ecuador) and E. Sanchez (Spain).
Women's Doubles.—Miss M. Navratilova and Miss P. Shriver (U.S.A.).
Mixed Doubles.—J. Lozano (Mexico) and Miss L. McNeil (U.S.A.).

DAVIS CUP, 1987
(Founder—Dwight Filley Davis (1879–1945))

Sweden beat India by 5 matches to 0.

WIGHTMAN CUP, 1987
(Williamsburg, U.S.A.)

U.S.A. beat G.B. by 5 matches to 2.

Youll Cup.—Repton.
Clark Cup.—Repton.

Prudential County Cup—Men: Yorkshire; *Women:* Surrey.

REAL TENNIS, 1987-88

Professional Doubles Championship.—C. and S. Ronaldson beat M. Gooding and C. Lumley, 2–1.

Women's Professional Doubles.—S. Jones and A. Warren-Piper beat K. Allen and L. Ronaldson, 2–0.

Amateur Singles Championship.—J. Snow beat I. Snell, 3–0.

Amateur Doubles Championship.—A. Lovell and M. Dean beat J. Snow and J. Male, 3–2.

British Open Singles Championship.—L. Deuchar beat W. Davies, 3–2.

British Open Doubles Championship.—W. Davies and L. Deuchar beat N. Cripps and P. Tabley, 3–1.

Women's Open Singles.—S. Jones beat A. Warren-Piper, 2–1.

Henry Leaf Cup.—Radley beat Winchester, 2–1.

BADMINTON, 1988

ENGLISH NATIONAL CHAMPIONSHIPS

Men's Singles.—D Hall.

Women's Singles.—Mrs S. Podger.

Men's Doubles.—M. Dew and A. Goode.

Women's Doubles.—Miss G. Clark and Miss G. Gowers.

Mixed Doubles.—M. Dew and Mrs. G. Gilks.

ALL-ENGLAND CHAMPIONSHIPS (WEMBLEY)

Men's Singles.—I. Frederiksen (Denmark).

Women's Singles.—Gu Jiaming (China).

Men's Doubles.—Li. Yongbo and Tian Bingyi (China).

Women's Doubles.—Chung So-Young and Kim Yun-Ja (S. Korea).

Mixed Doubles.—Wang Pengren and Shi Fangjing (China).

RACKETS, 1987-88

Celestion Amateur Singles Championship.—W. Boone beat J. Prenn, 3–0.
Celestion Amateur Doubles Championship.—J. Prenn and J. Male beat W. Boone and R. Crawley, 4–2.
Rank Xerox Professional Singles Championship.—N. Smith beat S. Hazell, 3–0.
Celestion British Open Singles Championship.—J. Male beat N. Smith, 4–0.
Celestion British Open Doubles Championship.—J. Prenn and J. Male beat W. Boone and R. Crawley, 4–2.
Noel Bruce Cup.—Radley (J. Male and J. Snow) beat Malvern (M. and P. Nicholls), 4–0.
Public Schools Doubles Championship.—Marlborough beat Tonbridge, 4–0.
Universities.—Oxford beat Cambridge, 3–0.

SQUASH RACKETS, 1987-88

World Open Championship 1987.—Jansher Khan (Pakistan) beat C. Dittmar (Australia), 3–1.
World Open Championship 1988.—Jahangir Khan (Pakistan) beat Jansher Khan (Pakistan), 3–0.
Women's World Open Championship 1988.—Miss S. Devoy (N.Z) beat Miss L. Opie (England), 3–0.
World Team Championship.—Pakistan.
Women's World Team Championship.—England.
British Open Championship.—Jahangir Khan (Pakistan) beat R. Martin (Australia), 3–1.
Women's British Open Championship.—Miss S. Devoy (N.Z.) beat Miss L. Irving (Australia), 3–0.
Men's National Championship.—D. Harris beat A. Naylor, 3–1.
Women's National Championship.—Miss L. Opie beat Miss L. Soutter, 3–2.
World Junior Open Championship.—D. Harris (England) beat A. Hill (Australia), 3–2.
Women's World Junior Open Championship.—Miss S. Fitzgerald (Australia) beat Miss D. Vardy (England), 3–0.

ALPINE SKI-ING 1987–88

WORLD CUP 1987–88

Men's:
Downhill.—P. Zurbriggen (Switzerland).
Slalom.—A. Tomba (Italy).
Giant Slalom.—A. Tomba (Italy).
Super Giant Slalom.—P. Zurbriggen (Switzerland).
Overall.—P. Zurbriggen (Switzerland).
Women's:
Downhill.—M. Figini (Switzerland).
Slalom.—R. Steiner (Austria).
Giant Slalom.—M. Svet (Yugoslavia).
Super Giant Slalom.—M. Figini (Switzerland).
Overall.—M. Figini (Switzerland).

British National Alpine Championships, 1988.
Men.—S. Langmuir.
Women.—I. Grant.

ICE SKATING, 1987–88

WORLD CHAMPIONSHIPS
(Budapest)

Men's Figure.—B. Boitano (U.S.A.).
Ladies' Figure.—Miss K. Witt (G.D.R.).
Pairs.—O. Vasiliev and Miss Y. Valova.
Ice Dancing.—A. Bukin and Miss N. Bestemianova (U.S.S.R.).

EUROPEAN CHAMPIONSHIPS
(Prague)

Men's Figure.—A. Fadeyev (U.S.S.R.).
Ladies' Figure.—Miss K. Witt (G.D.R.).
Pairs.—S. Grinkov and Miss E. Gordeyeva.
Ice Dancing.—A. Bukin and Miss N. Bestemianova (U.S.S.R.).

BRITISH CHAMPIONSHIPS

Men's Figure.—P. Robinson.
Ladies' Figure.—Miss J. Conway.
Pairs.—A. Naylor and Miss C. Peake.
Ice Dancing.—P. Askham and Miss S. Jones.

FENCING, 1987–88

British Championships:
Foil.—P. Harper (Salle Goodall).
Epée.—J. Llewellyn (Reading F.C.).
Ladies' Foil.—Miss L. Martin (Salle Paul).
Sabre.—M. Slade (Hemel Hempstead).
Sporting Record Cup.—Salle Paul.
Magrini Cup.—London Thames.
Savage Shield.—London Thames.
Martin Edmunds Cup.—Salle Boston.
Eden Cup.—A. Puccini (Italy).
Challenge Martini International Epée.—M. Poffet (Switzerland).

ETON FIVES, 1988

Amateur Championship (Kinnaird Cup).—B. C. Matthews and J. Reynolds.
Nat West County Championship.—Middlesex.
Holmwoods Schools Championships.—Harrow.
Alan Barber Cup.—Old Cholmeleians.
League Championship (Douglas Keeble Cup).—Village Club.

RUGBY FIVES, 1987–88

Amateur Singles Championship.—G. W. Enstone beat I. P. Fuller.
Amateur Doubles Championship.—I. P. Fuller and D. J. Hebden beat D. Parlby and J. Schroeter.
National Schools' Championships.—*Singles:* P. Newman (St. Dunstan's).
Doubles: St. Dunstan's.

TABLE TENNIS, 1988

ENGLISH NATIONAL CHAMPIONSHIPS
(Crawley)

Men's Singles: A. Cooke.
Women's Singles: Miss A. Gordon.
Men's Doubles: S. Andrew and N. Mason.
Women's Doubles: Miss F. Elliot and Miss L. Lomas.
Mixed Doubles: S. Andrew and Miss F. Elliot.

CYCLING, 1988

Tour de France.—P. Delgado (Spain).
Milk Race.—V. Zhdanov (U.S.S.R.).
World Professional Road Race Championship.—M. Fondriest (Italy).
British Professional Road Race Championship.—S. Joughin.
British Amateur Road Race Championship.—N. Hoban.
Tour of Britain.—M. Elliott.

BASKET BALL, 1987–8

MEN'S

Prudential National Cup, Polycell Kingston.
Carlsberg National League, H.F.S. Portsmouth.
Carlsberg National Championship, M. I. M. Livingston.

WOMEN'S

National Cup, Avon Northampton.
National League, Avon Northampton.
Carlsberg National Championship, Stockport Louvolite.

OXFORD AND CAMBRIDGE

PRINCIPAL EVENTS AND WINNERS, 1987–88

Event (with date of first meeting)	Summary of Results			Results 1987–88
	Ox.	Camb.	Drawn	
Athletics (1864)	57	50	7	Camb.
Boat Race (1829)	64	69	1	Oxford
Cricket (1827)	46	54	43	Aband.
Football—				
Association (1873–4)	38	45	21	Camb.
Rugby (1871–2)	45	48	13	Camb.
Golf (1878)	39	53	5	Camb.
Hockey (1890)	28	41	16	Camb.

OTHER UNIVERSITY EVENTS AND WINNERS, 1987–88

Cross Country	Oxford
Rackets	Oxford
Basket Ball	Oxford
Fencing	Cambridge
Boxing	Oxford
Judo	Cambridge
Volleyball	Cambridge

ANGLING

NATIONAL COARSE CHAMPIONSHIPS

Year	Venue	No. of teams	Individual Winner	Weight k. g.	Team Winners	Points	Division
1986	Oxford Canal	78	M. Stabler (Provincial)	3 820	I. Walton Stafford	815	1
	R. Trent	76	J. Howard (Bawtry)	18 110	Hull	813	2
	Royal Military Canal	74	P. Barber (Reddish A.C.)	34 270	Starlets	742	3
	R. Witham	75	P. Stanton (Wadsley Bridge)	7 790	Trevs	779	4
	Lancaster Canal	57	A. Holdsworth (Pendle)	5 400	Lansil	589	5
	Grand Union Canal	56	R. Stimpson (Oxford)	5 610	Milton Keynes	594	Jr. Ch.
1987	R. Trent	80	J. Robinson (Bawtry)	14 080	Nottingham & D.	773	1
	Oxford Canal	77	B. Mann (Tewkesbury Popular)	2 940	Weybridge	767	2
	R. Severn	79	S. Carr (North Staffs.)	17 660	Trevs A.S.	718	3
	R. Nene	72	C. Shortland (Crosby)	5 490	Earl Manvers	716	4
	Oxford Canal	70	T. May (Bedford A.C.)	4 030	Star A.C.	661	5
	Bristol Avon	36	P. Mason (Leighton Buzzard)	13 200	Bristol & West	326	Jr. Ch.

SWIMMING

WORLD SWIMMING RECORDS
(as at Aug. 31, 1988)

Men:
100 metres Freestyle.—M. Biondi (U.S.A.), 48·42 s.
200 metres Freestyle.—M. Gross (F.R.G.), 1 m. 47·44 s.
400 metres Freestyle.—A. Wojdat (Poland), 3 m. 47·38 s.
800 metres Freestyle.—V. Salnikov (U.S.S.R.), 7 m. 50·64 s.
1,500 metres Freestyle.—V. Salnikov (U.S.S.R.), 14 m. 54·76 s.
100 metres Breaststroke.—S. Lundquist (U.S.A.), 1 m. 01·65 s.
200 metres Breaststroke.—V. Davis (Canada), 2 m. 13·34 s.
100 metres Butterfly.—P. Morales (U.S.A.), 52·84 s.
200 metres Butterfly.—M. Gross (F.R.G.), 1 m. 56·24 s.
100 metres Backstroke.—D. Berkoff (U.S.A.), 54·91 s.
200 metres Backstroke.—I. Polyanski (U.S.S.R.), 1 m. 58·14 s.
200 metres Medley.—T. Darnyi (Hungary), 2 m.00·56 s.
400 metres Medley.—T. Darnyi (Hungary) 4 m.15·42 s.
4 × 100 metres Freestyle Relay.—U.S.A., 3 m. 17·08 s.
4 × 200 metres Freestyle Relay.—F.R.G., 7 m. 13·10 s.
4 × 100 metres Medley Relay.—U.S.A., 3 m. 38·28 s.

Women:
100 metres Freestyle.—K. Otto (G.D.R.), 54·73 s.
200 metres Freestyle.—H. Friedrich (G.D.R.), 1 m. 57·55 s.
400 metres Freestyle.—J. Evans (U.S.A.), 4 m. 05·45 s.
800 metres Freestyle.—J. Evans (U.S.A.), 8 m.17·12 s.
1,500 metres Freestyle.—J. Evans (U.S.A.), 15 m. 52·10 s.
100 metres Breaststroke.—S. Hörner (G.D.R.), 1 m.07·91 s.
200 metres Breaststroke.—A. Higson (Canada), 2 m. 27·27 s.
100 metres Butterfly.—M. Meagher (U.S.A.), 57·93 s.
200 metres Butterfly.—M. Meagher (U.S.A), 2 m. 05·96 s.
100 metres Backstroke.—I. Kleber (G.D.R.), 1 m. 00·59 s.
200 metres Backstroke.—B. Mitchell (U.S.A.), 2 m. 08·60 s.

200 metres Medley.—U. Geweniger (G.D.R.), 2 m. 11·73 s.
400 metres Medley.—P. Schneider (G.D.R.), 4 m. 36·10 s.
4 × 100 metres Freestyle Relay.—G.D.R., 3 m. 40·57 s.
4 × 200 metres Freestyle Relay.—G.D.R., 7 m. 55·47 s.
4 × 100 metres Medley Relay.—G.D.R., 4 m. 03·69 s.

NATIONAL SWIMMING CHAMPIONSHIPS
1988 (Leeds, July 27–31)

Men:

50 metres Freestyle.—M. Foster.
100 metres Freestyle.—A. Jameson.
200 metres Freestyle.—R. Lee.
400 metres Freestyle.—P. Howe.
1,500 metres Freestyle.—A. Day.
100 metres Breaststroke.—J. Parrack.
200 metres Breaststroke.—N. Gillingham.
100 metres Butterfly.—A. Jameson.
200 metres Butterfly.—T. Jones.
100 metres Backstroke.—N. Cochran.
200 metres Backstroke.—G. Binfield.
200 metres Medley.—N. Cochran.
400 metres Medley.—J. Davey.
4 × 100 metres Freestyle Relay.—City of Birmingham.
4 × 100 metres Medley Relay.—Beckenham.

Women:

50 metres Freestyle.—C. van Bentum (Neth.).
100 metres Freestyle.—C. van Bentum (Neth.).
200 metres Freestyle.—C. van Bentum (Neth.).
400 metres Freestyle.—R. Gilfillan.
800 metres Freestyle.—K. Mellor.
100 metres Breaststroke.—S. Brownsdon.
200 metres Breaststroke.—S. Brownsdon.
100 metres Butterfly.—C. van Bentum (Neth.).
200 metres Butterfly.—C. van Bentum (Neth.).
100 metres Backstroke.—K. Read.
200 metres Backstroke.—I. de Rover (Neth.)
200 metres Medley.—M. Muis (Neth.).
400 metres Medley.—T. Atkin.
4 × 100 metres Freestyle Relay.—Wigan Wasps.
4 × 100 metres Medley Relay.—Norwich Penguins.

ROWING

HENLEY ROYAL REGATTA, 1988

Grand Challenge Cup.—Leander/University of London beat Australian Institute of Sport by 1 foot.

Ladies Challenge Plate.—Mercantile (Australia) beat Leander by 1 length.

Princess Elizabeth Cup.—Hampton beat Eton by ¾ length.

*Thames Cup.*Thames R. C. "A" beat Univ. College, Galway (Galway disqualified).

Prince Philip Cup.—Vancouver (Canada) beat Syracuse University (U.S.A.) easily.

Queen Mother Cup.—Melbourne University/University of Queensland (Australia) beat Nautilus by 1 length.

Visitors' Cup.—University of Durham beat Imperial College London "A" by 2¼ lengths.

Wyfold Cup.—Nottinghamshire County "A" beat Nautilus by 2¼ lengths.

Britannia Challenge Cup.—University of London beat Lea by 2 lengths.

Stewards Cup.—Leander beat Penn Athletic (U.S.A.) easily.

Silver Goblets and Nickall's Cup.—T. S. Swinford and J. P. Riley (Penn Athletic—U.S.A.) beat S. J. Chilmaid and A. D. J. Butt (London) easily.

Double Sculls Cup.—A. C. Rudkin (Tideway Scullers) and A. P. S. Kittermaster (Barclays Bank) beat J. Scrivener and R. Henderson (Lea) by ⅓ length.

Diamond Sculls.—G. H. McGlashan (Melbourne University) beat A. H. Sudduth (Harvard) by 3½ lengths.

Special Schools Race.—Radley beat St. Edward's by 1½ lengths.

NATIONAL CHAMPIONSHIPS 1988

(Holme Pierrepont)

Men's:
Eights.—Tideway Scullers.
Coxed Fours.—Kingston.
Coxless Fours.—Leander.
Coxed Pairs.—Kingston.
Coxless Pairs.—Notts County.
Quad Sculls.—Notts County.
Double Sculls.—Tideway Scullers.
Single Sculls.—S. Larkin (Notts County).
Coastal Fours.—Eastbourne.
Coastal Pairs.—Dover.
Coastal Singles.—P. Mahoney (Southsea).

Women's:
Eights.—G.B. Squad.
Coxed Fours.—Tideway Scullers.
Coxless Pairs.—Strodes/Univ. of London.
Quad Sculls.—Thames Tradesmen "A".
Double Sculls.—Marlow/Thames Tradesmen.
Single Sculls.—A. Marden (Thames Tradesmen).
Coastal Fours.—Christchurch.

THE 134TH UNIVERSITY BOAT RACE
(Putney–Mortlake, 4 m. 1 f. 180 yds.)

Oxford beat Cambridge by 5½ lengths, 17 m 35 s.
(Cambridge have won 69 times, Oxford 64 and there has been 1 dead-heat. The record time is the 16 m 45 s rowed by Oxford in 1984.)

OTHER ROWING EVENTS

Oxford Summer Eights.—Oriel.
Oxford Torpids.—Oriel.
Cambridge Lents.—Downing.
Cambridge Mays.—Lady Margaret.
Doggett's Coat and Badge (Estab. 1715, 274th race, London Bridge–Chelsea, 4½ miles).—G. Hayes.
Head of the River.—A.R.A. National Squad II.

SHOOTING

BISLEY, 119th N.R.A., 1988

Queen's Prize.—1. J. Pugsley, 290 pts.; 2. D. Armstrong, 290 pts.; 3, C. Mallett, 290 pts.

Prince of Wales Prize.—1. Lt.-Col. H. J. Orpen-Smellie, 75 pts.

St. George's Challenge Vase.—1. Fl. Lt. C. Fitzpatrick, 149 pts.; 2. V. Robertshaw, 148 pts; 3. Miss A. Lennane, 148 pts.

All Comers Aggregate.—1. Sqn. Ldr. D. P. Calvert, 319 pts.; 2. Sgt. G. Tucker, 318 pts.; 3. A. Chown, 317 pts.

National Trophy.—1. England, 2,035 pts.; 2. Scotland, 2,008 pts.; 3. Ireland, 1,953 pts.

Kolapore Cup.—1. Great Britain, 1,165 pts.; 2. Canada, 1,145 pts.; 3. Jersey, 1,145 pts.

Chancellor's Challenge Plate.—1. Cambridge Univ., 1,114 pts.; 2. Oxford Univ., 1,101 pts.

Musketeers Cup.—1. Edinburgh Univ., 567 pts.; 2. London Univ., 565 pts.; 3. Exeter Univ., 560 pts.

Visianagram Trophy.—1. House of Lords, 661 pts.; 2. House of Commons, 616 pts.

County Long-Range Championship.—1. Devon, 289 pts.; 2. Surrey, 289 pts.; 3. Cheshire, 287 pts.

MacKinnon Challenge Cup.—1. England, 1,111 pts.; 2. Scotland, 1,096 pts.; 3. Canada, 1,088 pts.

CLAY PIGEON SHOOTING, 1988

International Cup (Down-the-Line).—England, 7,247/7,500.

British Open Down-the-Line Championship.—D. T. Williams, 299/300.

Mackintosh Trophy.—Australia, 7,393/7,500.

British Open Skeet Championship.—M. Elworthy, 100/100 + 175.

British Open Sporting Championship.—M. Rouse, 94/100.

Coronation Cup.—A. B. Hebditch.

EQUESTRIANISM, 1988

Badminton Horse Trials:
1. I. Stark—Sir Wattie (G.B.).
2. I. Stark—Glenburrie (G.B.).
3. Mrs. V. Leng—Master Craftsman (G.B.).

British Open Championship:
1. M. Todd—Charisma (N.Z.).
2. R. Lemieux—The Poser (G.B.).
3. I. Stark—Murphy Himself (G.B.).

Burghley Horse Trials:
1. Miss J. Thelwall—King's Jester (G.B.).
2. Miss M. Gurdon—Midnight March (G.B.).
3. Miss N. May—McDuff (G.B.).

Hickstead Derby.—N. Skelton (Apollo).

YACHTING, 1988

AMERICA'S CUP 1988
(San Diego, U.S.A.)

Final.—The defender *Stars and Stripes* (U.S.A.) beat the challenger *New Zealand* (N.Z.) by 2–0.

Transatlantic Yacht Race.—P. Poupon (France) *Fleury Michon. 1st woman.*—F. Arthaud (France) *Group Pierre.*

BOXING, 1987–88

A.B.A. CHAMPIONSHIPS (Winners)

Light-Fly (48 kg).—M. Cantwell; *Fly* (51 kg).—J. Lyon; *Bantam* (54 kg).—Sgt. K. Howlett; *Feather* (57 kg).—D. Anderson; *Light* (60 kg).—C. Kane; *Light-Welter* (63·5 kg).—A. Hall; *Welter* (67 kg).—M. McCreath; *Light-Middle* (71 kg).—W. Ellis; *Middle* (75 kg).—M. Edwards; *Light-Heavy* (81 kg).—H. Lawson; *Heavy* (91 kg).—H. Akinwande; *Super-Heavy* (91+ kg).—K. McCormack.

PROFESSIONAL BOXING

WORLD (W.B.C.) CHAMPIONS

Heavy.—M. Tyson (U.S.A.); *Cruiser.*—E. Holyfield (U.S.A.); *Light-Heavy.*—D. Lalonde (Canada); *Middle.*—I. Barclay (U.S.A.); *Light-Middle.*—G. Rosi (Italy); *Welter.*—L. Honeyghan (G.B.); *Light-Welter.*—R. Mayweather (U.S.A.); *Light.*—J.-L. Ramirez (Mexico); *Super-Feather.*—R. Dickie (G.B.); *Feather.*—J. Fenech (Australia); *Super-Bantam.*—D. Zaragoza (Mexico); *Bantam.*—M. Lora (Colombia); *Super-Fly.*—G. Roman (Mexico); *Fly.*—S. Chitilada (Thailand); *Light-Fly.*—J. Chang (Korea); *Straw.*—H. Ioka (Japan).

WORLD (W.B.A.) CHAMPIONS

Heavy.—M. Tyson (U.S.A.); *Cruiser.*—E. Holyfield (U.S.A.); *Light-Heavy.*—V. Hill (U.S.A.); *Super-Middle.*—Chong Pal Park (Korea); *Middle.*—S. Kalambay (Zaire); *Light-Middle.*—J. Jackson (Virgin Is.); *Welter.*—M. Starling (U.S.A.); *Light-Welter.*—J. Coggi (Argentina); *Light.*—J.-C. Chavez (Mexico); *Super-Feather.*—B. Mitchell (S. Africa); *Feather.*—A. Esparagoza (Venezuela); *Super-Bantam.*—D. Pinango (Venezuela); *Bantam.*—W. Vasquez (Puerto Rico); *Super-Fly.*—K. Galexi (Thailand); *Fly.*—F. Bassa (Colombia); *Light-Fly.*—M. W. Yuh (Korea); *Mini-Fly.*—R. Gamez (Venezuela).

INTERNATIONAL BOXING FEDERATION (I.B.F.) CHAMPIONS

Heavy.—M. Tyson (U.S.A.); *Cruiser.*—E. Holyfield (U.S.A.); *Light-Heavy.*—C. Williams (Nigeria); *Super-Middle.*—G. Rocchigiani (W. Germany); *Middle.*—F. Tate (U.S.A.); *Light-Middle.*—M. Hilton (Canada); *Welter.*—S. Brown (U.S.A.); *Light-Welter.*—B. McGirt (U.S.A.); *Light.*—G. Haugen (U.S.A.); *Super-Feather.*—R. Lockridge (U.S.A.); *Feather.*—C. Grove (U.S.A.); *Super-Bantam.*—(vacant); *Bantam.*—K. Seabrook (U.S.A.); *Super-Fly.*—E. Pical (Indonesia); *Fly.*—R. Bohol (Philippines); *Light-Fly.*—J. Choi (Korea); *Mini-Fly.*—S. Sithnarvepol (Thailand).

BRITISH CHAMPIONS

Heavy.—H. Notice; *Cruiser.*—G. McCrory; *Light-Heavy.*—T. Collins; *Middle.*—H. Graham; *Light-Middle.*—G. Cooper; *Welter.*—K. Laing; *Light-Welter.*—L. Christie; *Light.*—S. Boyle; *Super-Feather.*—F. Havard; *Feather.*—P. Hodkinson; *Bantam.*—B. Hardy; *Fly.*—P. Clinton.

COMMONWEALTH CHAMPIONS

Heavy.—H. Notice (G.B.); *Cruiser.*—G. McCrory (G.B.); *Light-Heavy.*—W. Featherstone (Canada); *Middle.*—N. Benn (G.B.); *Light-Middle.*—T. Waters (Australia); *Welter.*—G. Jacobs (G.B.); *Light-Welter.*—L. Ellis (Australia); *Light.*—M. Hussein (G.B.); *Super-Feather.*—J. Sichula (Zambia); *Feather.*—T. Downes (Trinidad); *Bantam.*—R. Minus (Bahamas); *Fly.*—N. Y. Konadu (Ghana).

EUROPEAN CHAMPIONS

Heavy.—F. Damiani (Italy); *Cruiser.*—S. Reeson (G.B.); *Light-Heavy.*—T. Collins (G.B.); *Middle.*—C.

Tiozzo (France); *Light-Middle.*—(vacant); *Welter.*—M. Martelli (Switzerland); *Light-Welter.*—T. N'Kalankete (France); *Light.*—R. Weller (W. Germany); *Super-Feather.*—P. Morelli (Italy); *Feather.*—J.-M. Renard (Belgium); *Bantam.*—L. Gomis (France); *Fly.*—D. McKenzie (G.B.).

MOTOR CYCLING, 1988

Senior Manx Grand Prix.—J. Dunlop (Honda).
Senior T.T., Isle of Man.—J. Dunlop (Honda).
Junior T.T., Isle of Man.—J. Dunlop (Honda).
British 500 c.c. Grand Prix (*Donington*).—W. Rainey (U.S.A.) (Yamaha).

MOTOR SPORT, 1988

FORMULA ONE MOTOR RACING

Grand Prix 1987:
Mexican (Mexico City)—1. N. Mansell (Williams); 2. N. Piquet (Williams); 3. R. Patrese (Brabham).
Japanese (Suzuka)—1. G. Berger (Ferrari); 2. A. Senna (Lotus); 3. S. Johansson (McLaren).
Australian (Adelaide)—1. G. Berger (Ferrari); 2. M. Alboreto (Ferrari); 3. T. Boutsen (Benetton).
FORMULA ONE CHAMPION, 1987.—N. Piquet (Williams) 73 pts.
Grand Prix 1988:
Brazilian (Rio)—1. A. Prost (McLaren); 2. G. Berger (Ferrari); 3. N. Piquet (Lotus).
San Marino (Imola)—1. A. Senna (McLaren); 2. A. Prost (McLaren); 3. N. Piquet (Lotus).
Monaco—1. A. Prost (McLaren); 2. G. Berger (Ferrari); 3. M. Alboreto (Ferrari).
Mexican (Rodriguez Circuit)—1. A. Prost (McLaren); 2. A. Senna (McLaren); 3. G. Berger (Ferrari).
Canadian (Montreal)—1. A. Senna (McLaren); 2. A. Prost (McLaren); 3. T. Boutsen (Benetton).
United States (Detroit)—1. A. Senna (McLaren); 2. A. Prost (McLaren); 3. T. Boutsen (Benetton).
French (Le Castellet)—1. A. Prost (McLaren); 2. A. Senna (McLaren); 3. M. Alboreto (Ferrari).
British (Silverstone)—1. A. Senna (McLaren); 2. N. Mansell (Williams); 3. A. Nannini (Benetton).
West German (Hockenheim)—1. A. Senna (McLaren); 2. A. Prost (McLaren); 3. G. Berger (Ferrari).
Hungarian (Budapest)—1. A. Senna (McLaren); 2. A. Prost (McLaren); 3. T. Boutsen (Benetton).
Belgian (Spa)—1. A. Senna (McLaren); 2. A. Prost (McLaren); 3. T. Boutsen (Benetton).
Italian (Monza)—1. G. Berger (Ferrari); 2. M. Alboreto (Ferrari); 3. E. Cheever (Arrows).
Portuguese (Estoril)—1. A. Prost (McLaren); 2. I. Capelli (March); 3. T. Boutsen (Benetton).
Spanish (Jerez)—1. A. Prost (McLaren); 2. N. Mansell (Williams); 3. A. Nannini (Benetton).

OTHER EVENTS

Birmingham Super-Prix.—R. Moreno (Reynolds).
Le Mans (*24-hour*).—A. Wallace, Lord Dumfries and J. Lammers (Jaguar XJR-9).
Lombard R.A.C. Rally, 1987.—J. Kankkunen (Lancia Delta).
Paris/Dakar Trans-Sahara Rally.—J. Kankkunen (Peugeot).
Safari Rally.—M. Biasion (Lancia Delta).
Circuit of Ireland Rally.—J. McRae (Sierra Cosworth).
Indianapolis 500.—R. Mears.

SPORTS REPRESENTATIVE BODIES

ANGLING.—National Anglers' Council, 11 Cowgate, Peterborough PE1 1LZ. *Exec. Dir.*, P. H. Tombleson, O.B.E.

ASSOCIATION FOOTBALL.—The Football Association. *Sec.*, E. A. Croker, 16 Lancaster Gate, W2 3LW.

ATHLETICS.—Amateur Athletic Association. *Gen. Sec.*, M. A. Farrell, Francis House, Francis Street, SW1P 1DL.

—Women's Amateur Athletic Association, Francis House, Francis Street, SW1P 1DE. *Hon. Sec.*, Miss M. Hartman, C.B.E.

BADMINTON.—Badminton Association of England, National Badminton Centre, Loughton Lodge, Bradwell Road, Milton Keynes MK8 9LA. *Chief Exec.*, Air Vice-Marshal G. C. Lamb, C.B., C.B.E., A.F.C.

BASKET BALL.—English Basket Ball Association. Calomax House, Lupton Avenue, Leeds LS9 6EE. *Sec.*, M. D. Welch.

BILLIARDS.—Billiards and Snooker Control Council. *Chair.*, S. Brooke, Coronet House, Queen Street, Leeds LS1 2TN.

BOBSLEIGH.—British Bobsleigh Association. *Sec.*, Mrs. B. Powe, 50 Sulivan Road, SW6 3DX.

BOWLS.—English Bowling Association, Lyndhurst Rd., Worthing, W. Sussex BN11 2AZ. *Sec.*, D. W. Johnson.

BOXING.—Amateur Boxing Association of England, Francis House, Francis Street, SW1P 1DE.—*Exec. Dir.*, C. J. Howe.

— British Boxing Board of Control, 70 Vauxhall Bridge Road, SW1V 2RP.—*Gen. Sec.*, J. Morris.

CANOEING.—British Canoe Union, Flexel House, 45–47 High Street, Addlestone, Weybridge, Surrey KT15 1TU.—*Dir.*, T. J. Bailey.

CRICKET.—M.C.C., Lords, NW8 8QN. *Pres.* Field Marshal Lord Bramall, G.C.B., O.B.E.; *Sec.*, Lt.-Col. J. R. Stephenson, O.B.E.

—T.C.C.B., Lord's, NW8 8QN. *Chairman* (1987–88), R. Subba Row; *Chief Exec.*, A. C. Smith.

—Cricket Council, Lord's, NW8 8QN. *Chairman*, R. Subba Row; *Sec.*, A. C. Smith.

CROQUET.—Croquet Association, c/o The Hurlingham Club, Ranelagh Gardens, SW6 3PR. *Sec.*, B. C. Macmillan.

CYCLING.—British Cycling Federation, 36 Rockingham Road, Kettering, Northants. NN16 8HG. *Sec.*, L. A. Unwin.

ETON FIVES.—Eton Fives Association.—*Hon. Sec.*, R. M. Knight, Saintbury Close, Saintbury, nr. Broadway, Worcs. WR12 7PX.

FENCING.—Amateur Fencing Association, 83 Perham Road, W. Kensington, W14 9SP. *Sec.*, Miss G. Kenneally.

GLIDING.—British Gliding Association, Kimberley House, Vaughan Way, Leicester LE1 4SE. *Sec.*, B. Rolfe.

GOLF.—Royal and Ancient Golf Club, St. Andrews, Fife KY16 9JD. *Sec.*, M. F. Bonallack, O.B.E.

— English Golf Union. 1–3 Upper King Street, Leicester LE1 6XF. *Sec.*, K. Wright.

— Ladies' Golf Union, The Scores, St. Andrews, Fife KY16 9AT.—*Gen. Administrator*, Mrs A. White.

GYMNASTICS.—British Amateur Gymnastics Association, 2 Buckingham Avenue East, Slough, Berks. SL1 3DZ. *Development Dir.*, A. L. Murdock.

HOCKEY.—Hockey Association, 16 Northdown Street, N1 9BG. *Chief Exec.*, S. P. Baines.

— All England Women's Hockey Association, 3rd Flr, Argyle House, 29–31 Euston Road, NW1 2SD. *Sec.*, Miss T. Morris.

JUDO.—British Judo Association, 16 Upper Woburn Place, WC1H 0QH. *Gen. Sec.*, Miss G. M. Kenneally.

LACROSSE.—English Lacrosse Union. *Hon. Sec.*, R. Balls, 70 High Road, Rayleigh, Essex SS6 7AD.

— All England Women's Lacrosse Association, Francis House, Francis Street, SW1P 1DE. *Chief Exec.*, Miss P. A. Barratt.

LAWN TENNIS.—Lawn Tennis Association, The Queen's Club, W. Kensington, W14 9EG. *Sec.*, J. C. U. James.

— International Tennis Federation, Palliser Rd., Barons Court, W14 9EN.

MOTOR CYCLING.—Auto-Cycle Union, Miller House, Corporation Street, Rugby, Warwicks. CV21 2DN. *Sec. Gen.*, D. G. Coleman.

NETBALL.—All England Netball Association Ltd., Francis House, Francis Street, SW1P 1DE. *Chief Exec.*, Mrs. E. Nicholl.

OLYMPICS.—British Olympic Association, 1 Wandsworth Plain, SW18 1EH. *Gen. Sec.*, R. Palmer.

ORIENTEERING.—British Orienteering Federation, "Riversdale", Dale Road North, Darley Dale, Matlock, Derbys. DE4 2HX. *Gen. Sec.*, R. Mason.

POLO.—The Hurlingham Polo Association, Ambersham Farm, Ambersham, Midhurst, W. Sussex GU29 0BX. *Hon. Sec.*, Lt.-Col. A. F. Harper, D.S.O.

RACING.—The Jockey Club (incorporating National Hunt Committee), 42 Portman Square, W1H 0EN *Sec.*, C. N. Foster.

RIFLE SHOOTING.—National Rifle Association. *Sec.*, Brig. P. G. A. Prescott, M.C., Bisley Camp, Brookwood, Woking, Surrey GU24 0PB.

—National Small-bore Rifle Association, Lord Roberts House, Bisley Camp, Brookwood, Woking GU24 0NP. *Sec.*, Gp. Capt. D. King, M.B.E.

ROWING.—Amateur Rowing Association, 6 Lower Mall, W6 9DJ. *Exec. Sec.*, I. W. Pratt.

RUGBY FIVES.—Rugby Fives Association. *Hon. Sec.*, P. J. Reeder, 12 Alexandra Cottages, Hardings Lane, SE20 7JJ.

RUGBY FOOTBALL.—The Rugby Football Union, Whitton Road, Twickenham, Middx. TW1 1DZ. *Sec.*, D. E. Wood.

— The Rugby Football League, 180 Chapeltown Road, Leeds LS7 4HT. *Sec. Gen.*, D. S. Oxley.

SKATING.—National Skating Association of Great Britain. *Gen. Administrator*, E. Waughray, 15–27 Gee Street, EC1V 2RU.

SKI-ING.—British Ski Federation. *Chairman*, T. Fitzpatrick, 118 Eaton Square, SW1W 9AF.

SQUASH RACKETS.—Squash Rackets Association. *Chief Executive*, R. I. Morris, Francis House, Francis Street, SW1P 1DE.

— Women's Squash Rackets Association. *Sec.*, Miss C. Myers, 345 Upper Richmond Road West, SW14 8QN.

SWIMMING.—Amateur Swimming Association, Harold Fern House, Derby Square, Loughborough, Leics. LE11 0AL. *Sec.*, D. A. Reeves.

TABLE TENNIS.—English Table Tennis Association, 21 Claremont, Hastings TN34 1HF. *Chief Exec.*, E. J. Wallbutton.

VOLLEYBALL.—English Volleyball Association, 13 Rectory Road, W. Bridgford, Nottingham NG2 6BE. *National Dir.*, G. Bulman.

WALKING.—Race Walking Association. *Gen. Sec.*, J. F. Keowm, 30 Maxwell Gardens, Orpington, Kent BR6 9QS.

WATER SKIING.—British Water Ski Federation, 390 City Road, EC1V 2QA. *Sec.*, Ms. G. Hill.

WEIGHTLIFTING.—British Amateur Weightlifters Association. *Hon. Sec.*, W. Holland, O.B.E., 3 Iffley Turn, Oxford OX4 4DU.

WRESTLING.—English Olympic Wrestling Association, 16 Choir Street, Cambridge Industrial Estate, Salford M7 9ZD; *Sec.*, H. I. Jacob, O.B.E.

YACHTING.—Royal Yachting Association, Victoria Way, Woking, Surrey GU21 1EQ. *Sec. Gen.*, R. Duchesne, O.B.E.

LITERATURE, 1987–88

Among the plethora of awards vying for coverage in the literary pages of newspapers, and despite the amounts of money on offer increasing faster than the rate of inflation, the Whitbread Prize is emerging as the winner among the book prizes. Long a second fiddle to the Booker, the revamped Whitbread risked losing all credibility with the new set-up adopted when it was relaunched a few years ago. The idea of the winners of five different categories (for best novel, first novel, poetry, biography and children's novel) competing with one another for an overall prize attracted criticism on the grounds that the judges would not be comparing like with like. However, the idea has captured public attention and increased the publicity for both the books and the prize itself.

With the previous overall winners, Douglas Dunn's *Elegies* and Kazuo Ishiguro's *An Artist of the Floating World*, coming from the poetry and novel categories, there was an air of inevitability about the latest winner being chosen from one of the other sections. The overall prize this year went to *Under the Eye of the Clock*, the life story of Christopher Nolan, the surprise winner of the biography prize which many had expected to go to Richard Ellman's *Oscar Wilde*.

Nolan's autobiography was a bold and imaginative choice by the Whitbread judges. One, Ben Pimlott, described the work by the 21-year-old Irish writer, who has been physically handicapped since birth, as "a moving and beautifully written account of the struggle for survival of a severely handicapped boy. We felt that, more than any other book, *Under the Eye of the Clock* made an important and original contribution to the writing of biography and autobiography." Competing for the £18,750 first prize (in addition to the £1,250 awarded to each category winner) against Ian McEwan for *The Child in Time*, Francis Wyndham's *The Other Garden*, Seamus Heaney's *The Haw Lantern* and Geraldine Mc-Caughrean's *A Little Lower than the Angels*, Christopher Nolan was a popular winner.

"Night for Laughing"

In his acceptance speech, read by his mother, Nolan said "Tonight crippled man is taking his place on the world literary stage. Tonight is my night for laughing, for crying tears of joy." He also made an eloquent plea for other handicapped people: "My brothers hobble after me hinting, 'What about silent us? Can we too have a voice?' Tonight I am speaking for them ... Can freedom now be denied to a handicapped man? Can yessing be so difficult that rather than give a baby a chance at life, man treads upon his brother and silences him before he can draw one breath of this world's fresh air?"

Nolan had given evidence of his exceptional talent at the age of 15 with a volume of poetry, *Dam-burst of Dreams*. John Carey, in a preface to the autobiography, wrote how Nolan "plummeted into language like an avalanche, as if it were his one escape route from death". Nolan himself, in the first chapter "A Modicum of Aloe", wrote of his *alter ego*: "poetry was his vehicle of expression and truth his hallmark. Best assessed messages lighted his writing, trying as

he was to solve the mystery surrounding spoilt manhood, birthed brain-damaged, but curiously, though seldom recognised, intellectually normal. Leaning on his family he cast down the gauntlet—accept me for what I am and I'll accept you for what you're accepted as. And so the battle was staged between a crippled, sane boy and a hostile, sane, secretly savage though sometimes merciful world."

Runners-Up

Ian McEwan was considered unfortunate not to have made the Booker shortlist also with *The Child in Time*, about a marriage broken up by grief at the loss of a child. For some its polemic against Thatcherite Britain in the near future, where beggars are licensed and children ruled with an iron rod under the aegis of the Government-produced "Authorized Childcare Handbook", detracted from the fine writing. Francis Wyndham's *The Other Garden*, winner of the first novel award, explores village life during the Second World War through the eyes of a young boy. It is a brief but beautifully constructed work, "almost flawlessly written" although some characters are overdrawn and tend towards caricature. Seamus Heaney's *The Haw Lantern* reveals "rare poetic intelligence". This new collection by the celebrated Northern Irish poet deals with the theme of loss, particularly the death of his mother, movingly described in a sonnet sequence. Geraldine Mc-Caughrean's *A Little Lower than the Angels* which won the children's novel category was an accomplished parable about Gabriel, an apprentice stonemason.

Lively Booker

The controversy surrounding the 1987 Booker Prize for Fiction (worth £15,000 to the winner) concerned changes to the judges' operation of the rules. Publishers in the past have submitted three of their lesser authors secure in the knowledge that the judges would always call in any notable absentees. However, this year the judges, under the chairmanship of crime writer P. D. James, restricted themselves to consideration of the 93 novels originally submitted, in accordance with the rules. No novels from the secondary list were called in, to the chagrin of many publishers, who pointed out that it is inequitable to allow those with only a limited fiction list to submit as many titles as publishing houses that specialize in fiction. Miss James commented: "The Booker is by tradition controversial, apart, of course, from the always controversial final choice."

Although no author has won the Booker twice, some have been shortlisted several times and this year's shortlist included the 1978 winner, Iris Murdoch. Her novel *The Book and the Brotherhood* concerns a group of Oxford graduates who support one of their number, Crimond, who "crammed with revolutionary virtue" has been working on "the book" for twenty years. Although never explained, the work in question is "a synthesis, it's immensely long, it's about everything", an apt description for Iris Murdoch's 600-page novel. Brian Moore's *The*

Colour of Blood is an intelligent and finely written thriller about Cardinal Stephen Bem, primate of a small Soviet bloc country who survives an assassination attempt. He puts aside his cardinal's robes (which give the novel its title) to try to find out who is trying to kill him. This "anti-terrorist" novel effectively conveys a sense of menace and Bem's awakening as he begins to see his people in a new light. Moore said the book was "about the impossibility of extreme situations, anywhere, and also about some of the things I think about Ireland . . . but find impossible to tackle directly".

Power and Illusions

Chinua Achebe's *Things Fall Apart* was widely acclaimed as a classic thirty years ago and his latest work, *Anthills of the Savannah*, was a worthy candidate on the Booker shortlist. Set in the backward West African state of Kangan, the novel is an accomplished political drama. It deals with the corrupting effect of power on a Sandhurst-trained army officer who becomes head of state after a military coup, and his relationships with two former schoolfriends, Chris Oriko, Commissioner for Information, and Ikem Osodie, editor of the *National Gazette*. Peter Ackroyd's *Hawksmoor* was omitted from the Booker shortlist a few years ago but nevertheless sold over 100,000 copies. His latest novel, *Chatterton*, was shortlisted this year but it is generally considered inferior to the previous work. Once again Ackroyd employs shifts of time, moving from the eighteenth to the nineteenth and twentieth centuries in his story about the child prodigy, Wordsworth's "marvellous boy", who committed suicide in 1776. Ackroyd is not interested in the past for its own sake but he is "interested in the way the present echoes the past". Thus, a contemporary, unsuccessful poet, Charles Wychwood, helped by an eccentric elderly novelist, Harriet Scrope, tries to discover the truth behind Chatterton's life and death. Ackroyd's theme is that "Thomas Chatterton believed he could explain the entire material and spiritual world in terms of imitation and forgery". Unfortunately, his characters become cyphers in the examination of what is real and what is false. Although clever use is made of Henry Wallis's famous painting of the death of Chatterton, for which the poet George Meredith posed, Ackroyd's immersion in the language of the past becomes tiresome, with pastiche substituted for original thought. *Circles of Deceit*, Nina Bawden's twentieth novel, also concerned imitation and art, in the story of a painter who copies old masters.

However, the winner of the Booker Prize for 1987 was *Moon Tiger* by Penelope Lively, shortlisted in 1977 for *The Road to Lichfield* and in 1984 for *According to Mark*. The successful novel was the story of Celia Hampton, an outspoken popular historian who considers writing a history of the world as she lies dying in hospital but instead tells her own life story. She remembers in particular her lost lover, a tank officer killed at El Alamein while she was stationed at Cairo; the title refers to a brand of mosquito repellent that burned in their bedroom at the Winter Palace at Luxor. The judges said: "This compact and beautifully controlled novel is an exciting story of war and action, which is also a modern love story, written without sentimentality: a splendid and moving achievement".

Nobel Prize

The 1987 Nobel Prize for Literature was awarded to the exiled Russian writer Joseph Brodsky. Born in Leningrad in 1940, he is a cult figure in the Soviet Union, but in 1964 was sentenced to five years' hard labour for "social parasitism" and for writing poetry without a licence. He was released after protests but in 1972 left his homeland unwillingly for Vienna, having been advised to depart by the police. The Swedish Academy praised Brodsky for the "great breadth in time and space" of his poetry. His work includes *A Part of Speech* (published in 1980), his second major collection containing poems written between 1965 and 1978, a collection of essays entitled *Less than One*, and his latest volume of poetry, *To Urania*.

Prizes New and Old

The new N.C.R. Award for Non-Fiction, worth £25,000 to the winner with runners-up awards of £1,000, was created to reward "originality of thought, elegance of expression, and the ability of the author to express his or her knowledge of the subject to the widest possible readership". Sadly, the winner of this colossal sum, David Thomson, died three months before his *Nairn in Darkness and Light* was chosen as the winner. The book describes his childhood in a small town on the Moray Firth in the 1920s. The chairman of the judges, Jeremy Isaacs, praised "the originality of its form, the elegance of its expression, its revelation of a character developing". The book also won the £5,000 McVitie's Prize for Scottish writer of the year. The shortlisted books for the N.C.R. Award, out of a total of 195 considered by the judges, were *Katherine Mansfield: A Secret Life* by Claire Tomalin, *The Korean War* by Max Hastings, *The Life of Kenneth Tynan* by Kathleen Tynan, *The Russian Album* by Michael Ignatieff and *Thy Hand, Great Anarch!* by Nirad C. Chaudhuri.

The W. H. Smith Literary Award, which has increased in value from £4,000 to £10,000, was awarded to Robert Hughes for his account of "the most successful form of penal rehabilitation that had ever been tried in English, American or European history', the transportation of some 140,000 convicts to Australia. *The Fatal Shore* was the thirtieth winner of a senior literary prize which has long rewarded excellence without the histrionics accompanying some of the more recent entrants to the prize-giving merry-go-round.

The new *Sunday Express* Book of the Year Award, for the "most stylish, literate and readable" work of fiction, is worth £20,000. The first winner was Brian Moore for *The Colour of Blood*, although reportedly one judge, Auberon Waugh, dissented. He preferred Mary Wesley's *Not That Sort of Girl*, finding the political message in Moore offensive, while Hammond Innes strongly objected to William Boyd's *The New Confessions*.

Without controversy, real or imagined, there would be little excitement in the mass of competing awards. Award-winning writers undoubtedly benefit from increased sales and the financial rewards must more than compensate for the paltry Public Lending Right handouts, but as indicators of literary merit awards must be treated with caution. Although several prizes have high publicity profiles, inconsistencies in the criteria of judgement and in the selection of judges means that none has achieved a status like that of the Prix Goncourt in France.

Young Writers

The Betty Trask Award for Romantic Fiction was shared by Alex Martin's as yet unpublished novel *The General Interruptor* and Candia McWilliam's *A Case of Knives*. The latter is a somewhat overwritten tale which hardly seems to qualify as a traditional novel although the author qualified on grounds of age. Both authors received £6,500, while runners-up awards of £2,000 each were made to Georgina Andrewes for *Behind the Waterfall*, James Friel for *Left of North*, Glenn Patterson for *Burning Your Own*, and Susan Webster for *Small Tales of a Town*.

Somerset Maugham Travel Awards, worth £4,000 each, were given to Jimmy Burns for *The Land that Lost its Heroes*, Carol Ann Duffy for *Selling Manhattan* and Matthew Kneale for *Whore Banquets*. The annual Cholmondeley Awards for Poetry (£2,000 each) went to John Heath-Stubbs, John Whitworth and Sean O'Brien, while the Eric Gregory Awards for writers under the age of 30 were awarded to Michael Symmons Roberts (£7,000), Gwyneth Lewis (£6,000), Adrian Blackledge (£5,000), Simon Armitage (£4,000) and Robert Crawford (£3,000). The first £10,000 Commonwealth Writers Prize was won by Olive Senior for *Summer Lightning*, the runner-up (£1,000) being Witi Ihimaera with *The Matriarch*.

The first Nelson Hurst and Marsh Biography Award, worth £2,000, went to Roland Huntford for *Shackleton*, and the £2,000 Constable Trophy for a Northern writer was given to Paul Sayer for *The Comfort of Madness*. The £1,000 David Higham Prize for a first work of fiction was won by Adam Zameenzad for *The Thirteenth House*, and the £500 John Llewellyn Rhys Memorial Prize went to Jeanette Winterson for *The Passion*. Derek Walcott was the first Commonwealth citizen to receive the Queen's Gold Medal for Poetry, for his recent collection *The Arkansas Testament*.

The Play's the Thing

Thomas Keneally, whose "faction" work *Schindler's Ark* stretched the Booker rules in 1982, drew on historical events again for his latest novel. *The Playmaker* concerns the first play ever to be performed in Australia, a production of Farquhar's *The Recruiting Officer* which was put on by a Royal Marine, Lt. Ralph Clark, on June 4, 1789 to honour the King's birthday. His cast are a motley collection of convicts at the penal settlement at Sydney Cove and Keneally marks the bicentenary of Australia by examining the lives and relationships of its first settlers. Based in part on *The Journals and Letters of Lieutenant Ralph Clark*, *The Playmaker* is dedicated "to Arabanoo [an Aborigine] and his brethren, still dispossessed".

William Boyd's *The New Confessions* was inspired by Jean-Jacques Rousseau's *The Confessions* and follows the life of a twentieth century Rousseau, John James Todd, born in 1899 in Edinburgh. "My first act in entering this world was to kill my mother", writes Todd, who becomes a film-maker, dedicating his life to filming Rousseau's memoirs. Ironically, he achieves a surprise success with *The Confessions: Part 1*, which is critically acclaimed, but robbed of popular success when his silent film is overtaken by talking pictures. *The New Confessions* is "One man's life in the 20th century"; if overlong at 460 pages, it is an amusing and cleverly worked tale.

Old Hands

Doris Lessing's first novel since the much-acclaimed *The Good Terrorist* is *The Fifth Child*, a tale of unmitigated horror about a couple who retreat to a rural idyll only to have their life destroyed when their fifth child turns out to be a monster. J. G. Ballard sets *The Day of Creation* in the desolate terrain of Central Africa; it is the narrative of Dr Mallory, who dreams of bringing water to the region. Clare Nonhebel won the Betty Trask award with her first novel *Cold Showers*; her third book, *Incentives*, is a well-written analysis of corporate life and affairs, which cleverly penetrates surface stereotypes. Graham Swift examines the nature of reality, and the modern obsession with viewing events through the television or camera lens, in *Out of this World*. In her seventh novel Anita Brookner reverts to the successful formula from which she deviated in *Family and Friends*, and examines the life of a single heroine through her effect on those around her. However, the novel, *A Friend from England*, suggests that the formula is becoming a little bit dull. Dennis Potter's *Blackeyes* is a disturbing and witty novel. It concerns "the lovely Jessica", who entertains her disgusting old Uncle Maurice with tales of her licentious past; he turns her stories into a novel which becomes a bestseller and a "favourite for the Booker", so to gain her revenge she rewrites the story her own way.

Malcolm Bradbury has lampooned the literary fashion for structuralism in the universities in his latest novel; *Mensonge* is the story of Henri Mensonge, supposed author of *La Fornication comme acte culturel*, a book which Bradbury brilliantly describes. Were it not that he possesses a copy of this work, no-one would believe in the existence of Mensonge for they cannot track him down. "The ultimate case of Deconstructionist Integrity", *Mensonge* is a good literary joke at the expense of some of Bradbury's colleagues in university English departments.

Emma Tennant's *The House of Hospitalites* is the first in a series of novels covering the lives of four friends from the time of the Coronation to the present. The action of the first novel takes place mostly over one weekend which the narrator, Jenny Carter, spends at Lovegrove, the country home of a schoolfriend who is a member of one of England's leading families.

American authors

Saul Bellow, Nobel Laureate in 1976, examines in *More Die of Heartbreak* two men with brilliant minds whose lives are ruined by the misery of their own emotions. The novel tells the story of Benn, a botanist of Russian-Jewish extraction, who specializes in lichens but is inexpert in human relationships. He was born "with that increasingly rare capacity. He would actually fall in love", but, unfortunately, with unsuitable partners. Narrated by his nephew Kenneth, the book consists mainly of conversations between the two characters. The title comes from Benn's assertion that "more die of heartbreak than radiation".

Gore Vidal's new novel, *Empire*, opens with the ending of the Spanish-American war at the end of the nineteenth century, and traces the beginning of the American empire. Through the lives of William Randolph Hearst, Henry Adams and Presidents William McKinley and Theodore Roosevelt, Vidal shows the development of modern America, paralleled by the decline of Britain as a world power. The novel ends with Roosevelt installed as President, a creature of the press mogul Hearst, "the true inventor of the modern world", who uses his newspapers to create a false reality to entertain or persuade the masses. Vidal also published *Armageddon?*, a collection of essays written from 1983 to 1987.

Kurt Vonnegut's *Bluebeard* is the hoax autobiography of Rabo Karabekian, a famous modern artist who is disgraced when the acrylic "Sateen Dura-Luxe" paint he used to create his expensive abstract paintings falls off the canvas. His life is transformed when an inquisitive widow, Circe Berman, moves into his house and provokes him into revealing his secrets. The pioneer of "new journalism", Tom Wolfe, made a brilliant debut as a novelist with *The Bonfire of the Vanities*. The story of Sherman McCoy, a top bond salesman with a Wall Street firm whose world collapses when he kills a black youth in the Bronx after taking a wrong turning in his car, the novel is an American *Crime and Punishment*. Wolfe sustains the story brilliantly throughout the 670 pages of the book, which is dominated by the "character" of the city of New York and the everyday tensions and obsession with money and status of its inhabitants.

Garrison Keillor, author of *Lake Wobegon Days*, is a born storyteller. In *Leaving Home: a Collection of Lake Wobegon Stories*, he returns to the Lutheran enclave in Minnesota which he created, where the life of the people revolves around the lake, the church and the land. Their trials and tribulations, such as the tomato frost of '68 or the virus which strikes the piglets, are whimsical and amusing without ever descending into pure sentiment.

Glasnost

The Arbat was the traditional heart of Moscow and was destroyed by Stalin. Anatoli Rybakov's novel *Children of the Arbat*, is a graphic account of the Great Terror. After being banned for twenty years, the spirit of *glasnost* has brought about the book's publication in the Soviet Union, where it has reportedly sold 1·5 million copies. The author has said that "this book is about power. Stalin was consciously aware of the uses of power, the abuses of power, how to get power and how to keep power." Like Gorbachev, Rybakov knows that until the Russians "eliminate the consequences of Stalinism

from the psychology of our people we cannot move further forward". Hence the publication of this novel, with the arts being used as a weapon in *perestroika*.

Lives and times

A. N. Wilson's *Tolstoy* is an excellent biography of the complex Russian genuis. Taking the view that "the most interesting thing about Tolstoy is his literary genuis" Wilson illuminates Tolstoy's works by revealing the man behind them. He is also perceptive on the character of the aristocrat who lived by extremes, on the one hand an inveterate gambler and womaniser, and on the other a soldier and social reformer who foresaw the revolution through the condition of the slums of Moscow. Tolstoy's funeral shows the effect that he had on the Russian people: as Wilson writes, it was "one of the most extraordinary demonstrations of public sympathy in the history of the world. No novelist has ever been given such a funeral, but it was not for his novels that they honoured him. It was for the deeds which now seem to us half mad and quixotic; it was for those volumes of his work which most readers now leave unread."

Ronald Clark's *Lenin: The Man behind the Mask* concentrates on the "charismatic personality, one of the most important keys to his success", and is full of interesting details, such as Lenin turning off the lights in the Kremlin because "Communism is Soviet power plus electrification". Alan Brien, who has studied Lenin for many years, spent a year in the Soviet Union researching *Lenin*, his novelized account of the Soviet leader's secret diaries.

Martin Gilbert has reached the end of the road with the eighth and final volume of the official biography of the last great British statesman. *Never Despair—Winston Churchill 1945-65* takes Churchill's story from the aftermath of victory, through the traumatic 1945 election defeat, the post-war premiership, illness and retirement to his death. The book shows Churchill's determination to make the West aware of the Soviet threat (he was the originator of the phrase "iron curtain"), although this was an unpopular stance to take at the time, and how he also wished to see the unification of Europe. The volume completes almost twenty years of work by Gilbert, who started as research assistant on the first two volumes, written by Randolph Churchill, and took over the work after Randolph's death.

Playwrights and Poets

Richard Ellman's *Oscar Wilde* is a meticulously researched and sensitive account of the man "who stood in symbolic relation to the art and culture of my age", as Wilde wrote in *De Profundis*. Sadly, Ellman, already respected for his studies of Yeats and Joyce, died after completing this work but it stands as a fine memorial to a distinguished American scholar. He is particularly illuminating on Wilde's life after his fall from grace when, snubbed and condemned to penury, he lived alone in Paris as Sebastian Melmoth. Ellman's conclusion on Wilde is that: "He belongs to our world more than to the Victorians. Now, beyond the reach of scandal, his best writings validated by time, he comes before us, a towering figure, laughing and weeping, with parables and paradoxes, so generous, so amusing, and so right."

Linda Wagner-Martin in her biography of Sylvia Plath relates the short, tragic life of the American poet. An obsessive perfectionist, Plath's life was dominated by the death of her father when she was eight years old and the book reveals that nothing ever filled the resulting void she felt. She first attempted suicide when aged 20 and was subsequently subjected to horrific electric shock treatment; she finally ended her life ten years later.

In *A Serious Character: The Life of Ezra Pound*, Humphrey Carpenter, biographer of Tolkien and Auden, has written a brilliant exposé of the literary titan who, in the words of William Carlos Williams, "hated humanity". Carpenter reveals how the man who influenced such brilliant figures as T. S. Eliot, Hemingway and Joyce was nevertheless a charlatan, an "agile and slippery character", riddled with anti-semitism. His trial for treason in 1946, at which the jury found him of unsound mind, led to his imprisonment for twelve years. After his release Pound lived out his days in Italy, an influential figure but such a flawed and misguided individual that Carpenter succeeds in demolishing any sympathy he might once have provoked.

First reports

In *The Faber Book of Reportage*, John Carey has collected eye-witness accounts of major historical events, from the account by Thucydides of the plague in Athens to James Fenton's description of the presidential palace in Manila after the downfall of the Marcos regime. His choice is primarily concerned "with the qualities of writing and observation displayed". Notable accounts include Dickens's description of a public execution in Rome in 1845, with many evocative images, such as Mary Queen of Scots' lap dog remaining with her when she was beheaded.

Children of the Siege is Dr. Pauline Cutting's moving account of her time in the Palestinian refugee camps of Beirut. Although the inmates suffered privation and the horrors of torture, shootings and murders daily, the resilience of the human spirit shines through the author's modestly described but nonetheless heroic achievements.

The fruit of 15 years' research, Susan Maclean Kybett's *Bonnie Prince Charlie* shows the romantic hero of the Jacobite Rebellion of 1745 to have been an unscrupulous adventurer of limited intelligence, concerned with his own future rather than the welfare of his potential subjects. The author had access to the Stuart archives in the Queen's private collection in producing a portrait that upsets popular conceptions. In *Young Betjeman*, Bevis Hillier examines the early life of the popular English poet, from his birth to marriage; for an essentially minor literary figure, the book is overlong, and indiscriminate in its obsessive relating of Betjeman trivia.

Spycatcher

The *cause célèbre* of the year in the book world was Peter Wright's *Spycatcher*, a poorly written and somewhat paranoid work by a former member of the security services. It achieved bestseller status in countries where it could be published, such as Australia and the U.S.A., because of the British Government's unsuccessful attempts to prevent its publication. Ironically, without the massive publicity generated by the Government's attempt to ban it, the book would probably have sunk into well-deserved oblivion.

Shakespeare was once again in the news, following claims by Professor Peter Levi that he had discovered 62 lines of verse written by Shakespeare but not previously attributed to him. The manuscript, pasted into a masque written by John Marston in 1607, was uncovered in the Huntington Library in California. The attribution to Shakespeare was treated with widespread scepticism by other scholars.

A literary curiosity was the publication of Stephen Spender's *The Temple*, written in 1929 when he was in his twenties. At the time it was considered both too libellous and too obscene for publication. Spender apparently sold the manuscript to Texas University in 1962, and was reminded of its existence in 1986 by John Fuller. Spender obtained a copy, and then rewrote the work. Although much of the material is familiar from Spender's autobiography *World within World*, the work is of interest, especially for its thinly disguised portraits of Auden and Isherwood.

Shaw Record

The craft of biography received a surprising boost with the news that Chatto had paid £625,000 for Michael Holroyd's as yet unfinished authorized life of George Bernard Shaw. The previous record was reported to have been the £90,000 paid for Ellman's *Oscar Wilde*. Chatto was not in fact the highest bidder for the work but was reported to have offered the author the best deal. Holroyd began the work some fifteen years ago, and it will take him another fifteen years to complete it. When finished it should comprise three volumes of biography, two of commentary and an academic source work.

Other books of note published during the year included: *The Clothes in the Wardrobe* by Alice Thomas Ellis; *The Hearts and Lives of Men* by Fay Weldon; *Oscar and Lucinda* by Peter Carey; *S* by John Updike; *Tell It Me Again* by John Fuller; *Love in the Time of Cholera* by Gabrial Garcia Marquez; *Where the Rivers Meet* by John Wain; *Olivier* by Anthony Holden; *A. E. Housman: Collected Poems and Selected Prose* edited by Christopher Ricks; *Elizabeth Barrett Browning* by Margaret Forster; *The Life of Kenneth Tynan* by Kathleen Tynan; *Penfriends from Porlock* by A. N. Wilson; *Recovery* by Stanley Middleton.

Public Lending Right

The total sum available for distribution to authors registered under the Public Lending Right scheme remained at £2.75 million in 1987, although an increase to £3·5 million has been announced for 1988. The amount per loan was 1·12p, down from 1·2p in 1986–87. The maximum payment of £5,000 went to 57 authors, 123 received between £2,501 and £5,000, 345 between £1,001 and £2,500 and 8,624 between £1 and

£99; 2,375 of the 14,635 writers registered received no payment. The list of the 100 most borrowed books at the 21 sampling libraries was headed by Catherine Cookson with 26 titles, plus two written under a pseudonym. She was followed by Dick Francis with twelve titles, Wilbur Smith with ten, Danielle Steel with seven, and Jeffrey Archer and Jack Higgins with six each.

Although authors welcome the acknowledgement that they should receive payments for library loans, criticism of the scheme has mounted. The intrinsic flaws are that those who earn the maximum payments tend least to need them. Public Lending Right favours the quickly-read potboiler, which has a rapid turn-over on library shelves, unlike the *magnum opus* over which the author has laboured long and which demands leisured reading or study. It was pointed out that the whole system of free library loans looks

increasingly anachronistic, when the public are apparently quite happy to pay between £1 and £2 a night to borrow a video tape. The Society of Authors, the Writers' Guild and the Crime Writers Association campaigned for an increase in the basic payment, saying that the figure of just over 1p per loan "looks startlingly ridiculous" compared with the royalties forgone by just one lost sale—about £1 for a hardback novel. As A. S. Byatt, chairman of the Society of Authors, said: "It is important to recognize that P.L.R. is not a state subsidy or welfare payment but a statutory right. It is a payment for services provided by authors whose books are extensively borrowed from libraries and is not susceptible to sponsorship or other 'incentive funding'." In August 1988, the Minister for the Arts, Mr. Richard Luce, proposed increasing the ceiling for payments under Public Lending Right from £5,000 to £6,000.

BOOKER PRIZEWINNERS

1969   *Something to Answer For*—P. H. Newby (Faber).
1970   *The Elected Member*—Bernice Rubens (Eyre & Spottiswoode).
1971   *In A Free State*—V. S. Naipaul (Andre Deutsch).
1972   *G*—John Berger (Weidenfeld).
1973   *The Siege of Krishnapur*—J. G. Farrell (Weidenfeld).
1974   *The Conservationist*—Nadine Gordimer (Cape).
       Holiday—Stanley Middleton (Hutchinson).
1975   *Heat and Dust*—Ruth Prawer Jhabvala (Murray).
1976   *Saville*—David Storey (Cape).
1977   *Staying On*—Paul Scott (Heinemann).
1978   *The Sea, The Sea*—Iris Murdoch (Chatto & Windus).
1979   *Offshore*—Penelope Fitzgerald (Collins).
1980   *Rites of Passage*—William Golding (Faber).
1981   *Midnight's Children*—Salman Rushdie (Cape).
1982   *Schindler's Ark*—Thomas Keneally (Hodder & Stoughton).
1983   *Life & Times of Michael K*—J. M. Coetzee (Secker & Warburg).
1984   *Hôtel du Lac*—Anita Brookner (Cape).
1985   *The Bone People*—Keri Hulme (Hodder & Stoughton).
1986   *The Old Devils*—Kingsley Amis (Hutchinson).
1987   *Moon Tiger*—Penelope Lively (Deutsch).

The finalists for the 1988 prize are:
The Beginning of Spring—Penelope Fitzgerald (Collins), *The Lost Father*—Marina Warner (Chatto), *Nice Work*—David Lodge (Secker & Warburg), *Oscar and Lucinda*—Peter Carey (Faber), *The Satanic Verses*—Salman Rushdie (Viking), *Utz*—Bruce Chatwin (Cape).

DRAMA 1987–88

An era ended at the National Theatre in the summer of 1988 when Sir Peter Hall bowed out as director. However, despite Hall's success in establishing the three-stage complex as a major artistic force in Britain financial worries continue to dog the National. The Government announced in December 1987 a 17 per cent increase in funding for the arts spread over three years, with a 10 per cent rise in 1988. According to the Minister for the Arts, Richard Luce, this is intended to create "a positive atmosphere in which we can move forward" but the Arts Council granted the National Theatre an increase of only 1·35 per cent. Sir Peter called the Arts Council "astonishingly ungracious" to his successors, and said the National Theatre was "being penalized for doing well".

For his finale, which he termed "a call to arms" rather than an elegy, Sir Peter directed three late Shakespeare plays, *The Tempest, Cymbeline* and *The Winter's Tale*. This was an immense undertaking which not surprisingly met with difficulties. Not the least of these was having to rehearse the three plays simultaneously on the National's smallest stage, the Cottesloe, with one set. There were also casting problems; Sarah Miles, considered a surprising choice as Imogen in *Cymbeline*, left the production one month before the opening, and another actor, Robert Eddison, was dropped from all three plays. However, the delays and difficulties were overcome and the productions received widespread acclaim—a fitting end to a distinguished theatrical reign.

Sir Peter was succeeded as director by his preferred heir, Richard Eyre. Eyre will run the theatre as a duopoly with David Aukin, who has assumed the role of executive director. Eyre announced that the National would operate as one company with five directors, ending Hall's system of 24 resident and part-time directors. He also intends the company to tour for 16 weeks a year, visiting regional outposts, and they will seek to raise £3 million a year in commercial sponsorship.

The Royal Shakespeare Company also faced a difficult period financially and artistically. At the beginning of 1988 artistic director Terry Hands said that the company was facing a "difficult summer", with the decline of the dollar against the pound affecting the number of foreign visitors to Stratford. With 24 per cent of its audience made up of foreign visitors, 17·5 per cent of them from the U.S.A., the R.S.C. feared a repeat of the disastrous summer of 1986, when Americans stayed at home for fear of reprisals in Europe after the bombing of Libya. Despite sponsorship of £1·1 million over three years from Royal Insurance, the number of new productions dropped from 25 in 1987 to 18 in 1988. Excluding the commercial sector, the R.S.C. planned to put on a total of 37 productions in all its venues and the link-up with the Mermaid Theatre in London, since March 1987 a base for transfers from the Swan, also ended. At Stratford, the company was reorganized into two groups of 40 actors, moving between the three theatres, with Adrian Noble in charge of the Stratford season, while Bill Alexander supervised the London productions.

Playing with fire

In February the R.S.C. undertook what at the time seemed a misguided venture into overtly commercial theatre, and in retrospect was a complete disaster. A musical adaptation of Stephen King's novel *Carrie* (already made into a successful film by Brian de Palma) was staged at Stratford for a four-week run prior to a transfer to Broadway. Set in Hicksville, Maine, this story of an adolescent girl with telekinetic powers seemed an unlikely choice for a musical. Terry Hands said the story had parallels with Greek tragedy, and he considered King a "great writer—in the Steinbeck tradition". Be that as it may, few would consider turning *The Grapes of Wrath* into a musical.

The cast was half British, half American, following an agreement between the British and American Equity unions. Hundreds of actresses were auditioned for the title role and an unknown, Linzi Hateley, was chosen to star, the R.S.C.'s youngest ever leading lady. Debbie Allen, well known from the film and television series *Fame* was brought in to choreograph the production, which was to have been "the first serious music drama since *West Side Story*", according to Hands.

The production was reputed to have cost the R.S.C. £350,000 of the total production cost of over £3 million. However, the R.S.C. was reportedly guaranteed £550,000 from the 25 performances at Stratford and no doubt hoped for a substantial profit from a successful Broadway run. The venture was underwritten by German impresario Friedrich Kurz.

At Stratford the critical reception was hostile. Barbara Cook, who played Carrie's mother, was dropped before the transfer after differences with Hands. The show was rewritten and its Broadway opening delayed in an attempt to save it but the New York theatre critics were unforgiving. One critic commented that the show "could become a new reference point for Broadway atrocities". Hands claimed it could have succeeded on Broadway if Kurz had had the money to see the show through, but despite standing ovations during its five-night run, *Carrie* failed to survive the critical battering. Curiously, Hands said the Broadway version was a "totally different show from the one at Stratford". Such radical rewriting suggests desperation, but the main question was what a subsidized company was doing involving itself in such a misconceived venture, totally unconnected with its *raison d'être*.

Follies and Fortune

Problems were faced in London by Harold Fielding's £3·5 million production of *Ziegfeld* at the Palladium, a musical about the famous American showman. The star, Len Cariou, resigned from the title role and Fielding brought in Tommy Steele as director to "doctor" the production. Steele replaced Joe Layton, who had conceived the musical, and Cariou's understudy Marc Urquhart took over the lead. It was said that Cariou was too serious for the role, which needed to be played "very light and frivolous". In July, the actor Topol was brought in as lead, with Wendy Toye as director, but in August it was announced that *Ziegfeld* would close. The most expensive production in London, it needed to run for at least a year to recover its costs. Ironically, *Ziegfeld* was by no means a bad musical. Reviews were mixed but not hostile, the chorus line was superb, and the score and songs were well above average. However, like *Sweeney Todd* before it, *Ziegfeld* lacked a vital ingredient to make it a success and unfortunately, no-one knew what this was.

More predictably, *Winnie* failed dismally. A musical about Sir Winston Churchill, it was only partially redeemed by Robert Hardy's by now familiar impersonation of the great man. A late night revue at the Fortune Theatre called *After the Show* was cancelled by the management after the first dress rehearsal, for being "not good enough". However, a revival of *South Pacific* at the Fortune was a deserved success with a strong cast led by Gemma Craven as Ensign Nelly Forbush, Emile Belcourt, and Bertice Reading as Bloody Mary.

Dramatic Returns

The Playhouse Theatre reopened after a £2 million renovation. This 800-seat theatre closed in 1951, and spent 35 years as a B.B.C. theatre. The opening production, *Girlfriends*, was not a success, however: in April 1988 author, and now playwright, Jeffrey Archer bought a controlling interest. Archer's first play, *Beyond Reasonable Doubt*, was a dated, unoriginal courtroom melodrama with a creaking and predictable plot. After being slated in its out-of-town try-outs and given a critical thumbs-down in the West End, it settled in at the Queens Theatre for a lengthy run. Whether Mr. Archer's well-publicized libel action against a daily newspaper had helped or not, the play, like his novels, showed that there is no accounting for public taste. Indeed, the dire comedy *No Sex Please, We're British* had only just closed after a 16-year run.

The Royalty Theatre also returned to staging drama after serving first as a cinema, and then as a home for Thames Television shows such as *This Is Your Life*. Under administrative director Martin Tickner, the theatre's avowed policy is to present late Victorian and 20th century revivals for six-week runs. It hopes thereby to attract well-known film and television actors to appear who would be reluctant to commit themselves to long runs. The first production, Oscar Wilde's *The Importance of Being Earnest*, was well received; directed by Donald Sinden, the cast featured Wendy Hiller, Clive Francis and Denis Lawson. This was followed by the first West End production since 1953 of Graham Greene's play *The Living Room*, which he had written soon after the novel *The End of the Affair*. The production was praised, although defects in this drama about adultery in middle age were only too apparent. Also at the Royalty, a fresh light was shed on Rattigan's double bill, *The Browning Version* and *Harlequinade*, by reversing the traditional order in which the two are played. The distinguished cast included Paul Eddington, Dorothy Tutin, Anna Quayle and Jack Watling.

Sir John Gielgud made a welcome return to the stage after an absence of nearly ten years in Hugh Whitemore's *The Best of Friends*. This related the story of the somewhat unlikely but most productive 25-year correspondence between George Bernard Shaw, Dame Laurentia McLachlan, Abbess of Stanbrook, and Sir Sydney Cockerell, director of the Fitzwilliam Museum. *The Best of Friends* was not so much a play as a dramatic dialogue based on the letters between the friends, in which Gielgud was joined in a brilliantly-acted three-hander by Rosemary Harris and Ray McAnally.

At the Old Vic, Jonathan Miller returned to the theatre for a season as artistic director. His first production was Racine's *Andromache*. Although it featured Janet Suzman and Penelope Wilton, the production was not wholly successful. The second play in the season was Reinhold Lenz's *The Tutor*, but unfortunately this was not the author's version but Brecht's adaption. It was followed by N. F. Simpson's surreal comedy *One Way Pendulum* and the season seemed to be heading for disaster as the audiences continued to stay away in droves. Fortunately for the theatre the next production, *Too Clever by Half* by Alexander Ostrovsky, proved a triumph, with richly comic characters and a dazzling performance by Alex Jennings.

Renaissance

Kenneth Branagh's Renaissance Theatre Company, which achieved critical and popular acclaim with its first season, enhanced its reputation with a three-month Shakespeare season at the Birmingham Repertory Theatre. The company took the bold step of letting experienced actors direct the plays, Judi Dench starting with *Much Ado About Nothing*, followed by Geraldine McEwan with *As You Like It* and Derek Jacobi with *Hamlet*.

In March agreement was reached between the Turnstyle Group, the Jujamcyn Group of New York, which owns five Broadway theatres, and Pace Theatrical, owners of many American theatres. The agreement will allow hit shows to cross the Atlantic. The group is headed by Michael Attenborough, formerly artistic director of the Hampstead Theatre, with the actor Simon Callow and Simon Stokes, formerly of the Bush Theatre, as artistic associates. A £200,000 fund was set up to encourage writers and directors to develop new ideas. A levy on productions is to be used to boost the fund.

Tom Stoppard's first new play since *The Real Thing* five years ago opened at the Aldwych. A convoluted spy thriller, *Hapgood* was much less accessible than recent Stoppard works. Eugene O'Neill's *A Touch of the Poet* received its first ever London production at the Young Vic. Featuring Vanessa Redgrave and Timothy Dalton, this much-praised production subsequently transferred to the Comedy.

In April, Peter Brook's nine-hour epic. *The Mahabharata*, featuring a multi-national company, was produced in the old Museum of Transport in Glasgow. Based on a 100,000 stanza Sanskrit poem, it had been nine years in preparation and nine months in rehearsal; unfortunately, the drama proved flat and undramatic. At Birmingham Repertory Peter Nicholls' 1977 hit, *Privates on Parade*, reappeared in a revised less glamorous version. An early Ayckbourn,

How the Other Half Loves, was revived at Greenwich, and transferred to the West End.

Hits and Misses

At the National, Boucicault's 1874 play *The Shaughraun*—meaning wanderer—proved another worthy revival. William Dudley created a spectacular set for it, consisting of a ruined castle, cottages, cliffs and seascape. The first National Theatre production of Beckett's *Waiting for Godot* used the playwright's revised text, which differs from the standard version, mostly in the scenes involving Pozzo. John Alderton, transcending his sit-com image, matched Alec Mc-Cowen's excellent performance in what was overall a fine production. Eric Porter made a welcome return to the stage, after an absence of over ten years, as Big Daddy in a revival of Tennessee Williams's 1955 modern classic, *Cat on a Hot Tin Roof.* Mike Alfreds adapted and directed three short comedies by Carlo Goldoni, the 18th century playwright who introduced social realism into the Italian theatre, and presented them successfully as *Countrymania.* Alan Ayckbourn's half-hearted production of John Ford's Jacobean tragedy *'Tis Pity She's a Whore* failed to satisfy the critics, who were particularly scathing about the casting of Suzen Sylvester and Rupert Graves. Middleton and Rowley's *The Changeling,* directed by Richard Eyre, attracted mixed reviews.

At the Swan in Stratford, John Caird resuscitated—briefly—Ben Jonson's greatest failure, *The New Inn.* Hissed at its first, and apparently only previous, performance in 1629, the play marked Jonson's return to the public theatre after composing courtly masques, the techniques of which he brought unsuccessfully to this curiosity. More impressive was Nicholas Hytner's directorial debut at Stratford, a powerful reading of *Measure for Measure.* The new Stratford season opened in April 1988 with a production of *Much Ado About Nothing* directed by Di Trevis, the first woman to direct a play on the main Stratford stage since the late Buzz Goodbody in 1975. Dame Wendy Hiller continued her distinguished career in a less than distinguished play, Alfred Uhry's Pulitzer Prize-winning *Driving Miss Daisy.* Another veteran actor, Rex Harrison, featured in J. M. Barrie's role reversal satire, *The Admirable Crichton.* Despite an exemplary performance from Edward Fox, the production lacked pace and variety. Richard Briers also escaped the confines of sit-com as a notable Malvolio in Kenneth Branagh's production of *Twelfth Night* at the Riverside Studios: while Ian McKellen turned his professional experience to charitable purposes in an acclaimed one-man show *Acting Shakespeare,* in aid of the London Lighthouse Centre.

PRODUCTIONS

London productions between September 1, 1987, and August 31, 1988, included the following:

ALBERY: St Martin's Lane, WC2. (1987) Sept. 21. *The Big Knife* by Clifford Odets, with James B. Sikking, Gayle Hunnicut, David de Keyser and Martin Shaw, dir. by Robin Lefevre, des. by Grant Hicks. Oct. 29. *The Life of Napoleon,* devised, written and performed by John Sessions, dir. by Kenneth Branagh (Renaissance Co. prodn., trans. from River-side Studios). Dec. 15. *The Foreigner* by Larry Shue, with Nicholas Lyndhurst, Doreen Mantle, Melinda McGraw and Stuart Milligan, dir. by Nick Broadhurst. (1988) *Blood Brothers* by Willy Russell, with Kiki Dee, Robert Locke and Con O'Neill, dir. by Bob Thomson.

ALDWYCH: WC2. (1987) *A View from the Bridge* by Arthur Miller, with Michael Gambon, dir. by Alan Ayckbourn (National Theatre prodn.). (1988) March 8. *Hapgood* by Tom Stoppard, with Nigel Hawthorne, Felicity Kendal and Roger Rees, dir. by Peter Wood, des. by Carl Toms.

ALMEIDA: Almeida St., N1. (1987) Nov. 18. *Nana* by Emile Zola, with Belinda Davison, dir. by Jane Gibson, Sue Lefton, des. by John Joyne, Lorna Heilbron (Shared Experience prodn.). Dec. 9. *The Traveller* by Jean-Claude van Italie, with David Threlfall and Morag Hood. (1988) Jan. 28. *Venus and Lucrece* by Shakespeare, with David Lansbury and Sarah Woodward, dir. by Bardy Thomas, des. by David Lewis. Feb. 25. *The Possibilities* by Howard Barker, with Nicholas Woodeson, Katharine Rogers, Suzanne Burden, Douglas Hodge, Heather Canning and Michael Grandage, dir. by Ian McDiarmid, des. by Julian McGowan (Not the RSC Group prodn.). May 5. *Moon on a Rainbow Shawl* by Errol John, with Ellen Thomas, Claire Benedict and Ram John Holder, dir. by Maya Angelou (Akintunde Co. prodn.). Aug. 4. *Hello and Goodbye* by Athol Fugard, with Antony Sher and Estelle Kohler, dir. by Janice Honeyman (R.S.C. prodn. with Market Theatre, Johannesburg). Aug. 11. *Keeping Tom Nice* by Lucy Gannon, with Linus Roache, Shirley King, Richard Conway and Mike Dowling, dir. Bill Buffery, des. by Louise Belson. Aug. 18. *Oedipus* by Seneca (translated by Ted Hughes), with John Shrapnel, Julie Legrand, Stella Gonet and Phil Daniels, dir. by Donald Sumpter, des. by Louise Belson.

APOLLO: Shaftesbury Ave., W1. (1987) Sept. 9. *Thursday's Ladies* by Loleh Bellon, with Siân Phillips, Dorothy Tutin, Eileen Atkins and Albert Welling, dir. by Frank Hauser, des. by Peter Rice. Nov. 9. *Dangerous Obsession* by N. J. Crisp, with Dinsdale Landen, Carol Drinkwater and Jeremy Bulloch, dir. by Roger Smith. (1988) Feb. 10. *The Best of Friends* by Hugh Whitemore, with John Gielgud, Rosemary Harris and Ray McAnally, dir. by James Roose-Evans, des. by Julia Trevelyan Oman. June 8, *Driving Miss Daisy* by Alfred Uhry, with Wendy Hiller, Barry Foster and Clarke Peters, dir. by Ron Lagomarsino, des. by Thomas Lynch.

ARTS: Great Newport St., WC1. (1988) Jan. 12. *Candida* by G. B. Shaw, with Maureen O'Brien, David Rintoul, Grant Thatcher and Christopher Hancock, dir. by Frank Hauser, des. by Claire Lyth. April 27. *Teechers* by John Godber, with Paul Rider, Shirley-Anne Selby and Gillian Tompkins (Hull Truck Co. prodn.).

BARBICAN: EC2. (1987) Dec. 10. *The Wizard of Oz* by L. Frank Baum, adapted from screenplay by John Kane, music and lyrics by Harold Arlen and E. Y. Harburg, with Imelda Staunton, Paul Greenwood, John Bowe, Dilys Laye and Tony Church, dir. by Ian Judge. (1988) March 23. *The Jew of Malta* by Christopher Marlowe, with Alun Armstrong and John Carlisle, dir. by Barry Kyle. April 8. Shakespeare's *Twelfth Night,* with Harriet Walter, Roger Allam, David Bradley, Donald Sumpter, Deborah Findlay, John Carlisle and Bruce Alexander, dir. by Bill Alexander, des. by Deirdre Clancy and Kit Surrey. April 26. Shakespeare's *The Merchant of Venice,* with Antony Sher, Deborah Findlay, Nicholas Farrell and John Carlisle, dir. by Bill Alexander, des. by Kit Surrey. June 14. Shakespeare's *Julius*

Caesar, with Roger Allam, Sean Baker, Joseph O'Conor and Linus Roache, dir. by Terry Hands. Aug. 9. *Three Sisters* by Anton Chekhov, with Bruce Alexander, David Bradley, Brian Cox, Nicholas Farrell, Deborah Findlay, Stella Gonet, Pippa Guard, Joseph O'Conor and Harriet Walter, dir. by John Barton, des. by Timothy O'Brien.

BARBICAN PIT : (1987) Oct. 24. *Death Watch* and *The Maids* by Jean Genet (translated by David Rudkin), with Gerard Murphy, Miles Anderson and Patrick Bailey, dir. by Gerard Murphy, des. by Ultz. Dec. 15. *Speculators* by Tony Marchant, with Gary Love, Robert Demeger, Gerard Murphy, Amanda Harris and Simon Russell Beale, dir. by Barry Kyle, des. by Fotini Dimou. (1988) March 22. Shakespeare's *Cymbeline*, with Harriet Walter, Nicholas Farrell, Donald Sumpter, David Bradley, Julie Legrand and Bruce Alexander, dir. by Bill Alexander, des. by Ilona Sekacz. April 25. *Temptation* by Vaclav Havel, with Julie Legrand, John Shrapnel, Paul Webster and David Bradley, dir. by Roger Michell. May 23. *The Revenger's Tragedy* by Cyril Tourneur, with Antony Sher, Nicholas Farrell, Sean Baker and Stella Gonet, dir. by Di Trevis, des. by Michael Levine. July 4. Shakespeare's *Titus Andronicus*, with Brian Cox, Donald Sumpter, Estelle Kohler, Sonia Ritter, Piers Ibbotson, Richard McCabe and Peter Polycarpou, dir. by Deborah Warner. Aug. 8. *Hyde Park* by James Shirley, with Fiona Shaw, Alex Jennings, Felicity Dean, John Carlisle and James Fleet, dir. by Barry Kyle.

BUSH : Shepherd's Bush Green, W12. (1988) Feb. 16. *A Handful of Stars* by Billy Roche, with Gary O'Brien, Breffni McKenna and Aidan Murphy, dir. by Robin Lefevre. March 29. *Raping the Gold* by Lucy Gannon, with Trevor Peacock, Paul Copley, Sophie Thursfield and Paterson Joseph, dir. by Debbie Shewell, des. by Paul Brown.

CAMBRIDGE : Earlham St., WC2. (1988) Feb. *The Rink* by Kandor and Ebb, with Diane Langton and Josephine Blake, dir. and chor. by Paul Kerryson, des. by Chris Kinman.

COMEDY : Panton St., W1. (1987) Sept. 16. *Groucho : A Life in Revue* by Arthur Marx and Robert Fisher, with Frank Ferrante, Les Marsden and Marguerite Lowell, dir. by Arthur Marx. Dec. 8. *Separation* by Tom Kempinski, with David Suchet and Saskia Reeves, dir. by Michael Attenborough (Hampstead Theatre prodn.). (1988) March 10. *A Touch of the Poet* by Eugene O'Neill (trans. from Young Vic). July 7. *Exclusive Yarns* by Gary Lyons and Stewart Permutt, with Pam Ferris, Susie Blake, Colette Gleason, Lesley Joseph and Brian Deacon, dir. by Gary Lyons, des. by Dermot Hayes.

DONMAR WAREHOUSE : Earlham St., WC2. (1987) Oct. 13. *Conversations on a Homecoming* by Tom Murphy, with Maurice O'Donoghue, Sean McGinley and Ray McBride, dir. by Gary Hynes (Druid Theatre Co. prodn.). Nov. 17. Shakespeare's *Macbeth* with Keith Bartlett, Leslee Udwin and Timothy Walker, dir. by Declan Donnellan (Cheek by Jowl Co. prodn.). Dec. 10. *Brel*, compiled and dir. by Bill Bryden, with Siân Phillips, Alexander Hanson and Kelly Hunter. (1988) Jan 19. *Company* by Samuel Beckett, with Julian Curry, dir. by Tim Pigott-Smith. March 29. *Exit Entrance* by Aidan C. Mathews, with Ingrid Craigie, Malcolm Douglas, Denys Hawthorne and Joan O'Hara, dir. by Ben Barnes. April 2. *A Family Affair* by Alexander Ostrovsky (adapted by Nick Dear), with Marcia Warren, Adam Kotz, Timothy Walker and Lesley Sharp, dir. by Declan Donnellan (Cheek by Jowl Co. prodn.). June 22. *Simplicity* by Marivaux (trans. by Lady Mary Wortley Montagu), with Elizabeth Rider, Christopher Villiers, Joanna

Hole and Norman Bowler, dir. by Sonia Fraser, des. by Meg Surrey. Aug. 4. *Don't Go Away Mad* by William Saroyan, with Michael Moriarty, Nick Edmett, David Yip and Barrie Houghton, dir. by Keith Hack, des. by Voytek.

DUKE OF YORK's : St. Martin's Lane, WC2: (1987) Oct. 7. *And Then There Were None* by Agatha Christie, with Glynis Barber, Rodney Bewes, Geoffrey Davies, Jack Hedley and Miriam Karlin, dir. by Kenneth Alan Taylor, des. by Robert Jones. (1988) June 14. *How the Other Half Loves* by Alan Ayckbourn (Greenwich Theatre prodn.).

FORTUNE : Russell St., WC2. (1988) Jan. 28. *Dangerous Obsession* by N. J. Crisp (trans. from Apollo).

GARRICK : Charing Cross Rd., WC2 (1988) April 21. *Easy Virtue* by Noel Coward (King's Head Theatre prodn.).

GLOBE : Shaftesbury Ave., W1. (1987) Oct. 27 *Lettice and Lovage* by Peter Shaffer, with Maggie Smith, Margaret Tyzack and Richard Pearson, dir. by Michael Blakemore, des. by Alan Tagg.

GREENWICH : Croom's Hill, SE10. (1987) Oct. 23. *A Collier's Friday Night* by D. H. Lawrence, with Alfred Lynch, Annette Crosbie, Neil Dudgeon and Claire Parker, dir. by John Dove, des. by Kenny Miller. Dec. 3. *The Bells are Ringing* by Jule Styne, Betty Comden and Adolph Green, with Leslie Mackie, Ray Lonnen and Gary Yershon, dir. by John Doyle. (1988) Feb. 5. *How the Other Half Loves* by Alan Ayckbourn, with Gabrielle Drake, Christopher Benjamin, Lavinia Bertram and Richard Kane, dir. by Alan Strachan, des. by Michael Pavelka. March 28. *The Musical Comedy Murders of 1940* by John Bishop, with Simon Cadell, Tom Baker, Margaret Courtenay and Sheila Steafel, dir. by Peter Farago. May 16. *Mary Stuart* by Friedrich Schiller (translated by Robert David MacDonald), with Paola Dionisotti and Fiona Shaw, dir. by Tim Albery. July 4. *To Kill a Mocking Bird* by Harper Lee (adapted by Christopher Sergel), with Jane Hazlegrove, Mark Chatterton, Francesca Ryan and James Quinn, dir. by Anthony Clark.

HALF MOON : Mile End Road, E1. (1987) Dec. 2. *Private Members* by "The Go-Go Boys" (Andrew Alty and Howard Lester).

HAMPSTEAD : Swiss Cottage, NW3. (1987) Sept. 7. *Curtains* by Stephen Bill, with Alfred Lynch, Gwen Nelson, Ralph Nossek and Bridget Turner, dir. by Stuart Burge. Oct.15. *Separation* by Tom Kempinski, with Saskia Reeves and David Suchet, dir. by Michael Attenborough, des. by Sue Plummer, Dec. 16. *Between East and West* by Richard Nelson, with John Woodvine and Sheila Allen, dir. by David Jones. (1988) Feb. 4. *Film Society* by Jon Robin Baitz, with Denis Lawson, Dinah Stabb, John Rogan and Alan MacNaughton, dir. by Michael Attenborough. April 6. *Danger : Memory! (I Can't Remember Anything and Clara)* by Arthur Miller, with John Bennett, Betsy Blair, Paul Rogers, Stephen Hoye and Sarah Keller, dir. by Jack Gold. June 2. *Aristocrats* by Brian Friel, with Niall Buggy, Sinead Cusack, Charlotte Cornwell and Peter Caffrey, dir. by Robin Lefevre. July 14. *Sophiatown* dir. by Malcolm Purkey (Junction Avenue and Market Theatre Johannesburg prodn.). Aug. 17. *The Fancy Man* by Mike Stott, with Julia Lane, Ian Mercer and Bernard Gallagher, dir. by Alan Dossor.

KING'S HEAD : Upper St., N1. (1987) Dec. 31. *Easy Virtue* by Noel Coward, with Ronnie Stevens, Jane How, Avril Angers, and John Michie, dir. by Tim Luscombe, des. by Graham Wynne.

LYRIC : Hammersmith, W6. (1987) Oct. 13. *The Hypochondriac* by Moliere (translated by Alan

Drury), with Tom Courtenay, Kathryn Hunter, Brian Glover, Mary Maddox and Marilyn Cutts, dir. by Nancy Meckler. Nov. *Faustus* by Christopher Marlowe, with Peter Lindford, George Anton and David Westhead, adapted and dir. by Mark Brickman (Actors Touring Co. prodn.). (1988) April 6 and 11. *Faust (Part 1)* and *Faust (Part 2)* by Goethe (translated by Robert David MacDonald), with Simon Callow, Peter Lindford, Alyson Spiro and Caroline Bliss, dir. by David Freeman, des. by David Royer. July 12. *Busman's Honeymoon* by Dorothy L. Sayers and Muriel St. Clare Byrne, with Edward Petherbridge, Emily Richard and Sharon Bower.

LYRIC STUDIO: Hammersmith, W6. (1987) Sept. 2. *The Light of Day* by Graham Swannell, with Nicola Pagett, Nigel Terry and Claire Hackett, dir. by Peter James. (1988) March 3. *Tales from a Long Room* by Peter Tinniswood, with William Rushton and Sam Kelly, dir. by Peter James. June 22. *Facades* by William Humble, with Frances de la Tour, Graham Crowden, Sheila Reid and Aubrey Morris, dir. by Simon Callow, des. by Bruno Santini.

LYRIC: Shaftesbury Ave., W1. (1987) Oct. 21. *One for the Road* by Willy Russell, with Russ Abbot, Michael Angelis, Elizabeth Bennett, and Janet Dale, dir. by William Gaunt, des. by Bruno Santini. (1988) May 9. *Emerald City* by David Williamson, with Garry McDonald, Andrea Moor, Max Cullen and Robyn Nevin, dir. by Richard Wherrett, des. by Laurence Eastwood.

MERMAID: Puddle Dock, Blackfriars, EC4. (1987) Nov. 4. *The Rover* by Aphra Behn, with Jeremy Irons, Imogen Stubbs, Tony Armatrading, David Troughton, Geraldine Fitzgerald and Stephanie Beacham, dir. by John Barton (R.S.C. Swan prodn.). (1988) June 7. *Le Cirque Imaginaire* with Jean-Baptiste Thieree and Victoria Chaplin.

NATIONAL THEATRE: South Bank, SE1. COTTESLOE: (1987) Sept. 23. *Ting Tang Mine* by Nick Darke, with Robert Glenister, and Barbara Jefford, dir. by Michael Rudman, des. by Carl Toms. Oct. 15. *Entertaining Strangers* by David Edgar, with Tim Pigott-Smith and Judi Dench, dir. by Peter Hall, des. by William Dudley. (1988) Feb. 16. *A Place with the Pigs* by Athol Fugard, with Jim Broadbent and Linda Bassett, dir. by Athol Fugard. May 18. Shakespeare's *The Winter's Tale*, with Eileen Atkins, Sally Dexter, Shirley Henderson, Tim Pigott-Smith, Basil Henson and Peter Woodward, dir. by Peter Hall, des. by Alison Chitty. May 19. Shakespeare's *The Tempest*, with Michael Bryant, Tony Haygarth, Steven Mackintosh, Jennifer Hall, Peter Woodward and Tim Pigott-Smith, dir. by Peter Hall. May 20. Shakespeare's *Cymbeline*, with Peter Woodward, Tim Pigott-Smith, Geraldine James, Tony Church and Eileen Atkins, dir. by Peter Hall.

LYTTELTON: (1987) Nov. 25. *Waiting for Godot* by Samuel Beckett, with John Alderton, Alec McCowen, Colin Welland and Peter Wight, dir. by Michael Rudman, des. by William Dudley. (1988) Feb. 3. *Cat on a Hot Tin Roof* by Tennessee Williams, with Ian Charleson, Lindsay Duncan, Colin Jeavons, Eric Porter, Alison Steadman and Barbara Leigh-Hunt, dir. by Howard Davies. June 21. *The Strangeness of Others*, written and dir. by Nick Ward, with David Burke, Trevor Peacock, Peter Hugo-Daly, Cheryl Maiker and David Bamber. June 23. *The Changeling* by Thomas Middleton and William Rowley, with Miranda Richardson, George Harris, Henry Goodman, Paul Jesson, Caroline Lee Johnson and David Ryall, dir. by Richard Eyre, des. by William Dudley. Aug. 10. *Mrs. Klein* by Nicholas Wright, with Gillian Barge, Francesca Annis and Zoe Wanamaker, dir. by Peter Gill.

OLIVIER: (1987) Dec. 12. *Countrymania* by Carlo Goldoni, adapted and dir. by Mike Alfreds, with Sylvestra le Touzel, Maggie Wells, Pip Donaghy, Mark Rylance, Siân Thomas and James Smith, des. by Paul Dart. (1988) March 3. *'Tis Pity She's a Whore* by John Ford, with Suzan Sylvester, Rupert Graves, Clive Francis, Polly Adams and Russell Dixon, dir. by Alan Ayckbourn, des. by Roger Glossop. May 11. *The Shaughran* by Dion Boucicault, with Stephen Moore, Stephen Rea, Julia Dearden, Anthony O'Donnell and Gillian Barge, dir. by Howard Davies, des. by William Dudley, music by Dominic Muldowney.

NEW END: Hampstead, NW3. (1988) July 20. *Exceptions* by Geraldine Sherman, with Jill Bennett, Julia Swift, Esther Freud and Michael Mueller, dir. by Sean Mathias, des. by Michael Vale.

OLD VIC: The Cut, SE1. (1988) Jan. 19. *Andromache* by Racine (translated by Eric Korn), with Janet Suzman, Penelope Wilton, Kevin McNally, Peter Eyre and John Barron, dir. by Jonathan Miller, des. by Richard Hudson. March 11. *The Tutor* by Reinhold Lenz, adapted by Bertolt Brecht, with Kevin McNally, Sheila Reid, Niamh Cusack, Windsor Davis, Frank Thornton and John Lynch, dir. by Angelika Hurwicz, des. by A. Christian Steiof. May 3. *One Way Pendulum* by N. F. Simpson, with Peter Bayliss, Ann Way, Andrew St. Clair, Brenda Bruce, John Savident and Graham Crowden, dir. by Jonathan Miller, des. by Richard Hudson. June 29. *Too Clever by Half* by Alexander Ostrovsky (translated by Rodney Ackland), with Alex Jennings, Peter Wear, Linda Marlowe, Aden Gillett and Janet Henfrey, dir. by Richard Jones, des. by Richard Hudson.

OPEN AIR: Regent's Park, W1. (1988) June 1. Shakespeare's *The Winter's Tale*, with Carolyn Pickles, Jane Arden, Paul Rattigan, Cliff Howells, Sheila Allen, Clive Arrindell and David Henry, dir. by David Gilmore, des. by Fran Thompson. June 15. Shakespeare's *A Midsummer Night's Dream*, with Clive Arrindell, Ian Talbot, Carol Royle and Cliff Howells, dir. by Caroline Smith. August 5. *Babes in Arms* by Rodgers and Hart, with Briony Glassco, Jessica Martin, Sheila Allen, Paul Reeves and Cliff Howells, dir. by Ian Talbot.

PALLADIUM: Argyll St., W1. (1988) April 26. *Ziegfeld* by Ned Sherrin, Alistair Beaton, score by Michael Reed, with Len Cariou, Geoffrey Hutchings, Amanda Rickard, Haydn Gwynne, Louise Gold and Fabienne Guyen, choreog. and dir. by Joe Layton, des. by Robin Don, costumes by Theoni V. Aldredge.

PHOENIX: Charing Cross Rd., WC2. (1987) Nov. 18. *J. J. Farr* by Ronald Harwood, with Albert Finney, Bob Peck, Bernard Lloyd, Hugh Paddick, Trevor Peacock and Dudley Sutton, dir. by Ronald Eyre, des. by Jocelyn Herbert. (1988) April 7. *The Common Pursuit* by Simon Gray, with Rik Mayall, John Sessions, Stephen Fry, John Gordon Sinclair and Sarah Berger, dir. by Simon Gray (Watford Palace Theatre prodn.).

PLAYHOUSE: Northumberland Ave., WC2. (1987) Oct. 16. *Girlfriends* by Howard Goodall, with Hazel O'Connor, David Easter and Clare Burt, dir. by John Retallack, des. by William Dudley. Dec. 14. *Acting Shakespeare*, with Ian McKellen. (1988) Feb. 27. *Nite Club Confidential* by Dennis Deal and Albert Evans, with Ruth Madoc, Kathryn Evans and Stuart Milligan.

PRINCE OF WALES: Coventry St., W1. (1987) Sept. 22. *'Allo 'Allo!* by Jeremy Lloyd and David Croft. (1988) Jan. 20. *South Pacific* by Rodgers and Hammerstein, with Gemma Craven, Emile Belcourt, Bertice Reading, Andrew C. Wadsworth, dir. by Roger Redfarn, des. by Terry Parsons.

QUEENS: Shaftesbury Ave., W1. (1987) Sept. 22. *Beyond Reasonable Doubt* by Jeffrey Archer, with Frank Finlay, Wendy Craig, Andrew Cruickshank, David Langton and Jeffry Wickham, dir. by David Gilmore, des. by Tim Goodchild.

RIVERSIDE STUDIOS: Hammersmith, W6. (1987) Nov. 9. *Last Summer in Chulimsk* by Alexander Vampilov, with Sylvia Sims and Andy Lucas, dir. by Bill Pryde. Nov. 26. Shakespeare's *Twelfth Night*, with Frances Barber, Caroline Langrishe, Anton Lesser and Richard Briers, dir. by Kenneth Branagh, des. by Bunny Christie (Renaissance Theatre Co. prodn.).

ROYAL COURT: Sloane Square, SW1. (1987) *The Emperor* by Ryszard Kapuscinski, with Nabil Shaban, dir. by Jonathan Miller, des. by Richard Hudson. Oct. 14. *A Lie of the Mind* by Sam Shepard, with Will Patton, Miranda Richardson, Geraldine McEwan, Tony Haygarth and Paul McGann, dir. by Simon Curtis, des. by Paul Brown. (1988) Jan. 28. *A Wholly Healthy Glasgow* by Iain Heggie, with Gerard Kelly, Paul Higgins and Tom Watson, dir. by Richard Wilson, des. by Sue Plummer (Royal Exchange Theatre prodn.). March 9. *The Last Supper* by Howard Barker, with Philip Sayer and Meg Davies, dir. by Kenny Ireland (co-prod. with Leicester Haymarket). April 12. *Bloody Poetry* by Howard Brenton, with Mark Rylance, Nigel Terry, Robin Hooper, Siân Thomas and Lizzy McInnerny, dir. by Max Stafford-Clark, des. by Kenny Miller. June 1. *Greenland* by Howard Brenton, with Sheila Hancock, Jane Lapotaire, Janet McTeer, Ben Onwukwe and Lesley Sharp, dir. by Simon Curtis. July 26. *The Recruiting Officer* by George Farquhar, with Lesley Sharp, Ron Cook, Mossie Smith, David Haig, Linda Bassett and Jim Broadbent, dir. by Max Stafford-Clark, des. by Peter Hartwell.

ROYALTY: Drury Lane, WC2. (1987) Sept. 11. *The Importance of Being Earnest* by Oscar Wilde, with Clive Francis, Denis Lawson, Gabrielle Drake, Natalie Ogle and Wendy Hiller, dir. by Donald Sinden, des. by Carl Toms. Oct. 22. *The Living Room* by Graham Greene, with Peter Blythe, Judy Campbell, Dulcie Gray, Jennie Linden, Katharine Schlesinger and Paul Daneman, dir. by Bryan Forbes. (1988) March 17. *Harlequinade* and *The Browning Version* by Terence Rattigan, with Jean Anderson, John Duttine, Paul Eddington, Anna Quayle, Dorothy Tutin and Jack Watling, dir. by Tim Luscombe.

SAVOY: Strand, WC2. (1987) Oct. 19. *A Man for All Seasons* by Robert Bolt, with Charlton Heston, Gwen Watford, Benjamin Whitrow and Roy Kinnear, dir. by Frank Hauser, des. by Julia Trevelyan Oman (Chichester Festival prodn.). Aug. 31. *Sugar Babies* with Mickey Rooney and Ann Miller.

SHAW: Euston Rd., NW1. (1988) Feb. 9. *The Quartered Man*, written and dir. by Donald Freed, with Barry Foster, Frank Grimes, Don Fellows and Andy de la Tour.

STRAND: Aldwych, WC2. (1987) Nov. 17. *Back with a Vengeance!* with Barry Humphries.

THEATRE ROYAL: Haymarket, SW1. (1987) Dec. 18. *You Never Can Tell* by G. B. Shaw, with Michael Hordern, Irene Worth, Jenny Quayle, Derek Waring, Michael Denison and Frank Middlemass, dir. by Tony Robertson, des. by Saul Radomsky (Theatre Clwyd prodn.). (1988) May 26. *The Deep Blue Sea* by Terence Rattigan, with Penelope Keith, Anthony Bate, John Normington and David Yelland, dir. by Alan Strachan, des. by Eileen Diss. Aug. 8. *The Admirable Crichton* by J. M. Barrie, with Rex Harrison, Edward Fox, Margaret Courtenay and Niamh Cusack, dir. by Frith Banbury, des. by Hayden Griffin (Theatre Clwyd prodn.).

THEATRE ROYAL: Stratford East, E15. (1988) Jan. 28. *King of England* by Barrie Keeffe, with Rudolph Walker, Paul Barber and Larry Dann, dir. by Philip Hedley. March 7. Shakespeare's *Twelfth Night*, with Winston Crooke, Alan Cowan, Josephine Welcome and Helen Atkinson Wood, dir. by Jeff Teare.

VAUDEVILLE: Strand, WC2. (1988) Jan. 21. *Shirley Valentine* by Willy Russell, with Pauline Collins, dir. by Simon Callow, des. by Bruno Santini. May 24. *Uncle Vanya* by Anton Chekhov (translated by Michael Frayn), with Michael Gambon, Jonathan Pryce, Imelda Staunton, Benjamin Whitrow, and Greta Scacchi, dir. by Michael Blakemore, des. by Tanya McCallin.

VICTORIA PALACE: SW1. (1988) May 31. *Winnie* by Robin Hardy, with Robert Hardy, Virginia McKenna and Frank Thornton, dir. by Albert Marre, des. by Simon Higlett.

WESTMINSTER: Palace St., SW1. (1988) March 9. *The Miracle Worker* by William Gibson, with Daryl Bach, Hildegard Neil, Ian Lavender and Sally Osborn, dir. by Adrian Reynolds (Byre Theatre, St Andrews prodn.).

WHITEHALL: SW1. (1987) Nov. 2. *The Importance of Being Earnest* by Oscar Wilde, adapted and dir. by Lou Stein, with Hinge and Brackett, des. by Norman Coates. (1988) Feb. 22. *Curtains* by Stephen Bill, with Annette Crosbie, Sheila Ballantine, Gwen Nelson and Alfred Lynch, dir. by Stuart Burge (Hampstead Theatre prodn.). April 19. *Journey's End* by R. C. Sherriff, with Jason Connery, Nicky Henson and Andrew Castell, dir. by Justin Greene (Nuffield Theatre, Southampton prodn.).

WYNDHAM'S: Charing Cross Rd., WC2. (1988) May 12. *Married Love* by Peter Luke, with Susan Hampshire, John Moffatt, Michael Cochrane and Moray Watson, dir. by Joan Plowright, des. by Bunny Christie. June 29. *Greek* written, dir. and performed by Steven Berkoff, with Georgia Brown, Gillian Eaton and Bruce Payne. July 18. *The Foreigner* by Larry Shue (trans. from the Albery).

YOUNG VIC: The Cut, SE1. (1987) Sept. 22. *Comedians* by Trevor Griffiths, with Bert Parnaby, Mark McGann, Matthew Marsh and Mick Kemp, dir. by David Thacker, des. by Fran Thompson. Oct. 26. Shakespeare's *Romeo and Juliet*, with Sarah-Jane Fenton, Richard Huw, Rudolph Walker, Annette Badland and Anthony Wellington, dir. by David Thacker. (1988) Jan. 29. *A Touch of the Poet* by Eugene O'Neill, with Vanessa Redgrave, Timothy Dalton, Rudi Davies, Joely Richardson, John McEnery, Amanda Boxer and Malcolm Tierney, dir. by David Thacker. April 29. *Doctor Faustus* by Christopher Marlowe, with Peter Guinness, Stephen Jenn and Jon Strickland, dir. by Anthony Clark, des. by Kate Burnett.

Productions outside London included the following:

STRATFORD MEMORIAL THEATRE (Royal Shakespeare Company): (1987) Sept. 8. *The Taming of the Shrew* with Brian Cox, Fiona Shaw, Felicity Dean, Alex Jennings, James Fleet and Barry Rutter, dir. by Jonathan Miller, des. by Stefanos Lazaridis. Nov. 12. *Measure for Measure* with Josette Simon, Sean Baker, Roger Allam, Alex Jennings and Mark Dignam, dir. by Nicholas Hytner, des. by Mark Thompson. (1988) Feb. 13. *Carrie* by Stephen King, music by Michael Gore, lyrics by Dean Pitchford, book by Lawrence Cohen, with Linzi Hateley, Barbara Cook and Gene Anthony Ray, dir. by Terry Hands, des. by Ralph Koltai. April 14. *Much Ado About Nothing* with Clive Merrison, Maggie Steed, Ralph Fiennes, Julia Ford, David Lyon and David Waller, dir. by Di Trevis, des.

by Mark Thompson. May 4. *Macbeth* with Miles Anderson, Amanda Root, Tony Armatrading, Colin McCormack and Duncan Bell, dir. by Adrian Noble, des. by Bob Crowley. July 14. *The Tempest* with John Wood, Duncan Bell, John Kane, Desmond Barrit, Melanie Thaw and James Purefoy, dir. by Nicholas Hytner, des. by David Fielding.

OTHER PLACE: (1987) Sept. 10. *A Question of Geography* by John Berger and Nella Bielski, with Harriet Walter, Clive Russell and Linus Roache, dir. by John Caird. Nov. 4. *Cymbeline* with Nicholas Farrell, Harriet Walter, David Bradley, Julie Legrand and Donald Sumpter, dir. by Bill Alexander, des. by Ilona Sekacz. (1988) April 29. *Across Oka* by Robert Holman, with Edward Rawle-Hicks, Timothy Stark, Alfred Burke and Patricia Lawrence. May 11. *King John* with David Lyon, Nicholas Woodeson, Robert Demeger, Susan Engel and David Morrissey, dir. by Deborah Warner, des. by Sue Blane.

SWAN: (1987) Sept. 11. *The Revenger's Tragedy* by Cyril Tourneur, with Antony Sher, Sean Baker, Nicholas Farrell and Stella Gonet, dir. by Di Trevis. Nov. 10. *The New Inn* by Ben Jonson, with Fiona Shaw, John Carlisle, Clive Russell, Deborah Findlay, Joseph O'Conor and Richard McCabe, dir. by John Caird. (1988) April 5. *The Constant Couple* by George Farquhar, with Pip Donaghy, Amanda Root, Tony Armatrading, Simon Russell Beale, Joe Melia, and Maureen Beattie, dir. by Roger Michell, des. by Ultz. April 27. *The Plain Dealer* by William Wycherley, with David Calder, Mark Hadfield, Marjorie Yates, Geraldine Alexander and Joanne Pearce, dir. by Ron Daniels, des. by David Fielding. July 13. *The Man of Mode* by George Etherege, with Simon Russell Beale, Miles Anderson, Pip Donaghy, Amanda Root, Patricia Lawrence and Joe Melia, dir. by Garry Hynes, des. by Ultz.

BIRMINGHAM REPERTORY: (1988) April 20. *Privates on Parade* by Peter Nicholls, with Paul Greenwood and Eric Allen, dir. by Derek Nicholls. Renaissance

Co. Shakespeare season: May 3. *Much Ado About Nothing*, with Samantha Bond, Tam Hoskyns, Kenneth Branagh, Richard Easton and James Larkin, dir. by Judi Dench. May 4. *As You Like It* with Tam Hoskyns, Sophie Thompson, James Larkin, Richard Clifford, Kenneth Branagh, Robert Easton and David Lloyd Meredith, dir. by Geraldine McEwan. May 24. *Hamlet* with Kenneth Branagh, Sophie Thompson, Richard Easton and Dearbhla Molloy, dir. by Derek Jacobi.

CHICHESTER FESTIVAL THEATRE: (1988) May 2. *Hay Fever* by Noel Coward, with Googie Withers, John McCallum, Jan Francis and Christopher Godwin, dir. by Tony Britton. May 18. *Major Barbara* by G. B. Shaw, with Donald Sinden, Anna Carteret, Paul Shelley and Marc Sinden, dir. by Christopher Morahan, des. by Gerard Howland. July 13. *The Royal Baccarat Scandal* by Royce Ryton, with Keith Michell, Gerald Harper, Fiona Fullerton, Gary Bond and John McCallum, dir. by Val May. Aug. 3. *Ring Round the Moon* by Jean Anouilh (translated by Christopher Fry), with Jose Ferrer, Holly Aird, Googie Withers, Michael Denison, Michael Sibery, June Whitfield, Linda Thorson and Christopher Godwin, dir. by Elijah Moshinsky, des. by Saul Radomsky.

MANCHESTER ROYAL EXCHANGE: (1987) *Loot* by Joe Orton, with Bernard Gallagher, Patrick Barlow, Stephen McGann, Susan Tracy and Patrick Field, dir. by Paul Unwin. Dec. 17. *The Cabinet Minister* by Pinero, with Frank Thornton, Susan Fleetwood and Dilys Hamlett, dir. by Braham Murray. (1988) Feb. 26. *All My Sons* by Arthur Miller, with John Thaw, Lynn Farleigh, Michael Maloney and Joanna Foster, dir. by Gregory Hersov, des. by Michael Holt. April 14. *Don Juan* by Moliere, with Jonathan Kent, Bernard Bresslaw, Paul Ratlee and Marcus Hutton, dir. by Ian McDiarmid, des. by Julian McGowan. July 1. *Born Yesterday* by Garson Kanin, with Derrick O'Connor, Brenda Blethyn, Terrence Wilton and Tom Watson, dir. by Gregory Hersov.

THE ACADEMY AWARDS 1987

Best Picture: *The Last Emperor.*
Best Director: Bernardo Bertolucci, *The Last Emperor.*
Best Actor: Michael Douglas, *Wall Street.*
Best Actress: Cher, *Moonstruck.*
Best Supporting Actor: Sean Connery, *The Untouchables.*
Best Supporting Actress: Olympia Dukakis, *Moonstruck.*
Best Original Screenplay: John Shanley, *Moonstruck.*
Best Adapted Screenplay: Bernardo Bertolucci and Mark Peploe, *The Last Emperor.*
Best Foreign Language: *Babette's Gaestebud* (Babette's Feast).
Best Original Score: Ryuichi Sakamoto, David Byrne and Cong Su, *The Last Emperor.*
Best Original Song: "(I've Had) The Time of My Life", *Dirty Dancing.*

Best Cinematography: Vittorio Storaro, *The Last Emperor.*
Best Art Direction: Ferdinando Scarfiotti and Bruno Cesari, *The Last Emperor.*
Best Costume Design: James Acheson, *The Last Emperor.*
Best Film Editing: Gabriella Christiani, *The Last Emperor.*
Best Sound: Bill Rowe and Ivan Sharrock, *The Last Emperor.*
Best Visual Effects: Denis Muren, William George, Harley Jessup and Kenneth Smith, *Innerspace.*
Best Make-up: Rick Baker, *Harry and the Hendersons.*
Best Animated Short: *The Man Who Planted Trees.*
Best Short Documentary: *Young at Heart.*
Best Documentary Feature: *The Ten-Year Lunch: The Wit and Legend of the Algonquin Round Table.*
Best Live Action Short: *Ray's Male Heterosexual Dance Hall.*

OPERA AND DANCE 1987–88

For some years our major opera and dance companies have been contending with the problems caused by the failure of government funding to keep pace with inflation. The problem has been exacerbated by uncertainty over future levels of funding because grants were provided only for one financial year at a time. The hand-to-mouth existence created by this arrangement has prevented long-term planning, making it difficult for companies to make the most efficient use of their resources. So the announcement by the Minister for the Arts in late 1987 that in future grants would be made on a three-year basis was welcomed by the Arts Council's clients. Mr. Luce also announced the creation of "incentive" funding, intended to reward with extra public funding those companies which raise additional money from private sources. A promised increase in funding of 17 per cent over three years, with the bulk of the increase in the first year, seemed likely to compensate for the effects of inflation, even though some of the extra money was intended for the incentive scheme. However, the reaction to the announcement of the 1988–89 grants was one of shock and dismay, for the Arts Council, with an increase of 8·4 per cent in funding at its disposal, had awarded the four national companies increases of only about 2·5 per cent—less than the rate of inflation and so in real terms a cut. As the companies concerned have made strenuous efforts to increase their revenue from box-office receipts and private sponsorship over the last three years, it was a particularly bitter blow to find themselves apparently penalized for adapting successfully to the requirements of "mixed-economy" arts funding. The Arts Council was accused of failing its principal clients and a campaign was launched by Peter Jonas, managing director of English National Opera, for the national companies to be funded directly by the Government.

Kent Reprieve

The requirement that companies derive a proportion of their income from private sources had left Kent Opera in an uncertain situation in the latter part of 1987. The Arts Council had threatened to discontinue funding the company unless it increased its income from sources other than the box office by at least £200,000 a year. After six months the company had raised £90,000 in donations and sponsorship and in January 1988 the Arts Council announced that funding would continue.

A considerable increase in private sponsorship enabled the Royal Opera House to announce in July 1988 that its deficit for 1987–88 was £522,000, less than half of the anticipated deficit of £1·2 million. Much of the deficit was due to the cost of touring overseas, a particularly heavy expense in 1987–88. From 1988 Arts Council funding will meet these costs: had this arrangement applied for 1987–88 the Royal Opera House would have been in the happy position of breaking even. However, this situation was viewed as no cause for complacency by Jeremy Isaacs, the former chief executive of Channel 4 television who replaces Sir John Tooley as general director of the Royal Opera House in September 1988.

New Brooms

Isaacs heads a relatively new team: Bernard Haitink took over as musical director of the Royal Opera at the start of the 1987–88 season and Paul Findlay was appointed opera director in October 1987. The advent of this new team, and particularly of Isaacs, seems likely to set in progress some dramatic and necessary changes. The Royal Opera House has attracted much criticism in recent years. This has centred on standards of performances, on the age and decrepitude of some of the productions, and on the level of seat prices. These problems have been due in part to the diminishing number of world-class singers available to meet a demand which has grown considerably in the past few decades, and in part to the decline in the level of funding.

At a press conference in May 1988, Isaacs and his team acknowledged the justice of much of the criticism and committed themselves to remedying the faults. They unveiled a five-year plan for the Royal Opera based on the development of more British talent (whilst leaving room in the schedules for singers of the status of Domingo, etc.) and the development of themes in the repertoire of productions undertaken. A practical step was taken towards ensuring the proper rehearsal of revivals by appointing John Cox as production director and Patrick Carnegy as dramaturg. Isaacs also said that future productions would not remain in the repertoire as long as the present ones: some of the productions still performed were first mounted in the 1950s and now look tired and dated.

The old problem of funding overshadows all these plans, however. Isaacs has no illusions about the level of public funding which can be expected in the future or the need to find ever-increasing amounts of private funding. He is prepared to grasp the nettle of raising seat prices but wishes to continue to use the subsidy to keep down the prices of the cheaper seats.

Plans Afoot

The question of money will become even more acute for the Royal Opera House in the coming year. The Royal Opera House has sought and, after a lengthy legal battle, obtained planning permission to redevelop a site adjacent to the Royal Opera House in Covent Garden. The redevelopment will improve backstage facilities and provide rehearsal and other facilities at Covent Garden for the Royal Ballet. Rebuilding work will necessitate the closure of the Royal Opera House for three seasons from 1993. As yet neither the method of financing the redevelopment nor the activities of the Royal Opera and Royal Ballet during the closure have been decided. One proposal is that the two companies should spend the 1993–96 period at either Birmingham or Manchester.

The more permanent transfer of Sadler's Wells Royal Ballet to Birmingham was also broached during the past season. The Birmingham Hippodrome has been the company's second home for a few seasons, and in December 1987 the Birmingham Hippodrome and Birmingham City Council invited the company to make the Hippodrome its main base. The board of the Royal Opera House and Birmingham decided to commission a report into the advantages and disadvantages of the proposal from an independent consultant, David Allen, before making a decision. The report is expected to be completed by autumn 1988 and a decision taken by the end of the year.

Sadler's Wells Theatre, the present base of the Sadler's Wells Royal Ballet, was galvanized by the competition from Birmingham into mounting an appeal for £1 million to widen the theatre's stage. The existing space is too small for the SWRB's large-scale productions, e.g. Swan Lake, and has its limitations for visiting companies. A few years ago the theatre had plans for more ambitious improvements but abandoned these when it seemed that the former Lyceum theatre was to be turned into a large-scale theatre for dance. The subsequent inaction and confusion over the Lyceum's future not only scuppered Sadler's Wells original plans but also highlighted the lack of any co-ordinated planning of arts provision in the capital.

Good Home Needed

The need to provide a home for dance in London was a conclusion of the Drummond inquiry set up by the Arts Council in the early 1980s. The Lyceum emerged as a possible venue about three years ago and since then members of the dance world have lobbied for the restoration of the building after over 40 years as a Mecca dance hall. The project has also received the backing of the City of Westminster Council which gives financial support to London Festival Ballet and would like its protégée to have a proper London base. With Mecca's lease about to run out, the future of the Lyceum has been much in the news in recent months. Mecca failed in its attempt to obtain a new lease but was one of the bidders when the lease was put on sale. The decision of the leaseholders, the London Residuary Body, to offer the lease to the Brent Walker company, who intend using the Lyceum for cabaret, caused widespread anger. Brent Walker have said that the theatre will not be used solely for cabaret but its availability for dance performances has yet to be discussed.

The lack of theatres in London which can accommodate large-scale productions caused congestion at the few suitable venues this summer, as visiting companies timed their appearances in London for the few weeks when the resident companies at the Royal Opera House and the Coliseum were taking a break between seasons. London Festival Ballet undertook its usual fortnight of performances at the Coliseum before moving to the Royal Festival Hall (where the company performs in a converted concert hall). Then the Coliseum was host for a week to the Kirov Ballet, which was followed at the theatre by the Dance Theatre of Harlem. Meanwhile, the Royal Opera House was host to the Australian Ballet for two weeks, and then to the Kirov Ballet for its final week in Britain. Between its appearances at the Coliseum and the Royal Opera House, the Kirov Ballet had spent a week performing at the Business Design Centre in Islington, a vast arena converted temporarily into a 4,000 seat theatre. When the Moscow Ballet arrived for its two-week visit to London in early

August, the Business Design Centre was the only venue available for its performances. Many were annoyed that the lack of facilities in London prevented visits by foreign companies being spread throughout the season. There were also fears that the simultaneous presence of so many world-class companies would lead to competition for audiences and depress attendances. In the event, no performances had less than a 75 per cent attendance and many were sold out. This evidence of a huge demand reinforced calls for a theatre dedicated to dance which would allow both international and British companies a proper showplace for their talents.

Persistence

The temporary conversion of the Business Design Centre was undertaken by the Enterprise Corporation, which had organized the visits of the Kirov, Harlem and Moscow companies. Although better known as a promoter of pop concerts, the corporation has tried persistently to remedy the lack of dance venues in London. Early in 1988 it applied for planning permission for a theatre in Battersea Park, the site of the Big Top used by the Sadler's Wells Royal Ballet for the past few summers. Protests at the loss of open space, lack of access and inconvenience to local residents caused the council to refuse planning permission but, nothing daunted, the Enterprise Corporation then proposed that the theatre be built on the South Bank. The drawback with this new site is that the scheme is linked to plans for adapting County Hall into a hotel and flats, and the proposal seems likely to be opposed by the planning authority.

End of an Era

The 1987–88 season came to a sad close with the death of Sir Frederick Ashton on August 18 at the age of 83. Ashton started his career as a dancer, studying first with Massine and then with Rambert, and it was whilst working with Rambert's company that he choreographed his first work, A Tragedy of Fashion (1926). He made nearly a score of works for the company, including his first major work, Façade (1931), in the next nine years. In 1935 Ashton moved to the Vic-Wells Ballet (later the Royal Ballet) as principal choreographer and spent 35 years in this post, seven of them as artistic director of the company. The works made for the company in the pre-war period include The Wedding Bouquet and Les Patineurs, which are still part of the repertoire. The Royal Ballet's transfer to Covent Garden in 1946 led to the creation of Symphonic Variations and this work heralded a series of plotless lyrical ballets, notably Scènes de Ballet, Valses nobles et sentimentales and Monotones. The late 1940s also saw the creation of Cinderella, the first of Ashton's large-scale dramatic works in the 19th century classical tradition. It was followed by Romeo and Juliet, Ondine, La Fille mal gardée, The Two Pigeons, Daphnis and Chloe and Marguerite and Armand, as well as many shorter works. Ashton's was a seminal role in the development of the company and in the creation of a native tradition and style of dance.

Although many of Ashton's works have never left the repertoire, some of his earlier works were feared lost. However, in the past three years two of the works created in his prime have been revived with the choreographer's assistance. Ashton's *Romeo and Juliet* was originally created for the Royal Danish Ballet but had not been performed for about 20 years by that company and had never been seen in London. The idea of reviving the ballet was that of Peter Schaufuss, director of London Festival Ballet, whose parents appeared as Juliet and Mercutio in the original production. The premiere of the reconstructed ballet was given in July 1985 and it has featured in the company's repertoire in every season since its revival. Schaufuss's success with *Romeo and Juliet* inspired Anthony Dowell when he took over as director of the Royal Ballet to revive his 1958 ballet *Ondine*. Dowell danced in the corps de ballet during performances of the ballet in the early 1960s and never lost his admiration for the work. With the assistance of Ashton and members of the original cast, including Michael Somes (Palemon to Fonteyn's Ondine in the original production), the ballet re-entered the repertoire of the Royal Ballet in May 1988 (*see* below).

Scottish Loss

Another loss to the dance world was Peter Darrell, founder-director of Scottish Ballet and choreographer, who died suddenly on December 2, 1987 at the age of 58. Darrell started his career as a dancer with the Sadler's Wells Ballet. The opportunity to break into choreography, an early ambition, was provided with the founding of Ballet Workshop and by 1956, when he was 27, Darrell had made over a dozen ballets. In 1957 Darrell and Elizabeth West set up Western Theatre Ballet. Although joint directors and choreographers, West provided the administrative genius which kept the company on the road, and Darrell the creative imagination which gave the company and repertoire their individuality. Darrell's choreographic work during this period included *The Prisoners*, *Chiaroscuro* and *A Wedding Present*. All broke new ground in combining classical technique with contemporary themes, and particularly in recognizing and responding to the influence of the other arts and of psychology.

Elizabeth West's death in an accident in 1962 led to Darrell assuming sole responsibility for the company. Although reluctant to take on duties which interfered with his choreography, he proved an able administrator and excellent at foreseeing and bringing out the latent talent of his dancers. In 1969 Darrell and some of the dancers from Western Theatre Ballet moved to Scotland at the Arts Council's suggestion and founded the Scottish Theatre Ballet (renamed Scottish Ballet in 1974).

Although small initially, the new company gradually expanded and built up a repertoire of classical ballets alongside its modern works. Other choreographers were brought in to create works for the company and Darrell also instituted workshops to provide his dancers with the opportunity to try their hand at choreography. His own work was concentrated now on large-scale dramatic ballets with two

or three acts which helped to bring in the audiences. These included *The Tales of Hoffmann*, *Cinderella*, *Carmen*, *Beauty and the Beast* and *The Nutcracker*.

After directing ballet companies for 24 years, 17 of them with Scottish Ballet, Darrell announced in 1986 his wish to step down as director. The search for a replacement had not been completed at the time of his sudden death. The company subsequently decided not to appoint a new artistic director, but Elaine McDonald, a founder member of the company and its principal dancer, became artistic controller.

OPERA PRODUCTIONS

ROYAL OPERA (1946)
Royal Opera House, Covent Garden, WC2E 9DD

Productions from the repertoire were *Tannhäuser* (1984), *Falstaff* (1982), *La Bohème* (1974), *Tosca* (1964), *L'elisir d'amore* (1975), *Jenůfa* (1986), *Un ballo in maschera* (1975), *Eugene Onegin* (1971), *Lucia di Lammermoor* (1959), *Peter Grimes* (1975), *Macbeth* (1981), *Lohengrin* (1977), *Elektra* (1953), *Don Giovanni* (1981) and *Boris Godunov* (1983).

New productions were:
Oct. 8, 1987. **Le nozze di Figaro** (Mozart). *Conductor*, Bernard Haitink; *producer*, Johannes Schaaf; *set designer*, Xenia Hausner; *costumes*, Peter Pabst.
Figaro, Claudio Desderi; *Susanna*, Marie McLaughlin; *Count Almaviva*, Thomas Allen; *Countess Almaviva*, Karita Mattila; *Cherubino*, Stella Kleindienst.

Nov. 9, 1987. **Die Entführung aus dem Serail** (Mozart). *Conductor*, Georg Solti; *producer*, Elijah Moshinsky; *scenery*, Sidney Nolan, Timothy O'Brien; *costumes*, Timothy O'Brien.
Constanze, Inga Nielsen; *Blonde*, Lillian Watson; *Belmonte*, Deon van der Walt; *Osmin*, Kurt Moll; *Pedrillo*, Lars Magnusson; *Pasha Selim*, Oliver Tobias.

Jan. 2. **L'Italiana in Algeri** (Rossini), in association with Vienna State Opera. *Conductor*, Gabriele Ferro; *producer and designer*, Jean-Pierre Ponnelle; *producer of restaging*, Sonja Frisell.
Isabella, Agnes Baltsa; *Elvira*, Judith Howarth; *Lindoro*, Deon van der Walt; *Mustafa*, Paolo Montarsolo; *Taddeo*, Alessandro Corbelli.

Jan. 28. **Parsifal** (Wagner). *Conductor*, Bernard Haitink; *producer*, Bill Bryden; *designer*, Hayden Griffin; *choreographer*, David Toguri.
Parsifal, Peter Seiffert; *Kundry*, Waltraud Meier; *Klingsor*, Willard White; *Gurnemanz*, Robert Lloyd; *Amfortas*, Simon Estes; *Titurel*, John Connell.

April 8. **Salome** (Strauss), in association with Los Angeles Opera. *Conductor*, Christoph von Dohnányi; *producer*, Peter Hall; *designer*, John Bury; *choreographer*, Elizabeth Keen.
Salome, Maria Ewing; *Herod*, Robert Tear; *Herodias*, Helga Dernesch; *Narraboth*, Robin Leggate; *Jokanaan*, Robert Hale.

April 29. **The Knot Garden** (Tippett). *Conductor*, Sian Edwards; *producer*, Nicholas Hytner; *designer*, Bob Crowley.
Faber, Rodney Macann; *Thea*, Anne Howells; *Flora*, Linda Kitchen; *Denise*, Anna Steiger; *Mel*, Arthur Thompson; *Dov*, Christopher Gillett; *Mangus*, Alan Opie.

May 30. **Anna Bolena** (Donizetti), in association with the State Theatre, Stuttgart/Bregenz Festival. *Conductor*, Richard Bonynge; *producer and designer*, John Pascoe.

Anna Bolena, Joan Sutherland; *Giovanna Sey-mour*, Susanne Mentzer; *Enrico VIII*, Dimitri Kavrakos; *Lord Riccardo Percy*, John Aler; *Smeton*, Eirian James.

ENGLISH NATIONAL OPERA (1931)
London Coliseum, St. Martin's Lane, WC2

Productions from the repertoire were: *Salome* (1975), *Rigoletto* (1982), *Der Rosenkavalier* (1975), *Madam Butterfly* (1984), *Orpheus in the Underworld* (1985), *Cavalleria Rusticana/Pagliacci* (1986), *The Makropulos Case* (1982), *Così fan tutte* (1980), *Xerxes* (1985) and *Fidelio* (1980).

New productions were:
Sept. 10, 1987. The British premiere of **Pacific Overtures** (Sondheim). *Conductor*, James Holmes; *producer*, Keith Warner; *designer*, Ralph Koltai; *costumes*, Marie-Jeanne Lecca; *choreographer*, David Toguri.

Lord Abe, John Kitchiner; *Reciter*, Richard Angas; *Manjiro*, Christopher Booth-Jones; *Kayama*, Malcolm Rivers; *Commodore Perry*, Graham Fletcher; *other parts* played by Leon Berger, Edward Byles, John Cashmore, Gordon Christie, Ian Comboy, Terry Jenkins, Simon Masterton-Smith, Harry Nicoll, Eric Roberts, Michael Sadler, Paul Strathearn and Alan Woodrow.

Sept. 21, 1987. The **Pearl Fishers** (Bizet). *Conductor*, Charles Mackerras; *producer and designer*, Philip Prowse; *choreographer*, Imogen Claire.

Leila, Valerie Masterson; *Nadir*, Adrian Martin; *Zurga*, Sergei Leiferkus.

Oct. 7, 1987. **Werther** (Massenet), a restaging of the 1977 production. *Conductor*, Mark Elder; *producer*, Keith Warner; *designer*, Stefanos Lazaridis; *costumes*, Michael Stennett.

Werther, Arthur Davies; *Charlotte*, Ann Murphy; *Albert*, Steven Page.

Nov. 18, 1987. The **Barber of Seville** (Rossini). *Conductor*, Mark Elder; *producer*, Jonathan Miller; *designer*, Tanya McCallin.

Rosina, Della Jones; *Count Almaviva*, Patrick Power; *Figaro*, Alan Opie; *Dr. Bartolo*, Rodney Macann; *Berta*, Jane Eaglen; *Basilio*, John Connell.

Dec. 16, 1987. **Hansel and Gretel** (Humperdinck). *Conductor*, Mark Elder; *producer*, David Pountney; *designer*, Stefanos Lazaridis.

Hansel, Ethna Robinson; *Gretel*, Cathryn Pope; *The Mother/Witch*, Felicity Palmer; *The Father*, Norman Bailey; *The Sandman*, Susan Bullock; *The Dew Fairy*, Janis Kelly.

Feb. 24. **Billy Budd** (Britten). *Conductor*, David Atherton; *producer*, Tim Albery; *designers*, Antony McDonald, Tom Cairns.

Billy Budd, Thomas Allen; *Capt. Vere*, Philip Langridge; *Claggart*, Richard Van Allen.

March 30. The **Magic Flute** (Mozart), a co-production with De Nederlandse Operastichting. *Conductor*, Ivan Fischer; *producer*, Nicholas Hytner; *designer*, Bob Crowley.

Pamina, Helen Field; *Tamino*, Thomas Randle; *Papageno*, John Rawnsley; *Queen of the Night*, Nan Christie; *Sarastro*, Gwynne Howell; *Speaker*, Richard Van Allen; *Papagena*, Lesley Garrett; *Monostatos*, Alexander Oliver.

June 9. The **Cunning Little Vixen** (Janáček), a co-production of Welsh National Opera and Scottish Opera. *Conductor*, Mark Elder; *producer*, David Pountney; *designer*, Marie Bjørnson; *choreographer*, Stuart Hopps.

Vixen, Anne Dawson; *Fox*, Rita Cullis; *Forester*, Norman Bailey; *Schoolmaster*, Terry Jenkins;

Badger, John Tranter; *Cock*, Alan Woodrow; *Poacher*, Alastair Miles; *Parson*, Arwel Huw Morgan.

NEW SADLER'S WELLS OPERA (1982)
Sadler's Wells Theatre, Rosebery Ave., EC1

Performances of *H.M.S. Pinafore* (1984) were given in a two-week season at Sadler's Wells Theatre and subsequently on tour at Aberdeen, Birmingham, Bath, Southampton, Sunderland, Nottingham and Oxford.

A new production of *Bitter Sweet* was presented at Plymouth, London (Sadler's Wells Theatre), Aberdeen, Glasgow, Oxford, Bath, Southampton, Canterbury, Bradford, Sunderland, Manchester, Birmingham and Liverpool.

Feb. 24. **Bitter Sweet** (Coward). *Director*, Ian Judge; *musical director*, Michael Reed; *set designer*, Russell Craig; *costumes*, Deirdre Clancy; *choreographer*, Sheila Falconer; *conductor*, Stuart Hutchinson.

Sari, Valerie Masterson/Ann Mackay; *Carl Linden*, Martin Smith; *Manon*, Rosemary Ashe; *Capt. Schensi*, Gordon Sandison.

WELSH NATIONAL OPERA (1946)
John Street, Cardiff CF1 4SP

Productions from the repertoire were *Fidelio* (1981), *The Cunning Little Vixen* (1980), *The Marriage of Figaro* (1986), *Eugene Onegin* (1980), *Tosca* (1980) and *Don Giovanni* (1984).

New productions were:
Sept. 9, 1987. **Die Fledermaus** (Strauss). *Conductor*, György Fischer; *producer*, Helmut Polixa; *set designer*, Kathrin Kegler; *costumes*, Marie Therese Cramer.

Rosalinde, Suzanne Murphy; *Adele*, Andrea Bolton; *Eisenstein*, Laurence Dale; *Falke*, Henry Newman; *Prince Orlofsky*, Deborah Stuart-Rogers; *Alfred*, Peter Bronder; *Frank*, Donald Adams; *Frosch*, Sebastian Shaw.

March 25. **Salome** (Strauss). *Conductor*, Charles Mackerras; *producer*, André Engel; *set designer*, Nick Rieti; *costumes*, Elizabeth Neumuller; *choreographer*, Françoise Grès.

Salome, Stephanie Sundine; *Herod*, Robert Tear; *Herodias*, Della Jones; *Narraboth*, Peter Bronder; *Jokanaan*, Phillip Joll.

June 4. **La traviata** (Verdi). *Conductor*, Charles Mackerras; *producer*, Göran Järvefelt; *designer*, Carl Friedrich Oberle.

Violetta, Susan Patterson; *Alfredo*, Laurence Dale; *Germont*, Barry Mora.

The company began the season at the Grand Theatre, Swansea, as their usual base, the New Theatre, Cardiff, was closed for renovation. Performances were given on tour at Birmingham, Liverpool, Bristol, Mold, Oxford, Southampton and Plymouth. A tour of smaller venues, with *The Marriage of Figaro*, was also undertaken.

SCOTTISH OPERA (1962)
Theatre Royal, Hope Street, Glasgow 2

Productions from the repertoire during the company's Silver Jubilee season were *The Seraglio* (1978), *La Vie Parisienne* (1985), *The Pearl Fishers* (1981), *Eugene Onegin* (1979) and *Death in Venice* (1983).

New productions were:
Sept. 15, 1987. **Aida** (Verdi). *Conductor*, John Mauceri; *producer*, Gilbert Deflo; *designer*, William Orlandi.

Aida, Janice Cairns; *Amneris*, Ambra Vespasiani; *Radames*, John Treleaven; *Amonasro*, Ljubomir Videnov; *The King*, John Tranter; *Ramfis*, Roderick Kennedy.

Oct. 21, 1987. **Lulu** (Berg), a co-production with Opera North. *Conductor*, John Mauceri; *producer*, John Cox; *designers*, John and Elizabeth Bury.

Lulu, Beverly Morgan; *Countess Geschwitz*, Delia Wallis; *Alwa*, Eduardo Alvares; *Marquis/Prince/ Manservant*, Hugh Hetherington; *Professor/Doctor*, Ian McKinven; *Dr. Schön/Jack the Ripper*, Chester Ludgin; *Painter/African*, Justin Lavender; *Prologue/ Acrobat*, Roderick Kennedy; *Schigolch*, Roger Bryson; *Schoolboy*, Fiona Kimm.

Jan. 26. **The Pearl Fishers** (Bizet). *Conductor*, Peter Robinson; *producer*, Stephen Lawless; *designer*, Lez Brotherston; *choreographer*, Eleanor Fazan.

Leila, Rita Cullis; *Nadir*, Kim Begley; *Zurga*, Patrick Wheatley.

Feb. 6. **Così fan tutte** (Mozart). *Conductor*, Graeme Jenkins; *producer*, Richard Jones; *designer*, Nigel Lowery.

Fiordiligi, Marie Slorach; *Dorabella*, Clare Shearer; *Despina*, Elizabeth Gale; *Ferrando*, Maldwyn Davies; *Guglielmo*, Steven Page; *Don Alfonso*, Andrew Shore.

May 10. **La Bohème** (Puccini). *Conductor*, John Mauceri; *producer*, Elijah Moshinsky; *designer*, Michael Yeargan.

Mimi, Jane Eaglen; *Rudolfo*, Jorge Pita; *Musetta*, Susan Burghardt; *Marcello*, Steven Page; *Colline*, Jonathan Best; *Schaunard*, Geoffrey Dolton; *Benoit/ Alcindoro*, William McCue.

May 19. **Candide** (Bernstein). *Conductor*, John Mauceri; *producers*, Jonathan Miller, John Wells; *designer*, Richard Hudson.

Candide, Mark Beudert; *Voltaire/Pangloss*, Nickolaus Grace; *Cunégonde*, Marilyn Hill Smith; *Paquette*, Gaynor Miles; *Old Lady*, Ann Howard; *Governor/Captain*, Bonaventura Bottone; *Maximilian*, Mark Tinkler; *Baron*, Leon Greene.

Performances were also given on tour at Edinburgh, Aberdeen, Newcastle upon Tyne and Liverpool. *Candide* will be performed for a season at the Old Vic, London.

Scottish Opera Go Round toured smaller venues in Scotland and Wales with a small-scale production of *La Bohème*.

OPERA NORTH (1978)
Grand Theatre, New Briggate, Leeds LS1 6NZ

Productions from the repertoire were *Rebecca* (1983), *The Merry Widow* (1979) and *Katya Kabanova* (1983).

The company opened its season with *The Trojans in Carthage*, the final three acts of Berlioz's *The Trojans*. A co-production of Opera North, Scottish Opera and Welsh National Opera, *The Trojans* was given in its entirety by the latter company in the 1986–87 season.

Sept. 18, 1987. **The Trojans in Carthage** (Berlioz). *Conductor*, David Lloyd-Jones; *producer*, Tim Albery; *designers*, Tom Cairns, Antony McDonald.

Dido, Sally Burgess; *Anna*, Patricia Bardon; *Aeneas*, William Lewis; *Ascanius*, Doreen O'Neill; *Narbal*, Matthew Best; *Iopas*, Barry Banks; *Hylas*, Paul Nilon.

Oct. 8, 1987. **The Marriage of Figaro** (Mozart). *Conductor*, Stephen Barlow; *producer*, Peter Gill; *designer*, Alison Chitty.

Susanna, Helen Field; *Figaro*, Robert Hayward; *Countess Almaviva*, Ida-Maria Turri; *Count Almaviva*, Peter Savidge; *Cherubino*, Beverley Mills.

Oct. 12, 1987. **Macbeth** (Verdi). *Conductor*, John Pryce-Jones; *producer*, Ian Judge; *set designer*, John Gunter; *costumes*, Deirdre Clancy.

Macbeth, Brent Ellis; *Lady Macbeth*, Josephine

Barstow; *Banquo*, Clive Bayley; *Duncan*, Trefor Glenn; *Macduff*, Gardar Cortes; *Malcolm*, Peter Bodenham.

Dec. 15, 1987. **Carmen** (Bizet). *Conductor*, Alexander Rahbari; *producer*, Richard Jones; *designer*, Nigel Lowery.

Carmen, Cynthia Buchan; *Micaëla*, Marie Slorach; *Don José*, Dennis O'Neill; *Escamillo*, Anthony Michaels-Moore; *Zuniga*, John Hall; *Moralès*, Adrian Clarke.

April 6. **Tosca** (Puccini). *Conductor*, Clive Timms; *producer*, Ian Judge; *designer*, Gerard Howland.

Tosca, Mary Jane Johnson; *Cavaradossi*, John Treleaven; *Scarpia*, Sergei Leiferkus.

April 28. **Fidelio** (Beethoven). *Conductor*, David Lloyd-Jones; *producer*, Michael McCarthy, *designer*, Peter Mumford.

Leonore, Janice Cairns; *Marzelline*, Jane Leslie Mackenzie; *Florestan*, Jeffrey Lawton; *Rocco*, Mark Munkittrick; *Pizarro*, Donald Maxwell; *Jaquino*, Adrian Martin.

Performances were also given on tour at Hull, Nottingham, Manchester, Sheffield and Bradford. The company also performed *Acis and Galatea* at the Cheltenham Festival.

KENT OPERA (1969)
Pembles Cross, Egerton, Ashford, Kent

Productions from the repertoire were *A Night at the Chinese Opera* (1987), *The Magic Flute* (1987), *Pygmalion/Dido and Aeneas* double bill and *Don Giovanni* (1983).

New productions were:

Sept. 26, 1987. **Il re pastore** (Mozart). *Conductor*, Ivan Fischer; *producer*, Michael McCarthy; *designer*, Roger Butlin.

Aminta, Jill Gomez; *Alexander the Great*, Martyn Hill; *Elisa*, Louisa Kennedy; *Tamiri*, Patricia Rozario; *Agenore*, Neill Archer.

May 4. **Count Ory** (Rossini). *Conductor*, Ivan Fischer; *producer*, Richard Jones; *designer*, Richard Hudson.

Countess Adèle, Patricia Rozario; *Count Ory*, Neil Jenkins; *Ragonde*, Enid Hartle; *Isolier*, Katherine Steffan; *Raimbaud*, Alan Watt.

Performances were given at the Queen Elizabeth Hall, London, Tunbridge Wells, Canterbury, Southsea, Dartford, Norwich, Northampton, Plymouth and Eastbourne.

GLYNDEBOURNE FESTIVAL OPERA (1934)
Glyndebourne, Lewes, Sussex BN8 5UU

The 1988 Festival ran from May 16 to August 18; the orchestra was the London Philharmonic Orchestra. Seven operas (including a double bill) were presented, of which four were revivals: *Die Entführung aus dem Serail* (1980), *La traviata* (1987) and *L'heure espagnole/L'enfant et les sortilèges* (1987).

The new productions were:

May 19. **Katya Kabanova** (Janáček). *Conductor*, Andrew Davis; *director*, Nikolaus Lehnhoff; *designer*, Tobias Hoheisel.

Katya, Nancy Gustafson; *Tichon*, Ryland Davies; *Kabanicha*, Felicity Palmer; *Boris*, Barry McCauley; *Varvara*, Louise Winter; *Kudrjaš*, John Graham-Hall; *Dikoy*, Donald Adams.

June 5. **The Electrification of the Soviet Union** (Osborne), commissioned for Glyndebourne Festival by the B.B.C. *Conductor*, Elgar Howarth; *director*, Peter Sellars; *set designer*, George Tsypin; *costumes*, Duná Ramicová.

Anna, Elizabeth Laurence; *Sashka*, Helen Williams; *Natasha*, Hyacinth Nicholls; *Mrs. Frestln*, Penelope Walmsley-Clark; *Pasternak*, Henry Her-ford; *Serezha*, Omar Ebrahim; *Lemokh*, Jonathan Veira; *Frestln*, Philip O'Reilly; *Fardybassov*, Wout Oosterkamp; *Harry Frestln*, Jamie Gates. (The world premiere of this work was given at Glyndebourne by the Glyndebourne Touring Opera on Oct. 5, 1987.)

June 29. **Falstaff** (Verdi). *Conductor*, Bernard Haitink; *director*, Peter Hall; *designer*, John Gunter.

Falstaff, Claudio Desderi; *Mistress Ford*, Yvonne Kenny; *Mistress Page*, Anne Howells; *Mistress Quickly*, Felicity Palmer; *Ford*, Robert McFarland; *Nannetta*, Eva Lind; *Fenton*, Gianluco Sorrentino.

The Glyndebourne Touring Opera visited Oxford, Southampton, Plymouth, Manchester and Norwich in autumn 1988.

DANCE PRODUCTIONS

ROYAL BALLET (1931)
Royal Opera House, Covent Garden, WC2E 9DD

Full-length ballets from the repertoire performed in the 1987–88 season were *Swan Lake* (Petipa/Ivanov; Dowell, 1987), *Giselle* (Petipa, after Coralli and Perrot; Wright, 1985) and *Manon* (MacMillan, 1974).

Programmes also included the following shorter ballets from the repertoire: *The Fire Bird* (Fokine), *Scènes de ballet* (Ashton), *The Rite of Spring* (MacMillan), *The Dream* (Ashton), *Galanteries* (Bintley), *The Concert* (Robbins), *Pursuit* (Page), *The Sons of Horus* (Bintley), *Symphonic Variations* (Ashton), *La Fin du Jour* (MacMillan) and *Serenade* (Balanchine).

New productions were:
Dec. 16, 1987. **Cinderella**. *Choreography*, Ashton; *music*, Prokofiev; *designer*, David Walker. The cast at the premiere was led by Maria Almeida and Jonathan Cope.

March 9. **Bugaku**, introduced into the company's repertoire. *Choreography*, Balanchine; *music*, Toshiro Mayuzumi; *scenery*, David Hays; *costumes*, Karinska.

May 10. **Ondine**, a revival of Ashton's 1958 ballet; *music*, Hans Werner Henze; *designer*, Lila de Nobili. The cast at the premiere was led by Maria Almeida and Anthony Dowell.

A new ballet was:
March 9. **'Still Life' at the Penguin Café**. *Choreography*, David Bintley; *music*, Simon Jeffes; *designer*, Hayden Griffin. The cast at the premiere included Fiona Brockway, Phillip Broomhead, Deborah Bull, Jonathan Cope, Cynthia Harvey, Stephen Jefferies, Sonia Noy, Nicola Roberts and Bruce Sansom.

In addition to performances at Covent Garden, the Royal Ballet also took productions to Birmingham and Manchester The company spent July 1988 on tour in Australia as part of Australia's bicentenary celebrations, with a repertoire of *Swan Lake*, *The Dream*, *Rhapsody*, *A Month in the Country*, *Manon*, *The Rite of Spring*, and a new Bintley ballet premiered in Brisbane.

SADLER'S WELLS ROYAL BALLET (1931)
Sadler's Wells Theatre, Rosebery Avenue, EC1R 4TN

Full-length ballets from the repertoire performed this season were *Swan Lake* (Petipa/Ivanov/Wright; Wright, Samsova, 1980), *Coppélia* (Petipa/Cecchetti/Wright; Wright, 1979), *La Fille mal gardée* (Ashton; 1960), *The Snow Queen* (Bintley; 1986) and *The Sleeping Beauty* (Petipa/Wright; Wright, 1984).

Programmes also included the following shorter ballets: *Paquita* (Petipa), *The Picture of Dorian Gray* (Deane), *Façade* (Ashton), *Paramour* (Lister), *Capriol Suite* (Ashton), *Valses nobles et sentimentales* (Ashton), *Private City* (Crow), *Allegri Diversi* (Bin-

tley), *Flowers of the Forest* (Bintley) and *Elite Syncopations* (MacMillan).

New ballets were:
Nov. 13, 1987. **Gloriana**. *Choreography*, Michael Corder; *music*, Britten; *designer*, Philip Prowse. The cast at the premiere was led by Galina Samsova (*Elizabeth I*) and Joseph Cipolla (*Essex*).

Jan. 14. **The Edge of Silence**. *Choreography*, Graham Lustig; *music*, Alfred Schnittke; *designer*, Nadine Baylis. At this performance members of the Prague Chamber Ballet gave the British premiere of *Kreutzer Sonata* (choreographer, Pavel Smok).

June 24. **Bastet**. *Choreography*, Lynn Seymour; *music*, Michael Berkeley; *designer*, Andrew Logan. The cast at the premiere was led by June Highwood, Susan Lucas and Petter Jacobsson.

In addition to seasons at Sadler's Wells Theatre the company gave performances on tour at Leeds Castle, Maidstone (a Big Top season), Bristol, Northampton, Sunderland, Birmingham, Leeds, Southampton, Oxford, Liverpool, Plymouth, Cambridge (a Big Top season), Birmingham and Scarborough (a Big Top season). The company also undertook an eight-week tour of the Far East in March and April 1988. They visited Thailand, South Korea, China, Hong Kong and Japan with a repertoire of *La Fille mal gardée*, *Swan Lake*, *Flowers of the Forest*, *Checkmate* and *Elite Syncopations*.

LONDON FESTIVAL BALLET (1950)
Festival Ballet House, 39 Jay Mews, SW7 2ES

Performances of full-length ballets from the repertoire included *The Nutcracker* (Schaufuss, 1986), *Onegin* (Cranko, 1983), *Romeo and Juliet* (Ashton, 1985) and *La Sylphide* (Schaufuss after Bournonville, 1979).

On April 12 a new production was premiered of *Swan Lake*: *choreography*, Petipa, Ivanov, Ashton; *producer*, Natalia Makarova; *designers*, Gunther Schneider-Siemsson, Dietmar Solt. The cast at the premiere was led by Patrick Armand (*Siegfried*), Trinidad Sevillano (*Odette*) and Susan Hogard (*Odile*).

Programmes of shorter ballets performed by the company included: *Night Creature* (Ailey), *Carmen* (Petit), *Les Sylphides* (Fokine), *Corsair* pas de deux (Petipa), *Dances from Napoli* (Bournonville), *Etudes* (Lander), *La Bayadère* (Makarova after Petipa), *Aureole* (Taylor), *Songs of a Wayfarer* (Béjart), *The Dream is Over* (Bruce), *Apollo* (Balanchine), *L'Arlésienne* (Petit), *Symphony in C* (Balanchine), *Bolero* (Béjart), *Petrushka* (Fokine), *Land* (Bruce), and *Sphinx* (Tetley).

The company introduced into its repertoire *Cruel Garden* (May 24: choreographer, Christopher Bruce) and the new work premiered this season was by the same composer.

Dec. 8, 1987. **Swansong** *Choreography*, Christopher Bruce; *music*, Philip Chambon; *performed* by Matz Skoog, Koen Onzia and Kevin Richmond.

The company performed in London at the Royal Festival Hall, Sadler's Wells Theatre and the Coliseum, and on tour at Bradford, Canterbury, Manchester, Bristol, Birmingham, Jersey, Guernsey, Oxford, Eastbourne and Southampton.

RAMBERT DANCE COMPANY (1926)
94 Chiswick High Road, W4 1SH

Works from the repertoire performed during the season were *Swamp* (Clark), *Wolfy* (Seymour), *Pulcinella* (Alston), *Dutiful Ducks* (Alston), *Strong Language* (Alston), *Dancing Day* (Bruce), *Rushes* (Davies), *Pierrot Lunaire* (Tetley) and *Dangerous Liaisons* (Alston).

Works introduced into the repertoire this season

were *Septet* (Nov. 20, 1987: choreography, Merce Cunningham) and the Antony Tudor work *Dark Elegies*, created for the Rambert company in 1937, which was revived in May 1988.

New works included:
March 3. **Rhapsody in Blue**. *Choreography*, Richard Alston; *music*, Gershwin; *designer*, Victor Edelstein.

April 28. **Trace**, for six dancers. *Choreography*, Mary Evelyn; *music*, Simon Bainbridge; *designer*, Stephen Buckley.

June 8. **Mates**. *Choreography*, David Gordon; *music*, Chuck Hammer; *designer*, Antony McDonald.

During the 1987–88 season the company performed on tour at Bath, Nottingham, Plymouth, Oxford, Swansea, Glasgow, Birmingham, Leicester, Southampton, the Royal Northern College of Music in Manchester, Mold and at Sadler's Wells Theatre, London. In December 1987 the company also performed in Brussels and in East Berlin.

LONDON CONTEMPORARY DANCE THEATRE (1967)
The Place, 16 Flaxman Terrace, WC1H 9AT

Performances from the repertoire were *Red Steps* (Davies), *Fabrications* (North), *And do they do* (Davies), *Irma Vep* (Ezralow), *Forest* (Cohan), duet from *Nympheas* (Cohan), *Songs, Lamentations and Praises* (Cohan).

The company opened the season with a two-act "entertainment" **The Phantasmagoria**, premiered on Sept. 29, 1987, with choreography by Robert Cohan, Tom Jobe and Darshan Singh Buller. Other new works included:

Nov. 24, 1987. **John Somebody**. *Choreography*, Rosalind Newman; *music*, Scott Johnson; *designer*, Antony McDonald.
and **Hang Up**. *Choreography*, Jonathan Lunn; *text* by Anthony Mingella, spoken by Juliet Stevenson and David Threlfall; *performed* by Jonathan Lunn and Lauren Potter.

Dec. 1, 1987. **Maybe Tomorrow**, for eight dancers. *Choreography*, Christopher Bannerman and Paul Chamberlain; *music*, Man Jumping; *designer*, Colin Winslow.

Feb. 11. **Exquisite Corpse**; *choreography*, Jonathan Lunn; and **Stand By Your Man**; *choreography*, Aletta Collins.

Feb. 26. **Futures**—a four-part work created in collaboration with local school and community dance groups in Leeds. Choreography, music and design were created locally, and young dancers and musicians appeared at the performances.

The company performed on tour at Birmingham, Leicester, Liverpool, Norwich, Leeds, Bristol, Warwick, Swindon, Plymouth, Northampton, Swansea, Oxford, Canterbury and at Sadler's Wells Theatre London. In June the company performed *The Annunciation* (North), *Stabat Mater* (Cohan) and *Songs, Lamentations and Praises* (Cohan) at the York Festival.

THE SCOTTISH BALLET (1969)
261 West Princes Street, Glasgow G4 9EE

Productions from the repertoire were *Carmen* (Darrell: 1985), *The Nutcracker* (Darrell after Ivanov: 1973), *Romeo and Juliet* (Cranko: 1982) and the shorter works *Les Sylphides* (Fokine), *Three Dances to Japanese Music* (Carter), *Corsair* pas de deux (Petipa), *Economy in strait jacket but still room for movement* (Darrell), *The Prisoners* (Darrell), *Vespri* (Prokovsky), *The Water's Edge* (North). *Chéri*, *Five Rückert Songs* and excerpts from other Darrell ballets were performed in tribute to the company's founder–director, Peter Darrell, after his death in December 1987.

Introduced into the repertoire was *La Bayadère* Act III (Nov. 5, 1987: choreography, Petipa; producer, Cecilia Barrett).

New works, premiered on Nov. 26, 1987, were: **For you were mine**; *choreography*, Lloyd Emberton; *music*, Sibelius: **Libera me**; *choreography*, Paolo Lopez; *music*, Rachmaninov: and **Just Stepping Along**; *choreography*, Jane Jewel; *music*, songs by Reynaldo Hahn performed by Alan Watt.

The company began the season at the new studio theatre attached to its headquarters at West Princes Street. Larger-scale works were performed at the Theatre Royal, Glasgow, and also on tour at Aberdeen, Newcastle, Edinburgh, Belfast, Hull and Inverness. In September 1987 small-scale productions were performed at a number of small venues in Scotland.

FILM AND CINEMA, 1987–88

The year for films and the cinema was one of highs and lows, spectacular flops and unexpected successes, disillusionment and belated triumph. David Puttnam left Hollywood in near humiliation, but at the Oscar ceremony soon after his departure he received confirmation that his policies had been proved right even if his politics had not.

Puttnam, the first Briton to head a major American studio, had been enticed to Hollywood by a reported $2 million a year salary and the guarantee of total creative freedom. After a troubled year's reign, he resigned in September 1987, his position having become untenable. Puttnam had said that he hoped "to make films that are humanist without being sentimental, and commercial without being condescending". He particularly deplored films such as Stallone's *Rambo*, which he considered exploitative. However, without his knowledge Columbia merged with a smaller company, Tri-Star Pictures, whose greatest cinematic success has been *Rambo*. Tri-Star's chairman Victor Kaufman was then placed in charge of the new company: Puttnam first read of the deal in a newspaper.

David Puttnam had always considered himself an outsider in Hollywood and was proud of the fact. However, it appears that he seriously under-estimated the hostility aroused first by his appointment and then by his outspoken condemnation of a system that developed films around box office stars commanding fantastic salaries, frequently to the detriment of the finished product. A prime example of this was Columbia's own *Ishtar* (begun before Puttnam took control). A star vehicle for Warren Beatty and Dustin Hoffman, the film cost a reputed $40 million and seems unlikely to recoup even a fraction of that amount. Written and directed by Elaine May, this supposed comedy was an unmitigated disaster that could have been made for a fraction of its final cost. It was a monument to the worst excesses of Hollywood and exactly the sort of thing that Puttnam wished to stamp out, but he had reckoned without the power of a system that could condone such disasters. Puttnam had said that his reign should not be judged before the spring of 1989, when his policies would have had time to take effect and the films that he commissioned would begin to be released. However, he was partially vindicated a year earlier at the Oscar awards, where two of his first four productions (significantly—to Hollywood—all directed by Europeans) were prominent in the nominations.

Elstree Sale

In October 1987, the Cannon group's incursion into British cinema ran into further trouble. It was announced that Cannon would sell its British cinemas and the Elstree film studios to a Spanish company, Renta Immobiliaria, for some $300 million and then lease them back. However, in June 1988, Cannon sold Elstree studios to property developers. The move was widely condemned by film companies, which protested that they should have been given a chance to buy the studios as a going concern. Steven Spielberg, who has made eight successful films at Elstree, was among those who felt that the loss of the studios' ten stages

would be a severe blow to British and international film-making.

Cannon had a deal with Warner Communications to allow Warner an option to buy half of Cannon's European cinema circuit for $50 million. This was cancelled by Cannon's agreement with Renta Immobiliaria. However, Warner Brothers announced in August 1988 that it would be introducing the American concept of "multiplex" cinema complexes into the United Kingdom. Within three to four years, the company hopes to open 30 such complexes at a cost of around £120 million. Each would have at least eight auditoria, and up to 4,000 seats. The Cineplex Odeon Corporation also revealed plans to develop a chain of new cinemas: their intention is to have 110 screens in 20 locations by 1990.

"Emperor" First

At the 60th annual Academy Awards there were four main contenders for the most prestigious awards. Bertolucci's *The Last Emperor* led the field with nine nominations, followed by *Broadcast News* with seven, *Empire of the Sun* and *Moonstruck* with six, and *Hope and Glory* with five. The clear winner was *The Last Emperor*, which won all the categories for which it had been nominated. These included the premier awards of best picture and best director. The film was the most expensive ever to be made independently; the $25 million it cost to produce was raised by a consortium led by the London merchant bankers Hill Samuel. Producer Jeremy Thomas spent four years on the project, which was rejected by all the Hollywood studios although Columbia, under Puttnam, became involved in its distribution.

The Last Emperor told the remarkable story of Pu Yi, who at the age of three was taken to Peking's Forbidden City to succeed the Dowager Empress of China. Although China became a republic in 1912 his cloistered and pampered life carried on much as before until the revolution in 1949. After the revolution he spent nearly ten years in jail, where he was re-educated by an enlightened prison governor, before being pardoned and released to work as a gardener. Pu Yi died in 1967 of cancer. His remarkable history is brilliantly realized by Bertolucci, the epic scale of the film perfectly matching the story. Four actors played Pu Yi in the film, with John Lone particularly impressive as the adult Emperor. *The Last Emperor* also featured Peter O'Toole and Joan Cheng.

In addition to best film and best director *The Last Emperor* won Oscars for best screenplay adaptation (Bernardo Bertolucci and Mark Peploe), best original score (Ryuichi Sakamoto, David Byrne and Cong Su), cinematography (Vittorio Storaro), art direction (Ferdinando Scarfiotti and Bruno Cesari), costume design (James Acheson), editing (Gabriella Cristiani), and sound (Bill Rowe and Ivan Sharrock). *The Last Emperor* also won four Golden Globe awards—best dramatic picture, best direction, best screenplay and best original score.

Michael Douglas won the Oscar for best actor for his portrayal of the unscrupulous, amoral, Gekko in Oliver Stone's *Wall Street*. Although the film was

not popular with stockbrokers in America or Britain,
it struck a chord with a public mindful of the insider-
dealing scandals that have struck stock exchanges
on both sides of the Atlantic. "Greed is good" was
Gekko's motto, and Douglas's study of corruption
was a worthy winner of an award. *Wall Street* also
featured Charlie Sheen and Martin Sheen, who
played father and son in the film.

Moonstruck

Moonstruck received six Oscar nominations and
won three awards, including best actress for Cher.
Directed by Norman Jewison, the film is a moving
love story set among the Italian community in New
York's Bronx area and was deservedly popular.
Olympia Dukakis received the award for best supporting actress for the same film, and John Shapley
won the award for the best original screenplay.

Brian de Palma's *The Untouchables* was the story
of F.B.I. agent Eliot Ness, the man who succeeded in
having Al Capone convicted and sentenced for tax
fraud. A series of the same name had been popular on
television. Robert de Niro gave a brilliant cameo
portrayal as Capone, but the film was notable for
gaining Sean Connery his first Oscar. He won the
award for best supporting actor for his role as an
honest policeman who helps Ness in his battle against
the Prohibition-era gangsters.

Two years previously *Out of Africa*, the story of
Karen Blixen, won the Oscar for best film and a film
adaptation of a story by Blixen (written under her
penname of Isak Dinesen) won the award this year
for best foreign language film. *Babette's Feast*,
adapted and directed by Gabriel Axel, featured
Stephane Audran and, true to the original story,
culminated in a splendid epicurean banquet.

Other main Oscar winners were: best original
song, "I've had the time of my life" (*Dirty Dancing*);
visual effects, Denis Muren, William George, Harley
Jessup and Kenneth Smith (*Innerspace*); make-up,
Rick Baker (*Harry and the Hendersons*); animated
short, *The Man Who Planted Trees*; short documen-
tary, *Young at Heart*; documentary feature, *The Ten-
Year Lunch: The Wit and Legend of the Algonquin
Round Table*; and live action short, *Ray's Male
Heterosexual Dance Hall*.

British Awards

At the British Academy of Film and Television
Awards, the distinguished Swedish director Ingmar
Bergman was awarded a fellowship and the Michael
Balcon Award for Outstanding British Contribution
to Cinema was presented to the Monty Python team.
The best film award went to Claude Berri's *Jean de
Florette*, and Oliver Stone won best director for
Platoon, the previous year's Oscar winner. The best
original screenplay was awarded to David Leland for
Wish You Were Here, which was based on the early
life of Cynthia Payne. The film featured an impressive
debut by Emily Lloyd as the bored teenager growing
up too fast in an English seaside town, with Tom Bell
as her older lover. Best adapted screenplay was *Jean
de Florette* (Claude Berri and Gerard Brach), and
Daniel Auteuil was judged best supporting actor in
the same film. Sean Connery won the best actor prize

for his role as a medieval monk turned detective in
The Name of the Rose, based on Umberto Eco's novel
about murders at a monastery. Ann Bancroft was
awarded best actress for her role as Helene Hanff in
84 Charing Cross Road, the sentimental tale of a New
York writer's long-distance love affair with a London
bookshop and its staff. Best supporting actress went
to Susan Wooldrige for *Hope and Glory*, John
Boorman's semi-autobiographical account of growing
up in suburbia during the Second World War.
Boorman spent £750,000 on recreating Rosehill
Avenue, the setting for the film, at a disused airfield.
This concern for detail, coupled with excellent
performances from a cast which also included Sarah
Miles, Sebastian Rice-Edwards and Ian Bannen, all
contributed to the film's success.

Ennio Morricone's score for *The Untouchables* won
a B.A.F.T.A. award, with further prizes going to
Anna-Lena Wibom and Andrei Tarkovsky for best
foreign language film (*The Sacrifice*) and to Jonas
Grimas for best short film (*Artisten*). The Flaherty
Documentary Award was given to Phil Agland for
Baka—People of the Rainforest, and best animated
film was Bridget Appleby's *The Reluctant Dragon*.

Film craft awards were presented to Bruno Nuyt-
ten for cinematography in *Jean de Florette*; Claire
Simpson for the editing of *Platoon*; Jonathan Bates,
Simon Kaye and Gerry Humphreys for sound in *Cry
Freedom*; Santo Loquasto for production design on
Radio Days, and Jeffrey Kurland for costume design;
Hasso von Hugo for make-up in *The Name of the
Rose*; and the special effects award went to the team
which worked on *The Witches of Eastwick*. The
Academy also paid a special tribute to Sir John Mills
on his 80th birthday for his outstanding contribution
to the film industry.

Glasnost in London

Controversy surrounded the opening of the London
Film Festival after *A Prayer for the Dying* was
dropped. Based on an unremarkable Jack Higgins
story about a reformed I.R.A. terrorist, the film was
withdrawn following the Remembrance Day bombing
at Enniskillen, in the light of which screening was
considered insensitive. Director Mike Hodges also
complained that the film had been re-edited without
his knowledge, but it was not clear whether this
accounted for the poor dialogue and underdeveloped
characterization, with Bob Hoskins notably miscast
as a priest and Mickey Rourke as the terrorist.

The Festival was more memorable for its wide and
imaginative programme of some 140 feature films,
plus shorts and videos, from 40 countries. The
programme included 40 new British films, and
Eastern Europe was also particularly well represented, with some of the recent cinematic fruits of
glasnost on display. Although completed in 1982,
Tenghis Abuladze's *Repentance* had only recently
been released. The story of a corrupt commissar in a
Georgian town, with its echoes of Stalin, had
originally touched a raw nerve, but the more
enlightened current régime decided that there is
much to gain from exposing artistically the excesses
of the past. In *Repentance* Avtandil Makharadze
gave a brilliant performance as Commissar Varlam.
The film had previously won the Special Grand Prize

at the 40th Cannes Film Festival. Also shown at the London Festival was Gennadi Poloka's *Intervention*, a celebration of the October Revolution that had been suppressed for twenty years.

Restored classics on show in London included Raoul Walsh's 1930 film *The Big Trail*, which featured John Wayne. This classic Western was restored from the decaying nitrate originals after apparently not being shown for fifty years. Also shown were Eisenstein's *Battleship Potemkin*, with the original score by Edmund Meisel, and the silent film version of *Ben Hur*, a masterpiece dating from 1925.

The 41st Cannes Film Festival again produced a rank outsider as winner of the *Palme d'Or*. The premier award went to *Pelle the Conqueror*, Bille August's Danish story of rural hardship at the turn of the century, starring Max von Sydow. Chris Menges' cinematography has long been admired and brought him Oscars in recent years for *The Mission* and *The Killing Fields*. His first directorial effort, *A World Apart*, won the Grand Prix of the Jury. The film concerns apartheid in South Africa in the 1960s and the strength of the acting was recognized by the best actress prize being awarded jointly to its three leading players, Barbara Hershey, Johdi May and Linda Mvusi. Forest Whitaker received the prize for best actor for his role in *Bird*, Clint Eastwood's film about the life of jazz saxophonist Charlie Parker, and Peter Greenaway took the prize for best artistic contribution for his *Drowning by Numbers*.

Lions and Bears

At Venice, the Golden Lion went to Louis Malle's *Au Revoir, les Enfants*, while the Silver Lion was shared between Ivory and Merchant's *Maurice* and Ermanno Olmi's *Long Life to the Lady*. The Special Jury Prize was awarded to Kjell Grede's *Hip, Hip, Hurra!* and the Prize of the Republic to Vadim Abdrashitov's *Plumbum*. James Wilby and Hugh Grant shared the best actor award for their roles in *Maurice*, the twenty-fifth collaboration between producer Ismail Merchant and director James Ivory. They achieved widespread acclaim for their masterly screen version of E. M. Forster's *A Room with a View*, a more readily accessible novel than *Maurice*, a story of homosexual love written in 1914 but not published until after Forster's death. With a script by Kit Hesketh-Harvey and James Ivory, the film had much to recommend it, including fine performances from Rupert Graves, Denholm Elliott and Ben Kingsley.

John Huston's last film, marking the end of a varied and brilliant career in the cinema, was given its world premiere at Venice a week after his death in August 1987. *The Dead* was based on the last of James Joyce's fifteen stories of Dublin life, *The Dubliners*, first published in 1914. An almost flawless film, it will rank in the Huston canon alongside *The Maltese Falcon* as the work of a true genius. The distinguished cast included Helena Carroll, Cathleen Delany, Donal Donnelly and Huston's daughter Angelica. The script was written by his son Tony.

At Berlin, the Silver Bear Award was won by Alexander Askoldov's *The Commissar*, released for distribution after having been suppressed for twenty years. The director made a brave public protest at a conference on *glasnost* in Moscow about the banning of his film, the making of which had forced him out of the industry. The protest succeeded, and the film was not only screened in Moscow but also achieved belated and much-deserved success abroad.

American Productions

Popular successes at the box office in America reflected a variety of preoccupations, with films featuring babies scoring well and adultery apparently a thing of the past following *Fatal Attraction*. *Three Men and a Baby* reportedly grossed $150 million in its first 150 days on release in the U.S.A., although like most remakes of French films it was far inferior to its French original, *Trois Hommes et un Couffin*. A rather limp comedy about three bachelors bringing up a baby, it contained much predictable lavatorial humour. It success was probably attributable to the box office appeal of its stars, Tom Selleck and Ted Danson who, together with Steve Guttenberg, comprised the unlikely trio. The film was directed by Leonard Nimoy.

Fatal Attraction starred Michael Douglas, Glenn Close and Anne Archer in a reworking of the eternal triangle theme. Like *Play Misty for Me*, directed some years ago and to better effect by Clint Eastwood, *Fatal Attraction* featured a revenge twist to the plot. The "other woman" refused to leave the errant husband alone after their affair ended, her obsession turning finally to violence. The plot was predictable and shallow but caught the mood of prevailing sexual mores. Directed by Adrian Lyne, who was responsible for the popular *Flashdance*, the film's ending was changed as the first version was not liked by preview audiences.

Another successful American film was *Coming to America*, also the result of the box office appeal of its star, Eddie Murphy, rather than any intrinsic merit. The film is a modern fairy tale of an African prince visiting New York to find true love before having to accept an arranged marriage back home. Directed by John Landis, it also featured Arsenio Hall and James Earl Jones.

Broadcast News, while missing out on the Academy Awards, was nevertheless an intelligently-made film about the struggle for success in the newsroom of an American television station. William Hurt, who won an Oscar for his role in *Kiss of the Spider Woman*, gave another fine performance, ably supported by Holly Hunter and Albert Brooks; the film was directed by James L. Brooks.

Barfly, written by Charles Bukowski and directed by Barbet Schroeder, starred Mickey Rourke and Faye Dunaway as habitués of Californian lowlife existing in a perpetual alcoholic haze. *La Bamba* celebrated the brief but eventful life of the singer Ritchie Valens, who had a meteoric rise to fame and died in the same aeroplane crash which killed Buddy Holly.

Bill Forsyth's first feature to be made outside his native Scotland was filmed in British Columbia. *Housekeeping* was an evocative, mythical story based on a novel by Marilynne Robinson and starred Christine Lahti and Sara Walker. George Miller directed *The Witches of Eastwick*, a film version of John Updike's novel about devilish goings-on in New England. A bravura performance from Jack Nicholson was well supported by Cher, Michelle Pfeiffer and Susan Sarandon as the witches.

Since the spectacular success of his early *Star Wars* trilogy George Lucas appears to have lost his magic touch. *Howard the Duck* and *Labyrinth* were hardly notable successes but his latest film, *Willow*, threatened to dwarf even the disastrous *Ishtar* as the flop of the year. This derivative and stale fantasy cost $35 million and had a further $50 million's worth of promotional material and tie-ins riding on its success, which seems improbable.

Crocodile Dundee II obeyed the law of diminishing returns for sequels; although very successful, it failed to match the appeal, cinematically or in the box office, of its predecessor. Paul Hogan again starred with Linda Kozlowski. The inventive American comedian Steve Martin updated the *Cyrano de Bergerac* story in *Roxanne*. He played a fire chief in a small ski resort in Washington State handicapped romantically by his large nose but helping out his rival in love.

Lindsay Anderson effected a remarkable screen pairing in *The Whales of August*. The film brought together the 80-year-old veteran Bette Davis and the 92-year-old star of the silent screen Lillian Gish, with support from the comparatively youthful Vincent Price. Steven Spielberg directed *The Empire of the Sun*, which was based on J. G. Ballard's autobiographical novel. Scripted by Tom Stoppard, the film featured Christian Bale as 11-year-old Jim Graham. He was chosen from 4,000 prospective young actors to star with John Malkovich, Miranda Richardson and Nigel Havers in a story about the experiences of a young boy as a Japanese prisoner-of-war.

British Films

Richard Attenborough's film *Cry Freedom* was based on the relationship between Steve Biko, the Black Consciousness leader who was killed in captivity by the South African police, and liberal newspaper editor Donald Woods. The film was a damning indictment of apartheid and oppression in South Africa, with fine performances from Denzel Washington as Biko and Kevin Kline as Woods. Once again

Attenborough's fine directorial control was demonstrated, particularly in the scene of Biko's funeral, which featured 20,000 extras. The film came in under budget at $20 million.

Hanif Kureishi and Stephen Frears, who collaborated on the successful *My Beautiful Laundrette*, set another film, *Sammy and Rosie Get Laid* in London's Asian community. It featured Frances Barber, Ayub Khan Din, Shashi Kapoor and Claire Bloom. Peter Greenaway's most accessible film yet was *The Belly of an Architect*, which featured a superb performance from Brian Dennehy. He played American architect Stourley Kracklite, who becomes obsessed with an exhibition he is organizing in Rome dedicated to the 18th century visionary architect Etienne-Louis Boullee. Brilliantly filmed by Sacha Vierny, the drama is played out against a superb backdrop of Roman architecture. The cast also included Lambert Wilson, Stefania Casini and Sergio Fantoni.

The real-life murder of the philandering Earl of Erroll in Kenya in 1941 was the subject of *White Mischief*. Directed by Michael Radford, the story seemed muddled and unconvincing although the film featured a distinguished cast, including Joss Ackland, Geraldine Chaplin, Charles Dance, Trevor Howard, John Hurt, Sarah Miles and Greta Scacchi. *Track 29* was directed by Nicholas Roeg from a Dennis Potter script. This enigmatic but powerful tale of complex relationships, played out against the unlikely but effective background of a model railway set, featured Theresa Russell, Gary Oldman and Christopher Lloyd.

Other notable productions included *A Handful of Dust*, directed by Charles Sturridge from the novel by Evelyn Waugh, which featured James Wilby, Rupert Graves, Kristin Scott Thomas, Alec Guinness and Judi Dench. Alec Guinness also appeared in *Little Dorrit*, adapted from the Dickens novel by Christine Edzard and filmed in two parts, totalling six hours in length. Sarah Pickering took the title role and the film also starred Derek Jacobi. *The Unbearable Lightness of Being* was adapted from Milan Kundera's 1984 novel; directed by Philip Kaufman, it featured Daniel Day-Lewis, Linda Olin and Juliette Binoche.

FILM CERTIFICATES

The British Board of Film Classification issues the following categories of film certificates:

U   Universal: suitable for all.
PG   Parental Guidance: some scenes may be unsuitable for young children.
15   Passed only for persons of fifteen years and over.
18   Passed only for persons of eighteen years and over.
R18 For Restricted Distribution Only (through segregated premises to which no one under the age of eighteen is admitted).

The classifications of video tapes differ slightly:

U   Universal: suitable for all.
Uc   Universal: particularly suitable for children.
PG   Parental Guidance: general viewing, but some scenes may be unsuitable for young children.
15   Suitable only for persons of 15 years and over.
18   Suitable only for persons of 18 years and over.
R18 Restricted: to be supplied only in licensed sex shops to persons of not less than 18 years.

TELEVISION, 1987–88

After the torrid period of the past few years, the BBC began to show signs of renewed confidence as its new management team settled in and the apparent threat posed by the Peacock report receded. In September 1987, the director-general of the BBC, Michael Checkland, said in an address to the Royal Television Society, "We have put away our begging bowl". He went on to say that the Corporation was examining radical ways of raising revenue, including subscription services, sponsorship and magazines.

Soon after Mr. Checkland's speech, the BBC said that it was interested in broadcasting a night-time subscription service on BBC2 which would contain coded news and information for doctors. The project would be run jointly with British Direct Television Ltd., and a decoder costing £40 would be necessary for those wishing to receive the service. There would be no charge for the programmes, the cost of which would be covered by advertising, estimated at £3 million per year. There was some concern about the BBC in effect selling off parts of its airtime to outside companies, and the Home Office said that such a service would need to be covered by new legislation. However, at the end of January 1988 the scheme was given the go-ahead for a two-year trial period, commencing in late 1988. Similar services might be undertaken for other professions, such as architects, lawyers and accountants, if the trial scheme proves successful. In the meantime, the BBC's revenues continue to depend mostly on licence fees, which rose on April 1, 1988, to £62·50 for colour television and to £21 for black and white. The licence fee is now index-linked.

Although the BBC faced controversy over some of its programmes in the course of the year, the only serious embarrassment was the premature publication in certain tabloid newspapers of the contents of the Queen's Christmas broadcast to the Commonwealth. The BBC's Court correspondent had discussed the prerecorded broadcast with fellow journalists at a private luncheon, not expecting his confidences to be leaked. He was moved to another position, and in August 1988 left the Corporation after twenty years' service.

Settling Down

Some friction arose as the new management team started to introduce changes. In December the director-general exerted his editorial control when he announced to a press conference that BBC2's current affairs flagship *Newsnight* would in future be scheduled to start at 10.30 p.m. every night. The programme had never received the viewing figures it deserved because of its constantly changing starting times. The director-general's intervention ended a dispute between the deputy director-general John Birt and the controllers of BBC1 and BBC2, who wanted to retain flexibility in their scheduling.

The management team was further enhanced in March with the appointment of Paul Fox as managing director of BBC Television. At the time of his appointment Mr. Fox was managing director of Yorkshire Television and chairman of ITN, though his early experience included a spell as controller of BBC1 from 1967–73. Mr. Fox replaced Bill Cotton,

whose successor had been expected to be Michael Grade until he left the BBC for Channel 4 in November, reportedly unable to get on with John Birt.

See for Yourself

In November the BBC published a "slimmed down" version of its Annual Report and Accounts. In the report the director-general said that the BBC saw itself as a modern, £1,000 million company that was adapting to competition "as other companies in this country have had to do ... If it was once seen as bureaucratic and a stout defender of the status quo, it is now increasingly seen as willing to listen, to admit mistakes, and to come to terms with change".

This desire for greater openness manifested itself in "See for Yourself". Instead of producing the traditional BBC Handbook in 1988, a supplement to the *Radio Times* entitled "See for Yourself" was published. In addition a two-hour peak-time television programme with the same title reported to viewers on such matters as what the BBC was doing, the cost of making programmes, the amalgamation of news and current affairs, and mistakes that had been made. The chairman, Marmaduke Hussey, and director-general Michael Checkland answered questions from viewers for 45 minutes in a live discussion programme after "See for Yourself". The director-general said that it was essential to "open up the BBC, and make ourselves more accountable to the 20 million homes that are funding us, and whom we wish to continue to fund us through the licence fee system". Some felt that the programme was rather cosy and self-satisfied in its outlook and gave the impression that the BBC is a huge and unwieldy organization, but a valuable precedent had been set.

The "See for Yourself" magazine also provoked fears that the Corporation might be going too far downmarket in its new-found desire to be held accountable. In his statement the Chairman wrote: "We are much more pleased that our share of television audiences has been increasing—a great tribute to the quality of our programmes. Last Christmas, for instance, over half the population watched the special double *EastEnders*."

The director-general wrote: "1987 has been a year of great change and challenge for the BBC. A tighter and more coherent management structure has made us a stronger and more confident broadcasting organization, geared up to face the new broadcasting era of the 1990s. The merger of news and current affairs across radio and television and the strengthening of our regional operation are two of the most significant achievements of the year. The decision to complete our chain of local radio stations in England with the last seven stations to be funded entirely out of savings is another landmark."

Mr. Checkland continued: "Faced with the challenge of new broadcasting technologies, our position is absolutely clear. Despite what you have heard or read, we have no imperial mission to expand and manage any of the new services for viewers, like cable and satellite. We have neither the funds nor the right to be part of every new broadcasting development. But we can certainly sell to these new services some of our programmes—quality programmes . . . The growth of cable and satellite is not a threat—I see it as a marvellous opportunity for the BBC to be a supplier to these new transmission systems, and a way of supplementing the licence fee with extra income."

"The most striking leap forward is the move to independent production. We have already set aside £24 million for independent television production so that by 1990 we will be commissioning 600 hours of programmes from the independent sector."

External Services

In February 1988, an all-party group of M.P.s nominated BBC External Services for the 1988 Nobel Peace Prize for their work "providing an objective, unbiased, factual and accurate service of world news". In 1987 External Services received 530,000 letters, many coming from China after the opening of a transmitter in Hong Kong. With programmes broadcast in English and Mandarin, the BBC is now reaching a potential audience of 1 billion in China. In March the Government said that no public funds would be made available for BBC External Services to launch a world television news service.

Decent Media

The BBC's deputy director-general John Birt in April called for a reverse to declining standards of British journalism before Parliament imposed sanctions to curb the excesses of the media. Delivering the Royal Television Society's Fleming Memorial Lecture, entitled "Decent Media", he said there was a need for a "determined and radical move towards self-regulation". The BBC was, he said, reviewing its own guidelines, and having updated them they would be published so the public knew exactly where the BBC stood. Later, the Corporation said that is was considering the appointment of an independent ombudsman, preferably a public figure, to deal with complaints from viewers and listeners.

In October 1987 the BBC said that it was planning staff cost reductions of over five per cent by 1993 and the introduction of measures to improve efficiency. By 1993 the BBC hopes to have fulfilled the Government's requirement that 25 per cent of programmes should be made by independent production companies. It is envisaged that changes affecting radio will include the provision of education and sports stations, and the streamlining of frequencies.

The BBC announced in April that it would be spending an extra £40 million a year on radio and television programmes during each of the next five years, due to savings made through job losses and through increased efficiency. An extra 40 per cent will be allocated to the news and current affairs budget. In revealing planned expenditure of £6,000 million, the director-general said that the aim is to establish the Corporation's pre-eminence in the forthcoming broadcasting revolution. The "core element of BBC services in the 1990s . . . has to be a very authoritative and powerful news and current affairs service". In August 1988 the BBC said that its weekday television news programmes now attract 59 per cent of the viewing audience, 18 per cent more than ITN, suggesting that John Birt's drive for

improved news coverage is beginning to pay dividends.

In August the BBC said that is was seeking an end to restrictive practices by actors and musicians which prevent the commercial exploitation of past programmes: its library has 150,000 video tapes and 500,000 cans of film. For example, the BBC cannot sell programmes to South Africa or to cable and satellite services because of the terms of its agreements with members of Equity, the Musicians' Union and the Writers' Guild. Equity said that it would never allow unrestricted rights over recorded works.

Independent Television

With the BBC emerging from the doldrums, the focus of attention shifted during the year to the independent television companies. For the independent sector, the year was dominated by labour troubles and threats to their income from advertising revenue.

As with the newspaper industry, the television companies took advantage of a high-profile stand by one company (in this case TV-am) against restrictive union practices to force through their own sweeping changes with far less publicity or bloodletting. A dispute involving 34 electricians at Tyne Tees was resolved after some months when they accepted changes to work practices as part of the "new realism" facing television unions. Thames Television warned members of the Broadcasting and Entertainment Trades Alliance to accept new working conditions or face dismissal: ACTT members at Thames had already accepted the new deal, introduced initially for production of *The Bill* when it became a twice-weekly serial.

London Weekend said in December 1987 that it was seeking 200 redundancies and the end to "Spanish customs". It hoped for voluntary agreement, but made clear that the move was essential to the company's success in the face of increased commercial pressures. In March LWT said that 239 jobs would be lost over 12 months and that cost reductions would be made through the ending of "sudden hours" overtime payments and the introduction of new technology. In June, LWT said that 100 staff had taken voluntary redundancy, and that the other jobs would be lost through unfilled vacancies, retirements and non-replacement of staff.

Three hundred ACTT members at Scottish TV agreed to reforms of restrictive practices after 16 months of talks. ITN announced that it wanted to lose 142 jobs and to save £5 million a year through changes to working practices and the use of new technology, such as the introduction of Japanese cameras which provide sound and lighting as well as pictures. TVS demanded radical changes in working practices though it plans no job losses.

TV-am

The IBA's Annual Report 1987–88 contained trenchant criticism of the independent breakfast television station TV-am. In his review director-general John Whitney said: "TV-am's year has been dominated by the dispute with its technical staff which began in late November. During the period of the dispute and its aftermath, TV-am has continued to transmit a service produced by journalists and management which has fallen below the overall standards the IBA would normally seek and which the station would wish to provide. The company has expressed confidence and optimism about its ability to restore a normal programme service as soon as possible. We have told TV-am that we require standards on screen to show further improvements over the coming months. We shall continue to monitor TV-am's output closely."

In August the IBA again expressed dissatisfaction with TV-am's service. At a meeting, TV-am's managing director Bruce Gyngell told the IBA of TV-am's plans to expand news coverage at the weekends, to extend David Frost's Sunday programme and to establish a department to supervise children's programmes. The IBA said that in the light of the assurances given by TV-am, it had asked the company "to report back on what steps they propose to take to return to normal programming".

TV-am's year of crisis began with a dispute over its "Caring Christmas" charity show. The company could not agree manning levels with the ACTT and so the technicians were locked out. They were informed they would not be reinstated unless they agreed to a ten-point plan produced by management which demanded the end to restrictive practices. The technicians picketed the station's studios but, although the live breakfast show was off the air for two weeks, TV-am continued broadcasting. Ironically the station actually increased its audience in this period by screening repeats of programmes such as *Batman*. When the IBA told the company to improve its service, management and staff began producing shows without the assistance of any technicians.

Although the ACTT threatened to call a national strike over the dispute, it never materialized, and journalists at TV-am voted to continue to work normally. With no prospect of the ten-point plan proving acceptable, dismissal notices were sent to the striking staff and in April TV-am informed the IBA that the dispute had ended. However, only 45 non-union studio staff had been taken on by August 1988 to replace the dismissed technicians, and the IBA were still not satisfied that TV-am was fulfilling its contractual obligations. The renewal of its franchise was thus placed seriously in doubt.

Selling and Buying

Apart from the dispute, TV-am suffered further damaging publicity and conflict with the IBA, when it was revealed in February that a Saudi Arabian company had bought a 15 per cent interest in TV-am in 1981. Under IBA rules, the IBA should have been informed of the shareholding by a non-E.E.C. organization. The IBA demanded that the stake be reduced to less than 10 per cent immediately and that chairman Timothy Aitken and director Jonathan Aitken, both of whom resigned following the disclosure, should lose their voting rights. The IBA said that "failure to carry out these procedures ... would place the contract between TV-am and the IBA in jeopardy".

In July, Television South became Britain's largest television company and one of the ten major suppliers of programmes in the U.S.A. through its purchase of MTM Entertainment. An American television com-

pany founded by Mary Tyler Moore, MTM Entertainment is responsible for such popular and highly acclaimed programmes as *Lou Grant*, *Hill Street Blues* and *St Elsewhere*. TVS paid £190 million for MTM, and gained access to its library of 1,000 hours of programmes.

The two principal broadcasting unions, the ACTT and the BETA, announced plans to merge to form one 60,000-strong super-union in order to resist Government and ITV companies' attacks on their members. However, a wind of change had swept through the independent companies which had for too long, in the Prime Minister's words, been "the last bastion of restrictive practices in British industry".

Levy

Although wary of Government hints that franchises would in future be put up to auction, more immediate threats were posed by Council of Europe and European Community proposals on advertising, and changes to the method by which the Government levy was calculated.

In January it was estimated that the Exchequer had lost £19 million in revenue from independent television companies due to poor calculations by the Home Office. The levies were assessed on results the companies achieved in 1985 and 1986, which are now regarded as unrepresentative years. The £63 million which the IBA collected for the Government would, under the old method of assessment, have been £82 million.

In June the Government said that in future the levy would be based on the companies' net advertising revenue for the years 1990 to 1992, when franchises are due to be renewed. This caused uproar, as it was estimated that it would in effect mean that the five largest companies faced a 100 per cent increase in their payments. In 1990 all 15 companies will pay between £150–200 million on the new basis, compared with £87 million in 1988. One likely effect is that the companies will have to increase their advertising rates at a time when these are widely regarded as too high. The imminent prospect of competition from satellite stations threatens revenue still further.

Council of Europe Proposals

The proposals on advertising of the two European organizations were first mooted in January, when IBA chairman Lord Thomson of Monifieth said they were "disastrous". Controversy surrounded the proposal that: "With the exception of feature films, which may only be interrupted once, the transmission of audio-visual works such as films made for television, including serials and documentaries, provided their duration is more than 45 minutes, may be interrupted once for each complete period of 45 minutes". No commercial breaks would be permitted in news and current affairs programmes, or children's programmes lasting for less than 30 minutes.

Although the Council of Europe Convention would only be binding on member states that signed it, the proposal could also become part of a European Community Broadcasting Directive if taken up by the European Parliament. This would require compliance by all member states. The effect of such a restriction on advertising breaks would be that blocks of advertisements lasting for up to 15 minutes each hour would be transmitted, which companies fear most British viewers would find unacceptable.

Channel 4

Jeremy Isaacs, "the architect of Channel 4", left the station at the end of 1987 to become general director of the Royal Opera House. He was succeeded as chief executive by Michael Grade, formerly BBC Television's director of programmes. Channel 4 faces an uncertain future, as the Government is reported to be considering alterations to the formula whereby it receives its income through a levy of 17 per cent annually in arrears on the net advertising proceeds of the independent television companies. There is concern that specialist and minority interest programmes would be at risk if Channel 4 has to sell its own advertising airtime.

Also of concern to Channel 4 is the possibility of a fifth terrestrial television channel. In his statement in the IBA's annual report, Channel 4's chairman Sir Richard Attenborough said: "The revelation of such a channel's availability must radically alter all previously accepted criteria for the future of commercial television broadcasting in the United Kingdom. (It) will screen mass entertainment which is advertising-financed in order to meet the unsatisfied demand caused by the present shortage of airtime. This being so, it will be even more vital that minority interests, unrepresented elsewhere, continue to be served by the one channel which has a statutory duty to do so."

In July 1988 Channel 4 announced that it would be launching an up-market breakfast television service in the spring of 1989. Programmes will be made by independent producers and advertising sold by TV-am, the relevant franchise holder. With a budget of around £10 million, Channel 4 is aiming to provide "distinctive and different programming in the early morning".

Cable and Satellite

Cable television services have been slow to take off; although 25 franchises had been awarded by July 1988, only ten were operational. Nevertheless, satellite services look set to revolutionize broadcasting in the United Kingdom. The only foreseeable brake to development is that the two competing systems, Astra and British Satellite Broadcasting, will be using incompatible technology. Potential viewers will have to purchase separate receiving dishes or settle for just one service.

The medium-power Astra system is due to be launched in late 1988. It is run by the Société Européenne des Satellites in Luxembourg and backed by financial institutions as well as Thames Television, Ulster Television and TSW. The 16-channel system received a valuable boost in June when Rupert Murdoch, head of News International, announced that his Sky Television service would be using the Astra satellite to beam four channels to Britain from early 1989. Sky Channel, Sky News, Sky Movies and Eurosport will be free to viewers who purchase a dish receiver for approximately £200. With advertising rates lower than those charged by independent television companies, Astra poses a serious threat to their future.

British Satellite Broadcasting, which won the IBA satellite franchise, is not scheduled to be launched until autumn 1989. However, the high-powered satellite, backed by Granada, Pearson, Virgin, the Bond Corporation and Reed International, offers several potential advantages over Astra's PAL transmission system. Using the sophisticated D-MAC system, BSB will be able to offer enhanced picture quality, stereo sound and signal encryption, which will enable the satellite to provide also subscription television services. BSB also demonstrated a lightweight antenna, under one foot square and one-quarter the size of the Sky dish, which it estimates will retail at about £250.

How readily the public will accept the competing satellite services remains to be seen. Dissatisfaction with the existing land-based services will probably be the major factor deciding the extent to which satellite services are taken up. However, viewers may wait until both satellite services are operational before deciding to opt for one or the other. Dr. Michael Tracey, head of the Broadcasting Research Unit, called in January for a European-wide investigation to discover if the public wants the host of new channels promised by the satellite revolution. The comparatively low budgets of the new channels, in relation to the resources of the BBC and ITV, means that their programmes will consist largely of films, mini-series, soap operas and imports, which might not attract viewers.

However, the success of the video recorder in Britain suggests that the viewing public is prepared to accept alternatives to the existing television services, and there is evidence of widespread dissatisfaction with their tired and unimaginative scheduling, particularly in the summer months.

As the independent television companies trim their staff and costs and the BBC plans to do likewise, competition from satellite television may provide the impetus needed to encourage the established companies to improve their output or risk losing their traditional audiences. If improved quality and more choice are the result, viewers will benefit from the impending revolution.

Future of Broadcasting

The Government's long-awaited White Paper on the future of broadcasting was still awaited in autumn 1988. The Government appeared to be unable to decide what its policy should be, while behind the scenes an unseemly wrangle continued between the Home Office and the Department of Trade and Industry about which of them is responsible for broadcasting policy.

At times the debate on broadcasting descended to the level of farce as various factions floated ideas which had not been properly thought through. For example, it was suggested in June that BBC2 and Channel 4 should be broadcast on two channels on British Satellite Broadcasting, releasing their current frequencies for two new land-based stations which would be financed by advertising. After widespread opposition, the proposal was dropped because of "practical and other difficulties". Similarly, an apparently serious proposal that home video tapes of television programmes must be erased within 28 days of recording was regarded as totally unenforceable and liable to bring the law into disrepute if enacted. It was soon scrapped, and the Government said that instead home taping would be legalized.

In April the IBA produced a major policy statement, *Independent Television in the 1990s*, as part of the debate on broadcasting in advance of the publication of the Government White Paper. The IBA expressed opposition to selling off independent television franchises to the highest bidder in 1992, saying that this would "undermine public service broadcasting on ITV". It also opposed allowing Channel 4 to sell its own advertising airtime and the establishment of the Broadcasting Standards Council, which it said was "not an effective means of enforcing standards". The IBA said that it preferred a system of warnings and fines for breaches of accepted standards of taste, decency or impartiality, with termination of an offending company's contract as the ultimate sanction. It was unfortunate for the IBA that three days after the publication of its policy statement it should be embroiled with the Government in a dispute over its role in the Thames Television programme *Death on the Rock*, about the shooting of IRA terrorists in Gibraltar.

In July the House of Commons home affairs committee published a report entitled *The Future of Broadcasting* which the Home Secretary, Mr. Douglas Hurd, welcomed as an "interesting and challenging contribution" to the debate. Among its recommendations the committee said that: the BBC and Channel 4 should remain as high quality public service broadcasting stations, and the BBC's funding and regulatory framework should not be changed; a new commercial television authority should be set up to control commercial, cable and satellite broadcasting; independent television franchises should be awarded by competitive tendering with incentives for quality; a franchise should be awarded for a nighttime service on ITV; a fifth channel should be set up, funded by advertising and based on a local station network; sponsorship of arts and sports programmes on BBC should be permitted.

Mr. Hurd had already given an indication of the future direction of government broadcasting policy in June. He said in a speech that the BBC licence fee might be replaced in the 1990s by a form of pay-as-you-view, as suggested by the Peacock report. He also forecast the end of the IBA, to be replaced by a new television authority with responsibility for cable, satellite, ITV and Channel 4. He expected that the courts would uphold the standards of the individual companies as set out in their contracts. Whatever the final shape of the Government's broadcasting proposals, it is apparent that the broadcasting industry in Britain is about to face its most radical period for years, with no part of it unaffected by the impending revolution.

Sex and Violence

With the future of broadcasting yet to be determined, the Government's more immediate concern seemed to be with the level of sex and violence transmitted in television programmes. Mr. Hurd

called in the chairmen of the BBC and IBA to ask them to explain why so many programmes still contained unacceptable scenes. This meeting was prompted by the broadcasting before 9 p.m. of an ITV mini-series starring Joan Collins which had caused uproar in September 1987, leading IBA director-general John Whitney to reprimand ITV chiefs for a "serious mistake" in allowing material unsuitable for children to be screened in peak-time. Mr. Hurd subsequently announced that a public organization, the Broadcasting Standards Council, would be set up to deal with complaints about offensive sex and violence on television: the Council will operate outside the scope of the existing broadcasting authorities.

The move was in line with the Government's manifesto pledge for "stronger and more effective arrangements" to cater for "deep public concern" over such matters. The BBC's annual report, published in November 1987, had recorded this concern. It said that "Correspondence generally showed a notable tendency for people to look to drama and entertainment to convey the feeling of a changing, and stricter, code of sexual conduct". Of the 755 letters the Corporation had received about Dennis Potter's *The Singing Detective*, 652 were critical, especially of "one scene of sexual behaviour". However, a report by the IBA, *Attitudes to Broadcasting in 1987*, revealed that viewers are more concerned about bad language in television programmes than by portrayals of sex and violence.

Broadcasting Standards Council

Sir William Rees-Mogg, chairman of the Arts Council and a former editor of *The Times* and governor of the BBC, was appointed chairman of the Broadcasting Standards Council in May. The appointment and terms of reference caused widespread disquiet in the industry, which recalled Sir William's part in the BBC's *Real Lives* documentary debacle in 1985. Sir William, who became a life peer in the Queen's Birthday Honours, said that he wanted statutory powers granting the Council the right to preview imported programmes, a demand supported by the Home Secretary but strongly resisted by the BBC and the IBA. Sir William said: "The crucial thing to do is to see that the violence aspect of U.S. television culture is not bought in cheaply to British television. That is why I want to have the preview right". However, Sir William later conceded that he would be prepared to keep the power to preview in reserve if television chiefs prove that they can keep unacceptable sex and violence off the screen.

Although set up initially on a non-statutory basis, the Broadcasting Standards Council will be given statutory powers when the Government eventually brings in its Broadcasting Bill. The Council intends to draw up a code on the portrayal of sexual activity and violence, to monitor programmes containing such scenes and to commission research into the effects of sex and violence on behaviour. It will have the power to order the screening of critical findings, and will report annually.

Televising the Commons

A renewed campaign to televise the proceedings of the House of Commons was launched in November

1987 by an all-party group led by former Labour Home Secretary Merlyn Rees. In spite of continued opposition from the Prime Minister, the House of Commons voted in January by a majority of 54 in favour of televising its proceedings for a six-month trial period. A committee was set up to consider the details and prepare a report. It was hoped initially that the televising of proceedings would begin with the State Opening of Parliament in 1988 but the matter was more complex than originally anticipated, and the start of the trial period has been delayed until late 1989.

Controversy

Both the BBC and ITV aroused the Government's wrath over the screening of certain programmes. Those about the shooting of IRA terrorists in Gibraltar caused the most controversy. The Foreign Secretary, Sir Geoffrey Howe, twice requested that the IBA postpone Thames Television's *This Week* programme, 'Death on the Rock', until after the inquest on the deaths. Sir Geoffrey said that there was "no justification" for screening it and the Commissioner for Police in Gibraltar claimed that the programme posed a risk to the fairness of the inquest, but their requests were not heeded by the IBA. Lord Thomson of Monifieth, the chairman of the IBA, said that the documentary makers were "simply doing a normal, professional journalistic job and one they were fully entitled, in our view, to do". The IBA's demonstration of independence won it few friends in government and was unfortunately timed, coming soon after the publication of its policy document on Independent Television in the 1990s.

The BBC also rejected the Government's request not to screen a *Spotlight* documentary in Northern Ireland which contained interviews with witnesses to the shootings in Gibraltar. Sir Geoffrey Howe said the programme was "precisely calculated to contaminate the evidence", but director-general Michael Checkland personally authorized its broadcast.

In June the BBC infuriated the South African Government when it broadcast a film entitled *Suffer Little Children* which dealt with the mistreatment of black children in detention in South Africa. The South African Government and some Conservative Members of Parliament were also annoyed by the BBC broadcasting the Nelson Mandela 70th birthday concert at Wembley Stadium in the summer.

Thames Television's "trial" of Austrian President Kurt Waldheim on Channel 4 also raised questions of ethics and taste. Although eminent lawyers were involved, the programme failed to shed much light on a delicate and controversial subject. A BBC play, *Airbase*, which depicted American pilots at a British base under the influence of drugs and drink, was widely condemned for distortion, and for purporting to be based on fact. BBC chairman Marmaduke Hussey said later that it had "little merit".

Also controversial, but a powerful and moving production, was BBC's *Tumbledown*. The drama was written by Charles Wood and based on the exploits of a 21-year-old Scots Guards officer, Robert Lawrence, during the Falklands conflict. The Defence Secretary, George Younger, said that the film would cause "grave offence" to those involved in the battle, and

before transmission a twelve-second scene was cut following legal submissions. The scene was one in which a platoon commander told Lawrence not to proceed and to shoot anyone who tried to make him, and was opposed by an individual who disputed the film's version of events. Directed by Richard Eyre, and featuring Colin Firth as Lawrence, *Tumbledown* was well-made and well-acted. The play raised yet again, though, "issues about drama based on real life which the BBC will have to consider seriously", according to Chairman Marmaduke Hussey in a mid-year BBC review issued to M.P.s, Civil Servants and leading companies. He mentioned the possibility that stricter guidelines for "faction" would have to be drawn up to avoid causing offence to characters represented in such plays.

Programmes

ITV dropped its soap opera *Crossroads* after 23 years and 4,510 episodes. Long derided as television at its worst, its ratings had dropped from a peak of 20 million to around 12 million. Ironically, the BBC scored a triumph in the viewing ratings by showing an Australian soap opera, *Neighbours*, in the early evening five days a week. ITV also dropped its current affairs flagship, *Weekend World*, after 16 years, and said that it would cease to televise wrestling. The future of darts, gymnastics and bowls was also in doubt due to declining audience figures. Meanwhile, Channel 4 screened a series on Japanese Sumo wrestling which brought out the skill and ritual in the event without making it seem ridiculous.

In the summer ITV brought back Sunday evening drama with a season of eight 90-minute films, and promised an investment of £30 million on 56 hours of drama in the forthcoming viewing season. In July Thames Television's *The Bill*, originally a weekly one-hour police drama series, was brought back as a twice-weekly half-hour show. The change was an attempt to capture the BBC's audience of *EastEnders* viewers. On BBC2 Andrew Davies's *A Very Peculiar Practice*, a brilliant satire on contemporary Britain set in the imaginary Lowlands University, returned for a second series which maintained the very high standards of the first. On Channel 4 Alan Plater adapted Chris Mullin's story of an establishment plot against a left-wing British Government in *A Very British Coup*. Ray McAnally played the Labour Prime Minister Harry Perkins in an idealistic tale which was well paced and eminently watchable.

A £4·5 million drama series, *Betty*, commissioned by London Weekend Television and starring Twiggy, was scrapped because of a dispute involving Equity and the Musicians' Union. This prompted the Secretary of State for Employment, Mr. Norman Fowler, to order the Monopolies and Mergers Commission to investigate working practices in film and television production. He felt union practices might "unduly hinder the efficient use of labour" by restrictive practices which threatened competition.

Football Coverage

The arrangements for football coverage on television almost caused the break-up of the Football League when ITV attempted to deal directly with top First Division clubs. It offered the clubs £10 million in return for exclusive coverage of matches over two seasons. The competition to provide coverage became intense when the BBC, changing its principles, joined with British Satellite Broadcasting to bid for joint coverage of football matches at a cost of at least £40 million over four years.

Eventually, the BBC and BSB signed a deal with the Football Association worth £3 million a year for exclusive rights to FA Cup ties (but not the Final, which will still be shared with ITV) for five years, and internationals, with an option on a live World Cup qualifying match. BSB will screen cup replays and midweek internationals. The BBC and BSB withdrew their offer for Football League matches and the League clubs accepted an ITV offer worth £44 million over four years for coverage of 20 live matches. Of the sum, 75 per cent will be allocated to First Division clubs.

The entry of satellite services into what had previously been the exclusive domain of BBC and ITV gave an indication of the influence that extra-terrestrial broadcasting will have on many aspects of traditional television. The televising of other major sporting events, such as rugby and cricket matches, will probably also be affected by the new era as organizing bodies become aware of the possibility of both improved coverage and greatly increased revenue.

Awards

At the Prix Italia Festival, Simon Gray's *After Pilkington* (BBC) won a drama prize, and Geoffrey Case's *Scub* (Yorkshire) received a special award. A special prize for music programmes was awarded to Channel 4's *Behind the Mask: Perspectives on the Music of Harrison Birtwistle*, and the BBC won an ecology prize for *Vanishing Earth: Soil*. At the American Academy of Television Arts and Sciences awards, four of the Emmys for foreign programmes were awarded to *Alas Smith and Jones*, *The Sword of Islam*, *Porterhouse Blue* and *The Belle of Islam*.

At the BAFTA Awards for television production and performance, the Desmond Davis Award for outstanding creative contribution to television was presented to Julia Smith, producer of *EastEnders*. Best single drama was Mick Jackson's *Lifestory*, and best drama series Andy Park's and Tony Smith's *Tutti Frutti*. Best factual series was *The Duty Men*, and best light entertainment programme *Victoria Wood on TV*. Best comedy series was *Blackadder the Third*, best children's drama programme *A Little Princess*, and best children's documentary *The Really Wild Show*. Stewart Purvis received the award for best news or outside broadcast for the special edition of *Channel 4 News* covering the Zeebrugge disaster.

David Jason was best actor (*Porterhouse Blue*) and Emma Thompson best actress (*Fortunes of War* and *Tutti Frutti*). Nigel Hawthorne won the prize for best light entertainment performance for *Yes, Prime Minister*; the Huw Weldon Award was given to Ian Squires and Gillian Lynne for *A Simple Man*; the writer's award went to Jonathan Lynn and Anthony Jay for *Yes, Prime Minister*; the Richard Dimbleby Award was presented to Esther Rantzen, and the 1987 Television Award for Originality to Channel 4's *Network 7*. An independent production for Channel 4, *The Comic Strip presents ... The Strike* won the prestigious Golden Rose of Montreux light entertainment award.

ARCHITECTURE 1987–88

PRINCES SQUARE SHOPPING CENTRE, GLASGOW

Architect: Hugh Martin and Partners
Interior Design Consultant: The Design Solution

The last few years have witnessed a remarkable cultural and commercial renaissance in Glasgow in the wake of widespread decay and the destruction wrought in the name of progress in the 1960s and 1970s. Nowhere is this more evident than in the many cleaned and restored Victorian buildings which now grace the city centre. Renewed economic activity and a thriving tourist trade generated by cultural attractions such as the Burrell Gallery and, during the summer of 1988, the Glasgow Garden Festival, have brought in their wake pressures for improvements in the quantity and choice of top quality retailing.

The new Princes Square Shopping Centre is located on Buchanan Street, one of the City's major pedestrianized shopping streets. It satisfies the demand for high quality specialist shopping outlets within an elegant architectural framework, and provides today's Glaswegians with a new place to visit and be seen that rivals the popularity of the once famous tearooms of Miss Cranston. The architect has successfully realized a concept of the centre as a setting for people to meet, a Glaswegian version of the Venice "Rialto", in which shopping is closely interlinked with entertainment and leisure activities, a market place and theatre combined.

Princes Square has been skilfully created from the bones of a mid-19th century courtyard building. The cobbled courtyard has been excavated to form a new lower "courtyard" level, while the existing yellow sandstone courtyard elevations dating from 1844 have been retained and restored, with window openings adapted and opened up to form new doorways and frontages to the shop units. Within the courtyard space a new and completely independent steel structure has been inserted to support a pitched glazed roof extending over the whole square, generating a grand and elegantly proportioned internal space some six storeys high.

The structural frame takes the form of linked clusters of white-painted tubular steel columns, each cluster comprising a triangular arrangement of three columns. The column clusters are set well forward of the sandstone courtyard walls and provide support for the new balconies and walkways that encircle the courtyard space. These act as a sort of perimeter mall linking the shop units, which are placed within the depth of the old building, and provide spacious seating areas for the food court situated at the uppermost level.

From each cluster, the leading pair of columns rises and curves forward in an uninterrupted line to create the main vault of the roof in a flattened arch form. The third column, to the rear, arches in the opposite direction to link the new structure with the line of the original walls. Further subsidiary arches, all in white-painted tubular steel, link the clusters together and also act as supports for large decorative open metalwork lighting globes that contain powerful

theatrical spot-lights for night-lighting. The resulting division of space produces what is effectively a central nave and side aisles. The ecclesiastical reference is completed at the Buchanan Street end of the centre where the structure condenses to a series of single shaft columns. These are arranged in a semicircle, suggesting the form of an apse and ambulatory, and support the domed end of the fully-glazed pitched roof.

With the proposed development requiring retailing and associated functions on four levels and pedestrian access available only from street level in Buchanan Street, the architect had to develop ingenious and effective methods for ensuring that good pedestrian flow was generated in all parts of the centre. Efficient vertical circulation was of paramount importance. The solution adopted was to devote one of the three street level entrances to a direct escalator link with the second floor "terrace", and in addition to provide six further escalators, six staircases and two feature lifts.

The six escalators connect the four levels together at one end of the square, and are splayed alternately in pairs so that shoppers travelling between floors are presented with interesting oblique views up and down and out into the courtyard. This arrangement has the advantage of making the escalator group, when seen from elsewhere in the scheme, transcend its merely functional purpose and become a powerful sculptural statement in its own right.

In keeping with the theatrical ambience of the centre, the main staircase, flanked by two freestanding feature lifts in tubular steel enclosures, has developed into the grandest of gestures with a sweep and bravura suggestive of a Hollywood stage set. It is arranged in the form of a double helix with generous curved half-landings between each flight. But perhaps the most memorable design feature of the entire scheme is the exquisitely wrought metalwork of the balcony and staircase balustrades and of the lamp standards.

Throughout the scheme there has been a conscious attempt to recall the architectural and artistic glories of the golden age just before the turn of the century when Glasgow was the "second city of the Empire". In the event, the style evoked owes more to the wider European influences of the Art Nouveau and Vienna Secession schools than homage to Glasgow's own Charles Rennie Mackintosh.

The interior design theme is of the "Tree of Life". This has found inspired expression in the sinuous and stylized plant forms developed in the wrought iron balcony railings and etched into the glass panels of the balustrades and of the glass panels enclosing the freestanding feature lifts. Over each of the three pedestrian entrances from Buchanan Street a modestly-scaled but stylish metal and glass canopy projects. These show more of the sinuous and organic lines and forms and a stylized peacock decorative motif, with yet more inventive reinterpretation of the theme in the massive metal security gates that flank each entrance.

Such artistic skill and craftsmanship does not come cheap and the 75,000 square feet development has cost £20 million to complete. However, the joint developers, Teesland Development Co. and Guardian Royal Exchange, are confident that their committment to quality, demonstrated in the solid oak finishes, high quality ceramic floor tiling and the extensive use of handcrafted elements, will ensure that their investment is rewarded with success in the long term.

A notable feature of this attempt to raise the quality of the retail environment is the confidence with which a wide-ranging aesthetic vocabulary has been introduced and co-ordinated. Too often the use of historical styles out of context is indicative of a lack of design integrity, a common characteristic of commercial undertakings as ruthless as retailing. Here, however, the tubular steel columns to the glazed roof, which might seem to some out of context amongst the mellow stonework facades, echo the functional but elegant structures of winter gardens and conservatories of an earlier age and harmonize happily with the handcrafted glass and metalwork of the balustrades. The extension of the tubular steel aesthetic into the supporting cages of the feature lifts produces a rather different effect, but effort has been made to incorporate decorative elements which respond to the craft-based aesthetic of the visible fabric of the centre.

The perception of the relationship between new and old and of the stylistic quotations are matters of personal taste, and it is clear that this innovative new centre is to the taste of the people of Glasgow. Despite the fact that only a handful of the shop units were trading when the centre opened to the public in November 1987, the popularity of the food court has already made Princes Square a resounding success: indeed, it has proved so popular on occasions that the numbers of visitors entering the centre has had to be controlled to avoid overcrowding.

LANSDOWNE HOUSE, BERKELEY SQUARE, LONDON

Architect: Chapman Taylor Partners

The magnificent plane trees of Berkeley Square, planted by Edward Bouverie in 1789, survived the October 1987 hurricane virtually unscathed and now form the impressive setting for a new office development on the south side of the square. As recently as 1930 the site was still open and green. It was then the garden of Lansdowne House, named after the first Marquess of Lansdowne. The house was originally built to the design of Robert Adam for the Earl of Bute in 1762. The facade of this house, much adapted and rebuilt between 1930–35, is now the frontage of the Lansdowne Club in Fitzmaurice Place.

It was in the 1930s that the garden was built over and the second "Lansdowne House", a brick building, was completed to the design of Wimperis Simpson and Guthrie for residential and retail use. By the early 1980s it was clear that the accommodation was not up to current office standards and proposals were put in hand for a new Lansdowne House by the Legal and General Assurance Society Ltd., the new owners of the site.

Opposition to demolition of the 1930s building led to a public inquiry, but planning permission was granted in late 1983 after the Inspector had concluded that the proposed design "is innovative and would provide a building of excellence". After a preliminary contract to permit the retention of the Lansdowne Row shops, which were integral to the old building, construction work commenced in September 1985 on a two and a half year building contract, to provide 175,000 square feet of high quality office space on seven floors above ground and one below, with basement car parking, and a proportion of the space at ground and lower ground levels allocated to retail use on the three exposed frontages.

The form and mass of the new building follow that of its U-shaped predecessor, though the Berkeley Square frontage has been completed with a central "gatehouse". A monumental central arch, forming the main entrance, leads to a grand atrium rising from lower ground level through seven storeys. The organization of the circulation through the building ensures that this magnificent internal court is traversed by everyone wishing to enter the building, as it connects the main entrance lobby with the central lift core, which in turn gives access to the individual floor areas.

The gatehouse, atrium and central core areas exhibit the extensive use of a variety of natural stones. These include both marble and granite, in particular Juperana granites from India and Brazil, Paradiso granite from India, and, most notably, the exotic Blue Bahia granite from Brazil. The latter is used sparingly but to great effect in the central roundels of the floor pattern.

A dark red granite is used as a principal band course to pick out the essential form and axes of the three principal areas, and as a skirting and plinth course in the central lift core and staircase. The parallel bands link the revolving door at the main entrance with adjoining reception and waiting areas, and define the main route through to the lifts across the atrium floor. A secondary cross-axis is similarly highlighted linking the two projecting porches in the centre of the atrium. The ensuing cruciform pattern is echoed in the dramatic structure of the glazed atrium roof overhead, where suspended walkways provide dramatic views for those with a head for heights.

The walls and columns of the atrium and gatehouse are clad in a honey-coloured limestone, known as Perlato Svevo Royale, which is quarried near Trani in southern Italy. It is light enough in tone to generate a light and airy feeling at the lower levels, particularly when sunlight pours in through the roof, yet has enough life in its structure and warmth of colour to prevent the large areas of polished stone appearing too cold and impersonal.

The *pièce de résistance* of this stunning space is the introduction of four separate clumps of mature bamboo (of the type *Arundinaria Nigra*) as the sole use of planting in the atrium. The highest canes rise to a height of some ten metres and the delicate leafy canopy offers a pleasing counterpoint to the strong architectural style and highly polished finishes of the atrium.

In the four corners of the atrium, beyond the clumps of bamboo, the floor level drops another storey, to enable daylight to penetrate the central areas of the lower ground floor. At the same time exciting vistas diagonally up and across the atrium are provided from what would otherwise have been traditional basement office areas, always less attractive to prospective tenants. Here, at the lowest level, decorative carved granite water cascades and pool features enliven the immediate outlook from the lower ground floor office areas, and also provide an appropriate habitat for a pair of flamingoes (life-size bronze sculptures from India).

The use of stone reaches its most exuberant levels in the central lift core where six passenger lifts, including two wallclimber lifts facing into the atrium, are grouped around a central staircase. Visibility from the central lift call point, which is incorporated in a free-standing stone pedestal, is assisted by the angled setting out of the lobby walls, a geometrical feature that is fortuitously generated by the angle of the rear facade along Lansdowne Row. The volume of the central staircase, which has a rounded rear wall faced in polished Perlato Svevo stone, breaks forward beyond the angled returns of the lift lobby, and the implied half-landing radius is highlighted by four full-height granite columns. These columns enable the stepped ceiling to follow the course of the stair from flight to flight and complete the definition of the stair volume, but permit the space, and people, to flow through and round, binding together most successfully the angled lobby space and the flat oval of the stair.

The full-height columns, some 2·6 metres long, are each turned from single blocks of Indian Juperana granite and display the life and vitality of its graining to telling effect. The floor pattern picks up the centrelines of the semicircular band of columns with radiating lines picked out in white Carrara marble, which develop as a series of panels in the main Brazilian Juperana floor material. Throughout the ground floor the white Carrara is used in narrow bands to define and separate areas of different stone colours. This enables a feeling of great richness to develop without the uncomfortable colour clashes that might otherwise be generated.

The external elevations are clad in Whitbed Portland stone, with a textured and rusticated base in Hantergantick Cornish Grey granite. The use of Blue Bahia granite for the head and sill stones to the showcase windows of the ground floor retail units is intended to highlight the strongly modelled lower stages and, with the help of precisely carved decorative geometric patterns, add interest and colour at pedestrian level.

At the upper levels, the use of grey anodized aluminium curtain walling for the top two storeys brings the effective height of the building down to a "cornice" level related to the height of the older houses of the west side of Berkeley square. The projecting stone-clad windows at the sixth floor also reflect the roof dormers and other features of the earlier buildings and enable the Portland stone cladding to dovetail with the curtain walling, thus avoiding a "layer-cake" of different materials.

A similar dovetailing device is employed at the junction between the granite base and the Portland stone, while along the rear of the building, facing Lansdowne Row, the curtain walling steps down to occupy the whole of the central section. This device reduces the scale and avoids the overpowering effect of a stone facade towering over the single-storey shops.

Internally, an exceptionally high quality of finish has been achieved, with European and American oak joinery, doors inlaid with wenge hardwood from Africa, and a specially designed ceiling system which has required high standards of workmanship and adherence to strict tolerances. The building is fully air-conditioned throughout, and external windows are triple-glazed for energy conservation and to achieve a high degree of acoustic performance; so that occupants will be largely unaware of the incessant traffic flow around the site. The services installation boasts a state-of-the-art building management system with computer-controlled monitoring, fault-reporting facilities and sophisticated security controls.

This is a building constructed to the highest standards and with committment to quality. The design is notable for the thoroughness of the detailing and for the care with which a wide range of design motifs and ideas have been co-ordinated into a consistent vocabulary. The facade echoes the classical form of the earlier Adam building but nevertheless encompasses a truly modern building designed to accommodate business needs into the next century. The new Lansdowne House is a distinguished companion to the historic houses that have graced Berkeley Square for the last 200 years.

THE TATE GALLERY, ALBERT DOCK, LIVERPOOL

Architect: Stirling, Wilford and Associates

The last few decades have seen an enormous upsurge in the numbers of historic buildings undergoing conversion in order to accommodate new uses. An area in which this transformation process has been particularly evident is our unique heritage of industrial architecture, from the humblest mill to the grandest warehouse, in the great manufacturing centres of the industrial revolution and in our ports.

Perhaps the finest surviving group of warehouses in the country is to be found at Liverpool's Albert Dock, once the focus of the thriving nineteenth century port. Recently the buildings have been undergoing a typical variety of restoration and conversion projects, with their new functions ranging from fashionable and expensive flats to wine bars and restaurants. This range now extends to the accommodation of a new gallery committed to the presentation of modern art, the Liverpool extension of London's Tate Gallery.

Designed in the early 1840s by the dock engineer Jesse Hartley and built between 1841-5, the Albert Dock is a magnificent example of metal and masonry architecture. At the time the dock was a pioneering building in its development of construction techniques and its planning. The design clearly owes a debt to London's St. Katharine's Dock by Thomas Telford, built in 1827-29.

In common with its earlier counterpart the Albert Dock presents the fronts of the warehouses, with their monumental brickwork walls supported on a sturdy colonnade of cast iron Tuscan columns, directly to the edge of the dock basin to enable the direct transfer of goods from the ships into the warehouses. The elevations of the Hartley building, however, introduce large semi-elliptical arches into the brickwork over the colonnade at intervals, and the leaping rhythms of the arches provide a welcome modulation to the forbiddingly regular geometry of the squat brick arched window openings and chunky columns. Hartley's warehouses were also innovatory for their fireproof construction, dispensing with the timber floors typical of the time. Inside the masonry exterior a regular grid of cast iron columns and arched beams with interconnecting tie-rods supports the brick vaulted floors, with the overall volume divided into several separate areas by means of thick brick walls.

Such a building might at first sight seem ideal for conversion into an art gallery, but so rigorous and disciplined a structure presented a considerable architectural challenge. The conversion had to accommodate the complex modern services necessary for the strict environmental criteria and controlled lighting techniques required by any modern gallery displaying collections of international significance. It is a tribute to the skill of the architect in resolving these problems that the new work creates such a minimal impact with the fabric of the building. The plan arrangement is deceptively simple and generates a pattern of circulation that is both straightforward and easily comprehensible to the visitor.

The central fire wall, which divided the deepest section of the warehouse in two longitudinally, has been enlarged by the depth of one structural bay to form a linear central core. This contains all the necessary vertical services risers and ducts, linking the basement plant room areas with air handling units on the third floor, together with the main and escape staircases, lifts and lavatories. The centralized location of the vertical circulation thus ensures the most economical use of space and simple access into the open gallery spaces at the front and rear.

The desirability of maintaining the visual qualities of the existing metal and masonry structure, and the lack of sufficient floor to ceiling height for either suspended ceiling systems or raised cavity floors, proved to be the determining factors in the design of the services distribution system for the gallery spaces themselves. The gallery walls are lined out, with a supporting timber frame spaced a short distance away from the structure to permit horizontal service runs to pass behind. This also avoids any intrusion on the existing fabric due to the hanging of pictures or other fixtures. Down the centre of each of the shallow brick vaults is suspended a multi-purpose services housing, which accommodates the air-conditioning ducts and inlets, electrical supplies, sprinklers, loudspeakers, smoke detectors and all artificial lighting. The suspended ducts are fed from both ends to reduce the overall cross-sectional area as much as possible. Given the inevitable complexity of such arrangements it is a neat and elegant solution: the suspension of the housing on rods clear of the brickwork soffit permits the original building, with its clearly expressed structure, to be easily assimilated, although

where the ceiling heights are lower, as on the upper floors, they remain a dominant feature.

It is in the approach to the building and in the main entrance foyer that the new insertions are most clearly manifest. The main entrance to the gallery is centred on one of the large arches punctuating the colonnade. It comprises a pair of revolving door drums in bright orange metalwork set within a glazed screen which runs full-height for the whole length of the foyer space, again framed in bright orange metalwork. Either side of the main entrance screen the framing continues as a solid enclosing wall with brilliant blue infill panels, leaving the first bay of cast iron columns exposed to the colonnade. To the right of the entrance, the panels are subdivided into four with central porthole windows admitting light to the reception counter, reading room and office areas. Bold three-dimensional illuminated orange lettering announcing the gallery's name is mounted on the exposed mezzanine edge beam. The porthole windows and bright colours impart a distinctly nautical flavour which is also apparent in some of the interior detailing and is an appropriate reference to the gallery's waterside location.

The entrance foyer itself is a long, tall space created by the removal of the existing mezzanine floor. Much of the mezzanine level which existed between the ground and first floors has been removed to generate a series of double-height ground floor galleries. It was discovered as work progressed that this possibility had been allowed for in the original structure by the provision of integral support flanges at the mid-point of the double-height cast iron columns to take the intermediate mezzanine beams. The floor has been retained to one side of the foyer and the lower headroom accommodates the reception desk and reading room at ground level, with a small kitchen and office at the upper level. Projecting into the foyer space at the mezzanine level are the bulbous curves of a double bow-fronted balcony which is the location for a book shop and coffee shop. The solid balustrades are again picked out in the bright blue and orange livery of the entry screen. Below each of the curving balconies, and echoing their simple geometry, a free-standing semi-circular bench seat wraps round one of the supporting columns. Each seat is made up as a layer cake of unorthodox materials, slate, copper and stainless steel, looking like an exhibit on loan from a modern sculpture gallery.

By contrast with the aggressive colours and bold forms of the foyer and entrance, the galleries themselves are restrained and peaceful. With wood-strip floors, white-painted walls and vaults and with all metalwork painted grey, they form a pleasing and receptive background for the exhibitions of sculpture and painting. The overall impression is that despite the extensive servicing requirements very little has been done to alter the appearance of the original building, which still displays the clarity of its industrial aesthetic.

Later phases are planned to complete the conversion of all the available space, including the conversion of the roof space to incorporate further galleries and studios, a restaurant and a space for performances. The possibility of extending the range of artistic expression into that of the performing arts would seem to indicate a healthy and creative future for the gallery, and help continue what has been a successful opening season. On the architectural front, this sensitive adaptation of an outstanding Grade 1 listed building is proof that with care and ingenuity our surviving architectural heritage can be given a new relevance to society and more than a merely temporary stay of execution.

THE PAVILIONS SHOPPING CENTRE, BIRMINGHAM
Architect: Chapman Taylor Partners

The current boom in high street retailing is producing an equivalent surge in the number of new shopping centres being created both in city centre and out-of-town locations. While the latest out-of-town centres can be seen to reflect the principal characteristics of their immediate predecessors in North America, many of Britain's city centre schemes present designers with particular problems of access, physical integration and architectural context peculiar to this country. Birmingham, now ranking second only to London for the extent and range of its shops and stores, has a large and impressive prime shopping area centred on New Street, High Street, Union Street and Corporation Street. However, even here a need to reinforce the quality and variety of the shopping and breathe new life and activity into the centra area was perceived.

It was against this background that the site of the former Greater Midlands Co-operative Society building was acquired as a joint venture by Bryant Properties P.L.C. and Royal Life Insurance Ltd. in an open competition between developers in July 1984. The prime position of the site, at the heart of Birmingham's most important shopping area, offered enormous potential for retail development, fronting the High Street and adjacent to a leading Marks and Spencer store. Believed to be this country's first four-storey shopping centre, The Pavilions provides approximately 155,000 square feet of retail space and realizes the maximum value of the location for the developer by exploiting the physical characteristics of the site with an exciting and imaginative use of changes in level.

Following the initial purchase of the site, additional parcels of land were acquired and a road closure order was obtained to enable the proposed development to proceed. The latter also permitted the new building to connect directly into the existing Marks and Spencer store at three levels. Planning permission for the £75 million development was granted in June 1985 and work started almost immediately afterwards.

The primary design considerations in developing the layout of the shopping malls were to make the most advantageous use of the prime frontage onto the High Street and the pedestrian flow generated by the Marks and Spencer store, and to ensure as good a level of pedestrian access and circulation over the various levels of the centre as possible. The concept which emerged was to provide two ground floors, lower and upper, both directly related to the pavement level in the High Street.

The upper ground floor mall links the first floor of Marks and Spencer to the pavement level in the High Street with a long gentle gradient, while the ground floor of the store is linked to the pavement level via the lower ground floor mall and a pair of escalators at the High Street entrance. By this means a circuit is generated which takes shoppers through the new centre and back onto the High Street via the Marks and Spencer main entrance. At the lowest level, escalators lead directly down to a third mall level which connects directly with Marks and Spencer's lower ground trading floor, and this also has ground level access at the rear of the store. At the upper level, a staircase and escalators lead to the first floor where the Food Gallery is located together with other speciality shopping units. The Food Gallery is a food court which provides seating for 450 people and is served by nine food kiosks each providing a specific and different choice of menu.

Goods servicing is effected from a basement service area with vehicular access from the rear from Moor Street Ringway. Goods hoists rise from a number of points around the basement floor with either direct or corridor access to the unloading docks in the central service area, and at the upper levels these give access onto trolley ways servicing the rear of all the shop units.

The existing relationship between the High Street entrance and the side entrance into Marks and Spencer was the one determining factor in the design of the great central concourse, which has to effect a 90° turn through its length. The other factor was the need to make the various levels and circulation possibilities apparent to the incoming shopper at the earliest possible moment, providing a choice of routes and thereby spreading people throughout the centre.

The first indications of the nature of the spaces inside are given by the elevational treatment of the High Street frontage. The columns and walls on either side of the main entrance are clad with pinkish-grey granite panels. String courses and highlights are picked out in a darker maroon-coloured stone, while the upper levels of the elevation are clad with a gridded reflective glass curtain wall in two colours, limestone and blue. At the main entrance, however, the curtain wall steps down and sets back to a square grid of clear glazed panels, while the solid granite-faced walls are cut away completely in an extravagant outburst of modelling. Free-standing columns and a cut-away projecting curved canopy focus attention on the segmental framing over the glazed entrance doors and a secondary canopy in mirror polished stainless steel panels. The transition to clear glazing at and over the entrance provides dramatic views into the heart of the scheme and reveals the simple angled profile of the continuous glazed rooflight which encloses the mall interiors.

When the shopper moves through the entrance, up a gentle ramp, the whole of the concourse comes into view. It is a complex and very dynamic space with its changes in level and angled plan shape. It appears lofty and light, being five storeys high under the central glazed rooflight which allows good natural light to spill down even to the lowest levels. This enables displays of natural planting to flourish and is subtly enhanced by the creative use of artificial lighting to impart a changing visual quality at night and on dull days.

Once through the main entrance, the shopper is immediately presented with a choice of directions, and is able at a glance to understand how the centre is laid out. The different levels of the balcony malls present a visual guide to the routes around all the shops and are accentuated by the strongly-modelled white plaster fascias at the edges of the slabs. Escalators, stairs, ramps and lifts are all visible, suggesting that movement around the centre will be both easy and visually stimulating. Two glass feature lifts rise in the centre of the space, and the movement of the lift cars combines with the bubbling movement and reflections of a pool and fountain at the lowest level to create a dynamic centrepiece and focal point for the scheme. This vertical element also helps to draw the attention of shoppers to each and every level, and in particular to the Food Court at the upper level. This is not as immediately visible as the lower retailing levels because of the cut-off of sight lines and because this level is the most remote from the main entrance due to the fall in level to the High Street.

While the shop units themselves are clearly intended to be the stars of the show, the malls benefit from detailed high quality finishes, including polished granite, stainless steel and mirror. The ceilings below the balcony malls are finished with a silvered metallic eggcrate ceiling tile, which adds to the sparkle by reflecting the spotlights and displays in the shop windows. The dozens of high quality centres in America and the increasing pace of High Street competition for customers has improved standards of shop fitting. The best now offer dramatic architectural experiences of their own, particularly in situations such as The Pavilions where the changing levels allow intermediate mezzanine floors within double-height retail units.

Such elements add further interest to what is already a stimulating and successful shopping environment with a predominantly high-class fashion flavour. First opened to the public in October 1987 after a 28 month construction period, The Pavilions' success has already been recognized with the conferment in March 1988 of the International Council of Shopping Centres' European Award for the best large shopping centre.

RICHMOND RIVERSIDE, RICHMOND, SURREY
Architect: Quinlan Terry

The view of Richmond Hill from the towpath alongside the River Thames and Petersham Meadows has long been one of the glories of the Thames Valley. In recent years, however, the riverside views downstream from Richmond Bridge have presented a depressing contrast, blighted by the decaying condition of the terraces of old houses built high upon the river bank; the long-term survival of this substantial and historic part of Richmond's town centre in a form and scale sympathetic to the town's size and character appeared to be at risk.

On a huge site bounded by Water Lane to the north, Hill Street to the east, Bridge Street to the

south and the River Thames on the fourth side, there has recently been completed a £20 million mixed development. This comprises a substantial area of offices, shops, flats, restaurants and car parking, and incorporates all the modern technical accoutrements of air-conditioning, computer floors, modern lifts and open-plan office areas. In itself this is not remarkable: what is out of the ordinary is that the entire scheme has been carried out in what might be generalized as "the Classical style", utilizing "traditional" forms of construction, at least as far as the public exterior elevations are concerned. In the current debate about style in modern architecture, the architect of this extraordinary development is one of the leaders of a burgeoning Classical revival which subscribes to the aesthetic and moral values of Classical architecture based firmly on the disciplines of the ancient classical orders.

Although designed in a Classical style, the development does not stamp too rigid a discipline on its neighbours. It responds with great sensitivity to its site and to the variety of architecture to be found in Richmond, taking a picturesque and assymetrical form such as might have arisen naturally in the organic and piecemeal development of a typical English town.

The planning brief for the site, laid down by the developer Haslemere Estates, established a requirement for approximately 106,000 square feet of office space, two restaurants, 28 flats and parking spaces for 135 cars. In laying out the scheme, the architect has retained and incorporated a number of old buildings of various periods which were already on the site. These included a run-down stucco-clad Regency coaching inn known as The Castle; the town hall of 1893 by W. J. Ancell; Heron House, a Georgian house dating from 1716; and a terrace of dilapidated mid-nineteenth century stucco houses. Among the latter is Laxton's Italianate Tower House of 1856, a well-known landmark whose tall tower stands as an ideal complement to the long wide arches of Richmond Bridge. The facades of all these buildings have been kept and restored or adapted in the new scheme.

The plan form of the development derives principally from the location of the retained buildings and the reinstatement of the terraces fronting on to Hill Street and Bridge Street. The rear elevations of these buildings have been developed in their own mix of styles to create a new sequence of open courtyard spaces, with the two existing streets linked to the landscaped riverside terraces via a new "Town Square". The new terraced structures are composed of a series of buildings of traditional depth and width of frontage, but they have been consciously elevated in a wide variety of styles to give the impression that here is a motley collection of buildings that has grown organically over a considerable period of time. A number of historical styles have been quoted, including Neo-Palladian, Neo-Classical, Renaissance, Greek Revival, Georgian domestic and even Venetian Gothic.

The most impressive and, from a townscape point of view, the most important aspect is the riverside frontage and the broad view over the sweep of the Thames from the opposite bank and Richmond Bridge. From this vantage point is revealed a dramatic congregation of buildings, complex in its variety of styles, yet consistent in scale. With its suggestion of grander spaces within and beyond, its busy skyline and constant shifts of plane, it presents a dynamic composition of surprising richness.

The frontage comprises new and old, with the retained stucco terraces up to the Tower House and the restored brickwork of Heron House framing a small and charming new insert. This is in the Palladian style, with two Venetian windows set one over the other, supported by a Venetian arch, and through which a flight of steps leads up into the new "Town Square". Immediately flanking this group is another and much larger new structure, Hotham House, designed on a grand scale in the Georgian domestic manner. It has a huge overhanging cornice and central pediment below a slate-covered roof and a pepperpot-style turret set within a balustrade. Beyond, on the north side of a new square, sits the long stucco terrace of The Castle, poised at right angles to the riverside with its east end disappearing beyond the restored Town Hall. Fortuitously, an impression of great depth is given to the overall massing which would not have been enjoyed had the riverside frontage been completed across the square with new buildings.

Tucked into the corner of the site, and fronting on to the towpath immediately next to two existing old houses, lies perhaps the most striking of the new structures. This is a square building of two principal storeys on a rusticated base. The exposed facades are completely given over to arcades of huge arched windows under a hipped roof and it is surmounted by a cupola, also with miniature arched openings in the same style. This confident essay in the Palladian style appears like some Venetian palace, with a generous balcony one bay deep overlooking the towpath and riverside. It is intended to function as a restaurant and is the perfect location for this with superb views up and down the river, and appropriately festive in spirit. Its strong, simple form, pinpointed by the decorative cupola, acts as a perfect counterfoil to the Tower House at the other end of the riverside frontage, and both combine to anchor the whole composition firmly on to the sloping site.

Many of the same qualities are to be found in the other facades. The central courtyard and the elevations to Hill Street and Bridge Street present an equally resourceful yet cohesive display of Classically-based styles, though with a more restrained palette of materials and of a consistent height. Along each of the streets there is an arcade, each block or "house" supported on columns of a different order. All these new buildings, on the exterior at least, are constructed with traditional load-bearing walls, i.e. solid brickwork as much as 18 to 24 inches thick, without cavities and bonded together in lime mortar. Because of the flexibility arising from the composition of the mortar (modern cement mortar is hard and brittle) and because of the solidity and mass of the external walls, the architect has been able to avoid the need to incorporate expansion joints at frequent intervals throughout the structure. However, as a compromise to the needs of the developer for quick construction and efficient use of space, the internal structure of floors and columns is fabricated in reinforced concrete, as are the underground car parking structures.

The depth of the exterior walls is one of the factors which has enabled the architect to achieve the appearance of authenticity in the facades. Inevitably, one of the enduring criticisms of the scheme derives from the functions which these overly domestic exteriors are supposed to encompass; there can be no avoiding the fact that the richness of the classical vocabulary stops abruptly with the onset of the bland, open plan office interiors, all too familiar as "developers speculative offices". While this may trouble the architectural purists of both Classical and Modern persuasions, it is unlikely to bother the inhabitants of Richmond. They will doubtless derive lasting pleasure from its charm, richness and complexity, and to judge from the prompt letting of the office spaces themselves, there are many others for whom the aesthetic contradictions are not insurmountable. Although this unique scheme falls some way short of being a wholly consistent exemplar of how a twentieth century classical architecture might develop, it remains a remarkable achievement for which the architect and the developer are to be congratulated.

ARCHAEOLOGY 1987–88

One of the few recent archaeological discoveries to make front-page news was the discovery of the Roman amphitheatre in the heart of London. The remains are located at the east side of the Guildhall Yard, an open space which lies to the south of the medieval Guildhall of the City of London, beneath the site of the 15th century Guildhall Chapel. Excavations have revealed a curved wall of Roman date, together with the remains of the eastern entrance of the structure. The discovery of the curved wall recalled for archaeologists the earlier uncovering of curved walling in Gresham Street to the south of the 1988 excavation area. The curved walling in the Guildhall Yard is now seen as the inner, and the remains in Gresham Street as the outer, walls of the amphitheatre. The floor of the arena appears to be in the best state of preservation, complete with a central drain which retained its wooden lining.

As so often on archaeological sites it is coins which provide the best clues for dating purposes. In this case Trajan seems to be the earliest Emperor recognized and the latest coin was dated to about A.D. 367, the amphitheatre itself being demolished in the fourth century.

The location of the amphitheatre in the city is interesting, for this type of structure was, like cemeteries, generally placed outside rather than inside Roman town walls. The explanation would seem to be that the amphitheatre was constructed before the town walls were built and stood just beyond the eastern side of Cripplegate Fort at the then outer limit of the Roman settlement of Londinium.

Roman Britain

For an informative summary of archaeological excavations and discoveries relating to the Roman period reference must be made to *Britannia*, Vol. XVIII for 1987, from which may be noted the discovery from the air of a pentagonal fort or stores-compound at Llansanffraid-ym-Mechain, Powys. Elsewhere in the principality, at Bassaleg in Gwent, a hoard of 904 coins was discovered, made up of one denarius of Maximinus I and 903 antoniniani ranging in date from Gordian III to Victorinus, the latest coin being of about A.D. 270; also discovered were traces of a possible pewter container. Another hoard of 51 antoniniani was among the discoveries at Caerleon; the coins ranged in date from Volusian to Victorinus with the latest coin dating to about A.D. 270. The usefulness of coin evidence is demonstrated by excavations at Caerwent, Gwent, the third season of investigations in Insula IX: "In the earliest phase a N.-S. metalled street c.18 m. wide separated the insula from the forum; on its east side stood a timber building with veranda, in which three rooms have been examined. Each had a clay floor renewed at least once, and the veranda was rebuilt slightly to the east of its predecessor. A coin of 86 dated either the original building or the reconstruction. Later a second timber building replaced the first and later still a stone strip-building was erected with forecourt encroaching on the street to its west; this shop was rebuilt on four occasions, gradually encroaching on the main street to the south. In Period 3 the shop at the south end was backed by a work room containing bowl hearths, behind which lay a hypocaust and other living-rooms. In Period 4, which also saw the erection of the temple on the west side of this building, greatly reducing the width of the street, the level of the whole area was raised by up to 1 m. and a coin of 330-5, sealed by the make-up in the workroom, gives a *terminus post quem* for both buildings."

On Tayside the last season of the fourteen-year excavation at Strageath Fort was completed, demonstrating that it had three main phases belonging to the Flavian, Antonine I and II periods. Elginhaugh Fort at Dalkeith is reported as being completely stripped and having its Flavian date confirmed. The latest coin found was a sestertius of 86 as well as a hoard of 41 denarii including many Republican issues; the latest coin was a slightly worn one of A.D. 77–8. The buildings of the Fort are reported to be of one period only although three of the gates seem to have been rebuilt. "Occupation ended with thorough demolition; burnt daub appeared in localized concentrations, often in demolition-pits".

Hadrian's Wall continues to attract the dedicated attention of archaeologists. During excavations at Chesterholm "A further 180 fragments of writing-tablets were found of which 20 were stylus tablets, the others ink-leaf, together with two fragmentary ink pens and nine styli."

An interesting chronological sequence has been revealed during excavations at Rocester Fort, Staffs., which "showed three principal phases of Roman occupation: (a) Two V-shaped ditches c.5 m. wide and up to 2 m. deep belonged to the defences of a Neronian military site. (b) The northern part of a barrack in the late first-century fort consisted of the officers' quarters with attached latrine and some *contubernia*. In the *intervallum* space a timber building was thought to be a cook-house. The fort was abandoned by the mid-second century: finds include cavalry trappings and mould-fragments for decorative metal-work. (c) Civilian occupation of the late second to third centuries was represented by metalled surfaces and wall-trenches. Ten metres of the second phase of the northern rampart were examined; the dating evidence seemed to confirm its previously proposed Antonine date."

In Hereford and Worcester a discovery at Castle Field Farm in Kentchurch is reported: "A suspected Roman Fort has been located in the Monnow Valley: the site partly survives in earthwork form, and has yielded Claudio-Neronian samian. Excavation showed evidence of two periods of timber buildings similarly aligned. The site lies well off the road from Abergavenny to Kenchester but may be associated with a possible road from Clifford to Monmouth."

Part of a cemetery at Upper Walls Common in Baldock, Herts., at the junction of the Icknield Way and the road to Verulamium was investigated: "Totals of 248 cremations and 12 inhumations were recovered. Of the former only 44 were in urns, a ratio of barely 1:3 urned to unurned which contrasts with 1:19 in the broadly contemporary cemetery excavated in 1982 on the south side of the same field." It is noted that "In 1986 several cremations appeared to be in wooden boxes, but grave-goods were few." Also discovered was the site of a possible pyre.

At Great Walsingham, Norfolk, the discovery of "two bronze statuettes of Mercury together with a patera-handle, coins of the second to fourth centuries and building-tiles may mark a temple site." There were many individual finds in Suffolk but particularly significant was the discovery of two miniature bronze votive axes at Wattisfield and two Icenian coins as well as a small bronze bust of Mercury at Wetheringsett.

Colchester was the site of an important Roman colony and at the continuing excavations at Angel Yard in the south west corner of Insula 28, parts of two second or third century town houses were examined: "two ranges of rooms were divided by a party wall; foundations were of mortared gravel. Despite damage by later pits, areas of mortar floor were seen in four rooms; one building had a room containing an oven 1·8 m in diameter; next to this was a cellar filled with rubble and wall-plaster, most of which lay outside the area of excavation. Thirteen votive pots, some still intact, were set in the floors. In the N.W. corner of the site part of the street on the W. side of the insula was noted. Dark earth sealing the remains yielded many late Roman coins, possibly a scattered hoard."

At the airport development at Stansted, Essex, an examination of the airport catering site has "located a settlement of the Iron Age and Roman period. A ditch 2–4 m. wide bisects the site; on either side were timber round houses, seven in all, the most complete of which was *c*.11 m. in diameter; another had a central hearth. The main occupation was in the late first century A.D., but residual Belgic and late Iron Age material was present".

So important did London become during the Roman period that excavations are continuously producing more information about the city of that time. The excavations at Gracechurch Street/Whittington Avenue are of "a large site near the N.E. corner of the Hadrianic forum." The summary continues: "Early quarry-pits, ditches and post-holes of a building were sealed by a thick layer of burning, above which lay six buildings with brick earth walls associated with pottery of *c*.60–80 A.D. These were replaced by the range of rooms flanking the north side of the Hadrianic basilica, north of which ran an E.–W. street with brick earth and timber buildings beyond. Much pottery of Flavian to fourth-century date included unusual or imported types; among glass finds were chariot and athletes cups and a scyphos. After nine resurfacings the street was sealed by silt into which Saxon pits were cut."

In the West Country rescue excavation at King's School playing field, Kingsholm, Glos., in advance of an inner relief road, uncovered the remains of a cobbled courtyard of a substantial building. It is reported that "finds suggested that this had possessed a colonnaded veranda. The site became derelict in the third century. A third-century gold ear-ring with pearl droplets was found." At Somerford Keynes, Glos., "large numbers of coins, including two Dobunnic, one Republican and many of the first and second centuries, together with many brooches, were found with building-debris during field-walking. The settlement, 7 km. south of Cirencester, where the road to the tile-making site of Minety crosses the Thames, extends over three gravel platforms, or "islands" and was bounded by straight triple drain-age-ditches to north and south. A trackway forms a T-junction on the summit, beside which an aisled building measuring 27 by 9 m., with 10 pairs of posts, was excavated before winter flooding. The great quantity and variety of unused tile found around the building suggests a depot for tiles from Minety, 3 km. to the south. A curving enclosure-ditch to the east yielded three sculptured fragments of limestone; these consisted of part of an altar, an eagle, and part of a shield with drapery attached to the rear side."

The cutting of a water main trench west of the city of Dorchester enabled the cemetery at Poundbury to be investigated. Of five inhumation burials, four were of adults in wooden coffins on a west–east orientation, while the fifth was "an adult gypsum burial similarly orientated in a lead coffin within a substantial coffin of greensand. This is the first lead-lined stone coffin, and the first greensand coffin recorded in the Poundbury cemetery; earlier finds have been of Ham Hill stone coffins or lead-lined wooden coffins. No grave-goods were present." In the vicinity "At the western end two roundhouses and a pit of Iron Age date were located; two ditches may have represented a surrounding enclosure. Nine more burials were found. A crouched adult inhumation of the late first century A.D. was accompanied by

a Black-burnished dish and meat bones. The other eight (two juveniles and six adults) belonged to the late Roman cemetery; seven were in wooden coffins, the eighth lay prone and uncoffined. One child and one adult were buried with hobnail boots."

At Wareham, Dorset, investigations of a bypass site showed an extensive system of ditched enclosures of between late Iron Age and late third century A.D. date. Although it is reported that "There was some evidence for iron-smithing during the Iron Age; from the mid second century activity switched to the production of Black-burnished ware. Evidence included a large quarry-pit producing fine white clay, a small rectangular preparation-trough, and a possible pit-clamp. Five kilns were excavated, all of a single-chamber, single-flue design, with no permanent raised floor or portable kiln-furniture; one kiln contained its final load."

In concluding this brief summary of discoveries of the Roman period, mention must be made of the most interesting discovery at St. Peter Port, Guernsey, where the "remains of a Gallo-Roman ship of the late third century were surveyed in the harbour, and a section of hull below the waterline, 18 m. long was recovered for conservation; the vessel is thought to have been *c*.23–25 m. long and 5–6 m. wide. It was a single-masted sailing ship, frame-built with carvel planking fastened to massive floor-timbers by iron nails. All timbers were of oak and the planks were caulked with crushed twigs. Moss grommets were used to provide a waterproof seating beneath the cone-shaped heads of the nails ... the mast was stepped into a raised central portion of a floor-timber with raised medial ridges extending away from the step on each side."

The Medieval Period

A comprehensive summary of recent work connected with the medieval period is to be found in *Medieval Archaeology*, Vol. XXXI for 1987. Of particular interest is the new excavation at Acton Court, Avon, of a Tudor mansion erected about 1535–1555 by Sir Nicholas Poyntz on the site of an earlier manor house. Work concentrated on the demolished part of the Tudor house and a twelfth century pottery group with a short-cross penny was recovered, as was 13th century pottery. It is reported that the Period I structure "appeared to be a hall or chapel, certainly in existence by the 14th century, and possibly Norman in origin. In Period 2 a block was added on its N. side, probably in the 14th century, with a large garderobe and vaulted drain at its W. end. It presumably formed part of one range of a much larger house. When the S. and E. ranges were constructed in the 1530s, most if not all the medieval house remained standing, and was linked to the new work by a short, narrow N. range. The earlier house was only demolished in the 1540s, when the W. range and a new N. range were built. Surprisingly, the Period I structure was incorporated in the Tudor house, and actually outlived it, since it was converted into a barn in the late 17th century and survived until the mid/late 18th century."

Excavations at St. Neots Priory, Cambs., were undertaken during redevelopment and "Two stone coffins were discovered when in one small square excavations were taken down to medieval levels, at *c.*2 m. Both coffins could be dated by the decoration of their lids to the 13th century and both contained females who, judging by the skeletons, had been well nourished with a refined diet and had never been involved in heavy manual work. As they were buried in the cloister they were presumably benefactors of the priory."

Saxon levels were found during work at Cuppin

Street, Chester, where one of the pits of Saxon date contained a broken stone mould for casting silver ingots; the find was less than fifty metres away from the location of a major Saxon hoard including silver ingots found in 1950. Work was completed at Guisborough Priory, Cleveland, where "six phases of activity were recorded, commencing in the late Saxon period (post-holes of a timber building) and including an episode of agricultural use, three monastic building phases and the Dissolution destruction. The major discovery was the location of the first stone church (c.1120), one of the earliest excavated examples of an Augustinian church in the country."

In the south-west the need for cliff stabilization work enabled further investigations to be carried out at Tintagel Castle, Cornwall. In one of the trenches Dark Age material was found; "Associated with the Dark Age occupation were over a hundred stake-holes, evidence for wattle-and-daub structures, a succession of hearths, much charcoal, butchered bones and imported Mediterranean pottery." The summary concludes: "Perhaps the most interesting discovery was evidence for timber structures in close association with a large collection (considering the size of the trench) of imported pottery. This is the first real evidence for a timber phase at Tintagel, contemporary with the use of these wares. It is also significant that this discovery was made on the mainland, rather than the Island. It would appear that during the 5th to 7th centuries settlement at Tintagel was more extensive than has hitherto been supposed; during excavation two previously unrecognised potential terrace sites, below the castle ward on the mainland, were noted."

Investigations at the Old Fire Station in Coggesh all, Essex, noted "This part of the town which is low-lying and susceptible to flooding, was only built up in the later medieval period, and that its shift to the present site was influenced by the Abbey which controlled the market." At Angel Yard in Colchester excavation in advance of redevelopment revealed that "pits appear to date from the 11th century onwards. Though early Saxon pottery does occur, more significant is the presence of Thetford-type pottery of late Saxon date. The latter, coupled with the lack of mid-Saxon pottery, tends to confirm the theory that Colchester did not become an important settlement until the 10th century."

In Rochford, Essex, small-scale excavation and a watching brief on the site of a 19th century butchers shop demonstrated that the latter incorporated two 15th–16th-century timber-framed buildings and showed further that the earliest levels were "gravelled surfaces from the 13th-/14th-century pottery, probably associated with the medieval market place. From about the 15th century structures were erected on the site, and in some places as many as six superimposed floor levels, from timber buildings predating the standing structure, were recorded. Since none of the structures could have had a very long life-span, it suggests classic market-place infill".

At the Barking Abbey Industrial Estate, London, there was "continued work on the mid Saxon site of Barking Abbey revealing three hall-type wooden buildings, three Saxon wells and a rivetted water channel. Important finds included a large collection of Ipswich-type pottery and imported wares, a range of glass vessel fragments and over 100 timbers showing clear tool marks, many suitable for dendrochronology. A section of road lying between the Abbey Church and the Industrial Estate excavation site was relayed. The continuation of the medieval wall screening the church from the area of the precinct running down to Barking Creek was recorded. The corner of a building to the W. of this wall was also noted. The wall lines of the main drain

from the reredorter were revealed briefly and appear to be badly damaged."

Of the substantial programme of work undertaken in London, excavations in the City revealed that "Much structural evidence survived of the 15th-century Leadenhall market, as the trenches straddled the N. part of the quadrangular market building, locating its truncated foundations. A fragment of the exterior wall of the W. range survived to a height of 11·2 m. between modern buildings. It displayed evidence for an open round floor for trade and, above, two floors for storage of wheat. Cellars built on the site of the N. wing, after its demolition in 1795, incorporated over 100 dressed mouldings and blocks from the superstructure of the building. This information, coupled with the large body of documentary/pictorial records preserved in the Guildhall, will make possible a detailed reconstruction of this unique medieval building."

At Kingston upon Thames work was undertaken on the site of the medieval bridge across the Thames. "The excavation revealed an original bridge construction of a landward abutment and four free-standing piers, spanning some 30 m. E. of the present riverbank. The first known reference to the bridge dates from 1193; dendrochronological samples indicate a construction date of c.1170. The first phase foundations were of dressed Reigate stone masonry enclosing a solid flint rubble core which may have supported a timber superstructure. The piers were boat-shaped, narrow and pointed at each end. The foundations of all but the first had been embanked with timber piles—most commonly beech—and evidently stood within the contemporary river. Between c.1200 and 1400 the Kingston end of the bridge underwent major redevelopment: the resultant structure was to survive in its general form until 1828. Substantial masonry walls were constructed to link the landward abutment with the first and (subsequently) second piers, creating a continuous causeway some 15 m. in length. The two further piers remained free-standing but were largely rebuilt in the mid to late 14th century, most likely as part of a single programme; from this date both piers retained the springing for stone arches, the outer spanning c.5·5 m. The westernmost arch was subsequently rebuilt, probably in the mid 16th century. Both arches had become dry by the 17th century and were then blocked off for storage purposes."

On the other side of London exploratory excavations at Cathay Street, Rotherhithe, "revealed a well-preserved stone building, thought to be the mid 14th-century moated manor house of Edward III. The building, a standing wall of which survived in 1907, is c.30 × 20 m., and is surrounded by a moat 8 m. wide. The external walls stand over 3 m. high, and internal walls and floor surfaces also survive. A clay wall, which may have enclosed an outer-court range of buildings and the precinct entrance, has also been found."

North of the Thames, at East Smithfield, the redevelopment of the Old Royal Mint Site has permitted the investigation of the Cistercian Abbey of St. Mary Graces which was founded in 1350. The work has "revealed the S. side of the cloister, the warming house, frater, the reredorter, (?) dorter/chapter house and infirmary. A single phased cemetery, perhaps of the Black Death period, has been located E. of the Abbey complex. To the N. of the Abbey another cemetery, possibly the Abbey hospital burying ground, has also been identified. The post-medieval Royal Navy Victualling Yards which occupied the Abbey buildings have been examined."

At Westminster Abbey the late 11th-century undercroft was investigated and it is reported that: "The site lay on the E. side of the cloisters near the S. edge of Thorney Island, the gravel eyot upon which the Abbey stands. Stratified deposits up to 20 m. deep were uncovered showing occupation from the 10th century onwards and residual Roman material. A large irregular feature, probably a quarry, was found on the S. edge of the site. It silted up in the late 10th century and was sealed further by *c.*0·5 m. of water-lain, possibly riverine, deposits. Cut through these deposits was a ditch 7 m. wide and 2 m. deep which turned 90° within the excavation, possibly defining the S. limit of the Abbey precinct. Much environmental material and 11th-century pottery were recovered; other finds include a fine book clasp and much window glass. Possibly contemporary with the ditch was a rammed gravel surface that may have been a road; the surface was renewed twice. The ditch top was backfilled with clay and sand. That capping was cut by a series of post-pits for a timber building 6 m. wide and over 10 m. long. Most of the occupation levels had been destroyed but it was probably built in the mid 11th century. After it had been removed a shallow ditch was cut through the centre of the structure; a polychrome tile was found in its fill. About 1060 the present undercroft was begun. Its original purpose was probably storage, but alterations between the 12th century onwards converted it into a series of rooms, including a warming house. This entailed reducing the floor level by *c.*0·75 m., removing earlier deposits."

A quite different kind of site was investigated at Brighton Hill South, Farleigh Wallop, Hants. during excavation of the lost Domesday settlement of Hatch. The work included the machine stripping of about two hectares of land down to the chalk surface, which exposed many features including all of the church-yard. "The churchyard contained 264 burials. More graves were revealed within the church, which was completely uncovered. It was found to be of a two-cell plan, with at least two constructional episodes, the chancel having been substantially enlarged."

Investigations in Southampton included one of the Conduit House: "the building, which is situated close to several springs, was constructed to supply water to the Franciscan Friary by *c.*1310. In 1420 the borough purchased the water course, and the Conduit House contributed to the municipal water supply until the first half of this century. Several pipe trenches, three of which contained post-medieval pipes *in situ*, were excavated. Evidence for the existence of medieval water pipes consisted of a backfilled trench which led to brick blocking in the N. wall of the Conduit House, and several fragments of ceramic water pipe from later features." Another excavation in Southampton took place at St. Michael's Square, an area which appears to have been densely populated with seven properties erected respecting a previously unrecorded road, the latter being in use for a considerable period of time. "By the mid 13th century the road had gone out of use and the area to the S. had been given over to an open-air fish market. In the mid 15th century the site was levelled and a large, two-storey arcaded building was erected. The top storey was used as the town cloth hall, the bottom floor as a covered fish-market. In the mid 17th century the derelict shell was dismantled and re-erected next to the West Gate, where it is now erroneously known as the Tudor Merchant's Hall."

At Beverley, Humberside, excavations included one in Beck View Road of a medieval clay roof-tile factory complex in a medieval industrial suburb of Beverley along the course of the Beverley Beck. "The remains of six kilns in all were identified. Five were tile-built, twin-flued, rectangular structures of which two survived complete in plan. The sixth was twin-flued and of clay construction. All the kilns were orientated N.E.–S.W. and lay in the S. half of the site close to the Beck. The best preserved examples had projecting wing walls of tile around the stoking point

at the N.E. side, and evidence for at least two phases of kiln rebuilding was found." Traces of various buildings were found: "The sheds were timber-built on padstone supports or post-holes without intermediate walling, showing them to be open-sided structures, probably drying sheds from which the tiles would be loaded directly into the kiln. Part of a more substantial timber building of padstone and sill wall construction lay next to the Beck and contained evidence for two circular hearth or brazier positions within."

The kilns produced mainly flat roof tiles in two sizes as well as hip and ridge tiles. As to dating it is noted that "Pottery finds were sparse but of early to mid 14th-century date, and a penny of 1351–77 recovered from the surface of one of the yards suggests production into the second half of the century. No evidence of contemporary clay pits was found but later pits cutting through one of the kilns at the W. end of the site contained brick and tile wasters, indicating that a later period of production expanding into brickmaking took place. No evidence for brick kilns was found, however."

At Kingston-upon-Hull excavations were undertaken on the site of the Beverley Gate, with a view to finding and exposing the remains as part of a scheme to incorporate the monument into the pedestrianization of the city centre. The Beverley Gate stood at the N.W. angle of the defensive wall circuit which from the 14th century onward protected the landward side of the medieval port of Hull, the gate being the principal entrance into the town: it survived until 1776. The investigation revealed: "Pottery from the construction levels in front of the Beverley Gate indicates that it was probably built after 1350, some thirty years after grant of a licence to crenellate. Documentary references to works on the defences before 1350 therefore suggest that the earliest activity was concentrated elsewhere in the circuit, probably on the sea-wall at the Humber foreshore."

Investigations at Christchurch College, Canterbury, "produced evidence for mid Saxon occupation, possibly the site of a small secular settlement established soon after the founding of the Abbey of St. Augustine *c.* A.D. 598 and continuing until the late 9th century ... Features included a track with shallow side ditches and pits of 8th to 9th century date, many containing metalworking debris. Some yielded boss decorated Ipswich wares."

The usefulness of aerial photography combined with survey was demonstrated by the identification of the site of an apsidal-ended church, some 20 × 56 feet, associated with a hall-like building to the south, at Itteringham, Norfolk. "Pottery sherds and tile from the site of the 'hall' suggest a date not later than the 15th century." From documentary research it seems that "the church is most likely to be the Chapel of St. Nicholas and the hall that of the lost Nower's Manor, which belonged to King Harold in 1066, thereafter passing to the see of Thetford/Norwich. The chapel was apparently still in existence in 1430."

In Oxford excavations have been carried out at the Christ Church Cathedral cloister. Four of the burials found are of a sufficiently early date to "give considerable support to the view that this was the site of Oxford's minster church, which legend tells us was founded by St. Frideswide before 727. The early burials had no datable grave furniture, but later examples had stone 'ear-muffs', and the 12th-century burials were in mortared stone cists familiar elsewhere in Oxford at this time. Two graves had beds of charcoal. The latest burials perhaps belong to the period when the minster had been refounded as an Augustinian priory in 1122, and regular burial may only have ended when this area was subsequently enclosed by a cloister before 1190, the year of a major fire which left its mark on the Chapter House, and on the plain Romanesque doorway of a night-stair at the N. end of the E. range."

Also in Oxford the investigation of the building standing at 26–27 Cornmarket Street showed it to have much of the timber frame of the New Inn of about 1390. "It is clear that the inn originally comprised five shops facing the Cornmarket, jettied at first- and second-floor levels. To the rear it had a gallery with crown-post roof. The gallery overlooked a long narrow courtyard formed by ranges which can be largely reconstructed from the drawings of J. C. Buckler (c.1860s) and W. Allfrey (c.1900). Part of the N. range survives as an open hall at first floor level, with two doors at its W. end opening onto the N. end of the gallery. The courtyard entry from Ship Street comes in beneath this point, opening awkwardly under the gallery. Excavation showed that the inn of 1390 replaced a similar courtyard arrangement of the earlier 14th century, from which the stone walls had been reused."

At Wenlock Priory in Shropshire excavations showed that: "The earliest building was Roman; a layer of collapsed wall plaster represents the abandonment of the building; the plaster layer was sealed by a layer of midden, dated by radiocarbon determination to A.D. 660. This layer represents the reoccupation of the abandoned Roman building for use as part of a double monastery. Above the 7th-century midden layer was a cemetery for which five radiocarbon determinations gave a date span of 860 × 1140. The Roman building was demolished by Roger de Montgomery to make way for a Romanesque church in 1076–87. The N. and S. aisles of his basilica were excavated. There was no crossing."

Excavations were undertaken at Sandwell Priory, Coventry, and the summary reports that: "The church was shown to have originally consisted of a nave, S. aisle, crossing, N. and S. transepts, chancel and two N. and two S. chapels. The chancel and chapels each had an apsidal E. end. In the centre of the chancel there was a stone coffin which had probably been covered by a life-sized stone effigy of a knight in chain-mail; the head of this effigy was found in demolition rubble nearby. In the 15th century the entrances to the S. chapels were blocked off and tiled floors were laid in the chancel and N. and S. transepts. Graves were dug in the S. transept, crossing and chancel. In each a wooden staff had been laid on the right-hand side of the body, and some of the bodies wore leather boots. The staffs may indicate that the individuals had undertaken a pilgrimage during their lifetime. At a later stage a timber-lined drain was constructed across the crossing."

In York excavations on the site of the Redfearn National Glassworks exposed part of an Anglian settlement including at least six timber halls. "Occupation levels and associated rubbish pits and latrines produced an important corpus of finds including 32 coins dating between the 8th and mid 9th century, and pottery including local wares and imports from East Anglia and the Continent. All primary Anglian deposits (over 50 tonnes) were sieved to provide environmental data. The settlement is probably part of an extensive area of occupation, c.25 hectares in size, stretching from Fishergate to Walmgate Bar. It presumably represents Eoforwic, perhaps the commercial and industrial area of the Anglian settlement at York, on a new site well outside the area of Roman Eboracum. Occupation seems to have ceased at about the time of the Viking attack on York in 866–67."

In Scotland particularly interesting excavations were undertaken at Whithorn Priory in Dumfries and Galloway. It is reported that there were five main phases of activity; Early Christian (c.400–700),

Anglian (c.700–850), Anglo-Norse (c.850–1125), High Medieval (1125–1560) and Post Reformation (1560–present). For all of these periods information was produced but of particular interest was the Anglo-Norse Period, of which it is reported: "Whithorn has no reliable historical records between 802 and 1125 but excavation has produced abundant evidence dating to this obscure period. The deposits are deepest in the low ground between priory and town. This area has revealed two small, single-room houses similar to buildings from Viking Dublin. Deposits overlying the houses have produced substantial quantities of manufacturing debris and a scatter of artefacts. Manufacturing activities include leatherwork, antlerwork (combs and possibly tine handles), ironwork and smithing, leadworking and copperworking. Artefacts include combs; stick-pins; 'Saxo-Norman' pottery; querns; waisted, grooved hones; a decorated lead weight; a piece of steatite bowl; two large lead vessels; a boat-shaped net-sinker and a Hiberno-Norse coin of c.1050. The area towards the top of the hill produced artefacts but little manufacturing debris. The houses probably comprised part of a secular settlement on the fringes of the ecclesiastical site. The associated finds suggest its function as a trading post. The culturally diagnostic finds are consistently Norse."

The Post-Medieval Period

Useful summaries of work relating to more recent centuries may be found in *Post-Medieval Archaeology*, Vol. 21 for 1987. The work described includes the continuing excavations at Dudley Castle in the West Midlands: "Two medieval garderobes containing Civil War material were excavated within the keep. The deposits within the garderobes were anaerobic enough to preserve organic matter, among which were leather, seeds, insect pupae, a wooden lid with bronze attachments, textile fragments, and five condoms of animal membrane, probably of 17th century date, which are currently being investigated. Pottery, glass (including a urinal and wine glass) and two iron shovels were also found."

At Pontefract in West Yorkshire a ditch was investigated in Tanners Row which was filled with musket balls, suggesting "that it was associated with one of the three sieges of the castle during the Civil War." The diary of Nathan Drake (a defender during the second siege) records a ditch cut from the castle to the churchyard, to provide a covered way from the castle to collect fodder under fire. This ditch, dug on June 13, 1645, appears to be identifiable with that recorded in the excavation."

In Aberdeen excavations between Gallowgate and Loch Street showed that: "During the 15th and 16th centuries the area was divided into three tenements and the first yard boundaries were established. This presumably marked the beginning of domestic occupation on the frontages. The yard surfaces from this period produced Raeren and Langerwhehe stonewares. Later 16th- or early 17th-century activity was represented by a well, a large cess-pit and several smaller hollows for extracting building materials. The fill of the cess-pit included several shoes and a fragment of Venetian type glass."

In London excavations were undertaken in advance of housing development in Isleworth on the moated site of a medieval manor. "Among the principal features recorded were the brick foundations and cellars of a house thought to have been built in 1645 by Sir John Offley, Gentleman of the Bedchamber to James I. Substantial groups of tin-glazed pottery and leather off-cuts, dating to c.1700, were recovered from the infilling of the moat." At Uxbridge the remains of a brick-built hexagonal gate tower were found. "This was originally one of a pair which formed the gatehouse of the 16th-century mansion house known as 'The Place' (one wing of the house still survives in the Crown and Treaty public house). With the construction of the Grand Union Canal and the realignment of the Oxford Road in the late 1780s, the gate tower became incorporated in a coal wharf associated with the adjacent canal dock. A brick-wall extension at the rear of the tower relates to the use of the building as a cottage until the 1850s, when it appears to have been finally demolished." In central London excavation was carried out on the Thames foreshore immediately to the south of the Tower of London; work had to be related to the times of the tides. The intention was to find out whether stratified deposits existed and if the material related to Royal Ordnance workshops located there. A series of compacted foreshore surfaces was uncovered; these ranged in date from the 16th century to the present day. They were all gently sloping, and would have been ideal for beaching flat-bottomed boats. A wooden structure of 16th- or 17th-century date, interpreted as the remains of a timber revetment, or perhaps the footings of a jetty or stair, was found adjacent to the river wall. Finds recovered with the help of metal detectors included a range of gun parts (some unfinished) and tools—presumably associated with the workshops, five buttons bearing the Board of Ordnance arms, and a 17th- or 18th-century ring sundial."

South of the Thames excavations at Platform Wharf/Cathay Street in Rotherhithe on the site of the medieval manor house "showed that in the early 17th century the manufacture of tin-glazed earthenware was established in the surviving parts of the former royal residence. The brick base of a rectangular kiln was found cut into the walls of the N.W. tower, and two brick-lined puddling pits had been dug into the E. wall and the backfilled moat. Also at this time, much of the W. wall was refaced in brick. The industrial activity appears to have ceased by the end of the 17th century and a metre-thick layer of kiln waste was dumped over the moat area."

At Polesworth in Warwick there have been recovered "large quantities of pottery waste, kiln bricks, kiln bobs, saggars, ash, coal and burnt clay from a building site. This is the first evidence for the range of products of the local industry, which seems to have been active especially in the 18th century. The following products have been identified: blackwares with orange-red fabric and iron-rich red slip under a lead glaze—vessels included cups, jugs, a pancheon, a cistern, a butter pot and a flower pot; slipwares with orange-red fabric press moulded dishes, on which various decorative techniques were used, with patterns in two or three colours; yellowwares cups, bowls and jars, with some decoration. A cistern inscribed "Polesworth Pottery May 6th 1 . . ." confirms the name of the industry."

The salt production industry was the subject of the excavation at Port Eynon, West Glamorgan, where the Salt House was excavated because of severe damage to the site from sea erosion. "The site, which consists of standing remains of buildings on a low cliff, and associated structures on the adjacent beach close to Port Eynon Point, is reputed to have been the fortified residence of the pirate and smuggler John Lucas in the 16th century. Documentary evidence suggests that it also operated as a sea-salt works until the mid 17th century. The site was later occupied by oyster-fishermens' cottages. Excavation of the building has confirmed that they are, at least in part, a fortified house. Associated structures are three masonry-lined chambers, set into the beach. The largest of these measures 20 × 3 m. and 3 m. deep, and is thought to be a reservoir, fed by the high tide, from which sea-water was pumped by means of a wooden pump (of which the remains were found) to a higher level. Here the water would have been evaporated in shallow pans by artificial heat. This level of technology is not recorded elsewhere before the early 18th century."

THE NOBEL PRIZES

For prize winners for the years 1901–1984, *see* earlier editions of WHITAKER'S ALMANACK.

The Nobel Prizes are awarded each year from the income of a trust fund established by the Swedish scientist Alfred Nobel, the inventor of dynamite, who died on December 10, 1896, leaving a fortune of £1,750,000. They are awarded to those who have contributed most to the common good in the domain of (*a*) Physics, awarded by the Royal Swedish Academy of Sciences; (*b*) Chemistry, awarded by the Royal Swedish Academy of Sciences; (*c*) Physiology or Medicine, awarded by the Karolinska Institute; (*d*) Literature, awarded by the Swedish Academy of Arts; (*e*) Peace, awarded by a five-person committee elected by the Norwegian Storting; (*f*) Economic Sciences (instituted 1969), awarded by the Royal Swedish Academy of Sciences. The first awards were made in 1901 on the fifth anniversary of Nobel's death.

The Trust is administered by the Board of Directors of the Nobel Foundation, Stockholm, consisting of five members and three deputy members. The Swedish Government appoints a chairman and a deputy chairman, the remaining members being appointed by the awarding authorities.

Prize	1985	1986	1987
PHYSICS	Prof. K. von Klitzing (German)	Dr. G. Binnig (German) Dr. H. Rohrer (Swiss) Prof. E. Ruska (German)	Dr. J. G. Bednorz (German) Dr. K. A. Müller (Swiss)
CHEMISTRY	Prof. H. A. Hauptman (American) Prof. J. Karle (American)	Prof. D. Herschbach (American) Prof. Y. T. Lee (American) Prof. J. C. Polanyi (Canadian)	Prof. D. Cram (American) Prof. J.-M. Lehn (France) C. J. Pedersen (U.S.A.)
PHYSIOLOGY OR MEDICINE	Dr. M. S. Brown (American) Dr. J. L. Goldstein (American)	Prof. S. Cohen (American) Prof. R. Levi-Montalcini (Italian)	S. Tonegawa (Japanese)
LITERATURE	C. Simon (French)	Prof. Wole Soyinka (Nigerian)	J. Brodsky (American)
PEACE	International Physicians for the Prevention of Nuclear War	Prof. E. Wiesel (American)	Pres. O. Arias (Costa Rican)
ECONOMICS	F. Modigliani (American)	Prof. J. M. Buchanan (American)	Prof. R. M. Solow (American)

The awards have been distributed as follows:

PHYSICS.—American 48; British 20; German 18; French 9; Russian 7; Dutch 6; Swedish 4; Austrian 3; Danish 3; Italian 3; Japanese 3; Chinese 2; Swiss 2; Indian 1; Irish 1; Pakistani 1.

CHEMISTRY.—American 33; German 24; British 23; French 7; Swedish 4; Swiss 4; Canadian 2; Dutch 2; Argentinian 1; Austrian 1; Belgian 1; Czech 1; Finnish 1; Hungarian 1; Italian 1; Japanese 1; Norwegian 1; Russian 1.

PHYSIOLOGY/MEDICINE.—American 61; British 21; German 12; French 7; Swedish 7; Danish 5; Swiss 5; Austrian 4; Belgian 4; Italian 3; Australian 2; Canadian 2; Dutch 2; Hungarian 2; Russian 2; Argentinian 1; Japanese 1; Portuguese 1; S. African 1; Spanish 1.

LITERATURE.—French 12; American 9; British 8; German 7; Swedish 6; Italian 5; Spanish 4; Danish 3; Norwegian 3; Russian 3; Chilean 2; Greek 2; Irish 2; Polish 2; Swiss 2; Australian 1; Belgian 1; Colombian 1; Czech 1; Finnish 1; Guatemalan 1; Icelandic 1; Indian 1; Israeli 1; Japanese 1; Nigerian 1; Yugoslav 1; Stateless 1.

PEACE.—American 17; Institutions 15; British 9; French 9; Swedish 5; German 4; Belgian 3; Swiss 3; Argentinian 2; Austrian 2; Norwegian 2; S. African 2; Canadian 1; Costa Rican 1; Danish 1; Dutch 1; Egyptian 1; Irish 1; Israeli 1; Italian 1; Japanese 1; Mexican 1; Polish 1; Russian 1; Vietnamese 1; Yugoslav 1.

ECONOMICS.—American 15; British 5; Swedish 2; Dutch 1; Norwegian 1; Russian 1.

SCIENCE AND DISCOVERY, 1987–88

Blue-Schists Explained.—Dense blue rocks called blue-schists are thought to have been formed at least 25 km. down in the Earth's crust. However, they do appear on the Earth's surface and scientists have been unable to explain this. In 1986 John Platt of Oxford University proposed that they reached the surface through long horizontal fractures in the crust, these features being known as extensional faults. He suggested that when one crustal plate is subducted under another, a large stable wedge of material develops in front of the upper plate in the same way that wood shavings collect in front of a plane. As the lower plate is subducted material also gets caught up beneath the wedge, causing instability. In time cracks appear in the wedge and the wedge then collapses in on itself. This stretches the wedge, causing more faults to develop, and the wedge moves forward, taking the blue-schist to the surface.

Clark Blake of the U.S. Geological Survey and David Jones of the University of California at Berkeley looked for extensional faults in California and in the Japanese islands of Honshu and Kyushu. They discovered blue-schists at both sites. In some places, layers of rock which were once 10 to 15 km. apart were found lying directly on top of each other. It is now realized that extensional faults often occur where the crust is thinning and where plates are diverging. They are not generally thought to occur in mountain systems formed by compression, although field work has shown them to be present in the mountain systems of both California and Japan. Difficulties with Platt's theory remain, however. According to Platt, the extensional faults in California should move westwards towards the ocean but they are moving eastwards. This discrepancy has yet to be explained.

Brown Dwarf Stars.—Two American astronomers, Benjamin Zuckerman of the University of California, Los Angeles, and Eric Becklin of the University of Hawaii, think they may have discovered a new class of star, which they have named brown dwarf stars. The existence of such objects was predicted some twenty years ago but there has been difficulty locating them because they are exceedingly dim.

The new object, which has a mass between that of Jupiter and the smallest star previously known, is thought to be a companion star to the white dwarf Giclas 29–38. The spectrum of Giclas 29–38 has an infra-red radiation in excess of that normally expected from a white dwarf. The infra-red colour temperature of the excess radiation is about 1,200 K. In view of the distance of the white dwarf, this corresponds to a total luminosity only 0·05 per cent that of the Sun. If the body responsible for the radiation is a star then its radius would be less than one sixth that of the Sun, and its mass only a few per cent of that of the Sun. This is in complete agreement with the predicted properties of such objects.

Other American astronomers, using the infra-red facility at Mauna Kea, Hawaii, have obtained a photograph of another star, labelled Gliese 569B, which could be the first confirmed case of a brown dwarf. It lies 34 light years away in the constellation Bootes. It has been realized for some time that the dynamics of star systems and of the Milky Way as a whole can only be explained satisfactorily if there exist huge quantities of invisible matter which have yet to be discovered. The discovery of the brown dwarfs may be the forerunner of discoveries of many objects in this class.

Carbon Dioxide and the Ice Ages.—The snow that falls in the Antarctic forms each year a distinctive layer in ice-cores, which can be dated in the same way as tree rings. Each layer contains a record of the conditions existing at the time of the snowfall in the form of deuterium (heavy hydrogen). The amount of deuterium is a guide to temperature because water molecules containing heavy hydrogen evaporate more slowly than water which contains the ordinary, much lighter, form of hydrogen. The ratio of hydrogen to deuterium gives an estimate of the average temperature at the time the ice was formed. In addition the small air bubbles trapped in the ice-core record the proportion of carbon dioxide in the air at the time.

Work carried out by a team of French and Soviet scientists has shown that there is a link between changes in the carbon dioxide content in the atmosphere and the cycle of ice ages to which the Earth has been subjected. The evidence was obtained from an ice-core drilled into the Antarctic ice cap which took from 1980 to 1985 to extract. At over 2,000 metres long, this is the deepest ice-core ever drilled. The core, known as the Vostok core, spans a period of more than 160,000 years covering the two most recent ice ages and the warmer interglacial period between them.

The analysis of the carbon dioxide content has shown that there were substantial increases in the gas, from about 190 to 280 parts per million by volume at the end of the ice ages. There was a fall in the concentration of carbon dioxide at the beginning of the ice age but this lagged behind the corresponding fall in temperature by about 10,000 years. The temperature record registered two regular variations over periods of about 20,000 and 40,000 years. These are in step with the changes in the orientation of the Earth to the Sun, the so-called Milankovitch cycles. The 20,000 year deuterium cycle is also present in the carbon dioxide cycle, though the 40,000 year period is not evident. Scientists are hoping that the study of changes in the carbon dioxide content may throw more light on why such small variations in the heat reaching the Earth could have such dramatic effects.

Dinosaur Embryos Found.—Preserved embryos in a dinosaur's nest have been discovered by American scientists in sediments in the Two Medicine formation near Egg Mountain in Montana. The deposits are about 75 million years old. Previously the scientists had found in the area eggs, nests and colonial nesting sites of the eight-metre long hadrosaur, a bipedal and herbivorous dinosaur belonging to the genus Maiasaura. The new discovery includes the remains of Maiasaura embryos and also of the hysilophodonrid Orodromeus. This latter dinosaur is similar but smaller, only 2·5 metres long, and until this discovery very little was known about it.

The scientists found a nest of 19 unhatched eggs and the remains of the Orodromeus, together with Maiasaur remains, as scattered embryonic bones within a nest mound. Careful analysis of the bones showed differences between the two types of dinosaur. The joint surfaces of the limbs in the smaller Orodromeus were well formed and composed of calcified cartilage, while those of the larger hadrosaur were poorly finished off. A possible explanation of this is that the smaller hadrosaur could scamper about in search of food immediately after hatching, whereas the larger Maiasaur spent a long time in the nest being fed by its parents. The study has also revealed that certain bony processes for muscle attachment do not seem to have ossified until after the dinosaur hatched and the muscles became active. Also, the denticles (coarse projections) which run down the edges of the teeth in the mature Orodromeus are completely lacking in the early stages. The discovery of the remains of eggs, embryos, juveniles and adults at one site will add greatly to knowledge about these dinosaurs.

Dinosaurs in China.—The Canadian and Chinese governments recently signed a four year agreement which allows Canadian researchers to work with the Chinese on a number of projects. One of these was to learn more about the existence of dinosaurs in the Chinese landmass and the discoveries have increased understanding of the behaviour and movements of dinosaurs.

During an expedition into the Gobi desert the research team unearthed the largest dinosaur ever found in Asia. With a neckbone measuring 3·6 metres long, the creature, a sauropod, must have been about 30 metres long overall and weighed about 25 tonnes. The expedition also located the well-preserved skull and feet of an eight-metre long carnivorous dinosaur called a Jiangjun-miaosaurus. Both the discoveries are of previously unknown species. The team also found dinosaur eggshells and the footprints of fossilized turtles, the oldest crocodiles from China and small plant-eating dinosaurs. In one day a survey in Inner Mongolia found 23 specimens of Protoceratops, a horned dinosaur.

The conditions under which dinosaurs existed in China are in total contrast to those in America. In the latter the environment was lush and well-watered whereas in China conditions were much harsher, not unlike the Great Salt Lake basin in Utah. One of the purposes of the project is to determine if dinosaurs migrated in herds between Asia and America when the two continents were joined by a land bridge about 80 million years ago. Certainly there are similar finds in both continents: at Sabusamu in southern Inner Mongolia, dinosaur footprints were found which show great similarity to some discovered in British Columbia.

Distant Galaxies.—It is generally thought that the universe started from the "Big Bang" about 15 thousand million years ago, although this date is by no means well defined. According to the "cold dark matter" theory, the universe consists mainly of

matter which cannot as yet be detected, but which can be pulled together by gravitational forces to form galaxies. This theory suggests that it takes about four to five thousand million years for a galaxy to be formed. However, a newly discovered galaxy, known as 0902+34, has been discovered which is so old that some of its stars were formed within a thousand million years of the Big Bang. This new galaxy, about ten times larger than our own Milky Way galaxy is 12 thousand million light years away, but most of its brightness is thought to originate from stars formed up to two thousand million years earlier. These older stars, which account for up to 90 per cent. of the mass of the galaxy, have been detected at infra-red wavelengths.

The galaxy was first discovered in 1982 as a radio source. For the past three years a British astronomer, Simon Lilly, has used the 3·8 metre U.K. Infra-red telescope and the 3·6 metre telescope on Mauna Kea, Hawaii, to find infra-red and optical emissions from this radio source. He discovered an object with a red shift of 3·4, a value nearly twice that of the most distant galaxies known at the time. The size of the object and the characteristics of the light emission eliminated the possibility of a quasar, some of which have red shifts as high as 4·5.

Astronomers in California confirmed the find and a concerted effort was made to find out whether the galaxy was unique or whether there are other objects at the same or even greater distances. At the International Astronomical Union's Congress in Baltimore in August 1988 the discovery of an even more distant galaxy than 0902+34 was reported. This new object, known as 4C41.17, is the same size as our own Milky Way galaxy, about 100,000 light years across, but nothing like it in appearance. It is surrounded by a halo of hot glowing hydrogen gas which is 300,000 light years in diameter and as bright as all the stars in our galaxy.

It has a red-shift of 3·8, which indicates that it is at a distance of 15 thousand million light years. This means that the light from it started travelling to us very soon after the universe was formed.

The discovery was made by a team of astronomers working in New Mexico, U.S.A. Some years ago they started investigating radio sources which had abnormally high energy at long wavelengths. Precise positions were found for quite a few sources, amongst which was galaxy 4C41.17. It was then identified optically using the 4 metre Mayall telescope at Kitt Peak, Arizona.

Whether 4C41.17 is a member of a new class of object or whether it is just a very early stage in the general evolution of galaxies has yet to be determined. Much will depend on whether similar objects are identified in the outer regions of the universe. If more are discovered and it is found that they are normal galaxies in the early stages of development, the cold dark matter theory, in its present form at least, will have to be discarded.

Earthquake Waves in Turmoil.—Scientists at the California Institute of Technology (Caltech) have found that shock waves generated by earthquakes travel through the Earth faster when moving in a north–south direction than when travelling in an east–west direction. The scientists report that the difference in time for a seismic wave to reach the other side of the Earth is as much as two seconds. This result takes full account of the Earth's equatorial bulge.

At the moment there appears to be no logical explanation for this difference. A group from Harvard University has put forward the idea that the speed of the waves depends on the direction the waves pass through the core of the Earth. If the core behaves like a single pure iron crystal the direction through this crystal taken by the wave would affect its speed. This explanation, however, is insufficient to account for the recorded difference in time. Nor does it account for a time difference existing even when the wave passes only through the liquid outer core of the Earth, not through the solid core. This presents a further problem because a liquid should be isotropic, i.e. the speed should be the same no matter what the direction of the wave travelling through it. Another explanation put forward involves fluid motions of the core but calculations have shown that the motions would have to be so fast as to make the idea untenable.

Donald Anderson, director of the seismological laboratory at Caltech, suggests that the least unlikely explanation for the anomaly is that the outer core is not a pure liquid but similar to a slurry containing small solid particles of iron, like iron filings: these would line up with the Earth's axis rather than the equatorial plane. Another suggestion involves a super magnetic field, as strong as that in some of the stars, but no such magnetic field has been detected. More work will be necessary before a satisfactory explanation is found.

A Fundamental Fifth Force?—There is increasing support among scientists for the possibility that a fifth fundamental force may exist (the four known ones are gravity, electromagnetic and the strong and weak nuclear forces). At present there is no firm evidence of such a force but there are serious difficulties in explaining observed phenomena in terms of the four known forces. Work carried out to identify a fifth force has produced evidence that there are deviations from Newton's law of gravity over distances of up to a few hundred metres. These deviations seem to affect all objects equally and some feel that the deviations may be the result of a fifth force which is a repulsive and an attractive one.

Fifteen years ago a Japanese scientist suggested that one way of combining gravity with the mathematical description of the three other forces would be to add a so-called "Yukawa term" to the equation describing gravitational potential. This term involves two constants, one defining the strength of an extra component of gravity and the other giving an indication of the way this extra component is affected by distance. This work was taken up by Australian Frank Stacey, who carried out experiments at different levels in mines. First Stacey and then others found the constant of gravity (G) to be about 1 per cent. less than that obtained by traditional methods. Ephraim Fischbach of the University of Washington, Seattle, then questioned the accuracy of the work carried out by Roland von Eotvos, and a

reanalysis showed that there was a slight deviation from Newton's law. This appeared to be caused by a small repulsive force which varied for different materials, suggesting that the strength of the fifth force might be related to the number of particles in the nucleus of the atoms of the materials. More recent work does not support this but there is support for the existence of a new force which has a range of only a few hundred metres. Whether there is a fifth force, or two components, or even an entirely new explanation of the reported deviations, remains to be seen.

Galaxies Still Being Formed.—It is generally thought that most galaxies were formed soon after the Big Bang. If this were so, and if all matter in the universe were concentrated in the bright stars, then the overall density of the universe would be too low for galaxies still to form. And because light travels at a finite speed, astronomers would expect to find the youngest galaxies furthest from our own Milky Way galaxy. However, Swedish astronomers working at the European Southern Observatory in Chile have discovered what is thought to be a new galaxy close to the Milky Way galaxy. The new object is a dwarf galaxy known as ES0400-G43 which is in the process of forming its first generation of stars. It is classed as a blue compact galaxy, a type characterized by a compact appearance and a very blue colour indicative of a high rate of star formation. The relatively low amounts of metals in the spectrum suggest either that the galaxy is very young or that the star formation takes place in bursts.

This new discovery provides strong evidence for the cold dark matter theory which says that 90 per cent. of all the matter in the universe is in the form of particles left over from the Big Bang and that only a small amount has been converted into stars and galaxies. The cold dark matter theory allows for the presence of sufficient material to generate high enough densities for a few irregular galaxies to be formed at a late stage in the evolution of the universe. The new discovery is completely in line with these ideas. Optical observations indicate a predominantly young stellar population and an extremely low mass to light ratio. The luminous stars are concentrated in a rapidly spinning central disk but dark matter seems to be dominant in the outer regions—another feature that accords with the cold dark matter theory.

Geminga Identified.—In the early 1970s the *SAS 2* satellite detected 121 gamma-ray photons coming from the direction of the Crab Nebula. Observations by the *COS-B* satellite recorded 1,000 gamma rays and narrowed down their area of origin to a region of $0°.8$ across near to the star 20 Geminorum. The source was called Geminga and it is unusual because it emits almost all its energy in the form of high-energy gamma rays.

It was assumed that a strong gamma-ray source would also be a strong X-ray source. The use of the *Einstein* X-ray satellite enabled astronomers to locate a strong X-ray source almost at the centre of the region identified by the *COS-B* satellite, giving a position to within 3 arc seconds. The identification of the source was the result of work by Jules Halern and David Tytler of Columbia University. They made multicolour C.C.D. observations of the stars in the region of the gamma ray source using the 200 inch telescope at Mount Palomar. The colours and magnitudes of 93 stars were then plotted on a colour-magnitude diagram and it was obvious immediately that one star did not fit the general picture: it was unusually blue compared with the other stars in the field. Subsequent analysis has shown it to be an isolated neutron star with a surface temperature between 500,000 and 1,200,000 K. at a distance between 1,500 and 3,000 light years away. No radio pulses are received from it on Earth, which suggests that the radio beams are not pointing towards the Earth.

The astronomers believe it to be a relatively young pulsar, similar to the one at the centre of the Vela supernova remnant. It is thought that other unidentified gamma-ray sources found by *COS-B* may be similar pulsars.

Halley's Comet.—The European Space Agency spacecraft *Giotto* encountered Halley's comet on March 13, 1986, and photographed the nucleus of the comet using a Multicolour camera. The images taken by the camera were improved by careful calibration and image-processing methods to reveal surface features a few hundred metres across. The nucleus of the comet is peanut-shaped (dimensions $16 \times 8 \times 8$ km.), rotating about an axis approximately perpendicular to the long axis over a period of about 54 hours. The surface details and the variations of the limb suggest that the nucleus has a hilly surface with a coarse roughness, at least down to the half kilometre resolution.

Smaller features were visible only around the active northern area, where a small finger-like patch about 1·4 km. long and about 550 m. wide can be discerned. This is separated from the main area of the dark surface by a bright patch some 600 m. across. One of the prominent features is about 2 km. across and about 150 m. deep and crater-like in appearance, but it is not clear whether the "crater" is really a coherent feature: it is thought that it may be associated with particularly strong activity, possibly in the past. Running almost north–south along the terminator lies a chain of at least four regularly-spaced hills with dimensions of about 0·5 km.

The most prominent feature is a bright, sharply defined patch (the "mountain") towards the centre of the observed nucleus. The spot could not be resolved, which puts an upper limit of 0·2 km. on its size. If it is due to the top of a hill being illuminated by the morning sun it could have a height of up to 1 km. A central depression, located in the middle of the elongated nucleus, surrounds it like a waist. A broad valley tapers from the limb towards the mountain.

It appears that dust emission is concentrated at certain parts of the nucleus, with the strongest observed area located on the northern sunward tip. High resolution images show fine structure in the global dust streamers and in some cases can follow them out to a distance of over 100 km. However, these dust filaments, about 0·5 km. across near the nucleus, contribute only about 30 per cent to the overall dust density.

During the visit of the comet, two Russian *Vega* probes were also sent to penetrate the comet and send back data. One of these, *Vega 1*, collected for analysis dust grains emitted by the nucleus. *Vega 1* flew through the comet at 68 km. per second. As it did so, dust particles hit a metallic target, exploding in a puff of gas, and the composition of this gas was then recorded using a mass spectrometer.

The experiment was set up by a team of physicists led by Jochen Kissel of the Max Planck Institute for Nuclear Physics in Heidelberg, and they were able to identify 17 different elements in the 79 dust grains which hit the plate. Of the 79 grains, 21 had a rocky composition and fell into two distinct types. One type had a high iron content, whilst the other was rich in silicon and magnesium. Both types had few CHON elements (i.e. carbon, hydrogen, oxygen, nitrogen). Other elements were found to be present in amounts similar to the composition of carbonaceous chondrites, the oldest type of meteorite. But on average, Halley's comet contains greater amounts of the CHON elements than meteorites, although they occurred in different proportions in the different dust grains.

The physicists identified five main types of grains, based on the proportion of CHON elements. Two grains consisted of over 90 per cent hydrogen, ten had about 65 per cent carbon and another 15 consisted mainly of oxygen. These dust grains have altered very little since the comet, and the solar system, was formed over four thousand million years ago. They therefore provide a sample of the dust particles that formed the planets and direct evidence of the composition of interstellar space.

More Evidence for Darwinism.—From time to time ideas are proposed which challenge Darwin's theory of evolution, the theory of punctuated equilibria being one that has received considerable publicity. This theory asserts that the fossil record shows that evolutionary changes are not gradual and continuous, but that for long periods there is little change (statis), these periods being interrupted by sudden changes (punctuation). However, recent work by Peter Sheldon of Trinity College, Dublin, has shown that in the case of Ordovician trilobites the punctuation theory does not hold.

Sheldon's results are based on the study of about 15,000 specimens covering eight genera. He collected samples from seven sections and 400 sampling sites in central Wales, covering a period of about three million years. He was able to count the ribs of about 3,500 specimens and found that in all eight genera the number of ribs increased during the period, although there were changes of rate and several short period reversals. Previously the earliest and latest populations of trilobites had been placed in different species, and in one case in different genera. Sheldon concluded that no evidence could be found for any punctuational effect. He found that most of the populations were at an intermediate stage between the previously described species, while others were sufficiently variable to have been placed in different species under the previous classification.

Sheldon's work has important implications for the method of naming fossils. The well-established Linnaean nomenclature permitted the trilobites to be assigned to differing linnean species. Sheldon commented that this could have been interpreted as evidence for statis and punctuation, an interpretation which his work has shown to be unjustified. He says that statements about rates and patterns of evolution should be made on the basis of a statistical analysis of populations and not on the presence or absence of named species or genera.

Mysterious Pluto.—Pluto, the most distant planet in our solar system, continues to confound expectations of planetary behaviour derived from studies of the other planets. Its diameter is only 2,400 km., about two thirds of that of our Moon. Since the Moon is too small a body to hold an atmosphere, it seemed logical to assume that Pluto also lacked an atmosphere. But over the last few years observations of the planet, especially by the Infra-red Astronomical satellite, have suggested that it may support an atmosphere after all.

Further evidence of this was provided on June 9, 1988 when the planet occulted a faint star. This event had been predicted and astronomers despatched to observe the event in the southern hemisphere, mainly from locations in Australia and New Zealand. A team from the Massachusetts Institute of Technology (M.I.T.) watched the event from NASA's airborne Kuiper Observatory whilst flying over the south Pacific Ocean. The data collected showed that the light from the star was not cut off abruptly as astronomers would expect if the planet lacked an atmosphere, but that it dimmed gradually. Lawrence Wasserman of Lowell Observatory (the observatory which first discovered Pluto) commented that the light from a star can be recorded as being dimmed by an atmosphere when the atmospheric pressure is more than one millionth of the Earth's sea level pressure. The extent of the atmosphere will not be known until the data has been fully analysed but a spokesman from M.I.T. said that the atmosphere appears to extend for several hundred kilometres from the planet's surface.

New Species of Primate.—The island of Madagascar is of great significance in the study of biological development. It broke away from the African landmass 80 to 100 million years ago and for the last 60 million years its flora and fauna have evolved virtually in isolation. None of the mammals on the island are found elsewhere.

Of considerable interest are the lemurs, small members of the primate family. Zoologists have known for some time of the existence of two species of bamboo lemur. The grey gentle lemur exists in large numbers but the greater bamboo lemur was thought to have become extinct until some were found in a forest near Kianjavato in 1972. In 1985 more greater bamboo lemur were reported in an area near Ranamofana, living with grey lemurs. A West German zoologist, Bernhard Meier, with a team of Malagasy helpers, visited the area in 1986 and located the greater bamboo lemurs.

After seven months detailed study, Meier travelled to Kianjavato to compare the animals at Ranamofana with those discovered in 1972. To his surprise he found them to be entirely different. They are much bigger than the lemurs at Ranamofana, with huge masticatory muscles and flat snouts, and Meier said that they give alarm calls he had never heard before. It appears that the Kianjavato lemurs are the true greater bamboo lemurs, while the ones Meier had studied at Ranamofana are a new species. In 1987 all three species were found in the same place at Ranamofana.

Because of the colour of its fur the new species has been named the golden bamboo lemur. Its weight is about half way between that of the greater bamboo lemur and the grey gentle lemur. Skin samples revealed that it has 62 chromosomes whereas the greater lemur has 60 and the grey 54 to 58. Particularly important is the discovery of an inversion in one of the chromosomes of the golden bamboo lemur which would make it hard for the species to interbreed with the others. All three species feed on bamboo but they do not compete as the gold lemur eats bamboo exclusively but the others also eat fruit and other plants.

Nitrogen Fixation.—Although there is abundant nitrogen in the atmosphere, it is not in the form required by natural biological processes or by the chemical industry. Atmospheric nitrogen can be converted into a form which living organisms can assimilate either by lightning or by bacteria. Nitrogen fixation by bacteria involves the enzyme Nitrogenase, an iron-sulphur protein containing molybdenum. Experimental work showed that it was virtually impossible to fix nitrogen if molybdenum was excluded from the growth medium.

However, two years ago it was discovered that strains of *Azotobacter vinelandii* and *A. chroococcum* are capable of producing an alternative nitrogenase which contains vanadium but no molybdenum. Since then a nitrogenase has been identified in which iron replaces both molybdenum and vanadium. This ends the widely-held belief that nitrogen fixation by bacteria can only take place if molybdenum is present as a trace element.

Although the existence of non-molybdenum nitrobases had been suspected for some years, discovery of the new forms has been slow because they are not very active in the reduction of acetylene to ethylene, the standard method of detecting nitrogenase activity. So far the iron form has only been found in the *A. vinelandii* and it appears to be repressed if either molybdenum or vanadium is present in the growth medium.

All three forms are similar in that they are made up of a large protein, sometimes referred to as dinitrogenase, together with a smaller iron-sulphur protein dinitrogenase reductase. The Fe-form and the V-form also appear to contain a third component whose function is unknown. It has been possible to extract the inorganic co-factors termed Fe-Mo-co and Fe-Va-co and it seems that these are the keys to the actual process of nitrogen fixation.

Nitrogen Fixation and Acid Rain.—The formation of acid rain, with its implications for the ecology of the Earth, has been in the forefront of research during the last few decades. Attention has focussed on the burning of fossil fuels but recent work by Edward Franzblau and Carl Popp of the New Mexico Institute of Mining and Technology in Socorro suggests that the presence of nitric acid may be due to the fixation of nitrogen by lightning. Until recently laboratory experiments simulating lightning flashes had indicated that less than 10 per cent of the world's fixed nitrogen is formed by lightning. This new research seems to suggest that lightning is responsible for about 50 per cent.

Nitrogen is a relatively inactive molecule but the energies available during a lightning flash enable it to combine directly with atmospheric oxygen to form nitric oxide and nitrogen dioxide. These are washed out of the atmosphere when it rains, forming nitric acid. This in turn produces the nitrates in the soil. Franzblau and Popp were puzzled that this natural process accounted for only 10 per cent of nitrogen fixation. The amount of nitrogen dioxide produced in lightning flashes was measured using a correlation spectrometer. They measured one flash at close range and obtained readings of two storms each containing about 30 flashes. It was calculated that on average 10^{27} molecules of nitrogen were oxidized during each flash. As there are about 100 flashes every second worldwide, the result points to about half of the fixed nitrogen in the atmosphere being derived from electrical storms.

Origin of the Oceans.—Over the years the origins of the oceans have been the cause of much discussion. It is thought that comets originate from the so-called Oort cloud which forms a shell around the solar system at distances between 10 and 100 thousand astronomical units (A.U.). Perturbations by passing stars cause some of the vast number of comets to penetrate the inner regions of the solar system and a few of these collide with the Earth. Earlier calculations showed that the Earth could have acquired about four per cent of its water through these collisions.

Recent work by Christopher Chyba, of Cornell University, suggests that cometary impacts could have provided sufficient water to fill the oceans. Calculations by Chyba of the number of objects which struck the Moon, shown by crater density studies, during the early period of the solar system (4·5 to 3·8 thousand million years ago) indicate that the Earth during the same period would have acquired more than 10^{25} grams of material in the form of rock and cometary material. Chyba argues that if 10 per cent of the total impact material were cometary in nature and if 50 per cent of this consisted of water ice, then the cometary material could have supplied as much as 40 per cent of the present water in the oceans.

The difference between the four per cent of water suggested by earlier calculations and the 40 per cent calculated by Chyba may be explained by the modification of theories about the Oort cloud in recent years. It has been suggested that there existed originally an inner Oort cloud just beyond the orbit of Neptune which resulted in the inner regions of the solar system having a cometary flux some ten thousand times greater than exists today. This

version of the theory, although not yet proven, would suggest that an extraterrestrial source for a significant fraction of the Earth's oceans can no longer be dismissed out of hand.

Ozone Hole in the Arctic.—The existence of an ozone hole over the Arctic was first suggested in 1986 by Donald Heath of NASA's Goddard Space Flight Center. Because of difficulties in interpreting the data the idea was not widely accepted at the time. However, a recent re-examination of the data showed that the ozone layer in the northern hemisphere is thinning, though it is not clear how much of this thinning is due to ozone loss over the Arctic. Wayne Evans of Environment Canada, a Canadian government research establishment, has been studying the ozone layer over the Arctic since 1986 and has confirmed that a "hole" is appearing in the layer in late winter and early spring. He presented his findings at a meeting of the American Geophysical Union in Baltimore in May 1988.

The hole has a structure similar to that of the hole over the Antarctic but at the moment it is only half the size: it is about the size of Greenland whereas its southern counterpart covers the whole of the Antarctic continent. Evans found the Arctic hole more difficult to study than the southern hole because the more active weather systems in the northern hemisphere complicate the formation of the hole. His data was collected from special balloons, ozonesondes, at five stations in Canada, and results from the ozonesondes agree closely with the data collected by the *Nimbus 7* satellite.

Evans supports the claim that the hole has been caused by the chlorofluorocarbons (C.F.C.'s), used as propellants in aerosol sprays, in the manufacture of hamburger cartons and in refrigerators. Reduction of the ozone concentration will increase the amount of ultraviolet radiation reaching the Earth's surface, with serious repercussions for life on Earth.

Pioneer Probes Update.—The Jupiter probe *Pioneer 10*, launched in March 1972, is still sending back data about the solar wind. It is now about 45 astronomical units (A.U.) from the Earth. (An A.U. is the mean distance of the Earth from the Sun.) The probe, the first to reach the vicinity of Jupiter, took 21 months to reach the planet and since then has been travelling on towards the outer reaches of the solar system. At the moment radio signals from the probe are taking about twelve and a half hours to reach the Earth. Reports from NASA's Ames Research Center in California indicate that conditions on board are such that it may be possible to receive signals from the probe for another ten years.

It is hoped that during the coming decade data will be sent back about the boundary between the solar wind and the interstellar gases coming into the solar system. At the moment this boundary is thought to lie between 50 and 100 A.U. from the Earth. In addition to sending back this data, the spacecraft will be used in an attempt to verify the existence of Planet X. The theory that a planet exists outside the orbits of Neptune and Pluto is based on unexplained perturbations of the orbits of Uranus and Neptune. In an experiment at the end of 1989, the probe will be involved in trying to detect gravity waves. The existence of these was predicted by Einstein in his theory of relativity and it is possible that *Pioneer 10* may be able to detect waves at a lower frequency than has been possible so far.

Pioneer 11, launched in 1973, has also passed Jupiter but is now taking a different route out of the solar system. It also will be involved in the search for Planet X and in the gravity wave experiment. Currently it is at a distance of 26 A.U. but contact with this probe is not expected to last as long as with *Pioneer 10*.

The Platypus's Sixth Sense.—It has long been a mystery how the platypus locates its food. Whilst feeding in murky waters, it always shuts its eyes, ears and nose and yet it seemed unlikely that the animal could find its prey by touch alone. A German anatomist, Karl Andras, suggested that sensors located on the animal's bill are used to detect the flow of water: then in 1986 Henning Scheich, working with a research team from the Australian National University at Canberra, showed that the bill is so sensitive to electric fields that a platypus can pick up the tiny electrical signals passing between the nerves and muscles of a shrimp when it flicks its tail. Since 1986 physiologists at the Monash University, Melbourne, have found sensors on the left hand side of the animal's bill. It would appear that platypuses have a sixth sense used primarily for detecting faint electrical impulses generated by their prey. The research at Monash also showed that the animal can distinguish between different electrical sources and that the sensors are sensitive to both steady and alternating currents.

The Platypus and the echidna, or spiny anteater, are the only mammals known to lay eggs and also suckle their young. The Monash researchers suspect that the echidna also has electro-sensors but more research will be needed before this can be confirmed. No other mammal is known to possess a system of electro-receptors, though some fish, such as sharks, have them. The system existing in the platypus is, however, far more sophisticated, and the sensors in sharks are based on a different nerve, so it is believed that the two systems evolved independently.

Pterosaur Finds in Brazil.—Pterosaurs took to the air about 225 million years ago in the late Triassic period, some 70 million years earlier than birds and bats. Upper Triassic and Jurassic rocks have provided well-preserved specimens of pterosaurs but the Cretaceous period had not been so productive until the discovery of fossils in the Lower Cretaceous Santana formation in Brazil.

The Santana formation is a sequence of limestone and shale rich in fossils of both invertebrates and vertebrates. Plants have also been identified in what is thought to have been a large landlocked lagoon. It was in the early 1970s that the first pterosaur fragment was found and since then many more specimens have been collected. They vary in size, with wingspans from two to six metres and skulls up to 60 cm. long. The bony remains are very well-preserved and free from distortion: in one case part of the wing membrane has survived.

Ten species have so far been described but it is thought not all are valid. Fossils of at least four pterosaurs have been substantiated and they provide useful data for an improved understanding of pterosaurs in the Cretaceous period. A recent study, based on neck vertebrae, has revealed the existence of two distinct lineages of these creatures, one with short necks, culminating with the crested pterosaur Pteranodon, and the other with long necks, culminating with the large Quetzalcoatlus. Nevertheless, more research is required before a full understanding is achieved.

The Santorini Explosion.—An exact dating of the Santorini explosion (*see also* Whitaker's Almanack 1987) is of great interest to both scientists and historians. Archeologists consider it important because it is linked to the decline of the Cretan civilization. From a scientific point of view it provides an excellent opportunity for studying the effects of the sudden ejection into the atmosphere of huge quantities of dust and sulphur-laden particles. Studies of ice-cores from Greenland have shown traces of acidity which point to the explosion occurring within 20 years of 1645 B.C. Restricted growth of bristlecone pines in the U.S.A., shown by the narrowness of the tree rings, points to an interval between 1628 and 1626 B.C., indicating possible climatic changes caused by the event. In particular, the existence of a severe frost seems to point to 1626 B.C. as the critical year.

However, dates derived from carbon-14 and ice-core measurements are not very precise. A more exact date has been suggested, based not on relative dates but on absolute tree-ring chronology. Mike Baillie and Martin Munro of Queen's University, Belfast, have obtained a complete chronology of oak tree rings covering a period of 7,272 years. Their work was carried out on two trees from the Garry Bog in the north of County Antrim. These showed a significant concentration of extremely narrow rings within a period of less than 20 years and one of the rings in particular corresponds to a short period beginning in 1628 B.C. This date, the investigators believe, was the date of the Santorini explosion.

A Stable Sun.—During the 17th and 18th centuries there appears to have been a mini ice age. Europe suffered many very severe winters and records show that at one stage the Thames froze over. It has been suggested that the cold spell was due to irregularities in the behaviour of the Sun. This idea has been strengthened by the recent work of Elizabeth Ribes and colleagues at the Paris Observatory. They base their beliefs on the analysis of records of measurements made at the Observatory at the time. The analysis has led the astronomers to suggest that the Sun was bigger than it is today by as much as four arcseconds, about 0·4 per cent larger. It is suggested that the expansion produced a small drop in the temperature of the Sun. This idea appears to agree with the fact that the Sun was rotating more slowly than it does today, as would be expected by the law of conservation of angular momentum.

However, this neat theory about the Sun has been thrown into doubt by the work of a group of British astronomers who have also been analyzing past records. Their results are based on observations of a total solar eclipse in 1715 which was visible from England. It is possible from these records to obtain very precise values for the size of the oval cast by the Moon's shadow as the Moon passed in front of the Sun. This shadow moved across England from the south west. At Lewes, Sussex, a total eclipse was recorded but at Darlington, Durham, the eclipse was not total: a sliver of the Sun reportedly being unobscured which was about the size of Mars. Calculations have shown that the size of the Sun at that time was within 0·1 arcseconds of its present value. A Sun as large as that suggested by Ribes would have produced a narrower totality track and would have put outside the totality belt Lewes and a number of other places where totality was reported.

Sunspot Studies.—One problem which hampers all aspects of astronomical studies from earthbound observatories is atmospheric turbulence and the resulting distortion of images. These problems have been virtually overcome by observing from orbiting satellites and the results are often staggering. Data collected during the *Spacelab 2* mission on a *Challenger* shuttle flight in 1985 has been processed recently and the computer-generated images have revealed details of sunspot structure hitherto unknown.

In 1985 solar activity was near minimum but during the mission there was one medium-sized sunspot, which was studied in detail. The longest uninterrupted sequence contained 28 minutes of data with a frame every two seconds. The pictures showed features only 350 km. across and several new phenomena were seen. There was a flow of material outwards from the dark spot with velocities between 0·2 and 1·5 km. per second. This agreed with earlier observations of an outward flow in regions away from the centre of the spot. The frames also revealed dark "clouds" moving outwards and bright jets which seemed to be ejected into the photosphere, the normal bright surface of the Sun surrounding the spot, at speeds of about 2·7 km. per second. In one frame a large expanding bubble of material was apparent, possibly having been ejected above the photosphere. Also recorded were filamentary structures around the spot which seemed to expand and contract at the rate of a few km. per second. This is thought to be a visible indication of waves passing through the region.

A sunspot maximum is approaching, providing astronomers with the opportunity to study sunspots in detail. The results of observations will be of interest beyond the field of astronomy because of the marked effect that sunspots, and their associated flares, have on the terrestrial environment. For a long time it has been suspected that the eleven-year sunspot cycle has an effect on the global weather system. Much of the evidence put forward has been centred on such features as the growth of tree rings, ice layers and sedimentary rock deposits. However, because of the lack of accurate sunspot records in earlier periods, theories of correlation have been rather tentative and difficult to sustain.

Recent discoveries have altered the situation completely. About eight years ago, two University of Washington scientists found that the strengths and temperatures of the stratospheric winds above the North Pole were related to similar winds over the equator, but the latter were known to reverse their direction every few years. They found that when the equatorial winds blew from the west the polar winds speeded up and became cooler. Now Karin Labitzke of Free University, Berlin, and Harry van Loon of the National Center for Atmospheric Research in the U.S.A. have discovered a very strong correlation between sunspot activity and the behaviour of the upper atmosphere.

Labitzke observed that the average temperature of the polar stratosphere in January and February varied in line with sunspot activity. The air moved fastest and was coldest at sunspot minimum. At the moment no physical process can be put forward to explain the correlation and a statistical analysis of temperature and sunspot numbers has found that a chance agreement is highly unlikely. However, the work is continuing as the data used so far covers only three sunspot cycles.

Superconductivity.—Progress in the search for compounds which are superconducting at temperatures close to room temperature has been rapid in the past year. In 1987 compounds were made consisting of yttrium, barium and copper which lost their electrical resistance when cooled below 90 K., 13 K. above the boiling point of liquid nitrogen. Since then research workers have produced compounds in which the yttrium and barium have been replaced by other elements, mainly rare earths.

More recently, a new family of superconducting compounds has been developed in which the superconductivity begins to manifest itself at about 130 K., reaching zero resistance by 117 K. These compounds have a completely new structure and involve bismuth, strontium and calcium. They were first made by Japanese scientists at the Institute of Metallic Material Research at Tsukuba. American workers carried on the research and have unravelled the structure of the compounds. Unlike earlier compounds, the bismuth compounds produce flexible sheets similar to mica, and this property permits easier manufacture.

Research in the U.S.A. has produced a new class of thallium-based materials that superconduct at temperatures up to 125 K., and there are reports that temperatures as high as 200 K. are within reach. The first of the thallium compounds were discovered in May 1987 and consisted of thallium, barium, copper and oxygen. Later that year calcium was added and the critical temperature rose to 105 K. Bob Hazen of the Geophysical Laboratory at the Carnegie Institute, Washington, discovered that the new compound consisted of two superconductors and when these were separated he found that one of the components superconducted at 123 K. Research has shown that critical temperature increases with the number of copper oxide layers. The original compound had one layer but when three layers were used the critical temperature rose to 125 K. If theories are correct, a four-layer compound would have a critical temperature of 150 K. and ten-layer material might reach 200 K.

Supernova 1987A.—The supernova which erupted in the Large Magellanic Cloud on February 24, 1987 is one of the most important events in recent astronomy. It has added greatly to our understanding of stellar evolution and the formation of heavy elements, though there are still unexplained features.

Some aspects of the event are developing as predicted, e.g. the prediction that light echoes would be observed. Because light travels at such a high speed, the only way in which light can be reflected and the echo observed is when an astronomical event such as this occurs. Such a phenomenon has been recorded only on two previous occasions, from the ordinary novae Nova Persei 1901 and Nova Sagitarii 1936.

On March 4, 1988, Arlin Crotts of the University of Texas photographed two glowing arcs 32 arc-seconds and 47 arcseconds from the supernova. These glows come from clouds situated about 440 and 950 light years in front of the supernova as seen from the Earth. A re-examination of photographs taken on February 13 at the European Southern Observatory also revealed the arcs. It appears that the arcs are expanding at a rate of 2 arcseconds per month; given the distance of the Large Magellanic Cloud, this indicates an apparent velocity about 20 times that of light.

One observation which is baffling astronomers is the record of neutrinos received when the star first erupted. Two stations, one in Japan and one in the U.S.A., detected independently a burst of neutrinos lasting a few seconds, and these were considered to have come from the supernova. A burst which arrived about four and a half hours earlier was detected at Mont Blanc at the same time as gravity-wave detectors in Europe and America were set vibrating. Until recently this was dismissed as a coincidence. However, the probability that gravity-wave detectors in Rome and in Maryland both observed disturbances simultaneously, and both at the same time as the neutrino burst recorded at Mont Blanc is so small that coincidence can be confidently dismissed. No satisfactory explanation of this earlier disturbance is available at the moment.

Synthesis of Heavy Elements.—The formation of the lighter elements during the normal evolution of stars is understood but very little observational evidence has been available to explain the formation of the heavier elements which make up much of the Earth. Theories have been developed that these elements are formed during supernova explosions and the supernova explosion 1987A in the Large Magellanic Cloud has provided useful observational confirmation of many ideas.

Stanford Woosley of the University of California at Santa Cruz predicted that the fall in brightness after the initial burst would be irregular. He had constructed a model in which the initial explosion would generate large amounts of cobalt-56, which has a half life of 77 days. In decaying the cobalt emits gamma rays, and Woosley predicted that the supernova would brighten when its outer shell had

expanded sufficiently to allow the gamma rays, attenuated into visible light, to escape. Observations showed that after a gradual fall in brightness after the burst on February 24, 1987, the supernova brightened from mid-March to late May and then faded at a rate which appeared to match the decay of the cobalt-56.

Woosley also predicted that as the outer shell became more transparent it would be possible to record the decay of the cobalt, first as X-rays and then as gamma rays. This was vindicated by the recording of X-rays by the Soviet space station *Mir* and the Japanese satellite *Ginga* in October and by the detection of gamma rays a few weeks later by the American satellite *Solar Maximum Mission* and by balloons launched from Australia. During flights in November NASA's Kuiper Airborne Observatory detected infra-red emissions of the elements cobalt, nickel, silicon, sulphur and argon. Observational work is still continuing.

Tectonic Activity on Venus.—Geologists have gradually come to the view that tectonic activity on the planet Venus is minimal or absent. Because Venus is roughly the same size as the Earth, early ideas favoured the view of possible plate movements, but detailed analysis has shown very little evidence for crustal spreading. Some ridges and rifts are present on the surface but they were considered to be localized features of minor significance.

Recently, however, two Brown University geologists, James Head and Larry Crumpler, have studied the problem in detail, concentrating on topographical data for Aphrodite Terra, a highland plateau situated on the equator and about the size of Africa. Head and Crumpler discovered characteristics similar to those of crustal movement on the Earth, including a widespread system of fractures. They also examined cross-sections of the ridges and identified an elevated central trough flanked by symmetrical topography, similar to that of mid-oceanic ridges on the Earth. This, they claim, is evidence of tectonic activity either at present or in the past.

The two scientists predict that the expansion of the equatorial regions will make it possible to identify squeezed areas in the polar regions, where the terrain is already known to be higher and more rugged. Other work has suggested that the equatorial crust is less than a thousand million years old and that the terrain nearer the poles, which is more heavily cratered, must be older.

The Tunguska Event.—An explanation of what happened in the Tunguska region of Siberia on June 30, 1908, has eluded scientists for over half a century. It is generally acknowledged that an object from space exploded in the lower atmosphere over Tunguska but none of the many theories put forward have been substantiated. No crater was formed and over the years much effort has been expended in trying to find fragments which could provide information.

Recently Soviet scientists identified an excess of iridium in core samples taken in the area. The iridium excess occurs in a peat layer at a depth of just over 40 cm. below the present ground level, and according to the investigators this was formed at the period of the explosion.

To produce the observed increase in iridium content in the Tunguska samples, the object that exploded must have weighed many millions of tons. This is in line with estimates derived from studies based on the kinetic energy generated at the time. As present ideas on the constitution of comets indicate that they consist mainly of ice, the evidence points to a stony object being responsible. However, it has been suggested that an incoming comet would have been accompanied by a cloud of dust particles. This idea is supported by reports of bright sky glows over Europe for a few nights after the event. So the main debate about the event continues to centre on whether the object was an asteroid or a comet.

23,000 year-old Polish Boomerang.—It is commonly believed that the boomerang is uniquely Australian. However, although used by the Aborigines for centuries—9,000–10,000 year-old specimens have been recovered from Wyrie Swamp, South Australia—boomerangs and killing sticks have been found on five continents. Paintings of them have been found in North Africa which date from about 7,000 B.C. There is evidence to show that some form of throwing stick was used by the Eskimos, Hopi Indians and Polynesians.

Early finds in Europe include an oak specimen preserved in a bog in Holland which dates from 300 B.C. and a find in Jutland from an Iron Age settlement dated 5,000 B.C. A new find, a curved piece of mammoth tusk found in a cave in Poland, has been dated at about 21,000 B.C., making it the oldest known boomerang in the world. Scientists from the Polish Academy of Sciences found the instrument amongst other artifacts and human food debris: it is thought that the cave was inhabited by Upper Palaeolithic people who hunted reindeer.

The boomerang has a span of 70 cm. with a maximum width of 6 cm. and thickness of about 1·5 cm. One side has the natural curve of the external convex tusk but the other side has been polished until more or less flat and shows several scratch lines without any decorative pattern. At one end small transverse lines are visible on both sides and are thought to have been made during its manufacture. The overall shape and general characteristics make it fairly certain that it was used as a boomerang and its find furthers understanding of early man's techniques in killing animals.

ELEMENTS

Element	Symbol	Atomic Number	Element	Symbol	Atomic Number	Element	Symbol	Atomic Number
Actinium	Ac	89	Hafnium	Hf	72	Promethium	Pm	61
Aluminium	Al	13	Helium	He	2	Protactinium	Pa	91
Americium	Am	95	Holmium	Ho	67	Radium	Ra	88
Antimony	Sb	51	Hydrogen	H	1	Radon	Rn	86
Argon	A	18	Indium	In	49	Rhenium	Re	75
Arsenic	As	33	Iodine	I	53	Rhodium	Rh	45
Astatine	At	85	Iridium	Ir	77	Rubidium	Rb	37
Barium	Ba	56	Iron	Fe	26	Ruthenium	Ru	44
Berkelium	Bk	97	Krypton	Kr	36	Samarium	Sm	62
Beryllium	Be	4	Lanthanum	La	57	Scandium	Sc	21
Bismuth	Bi	83	Lawrencium	Lr	103	Selenium	Se	34
Boron	B	5	Lead	Pb	82	Silicon	Si	14
Bromine	Br	35	Lithium	Li	3	Silver	Ag	47
Cadmium	Cd	48	Lutetium	Lu	71	Sodium	Na	11
Caesium	Cs	55	Magnesium	Mg	12	Strontium	Sr	38
Calcium	Ca	20	Manganese	Mn	25	Sulphur	S	16
Californium	Cf	98	Mendelevium	Md	101	Tantalum	Ta	73
Carbon	C	6	Mercury	Hg	80	Technetium	Tc	43
Cerium	Ce	58	Molybdenum	Mo	42	Tellurium	Te	52
Chlorine	Cl	17	Neodymium	Nd	60	Terbium	Tb	65
Chromium	Cr	24	Neon	Ne	10	Thallium	Tl	81
Cobalt	Co	27	Neptunium	Np	93	Thorium	Th	90
Copper	Cu	29	Nickel	Ni	28	Thulium	Tm	69
Curium	Cm	96	Niobium	Nb	41	Tin	Sn	50
Dysprosium	Dy	66	Nitrogen	N	7	Titanium	Ti	22
Einsteinium	Es	99	Nobelium	No	102	Tungsten	W	74
Erbium	Er	68	Osmium	Os	76	(Wolfram)		
Europium	Eu	63	Oxygen	O	8	Uranium	U	92
Fermium	Fm	100	Palladium	Pd	46	Vanadium	V	23
Fluorine	F	9	Phosphorus	P	15	Xenon	Xe	54
Francium	Fr	87	Platinum	Pt	78	Ytterbium	Yb	70
Gadolinium	Gd	64	Plutonium	Pu	94	Yttrium	Y	39
Gallium	Ga	31	Polonium	Po	84	Zinc	Zn	30
Germanium	Ge	32	Potassium	K	19	Zirconium	Zr	40
Gold	Au	79	Praseodymium	Pr	59			

CONSERVATION AND HERITAGE, 1987-88

ABERNETHY FOREST ESTATE

In February 1988 the Royal Society for the Protection of Birds announced that it had purchased the Abernethy Forest estate in the Highlands of Scotland. The 30 square mile estate contains the most substantial surviving element of an ancient pine forest as well as moorland and the mountain of Cairngorm. The area is rich in wildlife, particularly birdlife, which includes golden eagles, peregrine falcons, capercaillie, crested tits, dotterels and snow buntings.

The new reserve is the largest-ever land purchase by a voluntary conservation organization in Europe and cost the R.S.P.B. £1·8 million. The Nature Conservancy Council and the National Heritage Memorial Fund have pledged £1 million towards the purchase but the R.S.P.B. will have to raise the remainder.

BOOK CONSERVATION

The natural process of decay affects all works of art that are created using organic raw materials, be they architecture, murals, stained glass, film (threatened by the instability of nitrates) or books. Not all books are affected, but there is a growing conservation problem with books published in the past 150 years.

Publications prior to 1850 were generally produced on handmade paper of which cotton rags were the basic constituent. Such paper was thick and durable but slow and expensive to manufacture, and the demands of a burgeoning publishing industry in the nineteenth century led to an almost universal reliance on paper made of wood pulp. The nature of wood pulp fibres combined with the effect of machinery and of the alum-rosin sizing compound used to treat the paper, leads over time to a build-up of acids which cause the disintegration of the pages. The effect of the acids is often exacerbated by environmental factors such as sunlight, overheating or pollution. The British Library estimates that some two million of its 16 million volumes may be at risk in this way.

Until recently book conservation has been a laborious process that costs about £50 per volume. The volume has to be unbound, each page separately washed and then dried between tissues. However, scientists at the University of Surrey, who were asked to examine the problem by the British Library in 1979, have now come up with an alternative conservation process. This is called graft-polymerization and using this method books can be left bound and even closed. Books are placed in a nitrogen container for several hours and coated with acrylic monomers. Afterwards they are irradiated, which converts the monomers to polymers, increasing the paper strength by ten times. There is no perceptible surface change.

As the threat to books has become more widely-known in recent years there has been a move towards giving paper coatings and sizings an alkaline base. However, at present only a small number of books are produced on acid-free paper: unless the proportion increases, book conservation will become an increasingly serious problem.

THE BROADS AUTHORITY

The Norfolk and Suffolk Broads Act was passed in 1988. It creates a new Broads Authority with a statutory duty to co-ordinate the protection of the Norfolk Broads (which also cover north Suffolk). It will enjoy a status similar to that of the ten National Park Authorities, although its brief is not only to conserve the countryside but also to encourage agriculture and commerce.

The Broads constitute England's greatest area of lowland river valley grassland. They already include three national nature reserves (at Bure Marshes, Hickling Broad and Ludham Marshes) and twenty four Sites of Special Scientific Interest. Since 1985 they have been also an Environmentally Sensitive Area, with financial incentives offered to farmers to maintain riverbanks and hedgerows and to inhibit the application of chemicals to the land.

The Broads Plan published in 1987 laid down about 100 policy recommendations for the Broads Authority. A priority will be the reduction of water pollution. This venture will require close co-operation with Anglian Water Authority, which retains statutory responsibility for water cleanliness. The tourist industry, centred on the hiring of boats, will not be allowed to debase the settings of the rivers, and the Authority's planning powers also preclude undesirable development on the dry areas of land. The traditional supervisors of all matters navigational, the Great Yarmouth Port and Haven Commissioners, retain their powers but will work in co-operation with the new Authority.

COMMON SEAL VIRUS

In August 1988 the international conservation organization Greenpeace and Queen Mary College, London, organized a two-day seminar for scientists to consider the outbreak of a mysterious disease among common seals in the North Sea. The disease was first noticed in April among seals off Anholt Island, Denmark, and then further north off the Norwegian coast. It killed about 7,000 out of the continental population of 16,000 common seals. By August the disease had reached the colonies off the East Anglian coast and it was feared that a further 20,000 seals might die.

Many environmentalists tended to blame pollution in the North Sea for the outbreak of the disease. However, scientists believed that a virus was the most likely cause of the epidemic. Researchers had ruled out a herpes virus and a form of foot and mouth disease when Dutch scientists claimed that they had isolated the virus. Dr. Albert Osterhaus of the Dutch National Institute of Public Health and Environmental Hygiene announced on August 29 that the infection killing the seals was canine distemper.

Researchers suspect that the epidemic among seals could be connected to an outbreak of canine distemper among huskies in Greenland in December 1987. It is believed that the huskies came into contact with seals during seal hunts. Harp seals, which live in Arctic waters, migrated further south than usual this year and may have infected common seals in the North Sea and the Baltic Sea.

A vaccine has been developed by Dutch scientists but even so the total number of deaths is expected to run to several thousand: in August alone 250 seals were found dead on the British coast. Although pollution was ruled out as the cause of the disease, most scientists felt that it has been a major contributory factor in the spread of the epidemic by lowering the seals' resistance to infection. As a consequence of the outbreak a number of governments in countries bordering the North Sea have funded research into the effect of pollution on the marine ecology.

THE FLOW COUNTRY

The area known as the Flow Country extends through east Sutherland and Caithness in the far north of Scotland. It is a vast moorland of peat bogs, small pools, surface mosses and occasional low hills, which has been compared to tundra. There is a tradition of human occupation but the land is too hostile for cultivation on a larger scale than crofting.

Generally the area is the preserve of a rich array of birdlife and flora: 35 per cent of the European population of dunlin nest there, as do golden plovers, snipe, sandpipers and 70 per cent of the British population of greenshank. As well as more common birds such as meadow pipits and skylarks, there are rarer species such as the common scoter and the black-throated diver, and predators like the golden eagle, peregrine, hen harrier and merlin. The flora includes orchids, heathers, sedges and lichens. The ecological significance of the area is recognized by four international treaties, all of which Britain has signed.

About 4,000 years ago the Flow Country was forested but since prehistoric times there has been no significant intrusion by trees because of the water-logged soil and lack of shelter. However, the system of grants for afforestation and the tax relief available have encouraged private investors in recent years to plant conifers, mainly sitka spruce, on marginal land. The incursion of conifer planting has affected the ecological balance of the Flow Country. The argument put forward in favour of the plantings was the economic benefit to the area of the new jobs which would be created.

In July 1987 the protest of environmentalists came to a head with a Nature Conservancy Council report tabulating the threat to birdlife and urging the end to further planting over the 400,000 hectares of the Flow Country. Although the main company involved had acquired 40,000 hectares of land in the Flow Country at the beginning of 1987, the physical difficulties facing the foresters were also becoming apparent, the effects of windblow and the attacks of the pine beauty moth adding to the general hostility of the climate.

The report on the ecological damage to the area followed close scrutiny and criticism of the expense to the taxpayer by the National Audit Office in 1986. The scrutiny tended to the conclusion that tax relief should be ended, calculating that since 1946 some £2,058 million of Government money had produced a forestry estate worth only £1,452 million (at 1984–85 prices). It also estimated that forestry jobs cost twice

as much to create in the north of Scotland as jobs in agriculture. Certainly the expected 2,000 forestry jobs in the Flow Country have not materialized.

The Government's response was forthright. In January 1988 the Secretary of State for Scotland declared nearly half of the Flow Country a Site of Special Scientific Interest. He coupled this announcement, however, with permission to plant 5,727 acres and a reaffirmation of the commitment to 33,000 hectares of conifer planting in Scotland each year. Forestry planting grants were increased but with incentives to use broad-leaved species.

At the same time the Secretary of State for the Environment announced a ban on new conifer planting in England's uplands, protecting from further encroachment areas such as the Pennines and the Lake District. Moreover, the Forestry Commission was asked to introduce more varieties of species when replanting existing conifer forests in such areas.

The financial incentive to plant conifers was removed in the Budget in March 1988. The Chancellor announced that the cost of planting, maintaining and selling trees could no longer be set against income tax, reversing government policy of some 70 years standing.

LAND USE

The Common Agricultural Policy of the E.E.C. has long been synonymous in the public mind with butter mountains, wine lakes and other surpluses produced by the subsidies that guarantee farmers' incomes. The members of the Community have been aware of the unsatisfactoriness of the situation but only recently have steps been taken to tackle the problems of overproduction.

In 1987 Community members agreed to reduce by one fifth the production of cereals. Since then the British Government has had to find ways of softening the blow for farmers and managing the effects the change will have on the countryside. The Alternative Land Uses and Rural Employment committee was set up to produce policies encouraging farmers to take agricultural land out of commission and find other uses for it. Suggested alternatives included afforestation, tourism, recreation (such as golf courses) or keeping the land fallow. "Set-aside" land put to no productive use will attract £80 an acre in government grants. Estimates put the likely amount of land to be set aside at one million acres.

The most irreversible of alternative land uses is use for building. The set-aside policy coincided in 1988 with much public debate about building in Green Belt areas. The economic boom in south-east England has led to a demand for housing which has not only pushed up the prices of existing property but also increased pressure for new housing to be built on greenfield sites. This pressure is reflected in the 1987 figure for new house starts which, at 94,000, is the largest total for 14 years.

It is too early to say how much the set-aside policy will cost the taxpayer but the interest expressed by farmers by August 1988 was higher than expected. It is, however, a policy that is policed: a Ministry of Agriculture inspection of the land surface is carried out by satellite each month.

THE LYNDHURST BYPASS

Lyndhurst, a small town in the New Forest, suffers like many other small towns from excessive through traffic. Plans for a relief road have been put forward on two occasions but following public inquiries, in 1975 and 1983, both alternatives failed to win planning permission. In 1988 Hampshire County Council decided to try to bypass normal planning procedures and win approval for a relief road by promoting a private Act of Parliament.

The Bill was sponsored by Mr. Keith Mans, the Conservative M.P. for Wyre (Lancs.), the local M.P. Mr. Patrick McNair-Wilson having refused. It proposed a single, two-lane carriageway, constructed in an arc to the east of the town. Opposition to the Bill was spearheaded by the Council for the Protection of Rural England which claimed that the proposal threatened the Forest ecologically and visually. The New Forest provides a habitat for over 1,000 types of butterflies and moths, 1,540 species of beetle, 29 species of dragonfly, 46 types of rare plant, and birds such as the woodlark, crossbill, firecrest, stonechat and nightjar whose populations are much depleted elsewhere.

Like many private Bills, the Bill failed to pass through Parliament.

STORM DAMAGE

The ferocious winds which hit south-east England on the night of October 15–16 were indirectly caused by Hurricane Floyd off the Florida coast. Buildings both grand and humble were damaged: many houses in the path of the storm lost their roof, while churches at Minster, Kent, and Rotherfield, Sussex, lost their spires. Two churches, the modern St. Justus at Rochester and the older Baptist chapel at Cransford, Sussex, were destroyed completely. Fifteen listed barns were severely damaged or destroyed. In addition half of Shanklin Pier on the Isle of Wight was blown down and at Brighton Pavilion a pinnacle fell through the roof of the Music Room.

The greatest losses, however, were the trees. In 1980 the Forestry Commission recorded 100 million trees in Britain: in the one night some 15 million were lost, half of them deciduous, the worst casualties being oaks and beeches. A Countryside Commission estimate in mid-November 1987 categorized the losses as 70 per cent on corporate woodland, 25 per cent on Forestry Commission land and five per cent in parks and gardens. The National Trust put its total casualties at 250,000.

In the worst-hit counties of West and East Sussex, Kent and Suffolk, about 20 per cent of all trees were blown down and millions more were damaged. Two million were felled in the Sevenoaks district alone, including six of the town's eponymous seven oaks. Five per cent of Britain's fruit trees were casualties, either blown down or poisoned by wind-blown salt. London lost 250,000 trees and Essex 40 per cent of the willows used for cricket bats.

In certain gardens the word "disaster" was no exaggeration. Kew Gardens lost 500 trees, including the Tree of Heaven. The avenues of chestnuts at Hever, of limes at Chilham in Kent, and of oaks at Helmingham in Suffolk were devastated. At the great 18th century landscape garden at Painshill, Surrey, where a comprehensive scheme of recreation was only half-completed, much of the work of recent years was undone. Nor did Britain alone suffer—Brittany lost twenty per cent of its timber in the storm.

The Association of British Insurers estimated that about £835 million would be paid out to meet the cost of damage to property caused by storms during the winter of 1987–88. However, damage to trees is not covered in most cases and English Heritage and the Countryside Commission offered emergency grants. The National Trust launched an appeal for £1·5 million to finance the repair work at its properties.

WATER AUTHORITIES

The present government is committed to privatizing as many public bodies as possible and one candidate is the water industry. The government first published proposals in 1986 but these were met with criticism from bodies as diverse as the Council for the Protection of Rural England and the Country Landowners Association. The proposals included the transfer to the private sector of all the present powers of the regional water authorities, i.e. their supervision of land drainage, river pollution control, flood protection and the management of fisheries, as well as their principal tasks of providing water and disposing of sewage. Legal opinion taken by the C.P.R.E. was that the placing of water pollution control in the hands of private companies would be illegal under European Community law.

The Government withdrew these proposals and published revised plans in December 1987. These provide for the creation of a National Rivers Authority which would be the regulatory body of the ten private companies that will run the industry after privatization. The need for effective supervision was emphasized by the publication of figures that suggested that the cleanliness of rivers has declined since 1985.

Legislation is to be introduced in the 1988–89 session of Parliament. If the Bill has been passed by summer 1989, privatization of the water boards will go ahead in autumn 1989.

ARCHITECTURAL CONSERVATION

Over the past few years the numbers of applications to demolish listed buildings in England and Wales have been fairly consistent—547 in 1982, 480 in 1983, 509 in 1984, 557 in 1985 and 566 in 1986. In 1987 the figure leapt to 649. However, the increase is largely a reflection of the many additions to the lists prompted by the resurvey of listed buildings that was finally concluded in 1988. By June 30, 1988 the total of listed buildings in England alone stood at 418,860. The increase in protection must to some extent be a factor in the increase in applications to demolish.

The applications certainly demonstrate the catholicity of the definition of a "listed building". The 1987 applications threatened two signal boxes, two railway viaducts, two seaside piers, ten telephone kiosks (nine of them at Gravesend), 23 barns, a pumping station at Wisbech, Cambs., a range of barracks at Shoeburyness, Essex, an airport observation tower at Shoreham, Sussex, a gingan for threshing corn at Netherwitton, Northumberland, the Odeon cinema at Worthing (later delisted), five dovecotes (two of them to be resited), a bandstand at Grange-over-Sands, Cumbria (the application was later withdrawn), the reinforced concrete CWS warehouse of 1892 on the Quayside, Newcastle-upon-Tyne, a number of mills including the Lintzford Mill at Rowlands Gill, Durham, of c.1840 (later proposed for residential conversion), a forge in Lynsted, Kent, and a Freemasons Hall at Halifax. The last was one of the most bizarre applications of the year, proposing to retain and cocoon the stone facade of the hall within a huge extension to the headquarters of a building society.

Listed chapels continue to be threatened at the rate of one every three weeks. Applications to demolish were received for 19 Nonconformist chapels in 1987. Perhaps the most serious threat was the application to demolish St. John's Methodist Chapel and Manse at Birstall, W. Yorks., a fine Classical composition which includes in its churchyard the 18th century study of the preacher John Nelson. The application to demolish the Grade II* listed Friends Meeting House of 1823 at Malton, N. Yorks. was rejected after a public inquiry. The single largest compendium of applications proposed to sweep away 17 listed buildings at Manningham, Bradford, to clear a route for an inner relief road, and 15 buildings in Cheltenham for replacement by a shopping centre. (The scheme was modified in 1988 to allow most of these buildings to remain). Perhaps the most outrageous application was that to demolish Harrison of Chester's Grade II* listed Lyceum Club in Bold Street, Liverpool. This came only a matter of weeks after the Council itself had proposed to demolish the Grade II* listed terrace of 1765 in Duke Street and was swiftly refused.

So far in 1988 threatened buildings have included a purpose-built music hall of 1868 at Barrow-in-Furness, Cumbria; a number of "mud and stud" cottages in Lincolnshire; St. Hilda's Church, Darlington, a nobly proportioned slum church by J. L. Pearson of 1883; Our Lady of the Immaculate Conception Church, Everton, Liverpool, which was begun in 1856 by E. W. Pugin as the intended Roman Catholic Cathedral for the diocese; and a red sandstone rubble structure at Rowton, Cheshire, said to have been used as a hospital for the wounded after the battle of Rowton Moor in 1645. The Unitarian Chapel at Trowbridge in Wiltshire of 1856 was destroyed without benefit of listed building consent on the grounds that it was dangerous.

The year under review did not see any legislative change apart from an abortive attempt to introduce greater control over cathedrals. The Care of Cathedrals Measure would have curtailed to a limited extent the absolute freedom which Deans and Chapters at present enjoy to alter cathedrals in any way they wish. The Measure was thrown out by the General Synod following an almost unanimous revolt by the Deans.

Conservation organizations established during the year included the British Dovecote Society, and a meeting was held to consider an equivalent body to study nonconformist chapels. A "Brunel in Devon Trust" was established at Watcombe Park near Torquay, the home of Isambard Kingdom Brunel. The Trust aims to conserve the estate and open a Brunel Centre where "the major theme is to be inspiration for the future rather than reverence for the past". The National Waterways Museum opened in Gloucester Docks in April 1988, and an endowment of around £2 million from the Department of the Environment helped to secure the future of the Ironbridge Gorge Museum in Shropshire. The Old Grammar School in Hull opened to the public in March as an educational museum. The late Georgian terrace at Notintone Place, Nottingham, where William Booth, the founder of the Salvation Army was born, opened after restoration as the William Booth Memorial Complex.

Money matters

Money oils the wheels in conservation as in other things and the Government announcement of an 11·5 per cent increase in grants to the ten National Parks in England and Wales, mainly to assist in the care of archaeological sites and historic buildings, was very welcome. The grant scheme operated by the Council for Small Industries in Rural Areas, which offers assistance towards the cost of renovating or modernizing redundant rural buildings in certain priority areas, has now been extended to cover conversion to tourist and recreational use. In April English Heritage introduced a number of changes to its grant system. These included the abolition of the rule preventing new purchasers from applying for grants within four years of acquisition.

THE NATIONAL PARKS

The ten National Parks described below in their order of designation have been established in England and Wales. These areas are not public property and although many public paths exist and some areas of open land are available for walking, visitors are not free to wander over private land within the Park boundaries. They have been marked out for special care aimed at two prime purposes: to conserve and enhance their natural beauty, and to promote their enjoyment by the public.

Peak District National Park (542 sq. miles).— Mainly in Derbyshire but extending into Staffordshire, Cheshire, South Yorkshire, West Yorkshire and Greater Manchester. There are information centres at Bakewell, Edale (open all year), Fairholmes and Castleton (April–October and winter weekends), and information points in Goyt Valley and at Hartington (summer weekends and Bank Holidays). An information caravan tours the Park and there is a residential study centre at Losehill Hall.

Lake District National Park (880 sq. miles).—In Cumbria. The area includes England's highest mountains (Scafell Pike, Helvellyn and Skiddaw) and largest lakes. There are information centres at Keswick, Waterhead, Hawkshead, Seatoller, Bowness, Grasmere, Coniston, Glenridding and Pooley Bridge, and an information van at Gosforth. At Brockhole, on the shore of Windermere, there is a National Park centre.

Snowdonia National Park (838 sq. miles).—In Gwynedd, North Wales. There are information centres at Aberdyfi, Bala, Betws y Coed, Blaenau Ffestiniog, Conwy, Harlech, Dolgellau and Llanberis. Plas Tan y Bwlch is a residential study centre.

Dartmoor National Park (365 sq. miles).—In Devon. The Park is rich in prehistoric relics. Information centres are sited at Newbridge, Tavistock, Bovey Tracey, Steps Bridge, Princeton and Postbridge.

Pembrokeshire Coast National Park (225 sq. miles).—In South Wales. In the north is Mynydd Preseli, abounding in prehistoric relics. There are information centres at Tenby, St. David's, Pembroke, Newport, Kilgetty, Haverfordwest and Broad Haven.

North York Moors National Park (553 sq. miles).—In North Yorkshire and Cleveland, stretching from the Hambleton Hills to the coastline above Scarborough. There are information centres at Danby, Pickering, Sutton Bank, Ravenscar, Helmsley and Hutton-le-Hole, and a day study centre at Danby (The Moors Centre).

Yorkshire Dales National Park (680 sq. miles).— Mostly in North Yorkshire but extending into Cumbria. The three peaks of Ingleborough, Whernside and Pen-y-Ghent are included. There are information centres at Clapham, Grassington, Hawes, Aysgarth Falls, Malham and Sedbergh, and an outdoor recreation and study centre at Whernside Manor.

Exmoor National Park (265 sq. miles).—Mainly in Somerset but extending into Devon. There are information centres at Lynmouth, County Gate, Dulverton and Combe Martin.

Northumberland National Park (398 sq. miles).—Stretching from Hadrian's Wall to the Scottish Border. There are information centres at Ingram, Once Brewed, Rothbury, Housesteads, Harbottle and Kielder. An information caravan is sited at Cawfields.

Brecon Beacons National Park (519 sq. miles).— Mostly in southern Powys but extending into Dyfed and Gwent and a small area of Mid Glamorgan. The Park is centred on "The Beacons", Pen y Fan, Corn Du and Cribyn, but includes the Black Mountains to the east and the Black Mountain to the west. There are information centres at Brecon, Craig-y-nos Country Park, Abergavenny, Llandovery, a study centre at Danywenallt and a day visitor centre near Libanus, Brecon.

AREAS OF OUTSTANDING NATURAL BEAUTY

These are designated solely for landscape conservation purposes. They are listed below, in alphabetical order, having been designated between December, 1956 and July, 1985.

Anglesey (83 sq. miles).—The designated area extends along the entire coastline of the island, except for breaks around the urban areas and in the vicinity of Wylfa.

Arnside and Silverdale (29 sq. miles).—The area embraces the upper half of Morecambe Bay, the Kent estuary, and includes extensive tidal flats in the Bay.

Cannock Chase (26 sq. miles).—An area of high heathland in Staffordshire. Deer continue to roam over the Chase.

Chichester Harbour (29 sq. miles).—The area extends from Hayling Island to Apuldram and includes Thorney Island.

Chilterns (309 sq. miles).—Chalk downlands running from South Oxfordshire northeastwards to Bedfordshire, including the outlying group of hills beyond Luton.

Clwydian Range (60 sq. miles).—A prominent ridge extending southwards from Prestatyn on the North Wales coast. Offa's Dyke runs along the crest of the Range.

Cornwall (360 sq. miles).—A number of separate areas including Bodmin Moor; most of the Land's

End peninsula; the coast between St. Michael's Mount and St. Austell (with Falmouth omitted); the Fowey Estuary: in north Cornwall most of the coast to Bedruthan Steps and between Perranporth and Godrevy Towans, plus 10 sq. miles of the Camel Estuary.

Cotswolds (582 sq. miles).—The area of limestone hills above the Vales of Gloucester and Evesham.

Cranborne Chase and West Wiltshire Downs (370 sq. miles).—A chalkland area, covering parts of Wiltshire, Dorset, Hampshire and Somerset, including the wooded remnants of the ancient Chase.

Dedham Vale (28 sq. miles).—The area bordering Essex and Suffolk, where John Constable painted.

East Devon (103 sq. miles).—The coastline between Exmouth and Lyme Regis, with Sidmouth, Beer and Seaton omitted. Inland Gittisham Hill, East Hill and Woodbury and Aylebeare Commons are included.

North Devon (66 sq. miles).—Includes most of the N. Devon coastline, from just north of Bude to the boundary of the Exmoor National Park.

South Devon (128 sq. miles).—Includes the coast between Bolt Head and Bolt Tail, Salcombe, Slapton Sands and Dartmouth, and the estuaries and valleys of the Yealm, Erme, Avon and Dart.

Dorset (400 sq. miles).—The coastline between Lyme Regis and Poole, with the Isle of Portland and

Weymouth omitted, stretching inland to include the Purbeck Hills and the downs, of the Hardy country.

Forest of Bowland (310 sq. miles).—A moorland area mostly in Lancashire running westward from the River Ribble, with a small outlying area east of the Ribble which includes Pendle Hill.

Gower (73 sq. miles).—A peninsula in West Glamorgan, South Wales, known for its coastline.

East Hampshire (151 sq. miles).—A chalkland area stretching from the outskirts of Winchester to the Sussex border at a distance of about 10 miles inland.

South Hampshire Coast (30 sq. miles).—14 miles of coastline between Hurst Castle and Calshot Castle, extending inland up the Beaulieu River for about six miles.

High Weald (560 sq. miles).—The area covers parts of East and West Sussex, Kent and Surrey. It is predominantly wooded, and includes larger heathland areas like Ashdown Forest, the remnants of the old Wealden forests.

Howardian Hills (80 sq. miles).—Wooded hills which rise above the Vales of York and Pickering (*designation to be confirmed*).

Kent Downs (326 sq. miles).—Running east and south-east from the Surrey border near Westerham to the coast near Dover and Folkestone, with a coastal outlier at South Foreland and a narrow strip of the old sea cliff escarpment west of Hythe overlooking Romney Marsh.

Lincolnshire Wolds (216 sq. miles).—The area extends in a south-east direction from Laceby and Caistor in the north to the region of Spilsby, about ten miles west of the coast.

Lleyn (60 sq. miles).—An isolated peninsula in Gwynedd, North Wales.

Malvern Hills (40 sq. miles).—The whole range of the Malvern Hills in the county of Hereford and Worcester, just touching Gloucestershire.

Mendip Hills (78 sq. miles).—Comprising over half of the Mendip Hills, the area stretches from Bleadon Hill to the A39 road north of Wells and includes Cheddar Gorge and Wookey Hole.

Norfolk Coast (174 sq. miles).—An almost continuous coastal strip three to five miles in depth from Hunstanton to Bacton, with a further small strip between Sea Palling and Winterton-on-Sea. The area includes part of the Sandringham Estate.

Northumberland Coast (50 sq. miles).—Stretches from just south of Berwick to Amble and includes Holy Island and the Farne Islands.

Quantock Hills (38 sq. miles).—A range of sandstone hills in Somerset.

Isles of Scilly (6 sq. miles).—About 140 islands and skerries in the Scillies group of which only five are inhabited. There are a number of sites of special scientific interest.

Shropshire Hills (300 sq. miles).—Most of south-west Shropshire between the Welsh border and the boundary with Hereford and Worcester, including the region around Clun, the area of the Stiperstones, the Long Mynd and Wenlock Edge, with the tongues of land running north-east to the Wrekin and south towards Ludlow.

Solway Coast (41 sq. miles).—A stretch of coastline in Cumbria from Maryport to the estuaries of the Rivers Eden and Esk (with Silloth omitted) backed by the Solway Plain.

Suffolk Coast and Heaths (151 sq. miles).—The area includes 38 miles of coastline and parts of the Stour and Orwell estuaries, while the Deben, Alde and Blyth flow through it.

Surrey Hills (160 sq. miles).—An area of hills to the east and south of Guildford, including the Hog's Back and the ridge of the North Downs.

Sussex Downs (379 sq. miles).—The area includes the chalk escarpment of the South Downs from Beachy Head to the Hampshire border, and stretches down to the coast between Eastbourne and Seaford.

North Wessex Downs (671 sq. miles).—An upland area in Hampshire, Wiltshire, Oxfordshire and Berkshire, bounded by the Marlborough and Lambourn Downs in the west and the Chiltern Hills in the east. Salisbury Plain forms the southern limit of what is so far the largest area designated.

Isle of Wight (73 sq. miles).—A number of separate areas comprising stretches of coastline, the Yar Valley, the high downland behind Ventnor and the chalk ridge which runs from Newport to Culver Cliff and Foreland.

Wye Valley (125 sq. miles).—The river valley running through the counties of Gwent, Gloucestershire and Hereford and Worcester.

HISTORIC MONUMENTS

England

A select list of monuments under the control, since its creation in April 1984, of the Historic Buildings and Monuments Commission for England.

Charges for admission represent the figures obtaining in 1988–9. Concessionary rates are available for children etc.

Annual membership passes are available at £10 for adults, £6 for pensioners and £4 for children upon application to P.O. Box 43, Ruislip, Middx., HA4 0XW.

Standard hours of opening (marked *) are as follows:

	Weekdays	Sundays
March 15–Oct. 15	9.30–6.30	2.00–6.30
Oct. 16–March 14	9.30–4.00	2.00–4.00

Monuments not marked * open April–Sept. only.

Those marked † open on Sundays at 9.30 a.m. from April–Sept. inclusive.

All monuments are closed on Christmas Eve, Christmas Day, Boxing Day and New Year's Day. Some smaller sites may close for the lunch-hour, which is normally 1–2 p.m.

BEESTON CASTLE, Cheshire. £1.25*. Thirteenth-century inner ward with gatehouse and towers, and considerable remains of large outer ward.

BERKHAMSTED CASTLE, Hertfordshire*. Extensive remains of a large 11th century motte-and-bailey castle.

BOLSOVER CASTLE, Derbyshire. £1.25*. Notable for its exceptionally interesting 17th century buildings.

BOSCOBEL HOUSE, Salop. 75p*. Timber-framed early 17th century hunting lodge with later alterations. Charles II's "Royal Oak" is nearby.

BRINKBURN PRIORY, Northumberland. 75p*. A house of Augustinian canons; the church (*c.* 1200, repaired in 1858) and parts of the cloister buildings survive.

BROUGHAM CASTLE, Cumbria. 75p†*. Extensive remains of the 13th century keep, and of other buildings of periods up to the 17th century.

BYLAND ABBEY, North Yorkshire. 75p*. Considerable remains of church and conventual buildings date from the abbey's foundation in 1177 by the Cistercians.

CARISBROOKE CASTLE, Isle of Wight. £2†*. Norman castle, the prison of Charles I from 1647–1648.

CARLISLE CASTLE, Cumbria. £1.75†*. The Castle was begun by William Rufus. Inner and outer wards enclosing a 12th century keep.

CASTLE ACRE PRIORY, Norfolk. £1*. (closed Mon. and Tue. in winter). Extensive remains include the 12th century church and the prior's lodgings.

CASTLE RISING, Norfolk. 75p† (standard, and Sun. mornings all year). A 12th-century keep standing in a massive earthwork with its gatehouse and bridge.

CHESTERS ROMAN FORT, Northumberland. £1†*. Fine example of a bath house.

CHYSAUSTER ANCIENT VILLAGE, Cornwall. 75p* (closed Thur. and Fri. in winter). 2nd century B.C. Iron Age village of courtyard houses.

CLEEVE ABBEY, Somerset. £1*. Much of the claustral buildings survive including timber-roofed frater, but only foundations of the church.

CORBRIDGE ROMAN SITE, Northumberland. £1·25*. Excavations have revealed the central area of a Roman town and successive military bases.

DEAL CASTLE, Kent. £1*. The largest and most complete of the castles erected by Henry VIII for coastal defence.

DOVER CASTLE, Kent. £2.20†* (Sun. mornings all year). (Underground Works closed in Winter.) One of the largest and most important English castles.

DUNSTANBURGH CASTLE, Northumberland. 75p†*. The 14th century castle standing on a cliff above the sea, has an unusual gatehouse-keep.

FARLEIGH HUNGERFORD CASTLE, Somerset. 75p* (closed Tues. and Thurs. morning in winter). Late 14th century castle of two courts. The chapel contains fine tomb of Sir Thomas Hungerford.

FARNHAM CASTLE, Surrey. 75p. Built by the Bishops of Winchester, the motte of the castle is enclosed by a large 12th century shell keep. Foundations of a Norman tower.

FINCHALE PRIORY, Durham. 75p* (free in Winter). Benedictine priory on banks of River Wear with considerable 13th century remains.

FRAMLINGHAM CASTLE, Suffolk. £1†*. Impressive castle (c. 1200) with high curtain-walls enclosing a poor-house of 1639.

FURNESS ABBEY, Cumbria. £1†*. Founded in 1123 by Stephen, afterwards King of England; extensive remains of church and conventual buildings.

GOODRICH CASTLE, Hereford and Worcester. £1†*. Extensive remains of beautiful 13th and 14th century castle incorporating 12th century keep.

GRIMES GRAVES, Norfolk. 75p†*. Extensive group of flint mines dating from the Neolithic period. Several shafts can be inspected.

HAILES ABBEY, Gloucestershire. £1* (closed Tues., Wed., Thurs. in winter). Ruins of a Cistercian monastery founded in 1246. Museum contains some fine architectural fragments.

HELMSLEY CASTLE, North Yorkshire. £1†*. Twelfth century keep and curtain wall with 16th century domestic buildings. Spectacular earthwork defences.

HOUSESTEADS ROMAN FORT, Northumberland. £1.25†*. Excavation has exposed this infantry fort on Hadrian's Wall with its extra-mural civilian settlement.

KENILWORTH CASTLE, Warwickshire. £1†*. One of the finest and most extensive castles in England, showing many styles of building from 1155 to 1649.

LANERCOST PRIORY, Cumbria. 75p. The nave of the Augustinian priory church, c. 1166, is still used and there are remains of other claustral buildings.

LINDISFARNE PRIORY, Northumberland. £1†*. The bishopric of the Northumbrian Kingdom destroyed by the Danes; re-established in 11th century as a Benedictine priory, now ruined.

LULLINGSTONE ROMAN VILLA, Kent. £1·20†*. A large villa occupied through much of the Roman period; fine mosaics. (*Closed until Spring 1989 for refurbishment.*)

MIDDLEHAM CASTLE, North Yorkshire. 75p*. The 12th century keep stands within later fortifications and domestic buildings.

MOUNT GRACE PRIORY, North Yorkshire. £1*. Carthusian monastery, founded 1398, with remains of monastic buildings.

NETLEY ABBEY, Hampshire. 75p* (weekends only in winter). Extensive remains of Cistercian abbey, founded 1239, with remarkable Tudor house.

OLD SARUM, Wiltshire. 75p†*. Large earthworks enclosing the excavated remains of the castle and the first Salisbury cathedral.

ORFORD CASTLE, Suffolk. 75p* (closed all day Thurs. and Fri. mornings in winter). Circular keep of c. 1170 and remains of coastal defence castle built by Henry II.

PENDENNIS CASTLE, Cornwall. £1†*. Well-preserved castle erected by Henry VIII for coastal defence.

PEVENSEY CASTLE, East Sussex. £1*. Walls of a 4th century Roman fort enclosing remains of an 11th century castle.

PEVERIL CASTLE, Derbyshire. 75p*. In a picturesque and nearly impregnable position, this 12th century castle is defended on two sides by precipitous rocks.

PORTCHESTER CASTLE, Hampshire. £1*. Walls of a late-Roman fort enclosing a Norman keep and an Augustinian priory church.

RECULVER TOWERS and ROMAN FORT, Kent. 75p* (June–Aug.). Remains of Saxon and Norman church with 12th century towers, standing in a Roman fort.

RICHBOROUGH CASTLE, Kent. 75p*. The landing-site of the Claudian invasion in 43 A.D., with massive 3rd century stone walls.

RICHMOND CASTLE, North Yorkshire. £1†*. This 12th century keep, with 11th century curtain-wall and gatehouse, commands Swaledale.

RIEVAULX ABBEY, North Yorkshire. £1.25†*. Founded c. 1132. Extensive remains include an early Cistercian nave and fine 13th century choir and claustral buildings.

ROCHESTER CASTLE, Kent. £1*†. Eleventh century wall, partly overlying the Roman city wall, encloses square keep of c. 1130.

ST. AUGUSTINE'S ABBEY, Kent. 75p*. Remains of Benedictine monastry, with Norman church, on site of abbey founded by St. Augustine in 598.

ST. MAWES CASTLE, Cornwall. 75p†*. Coast defence castle built by Henry VIII consisting of central tower and three bastions.

SCARBOROUGH CASTLE, North Yorkshire. £1†*. Remains of 12th century keep and curtain-walls dominating the town.

STONEHENGE, Wiltshire. £1.50†*. Prehistoric monument consisting of central stone circles surrounded by ditch and bank.

TILBURY FORT, Essex. 75p* (opens 30 mins. late and closes 30 mins. early). One of Henry VIII's coastal ports, extended by Charles II.

TINTAGEL CASTLE, Cornwall. £1.25†*. 12th century castle on cliff-top Dark Age settlement site.

TYNEMOUTH PRIORY and CASTLE, Tyne and Wear. 75p†* (closed Tues. and alternate Wed. in winter). Remains of a Benedictine priory, founded 1090, on Saxon monastic site. Coastal batteries with reconstructed First World War magazine.

WALMER CASTLE, Kent. £1.50*. (Closed Mon. except Bank Hols and when Lord Warden is in residence). One of Henry VIII's coast defence castles, now the residence of the Lord Warden of the Cinque Ports.

WARKWORTH CASTLE, Northumberland. 75p†*. 15th century keep amidst earlier ruins. 14th century hermitage upstream.

WHITBY ABBEY, North Yorkshire. 75p†*. 13th and 14th century Benedictine church on site of monastery founded in 657.

WROXETER ROMAN CITY, Shropshire. 75p*. The 2nd century public baths and part of the forum remain of the Roman town of Viroconium.

Wales

A select list of monuments under the control of Cadw: Welsh Historic Monuments. Charges for admission (subject to alteration) are given below. Concessionary rates are available for children, etc. Standard hours of admission:

	Weekdays	Sundays
March 15–Oct. 15	9.30–6.30	2.00–6.30
Oct. 16–March 14	9.30–4.00	2.00–4.00

All monuments are closed on Christmas Eve, Christmas Day, Boxing Day and New Year's Day.

BEAUMARIS CASTLE, Anglesey, Gwynedd. £1. The finest example of the concentrically planned castle in Britain, it is still almost intact.

CAERLEON ROMAN AMPHITHEATRE, Gwent. 75p. Late 1st-century oval arena surrounded by bank for spectators with entrance passages.

CAERLEON ROMAN FORTRESS BATHS, Gwent. 75p. Rare example of a legionary bath-house.

CAERNARFON CASTLE, Gwynedd. £2, Family Ticket £5. The most important of the Edwardian castles, built together with the town wall between 1283 and 1330.

CAERPHILLY CASTLE, Mid-Glamorgan. £1. Concentrically planned castle (c. 1270) notable for its great scale and use of water defences.

CASTELL COCH, S. Glamorgan. £1. Rebuilt 1875–90 on medieval foundations.

CHEPSTOW CASTLE, Gwent. 75p. Fine rectangular keep in the middle of extensive fortifications.

CONWY CASTLE, Gwynedd. £1. Built by Edward I to guard the Conway ferry.

CRICCIETH CASTLE, Gwynedd. £1.50. A native Welsh castle of the early 13th century, much altered by Edward I.

DENBIGH CASTLE, Clwyd. 75p. The remains of the castle, which dates from 1282–1322, includes an unusual triangular gatehouse.

HARLECH CASTLE, Gwynedd. £1. Well preserved Edwardian castle with a concentric plan sited on rocky outcrop above the former shore-line.

RAGLAN CASTLE, Gwent. £1. Extensive remains of 15th-century castle with moated hexagonal keep.

ST. DAVID'S, BISHOP'S PALACE, Dyfed. £1.50. Extensive remains of principal residence of Bishop of St. David's dating from 1280–1350.

TINTERN ABBEY, Gwent. £1. Extensive remains of 13th-century church and conventual buildings of this Cistercian monastery.

TRETOWER COURT, Powys. £1. Medieval house with remains of castle nearby.

Scotland

A select list of monuments under the control of Historic Buildings and Monuments, Scottish Development Department.

Charges for admission are those obtaining in 1988. Except where indicated differently, charges are adults 50p, concessions (con.) 25p.

Standard hours of opening (marked S.) are as follows:

	Weekdays	Sundays
April–Sept.	9.30–7.00	2.00–7.00
Oct.–March	9.30–4.00	2.00–4.00

Monuments open at any reasonable time are indicated by A.

ABERLEMNO, Tayside. A. Closed in winter. Adm. free. Four Pictish stones.

ANTONINE WALL, Central and Strathclyde Regions. A. Adm. free.

ARNOL BLACKHOUSE, Western Isles. S. Closed Sun. Traditional Hebridean dwelling.

BONAWE, Strathclyde. S. Closed in winter. Mid-18th century iron-furnace.

BROUGH OF BIRSAY, Orkney. S. Closed Mon., Tues. a.m. in winter. Remains of the Norse period.

BROWN AND WHITE CATERTHUNS, Tayside. A. Adm. free. Iron Age hill forts.

CAERLAVEROCK CASTLE, Dumfries and Galloway. S.

CAIRNPAPPLE HILL, Lothian. S. Closed in winter. A prehistoric ritual complex and Bronze Age cairn.

CALLANISH, Western Isles. A. Adm. free. Standing Stones.

CAMSTER CAIRNS, Highland. A. Adm. free.

CLAVA CAIRNS, Highland. A. Adm. free.

DRYBURGH ABBEY, Borders. S. £1, con. 50p.

EARLS AND BISHOPS PALACES, Kirkwall, Orkney. S. Closed in winter.

EDINBURGH CASTLE, including Scottish National War Memorial, Scottish United Services Museum and Historic Apartments. Open winter: Jan. 4–March 31 and Oct. 1–Dec. 31, Mon.–Sat. 9.30–4.20, Sun. 12.30–3.35. Summer: April 1–Sept. 30, Mon.–Sat. 9.30–5.05, Sun. 11–5.05. Alterations may be made to opening hours during the Tattoo, State and Military events. Adm. to War Memorial, free; to all other areas £2.20 con. £1.10 Family Ticket £5.

EDZELL CASTLE, Tayside. S. Closed Tues., Thurs. a.m.

ELGIN CATHEDRAL, Grampian. S.

FORT GEORGE, Highland. S. £1.50 con. 75p.

GLASGOW CATHEDRAL, Strathclyde. S. Adm. free.

GLENELG BROCHS, Highland. A. Adm. free.

HERMITAGE CASTLE, Borders. S.

HUNTLY CASTLE, Grampian. S.

JARLSHOF, Shetland. S. Closed Tues., Wed. p.m. in winter. Remains of villages from Bronze Age to Viking times.

JEDBURGH ABBEY, Borders. S. Closed Thurs. p.m. and Fri. in Winter. £1, con. 50p.

KELSO ABBEY, Borders. S. Adm. free.

LINLITHGOW PALACE, Lothian. S. £1, con. 50p.

LOANHEAD STONE CIRCLE, Grampian. A. Adm. free.

MAES HOWE, Orkney. S. £1, con. 50p. Prehistoric tomb.

MEIGLE MUSEUM, Tayside. S. Closed Sun. Pictish stones.

MELROSE ABBEY, Borders. S. £1, con. 50p.

MOUSA BROCH, Shetland. A. Adm. free.

NETHER LARGIE CAIRNS, Strathclyde. A. Adm. free.

NEW ABBEY CORN MILL, Dumfries and Galloway. S. Closed Wed. p.m., Thurs.

RING OF BROGAR, Orkney. A. Adm. free.

RUTHWELL CROSS, Dumfries and Galloway. A. Adm. free.

ST. ANDREWS' CASTLE AND CATHEDRAL, Fife. S.

SKARA BRAE, Orkney. S. £1.20, con. 60p. Prehistoric village.

SMAILHOLM TOWER, Borders. S. Closed in winter.

STIRLING CASTLE, Central. Open winter: Jan. 4–March 31 and Oct. 1–Dec. 31, Mon.–Sat. 9.30–4.20, Sun. 12.30–3.35; summer: April 1–Sept. 30, Mon.–Sat. 9.30–5.15, Sun. 10.30–4.45. £1·50, Con. 75p, Family Ticket £4.

TANTALLON CASTLE, Lothian. S. £1. Closed Wed., Thurs. a.m. in Winter.

THREAVE CASTLE, Dumfries and Galloway. S. Adm. 60p, con. 25p, including ferry.

HOUSES OPEN TO THE PUBLIC

Times of summer opening and admission fees shown are those which obtained in 1988, and are subject to modification. Space permits only a selection of some of the more noteworthy houses in the U.K. which are open to the public. (*Property of the National Trust; Adm. admission; con. concessionary rates).

A LA RONDE, Exmouth.—April 1–Sept. 30. Times vary. Adm. £1.50.

ALNWICK CASTLE, Northumberland. Seat of the Duke of Northumberland.—April 30—Sept. 30 daily (except Sat and Bank Hol. weekends) 1–5. Adm. £2.

ALTHORP, Northampton.—Daily 1–5. July, Aug., Sept. 1–6. Bank Hol. Suns and Mons. 11–6. Adm. £2.50, Weds. £3.50 (Connoisseurs' Day). Gardens 50p.

*ANGLESEY ABBEY, Cambs.—Easter Sat.–Oct. 16. Wed.–Sun. and Bank Hol. Mons. 1.30–5.30. Adm. £3.50. Gardens only April 2–July 3 Sat., Sun. and Bank Hol. Mons. 12–5.30, July 4–Oct. 16 daily, 1.30–5.30.

ARUNDEL CASTLE, W. Sussex. Seat of the Duke of Norfolk.—April 1–Oct. 28 daily (not Sat.) 1–5, June–Aug. and Bank Hols. 12–5. Adm. Charge.

*BASILDON PARK, Berks.—April–Oct. Wed.–Sat. 2–6, Suns. and Bank Hol. Mons. 12–6. Adm. £2.

BEAULIEU, Hants.—May–Sept. daily 10–6. Oct.–May, daily 10–5 (see also page 1156).

*BELTON HOUSE, Grantham.—April 2–Oct. 31 Wed.–Sun. and Bank Hol. Mons. 1–5.30. Adm. £2.60.

BELVOIR CASTLE, nr. Grantham. Seat of the Duke of Rutland.—March 19–Oct. 2 Tues., Wed., Thurs., Sat. and Good Friday, 12–6, Bank Hol. Mons. 11–7, Sun., 12–7. (Oct. Sun., 2–6.) Adm. £2.50.

BERKELEY CASTLE, Glos.—April, Sept. daily (not Mon.) 2–5, May–Aug. Tues.–Sat. 11–5, Sun. 2–5, Oct. Sun. only 2–4.30, Bank Hol. Mons. 11–5. Adm. charge.

BLAIR CASTLE, Tayside. Seat of the Duke of Atholl.—March 31–Oct. 16. Mon.–Sat. 10–6, Sun. 2–6. Adm. £2.50.

BLENHEIM PALACE, Oxon. Seat of the Duke of Marlborough.—March 16–Oct. 31 daily 10.30–6. Adm. charge.

BOUGHTON HOUSE, Northants. Seat of the Duke of Buccleuch & Queensberry.—July 30–Aug. 29 daily, Grounds 12–6, House 2–5. April 30–Oct. 2. Grounds daily (not Fri.) 12–5. Adm. £2.50, Grounds only, 80p.

BOWHILL, Selkirk.—House July 9–Aug. 21 daily 1–4.30 (Sun. 2–6); Grounds April 30–Aug. 29 daily (not Fri.) 12–5, Sun. 2–6. Adm. £2.50, Grounds only, £1.

BROADLANDS, Hants.—April–Sept. daily (closed Mon., except Aug., Sept. and Bank Hols.), 10–6. Adm. £3.

BRONTË PARSONAGE, Haworth, West Yorks.—Daily, April–Sept. 11–5.30, Oct.–March 11–4.30. Adm. £1.

BROUGHTON CASTLE, Oxon.—May 18–Sept. 14 Wed., Sun. (also Thurs. in July and Aug.) and Bank Hol. Suns and Mons. 2–5. Adm. £1.90.

*BUCKLAND ABBEY, Devon. Re-opened Summer 1988. Adm. £2.80.

BURGHLEY HOUSE, Stamford.—Good Friday–Oct. 9 (closed Sept. 10) daily 11–5 (Good Friday 2–5). Adm. £3.

*CALKE ABBEY, Derbyshire.—Gardens open all year. House opens April 1989.

CARDIFF CASTLE.—May–Sept. daily 10–6, Nov.–Feb. daily, 10–4.30, March, April, Oct. daily, 10–5.

CARLTON TOWERS, Humberside.—May to Sept. Sun. only, Bank Hol. weekends 1–5. Adm. £1.75.

*CASTLE COOLE, Enniskillen.—House open from June 1. Parklands open April–Sept.

*CASTLE DROGO, Devon.—April–Oct. daily 11–6. Adm. £2.60.

CASTLE HOWARD, N. Yorks.—March 25–Oct. daily 11–4.30. Adm. charge.

CAWDOR CASTLE, Inverness.—May–Oct. 2, daily 10–5.30. Adm. £2.40.

*CHARTWELL, Kent. Home of Sir Winston Churchill.—March and Nov. Sat., Sun., Wed. 11–4, April–Oct. 30 Tues., Wed., Thurs. 12–5, Sat., Sun. and Bank Hol. Mon., 11–5. (Closed Good Friday and Tues. after Bank Hols.). Adm. £2.70.

CHATSWORTH, Derbyshire. Seat of the Duke of Devonshire.—March 27–Oct. 30 daily 11.30–4.30. Adm. charge.

CHICHELEY HALL, Newport Pagnell.—April 1–Sept. 25 Sun. and Bank Hols. 2.30–6. Adm. £2.

*CLIVEDEN, Maidenhead.—House, April 3–Oct. 30, Thurs. and Sun. 3–6. Gardens, daily 11–6 (closed Jan. and Feb.); Adm. £2.20, 80p extra for House.

*COMPTON CASTLE, nr. Paignton.—April–Oct. Mon., Wed., Thurs. 10–12.15, 2–5. Adm. £1.30.

*CROFT CASTLE, Herefordshire.—Easter Bank Hol. weekend, May–Sept. Wed.–Sun. and Bank Hol. Mons. 2–6, April and Oct. Weekends 2–5. Adm. £1.70.

DOWN HOUSE, Downe, Kent. Home of Charles Darwin.—March–Jan. 31, 1–6, not Mon. (except Bank Hols.) or Fri. Adm. £1·50.

DRUMLANRIG CASTLE, Dumfries.—April 30–June 30, daily (not Fri.) 1.30–5, July 1–Aug. 21, daily (not Fri.) 11–5, Sun. 2–6. Adm. £2.50.

HADDON HALL, Derbyshire.—April–Sept. Tues.–Sat., and Bank Hols. 11–6. Closed Sun. in July and Aug. (except Bank Hol. weekends). Adm. £2.50.

*HARDWICK HALL, Derbyshire.—April 2–Oct. House Wed., Thurs., Sat., Sun., Bank Hol. Mons. 1–5.30. Garden daily 12–5.30. Adm. £3, Garden only, £1.30.

HAREWOOD HOUSE, Leeds.—April–Oct. daily from 11. Sun. only, Feb., March, and Nov.

HATFIELD HOUSE, Herts.—March 25–Oct. 9 daily (except Mon. and Good Friday) 12–5, Sun. 2–5.30, Bank Hols. 11–5. Adm. £2.95.

HEVER CASTLE, Kent.—March 29–Nov. 6 daily 12–6.

HOLKER HALL, Cumbria.—Easter Sun.-last Sun. in Oct. daily (not Sat.), 10.30–4.30.

HOLKHAM HALL, Norfolk.—Late May–Sept. Sun.-Thurs. 1.30–5. Spring and Summer Bank Holidays 11.30–5. Adm. £1.70. Also Bygones Collection £1.30.

HOPETOUN HOUSE, nr. Edinburgh.—Easter, then April 30–Sept. 19, daily 11–5.30. Adm. £2.50.

HOUGHTON HALL, Norfolk.—Easter Sun.-Sept. 25, Sun., Thurs. and Bank Hols. 1–5.30. Adm. £2.50.

*HUGHENDEN MANOR, High Wycombe. Disraeli's home.—April–Oct. Wed.-Sat. 2–6, Sun. and Bank Hol. Mons. 12–6. March weekends 2–6 or dusk. Adm. £2.

INVERARAY CASTLE, Argyll. Seat of the Dukes of Argyll.—1st Sat. in April–2nd Sun. in Oct. daily (not Fri.) 10–6, Sun. 1–6. Woods open all year.

JANE AUSTEN'S HOUSE, Chawton, Hants.—April–Oct. daily, Jan. and Feb. weekends, Nov., Dec. and March, Wed.–Sun. 11–4.30. Adm. £1.

KELMSCOTT MANOR, nr. Lechlade.—Tues., Wed., Thurs. (on written application). Adm. £2.50.

*KINGSTON LACY HOUSE, Dorset.—April 2–Oct.30 Sat.–Wed. 1–5. Adm. £3.

KNEBWORTH HOUSE, Herts.— March 26–May 22, Sat., Sun., School and Bank Hols., May 28–Sept. 11 daily (not Mon.) 12–5. Adm. £2.50.

*KNOLE, Kent.—April–Oct. Wed.–Sat. and Bank Hol. Mons. 11–5, Sun. 2–5. Adm. £2.20.

LEEDS CASTLE, Kent.—April–Oct. daily 11–5. Nov.–March, weekends only, 12–4. Castle closed for restoration Winter 1988–89.

*LITTLE MORETON HALL, Cheshire.—April–Sept. daily (not Tues.), March and Oct. weekends, 1.30–5.30. Closed Good Friday. Adm. £1.60. Weekends and Bank Hols. £2.

LONGLEAT HOUSE, Warminster.—Easter–Sept. daily 10–6, Oct.–Easter daily 10–4.

LUTON HOO, Beds.—Easter, then April 16–Oct. 16 daily 2–5.45 (not Mon. except Bank Hols.). Adm. £2.50.

MELBOURNE HALL, Derbyshire.—June 1–Oct. 5 Wed. 2–5. Adm. £1.50.

MICHELHAM PRIORY, E. Sussex.—March 25–Oct. 31 daily 11–5.30. Adm. £2.

*MONTACUTE HOUSE, Yeovil.—April 2–Oct. 30 daily (not Tues.) 12.30–5.30. Adm. £2.80.

*MOUNT STEWART, Co. Down.—April, Sept., Oct. weekends 2–6; Easter weekend 2–6, May Wed.–Sun. 2–6, June–Aug. daily (not Mon.). 12–6. Adm. £2.

OSBORNE HOUSE, I.O.W. —April–Oct. daily. Adm. £2.50.

*PENRHYN CASTLE, Bangor.— March 31–Oct. 30 daily (not Tues.) 12–5. (July–Aug. 11–5). Adm. £2.20.

PENSHURST PLACE, Kent.—April 1–Oct. 2 daily (not Mon. except Bank Hols.) 1–5.30. Adm. charge.

*PETWORTH HOUSE, W. Sussex.—April–Oct. Tues., Wed., Thurs., Sat., Sun., Bank Hol. Mons. 1–5. Adm. £3.

PORTMEIRION, Gwynedd.—April–Oct. daily 9.30–5.30. Admission charge.

POWDERHAM CASTLE, Exeter.—May 22–Sept. 15 Sun.–Thurs. 2–5.30.

*POWIS CASTLE, Powys.—April 2–June 30, Sept., Oct. Wed.–Sun. and Bank Hol. Mons. 12–5, July and Aug. daily (not Mon. except Bank Hol.) 11–6, Adm. £2.50.

RABY CASTLE, Durham.—Easter (Sat.–Wed.), April 30–June 30 Wed. and Sun., July–Sept. daily (not Sat.) 1–5. Also Bank Hol. weekends. Adm. £2.

RAGLEY HALL, Warwicks. April 2–Oct. 2 daily (not Mon., Fri.). Open Bank Hols. Adm. £2.90.

ROCKINGHAM CASTLE, Corby.—Easter Sunday–Sept. Sun., Thurs., (Mon. and Tues.) 2–6. Adm. £2.20.

*RUFFORD OLD HALL, Lancashire—April 2–Oct. daily (not Fri.) 1–5, Sun. 2–5. Adm. £1.50.

SANDRINGHAM, Norfolk.—April 3–Sept. 29 (closed July 18–Aug. 6) Mon.-Thurs., 11–4.45, Sun. 12–4.45. Adm. £2.

SCONE PALACE, Perth.—Good Friday-mid Oct. Mon.–Sat. 9.30–5, Sun. 1.30–5 (July and Aug. 10–5). Adm. £2.50.

SHERBORNE CASTLE, Dorset.—Easter Sat.–Sept. Thurs., Sat., Sun. and Bank Hol. Mons. 2–6. Adm. charge.

*SHUGBOROUGH, Staffs.—April–Sept. daily 11–5, Oct. 1–Dec. 24 daily 11–4. Adm. £4.

SKIPTON CASTLE, N. Yorks.—Open all year. Adm. £1.40

*SMALLHYTHE PLACE, Kent. Dame Ellen Terry's home.—April–Oct. Sat.–Wed. 2–6. Adm. £1.30.

STANFORD HALL, Leics.—Easter Sunday–Sept. Thurs., Sat., Sun., Bank Hols. (Mon. and Tues.) 2.30–6. Adm. £1.90.

STONELEIGH ABBEY, Warwicks.—April–May, Sun. and Bank Hols., June–Aug. Sun.–Thurs., Sept. Sun. only. 1–5.

STONOR PARK, Oxon.—April Sun. only, May–Sept. Wed., Thurs., Sun. (also Sat. in Aug.) 2–5.30. Bank Hol. Mons. 11–5.30. Adm. £1.90.

*STOURHEAD, Wilts.—May–Sept. Sat.–Thurs., April and Oct. Sat.–Wed. 2–6. Adm. £2. Gardens, daily 8–7 or dusk. Adm. £1.50.

STRATFIELD SAYE HOUSE, Reading.—Easter Sat., Sunday and Mon., April weekends, then May–last Sun. in Sept. daily (not Fri.) 11.30–5. Adm. £3.60.

*SUDBURY HALL, Derbys.—April 2–Oct. Wed.–Sun. and Bank Hol. Mons. 1–5.30. Adm. £2.20.

SUDELEY CASTLE, Glos.—April–Oct. daily 12–5. Adm. £3.25.

SULGRAVE MANOR, Northants. Home of the Washington family.—Feb.–Dec. daily (not Wed.) 10.30–5.30 (Feb., March, Oct.–Dec. 10.30–4). Adm. £1.

*TRERICE, Cornwall.—April–Oct. daily 11–6. Adm. £2.40.

*THE VYNE, Basingstoke.—April–Oct. 16 daily (not Mon. and Fri.) 1.30–5.30, Bank Hol. Mons. 11–5.30. (Closed Tues. following Bank Hol. Mons.). Adm. £2.20 (Sun. and Bank Hol. Mons. £2.50).

TYN-Y-RHOS HALL, Shropshire—May–Sept. Wed., Thurs., Sat., Sun. and Bank Hol. Mons. 2.30–6. Adm. £1.

*WADDESDON MANOR, Bucks.—March 23–Oct. 30, Wed. (except after Bank Hol.)–Sun. 1–5 (1–6 weekends May–Sept.) Bank Hols. 11–6. Adm. £3.

WARWICK CASTLE.—March–Oct. daily 10–5.30, Nov.–Feb. daily 10–4.30. Adm. charge.

WILTON HOUSE, Wilts.—March 29–Oct. 16 Tues-Sat. and Bank Hol. Mons. 11–6, Sun. 1–6. Adm. £3.35.

*WIMPOLE HALL, Cambs.—April 2–Oct. 30 daily (not Mon., Fri.) 1–5, Bank Hol. Mons. 11–5. Adm. £3.

WOBURN ABBEY, Beds. Seat of the Duke of Bedford.—March 28–Oct. 30 daily 11–5.45 (Sun. 11–6.15). Jan. 1–Mar. 27 weekends only 11–4.45. Adm. charge.

MUSEUMS AND ART GALLERIES OUTSIDE LONDON

(For National Art Galleries and Museums in London see pages 302–3 and 345–50.)

(Adm. admission; con. concessionary rates)

Barnard Castle, Co. Durham.—*The Bowes Museum.* Important collections of British and European fine art, from medieval period to 19th century. Fine porcelain and glass, tapestries and furniture. Music and costume galleries. English period rooms from Elizabeth I to Victoria; French decorative arts of 18th and 19th centuries; local antiquities. Temporary exhibitions. Open weekdays: May–Sept., 10–5.30, March, April, Oct., 10–5, Nov.–Feb., 10–4. Sun.: 2–5 (summer); 2–4 (winter). Adm. £1·50, con. 50p.

Bath.—*Roman Baths Museum.* Roman Baths complex of 1st century A.D. Adm. (including adjoining 18th-century Pump Room), £2.50, con. £1.50. *Museum of Costume*, Assembly Rooms. Fashion from 16th century to current year. Closed for building repairs until 1991. *American Museum in Britain*, Claverton Manor. American decorative arts from late 17th to mid 19th centuries. Open April 1–Oct. 30, daily (except Mon.), 2–5, Bank Hol. Mons. and preceding Suns. 11–5. During winter only on application. Adm. charge. *Victoria Art Gallery*, Bridge Street. Open Mon.–Fri. 10–6, Sat. 10–5. Closed Sun., Bank Hols. Adm. free.

Beamish.—*North of England Open Air Museum*, Chester-le-Street, Co. Durham. Re-creates Northern life around the turn of the century. Buildings from the region have been rebuilt and furnished, including old Town Street with houses, shops, etc., colliery with drift mine and cottages, station and steam locomotives, farm with farmhouse, agricultural machinery and animals. Open daily (except Mon. in winter): summer 10–6, winter 10–5.

Beaulieu.—*National Motor Museum.* Displays of vehicles dating from 1895 to present day. Open daily 10–6 (winter, 10–5). Adm. charge.

Belfast.—*Ulster Museum*, Botanic Gardens. Collections of Irish antiquities, natural and local history, fine and applied arts. Open Mon.–Fri. 10–5, Sat. 1–5, Sun. 2–5. *Ulster Folk and Transport Museum*, Holywood. Indoor and outdoor exhibits of all aspects of Ulster folklife. Open Oct.–April, weekdays 11–5, Sun. 2–5 (May–Sept. 2–6). May–June (Wed. only) 11–9. Adm. £1, con. 50p. *Transport Museum*, Holywood and Witham Street. History of land, sea and air transport in Ireland and road, rail and sea vehicles. Holywood site—open as for Folk Museum. Witham Street site open weekdays 10–5. Adm. 30p, children 20p, other con. 15p. Special arrangements apply at both museums over Christmas and Easter.

Beverley, N. Humberside.—*Museum of Army Transport.* Exhibits include field workshop, amphibious assault landing, railway section and aircraft. Open daily 10–5. Adm. £1.80, con., 90p.

Birmingham.—*City Museum and Art Gallery.* British and European masters from 14th to 20th centuries (particularly of the Pre-Raphaelite movement), sculpture, European gold, silver and jewellery, metalwork, glass, pottery and porcelain, furniture, textiles and costume, archaeology, local and natural history. Open Mon.–Sat. 9.30–5, Sun. 2–5. Closed Christmas Day, Boxing Day, New Year's Day and Good Friday. Adm. free.
Museum of Science and Industry, Newhall Street. The history of science from the Industrial Revolution to the present; many working machines under steam, gas, etc. Open Mon.–Sat. 9.30–5, Sun. 2–5. Adm. free. Also *Aston Hall, Blakesley Hall, Birmingham Nature Centre, Sarehole Mill*, and *Weoley Castle.*

Bradford.—*Cartwright Hall*, Lister Park. Contains mainly British 19th and 20th century fine art.

Bolling Hall, off Wakefield Road, a furnished period house, mainly 17th and 18th century. *Industrial Museum*, Moorside Road, illustrates the local wool and worsted industries and transport in an old mill, with mill owner's house. *Cliffe Castle*, Keighley. Natural and local history, minerals and gem display, and period rooms. *Manor House*, Ilkley. Archaeology, local history and contemporary fine art. Open 10–5 (April–Sept. 10–6, except Industrial museum). Closed Good Friday, Christmas Day, Boxing Day and Mons. (except Bank Hols.). Adm. free.

Brighton.—*The Royal Pavilion, Palace of George IV.* Chinoiserie interiors, much of the original furniture returned on loan from H.M. the Queen. Open daily 10–5 (June–Sept. 10–6). Closed Christmas Day and Boxing Day. Adm. £2.30.
Museum and Art Gallery, Church Street (adjacent Royal Pavilion). Old master paintings; Willett pottery and porcelain collection, 20th-century art and furniture, ethnography, archæology, local history, musical instruments, costume gallery. Open Tues.–Sat. 10–5.45, Sun. 2–5. Closed Christmas Day, Boxing Day, Good Friday, Mons and Jan. 1. Adm. free.
Preston Manor, Preston Park. Thomas-Stanford: Macquoid bequests of English period furniture, furnishings, china and silver. Open Tues.–Sun. 10–5; Tues. and Sun. 10–1, 2–5. Adm. £1.50. Closed Christmas Day, Boxing Day, Good Friday, Mons. Gardens open, free.
The Grange, Art Gallery and Museum, Rottingdean. Sussex Room, Kipling Room and collections of National Toy Museum. Open Mon., Thurs., Sat. 10–5, Tues. and Fri. 10–1, 2–5, Sundays, 2–5. Closed Christmas Day, Boxing Day, Good Friday, Weds. and Jan. 1. Adm. free.
The Booth Museum of Natural History, Dyke Road. Open 10–5, Sun. 2–5. Closed Christmas Day, Boxing Day, Good Friday, Thursdays and Jan. 1. Adm. free.

Bristol.—*City Museum and Art Gallery.* Collections of Egyptology, British archæology, natural and local history. Collection of Old Masters, 19th century and modern paintings, Chinese ceramics and glass, English silver, glass, porcelain and delftware, English and foreign embroideries. Open weekdays, 10–5. *Bristol Industrial Museum*, Prince's Wharf. Collections of manufacturing equipment and transport, including unique steam carriage and Bristol-built aero-engines. Open daily (except Thurs. and Fri.) 10–1, 2–5. *Maritime Heritage Centre* including *SS Great Britain*, open daily 10–6 (winter 10–5). Closed Christmas Eve and Day. Also *Red Lodge, Blaise Castle House Museum, Kingsweston Roman Villa, Georgian House* and *St. Nicholas Church Museum.*
National Life-boat Museum, Princes Wharf, Wapping Road. Displays of life-boats, models and equipment. Open daily 10.30–4.30. Adm. £1.50, con. 75p.

Cambridge.—*Fitzwilliam Museum.* Egyptian, Greek, Near Eastern and Roman antiquities, coins and medals, medieval manuscripts, paintings and drawings, prints, sculpture, Oriental and Occidental fans, pottery and porcelain, textiles, arms and armour, medieval and renaissance objects of art, and a library. Open Tues.–Sat., Lower Galleries 10–2, Upper Galleries 2–5; Sun. 2.15–5. Closed Dec. 24–Jan. 1 and Good Friday. Closed Mons. incl. May Day Bank Hol. but not Easter and Bank Hol. Mons. Permanent exhibitions free.

Canterbury.—*Royal Museum and Art Gallery, and Buffs Regimental Museum.* Collections include archaeology, porcelain, prints and pictures. Open free weekdays, 10–5. *Canterbury Heritage*, a timewalk museum of the city's history. Open Mon.–Sat.

10.30–4, Sun. (June–Oct.) 1.30–4. Adm. £1, con. 50p. *Roman Mosaic Museum.* Roman material from postwar excavations of Canterbury. *West Gate Tower Museum.* Arms and armour and display of city walls and gates. Roman and West Gate Museums open 10–1, 2–5 (Oct.–March, 2–4). Adm. 30p, con. 15p.

Carlisle.—*Carlisle Museum and Art Gallery,* Tullie House, Castle Street. Collections of archæology, natural and social history, fine and decorative arts in Jacobean house. Open Mon.–Sat. 9–5, Spring and Summer Bank Hols and Sun. June–Aug. 10–4. *Guildhall,* Greenmarket. Civic and Guild history and artefacts. Contact Tullie House Museum for opening information.

Chester.—*Grosvenor Museum,* Grosvenor Street. Collection of Roman antiquities from legionary fortress; natural history, art and folk-life. Open weekdays 10.30–5, Sun. 2–5. *The Georgian House,* Castle Street. Period room displays, costume and musical instruments. Open weekdays, 10.30–5, Sun., 2–5. *King Charles Tower* on City Walls. Civil War displays. Open daily (summer), weekends (winter), times vary. Adm. charge.

Colchester.—*Colchester and Essex Museum, The Castle* contains local archæological antiquities, especially those from Roman Colchester. The *Holly Trees Mansion* (1718) covers social life of the 18th and 19th centuries. *Natural History Museum,* All Saints Church. Natural history of Essex. *Museum of Social History,* Holy Trinity Church. Domestic life and crafts. Open Mon.–Sat. 10–5 (Oct.–March Sat. 10–4). Castle only, Sun. 2.30–5 (April–Sept.). Adm. 85p, con. 45p. *Tymperleys Clock Museum.* Open April–Oct. Tues.–Sat. 10–5 (10–4 Sats in Oct.). Closed Mon. except Bank Holidays. Adm. 40p, con. 20p.

Coventry.—*Herbert Art Gallery and Museum,* Jordan Well. Archæology, natural and local history, fine and decorative arts. Open weekdays 10–5.30, Sun. 2–5. Closed Good Friday and Christmas period. *Museum of British Road Transport,* St. Agnes Lane, Hales Street. Open April–Sept., Mon.–Fri. 10–4, Sat., Sun. 10–5.30; Oct.–March, Fri., Sat. and Sun. only. Adm. £1., con. 50p. *Lunt Roman Fort,* Baginton. June–Sept., 12–6 (closed Mon. and Thurs.). Adm. 50p, con. 25p. *Whitefriars Museum.* Open Thurs., Fri., Sat., and some Bank Hols, 10–5.30.

Crich, Nr. Matlock, Derbyshire—*National Tramway Museum.* Open air working museum with collection of trams from Britain and abroad. Open April Oct. weekends and Bank Holidays 10–6.30. April–Sept. also open daily (except Fri.) 10–5.30, also Fris. during summer holidays.

Derby.—*Museum and Art Gallery,* Strand. Archaeology, military, social history, natural history, collections of paintings by Joseph Wright of Derby, Derby porcelain, costume, model theatres. Open Tues.–Sat. 10–5. *Industrial Museum,* Silk Mill, Full Street, Rolls Royce collection of aero engines, a railway engineering gallery. Tues.–Fri. 10–5. Sat. 10–4.45. Closed on all Bank Hols.

Dorchester.—*Dorset County Museum.* Geology, archæology, local and natural history and rural crafts of Dorset. Collection of Thomas Hardy's manuscripts, books, notebooks, drawings, etc. Open Mon.–Sat. 10–5, closed Christmas Day, Boxing Day and Good Friday. Adm. £1, con. 50p.

Durham.—*Light Infantry Museum and Arts Centre.* County Regiment's 200 year history displayed, arts and crafts exhibitions. Open weekdays (except Mon.) 10–5, Sun. and Bank Hol. Mon. 2–5. Closed Christmas Day and Boxing Day. Adm. 60p, con. 25p. *Oriental Museum,* The University. Collections ranging from Ancient Egypt to China and Japan. Open weekdays: 9.30–5. Weekends: Nov.–

Feb. closed; March–Oct. Sat. 9.30–5, Sun. 2–5. *Cathedral Treasury.* Relics of St. Cuthbert, church plate, medieval seals, manuscripts and vestments. Open weekdays 10–4.30, Sun. 2–4.30. Adm. 60p, con. 10p. *Old Fulling Mill Museum.* Archaeological material from local excavations. Open Nov.–March, daily 2–4, April–Oct., Mon.–Fri. 10–4, Sat. and Sun., 2–4. Adm. free.

Edinburgh.—*City Art Centre,* 2 Market Street. Late 19th and 20th century art, mostly Scottish, and temporary exhibitions. Open weekdays 10–5 (June–Sept. 10–6). Adm. free. *Canongate Tolbooth,* 163 Canongate. Courthouse and prison, now museum. Open weekdays 10–5 (June–Sept. 10–6). Adm. free. *Huntly House,* 142 Canongate. Local history, collections of Edinburgh silver, glass and Scottish pottery. Open weekdays 10–5 (June–Sept. 10–6). Adm. free. *Lady Stair's House,* Lawnmarket. Mon. Sat. 10–5 (June–Sept. 10–6). *Lauriston Castle,* Cramond Road South, April–Oct. daily (except Fri.), 11–5; Nov.–March, weekends only. *Museum of Childhood,* 42 High Street. Open weekdays 10–5 (June–Sept. 10–6). Adm. free.

Exeter.—*Royal Albert Memorial Museum and Art Gallery,* Queen Street. Fine art, Exeter silver, ceramics and glass, natural and local history. Open Tues.–Sat. 10–5.15. Adm. free. *Exeter Maritime Museum,* The Haven. Collection of working boats. Open daily 10–5 (July–Aug. 10–6). Adm. charge. *Underground Passages,* Princesshay. Medieval aqueducts. Closed in 1989. *Rougemont House Museum of Costume and Lace,* Castle Street. Open Mon.–Sat. 10–5.

Fort William.—*West Highland Museum,* Cameron Square. Historical, natural history and folk exhibits, including those of the 1745 Rising. Daily (except Sun.) 10–5; June and Sept. 9.30–5.30; July and Aug. 9.30–9.

Glasgow.—*Art Gallery and Museum,* Kelvingrove. Old Masters, 19th century French paintings; archæology and natural history, collection of armour. *People's Palace,* Glasgow Green. History of city from 1175 to present. *The Burrell Collection,* Pollok Park. Textiles, furniture, ceramics, stained glass, silver and other art objects, paintings, especially 19th century French. *Pollok House,* Pollok Park. Spanish paintings, furniture, silver, ceramics. *Haggs Castle Museum,* St. Andrews Drive. Children's museum with activity workshops. *Provand's Lordship,* Castle Street. Oldest house in Glasgow, period furniture displays. *Rutherglen Museum,* King Street. History of former royal burgh of Rutherglen. *Museum of Transport,* Kelvin Hall. All open weekdays 10–5, Sun. 2–5. Adm. free.

Hull.—*Ferens Art Gallery.* European art, especially Dutch 17th century, British portraits of 18th–20th centuries, Humberside marine paintings, contemporary art and changing exhibitions. *Wilberforce House.* Jacobean merchant's house, birthplace of Wilberforce; collection of slavery relics, period furniture, costume and ceramics. *Transport and Archæology Museum.* Veteran cars, trams, coaches and velocipedes; archæological finds from Humberside, including Roman mosaics. *Town Docks Museum.* Whaling, fishing, trawling, ships and shipping. *Old Grammar School.* Hull's oldest building with city history display. *Spurn Lightship,* built 1927, restored 1986. Closed Mon. and Tues. in winter. All open Mon.–Sat. 10–5, Sun. 1.30–4.30. *Posterngate Gallery.* Exhibitions and one-man shows. Tues.–Sat. 10–5.30.

Huntingdon.—*Cromwell Museum.* Remaining portion of the 12th century Hospital of St. John housing portraits of Cromwell, his family and Parliamentary notables, and Cromwelliana—documents, armour, coins, etc. Open April–Oct. Tues.–Fri. 11–5, Sat, Sun. 11–4; Nov.–March, Tues.–Fri. 2–5, Sat. 11–4, Sun. 2–4. Closed Bank Hols other than Good Friday. Adm. free.

Ipswich.—*Ipswich Museum.* Collections of Suffolk geology, archæology and natural history and ethnology. Temporary exhibitions. Open Mon.–Sat. 10–5. Closed Bank Hols. *Christchurch Mansion.* Tudor house contains furniture, Suffolk portraits, English porcelain, pottery and glass. *Wolsey Art Gallery,* attached, houses Borough collections of paintings (local artists, Gainsborough, Constable), modern prints, sculpture. Open Mon.–Sat. 10–5, Sun. 2.30–4.30. Closed Good Friday, Dec. 24, 25, 26.

Leeds.—*City Art Gallery.* English watercolours. British and European painting, modern sculpture, incl. Henry Moore gallery. Print Room contains study collection of drawings and prints. Open weekdays, 10–6, Suns., 2–5.

Temple Newsam House. Tudor/Jacobean house, furnished in style of 17th and 18th centuries, with silver, European porcelain and pottery, pictures, etc. Open daily (except Mon.) 10.30–6.15 or dusk, Weds. (May–Sept.) 10.30–8.30, all Bank Hols (except Christmas). Adm. 65p, con. 30p. (Free adm. to farm). *Lotherton Hall,* Gascoigne art and silver collection, oriental gallery, costume collection, 19th century furniture, ceramics, park and gardens. Open daily (except Mon.) 10.30–6.15 or dusk, Thurs. (May–Sept.) 10.30–8.30, all Bank Hols (except Christmas). Adm. 65p, con. 30p. (Free adm. bird garden.) *Abbey House Museum.* Folk museum including three full-sized streets. Open Oct.–March weekdays 10–5, Sun. 2–5 (April–Sept. 2–6). *Industrial Museum.* Open April–Sept. Tues.–Sat. 10–5, Sun. 2–5 (Oct.–March 2–4). Open Bank Hols.

Leicester.—*Leicestershire Museum and Art Gallery,* New Walk. Natural history, geology, Egyptology, 18th–20th century English paintings, ceramics, silver. *Newarke Houses,* The Newarke. Social history of Leicestershire from 1500 A.D., musical instruments, local clocks. *Jewry Wall Museum,* St. Nicholas Circle. Archaeology (prehistoric–1500). Roman Jewry Wall and Baths, mosaics. *Belgrave Hall,* Church Road. A Queen Anne house with furniture and garden of note. Coaches and agricultural collection. *Museum of the Royal Leicestershire Regiment,* The Magazine, Oxford Street. *Museum of Technology,* Corporation Road. Knitting industry and Power galleries. Horse-drawn and motor vehicles, beam engines. *Wygston's House Museum of Costume,* Applegate. Costume from 1789–1924. All museums open weekdays (except Fri.) 10–5.30, Sun. 2–5.30. Closed Christmas Day, Boxing Day and Good Friday.

Lewes.—*Museum of Sussex Archæology,* Barbican House, near Castle. Prehistoric, Roman, Saxon and mediæval collections relating to Sussex; local pictures and prints. Open weekdays, 10–5.30, Sun. (April–Oct.) 11–5.30. Adm. £1.30, con. 65p.

Anne of Cleves House, Southover. Local history and folk museum. Open weekdays (mid. Feb.–mid. Nov.) 10–5.30. Sun. (April–Oct.) 2–5.30. Adm. £1.10, con. 55p.

Lincoln.—*Usher Gallery.* Watches, miniatures, porcelain, silver, etc., Peter de Wint collection of oils and watercolours, Lincolnshire topographical drawings, *personalia* associated with Tennyson family. Open weekdays 10–5.30, Sun. 2.30–5. *City and County Museum,* The Greyfriars. Geology, natural history and archæology of Lincolnshire. Open weekdays 10–5.30, Sun. 2.30–5. *Museum of Lincolnshire Life.* Collections illustrate life and work in Lincolnshire over the last 200 years. Includes large agricultural collection. Open weekdays 10–5.30, Sun. 2–5.30. *National Cycle Museum,* Brayford Wharf North.

Collection of vintage cycles. Open Easter to Oct. 10–5 daily; Oct. to Easter Fri., Sat., and Sun. 10–5.

Manchester.—*City Art Gallery,* Mosley Street. Old Masters, Turner, Pre-Raphaelites; sculpture, porcelain, silver. Mon.–Sat. 10–6, Sun. 2–6. *Athenaeum Gallery,* Princess Street. Adm. free. *Whitworth Art Gallery,* University of Manchester, Oxford Road. Watercolours, drawings, prints, textiles and wallpapers collections, and 20th century British art. Mon.–Sat. 10–5 (Thurs. 10–9), closed Suns. *Greater Manchester Museum of Science and Industry,* Liverpool Road Station. Working machinery and displays in world's oldest passenger railway station. Open daily 10–5. *Gallery of English Costume,* Platt Hall, Rusholme. Exhibits from 16th century to present. Open daily (not Tues.) 10–6, Sun. 2–6 (closes 4, Nov.–April). Also *Heaton Hall,* Prestwich, *Wythenshawe Hall,* Northenden and *Fletcher Moss Museum,* Didsbury. Open April–Sept. daily (not Tues.) 10–6, Sun. 2–6.

Newcastle upon Tyne.—*Laing Art Gallery,* Higham Place. Fine art from 17th century, pottery, glass, silver and metalwork. Open Tues.–Fri. 10–5.30, Sat. 10–4.30, Sun. 2.30–5.30. *Keep Museum,* St. Nicholas Street. History of site. Oct.–March, Mon.–Sat. 10–4.30 (April–Sept. 10–5.30). *Trinity Maritime Centre* and *Trinity House,* Broad Chare. Centre open April–Sept. Tues.–Fri. 10.30–4; Oct.–March, Tues.–Thurs. 11–3. Trinity House April–Oct., Tues., Wed., Thurs. 2–4. *Military Vehicle Museum,* Exhibition Park. Open daily 10.15–4.30. *Museum of Science and Engineering,* West Blandford Square. Tues.–Fri. 10–5.30, Sat. 10–4.30. *Newburn Hall Motor Museum,* Townfield Gdns. Tues.–Sat. 10–8.

Newmarket.—*National Horseracing Museum.* Five galleries of displays relating to the development of horseracing and to the horses and people connected with the sport. Equine Tours. Open April 2–Dec. 4, Tues.–Sat. 10–5, Sun. 2–5. Closed Mon. except Aug. and Bank Hols. Adm. £1.60, con. 80p.

Norwich.—*Castle Museum.* Exhibits of art (including Norwich School), local archæology, social and natural history, pottery and glass. Open, Mon.–Sat., 10–5, Sun. 2–5. *Strangers' Hall,* Charing Cross. Late medieval mansion furnished as a museum of urban domestic life, 16th–19th centuries. Open, Mon.–Sat. 10–5. *Bridewell Museum of Local Industries,* Bridewell Alley. Transport, crafts and industries of Norwich. Open Mon.–Sat. 10–5. *St. Peter Hungate Church Museum,* Princes Street. 15th century church used for display of church art and antiquities. Open Mon.–Sat. 10–5.

Nottingham.—*Castle Museum and Art Gallery.* English and Dutch paintings and drawings 17th–20th centuries, special collections of Bonington and Paul Sandby. Ceramics, silver, glass, medieval Nottingham alabaster carvings, local historical and archaeological displays, classical, oriental and ethnographical antiquities, the regimental collection of the Sherwood Foresters. Open Summer, 10–5.45, Winter, 10–4.45. Closed Christmas Day. Adm. free, small charge on Sun. and Bank Hols.

Industrial Museum, Wollaton Park. Industrial, lacemaking machinery, steam engines, transport. Open April–Sept. Mon.–Sat. 10–6, Sun. 2–6; Oct.–April, Thurs., Sat. 10–4.30, Sun. 1.30–4.30. Closed Christmas Day. Adm. free, small charge on Sun. and Bank Hols.

Canal Museum, Canal Street. Open Easter–Oct. Wed.–Sat. 10–5.45, Sun. 1–5.45; Oct.–Easter, Wed.–Sat. 1–5, Sun. 1–5. Adm. free.

Natural History Museum, Wollaton Hall. Open summer 10–7, Sun. 2–5; winter 10 till dusk (Sun. 1.30–4.30). Closed Christmas Day. Adm. free except Sun. and Bank Hols.

Castlegate Museum of Costumes and Textiles. Open daily 10–5. Closed Christmas Day. Adm. free.

Brewhouse Yard Museum, Castle Boulevard. Everyday life from the 17th century to present. Open daily 10–5. Adm. free. Closed Christmas Day.

Green's Mill and Science Centre, Sneinton. Working windmill and museum with models, displays about George Green. Open daily, Wed.–Sun. 10–5. Closed Christmas Day. Adm. free.

Oakham, *Rutland County Museum,* Catmos Street.—Archæology, local history, craft tools and agricultural implements. Open Tues.–Sat. 10–5, Sun. (April–Oct.) 2–5, and Bank Hol. Mons.

Oxford, *Ashmolean Museum,* Beaumont Street.— The University's collections of European and Oriental fine and applied arts, Classical and Near-Eastern archaeology and Numismatics. Open Tues.–Sat. 10–4, Sun. 2–4. Bank Hol. Mons. 2–5. Adm. free.

Plymouth.—*City Museum and Art Gallery,* Drake Circus. Fine art, including Cottonian collection and Reynolds' portraits, Plymouth porcelain, archaeology, local and natural history. Tues.–Sat. 10–5.30, Sun. 2–5. Also Bank Holiday Mons. Adm. free. The 16th century *Elizabethan House,* 32 New Street. Also *Merchant's House,* 33 St. Andrew's Street, dating from the 16th and early 17th centuries.

Portsmouth.—*City Museum and Art Gallery,* Museum Road. *Cumberland House Natural Science Museum and Butterfly House,* Eastern Parade. *Southsea Castle and Museum,* Clarence Esplanade. *D-Day Museum,* Clarence Esplanade. All open daily 10.30–5.30, except Dec. 24–26. Adm. charge. *Charles Dickens' Birthplace Museum,* Old Commercial Road. Open March 1–Oct. 31, daily 10.30–5.30. Adm. charge. *Eastney Pumping Station,* Henderson Road. Open April–Sept. daily 1.30–5.30; Oct.–March 1st Sun. of month. Adm. charge. *Fort Widley,* Portsdown Hill. Open April–Sept. Sat., Sun., Bank Hols. 1.30–5.50. Adm. charge. *Naval Heritage Area.* Tells the story of the Royal Navy using Henry VIII's *Mary Rose,* H.M.S. *Victory* (Nelson's flagship), and the Victorian ironclad, H.M.S. *Warrior* (1860). These are presented against a backdrop of the history of the modern Navy from earliest times to the Falklands Campaign related in the Royal Naval Museum. Open daily (except Christmas Day). Adm. charge.

St. Albans.—*City Museum,* Hatfield Road. Natural history, geology, craft and trade tools. Open weekdays 10–5. Admission free. *Verulamium Museum,* St. Michael's. Roman and Belgic material including mosaics, one *in situ* in Hypercaust annexe. Open weekdays 10–4, Sun. 2–4 (10–5.30 and 2–5.30 in summer). Adm. 70p, con. 40p.

Sheffield.—*City Museum, Weston Park.* Includes the Bateman Collection of antiquities from Peak District Bronze Age barrows, cutlery and old Sheffield plate. *Mappin Art Gallery,* Weston Park. Paintings and sculpture of 18th–20th centuries (mainly British School) and contemporary works, *Abbeydale Industrial Hamlet,* Abbeydale Road South. A late 18th–early 19th century scythe and steel works with associated housing. *Kelham Island Industrial Museum.* *Shepherd Wheel,* Whiteley Wood. Water-powered cutlery grinding establishment. *Bishops' House, Meersbrook Park.* Museum of local history in timber-framed domestic building. Opening times vary.

Stoke-on-Trent.—*City Museum and Art Gallery,* Bethesda Street, Hanley. Major ceramic collections.

Open daily 10.30–5, Sun. 2–5. *Chatterley Whitfield Mining Museum,* Tunstall. Guided tours underground. *Gladstone Pottery Museum,* Longton. A working Victorian pottery.

Pottery Factory Tours: Tours are available at the following: *Minton,* London Road, Stoke; *Royal Doulton,* Nile Street, Burslem; *Spode,* Church Street, Stoke, *Beswick,* Gold Street, *Melba-Wain,* Heathcote Road, *Parkhall China,* Weston Coyney Road, Longton, *Coalport and Crown Staffordshire,* Park Street, Fenton and *Wedgwood's* at Barlaston.

Stratford-upon-Avon.—*Shakespeare's Birthplace.* Period furniture, rare books, MSS and objects of Shakespearean interest with new Shakespeare Centre nearby. *Anne Hathaway's Cottage,* Shottery, early home of Shakespeare's wife. *Mary Arden's House,* Wilmcote, Tudor farmhouse home of Shakespeare's mother with Countryside Museum. *New Place,* where Shakespeare died. *Hall's Croft,* half-timbered home of Shakespeare's daughter and her family. *Grammar School* attended by Shakespeare. *Royal Shakespeare Theatre* burnt down 1926, rebuilt 1932. New *Swan Theatre* opened in 1986.

Styal.—*Quarry Bank Mill,* Cheshire. History of the cotton industry, weaving demonstrations. Giant iron waterwheel. Restored Apprentice House. Open all year. Closed Mon. Oct.–March. Open Bank Hols. Adm. £3.75, con £2.75.

Winchester.—*City Museum.* Weekdays 10–5, Sun. 2–5 (closed Mon. in winter). *Cathedral Library.* MSS and other exhibits from 10th century onwards. Open weekdays. Adm. free. *Cathedral Treasury.* Exhibition of church silver and other pieces. Open May–Sept. Adm. charge.

Worcester.—*City Museum and Art Gallery.* Natural history of Worcestershire and temporary art exhibitions; also museum of the Worcestershire Regiment and the Worcester Yeomanry Cavalry. Open Mon.–Wed., Fri. 9.30–6, Sat. 9.30–5. Closed Thurs., Sun. *The Commandery,* Sidbury. Civil War Centre, costume, industrial history. Weekdays 10.30–5, Sun. 2–5. *Tudor House Museum,* Friar Street. Local domestic and social history. Mon.–Wed., Fri., Sat. 10.30–5. *Dyson Perrins Museum of Worcester Porcelain,* Severn Street. Mon. to Fri. 9.30–5, Sat. 10–5.

York.—*Castle Museum.* Museum of everday life of the last three centuries. Open weekdays 9.30–5.30, Sun. 10–5.30 (closes 6.30 April–Oct.). Adm. £2.25, con. £1.25.

Jorvik Viking Centre, Coppergate. Reconstruction of Viking York and display of artifacts. Open daily. Adm. £2.50, con. £2/£1.25.

Yorkshire Museum and Gardens, Museum Street, Roman Life gallery, archæology, decorative arts, geology, natural history. Open weekdays 10–5, Sun. 1–5. Adm. £1.50, con. 75p, Family Ticket £4. Gardens, Roman, Anglian and medieval ruins. Open weekdays 7.30–dusk (summer 7.30–8), Sun. 10–dusk. *The York Story,* Castlegate. Open weekdays 10–5, Sun. 1–5. Adm. 80p, con. 40p.

Art Gallery, Exhibition Square. European paintings, 14th–20th century; watercolours and prints of Yorkshire; modern English stoneware pottery. Open weekdays 10–5, Sun. 2.30–5.

Treasurer's House (National Trust). Chapter House Street. Open April–Oct. 10.30–5 (closed Good Friday). Adm. charge.

WILDLIFE

PROTECTED SPECIES

The Wildlife and Countryside Act 1981 gives legal protection to a wide range of wild animals.

Under Schedule 5 of the Act it is normally an offence to kill, injure, take, possess or sell any of the animals mentioned below (whether alive or dead) and to disturb its place of shelter and protection or to destroy that place.

*Adder	Moth, Black-veined
Anemone, Ivell's Sea	Moth, Essex Emerald
Anemone, Startlet Sea	Moth, New Forest
Apus	Burnet
Bat, Horseshoe	Moth, Reddish Buff
Bat, Typical	Moth, Viper's Bugloss
Beetle, Rainbow Leaf	Newt, Great Crested
Beetle, Violet Click	(or Warty)
Burbot	*Newt, Palmate
Butterfly, Heath	*Newt, Smooth
Fritillary	Otter, Common
Butterfly, Large Blue	Porpoise
Butterfly, Swallowtail	Sandworm, Lagoon
Cat, Wild	Sea-Mat, Trembling
Cicada, New Forest	Shrimp, Fairy
**Crayfish, Atlantic	Shrimp, Lagoon Sand
Stream	†Slow-worm
Cricket, Field	Snail, Glutinous
Cricket, Mole	Snail, Sandbowl
Dolphin	†Snake, Grass
Dormouse	Snake, Smooth
Dragonfly, Norfolk	Spider, Fen Raft
Aeshna	Spider, Ladybird
*Frog, Common	Squirrel, Red
Grasshopper, Wart-	*Toad, Common
biter	Toad, Natterjack
Leech, Medicinal	Turtle, Marine
Lizard, Sand	Vendace
†Lizard, Viviparous	Walrus
Marten, Pine	Whale
Moth, Barberry Carpet	Whitefish

* the offence relates to "sale" only.
** the offence relates to "taking" and "sale" only.
† the offence relates to "killing, injuring and sale".

CLOSE SEASONS AND TIMES
Hunting and Ground Game

There is no statutory close-time for fox-hunting or rabbit-shooting, nor for hares: but by an Act passed in 1892 the *sale* of hares or leverets in Great Britain is prohibited from March 1 to July 31 inclusive under a penalty of a pound. November 1 is the recognized date for the opening of the fox-hunting season, which continues till the following April.

Deer

The statutory close seasons for deer (all dates inclusive) are:

	England and Wales	Scotland
Fallow deer		
Male	May 1–July 31	May 1–July 31
Female	Mar. 1–Oct. 31	Feb. 16–Oct. 20
Red deer		
Male	May 1–July 31	Oct. 21–June 30
Female	Mar. 1–Oct. 31	Feb. 16–Oct. 20
Roe deer		
Male	Nov. 1–Mar. 31	Oct. 21–Mar. 31
Female	Mar. 1–Oct. 31	April 1–Oct. 20
Sika deer		
Male	May 1–July 31	Oct. 21–June 30
Female	Mar. 1–Oct. 31	Feb. 16–Oct. 20

	England and Wales	Scotland
Red/Sika hybrids		
Male		Oct. 21–June 30
Female		Feb. 16–Oct. 20

Wild Birds

The Wildlife and Countryside Act, 1981, lays down a close season for wild birds (other than game birds) from February 1 to August 31 inclusive, each year. Exceptions to these dates are made for—
Capercaillie and (except Scotland) *Woodcock*, Feb. 1—Sept. 30.
Snipe, Feb. 1—Aug. 11.
Wild Duck and *Wild Goose* (below high water mark), Feb. 21—Aug. 31.

Birds which may be killed or taken outside the close season (except on Sundays and on Christmas Day in Scotland, and on Sundays in prescribed areas of England and Wales) are the above and coot, certain wild duck (gadwall, goldeneye, mallard, pintail, pochard, shoveler, teal, tufted duck, wigeon), certain wild geese (Canada, greylag, pink-footed, white-fronted (in England and Wales only)), moorhen, golden plover and woodcock.

Certain wild birds may be killed or taken at any time by authorized persons—crow, collared dove, gull (great and lesser black-backed or herring), jackdaw, jay, magpie, pigeon (feral or wood), rook, sparrow (house), and starling.

All other British birds are fully protected by law throughout the year.

Game Birds
In each case the dates are inclusive:—

Black Game—Dec. 11 to Aug. 19 (Aug. 31 in Somerset, Devon, and New Forest).
**Grouse*—Dec. 11 to Aug. 11.
**Partridge*—Feb. 2 to Aug. 31.
**Pheasant*—Feb. 2 to Sept. 30.
**Ptarmigan*—(Scotland only) Dec. 11 to Aug. 11.
It is also unlawful (in *England* and *Wales*) to kill the game marked * above on a Sunday or Christmas Day.

Angling

Close seasons (dates inclusive) are:
Coarse fishing.—Yorkshire, last day in Feb. to May 31; South West, none; rest of country, March 15 to June 15.
Game fishing.—Trout, Oct. 1 to last day of Feb.*; Salmon, Nov. 1 to Jan. 31*.

* The above dates are statutory close times. Particularly with salmon, migratory trout and trout, close seasons vary in accordance with water authority local by-laws. In all cases, it is best to check with the water authority concerned.

THE COUNTRY CODE

The following are the points of The Country Code, issued by the Countryside Commission:
(a) Enjoy the countryside and respect its life and work; (b) Guard against all risks of fire; (c) Fasten all gates; (d) Keep your dogs under close control; (e) Keep to public paths across farmland; (f) Use gates and stiles to cross fences, hedges and walls; (g) Leave livestock, crops and machinery alone; (h) Take your litter home; (i) Help to keep all water clean; (j) Protect wildlife, plants and trees; (k) Take special care on country roads; (l) Make no unnecessary noise.

HALLMARKS ON GOLD, SILVER AND PLATINUM WARES
London (Goldsmiths' Hall) Date Letters
From 1498

Style	Period	Style	Period
Black letter, small	1498–9 to 1517–8	Roman letter, small....	1739–40 to 1755–6
Lombardic	1518–9 „ 1537–8	Old English, capitals ..	1756–7 to 1775–6
Roman and other capitals	1538–9 „ 1557–8	Roman letter, small ...	1776–7 „ 1795–6
Black letter, small	1558–9 „ 1577–8	Roman letter, capitals .	1796–7 „ 1815–6
Roman letter, capitals .	1578–9 „ 1597–8	Roman letter, small ...	1816–7 „ 1835–6
Lombardic, external cusps	1598–9 „ 1617–8	Old English, capitals ..	1836–7 „ 1855–6
Italic letter, small	1618–9 „ 1637–8	Old English, small	1856–7 „ 1875–6
Court hand	1638–9 „ 1657–8	Roman letter, capitals [A to M *square* shield N to Z as shown]	1876–7 „ 1895–6
Black letter, capitals ..	1658–9 „ 1677–8	Roman letter, small ...	1896–7 „ 1915–6
Black letter, small	1678–9 „ 1696–7	Black letter, small	1916–7 „ 1935–6
Court hand	1697 „ 1715–6	Roman letter, capitals .	1936–7 „ 1955–6
Roman letter, capitals	1716–7 „ 1735–6	Italic letter, small	1956–7 „ 1974
Roman letter, small ...	1736–7 „ 1738–9	Italic letter, capitals ..	1975 „ ...

Hallmarks are the symbols stamped on gold, silver, or platinum articles to indicate that they have been chemically tested and that they conform to one of the legal standards. With certain exceptions, all gold, silver, or platinum articles are required by law to be hallmarked before they are offered for sale. Hallmarking was instituted in 1300 υ der a statute of Edward I.

Normally a complete modern hallmark consists of four symbols—the maker's mark or sponsor's mark, assay office mark, standard mark and date letter.

Additional marks have been authorized from time to time.

Maker's Mark.—Instituted in 1363, the maker's mark was originally a device such as a bird or *fleur-de-lys* and now consists invariably of the initial letters of the name or names of the maker or sponsor, or of the firm.

Assay Office Mark.—The existing assay offices and their distinguishing marks are:—

LONDON (Goldsmiths' Hall).
A leopard's head (uncrowned from 1300 to 1478–9, when it became crowned until 1821, since when it has been uncrowned). From 1697 to 1974 a lion's head erased was used on silver of the higher (Britannia) standard.

BIRMINGHAM (Newhall Street, B3 1SB) . An anchor
SHEFFIELD (137 Portobello Street, S1 4DS) . . A rose
EDINBURGH (9 Granton Road, EH5 3QJ) .. A castle

Offices formerly existed in other towns, e.g. Chester, Glasgow, Newcastle, Exeter, York and Norwich, each having its own distinguishing mark.

Standard Mark.—Instituted in 1544. The current legal standards and their marks are as follows:—

PLATINUM

SILVER.—Sterling silver (92·5 per cent. silver) is marked by English assay offices with a *lion passant* and by the Edinburgh Assay Office with a *lion rampant*. A full-length figure of *Britannia* was impressed on silver of a higher standard (95·84 per cent. silver) between 1697 and 1720 and this mark is still used occasionally by all British assay offices.

GOLD.—Since 1975 gold articles are marked with a crown followed by the millesimal figure for the standard, i.e. 916 for 22 carat, 750 for 18 carat, 585 for 14 carat and 375 for 9 carat.

PLATINUM.—Hallmarking of platinum articles began in 1975. The only standard permitted contains at least 95 per cent. platinum.

Date Letter.—Instituted in 1478. The date letter denotes the year in which an article was assayed and hallmarked. Each alphabetical cycle has a distinctive style of lettering or shape of shield. The date letters were different at the various assay offices and the particular office must be established from the assay office mark before reference is made to tables of date letters. Specimen shields and letters used by the London Office on silver articles in each period from

1498 to date are shown on the previous page. The same letters are found on gold articles but the surrounding shield may differ. Since Jan. 1, 1975 each Office has used the same style of date letter and shield for all articles.

OTHER MARKS

Duty Mark.—In 1784 an additional mark of the reigning sovereign's head was introduced to signify that the excise duty had been paid. The mark became obsolete on the abolition of the duty in 1890.

Commemorative Marks.—There are three other marks to commemorate special events, the Silver Jubilee of King George V and Queen Mary in 1935, the Coronation of Queen Elizabeth II in 1953 and her Silver Jubilee in 1977.

Foreign Wares.—Since 1842 foreign wares imported into Great Britain have been required to be hallmarked before sale. The marks consist of the importer's mark, a special assay office mark (*see below*), the figures denoting fineness and the annual date letter. The current assay office marks for foreign wares are as follows:—

LONDON.—The sign of the Constellation Leo.
BIRMINGHAM.—Equilateral triangle.
SHEFFIELD.—The sign of the Constellation Libra.
EDINBURGH.—St. Andrew's Cross.

Common Control Mark.—Special marks at authorized Assay Offices of the signatory countries of the International Convention—United Kingdom, Austria, Denmark, Finland, Ireland, Portugal, Norway, Sweden and Switzerland—are legally recognized in the United Kingdom as approved hallmarks. These marks consist of a Sponsor's Mark, a Common Control Mark, a Fineness Mark (arabic numerals showing the standard in parts per thousand) and an Assay Office Mark. There is no date letter.

POETS LAUREATE

Samuel Daniel	1599	Rev. Laurence Eusden	1718	Lord Tennyson	1850
Ben Jonson	1619	Colley Cibber	1730	Alfred Austin	1890
Sir William D'Avenant	1637	William Whitehead	1757	Robert Bridges	1913
John Dryden	1670	Rev. Thomas Warton	1785	John Masefield	1930
Thomas Shadwell	1688	Henry James Pye	1790	Cecil Day Lewis	1967
Nahum Tate	1692	Robert Southey	1813	Sir John Betjeman	1972
Nicholas Rowe	1715	William Wordsworth	1843	Edward (Ted) Hughes	1984

MASTERS OF THE QUEEN'S/KING'S MUSIC

	Apptd.		Apptd.
Nicholas Lanier	1626	Francois (Franz) Cramer	1834
Louis Grabu	1666	George Frederick Anderson	1848
Nicholas Staggins	1674	Sir William George Cusins	1870
John Eccles	1700	Sir Walter Parratt	1893
Maurice Greene	1735	Sir Edward Elgar	1924
William Boyce	1755 (1757)	Sir Henry Walford Davies	1934
John Stanley	1779	Sir Arnold Edward Trevor Bax	1941
Sir William Parsons	1786	Sir Arthur Bliss	1953
William Shield	1817	Malcolm Williamson	1975
Christian Kramer	1829		

WEIGHTS AND MEASURES

The Weights and Measures Act, 1985, enacts the legal measures for the United Kingdom. The United Kingdom primary standards are the yard or the metre as the unit of measurement of length, and the pound or the kilogram as the unit of measurement of mass. Other units of measurement are defined by reference to the primary standards. Responsibility for the maintenance of the primary standards and for the determination or redetermination of their value rests with the Secretary of State for Trade and Industry.

The definition of the U.K. primary standards is as follows:

YARD = 0·9144 metre.
METRE is the length of the path travelled by light in vacuum during a time interval of 1/299 792 458 of a second.
POUND = 0·453 592 37 kilogram.
KILOGRAM is equal to the mass of the international prototype of the kilogram.

The following list shows the definitions of measures set out in Schedule 1 of the Weights and Measures Act, 1985.

Measurement of Length

Imperial Units
Mile = 1,760 yards.
YARD (yd.) = 0·9144 metre.
Foot (ft.) = 1/3 yard.
Inch (in.) = 1/36 yard.

Metric Units
Kilometre (km.) = 1,000 metres.
METRE (m.) is the length of the path travelled by light in vacuum during a time interval of 1/299 792 458 of a second.
Decimetre (dm.) = 1/10 metre.
Centimetre (cm.) = 1/100 metre.
Millimetre (mm.) = 1/1000 metre.

Measurement of Area

Imperial Units
Acre = 4,840 square yards.
SQUARE YARD = a superficial area equal to that of a square each side of which measures one yard.
Square foot = 1/9 square yard.

Metric Units
Hectare (ha.) = 100 ares.
Decare = 10 ares.
Are (a.) = 100 square metres.
SQUARE METRE = a superficial area equal to that of a square each side of which measures one metre.
Square decimetre = 1/100 square metre.
Square centimetre = 1/100 square decimetre.
Square millimetre = 1/100 square centimetre.

Measurement of Volume

Metric Units
CUBIC METRE (m^3) = a volume equal to that of a cube each edge of which measures one metre.
Cubic decimetre = 1/1000 cubic metre.
Cubic centimetre = 1/1000 cubic decimetre.
Hectolitre = 100 litres.
LITRE = a cubic decimetre.
Decilitre = 1/10 litre.
Centilitre = 1/100 litre.
Millilitre = 1/1000 litre.

Measurement of Capacity

Imperial Units
GALLON = 4·546 09 cubic decimetres.
Quart = 1/4 gallon.

Pint (pt.) = 1/2 quart.
Gill = 1/4 pint.
Fluid ounce (fl. oz.) = 1/20 pint.

Metric Units
Hectolitre (hl.) = 100 litres.
LITRE (l.) = a cubic decimetre.
Decilitre = 1/10 litre.
Centilitre (cl.) = 1/100 litre.
Millilitre (ml.) = 1/1000 litre.

Measurement of Mass or Weight

Imperial Units
POUND (lb.) = 0·453 592 37 kilogram.
Ounce (oz.) = 1/16 pound.
*Ounce troy = 12/175 pound.

Metric Units
Tonne, metric tonne (t.) = 1000 kilograms.
KILOGRAM (kg.) is the unit of mass; it is equal to the mass of the international prototype of the kilogram.
Hectogram (hg.) = 1/10 kilogram.
Gram (g.) = 1/1000 kilogram.
**Carat (metric) = 1/5 gram.
Milligram (mg.) = 1/1000 gram.

*used only for transactions in gold, silver or other precious metals, and articles made therefrom.
**used only for transactions in precious stones or pearls.

Certain units of measurement may no longer be used for trade although the measure may still be used, *e.g.* it is legal to sell a 112 lb quantity of a commodity but it must be referred to in invoices, etc., as 112 lb, not as a cwt. These units are defined as follows:

Measurement of Length

Furlong = 220 yards.
Chain = 22 yards.

Measurement of Area

Square mile = 640 acres.
Rood = 1210 square yards.
Square inch = 1/144 square foot.

Measurement of Volume

Cubic yard = a volume equal to that of a cube each edge of which measures one yard.
Cubic foot = 1/27 cubic yard.
Cubic inch = 1/1728 cubic foot.

Measurement of Capacity

Bushel = 8 gallons.
Peck = 2 gallons.
Fluid drachm = 1/8 fluid ounce.
Minim (min.) = 1/60 fluid drachm.

Measurement of Mass or Weight

Ton = 2,240 pounds.
Hundredweight (*cwt.*) = 112 pounds.
Cental = 100 pounds.
Quarter = 28 pounds.
Stone = 14 pounds.
Dram (*dr.*) = 1/16 ounce.
Grain (*gr.*) = 1/7000 pound.
Pennyweight (*dwt.*) = 24 grains.
Ounce apothecaries = 480 grains.
Drachm (ʒl) = 1/8 ounce apothecaries.
Scruple(ʒl) = 1/3 drachm.

Metric ton = 1,000 kilograms.
Quintal (*q.*) = 100 kilograms.

Measurement of Electricity

Units of measurement of electricity are defined by the Weights and Measures Act, 1985, as follows:

An AMPERE (*A.*) is that constant current which, if maintained in two straight parallel conductors of infinite length, of negligible circular cross-section and placed 1 metre apart in vacuum, would produce between these conductors a force equal to 2×10^{-7} newton per metre of length.

An OHM (Ω) is the electric resistance between two points of a conductor when a constant potential difference of 1 volt, applied between the two points, produces in the conductor a current of 1 ampere, the conductor not being the seat of any electromotive force.

A VOLT (*V.*) is the difference of electric potential between two points of a conducting wire carrying a constant current of 1 ampere when the power dissipated between these points is equal to 1 watt.

A WATT (*W.*) is the power which in one second gives rise to energy of 1 joule.

Kilowatt (*kW.*) = 1,000 watts.
Megawatt (*MW.*) = one million watts.

Water Measures

1 cubic foot = 62·321 lb.
1 gallon = 160 fluid ounces.
     = 10 lb. (distilled).
1 cubic cm. = 1 gram.
1,000 cubic cm. = 1 litre; 1 kilogram.
1 cubic metre = 1,000 litres; 1,000 kg.; 1 tonne.
     An inch of rain on the surface of an acre (43,560 sq. ft.) = 3,630 cubic ft. = 100·992 tons.
     Cisterns: A cistern $4 \times 2\frac{1}{2}$ feet and 3 feet deep will hold brimful 186·963 gallons, weighing 1,869·63 lbs. in addition to its own weight.

Water for Ships
Kilderkin = 18 gallons.
Barrel = 36 gallons.
Puncheon = 72 gallons.
Butt = 110 gallons.
Tun = 210 gallons.

Bottles of Wine
Equivalent in standard champagne bottles (litres in brackets)
Magnum = 2 (1·6).
Jeroboam = 4 (3·2).
Rehoboam = 6 (4·8).
Methuselah = 8 (6·4).
Salmanazar = 12 (9·6).
Balthazar = 16 (12·8).
Nebuchadnezzar = 20 (16).
A quarter of a bottle is known as a *nip*.

NAUTICAL MEASURES

Distance at sea is measured in nautical miles. The British standard nautical mile was 6,080 feet (the length of a minute of an arc of a great circle of the earth, rounded off to a mean value to allow for the length varying at different latitudes). This measure has been obsolete since 1970 when the international nautical mile of 1,852 metres was adopted by the Hydrographic Department of the Ministry of Defence as a result of a recommendation by the International Hydrographic Bureau.

The cable (600 feet or 100 fathoms) was a measure approximately one tenth of a nautical mile. Such distances are now expressed in decimal parts of a sea mile or in metres.

Soundings at sea were recorded in fathoms (6 feet). Depths are now expressed in metres on new Admiralty charts.

Speed is measured in nautical miles per hour, called knots. A ship moving at the rate of 30 nautical miles per hour is said to be doing 30 knots.

Knots	m.p.h.	Knots	m.p.h.
1	1·1515	9	10·3636
2	2·3030	10	11·5151
3	3·4545	15	17·2727
4	4·6060	20	23·0303
5	5·7575	25	28·7878
6	6·9090	30	34·5454
7	8·0606	35	40·3030
8	9·2121	40	46·0606

The tonnage of a vessel is measured in tons of 100 cubic feet.
Gross tonnage = the total volume of all the enclosed spaces of a vessel.
Net tonnage = gross tonnage less deductions for crew space, engine room, water ballast and other spaces not used for passengers or cargo.

Million, Billion, etc.

Value in the United Kingdom

Million . . . . thousand × thousand (10^6)
Billion . . . . million × million (10^{12})
Trillion . . . . million × billion (10^{18})
Quadrillion . . . . million × trillion (10^{24})

Value in U.S.A.

Million . . . . thousand × thousand (10^6)
Billion . . . . thousand × million (10^9)
Trillion . . . . million × million (10^{12})
Quadrillion . . . . million × billion U.S. (10^{15})

Angular or Circular Measures

60 seconds (″) = 1 minute (′).
60 minutes = 1 degree (°).
90 degrees = 1 right angle or quadrant.
Diameter of circle × 3·141 6 = circumference.
Diameter squared × 0·7854 = area of circle.
Diameter squared × 3·141 6 = surface of sphere.
Diameter cubed × 0·523 = solidity of sphere.
One degree of circumference × 57·3 = radius.*
Diameter of cylinder × 3·141 6; product by length or height, gives the surface.
Diameter squared × 0·7854; product by length or height, gives solid content.

* Or, one radian (the angle subtended at the centre of a circle by an arc of the circumference equal in length to the radius) = 57·3 degrees, nearly.

THERMOMETER COMPARISONS
Comparison between Scales of Fahrenheit, Réaumur and Centigrade

$$F = C + R + 32$$
$$R = \frac{4(F-32)}{9}$$

$$F = \frac{9R}{4} + 32$$

$$*F = \frac{9C}{5} + 32$$
$$C = \frac{5(F-32)}{9}$$

CONVERSION
Let F = Fahr.
  " C = Cent.
  " R = Réaumur.

Note.—The normal temperature of the human body is 98·4°F., or 37° (36·9°) C., or 29·5° R. Freezing point=32°F.=0°C.=0°R.; Boiling point=212° F.=100° C.=80° R. "Absolute" Temperature is Temperature reckoned from "Absolute Zero," which is at 273° C. below 0° C., 459·4° below 0° F., and 218·4° below 0° R. and is denoted by the letter "K." * Below 32° F. subtract 32.

CENT.	FAH'T.	RMR.	CENT.	FAH'T.	RMR.
100B.	212B.	80B.	25	77	20
99	210·2	79·2	24	75·2	19·2
98	208·4	78·4	23	73·4	18·4
97	206·6	77·6	22	71·6	17·6
96	204·8	76·8	21	69·8	16·8
95	203	76	20	68	16
94	201·2	75·2	19	66·2	15·2
93	199·4	74·4	18	64·4	14·4
92	197·6	73·6	17	62·6	13·6
91	195·8	72·8	16	60·8	12·8
90	194	72	15	59	12
89	192·2	71·2	14	57·2	11·2
88	190·4	70·4	13	55·4	10·4
87	188·6	69·6	12	53·6	9·6
86	186·8	68·8	11	51·8	8·8
85	185	68	10	50	8
84	183·2	67·2	9	48·2	7·2
83	181·4	66·4	8	46·4	6·4
82	179·6	65·6	7	44·6	5·6
81	177·8	64·8	6	42·8	4·8
80	176	64	5	41	4
79	174·2	63	4	39·2	3·2
78	172·4	62·4	3	37·4	2·4
77	170·6	61·6	2	35·6	1·6
76	168·8	60·8	1	33·8	0·8
75	167	60	zero	32	zero
74	165·2	59·2	1	30·2	0·8
73	163·4	58·4	2	28·4	1·6
72	161·6	57·6	3	26·6	2·4
71	159·8	56·8	4	24·8	3·2
70	158	56	5	23	4
69	156·2	55·2	6	21·2	4·8
68	154·4	54·4	7	19·4	5·6
67	152·6	53·6	8	17·6	6·4
66	150·8	52·8	9	15·8	7·2
65	149	52	10	14	8
64	147·2	51·2	11	12·2	8·8
63	145·4	50·4	12	10·4	9·6
62	143·6	49·6	13	8·6	10·4
61	141·8	48·8	14	6·8	11·2
60	140	48	15	5	12
59	138·2	47·2	16	3·2	12·8
58	136·4	46·4	17	1·4	13·6
57	134·6	45·6	18	0·4	14·4
56	132·8	44·8	19	2·2	15·2
55	131	44	20	4	16
54	129·2	43·2	21	5·8	16·8
53	127·4	42·4	22	7·6	17·6
52	125·6	41·6	23	9·3	18·4
51	123·8	40·8	24	11·2	19·2
50	122	40	25	13	20
49	120·2	39·2	26	14·8	20·8
48	118·4	38·4	27	16·6	21·6
47	116·6	37·6	28	18·4	22·4
46	114·8	36·8	29	20·2	23·2
45	113	36	30	22	24
44	111·2	35·2	31	23·8	24·8
43	109·4	34·4	32	25·6	25·6
42	107·6	33·6	33	27·4	26·4
41	105·8	32·8	34	29·2	27·2
40	104	32	35	31	28
39	102·2	31·2	36	32·8	28·8
38	100·4	30·4	37	34·6	29·6
37	98·6	29·6	38	36·4	30·4
36	96·8	28·8	39	38·2	31·2
35	95	28	40	40	32
34	93·2	27·2	41	41·8	32·8
33	91·4	26·4	42	43·6	33·6
32	89·6	25·6	43	45·4	34·4
31	87·8	24·8	44	47·2	35·2
30	86	24	45	49	36
29	84·2	23·2	46	50·8	36·8
28	82·4	22·4	47	52·6	37·6
27	80·6	21·6	48	54·4	38·4
26	78·8	20·8	49	56·2	39·2

PAPER MEASURES

Writing Paper	Printing Paper
480 sheets = 1 ream	516 sheets = 1 ream
24 sheets = 1 quire	2 reams = 1 bundle
20 quires = 1 ream	5 bundles = 1 bale

Sizes of Writing and Drawing Papers

Emperor	=	72 × 48	inches
Antiquarian	=	53 × 31	,,
Double Elephant	=	40 × 27	,,
Grand Eagle	=	42 × 28¾	,,
Atlas	=	34 × 26	,,
Colombier	=	34¾ × 23½	,,
Imperial	=	30 × 22	,,
Elephant	=	28 × 23	,,
Cartridge	=	26 × 21	,,
Super Royal	=	27 × 19	,,
Royal	=	24 × 19	,,
Medium	=	22 × 17½	,,
Large Post	=	21 × 16½	,,
Copy or Draft	=	20 × 16	,,
Demy	=	20 × 15½	,,
Post	=	19 × 15¼	,,
Pinched Post	=	18½ × 14¾	,,
Foolscap	=	17 × 13½	,,
Double Foolscap	=	26½ × 16½	,,
Double Post	=	30½ × 19	,,
Double Large Post	=	33 × 21	,,
Double Demy	=	31 × 20	,,
Brief	=	16½ × 13½	,,
Pott	=	15 × 12½	,,

Sizes of Printing Papers

Foolscap	=	17 × 13½	inches
Double Foolscap	=	27 × 17	,,
Quad Foolscap	=	34 × 27	,,
Crown	=	20 × 15	,,
Double Crown	=	30 × 20	,,
Quad Crown	=	40 × 30	,,
Double Quad Crown	=	60 × 40	,,
Post	=	19¼ × 15¼	,,
Double Post	=	31¼ × 19¼	,,
Double Large Post	=	33 × 21	,,
Demy	=	22½ × 17½	,,
Double Demy	=	35 × 22½	,,
Quad Demy	=	45 × 35	,,
Music Demy	=	20 × 15½	,,
Medium	=	23 × 18	,,
Royal	=	25 × 20	,,
Super Royal	=	27½ × 20½	,,
Elephant	=	28 × 23	,,
Imperial	=	30 × 22	,,

Sizes of Brown Papers

Casing	=	46 × 36	inches
Double Imperial	=	45 × 29	,,
Elephant	=	34 × 24	,,
Double Four Pound	=	31 × 21	,,
Imperial Cap	=	29 × 22	,,
Haven Cap	=	26 × 21	,,
Bag Cap	=	24 × 19½	,,
Kent Cap	=	21 × 18	,,

INTERNATIONAL PAPER SIZES

The basis of the international series of paper sizes is a rectangle having an area of one square metre, the sides of which are in the proportion of 1:√2. The proportions 1:√2 have a geometrical relationship, the side and diagonal of any square being in this proportion. The effect of this arrangement is that if the area of the sheet of paper is doubled or halved, the shorter side and the longer side of the new sheet are still in the same proportion 1:√2. This feature is useful where photographic enlargement or reduction is used, as the proportions remain the same.

Description of the A series is by capital A followed by a figure. The basic size has the description A0 and the higher the figure following the letter, the greater is the number of sub-divisions and therefore the smaller the sheet. Half A0 is A1 and half A1 is A2. Where larger dimensions are required the A is *preceded* by a figure. Thus 2A means twice the size A0; 4A is four times the size of A0.

Subsidiary Series.—A series of B sizes has been devised for use in exceptional circumstances when sizes intermediate between any two adjacent sizes of the A series are needed.

In addition there is a series of C sizes which is used much less. A is for magazines and books, B for posters, wall charts and other large items, C for envelopes particularly where it is necessary for an envelope (in C series) to fit into another envelope. The size recommended for business correspondence is A4.

Long Sizes.—Long sizes are obtainable by dividing any appropriate sizes from the two series above into three, four or eight equal parts parallel with the shorter side in such a manner that the proportions mentioned in paragraph 2 (above) are not maintained, the ratio between the longer and the shorter sides being greater than √2:1. In practice long sizes should be produced from the A series only.

It is an essential feature of these series that the dimensions are of the trimmed or finished size.

'A' Series

	mm	inches
A0	841 × 1189	33·11 × 46·81
A1	594 × 841	23·39 × 33·11
A2	420 × 594	16·54 × 23·39
A3	297 × 420	11·69 × 16·54
A4	210 × 297	8·27 × 11·69
A5	148 × 210	5·83 × 8·27
A6	105 × 148	4·13 × 5·83
A7	74 × 105	2·91 × 4·13
A8	52 × 74	2·05 × 2·91
A9	37 × 52	1·46 × 2·05
A10	26 × 37	1·02 × 1·46

'B' Series

	mm	inches
B0	1000 × 1414	39·37 × 55·67
B1	707 × 1000	27·83 × 39·37
B2	500 × 707	19·68 × 27·83
B3	353 × 500	13·90 × 19·68
B4	250 × 353	9·84 × 13·90
B5	176 × 250	6·93 × 9·84
B6	125 × 176	4·92 × 6·93
B7	88 × 125	3·46 × 4·92
B8	62 × 88	2·44 × 3·46
B9	44 × 62	1·73 × 2·44
B10	31 × 44	1·22 × 1·73

SIZES OF BOUND BOOKS

The book sizes most commonly used are listed below. Approximate centimetre equivalents are in brackets. International sizes are converted to their nearest Imperial Size (*e.g.* A4 = D4; A5 = D8).

		inches	cms
Crown 32mo	C32	2½ × 3½	6 × 6
Crown 16mo	C16	3½ × 5	9 × 13
Foolscap 8vo	F8	4¼ × 6¾	11 × 17
Demy 16mo	D16	4⅜ × 5⅞	11 × 14
Crown 8vo	C8	5 × 7½	13 × 19
Demy 8vo	D8	5⅝ × 8¾	14 × 22
Medium 8vo	M8	5½ × 9	15 × 23
Royal 8vo	R8	6¼ × 10	16 × 25
Super Royal 8vo	suR8	6¾ × 10	17 × 25
Foolscap 4to	F4	6¾ × 8½	17 × 22
Crown 4to	C4	7½ × 10	19 × 25
Imperial 8vo	Imp8	7½ × 11	19 × 28
Demy 4to	D4	8½ × 11¼	22 × 29
Royal 4to	R4	10 × 12¼	25 × 31
Super Royal 4to	suR4	10 × 13½	25 × 34
Crown Folio	Cfol	10 × 15	25 × 38
Imperial Folio	Impfol	11 × 15	28 × 38

Folio means a sheet folded in half, *quarto* (4to) folded into four, *octavo* (8vo) folded into eight. Books are usually bound up in sheets of 16 or 32 pages. Octavo books are generally printed 64 pages at a time—32 pages on each side of a sheet of quad.

A TABLE OF THE NUMBER OF DAYS FROM ANY DAY IN ONE MONTH TO THE SAME IN ANY OTHER MONTH IN ORDINARY YEARS

	Jan.	Feb.	Mar.	April	May	June	July	Aug.	Sept.	Oct.	Nov.	Dec.
January	365	31	59	90	120	151	181	212	243	273	304	334
February	334	365	28	59	89	120	150	181	212	242	273	303
March	306	337	365	31	61	92	122	153	184	214	245	275
April	275	306	334	365	30	61	91	122	153	183	214	244
May	245	276	304	335	365	31	61	92	123	153	184	214
June	214	245	273	304	334	365	30	61	92	122	153	183
July	184	215	243	274	304	335	365	31	62	92	123	153
August	153	184	212	243	273	304	334	365	31	61	92	122
September	122	153	181	212	242	273	303	334	365	30	61	91
October	92	123	151	182	212	243	273	304	335	365	31	61
November	61	92	120	151	181	212	242	273	304	334	365	30
December	31	62	90	121	151	182	212	243	274	304	335	365

CONVERSION TABLES FOR WEIGHTS AND MEASURES

NOTE.—The central figures in heavy type represent either of the two columns beside them, as the case may be. *Examples:*—1 centimetre = 0·394 inch and 1 inch = 2·540 centimetres. 1 metre = 1·094 yards and 1 yard = 0·914 metre. 1 kilometre = 0·621 mile and 1 mile = 1·609 kilometres.

Length			Area			Volume			Weight (Mass)		
Centimetres		Inches	Square Centimetres		Square Inches	Cubic Centimetres		Cubic Inches	Kilograms		Pounds
2·540	**1**	0·394	6·452	**1**	0·155	16·387	**1**	0·061	0·454	**1**	2·205
5·080	**2**	0·787	12·903	**2**	0·310	32·774	**2**	0·122	0·907	**2**	4·409
7·620	**3**	1·181	19·355	**3**	0·465	49·161	**3**	0·183	1·361	**3**	6·614
10·160	**4**	1·575	25·806	**4**	0·620	65·548	**4**	0·244	1·814	**4**	8·819
12·700	**5**	1·969	32·258	**5**	0·775	81·936	**5**	0·305	2·268	**5**	11·023
15·240	**6**	2·362	38·710	**6**	0·930	98·323	**6**	0·366	2·722	**6**	13·228
17·780	**7**	2·756	45·161	**7**	1·085	114·710	**7**	0·427	3·175	**7**	15·432
20·320	**8**	3·150	51·613	**8**	1·240	131·097	**8**	0·488	3·629	**8**	17·637
22·860	**9**	3·543	58·064	**9**	1·395	147·484	**9**	0·549	4·082	**9**	19·842
25·400	**10**	3·937	64·516	**10**	1·550	163·871	**10**	0·610	4·536	**10**	22·046
50·800	**20**	7·874	129·032	**20**	3·100	327·742	**20**	1·220	9·072	**20**	44·092
76·200	**30**	11·811	193·548	**30**	4·650	491·613	**30**	1·831	13·608	**30**	66·139
101·600	**40**	15·748	258·064	**40**	6·200	655·484	**40**	2·441	18·144	**40**	88·185
127·000	**50**	19·685	322·580	**50**	7·750	819·355	**50**	3·051	22·680	**50**	110·231
152·400	**60**	23·622	387·096	**60**	9·300	983·226	**60**	3·661	27·216	**60**	132·277
177·800	**70**	27·559	451·612	**70**	10·850	1147·097	**70**	4·272	31·752	**70**	154·324
203·200	**80**	31·496	516·128	**80**	12·400	1310·968	**80**	4·882	36·287	**80**	176·370
228·600	**90**	35·433	580·644	**90**	13·950	1474·839	**90**	5·492	40·823	**90**	198·416
254·000	**100**	39·370	645·160	**100**	15·500	1638·710	**100**	6·102	45·359	**100**	220·464

Metres		Yards	Square Metres		Square Yards	Cubic Metres		Cubic Yards	Metric Tonnes		Tons (U.K.)
0·914	**1**	1·094	0·836	**1**	1·196	0·765	**1**	1·308	1·016	**1**	0·984
1·829	**2**	2·187	1·672	**2**	2·392	1·529	**2**	2·616	2·032	**2**	1·968
2·743	**3**	3·281	2·508	**3**	3·588	2·294	**3**	3·924	3·048	**3**	2·953
3·658	**4**	4·374	3·345	**4**	4·784	3·058	**4**	5·232	4·064	**4**	3·937
4·572	**5**	5·468	4·181	**5**	5·980	3·823	**5**	6·540	5·080	**5**	4·921
5·486	**6**	6·562	5·017	**6**	7·176	4·587	**6**	7·848	6·096	**6**	5·905
6·401	**7**	7·655	5·853	**7**	8·372	5·352	**7**	9·156	7·112	**7**	6·889
7·315	**8**	8·749	6·689	**8**	9·568	6·116	**8**	10·464	8·128	**8**	7·874
8·230	**9**	9·843	7·525	**9**	10·764	6·881	**9**	11·772	9·144	**9**	8·858
9·144	**10**	10·936	8·361	**10**	11·960	7·646	**10**	13·080	10·161	**10**	9·842
18·288	**20**	21·872	16·723	**20**	23·920	15·291	**20**	26·159	20·321	**20**	19·684
27·432	**30**	32·808	25·084	**30**	35·880	22·937	**30**	39·239	30·481	**30**	29·526
36·576	**40**	43·745	33·445	**40**	47·840	30·582	**40**	52·318	40·642	**40**	39·368
45·720	**50**	54·681	41·806	**50**	59·799	38·228	**50**	65·398	50·802	**50**	49·210
54·864	**60**	65·617	50·168	**60**	71·759	45·873	**60**	78·477	60·963	**60**	59·052
64·008	**70**	76·553	58·529	**70**	83·719	53·519	**70**	91·557	71·123	**70**	68·894
73·152	**80**	87·489	66·890	**80**	95·679	61·164	**80**	104·636	81·284	**80**	78·737
82·296	**90**	98·425	75·251	**90**	107·639	68·810	**90**	117·716	91·444	**90**	88·579
91·440	**100**	109·361	83·613	**100**	119·599	76·455	**100**	130·795	101·605	**100**	98·421

Kilometres		Miles	Hectares		Acres	Litres		Gallons	Metric Tonnes		Tons (U.S.)
1·609	**1**	0·621	0·405	**1**	2·471	4·546	**1**	0·220	0·907	**1**	1·102
3·219	**2**	1·243	0·809	**2**	4·942	9·092	**2**	0·440	1·814	**2**	2·205
4·828	**3**	1·864	1·214	**3**	7·413	13·638	**3**	0·660	2·722	**3**	3·305
6·437	**4**	2·485	1·619	**4**	9·844	18·184	**4**	0·880	3·629	**4**	4·409
8·047	**5**	3·107	2·023	**5**	12·355	22·730	**5**	1·100	4·536	**5**	5·521
9·656	**6**	3·728	2·428	**6**	14·826	27·276	**6**	1·320	5·443	**6**	6·614
11·265	**7**	4·350	2·833	**7**	17·297	31·822	**7**	1·540	6·350	**7**	7·716
12·875	**8**	4·971	3·327	**8**	19·769	36·368	**8**	1·760	7·257	**8**	8·818
14·484	**9**	5·592	3·642	**9**	22·240	40·914	**9**	1·980	8·165	**9**	9·921
16·093	**10**	6·214	4·047	**10**	24·711	45·460	**10**	2·200	9·072	**10**	11·023
32·187	**20**	12·427	8·094	**20**	49·421	90·919	**20**	4·400	18·144	**20**	22·046
48·280	**30**	18·641	12·140	**30**	74·132	136·379	**30**	6·599	27·216	**30**	33·069
64·374	**40**	24·855	16·187	**40**	98·842	181·839	**40**	8·799	36·287	**40**	44·092
80·467	**50**	31·069	20·234	**50**	123·555	227·298	**50**	10·999	45·359	**50**	55·116
96·561	**60**	37·282	24·281	**60**	148·263	272·758	**60**	13·199	54·431	**60**	66·139
112·654	**70**	43·496	28·328	**70**	172·974	318·217	**70**	15·398	63·503	**70**	77·162
128·748	**80**	49·710	32·375	**80**	197·684	363·677	**80**	17·598	72·575	**80**	88·185
144·841	**90**	55·923	36·422	**90**	222·395	409·137	**90**	19·798	81·647	**90**	99·208
160·934	**100**	62·137	40·469	**100**	247·105	454·596	**100**	21·998	90·719	**100**	110·231

DIARY OF EVENTS IN 1989

This diary is based on information (available at the time of going to press) supplied by the British Tourist Authority, *inter alia*. The horse-racing fixtures are the copyright of The Jockey Club.

SHOWS, PAGEANTS AND EXHIBITIONS

Jan. 4–15	London International Boat Show	Earls Court, London
Feb. 9–12	Cruft's Dog Show	Earls Court, London
March 7–April 2	*Daily Mail* Ideal Home Exhibition	Earls Court, London
April 3–5	London International Book Fair	Olympia, London
May 11–14	Royal Windsor Horse Show	Home Park, Windsor
May 25–26	Chelsea Flower Show	Royal Hospital, Chelsea, London
June 17	Trooping the Colour	Horse Guards Parade, London
July 3–6	Royal International Agricultural Show	Stoneleigh, Warwicks.
July 12–29	Royal Tournament	Earls Court, London
Aug. 10	Battle of Flowers	Jersey
Aug. 11–Sept. 2	Edinburgh Military Tattoo	Edinburgh Castle
Sept. 2	Braemar Royal Highland Gathering	Braemar, Grampian
Sept. 15–23	Southampton International Boat Show	Mayflower Park, Southampton
Nov. 5	London to Brighton Veteran Car Run	Hyde Park to Brighton
Nov. 11	Lord Mayor's Procession and Show	City of London
Dec. 3–7	Royal Smithfield Show and Agricultural Machinery Exhibition	Earls Court, London

MUSIC AND DRAMA FESTIVALS

May 19–Aug. 23	Glyndebourne Festival Opera season	Glyndebourne, nr. Lewes
May 29–June 11	Bath Festival	Bath, Avon
May–Sept.	Chichester Festival Theatre season	Chichester, W. Sussex
June 9–25	Aldeburgh Festival	Aldeburgh, Suffolk
July 21–Sept. 16	Promenade Concerts season	Royal Albert Hall
Aug. 5–12	Royal National Eisteddfod of Wales	Newport, Gwent
Aug. 13–Sept. 2	Edinburgh International Festival	Edinburgh
Aug. 19–26	Three Choirs Festival	Gloucester

HORSE RACING

March 16	Cheltenham Gold Cup	Cheltenham
March 25	Lincoln Handicap	Doncaster
April 8	Grand National	Aintree
May 4	One Thousand Guineas	Newmarket
May 6	Two Thousand Guineas	Newmarket
June 7	The Derby	Epsom
June 8	Coronation Cup	Epsom
June 10	The Oaks	Epsom
June 20–23	Royal Ascot	Ascot
July 22	King George VI and Queen Elizabeth Diamond Stakes	Ascot
Sept. 17	St. Leger	Doncaster
Oct. 7	Cambridgeshire	Newmarket
Oct. 14	Cesarewitch	Newmarket

OTHER SPORTS

Jan. 21	Rugby Union: Scotland v. Wales	Murrayfield, Edinburgh
Feb. 4	Rugby Union: England v. Scotland	Twickenham, London
Feb. 4	Rugby Union: Wales v. Ireland	Cardiff Arms Park
March 4	Rugby Union: England v. France	Twickenham, London
March 4	Rugby Union: Scotland v. Ireland	Murrayfield, Edinburgh
March 18	Rugby Union: Wales v. England	Cardiff Arms Park
April 23	London Marathon	London
May 4–7	Badminton Horse Trials	Badminton, Avon
May 20	Football: F.A. Cup Final	Wembley Stadium, London
June 3, 5, 7, 9	International TT Motorcycle Races	Isle of Man
June 5–10	Golf: British Amateur Championship	Royal Birkdale, Southport
June 26–July 9	Lawn Tennis Championships	Wimbledon, London
June 28–July 2	Henley Royal Regatta	Henley-on-Thames
July 20–23	Golf: Open Championship	Royal Troon, Strathclyde
July 29–Aug. 6	Cowes Week	Cowes, Isle of Wight
Oct. 2–7	Horse of the Year Show	Wembley Arena, London

INDEX

AB

AL

THE SCHOOL OF S. HELEN AND S. KATHARINE, ABINGDON

C. of E. day and weekly boarding school with 500 girls, 140 in the 6th form.

Academically selective with strong music and art departments.

Government assisted places and music scholarships available.

Entry at 11+ and 16+ and other years by arrangement.

Enquiries to the Headmistress
Abingdon, Oxon. OX14 1BE
Tel: (0235) 20173

Help us Build New Foundations for Shattered Lives

For men and women like Doris, who has never walked since a severe spinal injury while serving with the WRAF.

She despaired of finding a home suited to her needs.

Now she is happily installed in a cottage specially designed for the disabled.

Her home is one of 35 cottages purpose-built and owned by The Forces Help Society as part of OPERATION NEW FOUNDATIONS, set up to provide housing help for people like Doris and her neighbours, one of whom lost both legs while serving in World War II, another was rendered paraplegic by a sniper's bullet in Palestine in 1948, and yet another lost a leg and an arm in Ulster two years ago. Many more, of all ages, need such accommodation. All who have served at any time in H.M. Forces are equally considered, whether or not their disabilities result from their service.

To build more purpose-built homes OPERATION NEW FOUNDATIONS needs more money. We receive no direct State aid, so depend on public support through donations, covenants and legacies. Please help us to expand our work of building NEW FOUNDATIONS.

The Forces Help Society
and Lord Roberts Workshops
122 Brompton Road, London SW3 1JE
Tel: 01-589 3243

INDEX TO ADVERTISEMENTS

OLYMPIC GOLD MEDALLISTS 1988

The Games took place at Seoul, Korea, from September 17 to October 2. New world records are indicated by *. Fastest times that are not records because of wind assistance are indicated †.

Archery

		pts.
Men:		
Individual	J. Barrs (U.S.A.)	338
Team	South Korea	986
Women:		
Individual	Kim Soo-Nyung (S. Korea)	344
Team	South Korea	982

Athletics

		hr.	min.	sec.
Men:				
100 m.	C. Lewis (U.S.A.)			9·92
200 m.	J. DeLoach (U.S.A.)			19·75
400 m.	S. Lewis (U.S.A.)			43·87
800 m.	P. Ereng (Kenya)		1	43·45
1,500 m.	P. Rono (Kenya)		3	35·96
5,000 m.	J. Ngugi (Kenya)		13	11·70
10,000 m.	B. Boutayeb (Morocco)		27	21·46
Marathon	G. Bordin (Italy)	2	10	32
3,000 m. Steeple chase.	J. Kariuki (Kenya)		8	05·51
110 m. Hurdles	R. Kingdom (U.S.A.)			12·98
400 m. Hurdles	A. Phillips (U.S.A.)			47·19
20 km. Walk	J. Pribilinec (Czechoslovakia)	1	19	57
50 km. Walk	V. Ivanenko (U.S.S.R.)	3	38	29
4 × 100 m. Relay	U.S.S.R.			38·19
4 × 400 m. Relay	U.S.A.		2	56·16*
				metres
High Jump	G. Avdeyenko (U.S.S.R.)			2·38
Pole Vault	S. Bubka (U.S.S.R.)			5·90
Long Jump	C. Lewis (U.S.A.)			8·72
Triple Jump	K. Markov (Bulgaria)			17·61
Shot	U. Timmermann (G.D.R.)			22·47
Discus	J. Schult (G.D.R.)			68·82
Hammer	S. Litvinov (U.S.S.R.)			84·80
Javelin	T. Korjus (Finland)			84·28
Decathlon	G. Schenk (G.D.R.)			8,488 pts.

		hr.	min.	sec.
Women:				
100 m.	F. Griffith Joyner (U.S.A.)			10·54†
200 m.	F. Griffith Joyner (U.S.A.)			21·34*
400 m.	O. Bryzgina (U.S.S.R.)			48·65
800 m.	S. Wodars (G.D.R.)		1	56·10
1,500 m.	P. Ivan (Romania)		3	53·96
3,000 m.	T. Samolyenko (U.S.S.R.)		8	26·53
10,000 m.	O.Bondarenko (U.S.S.R.)	31	05·21	
Marathon	R. Mota (Portugal)	2	25	40
100 m. Hurdles	Y. Donkova (Bulgaria)			12·38
400 m. Hurdles	D. Flintoff-King (Australia)			53·17
4 × 100 m. Relay	U.S.A.			41·98
4 × 400 m. Relay	U.S.S.R.		3	15·18*
				metres
High Jump	L. Ritter (U.S.A.)			2·03
Long Jump	J. Joyner-Kersee (U.S.A.)			7·40
Shot	N. Lisovskaya (U.S.S.R.)			22·24
Discus	M. Hellmann (G.D.R.)			72·30
Javelin	P. Felke (G.D.R.)			74·68
Heptathlon	J. Joyner-Kersee (U.S.A.)			7,291 pts.*

Basketball

Men	U.S.S.R.
Women	U.S.A.

Boxing

Super Heavyweight	L. Lewis (Canada)
Heavyweight	R. Mercer (U.S.A.)
Light Heavyweight	A. Maynard (U.S.A.)
Middleweight	H. Maske (G.D.R.)
Light Middleweight	Park Si-Hun (S. Korea)
Welterweight	R. Wangila (Kenya)
Light Welterweight	V. Yanovsky (U.S.S.R.)
Lightweight	A. Zuelow (G.D.R.)
Featherweight	G. Parisi (Italy)
Bantamweight	K. McKinney (U.S.A.)
Flyweight	Kim Kwang-Sun (S. Korea)
Light Flyweight	I. Hristov (Bulgaria)

Canoeing

		min.	sec.
Men:			
Kayak Singles			
(K1) 500 m.	Z. Gyulay (Hungary)	1	44·82
Kayak Pairs			
(K2) 500 m.	New Zealand	1	33·98
Kayak Singles			
(K1) 1,000 m.	G. Barton (U.S.A.)	3	55·27
Kayak Pairs			
(K2) 1,000 m.	U.S.A.	3	32·42
Kayak Fours			
(K4) 1,000 m.	Hungary	3	00·20
Canadian Singles			
(C1) 500 m.	O. Heukrodt (G.D.R.)	1	56·42
Canadian Pairs			
(C2) 500 m.	U.S.S.R.	1	41·77
Canadian Singles			
(C1) 1,000 m.	I. Klementiev (U.S.S.R.)	4	12·78
Canadian Pairs			
(C2) 1,000 m.	U.S.S.R.	3	48·36
Women:		min.	sec.
Kayak Singles			
(K1) 500 m.	V. Guecheva (Bulgaria)	1	55·19
Kayak Pairs			
(K2) 500 m.	G.D.R.	1	43·46
Kayak Fours			
(K4) 500 m.	G.D.R.	1	40·78

Cycling

		hr.	min.	sec.
Men:				
1,000 m. Time Trial	A. Kirichenko (U.S.S.R.)		1	04·499
1,000 m. Sprint	L. Hesslich (G.D.R.)			
4,000 m. Individual Pursuit	G. Umaras (U.S.S.R.)		4	32·00
4,000 m. Team Pursuit	U.S.S.R.		4	13·31
Individual Points Race	D. Frost (Denmark)			
Individual Road Race	O. Ludwig (G.D.R.)	4	32	22
Road Team Time Trial	G.D.R.	1	57	47·70
Women:		hr.	min.	sec.
Individual Road Race	M. Knol (Netherlands)	2	00	52
1,000 m. Sprint	E. Saloumiae (U.S.S.R.)			

Diving

		pts.
Men:		
Springboard	G. Louganis (U.S.A.)	730·80
Platform	G. Louganis (U.S.A.)	638·61
Women:		pts.
Springboard	Gao Min (China)	580·23
Platform	Xu Yanmei (China)	445·20

Équestrianism

		pts.
Individual Dressage	N. Uphoff (F.R.G.)	1,521
Team Dressage	F.R.G.	4,302
Individual Three-Day Event	M. Todd (N.Z.)	42·60
Team Three-Day Event	F.R.G.	225·95
Individual Show Jumping	P. Durand (France)	
Team Show Jumping	F.R.G.	17·25

Fencing

Men:	
Individual Foil	S. Cerioni (Italy)
Team Foil	U.S.S.R.
Individual Epee	A. Schmitt (F.R.G.)
Team Epee	France
Individual Sabre	J-F. Lamour (France)
Team Sabre	Hungary
Women:	
Individual Foil	A. Fichtel (F.R.G.)
Team Foil	F.R.G.

Football

Winners	U.S.S.R.

Gymnastics

		pts.
Men:		
Team	U.S.S.R.	593·350
Individual		
All-round	V. Artemov (U.S.S.R.)	119·125
Floor	S. Kharkov (U.S.S.R.)	19·925
Pommel Horse	L. Gueraskov (Bulgaria)	
	Z. Borkai (Hungary)	
	D. Bilozerchev (U.S.S.R.)	19·950
Rings	H. Behrendt (G.D.R.)	
	D. Bilozerchev (U.S.S.R.)	19·925
Vault	Lou Yun (China)	19·875
Parallel Bars	V. Artemov (U.S.S.R.)	19·925
Horizontal Bar	V. Artemov (U.S.S.R.)	
	V. Lyukin (U.S.S.R.)	19·900
Women:		pts.
Team	U.S.S.R.	395·475
Individual		
All-Round	Y. Shushunova (U.S.S.R.)	79·662
Vault	S. Boginskaya (U.S.S.R.)	19·905
Asymmetric Bars	D. Silivas (Romania)	20·000
Beam	D. Silivas (Romania)	19·924
Floor	D. Silivas (Romania)	19·937
Modern Rhythmic	M. Lobach (U.S.S.R.)	60·000

Handball

Men	U.S.S.R.
Women	South Korea

Hockey

Men	Great Britain
Women	Australia

Judo

Over 95 kg.	H. Saito (Japan)
Up to 95 kg.	A. Miguel (Brazil)
Up to 86 kg.	P. Seisenbacher (Austria)
Up to 78 kg.	W. Legien (Poland)
Up to 71 kg.	M. Alexandre (France)
Up to 65 kg.	Lee Kyung-Keun (S. Korea)
Up to 60 kg.	Kim Jae-Yup (S. Korea)

Modern Pentathlon

Individual	J. Martinek (Hungary)	5,404 pts.
Team	Hungary	15,886 pts.

Rowing

		min. sec.
Men:		
Single Sculls	T. Lange (G.D.R.)	6 49·86
Double Sculls	Netherlands	6 21 13
Coxless Quadruple Sculls	Italy	5 53·37
Coxless Pairs	Great Britain	6 36·84
Coxed Pairs	Italy	6 58·79
Coxless Fours	G.D.R.	6 03·11
Coxed Fours	G.D.R.	6 10·74
Eights	F.R.G.	5 46·05
Women:		min. sec.
Single Sculls	J. Behrendt (G.D.R.)	7 47·19
Double Sculls	G.D.R.	7 00·48
Coxless Pairs	Romania	7 28·13
Coxless Quadruple Sculls	G.D.R.	6 21·06
Coxed Fours	G.D.R.	6 56·00
Eights	G.D.R.	6 15·17

Shooting

		pts.
Men:		
Free Pistol	S. Babii (Romania)	660
Rapid-Fire Pistol	A. Kouzmine (U.S.S.R.)	698 *
Small-Bore Rifle (3 positions)	M. Cooper (G.B.)	1,279·3
Small-Bore Rifle (prone)	M. Varga (Czechoslovakia)	703·9
Running Game Target	T. Heiestad (Norway)	689
Air Rifle	G. Maksimovic (Yugoslavia)	695·6
Air Pistol	T. Kiriakov (Bulgaria)	687·9
Women:		pts.
Sport Pistol	N. Saloukvadze (U.S.S.R.)	690
Standard Rifle	S. Sperber (F.R.G.)	685·6
Air Rifle	I. Shilova (U.S.S.R.)	498·5
Air Pistol	J. Sekaric (Yugoslavia)	489·5*
Open:		pts.
Trap	D. Monakov (U.S.S.R.)	222
Skeet	A. Wegner (G.D.R.)	222

Swimming

		min. sec.
Men:		
50 m. Freestyle	M. Biondi (U.S.A.)	22·14*
100 m. Freestyle	M. Biondi (U.S.A.)	48·63
200 m. Freestyle	D. Armstrong (Australia)	1 47·25*
400 m. Freestyle	U. Dassler (G.D.R.)	3 46·95*
1,500 m. Freestyle	V. Salnikov (U.S.S.R.)	15 00·40
100 m. Breaststroke	A. Moorhouse (G.B.)	1 02·04
200 m. Breaststroke	J. Szabo (Hungary)	2 13·52
100 m. Butterfly	A. Nesty (Suriname)	53·00
200 m. Butterfly	M. Gross (F.R.G.)	1 56·94
100 m. Backstroke	D. Suzuki (Japan)	55·05
200 m. Backstroke	I. Polyansky (U.S.S.R.)	1 59·37
200 m. Medley	T. Darnyi (Hungary)	2 00·17*
400 m. Medley	T. Darnyi (Hungary)	4 14·75*
4 × 100 m. Freestyle	U.S.A.	3 16·53*
4 × 200 m. Freestyle	U.S.A.	7 12·51*
4 × 100 m. Medley	U.S.A.	3 36·93*
Women:		min. sec.
50 m. Freestyle	K. Otto (G.D.R.)	25·49
100 m. Freestyle	K. Otto (G.D.R.)	54·93
200 m. Freestyle	H. Friedrich (G.D.R.)	1 57·65
400 m. Freestyle	J. Evans (U.S.A.)	4 03·85*
800 m. Freestyle	J. Evans (U.S.A.)	8 20·20
100 m. Breaststroke	T. Dangalakova (Bulgaria)	1 07·95
200 m. Breaststroke	S. Hörner (G.D.R.)	2 26·71*
100 m. Butterfly	K. Otto (G.D.R.)	59·00

200 m. Butterfly	K. Nord (G.D.R.)	2	09·51
100 m. Backstroke	K. Otto (G.D.R.)	1	00·89
200 m. Backstroke	K. Egerszegi (Hungary)	2	09·29
200 m. Medley	D. Hunger (G.D.R.)	2	12·59
400 m. Medley	J. Evans (U.S.A.)	4	37·76
4 × 100 m. Freestyle	G.D.R.	3	40·63
4 × 100 m. Medley	G.D.R.	4	03·74

		pts.
Synchronized Solo	C. Waldo (Canada)	200·150
Synchronized Duet	Canada	197·717

Table Tennis

Men's Singles	Yoo Nam-Kyu (S. Korea)
Men's Doubles	China
Women's Singles	Chen Jing (China)
Women's Doubles	South Korea

Tennis

Men's Singles	M. Mecir (Czechoslovakia)
Men's Doubles	U.S.A.
Women's Singles	S. Graf (F.R.G.)
Women's Doubles	U.S.A.

Volleyball

Men	U.S.A.
Women	U.S.S.R.

Water Polo

Winners	Yugoslavia

Weightlifting

		kg.
Over 110 kg.	A. Kurlovich (U.S.S.R.)	462·5
Up to 110 kg.	Y. Zakharevich (U.S.S.R.)	455·0*
Up to 100 kg.	P. Kuznetsov (U.S.S.R.)	425·0
Up to 90 kg.	A. Khrapaty (U.S.S.R.)	412·5
Up to 82·5 kg.	I. Arsamakov (U.S.S.R.)	377·5
Up to 75 kg.	B. Guidikov (Bulgaria)	375·0
Up to 67·5 kg.	J. Kunz (G.D.R.)	340·0
Up to 60 kg.	N. Suleymanoglu (Turkey)	342·5
Up to 56 kg.	O. Mirzoian (U.S.S.R.)	292·5
Up to 52 kg.	S. Marinov (Bulgaria)	270·0*

Wrestling

Freestyle:

Over 100 kg.	D. Gobedzhishvili (U.S.S.R.)
100 kg.	V. Puscasu (Romania)
90 kg.	M. Khadartsev (U.S.S.R.)
82 kg.	Han Myung-Woo (S. Korea)
74 kg.	K. Monday (U.S.A.)
68 kg.	A. Fadzaev (U.S.S.R.)
62 kg.	J. Smith (U.S.A.)
57 kg.	S. Beloglazov (U.S.S.R.)
52 kg.	M. Sato (Japan)
48 kg.	T. Kobayashi (Japan)

Greco-Roman:

Over 100 kg.	A. Karelin (U.S.S.R.)
100 kg.	A. Wronski (Poland)
90 kg.	A. Komchev (Bulgaria)
82 kg.	M. Mamiachvili (U.S.S.R.)
74 kg.	Kim Young-Nam (S. Korea)
68 kg.	L. Dzhulfalakyan (U.S.S.R.)
62 kg.	K. Madyidov (U.S.S.R.)
57 kg.	A. Sike (Hungary)
52 kg.	J. Ronningen (Norway)
48 kg.	V. Maenza (Italy)

Yachting

Men:		pts.
Soling	G.D.R.	11·7
Star	Great Britain	45·7
Flying Dutchman	Denmark	31·4
470 Class	France	34·7
Finn	J. Doreste (Spain)	38·1
Tornado	France	16·0
Division 2	B. Kendall (N.Z.)	35·4

Women:		pts.
470 Class	U.S.A.	26·7

MEDAL TABLE

	Gold	Silver	Bronze	Total
U.S.S.R.	55	31	46	132
G.D.R.	37	35	30	102
U.S.A.	36	31	27	94
F.R.G.	11	14	15	40
Bulgaria	10	12	13	35
South Korea	12	10	11	33
China	5	11	12	28
Romania	7	11	6	24
Great Britain	5	10	9	24
Hungary	11	6	6	23
France	6	4	6	16
Poland	2	5	9	16
Italy	6	4	4	14
Japan	4	3	7	14
Australia	3	6	5	14
New Zealand	3	2	8	13
Yugoslavia	3	4	5	12
Sweden	0	4	7	11
Canada	3	2	5	10
Kenya	5	2	2	9
Netherlands	2	2	5	9
Czechoslovakia	3	3	2	8
Brazil	1	2	3	6
Norway	2	3	0	5
Denmark	2	1	1	4
Finland	1	1	2	4
Spain	1	1	2	4
Switzerland	0	2	2	4
Morocco	1	0	2	3
Turkey	1	1	0	2
Jamaica	0	2	0	2
Argentina	0	1	1	2
Belgium	0	0	2	2
Mexico	0	0	2	2
Austria	1	0	0	1
Portugal	1	0	0	1
Suriname	1	0	0	1
Chile	0	1	0	1
Costa Rica	0	1	0	1
Indonesia	0	1	0	1
Iran	0	1	0	1
Netherlands Antilles	0	1	0	1
Peru	0	1	0	1
Senegal	0	1	0	1
U.S. Virgin Isles	0	1	0	1
Colombia	0	0	1	1
Djibouti	0	0	1	1
Greece	0	0	1	1
Mongolia	0	0	1	1
Pakistan	0	0	1	1
Philippines	0	0	1	1
Thailand	0	0	1	1
	241	234	264	739

The following countries did not compete at Seoul: Albania, Cuba, Ethiopia, Madagascar, Nicaragua, North Korea and Seychelles.